2019
Directory of
California
Wholesalers and Service
Companies

Exclusive Provider of
Dun & Bradstreet Library Solutions

dun & bradstreet

Published January 2019 next update January 2020

Publisher

Mergent Inc.

444 Madison Ave

New York, NY 10022

©Mergent Inc All Rights Reserved

2019 Mergent Business Press

ISSN 1080-2614

ISBN 978-1-64141-176-9

MERGENT
BUSINESS PRESS
by FTSE Russell

TABLE OF CONTENTS

SUMMARY OF CONTENTS

Number of Companies.. 27,965
Number of Decision Makers 72,321
Minimum Number of Employees 50

EXPLANATORY NOTES

How to Cross-Reference in This Directory

Sequential Entry Numbers. Each establishment in the Products & Services Section is numbered sequentially (P-00000). The number assigned to each establishment is referred to as its Entry Number. To make cross-referencing easier, each listing in the Products & Services, Alphabetic and Geographic Sections includes the establishment's entry number. To facilitate locating an entry in the Products & Services Section, the entry numbers for the first listing on the left page and the last listing on the right page are printed at the top of the page next to the Standard Industrial Classification (S.I.C.) description.

Source Suggestions Welcome

Although all known sources were used to compile this directory, it is possible that companies were inadvertently omitted. Your assistance in calling attention to such omissions would be greatly appreciated. A special form on the facing page will help you in the reporting process.

Analysis

Every effort has been made to contact all firms to verify their information. The one exception to this rule is the annual sales figure, which is considered by many companies to be confidential information. Therefore, estimated sales have been calculated by multiplying the nationwide average sales per employee for the firm's major SIC/NAICS code by the firm's number of employees. Nationwide averages for sales per employee by SIC/NAICS codes are provided by the U.S. Department of Commerce and are updated annually. All sales—sales (est)—have been estimated by this method. The exceptions are parent companies (PA), division headquarters (DH) and headquarter locations (HQ) which may include an actual corporate sales figure—sales (corporate-wide) if available.

Types of Companies

Descriptive and statistical data are included for companies in the entire state. These comprise manufacturers, machine shops, fabricators, assemblers and printers. Also identified are corporate offices in the state.

Employment Data

This directory contains companies with 50 or more employees. The employment figure shown in the Products & Services Section includes male and female employees and embraces all levels of the company: administrative, clerical, sales and maintenance. This figure is for the facility listed and does not include other plants or offices. It should be recognized that these figures represent an approximate year-round average. These employment figures are broken into codes A through E and used in the Alphabetic and Geographic Sections to further help you in qualifying a company. Be sure to check the footnotes at the bottom of the page for the code breakdowns.

Standard Industrial Classification (SIC)

The Standard Industrial Classification (SIC) system used in this directory was developed by the federal government for use in classifying establishments by the type of activity they are engaged in. The SIC classifications used in this directory are from the 1987 edition published by the U.S. Government's Office of Management and Budget. The SIC system separates all activities into broad industrial divisions (e.g., manufacturing, mining, retail trade). It further subdivides each division. The range of manufacturing industry classes extends from two-digit codes (major industry group) to four-digit codes (product).

For example:

Industry Breakdown	Code	Industry, Product, etc.
*Major industry group	20	Food and kindred products
Industry group	203	Canned and frozen foods
*Industry	2033	Fruits and vegetables, etc.

*Classifications used in this directory

Only two-digit and four-digit codes are used in this directory.

Arrangement

1. The **Product & Services Section** contains complete in-depth corporate data. This section lists companies under their primary SIC. SIC codes are in numerical order with companies listed alphabetically under each code. A numerical and alphabetical index precedes this section.

IMPORTANT NOTICE: It is a violation of both federal and state law to transmit an unsolicited advertisement to a facsimile machine. Any user of this product that violates such laws may be subject to civil and criminal penalties, which may exceed $500 for each transmission of an unsolicited facsimile. Mergent Inc. provides fax numbers for lawful purposes only and expressly forbids the use of these numbers in any unlawful manner.

2. The **Alphabetic Section** lists all companies with their full physical or mailing addresses and telephone number.

3. The **Geographic Section** is sorted by cities listed in alphabetic order and companies listed alphabetically within each city.

USER'S GUIDE TO LISTINGS

PRODUCT & SERVICES SECTION

Standard Industrial Classification (SIC) description

Sequential entry number

Division

Physical address

Fax number

Decision-makers

Employment at this location

Foreign trade
▲= Import ▼= Export
◆= Import/Export

Publicly or privately owned

Web address

Primary SIC code & secondary SIC codes

HQ = Headquarters
DH = Division headquarters
PA = Parent company

New business established in last 2 years

Designates this location as a headquarters

Mailing address

Business phone

Toll free number

Year established

Industry specific information square footage admissions (educational institutions)

Estimated annual sales K=Thousands; MM=Millions

Actual corporate wide sales M=Millions; B=Billions

Product description

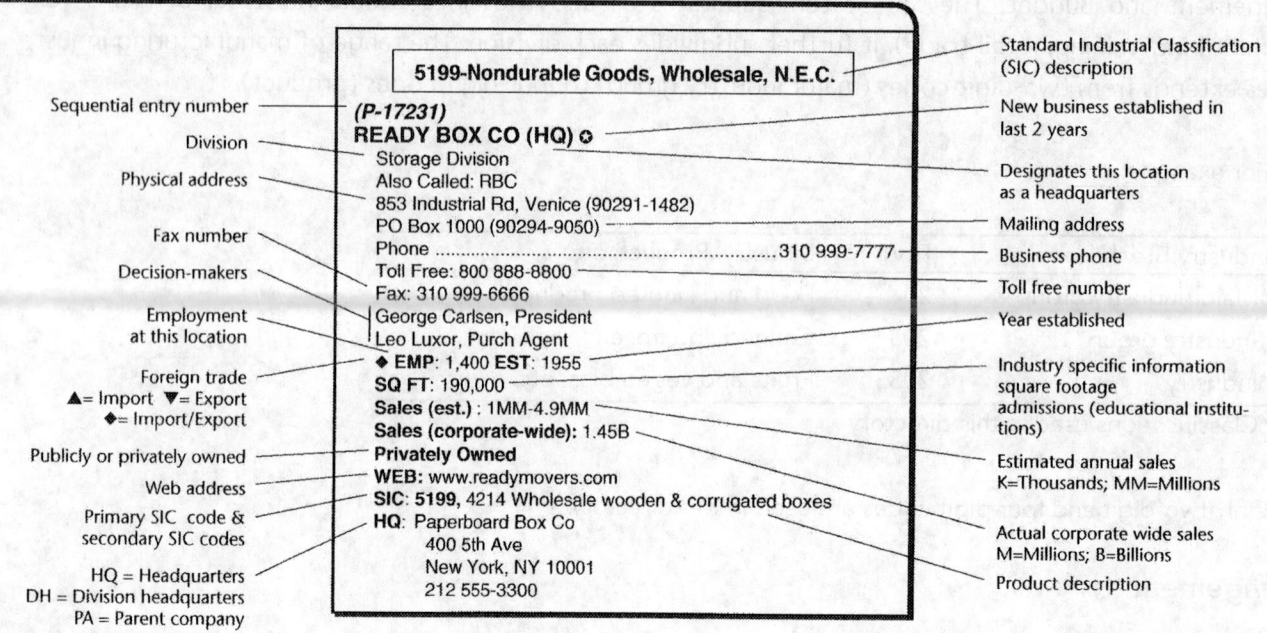

```
5199-Nondurable Goods, Wholesale, N.E.C.

(P-17231)
READY BOX CO (HQ) ✆
   Storage Division
   Also Called: RBC
   853 Industrial Rd, Venice (90291-1482)
   PO Box 1000 (90294-9050)
   Phone ....................................................... 310 999-7777
   Toll Free: 800 888-8800
   Fax: 310 999-6666
   George Carlsen, President
   Leo Luxor, Purch Agent
   ◆ EMP: 1,400 EST: 1955
   SQ FT: 190,000
   Sales (est.): 1MM-4.9MM
   Sales (corporate-wide): 1.45B
   Privately Owned
   WEB: www.readymovers.com
   SIC: 5199, 4214 Wholesale wooden & corrugated boxes
   HQ: Paperboard Box Co
       400 5th Ave
       New York, NY 10001
       212 555-3300
```

ALPHABETIC SECTION

Address, city & ZIP

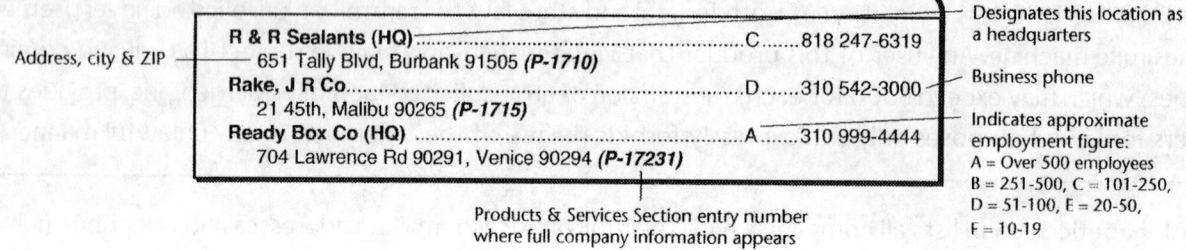

```
R & R Sealants (HQ) ........................................ C ...... 818 247-6319
   651 Tally Blvd, Burbank 91505 (P-1710)
Rake, J R Co .................................................... D ...... 310 542-3000
   21 45th, Malibu 90265 (P-1715)
Ready Box Co (HQ) ......................................... A ...... 310 999-4444
   704 Lawrence Rd 90291, Venice 90294 (P-17231)
```

Designates this location as a headquarters

Business phone

Indicates approximate employment figure:
A = Over 500 employees
B = 251-500, C = 101-250,
D = 51-100, E = 20-50,
F = 10-19

Products & Services Section entry number where full company information appears

GEOGRAPHIC SECTION

City, State & County

HQ = Headquarters
DH = Division headquarters
PA = Parent company

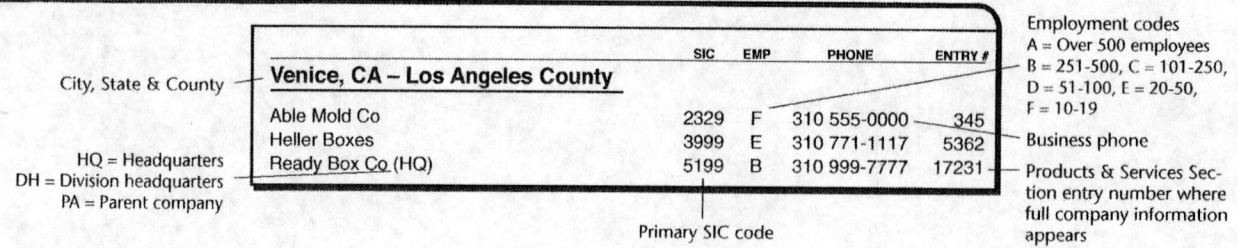

Venice, CA – Los Angeles County	SIC	EMP	PHONE	ENTRY #
Able Mold Co	2329	F	310 555-0000	345
Heller Boxes	3999	E	310 771-1117	5362
Ready Box Co (HQ)	5199	B	310 999-7777	17231

Primary SIC code

Employment codes
A = Over 500 employees
B = 251-500, C = 101-250,
D = 51-100, E = 20-50,
F = 10-19

Business phone

Products & Services Section entry number where full company information appears

Standard Industrial Classification (SIC)

The Standard Industrial Classification (SIC) system used in this directory was developed by the federal government for use in classifying establishments by the type of activity they are engaged in. The SIC classifications used in this directory are from the 1987 edition published by the U.S. Government's Office of Management and Budget. The SIC system separates all activities into broad industrial divisions (e.g., manufacturing, mining, retail trade). It further subdivides each division. The range of manufacturing industry classes extends from two-digit codes (major industry group) to four-digit codes (product).

For example:

Industry Breakdown	Code	Industry, Product, etc.
*Major industry group	20	Food and kindred products
Industry group	203	Canned and frozen foods
*Industry	2033	Fruits and vegetables, etc.

*Classifications used in this directory

Only two-digit and four-digit codes are used in this directory.

Arrangement

1. The **Product & Services Section** contains complete in-depth corporate data. This section lists companies under their primary SIC. SIC codes are in numerical order with companies listed alphabetically under each code. A numerical and alphabetical index precedes this section.

IMPORTANT NOTICE: It is a violation of both federal and state law to transmit an unsolicited advertisement to a facsimile machine. Any user of this product that violates such laws may be subject to civil and criminal penalties, which may exceed $500 for each transmission of an unsolicited facsimile. Mergent Inc. provides fax numbers for lawful purposes only and expressly forbids the use of these numbers in any unlawful manner.

2. The **Alphabetic Section** lists all companies with their full physical or mailing addresses and telephone number.

3. The **Geographic Section** is sorted by cities listed in alphabetic order and companies listed alphabetically within each city.

USER'S GUIDE TO LISTINGS

PRODUCT & SERVICES SECTION

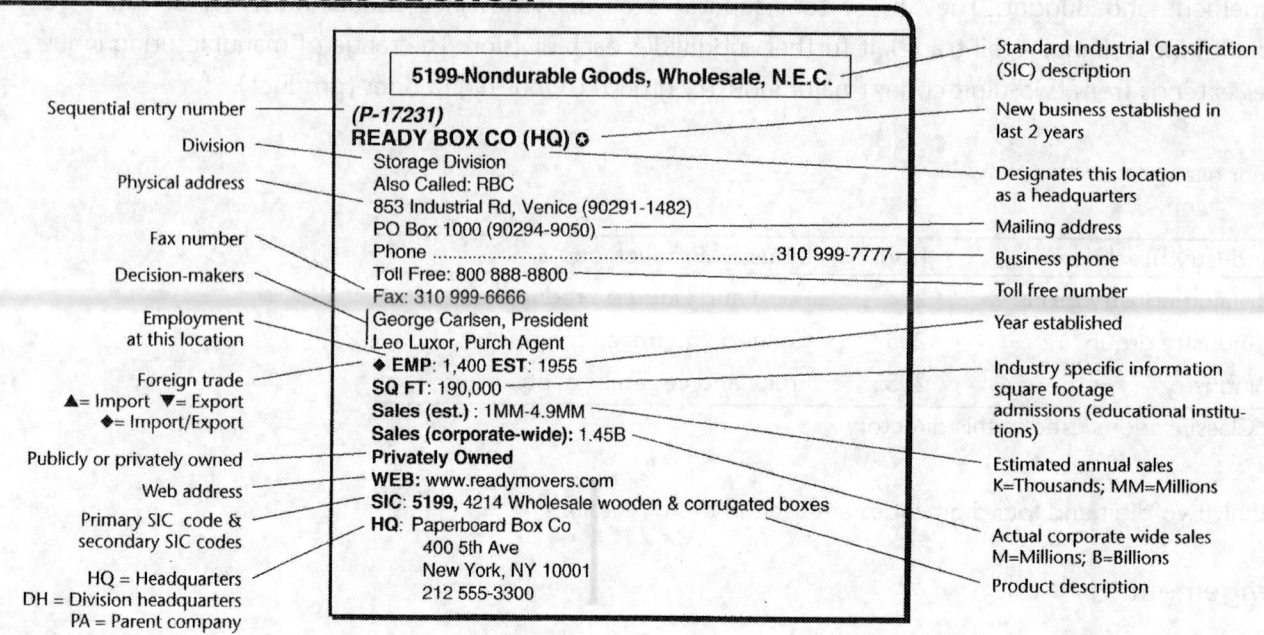

Sequential entry number
Division
Physical address
Fax number
Decision-makers
Employment at this location
Foreign trade
▲= Import ▼= Export
◆= Import/Export
Publicly or privately owned
Web address
Primary SIC code & secondary SIC codes
HQ = Headquarters
DH = Division headquarters
PA = Parent company

5199-Nondurable Goods, Wholesale, N.E.C.

(P-17231)
READY BOX CO (HQ) ✪
Storage Division
Also Called: RBC
853 Industrial Rd, Venice (90291-1482)
PO Box 1000 (90294-9050)
Phone 310 999-7777
Toll Free: 800 888-8800
Fax: 310 999-6666
George Carlsen, President
Leo Luxor, Purch Agent
◆ **EMP**: 1,400 **EST**: 1955
SQ FT: 190,000
Sales (est.) : 1MM-4.9MM
Sales (corporate-wide): 1.45B
Privately Owned
WEB: www.readymovers.com
SIC: 5199, 4214 Wholesale wooden & corrugated boxes
HQ: Paperboard Box Co
400 5th Ave
New York, NY 10001
212 555-3300

Standard Industrial Classification (SIC) description
New business established in last 2 years
Designates this location as a headquarters
Mailing address
Business phone
Toll free number
Year established
Industry specific information square footage admissions (educational institutions)
Estimated annual sales K=Thousands; MM=Millions
Actual corporate wide sales M=Millions; B=Billions
Product description

ALPHABETIC SECTION

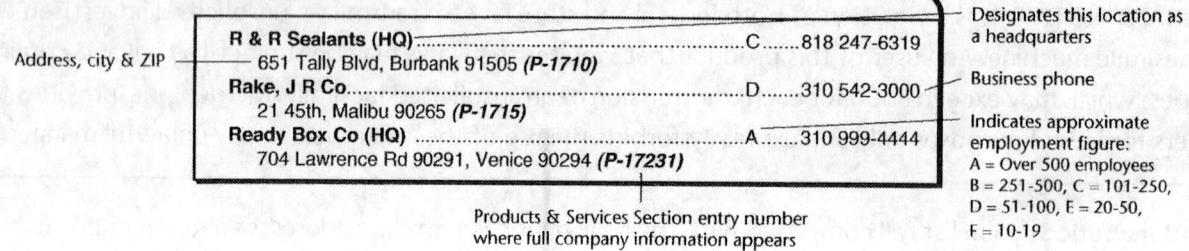

Address, city & ZIP

R & R Sealants (HQ) ....C......818 247-6319
651 Tally Blvd, Burbank 91505 **(P-1710)**
Rake, J R Co...D.......310 542-3000
21 45th, Malibu 90265 **(P-1715)**
Ready Box Co (HQ) ....A.......310 999-4444
704 Lawrence Rd 90291, Venice 90294 **(P-17231)**

Designates this location as a headquarters
Business phone
Indicates approximate employment figure:
A = Over 500 employees
B = 251-500, C = 101-250,
D = 51-100, E = 20-50,
F = 10-19

Products & Services Section entry number where full company information appears

GEOGRAPHIC SECTION

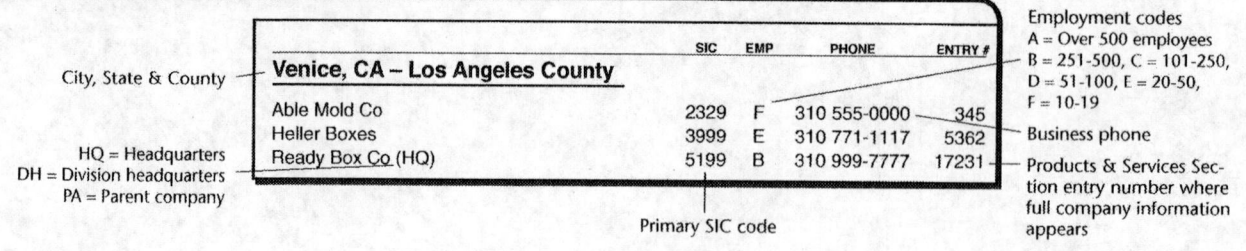

City, State & County
HQ = Headquarters
DH = Division headquarters
PA = Parent company

Venice, CA – Los Angeles County

	SIC	EMP	PHONE	ENTRY #
Able Mold Co	2329	F	310 555-0000	345
Heller Boxes	3999	E	310 771-1117	5362
Ready Box Co (HQ)	5199	B	310 999-7777	17231

Employment codes
A = Over 500 employees
B = 251-500, C = 101-250,
D = 51-100, E = 20-50,
F = 10-19
Business phone
Products & Services Section entry number where full company information appears

Primary SIC code

6

NUMERICAL INDEX of SIC DESCRIPTIONS
ALPHABETICAL INDEX of SIC DESCRIPTIONS

PRODUCTS & SERVICES SECTION
Companies listed alphabetically under thier primary SIC
In-depth company data listed

ALPHABETIC SECTION
Company listings in alphabetical order

GEOGRAPHIC INDEX
Companies sorted by city in alphabetical order

California
County Map

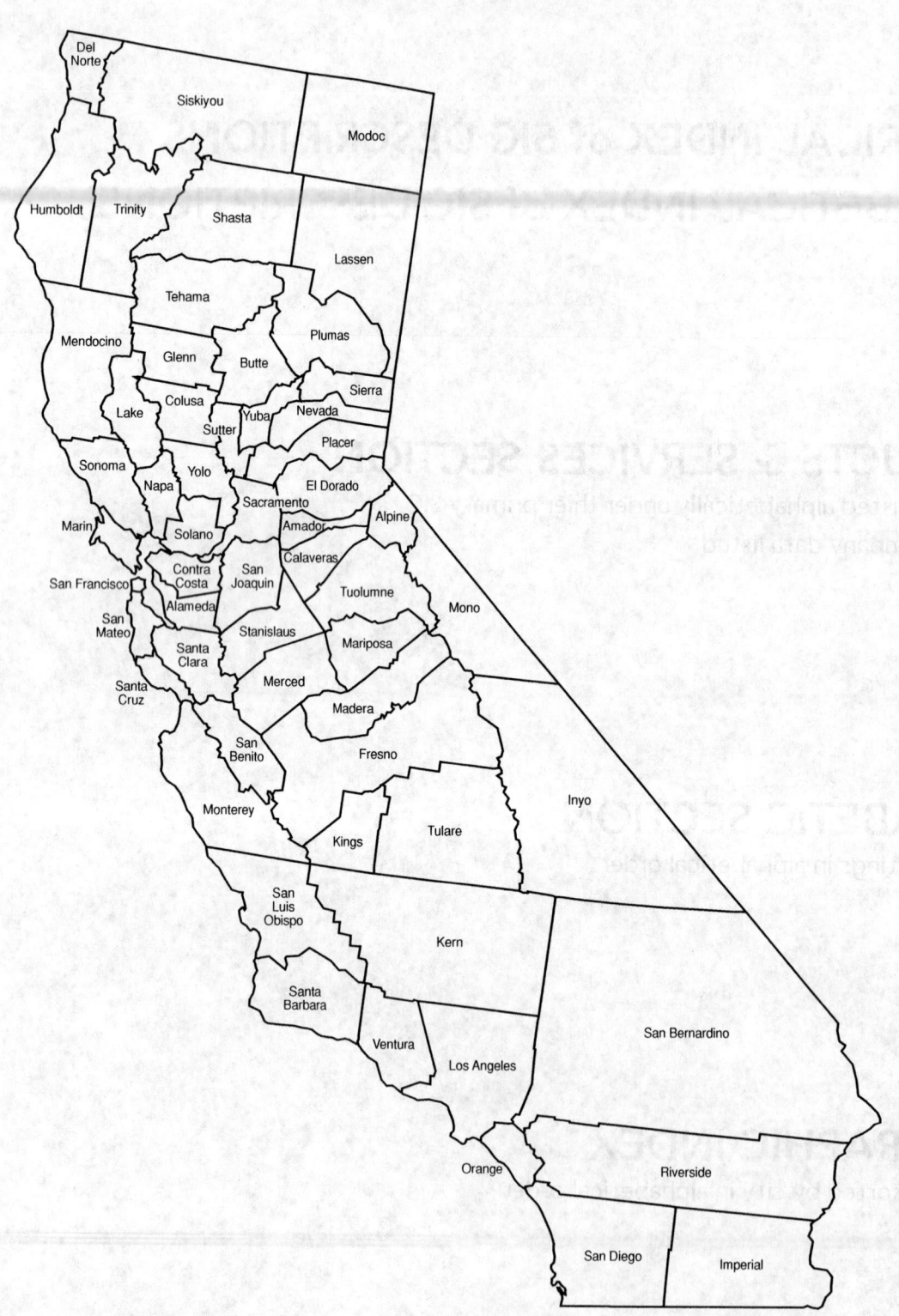

SIC INDEX

Standard Industrial Classification Numerical Index

SIC NO	PRODUCT

01 AGRICULTURAL PRODUCTION-CROPS

0111 Wheat
0112 Rice
0115 Corn
0131 Cotton
0134 Irish Potatoes
0139 Field Crops, Except Cash Grains, NEC
0161 Vegetables & Melons
0171 Berry Crops
0172 Grapes
0173 Tree Nuts
0174 Citrus Fruits
0175 Deciduous Tree Fruits
0179 Fruits & Tree Nuts, NEC
0181 Ornamental Floriculture & Nursery Prdts
0182 Food Crops Grown Under Cover
0191 Crop Farming, Misc

02 AGRICULTURAL PRODUCTION-LIVESTOCK AND ANIMAL SPECIALTIES

0211 Beef Cattle Feedlots
0212 Beef Cattle, Except Feedlots
0213 Hogs
0214 Sheep & Goats
0241 Dairy Farms
0252 Chicken Egg Farms
0253 Turkey & Turkey Egg Farms
0254 Poultry Hatcheries
0259 Poultry & Eggs Farms, NEC
0279 Animal Specialties, NEC
0291 Animal Production, NEC

07 AGRICULTURAL SERVICES

0711 Soil Preparation Svcs
0721 Soil Preparation, Planting & Cultivating Svc
0722 Crop Harvesting By Machine
0723 Crop Preparation, Except Cotton Ginning
0742 Veterinary Animal Specialties
0751 Livestock Svcs, Except Veterinary
0752 Animal Specialty Svcs, Exc Veterinary
0761 Farm Labor Contractors & Crew Leaders
0762 Farm Management Svcs
0781 Landscape Counseling & Planning
0782 Lawn & Garden Svcs
0783 Ornamental Shrub & Tree Svc

08 FORESTRY

0811 Timber Tracts
0851 Forestry Svcs

09 FISHING, HUNTING, AND TRAPPING

0971 Hunting & Trapping

10 METAL MINING

1041 Gold Ores

12 COAL MINING

1221 Bituminous Coal & Lignite: Surface Mining
1241 Coal Mining Svcs

13 OIL AND GAS EXTRACTION

1311 Crude Petroleum & Natural Gas
1381 Drilling Oil & Gas Wells
1382 Oil & Gas Field Exploration Svcs
1389 Oil & Gas Field Svcs, NEC

14 MINING AND QUARRYING OF NONMETALLIC MINERALS, EXCEPT FUELS

1422 Crushed & Broken Limestone
1423 Crushed & Broken Granite
1429 Crushed & Broken Stone, NEC
1442 Construction Sand & Gravel
1446 Industrial Sand
1479 Chemical & Fertilizer Mining
1481 Nonmetallic Minerals Svcs, Except Fuels
1499 Miscellaneous Nonmetallic Mining

15 BUILDING CONSTRUCTION-GENERAL CONTRACTORS AND OPERATIVE BUILDERS

1521 General Contractors, Single Family Houses
1522 General Contractors, Residential Other Than Single Family
1531 Operative Builders
1541 General Contractors, Indl Bldgs & Warehouses

1542 General Contractors, Nonresidential & Non-indl Bldgs

16 HEAVY CONSTRUCTION OTHER THAN BUILDING CONSTRUCTION-CONTRACTORS

1611 Highway & Street Construction
1622 Bridge, Tunnel & Elevated Hwy Construction
1623 Water, Sewer & Utility Line Construction
1629 Heavy Construction, NEC

17 CONSTRUCTION-SPECIAL TRADE CONTRACTORS

1711 Plumbing, Heating & Air Conditioning Contractors
1721 Painting & Paper Hanging Contractors
1731 Electrical Work
1741 Masonry & Other Stonework
1742 Plastering, Drywall, Acoustical & Insulation Work
1743 Terrazzo, Tile, Marble & Mosaic Work
1751 Carpentry Work
1752 Floor Laying & Other Floor Work, NEC
1761 Roofing, Siding & Sheet Metal Work
1771 Concrete Work
1781 Water Well Drilling
1791 Structural Steel Erection
1793 Glass & Glazing Work
1794 Excavating & Grading Work
1795 Wrecking & Demolition Work
1796 Installation Or Erection Of Bldg Eqpt & Machinery, NEC
1799 Special Trade Contractors, NEC

40 RAILROAD TRANSPORTATION

4011 Railroads, Line-Hauling Operations
4013 Switching & Terminal Svcs

41 LOCAL AND SUBURBAN TRANSIT AND INTERURBAN HIGHWAY PASSENGER TRANSPORTATION

4111 Local & Suburban Transit
4119 Local Passenger Transportation: NEC
4121 Taxi Cabs
4131 Intercity & Rural Bus Transportation
4141 Local Bus Charter Svc
4142 Bus Charter Service, Except Local
4151 School Buses
4173 Bus Terminal & Svc Facilities

42 MOTOR FREIGHT TRANSPORTATION AND WAREHOUSING

4212 Local Trucking Without Storage
4213 Trucking, Except Local
4214 Local Trucking With Storage
4215 Courier Svcs, Except Air
4221 Farm Product Warehousing & Storage
4222 Refrigerated Warehousing & Storage
4225 General Warehousing & Storage
4226 Special Warehousing & Storage, NEC
4231 Terminal & Joint Terminal Maint Facilities

44 WATER TRANSPORTATION

4412 Deep Sea Foreign Transportation Of Freight
4424 Deep Sea Domestic Transportation Of Freight
4449 Water Transportation Of Freight, NEC
4481 Deep Sea Transportation Of Passengers
4489 Water Transport Of Passengers, NEC
4491 Marine Cargo Handling
4492 Towing & Tugboat Svcs
4493 Marinas
4499 Water Transportation Svcs, NEC

45 TRANSPORTATION BY AIR

4512 Air Transportation, Scheduled
4513 Air Courier Svcs
4522 Air Transportation, Nonscheduled
4581 Airports, Flying Fields & Terminal Svcs

46 PIPELINES, EXCEPT NATURAL GAS

4613 Refined Petroleum Pipelines
4619 Pipelines, NEC

47 TRANSPORTATION SERVICES

4724 Travel Agencies
4725 Tour Operators
4729 Passenger Transportation Arrangement, NEC
4731 Freight Forwarding & Arrangement
4783 Packing & Crating Svcs
4785 Fixed Facilities, Inspection, Weighing Svcs Transptn
4789 Transportation Svcs, NEC

48 COMMUNICATIONS

4812 Radiotelephone Communications
4813 Telephone Communications, Except Radio
4822 Telegraph & Other Message Communications
4832 Radio Broadcasting Stations
4833 Television Broadcasting Stations
4841 Cable & Other Pay TV Svcs
4899 Communication Svcs, NEC

49 ELECTRIC, GAS, AND SANITARY SERVICES

4911 Electric Svcs
4922 Natural Gas Transmission
4923 Natural Gas Transmission & Distribution
4924 Natural Gas Distribution
4931 Electric & Other Svcs Combined
4932 Gas & Other Svcs Combined
4939 Combination Utilities, NEC
4941 Water Sply
4952 Sewerage Systems
4953 Refuse Systems
4959 Sanitary Svcs, NEC
4961 Steam & Air Conditioning Sply
4971 Irrigation Systems

50 WHOLESALE TRADE¨DURABLE GOODS

5012 Automobiles & Other Motor Vehicles Wholesale
5013 Motor Vehicle Splys & New Parts Wholesale
5014 Tires & Tubes Wholesale
5015 Motor Vehicle Parts, Used Wholesale
5021 Furniture Wholesale
5023 Home Furnishings Wholesale
5031 Lumber, Plywood & Millwork Wholesale
5032 Brick, Stone & Related Construction Mtrls Wholesale
5033 Roofing, Siding & Insulation Mtrls Wholesale
5039 Construction Materials, NEC Wholesale
5043 Photographic Eqpt & Splys Wholesale
5044 Office Eqpt Wholesale
5045 Computers & Peripheral Eqpt & Software Wholesale
5046 Commercial Eqpt, NEC Wholesale
5047 Medical, Dental & Hospital Eqpt & Splys Wholesale
5048 Ophthalmic Goods Wholesale
5049 Professional Eqpt & Splys, NEC Wholesale
5051 Metals Service Centers
5052 Coal & Other Minerals & Ores Wholesale
5063 Electrl Apparatus, Eqpt, Wiring Splys Wholesale
5064 Electrical Appliances, TV & Radios Wholesale
5065 Electronic Parts & Eqpt Wholesale
5072 Hardware Wholesale
5074 Plumbing & Heating Splys Wholesale
5075 Heating & Air Conditioning Eqpt & Splys Wholesale
5078 Refrigeration Eqpt & Splys Wholesale
5082 Construction & Mining Mach & Eqpt Wholesale
5083 Farm & Garden Mach & Eqpt Wholesale
5084 Industrial Mach & Eqpt Wholesale
5085 Industrial Splys Wholesale
5087 Service Establishment Eqpt & Splys Wholesale
5088 Transportation Eqpt & Splys, Except Motor Vehicles Wholesale
5091 Sporting & Recreational Goods & Splys Wholesale
5092 Toys & Hobby Goods & Splys Wholesale
5093 Scrap & Waste Materials Wholesale
5094 Jewelry, Watches, Precious Stones Wholesale
5099 Durable Goods: NEC Wholesale

51 WHOLESALE TRADE¨NONDURABLE GOODS

5111 Printing & Writing Paper Wholesale
5112 Stationery & Office Splys Wholesale
5113 Indl & Personal Svc Paper Wholesale
5122 Drugs, Drug Proprietaries & Sundries Wholesale
5131 Piece Goods, Notions & Dry Goods Wholesale
5136 Men's & Boys' Clothing & Furnishings Wholesale
5137 Women's, Children's & Infants Clothing Wholesale
5139 Footwear Wholesale
5141 Groceries, General Line Wholesale
5142 Packaged Frozen Foods Wholesale
5143 Dairy Prdts, Except Dried Or Canned Wholesale
5144 Poultry & Poultry Prdts Wholesale
5145 Confectionery Wholesale
5146 Fish & Seafood Wholesale
5147 Meats & Meat Prdts Wholesale
5148 Fresh Fruits & Vegetables Wholesale
5149 Groceries & Related Prdts, NEC Wholesale
5153 Grain & Field Beans Wholesale

SIC NO	PRODUCT

5154 Livestock Wholesale
5159 Farm-Prdt Raw Mtrls, NEC Wholesale
5162 Plastics Materials & Basic Shapes Wholesale
5169 Chemicals & Allied Prdts, NEC Wholesale
5171 Petroleum Bulk Stations & Terminals
5172 Petroleum & Petroleum Prdts Wholesale
5181 Beer & Ale Wholesale
5182 Wine & Distilled Alcoholic Beverages Wholesale
5191 Farm Splys Wholesale
5192 Books, Periodicals & Newspapers Wholesale
5193 Flowers, Nursery Stock & Florists' Splys Wholesale
5194 Tobacco & Tobacco Prdts Wholesale
5198 Paints, Varnishes & Splys Wholesale
5199 Nondurable Goods, NEC Wholesale

60 DEPOSITORY INSTITUTIONS

6011 Federal Reserve Banks
6021 National Commercial Banks
6022 State Commercial Banks
6029 Commercial Banks, NEC
6035 Federal Savings Institutions
6036 Savings Institutions, Except Federal
6061 Federal Credit Unions
6062 State Credit Unions
6081 Foreign Banks, Branches & Agencies
6082 Foreign Trade & Intl Banks
6091 Nondeposit Trust Facilities
6099 Functions Related To Deposit Banking, NEC

61 NONDEPOSITORY CREDIT INSTITUTIONS

6111 Federal Credit Agencies
6141 Personal Credit Institutions
6153 Credit Institutions, Short-Term Business
6159 Credit Institutions, Misc Business
6162 Mortgage Bankers & Loan Correspondents
6163 Loan Brokers

62 SECURITY AND COMMODITY BROKERS, DEALERS, EXCHANGES, AND SERVICES

6211 Security Brokers & Dealers
6221 Commodity Contracts Brokers & Dealers
6231 Security & Commodity Exchanges
6282 Investment Advice
6289 Security & Commodity Svcs, NEC

63 INSURANCE CARRIERS

6311 Life Insurance Carriers
6321 Accident & Health Insurance
6324 Hospital & Medical Svc Plans Carriers
6331 Fire, Marine & Casualty Insurance
6351 Surety Insurance Carriers
6361 Title Insurance
6371 Pension, Health & Welfare Funds
6399 Insurance Carriers, NEC

64 INSURANCE AGENTS, BROKERS, AND SERVICE

6411 Insurance Agents, Brokers & Svc

65 REAL ESTATE

6512 Operators Of Nonresidential Bldgs
6513 Operators Of Apartment Buildings
6514 Operators Of Dwellings, Except Apartments
6515 Operators of Residential Mobile Home Sites
6519 Lessors Of Real Estate, NEC
6531 Real Estate Agents & Managers
6541 Title Abstract Offices
6552 Land Subdividers & Developers
6553 Cemetery Subdividers & Developers

67 HOLDING AND OTHER INVESTMENT OFFICES

6712 Offices Of Bank Holding Co's
6719 Offices Of Holding Co's, NEC
6722 Management Investment Offices
6726 Unit Investment Trusts, Face-Amount Certificate Offices
6732 Education, Religious & Charitable Trusts
6733 Trusts Except Educational, Religious & Charitable
6794 Patent Owners & Lessors
6798 Real Estate Investment Trusts
6799 Investors, NEC

70 HOTELS, ROOMING HOUSES, CAMPS, AND OTHER LODGING PLACES

7011 Hotels, Motels & Tourist Courts

7021 Rooming & Boarding Houses
7032 Sporting & Recreational Camps
7033 Trailer Parks & Camp Sites
7041 Membership-Basis Hotels

72 PERSONAL SERVICES

7211 Power Laundries, Family & Commercial
7212 Garment Pressing & Cleaners' Agents
7213 Linen Sply
7215 Coin Operated Laundries & Cleaning
7216 Dry Cleaning Plants, Except Rug Cleaning
7217 Carpet & Upholstery Cleaning
7218 Industrial Launderers
7219 Laundry & Garment Svcs, NEC
7221 Photographic Studios, Portrait
7231 Beauty Shops
7241 Barber Shops
7251 Shoe Repair & Shoeshine Parlors
7261 Funeral Svcs & Crematories
7291 Tax Return Preparation Svcs
7299 Miscellaneous Personal Svcs, NEC

73 BUSINESS SERVICES

7311 Advertising Agencies
7312 Outdoor Advertising Svcs
7313 Radio, TV & Publishers Adv Reps
7319 Advertising, NEC
7322 Adjustment & Collection Svcs
7323 Credit Reporting Svcs
7331 Direct Mail Advertising Svcs
7334 Photocopying & Duplicating Svcs
7335 Commercial Photography
7336 Commercial Art & Graphic Design
7338 Secretarial & Court Reporting Svcs
7342 Disinfecting & Pest Control Svcs
7349 Building Cleaning & Maintenance Svcs, NEC
7352 Medical Eqpt Rental & Leasing
7353 Heavy Construction Eqpt Rental & Leasing
7359 Equipment Rental & Leasing, NEC
7361 Employment Agencies
7363 Help Supply Svcs
7371 Custom Computer Programming Svcs
7372 Prepackaged Software
7373 Computer Integrated Systems Design
7374 Data & Computer Processing & Preparation
7375 Information Retrieval Svcs
7376 Computer Facilities Management Svcs
7377 Computer Rental & Leasing
7378 Computer Maintenance & Repair
7379 Computer Related Svcs, NEC
7381 Detective & Armored Car Svcs
7382 Security Systems Svcs
7383 News Syndicates
7384 Photofinishing Labs
7389 Business Svcs, NEC

75 AUTOMOTIVE REPAIR, SERVICES, AND PARKING

7513 Truck Rental & Leasing, Without Drivers
7514 Passenger Car Rental
7515 Passenger Car Leasing
7519 Utility Trailers & Recreational Vehicle Rental
7521 Automobile Parking Lots & Garages
7532 Top, Body & Upholstery Repair & Paint Shops
7534 Tire Retreading & Repair Shops
7536 Automotive Glass Replacement Shops
7537 Automotive Transmission Repair Shops
7538 General Automotive Repair Shop
7539 Automotive Repair Shops, NEC
7542 Car Washes
7549 Automotive Svcs, Except Repair & Car Washes

76 MISCELLANEOUS REPAIR SERVICES

7622 Radio & TV Repair Shops
7623 Refrigeration & Air Conditioning Svc & Repair Shop
7629 Electrical & Elex Repair Shop, NEC
7631 Watch, Clock & Jewelry Repair
7641 Reupholstery & Furniture Repair
7692 Welding Repair
7699 Repair Shop & Related Svcs, NEC

78 MOTION PICTURES

7812 Motion Picture & Video Tape Production

7819 Services Allied To Motion Picture Prdtn
7822 Motion Picture & Video Tape Distribution
7829 Services Allied To Motion Picture Distribution
7832 Motion Picture Theaters, Except Drive-In
7833 Drive-In Motion Picture Theaters
7841 Video Tape Rental

79 AMUSEMENT AND RECREATION SERVICES

7911 Dance Studios, Schools & Halls
7922 Theatrical Producers & Misc Theatrical Svcs
7929 Bands, Orchestras, Actors & Entertainers
7933 Bowling Centers
7941 Professional Sports Clubs & Promoters
7948 Racing & Track Operations
7991 Physical Fitness Facilities
7992 Public Golf Courses
7993 Coin-Operated Amusement Devices & Arcades
7996 Amusement Parks
7997 Membership Sports & Recreation Clubs
7999 Amusement & Recreation Svcs, NEC

80 HEALTH SERVICES

8011 Offices & Clinics Of Doctors Of Medicine
8021 Offices & Clinics Of Dentists
8031 Offices & Clinics Of Doctors Of Osteopathy
8041 Offices & Clinics Of Chiropractors
8042 Offices & Clinics Of Optometrists
8049 Offices & Clinics Of Health Practitioners, NEC
8051 Skilled Nursing Facilities
8052 Intermediate Care Facilities
8059 Nursing & Personal Care Facilities, NEC
8062 General Medical & Surgical Hospitals
8063 Psychiatric Hospitals
8069 Specialty Hospitals, Except Psychiatric
8071 Medical Laboratories
8072 Dental Laboratories
8082 Home Health Care Svcs
8092 Kidney Dialysis Centers
8093 Specialty Outpatient Facilities, NEC
8099 Health & Allied Svcs, NEC

81 LEGAL SERVICES

8111 Legal Svcs

83 SOCIAL SERVICES

8322 Individual & Family Social Svcs
8331 Job Training & Vocational Rehabilitation Svcs
8351 Child Day Care Svcs
8361 Residential Care
8399 Social Services, NEC

84 MUSEUMS, ART GALLERIES, AND BOTANICAL AND ZOOLOGICAL GARDENS

8412 Museums & Art Galleries
8422 Arboreta, Botanical & Zoological Gardens

86 MEMBERSHIP ORGANIZATIONS

8611 Business Associations
8621 Professional Membership Organizations
8631 Labor Unions & Similar Organizations
8641 Civic, Social & Fraternal Associations
8651 Political Organizations
8699 Membership Organizations, NEC

87 ENGINEERING, ACCOUNTING, RESEARCH, MANAGEMENT, AND RELATED SERVICES

8711 Engineering Services
8712 Architectural Services
8713 Surveying Services
8721 Accounting, Auditing & Bookkeeping Svcs
8731 Commercial Physical & Biological Research
8732 Commercial Economic, Sociological & Educational Research
8733 Noncommercial Research Organizations
8734 Testing Laboratories
8741 Management Services
8742 Management Consulting Services
8743 Public Relations Svcs
8744 Facilities Support Mgmt Svcs
8748 Business Consulting Svcs, NEC

89 SERVICES, NOT ELSEWHERE CLASSIFIED

8999 Services Not Elsewhere Classified

SIC INDEX

Standard Industrial Classification Alphabetical Index

SIC NO	PRODUCT

A

6321 Accident & Health Insurance
8721 Accounting, Auditing & Bookkeeping Svcs
7322 Adjustment & Collection Svcs
7311 Advertising Agencies
7319 Advertising, NEC
4513 Air Courier Svcs
4522 Air Transportation, Nonscheduled
4512 Air Transportation, Scheduled
4581 Airports, Flying Fields & Terminal Svcs
7999 Amusement & Recreation Svcs, NEC
7996 Amusement Parks
0291 Animal Production, NEC
0279 Animal Specialties, NEC
0752 Animal Specialty Svcs, Exc Veterinary
8422 Arboreta, Botanical & Zoological Gardens
8712 Architectural Services
7521 Automobile Parking Lots & Garages
5012 Automobiles & Other Motor Vehicles Wholesale
7536 Automotive Glass Replacement Shops
7539 Automotive Repair Shops, NEC
7549 Automotive Svcs, Except Repair & Car Washes
7537 Automotive Transmission Repair Shops

B

7929 Bands, Orchestras, Actors & Entertainers
7241 Barber Shops
7231 Beauty Shops
0211 Beef Cattle Feedlots
0212 Beef Cattle, Except Feedlots
5181 Beer & Ale Wholesale
0171 Berry Crops
1221 Bituminous Coal & Lignite: Surface Mining
5192 Books, Periodicals & Newspapers Wholesale
7933 Bowling Centers
5032 Brick, Stone & Related Construction Mtrls Wholesale
1622 Bridge, Tunnel & Elevated Hwy Construction
7349 Building Cleaning & Maintenance Svcs, NEC
4142 Bus Charter Service, Except Local
4173 Bus Terminal & Svc Facilities
8611 Business Associations
8748 Business Consulting Svcs, NEC
7389 Business Svcs, NEC

C

4841 Cable & Other Pay TV Svcs
7542 Car Washes
1751 Carpentry Work
7217 Carpet & Upholstery Cleaning
6553 Cemetery Subdividers & Developers
1479 Chemical & Fertilizer Mining
5169 Chemicals & Allied Prdts, NEC Wholesale
0252 Chicken Egg Farms
8351 Child Day Care Svcs
0174 Citrus Fruits
8641 Civic, Social & Fraternal Associations
5052 Coal & Other Minerals & Ores Wholesale
1241 Coal Mining Svcs
7215 Coin Operated Laundries & Cleaning
7993 Coin-Operated Amusement Devices & Arcades
4939 Combination Utilities, NEC
7336 Commercial Art & Graphic Design
6029 Commercial Banks, NEC
8732 Commercial Economic, Sociological & Educational Research
5046 Commercial Eqpt, NEC Wholesale
7335 Commercial Photography
8731 Commercial Physical & Biological Research
6221 Commodity Contracts Brokers & Dealers
4899 Communication Svcs, NEC
7376 Computer Facilities Management Svcs
7373 Computer Integrated Systems Design
7378 Computer Maintenance & Repair
7379 Computer Related Svcs, NEC
7377 Computer Rental & Leasing
5045 Computers & Peripheral Eqpt & Software Wholesale
1771 Concrete Work
5145 Confectionery Wholesale
5082 Construction & Mining Mach & Eqpt Wholesale
5039 Construction Materials, NEC Wholesale
1442 Construction Sand & Gravel
0115 Corn
0131 Cotton

4215 Courier Svcs, Except Air
6159 Credit Institutions, Misc Business
6153 Credit Institutions, Short-Term Business
7323 Credit Reporting Svcs
0191 Crop Farming, Misc
0722 Crop Harvesting By Machine
0723 Crop Preparation, Except Cotton Ginning
1311 Crude Petroleum & Natural Gas
1423 Crushed & Broken Granite
1422 Crushed & Broken Limestone
1429 Crushed & Broken Stone, NEC
7371 Custom Computer Programming Svcs

D

0241 Dairy Farms
5143 Dairy Prdts, Except Dried Or Canned Wholesale
7911 Dance Studios, Schools & Halls
7374 Data & Computer Processing & Preparation
0175 Deciduous Tree Fruits
4424 Deep Sea Domestic Transportation Of Freight
4412 Deep Sea Foreign Transportation Of Freight
4481 Deep Sea Transportation Of Passengers
8072 Dental Laboratories
7381 Detective & Armored Car Svcs
7331 Direct Mail Advertising Svcs
7342 Disinfecting & Pest Control Svcs
1381 Drilling Oil & Gas Wells
7833 Drive-In Motion Picture Theaters
5122 Drugs, Drug Proprietaries & Sundries Wholesale
7216 Dry Cleaning Plants, Except Rug Cleaning
5099 Durable Goods: NEC Wholesale

E

6732 Education, Religious & Charitable Trusts
4931 Electric & Other Svcs Combined
4911 Electric Svcs
7629 Electrical & Elex Repair Shop, NEC
5064 Electrical Appliances, TV & Radios Wholesale
1731 Electrical Work
5063 Electrl Apparatus, Eqpt, Wiring Splys Wholesale
5065 Electronic Parts & Eqpt Wholesale
7361 Employment Agencies
8711 Engineering Services
7359 Equipment Rental & Leasing, NEC
1794 Excavating & Grading Work

F

8744 Facilities Support Mgmt Svcs
5083 Farm & Garden Mach & Eqpt Wholesale
0761 Farm Labor Contractors & Crew Leaders
0762 Farm Management Svcs
4221 Farm Product Warehousing & Storage
5191 Farm Splys Wholesale
5159 Farm-Prdt Raw Mtrls, NEC Wholesale
6111 Federal Credit Agencies
6061 Federal Credit Unions
6011 Federal Reserve Banks
6035 Federal Savings Institutions
0139 Field Crops, Except Cash Grains, NEC
6331 Fire, Marine & Casualty Insurance
5146 Fish & Seafood Wholesale
4785 Fixed Facilities, Inspection, Weighing Svcs Transptn
1752 Floor Laying & Other Floor Work, NEC
5193 Flowers, Nursery Stock & Florists' Splys Wholesale
0182 Food Crops Grown Under Cover
5139 Footwear Wholesale
6081 Foreign Banks, Branches & Agencies
6082 Foreign Trade & Intl Banks
0851 Forestry Svcs
4731 Freight Forwarding & Arrangement
5148 Fresh Fruits & Vegetables Wholesale
0179 Fruits & Tree Nuts, NEC
6099 Functions Related To Deposit Banking, NEC
7261 Funeral Svcs & Crematories
5021 Furniture Wholesale

G

7212 Garment Pressing & Cleaners' Agents
4932 Gas & Other Svcs Combined
7538 General Automotive Repair Shop
1541 General Contractors, Indl Bldgs & Warehouses
1542 General Contractors, Nonresidential & Non-indl Bldgs
1522 General Contractors, Residential Other Than Single Family

1521 General Contractors, Single Family Houses
8062 General Medical & Surgical Hospitals
4225 General Warehousing & Storage
1793 Glass & Glazing Work
1041 Gold Ores
5153 Grain & Field Beans Wholesale
0172 Grapes
5149 Groceries & Related Prdts, NEC Wholesale
5141 Groceries, General Line Wholesale

H

5072 Hardware Wholesale
8099 Health & Allied Svcs, NEC
5075 Heating & Air Conditioning Eqpt & Splys Wholesale
7353 Heavy Construction Eqpt Rental & Leasing
1629 Heavy Construction, NEC
7363 Help Supply Svcs
1611 Highway & Street Construction
0213 Hogs
5023 Home Furnishings Wholesale
8082 Home Health Care Svcs
6324 Hospital & Medical Svc Plans Carriers
7011 Hotels, Motels & Tourist Courts
0971 Hunting & Trapping

I

8322 Individual & Family Social Svcs
5113 Indl & Personal Svc Paper Wholesale
7218 Industrial Launderers
5084 Industrial Mach & Eqpt Wholesale
1446 Industrial Sand
5085 Industrial Splys Wholesale
7375 Information Retrieval Svcs
1796 Installation Or Erection Of Bldg Eqpt & Machinery, NEC
6411 Insurance Agents, Brokers & Svc
6399 Insurance Carriers, NEC
4131 Intercity & Rural Bus Transportation
8052 Intermediate Care Facilities
6282 Investment Advice
6799 Investors, NEC
0134 Irish Potatoes
4971 Irrigation Systems

J

5094 Jewelry, Watches, Precious Stones Wholesale
8331 Job Training & Vocational Rehabilitation Svcs

K

8092 Kidney Dialysis Centers

L

8631 Labor Unions & Similar Organizations
6552 Land Subdividers & Developers
0781 Landscape Counseling & Planning
7219 Laundry & Garment Svcs, NEC
0782 Lawn & Garden Svcs
8111 Legal Svcs
6519 Lessors Of Real Estate, NEC
6311 Life Insurance Carriers
7213 Linen Sply
0751 Livestock Svcs, Except Veterinary
5154 Livestock Wholesale
6163 Loan Brokers
4111 Local & Suburban Transit
4141 Local Bus Charter Svc
4119 Local Passenger Transportation: NEC
4214 Local Trucking With Storage
4212 Local Trucking Without Storage
5031 Lumber, Plywood & Millwork Wholesale

M

8742 Management Consulting Services
6722 Management Investment Offices
8741 Management Services
4493 Marinas
4491 Marine Cargo Handling
1741 Masonry & Other Stonework
5147 Meats & Meat Prdts Wholesale
7352 Medical Eqpt Rental & Leasing
8071 Medical Laboratories
5047 Medical, Dental & Hospital Eqpt & Splys Wholesale
8699 Membership Organizations, NEC
7997 Membership Sports & Recreation Clubs
7041 Membership-Basis Hotels
5136 Men's & Boys' Clothing & Furnishings Wholesale

S I C

PRODUCTS & SERVICES SECTION

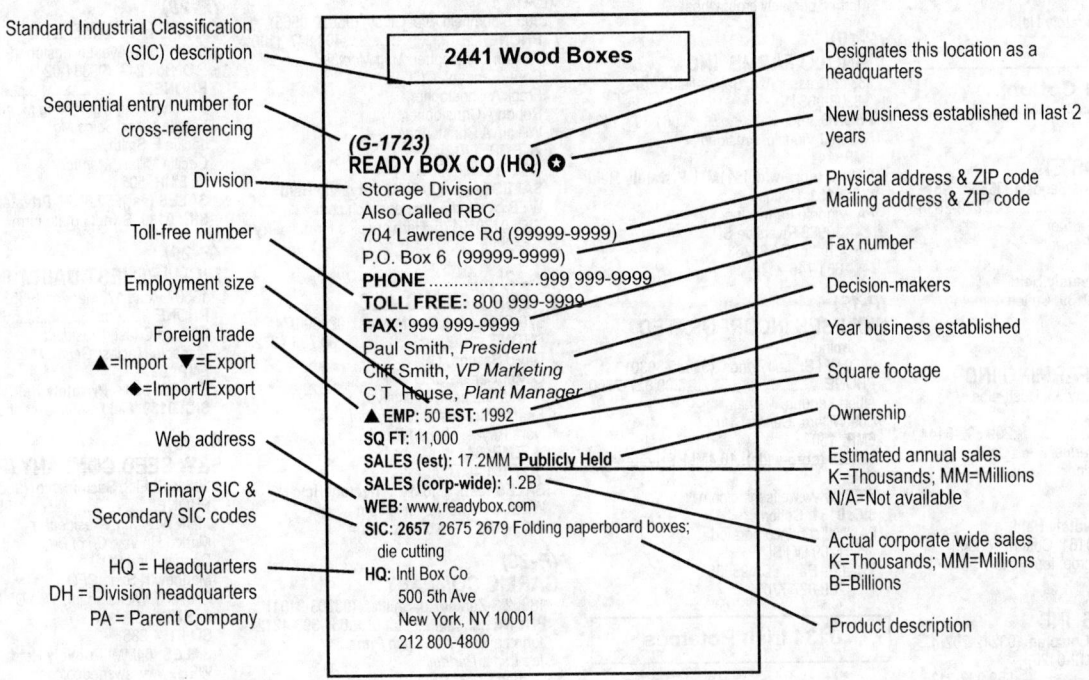

2441 Wood Boxes

Standard Industrial Classification (SIC) description

Sequential entry number for cross-referencing

Division

Toll-free number

Employment size

Foreign trade
▲=Import ▼=Export
◆=Import/Export

Web address

Primary SIC & Secondary SIC codes

HQ = Headquarters
DH = Division headquarters
PA = Parent Company

Designates this location as a headquarters

New business established in last 2 years

Physical address & ZIP code
Mailing address & ZIP code

Fax number

Decision-makers

Year business established

Square footage

Ownership

Estimated annual sales
K=Thousands; MM=Millions
N/A=Not available

Actual corporate wide sales
K=Thousands; MM=Millions
B=Billions

Product description

(G-1723)
READY BOX CO (HQ) ✪
Storage Division
Also Called RBC
704 Lawrence Rd (99999-9999)
P.O. Box 6 (99999-9999)
PHONE 999 999-9999
TOLL FREE: 800 999-9999
FAX: 999 999-9999
Paul Smith, *President*
Cliff Smith, *VP Marketing*
C T House, *Plant Manager*
▲ **EMP:** 50 **EST:** 1992
SQ FT: 11,000
SALES (est): 17.2MM **Publicly Held**
SALES (corp-wide): 1.2B
WEB: www.readybox.com
SIC: 2657 2675 2679 Folding paperboard boxes; die cutting
HQ: Intl Box Co
500 5th Ave
New York, NY 10001
212 800-4800

- Companies in this section are listed numerically under their primary SIC Companies are in alphabetical order under each code.
- A numerical and alphabetcal index precedes this section.
- **Sequential Entry Numbers.** Each establishment in this section is numbered sequentially. The number assigned to each establishment's Entry Number. To make cross-referencing easier, each listing in the Product's & Services, Alphabetic and Geographical Section includes the establishment's entry number. To facilitate locating an entry in this section, the entry numbers for the first listing on the left page and the last listing on the right page are printed at the top of the page next to the Standard Industrial Classification (SIC) description.
- Further information can be found in the Explanatory Notes starting on page 5.
- See the footnotes for symbols and abbreviations.

IMPORTANT NOTICE: It is a violation of both federal and state law to transmit an unsolicited advertisement to a facsimile machine. Any user of this product that violates such laws may be subject to civil and criminal penalties which may exceed $500 for each transmission of an unsolicited facsimile. Harris InfoSource provides fax numbers for lawful purposes only and expressly forbids the use of these numbers in any unlawful manner.

0111 Wheat

(P-1)
B E GIOVANNETTI & SONS (PA)
Also Called: Half Moon Fruity and Prod Co
403 Court St, Woodland (95695-3421)
PHONE 530 662-1729
Blaise E Giovannetti, *Partner*
John B Giovannetti, *Partner*
Ronald Giovannetti, *Partner*
EMP: 50 EST: 1979
SQ FT: 3,000
SALES (est): 4.3MM **Privately Held**
SIC: **0111** 0112 0131 0139 Wheat; rice; cotton; alfalfa farm; vegetables & melons; melon farms; lettuce & leaf vegetable farms; walnut grove

(P-2)
MULLER RANCH LLC
15810 County Road 95, Woodland (95695-9222)
PHONE 530 662-0105
Frank Muller, *Partner*
Thomas Muller, *Partner*
EMP: 85
SALES (est): 12.3MM **Privately Held**
WEB: www.joemuller.com
SIC: **0111** 0115 0161 Wheat; corn; tomato farm

(P-3)
T & P FARMS
1241 Putnam Way, Arbuckle (95912)
P.O. Box 83 (95912-0083)
PHONE 530 476-3038
Perry Charter, *Partner*
Tom Charter, *Partner*
Shelby Nation, *Bookkeeper*
EMP: 100
SALES (est): 16.8MM **Privately Held**
SIC: **0111** 0112 0181 0161 Wheat; rice; seeds, vegetable: growing of; tomato farm; general farms, primarily crop; food crops grown under cover

---

0112 Rice

(P-4)
CATTAIL FARMS INC
3970 Cr95b, Knights Landing (95645)
P.O. Box 1024 (95645-1024)
PHONE 916 207-6580
Sawyer Y Monckton, *CEO*
EMP: 99
SALES: 35K **Privately Held**
SIC: **0112** Rice

(P-5)
HALF MOON FRUIT & PRODUCE CO (PA)
Also Called: Giovannetti Equipment Sales
403 Court St, Woodland (95695-3421)
PHONE 530 662-1727
John B Giovannetti, *President*
Harold Dickerson, *Corp Secy*
Ronald Giovannetti, *Vice Pres*
EMP: 74
SQ FT: 60,000
SALES (est): 5.6MM **Privately Held**
SIC: **0112** 0131 0111 0119 Rice; cotton; wheat; barley farm; alfalfa farm; lettuce farm

(P-6)
MCFADDEN FARM
16000 Powerhouse Rd, Potter Valley (95469-8771)
PHONE 707 743-1122
Eugene McFadden, *Owner*
Andrea Caldwell, *Manager*
Luke Miller, *Manager*
EMP: 50
SQ FT: 1,000
SALES: 1.5MM **Privately Held**
WEB: www.mcfaddenfarm.com
SIC: **0112** 0172 0139 2099 Rice; grapes; herb or spice farm; food preparations

(P-7)
SUN WEST WILD RICE FACILITY
Vance Ave, Biggs (95917)
P.O. Box 305 (95917-0305)
PHONE 530 868-5188
Ralph Velasquez, *Manager*
EMP: 50
SALES (est): 1.1MM **Privately Held**
SIC: **0112** Rice

0115 Corn

(P-8)
JOE HEIDRICK ENTERPRISES INC
36826 County Road 24, Woodland (95695-9355)
PHONE 530 662-2339
Joe Heidrick, *President*
EMP: 50
SQ FT: 1,500
SALES (est): 6.4MM **Privately Held**
SIC: **0115** 0111 0161 0139 Corn; wheat; tomato farm; alfalfa farm

(P-9)
SIMONI & MASSONI FARMS
2510 Taylor Ln, Byron (94514)
P.O. Box 399 (94514-0399)
PHONE 925 634-2304

Diane Simoni, *Partner*
Anthony Massoni, *Partner*
Paul Simoni, *Partner*
EMP: 50
SALES: 5MM **Privately Held**
SIC: 0115 Corn

0131 Cotton

(P-10)
AL BARCELLOS ET
17599 Ward Rd, Los Banos (93635-9595)
PHONE..................209 826-2636
Aaron Barcellos, *Partner*
Arnold Barcellos, *Partner*
EMP: 50
SALES: 2MM **Privately Held**
SIC: 0131 0161 0139 Cotton; tomato farm; alfalfa farm

(P-11)
CLARK BROS FARMING INC
19772 State Highway 33, Dos Palos (93620-9621)
PHONE..................209 392-6144
Norman L Clark, *Partner*
Allan W Clark, *Partner*
EMP: 50
SQ FT: 5,000
SALES: 8MM **Privately Held**
SIC: 0131 0191 0161 Cotton; general farms, primarily crop; tomato farm

(P-12)
GILKEY FARMS INC
2411 Whitley Ave, Corcoran (93212-2025)
P.O. Box 426 (93212-0426)
PHONE..................559 992-2136
Donald Gilkey, *President*
Brent Gilkey, *Vice Pres*
Kirk Gilkey, *Vice Pres*
Matt Gilkey, *Vice Pres*
Ralph Gilkey Jr, *Vice Pres*
EMP: 60
SQ FT: 4,500
SALES (est): 5.1MM **Privately Held**
SIC: 0131 0139 0111 0119 Cotton; alfalfa farm; hay farm; wheat; safflower farm

(P-13)
J G BOSWELL COMPANY
21101 Bear Mountain Blvd, Bakersfield (93311-9412)
P.O. Box 9759 (93389-9759)
PHONE..................661 327-7721
Dave Cosyns, *Manager*
EMP: 200
SALES (corp-wide): 540.4MM **Privately Held**
SIC: 0131 0111 0724 Cotton; wheat; cotton ginning
PA: J. G. Boswell Company
101 W Walnut St
Pasadena CA 91103
626 583-3000

(P-14)
J G BOSWELL COMPANY
Also Called: Ranching Shop
28001 S Dairy Ave, Corcoran (93212)
P.O. Box 877 (93212-0877)
PHONE..................559 992-5141
Paul Athorp, *Branch Mgr*
Vern Mullins, *Purch Agent*
Hugh Bello, *Manager*
EMP: 500
SALES (corp-wide): 540.4MM **Privately Held**
SIC: 0131 0724 0182 Cotton; cotton ginning; food crops grown under cover
PA: J. G. Boswell Company
101 W Walnut St
Pasadena CA 91103
626 583-3000

(P-15)
STONE LAND COMPANY (PA)
Also Called: Stone Ranch
28521 Nevada Ave, Stratford (93266)
PHONE..................559 947-3185
Jack G Stone, *President*
Sally Moreno, *Corp Secy*
William Stone, *Vice Pres*
▲ **EMP:** 100
SQ FT: 2,000

SALES: 1MM **Privately Held**
WEB: www.jgslc.com
SIC: 0131 0191 0111 Cotton; general farms, primarily crop; wheat

(P-16)
VIGNOLO FARMS INC
33342 Dresser Ave, Bakersfield (93308-9634)
PHONE..................661 393-1431
Robert J Vignolo, *President*
EMP: 141
SALES (corp-wide): 11MM **Privately Held**
SIC: 0131 Cotton
PA: Vignolo Farms, Inc.
30988 Riverside St
Shafter CA 93263
661 746-2148

(P-17)
WOLFSEN INCORPORATED
Sjr Farming
1269 W I St, Los Banos (93635-3930)
PHONE..................209 827-7700
Albert Laguna, *Manager*
Don Willard, *General Mgr*
EMP: 150
SALES (corp-wide): 16.4MM **Privately Held**
WEB: www.wolfseninc.com
SIC: 0131 Cotton
PA: Wolfsen Incorporated
1269 W I St
Los Banos CA 93635
209 827-7700

0134 Irish Potatoes

(P-18)
GIUMARRA FARMS INC
11220 Edison Hwy, Edison (93220)
PHONE..................661 395-7000
Salvadore Giumarra, *President*
EMP: 100
SQ FT: 15,000
SALES (est): 7MM **Privately Held**
SIC: 0134 0174 0161 0175 Irish potatoes; orange grove; carrot farm; plum orchard

(P-19)
JOHNSTON FARMS
13031 E Packinghouse Rd, Edison (93220)
PHONE..................661 366-3201
Tari Johnston, *Principal*
Terry Henderson, *Principal*
Dennis B Johnston, *Principal*
Gerald Johnston, *Principal*
Kevin Johnston, *Principal*
▲ **EMP:** 65 **EST:** 1953
SQ FT: 100,000
SALES (est): 7.9MM **Privately Held**
WEB: www.johnstonfarms.com
SIC: 0134 0174 Irish potatoes; orange grove

0139 Field Crops, Except Cash Grains, NEC

(P-20)
AMERICAN FARMS LLC
1107 Harkins Rd, Salinas (93901-4435)
P.O. Box 599 (93902-0599)
PHONE..................831 424-1815
David Gill,
Steven Gill,
EMP: 100
SQ FT: 3,000
SALES (est): 23.9MM
SALES (corp-wide): 26.6MM **Privately Held**
WEB: www.americanfarms.net
SIC: 0139 0161 Feeder crops; lettuce farm
PA: Mesa Packing Llc
510 Broadway St
King City CA 93930
831 385-9173

(P-21)
CHRISTOPHER RANCH LLC (PA)
305 Bloomfield Ave, Gilroy (95020-9565)
PHONE..................408 847-1100
William Christopher, *Mng Member*
Corey Tennant, *CIO*
Frank A Christopher,
Robert A Christopher,
William A Christopher,
▲ **EMP:** 170
SQ FT: 220,000
SALES (est): 103.5MM **Privately Held**
WEB: www.christopher-ranch.com
SIC: 0139 0175 Herb or spice farm; cherry orchard

(P-22)
FRESH ORIGINS LLC
570 Quarry Rd, San Marcos (92069-9744)
PHONE..................760 736-4072
David Sasuga, *CPA*
Olivier Canler, *CFO*
Norma Stamant, *Executive*
Sharon McIntosh, *Accountant*
Nora Reyes, *Human Res Mgr*
▲ **EMP:** 344
SQ FT: 1,400,000
SALES (est): 11.6MM **Privately Held**
WEB: www.freshorigins.com
SIC: 0139 Herb or spice farm

(P-23)
GARLIC COMPANY
18602 S Zerker Rd, Shafter (93263-9101)
PHONE..................661 393-4212
John Layous, *Managing Prtnr*
Joe Lane, *Partner*
Gordan Cook, *CFO*
Anthony Kelly, *Human Res Mgr*
John Merkle, *Plant Mgr*
▲ **EMP:** 125
SQ FT: 150,000
SALES (est): 53.8MM **Privately Held**
WEB: www.thegarliccompany.com
SIC: 0139 2099 0191 Herb or spice farm; food preparations; general farms, primarily crop

(P-24)
GENE M ACCITO
331 Pelican Pl, Yuba City (95993-7100)
P.O. Box 3322 (95992-3322)
PHONE..................530 674-3179
Gene M Accito, *Owner*
EMP: 80
SALES (est): 1.5MM **Privately Held**
SIC: 0139 Food crops

(P-25)
HAYDAY FARMS INC
15500 S Commercial St, Blythe (92225-2750)
P.O. Box 1226 (92226-1226)
PHONE..................760 922-4713
Atsuya Ichida, *President*
Dale Tyson, *Vice Pres*
◆ **EMP:** 75
SQ FT: 2,160
SALES: 17.4MM **Privately Held**
SIC: 0139 0722 0723 Hay farm; hay, machine harvesting services; field crops, except cash grains, market preparation services

(P-26)
HERB THYME FARM INC
7909 Crossway Dr, Pico Rivera (90660-4449)
PHONE..................603 542-3690
Mary Lord, *Principal*
EMP: 70
SALES (est): 1.2MM **Privately Held**
SIC: 0139

(P-27)
JOHNSON & JOHNSON PISTACCIOS
Also Called: Johnson/Johnson
1720 Ben Lomond Dr, Glendale (91202-1006)
PHONE..................818 242-7853
Lee Johnson, *President*
EMP: 50

SALES (est): 1.2MM **Privately Held**
SIC: 0139 Peanut farm

(P-28)
QUAIL H FARMS LLC
5301 Robin Ave, Livingston (95334-9317)
P.O. Box 247 (95334-0247)
PHONE..................209 394-8001
J Michael Hennigan, *Mng Member*
Larelle Miller, *Sales Mgr*
Jackie E Smith,
Cecilia Millan, *Manager*
▼ **EMP:** 505
SALES (est): 52.8MM **Privately Held**
SIC: 0139 Sweet potato farm

(P-29)
RICHARD IEST DAIRY INC
13507 Road 17, Madera (93637-9040)
PHONE..................559 673-2635
Richard C Iest, *President*
Marisela Macias, *General Mgr*
EMP: 99
SALES: 950K **Privately Held**
SIC: 0139 Field crops, except cash grain

(P-30)
S&W SEED COMPANY (PA)
106 K St Fl 3, Sacramento (95814-3218)
PHONE..................559 884-2535
Mark W Wong, *President*
Mark J Harvey, *Ch of Bd*
Dennis Jury, *COO*
Matthew K Szot, *CFO*
Grover T Wickersham, *Vice Ch Bd*
◆ **EMP:** 50
SQ FT: 4,885
SALES: 64MM **Publicly Held**
WEB: www.swseedco.com
SIC: 0139 0723 Alfalfa farm; seed cleaning

(P-31)
YAGI BROS INC
Also Called: Yagi Bros Produce
5614 Lincoln Blvd, Livingston (95334-9642)
P.O. Box 515 (95334-0515)
PHONE..................209 394-7311
Blaine Yagi, *President*
Ben Yagi, *Vice Pres*
George Yagi, *Admin Sec*
Duane Hutton, *Manager*
EMP: 55
SQ FT: 31,000
SALES: 1.5MM **Privately Held**
WEB: www.yagibros.com
SIC: 0139 Sweet potato farm

0161 Vegetables & Melons

(P-32)
ABE-EL PRODUCE
42143 Road 120, Orosi (93647-9714)
PHONE..................559 528-3030
Franklin Abe, *Partner*
Herbert Abe, *Partner*
EMP: 350 **EST:** 1964
SALES (est): 7MM **Privately Held**
SIC: 0161 0174 Vegetables & melons; citrus fruits

(P-33)
ACE TOMATO COMPANY INC
777 N Pershing Ave Ste 1a, Stockton (95203-2153)
PHONE..................209 982-0734
Kathleen Lagorio Janssen, *CEO*
Tom McMillen, *CFO*
Dean Janssen, *Corp Secy*
Henry K Cole, *Vice Pres*
EMP: 60
SQ FT: 300,000
SALES (est): 4.2MM **Privately Held**
SIC: 0161 0723 Tomato farm; vegetable packing services

(P-34)
BALLETTO RANCH INC (PA)
5700 Occidental Rd, Santa Rosa (95401-5533)
P.O. Box 2579, Sebastopol (95473-2579)
PHONE..................707 568-2455
John Balletto, *President*

Monica Hunter, *Advt Staff*
▲ EMP: 70
SALES (est): 9.8MM **Privately Held**
WEB: www.ballettoranch.com
SIC: 0161 Lettuce farm; squash farm

(P-35)
BALOIAN PACKING CO INC (PA)
Also Called: Baloian Farm
446 N Blythe Ave, Fresno (93706-1003)
P.O. Box 11337 (93772-1337)
PHONE..................559 485-9200
Edward Baloian, *Ch of Bd*
Timothy Baloian, *President*
Yosh Kamine, *General Mgr*
Emily Baloian, *Admin Sec*
Eric Gilmore, *QC Mgr*
▲ EMP: 59
SQ FT: 35,000
SALES (est): 26.9MM **Privately Held**
WEB: www.baloianpacking.com
SIC: 0161 0723 Broccoli farm; pepper farm, sweet & hot (vegetables); cucumber farm; squash farm; vegetable packing services

(P-36)
BALOIAN PACKING CO INC
Also Called: Baloian Farms
3138 W Whites Bridge Ave, Fresno (93706-1125)
PHONE..................559 441-7043
Glen Yemoto, *Branch Mgr*
Maria Guzman, *Clerk*
EMP: 91
SALES (corp-wide): 26.9MM **Privately Held**
SIC: 0161 0723 Broccoli farm; pepper farm, sweet & hot (vegetables); cucumber farm; squash farm; vegetable packing services
PA: Baloian Packing Co., Inc.
446 N Blythe Ave
Fresno CA 93706
559 485-9200

(P-37)
BLACK DOG FARMS OF CALIFORNIA
530 W 6th St, Holtville (92250-1023)
P.O. Box 57 (92250-0057)
PHONE..................760 356-2951
Kenneth Peterson, *President*
Dora Saikhon, *Shareholder*
Carol Saikhon, *Vice Pres*
Carmen Lizaola, *Human Res Dir*
EMP: 150
SQ FT: 4,000
SALES (est): 15.3MM **Privately Held**
WEB: www.blackdogfarms.com
SIC: 0161 Vegetables & melons

(P-38)
BOLTHOUSE FARMS
3200 E Brundage Ln, Bakersfield (93304)
PHONE..................661 366-7205
William Bolthouse, *Owner*
◆ EMP: 2300
SALES (est): 25.7MM
SALES (corp-wide): 8.6B **Publicly Held**
SIC: 0161 Carrot farm
HQ: Wm. Bolthouse Farms, Inc.
7200 E Brundage Ln
Bakersfield CA 93307
661 366-7209

(P-39)
BOSKOVICH FARMS INC
4224 Pleasant Valley Rd, Camarillo (93012-8533)
P.O. Box 1352, Oxnard (93032-1352)
PHONE..................805 987-1443
Ken Mumford, *Opers Staff*
Yolanda Erazo, *Receptionist*
EMP: 300
SALES (corp-wide): 76.9MM **Privately Held**
WEB: www.boskovichfarms.com
SIC: 0161 0115 Vegetables & melons; corn
PA: Boskovich Farms, Inc.
711 Diaz Ave
Oxnard CA 93030
805 487-2299

(P-40)
C & G FARMS INC
Also Called: AMARAL RANCHES
25453 Iverson Rd, Chualar (93925)
P.O. Box 2216, Gonzales (93926-2216)
PHONE..................831 679-2978
Carlos Amaral, *President*
George Amaral, *Admin Sec*
▼ EMP: 200 EST: 1996
SQ FT: 2,000
SALES (est): 44.7MM **Privately Held**
WEB: www.cgfarms.com
SIC: 0161 Lettuce & leaf vegetable farms; broccoli farm; cabbage farm

(P-41)
CALIFORNIA WATERCRESS INC (PA)
550 E Telegraph Rd, Fillmore (93015-9667)
P.O. Box 874 (93016-0874)
PHONE..................805 524-4808
Alfred C Beserra, *President*
Teresa Beserra, *Admin Sec*
EMP: 65
SQ FT: 1,000
SALES (est): 5MM **Privately Held**
SIC: 0161 Vegetables & melons

(P-42)
CERUTTI BROS INC
26118 Mcclintock Rd, Newman (95360-9746)
P.O. Box 550 (95360-0550)
PHONE..................209 862-2249
Patrick Cerutti, *CEO*
EMP: 60
SALES (est): 950K **Privately Held**
SIC: 0161 Vegetables & melons

(P-43)
CHRISTENSEN & GIANNINI LLC
1588 Moffett St Ste B, Salinas (93905-3365)
PHONE..................831 449-2494
Sam Daoro,
Shelley Daroro, *Partner*
Dirk Giannini, *Partner*
Lori Giannini, *Partner*
Renea Wood, *Controller*
EMP: 54
SALES (est): 6.9MM **Privately Held**
SIC: 0161 Vegetables & melons

(P-44)
COAST FARMS INC
645 Laguna Rd, Camarillo (93012-8523)
P.O. Box 3297 (93011-3297)
PHONE..................805 383-0455
Roy Chikasawa, *President*
Don Chikasawa, *Treasurer*
Martha Chikasawa, *Admin Sec*
EMP: 100 EST: 1963
SALES (est): 3.6MM **Privately Held**
SIC: 0161 Vegetables & melons

(P-45)
COSTA SONS
36817 Foothill Rd, Soledad (93960-9656)
PHONE..................831 678-0799
Tony Costa, *Co-Owner*
David Costa, *Co-Owner*
Diane Costa, *Co-Owner*
Elsie Costa, *Co-Owner*
Michael Costa, *Co-Owner*
EMP: 50 EST: 1958
SALES (est): 3.2MM **Privately Held**
WEB: www.costafarmsinc.com
SIC: 0161 Broccoli farm

(P-46)
DAN AVILA AND SONS
2718 Roberts Rd, Ceres (95307-9627)
PHONE..................209 495-3899
Daniel Avila, *Owner*
EMP: 60
SALES: 16MM **Privately Held**
SIC: 0161 0139 Watermelon farm; sweet potato farm

(P-47)
DARRIGO BROSCOOF CALIFORNIA (PA)
Also Called: Andy Boy
21777 Harris Rd, Salinas (93908-8609)
P.O. Box 850 (93902-0850)
PHONE..................831 455-4500
Andrew A D'Arrigo, *Ch of Bd*
John C D'Arrigo, *President*
E John Culligan, *Corp Secy*
Chad Amaral, *Vice Pres*
Michelle Penny, *Office Mgr*
EMP: 50
SQ FT: 13,000
SALES (est): 239.1MM **Privately Held**
SIC: 0161 Broccoli farm; carrot farm; lettuce farm; celery farm

(P-48)
DIMARE ENTERPRISES INC (PA)
Also Called: Dimare Company
1406 N St, Newman (95360-1309)
P.O. Box 517 (95360-0517)
PHONE..................209 827-2900
Thomas F Dimare, *President*
Paul J Dimare, *Treasurer*
EMP: 250
SQ FT: 20,000
SALES (est): 51.7MM **Privately Held**
WEB: www.dimare-ca.com
SIC: 0161 0174 Vegetables & melons; citrus fruits

(P-49)
DOBLER & SONS LLC
174 Struve Rd, Moss Landing (95039-9661)
P.O. Box 1660, Watsonville (95077-1660)
PHONE..................831 724-6727
Carl Dobler, *Mng Member*
Jacob Dobler, *Prgrmr*
Craig Dobler,
Kenneth Dobler,
Michael Dobler,
EMP: 350
SALES (est): 42MM **Privately Held**
WEB: www.doblerandsons.com
SIC: 0161 Cabbage farm; lettuce farm

(P-50)
DONALD VALPREDO FARMING INC
Also Called: Db Custom Farming
2101 Mttler Frontage Rd E, Bakersfield (93307-9649)
PHONE..................661 858-2245
Donald Valpredo, *President*
Perry Eastin, *CFO*
Susan Gardner, *Human Resources*
EMP: 60
SALES (est): 8.2MM **Privately Held**
WEB: www.valpredofarms.com
SIC: 0161 Tomato farm; onion farm

(P-51)
DRESICK FARMS INC (PA)
19536 Jayne Ave, Huron (93234)
P.O. Box 1260 (93234-1260)
PHONE..................559 945-2513
Michael L Dresick, *CEO*
Jan Dresick, *Vice Pres*
EMP: 51
SQ FT: 3,500
SALES (est): 32.9MM **Privately Held**
WEB: www.dresickfarms.com
SIC: 0161 Lettuce farm; cantaloupe farm; tomato farm; rooted vegetable farms

(P-52)
FREITAS BROTHERS
Hwy 1, Guadalupe (93434)
P.O. Box 895 (93434-0895)
PHONE..................805 343-3134
Eric Freitas, *Partner*
Jon Freitas, *Partner*
▼ EMP: 50
SQ FT: 1,500
SALES (est): 3.6MM **Privately Held**
WEB: www.freitasfarms.com
SIC: 0161 Vegetables & melons

(P-53)
FRESH FARMS INC
700 Airport Rd, King City (93930-2501)
P.O. Box 1600 (93930-1600)
PHONE..................831 385-3285
Jerry J Rava II, *President*
▲ EMP: 50 EST: 1994
SALES (est): 2.8MM **Privately Held**
SIC: 0161 Spinach farm

(P-54)
FRESH LEAF FARMS LLC (DH)
1250 Hansen St, Salinas (93901-4552)
PHONE..................831 422-7405
Mann Packing, *Partner*
Anthony Costa Sons, *Partner*
Joe Nucci, *President*
EMP: 50
SALES (est): 20.4MM **Privately Held**
SIC: 0161 Lettuce & leaf vegetable farms
HQ: Mann Packing Co., Inc.
1333 Schilling Pl
Salinas CA 93901
831 422-7405

(P-55)
FRESH VENTURE FARMS LLC
1181 S Wolff Rd, Oxnard (93033-2105)
PHONE..................805 754-4449
Robert Boelts,
EMP: 80
SQ FT: 4,000
SALES (est): 8MM **Privately Held**
SIC: 0161 0191 Vegetables & melons; general farms, primarily crop

(P-56)
GEORGE AMARAL RANCHES INC
25453 Iverson Rd, Gonzales (93926-9403)
P.O. Box 3035 (93926-3035)
PHONE..................831 679-2977
George Amaral, *President*
Cathy Amaral, *Finance Mgr*
Mike Amaral, *Accountant*
▼ EMP: 100
SQ FT: 3,000
SALES (est): 49.6MM **Privately Held**
WEB: www.amaralranches.com
SIC: 0161 Lettuce & leaf vegetable farms; broccoli farm; cabbage farm; celery farm

(P-57)
GEORGE CHIALA FARMS INC
Also Called: Chiala, George Packing
15500 Hill Rd, Morgan Hill (95037-9516)
PHONE..................408 778-0562
George Chiala Sr, *President*
Alice Chiala, *CFO*
George Chiala Jr, *Vice Pres*
▲ EMP: 120
SQ FT: 14,000
SALES (est): 51.3MM **Privately Held**
WEB: www.gcfarmsinc.com
SIC: 0161 0723 Vegetables & melons; vegetable crops market preparation services

(P-58)
GIUSTI FARMS LLC
1800 Higgins Canyon Rd, Half Moon Bay (94019-2573)
PHONE..................650 726-9221
Aldo Giusti,
John Giusti,
EMP: 50
SQ FT: 145
SALES (est): 2.1MM **Privately Held**
SIC: 0161 Artichoke farm; pea & bean farms; brussels sprout farm

(P-59)
GIVENS JOHN
Also Called: Givens Farms
1133 N Fairview Ave, Goleta (93117-1822)
PHONE..................805 964-4477
John Givens, *Owner*
EMP: 70
SALES (est): 1.9MM **Privately Held**
SIC: 0161 Vegetables & melons

(P-60)
GOLDEN ACRES FARMS
87770 62nd Ave, Thermal (92274-9263)
P.O. Box 371 (92274-0371)
PHONE..........................760 399-1923
Joe Kitagawa, *President*
Kiyoko Kitagawa, *Corp Secy*
EMP: 50
SQ FT: 500
SALES (est): 2.3MM **Privately Held**
SIC: 0161 Vegetables & melons

(P-61)
HENRY HIBINO FARMS
106 Rico St, Salinas (93907-2101)
PHONE..........................831 757-3081
Henry Hibino, *Owner*
EMP: 75 EST: 1950
SQ FT: 20,000
SALES (est): 6.8MM **Privately Held**
SIC: 0161 Vegetables & melons

(P-62)
J MARCHINI & SON INC
8736 Minturn Rd, Le Grand (95333-9711)
PHONE..........................559 665-9710
Joseph Marchini, *Branch Mgr*
EMP: 93
SALES (corp-wide): 29.7MM **Privately Held**
SIC: 0161 Rooted vegetable farms
PA: J. Marchini & Son, Inc.
　　8736 Minturn Rd
　　Le Grand CA 95333
　　559 665-2944

(P-63)
JAY FISHER FARMS INC
2251 W Central Ave, Lompoc (93436)
PHONE..........................805 735-1598
Elmer Fisher, *President*
Patricia Fisher, *Corp Secy*
Jay Fisher, *Vice Pres*
EMP: 50
SALES (est): 1.8MM **Privately Held**
SIC: 0161 0181 Vegetables & melons;
　flowers grown in field nurseries

(P-64)
KELOMAR INC
3949 Austin Rd, Brawley (92227-9702)
PHONE..........................760 344-5253
Michael W Morgan, *President*
Joseph Johnson, *CFO*
EMP: 120
SQ FT: 3,000
SALES (est): 8.3MM **Privately Held**
WEB: www.kelomar.com
SIC: 0161 Vegetables & melons

(P-65)
KONO FARMS INCORPORATED
87481 Avenue 74, Thermal (92274)
PHONE..........................760 397-7110
Emerson Kono, *President*
Barbara Kono, *Treasurer*
Edward Kono, *Vice Pres*
Ronald Kono, *Vice Pres*
Spencer Kono, *Vice Pres*
▲ EMP: 150 EST: 1952
SQ FT: 20,000
SALES: 1.9MM **Privately Held**
SIC: 0161 Vegetables & melons

(P-66)
LA GRANDE FARM
P.O. Box 370 (95987-0370)
PHONE..........................530 473-5923
Ron La Grande, *Partner*
Mike La Grande, *Partner*
EMP: 70
SQ FT: 8,000
SALES (est): 3.9MM **Privately Held**
SIC: 0161 0191 0111 Tomato farm; general farms, primarily crop; wheat

(P-67)
LUCKY FARMS INC
1194 E Brier Dr, San Bernardino (92408-2838)
P.O. Box 985, Loma Linda (92354-0985)
PHONE..........................909 799-6688
Wen S Liaou, *President*
Gary Liaou, *Vice Pres*
▲ EMP: 60
SQ FT: 28,000

SALES (est): 8.1MM **Privately Held**
WEB: www.luckyfarms.com
SIC: 0161 Corn farm, sweet

(P-68)
MICHAEL W MORGAN
3949 Austin Rd, Brawley (92227-9702)
PHONE..........................760 344-5253
Michael W Morgan, *Owner*
EMP: 50
SALES (est): 2.4MM **Privately Held**
SIC: 0161 Vegetables & melons

(P-69)
MIKAELIAN & SONS INC
10368 Avenue 400, Dinuba (93618-9558)
PHONE..........................559 591-6324
Mike Mikaelian, *President*
Carol Mikaelian, *Corp Secy*
EMP: 120 EST: 1953
SALES: 1MM **Privately Held**
SIC: 0161 0175 0172 Watermelon farm;
　deciduous tree fruits; grapes

(P-70)
MURANAKA FARM
11018 W Los Angeles Ave, Moorpark (93021-9744)
P.O. Box 189 (93020-0189)
PHONE..........................805 529-0201
Greg EMI, *President*
EMP: 230
SALES (corp-wide): 42.9MM **Privately Held**
WEB: www.muranakafarm.com
SIC: 0161 Lettuce & leaf vegetable farms
PA: Muranaka Farm
　　11018 E Los Angeles Ave
　　Moorpark CA 93021
　　805 529-0201

(P-71)
NEIL BASSETTI FARMS
41715 Espinosa Rd, Greenfield (93927-6101)
P.O. Box 429 (93927-0429)
PHONE..........................831 674-2040
Maryanne Martinus, *Partner*
Adrienne Bassetti, *Partner*
Patrick Bassetti, *Partner*
Allison Fierro, *Partner*
Mary Ann Martinus, *Partner*
EMP: 50 EST: 1939
SALES (est): 6.3MM **Privately Held**
WEB: www.nbassetti.com
SIC: 0161 Vegetables & melons

(P-72)
OCEAN MIST FARMING COMPANY (PA)
Also Called: Ocean Mist Farms
10855 Ocean Mist Pkwy A, Castroville (95012-3232)
PHONE..........................831 633-2144
C Edward Boutonnet, *CEO*
Ed Bouponnet, *President*
Les Tottino, *Bd of Directors*
Don Bracco, *Vice Pres*
Joseph Micheli, *Vice Pres*
EMP: 150
SQ FT: 2,000
SALES (est): 45.9MM **Privately Held**
SIC: 0161 Lettuce & leaf vegetable farms;
　artichoke farm

(P-73)
OCEANVIEW PRODUCE COMPANY
3000 E Hueneme Rd, Oxnard (93033-8112)
PHONE..........................805 488-6401
David H Murdock, *President*
EMP: 60
SALES (est): 3.6MM **Privately Held**
SIC: 0161 5148 Celery farm; lettuce farm;
　fresh fruits & vegetables

(P-74)
OPAL FRY AND SON
Also Called: Fry, Opal W & Son Farming
Maricopa Hwy, Bakersfield (93307)
PHONE..........................661 858-2523
Jack Fry, *Partner*
George Fry, *Partner*
EMP: 50
SQ FT: 400

SALES (est): 2.4MM **Privately Held**
SIC: 0161 0131 Vegetables & melons; cotton

(P-75)
PAYNE BROTHERS RANCHES
13330 County Road 102, Woodland (95776-9119)
PHONE..........................530 662-2354
William A Payne, *Partner*
Robert B Payne, *Partner*
EMP: 100
SALES (est): 4.7MM **Privately Held**
WEB: www.paynefarms.com
SIC: 0161 0191 Tomato farm; general farms, primarily crop

(P-76)
PFYFFER ASSOCIATES INC
2611 Mission St, Santa Cruz (95060-5702)
P.O. Box 879 (95061-0879)
PHONE..........................831 423-8572
Ernie Bontadelli, *President*
Steve Bontadelli, *Vice Pres*
Charlie Bontadelli, *Principal*
EMP: 50
SALES (est): 3.2MM **Privately Held**
SIC: 0161 Brussels sprout farm

(P-77)
ROBERT CECCHINI INC
Also Called: Cecchini & Cecchini
5301 Orwood Rd, Brentwood (94513-5245)
P.O. Box 1150, Discovery Bay (94505-7150)
PHONE..........................925 634-4400
Robert L Cecchini, *President*
EMP: 100 EST: 1933
SALES (est): 8.5MM **Privately Held**
SIC: 0161 0115 0111 0139 Asparagus farm; corn; wheat; alfalfa farm

(P-78)
ROYAL PACKING DCF
Also Called: Doll Fresh Vegesable
32839 S Lassen Ave, Huron (93234)
PHONE..........................559 945-2537
Jack Shiyomura, *Manager*
EMP: 60
SALES (est): 2.2MM **Privately Held**
SIC: 0161 Lettuce farm

(P-79)
SAN MIGUEL PRODUCE INC
Also Called: Cut N Clean Greens
4444 Navalair Rd, Oxnard (93033-8298)
PHONE..........................805 488-0981
Roy I Nishimori, *CEO*
Jan Berk, *COO*
Karina Magallon, *Prdtn Mgr*
Elias Moo, *Opers Staff*
Rory Richmond, *Marketing Staff*
▲ EMP: 500
SQ FT: 25,000
SALES: 53.2MM **Privately Held**
WEB: www.cutnclean.com
SIC: 0161 0723 4212 Vegetables & melons; vegetable packing services; farm to market haulage, local

(P-80)
SANTA BARBARA FARMS LLC (PA)
1200 Union Sugar Ave, Lompoc (93436-9740)
PHONE..........................805 736-9776
Robert M Witt, *CEO*
Charles Witt, *COO*
RC Gerber, *CFO*
▲ EMP: 60
SQ FT: 2,800
SALES (est): 39.5MM **Privately Held**
WEB: www.oceanviewflowers.com
SIC: 0161 0181 Vegetables & melons;
　florists' greens & flowers

(P-81)
SCARBOROUGH FARMS INC
731 Pacific Ave, Oxnard (93030-7322)
P.O. Box 1267 (93032-1267)
PHONE..........................805 483-9113
Ann Stein, *President*
Wayne G Jansen, *President*
Sylvia Hague, *Human Res Mgr*
Jeff Stein, *Sales Mgr*
Elvia Alvarado, *Sales Staff*

EMP: 150
SALES (est): 21.6MM **Privately Held**
SIC: 0161 Vegetables & melons

(P-82)
SILVA FARMS LLC (PA)
111 Alpine Dr, Gonzales (93926)
PHONE..........................831 675-2327
Ed Silva, *Owner*
▼ EMP: 280
SQ FT: 30,000
SALES (est): 13.1MM **Privately Held**
WEB: www.edsilva.com
SIC: 0161 Broccoli farm; cabbage farm;
　lettuce farm

(P-83)
SUN AND SANDS ENTERPRISES LLC (PA)
Also Called: Prime Time International
86705 Avenue 54 Ste A, Coachella (92236-3814)
PHONE..........................760 399-4278
Carl S Maggio,
Kathy Jones, *Administration*
Jim Detty, *Credit Mgr*
Stacy Macmillan, *Asst Controller*
Patricia McManus, *Controller*
▲ EMP: 100
SQ FT: 7,500
SALES: 123.9MM **Privately Held**
WEB: www.primetimeproduce.com
SIC: 0161 Lettuce farm; snap bean farm (bush & pole); cantaloupe farm; watermelon farm

(P-84)
TANIMURA ANTLE FRESH FOODS INC (PA)
1 Harris Rd, Salinas (93908-8608)
P.O. Box 4070 (93912-4070)
PHONE..........................831 455-2950
Rick Antle, *President*
Ken Silveira, *COO*
Vic Feuerstein, *CFO*
Gary Tanimura, *Exec VP*
Mike Antle, *Vice Pres*
▲ EMP: 100
SQ FT: 135,000
SALES (est): 682.4MM **Privately Held**
WEB: www.taproduce.com
SIC: 0161 0182 0723 2099 Lettuce farm;
　celery farm; cauliflower farm; food crops grown under cover; vegetable packing services; food preparations

(P-85)
TEIXEIRA FARMS INC
2600 Bonita Lateral Rd, Santa Maria (93458-9798)
PHONE..........................805 928-3801
Allan Teixeira, *President*
Chris Wong, *CFO*
Glenn Teixeira, *Treasurer*
Marvin Teixeira, *Vice Pres*
Pam Lind, *Office Mgr*
EMP: 188
SALES (est): 14.2MM **Privately Held**
WEB: www.teixeirafarms.com
SIC: 0161 Broccoli farm; cabbage farm;
　cauliflower farm; celery farm

(P-86)
TELESIS ONION CO (PA)
3265 W Figarden Dr, Fresno (93711-3912)
P.O. Box 9050 (93790-9050)
PHONE..........................559 884-2441
Martin Britz, *Partner*
EMP: 121
SALES (est): 6.8MM **Privately Held**
SIC: 0161 0723 5148 Onion farm; vegetable packing services; fruits, fresh

(P-87)
TERRA FIRMA FARM CORP
Also Called: Terra Firma Farms
4713 Baker Rd, Winters (95694-9613)
P.O. Box 836 (95694-0836)
PHONE..........................530 795-2473
Paul Underhill, *CEO*
Paul Holmes, *Treasurer*
Hector Melendes, *Admin Sec*
EMP: 50
SQ FT: 800

▲ = Import ▼=Export
◆ =Import/Export

SALES: 1.4MM **Privately Held**
WEB: www.terrafirmafarm.com
SIC: 0161 0174 0173 0175 Rooted vegetable farms; citrus fruits; tree nuts; deciduous tree fruits

(P-88)
UESUGI FARMS INC (PA)
1020 State Highway 25, Gilroy
(95020-8074)
PHONE...................408 842-1294
Joseph Aiello, *President*
Dennis Humphries, *Vice Pres*
Kathy Carlson, *Office Mgr*
Diane Zent, *Office Mgr*
Virginia Haro, *Accounting Mgr*
EMP: 69 EST: 1979
SALES (est): 46.3MM **Privately Held**
SIC: 0161 Vegetables & melons

(P-89)
WM BOLTHOUSE FARMS INC (DH)
7200 E Brundage Ln, Bakersfield
(93307-3016)
PHONE...................661 366-7209
Jeff Dunn, *President*
Marty Buck, *Treasurer*
Timothy McCorkle, *Vice Pres*
Kevin Cook, *IT/INT Sup*
Thomas Salem, *Human Res Dir*
◆ EMP: 1477
SQ FT: 700,000
SALES (est): 1B
SALES (corp-wide): 8.6B **Publicly Held**
SIC: 0161 2099 0723 Carrot farm; onion farm; ready-to-eat meals, salads & sandwiches; crop preparation services for market

0171 Berry Crops

(P-90)
APTOS BERRY FARMS INC
730 S A St, Oxnard (93030-7138)
PHONE...................831 726-3256
Garland Reiter, *CEO*
Joseph M Reiter Jr, *President*
EMP: 70
SQ FT: 5,000
SALES (est): 4MM **Privately Held**
SIC: 0171 Strawberry farm; raspberry farm

(P-91)
B & E FARMS INC
Also Called: Ito Farms
9112 Mcfadden Ave, Westminster
(92683-6533)
PHONE...................714 893-8166
Bill Ito, *President*
Ed Ito, *Vice Pres*
EMP: 50
SQ FT: 2,000
SALES (est): 3.4MM **Privately Held**
SIC: 0171 Strawberry farm

(P-92)
CARDENAS BROS FARMING COMPANY
1141 Tama Ln, Santa Maria (93455-1127)
PHONE...................805 928-1559
Alberto Cardenas, *President*
Delfina Cardenas, *Vice Pres*
EMP: 100
SALES (est): 5.1MM **Privately Held**
SIC: 0171 Strawberry farm

(P-93)
CBS FARMS LLC
80 Sakata Ln, Watsonville (95076-5132)
P.O. Box 1825 (95077-1825)
PHONE...................831 724-0700
Ed Kelly, *Mng Member*
Carl Hamona,
Brad Peterson,
Bob Rigor,
EMP: 50
SALES: 1MM **Privately Held**
SIC: 0171 Strawberry farm

(P-94)
CJJ FARMING INC
125 W Mill St, Santa Maria (93458-4325)
PHONE...................805 739-1723

Juan Cisneros, *President*
Jesus Cisneros, *Admin Sec*
EMP: 50
SALES (est): 3.1MM **Privately Held**
SIC: 0171 0161 Strawberry farm; squash farm; broccoli farm; lettuce farm; romaine farm

(P-95)
CONROY FARMS INC
520 Maulhardt Ave, Oxnard (93030-8914)
P.O. Box 1467, Camarillo (93011-1467)
PHONE...................805 981-0537
Michael P Conroy, *President*
Willaine Conroy, *Chairman*
Alice Menchaca, *Manager*
EMP: 325
SQ FT: 700
SALES: 3MM **Privately Held**
SIC: 0171 Strawberry farm

(P-96)
DARENSBERRIES LLC
Also Called: D B Specialty Farms
714 S Blosser Rd, Santa Maria
(93458-4914)
P.O. Box 549 (93456-0549)
PHONE...................805 937-8000
Daren Gee,
EMP: 250
SQ FT: 1,500
SALES (est): 14.4MM **Privately Held**
SIC: 0171 Strawberry farm

(P-97)
ECLIPSE BERRY FARMS LLC
11812 San Vicente Blvd # 250, Los Angeles
(90049-6632)
PHONE...................310 207-7879
Norman Gilfenbain, *Bd of Directors*
Robert Wiviott, *General Mgr*
Sharon Fuller, *Administration*
Precy Estanislao, *Controller*
Ventura Strawberry,
▼ EMP: 100
SQ FT: 2,500
SALES (est): 52.8MM **Privately Held**
SIC: 0171 5148 Berry crops; fresh fruits & vegetables

(P-98)
ETCHANDY FARMS LLC
4324 E Vineyard Ave, Oxnard
(93036-1056)
P.O. Box 5770 (93031-5770)
PHONE...................805 983-4700
Michael Etchandy,
EMP: 99 EST: 2014
SQ FT: 400
SALES (est): 1.6MM **Privately Held**
SIC: 0171 Strawberry farm

(P-99)
FRESHWAY FARMS LLC
2165 W Main St, Santa Maria
(93458-9739)
P.O. Box 5369 (93456-5369)
PHONE...................805 349-7170
Paul M Allen, *Mng Member*
EMP: 150 EST: 2014
SALES (est): 22MM **Privately Held**
SIC: 0171 0161 Strawberry farm; broccoli farm

(P-100)
GAMA BERRY FARMS LLC
730 S A St, Oxnard (93030-7138)
PHONE...................805 483-1000
Garland Reider, *CEO*
EMP: 60
SALES (est): 1.1MM **Privately Held**
SIC: 0171 Strawberry farm

(P-101)
GUY GEORGE
Also Called: King George Cabbage
315 2nd St Ste A, Watsonville
(95076-5112)
P.O. Box 40 (95077-0040)
PHONE...................831 728-2410
Guy George, *Partner*
EMP: 50
SALES (est): 794.8K **Privately Held**
WEB: www.guygeorge.com
SIC: 0171 0161 Strawberry farm; cabbage farm; lettuce farm

(P-102)
JAL BERRY FARMS LLC
1767 San Juan Rd, Aromas (95004-9028)
PHONE...................831 763-7200
Jose Lopez,
Robert F Dunaven Jr,
Hernando Ramirez,
EMP: 99
SALES (est): 2.5MM **Privately Held**
SIC: 0171 Strawberry farm

(P-103)
KUSUMOTO FARMS
6535 Stonehill Dr, San Jose (95120-1619)
PHONE...................408 927-8348
Mel Kusumoto, *Owner*
EMP: 90
SALES (est): 1.3MM **Privately Held**
SIC: 0171 Strawberry farm

(P-104)
LACUESTA FARMING INC
1141 Tama Ln, Santa Maria (93455-1127)
PHONE...................805 349-1940
Fernando Contreras, *President*
Dalila Contreras, *Corp Secy*
EMP: 100
SALES (est): 5.1MM **Privately Held**
SIC: 0171 Strawberry farm

(P-105)
LASSEN CANYON NURSERY INC
14735 Big Springs Rd, Weed (96094-9665)
PHONE...................530 938-4720
Kenneth Elwood, *President*
EMP: 100
SALES (corp-wide): 93.1MM **Privately Held**
WEB: www.lassencanyonnursery.com
SIC: 0171 Strawberry farm
PA: Lassen Canyon Nursery, Inc.
1300 Salmon Creek Rd
Redding CA 96003
530 223-1075

(P-106)
LASSEN CANYON NURSERY INC
11651 Palm Ln, Ripon (95366)
PHONE...................209 599-7777
Kenneth Elwood, *President*
EMP: 100
SALES (corp-wide): 93.1MM **Privately Held**
WEB: www.lassencanyonnursery.com
SIC: 0171 Strawberry farm
PA: Lassen Canyon Nursery, Inc.
1300 Salmon Creek Rd
Redding CA 96003
530 223-1075

(P-107)
MARIZ BERRY FARMS
1650 E Gonzales Rd, Oxnard
(93036-3700)
PHONE...................805 981-9908
Victor Lopez, *Partner*
Donald Driscoll, *Partner*
Keith Ford, *Partner*
EMP: 105
SALES (est): 3.9MM **Privately Held**
SIC: 0171 Strawberry farm

(P-108)
MENDOZA FARMS INC
527 W Fesler St Apt A, Santa Maria
(93458-4052)
PHONE...................805 352-1070
Hector M Mendoza, *President*
Alex Mendoza, *Partner*
Hector Mendoza, *President*
EMP: 50
SALES (est): 1.6MM **Privately Held**
SIC: 0171 Strawberry farm

(P-109)
MORGAN FARM LLC
201 Vista Dr, Watsonville (95076-1754)
P.O. Box 758 (95077-0758)
PHONE...................831 726-5120
Jason Morgan, *President*
EMP: 70
SALES: 3MM **Privately Held**
SIC: 0171 7389 Strawberry farm;

(P-110)
NORTH RIVER RANCH LLC
3601 W Pendleton Ave, Santa Ana
(92704-3814)
PHONE...................714 556-6244
George Murai, *Partner*
Mark Murai, *Partner*
Triple M Packing, *Partner*
EMP: 50
SQ FT: 25,000
SALES: 7MM **Privately Held**
SIC: 0171 Strawberry farm; raspberry farm

(P-111)
ORANGE COUNTY PRODUCE LLC
11405 Jeffrey Rd, Irvine (92602-0503)
PHONE...................949 451-0880
Matthew K Kawamura, *Mng Member*
Ana Lozoya, *Administration*
Blanca Bermudez, *Human Resources*
Arthur Kawamura,
Luis Bermudez, *Mng Member*
EMP: 100
SQ FT: 1,000
SALES (est): 42.4MM **Privately Held**
SIC: 0171 Strawberry farm

(P-112)
PENDLETON FARMS
307 Wilshire Rd, Oceanside (92057-2902)
P.O. Box 522, San Luis Rey (92068-0522)
PHONE...................760 754-2359
Donald Stickles, *Owner*
EMP: 55
SALES (est): 845.7K **Privately Held**
SIC: 0171 Strawberry farm

(P-113)
RED BLOSSOM SALES INC
865 Black Rd, Santa Maria (93458-9701)
PHONE...................805 349-9404
Ruben Trevino, *Manager*
EMP: 500 **Privately Held**
SIC: 0171 Strawberry farm
PA: Red Blossom Sales, Inc.
400 W Ventura Blvd # 140
Camarillo CA 93010

(P-114)
RED BLOSSOM SALES INC (PA)
400 W Ventura Blvd # 140, Camarillo
(93010-9139)
P.O. Box 527, Los Olivos (93441-0527)
PHONE...................805 686-4747
Craig A Casca, *CEO*
David Lawrence, *President*
EMP: 1046
SQ FT: 1,200
SALES: 154.8MM **Privately Held**
WEB: www.redblossom.com
SIC: 0171 Strawberry farm

(P-115)
REITER AFFL COMPANIES LLC
124 Carmen Ln Ste A, Santa Maria
(93458-7768)
PHONE...................805 925-8577
Mario Pena, *Manager*
EMP: 101
SALES (corp-wide): 60.1MM **Privately Held**
SIC: 0171 Berry crops
PA: Reiter Affiliated Companies, Llc
730 S A St
Oxnard CA 93030
805 483-1000

(P-116)
REITER AFFL COMPANIES LLC
Also Called: Reiter Berry Watsonville
140 Westridge Dr, Watsonville
(95076-6602)
PHONE...................831 786-4244
EMP: 87
SALES (corp-wide): 60.1MM **Privately Held**
SIC: 0171 Raspberry farm
PA: Reiter Affiliated Companies, Llc
730 S A St
Oxnard CA 93030
805 483-1000

PRODUCTS & SVCS

(P-117)
REITER AFFL COMPANIES LLC
(PA)
730 S A St, Oxnard (93030-7138)
PHONE..................805 483-1000
Garland Reiter, *CEO*
Andy Rice, *Vice Pres*
Victor Rodriguez, *Vice Pres*
Shar Hotzler, *Accounting Mgr*
Ally Sorensen, *Accountant*
EMP: 50
SALES (est): 60.1MM **Privately Held**
SIC: 0171 Raspberry farm

(P-118)
RINCON PACIFIC LLC
1312 Del Norte Rd, Camarillo
(93010-8502)
PHONE..................805 986-8806
Kenneth Hasegawa,
EMP: 100
SALES (est): 10.4MM **Privately Held**
SIC: 0171 Strawberry farm

(P-119)
RIO MESA FARMS LLC
75 Sakata Ln, Watsonville (95076-5132)
P.O. Box 1359 (95077-1359)
PHONE..................831 728-1965
Mary Gregg, *Administration*
EMP: 99
SALES (est): 3.6MM **Privately Held**
SIC: 0171 Strawberry farm

(P-120)
SANTA ROSA BERRY FARMS
LLC
3500 Camino Ave Ste 250, Oxnard
(93030-7999)
PHONE..................805 981-3060
Bryan D Fiscalini,
Sarah Blacklock, *Bookkeeper*
EMP: 300
SQ FT: 3,500
SALES: 10MM **Privately Held**
SIC: 0171 Berry crops

(P-121)
SIERRA CASCADE
BLUEBERRIES
12753 Doe Mill Rd, Forest Ranch (95942)
PHONE..................530 894-8728
John Carlon, *Owner*
John Carlo, *Owner*
EMP: 50
SALES: 300K **Privately Held**
SIC: 0171 Blueberry farm

(P-122)
SOLIMAR FARMS INC
1312 Del Norte Rd, Camarillo
(93010-8502)
PHONE..................805 986-8806
Glen Hasegawa, *President*
Ken Hasegawa, *Vice Pres*
EMP: 80
SQ FT: 2,000
SALES (est): 14.4MM **Privately Held**
SIC: 0171 Strawberry farm

(P-123)
SUPERIOR FRUIT LLC
4324 E Vineyard Ave, Oxnard
(93036-1056)
PHONE..................805 485-2519
Robert Jones,
Richard Jones,
EMP: 200 EST: 2017
SQ FT: 6,000
SALES: 200MM **Privately Held**
SIC: 0171 Strawberry farm

(P-124)
T T MIYASAKA INC
209 Riverside Rd, Watsonville
(95076-3656)
PHONE..................831 722-3871
Tim Miyasaka, *President*
EMP: 400
SQ FT: 500
SALES (est): 10.8MM **Privately Held**
SIC: 0171 Strawberry farm

(P-125)
UYEDA FARM
656 Lakeview Rd, Watsonville
(95076-2228)
P.O. Box 1045, Freedom (95019-1045)
PHONE..................831 722-6345
Norman Uyeda, *Owner*
Darrell Uyeda, *Owner*
EMP: 50
SALES (est): 1.1MM **Privately Held**
SIC: 0171 Strawberry farm

(P-126)
UYEMATSU INC
1004 E Lake Ave, Watsonville
(95076-3406)
PHONE..................831 724-2200
Richard Uyematsu, *President*
Alan Uyematsu, *Vice Pres*
EMP: 65
SQ FT: 1,650
SALES (est): 2.1MM **Privately Held**
SIC: 0171 Strawberry farm

0172 Grapes

(P-127)
7TH STANDARD RANCH
COMPANY
Also Called: Sun Pacific Farming
33374 Lerdo Hwy, Bakersfield
(93308-9782)
PHONE..................661 399-0416
Berne Evans, *Partner*
Robert Reniers, *Partner*
Emily Ybarra, *VP Human Res*
EMP: 500
SQ FT: 140,000
SALES (est): 13.6MM **Privately Held**
SIC: 0172 4222 Grapes; refrigerated
warehousing & storage

(P-128)
ALEXANDER DELU
15175 N Devries Rd, Lodi (95242-9217)
PHONE..................209 334-6660
EMP: 80
SALES (est): 2.8MM **Privately Held**
SIC: 0172 0722

(P-129)
ANTHONY VINEYARDS INC (PA)
5512 Valpredo Ave, Bakersfield
(93307-9178)
P.O. Box 9578 (93389-9578)
PHONE..................661 858-6211
Domenick T Bianco, *President*
Paul A Loeffel, *CFO*
Robert O Bianco, *Senior VP*
Justin McGowan, *Administration*
Jonathan Gist, *Sales Staff*
▼ EMP: 150
SQ FT: 125,000
SALES: 142.5MM **Privately Held**
WEB: www.anthonyvineyards.com
SIC: 0172 0174 Grapes; grapefruit grove;
tangerine grove

(P-130)
BAZAN MARIO AG SERVICES &
VINE
Also Called: Bazan Mrio Vinyrd Mgmt AG
Svcs
1984 Yountville Cross Rd, Yountville
(94599-1291)
P.O. Box 864, NAPA (94559-0864)
PHONE..................707 945-0718
Mario Bazan, *Owner*
Lori Valdivia, *Controller*
▲ EMP: 62 EST: 1997
SALES: 1.3MM **Privately Held**
SIC: 0172 Grapes

(P-131)
BEDROSIAN FARMS INC
8333 S Sunnyside Ave, Fowler
(93625-9659)
P.O. Box 219 (93625-0219)
PHONE..................559 834-5981
Ernest Bedrosian, *President*
Kenneth Bedrosian, *Vice Pres*
Krikor Bedrosian, *Vice Pres*
EMP: 50

SALES (est): 3.2MM **Privately Held**
SIC: 0172 Grapes

(P-132)
BROCCHINI FARMS INC
27011 S Austin Rd, Ripon (95366-9627)
PHONE..................209 599-4229
Robert Brocchini, *President*
Steve Brocchini, *Principal*
EMP: 50
SALES (est): 4.3MM **Privately Held**
WEB: www.brocchinifarms.com
SIC: 0172 0173 0139 Grapes; almond
grove; alfalfa farm

(P-133)
CEDERLIND FARMS LP
2514 Kenney Ave, Winton (95388-9745)
PHONE..................209 606-8586
Jeff Cederlind, *Partner*
EMP: 99
SALES (est): 759.4K **Privately Held**
SIC: 0172 Grapes

(P-134)
CHAPPELLET VINEYARD
1581 Sage Canyon Rd, Saint Helena
(94574-9628)
PHONE..................707 286-4219
Donn Chappellet,
Andrew Opatz,
EMP: 50
SALES (est): 2.3MM **Privately Held**
SIC: 0172 Grapes

(P-135)
CIRCLE K RANCH
8640 E Manning Ave, Selma (93662-9763)
PHONE..................559 834-1571
Melvin Kazarian, *General Ptnr*
Ronald Kazarian, *Partner*
Charles Kazarian, *Info Tech Mgr*
EMP: 60 EST: 1971
SQ FT: 25,000
SALES (est): 3.8MM **Privately Held**
WEB: www.circlekranch.com
SIC: 0172 Grapes

(P-136)
CLARBEC INC
Also Called: Madrone Vineyard Management
19368 Orange Ave, Sonoma (95476-6249)
PHONE..................707 996-4012
Rebecca Jenkins, *Principal*
Clarence A Jenkins Jr, *President*
EMP: 50
SQ FT: 1,600
SALES (est): 3.6MM **Privately Held**
SIC: 0172 Grapes

(P-137)
CLENDENEN VINEYARD MGT
LLC
9235 W Dry Creek Rd, Healdsburg
(95448-9134)
P.O. Box 69 (95448-0069)
PHONE..................707 473-0881
John Clendenen,
Catherine Clendenen,
EMP: 60 EST: 1993
SALES (est): 3.6MM **Privately Held**
SIC: 0172 Grapes

(P-138)
DELMART FARMS INC
30988 Riverside Cntrl Vly, Shafter (93263)
PHONE..................661 746-2148
EMP: 100
SQ FT: 1,000
SALES (est): 2.5MM **Privately Held**
SIC: 0172 0131 0134 0724

(P-139)
DIRT FARMER & CO INC
9725 Los Guilicos Ave, Kenwood (95452)
P.O. Box 638 (95452-0638)
PHONE..................707 833-2054
Keith Kunde, *President*
EMP: 53
SALES (est): 500K **Privately Held**
SIC: 0172 0761 Grapes; farm labor con-
tractors

(P-140)
DOMAINE CARNEROS LTD
1240 Duhig Rd, NAPA (94559-9713)
P.O. Box 5420 (94581-0420)
PHONE..................707 257-0101
Eileen Crane, *Principal*
Debra Smith, *Executive Asst*
Kristen Guiducci, *Controller*
Fernanda Castro, *Hum Res Coord*
Nicole Hamill, *Buyer*
▲ EMP: 80
SQ FT: 50,000
SALES (est): 7.5MM **Privately Held**
WEB: www.domainecarneros.com
SIC: 0172 2084 Grapes; wines

(P-141)
DRAKE LARSON RANCHS
Also Called: Larson, Drake Sales
89780 Ave 60, Thermal (92274)
P.O. Box 355 (92274-0355)
PHONE..................760 399-5494
Drake Larson, *Partner*
Pamela Larson, *Partner*
EMP: 200
SQ FT: 3,000
SALES (est): 3.9MM **Privately Held**
SIC: 0172 0161 4222 Grapes; vegetables
& melons; refrigerated warehousing &
storage

(P-142)
E & J GALLO WINERY
Also Called: J Vineyards & Winery
11447 Old Redwood Hwy, Healdsburg
(95448-9523)
PHONE..................707 431-5400
Joseph Gallo, *CEO*
Nicole Mitchell, *Admin Asst*
Bill Richards, *Maint Spvr*
Jennifer Lukens, *Supervisor*
EMP: 52
SALES (corp-wide): 2.6B **Privately Held**
SIC: 0172 2084 Grapes; wines
PA: E. & J. Gallo Winery
600 Yosemite Blvd
Modesto CA 95354
209 341-3111

(P-143)
ENTERPRISE VINEYARDS
16600 Norrbom Rd, Sonoma (95476-4780)
P.O. Box 233, Vineburg (95487-0233)
PHONE..................707 996-6513
Philip Coturri, *President*
Arden Kremer, *Vice Pres*
EMP: 50
SALES (est): 5MM **Privately Held**
SIC: 0172 Grapes

(P-144)
GALLEANO ENTERPRISES INC
4231 Wineville Ave, Mira Loma
(91752-1412)
PHONE..................951 685-5376
Donald Galleano, *President*
Charlene Galleano, *Vice Pres*
EMP: 100
SALES (est): 3.5MM **Privately Held**
SIC: 0172 Grapes

(P-145)
GIUMARRA VINEYARDS
CORPORATION
Giumarra Winery
11220 Edison Hwy, Bakersfield
(93307-8431)
P.O. Box 1969 (93303-1969)
PHONE..................661 395-7071
Barry Douglas, *Manager*
EMP: 55
SALES (corp-wide): 162.4MM **Privately
Held**
SIC: 0172 Grapes
PA: Giumarra Vineyards Corporation
11220 Edison Hwy
Edison CA 93220
661 395-7000

(P-146)
GIUMARRA VINEYARDS
CORPORATION (PA)
11220 Edison Hwy, Edison (93220)
P.O. Box 1969, Bakersfield (93303-1969)
PHONE..................661 395-7000

Wayne Childress, *CEO*
William Butler, *CFO*
Jeffrey Giumarra, *CFO*
Johnathan Giumarra, *Treasurer*
Mimi Corsaro-Dorsey, *Admin Sec*
▲ **EMP:** 500 **EST:** 1946
SQ FT: 10,000
SALES: 162.4MM **Privately Held**
SIC: 0172 2084 2086 Grapes; wines; fruit drinks (less than 100% juice): packaged in cans, etc.; tea, iced: packaged in cans, bottles, etc.

(P-147)
H & R GUNLUND RANCHES INC
3510 W Saginaw Ave, Caruthers (93609-9568)
PHONE....................................559 864-8186
EMP: 220
SALES: 5.4MM **Privately Held**
SIC: 0172

(P-148)
JACK NEAL & SON INC
360 Lafata St, Saint Helena (94574-1410)
PHONE....................................707 963-7303
Mark J Neal, *President*
Tina Galambos, *Vice Pres*
EMP: 200
SQ FT: 20,000
SALES (est): 14.9MM **Privately Held**
SIC: 0172 Grapes

(P-149)
JAKOV P DULCICH & SONS
31956 Peterson Rd, Mc Farland (93250-9606)
PHONE....................................661 792-6360
Jakov Dulcich, *Owner*
Mayra Contreras, *Executive*
Mary Bisogno, *Accounting Mgr*
▲ **EMP:** 250
SALES: 12.7MM **Privately Held**
SIC: 0172 Grapes

(P-150)
JANE MCCLURG
4584 E Floral Ave, Selma (93662-9624)
PHONE....................................559 834-3080
Jane McClurg, *Owner*
EMP: 75
SALES (est): 1.2MM **Privately Held**
SIC: 0172 Grapes

(P-151)
KANDARIAN AGRI ENTERPRISES
Also Called: Agrichem
116 W Adams Ave, Fowler (93625-9614)
P.O. Box 278 (93625-0278)
PHONE....................................559 834-1501
Eugene Kandarian, *President*
Yvonne Kandarian, *Vice Pres*
EMP: 180
SQ FT: 6,500
SALES (est): 11.2MM **Privately Held**
SIC: 0172 4213 5191 Grapes; contract haulers; chemicals, agricultural; fertilizer & fertilizer materials; pesticides

(P-152)
KARAM BATH
1673 W Kamm Ave, Caruthers (93609-9797)
PHONE....................................559 864-3868
Karam Bath, *Owner*
EMP: 50 **EST:** 1983
SALES (est): 1MM **Privately Held**
SIC: 0172 Grapes

(P-153)
KAUTZ VINEYARDS INC (PA)
Also Called: Kautz Ironstone Vineyards
1894 6 Mile Rd, Murphys (95247-9543)
PHONE....................................209 728-1251
John K Kautz, *CEO*
Stephen Kautz, *President*
Kurt Kautz, *Treasurer*
Gail Kautz, *Vice Pres*
Joan Kautz, *Vice Pres*
◆ **EMP:** 100
SQ FT: 75,000
SALES (est): 13.2MM **Privately Held**
WEB: www.ironstonevineyards.com
SIC: 0172 5812 Grapes; eating places

(P-154)
KLEIN FOODS INC
Also Called: Rodney Strong Vineyards
11455 Old Redwood Hwy, Healdsburg (95448-9523)
P.O. Box 6010 (95448-6010)
PHONE....................................707 431-1533
Thomas B Klein, *President*
Tobin Ginter, *CFO*
▲ **EMP:** 100
SQ FT: 20,000
SALES (est): 21.5MM **Privately Held**
WEB: www.rodneystrong.com
SIC: 0172 2084 5182 Grapes; wines; wine & distilled beverages

(P-155)
KVL HOLDINGS INC (PA)
Also Called: Saint Nicolas Vineyard
37700 Foothill Rd, Soledad (93960-9620)
P.O. Box C (93960-0167)
PHONE....................................831 678-2132
Nicholaus Hahn, *CEO*
EMP: 50
SQ FT: 30,000
SALES (est): 19.7MM **Privately Held**
SIC: 0172 2084 6719 Grapes; wines; investment holding companies, except banks

(P-156)
LAMANUZZI & PANTALEO LLC (PA)
11767 Road 27 1/2, Madera (93637-9108)
PHONE....................................559 432-3170
Frank P Pantaleo,
Karol Ryals, *Accountant*
Gary Kalajian, *Sales Staff*
Tina Baer,
Patricia Benneyan,
▲ **EMP:** 64
SQ FT: 1,000
SALES (est): 30.8MM **Privately Held**
SIC: 0172 4222 Grapes; warehousing, cold storage or refrigerated

(P-157)
LANGETWINS INC
1298 E Jahant Rd, Acampo (95220)
PHONE....................................209 339-4055
Randy Lange, *President*
Brad Lange, *CFO*
Charlene Lange, *Vice Pres*
Susan Lange, *Admin Sec*
EMP: 75
SALES (est): 7.3MM **Privately Held**
WEB: www.langetwins.com
SIC: 0172 Grapes

(P-158)
LANZA VINEYARDS INC
Also Called: Wooden Valley Farms
4756 Suisun Valley Rd, Fairfield (94534-3114)
PHONE....................................707 864-0730
Richard Lanza, *President*
Adrienne Lanza, *Treasurer*
Kenneth Lee Lanza, *Vice Pres*
Lawrence Dean Lanza, *Vice Pres*
Mario Richard Lanza Jr, *Vice Pres*
EMP: 50
SQ FT: 1,300
SALES (est): 4.7MM **Privately Held**
WEB: www.woodenvalley.com
SIC: 0172 2084 Grapes; wines

(P-159)
M CARATAN INC (PA)
Also Called: Caliente Farms
33787 Cecil Ave, Delano (93215-9597)
PHONE....................................661 725-2566
Martin Caratin, *CEO*
Jerry Meadows, *Controller*
Renee Massey, *Human Res Dir*
Don Johnston, *Payroll Mgr*
Melissa Michelau, *Opers Mgr*
▼ **EMP:** 150
SQ FT: 6,000
SALES (est): 18.8MM **Privately Held**
WEB: www.mcaratan.com
SIC: 0172 0174 0723 Grapes; orange grove; almond hulling & shelling services

(P-160)
M CARATAN INC
33787 Cecil Ave, Delano (93215-9597)
PHONE....................................661 725-1777
Chris Caratan, *Principal*
EMP: 109
SALES (corp-wide): 18.8MM **Privately Held**
SIC: 0172 Grapes
PA: M. Caratan, Inc.
33787 Cecil Ave
Delano CA 93215
661 725-2566

(P-161)
MCCUTCHEON ENTERPRISES INC
604 W Nebraska Ave, Fresno (93706-9280)
P.O. Box 188, Caruthers (93609-0188)
PHONE....................................559 864-3200
Mike D Mc Cutcheon, *President*
EMP: 100
SQ FT: 4,200
SALES: 550K **Privately Held**
SIC: 0172 0173 Grapes; pistachio grove

(P-162)
MIRABELLA FARMS INC
5551 S Orange Ave, Fresno (93725-9505)
PHONE....................................559 237-4495
Paquerette Markarian, *President*
Philip Markarian, *Treasurer*
Joseph Markarian, *Vice Pres*
EMP: 75
SALES (est): 2.2MM **Privately Held**
WEB: www.mirabellafarms.com
SIC: 0172 Grapes

(P-163)
NESTOR ENTERPRISES LLC
13852 E Peltier Rd, Acampo (95220-9342)
PHONE....................................209 727-5711
Fransico Ilayala,
EMP: 50
SALES (est): 2.8MM **Privately Held**
WEB: www.nestorenterprises.com
SIC: 0172 Grapes

(P-164)
ONEILL BEVERAGES CO LLC (PA)
Also Called: O'Neill Vintners & Distillers
101 Larkspur Landing Cir, Larkspur (94939-1746)
PHONE....................................844 825-6600
Jeffrey B O'Neill, *CEO*
Mark Federighi, *Senior VP*
Ryan Davis, *Vice Pres*
Mike Drobnick, *Vice Pres*
Brendan O'Mahoney, *Division Mgr*
◆ **EMP:** 63
SQ FT: 5,000
SALES (est): 23MM **Privately Held**
SIC: 0172 2084 Grapes; wines

(P-165)
PANDOL & SONS
401 Road 192, Delano (93215-9598)
PHONE....................................661 725-3755
Cheri Diebel, *CEO*
Jack V Pandol, *Partner*
Lucy Pandol, *Partner*
Steve Pandol III, *Partner*
Sherry Dibdel, *CFO*
EMP: 50 **EST:** 1930
SQ FT: 10,000
SALES: 13.9MM **Privately Held**
SIC: 0172 0723 Grapes; fruit (fresh) packing services

(P-166)
R H PHILLIPS INC (HQ)
Also Called: R H Phillips Vineyard
26836 County Road 12a, Esparto (95627-2139)
PHONE....................................530 757-5557
John Giguiere, *Ch of Bd*
EMP: 245
SQ FT: 4,500
SALES (est): 11.9MM
SALES (corp-wide): 7.5B **Publicly Held**
SIC: 0172 2084 5182 Grapes; wines; wine & distilled beverages

PA: Constellation Brands, Inc.
207 High Point Dr # 100
Victor NY 14564
585 678-7100

(P-167)
RICHARD BAGDASARIAN INC
65500 Lincoln St, Mecca (92254-6500)
P.O. Box 698 (92254-0698)
PHONE....................................760 396-2168
Nicholas L Bozick, *CEO*
Michael Bozick, *President*
Darrell Billings, *CFO*
Tim Graven, *CFO*
Bobbie Bozick, *Exec VP*
▲ **EMP:** 60
SQ FT: 40,000
SALES (est): 14MM **Privately Held**
WEB: www.bagdasarianinc.com
SIC: 0172 0174 Grapes; citrus fruits

(P-168)
RICHARDS GROVE SARALEES VINYRD
1998 Jones Rd, Windsor (95492-7758)
PHONE....................................707 837-9200
Saralee McClelland Kunde, *President*
EMP: 65
SQ FT: 10,333
SALES (est): 1.2MM **Privately Held**
WEB: www.saraleesvineyards.com
SIC: 0172 Grapes

(P-169)
RIOS FARMING COMPANY LLC
3851 Chiles Pope Vly Rd, Saint Helena (94574-9588)
PHONE....................................707 965-2587
Manuel Rios,
EMP: 140
SQ FT: 1,500
SALES (est): 6.7MM **Privately Held**
SIC: 0172 0762 Grapes; vineyard management & maintenance services

(P-170)
ROBERT ALVES FARMS INC
Also Called: Alves, Robert L
10642 E Dinuba Ave, Selma (93662-9783)
PHONE....................................559 896-3309
Robert Alves, *Owner*
Rita Garza, *Bookkeeper*
EMP: 70
SALES (est): 2.1MM **Privately Held**
SIC: 0172

(P-171)
RON D & SHELLEY N HORN
3719 E Floral Ave, Fresno (93725-9651)
PHONE....................................559 834-2118
Ronald Horn, *Owner*
EMP: 50
SALES (est): 877.1K **Privately Held**
SIC: 0172 Grapes

(P-172)
SAN BERNABE VINEYARDS
53001 Oasis Rd, King City (93930-9667)
PHONE....................................831 385-4897
Claude Hoover, *President*
Dorothy Indelicato, *Treasurer*
Frank Indelicato, *Admin Sec*
EMP: 65
SQ FT: 15,000
SALES (est): 4.5MM
SALES (corp-wide): 46.5MM **Privately Held**
WEB: www.winequest.com
SIC: 0172 2084 Grapes; wines, brandy & brandy spirits
PA: Delicato Vineyards
12001 S Highway 99
Manteca CA 95336
209 824-3600

(P-173)
SANDRINI FARMS
29794 Schuster Rd, Mc Farland (93250-9784)
PHONE....................................661 792-3192
Mae Sandrini, *Owner*
EMP: 60
SALES (est): 1MM **Privately Held**
SIC: 0172 Grapes

PRODUCTS & SVCS

(P-174)
SCHEID VINEYARDS CAL INC
305 Hilltown Rd, Salinas (93908-8902)
PHONE.....................831 385-4801
Kurt Gollnick, *Branch Mgr*
Pete Garibay, *Maintence Staff*
EMP: 90
SALES (corp-wide): 59MM **Publicly Held**
WEB: www.scheidvineyards.com
SIC: 0172 5813 Grapes; drinking places
HQ: Scheid Vineyards California Inc.
305 Hilltown Rd
Salinas CA 93908
831 455-9990

(P-175)
SCHEID VINEYARDS INC (PA)
305 Hilltown Rd, Salinas (93908-8902)
PHONE.....................310 301-1555
Scott D Scheid, *President*
Alfred G Scheid, *Ch of Bd*
Kurt J Gollnick, *COO*
Michael S Thomsen, *CFO*
Heidi M Scheid, *Treasurer*
EMP: 78
SQ FT: 6,700
SALES (est): 59MM **Publicly Held**
SIC: 0172 2084 Grapes; wines

(P-176)
SCHEID VINEYARDS INC
373 Healdsburg Ave, Healdsburg
(95448-4137)
PHONE.....................707 433-1858
EMP: 107
SALES (corp-wide): 56.4MM **Publicly Held**
SIC: 0172
PA: Scheid Vineyards Inc.
305 Hilltown Rd
Salinas CA 93908
310 301-1555

(P-177)
SCHRAMSBERG VINEYARDS COMPANY
1400 Schramsberg Rd, Calistoga
(94515-9624)
PHONE.....................707 942-4558
Hugh Davies, *President*
Jack Bittner, *Bd of Directors*
William P Davies, *Bd of Directors*
Jenn North, *Admin Sec*
Doug Francisco, *HR Admin*
◆ EMP: 50
SQ FT: 20,000
SALES (est): 5.8MM **Privately Held**
WEB: www.schramsberg.com
SIC: 0172 2084 Grapes; wines

(P-178)
STAGECOACH VINEYARDS
1345 Hestia Way, NAPA (94558-2105)
PHONE.....................707 255-5459
Jan Krupp, *Partner*
▲ EMP: 100
SALES (est): 7.4MM **Privately Held**
WEB: www.stagecoachvineyard.com
SIC: 0172 Grapes

(P-179)
SUN-MAID GROWERS CALIFORNIA
Also Called: Valley Fig Growers
4683 Chabot Dr Ste 100, Pleasanton
(94588-3863)
P.O. Box 9106 (94566-9105)
PHONE.....................800 752-9277
John Slinkard, *Vice Pres*
Frank Ferraris, *Vice Pres*
David Joseph, *Vice Pres*
Doug Nesbit, *Vice Pres*
Joe Ponder, *Vice Pres*
EMP: 50
SALES (corp-wide): 360.8MM **Privately Held**
SIC: 0172 5149 5148 Grapes; groceries & related products; fresh fruits & vegetables
PA: Sun-Maid Growers Of California
13525 S Bethel Ave
Kingsburg CA 93631
559 897-6235

(P-180)
TREASURY WINE ESTATES AMERICAS
Also Called: Meridian Vineyards
7000 E Highway 46, Paso Robles
(93446-7390)
PHONE.....................805 237-6000
Jim Schaefer, *Manager*
EMP: 120 **Privately Held**
WEB: www.stclement.com
SIC: 0172 2084 Grapes; wines, brandy & brandy spirits
HQ: Treasury Wine Estates Americas Company
555 Gateway Dr
Napa CA 94558
707 259-4500

(P-181)
V SANGIACOMO & SONS
Also Called: Sangiacomo Vineyards
21543 Broadway, Sonoma (95476-8205)
PHONE.....................707 938-5503
Victor F Sangiacomo, *Partner*
Angelo C Sangiacomo, *Partner*
Lorraine J Sangiacomo, *Partner*
EMP: 180
SQ FT: 1,200
SALES (est): 14.3MM **Privately Held**
WEB: www.sangiacomo-vineyards.com
SIC: 0172 Grapes

(P-182)
VINCENT B ZANINOVICH SONS INC
Also Called: V B Z
20715 Ave 8, Richgrove (93261)
P.O. Box 1000 (93261-1000)
PHONE.....................661 720-9031
John V Zaninovich, *CEO*
Vincent Zaninovich, *President*
Andrew Zaninovich, *Vice Pres*
Tom Nguyen, *Technology*
Joe Butkiewicz, *Controller*
◆ EMP: 1000
SQ FT: 15,450
SALES (est): 24.1MM **Privately Held**
SIC: 0172 Grapes

(P-183)
VINCENT V ZANINOVICH & SONS
2480 E Washington St, Earlimart
(93219-9694)
PHONE.....................661 849-2613
INA Zaninovich, *Partner*
Estate of Vincent V Zaninovich, *Partner*
EMP: 99
SALES (est): 3.2MM **Privately Held**
SIC: 0172 0139 0131 Grapes; alfalfa farm; cotton

0173 Tree Nuts

(P-184)
AGRESERVES INC
Also Called: Deseret Farms of California
6100 Wilson Landing Rd, Chico
(95973-8902)
PHONE.....................530 343-5365
Travis Reid, *Branch Mgr*
Sherry Andersen, *Controller*
EMP: 75
SALES (corp-wide): 225.1MM **Privately Held**
WEB: www.dlandl.com
SIC: 0173 0175 Almond grove; walnut grove; prune orchard
HQ: Agreserves, Inc.
79 S Main St Ste 1100
Salt Lake City UT 84111

(P-185)
CHARANJIT SINGH BATTH
Also Called: Batth Farms
5434 W Kamm Ave, Caruthers
(93609-9400)
PHONE.....................559 864-9421
Charanjit Singh Batth, *Owner*
EMP: 90
SQ FT: 1,200

SALES (est): 7.3MM **Privately Held**
SIC: 0173 0175 0172 2034 Almond grove; prune orchard; grapes; raisins

(P-186)
DE BENEDETTO FARMS INC
Also Called: D'Best Produce
1547 N Marks Ave, Fresno (93722-5723)
P.O. Box 9760 (93794-9760)
PHONE.....................559 276-2400
Maurice De Benedetto, *President*
Mark De Benedetto, *Shareholder*
Mathew De Benedetto, *Shareholder*
Maury De Benedetto, *Shareholder*
EMP: 80
SQ FT: 2,000
SALES (est): 2.4MM **Privately Held**
SIC: 0173 Pecan grove; almond grove

(P-187)
ED THOMING & SONS INC
33600 S Koster Rd, Tracy (95304-8996)
PHONE.....................209 835-2792
John Thoming, *President*
James L Thoming, *Vice Pres*
EMP: 100
SQ FT: 800
SALES (est): 4.8MM **Privately Held**
SIC: 0173 0175 Almond grove; deciduous tree fruits

(P-188)
FARMERS INTERNATIONAL INC
1260 Muir Ave, Chico (95973-8644)
PHONE.....................530 566-1405
Don Wada, *CEO*
Mohnish Seth, *Principal*
◆ EMP: 50
SALES (est): 10.2MM **Privately Held**
WEB: www.farmersinternational.com
SIC: 0173 Almond grove

(P-189)
FRAZIER NUT FARMS INC
10830 Yosemite Blvd, Waterford
(95386-9637)
PHONE.....................209 522-1406
Jim Frazier Jr, *President*
Heidi Frazier-Slacks, *Corp Secy*
Steve Slacks, *Vice Pres*
Sherry Frazier, *Telecom Exec*
▼ EMP: 50
SALES (est): 4.7MM **Privately Held**
SIC: 0173 Walnut grove

(P-190)
INTERNATIONAL ALMOND EXCHANGE
144 W Lake Ave, Watsonville (95076-4573)
PHONE.....................831 728-4534
Jagjit Tut, *CEO*
Rajveer Tut, *Vice Pres*
▼ EMP: 50
SQ FT: 653,400
SALES: 1MM **Privately Held**
SIC: 0173 Almond grove

(P-191)
KEENAN FARMS INC
31510 Plymouth Ave, Kettleman City
(93239-9721)
P.O. Box 99, Avenal (93204-0099)
PHONE.....................559 945-1400
Robert M Keenan, *CEO*
Charles J Keenan III, *Vice Pres*
Catherine Underwood, *Office Mgr*
Manny Guerrero, *VP Opers*
Peter Theodore, *Plant Mgr*
◆ EMP: 100
SALES (est): 23.2MM **Privately Held**
SIC: 0173 2068 Pistachio grove; nuts: dried, dehydrated, salted or roasted

(P-192)
MARIANI NUT COMPANY INC (PA)
709 Dutton St, Winters (95694-1748)
P.O. Box 809 (95694-0809)
PHONE.....................530 795-3311
Jack Norman Marlani, *CEO*
Martin Mariani, *Treasurer*
Dennis Mariani, *Vice Pres*
Matt Messer, *Executive*
Tom Biggs, *Database Admin*
◆ EMP: 110
SQ FT: 30,000

SALES (est): 59.9MM **Privately Held**
WEB: www.marianinut.com
SIC: 0173 Walnut grove; almond grove

(P-193)
MARIANI NUT COMPANY INC
12 Baker St, Winters (95694-1704)
P.O. Box 808 (95694-0808)
PHONE.....................530 795-2225
Jef McDowell, *Manager*
EMP: 70
SALES (corp-wide): 59.9MM **Privately Held**
WEB: www.marianinut.com
SIC: 0173 Walnut grove
PA: Mariani Nut Company, Inc.
709 Dutton St
Winters CA 95694
530 795-3311

(P-194)
RAMOS ORCHARDS
9192 Boyce Rd, Winters (95694-9625)
P.O. Box 488 (95694-0488)
PHONE.....................530 795-4748
Fred Ramos, *Owner*
EMP: 67
SQ FT: 9,600
SALES (est): 3.5MM **Privately Held**
SIC: 0173 0175 Walnut grove; prune orchard

(P-195)
RICHARD SWANSON INC
17659 Swanson Rd, Delhi (95315-9636)
P.O. Box 244 (95315-0244)
PHONE.....................209 632-3883
Timothy Swanson, *President*
Erline Swanson, *Treasurer*
Richard Swanson, *Vice Pres*
EMP: 60
SALES: 1.5MM **Privately Held**
SIC: 0173 0175 0252 Almond grove; peach orchard; chicken eggs

(P-196)
TEJON RANCH CO (PA)
4436 Lebec Rd, Lebec (93243-9705)
P.O. Box 1000 (93243-1000)
PHONE.....................661 248-3000
Gregory S Bielli, *President*
Norman J Metcalfe, *Ch of Bd*
Allen E Lyda, *CFO*
Hugh McMahon, *Exec VP*
Joseph N Rentfro, *Exec VP*
EMP: 83 EST: 1936
SALES: 35.6MM **Publicly Held**
WEB: www.tejonfilm.com
SIC: 0173 0172 6531 Almond grove; pistachio grove; walnut grove; grapes; real estate brokers & agents

(P-197)
WONDERFUL ORCHARDS LLC (HQ)
Also Called: Paramount Farming
6801 E Lerdo Hwy, Shafter (93263-9610)
PHONE.....................661 399-4456
Craig Cooper,
Joseph Mac Ilvaine,
William Phillimore,
Stuart Resnick,
▲ EMP: 150
SQ FT: 10,000
SALES (est): 171.6MM
SALES (corp-wide): 1.5B **Privately Held**
SIC: 0173 0179 Almond grove; olive grove
PA: The Wonderful Company Llc
11444 W Olympic Blvd # 210
Los Angeles CA 90064
310 966-5700

(P-198)
WONDERFUL ORCHARDS LLC
Also Called: Wonderfulpistachiosandalmonds
13646 Highway 33, Lost Hills (93249-9719)
P.O. Box 400 (93249-0400)
PHONE.....................661 797-6400
Dennis Elam, *Branch Mgr*
EMP: 150
SALES (corp-wide): 1.5B **Privately Held**
SIC: 0173 0191 Almond grove; general farms, primarily crop

▲ = Import ▼=Export
◆ =Import/Export

HQ: Wonderful Orchards Llc
6801 E Lerdo Hwy
Shafter CA 93263
661 399-4456

0174 Citrus Fruits

(P-199)
ACEMI NURSERY INC
3626 N Howard Ave, Kerman (93630)
PHONE......................559 842-7766
Alvaro Garcia, *President*
Carmen Garcia, *Vice Pres*
EMP: 80
SALES: 5MM **Privately Held**
SIC: 0174 Citrus fruits

(P-200)
ACMPC CALIFORNIA 3 LLC
Also Called: Suntreat Packing & Shipping Co
38773 Rd 48, Lindsay (93247)
PHONE......................559 591-6140
Darren Silkins, *CEO*
Tracy Saiki, *Exec VP*
Rick Johnston, *VP Sales*
EMP: 200 EST: 2015
SALES (est): 3MM **Privately Held**
SIC: 0174 Citrus fruits

(P-201)
AIRDROME ORCHARDS INC (PA)
111 E Alma Ave, San Jose (95112-2792)
PHONE......................408 297-6461
Charles Fumia, *CEO*
John Fumia Jr, *CFO*
Anthony Buldo, *Vice Pres*
Paul Buldo, *Vice Pres*
Tony Buldo, *Vice Pres*
▼ EMP: 50
SQ FT: 30,000
SALES (est): 8.5MM **Privately Held**
SIC: 0174 0175 Orange grove; pear orchard

(P-202)
BADGER FARMING COMPANY INC
150 W Pine St, Exeter (93221-1613)
PHONE......................559 592-5520
Oleah Wilson, *President*
James Wilson, *President*
EMP: 60
SALES (est): 2.8MM **Privately Held**
SIC: 0174 Citrus fruits

(P-203)
BERESFORD CORP
582 Market St Ste 912, San Francisco (94104-5310)
PHONE......................415 981-7386
Christopher D Lange, *President*
EMP: 145
SALES (est): 8.3MM **Privately Held**
SIC: 0174 Citrus fruits

(P-204)
CALIFORNIA CITRUS COOPERATIVE
859 Center St, Riverside (92507-1408)
PHONE......................951 683-4045
Larry Topham, *Manager*
David Prior, *CFO*
EMP: 65
SQ FT: 2,000
SALES (est): 5.5MM **Privately Held**
SIC: 0174 Grapefruit grove; orange grove

(P-205)
HAMILTON FAMILY RANCH
2562 Doville Ranch Rd, Fallbrook (92028-9138)
PHONE......................760 728-1358
Dorothy Hamilton, *Partner*
Alexander Hamilton, *Partner*
Meade Hamilton, *Partner*
Michelle Hamilton, *Partner*
EMP: 70
SALES (est): 1MM **Privately Held**
SIC: 0174

(P-206)
HRONIS INC A CALIFORNIA CORP (PA)
10443 Hronis Rd, Delano (93215-9556)
PHONE......................661 725-2503
Kosta Hronis, *President*
Pete Hronis, *Vice Pres*
Ruben Galaviz, *Manager*
Sonia Ponce, *Manager*
▼ EMP: 54
SQ FT: 150,000
SALES (est): 50.3MM **Privately Held**
WEB: www.hronis.net
SIC: 0174 0172 Citrus fruits; grapes

(P-207)
MARLAND CO LP
444 S Flower St Ste 1200, Los Angeles (90071-2977)
PHONE......................213 614-6171
Chirstopher Martin, *Partner*
Oliver Santos, *Admin Sec*
EMP: 50
SQ FT: 200
SALES (est): 888.7K **Privately Held**
SIC: 0174 Orange grove

(P-208)
PADILLA FARM LABOR INC
20486 Road 196, Lindsay (93247-9426)
PHONE......................559 562-1166
David Padilla, *President*
Rosie Padilla, *Corp Secy*
EMP: 200
SALES (est): 5.8MM **Privately Held**
SIC: 0174 Orange grove

(P-209)
SATICOY LEMON ASSOCIATION
Also Called: Saticoy Fruit Exchange
7560 Bristol Rd, Ventura (93003-7027)
P.O. Box 46, Santa Paula (93061-0046)
PHONE......................805 654-6500
John Elliott, *Branch Mgr*
EMP: 100
SALES (corp-wide): 171MM **Privately Held**
SIC: 0174 Lemon grove
PA: Saticoy Lemon Association
103 N Peck Rd
Santa Paula CA 93060
805 654-6500

(P-210)
WONDERFUL CITRUS PACKING LLC
Also Called: Fillmore Farm Management
2707 W Telegraph Rd, Fillmore (93015-9647)
PHONE......................805 525-3818
EMP: 100
SALES (corp-wide): 1.5B **Privately Held**
WEB: www.paramountcitrus.com
SIC: 0174 Citrus fruits
HQ: Wonderful Citrus Packing Llc
1901 S Lexington St
Delano CA 93215
661 720-2400

(P-211)
WONDERFUL COMPANY LLC
Also Called: Paramount Citrus
1901 S Lexington St, Delano (93215-9207)
PHONE......................661 720-2400
Freddie Hernandez, *Manager*
Matthew Mitchell, *Network Enginr*
EMP: 273
SALES (corp-wide): 1.5B **Privately Held**
SIC: 0174 3911 Citrus fruits; jewelry, precious metal
PA: The Wonderful Company Llc
11444 W Olympic Blvd # 210
Los Angeles CA 90064
310 966-5700

(P-212)
YOUNG DOWLIN L
Also Called: Young's Nursery
101 Clay St, San Francisco (94111-2033)
PHONE......................760 397-4104
Dowlin L Young, *Owner*
Daisy Young, *Co-Owner*
EMP: 50
SQ FT: 1,000

SALES: 2.5MM **Privately Held**
SIC: 0174 Citrus fruits

0175 Deciduous Tree Fruits

(P-213)
ANTHONY BOTELHO
382 Olympia Ave, San Juan Bautista (95045-9501)
PHONE......................831 623-4228
Anthony Botelho, *Owner*
EMP: 60 EST: 1998
SALES (est): 1.3MM **Privately Held**
WEB: www.botelhoforsupervisor.com
SIC: 0175 Apple orchard

(P-214)
ASHLEY LANE CHERRY ORCHARDS LP
500 N Jack Tone Rd, Stockton (95215-9725)
P.O. Box 659, Linden (95236-0659)
PHONE......................209 546-0426
Henry J Foppiano, *Partner*
Diane Lechich, *Administration*
EMP: 50
SALES (est): 1.6MM **Privately Held**
SIC: 0175 Cherry orchard

(P-215)
BT HOLDINGS INC
Also Called: Quercus Ranch
4150 Soda Bay Rd, Kelseyville (95451)
P.O. Box 548 (95451-0548)
PHONE......................707 279-4317
EMP: 50 EST: 1979
SQ FT: 120,000
SALES (est): 500K **Privately Held**
SIC: 0175 0172

(P-216)
ENNS PACKING COMPANY INC
Also Called: Enns Farms
1911 Bergren Ct, Kingsburg (93631-2705)
PHONE......................559 897-7700
Melvin Enns, *President*
Kenneth Enns, *Treasurer*
Eugene Enns, *Principal*
Mike Enns, *Admin Sec*
EMP: 50
SQ FT: 4,200
SALES: 36.9K **Privately Held**
SIC: 0175 4222 0723 Deciduous tree fruits; storage, frozen or refrigerated goods; fruit (fresh) packing services

(P-217)
FARMINGTON FRESH SALES LLC (PA)
7735 S Highway 99, Stockton (95215-9623)
P.O. Box 951 (95201-0951)
PHONE......................209 983-9700
Ernie Pascua, *CEO*
Nick Rajkovich, *President*
Hugh Rice, *Administration*
Garrison Rajkovich, *Marketing Mgr*
Velda Redmond, *Sales Staff*
EMP: 250
SQ FT: 132,000
SALES: 25.8MM **Privately Held**
WEB: www.farmingtonfresh.com
SIC: 0175 4731 Apple orchard; pear orchard; agents, shipping

(P-218)
HAMLOW RANCHES INC
4018 Swanson Rd, Denair (95316-9733)
P.O. Box 898 (95316-0898)
PHONE......................209 632-2873
Karen Hamlow, *CEO*
EMP: 50 EST: 1951
SALES (est): 2MM **Privately Held**
SIC: 0175 0173 Peach orchard; almond grove

(P-219)
HILDRETH FARM INCORPORATED
1520 Rddick Cunningham Rd, Ukiah (95482-9638)
PHONE......................707 462-0648
Michael L Hildreth, *President*
Susan Hildreth, *Vice Pres*

EMP: 56
SALES (est): 2.3MM **Privately Held**
SIC: 0175 0172 Pear orchard; grapes

(P-220)
J & P SOLARI
6302 Foppiano Ln, Stockton (95212-9407)
PHONE......................209 931-1765
Joe S Solari, *Partner*
Joseph Solari I I I, *Partner*
Phillip Solari, *Partner*
Raymond Solari, *Partner*
EMP: 100
SALES (est): 1.4MM **Privately Held**
SIC: 0175 0173 0811 Cherry orchard; walnut grove; almond grove; timber tracts

(P-221)
KAY DIX INC
14400 Andrus Island Rd, Isleton (95641-9804)
P.O. Box 248, Walnut Grove (95690-0248)
PHONE......................916 776-1701
Daniel M Wilson, *President*
Darrell Wilson, *Treasurer*
Daniel Wilson, *General Mgr*
Angela Gonzalez, *Office Mgr*
Chiles Wilson, *Admin Sec*
EMP: 50
SQ FT: 1,000
SALES (est): 1MM **Privately Held**
SIC: 0175 0115 0111 Pear orchard; corn; wheat

(P-222)
KINGSBURG APPLE PARTNERS LP
10363 Davis Ave, Kingsburg (93631-9539)
P.O. Box 456 (93631-0456)
PHONE......................559 897-5132
Colleen Jackson, *Ltd Ptnr*
Susan Jackson Diepersloot, *Ltd Ptnr*
Brent Jackson, *Ltd Ptnr*
▼ EMP: 100
SQ FT: 140,000
SALES (est): 5.8MM **Privately Held**
WEB: www.kingsburgorchards.com
SIC: 0175 Apple orchard; pear orchard

(P-223)
KOZUKI FARMING INC
16518 E Adams Ave, Parlier (93648-9718)
PHONE......................559 646-2652
EMP: 60
SALES: 2.2MM **Privately Held**
SIC: 0175 0172

(P-224)
MALLOY ORCHARDS INC
925 Koch Ln, Live Oak (95953-9602)
PHONE......................530 695-1861
William A Filter Jr, *President*
EMP: 200
SALES (est): 4.1MM **Privately Held**
SIC: 0175 0173 0761 Peach orchard; prune orchard; walnut grove; farm labor contractors

(P-225)
MICHELI FARMS INC
6005 Highway 99, Live Oak (95953-9749)
PHONE......................530 695-9022
John Micheli, *President*
Justin Micheli, *Admin Sec*
EMP: 50
SQ FT: 108,000
SALES (est): 2.6MM **Privately Held**
WEB: www.lomocold.com
SIC: 0175 0173 Peach orchard; prune orchard; walnut grove

(P-226)
MIKE JENSEN FARMS
13138 S Bethel Ave, Kingsburg (93631-9216)
PHONE......................559 897-4192
Mike Jensen, *Owner*
EMP: 200
SQ FT: 14,000
SALES (est): 6.3MM **Privately Held**
SIC: 0175 2033 2099 Apricot orchard; nectarine orchard; peach orchard; plum orchard; fruits: packaged in cans, jars, etc.; food preparations

PRODUCTS & SVCS

(P-227)
PETERSON FAMILY INC
38694 Road 16, Kingsburg (93631-9106)
PHONE..............................559 897-5064
Vernon E Peterson, *Owner*
EMP: 100
SALES (est): 5.4MM **Privately Held**
WEB: www.peterson.org
SIC: 0175 0174 Deciduous tree fruits; citrus fruits

(P-228)
PHILLIPS FARMS
33771 Road 156, Visalia (93292-9153)
PHONE..............................559 798-1871
Douglas Phillips, *Owner*
Bobby Chavez, *Finance Mgr*
◆ **EMP:** 50
SALES (est): 3.3MM **Privately Held**
SIC: 0175 0723 Deciduous tree fruits; fruit (fresh) packing services

(P-229)
SACRAMENTO PACKING INC (PA)
833 Tudor Rd, Yuba City (95991-9532)
P.O. Box 3540 (95992-3540)
PHONE..............................530 671-4488
Jaswant S Bains, *President*
Satwant Bains, *General Mgr*
◆ **EMP:** 50
SQ FT: 80,000
SALES (est): 19.2MM **Privately Held**
WEB: www.sacramentopacking.com
SIC: 0175 Deciduous tree fruits

(P-230)
SMITH RANCH
1671 Campbell Rd, Live Oak (95953-9707)
PHONE..............................530 695-2521
Dale Smith, *Partner*
Dean Smith, *Partner*
Gail Hebert, *Principal*
EMP: 50
SALES (est): 3.2MM **Privately Held**
SIC: 0175 0173 Peach orchard; prune orchard; walnut grove

(P-231)
VIRGINIA SARABIAN
Also Called: Sarabian Farms
2816 S Leonard Ave, Sanger (93657-9754)
PHONE..............................559 493-2900
Michael Sarabian, *Owner*
Sarkis Sarabian, *Owner*
Virginia Sarabian, *Owner*
David Sarabian, *COO*
Maribel Rios, *Administration*
EMP: 50
SQ FT: 1,200
SALES: 15MM **Privately Held**
SIC: 0175 0172 4222 2033 Nectarine orchard; peach orchard; plum orchard; grapes; warehousing, cold storage or refrigerated; fruits: packaged in cans, jars, etc.

0179 Fruits & Tree Nuts, NEC

(P-232)
AGRILAND HOLDING INC
23400 Road 24, Chowchilla (93610-9558)
PHONE..............................559 665-2100
James Maxwell, *President*
Sandra Bain, *Admin Sec*
EMP: 85
SQ FT: 7,500
SALES (est): 2.9MM **Privately Held**
SIC: 0179 0173 Fig orchard; tree nuts

(P-233)
CHIQUITA FRESH NORTH AMER LLC
1440 E 3rd St, Oxnard (93030-6106)
PHONE..............................954 924-5642
Junior Cutrale, *Mng Member*
EMP: 300
SQ FT: 1,500
SALES: 50MM **Privately Held**
SIC: 0179 Banana grove

(P-234)
DOLE FOOD COMPANY INC (HQ)
1 Dole Dr, Westlake Village (91362-7300)
PHONE..............................818 874-4000
David H Murdock, *Ch of Bd*
Johan Linden, *President*
Johan Malmqvist, *CFO*
Yoon J Hugh, *Senior VP*
Charlene Mims, *Senior VP*
◆ **EMP:** 188
SALES (est): 1B
SALES (corp-wide): 11.7B **Privately Held**
WEB: www.dole.com
SIC: 0179 0174 0175 0161 Pineapple farm; banana grove; citrus fruits; deciduous tree fruits; lettuce farm; celery farm; cauliflower farm; broccoli farm; fruits; vegetables; fruit juices: fresh; fruit juices: packaged in cans, jars, etc.
PA: Dfc Holdings, Llc
1 Dole Dr
Westlake Village CA 91362
818 879-6600

(P-235)
DOLE HOLDING COMPANY LLC
1 Dole Dr, Westlake Village (91362-7300)
PHONE..............................818 879-6600
David H Murdock, *Ch of Bd*
EMP: 49207
SALES: 57.6MM **Privately Held**
SIC: 0179 0174 0175 0161 Pineapple farm; banana grove; citrus fruits; deciduous tree fruits; lettuce farm; celery farm; cauliflower farm; broccoli farm; fruits; vegetables; fruit juices: fresh; fruit juices: packaged in cans, jars, etc.
PA: Dhm Holding Company, Inc
1 Dole Dr
Westlake Village CA 91362
-

(P-236)
HENRY AVOCADO CORPORATION (PA)
2208 Harmony Grove Rd, Escondido (92029-2054)
P.O. Box 300867 (92030-0867)
PHONE..............................760 745-6632
Philip Henry, *President*
Rick Opel, *Vice Pres*
Lori Deaver, *Office Mgr*
Bill Pankey, *Applctn Conslt*
Terry Adams, *Accounting Mgr*
◆ **EMP:** 70
SQ FT: 35,000
SALES: 301.4MM **Privately Held**
SIC: 0179 4213 Avocado orchard; trucking, except local

(P-237)
IRVINE VALENCIA GROWERS
11501 Jeffrey Rd, Irvine (92602-0503)
PHONE..............................949 936-8000
Peter Changala, *President*
Brian Thompson, *Treasurer*
Scott Starkey, *Regional*
EMP: 75
SQ FT: 10,000
SALES (est): 2.9MM **Privately Held**
SIC: 0179 0723 Avocado orchard; fruit (fresh) packing services

(P-238)
MUNGER BROS LLC
Also Called: Munger Farm
786 Road 188, Delano (93215-9508)
PHONE..............................661 721-0390
Baldev K Munger,
Kewel K Munger,
▲ **EMP:** 600
SQ FT: 50,000
SALES: 10MM **Privately Held**
SIC: 0179 Avocado orchard

(P-239)
SUNDANCE NATURAL FOODS COMPANY
2231 Willowbrook Dr, Oceanside (92056-2506)
P.O. Box 5358 (92052-5358)
PHONE..............................760 945-9898
K Jacob Hoffnagle, *CEO*
Mary Hahlbohm, *Treasurer*

Lorena Estrada, *Chief Mktg Ofcr*
Lonnie Graves, *Purch Agent*
EMP: 50
SQ FT: 40,000
SALES (est): 7.3MM **Privately Held**
WEB: www.sundancenaturalfoodscompany.com
SIC: 0179 0723 Avocado orchard; fruit (fresh) packing services

(P-240)
WILLIAM C ARTERBERRY
40147 Calle Roxanne, Fallbrook (92028-9701)
PHONE..............................760 728-9096
William Arterberry, *Owner*
EMP: 62
SALES (est): 1.1MM **Privately Held**
SIC: 0179 Avocado orchard

0181 Ornamental Floriculture & Nursery Prdts

(P-241)
3-WAY FARMS (PA)
428 Browns Valley Rd, Watsonville (95076-0330)
PHONE..............................831 722-0748
Delbert Herschbach, *President*
Lorraine Stern, *Treasurer*
Rosemarie Herschbach, *Admin Sec*
EMP: 50
SALES (est): 3.8MM **Privately Held**
SIC: 0181 3999 Ornamental nursery products; flowers, artificial & preserved

(P-242)
AZALEA & ROSE CO
1420 N Campus Ave, Upland (91786-2317)
PHONE..............................909 949-2442
Mike Tolle, *President*
EMP: 50
SALES (est): 676.7K **Privately Held**
SIC: 0181 Roses, growing of

(P-243)
BALL HORTICULTURAL COMPANY
400 Obispo St, Guadalupe (93434-1632)
PHONE..............................805 343-2723
John Sorell, *Branch Mgr*
EMP: 117
SALES (corp-wide): 626.6MM **Privately Held**
SIC: 0181 Bulbs & seeds
PA: Ball Horticultural Company
622 Town Rd
West Chicago IL 60185
630 231-3600

(P-244)
BALL TAGAWA GROWERS
819 Zenon Way, Arroyo Grande (93420-5855)
P.O. Box 2440, Pismo Beach (93448-2440)
PHONE..............................805 481-7526
Randy Tagawa, *Partner*
Ann Ball, *Partner*
EMP: 50
SQ FT: 120,000
SALES (est): 1.1MM **Privately Held**
SIC: 0181 Nursery stock, growing of

(P-245)
BARCELO ENTERPRISES INC
4400 Macarthur Blvd # 980, Newport Beach (92660-2054)
PHONE..............................760 728-3444
Antonio C Barcelo Sr, *President*
Antonio Barcelo Jr, *Vice Pres*
Rosa H Barcelo, *Vice Pres*
▲ **EMP:** 100 **EST:** 1997
SALES (est): 7.9MM **Privately Held**
WEB: www.alivingfossil.com
SIC: 0181 Nursery stock, growing of

(P-246)
BAY CITY FLOWER CO
1450 Cabrillo Hwy S, Half Moon Bay (94019-2243)
PHONE..............................650 712-8147
Harrison Higaki, *Principal*
EMP: 224

SALES (corp-wide): 74.5MM **Privately Held**
SIC: 0181 Plants, potted: growing of
PA: Bay City Flower Co.
2265 Cabrillo Hwy S
Half Moon Bay CA 94019
650 726-5535

(P-247)
BLX GROUP INC
71534 Sahara Rd, Rancho Mirage (92270-4340)
PHONE..............................760 776-6622
Timothy Blixseth, *President*
EMP: 95
SALES (est): 2MM **Privately Held**
SIC: 0181

(P-248)
BROKAW NURSERY LLC
5501 Elizabeth Rd, Ventura (93004-1002)
P.O. Box 4818 (93007-0818)
PHONE..............................805 647-2262
Ellen Brokaw, *President*
Kay Mendel, *CFO*
Robert C Brokaw, *Vice Pres*
Marge Apodaca, *Principal*
Consuelo Fernandez, *Research*
EMP: 52
SQ FT: 5,000
SALES (est): 6.5MM **Privately Held**
WEB: www.brokawnursery.com
SIC: 0181 0179 Nursery stock, growing of; avocado orchard

(P-249)
CALIFORNIA PAJAROSA
133 Hughes Rd, Watsonville (95076-9458)
PHONE..............................831 722-6374
John Furman, *President*
Albert Furman, *Shareholder*
Betty Mitchell, *Shareholder*
Alan Mitchell, *Vice Pres*
EMP: 52
SQ FT: 17,000
SALES (est): 1.7MM **Privately Held**
SIC: 0181 Roses, growing of; flowers grown in field nurseries

(P-250)
CAMFLOR INC
2364 Riverside Rd, Watsonville (95076-9430)
PHONE..............................831 726-1330
Daniel Campos, *President*
Zandra Campos, *CFO*
Gil Campos, *Info Tech Mgr*
Jose Campos, *Financial Exec*
Javier Zamora, *Prdtn Mgr*
▲ **EMP:** 110
SALES (est): 5.1MM **Privately Held**
WEB: www.camflor.com
SIC: 0181 Nursery stock, growing of

(P-251)
COAST NURSERIES INC (PA)
5870 E Los Angeles Ave, Somis (93066-9752)
PHONE..............................805 386-4253
Samuel F Fujimoto, *CEO*
Steven Fujimoto, *President*
Iyako Fujimoto, *Corp Secy*
EMP: 140
SALES (est): 5.9MM **Privately Held**
WEB: www.coastnurseries.com
SIC: 0181 5083 0191 Nursery stock, growing of; landscaping equipment; general farms, primarily crop

(P-252)
DAVE WILSON NURSERY INC (PA)
Also Called: Dwn
19701 Lake Rd, Hickman (95323-9706)
P.O. Box 429 (95323-0429)
PHONE..............................209 874-1821
Robert B Woolley, *CEO*
Dennis Tarry, *President*
Dave Wilson, *Principal*
EMP: 50
SQ FT: 8,000
SALES (est): 17.7MM **Privately Held**
SIC: 0181 Nursery stock, growing of

(P-253)
DLT GROWERS INC
13131 S Bon View Ave, Ontario
(91761-8226)
PHONE..................................909 947-8198
Jaime Delatorre, *President*
Ricardo Delatorre, *Vice Pres*
EMP: 50
SQ FT: 400
SALES (est): 3.6MM **Privately Held**
SIC: 0181 5193 Plants, foliage & shrubberies; flowers & nursery stock

(P-254)
DUARTE NURSERY INC
23456 E Flood Rd, Linden (95236-9429)
PHONE..................................209 887-3409
Jim Duarte, *Manager*
EMP: 350
SQ FT: 1,558
SALES (corp-wide): 57.6MM **Privately Held**
WEB: www.duartenursery.com
SIC: 0181 Nursery stock, growing of
PA: Duarte Nursery, Inc.
    1555 Baldwin Rd
    Hughson CA 95326
    209 531-0351

(P-255)
DUARTE NURSERY INC (PA)
Also Called: Duarte Properties
1555 Baldwin Rd, Hughson (95326-9522)
PHONE..................................209 531-0351
John Duarte, *President*
Anita Duarte, *Treasurer*
Jeff Duarte, *Vice Pres*
Jena Dotson, *VP Finance*
Chris Yates, *Human Resources*
EMP: 400
SALES (est): 57.6MM **Privately Held**
WEB: www.duartenursery.com
SIC: 0181 Nursery stock, growing of

(P-256)
EARLY MORNING LLC
Also Called: Weeks Roses
30135 Mc Combs Rd, Wasco
(93280-9416)
PHONE..................................503 912-5261
Jim Holding,
EMP: 52
SALES (corp-wide): 12.2MM **Privately Held**
SIC: 0181 Nursery stock, growing of; florists' greens cultivated: growing of
PA: Early Morning Llc
    30590 Se Kelso Rd
    Boring OR 97009
    503 912-5261

(P-257)
EVERGREEN DISTRIBUTORS INC (PA)
Also Called: Evergreen Nursery
13650 Carmel Valley Rd, San Diego
(92130-5624)
P.O. Box 9830, Rancho Santa Fe (92067-4830)
PHONE..................................858 481-0622
Mark L Collins, *President*
Deborah Robertson, *Corp Secy*
Michael Chamberlin, *Vice Pres*
▲ EMP: 50
SQ FT: 3,000
SALES (est): 26.5MM **Privately Held**
SIC: 0181 Nursery stock, growing of

(P-258)
FLYNN INDUSTRIES INC (PA)
Also Called: One Flynn Center
825 Van Ness Ave Ste 501, San Francisco
(94109-7893)
PHONE..................................415 776-7337
Aurea C Knoedler, *Admin Sec*
EMP: 51
SQ FT: 2,500
SALES (est): 1.1MM **Privately Held**
WEB: www.flynnindustries.com
SIC: 0181 5812 Ornamental nursery products; fast-food restaurant, independent

(P-259)
FRANTZ WHOLESALE NURSERY LLC
12161 Delaware Rd, Hickman
(95323-9602)
PHONE..................................209 874-1459
Michael Frantz,
Mitzi Frantz,
▲ EMP: 150
SALES (est): 8.7MM **Privately Held**
WEB: www.frantznursery.com
SIC: 0181 Nursery stock, growing of

(P-260)
GALLUP & STRIBLING ORCHIDS LLC
Also Called: Gallup and Stribling Holdings
3450 Via Real, Carpinteria (93013-3047)
PHONE..................................805 684-1998
Alexander L Stribling, *CEO*
Michael E Pfau, *Admin Sec*
▲ EMP: 50
SQ FT: 1,400,000
SALES (est): 3MM **Privately Held**
SIC: 0181 Flowers grown in field nurseries

(P-261)
GLAD-A-WAY GARDENS INC
2669 E Clark Ave, Santa Maria
(93455-5815)
P.O. Box 2550 (93457-2550)
PHONE..................................805 938-0569
Brian Caird, *President*
Lance Runels, *Vice Pres*
Erin Caird, *Admin Sec*
▲ EMP: 172
SQ FT: 15,000
SALES (est): 18.1MM **Privately Held**
WEB: www.gladaway.net
SIC: 0181 Flowers grown in field nurseries

(P-262)
GOLD COAST FARMS LLC
32701 Road 204, Woodlake (93286-9625)
PHONE..................................559 564-6316
Jim Means,
EMP: 50
SALES (est): 1.8MM **Privately Held**
SIC: 0181 Nursery stock, growing of

(P-263)
GOLDEN STATE HERBS (PA)
60125 Polk St, Thermal (92274-8944)
P.O. Box 756 (92274-0756)
PHONE..................................760 342-7117
Sam Vince, *President*
Jack Vince, *Corp Secy*
Curtis Vince, *Vice Pres*
Sylvia Garza, *Sales Mgr*
▲ EMP: 50
SQ FT: 50,000
SALES (est): 6.7MM **Privately Held**
WEB: www.goldenstateherbs.com
SIC: 0181 Ornamental nursery products

(P-264)
GRAND VIEW GERANIUM GRDNS INC
18307 Central Ave, Carson (90746-4017)
PHONE..................................310 217-0490
Fax: 310 217-0536
EMP: 60
SQ FT: 2,500
SALES (est): 3.2MM **Privately Held**
WEB: www.gvgeranium.com
SIC: 0181

(P-265)
GROVER LANDSCAPE SERVICES INC
6224 Stoddard Rd, Modesto (95356-9198)
PHONE..................................209 545-4401
Mark Grover, *President*
Lorraine Grover, *Corp Secy*
Ruth Jupe, *Accounting Mgr*
EMP: 100 EST: 1970
SQ FT: 10,850
SALES: 14.9MM **Privately Held**
SIC: 0181 0782 0783 0781 Ornamental nursery products; landscape contractors; tree trimming services for public utility lines; landscape planning services

(P-266)
HERITAGE LAND COMPANY INC
Also Called: Delta Growers
111 N Zuckerman Rd, Stockton (95206)
P.O. Box 487 (95201-0487)
PHONE..................................209 444-1700
Dennis Gardenmeyer, *CEO*
EMP: 50
SALES (est): 4.4MM **Privately Held**
SIC: 0181 Sod farms

(P-267)
HMCLAUSE INC (DH)
260 Cousteau Pl Ste 210, Davis
(95618-5490)
PHONE..................................800 320-4672
Remi Bastien, *CEO*
Matthew M Johnston, *President*
Andre Cariou, *Vice Pres*
Agnes Mistretta, *Vice Pres*
John Lindbo, *Research*
◆ EMP: 133 EST: 1856
SQ FT: 200,000
SALES (est): 115.8MM
SALES (corp-wide): 185.5MM **Privately Held**
WEB: www.harrismoran.com
SIC: 0181 Seeds, vegetable: growing of
HQ: Groupe Limagrain Holding
    Clermont Limagne Rue Henri Moudor
    Saint Beauzire 63360
    475 828-101

(P-268)
HMCLAUSE INC
42 Glenshire Ln, Chico (95973-1093)
PHONE..................................530 713-5838
EMP: 70
SALES (corp-wide): 185.5MM **Privately Held**
SIC: 0181 Seeds, vegetable: growing of
HQ: Hm.Clause, Inc.
    260 Cousteau Pl Ste 210
    Davis CA 95618
    800 320-4672

(P-269)
HOLLAND AMERICA FLOWERS LLC
808 Albert Way, Arroyo Grande
(93420-5828)
PHONE..................................805 343-4004
Benno Dobbe, *CEO*
▲ EMP: 83
SQ FT: 1,700
SALES (est): 6.5MM
SALES (corp-wide): 13.5MM **Privately Held**
SIC: 0181 Flowers grown in field nurseries
PA: Holland America Bulb Farms, Inc.
    1066 S Pekin Rd
    Woodland WA 98674
    360 225-4512

(P-270)
J ROBERT ECHTER
Also Called: Robert J Echter Foxpoint Farms
1150 Quail Gardens Dr, Encinitas
(92024-2365)
PHONE..................................760 436-0188
Robert J Echter, *Owner*
Robert Echter, *Owner*
Eva Espinoza, *Human Res Mgr*
EMP: 50 EST: 2015
SALES (est): 868.9K **Privately Held**
SIC: 0181 Ornamental nursery products

(P-271)
JIMENEZ NURSERY INC
Also Called: Jimenez Nursery and Landscapes
3800 Via Real, Carpinteria (93013-3051)
P.O. Box 2460, Santa Barbara (93120-2460)
PHONE..................................805 684-7955
Manuel Jimenez, *CEO*
Alicia Jimenez, *Treasurer*
EMP: 100
SALES (est): 80.8K **Privately Held**
SIC: 0181 Nursery stock, growing of

(P-272)
JOHANNES FLOWERS INC
4990 Foothill Rd, Carpinteria (93013-3085)
PHONE..................................805 684-5686
Johannes A P Persoon, *President*

Madalenne Leanoard, *Vice Pres*
Jan Persoon, *Vice Pres*
Wilbert Q J Persoon, *Vice Pres*
▲ EMP: 60 EST: 1970
SALES (est): 5.3MM **Privately Held**
WEB: www.johannesflowers.com
SIC: 0181 5992 Flowers grown in field nurseries; florists

(P-273)
KAWAHARA NURSERY INC
698 Burnett Ave, Morgan Hill (95037-9022)
P.O. Box 1358 (95038-1358)
PHONE..................................408 779-2400
David Kawahara, *President*
Josh Kawahara, *Vice Chairman*
John Kawahara, *Vice Pres*
Paul Vollmer, *Accounts Mgr*
▲ EMP: 240 EST: 1947
SALES (est): 13MM **Privately Held**
WEB: www.kawaharanursery.com
SIC: 0181 5193 Nursery stock, growing of; flowers & florists' supplies

(P-274)
KENDALL FARMS LP
4230 White Lilac Rd, Fallbrook
(92028-8802)
PHONE..................................760 731-0681
Jason Kendall, *Managing Prtnr*
Tony Mungo, *Admin Asst*
Cindy Fuentes, *Accountant*
Katia McLaughlin, *Production*
Cathy McClintock, *Sales Dir*
EMP: 50
SALES (est): 4.2MM **Privately Held**
WEB: www.kendall-farms.com
SIC: 0181 Flowers grown in field nurseries

(P-275)
KITAYAMA BROS INC
481 San Andreas Rd, Watsonville
(95076-9524)
P.O. Box 537, Brighton CO (80601-0537)
PHONE..................................831 722-2912
Michael Deardorff, *President*
Stuart Kitayama, *Opers Mgr*
EMP: 80
SALES (corp-wide): 25.4MM **Privately Held**
SIC: 0181 5193 Flowers grown in field nurseries; flowers & florists' supplies
PA: Kitayama Bros., Inc.
    540 E Bridge St Ste A
    Brighton CO 80601
    303 659-8005

(P-276)
KITAYAMA BROTHERS INC
Also Called: Kitayama Flowers
481 San Andreas Rd, Watsonville
(95076-9524)
PHONE..................................831 722-8118
Winston Moore, *Branch Mgr*
EMP: 73
SALES (corp-wide): 5MM **Privately Held**
SIC: 0181 5261 5193 Flowers grown in field nurseries; roses, growing of; nurseries & garden centers; flowers & florists' supplies
PA: Kitayama Bros., Inc.
    540 E Bridge St Ste A
    Brighton CO 80601
    303 659-8000

(P-277)
KOBATA GROWERS INC (PA)
17622 Van Ness Ave, Torrance
(90504-3530)
PHONE..................................310 323-0662
Jack Mayesh, *President*
Sol Mayesh, *Shareholder*
Harry Mayesh, *Corp Secy*
EMP: 53
SALES (est): 4.5MM **Privately Held**
WEB: www.kobatagrowers.com
SIC: 0181 Nursery stock, growing of

(P-278)
L E COOKE CO
26333 Road 140, Visalia (93292-9452)
PHONE..................................559 732-9146
David Henry Cox, *CEO*
Ron Ludekens, *President*
Phillip Cox, *Admin Sec*
Deanna Felix, *Bookkeeper*

PRODUCTS & SVCS

Rosie Frias, *Sales Mgr*
▲ EMP: 200
SQ FT: 6,000
SALES (est): 9.6MM **Privately Held**
WEB: www.lecooke.com
SIC: 0181 Nursery stock, growing of

(P-279)
L J T FLOWERS INC
2425 Bonita School Rd, Nipomo
(93444-9728)
PHONE.................................805 310-6036
Grace Cruz, *Principal*
EMP: 94
SALES (corp-wide): 29.6MM **Privately
Held**
SIC: 0181 5191 Flowers grown in field
  nurseries; flower & field bulbs
PA: L J T Flowers Inc.
  2425 Bonita School Rd
  Nipomo CA 93444
  877 929-2476

(P-280)
LA VERNE NURSERY INC
3653 Center St, Piru (93040)
P.O. Box 410 (93040-0410)
PHONE.................................805 521-0111
Richard Wilson, *CEO*
EMP: 90 EST: 1980
SQ FT: 16,000
SALES (est): 5.4MM **Privately Held**
SIC: 0181 Nursery stock, growing of; fruit
  stocks, growing of

(P-281)
MARATHON LAND INC (PA)
2599 E Hueneme Rd, Oxnard
(93033-8112)
P.O. Box 579, Port Hueneme (93044-0579)
PHONE.................................805 488-3585
Jurgen Gramckow, *President*
EMP: 125
SQ FT: 3,000
SALES (est): 7.4MM **Privately Held**
WEB: www.sod.com
SIC: 0181 Sod farms

(P-282)
MARTINEZ FARMS INC
2433 Cactus Rd, San Diego (92154-8008)
PHONE.................................619 661-6571
Richard Martinez, *President*
Jose Martinez, *Ch of Bd*
EMP: 400
SALES (est): 16MM **Privately Held**
WEB: www.certseedpotato.com
SIC: 0181 Nursery stock, growing of

(P-283)
MATSUI NURSERY INC (PA)
1645 Old Stage Rd, Salinas (93908-9737)
PHONE.................................831 422-6433
Toshikiyo Matsui, *President*
Jose Renteria, *Human Resources*
Hillary Fish, *Marketing Mgr*
▲ EMP: 58 EST: 1967
SQ FT: 3,000,000
SALES (est): 22.8MM **Privately Held**
SIC: 0181 Nursery stock, growing of

(P-284)
MONROVIA NURSERY
COMPANY (PA)
Also Called: Monrovia Growes
817 E Monrovia Pl, Azusa (91702-6297)
P.O. Box 1385 (91702-1385)
PHONE.................................626 334-9321
Miles R Rosedale, *CEO*
William B Usrey, *President*
Richard Van Landinghan, *President*
Dennis Conner, *Vice Pres*
Richard Van Landingham, *Director*
▲ EMP: 567
SQ FT: 50,000
SALES (est): 438.7MM **Privately Held**
WEB: www.monrovia.com
SIC: 0181 5193 5261 Nursery stock,
  growing of; flowers & florists' supplies;
  nurseries & garden centers

(P-285)
MULROSES USA INC
741 S San Pedro St, Los Angeles
(90014-2417)
PHONE.................................213 489-1761

Patricio Nasser, *Manager*
EMP: 100
SALES (est): 2MM **Privately Held**
SIC: 0181 Roses, growing of

(P-286)
MYRIAD FLOWERS
INTERNATIONAL
4601 Foothill Rd, Carpinteria (93013-3097)
PHONE.................................805 684-8079
Harry Van Wingerden, *President*
Michelle Van Wingerden, *Vice Pres*
Erik Van Winderden, *Executive*
Erik Wingerden, *Office Mgr*
▲ EMP: 65
SQ FT: 2,000
SALES: 5MM **Privately Held**
WEB: www.myriadflowers.com
SIC: 0181 Flowers grown in field nurseries

(P-287)
NAUMES INC
3792 Feather River Blvd, Olivehurst
(95961-9688)
PHONE.................................530 743-2055
Bob Cosey, *General Mgr*
EMP: 50
SQ FT: 66,646
SALES (corp-wide): 57.6MM **Privately
Held**
WEB: www.naumes.com
SIC: 0181 0723 4731 Fruit stocks, grow-
  ing of; fruit (farm-dried) packing services;
  agents, shipping
PA: Naumes, Inc.
  2 W Barnett St
  Medford OR 97501
  541 772-6268

(P-288)
OCEAN BREEZE
INTERNATIONAL
Also Called: Mobis Wholesale
3910 Via Real, Carpinteria (93013-1266)
PHONE.................................805 684-1747
Rene Van Wingerden, *President*
June Van Wingerden, *Vice Pres*
Cagney Miller, *General Mgr*
Casey Martin, *Office Mgr*
▲ EMP: 60 EST: 1974
SQ FT: 900,000
SALES (est): 9.8MM **Privately Held**
WEB: www.oceanbreezeintl.com
SIC: 0181 Flowers: grown under cover
  (e.g. greenhouse production)

(P-289)
OCEAN VIEW FLOWERS LLC
1105 Union Sugar Ave, Lompoc
(93436-9737)
PHONE.................................800 736-5608
Robert M Witt,
John Donati,
EMP: 175
SALES (est): 322.5K **Privately Held**
SIC: 0181 Florists' greens & flowers;
  florists' greens cultivated: growing of

(P-290)
OLIVE HILL GREENHOUSES
3508 Olive Hill Rd, Fallbrook (92028-8296)
P.O. Box 1510 (92088-1510)
PHONE.................................760 728-4596
George A Godfrey, *Owner*
William McGregor, *Technology*
Shelley Demitsas, *Human Res Dir*
Denise Godfrey, *Sales Executive*
▲ EMP: 100
SQ FT: 2,000
SALES (est): 7MM **Privately Held**
WEB: www.olivehill.net
SIC: 0181 Nursery stock, growing of

(P-291)
PACIFIC EARTH RESOURCES
(PA)
Also Called: Pacific Sd/Pcfic Arbor Nrsries
305 Hueneme Rd, Camarillo (93012-8522)
PHONE.................................805 986-8277
Richard Rogers, *Owner*
Elizabeth Rogers, *Partner*
EMP: 80
SQ FT: 8,000

SALES (est): 21.9MM **Privately Held**
SIC: 0181 Sod farms; nursery stock, growing of

(P-292)
PLUG CONNECTION INC
2627 Ramona Dr, Vista (92084-1634)
PHONE.................................760 631-0992
Tim Wada, *President*
Jim Peterson, *CFO*
Bradley Rhoads, *CFO*
Juan St Amant, *VP Mktg*
Maria Rojas,
▲ EMP: 80
SQ FT: 350,000
SALES (est): 7.5MM **Privately Held**
WEB: www.plugconnection.com
SIC: 0181 Ornamental nursery products

(P-293)
PYRAMID FLOWERS INC
3813 Doris Ave, Oxnard (93030-4706)
PHONE.................................805 382-8070
Fred Van Wingerden, *President*
Edith Van Wingerden, *Vice Pres*
Marcos Van Wingerden, *Prdtn Mgr*
▲ EMP: 120
SQ FT: 900,000
SALES (est): 17.8MM **Privately Held**
WEB: www.pyramidflowers.com
SIC: 0181 Flowers grown in field nurseries

(P-294)
RICHARD WILSON
WELLINGTON
Also Called: Colorama Wholesale Nursery
1025 N Todd Ave, Azusa (91702-1602)
P.O. Box 1328, Glendora (91740-1328)
PHONE.................................626 812-7881
Richard Wilson, *Owner*
Steve Haston, *Opers Staff*
Spike Mitchell, *Sales Executive*
▲ EMP: 100
SQ FT: 70,000
SALES (est): 9.6MM **Privately Held**
SIC: 0181 5193 Nursery stock, growing of;
  nursery stock

(P-295)
RIVER RIDGE FARMS INC
3135 Los Angeles Ave, Oxnard
(93036-1010)
PHONE.................................805 647-6880
Rieuwert Jan Vis, *President*
▲ EMP: 95
SQ FT: 440
SALES: 13.8MM **Privately Held**
SIC: 0181 5193 Flowers grown in field
  nurseries; flowers: grown under cover
  (e.g. greenhouse production); plants, pot-
  ted

(P-296)
ROCKET FARMS INC (PA)
2651 Cabrillo Hwy N, Half Moon Bay
(94019-1357)
P.O. Box 3756, Salinas (93912-3756)
PHONE.................................800 227-5229
Charles Kosmont, *CEO*
Mark Clark, *Vice Pres*
▲ EMP: 113
SQ FT: 1,500,000
SALES (est): 49.8MM **Privately Held**
SIC: 0181 Flowers: grown under cover
  (e.g. greenhouse production)

(P-297)
ROSE THOMPSON COMPANY
949 Cassou Rd, San Marcos (92069-9715)
PHONE.................................760 736-6020
David Thompson, *President*
Scott Thompson, *Corp Secy*
Karen Thompson, *Vice Pres*
Chris Beck, *Office Mgr*
Joe Blair, *Technology*
EMP: 54
SQ FT: 1,704
SALES (est): 2.2MM **Privately Held**
WEB: www.thomprose.com
SIC: 0181 Nursery stock, growing of

(P-298)
SAN GABRIEL NURSERY AND
FLOR (PA)
632 S San Gabriel Blvd, San Gabriel
(91776-2798)
PHONE.................................626 286-0787
Margie Yoshihashi, *President*
Mary Swanton, *Treasurer*
Saburo Ishihara, *Vice Pres*
Dianne Yoshimura, *Admin Sec*
EMP: 73
SQ FT: 5,000
SALES (est): 5.2MM **Privately Held**
WEB: www.sgnursery.com
SIC: 0181 Nursery stock, growing of

(P-299)
SG PERSONNEL LLC
420 Espinosa Rd, Salinas (93907-8894)
PHONE.................................831 444-0523
Michael F Vukelich, *Manager*
Sarah Schmale, *Sales Staff*
EMP: 270
SALES (corp-wide): 437.7MM **Privately
Held**
WEB: www.colorspot.com
SIC: 0181 Plants, potted: growing of
HQ: Csn Winddown, Inc.
  27368 Via Industria
  Temecula CA 92590

(P-300)
SG PERSONNEL LLC
Also Called: Color Spot Lodi
5400 E Harney Ln, Lodi (95240-6903)
PHONE.................................209 369-3018
David Barrett, *President*
EMP: 60
SALES (corp-wide): 437.7MM **Privately
Held**
WEB: www.colorspot.com
SIC: 0181 5193 Plants, potted: growing of;
  flowers & florists' supplies
HQ: Csn Winddown, Inc.
  27368 Via Industria
  Temecula CA 92590

(P-301)
SIERRA GOLD NURSERIES INC
5320 Garden Hwy, Yuba City (95991-9499)
PHONE.................................530 674-1145
Jack Poukish, *CEO*
Brian Berg, *Vice Pres*
Ellen Berg, *Vice Pres*
Harold Foster, *Safety Mgr*
Matthew Haddon, *Marketing Staff*
▲ EMP: 86
SQ FT: 2,500
SALES (est): 10.6MM **Privately Held**
WEB: www.sierragoldtrees.com
SIC: 0181 Nursery stock, growing of

(P-302)
SIERRA-CASCADE NURSERY
INC (PA)
472-715 Johnson Rd, Susanville
(96130-8727)
PHONE.................................530 254-6867
Steve Fortin, *President*
Randy Jertberg, *COO*
Robert Akeson, *Vice Pres*
Beth Jertberg, *Vice Pres*
Robert Murie, *Vice Pres*
▼ EMP: 400
SQ FT: 2,600
SALES (est): 108.3MM **Privately Held**
SIC: 0181 Nursery stock, growing of

(P-303)
SUN VALLEY GROUP INC (PA)
3160 Upper Bay Rd, Arcata (95521-9690)
PHONE.................................707 822-2885
Leendert De Vries, *President*
Casey Razma, *CFO*
Debbie Hartman, *Regional Mgr*
Kyle Sharp, *Administration*
Roxanne McGuire, *Sr Software Eng*
▲ EMP: 350
SQ FT: 8,700

SALES (est): 135.7MM **Privately Held**
WEB: www.thesunvalleygroup.com
SIC: 0181 Flowers: grown under cover
(e.g. greenhouse production); flowers
grown in field nurseries; bulbs, growing of

(P-304)
SUNRISE RANCH
3623 Etting Rd, Oxnard (93033-5813)
PHONE.....................................805 488-0813
George Mimaki, *Partner*
Lori Kamei, *Partner*
Bryan Mimaki, *Partner*
Bob Suzuki, *Prdtn Mgr*
EMP: 90
SQ FT: 750
SALES (est): 5.2MM **Privately Held**
SIC: 0181 Flowers grown in field nurseries

(P-305)
SUPERIOR SOD I LP
17821 17th St Ste 165, Tustin
(92780-2172)
P.O. Box 1911, Tehachapi (93581-5911)
PHONE.....................................909 923-5068
Michael Considine, *Partner*
Richard H Considine, *Partner*
Trudy Considine, *Partner*
Peter Moore, *Partner*
EMP: 125
SQ FT: 1,400
SALES (est): 6.4MM **Privately Held**
WEB: www.superiorsod.com
SIC: 0181 0782 Sod farms; lawn & garden
services

(P-306)
TOPSTAR FLORAL INC
4255 W Gonzales Rd, Oxnard
(93036-7786)
PHONE.....................................805 984-7972
Steve Van Wingerden, *President*
EMP: 50
SQ FT: 6,500
SALES (est): 5.6MM **Privately Held**
WEB: www.topstarfloral.com
SIC: 0181 Flowers grown in field nurseries

(P-307)
WEST COAST TURF (PA)
42540 Melanie Pl, Palm Desert
(92211-5127)
P.O. Box 4563 (92261-4563)
PHONE.....................................760 340-7300
John M Foster, *President*
Joe Foster, *Vice Pres*
John Foster, *Principal*
EMP: 50
SQ FT: 2,000
SALES (est): 38MM **Privately Held**
WEB: www.westernsod.com
SIC: 0181 Sod farms

(P-308)
WEST FLOWER GROWERS
3623 Etting Rd, Oxnard (93033-5813)
PHONE.....................................805 488-0814
Bryan H Mimaki, *President*
EMP: 70
SALES (est): 2.1MM **Privately Held**
SIC: 0181 Ornamental nursery products

0182 Food Crops Grown Under Cover

(P-309)
CHANNEL ISLNDS VGTBLE FRMS INC (PA)
595 Victoria Ave, Oxnard (93030-4710)
PHONE.....................................805 984-1910
Steve Nishimori, *President*
Karen Nishimori, *Vice Pres*
EMP: 60
SQ FT: 2,000
SALES (est): 6.8MM **Privately Held**
SIC: 0182 Vegetable crops grown under
cover

(P-310)
COUNTRYSIDE MUSHROOMS INC
11300 Center Ave, Gilroy (95020-9257)
PHONE.....................................408 683-2748
Donald W Hordness, *President*

Lewis Di Cecco, *Vice Pres*
EMP: 70
SALES (est): 7MM **Privately Held**
SIC: 0182 Mushrooms grown under cover

(P-311)
FITZ FRESH INC
211 Lee Rd, Watsonville (95076-9447)
P.O. Box 1450, Freedom (95019-1450)
PHONE.....................................831 763-4440
Patrick J Fitz, *President*
Holly Pedemonte, *Manager*
▲ **EMP:** 50
SQ FT: 2,000
SALES: 5MM **Privately Held**
WEB: www.fitzfresh.com
SIC: 0182 Mushrooms grown under cover

(P-312)
FUJI NATURAL FOODS INC (HQ)
13500 S Hamner Ave, Ontario
(91761-2605)
P.O. Box 3728 (91761-0973)
PHONE.....................................909 947-1008
Katsuhiro Nakagawa, *CEO*
Ikuzo Sugiyama, *President*
▲ **EMP:** 77
SQ FT: 65,000
SALES (est): 11.1MM
SALES (corp-wide): 7.3MM **Privately Held**
SIC: 0182 Bean sprouts grown under
cover
PA: Taiyo Shokuhin Kogyo K.K.
2618-6, Naegicho
Tatebayashi GNM 374-0
276 722-551

(P-313)
GROWERS TRANSPLANTING INC (HQ)
360 Espinosa Rd, Salinas (93907-8895)
P.O. Box 3756 (93912-3756)
PHONE.....................................831 449-3440
Charles I Kosmont, *CEO*
Leslie Surber, *CFO*
Kevin Doyle, *Vice Pres*
Bill Rover, *Vice Pres*
▲ **EMP:** 83 EST: 1981
SQ FT: 4,000,000
SALES (est): 37.4MM **Privately Held**
WEB: www.growerstrans.com
SIC: 0182 Vegetable crops grown under
cover

(P-314)
HOLLANDIA PRODUCE LP
1545 Santa Monica Rd, Carpinteria
(93013-3067)
P.O. Box 1327 (93014-1327)
PHONE.....................................805 684-8739
Pete Overgaag, *Partner*
Ellen Seyle, *Controller*
Guido Daniels, *Prdtn Mgr*
Renee Cooper, *Marketing Mgr*
Anne Fortuna, *Sales Staff*
▲ **EMP:** 160
SQ FT: 16,000
SALES (est): 42.5MM **Privately Held**
WEB: www.hollandiaflowers.com
SIC: 0182 Vegetable crops grown under
cover

(P-315)
MONTEREY MUSHROOMS INC (PA)
260 Westgate Dr, Watsonville
(95076-2452)
PHONE.....................................831 763-5300
Shah Kazemi, *President*
Robert V Jenkins, *CFO*
Joe Caldwell, *Vice Pres*
Michael O'Brien, *Vice Pres*
Laurie Heath, *Info Tech Dir*
▲ **EMP:** 50
SALES (est): 531MM **Privately Held**
WEB: www.montereymushrooms.com
SIC: 0182 Mushrooms grown under cover

(P-316)
MONTEREY MUSHROOMS INC
Also Called: Monterey Mushrooms-Morgan
Hill
642 Hale Ave, Morgan Hill (95037-9221)
P.O. Box 818 (95038-0818)
PHONE.....................................408 779-4191

Clark Smith, *Branch Mgr*
EMP: 350
SQ FT: 5,000
SALES (corp-wide): 531MM **Privately
Held**
WEB: www.montereymushrooms.com
SIC: 0182 Mushrooms grown under
cover; dehydrated fruits, vegetables,
soups
PA: Monterey Mushrooms, Inc.
260 Westgate Dr
Watsonville CA 95076
831 763-5300

(P-317)
MONTEREY MUSHROOMS INC
777 Maher Ct, Royal Oaks (95076-9014)
PHONE.....................................831 728-8300
Wayne Batista, *Branch Mgr*
Miguel Calero, *Manager*
EMP: 501
SALES (corp-wide): 531MM **Privately
Held**
WEB: www.montereymushrooms.com
SIC: 0182 Mushrooms grown under cover
PA: Monterey Mushrooms, Inc.
260 Westgate Dr
Watsonville CA 95076
831 763-5300

(P-318)
MOUNTAIN MEADOW MUSHROOMS INC
26948 N Broadway, Escondido
(92026-8315)
PHONE.....................................760 749-1201
Bob Crouch, *President*
Elizabeth Crouch, *Vice Pres*
Roberto Ramirez, *Vice Pres*
Manuel Zuniga, *Vice Pres*
EMP: 72
SQ FT: 110,000
SALES (est): 9MM **Privately Held**
SIC: 0182 Mushrooms grown under cover

(P-319)
NORTH SHORE GREENHOUSES INC
Also Called: North Shore Living Herbs
82900 Johnson St, Thermal (92274-9319)
PHONE.....................................760 397-0400
Leonardus Overgaag, *President*
Suzette Overgaag, *Vice Pres*
▲ **EMP:** 110
SALES (est): 11MM **Privately Held**
WEB: www.northshoregreenhouses.com
SIC: 0182 Food crops grown under cover

(P-320)
PLEASANT VALLEY FLOWERS INC
3132 E Pleasant Valley Rd, Oxnard
(93033-4112)
PHONE.....................................805 986-2776
Lane Devries, *President*
▲ **EMP:** 335
SQ FT: 7,500
SALES (est): 9MM **Privately Held**
WEB: www.pleasantvalleyflowers.com
SIC: 0182 Food crops grown under cover
PA: The Sun Valley Group Inc
3160 Upper Bay Rd
Arcata CA 95521

(P-321)
PREMIER MUSHROOMS LP
2847 Niagara Ave, Colusa (95932)
PHONE.....................................530 458-2700
Jose Flores, *Plant Mgr*
EMP: 165 **Privately Held**
SIC: 0182 Mushrooms grown under cover
PA: Premier Mushrooms, L.P.
2880 Niagara Ave
Colusa CA 95932

(P-322)
ROYAL OAKS ENTERPRISES INC
Also Called: Royal Oaks Mushroom
15480 Watsonville Rd, Morgan Hill
(95037-5921)
P.O. Box 447 (95038-0447)
PHONE.....................................408 779-2362

Don Hordness, *President*
Deanne Arellano, *President*
Linda Abdella, *Treasurer*
Joseph Andrighetto, *Vice Pres*
Don Hordeness, *Vice Pres*
EMP: 50
SQ FT: 1,600
SALES (est): 3.9MM **Privately Held**
SIC: 0182 Mushrooms grown under cover

0191 Crop Farming, Misc

(P-323)
ARNAUDO BROS TRANSPORT INC (PA)
Also Called: Arnaudo Bros Trucking
16505 S Tracy Blvd, Tracy (95304-9436)
PHONE.....................................209 835-0406
Steve Arnaudo, *President*
Leo Arnaudo, *Vice Pres*
Ed Arnaudo, *Admin Sec*
EMP: 100 EST: 1947
SQ FT: 1,200
SALES (est): 17.7MM **Privately Held**
SIC: 0191 4212 General farms, primarily
crop; local trucking, without storage

(P-324)
BLACKJACK FARMS DE LA COSTA CN
Also Called: Black Jack Farms
2385 A St, Santa Maria (93455-1073)
PHONE.....................................805 347-1333
Jose Garcia, *CEO*
Pat Iniguez, *Administration*
EMP: 140
SALES (est): 52.8K **Privately Held**
SIC: 0191 General farms, primarily crop

(P-325)
BOWLES FARMING CO INC
11609 Hereford Rd, Los Banos
(93635-9514)
PHONE.....................................209 827-3000
Phillip Bowles, *President*
EMP: 50
SALES (corp-wide): 25MM **Privately
Held**
WEB: www.bfarm.com
SIC: 0191 General farms, primarily crop
PA: Bowles Farming Company, Inc.
545 Sansome St Ste 825
San Francisco CA 94111
415 421-4800

(P-326)
BURFORD FAMILY FARMING CO LP (PA)
Also Called: Burford Ranch
1443 W Sample Ave, Fresno (93711-1948)
PHONE.....................................559 431-0902
Jill Burford, *Managing Prtnr*
EMP: 130
SQ FT: 2,000
SALES (est): 20.7MM **Privately Held**
SIC: 0191 0131 0173 0111 General
farms, primarily crop; cotton; almond
grove; wheat; tomato farm; alfalfa farm

(P-327)
BUTTON & TURKOVICH
24604 Buckeye Rd, Winters (95694-9001)
PHONE.....................................530 795-2090
Tony Turkovich, *Partner*
Estate of Robert L Button, *Partner*
EMP: 100
SQ FT: 1,500
SALES (est): 7.1MM **Privately Held**
SIC: 0191 General farms, primarily crop

(P-328)
CALIFIA FARMS LLC
33502 Lerdo Hwy, Bakersfield
(93308-9438)
PHONE.....................................661 679-1000
Evans Berne, *Branch Mgr*
Greg Steltenpohl, *Officer*
Dan Newbold, *Software Dev*
Jim Whitaker, *VP Sales*
Mari Salazar, *Sales Staff*
EMP: 100
SALES (corp-wide): 100MM **Privately
Held**
SIC: 0191 General farms, primarily crop

PRODUCTS & SVCS

PA: Califia Farms, Llc
1321 Palmetto St
Los Angeles CA 90013
213 694-4667

(P-329)
CAMPOS FAMILY FARMS LLC
4726 W Jacquelyn Ave, Fresno
(93722-6406)
PHONE..............................559 275-3000
Fermin Campos,
Randy Bishop, *Manager*
EMP: 60 **EST:** 2011
SALES (est): 2.4MM **Privately Held**
SIC: 0191 General farms, primarily crop

(P-330)
CB NORTH LLC
480 W Beach St, Watsonville (95076-4555)
PHONE..............................831 786-1642
Richard Dahl,
Jeffrey Conner,
Beth Potillo,
Bob Ritts,
EMP: 1000
SALES (est): 10.4MM **Privately Held**
SIC: 0191 General farms, primarily crop

(P-331)
COELHO WEST CUSTOM
FARMING
26979 S Butte Ave, Five Points (93624)
P.O. Box 434 (93624-0434)
PHONE..............................559 884-2566
Anthony P Coelho Jr, *President*
EMP: 58
SALES (est): 4.7MM **Privately Held**
SIC: 0191 General farms, primarily crop

(P-332)
CRYSTAL ORGANIC FARMS
LLC
6900 Mountain View Rd, Bakersfield
(93307-9627)
PHONE..............................661 845-5200
Jeff Meger, *President*
EMP: 456
SALES (est): 13.9MM
SALES (corp-wide): 2.1B **Privately Held**
SIC: 0191 General farms, primarily crop
PA: Grimmway Enterprises, Inc.
14141 Di Giorgio Rd
Arvin CA 93203
800 301-3101

(P-333)
DAN R COSTA INC
17239 Louise Ave, Escalon (95320-8732)
PHONE..............................209 234-2004
Dan R Costa, *President*
Shirley Costa, *Treasurer*
EMP: 250
SALES (est): 3.5MM **Privately Held**
WEB: www.dannysfalldecor.com
SIC: 0191 0115 0723 General farms, pri-
marily crop; corn; vegetable packing serv-
ices; fruit (fresh) packing services

(P-334)
DELTA BREEZE FARMING INC
Also Called: Courtland Farming
11566 State Highway 160, Courtland
(95615-9732)
PHONE..............................916 775-2055
Mahinder S Shaliwal, *President*
Mahinder S Dhaliwal, *President*
Tawnya Dhaliwal, *Corp Secy*
EMP: 210
SQ FT: 4,000
SALES (est): 2MM **Privately Held**
SIC: 0191 General farms, primarily crop

(P-335)
DICK ANDERSON & SONS
FARMING
Also Called: Vasto Valle Farms
15900 W Dorris Ave, Huron (93234)
P.O. Box 10 (93234-0010)
PHONE..............................559 945-2511
Richard Anderson, *President*
Robert Anderson, *Corp Secy*
Craig Anderson, *Vice Pres*
EMP: 135 **EST:** 1968
SQ FT: 1,000

SALES (est): 10.8MM **Privately Held**
SIC: 0191 General farms, primarily crop

(P-336)
DON GRAGNANI FARMS
Also Called: Universal Custom Farming Co
12910 S Napa Ave, Tranquillity (93668)
P.O. Box 128 (93668-0128)
PHONE..............................559 693-4352
Donald Gragnani, *Partner*
Irene Gragnani, *Partner*
Jerry Gragnani, *Partner*
Jeanne Gragnani-Lloyd, *Partner*
Jerry Batistia, *Purch Mgr*
EMP: 80
SQ FT: 3,000
SALES (est): 8.9MM **Privately Held**
WEB: www.gragnanifarms.com
SIC: 0191 General farms, primarily crop

(P-337)
DV CUSTOM FARMING LLC
2101 Mettler Frontage E, Bakersfield
(93307-9649)
PHONE..............................661 858-2888
Donald J Valpredo,
EMP: 80
SALES (est): 76.3K **Privately Held**
SIC: 0191 General farms, primarily crop

(P-338)
DW BERRY FARMS LLC
3960 N Rose Ave, Oxnard (93036-1820)
P.O. Box 1029 (93032-1029)
PHONE..............................805 795-8403
Dean Walsh, *Mng Member*
EMP: 300 **EST:** 2010
SALES (est): 12.4MM **Privately Held**
SIC: 0191 General farms, primarily crop

(P-339)
E W MERRITT FARMS (PA)
11188 Road 192, Porterville (93257-9302)
PHONE..............................559 784-8916
Earl Merritt, *Partner*
Eric Merritt, *Partner*
Mark Merritt, *Partner*
Sarah Reid, *Manager*
EMP: 70
SALES (est): 8.5MM **Privately Held**
SIC: 0191 0131 0111 0119 General
farms, primarily crop; cotton; wheat; milo
farm; corn; vegetables & melons

(P-340)
EDWARD J KELLY
Also Called: E K T Farms
959 Riverside Rd, Watsonville
(95076-9412)
P.O. Box 794 (95077-0794)
PHONE..............................831 724-0832
Edward J Kelly, *Owner*
Jean Kelly, *Co-Owner*
EMP: 220
SALES (est): 11.5MM **Privately Held**
SIC: 0191 General farms, primarily crop

(P-341)
ELKHORN BERRY FARMS LLC
262 E Lake Ave, Watsonville (95076-4718)
PHONE..............................831 722-2472
Thomas Amrhein, *General Mgr*
▲ **EMP:** 95
SALES (est): 5.6MM **Privately Held**
SIC: 0191 0171 General farms, primarily
crop; strawberry farm

(P-342)
EMPRESAS DEL BOSQUE INC
51481 W Shields Ave, Firebaugh
(93622-9579)
P.O. Box 2455, Los Banos (93635-2455)
PHONE..............................209 364-6428
Joe L Del Bosque Jr, *President*
EMP: 325
SQ FT: 1,600
SALES (est): 11MM **Privately Held**
SIC: 0191 General farms, primarily crop

(P-343)
FARM FRESH TO YOU (PA)
Also Called: Capay Organic
3880 Seaport Blvd, West Sacramento
(95691-3449)
PHONE..............................916 303-7145
Freeman Barsotti, *CEO*

James Hubbard, *Principal*
EMP: 180
SALES (est): 37.7MM **Privately Held**
SIC: 0191 General farms, primarily crop

(P-344)
GENE WHEELER FARMS INC
444 W Avenue H6, Lancaster
(93534-1634)
P.O. Box 10029 (93584-2029)
PHONE..............................661 951-2100
Gene Wheeler, *President*
▼ **EMP:** 250
SALES (est): 17.7MM **Privately Held**
WEB: www.GeneWheelerfarms.com
SIC: 0191 General farms, primarily crop

(P-345)
GREENHEART FARMS INC (PA)
902 Zenon Way, Arroyo Grande
(93420-5807)
P.O. Box 1510 (93421-1510)
PHONE..............................805 481-2234
Hoy Buell, *CEO*
Leo Wolf, *Treasurer*
Henry Katzenstein, *Vice Pres*
Melody Fair, *Info Tech Mgr*
Jennifer Alexander, *Accounting Dir*
▲ **EMP:** 350
SQ FT: 225,000
SALES (est): 36.4MM **Privately Held**
WEB: www.greenheartfarms.com
SIC: 0191 General farms, primarily crop

(P-346)
GRIMMWAY ENTERPRISES INC
Also Called: Premiere Packing
6301 S Zerker Rd, Shafter (93263)
P.O. Box 81498, Bakersfield (93380-1498)
PHONE..............................661 399-0844
Randy Mower, *Vice Pres*
EMP: 400
SALES (corp-wide): 2.1B **Privately Held**
SIC: 0191 0174 General farms, primarily
crop; citrus fruits
PA: Grimmway Enterprises, Inc.
14141 Di Giorgio Rd
Arvin CA 93203
800 301-3101

(P-347)
GRIMMWAY FARMS
2105 Anderholt Rd, Holtville (92250)
PHONE..............................760 356-2513
Rancho Riddle, *Owner*
EMP: 70
SALES (est): 1.4MM **Privately Held**
SIC: 0191 General farms, primarily crop

(P-348)
HALL COMPANY
44328 W Nees Ave, Firebaugh
(93622-9647)
PHONE..............................209 364-0070
Tim Hall, *Partner*
Laurie Hall, *Partner*
Jason Hall, *Marketing Staff*
EMP: 70
SALES (est): 7.8MM **Privately Held**
WEB: www.orolomaranch.com
SIC: 0191 General farms, primarily crop

(P-349)
HAMMONDS RANCH INC
47375 W Dakota Ave, Firebaugh
(93622-9516)
PHONE..............................209 364-6185
James M Hammonds, *President*
William E Hammond, *Chairman*
Mary Hicks, *Corp Secy*
EMP: 100 **EST:** 1929
SQ FT: 3,500
SALES (est): 12.4MM **Privately Held**
SIC: 0191 General farms, primarily crop

(P-350)
HANSEN RANCHES
7124 Whitley Ave, Corcoran (93212-9669)
P.O. Box 398 (93212-0398)
PHONE..............................559 992-3111
James Hansen, *Partner*
EMP: 60
SQ FT: 4,000
SALES (est): 20.6MM **Privately Held**
SIC: 0191 General farms, primarily crop

(P-351)
HARRIS FARMS INC
Also Called: Harris Farm Horse Division
27366 W Oakland Ave, Coalinga
(93210-9627)
PHONE..............................559 884-2203
Dave McGlothlin, *Sales/Mktg Mgr*
EMP: 50
SALES (corp-wide): 4.5B **Privately Held**
WEB: www.harrisfarms.com
SIC: 0191 0752 General farms, primarily
crop; boarding services, horses: racing &
non-racing
PA: Harris Farms, Inc.
29475 Fresno Coalinga Rd
Coalinga CA 93210
559 884-2435

(P-352)
HARRIS FARMS INC
Harris Ranch Inn & Restaurant
24505 W Dorris Ave, Coalinga
(93210-9667)
PHONE..............................559 935-0717
Jonathan Farrington, *General Mgr*
Jack Brown, *Maintenance Dir*
EMP: 340
SALES (corp-wide): 4.5B **Privately Held**
WEB: www.harrisfarms.com
SIC: 0191 7011 5813 5812 General
farms, primarily crop; hotels & motels;
drinking places; eating places
PA: Harris Farms, Inc.
29475 Fresno Coalinga Rd
Coalinga CA 93210
559 884-2435

(P-353)
HARRIS FARMS INC
23300 W Oakland Ave, Coalinga
(93210-9804)
PHONE..............................559 884-2477
John Harris, *President*
EMP: 300
SALES (corp-wide): 4.5B **Privately Held**
WEB: www.harrisfarms.com
SIC: 0191 0182 0161 General farms, pri-
marily crop; food crops grown under
cover; vegetables & melons
PA: Harris Farms, Inc.
29475 Fresno Coalinga Rd
Coalinga CA 93210
559 884-2435

(P-354)
HIGARD FARMS LLC
6 Quail Run Cir, Salinas (93907-2345)
PHONE..............................831 753-5982
Gary Higl,
EMP: 96
SALES (est): 1.6MM **Privately Held**
SIC: 0191 General farms, primarily crop

(P-355)
J & J FARMS
36245 W Ashlan Ave, Firebaugh (93622)
P.O. Box 155 (93622-0155)
PHONE..............................559 659-1457
Bill Jones, *Owner*
Darcy Villere, *General Mgr*
Linda Dudley, *Manager*
EMP: 50
SALES (est): 3.8MM **Privately Held**
SIC: 0191 General farms, primarily crop

(P-356)
J & S FARM
803 W Kimball Ave, Visalia (93277-6567)
PHONE..............................559 308-0294
Sasha Gonzales, *Principal*
James B Reese, *Principal*
EMP: 60
SALES (est): 650.6K **Privately Held**
SIC: 0191 General farms, primarily crop

(P-357)
J CRECELIUS INC
Also Called: Montetisea Framing
5043 N Montpelier Rd, Denair
(95316-9608)
P.O. Box 579 (95316-0579)
PHONE..............................209 883-4826
Jim Crecelius, *President*
Robert McClain, *CFO*
EMP: 100

▲ = Import ▼=Export
◆ =Import/Export

SALES (est): 2.4MM **Privately Held**
SIC: 0191 0173

(P-358)
J H MEEK & SONS INC
22075 County Road 99, Woodland
(95695-9313)
P.O. Box 299 (95776-0299)
PHONE...................................530 662-1106
Steve Meek, *President*
John J Meek Jr, *President*
EMP: 50
SALES (est): 2.5MM **Privately Held**
SIC: 0191 General farms, primarily crop

(P-359)
J MARCHINI & SON INC
12000 Le Grand Rd, Le Grand
(95333-9708)
PHONE...................................559 665-2944
EMP: 93
SALES (corp-wide): 29.7MM **Privately Held**
SIC: 0191 General farms, primarily crop
PA: J. Marchini & Son, Inc.
8736 Minturn Rd
Le Grand CA 95333
559 665-2944

(P-360)
JACOBS FARM/DEL CABO INC
390 Swift Ave Ste 8, South San Francisco
(94080-6221)
PHONE...................................650 827-1133
Ted Witt, *Manager*
EMP: 75
SALES (corp-wide): 68.2MM **Privately Held**
SIC: 0191 General farms, primarily crop
PA: Jacobs Farm/Del Cabo, Inc.
2450 Stage Rd
Pescadero CA 94060
650 879-0580

(P-361)
JOHN GRIZZLE FARMING
1395 Bonds Corner Rd, Holtville
(92250-9736)
PHONE...................................760 356-4381
John Grizzle, *Owner*
Imala Rodriguez, *Owner*
EMP: 50
SALES (est): 3.7MM **Privately Held**
SIC: 0191 0212 General farms, primarily crop; beef cattle except feedlots

(P-362)
JOSE VRAMONTES
Also Called: V and V Farms
14345 N Highway 88, Lodi (95240-9312)
PHONE...................................209 810-5384
EMP: 50
SALES: 700K **Privately Held**
SIC: 0191

(P-363)
KG BERRY FARMS LLC
1660 Philbric Rd, Santa Maria
(93454-8027)
P.O. Box 1087 (93456-1087)
PHONE...................................805 680-6751
Kevin John Guggia, *Mng Member*
Nicole Lea Guggia,
EMP: 115
SQ FT: 1,000
SALES (est): 5.4MM **Privately Held**
SIC: 0191 General farms, primarily crop

(P-364)
KIRSCHENMAN ENTERPRISES INC
10100 Digiorgio Rd, Bakersfield (93307)
P.O. Box 27, Edison (93220-0027)
PHONE...................................661 366-5736
Wayne Kirschenman, *CEO*
Norma Rapp, *Admin Sec*
▼ EMP: 60
SQ FT: 25,000
SALES (est): 9.7MM **Privately Held**
SIC: 0191 General farms, primarily crop

(P-365)
L & J FARMS CARACCIOLI LLC
27905 Corda Rd, Gonzales (93926)
P.O. Box H (93926-0239)
PHONE...................................831 675-7901

Phil Caraecioli,
Gary Caraccioli,
EMP: 50
SALES (est): 4.5MM **Privately Held**
SIC: 0191 General farms, primarily crop

(P-366)
LION RAISINS INC
Also Called: Lion Brothers Farms-Newstone
12555 Road 9, Madera (93637-9089)
P.O. Box 1350, Selma (93662-1350)
PHONE...................................559 662-8686
Jeff Bergeron, *Manager*
EMP: 200
SALES (corp-wide): 105.8MM **Privately Held**
WEB: www.lionraisins.com
SIC: 0191 General farms, primarily crop
PA: Lion Raisins, Inc.
9500 S De Wolf Ave
Selma CA 93662
559 834-6677

(P-367)
LONE OAK FARMS
2911 Hanford Armona Rd, Hanford
(93230-9379)
PHONE...................................559 583-1277
Bernard Teveld, *Owner*
EMP: 110
SALES (est): 3.7MM **Privately Held**
SIC: 0191 General farms, primarily crop

(P-368)
LS FARMS LLC
29794 Schuster Rd, Mc Farland
(93250-9784)
PHONE...................................661 792-3192
Antonette Anich, *Mng Member*
EMP: 500
SALES: 10.8MM **Privately Held**
SIC: 0191 General farms, primarily crop

(P-369)
LUCICH SANTOS FARMS
12631 Rogers Rd, Patterson (95363-8511)
P.O. Box 637 (95363-0637)
PHONE...................................209 892-6500
Peter Lucich, *Partner*
David Santos, *Partner*
EMP: 120
SQ FT: 20,000
SALES (est): 8.4MM **Privately Held**
SIC: 0191 General farms, primarily crop

(P-370)
MARCHINI INC
12006 Le Grand Rd, Le Grand
(95333-9708)
PHONE...................................209 389-4566
Richard Marchini, *President*
Judy Marchini, *Vice Pres*
EMP: 50
SQ FT: 1,200
SALES (est): 2.8MM **Privately Held**
SIC: 0191 0173 General farms, primarily crop; almond grove

(P-371)
MOON MOUNTAIN FARMS LLC
3846 E Telegraph Rd, Fillmore
(93015-9779)
PHONE...................................805 521-1742
Les Blake, *Mng Member*
EMP: 50
SALES (est): 1.8MM **Privately Held**
SIC: 0191 General farms, primarily crop

(P-372)
OSCAR VALERO
Also Called: Valero Labor
1685 Jones St, Woodland (95776-6380)
PHONE...................................530 668-4342
Oscar Valero, *Owner*
EMP: 50
SALES: 100K **Privately Held**
SIC: 0191 General farms, primarily crop

(P-373)
PITMAN FAMILY FARMS (PA)
Also Called: Pitman Farms
1075 North Ave, Sanger (93657-3539)
PHONE...................................559 875-9300
Richard J Pitman, *President*
EMP: 90
SQ FT: 1,000

SALES (est): 57.6MM **Privately Held**
WEB: www.marysturkeys.com
SIC: 0191 General farms, primarily crop

(P-374)
RAINBOW RANCHES INC
13650 Copus Rd, Bakersfield
(93313-9676)
PHONE...................................661 858-2266
Michael Andrews, *CEO*
Marina Quintana, *Admin Sec*
EMP: 210
SALES (est): 6.9MM **Privately Held**
SIC: 0191 General farms, primarily crop

(P-375)
RANCHO LAGUNA FARMS LLC
2410 W Main St, Santa Maria
(93458-9712)
P.O. Box 6617 (93456-6617)
PHONE...................................805 925-7805
Larry Ferini, *Mng Member*
Tracy Ferini,
EMP: 100
SALES (est): 3.2MM **Privately Held**
WEB: www.lagunaproduce.com
SIC: 0191 General farms, primarily crop

(P-376)
RED BLOSSOM SALES INC
Also Called: Red Blossom Farms
9 Harris Pl, Salinas (93901-4586)
PHONE...................................831 751-9169
Michelle Huber, *Manager*
Velasco Adrian, *District Mgr*
EMP: 503 **Privately Held**
SIC: 0191 General farms, primarily crop
PA: Red Blossom Sales, Inc.
400 W Ventura Blvd # 140
Camarillo CA 93010
-

(P-377)
ROCKET FARMS HERBS INC
370 Espinosa Rd, Salinas (93907-8895)
P.O. Box 398104, San Francisco (94139-8104)
PHONE...................................562 340-5108
Don Barnett, *CEO*
EMP: 493
SALES (est): 26.8MM **Privately Held**
SIC: 0191 General farms, primarily crop

(P-378)
SAFARI HARVSTG & FARMING LLC
313 Plaza Dr Ste B12, Santa Maria
(93454-6931)
PHONE...................................805 925-2600
Robert T Sheehy,
EMP: 300
SALES (est): 9.3MM **Privately Held**
SIC: 0191 0722 General farms, primarily crop; crop harvesting

(P-379)
SCHULTE RANCHES
Also Called: Dos Pueblos Ranch
Rr 1 Box 228, Goleta (93117)
PHONE...................................805 563-0821
Rudolph Schulte, *Owner*
EMP: 70
SQ FT: 600
SALES (est): 1.8MM **Privately Held**
SIC: 0191 0179 General farms, primarily crop; avocado orchard

(P-380)
SERIMIAN M S D L RANCH
Also Called: D & L Produce
10463 S Del Rey Ave, Selma (93662-9706)
PHONE...................................559 896-1517
Donald Serimian, *Partner*
Lionel Serimian, *Partner*
EMP: 50 EST: 1961
SALES (est): 1.1MM **Privately Held**
SIC: 0191 General farms, primarily crop

(P-381)
SHELDON RANCHES
25140 Burr Dr, Lindsay (93247-9786)
P.O. Box 668 (93247-0668)
PHONE...................................559 562-3978
Charles H Sheldon, *President*
EMP: 60

SALES (est): 2.5MM **Privately Held**
SIC: 0191 General farms, primarily crop

(P-382)
SUN WORLD INTERNATIONAL LLC
5701 Truxtun Ave Ste 200, Bakersfield
(93309-0651)
P.O. Box 80298 (93380-0298)
PHONE...................................661 392-5000
Merrill N Dibble, *President*
David Hostetter, *CFO*
Keith Mitchell, *CFO*
Michael J Aiton, *Senior VP*
Reed E Fullmer, *Vice Pres*
▲ EMP: 450
SALES (est): 57.6MM **Privately Held**
WEB: www.sun-world.com
SIC: 0191 General farms, primarily crop
PA: Sun World International, Inc.
16351 Driver Rd
Bakersfield CA 93308

(P-383)
SWANTON BERRY FARMS INC
25 Swanton Rd, Davenport (95017-9742)
P.O. Box 308 (95017-0308)
PHONE...................................831 425-8919
James Cochran, *President*
EMP: 50
SALES (est): 3.3MM **Privately Held**
SIC: 0191 General farms, primarily crop

(P-384)
TAPIA FARMS
8425 W Ave 8, Rosamond (93560)
PHONE...................................661 256-4401
Charlie Tapia, *Owner*
EMP: 50
SALES (est): 817.5K **Privately Held**
WEB: www.tapiafarms.com
SIC: 0191 General farms, primarily crop

(P-385)
TERRA LINDA FARMS 1
17625 S Marks Ave, Riverdale
(93656-9559)
P.O. Box 758 (93656-0758)
PHONE...................................559 867-3400
Joe Coelho, *Partner*
EMP: 50
SALES (est): 1.6MM **Privately Held**
SIC: 0191 General farms, primarily crop

(P-386)
TERRANOVA RANCH INC
16729 W Floral Ave, Helm (93627)
P.O. Box 130 (93627-0130)
PHONE...................................559 866-5644
Diego Lissi, *President*
Don Cameron, *Vice Pres*
Annette Bauer, *Info Tech Mgr*
EMP: 50
SQ FT: 5,000
SALES (est): 5.8MM **Privately Held**
SIC: 0191 0172 General farms, primarily crop; grapes

(P-387)
THOMPSON FAMILY FARMS LLC
16478 Beach Blvd Ste 391, Westminster
(92683-7860)
PHONE...................................714 848-7536
Robert Thompson, *Mng Member*
EMP: 50
SALES (est): 665.5K **Privately Held**
SIC: 0191 General farms, primarily crop

(P-388)
TRAVIS JAMES WATTS
9631 Harvey Rd, Galt (95632-8861)
PHONE...................................209 810-6159
Travis James Watts, *Owner*
EMP: 200
SALES: 150K **Privately Held**
SIC: 0191 General farms, primarily crop

(P-389)
V&V FARM LABOR CONTRACTOR
18396 S Wagner Ave, Ripon (95366-9720)
PHONE...................................209 599-4834
Jose Villanueva, *President*

P
R
O
D
U
C
T
S

&

S
V
C
S

EMP: 50
SALES (est): 2MM **Privately Held**
SIC: 0191 General farms, primarily crop

(P-390)
VAN GRONINGEN & SONS INC
15100 Jack Tone Rd, Manteca
(95336-9729)
PHONE..................................209 982-5248
Robert Van Groningen, *President*
Monica Kuil, *CFO*
Dan Vangroningen, *Vice Pres*
Paul Hiemstra, *Plant Mgr*
Carlos Mata, *QC Mgr*
▼ EMP: 360
SQ FT: 3,000
SALES (est): 57.6MM **Privately Held**
WEB: www.vgandsons.com
SIC: 0191 0762 General farms, primarily
crop; farm management services

(P-391)
VAQUERO FARMS INC
43405 W Panoche Rd, Firebaugh
(93622-9720)
PHONE..................................559 659-2790
Havier Rodriquez, *Manager*
EMP: 60
SQ FT: 150
SALES (corp-wide): 7.4MM **Privately
Held**
SIC: 0191 General farms, primarily crop
PA: Vaquero Farms, Inc.
2800 W March Ln Ste 330
Stockton CA 95219
209 476-0002

(P-392)
VICTORIA ISLAND FARMS
16021 E Hwy 4, Holt (95234)
P.O. Box 87 (95234-0087)
PHONE..................................209 465-5609
Eileen Nichols, *Owner*
▲ EMP: 70 EST: 1998
SQ FT: 1,484
SALES (est): 7.6MM **Privately Held**
SIC: 0191 General farms, primarily crop

(P-393)
VINO FARMS INC
51375 S Netherlands Rd, Clarksburg
(95612-5019)
PHONE..................................916 775-4095
John Ledbetter, *Owner*
EMP: 116
SALES (corp-wide): 59.3MM **Privately
Held**
SIC: 0191 General farms, primarily crop
PA: Vino Farms, Inc.
1377 E Lodi Ave
Lodi CA 95240
209 334-6975

(P-394)
WILLOW FARMS LLC
9452 Telephone Rd Pmb 142, Ventura
(93004-2600)
PHONE..................................805 647-0720
George Ito, *Owner*
EMP: 60
SALES (est): 2.1MM **Privately Held**
WEB: www.willowfarms.com
SIC: 0191 General farms, primarily crop

(P-395)
**WOOLF FARMING CO CAL INC
(PA)**
Also Called: Lansing Farming Co
7041 N Van Ness Blvd, Fresno
(93711-7169)
PHONE..................................559 945-9292
Stuart P Woolf, *President*
John L Woolf III, *Chairman*
Michael T Woolf, *Treasurer*
Bernice Woolf, *Vice Pres*
Anne A Delaware, *Admin Sec*
EMP: 624 EST: 1974
SQ FT: 4,500
SALES (est): 33.8MM **Privately Held**
WEB: www.woolffarming.com
SIC: 0191 General farms, primarily crop

0211 Beef Cattle Feedlots

(P-396)
BRANDT CO INC
Also Called: Brandt Cattle
7015 Brandt Rd, Calipatria (92233-9761)
PHONE..................................760 348-2295
William Brent, *Manager*
EMP: 53
SALES (corp-wide): 7.9MM **Privately
Held**
WEB: www.brandtco.com
SIC: 0211 0139 Beef cattle feedlots; al-
falfa farm; grass seed farm
PA: Brandt Co., Inc.
299 W Main St
Brawley CA 92227
760 344-3430

(P-397)
MENDES CALF RANCH
13356 Avenue 168, Tipton (93272-9749)
PHONE..................................559 688-4708
Victor Mendes, *Owner*
EMP: 90
SALES (est): 3MM **Privately Held**
SIC: 0211 Beef cattle feedlots

(P-398)
**SUPERIOR CATTLE FEEDERS
LLC (PA)**
551 S Industrial Ave, Calipatria (92233)
P.O. Box 1828 (92233-1828)
PHONE..................................760 348-2218
Dmingue Antchagno,
Robert A Lofton,
EMP: 55 EST: 1996
SALES (est): 7.5MM **Privately Held**
SIC: 0211 Beef cattle feedlots

**0212 Beef Cattle, Except
Feedlots**

(P-399)
**FULLMER CATTLE NTHRN CAL
LLC**
16600 Hellman Ave, Corona (92880-9722)
PHONE..................................909 597-3274
Que J Fullmer,
Que Fullmer, *Owner*
EMP: 120
SQ FT: 100,000
SALES (est): 4.7MM **Privately Held**
SIC: 0212 Beef cattle except feedlots

(P-400)
M & T CALF RANCH
Also Called: Tuls Cattle
14998 Avenue 192, Tulare (93274-9074)
PHONE..................................559 686-7663
Sid Tuls, *Partner*
Mike Frings, *Partner*
Jason Tuls, *Partner*
EMP: 60
SQ FT: 1,800
SALES (est): 2MM **Privately Held**
SIC: 0212 Beef cattle except feedlots

(P-401)
ROBINSON & SONS
Also Called: Robinson and Enterprises
293 Lower Grass Valley Rd # 201, Nevada
City (95959-3120)
PHONE..................................530 265-5844
Lowell Robinson, *Partner*
Neil Robinson, *Partner*
EMP: 70
SQ FT: 2,000
SALES (est): 1.3MM **Privately Held**
WEB: www.timrobinson.com
SIC: 0212 Beef cattle except feedlots

(P-402)
**WESTERN MEAT PROCESSORS
INC**
Also Called: Agri-Feed Industries
502 E Barioni Blvd, Imperial (92251-1776)
P.O. Box 728 (92251-0728)
PHONE..................................760 355-1175
Philip E Bauer, *Principal*
EMP: 50

SALES (est): 1.8MM **Privately Held**
SIC: 0212 0723 Beef cattle except feedlots; grain milling, custom services

---

0213 Hogs

(P-403)
LINDA TERRA FARMS (PA)
5494 W Mount Whitney Ave, Riverdale
(93656-9329)
PHONE..................................559 867-3473
John Coelho, *CEO*
EMP: 170
SQ FT: 1,014
SALES (est): 20.7MM **Privately Held**
SIC: 0213 0182 0172 Hogs; fruits grown
under cover; grapes

(P-404)
SEABOARD CORPORATION
Also Called: Texas Farm
10350 Hritg Pk Dr Ste 111, Santa Fe
Springs (90670)
PHONE..................................806 435-5935
Steven J Bresky, *CEO*
EMP: 300
SALES (corp-wide): 5.8B **Publicly Held**
SIC: 0213 Hogs
PA: Seaboard Corporation
9000 W 67th St
Merriam KS 66202
913 676-8800

0214 Sheep & Goats

(P-405)
ETCHEGARAY FARMS LLC
32324 Famoso Rd, Mc Farland (93250)
P.O. Box 964, Visalia (93279-0964)
PHONE..................................661 393-0920
Sam Etchegaray,
Sam Etcegaray, *General Mgr*
EMP: 50 EST: 1985
SQ FT: 8,000
SALES (est): 845.1K **Privately Held**
SIC: 0214 0172 0179 0174 Lamb feedlot;
grapes; avocado orchard; grapefruit grove

0241 Dairy Farms

(P-406)
B & R TEVELDE
2911 Hanford Armona Rd, Hanford
(93230-9379)
PHONE..................................559 583-1277
Bernard Tevelde, *Owner*
Nico Slabber, *Principal*
EMP: 52
SALES: 950K **Privately Held**
SIC: 0241 0111 Dairy farms; wheat

(P-407)
BOSMAN DAIRY LLC
6802 Avenue 120 A, Tipton (93272-9525)
PHONE..................................559 752-7018
Clarence Bosman, *Partner*
Frank Bosman, *Partner*
EMP: 130 EST: 1959
SALES (est): 17.3MM **Privately Held**
SIC: 0241 Dairy farms

(P-408)
CASE VLOTT CATTLE
Also Called: Vlot Brothers
20330 Road 4, Chowchilla (93610-9489)
P.O. Box 309 (93610-0309)
PHONE..................................559 665-7399
EMP: 50
SALES (est): 2MM **Privately Held**
SIC: 0241

(P-409)
COSTA VIEW FARMS
Also Called: Costa View Farms Shop
16800 Road 15, Madera (93637-9445)
PHONE..................................559 675-3131
Darryl Azevedo, *Partner*
Linda Azevedo, *Partner*
Teresa Carr, *Partner*
William Carr, *Partner*
▲ EMP: 50 EST: 1999

SALES (est): 10.9MM **Privately Held**
SIC: 0241 0115 0211 Dairy farms; corn;
beef cattle feedlots

(P-410)
CURTI FAMILY INC
3235 Avenue 199, Tulare (93274-8909)
PHONE..................................559 688-8323
Phillip A Curti, *President*
Preston Nicholas Curti, *Shareholder*
Phillip Curti, *Treasurer*
Phillip Justin Curti, *Corp Secy*
EMP: 54
SALES (est): 6.3MM **Privately Held**
SIC: 0241 Dairy farms

(P-411)
**FERN OAKS FRMS A CAL GEN
PRTNR**
17001 Avenue 160, Porterville
(93257-9258)
PHONE..................................559 684-8220
Greg Fernandes, *Partner*
Gregory Fernandes, *Partner*
EMP: 50 EST: 2017
SQ FT: 3,000
SALES (est): 972.1K **Privately Held**
SIC: 0241 Milk production

(P-412)
FOSTER DAIRY FARMS (PA)
Also Called: Crystal Creamery
529 Kansas Ave, Modesto (95351-1515)
PHONE..................................209 576-3400
Frank Otis, *CEO*
Mark Shaw, *CFO*
Dennis Roberts, *Vice Pres*
▼ EMP: 800 EST: 1958
SALES (est): 320.5MM **Privately Held**
SIC: 0241 Milk production

(P-413)
**FRANK J GOMES DAIRY A
CALIFO**
Also Called: F and A Farms
5301 Deangelis Rd, Stevinson
(95374-9726)
PHONE..................................209 669-7978
Frank J Gomes, *Partner*
Albert Xavier, *Partner*
EMP: 58
SALES (est): 8.5MM **Privately Held**
SIC: 0241 Dairy farms

(P-414)
**GALLO CATTLE CO A LTD
PARTNR**
Also Called: Joseph Farms Cheese
10561 State Highway 140, Atwater
(95301-9309)
P.O. Box 775 (95301-0775)
PHONE..................................209 394-7984
Michael Gallo, *CEO*
Micah Gallo, *Partner*
Tiffanie Gallo, *Partner*
Linda Jelacich, *Partner*
EMP: 500
SQ FT: 6,000
SALES (est): 57.6MM **Privately Held**
SIC: 0241 2022 Milk production; cheese,
natural & processed

(P-415)
HIGH PLAINS RANCH LLC (PA)
2911 Hanford Armona Rd, Hanford
(93230-9379)
PHONE..................................559 583-1277
Bernard Te Velde, *Mng Member*
EMP: 120
SQ FT: 2,000
SALES (est): 17.4MM **Privately Held**
SIC: 0241 Dairy farms

(P-416)
HOLLANDIA DAIRY INC (PA)
622 E Mission Rd, San Marcos
(92069-1999)
PHONE..................................760 744-3222
Arie H Dejong, *President*
Peter De Jong, *Vice Pres*
Rudy De Jong, *Vice Pres*
Ken May, *Sales Staff*
Bob Hodge, *Manager*
EMP: 200
SQ FT: 20,000

SALES (est): 57.6MM **Privately Held**
WEB: www.hollandiadairy.com
SIC: **0241** Milk production

(P-417)
IEST FAMILY FARMS
Also Called: Richard Iest Dairy
14576 Avenue 14, Madera
PHONE.............................559 674-9417
Richard Iest, *Partner*
Danny Iest, *Partner*
Gerrlyn Iest, *Partner*
Linda Wedel, *General Mgr*
EMP: 70
SALES (est): 11.3MM **Privately Held**
SIC: **0241** Dairy farms

(P-418)
JAMES J STEVINSON A CORP (PA)
Also Called: Anchor J Dairy
25079 River Rd, Stevinson (95374-9724)
P.O. Box 818, Newman (95360-0818)
PHONE.............................209 632-1681
Robert Kelley, *President*
Kevin F Kelley, *Treasurer*
George Kelley, *Vice Pres*
EMP: 50
SQ FT: 1,500
SALES: 5MM **Privately Held**
SIC: **0241 0191** Dairy farms; general farms, primarily crop

(P-419)
MADDOX DAIRY LLC
3899 W Davis Ave, Riverdale (93656-9417)
PHONE.............................559 867-3545
Stephen Maddox,
Julia Maddox Chow, *CFO*
EMP: 73
SALES (est): 6.6MM **Privately Held**
SIC: **0241** Milk production

(P-420)
MADDOX DAIRY A LTD PARTNERSHIP (PA)
3899 W Davis Ave, Riverdale (93656-9417)
PHONE.............................559 867-3545
Steven Maddox, *Partner*
Douglas Maddox, *Partner*
Patrick Maddox, *Partner*
EMP: 60
SQ FT: 8,700
SALES (est): 10.2MM **Privately Held**
SIC: **0241** Milk production

(P-421)
MADDOX DAIRY A LTD PARTNERSHIP
Also Called: Ruann Dairy
7285 W Davis Ave, Riverdale (93656-9735)
PHONE.............................559 867-4457
Patrick Maddox, *Manager*
EMP: 50
SALES (corp-wide): 10.2MM **Privately Held**
SIC: **0241** Milk production
PA: Maddox Dairy, A Limited Partnership
3899 W Davis Ave
Riverdale CA 93656
559 867-3545

(P-422)
MADDOX DAIRY A LTD PARTNERSHIP
12863 W Kamm Ave, Riverdale (93656-9231)
PHONE.............................559 866-5624
Steve Maddox, *Partner*
EMP: 70
SALES (corp-wide): 10.2MM **Privately Held**
SIC: **0241** Milk production
PA: Maddox Dairy, A Limited Partnership
3899 W Davis Ave
Riverdale CA 93656
559 867-3545

(P-423)
NIELSENS CREAMERY (PA)
Also Called: Hoffman Farms
21346 Road 140, Tulare (93274-9363)
P.O. Box 579 (93275-0579)
PHONE.............................559 686-4744
Chase Hoffman, *Partner*

Marion N Hoffman, *Partner*
EMP: 57
SQ FT: 11,000
SALES (est): 4.6MM **Privately Held**
SIC: **0241** Milk production

(P-424)
ORGANIC PASTURES DAIRY CO LLC
7221 S Jameson Ave, Fresno (93706-9386)
PHONE.............................559 846-9732
Mark L McAfee, *Mng Member*
ADM McAfee,
Eric McAfee,
EMP: 50
SALES (est): 25.4MM **Privately Held**
SIC: **0241** Dairy farms

(P-425)
P H RANCH INC
Also Called: Veldhuis Dairy
6335 Oakdale Rd, Winton (95388-9648)
PHONE.............................209 358-5111
Ray Veldhuis, *President*
Jeanette Veldhuis, *Corp Secy*
Ray Veldhuis Jr, *Vice Pres*
EMP: 50
SALES (est): 7MM **Privately Held**
WEB: www.phranch.com
SIC: **0241** Milk production

(P-426)
VLOT BROTHERS TRUCKING CO INC
Also Called: Vlot Brothers Dairy
3197 Avenue 21, Chowchilla (93610-9294)
P.O. Box 309 (93610-0309)
PHONE.............................559 665-7399
Dirk J Vlot, *Partner*
Case Vlot, *Partner*
Valerie Vlot, *Partner*
EMP: 80
SALES (est): 8.8MM **Privately Held**
SIC: **0241** Dairy farms

(P-427)
WITHROW CATTLE
Also Called: Withrow Dairy
5301 Pleasant Grove Rd, Pleasant Grove (95668-9752)
PHONE.............................916 780-0364
Shane Johnson, *Manager*
EMP: 65
SALES (corp-wide): 2.6MM **Privately Held**
WEB: www.withrowdairy.com
SIC: **0241** Dairy farms
PA: Withrow Cattle
5301 Pleasant Grove Rd
Pleasant Grove CA 95668
916 780-0364

(P-428)
ZONNEVELD DAIRIES INC
1560 Cerini Ave, Laton (93242-9700)
PHONE.............................559 923-4546
John Zonneveld Sr, *President*
Frank Zonneveld, *Corp Secy*
EMP: 60
SALES (est): 10.9MM **Privately Held**
WEB: www.cainhibbard.com
SIC: **0241** Dairy farms

(P-429)
ZONNEVELD FARMS
1560 Cerini Ave, Laton (93242-9700)
PHONE.............................559 923-4546
Andrew Zonneveld, *Partner*
Craig Wierenga, *Project Mgr*
EMP: 99
SALES (est): 3.5MM **Privately Held**
SIC: **0241 0191** Dairy farms; general farms, primarily crop

---

0252 Chicken Egg Farms

(P-430)
DEMLER EGG RANCH
28198 Gromer Ave, Wasco (93280-9558)
P.O. Box 207 (93280-0207)
PHONE.............................661 758-4577
David Demler, *Partner*
Sharman Demler, *Partner*

EMP: 50
SALES (est): 1.4MM **Privately Held**
SIC: **0252** Chicken eggs

(P-431)
FOSTER FARMS LLC
770 N Plano St, Porterville (93257-6329)
PHONE.............................559 793-5501
Paul Bravinder, *Manager*
Tom Farrell, *Plant Mgr*
Chris Jones, *Maintence Staff*
Dave Gilpin, *Manager*
Claudia Ramos, *Manager*
EMP: 300
SQ FT: 81,000
SALES (corp-wide): 1.4B **Privately Held**
SIC: **0252** 2015 Chicken eggs; poultry slaughtering & processing
PA: Foster Farms, Llc
1000 Davis St
Livingston CA 95334
209 394-7901

(P-432)
GEMPERLE ENTERPRISES
Also Called: Gemperle Farms
10218 Lander Ave, Turlock (95380-9627)
PHONE.............................209 667-2651
Steve Gemperle, *Mng Member*
▲ EMP: 90 EST: 1952
SQ FT: 8,000
SALES (est): 6.8MM **Privately Held**
SIC: **0252** 5144 Chicken eggs; eggs

(P-433)
NORCO RANCH INC (DH)
12005 Cabernet Dr, Fontana (92337-7703)
PHONE.............................951 737-6735
Ric Sundal, *CEO*
Michael Lemire, *Controller*
EMP: 350
SQ FT: 120,000
SALES (est): 36MM
SALES (corp-wide): 12.8B **Privately Held**
WEB: www.norcoeggs.com
SIC: **0252** Chicken eggs
HQ: Moark, Llc
28 Under The Mountain Rd
North Franklin CT 06254
951 332-3300

(P-434)
S K S ENTERPRISES INC (PA)
11830 French Camp Rd, Manteca (95336-9732)
PHONE.............................209 599-4095
Wen Chang Su, *President*
EMP: 60
SALES (est): 3.6MM **Privately Held**
SIC: **0252** 2015 Chicken eggs; poultry slaughtering & processing

(P-435)
VALLEY FRESH FOODS INC
Nest Best Egg Company
3600 E Linwood Ave, Turlock (95380-9109)
P.O. Box 370, Rochester WA (98579-0370)
PHONE.............................209 669-5600
Duane Olsen, *Branch Mgr*
EMP: 61
SALES (corp-wide): 1.2B **Privately Held**
SIC: **0252** 2048 Chicken eggs; prepared feeds
PA: Valley Fresh Foods, Inc.
3600 E Linwood Ave
Turlock CA 95380
209 669-5600

(P-436)
VALLEY FRESH FOODS INC
Also Called: Rainbow Farms
1220 Hall Rd, Denair (95316-9617)
P.O. Box 910, Turlock (95381-0910)
PHONE.............................209 669-5510
Danny O'Day, *Manager*
Victor Maderiros, *CTO*
EMP: 100
SQ FT: 1,216
SALES (corp-wide): 1.2B **Privately Held**
SIC: **0252** 2015 Started pullet farm; poultry slaughtering & processing
PA: Valley Fresh Foods, Inc.
3600 E Linwood Ave
Turlock CA 95380
209 669-5600

0253 Turkey & Turkey Egg Farms

(P-437)
DIESTEL TURKEY RANCH
14111 High Tech Dr C, Jamestown (95327)
P.O. Box 4314, Sonora (95370-1314)
PHONE.............................209 984-0826
Tim Diestel, *Owner*
Joan Diestel, *Co-Owner*
EMP: 150
SALES (est): 5.9MM **Privately Held**
SIC: **0253** 2015 Turkey farm; poultry slaughtering & processing

(P-438)
DIESTEL TURKEY RANCH (PA)
22200 Lyons Bald Mtn Rd, Sonora (95370-8772)
P.O. Box 4314 (95370-1314)
PHONE.............................209 532-4950
Timothy Diestel, *CEO*
Dave Harmer, *CFO*
David Harmer, *CFO*
Jared Orrock, *Officer*
Joan Diestel, *Vice Pres*
EMP: 130
SQ FT: 5,000
SALES (est): 21.6MM **Privately Held**
SIC: **0253** Turkey farm

(P-439)
SWANSON FARMS
5213 W Main St, Turlock (95380-9413)
P.O. Box 2367 (95381-2367)
PHONE.............................209 667-2002
Richard E Swanson, *President*
Larry Pickering, *Vice Pres*
EMP: 65 EST: 1942
SQ FT: 5,000
SALES (est): 4.5MM **Privately Held**
WEB: www.associatedfeed.com
SIC: **0253 0173** Turkey farm; almond grove

0254 Poultry Hatcheries

(P-440)
FOSTER POULTRY FARMS
843 Davis St, Livingston (95334-1525)
P.O. Box 457 (95334-0457)
PHONE.............................209 394-7901
Richie King, *Branch Mgr*
EMP: 3000
SALES (corp-wide): 3B **Privately Held**
WEB: www.fosterfarms.com
SIC: **0254** 2015 Poultry hatcheries; poultry, processed
PA: Foster Poultry Farms
1000 Davis St
Livingston CA 95334
209 394-6914

(P-441)
FOSTER POULTRY FARMS
Also Called: Foster Turkey Live Haul
1033 S Center St, Turlock (95380-5568)
PHONE.............................209 668-5922
Steve Page, *Manager*
EMP: 100
SALES (corp-wide): 3B **Privately Held**
WEB: www.fosterfarms.com
SIC: **0254** Poultry hatcheries
PA: Foster Poultry Farms
1000 Davis St
Livingston CA 95334
209 394-6914

(P-442)
FOSTER POULTRY FARMS
900 W Belgravia Ave, Fresno (93706-3909)
PHONE.............................559 265-2000
Jessi Amezcua, *Branch Mgr*
Andy Rutherford, *Foreman/Supr*
Maggie Saragoza, *Legal Staff*
EMP: 567

SALES (corp-wide): 3B **Privately Held**
WEB: www.fosterfarms.com
SIC: 0254 2015 5812 0173 Chicken slaughtering & processing; turkey processing & slaughtering; chicken restaurant; almond grove; animal feeds; local trucking, without storage; chicken hatchery
PA: Foster Poultry Farms
　　1000 Davis St
　　Livingston CA 95334
　　209 394-6914

(P-443)
FOSTER POULTRY FARMS
Also Called: Foster Farms
2960 S Cherry Ave, Fresno (93706-5445)
PHONE...................(559) 442-3771
Bob Hansen, *Manager*
Tracy Bianchi, *Accounting Mgr*
Rebeca Reyes, *Human Res Mgr*
Donna Machado, *Buyer*
Michael Montero, *Maint Spvr*
EMP: 700
SALES (corp-wide): 3B **Privately Held**
WEB: www.fosterfarms.com
SIC: 0254 Poultry hatcheries
PA: Foster Poultry Farms
　　1000 Davis St
　　Livingston CA 95334
　　209 394-6914

0259 Poultry & Eggs Farms, NEC

(P-444)
REICHARDT DUCK FARM INC
3770 Middle Two Rock Rd, Petaluma (94952-4625)
PHONE...................707 762-6314
John T Reichardt, *President*
Kathy Shaw, *CFO*
▼ **EMP:** 95
SQ FT: 1,296
SALES (est): 3.6MM **Privately Held**
WEB: www.reichardtduckfarm.com
SIC: 0259 Duck farm

0279 Animal Specialties, NEC

(P-445)
BELCAMPO GROUP INC (PA)
65 Webster St, Oakland (94607-3720)
PHONE...................510 250-7810
Anya Fernald, *CEO*
Nate Morr, *COO*
Talia Dillman, *Project Mgr*
Jeremy Fisher, *Project Mgr*
Mary Torres, *Human Res Mgr*
◆ **EMP:** 70 **EST:** 2011
SALES (est): 17.4MM **Privately Held**
SIC: 0279 2011 2015 5812 Domestic animal farms; beef products from beef slaughtered on site; poultry slaughtering & processing; family restaurants; office management

(P-446)
SAN BERNARDINO MTNS WILDLIFE
Also Called: WILDHAVEN RANCH
29450 Pine Ridge Dr, Cedar Glen (92321)
P.O. Box 1782, Lake Arrowhead (92352-1782)
PHONE...................909 226-6189
Diane Dragotto Williams, *CEO*
EMP: 50 **EST:** 1995
SALES: 550.4K **Privately Held**
SIC: 0279 Bird sanctuaries

0291 Animal Production, NEC

(P-447)
BOOTH RANCHES LLC
440 Anchor Ave, Orange Cove (93646-2200)
PHONE...................559 626-4472
Otis Booth Jr, *Branch Mgr*

Edgar Rodriguez, *Manager*
EMP: 76
SALES (corp-wide): 16.2MM **Privately Held**
SIC: 0291 General farms, primarily animals
PA: Booth Ranches Llc
　　12201 Avenue 480
　　Orange Cove CA 93646
　　559 626-4732

(P-448)
DOUGLAS RANCH LLC
33200 E Carmel Valley Rd, Carmel Valley (93924-9396)
PHONE...................949 500-7009
Joy Berry, *Principal*
EMP: 50
SALES (est): 639.9K **Privately Held**
SIC: 0291 General farms, primarily animals

(P-449)
E & T FOODS INC
Also Called: Monrovia Ranch Market
14827 Seventh St, Victorville (92395-4023)
P.O. Box 661912, Arcadia (91066-1912)
PHONE...................760 843-7730
Franco Duenas, *Branch Mgr*
EMP: 330
SALES (corp-wide): 66.2MM **Privately Held**
SIC: 0291 General farms, primarily animals
PA: E & T Foods, Inc.
　　328 W Huntington Dr
　　Monrovia CA 91016
　　626 357-5051

(P-450)
HALEAKALA RANCH LLC
9923 Tyler Rd, Gerber (96035)
PHONE...................530 529-6651
Daniel James Davidson, *Mng Member*
▼ **EMP:** 50
SALES (est): 1.2MM **Privately Held**
SIC: 0291 General farms, primarily animals

(P-451)
LAGUNA BCH GOLF BNGLOW VLG LLC
Also Called: Ranch At Laguna Beach, The
31106 Coast Hwy, Laguna Beach (92651-8130)
PHONE...................949 499-2271
Mark Christy, *Principal*
Kurt Bjorkman, *General Mgr*
Lindsey Kenworthy, *Sales Staff*
Grace Guido, *Manager*
Sean Laurino, *Manager*
EMP: 50
SALES (est): 1.3MM **Privately Held**
SIC: 0291 General farms, primarily animals

(P-452)
MIGUEL RAMOS
196 San Andreas Rd, Watsonville (95076-9522)
PHONE...................831 761-9941
Miguel Ramos, *Owner*
EMP: 60
SALES (est): 2.9MM **Privately Held**
WEB: www.miguelramon.com
SIC: 0291 General farms, primarily animals

(P-453)
OAK GROVE INST FOUNDATION INC
1251 N A St, Perris (92570-1911)
PHONE...................951 238-6022
EMP: 311
SALES (corp-wide): 19MM **Privately Held**
SIC: 0291 General farms, primarily animals
PA: Oak Grove Institute Foundation, Inc.
　　24275 Jefferson Ave
　　Murrieta CA 92562
　　951 677-5599

(P-454)
R RANCH MARKET
1112 Walnut Ave, Tustin (92780-5607)
PHONE...................714 573-1182
Jubira Martinez, *Owner*
EMP: 709
SALES (est): 4MM
SALES (corp-wide): 128.4MM **Privately Held**
SIC: 0291 General farms, primarily animals

PA: R-Ranch Market, Incorporated
　　13985 Live Oak Ave
　　Irwindale CA 91706
　　626 814-2900

(P-455)
RAVA RANCHES INC
700 Airport Rd, King City (93930-2501)
P.O. Box 1600 (93930-1600)
PHONE...................831 385-3285
Jerry J Rava Sr, *President*
EMP: 50 **EST:** 1987
SALES (est): 4.8MM **Privately Held**
SIC: 0291 General farms, primarily animals

(P-456)
RIO BRAVO RANCH SHOP
15701 Highway 178, Bakersfield (93306-9500)
PHONE...................661 872-5050
Jim Nickel, *Partner*
EMP: 50
SALES (est): 845.6K **Privately Held**
SIC: 0291 General farms, primarily animals

(P-457)
SCHOOLSFIRST FEDERAL CREDIT UN
8865 Foothill Blvd, Rancho Cucamonga (91730-3577)
PHONE...................800 462-8328
EMP: 51
SALES (corp-wide): 413.4MM **Privately Held**
SIC: 0291 General farms, primarily animals
PA: Schoolsfirst Federal Credit Union
　　2115 N Broadway
　　Santa Ana CA 92706
　　714 258-4000

0711 Soil Preparation Svcs

(P-458)
BIO INDUSTRIES INC
2060 Montgomery Rd, Red Bluff (96080-4613)
PHONE...................530 529-3290
Ben Sale, *President*
EMP: 50
SQ FT: 400
SALES (est): 100K **Privately Held**
SIC: 0711 Soil preparation services

(P-459)
MEE INDUSTRIES INC
16021 Adelante St, Irwindale (91702-3255)
PHONE...................626 359-4550
John Mee, *Principal*
EMP: 68
SALES (corp-wide): 12.4MM **Privately Held**
WEB: www.meefog.com
SIC: 0711 Soil preparation services
PA: Mee Industries Inc.
　　16021 Adelante St
　　Irwindale CA 91702
　　626 359-4550

0721 Soil Preparation, Planting & Cultivating Svc

(P-460)
CALIFORNIA VALLEY LAND CO INC (PA)
Also Called: Woolf Enterprises
18036 Gale, Huron (93234)
P.O. Box 219 (93234-0219)
PHONE...................559 945-9292
Stuart P Woolf, *President*
Michael T Woolf, *Treasurer*
John L Woolf, *Vice Ch Bd*
Susan Hornor, *Asst Controller*
EMP: 93
SQ FT: 4,500
SALES (est): 48MM **Privately Held**
SIC: 0721 Planting services; crop cultivating services; crop protecting services

(P-461)
CHUCK JONES FLYING SERVICE (PA)
Also Called: Aerial Applicators
216 W Hamilton Rd, Biggs (95917-9793)
P.O. Box 497 (95917-0497)
PHONE...................530 868-5798
Dale Jones, *President*
Lori A Jones, *Treasurer*
Alan Jones, *Vice Pres*
EMP: 50
SQ FT: 25,000
SALES: 3.2MM **Privately Held**
SIC: 0721 Crop dusting services

(P-462)
GERAWAN FARMING PARTNERS INC
15749 E Ventura Ave, Sanger (93657-9657)
P.O. Box 67 (93657-0067)
PHONE...................559 787-8780
Dan Gerawan, *President*
EMP: 300
SALES (est): 10.4MM **Privately Held**
SIC: 0721 0172 Tree orchards, cultivation of; grapes

(P-463)
JOHN H KAUTZ FARMS
5490 Bear Creek Rd, Lodi (95240-7213)
PHONE...................209 334-4786
John H Kautz, *Co-Owner*
Gail Kautz, *Owner*
EMP: 50 **EST:** 1952
SQ FT: 3,000
SALES (est): 5.7MM **Privately Held**
SIC: 0721 Orchard tree & vine services

(P-464)
OAKRIDGE LANDSCAPE INC (PA)
28064 Avenue Stanford K, Valencia (91355-1158)
PHONE...................661 295-7228
Jeffrey E Myers, *CEO*
Andrea Fisher, *Administration*
Len Poloniato, *VP Finance*
Nancy Orduno, *Purch Mgr*
Eileen Vansickle-Valle, *Purch Agent*
EMP: 50
SALES (est): 31.3MM **Privately Held**
WEB: www.oakridgelandscape.com
SIC: 0721 0781 Irrigation system operation, not providing water; landscape services

(P-465)
PLANT TAPE USA INC
Also Called: Tanimura & Antle
1 Harris Rd Fl 1 # 1, Salinas (93908-8608)
P.O. Box 4070 (93912-4070)
PHONE...................831 455-2255
Brian Antle, *President*
▼ **EMP:** 50
SALES: 3.1MM
SALES (corp-wide): 810K **Privately Held**
SIC: 0721 Planting services
PA: Plant Tape Altea Sl
　　Calle Llobatona, 6 - Nave D
　　Viladecans 08840
　　936 379-892

(P-466)
S & S RANCH INC
Also Called: Stamoules Produce Company
904 S Lyon Ave, Mendota (93640-9735)
PHONE...................559 655-3491
Pagona Stefanopoulos, *CEO*
Athanasios Stefanopoulos, *Vice Pres*
▼ **EMP:** 85
SQ FT: 500
SALES (est): 10.6MM **Privately Held**
SIC: 0721 Planting services; crop cultivating services; crop protecting services

(P-467)
SEAMAN NURSERIES INC
336 Robertson Blvd Ste A, Chowchilla (93610-2867)
PHONE...................559 665-1860
William Seaman, *President*
EMP: 70

SALES (est): 5.7MM **Privately Held**
SIC: 0721 0762 5261 Orchard tree & vine services; farm management services; nurseries

(P-468)
SUNRIDGE NURSERIES INC
441 Vineland Rd, Bakersfield (93307-9556)
PHONE...........................661 363-8463
Craig Stoller, *CEO*
Glen Stoller, *President*
Tom Bracken, *COO*
Terrie Stoller, *Treasurer*
Leo Villanueva, *Prdtn Mgr*
EMP: 70
SQ FT: 60,000
SALES (est): 14MM **Privately Held**
WEB: www.sunridgenurseries.com
SIC: 0721 Vines, cultivation of

(P-469)
THIARA SUKHWANT
Also Called: Thiara Orchards
1537 Atkinson Ct, Yuba City (95993-9679)
PHONE...........................530 673-1581
Sukhwant Thiara, *Owner*
Ravi Thiara, *Principal*
EMP: 50
SALES (est): 3.3MM **Privately Held**
SIC: 0721 Tree orchards, cultivation of

(P-470)
VISTA VERDE FARMS INC
7124 Whitley Ave, Corcoran (93212-9669)
P.O. Box 398 (93212-0398)
PHONE...........................559 992-3111
Jim Hansen, *President*
Kendell W Gardner, *Corp Secy*
Jess Hansen, *Vice Pres*
EMP: 70
SQ FT: 3,000
SALES: 3.1MM **Privately Held**
SIC: 0721 0173 Crop planting & protection; almond grove

0722 Crop Harvesting By Machine

(P-471)
A & G GROVE SERVICE
32731 Mesa Lilac Rd, Escondido (92026-4402)
P.O. Box 1752, Fallbrook (92088-1752)
PHONE...........................760 728-5447
Angel Huerta, *Owner*
EMP: 100
SALES (est): 6.1MM **Privately Held**
SIC: 0722 Crop harvesting

(P-472)
ANTHONY HARVESTING INC
401 S Vanderhurst Ave, King City (93930-2934)
P.O. Box 608 (93930-0608)
PHONE...........................831 385-6460
Scott Anthony, *President*
EMP: 110
SALES (est): 7.1MM **Privately Held**
SIC: 0722 Crop harvesting

(P-473)
AZCONA HARVESTING LLC
44 El Camino Real Unit A, Greenfield (93927-5637)
P.O. Box 3310 (93927-3310)
PHONE...........................831 674-2526
Nick Azcona,
Pier Azcona,
EMP: 200
SQ FT: 1,000
SALES: 17.2MM **Privately Held**
SIC: 0722 Crop harvesting

(P-474)
BARNES AND BERGER
1091 S Intake Blvd, Blythe (92225-8209)
PHONE...........................760 922-6136
Euell Barnes, *Partner*
Duane Berger, *Partner*
Beverly Siegal, *Regional Mgr*
EMP: 50
SQ FT: 8,900

SALES: 3MM **Privately Held**
WEB: www.barnesandberger.com
SIC: 0722 Cotton, machine harvesting services

(P-475)
BYRD HARVEST INC
Also Called: Byrd Produce
192 Guadalupe St, Guadalupe (93434-1514)
P.O. Box 60 (93434-0060)
PHONE...........................805 343-1608
Joe George, *President*
Barbara Stanley, *Treasurer*
EMP: 300
SQ FT: 5,000
SALES (est): 20.3MM **Privately Held**
SIC: 0722 Field crops, except cash grains, machine harvesting services

(P-476)
DANELL CUSTOM HARVESTING LLC
8265 Hanford Armona Rd, Hanford (93230-9344)
PHONE...........................559 582-1251
Rance Danell,
EMP: 150
SALES (est): 12.4MM **Privately Held**
SIC: 0722 Crop harvesting

(P-477)
DARR & PITCAIRN AG INC
16674 Wasco Ave, Wasco (93280-7404)
PHONE...........................661 758-5156
Mike Pitcairn, *Partner*
Jim Darr, *Partner*
EMP: 50
SQ FT: 2,400
SALES (est): 1.5MM **Privately Held**
SIC: 0722 5083 6799 Cotton, machine harvesting services; tractors, agricultural; investors

(P-478)
I S A CONTRACTING SVCS INC
958 O St, Firebaugh (93622-2221)
PHONE...........................559 659-1080
Ileana Arvizu, *President*
EMP: 600
SQ FT: 5,000
SALES: 10MM **Privately Held**
SIC: 0722 Crop harvesting

(P-479)
LOPEZ HARVESTING
24079 Avenue 196, Strathmore (93267-9633)
PHONE...........................559 568-2553
Danny Lopez, *Owner*
EMP: 80
SALES (est): 2.1MM **Privately Held**
SIC: 0722 Crop harvesting

(P-480)
LOS DOS VALLES HARVSTG & PKG
2365 Westgate Rd, Santa Maria (93455-1045)
P.O. Box 1942 (93456-1942)
PHONE...........................805 739-1688
Felipe C Zepeda, *President*
EMP: 150
SQ FT: 4,500
SALES (est): 11.4MM **Privately Held**
SIC: 0722 0723 Vegetables & melons, machine harvesting services; vegetable packing services

(P-481)
NEW HOPE HARVESTING LLC
918 Nita Ct, Santa Maria (93454-3122)
PHONE...........................805 478-4469
Guadalupe Gaspar, *Principal*
Eugenia Martinez, *Principal*
EMP: 60
SALES (est): 4MM **Privately Held**
SIC: 0722 Crop harvesting

(P-482)
NOBLESSE OBLIGE INC
Also Called: Eight Star Equipment
2015 Silsbee Rd, El Centro (92243-9671)
PHONE...........................760 353-3336
Alex Abatti Jr, *President*

Tim Castelli, *CFO*
David Wells, *CFO*
Sid Swarthout, *Admin Sec*
EMP: 1200
SALES (est): 21.2MM **Privately Held**
WEB: www.noblesseoblige.com
SIC: 0722 Combining services; cotton, machine harvesting services; hay, machine harvesting services; vegetables & melons, machine harvesting services

(P-483)
PREMIUM PACKING INC
Also Called: Premium Harvesting
449 Harrison Rd, Salinas (93907-1617)
P.O. Box 4500 (93912-4500)
PHONE...........................831 443-6855
Jesus Alderete Jr, *President*
Marlene Alderete, *Corp Secy*
Ronnie Alderete, *General Mgr*
Yesenia Marquez, *Human Resources*
EMP: 130
SALES (est): 13.4MM **Privately Held**
WEB: www.premiumpacking.com
SIC: 0722 7361 Crop harvesting; labor contractors (employment agency)

(P-484)
R & G ENTERPRISES
627 N Main St, Porterville (93257-2358)
P.O. Box 230 (93258-0230)
PHONE...........................559 781-1351
Val B Guzman, *Partner*
Jose M Rios, *Partner*
EMP: 200
SQ FT: 1,500
SALES: 3MM **Privately Held**
SIC: 0722 0761 Crop harvesting; farm labor contractors

(P-485)
RC PACKING LLC
26769 El Camino Real, Gonzales (93926-9405)
PHONE...........................831 675-0308
Dennis Caprara, *Mng Member*
EMP: 300
SALES (est): 27.2MM **Privately Held**
WEB: www.rcpacking.com
SIC: 0722 Crop harvesting

(P-486)
TRI VALLEY VEGETABLE HARVSTG
123 N Depot St, Santa Maria (93458-3907)
P.O. Box 1969 (93456-1969)
PHONE...........................805 928-2727
Robert Espinola, *President*
Ronald Burke, *Treasurer*
EMP: 80
SQ FT: 600
SALES (est): 5.1MM **Privately Held**
SIC: 0722 Vegetables & melons, machine harvesting services

(P-487)
VALLEY PRIDE INC
86120 Tyler Ln, Coachella (92236-3123)
PHONE...........................760 398-1353
Tom Spulding, *Manager*
Mercedes Zepeda, *Manager*
EMP: 60
SALES (corp-wide): 2.2MM **Privately Held**
WEB: www.valleyprideinc.com
SIC: 0722 Crop harvesting
PA: Valley Pride, Inc.
  10855 Ocean Mist Pkwy D
  Castroville CA 95012
  831 633-5883

0723 Crop Preparation, Except Cotton Ginning

(P-488)
ADOBE PACKING COMPANY (PA)
367 W Market St, Salinas (93901-1423)
P.O. Box 4026 (93912-4026)
PHONE...........................831 753-6195
Jose G Esquivel, *President*
Basil Mills, *Shareholder*
Roger Mills, *Shareholder*
Mary Esquivel, *Treasurer*

Susan Mills, *Vice Pres*
EMP: 225
SQ FT: 2,500
SALES (est): 11.1MM **Privately Held**
WEB: www.millsfamilyfarms.com
SIC: 0723 4783 Vegetable packing services; packing & crating

(P-489)
AGRO-JAL FARMS INC
257 Kathleen Ct, Santa Maria (93458-4953)
P.O. Box 1862 (93456-1862)
PHONE...........................805 928-2682
Abel O Maldonado Jr, *President*
Frank Maldonado, *Vice Pres*
Patty Ponce, *Sales Executive*
David Murray, *Sales Staff*
EMP: 100
SALES (est): 7.7MM **Privately Held**
SIC: 0723 Vegetable crops market preparation services; vegetable precooling services

(P-490)
ALL STAR SEED (PA)
Also Called: Eight Star Commodities
2015 Silsbee Rd, El Centro (92243-9671)
PHONE...........................760 482-9400
Alex Abatti Jr, *President*
Tim Castelli, *CFO*
Sid Swarthout, *Vice Pres*
◆ EMP: 55
SALES (est): 59.4MM **Privately Held**
WEB: www.abatti.com
SIC: 0723 Seed cleaning

(P-491)
ALLDRIN BROTHERS INC
Also Called: Alldrin Brothers Almonds
584 Hi Tech Pkwy, Oakdale (95361-9371)
PHONE...........................855 667-4231
Gary Alldrin, *President*
Grant Neil Alldrin, *Mktg Dir*
◆ EMP: 50
SQ FT: 5,000
SALES (est): 9.5MM **Privately Held**
WEB: www.alldrinbros.com
SIC: 0723 Almond hulling & shelling services

(P-492)
ANDERSEN & SONS SHELLING INC
4530 Rowles Rd, Vina (96092)
P.O. Box 100 (96092-0100)
PHONE...........................530 839-2236
Patrick Knudt Andersen, *President*
Franklin Andersen, *Vice Pres*
Michael Andersen, *Vice Pres*
Jeff West, *Controller*
◆ EMP: 100
SALES (est): 38.4MM **Privately Held**
SIC: 0723 0762 Walnut hulling & shelling services; farm management services

(P-493)
ANDERSEN NUT COMPANY
Also Called: Gustine Mini Storage
3050 S Hunt Rd, Gustine (95322)
P.O. Box 445 (95322-0445)
PHONE...........................209 854-6820
Brian Anderson, *Partner*
Dan Anderson, *Partner*
◆ EMP: 50
SQ FT: 26,500
SALES: 5MM **Privately Held**
SIC: 0723 Walnut hulling & shelling services

(P-494)
BAIRD-NEECE PACKING CORP
60 S E St, Porterville (93257-4721)
P.O. Box 791 (93258-0791)
PHONE...........................559 784-3393
Dick Neece, *President*
EMP: 180
SQ FT: 37,249
SALES (est): 16.5MM **Privately Held**
WEB: www.bairdneece.com
SIC: 0723 Fruit (fresh) packing services

PRODUCTS & SVCS

(P-495)
BLUE BANNER COMPANY INC (PA)
Also Called: National Organic Packing
2601 3rd St, Riverside (92507-3310)
P.O. Box 226 (92502-0226)
PHONE..............................951 682-6183
Thomas L Mazzetti, *CEO*
Vincent Mazzetti, *Officer*
Jim Layes, *Info Tech Mgr*
EMP: 60
SQ FT: 38,650
SALES (est): 12.2MM **Privately Held**
SIC: 0723 0174 Fruit (fresh) packing services; citrus fruits

(P-496)
BLUE DIAMOND GROWERS
4800 Sisk Rd, Modesto (95356-8730)
PHONE..............................209 545-6221
Bruce Mickelson, *Manager*
Brian Barczak, *Senior VP*
Laura Lutz, *Executive Asst*
Mary Bolanos, *Planning*
Juan Moreno, *Planning*
EMP: 200
SALES (corp-wide): 1.6B **Privately Held**
WEB: www.bluediamond.com
SIC: 0723 2068 Almond hulling & shelling services; nuts: dried, dehydrated, salted or roasted
PA: Diamond Blue Growers
1802 C St
Sacramento CA 95811
916 442-0771

(P-497)
BOSKOVICH FARMS INC (PA)
711 Diaz Ave, Oxnard (93030-7247)
P.O. Box 1352 (93032-1352)
PHONE..............................805 487-2299
George S Boskovich Jr, *CEO*
Philip J Boskovich Jr, *President*
Andrew Costales, *Info Tech Mgr*
Manuel Villafana, *Technology*
Linda Grayson, *Controller*
▲ **EMP:** 205
SQ FT: 7,000
SALES (est): 76.9MM **Privately Held**
WEB: www.boskovichfarms.com
SIC: 0723 5812 0161 Crop preparation services for market; eating places; rooted vegetable farms; lettuce & leaf vegetable farms

(P-498)
CAL CITRUS PACKING CO
111 N Mount Vernon Ave, Lindsay (93247-2438)
P.O. Box 637 (93247-0637)
PHONE..............................559 562-2536
Jerry Luallen, *President*
Lori Leer, *Marketing Staff*
▼ **EMP:** 68
SQ FT: 30,000
SALES (est): 5.3MM **Privately Held**
WEB: www.calcitruspacking.com
SIC: 0723 Fruit (fresh) packing services

(P-499)
CALIFORNIA ARTICHOKE & VEGETAB
Also Called: Ocean Mist Farms
10855 Ocean Mist Pkwy, Castroville (95012-3232)
PHONE..............................831 633-2144
Edward Boutonnet, *President*
Albert Pieri, *Shareholder*
Don Reasons, *Treasurer*
Dale Huss, *Vice Pres*
Leslie Tottino, *Admin Sec*
EMP: 60
SALES (est): 15.4MM **Privately Held**
WEB: www.oceanmist.com
SIC: 0723 Vegetable packing services

(P-500)
CARMEL VALLEY PACKING INC
26965 Encinal Rd, Salinas (93908-9539)
P.O. Box 3723 (93912-3723)
PHONE..............................831 771-8860
Oscar Gardea, *President*
EMP: 150
SALES (est): 3MM **Privately Held**
SIC: 0723 Vegetable packing services

(P-501)
CECELIA PACKING CORPORATION
24780 E South Ave, Orange Cove (93646-9426)
PHONE..............................559 626-5000
James J Cotter, *CEO*
David G Roth, *President*
Randy Jacobson, *Sales Staff*
◆ **EMP:** 130
SQ FT: 55,000
SALES (est): 14.3MM **Privately Held**
SIC: 0723 Fruit (fresh) packing services

(P-502)
CENTRAL VALLEY AG TRNSPT INC
Also Called: Central Valley AG Transload
5509 Langworth Rd, Oakdale (95361-7909)
PHONE..............................209 544-9246
Michael Barry, *President*
Ryan Hogan, *CFO*
Paul Konzen, *Admin Sec*
EMP: 93
SALES (est): 8.3MM
SALES (corp-wide): 24.5MM **Privately Held**
SIC: 0723 1629 Field crops, except cash grains, market preparation services; railroad & railway roadbed construction
PA: Central Valley Ag Grinding, Inc.
5509 Langworth Rd
Oakdale CA 95361
209 869-1721

(P-503)
CHOOLJIAN & SONS INC (PA)
Also Called: Del Rey Packing Co
5287 S Del Rey Ave, Del Rey (93616-9700)
P.O. Box 160 (93616-0160)
PHONE..............................559 888-2031
Gerald Chooljian, *CEO*
Courtney Chooljian, *Corp Secy*
Kathleen Merlo, *Vice Pres*
Kathy Merlo,
◆ **EMP:** 69
SQ FT: 14,400
SALES: 29.1MM **Privately Held**
SIC: 0723 Fruit (farm-dried) packing services

(P-504)
CORONA - COLLEGE HEIGHTS ORA
8000 Lincoln Ave, Riverside (92504-4343)
PHONE..............................951 359-6451
John Demshki, *President*
Jennie Sistos, *Controller*
Keith French, *Export Mgr*
Jared Bray, *Sales Staff*
▼ **EMP:** 300 **EST:** 1905
SQ FT: 180,000
SALES (est): 38.8MM **Privately Held**
WEB: www.cchcitrus.com
SIC: 0723 Fruit (fresh) packing services

(P-505)
CRISP WAREHOUSE INC
Also Called: Crisp California Walnuts
20500 Main St, Stratford (93266-9758)
P.O. Box 490, Lemoore (93245-0490)
PHONE..............................559 947-9221
James R Crisp, *President*
Stacie Annon, *CFO*
◆ **EMP:** 67
SQ FT: 50,000
SALES (est): 5.5MM **Privately Held**
SIC: 0723 Walnut hulling & shelling services

(P-506)
DESERT VALLEY DATE INC
86740 Industrial Way, Coachella (92236-2718)
PHONE..............................760 398-0999
George Kirkjan, *President*
Tamara Kirkjan, *Vice Pres*
◆ **EMP:** 50
SQ FT: 42,000
SALES (est): 9.7MM **Privately Held**
WEB: www.desertvalleydate.com
SIC: 0723 Crop preparation services for market

(P-507)
DOLE FRESH VEGETABLES INC
16199 9th St, Huron (93234)
PHONE..............................559 945-2591
Luis Perez, *Principal*
EMP: 118
SALES (corp-wide): 11.7B **Privately Held**
SIC: 0723 Crop preparation services for market
HQ: Dole Fresh Vegetables, Inc.
2959 Salinas Hwy
Monterey CA 93940
831 422-8871

(P-508)
EARTHBOUND FARM LLC (DH)
1721 San Juan Hwy, San Juan Bautista (95045-9780)
PHONE..............................831 623-7880
Kevin C Yost, *President*
Miguel Bueno, *Human Res Mgr*
Veronica Sanchez, *Human Resources*
Katie Seldomridge, *Purch Mgr*
Sonia Manzo, *Opers Staff*
▲ **EMP:** 995
SQ FT: 15,000
SALES (est): 288.1MM
SALES (corp-wide): 718.1MM **Privately Held**
SIC: 0723 2037 2099 Vegetable packing services; fruit crops market preparation services; frozen fruits & vegetables; food preparations
HQ: Earthbound Holdings Iii, Llc
1721 San Juan Hwy
San Juan Bautista CA 95045
831 623-7880

(P-509)
ECO FARMS AVOCADOS INC (PA)
28790 Las Haciendas St, Temecula (92590-2614)
PHONE..............................951 694-3013
Steve Taft, *CEO*
Norman Traner, *Corp Secy*
Gahl Crane, *Sales Dir*
Miguel Hernandez, *Manager*
▲ **EMP:** 55
SQ FT: 20,000
SALES (est): 13.2MM **Privately Held**
SIC: 0723 Vegetable packing services

(P-510)
EXETER ENGINEERING INC
Also Called: TTI Technologies
109 W Pine St, Exeter (93221-1612)
P.O. Box 457 (93221-0457)
PHONE..............................559 592-3161
Jeffrey Batchman, *CEO*
Boomer Batchman, *General Mgr*
Jack Bedwell, *General Mgr*
Carlotta Spurger, *Purchasing*
Steve Lyon, *Purch Agent*
▲ **EMP:** 70
SQ FT: 20,000
SALES (est): 17.5MM **Privately Held**
SIC: 0723 Vegetable sorting services; fruit sorting services

(P-511)
EXETER PACKERS INC (PA)
Also Called: Sun Pacific Packers
1250 E Myer Ave, Exeter (93221-9345)
P.O. Box 217 (93221-0217)
PHONE..............................559 592-5168
Berne H Evans III, *CEO*
Robert Reniers, *President*
Ernie Larsen, *CFO*
Jeanne Wilkinson, *Controller*
Heidi Hill, *Clerk*
◆ **EMP:** 585
SQ FT: 70,000
SALES (est): 57.6MM **Privately Held**
SIC: 0723 Fruit (fresh) packing services

(P-512)
EXETER PACKERS INC
Also Called: Euclid Parking
23744 Avenue 181, Porterville (93257-9579)
PHONE..............................559 784-8820
Lenard Shelton, *General Mgr*
EMP: 150

SALES (corp-wide): 57.6MM **Privately Held**
SIC: 0723 Fruit (fresh) packing services
PA: Exeter Packers, Inc.
1250 E Myer Ave
Exeter CA 93221
559 592-5168

(P-513)
EXETER-IVANHOE CITRUS ASSN
901 Rocky Hill Dr, Exeter (93221-1322)
PHONE..............................559 592-3141
Kevin Riddle, *President*
Terry Orr, *General Mgr*
EMP: 75
SQ FT: 30,000
SALES (est): 11MM **Privately Held**
WEB: www.exetercitrus.com
SIC: 0723 Fruit (fresh) packing services

(P-514)
FAIR TRADE CORNER INC
11591 Meridian Rd, Chico (95973-9601)
PHONE..............................530 566-1405
D N Wadhwa, *President*
Mohnish Seth, *CFO*
▼ **EMP:** 50
SALES (est): 3.4MM **Privately Held**
SIC: 0723 0173 5145 Almond hulling & shelling services; almond grove; nuts, salted or roasted

(P-515)
FIENO INC
11583 Big Canyon Ln, San Diego (92131-4308)
PHONE..............................760 352-2996
Chris B Jackson, *President*
Mary A Jackson, *Vice Pres*
EMP: 55
SALES (est): 3.4MM **Privately Held**
SIC: 0723

(P-516)
FISHER RANCH LLC
10610 Ice Plant Rd, Blythe (92225-2757)
PHONE..............................760 922-4151
Dana B Fisher,
Meloni Carnes, *Manager*
Mike George, *Manager*
EMP: 99
SALES (est): 17.1MM **Privately Held**
SIC: 0723 Field crops, except cash grains, market preparation services

(P-517)
FOWLER PACKING COMPANY INC
Also Called: Telemarketing
8570 S Cedar Ave, Fresno (93725-8905)
PHONE..............................559 834-5911
Dennis Parnagian, *CEO*
Randy Parnagian, *Treasurer*
Kenneth Parnagian, *Vice Pres*
Philip Parnagian, *Admin Sec*
◆ **EMP:** 125
SQ FT: 6,300
SALES (est): 57.6MM **Privately Held**
WEB: www.fowlerpacking.com
SIC: 0723 4783 5148 Fruit (fresh) packing services; packing & crating; fresh fruits & vegetables

(P-518)
GILLETTE CITRUS COMPANY
10175 S Anchor Ave, Dinuba (93618-9204)
PHONE..............................559 626-4236
Jay Gillette, *Partner*
Dean Gillette, *Partner*
Mark Gillette, *Partner*
EMP: 60
SQ FT: 14,000
SALES (est): 5.8MM **Privately Held**
SIC: 0723 Fruit (fresh) packing services

(P-519)
GOLDEN VALLEY CITRUS INC
19875 Meredith Dr, Strathmore (93267-9691)
P.O. Box L (93267-4012)
PHONE..............................559 568-1768
Martine Mittman, *President*
Gerald Denni, *Vice Pres*
EMP: 75
SQ FT: 25,000

▲ = Import ▼=Export
◆ =Import/Export

SALES (est): 13.2MM **Privately Held**
SIC: 0723 Fruit (fresh) packing services

(P-520)
GRIDLEY PACKING INC
1366 Larkin Rd, Gridley (95948-9708)
PHONE.............................530 846-3753
James D Sanderson, *President*
Becky Sanderson, *Vice Pres*
▲ EMP: 150
SQ FT: 25,800
SALES (est): 2.6MM **Privately Held**
SIC: 0723 Fruit (fresh) packing services

(P-521)
GRIMMWAY ENTERPRISES INC
6101 S Zerker Rd, Shafter (93263-9611)
P.O. Box 81498, Bakersfield (93380-1498)
PHONE.............................661 393-3320
Bob Grimm, *Principal*
Dave Eagle, *Manager*
EMP: 233
SALES (corp-wide): 2.1B **Privately Held**
SIC: 0723 Vegetable packing services
PA: Grimmway Enterprises, Inc.
14141 Di Giorgio Rd
Arvin CA 93203
800 301-3101

(P-522)
GRIMMWAY ENTERPRISES INC
Also Called: Grimmway Frozen Foods
830 Sycamore Rd, Arvin (93203-2132)
P.O. Box 81498, Bakersfield (93380-1498)
PHONE.............................661 854-6250
Brandon Grimm, *Manager*
Shawna Uwaine, *Purchasing*
EMP: 400
SALES (corp-wide): 2.1B **Privately Held**
SIC: 0723 Vegetable packing services
PA: Grimmway Enterprises, Inc.
14141 Di Giorgio Rd
Arvin CA 93203
800 301-3101

(P-523)
GRIMMWAY ENTERPRISES INC
Also Called: Grimmway Farms
11412 Malaga Rd, Arvin (93203-9641)
P.O. Box 81498, Bakersfield (93380-1498)
PHONE.............................661 854-6200
Mike Anspach, *Vice Pres*
Todd Janssen, *Technical Mgr*
Gisela Gomez, *Technology*
Gerado Raya, *Purch Mgr*
Matthew Hammons, *Buyer*
EMP: 100
SALES (corp-wide): 2.1B **Privately Held**
SIC: 0723 4783 Vegetable packing services; containerization of goods for shipping
PA: Grimmway Enterprises, Inc.
14141 Di Giorgio Rd
Arvin CA 93203
800 301-3101

(P-524)
GRIMMWAY ENTERPRISES INC
Also Called: Grimmway Farms
6900 Mountain View Rd, Bakersfield (93307-9627)
P.O. Box 81498 (93380-1498)
PHONE.............................661 845-5200
Bob Grimm, *Owner*
Brian Spaulding, *Senior VP*
Mark Valpredo, *General Mgr*
Margaret Palmerin, *Admin Asst*
Gary Bumgarner, *Info Tech Dir*
EMP: 200
SALES (corp-wide): 2.1B **Privately Held**
SIC: 0723 Vegetable packing services
PA: Grimmway Enterprises, Inc.
14141 Di Giorgio Rd
Arvin CA 93203
800 301-3101

(P-525)
GROWER DIRECT NUT COMPANY INC
2288 Geer Rd, Hughson (95326-9614)
PHONE.............................209 883-4890
Aaron Martella, *President*
Kevin Chiesa, *COO*
Danny Jenkins, *Vice Pres*
Lucio Salazar, *Vice Pres*
Jennifer Martella, *Admin Sec*

▼ EMP: 50
SALES (est): 47.8MM **Privately Held**
WEB: www.grower-direct.com
SIC: 0723 Walnut hulling & shelling services

(P-526)
GROWERS STREET COOLING LLC
1080 Growers St, Salinas (93901-4445)
P.O. Box 2162 (93902-2162)
PHONE.............................831 424-2929
Ronald Mondo, *Mng Member*
EMP: 53
SQ FT: 20,000
SALES (est): 7.2MM **Privately Held**
SIC: 0723 Vegetable precooling services

(P-527)
GUERRA NUT SHELLING COMPANY
190 Hillcrest Rd, Hollister (95023-4944)
P.O. Box 1117 (95024-1117)
PHONE.............................831 637-4471
Frank Guerra, *President*
Jeff Guerra, *CFO*
▼ EMP: 55
SQ FT: 20,000
SALES (est): 8.1MM **Privately Held**
WEB: www.guerranut.com
SIC: 0723 Walnut hulling & shelling services

(P-528)
HARRIS WOOLF CAL ALMONDS LLC (PA)
26060 Colusa Ave, Coalinga (93210-9245)
P.O. Box 49, Ballico (95303-0049)
PHONE.............................559 884-2147
Joel Perkins, *CEO*
Stuart Woolf, *Managing Prtnr*
Brian Staggs, *CFO*
◆ EMP: 150
SQ FT: 110,000
SALES (est): 54.5MM **Privately Held**
WEB: www.harriswoolfalmonds.com
SIC: 0723 Tree nut crops market preparation services; almond hulling & shelling services

(P-529)
HILLTOP RANCH INC
Also Called: Hilltop Trading
13890 Looney Rd, Ballico (95303-9710)
PHONE.............................209 874-1875
David Harrison Long, *CEO*
Brad Filbrun, *CFO*
Christine Long, *Vice Pres*
Dave Long Jr, *Vice Pres*
David Long, *Vice Pres*
◆ EMP: 175
SQ FT: 134,800
SALES (est): 45MM **Privately Held**
WEB: www.hilltopranch.com
SIC: 0723 5441 Almond hulling & shelling services; candy, nut & confectionery stores

(P-530)
HILLTOWN PACKING CO INC
9 Harris Pl A, Salinas (93901-4586)
PHONE.............................831 784-1931
Chris Huntington, *President*
Louis Huntington Sr, *Shareholder*
Louis Huntington Jr, *Treasurer*
▼ EMP: 300
SALES (est): 30.3MM **Privately Held**
SIC: 0723 Vegetable packing services

(P-531)
J G BOSWELL COMPANY
Also Called: Processing Office
710 Bainum Ave, Corcoran (93212-9603)
P.O. Box 457 (93212-0457)
PHONE.............................559 992-2141
Fransico Alvarez, *Executive*
Darren Osterland, *General Mgr*
Dan Boswell, *Executive Asst*
Janice Salgado, *Info Tech Mgr*
Tom Gaffney, *Chief Engr*
EMP: 100
SALES (corp-wide): 540.4MM **Privately Held**
SIC: 0723 Crop preparation services for market

PA: J. G. Boswell Company
101 W Walnut St
Pasadena CA 91103
626 583-3000

(P-532)
JLG HARVESTING INC
27 Zabala Rd, Salinas (93908-7702)
P.O. Box 5205, Yuma AZ (85366-2461)
PHONE.............................831 422-7871
Jose Luis Garcia, *President*
EMP: 400 **Privately Held**
SIC: 0723 Crop preparation services for market
PA: Jlg Harvesting, Inc.
1450 S Atlantic Ave
Yuma AZ 85365

(P-533)
KERN RIDGE GROWERS LLC
25429 Barbara St, Arvin (93203-9748)
P.O. Box 455 (93203-0455)
PHONE.............................661 854-3141
Robert Giragosian,
▼ EMP: 500
SQ FT: 53,000
SALES: 43.2MM **Privately Held**
WEB: www.kernridge.com
SIC: 0723 5148 Vegetable packing services; vegetables, fresh

(P-534)
KIRSCHENMAN PACKING INC
12826 Edison Hwy, Edison (93220)
PHONE.............................661 366-5736
Wayne Kirschenman, *President*
Paul Sandoval, *Shareholder*
Herb Spitzer, *Vice Pres*
EMP: 120
SQ FT: 25,000
SALES (est): 4.4MM **Privately Held**
SIC: 0723 Vegetable packing services

(P-535)
KLINK CITRUS ASSOCIATION
Also Called: Klink Citrus Exchange
32921 Road 159, Ivanhoe (93235-1455)
P.O. Box 188 (93235-0188)
PHONE.............................559 798-1881
Eric Meling, *CEO*
EMP: 170
SQ FT: 50,000
SALES (est): 17MM **Privately Held**
SIC: 0723 Fruit (fresh) packing services

(P-536)
LIMONEIRA COMPANY (PA)
1141 Cummings Rd Ofc, Santa Paula (93060-9783)
PHONE.............................805 525-5541
Harold S Edwards, *President*
Gordon E Kimball, *Ch of Bd*
Mark Palamountain, *CFO*
Robert M Sawyer, *Vice Ch Bd*
Alex M Teague, *Senior VP*
◆ EMP: 188 EST: 1893
SALES: 121.3MM **Publicly Held**
WEB: www.limoneira.com
SIC: 0723 0174 0179 6531 Fruit (fresh) packing services; citrus fruits; lemon grove; orange grove; avocado orchard; real estate agents & managers; real estate leasing & rentals; commodity investors

(P-537)
LO BUE BROS INC
Also Called: Lo Bue Bros East
713 E Hermosa St, Lindsay (93247-2204)
PHONE.............................559 562-6367
Fred Lobue, *Branch Mgr*
EMP: 200
SALES (corp-wide): 40.7MM **Privately Held**
WEB: www.lobuebros.com
SIC: 0723 5148 0174 Crop preparation services for market
PA: Lo Bue Bros., Inc.
201 S Sweetbriar Ave
Lindsay CA 93247
559 562-2548

(P-538)
MAGARRO FARMS
23322 Peralta Dr Ste 3, Laguna Hills (92653-1713)
PHONE.............................949 859-6506
John Magarro, *Owner*
EMP: 80
SQ FT: 30,000
SALES (est): 3.4MM **Privately Held**
SIC: 0723 0171 Fruit precooling services; strawberry farm

(P-539)
MANN PACKING CO INC (DH)
1333 Schilling Pl, Salinas (93901-4535)
P.O. Box 690 (93902-0690)
PHONE.............................831 422-7405
Lorri Koster, *CEO*
Michael Jarrod, *President*
William Beaton, *CFO*
Richard Ramsey, *Chairman*
EMP: 450
SQ FT: 90,000
SALES (est): 170.6MM **Privately Held**
WEB: www.broccoli.com
SIC: 0723 4783 0722 Vegetable packing services; packing & crating; crop harvesting
HQ: Del Monte Fresh Produce N.A., Inc.
241 Sevilla Ave Ste 200
Coral Gables FL 33134
305 520-8400

(P-540)
MARIANI PACKING CO INC (PA)
500 Crocker Dr, Vacaville (95688-8706)
PHONE.............................707 452-2800
Mark A Mariani, *CEO*
George Sousa Jr, *Vice Chairman*
Forrest Chandler, *CFO*
Marian Ciabattari, *Corp Secy*
Craig Mackley, *Exec VP*
◆ EMP: 275 EST: 1982
SALES (est): 109.2MM **Privately Held**
WEB: www.marianifruit.com
SIC: 0723 2034 5148 Fruit (farm-dried) packing services; fruit drying services; dried & dehydrated fruits; fresh fruits & vegetables

(P-541)
MONARCH NUT COMPANY LLC
Also Called: Munger Farms
786 Road 188, Delano (93215-9508)
PHONE.............................661 725-6458
Kamie Munger, *Mng Member*
David Munger,
◆ EMP: 250 EST: 1986
SQ FT: 20,000
SALES (est): 51.8MM **Privately Held**
WEB: www.mungerfarms.com
SIC: 0723 Tree nuts (general) hulling & shelling services

(P-542)
MONTPELIER ORCHARDS MGT CO INC
Montpelier Nut Company
4931 S Montpelier Rd, Denair (95316-9663)
PHONE.............................209 883-4079
Lupe Dalvinos, *Manager*
EMP: 50
SALES (corp-wide): 7.3MM **Privately Held**
SIC: 0723 Crop preparation services for market
PA: Montpelier Orchards Management Company, Inc.
1131 12th St
Modesto CA 95354
209 577-2804

(P-543)
MOONEY FARMS
1220 Fortress St, Chico (95973-9029)
PHONE.............................530 899-2661
Mary Mooney, *President*
Steve Mooney, *Vice Pres*
Steve Lansdown, *QC Mgr*
▲ EMP: 50
SQ FT: 100,000

PRODUCTS & SVCS

SALES (est): 30.2MM **Privately Held**
WEB: www.mooneyfarms.com
SIC: 0723 2034 2033 Fruit crops market preparation services; dried & dehydrated fruits; canned fruits & specialties

(P-544)
MORADA PRODUCE COMPANY LP
500 N Jack Tone Rd, Stockton (95215-9725)
P.O. Box 659, Linden (95236-0659)
PHONE...............................209 546-0426
Henry Foppiano, *Partner*
Sandy Haswell, *Controller*
Ana Garibay, *Director*
Linda Jenkins, *Manager*
Kristi Friis, *Supervisor*
▲ **EMP:** 1500
SQ FT: 98,000
SALES (est): 57.6MM **Privately Held**
SIC: 0723 Fruit (fresh) packing services; vegetable packing services

(P-545)
NATIONAL CUSTOM PACKING INC
13526 Blackie Rd, Castroville (95012-3212)
PHONE...............................831 724-2026
Jonathon Thornton, *President*
Fred J Haas, *Ch of Bd*
Ron Marker, *CFO*
Louise McNary, *Corp Secy*
Jonathan Thornton, *Principal*
EMP: 50
SQ FT: 12,000
SALES (est): 5.1MM
SALES (corp-wide): 349.1MM **Privately Held**
WEB: www.nationalpacking.com
SIC: 0723 Fruit (fresh) packing services
PA: The Vps Companies Inc
310 Walker St
Watsonville CA 95076
831 724-7551

(P-546)
NEWSTAR FRESH FOODS LLC
126 Sun St, Salinas (93901-3751)
PHONE...............................831 758-7800
Brian McLaughlin, *Controller*
EMP: 100
SALES (corp-wide): 75MM **Privately Held**
WEB: www.newstarfreshfoods.com
SIC: 0723 Vegetable crops market preparation services
PA: Newstar Fresh Foods, Llc
850 Work St Ste 101
Salinas CA 93901
888 782-7220

(P-547)
NEWSTAR FRESH FOODS LLC (PA)
850 Work St Ste 101, Salinas (93901-4378)
P.O. Box 2627 (93902-2627)
PHONE...............................888 782-7220
Anthony Vasquez, *CEO*
Carl Wiseman, *CFO*
Mitch Secondo, *Vice Pres*
Jason McFadden, *Technology*
John Killeen, *VP Sales*
▼ **EMP:** 200
SQ FT: 1,300,000
SALES: 75MM **Privately Held**
WEB: www.newstarfreshfoods.com
SIC: 0723 Vegetable crops market preparation services

(P-548)
NORALCO INC
Also Called: H Naraghi Farms
20001 Mchenry Ave, Escalon (95320-9614)
P.O. Box 602, Denair (95316-0602)
PHONE...............................209 551-4545
Haslem Naraghi, *President*
◆ **EMP:** 125
SQ FT: 120,000
SALES (est): 3.1MM **Privately Held**
SIC: 0723 5145 Almond hulling & shelling services; walnut hulling & shelling services; nuts, salted or roasted

(P-549)
NUNES COOLING INC
925 Johnson Ave, Salinas (93901-4327)
P.O. Box 1585 (93902-1585)
PHONE...............................831 751-7510
Frank R Nunes Jr, *President*
Mike Scarr, *CFO*
EMP: 50
SALES (est): 4.5MM **Privately Held**
SIC: 0723 Vacuum cooling

(P-550)
OLAM AMERICAS INC (DH)
25 Union Pl Ste 3, Fresno (93720)
PHONE...............................559 447-1390
Gregory C Estep, *CEO*
Joe Kenny, *Managing Dir*
Jerry Block, *Research*
Jim Hastings, *Research*
Mihir Vasavada, *Research*
◆ **EMP:** 1000
SALES (est): 1.2B
SALES (corp-wide): 19.3B **Privately Held**
SIC: 0723 Crop preparation services for market
HQ: Olam Us Holdings Inc
2077 Convention Ctr 150
College Park GA 30337
404 209-2676

(P-551)
OLAM WEST COAST INC (DH)
Also Called: Olam Spces Vgtable Ingredients
205 E Rver Pk Cir Ste 310, Fresno (93720)
PHONE...............................559 447-1390
John Gibbons, *President*
◆ **EMP:** 188
SALES (est): 482.4MM
SALES (corp-wide): 19.3B **Privately Held**
SIC: 0723 Crop preparation services for market

(P-552)
OMEGA WALNUT INC
7233 County Road 24, Orland (95963-9777)
PHONE...............................530 865-0136
Todd J Southam, *CEO*
Marsha Squier, *Office Mgr*
▼ **EMP:** 50
SALES (est): 7MM **Privately Held**
SIC: 0723 Walnut hulling & shelling services

(P-553)
PEARL CROP INC (PA)
Also Called: Linden Nut
1550 Industrial Dr, Stockton (95206-3929)
PHONE...............................209 808-7575
Halil Ulas Turkhan, *President*
Hulya Dayac, *Shareholder*
Negaar Turkhan, *Vice Pres*
Scott Donald, *Executive*
◆ **EMP:** 75 **EST:** 2007
SQ FT: 126,000
SALES: 140MM **Privately Held**
SIC: 0723 Crop preparation services for market

(P-554)
PHELAN & TAYLOR PRODUCE CO
1860 Pacific Coast Hwy, Oceano (93445)
P.O. Box 458 (93475-0458)
PHONE...............................805 489-2413
John Taylor, *President*
EMP: 150
SQ FT: 20,000
SALES (est): 5.9MM **Privately Held**
SIC: 0723 0161 4213 Crop preparation services for market; vegetables & melons; trucking, except local

(P-555)
R & N PACKING CO
47920 W Nees Ave, Firebaugh (93622-9593)
P.O. Box 130, Turlock (95381-0130)
PHONE...............................209 364-6101
Leo Rolandelli, *President*
EMP: 250
SALES (est): 7.5MM **Privately Held**
SIC: 0723 Vegetable packing services

(P-556)
RAMCO ENTERPRISES LP
Also Called: Ramco Employment Services
520 E 3rd St Ste B, Oxnard (93030-0182)
PHONE...............................805 486-9328
Jesse Espinoza, *Branch Mgr*
EMP: 743
SALES (corp-wide): 85MM **Privately Held**
SIC: 0723 Crop preparation services for market
PA: Ramco Enterprises, L.P.
710 La Guardia St
Salinas CA 93905
831 758-5272

(P-557)
READY ROAST NUT COMPANY LLC (PA)
Also Called: Madera Quality Nut
2805 Falcon Dr, Madera (93637-9287)
PHONE...............................559 661-1696
Thomas Finn, *Mng Member*
Tyler Angle,
Ann Billek,
◆ **EMP:** 75
SQ FT: 144,000
SALES (est): 16.2MM **Privately Held**
SIC: 0723 Tree nut crops market preparation services

(P-558)
RED TOP RICE GROWERS
3200 8th St, Biggs (95917)
P.O. Box 477 (95917-0477)
PHONE...............................530 868-5975
John Adams, *President*
Doug Rudd, *Corp Secy*
Steve Cribari, *Vice Pres*
EMP: 50
SALES (est): 5.2MM **Privately Held**
SIC: 0723 Rice drying services

(P-559)
REDLANDS FOOTHILL GROVES
304 9th St, Redlands (92374-3404)
PHONE...............................909 793-2164
Robert Knight, *Plant Mgr*
EMP: 50
SQ FT: 48,000
SALES (est): 7.1MM **Privately Held**
SIC: 0723 Fruit (fresh) packing services

(P-560)
REDWOOD EMPIRE PACKING INC
8801 Old River Rd, Ukiah (95482-9659)
PHONE...............................707 462-5521
Randall Ruddick, *President*
EMP: 150
SALES (est): 6.9MM **Privately Held**
SIC: 0723 Fruit (fresh) packing services

(P-561)
RIVER MAID LAND CO A CAL LI (PA)
6011 E Pine St, Lodi (95240-0815)
P.O. Box 350 (95241-0350)
PHONE...............................209 369-3586
Chiles Wilson, *President*
Ken Carter, *Chief Mktg Ofcr*
Wolfgang Rochert, *Opers Staff*
John Lucchetti, *Production*
Brian Machado, *Marketing Staff*
EMP: 340
SALES (est): 10.6MM **Privately Held**
SIC: 0723 Fruit (fresh) packing services; vegetable packing services

(P-562)
S & J RANCHES LLC
39639 Avenue 10, Madera (93636-8845)
P.O. Box 3347, Pinedale (93650-3347)
PHONE...............................559 437-2600
James M Burkhart, *President*
Jim Burkhart,
Kevin Olsen,
EMP: 60 **EST:** 1950
SQ FT: 5,133
SALES (est): 2.1MM
SALES (corp-wide): 1.5B **Privately Held**
WEB: www.paramountcitrus.com
SIC: 0723 0762 Fruit (fresh) packing services; citrus grove management & maintenance services

HQ: Wonderful Citrus Packing Llc
1901 S Lexington St
Delano CA 93215
661 720-2400

(P-563)
S STAMOULES INC
Also Called: Stamoules Produce Co
904 S Lyon Ave, Mendota (93640-9735)
PHONE...............................559 655-9777
Peggy Stefanopoulos, *President*
Chrisopher S Stefanopoulos, *Treasurer*
Danny Stefanopoulos, *Vice Pres*
Tom Stefanopoulos, *Vice Pres*
Elena Stefanopoulos, *Admin Sec*
▼ **EMP:** 1000
SQ FT: 40,000
SALES: 100MM **Privately Held**
WEB: www.stamoules.com
SIC: 0723 Fruit (fresh) packing services; vegetable packing services

(P-564)
SAN JOAQUIN FIGS INC
Also Called: Nutra-Figs
3564 N Hazel Ave, Fresno (93722-4912)
P.O. Box 9547 (93793-9547)
PHONE...............................559 224-4492
Keith Jura, *President*
Mary Jura, *Treasurer*
Roy Jura,
▼ **EMP:** 50
SQ FT: 18,000
SALES (est): 9.3MM **Privately Held**
WEB: www.nutrafig.com
SIC: 0723 Fruit (fresh) packing services

(P-565)
SATICOY LEMON ASSOCIATION (PA)
Also Called: Saticoy Fruit Exchange
103 N Peck Rd, Santa Paula (93060-3099)
P.O. Box 46 (93061-0046)
PHONE...............................805 654-6500
Glenn A Miller, *President*
Jerry Pogorzelski, *CFO*
Jima Garrett, *Admin Sec*
▲ **EMP:** 100 **EST:** 1933
SALES: 171MM **Privately Held**
SIC: 0723 Fruit (fresh) packing services

(P-566)
SEED DYNAMICS INC
1081b Harkins Rd, Salinas (93901-4406)
P.O. Box 6069 (93912-6069)
PHONE...............................831 424-1177
David Holly, *CEO*
Curtis J Vaughan, *COO*
Mel Bachman, *Risk Mgmt Dir*
EMP: 53
SQ FT: 34,000
SALES (est): 6.4MM **Privately Held**
WEB: www.seeddynamics.com
SIC: 0723 3999 Crop preparation services for market; seeds, coated or treated, from purchased seeds

(P-567)
SEQUOIA ORANGE CO INC (PA)
150 W Pine St, Exeter (93221-1699)
PHONE...............................559 592-9455
Marvin Wilson, *President*
Oleah Wilson, *Treasurer*
Linda Pescosolido, *Vice Pres*
EMP: 100
SQ FT: 5,100
SALES (est): 9.2MM **Privately Held**
WEB: www.sequoiaorange.com
SIC: 0723 5148 Fruit (fresh) packing services; fresh fruits & vegetables

(P-568)
SIMONE FRUIT CO INC
8008 W Shields Ave, Fresno (93723-9657)
PHONE...............................559 275-1368
Mauro Simone, *President*
Margaret Simone, *Admin Sec*
▼ **EMP:** 50
SQ FT: 2,400
SALES (est): 3MM **Privately Held**
SIC: 0723 2034 0179 Avocado orchard

(P-569)
SUMA FRUIT INTL USA INC
1810 Academy Ave, Sanger (93657-3739)
PHONE...............................559 875-5000

▲ = Import ▼=Export
◆ =Import/Export

Ralph Hackett, *CEO*
▼ **EMP:** 50
SQ FT: 60,000
SALES (est): 3.5MM **Privately Held**
SIC: 0723 Fruit (fresh) packing services
HQ: Del Monte Fresh Produce N.A., Inc.
   241 Sevilla Ave Ste 200
   Coral Gables FL 33134
   305 520-8400

(P-570)
SUN PACIFIC MARICOPA
Also Called: Maricopa Packers
31452 Old River Rd, Bakersfield
(93311-9621)
PHONE..............................661 847-1015
Bern Evans, *Managing Prtnr*
EMP: 400
SQ FT: 450,000
SALES (est): 23.2MM **Privately Held**
SIC: 0723 Fruit (fresh) packing services

(P-571)
SUN RICH FRESH FOODS USA INC (HQ)
515 E Rincon St, Corona (92879-1391)
PHONE..............................951 735-3800
Brian Tieszen, *President*
Carl Svangtun, *President*
Neville Israel, *CFO*
▲ **EMP:** 65
SQ FT: 33,000
SALES (est): 30.9MM **Privately Held**
SIC: 0723 Fruit (fresh) packing services
PA: Sun Rich Fresh Foods Inc
   22151 Fraserwood Way
   Richmond BC V6W 1
   604 244-8800

(P-572)
SUN WORLD INTERNATIONAL INC (PA)
16351 Driver Rd, Bakersfield (93308-9733)
P.O. Box 80298 (93380-0298)
PHONE..............................661 392-5000
Keith Brackpool, *Ch of Bd*
Timothy J Shaheen, *CEO*
◆ **EMP:** 2500
SQ FT: 160,000
SALES (est): 57.6MM **Privately Held**
SIC: 0723 0172 0174 0175 Vegetable
crops market preparation services; veg-
etable packing services; grapes; citrus
fruits; deciduous tree fruits; date orchard;
mango grove; melon farms; pepper farm,
sweet & hot (vegetables)

(P-573)
SUN WORLD INTERNATIONAL INC
52200 Industrial Way, Coachella
(92236-2705)
P.O. Box 1028 (92236-1028)
PHONE..............................760 398-9300
Dave Margulas, *General Mgr*
Jesse Calderon, *Manager*
EMP: 500 **Privately Held**
SIC: 0723 Fruit (fresh) packing services
PA: Sun World International, Inc.
   16351 Driver Rd
   Bakersfield CA 93308

(P-574)
SUNKIST GROWERS INC
531 W Poplar Ave, Tipton (93272-9646)
P.O. Box 3720, Ontario (91761-0993)
PHONE..............................909 983-9811
Owen Belletto, *Branch Mgr*
Bob C Atchley, *Vice Pres*
Pragnesh Patel, *Electrical Engi*
Dennis Wooldridge, *Mfg Mgr*
Don Conley, *Manager*
EMP: 221
SALES (corp-wide): 1.3B **Privately Held**
WEB: www.sunkist.com
SIC: 0723 5149 2099 Fruit crops market
preparation services; juices; food prepa-
rations
PA: Sunkist Growers, Inc.
   27770 Entertainment Dr # 120
   Valencia CA 91355
   661 290-8900

(P-575)
SUNKIST GROWERS INC
531 W Poplar Ave, Tipton (93272-9646)
P.O. Box 3720, Ontario (91761-0993)
PHONE..............................559 752-4256
Owen Belletto, *Vice Pres*
EMP: 221
SQ FT: 25,000
SALES (corp-wide): 1.3B **Privately Held**
WEB: www.sunkist.com
SIC: 0723 Fruit crops market preparation
services
PA: Sunkist Growers, Inc.
   27770 Entertainment Dr # 120
   Valencia CA 91355
   661 290-8900

(P-576)
TALLEY FARMS
2900 Lopez Dr, Arroyo Grande
(93420-4999)
P.O. Box 360 (93421-0360)
PHONE..............................805 489-2508
Brian Talley, *President*
Todd Talley, *Treasurer*
Rayn Talley, *Vice Pres*
Rosemary Talley, *Admin Sec*
EMP: 175
SQ FT: 2,000
SALES (est): 28.4MM **Privately Held**
SIC: 0723 0161 Vegetable packing serv-
ices; vegetables & melons

(P-577)
TANIMURA & ANTLE INC
Also Called: Salad Time Farms
4401 Foxdale St, Baldwin Park
(91706-2161)
P.O. Box 4070, Salinas (93912-4070)
PHONE..............................831 424-6100
Randy Sipled, *Manager*
EMP: 400
SALES (corp-wide): 682.4MM **Privately Held**
WEB: www.taproduce.com
SIC: 0723 Vegetable packing services
PA: Tanimura & Antle Fresh Foods, Inc.
   1 Harris Rd
   Salinas CA 93908
   831 455-2950

(P-578)
TAYLOR FARMS CALIFORNIA INC (HQ)
150 Main St Ste 500, Salinas (93901-3462)
P.O. Box 1649 (93902-1649)
PHONE..............................831 754-0471
Bruce Taylor, *Owner*
Steve Ish, *President*
Alec Leach, *President*
Tanya Mason, *President*
Thomas Bryan, *CFO*
◆ **EMP:** 50
SALES (est): 470MM **Privately Held**
SIC: 0723 Vegetable crops market prepa-
ration services

(P-579)
TAYLOR FRESH FOODS INC (PA)
150 Main St Ste 400, Salinas (93901-3442)
P.O. Box 1649 (93902-1649)
PHONE..............................831 676-9023
Bruce Taylor, *CEO*
Nicole Devincenzo, *Officer*
Craig Enos, *Vice Pres*
Ron Guzman, *Vice Pres*
Kirit Vashee, *Business Anlyst*
▲ **EMP:** 150
SQ FT: 2,500
SALES: 3B **Privately Held**
SIC: 0723 Vegetable crops market prepa-
ration services

(P-580)
TELESIS ONION CO
21484 S Colusa, Five Points (93624)
PHONE..............................559 884-2441
Dan Garcia, *Manager*
Paul Brooks, *Manager*
Danny Gracia, *Manager*
EMP: 50
SALES (corp-wide): 6.8MM **Privately Held**
SIC: 0723 Vegetable packing services

PA: Telesis Onion Co
   3265 W Figarden Dr
   Fresno CA 93711
   559 884-2441

(P-581)
TRINITY FRUIT PACKING COMPANY
18700 E South Ave, Reedley (93654-9711)
PHONE..............................559 743-3913
David E White, *President*
▲ **EMP:** 250
SQ FT: 300,000
SALES: 12MM **Privately Held**
SIC: 0723 Fruit (fresh) packing services

(P-582)
VALLEY FIG GROWERS
2028 S 3rd St, Fresno (93702-4156)
PHONE..............................559 237-3893
Gary Jue, *President*
Paul Mesple, *Chairman*
Linda Cain, *Vice Pres*
Michael N Emigh, *Principal*
◆ **EMP:** 50
SQ FT: 100,000
SALES (est): 24.8MM **Privately Held**
WEB: www.valleyfig.com
SIC: 0723 2033 Fruit (fresh) packing serv-
ices; fruits & fruit products in cans, jars,
etc.

(P-583)
VASQUEZ BROTHERS INC
Also Called: Central Coast Packing
157 Kidder St, Soledad (93960-3080)
P.O. Box 625 (93960-0625)
PHONE..............................831 678-8894
Carlos Vasquez, *President*
Arturo Vasquez, *Vice Pres*
EMP: 100
SQ FT: 10,000
SALES (est): 8.9MM **Privately Held**
WEB: www.centralcoastpacking.com
SIC: 0723 Vegetable packing services

(P-584)
VENTURA COUNTY LEMON COOPS
Also Called: Ventura Pacific Co
P.O. Box 6986, Oxnard (93031-6986)
PHONE..............................805 385-3345
Donald Dames, *President*
Milton Daily, *Ch of Bd*
Mark Jacobs, *CFO*
Jim Waters, *Treasurer*
James H Gill, *Admin Sec*
EMP: 80 **EST:** 1943
SQ FT: 87,000
SALES (est): 12.5MM **Privately Held**
WEB: www.venturapacific.net
SIC: 0723 Fruit crops market preparation
services

(P-585)
WAWONA PACKING CO LLC
12133 Avenue 408, Cutler (93615-2056)
PHONE..............................559 528-4000
Brent Smittcamp, *Mng Member*
Justin Birch, *President*
Georgia Griffin, *Office Mgr*
Tara Sondergaard, *Office Mgr*
Janet Ramirez, *Purch Mgr*
▼ **EMP:** 1400
SQ FT: 16,000
SALES (est): 57.6MM **Privately Held**
WEB: www.wawonapacking.com
SIC: 0723 Fruit (fresh) packing services

(P-586)
WESTERN PRECOOLING SYSTEMS (PA)
43990 Fremont Blvd, Fremont
(94538-6057)
P.O. Box 1338 (94538-0133)
PHONE..............................510 656-2220
Craig A Miller, *President*
Jerry C Nobis, *Treasurer*
Robert H Dench, *Vice Pres*
Floyd E Miller, *Vice Pres*
Joshua Miller, *Vice Pres*
EMP: 125
SQ FT: 4,800

SALES: 62.3MM **Privately Held**
WEB: www.wpsox.com
SIC: 0723 7359 Vegetable precooling
services; fruit precooling services; equipment rental & leasing

(P-587)
WILBUR PACKING COMPANY INC
1500 Eager Rd, Live Oak (95953)
P.O. Box 3730, Yuba City (95992-3730)
PHONE..............................530 671-4911
Richard G Wilbur, *President*
Randy Baucom, *Vice Pres*
Emily L Friend, *Admin Sec*
◆ **EMP:** 350
SQ FT: 60,650
SALES (est): 53.6MM **Privately Held**
WEB: www.wilburpacking.com
SIC: 0723 Crop preparation services for
market

(P-588)
WONDERFUL CITRUS PACKING LLC
36445 Road 172, Visalia (93292-9193)
PHONE..............................559 798-3100
David Smith, *Manager*
EMP: 89
SALES (corp-wide): 1.5B **Privately Held**
WEB: www.paramountcitrus.com
SIC: 0723 0174 Fruit (fresh) packing serv-
ices; orange grove
HQ: Wonderful Citrus Packing Llc
   1901 S Lexington St
   Delano CA 93215
   661 720-2400

(P-589)
WONDERFUL CITRUS PACKING LLC (HQ)
Also Called: Paramount Citrus Packing Co
1901 S Lexington St, Delano (93215-9207)
PHONE..............................661 720-2400
Craig B Cooper, *Mng Member*
◆ **EMP:** 273
SQ FT: 400,000
SALES (est): 259.6MM
SALES (corp-wide): 1.5B **Privately Held**
WEB: www.paramountcitrus.com
SIC: 0723 0174 2033 Fruit (fresh) pack-
ing services; orange grove; lemon grove;
fruit juices: fresh
PA: The Wonderful Company Llc
   11444 W Olympic Blvd # 210
   Los Angeles CA 90064
   310 966-5700

(P-590)
WONDERFUL CITRUS PACKING LLC
710 Del Norte Blvd, Oxnard (93030-8963)
PHONE..............................805 988-1456
Tom Hooten, *Manager*
EMP: 60
SALES (corp-wide): 1.5B **Privately Held**
WEB: www.paramountcitrus.com
SIC: 0723 0174 Fruit (fresh) packing serv-
ices; citrus fruits
HQ: Wonderful Citrus Packing Llc
   1901 S Lexington St
   Delano CA 93215
   661 720-2400

(P-591)
YOUNGSTOWN GRAPE DISTRS INC
1625 G St, Reedley (93654-3435)
P.O. Box 271 (93654-0271)
PHONE..............................559 638-2271
Michael J Forrest, *CEO*
Brian Forrest, *General Mgr*
▲ **EMP:** 206
SQ FT: 100,000
SALES (est): 26.7MM **Privately Held**
SIC: 0723 Fruit (fresh) packing services

PRODUCTS & SVCS

0742 Veterinary Animal Specialties

(P-592)
ACCESS SPCLTY ANIMAL HOSPITALS
9599 Jefferson Blvd, Culver City
(90232-2917)
PHONE..................................310 558-6100
Amy Gram, *Administration*
Jennifer Mederos, *Admin Asst*
Raul Corral, *Technician*
Leah Basinais, *Opers Staff*
Jeremy Oneill, *Surgeon*
EMP: 84
SALES (est): 3.4MM **Privately Held**
SIC: 0742 Animal hospital services, pets & other animal specialties

(P-593)
ADOBE ANIMAL HOSPITAL INC
4470 El Camino Real, Los Altos
(94022-1003)
PHONE..................................650 948-9661
Dave M Ross, *President*
Jerry Berg, *Vice Pres*
Barry Riddle, *Technology*
Summer Holmstrand, *Manager*
EMP: 100
SQ FT: 6,577
SALES (est): 9.4MM **Privately Held**
SIC: 0742 Animal hospital services, pets & other animal specialties

(P-594)
ADVANCED CRITICAL CARE EMERGE
20051 Ventura Blvd Ste I, Woodland Hills
(91364-2646)
PHONE..................................818 887-2262
Howard Liberson, *CEO*
Richard J Mills, *President*
EMP: 100 EST: 2012
SALES (est): 3.3MM **Privately Held**
SIC: 0742 Animal hospital services, pets & other animal specialties

(P-595)
ADVANCED VETERINARY CARE CTR
15926 Hawthorne Blvd, Lawndale
(90260-2644)
PHONE..................................310 542-8018
Bonnie Mc Garr, *Owner*
EMP: 56
SALES (est): 1.8MM **Privately Held**
WEB: www.advancedveterinarycarecenter.com
SIC: 0742 Animal hospital services, pets & other animal specialties

(P-596)
ANIMAL CARE CENTER
Also Called: Constance Dehaan Dvm
6470 Redwood Dr, Rohnert Park
(94928-2326)
PHONE..................................707 584-4343
Constance Dehaan, *Partner*
EMP: 60
SALES (est): 1.1MM **Privately Held**
SIC: 0742 Veterinarian, animal specialties

(P-597)
BISHOP RANCH VETERINARY CENTER (PA)
2000 Bishop Dr, San Ramon (94583-2344)
PHONE..................................925 743-9300
James Delano, *Partner*
Jay Kerr, *Partner*
James Pogrel, *Partner*
Frank Utchen, *Partner*
Summer Godfrey,
EMP: 85
SALES (est): 5MM **Privately Held**
SIC: 0742 Animal hospital services, pets & other animal specialties

(P-598)
BRADSHAW VETERINARY CLINIC
Also Called: Allison, Amanda Dvm
9609 Bradshaw Rd, Elk Grove
(95624-9490)
PHONE..................................916 685-2494
Michael Johnson, *Ch of Bd*
Thomas Zehnder, *President*
EMP: 75
SQ FT: 8,000
SALES: 3MM **Privately Held**
SIC: 0742 0741 Veterinarian, animal specialties; veterinarian, livestock

(P-599)
CAMP BOW WOW FRANCHISING INC
12401 W Olympic Blvd, Los Angeles
(90064-1022)
PHONE..................................310 571-6500
Robert Antin, *President*
EMP: 67
SALES (est): 141.6K
SALES (corp-wide): 2.5B **Privately Held**
SIC: 0742 Veterinary services, specialties
HQ: Vicar Operating, Inc.
12401 W Olympic Blvd
Los Angeles CA 90064
310 571-6500

(P-600)
CONTRA COSTA VET MED EMRGCY CL
1145 Turtle Rock Ln, Concord
(94521-3526)
PHONE..................................925 798-5830
Peter Mangold, *President*
EMP: 50
SQ FT: 3,500
SALES (est): 1.1MM **Privately Held**
SIC: 0742 Animal hospital services, pets & other animal specialties

(P-601)
CRUZ VETERINARY HOSPITAL
2585 Soquel Dr, Santa Cruz (95065-1937)
PHONE..................................831 475-5400
Macy Nichols, *Owner*
Blake Douglas, *Surgeon*
Terry Cullison, *Manager*
EMP: 80
SALES (est): 1.2MM **Privately Held**
SIC: 0742 Animal hospital services, pets & other animal specialties

(P-602)
HAPPY PET CO
Also Called: Very Important Pet Vaccine Svc
5813 Skylane Blvd, Windsor (95492-6836)
PHONE..................................707 586-8660
Will Santana, *CEO*
Ken Pecoraro, *CFO*
EMP: 50
SQ FT: 1,700
SALES (est): 1.2MM **Privately Held**
WEB: www.vipvaccine.com
SIC: 0742 Veterinarian, animal specialties

(P-603)
JAMES I MILLER
Also Called: J I Miller
17659 Chatsworth St, Granada Hills
(91344-5602)
PHONE..................................818 363-7444
James I Miller, *Owner*
EMP: 50 EST: 2001
SALES (est): 463.6K **Privately Held**
SIC: 0742 Veterinarian, animal specialties

(P-604)
MARINE MAMMAL CENTER (PA)
2000 Bunker Rd, Sausalito (94965-2697)
PHONE..................................415 339-0430
Jeffrey Roger Boehm, *CEO*
Marci Davis, *COO*
Karen Takamoto, *Database Admin*
Hanne Larsen, *Opers Staff*
Jennifer Morrow, *Government*
EMP: 50
SQ FT: 25,000

SALES: 12.4MM **Privately Held**
SIC: 0742 8299 8733 Animal hospital services, pets & other animal specialties; arts & crafts schools; noncommercial research organizations

(P-605)
MUELLER PET MEDICAL CENTER
Also Called: Mueller Grooming & Pet Sups
7625 Freeport Blvd, Sacramento
(95832-1084)
PHONE..................................916 428-9202
Ken Schenck, *President*
Margit Spencer, *Admin Asst*
EMP: 50 EST: 1955
SQ FT: 4,000
SALES (est): 1.9MM **Privately Held**
WEB: www.muellerpmc.com
SIC: 0742 5999 Animal hospital services, pets & other animal specialties; pets & pet supplies

(P-606)
NATIONAL VETERINARY ASSOC INC
2300 N State St, Ukiah (95482-3128)
PHONE..................................707 462-8625
EMP: 51
SALES (corp-wide): 831.8MM **Privately Held**
SIC: 0742 Veterinarian, animal specialties; animal hospital services, pets & other animal specialties
PA: National Veterinary Associates, Inc.
29229 Canwood St Ste 100
Agoura Hills CA 91301
805 777-7722

(P-607)
NATIONAL VETERINARY ASSOC INC (PA)
29229 Canwood St Ste 100, Agoura Hills
(91301-1503)
PHONE..................................805 777-7722
Greg Hartmann, *CEO*
Thomas Sawicki, *COO*
R James Woloshyn, *CFO*
Carol Henry, *Chief Mktg Ofcr*
Tracy Klauder, *Admin Asst*
EMP: 188
SQ FT: 5,000
SALES (est): 831.8MM **Privately Held**
SIC: 0742 Veterinarian, animal specialties

(P-608)
NICHOLAS B MACY DVM
2585 Soquel Dr, Santa Cruz (95065-1937)
PHONE..................................831 475-5400
Nicholas Macy, *Owner*
Jay Stone, *Co-Owner*
EMP: 70 EST: 1950
SALES (est): 950.5K **Privately Held**
SIC: 0742 Veterinarian, animal specialties

(P-609)
SUNSET PET HOSPITAL INC (PA)
Also Called: AMC
7751 Sunset Ave, Fair Oaks (95628-4899)
PHONE..................................916 967-7768
Jay Griffiths, *President*
Kathy Griffiths, *Vice Pres*
EMP: 100
SQ FT: 2,400
SALES (est): 4.7MM **Privately Held**
WEB: www.sunsetpethospital.com
SIC: 0742 Animal hospital services, pets & other animal specialties

(P-610)
TONY LA RUSSAS ANIMAL RES FND
2890 Mitchell Dr, Walnut Creek
(94598-1635)
P.O. Box 30215 (94598-9215)
PHONE..................................925 256-1273
Elena Bicker, *Exec Dir*
Holli Hargrove, *Social Dir*
Kai Glass, *Exec Dir*
Mandi Pike, *Finance Mgr*
Stephanie Erickson, *Opers Staff*
EMP: 70
SQ FT: 37,000

SALES: 8.5MM **Privately Held**
WEB: www.arf.net
SIC: 0742 8699 Veterinary services, specialties; animal humane society

(P-611)
VCA ANIMAL HOSPITALS INC
Also Called: VCA Holly Street
501 Laurel St, San Carlos (94070-2415)
PHONE..................................650 631-7400
Barbara Beebe, *Office Mgr*
EMP: 50
SALES (corp-wide): 2.5B **Privately Held**
SIC: 0742 Veterinarian, animal specialties
HQ: Vca Animal Hospitals, Inc.
12401 W Olympic Blvd
Los Angeles CA 90064
-

(P-612)
VCA ANIMAL HOSPITALS INC
Also Called: VCA Lmis Bsin Vterinary Clinic
3901 Sierra College Blvd, Loomis
(95650-7943)
PHONE..................................916 652-5816
Robert Antin, *CEO*
Tomas Fuller, *CFO*
Neil Tauber, *Senior VP*
Stephen Speredelozzi, *Manager*
EMP: 50
SALES (est): 1.1MM **Privately Held**
SIC: 0742 Animal hospital services, pets & other animal specialties

(P-613)
VCA ANIMAL HOSPITALS INC (DH)
Also Called: VCA TLC Animal Hospital
12401 W Olympic Blvd, Los Angeles
(90064-1022)
PHONE..................................310 571-6500
Robert Antin, *President*
Richard Joseph, *Managing Prtnr*
Tomas Fuller, *Treasurer*
Jennifer Craft, *Administration*
Kim Dudder, *Technical Mgr*
EMP: 188
SQ FT: 3,200
SALES (est): 63.1MM
SALES (corp-wide): 2.5B **Privately Held**
SIC: 0742 Animal hospital services, pets & other animal specialties
HQ: Vca Inc.
12401 W Olympic Blvd
Los Angeles CA 90064
310 571-6500

(P-614)
VCA ANTECH INC
12401 W Olympic Blvd, Los Angeles
(90064-1022)
PHONE..................................310 207-0781
Bob Antin, *President*
Susan Kimmel, *Director*
EMP: 362
SALES (est): 440.4K
SALES (corp-wide): 2.5B **Privately Held**
SIC: 0742 Animal hospital services, pets & other animal specialties
HQ: Vicar Operating, Inc.
12401 W Olympic Blvd
Los Angeles CA 90064
310 571-6500

(P-615)
VCA DESERT ANIMAL HOSPITALS
4299 E Ramon Rd, Palm Springs
(92264-1422)
PHONE..................................760 778-9999
Raymond Mestas, *Principal*
EMP: 54
SALES (est): 1.2MM **Privately Held**
SIC: 0742 Animal hospital services, pets & other animal specialties

(P-616)
VCA INC
1818 S Sepulveda Blvd, Los Angeles
(90025-4314)
PHONE..................................310 473-2951
Todd Tams, *Administration*
William Farber,
EMP: 80

▲ = Import ▼=Export
◆ =Import/Export

SALES (corp-wide): 2.5B **Privately Held**
WEB: www.vcawoodlands.com
SIC: 0742 Veterinarian, animal specialties
HQ: Vca Inc.
12401 W Olympic Blvd
Los Angeles CA 90064
310 571-6500

(P-617)
VCA INC
Also Called: VCA-Asher Animal Hospital
2505 Hilltop Dr, Redding (96002-0505)
PHONE..............................530 224-2200
Annette Hixenbau, *Director*
Larry Correia,
EMP: 55
SALES (corp-wide): 2.5B **Privately Held**
WEB: www.vcawoodlands.com
SIC: 0742 Veterinary services, specialties
HQ: Vca Inc.
12401 W Olympic Blvd
Los Angeles CA 90064
310 571-6500

(P-618)
VETERINARY SURGICAL
ASSOCIATES (PA)
1410 Monu Blvd Ste 100, Concord (94520)
PHONE..............................925 827-1777
Julie Smith, *Partner*
Elisabeth Richardson, *Partner*
Sharon Ullman, *Partner*
Charles Walls, *Partner*
Chuck Walls, *Partner*
EMP: 187
SALES (est): 6.1MM **Privately Held**
WEB: www.vsasurgery.com
SIC: 0742 Veterinary services, specialties

(P-619)
VETERNARY MED SRGCAL
GROUP INC
Also Called: Vmsg
2199 Sperry Ave, Ventura (93003-7426)
PHONE..............................805 339-2290
Kenneth A Bruecker, *CEO*
Daniel Rose, *Technical Staff*
Mary Dulisch,
Edward Maher,
Theresa Ortega, *Med Doctor*
EMP: 80
SQ FT: 6,500
SALES (est): 2.8MM **Privately Held**
WEB: www.vmsg.com
SIC: 0742 Animal hospital services, pets &
other animal specialties

(P-620)
VICAR OPERATING INC (DH)
Also Called: Veterinary Centers America VCA
12401 W Olympic Blvd, Los Angeles
(90064-1022)
PHONE..............................310 571-6500
Robert Antin, *President*
Todd Lavender, *President*
Arthur Antin, *COO*
Elizabeth Ho, *Officer*
Jeff Sonnenberg, *Senior VP*
EMP: 162 EST: 1985
SALES (est): 93.5MM
SALES (corp-wide): 2.5B **Privately Held**
WEB: www.vcaantech.com
SIC: 0742 Veterinarian, animal specialties
HQ: Vca Inc.
12401 W Olympic Blvd
Los Angeles CA 90064
310 571-6500

(P-621)
WEST RIVERSIDE VETERINARY
HOSP
5488 Mission Blvd, Riverside (92509-4514)
PHONE..............................951 686-2242
Michael Butchko, *President*
Ruby Butchko, *Vice Pres*
EMP: 50
SALES (est): 1.8MM **Privately Held**
WEB: www.drbutchko.org
SIC: 0742 Animal hospital services, pets &
other animal specialties

(P-622)
WILSHIRE ANIMAL HOSPITAL
2421 Wilshire Blvd, Santa Monica
(90403-5876)
PHONE..............................310 828-4587
Natoional Pet Care Center, *Owner*
Pernilla Edstrom, *Med Doctor*
Frank Lavac, *Director*
Mary Espelage, *Manager*
Frank Labuc, *Manager*
EMP: 50
SQ FT: 2,000
SALES (est): 1.8MM **Privately Held**
SIC: 0742 Animal hospital services, pets &
other animal specialties

0751 Livestock Svcs, Except
Veterinary

(P-623)
AMERICAN BEEF PACKERS INC
13677 Yorba Ave, Chino (91710-5059)
PHONE..............................909 628-4888
Lawrence Miller, *President*
Cinthia Hernandez, *Human Resources*
Henry Wong, *Sales Mgr*
EMP: 250
SALES: 200MM **Privately Held**
SIC: 0751 2011 5147 Slaughtering: cus-
tom livestock services; beef products from
beef slaughtered on site; meats & meat
products

(P-624)
PLEASANT VALLEY FARMS (PA)
Also Called: Jenkins Poultry Farms
30636 E Carter Rd, Farmington
(95230-9633)
P.O. Box 752, Ripon (95366-0752)
PHONE..............................209 886-1000
Richard Jenkins, *Mng Member*
John Dendulk,
Jerry Jenkins,
EMP: 70
SALES (est): 8.8MM **Privately Held**
SIC: 0751 Poultry services

(P-625)
STANDARD CATTLE LLC
Also Called: Standard Cattle Company
8105a S Lassen Ave, San Joaquin
(93660-9728)
PHONE..............................559 693-1977
Michael Vanderdussen, *Owner*
▲ EMP: 75 EST: 2005
SALES (est): 1.1MM **Privately Held**
SIC: 0751 Livestock services, except vet-
erinary

0752 Animal Specialty Svcs,
Exc Veterinary

(P-626)
CANINE CMPNONS FOR
INDPENDENCE (PA)
2965 Dutton Ave, Santa Rosa
(95407-5711)
P.O. Box 446 (95402-0446)
PHONE..............................707 577-1700
Paul Mundell, *CEO*
John D Miller, *Ch of Bd*
Alan Feinne, *CFO*
Megan Koester, *Exec Dir*
Elizabeth Stalker, *Administration*
EMP: 71
SQ FT: 40,000
SALES: 31.9MM **Privately Held**
SIC: 0752 Training services, pet & animal
specialties (not horses)

(P-627)
DEDICATION & EVERLASTING
LOVE
Also Called: D E L T A Rescue
6021 Shannon Valley Rd, Acton
(93510-1190)
P.O. Box 9, Glendale (91209-0009)
PHONE..............................661 269-4010
Leo Grillo, *President*
EMP: 60

SALES: 5.9MM **Privately Held**
SIC: 0752 Shelters, animal

(P-628)
GUIDE DOGS FOR BLIND INC
(PA)
Also Called: G D B
350 Los Ranchitos Rd, San Rafael
(94903-3606)
P.O. Box 151200 (94915-1200)
PHONE..............................415 499-4000
Chris Benninger, *CEO*
Cathy Martin, *CFO*
Kenneth Stupi, *CFO*
Janet Benjamin, *Officer*
Keith Rosenthal, *Officer*
EMP: 170 EST: 1942
SALES: 22.4MM **Privately Held**
WEB: www.guidedogs.com
SIC: 0752 8299 Animal training services;
educational service, nondegree granting;
continuing educ.

(P-629)
HANGTOWN KNNEL CLB
PLCRVLLE CA
100 Placerville Dr, Placerville (95667-3910)
P.O. Box 2176 (95667-2176)
PHONE..............................530 622-4867
Pam Bectel, *President*
Joe Barnes, *Corp Secy*
EMP: 75
SALES: 110K **Privately Held**
SIC: 0752 Training services, pet & animal
specialties (not horses)

(P-630)
LOS ANGELES EQUESTRIAN
CENTER
480 W Riverside Dr, Burbank (91506-3209)
PHONE..............................818 840-9063
Tim Behunin, *President*
Kenneth Mowry, *Admin Sec*
EMP: 75
SALES (est): 2.6MM **Privately Held**
WEB: www.la-equestriancenter.com
SIC: 0752 7999 Boarding services,
horses: racing & non-racing; horse shows

(P-631)
OJAI RAPTOR CENTER
370 Baldwin Rd, Ojai (93023-9705)
PHONE..............................805 649-6884
Kimberly Stroud, *Director*
EMP: 70
SALES: 208.6K **Privately Held**
SIC: 0752 Shelters, animal

(P-632)
PETCO ANIMAL SUPPLIES INC
(DH)
10850 Via Frontera, San Diego
(92127-1705)
PHONE..............................858 453-7845
Ron Coughlin, *CEO*
James M Myers, *Ch of Bd*
Brad Weston, *President*
James Lampassi, *CEO*
Michael M Nuzzo, *CFO*
◆ EMP: 500
SQ FT: 164,000
SALES (est): 10.3B
SALES (corp-wide): 264.1K **Privately
Held**
WEB: www.petco.com
SIC: 0752 5199 5999 Grooming services,
pet & animal specialties; pet supplies; pet
supplies
HQ: Petco Holdings, Inc. Llc
10850 Via Frontera
San Diego CA 92127
858 453-7845

(P-633)
SONOMA COUNTY HUMANE
SOCIETY
Also Called: Hssc
5345 Highway 12, Santa Rosa
(95407-6401)
P.O. Box 1296 (95402-1296)
PHONE..............................707 542-0882
Scott Anderson, *Director*
Don Malone, *Director*
EMP: 50

SALES (est): 743.9K **Privately Held**
SIC: 0752 Shelters, animal

(P-634)
TOWN CATS MORGAN HILL
RESCUE
195 San Pedro Ave Ste B, Morgan Hill
(95037-5141)
P.O. Box 1828 (95038-1828)
PHONE..............................408 779-5761
Rosi Mirko, *Director*
Petrica Aberu, *Director*
Petrica Guthrie, *Director*
Albert Mirko, *Director*
EMP: 50
SALES: 314.9K **Privately Held**
WEB: www.towncats.org
SIC: 0752 Shelters, animal

(P-635)
WAGS & WIGGLES DOG
DAYCARE LLC (PA)
23171 Arroyo Vis, Rcho STA Marg
(92688-2616)
PHONE..............................949 635-9655
Laurie Zurborg,
David Zurborg, *Managing Prtnr*
EMP: 56
SALES (est): 1.1MM **Privately Held**
SIC: 0752 Boarding services, kennels

0761 Farm Labor
Contractors & Crew Leaders

(P-636)
AGSOURCE SERVICES LLC
222 N Garden St Ste 400, Visalia
(93291-6328)
PHONE..............................559 735-9700
Fred Lagomarsino,
EMP: 50 EST: 1998
SALES (est): 2.4MM **Privately Held**
SIC: 0761 Farm labor contractors

(P-637)
ALICIA ARROYO INC
Also Called: Arroyo Labor Contracting Svc
800 Johnson Cyn Rd 4, Gonzales (93926)
P.O. Box 846 (93926-0846)
PHONE..............................831 675-2850
Alicia Arroyo, *President*
Debra Arroyo, *Treasurer*
Michael Arroyo, *Vice Pres*
EMP: 250
SQ FT: 500
SALES (est): 7MM **Privately Held**
SIC: 0761 Farm labor contractors

(P-638)
ARMANDO GONZALEZ
CONTRACTING
32380 Elmo Hwy, Mc Farland
(93250-9616)
P.O. Box 1540 (93250-0140)
PHONE..............................661 792-3785
Armando Gonzalez, *Owner*
EMP: 300
SALES (est): 3.6MM **Privately Held**
SIC: 0761 Crew leaders, farm labor: con-
tracting services

(P-639)
AZTEC HARVESTING
1075 N Broadway, Blythe (92225-1664)
P.O. Box 1080 (92226-1080)
PHONE..............................760 922-7348
Charles Garcia, *President*
Marilyn Garcia, *Vice Pres*
Steve Garcia, *Vice Pres*
Tina Garcia, *Admin Sec*
EMP: 800
SALES: 5MM **Privately Held**
SIC: 0761 4212 0722 Farm labor contrac-
tors; local trucking, without storage; crop
harvesting

(P-640)
BORJON ISCANDER
Also Called: Bvls
18586 Highway 49, Plymouth (95669)
P.O. Box 252 (95669-0252)
PHONE..............................209 245-6289
Iscandor Borjon, *Owner*

PRODUCTS & SVCS

Elana Borjon, *Co-Owner*
EMP: 250
SALES (est): 164.4K **Privately Held**
SIC: 0761 Farm labor contractors

(P-641)
COASTAL HARVESTING INC
503 S Palm Ave, Santa Paula
(93060-3364)
PHONE...............................805 525-6250
EMP: 300
SALES (est): 10.2MM **Privately Held**
SIC: 0761

(P-642)
EDWARDO Z GARCIA
Also Called: Z Garcia Farm Labor
380 Tucker St, Arvin (93203-1527)
PHONE...............................661 854-5414
Edwardo Z Garcia, *Owner*
EMP: 250
SALES (est): 4.3MM **Privately Held**
SIC: 0761 Crew leaders, farm labor: contracting services

(P-643)
EL CAMINO LABOR LLC
815 Broadway St, King City (93930-3304)
PHONE...............................831 809-9537
Armando Zavala Chavez,
EMP: 60
SALES (est): 508.9K **Privately Held**
SIC: 0761 Farm labor contractors

(P-644)
ELIOCO PRODUCE INC
Also Called: Preferred Produce
367 W Market St Ste A, Salinas
(93901-1423)
P.O. Box 5700 (93915-5700)
PHONE...............................831 424-5450
Robert Elliott, *President*
EMP: 105
SQ FT: 1,400
SALES (est): 6.5MM **Privately Held**
SIC: 0761 Farm labor contractors

(P-645)
ELISEO ESPARZA DELGADILLO
88 Wildflower Dr, Galt (95632-2329)
P.O. Box 431 (95632-0431)
PHONE...............................209 745-3937
Eliseo E Delgadillo, *President*
EMP: 50
SALES (est): 2.8MM **Privately Held**
SIC: 0761 Farm labor contractors

(P-646)
F & F CONTRACTING INC
4145 W Alamos Ave, Fresno (93722-3939)
PHONE...............................559 276-2418
Frank Echeverrie, *President*
EMP: 200
SQ FT: 500
SALES (est): 10.2MM **Privately Held**
SIC: 0761 Farm labor contractors

(P-647)
FIVE STAR PACKING LLC
437 W 5th St, Holtville (92250-1167)
P.O. Box 838 (92250-0838)
PHONE...............................760 356-4103
Marc Heraz,
John A Heraz, *Manager*
EMP: 737
SQ FT: 900
SALES (est): 14.7MM **Privately Held**
SIC: 0761 Farm labor contractors

(P-648)
FLORES LABOR CONTRACTING
501 6th St, Mc Farland (93250-1103)
PHONE...............................661 792-3061
Dora Flores, *Owner*
EMP: 300
SALES (est): 4.9MM **Privately Held**
SIC: 0761 Farm labor contractors

(P-649)
FRANK BARRAZA
Also Called: Barraza Farm Labor Contractor
147 E Alamo, Calipatria (92233)
P.O. Box 864 (92233-0864)
PHONE...............................760 348-7363
Frank Barraza, *Owner*
EMP: 99

SALES (est): 1.8MM **Privately Held**
SIC: 0761 Farm labor contractors

(P-650)
GOMEZ FARM LABOR CONTG INC
62610 Monroe St, Thermal (92274-9059)
PHONE...............................760 399-1994
Jose J Gomez, *President*
George Gomez, *Admin Sec*
EMP: 100
SQ FT: 900
SALES (est): 5.3MM **Privately Held**
SIC: 0761 Farm labor contractors

(P-651)
GONZALES SALVADOR LABOR CONTRS
217 4th St, Galt (95632-1955)
PHONE...............................209 745-2223
Salvador Gonzalez, *President*
Theresa Gonzalez, *Treasurer*
EMP: 100
SALES (est): 3.9MM **Privately Held**
SIC: 0761 Crew leaders, farm labor: contracting services

(P-652)
HALL AG ENTERPRISES INC
Also Called: Hall AG Services
759 S Madera Ave, Kerman (93630-1744)
PHONE...............................559 846-7360
Brad Hall, *President*
Loraine Garcia, *Corp Secy*
Mike Van Hooser, *Vice Pres*
EMP: 200
SALES (est): 5.6MM **Privately Held**
SIC: 0761 7361 Farm labor contractors; labor contractors (employment agency)

(P-653)
J A CONTRACTING INC
2209 W Tulare Ave, Visalia (93277-2137)
P.O. Box 2109, Tulare (93275-2109)
PHONE...............................559 733-4865
EMP: 300
SQ FT: 1,500
SALES (est): 9MM **Privately Held**
WEB: www.jacontracting.net
SIC: 0761

(P-654)
JACOBS TREE SPECIALIST INC
2209 W Tulare Ave, Visalia (93277-2137)
P.O. Box 684, Lemoore (93245-0684)
PHONE...............................559 639-7138
Gregorio Jacobo, *President*
EMP: 50
SALES: 900K **Privately Held**
SIC: 0761 Farm labor contractors

(P-655)
JJ RIOS FARM SERVICES INC
4890 E Acampo Rd, Acampo (95220-9601)
P.O. Box 550 (95220-0550)
PHONE...............................209 333-7467
Fax: 209 333-3715
EMP: 80
SQ FT: 4,800
SALES: 2MM **Privately Held**
WEB: www.jjrios.com
SIC: 0761

(P-656)
JORGE PIMENTAL DIAZ
348 Manzanita Dr, Delano (93215-4675)
PHONE...............................661 344-5139
Jorge Pimental Diaz, *Owner*
EMP: 120
SALES (est): 5.7MM **Privately Held**
SIC: 0761 Farm labor contractors

(P-657)
L&D FARM LABOR
53762 Sapphire Ln, Coachella
(92236-7335)
PHONE...............................760 408-6311
Tania Alonzo, *President*
EMP: 50 **Privately Held**
SIC: 0761 Farm labor contractors

(P-658)
LABOR ONE INC
575 Minnewawa Ave Ste 3, Clovis
(93612-6300)
PHONE...............................559 430-4202
Cheat Nuon, *President*
EMP: 70
SALES (est): 625.3K **Privately Held**
SIC: 0761 Farm labor contractors

(P-659)
MARIN LABOR SERVICES
277 Country View Ct, Santa Paula
(93060-3015)
PHONE...............................805 525-7730
Juan Llamas, *Owner*
EMP: 200
SALES (est): 3.9MM **Privately Held**
SIC: 0761 Crew leaders, farm labor: contracting services

(P-660)
MAYORAL BROS
420 Hillcrest Cir, Dixon (95620-3722)
PHONE...............................707 693-9111
Rosendo Mayoral, *Owner*
Ricardo Mayoral, *President*
Hector Mayoral, *CFO*
EMP: 400
SALES (est): 297.2K **Privately Held**
SIC: 0761 Farm labor contractors

(P-661)
MOUNTAIN VIEW AG SERVICES INC
13281 Avenue 416, Orosi (93647)
PHONE...............................559 528-6004
Leonard E Hutchinson, *President*
Leonard Hutchinson, *President*
Sonya Hutchinson, *Corp Secy*
EMP: 1200
SQ FT: 800
SALES (est): 6.2MM **Privately Held**
SIC: 0761 Farm labor contractors

(P-662)
MOYA JUAN FARM LABOR SERVICES
Also Called: Moya Farm Labor Services
7919 S Alta Ave, Reedley (93654-9538)
PHONE...............................559 638-9498
Rosa Moya, *President*
Juan Moya, *Vice Pres*
EMP: 150
SALES (est): 9.1MM **Privately Held**
SIC: 0761 Farm labor contractors

(P-663)
OMAR OROZCO
Also Called: Omar Orozco's Contracting
816 Gibson Rd, Woodland (95695-4935)
PHONE...............................530 723-0849
Omar Orozco, *Principal*
EMP: 55
SALES (est): 478.1K **Privately Held**
SIC: 0761 Farm labor contractors

(P-664)
PACIFIC SUN LABOR ●
350 G St, Brawley (92227-2413)
PHONE...............................760 556-5085
Alejandro Palacios, *President*
EMP: 52 **EST:** 2018
SALES (est): 459.3K **Privately Held**
SIC: 0761 Crew leaders, farm labor: contracting services

(P-665)
PALO ALTO VINEYARD MGT LLC
50 Adobe Canyon Rd, Kenwood
(95452-9044)
P.O. Box 1399 (95452-1399)
PHONE...............................707 996-7725
Beverly Ordaz,
Jesus Ordaz,
EMP: 90 **EST:** 1997
SQ FT: 1,000
SALES (est): 7MM **Privately Held**
SIC: 0761 Farm labor contractors

(P-666)
PETE SANTELLAN
Also Called: Santellan Farm Labor Contr
176 S Valencia Blvd Ste C, Woodlake
(93286-1723)
PHONE...............................559 564-3748
Pete Santellan, *Partner*
Ruben Santellan, *Partner*
EMP: 150
SALES (est): 2.5MM **Privately Held**
SIC: 0761 Crew leaders, farm labor: contracting services

(P-667)
PYRAMID PRODUCE INC
12826 Edison Hwy, Bakersfield (93307)
P.O. Box 27 (93302-0027)
PHONE...............................661 366-5736
Wayde Kirschenman, *CEO*
Norma Rapp, *Treasurer*
EMP: 250
SALES (est): 3.8MM **Privately Held**
SIC: 0761 Crew leaders, farm labor: contracting services

(P-668)
R AND R LABOR INC
710 Kirkpatric Ct, Hollister (95023-2817)
PHONE...............................831 638-0290
Ramiro Rodriguez Jr, *President*
Jose Rodriguez, *Vice Pres*
Elda Garcia, *Executive*
EMP: 300
SALES (est): 9.7MM **Privately Held**
SIC: 0761 Farm labor contractors

(P-669)
R MORA FARM LABOR
930 5th St, Wasco (93280-1348)
PHONE...............................661 746-2858
Roberto Mora, *Owner*
EMP: 50
SALES: 300K **Privately Held**
SIC: 0761 Farm labor contractors

(P-670)
RANCHO SALINAS PACKING INC
2376 Alisal Rd, Salinas (93908-9718)
P.O. Box 5307 (93915-5307)
PHONE...............................831 758-3624
Gilberto Jimenez, *President*
EMP: 150
SQ FT: 500,000
SALES: 2MM **Privately Held**
SIC: 0761 Crew leaders, farm labor: contracting services

(P-671)
RODGZ FARM LABOR CONTG LLC
4422 College Way, Olivehurst
(95961-4622)
PHONE...............................530 329-8403
Fidel Rodriguez,
EMP: 80
SALES (est): 625.5K **Privately Held**
SIC: 0761 Crew leaders, farm labor: contracting services

(P-672)
SALAZAR LABOR CONTRACTING
957 Sugarloaf Dr, Escondido (92026-2364)
P.O. Box 460448 (92046-0448)
PHONE...............................760 746-0805
Joe Salazar, *Owner*
EMP: 60 **EST:** 1998
SALES (est): 2.1MM **Privately Held**
SIC: 0761 Farm labor contractors

(P-673)
SALVADOR MARTINEZ
2049 N Newcomb St, Porterville
(93257-9284)
PHONE...............................559 781-5150
Salvador Martinez, *Owner*
EMP: 120
SALES (est): 1.3MM **Privately Held**
SIC: 0761 Farm labor contractors

(P-674)
SEIU LOCAL 1021
447 29th St, Oakland (94609-3510)
P.O. Box 2077 (94604-2077)
PHONE.....................................510 350-9811
Damita Davis-Howard, *Director*
EMP: 165
SALES (est): 43.1MM **Privately Held**
SIC: 0761 Farm labor contractors

(P-675)
SOUTHERN MNTRREY CNTY LBOR SUP
Also Called: Southern Mntrey Cnty Labor Sup
44 El Camino Real Unit A, Greenfield (93927-5637)
P.O. Box G (93927-0105)
PHONE.....................................831 674-2727
Nick Azcona, *President*
Pier Azcona, *Vice Pres*
EMP: 100
SQ FT: 1,000
SALES (est): 3.2MM **Privately Held**
SIC: 0761 Crew leaders, farm labor: contracting services

(P-676)
VALLEY PRIDE INC (PA)
10855 Ocean Mist Pkwy D, Castroville (95012-3232)
PHONE.....................................831 633-5883
Joseph T Pezzini, *President*
Troy Boutonnet, *Vice Pres*
EMP: 399
SQ FT: 1,500
SALES (est): 2.2MM **Privately Held**
WEB: www.valleyprideinc.com
SIC: 0761 Crew leaders, farm labor: contracting services

(P-677)
VELAZQUEZ PACKING INC
124 N I St, Lompoc (93436-6721)
P.O. Box 488 (93438-0488)
PHONE.....................................805 735-6477
Raul Velasquez Jr, *President*
EMP: 100
SALES (est): 3MM **Privately Held**
SIC: 0761 Farm labor contractors

(P-678)
VENEGAS FARMING LLC
8002 Balcom Canyon Rd, Somis (93066-2107)
PHONE.....................................805 529-5038
Guillermo Venegas,
EMP: 50
SALES (est): 446.5K **Privately Held**
SIC: 0761 Farm labor contractors

0762 Farm Management

(P-679)
AG-WISE ENTERPRISES INC (PA)
5100 California Ave # 209, Bakersfield (93309-0716)
P.O. Box 9729 (93389-9729)
PHONE.....................................661 325-1567
Bruce Berreta, *President*
Ed Ray, *CFO*
EMP: 150
SQ FT: 4,400
SALES (est): 32.3MM **Privately Held**
SIC: 0762 Farm management services

(P-680)
AGRI-WORLD COOPERATIVE
31545 Donald Ave, Madera (93636-1475)
PHONE.....................................559 673-1306
Devin Aviles, *General Mgr*
EMP: 50
SQ FT: 1,500
SALES (est): 4MM **Privately Held**
SIC: 0762 Farm management services

(P-681)
ARTHUR KUNDE & SONS INC
Also Called: Kunde Estate Winery
9825 Sonoma Hwy, Kenwood (95452)
PHONE.....................................707 833-5501
Jim Mickelson, *President*
Arthur Kunde Jr, *President*

William Kunde, *Corp Secy*
▲ EMP: 50
SQ FT: 2,000
SALES (est): 3.9MM **Privately Held**
WEB: www.kunde.com
SIC: 0762 2084 Vineyard management & maintenance services; wines, brandy & brandy spirits

(P-682)
BIANCHI AG SERVICES INC
3056 Colusa Hwy, Yuba City (95993-8931)
PHONE.....................................530 923-7675
Jim Bianchi, *Branch Mgr*
EMP: 88
SALES (corp-wide): 41.1MM **Privately Held**
SIC: 0762 Farm management services
PA: Bianchi Ag. Services, Inc.
1210 Richvale Hwy
Richvale CA 95974
530 882-4575

(P-683)
CLIMATE CORPORATION (DH)
201 3rd St Ste 1100, San Francisco (94103-3149)
PHONE.....................................415 363-0500
Mike Stern, *CEO*
Greg Smirin, *COO*
Daniel McCaffrey, *Vice Pres*
John Raines, *Vice Pres*
Brian Zimmer, *Vice Pres*
EMP: 79
SALES (est): 44.9MM
SALES (corp-wide): 41.2B **Privately Held**
SIC: 0762 Farm management services
HQ: Monsanto Company
800 N Lindbergh Blvd
Saint Louis MO 63167
314 694-1000

(P-684)
CUMMINGS-VIOLICH INC
Also Called: Cummings-Vlich Inc-Orchard MGT
1750 Dayton Rd, Chico (95928-6968)
PHONE.....................................530 894-5494
Dan Cummings, *President*
Paul Violich, *CFO*
EMP: 80
SQ FT: 3,400
SALES (est): 7.3MM **Privately Held**
WEB: www.cvinc.ws
SIC: 0762 Farm management services

(P-685)
D J FARM MANAGEMENT
11298 Magnolia Ave, Wasco (93280-9647)
P.O. Box 82395, Bakersfield (93380-2395)
PHONE.....................................661 792-6222
Jeff Fabry, *Owner*
EMP: 50 EST: 2010
SALES (est): 742K **Privately Held**
SIC: 0762 Farm management services

(P-686)
E & J GALLO WINERY
Also Called: Livingston Ranch
5953 Weir Ave, Livingston (95334-9509)
PHONE.....................................209 394-6271
Alan Reynolds, *Manager*
Jonathon Meikle, *Business Anlyst*
EMP: 100
SALES (corp-wide): 2.6B **Privately Held**
WEB: www.gallo.com
SIC: 0762 2084 Vineyard management & maintenance services; wines
PA: E. & J. Gallo Winery
600 Yosemite Blvd
Modesto CA 95354
209 341-3111

(P-687)
E & M AG SVC INC A CAL CORP
2446 W Border Links Dr, Visalia (93291-4316)
P.O. Box 7208 (93290-7208)
PHONE.....................................559 627-2724
Matt Bakke, *President*
Evett Bakke, *Vice Pres*
EMP: 50
SALES (est): 5.8MM **Privately Held**
SIC: 0762 Farm management services

(P-688)
EASTSIDE MANAGEMENT CO INC
1131 12th St Ste C, Modesto (95354-0813)
PHONE.....................................209 578-9852
Steven Zeff, *President*
EMP: 148 **Privately Held**
SIC: 0762 Farm management services
PA: Eastside Management Company, Inc.
1518 K St
Modesto CA 95354

(P-689)
ECO FARM FIELD INC
28790 Las Haciendas St, Temecula (92590-2614)
PHONE.....................................951 676-4047
Steven Taft, *President*
Norman Traner, *Corp Secy*
▲ EMP: 75
SQ FT: 20,000
SALES (est): 2.8MM **Privately Held**
SIC: 0762 6519 0722 4212 Farm management services; real property lessors; crop harvesting; local trucking, without storage

(P-690)
ENZENNAUER VINEYARD MANAGMENT
18501 Ida Clayton Rd, Calistoga (94515-9537)
P.O. Box 1776, Healdsburg (95448-1776)
PHONE.....................................707 433-0532
Phillip Enzennauer, *President*
Liz Langerman, *Manager*
EMP: 58
SALES (est): 1MM **Privately Held**
SIC: 0762 Vineyard management & maintenance services

(P-691)
ESPARZA ENTERPRISES INC
251 W Main St Ste G&F, Brawley (92227-2201)
PHONE.....................................760 344-2031
Luis Esparza, *Branch Mgr*
EMP: 453
SALES (corp-wide): 90.9MM **Privately Held**
SIC: 0762 Farm management services
PA: Esparza Enterprises, Inc.
3851 Fruitvale Ave
Bakersfield CA 93308
661 831-0002

(P-692)
FREY FARMING & TPSRY VINEYARDS
2203 Fallen Leaf Dr, Santa Maria (93455-5736)
PHONE.....................................805 937-1542
Jeff Frey, *Owner*
EMP: 90
SALES (est): 1.4MM **Privately Held**
SIC: 0762 Vineyard management & maintenance services

(P-693)
GLESS RANCH INC (PA)
18541 Van Buren Blvd, Riverside (92508-9261)
PHONE.....................................951 780-8458
John J Gless, *CEO*
EMP: 50 EST: 1961
SALES (est): 14.2MM **Privately Held**
WEB: www.glessranch.com
SIC: 0762 Orchard management & maintenance services

(P-694)
HANSEN EQUIPMENT COMPANY LLC
7124 Whitley Ave, Corcoran (93212-9669)
P.O. Box 398 (93212-0398)
PHONE.....................................559 992-3111
James B Hansen,
Betsy Hansen,
EMP: 50
SALES: 12MM **Privately Held**
SIC: 0762 Farm management services

(P-695)
J & R DEBENEDETTO ORCHARDS INC
Also Called: De Benedetto AG
26393 Road 22 1/2, Chowchilla (93610-9624)
PHONE.....................................559 665-1712
Richard De Benedetto, *Owner*
Janelle Eggert, *Office Spvr*
EMP: 75
SALES (est): 3.3MM **Privately Held**
SIC: 0762 Farm management services

(P-696)
LARRY JACINTO FARMING INC
9555 N Wabash Ave, Redlands (92374-2714)
P.O. Box 275, Mentone (92359-0275)
PHONE.....................................909 794-2276
Larry Jacinto, *President*
Dennis Drexler, *Corp Secy*
EMP: 100
SQ FT: 3,000
SALES (est): 1.6MM **Privately Held**
SIC: 0762 Farm management services

(P-697)
LASSEN LAND CO
320 E South St, Orland (95963-9111)
P.O. Box 607 (95963-0607)
PHONE.....................................530 865-7676
Roderick Minkler, *President*
Betty Minkler, *Admin Sec*
Bill Minkler, *Director*
EMP: 50 EST: 1969
SQ FT: 6,000
SALES (est): 5.3MM **Privately Held**
WEB: www.lassenland.com
SIC: 0762 Farm management services

(P-698)
MESA VINEYARD MANAGEMENT INC
2570 Prell Rd, Santa Maria (93454-9110)
P.O. Box 6565 (93456-6565)
PHONE.....................................805 925-7200
Callado Rodolfo, *Manager*
EMP: 75
SALES (corp-wide): 16.5MM **Privately Held**
SIC: 0762 Vineyard management & maintenance services
PA: Mesa Vineyard Management Inc
110 Gibson Rd
Templeton CA 93465
805 434-4100

(P-699)
MESA VINEYARD MANAGEMENT INC (PA)
110 Gibson Rd, Templeton (93465-9510)
P.O. Box 789 (93465-0789)
PHONE.....................................805 434-4100
Dana Merrill, *President*
EMP: 75
SQ FT: 3,200
SALES (est): 16.5MM **Privately Held**
SIC: 0762 Vineyard management & maintenance services

(P-700)
MITCHELL VINEYARDS LLC
Also Called: Mitchell Vineyard Management
1831 Sarahs Way, Saint Helena (94574-9506)
PHONE.....................................707 963-7050
Anthony B Mitchell,
EMP: 90
SALES (est): 5MM **Privately Held**
SIC: 0762 Vineyard management & maintenance services

(P-701)
MONTEREY PACIFIC INC (PA)
Also Called: McIntyre Vineyards
169 The Crossroads Blvd, Carmel (93923-8645)
PHONE.....................................831 678-4845
Steven McIntyre, *CEO*
Kimberly McIntyre, *Corp Secy*
Jackie King, *Sales Staff*
Sherry Richardson, *Manager*
Jackie Skinner, *Manager*
▲ EMP: 50
SQ FT: 3,000

SALES (est): 9.4MM **Privately Held**
WEB: www.montereypacific.com
SIC: 0762 Vineyard management & maintenance services

(P-702)
NEW CENTURY FARMS
1445 Jason Way, Santa Maria (93455-1011)
PHONE..........................805 928-2333
Griselda Landey, *President*
EMP: 50
SALES (est): 446.5K **Privately Held**
SIC: 0762 Farm management services

(P-703)
NISSEN VINEYARD SERVICES INC
1226 Spring St, Saint Helena (94574-2024)
PHONE..........................707 963-3480
Peter G Nissen, *President*
Anne Nissen, *Vice Pres*
EMP: 60
SQ FT: 1,760
SALES (est): 6.1MM **Privately Held**
SIC: 0762 Vineyard management & maintenance services

(P-704)
OXFORD FARMS INC
Also Called: Meyers Farming
901 N St Ste 103, Firebaugh (93622-2241)
P.O. Box 457 (93622-0457)
PHONE..........................559 659-3033
Marvin Meyers, *President*
Gregory Meyers, *Vice Pres*
EMP: 50
SQ FT: 250
SALES (est): 2.1MM **Privately Held**
SIC: 0762 Farm management services

(P-705)
P C A FARM MANAGEMENT LLC
1901 S Lexington St, Delano (93215-9207)
PHONE..........................661 720-2400
David Krause,
EMP: 700
SQ FT: 10,000
SALES (est): 5.7MM **Privately Held**
SIC: 0762 Farm management services

(P-706)
PENTERMAN FARMING CO INC
3851 Chiles Pope Vly Rd, Saint Helena (94574-9588)
PHONE..........................707 967-9977
Brian Penterman, *President*
EMP: 60
SALES (est): 3.4MM **Privately Held**
SIC: 0762 Farm management services

(P-707)
PEREZ CONTRACTING LLC
12620 Snow Rd, Bakersfield (93314-8021)
PHONE..........................661 399-2700
Fax: 805 239-8076
EMP: 150
SALES (est): 4.6MM **Privately Held**
SIC: 0762

(P-708)
PINA VINEYARD MANAGEMENT LLC
7960 Silverado Trl, NAPA (94558-9433)
P.O. Box 373, Oakville (94562-0373)
PHONE..........................707 944-2229
Davie Pina, *Owner*
Omar Cruz, *Human Resources*
EMP: 50
SQ FT: 290
SALES (est): 6.4MM **Privately Held**
WEB: www.pinavineyards.com
SIC: 0762 0723 2084 Vineyard management & maintenance services; crop preparation services for market; wines, brandy & brandy spirits

(P-709)
REDWOOD EMPIRE VINEYARD MGT
22000 Geyserville Ave, Geyserville (95441)
P.O. Box 729 (95441-0729)
PHONE..........................707 857-3401
Kevin W Barr, *President*
Nancy Barr, *Treasurer*

Linda Barr, *Corp Secy*
EMP: 100
SALES (est): 12.3MM **Privately Held**
WEB: www.revm.net
SIC: 0762 0172 Vineyard management & maintenance services; grapes

(P-710)
ROBERT YOUNG FAMILY LTD PARTNR
Also Called: Robert Young Vineyards
4950 Red Winery Rd, Geyserville (95441-9573)
PHONE..........................707 433-3228
Robert Young, *Partner*
Susan Sheehy, *Partner*
Fred Young, *Partner*
James Young, *Partner*
Joann Young, *Partner*
EMP: 60
SQ FT: 5,078
SALES (est): 3.3MM **Privately Held**
WEB: www.ryew.com
SIC: 0762 Vineyard management & maintenance services

(P-711)
ROTHFLEISCH RANCHES INC
129 S El Cerrito Dr, Brawley (92227-2203)
PHONE..........................760 344-1819
Joseph Rothfleisch, *President*
Kacie Cox, *Manager*
Allison Mainas, *Manager*
EMP: 60
SALES (est): 2.7MM **Privately Held**
SIC: 0762 Farm management services

(P-712)
SIERRA PACIFIC FARMS INC (PA)
Also Called: Somis Pacific AG Management
43406 Business Park Dr, Temecula (92590-5526)
P.O. Box 1537 (92593-1537)
PHONE..........................951 699-9980
Scott A McIntyre, *CEO*
Keri Calonder, *CFO*
Debbie McIntyre, *CFO*
EMP: 68
SQ FT: 3,000
SALES (est): 18.8MM **Privately Held**
SIC: 0762 Farm management services

(P-713)
SUN PACIFIC FARMING COOP INC (PA)
Also Called: Allied Farming Company
1250 E Myer Ave, Exeter (93221-9345)
P.O. Box 1125 (93221-7125)
PHONE..........................559 592-7121
Berne H Evans III, *President*
Bob Reniers, *Corp Secy*
Patty Richardson, *Office Spvr*
Mireya Zepeda, *Hum Res Coord*
Louis Biglieri, *Sales Staff*
EMP: 500
SQ FT: 70,000
SALES (est): 111.9MM **Privately Held**
SIC: 0762 Citrus grove management & maintenance services

(P-714)
T AND M AGRICULTURAL SVCS LLC
493 Dowdell Ln, Saint Helena (94574-1441)
P.O. Box 122 (94574-0122)
PHONE..........................707 963-3330
Samuel Turner,
Sam E Turner, *Sales Executive*
Dianne Martinez,
EMP: 120
SALES (est): 4.9MM **Privately Held**
SIC: 0762 Vineyard management & maintenance services

(P-715)
UNITED BIOSOURCE LLC
303 2nd St Ste S700, San Francisco (94107-3627)
PHONE..........................415 293-1340
Mike Borkowski, *Branch Mgr*
EMP: 80

SALES (corp-wide): 106.9MM **Privately Held**
SIC: 0762 Farm management services
PA: United Biosource Llc
920 Harvest Dr Ste 200
Blue Bell PA 19422
215 591-2880

(P-716)
VALLEY FARM MANAGEMENT INC
37500 Foothill Rd, Soledad (93960-9507)
PHONE..........................831 678-1592
Richard R Smith, *President*
Alice Smith, *Treasurer*
James E Smith, *Vice Pres*
Jason Smith, *Admin Sec*
EMP: 100
SQ FT: 2,880
SALES (est): 10.8MM **Privately Held**
SIC: 0762 Vineyard management & maintenance services

(P-717)
VIMARK INC
Also Called: Vimark Vineyards
19500 Geyserville Ave, Geyserville (95441-9310)
P.O. Box 576 (95441-0576)
PHONE..........................707 857-3588
Krishik Hicks, *Manager*
EMP: 60
SALES (corp-wide): 65.1MM **Privately Held**
SIC: 0762 Vineyard management & maintenance services
PA: Vimark, Inc.
101 D St Fl 2nd
Santa Rosa CA
707 542-3134

(P-718)
VINO FARMS INC (PA)
1377 E Lodi Ave, Lodi (95240-0840)
PHONE..........................209 334-6975
James D Ledbetter, *President*
John K Ledbetter, *Officer*
Kimberly Bronson, *Exec VP*
Craig Ledbetter, *Vice Pres*
Marissa Ledbetter, *Vice Pres*
EMP: 50
SQ FT: 6,000
SALES (est): 59.3MM **Privately Held**
SIC: 0762 8748 Vineyard management & maintenance services; agricultural consultant

(P-719)
VINO FARMS INC
10651 Eastside Rd, Healdsburg (95448-9490)
PHONE..........................707 433-8241
Roy Davis, *Manager*
EMP: 100
SALES (corp-wide): 59.3MM **Privately Held**
SIC: 0762 Vineyard management & maintenance services
PA: Vino Farms, Inc.
1377 E Lodi Ave
Lodi CA 95240
209 334-6975

(P-720)
VYBORNY VINEYARD MANAGEMENT
7327 Silverado Trl, Rutherford (94573)
P.O. Box 367 (94573-0367)
PHONE..........................707 944-9135
J Alex Vyborny, *President*
Thomas Gore, *Vice Pres*
James M Decker, *Admin Sec*
▲ **EMP:** 99
SQ FT: 16,000
SALES (est): 4.4MM **Privately Held**
WEB: www.vyborny.com
SIC: 0762 Vineyard management & maintenance services

(P-721)
WEST COAST GRAPE FARMING INC
800 E Keyes Rd, Ceres (95307-7539)
P.O. Box 488 (95307-0488)
PHONE..........................209 538-3131

Fred Franzia, *President*
John Franzia, *Vice Pres*
Joseph Franzia, *Admin Sec*
EMP: 2500
SQ FT: 2,093
SALES (est): 57.6MM **Privately Held**
SIC: 0762 Farm management services

(P-722)
WEST COTTON AG MANAGEMENT INC
15900 W Dorris, Huron (93234)
P.O. Box 10 (93234-0010)
PHONE..........................559 945-2511
Bob Anderson, *President*
Richard Anderson, *Ch of Bd*
Craig Anderson, *Admin Sec*
EMP: 200
SQ FT: 1,000
SALES (est): 4.4MM **Privately Held**
SIC: 0762 Farm management services

(P-723)
WHITE HILLS VINEYARD RANC
8385 Graciosa Rd, Santa Maria (93455-6105)
PHONE..........................805 934-1986
Dale Hampton, *President*
EMP: 58
SALES (est): 1.5MM **Privately Held**
SIC: 0762 Vineyard management & maintenance services

0781 Landscape Counseling & Planning

(P-724)
A GROWING CONCERN LANDSCAPES
17382 Gothard St, Huntington Beach (92647-6203)
PHONE..........................714 843-5137
Douglas Neal, *Owner*
EMP: 82
SALES (est): 5.5MM **Privately Held**
WEB: www.growingconcern.com
SIC: 0781 Landscape services

(P-725)
ABSHEAR LANDSCAPE DEVELOPMENT
3171b Rippey Rd, Loomis (95650-9504)
P.O. Box 1817 (95650-1817)
PHONE..........................916 660-1617
Barry Abshear, *Owner*
EMP: 50
SALES (est): 1.7MM **Privately Held**
WEB: www.abshearlandscapes.com
SIC: 0781 Landscape services

(P-726)
ALLIED LANDSCAPE SVCS S INC
5542 Monterey Hwy Ste 277, San Jose (95138-1529)
PHONE..........................408 310-8476
Filiberto Fonseca, *President*
Gino Borello, *Vice Pres*
EMP: 65
SALES (est): 1.1MM **Privately Held**
WEB: www.allied-1.com
SIC: 0781 Landscape services

(P-727)
AMERICAN LANDSCAPE INC
Also Called: American Golf Construction
7013 Owensmouth Ave, Canoga Park (91303-2006)
PHONE..........................818 999-2041
Gary Peterson, *President*
Pamela Edmiston, *Vice Pres*
Jamie Tsui, *Admin Sec*
Tim Dugan, *Project Mgr*
Sonia Hill, *Project Mgr*
▲ **EMP:** 250
SQ FT: 14,000
SALES (est): 31.7MM **Privately Held**
SIC: 0781 Landscape services

(P-728)
**AMERICAN LANDSCAPE
MANAGEMENT (PA)**
Also Called: Custom Lawn Services
7013 Owensmouth Ave, Canoga Park
(91303-2006)
PHONE.............................818 999-2041
Mickey Strauss, *President*
Gary Peterson, *Vice Pres*
Angelica Godfrey, *Info Tech Mgr*
EMP: 400
SQ FT: 14,000
SALES (est): 14.1MM **Privately Held**
SIC: 0781 Landscape services

(P-729)
**AMERINE SYSTEMS
INCORPORATED**
10866 Cleveland Ave, Oakdale
(95361-9709)
PHONE.............................209 847-5968
Gary Amerine, *President*
Ronald Amerine, *Admin Sec*
EMP: 50
SQ FT: 20,000
SALES (est): 6.1MM **Privately Held**
WEB: www.amerinesys.com
SIC: 0781 5084 5083 Landscape serv-
ices; pumps & pumping equipment; irriga-
tion equipment

(P-730)
BARAZANI OUTDOORS INC
14101 Valleyheart Dr # 104, Sherman Oaks
(91423-2864)
PHONE.............................818 701-6977
Aviva Barazani, *CEO*
Al Guadagno, *Principal*
EMP: 75
SALES (est): 2.4MM **Privately Held**
SIC: 0781 Landscape counseling & plan-
ning

(P-731)
**BELLAVISTA LANDSCAPE SVCS
INC**
340 Twin Pines Dr, Scotts Valley
(95066-3951)
PHONE.............................831 461-1761
Thomas Moore, *President*
Matt Moore, *VP Mktg*
EMP: 65
SQ FT: 4,000
SALES (est): 3.8MM **Privately Held**
SIC: 0781 Landscape services

(P-732)
BRIGHTVIEW COMPANIES LLC
2447 Stagecoach Rd, Stockton
(95215-7929)
PHONE.............................209 993-9277
EMP: 105
SALES (corp-wide): 2.8B **Publicly Held**
SIC: 0781 Landscape services
HQ: Brightview Companies, Llc
24151 Ventura Blvd
Calabasas CA 91302
818 223-8500

(P-733)
BRIGHTVIEW COMPANIES LLC
201 Longden Ave, Irwindale (91706-1329)
PHONE.............................626 574-3940
Richard Perder, *President*
EMP: 105
SALES (corp-wide): 2.8B **Publicly Held**
SIC: 0781 Landscape services
HQ: Brightview Companies, Llc
24151 Ventura Blvd
Calabasas CA 91302
818 223-8500

(P-734)
**BRIGHTVIEW LANDSCAPE DEV
INC (DH)**
24151 Ventura Blvd, Calabasas
(91302-1449)
PHONE.............................818 223-8500
Thomas Donnelly, *CEO*
Thomas C Donelly, *President*
Kenneth L Hutcheson, *President*
Andrew J Brennan, *COO*
Pamela L Stark, *Vice Pres*
◆ EMP: 50
SQ FT: 25,000

SALES (est): 755MM
SALES (est): 2.8B **Publicly Held**
SIC: 0781 Landscape counseling & plan-
ning
HQ: Brightview Companies, Llc
24151 Ventura Blvd
Calabasas CA 91302
818 223-8500

(P-735)
**BRIGHTVIEW LANDSCAPE DEV
INC**
1960 S Yale St, Santa Ana (92704-3929)
PHONE.............................714 546-7843
EMP: 54
SALES (corp-wide): 2.8B **Publicly Held**
SIC: 0781 Landscape services
HQ: Brightview Landscape Development,
Inc.
24151 Ventura Blvd
Calabasas CA 91302
818 223-8500

(P-736)
**BRIGHTVIEW LANDSCAPE
SVCS INC**
20551b Corsair Blvd, Hayward
(94545-1005)
PHONE.............................510 487-4826
Tom Stoutt, *Branch Mgr*
Tony Fargnoli, *Manager*
EMP: 50
SALES (corp-wide): 2.8B **Publicly Held**
SIC: 0781 Landscape services
HQ: Brightview Landscape Services, Inc.
24151 Ventura Blvd
Calabasas CA 91302
818 223-8500

(P-737)
**BRIGHTVIEW LANDSCAPE
SVCS INC**
8500 Miramar Pl, San Diego (92121-2530)
PHONE.............................858 458-1900
Patrick Ceatter, *Manager*
EMP: 200
SALES (corp-wide): 2.8B **Publicly Held**
SIC: 0781 Landscape services
HQ: Brightview Landscape Services, Inc.
24151 Ventura Blvd
Calabasas CA 91302
818 223-8500

(P-738)
**BRIGHTVIEW LANDSCAPE
SVCS INC**
4677 Pacheco Blvd, Martinez
(94553-3625)
PHONE.............................925 957-8831
Martin Becker, *Manager*
EMP: 80
SALES (corp-wide): 2.8B **Publicly Held**
SIC: 0781 Landscape services
HQ: Brightview Landscape Services, Inc.
24151 Ventura Blvd
Calabasas CA 91302
818 223-8500

(P-739)
**BRIGHTVIEW LANDSCAPE
SVCS INC**
1960 S Yale St, Santa Ana (92704-3929)
PHONE.............................714 546-7843
Dave Hanson, *Manager*
EMP: 100
SALES (corp-wide): 2.8B **Publicly Held**
SIC: 0781 0782 Landscape services; lawn
& garden services
HQ: Brightview Landscape Services, Inc.
24151 Ventura Blvd
Calabasas CA 91302
818 223-8500

(P-740)
**BRIGHTVIEW LANDSCAPE
SVCS INC**
5745 Alder Ave, Sacramento (95828-1107)
PHONE.............................916 381-2800
John Bianco, *Manager*
Lisa Stinhilver, *Office Mgr*
EMP: 100
SALES (corp-wide): 2.8B **Publicly Held**
SIC: 0781 Landscape services

HQ: Brightview Landscape Services, Inc.
24151 Ventura Blvd
Calabasas CA 91302
818 223-8500

(P-741)
**BRIGHTVIEW LANDSCAPE
SVCS INC**
7039 Commerce Cir Ste B, Pleasanton
(94588-8006)
PHONE.............................925 924-8900
Doug Lape, *Manager*
Leonel Vasquez, *Manager*
EMP: 80
SALES (corp-wide): 2.8B **Publicly Held**
SIC: 0781 0782 Landscape services; lawn
& garden services
HQ: Brightview Landscape Services, Inc.
24151 Ventura Blvd
Calabasas CA 91302
818 223-8500

(P-742)
**BRIGHTVIEW LANDSCAPE
SVCS INC**
17813 S Main St Ste 105, Gardena
(90248-3542)
PHONE.............................310 327-8700
Andrea Musick, *Manager*
Tim Gravatt, *Accounts Mgr*
Uriel Rojas, *Accounts Mgr*
Tom Cutrono, *Contractor*
Manuel Bribiesca, *Supervisor*
EMP: 110
SQ FT: 1,530
SALES (corp-wide): 2.8B **Publicly Held**
SIC: 0781 0782 Landscape services; land-
scape contractors
HQ: Brightview Landscape Services, Inc.
24151 Ventura Blvd
Calabasas CA 91302
818 223-8500

(P-743)
**BRIGHTVIEW LANDSCAPES
LLC**
2420 Cougar Dr, Carlsbad (92010-8804)
PHONE.............................760 438-3551
Trey Dupont, *Manager*
EMP: 100
SALES (corp-wide): 2.8B **Publicly Held**
SIC: 0781 Landscape services
HQ: Brightview Landscapes, Llc
401 Plymouth Rd Ste 500
Plymouth Meeting PA 19462
484 567-7204

(P-744)
**BRIGHTVIEW LANDSCAPES
LLC**
9090 Birch St, Spring Valley (91977-4107)
PHONE.............................619 644-8584
Larry Neuhoff, *Manager*
EMP: 80
SALES (corp-wide): 2.8B **Publicly Held**
SIC: 0781 Landscape services
HQ: Brightview Landscapes, Llc
401 Plymouth Rd Ste 500
Plymouth Meeting PA 19462
484 567-7204

(P-745)
CICILEO LANDSCAPES
4565 Hollister Ave, Santa Barbara
(93110-1709)
P.O. Box 60912 (93160-0912)
PHONE.............................805 967-3939
Michael J Cicileo, *President*
EMP: 50
SALES (est): 4.4MM **Privately Held**
WEB: www.cicileolandscapes.com
SIC: 0781 0782 Landscape planning serv-
ices; garden maintenance services

(P-746)
**COASTAL MIRAGE
LANDSCAPES**
26362 Via De Anza, San Juan Capistrano
(92675-4723)
PHONE.............................949 496-7070
Joe A Malagon, *President*
Rachel Malagon, *Vice Pres*
EMP: 60
SQ FT: 700

SALES (est): 2.6MM **Privately Held**
WEB: www.coastalmirage.com
SIC: 0781 Landscape services

(P-747)
**COMET BUILDING
MAINTENANCE INC**
21 Commercial Blvd Ste 12, Novato
(94949-6109)
P.O. Box 2163, San Rafael (94912-2163)
PHONE.............................415 383-1035
Richard J Brasile, *CEO*
EMP: 70
SQ FT: 1,800
SALES (est): 4.9MM **Privately Held**
SIC: 0781 7349 Landscape services; jani-
torial service, contract basis

(P-748)
COMMERCIAL LANDSCAPE SVC
1821 Reynolds Ave, Irvine (92614-5713)
PHONE.............................949 660-8655
Mark Fitt, *President*
Joann Fitt, *Corp Secy*
Tim Skeen, *Vice Pres*
EMP: 91
SQ FT: 8,400
SALES (est): 2.1MM **Privately Held**
SIC: 0781 Landscape services

(P-749)
**DESERT CNCPTS LDSCPG
MAINT INC**
79469 Country Club Dr I, Bermuda Dunes
(92203-1206)
PHONE.............................760 200-9007
Julio Castro, *President*
Frank Castro, *Vice Pres*
EMP: 120
SQ FT: 1,100
SALES (est): 3.4MM **Privately Held**
WEB: www.desertconcepts.net
SIC: 0781 Landscape services

(P-750)
DL LONG LANDSCAPING INC
5475 G St, Chino (91710-5233)
PHONE.............................909 628-5531
David L Long, *President*
EMP: 100
SQ FT: 1,550
SALES: 6.9MM **Privately Held**
WEB: www.dllong.com
SIC: 0781 Landscape architects

(P-751)
**DREAMSCAPE LDSCP & MAINT
INC**
7192 Mission Gorge Rd, San Diego
(92120-1131)
PHONE.............................619 583-4439
Thomas Bjorstrom, *President*
Katie Wallace, *Purchasing*
Jayme Wessels, *Opers Staff*
EMP: 50
SQ FT: 1,200
SALES (est): 3.9MM **Privately Held**
SIC: 0781 0782 Landscape planning serv-
ices; landscape contractors

(P-752)
EDAW INC
401 W A St Ste 1200, San Diego
(92101-7905)
PHONE.............................619 233-1454
Michael Downs, *Branch Mgr*
EMP: 80
SALES (corp-wide): 20.1B **Publicly Held**
WEB: www.edaw.com
SIC: 0781 8748 8712 Landscape coun-
seling & planning; business consulting;
architectural services
HQ: Edaw, Inc.
300 California St Fl 5
San Francisco CA 94104
415 955-2800

(P-753)
EDAW INC
2020 L St Ste 400, Sacramento
(95811-4267)
PHONE.............................916 414-5800
Curtis Alling, *Manager*
Joy Woo, *VP Sales*
EMP: 100

SALES (corp-wide): 20.1B **Publicly Held**
WEB: www.edaw.com
SIC: 0781 8711 8712 8748 Landscape architects; engineering services; architectural services; business consulting
HQ: Edaw, Inc.
300 California St Fl 5
San Francisco CA 94104
415 955-2800

(P-754)
ELS INVESTMENTS
Also Called: Environmental Ldscp Solutions
9980 Horn Rd, Sacramento (95827-1905)
PHONE..................916 388-0308
Darryl Alan Thompson Jr, *President*
Shawna Thompson, *Vice Pres*
EMP: 110 EST: 2008
SQ FT: 7,200
SALES (est): 16.3MM **Privately Held**
SIC: 0781 1771 Landscape services; concrete work

(P-755)
FC LANDSCAPE INC
43216 Madison St, Indio (92201-1944)
PHONE..................760 347-6600
Francisco Corona, *President*
EMP: 75
SALES (est): 2.7MM **Privately Held**
SIC: 0781 Landscape services

(P-756)
GARDEN VIEW INC
417 E Huntington Dr, Monrovia
(91016-3632)
PHONE..................626 303-4043
Mark Meahl, *President*
EMP: 50
SQ FT: 1,500
SALES (est): 4MM **Privately Held**
SIC: 0781 0782 Landscape architects; garden services; landscape contractors

(P-757)
GOTHIC LANDSCAPING INC
Also Called: Gothic Grounds Mgmt
27413 Tourney Rd Ste 200, Valencia
(91355-5606)
PHONE..................661 257-5085
Ron Georgio, *President*
EMP: 500
SALES (corp-wide): 143.4MM **Privately Held**
WEB: www.gothiclandscape.com
SIC: 0781 0782 Landscape services; lawn & garden services
PA: Gothic Landscaping, Inc.
27502 Avenue Scott
Valencia CA 91355
661 257-1266

(P-758)
HAROLD JONES LANDSCAPE INC
530 New Los Angeles Ave, Moorpark
(93021-2081)
PHONE..................805 582-7443
Constance Wilson, *President*
EMP: 50
SALES (est): 3.9MM **Privately Held**
SIC: 0781 Landscape counseling & planning

(P-759)
HART HOWERTON LTD (PA)
1 Union St Fl 3, San Francisco
(94111-1223)
PHONE..................415 439-2200
Dave Howerton, *CEO*
Roland Aberg, *Vice Pres*
Diane Nielson, *Executive Asst*
Anne Haley Howerton, *Admin Sec*
Tony Hwang, *Info Tech Mgr*
EMP: 90
SQ FT: 20,000
SALES (est): 10.1MM **Privately Held**
SIC: 0781 8712 Landscape architects; architectural services

(P-760)
HERITAGE LANDSCAPE INC
7949 Deering Ave, Canoga Park
(91304-5009)
PHONE..................818 999-2041
William Leighton Knell, *President*

EMP: 130
SALES (est): 2.8MM **Privately Held**
SIC: 0781 0782 Landscape services; landscape contractors

(P-761)
HUPPE LANDSCAPE COMPANY INC (HQ)
9350 Viking Pl, Roseville (95747-9713)
PHONE..................916 784-7666
Chris Huppe, *President*
Gina Huppe, *Admin Sec*
EMP: 68
SQ FT: 215,000
SALES (est): 6.7MM
SALES (corp-wide): 115.4MM **Privately Held**
SIC: 0781 0782 Horticulture services; lawn & garden services
PA: Jensen Corporate Holdings, Inc.
1983 Concourse Dr
San Jose CA 95131
408 446-1118

(P-762)
I PWLC INC
408 Olive Ave, Vista (92083-3438)
P.O. Box 3557 (92085-3557)
PHONE..................760 630-0231
Richard Ruiz, *CEO*
Erika Roa, *Administration*
EMP: 90
SQ FT: 1,000
SALES (est): 4.6MM **Privately Held**
SIC: 0781 Landscape services

(P-763)
KEVIN PERSONS INC
Also Called: Ground Maintenance Services
2977 Los Feliz Dr, Thousand Oaks
(91362-3411)
P.O. Box 879, Newbury Park (91319-0879)
PHONE..................805 371-8746
Kevin Persons, *President*
EMP: 50
SALES (est): 5MM **Privately Held**
SIC: 0781 Landscape services

(P-764)
LAZAR LANDSCAPE DESIGN & CNSTR
2884 Ettie St, Oakland (94608-4009)
PHONE..................510 444-5195
Pam Cosce, *President*
Asa Sanchez, *CFO*
EMP: 55
SALES (est): 2.6MM **Privately Held**
WEB: www.lazarlandscape.com
SIC: 0781 7389 Landscape services; design services

(P-765)
LIBERTY LANDSCAPING INC
5212 El Rivino Rd, Riverside (92509-1807)
PHONE..................951 683-2999
Alejandro Casillas, *President*
Rose Casillas, *Vice Pres*
EMP: 100 EST: 1998
SALES: 7.7MM **Privately Held**
SIC: 0781 Landscape services

(P-766)
MALIBU CANYON LDSCP & MAINT
2046 Tierra Rejada Rd, Moorpark
(93021-9769)
PHONE..................805 523-2676
David S Bateman, *President*
D Brooke Bateman, *CFO*
Lee A Tarbet, *Admin Sec*
EMP: 55
SQ FT: 1,500
SALES (est): 1.9MM **Privately Held**
WEB: www.malibulandscape.com
SIC: 0781 Landscape services

(P-767)
MARINA LANDSCAPE INC
3707 W Garden Grove Blvd, Orange
(92868-4803)
PHONE..................714 939-6600
Robert B Cowan, *Manager*
EMP: 60

SALES (corp-wide): 63.9MM **Privately Held**
SIC: 0781 Landscape services
PA: Marina Landscape, Inc.
3707 W Garden Grove Blvd
Orange CA 92868
714 939-6600

(P-768)
MARINA LANDSCAPE MAINT INC
1900 S Lewis St, Anaheim (92805-6718)
PHONE..................714 939-6600
Robert B Cowan, *CEO*
EMP: 450
SALES (est): 68.1K
SALES (corp-wide): 2.8B **Publicly Held**
SIC: 0781 Landscape services
HQ: Brightview Landscapes, Llc
401 Plymouth Rd Ste 500
Plymouth Meeting PA 19462
484 567-7204

(P-769)
MASUDAS LANDSCAPE SERVICES
423 Salmar Ave, Campbell (95008-1413)
PHONE..................408 379-7100
Ken Masuda, *Owner*
EMP: 100
SALES (est): 7.2MM **Privately Held**
SIC: 0781 Landscape architects

(P-770)
MEDALLION LANDSCAPE MGT INC (PA)
10 San Bruno Ave, Morgan Hill
(95037-9214)
P.O. Box 1768 (95038-1768)
PHONE..................408 782-7500
John Gates, *CEO*
Joyce Dawson, *President*
Roger Green, *President*
Ildefonso Fonsie Bettencourt, *COO*
Robert Rosenberg, *CFO*
EMP: 65
SALES (est): 25.2MM **Privately Held**
WEB: www.mlmi.com
SIC: 0781 Landscape counseling services; landscape planning services

(P-771)
NATURES IMAGE INC
20361 Hermana Cir, Lake Forest
(92630-8701)
PHONE..................949 680-4400
Michelle M Caruana, *CEO*
John Caruana, *Vice Pres*
Sara Koenig, *Administration*
Dan Slinger, *Analyst*
Isabel Castillo, *Human Resources*
EMP: 95
SQ FT: 13,800
SALES (est): 9.4MM **Privately Held**
WEB: www.naturesimage.net
SIC: 0781 0782 Landscape services; landscape contractors

(P-772)
OUTSIDE LINES INC
2150 S Towne Cntre Pl 1, Anaheim (92806)
PHONE..................714 637-4747
John Wickham Zimmerman, *CEO*
Hugh F Hughes, *President*
EMP: 50
SALES (est): 13.5MM **Privately Held**
WEB: www.otl-inc.com
SIC: 0781 Landscape counseling & planning

(P-773)
PACHECO BROTHERS GARDENING INC (PA)
20973 Cabot Blvd, Hayward (94545-1155)
PHONE..................510 732-6330
George A Pacheco Jr, *CEO*
Lynn Pacheco, *Corp Secy*
Gary Pacheco, *Vice Pres*
EMP: 90
SQ FT: 12,000
SALES (est): 13.8MM **Privately Held**
WEB: www.pachecobrothers.com
SIC: 0781 0782 Landscape services; landscape contractors

(P-774)
PACIFIC COAST LDSCP MGT INC
3960 Holway Dr, Byron (94514)
P.O. Box 757 (94514-0757)
PHONE..................925 513-2310
Alvaro Beltran, *President*
Robin Rowley, *Office Mgr*
EMP: 60
SALES (est): 6.8MM **Privately Held**
WEB: www.pacificcoastlandscape.net
SIC: 0781 0782 Landscape services; lawn & garden services; garden services; landscape contractors

(P-775)
PACIFIC RESTORATION GROUP INC
325 E Ellis Ave, Perris (92570-8413)
P.O. Box 429 (92572-0429)
PHONE..................951 940-6069
John Richards, *President*
Daniel Richards, *CFO*
Patricia Richards, *Admin Sec*
EMP: 50
SQ FT: 10,000
SALES (est): 4.7MM **Privately Held**
SIC: 0781 Landscape services

(P-776)
PARKER LANDSCAPE DEV INC
6011 Franklin Blvd, Sacramento
(95824-2517)
PHONE..................916 383-4071
Timothy J Parker, *President*
Conney Parker, *Admin Sec*
EMP: 50
SALES (est): 4.6MM **Privately Held**
SIC: 0781 Landscape services

(P-777)
PIERRE LANDSCAPE INC
5455 2nd St, Irwindale (91706-2072)
PHONE..................818 373-0023
Harold Young, *CEO*
Joseph Lowden, *President*
Monty Khouri, *CFO*
Seana Smith, *Vice Pres*
Scott Horner, *Project Mgr*
EMP: 200
SQ FT: 9,425
SALES (est): 26.6MM **Privately Held**
SIC: 0781 Landscape architects; landscape services

(P-778)
PLATINUM LANDSCAPE INC
42575 Melanie Pl Ste C, Palm Desert
(92211-5162)
PHONE..................760 200-3673
Christopher Johnson, *President*
Cherie Johnson, *Vice Pres*
EMP: 150
SQ FT: 3,000
SALES: 18MM **Privately Held**
WEB: www.platinumlandscape.com
SIC: 0781 Landscape services

(P-779)
PRO PONDS WEST INC
Also Called: Pacific Outdoor Living
8309 Tujunga Ave Unit 201, Sun Valley
(91352-3216)
PHONE..................818 244-4000
Terry Morrill, *CEO*
Jerry McMahon, *Principal*
EMP: 100
SALES (est): 3.2MM **Privately Held**
SIC: 0781 Landscape services

(P-780)
PROFESSNL LDSCP SOLUTIONS INC
6108 27th St Ste C, Sacramento
(95822-3711)
PHONE..................916 424-3815
Michael E Parker, *President*
Chad Bush, *Vice Pres*
Penny Parker, *Admin Sec*
EMP: 50
SQ FT: 11,000
SALES (est): 3.2MM **Privately Held**
SIC: 0781 Landscape services

(P-781)
RANCHO DEL ORO LDSCP MAINT INC
4167 Avenida De La Plata, Oceanside (92056-6032)
P.O. Box 4608 (92052-4608)
PHONE..........................760 726-0215
Uriel Espinoza, *President*
Richard Kirk, *CFO*
Albertano Cardenas, *Vice Pres*
EMP: 73
SQ FT: 1,400
SALES (est): 4.2MM **Privately Held**
WEB: www.rancho.sdcoxmail.com
SIC: 0781 Landscape services

(P-782)
RICH MEIERS LANDSCAPING INC (PA)
652 W Avenue L14, Lancaster (93534-7135)
P.O. Box 3327 (93586-0327)
PHONE..........................661 723-2220
Richard A Meier, *President*
Annamarie Meier, *Vice Pres*
EMP: 80
SALES: 3.9MM **Privately Held**
SIC: 0781 Landscape services

(P-783)
ROCKEY MURATA LANDSCAPING
15417 Cornet St, Santa Fe Springs (90670-5533)
PHONE..........................562 921-3210
Rockey Murata, *President*
Andie Murata, *Corp Secy*
EMP: 60 **EST:** 1951
SQ FT: 10,000
SALES (est): 3.3MM **Privately Held**
SIC: 0781 Landscape services

(P-784)
SAN DIEGO LAND SYSTEMS
8720 Miramar Pl, San Diego (92121-2551)
PHONE..........................858 558-0542
Stewart C Frederick, *President*
Yevette Deboer, *Executive*
Kari Conradie, *Project Mgr*
Damon Follen, *Opers Mgr*
Matt Shaffer, *Opers Mgr*
EMP: 50
SQ FT: 11,700
SALES (est): 5.3MM **Privately Held**
WEB: www.landsystems.biz
SIC: 0781 Landscape services

(P-785)
SAN VAL CORP (PA)
Also Called: San Val Alarm System
72203 Adelaid St, Thousand Palms (92276-2321)
P.O. Box 12860, Palm Desert (92255-2860)
PHONE..........................760 346-3999
Robert L Sandifer, *President*
Carolina Felix, *Office Mgr*
Sharon L Sandifer, *Admin Sec*
EMP: 425
SALES (est): 32.8MM **Privately Held**
WEB: www.cvwebs.com
SIC: 0781 7381 Landscape services; burglary protection service

(P-786)
SEQUOIA ENVIRONMENTAL SVCS INC
1 University Dr, Aliso Viejo (92656-8081)
PHONE..........................949 480-4742
Danny McNamara, *CEO*
Scott Collins, *Treasurer*
Wendy Chen, *Office Mgr*
Malcolm Thomas, *Admin Sec*
EMP: 64
SALES (est): 2.5MM **Privately Held**
SIC: 0781 7349 Landscape services; janitorial service, contract basis

(P-787)
SHOOTER & BUTTS INC
3768 Old Santa Rita Rd, Pleasanton (94588-3457)
PHONE..........................925 460-5155
James E Butts, *President*
Richard Kusaba, *Project Mgr*

Keith Hollon, *Manager*
EMP: 50
SQ FT: 1,800
SALES (est): 5.1MM **Privately Held**
WEB: www.shooterandbutts.com
SIC: 0781 Landscape services

(P-788)
SIERRA LANDSCAPE & MAINTENANCE
546 Hickory St, Chico (95928-4811)
PHONE..........................530 895-0263
Catherine S Gurney, *Principal*
Syndi Winter, *Administration*
EMP: 52
SQ FT: 8,000
SALES (est): 4.7MM **Privately Held**
WEB: www.sierralandscapeinc.com
SIC: 0781 Landscape services

(P-789)
SLADE INDUSTRIAL LANDSCAPE INC
8838 Zelzah Ave, Sherwood Forest (91325-3139)
P.O. Box 571960, Tarzana (91357-1960)
PHONE..........................818 885-1916
David Slade, *President*
Sylvia Slade, *Corp Secy*
Jesse Slade, *Vice Pres*
EMP: 55
SALES (est): 4.4MM **Privately Held**
SIC: 0781 0782 Landscape planning services; landscape contractors; garden maintenance services; lawn services

(P-790)
SWA GROUP (PA)
2200 Bridgeway, Sausalito (94965-1750)
P.O. Box 5904 (94966-5904)
PHONE..........................415 332-5100
Gerdo Aquino, *CEO*
Kevin Shanley, *President*
Lawrence Reed, *CEO*
Scott Cooper, *CFO*
Jessica Reyes, *Admin Mgr*
EMP: 200 **EST:** 1957
SQ FT: 12,000
SALES (est): 21.6MM **Privately Held**
SIC: 0781 Landscape architects

(P-791)
TERRA PACIFIC LANDSCAPE (HQ)
1627 E Wilshire Ave, Santa Ana (92705-4504)
PHONE..........................714 567-0177
Rich Wingard, *President*
Wendy Garcia, *Administration*
Brenda Polk, *Manager*
EMP: 89
SQ FT: 6,000
SALES (est): 26.7MM
SALES (corp-wide): 143.4MM **Privately Held**
WEB: www.terrapac.com
SIC: 0781 Landscape services
PA: Gothic Landscaping, Inc.
27502 Avenue Scott
Valencia CA 91355
661 257-1266

(P-792)
VALENCIA TREE LANDSCAPE
321 N Quarantina St, Santa Barbara (93103-3228)
P.O. Box 4554 (93140-4554)
PHONE..........................805 965-4244
Rossendo Valencia, *Owner*
EMP: 50
SALES (est): 1.7MM **Privately Held**
SIC: 0781 Landscape services

(P-793)
VALLEYCREST LDSCP MAINT VCC
24121 Ventura Blvd, Calabasas (91302-1449)
PHONE..........................800 466-8510
Jon Pinkus, *President*
Aaron Pinkus, *Vice Pres*
Lillian Pinkus, *Vice Pres*
Tom Powell, *Vice Pres*
Po-Sun Chen, *Managing Dir*
EMP: 50 **EST:** 1951

SQ FT: 6,000
SALES (est): 3.6MM
SALES (corp-wide): 8.7MM **Privately Held**
SIC: 0781 Landscape services
PA: Nortex Wholesale Nursery, Inc.
7700 Northaven Rd
Dallas TX 75230
214 363-6715

0782 Lawn & Garden Svcs

(P-794)
AD LAND VENTURE LP
3217 Fitzgerald Rd, Rancho Cordova (95742-6813)
P.O. Box 65, Folsom (95763-0065)
PHONE..........................916 853-9015
Gregory Houck, *Partner*
EMP: 100
SQ FT: 8,000
SALES: 14MM **Privately Held**
SIC: 0782 Landscape contractors

(P-795)
ALL COMMERCIAL LANDSCAPE SVC
5213 E Pine Ave, Fresno (93727-2110)
PHONE..........................559 453-1670
Jack Murray, *President*
Carol Osborn, *Corp Secy*
Tom Delny, *Vice Pres*
EMP: 50
SQ FT: 22,500
SALES (est): 4.7MM **Privately Held**
WEB: www.acls.bz
SIC: 0782 Landscape contractors; lawn services

(P-796)
ALVIZIA LANDSCAPE CO LLC
2520 Cactus Rd, San Diego (92154-8009)
PHONE..........................619 661-6557
Jose Alexander Jr, *President*
Velda Pacheco, *Vice Pres*
EMP: 160
SQ FT: 1,151
SALES (est): 6.6MM **Privately Held**
SIC: 0782 Landscape contractors

(P-797)
AMERICAN LANDSCAPE MANAGEMENT
Also Called: Custom Lawn Services
1607 Los Angeles Ave I, Ventura (93004-3237)
PHONE..........................805 647-5077
Armondo Bello, *Manager*
EMP: 50
SALES (est): 747.7K **Privately Held**
SIC: 0782 0783 0781 Landscape contractors; ornamental shrub & tree services; landscape planning services
PA: American Landscape Management Inc
7013 Owensmouth Ave
Canoga Park CA 91303

(P-798)
ARAGON COMMERCIAL LDSCPG INC
2305 S Vasco Rd, Livermore (94550-9681)
PHONE..........................408 998-0600
Scott Tabler, *President*
Julie Tabler, *Manager*
EMP: 135
SQ FT: 7,000
SALES (est): 8.5MM **Privately Held**
SIC: 0782 0781 Landscape contractors; landscape services

(P-799)
ARREOLAS COMPLETE LDSCP SVC
Also Called: Arreolas Complete Ldscp Svc
8671 Morrison Creek Dr # 100, Sacramento (95828-1862)
PHONE..........................916 387-6777
Humberto Arreola, *Owner*
EMP: 50
SQ FT: 10,000
SALES (est): 2.4MM **Privately Held**
SIC: 0782 Lawn & garden services

(P-800)
ARTISTIC MAINTENANCE INC
603 S Milliken Ave Ste A, Ontario (91761-8102)
PHONE..........................909 390-5156
Monica Sanchez, *Manager*
EMP: 65
SALES (corp-wide): 26.3MM **Privately Held**
SIC: 0782 Garden maintenance services; lawn care services
HQ: Artistic Maintenance, Inc.
15510 Rockfield Blvd C200
Irvine CA 92618
949 581-9817

(P-801)
ARTISTIC MAINTENANCE INC
16092 Construction Cir E, Irvine (92606-4401)
PHONE..........................949 733-8690
Rudy Moracco, *Manager*
EMP: 150
SALES (corp-wide): 26.3MM **Privately Held**
SIC: 0782 Landscape contractors; garden maintenance services
HQ: Artistic Maintenance, Inc.
15510 Rockfield Blvd C200
Irvine CA 92618
949 581-9817

(P-802)
AZTEC LANDSCAPING INC (PA)
7980 Lemon Grove Way, Lemon Grove (91945-1820)
PHONE..........................619 464-3303
Genaro Garcia, *President*
Rafael Aguilar, *Treasurer*
Ramon Aguilar, *Vice Pres*
Ramon E Aguilar, *Vice Pres*
EMP: 220
SQ FT: 30,000
SALES (est): 22.5MM **Privately Held**
WEB: www.azteclandscaping.com
SIC: 0782 0783 7349 Landscape contractors; ornamental shrub & tree services; janitorial service, contract basis

(P-803)
BENCHMARK LANDSCAPE INC
12575 Stowe Dr, Poway (92064-6805)
PHONE..........................858 513-7190
John A Mohns, *President*
Sharon R Mohns, *Admin Sec*
EMP: 220
SQ FT: 18,000
SALES (est): 24.1MM **Privately Held**
WEB: www.benchmarklandscape.com
SIC: 0782 Landscape contractors

(P-804)
BENNETT ENTERPRISES A CA
Also Called: Bennett Landscape
25889 Belle Porte Ave, Harbor City (90710-3393)
PHONE..........................310 534-3543
Sean Bennett, *President*
Joe B Manalastas, *Manager*
EMP: 90
SQ FT: 10,500
SALES (est): 6.6MM **Privately Held**
SIC: 0782 Landscape contractors

(P-805)
BLOSSOM VALLEY CNSTR INC
1125 Mabury Rd, San Jose (95133-1029)
P.O. Box 611537 (95161-1537)
PHONE..........................408 993-0766
Mark Collishaw, *President*
Robert Jimenez, *CEO*
EMP: 60
SQ FT: 5,000
SALES (est): 5MM **Privately Held**
SIC: 0782 Landscape contractors

(P-806)
C J VANDERGEEST LDSCP CARE INC
2476 Palma Dr Ste G, Ventura (93003-5760)
PHONE..........................805 650-0726
Joanne Smith, *President*
Dusty Smith, *Vice Pres*
EMP: 84
SQ FT: 2,000

P R O D U C T S & S V C S

SALES (est): 3.8MM **Privately Held**
SIC: 0782 Landscape contractors

(P-807)
CACHO LANDSCAPE MAINTENANCE CO
711 Truman St, San Fernando
(91340-3314)
P.O. Box 922764, Sylmar (91392-2764)
PHONE..........................818 365-0773
Eddie Cacho, *President*
Diana Cacho, *CFO*
Genaro Gutierrez, *Vice Pres*
EMP: 50
SQ FT: 3,184
SALES (est): 3MM **Privately Held**
SIC: 0782 Landscape contractors

(P-808)
CAL-WEST NURSERIES INC
138 North Dr, Norco (92860-1637)
PHONE..........................951 270-0667
Michael Whiting, *President*
Marc Keck, *Project Mgr*
Steve Sidwell, *Project Mgr*
Matt Whiting, *Purch Agent*
Jerry Gonzalez, *Maint Spvr*
EMP: 150
SQ FT: 1,700
SALES (est): 14.9MM **Privately Held**
WEB: www.calwestlandscape.com
SIC: 0782 0181 Landscape contractors; nursery stock, growing of

(P-809)
CALIFORNIA LDSCP & DESIGN INC
Also Called: CA Landscape and Design
273 N Benson Ave, Upland (91786-5614)
PHONE..........................909 949-1601
Joseph Ciaglia Jr, *CEO*
Margaret Mingura, *CFO*
Robert Luna, *Technology*
Andres Olguin, *Technology*
EMP: 120
SQ FT: 1,500
SALES (est): 21MM **Privately Held**
WEB: www.callandscape.com
SIC: 0782 Landscape contractors

(P-810)
CENTRESCAPES INC
165 Gentry St, Pomona (91767-2184)
PHONE..........................909 392-3303
Mark Marcus, *President*
Grace Loya, *Corp Secy*
EMP: 88
SQ FT: 7,000
SALES (est): 6.9MM **Privately Held**
WEB: www.centrescapes.com
SIC: 0782 Landscape contractors

(P-811)
CHAMPAGNE LANDSCAPE NURS INC
3233 N Cornelia Ave, Fresno (93722-4606)
P.O. Box 9755 (93794-9755)
PHONE..........................559 277-8188
Robert Champagne, *President*
Gail Champagne, *Treasurer*
Robert N Champagne, *Vice Pres*
Courtney Woody, *Admin Sec*
EMP: 87
SALES (est): 5.3MM **Privately Held**
SIC: 0782 0781 Garden maintenance services; landscape architects

(P-812)
CIELO AZUL INC
Also Called: Blue Skies Landscape Maint
1545 Lake Dr, Encinitas (92024-5224)
PHONE..........................855 863-8503
Pedro Navarro Jr, *President*
Natali Navarro, *Treasurer*
Julie Navarro, *Admin Sec*
EMP: 75
SALES (est): 4.2MM **Privately Held**
WEB: www.blueskieslandscape.com
SIC: 0782 Landscape contractors

(P-813)
CITY II ENTERPRISES INC
Also Called: Flora Terra Landscape MGT
845 Earle Ave, San Jose (95126-3404)
PHONE..........................408 275-1200

Gene E Ebertowski, *President*
Kimberly Garcia, *Admin Sec*
EMP: 50
SQ FT: 40,000
SALES (est): 3MM **Privately Held**
WEB: www.floraterra.com
SIC: 0782 Landscape contractors

(P-814)
COHEN RICHARD LDSCP & CNSTR
20795 Canada Rd, El Toro (92630-7702)
PHONE..........................949 768-0599
Richard Cohen, *President*
Linda Cohen, *Treasurer*
EMP: 50 **EST:** 1976
SQ FT: 1,000
SALES (est): 2.2MM **Privately Held**
WEB: www.richardcohenlandscape.com
SIC: 0782 Landscape contractors

(P-815)
COMPLETE LANDSCAPE CARE INC
13316 Leffingwell Rd, Whittier
(90605-4136)
PHONE..........................562 946-4441
Tom Murray, *President*
EMP: 57
SQ FT: 26,000
SALES (est): 5MM **Privately Held**
WEB: www.completelandscapecareinc.com
SIC: 0782 1711 Landscape contractors; irrigation sprinkler system installation

(P-816)
D & H LANDSCAPING INC
4221 Appian Way, El Sobrante
(94803-2203)
P.O. Box 57, Pinole (94564-0057)
PHONE..........................510 223-6597
David Treas, *President*
EMP: 60
SALES (est): 4.7MM **Privately Held**
WEB: www.dandhlandscaping.com
SIC: 0782 0781 Lawn care services; landscape planning services

(P-817)
D AND S LANDSCAPING INC
26901 Hansen Rd, Tracy (95377-8847)
PHONE..........................925 455-4630
Ben Hansen, *Principal*
EMP: 130
SALES (est): 5.3MM **Privately Held**
SIC: 0782 Landscape contractors

(P-818)
DANS LANDSCAPE SERVICE INC
718 Aleppo St, Newport Beach
(92660-4122)
PHONE..........................714 241-9591
Dan Seminario, *President*
Myrna Seminario, *Vice Pres*
EMP: 65
SQ FT: 16,000
SALES (est): 3.3MM **Privately Held**
WEB: www.danslandscapeservice.com
SIC: 0782 Lawn & garden services

(P-819)
DAVID OLLIS LANDSCAPE DEV INC
450 Kansas St Ste 104, Redlands
(92373-1481)
PHONE..........................909 307-1911
David Ollis, *President*
EMP: 50
SALES (est): 3.8MM **Privately Held**
WEB: www.davidollis.com
SIC: 0782 Landscape contractors

(P-820)
DE LA TORRE LANDSCAPE & MAINT
656 Paseo Grande, Corona (92882-2837)
P.O. Box 3018 (92878-3018)
PHONE..........................951 549-3525
Robert De La Torre, *President*
Socorro De La Torre, *Vice Pres*
Veronica De La Torre, *Admin Sec*
Veronica Dela Torre, *Controller*
EMP: 230
SQ FT: 1,108

SALES (est): 9.3MM **Privately Held**
SIC: 0782 Landscape contractors

(P-821)
DECKER LANDSCAPING INC
13265 Bill Francis Dr, Auburn
(95603-9022)
PHONE..........................916 652-1780
Christopher Decker, *President*
Dan McElvin, *CFO*
Tom Decker, *Vice Pres*
EMP: 75
SQ FT: 2,500
SALES (est): 7.9MM **Privately Held**
SIC: 0782 0781 Landscape contractors; landscape architects

(P-822)
DEL CONTES LANDSCAPING INC
41900 Boscell Rd, Fremont (94538-3196)
PHONE..........................510 353-6030
Tom Del Conte, *CEO*
Amy Pacheco, *CFO*
Mario Camacho, *Division Mgr*
John Soriano, *Facilities Mgr*
Robert Papagni, *Director*
EMP: 100
SQ FT: 960
SALES (est): 11.4MM **Privately Held**
WEB: www.dclandscaping.com
SIC: 0782 Landscape contractors

(P-823)
DEMARIA LANDTECH
5631 Palmer Way Ste C, Carlsbad
(92010-7243)
PHONE..........................858 481-5500
John Demaria, *CEO*
EMP: 50 **EST:** 2016
SALES (est): 925K **Privately Held**
SIC: 0782 Landscape contractors

(P-824)
DEMARIA LANDTECH INC
2789 High Mead Cir, Vista (92084-1830)
PHONE..........................858 481-5500
John Demaria, *Owner*
EMP: 50
SALES (est): 1.2MM **Privately Held**
WEB: www.demarialandtech.com
SIC: 0782 Landscape contractors

(P-825)
DESERT HAVEN ENTERPRISES INC (PA)
43437 Copeland Cir, Lancaster
(93535-4672)
P.O. Box 2110 (93539-2110)
PHONE..........................661 948-8402
Jenni C Moran, *CEO*
Roberta Terry, *CFO*
Tiffany Russell, *Manager*
Jeff Whiteford, *Manager*
EMP: 536
SQ FT: 15,000
SALES (est): 8MM **Privately Held**
WEB: www.deserthaven.org
SIC: 0782 8331 Lawn & garden services; work experience center

(P-826)
DESERT HAVEN ENTERPRISES INC
43437 Copeland Cir, Lancaster
(93535-4672)
P.O. Box 2110 (93539-2110)
PHONE..........................661 948-8402
Jennie Moran, *Branch Mgr*
EMP: 278
SALES (corp-wide): 8MM **Privately Held**
WEB: www.deserthaven.org
SIC: 0782 8331 Lawn & garden services; job training & vocational rehabilitation services
PA: Desert Haven Enterprises, Inc
43437 Copeland Cir
Lancaster CA 93535
661 948-8402

(P-827)
DIABLO LANDSCAPE INC
1655 Berryessa Rd, San Jose
(95133-1082)
PHONE..........................408 487-9620

Fax: 408 487-9621
EMP: 80
SQ FT: 38,000
SALES (est): 6.9MM
SALES (corp-wide): 32.2MM **Privately Held**
WEB: www.diablolandscape.com
SIC: 0782
PA: The Celtis Group Inc
1655 Berryessa Rd Ste A
San Jose CA
408 487-9620

(P-828)
DIVERSCAPE INC
Also Called: Diversified Landscape Co
21730 Bundy Canyon Rd, Wildomar
(92595-8780)
PHONE..........................951 245-1686
Vicki Moralez, *President*
Paul Moralez, *Vice Pres*
Anthony Rodriguez, *Area Mgr*
Juan Martinez, *Project Mgr*
EMP: 90
SQ FT: 4,000
SALES: 12.5MM **Privately Held**
WEB: www.diversifiedlandscape.com
SIC: 0782 1611 Garden maintenance services; landscape contractors; general contractor, highway & street construction

(P-829)
DMA GREENCARE CONTRACTING INC
3000 E Coronado St, Anaheim
(92806-2602)
PHONE..........................714 630-9470
Dennis Aldridge, *CEO*
Darin Doucette, *Vice Pres*
EMP: 50
SQ FT: 5,000
SALES (est): 8.2MM **Privately Held**
SIC: 0782 Landscape contractors

(P-830)
DOMINGUEZ LANDSCAPE SVCS INC
8376 Rovana Cir, Sacramento
(95828-2527)
P.O. Box 292727 (95829-2727)
PHONE..........................916 381-8855
Robert Dominguez, *President*
Bonnie J Dominguez, *Vice Pres*
EMP: 78
SQ FT: 7,200
SALES (est): 5.1MM **Privately Held**
SIC: 0782 Landscape contractors

(P-831)
DOOSE LANDSCAPE INCORPORATED
785 E Mission Rd, San Marcos
(92069-1903)
PHONE..........................760 591-4500
Robert J Doose, *President*
Shelley Nolet, *Treasurer*
Tom Doose, *Vice Pres*
Susan Daugherty, *Admin Sec*
EMP: 85
SQ FT: 11,300
SALES (est): 6.8MM **Privately Held**
WEB: www.dooselandscape.com
SIC: 0782 Landscape contractors

(P-832)
DULEYS LANDSCAPE INC
28876 Topaz Rd, Tollhouse (93667-9712)
P.O. Box 390, Prather (93651-0390)
PHONE..........................559 855-5090
Robert Duley, *President*
Debbie Duley, *Vice Pres*
EMP: 50
SALES (est): 4MM **Privately Held**
SIC: 0782 Landscape contractors

(P-833)
DWIW INC
Also Called: Land Scapes
700 W 16th St, Costa Mesa (92627-4303)
PHONE..........................949 574-7147
John Duley, *President*
Pam Duley, *Vice Pres*
EMP: 50
SQ FT: 5,000

SALES (est): 2.3MM **Privately Held**
WEB: www.dwiw.com
SIC: 0782 Landscape contractors

(P-834)
ECHO LANDSCAPE
2401 Grant Ave, San Lorenzo
(94580-1807)
P.O. Box 20926, Castro Valley (94546-8926)
PHONE....................510 481-8614
Troy Deherrera, *President*
EMP: 60
SQ FT: 1,600
SALES (est): 2.5MM **Privately Held**
WEB: www.scyence.com
SIC: 0782 Landscape contractors

(P-835)
ELITE LANDSCAPING INC
2972 Larkin Ave, Clovis (93612-3986)
PHONE....................559 292-7760
Guy Stockbridge, *President*
Jill Stockbridge, *CFO*
EMP: 150
SQ FT: 20,000
SALES (est): 7.6MM **Privately Held**
WEB: www.elitelandscapinginc.com
SIC: 0782 Landscape contractors

(P-836)
EMERALD LANDSCAPE SERVICES
1041 N Kemp St, Anaheim (92801-2518)
PHONE....................714 844-2200
John C Croul, *President*
Pam McIntyre, *Controller*
Pam Mc Entire, *Consultant*
EMP: 70
SALES (est): 4.1MM **Privately Held**
SIC: 0782 0781 Landscape contractors;
landscape planning services

(P-837)
ENHANCED LANDSCAPE MGT INC
1938 E Thousand Oaks Blvd, Thousand Oaks (91362-2913)
PHONE....................805 557-2737
Gregory Epstein, *President*
Miguel Estrada, *Area Mgr*
EMP: 65
SALES (est): 3MM **Privately Held**
SIC: 0782 0721 Landscape contractors;
crop related entomological services (insect control)

(P-838)
ESQUIRE LANDSCAPE INC
8380 Miralani Dr Ste B, San Diego
(92126-4304)
PHONE....................858 530-2949
William A Behl, *President*
EMP: 50
SQ FT: 1,500
SALES (est): 2.2MM **Privately Held**
SIC: 0782 Landscape contractors

(P-839)
EXCEL LANDSCAPE INC
710 Rimpau Ave Ste 108, Corona
(92879-5724)
P.O. Box 77995 (92877-0133)
PHONE....................951 735-9650
Jose Alfaro, *President*
▲ EMP: 120
SQ FT: 1,200
SALES (est): 7.5MM **Privately Held**
WEB: www.excellandscape.com
SIC: 0782 Lawn care services; garden
maintenance services

(P-840)
EXECUTIVE LANDSCAPE INC
2131 Huffstatler St, Fallbrook (92028-8861)
P.O. Box 1075 (92088-1075)
PHONE....................760 731-9036
Edwin Earle, *CEO*
Walter Earle, *Treasurer*
Kathleen D Earle, *Vice Pres*
Mike Lindmark, *Controller*
EMP: 230
SQ FT: 1,800
SALES (est): 24.2MM **Privately Held**
WEB: www.executivelandscapeinc.com
SIC: 0782 Landscape contractors

(P-841)
FENDERSCAPE INC
Also Called: Proscape Landscape
1446 E Hill St, Signal Hill (90755-3527)
PHONE....................562 988-2228
David Fender, *President*
Linda Fender, *Treasurer*
Nikki Dagel, *Controller*
Joe Rocha, *Supervisor*
EMP: 127
SQ FT: 1,893
SALES: 1MM **Privately Held**
SIC: 0782 Landscape contractors

(P-842)
FRANK CARSON LDSCP & MAINT INC
Also Called: CARSON LANDSCAPE INDUSTRIES
9530 Elder Creek Rd, Sacramento
(95829-9306)
PHONE....................916 856-5400
Frank M Carson, *CEO*
Kathy Pipis, *Admin Sec*
EMP: 200
SQ FT: 36,000
SALES: 15.2MM **Privately Held**
SIC: 0782 Landscape contractors

(P-843)
FS COMMERCIAL LANDSCAPE INC (PA)
5151 Pedley Rd, Riverside (92509-3937)
PHONE....................951 360-7070
G John Wood, *President*
Juan Vargas, *Accounts Mgr*
EMP: 75
SQ FT: 1,500
SALES (est): 7.6MM **Privately Held**
WEB: www.fslandscapes.com
SIC: 0782 Landscape contractors

(P-844)
GACHINA LANDSCAPE MGT INC
1130 Obrien Dr, Menlo Park (94025-1411)
PHONE....................650 853-0400
John P Gachina, *CEO*
Stacie Callaghan, *Business Dir*
William Cruz, *Branch Mgr*
Sylvia Espinoza, *Admin Asst*
Xabier Flores, *Info Tech Mgr*
EMP: 269
SQ FT: 12,000
SALES (est): 26.2MM **Privately Held**
WEB: www.gachina.com
SIC: 0782 Landscape contractors

(P-845)
GARDENERS GUILD INC
2780 Goodrick Ave, Richmond
(94801-1110)
PHONE....................415 457-0400
Kevin Davis, *President*
Mike Davidson, *Vice Pres*
Ginny Kuhel, *Director*
Paul Swanson, *Director*
EMP: 140
SQ FT: 25,000
SALES (est): 14.8MM **Privately Held**
WEB: www.gardenersguild.com
SIC: 0782 Landscape contractors; lawn
services; garden services

(P-846)
GATEWAY LANDSCAPE CNSTR INC
6735 Sierra Ct Ste A, Dublin (94568-2656)
PHONE....................925 875-0000
Corey Pontrelli, *President*
David J Garcia, *Vice Pres*
Hali Pontrelli, *Purchasing*
EMP: 75
SQ FT: 3,000
SALES (est): 5.9MM **Privately Held**
WEB: www.gatewaylci.com
SIC: 0782 1711 Landscape contractors; irrigation sprinkler system installation

(P-847)
GOTHIC LANDSCAPING INC (PA)
Also Called: Gothic Ground Management
27502 Avenue Scott, Valencia
(91355-3484)
PHONE....................661 257-1266

Jon S Georgio, *President*
Ronald Georgio, *Vice Pres*
Mike Georgio, *Principal*
Allyson Beckwith, *Admin Asst*
Alexis Walker, *Marketing Staff*
EMP: 200
SQ FT: 5,000
SALES (est): 143.4MM **Privately Held**
WEB: www.gothiclandscape.com
SIC: 0782 Landscape contractors; lawn
services

(P-848)
GRANTS LANDSCAPE SERVICES INC
3046 Orange Ave, Santa Ana (92707-4248)
PHONE....................714 444-1903
Kenneth Grant, *Vice Pres*
Harold Grant, *Vice Pres*
EMP: 75
SQ FT: 4,000
SALES: 1.6MM **Privately Held**
SIC: 0782 Landscape contractors

(P-849)
GREEN AGAIN LDSCPG & CON INC
851 Charter St, Redwood City
(94063-3004)
PHONE....................650 368-9304
Frederick C Nurisso, *President*
EMP: 55
SQ FT: 1,400
SALES (est): 1.4MM **Privately Held**
WEB: www.greenagain.com
SIC: 0782 Landscape contractors

(P-850)
GREEN SCENE LANDSCAPE INC
21220 Devonshire St # 102, Chatsworth
(91311-2300)
PHONE....................818 280-0420
Scott Cohen, *CEO*
Lisa Cohen, *Vice Pres*
EMP: 58
SQ FT: 1,100
SALES (est): 1.9MM **Privately Held**
WEB: www.greenscenelandscape.com
SIC: 0782 Landscape contractors; lawn
care services

(P-851)
GREENBRIER LAWN TREE EXPRT CO
3616 Bancroft Dr, Spring Valley
(91977-2116)
PHONE....................619 469-8720
Bill Gibson, *President*
George Villanueva, *Accounts Mgr*
EMP: 60
SQ FT: 6,000
SALES (est): 2.7MM **Privately Held**
SIC: 0782 Landscape contractors

(P-852)
GROWING COMPANY INC
4 Wayne Ct Ste 3, Sacramento
(95829-1305)
PHONE....................916 379-9088
Bruno Sandoval, *President*
Anne Sandoval, *Vice Pres*
Gualberto Cardenas, *Area Spvr*
Modesto Gonzalez, *Area Spvr*
Dionisio Corona, *Production*
EMP: 100
SQ FT: 10,000
SALES (est): 10.5MM **Privately Held**
WEB: www.thegrowingcompany.net
SIC: 0782 Landscape contractors; garden
maintenance services

(P-853)
GS BROTHERS INC (PA)
2215 N Gaffey St, San Pedro (90731-1238)
PHONE....................310 833-1369
Alan M Gaudenti, *President*
Robert M Gaudenti, *Corp Secy*
Marge Gonzalez, *Manager*
Mary Barantis, *Accounts Mgr*
EMP: 190
SQ FT: 7,000
SALES (est): 19.7MM **Privately Held**
SIC: 0782 Landscape contractors

(P-854)
HABITAT RSTRATION SCIENCES INC (PA)
1217 Distribution Way, Vista (92081-8817)
PHONE....................760 479-4210
Mark Girard, *President*
June Collins, *President*
EMP: 65
SALES (est): 11MM **Privately Held**
SIC: 0782 Landscape contractors

(P-855)
HABITAT RSTRATION SCIENCES INC
Also Called: Restoration Resources Hrs
3888 Cincinnati Ave, Rocklin (95765-1312)
PHONE....................916 408-2990
Mark Girard, *President*
Michael Titus, *Manager*
EMP: 50
SALES (corp-wide): 11MM **Privately Held**
SIC: 0782 Landscape contractors
PA: Habitat Restoration Sciences, Inc.
1217 Distribution Way
Vista CA 92081
760 479-4210

(P-856)
HARVEST LANDSCAPE ENTPS INC
Also Called: Harvest Landscape Maintenance
2339 N Batavia St, Orange (92865-2001)
P.O. Box 3877 (92857-0877)
PHONE....................714 693-8100
Stephen G Schinhofen, *CEO*
Shelley Fajardo, *CFO*
Karolyna Sandoval, *Admin Asst*
Victoria Vasquez, *Human Res Dir*
Cody Harkins, *Accounts Mgr*
EMP: 160
SALES (est): 16.5MM **Privately Held**
SIC: 0782 Landscape contractors

(P-857)
HE JULIEN & ASSOCIATES INC
Also Called: C&R Maintnce
2275 E Hueneme Rd, Oxnard
(93033-8112)
P.O. Box 817, Port Hueneme (93044-0817)
PHONE....................805 488-8342
Harvey E Julien, *President*
EMP: 50
SQ FT: 3,568
SALES (est): 1.4MM **Privately Held**
SIC: 0782

(P-858)
HEAVILAND ENTERPRISES INC (PA)
2180 La Mirada Dr, Vista (92081-8815)
PHONE....................760 598-7065
Thomas J Heaviland, *CEO*
EMP: 154
SQ FT: 2,500
SALES (est): 11.4MM **Privately Held**
WEB: www.heaviland.net
SIC: 0782 1542 Landscape contractors;
commercial & office buildings, renovation
& repair

(P-859)
HEMINGTON LANDSCAPE SVCS INC
4170 Business Dr, Cameron Park
(95682-7230)
PHONE....................530 677-9290
Mark E Hemington, *President*
Jill Hemington, *Corp Secy*
EMP: 100
SALES (est): 8.3MM **Privately Held**
WEB: www.hemington.com
SIC: 0782 Landscape contractors

(P-860)
HORT TECH INC
78355 Darby Rd, Bermuda Dunes
(92203-9661)
P.O. Box 3284, Palm Desert (92261-3284)
PHONE....................760 360-9000
Bryan Jensen, *President*
Linda Gurrola, *Admin Sec*
EMP: 160
SQ FT: 8,000

SALES (est): 7MM **Privately Held**
SIC: 0782 Landscape contractors

(P-861)
IKES LANDSCAPING & MAINTENANCE
2700 Tiber Ave, Davis (95616-2958)
PHONE....................530 758-1698
Eric Aichwalder, *President*
Don Kearney, *Vice Pres*
Aletha Aichwalder, *Admin Sec*
EMP: 80
SQ FT: 2,000
SALES (est): 3MM **Privately Held**
SIC: 0782 5992 Landscape contractors; lawn care services; plants, potted

(P-862)
IRRI-SCAPE CONSTRUCTION INC
20182 Carancho Rd, Temecula (92590-4348)
PHONE....................951 694-6936
Robert Smith, *President*
EMP: 100
SQ FT: 1,500
SALES (est): 7MM **Privately Held**
SIC: 0782 Landscape contractors

(P-863)
J REDFERN INC
Also Called: Golden State Landscaping
164 N L St, Livermore (94550-2118)
P.O. Box 2091 (94551-2091)
PHONE....................925 371-3300
John E Redfern, *President*
Rashelle Redfern, *Controller*
Michael Walker, *Director*
EMP: 108
SALES (est): 7.7MM **Privately Held**
WEB: www.jredfern.com
SIC: 0782 Landscape contractors

(P-864)
J VITALE LANDSCAPE & MAINT
8801 Cottonwood Ave, Santee (92071-4460)
PHONE....................619 938-2435
Jim Vitale, *President*
EMP: 90
SALES (est): 7MM **Privately Held**
SIC: 0782 Landscape contractors

(P-865)
JAMES H COWAN & ASSOCIATES INC
5126 Clareton Dr Ste 200, Agoura Hills (91301-4529)
PHONE....................310 457-2574
Clark J Cowan, *President*
Kendall Whitney, *Admin Sec*
EMP: 95
SQ FT: 3,500
SALES (est): 8.6MM **Privately Held**
WEB: www.jhcowan.com
SIC: 0782 Landscape contractors

(P-866)
JENSEN CORP LANDSCAPE CONTR
1983 Concourse Dr, San Jose (95131-1708)
PHONE....................408 446-4881
John Vlay, *CEO*
Shamina Edwards, *Admin Sec*
EMP: 150 EST: 2008
SALES: 10MM **Privately Held**
SIC: 0782 1521 Landscape contractors; single-family housing construction

(P-867)
JENSEN CORPORATE HOLDINGS INC (PA)
1983 Concourse Dr, San Jose (95131-1708)
PHONE....................408 446-1118
John Vlay, *CEO*
Quang Trinh, *CFO*
Donald Defever, *Division Pres*
Glenn Berry, *Vice Pres*
Kirk Brown, *Vice Pres*
EMP: 117
SQ FT: 13,000

SALES (est): 115.4MM **Privately Held**
WEB: www.jensencorp.com
SIC: 0782 Landscape contractors

(P-868)
JENSEN LANDSCAPE SERVICES INC
Also Called: Jensen Corp Landscape Contrs
1983 Concourse Dr, San Jose (95131-1708)
PHONE....................408 446-1118
John Vlay, *CEO*
Anthony Whalls, *President*
Paul Johnson, *CFO*
Glenn Berry, *Vice Pres*
Darren Nosseck, *Regional Mgr*
EMP: 163
SALES (est): 8.8MM
SALES (corp-wide): 115.4MM **Privately Held**
WEB: www.jensencorp.com
SIC: 0782 Landscape contractors
PA: Jensen Corporate Holdings, Inc.
1983 Concourse Dr
San Jose CA 95131
408 446-1118

(P-869)
JLP LANDSCAPE CONTRACTING
901 7th St, Santa Rosa (95404-4255)
PHONE....................707 526-6285
John Prior, *President*
Alicia Lene Ruppell Prior, *Treasurer*
EMP: 50
SQ FT: 2,000
SALES: 3.1MM **Privately Held**
SIC: 0782 0781 Landscape contractors; landscape planning services

(P-870)
JMA INVESTMENTS LTD
Also Called: Ahrens Landscape & Maintenance
9265 Beatty Dr, Sacramento (95826-9702)
P.O. Box 279199 (95827-9199)
PHONE....................916 685-1355
Jeff Ahrens, *President*
Michele Ahrens, *Vice Pres*
EMP: 99
SQ FT: 2,000
SALES: 14MM **Privately Held**
SIC: 0782 Lawn care services

(P-871)
JPA LANDSCAPE & CNSTR INC
256 Boeing Ct, Livermore (94551-9258)
P.O. Box 1292, Pleasanton (94566-0129)
PHONE....................925 960-9602
Ed Morrissey, *President*
Jody Morrissey, *Treasurer*
Frances Morrissey, *Exec Dir*
John Morrissey, *Opers Mgr*
Deanna Wallace, *Cust Mgr*
EMP: 75
SQ FT: 9,000
SALES: 3.9MM **Privately Held**
WEB: www.jpalandscape.com
SIC: 0782 Landscape contractors

(P-872)
KIRKPATRICK LDSCPG SVCS INC
43752 Jackson St, Indio (92201-2540)
P.O. Box 10430 (92202-2542)
PHONE....................760 347-6926
Steven Kirkpatrick, *President*
EMP: 200
SQ FT: 5,000
SALES (est): 10.9MM **Privately Held**
SIC: 0782 Lawn care services; garden maintenance services

(P-873)
KITSON LANDSCAPE MGT INC
5787 Thornwood Dr, Goleta (93117-3801)
PHONE....................805 681-9460
Sarah Kitson, *President*
Dave Fudurich, *CFO*
David Fudurich, *Treasurer*
Brent Kitson, *Vice Pres*
Sally Kitson, *Admin Sec*
EMP: 80
SQ FT: 52,272

SALES (est): 5.4MM **Privately Held**
WEB: www.kitsonlandscape.com
SIC: 0782 Landscape contractors

(P-874)
L A SWIKARD INC
Also Called: Terra Firma Landscape Company
9520 Candida St, San Diego (92126-4540)
PHONE....................858 408-3700
Larry A Swikard, *President*
Cindy A Swikard, *CFO*
Mike Swikard, *VP Opers*
John Savallo, *Sales Staff*
EMP: 225 EST: 1981
SQ FT: 20,000
SALES (est): 15.8MM **Privately Held**
SIC: 0782 Landscape contractors

(P-875)
L BARRIOS & ASSOCIATES INC
302 E Fthill Blvd Ste 101, San Dimas (91773)
P.O. Box 3948 (91773-7948)
PHONE....................626 960-2934
Henry Barrios, *President*
EMP: 50 EST: 1955
SALES (est): 3MM **Privately Held**
SIC: 0782 1711 Landscape contractors; lawn services; irrigation sprinkler system installation

(P-876)
LANDCARE USA LLC
Also Called: Trugreen
216 N Clara St, Santa Ana (92703-3518)
PHONE....................949 559-7771
Kenny Stites, *Branch Mgr*
EMP: 80
SALES (corp-wide): 150MM **Privately Held**
SIC: 0782 Lawn care services
PA: Landcare Usa L.L.C.
5295 Westview Dr Ste 100
Frederick MD 21703
301 874-3300

(P-877)
LANDCARE USA LLC
Also Called: Trugreen
770 Metcalf St, Escondido (92025-1667)
PHONE....................760 747-1174
Brett Horan, *Branch Mgr*
EMP: 80
SALES (corp-wide): 150MM **Privately Held**
SIC: 0782 Lawn care services
PA: Landcare Usa L.L.C.
5295 Westview Dr Ste 100
Frederick MD 21703
301 874-3300

(P-878)
LANDCARE USA LLC
Also Called: Trugreen
1196 Patricia Ave, Simi Valley (93065-2809)
PHONE....................805 520-9394
Noe Alcaraz, *Branch Mgr*
EMP: 125
SALES (corp-wide): 150MM **Privately Held**
SIC: 0782 Lawn care services
PA: Landcare Usa L.L.C.
5295 Westview Dr Ste 100
Frederick MD 21703
301 874-3300

(P-879)
LANDCARE USA LLC
930 Shiloh Rd Bldg 44-B, Windsor (95492-9664)
PHONE....................707 836-1460
Scott Hall, *Branch Mgr*
EMP: 60
SALES (corp-wide): 150MM **Privately Held**
SIC: 0782 Landscape contractors
PA: Landcare Usa L.L.C.
5295 Westview Dr Ste 100
Frederick MD 21703
301 874-3300

(P-880)
LANDCARE USA LLC
Also Called: Trugreen Lndcare Michael Bogan
15606 Cornet St, Santa Fe Springs (90670-5514)
PHONE....................714 936-9512
EMP: 133
SALES (corp-wide): 150MM **Privately Held**
SIC: 0782 Landscape contractors
PA: Landcare Usa L.L.C.
5295 Westview Dr Ste 100
Frederick MD 21703
301 874-3300

(P-881)
LANDCARE USA LLC
1315 W 130th St, Gardena (90247-1503)
PHONE....................310 719-1008
Don Cully, *Branch Mgr*
EMP: 56
SALES (corp-wide): 150MM **Privately Held**
SIC: 0782 Landscape contractors; lawn services
PA: Landcare Usa L.L.C.
5295 Westview Dr Ste 100
Frederick MD 21703
301 874-3300

(P-882)
LANDCARE USA LLC
4134 Temple City Blvd, Rosemead (91770-1550)
PHONE....................310 354-1520
Joe Espinoza, *Branch Mgr*
EMP: 56
SALES (corp-wide): 150MM **Privately Held**
SIC: 0782 Landscape contractors; lawn services
PA: Landcare Usa L.L.C.
5295 Westview Dr Ste 100
Frederick MD 21703
301 874-3300

(P-883)
LANDCARE USA LLC
Also Called: Trugreen
1323 W 130th St, Gardena (90247-1503)
PHONE....................310 354-1520
Dave Evans, *Branch Mgr*
Jose Udave, *Accounts Mgr*
EMP: 170
SALES (corp-wide): 150MM **Privately Held**
SIC: 0782 7342 Lawn care services; disinfecting & pest control services
PA: Landcare Usa L.L.C.
5295 Westview Dr Ste 100
Frederick MD 21703
301 874-3300

(P-884)
LANDCARE USA LLC
Also Called: Trugreen
3213 Fitzgerald Rd, Rancho Cordova (95742-6813)
PHONE....................916 635-0936
Kevin Arnett, *Branch Mgr*
EMP: 100
SALES (corp-wide): 150MM **Privately Held**
SIC: 0782 Lawn care services
PA: Landcare Usa L.L.C.
5295 Westview Dr Ste 100
Frederick MD 21703
301 874-3300

(P-885)
LANDCARE USA LLC
Also Called: Trugreen
5248 Governor Dr, San Diego (92122-2800)
PHONE....................858 453-1755
Craig Gerber, *VP Finance*
Jasmine Sutherland, *Administration*
Jim Clifford, *Manager*
Krista Jimenez, *Manager*
EMP: 112
SALES (corp-wide): 150MM **Privately Held**
SIC: 0782 Lawn care services

PA: Landcare Usa L.L.C.
5295 Westview Dr Ste 100
Frederick MD 21703
301 874-3300

(P-886)
LANDCARE USA LLC
Also Called: Trugreen
7755 Deering Ave, Canoga Park
(91304-5653)
PHONE.................................818 346-7552
Raul Sanchez, *Branch Mgr*
EMP: 150
SALES (corp-wide): 150MM **Privately Held**
SIC: 0782 Lawn care services; landscape contractors
PA: Landcare Usa L.L.C.
5295 Westview Dr Ste 100
Frederick MD 21703
301 874-3300

(P-887)
LANDCARE USA LLC
Also Called: Trugreen
85 Old Tully Rd, San Jose (95111-1910)
PHONE.................................408 727-4099
Jeff Kunkel, *Branch Mgr*
EMP: 75
SALES (corp-wide): 150MM **Privately Held**
SIC: 0782 Landscape contractors
PA: Landcare Usa L.L.C.
5295 Westview Dr Ste 100
Frederick MD 21703
301 874-3300

(P-888)
LANDCO
7333 Clybourn Ave, Sun Valley
(91352-5143)
PHONE.................................818 612-0118
Martin Stowell, *Owner*
▲ **EMP:** 100
SALES (est): 1.7MM **Privately Held**
SIC: 0782 Landscape contractors

(P-889)
LANDESIGN CNSTR & MAINT INC
1328 Airport Blvd, Santa Rosa
(95403-1009)
P.O. Box 2326 (95405-0326)
PHONE.................................707 578-2657
John Fitzgerald, *Owner*
Denise Fitzgerald, *Co-Owner*
EMP: 90
SQ FT: 1,000
SALES: 5MM **Privately Held**
SIC: 0782 Landscape contractors

(P-890)
LANDSCAPE DEVELOPMENT INC (PA)
28447 Witherspoon Pkwy, Valencia
(91355-4174)
PHONE.................................661 295-1970
Gary Horton, *CEO*
Jenny Lunde, *CFO*
Tim Myers, *CFO*
Casper Correll, *Vice Pres*
Patrick Reinoso, *Office Mgr*
▲ **EMP:** 500
SALES (est): 57.6MM **Privately Held**
WEB: www.landscapedevelopment.com
SIC: 0782 5039 Landscape contractors; soil erosion control fabrics

(P-891)
LAWNMAN II INC
4300 82nd St Ste C, Sacramento
(95826-4730)
PHONE.................................916 739-1420
Burnie Lenau, *President*
▲ **EMP:** 60
SQ FT: 3,000
SALES: 3MM **Privately Held**
WEB: www.lawnmansac.com
SIC: 0782 Landscape contractors

(P-892)
LEONARD ANTHONY VALENTI INC
9110 Marcella Ave, Gilroy (95020-9716)
P.O. Box 1179 (95021-1179)
PHONE.................................408 848-9688
Leonard A Valenti, *President*
EMP: 60
SALES (est): 2.1MM **Privately Held**
SIC: 0782 7349 1742 Landscape contractors; building maintenance, except repairs; plastering, drywall & insulation

(P-893)
MACKENZIE LANDSCAPE A CAL CORP
33380 Bailey Park Blvd, Menifee
(92584-9585)
PHONE.................................951 679-5477
Michael Mackenzie, *President*
Judy Mackenzie, *CFO*
EMP: 100
SQ FT: 1,500
SALES (est): 2.9MM **Privately Held**
SIC: 0782 Landscape contractors; highway lawn & garden maintenance services

(P-894)
MARIPOSA LANDSCAPES INC (PA)
Also Called: Mariposa Horticultural Entps
6232 Santos Diaz St, Irwindale
(91702-3267)
PHONE.................................626 960-0196
Terry Noriega, *President*
Antonio Valenzuela, *Vice Pres*
James Olsen, *Opers Staff*
Michael Williams, *Maintence Staff*
Jesus Ramirez, *Accounts Mgr*
EMP: 61
SQ FT: 2,000
SALES (est): 49.9MM **Privately Held**
WEB: www.mariposahorticultural.com
SIC: 0782 Garden maintenance services; lawn care services; landscape contractors

(P-895)
MARTINA LANDSCAPE INC
811 Camden Ave, Campbell (95008-4103)
PHONE.................................408 871-8800
Joe Martina, *President*
EMP: 80
SQ FT: 2,000
SALES (est): 5.2MM **Privately Held**
SIC: 0782 Landscape contractors

(P-896)
MEDLIN DEVELOPMENT
320 Tropicana Ranch Rd, Colton
(92324-3605)
PHONE.................................909 825-5296
EMP: 50
SQ FT: 1,800
SALES (est): 1.5MM **Privately Held**
SIC: 0782

(P-897)
MIDORI LANDSCAPE INC
Also Called: Midori Landscaping
3231 S Main St, Santa Ana (92707-4405)
PHONE.................................714 751-8792
Naga Hamamoto, *President*
EMP: 80
SQ FT: 8,200
SALES (est): 5.2MM **Privately Held**
SIC: 0782 Landscape contractors

(P-898)
MIKE MCCALL LANDSCAPE INC
4749 Clayton Rd, Concord (94521-2936)
PHONE.................................925 363-8100
Mike McCall, *President*
Mark Tate, *COO*
Nana David, *Human Res Mgr*
Garrett McCall, *Purch Dir*
Rob Scott, *Manager*
EMP: 140
SQ FT: 1,000
SALES (est): 12.3MM **Privately Held**
WEB: www.mikemccalllandscape.com
SIC: 0782 Landscape contractors

(P-899)
MISSION LANDSCAPE SERVICE
952 E Francis St, Ontario (91761-5630)
PHONE.................................909 947-7290
David Dubois, *Owner*
Rocco Campanozzi, *Vice Pres*
Stephen Natalo, *Sr Project Mgr*
Chris Grogan, *Director*
Roberto Iniestra, *Accounts Mgr*
EMP: 80
SALES (est): 3.4MM **Privately Held**
SIC: 0782 Landscape contractors

(P-900)
MISSION LDSCP COMPANIES INC
536 E Dyer Rd, Santa Ana (92707-3737)
P.O. Box 15026 (92735-0026)
PHONE.................................714 545-9962
David Dubois, *CEO*
Kristen Parkins, *President*
Beth Du Boise, *Treasurer*
Beatrice Campos, *Vice Pres*
Cindy Clark, *Admin Sec*
EMP: 200
SQ FT: 11,000
SALES (est): 15.9MM **Privately Held**
WEB: www.missionlandscape.com
SIC: 0782 Landscape contractors

(P-901)
MONARCH LANDSCAPE HOLDINGS LLC (PA)
550 S Hope St Ste 1675, Los Angeles
(90071-2692)
PHONE.................................213 816-1750
Tony W Lee, *Mng Member*
Michael Hope, *Manager*
EMP: 150 **EST:** 2015
SALES (est): 7.9MM **Privately Held**
SIC: 0782 Garden services

(P-902)
MONUMENT CONSTRUCTION INC
Also Called: Techcon
16200 Vineyard Blvd # 100, Morgan Hill
(95037-7164)
PHONE.................................408 778-1350
Paul Maxwell Swing, *President*
Diane Swing, *CFO*
EMP: 90
SQ FT: 6,000
SALES (est): 8.7MM **Privately Held**
SIC: 0782 Landscape contractors

(P-903)
MPL ENTERPRISES INC
Also Called: Mike Parker Landscape
2302 S Susan St, Santa Ana (92704-4421)
PHONE.................................714 545-1717
Michael Parker, *President*
EMP: 90
SQ FT: 2,000
SALES (est): 5MM **Privately Held**
WEB: www.mikeparkerlandscape.com
SIC: 0782 Landscape contractors

(P-904)
N V LANDSCAPE INC
24400 Walnut St Ste D, Newhall
(91321-2855)
P.O. Box 4082, Sequim WA (98382-4353)
PHONE.................................661 286-8888
Jeff Brown, *President*
Holly Brown, *Corp Secy*
EMP: 60
SALES (est): 1.6MM **Privately Held**
WEB: www.nvlandscape.com
SIC: 0782 Landscape contractors

(P-905)
NATIVE SONS LANDSCAPING INC
25 Beta Ct Ste L, San Ramon
(94583-1245)
PHONE.................................925 837-8175
Mike Hertel, *President*
Louise Hertel, *Vice Pres*
EMP: 50
SQ FT: 1,800
SALES (est): 4.5MM **Privately Held**
WEB: www.nativesons.net
SIC: 0782 0781 Landscape contractors; landscape counseling & planning

(P-906)
NEW EARTH ENTERPRISES INC
3790 Manchester Ave, Encinitas
(92024-4935)
PHONE.................................760 942-1298
James R Williams, *President*
Carlos Delval, *Vice Pres*
Jessie Wilhoite, *Vice Pres*
EMP: 60
SQ FT: 192
SALES (est): 1.7MM **Privately Held**
SIC: 0782 Landscape contractors

(P-907)
NEW IMAGE LANDSCAPE COMPANY
3250 Darby Cmn, Fremont (94539-5601)
PHONE.................................510 226-9191
Brian Takehara, *President*
Gerardo Roque, *Division Mgr*
Irene Briggs, *Controller*
Carlos Barajas, *Manager*
Russell Takehara, *Accounts Mgr*
EMP: 55
SQ FT: 4,000
SALES (est): 3.6MM **Privately Held**
WEB: www.newimagelandscape.com
SIC: 0782 Lawn & garden services

(P-908)
NEW VIEW LANDSCAPE INC
24860 Calabasas Rd, Calabasas
(91302-1429)
PHONE.................................818 222-8972
Lance Lortscher, *President*
Mike Stell, *Treasurer*
EMP: 60
SQ FT: 1,200
SALES (est): 2.8MM **Privately Held**
WEB: www.newviewlandscape.com
SIC: 0782 Garden maintenance services; turf installation services, except artificial

(P-909)
NEW WAY LANDSCAPE & TREE SVCS
7485 Ronson Rd, San Diego (92111-1507)
PHONE.................................858 505-8300
Randy Newhard, *CEO*
Kathryn Dejong, *President*
Bob Rogers, *President*
Dan Suhovecky, *CFO*
Kevin Hall, *Vice Pres*
EMP: 175
SQ FT: 6,400
SALES (est): 20.3MM **Privately Held**
WEB: www.newwaypro.com
SIC: 0782 Landscape contractors

(P-910)
NIEVES LANDSCAPE INC
1629 E Edinger Ave, Santa Ana
(92705-5001)
PHONE.................................714 835-7332
Gregorio Nieves, *President*
Patricia White, *Admin Sec*
EMP: 150
SALES (est): 13.4MM **Privately Held**
SIC: 0782 Landscape contractors

(P-911)
NITTANY LION LANDSCAPING INC
Also Called: Nl Services
14770 Firestone Blvd # 203, La Mirada
(90638-5917)
PHONE.................................714 635-1788
Sam Aldrich, *President*
Don G Abbey, *Ch of Bd*
EMP: 63 **EST:** 1994
SQ FT: 7,300
SALES: 6.5MM **Privately Held**
SIC: 0782 Landscape contractors

(P-912)
NORTHWEST LANDSCAPE MAINT CO
283 Kinney Dr, San Jose (95112-4433)
PHONE.................................408 298-6489
Warren Nakamura, *President*
Douglas Nakamura, *Corp Secy*
Paul Nakamura, *Vice Pres*
EMP: 50
SQ FT: 4,808

SALES (est): 3.3MM **Privately Held**
WEB: www.northwestlandscapemc.com
SIC: 0782 Landscape contractors

(P-913)
OCONNELL LANDSCAPE MAINT INC
4600 Leisure Village Way, Oceanside (92056-5147)
PHONE..........................760 630-4963
Glen Foreman, *Branch Mgr*
EMP: 50
SALES (corp-wide): 147.9MM **Privately Held**
SIC: 0782 Landscape contractors
PA: O'connell Landscape Maintenance Inc.
23091 Arroyo Vis
Rcho Sta Marg CA 92688
949 589-2007

(P-914)
PAC WEST LAND CARE INC
Also Called: Pacific West Tree Service
408 Olive Ave, Vista (92083-3438)
P.O. Box 99 (92085-0099)
PHONE..........................760 630-0231
Barry Blue, *President*
EMP: 130
SQ FT: 3,000
SALES (est): 4.4MM **Privately Held**
SIC: 0782 Landscape contractors

(P-915)
PACIFIC GREEN LANDSCAPE INC (PA)
8834 Winter Gardens Blvd, Lakeside (92040-5419)
PHONE..........................619 390-1546
Michael C Regan, *President*
Ron Zaccaro, *Regional Mgr*
Mark Mazalewski, *Branch Mgr*
Chad Rogers, *Branch Mgr*
Maria Irvine, *Controller*
EMP: 110
SQ FT: 1,450
SALES (est): 8.4MM **Privately Held**
WEB: www.pacificgreenlandscape.com
SIC: 0782 Landscape contractors; lawn services

(P-916)
PARK LANDSCAPE MAINTENANCE (PA)
Also Called: Park Landscape Maint 1-2-3-4
22421 Gilberto Ste A, Rcho STA Marg (92688-2104)
PHONE..........................949 546-8300
Robert Morrison, *President*
Tom Tracy, *Shareholder*
Mike Tracy, *CEO*
Tom England, *CFO*
EMP: 300
SQ FT: 10,000
SALES (est): 12.9MM **Privately Held**
SIC: 0782 Lawn care services; lawn services; landscape contractors

(P-917)
PARK WEST RESCOM INC
22421 Gilberto, Rcho STA Marg (92688-2104)
PHONE..........................949 546-8300
Michael S Tracy, *CEO*
Bart Ryder, *President*
EMP: 101
SQ FT: 10,000
SALES (est): 4.8MM **Privately Held**
SIC: 0782 Landscape contractors

(P-918)
PARKWOOD LANDSCAPE MAINT INC
16443 Hart St, Van Nuys (91406-4608)
PHONE..........................818 988-9677
David Melito, *President*
EMP: 95 EST: 1988
SQ FT: 1,500
SALES (est): 6MM **Privately Held**
WEB: www.parkwoodlandscape.com
SIC: 0782 Landscape contractors

(P-919)
PENNEY LAWN SERVICE INC
Also Called: Penny Lawn Service
4000 Allen Rd, Bakersfield (93314-9091)
PHONE..........................661 587-4788
Dan Penny, *Owner*
Sandy Penny, *Owner*
Dan Penney, *Manager*
EMP: 100
SQ FT: 1,275
SALES (est): 8.7MM **Privately Held**
SIC: 0782 Landscape contractors

(P-920)
PETALON LANDSCAPE MGT INC
1766 Rogers Ave, San Jose (95112-1109)
PHONE..........................408 453-3998
Rudy Sotelo, *CEO*
John Linn, *President*
EMP: 65
SQ FT: 5,000
SALES (est): 5.1MM **Privately Held**
SIC: 0782 Landscape contractors

(P-921)
PINELANDS PRESERVATION INC
4501 Auburn Blvd Ste 201, Sacramento (95841-4213)
PHONE..........................609 703-0359
Christopher Carlino, *CEO*
EMP: 60
SALES (est): 1.9MM **Privately Held**
SIC: 0782 8741 Landscape contractors; management services

(P-922)
PLANTASIA INC
Also Called: Plantasia Landscaping
2550 Via Tejon Ste 3f, Palos Verdes Estates (90274-6809)
PHONE..........................310 375-0387
Alex Colovic, *President*
Kris Colin, *Executive*
Lily Colovic, *Project Mgr*
EMP: 75 EST: 1973
SALES (est): 5.3MM **Privately Held**
SIC: 0782 1629 Landscape contractors; irrigation system construction

(P-923)
PLOWBOY LANDSCAPES INC
2190 N Ventura Ave, Ventura (93001-1343)
P.O. Box 1802 (93002-1802)
PHONE..........................805 643-4966
Douglas Wasson, *President*
EMP: 55
SQ FT: 3,500
SALES (est): 4.9MM **Privately Held**
WEB: www.plowboyinc.com
SIC: 0782 Landscape contractors

(P-924)
PRO SCAPE INC
510 Venture St, Escondido (92029-1212)
PHONE..........................760 480-1544
Michael Helms, *President*
Jay Helms, *Vice Pres*
Aleah Helms, *Admin Sec*
EMP: 50
SQ FT: 2,600
SALES (est): 2.5MM **Privately Held**
SIC: 0782 Landscape contractors; garden maintenance services

(P-925)
PROCIDA LANDSCAPE INC
8465 Specialty Cir, Sacramento (95828-2523)
PHONE..........................916 387-5296
John Procida Jr, *President*
Toni Saenz, *Admin Asst*
Steve Detherage, *Manager*
EMP: 160
SQ FT: 15,000
SALES (est): 10.3MM **Privately Held**
SIC: 0782 Lawn care services; lawn services; garden planting services

(P-926)
R NAVARRO LANDSCAPE SERVICES
359 West Rd, La Habra Heights (90631-8048)
PHONE..........................562 690-6414

Raul Navarro, *President*
Dana Navarro, *Vice Pres*
EMP: 60
SALES (est): 1.5MM **Privately Held**
SIC: 0782 Landscape contractors

(P-927)
RANCHO CALIFORNIA LANDSCAPING
13801 S Western Ave, Gardena (90249-2517)
PHONE..........................310 768-1680
Sal Mora, *President*
Lidia Mora, *Office Mgr*
Ramon Sandoval, *Opers Staff*
Mike Barajas, *Supervisor*
EMP: 50
SQ FT: 33,610
SALES (est): 3.5MM **Privately Held**
WEB: www.ranchocalifornia.biz
SIC: 0782 Landscape contractors

(P-928)
RANCHO WEST LANDSCAPE
39140 Pala Vista Dr, Temecula (92591-7213)
PHONE..........................951 301-3979
Greg Duncan, *Owner*
Osvaldo Abarca, *Project Mgr*
Robert Calzada, *Maintence Staff*
EMP: 50
SALES (est): 4.9MM **Privately Held**
SIC: 0782 Landscape contractors

(P-929)
RELIABLE GARDENS INC
7837 Burnet Ave, Van Nuys (91405-1046)
PHONE..........................818 904-9801
Steven Selden, *CEO*
Debra Selden, *CFO*
Laurie Levavi, *Vice Pres*
EMP: 60
SALES (est): 3.1MM **Privately Held**
SIC: 0782 Garden planting services; garden maintenance services; landscape contractors; lawn services

(P-930)
RESCOM SERVICES INC
1637 Kings Way, Vista (92084-3641)
PHONE..........................760 930-3900
Mark Sutton, *President*
EMP: 92
SALES (est): 6.3MM **Privately Held**
WEB: www.rescomservices.com
SIC: 0782 Lawn & garden services

(P-931)
RESIDENT GROUP SERVICES INC (PA)
Also Called: Rgs Services
1156 N Grove St, Anaheim (92806-2109)
PHONE..........................714 630-5300
James M Gilly, *President*
Michael K Hayde, *CEO*
EMP: 149
SQ FT: 15,000
SALES (est): 19.8MM **Privately Held**
WEB: www.rgsservices.com
SIC: 0782 Landscape contractors

(P-932)
RMT LANDSCAPE CONTRACTORS INC
421 Pendleton Way, Oakland (94621-2122)
PHONE..........................510 568-3208
Rick Deherrera, *President*
Julie Briggs, *Vice Pres*
Sally Lipska, *Admin Sec*
Patrick Laake, *Accounting Mgr*
David Deherrera, *Director*
EMP: 50
SQ FT: 12,000
SALES (est): 5.4MM **Privately Held**
WEB: www.rmtlandscape.com
SIC: 0782 Landscape contractors

(P-933)
S G D ENTERPRISES
Also Called: Four Seasons Landscaping
14937 Delano St, Van Nuys (91411-2123)
PHONE..........................323 658-1047
Stephen G Darrison, *President*
EMP: 50
SQ FT: 1,800

SALES (est): 5.2MM **Privately Held**
SIC: 0782 6512 6513 Landscape contractors; nonresidential building operators; apartment building operators

(P-934)
SANSEI GARDENS INC
3250 Darby Cmn, Fremont (94539-5601)
PHONE..........................510 226-9191
Brian Takehara, *President*
EMP: 110
SQ FT: 3,000
SALES (est): 10.6MM **Privately Held**
WEB: www.sanseigardens.com
SIC: 0782 Landscape contractors

(P-935)
SCOTTS PLANT SERVICE CO
6206 Carver Rd, Modesto (95356-9177)
P.O. Box 3723 (95352-3723)
PHONE..........................209 545-0903
Scott Reis, *President*
EMP: 67
SALES (est): 350K **Privately Held**
SIC: 0782 Landscape contractors

(P-936)
SERPICO LANDSCAPING INC
1764 National Ave, Hayward (94545-1722)
PHONE..........................510 293-0341
Sharon Serpico Hanson, *CEO*
Richard Hanson, *Admin Sec*
EMP: 50
SQ FT: 1,000
SALES (est): 5.9MM **Privately Held**
WEB: www.serpicolandscaping.com
SIC: 0782 Landscape contractors

(P-937)
SHASTA LANDSCAPING INC
1340 Descanso Ave, San Marcos (92069-1306)
PHONE..........................760 744-6551
Leonard R Hogan, *CEO*
Daniel Hogan, *President*
Susan Hogan, *CFO*
Debara Prescott, *Corp Secy*
EMP: 75
SQ FT: 6,000
SALES (est): 3.9MM **Privately Held**
WEB: www.shastalandscaping.com
SIC: 0782 Landscape contractors

(P-938)
SHINSUKE CLIFFORD YAMAMOTO
Also Called: S C Yamamoto
2031 Emery Ave, La Habra (90631-5777)
PHONE..........................714 992-5783
Shinsuke C Yamamoto, *President*
EMP: 100
SQ FT: 7,660
SALES (est): 8MM **Privately Held**
WEB: www.scyamamoto.com
SIC: 0782 Garden maintenance services; landscape contractors

(P-939)
SHORELINE LAND CARE INC
Also Called: Landcare Logic
7348 Trade St Ste B, San Diego (92121-3434)
PHONE..........................858 560-8555
Craig Gerber, *CEO*
John Crawford, *COO*
Jalin Gerber, *Vice Pres*
Michelle Ferraro, *Administration*
EMP: 64 EST: 2007
SALES (est): 3.9MM **Privately Held**
SIC: 0782 Landscape contractors

(P-940)
SIERRA VIEW LANDSCAPE INC
Also Called: Restoration Resources
3888 Cincinnati Ave, Rocklin (95765-1312)
PHONE..........................916 408-2990
Fax: 916 408-2999
EMP: 50
SALES (est): 7MM **Privately Held**
SIC: 0782

(P-941)
SILVERWOOD LANDSCAPE CNSTR INC
2209 S Lyon St, Santa Ana (92705-5305)
PHONE..................714 427-6134
Steven Paul Lancaster, *President*
Marsha Lancaster, *CFO*
EMP: 50
SALES (est): 5.3MM **Privately Held**
SIC: 0782 Landscape contractors

(P-942)
SOTO COMPANY INC
34275 Camino Capistrano A, Capistrano Beach (92624-1917)
PHONE..................949 493-9403
Joe Soto, *President*
Carol Soto, *Corp Secy*
Jessica Solis, *Admin Mgr*
EMP: 75
SQ FT: 4,000
SALES (est): 3.7MM **Privately Held**
WEB: www.sotocompany.com
SIC: 0782 Landscape contractors

(P-943)
SOUTHWEST LANDSCAPE INC
2205 S Standard Ave, Santa Ana (92707-3036)
P.O. Box 15611 (92735-0611)
PHONE..................714 545-1084
Dan Hansen, *President*
Robert Hansen, *Vice Pres*
Todd Shaw, *General Mgr*
Casey Silva, *Marketing Staff*
Bryan Hansen, *Accounts Exec*
EMP: 80
SQ FT: 7,800
SALES (est): 5.7MM **Privately Held**
WEB: www.southwestlandscapeinc.com
SIC: 0782 Landscape contractors

(P-944)
SPECIALIZED LANDSCAPE MGT SVCS
Also Called: SLM Services
4212 Peast Los Angeles, Simi Valley (93063)
PHONE..................805 520-7590
Rene Emeterio, *President*
Wendy Emeterio, *Corp Secy*
EMP: 77
SALES (est): 3.4MM **Privately Held**
SIC: 0782 Landscape contractors

(P-945)
STONE TREE LANDSCAPE CORP
5757 Wilshire Blvd # 505, Los Angeles (90036-5810)
PHONE..................323 965-0944
Jerome Steinbaum, *President*
EMP: 50
SALES (est): 1.1MM **Privately Held**
SIC: 0782 Landscape contractors

(P-946)
SUNSET LANDSCAPE MAINTENANCE
27201 Burbank, El Toro (92610-2500)
PHONE..................949 455-4636
James Roughan, *President*
Claudia Roughan, *Corp Secy*
Laurie Savolainen, *Office Mgr*
EMP: 100
SQ FT: 6,300
SALES (est): 5.9MM **Privately Held**
SIC: 0782 Lawn & garden services

(P-947)
TED COOPER/COOPER INDUSTRIES
P.O. Box 36007 (95158-6007)
PHONE..................408 358-3060
Ted Cooper, *Owner*
EMP: 50
SALES (est): 1.6MM **Privately Held**
WEB: www.coopindustries.com
SIC: 0782 1799 Landscape contractors; parking facility equipment & maintenance

(P-948)
TRANSPORTATION CALIFORNIA DEPT
1490 George Dr, Redding (96003-1460)
PHONE..................530 225-3349
Frank Herrman, *Manager*
EMP: 70 **Privately Held**
SIC: 0782 Highway lawn & garden maintenance services
HQ: California Dept Of Transportation
1120 N St
Sacramento CA 95814

(P-949)
TREE SCULPTURE GROUP
Also Called: Tarra Landscape
463 Roland Way, Oakland (94621-2014)
PHONE..................510 562-4000
Craig Lundin, *President*
Cassidy Lundin, *Vice Pres*
Paulette Roddy, *Executive*
Dan Dachauer, *Manager*
EMP: 60
SALES (est): 4MM **Privately Held**
WEB: www.treesculpture.com
SIC: 0782 Landscape contractors

(P-950)
TREEBEARD LANDSCAPE INC
9917 Campo Rd, Spring Valley (91977-1609)
P.O. Box 2777 (91979-2777)
PHONE..................619 697-8302
Tim Hillman, *President*
Craig Des Lauriers, *Vice Pres*
EMP: 100
SQ FT: 2,500
SALES (est): 5.8MM **Privately Held**
SIC: 0782 Garden maintenance services; lawn services

(P-951)
TROPICAL PLAZA NURSERY INC
9642 Santiago Blvd, Villa Park (92867-2521)
PHONE..................714 998-4100
Leslie T Fields, *President*
Mike Feilds, *Vice Pres*
EMP: 100
SQ FT: 5,000
SALES (est): 2.6MM **Privately Held**
SIC: 0782 Landscape contractors

(P-952)
TRU GREEN LANDCARE INC
5248 Governor Dr, San Diego (92122-2800)
PHONE..................602 276-4311
David M Flott, *President*
Joseph Hanks, *Vice Pres*
EMP: 450
SQ FT: 3,000
SALES (est): 9.2MM
SALES (corp-wide): 2.9B **Publicly Held**
WEB: www.landcareusa.com
SIC: 0782 Landscape contractors
HQ: Landcare Usa, Inc
2603 Augusta Dr Ste 1300
Houston TX 77057
713 692-6371

(P-953)
TRUGREEN LIMITED PARTNERSHIP
Also Called: Tru Green-Chemlawn
1130 Palmyrita Ave # 300, Riverside (92507-1714)
P.O. Box 1359, Rancho Cucamonga (91729-1359)
PHONE..................951 231-2760
Jeff Martinau, *Manager*
EMP: 50
SALES (corp-wide): 3.4B **Privately Held**
SIC: 0782 Lawn care services
HQ: Trugreen Limited Partnership
1790 Kirby Pkwy
Memphis TN 38138
901 251-4128

(P-954)
ULTIMATE LANDSCAPING MGT
700 E Sycamore St, Anaheim (92805-2831)
PHONE..................714 502-9711
James Berne, *President*
Angelica Herrera, *Accounts Mgr*
EMP: 80
SALES (est): 4.6MM **Privately Held**
SIC: 0782 Landscape contractors

(P-955)
UNITED LANDSCAPE RESOURCE INC
Also Called: Botanica Landscapes
5411 Colusa Hwy, Yuba City (95993-9311)
P.O. Box 569 (95992-0569)
PHONE..................530 671-1029
Bill Lucich, *President*
Edmund Clavel III, *President*
Tim Corey, *COO*
Candice Lucich, *Corp Secy*
EMP: 65
SQ FT: 2,000
SALES (est): 3.7MM **Privately Held**
WEB: www.botanica.net
SIC: 0782 Landscape contractors; lawn care services

(P-956)
VALLEY LANDSCAPING & MAINT INC
12900 N Lwer Scramento Rd, Lodi (95242)
PHONE..................209 334-3659
Don Oliver, *President*
Lori Peck, *Treasurer*
Jed Phelps, *Vice Pres*
EMP: 120
SQ FT: 5,000
SALES (est): 7.4MM **Privately Held**
SIC: 0782 Landscape contractors

(P-957)
VENCO WESTERN INC (PA)
2400 Eastman Ave, Oxnard (93030-5187)
PHONE..................805 981-2400
Linda Del Nagro Burr, *President*
Bill Barrett, *Manager*
Craig Owen, *Accounts Mgr*
EMP: 150
SQ FT: 15,000
SALES (est): 12.7MM **Privately Held**
WEB: www.vencowestern.com
SIC: 0782 Landscape contractors

(P-958)
VINTAGE ASSOCIATES INC
Also Called: Vintage Nursery
78755 Darby Rd, Bermuda Dunes (92203-9621)
P.O. Box 5250, La Quinta (92248-5250)
PHONE..................760 772-3673
Gregory Gritters, *President*
Yvonne Leque, *Controller*
Al Hollinger, *Opers Mgr*
Rob Downing, *Manager*
Joe Elkins, *Manager*
EMP: 160
SQ FT: 1,000
SALES (est): 14MM **Privately Held**
SIC: 0782 5193 5261 Landscape contractors; nursery stock; nurseries

(P-959)
W B STARR INC
20602 Canada Rd, Lake Forest (92630-8100)
PHONE..................949 770-8835
William B Starr, *President*
Martha L Starr, *Vice Pres*
EMP: 65
SQ FT: 10,000
SALES (est): 3.6MM **Privately Held**
WEB: www.wbstarr.com
SIC: 0782 Garden maintenance services

(P-960)
WATKIN & BORTOLUSSI INC
726 Alfred Nobel Dr, Hercules (94547-1805)
PHONE..................415 453-4675
Phillip Bortolussi, *President*
Peggy Bortolussi, *Vice Pres*
EMP: 60
SQ FT: 1,000

SALES (est): 3.2MM **Privately Held**
SIC: 0782 Landscape contractors

(P-961)
WENDT LANDSCAPE SERVICES INC
Also Called: Pacific Coast Sweeping
29714 Avenida De Las, Rancho Santa Margari (92688)
PHONE..................949 589-8680
Richard Wendt, *President*
EMP: 70 EST: 1980
SQ FT: 6,600
SALES (est): 2.7MM **Privately Held**
SIC: 0782 Landscape contractors

(P-962)
WM VANDERGEEST LANDSCAPE CARE
3342 W Castor St, Santa Ana (92704-3908)
PHONE..................714 545-8432
Allan M Curr, *President*
Sherry Curr, *Treasurer*
Chris Curr, *Vice Pres*
EMP: 100 EST: 1974
SQ FT: 10,000
SALES (est): 3.4MM **Privately Held**
SIC: 0782 Landscape contractors

(P-963)
WURZEL LANDSCAPE MAINTENANCE
Also Called: Canyon Way Nursery
3214 Oakdell Rd, Studio City (91604-4221)
PHONE..................818 762-8653
Marc W Wurzel, *Partner*
Doris Wurzel, *Partner*
EMP: 50
SALES (est): 1.3MM **Privately Held**
SIC: 0782 Garden maintenance services; landscape contractors

(P-964)
YEAR ROUND LANDSCAPE MAINT INC
15189 Sierra Bonita Ln, Chino (91710-8904)
PHONE..................909 597-7734
Larry M Sweeden, *President*
EMP: 50
SQ FT: 5,700
SALES (est): 1.8MM **Privately Held**
SIC: 0782 Garden maintenance services

0783 Ornamental Shrub & Tree Svc

(P-965)
ARBORWELL INC (PA)
2337 American Ave, Hayward (94545-1807)
PHONE..................510 881-4260
Alvin Foye Sortwell, *President*
Brad Carson, *CFO*
Dennis Shanagher, *Corp Secy*
Andy Lavelle, *Vice Pres*
Ann B Sortwell, *Vice Pres*
▲ EMP: 75
SQ FT: 5,000
SALES (est): 30.6MM **Privately Held**
WEB: www.arborwell.com
SIC: 0783 Planting, pruning & trimming services

(P-966)
ASPLUNDH TREE EXPERT CO
Also Called: Utility Tree Services
6100 Francis Botello Rd C, Goleta (93117-3259)
PHONE..................805 964-9216
Alex Ramos, *Business Mgr*
EMP: 99
SALES (corp-wide): 4.3B **Privately Held**
WEB: www.asplundh.com
SIC: 0783 Tree trimming services for public utility lines
PA: Asplundh Tree Expert, Llc
708 Blair Mill Rd
Willow Grove PA 19090
215 784-4200

(P-967)
ASPLUNDH TREE EXPERT LLC
2055 N Ventura Ave, Ventura (93001-1308)
PHONE...................................805 641-0528
Tony Ortiz, *Branch Mgr*
EMP: 94
SALES (corp-wide): 4.3B **Privately Held**
SIC: 0783 Tree trimming services for public
   utility lines
PA: Asplundh Tree Expert, Llc
   708 Blair Mill Rd
   Willow Grove PA 19090
   215 784-4200

(P-968)
ASPLUNDH TREE EXPERT LLC
6101 Gateway Dr, Cypress (90630-4841)
PHONE...................................714 893-2405
Joseph Guerrero, *Branch Mgr*
EMP: 150
SALES (corp-wide): 4.3B **Privately Held**
WEB: www.asplundh.com
SIC: 0783 Tree trimming services for public
   utility lines
PA: Asplundh Tree Expert, Llc
   708 Blair Mill Rd
   Willow Grove PA 19090
   215 784-4200

(P-969)
BROOKER ASSOCIATES
16372 Cnstr Cir E 5, Irvine (92618)
PHONE...................................949 559-4877
Ray Duval, *Branch Mgr*
EMP: 52
SALES (corp-wide): 5.4MM **Privately
Held**
WEB: www.brookerassociates.com
SIC: 0783 1721 1542
PA: Brooker Associates
   2331 E Lambert Rd
   La Habra CA 90631
   714 773-9490

(P-970)
**CLS LANDSCAPE
MANAGEMENT INC**
4711 Schaefer Ave Unit A, Chino
(91710-5544)
PHONE...................................909 628-3005
Kevin L Davis, *President*
Gloria Gonzalez, *Office Mgr*
Kimberly Davis, *Admin Sec*
EMP: 325
SQ FT: 2,500
SALES: 16.3MM **Privately Held**
WEB: www.clslandscape.com
SIC: 0783 0782 Ornamental shrub & tree
   services; lawn & garden services

(P-971)
**DAVEY TREE SURGERY
COMPANY**
6915 Eastside Rd Ste 94, Anderson
(96007-9401)
PHONE...................................530 378-2674
Dennis Dodson, *Manager*
EMP: 60
SALES (corp-wide): 915.9MM **Privately
Held**
SIC: 0783 Surgery services, ornamental
   tree
HQ: Davey Tree Surgery Company
   2617 S Vasco Rd
   Livermore CA 94550
   925 443-1723

(P-972)
**DAVEY TREE SURGERY
COMPANY (HQ)**
2617 S Vasco Rd, Livermore (94550)
P.O. Box 5015 (94551-5015)
PHONE...................................925 443-1723
Karl J Warnke, *CEO*
R Douglas Cowan, *President*
David Adante, *CFO*
Howard Bowles, *Senior VP*
Rick Edson, *Admin Sec*
EMP: 873
SQ FT: 5,000
SALES: 12.4MM
SALES (corp-wide): 915.9MM **Privately
Held**
SIC: 0783 Tree trimming services for public
   utility lines

PA: The Davey Tree Expert Company
   1500 N Mantua St
   Kent OH 44240
   330 673-9511

(P-973)
**DAVEY TREE SURGERY
COMPANY**
1914 Mission Rd Ste N, Escondido
(92029-1116)
PHONE...................................760 975-0225
Brian Friedrich, *Branch Mgr*
EMP: 100
SALES (corp-wide): 915.9MM **Privately
Held**
SIC: 0783 Surgery services, ornamental
   tree
HQ: Davey Tree Surgery Company
   2617 S Vasco Rd
   Livermore CA 94550
   925 443-1723

(P-974)
**GREAT SCOTT TREE SERVICE
INC (PA)**
10761 Court Ave, Stanton (90680-2435)
PHONE...................................714 826-1750
Scott Griffiths, *President*
Jacob Griffiths, *Vice Pres*
Steve Guzonski, *Administration*
EMP: 120
SQ FT: 28,675
SALES (est): 13.4MM **Privately Held**
WEB: www.gstsinc.com
SIC: 0783 Pruning services, ornamental
   tree

(P-975)
LEONARD CHAIDEZ INC
Also Called: Leonard Chaidez Tree Service
2298 N Batavia St, Orange (92865-3106)
P.O. Box 29, Anaheim (92815-0029)
PHONE...................................714 279-8173
Leonard Chaidez, *President*
Deborah Foushee, *Admin Sec*
Jamie Lance, *Manager*
EMP: 60
SQ FT: 2,000
SALES (est): 3.5MM **Privately Held**
SIC: 0783 0781 8748 0782 Ornamental
   shrub & tree services; landscape serv-
   ices; environmental consultant; lawn &
   garden services

(P-976)
**ORIGINAL MOWBRAYS TREE
SVC INC (PA)**
1845 Bus Ctr Dr Ste 215, San Bernardino
(92408)
PHONE...................................909 383-7009
Dwight Anderson, *Principal*
Rhonda Ramirez, *General Mgr*
EMP: 200
SQ FT: 1,000
SALES: 12MM **Privately Held**
WEB: www.mowbrays.org
SIC: 0783 Tree trimming services for public
   utility lines

(P-977)
PACIFIC SLOPE TREE COOP INC
11201 State Rte One 201, Point Reyes Sta-
tion (94956)
P.O. Box 400 (94956-0400)
PHONE...................................415 663-1300
Thomas Kent, *President*
Elan Whitney, *Corp Secy*
EMP: 50
SALES: 4MM **Privately Held**
WEB: www.pacificslopetree.com
SIC: 0783 Planting, pruning & trimming
   services

(P-978)
SP MCCLENAHAN CO
Also Called: McClenahan S P Co Tree Serv-
ice
1 Arastradero Rd, Portola Valley
(94028-8012)
PHONE...................................650 326-8781
James M Mc Clenahan, *President*
Joshua McClenahan, *Risk Mgmt Dir*
Miguel Berumen, *Reverend*
EMP: 56
SQ FT: 5,000

SALES (est): 4.8MM **Privately Held**
SIC: 0783 Planting, pruning & trimming
   services

(P-979)
TONY GOMEZ TREE SERVICE
700 N Johnson Ave Ste H, El Cajon
(92020-2521)
PHONE...................................619 593-1552
Antonio Gomez, *Owner*
EMP: 60
SALES (est): 2.7MM **Privately Held**
SIC: 0783 Ornamental shrub & tree serv-
   ices

(P-980)
TRAVERS TREE SERVICE INC
1811 Lomita Blvd, Lomita (90717-1905)
P.O. Box 411 (90717-0411)
PHONE...................................310 545-5816
Richard Travers, *President*
Don Lorenzen, *Vice Pres*
Susan Travers, *Admin Sec*
Mary Keyse, *Manager*
EMP: 50
SQ FT: 2,000
SALES (est): 5.1MM **Privately Held**
SIC: 0783 Planting, pruning & trimming
   services

(P-981)
TREEPEOPLE INC
12601 Mulholland Dr, Beverly Hills
(90210-1332)
PHONE...................................818 753-4600
Walt Burkley, *Ch of Bd*
Andy Lipkis, *President*
Gwyn Quillen, *Treasurer*
Sarah Kern, *Officer*
Paul Bergman, *Admin Sec*
EMP: 50
SQ FT: 21,000
SALES: 4.4MM **Privately Held**
WEB: www.treepeople.org
SIC: 0783 8641 Planting, pruning & trim-
   ming services; environmental protection
   organization

(P-982)
**UTILITY TREE SERVICE LLC
(DH)**
Also Called: Utility Tree Service, Inc.
1884 Keystone Ct Ste A, Redding
(96003-4870)
PHONE...................................530 226-0330
Scott Asplundh, *President*
Joseph P Dwyer, *Corp Secy*
Brent D Asplundh, *Vice Pres*
Carl Asplundh III, *Vice Pres*
Gregg Asplundh, *Vice Pres*
EMP: 50
SALES (est): 11.8MM
SALES (corp-wide): 4.3B **Privately Held**
SIC: 0783 Tree trimming services for public
   utility lines

(P-983)
WEST COAST ARBORISTS INC
21718 Walnut Ave, Grand Terrace
(92313-4437)
PHONE...................................909 783-6544
Patrick Mahoney, *President*
EMP: 50
SALES (est): 758K
SALES (corp-wide): 57.6MM **Privately
Held**
SIC: 0783 Planting, pruning & trimming
   services
PA: West Coast Arborists, Inc.
   2200 E Via Burton
   Anaheim CA 92806
   714 991-1900

0811 Timber Tracts

(P-984)
**BOETHING TREELAND FARMS
INC**
2923 Alpine Rd, Portola Valley
(94028-7546)
PHONE...................................650 851-4770
Richard Hanley, *Branch Mgr*
EMP: 700

SALES (corp-wide): 75.8MM **Privately
Held**
WEB: www.boethingtreeland.com
SIC: 0811 5193 0181 Tree farm; nursery
   stock; nursery stock, growing of
PA: Boething Treeland Farms, Inc.
   23475 Long Valley Rd
   Woodland Hills CA 91367
   818 883-1222

(P-985)
**BOETHING TREELAND FARMS
INC (PA)**
23475 Long Valley Rd, Woodland Hills
(91367-6006)
PHONE...................................818 883-1222
Bruce Edgar Pherson, *CEO*
Marjorie Boething Arnold, *Shareholder*
Sally Boething Hilton, *Shareholder*
Cathy Boething Pherson, *Shareholder*
Marji Boething, *CFO*
EMP: 60
SQ FT: 1,500
SALES: 75.8MM **Privately Held**
WEB: www.boethingtreeland.com
SIC: 0811 5261 Tree farm; nurseries

(P-986)
**BOETHING TREELAND FARMS
INC**
Also Called: Boething Treeland Nursery
20601 E Kettleman Ln, Lodi (95240-9756)
PHONE...................................209 727-3741
Seilpe Gomez, *Branch Mgr*
Desiree Archuleta, *Sales Staff*
EMP: 175
SALES (est): 3.3MM
SALES (corp-wide): 75.8MM **Privately
Held**
WEB: www.boethingtreeland.com
SIC: 0811 Tree farm
PA: Boething Treeland Farms, Inc.
   23475 Long Valley Rd
   Woodland Hills CA 91367
   818 883-1222

(P-987)
BRIGHTVIEW TREE COMPANY
Also Called: Specimen Contracting
9500 Foothill Blvd, Sunland (91040-1857)
PHONE...................................818 951-5500
Tadd Russikoff, *Manager*
EMP: 115
SALES (corp-wide): 2.8B **Publicly Held**
WEB: www.vctree.com
SIC: 0811 Tree farm
HQ: Brightview Tree Company
   24151 Ventura Blvd
   Calabasas CA 91302
   818 223-8500

(P-988)
BRIGHTVIEW TREE COMPANY
Also Called: Environmental Industries
3200 W Telegraph Rd, Fillmore
(93015-9623)
PHONE...................................714 546-7975
Susan Flores, *Branch Mgr*
EMP: 160
SALES (corp-wide): 2.8B **Publicly Held**
WEB: www.vctree.com
SIC: 0811 0782 Tree farm; lawn services
HQ: Brightview Tree Company
   24151 Ventura Blvd
   Calabasas CA 91302
   818 223-8500

(P-989)
BRIGHTVIEW TREE COMPANY
8501 Calaveras Rd, Sunol (94586-9434)
PHONE...................................925 862-2485
John Serviss, *Branch Mgr*
Nancy Kennedy, *Office Mgr*
EMP: 100
SALES (corp-wide): 2.8B **Publicly Held**
WEB: www.vctree.com
SIC: 0811 Tree farm
HQ: Brightview Tree Company
   24151 Ventura Blvd
   Calabasas CA 91302
   818 223-8500

▲ = Import ▼=Export
◆ =Import/Export

(P-990)
BRIGHTVIEW TREE COMPANY
28915 E Funck Rd, Farmington
(95230-9567)
PHONE.....................209 886-5511
Gina Mortenson, *Executive*
EMP: 85
SQ FT: 784
SALES (corp-wide): 2.8B **Publicly Held**
WEB: www.vctree.com
SIC: 0811 Tree farm
HQ: Brightview Tree Company
24151 Ventura Blvd
Calabasas CA 91302
818 223-8500

(P-991)
GREEN DIAMOND RESOURCE COMPANY
900 Riverside Rd, Korbel (95550)
P.O. Box 68 (95550-0068)
PHONE.....................707 668-4400
Neal Ewald, *Manager*
EMP: 100
SALES (est): 4MM
SALES (corp-wide): 228.8MM **Privately Held**
SIC: 0811 0851 Timber tracts; forestry services
HQ: Diamond Green Resource Company
1301 5th Ave Ste 2700
Seattle WA 98101
206 224-5800

(P-992)
M & M ENTERPRISES
3732 Hacienda Rd, Cottonwood
(96022-9765)
PHONE.....................530 347-3238
Mark Green, *Owner*
EMP: 100 EST: 2001
SALES (est): 1.1MM **Privately Held**
SIC: 0811 Christmas tree farm

(P-993)
MENDOCINO REDWOOD COMPANY LLC (PA)
850 Kunzler Ranch Rd, Ukiah
(95482-7294)
P.O. Box 996 (95482-0996)
PHONE.....................707 463-5110
Richard Higgenbottom, *Mng Member*
Patrick Orourke, *Info Tech Mgr*
Elaine Smith, *Controller*
Betty Pierce, *Purchasing*
Henry Long, *VP Opers*
EMP: 400
SALES (est): 13.2MM **Privately Held**
WEB: www.mrc.com
SIC: 0811 Timber tracts, hardwood; timber tracts, softwood

(P-994)
PINERY LLC
13701 Highland Valley Rd, Escondido
(92025-2300)
P.O. Box 2484, Rancho Cucamonga
(91729-2484)
PHONE.....................858 675-3575
Philip C Guardia,
Dennis Anderson, *COO*
Lisa Bryant, *Sales Staff*
Donna Davidson, *Sales Staff*
Diana Radestock, *Sales Staff*
▲ EMP: 60
SQ FT: 2,800
SALES (est): 4.9MM **Privately Held**
SIC: 0811 Christmas tree farm

(P-995)
WEYERHAEUSER COMPANY
800 Pier T Ave, Long Beach (90802-6236)
PHONE.....................562 983-6589
EMP: 77
SALES (corp-wide): 7.2B **Publicly Held**
SIC: 0811 Timber tracts
PA: Weyerhaeuser Company
220 Occidental Ave S
Seattle WA 98104
206 539-3000

(P-996)
YEW BIO-PHARM GROUP INC
9460 Telstar Ave Ste 6, El Monte
(91731-2904)
PHONE.....................626 401-9588
Zhiguo Wang, *Ch of Bd*
Guifang Qi, *Admin Sec*
EMP: 86 EST: 1996
SALES: 40.5MM **Privately Held**
SIC: 0811 Tree farm

0851 Forestry Svcs

(P-997)
CALIFORNIA SILVER-AGRICULTURE
831 Ash Ave, Lindsay (93247-1449)
PHONE.....................559 562-3795
Raul L Acevedo, *Owner*
EMP: 50
SALES: 50K **Privately Held**
SIC: 0851 Forestry services

(P-998)
FORESTRY AND FIRE PROTECTION
Also Called: Shasta-Trinity Ranger Unit
875 Cypress Ave, Redding (96001-2719)
PHONE.....................530 225-2418
Mike Chuchel, *Manager*
EMP: 150 **Privately Held**
WEB: www.calopps.org
SIC: 0851 Fire prevention services, forest
HQ: Forestry And Fire Protection California Department Of
1416 9th St Ste 1535
Sacramento CA 95814
-

(P-999)
RCO REFORESTING INC
Also Called: R C O Reforesting
1332 Fairlane Rd Ste A, Yreka
(96097-8504)
P.O. Box 1370 (96097-1370)
PHONE.....................530 842-7647
Roberto C Ochoa, *President*
EMP: 50
SALES (est): 1.2MM **Privately Held**
SIC: 0851 Reforestation services; fire prevention services, forest

(P-1000)
REDDING TREE GROWERS CORP
18985 Avenue 256 Apt A, Exeter
(93221-9558)
PHONE.....................559 594-9299
Francisco Acevedo, *President*
Amelia Acevedo, *Vice Pres*
EMP: 100
SALES: 2MM **Privately Held**
SIC: 0851 Reforestation services

(P-1001)
UNITED STATES FOREST SERVICE
17696 State Highway 89, Hat Creek
(96040-9431)
P.O. Box 220, Fall River Mills (96028-0220)
PHONE.....................530 335-4103
Carol Chandler, *Director*
EMP: 50
SALES (est): 722.9K **Privately Held**
SIC: 0851 Forestry services

(P-1002)
USDA FOREST SERVICE
100 Forni Rd, Placerville (95667-5310)
PHONE.....................530 626-1546
Lawrence Crabtree, *Principal*
EMP: 53 **Publicly Held**
SIC: 0851 Forestry services
HQ: Us Dept Of Agriculture Forest Service
201 14th St Sw
Washington DC 20024

0971 Hunting & Trapping

(P-1003)
DUCKS UNLIMITED INC
Also Called: Western Regional Office
3074 Gold Canal Dr, Rancho Cordova
(95670-6116)
PHONE.....................916 852-2000
Rudy Rosses, *Director*
Anita Tyler, *Director*
EMP: 50
SALES (corp-wide): 62.8MM **Privately Held**
WEB: www.ducks.org
SIC: 0971 Wildlife management
PA: Ducks Unlimited, Inc.
1 Waterfowl Way
Memphis TN 38120
901 758-3825

1041 Gold Ores

(P-1004)
BARRICK GOLD CORPORATION
Also Called: Mc Laughlin Mine
26775 Morgan Valley Rd, Lower Lake
(95457-9411)
PHONE.....................707 995-6070
Pat Purtell, *Branch Mgr*
EMP: 100
SALES (est): 11.8MM
SALES (corp-wide): 8.3B **Privately Held**
WEB: www.barrick.com
SIC: 1041 Gold ores
PA: Barrick Gold Corporation
161 Bay St Suite 3700
Toronto ON M5J 2
416 861-9911

(P-1005)
GOLDEN QUEEN MINING CO LLC
2818 Silver Queen Rd, Mojave
(93501-7021)
P.O. Box 1030 (93502-1030)
PHONE.....................661 824-4300
Thomas Clay, *Ch of Bd*
Robert Walish, *President*
Andree St-Germain, *CFO*
Brenda Dayton, *Admin Sec*
Ken Mann, *Administration*
EMP: 180
SQ FT: 2,500
SALES (est): 70MM **Privately Held**
SIC: 1041 Gold ores mining

(P-1006)
MERIDIAN GOLD INC
Also Called: Royal Mountain King
4461 Rock Creek Rd, Copperopolis
(95228)
PHONE.....................209 785-3222
Edgar Smith, *Branch Mgr*
EMP: 160
SALES (corp-wide): 1.8B **Privately Held**
SIC: 1041 Gold ores
HQ: Meridian Gold Inc.
4635 Longley Ln Ste 110
Reno NV 89502
-

(P-1007)
STAVATTI INDUSTRIES LTD
1443 S Gage St, San Bernardino
(92408-2835)
P.O. Box 211258, Eagan MN (55121-2658)
PHONE.....................651 238-5369
Christopher R Beskar, *Branch Mgr*
Christopher Beskar, *CEO*
EMP: 60
SALES (corp-wide): 2MM **Privately Held**
SIC: 1041 1081 3511 3533 Gold ores mining; metal mining exploration & development services; turbines & turbine generator set units, complete; oil & gas field machinery; truck trailers
PA: Stavatti Industries Ltd
1061 Tiffany Dr
Eagan MN 55123
651 238-5369

1221 Bituminous Coal & Lignite: Surface Mining

(P-1008)
CHEVRON MINING INC
Moly
67750 Bailey Rd, Mountain Pass (92366)
PHONE.....................760 856-7625
Allen Randle, *Branch Mgr*
EMP: 400
SALES (corp-wide): 141.7B **Publicly Held**
SIC: 1221 Surface mining, bituminous
HQ: Chevron Mining Inc.
116 Invrneco Dr E Ste 207
Englewood CO 80112
303 930-3600

1241 Coal Mining Svcs

(P-1009)
GREKA INC
1791 Sinton Rd, Santa Maria (93458-9708)
P.O. Box 5489 (93456-5489)
PHONE.....................805 347-8700
Andy Devegvar, *President*
Randeep Grewal, *CEO*
EMP: 150
SQ FT: 3,000
SALES: 40MM **Privately Held**
SIC: 1241 1081 Coal mining services; metal mining services

(P-1010)
RIO TINTO MINERALS INC
Also Called: Reno Tenco
14486 Borax Rd, Boron (93516-2017)
PHONE.....................760 762-7121
Xiaoling Liu, *CEO*
Preston Chiaro, *President*
Hugo Bague, *Principal*
Brett Horton, *Engineer*
Trevor Plote, *Engineer*
▼ EMP: 150
SALES (est): 17.1MM
SALES (corp-wide): 40B **Privately Held**
SIC: 1241 Coal mining services
HQ: U.S. Borax Inc.
8051 E Maplewood Ave # 100
Greenwood Village CO 80111
303 713-5000

(P-1011)
TAFT PRODUCTION COMPANY
950 Petroleum Club Rd, Taft (93268-9748)
PHONE.....................661 765-7194
Daniel S Jaffee, *President*
EMP: 95
SALES (est): 6.9MM
SALES (corp-wide): 262.3MM **Publicly Held**
WEB: www.oildri.com
SIC: 1241 1081 Coal mining services; metal mining services
PA: Oil-Dri Corporation Of America
410 N Michigan Ave Fl 4
Chicago IL 60611
312 321-1515

1311 Crude Petroleum & Natural Gas

(P-1012)
BENTLEY-SIMONSON INC
1746 S Victoria Ave Ste F, Ventura
(93003-6190)
PHONE.....................805 650-2794
James Bentley, *Ch of Bd*
Theodore Bentley, *Ch of Bd*
Clifton O Simonson, *President*
Petter Romming, *Vice Pres*
EMP: 100
SQ FT: 1,000
SALES (est): 4.1MM **Privately Held**
SIC: 1311 Crude petroleum & natural gas production

(P-1013)
BERRY PETROLEUM COMPANY LLC (HQ)
5201 Truxtun Ave Ste 100, Bakersfield
(93309-0422)
PHONE..................................661 616-3900
Trem Smith, *President*
EMP: 65
SALES (est): 641.6MM **Publicly Held**
WEB: www.bry.com
SIC: 1311 Crude petroleum production;
natural gas production
PA: Berry Petroleum Corporation
5201 Truxtun Ave Ste 100
Bakersfield CA 93309
661 616-3900

(P-1014)
BP WEST COAST PRODUCTS LLC
22600 Wilmington Ave, Carson
(90745-4307)
PHONE..................................310 816-8787
EMP: 310
SALES (corp-wide): 240.2B **Privately Held**
SIC: 1311 Crude petroleum & natural gas
HQ: Bp West Coast Products Llc
4519 Grandview Rd
Blaine WA 98230
310 549-6204

(P-1015)
BP WEST COAST PRODUCTS LLC
1306 Canal Blvd, Richmond (94804-3556)
PHONE..................................510 231-4724
Fred Glueck, *Vice Pres*
EMP: 310
SQ FT: 4,550
SALES (corp-wide): 240.2B **Privately Held**
SIC: 1311 Crude petroleum production
HQ: Bp West Coast Products Llc
4519 Grandview Rd
Blaine WA 98230
310 549-6204

(P-1016)
BREITBURN GP LLC
707 Wilshire Blvd # 4600, Los Angeles
(90017-3501)
PHONE..................................213 225-5900
Halbert S Washburn, *CEO*
EMP: 833
SALES (est): 16.6MM **Privately Held**
SIC: 1311 Crude petroleum & natural gas
PA: Breitburn Energy Partners Lp
707 Wilshire Blvd # 4600
Los Angeles CA 90017

(P-1017)
CALIFORNIA RESOURCES CORP
111 W Ocean Blvd Ste 800, Long Beach
(90802-7930)
PHONE..................................562 624-3400
EMP: 103
SALES (corp-wide): 2B **Publicly Held**
SIC: 1311 Crude petroleum production
PA: California Resources Corporation
9200 Oakdale Ave Ste 900
Chatsworth CA 91311
888 848-4754

(P-1018)
CALIFORNIA RESOURCES PROD CORP
3450 E 5th St, Oxnard (93033-2100)
PHONE..................................805 483-8017
EMP: 83
SALES (corp-wide): 2.4B **Publicly Held**
SIC: 1311 1382
HQ: California Resources Production Cor-
poration
11109 River Run Blvd
Bakersfield CA 93311
661 869-8000

(P-1019)
CALIFORNIA RESOURCES PROD CORP (HQ)
Also Called: Vintage Production California
11109 River Run Blvd, Bakersfield
(93311-8957)
PHONE..................................661 869-8000
Todd A Stevens, *Principal*
Richard Oringderff, *President*
Todd Stevens, *CEO*
EMP: 125
SALES (est): 92.1MM
SALES (corp-wide): 2B **Publicly Held**
WEB: www.oxy.com
SIC: 1311 1382 Crude petroleum produc-
tion; oil & gas exploration services
PA: California Resources Corporation
9200 Oakdale Ave Ste 900
Chatsworth CA 91311
888 848-4754

(P-1020)
CARBON CALIFORNIA COMPANY LLC
270 Quail Ct Ste B, Santa Paula
(93060-9204)
PHONE..................................805 933-1901
Patrick R McDonald, *CEO*
Mark D Pierce, *President*
Kevin D Struzeski, *CFO*
EMP: 72 EST: 2016
SALES (est): 841.9K
SALES (corp-wide): 22.4MM **Publicly Held**
SIC: 1311 Crude petroleum & natural gas
PA: Carbon Energy Corporation
1700 Broadway Ste 1170
Denver CO 80290
720 407-7043

(P-1021)
CHEVRON USA INC
6001 Bollinger Canyon Rd, San Ramon
(94583-5737)
P.O. Box 6017 (94583-0717)
PHONE..................................925 842-0855
Kim Smith, *Branch Mgr*
Bruce Lincoln, *Supervisor*
EMP: 100
SALES (corp-wide): 141.7B **Publicly Held**
SIC: 1311 2911 Crude petroleum & natural
gas; petroleum refining
HQ: Chevron U.S.A. Inc.
6001 Bollinger Canyon Rd D1248
San Ramon CA 94583
925 842-1000

(P-1022)
E & B NTRAL RESOURCES MGT CORP (PA)
1600 Norris Rd, Bakersfield (93308-2234)
PHONE..................................661 679-1714
Steve Layton, *President*
Ronkese Frank, *CFO*
Frank J Ronkese, *CFO*
Jeff Blesener, *Senior VP*
Joyce Holtzclaw, *Senior VP*
EMP: 65
SALES: 326.3MM **Privately Held**
WEB: www.ebresources.com
SIC: 1311 Crude petroleum & natural gas

(P-1023)
FREEPORT-MCMORAN OIL & GAS LLC
1200 Discovery Dr Ste 500, Bakersfield
(93309-7038)
PHONE..................................661 322-7600
Kiran Leal, *Manager*
EMP: 60
SALES (corp-wide): 16.4B **Publicly Held**
SIC: 1311 Crude petroleum & natural gas
HQ: Freeport-Mcmoran Oil & Gas Llc
700 Milam St Ste 3100
Houston TX 77002
713 579-6000

(P-1024)
LINNCO LLC
5201 Truxtun Ave, Bakersfield
(93309-0421)
PHONE..................................661 616-3900
Gordon Beagley, *Technician*
Greg Williams, *Technology*

Jared Gilarducci, *Engineer*
Dom Sylvester, *VP Opers*
EMP: 1432
SALES (corp-wide): 40.7MM **Publicly Held**
SIC: 1311 Crude petroleum & natural gas
PA: Linnco, Llc
600 Travis St Ste 5100
Houston TX 77002
281 840-4000

(P-1025)
OXY USA INC
9600 Ming Ave Ste 300, Bakersfield
(93311-1365)
PHONE..................................661 869-8000
Gary O Lee Jr, *Credit Mgr*
EMP: 125
SALES (corp-wide): 13.2B **Publicly Held**
SIC: 1311 Crude petroleum & natural gas
HQ: Oxy Usa Inc.
1001 S County Rd W
Odessa TX 79763
432 335-0995

(P-1026)
PETROLEUM SALES INC
2066 Redwood Hwy, Greenbrae
(94904-2467)
PHONE..................................415 256-1600
Stephanie Shimk, *Branch Mgr*
EMP: 70
SALES (corp-wide): 31.7MM **Privately Held**
SIC: 1311 Crude petroleum & natural gas
PA: Petroleum Sales Inc
1475 2nd St
San Rafael CA 94901
415 256-1600

(P-1027)
QUANTUM TECHNOLOGIES INC
25242 Arctic Ocean Dr, Lake Forest
(92630-8821)
PHONE..................................949 399-4500
Dean K Aoki, *CEO*
Alan Niedzwiecki, *President*
Bradley J Timon, *CFO*
Mark Arold, *Vice Pres*
Neel Sirosh, *Principal*
EMP: 140
SALES (est): 38.2MM **Privately Held**
SIC: 1311 Crude petroleum & natural gas

(P-1028)
SAMEDAN OIL CORPORATION
Also Called: Noble Energy
1360 Landing Ave, Seal Beach
(90740-6525)
PHONE..................................661 319-5038
EMP: 336
SALES (corp-wide): 34.8MM **Privately Held**
SIC: 1311 Crude petroleum production
PA: Samedan Oil Corporation
1001 Noble Energy Way
Houston TX 77070
580 223-4110

(P-1029)
STRAND ENERGY COMPANY
Also Called: Breitburn Energy Co
10350 Heritage Park Dr, Santa Fe Springs
(90670-3787)
PHONE..................................562 944-9580
EMP: 227
SALES (corp-wide): 394.4MM **Privately Held**
SIC: 1311 Crude petroleum & natural gas
PA: The Strand Energy Company
515 S Flower St Ste 4800
Los Angeles CA 90071
213 225-5900

(P-1030)
UNOCAL CORPORATION (HQ)
6001 Bollinger Canyon Rd, San Ramon
(94583-2324)
PHONE..................................310 726-7600
Charles R Williamson, *Ch of Bd*
Terry G Dallas, *CFO*
John W Creighton Jr, *Vice Ch Bd*
Samuel H Gillespie III, *Vice Pres*
Douglas M Miller, *Vice Pres*
EMP: 350

SALES (est): 486.7MM
SALES (corp-wide): 141.7B **Publicly Held**
WEB: www.unocal.com
SIC: 1311 2873 2911 4612 Crude petroleum production; natural gas production;
nitrogenous fertilizers; coke, petroleum;
crude petroleum pipelines; refined petroleum pipelines; geothermal drilling
PA: Chevron Corporation
6001 Bollinger Canyon Rd
San Ramon CA 94583
925 842-1000

(P-1031)
VAQUERO ENERGY INCORPORATED
15545 Hermosa Rd, Bakersfield
(93307-9477)
PHONE..................................661 363-7240
Ken Hunter, *President*
EMP: 50
SALES (est): 953.9K **Privately Held**
SIC: 1311 Crude petroleum production

1381 Drilling Oil & Gas Wells

(P-1032)
AERA ENERGY LLC (HQ)
10000 Ming Ave, Bakersfield (93311-1301)
P.O. Box 11164 (93389-1164)
PHONE..................................661 665-5000
Christina S Sistrunk, *President*
Bill Hanson, *Exec VP*
Robert C Alberstadt, *Senior VP*
Brent D Carnahan, *Senior VP*
Lynne J Carrithers, *Senior VP*
EMP: 800
SALES (est): 2.1B
SALES (corp-wide): 305.1B **Privately Held**
WEB: www.aeraenergy.com
SIC: 1381 Directional drilling oil & gas
wells
PA: Royal Dutch Shell Plc
Shell Centre
London SE1 7
207 934-1234

(P-1033)
AERA ENERGY LLC
Also Called: Aera Energy South Midway
29235 Highway 33, Maricopa
(93252-9793)
PHONE..................................661 665-3200
Andy Anderson, *Manager*
Bob Alberstadt, *Vice Pres*
Joshua Boling, *Purch Agent*
Jay Licata, *Production*
Richard Stringer, *Manager*
EMP: 60
SALES (corp-wide): 305.1B **Privately Held**
WEB: www.aeraenergy.com
SIC: 1381 Directional drilling oil & gas
wells
HQ: Aera Energy Llc
10000 Ming Ave
Bakersfield CA 93311
661 665-5000

(P-1034)
ALUMATEC INC
18411 Sherman Way, Reseda
(91335-4319)
PHONE..................................818 609-7460
Francesco Chinaglia, *President*
Yazmin Ibarlucea, *Treasurer*
Laura Chinaglia, *Admin Sec*
EMP: 80
SALES (est): 7.1MM **Privately Held**
WEB: www.alumatec.us
SIC: 1381 Drilling oil & gas wells

(P-1035)
ELYSIUM JENNINGS LLC
1600 Norris Rd, Bakersfield (93308-2234)
PHONE..................................661 679-1700
Steve Layton, *EMP: 200*
EMP: 200
SALES (est): 8.7MM **Privately Held**
SIC: 1381 Drilling oil & gas wells

PA: E & B Natural Resources Management
Corporation
1600 Norris Rd
Bakersfield CA 93308

(P-1036)
EXCALIBUR WELL SERVICES CORP (PA)
22034 Rosedale Hwy, Bakersfield
(93314-9704)
PHONE...............................661 589-5338
Stephen Layton, *President*
Frachsco Galesi, *President*
Gordon Isbel, *Vice Pres*
Mary Telupessy, *Business Mgr*
EMP: 78
SALES (est): 40.3MM **Privately Held**
SIC: 1381 1389 Drilling oil & gas wells;
fishing for tools, oil & gas field

(P-1037)
GOLDEN STATE DRILLING INC
3500 Fruitvale Ave, Bakersfield
(93308-5106)
PHONE...............................661 589-0730
Philip F Phelps, *President*
James Phelps, *Treasurer*
Velma Phelps, *Vice Pres*
Russ Lueck, *Manager*
Mike McCutcheon, *Manager*
EMP: 75
SALES (est): 14.1MM **Privately Held**
WEB: www.gsdrilling.com
SIC: 1381 Directional drilling oil & gas
wells

(P-1038)
NABORS WELL SERVICES CO
1025 Earthmover Ct, Bakersfield
(93314-9529)
PHONE...............................661 588-6140
Tom Jaquez, *Manager*
EMP: 160 **Privately Held**
SIC: 1381 Drilling oil & gas wells
HQ: Nabors Well Services Co.
515 W Greens Rd Ste 1000
Houston TX 77067
281 874-0035

(P-1039)
PAUL GRAHAM DRILLING & SVC CO
2500 Airport Rd, Rio Vista (94571-1034)
P.O. Box 669 (94571-0669)
PHONE...............................707 374-5123
Kevin P Graham, *President*
Jill Graham, *CFO*
Clarence Santos, *Vice Pres*
Eddie Woodruff, *General Mgr*
Alyssa Graham, *Graphic Designe*
EMP: 170
SQ FT: 30,000
SALES (est): 30MM **Privately Held**
SIC: 1381 7389 7359 Drilling oil & gas
wells; crane & aerial lift service; industrial
truck rental

1382 Oil & Gas Field Exploration Svcs

(P-1040)
CALIFORNIA RESOURCES CORP (PA)
9200 Oakdale Ave Ste 900, Chatsworth
(91311-6559)
PHONE...............................888 848-4754
Todd A Stevens, *President*
William E Albrecht, *Ch of Bd*
Marshall D Smith, *CFO*
Justin Gannon, *Bd of Directors*
Ronald Havner, *Bd of Directors*
EMP: 77
SALES: 2B **Publicly Held**
SIC: 1382 Oil & gas exploration services

(P-1041)
DCOR LLC (PA)
290 Maple Ct Ste 290 # 290, Ventura
(93003-9144)
P.O. Box 3401 (93006-3401)
PHONE...............................805 535-2000
Bill Templeton,

Andrew Prestridge, *President*
Alan C Templeton, *CFO*
Greg Cavette, *Vice Pres*
Dennis Conley, *Vice Pres*
EMP: 76
SALES (est): 154.1MM **Privately Held**
WEB: www.dcor.com
SIC: 1382 Oil & gas exploration services

(P-1042)
DCOR LLC
290 Maple Ct Ste 290, Ventura
(93003-9144)
PHONE...............................805 576-1200
Stephanie Rice, *Branch Mgr*
EMP: 56
SALES (corp-wide): 154.1MM **Privately Held**
SIC: 1382 Oil & gas exploration services
PA: Dcor, L.L.C.
290 Maple Ct Ste 290 # 290
Ventura CA 93003
805 535-2000

(P-1043)
DEMENNO KERDOON
2000 N Alameda St, Compton
(90222-2799)
PHONE...............................310 537-7100
Shane Bamelin, *Principal*
Jim Tice, *Principal*
Jim Ennis, *Director*
EMP: 125
SQ FT: 11,614
SALES (est): 25.6MM **Privately Held**
WEB: www.demennokerdoon.com
SIC: 1382 Oil & gas exploration services

(P-1044)
E AND B NATURAL RESOURCES
1600 Norris Rd, Bakersfield (93308-2234)
PHONE...............................661 679-1700
Francesco Galesi, *CEO*
EMP: 51
SALES (est): 8.5MM **Privately Held**
SIC: 1382 Oil & gas exploration services

(P-1045)
NATIONS PETROLEUM CAL LLC
9600 Ming Ave Ste 300, Bakersfield
(93311-1365)
PHONE...............................661 387-6402
Phil Sorvet,
EMP: 60
SALES (est): 4MM **Privately Held**
SIC: 1382 Oil & gas exploration services
PA: Nations Petroleum Company Ltd
255 5 Ave Sw Suite 750
Calgary AB T2P 3
403 206-1420

(P-1046)
QRE OPERATING LLC
707 Wilshire Blvd # 4600, Los Angeles
(90017-3501)
PHONE...............................213 225-5900
Alan L Smith, *Mng Member*
EMP: 208
SALES (est): 708K **Privately Held**
SIC: 1382 Oil & gas exploration services
HQ: Qr Energy, Lp
707 Wilshire Blvd # 4600
Los Angeles CA 90017

(P-1047)
R W LYALL & COMPANY INC (DH)
2665 Research Dr, Corona (92882-6918)
P.O. Box 2259 (92878-2259)
PHONE...............................951 270-1500
Jeffrey W Lyall, *President*
Jennifer Fritchle, *COO*
Bruce Lange, *COO*
Tony Mauer, *CFO*
▲**EMP:** 168
SQ FT: 70,000
SALES (est): 152.4MM
SALES (corp-wide): 3.6B **Publicly Held**
WEB: www.rwlyall.com
SIC: 1382 Oil & gas exploration services

1389 Oil & Gas Field Svcs, NEC

(P-1048)
BAKER HGHES OLFLD OPRTIONS LLC
5700 Doolittle Ave, Shafter (93263-4035)
PHONE...............................661 834-9654
Bob Ledet, *Manager*
EMP: 50
SALES (corp-wide): 122B **Publicly Held**
WEB: www.bot.bhi-net.com
SIC: 1389 7353 5084 Oil field services; oil
field equipment, rental or leasing; drilling
bits
HQ: Baker Hughes Oilfield Operations Llc
17021 Aldine Westfield Rd
Houston TX 77073
713 879-1000

(P-1049)
BAKER HUGHES A GE COMPANY LLC
1127 Carrier Parkway Ave, Bakersfield
(93308-9666)
PHONE...............................661 387-1010
Charles Laymance, *Branch Mgr*
EMP: 87
SALES (corp-wide): 122B **Publicly Held**
SIC: 1389 Oil field services
HQ: Baker Hughes, A Ge Company, Llc
17021 Aldine Westfield Rd
Houston TX 77073
713 439-8600

(P-1050)
BAKER HUGHES A GE COMPANY LLC
3901 Fanucchi Way, Shafter (93263-9539)
PHONE...............................661 831-7686
Richard Mounts, *Manager*
EMP: 70
SALES (corp-wide): 122B **Publicly Held**
WEB: www.bjservices.com
SIC: 1389 Oil field services
HQ: Baker Hughes, A Ge Company, Llc
17021 Aldine Westfield Rd
Houston TX 77073
713 439-8600

(P-1051)
BAKER HUGHES A GE COMPANY LLC
5145 Boylan St, Bakersfield (93308-4511)
PHONE...............................800 229-7447
Lori Robinson, *Manager*
Doug Thomas, *General Mgr*
Sebastian Jung,
EMP: 87
SALES (corp-wide): 122B **Publicly Held**
WEB: www.bakerhughes.com
SIC: 1389 Oil field services
HQ: Baker Hughes, A Ge Company, Llc
17021 Aldine Westfield Rd
Houston TX 77073
713 439-8600

(P-1052)
BAKER PETROLITE LLC
5125 Boylan St, Bakersfield (93308-4511)
PHONE...............................661 325-4138
Doug Thomas, *Manager*
EMP: 60
SALES (corp-wide): 122B **Publicly Held**
WEB: www.bakerpetrolite.com
SIC: 1389 Oil field services
HQ: Baker Petrolite Llc
12645 W Airport Blvd
Sugar Land TX 77478
281 276-5400

(P-1053)
CALIFRNIA RSURCES LONG BCH INC
111 W Ocean Blvd Ste 800, Long Beach
(90802-7930)
PHONE...............................562 624-3204
Frank Komin, *CEO*
EMP: 137
SALES (est): 1.6MM
SALES (corp-wide): 2B **Publicly Held**
SIC: 1389 Oil field services

PA: California Resources Corporation
9200 Oakdale Ave Ste 900
Chatsworth CA 91311
888 848-4754

(P-1054)
CL KNOX INC
Also Called: Advanced Industrial Services
34933 Imperial St, Bakersfield (93308)
PHONE...............................661 837-0477
Leslie Knox, *President*
Chris Knox, *Corp Secy*
EMP: 80
SALES (est): 10.6MM **Privately Held**
SIC: 1389 8742 Oil field services; indus-
trial consultant

(P-1055)
CUMMINGS VACUUM SERVICE INC
Also Called: Cummings Transportation
19605 Broken Ct, Shafter (93263-9583)
PHONE...............................661 746-1786
Pam Cummings, *President*
Ted Cummings, *Vice Pres*
Shiloh Smith, *Engineer*
Dave Stitt, *Maint Spvr*
EMP: 60
SQ FT: 3,000
SALES (est): 7.6MM **Privately Held**
SIC: 1389 Oil field services

(P-1056)
DWAYNES ENGINEERING & CNSTR
3655 Addie Ave, Mc Kittrick (93251)
P.O. Box 116 (93251-0116)
PHONE...............................661 762-7261
Dwayne Emfinger, *President*
EMP: 78
SALES (est): 7.8MM **Privately Held**
WEB: www.dwayneseng.com
SIC: 1389 Construction, repair & disman-
tling services

(P-1057)
ENGINEERED WELL SVC INTL INC
3120 Standard St, Bakersfield
(93308-6241)
PHONE...............................866 913-6283
Paul Sturgeon, *CEO*
John E Powell Jr, *Principal*
EMP: 125 **EST:** 2009
SALES (est): 44MM **Privately Held**
SIC: 1389 Oil field services

(P-1058)
ETHOSENERGY FIELD SERVICES LLC (DH)
Also Called: Wg
10455 Slusher Dr Bldg 12, Santa Fe
Springs (90670-3750)
PHONE...............................310 639-3523
Rob Duby, *President*
Patricia Lelito, *CFO*
Mike Fieldhouse, *Vice Pres*
Mary Ros, *General Mgr*
Gary Goddard, *Sales Staff*
EMP: 75
SALES (est): 29.9MM
SALES (corp-wide): 5.3B **Privately Held**
WEB: www.woodgroupgts.com
SIC: 1389 8711 3462 Oil consultants; in-
dustrial engineers; pump, compressor &
turbine forgings

(P-1059)
FIELD FOUNDATION
15306 Carmenita Rd, Santa Fe Springs
(90670-5606)
P.O. Box 4236, Cerritos (90703-4236)
PHONE...............................562 921-3567
Irwin Field, *Owner*
EMP: 50
SALES: 24.3K **Privately Held**
SIC: 1389 Oil sampling service for oil com-
panies

(P-1060)
GENE WATSON CONSTRUCTION A CA
801 Kern St, Taft (93268-2734)
PHONE...............................661 763-5254
Gene Watson, *Ltd Ptnr*

Patricia Watson, *Ltd Ptnr*
EMP: 530
SALES (est): 11.2MM **Privately Held**
WEB: www.gwc-ltd.com
SIC: 1389 1382 Oil field services; oil & gas exploration services

(P-1061)
GRAYSON SERVICE INC
1845 Greeley Rd, Bakersfield
(93314-9547)
PHONE..................661 589-5444
Carol A Grayson, *President*
Cheryl Grayson, *Vice Pres*
EMP: 150
SALES (est): 5.7MM **Privately Held**
SIC: 1389 Servicing oil & gas wells

(P-1062)
HALLIBURTON COMPANY
34722 7th Standard Rd, Bakersfield
(93314-9435)
PHONE..................661 393-8111
Dennis Lovett, *Branch Mgr*
Mark Hansen, *Technical Staff*
Patty Drew, *Human Res Mgr*
Rocky Lawrence, *Manager*
EMP: 87 **Publicly Held**
SIC: 1389 Oil field services
PA: Halliburton Company
3000 N Sam Houston Pkwy E
Houston TX 77032

(P-1063)
HILLS WLDG & ENGRG CONTR INC
Also Called: Hwe Mechanical
22038 Stockdale Hwy, Bakersfield
(93314-8889)
PHONE..................661 746-5400
Debora M Hill, *Vice Pres*
Robert Hill, *Shareholder*
EMP: 92
SALES (est): 7.1MM **Privately Held**
SIC: 1389 Testing, measuring, surveying & analysis services

(P-1064)
HIRSH INC
Also Called: Better Mens Clothes
860 S Los Angeles St # 900, Los Angeles
(90014-3311)
PHONE..................213 622-9441
Mistie Banks, *General Mgr*
Stanley Hirsh, *President*
EMP: 50
SALES (est): 1MM **Privately Held**
SIC: 1389 Lease tanks, oil field: erecting, cleaning & repairing

(P-1065)
HUNTING ENERGY SERVICES INC
Also Called: Hunting-Vinson
4900 California Ave 100a, Bakersfield
(93309-7024)
PHONE..................661 633-4272
Bobby Ford, *Branch Mgr*
EMP: 76
SALES (corp-wide): 722.9MM **Privately Held**
WEB: www.hunting-inc.com
SIC: 1389 Oil field services
HQ: Hunting Energy Services, Inc.
16825 Northchase Dr # 600
Houston TX 77060

(P-1066)
HVI CAT CANYON INC
2617 E Clark Ave, Santa Maria
(93455-5815)
PHONE..................805 621-5800
Randeep S Grewal, *President*
Ken Miller, *CFO*
Susan Whalen, *Vice Pres*
EMP: 125
SALES (est): 9.6MM **Privately Held**
SIC: 1389 Oil field services

(P-1067)
JERRY MELTON & SONS CNSTR
Also Called: Jerry Melton & Sons Cnstr
100 Jamison Ln, Taft (93268-4329)
PHONE..................661 765-5546

Jerry W Melton, *President*
Karen Melton, *Treasurer*
Judy Melton, *Vice Pres*
Steven Melton, *Admin Sec*
EMP: 85
SALES (est): 11.6MM **Privately Held**
WEB: www.jerrymelton.com
SIC: 1389 Oil & gas wells: building, repairing & dismantling; grading oil & gas well foundations

(P-1068)
KATERRA INC (PA)
2494 Sand Hill Rd Ste 100, Menlo Park
(94025-6981)
PHONE..................650 422-3572
Brad Knight, *CEO*
Ben Janofsky, *Vice Pres*
Ravi Naik, *Vice Pres*
Robert Wagner, *Vice Pres*
Steve Weilbach, *Vice Pres*
EMP: 100 **EST:** 2015
SALES: 125MM **Privately Held**
SIC: 1389 8741 8711 Construction, repair & dismantling services; construction management; construction & civil engineering

(P-1069)
MMI SERVICES INC
4042 Patton Way, Bakersfield
(93308-5030)
PHONE..................661 589-9366
Steve McGowan, *President*
Mel McGowan, *CEO*
Eric Olson, *Vice Pres*
Roxanne Campbell, *Info Tech Dir*
Erick Olson, *Human Res Dir*
EMP: 250
SQ FT: 4,500
SALES (est): 51.3MM **Privately Held**
WEB: www.mmi-services.com
SIC: 1389 Oil field services

(P-1070)
NABORS WELL SERVICES CO
7515 Rosedale Hwy, Bakersfield
(93308-5727)
PHONE..................661 589-3970
Alan Pounds, *Sales Executive*
Melanie Mendoza, *Maintence Staff*
EMP: 270 **Privately Held**
SIC: 1389 1382 Servicing oil & gas wells; oil & gas exploration services
HQ: Nabors Well Services Co.
515 W Greens Rd Ste 1000
Houston TX 77067
281 874-0035

(P-1071)
NABORS WELL SERVICES CO
19431 S Santa Fe Ave, Compton
(90221-5912)
PHONE..................310 639-7074
Bernie Fish, *Manager*
Juan Landron, *Technology*
Gary Kaufman, *Human Res Mgr*
EMP: 230 **Privately Held**
SIC: 1389 Gas field services; oil field services
HQ: Nabors Well Services Co.
515 W Greens Rd Ste 1000
Houston TX 77067
281 874-0035

(P-1072)
NABORS WELL SERVICES CO
1954 James Rd, Bakersfield (93308-9749)
PHONE..................661 392-7668
Dave Warner, *District Mgr*
EMP: 76 **Privately Held**
SIC: 1389 Oil field services
HQ: Nabors Well Services Co.
515 W Greens Rd Ste 1000
Houston TX 77067
281 874-0035

(P-1073)
OIL WELL SERVICE COMPANY (PA)
10840 Norwalk Blvd, Santa Fe Springs
(90670-3826)
PHONE..................562 612-0600
Jack Frost, *President*
Connie Laws, *Treasurer*
Richard Laws, *Vice Pres*
Matt Hensley, *Admin Sec*

EMP: 225
SQ FT: 9,000
SALES (est): 35.5MM **Privately Held**
WEB: www.ows1.com
SIC: 1389 Oil field services

(P-1074)
PACIFIC PROCESS SYSTEMS INC (PA)
7401 Rosedale Hwy, Bakersfield
(93308-5736)
PHONE..................661 321-9681
Jerry Wise, *CEO*
Robert Peterson, *CFO*
Alan George, *Corp Secy*
Terry Alberts, *Purchasing*
Curt Avis, *Opers Mgr*
▼ **EMP:** 90
SQ FT: 7,000
SALES (est): 262.1MM **Privately Held**
WEB: www.pps-equipment.com
SIC: 1389 7353 5082 Testing, measuring, surveying & analysis services; oil field equipment, rental or leasing; oil field equipment

(P-1075)
PC MECHANICAL INC
2803 Industrial Pkwy, Santa Maria
(93455-1811)
PHONE..................805 925-2888
Lew Parker, *President*
Brandon Burginger, *COO*
Mary Parker, *Exec VP*
Mitch Caron, *Vice Pres*
Diane Caron, *Admin Asst*
EMP: 50
SQ FT: 67,000
SALES (est): 11.3MM **Privately Held**
WEB: www.pcmechanical.com
SIC: 1389 Oil field services

(P-1076)
PROS INCORPORATED
3400 Patton Way, Bakersfield
(93308-5722)
P.O. Box 20996 (93390-0996)
PHONE..................661 589-5400
Robert Lewis, *President*
Lori Buller, *Human Resources*
Randy Dubois, *Manager*
EMP: 58
SALES (est): 19.7MM **Privately Held**
SIC: 1389 Oil field services

(P-1077)
SCHLUMBERGER TECHNOLOGY CORP
Also Called: Schlumberger Well Services
2841 Pegasus Dr, Bakersfield
(93308-6896)
PHONE..................661 864-4750
Fax: 661 642-2065
EMP: 70 **Privately Held**
SIC: 1389 1382
HQ: Schlumberger Technology Corp
100 Gillingham Ln
Sugar Land TX 77478
281 285-8500

(P-1078)
SCHLUMBERGER TECHNOLOGY CORP
Schlumberger, Well Completions
12131 Industry St, Garden Grove
(92841-2813)
PHONE..................714 379-7332
Gene Barnett, *Systems Mgr*
EMP: 51 **Publicly Held**
SIC: 1389 3561 Oil & gas wells: building, repairing & dismantling; pumps & pumping equipment
HQ: Schlumberger Technology Corp
100 Gillingham Ln
Sugar Land TX 77478
281 285-8500

(P-1079)
SMITH INTERNATIONAL INC
Also Called: Omni Seals, Inc.
11031 Jersey Blvd Ste A, Rancho Cucamonga (91730-5150)
PHONE..................909 906-7900
Monte Russell, *Managing Dir*
EMP: 130 **Publicly Held**

SIC: 1389 Oil field services
HQ: Smith International, Inc.
1310 Rankin Rd
Houston TX 77073
281 443-3370

(P-1080)
SOLI-BOND INC
4230 Foster Ave, Bakersfield (93308-4559)
PHONE..................661 631-1633
Dwight Hartley, *President*
EMP: 50
SALES (corp-wide): 34.8MM **Privately Held**
SIC: 1389 Oil field services
PA: Soli-Bond, Inc.
2377 2 Mile Rd
Bay City MI 48706
989 684-9611

(P-1081)
TOTAL-WESTERN INC (HQ)
8049 Somerset Blvd, Paramount
(90723-4396)
PHONE..................562 220-1450
Paul F Conrad, *CEO*
Kris Schramm, *President*
Mary A Pool, *CFO*
Leonard Crespo, *Vice Pres*
Earl Grebing, *Vice Pres*
EMP: 50
SQ FT: 13,000
SALES (est): 123.6MM
SALES (corp-wide): 337.2MM **Privately Held**
WEB: www.total-western.com
SIC: 1389 Oil field services; construction, repair & dismantling services; excavating slush pits & cellars; grading oil & gas well foundations
PA: Bragg Investment Company, Inc.
6251 N Paramount Blvd
Long Beach CA 90805
562 984-2400

(P-1082)
TRUITT OILFIELD MAINT CORP
1051 James Rd, Bakersfield (93308-9753)
P.O. Box 5066 (93388-5066)
PHONE..................661 871-4099
Kimberly Sue New, *President*
Steve New, *Vice Pres*
EMP: 300
SQ FT: 3,000
SALES (est): 51.3MM **Privately Held**
SIC: 1389 Oil field services

(P-1083)
TRYAD SERVICE CORPORATION
5900 E Lerdo Hwy, Shafter (93263-4023)
PHONE..................661 391-1524
James Varner, *President*
Estate of Burl G Varner, *Shareholder*
Danny Seely, *Vice Pres*
▲ **EMP:** 90
SALES (est): 9.7MM **Privately Held**
SIC: 1389 Oil & gas wells: building, repairing & dismantling

(P-1084)
U S WEATHERFORD L P
2815 Fruitvale Ave, Bakersfield
(93308-5907)
PHONE..................661 589-9483
Rick Benton, *Branch Mgr*
EMP: 100 **Privately Held**
WEB: www.gaslift.com
SIC: 1389 Oil field services
HQ: U S Weatherford L P
179 Weatherford Dr
Schriever LA 70395
985 493-6100

(P-1085)
WEATHERFORD INTERNATIONAL LLC
1880 Santa Barbara Ave # 220, San Luis Obispo (93401-4481)
PHONE..................805 781-3580
Chris Smith, *Principal*
EMP: 73 **Privately Held**
SIC: 1389 Oil field services
HQ: Weatherford International, Llc
2000 Saint James Pl
Houston TX 77056
713 693-4000

(P-1086)
WEATHERFORD INTERNATIONAL LLC
Also Called: Coroc
21728 Rosedale Hwy, Bakersfield
(93314-9787)
PHONE..................................661 587-9753
Mark Sarcen, *Branch Mgr*
EMP: 60 **Privately Held**
WEB: www.weatherford.com
SIC: **1389** Oil field services
HQ: Weatherford International, Llc
2000 Saint James Pl
Houston TX 77056
713 693-4000

1422 Crushed & Broken Limestone

(P-1087)
SPECIALTY MINERALS INC
Minerals Technology
6565 Meridian Rd, Lucerne Valley
(92356-8602)
P.O. Box 558 (92356-0558)
PHONE..................................760 248-5300
Doug Mayger, *Branch Mgr*
EMP: 150 **Publicly Held**
WEB: www.specialtyminerals.com
SIC: **1422** Crushed & broken limestone
HQ: Specialty Minerals Inc.
622 3rd Ave Fl 38
New York NY 10017
212 878-1800

(P-1088)
SYAR INDUSTRIES INC
885 Lake Herman Rd, Vallejo
(94591-8324)
P.O. Box 2540, NAPA (94558-0524)
PHONE..................................707 643-3261
Mike Burneson, *Manager*
EMP: 100
SALES (corp-wide): 100.2MM **Privately Held**
WEB: www.syar.com
SIC: **1422** **5211** Crushed & broken limestone; cement
PA: Syar Industries, Inc.
2301 Napa Vallejo Hwy
Napa CA 94558
707 252-8711

1423 Crushed & Broken Granite

(P-1089)
JUNIPER ROCK CORPORATION
Also Called: ARB
26000 Commercentre Dr, Lake Forest
(92630-8816)
PHONE..................................949 500-1797
Eric Amlee, *General Mgr*
EMP: 409
SALES (est): 54.3MM
SALES (corp-wide): 2.3B **Publicly Held**
SIC: **1423** Crushed & broken granite
PA: Primoris Services Corporation
2100 Mckinney Ave # 1500
Dallas TX 75201
214 740-5600

1429 Crushed & Broken Stone, NEC

(P-1090)
SAN RAFAEL ROCK QUARRY INC (HQ)
Also Called: Dutra Materials
1000 Point San Pedro Rd, San Rafael
(94901-8312)
PHONE..................................415 459-7740
Bill Toney Dutra, *CEO*
EMP: 70
SALES (est): 70MM
SALES (corp-wide): 145.1MM **Privately Held**
SIC: **1429** **1629** Basalt, crushed & broken-quarrying; marine construction

PA: The Dutra Group
2350 Kerner Blvd Ste 200
San Rafael CA 94901
415 258-6876

1442 Construction Sand & Gravel

(P-1091)
GRANITE ROCK CO (PA)
350 Technology Dr, Watsonville
(95076-2488)
P.O. Box 50001 (95077-5001)
PHONE..................................831 768-2000
Thomas H Squeri, *CEO*
Bruce G Woolpert, *Vice Chairman*
Mary E Woolpert, *Chairman*
Todd Barreras, *Officer*
Greg Diehl, *Vice Pres*
EMP: 100
SQ FT: 10,000
SALES (est): 1.1B **Privately Held**
WEB: www.graniterock.com
SIC: **1442** **3273** **5032** **2951** Gravel mining; construction sand mining; ready-mixed concrete; sand, construction; stone, crushed or broken; asphalt & asphaltic paving mixtures (not from refineries); highway & street paving contractor; concrete block & brick

(P-1092)
GRANITE ROCK CO
Also Called: AR Wilson Quarry
Quarry Rd, Aromas (95004)
P.O. Box 699 (95004-0699)
PHONE..................................831 768-2300
Bruce Wollepert, *President*
EMP: 100
SALES (corp-wide): 1.1B **Privately Held**
WEB: www.graniterock.com
SIC: **1442** **2951** Gravel mining; asphalt paving mixtures & blocks
PA: Granite Rock Co.
350 Technology Dr
Watsonville CA 95076
831 768-2000

(P-1093)
HANSEN BROS ENTERPRISES (PA)
Also Called: Hbe Rental
11727 La Barr Meadows Rd, Grass Valley
(95949-7722)
P.O. Box 1599 (95945-1599)
PHONE..................................530 273-3100
Orson Hansen, *President*
Frank Bennallack, *Treasurer*
Helen Hansen, *Vice Pres*
Sue Peterson, *Vice Pres*
Brandon Hall, *Project Mgr*
EMP: 90
SQ FT: 20,000
SALES (est): 36.2MM **Privately Held**
WEB: www.gohbe.com
SIC: **1442** **3273** **1794** **7359** Gravel mining; ready-mixed concrete; excavation work; equipment rental & leasing

(P-1094)
LEGACY VULCAN LLC
San Bernardino Division
2400 W Highland Ave, San Bernardino
(92407-6408)
PHONE..................................909 875-1150
Darryl Charleson, *Sales/Mktg Dir*
Allyson Noah, *Manager*
Floyd Sibole, *Manager*
EMP: 50 **Publicly Held**
WEB: www.vulcanmaterials.com
SIC: **1442** **3273** Sand mining; ready-mixed concrete
HQ: Legacy Vulcan, Llc
1200 Urban Center Dr
Vestavia AL 35242
205 298-3000

(P-1095)
NEVOCAL ENTERPRISES INC
Also Called: Kh Construction
5320 N Barcus Ave, Fresno (93722-5050)
PHONE..................................559 277-0700
Frank Cornell, *President*
EMP: 75

SQ FT: 4,575
SALES (est): 4.2MM **Privately Held**
SIC: **1442** Construction sand & gravel

(P-1096)
WEST COAST AGGREGATE SUPPLY
Also Called: Aggregate West Coast
92500 Airport Blvd, Thermal (92274)
P.O. Box 790 (92274-0790)
PHONE..................................760 342-7598
Marvin Struiksma, *President*
EMP: 50
SALES (est): 5.4MM **Privately Held**
SIC: **1442** Common sand mining

1446 Industrial Sand

(P-1097)
PIONEER SANDS LLC
31302 Ortega Hwy, San Juan Capistrano
(92675)
PHONE..................................949 728-0171
Mike Miclette, *Branch Mgr*
EMP: 53
SALES (corp-wide): 5.4B **Publicly Held**
SIC: **1446** Silica sand mining
HQ: Pioneer Sands Llc
5205 N O Connor Blvd # 200
Irving TX 75039
972 444-9001

(P-1098)
PW GILLIBRAND CO INC
4537 Ish Dr, Simi Valley (93063-7667)
P.O. Box 1019 (93062-1019)
PHONE..................................805 526-2195
Celine Gillibrand, *CEO*
Richard Valencia, *President*
Jim Costello, *Corp Secy*
EMP: 75
SQ FT: 11,000
SALES (est): 30MM **Privately Held**
WEB: www.pwgcoinc.com
SIC: **1446** Grinding sand mining; foundry sand mining

1479 Chemical & Fertilizer Mining

(P-1099)
SEARLES VALLEY MINERALS INC
80201 Trona Rd, Trona (93562)
PHONE..................................760 372-2259
Burnell Blanchard, *Vice Pres*
EMP: 600
SALES (corp-wide): 703.3MM **Privately Held**
SIC: **1479** Salt & sulfur mining
HQ: Searles Valley Minerals Inc.
9401 Indn Crk Pkwy # 1000
Overland Park KS 66210
913 344-9500

1481 Nonmetallic Minerals Svcs, Except Fuels

(P-1100)
IMERYS MINERALS CALIFORNIA INC
Also Called: Imerys Filtration Minerals
2500 Miguelito Canyon Rd, Lompoc
(93436)
PHONE..................................805 736-1221
Kenneth Schweibert, *Manager*
EMP: 346
SALES (corp-wide): 2.6MM **Privately Held**
SIC: **1481** **3295** Nonmetallic mineral services; minerals, ground or treated
HQ: Imerys Minerals California, Inc.
2500 San Miguelito Rd
Lompoc CA 93436

(P-1101)
MP MINE OPERATIONS LLC
67750 Bailey Rd, Mountain Pass (92366)
PHONE..................................702 277-0848

Michael Rosethal, *Mng Member*
James H Litinsky,
EMP: 108
SALES (est): 220.2K **Privately Held**
SIC: **1481** Mine exploration, nonmetallic minerals

1499 Miscellaneous Nonmetallic Mining

(P-1102)
DICAPERL CORPORATION (DH)
Also Called: Grefco Dicaperl
23705 Crenshaw Blvd, Torrance
(90505-5236)
PHONE..................................610 667-6640
Ray Perelman, *CEO*
Glenn Jones, *President*
Mike Cull, *Treasurer*
Barry Katz, *Senior VP*
▼ EMP: 90
SQ FT: 5,000
SALES (est): 9.5MM **Privately Held**
SIC: **1499** **3677** Perlite mining; filtration devices, electronic
HQ: Grefco Minerals Inc.
1 Bala Ave Ste 310
Bala Cynwyd PA 19004
610 660-8820

(P-1103)
IMERYS FILTRATION MINERALS INC (DH)
1732 N 1st St Ste 450, San Jose
(95112-4579)
PHONE..................................805 562-0200
Douglas A Smith, *CEO*
John Oskan, *President*
Fred Weber, *Treasurer*
Paul Woodberry, *Vice Ch Bd*
Bob Wood, *Administration*
◆ EMP: 50
SQ FT: 11,600
SALES (est): 1.2B
SALES (corp-wide): 2.6MM **Privately Held**
SIC: **1499** Diatomaceous earth mining
HQ: Imerys Usa, Inc.
100 Mansell Ct E Ste 300
Roswell GA 30076
770 645-3300

(P-1104)
IMERYS MINERALS CALIFORNIA INC (DH)
2500 San Miguelito Rd, Lompoc
(93436-9743)
P.O. Box 519 (93438-0519)
PHONE..................................805 736-1221
Douglas A Smith, *President*
John Oskam, *CEO*
John Leichty, *CFO*
Bruno Van Herpen, *Vice Pres*
Bill Kinman, *Administration*
▼ EMP: 70
SQ FT: 11,600
SALES (est): 1B
SALES (corp-wide): 2.6MM **Privately Held**
SIC: **1499** **3295** Diatomaceous earth mining; minerals, ground or treated

(P-1105)
MONARCHY DIAMOND INC
550 S Hill St Ste 1088, Los Angeles
(90013-2417)
PHONE..................................213 924-1161
Rajnikumar Patel, *President*
EMP: 425
SALES (est): 12.3MM **Privately Held**
SIC: **1499** Gem stones (natural) mining

1521 General Contractors, Single Family Houses

(P-1106)
A & W MAINTENANCE
7573 Cibola Trl, Yucca Valley (92284-3255)
PHONE..................................310 619-8694
Alesia Ellis, *Owner*
EMP: 54
SQ FT: 3,400

(PA)=Parent Co (HQ)=Headquarters (DH)=Div Headquarters
✪ = New Business established in last 2 years
2019 Directory of California
Wholesalers and Services Companies
55

P
R
O
D
U
C
T
S
&
S
V
C
S

SALES (est): 1.6MM **Privately Held**
SIC: 1521 7349 Townhouse construction; building maintenance, except repairs

(P-1107)
A I T DEVELOPMENT CORP
Also Called: Mega Builders
21021 Devonshire St # 205, Chatsworth (91311-8240)
PHONE..................818 407-5533
Alon A Toker, *President*
Isabell Toker, *Corp Secy*
EMP: 66
SQ FT: 3,300
SALES (est): 4MM **Privately Held**
SIC: 1521 General remodeling, single-family houses

(P-1108)
A M ORTEGA CONSTRUCTION INC
58 Kellogg St, Ventura (93001-1732)
PHONE..................951 360-1352
Archie Maurice Ortega, *Branch Mgr*
EMP: 52
SALES (corp-wide): 47.7MM **Privately Held**
SIC: 1521 Single-family housing construction
PA: A. M. Ortega Construction, Inc.
10125 Channel Rd
Lakeside CA 92040
619 390-1988

(P-1109)
A W PROPERTIES WEST LLC
16236 San Dieguito Rd # 310, Rancho Santa Fe (92091-9802)
P.O. Box 9296 (92067-4296)
PHONE..................858 832-1462
Danny Hampel,
EMP: 68
SALES (est): 3.3MM **Privately Held**
SIC: 1521 New construction, single-family houses

(P-1110)
ACE INDUSTRIAL SUPPLY INC (PA)
7535 N San Fernando Rd, Burbank (91505-1044)
PHONE..................818 252-1981
Tim Stearns, *Principal*
Paola Aviles, *Admin Asst*
Nancy Barrera, *Admin Asst*
Larry Lawrence, *Data Proc Dir*
Jesse Romo, *Human Res Mgr*
◆ **EMP:** 50
SQ FT: 25,000
SALES (est): 35.8MM **Privately Held**
SIC: 1521 Single-family housing construction

(P-1111)
ALL-PRO REMODELING
706 N Tustin St, Orange (92867-7149)
PHONE..................714 288-1314
Dale Terry, *President*
John Johnston, *General Mgr*
▲ **EMP:** 56
SQ FT: 5,000
SALES (est): 6.6MM **Privately Held**
WEB: www.allproremodeling.com
SIC: 1521 General remodeling, single-family houses

(P-1112)
ALLSTATE CONSTRUCTION CO
1364 Londonderry Pl, Los Angeles (90069-1335)
PHONE..................310 652-6942
Morris Bardoff, *President*
EMP: 50
SALES: 4.5MM **Privately Held**
SIC: 1521 General remodeling, single-family houses

(P-1113)
ALPHA-WINFIELD CONTRACTORS INC
Also Called: Winfield Construction
1096 Yerba Buena Ave, Emeryville (94608-3836)
PHONE..................510 652-4712
Kenneth J Winfield, *President*

EMP: 100
SQ FT: 1,200
SALES (est): 7.4MM **Privately Held**
SIC: 1521 1542 New construction, single-family houses; general remodeling, single-family houses; commercial & office buildings, renovation & repair

(P-1114)
AMERICAN DREAM
300 Portinao Cir, Sacramento (95831-2952)
PHONE..................916 613-4917
Conway Phillips, *Principal*
EMP: 60
SALES: 500K **Privately Held**
SIC: 1521 Single-family housing construction

(P-1115)
AMERICAN SOLAR SOLUTION INC
6400 Laurel Canyon Blvd # 550, North Hollywood (91606-1563)
PHONE..................877 946-8855
Nicki Zvik, *President*
Shay Yavor, *COO*
Jerry Goldman, *Principal*
Julihta Gershomov-Rivas, *General Mgr*
EMP: 70
SALES (est): 4.4MM **Privately Held**
SIC: 1521 1711 1522 General remodeling, single-family houses; solar energy contractor; residential construction

(P-1116)
AMERICAN TECHNOLOGIES INC (PA)
Also Called: ATI
210 W Baywood Ave, Orange (92865-2603)
PHONE..................714 283-9990
Gary Moore, *President*
Cindy Helmstead, *Executive*
Robert Sparks, *Executive*
Aaron Murray, *Branch Mgr*
Jeff Moore, *General Mgr*
▲ **EMP:** 128
SQ FT: 57,000
SALES: 236.5MM **Privately Held**
WEB: www.amer-tech.com
SIC: 1521 1541 1742 1731 Repairing fire damage, single-family houses; industrial buildings & warehouses; plastering, drywall & insulation; electrical work; painting & paper hanging; plumbing, heating, air-conditioning contractors

(P-1117)
AMERICAN TECHNOLOGIES INC
Also Called: American Restoration Services
2688 Westhills Ct, Simi Valley (93065-6234)
PHONE..................818 700-5060
Doug Waters, *Branch Mgr*
Pauline Maclean, *Executive*
Julie Marcus, *Office Mgr*
Joanne Kelley, *Admin Asst*
Matt Kittleson, *Project Mgr*
EMP: 50
SALES (corp-wide): 236.5MM **Privately Held**
WEB: www.amer-tech.com
SIC: 1521 1799 Single-family home remodeling, additions & repairs; repairing fire damage, single-family houses; asbestos removal & encapsulation; decontamination services
PA: American Technologies Inc.
210 W Baywood Ave
Orange CA 92865
714 283-9990

(P-1118)
ANDREW CHEKENE ENTERPRISES INC
Also Called: AC Enterprises
21965 Meekland Ave, Hayward (94541-3862)
PHONE..................650 588-1001
Andrew Chekene, *President*
Rafael Munoz, *Admin Sec*
Helen Troosh, *Manager*
EMP: 215 **EST:** 2007
SQ FT: 3,000

SALES (est): 7.5MM **Privately Held**
SIC: 1521 Single-family housing construction

(P-1119)
ARRAND PROPERTIES LLC
5032 Westside Dr, San Ramon (94583-9125)
P.O. Box 2212, Dublin (94568-0221)
PHONE..................925 289-1032
Celia Arrand,
Ali Adams,
EMP: 50 **EST:** 2013
SALES (est): 2.3MM **Privately Held**
SIC: 1521 1522 1541 General remodeling, single-family houses; hotel/motel & multi-family home renovation & remodeling; renovation, remodeling & repairs: industrial buildings

(P-1120)
ARYA GROUP INC
Also Called: Arya Design Group
10490 Santa Monica Blvd, Los Angeles (90025-5033)
PHONE..................310 446-7000
Ardie Tavangarian, *President*
EMP: 50
SQ FT: 3,000
SALES (est): 8.2MM **Privately Held**
SIC: 1521 1542 New construction, single-family houses; commercial & office building, new construction

(P-1121)
AWT CONSTRUCTION GROUP INC
4740 E 2nd St Ste 22, Benicia (94510-1024)
PHONE..................707 746-7500
James Kint, *President*
Gregory W Smith, *Vice Pres*
Julie Duggin, *Manager*
EMP: 65
SQ FT: 3,000
SALES: 4MM **Privately Held**
SIC: 1521 1542 Single-family housing construction; single-family home remodeling, additions & repairs; commercial & office building contractors

(P-1122)
BERRY & BERRY INC (PA)
Also Called: Berry Construction
413 W Yosemite Ave # 106, Madera (93637-4574)
P.O. Box 278 (93639-0278)
PHONE..................559 674-2491
David Berry, *Owner*
Gwen Cain, *Shareholder*
Pablo Aleman, *CFO*
Todd Phillips, *Project Mgr*
EMP: 52
SQ FT: 20,000
SALES (est): 8.3MM **Privately Held**
SIC: 1521 6552 1531 6513 New construction, single-family houses; land subdividers & developers, commercial; land subdividers & developers, residential; speculative builder, single-family houses; apartment building operators

(P-1123)
BILL BROWN CONSTRUCTION CO
242 Phelan Ave, San Jose (95112-6109)
PHONE..................408 297-3738
William E Brown, *President*
EMP: 70
SQ FT: 1,650
SALES (est): 4.3MM **Privately Held**
WEB: www.bbrownconstruction.com
SIC: 1521 1794 1791 Single-family housing construction; excavation work; structural steel erection

(P-1124)
BLU HOMES INC
1015 Walnut Ave, Vallejo (94592-1190)
PHONE..................415 625-0809
William M Haney III, *CEO*
EMP: 178 **Privately Held**
SIC: 1521 New construction, single-family houses

PA: Blu Homes, Inc.
1015 Walnut Ave
Vallejo CA 94592

(P-1125)
BOLIN BUILDERS INC
3848 Berkesey Ln, Valley Springs (95252-9506)
P.O. Box 1437 (95252-1437)
PHONE..................209 772-9721
Benton Bolin, *President*
Thelma Bolin, *Corp Secy*
William Bolin, *Vice Pres*
EMP: 50 **EST:** 1998
SALES (est): 5MM **Privately Held**
SIC: 1521 New construction, single-family houses

(P-1126)
BREHM COMMUNITIES (PA)
1935 Camino Vida Roble # 200, Carlsbad (92008-5568)
PHONE..................760 448-2420
Forrest W Brehm, *President*
EMP: 80
SQ FT: 5,984
SALES (est): 4.7MM **Privately Held**
SIC: 1521 New construction, single-family houses

(P-1127)
BREHM COMMUNITIES LLC (PA)
1825 Aston Ave Ste B, Carlsbad (92008-7341)
PHONE..................760 448-2420
Forrest Brehm, *Managing Prtnr*
EMP: 60
SALES (est): 4.7MM **Privately Held**
SIC: 1521 New construction, single-family houses

(P-1128)
BRIECK RESTORATION INC
13750 Danielson St, Poway (92064-8889)
PHONE..................858 679-9928
Dorothy Ledesma, *CEO*
Leanne Ledesma, *Controller*
EMP: 50
SALES (est): 3MM **Privately Held**
SIC: 1521 Single-family home remodeling, additions & repairs

(P-1129)
BROOKFELD STHLAND HOLDINGS LLC
Also Called: Brookfield Residential
3200 Park Center Dr # 1000, Costa Mesa (92626-7163)
PHONE..................714 427-6868
Edrian Soley,
Dave Bartlett, *Vice Pres*
Chris Ball, *Executive Asst*
Thomas Lui, *Controller*
Mike Mullennix, *Site Mgr*
EMP: 160
SALES: 21.8MM
SALES (corp-wide): 31.9B **Publicly Held**
SIC: 1521 Single-family housing construction
HQ: Brookfield Homes Corporation
3201 Jermantown Rd # 150
Fairfax VA 22030
703 270-1400

(P-1130)
BROOKFIELD HOMES OF CALIFORNIA
Also Called: Brookfield 1996 California
12865 Pointe Del Mar Way # 200, Del Mar (92014-3860)
PHONE..................858 481-8500
Steven Doyle, *President*
EMP: 50 **EST:** 1996
SALES (est): 2.1MM **Privately Held**
SIC: 1521

(P-1131)
BROOKFIELD HOMES PACIFIC INC (HQ)
12865 Pointe Del 200, Del Mar (92014)
PHONE..................858 481-8500
Steven Doyle, *CEO*
Larry Cortes, *CFO*
Randy Johnson, *Exec VP*

Laura Bell, *Administration*
Kim Moodey, *Pub Rel Mgr*
EMP: 81
SQ FT: 14,000
SALES (est): 25.9MM
SALES (corp-wide): 2.1B **Privately Held**
WEB: www.onewfc.com
SIC: 1521 New construction, single-family
houses
PA: Brookfield Office Properties Inc
181 Bay St Suite 330
Toronto ON M5J 2
416 369-2300

(P-1132)
BRUCE OLSON CONSTRUCTION INC
7320 River Rd, Olympic Valley (96146)
PHONE..................530 581-1087
Bruce W Olson, *CEO*
Steve Morgan, *Foreman/Supr*
EMP: 145
SQ FT: 3,000
SALES (est): 12MM **Privately Held**
SIC: 1521 New construction, single-family
houses

(P-1133)
BX CONSTRUCTION LLC
11671 Sterling Ave Ste K, Riverside
(92503-4971)
PHONE..................951 509-9412
Aofan Wang,
Annie Naguillan,
EMP: 60
SQ FT: 1,100
SALES: 795K **Privately Held**
SIC: 1521 6552 6799 New construction,
single-family houses; land subdividers &
developers, residential; real estate in-
vestors, except property operators

(P-1134)
CALATLANTIC GROUP INC
Also Called: Standard Pacific Homes
5750 Fleet St Ste 200, Carlsbad
(92008-4709)
PHONE..................760 602-6824
Brian L Utsler, *Regional Mgr*
EMP: 140
SALES (corp-wide): 12.6B **Publicly Held**
WEB: www.standardpacifichomes.com
SIC: 1521 New construction, single-family
houses
HQ: Calatlantic Group, Inc.
1100 Wilson Blvd Ste 2100
Arlington VA 22209
240 532-3806

(P-1135)
CALATLANTIC GROUP INC
Southern Cal Inland Empire Div
355 E Rincon St Ste 300, Corona
(92879-1372)
PHONE..................951 898-5500
Douglas Krah, *Manager*
EMP: 53
SALES (corp-wide): 12.6B **Publicly Held**
SIC: 1521 New construction, single-family
houses
HQ: Calatlantic Group, Inc.
1100 Wilson Blvd Ste 2100
Arlington VA 22209
240 532-3806

(P-1136)
CALATLANTIC GROUP INC
Also Called: Standard Pacific Homes Ventura
757 Nile River Dr, Oxnard (93036-5354)
PHONE..................805 379-6600
David Rivas, *Branch Mgr*
EMP: 55
SQ FT: 1,200
SALES (corp-wide): 12.6B **Publicly Held**
WEB: www.standardpacifichomes.com
SIC: 1521 New construction, single-family
houses
HQ: Calatlantic Group, Inc.
1100 Wilson Blvd Ste 2100
Arlington VA 22209
240 532-3806

(P-1137)
CALATLANTIC GROUP INC
Also Called: Calatlantic Homes
15360 Barranca Pkwy, Irvine (92618-2215)
PHONE..................949 789-1600
Jason Dosek, *Officer*
Jackie Moore, *Officer*
Jeffrey McCall, *Exec VP*
Paul Carey, *Vice Pres*
Stan Deringer, *Vice Pres*
EMP: 60
SALES (corp-wide): 12.6B **Publicly Held**
WEB: www.standardpacifichomes.com
SIC: 1521 New construction, single-family
houses
HQ: Calatlantic Group, Inc.
1100 Wilson Blvd Ste 2100
Arlington VA 22209
240 532-3806

(P-1138)
CALATLANTIC GROUP INC
13200 Fiji Way, Marina Del Rey (90292)
PHONE..................310 821-9843
EMP: 59
SALES (corp-wide): 2.4B **Publicly Held**
SIC: 1521
PA: Calatlantic Group, Inc.
15360 Barranca Pkwy
Irvine CA 22209
949 789-1600

(P-1139)
CALATLANTIC GROUP INC
26 Technology Dr, Irvine (92618-2380)
PHONE..................949 789-1600
EMP: 59
SALES (corp-wide): 12.6B **Publicly Held**
WEB: www.standardpacifichomes.com
SIC: 1521 New construction, single-family
houses
HQ: Calatlantic Group, Inc.
1100 Wilson Blvd Ste 2100
Arlington VA 22209
240 532-3806

(P-1140)
CALHOUN CONSTRUCTION INC
110 Gateway Dr Ste 260, Lincoln
(95648-3307)
PHONE..................916 434-8356
Robert F Calhoun, *CEO*
Thomas Calhoun, *President*
EMP: 175 EST: 2001
SALES (est): 13.6MM **Privately Held**
WEB: www.calhounconstruction.org
SIC: 1521 Single-family housing construc-
tion

(P-1141)
CALIFORNIA PREFERRED BLDRS INC
20335 Ventura Blvd # 422, Woodland Hills
(91364-2444)
PHONE..................818 402-3345
Jacob Sherf, *President*
EMP: 50 EST: 2010
SALES (est): 2.7MM **Privately Held**
SIC: 1521 New construction, single-family
houses

(P-1142)
CARROLLCO INC
3104 N Miami Ave, Fresno (93727-8069)
P.O. Box 13039 (93794-3039)
PHONE..................559 396-3939
Benjamin Carroll, *CEO*
EMP: 50 EST: 2010
SQ FT: 10,000
SALES (est): 4.8MM **Privately Held**
SIC: 1521 0782 1711 Single-family home
remodeling, additions & repairs; land-
scape contractors; warm air heating & air
conditioning contractor

(P-1143)
CENTEX HOMES INC
27401 Los Altos Ste 400, Mission Viejo
(92691-8550)
PHONE..................949 453-0113
Bryan Swindell, *Branch Mgr*
EMP: 200
SALES (corp-wide): 8.5B **Publicly Held**
WEB: www.centexhomes.com
SIC: 1521 New construction, single-family
houses

HQ: Centex Homes, Inc.
2728 N Harwood St
Dallas TX 75201
800 777-8583

(P-1144)
CENTEX HOMES INC
250 Commerce Ste 100, Irvine
(92602-1341)
PHONE..................949 453-0113
Richard Douglass, *Branch Mgr*
EMP: 108
SALES (corp-wide): 8.5B **Publicly Held**
WEB: www.centexhomes.com
SIC: 1521 New construction, single-family
houses
HQ: Centex Homes, Inc.
2728 N Harwood St
Dallas TX 75201
800 777-8583

(P-1145)
CLYDE MILES CNSTR CO INC
1110 Burnett Ave Ste C, Concord
(94520-5611)
PHONE..................925 427-4473
Clyde E Miles, *President*
EMP: 100
SALES (est): 8.9MM **Privately Held**
SIC: 1521 New construction, single-family
houses

(P-1146)
COASTLINE CNSTR & AWNG CO INC
5742 Research Dr, Huntington Beach
(92649-1617)
PHONE..................714 891-9798
John W Almquist, *President*
John Almquist, *CIO*
EMP: 100
SQ FT: 1,600
SALES (est): 9.2MM **Privately Held**
SIC: 1521 Mobile home repair, on site

(P-1147)
CONSTRUCTION CUSTOMER SERVICE
1320 N Hancock St Ste A, Anaheim
(92807-1991)
PHONE..................714 701-1858
Jackie Roth, *President*
EMP: 50
SQ FT: 3,600
SALES (est): 3.1MM **Privately Held**
WEB: www.constructionserviceinc.com
SIC: 1521 8711 7361 Single-family hous-
ing construction; building construction
consultant; labor contractors (employment
agency)

(P-1148)
CORONEL CONSTRUCTION INC
2328 Venice Dr, Delano (93215-9241)
PHONE..................661 725-4400
Samuel Coronel, *President*
Ramona Coronel, *Treasurer*
EMP: 85
SALES (est): 6.4MM **Privately Held**
SIC: 1521 Single-family housing construc-
tion

(P-1149)
COUNTY OF RIVERSIDE
Facilities Mgmt
3133 Mission Inn Ave, Riverside
(92507-4199)
PHONE..................951 955-4800
Michael Sylvester, *Director*
EMP: 325 **Privately Held**
SIC: 1521 9532 7349 Single-family housing construction; urban & community development ; building maintenance
services
PA: County Of Riverside
4080 Lemon St Fl 11
Riverside CA 92501
951 955-1110

(P-1150)
CRAFTMAN CONCRETE
755 N Peach Ave Ste F11, Clovis
(93611-7259)
PHONE..................559 298-8864
Clyde E Been, *Partner*
David Been, *Partner*

EMP: 75
SALES (est): 3.6MM **Privately Held**
SIC: 1521 0782 New construction, single-
family houses; landscape contractors

(P-1151)
CUSTOM BUILDING PRODUCTS INC
7711 Center Ave Ste 500, Huntington
Beach (92647-3076)
PHONE..................562 598-8808
Thomas Nieto, *Manager*
EMP: 50 **Privately Held**
WEB: www.custombuildingproducts.com
SIC: 1521 3546 3423 New construction,
single-family houses; power-driven hand-
tools; hand & edge tools
HQ: Custom Building Products, Inc.
7711 Center Ave Ste 500
Huntington Beach CA 92647
800 272-8786

(P-1152)
DAIWA HOUSE CALIFORNIA INC
1901 Avenue Of The Stars # 264, Los An-
geles (90067-6001)
PHONE..................310 228-5675
Keiichi Yoshi, *President*
EMP: 297
SALES: 107.6MM **Privately Held**
SIC: 1521 General remodeling, single-fam-
ily houses

(P-1153)
DE MATTEI CONSTRUCTION INC
1794 The Alameda, San Jose
(95126-1729)
PHONE..................408 295-7516
Mark De Mattei, *President*
John Hinton, *CFO*
▲ **EMP:** 60
SQ FT: 5,000
SALES (est): 9.4MM **Privately Held**
WEB: www.demattei.com
SIC: 1521 1542 New construction, single-
family houses; commercial & office build-
ing contractors

(P-1154)
DENNIS ALLEN ASSOCIATES (PA)
201 N Milpas St, Santa Barbara
(93103-3201)
PHONE..................805 884-8777
Dennis W Allen, *President*
Ian Cronshaw, *Vice Pres*
Steve Nelson, *Area Mgr*
Jessica Dias, *Executive Asst*
Jennifer Cushnie, *Admin Sec*
EMP: 95
SALES (est): 35.3MM **Privately Held**
WEB: www.dennisallenassociates.com
SIC: 1521 1542 General remodeling, sin-
gle-family houses; new construction, sin-
gle-family houses; commercial & office
buildings, renovation & repair; commercial
& office building, new construction

(P-1155)
DENNIS HYDE CONSTRUCTION INC
7112 Darrin Ave, Bakersfield (93308-3775)
PHONE..................661 393-1077
Dennis Hyde, *President*
Julie Hyde, *Vice Pres*
EMP: 60
SALES (est): 5MM **Privately Held**
SIC: 1521 Single-family housing construc-
tion

(P-1156)
DEWHURST & ASSOCIATES
7533 Girard Ave, La Jolla (92037-5102)
P.O. Box 574 (92038-0574)
PHONE..................858 456-5345
Donald Dewhurst, *Chairman*
Doug Dewhurst, *President*
Dave Dewhurst, *CEO*
Dan Sehlhorst, *Architect*
EMP: 70
SQ FT: 1,200

PRODUCTS & SVCS

SALES: 6.5MM **Privately Held**
WEB: www.dewhurst.com
SIC: 1521 New construction, single-family houses

(P-1157)
DOMUS CONSTRUCTION & DESIGN
Also Called: Statewide
8864 Fruitridge Rd, Sacramento
(95826-9708)
PHONE.....................916 381-7500
Maksim R Yurtsan, *CEO*
EMP: 50 **EST:** 2008
SALES (est): 7MM **Privately Held**
SIC: 1521 Repairing fire damage, single-family houses

(P-1158)
E & E CO LTD
Also Called: Jla Home
2222 E Beamer St, Woodland
(95776-6226)
PHONE.....................530 669-5991
EMP: 393 **Privately Held**
SIC: 1521 Single-family housing construction
PA: E & E Co., Ltd.
45875 Northport Loop E
Fremont CA 94538

(P-1159)
EBC INC (PA)
Also Called: Ellis Building Contractors
219 Manhattan Beach Blvd, Manhattan Beach (90266-5324)
PHONE.....................310 753-6407
Brad Ellis, *President*
Patricia Ellis, *Admin Sec*
EMP: 97
SALES: 922K **Privately Held**
SIC: 1521 1542 New construction, single-family houses; commercial & office building, new construction

(P-1160)
ELLIOTT HOMES INC (PA)
340 Palladio Pkwy Ste 521, Folsom
(95630-8832)
PHONE.....................916 984-1300
Harry C Elliott III, *CEO*
Steve Hemington, *CFO*
Stephen Hemington, *Corp Secy*
Wayne Eide, *General Mgr*
Rebecca Coker, *Asst Controller*
EMP: 150
SQ FT: 10,000
SALES (est): 36.5MM **Privately Held**
WEB: www.elliotthomes.com
SIC: 1521 New construction, single-family houses

(P-1161)
EMERCON CONSTRUCTION INC (PA)
2906 E Coronado St, Anaheim
(92806-2501)
PHONE.....................714 630-9615
Richard Anderson, *President*
Joan E Anderson, *Exec VP*
Frank Brady, *Exec VP*
Michael Barlow, *Project Mgr*
Joseph Gildner, *Project Mgr*
EMP: 60
SQ FT: 30,000
SALES (est): 12.6MM **Privately Held**
WEB: www.emercon.com
SIC: 1521 Repairing fire damage, single-family houses

(P-1162)
EXCEL CONTRACTORS INC
Also Called: PROGRESSIN DRYWALL
348 E Avenue K8 Ste B, Lancaster
(93535-4514)
PHONE.....................661 942-6944
John Rockey, *President*
Rose Rockey, *Vice Pres*
EMP: 100

SALES: 17.9MM **Privately Held**
SIC: 1521 1742 1542 Single-family home remodeling, additions & repairs; new construction, single-family houses; drywall; commercial & office building, new construction; commercial & office buildings, renovation & repair

(P-1163)
F R GHIANNI ENTERPRISES INC
Also Called: F R Ghianni Drywall Cnstr Co
1937 Friendship Dr Ste A, El Cajon
(92020-1137)
PHONE.....................619 279-1073
Frank R Ghianni, *President*
Debby Weklem, *Admin Sec*
EMP: 100
SQ FT: 1,600
SALES (est): 5.6MM **Privately Held**
SIC: 1521 1771 1742 Single-family housing construction; concrete work; drywall

(P-1164)
FIELDSTONE COMMUNITIES INC
16 Technology Dr Ste 125, Irvine
(92618-2325)
PHONE.....................949 790-5400
Frank S Foster, *President*
Chantelle Miles, *Accountant*
EMP: 50
SALES (est): 4.8MM **Privately Held**
SIC: 1521 New construction, single-family houses

(P-1165)
FORT HILL CONSTRUCTION (PA)
12711 Ventura Blvd # 390, Studio City
(91604-2491)
PHONE.....................323 656-7425
George Peper, *President*
Gordon Foote, *CFO*
James Kweskin, *Vice Pres*
Mike Mc Grail, *Vice Pres*
Joseph Goldfarb, *Admin Sec*
▲ **EMP:** 70
SQ FT: 4,000
SALES (est): 14.3MM **Privately Held**
WEB: www.forthill.com
SIC: 1521 New construction, single-family houses

(P-1166)
FROMER INC
22225 Acorn St, Chatsworth (91311-4724)
PHONE.....................818 341-3896
Kim Fromer, *President*
Guy Zimmerman, *Vice Pres*
EMP: 70
SQ FT: 1,200
SALES (est): 6MM **Privately Held**
SIC: 1521 1522 Single-family housing construction; multi-family dwelling construction

(P-1167)
FRONTIER LAND COMPANIES
Also Called: Frontrs-Frnters Land Companies
10100 Trinity Pkwy # 420, Stockton
(95219-7238)
PHONE 209 957-8112
Thomas Doucette, *President*
Phillip Russell, *CFO*
George K Gibson, *Vice Pres*
EMP: 50
SQ FT: 3,000
SALES (est): 6MM **Privately Held**
SIC: 1521 8742 6552 Single-family housing construction; real estate consultant; subdividers & developers

(P-1168)
G I L C INC
585 W Beach St, Watsonville (95076-5123)
P.O. Box 50085 (95077-5085)
PHONE.....................831 724-1011
David Wats, *President*
EMP: 50 **EST:** 1922
SALES (est): 4.6MM **Privately Held**
SIC: 1521 Single-family housing construction

(P-1169)
GALLAHER CONSTRUCTION INC
220 Concourse Blvd, Santa Rosa
(95403-8210)
PHONE.....................707 535-3200
William P Gallaher, *President*
Cynthia J Gallaher, *Admin Sec*
EMP: 50
SQ FT: 11,000
SALES: 30MM **Privately Held**
WEB: www.dflow.com
SIC: 1521 6552 New construction, single-family houses; land subdividers & developers, residential; land subdividers & developers, commercial

(P-1170)
GENE A GARCIA CONSTRUCTION
1663 E Poppy Hills Dr, Fresno
(93730-4510)
PHONE.....................559 352-6173
Gene Aaron Garcia, *Principal*
EMP: 50 **EST:** 2010
SALES (est): 495K **Privately Held**
SIC: 1521 New construction, single-family houses

(P-1171)
GENERATION CONTRACTING & EMERG
13685 Stowe Dr Ste B, Poway
(92064-8824)
PHONE.....................858 679-9928
Dorothy Ledesma, *President*
Paul Brieck, *Admin Sec*
Jeremy Dacosta, *Project Mgr*
EMP: 50
SALES (est): 4.6MM **Privately Held**
WEB: www.contractorforlife.com
SIC: 1521 1542 Single-family home remodeling, additions & repairs; nonresidential construction

(P-1172)
GOODFELLOW BROS CALIFORNIA LLC
50 Contractors St, Livermore (94551-4863)
PHONE.....................925 245-2111
Brian Gates,
Frank Williams,
EMP: 387
SALES (est): 4MM **Privately Held**
SIC: 1521 Single-family housing construction

(P-1173)
GRANTS CUSTOM CABINETS
7310 Kingsbury Rd, Templeton
(93465-8304)
PHONE.....................805 466-9680
Grant Moore, *Owner*
EMP: 185
SALES (est): 4.5MM **Privately Held**
SIC: 1521

(P-1174)
GRANVILLE HOMES INC
1396 W Herndon Ave # 101, Fresno
(93711-7126)
PHONE.....................559 268-2000
Darius Assemi, *CEO*
Farid Assemi, *President*
Derek Hayashi, *CFO*
Jesse Buglione, *Creative Dir*
Steve Rau, *Admin Sec*
EMP: 60
SQ FT: 5,000
SALES (est): 17.7MM **Privately Held**
WEB: www.sommervilleestates.com
SIC: 1521 New construction, single-family houses

(P-1175)
GREYSTONE HOMES INC
6121 Bollinger Canyon Rd # 500, San Ramon (94583-5287)
PHONE.....................925 242-0811
Dale Billy, *President*
EMP: 250
SALES (corp-wide): 12.6B **Publicly Held**
SIC: 1521 Single-family housing construction

HQ: Greystone Homes, Inc
25 Enterprise
Aliso Viejo CA 92656

(P-1176)
HAMBURGER HOME
3701 Wilshire Blvd # 900, Los Angeles
(90010-2804)
PHONE.....................213 637-5000
Sandra Cohen, *Principal*
EMP: 52
SALES (corp-wide): 18.8MM **Privately Held**
SIC: 1521 Single-family housing construction
PA: Hamburger Home
7120 Franklin Ave
Los Angeles CA 90046
323 876-0550

(P-1177)
HANOVER BUILDERS INC
141 Duesenberg Dr Ste 6, Westlake Village
(91362-3471)
PHONE.....................818 706-2279
Donald Hanover, *President*
EMP: 50
SALES (est): 2.2MM **Privately Held**
WEB: www.hanoverbuildersinc.com
SIC: 1521 New construction, single-family houses

(P-1178)
HINERFELD-WARD INC
8931 Ellis Ave Ste B1, Los Angeles
(90034-3336)
PHONE.....................310 842-7929
Tom Hinerfeld, *President*
Peter Borrego, *Vice Pres*
EMP: 70
SALES (est): 5.7MM **Privately Held**
WEB: www.hinerfeld-ward.com
SIC: 1521 Single-family housing construction

(P-1179)
HOWARD CDM
Also Called: Howard Construction
3750 Long Beach Blvd, Long Beach
(90807-3310)
PHONE.....................562 427-4124
Martin D Howard, *President*
William G Burkett, *CFO*
Steven C Phillips, *Exec VP*
Scott Peterson, *Project Mgr*
Parker Cole, *Project Engr*
◆ **EMP:** 50
SQ FT: 7,000
SALES (est): 11.5MM **Privately Held**
WEB: www.howardcdm.net
SIC: 1521 Single-family housing construction

(P-1180)
JDF CONSTRUCTION INC
201 Gemini Ave, Brea (92821-3704)
PHONE.....................714 526-1120
John Fitzmaurice, *President*
▲ **EMP:** 50
SALES (est): 3.5MM **Privately Held**
SIC: 1521 Single-family housing construction

(P-1181)
JF SHEA CONSTRUCTION INC
17400 Clear Creek Rd, Redding
(96001-5113)
P.O. Box 494519 (96049-4519)
PHONE.....................530 246-4292
Ed Kernaghan, *Vice Pres*
EMP: 60
SALES (corp-wide): 2.2B **Privately Held**
WEB: www.jfshea.com
SIC: 1521 New construction, single-family houses
HQ: J.F. Shea Construction, Inc.
655 Brea Canyon Rd
Walnut CA 91789
909 595-4397

(P-1182)
JF SHEA CONSTRUCTION INC
Also Called: Shea Homes
2 Ada Ste 200, Irvine (92618-5325)
PHONE.....................949 526-8792

Bob Yoder, *President*
EMP: 75
SALES (corp-wide): 2.2B **Privately Held**
WEB: www.jfshea.com
SIC: 1521 Single-family housing construction
HQ: J.F. Shea Construction, Inc.
655 Brea Canyon Rd
Walnut CA 91789
909 595-4397

(P-1183)
JF SHEA CONSTRUCTION INC
Shea Business Properties
675 Brea Canyon Rd Ste 8, Walnut (91789-3065)
PHONE............................909 594-0998
Bill Gaboury, *President*
EMP: 50
SQ FT: 1,500
SALES (corp-wide): 2.2B **Privately Held**
WEB: www.jfshea.com
SIC: 1521 New construction, single-family houses
HQ: J.F. Shea Construction, Inc.
655 Brea Canyon Rd
Walnut CA 91789
909 595-4397

(P-1184)
JF SHEA CONSTRUCTION INC
Also Called: Shea Homes
6130 Monterey Hwy Ofc, San Jose (95138-1797)
PHONE............................408 225-1475
Alfonso Garcia, *Manager*
EMP: 344
SQ FT: 3,500
SALES (corp-wide): 2.2B **Privately Held**
WEB: www.jfshea.com
SIC: 1521 New construction, single-family houses
HQ: J.F. Shea Construction, Inc.
655 Brea Canyon Rd
Walnut CA 91789
909 595-4397

(P-1185)
JF SHEA CONSTRUCTION INC
Also Called: Shea Homes
2580 Shea Center Dr, Livermore (94551-7547)
PHONE............................925 245-3660
Layne Marceau, *President*
Darryl Schrick, *Cust Mgr*
EMP: 150
SALES (corp-wide): 2.2B **Privately Held**
WEB: www.jfshea.com
SIC: 1521 New construction, single-family houses
HQ: J.F. Shea Construction, Inc.
655 Brea Canyon Rd
Walnut CA 91789
909 595-4397

(P-1186)
JUAN LOPEZ
Also Called: All Types of Baseboard
3065 Beyer Blvd Ste B106, San Diego (92154-3499)
PHONE............................619 428-3138
Juan Lopez, *Owner*
EMP: 100
SALES (est): 4.6MM **Privately Held**
SIC: 1521 1542 Single-family housing construction; commercial & office building contractors

(P-1187)
K HOVNANIAN COMPANIES CAL INC (HQ)
Also Called: K Hovnanian
400 Exchange Ste 200, Irvine (92602-1340)
PHONE............................714 368-4500
Nicholas Pappas, *President*
EMP: 65
SALES (est): 81.1MM
SALES (corp-wide): 2.4B **Publicly Held**
SIC: 1521 Single-family housing construction
PA: Hovnanian Enterprises, Inc.
90 Matawan Rd Fl 5
Matawan NJ 07747
732 747-7800

(P-1188)
KB HOME GRATER LOS ANGELES INC (HQ)
10990 Wilshire Blvd # 700, Los Angeles (90024-3913)
PHONE............................310 231-4000
Bruce Karatz, *CEO*
EMP: 90
SQ FT: 40,000
SALES (est): 71.5MM
SALES (corp-wide): 4.3B **Publicly Held**
SIC: 1521 Single-family home remodeling, additions & repairs; multi-family dwelling construction
PA: Kb Home
10990 Wilshire Blvd Fl 5
Los Angeles CA 90024
310 231-4000

(P-1189)
KITCHEN MART INC
4381 Granite Dr Ste C, Rocklin (95677-2173)
PHONE............................916 315-3535
Dave Hollars, *President*
EMP: 65
SALES (corp-wide): 10.1MM **Privately Held**
SIC: 1521 General remodeling, single-family houses
PA: Kitchen Mart, Inc.
3742 Bradview Dr
Sacramento CA
916 362-7080

(P-1190)
LACONSTRUCTORA CO INC
2030 Broadway, Oceanside (92054-6516)
PHONE............................760 439-7686
Fabio Marchi, *President*
EMP: 50 **EST:** 1997
SALES (est): 2.1MM **Privately Held**
SIC: 1521 Single-family housing construction

(P-1191)
LARGO CONCRETE INC
1650 Hotel Cir N, San Diego (92108-2816)
PHONE............................619 356-2142
EMP: 219
SALES (corp-wide): 150.8MM **Privately Held**
SIC: 1521 Single-family housing construction
PA: Largo Concrete, Inc.
2741 Walnut Ave Ste 110
Tustin CA 92780
714 731-3600

(P-1192)
LENNAR HOMES CALIFORNIA INC (DH)
Also Called: Lennar Builders
25 Enterprise Ste 400, Aliso Viejo (92656-2712)
PHONE............................949 349-8000
Brent Reed, *Planning*
Kathy Dale, *Asst Controller*
EMP: 124
SQ FT: 12,000
SALES (est): 145.6MM
SALES (corp-wide): 12.6B **Publicly Held**
SIC: 1521 6552 New construction, single-family houses; subdividers & developers
HQ: Lennar Homes, Inc.
700 Nw 107th Ave Ste 115
Miami FL 33172
305 559-4000

(P-1193)
M K S CONSTRUCTION INC
Also Called: Schetter Electric
471 Bannon St, Sacramento (95811-0203)
P.O. Box 1377 (95812-1377)
PHONE............................916 446-2521
Frank Schetter, *President*
EMP: 152
SQ FT: 7,800
SALES (est): 6.3MM **Privately Held**
SIC: 1521 Single-family housing construction

(P-1194)
MACARTHUR TRANSIT COMMUNITY
345 Spear St Ste 700, San Francisco (94105-6136)
P.O. Box 190220 (94119-0220)
PHONE............................415 989-1111
Susan Johnson, *Vice Pres*
EMP: 200
SALES (est): 1.1MM **Privately Held**
SIC: 1521 Single-family housing construction
PA: Bridge Economic Development Corporation
345 Spear St Ste 700
San Francisco CA 94105

(P-1195)
MACHADO & SONS CNSTR INC
1000 S Kilroy Rd, Turlock (95380-9589)
PHONE............................209 632-5260
Manuel B Machado, *President*
Jason Machado, *Vice Pres*
Matt Machado, *Project Mgr*
EMP: 50
SALES (est): 10.7MM **Privately Held**
WEB: www.machadoandsons.com
SIC: 1521 1542 1771 1541 New construction, single-family houses; commercial & office building, new construction; patio construction, concrete; industrial buildings & warehouses

(P-1196)
MARK R EGGEN CONSTRUCTION INC
34145 Pacific Coast Hwy # 325, Dana Point (92629-2808)
PHONE............................949 661-2674
Mark Eggen, *President*
EMP: 50
SALES: 7.5MM **Privately Held**
SIC: 1521 New construction, single-family houses

(P-1197)
MATRIX GROUP INTERNATIONAL INC
1520 W Cameron Ave, West Covina (91790-2713)
PHONE............................626 960-6205
David Voyticky, *President*
Joseph Voyticky, *Treasurer*
EMP: 70
SALES (est): 2.7MM **Privately Held**
SIC: 1521

(P-1198)
MCCLONE CONSTRUCTION COMPANY
4340 Product Dr, Cameron Park (95682-8492)
PHONE............................559 431-9411
Scott McClone, *Branch Mgr*
Kim Wagner, *Office Mgr*
Nate Orr, *Project Mgr*
Gabe Lewis, *Project Engr*
Michelle Wilcox, *Bookkeeper*
EMP: 216 **Privately Held**
SIC: 1521 Single-family housing construction
PA: Mcclone Construction Company
5170 Hillsdale Cir Ste B
El Dorado Hills CA 95762

(P-1199)
MCMILLIN COMMUNITIES INC
Also Called: Temeku Hills
41687 Temeku Dr, Temecula (92591-3909)
PHONE............................951 506-3303
Sonia Howard, *Branch Mgr*
EMP: 944
SALES (corp-wide): 97.8MM **Privately Held**
SIC: 1521 Single-family housing construction
PA: Mcmillin Communities, Inc.
2750 Womble Rd Ste 200
San Diego CA 92106
619 561-5275

(P-1200)
MCMILLIN CONSTRUCTION SVCS LP
2750 Womble Rd, San Diego (92106-6114)
PHONE............................619 477-4170
Mark McMillin, *CEO*
Gary Arnold, *President*
Gary Beason, *CFO*
Joe Shiely, *Exec VP*
EMP: 50
SQ FT: 29,000
SALES (est): 2.3MM **Privately Held**
SIC: 1521

(P-1201)
MERCEDES DIAZ HOMES INC
7239 Washington Ave # 100, Whittier (90602-1432)
PHONE............................562 945-4576
Mercedes Diaz, *President*
Ramon Diaz, *Vice Pres*
EMP: 60
SALES (est): 8.2MM **Privately Held**
SIC: 1521 General remodeling, single-family houses

(P-1202)
MICHAEL BRUINGTON
9 Soledad Dr Ste E, Monterey (93940-6036)
PHONE............................831 663-1772
Michael Bruington, *Exec VP*
EMP: 50
SALES (est): 1.8MM **Privately Held**
SIC: 1521 Single-family housing construction

(P-1203)
MIDSTATE CONSTRUCTION CORP
1180 Holm Rd Ste A, Petaluma (94954-7120)
PHONE............................707 762-3200
Roger Nelson, *President*
Jim Debolt, *CFO*
Wesley Barry II, *Vice Pres*
Patrick Draeger, *Vice Pres*
Richard Oberdorfer, *Vice Pres*
EMP: 80
SQ FT: 18,928
SALES (est): 29.5MM **Privately Held**
SIC: 1521 1541 1542 New construction, single-family houses; general remodeling, single-family houses; industrial buildings, new construction; renovation, remodeling & repairs: industrial buildings; commercial & office building, new construction; commercial & office buildings, renovation & repair

(P-1204)
MIKE ROVNER CONSTRUCTION INC (PA)
Also Called: MRC
5400 Tech Cir, Moorpark (93021-1792)
PHONE............................805 584-5961
Mike Rovner, *President*
Janet Rovner, *Shareholder*
Thomas McBride, *Business Dir*
June Radley, *Executive Asst*
Kristen Abrams, *Administration*
EMP: 300
SQ FT: 2,500
SALES (est): 76.3MM **Privately Held**
WEB: www.rovnerconstruction.com
SIC: 1521 Single-family housing construction

(P-1205)
MILES CONSTRUCTION GROUP INC
42020 Winchester Rd, Temecula (92590-4804)
PHONE............................951 260-2504
Adam Miles, *President*
S Parkinson, *Corp Secy*
G King, *Vice Pres*
Scott King, *Vice Pres*
Mike Stevens, *General Mgr*
EMP: 50
SQ FT: 8,000
SALES: 3.7MM **Privately Held**
SIC: 1521 Single-family housing construction

(P-1206)
MILLENIA DEVELOPMENT
929 Bettina Way, San Jacinto
(92582-2507)
PHONE....................................951 660-5691
Brett Stucker, *Owner*
EMP: 50
SALES: 2MM **Privately Held**
SIC: 1521 Single-family housing construction

(P-1207)
MJD CONSTRUCTION CORP
Also Called: M J D Concrete Works
28244 Dorothy Dr, Agoura Hills
(91301-2605)
PHONE....................................818 575-9864
Mathias Di Cecco, *President*
EMP: 60
SQ FT: 1,500
SALES (est): 7.4MM **Privately Held**
SIC: 1521 Single-family housing construction

(P-1208)
NICHOLAS LANE CONTRACTORS INC
1157 N Red Gum St, Anaheim
(92806-2515)
PHONE....................................714 630-7630
Scott N Shaddix, *President*
Jo Ann Shaddix, *Corp Secy*
EMP: 400
SQ FT: 5,000
SALES: 26MM **Privately Held**
WEB: www.nicholaslane.com
SIC: 1521 1542 New construction, single-family houses; commercial & office buildings, renovation & repair

(P-1209)
NORTH WIND CNSTR SVCS LLC
730 Howe Ave Ste 700, Sacramento
(95825-4641)
PHONE....................................916 333-3015
Brent Brooks,
EMP: 69 **EST:** 2011
SALES (est): 1.7MM **Privately Held**
SIC: 1521 Single-family housing construction

(P-1210)
OLSON COMPANY LLC (PA)
Also Called: Olson Homes
3010 Old Ranch Pkwy # 100, Seal Beach
(90740-2750)
PHONE....................................562 596-4770
Steve Olson,
Karen Hoover, *President*
John Reischl, *Vice Pres*
Gabriel Chang, *Admin Asst*
Campbell Chris, *Project Mgr*
EMP: 99
SALES: 46.9MM **Privately Held**
SIC: 1521 Single-family housing construction

(P-1211)
PACIFIC BAY PROPERTIES (PA)
4041 Macarthur Blvd # 500, Newport Beach
(92660-2512)
PHONE....................................949 440-7200
Malcolm S McDonald, *President*
EMP: 50
SALES (est): 9.5MM **Privately Held**
SIC: 1521 Single-family housing construction

(P-1212)
PACIFIC DESIGN DIRECTIONS INC
Also Called: Pacific Interior Design
8171 E Kaiser Blvd, Anaheim
(92808-2214)
PHONE....................................714 685-7766
Susan S Stoneburner, *President*
Kristen S Stolle, *Division Mgr*
Kristen Stolle, *Division Mgr*
Reed Stoneburner, *Division Mgr*
Kristen Stoneburner, *Manager*
EMP: 50
SQ FT: 8,600

SALES: 15MM **Privately Held**
WEB: www.pacdesign.com
SIC: 1521 1731 7389 8712 Single-family housing construction; general electrical contractor; interior designer; architectural services

(P-1213)
PAGLIA & ASSOCIATES CNSTR
Also Called: Protech Construction
2790 E Regal Park Dr, Anaheim
(92806-2417)
PHONE....................................714 982-5151
Vince Paglia, *President*
Kimm Paglia, *CFO*
▲ **EMP:** 65
SQ FT: 6,500
SALES: 13.1MM **Privately Held**
WEB: www.protechconst.com
SIC: 1521 1542 New construction, single-family houses; commercial & office building, new construction

(P-1214)
PENINSULA CUSTOM HOMES INC
1401 Old County Rd, San Carlos
(94070-5202)
PHONE....................................650 574-0241
Richard L Breaux, *CEO*
Bryan Murphy, *President*
EMP: 60 **EST:** 1979
SALES (est): 9.9MM **Privately Held**
WEB: www.pchi.com
SIC: 1521 New construction, single-family houses

(P-1215)
PETERSEN BUILDERS INC
7706 Bell Rd Ste A, Windsor (95492-8546)
PHONE....................................707 838-3035
Talbert Petersen, *President*
Rex Petersen, *Treasurer*
Dwight Petersen, *Admin Sec*
▲ **EMP:** 50
SQ FT: 1,300
SALES (est): 7.5MM **Privately Held**
SIC: 1521 1522 1542 1541 New construction, single-family houses; multi-family dwellings, new construction; commercial & office building, new construction; school building construction; food products manufacturing or packing plant construction

(P-1216)
PINNACLE BUILDERS INC
1911 Douglas Blvd Ste 85, Roseville
(95661-3811)
PHONE....................................916 372-5000
EMP: 300
SQ FT: 3,000
SALES (est): 11.5MM **Privately Held**
WEB: www.pinnaclebuildersinc.com
SIC: 1521 1542 1751

(P-1217)
PORTER CONSTRUCTION CO INC
18931 Portola Dr Ste A, Salinas
(93908-1295)
PHONE....................................831 455-3020
Daniel Porter, *President*
Debra Porter, *Corp Secy*
EMP: 240
SALES (est): 11.2MM **Privately Held**
SIC: 1521 1542 New construction, single-family houses; commercial & office building, new construction

(P-1218)
PRIMECARE QUALITY HM CARE INC
2372 Morse Ave, Irvine (92614-6234)
PHONE....................................949 681-3515
EMP: 99
SALES (est): 3.6MM **Privately Held**
SIC: 1521

(P-1219)
PULTE HOME COMPANY LLC
6210 Stoneridge Mall Rd, Pleasanton
(94588-3268)
PHONE....................................925 249-3200
Can Carrol, *Manager*

Vicky Bullard, *General Mgr*
EMP: 65
SQ FT: 12,000
SALES (corp-wide): 8.5B **Publicly Held**
SIC: 1521 New construction, single-family houses
HQ: Pulte Home Company, Llc
3350 Peachtree Rd Ne # 150
Atlanta GA 30326
248 647-2750

(P-1220)
QUALITY GROUP HOMES INC
Also Called: Consortium For Community Svcs
250 Dos Rios St Ste A1, Sacramento
(95811-0442)
PHONE....................................916 930-0066
Sarah Thomas, *Director*
EMP: 184
SALES (corp-wide): 8MM **Privately Held**
SIC: 1521 New construction, single-family houses
PA: Quality Group Homes, Inc.
4928 E Clinton Way # 108
Fresno CA 93727
559 255-8519

(P-1221)
R J DAILEY CONSTRUCTION CO
401 1st St, Los Altos (94022-3607)
PHONE....................................650 948-5196
Robert J Dailey, *President*
Christine Dailey, *Treasurer*
Carol Lopez, *Admin Asst*
Aaron Ackerman, *Project Mgr*
Jeff Del Conte, *Project Mgr*
▲ **EMP:** 70
SQ FT: 2,000
SALES (est): 12.5MM **Privately Held**
SIC: 1521 New construction, single-family houses; general remodeling, single-family houses

(P-1222)
REDHORSE CONSTRUCTORS INC
36 Professional Ctr Pkwy, San Rafael
(94903-2703)
PHONE....................................415 492-2020
David J Warner, *President*
Jay Blumenfeld, *General Mgr*
Thomas Bates, *Project Mgr*
Michael Houts, *Project Mgr*
Craig Smith, *Project Mgr*
▲ **EMP:** 75
SQ FT: 3,500
SALES: 37.8MM **Privately Held**
WEB: www.redhorseconstructors.com
SIC: 1521 General remodeling, single-family houses; new construction, single-family houses

(P-1223)
REGIONAL CONNECTOR CONSTRS
1995 Agua Mansa Rd, Riverside
(92509-2405)
PHONE....................................951 368-6400
Patty Macias, *Office Mgr*
EMP: 50
SALES (est): 3MM **Privately Held**
SIC: 1521 New construction, single-family houses

(P-1224)
REYNEN & BARDIS CONSTRUCTION (PA)
10630 Mather Blvd, Mather (95655-4125)
PHONE....................................916 366-3665
Chris Bardis, *President*
John Reynen, *Admin Sec*
EMP: 120
SALES (est): 43.5MM **Privately Held**
WEB: www.rbhome.us
SIC: 1521 6552 New construction, single-family houses; land subdividers & developers, residential

(P-1225)
RICHMOND AMERICAN HOMES
16600 Sherman Way Ste 180, Van Nuys
(91406-3725)
PHONE....................................818 908-3267
Bob Shiota, *Exec VP*
EMP: 50

SALES (corp-wide): 2.5B **Publicly Held**
SIC: 1521 Single-family housing construction
HQ: Richmond American Homes
5171 California Ave # 120
Irvine CA 92617
949 467-2600

(P-1226)
RIDGESIDE CONSTRUCTION INC
Also Called: Ridgeside Finishing
4345 E Lowell St Ste A, Ontario
(91761-2223)
P.O. Box 1237 (91762-0237)
PHONE....................................909 218-7593
Dan Zita, *President*
Kevin Hammond, *Vice Pres*
EMP: 65
SALES: 125.2MM **Privately Held**
SIC: 1521 Single-family housing construction

(P-1227)
ROBERT MORKEN CONSTRUCTION
1300 Regency Way Ste 59, Kings Beach
(96143)
PHONE....................................530 386-1512
Robert Morken, *President*
EMP: 50
SALES: 10MM **Privately Held**
SIC: 1521 1542 New construction, single-family houses; commercial & office building, new construction

(P-1228)
RYLAND HMES INLND EMPIRE CSTMR
Also Called: Home Building
1250 Corona Pointe Ct # 100, Corona
(92879-2099)
PHONE....................................951 273-3473
Linda Edwards, *President*
EMP: 80
SALES (est): 6.2MM **Privately Held**
SIC: 1521 New construction, single-family houses

(P-1229)
S TAYLOR CONSTRUCTION INC
23905 Clinton Keith Rd, Wildomar
(92595-7897)
PHONE....................................310 291-4505
Steve Taylor, *President*
EMP: 103
SALES: 1MM **Privately Held**
SIC: 1521 Single-family housing construction

(P-1230)
SAVOY CONTRACTORS GROUP INC
Also Called: Ritz Companies
8905 Research Dr, Irvine (92618-4237)
PHONE....................................949 753-1919
Robert Ritz Sadeghi, *Ch of Bd*
Shadi Sepehrband, *Controller*
EMP: 175
SQ FT: 2,000
SALES (est): 12.8MM **Privately Held**
WEB: www.theritzcompanies.com
SIC: 1521 7349 Single-family housing construction; building maintenance services

(P-1231)
SEARS HOME IMPRV PDTS INC
9586 Dist Ave Ste F, San Diego (92121)
PHONE....................................858 790-7721
Jerry Hanosh, *Branch Mgr*
EMP: 52
SALES (corp-wide): 16.7B **Publicly Held**
SIC: 1521 General remodeling, single-family houses
HQ: Sears Home Improvement Products, Inc.
1024 Florida Central Pkwy
Longwood FL 32750
407 767-0990

(P-1232)
SELIG CONSTRUCTION CORP
337 Huss Dr, Chico (95928-8209)
PHONE....................................530 893-5898

▲ = Import ▼=Export
◆ =Import/Export

M Scott Selig, *President*
Erik Palo, *Vice Pres*
▲ EMP: 50
SALES (est): 5.8MM **Privately Held**
WEB: www.seligconstruction.com
SIC: 1521 General remodeling, single-family houses

(P-1233)
SHAPELL INDUSTRIES LLC
Also Called: Shapell's Home Center
11280 Corbin Ave, Northridge
(91326-4120)
PHONE.................................818 366-1132
Nathan Shapell, *Ch of Bd*
EMP: 50
SALES (corp-wide): 5.8B **Publicly Held**
WEB: www.shapell.com
SIC: 1521 New construction, single-family houses
HQ: Shapell Industries, Llc
8383 Wilshire Blvd # 700
Beverly Hills CA 90211
323 655-7330

(P-1234)
SHEA HOMES AT MONTAGE LLC
655 Brea Canyon Rd, Walnut
(91789-3078)
PHONE.................................909 594-9500
John C Morrissey, *Principal*
EMP: 51 **EST:** 2013
SALES (est): 2.9MM
SALES (corp-wide): 2.2B **Privately Held**
SIC: 1521 Single-family housing construction
HQ: Shea Homes Limited Partnership, A California Limited Partnership
655 Brea Canyon Rd
Walnut CA 91789

(P-1235)
SHEA HOMES LMTD PARTNERSHIP A (HQ)
655 Brea Canyon Rd, Walnut
(91789-3078)
PHONE.................................909 594-9500
Jim Shontere, *Partner*
John F Shea LP, *Partner*
EMP: 50
SQ FT: 29,000
SALES: 1.1B
SALES (corp-wide): 2.2B **Privately Held**
WEB: www.highlandsranch.com
SIC: 1521 Single-family housing construction
PA: J. F. Shea Co., Inc.
655 Brea Canyon Rd
Walnut CA 91789
909 594-9500

(P-1236)
SHEEHAN CONSTRUCTION INC
477 Devlin Rd Ste 108, NAPA
(94558-7511)
PHONE.................................707 603-2610
Steve Mosiman, *President*
Tom Sheehan, *Vice Pres*
Lori Scott, *Human Res Mgr*
EMP: 500
SALES (est): 42.2MM **Privately Held**
WEB: www.sheehanconstruction.com
SIC: 1521 Single-family housing construction

(P-1237)
SKYVA CONSTRUCTION INC
5781 Old Antelope N Rd, Antelope
(95843-3962)
P.O. Box 8094, Citrus Heights (95621-8094)
PHONE.................................916 726-4999
Vladimir Andrichuk, *President*
EMP: 50
SALES (est): 4.9MM **Privately Held**
WEB: www.skyvaconstruction.com
SIC: 1521 General remodeling, single-family houses

(P-1238)
SMA BUILDERS INC
16134 Leadwell St, Van Nuys
(91406-3424)
PHONE.................................818 994-8306

Shawn Antin, *President*
Diana Antin, *Vice Pres*
EMP: 50
SALES (est): 9.1MM **Privately Held**
SIC: 1521 Single-family housing construction

(P-1239)
STEVEN N LEDSON
Also Called: Ledson Winery & Vineyards
7335 Sonoma Hwy, Santa Rosa
(95409-6269)
P.O. Box 653, Kenwood (95452-0653)
PHONE.................................707 537-3810
Steven N Ledson, *Owner*
Steven Ledson, *General Mgr*
EMP: 60
SALES (est): 5MM **Privately Held**
SIC: 1521 2084 Single-family housing construction; wines

(P-1240)
STOCKER & ALLAIRE INC
21 Mandeville Ct, Monterey (93940-5745)
PHONE.................................831 375-1890
David Stocker, *President*
David Allaire, *CFO*
Will Gaccione, *Project Mgr*
Jared Kemp, *Foreman/Supr*
EMP: 50
SQ FT: 3,200
SALES (est): 9.2MM **Privately Held**
WEB: www.stockerallaire.com
SIC: 1521 General remodeling, single-family houses

(P-1241)
SUMMERHILL CONSTRUCTION CO
Also Called: Summerhill Homes
3000 Executive Pkwy # 450, San Ramon
(94583-4255)
PHONE.................................925 244-7520
Roger Menard, *President*
EMP: 50
SQ FT: 45,000
SALES (est): 3.8MM
SALES (corp-wide): 90.7MM **Privately Held**
WEB: www.summerhillhomes.com
SIC: 1521 New construction, single-family houses
HQ: Summerhill Homes Llc
3000 Executive Pkwy # 450
San Ramon CA 94583
925 244-7500

(P-1242)
SUPERIOR CONSTRUCTION INC
265 N Joy St, Corona (92879-0600)
P.O. Box 1148 (92878-1148)
PHONE.................................951 808-8780
Kenneth Day, *President*
Don Mc Lellan, *Sls & Mktg Exec*
Darren Smith, *Accounts Mgr*
EMP: 100
SQ FT: 3,000
SALES (est): 8.7MM **Privately Held**
SIC: 1521 1542 New construction, single-family houses; commercial & office building, new construction

(P-1243)
SUPPORT FOR HOME INC
1333 Howe Ave Ste 206, Sacramento
(95825-3362)
PHONE.................................530 792-8484
Bert Cave, *Principal*
Carlotta Sanchez, *Principal*
EMP: 50
SALES (est): 3.2MM **Privately Held**
SIC: 1521 Single-family housing construction

(P-1244)
SWINERTON BUILDERS INC
2300 Clayton Rd Ste 800, Concord
(94520-2166)
PHONE.................................925 602-6400
Jeffrey Hoopes, *CEO*
Gary Rafferty, *President*
Linda Schowalter, *CFO*
Charlene Atkinson, *Principal*
EMP: 79

SALES (est): 24.4MM **Privately Held**
SIC: 1521 New construction, single-family houses

(P-1245)
T B PENICK & SONS INC
41892 Enterprise Cir S, Temecula
(92590-4822)
PHONE.................................951 719-1492
EMP: 122
SALES (corp-wide): 139.2MM **Privately Held**
SIC: 1521 General remodeling, single-family houses
PA: T. B. Penick & Sons, Inc.
15435 Innovation Dr # 100
San Diego CA 92128
858 558-1800

(P-1246)
TIM MELLO CONSTRUCTION
464 Lamarque Ct, Grass Valley
(95945-7061)
PHONE.................................530 205-8588
Timothy Mello, *Principal*
EMP: 50 **EST:** 2011
SALES (est): 210.8K **Privately Held**
SIC: 1521 Single-family housing construction

(P-1247)
TIMBER WORKS CONSTRUCTION INC
7031 Roseville Rd Ste A, Sacramento
(95842-1670)
PHONE.................................916 786-6666
Scott D Robbins, *President*
EMP: 125 **EST:** 2008
SALES (est): 13.5MM **Privately Held**
SIC: 1521 1542 Single-family housing construction; nonresidential construction

(P-1248)
TOLL BROTHERS INC
Also Called: Toll Brothers Division Office
6800 Koll Center Pkwy # 320, Pleasanton
(94566-7053)
PHONE.................................925 855-0260
Rick Nelson, *Branch Mgr*
EMP: 60
SALES (corp-wide): 5.8B **Publicly Held**
WEB: www.tollbros.com
SIC: 1521 New construction, single-family houses; townhouse construction
PA: Toll Brothers, Inc.
250 Gibraltar Rd
Horsham PA 19044
215 938-8000

(P-1249)
TORRES GENERAL INC
9484 Mission Park Pl, Santee
(92071-5610)
PHONE.................................619 448-8900
Carlos Torres Jr, *President*
Maria Morfin, *Financial Exec*
EMP: 100
SALES (est): 7.5MM **Privately Held**
SIC: 1521 New construction, single-family houses

(P-1250)
TUPAZ HOMES LLC
2038 Biarritz Pl, San Jose (95138-2259)
PHONE.................................408 377-1622
Rosario Tupaz, *Mng Member*
Beebe Tupaz, *CFO*
EMP: 100
SALES (est): 357K **Privately Held**
SIC: 1521 Single-family housing construction

(P-1251)
TURNER CONSTRUCTION COMPANY
555 S Flower St Ste 4220, Los Angeles
(90071-2438)
PHONE.................................213 891-3000
Michael O'Brien, *Senior VP*
Mauricio Romero, *Project Mgr*
EMP: 70
SALES (corp-wide): 579.6MM **Privately Held**
SIC: 1521 Single-family housing construction

HQ: Turner Construction Company Inc
375 Hudson St Fl 6
New York NY 10014
212 229-6000

(P-1252)
US BEST REPAIR SERVICE INC
Also Called: US Best Repairs
2004 Mcgaw Ave, Irvine (92614-0911)
PHONE.................................888 750-2378
Mark Zaverl, *CEO*
Brian Craycraft, *CFO*
David Lopez, *Info Tech Mgr*
Samuel Tucci, *Business Mgr*
Johanna Avalos, *Maintence Staff*
EMP: 101
SALES (est): 14.2MM **Privately Held**
WEB: www.usbestrepairs.com
SIC: 1521 1522 1542 Single-family home remodeling, additions & repairs; remodeling, multi-family dwellings; commercial & office buildings, renovation & repair

(P-1253)
VALLEYWIDE CONSTRUCTION INC
284 W Lester Ave, Clovis (93619-3788)
PHONE.................................559 834-6212
Christina Birdsell, *President*
John Birdsell, *Treasurer*
EMP: 150
SQ FT: 5,000
SALES: 6.8MM **Privately Held**
SIC: 1521 1751 New construction, single-family houses; framing contractor

(P-1254)
VAN ACKER CNSTR ASSOC INC
1060 Redwood Hwy Frntg Rd, Mill Valley
(94941-1613)
PHONE.................................415 383-5589
Gary Van Acker, *President*
Pamela Blier, *Vice Pres*
Heide Vasquez, *Administration*
Allison Ewald, *Project Mgr*
Noel Manerud, *Project Mgr*
▲ EMP: 134
SQ FT: 15,000
SALES (est): 29.8MM **Privately Held**
WEB: www.vanacker.com
SIC: 1521 New construction, single-family houses

(P-1255)
VASONA MANAGEMENT INC
Also Called: Vasonic Construction
37390 Central Mont Pl, Fremont (94538)
PHONE.................................510 413-0091
Dan Scharnow, *Vice Pres*
EMP: 80
SALES (corp-wide): 29.1MM **Privately Held**
WEB: www.vasonamanagement.com
SIC: 1521 Single-family housing construction
PA: Vasona Management, Inc.
18 E Main St
Los Gatos CA 95030
408 354-4200

(P-1256)
VENTURA STREETS DEPT
Also Called: City Hall
336 San Jon Rd, Ventura (93001-3233)
PHONE.................................805 652-4515
Ron Calkins, *Director*
EMP: 100 **EST:** 1998
SALES (est): 2.7MM **Privately Held**
SIC: 1521 1611 General remodeling, single-family houses; highway & street construction

(P-1257)
VORWALLER & BROOKS INC
72182 Corporate Way, Thousand Palms
(92276-3324)
PHONE.................................760 262-6300
Eugene Sheldon Vorwaller, *President*
Jason Brooks, *Vice Pres*
EMP: 55
SALES (est): 7.9MM **Privately Held**
SIC: 1521 New construction, single-family houses

PRODUCTS & SVCS

(P-1258)
WARMINGTON RESIDENTIAL CAL INC
3090 Pullman St, Costa Mesa (92626-5901)
PHONE.....................714 557-5511
James Warmington Jr, *President*
Mike Riddlesberger, *CFO*
Matt Tingler, *Vice Pres*
Mario Santos, *Information Mgr*
Jennifer Bell, *Marketing Staff*
EMP: 150
SALES (est): 24.4MM **Privately Held**
SIC: **1521** Single-family housing construction

(P-1259)
WESTCOR CONSTRUCTION OF CAL
2351 W Lugonia Ave Ste D, Redlands (92374-5014)
PHONE.....................909 796-8900
Michael A Coronado, *President*
Kevin R Booth, *CFO*
James D Hammer, *Treasurer*
Robert Keele, *General Mgr*
EMP: 120
SQ FT: 4,600
SALES: 13.9MM
SALES (corp-wide): 30.5MM **Privately Held**
SIC: **1521** New construction, single-family houses
PA: Westcor Construction
5620 Stephanie St
Las Vegas NV 89122
702 433-1414

(P-1260)
WOOD CASTLE CONSTRUCTION INC
770 W Golden Grove Way, Covina (91722-3255)
PHONE.....................626 966-8600
Daniel Toro, *President*
Victor Quintana, *Treasurer*
Julio Toro, *Vice Pres*
EMP: 50
SALES (est): 5.9MM **Privately Held**
SIC: **1521** Single-family housing construction

(P-1261)
XL CONSTRUCTION CORPORATION
1810 13th St Ste 110, Sacramento (95811-7149)
PHONE.....................916 282-2900
Eric Raff, *Branch Mgr*
Silas Nigam, *Executive*
Kim Prock, *Engineer*
EMP: 75 **Privately Held**
SIC: **1521** Single-family housing construction
PA: XL Construction Corporation
851 Buckeye Ct
Milpitas CA 95035

(P-1262)
ZOHAR CONSTRUCTION INC
Also Called: Quality Construction
4272 Pasadero Pl, Tarzana (91356-5218)
P.O. Box 4522, Valley Village (91617-0522)
PHONE.....................818 609-7473
Zohar Haykeen, *President*
Itzik Valigura, *Supervisor*
EMP: 100 EST: 2011
SALES (est): 5.1MM **Privately Held**
SIC: **1521** Single-family housing construction

1522 General Contractors, Residential Other Than Single Family
---

(P-1263)
APEX DEVELOPMENT INC
23679 Calabasas Rd # 764, Calabasas (91302-1502)
PHONE.....................818 887-0400

Anthony A Nowaid, *President*
EMP: 138
SALES (est): 8.1MM **Privately Held**
SIC: **1521** 1521 1541 1542 Residential construction; single-family housing construction; industrial buildings & warehouses; nonresidential construction; highway & street construction; bridge, tunnel & elevated highway

(P-1264)
ARNEL DEVELOPMENT COMPANY
3146 Tiger Run Ct Ste 108, Carlsbad (92010-6696)
PHONE.....................760 599-6111
Carol Cole, *Principal*
EMP: 62
SALES (corp-wide): 16.6MM **Privately Held**
SIC: **1522** Residential construction
PA: Arnel Development Company
949 S Coast Dr Ste 600
Costa Mesa CA 92626
714 481-5000

(P-1265)
ASHWOOD CONSTRUCTION INC
5755 E Kings Canyon Rd # 110, Fresno (93727-4744)
PHONE.....................559 253-7240
Michael J Conway Jr, *President*
EMP: 50
SQ FT: 1,200
SALES (est): 11.1MM **Privately Held**
WEB: www.ashwoodco.com
SIC: **1522** Multi-family dwellings, new construction

(P-1266)
AV BUILDER CORP (PA)
6373 Nancy Ridge Dr, San Diego (92121-2247)
PHONE.....................858 622-9200
A V Tony Madureira, *President*
Sarah McNamara, *CFO*
Laura Dusina, *Prgrmr*
EMP: 75
SQ FT: 7,140
SALES (est): 11.6MM **Privately Held**
SIC: **1522** 8711 Hotel/motel & multi-family home renovation & remodeling; building construction consultant

(P-1267)
AXIS SERVICES INC
Also Called: Axis Construction
2566 Barrington Ct, Hayward (94545-1133)
PHONE.....................510 732-6111
Bizhan Mahallati, *CEO*
Parisa Mahallati, *Vice Pres*
Conor Meyers, *Vice Pres*
Jeannie Cuevas, *Admin Asst*
Mario Flores, *Project Mgr*
EMP: 110
SQ FT: 10,000
SALES (est): 19.1MM **Privately Held**
WEB: www.axisconstruction.com
SIC: **1522** Residential construction

(P-1268)
BERNARDS BUILDERS INC
555 1st St, San Fernando (91340-3051)
PHONE.....................818 898-1521
Doug Bernards, *Chairman*
Greg Simons, *President*
Jeffrey G Bernards, *CEO*
Ken Menager, *CFO*
EMP: 270
SALES (est): 488.8K
SALES (corp-wide): 158.6MM **Privately Held**
SIC: **1522** Residential construction
PA: Bernards Bros. Inc.
555 1st St
San Fernando CA 91340
818 898-1521

(P-1269)
BILL BROWN CONSTRUCTION CO
242 Phelan Ave, San Jose (95112-6109)
PHONE.....................408 297-3738
Bill Brown, *Principal*

William Brown, *President*
EMP: 100
SALES (est): 15.1MM **Privately Held**
SIC: **1522** 1771 Hotel/motel & multi-family home construction; concrete work

(P-1270)
BLH CONSTRUCTION COMPANY
21031 Ventura Blvd # 200, Woodland Hills (91364-6517)
PHONE.....................818 905-3837
Charles Brumbaugh, *CEO*
Brian Holland, *COO*
EMP: 150
SALES (est): 26.5MM **Privately Held**
WEB: www.blhconstruction.com
SIC: **1522** Apartment building construction

(P-1271)
BRUCE OLSON CONSTRUCTION INC
7320 River Rd, Tahoe City (96145)
PHONE.....................530 581-1087
Bruce Olson, *President*
EMP: 90
SQ FT: 3,050
SALES (est): 5.9MM **Privately Held**
WEB: www.bruceolsonconstruction.com
SIC: **1522** Residential construction

(P-1272)
CABRILLO ECONOMIC DEV CORP (PA)
702 County Square Dr # 100, Ventura (93003-5450)
PHONE.....................805 659-3791
Rodney Fernandez, *CEO*
Maria Hernandez, *Bd of Directors*
Laura Cuellar, *General Mgr*
Eileen Panter, *Assistant*
EMP: 72
SQ FT: 22,000
SALES (est): 6.4MM **Privately Held**
SIC: **1522** Residential construction

(P-1273)
CASTLE & COOKE INC
17600 Collier Ave C120, Lake Elsinore (92530-2633)
PHONE.....................951 245-0476
Al Tomlinson, *Branch Mgr*
EMP: 5000
SALES (corp-wide): 911.7MM **Privately Held**
SIC: **1522** Residential construction
PA: Castle & Cooke, Inc.
1 Dole Dr
Westlake Village CA 91362
310 374-3952

(P-1274)
CJ CONSTRUCTION & DEV INC
78206 Varner Rd Ste D, Palm Desert (92211-4136)
PHONE.....................760 247-6868
Lloyd James, *President*
EMP: 52 EST: 2009
SQ FT: 2,200
SALES: 5MM **Privately Held**
SIC: **1522** Apartment building construction

(P-1275)
CKL CONSTRUCTION INC
967 W Hedding St, San Jose (95126-1257)
PHONE.....................408 244-7042
Cortland C Lanning Jr, *President*
EMP: 300
SQ FT: 3,133
SALES (est): 16.9MM **Privately Held**
SIC: **1522** 1611 Condominium construction; general contractor, highway & street construction

(P-1276)
COBALT CONSTRUCTION COMPANY
2259 Ward Ave Ste 200, Simi Valley (93065-1880)
PHONE.....................805 577-6222
Darin Kruse, *CEO*
Dru Guillot, *Business Dir*
Debra White, *Admin Asst*
David Strong, *Info Tech Mgr*
Chuck Lima, *Project Mgr*
▲ EMP: 70

SQ FT: 43,000
SALES (est): 29.6MM **Privately Held**
SIC: **1522** 8711 1542 Multi-family dwellings, new construction; construction & civil engineering; commercial & office building, new construction; specialized public building contractors

(P-1277)
COUNTRY BUILDERS INC
Also Called: Country Builders Construction
5915 Graham Ct, Livermore (94550-9710)
PHONE.....................925 373-1020
Weldon Offill, *President*
EMP: 150
SQ FT: 5,000
SALES (est): 14.7MM **Privately Held**
WEB: www.countrybuilders.com
SIC: **1522** Apartment building construction; remodeling, multi-family dwellings

(P-1278)
COVE BUILDERS INC
2264 Arroyo Dr, Riverside (92506-1507)
PHONE.....................714 436-2973
Ed Holmes II, *President*
EMP: 120
SALES (est): 7.4MM **Privately Held**
SIC: **1522** 1542 1521 Residential construction; nonresidential construction; single-family housing construction

(P-1279)
DANCO BUILDERS INC
5251 Ericson Way Ste A, Arcata (95521-9274)
PHONE.....................707 822-9000
Daniel J Johnson, *President*
Kendra Johnson, *Shareholder*
Kirk Heberly, *Vice Pres*
Kira Sandoval, *Administration*
Chuck Barnhart, *Technology*
EMP: 100
SQ FT: 15,000
SALES (est): 15.3MM **Privately Held**
WEB: www.dancobuilders.com
SIC: **1522** 1542 Apartment building construction; nonresidential construction; commercial & office building contractors

(P-1280)
DINYARI CONSTRUCTION INC
500 Phelan Ave, San Jose (95112-2506)
PHONE.....................408 289-5400
Toll Free:.....................888 -
Farbod Buck Dinyari, *President*
Katayoon Dinyari, *Vice Pres*
EMP: 50
SQ FT: 12,000
SALES (est): 5.5MM **Privately Held**
WEB: www.dinyari.com
SIC: **1522** 1542 Residential construction; commercial & office building contractors

(P-1281)
DOUGLAS ROSS CONSTRUCTION INC
900 E Hamilton Ave # 140, Campbell (95008-0665)
PHONE.....................408 429-7700
J Douglas Ross, *President*
Andrew Maurer, *CFO*
Jeff Jelniker, *Vice Pres*
Jeffrey Jelniker, *Vice Pres*
Mike Brophy, *Project Mgr*
EMP: 55
SQ FT: 7,158
SALES (est): 9.6MM **Privately Held**
SIC: **1522** Hotel/motel & multi-family home renovation & remodeling

(P-1282)
EDEN HOUSING INC (PA)
22645 Grand St, Hayward (94541-5031)
PHONE.....................510 582-1460
John Gaffney, *CEO*
Linda Mandolini, *President*
Jan Peters, *COO*
Olivia Dequzman, *Principal*
Julia Cerna, *Manager*
EMP: 58
SQ FT: 10,000
SALES: 32.9MM **Privately Held**
SIC: **1522** Multi-family dwellings, new construction

(P-1283)
EDEN HOUSING INC
3428 Mt Diablo Blvd, Lafayette (94549-4083)
PHONE....................925 297-4297
EMP: 92
SALES (corp-wide): 32.9MM **Privately Held**
SIC: 1522 Multi-family dwellings, new construction
PA: Eden Housing, Inc.
22645 Grand St
Hayward CA 94541
510 582-1460

(P-1284)
FAIRFIELD DEVELOPMENT INC (PA)
Also Called: Ffd II
5510 Morehouse Dr Ste 200, San Diego (92121-3722)
PHONE....................858 457-2123
Christopher E Hashioka, *Principal*
Greg Pinkalla, *COO*
James A Hribar, *CFO*
James L Bosler, *Chairman*
Ted Bradford, *Senior VP*
▲ **EMP:** 225
SALES (est): 364.1MM **Privately Held**
WEB: www.westbrook-apts.com
SIC: 1522 Multi-family dwelling construction

(P-1285)
FRAMING ASSOCIATES INC
1320 Coolidge Ave, National City (91950-4334)
PHONE....................619 336-9991
Bruce Mc Dowell, *CEO*
Ruth Jaffe, *Administration*
EMP: 150
SALES (est): 11.6MM **Privately Held**
SIC: 1522 Residential construction

(P-1286)
G B GROUP INC (PA)
8921 Murray Ave, Gilroy (95020-3633)
PHONE....................408 848-8118
Gregory D Brown, *CEO*
Mark Greening, *President*
Jeffery Dame, *CFO*
Regan L Brown, *Corp Secy*
Pat Falconio, *Exec VP*
EMP: 79
SQ FT: 4,300
SALES (est): 56.1MM **Privately Held**
WEB: www.gbgroupinc.com
SIC: 1522 1542 8322 1541 Hotel/motel & multi-family home renovation & remodeling; condominium construction; nonresidential construction; rehabilitation services; renovation, remodeling & repairs: industrial buildings; construction management

(P-1287)
HAMMER DOWN DAVILA CNSTR
Also Called: Hdd Construction
2338 W Erie St, Caruthers (93609-9529)
P.O. Box 642 (93609-0642)
PHONE....................559 864-2001
David Davila, *Owner*
EMP: 85 **EST:** 1998
SQ FT: 2,400
SALES (est): 4.7MM **Privately Held**
SIC: 1522 Residential construction

(P-1288)
HEIDI CORPORATION
Also Called: Donald J Schefflers Cnstr
727 N Vernon Ave, Azusa (91702-2232)
PHONE....................626 333-6317
Donald J Scheffler, *President*
▲ **EMP:** 75
SQ FT: 15,000
SALES (est): 10.5MM **Privately Held**
SIC: 1522 Residential construction

(P-1289)
HILLCREST SENIOR HOUSING CORP
35 Hillcrest Dr, Daly City (94014-1098)
PHONE....................650 757-1737
Susan Ruan, *Principal*
David A Grant, *Principal*

EMP: 260 **EST:** 2005
SALES (est): 468.6K
SALES (corp-wide): 178.8MM **Privately Held**
SIC: 1522 Apartment building construction
HQ: Humangood Affordable Housing
6120 Stoneridge Mall Rd # 100
Pleasanton CA 94588
925 924-7163

(P-1290)
HURLEY CONSTRUCTION INC
1801 I St Ste 200, Sacramento (95811-3000)
PHONE....................916 446-7599
Peter H Geremia, *CEO*
Steven Eggert, *Vice Pres*
EMP: 80
SQ FT: 2,500
SALES (est): 11.6MM **Privately Held**
WEB: www.antonllc.com
SIC: 1522 Multi-family dwellings, new construction

(P-1291)
JAMES E ROBERTS-OBAYASHI CORP
20 Oak Ct, Danville (94526-4006)
PHONE....................925 820-0600
Larry R Smith, *CEO*
Obayashi Corporation, *Principal*
Tim Clark, *Project Mgr*
Jeanine Kaufman, *Project Mgr*
Jeffrey Marek, *Project Mgr*
EMP: 110
SQ FT: 4,000
SALES (est): 30.7MM **Privately Held**
WEB: www.jerocorp.com
SIC: 1522 1542 Multi-family dwellings, new construction; commercial & office building, new construction

(P-1292)
JAMES MCCUTCHEON
17521 Walker Basin Rd, Caliente (93518-1407)
PHONE....................661 867-1810
Mg Taylor, *President*
EMP: 50
SALES (est): 2.6MM **Privately Held**
SIC: 1522 Residential construction

(P-1293)
JUDSON ENTERPRISES INC (PA)
Also Called: K-Designers
2440 Gold River Rd # 100, Rancho Cordova (95670-6390)
PHONE....................916 596-6721
Larry D Judson, *President*
Tony Tobia, *CFO*
Michael Burgess, *Vice Pres*
Brian Vidlock, *Vice Pres*
Lane Black, *Office Admin*
▲ **EMP:** 265
SQ FT: 28,000
SALES (est): 86.2MM **Privately Held**
WEB: www.k-designers.com
SIC: 1522 Residential construction

(P-1294)
JWC CONSTRUCTION INC (PA)
Also Called: Jon Wayne Construction
2580 Fortune Way, Vista (92081-8441)
PHONE....................760 727-2494
Jon Wayne, *CEO*
Mario Alesi, *Project Mgr*
Tomasa Collazo, *Accountant*
Matt Friedman, *Director*
David Dillon, *Manager*
EMP: 50
SQ FT: 7,000
SALES (est): 25.7MM **Privately Held**
SIC: 1522 1521 Residential construction; new construction, single-family houses

(P-1295)
JWC CONSTRUCTION INC
4570 Campus Dr, Newport Beach (92660-8809)
PHONE....................949 252-2107
William V Gennusa, *Principal*
EMP: 50

SALES (corp-wide): 25.7MM **Privately Held**
SIC: 1522 1521 Residential construction; new construction, single-family houses
PA: Jwc Construction, Inc.
2580 Fortune Way
Vista CA 92081
760 727-2494

(P-1296)
K&M CONSTRUCTION
642 Pine Ave, Pacific Grove (93950-3347)
PHONE....................831 643-2819
Kevin Ralph, *Partner*
EMP: 70
SALES (est): 3.3MM **Privately Held**
SIC: 1522 Residential construction

(P-1297)
KB HOME SOUTH BAY INC
5000 Executive Pkwy # 125, San Ramon (94583-4210)
PHONE....................925 983-2500
Chris Apostolopoulos, *CEO*
Robert Freed, *President*
Joe Gregorich, *Vice Pres*
Andrew Kusnick, *Vice Pres*
Jeffrey McMullen, *Vice Pres*
EMP: 140
SQ FT: 5,500
SALES (est): 16MM
SALES (corp-wide): 4.3B **Publicly Held**
SIC: 1522 1521 Residential construction; single-family housing construction
HQ: Kb Home Greater Los Angeles Inc.
10990 Wilshire Blvd # 700
Los Angeles CA 90024
310 231-4000

(P-1298)
KENNARD DEVELOPMENT GROUP
Also Called: Kdg Construction Consulting
520 N Central Ave Ste 715, Glendale (91203-3959)
PHONE....................818 241-0800
Lydia Kennard, *CEO*
Jeffrey Lilly, *Finance*
Tess Da Silva, *Director*
EMP: 50
SQ FT: 2,500
SALES (est): 3MM **Privately Held**
SIC: 1522 1541 1623 1611 Residential construction; industrial buildings & warehouses; water, sewer & utility lines; highway & street construction; bridge, tunnel & elevated highway

(P-1299)
KERN 2008 CMNTY PARTNERS LP
Also Called: Desert Oaks Apartments
1219 N Plaza Dr, Visalia (93291-8837)
PHONE....................559 651-3559
Terry Coyne, *General Ptnr*
EMP: 85
SALES: 950K **Privately Held**
SIC: 1522 Residential construction

(P-1300)
LAKE MERRITT HOTEL ASSOCIATES
1800 Madison St, Oakland (94612-4638)
PHONE....................510 832-2300
Randall C Berger, *Partner*
Cheryl Berger, *Partner*
Johanna Leonard, *Manager*
EMP: 50
SQ FT: 44,155
SALES (est): 3.4MM **Privately Held**
WEB: www.lakemerritthotel.com
SIC: 1522 7011 Apartment building construction; hotels & motels

(P-1301)
MARK SCOTT CONSTRUCTION INC
241 Frank West Cir # 200, Stockton (95206-4012)
PHONE....................209 982-0502
Mark Scott, *Principal*
EMP: 74 **Privately Held**
SIC: 1522 1521 Residential construction; single-family housing construction

PA: Mark Scott Construction, Inc.
2835 Contra Costa Blvd
Pleasant Hill CA 94523

(P-1302)
NANCY SMITH CONSTRUCTION INC
47 Yorkshire Dr, Oakland (94618-2021)
PHONE....................510 923-1671
Ronald Smith, *President*
Christy Smith, *Treasurer*
Kristie Smith, *Treasurer*
Randal Smith, *Vice Pres*
EMP: 50
SALES: 15.3MM **Privately Held**
SIC: 1522 Apartment building construction

(P-1303)
NIBBI BROS ASSOCIATES INC
Also Called: Nibbi Bros Concrete
1000 Brannan St Ste 102, San Francisco (94103-4888)
PHONE....................415 863-1820
Robert L Nibbi, *President*
Larry Nibbi, *CEO*
Richard Fedick, *CFO*
Mike Nibbi, *Vice Pres*
Jeff Hartman, *Division Mgr*
EMP: 150
SALES (est): 12.6MM **Privately Held**
SIC: 1522 1542 Residential construction; custom builders, non-residential

(P-1304)
OLEN RESIDENTIAL REALTY CORP (HQ)
Also Called: Olen Companies, The
7 Corporate Plaza Dr, Newport Beach (92660-7904)
PHONE....................949 644-6536
Igor M Olenicoff, *President*
EMP: 70
SALES (est): 63.4MM **Privately Held**
SIC: 1522 Multi-family dwellings, new construction

(P-1305)
PARKHURST TERRACE
100 Parkhurst Cir, Aptos (95003-9657)
PHONE....................831 685-0800
Cheryl Digrazia, *Principal*
EMP: 93
SALES (est): 3.6MM
SALES (corp-wide): 41.9K **Privately Held**
SIC: 1522 Apartment building construction
HQ: Midpen Property Management Corporation
303 Vintage Park Dr # 250
Foster City CA 94404
650 356-2900

(P-1306)
PRC BUILDERS INC
26616 Mission St, San Juan Capistrano (92675-3122)
PHONE....................949 529-7011
David P Fitts, *President*
Jason Pammer, *Vice Pres*
EMP: 90 **EST:** 1997
SALES: 12MM **Privately Held**
SIC: 1522 Residential construction

(P-1307)
PRIDE INDUSTRIES
Cbc Base Bldg 19 43rd St, Port Hueneme (93041)
PHONE....................805 985-8481
Dennis Carter, *Branch Mgr*
EMP: 140
SALES (corp-wide): 290.6MM **Privately Held**
SIC: 1522 Residential construction
PA: Pride Industries
10030 Foothills Blvd
Roseville CA 95747
916 788-2100

(P-1308)
PROPATH INC
17891 Cartwright Rd # 100, Irvine (92614-4255)
PHONE....................949 341-8000
Doug Wooley, *Regional Mgr*
EMP: 50

P
R
O
D
U
C
T
S

&

S
V
C
S

SALES (est): 177.4K **Privately Held**
SIC: 1522 Residential construction

(P-1309)
PSLQ INC
28910 Rancho California R, Temecula
(92590-1870)
PHONE..........................951 795-4260
John P Swensen, *President*
Lee Quigley, *Vice Pres*
Danny Perez, *Manager*
EMP: 75
SQ FT: 800
SALES (est): 11.8MM **Privately Held**
SIC: 1522 0781 Residential construction; landscape services

(P-1310)
RDR BUILDERS LP
Also Called: Rdr Production Builders
1806 W Kettleman Ln Ste F, Lodi
(95242-4316)
PHONE..........................209 368-7561
Ron Dos Reis, *Partner*
Mark Barbieri, *Partner*
Ed Dos Reis, *Partner*
Ron Dos-Reis, *President*
EMP: 85
SQ FT: 1,400
SALES: 18MM **Privately Held**
SIC: 1522 1542 Multi-family dwellings, new construction; hotel/motel & multi-family home renovation & remodeling; commercial & office building, new construction; commercial & office buildings, renovation & repair

(P-1311)
REEGS INC
Also Called: Monterey Construction Company
88 Monterey Salinas Hwy A, Salinas
(93908-8976)
PHONE..........................831 455-7931
Richard Benjamin Rega, *President*
EMP: 65
SALES (est): 2.7MM **Privately Held**
SIC: 1522 Residential construction

(P-1312)
REGIONAL INVESTMENT & MGT LLC
4640 Admiralty Way # 1050, Marina Del Rey (90292-6642)
PHONE..........................310 821-1945
Alicia Miller,
EMP: 50
SALES (est): 3.3MM **Privately Held**
SIC: 1522 6798 Multi-family dwellings, new construction; real estate investment trusts

(P-1313)
RRM CONSTRUCTION INC
9135 Cord Ave, Downey (90240-2433)
PHONE..........................562 440-3539
Cesar Montano, *CEO*
EMP: 50
SALES (est): 702.9K **Privately Held**
SIC: 1522 Residential construction

(P-1314)
SAARMAN CONSTRUCTION LTD
683 Mcallister St, San Francisco
(94102-3111)
PHONE..........................415 749-2700
Jeffrey M Saarman, *President*
Steven P Saarman, *CEO*
Paul Saarman, *General Mgr*
Irma Saarman, *Admin Sec*
Karl Tahir, *Info Tech Dir*
EMP: 250
SQ FT: 4,500
SALES (est): 38MM **Privately Held**
WEB: www.saarman.com
SIC: 1522 1521 Condominium construction; apartment building construction; general remodeling, single-family houses; new construction, single-family houses

(P-1315)
SHEA HOMES VANTIS LLC
655 Brea Canyon Rd, Walnut
(91789-3078)
PHONE..........................909 594-9500
EMP: 51

SALES (est): 3.1MM
SALES (corp-wide): 2.2B **Privately Held**
SIC: 1522 Apartment building construction
HQ: Shea Homes Limited Partnership, A California Limited Partnership
655 Brea Canyon Rd
Walnut CA 91789

(P-1316)
SILICONSAGE CONSTRUCTION INC
560 S Mathilda Ave, Sunnyvale
(94086-7607)
PHONE..........................408 916-3205
Sanjeev Acharya, *CEO*
Hassan Nabousli, *Info Tech Mgr*
EMP: 200 EST: 2014
SALES: 50MM **Privately Held**
SIC: 1522 Multi-family dwellings, new construction

(P-1317)
STRATHAM HOMES INC
2201 Dupont Dr Ste 300, Irvine
(92612-7509)
PHONE..........................949 833-1554
Ali Razi, *President*
David Lamb, *Shareholder*
Mehrdad Rassekh, *Shareholder*
Karen Evans, *CFO*
Pat Potts, *Project Mgr*
EMP: 100
SQ FT: 7,000
SALES: 30MM **Privately Held**
SIC: 1522 Residential construction

(P-1318)
SWINERTON INCORPORATED
2300 Clayton Rd Ste 800, Concord
(94520-2166)
PHONE..........................925 689-2336
Lawrence Mathews, *Branch Mgr*
EMP: 97 **Privately Held**
SIC: 1522 8741 Residential construction; construction management
PA: Swinerton Incorporated
260 Townsend St
San Francisco CA 94107

(P-1319)
THOMPSON BUILDERS CORPORATION
250 Bel Marin Keys Blvd A, Novato
(94949-5727)
PHONE..........................415 456-8972
Paul Thompson, *President*
F Joseph Hass, *Vice Pres*
Peter Hopkins, *Project Mgr*
David Girdley, *Project Engr*
Alex Diaz, *Manager*
▲ **EMP:** 170
SQ FT: 6,000
SALES: 72.7MM **Privately Held**
WEB: www.westbaybuilders.com
SIC: 1522 1542 8711 7389 Multi-family dwelling construction; commercial & office building, new construction; construction & civil engineering; design services; general contractor, highway & street construction

(P-1320)
TONNER HILLS HSING PARTNERS LP
17701 Cowan Ste 200, Irvine (92614-6840)
PHONE..........................949 263-8676
Laura Archuleta, *Partner*
Marcy Finamore, *Info Tech Mgr*
EMP: 50
SALES (est): 4.6MM **Privately Held**
SIC: 1522 Apartment building construction

(P-1321)
TOSCANA HOMES LP
Also Called: Toscana Country Club
300 Eagle Dance Cir, Palm Desert
(92211-7440)
PHONE..........................760 772-7227
William Bone, *Partner*
Jane Hauck, *VP Opers*
EMP: 50
SQ FT: 6,000

SALES (est): 3.5MM **Privately Held**
WEB: www.sunrisemis.com
SIC: 1522 Residential construction

(P-1322)
TOTAL-WESTERN INC
2811 Fruitvale Ave Ste A, Bakersfield
(93308-5947)
PHONE..........................661 589-5200
Jeff Jordan, *Administration*
Ed Harper, *Manager*
Bill Reynolds, *Manager*
EMP: 80
SALES (corp-wide): 337.2MM **Privately Held**
WEB: www.total-western.com
SIC: 1522 1542 Residential construction; nonresidential construction
HQ: Total-Western, Inc.
8049 Somerset Blvd
Paramount CA 90723
562 220-1450

(P-1323)
TRI POINTE HOMES INC (HQ)
19520 Jamboree Rd Ste 300, Irvine
(92612-2429)
P.O. Box 57088 (92619-7088)
PHONE..........................949 438-1400
Barry S Sternlicht, *Ch of Bd*
Darren Dupree, *President*
Thomas J Mitchell, *President*
Kevin Wilson, *President*
Douglas F Bauer, *CEO*
EMP: 134
SALES: 1.7B
SALES (corp-wide): 2.8B **Publicly Held**
SIC: 1522 Residential construction
PA: Tri Pointe Group, Inc.
19540 Jamboree Rd Ste 300
Irvine CA 92612
949 438-1400

(P-1324)
V DEVELOPMENT INC
Also Called: Capital Builders
550 Harvest Park Dr Ste A, Brentwood
(94513-4058)
PHONE..........................925 634-8890
Manuel Vierra, *President*
EMP: 75
SQ FT: 2,300
SALES: 5MM **Privately Held**
SIC: 1522 Residential construction

(P-1325)
WERMERS MULTI-FAMILY CORP
5120 Shoreham Pl Ste 150, San Diego
(92122-5959)
PHONE..........................858 535-1475
Thomas W Wermers, *President*
Jeff Bunker, *President*
Tom Wermers, *CEO*
Richard Lemmel, *CFO*
Barry Weber, *Vice Pres*
EMP: 130
SQ FT: 7,000
SALES (est): 28.6MM **Privately Held**
WEB: www.wermerscontractors.com
SIC: 1522 Hotel/motel & multi-family home construction

(P-1326)
WESTERN NATIONAL PROPERTIES (PA)
Also Called: Arkebauer Properties
8 Executive Cir, Irvine (92614-6746)
P.O. Box 19528 (92623-9528)
PHONE..........................949 862-6200
David Stone, *Ch of Bd*
Rex Delong, *President*
Michael K Hayde, *CEO*
Jeffrey R Scott, *CFO*
Debra Meute, *Vice Pres*
▲ **EMP:** 129 EST: 1981
SQ FT: 37,000
SALES (est): 64.3MM **Privately Held**
WEB: www.wng.com
SIC: 1522 6513 6512 6531 Apartment building construction; apartment building operators; nonresidential building operators; real estate agents & managers

(P-1327)
WL BUTLER INC
1629 Main St, Redwood City (94063-2121)
PHONE..........................650 361-1270
William Butler, *CEO*
Frank York, *President*
David A Nevens Jr, *COO*
Gina Henson, *CFO*
Gina Tankersley, *Vice Pres*
EMP: 250
SALES (est): 32.2MM **Privately Held**
SIC: 1522 Residential construction

(P-1328)
ZASTROW CONSTRUCTION INC
Also Called: Reliance Company
3267 Verdugo Rd, Los Angeles
(90065-2035)
PHONE..........................323 478-1956
Mark Zastrow, *President*
Patti Eldridge, *Treasurer*
Kai Wilson, *Vice Pres*
EMP: 115 EST: 1976
SQ FT: 2,000
SALES (est): 13MM **Privately Held**
SIC: 1522 Multi-family dwelling construction; multi-family dwellings, new construction

---

1531 Operative Builders

(P-1329)
ALBERT D SEENO CNSTR CO INC
4021 Port Chicago Hwy, Concord
(94520-1122)
P.O. Box 4113 (94524-4113)
PHONE..........................925 671-7711
Albert D Seeno Jr, *CEO*
Richard B Seeno, *Principal*
Thomas A Seeno, *Principal*
EMP: 80
SQ FT: 30,000
SALES (est): 26.9MM **Privately Held**
WEB: www.seenohomes.com
SIC: 1531 Speculative builder, single-family houses

(P-1330)
BARA CONSTRUCTION SERVICES
2678 Bishop Dr Ste 116, San Ramon
(94583-4455)
PHONE..........................925 790-0130
Selina Singh, *Principal*
EMP: 50
SQ FT: 1,500
SALES (est): 4.6MM **Privately Held**
SIC: 1531 1799 1711 ; coating, caulking & weather, water & fireproofing; heating systems repair & maintenance

(P-1331)
BENJAMIN KURZBAN SON CTRL INC
24533 Stagg St, Canoga Park
(91304-6124)
PHONE..........................347 227-3425
Mitchell Kurzban, *President*
Sharlene Vadal, *Manager*
EMP: 50
SQ FT: 9,000
SALES (est): 7.5MM **Privately Held**
WEB: www.kurzban.com
SIC: 1531 Operative builders

(P-1332)
CALATLANTIC GROUP INC
3825 Hopyard Rd Ste 195, Pleasanton
(94588-8529)
PHONE..........................925 847-8700
Glen Martin, *Manager*
EMP: 50
SQ FT: 5,000
SALES (corp-wide): 12.6B **Publicly Held**
WEB: www.standardpacifichomes.com
SIC: 1531 1521 Operative builders; single-family housing construction
HQ: Calatlantic Group, Inc.
1100 Wilson Blvd Ste 2100
Arlington VA 22209
240 532-3806

(P-1333)
CALATLANTIC GROUP INC
Also Called: Ryland Homes
5740 Fleet St Ste 200, Carlsbad
(92008-4704)
PHONE...................................760 931-4414
Karen Carter, *Manager*
EMP: 55
SALES (corp-wide): 12.6B **Publicly Held**
WEB: www.ryland.com
SIC: **1531** Speculative builder, single-fam-
ily houses
HQ: Calatlantic Group, Inc.
1100 Wilson Blvd Ste 2100
Arlington VA 22209
240 532-3806

(P-1334)
**CALIFORNIA PACIFIC HOMES
INC (PA)**
16530 Bake Pkwy Ste 200, Irvine
(92618-4685)
PHONE...................................949 833-6000
Cary Bren, *CEO*
Lyle McColloch, *CFO*
Richard Lyle McColloch, *CFO*
Brian Blain, *Vice Pres*
Janet Loyd, *Office Mgr*
▲ EMP: 93
SQ FT: 6,000
SALES (est): 25.8MM **Privately Held**
WEB: www.californiapacifichomes.com
SIC: **1531** Speculative builder, multi-family
dwellings; speculative builder, single-fam-
ily houses

(P-1335)
**DE ANZA SQUARE SHOPPING
CENTER**
1306 S Mary Ave 1370, Sunnyvale
(94087-3130)
PHONE...................................408 738-4444
Rosanna Callegari, *Principal*
EMP: 99
SALES: 950K **Privately Held**
SIC: **1531** Operative builders

(P-1336)
**DONALD LAWRENCE
FULBRIGHT CO**
Also Called: Donald Lawrence Company
32557 Road 138, Visalia (93292-9381)
P.O. Box 2622 (93279-2622)
PHONE...................................559 625-0762
Donald Fulbright, *President*
Jeffrey Englund, *Treasurer*
Mary Fulbright, *Vice Pres*
EMP: 62
SQ FT: 1,700
SALES (est): 4.8MM **Privately Held**
SIC: **1531** Speculative builder, single-fam-
ily houses

(P-1337)
DR HORTON INC
2280 Wardlow Cir Ste 100, Corona
(92880-2879)
PHONE...................................951 272-9000
Steve Fitzpatrick, *Branch Mgr*
Brad Paulsen, *President*
Daniel Boyd, *Vice Pres*
Diane Lyttle, *Vice Pres*
Nathan Simmons, *Info Tech Mgr*
EMP: 50
SALES (corp-wide): 13.7B **Publicly Held**
WEB: www.drhorton.com
SIC: **1531** Speculative builder, single-fam-
ily houses
PA: D.R. Horton, Inc.
1341 Horton Cir
Arlington TX 76011
817 390-8200

(P-1338)
EJM KYRENE LLC (PA)
Also Called: Ejm Property Management
9061 Santa Monica Blvd, Los Angeles
(90069-5520)
PHONE...................................310 278-1830
Eugene Monkarsh,
Jerrold Monkarsh,
EMP: 50 EST: 1999
SQ FT: 5,500

SALES (est): 9.2MM **Privately Held**
SIC: **1531** 6531 Condominium developers;
real estate managers

(P-1339)
**FIELDSTONE COMMUNITIES
INC (PA)**
16 Technology Dr Ste 125, Irvine
(92618-2325)
PHONE...................................949 790-5400
William H McFarland, *CEO*
Peter Ochs, *Ch of Bd*
Frank Foster, *President*
David Langlois, *Exec VP*
Jim Hanson, *Senior VP*
EMP: 130
SQ FT: 15,000
SALES (est): 23.3MM **Privately Held**
WEB: www.fieldstone-homes.com
SIC: **1531** Speculative builder, single-fam-
ily houses

(P-1340)
**GREENBRIAR HOMES
COMMUNITIES**
4340 Stevens Creek Blvd # 240, San Jose
(95129-1102)
PHONE...................................510 497-8200
Carol M Meyer, *Ch of Bd*
Gilbert M Meyer, *President*
EMP: 100
SQ FT: 12,000
SALES (est): 8.3MM **Privately Held**
SIC: **1531** Operative builders

(P-1341)
**GREENLAND US CONSULTING
INC**
515 S Figueroa St # 1703, Los Angeles
(90071-3301)
PHONE...................................213 362-9300
Ifei Chang, *CEO*
EMP: 99 EST: 2013
SALES (est): 4MM **Privately Held**
SIC: **1531**

(P-1342)
**GRUPE DEV
COMPANYNORTHERN CAL**
3255 W March Ln Ste 400, Stockton
(95219-2352)
P.O. Box 7576 (95267-0576)
PHONE...................................209 473-6000
Fritz Unruh, *CEO*
EMP: 127
SQ FT: 7,000
SALES (est): 6.2MM
SALES (corp-wide): 87.6MM **Privately
Held**
WEB: www.grupe.com
SIC: **1531** Speculative builder, single-fam-
ily houses; speculative builder, multi-fam-
ily dwellings; condominium developers
PA: The Grupe Company
3255 W March Ln Ste 400
Stockton CA 95219
209 473-6000

(P-1343)
**HWN MARIPOSA ASSOCIATES
LLC**
11150 Santa Monica Blvd # 760, Los Ange-
les (90025-3380)
PHONE...................................310 478-8757
Thomas B Wilson,
Thomas Wilson,
EMP: 99
SALES (est): 3.3MM **Privately Held**
SIC: **1531** Operative builders

(P-1344)
INLAND VALLEY CNSTR CO INC
18382 Slover Ave, Bloomington
(92316-2363)
PHONE...................................909 875-2112
Kenneth Caruso, *President*
Kelly Bird, *Treasurer*
Stacy Veggin, *Treasurer*
Tim Gaines, *Vice Pres*
Moe Badwan, *Project Mgr*
EMP: 75
SQ FT: 4,000
SALES (est): 19.1MM **Privately Held**
WEB: www.inlandvalleyconst.com
SIC: **1531** Operative builders

(P-1345)
KAUFMAN AND BROAD LIMITED
Also Called: Kaufman & Broad
10990 Wilshire Blvd Fl 7, Los Angeles
(90024-3907)
PHONE...................................310 231-4000
EMP: 151
SALES (est): 7.6MM
SALES (corp-wide): 3.5B **Publicly Held**
WEB: www.kbhomesutah.com
SIC: **1531**
PA: Kb Home
10990 Wilshire Blvd Fl 5
Los Angeles CA 90024
310 231-4000

(P-1346)
KB HOME COASTAL INC
10990 Wilshire Blvd Fl 7, Los Angeles
(90024-3907)
PHONE...................................310 231-4000
Jeff Nezger, *President*
Domenico Cecere, *CFO*
William Hollinger, *CFO*
Kelly Allred, *Vice Pres*
Cory Cohen, *Vice Pres*
▲ EMP: 90
SQ FT: 13,346
SALES (est): 10.3MM
SALES (corp-wide): 4.3B **Publicly Held**
WEB: www.kbhome.com
SIC: **1531** Operative builders
PA: Kb Home
10990 Wilshire Blvd Fl 5
Los Angeles CA 90024
310 231-4000

(P-1347)
KBSA INC
Also Called: Kaufman & Broad
10990 Wilshire Blvd 7th, Los Angeles
(90024-3913)
PHONE...................................310 231-4000
Roger Menard, *President*
Julia Ambrose, *Vice Pres*
Michael Carver, *Vice Pres*
Lacy Vinson, *Sales Staff*
EMP: 60
SQ FT: 40,000
SALES (est): 3.1MM
SALES (corp-wide): 4.3B **Publicly Held**
WEB: www.kbhome.com
SIC: **1531** Operative builders
PA: Kb Home
10990 Wilshire Blvd Fl 5
Los Angeles CA 90024
310 231-4000

(P-1348)
LENNAR CORPORATION
25 Enterprise Ste 400, Aliso Viejo
(92656-2712)
PHONE...................................949 349-8000
Jonathan Jaffe, *COO*
Jenny Masters, *Comms Dir*
Marlon Taylor, *Project Mgr*
Beth Beecher, *Accounting Dir*
Rhonda Lopez, *HR Admin*
EMP: 100
SALES (corp-wide): 12.6B **Publicly Held**
WEB: www.lennar.com
SIC: **1531** Speculative builder, single-fam-
ily home
PA: Lennar Corporation
700 Nw 107th Ave Ste 400
Miami FL 33172
305 559-4000

(P-1349)
LENNAR HOMES INC
3788 Edington Dr, Rancho Cordova
(95742-7829)
PHONE...................................916 517-4950
Brenda Coementson, *Principal*
EMP: 101
SALES (corp-wide): 12.6B **Publicly Held**
SIC: **1531** Condominium developers
HQ: Lennar Homes, Inc.
700 Nw 107th Ave Ste 115
Miami FL 33172
305 559-4000

(P-1350)
LENNAR HOMES INC
980 Montecito Dr Ste 300, Corona
(92879-1796)
PHONE...................................951 739-0267
Maureen Johnson, *Manager*
Monica Smith, *Controller*
Randy Schroeder, *Manager*
EMP: 200
SALES (corp-wide): 12.6B **Publicly Held**
SIC: **1531** Speculative builder, single-fam-
ily houses
HQ: Lennar Homes, Inc.
700 Nw 107th Ave Ste 115
Miami FL 33172
305 559-4000

(P-1351)
LEWIS COMPANIES (PA)
1156 N Mountain Ave, Upland
(91786-3633)
PHONE...................................909 985-0971
Richard A Lewis, *President*
Goldy S Lewis, *Principal*
Randall W Lewis, *Principal*
Robert E Lewis, *Principal*
Roger G Lewis, *Principal*
EMP: 380
SALES (est): 25.7MM **Privately Held**
WEB: www.lewishomes.com
SIC: **1531** Operative builders

(P-1352)
LYON PROMENADE LLC
4901 Birch St, Newport Beach
(92660-2114)
PHONE...................................949 252-9101
William Lyon,
Joanna Lizarraga, *Office Mgr*
Frank T Suryan,
EMP: 50
SALES (est): 2.7MM **Privately Held**
SIC: **1531** Operative builders

(P-1353)
M7 BUILDERS LLC
4225 Northgate Blvd, Sacramento
(95834-1233)
PHONE...................................916 317-3529
Israel Velasco,
EMP: 50
SALES (est): 197K **Privately Held**
SIC: **1531** Operative builders

(P-1354)
MANOR BELL L P
790 Sonoma Ave, Santa Rosa
(95404-4713)
PHONE...................................707 526-9782
Jose Luis Caballero,
Charles A Cornell,
EMP: 99
SALES (est): 5MM **Privately Held**
SIC: **1531** Condominium developers

(P-1355)
NEW HOME COMPANY INC (PA)
85 Enterprise Ste 450, Aliso Viejo
(92656-2680)
PHONE...................................949 382-7800
H Lawrence Webb, *Ch of Bd*
Leonard S Miller, *COO*
John M Stephens, *CFO*
John Stephens, *CFO*
Sam Bakhshandehpour, *Bd of Directors*
EMP: 61
SQ FT: 18,700
SALES: 751.1MM **Publicly Held**
SIC: **1531** Operative builders

(P-1356)
PACIFICA REFLECTIONS
Also Called: Pacifica Crossroads
405 Reflections Cir, San Ramon
(94583-5203)
PHONE...................................925 275-9800
Tracy Dalton, *Principal*
EMP: 50
SALES (est): 1.9MM **Privately Held**
SIC: **1531** Condominium developers

PRODUCTS & SVCS

(P-1357)
PORTER RANCH
DEVELOPMENT CO
8383 Wilshire Blvd # 700, Beverly Hills
(90211-2407)
PHONE.................323 655-7330
Nathan Shapell, *Partner*
I N S Corporation, *Partner*
EMP: 85 **EST:** 1976
SALES (est): 4.4MM
SALES (corp-wide): 5.8B **Publicly Held**
SIC: 1531 Speculative builder, single-fam-
ily houses
PA: Toll Brothers, Inc.
250 Gibraltar Rd
Horsham PA 19044
215 938-8000

(P-1358)
RYLAND HOMES OF TEXAS INC
15360 Barranca Pkwy, Irvine (92618-2215)
PHONE.................805 367-3800
Rene L Mentch, *President*
EMP: 132
SALES (est): 13.9MM **Privately Held**
SIC: 1531 Operative builders

(P-1359)
STRAUB - BRUTOCO A JOINT
VENTR
202 W College St Ste 201, Fallbrook
(92028-2970)
PHONE.................760 414-9000
Richard Straub, *Partner*
Robert Mhyre, *Partner*
Michael J Murphy, *Partner*
EMP: 150
SQ FT: 17,000
SALES (est): 4.8MM **Privately Held**
SIC: 1531 1541 ; ; industrial buildings &
warehouses; industrial buildings, new
construction; prefabricated building erec-
tion, industrial

(P-1360)
TRI POINTE CONTRACTORS LP
(HQ)
5 Peters Canyon Rd # 100, Irvine
(92606-1792)
PHONE.................949 478-8600
Doug Bauer, *Partner*
EMP: 100
SALES (est): 1MM
SALES (corp-wide): 2.8B **Publicly Held**
SIC: 1531 Speculative builder, single-fam-
ily houses
PA: Tri Pointe Group, Inc.
19540 Jamboree Rd Ste 300
Irvine CA 92612
949 438-1400

(P-1361)
US HOME CORPORATION
Also Called: US Home
980 Montecito Dr 302, Corona
(92879-1792)
PHONE.................951 817-3500
Mike Lutz, *Branch Mgr*
EMP: 50
SALES (corp-wide): 12.6B **Publicly Held**
WEB: www.ushome.com
SIC: 1531 Speculative builder, single-fam-
ily houses
HQ: U.S. Home Corporation
10707 Clay Rd
Houston TX 77041
305 559-4000

(P-1362)
VAN DAELE DEVELOPMENT
CORP
Also Called: Van Daele Homes
2900 Adams St Ste C25, Riverside
(92504-8312)
PHONE.................951 354-6800
Michael B Van Daele, *CEO*
Jeff Hack, *President*
Barbara Koenig, *Project Mgr*
EMP: 110
SQ FT: 6,000
SALES: 3.3MM **Privately Held**
WEB: www.vandaele.com
SIC: 1531 Speculative builder, single-fam-
ily houses

(P-1363)
VILLA LA ESPERANZA LP
3533 Empleo St, San Luis Obispo
(93401-7334)
PHONE.................805 781-3088
John Fowler, *Managing Prtnr*
Robin Bush, *Accounting Mgr*
EMP: 99
SALES (est): 3MM **Privately Held**
SIC: 1531 Cooperative apartment develop-
ers

(P-1364)
WARMINGTON HOMES (PA)
3090 Pullman St, Costa Mesa
(92626-7936)
PHONE.................714 434-4435
Timothy P Hogan, *President*
James P Warmington, *Ch of Bd*
Michael McClellan, *President*
Greg Oberling, *President*
Jack Schwellenbach, *President*
▲ **EMP:** 120
SQ FT: 40,000
SALES (est): 104.7MM **Privately Held**
SIC: 1531 Speculative builder, single-fam-
ily houses

(P-1365)
WARMINGTON HOMES
15615 Alton Pkwy Ste 150, Irvine
(92618-7302)
PHONE.................949 679-3100
EMP: 96
SALES (corp-wide): 104.7MM **Privately**
Held
SIC: 1531 Speculative builder, single-fam-
ily houses
PA: Warmington Homes
3090 Pullman St
Costa Mesa CA 92626
714 434-4435

(P-1366)
WARMINGTON HOMES
Also Called: Warmington Residental
2400 Camino Ramon Ste 234, San Ramon
(94583-4350)
PHONE.................925 866-6700
Larry Riggs, *Exec VP*
EMP: 159
SALES (corp-wide): 104.7MM **Privately**
Held
SIC: 1531 Speculative builder, single-fam-
ily houses
PA: Warmington Homes
3090 Pullman St
Costa Mesa CA 92626
714 434-4435

(P-1367)
WILLIAM LYON HOMES (PA)
4695 Macarthur Ct Ste 800, Newport Beach
(92660-1863)
PHONE.................949 833-3600
Matthew R Zaist, *President*
William H Lyon, *Ch of Bd*
Brian S Hale, *President*
Colin T Severn, *CFO*
Michael Barr, *Bd of Directors*
EMP: 151
SALES: 1.8B **Publicly Held**
WEB: www.lyonhomes.com
SIC: 1531 Speculative builder, single-fam-
ily houses

(P-1368)
WILLIAM LYON HOMES INC
(HQ)
4695 Macarthur Ct Ste 800, Newport Beach
(92660-1863)
P.O. Box 7520 (92658-7520)
PHONE.................949 833-3600
William H Lyon, *Ch of Bd*
Colin Severn, *CFO*
Doug Harris, *Senior VP*
Danny George, *Vice Pres*
Susan Menard, *Executive Asst*
EMP: 69
SQ FT: 30,000
SALES (est): 102.5MM **Publicly Held**
SIC: 1531 Operative builders

| **1541 General Contractors,** |
| **Indl Bldgs & Warehouses** |

(P-1369)
5 STAR POOL PLASTER INC
7275 National Dr Ste A, Livermore
(94550-8868)
PHONE.................209 599-3111
Juan C Munoz, *President*
Luz Munoz, *Vice Pres*
Christopher Newton, *Vice Pres*
EMP: 53 **EST:** 2008
SALES (est): 7.7MM **Privately Held**
SIC: 1531 1521 Renovation, remodeling &
repairs: industrial buildings; single-family
home remodeling, additions & repairs

(P-1370)
ACME CONSTRUCTION
COMPANY INC
1565 Cummins Dr, Modesto (95358-6401)
P.O. Box 4710 (95352-4710)
PHONE.................209 523-2674
Philip Mastagni, *President*
Judith Boydston, *CFO*
Ron Kettelman, *Vice Pres*
Michael A Mastagni, *Vice Pres*
Mike Mastagni, *Vice Pres*
EMP: 75
SQ FT: 12,000
SALES (est): 17.4MM **Privately Held**
WEB: www.acmeconstruction.com
SIC: 1541 1542 Industrial buildings, new
construction; commercial & office build-
ing, new construction

(P-1371)
ADIR INTERNATIONAL LLC
Also Called: La Curacao
4444 Ayers Ave, Vernon (90058-4317)
PHONE.................213 639-7716
Russell Yeager, *Branch Mgr*
EMP: 206
SALES (corp-wide): 500.7MM **Privately**
Held
SIC: 1541 Industrial buildings & ware-
houses
PA: Adir International, Llc
1605 W Olympic Blvd # 405
Los Angeles CA 90015
213 639-2100

(P-1372)
AHTNA-CDM JV
3200 El Camino Real, Irvine (92602-1378)
PHONE.................714 824-3470
Craig O'Rourke, *General Ptnr*
EMP: 50
SQ FT: 5,000
SALES (est): 1.5MM **Privately Held**
SIC: 1541 Industrial buildings, new con-
struction

(P-1373)
ANGELES CONTRACTOR INC
(PA)
783 Phillips, Rowland Heights
(91748-1147)
PHONE.................714 523-1021
Young W Kang, *President*
Ray Yoo, *Vice Pres*
Alex Cho, *Project Mgr*
Jake Choe, *Project Mgr*
Jae Lee, *Project Mgr*
EMP: 78
SQ FT: 30,000
SALES (est): 34.2MM **Privately Held**
WEB: www.angelescontractor.com
SIC: 1541 Industrial buildings, new con-
struction

(P-1374)
ARNTZ BUILDERS INC
431 Payran St Ste A, Petaluma
(94952-5935)
PHONE.................415 382-1188
Donald M Arntz, *CEO*
Brian Proteau, *President*
Thomas Artz, *Corp Secy*
Lisa Kentzell, *Controller*
EMP: 50

SALES (est): 14.7MM **Privately Held**
SIC: 1541 1542 Industrial buildings, new
construction; renovation, remodeling & repairs: industrial buildings; commercial &
office building, new construction; commercial & office buildings, renovation &
repair

(P-1375)
BCM CONSTRUCTION
COMPANY INC
2990 State Highway 32 # 100, Chico
(95973-8632)
PHONE.................530 342-1722
Kurtis Carman, *President*
Nancy Chinn, *Treasurer*
Matt Bowman, *Vice Pres*
Matthew Bowman, *Vice Pres*
Scott January, *Vice Pres*
EMP: 50
SQ FT: 1,700
SALES (est): 19.5MM **Privately Held**
WEB: www.bcmconstruction.com
SIC: 1541 Industrial buildings, new con-
struction

(P-1376)
BEAR VLY FBRCATORS STL
SUP INC
10700 Civic Center Dr 100c, Rancho Cuca-
monga (91730-3897)
PHONE.................760 247-5381
Judy Carlos, *President*
Tony Carlos, *Vice Pres*
EMP: 60
SQ FT: 25,000
SALES (est): 10.6MM **Privately Held**
SIC: 1541 1791 5051 Renovation, remod-
eling & repairs: industrial buildings; struc-
tural steel erection; steel

(P-1377)
BECK INTERNATIONAL INC
Also Called: Beck Group, The
9641 Sunset Blvd, Beverly Hills
(90210-2938)
PHONE.................310 281-2980
EMP: 300
SALES (corp-wide): 383.5MM **Privately**
Held
WEB: www.beckarchitecture.com
SIC: 1541 1542 Industrial buildings &
warehouses; nonresidential construction
PA: Beck International, Llc
1807 Ross Ave Ste 500
Dallas TX 75201
214 303-6200

(P-1378)
BLACH CONSTRUCTION
COMPANY (PA)
2244 Blach Pl Ste 100, San Jose
(95131-2041)
PHONE.................408 244-7100
Mike Blach, *President*
Juan Barroso, *Vice Pres*
Gaye Landau, *Vice Pres*
Daniel Rogers, *Vice Pres*
Ken Treadwell, *Vice Pres*
EMP: 80
SQ FT: 24,000
SALES (est): 50.3MM **Privately Held**
WEB: www.blach.com
SIC: 1541 Industrial buildings &
warehouses; commercial & office build-
ing, new construction

(P-1379)
BOMEL CONSTRUCTION CO
INC
Also Called: Unknown
701 Palomar Airport Rd # 270, Carlsbad
(92011-1047)
PHONE.................760 431-6360
Mike Lucio, *Branch Mgr*
Angela Byan, *Vice Pres*
EMP: 139
SALES (corp-wide): 99.5MM **Privately**
Held
SIC: 1541 Industrial buildings & ware-
houses
PA: Bomel Construction Co., Inc.
96 Corporate Park Ste 100
Irvine CA 92606
714 921-1660

(P-1380)
BOMEL CONSTRUCTION CO INC (PA)
96 Corporate Park Ste 100, Irvine (92606-3136)
PHONE.....................714 921-1660
Kent Matranga, *CEO*
Lisa McGinnis, *CFO*
Shawn Devine, *Vice Pres*
James Ure, *Vice Pres*
Jim Ure, *Vice Pres*
EMP: 51 EST: 1970
SQ FT: 8,000
SALES (est): 99.5MM **Privately Held**
WEB: www.bomelconstruction.com
SIC: 1541 Industrial buildings & warehouses

(P-1381)
BRANNON INC
Also Called: Smith Electric Service
1340 W Betteravia Rd, Santa Maria (93455-1030)
PHONE.....................805 621-5000
Michael Brannon, *President*
Sara Dalton, *Officer*
Larry Brannon, *Vice Pres*
Steve Fredette, *Vice Pres*
Joyce Gardner, *General Mgr*
EMP: 150
SQ FT: 10,000
SALES (est): 65.6MM **Privately Held**
WEB: www.smith-electric.com
SIC: 1541 1711 1731 1542 Industrial buildings, new construction; plumbing, heating, air-conditioning contractors; fire sprinkler system installation; fire detection & burglar alarm systems specialization; general electrical contractor; nonresidential construction

(P-1382)
C OVERAA & CO (PA)
Also Called: Overaa Construction
200 Parr Blvd, Richmond (94801-1191)
PHONE.....................510 234-0926
Jerry Overaa, *CEO*
Christopher Manning, *President*
Ellen Hoffman, *CFO*
Roy Samuelsz, *Officer*
Larry Etcheverry, *Vice Pres*
EMP: 151 EST: 1907
SQ FT: 20,000
SALES (est): 182.9MM **Privately Held**
WEB: www.overaa.com
SIC: 1541 Industrial buildings, new construction

(P-1383)
C OVERAA & CO
Also Called: Overaa Construction
2555 El Portal Dr, San Pablo (94806-3303)
PHONE.....................510 235-0540
EMP: 198
SALES (corp-wide): 182.9MM **Privately Held**
SIC: 1541 Industrial buildings & warehouses
PA: C. Overaa & Co.
200 Parr Blvd
Richmond CA 94801
510 234-0926

(P-1384)
CALIFORNIA SHTMTL WORKS INC
1020 N Marshall Ave, El Cajon (92020-1829)
PHONE.....................619 562-7010
Robin Hoffos, *President*
Joe Isom, *Vice Pres*
▲ EMP: 90
SQ FT: 15,000
SALES (est): 32.2MM **Privately Held**
WEB: www.califsheetmetal.com
SIC: 1541 3444 Renovation, remodeling & repairs: industrial buildings; sheet metal work

(P-1385)
CHALMERS CORPORATION
Also Called: C.E.G. Construction
7901 Crossway Dr, Pico Rivera (90660-4449)
PHONE.....................562 948-4850

Tracy John Chalmers, *CEO*
James N Devling, *CFO*
EMP: 55
SQ FT: 45,000
SALES (est): 17.6MM **Privately Held**
WEB: www.cegconstruction.com
SIC: 1541 8742 Industrial buildings & warehouses; management consulting services

(P-1386)
CLARION CONSTRUCTION INC
21067 Commerce Point Dr, Walnut (91789-3052)
PHONE.....................909 598-4060
Kelly Owen, *President*
Bruce Kidd, *Vice Pres*
Karen Snider, *Vice Pres*
Dana Spann, *Vice Pres*
Jessica Figueroa, *Admin Asst*
EMP: 50
SQ FT: 10,000
SALES (est): 14.6MM **Privately Held**
SIC: 1541 Industrial buildings & warehouses

(P-1387)
CLARK CNSTR GROUP-CALIFORNIA
18201 Von Karman Ave # 800, Irvine (92612-1000)
PHONE.....................714 754-0764
Richard M Heim, *President*
Brad Weisbecker, *Engineer*
Art Vasconcelos, *Superintendent*
EMP: 450
SALES (est): 40.2MM
SALES (corp-wide): 1.9B **Privately Held**
SIC: 1541 1542 Industrial buildings & warehouses; nonresidential construction
HQ: Clark Construction Group, Llc
7500 Old Georgetown Rd # 1500
Bethesda MD 20814
301 272-8100

(P-1388)
CONEJO PACIFIC TECHNOLOGIES
1560 Newbury Rd Ste 1, Newbury Park (91320-3448)
PHONE.....................805 498-5315
Scott Connelly, *President*
EMP: 65
SQ FT: 100
SALES (est): 4.3MM **Privately Held**
SIC: 1541 0782

(P-1389)
CUBIX CONSTRUCTION COMPANY (PA)
Also Called: Allsafe Selfstorage
5 Meadowbrook Ln, Danville (94526-1707)
PHONE.....................925 314-0770
Stanley Boersma, *President*
Geurtje Boersma, *Corp Secy*
EMP: 200
SALES (est): 27.5MM **Privately Held**
WEB: www.cubixcc.com
SIC: 1541 Warehouse construction

(P-1390)
DENVER D DARLING INC
Also Called: Darco Construction
8402 Katella Ave, Stanton (90680-3215)
PHONE.....................714 761-8299
Denver D Darling, *President*
Wayne Darling, *Vice Pres*
Kale Darling, *Project Mgr*
Ron Neilsen, *Project Mgr*
EMP: 75
SQ FT: 10,000
SALES (est): 11MM **Privately Held**
WEB: www.darcoconstruction.com
SIC: 1541 1771 Industrial buildings, new construction; concrete work

(P-1391)
DEVCON CONSTRUCTION INC (PA)
690 Gibraltar Dr, Milpitas (95035-6317)
PHONE.....................408 942-8200
Gary Filizetti, *President*
Justine Pereira, *CFO*
Brett Sisney, *CFO*
Jonathan Harvey, *Vice Pres*

Daisy Pereira, *Vice Pres*
EMP: 320
SQ FT: 45,000
SALES (est): 1.2B **Privately Held**
WEB: www.devcon-const.com
SIC: 1541 Industrial buildings, new construction

(P-1392)
DPR CONSTRUCTION INC
1510 S Winchester Blvd, San Jose (95128-4334)
PHONE.....................408 370-2322
Jim Carter, *Manager*
EMP: 50
SALES (corp-wide): 3.7B **Privately Held**
WEB: www.dprconstruction.com
SIC: 1541 1542 Industrial buildings & warehouses; nonresidential construction
PA: Dpr Construction, Inc.
1450 Veterans Blvd
Redwood City CA 94063
650 474-1450

(P-1393)
DPR CONSTRUCTION INC (PA)
1450 Veterans Blvd, Redwood City (94063-2617)
PHONE.....................650 474-1450
Douglas E Woods, *CEO*
Alison Lyons, *President*
George J Pfeffer, *President*
Michele Leiva, *CFO*
Ron J Davidowski, *Treasurer*
▲ EMP: 1200
SQ FT: 36,300
SALES (est): 3.7B **Privately Held**
WEB: www.dprconstruction.com
SIC: 1541 1542 Industrial buildings & warehouses; commercial & office building contractors

(P-1394)
DPR CONSTRUCTION INC
5010 Shoreham Pl Ste 100, San Diego (92122-6900)
PHONE.....................858 646-0757
Peter Salvati, *Director*
EMP: 300
SALES (corp-wide): 3.7B **Privately Held**
WEB: www.dprconstruction.com
SIC: 1541 1542 Industrial buildings & warehouses; commercial & office building contractors
PA: Dpr Construction, Inc.
1450 Veterans Blvd
Redwood City CA 94063
650 474-1450

(P-1395)
DPR CONSTRUCTION A GEN PARTNR
2480 Natomas Park Dr # 100, Sacramento (95833-2979)
PHONE.....................916 568-3434
EMP: 50
SALES (corp-wide): 3.7B **Privately Held**
SIC: 1541 Industrial buildings & warehouses
HQ: Dpr Construction, A General Partnership
1450 Veterans Blvd
Redwood City CA 94063

(P-1396)
DPR CONSTRUCTION A GEN PARTNR (HQ)
1450 Veterans Blvd, Redwood City (94063-2617)
PHONE.....................650 474-1450
Douglas E Woods, *President*
Michele Leiva, *CFO*
Ron J Davidowski, *Corp Secy*
James F Dolen, *Exec VP*
Michael Ford, *Exec VP*
EMP: 2300
SQ FT: 36,300
SALES (est): 2.6B
SALES (corp-wide): 3.7B **Privately Held**
SIC: 1541 Industrial buildings & warehouses
PA: Dpr Construction, Inc.
1450 Veterans Blvd
Redwood City CA 94063
650 474-1450

(P-1397)
EXCEL CONSTRUCTION SVCS INC (PA)
1950 Raymer Ave, Fullerton (92833-2513)
PHONE.....................714 680-9200
Karen Latzlaff, *CEO*
Dan Jurado, *President*
Todd London, *Vice Pres*
EMP: 54
SQ FT: 12,000
SALES (est): 31.1MM **Privately Held**
SIC: 1541 Industrial buildings & warehouses

(P-1398)
FRIZE CORPORATION
16605 Gale Ave, City of Industry (91745-1802)
PHONE.....................800 834-2127
James N Frize, *President*
Brad Daugherty, *Project Mgr*
Jon Oleinick, *Project Mgr*
Paul Nevarez, *Safety Mgr*
Jeff Barber, *Foreman/Supr*
EMP: 80
SQ FT: 25,000
SALES (est): 22.3MM **Privately Held**
WEB: www.frizecorp.com
SIC: 1541 1542 Industrial buildings & warehouses; commercial & office building contractors

(P-1399)
FULLMER CONSTRUCTION
1725 S Grove Ave, Ontario (91761-4530)
PHONE.....................909 947-9467
Robert A Fullmer, *President*
Gered Yetter, *CFO*
James Fullmer, *Corp Secy*
Brad Anderson, *Vice Pres*
Bradley J Anderson, *Vice Pres*
◆ EMP: 120
SQ FT: 20,000
SALES (est): 65.4MM **Privately Held**
SIC: 1541 Industrial buildings, new construction

(P-1400)
GEORGE RICHARD
P.O. Box 712002, Santee (92072-2002)
PHONE.....................619 805-6751
George Richards, *President*
EMP: 60
SALES (est): 2.5MM **Privately Held**
SIC: 1541 Renovation, remodeling & repairs: industrial buildings

(P-1401)
GERDAU REINFORCING STEEL (DH)
3880 Murphy Canyon Rd # 100, San Diego (92123-4410)
PHONE.....................858 737-7700
Christopher Ervin, *Principal*
▲ EMP: 50
SALES (est): 505.6MM **Privately Held**
WEB: www.pcsgp.com
SIC: 1541 Steel building construction
HQ: Gerdau Ameristeel Us Inc.
4221 W Boy Scout Blvd # 600
Tampa FL 33607
813 286-8383

(P-1402)
GRIMMWAY ENTERPRISES INC
Grimmway Farm
12020 Malaga Rd, Arvin (93203-9527)
PHONE.....................661 854-6240
Mike Blakley, *Supervisor*
EMP: 100
SALES (corp-wide): 2.1B **Privately Held**
SIC: 1541 1542 Industrial buildings & warehouses; nonresidential construction
PA: Grimmway Enterprises, Inc.
14141 Di Giorgio Rd
Arvin CA 93203
800 301-3101

(P-1403)
H C OLSEN CNSTR CO INC
710 Los Angeles Ave, Monrovia (91016-4250)
PHONE.....................626 359-8900
Linda Jacqueline Pearson, *CEO*
Karl Pearson, *Corp Secy*

(PA)=Parent Co (HQ)=Headquarters (DH)=Div Headquarters
✿ = New Business established in last 2 years
2019 Directory of California
Wholesalers and Services Companies
67

P R O D U C T S & S V C S

Mercedes Gray, *Administration*
Brenda Gutierrez, *Administration*
Marty Cranford, *Project Mgr*
EMP: 75 **EST:** 1946
SQ FT: 12,800
SALES (est): 27.8MM **Privately Held**
WEB: www.hcolsen.com
SIC: **1541** Industrial buildings, new construction

(P-1404)
HAL HAYS CONSTRUCTION INC (PA)
4181 Latham St, Riverside (92501-1729)
PHONE..................951 369-1008
Hal Hays, *President*
E Denise Hays, *CFO*
EMP: 113
SQ FT: 28,400
SALES: 76.6MM **Privately Held**
WEB: www.halhays.com
SIC: **1541 1542 1623 1629** Industrial buildings & warehouses; commercial & office buildings, renovation & repair; water, sewer & utility lines; dams, waterways, docks & other marine construction; highway & street paving contractor; concrete work

(P-1405)
HAMANN CONSTRUCTION
1000 Pioneer Way, El Cajon (92020-1923)
PHONE..................619 440-7424
Jeffrey C Hamann, *CEO*
Gregg Hamann, *Treasurer*
EMP: 75
SQ FT: 15,000
SALES (est): 17.7MM **Privately Held**
WEB: www.hamannco.com
SIC: **1541** Industrial buildings, new construction

(P-1406)
HASKELL COMPANY (INC)
478 Lindbergh Ave, Livermore (94551-9553)
PHONE..................925 960-1815
EMP: 185
SALES (corp-wide): 953.1MM **Privately Held**
SIC: **1541** Industrial buildings, new construction
HQ: The Haskell Company Inc
   111 Riverside Ave
   Jacksonville FL 32202
   904 791-4500

(P-1407)
HERRERO BUILDERS INCORPORATED (PA)
2100 Oakdale Ave, San Francisco (94124-1516)
PHONE..................415 824-7675
Mark D Herrero, *Ch of Bd*
Rick Herrero, *President*
Craig Braccia, *Vice Pres*
Saptarshi Desai, *Executive*
John Costa, *Info Tech Mgr*
▲ **EMP:** 128
SQ FT: 10,000
SALES (est): 75.6MM **Privately Held**
WEB: www.herrero.com
SIC: **1541** Industrial buildings, new construction

(P-1408)
HUGO ALONSO INC
Also Called: Alonso Construction
2820 Via Orange Way Ste J, Spring Valley (91978-1742)
PHONE..................619 660-6255
Hugo Alonso, *President*
Norma Alonso, *Treasurer*
Tom Fox, *Vice Pres*
EMP: 50
SQ FT: 13,000
SALES (est): 10.1MM **Privately Held**
WEB: www.hugoalonsoinc.com
SIC: **1541 1721** Industrial buildings & warehouses; industrial painting

(P-1409)
JACKSON CONSTRUCTION (PA)
155 Cadillac Dr, Sacramento (95825-5499)
PHONE..................916 381-8113
John Jackson Jr, *President*

Don Hanson, *CFO*
Lynda Jackson, *Treasurer*
Eric J Edelmayer, *Vice Pres*
Todd Kraenzel, *Vice Pres*
EMP: 50 **EST:** 1974
SQ FT: 10,000
SALES (est): 20.1MM **Privately Held**
WEB: www.jacksonprop.com
SIC: **1541 1542 6552 6531** Industrial buildings & warehouses; nonresidential construction; land subdividers & developers, residential; real estate agents & managers

(P-1410)
JH BRYANT JR INC (PA)
17217 S Broadway, Gardena (90248-3117)
PHONE..................310 532-1840
Barbara Bryant, *CEO*
John Bryant III, *President*
David Bryant, *COO*
Howe Rich, *CFO*
Joseph Perez, *Vice Pres*
EMP: 50
SQ FT: 6,500
SALES: 13MM **Privately Held**
WEB: www.jhbryant.com
SIC: **1541** Industrial buildings & warehouses

(P-1411)
JULIUS STEVE CONSTRUCTION INC
Also Called: S R J
230 Calle Pintoresco, San Clemente (92672-7503)
PHONE..................949 369-7820
Leigh Thornburg Julius, *CEO*
Pete Ferrarini, *President*
Shane Hankins, *General Mgr*
Ashley Daniels, *Project Mgr*
Donald Westad, *Project Mgr*
EMP: 50
SQ FT: 6,700
SALES: 12.9MM **Privately Held**
WEB: www.stevejuliusconstruction.com
SIC: **1541** Industrial buildings, new construction

(P-1412)
KAJIMA CONSTRUCTION SVCS INC
Also Called: Kajima International
250 E 1st St Ste 400, Los Angeles (90012-3820)
PHONE..................323 269-0020
Nori Ohashi, *Branch Mgr*
Larry Atwater, *Vice Pres*
Howard Craig, *Project Mgr*
William Kobayashi, *Business Mgr*
EMP: 50
SALES (corp-wide): 17.1B **Privately Held**
SIC: **1541 1542 8712** Industrial buildings, new construction; commercial & office building, new construction; house designer
HQ: Kajima Construction Services, Inc.
   3550 Lenox Rd Ne Ste 1850
   Atlanta GA 30326

(P-1413)
KAZARIAN/JEWETT INC
Also Called: Kcb Builders
6621 Pcf Cast Hwy Ste 120, Long Beach (90803)
PHONE..................562 594-5927
K C Kazarian, *President*
Bill Jewett, *Treasurer*
EMP: 50
SALES: 2MM **Privately Held**
SIC: **1541 1542** Industrial buildings & warehouses; commercial & office building contractors

(P-1414)
KEMP BROS CONSTRUCTION INC
10135 Geary Ave, Santa Fe Springs (90670-3253)
PHONE..................562 236-5000
Greg S Solaas, *President*
Steven Solaas, *President*
Darren Sagert, *CFO*
Steve Rosenfield, *Vice Pres*
Luis Cevallos, *Project Mgr*

EMP: 50
SQ FT: 15,500
SALES (est): 19.2MM **Privately Held**
SIC: **1541 1542** Industrial buildings, new construction; hospital construction

(P-1415)
KENDRICK CONSTRUCTION SERVICES
Also Called: Kendrick Co The
3010 Old Ranch Pkwy # 470, Seal Beach (90740-2789)
PHONE..................562 546-0200
Gregory T Hook, *President*
Randy Kendrick, *Shareholder*
Jud Leibee, *CFO*
Sandra Combee, *Admin Sec*
EMP: 55
SQ FT: 3,500
SALES (est): 6.4MM **Privately Held**
WEB: www.kendrickconstruction.com
SIC: **1541 1542** Industrial buildings & warehouses; nonresidential construction

(P-1416)
KERNEN CONSTRUCTION
2350 Glendale Dr, McKinleyville (95519-9205)
P.O. Box 1340, Blue Lake (95525-1340)
PHONE..................707 826-8686
Kurt Kernen, *Partner*
Scott Farley, *Partner*
EMP: 60
SQ FT: 120
SALES (est): 16.2MM **Privately Held**
WEB: www.kernenconstruction.com
SIC: **1541 1542** Industrial buildings, new construction; renovation, remodeling & repairs: industrial buildings; commercial & office building, new construction; commercial & office buildings, renovation & repair

(P-1417)
LEDCOR CMI INC
6405 Mira Mesa Blvd # 100, San Diego (92121-4120)
PHONE..................602 595-3017
David W Lede, *CEO*
EMP: 82
SALES (est): 104MM **Privately Held**
SIC: **1541 1611 1629 1623** Industrial buildings & warehouses; highway & street construction; mine loading & discharging station construction; industrial plant construction; pipeline construction; condominium construction; communication services

(P-1418)
LEVY PRMIUM FDSRVICE LTD PRTNR
Also Called: Levy Cncessions At Staples Ctr
1111 S Figueroa St, Los Angeles (90015-1300)
PHONE..................213 742-7867
Jeffrey Rosenbaugh, *Manager*
EMP: 70
SALES (corp-wide): 28.9B **Privately Held**
WEB: www.cafespiaggia.com
SIC: **1541** Industrial buildings & warehouses
HQ: Levy Premium Foodservice Limited
   Partnership
   980 N Michigan Ave # 400
   Chicago IL 60611
   312 664-8200

(P-1419)
MA STEINER CONSTRUCTION INC
2210 Plaza Dr Ste 300, Rocklin (95765-4406)
PHONE..................916 988-6300
Martin Steiner, *President*
EMP: 64
SALES (est): 13.5MM **Privately Held**
SIC: **1541 1794 1542 1611** Industrial buildings, new construction; excavation & grading, building construction; commercial & office building, new construction; highway & street construction; general contractor, highway & street construction

(P-1420)
MILLIE AND SEVERSON INC
3601 Serpentine Dr, Los Alamitos (90720-2440)
PHONE..................562 493-3611
Scott Feest, *President*
Robert E Wissmann, *Senior VP*
John Grossman, *Vice Pres*
Mark Huber, *Vice Pres*
Doran Boctor, *Executive*
EMP: 75 **EST:** 1945
SQ FT: 15,000
SALES: 288.6MM **Privately Held**
WEB: www.mandsinc.com
SIC: **1541** Industrial buildings, new construction; renovation, remodeling & repairs: industrial buildings; steel building construction; warehouse construction
PA: Severson Group Incorporated
   3601 Serpentine Dr
   Los Alamitos CA 90720

(P-1421)
MINSHEW BROTHERS STL CNSTR INC
12578 Vigilante Rd, Lakeside (92040-1112)
P.O. Box 1000 (92040-0902)
PHONE..................619 561-5700
James Minshew, *President*
Daniel P Minshew, *Treasurer*
John M Minshew, *Vice Pres*
EMP: 105
SQ FT: 22,000
SALES (est): 28.3MM **Privately Held**
SIC: **1541 1791** Steel building construction; structural steel erection

(P-1422)
MODERN BUILDING INC
3083 Southgate Ln, Chico (95928-7427)
P.O. Box 772 (95927-0772)
PHONE..................530 891-4533
L Gage Chrysler, *CEO*
Gary Fowler, *Corp Secy*
James Seegert, *Vice Pres*
Debbie Barnett, *Admin Asst*
Terry Wolkoff, *Administration*
EMP: 50
SQ FT: 5,000
SALES (est): 19.5MM **Privately Held**
WEB: www.modernbuildinginc.com
SIC: **1541 1542** Industrial buildings, new construction; commercial & office building, new construction

(P-1423)
NORTH COAST FABRICATORS INC
4801 West End Rd, Arcata (95521-9242)
PHONE..................707 822-4629
Paula E Crowley, *President*
Tim Crowley, *COO*
EMP: 50 **EST:** 1979
SQ FT: 12,000
SALES (est): 13.5MM **Privately Held**
SIC: **1541 1542 7699** Prefabricated building erection, industrial; commercial & office buildings, prefabricated erection; industrial machinery & equipment repair

(P-1424)
OLTMANS CONSTRUCTION CO (PA)
10005 Mission Mill Rd, Whittier (90601-1739)
P.O. Box 985 (90608-0985)
PHONE..................562 948-4242
Joseph O Oltmans II, *Ch of Bd*
John Gormly, *President*
Dan Schlothan, *CFO*
Tom Augustine, *Vice Pres*
Robert Larson, *Vice Pres*
▼ **EMP:** 85
SQ FT: 33,000
SALES (est): 259.2MM **Privately Held**
WEB: www.oltmans.com
SIC: **1541 1542** Industrial buildings, new construction; renovation, remodeling & repairs: industrial buildings; commercial & office building, new construction; commercial & office buildings, renovation & repair

(P-1425)
ORANGE COAST BUILDING SERVICES
2191 S Dupont Dr, Anaheim (92806-6102)
PHONE...................................714 453-6300
Kevin W Franklin, *President*
EMP: 115
SQ FT: 6,000
SALES (est): 26.9MM **Privately Held**
WEB: www.ocbsonline.com
SIC: 1541 1542 Industrial buildings, new construction; commercial & office building contractors

(P-1426)
OUT OF SHELL LLC
Also Called: Ling's
9658 Remer St, South El Monte (91733-3033)
PHONE...................................626 401-1923
Alice Liu,
Bing Yang,
EMP: 200
SALES (est): 24.2MM **Privately Held**
SIC: 1541 Food products manufacturing or packing plant construction

(P-1427)
PARSONS PROJECT SERVICES INC
100 W Walnut St, Pasadena (91124-0001)
PHONE...................................626 440-4000
Charles Harrington, *CEO*
Todd K Wager, *President*
EMP: 131
SALES (est): 5.2MM **Privately Held**
SIC: 1541 Industrial buildings & warehouses

(P-1428)
PCL INDUSTRIAL SERVICES INC
1500 S Union Ave, Bakersfield (93307-4144)
PHONE...................................661 832-3995
Joe W Carrieri, *CEO*
Gary L Basher, *Corp Secy*
Mark Schneider, *Project Engr*
Jose Rocha, *Manager*
EMP: 300
SALES (est): 85MM **Privately Held**
SIC: 1541 Industrial buildings, new construction

(P-1429)
PERFORMANCE CONTRACTING INC
1943 Rutan Dr, Livermore (94551-7646)
PHONE...................................925 273-3800
Mike Ligon, *Manager*
EMP: 50
SALES (corp-wide): 1.1B **Privately Held**
SIC: 1541 Industrial buildings, new construction
HQ: Performance Contracting, Inc.
    11145 Thompson Ave
    Lenexa KS 66219
    913 888-8600

(P-1430)
R Q CONSTRUCTION INC
3194 Lionshead Ave, Carlsbad (92010-4701)
PHONE...................................760 477-1199
George H Rogers III, *CEO*
Michael D Patterson, *President*
Craig Shadle, *CFO*
Donald M Rogers, *Vice Pres*
EMP: 140
SQ FT: 8,000
SALES (est): 30.2MM **Privately Held**
SIC: 1541 Industrial buildings, new construction

(P-1431)
RQ CONSTRUCTION LLC
3194 Lionshead Ave, Carlsbad (92010-4701)
PHONE...................................760 631-7707
George H Rogers III, *CEO*
Craig Shadle, *CFO*
Mary Baker, *Admin Sec*
Kirk Van Cleave, *Manager*
EMP: 170

SALES (est): 75.3MM **Privately Held**
SIC: 1541 1611 Industrial buildings, new construction; general contractor, highway & street construction

(P-1432)
SHAWS STRCTURES UNLIMITED INC
Also Called: Shaw Construction
2573 W Cambridge Ave, Fresno (93705-4737)
PHONE...................................559 275-3475
Paul W Shaw, *President*
Gloria Shaw, *Vice Pres*
Mildred Shaw, *Vice Pres*
EMP: 50
SQ FT: 7,850
SALES (est): 5.4MM **Privately Held**
SIC: 1541 1542 1791 Prefabricated building erection, industrial; commercial & office buildings, prefabricated erection; religious building construction; structural steel erection

(P-1433)
SHIMS BARGAIN INC
Also Called: JC Sales
7030 E Slauson Ave, Commerce (90040-3621)
PHONE...................................323 726-8800
Andy Kim, *Manager*
EMP: 210
SALES (corp-wide): 177.5MM **Privately Held**
SIC: 1541 Industrial buildings & warehouses
PA: Shims Bargain, Inc.
    2600 S Soto St
    Vernon CA 90058
    323 881-0099

(P-1434)
SIERRA BAY CONTRACTORS INC
4021 Port Chicago Hwy # 150, Concord (94520-1122)
PHONE...................................925 671-7711
Albert D Seeno Jr, *President*
Robert Coburn, *Vice Pres*
Thomas A Seeno, *Vice Pres*
EMP: 50
SQ FT: 2,000
SALES (est): 5.4MM **Privately Held**
WEB: www.sierrabayinc.com
SIC: 1541 6221 Industrial buildings & warehouses; commodity contracts brokers, dealers

(P-1435)
SILMAN VENTURE CORPORATION (PA)
Also Called: Silman Construction
1600 Factor Ave, San Leandro (94577-5618)
PHONE...................................510 347-4800
Tom Mangin, *CEO*
Rick Silva, *COO*
Alex Breitenbach, *Project Mgr*
Tammy Floyd, *Project Mgr*
Jason Hennessee, *Project Mgr*
EMP: 125 **EST:** 2007
SQ FT: 17,000
SALES: 40MM **Privately Held**
SIC: 1541 Industrial buildings, new construction

(P-1436)
SPRINKLES CUPCAKES INC
5916 Bowcroft St, Los Angeles (90016-4302)
PHONE...................................310 657-4102
Stephen Snyder, *Manager*
EMP: 59
SALES (corp-wide): 72.8MM **Privately Held**
SIC: 1541 Industrial buildings & warehouses
PA: Sprinkles Cupcakes Inc.
    9635 Santa Monica Blvd
    Beverly Hills CA 90210
    310 274-8765

(P-1437)
STANTRU RESOURCES INC
Also Called: Stantru Reinforcing Steel
11175 Redwood Ave, Fontana (92337-7137)
P.O. Box 310189 (92331-0189)
PHONE...................................909 587-1441
Ida Ichen, *President*
William M Klorman, *Manager*
EMP: 83
SALES (est): 6.3MM **Privately Held**
SIC: 1541 1542 Industrial buildings, new construction; pharmaceutical manufacturing plant construction; commercial & office building, new construction; school building construction; institutional building construction

(P-1438)
STEELTECH CONSTRUCTION SVCS
4081 E La Palma Ave Ste G, Anaheim (92807-1701)
PHONE...................................714 630-2890
Edward Campbell, *President*
EMP: 100
SQ FT: 2,200
SALES: 5MM **Privately Held**
SIC: 1541 Industrial buildings & warehouses

(P-1439)
SWINERTON BUILDERS (HQ)
Also Called: Swinerton MGT & Consulting
260 Townsend St, San Francisco (94107-1719)
PHONE...................................415 421-2980
Jeffrey C Hoopes, *Ch of Bd*
John T Capener, *President*
Gary J Rafferty, *President*
Linda G Schowalter, *CFO*
Frank Foellmer, *Exec VP*
▲ **EMP:** 200
SQ FT: 300,353
SALES: 3.3B **Privately Held**
SIC: 1541 1522 1542 Industrial buildings, new construction; steel building construction; hotel/motel, new construction; commercial & office building, new construction; commercial & office buildings, renovation & repair; specialized public building contractors

(P-1440)
SWINERTON BUILDERS
Swinerton Renewable Energy
16798 W Bernardo Dr, San Diego (92127-1904)
PHONE...................................858 622-4040
Don Adair, *Manager*
Jesse Blake, *Webmaster*
Carol Stevens, *Manager*
EMP: 65 **Privately Held**
SIC: 1541 Industrial buildings, new construction
HQ: Swinerton Builders
    260 Townsend St
    San Francisco CA 94107
    415 421-2980

(P-1441)
T B PENICK & SONS INC (PA)
15435 Innovation Dr # 100, San Diego (92128-3443)
PHONE...................................858 558-1800
Marc E Penick, *CEO*
Timothy Penick, *President*
John Boyd, *CFO*
Victor Klemaske, *Vice Pres*
Frank Klemaske, *VP Bus Dvlpt*
EMP: 151
SQ FT: 30,000
SALES: 139.2MM **Privately Held**
WEB: www.tbpenick.com
SIC: 1541 1542 Industrial buildings & warehouses; nonresidential construction

(P-1442)
TAISEI CONSTRUCTION CORP (HQ)
970 W 190th St Ste 920, Torrance (90502-1063)
PHONE...................................714 886-1530
Tetsuo Tawada, *CEO*
Takashi Uchida, *Treasurer*

Jason Van, *Director*
Heather Von Itter, *Manager*
▲ **EMP:** 52
SQ FT: 15,000
SALES (est): 37.8MM **Privately Held**
SALES (corp-wide): 14.8B **Privately Held**
SIC: 1541 1542 Industrial buildings & warehouses; nonresidential construction
PA: Taisei Corporation
    1-25-1, Nishishinjuku
    Shinjuku-Ku TKY 160-0
    333 481-111

(P-1443)
TCB INDUSTRIAL INC (PA)
2955 Farrar Ave, Modesto (95354-4118)
PHONE...................................209 571-0569
Dave Raybourn, *CEO*
Bruce Elliott, *CFO*
EMP: 160
SALES (est): 48.2MM **Privately Held**
WEB: www.Tcbindustrial.net
SIC: 1541 Industrial buildings, new construction

(P-1444)
TEKTETCO
Also Called: Tribal Tektet
5251 Ericson Way, Arcata (95521-9273)
PHONE...................................707 822-9000
Daniel Johnson,
Terry Wilson,
EMP: 65
SALES (est): 3MM **Privately Held**
SIC: 1541 1542 1522 Industrial buildings, new construction; commercial & office building, new construction; hotel/motel, new construction; multi-family dwellings, new construction

(P-1445)
TORRES CONSTRUCTION CORP (PA)
1370 N El Molino Ave, Pasadena (91104-5026)
PHONE...................................323 257-7460
Martha McGowin, *President*
Mael Torres, *Treasurer*
Esteban Torres, *Vice Pres*
Nick Porter, *Project Mgr*
Sergio Torres, *Project Mgr*
EMP: 60
SQ FT: 7,500
SALES (est): 26.6MM **Privately Held**
WEB: www.torresconstruction.com
SIC: 1541 Industrial buildings & warehouses

(P-1446)
TRI-TECH RESTORATION CO INC
3301 N San Fernando Blvd, Burbank (91504-2531)
PHONE...................................818 565-3900
Armine Bakmazian, *President*
Michael Boyd, *Admin Sec*
Sarkis Kouyoumdjian, *Manager*
EMP: 70
SQ FT: 35,000
SALES: 8MM **Privately Held**
WEB: www.tritechrestoration.com
SIC: 1541 Industrial buildings & warehouses

(P-1447)
TRILOGY RIO VISTA
Also Called: SHEA HOMES
1200 Clubhouse Dr, Rio Vista (94571-9801)
PHONE...................................707 374-1100
Steve Hextell, *Vice Pres*
EMP: 60
SALES: 62.2MM **Privately Held**
SIC: 1541 Industrial buildings, new construction

(P-1448)
UNIVERSAL DUST COLLECTOR (PA)
Also Called: UDC
1041 N Kraemer Pl, Anaheim (92806-2611)
PHONE...................................714 630-8588
Theresa A Shaffer, *CEO*
Curt Schendel, *President*
Deborah Huerta, *CFO*

PRODUCTS & SVCS

Curtis Schendel, *Vice Pres*
Shawn E Shaffer, *Vice Pres*
EMP: 59
SQ FT: 30,000
SALES (est): 28MM **Privately Held**
WEB: www.udccorporation.com
SIC: 1541 Industrial buildings, new construction

(P-1449)
WATSON CONTRACTORS INC
3185 Longview Dr, Sacramento (95821-7214)
PHONE..................916 481-6293
Greg Watson, *President*
EMP: 65
SALES (est): 4.1MM **Privately Held**
WEB: www.watsonroofing.com
SIC: 1541 Renovation, remodeling & repairs: industrial buildings

(P-1450)
WEST HILLS CONSTRUCTION INC
423 Jenks Cir Ste 101, Corona (92880-2540)
PHONE..................800 515-5270
Ross L Wood, *President*
Rusty Wood, *Vice Pres*
Stephanie Wood, *Director*
EMP: 50
SQ FT: 7,500
SALES (est): 7.1MM **Privately Held**
SIC: 1541 Industrial buildings, new construction

1542 General Contractors, Nonresidential & Non-indl Bldgs

(P-1451)
2H CONSTRUCTION INC
2653 Walnut Ave, Signal Hill (90755-1830)
PHONE..................562 424-5567
Sean Hitchcock, *President*
Ericka Hitchcock, *CFO*
Ronald Compton, *Vice Pres*
EMP: 70
SQ FT: 8,000
SALES: 50MM **Privately Held**
WEB: www.2hconstruction.com
SIC: 1542 Commercial & office building, new construction

(P-1452)
A RUIZ CNSTR CO & ASSOC INC
1601 Cortland Ave, San Francisco (94110-5716)
PHONE..................415 647-4010
Antonio Ruiz, *President*
Thomas Cotter, *Executive*
Victor Godinez, *Project Mgr*
Juan Gomez, *Project Mgr*
Henriette Ruiz, *Receptionist*
EMP: 50
SQ FT: 10,000
SALES (est): 14.9MM **Privately Held**
WEB: www.aruizconstruction.com
SIC: 1542 Commercial & office building, new construction; commercial & office building contractors

(P-1453)
AARDEX INC
1550 E Main St, Santa Maria (93454-4819)
PHONE..................805 928-7600
Shane Fowleror, *President*
EMP: 60
SALES (est): 3.4MM **Privately Held**
SIC: 1542 Commercial & office building, new construction

(P-1454)
ABHE & SVOBODA INC
880 Tavern Rd, Alpine (91901-3810)
PHONE..................619 659-1320
David Grant, *Manager*
Daniel Markwell, *Project Mgr*
Jim Ness, *Sr Project Mgr*
Rex Huffman, *Superintendent*
EMP: 58

SALES (corp-wide): 1.7MM **Privately Held**
SIC: 1542 Commercial & office building, new construction
PA: Abhe & Svoboda, Inc.
18100 Dairy Ln
Jordan MN 55352
952 447-6025

(P-1455)
ACCESS PACIFIC INC
755 E Washington Blvd, Pasadena (91104-5009)
PHONE..................626 792-0616
Tomas Torres, *President*
EMP: 50 **EST:** 2009
SALES (est): 14.9MM **Privately Held**
SIC: 1542 Nonresidential construction

(P-1456)
ADVANTAGE FRAMING SOLUTIONS
1965 N Beale Rd, Marysville (95901-6914)
PHONE..................530 742-7660
Joel Bueno, *CFO*
EMP: 50
SALES (est): 1.7MM **Privately Held**
SIC: 1542 Nonresidential construction

(P-1457)
AFA CONSTRCTN GRP/CAL INC JV
2040 Peabody Rd Ste 400, Vacaville (95687-6694)
PHONE..................707 446-7996
Ralph Hodges, *President*
Steven Essert, *COO*
Olivia Trudell, *Vice Pres*
EMP: 80
SALES (est): 4.3MM **Privately Held**
SIC: 1542 Nonresidential construction

(P-1458)
AHTNA GOVERNMENT SERVICES CORP
3100 Beacon Blvd, West Sacramento (95691-3483)
PHONE..................916 372-2000
Chris Smith, *President*
EMP: 60
SALES (corp-wide): 322.2MM **Privately Held**
WEB: www.ahtnagov.com
SIC: 1542 Nonresidential construction
HQ: Ahtna Government Services Corporation
3100 Beacon Blvd
West Sacramento CA 95691
916 372-2000

(P-1459)
AIS CONSTRUCTION COMPANY
713 Rincon Hill Rd, Santa Maria (93455)
P.O. Box 4209, San Luis Obispo (93403-4209)
PHONE..................805 928-9467
Andy Sheaffer, *President*
EMP: 85
SQ FT: 4,000
SALES (est): 12.5MM **Privately Held**
WEB: www.aisconstruction.com
SIC: 1542 Commercial & office building contractors

(P-1460)
AJW RESTORATION SERVICES LLC
7445 Raytheon Rd, San Diego (92111-1505)
PHONE..................858 429-5641
Arthur Candland, *CEO*
Warren Thompson, *President*
EMP: 50
SALES: 3MM **Privately Held**
SIC: 1542 Commercial & office building, new construction

(P-1461)
AK CONSTRUCTORS INC
Also Called: AK Electrical Services
1751 Jenks Dr, Corona (92880-2516)
PHONE..................951 280-0269
Kenneth G Dougher, *President*
Micheal Harrington, *Corp Secy*
Robert Griffin, *Principal*

Kurt Meyers, *Principal*
Mike Harrington, *General Mgr*
EMP: 65
SALES (est): 17.4MM **Privately Held**
WEB: www.akconstructors.com
SIC: 1542 Commercial & office building, new construction

(P-1462)
ALLEN L BENDER INC
6625 Quail Crossing Ln, Granite Bay (95746-7360)
PHONE..................916 372-2190
Blake Bender, *President*
Brian Bender, *CFO*
EMP: 120 **EST:** 1956
SQ FT: 22,000
SALES (est): 14.1MM **Privately Held**
WEB: www.allenlbender.com
SIC: 1542 8711 Commercial & office buildings, renovation & repair; engineering services

(P-1463)
ALSTON CONSTRUCTION CO INC (PA)
8775 Folsom Blvd Ste 201, Sacramento (95826-3725)
PHONE..................916 340-2400
Paul David Little, *CEO*
Adam Nickerson, *CFO*
Steve Beauchamp, *Vice Pres*
Ed Gorton, *Vice Pres*
Evan Hamilton, *Vice Pres*
EMP: 100 **EST:** 1998
SQ FT: 36,000
SALES: 865.5MM **Privately Held**
WEB: www.panconinc.com
SIC: 1542 1541 Commercial & office building contractors; industrial buildings & warehouses

(P-1464)
ALTEN CONSTRUCTION INC
1141 Marina Way S, Richmond (94804-3742)
PHONE..................510 234-4200
Robert Andrew Alten, *CEO*
Shannon M Alten, *Vice Pres*
EMP: 80
SQ FT: 14,000
SALES: 40.8MM **Privately Held**
WEB: www.altenconstruction.com
SIC: 1542 Commercial & office building, new construction

(P-1465)
ANDERSON BURTON CONSTRUCTION
1510 Oxley St Ste G, South Pasadena (91030-5745)
PHONE..................626 441-2464
Joanne Anderson, *President*
EMP: 99
SQ FT: 500
SALES (est): 3.2MM **Privately Held**
SIC: 1542 Commercial & office buildings, renovation & repair

(P-1466)
ANDREW L YOUNGQUIST CNSTR INC
3187 Red Hill Ave Ste 200, Costa Mesa (92626-3454)
PHONE..................949 862-5611
Andrew L Youngquist, *Ch of Bd*
James Lefler, *President*
Richard Lee Youngquist, *Vice Pres*
EMP: 90
SQ FT: 10,319
SALES (est): 8.9MM **Privately Held**
WEB: www.alyconstruction.com
SIC: 1542 1522 8741 Commercial & office building contractors; residential construction; construction management

(P-1467)
ARAGON CONSTRUCTION INC
5440 Arrow Hwy, Montclair (91763-1604)
PHONE..................909 621-2200
Joseph E Aragon, *President*
Regina Aragon, *General Mgr*
Lisa Lachowicz, *General Mgr*
Matt Aragon, *Project Mgr*
John Halbach, *Project Mgr*

EMP: 55
SALES (est): 24MM **Privately Held**
SIC: 1542 Institutional building construction; commercial & office buildings, renovation & repair; shopping center construction; specialized public building contractors

(P-1468)
ARB INC
50 Quint St, San Francisco (94124-1424)
PHONE..................415 206-1015
Chris Slack, *Branch Mgr*
EMP: 50
SALES (corp-wide): 2.3B **Publicly Held**
SIC: 1542 1623 Nonresidential construction; garage construction; oil & gas line & compressor station construction
HQ: Arb, Inc.
26000 Commercentre Dr
Lake Forest CA 92630
949 598-9242

(P-1469)
ASR CONSTRUCTORS INC
Also Called: Contractors Complete Surety
33891 Mission Trl, Wildomar (92595-8431)
PHONE..................951 779-6580
Alan Lee Rigotti, *President*
Stacey Rigotti, *Corp Secy*
EMP: 270 **EST:** 1999
SQ FT: 3,000
SALES (est): 47.5MM **Privately Held**
SIC: 1542 Nonresidential construction

(P-1470)
AT YOUR SVC HTG & COOLG LLC
333 H St Ste 5000, Chula Vista (91910-5561)
PHONE..................602 550-6946
Joe Lizarraga, *Manager*
EMP: 66
SALES: 950K **Privately Held**
SIC: 1542 Nonresidential construction

(P-1471)
B C C S INC (PA)
Also Called: South Bay Construction Company
1711 Dell Ave, Campbell (95008-6904)
PHONE..................408 379-5500
Richard Furtado, *Partner*
Veronica Mata, *Admin Asst*
Marcelo Estrada, *Software Engr*
Mark Avila, *Project Mgr*
John Machi, *Project Mgr*
EMP: 69
SQ FT: 10,100
SALES (est): 73.5MM **Privately Held**
WEB: www.sbci.com
SIC: 1542 Commercial & office buildings, prefabricated erection

(P-1472)
BALFOUR BEATTY CNSTR LLC
2335 Broadway Ste 300, Oakland (94612-2495)
PHONE..................510 903-2060
EMP: 186
SALES (corp-wide): 9.1B **Privately Held**
SIC: 1542 Commercial & office building, new construction
HQ: Balfour Beatty Construction, Llc
3100 Mckinnon St Fl 10
Dallas TX 75201
214 451-1000

(P-1473)
BALLIET BROS CONSTRUCTION CORP
390 Swift Ave Ste 14, South San Francisco (94080-6221)
PHONE..................650 871-9000
Robert F Balliet, *President*
Michael Warren, *Vice Pres*
Mike Warren, *Vice Pres*
Mareth Vedder, *Admin Sec*
EMP: 50
SQ FT: 9,000
SALES (est): 2.8MM **Privately Held**
WEB: www.ballietbros.com
SIC: 1542 1522 2434 2431 Commercial & office buildings, renovation & repair; remodeling, multi-family dwellings; wood kitchen cabinets; trim, wood

(P-1474)
BAYSIDE INSULATION & CNSTR
1635 Challenge Dr, Concord (94520-5206)
PHONE...................................925 288-8960
Shahram Ameli, *CEO*
Al Badakhshan, *Vice Pres*
EMP: 62
SQ FT: 10,000
SALES: 18.8MM **Privately Held**
WEB: www.baysideinsulation.com
SIC: 1542 Commercial & office building,
new construction

(P-1475)
BCCI CONSTRUCTION COMPANY (PA)
Also Called: Bcci Builders
1160 Battery St Ste 250, San Francisco
(94111-1216)
PHONE...................................415 817-5100
Michael Scribner, *President*
Hisham Mushasha, *CFO*
Michael Dean, *Vice Pres*
William Groth, *Vice Pres*
Dominic Sarica, *Vice Pres*
EMP: 121
SQ FT: 15,121
SALES (est): 65.6MM **Privately Held**
WEB: www.bcciconst.com
SIC: 1542 Commercial & office buildings,
renovation & repair

(P-1476)
BECHTEL ENTPS HOLDINGS INC
50 Beale St Bsmt 1, San Francisco
(94105-1819)
P.O. Box 193965 (94119-3965)
PHONE...................................415 768-6745
Dan Chao, *Director*
Paul Unruh, *Director*
EMP: 430
SALES (est): 14.8MM **Privately Held**
SIC: 1542 4581 Nonresidential construc-
tion; airport

(P-1477)
BEL ESPRIT BUILDERS INC
23112 Alcalde Dr Ste A, Laguna Hills
(92653-1458)
PHONE...................................949 709-3500
David K Jackson, *President*
Debra Jackson, *Admin Sec*
EMP: 50
SALES (est): 7.6MM **Privately Held**
SIC: 1542 Nonresidential construction

(P-1478)
BELMONT BRUNS CONSTRUCTION INC
1125 Mabury Rd, San Jose (95133-1029)
P.O. Box 612707 (95161-2707)
PHONE...................................408 977-1708
Mark A Collishaw, *CEO*
Paul J Helvik, *Vice Pres*
Jack Collishaw, *Admin Sec*
EMP: 55
SALES (est): 15.5MM **Privately Held**
SIC: 1542 1541 Commercial & office build-
ing, new construction; commercial & of-
fice buildings, renovation & repair;
industrial buildings & warehouses

(P-1479)
BENNATHON CORP (PA)
Also Called: Tudor Cnstr & Restoration
10278 Iron Rock Way, Elk Grove
(95624-1355)
P.O. Box 5426, Stockton (95205-0426)
PHONE...................................916 405-2100
David Urman, *President*
Tony Huynh, *CFO*
Peter Jones, *Vice Pres*
EMP: 60
SQ FT: 30,000
SALES (est): 12.6MM **Privately Held**
SIC: 1542 1541 1521 Commercial & of-
fice buildings, renovation & repair; reno-
vation, remodeling & repairs: industrial
buildings; repairing fire damage, single-
family houses

(P-1480)
BERGMAN KPRS LLC (PA)
2850 Saturn St Ste 100, Brea
(92821-1701)
PHONE...................................714 924-7000
Mark C Bergman,
Paul Kristedja,
Lev Rabinovich,
Joel H Stensby,
Daniel Medina, *Director*
EMP: 125
SQ FT: 7,500
SALES (est): 63.5MM **Privately Held**
WEB: www.thebergman.com
SIC: 1542 Restaurant construction; shop-
ping center construction

(P-1481)
BLAZONA CONCRETE CNSTR INC
525 Harbor Blvd Ste 10, West Sacramento
(95691-2246)
PHONE...................................916 375-8337
J Dennis Blazona, *CEO*
Karen Blazona, *Vice Pres*
Rhett Havner, *Vice Pres*
Randy Thayer, *General Mgr*
Mike Davis, *Project Mgr*
EMP: 100
SALES (est): 23.9MM **Privately Held**
WEB: www.blazona.com
SIC: 1542 Commercial & office building
contractors

(P-1482)
BOGART CONSTRUCTION INC
9980 Irvine Center Dr # 200, Irvine
(92618-4365)
PHONE...................................949 453-1400
Brad K Bogart, *President*
Amanda Gadde, *Administration*
Jason Flores, *Project Mgr*
Daniel Stone, *Project Mgr*
Alex Perette, *Project Engr*
EMP: 55
SQ FT: 10,000
SALES (est): 38.7MM **Privately Held**
WEB: www.bogartconstruction.com
SIC: 1542 Commercial & office building,
new construction

(P-1483)
BRADDOCK & LOGAN SERVICES INC
4155 Blackhawk Plaza Cir # 201, Danville
(94506-4613)
P.O. Box 5300 (94526-1076)
PHONE...................................925 736-4000
Joseph E Raphel, *CEO*
Thomas Thompson, *Officer*
Missy Castaneda, *Regional Mgr*
Kari Cartner, *Administration*
Jim Demartini, *Finance*
EMP: 200
SALES (est): 40.5MM **Privately Held**
SIC: 1542 1522 Nonresidential construc-
tion; residential construction

(P-1484)
BROWARD BUILDERS INC
1200 E Kentucky Ave, Woodland
(95776-5906)
PHONE...................................530 666-5635
Dennis Broward, *President*
Randy Cantrell, *Vice Pres*
EMP: 100
SQ FT: 7,000
SALES (est): 50.3MM **Privately Held**
WEB: www.browardbros.com
SIC: 1542 1531 School building construc-
tion; cooperative apartment developers

(P-1485)
BROWN CONSTRUCTION INC
1465 Entp Blvd Ste 100, West Sacramento
(95691)
P.O. Box 980700 (95798-0700)
PHONE...................................916 374-8616
Ron Brown, *President*
Ken Brown, *CFO*
Diana Houston, *CFO*
Kathryn Mc Guire, *Treasurer*
Matt Defazio, *Vice Pres*
EMP: 71
SQ FT: 11,000

SALES: 151.1MM **Privately Held**
WEB: www.brown-construction.com
SIC: 1542 1522 Nonresidential construc-
tion; apartment building construction

(P-1486)
BROWNCO CONSTRUCTION CO INC
1000 E Katella Ave, Anaheim (92805-6617)
PHONE...................................714 935-9600
Scot Alan Brown, *President*
Jeff Radtke, *Vice Pres*
Christine Moananu, *Admin Asst*
Michael Campbell, *Project Mgr*
Zoe Kelso, *Controller*
EMP: 87
SQ FT: 15,000
SALES (est): 23.9MM **Privately Held**
WEB: www.browncoinc.com
SIC: 1542 Commercial & office building
contractors

(P-1487)
BUILD GROUP INC (PA)
457 Minna St Ste 100, San Francisco
(94103-2914)
PHONE...................................415 367-9399
Ross Edwards, *President*
Eric Horn, *Ch of Bd*
Todd C Pennington, *President*
Ron Marano, *CFO*
Kenneth Jones, *Exec VP*
▲ EMP: 119 EST: 2006
SQ FT: 8,000
SALES: 187.4MM **Privately Held**
SIC: 1542 Commercial & office building,
new construction

(P-1488)
BUILD GROUP INC
Also Called: Build Sjc
1210 Coleman Ave, Santa Clara
(95050-4338)
PHONE...................................408 986-8711
EMP: 65
SALES (corp-wide): 187.4MM **Privately
Held**
SIC: 1542 Commercial & office building,
new construction
PA: Build Group, Inc.
457 Minna St Ste 100
San Francisco CA 94103
415 367-9399

(P-1489)
BURCH CONSTRUCTION COMPANY INC
405 Maple St Ste C-101, Ramona
(92065-1890)
P.O. Box 395 (92065-0395)
PHONE...................................760 788-9370
Nancy Burch, *CEO*
Mitchell Burch, *President*
EMP: 50
SQ FT: 4,000
SALES (est): 12.5MM **Privately Held**
SIC: 1542 Commercial & office building,
new construction

(P-1490)
BYCOR GENERAL CONTRACTORS INC
6490 Marindustry Dr Ste A, San Diego
(92121-5297)
PHONE...................................858 587-1901
Scott Kaats, *CEO*
Richard A Byer, *President*
Scott Hodges, *Vice Pres*
Gina Walker, *Vice Pres*
Brian Stanton, *Project Mgr*
EMP: 90
SQ FT: 10,041
SALES: 89MM **Privately Held**
WEB: www.bycor.com
SIC: 1542 Commercial & office building,
new construction; commercial & office
buildings, renovation & repair

(P-1491)
C & C CONSTRUCTION INC
7941 E Hidden Lakes Dr, Granite Bay
(95746-9539)
PHONE...................................916 434-5280
Paul Cavaghan, *CEO*
EMP: 50

SQ FT: 12,800
SALES (est): 10.1MM **Privately Held**
SIC: 1542 Commercial & office building
contractors

(P-1492)
C W DRIVER INCORPORATED (PA)
468 N Rosemead Blvd, Pasadena
(91107-3010)
PHONE...................................626 351-8800
Dana Roberts, *President*
Michael Byrne, *COO*
Bessie Kouvara, *CFO*
Robert Maxwell, *Senior VP*
Steven Nelson, *Vice Pres*
EMP: 60 EST: 1919
SQ FT: 14,000
SALES (est): 207.7MM **Privately Held**
WEB: www.cwdriver.com
SIC: 1542 Commercial & office building,
new construction

(P-1493)
CAHILL CONTRACTORS INC (PA)
425 California St # 2200, San Francisco
(94104-2207)
PHONE...................................415 986-0600
John E Cahill Jr, *CEO*
Chuck Palley, *President*
Darrell Diamond, *Corp Secy*
Kendra Gomez, *Admin Asst*
Gerald K Cahill, *Director*
▲ EMP: 86 EST: 1974
SALES: 233MM **Privately Held**
WEB: www.cahill-sf.com
SIC: 1542 Commercial & office building,
new construction

(P-1494)
CAHILL CONTRACTORS LLC
425 California St # 2200, San Francisco
(94104-2207)
PHONE...................................415 986-0600
Michael Grant, *CFO*
Trilce Farrugia, *Exec Sec*
EMP: 99
SALES (est): 4.9MM **Privately Held**
SIC: 1542 1522 Nonresidential construc-
tion; residential construction

(P-1495)
CAL-PACIFIC CONSTRUCTION INC
1009 Terra Nova Blvd, Pacifica
(94044-4308)
PHONE...................................650 557-1238
John Wah Chan, *President*
Kennedy Chan, *CEO*
EMP: 50
SQ FT: 4,500
SALES: 5.1MM **Privately Held**
SIC: 1542 1521 Commercial & office build-
ing contractors; general remodeling, sin-
gle-family houses

(P-1496)
CALIFORNIA STRL CONCEPTS INC
28358 Constellation Rd # 660, Valencia
(91355-5010)
PHONE...................................661 257-6903
Jeffrey Horne, *CEO*
Penny Horne, *Vice Pres*
EMP: 85 EST: 2006
SALES: 20.1MM **Privately Held**
SIC: 1542 Commercial & office building,
new construction

(P-1497)
CAPTURED SEA INC
5901 Warner Ave, Huntington Beach
(92649-4659)
PHONE...................................714 856-3358
Dave Wooten, *President*
EMP: 60
SQ FT: 24,000
SALES (est): 5.9MM **Privately Held**
WEB: www.capturedsea.com
SIC: 1542 Nonresidential construction

(P-1498)
CASTLE & COOKE CALAVERAS INC
1 Dole Dr, Westlake Village (91362-7300)
PHONE..................................310 208-3636
David H Murdock, *CEO*
EMP: 5000
SALES (est): 178.3K
SALES (corp-wide): 911.7MM **Privately Held**
SIC: 1542 Nonresidential construction
PA: Castle & Cooke, Inc.
1 Dole Dr
Westlake Village CA 91362
310 374-3952

(P-1499)
CELLO & MAUDRU CNSTR CO INC
2505 Oak St, NAPA (94559-2226)
P.O. Box 10106 (94581-2106)
PHONE..................................707 257-0454
William F Maudru, *CEO*
Michael Zatorski, *Partner*
Clint Simpson, *Regional Mgr*
Chela Ramos, *Admin Sec*
Melanie Troup, *Administration*
EMP: 50
SQ FT: 2,000
SALES (est): 26.1MM **Privately Held**
WEB: www.cello-maudru.com
SIC: 1542 1521 Commercial & office build-
ing, new construction; commercial & of-
fice buildings, renovation & repair; new
construction, single-family houses; gen-
eral remodeling, single-family houses

(P-1500)
CENTURY VISION DEVELOPERS INC
3000 Oak Rd Ste 360, Walnut Creek
(94597-7782)
P.O. Box 907, Concord (94522-0907)
PHONE..................................925 588-7390
John E Amaral, *CEO*
EMP: 50
SALES (est): 9.6MM **Privately Held**
SIC: 1542 6512 Commercial & office build-
ing, new construction; commercial & in-
dustrial building operation

(P-1501)
CHARLES E THOMAS COMPANY INC (PA)
Also Called: CETEC SOLUTIONS
13701 Alma Ave, Gardena (90249-2523)
PHONE..................................310 323-6730
Jerry Thomas, *President*
Brian Hurley, *Vice Pres*
Ann Thomas, *Vice Pres*
Greg Thomas, *Vice Pres*
▼ EMP: 60
SQ FT: 15,000
SALES (est): 61.1MM **Privately Held**
WEB: www.cethomas.net
SIC: 1542 7699 Design & erection, com-
bined: non-residential; service station
equipment repair

(P-1502)
CHARLES PANKOW BLDRS LTD A CAL (PA)
199 S Los Robles Ave # 300, Pasadena
(91101-2452)
PHONE..................................626 304-1190
Rik Kunnath, *Ch of Bd*
Kim Lum, *Partner*
Dick Walterhouse, *COO*
Kim Petersen, *CFO*
Lindsey Gray, *Project Engr*
EMP: 50
SQ FT: 40,000
SALES (est): 163.9MM **Privately Held**
WEB: www.pankow.com
SIC: 1542 Commercial & office building,
new construction

(P-1503)
CHARLES PANKOW BLDRS LTD A CAL
1111 Broadway Ste 200, Oakland
(94607-4171)
PHONE..................................510 893-5170
Scott Anderson, *Manager*

Dave Dwyer, *Executive*
EMP: 450
SALES (corp-wide): 163.9MM **Privately Held**
SIC: 1542 Commercial & office building
contractors
PA: Charles Pankow Builders, Ltd., A Cali-
fornia Limited Partnership
199 S Los Robles Ave # 300
Pasadena CA 91101
626 304-1190

(P-1504)
CIRKS CONSTRUCTION INC
Also Called: Kdc Construction
3300 Industrial Blvd, West Sacramento
(95691-5028)
PHONE..................................916 362-5460
Ryan Ferris, *Branch Mgr*
Dale Nelson, *Superintendent*
EMP: 89
SALES (corp-wide): 147.6MM **Privately Held**
SIC: 1542 Commercial & office building,
new construction
PA: Cirks Construction Inc.
2570 E Cerritos Ave
Anaheim CA 92806
714 632-6717

(P-1505)
CLAIM JUMPER RESTAURANT
Also Called: Cwn Management
27845 Snta Margarita Pkwy, Mission Viejo
(92691-6701)
PHONE..................................949 461-7170
Robert Ott, *Owner*
EMP: 110 EST: 1997
SALES (est): 8MM **Privately Held**
SIC: 1542 5813 5812 Restaurant con-
struction; drinking places; eating places

(P-1506)
CLARK & SULLIVAN BUILDERS INC
2024 Opportunity Dr # 150, Roseville
(95678-3026)
PHONE..................................916 338-7707
B J Sullivan, *President*
Kevin Stroupe, *CFO*
EMP: 150
SQ FT: 5,000
SALES (est): 17.2MM
SALES (corp-wide): 74.5MM **Privately Held**
SIC: 1542 1541 Commercial & office build-
ing, new construction; industrial buildings,
new construction
PA: C.S. General, Inc.
905 Industrial Way
Sparks NV 89431
775 355-8500

(P-1507)
CLARK CNSTR GRUP-CALIFORNIA LP
18201 Von Karman Ave, Irvine
(92612-1000)
PHONE..................................714 429-9779
Richard M Heim, *CEO*
EMP: 393
SQ FT: 5,000
SALES (est): 2.6MM
SALES (corp-wide): 1.9B **Privately Held**
WEB: www.clarkus.com
SIC: 1542 Commercial & office building,
new construction
HQ: Clark Construction Group, Llc
7500 Old Georgetown Rd # 1500
Bethesda MD 20814
301 272-8100

(P-1508)
CODDING CONSTRUCTION CO
1400 Valley House Dr # 100, Rohnert Park
(94928-4935)
P.O. Box 5800, Santa Rosa (95406-5800)
PHONE..................................707 795-3550
John Gordon, *CEO*
Reginald E Bayley, *Corp Secy*
Rick Freeman, *Vice Pres*
EMP: 50 EST: 1986
SQ FT: 5,000

SALES: 6.9MM
SALES (corp-wide): 21.6MM **Privately Held**
WEB: www.codding.com
SIC: 1542 Commercial & office building
contractors
PA: Codding Enterprises Lp
1400 Valley House Dr # 100
Rohnert Park CA 94928
707 795-3550

(P-1509)
CONNECT YOUR HOME LLC
Also Called: Dish Systems
1 Park Plz Ste 600, Irvine (92614-5987)
PHONE..................................949 777-0100
Brookhollow Marketing, *Principal*
EMP: 90 EST: 2010
SQ FT: 14,000
SALES (est): 9.3MM **Privately Held**
SIC: 1542 Commercial & office building
contractors

(P-1510)
CONTRACTOR WAREHOUSE
5950 N Paramount Blvd, Lakewood
(90805-3710)
PHONE..................................562 633-1428
Greg Inshinsha, *Manager*
EMP: 52
SALES (est): 2.7MM **Privately Held**
SIC: 1542 Commercial & office building
contractors

(P-1511)
CUSTOM DESIGN CO INC
20969 Ventura Blvd # 217, Woodland Hills
(91364-6617)
PHONE..................................818 507-5959
Mina Hamedani, *President*
Jalil Hamedani, *Vice Pres*
EMP: 50
SQ FT: 5,000
SALES (est): 4.2MM **Privately Held**
SIC: 1542 1751 1521 Nonresidential con-
struction; cabinet & finish carpentry; gen-
eral remodeling, single-family houses

(P-1512)
DAL CAIS INC
5101 Florin Perkins Rd, Sacramento
(95826-4817)
PHONE..................................916 381-8080
Tim Obrian, *President*
Phyllis O'Brien, *Corp Secy*
EMP: 80
SQ FT: 24,000
SALES (est): 5.5MM **Privately Held**
WEB: www.dalcais.com
SIC: 1542 6552 Commercial & office build-
ing, new construction; subdividers & de-
velopers

(P-1513)
DAVLOR COMPANY
Also Called: Davlor Constructio Corp
12 Oakbrook, Trabuco Canyon
(92679-4722)
P.O. Box 892799, Temecula (92589-2799)
PHONE..................................949 244-9748
Dave Fenton, *Owner*
EMP: 94
SALES (est): 5.6MM **Privately Held**
SIC: 1542 Commercial & office building
contractors

(P-1514)
DEACON CONSTRUCTION - CAL
7745 Greenback Ln Ste 250, Citrus Heights
(95610-5865)
PHONE..................................916 969-0900
Richard Smith, *President*
Steven D Deacon, *CEO*
Julie Rodrigues, *Controller*
EMP: 70
SQ FT: 5,000
SALES: 397.8K
SALES (corp-wide): 391.5MM **Privately Held**
SIC: 1542 Commercial & office building,
new construction
PA: Deacon Holdings, Inc.
7745 Greenback Ln Ste 250
Citrus Heights CA 95610
916 969-0900

(P-1515)
DEACON CORP
17880 Fitch, Irvine (92614-6002)
PHONE..................................949 222-9060
John Steffens, *Manager*
EMP: 60
SALES (corp-wide): 391.5MM **Privately Held**
WEB: www.deacon.com
SIC: 1542 Commercial & office building,
new construction
PA: Deacon Holdings, Inc.
7745 Greenback Ln Ste 250
Citrus Heights CA 95610
916 969-0900

(P-1516)
DEACON HOLDINGS INC (PA)
7745 Greenback Ln Ste 250, Citrus Heights
(95610-5865)
PHONE..................................916 969-0900
Steven D Deacon, *CEO*
Bob Miller, *Partner*
Richard Smith, *President*
Pete Snook, *Principal*
Curt Mills, *Administration*
EMP: 100
SQ FT: 5,000
SALES: 391.5MM **Privately Held**
WEB: www.deacon.com
SIC: 1542 Commercial & office building,
new construction

(P-1517)
DEL AMO CONSTRUCTION
23840 Madison St, Torrance (90505-6009)
PHONE..................................310 378-6203
Steve Donahue, *CEO*
Ed Hong, *CFO*
Susan Donahue, *Treasurer*
Jason Cave, *Vice Pres*
Harry Donahue, *Vice Pres*
EMP: 55
SQ FT: 4,000
SALES (est): 33.9MM **Privately Held**
SIC: 1542 1771 Commercial & office build-
ing, new construction; concrete work

(P-1518)
DESIGNED MBL SYSTEMS INDS INC
800 S State Highway 33, Patterson
(95363-9148)
PHONE..................................209 892-6298
David W Smith, *President*
Edward Smith, *Vice Pres*
EMP: 130
SQ FT: 100,000
SALES (est): 19.6MM **Privately Held**
WEB: www.dmsi-inc.com
SIC: 1542 2451 3448 2452 Design &
erection, combined: non-residential; mo-
bile classrooms; mobile buildings: for
commercial use; prefabricated metal
buildings; prefabricated wood buildings

(P-1519)
DIANI BUILDING CORP (PA)
351 N Blosser Rd, Santa Maria
(93458-4219)
P.O. Box 5757 (93456-5757)
PHONE..................................805 925-9533
Michael J Diani, *President*
Lowell Ledgerwood, *Treasurer*
Jeffrey Neal, *Senior VP*
Peter Hemesath, *Vice Pres*
Jason Diani, *Admin Sec*
EMP: 62
SQ FT: 11,000
SALES (est): 36.1MM **Privately Held**
SIC: 1542 Commercial & office building,
new construction

(P-1520)
DIEDE CONSTRUCTION INC
12393 N Hwy 99, Lodi (95240-7269)
P.O. Box 1007, Woodbridge (95258-1007)
PHONE..................................209 369-8255
Steven L Diede, *President*
Lillian Diede, *Corp Secy*
Bruce J Diede, *Vice Pres*
Wayne J Diede, *Vice Pres*
EMP: 100
SQ FT: 23,000

SALES (est): 68.8MM **Privately Held**
SIC: 1542 1771 1761 Commercial & office buildings, renovation & repair; foundation & footing contractor; roof repair

(P-1521)
DIVISION THREE CNSTR SVCS
30620 Plumas St, Lake Elsinore (92530-6915)
PHONE...............................951 609-3043
Steve Fisher, *President*
Randy Kendrick, *Shareholder*
EMP: 80
SALES (est): 5.7MM **Privately Held**
SIC: 1542 Commercial & office building contractors

(P-1522)
DMC CONSTRUCTION INCORPORATED
2110 Del Monte Ave, Monterey (93940-3712)
PHONE...............................831 656-1600
Dan McAweeney, *President*
Dan Mc Aweeney, *President*
EMP: 80
SQ FT: 3,500
SALES: 41MM **Privately Held**
SIC: 1542 1541 School building construction; hospital construction; commercial & office building, new construction; renovation, remodeling & repairs; industrial buildings; industrial buildings, new construction

(P-1523)
DPR CONSTRUCTION INC
2480 Natomas Park Dr # 100, Sacramento (95833-2979)
PHONE...............................916 568-3434
Trish Timothy, *Manager*
EMP: 300
SALES (corp-wide): 3.7B **Privately Held**
WEB: www.dprconstruction.com
SIC: 1542 Commercial & office building contractors
PA: Dpr Construction, Inc.
1450 Veterans Blvd
Redwood City CA 94063
650 474-1450

(P-1524)
DPR CONSTRUCTION INC
4665 Macarthur Ct Ste 100, Newport Beach (92660-1825)
PHONE...............................949 955-3771
Jim Washburn, *Regional Mgr*
EMP: 50
SALES (corp-wide): 3.7B **Privately Held**
WEB: www.dprconstruction.com
SIC: 1542 Commercial & office building contractors
PA: Dpr Construction, Inc.
1450 Veterans Blvd
Redwood City CA 94063
650 474-1450

(P-1525)
DRAGADOS/FLATIRON JOINT VENTR
14555 S Peach Ave, Selma (93662-9657)
PHONE...............................559 847-5388
EMP: 93
SALES (corp-wide): 19.1MM **Privately Held**
SIC: 1542 Nonresidential construction
PA: Dragados/Flatiron Joint Venture
1775 Park St Ste 75
Selma CA 93662
559 558-5213

(P-1526)
EAGLE LATH & PLASTER INC
4350 Warehouse Ct, North Highlands (95660-5809)
PHONE...............................916 925-1435
Robert P Milani, *President*
EMP: 100 EST: 2010
SQ FT: 10,000
SALES: 10MM **Privately Held**
SIC: 1542 Commercial & office building contractors

(P-1527)
ELEVEN WESTERN BUILDERS INC (PA)
2862 Executive Pl, Escondido (92029-1524)
PHONE...............................760 796-6346
Rick W Backus, *CEO*
Richard Huey, *CFO*
Jasen Boyens, *Project Mgr*
Gene Chesterton, *Project Mgr*
Doug Child, *Project Mgr*
EMP: 110
SQ FT: 20,000
SALES (est): 56.3MM **Privately Held**
SIC: 1542 Commercial & office building, new construction

(P-1528)
EMS CONSTRUCTION INC
12185 Dearborn Pl, Poway (92064-7111)
PHONE...............................858 679-8292
Charles S Speck, *President*
Sean Speck, *President*
Marybeth Edwards, *Vice Pres*
EMP: 75
SALES (est): 12.7MM **Privately Held**
SIC: 1542 Nonresidential construction

(P-1529)
ENVIRONMENTAL CONSTRUCTION INC
21550 Oxnard St Ste 1060, Woodland Hills (91367-7123)
PHONE...............................818 449-8920
Farid Soroudi, *CEO*
Zia Abhari, *President*
EMP: 90
SQ FT: 2,500
SALES (est): 37.3MM **Privately Held**
SIC: 1542 Commercial & office building contractors

(P-1530)
ERICKSON-HALL CONSTRUCTION CO (PA)
500 Corporate Dr, Escondido (92029-1517)
PHONE...............................760 796-7700
Dave Erickson, *CEO*
Mike Hall, *COO*
Michael Conroy, *CFO*
Mike Conroy, *CFO*
Chris Bartok, *Admin Sec*
EMP: 88
SALES (est): 45.5MM **Privately Held**
WEB: www.ericksonhall.com
SIC: 1542 Commercial & office building, new construction

(P-1531)
F & H CONSTRUCTION (PA)
1115 E Lockeford St, Lodi (95240-0878)
P.O. Box 2329 (95241-2329)
PHONE...............................209 931-3738
Charles Allen Ferrell, *President*
Dan Blackburn, *Partner*
Stephen Seibly, *Corp Secy*
Harold Jones, *Exec VP*
Harold Erwin Jones, *Vice Pres*
EMP: 75
SQ FT: 8,000
SALES: 81MM **Privately Held**
SIC: 1542 1541 Commercial & office building, new construction; industrial buildings, new construction

(P-1532)
FINE LINE GROUP INC
457 Minna St, San Francisco (94103-2914)
PHONE...............................415 777-4070
John S Santori, *Ch of Bd*
Robert M Helmers, *Exec VP*
EMP: 50
SQ FT: 7,000
SALES (est): 7.1MM **Privately Held**
WEB: www.finelinegroup.com
SIC: 1542 Commercial & office buildings, renovation & repair

(P-1533)
FRANK SCHIPPER CONSTRUCTION CO
Also Called: Fscc
610 E Cota St, Santa Barbara (93103-3166)
PHONE...............................805 963-4359

Frank Schipper, *President*
Arlan Schipper, *Vice Pres*
Paul Wieckowski, *Vice Pres*
Andrew Brenner, *Project Mgr*
Marc Cunningham, *Project Mgr*
EMP: 50
SQ FT: 2,200
SALES (est): 12.7MM **Privately Held**
SIC: 1542 8742 1611 Commercial & office buildings, renovation & repair; commercial & office building, new construction; business consultant; general contractor, highway & street construction

(P-1534)
GENERATION CONSTRUCTION INC
15650 El Prado Rd, Chino (91710-9108)
P.O. Box 991 (91708-0991)
PHONE...............................909 923-2077
Antwan De Paul, *President*
Tony Dakwar, *General Mgr*
Alicia Nash, *Financial Exec*
Melissa Torrez, *Sales Staff*
EMP: 150
SALES (est): 33.3MM **Privately Held**
SIC: 1542 Commercial & office buildings, renovation & repair

(P-1535)
GILBANE SMCC LLC
1655 Grant St 12f, Concord (94520-2600)
PHONE...............................925 946-3100
Lenoard Garner, *Admin Sec*
EMP: 99
SQ FT: 24,408
SALES (est): 3MM **Privately Held**
SIC: 1542 Nonresidential construction

(P-1536)
GOLDEN COAST CNSTR RESTORATION
4811 Chippendale Dr # 301, Sacramento (95841-2552)
PHONE...............................916 955-7461
Alex Kotyakov, *President*
Russ Stevenson, *General Mgr*
EMP: 68
SALES: 10MM **Privately Held**
SIC: 1542 1521 Commercial & office buildings, renovation & repair; new construction, single-family houses

(P-1537)
GRANI INSTALLATION INC (PA)
5411 Commercial Dr, Huntington Beach (92649-1231)
PHONE...............................714 898-0441
Gregory A Grani, *CEO*
Manisha Phanasgaonkar, *Officer*
Michael Liechty, *Project Mgr*
Garrett Price, *Project Mgr*
Henry Uranga, *Project Mgr*
EMP: 100
SQ FT: 6,000
SALES (est): 41.2MM **Privately Held**
SIC: 1542 1742 Commercial & office buildings, renovation & repair; acoustical & ceiling work

(P-1538)
GREEN VALLEY CORPORATION (PA)
Also Called: Swenson, Barry Builder
777 N 1st St Fl 5, San Jose (95112-6350)
PHONE...............................408 287-0246
C Barron Swenson, *Chairman*
Case Swenson, *President*
Lee Ann Woodard, *CFO*
Steven W Andrews, *Senior VP*
Ronald L Cot, *Senior VP*
▲ EMP: 50 EST: 1961
SQ FT: 12,000
SALES (est): 89.4MM **Privately Held**
WEB: www.barryswensonbuilder.com
SIC: 1542 1522 6512 Commercial & office building, new construction; multi-family dwelling construction; commercial & industrial building operation

(P-1539)
GSF ENTERPRISES INC
Also Called: Gsf Builders
700 N Valley St Ste B, Anaheim (92801-3824)
PHONE...............................714 524-9500
John Dunbar, *CEO*
Bob Mangold, *CFO*
Gary Viano, *Vice Pres*
EMP: 75
SQ FT: 1,500
SALES (est): 16.4MM **Privately Held**
WEB: www.woodframers.com
SIC: 1542 Commercial & office buildings, renovation & repair

(P-1540)
H2C2 & ASSOCIATES INC (PA)
6925 San Leandro St, Oakland (94621-3320)
PHONE...............................510 562-6181
Mike Christie, *President*
Richard Cleveland, *Corp Secy*
Marvin Henderson, *Vice Pres*
EMP: 50
SALES (est): 42.4MM **Privately Held**
SIC: 1542 1795 Commercial & office building contractors; demolition, buildings & other structures

(P-1541)
HARDISTY CONSTRUCTION ADMINIST
410 W 30th St Ste A, National City (91950-7269)
PHONE...............................619 245-6828
John T Hardisty, *President*
Wade Lindsay, *Vice Pres*
EMP: 70
SALES (est): 9MM **Privately Held**
SIC: 1542 1521 1522 Nonresidential construction; single-family housing construction; residential construction

(P-1542)
HARPER CONSTRUCTION CO INC (PA)
2241 Kettner Blvd Ste 300, San Diego (92101-1769)
PHONE...............................619 233-7900
Jeffrey A Harper, *CEO*
Jeff Harper, *CEO*
Ron Harper, *Chairman*
EMP: 140
SQ FT: 17,000
SALES (est): 81.5MM **Privately Held**
SIC: 1542 1521 Commercial & office building, new construction; single-family housing construction

(P-1543)
HARRIS CONSTRUCTION CO INC
5286 E Home Ave, Fresno (93727-2103)
PHONE...............................559 251-0301
Mike Spencer, *Vice Pres*
Richard F Spencer, *Chairman*
▲ EMP: 150 EST: 1914
SQ FT: 6,000
SALES (est): 65.8MM **Privately Held**
SIC: 1542 1541 Hospital construction; commercial & office building, new construction; food products manufacturing or packing plant construction

(P-1544)
HARVEY INC
Also Called: Harvey General Contracting
9455 Ridgehaven Ct # 200, San Diego (92123-1632)
PHONE...............................858 769-4000
Stephen Harvey, *CEO*
Debra Gillespie, *CFO*
Paul J Pietsch, *Vice Pres*
EMP: 125
SALES: 30.9MM **Privately Held**
SIC: 1542 Commercial & office building, new construction

(P-1545)
HATHAWAY DINWIDDIE CNSTR CO
565 Laurelwood Rd, Santa Clara (95054-2419)
PHONE...............................415 986-2718

PRODUCTS & SVCS

Greg Cosko, *President*
David A Lee, *Senior VP*
EMP: 100
SQ FT: 7,000
SALES (est): 18.6MM **Privately Held**
SIC: 1542 Commercial & office building, new construction

(P-1546)
HATHAWAY DINWIDDIE CNSTR CO
275 Battery St Ste 300, San Francisco (94111-3378)
PHONE....................415 986-2718
Greg Cosko, *CEO*
Paul Gregory Cosko, *President*
Stephen W McCoid, *Exec VP*
Gordon D Smith, *Senior VP*
Ed Conlon, *Vice Pres*
▲ **EMP:** 400
SQ FT: 21,000
SALES (est): 158.5MM **Privately Held**
WEB: www.hdcco.com
SIC: 1542 Commercial & office building, new construction; commercial & office buildings, renovation & repair
PA: Hathaway Dinwiddie Construction Group
275 Battery St Ste 300
San Francisco CA 94111

(P-1547)
HATHAWAY DINWIDDIE CNSTR GROUP (PA)
275 Battery St Ste 300, San Francisco (94111-3378)
PHONE....................415 986-2718
Greg Cosko, *CEO*
David Miller, *CFO*
Stephen E Smith, *Senior VP*
Stephen W McCoid, *Vice Pres*
EMP: 400
SQ FT: 18,000
SALES (est): 138.5MM **Privately Held**
SIC: 1542 Commercial & office building, new construction

(P-1548)
HBE CORPORATION
147 N Brent St, Ventura (93003-2809)
PHONE....................805 641-1305
Joe Thompson, *Director*
EMP: 50
SALES (est): 3.1MM **Privately Held**
SIC: 1542 Nonresidential construction

(P-1549)
HENSEL PHELPS CONSTRUCTION CO
5271 Viewridge Ct Frnt, San Diego (92123-1604)
PHONE....................858 266-7979
Scott Schilling, *Manager*
EMP: 60
SALES (corp-wide): 3.3B **Privately Held**
SIC: 1542 Commercial & office building, new construction
PA: Hensel Phelps Construction Co.
420 6th Ave
Greeley CO 80631
970 352-6565

(P-1550)
HENSEL PHELPS CONSTRUCTION CO
226 Airport Pkwy Ste 150, San Jose (95110-1024)
PHONE....................408 452-1800
Jon W Ball, *Vice Pres*
Todd Temple, *Opers Mgr*
EMP: 200
SALES (corp-wide): 3.3B **Privately Held**
WEB: www.henselphelps.com
SIC: 1542 1541 Commercial & office building contractors; industrial buildings & warehouses
PA: Hensel Phelps Construction Co.
420 6th Ave
Greeley CO 80631
970 352-6565

(P-1551)
HENSEL PHELPS CONSTRUCTION CO
9404 Genesee Ave Ste 140, La Jolla (92037-1353)
PHONE....................619 544-6828
Thom Diersbock, *Branch Mgr*
EMP: 70
SALES (corp-wide): 3.3B **Privately Held**
SIC: 1542 Commercial & office building contractors
PA: Hensel Phelps Construction Co.
420 6th Ave
Greeley CO 80631
970 352-6565

(P-1552)
HENSEL PHLPS GRNTE HNGR JV
18850 Von Karman 100, Irvine (92612)
PHONE....................949 852-0111
Cuyler R McGinley, *Vice Pres*
John A Franich, *Vice Pres*
Paul Ligocki, *Manager*
EMP: 200
SALES: 300MM **Privately Held**
SIC: 1542 1629 Nonresidential construction; heavy construction

(P-1553)
HILBERS INC
Also Called: HILBERS CONTRACTORS & ENGINEER
1210 Stabler Ln, Yuba City (95993-2620)
PHONE....................530 673-2947
Kurt G Hilbers, *President*
Doug Heacock, *COO*
Glenn Hilbers, *Treasurer*
Larry E Hilbers, *Vice Pres*
Tom Jones, *Vice Pres*
EMP: 75
SQ FT: 6,790
SALES: 121.7MM **Privately Held**
WEB: www.hilbersinc.com
SIC: 1542 1541 Commercial & office building, new construction; industrial buildings, new construction

(P-1554)
HOLBROOK CONSTRUCTION INC
9814 Norwalk Blvd Ste 200, Santa Fe Springs (90670-2992)
PHONE....................714 523-1150
Laurence A Holbrook, *President*
Richard Holbrook, *CFO*
Lisa Garcia, *Controller*
EMP: 75
SQ FT: 3,000
SALES (est): 4.4MM **Privately Held**
WEB: www.holbrookconstruction.net
SIC: 1542 Commercial & office building, new construction

(P-1555)
HOUALLA ENTERPRISES LTD
Also Called: Metro Bldrs & Engineers Group
2610 Avon St, Newport Beach (92663-4706)
PHONE....................949 515-4350
Fouad Houalla, *President*
Mustafa Mubaidin, *Project Mgr*
Ronald Blanchard, *Engineer*
Cameron Kosbab, *Assistant*
▲ **EMP:** 85
SQ FT: 1,200
SALES (est): 26MM **Privately Held**
SIC: 1542 Commercial & office building, new construction; specialized public building contractors

(P-1556)
HPM CONSTRUCTION LLC
17911 Mitchell S, Irvine (92614-6015)
PHONE....................949 474-9170
Karen Price, *President*
Cuyler McGinley, *Corp Secy*
Cindy McMackin, *Vice Pres*
Hensel Phelps Construction,
Morrow-Meadows Corporation,
EMP: 100 **EST:** 2012
SALES: 300MM
SALES (corp-wide): 3.3B **Privately Held**
SIC: 1542 Nonresidential construction

PA: Hensel Phelps Construction Co.
420 6th Ave
Greeley CO 80631
970 352-6565

(P-1557)
I WMI
17100 Pioneer Blvd # 230, Artesia (90701-2776)
PHONE....................562 977-4906
David T Gajdzik, *President*
Chris Gajdzik, *CFO*
EMP: 280
SALES: 40MM **Privately Held**
SIC: 1542 Commercial & office building contractors

(P-1558)
J B COMPANY
1825 Bell St Ste 100, Sacramento (95825-1020)
PHONE....................916 929-3003
EMP: 70
SQ FT: 24,000
SALES (est): 5.8MM **Privately Held**
SIC: 1542 1541

(P-1559)
J M C INTERNATIONAL LLC
1470 W Herndon Ave # 100, Fresno (93711-0552)
PHONE....................559 256-1300
Paul Owhadi,
EMP: 50
SQ FT: 14,000
SALES: 22MM **Privately Held**
SIC: 1542 1522 Commercial & office building contractors; residential construction

(P-1560)
J R ROBERTS CORP (HQ)
7745 Greenback Ln Ste 300, Citrus Heights (95610-5866)
PHONE....................916 729-5600
Robert Olsen, *CEO*
Robert C Hall Jr, *President*
Mike Vinks, *Vice Pres*
EMP: 100 **EST:** 1979
SQ FT: 9,000
SALES (est): 20.8MM
SALES (corp-wide): 391.5MM **Privately Held**
SIC: 1542 Commercial & office building, new construction
PA: Deacon Holdings, Inc.
7745 Greenback Ln Ste 250
Citrus Heights CA 95610
916 969-0900

(P-1561)
J R ROBERTS ENTERPRISES INC
7745 Greenback Ln Ste 300, Citrus Heights (95610-5866)
PHONE....................916 729-5600
Robert F Olsen, *Ch of Bd*
Robert C Hall Jr, *President*
James F Reilly, *Corp Secy*
EMP: 110
SALES (est): 11.6MM **Privately Held**
WEB: www.jrroberts.com
SIC: 1542 1522 Commercial & office building contractors; multi-family dwellings, new construction; remodeling, multi-family dwellings

(P-1562)
JACOBS ENGINEERING GROUP INC
4435 First St, Livermore (94551-4915)
PHONE....................925 423-7564
Arlene Emmert, *Branch Mgr*
EMP: 90
SALES (corp-wide): 10B **Publicly Held**
SIC: 1542 Commercial & office building, new construction
PA: Jacobs Engineering Group Inc.
1999 Bryan St Ste 1200
Dallas TX 75201
214 583-8500

(P-1563)
JAYNES CORPORATION CALIFORNIA
111 Elm St Fl 4, San Diego (92101-2649)
P.O. Box 26841, Albuquerque NM (87125-6841)
PHONE....................619 233-4080
Donald Power, *CEO*
Wayne Davenport, *Corp Secy*
Rick Marquardt, *Exec VP*
Richard Cohen, *Senior VP*
EMP: 105
SALES (est): 15.8MM
SALES (corp-wide): 12.3MM **Privately Held**
WEB: www.janescorp.com
SIC: 1542 Nonresidential construction
HQ: Jaynes Corporation
2906 Broadway Blvd Ne
Albuquerque NM 87107
505 345-8591

(P-1564)
JM STREAMLINE INC
Also Called: Streamline Construction
154 Scandling Ave, Grass Valley (95945-5816)
PHONE....................530 272-6806
Jesse McKenna, *President*
EMP: 55
SALES: 10.3MM **Privately Held**
SIC: 1542 Commercial & office building contractors

(P-1565)
JOHN F OTTO INC
Also Called: Otto Construction
1717 2nd St, Sacramento (95811-6214)
PHONE....................916 441-6870
Carl Barrett, *President*
Carol Otto, *Treasurer*
Rick McVey, *Vice Pres*
Allison Otto, *Vice Pres*
Elease Terry, *Vice Pres*
EMP: 120 **EST:** 1958
SQ FT: 10,000
SALES: 113.3MM **Privately Held**
WEB: www.ottoconstruction.com
SIC: 1542 1541 Commercial & office building, new construction; industrial buildings, new construction

(P-1566)
JOHN M FRANK CONSTRUCTION INC
Also Called: John M Frank Service Group
913 E 4th St, Santa Ana (92701-4748)
PHONE....................714 210-3600
John M Frank, *CEO*
Myra Mageo, *Executive*
Laurie Dawson, *Admin Sec*
Shaun Bell, *Safety Dir*
EMP: 80
SALES (est): 22.1MM **Privately Held**
WEB: www.cscconcreteservices.com
SIC: 1542 5411 5812 Commercial & office building, new construction; commercial & office buildings, renovation & repair; supermarkets; family restaurants; restaurant, lunch counter

(P-1567)
JOHN PLANE CONSTRUCTION INC
661 Hayne Rd, Hillsborough (94010-7006)
PHONE....................415 468-0555
John Plane, *President*
Paul Grech, *Vice Pres*
EMP: 120
SQ FT: 4,500
SALES: 8.7MM **Privately Held**
WEB: www.johnplane.com
SIC: 1542 Commercial & office building, new construction

(P-1568)
JR CONSTRUCTION INC
8123 Engineer Rd, San Diego (92111-1907)
PHONE....................858 505-4760
Ramon B Camacho, *President*
EMP: 70
SALES (est): 14.8MM **Privately Held**
WEB: www.jrconstruction.net
SIC: 1542 Nonresidential construction

(P-1569)
JUNE A GROTHE
CONSTRUCTION INC
Also Called: J G Construction
15632 El Prado Rd, Chino (91710-9108)
PHONE...............................909 993-9393
Jack Grothe, *Principal*
June A Grothe, *CEO*
Wally Clark, *Vice Pres*
Nan Richardson, *Mktg Dir*
EMP: 65
SQ FT: 15,500
SALES: 32.9MM **Privately Held**
SIC: 1542 Shopping center construction

(P-1570)
KADENA PACIFIC INC
3421 Gato Ct Ste A, Riverside
(92507-6819)
PHONE...............................951 990-7865
Fred Neff, *President*
Scott Bailey, *Treasurer*
Beverly Bailey, *Admin Sec*
EMP: 50
SALES (est): 4.9MM **Privately Held**
WEB: www.kadenapacific.com
SIC: 1542 Nonresidential construction

(P-1571)
KARSYN CONSTRUCTION INC
2740 N Sunnyside Ave, Fresno
(93727-1330)
PHONE...............................559 271-2900
Joseph C Parker, *President*
Judith Parnell, *CFO*
Kristin Parker, *Corp Secy*
EMP: 60
SQ FT: 5,000
SALES (est): 12.8MM **Privately Held**
WEB: www.karsyn.com
SIC: 1542 Commercial & office building,
new construction

(P-1572)
KEENAN HOPKINS SUDER &
STOWELL
Also Called: Khss Contractors
5109 E La Palma Ave Ste A, Anaheim
(92807-2066)
PHONE...............................714 695-3670
Doug Downing, *Manager*
EMP: 100
SALES (corp-wide): 253MM **Privately**
Held
SIC: 1542 1742 Nonresidential construc-
tion; drywall
PA: Keenan, Hopkins, Suder & Stowell
Contractors, Inc.
5109 E La Palma Ave Ste A
Anaheim CA 92807
714 695-3670

(P-1573)
KIE-CON INC
3551 Wilbur Ave, Antioch (94509-8530)
PHONE...............................925 754-9494
Allen Kung, *President*
Mike Porter, *Plant Supt*
EMP: 90
SALES (est): 13.6MM
SALES (corp-wide): 16.6B **Privately Held**
SIC: 1542 Commercial & office building
contractors
HQ: Kiewit Corporation
3555 Farnam St Ste 1000
Omaha NE 68131
402 342-2052

(P-1574)
KIEWIT CORPORATION
Also Called: Keiwit Infrastructure West Co
4650 Business Center Dr, Fairfield
(94534-6890)
PHONE...............................707 439-7300
Jeff Petersen, *Branch Mgr*
Matt Gardner, *Business Mgr*
Neil Murphy, *Human Res Mgr*
Paul Devaul, *Purchasing*
Brian Gardner, *Manager*
EMP: 65
SALES (corp-wide): 16.6B **Privately Held**
SIC: 1542 Nonresidential construction

HQ: Kiewit Corporation
3555 Farnam St Ste 1000
Omaha NE 68131
402 342-2052

(P-1575)
KIEWIT CORPORATION
10704 Shoemaker Ave, Santa Fe Springs
(90670-4040)
PHONE...............................907 222-9350
EMP: 80
SALES (corp-wide): 16.6B **Privately Held**
SIC: 1542 Nonresidential construction
HQ: Kiewit Corporation
3555 Farnam St Ste 1000
Omaha NE 68131
402 342-2052

(P-1576)
KLASSEN CORPORATION (PA)
2021 Westwind Dr, Bakersfield
(93301-3015)
PHONE...............................661 327-0875
Jerry D Klassen, *President*
Troy Fringer, *CFO*
Ed Childres, *Vice Pres*
Mark Delmarter, *Vice Pres*
Robbie Smith, *Business Dir*
EMP: 70
SQ FT: 7,981
SALES (est): 27.6MM **Privately Held**
WEB: www.klassencorp.com
SIC: 1542 Commercial & office building,
new construction

(P-1577)
KPRS CONSTRUCTION
SERVICES INC (PA)
2850 Saturn St Ste 110, Brea
(92821-1701)
PHONE...............................714 672-0800
Joel H Stensby, *President*
Lev Rabinovich, *Treasurer*
Paul Kristedja, *Vice Pres*
Jeanette Koga-Horen, *General Mgr*
Brie Costello, *Admin Asst*
EMP: 95 EST: 1995
SQ FT: 31,000
SALES: 546.9MM **Privately Held**
WEB: www.kprsinc.com
SIC: 1542 8711 Commercial & office build-
ing, new construction; building construc-
tion consultant

(P-1578)
LAMON CONSTRUCTION
COMPANY INC
871 Von Geldern Way, Yuba City
(95991-4215)
P.O. Box 632 (95992-0632)
PHONE...............................530 671-1370
Henry S Lamon, *President*
Steve Ithurum, *Vice Pres*
Ken Northon, *Vice Pres*
EMP: 50 EST: 1952
SQ FT: 3,200
SALES: 7.8MM **Privately Held**
WEB: www.lamonconstruction.com
SIC: 1542 Commercial & office building,
new construction

(P-1579)
LEDESMA & MEYER CNSTR CO
INC
9441 Haven Ave, Rancho Cucamonga
(91730-5844)
PHONE...............................909 297-1100
Joseph M Ledesma, *CEO*
Kris Meyer, *Vice Pres*
Colby Meyer, *Admin Asst*
Jennifer Johnson, *Project Mgr*
Tom Smith, *Opers Staff*
EMP: 55
SALES (est): 8.1MM **Privately Held**
SIC: 1542 School building construction

(P-1580)
LEVEL 10 CONSTRUCTION LP
1050 Entp Way Ste 250, Sunnyvale
(94089)
PHONE...............................408 747-5000
Dennis Giles, *President*
Jim Evans, *CFO*
Mike Castillo, *Executive*
Jason Antone, *Engineer*

John Bunje, *Sr Project Mgr*
EMP: 220 EST: 2011
SQ FT: 12,000
SALES: 200MM **Privately Held**
SIC: 1542 Commercial & office buildings,
renovation & repair

(P-1581)
LEVEL-IT INSTALLATIONS LTD
2443 Fillmore St, San Francisco
(94115-1814)
PHONE...............................604 942-2022
Colin Rimes, *CEO*
Todd Isackson, *Admin Sec*
Angie Marston, *Manager*
EMP: 50 EST: 2014
SQ FT: 15,000
SALES: 12MM **Privately Held**
SIC: 1542 Commercial & office building
contractors
PA: Level It Installations Ltd
1515 Broadway St Unit 802
Port Coquitlam BC V3C 6
604 942-2022

(P-1582)
LMC HOLLYWOOD HIGHLAND
Also Called: Lennar Multi Family Community
95 Enterprise Ste 200, Aliso Viejo
(92656-2611)
PHONE...............................949 448-1600
Todd Farrell, *CEO*
EMP: 500 EST: 2013
SALES (est): 24.3MM **Privately Held**
SIC: 1542 Commercial & office building
contractors

(P-1583)
M & M INTERIORS INC
3410 La Sierra Ave Ste F, Riverside
(92503-5205)
PHONE...............................951 279-9535
Mark A Maes, *President*
Mark Maes, *President*
EMP: 200
SQ FT: 8,000
SALES: 6MM **Privately Held**
WEB: www.mnminteriors.com
SIC: 1542 1742 Commercial & office build-
ing contractors; drywall

(P-1584)
M P M & ASSOCIATES INC
7011 Hayvenhurst Ave F, Van Nuys
(91406-3822)
PHONE...............................818 708-9676
Parviz Danesh, *General Mgr*
EMP: 100
SQ FT: 9,000
SALES: 2MM **Privately Held**
WEB: www.mpmassociates.com
SIC: 1542 Commercial & office building,
new construction; shopping center con-
struction

(P-1585)
MALLCRAFT INC
2225 Windsor Ave, Altadena (91001-5306)
P.O. Box 91983, Pasadena (91109-1983)
PHONE...............................626 765-9100
Gerald L Fishbein, *Ch of Bd*
Leslie E Hansen, *President*
Sheena E Pappas, *Vice Pres*
Sheena Pappas, *Vice Pres*
Jill Garber, *Admin Sec*
EMP: 50
SQ FT: 5,000
SALES (est): 12.4MM **Privately Held**
WEB: www.mallcraft.com
SIC: 1542 Commercial & office building,
new construction

(P-1586)
MARK DIVERSIFIED INC
650 Howe Ave Ste 1045, Sacramento
(95825-4700)
PHONE...............................916 923-6275
David Mark, *President*
Cecil J Mark, *Officer*
EMP: 50
SQ FT: 16,000
SALES: 30MM **Privately Held**
SIC: 1542 1541 Commercial & office build-
ing, new construction; industrial buildings,
new construction

(P-1587)
MARK SCOTT CONSTRUCTION
INC (PA)
Also Called: M S
2835 Contra Costa Blvd, Pleasant Hill
(94523-4221)
P.O. Box 4658, Walnut Creek (94596-
0658)
PHONE...............................925 944-0502
Mark A Scott, *CEO*
Joe Barale, *Project Mgr*
Michael Barham, *Project Mgr*
Arnie Corral, *Project Mgr*
Vince Curtis, *Project Mgr*
EMP: 50
SQ FT: 16,000
SALES (est): 65.2MM **Privately Held**
WEB: www.msconstruction.com
SIC: 1542 Commercial & office building,
new construction

(P-1588)
MATT-COLOMBO A JOINT
VENTURE
9814 Norwalk Blvd Ste 100, Santa Fe
Springs (90670-2997)
PHONE...............................562 903-2277
Paul Matt, *Partner*
Faron Vandissel, *Manager*
EMP: 99
SALES: 950K **Privately Held**
SIC: 1542 Commercial & office building,
new construction

(P-1589)
MATTHEW BURNS
Also Called: Act Associates
617 Flower Dr, Folsom (95630-4816)
PHONE...............................209 676-4940
EMP: 60
SALES (est): 6.2MM **Privately Held**
SIC: 1542 0851

(P-1590)
MCCARTHY BLDG COMPANIES
INC
20401 Sw Birch St Ste 200, Newport Beach
(92660-1796)
PHONE...............................949 851-8383
EMP: 347
SALES (corp-wide): 3.6B **Privately Held**
SIC: 1542 1541 Institutional building con-
struction; commercial & office building,
new construction; industrial buildings,
new construction
HQ: Mccarthy Building Companies, Inc.
1341 N Rock Hill Rd
Saint Louis MO 63124
314 968-3300

(P-1591)
MCCARTHY BLDG COMPANIES
INC
Southern California Division
20401 Sw Birch St Ste 300, Newport Beach
(92660-1798)
PHONE...............................949 851-8383
Randy Highland, *Branch Mgr*
EMP: 75
SALES (corp-wide): 3.6B **Privately Held**
WEB: www.mccarthy.com
SIC: 1542 Commercial & office building
contractors
HQ: Mccarthy Building Companies, Inc.
1341 N Rock Hill Rd
Saint Louis MO 63124
314 968-3300

(P-1592)
MCCUEN CONSTRUCTION INC
(PA)
3269 Swetzer Rd, Loomis (95650-7607)
PHONE...............................916 652-7824
Trenton B McCuen, *President*
Tobi Brown, *Manager*
EMP: 50
SQ FT: 1,300
SALES (est): 10.7MM **Privately Held**
WEB: www.mccueco.com
SIC: 1542 Commercial & office building
contractors

PRODUCTS & SVCS

(P-1593)
MENEMSHA DEVELOPMENT GROUP INC (PA)
Also Called: Menemsha Cnstr Solutions
20521 Earl St, Torrance (90503-3006)
PHONE..........................310 676-6591
John V Daigle, *CEO*
Laurie Collins, *COO*
Tom Speroni, *Treasurer*
EMP: 130
SQ FT: 10,000
SALES (est) 65.7MM **Privately Held**
SIC: 1542 8741 8712 7373 Commercial & office building contractors; construction management; architectural services; computer-aided design (CAD) systems service

(P-1594)
MICHAEL REYES
Also Called: Bender Miles Construction
577 N D St Ste 111a14, San Bernardino (92401-1324)
PHONE..........................909 444-0120
Michael Reyes, *Owner*
EMP: 125
SQ FT: 1,600
SALES: 300K **Privately Held**
SIC: 1542 Nonresidential construction

(P-1595)
MICON CONSTRUCTION CAL INC
1616 Sierra Madre Cir, Placentia (92870-6626)
PHONE..........................714 666-0203
Gene F Holle, *Principal*
EMP: 54
SQ FT: 9,000
SALES (est) 9.8MM **Privately Held**
WEB: www.miconconstruction.com
SIC: 1542 1771 0782 Nonresidential construction; concrete work; landscape contractors

(P-1596)
MOOREFIELD CONSTRUCTION INC (PA)
600 N Tustin Ave Ste 210, Santa Ana (92705-3781)
PHONE..........................714 972-0700
Ann Moorefield, *CEO*
Mike Moorefield, *President*
Hal Moorefield, *Vice Pres*
Larry Moorefield, *Vice Pres*
Noel Campos, *Project Engr*
EMP: 60
SQ FT: 8,490
SALES: 112.7MM **Privately Held**
WEB: www.moorefieldconst.com
SIC: 1542 Shopping center construction; commercial & office building, new construction

(P-1597)
MTM & THOMASVILLE CO
16035 Phoenix Dr, City of Industry (91745-1624)
PHONE..........................626 934-1112
Howard Lee, *Owner*
EMP: 51
SALES (est) 2.6MM **Privately Held**
SIC: 1542 Nonresidential construction

(P-1598)
MURPHY-TRUE INC
Also Called: Jim Murphy & Associates
464 Kenwood Ct Ste B, Santa Rosa (95407-5709)
PHONE..........................707 576-7337
Jim M Murphy, *CEO*
Leighton J True III, *Vice Pres*
Danny Arrow, *Project Mgr*
Andrew Supinger, *Project Mgr*
Steve Ronchelli, *Opers Mgr*
EMP: 60
SQ FT: 5,000
SALES: 35.1MM **Privately Held**
SIC: 1542 1521 Commercial & office building, new construction; new construction, single-family houses

(P-1599)
NATIONAL CONSTRUCTION & MAINT
Also Called: NCM
23846 Sunnymead Blvd # 10, Moreno Valley (92553-7737)
PHONE..........................909 888-7042
John Omar Blanco, *CEO*
EMP: 50
SQ FT: 600
SALES (est) 16.4MM **Privately Held**
SIC: 1542 Commercial & office building contractors

(P-1600)
NEAR-CAL CORP
512 Chaney St, Lake Elsinore (92530-2747)
PHONE..........................951 245-5400
Carl J Johnson, *Ch of Bd*
Mary Saenz, *Admin Sec*
Scott Harris, *Project Mgr*
Steven Lewis, *Project Mgr*
Steve E Sanderson, *Project Mgr*
EMP: 50
SQ FT: 10,000
SALES (est) 19.1MM **Privately Held**
WEB: www.nearcal.com
SIC: 1542 1541 Commercial & office building, new construction; factory construction

(P-1601)
NEXT VENTURE INC
Also Called: Sierra Group
560 Rverdale Drv Glendale, Glendale (91204)
PHONE..........................818 637-2888
Carl Frommer, *President*
Scott Martin, *CFO*
Richard Freeman, *Exec VP*
John Stenmo, *Division Mgr*
Warren Markar, *Admin Asst*
EMP: 55
SQ FT: 7,000
SALES: 14MM **Privately Held**
SIC: 1542 Commercial & office buildings, renovation & repair

(P-1602)
NORDBY CONSTRUCTION CO
Also Called: Nordby Wine Caves
1550 Airport Blvd Ste 101, Santa Rosa (95403-1095)
PHONE..........................707 526-4500
Wendell F Nordby Jr, *Ch of Bd*
Rick Shone, *President*
Nancy C Nordby, *Admin Sec*
EMP: 50 **EST:** 1977
SQ FT: 8,000
SALES (est) 10.6MM **Privately Held**
WEB: www.nordby.net
SIC: 1542 School building construction; commercial & office building, new construction; restaurant construction; shopping center construction

(P-1603)
NOVO CONSTRUCTION INC (PA)
1460 Obrien Dr, Menlo Park (94025-1432)
PHONE..........................650 701-1500
James C Fowler, *CEO*
Jim Fowler, *President*
Rob Volpentest, *President*
Doug Ballou, *Executive*
Chuck Flynn, *Executive*
EMP: 155 **EST:** 2000
SQ FT: 10,000
SALES: 603.8MM **Privately Held**
WEB: www.novoconstruction.com
SIC: 1542 Commercial & office buildings, renovation & repair

(P-1604)
OLIVER & COMPANY INC
1300 S 51st St, Richmond (94804-4628)
PHONE..........................510 412-9090
Steven Henri Oliver, *CEO*
Steve Cetrone, *Vice Pres*
Josh Oliver, *Vice Pres*
Jeff Shields, *Vice Pres*
Nicole Sprague, *Executive Asst*
▲ **EMP:** 90
SQ FT: 6,302

SALES (est) 45.8MM **Privately Held**
WEB: www.oliverandco.net
SIC: 1542 Commercial & office building, new construction

(P-1605)
PAAT & KIMMEL DEVELOPMENT INC
1490 S Vineyard Ave Ste D, Ontario (91761-8043)
PHONE..........................909 315-8074
Victor Paat, *CEO*
EMP: 60 **EST:** 2014
SALES (est) 12MM **Privately Held**
SIC: 1542 Commercial & office building, new construction

(P-1606)
PACIFIC BUILDING GROUP (PA)
9752 Aspen Creek Ct # 100, San Diego (92126-1082)
PHONE..........................858 552-0600
Gregory A Rogers, *CEO*
Jim Roherty, *President*
Lisa Hitt, *CFO*
Wayne Hickey, *Exec VP*
William Hansen, *Vice Pres*
▲ **EMP:** 190
SQ FT: 17,880
SALES: 52MM **Privately Held**
WEB: www.pacificbuildinggroup.com
SIC: 1542 Commercial & office building, new construction

(P-1607)
PACIFIC ENGINEERING BUILDERS
1009 Terra Nova Blvd, Pacifica (94044-4308)
PHONE..........................650 557-1238
John Chan, *President*
Kennedy Chan, *Treasurer*
Ada Lee, *Admin Sec*
EMP: 85
SALES (est) 7.3MM **Privately Held**
SIC: 1542 Commercial & office buildings, renovation & repair

(P-1608)
PACIFIC STTES ENVMTL CNTRS INC
11555 Dublin Blvd, Dublin (94568-2854)
P.O. Box 11357, Pleasanton (94588-1357)
PHONE..........................925 803-4333
Robert E McCarrick, *CEO*
Ernie Lampkin, *Treasurer*
Robert Ludden, *Foreman/Supr*
Jeff Moore, *Sr Project Mgr*
Robin Gomes, *Manager*
EMP: 50
SQ FT: 2,000
SALES (est) 16.1MM **Privately Held**
WEB: www.pacificstates.net
SIC: 1542 1791 1794 8744 Nonresidential construction; storage tanks, metal: erection; excavation & grading, building construction;

(P-1609)
PARAMOUNT BLDG SOLUTIONS LLC
4741 Pell Dr Ste 3, Sacramento (95838-2048)
PHONE..........................916 564-4102
Glen Kucera, *Branch Mgr*
EMP: 158
SALES (corp-wide): 149.9MM **Privately Held**
SIC: 1542 Commercial & office building contractors
PA: Paramount Building Solutions, Llc
10235 S 51st St Ste 185
Phoenix AZ 85044
480 348-1177

(P-1610)
PARKCO BUILDING COMPANY
3190 Airport Loop Dr F, Costa Mesa (92626-3408)
PHONE..........................714 444-1441
W Adrian Hoyle, *President*
Joel Templeton, *Project Mgr*
EMP: 99

SALES (est) 10.1MM **Privately Held**
SIC: 1542 1771 1799 Commercial & office building, new construction; garage construction; foundation & footing contractor; erection & dismantling of forms for poured concrete

(P-1611)
PARSONS GVRNMNT SVCS INTL INC
100 W Walnut St, Pasadena (91124-0001)
PHONE..........................626 440-6000
Thomas L Roell, *President*
Curtis A Bower, *Exec VP*
Gary L Stone, *Senior VP*
Laura York, *Executive Asst*
EMP: 268 **EST:** 1969
SALES: 408.1MM
SALES (corp-wide): 3.1B **Privately Held**
SIC: 1542 Commercial & office building, new construction
PA: The Parsons Corporation
100 W Walnut St
Pasadena CA 91124
626 440-2000

(P-1612)
PCL CONSTRUCTION SERVICES INC
500 N Brand Blvd Ste 1500, Glendale (91203-3938)
PHONE..........................818 246-3481
Dale Kain, *Manager*
Stamp Paula, *Business Mgr*
Dan Sliter, *Business Mgr*
Ashley Eighmy, *Receptionist*
EMP: 191
SQ FT: 17,619 **Privately Held**
SIC: 1542 Commercial & office building, new construction
HQ: Pcl Construction Services, Inc.
2000 S Colorado Blvd 2-500
Denver CO 80222
303 365-6500

(P-1613)
PENWAL INDUSTRIES INC
10611 Acacia St, Rancho Cucamonga (91730-5410)
PHONE..........................909 466-1555
Chris A Pennington, *Principal*
▲ **EMP:** 100
SQ FT: 65,000
SALES (est) 21.8MM **Privately Held**
WEB: www.penwal.com
SIC: 1542 3999 8742 3993 Shopping center construction; advertising display products; management consulting services; signs & advertising specialties

(P-1614)
PERRY COAST CONSTRUCTION INC
Also Called: West Coast Construction
14457 Meridian Pkwy, Riverside (92518-3007)
PHONE..........................951 774-0677
Robert Perry, *President*
Erin Perry, *Treasurer*
Britney Perry, *Admin Sec*
EMP: 105
SQ FT: 10,000
SALES: 21.3MM **Privately Held**
SIC: 1542 Restaurant construction

(P-1615)
PHILMONT MANAGEMENT INC
3450 Wilshire Blvd # 850, Los Angeles (90010-2211)
PHONE..........................213 380-0159
Monica Nam, *President*
EMP: 99 **EST:** 1997
SQ FT: 6,000
SALES: 5MM **Privately Held**
SIC: 1542 Commercial & office building, new construction

(P-1616)
PINNACLE CONTRACTING CORP
21800 Burbank Blvd # 210, Woodland Hills (91367-6470)
PHONE..........................818 888-6548
Mark Tieman, *CEO*
Mark A Tieman, *President*

▲ = Import ▼=Export
◆ =Import/Export

Iral Meyerhoff, *CFO*
Michael Grossman, *Chairman*
Susan Berson, *Vice Pres*
EMP: 50
SQ FT: 3,500
SALES (est): 11.3MM **Privately Held**
WEB: www.pincon.com
SIC: 1542 Commercial & office buildings, renovation & repair

(P-1617)
PINNER CONSTRUCTION CO INC (PA)
1255 S Lewis St, Anaheim (92805-6424)
PHONE................714 490-4000
John Pinner, *President*
Dirk Griffin, *CFO*
Johnny R Pinner, *Vice Pres*
Gary Myers, *Executive*
Teresa Parks, *Office Mgr*
▲ **EMP:** 75
SQ FT: 6,700
SALES: 99.4MM **Privately Held**
WEB: www.pinnerconstruction.com
SIC: 1542 Commercial & office building, new construction; hospital construction; stadium construction

(P-1618)
PLATINUM CONSTRUCTION INC
865 S East St, Anaheim (92805-5356)
PHONE................714 527-0700
Darrin W Streilein, *President*
Jim Hutchison, *Controller*
Jim Jensen, *Sls & Mktg Exec*
EMP: 100
SALES (est): 17MM **Privately Held**
SIC: 1542 1541 1742 Commercial & office building contractors; steel building construction; plastering, drywall & insulation

(P-1619)
PREFERRED CONSTRUCTION CO INC
5199 E Pacific Coast Hwy, Long Beach (90804-3309)
PHONE................714 630-3004
Thomas Cordova, *President*
▲ **EMP:** 60
SQ FT: 4,000
SALES (est): 7.5MM **Privately Held**
SIC: 1542 Commercial & office buildings, renovation & repair

(P-1620)
PRS/ROEBBELEN JV
4811 Tunis Rd, Sacramento (95835-1007)
PHONE................916 641-0324
EMP: 50
SALES (est): 5.2MM **Privately Held**
SIC: 1542

(P-1621)
QUIRING CORPORATION
5118 E Clinton Way # 201, Fresno (93727-2094)
PHONE................559 432-2800
Paul K Quiring, *President*
Greg Quiring, *Treasurer*
Kirk Miyake, *Controller*
Jim Kennedy, *Director*
Sue Kliewer, *Director*
EMP: 62
SQ FT: 4,000
SALES (est): 15.9MM **Privately Held**
WEB: www.quiring.com
SIC: 1542 Commercial & office building, new construction

(P-1622)
QUIRING GENERAL LLC
Also Called: Construction
5118 E Clinton Way # 201, Fresno (93727-2088)
PHONE................559 432-2800
Greg A Quiring, *Mng Member*
Paul Quiring, *CEO*
John Wood, *CFO*
Brian Reitz, *Asst Controller*
Kirk Miyake, *Controller*
EMP: 80
SQ FT: 6,200
SALES: 46MM **Privately Held**
SIC: 1542 Commercial & office building, new construction

(P-1623)
R J DAUM CONSTRUCTION CO (PA)
11581 Monarch St, Garden Grove (92841-1814)
PHONE................714 894-4300
Harold I Perong, *President*
Mark Perong, *CFO*
Christina M Perong, *Admin Sec*
Michelle A Perong, *Admin Sec*
EMP: 120
SQ FT: 10,000
SALES: 23.4MM **Privately Held**
SIC: 1542 Hospital construction; school building construction

(P-1624)
R J M CONSTRUCTION INC
224 Donna Dr, Redlands (92374-5526)
PHONE................909 794-8853
Belinda Marin, *Corp Secy*
Roger Marin, *President*
EMP: 50
SALES (est): 3.4MM **Privately Held**
SIC: 1542 Commercial & office building contractors

(P-1625)
RANCHWOOD CONTRACTORS INC
923 E Pacheco Blvd, Los Banos (93635-4327)
PHONE................209 826-6200
Greg Hostetler, *President*
Catherine Hostetler, *Corp Secy*
EMP: 80
SQ FT: 3,500
SALES (est): 14.6MM **Privately Held**
SIC: 1542 1521 Commercial & office building, new construction; new construction, single-family houses

(P-1626)
RANSOME COMPANY
1933 Williams St, San Leandro (94577-2303)
P.O. Box 2177 (94577-0217)
PHONE................510 686-9900
Myles Oberto, *Ch of Bd*
Geoff Raaka, *President*
Peter Scott, *Vice Pres*
EMP: 50
SALES (est): 8MM **Privately Held**
WEB: www.ransomeco.com
SIC: 1542 Nonresidential construction

(P-1627)
RED ONE - PSI JOINT VENTR LLC
310 W Murray Ave, Visalia (93291-4937)
PHONE................559 772-8264
Reynaldo Ruiz, *Partner*
Angelina Derossett, *Manager*
EMP: 50
SALES (est): 2.4MM **Privately Held**
SIC: 1542 1541 Commercial & office buildings, renovation & repair; hospital construction; school building construction; renovation, remodeling & repairs: industrial buildings

(P-1628)
REEVE-KNIGHT CONSTRUCTION INC
128 Ascot Dr, Roseville (95661-3422)
PHONE................916 786-5112
Robert H Reeve, *CEO*
Joe E Knight, *President*
Cynthia Knight, *Treasurer*
M Kathy Reeve, *Admin Sec*
Christine Tadlock, *Admin Asst*
EMP: 75
SQ FT: 9,200
SALES (est): 45.7MM **Privately Held**
WEB: www.reeve-knight.com
SIC: 1542 Commercial & office building, new construction; commercial & office buildings, renovation & repair

(P-1629)
RESOURCE ENVIRONMENTAL INC
6634 Schilling Ave, Long Beach (90805-1745)
PHONE................562 468-7000
Jared Sloan Cooper, *President*
Leticia Covarrubias, *Office Mgr*
EMP: 75
SQ FT: 4,400
SALES: 10MM **Privately Held**
SIC: 1542 Nonresidential construction

(P-1630)
RHC EQUIPMENT LLC
5237 Mallard Estates Rd, Chico (95973-9524)
PHONE................530 892-1918
Randy Hill, *Manager*
EMP: 50
SALES: 85K **Privately Held**
SIC: 1542 Nonresidential construction

(P-1631)
RMR CONSTRUCTION COMPANY
2424 Oakdale Ave, San Francisco (94124-1581)
PHONE................415 647-0884
Ray Reinertson Jr, *President*
Robert Reinertson, *Vice Pres*
Marie Reinertson, *Admin Sec*
EMP: 140
SQ FT: 12,000
SALES (est): 33.2MM **Privately Held**
SIC: 1542 Commercial & office buildings, renovation & repair

(P-1632)
RMS GROUP INC
17802 Mitchell N, Irvine (92614-6004)
PHONE................714 373-4882
Russel W McDaniel, *President*
EMP: 75 EST: 2000
SQ FT: 14,000
SALES (est): 8.3MM **Privately Held**
SIC: 1542 Commercial & office building, new construction

(P-1633)
ROBERT CLAPPER CNSTR SVCS INC
Also Called: RC Construction Services
2223 N Locust Ave, Rialto (92377-4113)
PHONE................909 829-3688
Robert W Clapper, *Principal*
Rebecca Clapper, *Corp Secy*
Howard Brissette, *Project Mgr*
Rich Negley, *Project Mgr*
Kimberly Hall, *Human Res Mgr*
EMP: 100
SALES: 35MM **Privately Held**
WEB: www.rcconstructionservices.com
SIC: 1542 Commercial & office building, new construction

(P-1634)
ROEBBELEN CONSTRUCTION INC
1241 Hawks Flight Ct, El Dorado Hills (95762-9648)
PHONE................916 939-4000
Hans J Roebbelen, *CEO*
Kenneth Roebbelen, *President*
Erin Anderson, *CFO*
Dennis Daniell, *CFO*
David Thuleen, *Exec VP*
EMP: 80
SQ FT: 25,000
SALES (est): 17.7MM **Privately Held**
SIC: 1542 1541 Commercial & office building, new construction; industrial buildings & warehouses

(P-1635)
ROEBBELEN CONTRACTING INC
1241 Hawks Flight Ct, El Dorado Hills (95762-9648)
PHONE................916 939-4000
Kenneth Wenham, *President*
Robert McLean, *COO*
Bruce Stimson, *CFO*
Dennis Daniell, *Officer*

Bob Kjome, *Exec VP*
EMP: 350
SQ FT: 28,000
SALES: 248MM **Privately Held**
SIC: 1542 1541 8741 Commercial & office building, new construction; industrial buildings & warehouses; construction management

(P-1636)
RORE INC (PA)
5151 Shoreham Pl Ste 260, San Diego (92122-5962)
PHONE................858 404-7393
Gita Murthy, *CEO*
Nandita Murthy, *Controller*
EMP: 64
SQ FT: 3,500
SALES: 16MM **Privately Held**
WEB: www.roreinc.com
SIC: 1542 1541 4959 Commercial & office building, new construction; commercial & office buildings, renovation & repair; renovation, remodeling & repairs: industrial buildings; toxic or hazardous waste cleanup

(P-1637)
RUDOLPH AND SLETTEN INC (HQ)
2 Circle Star Way Fl 4, San Carlos (94070-6200)
PHONE................650 216-3600
Martin B Sisemore, *President*
Dan Dolinar, *Exec VP*
Paul Aherne, *Vice Pres*
Jonathan Foad, *Vice Pres*
Michael Mohrman, *Vice Pres*
EMP: 100 EST: 1960
SQ FT: 47,000
SALES: 1.3B
SALES (corp-wide): 4.7B **Publicly Held**
WEB: www.rsconstruction.com
SIC: 1542 1541 Commercial & office building, new construction; industrial buildings & warehouses
PA: Tutor Perini Corporation
15901 Olden St
Sylmar CA 91342
818 362-8391

(P-1638)
S J AMOROSO CNSTR CO INC (PA)
390 Bridge Pkwy, Redwood City (94065-1061)
PHONE................650 654-1900
Dana McManus, *Ch of Bd*
Robert Erskine, *Vice Pres*
Kim Altamirano, *Executive*
Mike Cleveland, *Executive*
Sandra Bagoje, *Executive Asst*
EMP: 400
SQ FT: 22,500
SALES (est): 158.5MM **Privately Held**
SIC: 1542 Commercial & office building, new construction

(P-1639)
SAFEWAY STORES INCORPORATED
750 Walsh Ave, Santa Clara (95050-2613)
PHONE................408 719-9460
Marc Wilson, *Owner*
EMP: 73
SALES (corp-wide): 59.9B **Privately Held**
SIC: 1542 1522 Commercial & office building, new construction; residential construction
HQ: Safeway Stores, Incorporated
5918 Stoneridge Mall Rd
Pleasanton CA 94588
925 467-3000

(P-1640)
SAVANT CONSTRUCTION INC
13830 Mountain Ave, Chino (91710-9014)
P.O. Box 636 (91708-0636)
PHONE................909 614-4300
John L Aldridge, *President*
Brad Hastings, *Corp Secy*
Darren Nowicki, *Vice Pres*
Penny Rodela, *Admin Asst*
EMP: 52
SQ FT: 36,000

SALES (est): 22.8MM **Privately Held**
WEB: www.savantconst.com
SIC: **1542** Commercial & office building,
new construction

(P-1641)
SC BUILDERS INC (PA)
910 Thompson Pl, Sunnyvale
(94085-4517)
PHONE..............................408 328-0688
Samuel B Abbey, *CEO*
Chris Smither, *Vice Pres*
Sam Abbey, *Executive*
Joe Ascolese, *Project Mgr*
Greg Burda, *Project Mgr*
EMP: 55
SALES (est): 35.9MM **Privately Held**
WEB: www.scbuilders.com
SIC: **1542** 1611 8711 Custom builders,
non-residential; general contractor, high-
way & street construction; building con-
struction consultant

(P-1642)
SD DEACON CORP CALIFORNIA
7745 Greenback Ln Ste 250, Citrus Heights
(95610-5865)
PHONE..............................916 969-0900
Richard G Smith, *President*
Robert K Aroyan, *Vice Pres*
Paul B Cunha, *Vice Pres*
Brett Mykrantz, *Vice Pres*
EMP: 70
SALES (est): 5.3MM
SALES (corp-wide): 391.5MM **Privately Held**
SIC: **1542** Nonresidential construction
PA: Deacon Holdings, Inc.
7745 Greenback Ln Ste 250
Citrus Heights CA 95610
916 969-0900

(P-1643)
SERVICE FIRST CONTRACTORS
2510 N Grand Ave Ste 110, Santa Ana
(92705-8754)
PHONE..............................714 573-2200
Mark Bucher, *CEO*
Frank Vanderberg, *President*
Stan Hatch, *Treasurer*
Gary Bucher, *Admin Sec*
EMP: 50
SQ FT: 6,500
SALES (est): 14.1MM **Privately Held**
SIC: **1542** 1522 6512 Commercial & of-
fice building contractors; residential con-
struction; nonresidential building
operators

(P-1644)
SEVERSON GROUP INCORPORATED (PA)
3601 Serpentine Dr, Los Alamitos
(90720-2440)
PHONE..............................562 493-3611
Jonathan Edward Severson, *President*
Brian Cresap, *Treasurer*
Scott Feest, *Vice Pres*
Robert Severson, *Vice Pres*
EMP: 76
SQ FT: 15,000
SALES (est): 10MM **Privately Held**
WEB: www.millieseverson.com
SIC: **1542** 1541 Commercial & office build-
ing, new construction; hospital construc-
tion; institutional building construction;
industrial buildings, new construction

(P-1645)
SHAWMUT WOODWORKING & SUP INC
Also Called: Shawmut Design and Cnstr
11390 W Olympic Blvd Fl 2, Los Angeles
(90064-1607)
PHONE..............................323 602-1000
Leonard Porzio, *Principal*
EMP: 145
SALES (corp-wide): 1.1B **Privately Held**
SIC: **1542** Commercial & office building
contractors; commercial & office building,
new construction
PA: Shawmut Woodworking & Supply, Inc.
560 Harrison Ave Ste 200
Boston MA 02118
617 622-7000

(P-1646)
SIERRA PACIFIC WEST INC
2125 La Mirada Dr, Vista (92081-8830)
P.O. Box 231640, Encinitas (92023-1640)
PHONE..............................760 599-0755
Sandra L Brown, *CEO*
Tom Brown, *President*
Chad Sheridan, *Project Mgr*
Karen Gohringer, *Receptionist*
EMP: 56
SALES (est): 16.3MM **Privately Held**
WEB: www.sierrapacificwest.com
SIC: **1542** 1611 Nonresidential construc-
tion; highway & street construction

(P-1647)
SIGMA SERVICES INC (PA)
2140 Eastman Ave Ste 110, Ventura
(93003-7786)
P.O. Box 368, Goleta (93116-0368)
PHONE..............................805 642-8377
Vivian Solodkin, *President*
Louie Valenzuala, *CFO*
Benjamin Valenzuela Jr, *Vice Pres*
EMP: 60
SQ FT: 4,200
SALES (est): 12.8MM **Privately Held**
WEB: www.sigmaconstruction.net
SIC: **1542** 6531 7349 1731 Commercial
& office building contractors; real estate
managers; janitorial service, contract
basis; electrical work; facilities support
services

(P-1648)
SILVER CREEK INDUSTRIES INC
2830 Barrett Ave, Perris (92571-3258)
PHONE..............................951 943-5393
Brett D Bashaw, *CEO*
Micheal Rhodes, *Corp Secy*
Bill Bonnett, *Administration*
EMP: 175
SQ FT: 25,000
SALES (est): 89.1MM **Privately Held**
WEB: www.silver-creek.net
SIC: **1542** 2452 Commercial & office build-
ing contractors; prefabricated wood build-
ings; prefabricated buildings, wood

(P-1649)
SILVERLINE CONSTRUCTION INC
1421 W 132nd St, Gardena (90249-2105)
PHONE..............................310 464-8314
Michael Murphy, *CEO*
EMP: 220
SALES (est): 38.8MM **Privately Held**
WEB: www.pyramidbuilders.com
SIC: **1542** Commercial & office building,
new construction

(P-1650)
SIMMONS CONSTRUCTION INC
19252 Flypath Way, Bakersfield (93308)
PHONE..............................661 636-1321
Charles J Simmons, *President*
Evalee Simmons, *Vice Pres*
EMP: 50
SALES (est): 17.8MM **Privately Held**
SIC: **1542** Commercial & office building,
new construction

(P-1651)
SINANIAN DEVELOPMENT INC
18980 Ventura Blvd # 200, Tarzana
(91356-3228)
PHONE..............................818 996-9666
Antranik Sinanian, *CEO*
Harry Sinanian, *Shareholder*
Sinan Sinanian, *President*
Andy Sinanian, *Co-President*
EMP: 70
SQ FT: 4,000
SALES (est): 27.1MM **Privately Held**
SIC: **1542** 1522 6552 Commercial & of-
fice building, new construction; residential
construction; subdividers & developers

(P-1652)
SKYLINE COMMERCIAL INTERIORS (PA)
Also Called: Skyline Construction
505 Sansome St Fl 7, San Francisco
(94111-3108)
PHONE..............................415 908-1020
David Hayes, *CEO*
Rick Millitello, *President*
Randy Scott, *Senior VP*
Howard Fish, *Vice Pres*
Matt Slayen, *Executive*
EMP: 80
SQ FT: 9,000
SALES: 136MM **Privately Held**
WEB: www.skylineconst.com
SIC: **1542** Commercial & office buildings,
renovation & repair

(P-1653)
SMP CONSTRUCTION & MAINT INC (PA)
Also Called: Foundation Repair of CA
1813 Rutan Dr Ste A, Livermore
(94551-7639)
PHONE..............................925 961-9012
Mark Phelps, *CEO*
Matthew Phelps, *President*
Brett Parise, *Accountant*
EMP: 65
SALES (est): 9.1MM **Privately Held**
SIC: **1542** 1521 Commercial & office build-
ing contractors; single-family housing
construction

(P-1654)
SNYDER LANGSTON L P
Also Called: Snyder Langston
17962 Cowan, Irvine (92614-6026)
PHONE..............................949 863-9200
Stephen Jones, *Chm Emeritus*
Jason Rich, *President*
John F Rochford, *CEO*
Gary Campanaro, *CFO*
Richard Cavecche, *Vice Pres*
EMP: 70
SQ FT: 16,000
SALES: 413MM **Privately Held**
WEB: www.snyderlangston.com
SIC: **1542** 8742 1522 Commercial & of-
fice building, new construction; real estate
consultant; residential construction

(P-1655)
SO CALIFORNIA VENTURES LTD
1101 Richfield Rd, Placentia (92870-6790)
PHONE..............................714 524-0021
John T Palazzo, *President*
EMP: 80
SALES (est): 8.9MM **Privately Held**
SIC: **1542** Commercial & office building
contractors

(P-1656)
SOLPAC INC
Also Called: Soltek Pacific
2424 Congress St, San Diego
(92110-2819)
PHONE..............................619 296-6247
Stephen W Thompson, *CEO*
Dave Carlin, *President*
John Myers, *Senior VP*
Kevin Cammall, *Vice Pres*
Nicole Greed, *Business Dir*
EMP: 112
SQ FT: 7,386
SALES (est): 59.7MM **Privately Held**
SIC: **1542** Commercial & office building,
new construction; commercial & office
buildings, renovation & repair

(P-1657)
SOUTH COAST PIERING INC
Also Called: Saber
41357 Date St, Murrieta (92562-7030)
PHONE..............................800 922-2488
Franz M Froehlich, *CEO*
Brooke Morgan, *Marketing Staff*
EMP: 70
SALES: 8.5MM **Privately Held**
SIC: **1542** Commercial & office buildings,
renovation & repair

(P-1658)
SPAN CONSTRUCTION & ENGRG INC (PA)
1841 Howard Rd, Madera (93637-5122)
PHONE..............................559 661-1111
King F Husein, *CEO*
George Goddard, *President*
Firoz Mohamed Husein, *CEO*
Douglas M Standing, *Admin Sec*
▼ EMP: 100 EST: 1979
SQ FT: 120,000
SALES (est): 95.8MM **Privately Held**
WEB: www.spanconstruction.com
SIC: **1542** 1541 1791 Commercial & of-
fice buildings, prefabricated erection; agri-
cultural building contractors; industrial
buildings, new construction; structural
steel erection

(P-1659)
STREAMLINE FINISHES INC
26429 Rancho Pkwy S # 140, Lake Forest
(92630-8330)
PHONE..............................949 600-8964
William Seidel, *President*
EMP: 80 EST: 2004
SQ FT: 6,000
SALES (est): 13.9MM **Privately Held**
SIC: **1542** Commercial & office building
contractors

(P-1660)
STRONGHOLD ENGINEERING INC (PA)
2000 Market St, Riverside (92501-1769)
PHONE..............................951 684-9303
Beverly A Bailey, *President*
Scott Bailey, *Vice Pres*
Kamel Khalil, *Vice Pres*
Patricia McNicholas, *Risk Mgmt Dir*
Marco Morales, *Project Engr*
EMP: 250
SQ FT: 21,000
SALES (est): 156.7MM **Privately Held**
SIC: **1542** Specialized public building con-
tractors

(P-1661)
SUFFOLK CONSTRUCTION CO INC
550 S Hope St Ste 700, Los Angeles
(90071-2649)
PHONE..............................949 453-9400
Barbara Hescock, *Director*
Donald Fraser, *Vice Pres*
EMP: 90
SALES (corp-wide): 2.4B **Privately Held**
WEB: www.suffolkconstruction.com
SIC: **1542** Commercial & office building,
new construction
PA: Suffolk Construction Company, Inc.
65 Allerton St
Boston MA 02119
617 445-3500

(P-1662)
SUMMER SYSTEMS INC
28942 Hancock Pkwy, Valencia
(91355-1069)
PHONE..............................661 257-4419
Don London, *President*
Connie London, *Admin Sec*
EMP: 80
SQ FT: 20,000
SALES (est): 22.8MM **Privately Held**
WEB: www.summersystemsinc.com
SIC: **1542** Nonresidential construction

(P-1663)
SWINERTON BLDRS PACIFIC R
16798 W Bernardo Dr, San Diego
(92127-1904)
PHONE..............................619 954-8011
Mark Payne, *Principal*
EMP: 65
SALES (est): 8.6MM **Privately Held**
SIC: **1542** Nonresidential construction

(P-1664)
SWINERTON BUILDERS
865 S Figueroa St # 3000, Los Angeles
(90017-3009)
PHONE..............................213 896-3400
Gust Soteropulos, *Branch Mgr*
EMP: 100 **Privately Held**

▲ = Import ▼=Export
◆ =Import/Export

SIC: 1542 1541 Commercial & office building, new construction; industrial buildings & warehouses
HQ: Swinerton Builders
260 Townsend St
San Francisco CA 94107
415 421-2980

(P-1665)
SWINERTON BUILDERS HC
Also Called: HMH BUILDERS
15 Business Park Way # 101, Sacramento (95828-0959)
PHONE..................................916 383-4825
Gary J Rafferty, *Ch of Bd*
Eric M Foster, *President*
Leonard J Bischel, *CFO*
Frank Foellmer, *Exec VP*
Linda J Schowalter, *Senior VP*
EMP: 150
SQ FT: 25,000
SALES: 26.6MM **Privately Held**
WEB: www.hmh.com
SIC: 1542 Commercial & office building, new construction; hospital construction; institutional building construction
PA: Swinerton Incorporated
260 Townsend St
San Francisco CA 94107
-

(P-1666)
SWINERTON INCORPORATED (PA)
260 Townsend St, San Francisco (94107-1719)
PHONE..................................415 421-2980
Jeffrey C Hoopes, *CEO*
Gary J Rafferty, *President*
Linda G Showalter, *CFO*
Frank Foellmer, *Exec VP*
Eric M Foster, *Exec VP*
▲ EMP: 200
SQ FT: 66,943
SALES: 3.3B **Privately Held**
SIC: 1542 1541 6531 1522 Commercial & office building, new construction; industrial buildings & warehouses; real estate managers; residential construction

(P-1667)
TASLIMI CONSTRUCTION CO INC
1805 Colorado Ave, Santa Monica (90404-3411)
PHONE..................................310 447-3000
Shidan Taslimi, *Principal*
Mehran Taslimi, *Vice Pres*
Shawn Fatemi, *Executive*
Susanne Taslimi, *Admin Sec*
Thomas Aldrich, *Project Mgr*
EMP: 66
SQ FT: 8,500
SALES (est): 24.4MM **Privately Held**
SIC: 1542 Commercial & office building, new construction; commercial & office buildings, renovation & repair

(P-1668)
TAYLOR BAILEY INC
355 Lafata St Ste E, Saint Helena (94574-1413)
PHONE..................................707 967-8090
Mike Digiulio, *President*
Robert Covey, *Vice Pres*
Gerald Eastman, *Vice Pres*
EMP: 60
SQ FT: 2,000
SALES (est): 10.5MM **Privately Held**
WEB: www.baileyandtaylor.com
SIC: 1542 Agricultural building contractors

(P-1669)
TAYLOR STRUCTURES INC
905 Cotting Ln Ste 100, Vacaville (95688-8777)
PHONE..................................707 499-6870
Ridley Taylor, *President*
Scott Taylor, *Vice Pres*
EMP: 75
SQ FT: 3,000
SALES (est): 8.9MM **Privately Held**
SIC: 1542 Commercial & office building, new construction

(P-1670)
TCG BUILDERS INC
Also Called: Core Group, The
890 N Mccarthy Blvd # 100, Milpitas (95035-5127)
PHONE..................................408 321-6450
Andrew W Meade, *CEO*
Timothy Tempel, *President*
Jillian Dressel, *Corp Secy*
Robert Wagle, *Vice Pres*
EMP: 50
SQ FT: 6,000
SALES (est): 14.1MM **Privately Held**
SIC: 1542 Commercial & office building contractors; commercial & office building, new construction; commercial & office buildings, renovation & repair

(P-1671)
TECHNO COATINGS INC
795 Debra St, Anaheim (92805)
PHONE..................................714 774-4671
Michael Birney, *President*
EMP: 150
SALES (corp-wide): 109.2MM **Privately Held**
WEB: www.technocoatings.com
SIC: 1542 1629 1721 1799 Commercial & office buildings, renovation & repair; blasting contractor, except building demolition; painting & paper hanging; wallcovering contractors; coating of concrete structures with plastic; coating of metal structures at construction site; waterproofing
PA: Techno Coatings, Inc.
1391 S Allec St
Anaheim CA 92805
714 635-1130

(P-1672)
TEMALPAKH INC
Also Called: Works Floor & Wall, The
979 S Gene Autry Trl, Palm Springs (92264-3464)
PHONE..................................760 770-5778
Gerald A Flowers, *CEO*
Michael Collins, *Vice Pres*
Rusty Harling, *Admin Sec*
Steve Isen, *Contractor*
EMP: 65
SQ FT: 13,000
SALES (est): 14.5MM **Privately Held**
SIC: 1542 5713 5211 Commercial & office buildings, renovation & repair; floor covering stores; tile, ceramic

(P-1673)
THE NEVELL GROUP INC (PA)
Also Called: N G I
3001 Enterprise St # 200, Brea (92821-6210)
PHONE..................................714 579-7501
Michael J Nevell, *President*
Bryan Bodine, *CFO*
Therese Belisle, *Exec VP*
Bruce Pasqua, *Senior VP*
Greg Thomas, *Vice Pres*
EMP: 250
SQ FT: 35,000
SALES (est): 109.5MM **Privately Held**
SIC: 1542 Commercial & office building, new construction

(P-1674)
TILLER CONSTRUCTORS PARTNR INC
306 W Katella Ave Ste A, Orange (92867-4755)
PHONE..................................714 771-5600
Lin Lindstedt, *President*
Kerry Evert, *Vice Pres*
Patty Baker, *Manager*
Randy Abelar, *Supervisor*
EMP: 64
SQ FT: 4,000
SALES (est): 26.8MM **Privately Held**
WEB: www.tillerconstructors.com
SIC: 1542 Institutional building construction; commercial & office building contractors

(P-1675)
TOTAL BUILDING CARE INC
21228 Norwalk Blvd, Hawaiian Gardens (90716-1021)
PHONE..................................562 467-8333
Yong A Kim, *CEO*
Yong Kim, *CEO*
Colin Oconnell, *Vice Pres*
Tracy Bennett, *Regional Mgr*
Sean Simoskevitz, *Manager*
EMP: 70
SALES (est): 10.1MM **Privately Held**
WEB: www.totalbuildingcare.com
SIC: 1542 Commercial & office buildings, renovation & repair

(P-1676)
TRENDEX CORPORATION
9353 Eton Ave, Chatsworth (91311-5810)
PHONE..................................818 407-9600
William Vincent, *President*
Janet Ayers, *Treasurer*
April Helvig, *Office Mgr*
EMP: 60
SQ FT: 3,500
SALES: 11MM **Privately Held**
SIC: 1542 1742 Commercial & office building contractors; drywall

(P-1677)
TRICORP CONSTRUCTION INC (PA)
Also Called: Tricorp Hearn Construction
1030 G St, Sacramento (95814-0823)
PHONE..................................916 779-8010
Steve Hunter, *President*
Tony Moayed, *Vice Pres*
Jeannine H Long, *Business Dir*
Ken Cohen, *Principal*
Kasey Edling, *Assistant*
EMP: 60
SQ FT: 10,000
SALES (est): 28.6MM **Privately Held**
WEB: www.tricorpconstruction.com
SIC: 1542 1521 Commercial & office building, new construction; single-family housing construction

(P-1678)
TRITON STRUCTURAL CONCRETE INC
15435 Innovation Dr # 100, San Diego (92128-3443)
PHONE..................................858 866-2450
Tim Penick, *President*
Mitch Miller, *Project Mgr*
Khanna Tsymuk, *Project Mgr*
Mary Ann Wilson, *Controller*
Zulfecar McDoom, *QC Mgr*
EMP: 250
SALES: 57.5MM **Privately Held**
SIC: 1542 Commercial & office building, new construction

(P-1679)
TRUEBECK CONSTRUCTION INC (PA)
201 Redwood Shores Pkwy # 125, Redwood City (94065-1134)
PHONE..................................650 227-1957
David C Becker, *President*
Brad Bastian, *Shareholder*
Jeff Nielson, *Shareholder*
Kathy Reiner, *CFO*
Sean Truedale, *Vice Pres*
EMP: 50
SQ FT: 6,000
SALES (est): 21.1MM **Privately Held**
SIC: 1542 Commercial & office building, new construction; custom builders, non-residential

(P-1680)
TURELK INC
Also Called: Turelk San Diego
11622 El Camino Real # 100, San Diego (92130-2049)
PHONE..................................858 633-8085
Michael Turi, *Branch Mgr*
EMP: 85
SALES (corp-wide): 110MM **Privately Held**
SIC: 1542 Commercial & office buildings, renovation & repair

PA: Turelk, Inc.
3700 Santa Fe Ave Ste 200
Long Beach CA 90810
310 835-3736

(P-1681)
TURELK INC (PA)
3700 Santa Fe Ave Ste 200, Long Beach (90810-2169)
P.O. Box 93101 (90809-3101)
PHONE..................................310 835-3736
Michael G Turi, *CEO*
Michael R Paselk, *President*
Michael Paselk, *Exec VP*
Fred Capper, *Vice Pres*
Earl Lund, *Vice Pres*
EMP: 110
SQ FT: 14,000
SALES: 110MM **Privately Held**
WEB: www.turelk.com
SIC: 1542 Commercial & office building, new construction

(P-1682)
TURNER CONSTRUCTION COMPANY
1900 S State College Blvd # 200, Anaheim (92806-6197)
PHONE..................................714 940-9000
Bernie Morrissey, *Vice Pres*
Hugo Recinos, *Project Engr*
Michelle Smith-Ballard, *Director*
EMP: 300
SALES (corp-wide): 579.6MM **Privately Held**
WEB: www.tcco.com
SIC: 1542 Commercial & office building, new construction
HQ: Turner Construction Company Inc
375 Hudson St Fl 6
New York NY 10014
212 229-6000

(P-1683)
TURNER CONSTRUCTION COMPANY
2500 Venture Oaks Way # 200, Sacramento (95833-4222)
PHONE..................................916 444-4421
Donna Afflerdach, *Branch Mgr*
Frank D Zovi, *General Mgr*
Hayley Hintz, *Project Mgr*
Adrian Gonzalez, *Superintendent*
EMP: 75
SALES (corp-wide): 579.6MM **Privately Held**
WEB: www.tcco.com
SIC: 1542 Commercial & office building, new construction
HQ: Turner Construction Company Inc
375 Hudson St Fl 6
New York NY 10014
212 229-6000

(P-1684)
TURNER CONSTRUCTION COMPANY
300 Frank H Ogawa Plz # 510, Oakland (94612-2040)
PHONE..................................510 267-8100
Danny Cooke, *Branch Mgr*
Meade Hopkins, *Manager*
EMP: 50
SALES (corp-wide): 579.6MM **Privately Held**
WEB: www.tcco.com
SIC: 1542 8742 6531 Commercial & office building, new construction; management consulting services; real estate agents & managers
HQ: Turner Construction Company Inc
375 Hudson St Fl 6
New York NY 10014
212 229-6000

(P-1685)
TURNER CONSTRUCTION COMPANY
311 California St Ste 450, San Francisco (94104-2616)
PHONE..................................415 705-8900
Dan Wheeler, *Branch Mgr*
Leah Turner, *Project Engr*
Luis Vargas, *Superintendent*
EMP: 60

SALES (corp-wide): 579.6MM **Privately Held**
WEB: www.tcco.com
SIC: 1542 Commercial & office building, new construction
HQ: Turner Construction Company Inc
375 Hudson St Fl 6
New York NY 10014
212 229-6000

(P-1686)
TURNER CONSTRUCTION COMPANY
15378 Ave Of Science # 100, San Diego (92128-3451)
PHONE....................................858 320-4040
Richard C Bach, *Senior VP*
Tim Carter, *Project Engr*
Michael Daneshvar, *Engineer*
EMP: 61
SALES (corp-wide): 579.6MM **Privately Held**
WEB: www.tcco.com
SIC: 1542 Commercial & office building, new construction
HQ: Turner Construction Company Inc
375 Hudson St Fl 6
New York NY 10014
212 229-6000

(P-1687)
TURNER CONSTRUCTION COMPANY
2500 Venture Oaks Way # 200, Sacramento (95833-4222)
PHONE....................................916 444-4421
Frank Daizoi, *Branch Mgr*
EMP: 60
SALES (corp-wide): 579.6MM **Privately Held**
WEB: www.tcco.com
SIC: 1542 8741 Commercial & office building contractors; management services
HQ: Turner Construction Company Inc
375 Hudson St Fl 6
New York NY 10014
212 229-6000

(P-1688)
TUTOR PERINI CORPORATION (PA)
15901 Olden St, Sylmar (91342-1051)
PHONE....................................818 362-8391
Ronald N Tutor, *Ch of Bd*
James A Frost, *President*
Leonard J Rejcek, *President*
Gary G Smalley, *CFO*
Michael R Klein, *Vice Ch Bd*
EMP: 160 **EST:** 1894
SALES: 4.7B **Publicly Held**
WEB: www.perini.com
SIC: 1542 8741 1611 1791 Commercial & office building contractors; construction management; concrete construction: roads, highways, sidewalks, etc.; structural steel erection; concrete reinforcement, placing of; construction & civil engineering

(P-1689)
TUTOR-SALIBA CORPORATION (HQ)
15901 Olden St, Sylmar (91342-1051)
PHONE....................................818 362-8391
Ronald N Tutor, *CEO*
Jack Frost, *COO*
John D Barrett, *Senior VP*
David L Randall, *Senior VP*
William B Sparks, *Senior VP*
▲ **EMP:** 100
SQ FT: 20,000
SALES: 30MM
SALES (corp-wide): 4.7B **Publicly Held**
WEB: www.tutorsaliba.com
SIC: 1542 1629 7353 1799 Commercial & office building, new construction; subway construction; cranes & aerial lift equipment, rental or leasing; rigging & scaffolding; subdividers & developers
PA: Tutor Perini Corporation
15901 Olden St
Sylmar CA 91342
818 362-8391

(P-1690)
UNITED SEAL COATING SLURRYSEAL
3463 State St Ste 522, Santa Barbara (93105-2662)
PHONE....................................805 563-4922
Luis Rodriguez, *President*
Justin Rodriguez, *Treasurer*
Al Rodriguez, *Vice Pres*
Michelle Rodriguez, *Admin Sec*
EMP: 57
SQ FT: 2,500
SALES: 12.2MM **Privately Held**
WEB: www.unitedpavinginc.com
SIC: 1542 1522 7363 2951 Commercial & office building, new construction; residential construction; truck driver services; asphalt paving mixtures & blocks

(P-1691)
USS CAL BUILDERS INC
8051 Main St, Stanton (90680-2452)
PHONE....................................714 828-4882
Allen Othman, *CEO*
Jennifer Hotrum, *President*
Rabih El-Zein, *Vice Pres*
Rabih El Zein, *Vice Pres*
Arlene Bautista, *Office Mgr*
EMP: 135
SQ FT: 15,000
SALES (est): 93.3MM **Privately Held**
SIC: 1542 Specialized public building contractors

(P-1692)
VANCREST CONSTRUCTION CORP
7171 N Figueroa St, Los Angeles (90042-1279)
PHONE....................................323 256-0011
John T Van Dyke, *President*
Jim Van Dyke, *Vice Pres*
EMP: 50
SQ FT: 2,000
SALES (est): 10MM **Privately Held**
SIC: 1542 Commercial & office buildings, renovation & repair

(P-1693)
VILA CONSTRUCTION CO
Also Called: Richard H Vila
590 S 33rd St, Richmond (94804-4108)
PHONE....................................510 236-9111
Richard H Vila, *President*
Maria Elena Vila, *Office Mgr*
Bert Brendlinger, *Project Mgr*
EMP: 75 **EST:** 1946
SQ FT: 8,000
SALES: 30MM **Privately Held**
WEB: www.vilaconstruction.com
SIC: 1542 1751 1541 Commercial & office buildings, renovation & repair; carpentry work; industrial buildings & warehouses

(P-1694)
W L BUTLER CONSTRUCTION INC (PA)
735 Shasta St, Redwood City (94063-2124)
PHONE....................................650 361-1270
William L Butler, *CEO*
Frank York, *President*
Nick Shaw, *CFO*
Brett Crail, *Vice Pres*
Gina Tankersley, *Vice Pres*
EMP: 50
SQ FT: 13,500
SALES: 272.4MM **Privately Held**
SIC: 1542 Commercial & office building, new construction; commercial & office buildings, renovation & repair

(P-1695)
W M KLORMAN CONSTRUCTION CORP
23047 Ventura Blvd Fl 2, Woodland Hills (91364-1146)
PHONE....................................818 591-5969
William M Klorman, *President*
Tom Brull, *President*
Doug Fowler, *Vice Pres*
Ida Chen, *Controller*
Ryan Day, *Superintendent*
EMP: 65

SQ FT: 4,000
SALES: 50MM **Privately Held**
WEB: www.klorman.com
SIC: 1542 Commercial & office building, new construction; new construction; single-family houses

(P-1696)
WEBCOR CONSTRUCTION LP (DH)
Also Called: Webcor Builders
1751 Harbor Bay Pkwy # 200, Alameda (94502-3001)
PHONE....................................510 748-1900
Jes Pedersen, *CEO*
Margaret Austin, *President*
Julia Gray, *COO*
Rich Lamb, *COO*
Tim Lutz, *CFO*
EMP: 71
SALES (est): 66.2MM
SALES (corp-wide): 17.8B **Privately Held**
WEB: www.webcor.com
SIC: 1542 Commercial & office building, new construction
HQ: Obayashi Usa, Llc
577 Airport Blvd Ste 600
Burlingame CA 94010
650 952-4910

(P-1697)
WEINSTEIN CONSTRUCTION CORP
15102 Raymer St, Van Nuys (91405-1143)
PHONE....................................818 782-4000
Itzcik Weinstein, *President*
Johnathan Weinstein, *Vice Pres*
Ilana Nisnevich, *Human Res Mgr*
EMP: 50
SALES (est): 8.4MM **Privately Held**
WEB: www.weinsteinconstruction.com
SIC: 1542 1521 Commercial & office building, new construction; new construction; single-family houses

(P-1698)
WEST COAST CONTRACTORS INC
2320 Courage Dr Ste 111, Fairfield (94533-6743)
PHONE....................................541 267-7689
Alan Bond, *President*
Sharon Newcomer, *CFO*
Mark Dietlin, *Vice Pres*
James Latner, *Vice Pres*
EMP: 130
SQ FT: 15,000
SALES (est): 16.4MM **Privately Held**
WEB: www.westcoastcontractors.com
SIC: 1542 Specialized public building contractors; school building construction; commercial & office buildings, renovation & repair

(P-1699)
WESTGATE CNSTR & MAINT INC
5045 Fulton Dr Ste D, Fairfield (94534-1635)
PHONE....................................707 208-5763
Hilton Ham, *President*
Kelly Bishop, *Office Mgr*
EMP: 86
SALES: 1.8MM **Privately Held**
SIC: 1542 Commercial & office building, new construction; commercial & office buildings, renovation & repair; restaurant construction; shopping center construction

(P-1700)
WHITING-TURNER CONTRACTING CO
29209 Canwood St Ste 100, Agoura Hills (91301-1592)
PHONE....................................818 879-8100
Tavio Darchangelo, *Vice Pres*
EMP: 110
SALES (corp-wide): 6.1B **Privately Held**
SIC: 1542 Nonresidential construction
PA: The Whiting-Turner Contracting Company
300 E Joppa Rd Ste 800
Baltimore MD 21286
410 821-1100

(P-1701)
WHITING-TURNER CONTRACTING CO
1000 Wilshire Blvd 1850, Los Angeles (90017-2457)
PHONE....................................213 310-7900
Tavio Darchangelo, *Vice Pres*
EMP: 128
SALES (corp-wide): 6.1B **Privately Held**
SIC: 1542 1541 1629 8741 Nonresidential construction; industrial buildings & warehouses; dams, waterways, docks & other marine construction; construction management
PA: The Whiting-Turner Contracting Company
300 E Joppa Rd Ste 800
Baltimore MD 21286
410 821-1100

(P-1702)
WHITING-TURNER CONTRACTING CO
250 Commerce Ste 150, Irvine (92602-1345)
PHONE....................................949 863-0800
Len Cannatelli, *Exec VP*
Ryan Barry, *Project Mgr*
Eric Sullwold, *Project Mgr*
Sean Kaford, *Project Engr*
Casey Mulford, *Project Engr*
EMP: 50
SALES (corp-wide): 6.1B **Privately Held**
WEB: www.whiting-turner.com
SIC: 1542 1541 Commercial & office building, new construction; industrial buildings & warehouses
PA: The Whiting-Turner Contracting Company
300 E Joppa Rd Ste 800
Baltimore MD 21286
410 821-1100

(P-1703)
WIER CONSTRUCTION CORPORATION
16884 Old Survey Rd, Escondido (92025-3601)
PHONE....................................760 743-6776
Cathy Wier, *President*
Brian Wier, *Vice Pres*
EMP: 50
SQ FT: 10,000
SALES (est): 9.8MM **Privately Held**
WEB: www.wierconstruction.com
SIC: 1542 Specialized public building contractors

(P-1704)
WIMER CONSTRUCTION
10855 Wimer Country Rd, Sunland (91040-1348)
PHONE....................................818 848-0400
Rick Wimer, *Owner*
EMP: 50
SALES (est): 3.8MM **Privately Held**
WEB: www.wimerconstruction.com
SIC: 1542 Commercial & office building contractors

(P-1705)
WR CHAVEZ CONSTRUCTION INC
Also Called: Wr Chavez Company
12125 Kear Pl Ste A, Poway (92064-7131)
PHONE....................................858 375-2100
Wilfred R Chavez, *President*
Debbie L Chavez, *Treasurer*
EMP: 80
SQ FT: 15,000
SALES: 21.5MM **Privately Held**
SIC: 1542 1721 Commercial & office building, new construction; commercial painting

(P-1706)
WRIGHT CONTRACTING LLC
Also Called: Wright Contracting EPA
3020 Dutton Ave, Santa Rosa (95407-7886)
P.O. Box 1270 (95402-1270)
PHONE....................................707 528-1172
Mark Davis, *President*
Stephen M Wright, *COO*
Bryan Wright, *Vice Pres*

Dawn Neditch, *Director*
EMP: 60
SALES: 22MM **Privately Held**
SIC: 1542 Nonresidential construction

(P-1707)
XL CONSTRUCTION CORPORATION
343 Sansome St Ste 505, San Francisco (94104-5622)
PHONE.....................408 240-6312
Ron Paradies, *Vice Pres*
EMP: 65 **Privately Held**
SIC: 1542 Nonresidential construction
PA: Xl Construction Corporation
  851 Buckeye Ct
  Milpitas CA 95035

(P-1708)
XL CONSTRUCTION CORPORATION (PA)
851 Buckeye Ct, Milpitas (95035-7408)
PHONE.....................408 240-6000
Eric Raff, *President*
Tom Humbert, *CFO*
Dave Beck, *Exec VP*
Mario Wijtman, *Exec VP*
David Beck, *Vice Pres*
EMP: 111
SALES (est): 155.7MM **Privately Held**
WEB: www.xlconst.com
SIC: 1542 Commercial & office building, new construction; commercial & office buildings, renovation & repair

(P-1709)
ZUMWALT CONSTRUCTION INC
5520 E Lamona Ave, Fresno (93727-2276)
PHONE.....................559 252-1000
Kurt E Zumwalt, *President*
Teri Zumwalt, *Admin Sec*
Luiza Grinko, *Admin Asst*
Pamela Lacone, *Admin Asst*
Dana Hester, *Project Mgr*
EMP: 100
SQ FT: 2,000
SALES: 22.8MM **Privately Held**
WEB: www.zumwaltconst.com
SIC: 1542 1522 Commercial & office building, new construction; residential construction

1611 Highway & Street Construction

(P-1710)
A CSG-NOVA JOINT VENTURE
3960 Industrial Blvd # 500, West Sacramento (95691-3496)
P.O. Box 1505 (95691-1505)
PHONE.....................916 371-7303
Shelli Moreda, *Co-Venturer*
Scott Victor, *Co-Venturer*
EMP: 99
SALES (est): 3MM **Privately Held**
SIC: 1611 1623 1629 Airport runway construction; concrete construction: roads, highways, sidewalks, etc.; oil & gas pipeline construction; levee construction

(P-1711)
A J EXCAVATION INC
Also Called: American Fencing
514 N Brawley Ave, Fresno (93706-1014)
PHONE.....................559 408-5908
Alisa Emmett, *President*
EMP: 150
SALES (est): 200K **Privately Held**
SIC: 1611 Highway & street construction

(P-1712)
ADOPT-A-HIGHWAY MAINTENANCE
Also Called: Adopt-A-Beach
3158 Red Hill Ave Ste 200, Costa Mesa (92626-3416)
PHONE.....................800 200-0003
Peter Morin, *CEO*
Patricia Nelson, *President*
Dan Day, *CFO*
Dennis Day, *Admin Sec*
EMP: 104

SQ FT: 6,000
SALES (est): 17.5MM **Privately Held**
WEB: www.adoptabeach.com
SIC: 1611 4959 Highway & street maintenance; sanitary services

(P-1713)
AECOM ENERGY & CNSTR INC
Also Called: Washington Group
2850 Carmel Valley Rd, Del Mar (92014-3800)
PHONE.....................858 481-9502
EMP: 359
SALES (corp-wide): 20.1B **Publicly Held**
WEB: www.wgint.com
SIC: 1611 Highway & street construction
HQ: Aecom Energy & Construction, Inc.
  1999 Avenue Of The Stars
  Los Angeles CA 90067
  213 593-8100

(P-1714)
ALL AMERICAN ASPHALT (PA)
Also Called: All American Agrigate
400 E 6th St, Corona (92879-1521)
P.O. Box 2229 (92878-2229)
PHONE.....................951 736-7600
Mark Albert Luer, *President*
Mark Luer, *President*
Gordon Kline, *Project Mgr*
Bob Loth, *Human Res Mgr*
Gus Bogart, *Foreman/Supr*
EMP: 60
SALES (est): 172.6MM **Privately Held**
WEB: www.allamericanasphalt.net
SIC: 1611 5032 Highway & street paving contractor; brick, stone & related material

(P-1715)
ALL AMERICAN ASPHALT
All American Service and Sup
1776 All American Way, Corona (92879-2070)
P.O. Box 2229 (92878-2229)
PHONE.....................951 736-7617
Kim McGuire, *Manager*
EMP: 150
SALES (corp-wide): 172.6MM **Privately Held**
WEB: www.allamericanasphalt.net
SIC: 1611 Highway & street paving contractor
PA: All American Asphalt
  400 E 6th St
  Corona CA 92879
  951 736-7600

(P-1716)
ALL AMERICAN ASPHALT
Camco Construction Supply
1776 All American Way, Corona (92879-2070)
PHONE.....................951 736-7617
Kim McGuire, *Branch Mgr*
EMP: 150
SALES (corp-wide): 172.6MM **Privately Held**
WEB: www.allamericanasphalt.net
SIC: 1611 Highway & street paving contractor
PA: All American Asphalt
  400 E 6th St
  Corona CA 92879
  951 736-7600

(P-1717)
AMERICAN ASPHALT SOUTH INC
14436 Santa Ana Ave, Fontana (92337-7141)
P.O. Box 310036 (92331-0036)
PHONE.....................909 427-8276
Alan Henderson, *President*
Steve Aguirre, *COO*
Kim Henschel, *Vice Pres*
Jeff Petty, *Vice Pres*
Lyle Stone, *Admin Sec*
EMP: 65
SALES (est): 12.3MM **Privately Held**
WEB: www.americanasphaltsouth.com
SIC: 1611 Highway & street maintenance; surfacing & paving

(P-1718)
AMERICAN CIVIL CONST
Also Called: ACC West Coast
2990 Bay Vista Ct Ste D, Benicia (94510-1195)
PHONE.....................707 746-8028
Jeffrey Foerste, *President*
Clifford Barber, *Vice Pres*
David Wilkerson, *Vice Pres*
EMP: 75
SQ FT: 19,000
SALES (est): 13.5MM **Privately Held**
WEB: www.wcbridge.com
SIC: 1611 1622 Surfacing & paving; bridge construction
PA: American Civil Constructors Holdings, Inc.
  4901 S Windermere St
  Littleton CO 80120

(P-1719)
AMERICAN PAVING CO
Also Called: WM LYLES CO
315 N Thorne Ave, Fresno (93706-1444)
P.O. Box 4348 (93744-4348)
PHONE.....................559 268-9886
Steve Poindexter, *President*
Ross Jenkins, *Vice Pres*
EMP: 50
SQ FT: 9,000
SALES: 21.8MM
SALES (corp-wide): 33.7MM **Privately Held**
WEB: www.americanpavingco.com
SIC: 1611 1771 Highway & street paving contractor; curb construction; sidewalk contractor
PA: Lyles Diversified, Inc.
  1210 W Olive Ave
  Fresno CA 93728
  559 441-1900

(P-1720)
AMG CONSTRUCTION GROUP
1103 W Gardena Blvd # 201, Gardena (90248-5239)
PHONE.....................800 310-2609
Calvin Jackson, *CEO*
EMP: 69
SQ FT: 1,600
SALES (est): 2.8MM **Privately Held**
SIC: 1611 General contractor, highway & street construction

(P-1721)
AMS PAVING INC (PA)
11060 Rose Ave, Fontana (92337-7051)
PHONE.....................909 357-0711
William E Hawkins, *Principal*
Norma Swanson, *CFO*
EMP: 50
SQ FT: 4,000
SALES (est): 15.9MM **Privately Held**
WEB: www.amspaving.com
SIC: 1611 Highway & street paving contractor; surfacing & paving

(P-1722)
ANNUZZI CONCRETE SERVICE INC
85 Elmira St, San Francisco (94124-1910)
P.O. Box 27518 (94127-0518)
PHONE.....................415 468-2795
Carmello Annuzzi, *President*
Jack Annuzzi, *Vice Pres*
EMP: 50
SQ FT: 5,000
SALES (est): 6.9MM **Privately Held**
SIC: 1611 Concrete construction: roads, highways, sidewalks, etc.

(P-1723)
ANVIL BUILDERS INC
1475 Donner Ave, San Francisco (94124-3614)
PHONE.....................415 285-5000
Hien Manh Tran, *President*
Alan Guy, *COO*
Ann Hauer, *Vice Pres*
Richard Leider, *Admin Sec*
EMP: 125
SQ FT: 4,000

SALES: 28MM **Privately Held**
SIC: 1611 1623 General contractor, highway & street construction; water, sewer & utility lines

(P-1724)
ARCHER WESTERN CONTRACTORS LLC
9915 Mira Mesa Blvd # 230, San Diego (92131-7003)
PHONE.....................858 715-7200
Tim Gerken, *CFO*
EMP: 52
SALES (corp-wide): 3.6B **Privately Held**
WEB: www.walshgroup.com
SIC: 1611 Highway & street construction
HQ: Archer Western Contractors, Llc
  2410 Paces Ferry Rd Se # 600
  Atlanta GA 30339
  404 495-8700

(P-1725)
ARGONAUT CONSTRUCTORS
360 Sutton Pl, Santa Rosa (95407-8121)
P.O. Box 639 (95402-0639)
PHONE.....................707 542-4862
Michael D Smith, *CEO*
Michael A Smith, *Vice Pres*
EMP: 175 **EST:** 1957
SQ FT: 10,000
SALES: 28.1MM **Privately Held**
WEB: www.argonautconstructors.com
SIC: 1611 1623 Highway & street paving contractor; oil & gas pipeline construction

(P-1726)
ATKINSON CONSTRUCTION INC
18201 Von Karman Ave # 800, Irvine (92612-1092)
PHONE.....................303 410-2540
John O'Keefe, *President*
EMP: 450
SALES (est): 44.7MM
SALES (corp-wide): 1.9B **Privately Held**
SIC: 1611 1622 Highway & street construction; bridge, tunnel & elevated highway
HQ: Clark Construction Group, Llc
  7500 Old Georgetown Rd # 1500
  Bethesda MD 20814
  301 272-8100

(P-1727)
AVAR CONSTRUCTION INC
GMI
47375 Fremont Blvd, Fremont (94538-6521)
PHONE.....................510 354-2000
EMP: 79
SALES (corp-wide): 25MM **Privately Held**
SIC: 1611 Highway & street construction
PA: Avar Construction, Inc
  47375 Fremont Blvd
  Fremont CA 94538
  510 354-2000

(P-1728)
BASIC RESOURCES INC (PA)
928 12th St Ste 700, Modesto (95354-2330)
P.O. Box 3191 (95353-3191)
PHONE.....................209 521-9771
Jeffrey Reed, *CEO*
Wendell Reed, *President*
Leatha Wilson, *Admin Sec*
▲ **EMP:** 50
SALES (est): 197.8MM **Privately Held**
SIC: 1611 3273 2951 3532 Highway & street paving contractor; ready-mixed concrete; asphalt & asphaltic paving mixtures (not from refineries); mining machinery; construction machinery

(P-1729)
BEADOR CONSTRUCTION CO INC
26320 Lester Cir, Corona (92883-6399)
PHONE.....................951 674-7352
David A Beador, *President*
Jeff Barglowski, *Vice Pres*
Joe Beador, *General Mgr*
EMP: 80
SQ FT: 1,415

PRODUCTS & SVCS

SALES (est): 20.4MM **Privately Held**
SIC: 1611 General contractor, highway & street construction

(P-1730)
BECHO INC
15901 Olden St, Sylmar (91342-1051)
PHONE..............................818 362-8391
Tim Smith, *President*
Louis Lucido, *President*
William B Sparks, *Treasurer*
Steve Pavoggi, *Vice Pres*
Jim Tripp, *Vice Pres*
▲ **EMP:** 60 **EST:** 1979
SQ FT: 8,000
SALES: 9.4MM
SALES (corp-wide): 4.7B **Publicly Held**
WEB: www.bechoinc.com
SIC: 1611 Highway & street paving contractor; bridge construction; shoring & underpinning work
PA: Tutor Perini Corporation
15901 Olden St
Sylmar CA 91342
818 362-8391

(P-1731)
BENS ASPHALT & MAINT CO INC
Also Called: Medina Construction
2537 Rubidoux Blvd, Riverside (92509-2142)
PHONE..............................951 248-1103
EMP: 50
SALES (corp-wide): 21.6MM **Privately Held**
WEB: www.bensasphalt.com
SIC: 1611 Highway & street maintenance
PA: Ben's Asphalt & Maintenance Company, Inc.
2200 S Yale St Ste A
Santa Ana CA 92704
714 540-1700

(P-1732)
BRODERICK GEN ENGINNEERING INC
21750 8th St E Ste B, Sonoma (95476-9803)
PHONE..............................707 996-7809
John Benward, *President*
Earl G Broderick, *Vice Pres*
EMP: 50
SQ FT: 6,400
SALES (est): 12.9MM **Privately Held**
WEB: www.benwardco.com
SIC: 1611 Surfacing & paving

(P-1733)
BRUTOCO ENGRG & CNSTR INC
1272 Center Court Dr # 101, Covina (91724-3667)
PHONE..............................909 350-3535
Michael J Murphy, *President*
Mike Fenley, *Senior VP*
John Glanville, *Vice Pres*
Ron Neal, *Vice Pres*
Paul Sullivan, *Vice Pres*
EMP: 200
SQ FT: 5,000
SALES (est): 48.8MM **Privately Held**
WEB: www.brutoco.net
SIC: 1611 1629 1622 General contractor, highway & street construction; dams, waterways, docks & other marine construction; bridge construction, elevated

(P-1734)
BURTCH TRUCKING INC
Also Called: Burtch Construction
18815 Highway 65, Bakersfield (93308-9794)
P.O. Box 80546 (93380-0546)
PHONE..............................661 399-1736
Brenn Burtch McGowan, *President*
Linda Kay Burtch, *Principal*
EMP: 53
SQ FT: 4,000
SALES (est): 12.1MM **Privately Held**
WEB: www.burtchconstruction.com
SIC: 1611 Highway & street paving contractor

(P-1735)
CALIFORNIA PAV GRADING CO INC
3253 Verdugo Rd, Los Angeles (90065-2035)
P.O. Box 65966 (90065-0966)
PHONE..............................323 372-5920
Foster Dennis, *President*
Lee Sepielli, *Corp Secy*
EMP: 58
SQ FT: 1,600
SALES (est): 17.9MM **Privately Held**
WEB: www.calpave.com
SIC: 1611 Surfacing & paving

(P-1736)
CALIFORNIA PAVEMENT MAINT INC
Also Called: Rayner Equipment Systems
9390 Elder Creek Rd, Sacramento (95829-9326)
PHONE..............................916 381-8033
Gordon L Rayner, *CEO*
Richard Rayner, *President*
Mick Marchini, *Vice Pres*
Bruce Taylor, *Vice Pres*
Connie Morotti, *Executive*
EMP: 97 **EST:** 1979
SQ FT: 24,300
SALES: 11.9MM **Privately Held**
WEB: www.cpmamerica.com
SIC: 1611 Highway & street paving contractor; surfacing & paving

(P-1737)
CHIEF TRNSP & ENGRG CONTRS INC
Also Called: Chief Engineering Co
4056 Tamarind Rdg, Lake Elsinore (92530-2041)
P.O. Box 677 (92531-0677)
PHONE..............................951 258-6607
Jose Aceituno Jr, *CEO*
EMP: 78
SALES (est): 1.6MM **Privately Held**
SIC: 1611 Highway & street construction

(P-1738)
CHRISP COMPANY (PA)
43650 Osgood Rd, Fremont (94539-5631)
P.O. Box 1368 (94538-0136)
PHONE..............................510 656-2840
Robert P Chrisp, *CEO*
David Morris, *Vice Pres*
Roger Weisbrod, *Vice Pres*
Jake Chrisp, *Branch Mgr*
Marl Vincenzi, *Planning*
EMP: 140
SQ FT: 8,000
SALES (est): 69.3MM **Privately Held**
WEB: www.chrispco.com
SIC: 1611 Highway signs & guardrails

(P-1739)
CITY OF BURLINGAME
Also Called: Public Works and Highway Dept
1361 N Carolan Ave, Burlingame (94010-2401)
PHONE..............................650 558-7670
Rob Mallick, *Branch Mgr*
EMP: 50 **Privately Held**
SIC: 1611 Surfacing & paving
PA: City Of Burlingame
501 Primrose Rd
Burlingame CA 94010
650 558-7203

(P-1740)
CITY OF EL CENTRO
307 W Brighton Ave, El Centro (92243-3004)
PHONE..............................760 337-4505
Terry Heagan, *Principal*
EMP: 200 **Privately Held**
SIC: 1611 Highway & street construction
PA: City Of El Centro
1275 W Main St
El Centro CA 92243
760 337-4510

(P-1741)
CITY OF ENCINITAS
Also Called: Street Maintenance Department
160 Calle Magdalena, Encinitas (92024-3721)
PHONE..............................760 633-2850
Larry Watt, *Branch Mgr*
EMP: 50 **Privately Held**
WEB: www.cityofencinitas.org
SIC: 1611 Highway & street maintenance
PA: City Of Encinitas
505 S Vulcan Ave
Encinitas CA 92024

(P-1742)
CITY OF LA MESA
Also Called: Lamesa City Public Works
8152 Commercial St, La Mesa (91942-2926)
PHONE..............................619 667-1450
Eric Johnson, *Superintendent*
EMP: 50 **Privately Held**
SIC: 1611 Highway & street maintenance
PA: La Mesa, City Of (Inc)
8130 Allison Ave
La Mesa CA 91942
619 463-6611

(P-1743)
CITY OF LONG BEACH
Public Works Department
333 W Ocean Blvd Ste 9, Long Beach (90802-4664)
PHONE..............................562 570-6383
Raymond T Holland, *Director*
EMP: 500 **Privately Held**
SIC: 1611 Highway & street construction
PA: City Of Long Beach
333 W Ocean Blvd Fl 10
Long Beach CA 90802
562 570-6450

(P-1744)
CITY OF MILL VALLEY
Also Called: Department of Public Works
26 Corte Madera Ave, Mill Valley (94941-1830)
PHONE..............................415 388-4033
Don Hunter, *Manager*
EMP: 120 **Privately Held**
WEB: www.donnadacuti.com
SIC: 1611 Highway & street maintenance
PA: City Of Mill Valley
26 Corte Madera Ave
Mill Valley CA 94941
415 388-4033

(P-1745)
COMMERCIAL COATING COMPANY INC
Also Called: Commercial Paving
2809 W Avenue 37, Los Angeles (90065-3620)
P.O. Box 65557 (90065-0557)
PHONE..............................323 256-1331
Andrian Loera, *President*
William Emerson, *Treasurer*
EMP: 52
SQ FT: 10,000
SALES (est): 14.7MM **Privately Held**
SIC: 1611 Resurfacing contractor

(P-1746)
COUNTY OF ALAMEDA
Also Called: Public Works Dept
399 Elmhurst St, Hayward (94544-1307)
PHONE..............................510 670-5455
Daniel Woldesenbet, *Director*
Rohin Saleh, *General Mgr*
Art Carrera, *Engineer*
Alfred Harris, *Engineer*
Arthur Valderrama, *Engineer*
EMP: 300 **Privately Held**
WEB: www.co.alameda.ca.us
SIC: 1611 9199 Highway & street paving contractor; general government administration;
PA: County Of Alameda
1221 Oak St Ste 555
Oakland CA 94612
510 272-6691

(P-1747)
COUNTY OF CONTRA COSTA
Also Called: Administration of Public Works
255 Glacier Dr, Martinez (94553-4825)
PHONE..............................925 313-2000
Julia Bueren, *Director*
EMP: 250
SQ FT: 29,865 **Privately Held**
SIC: 1611 Highway & street maintenance
PA: County Of Contra Costa
625 Court St Ste 100
Martinez CA 94553
925 957-5280

(P-1748)
COUNTY OF GLENN
Also Called: Planning and Public Works Agcy
777 N Colusa St, Willows (95988-2211)
P.O. Box 1070 (95988-1070)
PHONE..............................530 934-6530
Dan Obermyer, *Manager*
Douglas Holvik, *Exec Dir*
EMP: 125 **Privately Held**
WEB: www.countyofglen.net
SIC: 1611 Highway & street maintenance
PA: County Of Glenn
516 N Sycamore St Fl 2
Willows CA 95988
530 934-6410

(P-1749)
COUNTY OF IMPERIAL
Also Called: Public Works
304 E 4th St, Imperial (92251-1725)
PHONE..............................760 355-1748
Willy Riven, *Manager*
EMP: 60 **Privately Held**
WEB: www.imperialcounty.net
SIC: 1611 Concrete construction: roads, highways, sidewalks, etc.
PA: County Of Imperial
940 W Main St Ste 208
El Centro CA 92243
760 482-4556

(P-1750)
COUNTY OF LOS ANGELES
Also Called: Public Works, Dept of
38126 Sierra Hwy, Palmdale (93550-4607)
PHONE..............................661 947-7173
Mark Caddick, *Manager*
EMP: 130 **Privately Held**
WEB: www.co.la.ca.us
SIC: 1611 9621 Highway & street maintenance; regulation, administration of transportation;
PA: County Of Los Angeles
500 W Temple St Ste 437
Los Angeles CA 90012
213 974-1101

(P-1751)
COUNTY OF LOS ANGELES
Also Called: Public Works, Dept of
1525 Alcazar St Bldg 1, Los Angeles (90033-1001)
PHONE..............................626 458-1700
Robert Scharf, *Opers Staff*
James Martinez, *Opers Spvr*
EMP: 250 **Privately Held**
WEB: www.co.la.ca.us
SIC: 1611 9511 Highway & street maintenance; sanitary engineering agency, government;
PA: County Of Los Angeles
500 W Temple St Ste 437
Los Angeles CA 90012
213 974-1101

(P-1752)
COUNTY OF MENDOCINO
Also Called: Transportation Dept
340 Lake Mendocino Dr, Ukiah (95482-9432)
PHONE..............................707 463-4363
Howard Dashiell, *Director*
EMP: 104 **Privately Held**
WEB: www.mcdss.org
SIC: 1611 8741 Highway & street construction; management services
PA: County Of Mendocino
501 Low Gap Rd Rm 1010
Ukiah CA 95482
707 463-4441

(P-1753)
COUNTY OF MONTEREY
Also Called: Monterey County Public Works
168 W Alisal St Fl 3, Salinas (93901-2487)
PHONE.................................831 755-4800
Yaz Emrani, *Director*
EMP: 300 **Privately Held**
WEB: www.montereycountyfarmbureau.org
SIC: **1611** Highway & street construction
PA: County Of Monterey
168 W Alisal St Fl 2
Salinas CA 93901
831 755-5040

(P-1754)
**D A MCCOSKER
CONSTRUCTION CO**
Also Called: Independent Construction Co
3911 Laura Alice Way, Concord
(94520-8544)
P.O. Box 5307 (94524-0307)
PHONE.................................925 686-1780
Brian Clay McCosker, *President*
David A Mc Cosker, *Ch of Bd*
Brian Cartmell, *Admin Sec*
Benito Sandoval, *Project Engr*
Dan Schuetz, *Safety Mgr*
EMP: 50 EST: 1910
SALES (est): 21.8MM **Privately Held**
SIC: **1611** Surfacing & paving; grading;
highway & street paving contractor

(P-1755)
**D W POWELL CONSTRUCTION
INC**
8555 Banana Ave, Fontana (92335-3019)
PHONE.................................909 356-8880
Doyle W Powell, *President*
Michael Powell, *General Mgr*
Suzanne Powell, *Admin Sec*
Kyle Baltes, *Project Engr*
Richard Wiley, *Manager*
EMP: 50
SQ FT: 2,000
SALES (est): 7MM **Privately Held**
SIC: **1611** General contractor, highway &
street construction

(P-1756)
**DENNIS M MCCOY & SONS INC
(PA)**
32107 Lindero Canyon Rd # 212, Westlake
Village (91361-4255)
PHONE.................................818 874-3872
Dennis McCoy, *CEO*
Morgan McCoy, *President*
Simone Brandon, *Manager*
EMP: 75
SQ FT: 3,000
SALES (est): 12.9MM **Privately Held**
WEB: www.mccoyandsons.com
SIC: **1611** Grading

(P-1757)
**DESILVA GATES
CONSTRUCTION LP**
7700 College Town Dr # 230, Sacramento
(95826-2303)
PHONE.................................916 386-9708
Edwin O Desilva, *Branch Mgr*
EMP: 124 **Privately Held**
SIC: **1611** General contractor, highway &
street construction
PA: Desilva Gates Construction L.P.
11555 Dublin Blvd
Dublin CA 94568

(P-1758)
**DESILVA GATES
CONSTRUCTION LP (PA)**
11555 Dublin Blvd, Dublin (94568-2854)
P.O. Box 2909 (94568-0909)
PHONE.................................925 361-1380
Edwin O Desilva, *President*
David Desilva, *Exec VP*
Richard B Gates, *Exec VP*
J Scott Archibald, *Vice Pres*
Pete Davos, *Vice Pres*
EMP: 100

SALES (est): 117.8MM **Privately Held**
WEB: www.desilvagates.com
SIC: **1611** 1794 1542 General contractor,
highway & street construction; excavation
& grading; building construction; nonresidential construction

(P-1759)
DISNEY CONSTRUCTION INC
533 Airport Blvd Ste 120, Burlingame
(94010-2007)
PHONE.................................650 689-5149
Richard L Disney, *President*
Tim Bennett, *Project Mgr*
Sean Lennan, *Project Engr*
Michael Birdsall, *Controller*
EMP: 60
SALES: 30MM **Privately Held**
SIC: **1611** Highway & street construction

(P-1760)
DOUMIT COMMUNICATION INC
25 Cadillac Dr Ste 134, Sacramento
(95825-8358)
PHONE.................................916 362-3519
Samir Doumit, *President*
Geralee Doumit, *Corp Secy*
EMP: 58 EST: 1996
SALES (est): 6.5MM **Privately Held**
SIC: **1611** 7389 General contractor, high-
way & street construction;

(P-1761)
**DRYCO CONSTRUCTION INC
(PA)**
42745 Boscell Rd, Fremont (94538-3106)
PHONE.................................510 438-6500
Daren R Young, *President*
David Henke, *CFO*
William McCrea, *Vice Pres*
Kevin Mitchell, *Vice Pres*
Rafael Torres, *Vice Pres*
EMP: 180
SQ FT: 3,700
SALES (est): 78.9MM **Privately Held**
WEB: www.dryco.com
SIC: **1611** 1721 5211 Highway & street
paving contractor; pavement marking
contractor; lumber & other building mate-
rials

(P-1762)
**EBS GENERAL ENGINEERING
INC**
1320 E 6th St Ste 100, Corona
(92879-1700)
PHONE.................................951 279-6869
Joe Nanci, *President*
Tom Nanci, *Controller*
Kathy Fairweather, *Human Res Mgr*
EMP: 80
SQ FT: 4,000
SALES (est): 13.2MM **Privately Held**
SIC: **1611** Highway & street construction

(P-1763)
ED SAFETY SERVICES INC
1040 W Kettleman Ln # 388, Lodi
(95240-6056)
PHONE.................................209 333-0807
Nicole Beadles, *President*
EMP: 112
SALES (est): 10.4MM **Privately Held**
SIC: **1611** Highway & street construction

(P-1764)
**FOOTH THE / EASTE TRANS
CORRI**
125 Pacifica Ste 100, Irvine (92618-3324)
PHONE.................................949 754-3400
Michael Kraman, *CEO*
Amy Potter, *CFO*
EMP: 70
SQ FT: 10,000
SALES: 214.4MM **Privately Held**
SIC: **1611** General contractor, highway &
street construction

(P-1765)
GCI CONSTRUCTION INC
1031 Calle Recodo Ste D, San Clemente
(92673-6269)
PHONE.................................714 957-0233
Terry Gillespie, *President*
Floyd Bennett, *Treasurer*

Richard Tirrell, *Vice Pres*
EMP: 50
SQ FT: 3,000
SALES (est): 8.3MM **Privately Held**
SIC: **1611** Highway & street construction

(P-1766)
GHILOTTI BROS INC
525 Jacoby St, San Rafael (94901-5370)
PHONE.................................415 454-7011
Dante W Ghilotti, *CEO*
Michael M Ghilotti, *President*
Daniel Y Chin, *CFO*
Thomas G Barr, *Vice Pres*
▲ EMP: 290 EST: 1914
SQ FT: 86,249
SALES (est): 112.4MM **Privately Held**
WEB: www.ghilottibros.com
SIC: **1611** 1794 1623 Surfacing & paving;
grading; highway & street paving contrac-
tor; excavation work; water, sewer & utility
lines

(P-1767)
**GHILOTTI CONSTRUCTION CO
INC**
600 S Napa Junction Rd, American Canyon
(94503-1277)
PHONE.................................707 556-9145
Mark Bower, *Branch Mgr*
EMP: 119 **Privately Held**
WEB: www.ghilotti.com
SIC: **1611** 1623 General contractor, high-
way & street construction; underground
utilities contractor
PA: Ghilotti Construction Company, Inc.
246 Ghillotti Ave
Santa Rosa CA 95407

(P-1768)
**GLENN CNTY PLG PUB WORKS
AGCY**
777 N Colusa St, Willows (95988-2211)
P.O. Box 1070 (95988-1070)
PHONE.................................530 934-6541
David Shoemaker, *Director*
EMP: 75
SALES (est): 6.1MM **Privately Held**
SIC: **1611** Highway & street construction

(P-1769)
GRAHAM CONTRACTORS INC
860 Lonus St, San Jose (95126-3713)
P.O. Box 26770 (95159-6770)
PHONE.................................408 293-9516
Gerald Graham Jr, *President*
Reed Graham, *Vice Pres*
Che Corlett, *Representative*
EMP: 50 EST: 1976
SQ FT: 1,200
SALES (est): 10.4MM **Privately Held**
WEB: www.grahamcontractors.com
SIC: **1611** Highway & street paving con-
tractor

(P-1770)
**GRANIT-BAYASHI 3 A JOINT
VENTR**
585 W Beach St, Watsonville (95076-5123)
P.O. Box 50085 (95077-5085)
PHONE.................................831 724-1011
Tobi Stonich, *Administration*
Rinkou Aki,
Jigisha Desai,
Mathew Tyler,
EMP: 50
SALES (est): 1.3MM **Privately Held**
SIC: **1611** 1542 Highway & street con-
struction; nonresidential construction

(P-1771)
**GRANITE CONSTRUCTION
COMPANY (HQ)**
585 W Beach St, Watsonville (95076-5123)
P.O. Box 50085 (95077-5085)
PHONE.................................831 724-1011
James H Roberts, *President*
Laurel Krzeminski, *Exec VP*
Christopher S Miller, *Exec VP*
Richard A Watts, *Vice Pres*
Mike Barker, *Controller*
▼ EMP: 200 EST: 1922
SQ FT: 39,000

SALES (est): 1.1B
SALES (corp-wide): 2.9B **Publicly Held**
WEB:
www.graniteconstructioncompany.com
SIC: **1611** 1622 Highway & street construction; general contractor, highway &
street construction; bridge construction;
tunnel construction
PA: Granite Construction Incorporated
585 W Beach St
Watsonville CA 95076
831 724-1011

(P-1772)
**GRANITE CONSTRUCTION
COMPANY**
3005 James Rd, Bakersfield (93308-9179)
P.O. Box 5127 (93388-5127)
PHONE.................................661 399-3361
Bruce McGowan, *Branch Mgr*
Timothy Findley, *Project Mgr*
EMP: 200
SALES (corp-wide): 2.9B **Publicly Held**
WEB: www.graniteconstruction.com
SIC: **1611** Highway & street construction
HQ: Granite Construction Company
585 W Beach St
Watsonville CA 95076
831 724-1011

(P-1773)
**GRANITE CONSTRUCTION
COMPANY**
Also Called: Southern California Regional
38000 Monroe St, Indio (92203-9500)
PHONE.................................760 775-7500
Jay McQuillen, *Manager*
Claes Bjork, *Bd of Directors*
William Dorey, *Bd of Directors*
EMP: 393
SALES (corp-wide): 2.9B **Publicly Held**
WEB:
www.graniteconstructioncompany.com
SIC: **1611** 1771 Highway & street con-
struction; concrete work
HQ: Granite Construction Company
585 W Beach St
Watsonville CA 95076
831 724-1011

(P-1774)
**GRANITE CONSTRUCTION
COMPANY**
5335 Debbie Rd, Santa Barbara
(93111-2001)
P.O. Box 6744 (93160-6744)
PHONE.................................805 964-9951
Bruce McGowan, *Manager*
EMP: 169
SQ FT: 65,396
SALES (corp-wide): 2.9B **Publicly Held**
WEB: www.graniteconstruction.com
SIC: **1611** Highway & street construction
HQ: Granite Construction Company
585 W Beach St
Watsonville CA 95076
831 724-1011

(P-1775)
**GRANITE CONSTRUCTION
COMPANY**
21541 E Bear Mtn Blvd, Arvin (93203)
PHONE.................................661 854-3051
Mike Hosley, *Branch Mgr*
EMP: 67
SALES (corp-wide): 2.9B **Publicly Held**
WEB: www.graniteconstruction.com
SIC: **1611** Highway & street construction
HQ: Granite Construction Company
585 W Beach St
Watsonville CA 95076
831 724-1011

(P-1776)
**GRANITE CONSTRUCTION
COMPANY**
Also Called: Palmdale Area
213 E Avenue M, Lancaster (93535-5335)
PHONE.................................661 726-4447
Steve Bridge, *Branch Mgr*
EMP: 150
SQ FT: 12,716

P R O D U C T S & S V C S

SALES (corp-wide): 2.9B **Publicly Held**
WEB: www.graniteconstruction.com
SIC: **1611** Highway & street paving contractor
HQ: Granite Construction Company
585 W Beach St
Watsonville CA 95076
831 724-1011

(P-1777)
GRANITE CONSTRUCTION COMPANY
715 Comstock St, Santa Clara (95054-3403)
PHONE.................................408 327-7000
Pat Traberso, *Manager*
EMP: 182
SQ FT: 22,902
SALES (corp-wide): 2.9B **Publicly Held**
WEB: www.graniteconstruction.com
SIC: **1611** 1622 1629 General contractor, highway & street construction; bridge construction; dams, waterways, docks & other marine construction
HQ: Granite Construction Company
585 W Beach St
Watsonville CA 95076
831 724-1011

(P-1778)
GRANITE CONSTRUCTION COMPANY
2716 S Granite Ct, Fresno (93706-5455)
PHONE.................................559 441-5700
Todd Hill, *Manager*
Eric Hammond, *IT Executive*
EMP: 225
SALES (corp-wide): 2.9B **Publicly Held**
SIC: **1611** General contractor, highway & street construction
HQ: Granite Construction Company
585 W Beach St
Watsonville CA 95076
831 724-1011

(P-1779)
GRANITE CONSTRUCTION INC
2095 Us Highway 111, El Centro (92243-9731)
PHONE.................................760 337-3030
Jeff Mercer, *Manager*
EMP: 120
SALES (corp-wide): 2.9B **Publicly Held**
WEB: www.graniteconstruction.com
SIC: **1611** General contractor, highway & street construction
PA: Granite Construction Incorporated
585 W Beach St
Watsonville CA 95076
831 724-1011

(P-1780)
GRANITE CONSTRUCTION INC
5 Justin Ct, Monterey (93940-5733)
P.O. Box 720, Watsonville (95077-0720)
PHONE.................................831 657-1700
Kurt Kniffin, *Principal*
EMP: 67
SALES (corp-wide): 2.9B **Publicly Held**
WEB: www.graniteconstruction.com
SIC: **1611** General contractor, highway & street construction
PA: Granite Construction Incorporated
585 W Beach St
Watsonville CA 95076
831 724-1011

(P-1781)
GRANITE CONSTRUCTION INC
4291 Bradshaw Rd, Sacramento (95827-3805)
PHONE.................................916 855-4495
Ryan Bingle, *Manager*
Sandy Smithers, *Executive Asst*
Amy Tobia, *Administration*
Brian Kotaska, *MIS Mgr*
Kelly Mitchell, *Business Mgr*
EMP: 67
SALES (corp-wide): 2.9B **Publicly Held**
WEB: www.graniteconstruction.com
SIC: **1611** General contractor, highway & street construction
PA: Granite Construction Incorporated
585 W Beach St
Watsonville CA 95076
831 724-1011

(P-1782)
GRANITE CONSTRUCTION INC
1324 S State St, Ukiah (95482-6414)
PHONE.................................707 467-4100
Dan Schuster, *Manager*
EMP: 67
SALES (corp-wide): 2.9B **Publicly Held**
WEB: www.graniteconstruction.com
SIC: **1611** General contractor, highway & street construction
PA: Granite Construction Incorporated
585 W Beach St
Watsonville CA 95076
831 724-1011

(P-1783)
GRANITE CONSTRUCTION INC
25485 Iverson Rd, Gonzales (93926-9403)
PHONE.................................831 763-5595
Eric Gaboury, *Manager*
EMP: 67
SALES (corp-wide): 2.9B **Publicly Held**
WEB: www.graniteconstruction.com
SIC: **1611** General contractor, highway & street construction
PA: Granite Construction Incorporated
585 W Beach St
Watsonville CA 95076
831 724-1011

(P-1784)
GRANITE CONSTRUCTION INC
1800 Felton Quarry Rd, Felton (95018-9153)
PHONE.................................831 335-3445
Eric Gaboury, *Manager*
EMP: 67
SALES (corp-wide): 2.9B **Publicly Held**
WEB: www.graniteconstruction.com
SIC: **1611** General contractor, highway & street construction
PA: Granite Construction Incorporated
585 W Beach St
Watsonville CA 95076
831 724-1011

(P-1785)
GRANITE ROCK CO
1900 Quarry Rd, Aromas (95004)
P.O. Box 699 (95004-0699)
PHONE.................................831 768-2330
Carey Wong, *Branch Mgr*
EMP: 151
SALES (corp-wide): 1.1B **Privately Held**
SIC: **1611** Surfacing & paving
PA: Granite Rock Co.
350 Technology Dr
Watsonville CA 95076
831 768-2000

(P-1786)
GRANITE ROCK CO
Also Called: Pavex Construction Company
355 Blomquist St, Redwood City (94063-2701)
PHONE.................................650 869-3370
John Franich, *Manager*
Wayne Holman, *Vice Pres*
John Holcomb, *Project Engr*
EMP: 300
SALES (corp-wide): 1.1B **Privately Held**
WEB: www.graniterock.com
SIC: **1611** Highway & street paving contractor
PA: Granite Rock Co.
350 Technology Dr
Watsonville CA 95076
831 768-2000

(P-1787)
GRIFFITH COMPANY (PA)
3050 E Birch St, Brea (92821-6248)
PHONE.................................714 984-5500
Thomas L Foss, *CEO*
Jim Waltze, *Ch of Bd*
Jaimie Angus, *COO*
Gordon Csutak, *CFO*
Dave Diaz, *Vice Pres*
EMP: 60 EST: 1922
SQ FT: 100,000
SALES (est): 141.6MM **Privately Held**
SIC: **1611** General contractor, highway & street construction

(P-1788)
GRIFFITH COMPANY
12200 Bloomfield Ave, Santa Fe Springs (90670-4742)
PHONE.................................562 929-1128
Dan Magrew, *Manager*
Elvira Arellano, *Admin Asst*
Luis Cervantes, *Project Mgr*
Dan Leeper, *Project Mgr*
Linda Hynds, *Project Engr*
EMP: 60
SQ FT: 4,036
SALES (corp-wide): 141.6MM **Privately Held**
SIC: **1611** 1622 General contractor, highway & street construction; bridge construction; tunnel construction
PA: Griffith Company
3050 E Birch St
Brea CA 92821
714 984-5500

(P-1789)
GSE CONSTRUCTION COMPANY INC
6950 Preston Ave, Livermore (94551-9545)
PHONE.................................925 447-0292
Orlando Gutierrez, *President*
Dennis Gutierrez, *Vice Pres*
Steve Mazza, *Vice Pres*
Irish Sosa, *Manager*
EMP: 90 EST: 1980
SQ FT: 52,000
SALES (est): 116.9K **Privately Held**
SIC: **1611** General contractor, highway & street construction

(P-1790)
HARDY & HARPER INC
1312 E Warner Ave, Santa Ana (92705-5416)
PHONE.................................714 444-1851
Daniel Thomas Maas, *CEO*
Fred T Maas Sr, *Director*
EMP: 50 EST: 1946
SQ FT: 3,000
SALES (est): 13.1MM **Privately Held**
WEB: www.hardyandharper.com
SIC: **1611** Surfacing & paving

(P-1791)
HILLCREST CONTRACTING INC
1467 Circle City Dr, Corona (92879-1668)
P.O. Box 1898 (92878-1898)
PHONE.................................951 273-9600
Glenn J Salsbury, *President*
E G Lindholm, *Vice Pres*
Amanda Gutierrez, *Administration*
Jason Jones, *Project Mgr*
Richard Sanchez, *Project Mgr*
EMP: 75
SQ FT: 11,600
SALES (est): 20.5MM **Privately Held**
SIC: **1611** General contractor, highway & street construction

(P-1792)
INTERNATIONAL PAVING SVCS INC
Also Called: I P S
1199 Opal Ave, Mentone (92359-1284)
P.O. Box 10458, San Bernardino (92423-0458)
PHONE.................................909 794-2101
Brent Rieger, *President*
EMP: 80 EST: 2007
SALES (est): 11.5MM **Privately Held**
SIC: **1611** Surfacing & paving

(P-1793)
J B BOSTICK COMPANY INC (PA)
2870 E La Cresta Ave, Anaheim (92806-1816)
PHONE.................................714 238-2121
James B Bostick, *President*
Jerry Hamlin, *Vice Pres*
Tony Imfeld, *Production*
EMP: 75
SQ FT: 2,870
SALES (est): 31.4MM **Privately Held**
WEB: www.jbbostick.net
SIC: **1611** 1771 Grading; highway & street paving contractor; concrete work

(P-1794)
J HARRIS SIM INC (PA)
9685 Via Excelencia # 200, San Diego (92126-7500)
PHONE.................................858 437-0190
James Coffman, *President*
John Palmer, *Vice Pres*
EMP: 85 EST: 2005
SQ FT: 10,000
SALES (est): 4.5MM **Privately Held**
SIC: **1611** General contractor, highway & street construction

(P-1795)
JACOBSSON ENGRG CNSTR INC
72310 Varner Rd, Thousand Palms (92276-3362)
P.O. Box 14430, Palm Desert (92255-4430)
PHONE.................................760 345-8700
Dan Jacobsson, *President*
Ingeborg Jacobsson, *Treasurer*
EMP: 75
SQ FT: 9,000
SALES (est): 11.3MM **Privately Held**
WEB: www.jacobssoninc.com
SIC: **1611** Highway & street construction

(P-1796)
JAMES MCMINN INC
21801 Barton Rd Ste B, Grand Terrace (92313-4402)
PHONE.................................909 514-1231
Jim McMinn, *President*
Rick Monge, *Vice Pres*
EMP: 50
SALES: 12MM **Privately Held**
SIC: **1611** Grading

(P-1797)
JJ FISHER CONSTRUCTION INC
261 W Dana St Ste 100, Nipomo (93444-9151)
P.O. Box 2219 (93444-2219)
PHONE.................................805 723-5220
Jayson Fisher, *CEO*
Mark Sczbecki, *CFO*
EMP: 65
SALES: 12MM **Privately Held**
SIC: **1611** 1771 1794 1761 Gravel or dirt road construction; concrete work; curb construction; blacktop (asphalt) work; excavation work; gutter & downspout contractor

(P-1798)
JOHN BRINK GENERAL CONTRACTOR
1760 W Lake Blvd Ste 3, Tahoe City (96145-1868)
P.O. Box 1902 (96145-1902)
PHONE.................................530 583-2005
John Brink, *Owner*
EMP: 50 EST: 1974
SALES (est): 4MM **Privately Held**
SIC: **1611** General contractor, highway & street construction

(P-1799)
KAD PAVING COMPANY
Also Called: Kad Engineering
32147 Dunlap Blvd Ste K, Yucaipa (92399-1757)
PHONE.................................909 790-3366
Donald S Wheeler Jr, *President*
EMP: 52
SQ FT: 11,000
SALES (est): 7.1MM **Privately Held**
SIC: **1611** Highway & street paving contractor; surfacing & paving

(P-1800)
KEC ENGINEERING
200 N Sherman Ave, Corona (92882-7162)
P.O. Box 909 (92878-0909)
PHONE.................................951 734-3010
James Elfring, *President*
Les Card, *Vice Pres*
EMP: 110
SQ FT: 9,600
SALES (est): 23.8MM **Privately Held**
WEB: www.kecengineering.com
SIC: **1611** General contractor, highway & street construction

(P-1801)
KIEWIT INFRASTRUCTURE WEST CO
1111 Broadway, Oakland (94607-4139)
PHONE..........................510 452-1400
William Silver, *Branch Mgr*
EMP: 54
SALES (corp-wide): 16.6B **Privately Held**
SIC: 1611 General contractor, highway & street construction
HQ: Kiewit Infrastructure West Co.
3555 Farnam St
Omaha NE 68131
402 342-2052

(P-1802)
KIEWIT INFRASTRUCTURE WEST CO
3200 Busch Rd, Pleasanton (94566)
PHONE..........................925 462-1088
Allan Kung, *General Mgr*
EMP: 80
SALES (corp-wide): 16.6B **Privately Held**
WEB: www.kiecon.com
SIC: 1611 General contractor, highway & street construction
HQ: Kiewit Infrastructure West Co.
3555 Farnam St
Omaha NE 68131
402 342-2052

(P-1803)
KIEWIT INFRASTRUCTURE WEST CO
10704 Shoemaker Ave, Santa Fe Springs (90670-4040)
PHONE..........................562 946-1816
Ken Riley, *Manager*
David Linderman, *Project Mgr*
Doug Collins, *Manager*
EMP: 125
SQ FT: 12,514
SALES (corp-wide): 16.6B **Privately Held**
WEB: www.kiecon.com
SIC: 1611 1542 1541 General contractor, highway & street construction; nonresidential construction; industrial buildings & warehouses
HQ: Kiewit Infrastructure West Co.
3555 Farnam St
Omaha NE 68131
402 342-2052

(P-1804)
KIEWIT INFRASTRUCTURE WEST CO
Also Called: Kie Con
3551 Wilbur Ave, Antioch (94509-8530)
PHONE..........................925 754-9494
John Burke, *Manager*
EMP: 50
SQ FT: 4,320
SALES (corp-wide): 16.6B **Privately Held**
WEB: www.kiecon.com
SIC: 1611 General contractor, highway & street construction
HQ: Kiewit Infrastructure West Co.
3555 Farnam St
Omaha NE 68131
402 342-2052

(P-1805)
LARRY JACINTO CONSTRUCTION INC
9555 N Wabash Ave, Redlands (92374-2714)
P.O. Box 615, Mentone (92359-0615)
PHONE..........................909 794-2151
Larry Frankland Jacinto, *CEO*
Steve Hopkins, *CFO*
Dennis Drexler, *Vice Pres*
EMP: 80
SQ FT: 8,500
SALES (est): 23.6MM **Privately Held**
SIC: 1611 Grading; highway & street paving contractor; sidewalk construction

(P-1806)
LEGACY PARTNERS LIMITED INC
Also Called: Legacy Paving
738 W Washington Ave A, Escondido (92025-1692)
PHONE..........................760 747-2711

EMP: 53
SALES (est): 4.4MM **Privately Held**
WEB: www.legacypaving.com
SIC: 1611

(P-1807)
LUND EQUIPMENT LP
5302 Roseville Rd, North Highlands (95660-5036)
PHONE..........................916 344-5800
Walter Martinez, *Principal*
Stephanie Hannah, *CFO*
Kevin Lund, *Vice Pres*
EMP: 50
SALES (est): 6.5MM **Privately Held**
SIC: 1611 General contractor, highway & street construction

(P-1808)
M F MAHER INC
Also Called: Maher M F Concrete Cnstr
490 Ryder St, Vallejo (94590-7217)
PHONE..........................707 552-2774
Malcolm F Maher, *President*
Janice K Maher, *Corp Secy*
Ronald Maher, *Vice Pres*
Steve Maher, *Executive*
Mike Maher, *Office Mgr*
EMP: 70
SQ FT: 4,000
SALES (est): 11.8MM **Privately Held**
WEB: www.mfmaher.com
SIC: 1611 General contractor, highway & street construction

(P-1809)
MACRO-Z-TECHNOLOGY COMPANY (PA)
Also Called: M Z T
841 E Washington Ave, Santa Ana (92701-3878)
PHONE..........................714 564-1130
Bryan J Zatica, *CEO*
Julie Moore, *Manager*
EMP: 97
SQ FT: 3,000
SALES (est): 45.8MM **Privately Held**
SIC: 1611 1542 8711 Concrete construction: roads, highways, sidewalks, etc.; commercial & office building contractors; engineering services

(P-1810)
MAMCO INC (PA)
Also Called: Alabbasi
764 Ramona Expy Ste C, Perris (92571-9716)
PHONE..........................951 776-9300
Marwan Alabbasi, *CEO*
Elizabeth Alabbasi, *President*
Rumzi Alabbasi, *Vice Pres*
EMP: 120
SQ FT: 2,200
SALES (est): 34.6MM **Privately Held**
SIC: 1611 General contractor, highway & street construction

(P-1811)
MANHOLE ADJUSTING CONTRS INC
9500 Beverly Rd, Pico Rivera (90660-2135)
PHONE..........................323 725-1387
John Corcoran, *President*
Maria E Corcoran, *Vice Pres*
Aung Win, *Controller*
EMP: 50
SALES (est): 10.8MM **Privately Held**
SIC: 1611 General contractor, highway & street construction; highway & street paving contractor

(P-1812)
MARATHON GENERAL INC
1728 Mission Rd, Escondido (92029-1111)
PHONE..........................760 738-9714
Mark Miller, *President*
Steven Gallant, *CFO*
Donald Tolen, *Vice Pres*
EMP: 80
SQ FT: 3,000
SALES (est): 18.5MM **Privately Held**
WEB: www.maragen.com
SIC: 1611 Grading; highway & street paving contractor

(P-1813)
MARTIN BROTHERS CONSTRUCTION (PA)
8801 Folsom Blvd Ste 260, Sacramento (95826-3250)
PHONE..........................916 386-1600
Felipe Martin, *President*
EMP: 75
SQ FT: 9,300
SALES (est): 26MM **Privately Held**
SIC: 1611 1794 1541 1795 General contractor, highway & street construction; surfacing & paving; highway & street paving contractor; excavation work; excavation & grading, building construction; industrial buildings, new construction; demolition, buildings & other structures

(P-1814)
MATICH CORPORATION (PA)
1596 E Harry Shepard Blvd, San Bernardino (92408-0197)
P.O. Box 10, Highland (92346-1010)
PHONE..........................909 382-7400
Stephen A Matich, *CEO*
Martin A Matich, *Chairman*
Randall Valadez, *Treasurer*
Patrick A Matich, *Exec VP*
Robert M Matich, *Exec VP*
EMP: 60 **EST:** 1918
SQ FT: 10,000
SALES (est): 58.7MM **Privately Held**
WEB: www.matichcm.com
SIC: 1611 2951 General contractor, highway & street construction; asphalt paving mixtures & blocks

(P-1815)
MATICH CORPORATION
13984 Apache Trl, Cabazon (92230-2143)
PHONE..........................951 849-8280
Nikolas Matich, *Branch Mgr*
EMP: 50
SALES (corp-wide): 58.7MM **Privately Held**
SIC: 1611 General contractor, highway & street construction
PA: Matich Corporation
1596 E Harry Shepard Blvd
San Bernardino CA 92408
909 382-7400

(P-1816)
MCCULLOUGH CONSTRUCTION
57 Alder Grove Rd, Arcata (95521-9276)
PHONE..........................707 825-1014
Jens Karlshoej, *Partner*
Dena McCullough, *Partner*
Hugh McCullough, *Partner*
Dan Schultz, *Partner*
Clay Hicks, *Foreman/Supr*
EMP: 80
SALES (est): 1.9MM **Privately Held**
SIC: 1611 1622 Highway & street construction; tunnel construction

(P-1817)
MCE CORPORATION (PA)
4000 Industrial Way, Concord (94520-1289)
P.O. Box 508 (94522-0508)
PHONE..........................925 803-4111
Jeff Core, *President*
Dan Furtado, *Vice Pres*
Steve Loweree, *Vice Pres*
Bill Macedo, *General Mgr*
Karen Briones, *Safety Mgr*
EMP: 65
SQ FT: 12,000
SALES (est): 53.6MM **Privately Held**
WEB: www.mce-corp.com
SIC: 1611 0782 General contractor, highway & street construction; lawn & garden services

(P-1818)
MESA CONTRACTING CORPORATION
22845 Savi Ranch Pkwy D, Yorba Linda (92887-4625)
PHONE..........................714 974-7300
Ronald Gene Smith, *CEO*
Ron McAmis, *Corp Secy*
Bill Bates, *Vice Pres*
EMP: 120

SQ FT: 4,518
SALES (est): 17.9MM **Privately Held**
SIC: 1611 Grading

(P-1819)
MGB CONSTRUCTION INC
91 Commercial Ave, Riverside (92507-1111)
PHONE..........................951 342-0303
Emily Beach, *President*
Emilly Beach, *President*
EMP: 150
SALES (est): 17MM **Privately Held**
SIC: 1611 Highway & street paving contractor

(P-1820)
MIDSTATE BARRIER INC
Also Called: MBI
3291 S Highway 99, Stockton (95215-8032)
P.O. Box 30550 (95213-0550)
PHONE..........................209 944-9565
Clark Ebinger, *President*
Stephen V Gifford, *Vice Pres*
EMP: 75
SQ FT: 20,000
SALES (est): 20MM **Privately Held**
WEB: www.hwysfty.com
SIC: 1611 Highway signs & guardrails; guardrail construction, highways

(P-1821)
MORRO BAY PUBLIC WORKS
Also Called: City of Morro Bay
955 Shasta Ave, Morro Bay (93442-1934)
PHONE..........................805 772-6261
Janice Peters, *Mayor*
Karen Sweeny, *Manager*
EMP: 100
SALES (est): 8.2MM **Privately Held**
SIC: 1611 Highway & street construction

(P-1822)
MUSE CONCRETE CONTRACTORS INC
8599 Commercial Way, Redding (96002-3902)
PHONE..........................530 226-5151
Boyce Muse, *President*
Joan Muse, *CFO*
EMP: 94
SALES (est): 18.1MM **Privately Held**
WEB: www.museconcrete.com
SIC: 1611 1771 Concrete construction: roads, highways, sidewalks, etc.; concrete work; curb construction

(P-1823)
MYERS & SONS CONSTRUCTION LP
4600 Northgate Blvd # 100, Sacramento (95834-1103)
PHONE..........................916 283-9950
Clinton C Myers, *Partner*
Clinton W Myers, *Partner*
Jenna Carlson, *Human Res Dir*
EMP: 250
SALES: 181.5MM **Privately Held**
SIC: 1611 Highway & street construction

(P-1824)
NATIONAL PAVING COMPANY INC
4361 Fort Dr, Riverside (92509-6784)
P.O. Box 3649 (92519-3649)
PHONE..........................951 369-1332
Richard J Lindholm, *President*
Lawrence Spicher, *CFO*
EMP: 78
SQ FT: 4,000
SALES (est): 15.1MM **Privately Held**
WEB: www.nationalpaving.com
SIC: 1611 Highway & street paving contractor; surfacing & paving

(P-1825)
NEHEMIAH CONSTRUCTION INC
12150 Tributary Ln P, Rancho Cordova (95670)
PHONE..........................707 746-6815
EMP: 50
SQ FT: 2,500

PRODUCTS & SVCS

SALES: 98.4K Privately Held
WEB: www.nehemiahconst.com
SIC: 1611

(P-1826)
NICHOLAS GRANT CORPORATION
Also Called: Daley
12570 Highway 67, Lakeside (92040-1159)
PHONE.................619 390-3900
John Daley Sr, *President*
Mark Thunder, *Exec VP*
▲ **EMP:** 100
SALES (est) 19.4MM **Privately Held**
SIC: 1611 Highway & street construction

(P-1827)
NORTH BAY CONSTRUCTION INC
431 Payran St, Petaluma (94952-5908)
P.O. Box 751389 (94975-1389)
PHONE.................707 283-0093
John E Barella, *President*
Steve Geney, *Vice Pres*
EMP: 80
SQ FT: 7,000
SALES (est): 8.2MM **Privately Held**
WEB: www.nbcinc.net
SIC: 1611 1623 Highway & street paving contractor; grading; sewer line construction

(P-1828)
O C JONES & SONS INC (PA)
1520 4th St, Berkeley (94710-1748)
PHONE.................510 526-3424
Kelly Kolander, *President*
Robert Pelascini, *Ch of Bd*
Rob Layne, *CEO*
Beth Yoshida, *CFO*
Jim Gallagher, *Area Mgr*
EMP: 150 **EST:** 1924
SQ FT: 80,000
SALES (est): 114.3MM **Privately Held**
WEB: www.ocjones.com
SIC: 1611 Grading; highway & street paving contractor

(P-1829)
OGRADY PAVING INC
2513 Wyandotte St, Mountain View (94043-2311)
PHONE.................650 966-1926
Thomas M O'Grady Jr, *President*
Celine Duran, *Corp Secy*
Craig Young, *Vice Pres*
Ryan Greene, *Manager*
Bob Taylor, *Manager*
EMP: 110
SQ FT: 3,200
SALES (est): 23.8MM **Privately Held**
WEB: www.ogradypaving.com
SIC: 1611 Highway & street paving contractor; grading

(P-1830)
ORTIZ ASPHALT PAVING INC
16588 Farmington St, Hesperia (92345-8825)
PHONE.................951 966-7060
Bruce Kevin Ortiz, *President*
EMP: 50
SQ FT: 1,000
SALES: 17MM **Privately Held**
SIC: 1611 Highway & street paving contractor

(P-1831)
ORTIZ ENTERPRISES INCORPORATED (PA)
6 Cushing Ste 200, Irvine (92618-4230)
PHONE.................949 753-1414
Patrick Ortiz, *President*
Jill Ortiz, *Vice Pres*
EMP: 80
SQ FT: 12,000
SALES: 31.5MM **Privately Held**
SIC: 1611 General contractor, highway & street construction

(P-1832)
PALP INC
Also Called: Excel Paving Co
2230 Lemon Ave, Long Beach (90806-5124)
P.O. Box 16405 (90806-0995)
PHONE.................562 599-5841
Curtis P Brown, *CEO*
George McRae, *Senior VP*
Bruce Flatt, *Vice Pres*
Darryl Rutledge, *General Mgr*
Michelle Drakulich, *Admin Sec*
EMP: 225 **EST:** 1976
SQ FT: 11,000
SALES (est): 59.9MM **Privately Held**
WEB: www.palp.com
SIC: 1611 8711 Highway & street paving contractor; grading; engineering services

(P-1833)
PAPICH CONSTRUCTION CO INC (PA)
398 Sunrise Ter, Arroyo Grande (93420-4419)
P.O. Box 2210, Pismo Beach (93448-2210)
PHONE.................805 473-3016
Jason William Papich, *President*
April Papich, *Admin Sec*
Craig Caballero, *Project Mgr*
Derek Todd, *Project Mgr*
EMP: 151
SQ FT: 6,000
SALES (est): 58.4MM **Privately Held**
WEB: www.papichconstruction.com
SIC: 1611 General contractor, highway & street construction

(P-1834)
PARSONS CORPORATION
44 Montgomery St Ste 880, San Francisco (94104-4620)
PHONE.................415 490-2400
Brad Braddock, *Manager*
EMP: 63
SALES (corp-wide): 3.1B **Privately Held**
SIC: 1611 Highway & street construction
PA: The Parsons Corporation
100 W Walnut St
Pasadena CA 91124
626 440-2000

(P-1835)
PARSONS CORPORATION
100 W San Fernando St # 450, San Jose (95113-2233)
PHONE.................626 440-2000
Joe Scarano, *Manager*
Carla Vincent, *Comp Spec*
EMP: 63
SALES (corp-wide): 3.1B **Privately Held**
SIC: 1611 Highway & street construction
PA: The Parsons Corporation
100 W Walnut St
Pasadena CA 91124
626 440-2000

(P-1836)
PAVE-TECH INC
2231 La Mirada Dr, Vista (92081-8828)
PHONE.................760 727-8700
Rudy Zavalani, *CEO*
Larry Keepers, *Shareholder*
EMP: 50
SALES (est): 14.6MM **Privately Held**
SIC: 1611 Highway & street paving contractor

(P-1837)
PENA GRADING & DEMOLITION INC
Also Called: Pena Trucking
11253 Vinedale St, Sun Valley (91352-3217)
PHONE.................818 768-5202
Orestes Pena, *President*
Irma Pena, *Vice Pres*
Michael Hernandez, *Opers Mgr*
EMP: 50
SQ FT: 8,000
SALES (est): 11.1MM **Privately Held**
SIC: 1611 4953 1795 1794 Grading; recycling, waste materials; wrecking & demolition work; demolition, buildings & other structures; excavation work; excavation & grading, building construction

(P-1838)
PETER KIEWIT SONS INC
1925 Wright Ave Ste C, La Verne (91750-5847)
PHONE.................909 962-6001
Rohit Shard, *Branch Mgr*
EMP: 177
SALES (corp-wide): 16.6B **Privately Held**
SIC: 1611 General contractor, highway & street construction
PA: Peter Kiewit Sons', Inc.
3555 Farnam St Ste 1000
Omaha NE 68131
402 342-2052

(P-1839)
QUAIL ENGINEERING INC
Also Called: Pacific Exteriors
11372 Trask Ave Ste 110, Garden Grove (92843-2605)
PHONE.................714 636-0612
Mark Kabarsky, *President*
▲ **EMP:** 50
SQ FT: 480
SALES (est): 4.4MM **Privately Held**
SIC: 1611 Grading

(P-1840)
REEVES TRACTOR SERVICE INC
5455 Blue Ridge Dr, Yorba Linda (92887-4234)
P.O. Box 702 (92885-0702)
PHONE.................714 692-4020
Jeffrey G Reeves, *President*
Laurie Reeves, *Manager*
EMP: 60
SALES (est): 4.4MM **Privately Held**
SIC: 1611 Grading

(P-1841)
RICK HAMM CONSTRUCTION INC
201 W Carleton Ave, Orange (92867-3607)
PHONE.................714 532-0815
Rick Hamm, *President*
Llana Hamm, *Corp Secy*
Cal Sistrunk, *Agent*
EMP: 90
SQ FT: 25,000
SALES (est): 19.6MM **Privately Held**
WEB: www.rickhamm.com
SIC: 1611 1771 1791 1741 General contractor, highway & street construction; patio construction, concrete; precast concrete structural framing or panels, placing of; masonry & other stonework; stone masonry; concrete block masonry laying; erection & dismantling of forms for poured concrete

(P-1842)
RJ NOBLE COMPANY (PA)
15505 E Lincoln Ave, Orange (92865-1015)
P.O. Box 620 (92856-9020)
PHONE.................714 637-1550
Michael J Carver, *President*
James N Ducote, *CFO*
Brenda Carver, *Vice Pres*
Craig Porter, *Vice Pres*
Terry McGill, *General Mgr*
EMP: 145 **EST:** 1950
SQ FT: 5,500
SALES (est): 60.2MM **Privately Held**
WEB: www.rjnoblecompany.com
SIC: 1611 Highway & street paving contractor

(P-1843)
ROMERO GENERAL CNSTR CORP
Also Called: ROMERO CONSTRUCTION
2150 N Centre City Pkwy I, Escondido (92026-1347)
PHONE.................760 489-8412
Keith Reilly, *President*
Troy Greer, *Vice Pres*
EMP: 175
SQ FT: 3,500
SALES: 17MM **Privately Held**
WEB: www.romerogc.com
SIC: 1611 Highway & street paving contractor

(P-1844)
ROY E LADD INC
Also Called: Ladd Construction Co
3724 Sunlight Ct, Redding (96001-0173)
PHONE.................530 241-6102
Craig Wiseman, *President*
Tom Capener, *Treasurer*
Mark Christopher, *Vice Pres*
Eric Ladd, *Vice Pres*
Bill Schoonmaker, *Vice Pres*
EMP: 50
SQ FT: 3,000
SALES: 20MM **Privately Held**
SIC: 1611 1622 Highway & street construction; bridge construction

(P-1845)
SAN JOAQUIN HILLS TRANSPORTTN (PA)
Also Called: JOINT POWERS AGENCY
125 Pacifica Ste 100, Irvine (92618-3324)
P.O. Box 53770 (92619-3770)
PHONE.................949 754-3400
Michael Kraman, *CEO*
Lance Maclean, *Executive*
Jim Rhodes, *Info Tech Dir*
Tracy Bowman, *Controller*
Patty Romo, *Exec Sec*
EMP: 51
SQ FT: 17,000
SALES: 198MM **Privately Held**
SIC: 1611 General contractor, highway & street construction

(P-1846)
SECURITY PAVING COMPANY INC (PA)
Also Called: Valley Base Materials
13170 Telfair Ave, Sylmar (91342-3573)
PHONE.................818 362-9200
Mike Mattivi, *CEO*
Albert Mattivi, *President*
Thomas J Mattivi, *Treasurer*
EMP: 100
SQ FT: 4,000
SALES (est): 50.3MM **Privately Held**
SIC: 1611 Surfacing & paving

(P-1847)
SEQUEL CONTRACTORS INC
13546 Imperial Hwy, Santa Fe Springs (90670-4821)
PHONE.................562 802-7227
Thomas S Pack, *CEO*
Abel Magellanes, *Vice Pres*
EMP: 50
SQ FT: 80,000
SALES (est): 8.6MM **Privately Held**
SIC: 1611 Highway & street construction

(P-1848)
SHELTON CONSTRUCTION COMPANY
5628 Spinnaker Bay Dr, Long Beach (90803-6806)
PHONE.................714 903-7853
William Shelton, *President*
EMP: 60
SQ FT: 3,200
SALES: 6MM **Privately Held**
WEB: www.sheltonconst.com
SIC: 1611 Grading

(P-1849)
SIALIC CONTRACTORS CORPORATION
Also Called: Shawnan
12240 Woodruff Ave, Downey (90241-5608)
PHONE.................562 803-9977
Shawn Smith, *President*
John Smith, *Admin Sec*
EMP: 68
SQ FT: 24,000
SALES (est): 6.1MM **Privately Held**
SIC: 1611 General contractor, highway & street construction

(P-1850)
SKANSKA USA CVIL W CAL DST INC (DH)
1995 Agua Mansa Rd, Riverside (92509-2405)
PHONE.................951 684-5360

Richard Cavallero, *CEO*
Michael Cobelli, *COO*
Joseph Nogues, *CFO*
Michael Aparicio, *Exec VP*
Lisa Picard, *Exec VP*
EMP: 700
SQ FT: 15,000
SALES (est): 289.1MM
SALES (corp-wide): 18.7B **Privately Held**
SIC: 1611 1622 1629 8711 General contractor, highway & street construction; bridge construction; highway construction, elevated; dam construction; engineering services; asphalt paving mixtures & blocks
HQ: Skanska Usa Civil Inc.
7520 Astoria Blvd Ste 200
East Elmhurst NY 11370
718 340-0777

(P-1851)
SKANSKA-RADOS A JOINT VENTURE
11390 W Olympic Blvd, Los Angeles (90064-1619)
PHONE................213 978-0600
Kent Percy, *Partner*
Michael Witz, *Partner*
EMP: 70
SALES (est): 1.2MM **Privately Held**
SIC: 1611 Highway & street construction

(P-1852)
SOUTH COAST STONE PAVING
Also Called: Hillside Contractor
2618 N Baker St, Santa Ana (92706-1511)
PHONE................714 835-0258
David Lopez, *Principal*
EMP: 65
SALES (est): 6MM **Privately Held**
SIC: 1611 Highway & street construction

(P-1853)
STEVE MANNING CONSTRUCTION INC
5211 Churn Creek Rd, Redding (96002-3914)
P.O. Box 491660 (96049-1660)
PHONE................530 222-0810
Steve Manning, *President*
Arlene T Litsey, *Treasurer*
Arlene Litsey, *Controller*
Jennie Davis, *Payroll Mgr*
EMP: 54
SQ FT: 2,200
SALES (est): 17.3MM **Privately Held**
SIC: 1611 Highway & street construction

(P-1854)
STEVENS CREEK QUARRY INC (PA)
12100 Stevens Canyon Rd, Cupertino (95014-5443)
PHONE................408 253-2512
Richard A Voss, *President*
Richard Voss, *President*
Bob Romano, *Principal*
Diana Voss, *Admin Sec*
EMP: 60
SALES (est): 20.3MM **Privately Held**
WEB: www.scqinc.com
SIC: 1611 7353 1442 General contractor, highway & street construction; highway & street maintenance; heavy construction equipment rental; construction sand mining

(P-1855)
SUDHAKAR COMPANY INTERNATIONAL
1450 N Fitzgerald Ave, Rialto (92376-8621)
PHONE................909 879-2933
Ashok Sudhakar, *President*
Betty Bogle, *Vice Pres*
EMP: 100 EST: 1998
SQ FT: 16,000
SALES: 21MM **Privately Held**
WEB: www.sudhakarco.com
SIC: 1611 Highway & street sign installation; highway reflector installation

(P-1856)
SULLY-MILLER CONTRACTING CO (DH)
Also Called: Blue Diamond Materials
135 S State College Blvd # 400, Brea (92821-5819)
PHONE................714 578-9600
John Harrington, *President*
Christian Ransinangue, *CFO*
Jon Layne, *Chief Mktg Ofcr*
Scott Bottomley, *Vice Pres*
William Boyd, *Vice Pres*
EMP: 306 EST: 1997
SALES: 189MM
SALES (corp-wide): 95.5MM **Privately Held**
WEB: www.thebluediamond.com
SIC: 1611 Highway & street construction
HQ: Colas Inc.
73 Headquarters Plz 10t
Morristown NJ 07960
973 290-9082

(P-1857)
SUPERIOR PAVING COMPANY INC
Also Called: United Paving Company
1880 N Delilah St, Corona (92879-1892)
PHONE................951 739-9200
Sabas Trujillo, *CEO*
EMP: 85
SQ FT: 3,000
SALES (est): 22.7MM **Privately Held**
WEB: www.united-paving.com
SIC: 1611 Highway & street paving contractor

(P-1858)
SYSTEMS PAVING INC (PA)
1570 Brookhollow Dr, Santa Ana (92705-5438)
PHONE................949 263-8301
Larry Green, *CEO*
Douglas Lueck, *President*
Steven Leuck, *Vice Pres*
EMP: 61
SQ FT: 13,000
SALES (est): 38.7MM **Privately Held**
SIC: 1611 Surfacing & paving

(P-1859)
TEAM GHILOTTI INC
2531 Petaluma Blvd S, Petaluma (94952-5523)
PHONE................707 763-8700
Glen Ghilotti, *President*
Glen C Ghilotti, *President*
Monica Bourdens, *Office Mgr*
EMP: 50
SQ FT: 5,900
SALES (est): 10MM **Privately Held**
WEB: www.teamghilotti.com
SIC: 1611 General contractor, highway & street construction

(P-1860)
TELFER OIL COMPANY (PA)
Also Called: Western Oil & Spreading
211 Foster St, Martinez (94553-1029)
P.O. Box 709 (94553-0151)
PHONE................925 228-1515
Michael S Telfer, *Owner*
John Telfer, *Owner*
EMP: 55
SQ FT: 5,000
SALES (est): 63.6MM **Privately Held**
WEB: www.telfercompanies.com
SIC: 1611 2951 4213 4212 Highway & street paving contractor; resurfacing contractor; paving mixtures; liquid petroleum transport, non-local; local trucking, without storage

(P-1861)
TNT GRADING INC
Also Called: T-N-T Grading
529 W 4th Ave B, Escondido (92025-4037)
PHONE................760 736-4054
EMP: 95
SQ FT: 2,500
SALES (est): 5.5MM **Privately Held**
WEB: www.tntgrading.com
SIC: 1611 Grading

(P-1862)
TORO ENTERPRISES INC
2101 Ventura Blvd, Oxnard (93036-8951)
P.O. Box 6285 (93031-6285)
PHONE................805 483-4515
Sean Castillo, *President*
Buffy Castillo, *Shareholder*
Teresa Ortega, *Shareholder*
Reuben Ortega, *Vice Pres*
Monica Ramirez, *Accountant*
EMP: 67
SALES (est): 21.5MM **Privately Held**
WEB: www.toroenterprises.com
SIC: 1611 Concrete construction: roads, highways, sidewalks, etc.

(P-1863)
TRANSPORTATION CALIFORNIA DEPT
Also Called: Maintenance Department
611 Payran St, Petaluma (94952-5910)
PHONE................707 762-6641
John Peterson, *Manager*
EMP: 110 **Privately Held**
WEB: www.caltip.org
SIC: 1611 9621 Highway & street maintenance; regulation, administration of transportation
HQ: California Dept Of Transportation
1120 N St
Sacramento CA 95814

(P-1864)
TRANSPORTATION CALIFORNIA DEPT
Also Called: Caltrans
2019 W Texas St, Fairfield (94533-4461)
P.O. Box 8 (94533-0084)
PHONE................707 428-2031
E L Poplin, *Branch Mgr*
EMP: 150 **Privately Held**
WEB: www.caltip.org
SIC: 1611 9621 Highway & street maintenance; regulation, administration of transportation
HQ: California Dept Of Transportation
1120 N St
Sacramento CA 95814

(P-1865)
TRANSPORTATION CALIFORNIA DEPT
Also Called: Caltrans Eastern Reg Rd Maint
1940 Workman Mill Rd, Whittier (90601-1414)
PHONE................562 692-0823
Edward Toledo, *Manager*
EMP: 200 **Privately Held**
WEB: www.caltip.org
SIC: 1611 9621 Highway & street maintenance; regulation, administration of transportation
HQ: California Dept Of Transportation
1120 N St
Sacramento CA 95814

(P-1866)
UNIVERSAL ASPHALT CO INC
10610 Painter Ave, Santa Fe Springs (90670-4091)
P.O. Box 2548 (90670-0548)
PHONE................562 941-0201
Daniel M Houck, *President*
EMP: 50
SQ FT: 22,000
SALES (est): 7.1MM **Privately Held**
SIC: 1611 Highway & street paving contractor

(P-1867)
VANCE CORPORATION
17761 Slover Ave, Bloomington (92316-2330)
PHONE................909 355-4333
Verner E Thomas, *CEO*
Darrel L Lohman, *CFO*
EMP: 50
SQ FT: 10,000
SALES (est): 10.3MM **Privately Held**
SIC: 1611 General contractor, highway & street construction

(P-1868)
VSS INTERNATIONAL INC (HQ)
Also Called: V S S
3785 Channel Dr, West Sacramento (95691-3421)
P.O. Box 981330 (95798-1330)
PHONE................916 373-1500
Jeffrey Reed, *President*
Ron Bolles, *Treasurer*
John Shoden, *Treasurer*
Alan Berger, *Vice Pres*
Diane Minor, *Admin Sec*
▲ **EMP:** 62
SQ FT: 5,000
SALES (est): 45MM
SALES (corp-wide): 197.8MM **Privately Held**
SIC: 1611 3531 2951 Highway & street paving contractor; construction machinery; asphalt paving mixtures & blocks
PA: Basic Resources Inc
928 12th St Ste 700
Modesto CA 95354
209 521-9771

(P-1869)
WESTERN PAVING CONTRACTORS INC
15533 Arrow Hwy, Irwindale (91706-2002)
PHONE................626 338-7889
Enrique Castillo, *CEO*
Henry Castillo, *President*
Rene Isenhart, *General Mgr*
John Gill, *Opers Staff*
EMP: 65
SQ FT: 3,200
SALES: 24.2MM **Privately Held**
SIC: 1611 Highway & street paving contractor; grading

(P-1870)
WESTERN RIM CONSTRUCTORS INC
621 S Andreasen Dr Ste B, Escondido (92029-1904)
PHONE................760 489-4328
Ray C Samuelson, *President*
Sandra Roth, *Manager*
EMP: 50
SALES (est): 10.5MM **Privately Held**
WEB: www.westernrim.net
SIC: 1611 General contractor, highway & street construction

(P-1871)
WR FORDE ASSOCIATES INC
984 Hensley St, Richmond (94801-2117)
PHONE................415 924-3072
Donald Russell, *CEO*
Donald J Russell, *Partner*
Dale Robbins, *Treasurer*
EMP: 55
SQ FT: 4,500
SALES: 11.8MM **Privately Held**
SIC: 1611 1622 1794 Grading; bridge construction; excavation & grading, building construction

---

1622 Bridge, Tunnel & Elevated Hwy Construction

(P-1872)
AECOM ENERGY & CNSTR INC (DH)
1999 Avenue Of The Stars, Los Angeles (90067-6022)
PHONE................213 593-8100
Thomas H Zarges, *CEO*
Robert Zaist, *President*
Judy L Rodgers, *Treasurer*
Randolph J Hill, *Senior VP*
H Thomas Hicks, *Principal*
◆ **EMP:** 151
SQ FT: 214,000
SALES (est): 5B
SALES (corp-wide): 20.1B **Publicly Held**
WEB: www.wgint.com
SIC: 1622 1629 1081 4953 Bridge, tunnel & elevated highway; oil refinery construction; metal mining services; refuse systems; engineering services

(P-1873)
AMERICAN BRDGE/FLUOR ENTPS INC
1390 Willow Pass Rd, Concord (94520-5200)
PHONE............................510 808-4623
Robert Luffy, *President*
David Degney, *Exec VP*
Douglas Fuller, *Vice Pres*
Donald Jones, *Vice Pres*
▲ EMP: 80
SALES (est): 14MM **Privately Held**
SIC: 1622 Bridge construction

(P-1874)
APW CONSTRUCTION INC (PA)
Also Called: Ace Fence Company
727 Glendora Ave, La Puente (91744-4014)
PHONE............................626 820-0812
Amy Tsui, *President*
Wayne Wong, *Treasurer*
Cristina Melgarejo, *Officer*
Jose Ramirez, *Vice Pres*
America Tang, *Vice Pres*
▲ EMP: 95
SQ FT: 8,000
SALES: 20MM **Privately Held**
WEB: www.acefencecompany.com
SIC: 1622 1799 Bridge, tunnel & elevated highway; fence construction

(P-1875)
AVAR CONSTRUCTION SYSTEMS INC (PA)
47375 Fremont Blvd, Fremont (94538-6521)
PHONE............................510 354-2000
Michael Anthony Pagano, *CEO*
Amy Winford, *Vice Pres*
▲ EMP: 50
SQ FT: 41,700
SALES (est): 11.5MM **Privately Held**
SIC: 1622 Bridge, tunnel & elevated highway

(P-1876)
COUNTY OF SACRAMENTO
Also Called: Municipal Svcs Agency
9700 Goethe Rd Ste D, Sacramento (95827-3558)
PHONE............................916 875-2711
Thor Lude, *Chief*
EMP: 100 **Privately Held**
WEB: www.sna.com
SIC: 1622 9199 Bridge, tunnel & elevated highway; general government administration;
PA: County Of Sacramento
700 H St Ste 7650
Sacramento CA 95814
916 874-5544

(P-1877)
FLATIRON WEST INC
2100 Goodyear Rd, Benicia (94510-1216)
PHONE............................707 742-6000
Richard Tradinski, *Manager*
Christina Newton, *HR Admin*
EMP: 150
SALES (corp-wide): 579.6MM **Privately Held**
SIC: 1622 1629 Bridge construction; industrial plant construction
HQ: Flatiron West, Inc.
1770 La Costa Meadows Dr
San Marcos CA 92078

(P-1878)
FLATIRON WEST INC
16341 Chino Corona Rd, Chino (91708-9233)
PHONE............................909 597-8413
Thomas J Rademacher, *Ch of Bd*
EMP: 95
SALES (corp-wide): 579.6MM **Privately Held**
SIC: 1622 1611 Bridge construction; highway & street construction
HQ: Flatiron West, Inc.
1770 La Costa Meadows Dr
San Marcos CA 92078

(P-1879)
FLUOR DANIEL CONSTRUCTION CO (DH)
3 Polaris Way, Aliso Viejo (92656-5338)
PHONE............................949 349-2000
Paul Buckham, *President*
EMP: 500
SALES: 3.3MM
SALES (corp-wide): 19.5B **Publicly Held**
SIC: 1622 Bridge, tunnel & elevated highway
HQ: Fluor Enterprises, Inc.
6700 Las Colinas Blvd
Irving TX 75039
469 398-7000

(P-1880)
GRANITE CONSTRUCTION INC (PA)
585 W Beach St, Watsonville (95076-5123)
P.O. Box 50085 (95077-5085)
PHONE............................831 724-1011
James H Roberts, *President*
Claes G Bjork, *Ch of Bd*
Christopher S Miller, *COO*
Laurel J Krzeminski, *CFO*
Kenneth B Olson, *Treasurer*
EMP: 250
SALES: 2.9B **Publicly Held**
WEB: www.graniteconstruction.com
SIC: 1622 1629 1442 1611 Bridge construction; tunnel construction; dam construction; canal construction; land leveling; construction sand & gravel; general contractor, highway & street construction

(P-1881)
HAZARD CONSTRUCTION COMPANY
6465 Marindustry Dr, San Diego (92121-2536)
P.O. Box 229000 (92192-9000)
PHONE............................858 587-3600
Jason Mordhorst, *President*
Noli Gavino, *Treasurer*
Klaus Guttau, *Vice Pres*
Charles White, *Vice Pres*
William Brownlow, *Project Mgr*
EMP: 100
SQ FT: 37,000
SALES (est): 37.3MM **Privately Held**
WEB: www.hazardconstruction.com
SIC: 1622 1611 Bridge construction; highway & street construction; grading; surfacing & paving; highway & street paving contractor

(P-1882)
JOHANN B GAROVI
Also Called: Garovibridge
109 Pinheiro Cir, Novato (94945-6817)
PHONE............................415 898-1801
Johann B Garovi, *Owner*
EMP: 50
SALES (est): 2.7MM **Privately Held**
SIC: 1622 Bridge, tunnel & elevated highway

(P-1883)
KIEWIT INFRASTRUCTURE WEST CO
12700 Stowe Dr Ste 180, Poway (92064-8883)
PHONE............................360 693-1478
R Michael Phelps, *President*
Mitchell Hoffman, *Technology*
Luke Spencer, *Manager*
EMP: 60
SALES (corp-wide): 16.6B **Privately Held**
SIC: 1622 Bridge, tunnel & elevated highway
HQ: Kiewit Infrastructure West Co.
3555 Farnam St
Omaha NE 68131
402 342-2052

(P-1884)
MCM CONSTRUCTION INC (PA)
6413 32nd St, North Highlands (95660-3001)
P.O. Box 620 (95660-0620)
PHONE............................916 334-1221
James A Carter, *President*
Harry D McGovern, *Vice Pres*
EMP: 70
SQ FT: 5,000
SALES: 150MM **Privately Held**
WEB: www.mcmconstructioninc.com
SIC: 1622 Bridge construction

(P-1885)
MCM CONSTRUCTION INC
19010 Slover Ave, Bloomington (92316-2459)
PHONE............................909 875-0533
Nella Flores, *Branch Mgr*
EMP: 180
SALES (corp-wide): 150MM **Privately Held**
WEB: www.mcmconstructioninc.com
SIC: 1622 Bridge construction
PA: M.C.M. Construction, Inc.
6413 32nd St
North Highlands CA 95660
916 334-1221

(P-1886)
OC 405 PARTNERS JOINT VENTURE
3100 W Lake Center Dr # 200, Santa Ana (92704-6917)
PHONE............................858 251-2200
EMP: 75
SQ FT: 69,000
SALES: 61MM
SALES (corp-wide): 829.8MM **Privately Held**
SIC: 1622 Bridge construction
HQ: Ohl Usa, Inc.
2615 Ulmer St
Flushing NY 11354

(P-1887)
R M HARRIS COMPANY INC
1000 Howe Rd Ste 200, Martinez (94553-3446)
PHONE............................925 335-3000
David R Harris, *CEO*
Mark Snapp, *Admin Sec*
Mauricio Mayora, *Technology*
John Tymo, *Technology*
Gayle Rabon, *Controller*
EMP: 100
SQ FT: 4,500
SALES (est): 18.4MM **Privately Held**
SIC: 1622 1611 Bridge, tunnel & elevated highway; highway & street construction

(P-1888)
SEMA CONSTRUCTION INC
6 Orchard Ste 150, Irvine (92618-4534)
PHONE............................949 330-4300
Steve Mills, *Manager*
EMP: 90
SALES (corp-wide): 293.3MM **Privately Held**
SIC: 1622 Bridge, tunnel & elevated highway
PA: Sema Construction, Inc.
7353 S Eagle St
Centennial CO 80112
303 627-2600

1623 Water, Sewer & Utility Line Construction

(P-1889)
A & H COMMUNICATIONS INC
1791 Reynolds Ave, Irvine (92614-5711)
PHONE............................949 250-4555
Brian Elliott, *President*
Brett Howard, *Vice Pres*
Galen Osborn, *Project Mgr*
Matt Vining, *Foreman/Supr*
Tom Howard, *Director*
EMP: 250 EST: 2000
SQ FT: 4,500
SALES (est): 20.8MM **Privately Held**
SIC: 1623 Cable laying construction

(P-1890)
ADVANCED CABLE TECHNOLOGIES
13400 Saticoy St Ste 30, North Hollywood (91605-7615)
PHONE............................818 262-6484
Yader V Gomez, *President*
Josh Neaf, *Vice Pres*
EMP: 50
SALES: 5.5MM **Privately Held**
SIC: 1623 Cable laying construction

(P-1891)
ARB INC
2235 N Ventura Ave, Ventura (93001-1311)
P.O. Box 1772 (93002-1772)
PHONE............................805 643-4188
David Cox, *Branch Mgr*
EMP: 50
SALES (corp-wide): 2.3B **Publicly Held**
WEB: www.arbinc.com
SIC: 1623 Oil & gas pipeline construction
HQ: Arb, Inc.
26000 Commercentre Dr
Lake Forest CA 92630
949 598-9242

(P-1892)
ARIZONA PIPELINE COMPANY (PA)
17372 Lilac St, Hesperia (92345-5162)
P.O. Box 401865 (92340-1865)
PHONE............................760 244-8212
Lowell Duane Moyers, *Chairman*
Nina Moyers, *CEO*
Tom Seals, *Corp Secy*
Ernie Bernard, *Vice Pres*
Connie Borden, *Executive*
EMP: 400
SQ FT: 5,000
SALES: 224.4MM **Privately Held**
SIC: 1623 Pipeline construction

(P-1893)
ARIZONA PIPELINE COMPANY
1745 Sampson Ave, Corona (92879-1864)
PHONE............................951 270-3100
John Guzlow, *Vice Pres*
Steve Lords, *CFO*
Steve Dilday, *Manager*
Bill Burris, *Superintendent*
John Reed, *Superintendent*
EMP: 200
SALES (corp-wide): 224.4MM **Privately Held**
SIC: 1623 8711 Underground utilities contractor; engineering services
PA: Arizona Pipeline Company
17372 Lilac St
Hesperia CA 92345
760 244-8212

(P-1894)
BALI CONSTRUCTION INC
9852 Joe Vargas Way, South El Monte (91733-3108)
PHONE............................626 442-8003
Ted Polich III, *President*
Michael E Brooks, *CEO*
Steven Tam, *Administration*
Kevin Delate, *Project Mgr*
Mark Hatfield, *Project Mgr*
EMP: 100
SQ FT: 7,000
SALES: 58MM **Privately Held**
WEB: www.baliconstruction.com
SIC: 1623 Underground utilities contractor

(P-1895)
BASILE CONSTRUCTION INC
7952 Armour St, San Diego (92111-3718)
PHONE............................858 278-2739
Allen Basile, *President*
Dawn Basile, *Admin Sec*
EMP: 50
SQ FT: 1,200
SALES (est): 10.1MM **Privately Held**
WEB: www.basile-dig.com
SIC: 1623 Water & sewer line construction

(P-1896)
BESS TESTLAB INC
2461 Tripaldi Way, Hayward (94545-5018)
PHONE............................408 988-0101
Juan Jose Bohorquez, *President*
Brandy Molina, *Manager*
EMP: 50
SALES (est): 9.2MM **Privately Held**
WEB: www.besstestlab.com
SIC: 1623 Water, sewer & utility lines

(P-1897)
BILL NLSON GEN ENGRG CNSTR INC
Also Called: Bill Nelson GEC
7600 N Ingram Ave Ste 126, Fresno
(93711-5852)
PHONE.................559 439-1756
Bill Nelson, *President*
Kristin Nelson, *Admin Sec*
EMP: 60
SQ FT: 1,200
SALES (est): 14.4MM **Privately Held**
SIC: 1623 Water, sewer & utility lines

(P-1898)
BLOIS CONSTRUCTION INC
3201 Sturgis Rd, Oxnard (93030-8931)
P.O. Box 672 (93032-0672)
PHONE.................805 485-0011
James B Blois, *President*
Steve Woodworth, *CFO*
Dan Schultz, *Vice Pres*
Palmer Douglas, *Info Tech Dir*
Mark Bower, *Project Dir*
EMP: 150
SQ FT: 10,000
SALES (est): 22MM **Privately Held**
WEB: www.bloisconstruction.com
SIC: 1623 Underground utilities contractor

(P-1899)
BURTECH PIPELINE INCORPORATED
102 2nd St, Encinitas (92024-3203)
PHONE.................760 634-2822
Dominic J Burtech, *President*
Julie Burtech, *Vice Pres*
EMP: 70
SQ FT: 3,000
SALES (est): 23.6MM **Privately Held**
WEB: www.burtechpipeline.com
SIC: 1623 Water main construction; sewer line construction; pipe laying construction

(P-1900)
C P CONSTRUCTION CO INC
105 N Loma Pl, Upland (91786-5620)
P.O. Box 1206, Ontario (91762-0206)
PHONE.................909 981-1091
Charles Pfister, *President*
Charles Michael Pfister, *Corp Secy*
Mark E Pfister, *Vice Pres*
Russel Pfister, *Vice Pres*
EMP: 50
SQ FT: 4,000
SALES: 13MM **Privately Held**
SIC: 1623 Sewer line construction; pipeline construction

(P-1901)
CA STATION MANAGEMENT INC
3200 E Guasti Rd Ste 100, Ontario
(91761-8661)
PHONE.................909 245-6251
Taqi Chaudry, *CEO*
EMP: 250 EST: 2016
SALES (est): 8.3MM **Privately Held**
SIC: 1623 7389 8082 Underground utilities contractor; telephone answering service; home health care services

(P-1902)
CAL SIERRA CONSTRUCTION INC
5904 Van Alstine Ave 1, Carmichael
(95608-5327)
PHONE.................916 416-7901
Joel Lucich, *President*
Greg Lucich, *Corp Secy*
Marco Lucich, *Vice Pres*
EMP: 80
SQ FT: 3,800
SALES (est): 12.9MM **Privately Held**
WEB: www.calsierra.net
SIC: 1623 8711 Underground utilities contractor; pipeline construction; sewer line construction; engineering services

(P-1903)
CAMERON INTRSTATE PIPELINE LLC
488 8th Ave, San Diego (92101-7123)
PHONE.................619 696-3110
Ryan O'Neal, *President*
EMP: 200

SALES: 20MM **Privately Held**
SIC: 1623 Oil & gas pipeline construction

(P-1904)
CASS CONSTRUCTION INC (PA)
1100 Wagner Dr, El Cajon (92020-3047)
P.O. Box 309 (92022-0309)
PHONE.................619 590-0929
Jimmie Nelson, *Ch of Bd*
Jerry Gaeir, *President*
Kyle P Nelson, *President*
Laura Nelson, *Vice Pres*
Breyon Maasch, *Administration*
EMP: 111
SQ FT: 5,700
SALES (est): 103.5MM **Privately Held**
WEB: www.cassconstruction.com
SIC: 1623 1611 Underground utilities contractor; grading

(P-1905)
CATANIA HIJAR CORPORATION
Also Called: Teldata
11487 Woodside Ave, Santee
(92071-4724)
PHONE.................800 400-3401
Doug Catania, *President*
Robb Hijar, *Vice Pres*
EMP: 103
SQ FT: 14,000
SALES (est): 10.6MM **Privately Held**
SIC: 1623 1731 Cable laying construction; telephone & telephone equipment installation; communications specialization; safety & security specialization; access control systems specialization

(P-1906)
CDM CONSTRUCTORS INC
9220 Cleveland Ave # 100, Rancho Cucamonga (91730-8560)
PHONE.................909 579-3500
Joyce Jackson, *Branch Mgr*
EMP: 90
SALES (corp-wide): 1.1B **Privately Held**
SIC: 1623 Water, sewer & utility lines
HQ: Cdm Constructors Inc.
75 State St Ste 701
Boston MA 02109
-

(P-1907)
CH2M HILL CONSTRUCTORS INC
2485 Natomas Park Dr # 600, Sacramento
(95833-2975)
PHONE.................916 920-0212
Craig Eldrich, *Branch Mgr*
EMP: 270
SALES (corp-wide): 10B **Publicly Held**
SIC: 1623 8711 Water, sewer & utility lines; engineering services
HQ: Ch2m Hill Constructors, Inc.
9189 S Jamaica St
Englewood CO 80112

(P-1908)
CITY HANFORD PUBLIC IMPRV CORP
900 S 10th Ave, Hanford (93230-5234)
PHONE.................559 585-2550
Gary Misenhimer, *Branch Mgr*
EMP: 54 **Privately Held**
SIC: 1623 9199 Water, sewer & utility lines;
PA: City Of Hanford
315 N Douty St 321
Hanford CA 93230
559 585-2515

(P-1909)
CMAC CONSTRUCTION COMPANY
Also Called: Cmac Cnstr Refinery & Pipeline
1450 Santa Fe Ave, Long Beach
(90813-1248)
PHONE.................562 435-5611
Michael L Mc Fadden, *CEO*
Mike Hosseini, *Project Mgr*
John Day, *Safety Dir*
EMP: 55
SQ FT: 3,000

SALES: 9.3MM **Privately Held**
WEB: www.cmac.us
SIC: 1623 Pipeline construction

(P-1910)
COLICH SONS
Also Called: Colich & Sons
547 W 140th St, Gardena (90248-1589)
PHONE.................323 770-2920
Tom Colich, *Partner*
John Colich, *Partner*
EMP: 160
SQ FT: 4,500
SALES (est): 9.9MM **Privately Held**
SIC: 1623 8711 Sewer line construction; engineering services

(P-1911)
CONSTRUCTION SPECIALTY SVC INC
Also Called: C S S
4550 Buck Owens Blvd, Bakersfield
(93308-4948)
P.O. Box 9429 (93389-9429)
PHONE.................661 864-7573
Daniel I George, *President*
Denise George, *CFO*
EMP: 53
SQ FT: 1,000
SALES (est): 13.5MM **Privately Held**
WEB: www.CSSIncorp.biz
SIC: 1623 Pipeline construction; concrete block & brick

(P-1912)
D S S COMPANY
655 W Clay St, Stockton (95206-1722)
P.O. Box 6099 (95206-0099)
PHONE.................209 948-0302
David C Barney, *CEO*
Phillip R Dunn, *President*
EMP: 50
SQ FT: 5,000
SALES: 8.7MM
SALES (corp-wide): 4.4B **Publicly Held**
WEB: www.dsscompany.com
SIC: 1623 1611 Sewer line construction; general contractor, highway & street construction
HQ: Knife River Corporation
1150 W Century Ave
Bismarck ND 58503
701 530-1400

(P-1913)
DALEO INC
550 E Luchessa Ave, Gilroy (95020-7068)
PHONE.................408 846-9621
David A Levisay, *Principal*
Susan Levisay, *Corp Secy*
EMP: 54
SALES (est): 11.1MM **Privately Held**
WEB: www.daleoinc.com
SIC: 1623 Cable television line construction

(P-1914)
DBI SERVICES INC
2775 Hollister St, Simi Valley (93065-4737)
PHONE.................805 523-7114
Derek Crombie, *President*
Bruce Sakamogo, *Shareholder*
EMP: 70
SALES (est): 7.2MM **Privately Held**
SIC: 1623 Telephone & communication line construction

(P-1915)
DIVERSIFIED UTILITY SVCS INC
3105 Unicorn Rd, Bakersfield
(93308-6858)
P.O. Box 80417 (93380-0417)
PHONE.................661 325-3212
Leigh Ann Anderson, *CEO*
Cody Anderson, *Shareholder*
William Mitchell, *Shareholder*
Steven S Anderson, *CFO*
Jeff Pylman, *VP Opers*
EMP: 272
SALES (est): 74.4MM **Privately Held**
SIC: 1623 Underground utilities contractor

(P-1916)
ELECTRIC TECH CONSTRUCTION INC
1910 Mark Ct Ste 130, Concord
(94520-1280)
PHONE.................925 849-5324
Tim Pessin, *Principal*
Dean Balough, *CFO*
Kathryn Balough, *Admin Sec*
EMP: 80
SQ FT: 5,000
SALES (est): 14.5MM **Privately Held**
SIC: 1623 1731 Telephone & communication line construction; electrical work

(P-1917)
FISHEL COMPANY
647 Young St, Santa Ana (92705-5633)
PHONE.................714 668-9268
Jeong Jeon, *Branch Mgr*
Fernando Rocha, *Division Mgr*
EMP: 86
SALES (corp-wide): 341.9MM **Privately Held**
SIC: 1623 Underground utilities contractor
PA: The Fishel Company
1366 Dublin Rd
Columbus OH 43215
614 274-8100

(P-1918)
FLOYD JOHNSTON CNSTR CO INC
2301 Herndon Ave, Clovis (93611-8911)
PHONE.................559 299-7373
Evelyn Johnston, *Principal*
Steve Little, *Executive*
EMP: 75
SQ FT: 6,000
SALES (est): 14.9MM **Privately Held**
SIC: 1623 Water main construction; sewer line construction; pipeline construction

(P-1919)
GD NIELSON CONSTRUCTION INC
147 Camino Oruga, NAPA (94558-6215)
PHONE.................707 253-8774
Diann Nielson, *President*
George S Nielson, *Corp Secy*
EMP: 60
SALES (est): 16.5MM **Privately Held**
WEB: www.nielsoninc.com
SIC: 1623 1629 1799 Sewer line construction; drainage system construction; boring for building construction

(P-1920)
GENERAL PRODUCTION SVC CAL INC
Also Called: G P S
1333 Kern St, Taft (93268-9700)
P.O. Box 344 (93268-0344)
PHONE.................661 765-5330
Charles Beard, *CEO*
Oreste Risi, *President*
Don Schock, *Top Exec*
Mike Smith, *Area Mgr*
George Harmer, *Safety Mgr*
EMP: 180
SALES (est): 54.5MM **Privately Held**
SIC: 1623 Oil & gas pipeline construction

(P-1921)
GEO TELECOM
252 Woodcrest Ln, Aliso Viejo
(92656-2134)
PHONE.................949 362-0921
Peter Skerlos, *Owner*
EMP: 50
SALES (est): 1.7MM **Privately Held**
SIC: 1623 Transmitting tower (telecommunication) construction

(P-1922)
GRANIT-BAYASHI 2 A JOINT VENTR
585 W Beach St, Watsonville (95076-5123)
PHONE.................831 724-1011
Jigisha Desai, *Partner*
Mathew Tyler, *Partner*
EMP: 60 EST: 2016
SALES (est): 1.5MM **Privately Held**
SIC: 1623 Water & sewer line construction

(PA)=Parent Co (HQ)=Headquarters (DH)=Div Headquarters
✪ = New Business established in last 2 years

(P-1923)
GSE CONSTRUCTION COMPANY INC (PA)
6950 Preston Ave, Livermore (94551-9545)
PHONE.................................925 447-0292
Orlando Gutierrez, *CEO*
Sue Gutierrez, *Admin Sec*
Cynthia Gutierrez, *Director*
EMP: 140
SQ FT: 23,400
SALES (est): 76MM **Privately Held**
SIC: **1623 1542** Water & sewer line construction; pipe laying construction; pipeline construction; nonresidential construction

(P-1924)
HCI INC (HQ)
Also Called: H C I
3166 Hrseless Carriage Rd, Norco (92860-3612)
P.O. Box 5389 (92860-8097)
PHONE.................................951 520-4200
Steven G Silagi, *President*
◆ EMP: 300 EST: 1981
SQ FT: 100,000
SALES (est): 85MM **Privately Held**
SIC: **1623** Telephone & communication line construction
PA: Lombardy Holdings, Inc.
151 Kalmus Dr Ste F6
Costa Mesa CA 92626
951 808-4550

(P-1925)
HENKELS & MCCOY INC
2840 Ficus St, Pomona (91766-6501)
PHONE.................................909 517-3011
Michael Giarratano, *Senior VP*
Pamela Aquino, *Administration*
Stephanie Degraff, *Administration*
Kara Stewart, *Analyst*
Jonathan Gray, *Marketing Staff*
EMP: 300
SALES (corp-wide): 1.5B **Privately Held**
SIC: **1623** Electric power line construction; transmitting tower (telecommunication) construction; oil & gas pipeline construction
HQ: Henkels & Mccoy, Inc
985 Jolly Rd
Blue Bell PA 19422
215 283-7600

(P-1926)
HENKELS & MCCOY INC
2840 Ficus St, Pomona (91766-6501)
PHONE.................................909 590-8419
Ed Campbell, *Manager*
EMP: 60
SALES (corp-wide): 1.5B **Privately Held**
WEB: www.henkels.com
SIC: **1623** Water, sewer & utility lines
HQ: Henkels & Mccoy, Inc
985 Jolly Rd
Blue Bell PA 19422
215 283-7600

(P-1927)
HERMAN WEISSKER INC (HQ)
1645 Brown Ave, Riverside (92509-1859)
PHONE.................................951 826-8800
Luis Alberto Armona, *CEO*
Ron Politte, *President*
Marty Mayeda, *CFO*
Brandi Green, *Admin Asst*
Katrina Suman, *Admin Asst*
EMP: 117 EST: 1959
SQ FT: 12,000
SALES (est): 136.6MM
SALES (corp-wide): 408.1MM **Privately Held**
WEB: www.hermanweissker.com
SIC: **1623 8711 1731** Underground utilities contractor; engineering services; electrical work
PA: Meruelo Enterprises, Inc.
9550 Firestone Blvd # 105
Downey CA 90241
562 745-2300

(P-1928)
HP COMMUNICATIONS INC
13341 Temescal Canyon Rd, Corona (92883-4980)
PHONE.................................951 572-1200

Nicholas Goldman, *President*
Chris Dotinga, *Shareholder*
Ahmad Olomi, *Exec VP*
Chris Price, *Vice Pres*
Marty Wilcox, *Area Mgr*
EMP: 240 EST: 1998
SQ FT: 130,680
SALES (est): 155.2MM **Privately Held**
SIC: **1623** Communication line & transmission tower construction

(P-1929)
HPS PLUMBING SERVICE INC
3100 E Belle Ter, Bakersfield (93307-6830)
PHONE.................................661 324-2121
Leslie Denherder, *President*
Jay Buenviaje, *Project Mgr*
EMP: 300
SALES (est): 21.2MM **Privately Held**
WEB: www.hpsmechanical.com
SIC: **1623 1711** Water, sewer & utility lines; plumbing contractors

(P-1930)
INSITUFORM TECHNOLOGIES LLC
19000 Macarthur Blvd # 800, Irvine (92612-1461)
PHONE.................................714 724-2324
Elva Alatorre, *Branch Mgr*
EMP: 50
SALES (corp-wide): 1.3B **Publicly Held**
SIC: **1623** Pipeline construction
HQ: Insituform Technologies, Llc
17988 Edison Ave
Chesterfield MO 63005
636 530-8000

(P-1931)
IRBY CONSTRUCTION COMPANY
100 W Keystone Rd, Brawley (92227-9741)
PHONE.................................760 344-4478
Pat Shouse, *Manager*
EMP: 66
SALES (corp-wide): 9.4B **Publicly Held**
WEB: www.irbyconst.com
SIC: **1623** Electric power line construction
HQ: Irby Construction Company
318 Old Highway 49 S
Richland MS 39218
601 709-4729

(P-1932)
IRISH COMMUNICATION COMPANY (DH)
2649 Stingle Ave, Rosemead (91770-3326)
P.O. Box 457 (91770-0457)
PHONE.................................626 288-6170
Gregory C Warde, *CEO*
Dan Mitchell, *President*
Pat D Furnare, *Chairman*
Dennis Brackney, *Vice Pres*
Larry Manke, *Vice Pres*
EMP: 100
SQ FT: 9,000
SALES (est): 62.5MM
SALES (corp-wide): 72.4MM **Privately Held**
WEB: www.irishteam.com
SIC: **1623 8748 1731** Telephone & communication line construction; telecommunications consultant; communications specialization
HQ: Irish Construction
2641 River Ave
Rosemead CA 91770
626 288-8530

(P-1933)
IRISH CONSTRUCTION (HQ)
2641 River Ave, Rosemead (91770-3392)
P.O. Box 579 (91770-0579)
PHONE.................................626 288-8530
Gregory C Warde, *Ch of Bd*
Ken West, *President*
William E Wilbanks, *President*
Randall W Dale, *Corp Secy*
Lonnie Gentry, *Vice Pres*
EMP: 150 EST: 1947
SQ FT: 15,000

SALES (est): 90.1MM
SALES (corp-wide): 72.4MM **Privately Held**
WEB: www.irishconstruction.com
SIC: **1623** Communication line & transmission tower construction; telephone & communication line construction
PA: Manhattan Capital Corporation
2641 River Ave
Rosemead CA 91770
626 288-8530

(P-1934)
IRISH CONSTRUCTION
19490 Monterey St, Morgan Hill (95037-2606)
PHONE.................................408 612-8440
Sue Nakagawa, *Manager*
EMP: 100
SQ FT: 18,004
SALES (est): 8.3MM
SALES (corp-wide): 72.4MM **Privately Held**
WEB: www.irishconstruction.com
SIC: **1623 1799** Telephone & communication line construction; athletic & recreation facilities construction
HQ: Irish Construction
2641 River Ave
Rosemead CA 91770
626 288-8530

(P-1935)
IRISH CONSTRUCTION
1329 Sweetwater Ln, Spring Valley (91977-4147)
P.O. Box 580, San Marcos (92079-0580)
PHONE.................................619 713-1991
Dave Watson, *Manager*
EMP: 60
SALES (est): 5.3MM
SALES (corp-wide): 72.4MM **Privately Held**
WEB: www.irishconstruction.com
SIC: **1623 1622** Telephone & communication line construction; bridge, tunnel & elevated highway
HQ: Irish Construction
2641 River Ave
Rosemead CA 91770
626 288-8530

(P-1936)
IRISH CONSTRUCTION
1028 Marchy Ln, Ceres (95307-6649)
PHONE.................................209 576-8766
Ron McMillan, *President*
EMP: 63
SALES (est): 4.1MM
SALES (corp-wide): 72.4MM **Privately Held**
SIC: **1623** Telephone & communication line construction
HQ: Irish Construction
2641 River Ave
Rosemead CA 91770
626 288-8530

(P-1937)
J & M INC
6700 National Dr, Livermore (94550-8804)
PHONE.................................925 724-0300
Manuel Marques III, *CEO*
Adrian Villeda, *Controller*
John Cooper, *Opers Mgr*
Steve Stoddard, *Manager*
EMP: 50
SQ FT: 2,000
SALES (est): 15.2MM **Privately Held**
SIC: **1623 1629** Underground utilities contractor; drainage system construction

(P-1938)
JMB CONSTRUCTION INC
132 S Maple Ave, South San Francisco (94080-6302)
PHONE.................................650 267-5300
Margaret P Burke, *President*
Cormac Hehir, *Project Mgr*
Sean Quinn, *Project Mgr*
Stephen Campbell, *Project Engr*
Ciaran Crossan, *Project Engr*
▲ EMP: 100
SALES (est): 36.5MM **Privately Held**
SIC: **1623** Water & sewer line construction

(P-1939)
JR FILANC CNSTR CO INC (PA)
740 N Andreasen Dr, Escondido (92029-1414)
PHONE.................................760 941-7130
Mark E Filanc, *CEO*
Harry S Cosmos, *President*
Kevin Elliot, *CFO*
Kevin Elliotts, *CFO*
Vincent L Diaz, *Vice Pres*
EMP: 100
SQ FT: 13,200
SALES (est): 123.5MM **Privately Held**
WEB: www.filanc.com
SIC: **1623 1629** Pumping station construction; waste water & sewage treatment plant construction

(P-1940)
K S FABRICATION & MACHINE INC
Also Called: KS Fabrication & Machine
6205 District Blvd, Bakersfield (93313-2141)
P.O. Box 41630 (93384-1630)
PHONE.................................661 617-1700
Kevin S Small, *CEO*
Becky Scott, *CFO*
EMP: 150
SALES (est): 39.6MM **Privately Held**
SIC: **1623** Water, sewer & utility lines

(P-1941)
K T A CONSTRUCTION INC
1920 Cordell Ct Ste 105, El Cajon (92020-0900)
PHONE.................................619 562-9464
Paul Michael Henderson, *CEO*
Mike Henderson, *President*
Marilyn L Henderson, *Vice Pres*
Brin Ragsdale, *Office Mgr*
Adam Ogden, *Sales Executive*
EMP: 62
SQ FT: 5,200
SALES (est): 18.1MM **Privately Held**
SIC: **1623** Sewer line construction; water main construction

(P-1942)
KANA PIPELINE INC
12620 Magnolia Ave, Riverside (92503-4636)
PHONE.................................714 986-1400
Dan Locke, *President*
EMP: 100
SQ FT: 55,000
SALES (est): 33.7MM **Privately Held**
WEB: www.kanapipeline.com
SIC: **1623 1629** Water main construction; sewer line construction; drainage system construction

(P-1943)
KENNEDY PIPELINE COMPANY
61 Argonaut, Laguna Hills (92656-1423)
PHONE.................................949 380-8363
Stuart P Trumble, *Owner*
Michael Trumble, *President*
Mark Trumble, *Vice Pres*
Matt Trumble, *Opers Mgr*
John Shoffeitt, *Superintendent*
EMP: 80 EST: 1969
SQ FT: 20,000
SALES (est): 15.4MM **Privately Held**
WEB: www.kennedypipeline.com
SIC: **1623** Oil & gas pipeline construction

(P-1944)
KS INDUSTRIES LP (PA)
Also Called: K S I
6205 District Blvd, Bakersfield (93313-2141)
P.O. Box 41630 (93384-1630)
PHONE.................................661 617-1700
Kevin Small, *CEO*
Scott Becky, *CFO*
Doug Erickson, *Vice Pres*
Neil Rice, *Project Mgr*
Ryan Turk-Bly, *Project Mgr*
EMP: 2000
SQ FT: 20,000
SALES (est): 367.2MM **Privately Held**
WEB: www.ksilp.com
SIC: **1623** Water, sewer & utility lines

(P-1945)
LARKIN LEASING INC
674 N Batavia St, Orange (92868-1221)
PHONE..................................714 528-3232
William Larkin, *President*
EMP: 80 **EST:** 2000
SQ FT: 15,000
SALES (est): 6.3MM **Privately Held**
SIC: 1623 Underground utilities contractor

(P-1946)
LIGHTBEAM POWER COMPANY GRIDLE
100 Century Center Ct # 100, San Jose (95112-4535)
PHONE..................................800 696-7114
John Fong,
Brendan Beasley,
John Gann,
EMP: 51
SALES (est): 1.6MM **Privately Held**
SIC: 1623 Electric power line construction

(P-1947)
LIGHTBEAM PWR GRIDLEY MAIN LLC
100 Century Center Ct # 100, San Jose (95112-4535)
PHONE..................................800 696-7114
John Fong,
Brendan Beasley,
John Gann,
EMP: 51
SALES (est): 1.7MM **Privately Held**
SIC: 1623 Electric power line construction

(P-1948)
LINKUS ENTERPRISES LLC
Also Called: Honeywell Authorized Dealer
5595 W San Madele Ave, Fresno (93722-5068)
PHONE..................................559 256-6600
Horacio Guzman, *CEO*
EMP: 295 **Privately Held**
SIC: 1623 Telephone & communication line construction
PA: Linkus Enterprises, Llc
18631 Lloyd Ln
Anderson CA 96007

(P-1949)
LINKUS ENTERPRISES LLC (PA)
18631 Lloyd Ln, Anderson (96007-8459)
PHONE..................................530 229-9197
Horacio Guzman, *CEO*
John Daily, *COO*
Dant Morris, *Vice Pres*
Jon Warren, *VP Finance*
Debbie Herrera, *Manager*
EMP: 133
SQ FT: 3,200
SALES (est): 133.5MM **Privately Held**
SIC: 1623 5731 4813 Telephone & communication line construction; antennas, satellite dish;

(P-1950)
LOMBARDY HOLDINGS INC (PA)
151 Kalmus Dr Ste F6, Costa Mesa (92626-5965)
P.O. Box 6019, Norco (92860-8034)
PHONE..................................951 808-4550
Marc Laulhere, *CEO*
Pam Laulhere, *Admin Sec*
EMP: 200
SQ FT: 80,000
SALES: 85MM **Privately Held**
SIC: 1623 5211 Telephone & communication line construction; cable television line construction; electrical construction materials

(P-1951)
LYLES DIVERSIFIED INC (PA)
Also Called: WM LYLES CO
1210 W Olive Ave, Fresno (93728-2816)
P.O. Box 4348 (93744-4348)
PHONE..................................559 441-1900
William Lyles IV, *CEO*
William M Lyles, *CEO*
Michael F Elkins, *CFO*
Richard E Amigh, *Vice Pres*
Gerald V Lyles, *Vice Pres*
EMP: 340 **EST:** 1946

SQ FT: 6,200
SALES: 33.7MM **Privately Held**
SIC: 1623 1629 1611 3494 Water & sewer line construction; water main construction; sewer line construction; power plant construction; highway & street paving contractor; sprinkler systems, field; apartment building operators

(P-1952)
MARGATE CONSTRUCTION INC
25007 Figueroa St, Carson (90745-6316)
P.O. Box 4507 (90749-4507)
PHONE..................................310 830-8610
Charles T Riegelhuth, *President*
EMP: 150 **EST:** 1965
SQ FT: 3,000
SALES (est): 9.7MM **Privately Held**
SIC: 1623 1541 Pumping station construction; industrial buildings & warehouses

(P-1953)
MATRIX SERVICE INC
500 W Collins Ave, Orange (92867-5510)
PHONE..................................714 289-4419
William Sullivan, *Manager*
EMP: 61
SALES (corp-wide): 1B **Publicly Held**
WEB: www.matrixservice.com
SIC: 1623 Oil & gas line & compressor station construction
HQ: Matrix Service Inc.
5100 E Skelly Dr Ste 700
Tulsa OK 74135

(P-1954)
MCELVANY INC
13343 Johnson Rd, Los Banos (93635-9704)
PHONE..................................209 826-1102
Charles McElvany, *President*
Holli McElvany, *Treasurer*
Isaac McElvany, *Vice Pres*
Helen McElvany, *Principal*
EMP: 52
SQ FT: 1,200
SALES (est): 10.8MM **Privately Held**
WEB: www.mcelvany.com
SIC: 1623 1629 Sewer line construction; land preparation construction

(P-1955)
MCGUIRE AND HESTER (PA)
2810 Harbor Bay Pkwy, Alameda (94502-3040)
PHONE..................................510 632-7676
Michael R Hester, *President*
Bruce Daseking, *Treasurer*
Robert Doud, *Exec VP*
Brock Grunt, *Area Mgr*
Kevin Hester, *Area Mgr*
EMP: 300
SQ FT: 22,000
SALES (est): 140.4MM **Privately Held**
WEB: www.mcguireandhester.com
SIC: 1623 7353 1611 0782 Underground utilities contractor; heavy construction equipment rental; general contractor, highway & street construction; garden planting services

(P-1956)
MGE UNDERGROUND INC
816 26th St, Paso Robles (93446-1243)
P.O. Box 4189 (93447-4189)
PHONE..................................805 238-3510
Michael Joe Goldstein, *President*
Summer Goldstein, *CFO*
Monica Castaneda, *Admin Mgr*
Summer Golstein, *Admin Sec*
Jedd Ingraham, *Project Mgr*
EMP: 85
SQ FT: 780
SALES: 18MM **Privately Held**
WEB: www.mgeunderground.com
SIC: 1623 Underground utilities contractor

(P-1957)
MLADEN BUNTICH CNSTR CO INC
1500 W 9th St, Upland (91786-5636)
PHONE..................................909 920-9977
Mladen Buntich Jr, *Ch of Bd*
Lee Roesner, *Vice Pres*
Scott Peterson, *Admin Sec*

Marcia Cogan, *Human Resources*
▲ **EMP:** 60
SQ FT: 4,000
SALES (est): 20MM **Privately Held**
WEB: www.buntich.com
SIC: 1623 8711 8322 Sewer line construction; pipeline construction; engineering services; individual & family services

(P-1958)
MOUNTAIN CASCADE INC (PA)
555 Exchange Ct, Livermore (94550-2400)
P.O. Box 5050 (94551-5050)
PHONE..................................925 373-8370
Michael L Fuller, *CEO*
Michael Duke Fuller, *President*
Schelly Frades, *Treasurer*
David Hicks, *Vice Pres*
Roger Williamson, *Vice Pres*
EMP: 250 **EST:** 1982
SQ FT: 15,000
SALES: 116.7MM **Privately Held**
WEB: www.mountaincascade.com
SIC: 1623 Pipeline construction; water & sewer line construction

(P-1959)
NOR-CAL PIPELINE SERVICES
1875 S River Rd, West Sacramento (95691-2896)
PHONE..................................530 673-3886
David Jaeger, *President*
David L Jaeger, *Vice Pres*
Craig Releford, *District Mgr*
William Jaeger, *Admin Sec*
Manny Badyal, *Project Mgr*
EMP: 70
SALES (est): 28.8MM **Privately Held**
SIC: 1623 Pipeline construction

(P-1960)
NOVA GROUP INC
185 Devlin Rd, NAPA (94558-6255)
P.O. Box 4050 (94558-0450)
PHONE..................................707 265-1100
Ronald M Fedrick, *Ch of Bd*
Scott R Victor, *President*
Scott Victor, *COO*
Carole Bionda, *Vice Pres*
Walter Birdsall, *Vice Pres*
EMP: 200 **EST:** 1957
SQ FT: 15,000
SALES: 2.9MM
SALES (corp-wide): 9.4B **Publicly Held**
SIC: 1623 Underground utilities contractor
PA: Quanta Services, Inc.
2800 Post Oak Blvd # 2600
Houston TX 77056
713 629-7600

(P-1961)
NOVA GRP INC -OBAYASHI CORP A
185 Devlin Rd, NAPA (94558-6255)
P.O. Box 4050 (94558-0450)
PHONE..................................707 265-1116
Ronald M Fedrick, *Manager*
EMP: 50
SALES: 32MM **Privately Held**
SIC: 1623 Pipeline construction

(P-1962)
NOVA-CPF INC
7411 Napa Vallejo Hwy, NAPA (94558-7501)
P.O. Box 4050 (94558-0450)
PHONE..................................707 257-3200
Charles Fedrick, *President*
Elbert C Lewey, *Treasurer*
David W Fedrick, *Vice Pres*
Ronald Fredrick, *Principal*
EMP: 200
SQ FT: 11,000
SALES (est): 9.3MM **Privately Held**
SIC: 1623 Underground utilities contractor

(P-1963)
NOVA/TIC GOV PROJ JV
185 Devlin Rd, NAPA (94558-6255)
P.O. Box 4050 (94558-0450)
PHONE..................................707 257-3200
Ronald M Fedrick, *President*
Scott R Victor, *President*
Carole L Bionda, *Vice Pres*
Walter M Birdsall, *Vice Pres*
Chris Mathies, *Vice Pres*

▲ **EMP:** 150
SQ FT: 15,000
SALES (est): 1.8MM **Privately Held**
SIC: 1623 Water, sewer & utility lines

(P-1964)
ORION CONSTRUCTION CORPORATION
2185 La Mirada Dr, Vista (92081-8830)
PHONE..................................760 597-9660
Richard Dowsing, *CEO*
Mark Dowsing, *Vice Pres*
EMP: 80
SQ FT: 7,000
SALES (est): 29.5MM **Privately Held**
WEB: www.orionconstruction.com
SIC: 1623 1629 1542 Water, sewer & utility lines; industrial plant construction; non-residential construction

(P-1965)
PACIFIC SOUTHWEST CNSTR & EQP
2308 Shaylene Way, Alpine (91901-3174)
PHONE..................................619 445-5190
Thomas L Scanlan, *President*
Kristina Scanlan, *Vice Pres*
EMP: 65
SALES (est): 5.4MM **Privately Held**
SIC: 1623 Underground utilities contractor

(P-1966)
PACIFIC W SPACE CMMNCTIONS INC
Also Called: P W C
900 W Gladstone St, San Dimas (91773-1734)
PHONE..................................909 592-4321
Sheryl F Patton, *CEO*
Joanna Patton, *CFO*
Betty Fonteno, *Corp Secy*
Rich Patton, *Vice Pres*
Jorge Curiel, *Opers Mgr*
EMP: 69 **EST:** 1981
SQ FT: 2,000
SALES (est): 21.5MM **Privately Held**
SIC: 1623 Communication line & transmission tower construction

(P-1967)
PAULUS ENGINEERING INC
2871 E Coronado St, Anaheim (92806-2504)
PHONE..................................714 632-3322
Ronald Paulus, *President*
Jason Paulus, *Vice Pres*
Roger Betten, *Project Mgr*
Mike Whipple, *Project Mgr*
Michelle Obermeier, *Asst Controller*
EMP: 60
SQ FT: 40,000
SALES (est): 10.3MM **Privately Held**
WEB: www.paulusengineering.com
SIC: 1623 Sewer line construction; pipeline construction

(P-1968)
PEARCE SERVICES LLC (HQ)
Also Called: Cross Rock
3720 La Cruz Way, Paso Robles (93446-5907)
P.O. Box 1708 (93447-1708)
PHONE..................................805 237-7480
Brett Forester, *CEO*
Kristen Osborne, *CFO*
Matt Gillette, *Exec VP*
Kullen Burk, *VP Opers*
EMP: 50 **EST:** 1998
SQ FT: 2,800
SALES (est): 31.6MM **Privately Held**
WEB: www.psixbox.com
SIC: 1623 Communication line & transmission tower construction; telephone & communication line construction
PA: Willcrest Partners, Llc
100 Spear St
San Francisco CA 94105
415 816-0086

(P-1969)
PRESTON PIPELINES INC (PA)
133 Bothelo Ave, Milpitas (95035-5325)
PHONE..................................408 262-1418
Michael D Preston, *President*
Ron Bianchini, *COO*

PRODUCTS & SVCS

Dave Heslop, *Vice Pres*
Rich Lewis, *Vice Pres*
Gary Menges, *Vice Pres*
EMP: 250
SQ FT: 12,000
SALES (est): 111.5MM **Privately Held**
WEB: www.prestonpipelines.com
SIC: 1623 Pipeline construction

(P-1970)
PRESTON PIPELINES INC A CAL
133 Bothelo Ave, Milpitas (95035-5325)
PHONE..........................408 262-6989
Michael Preston, *President*
Bob Chance, *CFO*
Emmanuel Rodriguez, *Project Engr*
EMP: 300
SQ FT: 1,000
SALES (est): 12.1MM **Privately Held**
SIC: 1623 Pipeline construction

(P-1971)
PRIMORIS SERVICES CORPORATION
26000 Commercentre Dr, Lake Forest
(92630-8816)
PHONE..........................949 598-9242
Peter J Moerbeek, *Principal*
EMP: 467
SALES (corp-wide): 2.3B **Publicly Held**
SIC: 1623 Pipeline construction
PA: Primoris Services Corporation
2100 Mckinney Ave # 1500
Dallas TX 75201
214 740-5600

(P-1972)
QUALITY TELECOM CONSULTANTS (PA)
Also Called: Quality Techniques Engrg Cnstr
3740 Cincinnati Ave, Rocklin (95765-1204)
P.O. Box 807, Loomis (95650-0807)
PHONE..........................916 315-0500
Scott Duncan, *President*
Candice Northam, *Treasurer*
Jacob Duncan, *Vice Pres*
Osh Duncan, *Admin Sec*
Ryan Kikel, *Manager*
EMP: 89
SALES (est): 23.6MM **Privately Held**
WEB:
www.qualitytelecomconsultantsinc.com
SIC: 1623 1731 4899 8748 Communication line & transmission tower construction; communications specialization; communication signal enhancement network system; telecommunications consultant

(P-1973)
RANGER PIPELINES INCORPORATED
1790 Yosemite Ave, San Francisco
(94124-2622)
P.O. Box 24109 (94124-0109)
PHONE..........................415 822-3700
Thomas Hunt, *President*
Mary Shea-Hunt, *Corp Secy*
Peter Cuddihy, *Vice Pres*
EMP: 101
SQ FT: 20,000
SALES (est): 37.9MM **Privately Held**
SIC: 1623 Pipeline construction

(P-1974)
ROBERT HEELY CONSTRUCTION LP (PA)
Also Called: Robert Heely Construction
5401 Woodmere Dr, Bakersfield
(93313-2777)
PHONE..........................661 617-1400
Robert Heely, *Chairman*
Craig Bonna, *President*
Kevin Couch, *Project Mgr*
Robert Hopkins, *Engineer*
Chrystal Abbott, *Human Res Mgr*
EMP: 350
SQ FT: 7,000
SALES (est): 93.6MM **Privately Held**
WEB: www.robertheely.com
SIC: 1623 Oil & gas pipeline construction

(P-1975)
S E C C CORPORATION
16224 Koala Rd, Adelanto (92301-3915)
PHONE..........................760 246-6218
Manuel Armenta, *Manager*
EMP: 56 **Privately Held**
SIC: 1623 Transmitting tower (telecommunication) construction
PA: S E C C Corporation
14945 La Palma Dr
Chino CA 91710
-

(P-1976)
S E PIPE LINE CONSTRUCTION CO
11832 Bloomfield Ave, Santa Fe Springs
(90670-4693)
PHONE..........................562 868-9771
Charles Rikel, *President*
James Doulames, *Vice Pres*
Thomas Tustin, *Admin Sec*
EMP: 100
SQ FT: 5,000
SALES (est): 39.6MM **Privately Held**
SIC: 1623 Gas main construction; electric power line construction; oil & gas pipeline construction

(P-1977)
SAM HILL & SONS INC
Also Called: WMS Transportation
2627 Beene Rd, Ventura (93003-7203)
P.O. Box 5670 (93005-0670)
PHONE..........................805 620-0828
Ronald Hill, *President*
Bobby Cardoza, *Vice Pres*
Kelly Orvis, *Executive*
Heather Jordan, *Controller*
Melisa Vickers, *Assistant*
EMP: 50
SQ FT: 1,000
SALES (est): 8.4MM **Privately Held**
WEB: www.samhillandsons.com
SIC: 1623 Underground utilities contractor

(P-1978)
SANCO PIPELINES INCORPORATED
727 University Ave, Los Gatos
(95032-7610)
PHONE..........................408 377-2793
David R Schrader, *Principal*
EMP: 50 **EST:** 1956
SQ FT: 3,000
SALES (est): 23MM **Privately Held**
WEB: www.sancopipelines.com
SIC: 1623 Pipeline construction

(P-1979)
SCHILLING PARADISE CORP
697 Greenfield Dr, El Cajon (92021-2983)
PHONE..........................619 449-4141
Jeff Platt, *President*
Michael Manos, *Principal*
Jackie Corbin, *Human Res Mgr*
Daniel J Shay, *Opers Staff*
Dale Holloway, *Foreman/Supr*
EMP: 175
SALES (est): 17.9MM **Privately Held**
SIC: 1623 1731 Underground utilities contractor; general electrical contractor

(P-1980)
SOLCOM INC
Also Called: Solcom Communications Inc
24801 Huntwood Ave, Hayward
(94544-1813)
PHONE..........................510 940-2490
Tony McMenamin, *President*
EMP: 500
SALES (est): 50MM **Privately Held**
SIC: 1623 Telephone & communication line construction

(P-1981)
SOLEX CONTRACTING INC
42146 Remington Ave, Temecula
(92590-2547)
PHONE..........................951 308-1706
Jerry Allen, *President*
Brandy Powell, *Manager*
EMP: 70
SQ FT: 12,000

SALES: 40.3MM **Privately Held**
SIC: 1623 1542 1541 Communication line & transmission tower construction; commercial & office building, new construction; renovation, remodeling & repairs: industrial buildings

(P-1982)
SOUTHWEST CONTRACTORS (PA)
Also Called: Bowman Pipeline Contractors
3235 Unicorn Rd, Bakersfield
(93308-6850)
PHONE..........................661 588-0484
Floyd E Bowman Jr, *CEO*
Kathy Bowman, *Vice Pres*
Donald Swank, *Project Mgr*
Amanda Diaz, *Accountant*
Gabe Perez, *Safety Dir*
EMP: 150
SQ FT: 10,000
SALES (est): 57MM **Privately Held**
SIC: 1623 3443 Oil & gas pipeline construction; industrial vessels, tanks & containers

(P-1983)
SPIESS CONSTRUCTION CO INC
Also Called: Scci
201 S Broadway St Ste 101, Orcutt
(93455-4612)
P.O. Box 2849, Santa Maria (93457-2849)
PHONE..........................805 937-5859
Scott A Coleman, *President*
Barry L Matchett, *Vice Pres*
Frank L Forthun, *Assistant VP*
EMP: 60
SALES (est): 33.1MM **Privately Held**
WEB: www.sccitanks.com
SIC: 1623 Sewer line construction; water main construction

(P-1984)
SPINIELLO COMPANIES
2650 Pomona Blvd, Pomona (91768-3220)
PHONE..........................909 629-1000
Priscilla Moyer, *Manager*
Abby Cruz, *Project Engr*
EMP: 100
SALES (corp-wide): 90MM **Privately Held**
SIC: 1623 Water, sewer & utility lines
PA: Spiniello Companies
354 Eisenhower Pkwy # 1200
Livingston NJ 07039
973 808-8383

(P-1985)
SRD ENGINEERING INC
3578 E Enterprise Dr, Anaheim
(92807-1627)
PHONE..........................714 630-2480
Deborah Denton, *CEO*
EMP: 65
SQ FT: 5,000
SALES (est): 8.8MM **Privately Held**
SIC: 1623 Water & sewer line construction

(P-1986)
SUKUT CONSTRUCTION LLC
4010 W Chandler Ave, Santa Ana
(92704-5202)
PHONE..........................714 540-5351
Michael Crawford, *Principal*
Paul Kuliev, *CFO*
Joe Philbin, *Principal*
Mike Zanaboni, *Principal*
EMP: 99 **EST:** 2014
SALES (est): 6.7MM **Privately Held**
SIC: 1623 1629 1611 Water, sewer & utility lines; pipe laying construction; earthmoving contractor; grading

(P-1987)
T C CONSTRUCTION COMPANY INC
10540 Prospect Ave, Santee (92071-4591)
PHONE..........................619 448-4560
Terry W Cameron, *CEO*
Austin Cameron, *President*
Jack Gieffels, *CFO*
Derek Franken, *Vice Pres*
Darren Tharp, *Vice Pres*
EMP: 150

SQ FT: 16,000
SALES: 62.2MM **Privately Held**
SIC: 1623 1611 Underground utilities contractor; highway & street paving contractor

(P-1988)
TRITON TOWER INC (PA)
3200 Jefferson Blvd, West Sacramento
(95691-5418)
PHONE..........................916 375-8546
Kevin Wingard, *President*
Mike Monroe, *Treasurer*
Rex Avakian, *Admin Sec*
EMP: 54
SALES: 2.5MM **Privately Held**
SIC: 1623 Transmitting tower (telecommunication) construction

(P-1989)
TURN AROUND COMMUNICATIONS INC
4400 Temple City Blvd, El Monte
(91731-1095)
P.O. Box 6121 (91734-2121)
PHONE..........................626 443-2400
Sayeid Kouhkan, *President*
Brad Adams, *Vice Pres*
Nick Fernandez, *Senior Mgr*
EMP: 170
SQ FT: 23,683
SALES (est): 7.6MM **Privately Held**
SIC: 1623 Telephone & communication line construction

(P-1990)
UNITED POWER CONTRACTORS INC
405 Maple St Ste A-103, Ramona
(92065-1890)
PHONE..........................760 735-8028
Andres A Canales, *President*
Jerome Reuben Rodriguez, *CEO*
Mark Walken, *Senior VP*
Reuben Rodriguez, *Vice Pres*
EMP: 117 **EST:** 2007
SALES (est): 15.3MM **Privately Held**
SIC: 1623 Electric power line construction

(P-1991)
UTAH PACIFIC CONSTRUCTION CO
40940 Eleanora Way, Murrieta
(92562-5946)
PHONE..........................951 677-9876
Craig R Young, *President*
Brian Keeline, *Vice Pres*
Jason Bent, *Safety Mgr*
Paula Durnford, *Manager*
Chris Medellin, *Manager*
EMP: 50
SQ FT: 5,000
SALES (est): 8.3MM **Privately Held**
SIC: 1623 Sewer line construction; water main construction; pipeline construction

(P-1992)
UTI LEAK SEEKERS
Also Called: Uti Underground Technology
1398 Monterey Pass Rd, Monterey Park
(91754-3619)
PHONE..........................323 724-0081
Lisa Pickareela, *Principal*
EMP: 70
SALES (est): 2.5MM **Privately Held**
SIC: 1623 Underground utilities contractor

(P-1993)
VADNAIS TRENCHLESS SVCS INC
26000 Commercentre Dr, Lake Forest
(92630-8816)
P.O. Box 5166 (92609-8666)
PHONE..........................858 550-1460
Paul Vadnais, *CEO*
EMP: 350 **EST:** 2014
SALES (est): 46.5MM
SALES (corp-wide): 2.3B **Publicly Held**
SIC: 1623 1622 Water, sewer & utility lines; tunnel construction
PA: Primoris Services Corporation
2100 Mckinney Ave # 1500
Dallas TX 75201
214 740-5600

(P-1994)

VADNAIS TRENCHLESS SVCS INC

2130 La Mirada Dr, Vista (92081-8815)
PHONE..................................858 550-1460
Paul Vadnais, *CEO*
Jesse Mangan, *CFO*
Jeff Anderson, *Vice Pres*
▲ EMP: 100
SALES (est): 21.8MM **Privately Held**
WEB: www.vadnaiscorp.com
SIC: **1623** Sewer line construction

(P-1995)

VALVERDE CONSTRUCTION INC

10936 Shoemaker Ave, Santa Fe Springs (90670-4533)
P.O. Box 3223 (90670-0223)
PHONE..................................562 906-1826
Joe A Valverde, *President*
Rose Valverde, *Treasurer*
Edward Valverde, *Vice Pres*
Christopher Valverde, *Admin Sec*
EMP: 75
SQ FT: 9,000
SALES (est): 32.6MM **Privately Held**
SIC: **1623** Water main construction; sewer line construction; telephone & communication line construction; cable laying construction

(P-1996)

VCI CONSTRUCTION LLC (HQ)

1921 W 11th St Ste A, Upland (91786-3508)
PHONE..................................909 946-0905
John Xanthos, *President*
Vic Marovish, *CFO*
Logan Teal, *Vice Pres*
Patrick Davies, *Division Mgr*
Gary Sharp, *Division Mgr*
EMP: 100
SQ FT: 29,500
SALES: 68MM
SALES (corp-wide): 3.1B **Publicly Held**
WEB: www.vcicom.com
SIC: **1623** Underground utilities contractor; transmitting tower (telecommunication) construction
PA: Dycom Industries, Inc.
    11780 Us Highway 1 # 600
    Palm Beach Gardens FL 33408
    561 627-7171

(P-1997)

W A RASIC CNSTR CO INC (PA)

4150 Long Beach Blvd, Long Beach (90807-2650)
PHONE..................................562 928-6111
Peter L Rasic, *CEO*
Shane Sato, *Division Mgr*
Wes Brodeur, *Project Mgr*
Richard Sahagun, *Engineer*
Corey Cossey, *Manager*
EMP: 151
SQ FT: 8,500
SALES (est): 151.4MM **Privately Held**
WEB: www.warasic.com
SIC: **1623** Sewer line construction; water main construction

(P-1998)

W M LYLES CO (HQ)

1210 W Olive Ave, Fresno (93728-2816)
P.O. Box 4377 (93744-4377)
PHONE..................................559 441-1900
David Dawson, *President*
Andrea Oliver, *President*
Dave Dawson, *Vice Pres*
Ken Strosnider, *Vice Pres*
Tony Mueller, *Executive*
EMP: 340
SQ FT: 6,200
SALES: 230MM
SALES (corp-wide): 33.7MM **Privately Held**
WEB: www.wmlyles.com
SIC: **1623** Pipeline construction; underground utilities contractor
PA: Lyles Diversified, Inc.
    1210 W Olive Ave
    Fresno CA 93728
    559 441-1900

(P-1999)

WATER & SEWER SERVICE

7051 Dublin Blvd, Dublin (94568-3018)
PHONE..................................925 828-8524
Berrt Michalzzyk, *General Mgr*
EMP: 80
SALES (est): 2.7MM **Privately Held**
SIC: **1623** Water, sewer & utility lines

(P-2000)

WATKINS CONSTRUCTION CO INC

Also Called: Johnston Vacuum Tank Service
112 E Cedar St, Taft (93268-9708)
P.O. Box 243 (93268-0243)
PHONE..................................661 763-5395
Eddie Watkins Sr, *President*
Mary King, *Manager*
EMP: 60 EST: 1967
SQ FT: 4,800
SALES (est): 9.9MM **Privately Held**
WEB: www.watkinsconstructionco.com
SIC: **1623** Oil & gas pipeline construction

(P-2001)

WDC EXPLRTION WELLS HOLDG CORP

1300 National Dr Ste 140, Sacramento (95834-1981)
PHONE..................................916 419-6043
Robert L Ruck, *CEO*
Ray Imbsen, *CFO*
EMP: 203
SQ FT: 8,788
SALES (est): 18.1MM **Privately Held**
SIC: **1623 1629** Pumping station construction; waste water & sewage treatment plant construction

(P-2002)

WEST STATES SKANSKA INC

1995 Agua Mansa Rd, Riverside (92509-2405)
PHONE..................................970 565-4903
Curtis Brotten, *President*
EMP: 150
SQ FT: 800
SALES (corp-wide): 18.7B **Privately Held**
SIC: **1623 1541** Water, sewer & utility lines; industrial buildings & warehouses
HQ: Skanska Usa Civil West Rocky Mountain District Inc.
    1995 Agua Mansa Rd
    Riverside CA 92509
    970 565-8000

(P-2003)

WEST VALLEY CNSTR CO INC (PA)

580 E Mcglincy Ln, Campbell (95008-4999)
PHONE..................................408 371-5510
Kevin Kelly, *CEO*
David Barnes, *CFO*
Jeff Boss, *Officer*
Jeff Azevedo, *Vice Pres*
James Vosburgh, *Vice Pres*
EMP: 150 EST: 1958
SQ FT: 9,000
SALES (est): 149.8MM **Privately Held**
WEB: www.westvalleyconstruction.com
SIC: **1623** Water main construction; telephone & communication line construction

(P-2004)

WHITTIER EQUIPMENT RENTALS

11832 Bloomfield Ave, Santa Fe Springs (90670-4610)
PHONE..................................562 863-0641
Charles Rikel, *President*
T C Tustin, *Treasurer*
James Doulames, *Vice Pres*
EMP: 85
SQ FT: 5,000
SALES (est): 4.3MM **Privately Held**
SIC: **1623** Pipeline construction

1629 Heavy Construction, NEC

(P-2005)

ALLOY CONSTRUCTION INC

701 Gardner Field Rd, Taft (93268)
P.O. Box 661 (93268-0661)
PHONE..................................661 203-2592
James Folkner, *President*
EMP: 60 EST: 1991
SQ FT: 300
SALES: 4.5MM **Privately Held**
WEB: www.alloyconstruction.com
SIC: **1629** Oil refinery construction

(P-2006)

AMERICAN CIVIL CONSTRS LLC

3701 Mallard Dr, Benicia (94510-1246)
PHONE..................................707 746-8028
Pete Wells, *Manager*
EMP: 150 **Privately Held**
WEB: www.americancivilconstructors.com
SIC: **1629 0783 0181** Land preparation construction; earthmoving contractor; golf course construction; dam construction; spraying services, ornamental bush; removal services, bush & tree; sod farms
HQ: American Civil Constructors Llc
    4901 S Windermere St
    Littleton CO 80120
    303 795-2582

(P-2007)

ANDERSON PCF ENGRG CNSTR INC

1390 Norman Ave, Santa Clara (95054-2047)
PHONE..................................408 970-9900
Peter E Anderson, *CEO*
Matthew Mirenda, *Vice Pres*
Ann Anderson, *Admin Sec*
Scott Anderson, *Project Mgr*
Michael Gossett, *Project Mgr*
EMP: 100
SQ FT: 3,000
SALES (est): 49.1MM **Privately Held**
WEB: www.andpac.com
SIC: **1629 1623** Dams, waterways, docks & other marine construction; pumping station construction; underground utilities contractor

(P-2008)

ARB INC (HQ)

26000 Commercentre Dr, Lake Forest (92630-8816)
PHONE..................................949 598-9242
Brian Pratt, *President*
John P Schauerman, *Corp Secy*
Timothy Healy, *Vice Pres*
Scott Summers, *Vice Pres*
John M Perisich, *Admin Sec*
▲ EMP: 140
SQ FT: 50,000
SALES (est): 159.5MM
SALES (corp-wide): 2.3B **Publicly Held**
WEB: www.arbinc.com
SIC: **1629 1623** Industrial plant construction; waste disposal plant construction; waste water & sewage treatment plant construction; oil & gas line & compressor station construction
PA: Primoris Services Corporation
    2100 Mckinney Ave # 1500
    Dallas TX 75201
    214 740-5600

(P-2009)

AUBURN CONSTRUCTORS INC

730 W Stadium Ln, Sacramento (95834-1130)
PHONE..................................916 924-0344
Dean Bailey, *President*
Bill Franceschini, *Corp Secy*
Kevin Couper, *Vice Pres*
EMP: 80
SQ FT: 5,500
SALES: 48.8MM **Privately Held**
WEB: www.auburnconstructors.com
SIC: **1629** Industrial plant construction; waste water & sewage treatment plant construction

(P-2010)

BECHTEL GROUP INC (PA)

50 Beale St Bsmt 1, San Francisco (94105-1819)
PHONE..................................415 768-1234
Brendan Bechtel, *Ch of Bd*
Paul Brown, *President*
Adrian Zaccaria, *President*
Catherine Hunt Ryan, *CFO*
Riley Bechtel, *Chairman*
◆ EMP: 2100
SQ FT: 300,000
SALES (est): 10.4B **Privately Held**
WEB: www.bechtelgroup.com
SIC: **1629 8742 8711** Industrial plant construction; construction project management consultant; civil engineering

(P-2011)

BELECTRIC INC (HQ)

951 Mariners Island Blvd, San Mateo (94404-1558)
PHONE..................................510 896-3940
David Taggart, *President*
David Johann, *Vice Pres*
Pat Christensen, *Executive Asst*
Bernhard Beck, *Finance Dir*
Matthew Lusk, *Financial Analy*
▲ EMP: 60
SQ FT: 29,198
SALES (est): 18.4MM
SALES (corp-wide): 112MM **Privately Held**
SIC: **1629** Power plant construction
PA: Apuron Holding Gmbh
    Grasleingasse 1
    Kolitzheim 97509
    938 171-0871

(P-2012)

BEMUS LANDSCAPE INC

1225 Puerta Del Sol # 500, San Clemente (92673-6312)
P.O. Box 74268 (92673-0143)
PHONE..................................714 557-7910
William Howard Bemus, *President*
Jonathon Parry, *Corp Secy*
Martine Bemus, *Vice Pres*
Kirk Hinshaw, *Vice Pres*
Spencer Bemus, *Branch Mgr*
EMP: 300
SQ FT: 7,000
SALES (est): 44.8MM **Privately Held**
WEB: www.bemuslandscape.com
SIC: **1629 0782** Drainage system construction; landscape contractors

(P-2013)

BILL PAPICH CONSTRUCTION INC

398 Sunrise Ter, Arroyo Grande (93420-4419)
PHONE..................................805 489-9420
Jason Papich, *President*
Marcia Papich, *Corp Secy*
EMP: 50
SALES (est): 787.8K **Privately Held**
SIC: **1629** Blasting contractor, except building demolition

(P-2014)

BRIGHTVIEW COMPANIES LLC (DH)

24151 Ventura Blvd, Calabasas (91302-1449)
PHONE..................................818 223-8500
John Feenan, *CEO*
Thomas C Donnelly, *President*
Jeff Herold, *President*
Shawn Rommerdahl, *Branch Mgr*
Karen Anderson, *Office Admin*
◆ EMP: 175
SQ FT: 25,000
SALES (est): 2.5B
SALES (corp-wide): 2.8B **Publicly Held**
WEB: www.valleycrest.com
SIC: **1629 0782 0781** Golf course construction; lawn & garden services; landscape services; landscape planning services
HQ: Brightview Landscapes, Llc
    401 Plymouth Rd Ste 500
    Plymouth Meeting PA 19462
    484 567-7204

(P-2015)
BRIGHTVIEW GOLF MAINT INC
405 Glen Annie Rd, Santa Barbara
(93117-1427)
PHONE..................................805 968-6400
Richard Hasah, *Manager*
EMP: 50
SALES (corp-wide): 2.8B **Publicly Held**
SIC: **1629** Golf course construction
HQ: Brightview Golf Maintenance, Inc.
24151 Ventura Blvd
Calabasas CA 91302
818 223-8500

(P-2016)
BRIGHTVIEW GOLF MAINT INC (DH)
24151 Ventura Blvd, Calabasas
(91302-1449)
PHONE..................................818 223-8500
Burton Sperber, *Ch of Bd*
Richard A Sperber, *Ch of Bd*
Gregory Pieschala, *President*
Andrew Mandell, *CFO*
Michael L Dingman, *Chairman*
EMP: 100
SQ FT: 80,000
SALES (est): 158.7MM
SALES (corp-wide): 2.8B **Publicly Held**
SIC: **1629** Golf course construction
HQ: Brightview Companies, Llc
24151 Ventura Blvd
Calabasas CA 91302
818 223-8500

(P-2017)
BRIGHTVIEW LANDSCAPE DEV INC
8450 Miramar Pl, San Diego (92121-2528)
PHONE..................................858 458-9900
Vince Germann, *Manager*
Michael Lyons, *General Mgr*
Dave Baty, *Sales Mgr*
EMP: 300
SQ FT: 16,050
SALES (corp-wide): 2.8B **Publicly Held**
SIC: **1629** Irrigation system construction;
land preparation construction
HQ: Brightview Landscape Development, Inc.
24151 Ventura Blvd
Calabasas CA 91302
818 223-8500

(P-2018)
BYROM-DAVEY INC
13220 Evnng Crk Dr S # 103, San Diego
(92128-4103)
PHONE..................................858 513-7199
Steve V Davey, *Owner*
Joanne Caspersen, *Treasurer*
Christine Butler, *Vice Pres*
Raul Gilbert, *Vice Pres*
Eric Jennings Sr, *Vice Pres*
EMP: 50
SQ FT: 2,200
SALES (est): 12.1MM **Privately Held**
WEB: www.byromdavey.com
SIC: **1629** 1611 Land preparation con-
struction; athletic field construction; high-
way & street construction

(P-2019)
C A RASMUSSEN INC (PA)
28548 Livingston Ave, Valencia
(91355-4171)
PHONE..................................661 367-9040
Charles A Rasmussen, *President*
D I C K Greenburg, *CFO*
Tim Macdonald, *Vice Pres*
Mike Medema, *Vice Pres*
Doug Misley, *Vice Pres*
EMP: 50
SQ FT: 20,000
SALES (est): 79.8MM **Privately Held**
WEB: www.carasmussen.com
SIC: **1629** 1611 Earthmoving contractor;
grading

(P-2020)
CAL WEST UNDERGROUND INC
951 6th St, Norco (92860-1442)
PHONE..................................951 371-6775
Jeffrey M Abernathy, *President*
EMP: 63

SQ FT: 1,200
SALES (est): 9.2MM **Privately Held**
SIC: **1629** Trenching contractor

(P-2021)
CATTRAC CONSTRUCTION INC
15030 Slover Ave, Fontana (92337-7237)
PHONE..................................909 355-1146
Stephanie A Jacinto, *CEO*
Greg Dineen, *Vice Pres*
EMP: 60
SQ FT: 5,000
SALES (est): 14.6MM **Privately Held**
WEB: www.cattrac.com
SIC: **1629** 7353 4213 Earthmoving con-
tractor; earth moving equipment, rental or
leasing; trucking, except local

(P-2022)
CE ALLENCOMPANY INC
2109 Gundry Ave, Long Beach
(90755-3517)
PHONE..................................562 989-6100
C E Peter Allen, *President*
EMP: 50
SQ FT: 1,277
SALES (est): 8.2MM **Privately Held**
SIC: **1629** 7353 Industrial plant construc-
tion; oil equipment rental services

(P-2023)
CITY OF LIVERMORE
Also Called: Water Resources Division
101 W Jack London Blvd, Livermore
(94551-7632)
PHONE..................................925 960-8100
Darren Greenwood, *Manager*
EMP: 50 **Privately Held**
SIC: **1629** Waste water & sewage treat-
ment plant construction
PA: City Of Livermore
1052 S Livermore Ave
Livermore CA 94550
925 960-4020

(P-2024)
COOPER CRANE & RIGGING INC (PA)
1175 Nimitz Ave Ste 104, Vallejo
(94592-1003)
P.O. Box 2540, Novato (94948-2540)
PHONE..................................707 765-4646
Russell Barnes, *President*
Barry K Cooper, *Vice Pres*
Karen Michalski, *Admin Sec*
▲ EMP: 51 EST: 1972
SQ FT: 6,000
SALES (est): 6.3MM **Privately Held**
WEB: www.coopercrane.com
SIC: **1629** Dams, waterways, docks &
other marine construction

(P-2025)
DOD CONSTRUCTORS A JV
185 Devlin Rd, NAPA (94558-6255)
PHONE..................................707 265-1100
Ronald Fedrick, *CEO*
Scott Victor, *President*
Walter Birdsall, *CFO*
Carole Bionda, *Vice Pres*
EMP: 99 EST: 2013
SALES (est): 2.6MM **Privately Held**
SIC: **1629** Dams, waterways, docks &
other marine construction

(P-2026)
DOD FUELING CONSTRUCTORS A JV
185 Devlin Rd, NAPA (94558-6255)
PHONE..................................707 265-1100
Ronald Fedrick, *Principal*
Walter Birdsall, *CFO*
Carole Bionda, *Principal*
Chris Mathies, *Principal*
Scott Victor, *Principal*
EMP: 99 EST: 2013
SALES (est): 2.4MM **Privately Held**
SIC: **1629** Dams, waterways, docks &
other marine construction

(P-2027)
DOD MARINE CONSTRUCTORS A JV
185 Devlin Rd, NAPA (94558-6255)
PHONE..................................707 265-1100

Ronald Fedrick, *Partner*
Carole Bionda, *Partner*
Walter Birdsall, *Partner*
Chris Mathies, *Partner*
Scott Victor, *Partner*
EMP: 99 EST: 2013
SQ FT: 18,000
SALES (est): 2.4MM **Privately Held**
SIC: **1629** Dams, waterways, docks &
other marine construction

(P-2028)
DUTRA DREDGING COMPANY (HQ)
2350 Kerner Blvd Ste 200, San Rafael
(94901-5595)
PHONE..................................415 721-2131
Bill T Dutra, *CEO*
EMP: 60
SQ FT: 2,000
SALES (est): 14MM
SALES (corp-wide): 145.1MM **Privately Held**
WEB: www.dutragroup.com
SIC: **1629** Dredging contractor
PA: The Dutra Group
2350 Kerner Blvd Ste 200
San Rafael CA 94901
415 258-6876

(P-2029)
DUTRA GROUP (PA)
Also Called: Dutra Dredging
2350 Kerner Blvd Ste 200, San Rafael
(94901-5595)
PHONE..................................415 258-6876
Bill T Dutra, *CEO*
Harry Stewart, *COO*
James Hagood, *CFO*
Leland R Selna, *Admin Sec*
Todd Bruce, *Project Mgr*
▲ EMP: 100
SQ FT: 22,000
SALES (est): 145.1MM **Privately Held**
SIC: **1629** 8711 1429 Marine construc-
tion; dredging contractor; earthmoving
contractor; civil engineering; igneous
rock, crushed & broken-quarrying

(P-2030)
DUTRA MANSON JV
1000 Point San Pedro Rd, San Rafael
(94901-8312)
PHONE..................................415 258-6876
Harry K Stewart, *Director*
James Hagood, *CFO*
Cliff Hunt, *Director*
EMP: 60
SALES (est): 2.3MM **Privately Held**
SIC: **1629** Marine construction

(P-2031)
ESOLAR INC (DH)
900 Glenneyre St, Laguna Beach
(92651-2707)
PHONE..................................818 303-9500
John Van Scoter, *CEO*
Bill Gross, *President*
Rayan Kassis, *President*
Linda Heller, *CFO*
Dale Rogers, *Exec VP*
▲ EMP: 78
SALES (est): 12.5MM
SALES (corp-wide): 169.2MM **Privately Held**
SIC: **1629** Power plant construction

(P-2032)
FORD CONSTRUCTION COMPANY INC
300 W Pine St, Lodi (95240-2022)
PHONE..................................209 333-1116
Richard Piombo, *Treasurer*
Nicholas B Jones, *President*
Scott Davis, *Technical Staff*
Vernon Silva, *Superintendent*
EMP: 100 EST: 1979
SQ FT: 8,500
SALES (est): 18.4MM **Privately Held**
WEB: www.ford-construction.com
SIC: **1629** 1623 Dam construction; earth-
moving contractor; water & sewer line
construction

(P-2033)
FOUNDATION CONSTRUCTORS INC (PA)
81 Big Break Rd, Oakley (94561-3081)
P.O. Box 97 (94561-0097)
PHONE..................................925 754-6633
Derek Halecky, *President*
Pete Brandl, *President*
Nikki Sjoblom, *Officer*
Don Hilton, *Vice Pres*
Mike Lindsay, *Vice Pres*
▲ EMP: 100
SQ FT: 6,000
SALES (est): 73.3MM **Privately Held**
SIC: **1629** Pile driving contractor

(P-2034)
GHILOTTI CONSTRUCTION CO INC (PA)
Also Called: Gcc
246 Ghillotti Ave, Santa Rosa
(95407-8152)
PHONE..................................707 585-1221
Richard W Ghilotti, *CEO*
EMP: 151
SQ FT: 9,000
SALES (est): 135.2MM **Privately Held**
WEB: www.ghilotti.com
SIC: **1629** Land preparation construction

(P-2035)
GRANITE CONSTRUCTION COMPANY
Also Called: Northern California Regional
4001 Bradshaw Rd, Sacramento
(95827-3800)
PHONE..................................916 855-4400
Wayne Cornelius, *Manager*
EMP: 61
SQ FT: 1,364
SALES (corp-wide): 2.9B **Publicly Held**
WEB:
www.graniteconstructioncompany.com
SIC: **1629** 1611 Land preparation con-
struction; highway & street construction
HQ: Granite Construction Company
585 W Beach St
Watsonville CA 95076
831 724-1011

(P-2036)
GREAT LAKES E & I/ INQUIP JV
6558 Lonetree Blvd, Rocklin (95765-5874)
P.O. Box 6277, Mc Lean VA (22106-6277)
PHONE..................................805 687-2007
Dominique Namy, *Principal*
Oscar Hensgen, *Principal*
Louay Owaidat, *Principal*
EMP: 99
SQ FT: 30,000
SALES (est): 1.9MM **Privately Held**
SIC: **1629** Dams, waterways, docks &
other marine construction; dam construc-
tion; levee construction

(P-2037)
HANS TECHNOLOGIES INC
1300 Clay St Ste 600, Oakland
(94612-1427)
PHONE..................................510 464-8018
Jerry Moseley, *President*
Craig Johns, *Vice Pres*
Kenneth Norcross III, *Vice Pres*
Weiping Xia, *Vice Pres*
James LI, *Admin Sec*
▲ EMP: 58
SQ FT: 6,500
SALES: 13.5MM **Privately Held**
SIC: **1629** Waste water & sewage treat-
ment plant construction

(P-2038)
HAT CREEK CNSTR & MTLS INC (PA)
24339 State Highway 89, Burney
(96013-9615)
PHONE..................................530 335-5501
Robert Thompson, *President*
Perry Thompson, *Treasurer*
Howard A Lakey Jr, *Vice Pres*
EMP: 50

SALES (est): 19.3MM **Privately Held**
WEB: www.hatcreekconstruction.com
SIC: **1629** 1771 1521 5032 Earthmoving
contractor; concrete work; single-family
housing construction; sand, construction;
gravel; highway & street construction

(P-2039)
JACOBS ENGINEERING GROUP INC
1111 S Arroyo Pkwy, Pasadena
(91105-3254)
P.O. Box 7084 (91109-7084)
PHONE...............................626 578-3500
Ford Hubbard, *President*
Dennis Rose, *Officer*
Patrick McFarlin, *Division VP*
Sy Exter, *Exec VP*
George Kunberger Jr, *Exec VP*
EMP: 89
SALES (corp-wide): 10B **Publicly Held**
SIC: **1629** Industrial plant construction
PA: Jacobs Engineering Group Inc.
1999 Bryan St Ste 1200
Dallas TX 75201
214 583-8500

(P-2040)
JACOBS FIELD SVCS N AMER INC
2600 Michelson Dr Ste 500, Irvine
(92612-6506)
P.O. Box 6025, Cypress (90630-0025)
PHONE...............................949 224-7585
Brandy Marquez, *Branch Mgr*
EMP: 250
SALES (corp-wide): 10B **Publicly Held**
WEB: www.jemcidecatur.com
SIC: **1629** Earthmoving contractor
HQ: Jacobs Field Services North America,
Inc.
5995 Rogerdale Rd
Houston TX 77072
832 351-6000

(P-2041)
JAMES-TIMEC INTERNATIONAL
155 Corporate Pl, Vallejo (94590-6968)
PHONE...............................707 642-2222
Anthony Marquez, *Manager*
EMP: 50
SALES (corp-wide): 571K **Privately Held**
SIC: **1629** Industrial plant construction
HQ: James-Timec International, Inc
2315 W Main St
Baytown TX 77520
281 471-3209

(P-2042)
JOHN S MEEK COMPANY INC
14732 S Maple Ave, Gardena
(90248-1934)
PHONE...............................310 830-6323
John S Meek, *President*
Jim Jilk, *General Mgr*
Chad Goodwin, *Project Mgr*
Lisa Paila, *Manager*
Michelle Kephart, *Receptionist*
EMP: 60
SQ FT: 5,000
SALES (est): 20.1MM **Privately Held**
WEB: www.johnsmeek.com
SIC: **1629** Marine construction

(P-2043)
K G WALTERS CNSTR CO INC
195 Concourse Blvd Ste A, Santa Rosa
(95403-8217)
P.O. Box 4359 (95402-4359)
PHONE...............................707 527-9968
Walt Johnson, *President*
David A Backman, *Senior VP*
Thomas Crotty, *Vice Pres*
Valerie Carmichael, *Admin Sec*
EMP: 55 EST: 1974
SQ FT: 4,000
SALES: 19.9MM **Privately Held**
WEB: www.kgwalters.com
SIC: **1629** Waste water & sewage treat-
ment plant construction

(P-2044)
MARCH INTERNATIONAL INC
Also Called: Wall Tech
1249 S Dmnd Bar Blvd 20, Diamond Bar
(91765-4122)
PHONE...............................909 821-5128
Frank Tilton, *CFO*
EMP: 50
SALES (est): 1.6MM **Privately Held**
SIC: **1629** Canal construction

(P-2045)
MILCO CONSTRUCTORS INC
3930b Cherry Ave, Long Beach
(90807-3727)
P.O. Box 2150 (90801-2150)
PHONE...............................562 595-1977
Charles Miller, *President*
Duane C Miller, *Corp Secy*
EMP: 50 EST: 1973
SQ FT: 17,000
SALES (est): 9.3MM **Privately Held**
WEB: www.milcoconstructors.com
SIC: **1629** Industrial plant construction

(P-2046)
MITCH BROWN CONSTRUCTION INC
14200 Road 284, Porterville (93257-9374)
PHONE...............................559 781-6389
Mitchell F Brown, *President*
Elizabeth Brown, *Corp Secy*
EMP: 60
SALES (est): 5MM **Privately Held**
SIC: **1629** Earthmoving contractor

(P-2047)
MONTEREY MECHANICAL CO (PA)
Also Called: Contra Costa Metal Fabricators
8275 San Leandro St, Oakland
(94621-1972)
PHONE...............................510 632-3173
Milton C Burleson, *CEO*
Jim Troup, *President*
Paul Moreira, *CFO*
Vy Nguyen, *Executive*
Karl Hoiser, *Project Mgr*
▲ EMP: 50
SQ FT: 40,000
SALES (est): 73.4MM **Privately Held**
WEB: www.montmech.com
SIC: **1629** 1711 1761 3444 Waste dis-
posal plant construction; waste water &
sewage treatment plant construction; me-
chanical contractor; boiler setting contrac-
tor; boiler maintenance contractor; sheet
metalwork; sheet metalwork; fabricated
structural metal; nonresidential construc-
tion

(P-2048)
NORDIC INDUSTRIES INC
1437 Furneaux Rd, Olivehurst
(95961-7404)
PHONE...............................530 742-7124
Jens Karlshoej, *President*
Inge Karlshoej, *Corp Secy*
Calvin Barnhill, *Project Mgr*
John Hicks, *Project Mgr*
Todd Lemmons, *Project Mgr*
EMP: 60
SQ FT: 5,000
SALES (est): 18.6MM **Privately Held**
WEB: www.nordicind.com
SIC: **1629** 4212 4213 Dam construction;
levee construction; local trucking, without
storage; trucking, except local

(P-2049)
NORDIC/GREAT LAKES E&I JV
1437 Furneaux Rd, Olivehurst
(95961-7404)
PHONE...............................530 742-7124
Louay Ouaidat, *Partner*
Jens Karlshoej, *Partner*
EMP: 99
SQ FT: 30,000
SALES (est): 2.2MM **Privately Held**
SIC: **1629** Dams, waterways, docks &
other marine construction; dam construc-
tion; levee construction

(P-2050)
NOVA ATL ELC A JOINT VENTR
185 Devlin Rd, NAPA (94558-6255)
PHONE...............................707 265-1100
Scott Victor, *Principal*
Carole Bionda, *Principal*
Dee Fedrick, *Principal*
Ronald Fedrick, *Principal*
Legrand Richardson, *Principal*
EMP: 99
SQ FT: 18,000
SALES (est): 1.9MM **Privately Held**
SIC: **1629** Pier construction

(P-2051)
NOVA BRINK A JOINT VENTURE
185 Devlin Rd, NAPA (94558-6255)
PHONE...............................707 265-1100
Ronld Fedrick, *Partner*
Brent Albrecht, *Partner*
Carole Bionda, *Partner*
Scott Victor, *Partner*
EMP: 99
SQ FT: 18,000
SALES (est): 2.1MM **Privately Held**
SIC: **1629** 1623 1622 Dams, waterways,
docks & other marine construction; water,
sewer & utility lines; tunnel construction

(P-2052)
NOVA LANE CONSTRUCTORS A JV
185 Devlin Rd, NAPA (94558-6255)
PHONE...............................707 265-1100
Ronald Fedrick, *CEO*
Carole Bionda, *Principal*
Walter Birdsall, *Principal*
Chris Mathies, *Principal*
Scott Victor, *Principal*
EMP: 99 EST: 2013
SALES (est): 2.4MM **Privately Held**
SIC: **1629** Dams, waterways, docks &
other marine construction

(P-2053)
PARSONS CORPORATION (PA)
100 W Walnut St, Pasadena (91124-0001)
PHONE...............................626 440-2000
Charles L Harrington, *Ch of Bd*
Mauseen Hayes, *President*
John A Scott, *President*
Carey A Smith, *President*
Ralph Steinhauser, *COO*
◆ EMP: 2000
SQ FT: 900,000
SALES (est): 3.1B **Privately Held**
SIC: **1629** 1611 8711 8741 Chemical
plant & refinery construction; highway &
street construction; industrial engineers;
chemical engineering; management serv-
ices

(P-2054)
PARSONS CORPORATION
1 Centerpointe Dr Ste 210, La Palma
(90623-2524)
PHONE...............................714 562-5725
EMP: 175
SALES (corp-wide): 3.1B **Privately Held**
SIC: **1629** Dams, waterways, docks &
other marine construction
PA: The Parsons Corporation
100 W Walnut St
Pasadena CA 91124
626 440-2000

(P-2055)
PATRICKS CONSTRUCTION CLEAN-UP
7851 14th Ave, Sacramento (95826-4301)
PHONE...............................916 452-5495
Patricio Mercado, *Owner*
Susan Lopez, *Accounting Mgr*
EMP: 100
SALES (est): 8.2MM **Privately Held**
SIC: **1629** Land clearing contractor

(P-2056)
POWERPLANT MINT SPCIALISTS INC
2900 Bristol St Ste H202, Costa Mesa
(92626-7917)
PHONE...............................714 427-6900
Jim McEachern, *CEO*
Richard G Engel, *President*

J Alexandra Barretto, *Vice Pres*
Dave Gatti, *Vice Pres*
Michael Medock, *Vice Pres*
EMP: 200
SQ FT: 3,300
SALES (est): 18.5MM **Privately Held**
WEB: www.pmsipower.com
SIC: **1629** Dams, waterways, docks &
other marine construction

(P-2057)
RAIN BIRD DISTRIBUTION CORP
1000 W Sierra Madre Ave, Azusa
(91702-1700)
P.O. Box 37 (91702-0037)
PHONE...............................626 963-9311
Anthony Lafetra, *CEO*
Anthony W Lafetra, *CEO*
Nick Kaleyias, *CFO*
Arthur Ludwick, *Treasurer*
EMP: 52
SQ FT: 20,000
SALES (est): 2MM **Privately Held**
SIC: **1629** 3523 Irrigation system con-
struction; fertilizing, spraying, dusting & ir-
rigation machinery

(P-2058)
RE LA MESA LLC
300 California St Fl 8, San Francisco
(94104-1416)
PHONE...............................415 675-1500
Arno Harris,
Greg Wilson,
EMP: 100
SALES (est): 2.7MM **Privately Held**
SIC: **1629** Land leveling

(P-2059)
SAN DIEGO HBR EXCURSIONS INC
1050 N Harbor Dr, San Diego
(92101-3316)
P.O. Box 120751 (92112-0751)
PHONE...............................619 234-4111
Arthur E Engel, *President*
EMP: 100
SALES: 15MM
SALES (corp-wide): 16.3MM **Privately
Held**
SIC: **1629** Harbor construction
PA: Star & Crescent Boat Company
1311 1st St
Coronado CA 92118
619 234-4111

(P-2060)
SCHWAGER DAVIS INC
198 Hillsdale Ave, San Jose (95136-1398)
PHONE...............................408 281-9300
Guido A Schwager, *President*
Robert Parkhurst, *CFO*
Michael Williams, *QA Dir*
Keith McKenna, *Project Mgr*
Mario Salice, *Project Mgr*
▲ EMP: 112
SQ FT: 12,000
SALES (est): 41.6MM **Privately Held**
SIC: **1629** 1622 Railroad & railway
roadbed construction; bridge construction

(P-2061)
SHIMMICK CONSTRUCTION CO INC (HQ)
8201 Edgewater Dr Ste 202, Oakland
(94621-2023)
PHONE...............................510 777-5000
Paul Cocotis, *Ch of Bd*
Paul Camaur, *President*
Scott Fairgrieve, *CFO*
Christian Fassari, *Exec VP*
Jeffrey Lessman, *Exec VP*
EMP: 151
SQ FT: 30,000
SALES: 319.6MM
SALES (corp-wide): 20.1B **Publicly Held**
SIC: **1629** 1623 Earthmoving contractor;
sewer line construction
PA: Aecom
1999 Avenue Of The Stars # 2600
Los Angeles CA 90067
213 593-8000

PRODUCTS & SVCS

(P-2062)
SIGMA INVESTMENT HOLDINGS LLC
2288 Villa Heights Rd, Pasadena
(91107-1141)
PHONE..................626 398-3098
Geoffrey G Ren, *Mng Member*
Asong Fu,
Chauan Ren,
Guang Ren,
▼ EMP: 50
SQ FT: 3,178
SALES: 50MM **Privately Held**
SIC: 1629 Industrial plant construction

(P-2063)
SKANSKA USA CIVIL WEST ROCKY M (DH)
Also Called: SKANSKA ROCKY MOUNTAIN DISTRICT
1995 Agua Mansa Rd, Riverside
(92509-2405)
PHONE..................970 565-8000
Curtis Broughton, *Senior VP*
Larry Casey, *Vice Pres*
David Sitton, *Vice Pres*
Tammy Hampton, *General Mgr*
Gary Moss, *Project Mgr*
EMP: 70
SQ FT: 22,500
SALES: 421.5K
SALES (corp-wide): 18.7B **Privately Held**
SIC: 1629 1611 1711 Dam construction;
general contractor, highway & street con-
struction; mechanical contractor
HQ: Skanska Usa Civil Inc.
　7520 Astoria Blvd Ste 200
　East Elmhurst NY 11370
　718 340-0777

(P-2064)
SLATER INC
11045 Rose Ave, Fontana (92337-7051)
P.O. Box 759 (92334-0759)
PHONE..................909 822-6800
Phillip S Slater, *CEO*
Edward Johnson, *CFO*
Steve David, *Vice Pres*
EMP: 97
SQ FT: 6,000
SALES (est): 13.4MM **Privately Held**
WEB: www.slaterinc.com
SIC: 1629 8711 Drainage system con-
struction; engineering services

(P-2065)
SOLTIS GOLF INCORPORATED
869 W 9th St, Upland (91786-4541)
P.O. Box 1309 (91785-1309)
PHONE..................909 822-7000
Christopher Soltis, *President*
EMP: 75
SALES (est): 6.3MM **Privately Held**
WEB: www.soltisgolf.com
SIC: 1629 Golf course construction

(P-2066)
TEAM WEST CONTRACTING CORP
2733 S Vista Ave, Bloomington
(92316-3269)
PHONE..................951 340-3426
Jerry R Pacheco, *President*
Steve Knehans, *CFO*
Michael Ellefson, *Officer*
Bryan Girard, *Officer*
Stephen Girard, *Officer*
EMP: 92
SQ FT: 7,200
SALES: 7.2MM **Privately Held**
SIC: 1629 1799 Railroad & railway
roadbed construction; fence construction

(P-2067)
TEICHERT/GREAT LAKES E&I JV
3500 American River Dr, Sacramento
(95864-5802)
P.O. Box 15002 (95851-0002)
PHONE..................916 484-3011
Louay Owaidat, *Partner*
Judson Riggs, *Partner*
EMP: 99
SQ FT: 30,000

SALES (est): 1.9MM **Privately Held**
SIC: 1629 Dams, waterways, docks &
other marine construction; dam construction; levee construction

(P-2068)
THOMAS CRANE AND TRCKG CO INC
18851 Stewart Ln, Huntington Beach
(92648-1520)
P.O. Box 640 (92648-0640)
PHONE..................562 592-2837
Michael Thomas, *CEO*
John Thomas, *Principal*
Mike Thomas, *Principal*
Linda Thomas, *Admin Sec*
EMP: 50 EST: 1962
SQ FT: 800
SALES (est): 8.4MM **Privately Held**
SIC: 1629 4212 Oil refinery construction;
light haulage & cartage, local

(P-2069)
TIMEC ACQUISITIONS INC (DH)
155 Corporate Pl, Vallejo (94590-6968)
PHONE..................707 642-2222
Pat McMahon, *President*
Gary Green, *COO*
Dennis Turnipseed, *CFO*
EMP: 850 EST: 1998
SQ FT: 25,000
SALES (est): 120.1MM
SALES (corp-wide): 571K **Privately Held**
SIC: 1629 Industrial plant construction;
chemical plant & refinery construction

(P-2070)
TIMEC COMPANIES INC (DH)
155 Corporate Pl, Vallejo (94590-6968)
PHONE..................707 642-2222
Denis Turnipseed, *President*
EMP: 350
SQ FT: 80,000
SALES (est): 120.1MM
SALES (corp-wide): 571K **Privately Held**
SIC: 1629 1799 Industrial plant construc-
tion; chemical plant & refinery construc-
tion; oil refinery construction; welding on
site
HQ: Timec Acquisitions Inc
　155 Corporate Pl
　Vallejo CA 94590
　707 642-2222

(P-2071)
TUTOR PERINI/ZACHRY/PARSONS
1401 Fulton St Ste 400, Fresno
(93721-1645)
PHONE..................559 385-7025
James Frost, *Partner*
Carol Einfalt, *Partner*
EMP: 99
SQ FT: 15,000
SALES (est): 7.2MM **Privately Held**
SIC: 1629 Railroad & railway roadbed con-
struction

(P-2072)
UNIVERSAL FIELD SERVICES INC
1630 E Shaw Ave Ste 163, Fresno
(93710-8108)
PHONE..................559 453-2901
Leslie Finnagin, *Principal*
EMP: 50
SALES (corp-wide): 54.1MM **Privately Held**
SIC: 1629 Cutting of right-of-way
PA: Universal Field Services, Inc.
　6737 S 85th East Ave
　Tulsa OK 74133
　918 494-7600

(P-2073)
VISTA STEEL CO INC
331 W Lewis St, Ventura (93001-1394)
PHONE..................805 653-1189
John Swaffar, *Branch Mgr*
EMP: 50
SALES (corp-wide): 7.9MM **Privately Held**
SIC: 1629 3449 Dams, waterways, docks
& other marine construction; miscella-
neous metalwork

PA: Vista Steel Co Inc
　6100 Francis Botello Rd C
　Goleta CA 93117
　805 964-4732

(P-2074)
WINDROW EARTH TRANSPORT INC
14032 Santa Ana Ave, Fontana
(92337-7035)
PHONE..................909 355-5531
Bruce Degler, *President*
Kim Pugmire, *Vice Pres*
EMP: 50
SQ FT: 1,100
SALES: 40MM
SALES (corp-wide): 28MM **Privately Held**
SIC: 1629 Earthmoving contractor
PA: Pro Loaders, Inc.
　14032 Santa Ana Ave
　Fontana CA 92337
　909 355-5531

(P-2075)
WOOD BROS INC
14147 18th Ave, Lemoore (93245-9741)
P.O. Box 216 (93245-0216)
PHONE..................559 924-7715
William S Wood, *CEO*
Donald T Wood, *Corp Secy*
Jerry Ghiglia, *General Mgr*
Bryon Barros, *Foreman/Supr*
Don Wood, *Marketing Staff*
EMP: 100
SQ FT: 30,000
SALES (est): 32MM **Privately Held**
SIC: 1629 Dredging contractor

1711 Plumbing, Heating & Air Conditioning Contractors

(P-2076)
20/20 PLUMBING & HEATING INC
Also Called: Honeywell Authorized Dealer
7343 Orangewood Dr Ste B, Riverside
(92504-1053)
PHONE..................951 396-2020
Thomas Lew Baker, *CEO*
Michael Mahony, *CFO*
EMP: 200
SALES (est): 32MM **Privately Held**
SIC: 1711 Plumbing contractors

(P-2077)
A & A MECHANICAL CONTRACTORS
2943 Daylight Way, San Jose (95111-3194)
PHONE..................408 225-1321
George A Reppas, *President*
Arthur G Reppas, *Ch of Bd*
Michael Reppas, *CFO*
EMP: 85
SQ FT: 32,000
SALES (est): 4.5MM **Privately Held**
SIC: 1711 Warm air heating & air condi-
tioning contractor

(P-2078)
A & D FIRE PROTECTION INC
Also Called: A & D General Contracting
11465 Woodside Ave Fl 1, Santee
(92071-4725)
PHONE..................619 258-7697
Andrew R Otero, *President*
Deborah Allard, *Admin Asst*
Rose Pullaro, *Administration*
Jeff Jukes, *Info Tech Mgr*
Owen Curtis, *Project Mgr*
EMP: 80
SQ FT: 10,000
SALES (est): 15.3MM **Privately Held**
WEB: www.adcompaniesinc.com
SIC: 1711 1542 Fire sprinkler system in-
stallation; nonresidential construction

(P-2079)
A A A FURNACE AC CO
1712 Stone Ave Ste 1, San Jose
(95125-1387)
PHONE..................408 293-4717
Jim Rendo, *President*
EMP: 60
SALES (est): 2MM **Privately Held**
SIC: 1711 Warm air heating & air condi-
tioning contractor

(P-2080)
A C RENTALS LLC
8540 Production Ave Ste A, San Diego
(92121-2263)
PHONE..................858 271-8571
EMP: 50
SALES (est): 1.8MM **Privately Held**
SIC: 1711

(P-2081)
A O REED & CO
4777 Ruffner St, San Diego (92111-1578)
P.O. Box 85226 (92186-5226)
PHONE..................858 565-4131
Steve Andrade, *Ch of Bd*
David Clarkin, *President*
John Norling, *President*
Craig Koehler, *CFO*
Martin Naranjo, *Vice Pres*
EMP: 400
SQ FT: 55,000
SALES (est): 158.5MM **Privately Held**
WEB: www.aoreed.com
SIC: 1711 Plumbing contractors

(P-2082)
AAA DRAIN PATROL
Also Called: Preferred Plumbing and Drain
3437 Myrtle Ave Ste 440, North Highlands
(95660-5147)
PHONE..................916 348-3098
Kathleen Graves, *Owner*
EMP: 50
SALES (est): 2.2MM **Privately Held**
SIC: 1711 Plumbing contractors

(P-2083)
ACCO ENGINEERED SYSTEMS INC
1133 Aladdin Ave, San Leandro
(94577-4311)
PHONE..................510 346-4300
Ron Krassensky, *Manager*
Robert Hammond, *Exec VP*
Steve Tuttle, *Vice Pres*
Teri Donnelly, *Admin Asst*
Sean Cua, *Design Engr*
EMP: 200
SALES (corp-wide): 768.2MM **Privately Held**
WEB: www.accoair.com
SIC: 1711 7623 Process piping contractor;
solar energy contractor; ventilation & duct
work contractor; warm air heating & air
conditioning contractor; air conditioning
repair
PA: Acco Engineered Systems, Inc.
　6265 San Fernando Rd
　Glendale CA 91201
　818 244-6571

(P-2084)
ACCUTHERM REFRIGERATON INC
Also Called: Accutherm Air Heating & Coolg
11264 Monarch St Ste A, Garden Grove
(92841-1449)
PHONE..................714 766-7800
Jeff Recker, *President*
EMP: 53
SQ FT: 6,800
SALES: 6.9MM **Privately Held**
WEB: www.accuthermrefrigeration.com
SIC: 1711 Refrigeration contractor

(P-2085)
ADEE PLUMBING AND HEATING INC (PA)
5457 Crenshaw Blvd, Los Angeles
(90043-2496)
PHONE..................323 296-8787
Jack Stephan, *President*
Jack Stephan Jr, *Vice Pres*
Russell Stephan, *Admin Sec*

EMP: 64
SQ FT: 18,000
SALES (est): 10.2MM **Privately Held**
SIC: **1711** Plumbing contractors; warm air heating & air conditioning contractor

(P-2086)
ADVANTAGE PLUMBING GROUP INC
3331 Orangewood Ave, Los Alamitos (90720-3813)
P.O. Box 733 (90720-0733)
PHONE.................714 898-6020
EMP: 67
SALES (est): 4.6MM **Privately Held**
SIC: **1711** 5074

(P-2087)
AEGIS ENTERPRISES INC
Also Called: Aegis Fire Systems
500 Boulder Ct Ste A, Pleasanton (94566-8311)
PHONE.................925 417-5550
Thomas J McKinnon, *President*
Timothy Higgins, *Vice Pres*
Sophia McKinnon, *Admin Sec*
Kelly Sleek, *Accounting Mgr*
Kristen Quintana, *Payroll Mgr*
EMP: 100
SALES (est): 17.6MM **Privately Held**
SIC: **1711** Fire sprinkler system installation

(P-2088)
AG AIR CONDITIONING & HTG INC
Also Called: AG Heating and AC
14620 Keswick St, Van Nuys (91405-1203)
PHONE.................818 988-5388
Yuval Giron, *CEO*
Yitchak Giron, *President*
EMP: 50
SALES: 3.6MM **Privately Held**
SIC: **1711** Warm air heating & air conditioning contractor

(P-2089)
AIR CONTROL SYSTEMS INC
1940 S Grove Ave, Ontario (91761-5615)
PHONE.................909 786-4230
Robert Leotaud, *President*
EMP: 50
SQ FT: 4,000
SALES: 15MM **Privately Held**
SIC: **1711** Warm air heating & air conditioning contractor; ventilation & duct work contractor

(P-2090)
AIR MECHANICAL INC
608 S Vicki Ln, Anaheim (92804-3207)
PHONE.................714 995-3947
Wallace Fox, *Principal*
EMP: 62
SALES (corp-wide): 21MM **Privately Held**
SIC: **1711** Warm air heating & air conditioning contractor
PA: Air Mechanical, Inc.
   16411 Aberdeen St Ne
   Anoka MN 55304
   763 434-7747

(P-2091)
AIR SYSTEMS SERVICE & CNSTR
10381 Old Placerville Rd # 100, Sacramento (95827-2558)
PHONE.................916 368-0336
Garry Westover, *CEO*
Kathleen Westover, *President*
Jim Meurer, *Vice Pres*
Eric Weymouth, *Manager*
EMP: 130
SQ FT: 10,000
SALES: 39.1MM **Privately Held**
WEB: www.airsystems1.com
SIC: **1711** 7623 Mechanical contractor; warm air heating & air conditioning contractor; ventilation & duct work contractor; plumbing contractors; refrigeration service & repair

(P-2092)
AIRCO MECHANICAL INC (PA)
Also Called: AMI Manufacturing
8210 Demetre Ave, Sacramento (95828-0919)
PHONE.................916 381-4523
Wyatt Jones, *CEO*
Joann Hillendrand, *CFO*
EMP: 122
SQ FT: 105,000
SALES: 40MM **Privately Held**
WEB: www.aircomech.com
SIC: **1711** 8711 Mechanical contractor; engineering services

(P-2093)
AIRCO MECHANICAL INC
401 13th St, San Francisco (94130-2003)
PHONE.................415 982-4726
EMP: 128
SALES (corp-wide): 40MM **Privately Held**
SIC: **1711** Plumbing, heating, air-conditioning contractors
PA: Airco Mechanical, Inc.
   8210 Demetre Ave
   Sacramento CA 95828
   916 381-4523

(P-2094)
AIRE-RITE AC & RFRGN INC
15122 Bolsa Chica St, Huntington Beach (92649-1025)
P.O. Box 3419 (92605-3419)
PHONE.................714 895-2338
Donald Langston, *Principal*
Carol Langston, *Corp Secy*
David Langston, *Vice Pres*
Bruce Coleman, *Manager*
Aaron Jonas, *Supervisor*
EMP: 97
SQ FT: 22,000
SALES: 16.6MM **Privately Held**
WEB: www.airerite.com
SIC: **1711** Refrigeration contractor

(P-2095)
ALDOC INC
304 N Townsend St Ste D, Santa Ana (92703-3539)
PHONE.................714 836-8477
P S Meckley, *President*
Philip Shurman Meckley, *President*
EMP: 60
SALES (est): 5.1MM **Privately Held**
SIC: **1711** Plumbing contractors

(P-2096)
ALISO MECHANICAL INCORPORATED
29736 A De Las Bandera, Rancho Santa Margari (92688)
PHONE.................949 544-1601
Christopher H Loftus, *CEO*
Jeffrey T Loftus, *President*
EMP: 150
SQ FT: 8,000
SALES (est): 9.7MM **Privately Held**
WEB: www.alisoair.com
SIC: **1711** Warm air heating & air conditioning contractor

(P-2097)
ALL AREA PLUMBING INC
5742 Venice Blvd, Los Angeles (90019-5016)
PHONE.................323 939-9990
Robert Felix, *President*
Beni Monaco, *CFO*
EMP: 235
SQ FT: 3,000
SALES: 1.1MM **Privately Held**
WEB: www.allareaco.com
SIC: **1711** Plumbing, heating, air-conditioning contractors

(P-2098)
ALL TMPERATURES CONTROLLED INC
Also Called: Honeywell Authorized Dealer
9720 Topanga Canyon Pl, Chatsworth (91311-4134)
PHONE.................818 882-1478
George Mego, *President*
Kathy Gomes, *Executive*

Nick Mego, *General Mgr*
Brent Brubaker, *Project Mgr*
Cheryl Piper, *Technology*
EMP: 72 EST: 1978
SQ FT: 13,481
SALES (est): 13.7MM **Privately Held**
SIC: **1711** Warm air heating & air conditioning contractor; heating & air conditioning contractors

(P-2099)
ALLAN AUTOMATIC SPRINKLER CORP
3233 Enterprise St, Brea (92821-6239)
PHONE.................714 993-9500
Jim Charrette, *Vice Pres*
EMP: 80
SQ FT: 40,000
SALES (est): 9.2MM
SALES (corp-wide): 7.6B **Publicly Held**
WEB: www.allansocal.com
SIC: **1711** 5084 Fire sprinkler system installation; industrial machinery & equipment
HQ: Shambaugh & Son, L.P.
   7614 Opportunity Dr
   Fort Wayne IN 46825
   260 487-7777

(P-2100)
ALLIED FIRE PROTECTION
555 High St, Oakland (94601-3989)
PHONE.................510 533-5516
Ted Vinther, *President*
Fritz Descovich, *Project Mgr*
Jim Crossley, *Sr Project Mgr*
EMP: 150
SQ FT: 29,000
SALES (est): 28.9MM **Privately Held**
WEB: www.alliedfire.com
SIC: **1711** Fire sprinkler system installation

(P-2101)
ALPHA MECHANICAL INC
4990 Greencraig Ln Ste A, San Diego (92123-1673)
PHONE.................858 278-3500
Boris Barshak, *Branch Mgr*
Cort Clifford, *Business Mgr*
EMP: 88 **Privately Held**
SIC: **1711** Fire sprinkler system installation
PA: Alpha Mechanical, Inc.
   4885 Greencraig Ln
   San Diego CA 92123

(P-2102)
ALPHA MECHANICAL INC (PA)
4885 Greencraig Ln, San Diego (92123-1664)
PHONE.................858 278-3500
Boris Barshak, *Principal*
Mark Futala, *Project Mgr*
John Genel, *Project Mgr*
Stacy Camacho, *Project Engr*
David Luhm, *Sr Project Mgr*
EMP: 97
SQ FT: 8,000
SALES (est): 42.6MM **Privately Held**
SIC: **1711** Fire sprinkler system installation

(P-2103)
AMERICAN AC DISTRS LLC
Also Called: Florida Conditioning
16900 Chestnut St, City of Industry (91748-1012)
PHONE.................407 850-0147
John Staples,
Kevin Lentz, *General Mgr*
John Scarsi,
Lori Thomas, *Mng Member*
▲ EMP: 92
SALES (est): 4.7MM **Privately Held**
SIC: **1711** Heating & air conditioning contractors

(P-2104)
AMERICAN CONTRACTORS INC
404 W Blueridge Ave, Orange (92865-4204)
PHONE.................714 282-5700
Gilbert L Wiggam, *CEO*
Christopher Wiggam, *Vice Pres*
EMP: 65
SQ FT: 11,000

SALES: 18.3MM **Privately Held**
SIC: **1711** 1623 Plumbing contractors; sewer line construction; water main construction

(P-2105)
AMERICAN INCORPORATED
Also Called: American Air
1345 N American St, Visalia (93291-9334)
PHONE.................559 651-1776
Corwyn Oldfield, *CEO*
Frank Saucedo, *CFO*
Lois Oldfield, *Vice Pres*
Nate Strable, *General Mgr*
Cassandra Frates, *Administration*
EMP: 425
SQ FT: 115,000
SALES: 75MM **Privately Held**
SIC: **1711** 1542 1541 1731 Warm air heating & air conditioning contractor; refrigeration contractor; plumbing contractors; commercial & office building contractors; industrial buildings & warehouses; electrical work

(P-2106)
AMERICAN LEAK DETECTION INC
304 N Townsend St Ste D, Santa Ana (92703-3539)
PHONE.................714 836-8477
Steve Lee, *Manager*
EMP: 50
SALES (corp-wide): 8.8MM **Privately Held**
SIC: **1711** Plumbing contractors
PA: American Leak Detection, Inc.
   888 E Research Dr Ste 100
   Palm Springs CA 92262
   203 433-2510

(P-2107)
AMERICAN RESIDENTIAL SVCS LLC
9895 Olson Dr Ste A, San Diego (92121-2841)
PHONE.................858 457-5547
Bonnie Bakken, *General Mgr*
Matt Harmon, *General Mgr*
EMP: 80
SALES (corp-wide): 2.4B **Privately Held**
WEB: www.ars.com
SIC: **1711** Plumbing contractors
PA: American Residential Services Llc
   965 Ridge Lake Blvd # 201
   Memphis TN 38120
   901 271-9700

(P-2108)
AMERICAN RESIDENTIAL SVCS LLC
15707 S Main St, Gardena (90248-2506)
PHONE.................310 808-0279
Daniel Dunduenabad, *Manager*
EMP: 50
SALES (corp-wide): 2.4B **Privately Held**
WEB: www.ars.com
SIC: **1711** Plumbing contractors
PA: American Residential Services Llc
   965 Ridge Lake Blvd # 201
   Memphis TN 38120
   901 271-9700

(P-2109)
AMERICAN RESIDENTIAL SVCS LLC
Also Called: ARS of San Diego-8112
6162 Nncy Rdge Dr Ste 100, San Diego (92121)
PHONE.................858 677-5445
Kevin Kellington, *General Mgr*
James McMahon, *CFO*
Myriam Roblebo, *Accounting Mgr*
EMP: 60
SALES (corp-wide): 2.4B **Privately Held**
WEB: www.ars.com
SIC: **1711** Heating & air conditioning contractors
PA: American Residential Services Llc
   965 Ridge Lake Blvd # 201
   Memphis TN 38120
   901 271-9700

(P-2110)
AMERICAN RESIDENTIAL SVCS LLC
P.O. Box 1592 (92022-1592)
PHONE............................858 292-4452
Ray Olsen, *Branch Mgr*
EMP: 59
SALES (corp-wide): 2.4B **Privately Held**
SIC: 1711 Plumbing contractors
PA: American Residential Services Llc
965 Ridge Lake Blvd # 201
Memphis TN 38120
901 271-9700

(P-2111)
AMERICAN RESIDENTIAL SVCS LLC
Also Called: Atlas Heating
1965 Kyle Park Ct, San Jose (95125-1029)
P.O. Box 610490 (95161-0490)
PHONE............................650 856-1612
EMP: 60
SALES (corp-wide): 2.4B **Privately Held**
SIC: 1711 Plumbing contractors
PA: American Residential Services Llc
965 Ridge Lake Blvd # 201
Memphis TN 38120
901 271-9700

(P-2112)
AMERICAN RESIDENTIAL SVCS LLC
Also Called: Rescue Rotter
1520 W Linden St, Riverside (92507-6808)
PHONE............................951 341-9371
Dave Slott, *COO*
EMP: 55
SALES (corp-wide): 2.4B **Privately Held**
WEB: www.ars.com
SIC: 1711 Plumbing contractors
PA: American Residential Services Llc
965 Ridge Lake Blvd # 201
Memphis TN 38120
901 271-9700

(P-2113)
AMERICAN RESIDENTIAL SVCS LLC
Also Called: Rescue Rooter Bay Area North
1618 Doolittle Dr, San Leandro (94577-2230)
PHONE............................510 729-6227
Larry Dehart, *General Mgr*
EMP: 59
SALES (corp-wide): 2.4B **Privately Held**
WEB: www.ars.com
SIC: 1711 Plumbing contractors
PA: American Residential Services Llc
965 Ridge Lake Blvd # 201
Memphis TN 38120
901 271-9700

(P-2114)
AMERICAN RESIDENTIAL SVCS LLC
Also Called: Rescue Rooter
29196 Simms Ct, Hayward (94544-6911)
P.O. Box 3098 (94540-3098)
PHONE............................510 657-7601
Chris Peterson, *Manager*
EMP: 70
SALES (corp-wide): 2.4B **Privately Held**
WEB: www.ars.com
SIC: 1711 Plumbing contractors
PA: American Residential Services Llc
965 Ridge Lake Blvd # 201
Memphis TN 38120
901 271-9700

(P-2115)
AMERICAN RESIDENTIAL SVCS LLC
Also Called: Rescue Rooter
740 N Hariton St, Orange (92868-1314)
PHONE............................714 634-1826
Dave Krol, *Manager*
EMP: 100
SALES (corp-wide): 2.4B **Privately Held**
WEB: www.ars.com
SIC: 1711 Plumbing contractors
PA: American Residential Services Llc
965 Ridge Lake Blvd # 201
Memphis TN 38120
901 271-9700

(P-2116)
AMERICAN RESIDENTIAL SVCS LLC
Also Called: Rescue Rooter
12507 San Fernando Rd, Sylmar (91342-5023)
PHONE............................818 833-6677
Darl Coopper, *General Mgr*
EMP: 60
SALES (corp-wide): 2.4B **Privately Held**
WEB: www.ars.com
SIC: 1711 Warm air heating & air conditioning contractor
PA: American Residential Services Llc
965 Ridge Lake Blvd # 201
Memphis TN 38120
901 271-9700

(P-2117)
AMGREEN SOLAR AND ELECTRICS
1367 Venice Blvd, Los Angeles (90006-5519)
PHONE............................213 388-5647
Minseon Ko, *CEO*
▲ **EMP:** 50
SALES (est): 2.5MM **Privately Held**
SIC: 1711 1731 Solar energy contractor; lighting contractor

(P-2118)
AMPAM PARKS MECHANICAL INC
17036 Avalon Blvd, Carson (90746-1206)
PHONE............................310 835-1532
Charles E Parks III, *CEO*
James C Wright, *CFO*
John D Parks, *Vice Pres*
Drew Defalle, *VP Bus Dvlpt*
Phil Borough, *Info Tech Mgr*
▲ **EMP:** 800
SQ FT: 16,000
SALES (est): 158.5MM **Privately Held**
WEB: www.parksmechanical.com
SIC: 1711 Plumbing contractors

(P-2119)
AMS AMERICAN MECH SVCS MD INC
2116 E Walnut Ave, Fullerton (92831-4845)
PHONE............................714 888-6820
Charles S Knight, *General Mgr*
Mitchell Haynam, *General Mgr*
Richard Salinger, *Manager*
EMP: 54
SALES (corp-wide): 2.4B **Privately Held**
SIC: 1711 Mechanical contractor
HQ: Ams American Mechanical Services Of Maryland, Inc.
13300 Mid Atlantic Blvd
Laurel MD 20708
301 206-5070

(P-2120)
ANDERSON ROWE & BUCKLEY INC
2833 3rd St, San Francisco (94107-3532)
PHONE............................415 282-1625
Robert E Buckley III, *President*
Rosy Zucchiatti, *Corp Secy*
Richard I Buckley Jr, *Vice Pres*
Hratch Krikorian, *Technology*
EMP: 170
SQ FT: 40,000
SALES (est): 55MM **Privately Held**
SIC: 1711 Mechanical contractor

(P-2121)
ANDERSON AIR CONDITIONING LP
2100 E Walnut Ave, Fullerton (92831-4845)
PHONE............................714 998-6850
Edward Dunn, *General Ptnr*
Mitchell J Haynam, *Partner*
EMP: 60
SALES (est): 11.5MM **Privately Held**
SIC: 1711 Warm air heating & air conditioning contractor; heating & air conditioning contractors
PA: Ams American Mechanical Services Of Maryland, L.L.C.
13300 Mid Atlantic Blvd
Laurel MD 20708

(P-2122)
ANDREWS GROUP INC (PA)
1801 Walters Ct, Fairfield (94533-2758)
P.O. Box 250 (94533-0450)
PHONE............................707 422-4844
Frank Andrews, *President*
Gary Andrews, *Vice Pres*
Jeff Andrews, *Vice Pres*
Dorothy Andrews, *Admin Sec*
Bill Fong, *VP Finance*
EMP: 70
SQ FT: 4,000
SALES (est): 4.1MM **Privately Held**
SIC: 1711 Mechanical contractor

(P-2123)
APEX MECHANICAL SYSTEMS INC
7440 Trade St Ste A, San Diego (92121-3412)
PHONE............................858 536-8700
Randall E Melhouse, *CEO*
Edward Draper, *Shareholder*
Blaine Stratton, *Shareholder*
David R Draper, *CFO*
Kathy Draper, *Admin Sec*
EMP: 79
SALES (est): 16.5MM **Privately Held**
SIC: 1711 Mechanical contractor

(P-2124)
APPRENTICE & JOURNEYMEN TRAINI
7850 Haskell Ave, Van Nuys (91406-1907)
PHONE............................818 464-4579
Leroy Riffel, *Director*
EMP: 99
SALES: 950K **Privately Held**
SIC: 1711 Plumbing contractors

(P-2125)
AQUALINE PIPING INC
Also Called: Plumbing
2108 Bering Dr Ste C, San Jose (95131-2029)
PHONE............................408 745-7100
Joshua B Moores, *CEO*
Chrystal L Steele, *Vice Pres*
EMP: 75
SALES (est): 11.9MM **Privately Held**
SIC: 1711 7389 Plumbing, heating, air-conditioning contractors;

(P-2126)
ARISE CONSTRUCTION INC
Also Called: Arise Solar
5390 E Pine Ave, Fresno (93727-2113)
PHONE............................559 449-8989
Paul Rutkowski, *CEO*
Glenn Siemens, *CEO*
Steve Saeger, *Sales Mgr*
EMP: 52
SALES (est): 6.7MM **Privately Held**
SIC: 1711 Solar energy contractor

(P-2127)
ARRAYCON LLC (PA)
1143 Blumenfeld Dr # 200, Sacramento (95815-3921)
PHONE............................916 925-0201
Rick Lavezzo, *Mng Member*
Donald Miller, *CFO*
Jeff Calabro, *Exec VP*
Mathew Ricci, *Exec VP*
Dan Hubiak, *Principal*
EMP: 50 **EST:** 2010
SQ FT: 50,000
SALES: 31.1MM **Privately Held**
SIC: 1711 8748 Solar energy contractor; business consulting

(P-2128)
ARS AMERICAN RESIDENTIAL (HQ)
Also Called: Southcoast Heating and Air
2373 La Mirada Dr, Vista (92081-7863)
PHONE............................760 941-7000
Ed Dunn, *President*
EMP: 100
SQ FT: 18,000
SALES (est): 24.6MM **Privately Held**
SIC: 1711 Warm air heating & air conditioning contractor

(P-2129)
ARTIC MECHANICAL INC (PA)
10440 Trademark St, Rancho Cucamonga (91730-5826)
PHONE............................909 980-2539
Daniel Hallisey, *President*
John Hadley, *CFO*
Ray Freeman, *Technician*
Devin Smith, *Technician*
Steve Pasqua, *Project Mgr*
EMP: 80
SQ FT: 15,500
SALES (est): 27.3MM **Privately Held**
WEB: www.arcticmechanical.com
SIC: 1711 Warm air heating & air conditioning contractor; refrigeration contractor

(P-2130)
ASI HASTINGS INC
Also Called: Asi Heating, Air and Solar
4870 Vewridge Ave Ste 200, San Diego (92123)
PHONE............................619 590-9300
Philip Justo, *President*
Kenneth Justo, *Vice Pres*
Steven Pea, *Office Mgr*
EMP: 120
SQ FT: 2,000
SALES: 23MM **Privately Held**
WEB: www.asihastings.com
SIC: 1711 Heating systems repair & maintenance; solar energy contractor

(P-2131)
ASSOCIATE MECHANICAL CONTRS
622 S Vinewood St, Escondido (92029-1925)
PHONE............................760 294-3517
Richard Reinholz, *President*
Laura Reinholz, *Admin Sec*
EMP: 70
SALES: 30MM **Privately Held**
SIC: 1711 Plumbing, heating, air-conditioning contractors

(P-2132)
AYOOB & PEERY PLUMBING CO INC
975 Indiana St, San Francisco (94107-3007)
PHONE............................415 550-0975
Peter Vincent McHugh, *CEO*
Lydia Lui, *Office Mgr*
Mylene Pabilona, *Admin Asst*
Elliott McHugh, *Manager*
EMP: 80
SQ FT: 20,000
SALES (est): 17.1MM **Privately Held**
WEB: www.ayoobpeery.com
SIC: 1711 Mechanical contractor

(P-2133)
B Z PLUMBING COMPANY INC
1901 Aviation Blvd, Lincoln (95648-9557)
PHONE............................916 645-1600
William J Zmrzel, *President*
Diane Zmrzel, *Corp Secy*
Sara Ladeas, *General Mgr*
Tom Brownell, *Sales Mgr*
Jennifer Todd, *Director*
EMP: 120
SQ FT: 12,000
SALES (est): 7.5MM **Privately Held**
WEB: www.bzplumbing.com
SIC: 1711 Plumbing contractors

(P-2134)
BAKERSFIELD KITCHEN & BATH
3529 Pegasus Dr, Bakersfield (93308-6856)
PHONE............................661 836-2284
Don Chminowski, *President*
EMP: 80
SALES (est): 3MM **Privately Held**
SIC: 1711 Plumbing contractors

(P-2135)
BARR ENGINEERING INC
12612 Clark St, Santa Fe Springs (90670-3950)
PHONE............................562 944-1722
Peter Buongiorno, *President*
Pamela Price-Recchia, *Corp Secy*
Mike Buongiorno, *Vice Pres*

Frank Pengal, *Vice Pres*
Dave Wilde, *Info Tech Dir*
EMP: 82 **EST:** 1958
SQ FT: 12,200
SALES (est): 14.7MM **Privately Held**
WEB: www.barrengineering.com
SIC: 1711 Warm air heating & air conditioning contractor

(P-2136)
BAY CITY MECHANICAL INC
4124 Lakeside Dr, Richmond (94806-1941)
PHONE 510 233-7000
Helge Theiss-Nyland, *President*
Chris Cochrane, *Treasurer*
Dominic Arnold, *Accountant*
Dan Denofrio, *Foreman/Supr*
David Lorenz, *Foreman/Supr*
EMP: 150
SQ FT: 6,000
SALES (est): 36.9MM **Privately Held**
WEB: www.baycitymech.com
SIC: 1711 Heating & air conditioning contractors

(P-2137)
BAYVIEW ENGRG & CNSTR CO INC
5040 Rbert J Mathews Pkwy, El Dorado Hills (95762-5702)
PHONE 916 939-8986
Robert Ellery, *CEO*
Pete Ellery, *Vice Pres*
Bart Wood, *Vice Pres*
Kyle Hergert, *Business Mgr*
EMP: 80
SQ FT: 6,000
SALES: 9MM **Privately Held**
SIC: 1711 8711 Boiler setting contractor; engineering services

(P-2138)
BDS PLUMBING INC
2125 Youngs Ct, Walnut Creek (94596-6319)
PHONE 925 939-1004
Brett M Stom, *President*
Dawn L Stom, *Corp Secy*
EMP: 100
SQ FT: 400
SALES (est): 11.4MM **Privately Held**
SIC: 1711 Plumbing contractors

(P-2139)
BELL PRODUCTS INC
722 Soscol Ave, NAPA (94559-3014)
P.O. Box 396 (94559-0396)
PHONE 707 255-1811
Paul D Irwin, *President*
Stan Foltz, *Corp Secy*
Casey Clark, *Project Mgr*
Nichole Egger, *Project Mgr*
Josh Gayski, *Project Mgr*
EMP: 74
SQ FT: 24,400
SALES (est): 21.4MM **Privately Held**
WEB: www.bellproducts.com
SIC: 1711 Ventilation & duct work contractor; warm air heating & air conditioning contractor; mechanical contractor

(P-2140)
BENICIA PLUMBING INC
265 W Channel Rd, Benicia (94510-1146)
P.O. Box 1095 (94510-4095)
PHONE 707 745-2930
William J Cawley Jr, *CEO*
Doug Kuznik, *President*
Karen Ramey, *Corp Secy*
William J Cawley III, *Vice Pres*
EMP: 55
SQ FT: 10,000
SALES (est): 13MM **Privately Held**
WEB: www.beniciaplumbing.com
SIC: 1711 Plumbing contractors

(P-2141)
BENNETT & BENNETT INC (PA)
Also Called: Bennett & Bennett Irrigation
955 S Commerce Way, Lemoore (93245-9001)
P.O. Box 190, Selma (93662-0190)
PHONE 559 582-9336
Tyler O Bennett, *CEO*
Gary R Bennett, *President*
Caron Ketchie, *CFO*

Scott Britten, *Vice Pres*
Adam Sabourin, *Manager*
EMP: 50 **EST:** 1929
SQ FT: 41,000
SALES (est): 18.9MM **Privately Held**
WEB: www.bennettbennett.com
SIC: 1711 3272 Irrigation sprinkler system installation; pipe, concrete or lined with concrete

(P-2142)
BERNEL INC
Also Called: Vfs Fire Protection Services
501 W Southern Ave, Orange (92865-3217)
PHONE 714 778-6070
Randy Roland Nelson, *CEO*
Kevin Berthoud, *Vice Pres*
Mario Lopez, *Vice Pres*
EMP: 105
SQ FT: 7,800
SALES (est): 19.5MM **Privately Held**
SIC: 1711 7382 Fire sprinkler system installation; security systems services; fire alarm maintenance & monitoring

(P-2143)
BFP FIRE PROTECTION INC
17 Janis Way, Scotts Valley (95066-3537)
PHONE 831 461-1100
Chris Amos, *President*
EMP: 60
SQ FT: 6,400
SALES (est): 12.8MM **Privately Held**
SIC: 1711 8711 Fire sprinkler system installation; engineering services

(P-2144)
BILL HOWE PLUMBING INC
Also Called: Am-PM Sewer & Drain Cleaning
9085 Aero Dr Ste B, San Diego (92123-2378)
PHONE 800 245-5469
William Howe, *President*
Tina Howe, *Vice Pres*
Sharon Wheeler, *Finance*
Bill Howe, *Opers Mgr*
Miguel Sanchez, *Manager*
EMP: 85
SQ FT: 21,000
SALES (est): 27.2MM **Privately Held**
WEB: www.billhowe.com
SIC: 1711 Plumbing contractors; septic system construction

(P-2145)
BLOCKA CONSTRUCTION INC
4455 Enterprise St, Fremont (94538-6306)
PHONE 510 657-3686
Bob Blocka, *President*
Jean Blocka, *CFO*
Mike Doerger, *Admin Dir*
Chad Blocka, *Project Mgr*
Aaron Croteau, *Project Mgr*
EMP: 70
SQ FT: 7,300
SALES (est): 39.3MM **Privately Held**
WEB: www.blockainc.com
SIC: 1711 1731 Mechanical contractor; general electrical contractor

(P-2146)
BLUE MOUNTAIN CNSTR SVCS INC
Also Called: Blue Mountain Air
707 Aldridge Rd Ste B, Vacaville (95688-9561)
PHONE 800 889-2085
Gregory S Owen, *President*
Jeff Farnsworth, *Project Mgr*
Miguel Martinez, *Project Mgr*
▲ **EMP:** 200
SQ FT: 37,000
SALES (est): 90.3MM **Privately Held**
WEB: www.bluemountainair.net
SIC: 1711 Heating & air conditioning contractors

(P-2147)
BONANZA PLUMBING INC (PA)
2259 Hamner Ave, Norco (92860-2608)
PHONE 951 360-8262
James Dean Potts, *President*
EMP: 80
SALES (est): 10.1MM **Privately Held**
SIC: 1711 Plumbing contractors

(P-2148)
BRIGHTVIEW LANDSCAPE DEV INC
13691 Vaughn St, San Fernando (91340-3072)
PHONE 818 838-4700
Greg Motschenbacher, *Branch Mgr*
EMP: 60
SALES (corp-wide): 2.8B **Publicly Held**
SIC: 1711 0781 Irrigation sprinkler system installation; landscape services
HQ: Brightview Landscape Development, Inc.
24151 Ventura Blvd
Calabasas CA 91302
818 223-8500

(P-2149)
BRIGHTVIEW LANDSCAPE DEV INC
11555 Cley Rver Cir Ste A, Fountain Valley (92708)
PHONE 714 546-7975
Gins Garmann, *Manager*
Greg Barker, *VP Opers*
Jeff Mutch, *Sales Staff*
Jeff Waltz, *Manager*
EMP: 450
SALES (corp-wide): 2.8B **Publicly Held**
SIC: 1711 0781 Irrigation sprinkler system installation; heating & air conditioning contractors; landscape services
HQ: Brightview Landscape Development, Inc.
24151 Ventura Blvd
Calabasas CA 91302
818 223-8500

(P-2150)
BROADSTREET SOLAR INC
Also Called: Broadstreet Power
16112 Hart St, Van Nuys (91406-3903)
PHONE 818 206-1464
Ahmad M Yakub, *CEO*
EMP: 50
SQ FT: 2,400
SALES: 6.9MM **Privately Held**
SIC: 1711 Solar energy contractor

(P-2151)
BROADWAY MECH - CONTRS INC
873 81st Ave, Oakland (94621-2509)
PHONE 510 746-4000
Fred Nurisso, *President*
Jill Demar, *Executive Asst*
Frank Yankey, *Info Tech Dir*
Ouma Moss, *Project Mgr*
Cliff Brown, *Project Engr*
EMP: 150
SALES (est): 41.6MM **Privately Held**
WEB: www.broadwaymechanical.com
SIC: 1711 Mechanical contractor

(P-2152)
C & L REFRIGERATION CORP
Also Called: HONEYWELL AUTHORIZED DEALER
4111 N Palm St, Fullerton (92835-1025)
P.O. Box 2319, Brea (92822-2319)
PHONE 800 901-4822
Ronald J Cassell Jr, *CEO*
Larry Jaslove, *Vice Pres*
Joe Knotts, *Info Tech Mgr*
Angel Sanchez, *Info Tech Mgr*
Andrew Morres, *Project Engr*
EMP: 150 **EST:** 1978
SQ FT: 18,000
SALES (est): 32.2MM **Privately Held**
SIC: 1711 Refrigeration contractor; warm air heating & air conditioning contractor

(P-2153)
CALIFORNIA COMFORT SYSTEMS USA
7740 Kenamar Ct, San Diego (92121-2425)
PHONE 858 564-1100
Kenneth Hoving, *CEO*
Roger Well, *President*
William George, *Vice Pres*
Trent McKenna, *Vice Pres*
Bo Macaraeg, *General Mgr*
EMP: 399

SALES (est): 5.1MM
SALES (corp-wide): 1.7B **Publicly Held**
SIC: 1711 Warm air heating & air conditioning contractor; heating & air conditioning contractors
PA: Comfort Systems Usa, Inc.
675 Bering Dr Ste 400
Houston TX 77057
713 830-9600

(P-2154)
CALIFORNIA COML SOLAR INC
Also Called: Calcom Solar
635 S Atwood St, Visalia (93277-8302)
PHONE 559 667-9200
Dylan Dupre, *CEO*
Rob Burkholder, *CFO*
Jordan Collins, *Vice Pres*
John Doyle, *Managing Dir*
Alison Baird, *Admin Sec*
EMP: 56
SQ FT: 7,000
SALES (est): 15.6MM **Privately Held**
SIC: 1711 Solar energy contractor

(P-2155)
CALIFORNIA UNITED MECH INC (PA)
2185 Oakland Rd, San Jose (95131-1574)
PHONE 408 232-9000
Tom Sosine, *CEO*
Dirk Durham, *Vice Chairman*
Jon Gundersen, *President*
Blaine Flickner, *Vice Pres*
Neal Fox, *Vice Pres*
EMP: 350
SQ FT: 40,000
SALES (est): 158.5MM **Privately Held**
WEB: www.umi1.com
SIC: 1711 Mechanical contractor

(P-2156)
CAN-AM PLUMBING INC
151 Wyoming St, Pleasanton (94566-6277)
PHONE 925 846-1833
Ronald Capilla, *President*
Karl Kyriss, *CFO*
Martin Ogara, *CFO*
Michael Capilla, *Vice Pres*
Rebecca Jose, *Supervisor*
EMP: 250
SQ FT: 16,000
SALES (est): 17.6MM **Privately Held**
WEB: www.canamplumbing.com
SIC: 1711 Plumbing contractors

(P-2157)
CASPIAN COMMERCIAL PLBG INC
711 Ivy St, Glendale (91204-1003)
PHONE 818 649-2500
Anahit Alexandrian, *President*
EMP: 65
SALES (est): 7.2MM **Privately Held**
SIC: 1711 Plumbing contractors

(P-2158)
CERTIFIED AIR CONDITIONING INC
12520 High Bluff Dr # 312, San Diego (92130-2041)
PHONE 858 292-5740
Brian Lynch, *President*
Terry Erickson, *Vice Pres*
▲ **EMP:** 150
SALES: 13.6MM **Privately Held**
WEB: www.certifiedair.net
SIC: 1711 Warm air heating & air conditioning contractor

(P-2159)
CFP FIRE PROTECTION INC
17461 Derian Ave Ste 114, Irvine (92614-5820)
PHONE 949 338-4280
Matt Krofcheck, *President*
Josh Hobgood, *Corp Secy*
EMP: 60
SQ FT: 2,000
SALES (est): 5.6MM **Privately Held**
SIC: 1711 Fire sprinkler system installation
PA: Mx Holdings Us, Inc.
153 Technology Dr Ste 200
Irvine CA 92618

P R O D U C T S   &   S V C S

(P-2160)
CIRCULATING AIR INC (PA)
Also Called: Honeywell Authorized Dealer
7337 Varna Ave, North Hollywood
(91605-4009)
PHONE....................818 764-0530
Joseph Gallagher, *CEO*
Susan Gallagher, *President*
Marcy Ahlstrom, *CFO*
Don Gallagher, *Vice Pres*
Tom Crossman, *Info Tech Dir*
EMP: 100
SQ FT: 13,000
SALES (est): 39MM **Privately Held**
WEB: www.circulatingair.com
SIC: 1711 Mechanical contractor; warm air heating & air conditioning contractor

(P-2161)
CITYWIDE PLUMBING HEATING
9825 Carroll Centre Rd, San Diego
(92126-6508)
PHONE....................619 231-2022
John Taylor, *Principal*
EMP: 50
SALES (est): 5.6MM **Privately Held**
SIC: 1711 Plumbing, heating, air-conditioning contractors

(P-2162)
CLAY DUNN ENTERPRISES INC
Also Called: Air-TEC
1606 E Carson St, Carson (90745-2504)
P.O. Box 5444 (90749-5444)
PHONE....................310 549-1698
Clayton N Dunn, *President*
Drew Mallad, *Info Tech Mgr*
Kurt Kredel, *Project Mgr*
Rafael Rodriguez, *Project Mgr*
Ken Yan, *Controller*
EMP: 120
SALES (est): 32.4MM **Privately Held**
WEB: www.airtecperforms.com
SIC: 1711 Warm air heating & air conditioning contractor

(P-2163)
CMA FIRE PROTECTION (PA)
Also Called: Rlh Fire Protection
4300 Stine Rd Ste 800, Bakersfield
(93313-2354)
P.O. Box 42470 (93384-2470)
PHONE....................661 322-9344
Terrence J Olson, *CEO*
Gary Stites, *Partner*
Michael Hardcastle, *Ch of Bd*
Jason Norton, *President*
Margaret McCarty, *Treasurer*
EMP: 75
SQ FT: 8,000
SALES (est): 29.4MM **Privately Held**
WEB: www.rlhfp.com
SIC: 1711 1542 Fire sprinkler system installation; nonresidential construction

(P-2164)
COLUMBIA SPECIALTY COMPANY INC (PA)
Also Called: PLUMBING WORLD
5875 Obispo Ave, Long Beach
(90805-3715)
PHONE....................562 634-6425
Michael Taylor, *CEO*
Tom Murphy, *Branch Mgr*
Jeff Warren, *Branch Mgr*
Erin Taylor, *Project Mgr*
Stacey SA, *Controller*
▲ EMP: 78
SQ FT: 44,000
SALES (est): 26.5MM **Privately Held**
WEB: www.plumbingworld.com
SIC: 1711 Process piping contractor

(P-2165)
COMFORT AIR INC
1607 French Camp Tpke, Stockton
(95206-1960)
P.O. Box 1969 (95201-1969)
PHONE....................209 466-4601
Steven J Evans, *President*
Gregory A Gaut, *Vice Pres*
Paulette Gaut, *Admin Sec*
EMP: 75 EST: 1946
SQ FT: 7,000

SALES: 11MM **Privately Held**
WEB: www.comfortairinc.com
SIC: 1711 Warm air heating & air conditioning contractor

(P-2166)
COMFORT SYSTEMS USA INC
4189 Santa Ana St Ste D, Ontario
(91761-1557)
PHONE....................909 390-6677
Joe Nichter, *Branch Mgr*
EMP: 83
SALES (corp-wide): 1.7B **Publicly Held**
SIC: 1711 Plumbing, heating, air-conditioning contractors
PA: Comfort Systems Usa, Inc.
675 Bering Dr Ste 400
Houston TX 77057
713 830-9600

(P-2167)
COMMERCIAL RFRGRN SPCALISTS LLC (HQ)
Also Called: CRS
3480 Arden Rd, Hayward (94545-3906)
PHONE....................510 784-8990
Todd Ernest, *CEO*
EMP: 102
SQ FT: 7,500
SALES (est): 24.7MM
SALES (corp-wide): 53.4MM **Privately Held**
WEB: www.crsref.com
SIC: 1711 5078 Heating & air conditioning contractors; refrigerators, commercial (reach-in & walk-in)
PA: Climate Pros Inc.
55 N Brandon Dr
Glendale Heights IL 60139
630 893-8511

(P-2168)
CONFORTI PLUMBING INC
6080 Pleasant Valley Rd C, El Dorado
(95623-4257)
P.O. Box 1090 (95623-1090)
PHONE....................530 622-0202
Marvin Collins, *President*
Jan Zygalinski, *CFO*
EMP: 1020
SQ FT: 1,000
SALES (est): 65.8MM **Privately Held**
WEB: www.confortiplumbing.com
SIC: 1711 Plumbing contractors

(P-2169)
CONTROL AC SVC CORP
5200 E La Palma Ave, Anaheim
(92807-2019)
PHONE....................714 777-8600
Kendrick Ellis, *President*
Greg Rummler, *CFO*
Stanley Ellis, *Vice Pres*
EMP: 51 EST: 1990
SALES (est): 4MM **Privately Held**
SIC: 1711 Plumbing, heating, air-conditioning contractors

(P-2170)
CONTROL AIR CONDITIONING CORP (PA)
Also Called: Honeywell Authorized Dealer
5200 E La Palma Ave, Anaheim
(92807-2019)
PHONE....................714 777-8600
Kendrick Ellis, *President*
Jay McEntire, *President*
Eileen Ellis, *Corp Secy*
Stan Ellis, *Vice Pres*
Jorge Norona, *Division Mgr*
EMP: 150
SALES (est): 110.3MM **Privately Held**
WEB: www.controlaircorp.com
SIC: 1711 3444 Warm air heating & air conditioning contractor; ducts, sheet metal

(P-2171)
COREY DELTA CONSTRUCTORS INC
261 Arthur Rd, Fairfield (94533)
PHONE....................925 370-9808
John T Weatherford, *CEO*
EMP: 88

SALES (est): 6.2MM
SALES (corp-wide): 53.1MM **Privately Held**
SIC: 1711 Mechanical contractor
PA: U.C.I. Construction, Inc.
261 Arthur Rd
Martinez CA 94553
800 245-6750

(P-2172)
COSCO FIRE PROTECTION INC
Also Called: 76
4990 Greencraig Ln, San Diego
(92123-1673)
PHONE....................858 444-2000
Alexander Hernandez, *Manager*
EMP: 75 **Privately Held**
WEB: www.coscofireprotection.com
SIC: 1711 Fire sprinkler system installation
HQ: Cosco Fire Protection, Inc.
29222 Rancho Viejo Rd # 205
San Juan Capistrano CA 92675
714 974-8770

(P-2173)
COSCO FIRE PROTECTION INC
1075 W Lambert Rd Ste D, Brea
(92821-2944)
PHONE....................714 989-1800
Barry Fielding, *Branch Mgr*
EMP: 193 **Privately Held**
SIC: 1711 Fire sprinkler system installation
HQ: Cosco Fire Protection, Inc.
29222 Rancho Viejo Rd # 205
San Juan Capistrano CA 92675
714 974-8770

(P-2174)
COUNTYWIDE MECH SYSTEMS INC
1400 N Johnson Ave # 114, El Cajon
(92020-1651)
PHONE....................619 449-9900
Paul Duke, *President*
David Cimpl, *CFO*
Lani Taylor, *Admin Asst*
Amy Scott, *Project Mgr*
Michael Garcia, *QC Mgr*
EMP: 230
SQ FT: 5,000
SALES (est): 51.2MM
SALES (corp-wide): 459.6MM **Privately Held**
SIC: 1711 Mechanical contractor
PA: Mmc Corp
10955 Lowell Ave Ste 350
Overland Park KS 66210
913 469-0101

(P-2175)
COUTS HEATING & COOLING INC
1693 Rimpau Ave, Corona (92881-3202)
PHONE....................951 278-5560
Jeff Lemke, *Branch Mgr*
EMP: 62
SALES (corp-wide): 29.3MM **Privately Held**
SIC: 1711 Heating & air conditioning contractors
PA: Couts Heating & Cooling, Inc.
1693 Rimpau Ave
Corona CA 92881
951 278-5560

(P-2176)
CRITCHFELD MECH INC STHERN CAL
1821 Mcgaw Ave, Irvine (92614-5733)
PHONE....................949 390-2900
Mike Pearlman, *CEO*
EMP: 100
SALES (est): 51.2MM **Privately Held**
SIC: 1711 Warm air heating & air conditioning contractor

(P-2177)
CRITCHFIELD MECHANICAL INC
4085 Campbell Ave, Menlo Park
(94025-1006)
PHONE....................650 321-7801
Joe Critchfield, *Chairman*
Jason Tran, *Project Engr*
EMP: 389

SALES (corp-wide): 162.2MM **Privately Held**
SIC: 1711 Mechanical contractor
PA: Critchfield Mechanical, Inc.
1901 Junction Ave
San Jose CA 95131
408 437-7000

(P-2178)
D & J PLUMBING INC
4341 Winters St, Sacramento
(95838-3031)
PHONE....................916 922-4888
Steve Waldron, *President*
Geri Richards, *Shareholder*
John Richards, *Shareholder*
Randy Golden, *Vice Pres*
EMP: 100
SQ FT: 5,000
SALES (est): 12.3MM **Privately Held**
SIC: 1711 Plumbing contractors

(P-2179)
D W NICHOLSON CORPORATION (PA)
24747 Clawiter Rd, Hayward (94545-2225)
P.O. Box 4197 (94540-4197)
PHONE....................510 887-0900
John L Nicholson, *Principal*
Cliff Schuch, *CFO*
Anna Curtis, *Executive Asst*
Joseph Santens, *Project Mgr*
Mari Duncan, *Accountant*
EMP: 250 EST: 1935
SQ FT: 12,000
SALES (est): 26.7MM **Privately Held**
WEB: www.dwnicholson.com
SIC: 1711 1731 8711 1796 Mechanical contractor; general electrical contractor; engineering services; millwright; residential construction; industrial buildings & warehouses

(P-2180)
D/K MECHANICAL CONTRACTORS INC
3870 E Eagle Dr, Anaheim (92807-1706)
PHONE....................714 970-0180
Gary Brubaker, *President*
Don Giarratano, *Vice Pres*
EMP: 200
SALES (est): 13.6MM **Privately Held**
WEB: www.dkmechanical.com
SIC: 1711 Plumbing contractors; warm air heating & air conditioning contractor

(P-2181)
DAART ENGINEERING COMPANY INC
1598 N H St, San Bernardino
(92405-4318)
PHONE....................909 888-8696
Timothy C Cantwell, *President*
James D Dunn, *Corp Secy*
Robert Pfeifer, *Admin Sec*
EMP: 70
SQ FT: 8,000
SALES: 9MM **Privately Held**
WEB: www.daarteng.com
SIC: 1711 Fire sprinkler system installation

(P-2182)
DAVE WILLIAMS PLBG & ELEC INC
75140 Saint Charles Pl C, Palm Desert
(92211-9044)
PHONE....................760 296-1397
Daniel Williams, *President*
Dave Williams, *Vice Pres*
EMP: 110 EST: 2008
SALES: 10MM **Privately Held**
SIC: 1711 Plumbing contractors; fire sprinkler system installation

(P-2183)
DC SOLAR SOLUTIONS INC
4901 Park Rd, Benicia (94510-1190)
PHONE....................925 203-1088
Jeffrey Paul Carpoff, *President*
Paulette Carpoff, *Vice Pres*
Greg Nelson, *Accounting Mgr*
Ryan Guidry, *Opers Staff*
EMP: 50
SALES (est): 15.7MM **Privately Held**
SIC: 1711 Solar energy contractor

▲ = Import ▼=Export
◆ =Import/Export

PA: Enerblu, Inc.
250 W Main St Ste 2100
Lexington KY 40507
562 270-0900

(P-2184)
DE HART PLUMBING HTG & A INC
311 Bitritto Way, Modesto (95356-9292)
PHONE......................................209 523-4578
Rod Dehart, *President*
Bryan Hardin, *Project Mgr*
Bryan Hansen, *Materials Mgr*
Steven Litt, *Consultant*
EMP: 50
SALES: 9.7MM **Privately Held**
WEB: www.dehartinc.com
SIC: 1711 Plumbing contractors; warm air heating & air conditioning contractor

(P-2185)
DESERT MECHANICAL INC
Also Called: Dmi
15870 Olden St, Sylmar (91342-1241)
PHONE......................................702 873-7333
Casey M Condron, *President*
Joseph Guglielmo, *Senior VP*
Andre Burnthon, *Vice Pres*
Alex L Hodson, *Vice Pres*
Dan Naylor, *Vice Pres*
EMP: 1100
SQ FT: 25,000
SALES: 43.4MM
SALES (corp-wide): 4.7B **Publicly Held**
WEB: www.lvdph.com
SIC: 1711 Plumbing contractors
PA: Tutor Perini Corporation
15901 Olden St
Sylmar CA 91342
818 362-8391

(P-2186)
DON BRANDEL PLUMBING INC
15100 Texaco Ave, Paramount
(90723-3916)
PHONE......................................562 408-0400
Greg Brandel, *President*
Dennis Castaldo, *Exec VP*
Jim Brandel, *Vice Pres*
Charron Castaldo, *Admin Sec*
Pam Evans, *Manager*
EMP: 50
SQ FT: 20,000
SALES (est): 10MM **Privately Held**
WEB: www.brandelplumbing.com
SIC: 1711 Plumbing contractors

(P-2187)
DONALD P DICK AC INC (PA)
Also Called: Mr Cool
1444 N Whitney Ave, Fresno (93703-4513)
PHONE......................................559 255-1644
James B Dick, *President*
David B Dick, *Vice Pres*
David Dick, *Vice Pres*
Jennifer Perea, *Office Admin*
Jeffrey Dick, *Admin Sec*
EMP: 80 EST: 1970
SQ FT: 30,000
SALES (est): 13.6MM **Privately Held**
WEB: www.mrcool4ac.com
SIC: 1711 Warm air heating & air conditioning contractor

(P-2188)
DRAIN DOCTOR
480 Aldo Ave, Santa Clara (95054-2304)
PHONE......................................408 970-3800
John Lin, *President*
Chris Choi, *Human Res Mgr*
▲ EMP: 50
SALES (est): 4.2MM **Privately Held**
SIC: 1711 8748 Plumbing contractors; business consulting

(P-2189)
DRAIN PATROL
7764 Arjons Dr, San Diego (92126-4391)
P.O. Box 503053 (92150-3053)
PHONE......................................858 560-1137
Scot Buck, *Manager*
EMP: 64
SALES (est): 4.9MM **Privately Held**
SIC: 1711 1623 Plumbing contractors; sewer line construction

(P-2190)
DYNAMIC PLUMBING COMMERCIAL
7343 Orangewood Dr Ste B, Riverside
(92504-1053)
PHONE......................................951 343-1200
Thomas L Baker, *President*
EMP: 84
SALES (est): 8.3MM **Privately Held**
SIC: 1711 Plumbing, heating, air-conditioning contractors

(P-2191)
DYNAMIC PLUMBING SYSTEMS INC
5920 Winterhaven Ave, Riverside
(92504-1048)
PHONE......................................951 343-1200
Thomas L Baker, *CEO*
EMP: 306 EST: 1999
SQ FT: 33,000
SALES (est): 35MM **Privately Held**
SIC: 1711 Plumbing, heating, air-conditioning contractors

(P-2192)
E L PAYNE HEATING COMPANY
Also Called: Payne, E L Company
226 S Lucerne Blvd, Los Angeles
(90004-3727)
PHONE......................................310 275-5331
Gordon Payne Jr, *President*
Gordon Payne Sr, *Ch of Bd*
EMP: 50
SQ FT: 1,200
SALES (est): 4.9MM **Privately Held**
SIC: 1711 Warm air heating & air conditioning contractor; heating & air conditioning contractors

(P-2193)
EAGLE SYSTEMS INTL INC
Also Called: Synergy Companies
28436 Satellite St, Hayward (94545-4863)
PHONE......................................510 259-1700
Steven R Shallenberger, *President*
Russell Jacobsen, *CFO*
EMP: 375
SQ FT: 6,962
SALES (est): 27.8MM **Privately Held**
SIC: 1711 1731 1742 1793 Warm air heating & air conditioning contractor; general electrical contractor; plastering, drywall & insulation; glass & glazing work

(P-2194)
ECB CORP (PA)
Also Called: Omniduct
6400 Artesia Blvd, Buena Park
(90620-1006)
PHONE......................................714 385-8900
Robert Brumleu, *President*
Steven G Philp, *CFO*
Sam Luk, *Project Leader*
Brian Daniels, *Sales Associate*
▲ EMP: 100
SQ FT: 56,000
SALES (est): 27.6MM **Privately Held**
WEB: www.omniduct.com
SIC: 1711 3444 Plumbing, heating, air-conditioning contractors; ducts, sheet metal

(P-2195)
ECONO AIR CONDITIONING INC
3366 E La Palma Ave, Anaheim
(92806-2814)
PHONE......................................714 630-3090
Mike Richard, *CEO*
EMP: 50
SALES (est): 2MM **Privately Held**
SIC: 1711 Warm air heating & air conditioning contractor

(P-2196)
ECOTECH RFRGN & HVAC INC
630 S Sunkist St Ste R, Anaheim (92806)
PHONE......................................888 833-8100
Erich Christopher Munzner, *CEO*
EMP: 60
SALES (est): 690.6K **Privately Held**
SIC: 1711 Heating & air conditioning contractors; refrigeration contractor

(P-2197)
EDF RENEWABLES INC (PA)
15445 Innovation Dr, San Diego
(92128-3432)
P.O. Box 504080 (92150-4080)
PHONE......................................858 521-3300
Tristan Grimbert, *President*
Luis Silva, *CFO*
Kara Vongphakdy, *Treasurer*
Ryan Pfaff, *Exec VP*
Larry Barr, *Vice Pres*
▲ EMP: 225
SALES (est): 569.6MM **Privately Held**
WEB: www.enxco.com
SIC: 1711 Solar energy contractor

(P-2198)
EDGEWATER PLUMBING OF BENICIA
5143 Port Chicago Hwy, Concord
(94520-1207)
PHONE......................................707 747-9204
Richard M Klauber, *Ch of Bd*
Steve Wilkerson, *President*
Lisa Wilkerson, *Corp Secy*
EMP: 50
SQ FT: 12,000
SALES (est): 5.5MM **Privately Held**
SIC: 1711 6531 Plumbing contractors; real estate leasing & rentals

(P-2199)
EMCOR FCLITIES SVCS N AMER INC
9505 Chesapeake Dr, San Diego
(92123-1304)
PHONE......................................858 712-4700
David Rastolich, *Vice Pres*
Ted Donald, *Manager*
EMP: 230
SALES (corp-wide): 7.6B **Publicly Held**
SIC: 1711 Heating & air conditioning contractors
HQ: Emcor Facilities Services Of North America, Inc.
306 Northern Ave Ste 5
Boston MA
-

(P-2200)
ENERGY ENTERPRISES USA INC (PA)
Also Called: Canopy Energy
6842 Van Nuys Blvd # 800, Van Nuys
(91405-4660)
PHONE......................................424 339-0005
Lior Agam, *CEO*
Frank Schwartz, *General Mgr*
Heather Pollock, *Project Mgr*
EMP: 100 EST: 2011
SQ FT: 11,000
SALES (est): 50MM **Privately Held**
SIC: 1711 Solar energy contractor

(P-2201)
ENERGY STORE OF CALIFORNIA INC
Also Called: Qc Wall Systems
14958 Venado Dr, Rancho Murieta
(95683-9322)
PHONE......................................916 825-8751
Dennis M Barsam, *President*
W Joe Mitchell, *Vice Pres*
EMP: 100
SALES (est): 3.5MM **Privately Held**
SIC: 1711 1742 Heating & air conditioning contractors; drywall

(P-2202)
ENVIRONMENTAL SYSTEMS INC (PA)
Also Called: Honeywell Authorized Dealer
3353 De La Cruz Blvd, Santa Clara
(95054-2633)
PHONE......................................408 980-1711
V C Enfantino, *President*
Lisa Enfantino, *Office Mgr*
Eugene L Enfantino, *Admin Sec*
Tammy Heimgartner, *Administration*
Bob Anthony, *Project Mgr*
EMP: 85
SQ FT: 13,800

SALES: 32.6MM **Privately Held**
SIC: 1711 7623 3444 Mechanical contractor; ventilation & duct work contractor; plumbing contractors; refrigeration service & repair; sheet metalwork

(P-2203)
ENVISE
12131 Western Ave, Garden Grove
(92841-2914)
PHONE......................................714 901-5800
Travis Feltcher, *Branch Mgr*
EMP: 63
SALES (corp-wide): 878.7MM **Privately Held**
SIC: 1711 Plumbing, heating, air-conditioning contractors
HQ: Envise
7390 Lincoln Way
Garden Grove CA 92841
800 613-6240

(P-2204)
ESS
Also Called: Evergreen Solar Services
5227 Dantes View Dr, Agoura Hills
(91301-2313)
PHONE......................................888 303-6424
Jacob Stephens, *President*
EMP: 100
SALES: 30.8MM **Privately Held**
SIC: 1711 Solar energy contractor

(P-2205)
F J HOOVER PLUMBING INC
Also Called: Pipeline Plumbing
2259 Hamner Ave, Norco (92860-2608)
PHONE......................................951 360-8262
Pamela Reno-Kemp, *President*
Hank Kemp, *Vice Pres*
James Dean Potts, *Principal*
EMP: 53
SQ FT: 1,500
SALES (est): 4.9MM **Privately Held**
SIC: 1711 Plumbing contractors

(P-2206)
FAMAND INC
1604 Airport Blvd, Santa Rosa
(95403-8204)
PHONE......................................707 255-9295
Charlie Butts, *Branch Mgr*
Stan Butts, *President*
Walt Yocum, *Vice Pres*
EMP: 80
SALES (corp-wide): 37.9MM **Privately Held**
SIC: 1711 Plumbing, heating, air-conditioning contractors
PA: Famand, Inc.
1512 Silica Ave
Sacramento CA 95815
916 988-8808

(P-2207)
FAULT LINE PLUMBING
7640 National Dr, Livermore (94550-8809)
PHONE......................................925 443-6450
Sean Collins, *President*
Karrie Collins, *Corp Secy*
EMP: 50
SALES (est): 7.8MM **Privately Held**
SIC: 1711 Plumbing contractors

(P-2208)
FERREIRA SERVICE INC (PA)
2600 Old Crow Canyon Rd # 100, San
Ramon (94583-1660)
PHONE......................................925 831-9330
Susan Ferreira, *CEO*
Albert Ferreira, *President*
Raymond Ferreira, *COO*
Josh Davis, *Sales Staff*
Al Ferreira, *Director*
EMP: 65 EST: 1978
SQ FT: 10,000
SALES (est): 10.9MM **Privately Held**
WEB: www.ferreira.com
SIC: 1711 Mechanical contractor

(P-2209)
FIDELITY HOME ENERGY INC (PA)
2235 Polvorosa Ave # 230, San Leandro
(94577-2249)
PHONE......................................858 220-7784

PRODUCTS & SVCS

Brad Smith, *Principal*
EMP: 73
SQ FT: 12,000
SALES (est): 20.7MM **Privately Held**
WEB: www.thesungate.com
SIC: 1711 1522 Solar energy contractor;
  remodeling, multi-family dwellings

(P-2210)
FIRE SAFE SYSTEMS INC
1312 Kingsdale Ave, Redondo Beach
(90278-3926)
PHONE.............................310 542-0585
Michael Moller, *CEO*
Joyce Moller, *President*
Sandra Marquez, *Office Mgr*
Mark Brancato, *Supervisor*
EMP: 60
SQ FT: 3,000
SALES (est): 9MM **Privately Held**
WEB: www.firesafesystems.com
SIC: 1711 Fire sprinkler system installation

(P-2211)
**FIRE SPRINKLER SYSTEMS INC
(PA)**
705 E Harrison St Ste 200, Corona
(92879-1398)
P.O. Box 2378 (92878-2378)
PHONE.............................800 915-3473
Harold Roger, *President*
Michael Kerby, *CFO*
Tammye Schillinger, *Administration*
Amy Descoteaux, *Engineer*
Juan Nieto, *Opers Mgr*
EMP: 86
SALES (est): 25.3MM **Privately Held**
WEB: www.fireinc.net
SIC: 1711 Fire sprinkler system installation

(P-2212)
FISCHER INC
1372 W 26th St, San Bernardino
(92405-3029)
PHONE.............................909 881-2910
Michael G Fischer, *President*
EMP: 70
SQ FT: 1,600
SALES (est): 8.7MM **Privately Held**
SIC: 1711 Plumbing contractors

(P-2213)
FREEDOM SOLAR SERVICES
43445 Bus Pk Dr Ste 110, Temecula
(92590-3671)
PHONE.............................951 696-9506
EMP: 150 EST: 2016
SALES (est): 13.4MM **Privately Held**
SIC: 1711 Solar energy contractor

(P-2214)
FRESCHI AIR SYSTEMS INC
Also Called: Freschi Service Experts
715 Fulton Shipyard Rd, Antioch
(94509-7557)
PHONE.............................925 827-9761
John R Freschi Jr, *President*
EMP: 55
SQ FT: 5,000
SALES (est): 5.9MM
SALES (corp-wide): 985.7MM **Privately
Held**
WEB: www.lennoxinternational.com
SIC: 1711 3444 Warm air heating & air
  conditioning contractor; sheet metalwork
HQ: Service Experts Llc
   3820 American Dr Ste 200
   Plano TX 75075

(P-2215)
**FRESNO PLUMBING & HEATING
INC (PA)**
Also Called: Ace Hardware
2585 N Larkin Ave, Fresno (93727-1357)
PHONE.............................559 294-0200
Larry Kumpe, *CEO*
Dean Kumpe, *Corp Secy*
Gary Kumpe, *Vice Pres*
Debbie Kumpe, *CIO*
Matt Kumpe, *Info Tech Mgr*
EMP: 202
SQ FT: 20,000

SALES (est): 43.4MM **Privately Held**
WEB: www.fphinc.com
SIC: 1711 5251 Plumbing contractors;
  hardware; door locks & lock sets; tools,
  hand; tools, power

(P-2216)
FRONTIER MECHANICAL INC
Also Called: Frontier Plumbing
6309 Seven Seas Ave, Bakersfield
(93308-5133)
PHONE.............................661 589-6203
Rick Palmer, *President*
Brenda Palmer, *Shareholder*
EMP: 93
SQ FT: 120,000
SALES (est): 14.6MM **Privately Held**
WEB: www.frontier-plumbing.com
SIC: 1711 1521 Plumbing contractors;
  new construction, single-family houses

(P-2217)
FW SPENCER & SON INC
Also Called: Brisbane Mechanical
99 S Hill Dr, Brisbane (94005-1274)
PHONE.............................415 468-5000
William D Spencer, *President*
Virgina Sevilla, *CFO*
Kevin Coyne, *Vice Pres*
Dan Everett, *Vice Pres*
Bob Latham, *Vice Pres*
EMP: 200 EST: 1903
SQ FT: 140,000
SALES (est): 38.6MM **Privately Held**
SIC: 1711 Plumbing contractors; warm air
  heating & air conditioning contractor

(P-2218)
GCL SOLAR ENERGY INC
1 Market Er 00 Steuart Tow, San Francisco
(94105-1596)
PHONE.............................415 362-2601
Peng Fang, *CEO*
Mac Moore, *Business Dir*
Emma Ye, *Admin Sec*
Quan Wang, *Info Tech Mgr*
Esther Clayson, *Human Res Dir*
▲ EMP: 54
SALES (est): 9.3MM **Privately Held**
SIC: 1711 Solar energy contractor
PA: Gcl Solar Energy Technology Holdings
  Limited
  Rm 1703b-1706 17/F International
  Commerce Ctr
  Yau Ma Tei KLN
  252 683-68

(P-2219)
**GENERAL ENGINEERING WSTN
INC (PA)**
Also Called: Thermal Air
1140 N Red Gum St, Anaheim
(92806-2516)
PHONE.............................714 630-3200
Stephen Weiss, *CEO*
Joseph Urban, *President*
EMP: 60
SQ FT: 10,000
SALES (est): 12.1MM **Privately Held**
SIC: 1711 Heating & air conditioning con-
  tractors; ventilation & duct work contractor

(P-2220)
GENERAL UNDERGROUND
701 W Grove Ave, Orange (92865-3213)
P.O. Box 29830, Anaheim (92809-0194)
PHONE.............................714 632-8646
Robert Anderson, *CEO*
Terry Householder, *President*
Karla Distrola, *Vice Pres*
Jason Stout, *Project Mgr*
Keith Kroeger, *Manager*
EMP: 110
SQ FT: 8,000
SALES (est): 22.2MM **Privately Held**
WEB: www.gufpinc.com
SIC: 1711 Fire sprinkler system installation

(P-2221)
**GEORGE M ROBINSON & CO
(PA)**
1461 Atteberry Ln, San Jose (95131-1409)
PHONE.............................510 632-7017
John P Joyce, *President*
Ned Raudsep, *Treasurer*
EMP: 100

SQ FT: 20,000
SALES (est): 5.6MM **Privately Held**
WEB: www.geomrobinson.com
SIC: 1711 3498 Fire sprinkler system in-
  stallation; fabricated pipe & fittings

(P-2222)
GRAYCON INC
232 S 8th Ave, City of Industry
(91746-3200)
PHONE.............................626 961-9640
Joseph F Klein, *CEO*
Sam Hitchcock, *CFO*
Brian Gavin, *Regional Mgr*
Jim Smith, *Regional Mgr*
Matt Guerrero, *Office Mgr*
EMP: 50
SQ FT: 12,000
SALES (est): 9.9MM **Privately Held**
WEB: www.graycon.net
SIC: 1711 Ventilation & duct work contrac-
  tor; warm air heating & air conditioning
  contractor

(P-2223)
**GREATER SAN DIEGO AC CO
INC**
Also Called: Honeywell Authorized Dealer
3883 Ruffin Rd Ste C, San Diego
(92123-4813)
PHONE.............................619 469-7818
Randy Baillargeon, *President*
Ryan Baillargeon, *Vice Pres*
Vanessa Tantay, *Human Res Mgr*
Eric Gage, *Manager*
Danielle Zuniga, *Accounts Mgr*
EMP: 115
SQ FT: 8,500
SALES (est): 12.3MM **Privately Held**
WEB: www.gsdac.com
SIC: 1711 Heating & air conditioning con-
  tractors; ventilation & duct work contractor

(P-2224)
GROWITH INC
Also Called: Mr Rooter
1069 Camero Way, Fremont (94539-3785)
PHONE.............................805 650-6650
Aung Oo, *CEO*
EMP: 68
SALES (est): 2.6MM **Privately Held**
SIC: 1711 Plumbing contractors

(P-2225)
H L MOE CO INC (PA)
Also Called: Keefe Plumbing Services
526 Commercial St, Glendale
(91203-2861)
PHONE.............................818 572-2100
Martha Tennyson, *CEO*
Michael C Davis, *President*
Bob Francis, *Vice Pres*
Robert Francis, *Vice Pres*
Jeff Hachey, *Vice Pres*
EMP: 130 EST: 1927
SALES (est): 38.7MM **Privately Held**
WEB: www.hlmoeco.com
SIC: 1711 Plumbing contractors

(P-2226)
HALDEMAN INC
2937 Tanager Ave, Commerce
(90040-2761)
PHONE.............................323 726-7011
Tom Haldeman, *Ch of Bd*
Mark O Donnell, *President*
Jeff Dandridge, *CFO*
Sue Haldeman, *Treasurer*
Holt Dandridge, *Vice Pres*
EMP: 50
SQ FT: 45,000
SALES (est): 3.6MM **Privately Held**
WEB: www.haldeman.com
SIC: 1711 Mechanical contractor

(P-2227)
HIBRID HOME LLC
10025 Mesa Rim Rd, San Diego
(92121-2913)
PHONE.............................844 442-7431
George Safonov, *Principal*
EMP: 200 EST: 2015
SALES (est): 5.1MM **Privately Held**
SIC: 1711 Solar energy contractor

(P-2228)
HPS MECHANICAL INC (PA)
3100 E Belle Ter, Bakersfield (93307-6830)
PHONE.............................661 397-2121
Les Denherder, *President*
Scott Denherder, *Vice Pres*
Jamie Ramos, *Executive Asst*
Renee Denesha, *Administration*
Roger Lane, *Project Mgr*
EMP: 127
SALES (est): 34.8MM **Privately Held**
SIC: 1711 Plumbing contractors

(P-2229)
HUMPHREY PLUMBING INC
880 S Kilroy Rd, Turlock (95380-9570)
PHONE.............................209 634-4626
Justin Humphrey, *President*
Robin Humphrey, *Corp Secy*
EMP: 75
SQ FT: 7,500
SALES (est): 9.5MM **Privately Held**
SIC: 1711 Plumbing contractors

(P-2230)
ICOM MECHANICAL INC
477 Burke St, San Jose (95112-4101)
P.O. Box 975 (95108-0975)
PHONE.............................408 292-4968
Donald George Isaacson, *CEO*
Dane Littleton, *President*
Elizabeth Wozniak, *CFO*
Alan Glace, *Vice Pres*
Al Grace, *Vice Pres*
EMP: 225
SQ FT: 24,000
SALES (est): 53.8MM **Privately Held**
WEB: www.icominc.com
SIC: 1711 Mechanical contractor

(P-2231)
INCOM MECHANICAL INC
975 Transport Way Ste 5, Petaluma
(94954-6860)
PHONE.............................707 586-0511
Charles J Lacoti, *President*
Gabrielle Candrian, *Treasurer*
Jeff Lacoti, *Vice Pres*
Phil Lacoti, *Vice Pres*
Jennifer Leavell, *Executive Asst*
EMP: 65
SQ FT: 7,000
SALES (est): 10.3MM **Privately Held**
WEB: www.incommechanical.com
SIC: 1711 Plumbing contractors; mechani-
  cal contractor

(P-2232)
**INDUSTRIAL COML SYSTEMS
INC**
Also Called: SAN MARCOS MECHANICAL
1165 Joshua Way, Vista (92081-7840)
PHONE.............................760 300-4094
Robin Sides, *President*
Matt Harbin, *Vice Pres*
Cindy Sides, *Admin Sec*
EMP: 160
SQ FT: 15,000
SALES: 29.8MM **Privately Held**
SIC: 1711 Ventilation & duct work contrac-
  tor; warm air heating & air conditioning
  contractor

(P-2233)
INFINITY ENERGY INC
1108 Tinker Rd Ste 150, Rocklin
(95765-1333)
PHONE.............................916 474-4723
EMP: 150
SALES (est): 261.3K **Privately Held**
SIC: 1711

(P-2234)
INFINITY SERVICE GROUP INC
Also Called: Allstar Home Services
9155 Archibald Ave # 302, Rancho Cuca-
monga (91730-5238)
P.O. Box 4229 (91729-4229)
PHONE.............................909 466-6237
Justin Speelman, *President*
Jason Carroll, *CFO*
Leighton Jenner, *Vice Pres*
James McNeeley, *Admin Sec*
EMP: 54
SQ FT: 3,200

102   2019 Directory of California
Wholesalers and Services Companies   ▲ = Import ▼=Export
◆ =Import/Export

SALES (est): 1.7MM **Privately Held**
SIC: **1711** Plumbing contractors

(P-2235)
INNOVATIVE MAINT SOLUTIONS INC
Also Called: IMS
725 Del Paso Rd, Sacramento
(95834-1106)
PHONE..................................916 568-1400
Roy L Hill, *CEO*
Roy Hill, *COO*
Roy A Hill, *COO*
Dennis Dalton, *CFO*
Mike Mayo, *Vice Pres*
EMP: 115
SQ FT: 5,400
SALES: 9.7MM **Privately Held**
WEB: www.imsfacilityservices.com
SIC: **1711** 0781 1731 7349 Heating & air conditioning contractors; landscape services; lighting contractor; janitorial service, contract basis

(P-2236)
INTECH MECHANICAL COMPANY LLC
7501 Galilee Rd, Roseville (95678-6905)
PHONE..................................916 797-4900
Richard B Chowdry,
Julie Chowdry, *Corp Secy*
Mike Friesen, *Vice Pres*
Corey Flissinger, *Project Mgr*
Martin Gatlin, *Project Mgr*
EMP: 150
SQ FT: 39,775
SALES: 40.6MM **Privately Held**
SIC: **1711** 8711 Plumbing contractors; heating & air conditioning contractors; mechanical contractor; process piping contractor; heating & ventilation engineering

(P-2237)
INTEGRATED MECH SYSTEMS INC
2390 Bateman Ave, Duarte (91010-3312)
PHONE..................................626 446-1854
John P Lynch, *CEO*
Vachik Armenian, *Shareholder*
Jack Lynch, *Shareholder*
Kevin Stiver, *Shareholder*
EMP: 50
SQ FT: 4,500
SALES (est): 14.9MM **Privately Held**
WEB: www.integratedmechanical.com
SIC: **1711** Mechanical contractor

(P-2238)
J & J AIR CONDITIONING INC
Also Called: Honeywell Authorized Dealer
1086 N 11th St, San Jose (95112-2927)
PHONE..................................408 920-0662
Jerry Hurwitz, *Owner*
Susan Borkin, *Treasurer*
Rynette Edwards, *Admin Asst*
Pam York, *Admin Asst*
Alex Alas, *Project Mgr*
EMP: 60
SQ FT: 10,000
SALES (est): 13.8MM **Privately Held**
WEB: www.jjair.com
SIC: **1711** Warm air heating & air conditioning contractor; ventilation & duct work contractor

(P-2239)
J M CARDEN SPRINKLER CO INC
2909 Fletcher Dr, Los Angeles
(90065-1479)
PHONE..................................323 258-8300
Michael Carden, *President*
Carroll B Carden, *Corp Secy*
Richard Wallace, *Vice Pres*
Kathy Delgado, *Office Mgr*
Harry Heck, *IT/INT Sup*
EMP: 60
SQ FT: 48,000
SALES (est): 9.7MM **Privately Held**
WEB: www.jmcfire.com
SIC: **1711** Fire sprinkler system installation

(P-2240)
J R PIERCE PLUMBING COMPANY
14481 Wicks Blvd, San Leandro
(94577-6711)
PHONE..................................510 483-5473
Richard Pierce, *President*
Dave Barich, *General Mgr*
Nick Glasco, *Warehouse Mgr*
EMP: 100
SQ FT: 4,000
SALES (est): 14MM **Privately Held**
SIC: **1711** Plumbing contractors

(P-2241)
JACKSON & BLANC
7929 Arjons Dr, San Diego (92126-4301)
PHONE..................................858 831-7900
Kirk Jackson, *CEO*
John Fusca, *President*
▲ EMP: 110
SQ FT: 36,000
SALES: 68.1MM **Privately Held**
WEB: www.jacksonandblanc.com
SIC: **1711** Mechanical contractor

(P-2242)
JCT COMPANY LLC
Also Called: Aliso Air Conditioning & Htg
29736 Avenida&Bandera, Rancho Santa
Margari (92688)
PHONE..................................949 589-2021
Jeffrey Loftus, *Vice Pres*
Monika Hall, *Department Mgr*
Lauren Barbarino, *Admin Asst*
Shawn Cooney, *Sales Staff*
Kc Fowler, *Manager*
EMP: 50
SALES (est): 5.4MM **Privately Held**
SIC: **1711** Heating & air conditioning contractors

(P-2243)
JEFF TRACY INC
Also Called: Land Forms Landscape Cnstr
15375 Barrancia Pkwy A110, Irvine
(92618-2203)
PHONE..................................949 582-0877
Jeff Thomas Tracy, *CEO*
Jon Gilmer, *President*
Brian Olsen, *President*
Sandy Wallace, *CFO*
EMP: 50
SQ FT: 1,608
SALES (est): 6.7MM **Privately Held**
SIC: **1711** 0782 Irrigation sprinkler system installation; landscape contractors

(P-2244)
JOHNSON CONTROLS
1868 Palma Dr, Ventura (93003-6300)
PHONE..................................805 642-0366
EMP: 64 **Privately Held**
SIC: **1711** Fire sprinkler system installation
HQ: Johnson Controls Fire Protection Lp
4700 Exchange Ct Ste 300
Boca Raton FL 33431
561 988-7200

(P-2245)
JOHNSON CONTROLS
3077 Wiljan Ct Ste B, Santa Rosa
(95407-5764)
PHONE..................................707 578-3212
John Becker, *Branch Mgr*
EMP: 61 **Privately Held**
WEB: www.simplexgrinnell.com
SIC: **1711** Fire sprinkler system installation
HQ: Johnson Controls Fire Protection Lp
4700 Exchange Ct Ste 300
Boca Raton FL 33431
561 988-7200

(P-2246)
JPI DEVELOPMENT GROUP INC
41205 Golden Gate Cir, Murrieta
(92562-6991)
PHONE..................................951 973-7680
Brad Janikowski, *President*
Dan Janikowski, *Vice Pres*
Lillian Hughes, *Manager*
EMP: 60
SQ FT: 6,000
SALES (est): 8.3MM **Privately Held**
SIC: **1711** Plumbing contractors

(P-2247)
JR PERCE PLBG INC SACRAMENTO
3610 Cincinnati Ave, Rocklin (95765-1203)
PHONE..................................916 434-9554
Dennis Pierce, *President*
EMP: 150 EST: 1927
SQ FT: 11,000
SALES (est): 38.3MM **Privately Held**
SIC: **1711** Plumbing contractors

(P-2248)
K & S AIR CONDITIONING INC
Also Called: K&S
143 E Meats Ave, Orange (92865-3309)
PHONE..................................714 685-0077
Steven Patz, *President*
Renee Patz, *Vice Pres*
Dave Guido, *Sales Staff*
Robert Herrera, *Sales Staff*
Hortensia Calvo, *Manager*
EMP: 140
SQ FT: 18,000
SALES: 28.9MM **Privately Held**
SIC: **1711** Warm air heating & air conditioning contractor

(P-2249)
KEN STARR INC
Also Called: Home Comfort USA
1120 N Tustin Ave, Anaheim (92807-1712)
PHONE..................................714 632-8789
Ken Starr, *President*
Paul Buono, *Vice Pres*
EMP: 80
SQ FT: 9,000
SALES: 14MM **Privately Held**
SIC: **1711** Warm air heating & air conditioning contractor; heating & air conditioning contractors

(P-2250)
KINCAID INDUSTRIES INC
31065 Plantation Dr, Thousand Palms
(92276-6623)
PHONE..................................760 343-5457
Scott Kincaid, *CEO*
Dave Seipel, *Project Mgr*
Tim Berg, *Sr Project Mgr*
EMP: 70
SQ FT: 7,000
SALES (est): 19.7MM **Privately Held**
WEB: www.kincaidplumbing.com
SIC: **1711** Plumbing contractors

(P-2251)
KINETIC SYSTEMS INC
1620 S Sunkist St, Anaheim (92806-5811)
PHONE..................................949 502-4856
Dan Naylor, *Opers Mgr*
EMP: 50
SALES (corp-wide): 232.2MM **Privately Held**
SIC: **1711** Mechanical contractor
HQ: Kinetic Systems, Inc.
3083 Independence Dr
Livermore CA 94551
510 683-6000

(P-2252)
KINETICS MECHANICAL SVC INC
6336 Patterson Pass Rd H, Livermore
(94550-9577)
PHONE..................................925 245-6200
Ralph E Dorotinsky, *President*
Craig Kirk, *Vice Pres*
EMP: 100 EST: 1997
SQ FT: 10,000
SALES: 14.3MM **Privately Held**
SIC: **1711** Mechanical contractor

(P-2253)
L A SERVICES INC
Also Called: George Brazil Plbg Htg & AC
9405 Jefferson Blvd, Culver City
(90232-2915)
PHONE..................................310 838-0408
Michael N Diamond, *President*
Goldyne Diamond, *Corp Secy*
Kenneth E Barbura, *Vice Pres*
EMP: 50
SQ FT: 4,000
SALES (est): 2.4MM **Privately Held**
SIC: **1711** Plumbing contractors

(P-2254)
L J KRUSE CO
Also Called: Honeywell Authorized Dealer
920 Pardee St, Berkeley (94710-2626)
P.O. Box 2900 (94702-0900)
PHONE..................................510 644-0260
David J Kruse, *President*
Karen Lown, *CFO*
Andrew S Kruse, *Exec VP*
Andrew Kruse, *Exec VP*
Janell Yates, *Vice Pres*
EMP: 60
SQ FT: 14,000
SALES (est): 12.3MM **Privately Held**
WEB: www.ljkruse.com
SIC: **1711** Plumbing contractors

(P-2255)
L&H AIRCO LLC
2530 Warren Dr, Rocklin (95677-2167)
PHONE..................................916 677-1000
Eric Crise, *President*
Jake Garcis, *Vice Pres*
John Harris, *Vice Pres*
Richard Racette, *Finance*
EMP: 80
SALES (est): 1.6MM **Privately Held**
SIC: **1711** 5084 Mechanical contractor; instruments & control equipment

(P-2256)
LADELL INC
Also Called: Johnson Air
605 N Halifax Ave, Clovis (93611-7270)
PHONE..................................559 650-2000
Steve Johnson, *President*
EMP: 50
SQ FT: 38,000
SALES (est): 6.4MM **Privately Held**
WEB: www.ladell.com
SIC: **1711** Warm air heating & air conditioning contractor

(P-2257)
LAWSON MECHANICAL CONTRACTORS (PA)
6090 S Watt Ave, Sacramento
(95829-1302)
P.O. Box 15224 (95851-0224)
PHONE..................................916 381-5000
Rodney Lawson, *President*
David Lawson, *Corp Secy*
Rod Barbour, *Vice Pres*
Stephen Humason, *Vice Pres*
Dean Schouweiler, *Engineer*
EMP: 100 EST: 1947
SQ FT: 31,000
SALES (est): 26.1MM **Privately Held**
WEB: www.lawsonmechanical.com
SIC: **1711** Plumbing contractors; heating & air conditioning contractors; mechanical contractor

(P-2258)
LDI MECHANICAL INC
3760 Happy Ln, Sacramento (95827-9731)
PHONE..................................916 361-3925
Shane Moser, *Manager*
EMP: 50
SALES (corp-wide): 88MM **Privately Held**
SIC: **1711** Mechanical contractor
PA: Ldi Mechanical, Inc.
1587 E Bentley Dr
Corona CA 92879
951 340-9685

(P-2259)
LDI MECHANICAL INC (PA)
Also Called: Honeywell Authorized Dealer
1587 E Bentley Dr, Corona (92879-1738)
PHONE..................................951 340-9685
Lloyd Smith, *President*
Derek Schaper, *Officer*
Mike Smith, *Senior VP*
Robert Smith, *Senior VP*
Steve Buren, *Vice Pres*
EMP: 151
SQ FT: 38,000
SALES (est): 88MM **Privately Held**
WEB: www.ldimechanical.com
SIC: **1711** Mechanical contractor

PRODUCTS & SVCS

(P-2260)
LED GLOBAL LLC
1010 Wilshire Blvd, Los Angeles
(90017-5662)
PHONE..................917 921-4315
Saila Smith,
EMP: 100
SALES: 10MM Privately Held
SIC: 1711 Solar energy contractor

(P-2261)
LEGACY MECH & ENRGY SVCS INC
3130 Crow Canyon Pl # 410, San Ramon
(94583-1346)
PHONE..................925 820-6938
Bill Longbotham, Vice Pres
Chip Eskildsen, Vice Pres
Jack Larkin, Vice Pres
Linda Jardin, General Mgr
David Zapf, Engineer
EMP: 100
SQ FT: 4,000
SALES (est): 26.2MM Privately Held
WEB: www.legacymechanical.com
SIC: 1711 Mechanical contractor

(P-2262)
LESCURE COMPANY INC
2301 Arnold Industrial Wa, Concord
(94520-5376)
P.O. Box 968, Lafayette (94549-0968)
PHONE..................925 283-2528
Michael Lescure, President
Allen Lescure, Vice Pres
Brian Lescure, Safety Mgr
Conrad Chin, Sales Mgr
Donna Burpee, Associate
EMP: 70
SQ FT: 10,000
SALES (est): 11.3MM Privately Held
WEB: www.lescurecompany.com
SIC: 1711 Plumbing contractors; mechanical contractor; warm air heating & air conditioning contractor

(P-2263)
LIMBACH COMPANY LP
Also Called: Western Air & Refrigeration
1709 Apollo Ct, Seal Beach (90740-5617)
PHONE..................714 653-7000
Charlie Bacon, CEO
John T Jordan Jr, CFO
Robert C Morgan, Vice Pres
Beverly Sullivan, Manager
Willie Whitaker, Manager
EMP: 167
SALES (est): 36.6MM Privately Held
SIC: 1711 Mechanical contractor
HQ: Limbach Company Llc
31 35th St
Pittsburgh PA 15201
412 359-2173

(P-2264)
LINDLEY FIRE PROTECTION CO
2220 E Via Burton, Anaheim (92806-1221)
PHONE..................714 535-5761
Leslie Lee Lindley II, President
Ann Lindley-Biship, Office Mgr
Ed Delgado, Engineer
Linda Kocher, Controller
Jefe F Rodriguez, Purchasing
EMP: 50
SQ FT: 5,000
SALES: 9MM Privately Held
SIC: 1711 Fire sprinkler system installation

(P-2265)
LITE SOLAR CORP
3553 Atlantic Ave, Long Beach
(90807-5606)
PHONE..................562 256-1249
Ranbir Sahni, CEO
EMP: 150
SALES (est): 11.5MM Privately Held
SIC: 1711 Solar energy contractor

(P-2266)
LOUIS LUSKIN & SONS INC
6004 Venice Blvd, Los Angeles (90034)
PHONE..................323 938-5142
Martin Luskin, President
Robert Luskin, Treasurer
EMP: 53
SQ FT: 7,000

SALES (est): 3.2MM Privately Held
SIC: 1711 Plumbing contractors

(P-2267)
LOVAZZANO MECHANICAL INC
189 Constitution Dr, Menlo Park
(94025-1106)
PHONE..................650 367-6216
Bruce Lovazzano Sr, CEO
Bruce Lovazzano Jr, President
Gary Lovazzano, Treasurer
EMP: 70
SQ FT: 3,100
SALES (est): 12.2MM Privately Held
SIC: 1711 Plumbing, heating, air-conditioning contractors

(P-2268)
LOZANO PLUMBING SERVICES INC
Also Called: Plumbing Master
3615 Presley Ave, Riverside (92507-4448)
P.O. Box 53137 (92517-4137)
PHONE..................951 683-4840
EMP: 130 EST: 2004
SALES (est): 13.2MM Privately Held
SIC: 1711

(P-2269)
LPSH HOLDINGS INC
Also Called: Horizon Solar Power
3570 W Florida Ave # 168, Hemet
(92545-3518)
PHONE..................951 926-1176
Zachary Allman, Accounts Mgr
EMP: 504
SALES (corp-wide): 16.5MM Privately Held
SIC: 1711 Solar energy contractor
PA: Lpsh Holdings, Inc.
27368 Via Industria
Temecula CA 92590
855 647-5061

(P-2270)
LUPPEN AND HAWLEY INC
6330 N Point Way, Sacramento
(95831-1067)
PHONE..................916 456-7831
John O'Connor, President
Terrence O'Connor, Vice Pres
Greg O'Connor, Admin Sec
EMP: 110 EST: 1920
SQ FT: 30,000
SALES (est): 14.3MM Privately Held
WEB: www.luppenandhawleyinc.com
SIC: 1711 1731 Plumbing contractors; warm air heating & air conditioning contractor; electrical work

(P-2271)
M & L PLUMBING CO INC
3540 N Duke Ave, Fresno (93727-7896)
PHONE..................559 291-5525
Fred C Ede III, President
Fred C Ede, President
EMP: 50
SQ FT: 6,000
SALES (est): 5MM Privately Held
SIC: 1711 Plumbing contractors

(P-2272)
M & M PLUMBING INC
6782 Columbus St, Riverside (92504-1118)
PHONE..................951 354-5388
Robert Malcom, President
Glenn Malcolm, Principal
EMP: 80
SALES (est): 5.9MM Privately Held
SIC: 1711 Plumbing contractors

(P-2273)
MARELICH MECHANICAL CO INC (HQ)
24041 Amador St, Hayward (94544-1201)
PHONE..................510 785-5500
Keith R Atteberry, President
Chad Johnston, Vice Pres
Terry J Kvochak, Vice Pres
Andrew Ostrowski, Vice Pres
John Powell, Vice Pres
EMP: 65
SQ FT: 40,000

SALES (est): 34.2MM
SALES (corp-wide): 7.6B Publicly Held
WEB: www.marelich.com
SIC: 1711 1623 3822 Mechanical contractor; pipeline construction; auto controls regulating residntl & coml environmt & applncs
PA: Emcor Group, Inc.
301 Merritt 7 Fl 6
Norwalk CT 06851
203 849-7800

(P-2274)
MARQUEE FIRE PROTECTION (PA)
710 W Stadium Ln, Sacramento
(95834-1130)
PHONE..................916 641-7997
Donna Awtrey, Principal
Jeff Awtrey, Vice Pres
Rick Awtrey, Vice Pres
Kimberly Reed, Vice Pres
EMP: 56
SQ FT: 5,400
SALES: 8.7MM Privately Held
WEB: www.marqueefire.com
SIC: 1711 Fire sprinkler system installation

(P-2275)
MASTERSERV INC
Also Called: Mastersev
560 Library St, San Fernando
(91340-2524)
PHONE..................818 356-4602
George Anderson, President
Cindy Anderson, Corp Secy
EMP: 50
SQ FT: 3,500
SALES (est): 6.8MM Privately Held
WEB: www.masterservinc.com
SIC: 1711 1731 Plumbing contractors; general electrical contractor

(P-2276)
MDDR INC
Also Called: Econo Air
555 Vanguard Way, Brea (92821-3933)
PHONE..................714 792-1993
Michael Richards, President
Rhonda Richards, Vice Pres
EMP: 110
SALES (est): 26.4MM Privately Held
WEB: www.e-conoair.com
SIC: 1711 1731 Warm air heating & air conditioning contractor; electrical work

(P-2277)
MEMEGED TEVUOT SHEMESH (PA)
Also Called: Titan Solar
5550 Topanga Canyon Blvd # 280, Woodland Hills (91367-7471)
PHONE..................866 575-1211
Ofir Haimoff, Owner
EMP: 152 EST: 2011
SQ FT: 20,000
SALES (est): 27.8MM Privately Held
SIC: 1711 5074 Solar energy contractor; heating equipment & panels, solar

(P-2278)
MESA ENERGY SYSTEMS INC (HQ)
Also Called: Emcor Services
2 Cromwell, Irvine (92618-1816)
PHONE..................949 460-0460
Robert A Lake, President
Steve Hunt, CFO
Kip Bagley, Vice Pres
Michael Ecshner, Vice Pres
Charles G Fletcher Jr, Vice Pres
EMP: 210
SQ FT: 55,000
SALES (est): 140.7MM
SALES (corp-wide): 7.6B Publicly Held
SIC: 1711 7623 Warm air heating & air conditioning contractor; refrigeration service & repair
PA: Emcor Group, Inc.
301 Merritt 7 Fl 6
Norwalk CT 06851
203 849-7800

(P-2279)
MESA ENERGY SYSTEMS INC
3980 N Chestnut Ave, Fresno
(93726-4730)
PHONE..................559 277-7900
Michael Echsner, Branch Mgr
EMP: 60
SALES (corp-wide): 7.6B Publicly Held
SIC: 1711 Warm air heating & air conditioning contractor
HQ: Mesa Energy Systems, Inc.
2 Cromwell
Irvine CA 92618
949 460-0460

(P-2280)
MESA ENERGY SYSTEMS INC
16130 Sherman Way, Van Nuys
(91406-3907)
PHONE..................818 756-0500
Craig Lacko, Manager
EMP: 104
SALES (corp-wide): 7.6B Publicly Held
SIC: 1711 Heating & air conditioning contractors
HQ: Mesa Energy Systems, Inc.
2 Cromwell
Irvine CA 92618
949 460-0460

(P-2281)
MIKE DIAMOND PLUMBING INC (PA)
Also Called: Diamond Mike Plbg Htg AC Elec
9405 Jefferson Blvd, Culver City
(90232-2915)
PHONE..................310 838-6197
Michael N Diamond, President
Goldyne Diamond, Corp Secy
Dave Diamond, Vice Pres
EMP: 66
SQ FT: 7,200
SALES (est): 5.7MM Privately Held
SIC: 1711 Plumbing contractors

(P-2282)
MONSTER MECHANICAL INC
1855 Norman Ave, Campbell (95008)
P.O. Box 6, Los Gatos (95031-0006)
PHONE..................408 727-8362
Jeffery Miller, President
EMP: 60
SQ FT: 10,000
SALES (est): 5.6MM Privately Held
WEB: www.monstermechanical.com
SIC: 1711 Mechanical contractor

(P-2283)
MOUNTING SYSTEMS INC
180 Promenade Cir Ste 300, Sacramento
(95834-2952)
PHONE..................916 374-8872
Kasim Ersoy, President
▲ EMP: 51
SALES: 8.4MM
SALES (corp-wide): 374.6MM Privately Held
SIC: 1711 Mechanical contractor
HQ: Mounting Systems Gmbh
Mittenwalder Str. 9a
Rangsdorf 15834
337 085-2910

(P-2284)
MUIR-CHASE PLUMBING CO INC
Also Called: M C
4530 Brazil St Ste 1, Los Angeles
(90039-1000)
PHONE..................818 500-1940
Don Chase, President
Jay Chase, Vice Pres
Grant Muir, Vice Pres
James M Muir, Vice Pres
Gail Comstock, Admin Sec
EMP: 90 EST: 1975
SQ FT: 5,000
SALES (est): 26.9MM Privately Held
WEB: www.muirchase.com
SIC: 1711 7699 Plumbing contractors; sewer cleaning & rodding

(P-2285)
MULTI MECHANICAL INC
Also Called: Honeywell Authorized Dealer
469 Blaine St, Corona (92879-1304)
PHONE................714 632-7404
Brandon Abblitt, *CEO*
Thomas Alvey, *Purch Mgr*
EMP: 75
SALES (est): 13.1MM **Privately Held**
WEB: www.multimechanical.com
SIC: 1711 Mechanical contractor; warm air heating & air conditioning contractor

(P-2286)
MUNI-FED ENERGY INC
192 N Marina Dr, Long Beach (90803-4601)
PHONE................714 321-3346
Phil Bowman, *President*
Clay Sandidge, *Treasurer*
Tim Shaw, *Exec VP*
Abbey Lam, *Principal*
EMP: 50 EST: 2011
SALES (est): 2.7MM **Privately Held**
SIC: 1711 8748 Solar energy contractor; systems analysis & engineering consulting services

(P-2287)
MURRAY PLUMBING AND HTG CORP (PA)
Also Called: Murray Company
18414 S Santa Fe Ave, E Rncho Dmngz (90221-5612)
P.O. Box 9061, Compton (90224-9061)
PHONE................310 637-1500
Kevan Steffey, *Chairman*
Jim Deflavio, *CEO*
Alvin Aeschlimann, *CFO*
Barbara Braymajor, *CFO*
Don Odom, *Vice Pres*
EMP: 1000
SQ FT: 26,000
SALES: 310.6MM **Privately Held**
SIC: 1711 Plumbing contractors; warm air heating & air conditioning contractor

(P-2288)
N V HEATHORN INC
Also Called: N V H
1155 Beecher St, San Leandro (94577-1251)
PHONE................510 569-9100
Edward W Heathorn, *President*
David A Heathorn, *CFO*
David Heathorn, *CFO*
Norman T R Heathorn, *Principal*
Stephen Griggs, *Project Mgr*
EMP: 59 EST: 1932
SQ FT: 57,500
SALES (est): 13.9MM **Privately Held**
WEB: www.nvheathorn.com
SIC: 1711 1629 Warm air heating & air conditioning contractor; plumbing contractors; ventilation & duct work contractor; waste water & sewage treatment plant construction

(P-2289)
NATIONAL AIR INC
Also Called: National Air and Energy
2053 Kurtz St, San Diego (92110-2014)
PHONE................619 299-2500
Jared M Wells, *CEO*
EMP: 110
SQ FT: 10,500
SALES: 20MM **Privately Held**
SIC: 1711 Warm air heating & air conditioning contractor

(P-2290)
NOVA PLUMBING INC
3111 W Central Ave, Santa Ana (92704-5302)
PHONE................714 556-6682
Rod Robbins, *President*
Kathryn Taylor, *Vice Pres*
EMP: 105
SQ FT: 13,000
SALES (est): 5.3MM **Privately Held**
SIC: 1711 Plumbing contractors

(P-2291)
NU FLOW AMERICA INC (PA)
7710 Kenamar Ct, San Diego (92121-2425)
PHONE................619 275-9130
Cameron Sean Manners, *President*
Steven Howe, *President*
Nicolas Ghosn, *Regional Mgr*
Dennis Persaud, *General Mgr*
Grant Duxbury, *Manager*
EMP: 53
SQ FT: 15,488
SALES (est): 24.2MM **Privately Held**
WEB: www.nuflowtech.com
SIC: 1711 3317 Plumbing contractors; steel pipe & tubes

(P-2292)
O C MCDONALD CO INC
1150 W San Carlos St, San Jose (95126-3440)
P.O. Box 26560 (95159-6560)
PHONE................408 295-2182
James Mc Donald, *President*
Heidi Dunn, *Admin Asst*
Jordan Taha, *Project Engr*
J Brennan, *Controller*
Eileen Allen, *Human Resources*
EMP: 150 EST: 1906
SQ FT: 10,500
SALES (est): 53.9MM **Privately Held**
WEB: www.ocmcdonald.com
SIC: 1711 3585 3541 3444 Mechanical contractor; refrigeration & heating equipment; machine tools, metal cutting type; sheet metalwork; plumbing fixture fittings & trim

(P-2293)
OHAGIN MANUFACTURING LLC
210 Classic Ct Ste 100, Rohnert Park (94928-1660)
PHONE................707 872-3620
Greg Daniels, *President*
Bruce Montoya, *Natl Sales Mgr*
Jake Carlson, *Marketing Staff*
EMP: 50 EST: 2013
SALES (est): 4.2MM **Privately Held**
SIC: 1711 Ventilation & duct work contractor

(P-2294)
OHAGINS INC
210 Classic Ct Ste 100, Rohnert Park (94928-1660)
PHONE................707 303-3660
Carolina O'Hagin, *CEO*
Greg Daniels, *CEO*
Mark Marquez, *COO*
Mike Fulton, *Technical Staff*
▲ EMP: 60
SQ FT: 57,000
SALES (est): 7.8MM **Privately Held**
WEB: www.ohaginvent.com
SIC: 1711 Ventilation & duct work contractor

(P-2295)
OMNIMENT INDUSTRIES INC (PA)
Also Called: Omni-Temp Refrigeration
9300 Hall Rd, Downey (90241-5309)
PHONE................562 923-9660
Hans Haasis Jr, *President*
Donald Durward, *Vice Pres*
Bonnie Edmunds, *Human Res Mgr*
EMP: 125
SQ FT: 6,000
SALES (est): 11.3MM **Privately Held**
WEB: www.omniteaminc.com
SIC: 1711 5078 Refrigeration contractor; commercial refrigeration equipment

(P-2296)
ON-TIME AC & HTG INC (PA)
Also Called: Service Champions
7020 Commerce Dr Ste C, Pleasanton (94588-8021)
PHONE................925 598-1911
Kevin J Comerford, *CEO*
John Cristiano, *CEO*
Gary Potts, *CFO*
Mark Stewart, *General Mgr*
Vincent Fernandes, *Manager*
EMP: 84

SALES (est): 25.2MM **Privately Held**
SIC: 1711 Warm air heating & air conditioning contractor

(P-2297)
ONE CALL PLUMBER SANTA BARBARA
1016 Cliff Dr Apt 309, Santa Barbara (93109-1784)
PHONE................805 364-6337
EMP: 100
SALES (est): 2.1MM **Privately Held**
SIC: 1711 Plumbing contractors

(P-2298)
ONTARIO REFRIGERATION SVC INC (PA)
635 S Mountain Ave, Ontario (91762-4114)
PHONE................909 984-2771
Phillip C Talleur, *President*
Scott Gray, *General Mgr*
Phil Talleur, *General Mgr*
Keri Vargas, *Controller*
Randy Parnell, *Foreman/Supr*
EMP: 158 EST: 1971
SQ FT: 5,300
SALES (est): 65.4MM **Privately Held**
SIC: 1711 Warm air heating & air conditioning contractor; heating & air conditioning contractors

(P-2299)
ORANGE COUNTY SERVICES INC
Also Called: George Brazil Plbg Htg & AC
3022 N Hesperian St, Santa Ana (92706-1151)
PHONE................714 541-9753
Mike Jones, *General Mgr*
EMP: 50
SALES (est): 2.3MM
SALES (corp-wide): 1.6MM **Privately Held**
SIC: 1711 1731 Plumbing, heating, air-conditioning contractors; electrical work
PA: Orange County Services Inc
9405 Jefferson Blvd
Culver City CA 90232
310 515-1001

(P-2300)
ORANGE PACIFIC PLUMBING INC
801 Panorama Rd, Fullerton (92831-1029)
PHONE................714 992-4547
Steven Hartshorn, *President*
Bonnie Hartshorn, *Corp Secy*
EMP: 66
SQ FT: 5,000
SALES (est): 3.9MM **Privately Held**
WEB: www.orangepacific.com
SIC: 1711 Plumbing contractors

(P-2301)
ORIGINAL SID BLACKMAN PLBG INC
1160 S 2nd St, El Centro (92243-3446)
PHONE................760 352-3632
Thomas Blackman, *President*
Monique Caldera, *Office Mgr*
Michael Wickline, *Admin Sec*
EMP: 68
SALES (est): 8.2MM **Privately Held**
WEB: www.blackmanplumbing.net
SIC: 1711 Plumbing contractors

(P-2302)
PACIFIC PRODUCTION PLUMBING (PA)
1584 Pioneer Way, El Cajon (92020-1638)
PHONE................951 509-3100
Daniel Whitt, *President*
Kim Whitt, *Treasurer*
Bruce Magellan, *Vice Pres*
Tobin Whitt, *Vice Pres*
Wes Whitt, *General Mgr*
EMP: 50
SQ FT: 3,000
SALES (est): 53.7MM **Privately Held**
SIC: 1711 Plumbing contractors

(P-2303)
PACIFIC RIM MECH CONTRS INC
1701 E Edinger Ave Ste F2, Santa Ana (92705-5028)
PHONE................714 285-2600
John Heusner, *Manager*
EMP: 61
SALES (corp-wide): 134.6MM **Privately Held**
WEB: www.prmech.com
SIC: 1711 Mechanical contractor
PA: Pacific Rim Mechanical Contractors, Inc.
7655 Convoy Ct
San Diego CA 92111
858 974-6500

(P-2304)
PACIFIC RIM MECH CONTRS INC (PA)
Also Called: HONEYWELL AUTHORIZED DEALER
7655 Convoy Ct, San Diego (92111-1103)
PHONE................858 974-6500
Joseph Mucher, *CEO*
Eric Bader, *CFO*
Craig Condon, *Vice Pres*
Colin Cook, *Vice Pres*
John Heusner, *Vice Pres*
EMP: 400
SQ FT: 50,000
SALES: 134.6MM **Privately Held**
WEB: www.prmech.com
SIC: 1711 Mechanical contractor

(P-2305)
PAN-PACIFIC MECHANICAL LLC (PA)
18250 Euclid St, Fountain Valley (92708-6112)
PHONE................949 474-9170
Cindy Lanette McMackin, *CEO*
Steve Sylvester, *CFO*
Ryan Cavanaugh, *Vice Pres*
Pat George, *Vice Pres*
Jon Houchin, *Vice Pres*
▲ EMP: 150
SQ FT: 60,000
SALES: 290MM **Privately Held**
WEB: www.panpacplumbing.com
SIC: 1711 Plumbing contractors

(P-2306)
PAN-PACIFIC MECHANICAL LLC
1205 Chrysler Dr, Menlo Park (94025-1134)
PHONE................650 561-8810
Tom Sakurai, *Manager*
EMP: 661
SALES (corp-wide): 290MM **Privately Held**
SIC: 1711 Plumbing contractors
PA: Pan-Pacific Mechanical Llc
18250 Euclid St
Fountain Valley CA 92708
949 474-9170

(P-2307)
PAN-PACIFIC MECHANICAL LLC
Also Called: Pan-Pacific Plumbing & Mech
11622 El Camino Real, San Diego (92130-2049)
PHONE................858 764-2464
EMP: 189
SALES (corp-wide): 290MM **Privately Held**
SIC: 1711 Mechanical contractor
PA: Pan-Pacific Mechanical Llc
18250 Euclid St
Fountain Valley CA 92708
949 474-9170

(P-2308)
PATTERN RENEWABLES 2 LP
Bay 3 Pier 1, San Francisco (94111)
PHONE................415 283-4000
EMP: 150
SQ FT: 10,000
SALES: 2MM **Privately Held**
SIC: 1711 Solar energy contractor

P
R
O
D
U
C
T
S
&
S
V
C
S

(P-2309)
PINASCO PLUMBING & HEATING INC
Also Called: Pinasco Mechinical
2145 E Taylor St, Stockton (95205-6337)
P.O. Box 55287 (95205-8787)
PHONE..................................209 463-7793
Tom Pinasco, *President*
John Pinasco, *Treasurer*
Joseph Pinasco, *Admin Sec*
EMP: 50
SQ FT: 1,000
SALES (est): 8.3MM **Privately Held**
SIC: 1711 Plumbing contractors; fire sprinkler system installation; warm air heating & air conditioning contractor

(P-2310)
PIPE RESTORATION INC
Also Called: Ace Duraflo Pipe Restoration
3122 W Alpine St, Santa Ana (92704-6912)
PHONE..................................714 564-7600
Larry Gillanders, *CEO*
Mike Carper, *Exec VP*
Ray Munguia, *VP Opers*
EMP: 50 EST: 2001
SQ FT: 6,000
SALES (est): 8.3MM **Privately Held**
WEB: www.restoremypipes.com
SIC: 1711 Plumbing contractors

(P-2311)
PIPELINE RESTORATION PLUMBING
2700 S Main St Ste E, Santa Ana (92707-3431)
PHONE..................................714 957-5836
EMP: 50 EST: 2015
SALES (est): 83.4K **Privately Held**
SIC: 1711 Plumbing contractors

(P-2312)
PLUMB TECH INC
1242 E Maple Ave, El Segundo (90245-3258)
PHONE..................................310 322-4925
Greg Misic, *President*
Jim Gonzales, *Vice Pres*
EMP: 57
SALES (est): 2.6MM **Privately Held**
SIC: 1711 Plumbing contractors

(P-2313)
PLUMBING PIPING & CNSTR INC
5950 Lakeshore Dr, Cypress (90630-3371)
PHONE..................................714 821-0490
Bruce Cook Jr, *President*
Mike McIsaac, *Manager*
EMP: 100 EST: 1960
SQ FT: 12,600
SALES (est): 29.9MM **Privately Held**
WEB: www.1ppc.com
SIC: 1711 Plumbing, heating, air-conditioning contractors

(P-2314)
PLUMBING SYSTEMS WEST INC
31491 Outer Highway 10, Redlands (92373-7568)
PHONE..................................909 794-3823
Bob Grable, *President*
EMP: 68
SALES (est): 1.4MM **Privately Held**
SIC: 1711 Plumbing contractors

(P-2315)
PPC ENTERPRISES INC
Also Called: Premier Plumbing Company
5920 Rickenbacker Ave, Riverside (92504-1042)
PHONE..................................951 354-5402
Jeffrey Geiger, *President*
Dawn Geiger, *CFO*
EMP: 125
SQ FT: 10,000
SALES (est): 15.3MM **Privately Held**
SIC: 1711 Plumbing contractors

(P-2316)
PRECISE AIR SYSTEMS INC
Also Called: Hvac Installation and Repair
5467 W San Fernando Rd, Los Angeles (90039-1014)
P.O. Box 39609 (90039-0609)
PHONE..................................818 240-1737

Toll Free:...........................877 -
Fred Khachekian, *President*
Greg Khachekian, *Executive*
Anahit Spight, *Admin Asst*
Shakeh Petrosian, *Info Tech Mgr*
Albert Shabandari, *Project Mgr*
EMP: 91
SQ FT: 3,200
SALES (est): 18.6MM **Privately Held**
WEB: www.preciseairsystems.com
SIC: 1711 Warm air heating & air conditioning contractor; heating & air conditioning contractors

(P-2317)
PRIBUSS ENGINEERING INC
523 Mayfair Ave, South San Francisco (94080-4509)
PHONE..................................650 588-0447
Bayardo Chamorro, *President*
John Pribuss, *CFO*
Michelle Lamlin, *Vice Pres*
Mark Walsh, *General Mgr*
Rick Bergamaschi, *Project Mgr*
EMP: 70
SQ FT: 16,000
SALES (est): 19.9MM **Privately Held**
WEB: www.pribuss.com
SIC: 1711 7623 Warm air heating & air conditioning contractor; fire sprinkler system installation; refrigeration service & repair

(P-2318)
PRO-CRAFT CONSTRUCTION INC
31597 Outer Highway 10 B, Redlands (92373-8626)
PHONE..................................909 790-5222
Timothy McFayden, *President*
Susan Mc Fayden, *CFO*
Chris McFayden, *Vice Pres*
Anthony Avila, *Project Mgr*
Greg House, *Project Mgr*
EMP: 60
SALES (est): 14.3MM **Privately Held**
SIC: 1711 Plumbing contractors

(P-2319)
PRODUCTION PLUS PLUMBING INC
2472 Grand Ave, Vista (92081-7804)
PHONE..................................760 597-0235
Robert Labaron, *President*
Cindy McIntosh, *Manager*
EMP: 124
SALES (corp-wide): 13.8MM **Privately Held**
WEB: www.productionplusplumbing.com
SIC: 1711 Plumbing contractors
PA: Production Plus Plumbing, Inc.
  312 Dawson Dr
  Camarillo CA
  760 597-0235

(P-2320)
PROGRESSIVE POWER GROUP INC
12552 Western Ave, Garden Grove (92841-4013)
PHONE..................................714 899-2300
Ross A Butcher, *CEO*
Don Hughes, *CFO*
Chris Staskewicz, *Executive*
Chris Hammerstone, *Principal*
Travis Mashin, *General Mgr*
EMP: 50
SQ FT: 12,000
SALES (est): 12.2MM **Privately Held**
SIC: 1711 5211 Solar energy contractor; solar heating equipment

(P-2321)
PURONICS RETAIL SERVICES INC
5775 Las Positas Rd, Livermore (94551-7819)
PHONE..................................925 456-7000
Scott A Batiste, *CEO*
Mark H Cosmez II, *CFO*
EMP: 60
SQ FT: 25,000
SALES (est): 4.6MM **Privately Held**
SIC: 1711 Plumbing contractors

(P-2322)
QUICK SYSTEMS INC
5042 Wilshire Blvd # 28533, Los Angeles (90036-4305)
PHONE..................................702 335-3574
Alma Roundy, *CEO*
Stewart Knudson, *CEO*
EMP: 50 EST: 2011
SQ FT: 6,000
SALES: 6.4MM **Privately Held**
SIC: 1711 Solar energy contractor

(P-2323)
R & R MECHANICAL CONTRS INC
1400 N Johnson Ave # 114, El Cajon (92020-1650)
PHONE..................................619 449-9900
Randall A Signore, *President*
Richard Signore, *Vice Pres*
Rose Signore, *Admin Sec*
EMP: 100
SQ FT: 13,900
SALES (est): 9MM **Privately Held**
WEB: www.countywidems.com
SIC: 1711 Heating & air conditioning contractors

(P-2324)
R A SCHREIBER PLUMBING
2358 Tavern Rd, Alpine (91901-3107)
P.O. Box 1315 (91903-1315)
PHONE..................................619 659-3101
R A Schreiber, *Owner*
EMP: 50 EST: 1986
SALES: 8MM **Privately Held**
SIC: 1711 Plumbing contractors

(P-2325)
R B SPENCER INC
Also Called: Honeywell Authorized Dealer
1188 Hassett Ave, Yuba City (95991-7212)
PHONE..................................530 674-8307
Robert B Spencer, *President*
Brigit Spencer, *CFO*
Kayce Wolcott, *Admin Asst*
Tom Dodd, *Project Mgr*
Sam Belcher, *Traffic Dir*
EMP: 52
SQ FT: 8,000
SALES (est): 10.2MM **Privately Held**
WEB: www.rbspencerinc.com
SIC: 1711 Warm air heating & air conditioning contractor

(P-2326)
RA HUGHES ENTERPRISES IN
9316 Abraham Way, Santee (92071-2861)
PHONE..................................619 390-4880
Ra Hughes, *Owner*
EMP: 50
SALES (est): 1.5MM **Privately Held**
SIC: 1711 Septic system construction

(P-2327)
RAM MECHANICAL INC
3506 Moore Rd, Ceres (95307-9402)
PHONE..................................209 531-9155
Neil Hodgson, *Principal*
Gary Broadwell, *Vice Pres*
Tom Bawdon, *Project Mgr*
Travis Hayes, *Project Mgr*
Greg Peden, *Project Mgr*
EMP: 60
SQ FT: 22,500
SALES: 15MM **Privately Held**
WEB: www.ram-mechanical.com
SIC: 1711 8711 3599 3535 Mechanical contractor; engineering services; custom machinery; conveyors & conveying equipment

(P-2328)
RANDO AAA HVAC INC
Also Called: A A A Furnace Company
1712 Stone Ave Ste 1, San Jose (95125-1309)
PHONE..................................408 293-4717
Jim Rando, *President*
Marrissa Rando, *Principal*
EMP: 50
SQ FT: 5,000

SALES (est): 8.7MM **Privately Held**
SIC: 1711 3444 3433 Warm air heating & air conditioning contractor; ventilation & duct work contractor; sheet metalwork; heating equipment, except electric

(P-2329)
RAPID PLUMBING INC (PA)
Also Called: Pullan Enterprises
3840 E Miraloma Ave, Anaheim (92806-2108)
PHONE..................................714 695-1800
Brian Pullan, *CEO*
Kate Pullan, *Exec VP*
EMP: 90
SQ FT: 13,000
SALES (est): 11.7MM **Privately Held**
SIC: 1711 Plumbing contractors

(P-2330)
RAWLINGS MECHANICAL CORP (PA)
11615 Pendleton St, Sun Valley (91352-2502)
P.O. Box 703 (91353-0703)
PHONE..................................323 875-2040
Robert S Bratton, *President*
Rex Horney, *Vice Pres*
Patricia Wood, *Admin Sec*
Ken Burton, *Project Mgr*
Troy Tervo, *Foreman/Supr*
EMP: 69
SQ FT: 22,000
SALES: 29.8MM **Privately Held**
SIC: 1711 Mechanical contractor

(P-2331)
RCR PLUMBING AND MECH INC (PA)
Also Called: Rcr Companies
12620 Magnolia Ave, Riverside (92503-4636)
PHONE..................................951 371-5000
Robert Richey, *President*
EMP: 150
SQ FT: 35,000
SALES: 46MM **Privately Held**
SIC: 1711 Plumbing contractors

(P-2332)
RE MILANO PLUMBING CORP
4881 Sunrise Dr Ste B, Martinez (94553-4304)
P.O. Box 1383 (94553-7383)
PHONE..................................925 500-1372
Leigha M Ramirez, *CEO*
Robert Romeo, *President*
EMP: 50
SQ FT: 7,000
SALES: 4MM **Privately Held**
SIC: 1711 Plumbing contractors

(P-2333)
RECURRENT ENERGY LLC (HQ)
3000 Oak Rd Ste 300, Walnut Creek (94597-7775)
PHONE..................................415 956-3168
David Brochu, *CEO*
Mitchell Randall, *President*
EMP: 55
SQ FT: 7,500
SALES (est): 23.9MM
SALES (corp-wide): 3.3B **Privately Held**
WEB: www.renewableenergyworld.com
SIC: 1711 Solar energy contractor
PA: Canadian Solar Inc
  545 Speedvale Ave W
  Guelph ON N1K 1
  519 837-1881

(P-2334)
REGENCY FIRE PROTECTION INC
7651 Densmore Ave, Van Nuys (91406-2043)
PHONE..................................818 982-0126
Jay Zohar Rapaport, *President*
Tal Dagan, *Vice Pres*
Ron Parsay, *Manager*
EMP: 60
SQ FT: 7,500

SALES (est): 11.4MM **Privately Held**
WEB: www.regencyfire.com
SIC: **1711** 7382 Fire sprinkler system installation; burglar alarm maintenance & monitoring; fire alarm maintenance & monitoring; protective devices, security

(P-2335)
RELIABLE ENERGY MANAGEMENT INC
Also Called: Honeywell Authorized Dealer
7201 Rosecrans Ave, Paramount (90723-2501)
PHONE..............................562 984-5511
George R Garcia, *President*
Judy Garcia, *Exec VP*
David Reyes, *Vice Pres*
Isabel Garibay, *Office Mgr*
Joyce Huang, *Controller*
EMP: 80
SQ FT: 6,000
SALES (est): 19.1MM **Privately Held**
WEB: www.relenergy.com
SIC: **1711** Heating & air conditioning contractors

(P-2336)
RENOVA ENERGY CORP
75181 Mediterranean, Palm Desert (92211-9094)
PHONE..............................760 568-3413
Vincent Battaglia, *Ch of Bd*
Matthew De La Torre, *President*
Marvin Roman, *President*
Lea Goodsell, *Exec VP*
Isaac Gamez, *Vice Pres*
EMP: 50
SQ FT: 5,200
SALES (est): 14.1MM **Privately Held**
WEB: www.renovasolar.com
SIC: **1711** Solar energy contractor

(P-2337)
RESIDENTIAL FIRE SYSTEMS INC
8085 E Crystal Dr, Anaheim (92807-2523)
PHONE..............................714 666-8450
Ty Maley, *President*
Ruben Hernandez, *Treasurer*
Cesar Anchondo, *Vice Pres*
Jack Maley, *Vice Pres*
Stephanie McKinney, *Technology*
EMP: 75 EST: 2000
SQ FT: 6,200
SALES: 19.5MM **Privately Held**
WEB: www.residentialfiresys.com
SIC: **1711** 5063 Fire sprinkler system installation; signaling equipment, electrical

(P-2338)
RITCHIE PLUMBING INC
11320 Lombardy Ln, Moreno Valley (92557-5739)
PHONE..............................949 709-7575
Lance Ritchie, *President*
EMP: 120
SQ FT: 7,500
SALES (est): 6.7MM **Privately Held**
WEB: www.ritchieplumbing.com
SIC: **1711** Plumbing contractors

(P-2339)
ROBINSON COMPANY CONTRS INC
Also Called: Robinson Electric
8871 Troy St, Spring Valley (91977-2638)
PHONE..............................619 697-6040
Thomas Petree, *CEO*
Donna Garrett, *Office Mgr*
Jaimee Russell, *Admin Asst*
Spencer Tilton, *Director*
EMP: 52
SQ FT: 1,200
SALES (est): 10MM **Privately Held**
WEB: www.robinsonelectric.com
SIC: **1711** 6513 Warm air heating & air conditioning contractor; apartment building operators

(P-2340)
RODDA ELECTRIC INC (PA)
380 Carrol Ct Ste L, Brentwood (94513-7353)
PHONE..............................925 240-6024
Raymond Rodda, *CEO*

James Mapalo, *Project Mgr*
EMP: 60
SQ FT: 21,000
SALES (est): 26.5MM **Privately Held**
SIC: **1711** 1731 Solar energy contractor; general electrical contractor

(P-2341)
ROUNTREE PLUMBING AND HTG INC
1624 Santa Clara Dr 130, Roseville (95661-3554)
PHONE..............................650 298-0300
Stephen Singewald, *President*
Pat Singewald, *Corp Secy*
EMP: 60
SQ FT: 10,000
SALES (est): 11.7MM **Privately Held**
WEB: www.rountreeinc.com
SIC: **1711** Plumbing contractors; warm air heating & air conditioning contractor

(P-2342)
RPM MECHANICAL - A JOINT VENTR
2919 E Victoria St, Compton (90221-5614)
PHONE..............................858 565-4131
Kevan Steffey, *President*
EMP: 100
SALES (est): 7.2MM **Privately Held**
SIC: **1711** Plumbing contractors

(P-2343)
RUSSELL MECHANICAL INC
3251 Monier Cir Ste A, Rancho Cordova (95742-6812)
PHONE..............................916 635-2522
Danny L Russell, *President*
Steve Russell, *Vice Pres*
Karen Russell, *Principal*
Terri Mosier, *Office Mgr*
Will Wakamiya, *Engrg Dir*
EMP: 90
SQ FT: 22,000
SALES (est): 18.9MM **Privately Held**
SIC: **1711** 1799 7389 3441 Mechanical contractor; welding on site; design services; fabricated structural metal

(P-2344)
S S W MECHANICAL CNSTR INC
Also Called: Ssw
670 S Oleander Rd, Palm Springs (92264-1502)
P.O. Box 3160 (92263-3160)
PHONE..............................760 327-1481
Sean Wood, *President*
W T Hayes, *Vice Pres*
Cary Miller, *Purch Dir*
EMP: 140
SQ FT: 7,000
SALES (est): 24.1MM **Privately Held**
WEB: www.sswmechanical.com
SIC: **1711** Plumbing contractors

(P-2345)
SABER PLUMBING INC
325 Market Pl, Escondido (92029-1302)
PHONE..............................760 480-5716
Glenn Phil Napierskie II, *President*
Annette Mott, *Admin Mgr*
Jim Kealy, *Purch Mgr*
Ron Jordan, *Sales Staff*
EMP: 60
SQ FT: 12,500
SALES (est): 11.1MM **Privately Held**
WEB: www.saberplumbing.com
SIC: **1711** Plumbing contractors

(P-2346)
SAHARGUN PLUMBING INC
Also Called: Sahargun Mechanical
2216 Stewart St, Stockton (95205-3232)
PHONE..............................209 474-2611
Roger Vincelet, *President*
Patrick Coon, *COO*
Lou Stewell, *Senior VP*
EMP: 70
SQ FT: 12,000
SALES (est): 9.3MM **Privately Held**
SIC: **1711** Mechanical contractor

(P-2347)
SAN BENITO HTG & SHTMTL INC
Also Called: Honeywell Authorized Dealer
1771 San Felipe Rd, Hollister (95023-2543)
P.O. Box 321 (95024-0321)
PHONE..............................831 637-1112
Robert Rodriguez, *President*
Enrique T Rodriguez, *Treasurer*
Araceli Rodriguez, *Vice Pres*
Priscilla Rodriguez, *Vice Pres*
EMP: 85
SQ FT: 12,000
SALES (est): 10.4MM **Privately Held**
SIC: **1711** 1761 Warm air heating & air conditioning contractor; sheet metalwork; roofing contractor

(P-2348)
SAWYERS HEATING & AC
5272 Jerusalem Ct Ste D, Modesto (95356-9278)
PHONE..............................209 416-7700
Derek Sawyer, *President*
Weston Sawyer, *Admin Sec*
EMP: 75
SQ FT: 10,000
SALES (est): 8MM **Privately Held**
SIC: **1711** Warm air heating & air conditioning contractor

(P-2349)
SCHMIDT FIRE PROTECTION CO INC
4760 Murphy Canyon Rd # 100, San Diego (92123-4334)
PHONE..............................858 279-6122
John J Durso, *President*
Greg Konold, *Vice Pres*
Leonard Moore, *Project Mgr*
Michael Davis, *Purch Agent*
EMP: 72
SQ FT: 13,800
SALES (est): 13.1MM **Privately Held**
WEB: www.schmidtfireprotection.com
SIC: **1711** Fire sprinkler system installation

(P-2350)
SCORPIO ENTERPRISES
Also Called: Airemasters Air Conditioning
12556 Mccann Dr, Santa Fe Springs (90670-3337)
PHONE..............................562 946-9464
Charles Everett Thompson, *CEO*
Linda Thompson, *Vice Pres*
▼ EMP: 55
SQ FT: 14,800
SALES (est): 11.6MM **Privately Held**
WEB: www.airemasters-ac.com
SIC: **1711** Warm air heating & air conditioning contractor; heating & air conditioning contractors

(P-2351)
SDG ENTERPRISES
Also Called: Century West Plumbing
822 Hampshire Rd Ste H, Westlake Village (91361-2850)
PHONE..............................805 777-7978
Nick Simili, *President*
Vincent Simili, *CFO*
Vincent Dipinto, *Vice Pres*
Robert Garcia, *Vice Pres*
EMP: 100
SQ FT: 3,000
SALES (est): 14.8MM **Privately Held**
SIC: **1711** Plumbing, heating, air-conditioning contractors

(P-2352)
SEEMS PLUMBING CO INC
5400 W Rosecrans Ave Lowr, Hawthorne (90250-6686)
PHONE..............................310 297-4969
Ed Hutcherson, *President*
EMP: 50
SALES (est): 7.4MM **Privately Held**
SIC: **1711** Plumbing contractors

(P-2353)
SERVI-TECH CONTROLS INC (PA)
2612 N Bus Park Ave # 101, Fresno (93727-8661)
PHONE..............................559 264-6679

Glenn L Johnson, *President*
Janelle R Silva, *Treasurer*
Nick Johnson, *Project Mgr*
Janelle Silva, *Mktg Dir*
EMP: 53
SQ FT: 4,500
SALES (est): 11.9MM **Privately Held**
WEB: www.servi-techcontrols.com
SIC: **1711** Warm air heating & air conditioning contractor; ventilation & duct work contractor

(P-2354)
SERVICE GENIUS LOS ANGELES INC
9761 Variel Ave, Chatsworth (91311-4315)
PHONE..............................818 200-3379
William Monk, *President*
EMP: 100
SALES (est): 10MM **Privately Held**
SIC: **1711** Heating & air conditioning contractors

(P-2355)
SHELDON MECHANICAL CORPORATION
26015 Avenue Hall, Santa Clarita (91355-1241)
PHONE..............................661 286-1361
Dan Boute, *President*
Beverly Nisenson, *Treasurer*
Stanley Nisenson, *Vice Pres*
Chrystal Bout'e, *Admin Sec*
Brian Valenzuela, *Project Engr*
EMP: 80
SQ FT: 45,000
SALES (est): 19.2MM **Privately Held**
SIC: **1711** Mechanical contractor; warm air heating & air conditioning contractor

(P-2356)
SHERWOOD MECHANICAL INC
6630 Top Gun St, San Diego (92121-4112)
PHONE..............................858 679-3000
Mitch Roberts, *President*
James Robert, *COO*
Bill Smyth, *CFO*
Art Ojeda, *Risk Mgmt Dir*
Glenn Fitzgerald, *Project Mgr*
EMP: 100
SALES (est): 17.8MM **Privately Held**
WEB: www.sherwoodmechanical.com
SIC: **1711** Mechanical contractor

(P-2357)
SILICON VALLEY MECHANICAL INC
2115 Ringwood Ave, San Jose (95131-1725)
P.O. Box 10415, Southport NC (28461-0415)
PHONE..............................408 943-0380
Blaine Flickner, *CEO*
Kevin Azpeitia, *Project Mgr*
Jeff Dreyer, *Foreman/Supr*
Ricky Suess, *Warehouse Mgr*
EMP: 89
SALES (est): 35MM **Privately Held**
SIC: **1711** Mechanical contractor; heating & air conditioning contractors

(P-2358)
SKYPOWER HOLDINGS LLC
4700 Wilshire Blvd, Los Angeles (90010-3853)
PHONE..............................323 860-4900
Kerry Adler, *CEO*
AVI Shemesh, *President*
EMP: 101 EST: 2010
SALES (est): 27MM **Privately Held**
SIC: **1711** Solar energy contractor

(P-2359)
SMART ENERGY SOLAR INC
Also Called: Smart Energy USA
1641 Comm St, Corona (92880)
PHONE..............................800 405-1978
Leo Joaquin Bautista, *Principal*
EMP: 120
SALES (est): 16.9MM **Privately Held**
SIC: **1711** Solar energy contractor

P R O D U C T S & S V C S

(P-2360)
SOLAR COMPANY INC
20861 Wilbeam Ave Ste 1, Castro Valley
(94546-5832)
PHONE.................510 888-9488
Mark Danenhower, *President*
Duane Redman, *CFO*
Adrian Hirt, *Web Dvlpr*
Rachelle Houle, *Human Res Mgr*
Scott McCoy, *Sales Associate*
EMP: 90
SQ FT: 4,000
SALES: 28MM **Privately Held**
SIC: 1711 Solar energy contractor

(P-2361)
SOLAR ENERGY LLC
21600 Oxnard St Ste 1200, Woodland Hills
(91367-4949)
PHONE.................818 449-5816
EMP: 80 EST: 2009
SALES (est): 7.2MM **Privately Held**
SIC: 1711

(P-2362)
SOLAR SPECTRUM LLC
Also Called: Sungevity
150 Linden St, Oakland (94607-2538)
PHONE.................844 777-6527
Patrick McGivern, *CEO*
William Nettles, *President*
David White, *CFO*
Sloane Morgan, *Officer*
Chris Murphy, *Vice Pres*
EMP: 266
SALES (est): 6.5MM **Privately Held**
SIC: 1711 8713 Solar energy contractor;
surveying services

(P-2363)
SOLCIUS LLC
12155 Magnolia Ave 12b, Riverside
(92503-4968)
PHONE.................951 772-0030
Bryan Jackson, *Branch Mgr*
Jason Knapp, *CFO*
Sam Taggart, *Vice Pres*
Dan White, *Software Dev*
Pedro Ortega, *Opers Staff*
EMP: 330
SALES (corp-wide): 45MM **Privately
Held**
SIC: 1711 Solar energy contractor
PA: Solcius, Llc
1555 N Freedom Blvd
Provo UT 84604
800 960-4150

(P-2364)
**SOLECON INDUSTRIAL CONTRS
INC**
1401 Mcwilliams Way, Modesto
(95351-1125)
PHONE.................209 572-7390
Jeffrey Grover, *President*
Allen Layman, *Treasurer*
Elaine Grover, *Vice Pres*
Will Grover, *Vice Pres*
Dave Hedrick, *Vice Pres*
EMP: 70
SQ FT: 15,000
SALES: 15.1MM **Privately Held**
WEB: www.soleconindustrial.com
SIC: 1711 Plumbing contractors

(P-2365)
SOLEEVA ENERGY INC
1938 Junction Ave, San Jose (95131-2102)
PHONE.................408 396-4954
Ahmad Qazi, *CEO*
Ralph Ahlgren, *President*
Jeff Anderson, *Consultant*
▲ EMP: 55
SQ FT: 17,000
SALES (est): 4.4MM **Privately Held**
SIC: 1711 Solar energy contractor

(P-2366)
**SOURCE RFRGN & HVAC INC
(PA)**
800 E Orangethorpe Ave, Anaheim
(92801-1123)
PHONE.................714 578-2300
Adam Coffey, *President*
Bradley Norman Howard, *Ch of Bd*

Steve Cook, *President*
Hal Kolp, *President*
Andrew Mandell, *COO*
EMP: 250
SALES (est): 385.1MM **Privately Held**
WEB: www.sourcerefrigeration.com
SIC: 1711 1731 Refrigeration contractor;
electrical work

(P-2367)
**SOUTH CHINA SHEET METAL
INC**
Also Called: General Restaurant Equipment
1740 Albion St, Los Angeles (90031-2520)
PHONE.................323 225-1522
Kam C Law, *CEO*
T K Yeung, *Vice Pres*
Tak Yeung, *Vice Pres*
▲ EMP: 65
SQ FT: 24,000
SALES (est): 7.3MM **Privately Held**
WEB: www.generalrestaurant.com
SIC: 1711 3589 3444 Ventilation & duct
work contractor; refrigeration contractor;
commercial cooking & foodwarming
equipment; sheet metalwork

(P-2368)
**SOUTH COAST MECHANICAL
INC**
2283 E Via Burton, Anaheim (92806-1222)
PHONE.................714 738-6644
James Reynolds, *CEO*
Zoltan Bulgozdi, *President*
EMP: 75
SQ FT: 19,000
SALES (est): 23.8MM **Privately Held**
WEB: www.southcoastmechanical.com
SIC: 1711 Mechanical contractor

(P-2369)
SOUTH VALLEY PLUMBING INC
3750 Charter Park Dr F, San Jose
(95136-1394)
PHONE.................408 265-5566
Robert Walker III, *President*
EMP: 150 EST: 1960
SQ FT: 19,000
SALES (est): 9.7MM **Privately Held**
SIC: 1711 Plumbing contractors; fire sprin-
kler system installation

(P-2370)
SOUTHLAND INDUSTRIES (PA)
7390 Lincoln Way, Garden Grove
(92841-1427)
PHONE.................800 613-6240
Theodore D Lynch, *Ch of Bd*
Charles M Allen, *COO*
Chuck Allen, *COO*
Kevin J Coghlan, *CFO*
Tony SF Wang, *Treasurer*
EMP: 50
SQ FT: 9,000
SALES: 878.7MM **Privately Held**
WEB: www.southlandind.com
SIC: 1711 Plumbing, heating, air-condition-
ing contractors

(P-2371)
SOUTHLAND INDUSTRIES
12131 Western Ave, Garden Grove
(92841-2914)
PHONE.................714 901-5800
Chris Taylor, *Manager*
Lisa Starr, *Officer*
Randee Guerry, *Vice Pres*
Victor Sanvido, *Vice Pres*
Phoebe Stowe, *General Mgr*
EMP: 200
SALES (corp-wide): 878.7MM **Privately
Held**
WEB: www.southlandind.com
SIC: 1711 Plumbing, heating, air-condition-
ing contractors
PA: Southland Industries
7390 Lincoln Way
Garden Grove CA 92841
800 613-6240

(P-2372)
STERLING PLUMBING INC
3111 W Central Ave, Santa Ana
(92704-5302)
PHONE.................714 641-5480
Rodney Robbins, *President*

Leslie Schaefer, *CFO*
Kyro Hudson, *Engineer*
EMP: 100
SALES (est): 13.5MM **Privately Held**
WEB: www.sterlingplumbinginc.com
SIC: 1711 Plumbing contractors

(P-2373)
STRATEGIC MECHANICAL INC
4661 E Commerce Ave, Fresno
(93725-2204)
PHONE.................559 291-1952
Lonnie F Petty, *President*
Donn Petty, *Treasurer*
Chad Petty, *Admin Sec*
Katherine Aldrich, *Controller*
EMP: 120
SQ FT: 60,000
SALES (est): 26MM **Privately Held**
SIC: 1711 3444 3441 Mechanical con-
tractor; awnings & canopies; fabricated
structural metal

(P-2374)
SUNBELT CONTROLS INC
735 N Todd Ave, Azusa (91702-2244)
PHONE.................626 610-2340
Jim Boyd, *Branch Mgr*
John Kaasa, *Bd of Directors*
Bryan Cooper, *Regional Mgr*
Cory McKnight, *Branch Mgr*
Scott Conley, *General Mgr*
EMP: 60
SALES (corp-wide): 814.8MM **Privately
Held**
SIC: 1711 Heating & air conditioning con-
tractors
HQ: Sunbelt Controls, Inc.
6265 San Fernando Rd
Glendale CA 91201

(P-2375)
**SUNPOWER CORPORATION
SYSTEMS (DH)**
Also Called: Powerlight
1414 Harbour Way S # 1901, Richmond
(94804-3606)
P.O. Box 3821, Sunnyvale (94088-3821)
PHONE.................510 260-8200
Thomas L Dinwoodie, *CEO*
Daniel S Shugar, *President*
Peter Aschenbrenner, *Exec VP*
Lisa Bodensteiner, *Exec VP*
Charles D Boynton, *Exec VP*
◆ EMP: 100
SQ FT: 5,000
SALES (est): 66.7MM
SALES (corp-wide): 8.3B **Publicly Held**
WEB: www.powerlight.com
SIC: 1711 Solar energy contractor
HQ: Sunpower Corporation
77 Rio Robles
San Jose CA 95134
408 240-5500

(P-2376)
SUNPRO SOLAR INC
34859 Frederick St # 101, Wildomar
(92595-7007)
PHONE.................951 678-7733
Adam Joshua Evans, *President*
Jason Green, *Vice Pres*
Burke Clyne, *Project Mgr*
Bob Kornmann, *Engineer*
Jennifer Dufresne, *Controller*
EMP: 64
SQ FT: 2,300
SALES: 4.7MM **Privately Held**
WEB: www.sunpro-solar.com
SIC: 1711 Solar energy contractor

(P-2377)
**SUNRISE PLUMBING & MECH
INC**
7581 Hazard Ave Ste C, Westminster
(92683-5351)
PHONE.................562 424-0332
Richard Hubbel, *CEO*
Garnet Hubbel, *Principal*
EMP: 50
SALES (est): 6.5MM **Privately Held**
SIC: 1711 Plumbing contractors

(P-2378)
**SUNRUN INSTALLATION SVCS
INC**
575 Dado St, San Jose (95131-1207)
PHONE.................408 746-3062
EMP: 2000 **Publicly Held**
SIC: 1711 Solar energy contractor
HQ: Sunrun Installation Services Inc.
775 Fiero Ln Ste 200
San Luis Obispo CA 93401
415 580-6900

(P-2379)
**SUPERIOR AUTOMATIC
SPRNKLR CO**
4378 Enterprise St, Fremont (94538-6305)
PHONE.................408 946-7272
Bob Lawson, *President*
Peter Hulin, *President*
Marci Kearney, *Vice Pres*
EMP: 100 EST: 1973
SQ FT: 15,000
SALES: 24.5MM **Privately Held**
WEB: www.superior-fire.com
SIC: 1711 Fire sprinkler system installation

(P-2380)
**SUTTLES PLUMBING & MECH
CORP**
21541 Nordhoff St Ste C, Chatsworth
(91311-6983)
PHONE.................818 718-9779
Stephanie Aguilar, *President*
Bryan Suttles, *Vice Pres*
Stephen Suttles, *Vice Pres*
Sheralyn Suttles, *Admin Sec*
Dan Boulais, *Manager*
EMP: 75 EST: 1970
SQ FT: 6,000
SALES: 12MM **Privately Held**
SIC: 1711 Plumbing contractors; warm air
heating & air conditioning contractor

(P-2381)
TAO MECHANICAL LTD
136 Wright Brothers Ave, Livermore
(94551-9240)
PHONE.................925 447-5220
Mitchell Ibsen, *President*
EMP: 50
SQ FT: 16,250
SALES (est): 8.7MM **Privately Held**
SIC: 1711 Plumbing contractors

(P-2382)
TARPY HEATING & AIR
Also Called: Tarpy Plumbing Heating and Air
9723 Roe Dr, Santee (92071-1451)
PHONE.................619 485-3311
Paul Tarpy, *President*
Jenee Tarpy, *Treasurer*
EMP: 50 EST: 2007
SQ FT: 2,100
SALES: 3MM **Privately Held**
SIC: 1711 Warm air heating & air condi-
tioning contractor; heating & air condition-
ing contractors

(P-2383)
**TESLA ENERGY OPERATIONS
INC (HQ)**
3055 Clearview Way, San Mateo
(94402-3709)
PHONE.................650 638-1028
Elon Musk, *Ch of Bd*
Jonathan Beamer, *Chief Mktg Ofcr*
Daniel Flanigan, *Exec VP*
Paul Brandt, *Exec VP*
Bryan Ellis, *Vice Pres*
EMP: 616
SQ FT: 68,025
SALES: 730.3MM
SALES (corp-wide): 11.7B **Publicly Held**
WEB: www.solarcity.com
SIC: 1711 Solar energy contractor
PA: Tesla, Inc.
3500 Deer Creek Rd
Palo Alto CA 94304
650 681-5000

(P-2384)
THERMAL MECHANICAL
425 Aldo Ave, Santa Clara (95054-2322)
P.O. Box 4730 (95056-4730)
PHONE.................408 988-8744

Richard Rood, *CEO*
David Rood, *President*
Noel Pascual, *Officer*
Martin Burke, *Department Mgr*
Jennifer Mosher, *Administration*
EMP: 77
SQ FT: 30,000
SALES: 20.7MM **Privately Held**
WEB: www.thermalmech.com
SIC: 1711 Mechanical contractor

(P-2385)
THERMALAIR INC (HQ)
1140 N Red Gum St, Anaheim
(92806-2516)
PHONE....................714 630-3200
Stephen C Weiss, *CEO*
William Reece, *President*
Rich Perez, *Exec VP*
Theresa Bransky, *Admin Asst*
Delena Leanza, *Admin Asst*
EMP: 67 **EST:** 1948
SQ FT: 8,500
SALES (est): 10.6MM
SALES (corp-wide): 12.1MM **Privately Held**
WEB: www.thermalair.com
SIC: 1711 Heating & air conditioning contractors; ventilation & duct work contractor; refrigeration contractor
PA: General Engineering Western, Inc.
1140 N Red Gum St
Anaheim CA 92806
714 630-3200

(P-2386)
THORPE DESIGN INC
410 Beatrice St Ct Ste A, Brentwood (94513)
P.O. Box 1149 (94513-3149)
PHONE....................925 634-0787
James Thorpe, *President*
Renee Thorpe, *Treasurer*
Kim Jones, *Executive*
Corey Gray, *Department Mgr*
Juan Munguia, *Manager*
EMP: 60
SQ FT: 500
SALES (est): 13.3MM **Privately Held**
WEB: www.thorpedesign.com
SIC: 1711 Fire sprinkler system installation

(P-2387)
TITAN SOLAR CONSTRUCTION
6711 Valjean Ave, Van Nuys (91406-5819)
PHONE....................866 575-1211
Ofir Haimof, *Principal*
EMP: 188
SALES (est): 3.1MM **Privately Held**
SIC: 1711 Solar energy contractor

(P-2388)
TONOPAH SOLAR ENERGY LLC
520 Broadway Fl 6, Santa Monica (90401-2420)
PHONE....................310 315-2200
Kevin Smith,
Rosie Sandoval, *General Mgr*
▲ **EMP:** 60
SALES (est): 5.8MM **Privately Held**
SIC: 1711 Solar energy contractor

(P-2389)
TRILOGY PLUMBING INC (PA)
1525 S Sinclair St, Anaheim (92806-5934)
PHONE....................714 441-2952
Dennis Burk, *President*
Linda Burk, *Vice Pres*
Tom Price, *Vice Pres*
EMP: 250
SQ FT: 18,000
SALES (est): 34MM **Privately Held**
WEB: www.trilogyplumbing.com
SIC: 1711 Septic system construction

(P-2390)
TRUE AIR MECHANICAL INC
Also Called: True Home Heating and AC
4 Faraday, Irvine (92618-2714)
PHONE....................888 316-0642
Scott Flora, *CEO*
Mont Flora, *General Mgr*
Steve Sippola, *Sales Staff*
EMP: 180

SALES (est): 18MM **Privately Held**
SIC: 1711 Heating & air conditioning contractors

(P-2391)
UNIVERSITY MARELICH MECH INC
1000 N Kraemer Pl, Anaheim (92806-2610)
PHONE....................714 632-2600
Scott Baker, *Senior VP*
Walter S Baker, *CEO*
John R Wycoff, *CFO*
John Ellis, *Vice Pres*
EMP: 150
SQ FT: 24,384
SALES (est): 15.3MM
SALES (corp-wide): 7.6B **Publicly Held**
WEB: www.umm-inc.com
SIC: 1711 Mechanical contractor
PA: Emcor Group, Inc.
301 Merritt 7 Fl 6
Norwalk CT 06851
203 849-7800

(P-2392)
UNIVERSITY MECHANICAL & (DH)
Also Called: Spira-Loc
1168 Fesler St, El Cajon (92020-1812)
PHONE....................619 956-2500
Steve Shirley, *President*
Peter Novak, *CFO*
John Modjeski, *Senior VP*
Steve Thompson, *Vice Pres*
Jennifer Reilly, *Executive Asst*
EMP: 151
SQ FT: 47,000
SALES: 94.8MM
SALES (corp-wide): 7.6B **Publicly Held**
WEB: www.umec-ca.com
SIC: 1711 1623 8741 Mechanical contractor; plumbing contractors; warm air heating & air conditioning contractor; pipeline construction; construction management

(P-2393)
V3 ELECTRIC INC
4925 Rj Mathews Pkwy 100, El Dorado Hills (95762)
PHONE....................916 597-2627
Joshua D Collette, *CEO*
EMP: 184
SQ FT: 15,000
SALES: 23.8MM **Privately Held**
SIC: 1711 Solar energy contractor

(P-2394)
VALLEY CLARK PLBG & HTG CO INC (PA)
Also Called: Clark Plumbing Co
7640 Gloria Ave Ste L, Van Nuys (91406-1800)
PHONE....................818 782-1047
Robert J Brunald, *President*
Traci Brunald, *Vice Pres*
EMP: 100
SQ FT: 8,000
SALES (est): 15MM **Privately Held**
WEB: www.clarkplumbing.com
SIC: 1711 Plumbing contractors

(P-2395)
VALLEY PROCESS SYSTEMS INC
3567 Benton St Ste 341, Santa Clara (95051-4404)
PHONE....................408 261-1277
Kenneth D Salazar, *CEO*
EMP: 66
SQ FT: 3,200
SALES (est): 7.6MM **Privately Held**
WEB: www.valleyprocessinc.com
SIC: 1711 Process piping contractor

(P-2396)
VALS PLUMBING AND HEATING INC
413 Front St, Salinas (93901-3690)
PHONE....................831 424-1633
Ray Spears, *President*
Valerio L Roberti, *Chairman*
Laura Roberti, *Vice Pres*
Delia Morales, *Manager*

EMP: 60
SQ FT: 12,500
SALES (est): 12.5MM **Privately Held**
SIC: 1711 5999 Warm air heating & air conditioning contractor; plumbing contractors; plumbing & heating supplies

(P-2397)
VENVEST BALLARD INC
3030 Myers St, Riverside (92503-5526)
PHONE....................951 276-9744
George E Donaldson, *CEO*
George McNeil, *CFO*
EMP: 100
SALES (est): 14.7MM **Privately Held**
SIC: 1711 1731 Plumbing, heating, air-conditioning contractors; general electrical contractor

(P-2398)
VILLARA CORPORATION (PA)
Also Called: Walk Through Video
4700 Lang Ave, McClellan (95652-2023)
PHONE....................916 646-2700
Calvin Rick Wylie, *Principal*
Gary Beutler, *CEO*
Elizabeth Vande, *CFO*
Tom Beutler, *Vice Pres*
John Chanda, *Vice Pres*
▲ **EMP:** 482
SALES (est): 147.1MM **Privately Held**
WEB: www.beutlerhvac.com
SIC: 1711 Warm air heating & air conditioning contractor

(P-2399)
VILLARA CORPORATION
Also Called: Comfort Zone
9828 Bus Park Dr Ste A1, Sacramento (95827-1739)
PHONE....................916 364-9370
Gary Beutler, *Branch Mgr*
EMP: 65
SALES (corp-wide): 147.1MM **Privately Held**
SIC: 1711 Heating & air conditioning contractors
PA: Villara Corporation
4700 Lang Ave
Mcclellan CA 95652
916 646-2700

(P-2400)
VILLARA CORPORATION
Also Called: Beutler Heating & AC
332 E Wetmore St, Manteca (95337-5741)
PHONE....................209 824-1082
Glen Hartsough, *General Mgr*
Rob Penrod, *Chief Engr*
Scott Eagle, *Opers Staff*
Dave Ostrander, *Manager*
EMP: 65
SALES (corp-wide): 147.1MM **Privately Held**
WEB: www.beutlerhvac.com
SIC: 1711 Mechanical contractor
PA: Villara Corporation
4700 Lang Ave
Mcclellan CA 95652
916 646-2700

(P-2401)
VILLARA CORPORATION
Also Called: Beutler Heating & Air
4700 Lang Ave, McClellan (95652-2023)
PHONE....................916 646-2222
Dana Coates, *Branch Mgr*
EMP: 65
SALES (corp-wide): 147.1MM **Privately Held**
SIC: 1711 Plumbing, heating, air-conditioning contractors
PA: Villara Corporation
4700 Lang Ave
Mcclellan CA 95652
916 646-2700

(P-2402)
W L HICKEY SONS INC
190 Commercial St, Sunnyvale (94085-4507)
P.O. Box 61209 (94088-1209)
PHONE....................408 736-4938
Edward Hickey, *CEO*
Michael N Hickey, *President*
Ed Calcany, *CFO*

Deborah Lopez, *General Mgr*
Michelle Bogomilsky, *Project Engr*
EMP: 150 **EST:** 1904
SQ FT: 10,000
SALES (est): 26.6MM **Privately Held**
WEB: www.wlhs.com
SIC: 1711 Plumbing contractors

(P-2403)
WALTER ANDERSON PLUMBING INC
Also Called: Anderson Plbg Htg A Condition
1830 John Towers Ave, El Cajon (92020-1134)
PHONE....................619 449-7646
Mary Jean Anderson, *CEO*
Kyle Anderson, *Vice Pres*
EMP: 125
SQ FT: 10,000
SALES (est): 27.9MM **Privately Held**
WEB: www.walterandersonplumbing.com
SIC: 1711 Plumbing contractors

(P-2404)
WAYNE MAPLES PLUMBING & HTG
317 W Cedar St, Eureka (95501-1698)
PHONE....................707 445-2500
Rodney Maples, *Partner*
Dale Maples, *Partner*
Mike Maples, *Partner*
Roger Maples, *Partner*
EMP: 55 **EST:** 1960
SQ FT: 7,000
SALES (est): 6.8MM **Privately Held**
WEB: www.maplesplumb.com
SIC: 1711 1623 Plumbing contractors; warm air heating & air conditioning contractor; underground utilities contractor

(P-2405)
WEEKS DRILLING AND PUMP CO (PA)
6100 Highway 12, Sebastopol (95472)
PHONE....................707 823-3184
Chris A Thompson, *CEO*
Charles Judson, *President*
EMP: 50
SQ FT: 13,000
SALES (est): 7.9MM **Privately Held**
SIC: 1711 5251 5084 3589 Plumbing, heating, air-conditioning contractors; pumps & pumping equipment; pumps & pumping equipment; water treatment equipment, industrial; water well servicing

(P-2406)
WEST COAST AC CO INC
1155 Pioneer Way Ste 101, El Cajon (92020-1964)
PHONE....................619 561-8000
David Dudley, *CEO*
James Clower, *Vice Pres*
Colin Fisher, *Vice Pres*
EMP: 150 **EST:** 1960
SQ FT: 24,000
SALES (est): 35.5MM **Privately Held**
WEB: www.wcac.com
SIC: 1711 Warm air heating & air conditioning contractor

(P-2407)
WESTATES MECHANICAL CORP INC
734 Whitney St, San Leandro (94577-1118)
PHONE....................510 635-9830
Nigel Cowan, *CEO*
Daniel Loeffler, *Senior VP*
William Bird, *Director*
EMP: 60
SQ FT: 20,000
SALES (est): 11.5MM **Privately Held**
WEB: www.westatesmechanical.com
SIC: 1711 Fire sprinkler system installation

(P-2408)
WESTERN ALLIED MECHANICAL INC
1180 Obrien Dr, Menlo Park (94025-1411)
PHONE....................650 326-8290
Angela Simon, *CEO*
Robert Dills, *Shareholder*
Peter Kelly, *Shareholder*
Richard Taipale, *Shareholder*
James A Muscarella, *President*

EMP: 175
SALES (est): 63MM **Privately Held**
SIC: 1711 3444 Mechanical contractor; sheet metalwork

(P-2409)
WESTERN STATES FIRE PROTECTION
4740 Northgate Blvd # 150, Sacramento (95834-1150)
PHONE.....................916 924-1631
Jack White, *Manager*
EMP: 80
SALES (corp-wide): 3B **Privately Held**
SIC: 1711 Fire sprinkler system installation
HQ: Western States Fire Protection Company Inc
7026 S Tucson Way
Centennial CO 80112
303 792-0022

(P-2410)
WHOLESALE SOLAR INC
412 N Mount Shasta Blvd, Mount Shasta (96067-2232)
P.O. Box 124 (96067-0124)
PHONE.....................800 472-1142
Alexandra Coleman, *CEO*
Jeremy Allen, *COO*
Charles Hirsh, *COO*
Michael Murray, *CFO*
Judith Roda, *Officer*
▼ EMP: 52
SQ FT: 5,000
SALES: 26.7MM **Privately Held**
WEB: www.wholesalesolar.com
SIC: 1711 Solar energy contractor

(P-2411)
WILMOR & SONS PLUMBING & CNSTR
8510 Thys Ct, Sacramento (95828-1007)
PHONE.....................916 381-9114
Terry Wilson, *President*
Gary Morrissette, *CEO*
EMP: 80
SQ FT: 6,000
SALES (est): 11.1MM **Privately Held**
WEB: www.wilmorplumbing.com
SIC: 1711 Plumbing contractors

(P-2412)
XAVIER PLUMBING AND MECH INC
2606 Mira Monte Dr, San Bernardino (92405-3042)
P.O. Box 90639 (92427-1639)
PHONE.....................909 883-9426
Anthony Bowers, *CEO*
Steven Bowers, *Principal*
EMP: 52
SQ FT: 6,000
SALES (est): 319.8K **Privately Held**
SIC: 1711 Mechanical contractor

(P-2413)
XCEL MECHANICAL SYSTEMS INC
1710 W 130th St, Gardena (90249-2004)
PHONE.....................310 660-0090
Kevin Michel, *President*
EMP: 175
SQ FT: 10,000
SALES: 30.1MM **Privately Held**
WEB: www.xcelmech.com
SIC: 1711 Mechanical contractor

(P-2414)
XL FIRE PROTECTION CO (PA)
3022 N Hesperian St, Santa Ana (92706-1151)
PHONE.....................714 554-6132
Gregory J Caniglia, *President*
Laura Himmelberg, *Vice Pres*
Debra Marin, *Project Mgr*
Jose Gutierrez, *Project Engr*
Angel George, *Accountant*
EMP: 65
SQ FT: 17,000
SALES (est): 23.5MM **Privately Held**
SIC: 1711 Fire sprinkler system installation

(P-2415)
ZERO ENERGY CONTRACTING INC
13850 Cerritos Corporate, Cerritos (90703-2467)
PHONE.....................626 701-3180
Michael Murphy, *Ch of Bd*
Paul Hanson, *CEO*
Jerry Suk, *CFO*
Maria Gill, *Human Resources*
David Perzynski,
EMP: 125
SQ FT: 8,000
SALES (est): 59.9MM **Privately Held**
SIC: 1711 Solar energy contractor

(P-2416)
ZERO ENERGY CONTRACTING LLC
13850 Cerritos Corporate, Cerritos (90703-2467)
PHONE.....................626 701-3180
Michael Murphy,
Brian Richwien, *Warehouse Mgr*
EMP: 93
SALES (est): 7.6MM **Privately Held**
SIC: 1711 Solar energy contractor

1721 Painting & Paper Hanging Contractors

(P-2417)
A-1 ELITE PAINTING INC
56409 Yuma Trl, Yucca Valley (92284-3614)
PHONE.....................760 365-6702
Charles Soffel, *President*
Ted Decicco, *Partner*
Glen Soffel, *Partner*
John Wright, *Partner*
Sharon Soffel, *Corp Secy*
EMP: 50
SALES: 2MM **Privately Held**
SIC: 1721 Painting & paper hanging

(P-2418)
ADVANCED INDUSTRIAL SVCS INC
Also Called: Advanced Industrial Svcs Cal
7831 Alondra Blvd, Paramount (90723-5005)
PHONE.....................562 940-8305
Rex Johnston Jr, *President*
EMP: 85
SALES (est): 13.3MM **Privately Held**
SIC: 1721 Industrial painting

(P-2419)
ADVANTAGE PNTG SOLUTIONS INC
14734 Yorba Ct, Chino (91710-9210)
PHONE.....................951 739-9204
Anthony Trujillo, *CEO*
Shevon Gonzales, *CFO*
EMP: 60
SALES: 3MM **Privately Held**
SIC: 1721 Commercial painting

(P-2420)
ANNA CORPORATION
Also Called: Jfp Company
2078 2nd St, Norco (92860-2804)
PHONE.....................951 736-6037
Anna L Degiacomo, *President*
Jaime Flores, *Vice Pres*
Luis Tull, *Project Mgr*
EMP: 50
SQ FT: 6,500
SALES (est): 2.9MM **Privately Held**
SIC: 1721 Commercial painting

(P-2421)
ARCHITECTURAL COATINGS INC
1565 E Edinger Ave, Santa Ana (92705-4907)
PHONE.....................714 701-1360
Sally K Rimmer, *President*
EMP: 50
SALES (est): 4.5MM **Privately Held**
SIC: 1721 Residential painting; commercial painting

(P-2422)
ARENA PAINTING CONTRACTORS INC
525 E Alondra Blvd, Gardena (90248-2903)
PHONE.....................310 316-2446
Wilson Grant, *CEO*
Guy Grant II, *President*
EMP: 100
SQ FT: 10,000
SALES (est): 12.7MM **Privately Held**
SIC: 1721 Commercial painting

(P-2423)
ARMSTRONG INSTALLATION SERVICE
Also Called: Armstrong Construction Co
4575 San Pablo Ave, Emeryville (94608-3325)
PHONE.....................408 777-1234
Mitchell Fine, *CEO*
Arthur Levine, *CFO*
EMP: 75
SQ FT: 8,000
SALES (est): 7.8MM **Privately Held**
WEB: www.armstrong1234.com
SIC: 1721 1761 1793 Exterior residential painting contractor; interior residential painting contractor; exterior commercial painting contractor; interior commercial painting contractor; roofing, siding & sheet metal work; glass & glazing work

(P-2424)
BORBON INCORPORATED
7312 Walnut Ave, Buena Park (90620-1760)
PHONE.....................714 994-0170
David Morales, *President*
EMP: 120
SQ FT: 7,400
SALES (est): 11.4MM **Privately Held**
WEB: www.borbon.net
SIC: 1721 Exterior residential painting contractor; wallcovering contractors

(P-2425)
C & O PAINTING INC
1500 N 4th St, San Jose (95112-4606)
PHONE.....................408 279-8011
Rick Ohlund, *President*
EMP: 50
SQ FT: 6,000
SALES (est): 4.3MM **Privately Held**
WEB: www.candopainting.com
SIC: 1721 Exterior commercial painting contractor; commercial wallcovering contractor

(P-2426)
C B B Z S INC
Also Called: Shapiro Ben Basat Painting
7015 Valjean Ave, Van Nuys (91406-3915)
PHONE.....................818 908-1900
Zvi Shapiro, *President*
Chaim B Basat, *Treasurer*
Raz Bronstein, *Project Mgr*
EMP: 55
SQ FT: 5,500
SALES (est): 3.7MM **Privately Held**
SIC: 1721 Interior commercial painting contractor

(P-2427)
CAL/PAC PAINTINGS & COATINGS
608 N Eckhoff St, Orange (92868-1004)
PHONE.....................714 628-1514
Dave Bedillion, *President*
Mike Stevenson, *CFO*
Lee Ann Green, *Controller*
EMP: 60
SQ FT: 2,000
SALES (est): 5.5MM **Privately Held**
WEB: www.calpacpainting.com
SIC: 1721 Residential painting

(P-2428)
CERTIFIED COATINGS COMPANY
2320 Cordelia Rd, Fairfield (94534-1600)
PHONE.....................707 639-4414
David Joseph Brockman, *CEO*
William Powell, *Vice Pres*
Pamela Langan, *Admin Sec*

EMP: 100
SQ FT: 8,000
SALES (est): 27.5MM
SALES (corp-wide): 292.1MM **Privately Held**
SIC: 1721 Industrial painting
PA: Muehlhan Ag
Schlinckstr. 3
Hamburg 21107
407 527-10

(P-2429)
CRAMER PAINTING INC
4080 Mission Blvd, Montclair (91763-6011)
PHONE.....................909 397-5770
Steven L Cramer, *President*
Anne McWeeney, *Admin Sec*
EMP: 50
SQ FT: 6,800
SALES (est): 3.6MM **Privately Held**
WEB: www.cramerpainting.com
SIC: 1721 Commercial painting

(P-2430)
D C VIENT INC (PA)
1556 Cummins Dr, Modesto (95358-6412)
P.O. Box D (95352-3668)
PHONE.....................209 578-1224
Darlene Vient, *President*
Danielle Bell, *Shareholder*
Douglas J Vient Jr, *Corp Secy*
Douglas C Vient, *Vice Pres*
Alex Rowell, *Manager*
EMP: 300
SQ FT: 12,000
SALES (est): 21.7MM **Privately Held**
WEB: www.dcvient.com
SIC: 1721 Commercial painting

(P-2431)
D P S INC
Also Called: Empire Community Painting
1682 Langley Ave, Irvine (92614-5620)
PHONE.....................714 564-7900
Jason Reid, *President*
Tracy Meneses, *CFO*
Jeff Gunhus, *Vice Pres*
Matt Stewart, *Vice Pres*
Spencer Pepe, *Admin Sec*
EMP: 91
SQ FT: 1,000
SALES: 2.8MM **Privately Held**
WEB: www.nsgmail.com
SIC: 1721 Painting & paper hanging
PA: National Services Group, Inc.
1682 Langley Ave
Irvine CA 92614

(P-2432)
DAPCON INC
877 Commercial St, San Jose (95112-1411)
PHONE.....................408 573-7200
Fernando Silva, *President*
Albert Gomes, *Vice Pres*
Lucia Silva, *Vice Pres*
EMP: 80
SQ FT: 6,000
SALES (est): 3.4MM **Privately Held**
WEB: www.dapconinc.com
SIC: 1721 1742 Residential painting; commercial painting; drywall

(P-2433)
DUGGAN & ASSOCIATES INC
1442 W 135th St, Gardena (90249-2218)
PHONE.....................323 965-1502
Chris M Duggan, *President*
◆ EMP: 65
SQ FT: 10,000
SALES (est): 7.9MM **Privately Held**
SIC: 1721 Interior commercial painting contractor; commercial wallcovering contractor

(P-2434)
EMPCC INC
Also Called: Empire Community Painting
1682 Langley Ave Fl 2, Irvine (92614-5620)
PHONE.....................714 564-7900
Jason Reid, *President*
Tracy Meneses, *CFO*
Jeff Gunhus, *Vice Pres*
Matt Stewart, *Vice Pres*
Spencer Pepe, *Admin Sec*

EMP: 59
SQ FT: 1,000
SALES: 1.1MM **Privately Held**
SIC: 1721 Painting & paper hanging
PA: Mjp Empire, Inc.
1682 Langley Ave Fl 2
Irvine CA 92614

(P-2435)
EUROPEAN PAVING DESIGNS INC
1474 Berger Dr, San Jose (95112-2701)
PHONE...................................408 283-5230
Randy Hays, *CEO*
Robyn Cerutti, *CFO*
Ismael Cortez, *Admin Asst*
Liz Schooler, *Administration*
Denton Bullard, *Project Engr*
EMP: 55
SQ FT: 3,000
SALES (est): 6.3MM **Privately Held**
SIC: 1721 Pavement marking contractor

(P-2436)
FREEDOM PAINTING INC
8822 Calmada Ave, Whittier (90605-2006)
PHONE...................................562 696-0785
Gerald Lundgren, *President*
Roselina Lundgren, *Corp Secy*
Beverly Lundgren, *Vice Pres*
Darren Lundgren, *Supervisor*
EMP: 50
SQ FT: 8,000
SALES: 4MM **Privately Held**
SIC: 1721 Residential painting

(P-2437)
GENERAL COATINGS CORPORATION
9349 Feron Blvd, Rancho Cucamonga (91730-4516)
PHONE...................................909 204-4150
Craig Kinsman, *Owner*
EMP: 250
SALES (corp-wide): 86.2MM **Privately Held**
SIC: 1721 Painting & paper hanging
PA: General Coatings Corporation
6711 Nancy Ridge Dr
San Diego CA 92121
858 587-1277

(P-2438)
GENERAL COATINGS CORPORATION
600 W Freedom Ave, Orange (92865-2537)
PHONE...................................858 587-1277
Craig Kinsman, *Branch Mgr*
EMP: 250
SQ FT: 7,047
SALES (corp-wide): 86.2MM **Privately Held**
WEB: www.gencoat.com
SIC: 1721 Painting & paper hanging
PA: General Coatings Corporation
6711 Nancy Ridge Dr
San Diego CA 92121
858 587-1277

(P-2439)
GENERAL COATINGS CORPORATION (PA)
6711 Nancy Ridge Dr, San Diego (92121-2231)
PHONE...................................858 587-1277
Craig A Kinsman, *CEO*
Andrew Fluken, *Vice Pres*
Hector Cueva, *Project Mgr*
Gary Vittori, *Project Mgr*
EMP: 250
SQ FT: 14,000
SALES (est): 86.2MM **Privately Held**
WEB: www.gencoat.com
SIC: 1721 1799 Painting & paper hanging; waterproofing

(P-2440)
GENERAL COATINGS CORPORATION
1220 E North Ave, Fresno (93725-1930)
PHONE...................................559 495-4004
Lee Morrison, *Principal*
EMP: 250

SALES (corp-wide): 86.2MM **Privately Held**
SIC: 1721 1799 Painting & paper hanging; coating of concrete structures with plastic
PA: General Coatings Corporation
6711 Nancy Ridge Dr
San Diego CA 92121
858 587-1277

(P-2441)
GEORGE E MASKER INC
Also Called: Masker Painting
7699 Edgewater Dr, Oakland (94621-3028)
PHONE...................................510 568-1206
Alan Bjerke, *President*
Claudia Ornelas, *Administration*
Dennis Gilreath, *Project Mgr*
Matt Johnson, *Project Mgr*
Newt Millward, *Project Mgr*
EMP: 100
SQ FT: 18,000
SALES (est): 9.1MM **Privately Held**
WEB: www.maskerpainting.com
SIC: 1721 Exterior commercial painting contractor; interior commercial painting contractor

(P-2442)
GIAMPOLINI & CO
Also Called: Giampolini/Courtney
1482 67th St, Emeryville (94608-1016)
PHONE...................................415 673-1236
Greg Quilici, *President*
Patrick Roland, *CFO*
Tom Quilici, *Vice Pres*
James Patrick Roland, *Principal*
EMP: 225
SQ FT: 9,720
SALES (est): 20MM **Privately Held**
WEB: www.giampolini.com
SIC: 1721 1542 1742 Exterior commercial painting contractor; interior commercial painting contractor; commercial & office buildings, renovation & repair; plastering, drywall & insulation

(P-2443)
GOLD COAST DESIGN INC
7667 Vickers St, San Diego (92111-1525)
PHONE...................................619 574-0111
David L Gash, *CEO*
Kathleen Gash, *Vice Pres*
EMP: 80
SQ FT: 7,331
SALES (est): 6.7MM **Privately Held**
SIC: 1721 Residential painting

(P-2444)
GONZALES PAINTING CORP
14437 Meridian Pkwy, Riverside (92518-3007)
PHONE...................................951 214-6400
John J Gonzales, *President*
EMP: 90
SALES (est): 3.1MM **Privately Held**
SIC: 1721 Interior residential painting contractor; exterior residential painting contractor; interior commercial painting contractor; exterior commercial painting contractor

(P-2445)
GPS PAINTING WALLCOVERING INC
1307 E Saint Gertrude Pl C, Santa Ana (92705-5228)
PHONE...................................714 730-8904
Eliot Schneider, *President*
David Cuevas, *Project Mgr*
Ed Lares, *Project Mgr*
EMP: 110
SALES (est): 9.6MM **Privately Held**
WEB: www.gpspainting.com
SIC: 1721 Painting & paper hanging

(P-2446)
HARRIS & RUTH PAINTING CONTG (PA)
2107 W San Bernardino Rd, West Covina (91790-1007)
PHONE...................................626 960-4004
Terry Cairy, *President*
Mark Heydorff, *COO*
Bruce Boyer, *VP Sales*
EMP: 82 EST: 1970
SQ FT: 1,000

SALES: 10.4MM **Privately Held**
WEB: www.harris-ruthpainting.com
SIC: 1721 Exterior commercial painting contractor; industrial painting

(P-2447)
J C FRENCH & COMPANY
2984 1st St Ste L, La Verne (91750-5675)
PHONE...................................909 596-1423
Sandra Perry, *President*
John C French, *CFO*
Robert French, *Corp Secy*
August Jacobson, *Senior VP*
EMP: 60 EST: 1977
SQ FT: 12,000
SALES (est): 4.8MM **Privately Held**
WEB: www.jcfrench.com
SIC: 1721 Residential painting

(P-2448)
J M V B INC
Also Called: Spc Building Services
12118 Severn Way, Riverside (92503-4804)
P.O. Box 614, Orange (92856-6614)
PHONE...................................714 288-9797
Benjamin J Rodriguez, *President*
EMP: 80 EST: 1993
SALES (est): 4.8MM **Privately Held**
SIC: 1721 Painting & paper hanging

(P-2449)
J P CARROLL CO INC
5707 Milton Ave, Whittier (90601-2420)
PHONE...................................323 660-9230
H B Fitzpatrick, *Ch of Bd*
Kevin Fitzpatrick, *President*
Rebecca Derry, *Vice Pres*
Barbara Fitzpatrick, *Admin Sec*
EMP: 60
SQ FT: 25,000
SALES (est): 2.6MM **Privately Held**
WEB: www.jpcarrollco.com
SIC: 1721 Residential painting; commercial painting; wallcovering contractors

(P-2450)
JD MILLER CONSTRUCTION INC
506 W Graham Ave Ste 202, Lake Elsinore (92530-3600)
PHONE...................................951 471-3513
Jeff Mosher, *CEO*
Jeffery D Miller, *President*
EMP: 50
SALES (est): 7.2MM **Privately Held**
SIC: 1721 Painting & paper hanging

(P-2451)
JEFFCO PAINTING & COATING INC
1260 Railroad Ave, Vallejo (94592-1012)
P.O. Box 1888 (94590-0655)
PHONE...................................707 562-1900
Steve Jeffress, *President*
Gene Glockner, *CFO*
Todd Anderson, *Vice Pres*
Paul Schoep, *Project Mgr*
Jacki Matejka, *Human Res Mgr*
EMP: 100 EST: 1978
SALES (est): 11.4MM **Privately Held**
WEB: www.jeffcoptg.com
SIC: 1721 3471 Industrial painting; sand blasting of metal parts

(P-2452)
JERRY THOMPSON & SONS PNTG INC
3 Simms St, San Rafael (94901-5414)
PHONE...................................415 454-1500
Stephen G Thompson, *President*
Dennis J Thompson, *Corp Secy*
Luke Thompson, *Division Mgr*
Tim Sasan, *Project Mgr*
Bob Williams, *Opers Mgr*
EMP: 140
SALES (est): 13.8MM **Privately Held**
SIC: 1721 Residential painting

(P-2453)
JOHNSON & TURNER PAINTING CO
8241 Electric Ave, Stanton (90680-2640)
PHONE...................................714 828-8282
Dale Bodwell, *President*

▲ EMP: 50 EST: 1955
SQ FT: 6,000
SALES: 4.1MM **Privately Held**
SIC: 1721 Residential painting

(P-2454)
LAWRENCE B BONAS COMPANY
3197 Arprt Loop Dr Ste C, Costa Mesa (92626)
PHONE...................................714 668-5250
Guy A Bonas, *President*
Doris A Bonas, *Treasurer*
EMP: 75
SQ FT: 7,200
SALES (est): 4.9MM **Privately Held**
SIC: 1721 Wallcovering contractors

(P-2455)
LIVING COLORS INC
16026 Rayen St, North Hills (91343-4814)
PHONE...................................818 893-5068
Raymond Sponsler, *President*
Paula Sponsler, *Treasurer*
Daniel Barton, *Sales Executive*
EMP: 60
SALES (est): 3.9MM **Privately Held**
WEB: www.livingcolorsinc.com
SIC: 1721 Residential painting

(P-2456)
M C BUILDER CORP
1251 Montalvo Way Ste L, Palm Springs (92262-5497)
PHONE...................................760 323-8010
Ernest Castro, *Owner*
EMP: 50
SQ FT: 2,800
SALES (est): 3.4MM **Privately Held**
SIC: 1721 Commercial painting; residential painting

(P-2457)
MEYER COATINGS INC
1844 W Bus Ctr Dr Ornge, Orange (92867)
PHONE...................................714 467-4600
Diana Meyer, *CEO*
Scott Meyer, *President*
Veronica Santoyo, *Vice Pres*
Kylie Suica, *Admin Asst*
John Beltran, *Project Mgr*
EMP: 50
SQ FT: 4,800
SALES (est): 6MM **Privately Held**
WEB: www.meyercoatings.com
SIC: 1721 Commercial painting

(P-2458)
MICKEY WALL PAINTING INC
250 East Ave, Turlock (95380-4941)
P.O. Box 3302 (95381-3302)
PHONE...................................209 669-0557
Mickey Wall, *President*
Kathy Wall, *CFO*
EMP: 50
SQ FT: 6,000
SALES (est): 3.7MM **Privately Held**
WEB: www.mickeywallpainting.com
SIC: 1721 Residential painting; exterior residential painting contractor; interior residential painting contractor

(P-2459)
MIKE CHAMPLIN
Also Called: Mike Champlin Painting
4374 Contractors Cmn, Livermore (94551-7544)
PHONE...................................925 961-1004
Mike Champlin, *Owner*
EMP: 100
SALES (est): 6MM **Privately Held**
SIC: 1721 Painting & paper hanging

(P-2460)
MJP EMPIRE INC (PA)
1682 Langley Ave Fl 2, Irvine (92614-5620)
PHONE...................................714 564-7900
Jason Reid, *President*
Tracy Meneses, *CFO*
Jeff Gunhus, *Vice Pres*
Matt Stewart, *Vice Pres*
Spencer Pepe, *Admin Sec*
EMP: 300
SALES (est): 5.8MM **Privately Held**
SIC: 1721 Painting & paper hanging

(P-2461)
NORCAL PAINTERS INC
Also Called: Certapro Painters
60 29th St 241, San Francisco
(94110-4929)
PHONE..................415 566-6800
Terrance Ladd, *President*
George Irving, *General Mgr*
EMP: 53
SALES (est): 2.8MM **Privately Held**
SIC: 1721 Residential painting

(P-2462)
NORTH ORANGE COAST PNTG INC
3969 Sierra Ave, Norco (92860-1390)
P.O. Box 520 (92860-0520)
PHONE..................951 279-2694
Fax: 951 279-9510
EMP: 100
SALES (est): 5MM **Privately Held**
SIC: 1721

(P-2463)
P B C PAVERS INC
Also Called: Peterson Bros Construction
1560 W Lambert Rd, Brea (92821-2826)
PHONE..................714 278-0488
Robert Peterson, *President*
Valerie Payne, *CFO*
Eldin Peterson, *Vice Pres*
Orlando Davila, *General Mgr*
Jeff Grise, *Project Mgr*
▲ EMP: 80
SALES (est): 7.4MM **Privately Held**
SIC: 1721 Pavement marking contractor

(P-2464)
PETERSON PAINTING INC
5750 La Ribera St, Livermore
(94550-9204)
PHONE..................925 455-5864
Raymond Peterson, *President*
John Peterson, *Vice Pres*
Kyle Peterson, *Opers Mgr*
EMP: 350
SQ FT: 10,000
SALES (est): 17.4MM **Privately Held**
WEB: www.petersonpainting.com
SIC: 1721 Residential painting

(P-2465)
PILOT PAINTING & CONSTRUCTION
5555 Corporate Ave, Cypress
(90630-4708)
P.O. Box 6377, Anaheim (92816-0377)
PHONE..................714 229-5900
Steve Gilkey, *President*
EMP: 60
SQ FT: 7,856
SALES (est): 3.3MM **Privately Held**
SIC: 1721 Residential painting

(P-2466)
PRIMECO PAINTING & CNSTR
220 Oceanside Blvd, Oceanside
(92054-4903)
PHONE..................760 967-8278
Brett Musgrove, *President*
Stacey Musgrove, *Admin Sec*
EMP: 90
SQ FT: 2,100
SALES (est): 8.4MM **Privately Held**
WEB: www.primecopainting.com
SIC: 1721 1542 Residential painting; commercial & office building contractors

(P-2467)
PS2 (PA)
17903 S Hobart Blvd, Gardena
(90248-3613)
PHONE..................310 243-2980
Peter Schmit, *President*
Peter Short, *Admin Sec*
Ryan Webb, *Project Mgr*
John Schmit, *VP Opers*
EMP: 68
SQ FT: 2,000
SALES (est): 11.6MM **Privately Held**
SIC: 1721 Residential painting

(P-2468)
PYRAMID PAINTING INC
2925 Bayview Dr, Fremont (94538-6520)
PHONE..................650 903-9791
Craig Ruybalid, *President*
EMP: 50
SQ FT: 6,240
SALES (est): 4.2MM **Privately Held**
WEB: www.pyramidpainting.com
SIC: 1721 Exterior commercial painting contractor; interior commercial painting contractor

(P-2469)
R & A PAINTING INC
11730 Sheldon Lake Dr, Elk Grove
(95624-9649)
P.O. Box 292730, Sacramento (95829-2730)
PHONE..................916 688-3955
Antonio Rodrigues, *President*
Cidalia Rodrigues, *Corp Secy*
EMP: 60
SALES (est): 2.5MM **Privately Held**
SIC: 1721 Commercial painting; residential painting

(P-2470)
R-BROS PAINTING INC
707 W Hedding St, San Jose (95110-1533)
PHONE..................408 291-6820
Rod Rodriquez, *President*
Paulina Tran, *Office Mgr*
Scott Allen, *Accounting Mgr*
▲ EMP: 50
SQ FT: 3,000
SALES (est): 5.2MM **Privately Held**
WEB: www.rbrothers.com
SIC: 1721 Commercial painting

(P-2471)
RANDALL MC-ANANY COMPANY
4935 Mcconnell Ave Ste 20, Los Angeles
(90066-6756)
PHONE..................310 822-3344
Timothy Mc Anany, *President*
Nancy Mc Anany, *Corp Secy*
Karl Keeney, *Exec VP*
Priscilla Dipierro, *Admin Asst*
Bill Dinh, *Project Mgr*
EMP: 60
SQ FT: 8,500
SALES (est): 5.5MM **Privately Held**
WEB: www.rmcompany.com
SIC: 1721 Commercial painting; commercial wallcovering contractor

(P-2472)
RC WENDT PAINTING INC
21612 Surveyor Cir, Huntington Beach
(92646-7068)
PHONE..................714 960-2700
Robert C Wendt, *President*
Jeri Wendt, *Corp Secy*
Scott Wendt, *Vice Pres*
EMP: 110 EST: 1980
SALES (est): 7.7MM **Privately Held**
WEB: www.wendtcompanies.com
SIC: 1721 Residential painting; commercial painting

(P-2473)
REDWOOD PAINTING CO INC
620 W 10th St, Pittsburg (94565-1806)
P.O. Box 1269 (94565-0126)
PHONE..................925 432-4500
Charles Duke Del Monte, *CEO*
George Del Monte, *Exec VP*
George D Monte, *Exec VP*
EMP: 110
SQ FT: 19,000
SALES (est): 27.7MM **Privately Held**
WEB: www.redwoodptg.com
SIC: 1721 Commercial painting; industrial painting

(P-2474)
RJP CONSTRUCTION & PAINTING (PA)
22600 Lambert St Ste 807, Lake Forest
(92630-1620)
PHONE..................949 707-5449
Raymond J Puzio, *President*
▲ EMP: 100
SQ FT: 2,400

SALES: 9.1MM **Privately Held**
WEB: www.rjpinc.net
SIC: 1721 Residential painting; commercial painting

(P-2475)
ROBERT MEUSCHKE COMPANY INC
Also Called: RMC Painting & Restoration
1039 Edwards Rd, Burlingame
(94010-2318)
PHONE..................650 342-3993
Bob Meuschke, *President*
Andy Smith, *Admin Sec*
EMP: 50
SQ FT: 1,200
SALES (est): 2.4MM **Privately Held**
WEB: www.rmcpainting.com
SIC: 1721 Exterior commercial painting contractor; interior commercial painting contractor

(P-2476)
RODIN & CO INC
7411 Laurel Canyon Blvd # 10, North Hollywood (91605-3160)
PHONE..................818 358-3427
Fred Rodin, *President*
Rowena Rodin, *Admin Sec*
EMP: 50
SQ FT: 4,400
SALES (est): 2.7MM **Privately Held**
WEB: www.rodincompany.com
SIC: 1721 Wallcovering contractors

(P-2477)
RTE ENTERPRISES INC
Also Called: Color Concepts
21530 Roscoe Blvd, Canoga Park
(91304-4144)
PHONE..................818 999-5300
Ron Evenhaim, *President*
EMP: 100
SQ FT: 2,000
SALES (est): 5.3MM **Privately Held**
WEB: www.colorconcepts.net
SIC: 1721 1742 Painting & paper hanging; plastering, drywall & insulation

(P-2478)
S W P T X INC
Also Called: Student Works Painting
1682 Langley Ave, Irvine (92614-5620)
PHONE..................714 564-7900
Matthew Stewart, *President*
EMP: 120
SALES (est): 2.8MM **Privately Held**
WEB: www.nsgmail.com
SIC: 1721 Painting & paper hanging
PA: National Services Group, Inc.
    1682 Langley Ave
    Irvine CA 92614
    -

(P-2479)
SANDERS & WOHRMAN CORPORATION
709 N Poplar St, Orange (92868-1013)
PHONE..................714 919-0446
John Thomas Wohrman, *Principal*
Todd Wohrman, *Treasurer*
Ray Wohrman, *Project Mgr*
Ron Edmonds, *Superintendent*
EMP: 150
SQ FT: 12,000
SALES (est): 18.1MM **Privately Held**
WEB: www.swpainting.com
SIC: 1721 Residential painting; industrial painting

(P-2480)
SCHAPER CONSTRUCTION INC (PA)
1177 N 15th St, San Jose (95112-1422)
PHONE..................408 437-0337
Leon Schaper, *CEO*
Curtis Schaper, *Vice Pres*
Greg Sipe, *General Mgr*
Jina Duncan, *Executive Asst*
Mark Scanlon, *Project Mgr*
EMP: 90
SQ FT: 8,400

SALES (est): 31.1MM **Privately Held**
WEB: www.schaperco.com
SIC: 1721 1611 1542 Exterior residential painting contractor; interior residential painting contractor; general contractor, highway & street construction; nonresidential construction

(P-2481)
SIGNATURE PAINTING & CNSTR INC
1565 3rd Ave, Walnut Creek (94597-2604)
PHONE..................925 287-0444
Brian Mitchell, *President*
Erik Oller, *Vice Pres*
Christian Cupolo, *Project Mgr*
Mike Witter, *Manager*
Charlie Johnson, *Superintendent*
EMP: 50
SALES (est): 6.3MM **Privately Held**
SIC: 1721 Painting & paper hanging

(P-2482)
SOCAL COATINGS INC
2820 Via Orange Way Ste J, Spring Valley
(91978-1742)
PHONE..................619 660-5395
Norma Alicia Alonso, *CEO*
John Thomas Fox, *Vice Pres*
EMP: 50
SALES (est): 2.7MM **Privately Held**
SIC: 1721 Residential painting

(P-2483)
STEGER INC
1938 N Batavia St Ste L, Orange
(92865-4140)
PHONE..................714 974-4383
Michael Steger, *President*
EMP: 50
SALES (est): 3.8MM **Privately Held**
WEB: www.steger.com
SIC: 1721 Residential painting; commercial painting

(P-2484)
STEVE BEATTIE INC
Also Called: Steve Beattie Painting
1766 Westridge Rd, Los Angeles
(90049-2516)
PHONE..................310 454-1786
Steve Beattie, *President*
Patricia H McGuire, *CEO*
EMP: 60 EST: 1986
SALES (est): 2.5MM **Privately Held**
SIC: 1721 Residential painting

(P-2485)
STUDENT WORKS PAINTING INC
1682 Langley Ave, Irvine (92614-5620)
PHONE..................714 564-7900
Spencer Pepe, *President*
Mathew Stewart, *Treasurer*
Matthew Stewart, *Treasurer*
Matthew Landauer, *Vice Pres*
Matthew Landauer, *Vice Pres*
EMP: 300
SALES (est): 6.7MM **Privately Held**
WEB: www.nsgmail.com
SIC: 1721 Residential painting
PA: National Services Group, Inc.
    1682 Langley Ave
    Irvine CA 92614

(P-2486)
T & R PAINTING CONSTRUCTION
7116 Valjean Ave, Van Nuys (91406-3901)
PHONE..................818 779-3800
Robin Rapaport, *President*
EMP: 110
SALES (est): 4.6MM **Privately Held**
WEB: www.tandrweb.com
SIC: 1721 Residential painting; commercial painting

(P-2487)
TRANS WORLD MAINTENANCE INC
Also Called: S A S
1590 Rollins Rd, Millbrae (94030)
PHONE..................650 455-2450
Theodore Siotos, *President*
Ted Siotos, *Vice Pres*

Costandinos Siotos, *Principal*
Alexandra Siotos, *Admin Sec*
EMP: 71
SQ FT: 5,700
SALES: 772.7K **Privately Held**
SIC: 1721 8742 1542 Residential painting; construction project management consultant; commercial & office buildings, renovation & repair

(P-2488)
TWI- TECHNO WEST INC
1391 S Allec St, Anaheim (92805-6304)
PHONE......................714 635-4070
Marcia Birney, *Chairman*
EMP: 85
SQ FT: 30,000
SALES (est): 4.1MM **Privately Held**
WEB: www.multipleplantservices.com
SIC: 1721 Commercial painting

(P-2489)
URBAN PAINTING INC
40 Lisbon St, San Rafael (94901-4709)
PHONE......................415 485-1130
Michael James Urban, *President*
Robert S Urban, *Shareholder*
James De Martini, *Vice Pres*
Chris Urban, *Vice Pres*
Martin Flores, *Human Res Mgr*
EMP: 60
SQ FT: 6,000
SALES (est): 4.9MM **Privately Held**
WEB: www.urbanco.com
SIC: 1721 Commercial painting; residential painting

(P-2490)
VERTEX COATINGS INC
1291 W State St, Ontario (91762-4015)
PHONE......................909 923-5795
Russ Phillips, *President*
Stacy Phillips, *Executive*
Randy Phillips, *Project Mgr*
EMP: 70
SQ FT: 11,000
SALES: 9.7MM **Privately Held**
WEB: www.vertexcoatings.com
SIC: 1721 Commercial painting

(P-2491)
WEST COAST INTERIORS INC
Also Called: West Coast Painting
1610 W Linden St, Riverside (92507-6810)
PHONE......................951 778-3592
Mark Herbert, *CEO*
Dan Slavin, *President*
Santos Garcia, *COO*
Keith Caneva, *Controller*
Colleen Butler, *Human Resources*
EMP: 600
SQ FT: 8,000
SALES (est): 39.6MM **Privately Held**
SIC: 1721 Wallcovering contractors

(P-2492)
WILLIAM M PERKINS COMPANY INC (PA)
Also Called: Perkins Pntg & Cstm Coatings
3148 Market St, San Diego (92102-3232)
PHONE......................619 236-0343
Paul Frankel, *President*
Jim Perkins, *Vice Pres*
Lori Wright, *Vice Pres*
EMP: 50
SQ FT: 2,500
SALES (est): 5.2MM **Privately Held**
SIC: 1721 Residential painting

(P-2493)
WILSON HAMPTON PNTG CONTRS INC
1524 W Mable St, Anaheim (92802-1097)
P.O. Box 9949 (92812-7949)
PHONE......................714 772-5091
Doug Hampton, *President*
Douglas J Hampton, *President*
Clifford C Hampton, *Vice Pres*
Robert D Hampton III, *Admin Sec*
EMP: 60
SQ FT: 44,000
SALES (est): 6.9MM **Privately Held**
WEB: www.wilsonhampton.com
SIC: 1721 7641 Residential painting; furniture repair & maintenance; office furniture repair & maintenance

(P-2494)
WM B SALEH CO
1364 N Jackson Ave, Fresno (93703-4624)
PHONE......................559 255-2046
Mark Saleh, *President*
Katherine Brusellas, *Corp Secy*
William B Saleh, *Vice Pres*
Connie York, *Admin Asst*
Dorothy Rivera, *Bookkeeper*
EMP: 75 **EST:** 1959
SQ FT: 6,800
SALES (est): 3.8MM **Privately Held**
SIC: 1721 Commercial painting; industrial painting; commercial wallcovering contractor

1731 Electrical Work

(P-2495)
A M ORTEGA CONSTRUCTION INC (PA)
Also Called: Western Rim Pipeline
10125 Channel Rd, Lakeside (92040-1703)
PHONE......................619 390-1988
Archie Maurice Ortega, *President*
Randy Michael, *Division Mgr*
Linda Ortega, *Admin Sec*
EMP: 110 **EST:** 1974
SQ FT: 10,000
SALES (est): 47.7MM **Privately Held**
WEB: www.amortega.com
SIC: 1731 Electrical work

(P-2496)
A-1 ELECTRIC SERVICE CO INC
4204 Sepulveda Blvd, Culver City (90230-4709)
P.O. Box 6453, Malibu (90264-6453)
PHONE......................310 204-1077
Linda Pieper, *CEO*
Scott Pieper, *Vice Pres*
Eric Cashman, *Technology*
EMP: 50
SQ FT: 5,000
SALES (est): 13.1MM **Privately Held**
WEB: www.a-1electric.com
SIC: 1731 Electrical work

(P-2497)
A-C ELECTRIC COMPANY (PA)
Also Called: AUTOMATED CONTROLS AND TECHNIC
2921 Hanger Way, Bakersfield (93308-1643)
P.O. Box 81977 (93380-1977)
PHONE......................661 410-0000
Thomas J Alexander, *Ch of Bd*
Daren T Alexander, *President*
Thomas P Zauder, *CFO*
David M Morton, *Exec VP*
David Morton, *Vice Pres*
EMP: 300 **EST:** 1945
SQ FT: 10,000
SALES (est): 66.6MM **Privately Held**
SIC: 1731 General electrical contractor

(P-2498)
AA/ACME LOCKSMITHS INC
1660 Factor Ave, San Leandro (94577-5618)
PHONE......................510 483-6584
Timothy J Whall, *CEO*
Jim Devries, *President*
Donald Young, *COO*
Jeff Likosar, *CFO*
P Gray Finney, *Senior VP*
EMP: 95
SQ FT: 20,000
SALES: 15.4MM
SALES (corp-wide): 2.9B **Publicly Held**
SIC: 1731 5999 Fire detection & burglar alarm systems specialization; alarm signal systems
PA: Adt Inc.
1501 W Yamato Rd
Boca Raton FL 33431
561 988-3600

(P-2499)
AAA ELCTRCAL CMMUNICATIONS INC (PA)
Also Called: AAA Property Services
25007 Anza Dr, Valencia (91355-3414)
PHONE......................800 892-4784

Joann Katinos, *CEO*
Brian Higgins, *President*
EMP: 160
SQ FT: 6,000
SALES: 17MM **Privately Held**
SIC: 1731 1711 7349 1721 General electrical contractor; plumbing, heating, air-conditioning contractors; building maintenance services; commercial painting; commercial & office buildings, renovation & repair

(P-2500)
ACCUNEX INC
Also Called: Accurate Electronics
20700 Lassen St, Chatsworth (91311-4507)
PHONE......................818 882-5858
Farid Jadali, *President*
Roxana Coronado, *Vice Pres*
▲ **EMP:** 50
SQ FT: 25,000
SALES (est): 6.9MM **Privately Held**
WEB: www.accurate-elec.com
SIC: 1731 Electrical work

(P-2501)
ACS COMMUNICATIONS INC
Also Called: Fiber Optic Technologies
680 Knox St Ste 150, Torrance (90502-1325)
PHONE......................310 767-2145
Robby Sawyer, *President*
Quint Cardwell, *Vice Pres*
Scott Kubenka, *Opers Staff*
EMP: 50
SALES (corp-wide): 774.6MM **Publicly Held**
WEB: www.acsdataline.com
SIC: 1731 Communications specialization
HQ: Acs Communications, Inc.
2535 Brockton Dr Ste 400
Austin TX 78758
512 837-4400

(P-2502)
AJ KIRKWOOD & ASSOCIATES INC
2752 Walnut Ave, Tustin (92780-7025)
PHONE......................714 505-1977
Arch Kirkwood, *Chairman*
James Klassen, *President*
Michael Hewson, *CFO*
Aidan Culligan, *Senior VP*
Sam Sandoval, *Vice Pres*
EMP: 275
SQ FT: 18,000
SALES (est): 108.7MM **Privately Held**
WEB: www.ajk-a.com
SIC: 1731 7389 8748 General electrical contractor; communications consulting; design services

(P-2503)
ALBD ELECTRIC AND CABLE
Also Called: A Lighting By Design
995 E Discovery Ln, Anaheim (92801-1147)
PHONE......................949 440-1216
Chad Lambert, *CEO*
James Black, *President*
EMP: 100
SQ FT: 12,000
SALES: 15MM **Privately Held**
SIC: 1731 3651 General electrical contractor; household audio & video equipment

(P-2504)
ALGONQUIN POWER AND UTILITIES
Also Called: Liberty Energy
933 Eloise Ave, South Lake Tahoe (96150-6470)
PHONE......................530 543-5288
Ian Robertson, *CEO*
David Bronicheski, *CFO*
EMP: 400 **EST:** 2011
SQ FT: 10,000
SALES (est): 20.3MM **Privately Held**
SIC: 1731 Electrical work

(P-2505)
ALL-GUARD ALARM SYSTEMS INC (PA)
Also Called: Grand Central Station
1306 Stealth St, Livermore (94551-9356)
PHONE......................800 255-4273
Denis Cooke, *President*
Michael Cooke, *Corp Secy*
Patricia Cooke, *Vice Pres*
Brendan Cooke, *Project Mgr*
Jodie L Osborne, *Controller*
EMP: 68
SQ FT: 12,600
SALES: 12.5MM **Privately Held**
SIC: 1731 7382 Fire detection & burglar alarm systems specialization; burglar alarm maintenance & monitoring

(P-2506)
AMERICAN ELECTRICAL SVCS INC
501 San Benito St Fl 3, Hollister (95023-3903)
PHONE......................831 638-1737
Ignacio Velazquez, *CEO*
Richard Champion, *President*
▲ **EMP:** 110
SQ FT: 1,700
SALES (est): 8.4MM **Privately Held**
SIC: 1731 General electrical contractor

(P-2507)
AMERICAN ENGRG CONTRS INC
Also Called: Budget Electric
25445 S Schulte Rd, Tracy (95377-9709)
PHONE......................209 229-1591
Larry Walling, *President*
Patricia Walling, *Corp Secy*
Joe Lorusso, *Superintendent*
EMP: 180
SQ FT: 4,000
SALES (est): 19MM **Privately Held**
WEB: www.budgete.com
SIC: 1731 General electrical contractor

(P-2508)
AMERICAN HOME ALARMS INC
1012 S Baldwin Ave Ste A, Arcadia (91007-7287)
PHONE......................888 531-5065
Jean Nguyen, *President*
Anthony Nguyen, *Vice Pres*
EMP: 120
SALES (est): 11.2MM **Privately Held**
SIC: 1731 7382 Fire detection & burglar alarm systems specialization; burglar alarm maintenance & monitoring; fire alarm maintenance & monitoring

(P-2509)
AMS ELECTRIC INC
6905 Sierra Ct Ste A, Dublin (94568-2708)
PHONE......................925 961-1600
William Breyton, *Principal*
Michael Stellato, *Treasurer*
John Modica, *Vice Pres*
Rich Corvello, *Project Mgr*
Sammy Peregrino, *Engineer*
EMP: 75
SQ FT: 25,000
SALES (est): 18.2MM **Privately Held**
WEB: www.amselectric.com
SIC: 1731 General electrical contractor

(P-2510)
ANDERSON & HOWARD ELECTRIC INC
Also Called: Anderson Howard
1791 Reynolds Ave, Irvine (92614-5711)
PHONE......................949 250-4555
Brian E Elliott, *President*
Charles B Howard, *Vice Pres*
Donna Elliot, *Office Mgr*
Tom Howard, *Admin Sec*
Brian Busch, *Sr Project Mgr*
EMP: 210
SQ FT: 10,500
SALES (est): 63.9MM **Privately Held**
WEB: www.aandh.com
SIC: 1731 General electrical contractor

(P-2511)
APOLLO ELECTRIC
330 N Basse Ln, Brea (92821-3906)
PHONE......................714 256-8414

PRODUCTS & SVCS

Leroy H Holt, *CEO*
Gregg L Holt, *Corp Secy*
Brent Holt, *Vice Pres*
Kelly Shay, *Vice Pres*
Joe St, *Project Mgr*
EMP: 60
SQ FT: 18,000
SALES (est): 13.6MM **Privately Held**
WEB: www.apolloelect.com
SIC: 1731 General electrical contractor

(P-2512)
ASSI SECURITY (PA)
1370 Reynolds Ave Ste 201, Irvine
(92614-5547)
PHONE............................949 955-0244
William Dominic Vuono, *President*
Michael Willey, *Vice Pres*
Micheal Willey, *Vice Pres*
Mark Kloman, *Technician*
Dan Gonzalez, *Project Mgr*
EMP: 67
SQ FT: 10,000
SALES (est): 17.5MM **Privately Held**
WEB: www.assisecurity.com
SIC: 1731 7382 Voice, data & video wiring
contractor; fire detection & burglar alarm
systems specialization; security systems
services; protective devices, security; bur-
glar alarm maintenance & monitoring;
confinement surveillance systems mainte-
nance & monitoring

(P-2513)
ATK AUDIOTEK
Also Called: Atk Services
28238 Avenue Crocker, Valencia
(91355-1248)
PHONE............................661 705-3700
Michael Murray Macdonald, *President*
James Harmala, *CFO*
Bill Lincoln, *CFO*
J Scott Harmala, *Vice Pres*
Erin Powell, *Program Mgr*
EMP: 85
SQ FT: 25,000
SALES (est): 23.6MM **Privately Held**
WEB: www.atkcorp.com
SIC: 1731 7359 Voice, data & video wiring
contractor; sound & lighting equipment
rental

(P-2514)
B F C INC
675 Davis St, San Francisco (94111-1903)
PHONE............................415 495-3085
John M Walsh, *President*
David Sellards, *COO*
Miles Luquingan, *Admin Asst*
Lindsay Rosecrans, *Admin Asst*
Chelsea Webb, *Admin Asst*
EMP: 110 **EST:** 1951
SQ FT: 6,300
SALES: 91MM **Privately Held**
WEB: www.cbfelectric.com
SIC: 1731 General electrical contractor

(P-2515)
BANISTER ELECTRICAL INC
2532 Verne Roberts Cir, Antioch
(94509-7904)
PHONE............................925 778-7801
Daniel T Pauline, *President*
Shovawn Barrera, *Controller*
EMP: 70
SALES (est): 2.3MM **Privately Held**
SIC: 1731 General electrical contractor

(P-2516)
BARNUM & CELILLO ELECTRIC INC (PA)
135 Main Ave Ste A, Sacramento
(95838-2090)
PHONE............................916 646-4661
Fred Troy Barnum, *CEO*
Paul Celillo, *Vice Pres*
John Aspling, *Project Mgr*
Dj Allis, *Purch Mgr*
Scott Teachout, *Purch Agent*
EMP: 89
SQ FT: 3,000
SALES (est): 50.5MM **Privately Held**
WEB: www.barnumcelillo.com
SIC: 1731 General electrical contractor

(P-2517)
BAY ALARM COMPANY (PA)
Also Called: S A S
5130 Commercial Cir, Concord
(94520-8522)
P.O. Box 8140, Walnut Creek (94596-
8140)
PHONE............................925 935-1100
Bruce A Westphal, *Ch of Bd*
Roger L Westphal, *CEO*
Graham Westphal, *Co-President*
Matt Westphal, *Co-President*
Shane Clary, *Vice Pres*
◆ **EMP:** 70
SQ FT: 12,000
SALES (est): 163.5MM **Privately Held**
WEB: www.bayalarm.com
SIC: 1731 7382 5063 Fire detection &
burglar alarm systems specialization; bur-
glar alarm maintenance & monitoring; fire
alarm maintenance & monitoring; electri-
cal apparatus & equipment

(P-2518)
BEAM VACUUMS CALIFORNIA INC
Also Called: Beam "easy Living" Center
422 Henderson St, Grass Valley
(95945-7311)
P.O. Box 1803 (95945-1803)
PHONE............................916 564-3279
Robert Medlyn, *President*
Julie Medlyn, *Planning*
Sean Pelling, *Technology*
Brian Obrien, *Sales Executive*
Venitia Sutton, *Representative*
EMP: 50
SQ FT: 13,000
SALES (est): 7.8MM **Privately Held**
WEB: www.beameasy.com
SIC: 1731 1799 5722 5731 Environmen-
tal system control installation; sound
equipment specialization; voice, data &
video wiring contractor; closet organizers,
installation & design; vacuum cleaners;
high fidelity stereo equipment; communi-
cation equipment; closet organizers &
shelving units

(P-2519)
BERGELECTRIC CORP (PA)
5650 W Centinela Ave, Los Angeles
(90045-1501)
PHONE............................310 337-1377
Thomas R Anderson, *Ch of Bd*
Alan Mashburn, *President*
William Wingrning, *CEO*
William M Wingerning, *Exec VP*
Edward P Billig, *Senior VP*
▲ **EMP:** 250
SQ FT: 14,600
SALES: 483.1MM **Privately Held**
WEB: www.bergelectric.com
SIC: 1731 General electrical contractor

(P-2520)
BERGELECTRIC CORP
650 Opper St, Escondido (92029-1020)
PHONE............................760 746-1003
Tom Anderson, *Branch Mgr*
Ed Billig, *Vice Pres*
George Stivers, *Vice Pres*
Kevin Anderson, *General Mgr*
Steve Stroder, *General Mgr*
EMP: 760
SALES (corp-wide): 483.1MM **Privately Held**
WEB: www.bergelectric.com
SIC: 1731 General electrical contractor
PA: Bergelectric Corp.
5650 W Centinela Ave
Los Angeles CA 90045
310 337-1377

(P-2521)
BERGELECTRIC CORP
11333 Sunrise Park Dr, Rancho Cordova
(95742-6532)
PHONE............................916 636-1880
Matt Ordway, *Branch Mgr*
Robert Trabert, *Sr Project Mgr*
Nick Rodriguez, *Supervisor*
EMP: 100

SALES (corp-wide): 483.1MM **Privately Held**
WEB: www.bergelectric.com
SIC: 1731 General electrical contractor
PA: Bergelectric Corp.
5650 W Centinela Ave
Los Angeles CA 90045
310 337-1377

(P-2522)
BERGELECTRIC CORP
1935 Deere Ave, Irvine (92606-4818)
PHONE............................949 250-7005
Mark Bauer, *Manager*
Randy Drinkward, *Branch Mgr*
Charles Anderson, *Project Mgr*
John Esraelo, *Technology*
Joyce Enderud, *Finance Mgr*
EMP: 95
SALES (corp-wide): 483.1MM **Privately Held**
WEB: www.bergelectric.com
SIC: 1731 General electrical contractor
PA: Bergelectric Corp.
5650 W Centinela Ave
Los Angeles CA 90045
310 337-1377

(P-2523)
BLACK DIAMOND ELECTRIC INC
2595 W 10th St, Antioch (94509-1374)
PHONE............................925 777-3440
Jason C Pauline, *CEO*
Mike Pauline, *General Mgr*
Greg Lloyd, *Administration*
Naila Viveros, *Administration*
Tim Pauline, *Project Mgr*
EMP: 100
SQ FT: 9,000
SALES (est): 21.1MM **Privately Held**
SIC: 1731 General electrical contractor

(P-2524)
BOCKMON & WOODY ELC CO INC
1528 El Pinal Dr, Stockton (95205-2643)
P.O. Box 1018 (95201-1018)
PHONE............................209 464-4878
Gary E Woody, *President*
Nick Woody, *Treasurer*
Jeff Bockmon, *Vice Pres*
Gary M Woody, *Vice Pres*
Wayne Johnson, *Project Mgr*
EMP: 190
SQ FT: 36,000
SALES: 40MM **Privately Held**
WEB: www.bockmonwoody.com
SIC: 1731 General electrical contractor

(P-2525)
BRAUN ELECTRIC COMPANY INC (HQ)
3000 E Belle Ter, Bakersfield (93307-7093)
PHONE............................661 633-1451
John A Braun, *President*
Kevin B Coghlin, *Vice Pres*
Todd Bradford, *Manager*
EMP: 400
SQ FT: 11,000
SALES: 55.5MM
SALES (corp-wide): 38.6MM **Privately Held**
WEB: www.braunelec.com
SIC: 1731 General electrical contractor
PA: C&B Holding Co., Inc.
3000 Belle Terrace
Bakersfield CA 93304
661 633-1451

(P-2526)
BRAUN ELECTRIC COMPANY INC
111 Main St, Taft (93268-3519)
PHONE............................661 763-1531
John Braun, *Manager*
EMP: 140
SALES (corp-wide): 38.6MM **Privately Held**
WEB: www.braunelec.com
SIC: 1731 General electrical contractor
HQ: Braun Electric Company, Inc.
3000 E Belle Ter
Bakersfield CA 93307
661 633-1451

(P-2527)
BRENNAN ELECTRIC INC
460 S Stoddard Ave Ste 3, San Bernardino
(92401-2039)
P.O. Box 1028, Rancho Cucamonga
(91729-1028)
PHONE............................909 772-2263
Robert Brennan, *President*
Jeff Deputy, *Vice Pres*
EMP: 180
SQ FT: 2,000
SALES (est): 13.7MM **Privately Held**
SIC: 1731 General electrical contractor

(P-2528)
BRIGGS ELECTRIC INC (PA)
14381 Franklin Ave, Tustin (92780-7010)
PHONE............................714 544-2500
Jeff Perry, *President*
Thomas J Perry, *President*
Todd Perry, *CFO*
▲ **EMP:** 100
SQ FT: 5,500
SALES: 91.7MM **Privately Held**
WEB: www.briggselectric.com
SIC: 1731 General electrical contractor

(P-2529)
BRUDVIK INC (PA)
Also Called: BRUDVIK RENTAL DIVISION
600 S Eugene Rd, Palm Springs
(92264-1514)
PHONE............................760 320-4429
John Brudvik, *President*
Veneita Brudvik, *Corp Secy*
Bo Ford, *Vice Pres*
EMP: 70
SQ FT: 1,000
SALES: 4.9MM **Privately Held**
WEB: www.brudvikelectric.com
SIC: 1731 8711 7359 5063 General elec-
trical contractor; electrical or electronic
engineering; stores & yards equipment
rental; lighting fixtures

(P-2530)
BUDGET ELECTRICAL CONTRS INC
25051 5th St, San Bernardino
(92410-5119)
PHONE............................909 381-2646
Danny E Guy, *CEO*
William Morris Diesel, *President*
EMP: 150
SQ FT: 5,000
SALES (est): 18MM **Privately Held**
WEB: www.becelectric.com
SIC: 1731 General electrical contractor

(P-2531)
BUILDING ELCTRONIC CONTRLS INC (PA)
2246 Lindsay Way, Glendora (91740-5398)
PHONE............................909 305-1600
Richard Taylor, *President*
Shelley Taylor, *Vice Pres*
EMP: 50
SQ FT: 13,000
SALES: 22.1MM **Privately Held**
WEB: www.becinc.net
SIC: 1731 3699 Electrical work; security
control equipment & systems; security de-
vices

(P-2532)
BUTTERFIELD ELECTRIC INC (PA)
2101 Freeway Dr Ste A, Woodland
(95776-9510)
P.O. Box 25 (95776-0025)
PHONE............................530 666-2116
Rick Butterfield, *President*
Rorie Butterfield, *Vice Pres*
Chris Morse, *Project Mgr*
EMP: 165
SQ FT: 14,000
SALES (est): 29MM **Privately Held**
WEB: www.butterfieldelectric.com
SIC: 1731 General electrical contractor

(P-2533)
C & R SYSTEMS INC (PA)
1835 Capital St, Corona (92880-1727)
PHONE............................951 270-0255
Pam Mosbaugh, *President*

▲ = Import ▼=Export
◆ =Import/Export

Robert V Cross, *Principal*
Martha Cardenas, *Technician*
Timothy Potts, *Senior Engr*
Linda Van Meter, *Sales Staff*
EMP: 50
SQ FT: 8,000
SALES (est): 15.9MM **Privately Held**
WEB: www.crsys.net
SIC: 1731 Communications specialization; telephone & telephone equipment installation; safety & security specialization; fire detection & burglar alarm systems specialization

(P-2534)
C H REYNOLDS ELECTRIC INC
Also Called: Ch Reynolds
1281 Wayne Ave, San Jose (95131-3599)
PHONE..................................408 436-9280
Charles Reynolds, *President*
EMP: 500
SQ FT: 25,000
SALES (est): 51MM **Privately Held**
WEB: www.chreynolds.com
SIC: 1731 General electrical contractor

(P-2535)
C T AND F INC
7228 Scout Ave, Bell Gardens (90201-4998)
PHONE..................................562 927-2339
Ruby Galland, *CEO*
Todd N Simmons, *Vice Pres*
Kent M Simmons, *Principal*
Judith L Simmons, *Admin Sec*
EMP: 80
SQ FT: 15,000
SALES (est): 11.8MM **Privately Held**
SIC: 1731 General electrical contractor

(P-2536)
CALENERGY LLC
7030 Gentry Rd, Calipatria (92233-9720)
PHONE..................................402 231-1527
Bill Fehrman, *President*
Joshua Hawk, *Safety Mgr*
Hector Corella, *Manager*
EMP: 350 EST: 2013
SALES (est): 30.3MM **Privately Held**
SIC: 1731 Electric power systems contractors

(P-2537)
CALIFORNIA AND NEVADA IBEW/NEC
Also Called: California Lmcc/Ibew-Neca
5934 Gibraltar Dr Ste 205, Pleasanton (94588-2792)
PHONE..................................925 828-6322
Bernie Kotlier, *Principal*
EMP: 99
SALES (est): 3.1MM **Privately Held**
SIC: 1731 Electrical work

(P-2538)
CAROL ELECTRIC COMPANY INC
3822 Cerritos Ave, Los Alamitos (90720-2420)
PHONE..................................562 431-1870
John R Fuqua, *Ch of Bd*
Allen Moffitt, *President*
Brian Moffitt, *Vice Pres*
Erik Anderson, *Project Mgr*
Jeff Fetters, *Project Mgr*
EMP: 90
SQ FT: 10,000
SALES (est): 17.4MM **Privately Held**
WEB: www.carolelectric.com
SIC: 1731 General electrical contractor

(P-2539)
CHAMPION ELECTRIC INC
3950 Garner Rd, Riverside (92501-1005)
PHONE..................................951 276-9619
Glenn Rowden, *President*
Cynthia D Rowden, *CFO*
Tom Rowden, *Vice Pres*
Liset Galv N, *Accountant*
EMP: 65
SQ FT: 12,000
SALES (est): 8MM **Privately Held**
WEB: www.championelec.com
SIC: 1731 General electrical contractor

(P-2540)
CHICO ELECTRIC INC
36 W Eaton Rd, Chico (95973-0160)
PHONE..................................530 891-1933
Norman Nielsen, *CEO*
Charlene Bellante, *Vice Pres*
Frank Vanskike, *Contractor*
EMP: 60
SQ FT: 8,500
SALES: 17.2MM **Privately Held**
SIC: 1731 General electrical contractor

(P-2541)
CLIMATEC LLC
13715 Stowe Dr, Poway (92064-6836)
PHONE..................................858 391-7000
Eince Scalise, *Branch Mgr*
EMP: 50
SALES (corp-wide): 261.7MM **Privately Held**
SIC: 1731 Environmental system control installation; energy management controls
HQ: Climatec, Llc
2851 W Kathleen Rd
Phoenix AZ 85053
602 944-3330

(P-2542)
COCKRELL ELECTRIC INC
79553 Country Club Dr B, Bermuda Dunes (92203-1283)
PHONE..................................760 864-6233
John Cockrell, *President*
Michele Cockrell, *Vice Pres*
Rick Valle, *General Mgr*
EMP: 85
SQ FT: 5,000
SALES (est): 9.1MM **Privately Held**
WEB: www.cockrellelectric.com
SIC: 1731 General electrical contractor

(P-2543)
COGAR INTERNATIONAL ENRGY CORP (PA)
5286 Industrial Dr, Huntington Beach (92649-1515)
P.O. Box 93967, Pasadena (91109-3967)
PHONE..................................626 494-8157
Gabriel Obadan, *President*
EMP: 50
SQ FT: 5,000
SALES (est): 2.4MM **Privately Held**
SIC: 1731 Electric power systems contractors

(P-2544)
COLLINS ELECTRICAL COMPANY INC (PA)
3412 Metro Dr, Stockton (95215-9440)
PHONE..................................209 466-3691
Eugene C Gini, *President*
Phil Asborno, *COO*
Brian Gini, *Vice Pres*
Craig Gini, *Vice Pres*
Dianne R Gini, *Vice Pres*
EMP: 310 EST: 1928
SQ FT: 80,000
SALES (est): 106.8MM **Privately Held**
WEB: www.collinselectric.com
SIC: 1731 General electrical contractor

(P-2545)
COLLINS ELECTRICAL COMPANY INC
1902 Channel Dr, West Sacramento (95691-3441)
PHONE..................................209 466-3691
Kevin Gini, *Branch Mgr*
Krishneel Prasad, *Technology*
Susan Rodriguez, *Human Res Mgr*
EMP: 108
SALES (corp-wide): 106.8MM **Privately Held**
WEB: www.collinselectric.com
SIC: 1731 General electrical contractor
PA: Collins Electrical Company, Inc.
3412 Metro Dr
Stockton CA 95215
209 466-3691

(P-2546)
COLLINS ELECTRICAL COMPANY INC
385 Reservation Rd, Marina (93933-3229)
PHONE..................................831 384-0114

Eric Tonnesen, *Branch Mgr*
EMP: 77
SALES (corp-wide): 106.8MM **Privately Held**
WEB: www.collinselectric.com
SIC: 1731 Electrical work
PA: Collins Electrical Company, Inc.
3412 Metro Dr
Stockton CA 95215
209 466-3691

(P-2547)
COMET ELECTRIC INC
21625 Prairie St, Chatsworth (91311-5833)
PHONE..................................818 340-0965
Adam Saitman, *Principal*
Keith Berson, *COO*
Jason Pennington, *CFO*
Tim Erno, *Vice Pres*
Steve Goad, *Vice Pres*
EMP: 150
SQ FT: 12,000
SALES (est): 41.1MM **Privately Held**
WEB: www.cometelectric.com
SIC: 1731 General electrical contractor

(P-2548)
COMMUNCTION WIRG SPCALISTS INC
Also Called: C W S
8909 Complex Dr Ste F, San Diego (92123-1418)
PHONE..................................858 278-4545
Eric Templin, *Owner*
Donna Templin, *Shareholder*
Richard Templin, *Vice Pres*
Barbara Gerardi, *Admin Asst*
Darren Waitley, *Admin Asst*
EMP: 80
SQ FT: 5,500
SALES: 8.5MM **Privately Held**
WEB: www.cwssandiego.com
SIC: 1731 Telephone & telephone equipment installation; voice, data & video wiring contractor

(P-2549)
COMTEL SYSTEMS TECHNOLOGY
1292 Hammerwood Ave, Sunnyvale (94089-2232)
PHONE..................................408 543-5600
Richard Nielsen, *President*
Andrea Nielsen, *Vice Pres*
Patricia Porazynski, *Administration*
Mike Wagner, *Project Mgr*
Nikki Soares, *Assistant*
EMP: 70
SQ FT: 10,760
SALES (est): 14MM **Privately Held**
WEB: www.comtelsys.com
SIC: 1731 Communications specialization; access control systems specialization; fire detection & burglar alarm systems specialization

(P-2550)
CONTRA COSTA ELECTRIC INC (DH)
825 Howe Rd, Martinez (94553-3441)
P.O. Box 2523 (94553-0317)
PHONE..................................925 229-4250
Michael Dias, *President*
Dave Galli, *CFO*
Charlie Hadsell, *Vice Pres*
Joey Ramirez, *Vice Pres*
Tom Tatro, *Vice Pres*
EMP: 300
SALES (est): 84.1MM
SALES (corp-wide): 7.6B **Publicly Held**
WEB: www.ccelectric.com
SIC: 1731 General electrical contractor

(P-2551)
CONTRA COSTA ELECTRIC INC
3208 Landco Dr, Bakersfield (93308-6156)
PHONE..................................661 322-4036
Richard Trainer, *Manager*
Matt Furrer, *Vice Pres*
Paul White, *Division Mgr*
EMP: 104
SALES (corp-wide): 7.6B **Publicly Held**
WEB: www.ccelectric.com
SIC: 1731 General electrical contractor

HQ: Contra Costa Electric, Inc.
825 Howe Rd
Martinez CA 94553
925 229-4250

(P-2552)
COSCO FIRE PROTECTION INC
7455 Longard Rd, Livermore (94551-8238)
PHONE..................................925 455-2751
Phil Raya, *Manager*
EMP: 96 **Privately Held**
SIC: 1731 3494 8711 7382 General electrical contractor; sprinkler systems, field; engineering services; security systems services; plumbing, heating, air-conditioning contractors
HQ: Cosco Fire Protection, Inc.
29222 Rancho Viejo Rd # 205
San Juan Capistrano CA 92675
714 974-8770

(P-2553)
COVE ELECTRIC INC
77971 Wildcat Dr Ste F, Palm Desert (92211-4133)
PHONE..................................760 568-9924
Charles Bojkovsky, *President*
Michele Bojkovsky, *Shareholder*
Jeannie Stewart, *CFO*
Steve Tavares, *Vice Pres*
EMP: 70
SQ FT: 4,500
SALES: 8.7MM **Privately Held**
WEB: www.coveelectric.com
SIC: 1731 General electrical contractor

(P-2554)
CSI ELECTRICAL CONTRACTORS INC
41769 11th St W Ste B, Palmdale (93551-1418)
PHONE..................................661 723-0869
Roland Tamayo, *General Mgr*
Andy Klein, *Vice Pres*
EMP: 90
SALES (est): 3.8MM
SALES (corp-wide): 110.1MM **Privately Held**
SIC: 1731 General electrical contractor
PA: Csi Electrical Contractors, Inc.
10623 Fulton Wells Ave
Santa Fe Springs CA 90670
562 946-0700

(P-2555)
CSI ELECTRICAL CONTRACTORS INC (PA)
Also Called: C S I
10623 Fulton Wells Ave, Santa Fe Springs (90670-3741)
P.O. Box 2887 (90670-0887)
PHONE..................................562 946-0700
Steven M Watts, *President*
Andy Klein, *President*
Chris Corder, *Vice Pres*
Craig Epperly, *Vice Pres*
Rick Salerno, *Executive*
EMP: 150
SALES (est): 110.1MM **Privately Held**
WEB: www.csielectric.com
SIC: 1731 General electrical contractor

(P-2556)
CUPERTINO ELECTRIC INC
350 Lenore Way, Felton (95018-8973)
P.O. Box 1517 (95018-1517)
PHONE..................................408 808-8260
EMP: 2038
SALES (corp-wide): 400MM **Privately Held**
SIC: 1731 General electrical contractor
PA: Cupertino Electric, Inc.
1132 N 7th St
San Jose CA 95112
408 808-8000

(P-2557)
CUPERTINO ELECTRIC INC (PA)
Also Called: Cei
1132 N 7th St, San Jose (95112-4438)
PHONE..................................408 808-8000
Tom Schott, *President*
Gene Ryley, *COO*
Marjorie Goss, *CFO*
Bill Slakey, *CFO*
Laura Latshaw, *Risk Mgmt Dir*

▲ **EMP:** 400
SQ FT: 90,000
SALES: 400MM **Privately Held**
WEB: www.cei.com
SIC: 1731 General electrical contractor

(P-2558)
CUPERTINO ELECTRIC INC
1740 Cesar Chavez Fl 2, San Francisco (94124-1134)
PHONE..............................415 970-3400
Adam Spillane, *Branch Mgr*
Brian Ward, *Admin Asst*
BJ Johnson, *Administration*
Bill Diekmann, *Info Tech Dir*
Johnny Santos, *Technician*
EMP: 55
SALES (corp-wide): 400MM **Privately Held**
WEB: www.cei.com
SIC: 1731 General electrical contractor
PA: Cupertino Electric, Inc.
1132 N 7th St
San Jose CA 95112
408 808-8000

(P-2559)
D M ELECTRIC INC
336 S Waterman Ave Ste K, San Bernardino (92408-1533)
PHONE..............................909 888-8639
Danny Moore, *President*
Michelle Moore, *Corp Secy*
EMP: 80
SQ FT: 1,000
SALES (est): 6.2MM **Privately Held**
SIC: 1731 Electrical work

(P-2560)
DAMON ELECTRICAL
7800 Bobbyboyar Ave, West Hills (91304-4418)
PHONE..............................818 426-3450
Zekrollah Ali, *Principal*
Ali Zekrollah, *Principal*
EMP: 65 **EST:** 2011
SALES (est): 3.1MM **Privately Held**
SIC: 1731 General electrical contractor

(P-2561)
DAN FREITAS ELECTRIC
983 E Levin Ave, Tulare (93274-6525)
PHONE..............................559 686-9572
Daniel Freitas, *President*
Jeanette Freitas, *Vice Pres*
EMP: 60
SQ FT: 14,460
SALES (est): 11.2MM **Privately Held**
WEB: www.danfreitaselectric.com
SIC: 1731 General electrical contractor

(P-2562)
DATA SPECIALTIES INC (PA)
8400 Kass Dr, Buena Park (90621-3808)
PHONE..............................714 523-8489
Phil Rafferty, *President*
Ric Maxson, *Vice Pres*
Tina Dixson, *Executive*
Krista Lopez, *Admin Asst*
Steve Clark, *Project Mgr*
EMP: 55
SALES: 25.8MM **Privately Held**
WEB: www.dataspecialtiesinc.com
SIC: 1731 Electrical work

(P-2563)
DECKER ELC CO INC ELEC CONTRS
147 Beacon St, South San Francisco (94080-6921)
PHONE..............................650 635-1390
David Chad, *Vice Pres*
Myra Garces, *Administration*
EMP: 100
SALES (est): 5.7MM
SALES (corp-wide): 112.3MM **Privately Held**
WEB: www.deckerelectric.com
SIC: 1731 General electrical contractor
PA: Decker Electric Co., Inc., Electrical Contractors
1282 Folsom St
San Francisco CA 94103
415 552-1622

(P-2564)
DEPLOYMENT SOLUTIONS LLC
332 Bandini Pl, Vista (92083-5903)
PHONE..............................317 281-9682
Jennifer Shaffer, *Partner*
Martin Keith, *Partner*
EMP: 50
SALES (est): 5.4MM **Privately Held**
WEB: www.deploymentsolutions.com
SIC: 1731 Electronic controls installation; communications specialization

(P-2565)
DYNALECTRIC COMPANY
668 Flinn Ave, Moorpark (93021-2077)
PHONE..............................805 517-1253
Frank Miller, *Vice Pres*
EMP: 127
SALES (corp-wide): 7.6B **Publicly Held**
SIC: 1731 General electrical contractor
HQ: Dynalectric Company
22930 Shaw Rd Ste 100
Dulles VA 20166
703 288-2866

(P-2566)
DYNALECTRIC COMPANY
9505 Chesapeake Dr, San Diego (92123-6393)
PHONE..............................858 712-4700
Daivd Rispolrch, *Manager*
Will Coyle, *Planning Mgr*
Matt Hammer, *Administration*
Eric Clevenger, *Project Mgr*
Miguel Tapia, *Foreman/Supr*
EMP: 300
SALES (corp-wide): 7.6B **Publicly Held**
WEB: www.dyna-fl.com
SIC: 1731 General electrical contractor
HQ: Dynalectric Company
22930 Shaw Rd Ste 100
Dulles VA 20166
703 288-2866

(P-2567)
DYNALECTRIC COMPANY
4462 Corporate Center Dr, Los Alamitos (90720-2539)
PHONE..............................714 236-2242
Christopher Pesavento, *Branch Mgr*
EMP: 127
SALES (corp-wide): 7.6B **Publicly Held**
WEB: www.dyna-fl.com
SIC: 1731 General electrical contractor
HQ: Dynalectric Company
22930 Shaw Rd Ste 100
Dulles VA 20166
703 288-2866

(P-2568)
DYNALECTRIC COMPANY
825 Howe Rd, Martinez (94553-3441)
PHONE..............................415 487-4700
David Raspolich, *Manager*
EMP: 150
SALES (corp-wide): 7.6B **Publicly Held**
SIC: 1731 General electrical contractor
HQ: Dynalectric Company
22930 Shaw Rd Ste 100
Dulles VA 20166
703 288-2866

(P-2569)
EDWARD STRALING
Also Called: Quality Electrical Services
2940 Grace Ln Ste C, Costa Mesa (92626-4133)
PHONE..............................760 887-3673
Edward Sterling, *Owner*
EMP: 50
SQ FT: 7,500
SALES (est): 4.1MM **Privately Held**
SIC: 1731 General electrical contractor

(P-2570)
EDWARDS TECHNOLOGIES INC
139 Maryland St, El Segundo (90245-4116)
PHONE..............................310 536-7070
Brian Edwards, *President*
▲ **EMP:** 51
SQ FT: 10,000
SALES (est): 17.3MM **Privately Held**
WEB: www.edwardstechnologies.com
SIC: 1731 Sound equipment specialization

(P-2571)
ELCOR ELECTRIC INC
3310 Bassett St, Santa Clara (95054-2702)
PHONE..............................408 986-1320
George Woodley, *General Mgr*
Clint Woodley, *Vice Pres*
EMP: 120
SQ FT: 5,000
SALES (est): 17.4MM **Privately Held**
SIC: 1731 General electrical contractor

(P-2572)
ELECTRCAL INSTRUMENTATION INTL
Also Called: E I I
6950 District Blvd, Bakersfield (93313-2012)
P.O. Box 40878 (93384-0878)
PHONE..............................661 836-9466
Gloria Tominaga-Minor, *President*
Barney J Blanchard, *Director*
Christopher P Minor, *Director*
EMP: 366
SQ FT: 2,000
SALES (est): 22.8MM **Privately Held**
SIC: 1731 General electrical contractor

(P-2573)
ELECTRIC SVC & SUP CO PASADENA
Also Called: Essco
2668 E Foothill Blvd, Pasadena (91107-3409)
PHONE..............................626 795-8641
Stanley R Lazarian, *President*
Nancy Rose, *Treasurer*
Iris Lazarian, *Vice Pres*
EMP: 70 **EST:** 1946
SALES (est): 7.1MM **Privately Held**
WEB: www.esscoelectric.com
SIC: 1731 General electrical contractor

(P-2574)
ELECTRIC USA
480 Aldo Ave, Santa Clara (95054-2304)
PHONE..............................800 921-1151
John Lim, *Owner*
EMP: 50
SALES (est): 1.4MM **Privately Held**
SIC: 1731 1711 General electrical contractor; plumbing contractors

(P-2575)
ELECTRICAL & INSTRUMENTATION
Also Called: Eiu of California
6950 District Blvd, Bakersfield (93313-2012)
P.O. Box 40878 (93384-0878)
PHONE..............................661 836-9466
Chris Minor, *President*
Barney J Blanchard, *Corp Secy*
Paul Labauve, *Exec VP*
EMP: 200
SQ FT: 10,000
SALES (est): 43.1MM **Privately Held**
WEB: www.eiucal.com
SIC: 1731 Electrical work

(P-2576)
ELECTRONIC CONTROL SYSTEMS LLC
Also Called: Albireo Energy
12575 Kirkham Ct Ste 1, Poway (92064-8844)
PHONE..............................858 513-1911
Dan Coler, *Mng Member*
Luis Ochoa, *Engineer*
Amanda Barry, *Controller*
EMP: 145
SQ FT: 17,000
SALES: 27MM
SALES (corp-wide): 55MM **Privately Held**
WEB: www.ecscontrols.com
SIC: 1731 7382 Energy management controls; security systems services
PA: Albireo Energy, Llc
3 Ethel Rd Ste 300
Edison NJ 08817
732 512-9100

(P-2577)
ELITE ELECTRIC
9415 Bellegrave Ave, Riverside (92509-2741)
PHONE..............................951 681-5811
Carl Eric Dawson, *President*
Marshall Hockersmith, *Project Mgr*
Tara Fogliasso, *Controller*
EMP: 80
SQ FT: 1,720
SALES (est): 8.8MM **Privately Held**
SIC: 1731 General electrical contractor

(P-2578)
ELITE POWER INC
6530 Asher Ln, Sacramento (95828-1832)
PHONE..............................916 739-1580
Walt Zacharias, *President*
Shannon Allen, *Accounting Mgr*
Todd May, *Opers Staff*
Mike Wilson, *Director*
EMP: 54 **EST:** 2001
SQ FT: 15,000
SALES (est): 9.7MM **Privately Held**
WEB: www.elitepower.com
SIC: 1731 General electrical contractor

(P-2579)
ENERPATH SERVICES INC
1758 Orange Tree Ln, Redlands (92374-2856)
PHONE..............................909 335-1699
Stephen Guthrie, *President*
Janina Guthrie, *Treasurer*
Jonathan Baty, *Admin Sec*
EMP: 100
SQ FT: 4,500
SALES (est): 16.9MM **Privately Held**
WEB: www.expertlighting.com
SIC: 1731 8748 Lighting contractor; lighting consultant

(P-2580)
EQUAL ACCESS INTERNATIONAL
1212 Market St Ste 200, San Francisco (94102-4817)
PHONE..............................415 561-4884
Ronni Goldfarb, *President*
Lisa Ellis, *COO*
Rebecca Chapman, *Officer*
Ashley Dumich, *Officer*
Dorothee Stangle, *Officer*
EMP: 52
SQ FT: 2,459
SALES: 12.2MM **Privately Held**
WEB: www.equalaccess.org
SIC: 1731 Communications specialization

(P-2581)
FAITH ELECTRIC LLC
12350 Hesperia Rd Ste 215, Victorville (92395)
PHONE..............................909 767-2682
Elijah Adams, *CEO*
EMP: 135
SQ FT: 5,000
SALES (est): 2.3MM **Privately Held**
SIC: 1731 Electrical work

(P-2582)
FAR WEST ELECTRIC INC
6094 Keswick Ave, Riverside (92506-3747)
PHONE..............................909 684-8661
Joe Ruzzamenti, *President*
Rick Ruzzamanti, *Vice Pres*
Judy Ruzzamanti, *Admin Sec*
EMP: 60
SQ FT: 2,100
SALES: 10MM **Privately Held**
SIC: 1731 General electrical contractor

(P-2583)
FEI ENTERPRISES INC
5242 W Adams Blvd, Los Angeles (90016-2628)
PHONE..............................323 937-0856
Gabriel Fedida, *CEO*
▲ **EMP:** 50
SQ FT: 3,900
SALES (est): 6.1MM **Privately Held**
WEB: www.feienterprises.com
SIC: 1731 5063 General electrical contractor; burglar alarm systems

(P-2584)
FIRST ALARM
1 Lower Ragsdale Dr # 3700, Monterey
(93940-5769)
PHONE 831 649-1111
David Hood, *Manager*
Krzysztof Supinski, *IT/INT Sup*
John La Fala, *Sales Executive*
John Lasalla, *Manager*
EMP: 869
SALES (corp-wide): 109.2MM **Privately
Held**
SIC: 1731 Fire detection & burglar alarm
systems specialization
PA: First Alarm
1111 Estates Dr
Aptos CA 95003
831 476-1111

(P-2585)
FIRST ALARM (PA)
1111 Estates Dr, Aptos (95003-3572)
PHONE 831 476-1111
Jarl E Saal, *Chairman*
David Hood, *President*
Chris Guzman, *COO*
Jon Dallimonti, *Officer*
Lex Dang, *Officer*
EMP: 120
SQ FT: 14,000
SALES (est): 109.2MM **Privately Held**
WEB: www.firstalarm.com
SIC: 1731 Fire detection & burglar alarm
systems specialization

(P-2586)
FISK ELECTRIC COMPANY
15870 Olden St, Sylmar (91342-1241)
PHONE 818 884-1166
Orvil Anthony, *Senior VP*
EMP: 165
SALES (corp-wide): 4.7B **Publicly Held**
SIC: 1731 General electrical contractor
HQ: Fisk Electric Company
10855 Westview Dr
Houston TX 77043
713 868-6111

(P-2587)
**FLATIRON ELECTRIC GROUP
INC**
15335 Fairfield Ranch Rd # 200, Chino Hills
(91709-8833)
PHONE 714 228-9631
Kurt Welter, *President*
John Diciurcio, *CEO*
Javier Sevilla, *COO*
Lars Leitner, *CFO*
EMP: 50
SALES (est): 5.8MM
SALES (corp-wide): 579.6MM **Privately
Held**
SIC: 1731 General electrical contractor
HQ: Flatiron West, Inc.
1770 La Costa Meadows Dr
San Marcos CA 92078

(P-2588)
FOSHAY ELECTRIC COINC
1555 Laurel Bay Ln, San Diego
(92154-7715)
PHONE 858 277-7676
Theresa M Faucher, *President*
Michael Beringhaus, *Vice Pres*
Mark Faucher, *Vice Pres*
EMP: 100
SQ FT: 8,000
SALES (est): 15.8MM **Privately Held**
WEB: www.foshayelectric.com
SIC: 1731 General electrical contractor

(P-2589)
FRANKE CON J ELECTRIC INC
317 N Grant St, Stockton (95202-2633)
PHONE 209 462-0717
Barry Frain, *President*
Diana Frain, *Corp Secy*
Lewis Frain, *Vice Pres*
Lori Cass, *Office Mgr*
Dave Forsyth, *Project Mgr*
EMP: 100 **EST:** 1925
SQ FT: 7,000
SALES (est): 24.2MM **Privately Held**
WEB: www.cjfranke.com
SIC: 1731 General electrical contractor

(P-2590)
GENERAL ELECTRIC COMPANY
428 Ballindine Dr, Vacaville (95688-9236)
PHONE 707 469-8346
EMP: 51
SALES (corp-wide): 122B **Publicly Held**
SIC: 1731 Electrical work
PA: General Electric Company
41 Farnsworth St
Boston MA 02210
617 443-3000

(P-2591)
**GLOBAL POWER GROUP INC
(PA)**
12060 Woodside Ave, Lakeside
(92040-2949)
PHONE 619 579-1221
Terry Mammen, *CEO*
Salvatore Martorana, *President*
Salvador Ceballos, *CFO*
EMP: 61
SQ FT: 10,000
SALES (est): 13.4MM **Privately Held**
SIC: 1731 Electric power systems contractors

(P-2592)
GRC ELECTRIC INC
Also Called: Wired Rite Electric
675 S Glenwood Pl, Burbank (91506-2819)
PHONE 818 242-9891
Glen Christensen, *Principal*
EMP: 80
SALES (est): 2.9MM **Privately Held**
SIC: 1731 Electrical work

(P-2593)
**GREATER ALARM COMPANY
INC (DH)**
3750 Schaufele Ave # 200, Long Beach
(90808-1779)
PHONE 949 474-0555
George De Marco, *President*
James De Marco, *Vice Pres*
EMP: 71
SQ FT: 11,500
SALES (est): 7.2MM
SALES (corp-wide): 86.1MM **Privately
Held**
SIC: 1731 Safety & security specialization
HQ: Interface Security Systems, Llc
3773 Corporate Centre Dr
Earth City MO 63045
314 595-0100

(P-2594)
GREGG ELECTRIC INC
608 W Emporia St, Ontario (91762-3709)
PHONE 909 983-1794
Randall F Fehlman, *President*
Victoria Mensen, *CFO*
James Fehlman, *Vice Pres*
Vicki Mensen, *Controller*
EMP: 150 **EST:** 1961
SQ FT: 15,000
SALES (est): 22.9MM **Privately Held**
WEB: www.greggelectric.com
SIC: 1731 General electrical contractor

(P-2595)
**GUILLEN ELECTRIC COMPANY
INC**
1485 Andrew Dr Ste D, Claremont
(91711-5766)
PHONE 909 480-3915
Julio Raymond Guillen, *CEO*
EMP: 50
SALES (est): 74.5K **Privately Held**
SIC: 1731 Electrical work

(P-2596)
H & D ELECTRIC
5237 Walnut Ave Ste 100, Sacramento
(95841-2694)
P.O. Box 41360 (95841-0360)
PHONE 916 332-0794
Mark E Cooper, *President*
EMP: 360
SQ FT: 14,400
SALES (est): 36.5MM **Privately Held**
WEB: www.hdelectric.com
SIC: 1731 General electrical contractor

(P-2597)
H A BOWEN ELECTRIC INC
2055 Williams St, San Leandro
(94577-2305)
P.O. Box 2153 (94577-0329)
PHONE 510 483-0500
Herbert A Bowen, *President*
EMP: 60 **EST:** 1979
SQ FT: 9,000
SALES: 33.7MM **Privately Held**
WEB: www.bowenelectric.com
SIC: 1731 General electrical contractor

(P-2598)
HACKNEY ELECTRIC INC (PA)
23286 Arroyo Vis, Rcho STA Marg
(92688-2610)
PHONE 949 264-4000
David J Hackney, *President*
Rebecca Hackney, *Vice Pres*
EMP: 65
SQ FT: 6,200
SALES: 15.5MM **Privately Held**
WEB: www.hackneyelectric.com
SIC: 1731 Electrical work

(P-2599)
**HAMILTON AND DILLON ELC
INC**
1128 Reno Ave, Modesto (95351-1128)
P.O. Box 581890 (95358-0033)
PHONE 209 529-6292
Bobby Hamilton, *President*
John Dillon, *Vice Pres*
Reggie Pena, *Project Mgr*
EMP: 60
SQ FT: 5,000
SALES (est): 7.7MM **Privately Held**
SIC: 1731 General electrical contractor

(P-2600)
HAROLD E NUTTER INC (PA)
Also Called: Harold E Nutter & Son
5930 Rosebud Ln, Sacramento
(95841-2989)
PHONE 916 334-4343
Norman Nutter, *President*
EMP: 70 **EST:** 1970
SQ FT: 16,000
SALES (est): 14.9MM **Privately Held**
WEB: www.henutter.com
SIC: 1731 General electrical contractor

(P-2601)
HARRIS L WOODS ELEC CONTR
Also Called: Woods Electric Company
9214 Norwalk Blvd, Santa Fe Springs
(90670-2924)
P.O. Box 2367 (90670-0367)
PHONE 562 945-8751
Sandra Woods, *President*
Ralph L Woods, *Admin Sec*
Jason Lomeli, *Purch Agent*
John Conlon, *Foreman/Supr*
Richard Orozco, *Foreman/Supr*
EMP: 55
SQ FT: 5,000
SALES (est): 9.2MM **Privately Held**
SIC: 1731 General electrical contractor

(P-2602)
HCI SYSTEMS INC (PA)
Also Called: Hcis
1354 S Parkside Pl, Ontario (91761-4555)
PHONE 909 628-7773
Hany Dimitry, *President*
Michael Peters, *President*
Andrew Fahrenhorst, *Senior VP*
Dan Downs, *Vice Pres*
Jeff Kresge, *Vice Pres*
EMP: 50 **EST:** 2008
SQ FT: 12,000
SALES (est): 16.7MM **Privately Held**
SIC: 1731 General electrical contractor

(P-2603)
HHS COMMUNICATIONS INC
2042 S Grove Ave, Ontario (91761-5617)
PHONE 909 230-5170
Royce S Jaime, *President*
EMP: 60 **EST:** 2007
SALES (est): 6.8MM **Privately Held**
SIC: 1731 Fiber optic cable installation

(P-2604)
HIGH-LIGHT ELECTRIC INC
6942 Ed Perkic St, Riverside (92504-1005)
P.O. Box 7339 (92513-7339)
PHONE 951 352-9646
Erwin Mendoza, *President*
Iris Leung, *Controller*
EMP: 60
SALES: 19.2MM **Privately Held**
WEB: www.mbe-hlj.com
SIC: 1731 General electrical contractor

(P-2605)
HILLS FLAT LUMBER CO (PA)
380 Railroad Ave, Grass Valley
(95945-5909)
P.O. Box 1630, Colfax (95713-1630)
PHONE 530 273-6171
Edward J Pardini Jr, *CEO*
Jason Pardini, *Vice Pres*
Kennan Pardini, *Vice Pres*
Sandra Pardini, *Vice Pres*
Peggy White, *Finance Mgr*
EMP: 80
SQ FT: 12,000
SALES (est): 26MM **Privately Held**
WEB: www.hillsflatlumber.com
SIC: 1731 5031 5193 5999 Electrical
work; doors & windows; nursery stock;
plumbing & heating supplies; general
merchandise, non-durable; equipment
rental & leasing

(P-2606)
HMT ELECTRIC INC
2340 Meyers Ave, Escondido (92029-1008)
PHONE 858 458-9771
Brian Hudak, *CEO*
Howard Powell, *Division Mgr*
Jeremy Arnold, *Project Mgr*
Joe Zapata, *Project Mgr*
Jay Guerrero, *Engineer*
EMP: 85
SQ FT: 2,000
SALES: 53.8MM **Privately Held**
SIC: 1731 General electrical contractor

(P-2607)
HODGES ELECTRIC INC
1239 Hoblitt Ave, Clovis (93612-2807)
PHONE 559 298-5533
Roger L Hidy, *President*
Janel M Hidy, *CFO*
EMP: 50
SQ FT: 5,000
SALES (est): 5.8MM **Privately Held**
SIC: 1731 General electrical contractor

(P-2608)
HOT LINE CONSTRUCTION INC
9020 Brentwood Blvd Ste H, Brentwood
(94513-4049)
PHONE 925 634-9333
Carol Bade, *President*
Kelly G Kutchera, *CFO*
Troy Myers, *Vice Pres*
EMP: 425
SQ FT: 4,000
SALES (est): 183MM **Privately Held**
WEB: www.hotlineconstructioninc.com
SIC: 1731 1799 Electric power systems
contractors; cable splicing service

(P-2609)
**HOTLINE
TELECOMMUNICATIONS (PA)**
528 Bethany Cir, Claremont (91711-2231)
PHONE 909 593-6575
Harold Hung Kim, *Co-Owner*
Helen Hehja Kim, *Co-Owner*
EMP: 100
SALES (est): 6.2MM **Privately Held**
WEB: www.hotlinetelecom.com
SIC: 1731 Telephone & telephone equipment installation

(P-2610)
**HOWE ELECTRIC
CONSTRUCTION INC**
4682 E Olive Ave, Fresno (93702-1689)
PHONE 559 255-8992
Todd Howe, *President*
Marjorie Montes, *Treasurer*
Ty Howe, *Vice Pres*
Monica Teare, *Admin Sec*

**P
R
O
D
U
C
T
S

&

S
V
C
S**

EMP: 140
SALES (est): 15MM **Privately Held**
SIC: 1731 General electrical contractor

(P-2611)
ICKLER ELECTRIC CORPORATION
13250 Kirkham Way, Poway (92064)
PHONE..........................858 486-1585
Kurt Ickler, *CEO*
Laurie Ickler, *Vice Pres*
EMP: 50
SQ FT: 5,435
SALES (est): 13.5MM **Privately Held**
WEB: www.icklerelectric.com
SIC: 1731 General electrical contractor

(P-2612)
ICS INTEGRATED COMM SYSTEMS
6680 Via Del Oro, San Jose (95119-1392)
PHONE..........................408 491-6000
Aaron Colton, *CEO*
Tammy Bailey, *Administration*
Carolyn Brown, *Administration*
Jason Meyer, *Prgrmr*
Trevor Hickey, *Technician*
▲ **EMP:** 65
SQ FT: 18,000
SALES: 22.1MM **Privately Held**
WEB: www.ceitronics.com
SIC: 1731 Fire detection & burglar alarm systems specialization; access control systems specialization; cable television installation; voice, data & video wiring contractor

(P-2613)
INTERIOR ELECTRIC INCORPORATED
747 N Main St, Orange (92868-1105)
PHONE..........................714 771-9098
Mark Beverly, *President*
Gus Baquerizo, *Vice Pres*
Mark Maskevich, *Vice Pres*
Glen Nielsen, *Vice Pres*
Chad Stewart, *Vice Pres*
EMP: 75
SQ FT: 10,000
SALES (est): 13.3MM **Privately Held**
WEB: www.interiorelectric.com
SIC: 1731 General electrical contractor

(P-2614)
IPITEK INC
2461 Impala Dr, Carlsbad (92010-7227)
P.O. Box 130878 (92013-0878)
PHONE..........................760 438-1010
Michael M Salour, *Ch of Bd*
EMP: 170
SQ FT: 40,000
SALES (est): 16.1MM **Privately Held**
WEB: www.ipitek.com
SIC: 1731 Fiber optic cable installation

(P-2615)
ITRON INC
1111 Broadway Ste 1800, Oakland (94607-4091)
PHONE..........................510 844-2800
Derek Hall, *Manager*
Robin Hill, *Administration*
Leslie Fergison, *Human Resources*
Wendy Lohkamp, *Marketing Staff*
David Yee, *Director*
EMP: 2000
SALES (corp-wide): 2B **Publicly Held**
WEB: www.siliconenergy.com
SIC: 1731 3571 Energy management controls; electronic computers
PA: Itron, Inc.
2111 N Molter Rd
Liberty Lake WA 99019
509 924-9900

(P-2616)
JAROTH INC
Also Called: Pacific Telemanagement Svcs
2001 Crow Canyon Rd # 200, San Ramon (94583-5368)
PHONE..........................925 553-3650
Thomas R Keane, *CEO*
Michael R Zumbo, *President*
Nancy Rossi, *CFO*
Doug Lubushkin, *General Mgr*

EMP: 130
SALES (est): 33.6MM **Privately Held**
WEB: www.pts-telecom.com
SIC: 1731 7349 Telephone & telephone equipment installation; telephone booth cleaning & maintenance

(P-2617)
JEEVA CORP
Also Called: Satellite Pros
750 E E St Unit B, Ontario (91764-3821)
PHONE..........................909 238-4073
Orlando Uranga, *CEO*
EMP: 50 **EST:** 2011
SQ FT: 1,800
SALES: 2.5MM **Privately Held**
SIC: 1731 Cable television installation

(P-2618)
JENSCO INC
Also Called: J M Electric
400 Griffin St, Salinas (93901-4344)
PHONE..........................831 422-7819
Frederick A Jensen, *President*
Chris Jensen, *CFO*
EMP: 50
SQ FT: 8,400
SALES (est): 8.2MM **Privately Held**
SIC: 1731 General electrical contractor

(P-2619)
JMG SECURITY SYSTEMS INC
17150 Newhope St Ste 109, Fountain Valley (92708-4273)
PHONE..........................714 545-8882
Ken Jacobs, *CEO*
Mike Christensen, *COO*
Michael Christensen, *Exec VP*
Gil Ledesma, *Exec VP*
Sue Tjelmeland, *Vice Pres*
EMP: 70
SQ FT: 14,000
SALES (est): 14.2MM **Privately Held**
SIC: 1731 5063 Safety & security specialization; burglar alarm systems

(P-2620)
JOE LUNARDI ELECTRIC INC
5334 Sebastopol Rd, Santa Rosa (95407-6423)
P.O. Box 120, Sebastopol (95473-0120)
PHONE..........................707 823-2129
Joseph I Lunardi, *Ch of Bd*
Jolene A Corcoran, *President*
Ronald J Lunardi, *Corp Secy*
Raymond J Lunardi, *Vice Pres*
EMP: 52
SQ FT: 12,000
SALES (est): 10.5MM **Privately Held**
WEB: www.lunardielectric.com
SIC: 1731 General electrical contractor

(P-2621)
JOIE DE VIVRE HOSPITALITY LLC
210 E Main St, Los Gatos (95030-6107)
PHONE..........................408 335-1700
EMP: 618
SALES (corp-wide): 231.8MM **Privately Held**
SIC: 1731 Electrical work
PA: Joie De Vivre Hospitality, Llc
1750 Geary Blvd
San Francisco CA 94115
415 835-0300

(P-2622)
KCS ELECTRIC INC
1585 N Harmony Cir, Anaheim (92807-6003)
P.O. Box 1478, Big Bear Lake (92315-1478)
PHONE..........................623 551-1500
Kenneth C Simonds, *President*
EMP: 60
SALES (est): 4.1MM **Privately Held**
WEB: www.kcselectric.com
SIC: 1731 Electrical work

(P-2623)
KDC INC (HQ)
Also Called: Kdc Systems
4462 Corporate Center Dr, Los Alamitos (90720-2539)
PHONE..........................714 828-7000
Johnny Menninga, *President*

William B Davenport, *CFO*
Dan Bennett, *General Mgr*
Geoff Scarp, *Technology*
Larry Barcelos, *Engineer*
EMP: 144
SQ FT: 57,000
SALES: 64.5MM
SALES (corp-wide): 7.6B **Publicly Held**
WEB: www.dyna-la.com
SIC: 1731 1611 3823 General electrical contractor; general contractor, highway & street construction; industrial instrmnts msrmnt display/control process variable
PA: Emcor Group, Inc.
301 Merritt 7 Fl 6
Norwalk CT 06851
203 849-7800

(P-2624)
KERTEL COMMUNICATIONS INC (HQ)
Also Called: Sebastian
7600 N Palm Ave Ste 101, Fresno (93711-5520)
PHONE..........................559 432-5800
William S Barcus, *CEO*
Ruth Barcus, *Vice Pres*
Ron Cato, *Vice Pres*
Sarah Gonzales, *Office Mgr*
Susan Moran, *Admin Sec*
EMP: 92
SQ FT: 9,436
SALES: 23.4MM
SALES (corp-wide): 51.4MM **Privately Held**
SIC: 1731 Communications specialization
PA: Sebastian Enterprises, Inc.
811 S Madera Ave
Kerman CA 93630
559 946-4954

(P-2625)
KITE ELECTRIC INC
Also Called: K E
2 Thomas, Irvine (92618-2512)
PHONE..........................949 380-7471
Tracy Adams, *President*
Irwin Guadalupe, *Purchasing*
EMP: 120
SALES (est): 14.9MM **Privately Held**
SIC: 1731 Electrical work

(P-2626)
KOSITCH ENTERPRISES INC
Also Called: MISSION ELECTRIC COMPANY
5700 Boscell Cmn, Fremont (94538-5111)
PHONE..........................510 657-4460
Jeffrey Kositch, *CEO*
Jeffrey A Kositch, *Treasurer*
Heather Hartel, *Controller*
Miles Goodman, *Manager*
Patrick Macones, *Manager*
EMP: 80
SQ FT: 9,000
SALES: 29.7MM **Privately Held**
WEB: www.mission-elec.com
SIC: 1731 General electrical contractor

(P-2627)
L TECH NETWORK SERVICES INC
9926 Pioneer Blvd Ste 101, Santa Fe Springs (90670-6248)
PHONE..........................562 222-1121
Robert O Lopez, *President*
EMP: 65
SQ FT: 4,060
SALES: 5MM **Privately Held**
WEB: www.ltechnet.com
SIC: 1731 Communications specialization

(P-2628)
LASER ELECTRIC INC
2250 Micro Pl 200, Escondido (92029-1011)
PHONE..........................760 658-6626
Denise Hartnett, *CEO*
Kevin Hartnett, *Vice Pres*
EMP: 50
SQ FT: 11,000
SALES: 18.3MM **Privately Held**
SIC: 1731 General electrical contractor

(P-2629)
LAZER ELECTRIC INC
4701 E Hunter Ave, Anaheim (92807-1940)
PHONE..........................714 777-4233
Rodney W Brewer, *President*
David Cameron, *Treasurer*
Richard Southern, *Vice Pres*
EMP: 85
SQ FT: 13,000
SALES: 6MM **Privately Held**
WEB: www.lazerelect.com
SIC: 1731 General electrical contractor

(P-2630)
LEED ELECTRIC INC
13138 Arctic Cir, Santa Fe Springs (90670-5508)
PHONE..........................562 270-9500
Seth Jamali, *President*
Ali Pakzad, *Vice Pres*
Annette Iribarren, *Manager*
EMP: 51
SQ FT: 7,000
SALES: 14.5MM **Privately Held**
WEB: www.leedelect.com
SIC: 1731 Electrical work

(P-2631)
LELAND STANFORD JUNIOR UNIV
Also Called: Department of Public Safety
711 Serra St, Stanford (94305-7203)
PHONE..........................650 723-9633
Laura Wilson, *Director*
EMP: 58
SQ FT: 10,000
SALES (corp-wide): 5.6B **Privately Held**
SIC: 1731 8221 Safety & security specialization; university
PA: Leland Stanford Junior University
450 Serra Mall
Stanford CA 94305
650 723-2300

(P-2632)
M & R JOINT VENTURE ELECTRICAL
Also Called: Marrow Meadows
231 Benton Ct, Walnut (91789-5213)
PHONE..........................909 598-7700
Robert E Meadows, *Vice Pres*
Morrow-Meadows Corporation, *Co-Venturer*
David Hill, *Vice Pres*
Chris Salorio, *Planning*
John Menicucci, *Project Mgr*
EMP: 60
SALES (est): 6.5MM **Privately Held**
SIC: 1731 General electrical contractor

(P-2633)
MARK III CONSTRUCTION INC (PA)
Also Called: Mark III Dvlpers Dsgn/Builders
5101 Florin Perkins Rd, Sacramento (95826-4817)
PHONE..........................916 381-8080
Daniel Carlton, *CEO*
Jennifer O'Brien Cooley, *President*
Michael O'Brien, *Treasurer*
Mark O'Brien, *Director*
Tim O'Brien, *Director*
EMP: 75
SQ FT: 11,000
SALES (est): 26.7MM **Privately Held**
SIC: 1731 1542 1711 General electrical contractor; electronic controls installation; commercial & office building, new construction; plumbing contractors; fire sprinkler system installation

(P-2634)
MARK LAND ELECTRIC INC
7876 Deering Ave, Canoga Park (91304-5005)
PHONE..........................818 883-5110
Lloyd Saitman, *CEO*
John Bennet, *CFO*
John Bennett, *CFO*
Don Dewhurst, *Vice Pres*
Stewart Franklin, *Vice Pres*
EMP: 75
SQ FT: 10,000
SALES: 27.7MM **Privately Held**
WEB: www.landmarkelec.com
SIC: 1731 Electrical work

(P-2635)
MARTICUS ELECTRIC INC
9266 Beatty Dr Ste D, Sacramento
(95826-9732)
PHONE...................................916 368-2186
Art Munoz, *President*
Susan Munoz, *Corp Secy*
Tim Collins, *Opers Spvr*
EMP: 80
SQ FT: 14,000
SALES (est): 7.3MM **Privately Held**
WEB: www.marticus.com
SIC: 1731 General electrical contractor

(P-2636)
**MASS ELECTRIC
CONSTRUCTION CO**
1925 Wright Ave Ste D, La Verne
(91750-5847)
PHONE...................................800 933-6322
Rohit Shard, *Branch Mgr*
H Richard Case, *Manager*
EMP: 100
SALES (corp-wide): 16.6B **Privately Held**
WEB: www.masselec.com
SIC: 1731 General electrical contractor
HQ: Mass. Electric Construction Co.
    400 Totten Pond Rd # 400
    Waltham MA 02451
    781 290-1000

(P-2637)
MATSON ALARM CO INC (PA)
581 W Fallbrook Ave # 100, Fresno
(93711-5519)
PHONE...................................559 438-8000
Larry E Matson, *President*
Mike Matson, *Vice Pres*
Ben Kiser, *Info Tech Mgr*
Tim Hovsepian, *Human Res Dir*
EMP: 50
SQ FT: 1,000
SALES (est): 13.9MM **Privately Held**
WEB: www.matsonalarm.com
SIC: 1731 Fire detection & burglar alarm
    systems specialization

(P-2638)
MAY-HAN ELECTRIC INC
Also Called: M & M Electric
1600 Auburn Blvd, Sacramento
(95815-1906)
PHONE...................................916 929-0150
Cecilia J Hanson, *CEO*
Audrey Daugherty, *President*
Connie Gisler, *Corp Secy*
EMP: 65
SQ FT: 16,000
SALES: 12.7MM **Privately Held**
WEB: www.sacmmelectric.com
SIC: 1731 Lighting contractor

(P-2639)
MB HERZOG ELECTRIC INC
15709 Illinois Ave, Paramount
(90723-4112)
PHONE...................................562 531-2002
Ryan M Herzog, *CEO*
Kevin Ryan, *Vice Pres*
Kevin Murphy, *Network Enginr*
Paul Perrizo, *Opers Mgr*
Ryan Herzog, *Sales Executive*
EMP: 200
SQ FT: 6,200
SALES: 45.1MM **Privately Held**
WEB: www.herzogelectric.com
SIC: 1731 General electrical contractor

(P-2640)
MCH ELECTRIC INC (PA)
7693 Longard Rd, Livermore (94551-8208)
PHONE...................................209 835-9755
James Humphrey, *President*
Christine Morris, *CFO*
Gary Tennyson, *Vice Pres*
Tyler Humphrey, *Project Mgr*
Jonathan Young, *Project Mgr*
EMP: 62 EST: 1999
SQ FT: 2,600
SALES (est): 24.8MM **Privately Held**
WEB: www.mchelec.com
SIC: 1731 Electrical work

(P-2641)
**MCMILLAN DATA
CMMNICATIONS INC**
1950 Cesar Chavez, San Francisco
(94124-1132)
PHONE...................................415 826-5100
Patrick J McMillan, *CEO*
Mark Mahoney, *Managing Prtnr*
Jim Murray, *Managing Prtnr*
Patrick McMillan, *CEO*
EMP: 55
SALES (est): 1.9MM **Privately Held**
SIC: 1731 Electrical work

(P-2642)
MCMILLAN ELECTRIC
1950 Cesar Chavez, San Francisco
(94124-1132)
PHONE...................................415 826-5100
William Musgrave, *President*
Russell Schmittou, *CFO*
David Auch, *Vice Pres*
Ryan Mahoney, *Vice Pres*
Michael McAlister, *Vice Pres*
▲ EMP: 280 EST: 1965
SQ FT: 30,000
SALES (est): 63.2MM **Privately Held**
SIC: 1731 General electrical contractor

(P-2643)
MDE ELECTRIC COMPANY INC
2166 Palou Ave, San Francisco
(94124-1503)
PHONE...................................415 552-2500
Marshall Goldman, *CEO*
Harry Goldman, *Corp Secy*
Aaron Jelovic, *Administration*
Ranfis Villatoro, *Purch Agent*
Rudy Cervantes, *Foreman/Supr*
EMP: 50
SQ FT: 5,000
SALES (est): 9.5MM **Privately Held**
WEB: www.mde-electric.com
SIC: 1731 General electrical contractor

(P-2644)
**MEDLEY COMMUNICATIONS
INC**
255 N Ash St, Escondido (92027-3068)
PHONE...................................760 294-4579
EMP: 82 **Privately Held**
WEB: www.medleycom.com
SIC: 1731 8748 Cable television installa-
    tion; communications consulting
PA: Medley Communications, Inc
    43015 Black Deer Loop # 203
    Temecula CA 92590

(P-2645)
**MEDLEY COMMUNICATIONS
INC (PA)**
43015 Black Deer Loop # 203, Temecula
(92590-3575)
PHONE...................................951 245-5200
Darrin Medley, *President*
EMP: 175
SALES (est): 20.2MM **Privately Held**
WEB: www.medleycom.com
SIC: 1731 8748 Cable television installa-
    tion; communications consulting

(P-2646)
**METROPOLITAN ELEC CNSTR
INC**
2400 3rd St, San Francisco (94107-3111)
PHONE...................................415 642-3000
Nick Dutto, *Principal*
Mark Friedeberg, *CFO*
Jeremy Senseney, *Project Mgr*
John Gallagher, *Warehouse Mgr*
Russell Wade, *Manager*
EMP: 210 EST: 1981
SQ FT: 23,000
SALES: 63MM **Privately Held**
WEB: www.metroelectric.com
SIC: 1731 General electrical contractor

(P-2647)
METROPOWER INC
941 Grand Ave, Long Beach (90804-5214)
PHONE...................................562 305-9617
Gary Evan Freenleaf, *Branch Mgr*
EMP: 85

SALES (corp-wide): 146.1MM **Privately
Held**
SIC: 1731 Electrical work
HQ: Metropower, Inc.
    798 21st Ave
    Albany GA 31701
    229 432-7345

(P-2648)
MIKE BROWN ELECTRIC CO
561a Mercantile Dr, Cotati (94931-3040)
PHONE...................................707 792-8100
James G Brown, *President*
Tiffany Howe, *Vice Pres*
Susan Allred, *Administration*
Arnold Gonzales, *Project Mgr*
Eric Nogleberg, *Project Mgr*
EMP: 65
SQ FT: 14,000
SALES: 22.3MM **Privately Held**
WEB: www.mbelectric.com
SIC: 1731 General electrical contractor

(P-2649)
MJ STAR-LITE INC
Also Called: Star - Lite Electric
9232 Independence Ave, Chatsworth
(91311-5931)
PHONE...................................818 717-0834
Michael Rios, *President*
EMP: 50
SALES (est): 3MM **Privately Held**
SIC: 1731 Electrical work

(P-2650)
ML ELECTRICWORKS INC
11325 Magnolia Ave, Riverside
(92505-3609)
P.O. Box 70962 (92513-0962)
PHONE...................................951 687-5078
Mark S Lowen, *President*
EMP: 67
SQ FT: 2,000
SALES: 5.5MM **Privately Held**
WEB: www.mlelectricworks.com
SIC: 1731 Electrical work

(P-2651)
**MODESTO INDUSTRIAL ELEC
CO INC (PA)**
1417 Coldwell Ave, Modesto (95350-5703)
PHONE...................................209 495-1597
David Howell, *President*
Michelle Howell, *Admin Sec*
Harold Dawson, *Project Mgr*
Joel Salinas, *Technology*
Tammy Dolberry, *Accounting Mgr*
EMP: 151
SQ FT: 21,000
SALES: 51MM **Privately Held**
WEB: www.i-e-c.net
SIC: 1731 5063 7694 General electrical
    contractor; motors, electric; electric motor
    repair

(P-2652)
**MORROW-MEADOWS
CORPORATION (PA)**
Also Called: Cherry City Electric
231 Benton Ct, City of Industry
(91789-5213)
PHONE...................................858 974-3650
Robert E Meadows, *Vice Pres*
Tim Langley, *CFO*
Bob Atkinson, *Vice Pres*
Craig Earley, *Vice Pres*
Rick Jarvis, *Vice Pres*
EMP: 2000 EST: 1964
SQ FT: 55,000
SALES (est): 158.5MM **Privately Held**
WEB: www.morrow-meadows.com
SIC: 1731 General electrical contractor

(P-2653)
**MORROW-MEADOWS
CORPORATION**
1050 Bing St, San Carlos (94070-5326)
PHONE...................................510 562-1980
Jim Goetz, *Manager*
Robert Meadows, *Exec VP*
Mike Cuthbertson, *Project Mgr*
Lance Slagle, *Director*
EMP: 200

SALES (corp-wide): 158.5MM **Privately
Held**
WEB: www.morrow-meadows.com
SIC: 1731 General electrical contractor
PA: Morrow-Meadows Corporation
    231 Benton Ct
    City Of Industry CA 91789
    858 974-3650

(P-2654)
MSL ELECTRIC INC
4938 E La Palma Ave, Anaheim
(92807-1912)
PHONE...................................714 693-4837
Warren L Moore, *President*
Sally Moore, *Admin Sec*
EMP: 60
SQ FT: 12,600
SALES (est): 11MM **Privately Held**
SIC: 1731 General electrical contractor

(P-2655)
MURRIETTA CIRCUITS
5000 E Landon Dr, Anaheim (92807-1978)
PHONE...................................714 970-2430
Andrew Murrietta, *CEO*
Albert G Murrietta, *President*
Albert A Murrieta, *COO*
Helen Murrietta, *Treasurer*
Josh Murrietta, *Vice Pres*
EMP: 75 EST: 1992
SQ FT: 48,500
SALES: 8.2MM **Privately Held**
WEB: www.murrietta.com
SIC: 1731 3672 8711 Closed circuit televi-
    sion installation; printed circuit boards;
    engineering services

(P-2656)
NATIONAL FAIL SAFE INC
Also Called: National Fail-Safe SEC Systems
6442 Industry Way, Westminster
(92683-3600)
PHONE...................................562 493-5447
Al Puskas, *President*
Kathy Puskas, *Vice Pres*
Cristyn Van Fossen, *Sales Staff*
EMP: 50 EST: 1972
SQ FT: 10,000
SALES (est): 8.3MM **Privately Held**
WEB: www.nf-s.com
SIC: 1731 7382 Fire detection & burglar
    alarm systems specialization; fire alarm
    maintenance & monitoring

(P-2657)
NAZZARENO ELECTRIC CO INC
1250 E Gene Autry Way, Anaheim
(92805-6716)
PHONE...................................714 712-4744
Paul Rick Nazzareno, *President*
Jimmy Marshall, *Project Mgr*
Andrew Mead, *Foreman/Supr*
EMP: 75
SQ FT: 10,000
SALES (est): 9.6MM **Privately Held**
SIC: 1731 General electrical contractor

(P-2658)
NEAL ELECTRIC CORP (HQ)
2790 Business Park Dr, Vista (92081-7860)
P.O. Box 1655, Poway (92074-1655)
PHONE...................................858 513-2525
Daniel Zupp, *President*
Alex Meruelo, *Treasurer*
Luis Armona, *Vice Pres*
Lance Neal, *Vice Pres*
Dennis Ramsey, *Vice Pres*
EMP: 75
SQ FT: 30,000
SALES (est): 54.4MM
SALES (corp-wide): 408.1MM **Privately
Held**
WEB: www.whitney.com
SIC: 1731 General electrical contractor
PA: Meruelo Enterprises, Inc.
    9550 Firestone Blvd # 105
    Downey CA 90241
    562 745-2300

(P-2659)
**NETRONIX INTEGRATION INC
(PA)**
2170 Paragon Dr, San Jose (95131-1305)
PHONE...................................408 573-1444
Craig E Jarrett, *President*

Steve Piechota, *CFO*
Terry Houk, *Program Mgr*
Dean Scoggins, *Branch Mgr*
Yvonne Zertuche, *Admin Asst*
EMP: 92
SQ FT: 13,500
SALES (est): 26.7MM **Privately Held**
SIC: 1731 General electrical contractor

(P-2660)
NETVERSANT - SILICON VLY INC (PA)
Also Called: Apex Communications
47811 Warm Springs Blvd, Fremont (94539-7400)
PHONE.................................510 771-1200
John Chelstowski, *President*
EMP: 125
SQ FT: 14,000
SALES (est): 12.2MM **Privately Held**
WEB: www.apexcommunications.com
SIC: 1731 7376 Communications specialization; telephone & telephone equipment installation; computer facilities management

(P-2661)
NEVADA REPUBLIC ELECTRIC N INC
11855 White Rock Rd, Rancho Cordova (95742-6603)
PHONE.................................916 294-0140
Eric Stafford, *President*
Jeff Stafford, *Treasurer*
Jerry Stafford, *Director*
Linda Stafford, *Director*
EMP: 140
SQ FT: 14,000
SALES (est): 16MM **Privately Held**
WEB: www.republicelectricwest.com
SIC: 1731 General electrical contractor

(P-2662)
NEW AGE ELECTRIC INC
1085 N 11th St, San Jose (95112-2928)
PHONE.................................408 279-8787
Kurt Rocklage, *President*
Vickie Roberts, *Office Mgr*
Josh Rocklage, *Technology*
Mathew Misterka, *Controller*
Nick Hughly, *Foreman/Supr*
EMP: 60
SQ FT: 8,500
SALES (est): 13.1MM **Privately Held**
SIC: 1731 General electrical contractor

(P-2663)
NORTH STATE ELEC CONTRS INC
11415 Sunrise Gold Cir # 1, Rancho Cordova (95742-6583)
PHONE.................................916 572-0571
Rodney Bingaman, *President*
Jason Alexander, *Project Mgr*
Larry Logue, *Project Mgr*
EMP: 80
SQ FT: 5,500
SALES (est): 16.6MM **Privately Held**
SIC: 1731 General electrical contractor

(P-2664)
NORTHLAND CONTROL SYSTEMS INC (PA)
1533 California Cir, Milpitas (95035-8101)
PHONE.................................510 226-1015
Pierre Trapanese, *CEO*
Jim Conley, *CFO*
Henry Hoyne, *Vice Pres*
Bill Byington, *Program Mgr*
Chris Hoover, *Program Mgr*
EMP: 93
SALES (est): 38MM **Privately Held**
WEB: www.northlandcontrols.com
SIC: 1731 7389 Fire detection & burglar alarm systems specialization; automobile recovery service

(P-2665)
NRG POWER INC
3011 S Shannon St, Santa Ana (92704-6320)
PHONE.................................714 424-6484
Than V Nguyen, *President*
John Toan Nguyen, *Vice Pres*
EMP: 57

SQ FT: 5,700
SALES (est): 6.3MM **Privately Held**
SIC: 1731 General electrical contractor

(P-2666)
OBRYANT ELECTRIC INC
9314 Eton Ave, Chatsworth (91311-5809)
PHONE.................................818 407-1986
Cathy O'Bryant, *President*
Steve O'Bryant, *Admin Sec*
Tony Olivas, *Project Mgr*
Carlos Salazar, *Foreman/Supr*
John Mellor, *Sr Project Mgr*
EMP: 200 **EST:** 1978
SQ FT: 25,000
SALES (est): 51.4MM **Privately Held**
WEB: www.obryantelectric.com
SIC: 1731 General electrical contractor

(P-2667)
OILFIELD ELECTRIC COMPANY
Also Called: Oilfield Electric & Motor
1801 N Ventura Ave, Ventura (93001-1597)
PHONE.................................805 648-3131
Alan Dale Fletcher, *CEO*
Jana Fletcher, *President*
Scott Wallis, *Controller*
EMP: 60
SQ FT: 10,000
SALES (est): 14.7MM **Privately Held**
SIC: 1731 7629 General electrical contractor; electrical repair shops

(P-2668)
ONLINE COMMUNICATIONS INC
3291 Swetzer Rd, Loomis (95650-7607)
PHONE.................................916 652-7253
Martin P Green, *President*
Christopher Green, *Vice Pres*
Marty Green, *Vice Pres*
EMP: 110
SALES (est): 6.9MM **Privately Held**
SIC: 1731 4813 8748 Fiber optic cable installation; telephone & telephone equipment installation; telephone communication, except radio; telecommunications consultant

(P-2669)
PACIFIC METRO ELECTRIC INC
3150 E Fremont St, Stockton (95205-3918)
P.O. Box 127 (95201-0127)
PHONE.................................209 939-3222
Glen Rigsbee, *President*
Jim Bohacek, *Project Mgr*
EMP: 60
SALES (est): 10.3MM **Privately Held**
WEB: www.pacificmetroelectric.com
SIC: 1731 General electrical contractor

(P-2670)
PACIFIC UTLTY INSTLLATION INC
1585 N Harmony Cir, Anaheim (92807-6003)
PHONE.................................714 970-6430
William B Pfeifer, *CEO*
Daniel Mole, *President*
▲ **EMP:** 65
SALES (est): 14.8MM **Privately Held**
SIC: 1731 1623 General electrical contractor; water, sewer & utility lines

(P-2671)
PAGANINI ELECTRIC CORPORATION
Also Called: Paganini Companies
190 Hubbell St Ste 200, San Francisco (94107-2240)
PHONE.................................415 575-3900
Kenneth A Paganini, *CEO*
Michael K Paganini, *President*
Benson Lee, *Info Tech Dir*
Ron Baxter, *Project Mgr*
Shane Brown, *Project Mgr*
EMP: 115
SQ FT: 20,000
SALES (est): 28.4MM **Privately Held**
WEB: www.pagcos.com
SIC: 1731 General electrical contractor

(P-2672)
PAR ELECTRICAL CONTRACTORS INC
525 Corporate Dr, Escondido (92029-1500)
PHONE.................................760 291-1192
Jay Taylor, *Vice Pres*
EMP: 58
SALES (corp-wide): 9.4B **Publicly Held**
SIC: 1731 General electrical contractor
HQ: Par Electrical Contractors, Inc.
　4770 N Belleview Ave # 109
　Kansas City MO 64116
　816 474-9340

(P-2673)
PAR ELECTRICAL CONTRACTORS INC
11276 5th St Ste 100, Rancho Cucamonga (91730-0922)
PHONE.................................909 854-2880
Jim Stapp, *Manager*
EMP: 100
SALES (corp-wide): 9.4B **Publicly Held**
WEB: www.parelectric.com
SIC: 1731 General electrical contractor
HQ: Par Electrical Contractors, Inc.
　4770 N Belleview Ave # 109
　Kansas City MO 64116
　816 474-9340

(P-2674)
PAR ELECTRICAL CONTRACTORS INC
1416 Midway Rd, Vacaville (95688-9437)
PHONE.................................707 693-1237
Kenny Bruce, *Vice Pres*
EMP: 80
SALES (corp-wide): 9.4B **Publicly Held**
WEB: www.parelectric.com
SIC: 1731 General electrical contractor
HQ: Par Electrical Contractors, Inc.
　4770 N Belleview Ave # 109
　Kansas City MO 64116
　816 474-9340

(P-2675)
PARADISE ELECTRIC INC
697 Greenfield Dr, El Cajon (92021-2983)
PHONE.................................619 449-4141
Mike Manos, *President*
Jeff Platt, *CFO*
EMP: 70
SQ FT: 7,000
SALES: 6MM
SALES (corp-wide): 96.6MM **Privately Held**
WEB: www.paradise-electric.com
SIC: 1731 General electrical contractor
HQ: Builders Tradesource Corp
　697 Greenfield Dr
　El Cajon CA 92021
　619 792-1795

(P-2676)
PATRIC COMMUNICATIONS INC (PA)
Also Called: Advanced Electronic Solutions
33 Hammond Ste 201, Irvine (92618-1637)
PHONE.................................619 579-2898
Sean P McDermott, *President*
Richard P Apgar, *Vice Pres*
Kathy Alford, *Admin Sec*
EMP: 70
SQ FT: 27,000
SALES (est): 8.1MM **Privately Held**
WEB: www.aes2.net
SIC: 1731 1751 3699 Fire detection & burglar alarm systems specialization; carpentry work; security devices

(P-2677)
PAVLETICH ELC CMMNICATIONS INC (PA)
6308 Seven Seas Ave, Bakersfield (93308-5132)
PHONE.................................661 589-9473
John Pavletich, *CEO*
Scott Pavletich, *President*
Andy Sweaney, *Manager*
Ryan Kurtz, *Supervisor*
EMP: 90
SQ FT: 15,000

SALES (est): 18MM **Privately Held**
WEB: www.pavelectric.com
SIC: 1731 General electrical contractor; fiber optic cable installation

(P-2678)
PETRELLI ELECTRIC INC
11615 Davenport Rd, Agua Dulce (91390-4690)
P.O. Box 801148, Santa Clarita (91380-1148)
PHONE.................................661 268-7312
Cindy Petrelli, *CEO*
Bill Murray, *Vice Pres*
Salvatore Petrelli, *Vice Pres*
Linda Pellico, *Office Mgr*
Katelyn Petrelli, *Admin Asst*
EMP: 66
SALES (est): 16.1MM **Privately Held**
SIC: 1731 7629 General electrical contractor; electrical equipment repair, high voltage

(P-2679)
PHASE 3 COMMUNICATIONS INC
224 N 27th St Ste B, San Jose (95116-1120)
PHONE.................................408 946-9011
Nicolas Dezubiria, *CEO*
Ruben N Yusi, *CFO*
Ruben Yusi, *CFO*
Juan Dezubiria, *Vice Pres*
Walid Azizi, *Engineer*
EMP: 70
SQ FT: 3,500
SALES (est): 7MM **Privately Held**
WEB: www.p3com.net
SIC: 1731 1799 Fiber optic cable installation; cable splicing service

(P-2680)
PINNACLE NETWORKING SVCS INC
Also Called: Pinnacle Communication Svcs
730 Fairmont Ave, Glendale (91203-1078)
PHONE.................................818 241-6009
Avo Amirian, *CEO*
Joe Licursi, *President*
Jose Aguirre, *Executive*
Carlos Barajas, *Admin Asst*
Roupen Dilan, *Administration*
EMP: 75
SQ FT: 10,000
SALES (est): 19.9MM **Privately Held**
SIC: 1731 Communications specialization; general electrical contractor; telephone & telephone equipment installation; computer installation

(P-2681)
PIVOT INTERIORS INC
Pivot Interiors-Receiving Only
3200 Park Center Dr # 100, Costa Mesa (92626-7104)
PHONE.................................949 988-5400
Ken Baugh, *CEO*
EMP: 60
SALES (corp-wide): 171MM **Privately Held**
WEB: www.pivotinteriors.com
SIC: 1731 Electrical work
PA: Pivot Interiors, Inc.
　3355 Scott Blvd Ste 110
　Santa Clara CA 95054
　408 432-5600

(P-2682)
PMD INDUSTRIES INC
Also Called: Eie Electric
703 Randolph Ave, Costa Mesa (92626-5917)
PHONE.................................949 222-0999
Phillip M Davis, *President*
Howard C Waters, *CFO*
John Davis, *Vice Pres*
Matt Engle, *Manager*
EMP: 50
SQ FT: 2,500
SALES (est): 7.7MM **Privately Held**
WEB: www.eieelectric.com
SIC: 1731 7373 Electrical work; computer integrated systems design

▲ = Import ▼=Export
◆ =Import/Export

(P-2683)
POINT ONE ELEC SYSTEMS INC
6751 Southfront Rd, Livermore
(94551-8218)
PHONE.....................925 667-2935
Michael G Curran, *President*
Thomas F Curran, *Vice Pres*
Ken Miller, *Vice Pres*
EMP: 60
SQ FT: 30,000
SALES: 15MM **Privately Held**
SIC: 1731 Electrical work

(P-2684)
PONDEROSA ELECTRIC INC
17155 Von Karman Ave # 101, Irvine
(92614-0906)
PHONE.....................949 253-3100
Dale Arnold, *President*
EMP: 60
SQ FT: 2,400
SALES: 4.8MM **Privately Held**
SIC: 1731 General electrical contractor

(P-2685)
PORTERMATT ELECTRIC INC
5431 Production Dr, Huntington Beach
(92649-1524)
PHONE.....................714 596-8788
Tim Matthews, *President*
John F Porter III, *Vice Pres*
EMP: 90
SQ FT: 5,300
SALES (est): 19.5MM **Privately Held**
SIC: 1731 1799 General electrical contractor; athletic & recreation facilities construction

(P-2686)
POWER PLUS SOLUTIONS CORP
1210 N Red Gum St, Anaheim
(92806-1820)
PHONE.....................714 507-1881
Steven Bray, *President*
EMP: 50
SALES (est): 1.8MM **Privately Held**
SIC: 1731 Electric power systems contractors
PA: Power Plus International, Inc.
1210 N Red Gum St
Anaheim CA 92806

(P-2687)
PROFESSNAL ELEC CNSTR SVCS INC
Also Called: Pecs
9112 Santa Anita Ave, Rancho Cucamonga
(91730-6143)
PHONE.....................909 373-4100
Diane Casey, *CEO*
Robert W Casey, *CFO*
Jeff Hager, *Supervisor*
EMP: 102
SQ FT: 15,000
SALES (est): 17.8MM **Privately Held**
SIC: 1731 General electrical contractor

(P-2688)
PS DEVELOPMENT CORPORATION
21625 Prairie St, Chatsworth (91311-5833)
PHONE.....................818 340-0965
Adam Saitman, *President*
EMP: 100
SQ FT: 5,000
SALES (est): 4.9MM **Privately Held**
SIC: 1731 General electrical contractor

(P-2689)
PYRO-COMM SYSTEMS INC (PA)
15531 Container Ln, Huntington Beach
(92649-1530)
PHONE.....................714 902-8000
Michael Donahue, *President*
Nanci Donahue, *Vice Pres*
Lisa Ayala, *Administration*
Melissa Tadlock, *Administration*
Margarita Hristeva, *Info Tech Mgr*
EMP: 150
SQ FT: 10,000

SALES (est): 45.4MM **Privately Held**
WEB: www.pyrocomm.com
SIC: 1731 5063 Safety & security specialization; fire alarm systems

(P-2690)
R & R ELECTRIC
2029 Century Park E A4, Los Angeles
(90067-1915)
PHONE.....................310 785-0288
Ricardo Ramos, *Owner*
Brenda Mitchell, *Office Admin*
Brishen Foley, *Technology*
Miguel Navarrete, *Purch Agent*
Mario Mata, *Superintendent*
EMP: 50
SQ FT: 5,000
SALES (est): 4.2MM **Privately Held**
SIC: 1731 General electrical contractor

(P-2691)
RADONICH CORP
Also Called: Cal Coast Telecom
886 Faulstich Ct, San Jose (95112-1361)
PHONE.....................408 275-8888
Rick M Radonich, *CEO*
David S Miguel, *Corp Secy*
William L Radonich Jr, *Vice Pres*
EMP: 50
SQ FT: 5,000
SALES: 18MM **Privately Held**
WEB: www.calcoasttelecom.com
SIC: 1731 Fiber optic cable installation; voice, data & video wiring contractor

(P-2692)
RANCHO PACIFIC ELECTRIC INC
9063 Santa Anita Ave, Rancho Cucamonga
(91730-6142)
PHONE.....................909 476-1022
Steve Robinson, *President*
Dave Robinson, *Corp Secy*
EMP: 50
SQ FT: 4,500
SALES (est): 2.8MM **Privately Held**
SIC: 1731 General electrical contractor

(P-2693)
RAYLEE ELECTRIC
1202 Tarapin Ln, Lincoln (95648-8138)
PHONE.....................916 408-7556
R George Alvarado, *President*
Raymond George Alvarado, *President*
Cindy Alvarado, *Vice Pres*
EMP: 50
SALES (est): 206K **Privately Held**
SIC: 1731 Electrical work

(P-2694)
RCI ELECTRIC INC
Also Called: Rayco Electric
3144 Fitzgerald Rd, Rancho Cordova
(95742-6802)
PHONE.....................916 858-8000
Raymond Alvarado, *President*
Jimmy Green, *Purch Mgr*
EMP: 99
SALES (est): 14.7MM **Privately Held**
WEB: www.raycoelectric.com
SIC: 1731 General electrical contractor

(P-2695)
RDM ELECTRIC CO INC
13867 Redwood Ave, Chino (91710-6010)
PHONE.....................909 591-0990
Robert McDonnell, *President*
Diane McDonnell, *Officer*
Anthony Gerdes, *Vice Pres*
Robert D McDonnell Jr, *Vice Pres*
Maria Bernabe, *Administration*
EMP: 75
SALES: 19MM **Privately Held**
SIC: 1731 General electrical contractor

(P-2696)
RED HAWK FIRE & SEC CA INC
4384 Enterprise Pl, Fremont (94538-6365)
PHONE.....................510 438-1300
Mack Katal, *President*
EMP: 90
SALES (corp-wide): 349.6MM **Privately Held**
SIC: 1731 Fire detection & burglar alarm systems specialization

HQ: Red Hawk Fire & Security (Ca), Inc.
7605 N San Fernando Rd
Los Angeles CA 90065

(P-2697)
RED HAWK FIRE & SEC CA INC
1640 N Batavia St, Orange (92867-3509)
PHONE.....................714 685-8100
Bob Berkery, *Manager*
EMP: 105
SALES (corp-wide): 349.6MM **Privately Held**
WEB: www.detectionlogic.com
SIC: 1731 Fire detection & burglar alarm systems specialization
HQ: Red Hawk Fire & Security (Ca), Inc.
7605 N San Fernando Rd
Los Angeles CA 90065

(P-2698)
RED HAWK FIRE & SEC CA INC (HQ)
7605 N San Fernando Rd, Los Angeles
(90065)
PHONE.....................818 683-1500
Sean Flint, *CEO*
EMP: 94
SQ FT: 15,500
SALES (est): 32.4MM
SALES (corp-wide): 349.6MM **Privately Held**
WEB: www.chubbfs.com
SIC: 1731 Fire detection & burglar alarm systems specialization
PA: Red Hawk Fire & Security, Llc
5100 Town Center Cir # 350
Boca Raton FL 33486
877 387-0188

(P-2699)
RED HAWK FIRE & SEC CA INC
920 S Andreasen Dr # 102, Escondido
(92029-1936)
PHONE.....................760 233-9787
Brad Mattonen, *Branch Mgr*
EMP: 68
SALES (corp-wide): 349.6MM **Privately Held**
SIC: 1731 Fire detection & burglar alarm systems specialization
HQ: Red Hawk Fire & Security (Ca), Inc.
7605 N San Fernando Rd
Los Angeles CA 90065

(P-2700)
REDWOOD ELECTRIC GROUP INC (PA)
2775 Northwestern Pkwy, Santa Clara
(95051-0947)
PHONE.....................707 451-7348
Victor Castello, *President*
Jeff Tarzwell, *CFO*
Gordon Armstrong, *Vice Pres*
Bruce Kelly, *Vice Pres*
EMP: 680 **EST:** 1974
SQ FT: 35,000
SALES (est): 190.2MM **Privately Held**
SIC: 1731 General electrical contractor

(P-2701)
REPUBLIC ELECTRIC INC
3820 Happy Ln, Sacramento (95827-9721)
PHONE.....................916 294-0140
Eric Stafford, *Manager*
EMP: 100
SALES (corp-wide): 29.6MM **Privately Held**
SIC: 1731 Electrical work
PA: Republic Electric, Inc.
3985 N Pecos Rd
Las Vegas NV 89115
702 643-2688

(P-2702)
REPUBLIC ELECTRIC WEST INC
3820 Happy Ln, Sacramento (95827-9721)
PHONE.....................916 294-0140
Eric J Stafford, *President*
Gerald Stafford, *CFO*
Hope Weber, *Executive*
Skip Harvey, *General Mgr*
Jerry Stafford, *Admin Sec*
EMP: 70

SALES (est): 10.3MM **Privately Held**
SIC: 1731 General electrical contractor

(P-2703)
REX MOORE GROUP INC
6001 Outfall Cir, Sacramento (95828-1020)
PHONE.....................916 372-1300
David Rex Moore, *President*
Doug Cuthbert, *President*
J Brock Littlejohn, *CFO*
James Brock Littlejohn, *CFO*
William C Hubbard, *Exec VP*
EMP: 450
SQ FT: 36,000
SALES (est): 121.2MM **Privately Held**
WEB: www.rmi-systems.com
SIC: 1731 8711 General electrical contractor; engineering services

(P-2704)
REX MORE ELEC CONTRS ENGINEERS (PA)
6001 Outfall Cir, Sacramento (95828-1020)
PHONE.....................916 372-1300
David R Moore, *CEO*
William C Hubbard, *Partner*
James B Littlejohn, *Partner*
Steven R Moore, *Partner*
Roberto Santos, *Telecom Exec*
EMP: 550
SQ FT: 36,000
SALES (est): 74.1MM **Privately Held**
WEB: www.rexmoore.com
SIC: 1731 General electrical contractor

(P-2705)
REX MORE ELEC CONTRS ENGINEERS
5803 E Harvard Ave, Fresno (93727-1366)
P.O. Box 7677 (93747-7677)
PHONE.....................559 294-1300
John Abele, *Manager*
Tristan Hankla, *Sr Project Mgr*
EMP: 70
SALES (est): 4.1MM
SALES (corp-wide): 74.1MM **Privately Held**
SIC: 1731 General electrical contractor
PA: Rex Moore Electrical Contractors & Engineers, Inc
6001 Outfall Cir
Sacramento CA 95828
916 372-1300

(P-2706)
REX MORE ELEC CONTRS ENGINEERS
6001 Outfall Cir, Sacramento (95828-1020)
PHONE.....................510 785-1300
Brent Iseman, *Manager*
EMP: 100
SALES (est): 4.6MM
SALES (corp-wide): 74.1MM **Privately Held**
SIC: 1731 General electrical contractor
PA: Rex Moore Electrical Contractors & Engineers, Inc
6001 Outfall Cir
Sacramento CA 95828
916 372-1300

(P-2707)
RFI ENTERPRISES INC (PA)
Also Called: RFI Communications SEC Systems
360 Turtle Creek Ct, San Jose
(95125-1389)
PHONE.....................408 298-5400
Dee Ann Harn, *President*
Michelle Brooks, *Vice Pres*
Dale Mac McComb, *Vice Pres*
Dale Mc Comb, *Vice Pres*
Brad J Wilson, *Principal*
EMP: 54
SQ FT: 30,000
SALES (est): 60.9MM **Privately Held**
SIC: 1731 7382 Safety & security specialization; communications specialization; security systems services

(P-2708)
RIIVOS INC
130 Battery St Fl 3, San Francisco
(94111-4905)
PHONE.....................415 813-1840

PRODUCTS & SVCS

Michele Wardell McGovern, *CEO*
EMP: 60
SALES (est): 86.8K **Privately Held**
SIC: 1731 Electrical work

(P-2709)
RIS ELECTRICAL CONTRS INC
7330 Sycamore Canyon Blvd # 1, Riverside
(92508-2317)
PHONE..............................951 688-8049
Bob Hayes, *President*
EMP: 50
SQ FT: 1,600
SALES (est): 7MM **Privately Held**
SIC: 1731 General electrical contractor

(P-2710)
RJB ENTERPRISES INC
Also Called: Ultimate Communication Systems
2579 W Woodland Dr, Anaheim
(92801-2608)
PHONE..............................714 484-3101
Robert Bohan, *President*
Don Averill, *Manager*
Donald Ramirez, *Manager*
EMP: 50
SQ FT: 3,500
SALES (est): 6.7MM **Privately Held**
WEB: www.ucomsys.com
SIC: 1731 Voice, data & video wiring contractor

(P-2711)
RK ELECTRIC INC
42021 Osgood Rd, Fremont (94539-5028)
PHONE..............................510 580-2850
Lonnie Robinson, *President*
Raul Real, *Vice Pres*
Dale Swanson, *Vice Pres*
Dan Yeggy, *Vice Pres*
Michael Wonderlin, *Info Tech Mgr*
EMP: 130
SQ FT: 11,500
SALES (est): 27.5MM **Privately Held**
SIC: 1731 General electrical contractor

(P-2712)
ROSENDIN ELECTRIC INC (PA)
880 Mabury Rd, San Jose (95133-1021)
P.O. Box 49070 (95161-9070)
PHONE..............................408 286-2800
Tom Sorley, *Ch of Bd*
Larry Beltramo, *President*
Lorne Rundquist, *CFO*
Sam Lamonica, *CIO*
Steve Collier, *Info Tech Mgr*
EMP: 3000 **EST:** 1919
SQ FT: 45,000
SALES (est): 2B **Privately Held**
WEB: www.rosendin.com
SIC: 1731 General electrical contractor

(P-2713)
ROSENDIN ELECTRIC INC
1730 S Anaheim Way, Anaheim
(92805-6537)
PHONE..............................714 739-1334
Cliff Thompson, *Branch Mgr*
Brian Smith, *Sr Project Mgr*
Susanne Beckwith, *Manager*
Jake Woodworth, *Manager*
EMP: 668
SALES (corp-wide): 2B **Privately Held**
SIC: 1731 General electrical contractor
PA: Rosendin Electric, Inc.
880 Mabury Rd
San Jose CA 95133
408 286-2800

(P-2714)
ROSENDIN ELECTRIC INC
2698 Orchard Pkwy, San Jose
(95134-2020)
PHONE..............................408 321-2200
Mary Marshall, *Principal*
EMP: 668
SALES (corp-wide): 2B **Privately Held**
SIC: 1731 General electrical contractor
PA: Rosendin Electric, Inc.
880 Mabury Rd
San Jose CA 95133
408 286-2800

(P-2715)
ROSENDIN ELECTRIC INC
2121 Oakdale Ave, San Francisco
(94124-1530)
PHONE..............................415 495-9300
Rick Shandrew, *Manager*
EMP: 213
SALES (corp-wide): 2B **Privately Held**
WEB: www.rosendin.com
SIC: 1731 General electrical contractor
PA: Rosendin Electric, Inc.
880 Mabury Rd
San Jose CA 95133
408 286-2800

(P-2716)
ROSENDIN ELECTRIC INC
1001 Potrero Ave, San Francisco
(94110-3518)
PHONE..............................415 495-9300
EMP: 668
SALES (corp-wide): 2B **Privately Held**
SIC: 1731 General electrical contractor
PA: Rosendin Electric, Inc.
880 Mabury Rd
San Jose CA 95133
408 286-2800

(P-2717)
ROWAN INCORPORATED
Also Called: Rowan Electric
2778 Loker Ave W, Carlsbad (92010-6611)
PHONE..............................760 692-0700
Paul J Rowan, *CEO*
Mark B Rowan, *Vice Pres*
EMP: 67
SQ FT: 6,000
SALES (est): 15MM **Privately Held**
WEB: www.rowanelectric.com
SIC: 1731 Electrical work

(P-2718)
RYE ELECTRIC INC
3940 Electric Ave, Laguna Hills (92653)
PHONE..............................949 441-0545
Christopher Dale Golden, *CEO*
EMP: 62
SALES (est): 235.4K **Privately Held**
SIC: 1731 Electrical work

(P-2719)
SABAH INTERNATIONAL INC (HQ)
5925 Stoneridge Dr, Pleasanton
(94588-2705)
PHONE..............................925 463-0431
Michele Sabah, *CEO*
Don Jones, *Division Mgr*
Jason Hughes, *Project Mgr*
Jay Keenan, *Project Mgr*
Lex Nadeau, *Project Mgr*
EMP: 51
SQ FT: 13,000
SALES (est): 15.3MM
SALES (corp-wide): 51.1MM **Privately Held**
WEB: www.sabah-intl.com
SIC: 1731 7382 Safety & security specialization; protective devices, security
PA: Sciens Building Solutions, Llc
500 Griswold St Ste 2700
Detroit MI 48226
313 962-5800

(P-2720)
SAGE ELECTRIC COMPANY
9144 Owensmouth Ave, Chatsworth
(91311-5851)
P.O. Box 1266, Agoura Hills (91376-1266)
PHONE..............................818 718-9080
Greg Stevens, *President*
Ilya Sitnitsky, *President*
Mark Custodero, *Treasurer*
Donald Huff, *Vice Pres*
Brad Pennington, *Admin Sec*
EMP: 75
SQ FT: 3,500
SALES (est): 11.7MM **Privately Held**
SIC: 1731 General electrical contractor

(P-2721)
SAN DIEGO BAY AREA ELC INC
13100 Kirkham Way Ste 205, Poway
(92064-7128)
PHONE..............................858 748-2060
Dennis P Phillips, *President*
EMP: 60
SQ FT: 3,500
SALES (est): 6.2MM **Privately Held**
SIC: 1731 Electrical work

(P-2722)
SANTA CRUZ WESTSIDE ELC INC
Also Called: Sandbar Solar and Electric
2119 Delaware Ave, Santa Cruz
(95060-5706)
PHONE..............................831 469-8888
Scott Laskey, *President*
EMP: 55 **EST:** 2004
SALES (est): 1.9MM **Privately Held**
SIC: 1731 Electrical work

(P-2723)
SATURN ELECTRIC INC
7552 Trade St Ste A, San Diego
(92121-2412)
PHONE..............................858 271-4100
Ron Dudek, *President*
Tim A Dudek, *President*
Thomas J Dudek, *Vice Pres*
Joe Fraire, *Administration*
EMP: 50
SQ FT: 7,000
SALES (est): 6.7MM **Privately Held**
WEB: www.saturnelectric.com
SIC: 1731 Electrical work

(P-2724)
SB PRODUCT GROUP LLC
1 Circle Star Way Fl 3, San Carlos
(94070-6288)
PHONE..............................650 562-8221
R Marcelo Claure, *Mng Member*
Kahori Matsui,
EMP: 200
SALES (est): 7MM **Privately Held**
SIC: 1731 Communications specialization

(P-2725)
SBE CONTRACTING
17256 Red Hill Ave, Irvine (92614-5628)
PHONE..............................714 544-5066
Jeff Wilson, *President*
EMP: 50
SALES (est): 10.4MM **Privately Held**
SIC: 1731 General electrical contractor

(P-2726)
SCHETTER ELECTRIC INC (PA)
471 Bannon St, Sacramento (95811-0296)
P.O. Box 1377 (95812-1377)
PHONE..............................916 446-2521
Frank E Schetter, *President*
Linda Schetter, *Shareholder*
Roger Ghilain, *CFO*
Vince Bernacchi, *Vice Pres*
Keith M Hoffman, *Executive*
EMP: 90
SQ FT: 7,800
SALES (est): 23MM **Privately Held**
WEB: www.schetter.com
SIC: 1731 General electrical contractor

(P-2727)
SEAL ELECTRIC INC
1162 Greenfield Dr, El Cajon (92021-3314)
PHONE..............................619 449-7323
Frank Bongiovanni, *President*
Joe Bongiovanni, *Vice Pres*
Roy Wheeler, *Technology*
Andrew Gonzalez, *Project Engr*
Marcia Reardon, *Accounting Mgr*
EMP: 145
SQ FT: 5,000
SALES (est): 23.6MM **Privately Held**
WEB: www.sealelectric.com
SIC: 1731 General electrical contractor

(P-2728)
SECURECOM INC
4822 Golden Foothill Pkwy, El Dorado Hills
(95762-9829)
PHONE..............................916 638-2855
Kevin McElwee, *President*
EMP: 50
SALES (est): 2.2MM **Privately Held**
WEB: www.securecom.net
SIC: 1731 Fire detection & burglar alarm systems specialization

PA: Securecom, Inc.
1940 Don St Ste 100
Springfield OR 97477
-

(P-2729)
SEMANS COMMUNICATIONS (PA)
112 Stonegate Rd, Portola Vally
(94028-7649)
PHONE..............................650 529-9984
Greg Semans, *President*
Roland Valtierra, *Vice Pres*
Bonnie Semans, *Admin Sec*
EMP: 80
SQ FT: 10,000
SALES (est): 6.6MM **Privately Held**
SIC: 1731 Telephone & telephone equipment installation

(P-2730)
SERRANO ELECTRIC INC
1705 Russell Ave, Santa Clara
(95054-2032)
PHONE..............................408 986-1570
Daniel Serrano, *President*
Harry Serrano, *Executive*
Leslie Nakamura, *Admin Sec*
Dave Haney, *Project Mgr*
Michael Serrano, *Project Mgr*
EMP: 50
SQ FT: 8,000
SALES (est): 10.4MM **Privately Held**
WEB: www.serranoelectric.com
SIC: 1731 General electrical contractor

(P-2731)
SERVICE 1ST ELECTRICAL SVCS
1092 N Armando St, Anaheim
(92806-2605)
PHONE..............................714 630-9699
James Graham, *President*
EMP: 50
SALES (est): 4.8MM **Privately Held**
SIC: 1731 Electrical work

(P-2732)
SFADIA INC
Also Called: Green Energy Innovations
10011 Pioneer Blvd, Santa Fe Springs
(90670-3221)
PHONE..............................323 622-1930
Pilje Park, *President*
Pil Soon Um, *Vice Pres*
▲ **EMP:** 86
SQ FT: 8,000
SALES (est): 9.6MM **Privately Held**
SIC: 1731 Energy management controls

(P-2733)
SHORELINE HOLDINGS INC (PA)
2505 Mira Mar Ave, Long Beach
(90815-1759)
PHONE..............................562 498-6444
Robert Yellin, *President*
EMP: 105
SQ FT: 15,000
SALES (est): 7.9MM **Privately Held**
SIC: 1731 8748 Fire detection & burglar alarm systems specialization; business consulting

(P-2734)
SIMPLEX TIME RECORDER LLC
Also Called: Simplex Time Recorder 480
9855 Carroll Canyon Rd, San Diego
(92131-1103)
PHONE..............................858 740-0100
Ross Larson, *Branch Mgr*
EMP: 100 **Privately Held**
WEB: www.comtec-alaska.com
SIC: 1731 5063 7382 Fire detection & burglar alarm systems specialization; electrical apparatus & equipment; security systems services
HQ: Simplex Time Recorder Llc
50 Technology Dr
Westminster MA 01441
978 731-2500

(P-2735)
SOUTHERN CONTRACTING COMPANY
559 N Twin Oaks Valley Rd, San Marcos (92069-1798)
P.O. Box 445 (92079-0445)
PHONE....................760 744-0760
Timothy R McBride, *CEO*
Richard W Mc Bride, *President*
Tim Mc Bride, *Vice Pres*
James Filanc, *Business Dir*
Robert Pangonis, *Project Mgr*
▲ EMP: 125
SQ FT: 8,400
SALES (est): 40.6MM **Privately Held**
WEB: www.southerncontracting.com
SIC: 1731 General electrical contractor

(P-2736)
SOUTHLAND ELECTRIC INC
4950 Greencraig Ln, San Diego (92123-1673)
PHONE....................858 634-5050
Leanne M Peterson, *President*
Marilyn Ciborski, *Office Mgr*
Allen Ruckle, *Project Mgr*
Dan Vickery, *Project Mgr*
Molina Mario, *Foreman/Supr*
EMP: 54
SQ FT: 18,000
SALES: 15.3MM **Privately Held**
SIC: 1731 General electrical contractor

(P-2737)
SPECIALTY CONSTRUCTION INC
645 Clarion Ct, San Luis Obispo (93401-8177)
PHONE....................805 543-1706
Rudolph Bachmann, *President*
Chris Teaford, *CFO*
Jeff Martin, *Senior VP*
Jeffrey Martin, *Senior VP*
Doug Clay, *Vice Pres*
EMP: 80
SQ FT: 8,000
SALES (est): 33.7MM **Privately Held**
WEB: www.specialtyconstruction.com
SIC: 1731 Telephone & telephone equipment installation

(P-2738)
SPECTRA I CALIFORNIA
Also Called: Spectra Industrial Electric
21818 S Wilmington Ave # 402, Carson (90810-1642)
PHONE....................310 835-0808
Michael J Merrill, *President*
Cliff Krueger, *CFO*
Richard Mangan, *Vice Pres*
Patricia Sandoval, *Finance Mgr*
Laura Carr, *Accountant*
EMP: 70
SQ FT: 20,000
SALES (est): 7.1MM **Privately Held**
WEB: www.spectrainc.com
SIC: 1731 Access control systems specialization

(P-2739)
SPRIG ELECTRIC CO (PA)
1860 S 10th St, San Jose (95112-4108)
PHONE....................408 298-3134
Medford Snyder, *CEO*
Mark Mandarelli, *President*
Laura Lacomble, *Officer*
Hossein Tofangsazan, *Officer*
Paula Harvey, *Analyst*
EMP: 151 EST: 1970
SQ FT: 24,100
SALES (est): 68.6MM **Privately Held**
WEB: www.sprigelectric.com
SIC: 1731 General electrical contractor

(P-2740)
SR BRAY LLC (PA)
Also Called: Power Plus
1210 N Red Gum St, Anaheim (92806-1820)
PHONE....................714 765-7551
Steven R Bray, *President*
Brian Schultz, *Vice Pres*
Michelle Lee, *Administration*
Shasta Wilson, *Administration*
Sandy Hicks, *Natl Sales Mgr*

EMP: 50
SQ FT: 60,000
SALES (est): 120.9MM **Privately Held**
SIC: 1731 7359 Standby or emergency power specialization; equipment rental & leasing

(P-2741)
ST DENIS ELECTRIC INC
734 Ralcoa Way, Arroyo Grande (93420-9620)
PHONE....................805 343-9999
Jeffery S St Denis, *President*
EMP: 50
SALES (est): 729.6K **Privately Held**
SIC: 1731 Electrical work

(P-2742)
ST FRANCIS ELECTRIC INC
975 Carden St, San Leandro (94577-1102)
P.O. Box 2057 (94577-0317)
PHONE....................510 639-0639
Robert Spinardi, *President*
Randy Krebs, *CFO*
Joseph Medeiros, *Vice Pres*
Guy Smith, *Vice Pres*
Eddie Montufar, *Project Mgr*
EMP: 250 EST: 1947
SQ FT: 32,500
SALES: 60MM **Privately Held**
SIC: 1731 General electrical contractor

(P-2743)
ST FRANCIS ELECTRIC LLC
975 Carden St, San Leandro (94577-1102)
P.O. Box 2057 (94577-0317)
PHONE....................510 750-8271
Guy Smith,
EMP: 250
SALES: 30MM **Privately Held**
SIC: 1731 Electrical work

(P-2744)
STADTNER CO INC
Also Called: Sierra Electric Co
3112 Geary Blvd, San Francisco (94118-3317)
PHONE....................415 752-2850
Rose Stadtner, *President*
David Stadtner, *Vice Pres*
Larry Stadtner, *Vice Pres*
Josephine Brennan, *Administration*
Maria McDowell, *Controller*
EMP: 50 EST: 1953
SQ FT: 2,500
SALES (est): 9.3MM **Privately Held**
SIC: 1731 General electrical contractor

(P-2745)
STC NETCOM INC (PA)
11611 Industry Ave, Fontana (92337-6931)
PHONE....................951 685-8181
Giuseppe Floro, *President*
Shawnda Letourneau, *Treasurer*
Jeffry Kinne, *Admin Sec*
Ramon Estrada, *Project Mgr*
Aaron Semenoff, *Manager*
EMP: 70
SQ FT: 6,000
SALES (est): 15.1MM **Privately Held**
WEB: www.stcnetcom.com
SIC: 1731 Fiber optic cable installation; telephone & telephone equipment installation

(P-2746)
STEINY AND COMPANY INC (PA)
221 N Ardmore Ave, Los Angeles (90004-4503)
PHONE....................626 962-1055
Susan Steiny, *CEO*
John O Steiny, *Ch of Bd*
Vincent Mauch, *CFO*
Gayle Kappelman, *Admin Sec*
Paul Narvaez, *Admin Asst*
EMP: 65 EST: 1956
SQ FT: 13,000
SALES (est): 58.1MM **Privately Held**
WEB: www.steinyco.com
SIC: 1731 General electrical contractor; safety & security specialization

(P-2747)
STEINY AND COMPANY INC
221 N Ardmore Ave, Los Angeles (90004-4503)
PHONE....................213 382-2331
Joan Schultz, *Branch Mgr*
EMP: 150
SALES (corp-wide): 58.1MM **Privately Held**
SIC: 1731 General electrical contractor
PA: Steiny And Company, Inc.
221 N Ardmore Ave
Los Angeles CA 90004
626 962-1055

(P-2748)
STOMMEL INC (PA)
Also Called: Lehr
4707 Northgate Blvd, Sacramento (95834-1120)
PHONE....................916 646-6626
Jim Stommel, *President*
Linda Stommel, *Vice Pres*
EMP: 50
SQ FT: 20,000
SALES: 16.2MM **Privately Held**
WEB: www.lehrauto.com
SIC: 1731 7539 5531 Safety & security specialization; electrical services; automotive parts

(P-2749)
SUMMIT TECHNOLOGY GROUP INC
Also Called: Summit Electric
2450c Bluebell Dr Ste C, Santa Rosa (95403-2509)
PHONE....................707 542-4773
Laurence W Dashiell, *President*
EMP: 50
SALES (est): 2.1MM **Privately Held**
SIC: 1731 Voice, data & video wiring contractor

(P-2750)
SUN ELECTRIC LP
2101 S Yale St Ste B, Santa Ana (92704-4424)
PHONE....................714 210-3744
Jeffery J Bernardino, *Ltd Ptnr*
Duncan Frederick, *Partner*
Another Lighting Service, *Principal*
EMP: 100 EST: 2003
SALES (est): 3.9MM **Privately Held**
SIC: 1731 General electrical contractor

(P-2751)
SUNBELT CONTROLS INC (HQ)
6265 San Fernando Rd, Glendale (91201-2214)
PHONE....................818 244-6571
Kenneth B Westphal, *CEO*
John Hansen, *President*
Bob Hamill, *Vice Pres*
Josh Reding, *Vice Pres*
Michael Ridout, *Vice Pres*
EMP: 300
SQ FT: 20,000
SALES (est): 18MM
SALES (corp-wide): 768.2MM **Privately Held**
SIC: 1731 Environmental system control installation
PA: Acco Engineered Systems, Inc.
6265 San Fernando Rd
Glendale CA 91201
818 244-6571

(P-2752)
SUNRUN INSTALLATION SVCS INC (HQ)
775 Fiero Ln Ste 200, San Luis Obispo (93401-7904)
PHONE....................415 580-6900
Lynn Jurich, *CEO*
Robert Komin Jr, *CFO*
Mark Bettis, *Vice Pres*
Mina Kim, *Admin Sec*
Greg Whittaker, *Administration*
▲ EMP: 151
SQ FT: 26,000
SALES (est): 148MM **Publicly Held**
WEB: www.recsolar.com
SIC: 1731 Electric power systems contractors

(P-2753)
SUNSHINE COMMUNICATIONS INC
350 Cypress Ln Ste D, El Cajon (92020-1664)
P.O. Box 3509, Apollo Beach FL (33572-1005)
PHONE....................619 448-7600
Robert Straub, *CEO*
EMP: 235
SALES (est): 19.8MM **Privately Held**
WEB: www.sunshinecom.com
SIC: 1731 Cable television installation

(P-2754)
SUNWEST ELECTRIC INC
3064 E Miraloma Ave, Anaheim (92806-1810)
PHONE....................714 630-8700
Brien Pariseau, *President*
Doug Lyvers, *CFO*
Jim Aaron, *Project Mgr*
Craig Ryan, *Project Mgr*
Barry Walters, *Project Mgr*
EMP: 175
SQ FT: 20,000
SALES (est): 32.7MM **Privately Held**
SIC: 1731 Electrical work

(P-2755)
SUPERIOR ELEC MECH & PLBG INC
8613 Helms Ave, Rancho Cucamonga (91730-4521)
PHONE....................909 357-9400
David A Stone Jr, *CEO*
Walt Schobel, *President*
Pam Metzer, *CFO*
EMP: 291
SQ FT: 50,000
SALES (est): 81.4MM **Privately Held**
SIC: 1731 1711 General electrical contractor; mechanical contractor

(P-2756)
SURGENER ELECTRIC INC
Also Called: McKee Electric
1406 N Chester Ave, Bakersfield (93308-3525)
P.O. Box 5399 (93388-5399)
PHONE....................661 399-3321
Lester C Surgener II, *CEO*
Josh Lancaster, *President*
R L Surgener, *President*
Diane Dansby, *Corp Secy*
Anthony Felix, *Project Mgr*
EMP: 85 EST: 1947
SQ FT: 5,000
SALES (est): 19.5MM **Privately Held**
SIC: 1731 General electrical contractor

(P-2757)
SWINFORD ELECTRIC INC
Also Called: A & R Electric
1150 E Elm Ave, Fullerton (92831-5024)
PHONE....................714 578-8888
Sharon Swinford, *President*
Michael Swinford, *Treasurer*
Ray Winford, *General Mgr*
EMP: 50
SQ FT: 5,400
SALES (est): 9.9MM **Privately Held**
SIC: 1731 General electrical contractor

(P-2758)
SYNCHRONOSS TECHNOLOGIES INC
60 S Market St Ste 700, San Jose (95113-2370)
PHONE....................800 575-7606
EMP: 316
SALES (corp-wide): 402.3MM **Publicly Held**
SIC: 1731 7379 7371 Computerized controls installation; access control systems specialization; cogeneration specialization; electronic controls installation; ; computer software development & applications
PA: Synchronoss Technologies, Inc.
200 Crossing Blvd Fl 8
Bridgewater NJ 08807
866 620-3940

(P-2759)
T BOYER COMPANY
1656 Babcock St, Costa Mesa
(92627-4330)
PHONE..............................949 642-2431
Thomas Boyer, *President*
Scott Lite, *Supervisor*
EMP: 50
SQ FT: 1,600
SALES (est): 6.9MM **Privately Held**
SIC: 1731 General electrical contractor

(P-2760)
T MCGEE ELECTRIC INC
2390 S Reservoir St, Pomona
(91766-6410)
P.O. Box 1111, Chino (91708-1111)
PHONE..............................909 591-6461
Trent L Mc Gee, *President*
EMP: 100
SALES (est): 10.2MM **Privately Held**
SIC: 1731 General electrical contractor

(P-2761)
T S J ELEC COMMUNICATIONS INC
Also Called: Masters Electric Telcom
7490 Jurupa Ave, Riverside (92504-1030)
PHONE..............................951 785-0921
Philip Schaefer, *President*
Lisa Schaefer, *Admin Sec*
EMP: 100
SQ FT: 33,000
SALES (est): 12.9MM **Privately Held**
WEB: www.mastersec.com
SIC: 1731 General electrical contractor

(P-2762)
TAFT ELECTRIC COMPANY (PA)
1694 Eastman Ave, Ventura (93003-5782)
P.O. Box 3416 (93006-3416)
PHONE..............................805 642-0121
Walter E Hartman, *Chairman*
James Marsh, *President*
Carol A Smith, *Admin Sec*
EMP: 127
SQ FT: 40,000
SALES (est): 54.9MM **Privately Held**
WEB: www.tecelect.com
SIC: 1731 1629 General electrical contractor; waste water & sewage treatment plant construction

(P-2763)
TEL TECH PLUS INC
Also Called: Ttp-US
393 Enterprise St, San Marcos
(92078-4374)
PHONE..............................760 510-1323
Gregory A Stearns, *President*
Cindy Stearns, *Admin Sec*
Rick Clawson, *Project Mgr*
EMP: 50
SQ FT: 10,268
SALES (est): 8.8MM **Privately Held**
SIC: 1731 1623 7382 Voice, data & video wiring contractor; telephone & communication line construction; security systems services

(P-2764)
TELECMMNCTONS MGT SLUTIONS INC
Also Called: T M S
570 Division St, Campbell (95008-6906)
PHONE..............................408 866-5495
Bruce Jaftok, *President*
Michael Finn, *Vice Pres*
Kelly Cox, *Project Mgr*
Jay Wiles, *Project Mgr*
EMP: 57
SALES (est): 11.5MM **Privately Held**
WEB: www.yru.com
SIC: 1731 Voice, data & video wiring contractor

(P-2765)
TELSTAR INSTRUMENTS (PA)
1717 Solano Way Ste 34, Concord
(94520-5478)
PHONE..............................925 671-2888
Robert S Marston Jr, *CEO*
John Gardiner, *Vice Pres*
Gary Dalton, *Division Mgr*
Mandy Hanks, *Office Mgr*

Chris Gaffga, *Info Tech Mgr*
EMP: 53 **EST:** 1981
SQ FT: 4,000
SALES (est): 23.9MM **Privately Held**
SIC: 1731 7629 General electrical contractor; electrical repair shops

(P-2766)
TENNYSON ELECTRIC INC
7275 National Dr, Livermore (94550-8869)
PHONE..............................925 606-1038
Michael A Tennyson, *CEO*
Cathleen Tennyson, *Treasurer*
EMP: 50
SQ FT: 26,000
SALES (est): 20.1MM **Privately Held**
SIC: 1731 Electrical work

(P-2767)
THOMA ELECTRIC INC
Also Called: Thoma Electric Co
3562 Empleo St Ste C, San Luis Obispo
(93401-7367)
P.O. Box 1167 (93406-1167)
PHONE..............................805 543-3850
William A Thoma, *President*
Edward C Thoma, *Vice Pres*
Sheri Budrow, *Administration*
Steve Arnold, *Project Mgr*
Mark Westley, *Project Mgr*
EMP: 55
SQ FT: 7,500
SALES (est): 10MM **Privately Held**
WEB: www.thomaelec.com
SIC: 1731 8711 General electrical contractor; electrical or electronic engineering

(P-2768)
TIGER ELECTRIC INC (PA)
650 N Berry St, Brea (92821-3011)
PHONE..............................714 529-8061
Stanley Longenecker, *President*
Carol Capon, *Office Mgr*
Mary D Longenecker, *Admin Sec*
Timica Lowe, *Admin Asst*
Mimi Lawson, *Sales Staff*
▲ **EMP:** 82
SQ FT: 12,500
SALES (est): 12.6MM **Privately Held**
WEB: www.tigerelectric.com
SIC: 1731 General electrical contractor

(P-2769)
TIME AND ALARM SYSTEMS (PA)
3828 Wacker Dr, Mira Loma (91752-1147)
PHONE..............................951 685-1761
Keith A Senn, *CEO*
Gilbert Contreras, *Comp Tech*
EMP: 53
SQ FT: 12,000
SALES (est): 12.4MM **Privately Held**
WEB: www.timeandalarm.com
SIC: 1731 Fire detection & burglar alarm systems specialization; communications specialization; telephone & telephone equipment installation

(P-2770)
TRI-SIGNAL INTEGRATION INC (PA)
Also Called: Honeywell Authorized Dealer
15853 Monte St Ste 101, Sylmar
(91342-7671)
PHONE..............................818 566-8558
Robert McKibben, *President*
Jason Meister, *President*
Michael Swisher, *COO*
Mike Swisher, *COO*
Dennis Furden, *CFO*
EMP: 100 **EST:** 1998
SQ FT: 16,000
SALES (est): 87.5MM **Privately Held**
WEB: www.tri-signal.com
SIC: 1731 Fire detection & burglar alarm systems specialization

(P-2771)
TRL SYSTEMS INCORPORATED
Also Called: T R L
9531 Milliken Ave, Rancho Cucamonga
(91730-6006)
PHONE..............................909 390-8392
Lynn Purdy, *Chairman*
Mark L Purdy, *President*
John Hadley, *CFO*

Patrick Lewis, *Vice Pres*
Jeff Purdy, *Vice Pres*
EMP: 100
SQ FT: 14,000
SALES (est): 55MM **Privately Held**
SIC: 1731 General electrical contractor

(P-2772)
TUCKER ELECTRIC CORPORATION
Also Called: Tucker Electrical
3365 Chestnut Ln, Santa Rosa Valley
(93012-8225)
PHONE..............................818 426-7645
Dean Tucker, *CEO*
Ray Marino, *Vice Pres*
EMP: 50
SQ FT: 1,500
SALES (est): 5.8MM **Privately Held**
SIC: 1731 General electrical contractor

(P-2773)
TURNUPSEED ELECTRIC SERVICE
1580 S K St, Tulare (93274-6400)
P.O. Box 26 (93275-0026)
PHONE..............................559 686-1541
Wallace J Nelson, *President*
Terri Grant, *Corp Secy*
David Turnupseed, *Vice Pres*
EMP: 55
SQ FT: 8,000
SALES (est): 9.3MM **Privately Held**
WEB: www.turnupseed.com
SIC: 1731 7694 5063 General electrical contractor; rewinding stators; electric motor repair; motors, electric

(P-2774)
UNISON ELECTRIC
16652 Gemini Ln, Huntington Beach
(92647-4429)
PHONE..............................714 375-5915
Lance E Charlesworth, *President*
Kristi Kirkenslager, *Corp Secy*
Gary Charlesworth, *Exec VP*
Sandra Martin, *Project Mgr*
EMP: 50
SQ FT: 6,000
SALES (est): 9.4MM **Privately Held**
WEB: www.unisonltd.com
SIC: 1731 General electrical contractor

(P-2775)
UNITED STATES INFO SYSTEMS INC
7621 Galilee Rd, Roseville (95678-6972)
PHONE..............................845 353-9224
EMP: 152
SALES (corp-wide): 126.5MM **Privately Held**
SIC: 1731 Communications specialization
PA: United States Information Systems Inc.
35 W Jefferson Ave
Pearl River NY 10965
845 358-7755

(P-2776)
VALLEY COMMUNICATIONS INC (PA)
6921 Roseville Rd, Sacramento
(95842-1660)
PHONE..............................916 349-7300
Ken Hurst, *President*
Robin Reid, *Officer*
Heather Sykes, *Officer*
Kate Dewitt, *Vice Pres*
Jeff Frydenlund, *Vice Pres*
EMP: 60
SQ FT: 12,000
SALES: 11.8MM **Privately Held**
SIC: 1731 3699 Voice, data & video wiring contractor; closed circuit television installation; security control equipment & systems

(P-2777)
VASKO ELECTRIC INC
4300 Astoria St, Sacramento (95838-3004)
PHONE..............................916 568-7700
Darryl A Vasko, *President*
Ron Gracik, *Vice Pres*
EMP: 80
SQ FT: 8,500

SALES: 20.9MM **Privately Held**
WEB: www.vasko.com
SIC: 1731 General electrical contractor

(P-2778)
VECTOR RESOURCES INC (PA)
Also Called: Vectorusa
3530 Voyager St, Torrance (90503-1666)
PHONE..............................310 436-1000
David Zukerman, *President*
D Zuckerman, *COO*
Matt Recknagel, *Officer*
Robert Messinger, *Exec VP*
John Schuman, *Exec VP*
EMP: 151
SQ FT: 20,000
SALES (est): 76.4MM **Privately Held**
SIC: 1731 3651 7373 Communications specialization; computer installation; clock radio & telephone combinations; video camera-audio recorders, household use; systems engineering, computer related; turnkey vendors, computer systems; value-added resellers, computer systems

(P-2779)
VECTOR SECURITY INC
5411 Valley Blvd, Los Angeles
(90032-3518)
PHONE..............................323 224-6700
John Murphy, *Manager*
EMP: 59
SALES (corp-wide): 396.9MM **Privately Held**
SIC: 1731 7382 Fire detection & burglar alarm systems specialization; burglar alarm maintenance & monitoring
HQ: Vector Security Inc.
2000 Ericsson Dr Ste 250
Warrendale PA 15086
724 741-2200

(P-2780)
W BRADLEY ELECTRIC INC
501 Seaport Ct Ste 103a, Redwood City
(94063-2776)
PHONE..............................650 701-1502
EMP: 125
SALES (corp-wide): 61.4MM **Privately Held**
SIC: 1731
PA: W. Bradley Electric, Inc.
90 Hill Rd
Novato CA 94945
415 898-1400

(P-2781)
W BRADLEY ELECTRIC INC (PA)
90 Hill Rd, Novato (94945-4506)
PHONE..............................415 898-1400
Leslie Murphy, *CEO*
Mike Murphy, *COO*
Ralph Greenwood, *CFO*
Bob Bourdet, *Vice Pres*
▲ **EMP:** 50 **EST:** 1977
SQ FT: 24,000
SALES (est): 54.7MM **Privately Held**
SIC: 1731 General electrical contractor; communications specialization

(P-2782)
WALKER COMMUNICATIONS INC
521 Railroad Ave, Suisun City
(94585-4244)
PHONE..............................707 421-1300
Gary Walker, *President*
EMP: 100
SQ FT: 2,200
SALES (est): 5.8MM **Privately Held**
SIC: 1731 3669 4812 Communications specialization; emergency alarms; radio telephone communication

(P-2783)
WALTON ELECTRIC CORPORATION
755 N Central Ave, Upland (91786-9474)
P.O. Box 1599, Claremont (91711-8599)
PHONE..............................909 981-5051
Tanyon D Dunkley, *CEO*
Don R Davis, *Exec VP*
Ron C Stickel, *Vice Pres*
Michael Brady, *Project Mgr*
EMP: 60
SQ FT: 10,150

SALES: 7MM **Privately Held**
SIC: 1731 3669 General electrical contractor; fire alarm apparatus, electric

(P-2784)
WB ELECTRIC INC
30611 Road 400, Coarsegold
(93614-9437)
P.O. Box 319 (93614-0319)
PHONE..............................408 842-7911
Randy Walker, *CEO*
Susan Walker, *CFO*
EMP: 60
SALES: 11.7MM **Privately Held**
WEB: www.wbelectric.com
SIC: 1731 General electrical contractor

(P-2785)
**WECKWORTH CONSTRUCTION
CO INC**
Also Called: Weckworth Electric Company
3941 Park Dr Ste 20-373, El Dorado Hills
(95762-4549)
PHONE..............................916 939-6636
Kristen Weckworth, *President*
EMP: 65
SALES (est): 6MM **Privately Held**
SIC: 1731 Switchgear & related devices installation

(P-2786)
WEST COAST LTG & ENRGY INC
18550 Minthorn St, Lake Elsinore
(92530-2784)
PHONE..............................951 296-0680
Johnny Odell Leach, *President*
Tammy Leach, *Corp Secy*
EMP: 90
SQ FT: 2,646
SALES (est): 13.1MM **Privately Held**
WEB: www.es-corp.com
SIC: 1731 General electrical contractor

(P-2787)
WESTECH SYSTEMS INC
827 Jefferson Ave, Clovis (93612-2260)
PHONE..............................559 298-5237
Larry Troglin, *President*
Helder Domingos, *Vice Pres*
Jeri Swenson, *General Mgr*
Marissa Bower, *Administration*
Darin Culbertson, *Project Mgr*
EMP: 60 **EST:** 1997
SQ FT: 10,000
SALES (est): 16.9MM **Privately Held**
SIC: 1731 Computer installation

(P-2788)
**WESTERN SUN ENTERPRISES
INC**
Also Called: Three D Electric
4690 E 2nd St Ste 4, Benicia (94510-1008)
PHONE..............................707 748-2542
David Alan Whitt, *President*
Laura Whitt, *Corp Secy*
EMP: 150
SQ FT: 4,700
SALES (est): 16.5MM **Privately Held**
WEB: www.threedelectric.com
SIC: 1731 General electrical contractor

(P-2789)
**WILD ELECTRIC
INCORPORATED**
4626 E Olive Ave, Fresno (93702-1660)
PHONE..............................559 251-7770
Fred Merlo, *President*
Jan Merlo, *Vice Pres*
Rick Merlo, *Project Mgr*
Jacqueline Bacorn, *Controller*
EMP: 55 **EST:** 1973
SQ FT: 3,750
SALES (est): 8MM **Privately Held**
WEB: www.wildelectric.net
SIC: 1731 General electrical contractor

(P-2790)
WOLTCOM INC
Also Called: W C I
2300 Tech Pkwy Ste 8, Hollister (95023)
PHONE..............................831 638-4900
Mona K Wolters, *President*
Lisa Scheufler, *Shareholder*
Pat Scheufler, *CFO*
Kimberly A Morgan, *Vice Pres*

EMP: 150
SQ FT: 2,250
SALES: 10.3MM **Privately Held**
SIC: 1731 Communications specialization

(P-2791)
WORLDWIND SERVICES LLC
915 Tehachapi Wllw Spgs, Tehachapi
(93561-8178)
PHONE..............................661 822-4877
Edward Cummings,
Ian Steele, *Opers Spvr*
Suzannah Cummings,
EMP: 51
SALES (est): 11.6MM **Privately Held**
SIC: 1731 1389 8742 Electrical work; construction, repair & dismantling services; maintenance management consultant

(P-2792)
**WP ELECTRIC
COMMUNICATIONS INC**
14198 Albers Way, Chino (91710-6938)
PHONE..............................909 606-3510
Debra Rooney, *President*
Jim Roche, *Vice Pres*
Robert Trimble, *Accounts Exec*
EMP: 50
SQ FT: 8,100
SALES: 6MM **Privately Held**
SIC: 1731 General electrical contractor

(P-2793)
**WPCS INTRNTIONAL-SUISUN CY
INC**
2208 Srra Madows Dr Ste B, Rocklin
(95677)
PHONE..............................916 624-1300
EMP: 60
SALES (corp-wide): 24.4MM **Publicly
Held**
SIC: 1731
HQ: Wpcs International-Suisun City, Inc.
521 Railroad Ave
Suisun City CA 94585
707 398-3421

(P-2794)
YOUNG ELECTRIC CO
Also Called: Young Communications
195 Erie St, San Francisco (94103-2416)
PHONE..............................415 648-3355
James P Young, *President*
Wayne Huie, *President*
Richard Green, *Corp Secy*
EMP: 120 **EST:** 1977
SQ FT: 5,000
SALES: 28MM **Privately Held**
WEB: www.youngelec.com
SIC: 1731 General electrical contractor

1741 Masonry & Other Stonework

(P-2795)
3M/PHARMACEUTICALS
19901 Nordhoff St, Northridge
(91324-3213)
PHONE..............................818 341-1300
Kathy Yamaoka, *Owner*
Gina Riddle, *General Mgr*
Dena Robertson, *General Mgr*
Ray Fritz, *QA Dir*
Kathren Pearce, *Info Tech Dir*
▼ **EMP:** 86
SALES (est): 10.3MM **Privately Held**
SIC: 1741 Masonry & other stonework

(P-2796)
**B&B INDUSTRIAL SERVICES
INC (PA)**
14549 Manzanita Dr, Fontana
(92335-5378)
PHONE..............................909 428-3167
Lyndon Brewer, *President*
Ted Brewer, *Vice Pres*
Tim Brewer, *Admin Sec*
EMP: 67
SQ FT: 12,000
SALES (est): 27.3MM **Privately Held**
WEB: www.bb-industrial.com
SIC: 1741 Refractory or acid brick masonry

(P-2797)
BARAZANI PAVE STONE INC
14546 Hamlin St Ste 201, Van Nuys
(91411-4194)
PHONE..............................818 701-6977
Yuval Barazani, *President*
Aviva Barazani, *Vice Pres*
EMP: 185
SQ FT: 20,000
SALES (est): 9.8MM **Privately Held**
WEB: www.barazani.com
SIC: 1741 1771 1611 Masonry & other stonework; driveway, parking lot & blacktop contractors; surfacing & paving

(P-2798)
BLEDSOE MASONRY INC
Also Called: RMC Transport
4680 Felspar St Ste A, Riverside
(92509-3086)
PHONE..............................951 360-6140
Dyana Bledsoe, *President*
Robert Bledsoe, *Corp Secy*
Cynthia Lacava, *Executive*
EMP: 60
SQ FT: 1,300
SALES: 1MM **Privately Held**
SIC: 1741 Masonry & other stonework

(P-2799)
BOSTON BRICK & STONE INC
2005 Lincoln Ave, Pasadena (91103-1322)
PHONE..............................626 269-2622
David Laverdiere, *President*
Karen Laverdiere, *CEO*
Dan Shay, *CEO*
Mark Peters, *Vice Pres*
EMP: 50
SALES (est): 5.6MM **Privately Held**
WEB: www.bostonbrick.com
SIC: 1741 Chimney construction & maintenance

(P-2800)
BRAD WATKINS MASONRY INC
10315 Woodley Ave Ste 130, Granada Hills
(91344-6953)
P.O. Box 8466, Mission Hills (91346-8466)
PHONE..............................818 360-3796
Brad Watkins, *President*
EMP: 70
SALES: 15MM **Privately Held**
SIC: 1741 Masonry & other stonework

(P-2801)
CLEVELAND MARBLE LP
219 E Bristol Ln, Orange (92865-2715)
PHONE..............................714 998-3280
Elias N Ghattas, *Partner*
Gale Chrostowski, *Controller*
▲ **EMP:** 50
SALES (est): 950K **Privately Held**
SIC: 1741 Masonry & other stonework

(P-2802)
DESIGN MASONRY INC
20703 Santa Clara St, Canyon Country
(91351-2424)
PHONE..............................661 252-2784
Scott Floyd, *President*
Randall Carpenter, *Vice Pres*
Marilyn Carpenter, *Executive*
EMP: 70
SALES (est): 7.8MM **Privately Held**
SIC: 1741 Stone masonry

(P-2803)
DJ SCHEFFLER INC (PA)
2500 Pomona Blvd, Pomona (91768-3218)
PHONE..............................909 595-2924
Dale J Scheffler, *President*
Mark Nye, *Vice Pres*
Cindy Scheffler, *Manager*
▲ **EMP:** 50
SALES (est): 10.8MM **Privately Held**
WEB: www.djscheffler.com
SIC: 1741 Foundation building

(P-2804)
EKEDAL CONCRETE INC
19600 Fairchild Ste 123, Irvine
(92612-2509)
PHONE..............................949 720-8011
Dave Ekedal, *Branch Mgr*
EMP: 84

SALES (corp-wide): 20MM **Privately
Held**
SIC: 1741 Masonry & other stonework
PA: Ekedal Concrete, Inc.
19600 Fairchild Ste 123
Irvine CA 92612
949 729-8082

(P-2805)
ELSTON MASONRY INC
1422 Santa Margarita Dr, Fallbrook
(92028-1634)
PHONE..............................760 728-3593
Paul Elston, *President*
Carol Elston, *Vice Pres*
EMP: 85
SALES: 10.4MM **Privately Held**
SIC: 1741 Bricklaying

(P-2806)
**ENGINEERED SOIL REPAIRS
INC**
1267 Springbrook Rd, Walnut Creek
(94597-3916)
PHONE..............................408 297-2150
Steve O'Connor, *President*
Mark Wilhite, *Treasurer*
Morgan Anderson, *Vice Pres*
Bill Gibson, *Vice Pres*
Donna Byrne, *Office Mgr*
EMP: 55
SQ FT: 3,000
SALES (est): 8.1MM **Privately Held**
SIC: 1741 1771 Foundation building; foundation & footing contractor

(P-2807)
FRANK S SMITH MASONRY INC
2830 Pomona Blvd, Pomona (91768-3224)
PHONE..............................909 468-0525
Frank E Smith, *President*
Kevin J Smith, *CFO*
Brian E Smith, *Vice Pres*
EMP: 100
SQ FT: 54,000
SALES (est): 10.4MM **Privately Held**
WEB: www.fssmi.com
SIC: 1741 Bricklaying; concrete block masonry laying

(P-2808)
**GBC CONCRETE MASNRY
CNSTR INC**
561 Birch St, Lake Elsinore (92530-2732)
PHONE..............................951 245-2355
Tom Daniel, *President*
EMP: 170
SQ FT: 8,000
SALES (est): 18.7MM **Privately Held**
WEB: www.gbcconstruction.com
SIC: 1741 1771 Foundation building; concrete work

(P-2809)
HARDROCK TILE & MARBLE INC
23151 Verdugo Dr Ste 111, Laguna Hills
(92653-1340)
PHONE..............................714 282-1766
Fax: 714 282-0501
EMP: 52
SQ FT: 1,400
SALES (est): 4.9MM **Privately Held**
WEB: www.hardrocktilemarble.com
SIC: 1741

(P-2810)
HBA INCORPORATED
421 E Cerritos Ave, Anaheim (92805-6320)
P.O. Box 25861 (92825-5861)
PHONE..............................714 635-8602
Gerald G Pyle, *President*
Joe Alessandrini, *CFO*
EMP: 100
SALES (est): 12.2MM **Privately Held**
SIC: 1741 Masonry & other stonework

(P-2811)
INDUSTRIAL MASONRY INC
3299 Horse Carri Rd Ste H, Norco (92860)
PHONE..............................951 284-0251
Greg E Wilson, *President*
Janice Tessier, *CFO*
Guy W Yocom, *CFO*
EMP: 100
SALES (est): 5.3MM **Privately Held**
SIC: 1741 Bricklaying

P R O D U C T S & S V C S

(P-2812)
J GINGER MASONRY LP (PA)
8188 Lincoln Ave Ste 100, Riverside
(92504-4329)
PHONE..............................951 688-5050
John L Ginger, *Partner*
Brad Fogg, *President*
EMP: 265
SALES (est): 47.6MM **Privately Held**
SIC: 1741 Masonry & other stonework

(P-2813)
JAMES FEDOR MASONRY INC
54859 Bodine Dr, Thermal (92274-8911)
P.O. Box 1397, La Quinta (92247-1397)
PHONE..............................760 772-3036
James Fedor, *President*
EMP: 70
SALES: 2MM **Privately Held**
WEB: www.jamesfedormasonryinc.com
SIC: 1741

(P-2814)
JOHN JACKSON MASONRY
5691 Power Inn Rd Ste B, Sacramento
(95824-2361)
PHONE..............................916 381-8021
Jeff Barber, *President*
Cheryl Lincoln, *Corp Secy*
Donald C Ekstrom, *Vice Pres*
Tom Sneed, *General Mgr*
Jim Loehr, *Director*
EMP: 60
SQ FT: 6,200
SALES: 13.9MM **Privately Held**
WEB: www.johnjacksonmasonry.com
SIC: 1741 Bricklaying

(P-2815)
JOHN L GINGER MASONRY INC
8188 Lincoln Ave Ste 100, Riverside
(92504-4329)
PHONE..............................951 688-5050
John L Ginger, *President*
EMP: 100
SQ FT: 8,000
SALES (est): 6.1MM **Privately Held**
WEB: www.gingermasonry.com
SIC: 1741 Masonry & other stonework

(P-2816)
MASONRY CONCEPTS INC
15408 Cornet St, Santa Fe Springs
(90670-5534)
PHONE..............................562 802-3700
Ronald O Udall, *President*
Peter Sturdivant, *Corp Secy*
Russell Knight, *Vice Pres*
Sharyl Narike, *Technology*
Dana Kemp, *Mktg Dir*
EMP: 100
SQ FT: 10,000
SALES (est): 9.9MM **Privately Held**
WEB: www.masonry-concepts.com
SIC: 1741 Masonry & other stonework

(P-2817)
MONTEREY BAY MASONRY INC
333 Phelan Ave, San Jose (95112-4104)
PHONE..............................408 289-8295
Casey Ricks, *President*
EMP: 50
SQ FT: 11,000
SALES (est): 1.3MM **Privately Held**
SIC: 1741 Concrete block masonry laying

(P-2818)
NIBBELINK MASONRY CNSTR CORP
2010 W Avenue K, Lancaster (93536-5229)
PHONE..............................661 948-7859
Troy Nibbelink, *President*
Gerald J Nibbelink, *Vice Pres*
Leann Fenner, *Office Mgr*
EMP: 60 EST: 1976
SQ FT: 2,000
SALES (est): 11.4MM **Privately Held**
SIC: 1741 1771 Masonry & other
stonework; exterior concrete stucco con-
tractor

(P-2819)
ORANGE COAST MASONRY ACQUISIT
601 N Batavia St, Orange (92868-1220)
P.O. Box 608 (92856-6608)
PHONE..............................714 538-4386
Todd Essenmacher, *President*
EMP: 100
SQ FT: 10,000
SALES: 16MM **Privately Held**
SIC: 1741 Masonry & other stonework

(P-2820)
PACIFIC SHORES MASONRY
1369 Walker Ln, Corona (92879-1775)
PHONE..............................951 371-8550
Jeff McAninch, *President*
EMP: 50
SALES (est): 5.2MM **Privately Held**
SIC: 1741 Stone masonry

(P-2821)
PENHALL COMPANY (DH)
2121 W Crescent Ave Ste A, Anaheim
(92801-3810)
P.O. Box 4609 (92803-4609)
PHONE..............................714 772-6450
Jeff Long, *CEO*
C George Bush, *President*
Lynn Behler, *CFO*
Bruce Lux, *CFO*
John Smith, *Officer*
EMP: 100
SQ FT: 8,000
SALES (est): 557.6MM
SALES (corp-wide): 2.5B **Privately Held**
SIC: 1741 1795 Foundation & retaining
wall construction; demolition, buildings &
other structures
HQ: Penhall International Corp.
7501 Esters Blvd Ste 150
Irving TX 75063
817 796-7150

(P-2822)
RAYCON CONSTRUCTION INC
1795 E Lemonwood Dr, Santa Paula
(93060-9651)
P.O. Box 910 (93061-0910)
PHONE..............................805 525-5256
Paul Reyes, *President*
Robert Reyes, *Treasurer*
Augie Reyes, *Vice Pres*
Chris Urrea, *Admin Sec*
EMP: 50
SQ FT: 6,000
SALES: 8MM **Privately Held**
SIC: 1741 Masonry & other stonework

(P-2823)
SMG STONE COMPANY INC
8460 San Fernando Rd, Sun Valley
(91352-3227)
PHONE..............................818 767-0000
Solomon Aryeh, *President*
▲ EMP: 80
SQ FT: 12,000
SALES (est): 11.2MM **Privately Held**
WEB: www.smgstone.com
SIC: 1741 8711 5032 Masonry & other
stonework; engineering services; marble
building stone

(P-2824)
SPECTRA COMPANY
2510 Supply St, Pomona (91767-2113)
PHONE..............................909 599-0760
Ray Adamyk, *CEO*
Tim Harris, *COO*
Ann Dresselhaus, *Admin Sec*
▲ EMP: 125
SQ FT: 7,000
SALES: 18.1MM **Privately Held**
WEB: www.spectracompany.com
SIC: 1741 1771 1743 1721 Masonry &
other stonework; concrete work; terrazzo,
tile, marble, mosaic work; painting &
paper hanging; carpentry work

(P-2825)
SUPERIOR MASONRY WALLS LTD
300 W Olive St Ste A, Colton (92324-1765)
PHONE..............................909 370-1800
Daniel Lee, *President*

Jeremiah Curtis, *CFO*
EMP: 75
SALES: 950K **Privately Held**
SIC: 1741 Masonry & other stonework

(P-2826)
VARIATIONS IN STONE INC
360 La Perle Pl, Costa Mesa (92627-3758)
PHONE..............................949 438-8337
Joseph Dorando, *CFO*
James Joseph Dorando, *President*
EMP: 75
SALES (est): 198.4K **Privately Held**
SIC: 1741 Masonry & other stonework

(P-2827)
VILLA PACIFIC CONTRACTORS INC
3303 Harbor Blvd Ste D6, Costa Mesa
(92626-1519)
PHONE..............................714 850-1640
Brad Gilbert, *President*
EMP: 50
SALES (est): 3MM **Privately Held**
SIC: 1741 Masonry & other stonework

(P-2828)
VINCENT CONTRACTORS INC
4501 E La Palma Ave # 200, Anaheim
(92807-1904)
PHONE..............................714 693-1726
Justin Erdtsieck, *President*
Kenny Vo, *Accounts Mgr*
EMP: 430
SQ FT: 5,538
SALES (est): 4.5MM **Privately Held**
SIC: 1741 1742 Masonry & other
stonework; plastering, drywall & insulation

(P-2829)
WILKIE MASONRY INC
4016 Hunter Oaks Ln, Loomis
(95650-9280)
P.O. Box 387 (95650-0387)
PHONE..............................916 652-0118
Brian Wilkie, *President*
EMP: 50
SQ FT: 700
SALES: 750K **Privately Held**
SIC: 1741 5082 Masonry & other
stonework; masonry equipment & sup-
plies

(P-2830)
WILLIAMS & SONS MASONRY INC
8531 Winter Gardens Blvd A, Lakeside
(92040-5475)
PHONE..............................619 443-1751
Darwin Todd Williams, *President*
Derrick Williams, *Admin Sec*
EMP: 70
SQ FT: 1,200
SALES (est): 4.5MM **Privately Held**
WEB: www.sons.sdcoxmail.com
SIC: 1741 Masonry & other stonework

(P-2831)
WINEGARDNER MASONRY INC
32147 Dunlap Blvd Ste A, Yucaipa
(92399-1757)
PHONE..............................909 795-9711
Carolyn Winegardner, *CEO*
Julie Salazar, *President*
Dean Saavedra, *Project Mgr*
EMP: 50
SQ FT: 7,500
SALES (est): 7.5MM **Privately Held**
SIC: 1741 Bricklaying; concrete block ma-
sonry laying

(P-2832)
WIRTZ QULTY INSTALLATIONS INC
7932 Armour St, San Diego (92111-3718)
PHONE..............................858 569-3816
Amber Fox, *President*
Ida Wirtz, *Vice Pres*
John Wirtz, *Vice Pres*
EMP: 65

SALES (est): 6MM **Privately Held**
SIC: 1741 1752 1743 1799 Masonry &
other stonework; floor laying & floor work;
wood floor installation & refinishing; terrazzo, tile, marble, mosaic work; cleaning
building exteriors

1742 Plastering, Drywall, Acoustical & Insulation Work

(P-2833)
A A GONZALEZ INC
13264 Ralston Ave, Sylmar (91342-7607)
P.O. Box 408, San Fernando (91341-0408)
PHONE..............................818 367-2242
Albert Gonzales, *President*
Aida Lepe, *Treasurer*
EMP: 100
SALES (est): 8MM **Privately Held**
SIC: 1742 Plastering, drywall & insulation

(P-2834)
A COLMENERO PLASTERING INC
1710 W San Madele Ave, Fresno
(93711-2929)
PHONE..............................559 435-3606
Augie Colmenero, *President*
EMP: 55
SALES (est): 4MM **Privately Held**
SIC: 1742 Plaster & drywall work

(P-2835)
ADERHOLT SPECIALTY COMPANY INC
1557 Cummins Dr, Modesto (95358-6413)
PHONE..............................209 526-2000
Herbert Aderholt, *Ch of Bd*
Sherry Lynette Aderholt, *CEO*
Helen Aderholt, *Admin Sec*
EMP: 100
SQ FT: 4,000
SALES (est): 8.5MM **Privately Held**
WEB: www.aderholt.com
SIC: 1742 1799 Drywall; plastering, plain
or ornamental; fireproofing buildings

(P-2836)
ADVANCED ACOUSTICS
3430 Golden Gate Way, Lafayette
(94549-4518)
PHONE..............................925 299-0515
Steve Bossert, *Partner*
Ron Bossert, *Partner*
EMP: 50
SQ FT: 850
SALES (est): 1.8MM **Privately Held**
WEB: www.advancedacoustics.net
SIC: 1742 Acoustical & ceiling work

(P-2837)
ALAN SMITH POOL PLASTERING INC
227 W Carleton Ave, Orange (92867-3607)
PHONE..............................714 628-9494
Stephen Scherer, *President*
Teresa Smith, *CFO*
Alan Smith, *Executive*
Ray Cassey, *Project Mgr*
Chris Smith, *Project Mgr*
▲ EMP: 78
SQ FT: 5,000
SALES (est): 9MM **Privately Held**
WEB: www.alansmithpools.com
SIC: 1742 Plastering, plain or ornamental

(P-2838)
ALERT INSULATION COMPANY INC
15913 Old Valley Blvd A, La Puente
(91744-5439)
PHONE..............................626 961-9113
Donald W Kent, *President*
Charles Klinakis, *Vice Pres*
Joe Rodriguez, *General Mgr*
Bruce Abott, *Project Mgr*
Jeff Chaffin, *Project Mgr*
EMP: 66
SQ FT: 4,500

SALES (est): 8.8MM **Privately Held**
WEB: www.alertinsulation.net
SIC: 1742 Insulation, buildings

(P-2839)
ALL PRO DRYWALL
22148 Buckeye Pl, Cottonwood
(96022-7701)
PHONE................................530 722-5182
EMP: 50
SALES: 3MM **Privately Held**
SIC: 1742

(P-2840)
**ALLEN DRYWALL &
ASSOCIATES**
380 Lang Rd, Burlingame (94010-2003)
PHONE................................650 579-0664
Richard Allen, *President*
Julie Allen, *Treasurer*
Bill Lorenzini, *Project Mgr*
Kelly Feist, *Controller*
Nick Allen, *Manager*
EMP: 60
SALES (est): 6.1MM **Privately Held**
SIC: 1742 Drywall

(P-2841)
ALLIANCE WALL SYSTEMS INC
4638 Skyway Dr, Marysville (95901)
PHONE................................530 740-7800
Gregory L Bolin, *President*
Shawn Shingler, *Vice Pres*
EMP: 50
SALES (est): 1.8MM **Privately Held**
SIC: 1742 Plastering, drywall & insulation

(P-2842)
ALTA INTERIORS INC
847 Palmyrita Ave, Riverside (92507-1805)
PHONE................................951 784-1400
Frank Apeldoorn, *CFO*
▲ EMP: 99 EST: 2012
SQ FT: 50,000
SALES (est): 4.6MM **Privately Held**
SIC: 1742 Drywall

(P-2843)
ANCCA CORPORATION
Also Called: N-U Enterprise
7 Goddard, Irvine (92618-4600)
PHONE................................949 553-0084
Nicole Hunt, *Corp Secy*
EMP: 99
SALES (est): 950K **Privately Held**
SIC: 1742 Plastering, drywall & insulation

(P-2844)
ANNING-JOHNSON COMPANY
22955 Kidder St, Hayward (94545-1670)
PHONE................................510 670-0100
R Todd Fearon, *Vice Pres*
Earl Kramer, *Manager*
EMP: 140
SQ FT: 16,000
SALES (corp-wide): 461.9MM **Privately Held**
SIC: 1742 Drywall; acoustical & ceiling work
HQ: Anning-Johnson Company
1959 Anson Dr
Melrose Park IL 60160
708 681-1300

(P-2845)
ANNING-JOHNSON COMPANY
13250 Temple Ave, City of Industry (91746-1583)
PHONE................................626 369-7131
Larry Domino, *Vice Pres*
Lazaro Mendez, *Manager*
Frank Valencia, *Superintendent*
EMP: 50
SALES (corp-wide): 461.9MM **Privately Held**
SIC: 1742 1761 1799 Acoustical & ceiling work; roofing, siding & sheet metal work; building site preparation
HQ: Anning-Johnson Company
1959 Anson Dr
Melrose Park IL 60160
708 681-1300

(P-2846)
ANSCHUTZ FILM GROUP
1888 Century Park E # 1400, Los Angeles (90067-1718)
PHONE................................310 887-1000
EMP: 5002
SALES (est): 4.9MM
SALES (corp-wide): 110.5MM **Privately Held**
SIC: 1742
PA: The Anschutz Corporation
555 17th St Ste 2400
Denver CO 80202
303 298-1000

(P-2847)
AYALA DRYWALL
2600 Alexander St, Oxnard (93033-4728)
PHONE................................805 487-3392
Abel Ayala, *Owner*
Abe Ayala, *Owner*
EMP: 50
SALES (est): 1.1MM **Privately Held**
SIC: 1742 Drywall

(P-2848)
B S I HOLDINGS INC
100 Clock Tower Pl # 200, Carmel (93923-8774)
PHONE................................831 622-1840
EMP: 2000
SQ FT: 1,400
SALES (est): 44.4MM
SALES (corp-wide): 7.1B **Publicly Held**
WEB: www.bsiholdings.com
SIC: 1742
PA: Masco Corporation
21001 Van Born Rd
Taylor MI 48152
313 274-7400

(P-2849)
BAYSIDE INTERIORS INC (PA)
3220 Darby Cmn, Fremont (94539-5601)
PHONE................................510 438-9171
Steven A Rivera, *CEO*
Tim Hogan, *President*
Michael Nicholson, *COO*
Jon Braden, *CFO*
Norma Nicholson, *Treasurer*
▲ EMP: 145
SQ FT: 20,000
SALES (est): 25.1MM **Privately Held**
WEB: www.baysideinteriors.com
SIC: 1742 Drywall

(P-2850)
BEST INTERIORS INC (PA)
2100 E Via Burton, Anaheim (92806-1219)
PHONE................................714 490-7999
Dennis Ayres, *President*
Michael Herrig, *CFO*
Mike Herrig, *CFO*
Elise Wright, *Administration*
Alex Briceno, *Project Mgr*
EMP: 150
SQ FT: 20,000
SALES (est): 26.3MM **Privately Held**
WEB: www.bestinteriors.net
SIC: 1742 Drywall

(P-2851)
BOYETT CONSTRUCTION INC (PA)
2404 Tripaldi Way, Hayward (94545-5017)
PHONE................................510 264-9100
Vernon H Boyett, *President*
James Roberts, *Corp Secy*
Cindy Le, *Admin Asst*
Cherise Serduke, *Admin Asst*
Dave Heagney, *Project Mgr*
EMP: 78
SQ FT: 2,600
SALES (est): 24MM **Privately Held**
SIC: 1742 1751 Drywall; acoustical & ceiling work; window & door installation & erection

(P-2852)
BRADY COMPANY/CENTRAL CAL
13540 Blackie Rd, Castroville (95012-3212)
PHONE................................831 633-3315
Allen D Larson, *President*

Keith Eshelman, *CFO*
Gregg Brady, *Admin Sec*
EMP: 200
SALES (est): 12.7MM **Privately Held**
SIC: 1742 Plastering, plain or ornamental; insulation, buildings; acoustical & ceiling work; drywall

(P-2853)
BRADY COMPANY/LOS ANGELES INC
1010 N Olive St, Anaheim (92801-2539)
P.O. Box 470 (92815-0470)
PHONE................................714 533-9850
William Saddler, *CEO*
John Dewey, *CFO*
Ron Brady, *Admin Sec*
EMP: 100
SALES (est): 6.7MM **Privately Held**
SIC: 1742 1791 Plaster & drywall work; metal lath & furring

(P-2854)
BRADY COMPANY/SAN DIEGO INC
8100 Center St, La Mesa (91942-2925)
P.O. Box 968 (91944-0968)
PHONE................................619 462-2600
Scott Brady, *CEO*
Larry McClure, *Opers Mgr*
EMP: 300
SQ FT: 4,000
SALES (est): 21.6MM **Privately Held**
SIC: 1742 1542 Plastering, plain or ornamental; insulation, buildings; acoustical & ceiling work; drywall; commercial & office buildings, renovation & repair

(P-2855)
BRADY SOCAL INCORPORATED
8100 Center St, La Mesa (91942-2925)
PHONE................................619 462-2600
Ricky Marshall, *President*
Scott Brady, *Senior VP*
Dana Ursino, *Office Mgr*
Kevin Rule, *Opers Mgr*
▲ EMP: 99
SALES (est): 8.8MM **Privately Held**
SIC: 1742 1751 Drywall; window & door installation & erection

(P-2856)
C A HOFMANN CONSTRUCTION INC
8923 Laramie Dr, Rancho Cucamonga (91737-1466)
P.O. Box 8463 (91701-0463)
PHONE................................909 484-5888
Clarence A Hofmann, *CEO*
EMP: 50
SALES (est): 3.8MM **Privately Held**
SIC: 1742 1751 7389 Drywall; framing contractor;

(P-2857)
C D R ENTERPRISES INC
42302 8th St E, Lancaster (93535-5440)
P.O. Box 507, Friant (93626-0507)
PHONE................................661 940-0344
Samuel D McDowell, *President*
Randy McDowell, *Vice Pres*
Audrey McDowell, *Admin Sec*
EMP: 70
SALES (est): 2.6MM **Privately Held**
SIC: 1742

(P-2858)
C R S DRYWALL INC
Also Called: Cr Drywall
135 San Jose Ave, San Jose (95125-1018)
PHONE................................408 998-4360
Carlos Silveria, *President*
Manuela Silveira, *CFO*
EMP: 80
SQ FT: 4,000
SALES (est): 5.4MM **Privately Held**
SIC: 1742 Drywall

(P-2859)
CALIFORNIA DRYWALL CO (PA)
2290 S 10th St, San Jose (95112-4114)
PHONE................................408 292-7500
Greg Eckstrom, *Vice Pres*
Kent Bowles, *President*
David Garrett, *COO*

Stephen Eckstrom, *Vice Pres*
Brian Bowles, *Project Mgr*
EMP: 250
SQ FT: 15,000
SALES (est): 56.6MM **Privately Held**
WEB: www.caldrywall.com
SIC: 1742 Drywall

(P-2860)
CANYON INSULATION INC
645 E Harrison St Ste 100, Corona (92879-1376)
PHONE................................951 278-9200
Gerald Volas, *CEO*
EMP: 70
SALES: 16.5MM
SALES (corp-wide): 1.9B **Publicly Held**
SIC: 1742 Insulation, buildings
PA: Topbuild Corp.
475 N Williamson Blvd
Daytona Beach FL 32114
386 304-2200

(P-2861)
CAPITAL CITY DRYWALL INC
6525 32nd St Ste B1, North Highlands (95660-3028)
PHONE................................916 331-9200
John Beers, *President*
Andrew Sellers, *Vice Pres*
EMP: 100 EST: 2000
SQ FT: 2,500
SALES (est): 9MM **Privately Held**
WEB: www.capitalcitydrywall.com
SIC: 1742 Drywall

(P-2862)
CAPITAL DRYWALL LP
333 S Grand Ave Ste 4070, Los Angeles (90071-1544)
PHONE................................909 599-6818
Frank Scardino, *President*
Art Toscano, *Vice Pres*
Angela Gates, *Admin Sec*
EMP: 150
SQ FT: 8,000
SALES (est): 7.9MM
SALES (corp-wide): 280MM **Privately Held**
SIC: 1742 Drywall
PA: U.S. Builder Services, Llc
272 E Deerpath Ste 308
Lake Forest IL 60045
847 735-2066

(P-2863)
CASTON INC
354 S Allen St, San Bernardino (92408-1508)
PHONE................................909 381-1619
James I Malachowski Jr, *President*
Mark Landon, *Project Mgr*
EMP: 100
SALES (est): 11.5MM **Privately Held**
SIC: 1742 Drywall

(P-2864)
CEN CAL PLASTERING INC
1256 W Lathrop Rd, Manteca (95336-9671)
P.O. Box 307 (95336-1125)
PHONE................................209 858-1045
Jeffery F Gann, *President*
Jeffrey F Gann, *President*
EMP: 450 EST: 2010
SALES: 17MM **Privately Held**
SIC: 1742 Plastering, plain or ornamental

(P-2865)
CHARLES CULBERSON INC
Also Called: Culberson Drywall
1084 Allen Way, Campbell (95008-4509)
P.O. Box 1954, Chester (96020-1954)
PHONE................................650 335-4730
Fax: 650 335-4736
EMP: 150
SQ FT: 8,000
SALES (est): 7.3MM **Privately Held**
SIC: 1742

(P-2866)
CHURCH & LARSEN INC
16103 Avenida Padilla, Irwindale (91702-3223)
PHONE................................626 303-8741
Raymond W Larsen, *President*

PRODUCTS & SVCS

Kenneth R Larsen, *Vice Pres*
Kenneth P Larsen, *Vice Pres*
EMP: 250
SQ FT: 10,800
SALES (est): 18.6MM **Privately Held**
SIC: 1742 Plaster & drywall work

(P-2867)
CLOVIS CUSTOM DRYWALL INC
Also Called: Custom Drywall Service
141 Sunnyside Ave Ste 108, Clovis
(93611-0570)
PHONE...................559 297-7073
Dan Ploy, *Owner*
D Ployangunsri, *President*
Khatiya Hanvongse, *Vice Pres*
EMP: 50
SQ FT: 5,000
SALES (est): 2.8MM **Privately Held**
SIC: 1742 Drywall

(P-2868)
COAST INSULATION CONTRS INC (DH)
Also Called: Coast Building Products
1341 Old Oakland Rd, San Jose
(95112-1317)
PHONE...................386 304-2222
Michael Raridon, *President*
EMP: 65
SQ FT: 10,000
SALES (est): 11.4MM
SALES (corp-wide): 1.9B **Publicly Held**
SIC: 1742 Insulation, buildings
HQ: American National Services, Inc.
475 N Williamson Blvd
Daytona Beach FL 32114
386 304-2200

(P-2869)
CUSTOM DRYWALL INC
1570 Gladding Ct, Milpitas (95035-6814)
PHONE...................408 263-1616
Gene Cox, *President*
Tom Knight, *Manager*
Craig Lammers, *Manager*
EMP: 90
SQ FT: 10,000
SALES (est): 7.5MM **Privately Held**
WEB: www.custom-drywall-inc.com
SIC: 1742 Drywall

(P-2870)
CUTTING EDGE DRYWALL INC
7046 Convoy Ct, San Diego (92111-1017)
PHONE...................858 408-0870
Robert Pearn, *President*
EMP: 50
SQ FT: 4,800
SALES (est): 4MM **Privately Held**
WEB: www.cuttingedgedrywall.net
SIC: 1742 Drywall

(P-2871)
DALEYS DRYWALL AND TAPING INC
960 Camden Ave, Campbell (95008-4104)
PHONE...................408 378-9500
Craig Spencer Daley, *President*
Brittni Daley, *CFO*
Chris Daley, *Vice Pres*
Adam Barbee, *Superintendent*
EMP: 550
SQ FT: 20,000
SALES (est): 84MM **Privately Held**
WEB: www.daleysdrywall.com
SIC: 1742 Drywall

(P-2872)
DEL MAR PLASTERING INC
7085 Jurupa Ave Ste 2, Riverside
(92504-1044)
PHONE...................951 343-5955
Dale Pratte, *President*
EMP: 100
SQ FT: 2,000
SALES (est): 12MM **Privately Held**
SIC: 1742 Plastering, plain or ornamental

(P-2873)
DEMKO DRYWALL & DEMOLITION CO
419 S Marshall Ave, El Cajon (92020-4210)
PHONE...................619 590-0025
Nicholas Demko, *President*

Debra Demko, *Corp Secy*
EMP: 50
SALES (est): 5.8MM **Privately Held**
WEB: www.demkodemolition.com
SIC: 1742 1751 1795 Drywall; framing
contractor; wrecking & demolition work

(P-2874)
DH SMITH COMPANY INC
6000 Hellyer Ave Ste 150, San Jose
(95138-1031)
P.O. Box 730189 (95173-0189)
PHONE...................408 532-7617
Daniel Smith III, *President*
Cheryl Smith, *Treasurer*
Steven Smith, *Vice Pres*
EMP: 85
SQ FT: 20,000
SALES (est): 9.1MM **Privately Held**
SIC: 1742 Plastering, plain or ornamental

(P-2875)
DIAZ PLASTERING INC
4900 California Ave 210b, Bakersfield
(93309-7024)
P.O. Box 11014 (93389-1014)
PHONE...................661 244-8228
Jovani Diaz, *President*
EMP: 60 **EST:** 2010
SALES: 8MM **Privately Held**
SIC: 1742 Plaster & drywall work

(P-2876)
DOVE CEILINGS INC (PA)
22991 Belquest Dr, Lake Forest
(92630-4007)
PHONE...................949 597-1794
David W Cowan, *CEO*
David Cowan, *President*
Carolyn Hacking, *CFO*
Mark Hacking, *Vice Pres*
EMP: 50 **EST:** 1981
SQ FT: 1,500
SALES (est): 3.8MM **Privately Held**
WEB: www.doveceilings.com
SIC: 1742 Acoustical & ceiling work

(P-2877)
DRY CREEK LATH & PLASTER INC
27940 Kennefick Rd, Galt (95632-8290)
P.O. Box 1051 (95632-1051)
PHONE...................209 367-8607
Ron Bohlender, *President*
EMP: 70
SQ FT: 6,000
SALES: 4MM **Privately Held**
SIC: 1742 Plaster & drywall work

(P-2878)
DRYWALL WORKS INC
5451 Whse Way Ste 105, Sacramento
(95826)
PHONE...................916 383-6667
Xavier Valdez, *President*
Michael A Rizo, *Treasurer*
EMP: 80
SQ FT: 26,000
SALES: 9MM **Privately Held**
SIC: 1742 Drywall

(P-2879)
EDCO DRYWALL INC
Also Called: Edco Drywall Company
7200 Hazard Ave, Westminster
(92683-5027)
PHONE...................714 799-9886
Dave Blunk, *President*
EMP: 50
SQ FT: 4,257
SALES (est): 2.4MM **Privately Held**
SIC: 1742 Drywall; acoustical & ceiling
work

(P-2880)
ELLJAY ACOUSTICS INC
511 Cameron St, Placentia (92870-6425)
PHONE...................714 961-1173
Ronald B Bishop, *President*
Tim Coggins, *Vice Pres*
Narda Reyes, *Admin Asst*
Matt Paul, *Project Mgr*
EMP: 70
SQ FT: 6,900

SALES (est): 8.2MM **Privately Held**
WEB: www.elljay.com
SIC: 1742 Acoustical & ceiling work

(P-2881)
ENERGETIC PNTG & DRYWALL INC (PA)
Also Called: Energetic Lath & Plaster
2929 Orange Grove Ave, North Highlands
(95660-5703)
PHONE...................916 488-8455
Edwin G Gerber, *President*
EMP: 250
SQ FT: 10,000
SALES: 12MM **Privately Held**
SIC: 1742 Drywall

(P-2882)
ERIC STARK INTERIORS INC
2284 Paragon Dr, San Jose (95131-1306)
PHONE...................408 441-6136
Eric Stark, *President*
EMP: 100
SQ FT: 10,000
SALES (est): 9.5MM **Privately Held**
WEB: www.ericstarkinteriors.com
SIC: 1742 Drywall

(P-2883)
FARWEST INSULATION CONTRACTING
Also Called: Pacific Insulation
2741 Yates Ave, Commerce (90040-2623)
PHONE...................310 634-2800
Linda Chadarria, *Manager*
Linda Chavarria, *Manager*
EMP: 50
SALES (corp-wide): 46.5MM **Privately
Held**
SIC: 1742 Insulation, buildings
PA: Farwest Insulation Contracting, Inc
1220 S Sherman St
Anaheim CA 92805
714 520-5600

(P-2884)
FOUNDATION BUILDING MTLS LLC (HQ)
2741 Walnut Ave Ste 200, Tustin
(92780-7063)
PHONE...................714 380-3127
Ruben Mendoza, *Mng Member*
Joe Kirkendall, *President*
Pete Welly, *COO*
Richard Tilley, *Vice Pres*
Tom Deberry, *Branch Mgr*
EMP: 94 **EST:** 2011
SALES (est): 591MM
SALES (corp-wide): 2B **Publicly Held**
SIC: 1742 Plastering, drywall & insulation
PA: Foundation Building Materials, Inc.
2741 Walnut Ave Ste 200
Tustin CA 92780
714 380-3127

(P-2885)
FUTURE ENERGY CORPORATION
4120 Avenida De La Plata, Oceanside
(92056-6001)
PHONE...................760 477-9700
Jeffrey Adkins, *Branch Mgr*
EMP: 89
SALES (corp-wide): 33MM **Privately
Held**
SIC: 1742 1521 Acoustical & insulation
work; single-family home remodeling, ad-
ditions & repairs
PA: Future Energy Corporation
8980 Grant Line Rd
Upland CA 91786
800 985-0733

(P-2886)
FUTURE ENERGY CORPORATION (PA)
Also Called: Future Energy Savers
8980 Grant Line Rd, Upland (91786)
P.O. Box 87, Wilton (95693-0087)
PHONE...................800 985-0733
Jeffrey Adkins, *CEO*
EMP: 224
SQ FT: 6,800

SALES (est): 33MM **Privately Held**
WEB: www.energysavers.com
SIC: 1742 Insulation, buildings

(P-2887)
G BROTHERS CONSTRUCTION INC
7070 Patterson Dr, Garden Grove
(92841-1438)
PHONE...................714 590-3070
Rick Gutierrez, *President*
Mike Gutierrez, *Vice Pres*
EMP: 50
SQ FT: 6,500
SALES (est): 6.6MM **Privately Held**
WEB: www.gbrothers.net
SIC: 1742 Drywall

(P-2888)
GIERAHN DRY WALL INC
28490 Westinghouse Pl # 150, Santa
Clarita (91355-0955)
PHONE...................661 257-7900
Henry Carl Gierahn, *President*
EMP: 50
SQ FT: 1,200
SALES (est): 3.8MM **Privately Held**
WEB: www.gierahn.com
SIC: 1742 Drywall

(P-2889)
GREYSTONE PLASTERING INC
1716 Stone Ave Ste B, San Jose
(95125-1308)
P.O. Box 41457 (95160-1457)
PHONE...................408 298-5934
Michael Stonehocker, *President*
EMP: 80
SQ FT: 1,500
SALES (est): 7.2MM **Privately Held**
SIC: 1742 Plaster & drywall work

(P-2890)
GYPSUM CONTRACTORS INC
23785 El Toro Rd Ste 135, Lake Forest
(92630-4762)
PHONE...................949 340-9100
Aram Fatourehchian, *CEO*
Aram Fatoure, *President*
EMP: 50 **EST:** 2012
SQ FT: 1,000
SALES (est): 2.8MM **Privately Held**
SIC: 1742 Insulation, buildings

(P-2891)
H B J CORPORATION
Also Called: Superior Pntg Drywall Fnshings
5806 Frontier Way, Carmichael
(95608-5137)
PHONE...................707 333-7066
Harry Boyajian Jr, *President*
EMP: 80
SQ FT: 2,000
SALES: 1.5MM **Privately Held**
SIC: 1742 Drywall

(P-2892)
HARRISON DRYWALL INC
447 10th St, San Francisco (94103-4303)
P.O. Box 508, Cotati (94931-0508)
PHONE...................415 821-9584
Jeff Harrison, *President*
Dan Harrison, *Project Mgr*
Erik Kristensen, *Project Engr*
Timothy Higgins, *Manager*
Tommy Shaw, *Manager*
EMP: 50
SQ FT: 5,000
SALES (est): 6.7MM **Privately Held**
WEB: www.harrisondrywallinc.com
SIC: 1742 Plastering, plain or ornamental;
drywall

(P-2893)
HUTCHISON CORPORATION
Also Called: Inner Space Constructors Div
6107 Obispo Ave, Long Beach
(90805-3799)
PHONE...................310 763-7991
Robert J Hutchison, *Ch of Bd*
Linda Mc Dannold, *Corp Secy*
Stephen Mc Dannold, *Vice Pres*
Norma Herrera, *Executive*
EMP: 80
SQ FT: 50,000

SALES (est): 20MM **Privately Held**
SIC: **1742** 1521 1542 Acoustical & ceiling work; single-family housing construction; commercial & office building, new construction

(P-2894)
INFINITY DRYWALL CONTG INC
225 S Loara St, Anaheim (92802-1019)
PHONE................................714 634-2255
Dennis Lafreniere, *President*
James Darling, *Vice Pres*
Liza Lafreniere, *Vice Pres*
EMP: 60
SALES (est): 6.5MM **Privately Held**
SIC: **1742** 1751 Drywall; framing contractor

(P-2895)
INNOVATIVE DRYWALL SYSTEMS INC
Also Called: Alta Drywall
116 Market Pl, Escondido (92029-1352)
P.O. Box 3268, Ramona (92065-0956)
PHONE................................760 743-0331
Doug Bellamy, *President*
Larry Johnson, *Director*
EMP: 80
SQ FT: 3,500
SALES (est): 4.5MM **Privately Held**
SIC: **1742** Drywall

(P-2896)
INSUL ACOUSTICS INC
1432 Chico Ave, El Monte (91733-2995)
PHONE................................323 686-2670
Roy W Tonks, *President*
Don C Tonks, *Vice Pres*
EMP: 200
SQ FT: 10,000
SALES (est): 9.1MM **Privately Held**
WEB: www.insulacoustics.com
SIC: **1742** Drywall; plastering, plain or ornamental; acoustical & ceiling work

(P-2897)
INTERIOR EXPERTS GENERAL BLDRS
4534 Carter Ct, Chino (91710-5060)
PHONE................................909 203-4922
Adam Lopez, *President*
EMP: 80
SQ FT: 9,000
SALES (est): 7.7MM **Privately Held**
WEB: www.expert-email.com
SIC: **1742** Drywall

(P-2898)
INTERWALL DEV SYSTEMS INC
17401 Armstrong Ave, Irvine (92614-5723)
PHONE................................949 553-9102
William Hunt, *President*
Cynthia Hunt, *Vice Pres*
Michelle Jaime, *Office Mgr*
EMP: 75
SQ FT: 2,100
SALES (est): 3.8MM **Privately Held**
WEB: www.wchuntco.com
SIC: **1742** Drywall

(P-2899)
IVO WALL EXPERTS INC
5359 Sheila St, Commerce (90040-2101)
PHONE................................323 246-4026
Ildefonso V Osorio, *President*
Frank Osorio, *Vice Pres*
Jose A Osorio, *Vice Pres*
Valentin Osorio, *Admin Sec*
EMP: 98
SQ FT: 7,200
SALES (est): 6.9MM **Privately Held**
SIC: **1742** Drywall

(P-2900)
J & J ACOUSTICS INC
2260 De La Cruz Blvd, Santa Clara (95050-3008)
PHONE................................408 275-9255
James Jean, *President*
Joseph Jean, *Vice Pres*
Marge Meide, *Admin Sec*
EMP: 140 EST: 1975
SALES (est): 20.1MM **Privately Held**
WEB: www.jjacoustics.com
SIC: **1742** Drywall; acoustical & ceiling work

(P-2901)
JADE INC
11126 Sepulveda Blvd B, Mission Hills (91345-1130)
PHONE................................818 365-7137
Steven Arteaga, *CEO*
Jay Arteaga, *President*
Cheryl Taylor, *Treasurer*
Michelle Vojtech, *Vice Pres*
Gail De Ande, *Admin Sec*
EMP: 75
SQ FT: 5,000
SALES (est): 7.3MM **Privately Held**
WEB: www.jade.net
SIC: **1742** Drywall

(P-2902)
JCV INC
1118 W Orangethorpe Ave, Fullerton (92833-4743)
P.O. Box 856 (92836-0856)
PHONE................................714 871-2007
Mario Valadez, *CFO*
Juan Valadez, *CEO*
EMP: 50
SQ FT: 1,900
SALES (est): 3.6MM **Privately Held**
SIC: **1742** Drywall

(P-2903)
JOHN JORY CORPORATION (PA)
2180 N Glassell St, Orange (92865-3308)
PHONE................................714 279-7901
Kenneth Johnson, *CEO*
Tim Harrison, *Vice Pres*
Jack Jory, *Admin Sec*
Sam Berry, *Project Mgr*
John Oliver, *Project Mgr*
EMP: 385
SALES (est): 53.6MM **Privately Held**
WEB: www.johnjorycorp.com
SIC: **1742** Drywall

(P-2904)
KEENAN HOPKINS SUDER & STOWELL (PA)
Also Called: Khs & S Contractors
5109 E La Palma Ave Ste A, Anaheim (92807-2066)
PHONE................................714 695-3670
David Suder, *President*
Philip Cherne, *COO*
Dennis Norman, *CFO*
John Platon, *Senior VP*
Mark Gill, *Vice Pres*
▲ EMP: 65
SALES (est): 253MM **Privately Held**
SIC: **1742** 1751 1743 1741 Plastering, plain or ornamental; carpentry work; terrazzo, tile, marble, mosaic work; masonry & other stonework; painting & paper hanging

(P-2905)
KENYON CONSTRUCTION INC
4667 N Blythe Ave, Fresno (93722-3908)
PHONE................................559 277-5645
Jose Valenzuela, *Manager*
EMP: 56
SQ FT: 9,182
SALES (corp-wide): 134.6MM **Privately Held**
SIC: **1742** Plastering, drywall & insulation
PA: Kenyon Construction, Inc.
4001 W Indian School Rd
Phoenix AZ 85019
602 484-0080

(P-2906)
KENYON CONSTRUCTION INC
Also Called: Kenyon Plastering
3223 E St, North Highlands (95660-4606)
P.O. Box 2077 (95660-8077)
PHONE................................916 514-9502
Carl Schmidt, *Principal*
EMP: 200
SALES (corp-wide): 134.6MM **Privately Held**
WEB: www.kenyonconstruction.com
SIC: **1742** Plastering, drywall & insulation
PA: Kenyon Construction, Inc.
4001 W Indian School Rd
Phoenix AZ 85019
602 484-0080

(P-2907)
KERDUS PLASTERING INC
575 6th St, Norco (92860-1540)
PHONE................................951 272-6720
Craig L Kerdus, *President*
Laura T Kerdus, *Corp Secy*
EMP: 165
SQ FT: 2,000
SALES (est): 16.4MM **Privately Held**
SIC: **1742** Stucco work, interior

(P-2908)
KURT MEISWINKEL INC
1407 E 3rd Ave, San Mateo (94401-2109)
PHONE................................650 344-7200
Kurt Meiswinkel, *President*
EMP: 50
SQ FT: 25,000
SALES: 3.3MM **Privately Held**
WEB: www.km.net
SIC: **1742** Drywall

(P-2909)
LANCASTER BURNS CNSTR INC
Also Called: L B Construction
8655 Washington Blvd, Roseville (95678-5945)
PHONE................................916 624-8404
Jordan Edward Burns, *President*
Christine Lancaster, *CFO*
Vance Lancaster, *Vice Pres*
EMP: 150
SQ FT: 43,000
SALES (est): 30.4MM **Privately Held**
SIC: **1742** 1751 1791 Drywall; framing contractor; building front installation metal

(P-2910)
LEAVY BROTHERS INCORPORATED
Also Called: Solid Drywall
4117 Elverta Rd Ste 102, Antelope (95843-4734)
PHONE................................916 773-5636
Joseph W Leavy, *CEO*
Masami Yoshieda, *Corp Secy*
Kevin Leavy, *Vice Pres*
EMP: 54
SALES: 500K **Privately Held**
SIC: **1742** Plastering, drywall & insulation

(P-2911)
MAGNUM DRYWALL INC
42027 Boscell Rd, Fremont (94538-3106)
PHONE................................510 979-0420
Gary Robinson, *President*
Jason Jordan, *Project Mgr*
EMP: 72
SQ FT: 3,200
SALES (est): 17.8MM **Privately Held**
WEB: www.magnumdrywall.com
SIC: **1742** Drywall

(P-2912)
MARTIN BROS/MARCOWALL INC (PA)
17104 S Figueroa St, Gardena (90248-3097)
P.O. Box 2089 (90247-0089)
PHONE................................310 532-5335
Mohammad Chahine, *CEO*
Raffi Ounanian, *Partner*
Dave Aguilera, *Vice Pres*
Damon Hoover, *Vice Pres*
Cody Nowak, *Research*
EMP: 150
SQ FT: 6,000
SALES (est): 25.7MM **Privately Held**
WEB: www.martinbros-marcowall.com
SIC: **1742** Plastering, drywall & insulation

(P-2913)
MARTIN INTEGRATED SYSTEMS
2330 N Pacific St, Orange (92865-2618)
PHONE................................714 998-9100
Marshall Hovivian, *President*
Anne Reizer, *Corp Secy*
Jeff Anderson, *Project Mgr*
EMP: 55
SQ FT: 5,540
SALES (est): 7MM **Privately Held**
SIC: **1742** Acoustical & ceiling work

(P-2914)
MASTER DESIGN DRYWALL INC
Also Called: Pacific Lath & Plaster
360 S Spruce St, Escondido (92025-4052)
P.O. Box 3058 (92033-3058)
PHONE................................760 480-9001
Mary Kathawa, *President*
EMP: 140
SALES (est): 8.7MM **Privately Held**
WEB: www.pacificlathandplaster.com
SIC: **1742** Plaster & drywall work

(P-2915)
MASTER DRYWALL INC
6727 Bucktown Ln, Vacaville (95688-9719)
PHONE................................707 448-8659
Joseph R Mendonca, *President*
Manuela Mendonc, *Vice Pres*
EMP: 125
SALES (est): 7.8MM **Privately Held**
WEB: www.masterdrywall.com
SIC: **1742** Drywall

(P-2916)
MELOS PLST LTHG & DRYWALL
2038 E Jensen Ave, Fresno (93706-5054)
PHONE................................559 237-0028
Carlos Melo, *President*
Maria Melo, *Vice Pres*
EMP: 100
SQ FT: 5,820
SALES (est): 5.5MM **Privately Held**
SIC: **1742** Plastering, plain or ornamental; plaster & drywall work; drywall

(P-2917)
MGM DRYWALL INC
1050 Coml St Ste 102, San Jose (95112)
PHONE................................408 292-4085
Miguel Guillen, *President*
Martina Guillen, *CFO*
Gonzalo Guillen, *Vice Pres*
Sal Madrigal, *Vice Pres*
William Guillen, *Project Engr*
EMP: 100
SALES (est): 5.1MM **Privately Held**
WEB: www.mgmdrywall.com
SIC: **1742** 1721 3446 Drywall; acoustical & insulation work; acoustical & ceiling work; residential painting; commercial painting; acoustical suspension systems, metal

(P-2918)
MICHAEL B MAYOCK INC
Also Called: A Complete Drywall Co
1945 Francisco Blvd E # 31, San Rafael (94901-5525)
PHONE................................415 456-9306
Michael B Mayock, *President*
Lisa Mayock, *Corp Secy*
EMP: 60 EST: 1977
SALES (est): 3.9MM **Privately Held**
SIC: **1742** 1751 Drywall; lightweight steel framing (metal stud) installation

(P-2919)
MID VALLEY PLASTERING INC
15300 Mckinley Ave, Lathrop (95330-8782)
PHONE................................209 858-9766
Jeff Gann, *President*
Kevin Gann, *Corp Secy*
Jeremy Gann, *Vice Pres*
EMP: 400
SQ FT: 5,000
SALES (est): 32.7MM **Privately Held**
WEB: www.midvalleyplastering.com
SIC: **1742** Plastering, plain or ornamental

(P-2920)
MOWERY THOMASON INC
1225 N Red Gum St, Anaheim (92806-1821)
PHONE................................714 666-1717
Robert J Heimerl, *President*
Toni Heimerl, *Corp Secy*
Todd Heimerl, *Vice Pres*
EMP: 175 EST: 1957
SQ FT: 8,000
SALES (est): 17.7MM **Privately Held**
WEB: www.mowerythomason.com
SIC: **1742** Drywall; plastering, plain or ornamental

PRODUCTS & SVCS

(P-2921)
NEW WEST PARTITIONS
2550 Sutterville Rd, Sacramento
(95820-1020)
PHONE............................916 456-8365
Kem P Modellas, *CEO*
Mark Modellas, *Admin Sec*
EMP: 120
SQ FT: 3,000
SALES (est): 9.8MM **Privately Held**
SIC: 1742 Drywall

(P-2922)
NOROGACHI CONSTRUCTION INC/CA
600 Industrial Dr Ste 100, Galt
(95632-8164)
PHONE............................916 236-4201
Anival Guerrero, *CEO*
Laura Guerrero, *Vice Pres*
Gerardo Guerrero, *Office Mgr*
EMP: 100
SALES (est): 9.1MM **Privately Held**
SIC: 1742 1541 1542 Drywall; acoustical & insulation work; acoustical & ceiling work; institutional building construction

(P-2923)
NORTH COUNTIES DRYWALL INC
20563 Broadway, Sonoma (95476-7590)
P.O. Box 260 (95476-0260)
PHONE............................707 996-0198
Diane Merlo, *President*
Richard Merlo, *President*
Fred Burbage, *Project Mgr*
Tony Rosales, *Project Mgr*
Olivia Acevedo, *HR Admin*
EMP: 50
SQ FT: 2,000
SALES (est): 7.1MM **Privately Held**
WEB: www.ncdinc.net
SIC: 1742 1542 1521 Drywall; commercial & office building, new construction; new construction, single-family houses

(P-2924)
OJ INSULATION LP
5820 Obata Way Unit B, Gilroy
(95020-7038)
PHONE............................408 842-6315
Griff Jenkins, *Branch Mgr*
EMP: 73
SALES (corp-wide): 32.8MM **Privately Held**
SIC: 1742 1751 1741 Insulation, buildings; carpentry work; masonry & other stonework
PA: Oj Insulation, L.P.
　　600 S Vincent Ave
　　Azusa CA 91702
　　626 812-6070

(P-2925)
OJ INSULATION LP
Also Called: Oj Insulation & Fireplaces
2061 Albergrov Ave, Escondido (92029)
PHONE............................760 839-3200
Tom Berry, *Manager*
EMP: 50
SALES (corp-wide): 32.8MM **Privately Held**
WEB: www.ojinc.com
SIC: 1742 Insulation, buildings
PA: Oj Insulation, L.P.
　　600 S Vincent Ave
　　Azusa CA 91702
　　626 812-6070

(P-2926)
OJ INSULATION LP
78 015 Wildcat Dr, Palm Desert (92211)
PHONE............................760 200-4343
Griff Jenkins, *Branch Mgr*
EMP: 73
SALES (corp-wide): 32.8MM **Privately Held**
SIC: 1742 1751 1741 Insulation, buildings; carpentry work; masonry & other stonework
PA: Oj Insulation, L.P.
　　600 S Vincent Ave
　　Azusa CA 91702
　　626 812-6070

(P-2927)
OJ INSULATION LP (PA)
Also Called: Abco Insulation
600 S Vincent Ave, Azusa (91702-5145)
PHONE............................626 812-6070
Pamela A Henson, *Partner*
Rocco Tannascoli, *Project Mgr*
Charlene Smith, *Human Res Dir*
Mike Shepherd, *Sales Staff*
EMP: 148
SQ FT: 12,000
SALES (est): 32.8MM **Privately Held**
WEB: www.ojinc.com
SIC: 1742 1751 1741 Insulation, buildings; carpentry work; masonry & other stonework

(P-2928)
ORANGE COUNTY PLST CO INC
3191 Arprt Loop Dr Ste B1, Costa Mesa
(92626)
PHONE............................714 957-1971
Robert G Smith, *President*
EMP: 128
SALES (est): 11.8MM **Privately Held**
WEB: www.ocplastering.com
SIC: 1742 Plastering, plain or ornamental; drywall

(P-2929)
P H B CONTRACTING INC
43180 Sunburst St, Indio (92201-2083)
PHONE............................760 347-7290
Dave Boggs, *President*
Nicholas Panzarini, *Vice Pres*
Laura Mariscal, *Office Mgr*
EMP: 225
SALES (est): 7.9MM **Privately Held**
SIC: 1742 Plaster & drywall work

(P-2930)
PACE INC
Also Called: Pace Drywall
2301 Arnold Industrial Wa, Concord
(94520-5375)
P.O. Box 573 (94522-0573)
PHONE............................925 602-0900
Alan D Mauldin, *President*
Patricia Mauldin, *Corp Secy*
EMP: 80
SQ FT: 17,000
SALES (est): 7.9MM **Privately Held**
WEB: www.pacedrywall.com
SIC: 1742 Drywall

(P-2931)
PACIFIC BUILDING GROUP
13541 Stoney Creek Rd, San Diego
(92129-2050)
PHONE............................858 552-0600
Jim Roherty, *Branch Mgr*
EMP: 100
SALES (corp-wide): 52MM **Privately Held**
SIC: 1742 Acoustical & ceiling work
PA: Pacific Building Group
　　9752 Aspen Creek Ct # 100
　　San Diego CA 92126
　　858 552-0600

(P-2932)
PACIFIC EXTERIORS INC
13911 Enterprise Dr Ste B, Garden Grove
(92843-4042)
PHONE............................714 265-1998
Frank Blasetti, *President*
Christine Blasetti, *CFO*
Mark Blasetti, *Treasurer*
EMP: 75
SALES (est): 6.1MM **Privately Held**
WEB: www.pacificexteriors.com
SIC: 1742 Plastering, plain or ornamental

(P-2933)
PACIFIC RIM CONTRACTORS INC
1315 E Saint Andrew Pl B, Santa Ana
(92705-4919)
PHONE............................714 641-7380
Jerry Tyner, *President*
Aaron Tyner, *Vice Pres*
Justin Tyner, *Opers Mgr*
Tina Feraco, *Manager*
EMP: 65
SQ FT: 3,000

SALES (est): 5.3MM **Privately Held**
WEB: www.pacificrimcontractors.com
SIC: 1742 1721 Drywall; painting & paper hanging

(P-2934)
PACIFIC SYSTEMS INTERIORS INC
190 E Arrow Hwy Ste D, San Dimas
(91773-3314)
PHONE............................310 436-6820
Jonathan Miasnik, *President*
EMP: 150
SQ FT: 30,000
SALES (est): 32.2MM **Privately Held**
SIC: 1742 Plastering, drywall & insulation

(P-2935)
PACIFIC WEST LATH & PLASTER
6853 Mccomber St, Sacramento
(95828-2515)
PHONE............................916 329-9028
Theodore Brown, *CEO*
Greg Brown, *President*
Paul Maples, *Vice Pres*
EMP: 50
SALES (est): 5.1MM **Privately Held**
SIC: 1742 Drywall

(P-2936)
PADILLA CONSTRUCTION COMPANY
Also Called: Garris Plastering
205 W Bristol Ln, Orange (92865-2605)
P.O. Box 2847 (92859-0847)
PHONE............................714 685-8500
Ralph Padilla, *Principal*
Tom Mattera, *Vice Pres*
Dennis Davies, *VP Opers*
EMP: 250
SQ FT: 5,000
SALES (est): 25.5MM **Privately Held**
WEB: www.padillaconstruction.com
SIC: 1742 Plastering, drywall & insulation

(P-2937)
PAUL PIETRZYK
Also Called: Pauls Drywall
1142 Acapulco Ct, Merced (95348-1859)
PHONE............................209 726-5034
Paul Pietryk, *President*
Loree Pietryk, *CFO*
EMP: 50
SALES (est): 2.5MM **Privately Held**
SIC: 1742 Drywall

(P-2938)
PETROCHEM INSULATION INC
19010 S Alameda St, Compton
(90221-6201)
PHONE............................310 638-6663
Erich Freudenthaler, *Manager*
Linda Lewis, *Executive*
Eric Freudenthaler, *Marketing Mgr*
EMP: 200
SALES (corp-wide): 2.8B **Privately Held**
WEB: www.petrocheminc.com
SIC: 1742 3531 Insulation, buildings; construction machinery
HQ: Petrochem Insulation, Inc.
　　2300 Clayton Rd Ste 1050
　　Concord CA 94520
　　707 644-7455

(P-2939)
PRE CON INDUSTRIES INC
4340 Viewridge Ave Ste B, San Diego
(92123-1682)
P.O. Box 5728, Santa Maria (93456-5728)
PHONE............................805 928-3397
John Amburgey, *President*
Anne Temple, *Principal*
EMP: 99
SALES (est): 3.5MM **Privately Held**
SIC: 1742 Drywall

(P-2940)
PRE CON INDUSTRIES INC
917 W Inyokern Rd Ste C, Ridgecrest
(93555-5602)
P.O. Box 5728, Santa Maria (93456-5728)
PHONE............................760 499-6176
John Amburgey, *President*
EMP: 99

SALES (est): 2.8MM **Privately Held**
SIC: 1742 Drywall

(P-2941)
PREMIER DRYWALL
725 Oak St, Santa Maria (93454-6215)
P.O. Box 57 (93456-0057)
PHONE............................805 928-3397
John Amburgey, *CEO*
Danny Amburgery, *Principal*
EMP: 99 EST: 1990
SALES (est): 5.3MM **Privately Held**
SIC: 1742 Drywall

(P-2942)
PREMIUM ROCK DRYWALL INC
31348 Via Colinas Ste 103, Westlake Village (91362-6805)
PHONE............................818 676-3350
Rick Cook, *President*
Stacy Cook, *Corp Secy*
EMP: 80
SQ FT: 800
SALES: 3MM **Privately Held**
SIC: 1742 Drywall

(P-2943)
PROWALL LATH AND PLASTER
360 S Spruce St, Escondido (92025-4052)
PHONE............................760 480-9001
Mary Kathawa, *President*
Lonnie Loutherback, *Vice Pres*
EMP: 99
SALES (est): 6.1MM **Privately Held**
SIC: 1742 Plastering, plain or ornamental

(P-2944)
QUALITY PRODUCTION SVCS INC
18711 S Broadwick St, Compton
(90220-6427)
PHONE............................310 406-3350
Arshak George Kotoyantz, *President*
EMP: 100
SALES (est): 11.4MM **Privately Held**
SIC: 1742 Drywall

(P-2945)
QUALITY WALL SYSTEMS INC
Also Called: Residential Wall Systems
104 S Maple St, Corona (92880-1704)
P.O. Box 2649 (92878-2649)
PHONE............................951 739-4409
Glenn L Crowther, *President*
EMP: 99
SALES (est): 5.9MM **Privately Held**
SIC: 1742 1721 Drywall; painting & paper hanging

(P-2946)
REDDING DRYWALL SYSTEMS INC
Also Called: High Performance Wall Systems
3092 Crossroads Dr, Redding
(96003-8058)
P.O. Box 494156 (96049-4156)
PHONE............................530 222-8767
Marvin O'Dell, *President*
EMP: 50
SQ FT: 3,800
SALES (est): 4.3MM **Privately Held**
WEB: www.drywallsystems.com
SIC: 1742 Drywall

(P-2947)
RFJ CORPORATION
Also Called: Rfj Meiswinkel
930 Innes Ave, San Francisco
(94124-2905)
PHONE............................415 824-6890
Joseph Meiswinkel, *President*
EMP: 60
SQ FT: 15,000
SALES (est): 8.8MM **Privately Held**
WEB: www.rfjmeiswinkel.com
SIC: 1742 Plastering, plain or ornamental; drywall

(P-2948)
RICE DRYWALL INC
919 E 6th St, Santa Ana (92701-4725)
PHONE............................714 543-5400
John H Laing, *President*
Keith Barakat, *Vice Pres*
Kim Riker, *Admin Sec*

EMP: 90
SQ FT: 8,000
SALES: 2.3MM **Privately Held**
SIC: 1742 Drywall

(P-2949)
RICHMOND PLASTERING INC
12102 Centralia Rd Ste B, Hawaiian Gardens (90716-1003)
PHONE.................................562 924-4202
Tim Richmond, *President*
Debbie Richmond, *Corp Secy*
Mark Nevin, *Vice Pres*
J Arroyo, *Technology*
Curtis Claude, *Opers Staff*
▲ EMP: 50 EST: 1979
SQ FT: 1,375
SALES (est): 5.6MM **Privately Held**
WEB: www.richmondplastering.com
SIC: 1742 Plastering, plain or ornamental

(P-2950)
RICK H HITCH PLASTERING INC
Also Called: Venture Lath and Plaster
3306 Orange Grove Ave, North Highlands (95660-5808)
PHONE.................................916 334-3591
Jason Wu, *President*
Loretta Hitch, *Vice Pres*
EMP: 125
SALES (est): 4.5MM **Privately Held**
WEB: www.venturelp.com
SIC: 1742 Plastering, plain or ornamental

(P-2951)
ROYAL WEST DRYWALL INC
2008 2nd St, Norco (92860-2804)
PHONE.................................951 271-4600
Paul Diguiseppe, *CEO*
EMP: 100
SQ FT: 20,473
SALES (est): 8.1MM **Privately Held**
WEB: www.westcoastdrywallinc.com
SIC: 1742 Drywall

(P-2952)
RUDY CARRILLO DRYWALL INC
1913 W Magnolia Blvd, Burbank (91506-1727)
PHONE.................................818 841-2011
Rudy Carrillo, *CEO*
Darcy Carrillo, *Vice Pres*
EMP: 80
SQ FT: 2,399
SALES (est): 5.3MM **Privately Held**
SIC: 1742 Drywall

(P-2953)
RUTHERFORD CO INC (PA)
2107 Crystal St, Los Angeles (90039-2901)
PHONE.................................323 666-5284
Paul Rutherford, *President*
James Rutherford, *Treasurer*
Brad Rutherford, *Vice Pres*
Sheila Rutherford, *Admin Sec*
Maricela Meza, *Manager*
EMP: 100
SQ FT: 15,000
SALES (est): 19MM **Privately Held**
SIC: 1742 Plastering, plain or ornamental

(P-2954)
S A CALI-U ACOUSTICS INC
Also Called: Acoustical Contractor
1111 Rancho Conejo Blvd # 501, Thousand Oaks (91320-1412)
PHONE.................................805 376-9300
Diego Velasquez, *President*
Anna Velasquez, *Vice Pres*
Federico Velasquez, *Project Mgr*
Tim Velasquez, *Technology*
EMP: 60
SQ FT: 3,000
SALES (est): 1.4MM **Privately Held**
WEB: www.caliusa.net
SIC: 1742 Acoustical & ceiling work; insulation, buildings

(P-2955)
SAN MARINO PLASTERING INC
4501 E La Palma Ave # 200, Anaheim (92807-1950)
PHONE.................................714 693-7840
Fred Erdtsieck, *President*
Edward Birn, *CFO*
EMP: 820

SALES (est): 30.6MM **Privately Held**
WEB: www.smcompanies.com
SIC: 1742 Plastering, plain or ornamental

(P-2956)
SERVICE LATHING COMPANY
1090 139th Ave, San Leandro (94578-2615)
PHONE.................................510 483-9732
Robert G Brown, *President*
Ernest Schorno, *Treasurer*
EMP: 50
SQ FT: 4,500
SALES (est): 4.5MM **Privately Held**
SIC: 1742 1751 Plastering, plain or ornamental; framing contractor

(P-2957)
SIERRA LATHING COMPANY INC
1189 Leiske Dr, Rialto (92376-8633)
PHONE.................................909 421-0211
Gary K Waldron, *CEO*
Connie Waldron, *Treasurer*
EMP: 200
SQ FT: 10,000
SALES (est): 14MM **Privately Held**
SIC: 1742 1751 Drywall; framing contractor

(P-2958)
SIERRA WES DRYWALL INC (PA)
3340 Swetzer Ct Ste A, Loomis (95650-9580)
PHONE.................................916 652-4491
Wayne E Stilwell, *President*
Chris Beloberk, *Vice Pres*
Diane M Stilwell, *Admin Sec*
Julie Chapman, *Bookkeeper*
Carl Haupt, *Prdtn Mgr*
EMP: 300
SALES (est): 14.4MM **Privately Held**
WEB: www.sierrawesdrywall.com
SIC: 1742 Drywall

(P-2959)
SNEARY CONSTRUCTION INC
1182 Monte Vista Ave # 2, Upland (91786-8204)
PHONE.................................909 982-1833
Montie Sneary, *President*
Nicole Van Gundy, *CFO*
Shawna Sneary, *Vice Pres*
Deborah Herring, *Manager*
EMP: 50
SALES (est): 3.4MM **Privately Held**
SIC: 1742 Drywall

(P-2960)
SPACETONE ACOUSTICS INC
1051 Serpentine Ln # 300, Pleasanton (94566-8451)
PHONE.................................925 931-0749
Robert A Libby, *President*
Joan Libby, *Vice Pres*
Robert Libby, *Vice Pres*
Katie Chan, *Office Mgr*
Dominic Sanchez, *Manager*
EMP: 50
SQ FT: 3,500
SALES (est): 7.5MM **Privately Held**
WEB: www.spacetoneacoustics.com
SIC: 1742 Acoustical & ceiling work

(P-2961)
SPECIALTY TEAM PLASTERING INC
4652 Vintage Ranch Ln, Santa Barbara (93110-2079)
PHONE.................................805 966-3858
Jaime Melgosa, *President*
Robin Melgosa, *Vice Pres*
EMP: 130
SQ FT: 1,000
SALES: 8.2MM **Privately Held**
SIC: 1742 Plastering, drywall & insulation

(P-2962)
STANDARD DRYWALL INC (HQ)
Also Called: S D I
9902 Channel Rd, Lakeside (92040-3042)
PHONE.................................619 443-7034
Robert E Caya, *Principal*
Blaine Caya, *Vice Pres*

EMP: 300
SQ FT: 4,500
SALES (est): 128.4MM **Privately Held**
WEB: www.standarddrywall.net
SIC: 1742 Drywall; acoustical & ceiling work

(P-2963)
STUCCO WORKS INC
5451 Whse Way Ste 105, Sacramento (95826)
PHONE.................................916 383-6699
Kevin Nelson, *President*
Anselmo Padilla, *Vice Pres*
Xavier Valdez, *Admin Sec*
EMP: 300
SQ FT: 26,000
SALES (est): 10.9MM **Privately Held**
SIC: 1742 Stucco work, interior

(P-2964)
SUNSHINE METAL CLAD INC
7201 Edison Hwy, Bakersfield (93307-9011)
PHONE.................................661 366-0575
James R Eudy, *President*
Linda Payne, *CFO*
Sandy Eudy, *Vice Pres*
Mark D Given, *Project Mgr*
Bill Lutz, *Project Mgr*
▲ EMP: 100
SQ FT: 50,000
SALES (est): 11.5MM **Privately Held**
WEB: www.smc3000.com
SIC: 1742 Insulation, buildings

(P-2965)
SUPERIOR CONTRACTING CORP
Also Called: Coast Building Products
45 N Main St, Salinas (93901-2892)
PHONE.................................831 757-1089
EMP: 50
SALES (corp-wide): 1.9B **Publicly Held**
SIC: 1742 Insulation, buildings
HQ: Superior Contracting Corporation
475 N Williamson Blvd
Daytona Beach FL 32114
386 304-2200

(P-2966)
SUPERIOR WALL SYSTEMS INC
Also Called: Sws
1232 E Orangethorpe Ave, Fullerton (92831-5224)
PHONE.................................714 278-0000
Ronald Lee Hudson, *CEO*
EMP: 500 EST: 1979
SQ FT: 40,000
SALES: 48.9MM **Privately Held**
SIC: 1742 Drywall

(P-2967)
TEMECULA VALLEY DRYWALL INC
Also Called: Timberlake Painting
41228 Raintree Ct, Murrieta (92562-7089)
PHONE.................................951 600-1742
Doug A Misemer, *CEO*
Sandy Villella, *Corp Secy*
Lorry Hales, *Vice Pres*
Eric Kazakoff, *Project Mgr*
EMP: 75
SQ FT: 8,000
SALES (est): 10.8MM **Privately Held**
SIC: 1742 1721 Drywall; painting & paper hanging

(P-2968)
THERMO POWER INDUSTRIES
10570 Humbolt St, Los Alamitos (90720-2439)
PHONE.................................562 799-0087
Edward Lydic, *CEO*
John G Carroll, *CFO*
EMP: 50
SQ FT: 5,500
SALES (est): 8.4MM **Privately Held**
WEB: www.thermopowerindustries.com
SIC: 1742 1721 3479 Insulation, buildings; commercial painting; coating, rust preventive

(P-2969)
TOMMY GUN PLASTERING INC
944 4th St, Calimesa (92320-1205)
PHONE.................................909 795-9966
Tommy Lucero, *CEO*
EMP: 60
SQ FT: 1,800
SALES (est): 4.7MM **Privately Held**
SIC: 1742 Plastering, plain or ornamental

(P-2970)
TONY MARQUEZ POOL PLST INC
14960 Foothill Blvd, Sylmar (91342-1301)
PHONE.................................818 833-5872
Antonio R Marquez, *President*
Tony Marquez, *President*
Georgette Marquez, *CFO*
Denise Tencza, *Marketing Mgr*
EMP: 63
SALES (est): 3.8MM **Privately Held**
SIC: 1742 1799 Plastering, plain or ornamental; swimming pool construction

(P-2971)
TOUCH-UP INC
Also Called: T & R Painting & Drywall
7116 Valjean Ave, Van Nuys (91406-3901)
PHONE.................................818 994-6166
Hagai Rapaport, *President*
EMP: 120
SQ FT: 2,500
SALES (est): 6.5MM **Privately Held**
SIC: 1742 1721 Drywall; painting & paper hanging

(P-2972)
TOWNE CONSTRUCTION INC
12115 Lakeside Ave, Lakeside (92040-1712)
PHONE.................................619 390-4557
Tom Towne, *President*
EMP: 60
SQ FT: 1,700
SALES (est): 6.8MM **Privately Held**
SIC: 1742 Drywall

(P-2973)
TRI-STAR DRYWALL LP
2479 Burgan Ave, Clovis (93611-4107)
P.O. Box 1081 (93613-1081)
PHONE.................................559 299-9858
Raymond William McGuire, *Partner*
EMP: 80
SALES (est): 3.2MM **Privately Held**
SIC: 1742 Drywall

(P-2974)
VANTAGE PLASTER & DRYWALL
79607 Country Club Dr, Bermuda Dunes (92203-1207)
PHONE.................................760 345-3622
Jim Morales, *President*
EMP: 85
SALES (est): 2.7MM **Privately Held**
SIC: 1742 Plastering, plain or ornamental

(P-2975)
VINEYARD PLASTERING INC
10335 Vineyard Dr, Fontana (92337-7458)
PHONE.................................909 357-3701
Ray Hays, *President*
EMP: 50
SALES (est): 2.3MM **Privately Held**
SIC: 1742 Plastering, drywall & insulation

(P-2976)
W F HAYWARD CO
629 Main St Ste 101, Placerville (95667-5752)
PHONE.................................530 303-3030
Daryll Hayward, *Vice Pres*
EMP: 70
SALES (corp-wide): 6.2MM **Privately Held**
SIC: 1742 Drywall
PA: W. F. Hayward Co.
1264 W 130th St
Gardena CA 90247
310 532-9501

PRODUCTS & SVCS

(P-2977)
W F HAYWARD CO (PA)
1264 W 130th St, Gardena (90247-1502)
PHONE..................310 532-9501
Dennis F Hayward, *CEO*
Robert D Hayward, *Corp Secy*
EMP: 100
SQ FT: 12,600
SALES: 6.2MM **Privately Held**
WEB: www.wfhayward.com
SIC: 1742 Drywall; plastering, plain or or-
namental

(P-2978)
WALL SYSTEMS INC
11975 Discovery Ct, Moorpark
(93021-7120)
PHONE..................805 523-9091
Kenyon Lee, *President*
Frank Bass, *Vice Pres*
Darrell Talavera, *Vice Pres*
EMP: 90
SQ FT: 6,200
SALES: 10MM **Privately Held**
SIC: 1742 Drywall; stucco work, interior

(P-2979)
**WEST COAST DRYWALL & CO
INC**
1610 W Linden St, Riverside (92507-6810)
PHONE..................951 778-3592
Mark Herbert, *CEO*
Dan Slavin, *President*
Santos Garcia, *Vice Pres*
Colleen Butler, *Human Resources*
EMP: 400
SQ FT: 18,962
SALES (est): 30.7MM **Privately Held**
WEB: www.westcoastpainting.com
SIC: 1742 Drywall

(P-2980)
**WESTERN BUILDING
MATERIALS CO (PA)**
4620 E Olive Ave, Fresno (93702-1660)
PHONE..................559 454-8500
Peter Hastrup, *President*
Pat Quigley, *Controller*
EMP: 60
SQ FT: 32,000
SALES: 17MM **Privately Held**
WEB: www.western-building.com
SIC: 1742 5211 Acoustical & ceiling work;
millwork & lumber

(P-2981)
WESTERN DRYWALL INC
4981 Salida Blvd, Salida (95368-9420)
P.O. Box 11130, Oakdale (95361-1025)
PHONE..................209 847-6401
Cecil Shatswell, *President*
John Shatswell, *Vice Pres*
Kevin Shatswell, *Vice Pres*
EMP: 70
SQ FT: 5,000
SALES: 3MM **Privately Held**
WEB: www.westerndrywall.com
SIC: 1742 Drywall

(P-2982)
WGG ENTERPRISES INC
Also Called: Pierce Enterprises
11340 Stewart St, El Monte (91731-2747)
PHONE..................626 442-5493
Weldon G Gainer, *President*
EMP: 150 EST: 1969
SQ FT: 25,000
SALES (est): 10.2MM **Privately Held**
SIC: 1742 Plastering, plain or ornamental

(P-2983)
WINEGARD ENERGY INC
2885 S Chestnut Ave, Fresno
(93725-2211)
PHONE..................559 441-0243
Wallas Winegard, *Owner*
Arnold Espinoza, *Project Dir*
EMP: 100 **Privately Held**
WEB: www.winegardenergy.com
SIC: 1742 Insulation, buildings
PA: Winegard Energy, Inc.
5354 Irwindale Ave Ste B
Irwindale CA 91706

(P-2984)
WINEGARD ENERGY INC
2159 Zeus Ct, Bakersfield (93308-6866)
PHONE..................661 393-9467
Jessica Landrum, *Manager*
Bryce Larson, *Manager*
EMP: 72
SALES (est): 2.1MM **Privately Held**
WEB: www.winegardenergy.com
SIC: 1742 Insulation, buildings
PA: Winegard Energy, Inc.
5354 Irwindale Ave Ste B
Irwindale CA 91706

(P-2985)
**WM ONEILL LATH AND PLST
CORP**
P.O. Box 60352 (94088-0352)
PHONE..................408 329-1413
William O'Neill, *President*
Sandra O'Neill, *Admin Sec*
EMP: 50 EST: 2009
SALES (est): 5.3MM **Privately Held**
SIC: 1742 Plastering, plain or ornamental

**1743 Terrazzo, Tile, Marble &
Mosaic Work**

(P-2986)
**AMERICAN TILE BRICK VENEER
INC**
1389 E 28th St, Signal Hill (90755-1841)
PHONE..................562 595-9293
Albert Weinstein, *President*
Taghi Nahidi, *CFO*
Andrew Nahidi, *Vice Pres*
Bardia Nahidi, *Vice Pres*
EMP: 50
SQ FT: 3,000
SALES: 6MM **Privately Held**
SIC: 1743 1741 Tile installation, ceramic;
bricklaying

(P-2987)
ARRIAGA USA INC
11831 Vose St, North Hollywood
(91605-5748)
PHONE..................818 982-9559
EMP: 75
SALES (corp-wide): 24.8MM **Privately
Held**
SIC: 1743 Tile installation, ceramic
PA: Arriaga Usa, Inc.
12000 Sherman Way
North Hollywood CA 91605
818 982-9559

(P-2988)
BREWSTER MARBLE CO INC
20801 Dearborn St, Chatsworth
(91311-5916)
PHONE..................818 834-2195
Teo Zeolla, *President*
Christina Elias, *Accountant*
▲ **EMP:** 50
SQ FT: 11,000
SALES (est): 3.9MM **Privately Held**
WEB: www.brewstermarble.net
SIC: 1743 Marble installation, interior

(P-2989)
CAL CUSTOM TILE
1300 Commerce Way, Sanger
(93657-8731)
PHONE..................559 875-1460
Rick Berry, *President*
Michele Berry, *Vice Pres*
Gerson Cruz, *Supervisor*
EMP: 95
SQ FT: 10,000
SALES (est): 10.2MM **Privately Held**
SIC: 1743 Tile installation, ceramic

(P-2990)
CERAMIC TILE ART INC
11601 Pendleton St, Sun Valley
(91352-2502)
PHONE..................818 767-9088
Itamar Levy, *President*
▲ **EMP:** 75

SALES (est): 6MM **Privately Held**
SIC: 1743 Tile installation, ceramic

(P-2991)
COASTAL TILE INC
Also Called: Coastal The
7403 Greenbush Ave, North Hollywood
(91605-4006)
PHONE..................818 988-6134
Roniq Yemini, *President*
Eyal Reguev, *Vice Pres*
▲ **EMP:** 100
SALES (est): 8.8MM **Privately Held**
SIC: 1743 Tile installation, ceramic

(P-2992)
D & J TILE COMPANY INC
1045 Terminal Way, San Carlos
(94070-3226)
PHONE..................650 632-4000
David Newman, *Principal*
Michael Brady, *Treasurer*
John Reich, *Admin Sec*
Jaleh Dale, *Project Mgr*
Victor Zamora, *Project Mgr*
▲ **EMP:** 100
SALES (est): 13.3MM **Privately Held**
WEB: www.djtile.com
SIC: 1743 Tile installation, ceramic

(P-2993)
DELLA MAGGIORE TILE INC
87 N 30th St, San Jose (95116-1124)
PHONE..................408 286-3991
Nick D Maggiore, *President*
Julie D Maggiore, *Admin Sec*
Luis Casas, *Manager*
Derol Briscoe, *Supervisor*
▲ **EMP:** 80
SQ FT: 20,000
SALES (est): 7.3MM **Privately Held**
WEB: www.slabshop.com
SIC: 1743 Tile installation, ceramic

(P-2994)
DENNETT TILE & STONE INC
4536 Bennett View Dr, Santa Rosa
(95404-6204)
PHONE..................707 541-3700
Rick Dennett, *President*
Bambi Dennett, *Admin Sec*
EMP: 50
SQ FT: 5,500
SALES (est): 6.2MM **Privately Held**
WEB: www.dennett-tile.com
SIC: 1743 Tile installation, ceramic

(P-2995)
ELEGANZA TILES INC (PA)
3125 E Coronado St, Anaheim
(92806-1915)
PHONE..................714 224-1700
Mike Darmawan, *Principal*
Vonny Purnama, *Vice Pres*
Robert Cordero, *Info Tech Mgr*
Dan Kort, *Opers Mgr*
Nicole Hillyard, *Sales Mgr*
◆ **EMP:** 100
SQ FT: 145
SALES (est): 27.3MM **Privately Held**
WEB: www.eleganzatiles.com
SIC: 1743 Tile installation, ceramic

(P-2996)
EMSER TILE LLC
5300 Shea Center Dr, Ontario
(91761-7883)
PHONE..................909 974-1600
Gabriel Castro, *Branch Mgr*
Scott Charlesworth, *Manager*
EMP: 60
SALES (corp-wide): 285.7MM **Privately
Held**
SIC: 1743 Tile installation, ceramic
PA: Emser Tile, Llc
8431 Santa Monica Blvd
Los Angeles CA 90069
323 650-2000

(P-2997)
**FISCHER TILE AND MARBLE
INC**
1800 23rd St, Sacramento (95816-7112)
PHONE..................916 452-1426
Jay H Fischer, *President*

Tara McCord, *Project Mgr*
Matthew Beauchamp, *Opers Mgr*
Charles Rich, *Contractor*
▲ **EMP:** 150
SQ FT: 22,000
SALES (est): 19.1MM **Privately Held**
WEB: www.fischertile.com
SIC: 1743 Tile installation, ceramic; marble
installation, interior

(P-2998)
GINO RINALDI INC
Also Called: Rinaldi Tile & Marble
51 Fremont St, Royal Oaks (95076-5213)
PHONE..................831 761-0195
Gino Rinaldi, *President*
Yvonne Rinaldi, *Corp Secy*
Rick Scurich, *Plant Mgr*
▲ **EMP:** 80
SQ FT: 10,000
SALES (est): 10.7MM **Privately Held**
WEB: www.rinalditileandmarble.com
SIC: 1743 Tile installation, ceramic

(P-2999)
GMG STONE INC
7988 Stromesa Ct, San Diego
(92126-4329)
P.O. Box 722917 (92172-2917)
PHONE..................619 258-6899
Jean Francois Hope, *President*
Robert Bruce, *Assistant*
EMP: 50
SALES (est): 4MM **Privately Held**
WEB: www.gmgstone.com
SIC: 1743 Marble installation, interior

(P-3000)
KDI ELEMENTS
79431 Country Club Dr, Bermuda Dunes
(92203-1200)
P.O. Box 14150, Palm Desert (92255-
4150)
PHONE..................760 345-9933
Paul Klein, *CEO*
Lauri Nichols, *Senior VP*
Jeanette Nichols, *Project Mgr*
Krista Rounds, *Purch Agent*
EMP: 250
SALES (est): 25.7MM **Privately Held**
WEB: www.kdistoneworks.com
SIC: 1743 5999 1741 Tile installation, ce-
ramic; monuments & tombstones; ma-
sonry & other stonework

(P-3001)
KELLY MOSES FLOORS
27430 Bostik Ct Ste 101, Temecula
(92590-5511)
PHONE..................951 296-5147
Moses Kelly, *Principal*
EMP: 50
SALES (est): 1.7MM **Privately Held**
SIC: 1743 Tile installation, ceramic

(P-3002)
LEGACY TILE AND STONE INC
26825 Jefferson Ave Ste D, Murrieta
(92562-8964)
PHONE..................951 296-1096
Robert Blackmore Jr, *President*
EMP: 50 EST: 2014
SALES: 3.7MM **Privately Held**
SIC: 1743 Tile installation, ceramic

(P-3003)
MARBLEWEST INC
Also Called: Marbleworks
7421 Vincent Cir, Huntington Beach
(92648-1246)
PHONE..................714 847-6472
Gordon Bair, *President*
Suzanne Bair, *Vice Pres*
▲ **EMP:** 50
SQ FT: 6,800
SALES (est): 3.5MM **Privately Held**
WEB: www.marbleworks.org
SIC: 1743 Marble installation, interior

(P-3004)
MATRIX SURFACES INC
5449 E La Palma Ave, Anaheim
(92807-2022)
PHONE..................714 696-5449
Jerry Eugene Jones, *CEO*
Laura J Jones, *Vice Pres*

▲ EMP: 60
SQ FT: 5,000
SALES (est): 8.8MM **Privately Held**
WEB: www.matrixtile.com
SIC: **1743** Tile installation, ceramic

(P-3005)
MTHURON INC
Also Called: Elite Tile
1903 Rutan Dr, Livermore (94551-7646)
PHONE..................................925 932-4101
Dennis Hourany, *President*
Estella Ortiz, *Human Res Dir*
EMP: 115 EST: 1976
SQ FT: 7,474
SALES (est): 7.8MM **Privately Held**
WEB: www.elitetileusa.com
SIC: **1743** Marble installation, interior; tile installation, ceramic

(P-3006)
PARAGON INDUSTRIES INC
19305 White Sage Trl, Desert Hot Springs (92241-7496)
PHONE..................................760 898-4716
EMP: 101
SALES (corp-wide): 294.7MM **Privately Held**
SIC: **1743** Tile installation, ceramic
PA: Paragon Industries Inc.
4285 N Golden State Blvd
Fresno CA 93722
559 275-5000

(P-3007)
PAUL WILLIAMS TILE CO INC
77570 Springfield Ln K, Palm Desert (92211-0473)
PHONE..................................760 772-7440
Randy Coulter, *President*
▲ EMP: 60
SQ FT: 10,000
SALES (est): 4.5MM **Privately Held**
WEB: www.paulwilliamstile.com
SIC: **1743** Tile installation, ceramic

(P-3008)
PREMIER TILE & MARBLE
15000 S Main St, Gardena (90248-1945)
PHONE..................................310 516-1712
Greg Games, *President*
Lilian Games, *Admin Sec*
EMP: 55
SALES: 15MM **Privately Held**
SIC: **1743** 5032 Tile installation, ceramic; ceramic wall & floor tile

(P-3009)
S C TILE COMPANY INC
Also Called: S C Tile and Surfaces
606 S Marshall Ave, El Cajon (92020-4215)
PHONE..................................619 669-1575
Scott Cowles, *President*
Scott H Cowles, *President*
▲ EMP: 50
SALES (est): 1.6MM **Privately Held**
SIC: **1743** Tile installation, ceramic

(P-3010)
SHERMN-LEHR CSTM TILE WRKS INC
5691 Power Inn Rd Ste A, Sacramento (95824-2361)
PHONE..................................916 386-0417
James P Loehr, *President*
Jane Sherman, *Treasurer*
Eber T Sherman, *Vice Pres*
Joyce Loehr, *Admin Sec*
EMP: 100
SQ FT: 3,400
SALES (est): 11.6MM **Privately Held**
SIC: **1743** Tile installation, ceramic

(P-3011)
SOSA GRANITE & MARBLE INC
Also Called: Sosa Tile Co
7701 Marathon Dr, Livermore (94550-9550)
PHONE..................................925 373-7675
Mario Sosa, *President*
Tracy Ruiz, *Accountant*
▲ EMP: 50
SQ FT: 16,000
SALES (est): 5.9MM **Privately Held**
WEB: www.sosagranite.com
SIC: **1743** Tile installation, ceramic

(P-3012)
TILE WEST INC (PA)
11 Hamilton Dr, Novato (94949-5602)
P.O. Box 5789 (94948-5789)
PHONE..................................415 382-7550
Carl E Jacobson, *President*
Julia M Ratto, *Corp Secy*
Cliff E Jacobson, *Vice Pres*
Wayne Jackson, *Project Mgr*
Alicia Isley, *Manager*
▲ EMP: 82
SQ FT: 5,000
SALES (est): 9.3MM **Privately Held**
WEB: www.tilewestinc.com
SIC: **1743** Tile installation, ceramic

(P-3013)
TRM CORPORATION (PA)
Also Called: Superior Tile Co
2378 Polvorosa Ave, San Leandro (94577-2218)
P.O. Box 2106, Oakland (94621-0006)
PHONE..................................510 895-2700
Tommy Conner, *CEO*
Robert Herman, *President*
Jerry T Sue, *CFO*
Patty Moore, *Vice Pres*
Danny Mullen, *Manager*
EMP: 170 EST: 1975
SQ FT: 12,000
SALES (est): 32.2MM **Privately Held**
SIC: **1743** Tile installation, ceramic; marble installation, interior

(P-3014)
U S PERMA INC
Also Called: California Tile Installers
1696 Rogers Ave, San Jose (95112-1105)
PHONE..................................408 436-0600
Jack O'Brien, *President*
Randall Sundberg, *Vice Pres*
Donald K O'Brien, *Admin Sec*
▲ EMP: 50
SQ FT: 9,000
SALES: 7MM **Privately Held**
WEB: www.usperma.com
SIC: **1743** Tile installation, ceramic

1751 Carpentry Work

(P-3015)
ALL SEASONS FRAMING CORP
644 N Eckhoff St, Orange (92868-1004)
PHONE..................................714 634-2324
Dave Karos, *President*
Gerado Rodarte, *Admin Sec*
EMP: 50
SQ FT: 3,600
SALES: 4MM **Privately Held**
WEB: www.allseasonspressed.com
SIC: **1751** Framing contractor

(P-3016)
ALLEN CONSTRUCTION INC
31356 Via Colinas Ste 107, Westlake Village (91362-6799)
PHONE..................................818 879-5334
Darrel Allen, *President*
Karen Scheneman, *Vice Pres*
EMP: 50
SALES (est): 3.5MM **Privately Held**
SIC: **1751** Framing contractor

(P-3017)
ALLIED FRAMERS INC
4990 Allison Pkwy, Vacaville (95688-9346)
PHONE..................................707 452-7050
Jakki Kutz, *President*
Dave Burrell, *Vice Pres*
Mark Johnson, *Vice Pres*
Mike Thomason, *Vice Pres*
Danielle Gregorich, *Controller*
EMP: 130
SQ FT: 6,000
SALES (est): 12.5MM **Privately Held**
WEB: www.alliedframers.com
SIC: **1751** Framing contractor

(P-3018)
BAY AREA CNSTR FRAMERS INC
1150 W Center St Ste 105, Manteca (95337-4313)
PHONE..................................925 454-8514

Fax: 925 454-0507
EMP: 175
SQ FT: 6,700
SALES (est): 14MM **Privately Held**
SIC: **1751** 1521

(P-3019)
BOB DILLON CONSTRUCTION INC
856 Calle Margarita, Thousand Oaks (91360-4852)
PHONE..................................805 495-2607
Bob Dillon, *President*
Tracy Dillon, *Admin Sec*
EMP: 150
SALES (est): 6.7MM **Privately Held**
SIC: **1751** Framing contractor

(P-3020)
CHATEAUX FRAMING INC
3701 Georgeann Pl, Ceres (95307-9317)
PHONE..................................209 537-6799
Steve Durossette, *President*
Derk Durossette, *Treasurer*
Jill Durossette, *Corp Secy*
William Durossette, *Vice Pres*
EMP: 150
SALES: 750K **Privately Held**
SIC: **1751** Framing contractor

(P-3021)
CLOSET WORLD INC
14438 Don Julian Rd, City of Industry (91746-3101)
PHONE..................................626 855-0846
EMP: 252 **Privately Held**
WEB: www.closetworld.net
SIC: **1751** 5211 Cabinet building & installation; closets, interiors & accessories
PA: Closet World, Inc.
3860 Capitol Ave
City Of Industry CA 90601

(P-3022)
COMMERCIAL DOOR COMPANY INC
1374 E 9th St, Pomona (91766-3831)
PHONE..................................714 529-2179
David O Holmes, *CEO*
Carol Holmes, *Treasurer*
Thomas Goodwin, *Project Mgr*
EMP: 60
SQ FT: 10,000
SALES (est): 9.9MM **Privately Held**
WEB: www.commercialdoorcompany.com
SIC: **1751** Garage door, installation or erection

(P-3023)
COOK CABINETS INC
6428 Capitol Ave, Diamond Springs (95619-9521)
PHONE..................................530 621-0851
Richard Gularte, *President*
Steve Gularte, *Vice Pres*
EMP: 65
SQ FT: 35,000
SALES (est): 3.5MM **Privately Held**
SIC: **1751** 5712 5031 2434 Cabinet building & installation; cabinet work, custom; lumber, plywood & millwork; wood kitchen cabinets

(P-3024)
CRAFTSMAN LATH AND PLASTER INC
8325 63rd St, Riverside (92509-6004)
PHONE..................................951 685-9922
Kevin Tunstill, *President*
EMP: 350 EST: 2015
SALES (est): 11.1MM **Privately Held**
SIC: **1751** Carpentry work

(P-3025)
CWP CABINETS INC
10007 Yucca Rd, Adelanto (92301-2242)
PHONE..................................760 246-4530
Michael Rodriguez, *CEO*
EMP: 115 EST: 2011
SALES (est): 5.3MM **Privately Held**
SIC: **1751** 2434 2541 5712 Cabinet building & installation; wood kitchen cabinets; wood partitions & fixtures; cabinet work, custom

(P-3026)
D F RIOS CONSTRUCTION INC
45847 Warm Springs Blvd, Fremont (94539-6779)
PHONE..................................510 226-7467
David F Rios, *President*
EMP: 75
SQ FT: 4,000
SALES (est): 4.1MM **Privately Held**
SIC: **1751** Framing contractor

(P-3027)
DAVIS BROTHERS FRAMING INC
8780 Prestige Ct, Rancho Cucamonga (91730-5138)
PHONE..................................909 944-4899
Randy Davis, *President*
George E Davis, *CEO*
EMP: 200
SALES (est): 10.1MM **Privately Held**
SIC: **1751** Framing contractor

(P-3028)
DAVIS FRAMING INC
8103 Commercial St, La Mesa (91942-2927)
PHONE..................................619 463-2394
Steve Davis, *President*
EMP: 50
SQ FT: 1,200
SALES (est): 3.9MM **Privately Held**
SIC: **1751** Carpentry work

(P-3029)
DAY STAR FIXTURES
1802 Riverford Rd, Tustin (92780-3950)
PHONE..................................714 838-4613
Dan Prigmore, *Owner*
EMP: 50
SALES (est): 1.7MM **Privately Held**
SIC: **1751** Cabinet building & installation

(P-3030)
DON KINZEL CONSTRUCTION INC
4300 Easton Dr Ste 2, Bakersfield (93309-9420)
PHONE..................................661 322-9105
Donald Kinzel, *President*
▲ EMP: 93
SQ FT: 2,700
SALES (est): 4.6MM **Privately Held**
SIC: **1751** 1542 Carpentry work; commercial & office building contractors

(P-3031)
ELLISON FRAMING INC
Also Called: Ellison Construction-Framing
160 Guthrie Ln Ste 13, Brentwood (94513-4060)
P.O. Box 580 (94513-0580)
PHONE..................................925 516-9269
Matthew M Ellison, *President*
Ron Kapphahn, *Treasurer*
EMP: 125
SQ FT: 15,000
SALES (est): 9.1MM **Privately Held**
WEB: www.ellisonframing.com
SIC: **1751** Framing contractor

(P-3032)
EMPIRE LEASING INC
Also Called: Alliance Construction
2045 Placentia Ave Ste A, Costa Mesa (92627-6239)
PHONE..................................949 646-7400
Fax: 949 645-3461
EMP: 75
SALES (est): 3.1MM **Privately Held**
WEB: www.empireleasinginc.com
SIC: **1751** 1795

(P-3033)
EPPINK OF CALIFORNIA INC
11900 Center St, South Gate (90280-7834)
PHONE..................................562 633-1275
Erik Eppink, *CEO*
Michael Hunter, *Vice Pres*
▲ EMP: 50
SQ FT: 20,000
SALES (est): 6.2MM **Privately Held**
WEB: www.davisandwells.com
SIC: **1751** Carpentry work

(PA)=Parent Co (HQ)=Headquarters (DH)=Div Headquarters
✪ = New Business established in last 2 years

(P-3034)
ERICKSON CONSTRUCTION LP
8350 Industrial Ave, Roseville
(95678-6239)
PHONE..........................916 774-1100
Randall Folts, *President*
Anthony D'Attomo, *CFO*
EMP: 200
SALES (est): 47.2MM
SALES (corp-wide): 7.6B **Publicly Held**
SIC: 1751 Carpentry work
PA: Masco Corporation
17450 College Pkwy
Livonia MI 48152
313 274-7400

(P-3035)
FENNEL INC
Also Called: Thompson Cnstr Sup Door
Frame
1169 Sherborn St, Corona (92879-5005)
P.O. Box 78300 (92877-0143)
PHONE..........................951 284-2020
Kenneth R Thompson, *CEO*
Robert Leos, *Vice Pres*
EMP: 65
SALES (est): 1.3MM **Privately Held**
SIC: 1751 5251 5999 Garage door, instal-
lation or erection; door locks & lock sets;
art, picture frames & decorations

(P-3036)
FORCE FRAMING INC
21520 Yorba Linda Blvd G, Yorba Linda
(92887-3764)
PHONE..........................714 970-3888
Donald Briscoe, *President*
Christina Matlack, *Controller*
EMP: 50
SQ FT: 2,400
SALES (est): 1.2MM **Privately Held**
SIC: 1751 Framing contractor

(P-3037)
GATEHOUSE MSI LLC
Also Called: McMurray Stern
15511 Carmenita Rd, Santa Fe Springs
(90670-5609)
PHONE..........................562 623-3000
Kenneth De Angelis, *Principal*
Dave Cagle, *Vice Pres*
Tom O'Neill, *Vice Pres*
Timothy Hill, *Principal*
Hank Miller, *Principal*
EMP: 50
SQ FT: 30,000
SALES (est): 15MM **Privately Held**
SIC: 1751 1771 Cabinet & finish carpen-
try; stucco, gunite & grouting contractors

(P-3038)
GRANT CONSTRUCTION INC
7702 Meany Ave Ste 103, Bakersfield
(93308-5199)
PHONE..........................661 588-4586
Grant Fraysier, *President*
EMP: 230 EST: 1994
SQ FT: 1,000
SALES (est): 31MM **Privately Held**
WEB: www.gciframing.com
SIC: 1751 1771 Framing contractor; con-
crete work

(P-3039)
HAKES SASH & DOOR INC
31945 Corydon St, Lake Elsinore
(92530-8524)
PHONE..........................951 674-2414
Allen J Hakes, *President*
Gaspar Santos, *Vice Pres*
Christina Rupp, *Office Mgr*
Charles Pumphrey, *Accountant*
Ricky Luper, *Opers Mgr*
EMP: 190
SQ FT: 2,000
SALES (est): 25.5MM **Privately Held**
SIC: 1751 3442 5211 Window & door in-
stallation & erection; window & door
frames; sash, wood or metal

(P-3040)
HARDWOOD CREATIONS (PA)
Also Called: H C I
1560 N Maple St, Corona (92880-1783)
PHONE..........................714 674-0527
Thomas Steele, *President*

Melvin Grimes, *CEO*
Jeremy Steele, *VP Sales*
EMP: 80
SQ FT: 8,000
SALES (est): 9.2MM **Privately Held**
WEB: www.hardwoodcreations.com
SIC: 1751 Carpentry work

(P-3041)
HERITAGE INTERESTS LLC (PA)
4300 Jetway Ct, North Highlands
(95660-5702)
P.O. Box 214609, Sacramento (95821-
0609)
PHONE..........................916 481-5030
Edward Zuckerman, *President*
Dennis Gardemeyer, *CFO*
Charlie Gardemeyer, *Vice Pres*
EMP: 90
SQ FT: 80,000
SALES (est): 89.5MM **Privately Held**
SIC: 1751 5031 2431 Cabinet & finish
carpentry; finish & trim carpentry; lumber,
plywood & millwork; windows & window
parts & trim, wood; louver windows, glass,
wood frame

(P-3042)
**HEWITT AND CANFIELD CNSTR
INC**
495 E Easy St Ste A, Simi Valley
(93065-1845)
PHONE..........................805 522-4426
Ron Hewitt, *President*
Liz Weigand, *Office Mgr*
Dale Canfield, *Admin Sec*
EMP: 80
SQ FT: 10,000
SALES: 13MM **Privately Held**
WEB: www.rondaleconstruction.com
SIC: 1751 Framing contractor

(P-3043)
HOME ORGANIZERS INC
Also Called: Closet World, The
3860 Capitol Ave, City of Industry
(90601-1733)
PHONE..........................562 699-9945
Frank Melkonian, *President*
EMP: 660
SALES (est): 27.5MM **Privately Held**
WEB: www.closetworld.com
SIC: 1751 2541 Cabinet building & instal-
lation; cabinets, lockers & shelving

(P-3044)
JAG FRAMING INC
16741 Los Alimos St, Granada Hills
(91344-5052)
PHONE..........................818 822-7110
Jose Antoio Guerra, *President*
EMP: 50 EST: 2008
SALES: 3.9MM **Privately Held**
SIC: 1751 Framing contractor

(P-3045)
JB FINISH INC
82750 Atlantic St, Indio (92203-9626)
P.O. Box 3093 (92202-3093)
PHONE..........................760 342-6300
John Broyles, *President*
EMP: 56
SQ FT: 12,500
SALES (est): 3.8MM **Privately Held**
WEB: www.johnbroyles.com
SIC: 1751 5211 Finish & trim carpentry;
lumber & other building materials

(P-3046)
JENCOR DOOR AND TRIM INC
26845 Oak Ave Ste 12, Canyon Country
(91351-6645)
PHONE..........................661 251-8161
Jeno Horvath, *President*
EMP: 50
SQ FT: 10,000
SALES (est): 2.8MM **Privately Held**
SIC: 1751 Finish & trim carpentry

(P-3047)
**JONCE THOMAS
CONSTRUCTION CO**
3390 Seldon Ct, Fremont (94539-5625)
P.O. Box 1856 (94538-0034)
PHONE..........................510 657-7171
Donna Jean Thomas, *President*

Jonce Thomas, *Vice Pres*
EMP: 50
SQ FT: 10,000
SALES (est): 3.5MM **Privately Held**
SIC: 1751 Framing contractor

(P-3048)
**KRC BUILDERS
INCORPORATED**
6141 W 4th St, Rio Linda (95673-4011)
PHONE..........................916 417-1200
Gene M Kindy, *CEO*
Jack E Ross, *Admin Sec*
EMP: 80
SALES (est): 3.6MM **Privately Held**
SIC: 1751 1521 Framing contractor; new
construction, single-family houses

(P-3049)
LAURENCE-HOVENIER INC
179 N Maple St, Corona (92880-1760)
PHONE..........................951 736-2990
Ronald Laurence, *President*
Fred Hovenier, *Vice Pres*
EMP: 190
SQ FT: 6,000
SALES (est): 23.9MM **Privately Held**
WEB: www.framingcontractor.com
SIC: 1751 Framing contractor

(P-3050)
**LEXINGTON SCENERY & PROPS
INC**
12800 Rangoon St, Arleta (91331-4321)
PHONE..........................818 768-5768
Richard Bencivengo, *CEO*
Frank Benchivengo, *President*
John Wright, *Principal*
EMP: 120
SALES (est): 4.9MM **Privately Held**
SIC: 1751 2542 3993

(P-3051)
**MCCARTHY FRAMING
CONSTRUCTION**
Also Called: McCarthy Construction
15133 Grevillea Ave, Lawndale
(90260-2017)
PHONE..........................310 219-3038
Patrick McCarthy, *Owner*
▲ EMP: 100
SALES (est): 7.2MM **Privately Held**
SIC: 1751 Framing contractor

(P-3052)
NORCAL INC
Also Called: Seeley Brothers
1400 Moonstone, Brea (92821-2801)
PHONE..........................714 224-3949
Michael Seeley, *Partner*
Joe Calvillo, *Partner*
Phil Norys, *Partner*
EMP: 175
SQ FT: 62,000
SALES (est): 25.2MM **Privately Held**
SIC: 1751 Finish & trim carpentry

(P-3053)
NORCAL INC
Also Called: Seeley Brothers
1400 Moonstone, Brea (92821-2801)
PHONE..........................714 224-3949
EMP: 105
SQ FT: 60,000
SALES (est): 4.5MM **Privately Held**
WEB: www.seeleybros.com
SIC: 1751

(P-3054)
OLIVIERI ENTERPRISES LP
Also Called: Olympic Construction
210 Estates Dr Ste 200, Roseville
(95678-2300)
P.O. Box 2490, Granite Bay (95746-2490)
PHONE..........................916 791-7857
John Olivieri, *Partner*
Teresa Olivieri, *Partner*
EMP: 200
SQ FT: 2,300
SALES (est): 6.1MM **Privately Held**
SIC: 1751 Framing contractor

(P-3055)
**ON TRAC OVERHEAD DOOR CO
INC**
1430 Richardson St, San Bernardino
(92408-2962)
PHONE..........................909 799-8555
Charles L Colton, *CEO*
Chuck Colton, *President*
Terri Colton, *Vice Pres*
EMP: 50
SQ FT: 16,600
SALES (est): 5MM **Privately Held**
WEB: www.ontracdoor.com
SIC: 1751 Garage door, installation or
erection

(P-3056)
**OVERHEAD DOOR
CORPORATION**
1617 N Orangethorpe Way, Anaheim
(92801-1228)
PHONE..........................714 680-0600
Dave Fowler, *Vice Pres*
EMP: 93
SALES (corp-wide): 3.6B **Privately Held**
SIC: 1751 Garage door, installation or
erection
HQ: Overhead Door Corporation
2501 S State Hwy 121 Ste
Lewisville TX 75067
469 549-7100

(P-3057)
PRE CON INDUSTRIES INC
950 Riata Ln, Nipomo (93444-9484)
P.O. Box 5728, Santa Maria (93456-5728)
PHONE..........................805 481-7305
John Amburgey, *President*
EMP: 50 **Privately Held**
SIC: 1751 1742 1542 Carpentry work;
drywall; commercial & office building con-
tractors
PA: Pre Con Industries, Inc.
725 Oak St
Santa Maria CA 93454

(P-3058)
PRECISION FRAMING INC
1504 Eureka Rd Ste 160, Roseville
(95661-3084)
PHONE..........................916 791-7464
William Peterson, *President*
EMP: 260
SQ FT: 1,100
SALES (est): 7.4MM **Privately Held**
SIC: 1751 Framing contractor

(P-3059)
PRIME TECH CABINETS INC
2652 White Rd, Irvine (92614-6248)
PHONE..........................714 558-4837
Hassan Farjamrad, *President*
Zahra Farjamrad, *Vice Pres*
Zora Farjamrad, *Vice Pres*
David Bondy, *Purch Agent*
Bobby Farjamrad, *Sales Staff*
EMP: 110
SALES (est): 12.8MM **Privately Held**
WEB: www.ptcabinets.com
SIC: 1751 Cabinet building & installation

(P-3060)
PRODUCTION FRAMING INC
2000 Opportunity Dr # 140, Roseville
(95678-3020)
PHONE..........................916 978-2843
Doyle Headrick, *President*
EMP: 99
SALES (est): 3.1MM **Privately Held**
SIC: 1751 Framing contractor

(P-3061)
**PRODUCTION FRAMING
SYSTEMS INC (PA)**
2000 Opportunity Dr # 140, Roseville
(95678-3020)
PHONE..........................916 978-2888
Steve J Benjamin, *President*
Kerry Palmer, *Vice Pres*
EMP: 150
SALES (est): 13.8MM **Privately Held**
WEB: www.productionframing.com
SIC: 1751 Framing contractor

(P-3062)
PROTEGE BUILDERS INC
4306 Pinell St, Sacramento (95838-2928)
PHONE......................................916 825-8478
Leah Rivera, *President*
Shelly Hinkle, *Corp Secy*
EMP: 50
SALES (est): 5.3MM **Privately Held**
WEB: www.protegebuilders.com
SIC: 1751 Framing contractor

(P-3063)
R D S UNLIMITED INC
14372 Olde Highway 80 E, El Cajon
(92021-2865)
P.O. Box 21066
PHONE......................................619 443-0221
Ronnie Swaim, *President*
EMP: 50
SQ FT: 3,000
SALES: 3.5MM **Privately Held**
SIC: 1751 Framing contractor

(P-3064)
R T FRAMING CORPORATION
299 W Hillcrest Dr # 212, Thousand Oaks
(91360-7838)
PHONE......................................805 496-3985
Lorene Fuess, *President*
Raymond Fuess, *Vice Pres*
EMP: 100
SQ FT: 1,000
SALES (est): 5.7MM **Privately Held**
SIC: 1751 Framing contractor

(P-3065)
RANCH HOUSE DOORS INC
Also Called: R H D
1527 Pomona Rd, Corona (92880-6959)
PHONE......................................951 278-2884
Michael James Neal, *CEO*
Sandra Neal, *President*
Cristian Neal, *CFO*
Steve Serrano, *Sales Staff*
Ralph Tan, *Sales Staff*
EMP: 70
SQ FT: 33,000
SALES (est): 7MM **Privately Held**
WEB: www.ranchhousedoors.com
SIC: 1751 Garage door, installation or
erection

(P-3066)
RH FRAMING INC
815 Quail Ridge Ln, Salinas (93908-8966)
PHONE......................................831 759-8860
Ryan Harrod, *President*
EMP: 150
SALES (est): 5.9MM **Privately Held**
SIC: 1751 Framing contractor

(P-3067)
RICHARD HANCOCK INC
Also Called: Rhi
1029 3rd St, Santa Rosa (95404-6635)
PHONE......................................707 528-4900
Bruce Lamar, *President*
EMP: 50
SQ FT: 1,600
SALES: 10MM **Privately Held**
SIC: 1751 Carpentry work

(P-3068)
ROCKY COAST BUILDERS INC
135 Market Pl, Escondido (92029-1353)
PHONE......................................760 489-7770
Douglas J Ladderbush, *CEO*
Cris Madsen, *Treasurer*
Amanda Kerins, *Admin Sec*
EMP: 60
SQ FT: 6,200
SALES (est): 8.7MM **Privately Held**
SIC: 1751 Framing contractor

(P-3069)
ROY E WHITEHEAD INC
Also Called: Rew Inc
2245 Via Cerro, Riverside (92509-2412)
PHONE......................................951 682-1490
David Whitehead, *CEO*
Chris Bagley, *President*
Dennis Whitehead, *Treasurer*
Dan Gilley, *Vice Pres*
Byron Mitchell, *Vice Pres*
EMP: 75
SQ FT: 36,000
SALES (est): 11.1MM **Privately Held**
WEB: www.royewhitehead.com
SIC: 1751 Cabinet building & installation

(P-3070)
RSI PROFESSIONAL CAB SOLUTIONS
11350 Riverside Dr Frnt, Mira Loma
(91752-3703)
PHONE......................................909 614-2900
Eric Vanderheyden, *President*
Robert Asman, *Planning Mgr*
Rosalind J Manning, *Executive Asst*
Audra Greenberg, *Credit Mgr*
Colby Mendelson, *Purchasing*
EMP: 250
SALES (est): 22.3MM
SALES (corp-wide): 1.2B **Publicly Held**
SIC: 1751 Cabinet & finish carpentry
HQ: Rsi Home Products, Inc.
400 E Orangethorpe Ave
Anaheim CA 92801
714 449-2200

(P-3071)
S I J INC
26035 Jefferson Ave, Murrieta
(92562-6983)
PHONE......................................951 304-9444
Briana Sather-Layfield, *President*
Joseph Sather, *Treasurer*
Patricia Sather, *Admin Sec*
EMP: 50
SALES: 5.5MM **Privately Held**
WEB: www.sicorp.us
SIC: 1751 Carpentry work

(P-3072)
S W CONSTRUCTION INC
Also Called: Wilson Stephen Construction Co
1145 E Stanford Ct, Anaheim (92805-6822)
PHONE......................................714 978-7871
Stephen L Wilson, *President*
EMP: 120
SQ FT: 7,500
SALES (est): 8.7MM **Privately Held**
SIC: 1751 Framing contractor

(P-3073)
SAN-MAR CONSTRUCTION CO INC
4875 E La Palma Ave # 601, Anaheim
(92807-1955)
PHONE......................................714 693-5400
Sandra Drew, *CEO*
Darren Drew, *Project Mgr*
Tamara Kennedy, *Human Res Dir*
Sue Moran, *Associate*
EMP: 200
SQ FT: 3,000
SALES (est): 20.6MM **Privately Held**
SIC: 1751 Carpentry work

(P-3074)
SANTA CLARITA VALLEY BLDRS INC
Also Called: Main Frame Construction
24307 Magic Mountain Pkwy # 122, Santa
Clarita (91355-3402)
PHONE......................................661 295-6722
Mike Spigno, *President*
Cheryl A Spigno, *Shareholder*
EMP: 225
SALES (est): 7.7MM **Privately Held**
SIC: 1751 7389 Framing contractor; inte-
rior design services

(P-3075)
SHOOK & WALLER CNSTR INC
7677 Bell Rd Ste 101, Windsor
(95492-7432)
PHONE......................................707 578-3933
Eddie Waller, *President*
Shawn Dolan, *CFO*
Steven Shook, *Corp Secy*
EMP: 64
SQ FT: 8,000
SALES (est): 26.5MM **Privately Held**
WEB: www.shookandwaller.com
SIC: 1751 1521 1542 Framing contractor;
new construction, single-family houses;
nonresidential construction

(P-3076)
SI INC
Also Called: Sather Installation
26035 Jefferson Ave, Murrieta
(92562-6983)
PHONE......................................951 304-9444
EMP: 50
SQ FT: 8,000
SALES (est): 4.7MM **Privately Held**
WEB: www.sicorp.us
SIC: 1751

(P-3077)
SIERRA LUMBER CO
Also Called: Sierra Lumber & Decking
1711 Senter Rd, San Jose (95112-2598)
PHONE......................................408 286-7071
Roger Burch, *President*
James Moblad, *Vice Pres*
Steve Miller, *Manager*
Todd Fernandez, *Supervisor*
EMP: 125
SQ FT: 22,000
SALES (est): 7.7MM
SALES (corp-wide): 191.1MM **Privately
Held**
WEB: www.sierrafence.com
SIC: 1751 5211 Carpentry work; lumber
products
PA: Pacific States Industries, Incorporated
10 Madrone Ave
Morgan Hill CA 95037
408 779-7354

(P-3078)
SIERRA WEST CONSTRUCTION INC
24744 Connie Ct, Auburn (95602-8525)
PHONE......................................530 268-7614
Richard T Ahrens, *President*
Melinda K Ahrens, *Treasurer*
Melinda Ahrens, *Corp Secy*
EMP: 50
SALES (est): 4.5MM **Privately Held**
SIC: 1751 Framing contractor

(P-3079)
SILVER STRAND
8945 Fullbright Ave, Chatsworth
(91311-6124)
PHONE......................................818 701-9707
David Meador, *Principal*
EMP: 50
SQ FT: 7,500
SALES (est): 5.8MM **Privately Held**
WEB: www.silverstrandinc.com
SIC: 1751 Cabinet & finish carpentry

(P-3080)
SLIDING DOOR COMPANY (PA)
Also Called: Sliding Door Co, The
20235 Bahama St, Chatsworth
(91311-6204)
PHONE......................................818 997-7855
Doron Polus, *President*
Sheryl Hai-AMI, *Officer*
Leilani Garcia, *Graphic Designe*
Amanda Redcloud, *Personnel Assit*
Kimberly Antillon, *Recruiter*
▲ EMP: 92
SQ FT: 22,000
SALES (est): 27.4MM **Privately Held**
WEB: www.slidingdoorco.com
SIC: 1751 Window & door installation &
erection

(P-3081)
SMITH BROS INC (PA)
Also Called: Smith Bros Finished Carpentry
2301 Townsgate Rd Ste A, Westlake Village
(91361-2502)
PHONE......................................805 449-2841
Dan Smith, *President*
Sue Christmann, *Controller*
Ani Reihs,
Darin Jackson, *Sr Project Mgr*
EMP: 60
SQ FT: 9,000
SALES (est): 4.3MM **Privately Held**
SIC: 1751 Finish & trim carpentry

(P-3082)
SR FREEMAN INC
2380 S Bascom Ave Ste 200, Campbell
(95008-4389)
PHONE......................................408 364-2200
Shone Freeman, *President*
Josie Freeman, *Admin Sec*
Shayne Freeman, *Manager*
EMP: 60 EST: 1992
SALES: 12.3MM **Privately Held**
WEB: www.srfreemaninc.com
SIC: 1751 Framing contractor

(P-3083)
STOCKHAM CONSTRUCTION INC
475 Portal St, Cotati (94931-3006)
PHONE......................................707 664-0945
Boyd L Stockham, *President*
Dani Stockham, *Treasurer*
EMP: 430
SQ FT: 15,301
SALES: 54.1MM **Privately Held**
WEB: www.stockhamconstruction.com
SIC: 1751 1742 Lightweight steel framing
(metal stud) installation; drywall; acousti-
cal & ceiling work

(P-3084)
SUNDANCE CONSTRUCTION INC
3500 W Lake Center Dr B, Santa Ana
(92704-6900)
PHONE......................................714 437-0802
Tim Boggess, *President*
Ernie Castro Sr, *CEO*
Mario Munoz, *Vice Pres*
Joshua Morales, *Safety Dir*
EMP: 200
SALES (est): 6.8MM **Privately Held**
WEB: www.woodsgrouparch.com
SIC: 1751 Framing contractor

(P-3085)
SURECRAFT DOOR AND HDWR INC
2875 Executive Pl, Escondido
(92029-1524)
PHONE......................................760 737-2120
Richard J Smerud, *President*
Scott Smerud, *CEO*
Paul Smarud, *Vice Pres*
Randy Stoddard, *Vice Pres*
EMP: 145
SQ FT: 33,000
SALES (est): 11.6MM **Privately Held**
SIC: 1751 Carpentry work

(P-3086)
TRUFORM CONSTRUCTION CORP
1041 N Shepard St, Anaheim
(92806-2817)
PHONE......................................714 630-7447
Dan Ruppe, *President*
EMP: 50
SQ FT: 1,400
SALES (est): 3.5MM **Privately Held**
SIC: 1751 1742 Lightweight steel framing
(metal stud) installation; drywall

(P-3087)
TWR ENTERPRISES INC
1661 Railroad St, Corona (92880-2503)
PHONE......................................951 279-2000
Thomas W Rhodes, *President*
Jordan Echt, *Project Mgr*
Deborah Dieter, *Finance*
Debbie Diter, *Controller*
Yesenia Salazar, *Human Res Mgr*
EMP: 200
SQ FT: 20,000
SALES (est): 18.3MM **Privately Held**
SIC: 1751 Framing contractor

(P-3088)
ULTIMATE CONSTRUCTION INC
8811 Alonzo Blvd, Long Beach (90805)
P.O. Box 571117, Tarzana (91357-1117)
PHONE......................................562 633-3389
Enrique Vera, *President*
Gloria Vera, *CFO*
EMP: 112
SQ FT: 10,000
SALES (est): 7MM **Privately Held**
SIC: 1751 1522 1541 1521 Carpentry
work; residential construction; industrial
buildings, new construction; new con-
struction, single-family houses

P R O D U C T S & S V C S

(P-3089)
WALTERS & WOLF INTERIORS (PA)
41450 Boscell Rd, Fremont (94538-3103)
PHONE..............................415 243-9400
Randall Alan Wolf, CEO
Michael Wolf, President
Jeff Belzer, CFO
▲ EMP: 80
SQ FT: 30,000
SALES (est): 13MM Privately Held
SIC: 1751 Carpentry work

(P-3090)
WESLAR INC
28310 Constellation Rd, Valencia (91355-5078)
PHONE..............................661 702-1362
Larry Kern, President
Wes Toy, Vice Pres
EMP: 100
SQ FT: 5,500
SALES (est): 9.1MM Privately Held
WEB: www.weslarinc.com
SIC: 1751 Framing contractor

(P-3091)
WIN-DOR INC (PA)
450 Delta Ave, Brea (92821-2935)
PHONE..............................714 576-2030
Gary Templin, CEO
Wolfgang Wirthgen, President
David May, General Mgr
Dwight Swearingen, Engineer
Eric Edwards, Sales Mgr
EMP: 170
SQ FT: 73,000
SALES (est): 25.2MM Privately Held
WEB: www.win-dor.com
SIC: 1751 3446 Window & door (prefabricated) installation; guards, made from pipe

(P-3092)
X-ACT FINISH & TRIM INC
248 Glider Cir, Corona (92880-2533)
PHONE..............................951 582-9229
Jessie A Moreno, President
EMP: 60
SALES (est): 9.2MM Privately Held
SIC: 1751 Finish & trim carpentry

1752 Floor Laying & Other Floor Work, NEC

(P-3093)
ACE FLOOR CO INC
Also Called: Naturally Aged Flooring
5155 Goldman Ave, Moorpark (93021-1759)
PHONE..............................805 955-9000
Jack Schoen, President
Angela Schoen, Vice Pres
▲ EMP: 55
SQ FT: 20,000
SALES (est): 12.4MM Privately Held
SIC: 1752 Floor laying & floor work

(P-3094)
ANTHONY TREVINO
Also Called: A&S Floors
938 Adams St Ste A, Benicia (94510-2948)
PHONE..............................707 747-4776
Anthony Trevino, Owner
EMP: 52 EST: 1993
SALES (est): 3.7MM Privately Held
SIC: 1752 Floor laying & floor work

(P-3095)
B T MANCINI CO INC (PA)
Also Called: B.T. Mancini Company
876 S Milpitas Blvd, Milpitas (95035-6311)
P.O. Box 361930 (95036-1930)
PHONE..............................408 942-7900
Brooks T Mancini Jr, President
Jim Evans, Vice Pres
Greg Hartwick, Vice Pres
Brooks T Mancini Sr, Vice Pres
Tom McGovern, Vice Pres
▲ EMP: 300
SQ FT: 36,000

SALES (est): 99.2MM Privately Held
WEB: www.btmancini.com
SIC: 1752 1761 Wood floor installation & refinishing; roofing, siding & sheet metal work; siding contractor

(P-3096)
BIG OAK HARDWOOD FLOOR CO INC
1731 Leslie St, San Mateo (94402-2409)
PHONE..............................650 591-8651
Richard Mack, President
Robert Connor, Treasurer
EMP: 58
SQ FT: 7,500
SALES (est): 4.7MM Privately Held
SIC: 1752 Wood floor installation & refinishing

(P-3097)
CAPITAL COMMERCIAL FLRG INC
3709 Bradview Dr Ste 100, Sacramento (95827-9737)
PHONE..............................916 569-1960
Douglas Vincent Lawson, CEO
Scott Fairley, CFO
Jenasis Fullmer, Executive
Diana Lawson, Admin Sec
Carlos Cabera, Data Proc Exec
EMP: 50
SQ FT: 14,000
SALES (est): 6.9MM Privately Held
WEB: www.ccfinc.net
SIC: 1752 Carpet laying

(P-3098)
CREATIVE DESIGN INTERIORS INC (PA)
Also Called: C D I
737 Del Paso Rd, Sacramento (95834-1106)
PHONE..............................916 641-1121
Ronald Lapp, President
Kathy Lapp, Vice Pres
Ron Lewis, Branch Mgr
EMP: 100
SQ FT: 10,000
SALES (est): 29MM Privately Held
SIC: 1752 Ceramic floor tile installation

(P-3099)
DAVENPORT DEVELOPMENT CORP
Also Called: Classic Hardwood Floors
8360 Clairemont Mesa Blvd # 111, San Diego (92111-1321)
PHONE..............................858 300-3333
Marc Davenport, President
Lisa Davenport, Admin Sec
▲ EMP: 50
SALES (est): 5.4MM Privately Held
SIC: 1752 Wood floor installation & refinishing

(P-3100)
DFS FLOORING INC (PA)
15651 Saticoy St, Van Nuys (91406-3234)
PHONE..............................818 374-5200
Richard Friedman, CEO
Greg Keyes, Vice Pres
Scott Sidlow, Vice Pres
Luisana Regla, Admin Asst
Maria Harrison, Project Mgr
EMP: 110
SQ FT: 19,865
SALES (est): 35.4MM Privately Held
WEB: www.dfsflooring.com
SIC: 1752 Wood floor installation & refinishing

(P-3101)
DT FLOORMASTERS INC
Also Called: Floormasters, The
31164 Huntwood Ave, Hayward (94544-7817)
PHONE..............................510 476-1000
Teresa Lau, CEO
Rick Curbelo, Vice Pres
Garrett Gollnick, Executive
Jeff Davis, Manager
Jennifer Pinkston, Accounts Exec
EMP: 70
SQ FT: 1,000

SALES (est): 14.6MM Privately Held
SIC: 1752 Wood floor installation & refinishing

(P-3102)
FASHIONCRAFT FLOORS INC (PA)
1630 Faraday Ave, Carlsbad (92008-7313)
PHONE..............................714 255-8400
Thomas R Roberts, President
Ken Hoffman, Vice Pres
EMP: 50
SQ FT: 10,000
SALES (est): 4.2MM Privately Held
WEB: www.fashioncraftfloors.com
SIC: 1752 Resilient floor laying; carpet laying; vinyl floor tile & sheet installation; wood floor installation & refinishing

(P-3103)
FLOORGATE INC
3350 N San Fernando Rd, Los Angeles (90065-1417)
PHONE..............................323 478-2000
Al Hembarsoonian, President
Gary Damadian, Project Mgr
Artin Hambarsoomian, Project Mgr
EMP: 55
SQ FT: 27,400
SALES: 3.2MM Privately Held
SIC: 1752 5713 Carpet laying; floor covering stores

(P-3104)
H V WELKER CO INC
Also Called: Welker Bros
970 S Milpitas Blvd, Milpitas (95035-6323)
PHONE..............................408 263-4400
Stuart Welker, President
Chuck Gulan, Shareholder
Stuart H Welker, President
Jack Sanguinitti, Exec VP
Vincent A Grana, Vice Pres
EMP: 65
SQ FT: 18,375
SALES: 33.8MM Privately Held
WEB: www.welkers.com
SIC: 1752 Floor laying & floor work

(P-3105)
HOEM & ASSOCIATES INC
951 Linden Ave, South San Francisco (94080-1753)
PHONE..............................650 871-5194
Russell William Hoem, CEO
Sean Hogan, President
Mike Valerio, Vice Pres
Al Dalessio, Executive
Lina Campi, Office Mgr
EMP: 85
SQ FT: 24,000
SALES: 38MM Privately Held
WEB: www.hoemschurba.com
SIC: 1752 Carpet laying; vinyl floor tile & sheet installation; wood floor installation & refinishing

(P-3106)
HOME CARPET INVESTMENT INC (PA)
Also Called: Americas Finest Carpet Co
730 Design Ct Ste 401, Chula Vista (91911-6160)
PHONE..............................619 262-8040
Carlos Ledesma, CEO
Veronica Mendoza, Plant Mgr
EMP: 81
SQ FT: 2,500
SALES (est): 21.5MM Privately Held
WEB: www.americasfinestcarpet.com
SIC: 1752 7217 Carpet laying; carpet & upholstery cleaning; carpet & upholstery cleaning on customer premises; carpet & upholstery cleaning plants

(P-3107)
HY-TECH TILE INC
1355 Palmyrita Ave, Riverside (92507-1601)
P.O. Box 5577 (92517-5577)
PHONE..............................951 788-0550
Michael Postolache, CEO
Tom Shoemaker, President
Narcis Postolache, CEO
Cristina Olteanu, CFO
Bryan Shoemaker, Project Mgr

EMP: 110
SQ FT: 12,000
SALES (est): 16.2MM Privately Held
WEB: www.hytechtile.com
SIC: 1752 5211 Ceramic floor tile installation; tile, ceramic

(P-3108)
ICS PROFESSIONAL SERVICES INC
7755 Center Ave Fl 11, Huntington Beach (92647-3007)
PHONE..............................714 868-3900
Jessie Croteau, CEO
Vance Cook, Vice Pres
▲ EMP: 123
SALES: 7.7MM Privately Held
SIC: 1752 Floor laying & floor work

(P-3109)
INTERIOR SPECIALISTS INC (HQ)
1630 Faraday Ave, Carlsbad (92008-7313)
P.O. Box 61929, Irvine (92602-6064)
PHONE..............................760 929-6700
Alan Davenport, President
Brian Reed, President
Lee Singer, President
Joe Terrana, President
Steve Tracy, President
▲ EMP: 75
SALES (est): 807MM
SALES (corp-wide): 385.6MM Privately Held
WEB: www.isidc.com
SIC: 1752 1799 Carpet laying; drapery track installation
PA: Faraday Holdings, Llc
1630 Faraday Ave
Carlsbad CA 92008
760 929-6700

(P-3110)
INTERIOR SPECIALISTS INC
9300 Hubbard Rd, Auburn (95602-7819)
PHONE..............................530 885-0632
Doug Ederer, Owner
EMP: 70
SALES (corp-wide): 385.6MM Privately Held
SIC: 1752 Floor laying & floor work
HQ: Interior Specialists, Inc.
1630 Faraday Ave
Carlsbad CA 92008
760 929-6700

(P-3111)
J W FLOOR COVERING INC (PA)
9881 Carroll Centre Rd, San Diego (92126-4554)
PHONE..............................858 536-8565
John Wallace, Owner
John S Wallace, President
Gary Morris, Branch Mgr
Ralph Schlotman, Division Mgr
Devon Abbate, Accountant
EMP: 140
SQ FT: 20,500
SALES (est): 44.1MM Privately Held
WEB: www.jwfloors.com
SIC: 1752 Floor laying & floor work

(P-3112)
KYA SERVICES LLC
1522 Brookhollow Dr Ste 3, Santa Ana (92705-5412)
PHONE..............................714 659-6476
John Leyds,
Derrick B Mendoza,
EMP: 50
SALES (est): 721.5K Privately Held
SIC: 1752 Carpet laying

(P-3113)
MAGNESITE SPECIALTIES INC
Also Called: American Deck Systems
8686 Production Ave Ste A, San Diego (92121-2207)
PHONE..............................858 578-4186
Curtis Tyree, President
Dwain Stratton, Shareholder
Vikki J Tyree, Corp Secy
EMP: 50
SQ FT: 2,500

SALES (est): 7.5MM **Privately Held**
WEB: www.magnesitespecialties.com
SIC: 1752 1521 1799 1743 Floor laying & floor work; patio & deck construction & repair; waterproofing; terrazzo, tile, marble, mosaic work

(P-3114)
NATIONAL APARTMENT FLRG LLC
3205 Ocean Park Blvd # 180, Santa Monica (90405-3233)
PHONE..................................800 773-6904
Richard Berle, *President*
Viridiana Acosta, *Sales Staff*
Jackie Lemus, *Director*
EMP: 75
SALES (est): 10.1MM **Privately Held**
SIC: 1752 Access flooring system installation

(P-3115)
PROGRESSIVE FLOOR COVERING INC
924 S Highland Ave, Fullerton (92832-2903)
PHONE..................................714 213-8805
Rita Spinella, *President*
Oanh Pham, *CFO*
Kevin Deehan, *Vice Pres*
EMP: 50
SQ FT: 17,500
SALES (est): 9.2MM **Privately Held**
WEB: www.progressivefloorcovering.com
SIC: 1752 Floor laying & floor work

(P-3116)
R E CUDDIE CO
1751 Junction Ave, San Jose (95112-1029)
PHONE..................................408 998-1250
Thomas Cuddie, *CEO*
Robert Cuddie, *Vice Pres*
Tish Allen, *Admin Sec*
Joanne Brock, *Manager*
EMP: 50
SQ FT: 30,000
SALES (est): 9.5MM **Privately Held**
WEB: www.recuddie.com
SIC: 1752 Floor laying & floor work

(P-3117)
SIGNATURE FLOORING INC
Also Called: Signature Floors
701 N Hariton St, Orange (92868-1313)
PHONE..................................714 558-9200
Jeffery Grimsley, *President*
Margaret Anderson, *COO*
Michael Gray, *Vice Pres*
Dave Garrett, *Project Mgr*
Blake Grimsley, *Sales Staff*
EMP: 65
SALES: 10.3MM **Privately Held**
WEB: www.floorsbysignature.com
SIC: 1752 Floor laying & floor work

(P-3118)
SIMAS FLOOR CO INC (PA)
Also Called: Simas Floor Co Design Center
3550 Power Inn Rd, Sacramento (95826-3892)
PHONE..................................916 452-4933
Ken Simas, *President*
David G Simas, *Vice Pres*
John U Simas, *Vice Pres*
EMP: 180
SQ FT: 10,000
SALES (est): 35.2MM **Privately Held**
SIC: 1752 5713 Floor laying & floor work; floor covering stores

(P-3119)
VINTAGE DESIGN INC (PA)
25200 Commercentre Dr, Lake Forest (92630-8810)
PHONE..................................714 974-4822
Timothy Patrick Buckley, *CEO*
Jennifer Buckley, *Admin Sec*
Marisol Robles, *Consultant*
EMP: 60
SQ FT: 16,000
SALES (est): 30MM **Privately Held**
WEB: www.vintagedesigninc.com
SIC: 1752 Carpet laying; vinyl floor tile & sheet installation; asphalt tile installation

(P-3120)
WIRTZ TILE & STONE INC
7932 Armour St, San Diego (92111-3718)
PHONE..................................858 569-3816
John David Wirtz, *President*
Ida F Wirtz, *Vice Pres*
EMP: 86 **EST:** 1974
SQ FT: 4,600
SALES (est): 6.4MM **Privately Held**
WEB: www.wirtztile.com
SIC: 1752 Ceramic floor tile installation

1761 Roofing, Siding & Sheet Metal Work

(P-3121)
ACETECK ROOFING CO INC
5830 Woodlawn Ave, Los Angeles (90003-1226)
PHONE..................................323 231-6060
Jay Kim, *President*
Song Kim, *Treasurer*
Jin Heo, *Project Mgr*
Tim Park, *Project Mgr*
EMP: 50
SALES (est): 5MM **Privately Held**
WEB: www.acetekroofing.com
SIC: 1761 Roofing contractor

(P-3122)
AEP SPAN INC
2110 Enterprise Blvd, West Sacramento (95691-3428)
PHONE..................................916 372-0933
Al Price, *Manager*
EMP: 85
SQ FT: 16,000
SALES (est): 2.9MM **Privately Held**
WEB: www.ascpacific.com
SIC: 1761 3448 3444 3443 Roofing contractor; prefabricated metal buildings; sheet metalwork; fabricated plate work (boiler shop)
HQ: Asc Profiles Llc
2110 Enterprise Blvd
West Sacramento CA 95691
916 372-6851

(P-3123)
ALCAL SPECIALTY CONTG INC (DH)
946 N Market Blvd, Sacramento (95834-1268)
PHONE..................................916 929-3100
Darren C Morris, *President*
Sonny Kooner, *CFO*
Arthur R Gardner, *Exec VP*
Richard Bledsoe, *Vice Pres*
Robert Colla, *Vice Pres*
EMP: 94
SALES (est): 31MM
SALES (corp-wide): 1.7B **Privately Held**
WEB: www.paccoast.com
SIC: 1761 1793 1742 1799 Roofing contractor; glass & glazing work; plastering; drywall & insulation; coating, caulking & weather, water & fireproofing; garage door, installation or erection

(P-3124)
ALL FAB PRCSION SHEETMETAL INC
1015 Timothy Dr, San Jose (95133-1050)
PHONE..................................408 279-1099
Son P Ho, *CEO*
Kelly T Ho, *CFO*
▲ **EMP:** 100
SQ FT: 58,000
SALES (est): 17.6MM **Privately Held**
SIC: 1761 3444 Sheet metalwork; sheet metalwork

(P-3125)
ALLIANCE ROOFING COMPANY INC (PA)
630 Martin Ave, Santa Clara (95050-2914)
PHONE..................................800 579-2595
Roderick Miller, *CEO*
Donna Miller, *Admin Sec*
William Logan, *Manager*
EMP: 50
SQ FT: 2,800

SALES (est): 34.3MM **Privately Held**
WEB: www.allianceroofingcal.com
SIC: 1761 1799 Roofing contractor; roof repair; waterproofing

(P-3126)
AZTEC SHEET METAL INC
11222 Woodside Ave N, Santee (92071-4716)
PHONE..................................619 937-0005
Dick Buxton, *President*
Tom Buxton, *CFO*
Larry Hendry, *Admin Sec*
EMP: 60
SALES (est): 4.1MM **Privately Held**
WEB: www.ltdsheetmetal.com
SIC: 1761 Architectural sheet metal work

(P-3127)
BEST CONTRACTING SERVICES INC
4301 Bettencourt Way, Union City (94587-1519)
PHONE..................................510 886-7240
Mohmmad Beigi, *Branch Mgr*
Mohammad Beigi, *General Mgr*
EMP: 75
SALES (corp-wide): 108.4MM **Privately Held**
SIC: 1761 Roofing contractor
PA: Best Contracting Services, Inc.
19027 S Hamilton Ave
Gardena CA 90248
310 328-9176

(P-3128)
BEST CONTRACTING SERVICES INC (PA)
19027 S Hamilton Ave, Gardena (90248-4408)
PHONE..................................310 328-9176
Sean Tabazadeh, *CEO*
Modjtaba Tabazadeh, *President*
Fatemeh Tabazadeh, *Treasurer*
Tony Esfahani, *Division Mgr*
Thomas Ryan, *Division Mgr*
▲ **EMP:** 400
SQ FT: 57,000
SALES (est): 108.4MM **Privately Held**
WEB: www.bestcontracting.com
SIC: 1761 Roofing contractor

(P-3129)
BEVEN-HERRON INC
14511 Industry Cir, La Mirada (90638-5865)
P.O. Box 848 (90637-0848)
PHONE..................................714 523-5870
J D Herron, *President*
Joseph A Herron, *Chairman*
EMP: 120 **EST:** 1959
SQ FT: 26,000
SALES (est): 11.8MM **Privately Held**
WEB: www.bevenherron.com
SIC: 1761 Roofing contractor

(P-3130)
BIGHAM TAYLOR ROOFING CORP
22721 Alice St, Hayward (94541-6401)
PHONE..................................510 886-0197
Stephen E Bigham, *CEO*
Stephen Bigham, *COO*
Laura Bigham, *Treasurer*
Laura Jo Bigham, *Corp Secy*
Don Taylor, *Vice Pres*
EMP: 70 **EST:** 1977
SQ FT: 10,000
SALES (est): 12.4MM **Privately Held**
WEB: www.btroof.com
SIC: 1761 Roofing contractor

(P-3131)
BYERS ENTERPRISES INC
Also Called: Byers Leafguard Gutter Systems
11773 Slow Poke Ln, Grass Valley (95945-8417)
PHONE..................................530 272-7777
Raymond W Byers Sr, *CEO*
Jeff Fierstein, *General Mgr*
Patty Moore, *General Mgr*
Michelle Stroud, *Manager*
EMP: 69
SQ FT: 2,400

SALES: 8MM **Privately Held**
WEB: www.byersleafguard.com
SIC: 1761 Sheet metalwork

(P-3132)
CANNON FABRICATION INC
Also Called: Canfab
182 Granite St Ste 101, Corona (92879-1288)
PHONE..................................951 278-1830
Donald J Prosser, *CEO*
Mary D Prosser, *President*
William Prosser Jr, *Vice Pres*
EMP: 61
SQ FT: 43,000
SALES (est): 10.3MM **Privately Held**
WEB: www.canfab.com
SIC: 1761 Sheet metalwork

(P-3133)
CARMEL ARCHITECTURAL SALES
2300 E Katella Ave # 370, Anaheim (92806-6046)
PHONE..................................714 630-7221
David Traino, *CEO*
James M Henry, *Vice Pres*
James Henry, *Vice Pres*
Patricia Dalton, *Admin Sec*
▲ **EMP:** 60
SQ FT: 10,500
SALES (est): 6.1MM **Privately Held**
WEB: www.carmelsales.com
SIC: 1761 Skylight installation; architectural sheet metal work

(P-3134)
CENTIMARK CORPORATION
Also Called: Questmark
1420 S Archibald Ave, Ontario (91761-7626)
PHONE..................................909 652-9280
Jong S Lee, *Manager*
EMP: 50
SALES (corp-wide): 670.5MM **Privately Held**
WEB: www.centimark.com
SIC: 1761 Roofing contractor
PA: Centimark Corporation
12 Grandview Cir
Canonsburg PA 15317
724 514-8700

(P-3135)
CENTIMARK CORPORATION
Also Called: Centimark Roofing Systems
2380 W Winton Ave, Hayward (94545-1102)
PHONE..................................510 921-5500
Anthony Zahteila, *President*
Rob Dennis, *Opers Mgr*
EMP: 108
SALES (corp-wide): 625.8MM **Privately Held**
WEB: www.centimark.com
SIC: 1761 1752 6331 Roofing contractor; floor laying & floor work; resilient floor laying; fire, marine & casualty insurance; automobile insurance; workers' compensation insurance
PA: Centimark Corporation
12 Grandview Cir
Canonsburg PA 15317
724 514-8700

(P-3136)
CHALLENGER SHEET METAL INC
9353 Abraham Way Ste A, Santee (92071-5641)
PHONE..................................619 596-8040
Joel Quinonez, *CEO*
Robert Basso, *CFO*
Roseann Marsh, *Accounting Mgr*
▲ **EMP:** 80
SQ FT: 18,000
SALES: 17MM **Privately Held**
WEB: www.challengersm.com
SIC: 1761 Sheet metalwork

(P-3137)
CITADEL ROOFING & SOLAR
4980 Allison Pkwy, Vacaville (95688-9346)
PHONE..................................707 446-5500
Dieter Folk, *CEO*
EMP: 150

SALES (est): 82.8K **Privately Held**
SIC: 1761 Roofing contractor

(P-3138)
CLAUD TOWNSLEY INC
Also Called: Central Roofing Company
555 W 182nd St, Gardena (90248-3400)
PHONE....................310 527-6770
William E Knapp, *President*
Jonathan Townsley, *CEO*
Janet Townsley, *Exec VP*
EMP: 60
SQ FT: 12,000
SALES (est): 7.6MM **Privately Held**
WEB: www.centralroof.com
SIC: 1761 Roofing contractor

(P-3139)
CMF INC
Also Called: Custom Metal Fabricators
1317 W Grove Ave, Orange (92865-4137)
PHONE....................714 637-2409
David Duclett, *CEO*
Vic Maynez, *President*
Darren Sagert, *CFO*
Mark Allen, *Vice Pres*
Rafael Moran, *Technician*
EMP: 100
SQ FT: 11,000
SALES (est): 22.5MM **Privately Held**
SIC: 1761 Siding contractor

(P-3140)
COMMERCIAL INDUS ROOFG CO INC
Also Called: C & I
9239 Olive Dr, Spring Valley (91977-2306)
PHONE....................619 465-3737
Barry Turnour, *President*
Ron Albrecht, *Project Mgr*
Barry Turenouer, *Technology*
EMP: 60
SQ FT: 4,500
SALES (est): 11MM **Privately Held**
SIC: 1761 Roof repair; roofing contractor

(P-3141)
COMMERCIAL ROOFING SYSTEMS INC
11735 Goldring Rd, Arcadia (91006-5894)
PHONE....................626 359-5354
Glenn Hiller, *President*
Allan Londo, *Superintendent*
EMP: 55 **EST:** 1989
SQ FT: 9,800
SALES (est): 7.7MM **Privately Held**
WEB: www.comroofsys.com
SIC: 1761 Roofing contractor

(P-3142)
COOL ROOFING SYSTEMS INC (PA)
1286 Dupont Ct, Manteca (95336-6003)
PHONE....................209 825-0818
Jamie Billman, *President*
Jesus Oliva, *Officer*
Daniel Edge, *Vice Pres*
Misty Beslanowitch, *Office Mgr*
Elizabeth Hansen, *Administration*
EMP: 55
SQ FT: 3,000
SALES (est): 25MM **Privately Held**
WEB: www.coolroofingsystems.net
SIC: 1761 Roofing contractor

(P-3143)
CROWNER SHEET METAL PDTS INC
14346 Arrow Hwy, Baldwin Park (91706-1335)
PHONE....................626 960-4971
Kim M Baier, *CEO*
Dennis Curran, *Vice Pres*
Russell Dunegan, *Admin Sec*
EMP: 50 **EST:** 1945
SQ FT: 9,000
SALES (est): 9.7MM **Privately Held**
WEB: www.crowner.net
SIC: 1761 Sheet metalwork

(P-3144)
CULVER CITY ROOFING COMPANY
5741 W Adams Blvd, Los Angeles (90016-2440)
PHONE....................323 930-1311
Brad Coyne, *President*
Paula Coyne, *Vice Pres*
EMP: 60
SQ FT: 13,000
SALES (est): 3.8MM **Privately Held**
WEB: www.culvercityroofing.biz
SIC: 1761 Roofing contractor

(P-3145)
CUSTOM PRODUCT DEV CORP
4603 Las Positas Rd Ste A, Livermore (94551-8845)
PHONE....................925 960-0577
Gerald John Ammirato, *President*
Delores Jumper, *Program Mgr*
Nancy Ammirato, *Admin Sec*
Ed Tahvilian, *Info Tech Mgr*
John Abate, *Technology*
▲ **EMP:** 55
SQ FT: 33,500
SALES (est): 14.7MM **Privately Held**
WEB: www.cpd-corp.com
SIC: 1761 Sheet metalwork

(P-3146)
D C TAYLOR CO
5060 Forni Dr Ste B, Concord (94520-8579)
PHONE....................925 603-1100
James Meyersieck, *Branch Mgr*
EMP: 50
SALES (corp-wide): 96.9MM **Privately Held**
WEB: www.dctaylorco.com
SIC: 1761 Roofing contractor
PA: D. C. Taylor Co.
312 29th St Ne
Cedar Rapids IA 52402
319 363-2073

(P-3147)
D7 ROOFING SERVICES INC
2851 Gold Tailings Ct, Rancho Cordova (95670-6189)
PHONE....................916 447-2175
Jeffrey Lyn Williamson, *CEO*
James J English Jr, *Vice Pres*
EMP: 70
SQ FT: 15,000
SALES (est): 11.1MM **Privately Held**
WEB: www.d7roofing.com
SIC: 1761 Roofing contractor

(P-3148)
DE MELLO ROOFING INC
45 Jordan St, San Rafael (94901-3918)
PHONE....................415 456-0741
Richard H Garzoli Jr, *President*
EMP: 55
SQ FT: 500
SALES (est): 5.2MM **Privately Held**
WEB: www.demelloroofing.com
SIC: 1761 Roofing contractor

(P-3149)
DESERT AIR CONDITIONING INC
Also Called: Honeywell Authorized Dealer
590 S Williams Rd, Palm Springs (92264-1551)
PHONE....................760 323-3383
Jeffrey Shaw, *CEO*
Todd Shaw, *President*
Valerie Botts, *Admin Sec*
EMP: 50 **EST:** 1954
SQ FT: 1,500
SALES (est): 9.6MM **Privately Held**
WEB: www.desertairconditioning.com
SIC: 1761 1711 Sheet metalwork; warm air heating & air conditioning contractor

(P-3150)
DUKE PACIFIC INC
13950 Monte Vista Ave, Chino (91710-5535)
P.O. Box 1800 (91708-1800)
PHONE....................909 591-0191
Gregory C Severson, *President*
Judith E Braaten, *Corp Secy*
James J Enright IV, *Vice Pres*
Karen Rowlands, *Human Res Dir*
Stan Little, *Sales Staff*
EMP: 100 **EST:** 1958
SQ FT: 10,000
SALES (est): 18.1MM **Privately Held**
WEB: www.dukepacific.com
SIC: 1761 Roofing contractor

(P-3151)
DWAYNE NASH INDUSTRIES INC
Also Called: Kodiak Roofing & Waterproofing
8825 Washington Blvd # 100, Roseville (95678-6213)
PHONE....................916 253-1900
Dwayne Nash, *CEO*
David Pope, *Vice Pres*
▲ **EMP:** 250
SQ FT: 23,617
SALES (est): 64.5MM **Privately Held**
WEB: www.kodiakroofing.com
SIC: 1761 Roofing contractor

(P-3152)
EHMCKE SHEET METAL CORP
840 W 19th St, National City (91950-5406)
P.O. Box 13010, San Diego (92170-3010)
PHONE....................619 477-6484
John F Cornell, *CEO*
Dennis Isaacs, *Treasurer*
Dennis Stainbrook, *Admin Sec*
Richard Parra, *Director*
Vi Tang, *Supervisor*
▲ **EMP:** 55
SQ FT: 25,000
SALES (est): 13.7MM **Privately Held**
WEB: www.ehmckesheetmetal.com
SIC: 1761 8712 3446 Sheet metalwork; architectural services; architectural metalwork

(P-3153)
ELITE & ASSOCIATES
Also Called: Elite Roofing Company
18605 Parthenia St, Northridge (91324-4028)
PHONE....................805 582-0353
Shawn Reeves, *Owner*
EMP: 80
SQ FT: 14,000
SALES (est): 3.1MM **Privately Held**
SIC: 1761 Roofing contractor

(P-3154)
ENTERPRISE ROOFING SERVICE INC
2400 Bates Ave, Concord (94520-1217)
P.O. Box 5130 (94524-0130)
PHONE....................925 689-8100
Lawrence T Reardon, *President*
Steven L Reardon, *President*
Aubrey Shehorn, *Treasurer*
Scott Lynd, *Vice Pres*
Lynda She Horn, *Admin Sec*
EMP: 80
SQ FT: 1,200
SALES (est): 17MM **Privately Held**
WEB: www.enterpriseroofing.com
SIC: 1761 Roofing contractor

(P-3155)
FIDELITY ROOF COMPANY (PA)
1075 40th St, Oakland (94608-3691)
PHONE....................510 547-6330
Montague M Upshaw Sr, *Ch of Bd*
Stephen H Cadet, *President*
Kenneth White, *COO*
Montague M Upshaw Jr, *Vice Pres*
Gustavo Sanchez II, *Commercial*
EMP: 60
SQ FT: 8,000
SALES (est): 13.8MM **Privately Held**
WEB: www.fidelityroof.com
SIC: 1761 Roofing contractor

(P-3156)
FIRST AVENUE INC
5105 Heintz St, Baldwin Park (91706-1820)
PHONE....................626 856-2076
Brett Maurer, *President*
EMP: 60
SALES (est): 4.1MM **Privately Held**
SIC: 1761 Roofing, siding & sheet metal work

(P-3157)
FOREVER FIREWOOD INC (PA)
Also Called: Warren Knox Roofing
46 El Pueblo Rd Ste A, Santa Cruz (95065-3544)
PHONE....................831 461-0634
Warren Knox, *President*
Mark Thenhaus, *Vice Pres*
EMP: 50
SALES (est): 5.6MM **Privately Held**
SIC: 1761 Roofing contractor

(P-3158)
FOUR CS SERVICE INC
1560 H St, Fresno (93721-1616)
PHONE....................559 237-3990
Preston Cross, *CEO*
Graydon Cross, *Vice Pres*
EMP: 80
SQ FT: 22,500
SALES (est): 12.4MM **Privately Held**
WEB: www.sheetmetalco.com
SIC: 1761 Sheet metalwork

(P-3159)
FRESNO ROOFING CO INC
5950 E Olive Ave, Fresno (93727-2710)
P.O. Box 7676 (93747-7676)
PHONE....................559 255-8377
Scott Logan Raypholtz, *CEO*
Michael Raypholtz, *Corp Secy*
Michael C Raypholtz, *General Mgr*
Edward Duarte, *Manager*
EMP: 60
SQ FT: 23,746
SALES (est): 8MM **Privately Held**
SIC: 1761 Roofing contractor; roof repair

(P-3160)
GARCIA ROOFING INC
201 Mount Vernon Ave, Bakersfield (93307-2741)
P.O. Box 70250 (93387-0250)
PHONE....................661 325-5736
Mike Garcia, *President*
Denise Roberts, *Corp Secy*
▲ **EMP:** 50 **EST:** 1975
SQ FT: 5,000
SALES (est): 7.7MM **Privately Held**
WEB: www.garciaroofinginc.com
SIC: 1761 Roofing contractor

(P-3161)
GRAHAM-PREWETT INC
2773 N Bus Park Ave # 101, Fresno (93727-8662)
PHONE....................559 291-3741
Sean Prewett, *President*
Gary Graham, *Vice Pres*
EMP: 50
SQ FT: 2,000
SALES (est): 13.1MM **Privately Held**
WEB: www.grahamprewett.com
SIC: 1761 Roofing contractor

(P-3162)
GUDGEL ROOFING INC
Also Called: Yancey Roofing
5321 84th St, Sacramento (95826-4803)
PHONE....................916 387-6900
Janet M Gudgel, *President*
Jason Gudgel, *Vice Ch Bd*
Stephen Reiland, *Exec VP*
Jason W Gudgel, *Vice Pres*
Catherine Youngblood, *Admin Sec*
EMP: 50
SQ FT: 6,000
SALES (est): 12.2MM **Privately Held**
WEB: www.yanceyroofing.com
SIC: 1761 Roofing contractor

(P-3163)
HERBERT MALARKEY ROOFING CO
9301 Garfield Ave, South Gate (90280-3804)
PHONE....................562 806-8000
John Stromme, *Manager*
EMP: 77
SALES (est): 5.2MM
SALES (corp-wide): 158.5MM **Privately Held**
SIC: 1761 Roofing contractor

PA: Herbert Malarkey Roofing Company
3131 N Columbia Blvd
Portland OR 97217
503 283-1191

(P-3164)
HILLCREST SHEET METAL INC
Also Called: Hillcrest AC & Shtmtl
2324 Perseus Ct, Bakersfield
(93308-6943)
PHONE.................................661 335-1500
Jim Barker, *President*
EMP: 67 **EST:** 1952
SQ FT: 14,010
SALES (est): 7.7MM
SALES (corp-wide): 7.6B **Publicly Held**
WEB: www.emcorgroup.com
SIC: 1761 1711 Sheet metalwork; heating
& air conditioning contractors; ventilation
& duct work contractor
HQ: Mesa Energy Systems, Inc.
2 Cromwell
Irvine CA 92618
949 460-0460

(P-3165)
HOWARD ROOFING COMPANY INC
245 N Mountain View Ave, Pomona
(91767-5629)
PHONE.................................909 622-5598
Larry K Malekow, *President*
Mitch T Caldwell, *Vice Pres*
Ron A Malekow, *Vice Pres*
Ron Malekow, *Vice Pres*
Rick Marion, *Project Mgr*
EMP: 70
SQ FT: 27,000
SALES (est): 11.3MM **Privately Held**
SIC: 1761 Roofing contractor

(P-3166)
HOYT ROOFS INC
1809 N Orangethorpe Park, Norco (92860)
PHONE.................................714 632-3939
Brian Hoyt, *CEO*
EMP: 50
SALES (est): 1.1MM **Privately Held**
SIC: 1761 Roofing contractor

(P-3167)
IRC TECHNOLOGIES INC (PA)
Also Called: Independent Roofing Cons
2901 Pullman St, Santa Ana (92705-5818)
PHONE.................................949 476-8626
Phillip L Penney, *President*
Jeff Starr, *CFO*
Michael A Wilsey, *Principal*
Mike Maneri, *Consultant*
▲ **EMP:** 70
SQ FT: 5,000
SALES (est): 6.7MM **Privately Held**
WEB: www.irctech.com
SIC: 1761 Roofing contractor

(P-3168)
J P WITHEROW ROOFING COMPANY
1083 N Cuyamaca St, El Cajon
(92020-1803)
PHONE.................................619 297-4701
Richard S Witherow, *President*
Charlie Walters, *General Mgr*
Linda Witherow, *Admin Sec*
EMP: 53 **EST:** 1935
SQ FT: 42,000
SALES (est): 13.8MM **Privately Held**
SIC: 1761 Roofing contractor

(P-3169)
JM ROOFING COMPANY INC
Also Called: Action Roofing
534 E Ortega St, Santa Barbara
(93103-3016)
PHONE.................................805 966-3696
John J Martin Jr, *President*
Sharon Fritz, *Corp Secy*
Peggy Martin, *Vice Pres*
Steve Martin, *Vice Pres*
Action Roofing, *General Mgr*
EMP: 70
SQ FT: 5,000
SALES (est): 10.2MM **Privately Held**
SIC: 1761 Roofing contractor

(P-3170)
KINGSPAN LIGHT & AIR LLC
401 Goetz Ave, Santa Ana (92707-3709)
PHONE.................................714 540-8950
Gene Murtagh,
Adam Toogood, *Technician*
EMP: 150 **EST:** 2016
SALES: 36.7MM **Privately Held**
SIC: 1761 Skylight installation

(P-3171)
L I METAL SYSTEMS
9041 Bermudez St, Pico Rivera
(90660-4505)
PHONE.................................562 948-5950
Anthony Chiovare, *President*
Peter Bueckert, *Treasurer*
Frank Lemmo, *Vice Pres*
▲ **EMP:** 50
SQ FT: 12,600
SALES (est): 5.1MM **Privately Held**
SIC: 1761 Gutter & downspout contractor

(P-3172)
LAWSON ROOFING CO INC
1495 Tennessee St, San Francisco
(94107-3420)
PHONE.................................415 285-1661
Frank E Lawson Sr, *Ch of Bd*
Frank E Lawson Jr, *President*
Richard Lawson, *Treasurer*
Richard J Lawson, *Vice Pres*
EMP: 70
SQ FT: 10,000
SALES (est): 12.6MM **Privately Held**
WEB: www.lawsonroofing.com
SIC: 1761 1799 Roofing contractor; water-
proofing

(P-3173)
LBC INC
1881 Duncan St, Simi Valley (93065-3411)
PHONE.................................805 581-1068
Luke Richard Bancroft, *Principal*
Bonnie McDaniel, *Bookkeeper*
EMP: 60
SALES (est): 3MM **Privately Held**
SIC: 1761 Roofing, siding & sheet metal
work

(P-3174)
LJC CONSTRUCTION INC
712 W Harding Rd, Turlock (95380-9743)
PHONE.................................209 668-2700
Lon Jones, *President*
EMP: 55 **EST:** 2000
SQ FT: 2,719
SALES (est): 3.5MM **Privately Held**
SIC: 1761 Roofing, siding & sheet metal
work

(P-3175)
LUCKY INSTALLATIONS
9041 Bermudez St, Pico Rivera
(90660-4505)
PHONE.................................562 948-5950
Frank Lemmo, *Owner*
EMP: 50
SALES (est): 1.6MM **Privately Held**
SIC: 1761 Roofing, siding & sheet metal
work

(P-3176)
MASTER ROOFING SYSTEMS INC
52 S Linden Ave Ste 5, South San Fran-
cisco (94080-6432)
PHONE.................................415 407-4450
Angela Sohn-Lee, *CEO*
Stephen Lee, *Director*
EMP: 60
SALES (est): 439.3K **Privately Held**
SIC: 1761 Roofing, siding & sheet metal
work

(P-3177)
MCCORMACK ROOFNG CONSTRCTN & E
1260 N Hancock St Ste 108, Anaheim
(92807-1951)
PHONE.................................714 777-4040
James McCormack, *Owner*
EMP: 60
SALES (est): 5.1MM **Privately Held**
SIC: 1761 Roofing contractor

(P-3178)
MCMURRAY & SONS INC (PA)
Also Called: M & S SUPPLY CO
1818 Allard Ave, Eureka (95503-5704)
P.O. Box 1111 (95502-1111)
PHONE.................................707 443-3088
David W McMurray, *CEO*
Heidi Bersin, *Shareholder*
Cathy Minkema, *Admin Sec*
Sachio Tanuma, *Supervisor*
EMP: 80
SQ FT: 14,500
SALES: 6.3MM **Privately Held**
SIC: 1761 1742 Roofing contractor; insu-
lation, buildings

(P-3179)
MID-PENINSULA ROOFING INC
1326 Marsten Rd, Burlingame
(94010-2406)
PHONE.................................650 375-7850
Matthew Greening, *President*
Ronald Stahl, *Vice Pres*
EMP: 55
SQ FT: 10,000
SALES (est): 9.4MM **Privately Held**
SIC: 1761 Roofing contractor

(P-3180)
MILAN CORPORATION
Also Called: Marco Roofing
43230 Osgood Rd, Fremont (94539-5607)
P.O. Box 1691 (94538-0169)
PHONE.................................510 656-6400
Michael Edward Creeden, *President*
EMP: 50
SQ FT: 20,000
SALES (est): 6.3MM **Privately Held**
SIC: 1761 Roofing contractor

(P-3181)
NUSHAKE INC
Also Called: Nushake Roofing
319 S Parallel Ave, Ripon (95366-2910)
PHONE.................................209 239-8616
Douglas Heath, *President*
Elizabeth Heath, *Vice Pres*
EMP: 60
SQ FT: 2,800
SALES (est): 7.2MM **Privately Held**
WEB: www.nushake.com
SIC: 1761 Roofing contractor

(P-3182)
OSSCIM INC
Also Called: Royal Roofing Construction Co
172 E Orangethorpe Ave, Placentia
(92870-6410)
PHONE.................................714 680-0015
Ronald Ossenberg, *President*
Curtis Ide, *General Mgr*
EMP: 50
SQ FT: 3,000
SALES: 3.7MM **Privately Held**
SIC: 1761 Roofing contractor

(P-3183)
PATTON SHEET METAL WORKS INC
Also Called: Patton Air Conditioning
272 N Palm Ave, Fresno (93701-1436)
PHONE.................................559 486-5222
Robert M Patton, *President*
Ellen D Patton, *Corp Secy*
Pat Shattuck, *Vice Pres*
Dawn Kelley, *Admin Asst*
Justin Fortmeyer, *Chief Engr*
▲ **EMP:** 50
SQ FT: 14,500
SALES (est): 10.8MM **Privately Held**
WEB: www.pattonac.com
SIC: 1761 1711 Sheet metalwork; warm
air heating & air conditioning contractor

(P-3184)
PENNY ROOFING COMPANY
2501 Exposition Blvd, Los Angeles
(90018-4299)
P.O. Box 18737 (90018-0737)
PHONE.................................323 731-5424
Lance Mahler, *President*
EMP: 50
SQ FT: 3,000
SALES (est): 4MM **Privately Held**
SIC: 1761 Roofing contractor

(P-3185)
PERFORMANCE SHEETS LLC
440 Baldwin Park Blvd, City of Industry
(91746-1407)
PHONE.................................626 333-0195
Mike Crosson, *President*
Forest Felvey,
Michael Feterik, *Mng Member*
Greg Hall, *Mng Member*
▲ **EMP:** 125
SALES (est): 10.6MM **Privately Held**
SIC: 1761 Sheet metalwork
HQ: Smurfit Kappa North America Llc
13400 Nelson Ave
City Of Industry CA 91746
626 333-6363

(P-3186)
PETERSEN-DEAN INC
Also Called: Petersendean
21616 Golden Triangle Rd # 101, Santa
Clarita (91350-3993)
PHONE.................................661 254-3322
EMP: 100
SALES (corp-wide): 335.8MM **Privately
Held**
WEB: www.needaroof.com
SIC: 1761
PA: Petersen-Dean, Inc.
39300 Civic Center Dr # 300
Fremont CA 94538
707 469-7470

(P-3187)
PETERSEN-DEAN INC
Petersendean
1705 Enterprise Dr, Fairfield (94533-5801)
PHONE.................................707 469-7470
Dieter Folk, *Senior VP*
Jim Petersen, *CEO*
EMP: 50
SALES (corp-wide): 369MM **Privately
Held**
WEB: www.needaroof.com
SIC: 1761 Roofing contractor
PA: Petersen-Dean, Inc.
39300 Civic Center Dr # 300
Fremont CA 94538
707 469-7470

(P-3188)
PETERSEN-DEAN INC
Also Called: Petersendean
2210 S Dupont Dr, Anaheim (92806-6104)
PHONE.................................714 629-9670
Greg O'Donnell, *Manager*
EMP: 202
SALES (corp-wide): 369MM **Privately
Held**
WEB: www.needaroof.com
SIC: 1761 Roofing contractor
PA: Petersen-Dean, Inc.
39300 Civic Center Dr # 300
Fremont CA 94538
707 469-7470

(P-3189)
PETERSEN-DEAN COMMERCIAL INC
Also Called: Petersendean
1705 Enterprise Dr, Fairfield (94533-5801)
PHONE.................................707 469-7470
James Petersen, *President*
David V Beek, *COO*
Jennifer Faircloth, *Sales Staff*
Paul Beckman, *Accounts Mgr*
Danilo Castillo, *Superintendent*
EMP: 170
SALES (est): 8.1MM
SALES (corp-wide): 369MM **Privately
Held**
WEB: www.needaroof.com
SIC: 1761 1711 Roofing contractor; solar
energy contractor
PA: Petersen-Dean, Inc.
39300 Civic Center Dr # 300
Fremont CA 94538
707 469-7470

(P-3190)
PLATINUM ROOFING INC
1900 Dobbin Dr, San Jose (95133-1758)
PHONE.................................408 280-5028
Bill Shevlin, *CEO*
Sean Marzola, *COO*
Rafael Lapizco, *VP Opers*

Jack Lanto, *Opers Mgr*
Izzy Jimenez, *Superintendent*
EMP: 80
SALES (est): 11.9MM **Privately Held**
SIC: 1761 Roofing contractor

(P-3191)
PROGRESSIVE SERVICES INC
Also Called: Progressive Roofing
3832 S Highway 99 Ste A, Stockton
(95215-8000)
PHONE..................................209 824-2837
John William, *Branch Mgr*
EMP: 95
SALES (corp-wide): 153.3MM **Privately Held**
SIC: 1761 Roof repair
PA: Progressive Services, Inc.
23 N 35th Ave
Phoenix AZ 85009
602 278-4900

(P-3192)
R HAUPT ROOFING CONSTRUCTION
1305 W 132nd St Fl 2, Gardena
(90247-1507)
PHONE..................................310 515-9709
Robert Haupt, *President*
Donna Haupt, *Principal*
EMP: 50
SALES (est): 5.2MM **Privately Held**
SIC: 1761 Roofing contractor

(P-3193)
R2G ENTERPRISES INC
Also Called: Advanced Fabrication Tech
31154 San Benito St, Hayward
(94544-7912)
PHONE..................................510 489-6218
Stephen Green, *President*
EMP: 65
SALES (est): 5.5MM **Privately Held**
SIC: 1761 Sheet metalwork

(P-3194)
RED POINTE ROOFING LP (PA)
1814 N Neville St, Orange (92865-4216)
PHONE..................................714 685-0010
Aaron Martin, *President*
Sean Brophy, *Partner*
John Patterson, *Vice Pres*
EMP: 85
SALES (est): 21.6MM **Privately Held**
SIC: 1761 Roofing contractor

(P-3195)
RED POINTE ROOFING LP
9542 Topanga Canyon Blvd, Chatsworth
(91311-4011)
PHONE..................................818 998-3857
EMP: 62
SALES (corp-wide): 21.6MM **Privately Held**
SIC: 1761 Roof repair
PA: Red Pointe Roofing, Lp
1814 N Neville St
Orange CA 92865
714 685-0010

(P-3196)
REINHARDT ROOFING INC
19258 Donna Ct, Morgan Hill (95037-9319)
P.O. Box 2230 (95038-2230)
PHONE..................................510 713-7014
Carole Lowrance, *President*
Ray Lowrance, *Vice Pres*
EMP: 60
SQ FT: 17,000
SALES (est): 4.1MM **Privately Held**
WEB: www.reinhardtroofing.net
SIC: 1761 Roofing contractor

(P-3197)
ROOFING CONSTRUCTORS INC
Also Called: Western Roofing Service
15002 Wicks Blvd, San Leandro
(94577-6600)
PHONE..................................415 648-6472
Mark F Santacrose, *Principal*
Robert Ferrando, *CFO*
George O'Neill, *Senior VP*
John Nolan, *Vice Pres*
Erica Mapp, *Admin Sec*
▼ **EMP:** 150
SQ FT: 3,000

SALES (est): 19.2MM
SALES (corp-wide): 24.5B **Privately Held**
WEB: www.westroof.com
SIC: 1761 Roofing contractor
HQ: Tecta America Corp.
9450 Bryn Mawr Ave
Rosemont IL 60018
847 581-3888

(P-3198)
ROYAL ROOFING & CNSTR CO
1144 N Armando St, Anaheim
(92806-2609)
PHONE..................................714 764-1100
Tom Beattie, *President*
EMP: 100
SQ FT: 20,000
SALES (est): 14.8MM **Privately Held**
SIC: 1761 Roofing contractor

(P-3199)
SBB ROOFING INC (PA)
Also Called: Bilt-Well Roofing & Mtl Co
3310 Verdugo Rd, Los Angeles
(90065-2845)
P.O. Box 65827 (90065-0827)
PHONE..................................323 254-2888
Bruce Radenbaugh, *President*
Steven Radenbaugh, *Vice Pres*
Jodi Burks, *Executive*
Lupe Diaz, *Executive*
EMP: 200
SQ FT: 5,000
SALES (est): 20MM **Privately Held**
SIC: 1761 Roofing contractor

(P-3200)
SONORAN ROOFING INC (PA)
4161 Citrus Ave, Rocklin (95677-4008)
PHONE..................................916 624-1080
John Daly, *CEO*
Jim Pelton, *Corp Secy*
Monica Dooling, *Executive*
EMP: 160
SQ FT: 5,000
SALES (est): 18.4MM **Privately Held**
SIC: 1761 Roofing contractor

(P-3201)
STATE ROOFING SYSTEMS INC
15444 Hesperian Blvd, San Leandro
(94578-3959)
PHONE..................................510 317-1477
Keith Symons, *President*
Jack White, *Corp Secy*
EMP: 100
SQ FT: 6,000
SALES (est): 22MM **Privately Held**
WEB: www.stateroofingsystems.com
SIC: 1761 Roofing contractor

(P-3202)
STRAIGHT LINE ROOFING & CNSTR
3811 Dividend Dr Ste A, Shingle Springs
(95682-8592)
PHONE..................................530 672-9995
John Borba, *President*
Rob Williams, *Project Mgr*
Brad Mosakowski, *Opers Mgr*
EMP: 50
SALES (est): 7MM **Privately Held**
WEB: www.straightlineroofing.com
SIC: 1761 Roofing contractor

(P-3203)
SYLVESTER ROOFING COMPANY INC
2593 Auto Park Way, Escondido
(92029-2088)
PHONE..................................760 743-0048
Anthony Zaffuto, *CEO*
Wesley Sylvester, *CFO*
Ivan Graham, *Project Mgr*
EMP: 50
SQ FT: 1,000
SALES (est): 21MM **Privately Held**
WEB: www.sylvesterroofing.com
SIC: 1761 Roofing contractor

(P-3204)
T&C ROOFING INC
Also Called: Town & Country Roofing
2155 Elkins Way Ste H, Brentwood
(94513-7365)
PHONE..................................925 513-8463

Jeff Tamayo, *President*
Sara Tamayo, *Corp Secy*
EMP: 75
SQ FT: 5,000
SALES (est): 12.7MM **Privately Held**
WEB: www.canawine.com
SIC: 1761 Roofing contractor

(P-3205)
TECTA AMERICA SOUTHERN CAL INC (DH)
1217 E Wakeham Ave, Santa Ana
(92705-4145)
PHONE..................................714 973-6233
Daniel L Klein, *CEO*
Javier Sarabia, *Foreman/Supr*
Debbie Klein, *Manager*
Frank Downing, *Superintendent*
EMP: 50 **EST:** 2002
SALES (est): 8.4MM
SALES (corp-wide): 24.5B **Privately Held**
WEB: www.laveyroofingservices.com
SIC: 1761 Roofing contractor
HQ: Tecta America Corp.
9450 Bryn Mawr Ave
Rosemont IL 60018
847 581-3888

(P-3206)
THORSENS INC
Also Called: Thorsens Plumbing & AC
2310 N Walnut Rd, Turlock (95382-8910)
PHONE..................................209 524-5296
Craig Vernon Pitau, *CEO*
Esther Thorsen, *Corp Secy*
Craig Vernon, *Agent*
EMP: 55
SQ FT: 19,500
SALES (est): 8.8MM **Privately Held**
WEB: www.thorsensinc.com
SIC: 1761 1711 5722 5075 Sheet metalwork; plumbing contractors; heating & air conditioning contractors; household appliance stores; warm air heating equipment & supplies; sheet metalwork

(P-3207)
TINCO SHEET METAL INC
958 N Eastern Ave, Los Angeles
(90063-1308)
PHONE..................................323 263-0511
Michael Nevarez, *CEO*
Mike Serrato, *President*
John Millan, *CFO*
▲ **EMP:** 100
SQ FT: 18,000
SALES (est): 24.2MM **Privately Held**
SIC: 1761 Roofing contractor

(P-3208)
TITAN SHEET METAL INC
180 Vander St, Corona (92880-1719)
PHONE..................................951 372-1362
Dale Auslander, *President*
Linda Sands, *Office Mgr*
EMP: 150
SALES (est): 8.5MM **Privately Held**
SIC: 1761 Sheet metalwork

(P-3209)
VILLARA CORPORATION
Also Called: Beutler Heating & AC
5005 Fulton Dr Ste F, Fairfield
(94534-1645)
PHONE..................................707 863-8222
Rod Schoppe, *General Mgr*
EMP: 50
SALES (corp-wide): 147.1MM **Privately Held**
WEB: www.beutlerhvac.com
SIC: 1761 1711 Sheet metalwork; heating & air conditioning contractors; warm air heating & air conditioning contractor
PA: Villara Corporation
4700 Lang Ave
Mcclellan CA 95652
916 646-2700

(P-3210)
WESTERN TEAR-OFF & DISPOSAL
Also Called: Western Waste Services
10920 Grand Ave, Temple City
(91780-3551)
P.O. Box 1794, Glendora (91740-1794)
PHONE..................................626 443-9984

Michael D Debarry, *President*
EMP: 70
SALES (est): 5.7MM **Privately Held**
SIC: 1761 Roofing contractor

(P-3211)
ZIMMERMAN ROOFING INC
3675 R St, Sacramento (95816-6624)
PHONE..................................916 454-3667
David Zimmerman, *President*
EMP: 65
SQ FT: 5,500
SALES: 12MM **Privately Held**
SIC: 1761 Roofing contractor; siding contractor; sheet metalwork

---

1771 Concrete Work

(P-3212)
ADORNO CONSTRUCTION INC
520 Westchester Dr Ste A, Campbell
(95008-5070)
PHONE..................................408 369-8675
Frank Adorno III, *President*
Frank Adorno Jr, *Treasurer*
Victor M Perez Jr, *Vice Pres*
Sherry Jackson, *Executive*
Monica Barreda, *Office Mgr*
EMP: 52
SQ FT: 1,300
SALES (est): 6MM **Privately Held**
SIC: 1771 Concrete work

(P-3213)
AMERICAN ASP REPR RSRFCING INC (PA)
24200 Clawiter Rd, Hayward (94545-2216)
P.O. Box 3367 (94540-3367)
PHONE..................................510 723-0280
Allan A Henderson, *CEO*
Steve Aguirre, *COO*
Kim Henschel, *Vice Pres*
Lisa Anderson, *Admin Asst*
Jackie Buckley, *Traffic Dir*
EMP: 100
SALES (est): 23.5MM **Privately Held**
SIC: 1771 Blacktop (asphalt) work

(P-3214)
AMERICAN CONCRETE
1125 Linda Vista Dr Ste 1, San Marcos
(92078-3819)
PHONE..................................760 471-9907
Anthony Cannariato, *President*
EMP: 90
SQ FT: 1,500
SALES (est): 5.1MM **Privately Held**
SIC: 1771 Concrete work

(P-3215)
ARCIERO BROTHERS INC
5614 E La Palma Ave, Anaheim
(92807-2110)
PHONE..................................714 238-6600
Philip Arciero, *President*
Karen Bouslog, *Vice Pres*
EMP: 130 **EST:** 1955
SALES (est): 11.6MM **Privately Held**
SIC: 1771 Concrete repair

(P-3216)
ASPHALT MANAGEMENT INC
7243 Somerset Blvd, Paramount
(90723-3998)
PHONE..................................562 630-6811
Fax: 562 529-5899
EMP: 50
SQ FT: 5,000
SALES (est): 2.7MM **Privately Held**
SIC: 1771

(P-3217)
AUS DECKING INC
2999 Promenade St Ste 100, West Sacramento (95691-6418)
P.O. Box 698 (95691-0698)
PHONE..................................916 373-5320
Eric Meissner, *President*
Patty Rawstron, *Accounting Mgr*
Matt Rugg, *Opers Mgr*
EMP: 57
SQ FT: 56,628
SALES (est): 6.5MM **Privately Held**
SIC: 1771 Concrete work

(P-3218)
B & M CONTRACTORS INC
4473 Cochran St, Simi Valley (93063-3065)
PHONE..................................805 581-5480
Dave C Moore, *CEO*
Randall Bilsland, *Vice Pres*
EMP: 68
SALES (est): 7.8MM **Privately Held**
WEB: www.bandmcontractors.com
SIC: 1771 Concrete work

(P-3219)
B S HAND & SONS INC
4450 Shopping Ln, Simi Valley
(93063-3451)
PHONE..................................818 983-1155
Gary B Hand, *President*
Todd Hand, *Vice Pres*
EMP: 50 **EST:** 1964
SQ FT: 4,300
SALES (est): 5.4MM **Privately Held**
WEB: www.bshand.com
SIC: 1771 1522 Concrete work; residential construction

(P-3220)
BALTAZAR CONSTRUCTION INC
236 E Arrow Hwy, Covina (91722-1817)
PHONE..................................626 339-8620
Baltazar Jimenez Siqueiros, *CEO*
EMP: 50
SALES (est): 12MM **Privately Held**
SIC: 1771 Blacktop (asphalt) work

(P-3221)
BAYMARR CONSTRUCTORS INC (PA)
6950 Mcdivitt Dr, Bakersfield (93313-2046)
PHONE..................................661 395-1676
Eric Recktenwald, *CEO*
Jack Whitney, *President*
Pat Howes, *Corp Secy*
Nick Almengor, *Superintendent*
EMP: 100
SQ FT: 10,000
SALES (est): 20.4MM **Privately Held**
WEB: www.baymarr.com
SIC: 1771 Concrete work

(P-3222)
BEDROCK COMPANY
2970 Myers St, Riverside (92503-5524)
PHONE..................................951 273-1931
Glenn E Jackson Jr, *CEO*
Carlene Jackson, *Admin Sec*
EMP: 70 **EST:** 1993
SQ FT: 5,000
SALES (est): 8MM **Privately Held**
SIC: 1771 Concrete work

(P-3223)
BEN F SMITH INC
Also Called: Concrete Construction
8655 Miramar Pl Ste B, San Diego
(92121-2567)
PHONE..................................858 271-4320
Stuart Shelton, *Manager*
Stuart Schouten, *Vice Pres*
EMP: 120
SALES (corp-wide): 21.9MM **Privately Held**
WEB: www.benfsmithinc.com
SIC: 1771 Concrete work
PA: Ben F. Smith, Inc.
4420 Baldwin Ave
El Monte CA 91731
626 444-2543

(P-3224)
BERKELEY CEMENT INC
1200 6th St, Berkeley (94710-1402)
PHONE..................................510 525-8175
Ron Fadelli, *CEO*
Andy A Fadelli, *President*
Ronald M Fadelli, *Vice Pres*
Ronald J Fadelli, *Vice Pres*
Scott Fadelli, *Admin Sec*
EMP: 140
SQ FT: 10,000
SALES (est): 29.9MM **Privately Held**
WEB: www.bciconcrete.com
SIC: 1771 Concrete pumping

(P-3225)
BITECH-ACE A JOINT VENTURE
7371 Walnut Ave, Buena Park
(90620-1759)
PHONE..................................714 521-1477
Benjamin Kim,
Simon Jeon, *Vice Pres*
EMP: 75
SALES (est): 1.9MM **Privately Held**
SIC: 1771 1522 1611 1623 Concrete work; remodeling, multi-family dwellings; general contractor, highway & street construction; water, sewer & utility lines; renovation, remodeling & repairs: industrial buildings

(P-3226)
BLUE ROSE CONCRETE CONTRS INC
14636 Ceres Ave, Fontana (92335-4204)
PHONE..................................909 823-6190
James Hernandez, *CEO*
Arthur Carrillo, *President*
EMP: 140
SALES (est): 7.5MM **Privately Held**
SIC: 1771 Concrete work

(P-3227)
BOGH ENGINEERING INC
401 W Fourth St, Beaumont (92223-2613)
PHONE..................................951 845-5130
Mark A Bogh, *President*
EMP: 56
SALES (est): 5.1MM **Privately Held**
SIC: 1771 Concrete work

(P-3228)
C TEAM CONSTRUCTION INC
1272 Greenfield Dr, El Cajon (92021-3316)
PHONE..................................619 579-6572
David Clarke, *President*
Alan Salherst, *Manager*
EMP: 70 **EST:** 1995
SQ FT: 2,000
SALES (est): 8.8MM **Privately Held**
WEB: www.teamcconstruction.com
SIC: 1771 Concrete work

(P-3229)
CAL-WEST CONCRETE CUTTING INC (PA)
3000 Tara Ct, Union City (94587-1508)
PHONE..................................510 656-0253
Marvin Weldon Birch, *CEO*
Weldon Birch, *President*
Barbara Birch, *Treasurer*
Jan Jeffreys, *Admin Sec*
EMP: 56
SQ FT: 100,000
SALES (est): 11.4MM **Privately Held**
WEB: www.calwestconcretecutting.com
SIC: 1771 Concrete repair

(P-3230)
CALMEX ENGINEERING INC
2764 S Vista Ave, Bloomington
(92316-3270)
PHONE..................................909 546-1311
Robert Stone, *President*
Rosie Lopez, *Director*
EMP: 51
SQ FT: 11,000
SALES (est): 8.5MM **Privately Held**
SIC: 1771 Blacktop (asphalt) work

(P-3231)
CASEY-FOGLI CON CONTRS INC
1970 National Ave, Hayward (94545-1710)
PHONE..................................510 887-0837
Vincent Ippolito, *CEO*
EMP: 100
SQ FT: 4,000
SALES (est): 11.1MM **Privately Held**
SIC: 1771 Concrete work

(P-3232)
CELL-CRETE CORPORATION
995 Zephyr Ave, Hayward (94544-7917)
PHONE..................................510 471-7257
Joe Barclay, *Branch Mgr*
EMP: 55
SALES (corp-wide): 37.1MM **Privately Held**
SIC: 1771 1761 Flooring contractor; roofing contractor

PA: Cell-Crete Corporation
135 Railroad Ave
Monrovia CA 91016
626 357-3500

(P-3233)
CEMENT CUTTING INC
3610 Hancock St Frnt Frnt, San Diego
(92110-4335)
PHONE..................................619 296-9592
Harold O Grafton, *CEO*
Steve Quinn, *Treasurer*
John Gregory Becker, *Vice Pres*
Steven Morgan, *Admin Sec*
Natalie Chastain, *Admin Asst*
EMP: 80
SQ FT: 7,000
SALES (est): 16.8MM **Privately Held**
WEB: www.cementcutting.com
SIC: 1771 Concrete work

(P-3234)
CM CONCRETE INC
650 E Easy St, Simi Valley (93065-1808)
PHONE..................................805 520-8100
Charles Melia, *President*
Joe Melia, *Vice Pres*
EMP: 125
SALES (est): 9.8MM **Privately Held**
SIC: 1771 Concrete work

(P-3235)
COAN CONSTRUCTION CO INC
1481 E Grand Ave, Pomona (91766-3806)
PHONE..................................909 868-6812
Jeffery Coan, *President*
Perry Coan, *Vice Pres*
Sharon Coan, *Admin Sec*
Ryan Granger, *Project Mgr*
John Rich, *Project Mgr*
EMP: 100
SQ FT: 4,300
SALES (est): 6.2MM **Privately Held**
WEB: www.coanconstruction.com
SIC: 1771 Foundation & footing contractor

(P-3236)
COASTAL PAVING INCORPORATED
1295 Norman Ave, Santa Clara
(95054-2027)
PHONE..................................408 988-5559
Anna Jarvis, *CEO*
Clifford Heaps, *Treasurer*
Ray Jarvis, *Vice Pres*
Clifford J Heaps, *General Mgr*
Rene Centeno, *Technology*
EMP: 52
SQ FT: 1,000
SALES (est): 10.1MM **Privately Held**
WEB: www.coastalpaving.com
SIC: 1771 1611 Blacktop (asphalt) work; surfacing & paving; concrete construction: roads, highways, sidewalks, etc.; sidewalk construction

(P-3237)
COFFMAN SPECIALTIES INC (PA)
9685 Via Excelencia # 200, San Diego
(92126-7500)
PHONE..................................858 536-3100
Colleen Coffman, *President*
Kevin Coffman, *Vice Pres*
Pablo Aranalde, *Project Mgr*
Greg Brown, *Project Mgr*
Gus Rios, *Project Mgr*
EMP: 151
SQ FT: 6,000
SALES (est): 72.7MM **Privately Held**
WEB: www.coffmanspecialties.com
SIC: 1771 Concrete work

(P-3238)
CONCO PUMPING
13052 Dahlia St, Fontana (92337-6926)
PHONE..................................909 350-0503
Doug Marquis, *Manager*
EMP: 60
SALES (est): 3.1MM **Privately Held**
SIC: 1771 Concrete pumping

(P-3239)
CONCRETE CONCEPTS INC
2317 Auto Park Way, Escondido
(92029-1218)
PHONE..................................760 737-5470
Chuck Clary, *President*
Christopher Bramwell, *Vice Pres*
EMP: 60
SQ FT: 8,000
SALES (est): 4MM **Privately Held**
SIC: 1771 Concrete work

(P-3240)
CONCRETE IMAGES INTERNATIONAL
17237 Saint Andrews Dr, Poway
(92064-1228)
PHONE..................................858 676-1253
Ernest Hoffman, *CEO*
Edward Stafford, *President*
EMP: 75
SALES (est): 6MM **Privately Held**
SIC: 1771 Concrete work

(P-3241)
CONCRETE NORTH INC
10274 Iron Rock Way, Elk Grove
(95624-1355)
PHONE..................................209 745-7400
James Grimes, *Owner*
Kim Grimes, *Principal*
Lisa Rodriguez, *Manager*
Ed Cowen, *Superintendent*
EMP: 75
SALES (est): 11MM **Privately Held**
SIC: 1771 Foundation & footing contractor

(P-3242)
CONDON-JOHNSON & ASSOC INC (PA)
480 Roland Way Ste 200, Oakland
(94621-2053)
P.O. Box 12368 (94604-2150)
PHONE..................................510 636-2100
Gerard Jerry Condon, *President*
George Burrough, *President*
Dominic Parmantier, *President*
Kenneth Welch, *COO*
Jeremy Condon, *Vice Pres*
▲ **EMP:** 50
SQ FT: 12,400
SALES (est): 67.3MM **Privately Held**
SIC: 1771 Concrete work

(P-3243)
CS CONCRETE SOLUTIONS INC
Also Called: Concrete Contractor
47 Goldbriar Way, Mission Viejo
(92692-5986)
PHONE..................................949 285-3122
Curt Stidham, *President*
EMP: 99
SALES (est): 4.1MM **Privately Held**
SIC: 1771 Concrete work

(P-3244)
D AND D CONCRETE CNSTR INC
13795 Blaisdell Pl # 201, Poway
(92064-8896)
PHONE..................................619 518-9737
Dereck Leffler, *President*
Diane Leffler, *Admin Sec*
EMP: 60 **EST:** 1989
SQ FT: 2,500
SALES (est): 7.9MM **Privately Held**
SIC: 1771 Foundation & footing contractor

(P-3245)
DAVID L AMADOR INC
Also Called: Amador Development
762 N Loren Ave, Azusa (91702-2255)
P.O. Box 907 (91702-0907)
PHONE..................................626 334-2011
David Amador, *President*
Debra Amador, *Corp Secy*
EMP: 55
SQ FT: 2,500
SALES (est): 6.7MM **Privately Held**
SIC: 1771 Curb construction

(P-3246)
DE OLIVIERA CONCRETE INC
14111 Soledad Canyon Rd, Santa Clarita
(91387-2224)
PHONE..................................661 252-7522

PRODUCTS & SVCS

Fred De Oliviera, *President*
Alfred Samora, *Vice Pres*
EMP: 50
SQ FT: 1,000
SALES (est): 3.7MM **Privately Held**
SIC: 1771 Concrete work

(P-3247)
DENNIS BLAZONA CONSTRUCTION
525 Harbor Blvd Ste 10, West Sacramento (95691-2246)
PHONE..............916 375-8337
J Dennis Balzona, *President*
Karin Blazona, *Admin Sec*
EMP: 65
SALES (est): 4.5MM **Privately Held**
SIC: 1771 Concrete work

(P-3248)
DEVINCENZI CONCRETE CNSTR
3276 Dutton Ave, Santa Rosa (95407-7866)
P.O. Box 508 (95402-0508)
PHONE..............707 568-4370
Gary Dahl, *President*
Gina Dahl, *Vice Pres*
Jean Dahl, *Vice Pres*
EMP: 50
SQ FT: 3,500
SALES (est): 11.6MM **Privately Held**
SIC: 1771 Curb construction; sidewalk contractor; driveway contractor; parking lot construction

(P-3249)
DISTINCTIVE CONCRETE INC
9320 Chesapeake Dr # 214, San Diego (92123-1021)
PHONE..............858 277-9707
Steven G Zoumaras, *President*
EMP: 50
SALES (est): 3.6MM **Privately Held**
SIC: 1771 Concrete work

(P-3250)
DOLAN CONCRETE CONSTRUCTION
3045 Alfred St, Santa Clara (95054-3303)
PHONE..............408 869-3250
Leo A Gutierrez, *President*
Dolores E Dolan, *Shareholder*
Benjamin C Newsom, *Corp Secy*
Robert F Dumesnil Jr, *Vice Pres*
EMP: 90
SQ FT: 8,500
SALES (est): 11MM **Privately Held**
WEB: www.dolanconcrete.com
SIC: 1771 Curb construction

(P-3251)
E & M CONCRETE CONSTRUCTION
2842 Sherwin Ave Ste A, Ventura (93003-7272)
P.O. Box 5600 (93005-0600)
PHONE..............805 658-2888
Edmundo Mendez, *President*
Mariel Mendez, *Admin Sec*
EMP: 80
SQ FT: 3,478
SALES (est): 8.6MM **Privately Held**
WEB: www.emconcrete.com
SIC: 1771 Concrete work

(P-3252)
EBS CONCRETE INC
1320 E 6th St Ste 100, Corona (92879-1700)
PHONE..............951 279-6869
Thomas Nanci, *President*
EMP: 50 **EST:** 2000
SQ FT: 3,000
SALES (est): 3.9MM **Privately Held**
SIC: 1771 Concrete work

(P-3253)
EMPIRE DEMOLITION INC
1623 Leeson Ln, Corona (92879-2061)
PHONE..............909 393-8300
Kris Huff, *CEO*
Collin Cumbee, *CFO*
EMP: 100 **EST:** 1997
SQ FT: 8,000

SALES (est): 11.9MM **Privately Held**
WEB: www.empiredemolition.com
SIC: 1771 Concrete work

(P-3254)
EPIDENDIO CONSTRUCTION INC
11325 Highway 29, Lower Lake (95457)
PHONE..............707 994-5100
Mike Epidendio, *President*
Joan Epidendio, *Corp Secy*
Anthony Epidendio, *Vice Pres*
Donald Epidendio, *Vice Pres*
EMP: 50 **EST:** 1973
SQ FT: 14,000
SALES (est): 6.2MM **Privately Held**
SIC: 1771 Blacktop (asphalt) work

(P-3255)
FORD PLASTERING INC
732 W Grove Ave, Orange (92865-3214)
PHONE..............714 921-0624
Gary L Ford, *President*
Darrell Ford, *Vice Pres*
EMP: 300
SQ FT: 1,200
SALES (est): 10.3MM **Privately Held**
WEB: www.fordplastering.com
SIC: 1771 1742 Stucco, gunite & grouting contractors; plastering, drywall & insulation

(P-3256)
GINO/GIUSEPPE INC
Also Called: G & G Construction Co
700 Enterprise Ct Ste A, Atwater (95301-9512)
PHONE..............209 358-0556
Giuseppe Castiglione, *CEO*
Giuseppe Castiglione, *CEO*
Gino Graziano, *CFO*
John Potts, *Supervisor*
EMP: 250
SQ FT: 7,600
SALES (est): 30MM **Privately Held**
WEB: www.ggconcrete.com
SIC: 1771 Foundation & footing contractor

(P-3257)
GOLDEN EMPIRE CONCRETE PDTS
Also Called: Structure Cast
8261 Mccutchen Rd, Bakersfield (93311-9407)
PHONE..............661 833-4490
Brent Dezember, *CEO*
Anna Dezember, *Admin Sec*
EMP: 60
SALES (est): 10MM **Privately Held**
SIC: 1771 Concrete work

(P-3258)
GOLDSMITH CONSTRUCTION CO INC
2683 Lime Ave, Signal Hill (90755-2709)
PHONE..............562 595-5975
William Goldsmith, *President*
Susan Goldsmith, *Corp Secy*
Kelly Goldsmith, *Vice Pres*
Kelly Mogg, *Office Mgr*
Sam Mounce, *Project Mgr*
EMP: 50
SQ FT: 6,000
SALES (est): 10.7MM **Privately Held**
SIC: 1771 1629 5082 Concrete work; oil refinery construction; construction & mining machinery

(P-3259)
GONSALVES & SANTUCCI INC (PA)
Also Called: Conco Cement Company
5141 Commercial Cir, Concord (94520-8523)
PHONE..............925 685-6799
Mathew Gonsalves, *Ch of Bd*
Steven Gonsalves, *President*
Barry Silberman, *CFO*
Holly Bertuccelli, *Vice Pres*
Joseph Santucci, *Vice Pres*
EMP: 1000
SQ FT: 35,000
SALES (est): 158.5MM **Privately Held**
WEB: www.theconcocompanies.com
SIC: 1771 Concrete work

(P-3260)
GRAHAM CONCRETE CNSTR INC
1323 Dayton Ave Ste 103, Clovis (93612-5869)
PHONE..............559 292-6571
James Graham, *President*
Jason Graham, *Admin Sec*
Heather Bender, *Admin Asst*
Tom Shields, *Project Mgr*
EMP: 75
SQ FT: 10,000
SALES (est): 9.7MM **Privately Held**
WEB: www.grahamconcrete.com
SIC: 1771 Concrete work

(P-3261)
GREG H CARPENTER CONCRETE INC
955 N Guild Ave, Lodi (95240-0877)
PHONE..............209 367-4224
Greg Carpenter, *President*
EMP: 50
SALES (est): 7.1MM **Privately Held**
SIC: 1771 Concrete work

(P-3262)
GROUNDWORKS INC
2145 Elkins Way Ste C, Brentwood (94513-7363)
PHONE..............925 513-0300
Bryan Lucay, *President*
Lalo Sanchez, *Opers Mgr*
EMP: 80
SQ FT: 2,500
SALES (est): 5.8MM **Privately Held**
SIC: 1771 1611 1629 Concrete work; grading; drainage system construction

(P-3263)
GUY YOCOM CONSTRUCTION INC (PA)
3299 Horseless Carriage R, Norco (92860-3604)
PHONE..............951 284-3456
Guy W Yocom, *Principal*
Greg Wilson, *CFO*
Richard Majestic, *Exec VP*
Dave Kent, *Vice Pres*
Shirley Kowalke, *Admin Sec*
EMP: 112
SQ FT: 41,000
SALES (est): 33.6MM **Privately Held**
WEB: www.yocominc.com
SIC: 1771 Concrete work

(P-3264)
HB PARKCO CONSTRUCTION INC (PA)
3190 Arprt Loop Dr Ste F, Costa Mesa (92626)
PHONE..............714 444-1441
Brett D Behrns, *CEO*
W Adrian Hoyle, *President*
Micheal Barry, *CFO*
EMP: 394
SQ FT: 4,000
SALES (est): 40.4MM **Privately Held**
WEB: www.hbparkco.com
SIC: 1771 Parking lot construction

(P-3265)
HOFFMAN CONCRETE COMPANY INC
102 E Grand Blvd, Corona (92879-1364)
PHONE..............951 372-8333
Dean Hoffman Jr, *President*
EMP: 50
SALES (est): 15MM **Privately Held**
SIC: 1771 Concrete work

(P-3266)
HOME FRANCHISE CONCEPTS LLC (PA)
Also Called: All American Decorative Con
19000 Macarthur Blvd # 100, Irvine (92612-1416)
PHONE..............949 404-1100
Chad Hallock, *President*
Todd Jackson, *COO*
Shirin Behzadi, *CFO*
Tom Hillebrandt, *CFO*
Tony Forbes, *Exec VP*
EMP: 90

SALES (est): 13.8MM **Privately Held**
SIC: 1771 6794 Concrete work; franchises, selling or licensing

(P-3267)
INLAND CC INC
Also Called: ICC
13820 Slover Ave, Fontana (92337-7037)
PHONE..............909 355-1318
Marvin Hawkins, *CEO*
Karen Hawkins, *President*
Dave Galban, *Manager*
EMP: 150
SALES (est): 16.7MM **Privately Held**
SIC: 1771 Foundation & footing contractor

(P-3268)
INTERNTNAL PVMENT SLUTIONS INC
1209 Van Buren St Ste 3, Thermal (92274-8800)
P.O. Box 10458, San Bernardino (92423-0458)
PHONE..............909 794-2101
Brent Rieger, *President*
Dennis Rieger, *Treasurer*
EMP: 80
SQ FT: 3,000
SALES (est): 5.7MM **Privately Held**
WEB: www.pavement-solutions.com
SIC: 1771 Blacktop (asphalt) work

(P-3269)
INTERSTATE CON PMPG CO INC
11180 Vallejo Ct, French Camp (95231-9783)
PHONE..............209 983-3092
Andy Paulazzo, *CEO*
Shawn Slate, *Treasurer*
Lisa Fernandez, *Payroll Mgr*
Mark Bobbitt, *Maintence Staff*
Ken Anderson, *Manager*
EMP: 52
SALES (est): 10.8MM **Privately Held**
WEB: www.icpumps.com
SIC: 1771 Concrete pumping

(P-3270)
J L S CONCRETE PUMPING INC
2055 N Ventura Ave, Ventura (93001-1308)
PHONE..............805 643-0766
Jeffrey L Switzer, *President*
Joel Silkett, *President*
Jeffrey Switzer, *Vice Pres*
▲ **EMP:** 75
SQ FT: 10,000
SALES (est): 5.4MM **Privately Held**
WEB: www.jlspumping.com
SIC: 1771 Concrete pumping

(P-3271)
JEZOWSKI & MARKEL CONTRS INC
749 N Poplar St, Orange (92868-1013)
PHONE..............714 978-2222
Leonard Michael Barth, *Principal*
Joseph Dean, *Vice Pres*
Dorothy Destefano, *Admin Sec*
EMP: 145
SQ FT: 4,500
SALES (est): 26.3MM **Privately Held**
SIC: 1771 Foundation & footing contractor

(P-3272)
JKB CORPORATION
561 S Walnut St, La Habra (90631-6035)
PHONE..............562 905-3477
John D Brown, *President*
Kathy Brown, *Vice Pres*
EMP: 50
SQ FT: 4,000
SALES (est): 5.8MM **Privately Held**
SIC: 1771 Concrete work

(P-3273)
JOHN KENNEY CONSTRUCTION INC
619 E Montecito St, Santa Barbara (93103-3217)
P.O. Box 40929 (93140-0929)
PHONE..............805 884-1579
Jonathan Kenney, *President*
EMP: 52
SQ FT: 5,000

SALES (est): 8.1MM **Privately Held**
SIC: **1771** Concrete work

(P-3274)
JOHNSEN CONSTRUCTION INC
6448 Capitol Ave, Diamond Springs
(95619-9393)
PHONE.........................530 642-2123
David W Johnsen, *President*
David W Johnson, *President*
EMP: 70
SQ FT: 300
SALES (est): 5.6MM **Privately Held**
WEB: www.johnsenconstruction.com
SIC: **1771** Concrete work

(P-3275)
JOSEPH J ALBANESE INC
851 Martin Ave, Santa Clara (95050-2903)
P.O. Box 667 (95052-0667)
PHONE.........................408 727-5700
Joseph J Albanese, *Principal*
Phillip Albanese, *Vice Pres*
John Franich, *Vice Pres*
Phil Roby, *Vice Pres*
Kevin Albanese, *Executive*
EMP: 700
SALES (est): 158.5MM **Privately Held**
WEB: www.jjalbanese.com
SIC: **1771** Foundation & footing contractor

(P-3276)
JT WIMSATT CONTG CO INC (PA)
28064 Avenue Stanford B, Valencia
(91355-1159)
PHONE.........................661 775-8090
John E Wimsatt III, *President*
Tricia Wimsatt, *Vice Pres*
Maria Dela Cruz, *Director*
EMP: 68
SALES (est): 40.5MM **Privately Held**
WEB: www.jtwimsatt.com
SIC: **1771** Concrete work

(P-3277)
JYG CONCRETE CONSTRUCTION INC
24841 Avenue Tibbitts, Valencia
(91355-3405)
PHONE.........................661 607-0337
John Stich, *President*
EMP: 110
SALES (est): 6.3MM **Privately Held**
WEB: www.jygconstruction.com
SIC: **1771** Concrete work

(P-3278)
K A R CONSTRUCTION INC
1306 Brooks St, Ontario (91762-3611)
PHONE.........................909 988-5054
Kurt Rothweiler, *President*
Peggy Rothweiler, *Corp Secy*
Todd Rothweiler, *Vice Pres*
Margaret Rothweiler, *Admin Sec*
EMP: 60
SQ FT: 2,700
SALES (est): 5.9MM **Privately Held**
WEB: www.karconstruction.com
SIC: **1771** 1541 1542 Concrete work; industrial buildings & warehouses; nonresidential construction

(P-3279)
KENYON CONSTRUCTION INC
Also Called: Kenyon Plastream
63 Trevarno Rd D, Livermore (94551-4931)
PHONE.........................925 371-8102
Laura Neil, *Manager*
EMP: 300
SALES (corp-wide): 134.6MM **Privately Held**
WEB: www.kenyonconstruction.com
SIC: **1771** 1742 Stucco, gunite & grouting contractors; plastering, plain or ornamental
PA: Kenyon Construction, Inc.
4001 W Indian School Rd
Phoenix AZ 85019
602 484-0080

(P-3280)
LARGO CONCRETE INC
1690 W Foothill Blvd B, Upland
(91786-8433)
PHONE.........................909 981-7844

Paul Burkel, *Principal*
Kristi Desormier, *Office Mgr*
Mark Curtis, *Superintendent*
EMP: 548
SALES (corp-wide): 150.8MM **Privately Held**
SIC: **1771** Concrete work
PA: Largo Concrete, Inc.
2741 Walnut Ave Ste 110
Tustin CA 92780
714 731-3600

(P-3281)
LARGO CONCRETE INC
891 W Hamilton Ave, Campbell
(95008-0402)
PHONE.........................408 874-2500
Ken Long, *Manager*
EMP: 658
SALES (corp-wide): 150.8MM **Privately Held**
SIC: **1771** Concrete work
PA: Largo Concrete, Inc.
2741 Walnut Ave Ste 110
Tustin CA 92780
714 731-3600

(P-3282)
LEONARDS CARPET SERVICE INC
6767 Nancy Ridge Dr, San Diego
(92121-2225)
PHONE.........................858 453-9525
Daniel Nagel, *Manager*
EMP: 50
SQ FT: 12,000
SALES (est): 1.8MM
SALES (corp-wide): 35.3MM **Privately Held**
WEB: www.lcsdesign.com
SIC: **1771** Flooring contractor
PA: Leonard's Carpet Service, Inc.
1121 N Red Gum St
Anaheim CA 92806
714 630-1930

(P-3283)
LOMBARDO DIAMND CORE DRLG INC
2225 De La Cruz Blvd, Santa Clara
(95050-3007)
PHONE.........................408 727-7922
Richard D Long, *President*
Dorothy Long, *Admin Sec*
EMP: 58 EST: 1961
SQ FT: 1,300
SALES (est): 11MM **Privately Held**
WEB: www.lombardodrilling.com
SIC: **1771** 1795 Concrete work; demolition, buildings & other structures

(P-3284)
MARNE CONSTRUCTION INC
Also Called: Newval Chemical
749 N Poplar St, Orange (92868-1013)
PHONE.........................714 935-0995
Charles Randolph, *President*
L Michael Barth, *Vice Pres*
Tony Naranjo, *VP Sales*
Yolanda Spedden, *Marketing Mgr*
EMP: 80
SQ FT: 10,000
SALES: 12.3MM **Privately Held**
WEB: www.marneconstruction.com
SIC: **1771** Concrete work

(P-3285)
MCGUIRE CONTRACTING INC
16579 Slover Ave, Fontana (92337-7508)
PHONE.........................909 357-1200
David McGuire, *President*
Kathie Vilas, *CEO*
Sandy McGuire, *Admin Sec*
EMP: 51
SQ FT: 1,800
SALES (est): 6.4MM **Privately Held**
WEB: www.mcguirecontracting.com
SIC: **1771** Concrete work

(P-3286)
MCM CONSTRUCTION INC
708 Pier A St, Wilmington (90744-6433)
PHONE.........................310 549-9207
EMP: 60

SALES (corp-wide): 150MM **Privately Held**
SIC: **1771** 1521 Concrete work; single-family housing construction
PA: M.C.M. Construction, Inc.
6413 32nd St
North Highlands CA 95660
916 334-1221

(P-3287)
MELO CONCRETE CONSTRUCTION
5820 Obata Way, Gilroy (95020-7038)
PHONE.........................408 842-3484
Manuel Melo, *President*
Maria Melo, *Vice Pres*
EMP: 80
SALES (est): 9MM **Privately Held**
WEB: www.meloconcrete.com
SIC: **1771** Concrete work

(P-3288)
MINEGAR CONTRACTING INC
925 Poinsettia Ave Ste 10, Vista
(92081-8452)
PHONE.........................760 598-5001
Michael Dahlquist, *President*
EMP: 50
SALES (est): 5.9MM **Privately Held**
SIC: **1771** Concrete work

(P-3289)
MITCHELL JONES CONCRETE INC
Also Called: Mitchell Concrete
3185 Fitzgerald Rd, Rancho Cordova
(95742-6801)
PHONE.........................916 638-6870
Mitchell L Jones, *President*
Peggy Jones, *Vice Pres*
Bob Miller, *Manager*
Larry McDaniel, *Superintendent*
EMP: 175
SQ FT: 7,200
SALES (est): 17.6MM **Privately Held**
WEB: www.mitchellconcrete.com
SIC: **1771** Concrete work

(P-3290)
MORLEY CONSTRUCTION COMPANY (HQ)
3330 Ocean Park Blvd # 101, Santa Monica
(90405-3202)
PHONE.........................310 399-1600
Mark Benjamin, *Ch of Bd*
Tod Paris, *CFO*
Bert Lewitt, *Exec VP*
Arun Asher, *Vice Pres*
Reginald Jackson, *Vice Pres*
▲ EMP: 80
SQ FT: 20,000
SALES (est): 30.2MM
SALES (corp-wide): 168.7MM **Privately Held**
WEB: www.morleybuilders.com
SIC: **1771** 1522 1542 Concrete work; condominium construction; commercial & office building, new construction
PA: Morley Builders, Inc.
3330 Ocean Park Blvd # 101
Santa Monica CA 90405
310 399-1600

(P-3291)
MORRISON CONCRETE INC
14114 Rosecrans Ave Ste C, Santa Fe
Springs (90670-5214)
PHONE.........................562 802-1450
Bradley Morrison, *President*
EMP: 50
SALES (est): 8MM **Privately Held**
SIC: **1771** Concrete work

(P-3292)
NED L WEBSTER CONCRETE CNSTR
8800 Grimes Canyon Rd, Moorpark
(93021-9768)
PHONE.........................805 529-4900
Ned Webster, *Principal*
EMP: 75
SALES (est): 7.2MM **Privately Held**
SIC: **1771** Concrete work

(P-3293)
NMN CONSTRUCTION INC
1077 Lakeville St, Petaluma (94952-3331)
P.O. Box 110244, Campbell (95011-0244)
PHONE.........................707 763-6981
Fax: 408 874-2574
EMP: 100
SALES (est): 4.5MM **Privately Held**
SIC: **1771**

(P-3294)
NOAH CONCRETE CORPORATION
5900 Rossi Ln, Gilroy (95020-7013)
PHONE.........................408 842-7211
Don Alvarez, *CEO*
Christine Morales, *Office Mgr*
Eugene Pacchetti, *Technology*
Jacob Alvarez, *Manager*
▲ EMP: 60
SALES (est): 8.6MM **Privately Held**
SIC: **1771** Concrete work

(P-3295)
NORTH BAY CONSTRUCTION INC
930 Shiloh Rd Bldg 46, Windsor
(95492-9679)
PHONE.........................707 836-8500
Lohrie Pardue, *President*
Robert Pardue, *Vice Pres*
EMP: 50
SQ FT: 10,000
SALES (est): 6.3MM **Privately Held**
SIC: **1771** Foundation & footing contractor

(P-3296)
NORTHSTATE PLASTERING INC
2210 Cordelia Rd, Fairfield (94534-1912)
PHONE.........................707 207-0950
Buck W Kimbriel Jr, *President*
Francisco Tolento, *Vice Pres*
EMP: 80
SALES (est): 6MM **Privately Held**
WEB: www.northstateplastering.com
SIC: **1771** Stucco, gunite & grouting contractors

(P-3297)
ODYSSEY LANDSCAPING CO INC
Also Called: Odyssey Environmental Services
5400 W Highway 12, Lodi (95242-9170)
PHONE.........................209 369-6197
Martin Gates, *President*
EMP: 80
SQ FT: 2,400
SALES (est): 11.5MM **Privately Held**
WEB: www.odysseylandscape.com
SIC: **1771** 0781 Concrete work; landscape architects

(P-3298)
OPTIMUM CON FUNDATIONS USA INC
6258 Rustic Ln, Jurupa Valley
(92509-7228)
PHONE.........................877 212-7994
Mario Garcia, *CEO*
Scott Cable, *President*
EMP: 55
SALES: 20MM **Privately Held**
SIC: **1771** Concrete work

(P-3299)
PACIFIC CONCRETE SPECIALTIES
101 Business Park Way, Atwater
(95301-9483)
PHONE.........................209 358-0741
Veryl Esau, *President*
Don Semans, *Vice Pres*
Josie Esau, *Admin Sec*
EMP: 75
SQ FT: 3,200
SALES (est): 6.4MM **Privately Held**
WEB: www.pacificconcretespecialties.com
SIC: **1771** Concrete work

(P-3300)
PACIFIC PAVINGSTONE INC
Also Called: Pacific Outdoor Living
8309 Tujunga Ave Unit 201, Sun Valley
(91352-3216)
PHONE................................818 244-4000
Terry Morrill, *President*
Trent Morrill, *Vice Pres*
Chad Morrill, *Admin Sec*
EMP: 115
SALES (est): 11.9MM **Privately Held**
WEB: www.pacificpavingstone.com
SIC: 1771 Driveway contractor

(P-3301)
PACIFIC STHWEST STRUCTURES INC
7845 Lemon Grove Way A, Lemon Grove
(91945-1880)
PHONE................................619 469-2323
Daniel Fitzgerald, *President*
EMP: 150
SQ FT: 7,500
SALES (est): 14.3MM **Privately Held**
WEB: www.pswsi.com
SIC: 1771 Concrete work

(P-3302)
PACIFIC STRUCTURES INC (PA)
3004 16th St Fl 2, San Francisco
(94103-3434)
PHONE................................415 970-5434
Ross Edwards, *Ch of Bd*
David E Williams, *President*
Ron Marano, *CFO*
Eric Horn, *Treasurer*
Pratik Jain, *Administration*
EMP: 249
SQ FT: 6,000
SALES: 137.7MM **Privately Held**
SIC: 1771 Concrete work

(P-3303)
PACIFIC STRUCTURES CNSTR INC
101 State Pl Ste E, Escondido
(92029-1365)
P.O. Box 502648, San Diego (92150-2648)
PHONE................................740 480-4133
Michael Meier, *President*
L Chris Meier, *CFO*
Andrew Meier III, *Vice Pres*
EMP: 50
SQ FT: 2,500
SALES (est): 5.8MM **Privately Held**
SIC: 1771 Concrete work

(P-3304)
PECK & HILLER COMPANY
870 Napa Valley Corp Way, NAPA (94558)
PHONE................................707 258-8800
Russell B Peck, *Principal*
Ben Kerr, *Vice Pres*
Tom H O'Connor, *Vice Pres*
Cindy Joy Westerberg, *Controller*
Axel Heredia, *Superintendent*
EMP: 100
SQ FT: 8,680
SALES (est): 22.4MM **Privately Held**
WEB: www.peckandhiller.com
SIC: 1771 Foundation & footing contractor

(P-3305)
PENHALL COMPANY
Also Called: Penhall San Leandro 153
13750 Catalina St, San Leandro
(94577-5502)
PHONE................................510 357-8810
Scott Hustad, *Manager*
EMP: 60
SALES (corp-wide): 2.5B **Privately Held**
SIC: 1771 Concrete work
HQ: Penhall Company
　　2121 W Crescent Ave Ste A
　　Anaheim CA 92801

(P-3306)
PERRY FLOOR SYSTEMS INC
963 Seaboard Ct, Upland (91786-4572)
PHONE................................909 949-1211
Brian Perry, *President*
Angela Perry, *Vice Pres*
EMP: 65
SQ FT: 6,000
SALES (est): 6.8MM **Privately Held**
SIC: 1771 Flooring contractor

(P-3307)
PETERSON BROS CONTRUCTION INC
Also Called: Pbc Companies
1560 W Lambert Rd, Brea (92821-2826)
PHONE................................714 278-0488
Elden Peterson, *CEO*
Robert K Peterson, *Ch of Bd*
Patrick Burns, *CFO*
Mike Hoefnagels, *Vice Pres*
Jack Saldate, *Vice Pres*
▲ EMP: 600
SQ FT: 24,000
SALES (est): 50.5MM **Privately Held**
SIC: 1771 3531 1741 Concrete work;
pavers; concrete block masonry laying

(P-3308)
POWERHOUSE BUILDING INC
4320 Redwood Hwy Ste 200, San Rafael
(94903-2151)
PHONE................................415 446-0188
David Hynes, *President*
Philip Hynes, *Vice Pres*
John Cotten, *Manager*
EMP: 60
SQ FT: 1,200
SALES (est): 5.3MM **Privately Held**
SIC: 1771 1522 Concrete work; residential
construction

(P-3309)
PRESTIGE CONCRETE
13507 Midland Rd, Poway (92064-4711)
PHONE................................858 679-2772
Jerry Green, *President*
EMP: 60
SALES (est): 7.2MM **Privately Held**
SIC: 1771 Concrete work

(P-3310)
PRESTIGE GUNITE CALIFORNIA INC
18300 Wood Edge Ln, Riverside
(92504-9580)
PHONE................................909 276-9096
Carl Pagel, *President*
William Huchton, *Vice Pres*
EMP: 50
SQ FT: 10,000
SALES (est): 3.2MM **Privately Held**
SIC: 1771 Gunite contractor

(P-3311)
R & R MAHER CNSTR CO INC
1324 Lemon St, Vallejo (94590-7250)
P.O. Box 3129 (94590-0668)
PHONE................................707 552-0330
Bradley V Maher, *Vice Pres*
Bradley Maher, *Vice Pres*
Richard D Maher, *Vice Pres*
Ken Scolavino, *Vice Pres*
EMP: 55 EST: 1970
SQ FT: 1,600
SALES (est): 6.1MM **Privately Held**
SIC: 1771 Concrete work

(P-3312)
R E MAHER INC
4545 Hess Rd, American Canyon
(94503-9727)
PHONE................................707 642-3907
Rod E Maher, *CEO*
EMP: 95
SQ FT: 1,000
SALES: 22MM **Privately Held**
SIC: 1771 Foundation & footing contractor

(P-3313)
RESCUE CONCRETE INC
9275 Beatty Dr, Sacramento (95826-9702)
P.O. Box 276812 (95827-6812)
PHONE................................916 852-2400
David Winn, *President*
EMP: 60 EST: 1995
SALES (est): 4MM **Privately Held**
WEB: www.rescueconcrete.com
SIC: 1771 Concrete work

(P-3314)
REY CON CONSTRUCTION INC
1795 E Lemonwood Dr, Santa Paula
(93060-9651)
P.O. Box 910 (93061-0910)
PHONE................................805 525-8134
Paul Reyes, *President*
Robert Reyes, *Treasurer*
Augie Reyes, *Vice Pres*
Chris Urrea, *Admin Sec*
EMP: 50
SQ FT: 5,000
SALES (est): 16.4MM **Privately Held**
SIC: 1771 1741 1751 Sidewalk contrac-
tor; masonry & other stonework; framing
contractor

(P-3315)
RJS & ASSOCIATES INC
1675 Sabre St, Hayward (94545-1013)
PHONE................................510 670-9111
Robert J Simmons, *President*
EMP: 225
SQ FT: 10,000
SALES (est): 29.5MM **Privately Held**
SIC: 1771 1521 Foundation & footing con-
tractor; single-family housing construction

(P-3316)
RMR INC (PA)
2311 S Oakley Ave Ste C, Santa Maria
(93455-1131)
P.O. Box 1715 (93456-1715)
PHONE................................805 928-4013
Mario Perea, *President*
Gloria Perea, *Vice Pres*
EMP: 60
SQ FT: 5,000
SALES (est): 5.7MM **Privately Held**
WEB: www.rmrinc.com
SIC: 1771 1389 Concrete work; oil field
services

(P-3317)
ROBERT A BOTHMAN INC (PA)
Also Called: B & B Concrete
2690 Scott Blvd, Santa Clara (95050-2511)
PHONE................................408 279-2277
Robert A Bothman, *CEO*
Saeed Yousuf, *COO*
Andy Bothman, *Vice Pres*
Brian Bothman, *Vice Pres*
Jim Brogoitti, *Vice Pres*
EMP: 118 EST: 1978
SQ FT: 20,000
SALES (est): 38.8MM **Privately Held**
WEB: www.bothman.com
SIC: 1771 0782 Concrete work; landscape
contractors

(P-3318)
RON NURSS INC
Also Called: Blueline Construction
11290 Sunrise Park Dr B, Rancho Cordova
(95742-6895)
PHONE................................916 631-9761
Ron Nurss, *President*
Darcy Nurss, *Admin Sec*
EMP: 65
SQ FT: 6,400
SALES (est): 5.3MM **Privately Held**
WEB: www.blueline-construction.com
SIC: 1771 Concrete work

(P-3319)
SACRAMENTO PRESTIGE GUNITE INC
8634 Antelope North Rd, Antelope
(95843-3930)
PHONE................................916 723-0404
George Wagner, *President*
EMP: 50
SQ FT: 1,100
SALES (est): 3.1MM **Privately Held**
WEB: www.sacgunite.com
SIC: 1771 Gunite contractor
HQ: Vcna Prestige Gunite Inc
　　8529 Suthpark Cir Ste 320
　　Orlando FL 32819
　　407 802-3540

(P-3320)
SANTA CLARITA CONCRETE
16164 Sierra Hwy, Santa Clarita
(91390-4733)
PHONE................................661 252-2012

Wayne Crawford, *President*
Keith Crawford, *Vice Pres*
Eric Stoh, *Vice Pres*
Eric Stroh, *Vice Pres*
Curtis Marzinzik, *Project Mgr*
EMP: 50
SQ FT: 5,000
SALES (est): 7.7MM **Privately Held**
SIC: 1771 Foundation & footing contractor

(P-3321)
SANTANA CONCRETE
18241 Slover Ave, Bloomington
(92316-2366)
PHONE................................909 421-2218
Jesse Santana, *Owner*
EMP: 60
SALES (est): 4.2MM **Privately Held**
SIC: 1771 Concrete work

(P-3322)
SCI INC
18501 Collier Ave B106, Lake Elsinore
(92530-2764)
PHONE................................951 245-7511
Mark A Dix, *President*
Jordan Mentz, *Controller*
EMP: 65
SQ FT: 3,000
SALES: 13MM **Privately Held**
WEB: www.tiltupsbysci.com
SIC: 1771 Concrete work

(P-3323)
SCOTT SILVA CONCRETE INC
11374 Gold Dredge Way, Rancho Cordova
(95742)
PHONE................................916 859-0593
Scott Silva, *President*
EMP: 100
SALES (est): 3.6MM **Privately Held**
SIC: 1771 Concrete work

(P-3324)
SERVICON SYSTEMS INC
3329 Jack Northrop Ave, Hawthorne
(90250-4426)
PHONE................................310 970-0700
Julio E Ramirez, *Branch Mgr*
Francisco Mancia, *District Mgr*
EMP: 1472
SALES (corp-wide): 98.4MM **Privately
Held**
SIC: 1771 Flooring contractor
PA: Servicon Systems, Inc.
　　3965 Landmark St
　　Culver City CA 90232
　　310 204-5040

(P-3325)
SIMPLE LUXURIES LLC
1560 N Sycamore Ave, Rialto
(92376-3666)
PHONE................................310 627-6514
Heather Tiger,
EMP: 50
SALES (est): 1.6MM **Privately Held**
SIC: 1771 7389 8712 Exterior concrete
stucco contractor; interior design serv-
ices; house designer

(P-3326)
SINCLAIR CONCRETE
7205 Church St, Penryn (95663-9411)
PHONE................................916 663-0303
Keith Sinclair, *Admin Sec*
Tina Pourfathi, *Office Admin*
Karin Sinclair, *Admin Sec*
EMP: 85
SALES (est): 7.6MM **Privately Held**
SIC: 1771 Foundation & footing contractor

(P-3327)
SOUTH COAST CONCRETE CNSTR
6770 Central Ave Ste B, Riverside
(92504-1443)
PHONE................................951 351-7777
Monica Perry, *President*
Bob Perry, *CFO*
Pedro Rico, *Vice Pres*
EMP: 50
SQ FT: 14,000
SALES (est): 8.7MM **Privately Held**
SIC: 1771 Concrete work

(P-3328)
SOUTHLAND PAVING INC
361 N Hale Ave, Escondido (92029-1798)
PHONE..............................760 747-6895
Richard Fleck, *CEO*
Anne Fleck, *Corp Secy*
Daniel Devlin, *Vice Pres*
Bob Kennedy, *Vice Pres*
Robert Kennedy, *Vice Pres*
EMP: 75
SQ FT: 35,000
SALES (est): 15.9MM **Privately Held**
WEB: www.southlandpaving.com
SIC: 1771 2951 Blacktop (asphalt) work;
asphalt paving mixtures & blocks; asphalt
paving blocks (not from refineries)

(P-3329)
SOUTHWEST CONSTRUCTION CO INC
2909 Rainbow Valley Blvd, Fallbrook
(92028-8859)
PHONE..............................760 728-4460
David Simon, *President*
Lorie Simon, *Vice Pres*
Paul Simon, *Admin Sec*
EMP: 60
SQ FT: 5,000
SALES (est): 8.5MM **Privately Held**
SIC: 1771 Concrete work

(P-3330)
STEFAN MERLI PLASTERING CO INC (PA)
Also Called: Merli Concrete Pumping
1230 W 130th St, Gardena (90247-1502)
PHONE..............................310 323-0404
Stefan R Merli, *President*
Adele Merli, *Treasurer*
Gunther Merli, *Admin Sec*
Millie McCarthy, *Admin Asst*
Ester Graf, *Manager*
EMP: 63
SQ FT: 5,000
SALES (est): 19.7MM **Privately Held**
SIC: 1771 Concrete pumping

(P-3331)
STEVE DUICH INC
Also Called: H & D Construction
1369 N Magnolia Ave, El Cajon
(92020-1619)
P.O. Box 12859 (92022-2859)
PHONE..............................619 444-6118
Steve Duich, *President*
Joyce Duich, *Vice Pres*
Ginger Poutous, *Administration*
Tuesdae Catalano, *Controller*
EMP: 50
SQ FT: 3,700
SALES (est): 6.8MM **Privately Held**
SIC: 1771 Sidewalk contractor

(P-3332)
STRUCTURES WEST INC
300 W Grand Ave Ste 201, Escondido
(92025-2617)
PHONE..............................760 737-2349
Jeff Steele, *President*
Robert Davidson, *CFO*
EMP: 100
SALES (est): 6.3MM **Privately Held**
SIC: 1771 Concrete work

(P-3333)
SUPERIOR GUNITE (PA)
12306 Van Nuys Blvd, Sylmar
(91342-6086)
PHONE..............................818 896-9199
Anthony L Federico, *President*
Steve Crawford, *Vice Pres*
David Bowers, *Admin Sec*
Gene McKay, *Info Tech Mgr*
Michael Ricci, *Project Engr*
EMP: 145
SQ FT: 5,000
SALES (est): 32.2MM **Privately Held**
WEB: www.shotcrete.com
SIC: 1771 Gunite contractor

(P-3334)
SURE FORMING SYSTEMS INC
10602 Humbolt St, Los Alamitos
(90720-2448)
PHONE..............................562 598-6348

Samuel F Shon, *President*
Wanda L Shon, *Treasurer*
EMP: 50
SQ FT: 6,200
SALES (est): 5.8MM **Privately Held**
SIC: 1771 Concrete work

(P-3335)
TEAM FINISH INC
155 Arovista Cir Ste A, Brea (92821-3842)
PHONE..............................714 671-9190
Thomas M Stangl, *President*
Mary Stangl, *CFO*
EMP: 80
SQ FT: 1,200
SALES (est): 12.6MM **Privately Held**
WEB: www.teamvelocity.org
SIC: 1771 Concrete work

(P-3336)
TERRY TUELL CONCRETE INC
287 W Fallbrook Ave # 105, Fresno
(93711-5805)
P.O. Box 3933 (93650-3933)
PHONE..............................559 431-0812
Terry Tuell, *President*
Matthew Tuell, *Treasurer*
Joel Stokes, *Supervisor*
EMP: 90
SQ FT: 3,000
SALES (est): 9MM **Privately Held**
SIC: 1771 Concrete work

(P-3337)
TRADEMARK CONCRETE SYSTEMS (PA)
4561 E Eisenhower Cir, Anaheim
(92807-1823)
PHONE..............................714 970-8200
Lance A Boyer, *President*
Carlos Rodriguez, *Shareholder*
Arthur Rodriguez, *Admin Sec*
EMP: 50
SQ FT: 6,000
SALES (est): 10.8MM **Privately Held**
SIC: 1771 Concrete pumping

(P-3338)
UNITED BROTHERS CONCRETE INC
41905 Boardwalk Ste K, Palm Desert
(92211-9091)
P.O. Box 756, Thousand Palms (92276-0756)
PHONE..............................760 346-1013
Lauro Barcenas, *President*
Oscar Barcenas, *Treasurer*
Luis Barcenas, *Vice Pres*
EMP: 150 EST: 1999
SQ FT: 2,000
SALES (est): 15.8MM **Privately Held**
SIC: 1771 Concrete work

(P-3339)
URATA & SONS CONCRETE INC
3430 Luyung Dr, Rancho Cordova
(95742-6871)
PHONE..............................916 638-5364
Charles Urata, *President*
Darrell Dwyer, *CFO*
Kelly Urata, *Corp Secy*
John Bell, *Vice Pres*
Susan Bigler, *Executive*
EMP: 125
SQ FT: 10,000
SALES: 71MM **Privately Held**
WEB: www.urataconcrete.com
SIC: 1771 Foundation & footing contractor

(P-3340)
VALENCIA BROS INC
Also Called: Valencia Brothers Concrete
257 Maple Ave, El Centro (92243-3311)
PHONE..............................760 353-2168
EMP: 80 EST: 2000
SQ FT: 1,700
SALES (est): 4.4MM **Privately Held**
SIC: 1771

(P-3341)
VALENTE CONCRETE
255 Benjamin Dr, Corona (92879-6509)
PHONE..............................951 279-2221
Matthew R Valente, *President*
EMP: 70
SQ FT: 3,600

SALES (est): 5.2MM **Privately Held**
WEB: www.valenteconcrete.com
SIC: 1771 Foundation & footing contractor

(P-3342)
VALLEY PACIFIC CONCRETE INC
27580 Tabb Ln, Menifee (92584-9521)
PHONE..............................951 672-6151
Chris Russo, *President*
Kristi Russo, *Vice Pres*
EMP: 110
SQ FT: 1,500
SALES (est): 11MM **Privately Held**
WEB: www.vpconcrete.com
SIC: 1771 Concrete work

(P-3343)
WAGNER CONSTRUCTION CO (PA)
12512 Ca 67, Lakeside (92040)
PHONE..............................619 873-2160
Lee James Wagner, *President*
Ed Brelling, *Vice Pres*
Suzanne Wagner, *Buyer*
EMP: 125 EST: 1974
SQ FT: 5,000
SALES (est): 7.3MM **Privately Held**
SIC: 1771 Foundation & footing contractor

(P-3344)
WAYNE E SWISHER CEM CONTR INC
2620 E 18th St, Antioch (94509-7229)
PHONE..............................925 757-3660
Wayne Swisher, *President*
Elma Swisher, *Vice Pres*
EMP: 75
SQ FT: 4,000
SALES (est): 12.5MM **Privately Held**
SIC: 1771 Foundation & footing contractor

(P-3345)
WESTERN CONCRETE PUMPING INC (PA)
2181 La Mirada Dr, Vista (92081-8830)
PHONE..............................760 598-7855
Charles D Reed, *President*
Brett Reid, *CFO*
Judy Reid, *Vice Pres*
Todd Termini, *Regional Mgr*
Mitch Straw, *Manager*
EMP: 55
SQ FT: 5,000
SALES (est): 39.9MM **Privately Held**
SIC: 1771 Concrete pumping

(P-3346)
WHITING CONSTRUCTION INC
Also Called: Whiting Concrete Construction
7281 Lone Pine Dr, Rancho Murieta
(95683-9715)
P.O. Box 887, Sloughhouse (95683-0887)
PHONE..............................916 354-2756
Tim Whiting, *President*
Sarah Hallam, *Manager*
EMP: 55
SALES (est): 5.2MM **Privately Held**
WEB: www.whitingcc.com
SIC: 1771 Concrete work

(P-3347)
Z-BEST CONCRETE INC
2575 Main St, Riverside (92501-2238)
PHONE..............................951 774-1870
Roger Crott, *President*
Jerry Faust, *Vice Pres*
EMP: 80
SQ FT: 2,400
SALES (est): 13.7MM **Privately Held**
SIC: 1771 1741 Concrete work; masonry
& other stonework

1781 Water Well Drilling

(P-3348)
BEKS ACQUISITION INC
Also Called: Bc2 Environmental
1150 W Trenton Ave, Orange (92867-3536)
PHONE..............................714 744-2990
Kurt Samuelson, *President*
EMP: 50

SALES (est): 3.8MM **Privately Held**
SIC: 1781 Water well drilling

(P-3349)
CASCADE DRILLING LP
1333 W 9th St, Upland (91786-5712)
PHONE..............................909 946-1605
Kirk McGeee, *Branch Mgr*
Andrew Hillstrand, *Business Mgr*
EMP: 50
SALES (corp-wide): 874.5MM **Privately Held**
SIC: 1781 Water well drilling
HQ: Cascade Drilling, L.P.
17270 Woodinville Redmond
Woodinville WA 98072

(P-3350)
GREGG DRILLING LLC (PA)
2726 Walnut Ave, Signal Hill (90755-1832)
PHONE..............................562 427-6899
John Gregg, *President*
Chris Christensen, *Vice Pres*
Patrick Keating, *Vice Pres*
Sonja De Keyser-Meurs, *Admin Sec*
Stacey Fuller, *Admin Asst*
EMP: 77
SQ FT: 17,000
SALES: 8MM **Privately Held**
SIC: 1781 Water well drilling

(P-3351)
GREGG DRILLING LLC
950 Howe Rd, Martinez (94553-3444)
PHONE..............................925 313-5800
Chris Christensen, *Branch Mgr*
EMP: 83
SALES (corp-wide): 8MM **Privately Held**
SIC: 1781 Water well drilling
PA: Gregg Drilling, Llc
2726 Walnut Ave
Signal Hill CA 90755
562 427-6899

(P-3352)
GREGG DRILLING & TESTING INC
Also Called: Gregg Dilling and Testing
950 Howe Rd, Martinez (94553-3444)
PHONE..............................925 313-5800
Chris Christensen, *Branch Mgr*
EMP: 61
SALES (corp-wide): 43.1MM **Privately Held**
WEB: www.greggdrilling.com
SIC: 1781 Water well drilling
PA: Gregg Drilling & Testing, Inc.
2726 Walnut Ave
Signal Hill CA 90755
562 427-6899

(P-3353)
HMS CONSTRUCTION INC (PA)
2885 Scott St, Vista (92081-8547)
PHONE..............................760 727-9808
Michael High, *President*
Ian High, *Vice Pres*
Sharon High, *Admin Sec*
Victoria Castellones, *Project Mgr*
Buck Hubbard, *Project Mgr*
EMP: 75
SQ FT: 5,200
SALES (est): 27.8MM **Privately Held**
WEB: www.hmsconstructioninc.com
SIC: 1781 8711 Geothermal drilling; engineering services

(P-3354)
MAGGIORA BROS DRILLING INC (PA)
595 Airport Blvd, Watsonville (95076-2094)
PHONE..............................831 724-1338
David T Maggiora, *CEO*
Mark Maggiora, *Treasurer*
Joanne Maggiora, *Vice Pres*
Michael Maggiora, *Admin Sec*
Robert Filippi, *Agent*
EMP: 70
SQ FT: 5,000
SALES (est): 13.4MM **Privately Held**
SIC: 1781 1711 Water well drilling; plumbing contractors

(P-3355)
PACIFIC BORING INCORPORATED
1985 W Mountain View Ave, Caruthers (93609-9701)
P.O. Box 727 (93609-0727)
PHONE....................559 864-9444
David Cline, *President*
James Gardner, *Vice Pres*
Calastro Terrasas, *Admin Sec*
EMP: 50
SQ FT: 750
SALES (est): 10.4MM **Privately Held**
WEB: www.pacificboring.com
SIC: 1781 Water well drilling

(P-3356)
YELLOW JACKET DRLG SVCS LLC
9460 Lucas Ranch Rd, Rancho Cucamonga (91730-5743)
PHONE....................909 989-8563
Richard Leblenc,
EMP: 51
SALES (corp-wide): 22.7MM **Privately Held**
SIC: 1781 Water well drilling
PA: Yellow Jacket Drilling Services, Llc
3445 E Illini St
Phoenix AZ 85040
602 453-3252

(P-3357)
ZIM INDUSTRIES INC
Bakersfield Well & Pump Co
7212 Fruitvale Ave, Bakersfield (93308-9529)
PHONE....................661 393-9661
John Zimmerer, *Manager*
EMP: 90
SALES (est): 12.9MM
SALES (corp-wide): 51.6MM **Privately Held**
SIC: 1781 7699 Water well servicing; pumps & pumping equipment repair
PA: Zim Industries, Inc.
4532 E Jefferson Ave
Fresno CA 93725
559 834-1551

1791 Structural Steel Erection

(P-3358)
ALLIED STEEL CO INC
1027 Palmyrita Ave, Riverside (92507-1701)
PHONE....................951 241-7000
Brian P Chapman, *President*
Nicky Chapman, *Treasurer*
Perry K Chapman, *Vice Pres*
Gary Chapman, *General Mgr*
Jeanette Chapman, *Admin Sec*
EMP: 60
SQ FT: 48,000
SALES (est): 15.9MM **Privately Held**
WEB: www.alliedsteelco.com
SIC: 1791 3441 Structural steel erection; fabricated structural metal

(P-3359)
ANDERSON CHRNESKY STRL STL INC
Also Called: Acss
353 Risco Cir, Beaumont (92223-2676)
PHONE....................951 769-5700
Kevin Charneskey, *President*
Kevin Charnesky, *President*
EMP: 72
SQ FT: 6,600
SALES (est): 21.6MM **Privately Held**
SIC: 1791 Structural steel erection

(P-3360)
ARTIMEX IRON COMPANY INC
315 Cypress Ln, El Cajon (92020-1695)
PHONE....................619 444-3155
Jose J Padilla, *President*
EMP: 116
SQ FT: 4,000
SALES (est): 14.3MM **Privately Held**
WEB: www.artimexiron.com
SIC: 1791 Iron work, structural

(P-3361)
BAJA CONSTRUCTION CO INC (PA)
223 Foster St, Martinez (94553-1029)
P.O. Box 3080 (94553-8080)
PHONE....................925 229-0732
Robert Hayworth, *Chairman*
Laura Daum, *President*
Brandon Morford, *CEO*
Robert J Hayworth, *Chairman*
Luis Fabian, *Vice Pres*
EMP: 90
SQ FT: 7,200
SALES: 26MM **Privately Held**
SIC: 1791 Structural steel erection

(P-3362)
BAPKO METAL INC
180 S Anita Dr, Orange (92868-3306)
PHONE....................714 639-9380
Fred Bagatourian, *President*
Clint Rieber, *CFO*
Heather Wiliams, *Admin Sec*
EMP: 80 **EST:** 1978
SQ FT: 4,000
SALES (est): 28.9MM **Privately Held**
WEB: www.bapko.com
SIC: 1791 3441 Structural steel erection; fabricated structural metal

(P-3363)
BELLIS STEEL COMPANY INC (PA)
8740 Vanalden Ave, Northridge (91324-3691)
PHONE....................818 886-5601
Theron Arthur Ghrist, *CEO*
Gail R Ghrist, *Vice Pres*
Alan Miley, *General Mgr*
Veronica Salazar, *Controller*
Andrea Cervantes, *HR Admin*
EMP: 52 **EST:** 1961
SQ FT: 2,500
SALES (est): 15.1MM **Privately Held**
WEB: www.bellissteel.com
SIC: 1791 5051 Concrete reinforcement, placing of; iron & steel (ferrous) products

(P-3364)
BLAZING INDUSTRIAL STEEL INC
9040 Jurupa Rd, Riverside (92509-3106)
PHONE....................951 360-8340
Fernando Herrera, *President*
Roberta Calderon, *Treasurer*
Mike Calderon, *Vice Pres*
Brad McGlothlin, *General Mgr*
EMP: 110
SQ FT: 100,000
SALES (est): 17.5MM **Privately Held**
SIC: 1791 Structural steel erection

(P-3365)
BONNEVILLE STEEL INC
13654 Live Oak Ln, Irwindale (91706-1317)
PHONE....................866 956-8323
Joe Wigginton, *President*
Kathryn Wigginton, *CFO*
Billie Wigginton, *Corp Secy*
Albert Vanderden, *Vice Pres*
EMP: 100
SQ FT: 6,000
SALES (est): 6.1MM **Privately Held**
SIC: 1791 Structural steel erection

(P-3366)
C M C STEEL FABRICATORS INC
Also Called: Fontana Steel
12451 Arrow Rte, Etiwanda (91739-9601)
P.O. Box 2219, Rancho Cucamonga (91729-2219)
PHONE....................909 899-9993
Deborah Marshall, *Manager*
Tim Folsom, *Manager*
EMP: 200
SQ FT: 70,348
SALES (corp-wide): 4.6B **Publicly Held**
WEB: www.cmcsg.com
SIC: 1791 3441 3496 Concrete reinforcement, placing of; fabricated structural metal; miscellaneous fabricated wire products

HQ: C M C Steel Fabricators, Inc.
1 Steel Mill Dr
Seguin TX 78155
830 372-8200

(P-3367)
C M C STEEL FABRICATORS INC
Also Called: CMC Rebar Fabricators
2755 S Willow Ave, Bloomington (92316-3260)
PHONE....................909 873-3060
Keith Dixon, *Branch Mgr*
EMP: 75
SQ FT: 45,032
SALES (corp-wide): 4.6B **Publicly Held**
WEB: www.cmcsg.com
SIC: 1791 Iron work, structural
HQ: C M C Steel Fabricators, Inc.
1 Steel Mill Dr
Seguin TX 78155
830 372-8200

(P-3368)
CAL-STATE STEEL CORPORATION
1801 W Compton Blvd, Compton (90220-2758)
P.O. Box 572034, Tarzana (91357-2034)
PHONE....................310 632-2772
Salvador Valenzuelam, *CEO*
Les Furdek, *CFO*
David Olson, *Corp Secy*
Reina Varela, *Office Mgr*
Jack Furdek, *Project Dir*
▲ **EMP:** 150
SQ FT: 10,000
SALES (est): 24.9MM **Privately Held**
WEB: www.calstatesteel.com
SIC: 1791 Iron work, structural

(P-3369)
CALIFRNIA ERCTORS BAY AREA INC
4500 California Ct, Benicia (94510-1021)
PHONE....................707 746-1990
David W McEuen, *CEO*
Dennis Mc Euen, *Ch of Bd*
Galen Jaeger, *Vice Pres*
EMP: 150
SQ FT: 16,000
SALES (est): 19.5MM **Privately Held**
WEB: www.calerectors.com
SIC: 1791 Iron work, structural; concrete reinforcement, placing of

(P-3370)
CENTRAL REINFORCING CORP
14166 Slover Ave, Fontana (92337-7162)
P.O. Box 4967, San Dimas (91773-8967)
PHONE....................909 773-0840
Eugene E Gutierrez, *President*
Patricia Cipriano, *CFO*
EMP: 60
SQ FT: 8,000
SALES: 6MM **Privately Held**
SIC: 1791 Concrete reinforcement, placing of

(P-3371)
CMC FONTANA STEEL
12451 Arrow Rte, Rancho Cucamonga (91739-9601)
P.O. Box 2219 (91729-2219)
PHONE....................909 899-9993
Paul D Ware, *Ch of Bd*
Donald G Ware, *President*
John E Ware, *Treasurer*
▲ **EMP:** 300 **EST:** 1946
SQ FT: 10,000
SALES (est): 20.5MM **Privately Held**
SIC: 1791 Concrete reinforcement, placing of

(P-3372)
CMC REBAR
12451 Arrow Rte, Rancho Cucamonga (91739-9601)
P.O. Box 11117, San Bernardino (92423-1117)
PHONE....................909 899-9993
Alfredo Bubion, *Owner*
▼ **EMP:** 63
SALES (est): 8.6MM **Privately Held**
SIC: 1791 Structural steel erection

(P-3373)
COAST IRON & STEEL CO
12300 Lakeland Rd, Santa Fe Springs (90670-3869)
P.O. Box 2846 (90670-0846)
PHONE....................562 946-4421
Greg White, *President*
Cyndi White Cramer, *Shareholder*
Carrie White, *Shareholder*
Jared White, *Shareholder*
Ronald G White, *CEO*
▲ **EMP:** 50 **EST:** 1953
SQ FT: 360,000
SALES (est): 11.4MM **Privately Held**
WEB: www.indiainfoline.com
SIC: 1791 3441 Structural steel erection; fabricated structural metal

(P-3374)
CONCORD IRON WORKS INC
Also Called: C I W
1501 Loveridge Rd Ste 15, Pittsburg (94565-2812)
PHONE....................925 432-0136
Jill Lee, *President*
Rita Gonsalves, *Corp Secy*
Jill M Lee, *Vice Pres*
Dave Maggi, *Vice Pres*
David Maggi, *Vice Pres*
EMP: 50
SQ FT: 65,000
SALES (est): 12.4MM **Privately Held**
WEB: www.concordiron.com
SIC: 1791 Iron work, structural

(P-3375)
GONSALVES & SANTUCCI INC
Also Called: Conco Cement Company
5141 Commercial Cir, Concord (94520-8523)
PHONE....................707 745-5019
Brent Alamillo, *Manager*
EMP: 250
SALES (corp-wide): 158.5MM **Privately Held**
SIC: 1791 Iron work, structural
PA: Gonsalves & Santucci, Inc.
5141 Commercial Cir
Concord CA 94520
925 685-6799

(P-3376)
HARRIS REBAR NORTHERN CAL INC
355 S Vasco Rd, Livermore (94550-5300)
PHONE....................925 373-0733
Tyler Keith, *President*
Connie Caisse, *CFO*
Ed Mize, *Vice Pres*
Lyle Sieg, *Vice Pres*
Margurite Dacey, *Administration*
▲ **EMP:** 250
SQ FT: 4,000
SALES (est): 41.8MM **Privately Held**
SIC: 1791 Structural steel erection

(P-3377)
INTEGRITY REBAR PLACERS
1345 Nandina Ave, Perris (92571-9402)
PHONE....................951 696-6843
Kenneth Negrete, *President*
Richard Rabay, *Vice Pres*
Jay Ferguson, *Technology*
Emily Webster, *Accounting Mgr*
Lester Otey, *Superintendent*
▲ **EMP:** 200
SALES (est): 29.5MM **Privately Held**
SIC: 1791 Structural steel erection

(P-3378)
IWORKS US INC
2501 S Malt Ave, Commerce (90040-3203)
PHONE....................323 278-8363
Eric Dortch, *CEO*
▲ **EMP:** 53
SQ FT: 35,000
SALES (est): 10.1MM **Privately Held**
WEB: www.interironwork.com
SIC: 1791 Iron work, structural

(P-3379)
JS REAL ESTATE PRPTS INC
134 W 168th St, Gardena (90248-2729)
PHONE....................310 856-6868
Gerry A Bustrum, *CEO*
Paul Schisino, *President*

EMP: 85
SQ FT: 4,000
SALES (est): 7.9MM **Privately Held**
WEB: www.juniorsteel.com
SIC: 1791 Structural steel erection

(P-3380)
KCB TOWERS INC
27260 Meines St, Highland (92346-4223)
P.O. Box 100 (92346-0100)
PHONE..............................909 862-0322
S Lynn Bogh, *CEO*
Sharon Bogh, *Corp Secy*
Miles Bogh, *Vice Pres*
EMP: 100
SQ FT: 12,000
SALES (est): 18.2MM **Privately Held**
WEB: www.kcbtowers.com
SIC: 1791 3441 Concrete reinforcement, placing of; fabricated structural metal

(P-3381)
KERN STEEL FABRICATION INC (PA)
627 Williams St, Bakersfield (93305-5445)
PHONE..............................661 327-9588
Tom Champness, *President*
Gene Panelli, *Vice Pres*
Blair Pruett, *Vice Pres*
Yolanda De, *Office Mgr*
Josh Perales, *Project Mgr*
◆ **EMP:** 80
SQ FT: 50,000
SALES (est): 30.3MM **Privately Held**
WEB: www.kernsteel.com
SIC: 1791 3441 3721 3728 Structural steel erection; fabricated structural metal; aircraft; aircraft parts & equipment; miscellaneous metalwork

(P-3382)
KWAN WO IRONWORKS INC
31628 Hayman St, Hayward (94544-7122)
PHONE..............................415 822-9628
Florence Kong, *President*
Ada Tang, *Office Mgr*
Fay Chu, *Admin Asst*
Shannel Cheung, *Project Engr*
Frank Wu, *Project Engr*
▲ **EMP:** 120
SQ FT: 32,000
SALES (est): 33.7MM **Privately Held**
SIC: 1791 Iron work, structural

(P-3383)
LA STEEL SERVICES INC
1760 California Ave # 201, Corona (92881-3396)
PHONE..............................951 393-2013
Pamela L Albright, *CEO*
Lee Albright, *President*
Richard Rabay, *Vice Pres*
Pamela Albright, *General Mgr*
EMP: 50
SALES (est): 1.3MM **Privately Held**
SIC: 1791 Structural steel erection

(P-3384)
LONG SWIMMING POOL STEEL INC
3920 E Coronado St # 205, Anaheim (92807-1623)
PHONE..............................714 524-8172
Larry E Long, *President*
EMP: 50 **EST:** 1971
SQ FT: 15,000
SALES (est): 6.3MM **Privately Held**
WEB: www.lspsinc.com
SIC: 1791 Concrete reinforcement, placing of

(P-3385)
M BAR C CONSTRUCTION INC
674 Rancheros Dr, San Marcos (92069-3005)
PHONE..............................760 744-4131
Jason Ianni, *CEO*
EMP: 85
SQ FT: 6,000
SALES (est): 42.3MM **Privately Held**
WEB: www.mbarcconstruction.com
SIC: 1791 1623 Structural steel erection; electric power line construction

(P-3386)
MCINTYRE COMPANY (PA)
2817 E Cedar St Ste 200, Ontario (91761-8568)
PHONE..............................909 962-6322
Roger Mc Intyre, *President*
Scott Mc Intyre, *Vice Pres*
EMP: 60
SQ FT: 10,000
SALES (est): 9.3MM **Privately Held**
WEB: www.justdeckit.com
SIC: 1791 Structural steel erection

(P-3387)
MECHANICAL INDUSTRIES INC
Also Called: M I I
314 Yampa St, Bakersfield (93307-2722)
PHONE..............................661 634-9477
Jerry L Nordine, *President*
Jerry Miranda, *Vice Pres*
Nicole Hernandez, *Administration*
Rick Martin, *Production*
EMP: 50
SQ FT: 43,000
SALES (est): 13MM **Privately Held**
SIC: 1791 Structural steel erection

(P-3388)
MID STATE STEEL ERECTION (PA)
1916 Cherokee Rd, Stockton (95205-2721)
PHONE..............................209 464-9497
Jerry Shipman, *President*
Patty Shipman, *Corp Secy*
Glenda Roe, *Technology*
Melissa Scott, *Technology*
EMP: 70
SALES (est): 14.3MM **Privately Held**
SIC: 1791 Structural steel erection

(P-3389)
PACIFIC REBAR INC
501 S Oaks Ave, Ontario (91762-4020)
PHONE..............................909 984-7199
Tim Herwehe, *President*
EMP: 60
SQ FT: 3,000
SALES (est): 7.8MM **Privately Held**
SIC: 1791 Concrete reinforcement, placing of

(P-3390)
PARCELL STEEL CORP (PA)
26365 Earthmover Cir, Corona (92883-5270)
PHONE..............................951 471-3200
Terry L Parcell, *President*
Ron J Parcell Sr, *Vice Pres*
Kristen Parcell, *Admin Sec*
EMP: 140
SQ FT: 3,500
SALES (est): 17.9MM **Privately Held**
WEB: www.parcellsteel.com
SIC: 1791 Structural steel erection

(P-3391)
PASO ROBLES TANK - BROWN-MINNE (PA)
825 26th St, Paso Robles (93446-1242)
P.O. Box 3229 (93447-3229)
PHONE..............................805 227-1641
Shawn P Owens, *CEO*
Robert Caldwell, *Vice Pres*
Waldon Davis, *Vice Pres*
Renee Cook, *Principal*
▲ **EMP:** 63
SALES (est): 39.1MM **Privately Held**
WEB: www.pasoroblestank.com
SIC: 1791 3795 Storage tanks, metal: erection; amphibian tanks, military

(P-3392)
QUALITY REINFORCING INC
13275 Gregg St, Poway (92064-7120)
PHONE..............................858 748-8400
Bryan Miller, *President*
Linda Stewart, *Manager*
▲ **EMP:** 85
SQ FT: 5,000
SALES (est): 11.2MM **Privately Held**
WEB: www.qualityreinforcing.com
SIC: 1791 Concrete reinforcement, placing of

(P-3393)
R & B REINFORCING STEEL CORP
13581 5th St, Chino (91710-5166)
PHONE..............................909 591-1726
David McDaniel, *CEO*
Robert Bessette, *President*
Dave McDaniel, *CFO*
Nancy Bessette, *Admin Sec*
EMP: 80
SQ FT: 30,000
SALES (est): 24MM **Privately Held**
SIC: 1791 Iron work, structural

(P-3394)
REBAR ENGINEERING INC
10706 Painter Ave, Santa Fe Springs (90670-4581)
P.O. Box 3986 (90670-1986)
PHONE..............................562 946-2461
Charles L Krebs, *President*
Jack Garroutte, *Exec VP*
EMP: 50
SQ FT: 6,500
SALES (est): 45MM **Privately Held**
WEB: www.rebareng.com
SIC: 1791 Concrete reinforcement, placing of

(P-3395)
RIKA CORPORATION
Also Called: Diversified Metal Works
332 W Brenna Ln, Orange (92867-5637)
PHONE..............................949 830-9050
John E Ferguson, *CEO*
Justin Ferguson, *Vice Pres*
▲ **EMP:** 100
SQ FT: 8,000
SALES: 15MM **Privately Held**
SIC: 1791 Structural steel erection

(P-3396)
SANTA CLARITA INTERIORS INC
25682 Springbrook Ave # 130, Santa Clarita (91350-2432)
PHONE..............................661 253-0861
Brian Schienle, *President*
Patty Schienle, *Treasurer*
EMP: 75
SQ FT: 10,000
SALES (est): 5.7MM **Privately Held**
SIC: 1791 1742 Iron work, structural; drywall

(P-3397)
SCHUFF STEEL COMPANY
2324 Navy Dr, Stockton (95206-1161)
PHONE..............................209 938-0869
Chase Abbott, *Branch Mgr*
EMP: 149 **Publicly Held**
SIC: 1791 3441 Structural steel erection; fabricated structural metal
HQ: Schuff Steel Company
3003 N Central Ave # 700
Phoenix AZ 85012
602 252-7787

(P-3398)
SO-CAL STRL STL FBRICATION INC
130 S Spruce Ave, Rialto (92376-9005)
PHONE..............................909 877-1299
Craig B Yates, *CEO*
Kim Yates, *Vice Pres*
EMP: 50
SQ FT: 40,000
SALES (est): 9.3MM **Privately Held**
SIC: 1791 Structural steel erection

(P-3399)
T L FABRICATIONS LP
2921 E Coronado St, Anaheim (92806-2502)
PHONE..............................562 802-3980
Ryan Kerrigan, *President*
Vic O'Mara, *Exec VP*
Michael Hsu, *Vice Pres*
Javier Hernandez, *Project Mgr*
▲ **EMP:** 60
SQ FT: 30,000
SALES (est): 8.8MM **Privately Held**
WEB: www.tlfab.com
SIC: 1791 Structural steel erection

(P-3400)
TAP RAM REINFORCING INC
11658 Excelsior Dr, Norwalk (90650-5826)
PHONE..............................562 484-0859
Maria G Tapia, *President*
EMP: 80
SALES (est): 810.1K **Privately Held**
SIC: 1791 Smoke stacks, steel: installation & maintenance

(P-3401)
TEXTURE SPECIALTIES INC
295 Mccreary Ave, Hanford (93230-2032)
PHONE..............................559 904-6047
Robert Tarlton, *President*
Mollie Pusich, *Principal*
EMP: 50
SALES (est): 950K **Privately Held**
SIC: 1791 1742 Metal lath & furring; plaster & drywall work

1793 Glass & Glazing Work

(P-3402)
BAGATELOS GLASS SYSTEMS INC (PA)
Also Called: Bagatlos Archtctral GL Systems
2750 Redding Ave, Sacramento (95820-2156)
PHONE..............................916 364-3600
Nick Bagatelos, *CEO*
Chris Bagatelos, *Admin Sec*
Karl Pavlik, *Project Mgr*
Jude Salgado, *Project Mgr*
▲ **EMP:** 65 **EST:** 1999
SQ FT: 50,000
SALES (est): 21MM **Privately Held**
WEB: www.bagatelos.com
SIC: 1793 Glass & glazing work

(P-3403)
CENTER GLASS CO NO 3
7853 El Cajon Blvd, La Mesa (91942-0621)
P.O. Box 1088 (91944-1088)
PHONE..............................619 469-6181
Jackson R Witte, *Ch of Bd*
Donald Witte, *Shareholder*
Ronald A Leaverton, *President*
David C Lawrenz, *Vice Pres*
Ron Leaverton, *Vice Pres*
EMP: 55 **EST:** 1963
SQ FT: 20,000
SALES: 6.4MM **Privately Held**
WEB: www.centerglass.com
SIC: 1793 Glass & glazing work

(P-3404)
DIVISION 8 INC
1920 Cordell Ct Ste 105, El Cajon (92020-0900)
PHONE..............................619 741-7552
Robert Hoyt, *President*
David W Vincent, *CFO*
Debra Hoyt, *Corp Secy*
Stephanie Lindsay, *Vice Pres*
Miguel Rodriguez, *Vice Pres*
EMP: 50
SQ FT: 5,000
SALES: 4MM **Privately Held**
WEB: www.division8inc.com
SIC: 1793 Glass & glazing work

(P-3405)
GIROUX GLASS INC (PA)
850 W Wash Blvd Ste 200, Los Angeles (90015-3359)
PHONE..............................213 747-7406
Anne M Murrell, *Ch of Bd*
Anne-Merelie Murrell, *Ch of Bd*
Jerod Allen, *President*
Nataline Lomedico, *CEO*
Stephanie Lamb, *COO*
▲ **EMP:** 120 **EST:** 1946
SALES: 25.2MM **Privately Held**
WEB: www.girouxglass.com
SIC: 1793 Glass & glazing work

(P-3406)
HABENICHT & HOWLETT A CORP
25 Patterson St, San Francisco (94124-1328)
PHONE..............................415 824-7040
Tom Bukard, *CEO*

EMP: 75
SALES (est): 2.4MM **Privately Held**
SIC: 1793 5231 Glass & glazing work;
glass

(P-3407)
PERFECTION GLASS INC
554 3rd St, Lake Elsinore (92530-2729)
PHONE...................951 674-0240
Richard L Warren, *President*
Dane Warren, *Treasurer*
Chris Bonnet, *Admin Sec*
EMP: 50
SQ FT: 4,200
SALES (est): 7.6MM **Privately Held**
SIC: 1793 Glass & glazing work

(P-3408)
PROGRESS GLASS CO INC (PA)
25 Patterson St, San Francisco
(94124-1377)
PHONE...................415 824-7040
Tom Burkard, *CEO*
Chuck Burkard, *President*
Thomas C Burkard III, *President*
Shirley Wallace, *Treasurer*
Jim Holmberg, *Senior VP*
▲ **EMP:** 105 **EST:** 1956
SQ FT: 16,250
SALES (est): 25.3MM **Privately Held**
WEB: www.progressglass.com
SIC: 1793 Glass & glazing work

(P-3409)
ROYAL GLASS COMPANY INC
3200 De La Cruz Blvd, Santa Clara
(95054-2602)
PHONE...................408 969-0444
John Maggiore, *CEO*
James Maggiore, *Vice Pres*
▲ **EMP:** 80
SALES (est): 22.6MM **Privately Held**
SIC: 1793 Glass & glazing work

(P-3410)
SAFECO DOOR & HARDWARE INC
Also Called: Safeco Glass
31054 San Antonio St, Hayward
(94544-7904)
PHONE...................510 429-4768
Mahboubeh Ahmadi, *President*
Milagors Missaghi, *Treasurer*
Ali Missaghi Akoub, *Vice Pres*
Hamid Ahmadi, *Admin Sec*
Alexis Wilson, *Project Engr*
EMP: 65
SQ FT: 13,000
SALES (est): 11.9MM **Privately Held**
SIC: 1793 Glass & glazing work

(P-3411)
TOWER GLASS INC
9570 Pathway St Ste A, Santee
(92071-4100)
PHONE...................619 596-6199
Evelyn Dee Swaim, *CEO*
Barry Swaim, *CFO*
Julie McConnaughy, *Admin Asst*
Greg Gates, *Project Mgr*
Carl Marquette, *Project Mgr*
EMP: 100
SQ FT: 15,000
SALES (est): 22MM **Privately Held**
WEB: www.towerglass.com
SIC: 1793 Glass & glazing work

(P-3412)
WALTERS & WOLF GLASS COMPANY (PA)
Also Called: Walter & Wolf
41450 Boscell Rd, Fremont (94538-3103)
PHONE...................510 490-1115
Randall A Wolf, *President*
Jeff Belzer, *CFO*
Jim O'Connor, *CFO*
Nick Kocelj, *Vice Pres*
Michelle Messersmith, *Office Mgr*
▲ **EMP:** 135 **EST:** 1977
SALES (est): 104.1MM **Privately Held**
WEB: www.waltersandwolf.com
SIC: 1793 Glass & glazing work

(P-3413)
WOODBRIDGE GLASS INC
14321 Myford Rd, Tustin (92780-7022)
PHONE...................714 838-4444
Virginia Siciliani, *President*
Jim Siciliani, *Corp Secy*
John Siciliani, *Vice Pres*
▲ **EMP:** 205
SQ FT: 8,500
SALES (est): 90MM **Privately Held**
WEB: www.woodbridgeglass.com
SIC: 1793 5231 Glass & glazing work;
glass, leaded or stained

1794 Excavating & Grading Work

(P-3414)
ANDREW M JORDAN INC
Also Called: A & B Construction
1350 4th St, Berkeley (94710)
PHONE...................510 999-6000
Andrew M Jordan, *President*
EMP: 90
SQ FT: 1,000
SALES: 30MM **Privately Held**
WEB: www.a-bconstruction.net
SIC: 1794 Excavation & grading, building
construction

(P-3415)
BAY CITIES PAV & GRADING INC
1450 Civic Ct Bldg B, Concord
(94520-5295)
PHONE...................925 687-6666
Ben L Rodriguez, *CEO*
Marlo Manqueros, *Vice Pres*
Kim Rodriguez, *Admin Sec*
Steven Caudill, *Human Res Mgr*
EMP: 250
SQ FT: 4,000
SALES (est): 63.3MM **Privately Held**
SIC: 1794 1611 7353 Excavation work;
highway & street construction; earth mov-
ing equipment, rental or leasing

(P-3416)
CALEX ENGINEERING INC
23651 Pine St, Newhall (91321-3106)
PHONE...................661 254-1866
Kenny Seitz, *Partner*
Mike Neilson, *CEO*
EMP: 70
SQ FT: 1,800
SALES (est): 14.2MM **Privately Held**
SIC: 1794 Excavation work

(P-3417)
CARONE & COMPANY INC
Also Called: Diablo Valley Rock
5009 Forni Dr Ste A, Concord
(94520-8525)
PHONE...................925 602-8800
Richard Lloyd Carone, *President*
EMP: 60
SQ FT: 48,000
SALES (est): 13.1MM **Privately Held**
SIC: 1794 Excavation work

(P-3418)
CHINO GRADING INC
3613 Philadelphia St, Chino (91710-2068)
PHONE...................909 364-8667
Norm Gorgone, *President*
Oscar Alegre, *Project Mgr*
Scott Thompson, *Project Mgr*
Dave Horn, *Superintendent*
EMP: 60
SALES (est): 4.9MM **Privately Held**
SIC: 1794 Excavation & grading, building
construction

(P-3419)
COASTAL GRADING AND EXCAVATING
756 Calle Plano, Camarillo (93012-8555)
PHONE...................805 445-6433
Thomas Staben Jr, *President*
Carrie Cox, *Office Mgr*
EMP: 50
SALES (est): 4.9MM **Privately Held**
SIC: 1794 Excavation work

(P-3420)
COMMERCIAL SITE IMPRVS INC
192 Poker Flat Rd, Copperopolis
(95228-9601)
PHONE...................209 785-1920
Kimberly Batch, *President*
Ron Batch, *Vice Pres*
EMP: 50
SALES (est): 1.4MM **Privately Held**
SIC: 1794 Excavation & grading, building
construction

(P-3421)
CREW INC
19618 S Susana Rd, Compton
(90221-5716)
PHONE...................310 608-6860
David M Lalonde, *President*
Darrin Lalonde, *Admin Sec*
Warren Duke, *Purch Mgr*
EMP: 60
SQ FT: 5,000
SALES (est): 14MM **Privately Held**
WEB: www.crew.net
SIC: 1794 Excavation & grading, building
construction

(P-3422)
DAVE SPURR EXCAVATING INC
Also Called: Spurr Co.
935 Riverside Ave Ste 18, Paso Robles
(93446-2649)
P.O. Box 1920 (93447-1920)
PHONE...................805 238-0834
David Spurr, *President*
EMP: 50
SQ FT: 1,000
SALES (est): 7.3MM **Privately Held**
SIC: 1794 Excavation & grading, building
construction

(P-3423)
EMERALD SITE SERVICES INC
9883 Kent St, Elk Grove (95624-4009)
PHONE...................916 685-7211
Kaycie Edwards, *President*
Mark Edwards, *Treasurer*
Austin Edwards, *Admin Sec*
Coleen Cortiz, *Controller*
Aaron Jerome, *VP Opers*
EMP: 55
SALES: 9.5MM **Privately Held**
SIC: 1794 1796 0782 Excavation & grad-
ing, building construction; pollution control
equipment installation; garden mainte-
nance services; turf installation services,
except artificial; highway lawn & garden
maintenance services

(P-3424)
ERRECAS INC
12570 Slaughter House, Lakeside (92040)
P.O. Box 640 (92040-0640)
PHONE...................619 390-6400
Charles M Erreca, *President*
Charmaine Bridwell, *Shareholder*
Mike Conroy, *CFO*
John East, *Vice Pres*
Scott Erreca, *Vice Pres*
EMP: 100
SQ FT: 48,450
SALES (est): 9.3MM **Privately Held**
WEB: www.erreca.com
SIC: 1794 1771 Excavation & grading,
building construction; concrete work

(P-3425)
FJ WILLERT CONTRACTING CO
1869 Nirvana Ave, Chula Vista
(91911-6117)
PHONE...................619 421-1980
Fred M Willert, *President*
EMP: 110 **EST:** 1972
SQ FT: 11,748
SALES: 37.9MM **Privately Held**
WEB: www.fjwillert.com
SIC: 1794 Excavation & grading, building
construction

(P-3426)
G AND L BROCK CNSTR CO INC
4145 Calloway Ct, Stockton (95215-2400)
PHONE...................209 931-3626
Lynne Brock, *President*
Gary Brock, *Vice Pres*
David Brock, *Project Mgr*

EMP: 50
SQ FT: 5,800
SALES (est): 9.6MM **Privately Held**
SIC: 1794 Excavation work

(P-3427)
GILLIAM & SONS INC
Also Called: Valco Construction
9831 Rosedale Hwy, Bakersfield
(93312-2604)
P.O. Box 9955 (93389-1955)
PHONE...................661 589-0913
Bill W Gilliam, *CEO*
Scott Gilliam, *Vice Pres*
Nancy Northern, *Controller*
Ken Spiker, *Human Res Dir*
EMP: 50
SQ FT: 2,500
SALES (est): 10.2MM **Privately Held**
WEB: www.gilliamandsons.com
SIC: 1794 Excavation & grading, building
construction

(P-3428)
GUINN CORPORATION
6533 Rosedale Hwy, Bakersfield
(93308-5903)
P.O. Box 1339 (93302-1339)
PHONE...................661 325-6109
Gary Guinn, *CEO*
Jeff Affonso, *Corp Secy*
Tim Guinn, *Vice Pres*
Adrienne Reitsma, *Controller*
Matt Morrow, *Opers Mgr*
EMP: 75
SQ FT: 3,600
SALES (est): 18MM **Privately Held**
WEB: www.guinnconstruction.com
SIC: 1794 Excavation & grading, building
construction

(P-3429)
HOWARD CONTRACTING INC
12354 Carson St, Hawaiian Gardens
(90716-1604)
PHONE...................562 596-2969
Frederick Stanley Howard, *CEO*
Viki R Howard, *Corp Secy*
Stanley L Howard, *Vice Pres*
Stanley Howard, *Vice Pres*
Denise Pontius, *Controller*
EMP: 50
SQ FT: 3,500
SALES (est): 9.2MM **Privately Held**
SIC: 1794 Excavation work

(P-3430)
INLAND EROSION CONTROL SVCS
42181 Avenida Alvarado A, Temecula
(92590-3429)
P.O. Box 728, Murrieta (92564-0728)
PHONE...................951 301-8334
Todd Close, *President*
Carlos Garcia, *Vice Pres*
Leo Rodriguez, *Controller*
EMP: 59
SQ FT: 1,000
SALES (est): 7.4MM **Privately Held**
SIC: 1794 Excavation & grading, building
construction

(P-3431)
JEFF CARPENTER INC
1380 W Oleander Ave, Perris (92571-7863)
PHONE...................951 657-5115
Jeff Carpenter, *President*
EMP: 60
SQ FT: 1,300
SALES (est): 10.1MM **Privately Held**
SIC: 1794 Excavation work

(P-3432)
LOVCO CONSTRUCTION INC
1300 E Burnett St, Signal Hill (90755-3512)
P.O. Box 90335, Long Beach (90809-0335)
PHONE...................562 595-1601
Terry C Lovingier, *President*
Katie Lovingier, *Treasurer*
Steve Barnett, *Vice Pres*
Matt Lovinger, *Vice Pres*
Terry Lovingier, *Vice Pres*
EMP: 125
SQ FT: 2,500

SALES (est): 33.5MM **Privately Held**
WEB: www.lovco.com
SIC: 1794 1771 1611 Excavation & grading, building construction; concrete work; highway & street construction; general contractor, highway & street construction

(P-3433)
LUPTON EXCAVATION INC
8467 Florin Rd, Sacramento (95828-2512)
PHONE.................................916 387-1104
Kenneth Lupton Jr, *President*
EMP: 75
SQ FT: 4,000
SALES (est): 9.9MM **Privately Held**
SIC: 1794 Excavation & grading, building construction

(P-3434)
MEYERS EARTHWORK INC
4150 Fig Tree Ln, Redding (96002-9315)
P.O. Box 493730 (96049-3730)
PHONE.................................530 365-8858
Jacob Meyers, *President*
Charleen Meyers, *Vice Pres*
Charlene Meyers, *General Mgr*
▼ **EMP:** 55
SQ FT: 2,000
SALES (est): 10.2MM **Privately Held**
SIC: 1794 Excavation & grading, building construction

(P-3435)
MITCHELL ENGINEERING
1395 Evans Ave, San Francisco (94124-1703)
P.O. Box 880308 (94188-0308)
PHONE.................................415 227-1040
Michael A Silva, *President*
Curtis F Mitchell, *Vice Pres*
Thelma Welch, *Manager*
▲ **EMP:** 50
SQ FT: 2,000
SALES (est): 12MM **Privately Held**
WEB: www.mitchell-engineering.com
SIC: 1794 1623 1622 1629 Excavation & grading, building construction; water main construction; pipeline construction; bridge, tunnel & elevated highway; railroad & subway construction

(P-3436)
MOZINGO CONSTRUCTION INC
751 Wakefield Ct, Oakdale (95361-7761)
PHONE.................................209 848-0160
Kurtis Mozingo, *CEO*
Doni Mozingo, *President*
Michael Freeman, *Vice Pres*
Philip Gianfortone, *Vice Pres*
Ruth A Brickner, *Executive*
EMP: 50
SALES (est): 11.2MM **Privately Held**
SIC: 1794 Excavation work

(P-3437)
PACIFIC EXCAVATION INC
9796 Kent St, Elk Grove (95624-4823)
PHONE.................................916 686-2800
Tim Paxin, *President*
Jim Paxin, *Vice Pres*
Brennon Aho, *Project Mgr*
EMP: 75
SQ FT: 30,000
SALES (est): 9.9MM **Privately Held**
WEB: www.pacexcavation.com
SIC: 1794 Excavation work

(P-3438)
REED THOMAS COMPANY INC
1025 N Santiago St, Santa Ana (92701-3800)
PHONE.................................714 558-7691
Harvey T Biegle, *President*
Sam Matthews, *Info Tech Dir*
Fulgencio Reynaga, *Foreman/Supr*
EMP: 90
SQ FT: 8,800
SALES (est): 13.2MM **Privately Held**
WEB: www.reedthomas.com
SIC: 1794 Excavation & grading, building construction

(P-3439)
STURGEON SON GRADING & PAV INC (PA)
3511 Gilmore Ave, Bakersfield (93308-6205)
P.O. Box 2840 (93303-2840)
PHONE.................................661 322-4408
John E Powell, *CEO*
Paul Sturgeon, *President*
Oliver Sturgeon, *Principal*
EMP: 180 **EST:** 1927
SQ FT: 3,500
SALES (est): 51.5MM **Privately Held**
WEB: www.sturgeonandson.com
SIC: 1794 8711 Excavation work; engineering services

(P-3440)
SUKUT CONSTRUCTION INC (PA)
4010 W Chandler Ave, Santa Ana (92704-5202)
PHONE.................................714 540-5351
Michael H Crawford, *President*
Paul Kuliev, *CFO*
Myron C Sukut, *Chairman*
Mike Zanaboni, *Vice Pres*
Kathie Kaiser, *General Mgr*
▲ **EMP:** 60
SQ FT: 12,000
SALES (est): 44.2MM **Privately Held**
WEB: www.sukut.com
SIC: 1794 1611 1623 1629 Excavation & grading, building construction; general contractor, highway & street construction; water & sewer line construction; dams, waterways, docks & other marine construction

(P-3441)
SWAN ENGINEERING INC
4470 Yankee Hill Rd # 200, Rocklin (95677-1632)
PHONE.................................916 474-5299
Justin Swanson, *President*
Krysta Swanson, *Bookkeeper*
Brendin Swanson, *Superintendent*
EMP: 54 **EST:** 2010
SALES (est): 3.6MM **Privately Held**
WEB: www.swanenginc.com
SIC: 1794 1623 1611 Excavation & grading, building construction; water & sewer line construction; telephone & communication line construction; gravel or dirt road construction

(P-3442)
TIDWELL EXCAV ACQUISITION INC
1691 Los Angeles Ave, Ventura (93004-3213)
PHONE.................................805 647-4707
Alex Miruello, *President*
Louis Armona, *Treasurer*
Timothy Wayne Goodwin, *Vice Pres*
EMP: 90 **EST:** 1956
SALES (est): 12.4MM
SALES (corp-wide): 408.1MM **Privately Held**
PA: Meruelo Enterprises, Inc.
9550 Firestone Blvd # 105
Downey CA 90241
562 745-2300

(P-3443)
TIM PAXINS PACIFIC EXCAVATION
9796 Kent St, Elk Grove (95624-4823)
PHONE.................................916 686-2800
Tim Paxin, *President*
EMP: 50
SQ FT: 2,500
SALES (est): 4.7MM **Privately Held**
SIC: 1794 Excavation & grading, building construction

(P-3444)
VANDER WEERD GENERAL CNSTR
837 Commercial Ave, Tulare (93274-7101)
PHONE.................................559 688-1099
Ron A Vander Weerd, *President*
Rosalinda Vander Weerd, *Corp Secy*

EMP: 65
SQ FT: 10,000
SALES (est): 4MM **Privately Held**
SIC: 1794 Excavation & grading, building construction

1795 Wrecking & Demolition Work

(P-3445)
AMERICAN CONCRETE CUTTING INC
Also Called: American Dmlton/Concrete Cutng
620 N Poinsettia St, Santa Ana (92701-3999)
PHONE.................................714 547-7181
F Richard Stewart, *President*
John Moore, *Vice Pres*
EMP: 100
SALES (est): 8.8MM **Privately Held**
WEB: www.americandemo.com
SIC: 1795 Concrete breaking for streets & highways

(P-3446)
AMERICAN WRECKING INC
2459 Lee Ave, South El Monte (91733-1407)
PHONE.................................626 350-8303
Jose Luis Galaviz, *President*
Jay Gonzalez, *COO*
Warne Galaviz, *Vice Pres*
Robert Hall, *Vice Pres*
EMP: 100
SQ FT: 1,000
SALES (est): 25.9MM **Privately Held**
WEB: www.americanwreckinginc.com
SIC: 1795 Demolition, buildings & other structures

(P-3447)
CAL EMPIRE ENGINEERING INC
628 E Edna Pl, Covina (91723-1312)
PHONE.................................626 915-8030
Greg Miller, *President*
Sheree Kaplan, *Administration*
Roy Mousel, *VP Opers*
Dan Gallet, *Manager*
EMP: 50 **EST:** 2016
SALES (est): 4MM **Privately Held**
SIC: 1795 1794 1623 Concrete breaking for streets & highways; demolition, buildings & other structures; excavation work; underground utilities contractor

(P-3448)
CASPER COMPANY
3825 Bancroft Dr, Spring Valley (91977-2122)
PHONE.................................619 589-6001
Roger Casper, *CEO*
William R Haithcock, *President*
Greg T Casper, *Vice Pres*
Steven Casper, *Vice Pres*
Isabel Ortiz Marocco, *Vice Pres*
EMP: 143
SQ FT: 6,000
SALES (est): 42.7MM **Privately Held**
SIC: 1795 Concrete breaking for streets & highways

(P-3449)
CLAUSS CONSTRUCTION
9911 Maine Ave, Lakeside (92040-3107)
PHONE.................................619 390-4940
Patrick Michael Clauss, *CEO*
Joe Clauss, *Vice Pres*
Briana Munoz, *Admin Asst*
Aaron Vincent, *Project Mgr*
Benny Garcia, *Purchasing*
EMP: 80
SALES (est): 18.1MM **Privately Held**
WEB: www.claussconstruction.com
SIC: 1795 1629 4959 Wrecking & demolition work; earthmoving contractor; toxic or hazardous waste cleanup

(P-3450)
CLEVELAND WRECKING COMPANY (DH)
Also Called: CWC Acquisition
999 W Town And Country Rd, Orange (92868-4713)
PHONE.................................626 967-4287
James Sheridan, *President*
Andrew Varga, *President*
EMP: 78
SQ FT: 60,000
SALES (est): 16.8MM
SALES (corp-wide): 20.1B **Publicly Held**
WEB: www.clevelandwrecking.com
SIC: 1795 1796 1799 Demolition, buildings & other structures; machinery dismantling; asbestos removal & encapsulation
HQ: Urs Group, Inc.
300 S Grand Ave Ste 1100
Los Angeles CA 90071
213 593-8000

(P-3451)
DANNY RYAN PRECISION CONTG INC
1818 N Orangethorpe Park, Anaheim (92801-1140)
PHONE.................................949 642-6664
Danny Ryan, *President*
EMP: 90
SQ FT: 10,000
SALES: 19MM **Privately Held**
SIC: 1795 1799 Demolition, buildings & other structures; asbestos removal & encapsulation

(P-3452)
DIRT CHEAP DEMOLITION INC
171 Mace St Ste A4, Chula Vista (91911-5861)
P.O. Box 1186, Bonita (91908-1186)
PHONE.................................619 426-9598
Dan Cannon, *President*
EMP: 50
SALES (est): 3.5MM **Privately Held**
SIC: 1795 Demolition, buildings & other structures

(P-3453)
GD HEIL INC
1031 Segovia Cir, Placentia (92870-7137)
PHONE.................................714 687-9100
James A Langford, *CEO*
Gary Heil, *President*
Steve Mc Clain, *Vice Pres*
Laura Heil, *Admin Sec*
EMP: 160
SQ FT: 20,770
SALES (est): 27.3MM **Privately Held**
WEB: www.gdheil.com
SIC: 1795 Demolition, buildings & other structures

(P-3454)
HULK CONSTRUCTION
4352 Lakeview Ave, Yorba Linda (92886-2422)
PHONE.................................714 701-9458
Ronald Short, *President*
EMP: 80
SALES (est): 3.2MM **Privately Held**
SIC: 1795 Dismantling steel oil tanks

(P-3455)
INTERIOR RMOVAL SPECIALIST INC
8990 Atlantic Ave, South Gate (90280-3505)
PHONE.................................323 357-6900
Carlos Herrera, *CEO*
Isabel Herrera, *Vice Pres*
Francesco Decarlo, *Info Tech Mgr*
Chuck Brode, *Project Mgr*
Roy Ludt, *Project Mgr*
EMP: 150
SALES (est): 24.2MM **Privately Held**
WEB: www.irsdemo.com
SIC: 1795 Demolition, buildings & other structures

PRODUCTS & SVCS

(P-3456)
KROEKER INC
4627 S Chestnut Ave, Fresno
(93725-9238)
PHONE...................................559 237-3764
Joyce Kroeker, *President*
Jeff Kroeker, *Corp Secy*
Ed Kroeker, *Vice Pres*
Rodney Ainsworth, *General Mgr*
John Ramirez, *Office Mgr*
EMP: 120
SQ FT: 9,000
SALES: 25MM **Privately Held**
SIC: **1795** 1629 4953 Wrecking & demoli-
tion work; land reclamation; earthmoving
contractor; recycling, waste materials

(P-3457)
MILLER ENVIRONMENTAL INC
1130 W Trenton Ave, Orange (92867-3536)
PHONE...................................714 385-0099
Gregg Miller, *President*
Rob Schaefer, *Vice Pres*
Lourdes Vargas, *Admin Asst*
Rosie Lizarraga, *Controller*
Dennis Parker, *Opers Staff*
EMP: 150
SQ FT: 3,000
SALES (est): 34.5MM **Privately Held**
WEB: www.millerenvironmental.com
SIC: **1795** 4953 Demolition, buildings &
other structures; hazardous waste collec-
tion & disposal

(P-3458)
**NORTHSTAR CONTG GROUP
INC**
13320 Cambridge St, Santa Fe Springs
(90670-4904)
PHONE...................................714 639-7600
John Leonard, *Vice Pres*
EMP: 60
SALES (corp-wide): 371.8MM **Privately
Held**
SIC: **1795** 1799 Wrecking & demolition
work; asbestos removal & encapsulation
HQ: Northstar Contracting Group, Inc.
2614-20 Barrington Ct
Hayward CA 94545
510 491-1330

(P-3459)
**NORTHSTAR DEM &
REMEDIATION LP (DH)**
404 N Berry St, Brea (92821-3104)
PHONE...................................714 672-3500
Jose Alonso, *General Mgr*
Subhas Khara, *President*
Duane Kerr, *CFO*
Donald B McGlamery, *Branch Mgr*
Jeni Sarvaiya, *Administration*
EMP: 174
SQ FT: 19,000
SALES (est): 115.4MM
SALES (corp-wide): 371.8MM **Privately
Held**
SIC: **1795** 1799 8744 Demolition, build-
ings & other structures; decontamination
services;
HQ: Northstar Group Services, Inc.
370 7th Ave Ste 1803
New York NY 10001
212 951-3660

(P-3460)
RANDAZZO ENTERPRISES INC
13550 Blackie Rd, Castroville
(95012-3200)
PHONE...................................831 633-4420
John Randazzo, *President*
Alice Randazzo, *CFO*
Mark Randazzo, *Vice Pres*
Sandy Lynch, *IT/INT Sup*
Ken Hepper, *Project Mgr*
EMP: 55 EST: 1965
SQ FT: 13,000
SALES (est): 11.2MM **Privately Held**
WEB: www.randazzoenterprises.com
SIC: **1795** Demolition, buildings & other
structures

(P-3461)
**SECA EQP REMOVAL &
DISMANTLE**
Also Called: Seca Eqp Removal & Disman-
tling
684 Bitritto Ct, Modesto (95356-9272)
PHONE...................................209 543-1600
Maria Carbenas, *President*
EMP: 50
SQ FT: 2,300
SALES (est): 3.1MM **Privately Held**
SIC: **1795** Wrecking & demolition work

(P-3462)
SIERRA RECYCLING & DEM INC
1620 E Brundage Ln Frnt, Bakersfield
(93307-2756)
PHONE...................................661 327-7073
Philip Sacco, *President*
EMP: 71
SQ FT: 20,000
SALES (est): 8.8MM **Privately Held**
SIC: **1795** Demolition, buildings & other
structures

(P-3463)
**SILVERADO CONTRACTORS
INC (PA)**
2855 Mandela Pkwy Fl 2, Oakland
(94608-4011)
PHONE...................................510 658-9960
Joseph M Capriola, *President*
Sue Capriola, *Treasurer*
Peter Knutch, *Vice Pres*
Richard Riggs, *Vice Pres*
Nancy Meesai, *Accountant*
EMP: 65
SALES (est): 18.3MM **Privately Held**
WEB: www.silveradocontractors.com
SIC: **1795** Demolition, buildings & other
structures

(P-3464)
STOMPER CO INC
7799 Enterprise Dr, Newark (94560-3408)
PHONE...................................510 574-0570
Donna R Rehrmann, *President*
George Rehrmann, *Vice Pres*
EMP: 60 EST: 1968
SQ FT: 15,000
SALES (est): 9.8MM **Privately Held**
WEB: www.stomper.org
SIC: **1795** Concrete breaking for streets &
highways

(P-3465)
TWO RIVERS DEMOLITION INC
2620 Mercantile Dr 100, Rancho Cordova
(95742-6519)
PHONE...................................916 638-6775
W Roderick Palon, *President*
EMP: 55
SALES (est): 11.7MM **Privately Held**
WEB: www.2riversdemo.com
SIC: **1795** Demolition, buildings & other
structures; concrete breaking for streets &
highways

(P-3466)
ULTIMATE REMOVAL INC
Also Called: ULTIMATE DEMO
2168 Pomona Blvd, Pomona (91768-3332)
P.O. Box 1220 (91769-1220)
PHONE...................................909 524-0800
John W Welch, *President*
Patrick Coleman, *CFO*
Derek Mireles, *Senior VP*
Eddie Somoza, *Project Mgr*
EMP: 124
SQ FT: 9,900
SALES: 9.4MM **Privately Held**
WEB: www.ultimateremoval.com
SIC: **1795** Demolition, buildings & other
structures

(P-3467)
VIKING EQUIPMENT CORP
Also Called: Viking Demolition
540 W Windsor Rd, Glendale
(91204-1812)
P.O. Box 251257 (91225-1257)
PHONE...................................818 500-9447
Berger Jostad, *President*
John Mike Tredick, *CFO*
Scott Tredick, *Corp Secy*

Tanner Tredick, *Engineer*
EMP: 65
SALES (est): 6.5MM **Privately Held**
WEB: www.vikingdemo.com
SIC: **1795** 1799 5932 Demolition, build-
ings & other structures; building mover,
including houses; building materials, sec-
ondhand

**1796 Installation Or Erection
Of Bldg Eqpt & Machinery,
NEC**

(P-3468)
ANDERSON & MARTELLA INC
1200 Mt Diablo Blvd # 400, Walnut Creek
(94596-4890)
PHONE...................................925 934-3831
Marc Anderson, *President*
EMP: 50
SQ FT: 1,000
SALES (est): 5.4MM **Privately Held**
SIC: **1796** Installing building equipment

(P-3469)
CLASSIC INSTALLS INC
22475 Baxter Rd, Wildomar (92595-9040)
PHONE...................................951 678-9906
Dirk Steffen, *CEO*
Brian Staub, *Project Mgr*
Nicole Steen, *Opers Staff*
Micaela Hilderbrand, *Manager*
EMP: 70
SALES: 75.5K **Privately Held**
SIC: **1796** Installing building equipment

(P-3470)
**FOSTER WHEELER ENERGY
SVCS INC**
9645 Scranton Rd Ste 230, San Diego
(92121-1790)
PHONE...................................800 500-1993
Ed Linck, *President*
EMP: 50
SALES (est): 3.1MM
SALES (corp-wide): 5.3B **Privately Held**
SIC: **1796** 1629 1731 4911 Power gener-
ating equipment installation; power plant
construction; electric power systems con-
tractors; cogeneration specialization; gen-
eration, electric power
HQ: Amec Foster Wheeler North America
Corp.
53 Frontage Rd
Hampton NJ 08827
936 448-6323

(P-3471)
HARELSON MECHANICAL INC
Also Called: Hmi Industrial Contractors Inc
3899 Security Park Dr, Rancho Cordova
(95742-6920)
PHONE...................................916 386-2586
Ruth Gilman, *CEO*
Don Gilman, *Vice Pres*
Debbie Carew, *Admin Mgr*
Ashley Crawford, *Admin Asst*
Casey Henke, *Project Mgr*
EMP: 62
SQ FT: 37,000
SALES: 15MM **Privately Held**
SIC: **1796** Millwright

(P-3472)
LLOYD W AUBRY CO INC (PA)
2148 Dunn Rd, Hayward (94545-2204)
P.O. Box 55426 (94545-0426)
PHONE...................................510 732-9038
Robert Butler, *President*
Robert J Butler, *President*
Jay Butler, *CFO*
Brian Phillips, *Project Mgr*
Nick Ayhens, *Superintendent*
EMP: 79
SQ FT: 27,000
SALES: 48.5MM **Privately Held**
WEB: www.lloydwaubry.com
SIC: **1796** 8711 Machinery installation;
mechanical engineering

(P-3473)
**MITSUBISHI ELECTRIC US INC
(DH)**
Also Called: Meus
5900 Katella Ave Ste A, Cypress
(90630-5019)
P.O. Box 6007 (90630-0007)
PHONE...................................714 220-2500
Hora Keijiro, *CEO*
Mike Corbo, *COO*
Makoto Kono, *Treasurer*
Perry Pappous, *Exec VP*
Erik Zommers, *Senior VP*
◆ EMP: 200
SQ FT: 10,400
SALES (est): 402MM
SALES (corp-wide): 41.5B **Privately Held**
WEB: www.diamond-vision.com
SIC: **1796** 3534 5065 3669 Elevator in-
stallation & conversion; escalators, pas-
senger & freight; electronic parts;
semiconductor devices; visual communi-
cation systems
HQ: Mitsubishi Electric Us Holdings, Inc.
5900 Katella Ave Ste A
Cypress CA 90630
714 220-2500

(P-3474)
OTIS ELEVATOR INTL INC
1358 14th St, Oakland (94607-2209)
PHONE...................................510 874-5129
Dennis Fuller, *Branch Mgr*
EMP: 58
SALES (corp-wide): 59.8B **Publicly Held**
WEB: www.otis.com
SIC: **1796** 7699 Elevator installation &
conversion; elevators: inspection, service
& repair
HQ: Otis Elevator Company
1 Carrier Pl
Farmington CT 06032
860 674-3000

(P-3475)
**PACIFIC COAST EQUIPMENT CO
INC (PA)**
3839 E Coronado St, Anaheim
(92807-1606)
PHONE...................................714 630-5957
David E Walker, *CEO*
Curtis Walker, *Vice Pres*
Larry Kalina, *Marketing Staff*
Scott Weseman, *Sales Staff*
EMP: 50
SQ FT: 67,500
SALES (est): 14.7MM **Privately Held**
WEB: www.walkerbro.com
SIC: **1796** Machine moving & rigging

(P-3476)
**TRANSBAY FIRE PROTECTION
INC (PA)**
2182 Rheem Dr, Pleasanton (94588-2796)
PHONE...................................925 846-9484
Charlie Marlin, *President*
Julie Schmidt, *CFO*
Hossein Tabatabai, *Vice Pres*
Toni Yerton, *Admin Asst*
Christian Gerbich, *Design Engr*
▲ EMP: 50
SQ FT: 17,000
SALES (est): 10.4MM **Privately Held**
WEB: www.transbayfire.com
SIC: **1796** 7389 Installing building equip-
ment; safety inspection service

(P-3477)
**UNITED RIGGERS & ERECTORS
INC (PA)**
4188 Valley Blvd, Walnut (91789-1446)
P.O. Box 728 (91788-0728)
PHONE...................................909 978-0400
Brian D Kelley, *CEO*
Thomas J Kruss, *COO*
Frank Cangey, *Engineer*
Tom Larsen, *Manager*
EMP: 120 EST: 1966
SQ FT: 58,000
SALES: 24MM **Privately Held**
SIC: **1796** Machinery installation

1799 Special Trade Contractors, NEC

(P-3478)
1ST LIGHT ENERGY INC (PA)
1869 Moffat Blvd, Manteca (95336-8944)
PHONE..................................209 824-5500
Justin Krum, *CEO*
Gregory Smith, *CFO*
John McIntosh, *Director*
Lena Kuntz, *Commercial*
EMP: 50
SQ FT: 6,300
SALES (est): 51.9MM **Privately Held**
SIC: 1799 1711 Hydraulic equipment, installation & service; solar energy contractor

(P-3479)
AAA RESTORATION INC
29850 2nd St, Lake Elsinore (92532-2420)
PHONE..................................951 471-5828
Kirk Munio, *President*
EMP: 50
SQ FT: 1,400
SALES (est): 3.8MM **Privately Held**
SIC: 1799 Home/office interiors finishing, furnishing & remodeling

(P-3480)
AJC SANDBLASTING INC
932 Schley Ave, Wilmington (90744-4060)
PHONE..................................562 436-3606
Lisa Charleston, *President*
Larry Dowling, *Treasurer*
EMP: 90
SQ FT: 10,000
SALES (est): 8MM **Privately Held**
SIC: 1799 Sandblasting of building exteriors; epoxy application

(P-3481)
ALCORN FENCE COMPANY (PA)
9901 Glenoaks Blvd, Sun Valley (91352-1089)
P.O. Box 1249 (91353-1249)
PHONE..................................818 983-0650
Thomas Joseph Stack, *CEO*
Greg Erickson, *President*
Oscar Mancialla, *CFO*
Bob Gibson, *Vice Pres*
Rick Sohns, *Project Mgr*
EMP: 150 **EST:** 1942
SQ FT: 18,000
SALES (est): 23MM **Privately Held**
SIC: 1799 Fence construction

(P-3482)
ALL STAR MAINTENANCE INC
12250 El Camino Real # 300, San Diego (92130-3076)
PHONE..................................858 259-0900
John Junge, *President*
EMP: 100
SALES (est): 5.3MM **Privately Held**
SIC: 1799 Building site preparation

(P-3483)
ALL STARS
Also Called: Sab Pacific
12250 El Camino Real # 300, San Diego (92130-3076)
PHONE..................................858 259-0900
John P Junge, *Partner*
John Jung, *Partner*
EMP: 300
SQ FT: 17,000
SALES (est): 10MM **Privately Held**
SIC: 1799 Home/office interiors finishing, furnishing & remodeling

(P-3484)
AMERICAN SYNERGY ASBESTOS REMO
Also Called: Synergy Environmental
28436 Satellite St, Hayward (94545-4863)
PHONE..................................510 444-2333
David C Clark, *President*
Douglas Price, *Manager*
EMP: 100
SQ FT: 6,000

SALES (est): 10MM **Privately Held**
WEB: www.synergyenvironmental.com
SIC: 1799 Asbestos removal & encapsulation

(P-3485)
AMERICAN TECHNOLOGIES INC
Also Called: American Restoration Services
25000 Industrial Blvd, Hayward (94545-2349)
PHONE..................................510 429-5000
Toll Free:.............................888 -
Kyle Picket, *Manager*
Dan Ward, *Branch Mgr*
Gina Artis-Coleman, *Accounts Exec*
EMP: 60
SALES (corp-wide): 236.5MM **Privately Held**
WEB: www.amer-tech.com
SIC: 1799 1521 Asbestos removal & encapsulation; decontamination services; single-family home remodeling, additions & repairs; repairing fire damage, single-family houses
PA: American Technologies Inc.
210 W Baywood Ave
Orange CA 92865
714 283-9990

(P-3486)
ANDRIAN INC
Also Called: Stations
1935 Lundy Ave, San Jose (95131-1848)
PHONE..................................408 434-0730
Andrew Lanier, *President*
Brian Fajardo, *CEO*
EMP: 50
SQ FT: 11,000
SALES (est): 6.6MM **Privately Held**
SIC: 1799 Office furniture installation

(P-3487)
ANDRIGHETTO PRODUCE INC
Also Called: Shasta Produce Co
155 Terminal Ct Stalls 15 Stalls, South San Francisco (94083)
P.O. Box 2328 (94083-2328)
PHONE..................................650 588-0930
Steven Andrighetto, *CEO*
David Andrighetto, *Owner*
Peter Carcione, *President*
Steven Hurwitz, *Treasurer*
Domenic Andrighetto, *Vice Pres*
EMP: 55
SQ FT: 10,000
SALES (est): 10.8MM **Privately Held**
SIC: 1799 5411 Bowling alley installation; supermarkets, chain

(P-3488)
APW CONSTRUCTION INC
15135 Salt Lake Ave, City of Industry (91746-3316)
PHONE..................................626 855-1720
America Tang, *Branch Mgr*
EMP: 65
SALES (corp-wide): 20MM **Privately Held**
SIC: 1799 Fence construction
PA: Apw Construction, Inc.
727 Glendora Ave
La Puente CA 91744
626 820-0812

(P-3489)
AQUA GUNITE INC
5830 S Naylor Rd, Livermore (94551-8308)
PHONE..................................408 271-2782
Jose G Aguayo, *CEO*
Fargio Garcia, *Vice Pres*
EMP: 50
SQ FT: 2,120
SALES (est): 5.2MM **Privately Held**
SIC: 1799 Swimming pool construction

(P-3490)
ASBESTOS INSTANT RESPONSE INC
3517 W Washington Blvd, Los Angeles (90018-1122)
PHONE..................................323 733-0508
Eric Chevasson, *President*
Steven Liedernan, *COO*
EMP: 65
SQ FT: 1,500

SALES (est): 7.8MM **Privately Held**
WEB: www.airinc.ws
SIC: 1799 Asbestos removal & encapsulation

(P-3491)
BARON POOL PLST STHERN CAL INC
495 Industrial Rd, San Bernardino (92408-3715)
PHONE..................................909 792-8891
Craig Bennion, *President*
EMP: 55
SQ FT: 5,000
SALES (est): 5.5MM **Privately Held**
WEB: www.baronpool.com
SIC: 1799 Swimming pool construction

(P-3492)
BAY AREA INSTALLATIONS INC (PA)
2481 Verna Ct, San Leandro (94577-4222)
PHONE..................................510 895-8196
Thomas Clark Mohamed, *President*
Herman B Chibnick, *Vice Pres*
Alta Clark, *Admin Sec*
Taj Chibnik, *Accounting Mgr*
Tom Mohamed, *Opers Mgr*
▲ **EMP:** 69
SQ FT: 25,000
SALES (est): 8.7MM **Privately Held**
WEB: www.baiinc.com
SIC: 1799 4212 Demountable partition installation; office furniture installation; delivery service, vehicular

(P-3493)
BEACHSIDE REALTORS
4197 Chino Hills Pkwy, Chino Hills (91709-2614)
PHONE..................................909 606-1299
Iris Tonti, *Manager*
EMP: 68
SALES (est): 1.7MM
SALES (corp-wide): 20.3MM **Privately Held**
WEB: www.mikelembeck.com
SIC: 1799 5084 7389 7331 Steam cleaning of building exteriors; cleaning equipment, high pressure, sand or steam; packaging & labeling services; mailing service; real estate agents & managers
PA: Beachside Realtors
19671 Beach Blvd Ste 101
Huntington Beach CA 92648
714 969-6100

(P-3494)
BLUEWATER ENVMTL SVCS INC
2075 Williams St, San Leandro (94577-2305)
PHONE..................................510 346-8800
Chris J Kirschenheuter, *CEO*
Todd Kirschenheuter, *Vice Pres*
EMP: 100
SQ FT: 15,000
SALES (est): 15MM **Privately Held**
WEB: www.bwserv.com
SIC: 1799 Asbestos removal & encapsulation

(P-3495)
BRAND SERVICES LLC
Also Called: Brand Scaffold Service
940 Hensley St, Richmond (94801-2106)
PHONE..................................510 231-9640
Art Cruz, *Branch Mgr*
EMP: 52
SALES (corp-wide): 3.1B **Privately Held**
WEB: www.brandscaffold.com
SIC: 1799 Scaffolding construction
HQ: Brand Shared Services Llc
1325 Cobb Intl Dr Nw
Kennesaw GA 30152
678 285-1400

(P-3496)
BRICKLEY CONSTRUCTION CO INC
Also Called: Brickley Environmental
957 Reece St, San Bernardino (92411-2356)
PHONE..................................909 888-2010
James L Brickley, *CEO*
Thomas Brickley, *President*

Annorr Gowdy, *CFO*
Shane Brickley, *Vice Pres*
Kathleen Herrera, *Admin Asst*
EMP: 50
SQ FT: 10,000
SALES (est): 7MM **Privately Held**
WEB: www.brickleyenv.com
SIC: 1799 4959 Asbestos removal & encapsulation; environmental cleanup services

(P-3497)
BURDICK PAINTING
705 Nuttman St, Santa Clara (95054-2623)
PHONE..................................408 567-1330
John C Cintas, *CEO*
EMP: 67
SQ FT: 8,000
SALES (est): 7MM **Privately Held**
SIC: 1799 1721 Paint & wallpaper stripping; coating, caulking & weather, water & fireproofing; coating of concrete structures with plastic; coating of metal structures at construction site; commercial painting

(P-3498)
C E TOLAND & SON
5300 Industrial Way, Benicia (94510-1025)
PHONE..................................707 747-1000
Clyde E Toland Jr, *Ch of Bd*
Blake Toland, *President*
Rey Trias, *Vice Pres*
Jeanette Vaiana, *Executive*
Lisa Castro, *Human Res Mgr*
▲ **EMP:** 120
SQ FT: 90,000
SALES (est): 20.4MM **Privately Held**
WEB: www.cetoland.com
SIC: 1799 Ornamental metal work

(P-3499)
CALIFORNIA ACCESS SCAFFOLD LLC
331 Vineland Ave, City of Industry (91746-2321)
PHONE..................................310 324-3388
Daniel Johnson, *CEO*
Daniel Styles, *CFO*
James Johnson, *Vice Pres*
Dennis Highstreet, *Admin Mgr*
Kevin Johnson, *Info Tech Mgr*
EMP: 56 **EST:** 2012
SALES: 5.6MM **Privately Held**
SIC: 1799 Scaffolding construction

(P-3500)
CALIFORNIA CLOSET CO O
42210 Cook St Ste E, Palm Desert (92211-5199)
PHONE..................................760 773-4784
Steve Coughlin, *Manager*
EMP: 83
SALES (corp-wide): 16MM **Privately Held**
SIC: 1799 Closet organizers, installation & design
PA: California Closet Co. Of Orange County/Long Beach, Inc.
5921 Skylab Rd
Huntington Beach CA 92647
714 899-4905

(P-3501)
CALIFRNIAS GNITE POOL PLST INC
510 Greenville Rd, Livermore (94550-9297)
PHONE..................................925 960-9500
Manuel Rodriguez, *President*
Jose Arellano, *Vice Pres*
Alvaro Lando, *Vice Pres*
Monroe Rodriguez, *Vice Pres*
EMP: 60
SQ FT: 15,625
SALES (est): 7.6MM **Privately Held**
SIC: 1799 Swimming pool construction

(P-3502)
CITY OF SANTA CLARA
Also Called: City of Santa Clra Parks Svc
2600 Benton St, Santa Clara (95051-4802)
PHONE..................................408 615-3770
George Friedenbach, *Manager*
EMP: 55 **Privately Held**

SIC: 1799 Parking facility equipment & maintenance
PA: City Of Santa Clara
1500 Warburton Ave
Santa Clara CA 95050
408 615-2200

(P-3503)
CITY SERVICE CONTRACTING INC (PA)
Also Called: City Service Paving
920 Lawrence St, Placentia (92870-7031)
PHONE..................714 632-6610
Mike Garvin, *CEO*
Jon Beach, *CFO*
George Puente, *Vice Pres*
EMP: 74
SALES: 23MM **Privately Held**
WEB: www.citypaving.com
SIC: 1799 Parking lot maintenance

(P-3504)
CLARO POOL SERVICES INC
42161 Beacon HI, Palm Desert (92211-5108)
PHONE..................760 341-3377
Stephen Little, *CEO*
EMP: 53
SQ FT: 8,000
SALES (est): 296.5K **Privately Held**
SIC: 1799 Swimming pool construction

(P-3505)
CLEANRITE INC (PA)
Also Called: Buildrite
1200 W East Ave, Chico (95926-3034)
PHONE..................530 891-0333
Danny J Andreasen, *President*
EMP: 95 **EST:** 1979
SQ FT: 6,300
SALES: 12.5MM **Privately Held**
WEB: www.cleanrite-buildrite.com
SIC: 1799 7349 Post-disaster renovations; janitorial service, contract basis

(P-3506)
COASTAL MARINE SERVICES INC (PA)
2255 National Ave, San Diego (92113-3614)
PHONE..................619 291-8176
Howard Gordon, *President*
Robert M Baugh, *Program Dir*
Robert R Baugh, *Program Dir*
EMP: 50
SQ FT: 10,500
SALES (est): 6.2MM **Privately Held**
WEB: www.coastalmarineservices.com
SIC: 1799 Insulation of pipes & boilers

(P-3507)
COURTNEY INC (PA)
16781 Millikan Ave, Irvine (92606-5009)
PHONE..................949 222-2050
George Courtney, *CEO*
Mildred Courtney, *Admin Sec*
EMP: 80
SALES (est): 32.6MM **Privately Held**
SIC: 1799 Waterproofing

(P-3508)
CROWN FENCE CO
12118 Bloomfield Ave, Santa Fe Springs (90670-4703)
PHONE..................562 864-5177
Eric Fiedler, *Principal*
Matt Brock, *COO*
Eric W Fiedler, *Vice Pres*
Blanca Del Valle, *Administration*
Murat Ortun, *Project Mgr*
▲ **EMP:** 96
SQ FT: 36,000
SALES (est): 34.6MM **Privately Held**
SIC: 1799 5039 Fence construction; wire fence, gates & accessories

(P-3509)
DAVE GROSS ENTERPRISES INC
Also Called: Adams Pool Specialties
7 Wayne Ct, Sacramento (95829-1300)
PHONE..................916 388-2000
David William Gross, *CEO*
Michel McDonnell, *Vice Pres*
Barbara Hall, *Controller*

EMP: 65
SQ FT: 25,000
SALES: 7MM **Privately Held**
SIC: 1799 Swimming pool construction

(P-3510)
DEHART INC
Also Called: California Closet Co
7550 Miramar Rd Ste 300, San Diego (92126-4217)
PHONE..................858 695-0882
Mike Cayheart, *President*
EMP: 72
SQ FT: 5,700
SALES (est): 5.3MM **Privately Held**
WEB: www.dehart.com
SIC: 1799 2541 2521 1751 Closet organizers, installation & design; wood partitions & fixtures; wood office furniture; carpentry work; wood television & radio cabinets

(P-3511)
EASYTURF INC (DH)
2750 La Mirada Dr, Vista (92081-8401)
PHONE..................760 745-7026
David Hartman, *CEO*
George Ballow, *Executive*
Sandi Kane, *Sales Staff*
Charles Colletti, *Director*
Jay Holguin, *Director*
◆ **EMP:** 79
SQ FT: 30,000
SALES (est): 10.4MM
SALES (corp-wide): 528.7K **Privately Held**
SIC: 1799 Artificial turf installation

(P-3512)
ENCORE AEROSPACE LLC
1729 Apollo Ct, Seal Beach (90740-5617)
PHONE..................562 344-1700
Tom McFarland,
EMP: 100
SALES (est): 3.9MM **Privately Held**
SIC: 1799 Renovation of aircraft interiors

(P-3513)
ENVIRONMENTS PLUS (PA)
1700 1st St, San Fernando (91340-2711)
PHONE..................805 375-5727
Regina Gomez, *Ch of Bd*
Mark Cordell, *President*
Brian Pang, *Software Engr*
Bryan Migdol, *Director*
EMP: 60
SQ FT: 9,000
SALES (est): 9.8MM **Privately Held**
WEB: www.epi-usa.com
SIC: 1799 Office furniture installation

(P-3514)
ERNIE & SONS SCAFFOLDING
Also Called: Unique Scaffold
1960 Olivera Rd, Concord (94520-5425)
PHONE..................925 446-4442
Ernesto Negrete Jr, *CEO*
Joe Garcia, *CFO*
John Soto, *Vice Pres*
EMP: 180 **EST:** 2010
SQ FT: 47,000
SALES: 21MM **Privately Held**
SIC: 1799 Scaffolding construction

(P-3515)
EXCEL MDULAR SCAFFOLD LSG CORP
2555 Birch St, Vista (92081-8433)
PHONE..................760 598-0050
Benjamin Bartlett, *Branch Mgr*
Chris Pearson, *Project Mgr*
Gary Munn, *Director*
Richard Williams, *Manager*
Maria Noto, *Accounts Mgr*
EMP: 1743 **Privately Held**
SIC: 1799 Rigging & scaffolding
PA: Excel Modular Scaffold And Leasing Corporation
720 Washington St Unit 5
Hanover MA 02339

(P-3516)
FARWEST CORROSION CONTROL CO (PA)
12029 Regentview Ave, Downey (90241-5517)
PHONE..................310 532-9524
Troy Gordon Rankin Jr, *CEO*
Roy Rankin Jr, *President*
Marian Rankin, *Treasurer*
Steve Sosa, *Principal*
◆ **EMP:** 173
SQ FT: 42,000
SALES (est): 100.6MM **Privately Held**
WEB: www.farwst.com
SIC: 1799 Corrosion control installation

(P-3517)
FENCECORP INC (HQ)
18440 Van Buren Blvd, Riverside (92508-9258)
PHONE..................951 686-3170
T Perrry Massie, *CEO*
Dale Marriott, *President*
Gary Hansen, *Vice Pres*
Jessi Cobb, *Office Admin*
Floyd Nixon, *Admin Sec*
EMP: 340
SQ FT: 5,000
SALES (est): 18.4MM
SALES (corp-wide): 121MM **Privately Held**
SIC: 1799 Fence construction
PA: Fenceworks, Inc.
870 Main St
Riverside CA 92501
951 788-5620

(P-3518)
FENCEWORKS INC
Also Called: Golden State Fence
2861 E La Cresta Ave, Anaheim (92806-1817)
PHONE..................714 238-0091
Steve Anderson, *Principal*
Ted Nesbitt, *Project Mgr*
EMP: 75
SALES (corp-wide): 121MM **Privately Held**
WEB: www.goldenstatefence.com
SIC: 1799 Fence construction
PA: Fenceworks, Inc.
870 Main St
Riverside CA 92501
951 788-5620

(P-3519)
FENCEWORKS INC (PA)
Also Called: Golden State Fence Co.
870 Main St, Riverside (92501-1016)
PHONE..................951 788-5620
Jason Ostrander, *CEO*
Mel Kay, *President*
Aaron Garcia, *CFO*
Elizabeth Olive, *Branch Mgr*
Dawn Smith, *Office Mgr*
▲ **EMP:** 250
SQ FT: 20,000
SALES (est): 121MM **Privately Held**
WEB: www.goldenstatefence.com
SIC: 1799 Fence construction

(P-3520)
FENCEWORKS INC
Also Called: Golden State Fence
891 Corporation St, Santa Paula (93060-3005)
PHONE..................661 265-0082
Pete Schank, *Manager*
Tony Masciola, *General Mgr*
EMP: 100
SALES (corp-wide): 121MM **Privately Held**
WEB: www.goldenstatefence.com
SIC: 1799 Fence construction
PA: Fenceworks, Inc.
870 Main St
Riverside CA 92501
951 788-5620

(P-3521)
FLUOR ENTERPRISES INC
1 Fluor Daniel Dr, Aliso Viejo (92698-1000)
PHONE..................469 398-7000
Scott Snyder, *Manager*
Gregory Amparano, *Vice Pres*
Gerald Stone, *Vice Pres*

Larry Grosskreuz, *Info Tech Mgr*
Denny LI, *Engineer*
EMP: 52
SALES (corp-wide): 19.5B **Publicly Held**
SIC: 1799 Building site preparation
HQ: Fluor Enterprises, Inc.
6700 Las Colinas Blvd
Irving TX 75039
469 398-7000

(P-3522)
FRESH AIR ENVIRONMENTAL SVCS
10675 Rush St, South El Monte (91733-3439)
PHONE..................323 913-1965
Kevan Stark, *President*
Erin McConnell, *Office Mgr*
Michael Davis, *Project Mgr*
David Delgado, *Project Mgr*
EMP: 60
SQ FT: 7,000
SALES (est): 4.4MM **Privately Held**
WEB: www.4freshair.biz
SIC: 1799 Asbestos removal & encapsulation

(P-3523)
G W SURFACES (PA)
Also Called: Showershapes
2432 Palma Dr, Ventura (93003-5732)
PHONE..................805 642-5004
James A Garver, *President*
Georgann Garver, *Corp Secy*
Tidus Gutierrez, *Vice Pres*
EMP: 170
SQ FT: 30,000
SALES (est): 18.8MM **Privately Held**
WEB: www.gwsurfaces.com
SIC: 1799 Counter top installation

(P-3524)
GARDNER POOL COMPANY INC (PA)
Also Called: Gardner Pool Plastering
801 Gable Way, El Cajon (92020-1910)
PHONE..................619 593-8880
Scott McKenna, *President*
EMP: 51 **EST:** 1967
SQ FT: 6,000
SALES (est): 17.5MM **Privately Held**
WEB: www.gardnerpoolplastering.com
SIC: 1799 Swimming pool construction

(P-3525)
GETTLER-RYAN INC (PA)
6805 Sierra Ct Ste G, Dublin (94568-2694)
PHONE..................925 551-7555
Jeffrey M Ryan, *CEO*
Dave Byron, *Vice Pres*
Janice Grant, *Admin Sec*
Desiree Walton, *Admin Asst*
Liddy McKenzie, *Design Engr*
EMP: 65
SQ FT: 20,000
SALES (est): 19.1MM **Privately Held**
WEB: www.grinc.com
SIC: 1799 Petroleum storage tanks, pumping & draining; service station equipment installation, maintenance & repair

(P-3526)
GLOBAL ENTERTAINMENT INDS INC
2948 N Ontario St, Burbank (91504-2016)
PHONE..................818 567-0000
Christopher Hyde, *President*
Teresa Harris, *Manager*
▲ **EMP:** 55
SQ FT: 65,000
SALES (est): 6.3MM **Privately Held**
WEB: www.globalentind.com
SIC: 1799 Prop, set or scenery construction, theatrical

(P-3527)
GREGG DRILLING & TESTING INC (PA)
2726 Walnut Ave, Signal Hill (90755-1832)
PHONE..................562 427-6899
John M Gregg, *President*
Chris Christensen, *Vice Pres*
Patrick Keating, *Vice Pres*
Peter Robertson, *Manager*
▲ **EMP:** 71

SQ FT: 17,000
SALES: 43.1MM **Privately Held**
WEB: www.greggdrilling.com
SIC: 1799 1781 Core drilling & cutting; water well drilling

(P-3528)
HAYWARD BAKER INC
1780 E Lemonwood Dr, Santa Paula (93060-9510)
PHONE...........................805 933-1331
Alan Ringen, *Branch Mgr*
Gary Taylor, *Senior VP*
Joseph Mann, *Project Mgr*
Lisheng Shao, *Chief Engr*
Robert Mendez, *Purch Agent*
EMP: 75
SALES (corp-wide): 2.7B **Privately Held**
WEB: www.haywardbaker.com
SIC: 1799 Building site preparation
HQ: Hayward Baker Inc
     7550 Teague Rd Ste 300
     Hanover MD 21076
     410 551-8200

(P-3529)
HEARN ENTERPRISE INC (PA)
Also Called: Hearn Construction
536 Davis St, Vacaville (95688-4605)
PHONE...........................707 446-5467
Jamie Healer, *CEO*
Fred J Hearn Jr, *Vice Pres*
EMP: 115
SQ FT: 6,000
SALES (est): 14.8MM **Privately Held**
SIC: 1799 Building board-up contractor

(P-3530)
HEAVENLY CONSTRUCTION INC
Also Called: Heavenly Greens
370 Umbarger Rd Ste A, San Jose (95111-2070)
PHONE...........................408 723-4954
Daniel Theis, *President*
EMP: 73
SQ FT: 75,000
SALES (est): 7.7MM **Privately Held**
WEB: www.heavenlygreens.com
SIC: 1799 Artificial turf installation

(P-3531)
HEINAMAN CONTRACT GLAZING INC (PA)
26981 Vista Ter Ste E, Lake Forest (92630-8127)
PHONE...........................949 587-0266
John L Heinaman, *President*
Gaye Howhannesian, *Treasurer*
Angela Heinaman, *Exec VP*
Mark Heinaman, *Vice Pres*
◆ **EMP:** 50
SQ FT: 4,950
SALES (est): 21.1MM **Privately Held**
SIC: 1799 1793 Window treatment installation; glass & glazing work

(P-3532)
HERZOG CONTRACTING CORP
2155 Hancock St, San Diego (92110-2012)
PHONE...........................619 849-6990
EMP: 747
SALES (corp-wide): 269MM **Privately Held**
SIC: 1799 Antenna installation
PA: Herzog Contracting Corp.
     600 S Riverside Rd
     Saint Joseph MO 64507
     816 233-9001

(P-3533)
HIGH END DEVELOPMENT INC
665 Stone Rd, Benicia (94510-1141)
PHONE...........................925 687-2540
Jim Metzger, *President*
Larry V Harmen, *CFO*
Anthony Froyd, *Admin Sec*
EMP: 60
SALES: 26.5MM **Privately Held**
SIC: 1799 Waterproofing

(P-3534)
HOME IMPROVEMENT COMPANY INC
1585 Creek St, San Marcos (92078-2442)
PHONE...........................760 744-4840
Chet Johnston, *President*
Ron Helmes, *CFO*
EMP: 50
SALES (est): 4.5MM **Privately Held**
SIC: 1799 1521 1541 Post-disaster renovations; general remodeling, single-family houses; renovation, remodeling & repairs: industrial buildings

(P-3535)
J PEREZ ASSOCIATES INC (PA)
Also Called: J. Perez & Associates
10833 Valley View St # 200, Cypress (90630-5046)
PHONE...........................562 801-5397
Joe Perez, *CEO*
Peter Beath, *Vice Pres*
Tony Perez, *Vice Pres*
Yusimil Perez, *Admin Asst*
Robert Adames, *Opers Mgr*
EMP: 55
SQ FT: 15,000
SALES (est): 16.5MM **Privately Held**
WEB: www.jperez.com
SIC: 1799 Sign installation & maintenance

(P-3536)
JANUS CORPORATION (PA)
1081 Shary Cir, Concord (94518-2407)
PHONE...........................925 969-9200
Mike Ely, *CEO*
Sean Tavernier, *President*
Craig M Uhle, *Vice Pres*
Barb Eaves, *Admin Sec*
EMP: 100
SQ FT: 15,000
SALES (est): 31.3MM **Privately Held**
WEB: www.januscorp.com
SIC: 1799 Asbestos removal & encapsulation; decontamination services

(P-3537)
JANUS CORPORATION
2025 Tandem, Norco (92860-3610)
PHONE...........................951 479-0700
Chad Chandler, *Manager*
EMP: 50
SQ FT: 21,780
SALES (corp-wide): 31.3MM **Privately Held**
WEB: www.januscorp.com
SIC: 1799 Asbestos removal & encapsulation
PA: Janus Corporation
     1081 Shary Cir
     Concord CA 94518
     925 969-9200

(P-3538)
JARKA ENTERPRISES INC
1059 Vine St Ste 108, Sacramento (95811-0339)
PHONE...........................916 491-6180
Ken Binsmore, *Branch Mgr*
EMP: 65
SALES (corp-wide): 16.2MM **Privately Held**
SIC: 1799 Office furniture installation
PA: Jarka Enterprises, Inc.
     675 Brennan St
     San Jose CA 95131
     408 325-5700

(P-3539)
JEFF KERBER POOL PLST INC
166 San Lorenzo St, Pomona (91766-2334)
PHONE...........................909 465-0677
Jeff Kerber, *President*
▲ **EMP:** 260
SQ FT: 77,100
SALES (est): 22.1MM **Privately Held**
WEB: www.jeffkerber.com
SIC: 1799 Swimming pool construction

(P-3540)
JOHNSON FINCH & MCCLURE CNSTR (PA)
Also Called: Jfm
9749 Cactus St, Lakeside (92040-4117)
PHONE...........................619 938-9727
Mark Finch, *CEO*
Scott McClure, *President*
Jim Johnson, *Chairman*
EMP: 146
SQ FT: 10,000
SALES (est): 24.6MM **Privately Held**
SIC: 1799 1742 Demountable partition installation; acoustical & ceiling work

(P-3541)
JONES/COVEY GROUP INCORPORATED
Also Called: Jones Covey Group
9595 Lucas Ranch Rd # 100, Rancho Cucamonga (91730-5725)
PHONE...........................888 972-7581
Bret Christopher Covey, *CEO*
Robert Christie, *Principal*
Ellen Collins, *Administration*
Sue Hulse, *Administration*
Jim Gonzales, *Project Mgr*
EMP: 63
SQ FT: 2,400
SALES (est): 23MM **Privately Held**
SIC: 1799 Service station equipment installation & maintenance

(P-3542)
KARCHER ENVIRONMENTAL INC (PA)
2300 E Orangewood Ave, Anaheim (92806-6112)
P.O. Box 7385, Orange (92863-7385)
PHONE...........................714 385-1490
Benjamin R Karcher, *President*
Mark Kavanaugh, *Sales Staff*
EMP: 120
SQ FT: 26,400
SALES (est): 9.7MM **Privately Held**
WEB: www.karcherenv.com
SIC: 1799 1742 Asbestos removal & encapsulation; insulation, buildings

(P-3543)
KERBER BROS INC
14006 Gracebee Ave, Norwalk (90650-4506)
PHONE...........................562 921-3447
Skip Hawkins, *President*
EMP: 236
SQ FT: 2,800
SALES (est): 10.8MM **Privately Held**
WEB: www.kerberbrothers.com
SIC: 1799 1742 Swimming pool construction; plastering, drywall & insulation

(P-3544)
L&G CABLE CONSTRUCTION
2776 E Miraloma Ave, Anaheim (92806-1701)
PHONE...........................714 630-6174
Lou Gentile, *President*
Joe Winek, *Supervisor*
EMP: 60
SALES (est): 5.5MM **Privately Held**
SIC: 1799 Cable splicing service

(P-3545)
LAYFIELD USA CORPORATION (DH)
2500 Sweetwater Springs B, Spring Valley (91978-2007)
PHONE...........................619 562-1200
Thomas Rose, *CEO*
Steve Palubiski, *CFO*
Rob Rempel, *Vice Pres*
Laura Quillen, *Executive*
Toni Smith, *Administration*
▲ **EMP:** 100
SQ FT: 1,000
SALES (est): 25.4MM **Privately Held**
SIC: 1799 Building board-up contractor
HQ: Layfield Group Limited
     11131 Hammersmith Gate
     Richmond BC V7A 5
     604 275-5588

(P-3546)
M GAW INC
Also Called: Jet Sets
6910 Farmdale Ave, North Hollywood (91605-6210)
PHONE...........................818 503-7997
Michael Gaw, *President*
EMP: 90
SQ FT: 15,000
SALES (est): 9.2MM **Privately Held**
SIC: 1799 Prop, set or scenery construction, theatrical

(P-3547)
MALCO MAINTENANCE INC
Also Called: Malco Services
3703 E Melville Way, Anaheim (92806-2122)
PHONE...........................714 630-0194
Duane Malone, *President*
Katie Goldsberry, *Manager*
EMP: 66
SQ FT: 15,000
SALES (est): 6.2MM **Privately Held**
SIC: 1799 Exterior cleaning, including sandblasting; cleaning building exteriors; cleaning new buildings after construction; steam cleaning of building exteriors

(P-3548)
MALCOLM DRILLING COMPANY INC (PA)
92 Natoma St Ste 400, San Francisco (94105-2685)
PHONE...........................415 901-4400
John M Malcolm, *CEO*
Jerry Riggs, *President*
Terry Tucker, *President*
Alec Bloem, *Vice Pres*
Heinrich Majewski, *Vice Pres*
▲ **EMP:** 151
SQ FT: 7,500
SALES (est): 657.6MM **Privately Held**
WEB: www.malcolmdrilling.com
SIC: 1799 Building site preparation; boring for building construction

(P-3549)
MATRIX ENVIRONMENTAL INC
2330 Cherry Indus Cir, Long Beach (90805-4417)
PHONE...........................562 236-2704
Jason McKeever, *President*
Duane Pate, *Vice Pres*
Taryn M Ryan, *Info Tech Mgr*
EMP: 60
SQ FT: 9,000
SALES: 21.9MM **Privately Held**
SIC: 1799 Athletic & recreation facilities construction

(P-3550)
MATRIX INDUSTRIES INC
2330 E Cherry Indus Cir, Long Beach (90805-4417)
PHONE...........................562 236-2700
Larry Larkin, *President*
Edwin Vargas, *Assistant*
EMP: 260
SQ FT: 10,000
SALES (est): 15.5MM **Privately Held**
SIC: 1799

(P-3551)
MEMO SCAFFOLDING INC
12722 Carmenita Rd, Santa Fe Springs (90670-4804)
PHONE...........................562 404-8600
Jose G Santos, *President*
Lynn Hollister, *CFO*
EMP: 100
SQ FT: 9,000
SALES (est): 7.8MM **Privately Held**
WEB: www.memoscaffolding.com
SIC: 1799 Scaffolding construction

(P-3552)
MOVER SERVICES INC
Also Called: ATLAS MOVER SERVICES
721 E Compton Blvd, Rancho Dominguez (90220-1153)
PHONE...........................310 868-5143
John Moses, *President*
Michelle Moses, *Vice Pres*
EMP: 50
SQ FT: 33,000

PRODUCTS & SVCS

SALES: 6.6MM **Privately Held**
WEB: www.msiatlas.com
SIC: 1799 4214 5712 Office furniture installation; household goods moving & storage, local; office furniture

(P-3553)
MP AERO LLC
7701 Woodley Ave, Van Nuys (91406-1732)
PHONE.................................818 901-9828
Christine Paschal, *CFO*
EMP: 85 **EST:** 2013
SQ FT: 165,000
SALES (est): 12.5MM **Privately Held**
SIC: 1799 Renovation of aircraft interiors

(P-3554)
MUEHLHAN CERTIFED COATINGS INC
2320 Cordelia Rd, Fairfield (94534-1600)
PHONE.................................707 639-4414
David Brockman, *President*
EMP: 150
SQ FT: 18,000
SALES (est): 5.6MM
SALES (corp-wide): 292.1MM **Privately Held**
SIC: 1799 Coating, caulking & weather, water & fireproofing; coating of metal structures at construction site; coating of concrete structures with plastic
HQ: Muehlhan Surface Protection Inc
2320 Cordelia Rd
Fairfield CA 94534
707 639-4421

(P-3555)
MY OFFICE INC
6060 Nncy Rdge Dr Ste 100, San Diego (92121)
PHONE.................................858 549-6700
Ronald D Harrell, *CEO*
▲ **EMP:** 65
SQ FT: 40,000
SALES (est): 18.7MM **Privately Held**
WEB: www.4myoffice.com
SIC: 1799 Office furniture installation

(P-3556)
NAVAL COATING INC
3475 E St, San Diego (92102-3335)
PHONE.................................619 234-8366
Alan Lerchbacker, *President*
EMP: 149
SQ FT: 50,000
SALES (est): 22.6MM **Privately Held**
WEB: www.navalcoating.com
SIC: 1799 1721 2851 Sandblasting of building exteriors; industrial painting; paints & allied products

(P-3557)
NORTH VALLEY CONSTRUCTION INC
4010 Raymond Rd, Livermore (94551-9776)
P.O. Box 2511 (94551-2511)
PHONE.................................925 373-1246
Charles E Inderbitzen, *President*
Sandra Inderbitzen, *Treasurer*
EMP: 70
SQ FT: 1,000
SALES (est): 4.7MM **Privately Held**
SIC: 1799 Construction site cleanup

(P-3558)
NORTHSTAR CONTG GROUP INC (DH)
2614-20 Barrington Ct, Hayward (94545)
PHONE.................................510 491-1330
Trip Turner, *President*
Michael Kinelski, *Co-President*
James Fredrickson, *Vice Pres*
Jack Hesotian, *Vice Pres*
John Leonard, *Vice Pres*
EMP: 59
SALES (est): 50.7MM
SALES (corp-wide): 371.8MM **Privately Held**
SIC: 1799 1795 Asbestos removal & encapsulation; wrecking & demolition work

HQ: Northstar Group Services, Inc.
370 7th Ave Ste 1803
New York NY 10001
212 951-3660

(P-3559)
PACIFIC AQUASCAPE INC
18685 Main St Ste 101, Huntington Beach (92648-1719)
PHONE.................................714 481-7260
Johan Perslow, *Chairman*
Cory M Severson, *President*
Kevin Curran, *COO*
Mark Krebs, *Vice Pres*
Bob Lobo, *Vice Pres*
EMP: 75
SQ FT: 21,000
SALES (est): 15.8MM **Privately Held**
SIC: 1799 Swimming pool construction

(P-3560)
PACIFIC HOME WORKS INC
20725 S Wstn Ave Ste 100, Torrance (90501)
PHONE.................................310 781-3012
Marcus Mac, *President*
Adam Konrad, *Vice Pres*
EMP: 195
SQ FT: 7,000
SALES (est): 18.8MM **Privately Held**
SIC: 1799 1751 Kitchen & bathroom remodeling; window & door installation & erection; window & door (prefabricated) installation

(P-3561)
PACIFIC LINE CLEAN-UP INC
27601 Forbes Rd Ste 29, Laguna Niguel (92677-1240)
P.O. Box 7765 (92607-7765)
PHONE.................................949 348-0245
Raul Rios, *President*
Fermina Rios, *Vice Pres*
EMP: 120
SQ FT: 1,000
SALES (est): 8.2MM **Privately Held**
SIC: 1799 Cleaning new buildings after construction

(P-3562)
PARC SPECIALTY CONTRACTORS
1400 Vinci Ave, Sacramento (95838-1716)
PHONE.................................916 992-5405
Greg Johnson, *President*
John Kimmel, *Vice Pres*
Laura Greer, *Division Mgr*
Paul Lane, *Admin Sec*
Mike Kidd,
EMP: 85
SQ FT: 10,000
SALES: 6MM **Privately Held**
SIC: 1799 Asbestos removal & encapsulation

(P-3563)
PARKING NETWORK INC
350 S Figueroa St Ste 420, Los Angeles (90071-1203)
PHONE.................................213 613-1500
Frank Zelaya, *CEO*
Rose Zelaya, *President*
Ron Parto, *Vice Pres*
Todd Wensley, *Vice Pres*
EMP: 120
SQ FT: 2,400
SALES: 4MM **Privately Held**
WEB: www.parkingnetwork.net
SIC: 1799 8748 Parking lot maintenance; business consulting

(P-3564)
PARTITIONS INSTALLATION INC
Also Called: Showcase Installations
13021 Leffingwell Ave, Santa Fe Springs (90670-6341)
PHONE.................................562 207-9868
Rick A Faist Jr, *President*
Debbie Galindo, *Project Mgr*
Carlos Mispireta, *Sr Project Mgr*
▲ **EMP:** 60
SQ FT: 60,000
SALES: 4MM **Privately Held**
WEB: www.showcaseinstall.com
SIC: 1799 Demountable partition installation

(P-3565)
PATRICK DEAN BRYAN
Also Called: Affordable Installations
12481 Lttle Deer Creek Ln, Nevada City (95959-8919)
PHONE.................................530 273-5484
Patrick Dean Bryan, *Owner*
Patricia Bryan, *Principal*
EMP: 60
SALES (est): 2.9MM **Privately Held**
SIC: 1799 Office furniture installation

(P-3566)
PEACE OFFICRS FOR A GRN ENVIRN
21800 Barton Rd Ste 108, Grand Terrace (92313-4438)
PHONE.................................951 824-7705
Patricia Gonzalez, *President*
EMP: 50
SALES (est): 3.5MM **Privately Held**
SIC: 1799 Appliance installation

(P-3567)
PREFERRED INSULATION CONTRS (PA)
1691 Jenks Dr, Corona (92880-2514)
PHONE.................................951 735-3725
Charles Steinhaus, *President*
Aj Newton, *Project Mgr*
Beleza Terrill, *Human Resources*
Kevin Panella, *Sales Associate*
EMP: 52
SALES (est): 6.9MM **Privately Held**
SIC: 1799 Insulation of pipes & boilers

(P-3568)
PREMIER POOLS AND SPAS LP (PA)
11250 Pyrites Way, Gold River (95670-4481)
PHONE.................................916 852-0223
Keith H Harbeck, *General Ptnr*
Paul Porter, *General Ptnr*
Karen Querido, *Technology*
Noona Synhorst, *Manager*
EMP: 90
SQ FT: 3,500
SALES (est): 25.7MM **Privately Held**
SIC: 1799 Spa or hot tub installation or construction; swimming pool construction

(P-3569)
PROJECT GO INCORPORATED
801 Vernon St, Roseville (95678-3149)
PHONE.................................916 782-3443
Linda Timbers, *Exec Dir*
Lillian Durbin, *Opers Staff*
EMP: 50
SQ FT: 3,000
SALES (est): 4.5MM **Privately Held**
SIC: 1799 Waterproofing

(P-3570)
PSG FENCING CORPORATION (PA)
Also Called: Soares Lumber Company
6630 Monterey Rd, Gilroy (95020-6644)
PHONE.................................831 726-2002
Frank Soares, *President*
EMP: 200
SQ FT: 5,000
SALES (est): 9.5MM **Privately Held**
SIC: 1799 5031 5211 Fence construction; lumber, plywood & millwork; lumber products

(P-3571)
PW STEPHENS ENVMTL INC (PA)
15201 Pipeline Ln Ste B, Huntington Beach (92649-5704)
PHONE.................................714 892-2028
Scott Johnson, *President*
EMP: 52
SALES (est): 27.6MM **Privately Held**
WEB: www.pwsei.com
SIC: 1799 Athletic & recreation facilities construction; asbestos removal & encapsulation

(P-3572)
PW STEPHENS ENVMTL INC
4047 Clipper Ct, Fremont (94538-6540)
PHONE.................................510 651-9506
Steve Macfarlane, *Principal*
EMP: 55
SALES (corp-wide): 27.6MM **Privately Held**
SIC: 1799 Athletic & recreation facilities construction
PA: P.W. Stephens Environmental, Inc.
15201 Pipeline Ln Ste B
Huntington Beach CA 92649
714 892-2028

(P-3573)
QUALITY SYSTEMS INSTALLATIONS
Also Called: Q S I
212 Shaw Rd Ste 3, South San Francisco (94080-6613)
PHONE.................................650 875-9000
Jon Chase, *President*
Daniel Castillo, *Vice Pres*
Robert W Lindstrom, *Vice Pres*
EMP: 60
SQ FT: 40,000
SALES (est): 4.3MM **Privately Held**
WEB: www.qsiltd.com
SIC: 1799 Office furniture installation

(P-3574)
RAINBOW WTRPROFING RESTORATION
600 Treat Ave, San Francisco (94110-2016)
PHONE.................................415 641-1578
Christopher Abel, *President*
Rob Browne, *Corp Secy*
Leticia Ramirez, *Admin Asst*
Alfredo Lopez, *Warehouse Mgr*
Ken Bengtson, *Manager*
EMP: 124
SALES: 18MM **Privately Held**
WEB: www.rainbow415.com
SIC: 1799 Waterproofing

(P-3575)
RAYCON ENVIRONMENTAL CNSTR
882 Patriot Dr Ste G, Moorpark (93021-3544)
PHONE.................................805 955-0900
Dennis Ray, *President*
EMP: 50
SALES: 5MM **Privately Held**
WEB: www.rayconenvironmental.com
SIC: 1799 Waterproofing

(P-3576)
REGENT AEROSPACE CORPORATION (PA)
28110 Harrison Pkwy, Valencia (91355-4109)
PHONE.................................661 257-3000
Reza Soltanianzadeh, *CEO*
Reza Soltanian, *President*
Everardo Guereca, *COO*
Tim Garvin, *Vice Pres*
Scott Wargo, *Vice Pres*
▲ **EMP:** 200
SQ FT: 90,000
SALES: 45MM **Privately Held**
WEB: www.regentaerospace.com
SIC: 1799 5088 Athletic & recreation facilities construction; aircraft & parts

(P-3577)
RESTEC CONTRACTORS INC
22955 Kidder St, Hayward (94545-1670)
PHONE.................................510 670-0100
John Andrzejewski, *President*
Freeman Boyett, *Treasurer*
R Todd Fearon, *Vice Pres*
David Brueggen, *Asst Sec*
EMP: 100
SALES (est): 9.9MM
SALES (corp-wide): 461.9MM **Privately Held**
WEB: www.resteccontractors.com
SIC: 1799 Asbestos removal & encapsulation

HQ: Vertecs Corporation
14700 Ne 95th St Ste 201
Redmond WA
425 885-1990

(P-3578)
REY-CREST ROOFG WATERPROOFING
Also Called: Rey-Crest Roofg Waterproofing
3065 Verdugo Rd, Los Angeles
(90065-2014)
PHONE..............................323 257-9329
George Reyes, *President*
Georgia Reyes, *Corp Secy*
Harold Lim, *Project Mgr*
Michael Reyes, *Project Mgr*
EMP: 80
SQ FT: 10,000
SALES (est): 8.8MM **Privately Held**
WEB: www.reycrest.com
SIC: 1799 1761 Waterproofing; roofing contractor

(P-3579)
SADDLE CORP (PA)
Also Called: Saddleback Waterproofing
23531 Ridge Route Dr C, Laguna Hills
(92653-1504)
PHONE..............................949 589-3422
Larry Goldenberg, *President*
Christee Grecco, *Office Mgr*
EMP: 60
SQ FT: 4,800
SALES (est): 7.7MM **Privately Held**
SIC: 1799 Waterproofing

(P-3580)
SCENIC ROUTE INC
13516 Desmond St, Pacoima
(91331-2315)
PHONE..............................818 896-6006
Ulf Henriksson, *President*
Sean Culhane, *Vice Pres*
Micheal Goglia, *Vice Pres*
Ron Gould, *Creative Dir*
John Giordano, *Info Tech Mgr*
▲ **EMP:** 50 **EST:** 1987
SQ FT: 25,000
SALES (est): 6.4MM **Privately Held**
WEB: www.the-scenic-route.com
SIC: 1799 Prop, set or scenery construction, theatrical

(P-3581)
SCHAEFER MARY-JUDITH
Also Called: Schaefer Parking Lot Service
7202 Petterson Ln, Paramount
(90723-2022)
PHONE..............................562 634-3164
Mary-Judith Schaefer, *Owner*
EMP: 55
SALES (est): 1.3MM **Privately Held**
SIC: 1799 Parking lot maintenance

(P-3582)
SELEX INC (PA)
Also Called: Borg Redwood Fences
442 Longfellow St, Livermore
(94550-7122)
P.O. Box 5430, Pleasanton (94566-1430)
PHONE..............................707 836-8836
Julie Borg, *CEO*
Reuben Borg, *President*
Dave Lamarre, *Vice Pres*
EMP: 100
SALES (est): 12.3MM **Privately Held**
WEB: www.borgfence.com
SIC: 1799 Fence construction

(P-3583)
SELEX INC
930 Shiloh Rd, Windsor (95492-9659)
PHONE..............................707 836-8836
Dave Boettger, *Branch Mgr*
EMP: 51
SALES (corp-wide): 12.3MM **Privately Held**
SIC: 1799 Fence construction
PA: Selex, Inc.
442 Longfellow St
Livermore CA 94550
707 836-8836

(P-3584)
SHADE STRUCTURES INC
1085 N Main St Ste C, Orange
(92867-5458)
PHONE..............................714 427-6981
John Saunders, *CEO*
Adam Auten, *Finance*
EMP: 349 **Publicly Held**
SIC: 1799 2394 Building site preparation; canvas & related products; shades, canvas: made from purchased materials
HQ: Shade Structures, Inc.
8505 Chancellor Row
Dallas TX 75247
214 905-9500

(P-3585)
SHORING ENGINEERS
Also Called: Shoring & Excavating
12645 Clark St, Santa Fe Springs
(90670-3951)
PHONE..............................562 944-9331
George A Woodley Sr, *Vice Pres*
George A Woodleysr, *President*
Ren Contreras, *Vice Pres*
Rene Contreras, *Vice Pres*
Jason E Weinstein, *Vice Pres*
▲ **EMP:** 60 **EST:** 1966
SALES (est): 14.1MM **Privately Held**
WEB: www.shoringengineers.com
SIC: 1799 8711 Shore cleaning & maintenance; engineering services

(P-3586)
SOUTH COAST FENCING CENTER
3518 W Lake Center Dr C, Santa Ana
(92704-6979)
PHONE..............................714 549-2946
Brenden Richard, *President*
Mary Rafanelli, *Office Mgr*
EMP: 60
SALES: 135.8K **Privately Held**
WEB: www.southcoastfencing.com
SIC: 1799 Fence construction

(P-3587)
SPECIAL SERVICE CONTRS INC
3580 Airport Rd, Paso Robles
(93446-9554)
P.O. Box 3121 (93447-3121)
PHONE..............................805 227-1081
Russell Wilson, *President*
EMP: 51
SQ FT: 1,600
SALES (est): 7.1MM **Privately Held**
WEB: www.sscinfo.com
SIC: 1799 Cable splicing service

(P-3588)
STUMBAUGH & ASSOCIATES INC (PA)
3303 N San Fernando Blvd, Burbank
(91504-2531)
PHONE..............................818 240-1627
Jeff Stumbaugh, *President*
Richard Stumbaugh, *Ch of Bd*
Tim Reardon, *Vice Pres*
Christine Dark, *Director*
EMP: 54 **EST:** 1965
SALES (est): 12.9MM **Privately Held**
WEB: www.stumbaugh.net
SIC: 1799 5046 Demountable partition installation; partitions

(P-3589)
SUNRIZE STAGING INC
1326 Mission Rd, Escondido (92029-1101)
P.O. Box 300067 (92030-0067)
PHONE..............................760 743-2043
Lucian Luly, *President*
EMP: 51
SQ FT: 600
SALES (est): 2.5MM **Privately Held**
WEB: www.sunrizestaging.com
SIC: 1799 Scaffolding construction

(P-3590)
TAILORED LIVING CHOICES LLC
1957 Sierra Ave, NAPA (94558-2840)
PHONE..............................707 259-0526
Vicki Robinson, *Mng Member*
Stacy Perez,
Connie Kirtlink, *Manager*

EMP: 112
SALES (est): 7.3MM **Privately Held**
SIC: 1799 Home/office interiors finishing, furnishing & remodeling

(P-3591)
TAIT ENVIRONMENTAL SVCS INC (PA)
701 Parkcenter Dr, Santa Ana
(92705-3541)
P.O. Box 11118 (92711-1118)
PHONE..............................714 560-8200
Thomas F Tait, *CEO*
Richard Tait, *President*
Nick Nyugen, *Project Mgr*
Chuck Bentley, *Manager*
Douglas Fenn, *Manager*
▲ **EMP:** 55
SQ FT: 8,900
SALES (est): 13.6MM **Privately Held**
SIC: 1799 8748 Gas leakage detection; environmental consultant

(P-3592)
TESERRA (PA)
Also Called: California Pools
86100 Avenue 54, Coachella (92236-3813)
P.O. Box 1280 (92236-1280)
PHONE..............................760 340-9000
Bob Smith, *President*
James Harebottle, *CFO*
EMP: 400
SQ FT: 10,000
SALES (est): 43.1MM **Privately Held**
SIC: 1799 Swimming pool construction

(P-3593)
THE TEECOR GROUP INC
Also Called: Key Environmental Services
1450 S Burlington Ave, Los Angeles
(90006-5409)
PHONE..............................213 632-2350
Kalani Childs, *President*
Eric Youssef, *Vice Pres*
EMP: 60
SQ FT: 5,000
SALES (est): 5.5MM **Privately Held**
WEB: www.teecor.com
SIC: 1799 Asbestos removal & encapsulation

(P-3594)
THUNDER MOUNTAIN ENTERPRISES (PA)
9335 Elder Creek Rd, Sacramento
(95829-9339)
P.O. Box 292821 (95829-2821)
PHONE..............................916 381-3400
Dave Smiley, *President*
Beth Smiley, *Treasurer*
Carrie Young, *Manager*
EMP: 61
SQ FT: 5,000
SALES: 7MM **Privately Held**
WEB: www.tme1.com
SIC: 1799 Corrosion control installation

(P-3595)
TOPBUILD SERVICES GROUP CORP
Also Called: Masco
1341 Old Oakland Rd, San Jose
(95112-1317)
PHONE..............................408 882-0411
Bob Colla, *Branch Mgr*
Rick Henson, *Contractor*
EMP: 75
SALES (corp-wide): 1.9B **Publicly Held**
WEB: www.galeind.com
SIC: 1799 Prefabricated fireplace installation
HQ: Topbuild Services Group Corp.
475 N Williamson Blvd
Daytona Beach FL 32114
386 304-2200

(P-3596)
TORRES FENCE CO INC
2357 S Orange Ave, Fresno (93725-1021)
P.O. Box 10137 (93745-0137)
PHONE..............................559 237-4141
Ralph Torres, *President*
Rebecca Torres, *Corp Secy*
Ralph Torres Jr, *Vice Pres*
Rene J Torres, *Vice Pres*

Mari Salas, *Admin Sec*
▲ **EMP:** 50
SQ FT: 6,000
SALES (est): 6.3MM **Privately Held**
WEB: www.torresfence.com
SIC: 1799 3315 3496 Fence construction; chain link fencing; barbed wire, made from purchased wire

(P-3597)
TOURNESOL SITEWORKS LLC (PA)
2930 Faber St, Union City (94587-1214)
PHONE..............................800 542-2282
Christopher J Lyon, *Mng Member*
Corina Ornelas, *Manager*
▲ **EMP:** 55
SQ FT: 10,000
SALES: 18MM **Privately Held**
WEB: www.plantertechnology.com
SIC: 1799 5023 3444 1521 Fiberglass work; home furnishings, wicker, rattan or reed; metal roofing & roof drainage equipment; patio & deck construction & repair; retaining wall construction; fountain repair

(P-3598)
TROYER CONTRACTING COMPANY INC
10122 Freeman Ave, Santa Fe Springs
(90670-3408)
PHONE..............................562 944-6452
Mark Troyer, *CEO*
▲ **EMP:** 55 **EST:** 1995
SQ FT: 15,208
SALES (est): 9.5MM **Privately Held**
SIC: 1799 1761 Waterproofing; roofing contractor

(P-3599)
UNITED SPECTRUM INC
Also Called: Spectrum Abatement
1910 N Lime St, Orange (92865-4123)
P.O. Box 5747 (92863-5747)
PHONE..............................714 283-1010
David Fischer, *President*
EMP: 50
SQ FT: 20,000
SALES (est): 5.3MM **Privately Held**
WEB: www.asbestos-removal.com
SIC: 1799 1795 Asbestos removal & encapsulation; demolition, buildings & other structures

(P-3600)
UP N DOWN SCAFFOLD COMPANY INC (PA)
5216 Naranja St, San Diego (92114-3521)
P.O. Box 300067, Escondido (92030-0067)
PHONE..............................619 266-0542
Sue A Luly, *CEO*
Paul Thomas, *Vice Pres*
EMP: 51
SQ FT: 1,200
SALES (est): 3MM **Privately Held**
SIC: 1799 Scaffolding construction

(P-3601)
VALENTINE CORPORATION
111 Pelican Way, San Rafael (94901-5519)
P.O. Box 9337 (94912-9337)
PHONE..............................415 453-3732
Toll Free:..........................877 -
Robert O Valentine, *CEO*
Robert Valentine Jr, *President*
Alan Hanley, *CFO*
Madeline Valentine, *Corp Secy*
David Levine, *Vice Pres*
EMP: 50
SQ FT: 3,000
SALES (est): 11.9MM **Privately Held**
SIC: 1799 8711 1622 Waterproofing; building construction consultant; bridge construction

(P-3602)
VALLEY SUN MECHANICAL CNSTR
4205 Atlas Ct, Bakersfield (93308-4510)
P.O. Box 515, Oxford IN (47971-0515)
PHONE..............................661 321-9070
Charles J Richmond, *President*
EMP: 64
SQ FT: 5,200

PRODUCTS & SVCS

SALES (est): 4.6MM **Privately Held**
WEB: www.vsmc.com
SIC: **1799** Food service equipment installation; welding on site

(P-3603)
VALLEY WATER PROOFING INC
825 Civic Center Dr Ste 6, Santa Clara
(95050-3961)
P.O. Box 20003, San Jose (95160-0003)
PHONE..........................408 985-7701
Donna O'Brien, *President*
Michael O'Brien, *Vice Pres*
Kevin Ruffoni, *General Mgr*
Jay Perez, *Project Mgr*
Mark Furtado, *Opers Mgr*
EMP: 80
SQ FT: 1,000
SALES (est): 9.2MM **Privately Held**
WEB: www.valleyh2o.com
SIC: **1799** Waterproofing

(P-3604)
VIKING POOLS LLC
121 Crawford Rd, Williams (95987)
PHONE..........................530 473-5319
Alan K Stahl, *Branch Mgr*
Angelo Saldana, *General Mgr*
EMP: 50 **Privately Held**
WEB: www.cpcpools.com
SIC: **1799** Swimming pool construction
HQ: Viking Pools, Llc
175 Viking Dr
Jane Lew WV 26378
530 473-5319

(P-3605)
WALTON ENGINEERING INC
3900 Commerce Dr, West Sacramento
(95691-2157)
P.O. Box 1025 (95691-1025)
PHONE..........................916 372-1888
Michael Walton, *President*
Richard Walton, *Vice Pres*
EMP: 65
SQ FT: 13,000
SALES (est): 13.4MM **Privately Held**
SIC: **1799** 1542 7389 Service station equipment installation, maintenance & repair; service station construction; drafting service, except temporary help

(P-3606)
WASHINGTON ORNA IR WORKS INC (PA)
Also Called: Washington Iron Works
17926 S Broadway, Gardena (90248-3540)
P.O. Box 460 (90247-0846)
PHONE..........................310 327-8660
Daniel Welsh, *CEO*
Chris Powell, *CFO*
Tom Pederson, *Treasurer*
Steve Simester, *Project Mgr*
Luke Welsh, *VP Opers*
EMP: 90 EST: 1966
SQ FT: 141,240
SALES (est): 24.6MM **Privately Held**
WEB: www.washingtoniron.com
SIC: **1799** 3446 Ornamental metal work; architectural metalwork

(P-3607)
WAYNE PERRY INC (PA)
8281 Commonwealth Ave, Buena Park
(90621-2537)
PHONE..........................714 826-0352
Wayne Perry, *President*
Tom Ritchie, *President*
Tom Wyper, *President*
Adam Leiter, *Treasurer*
Ed Smith, *Assoc VP*
EMP: 185
SQ FT: 4,000
SALES (est): 45.7MM **Privately Held**
WEB: www.wpinc.com
SIC: **1799** 8711 Decontamination services; petroleum storage tank installation, underground; engineering services

(P-3608)
WELL WITHIN SPA
417 Cedar St, Santa Cruz (95060-4304)
PHONE..........................831 458-9355
David Levan, *Owner*
Eric Heckert, *Co-Owner*
EMP: 60

SALES: 360K **Privately Held**
WEB: www.wellwithinspa.com
SIC: **1799** 7299 Spa or hot tub installation or construction; massage parlor & steam bath services

(P-3609)
WEST COAST FIRESTOPPING INC
1130 W Trenton Ave, Orange (92867-3536)
PHONE..........................714 935-1104
Karl Stoll, *President*
Lisa Stoll, *General Mgr*
Joe Riordan, *Marketing Staff*
Keith Stoll, *Sales Staff*
Megan Featherston,
EMP: 80
SALES (est): 6.9MM **Privately Held**
SIC: **1799** Fireproofing buildings

(P-3610)
WESTAR MANUFACTURING INC
Also Called: Fix Shore
13217 Laureldale Ave, Downey
(90242-5140)
PHONE..........................562 633-0581
Thomas Feldmar, *President*
EMP: 60
SALES (est): 1.7MM
SALES (corp-wide): 67.5MM **Privately Held**
SIC: **1799** 3531 Shoring & underpinning work; construction machinery
PA: Trench Plate Rental Co.
13217 Laureldale Ave
Downey CA 90242
562 602-1642

(P-3611)
WESTERN MAGNESITE INC
11927 Sherman Rd Unit 1, North Hollywood
(91605-3717)
PHONE..........................818 255-1150
Bernard Fainstein, *Owner*
EMP: 50 EST: 2000
SALES (est): 1.9MM **Privately Held**
WEB: www.westernmagnesite.com
SIC: **1799** Waterproofing

(P-3612)
WLMD (PA)
Also Called: Wellmade Products
1715 Kibby Rd, Merced (95341-9301)
PHONE..........................209 723-9120
Mark R Riley, *CEO*
Doug Bartman, *CFO*
Steve Squires, *General Mgr*
Jerry Yon, *Controller*
▲ EMP: 127
SQ FT: 120,000
SALES (est): 17.8MM **Privately Held**
WEB: www.wlmd.com
SIC: **1799** 1761 Lightning conductor erection; roofing, siding & sheet metal work

(P-3613)
WOODS MAINTENANCE SERVICES INC
Also Called: Hydro-Pressure Systems
7260 Atoll Ave, North Hollywood
(91605-4104)
PHONE..........................818 764-2515
Barry Woods, *President*
Diane Woods, *Principal*
Jeff Woods, *General Mgr*
Enrique Lopez, *Project Mgr*
Josh Woods, *Opers Staff*
EMP: 135
SQ FT: 26,000
SALES (est): 17.5MM **Privately Held**
WEB: www.graffiticontrol.com
SIC: **1799** Cleaning building exteriors

4011 Railroads, Line-Hauling Operations

(P-3614)
BNSF RAILWAY COMPANY
Also Called: Burlington Northern
740 Carnegie Dr, San Bernardino
(92408-3571)
PHONE..........................909 386-4002
EMP: 120

SALES (corp-wide): 242.1B **Publicly Held**
SIC: **4011**
HQ: Bnsf Railway Company
2650 Lou Menk Dr
Fort Worth TX 76131
800 795-2673

(P-3615)
BNSF RAILWAY COMPANY
Also Called: Burlington Northern
200 N Avenue H, Barstow (92311-2553)
PHONE..........................760 255-7803
Brandon Mabry, *Superintendent*
EMP: 110
SALES (corp-wide): 242.1B **Publicly Held**
WEB: www.billpurdy.com
SIC: **4011** 4111 4213 4225 Interurban railways; commuter rail passenger operation; trucking, except local; general warehousing; railroad freight agency; railroad property lessors
HQ: Bnsf Railway Company
2650 Lou Menk Dr
Fort Worth TX 76131
800 795-2673

(P-3616)
BNSF RAILWAY COMPANY
Also Called: Burlington Northern
6300 Sheila St, Commerce (90040-2411)
PHONE..........................323 869-3002
Julian Sanchez, *Superintendent*
EMP: 180
SALES (corp-wide): 242.1B **Publicly Held**
WEB: www.billpurdy.com
SIC: **4011** Railroads, line-haul operating
HQ: Bnsf Railway Company
2650 Lou Menk Dr
Fort Worth TX 76131
800 795-2673

(P-3617)
BNSF RAILWAY COMPANY
Also Called: Burlington Northern
3770 E Washington Blvd, Vernon
(90058-8125)
PHONE..........................323 267-4133
John Hynes, *Principal*
EMP: 200
SALES (corp-wide): 242.1B **Publicly Held**
WEB: www.billpurdy.com
SIC: **4011** Railroads, line-haul operating
HQ: Bnsf Railway Company
2650 Lou Menk Dr
Fort Worth TX 76131
800 795-2673

(P-3618)
CALIFRNIA HIGH SPEED RAIL AUTH
770 L St Ste 620, Sacramento
(95814-3385)
PHONE..........................916 324-1541
Dan Richard, *Ch of Bd*
EMP: 100
SALES (est): 8.4MM **Privately Held**
SIC: **4011** Railroads, line-haul operating
PA: State Of California
State Capital
Sacramento CA 95814
916 445-2864

(P-3619)
CSX CORPORATION
14863 Clark Ave, Hacienda Heights
(91745-1308)
PHONE..........................626 336-1377
EMP: 149
SALES (corp-wide): 12.6B **Publicly Held**
SIC: **4011**
PA: Csx Corporation
500 Water St Fl 15
Jacksonville FL 32202
904 359-3200

(P-3620)
NATIONAL RAILROAD PASS CORP
601 Marina Vista Ave, Martinez
(94553-1132)
PHONE..........................925 335-5180
EMP: 2046 **Publicly Held**

SIC: **4011** 4013 Interurban railways; railroad terminals
HQ: National Railroad Passenger Corporation
1 Massachusetts Ave Nw
Washington DC 20001
202 906-3741

(P-3621)
NATIONAL RAILROAD PASS CORP
Also Called: Amtrak
1050 Kettner Blvd Ste 1, San Diego
(92101-3339)
PHONE..........................619 239-9989
Debbi Dewfwood, *Branch Mgr*
EMP: 138 **Publicly Held**
WEB: www.amtrak.com
SIC: **4011** 9621 Interurban railways; regulation, administration of transportation;
HQ: National Railroad Passenger Corporation
1 Massachusetts Ave Nw
Washington DC 20001
202 906-3741

(P-3622)
PACIFIC HARBOR LINE INC (HQ)
705 N Henry Ford Ave, Wilmington
(90744-6716)
PHONE..........................310 834-4594
Peter Gilbertson, *Ch of Bd*
Otis L Cliatt, *President*
Bruce A Lieberman, *CFO*
R Scott Morgan, *Controller*
Mark Sidman, *General Counsel*
EMP: 150
SALES (est): 15.2MM
SALES (corp-wide): 49.5MM **Privately Held**
SIC: **4011** Railroads, line-haul operating
PA: Anacostia Rail Holdings Company
224 S Michigan Ave # 330
Chicago IL 60604
312 362-1888

(P-3623)
R R DONNELLEY & SONS COMPANY
Also Called: Moore Business Forms
1646 N Calif Blvd Ste 510, Walnut Creek
(94596-4171)
PHONE..........................925 951-1320
Wes McCracken, *Branch Mgr*
EMP: 50
SQ FT: 9,000
SALES (corp-wide): 6.9B **Publicly Held**
WEB: www.moore.com
SIC: **4011** 5943 Railroads, line-haul operating; office forms & supplies
PA: R. R. Donnelley & Sons Company
35 W Wacker Dr Ste 3650
Chicago IL 60601
312 326-8000

(P-3624)
SAN JOAQUIN VALLEY RAILROAD CO
221 N F St, Exeter (93221-1119)
P.O. Box 937 (93221-0937)
PHONE..........................559 592-1857
Randy Perry, *CEO*
Rex Bergholm, *President*
Richard McGowan, *Chief Mktg Ofcr*
Steve Coomes, *Vice Pres*
Joe Evans, *General Mgr*
EMP: 200
SQ FT: 1,100
SALES: 16.4MM
SALES (corp-wide): 2.2B **Publicly Held**
WEB: www.statesrail.com
SIC: **4011** Railroads, line-haul operating
HQ: Railamerica, Inc.
20 West Ave
Darien CT 06820

(P-3625)
SIERRA ENTERTAINMENT
341 Industrial Way, Woodland
(95776-6012)
PHONE..........................530 666-9646
David Magew, *President*
Robert Pinoli, *Vice Pres*

Torgny Nilsson, *Admin Sec*
EMP: 50
SALES (est): 83.7K **Privately Held**
SIC: 4011 Railroads, line-haul operating
PA: Sierra Railroad Company
  341 Industrial Way
  Woodland CA 95776

(P-3626)
UNION PACIFIC CORPORATION
9451 Atkinson St Ste 100, Roseville
(95747-9301)
P.O. Box 42 (95747)
PHONE.............................916 789-5311
Mike Evans, *President*
EMP: 503
SALES (corp-wide): 21.2B **Publicly Held**
SIC: 4011 Railroads, line-haul operating
PA: Union Pacific Corporation
  1400 Douglas St
  Omaha NE 68179
  402 544-5000

(P-3627)
UNION PACIFIC RAILROAD COMPANY
999 Paso Robles St, Paso Robles
(93446-2628)
PHONE.............................805 286-5851
Athey Roy, *Branch Mgr*
EMP: 80
SALES (corp-wide): 21.2B **Publicly Held**
SIC: 4011 Railroads, line-haul operating
HQ: Union Pacific Railroad Company Inc
  1400 Douglas St
  Omaha NE 68179
  402 544-5000

(P-3628)
UNION PACIFIC RAILROAD COMPANY
3135 N Weber Ave, Fresno (93705-3655)
PHONE.............................559 443-2244
Randy Esquiza, *Manager*
EMP: 125
SALES (corp-wide): 21.2B **Publicly Held**
WEB: www.uprr.com
SIC: 4011 Railroads, line-haul operating
HQ: Union Pacific Railroad Company Inc
  1400 Douglas St
  Omaha NE 68179
  402 544-5000

(P-3629)
UNION PACIFIC RAILROAD COMPANY
2000 S Sycamore Ave, Bloomington
(92316-2463)
PHONE.............................909 685-2710
EMP: 80
SALES (corp-wide): 21.2B **Publicly Held**
SIC: 4011 Railroads, line-haul operating
HQ: Union Pacific Railroad Company Inc
  1400 Douglas St
  Omaha NE 68179
  402 544-5000

(P-3630)
UNION PACIFIC RAILROAD COMPANY
9391 Atkinson St Ste 100, Roseville
(95747-9605)
PHONE.............................916 789-5930
Jack Huddleston, *Branch Mgr*
EMP: 80
SALES (corp-wide): 21.2B **Publicly Held**
SIC: 4011 Railroads, line-haul operating
HQ: Union Pacific Railroad Company Inc
  1400 Douglas St
  Omaha NE 68179
  402 544-5000

(P-3631)
UNION PACIFIC RAILROAD COMPANY
4341 E Washington Blvd, Commerce
(90023-4470)
PHONE.............................213 446-1900
Ramiro Barba, *Manager*
EMP: 80
SALES (corp-wide): 21.2B **Publicly Held**
SIC: 4011 Railroads, line-haul operating

HQ: Union Pacific Railroad Company Inc
  1400 Douglas St
  Omaha NE 68179
  402 544-5000

(P-3632)
UNION PACIFIC RAILROAD COMPANY
10031 Fthlls Blvd Ste 200, Roseville
(95747)
PHONE.............................916 789-6055
Karen Calli, *Manager*
Lynda Risucci, *Admin Asst*
Robert N Belt,
Michael L Johnson,
James C Spaulding,
EMP: 120
SALES (corp-wide): 21.2B **Publicly Held**
WEB: www.uprm.com
SIC: 4011 Railroads, line-haul operating
HQ: Union Pacific Railroad Company Inc
  1400 Douglas St
  Omaha NE 68179
  402 544-5000

(P-3633)
UNION PACIFIC RAILROAD COMPANY
Also Called: Southern Pacific Railroad
730 Sumner St, Bakersfield (93305)
PHONE.............................661 321-4604
Bill Gafford, *President*
EMP: 80
SALES (corp-wide): 21.2B **Publicly Held**
WEB: www.uprr.com
SIC: 4011 Railroads, line-haul operating
HQ: Union Pacific Railroad Company Inc
  1400 Douglas St
  Omaha NE 68179
  402 544-5000

4013 Switching & Terminal Svcs

(P-3634)
LOS ANGELES JUNCTION RLWY CO
4433 Exchange Ave, Vernon (90058-2622)
PHONE.............................323 277-2004
Chuck Potempa, *CEO*
Rob Rellyl, *President*
Rm Reilly, *Vice Pres*
EMP: 50 **EST:** 1922
SALES (est): 4.3MM
SALES (corp-wide): 242.1B **Publicly Held**
WEB: www.billpurdy.com
SIC: 4013 Switching & terminal services
HQ: Bnsf Railway Company
  2650 Lou Menk Dr
  Fort Worth TX 76131
  800 795-2673

4111 Local & Suburban Transit

(P-3635)
ACCESS SERVICES
Also Called: Access Paratransit
3449 Santa Anita Ave, El Monte
(91731-2424)
P.O. Box 5728 (91734-1728)
PHONE.............................213 270-6000
Doran J Barnes, *CEO*
Shelly Verrinder, *Exec Dir*
EMP: 80
SALES: 144.1MM **Privately Held**
SIC: 4111 Local & suburban transit

(P-3636)
AIRLINE COACH SERVICE INC (PA)
863 Malcolm Rd, Burlingame (94010-1406)
P.O. Box 282998, San Francisco (94128-2998)
PHONE.............................650 697-7733
Gregory Choo, *Ch of Bd*
Kyung C Lee, *President*
Alex Morrison, *Vice Pres*
EMP: 90
SQ FT: 7,000

SALES (est): 6.6MM **Privately Held**
SIC: 4111 Airport transportation services, regular route

(P-3637)
AIRPORT CONNECTION INC
Also Called: Roadrunner Shuttle
95 Dawson Dr, Camarillo (93012-8001)
PHONE.............................805 389-8196
Sumaia Sandlin, *CEO*
Desmond P Sandlin, *Admin Sec*
Nitin Pai, *Info Tech Dir*
Charles Sandlin, *Technology*
Roschelle Ayon, *Human Res Dir*
EMP: 180
SQ FT: 3,500
SALES (est): 23.7MM **Privately Held**
WEB: www.rrshuttle.com
SIC: 4111 4119 Airport transportation; airport transportation services, regular route; limousine rental, with driver

(P-3638)
ALAMEDA-CONTRA COSTA TRNST DST (PA)
Also Called: AC TRANSIT
1600 Franklin St, Oakland (94612-2806)
P.O. Box 28507 (94604-8507)
PHONE.............................510 891-4777
David J Armijo, *General Mgr*
Lewis Clinton, *CFO*
Kathleen Kelly, *Officer*
Nancy Skowbo, *General Mgr*
Lyell Amora, *Admin Asst*
EMP: 250
SQ FT: 100,000
SALES: 67.6MM **Privately Held**
WEB: www.actransit.org
SIC: 4111 Bus line operations

(P-3639)
ARCADIA TRANSIT INC
Also Called: Super Shuttle
7955 San Fernando Rd, Sun Valley
(91352-4614)
PHONE.............................818 252-0630
Tim Mardirossian, *President*
Patrick Voskian, *CFO*
Sedik Mardirossian, *Treasurer*
Rozan Mardosian, *Accounting Mgr*
EMP: 50
SQ FT: 25,000
SALES (est): 2.5MM **Privately Held**
SIC: 4111 Airport transportation services, regular route

(P-3640)
CALIFORNIA TRANSIT INC
3201 Hooper Ave, Los Angeles
(90011-2128)
PHONE.............................323 234-8750
Timmy Mardirossian, *President*
Eda Aghajanian, *Treasurer*
Carol Story, *Treasurer*
Petros Keshishian, *Principal*
Christina Pineda, *General Mgr*
EMP: 99 **EST:** 2008
SQ FT: 16,000
SALES (est): 3.1MM
SALES (corp-wide): 21.5MM **Privately Held**
SIC: 4111 Bus line operations
PA: San Gabriel Transit, Inc.
  3650 Rockwell Ave
  El Monte CA 91731
  626 258-1310

(P-3641)
CITY OF ARCADIA
240 W Huntington Dr, Arcadia
(91007-3401)
PHONE.............................626 574-5435
Dominic Lazzaietto, *Principal*
EMP: 300 **Privately Held**
SIC: 4111 Local & suburban transit
PA: City Of Arcadia
  240 W Huntington Dr
  Arcadia CA 91007
  626 574-5400

(P-3642)
CITY OF FRESNO
Fresno Area Express
2223 G St, Fresno (93706-1631)
PHONE.............................559 621-7433
Bruce Red, *General Mgr*

EMP: 460 **Privately Held**
WEB: www.fresnocitizencorps.org
SIC: 4111 Bus transportation
PA: City Of Fresno
  2600 Fresno St
  Fresno CA 93721
  559 621-7001

(P-3643)
CITY OF GARDENA
Also Called: Gardena Municipal Bus Lines
13999 S Western Ave, Gardena
(90249-3005)
PHONE.............................310 324-1475
Whitman Ballenger, *Director*
EMP: 97 **Privately Held**
WEB: www.gardenapd.org
SIC: 4111 9621 Bus line operations; regulation, administration of transportation;
PA: City Of Gardena
  1700 W 162nd St
  Gardena CA 90247
  310 217-9500

(P-3644)
CUSA AWC LLC
Also Called: All West Coachlines
7701 Wilbur Way, Sacramento
(95828-4929)
PHONE.............................916 423-4000
Linda King,
Craig Lentzch,
EMP: 50
SALES (est): 2.1MM **Privately Held**
SIC: 4111 Bus transportation

(P-3645)
DESTINATION SHUTTLE SVCS LLC
6150 W 96th St, Los Angeles (90045-5218)
PHONE.............................310 338-9466
Brian Clark,
Brian Lott,
Jack Lott,
EMP: 130
SALES (est): 4.1MM **Privately Held**
SIC: 4111 Airport transportation

(P-3646)
DIVERSIFIED TRANSPORTATION LLC
6053 W Century Blvd # 900, Los Angeles
(90045-6400)
PHONE.............................310 981-9500
Lisa Jasper, *Manager*
EMP: 58 **Privately Held**
SIC: 4111 4121 Airport transportation; taxicabs
HQ: Diversified Transportation Llc
  1400 E Mission Blvd
  Pomona CA
  909 622-1313

(P-3647)
EAST BAY CONNECTION INC
Also Called: East Bay Airport Shuttle
140 Mayhew Way Ste 1002, Pleasant Hill
(94523-4370)
PHONE.............................925 609-1920
Amid Alefi, *Manager*
EMP: 50
SQ FT: 11,600
SALES: 2MM **Privately Held**
WEB: www.eastbayconnection.net
SIC: 4111 Airport transportation

(P-3648)
EL DORADO COUNTY TRANSIT AUTH
Also Called: EDCTA
6565 Commerce Way Ste A, Diamond
Springs (95619-9454)
PHONE.............................530 642-5383
Mindy Jackson, *Exec Dir*
Brian James, *Planning*
Julie Petersen, *Financial Exec*
Alicia Kennedy, *Opers Spvr*
Robert O'Brien, *Opers Spvr*
EMP: 74
SQ FT: 174,240
SALES: 1.5MM **Privately Held**
WEB: www.eldoradotransit.com
SIC: 4111 Bus line operations

PRODUCTS & SVCS

(P-3649)
FIRST STUDENT INC
550 E C St, Dixon (95620-3634)
PHONE..............................707 678-8679
Valerie Salaun, *Branch Mgr*
EMP: 71
SALES (corp-wide): 8.9B **Privately Held**
SIC: 4111 Local & suburban transit
HQ: First Student, Inc.
600 Vine St Ste 1400
Cincinnati OH 45202

(P-3650)
FIRST STUDENT INC
Also Called: Community Transit Services
4337 Rowland Ave, El Monte (91731-1119)
PHONE..............................626 448-9446
John Desmond, *Branch Mgr*
EMP: 100
SALES (corp-wide): 8.9B **Privately Held**
WEB: www.leag.com
SIC: 4111 4119 Bus line operations; local
passenger transportation
HQ: First Student, Inc.
600 Vine St Ste 1400
Cincinnati OH 45202

(P-3651)
FIRST STUDENT INC
801 Wilbur Ave, Antioch (94509-7500)
PHONE..............................925 754-4878
Susan Hinson, *Branch Mgr*
EMP: 160
SALES (corp-wide): 8.9B **Privately Held**
WEB: www.leag.com
SIC: 4111 Bus line operations
HQ: First Student, Inc.
600 Vine St Ste 1400
Cincinnati OH 45202

(P-3652)
FIRST TRANSIT
Also Called: First Group of America
1303 Fairway Dr, Santa Maria
(93455-1407)
PHONE..............................805 925-5254
Mary McKinley, *Principal*
EMP: 71
SALES (est): 3.4MM **Privately Held**
SIC: 4111

(P-3653)
FIRST TRANSIT INC
2400 E Dominguez St, Long Beach
(90810-1012)
PHONE..............................310 515-8270
EMP: 54
SALES (corp-wide): 9.2B **Privately Held**
SIC: 4111
HQ: First Transit, Inc.
600 Vine St Ste 1400
Cincinnati OH 45202
513 241-2200

(P-3654)
FIRST TRANSIT INC
411 High St, Oakland (94601-3903)
PHONE..............................510 535-9192
Brian Nieman, *Branch Mgr*
EMP: 100
SALES (corp-wide): 8.9B **Privately Held**
WEB: www.firsttransit.com
SIC: 4111 Local & suburban transit
HQ: First Transit, Inc.
600 Vine St Ste 1400
Cincinnati OH 45202
513 241-2200

(P-3655)
FIRST TRANSIT INC
Also Called: Dispatch Office
407 High St, Oakland (94601-3903)
PHONE..............................510 437-8990
Harris, *Branch Mgr*
EMP: 54
SALES (corp-wide): 8.9B **Privately Held**
WEB: www.firsttransit.com
SIC: 4111 Bus transportation
HQ: First Transit, Inc.
600 Vine St Ste 1400
Cincinnati OH 45202
513 241-2200

(P-3656)
FOOTHILL TRANSIT SERVICE CORP (PA)
100 S Vincent Ave Ste 200, West Covina
(91790-2944)
PHONE..............................626 967-3147
Julie Austin, *CEO*
Doran Barnes, *Exec Dir*
Toran Barns, *Exec Dir*
Jon House, *Opers Staff*
Lawrence Hernandez, *Director*
EMP: 55
SQ FT: 9,626
SALES (est): 7.9MM **Privately Held**
SIC: 4111 Bus line operations

(P-3657)
FRESNO COUNTY RURAL TRNST AGCY (PA)
Also Called: Fcrta
2035 Tulare St, Fresno (93721-2004)
PHONE..............................559 233-6789
Barbara Goodwin, *Director*
Trinidad Rodriguez, *Ch of Bd*
Kristine Cai, *Planning*
EMP: 53
SALES (est): 1.5MM **Privately Held**
SIC: 4111 Bus transportation

(P-3658)
GOLDEN EMPIRE TRANSIT DISTRICT (PA)
Also Called: Get-A-Lift Handicap Bus Trnsp
1830 Golden State Ave, Bakersfield
(93301-1012)
PHONE..............................661 869-2438
Steven Woods, *CEO*
Karen King, *President*
Jill Smith, *Administration*
Jeanie Hill, *Human Res Mgr*
Bryan Haver, *Personnel Assit*
EMP: 232
SALES: 30.3MM **Privately Held**
WEB: www.getbus.org
SIC: 4111 Bus line operations

(P-3659)
IDEAL TRANSIT INC
13404 Waco St, Baldwin Park
(91706-4734)
PHONE..............................626 448-2690
Baldo M Paseta, *President*
Alicia Chavira, *Supervisor*
EMP: 50
SALES (est): 3.7MM **Privately Held**
SIC: 4111 Local & suburban transit

(P-3660)
KEOLIS TRANSIT AMERICA INC
14663 Keswick St, Van Nuys (91405-1204)
PHONE..............................818 616-5254
Steve Shaw, *President*
EMP: 175 **Privately Held**
SIC: 4111 Local & suburban transit
HQ: Keolis Transit America, Inc.
6053 W Century Blvd # 900
Los Angeles CA 90045

(P-3661)
KEOLIS TRANSIT AMERICA INC
4488 N Blackstone Ave, Fresno
(93726-1903)
PHONE..............................559 621-5783
Steve Shaw, *President*
Kim Jamron, *Accounting Mgr*
EMP: 100
SALES (est): 249.8K **Privately Held**
SIC: 4111 Local & suburban transit
HQ: Keolis Transit America, Inc.
6053 W Century Blvd # 900
Los Angeles CA 90045

(P-3662)
KEOLIS TRANSIT AMERICA INC
660 W Avenue L, Lancaster (93534-7117)
PHONE..............................661 341-3910
Steve Shaw, *President*
Kim Jamron, *Accounting Mgr*
EMP: 90
SALES (est): 133.3K **Privately Held**
SIC: 4111 Local & suburban transit

HQ: Keolis Transit America, Inc.
6053 W Century Blvd # 900
Los Angeles CA 90045
-

(P-3663)
KOTOBUKI-YA INC
Also Called: CPS
314 Lang Rd, Burlingame (94010-2003)
PHONE..............................650 344-7955
Koichi Suyama, *President*
EMP: 70
SQ FT: 1,000,000
SALES: 2MM **Privately Held**
WEB: www.kotobukiyausa.com
SIC: 4111 Airport transportation

(P-3664)
LONG BEACH PUBLIC TRNSP CO
1300 Gardenia Ave, Long Beach
(90813-2599)
PHONE..............................562 591-2301
Laurence Jackson, *Branch Mgr*
EMP: 325
SALES (est): 3.6MM
SALES (corp-wide): 49.2MM **Privately Held**
SIC: 4111 Bus line operations
PA: Long Beach Public Transportation Co Inc
1963 E Anaheim St
Long Beach CA 90813
562 591-8753

(P-3665)
LONG BEACH PUBLIC TRNSP CO (PA)
Also Called: Long Beach Public Transit
1963 E Anaheim St, Long Beach
(90813-3907)
P.O. Box 731 (90801-0731)
PHONE..............................562 591-8753
Laurence W Jackson, *President*
Kenneth A McDonald, *CEO*
Laverne David, *Executive*
Lee Burner, *Exec Dir*
William Henderson, *General Mgr*
EMP: 570
SQ FT: 10,000
SALES (est): 49.2MM **Privately Held**
SIC: 4111 Bus line operations

(P-3666)
LONG BEACH PUBLIC TRNSP CO
1963 E Anaheim St, Long Beach
(90813-3907)
P.O. Box 731 (90801-0731)
PHONE..............................562 591-8753
Larry Jackson, *Manager*
EMP: 80
SALES (corp-wide): 49.2MM **Privately Held**
SIC: 4111 Bus line operations
PA: Long Beach Public Transportation Co Inc
1963 E Anaheim St
Long Beach CA 90813
562 591-8753

(P-3667)
LOS ANGELES COUNTY MTA
9201 Canoga Ave, Chatsworth
(91311-5839)
PHONE..............................213 922-6308
Pat Orr, *Manager*
EMP: 217
SALES (corp-wide): 740.1MM **Privately Held**
WEB: www.mta.net
SIC: 4111 Bus line operations
PA: Los Angeles County Metropolitan
Transportation Authority
1 Gateway Plz Fl 25
Los Angeles CA 90012
323 466-3876

(P-3668)
LOS ANGELES COUNTY MTA
900 Lyon St, Los Angeles (90012-2913)
PHONE..............................213 922-5887
John Drayton, *Manager*
Casaundra Mangan, *Officer*
Wilson Chu, *Systems Analyst*

John Mirabal, *Purchasing*
EMP: 217
SALES (corp-wide): 740.1MM **Privately Held**
WEB: www.mta.net
SIC: 4111 Bus line operations
PA: Los Angeles County Metropolitan
Transportation Authority
1 Gateway Plz Fl 25
Los Angeles CA 90012
323 466-3876

(P-3669)
LOS ANGELES COUNTY MTA
Also Called: Division 1
1130 E 6th St, Los Angeles (90021-1108)
PHONE..............................213 922-6301
Ron Reedy, *Branch Mgr*
Aida Asuncion, *Officer*
EMP: 150
SALES (corp-wide): 740.1MM **Privately Held**
WEB: www.mta.net
SIC: 4111 Bus line operations
PA: Los Angeles County Metropolitan
Transportation Authority
1 Gateway Plz Fl 25
Los Angeles CA 90012
323 466-3876

(P-3670)
LOS ANGELES COUNTY MTA
630 W Avenue 28, Los Angeles
(90065-1502)
PHONE..............................213 922-6203
Cheryl Brown, *Manager*
EMP: 400
SALES (corp-wide): 740.1MM **Privately Held**
WEB: www.mta.net
SIC: 4111 Bus line operations
PA: Los Angeles County Metropolitan
Transportation Authority
1 Gateway Plz Fl 25
Los Angeles CA 90012
323 466-3876

(P-3671)
LOS ANGELES COUNTY MTA
Also Called: Los Angeles Cnty Mtro Trnspt
1 Gateway Plz, Los Angeles (90012-3745)
PHONE..............................213 922-6202
Maria Japardi, *Branch Mgr*
EMP: 217
SALES (corp-wide): 740.1MM **Privately Held**
WEB: www.mta.net
SIC: 4111 Bus line operations
PA: Los Angeles County Metropolitan
Transportation Authority
1 Gateway Plz Fl 25
Los Angeles CA 90012
323 466-3876

(P-3672)
LOS ANGELES COUNTY MTA (PA)
1 Gateway Plz Fl 25, Los Angeles
(90012-3745)
P.O. Box 512296 (90051-0296)
PHONE..............................323 466-3876
Philip Washington, *CEO*
Rick Thorpe, *CEO*
Nalini Ahuja, *CFO*
Bill Satterfield, *Officer*
Henry Solis, *Officer*
EMP: 900
SALES (est): 740.1MM **Privately Held**
WEB: www.mta.net
SIC: 4111 Bus line operations; subway operation

(P-3673)
LOS ANGELES COUNTY MTA
8800 Santa Monica Blvd, Los Angeles
(90069-4536)
PHONE..............................213 922-6207
Grant Myers, *Manager*
EMP: 700
SALES (corp-wide): 740.1MM **Privately Held**
WEB: www.mta.net
SIC: 4111 Bus line operations; local railway
passenger operation

PA: Los Angeles County Metropolitan
Transportation Authority
1 Gateway Plz Fl 25
Los Angeles CA 90012
323 466-3876

(P-3674)
LOS ANGELES COUNTY MTA
11900 Branford St, Sun Valley
(91352-1003)
PHONE..............................213 922-6215
Gary Stivack, *Manager*
EMP: 500
SALES (corp-wide): 740.1MM **Privately Held**
WEB: www.mta.net
SIC: 4111 Bus line operations
PA: Los Angeles County Metropolitan
Transportation Authority
1 Gateway Plz Fl 25
Los Angeles CA 90012
323 466-3876

(P-3675)
LOS ANGELES COUNTY MTA
720 E 15th St, Los Angeles (90021-2122)
PHONE..............................213 533-1506
Carla Aleman, *Branch Mgr*
EMP: 360
SALES (corp-wide): 740.1MM **Privately Held**
SIC: 4111 Bus line operations
PA: Los Angeles County Metropolitan
Transportation Authority
1 Gateway Plz Fl 25
Los Angeles CA 90012
323 466-3876

(P-3676)
LOS ANGELES COUNTY MTA
Also Called: Lacmta
470 Bauchet St, Los Angeles (90012-2907)
PHONE..............................213 922-5012
Jim Montoya, *Branch Mgr*
Angel Noriega, *Supervisor*
EMP: 217
SALES (corp-wide): 740.1MM **Privately Held**
WEB: www.mta.net
SIC: 4111 Bus transportation
PA: Los Angeles County Metropolitan
Transportation Authority
1 Gateway Plz Fl 25
Los Angeles CA 90012
323 466-3876

(P-3677)
LOS ANGELES COUNTY MTA
Also Called: Division 7
100 Sunset Ave, Venice (90291-2517)
PHONE..............................310 392-8636
John Adams, *Manager*
EMP: 120
SALES (corp-wide): 740.1MM **Privately Held**
WEB: www.mta.net
SIC: 4111 Bus transportation
PA: Los Angeles County Metropolitan
Transportation Authority
1 Gateway Plz Fl 25
Los Angeles CA 90012
323 466-3876

(P-3678)
LOS ANGELES COUNTY MTA
Also Called: Office of Inspector General
818 W 7th St Ste 500, Los Angeles
(90017-3463)
PHONE..............................213 244-6783
Arthur Sinai, *Manager*
Eva Rodriguez, *Administration*
EMP: 217
SALES (corp-wide): 740.1MM **Privately Held**
WEB: www.mta.net
SIC: 4111 Bus line operations
PA: Los Angeles County Metropolitan
Transportation Authority
1 Gateway Plz Fl 25
Los Angeles CA 90012
323 466-3876

(P-3679)
LOS ANGELES COUNTY MTA
320 S Santa Fe Ave, Los Angeles
(90013-1812)
P.O. Box 194 (90078-0194)
PHONE..............................213 626-4455
Julian Burke, *CEO*
Russell Bradshaw, *Engineer*
Annie Yang, *Manager*
EMP: 217
SALES (corp-wide): 740.1MM **Privately Held**
WEB: www.mta.net
SIC: 4111 Bus line operations
PA: Los Angeles County Metropolitan
Transportation Authority
1 Gateway Plz Fl 25
Los Angeles CA 90012
323 466-3876

(P-3680)
MARIN AIRPORTER INC (PA)
Also Called: Marin Airporter Chrtr & Tours
8 Lovell Ave, San Rafael (94901-3921)
PHONE..............................415 256-8833
Randy J Kokke, *President*
Sunhee Kim, *CFO*
Grace Hughes, *Vice Pres*
David Hughes, *General Mgr*
Margie Franklin, *Bookkeeper*
EMP: 70 **EST:** 1972
SQ FT: 2,160
SALES (est): 4MM **Privately Held**
SIC: 4111 4141 Airport transportation
services, regular route; local bus charter
service

(P-3681)
**MENDOCINO TRANSIT
AUTHORITY**
111 Boatyard Dr, Fort Bragg (95437-5709)
P.O. Box 556, Gualala (95445-0556)
PHONE..............................707 462-1422
Sam Kingsley, *Principal*
EMP: 60
SALES (corp-wide): 6.2MM **Privately Held**
WEB: www.4mta.org
SIC: 4111 4131 Bus line operations; inter-
city & rural bus transportation
PA: Mendocino Transit Authority
241 Plant Rd
Ukiah CA 95482
707 462-3881

(P-3682)
**METROPOLITAN TRNSP COMM
(PA)**
Also Called: M T C
375 Beale St Ste 800, San Francisco
(94105-2179)
PHONE..............................415 778-6700
Steve Hieminger, *Exec Dir*
Brian Mayhew, *CFO*
Jake Mackenzie, *Vice Ch Bd*
Therese McMillan, *Exec Dir*
Kenneth KAO, *Program Mgr*
EMP: 115 **EST:** 1970
SQ FT: 21,000
SALES: 313.1MM **Privately Held**
SIC: 4111 Bus line operations

(P-3683)
MONTEBELLO TRANSIT
400 S Taylor Ave, Montebello (90640-5057)
PHONE..............................323 887-4600
Allan Pollock, *Director*
EMP: 250
SALES (est): 3.6MM **Privately Held**
SIC: 4111 Local & suburban transit

(P-3684)
MV TRANSPORTATION INC
13690 Vaughn St, San Fernando
(91340-3017)
PHONE..............................323 666-0856
EMP: 78
SALES (corp-wide): 1.7B **Privately Held**
SIC: 4111 Local & suburban transit
PA: Mv Transportation, Inc.
2711 N Haskell Ave
Dallas TX 75204
214 265-3400

(P-3685)
MV TRANSPORTATION INC
1242 Los Angeles St, Glendale
(91204-2404)
PHONE..............................818 409-3387
Jesse Saavedra, *Branch Mgr*
EMP: 78
SALES (corp-wide): 1.7B **Privately Held**
SIC: 4111 Local & suburban transit
PA: Mv Transportation, Inc.
2711 N Haskell Ave
Dallas TX 75204
214 265-3400

(P-3686)
MV TRANSPORTATION INC
1250 S Wilson Way Ste A1, Stockton
(95205-7026)
PHONE..............................209 547-7879
Nick Harbut, *Branch Mgr*
EMP: 78
SALES (corp-wide): 1.7B **Privately Held**
SIC: 4111 Local & suburban transit
PA: Mv Transportation, Inc.
2711 N Haskell Ave
Dallas TX 75204
214 265-3400

(P-3687)
MV TRANSPORTATION INC
24 S Sacramento St, Lodi (95240-2150)
PHONE..............................209 339-1972
Elizabeth Davidiaz, *Manager*
EMP: 78
SALES (corp-wide): 1.7B **Privately Held**
SIC: 4111 Local & suburban transit
PA: Mv Transportation, Inc.
2711 N Haskell Ave
Dallas TX 75204
214 265-3400

(P-3688)
MV TRANSPORTATION INC
265 S Rancho Rd, Thousand Oaks
(91361-5222)
PHONE..............................805 557-7372
Cheryl Seafert, *Branch Mgr*
EMP: 76
SALES (corp-wide): 1.7B **Privately Held**
SIC: 4111 Local & suburban transit
PA: Mv Transportation, Inc.
2711 N Haskell Ave
Dallas TX 75204
214 265-3400

(P-3689)
MV TRANSPORTATION INC
479 Mason St Ste 221, Vacaville
(95688-4548)
PHONE..............................707 446-5573
Nigel Browne, *Manager*
EMP: 60
SALES (corp-wide): 1.7B **Privately Held**
WEB: www.mvtransit.com
SIC: 4111 Local & suburban transit
PA: Mv Transportation, Inc.
2711 N Haskell Ave
Dallas TX 75204
214 265-3400

(P-3690)
**NORTH COUNTY TRANSIT
DISTRICT (PA)**
Also Called: Nctd
810 Mission Ave, Oceanside (92054-2825)
PHONE..............................760 966-6500
Matt Tucker, *Exec Dir*
Luz Cofresihowe, *CFO*
Brian Helms, *Officer*
Bryan Killian, *Officer*
Karen Tucholski, *Officer*
EMP: 103
SQ FT: 7,000
SALES: 31.5MM **Privately Held**
SIC: 4111 Bus transportation

(P-3691)
NORWALK TRANSIT SYSTEM
Also Called: City of Norwalk
12650 Imperial Hwy, Norwalk (90650-3137)
PHONE..............................562 929-5550
James C Parker, *Director*
Barbara Esparza, *Admin Sec*
Theresa Clark, *Planning*
Vickie Yoshikawa, *Analyst*
Derek Donnell, *Opers Staff*

EMP: 99
SALES (est): 4.4MM **Privately Held**
SIC: 4111 Local & suburban transit

(P-3692)
OMNITRANS INC
4748 Arrow Hwy, Montclair (91763-1208)
PHONE..............................909 379-7100
John Steffon, *Branch Mgr*
EMP: 150
SALES (corp-wide): 13.6MM **Privately Held**
SIC: 4111 Bus line operations
PA: Omnitrans, Inc.
1700 W 5th St
San Bernardino CA 92411
909 379-7100

(P-3693)
ORANGE COUNTY TRNSP AUTH
11790 Cardinal Cir, Garden Grove
(92843-3839)
P.O. Box 14184, Orange (92863-1584)
PHONE..............................714 560-6282
Arthur Leahy, *CEO*
Carlos Ortiz, *Supervisor*
EMP: 1000
SALES (corp-wide): 611.9MM **Privately Held**
WEB: www.octa.net
SIC: 4111 Bus line operations
PA: Orange County Transportation Author-
ity
550 S Main St
Orange CA 92868
714 636-7433

(P-3694)
**ORANGE COUNTY TRNSP AUTH
(PA)**
Also Called: ORANGE COUNTY TRANSIT
DISTRICT
550 S Main St, Orange (92868-4506)
P.O. Box 14184 (92863-1584)
PHONE..............................714 636-7433
Darrell Johnson, *CEO*
Don Hansen, *Director*
Charles V Smith, *Director*
EMP: 350
SQ FT: 77,000
SALES: 611.9MM **Privately Held**
WEB: www.octa.net
SIC: 4111 8711 Bus line operations; con-
struction & civil engineering

(P-3695)
ORANGE COUNTY TRNSP AUTH
Also Called: Octa
600 S Main St Ste 910, Orange
(92868-4689)
PHONE..............................714 999-1726
Oscar Moreno, *Branch Mgr*
EMP: 600
SALES (corp-wide): 611.9MM **Privately Held**
WEB: www.octa.net
SIC: 4111 Bus line operations
PA: Orange County Transportation Author-
ity
550 S Main St
Orange CA 92868
714 636-7433

(P-3696)
OUTREACH & ESCORT INC (PA)
2221 Oakland Rd Ste 200, San Jose
(95131-1415)
P.O. Box 640910 (95164-0910)
PHONE..............................408 678-8585
Katheryn H Heatley, *President*
William Chawarz, *Vice Pres*
EMP: 79
SQ FT: 20,000
SALES: 9.9MM **Privately Held**
WEB: www.outreach1.org
SIC: 4111 Local & suburban transit

(P-3697)
**PENINSULA CRRDOR JINT
PWERS BD**
Also Called: CALTRAIN
1250 San Carlos Ave, San Carlos
(94070-2468)
P.O. Box 3006 (94070-1306)
PHONE..............................650 508-6200
Michael J Scanlon, *Exec Dir*

Virginia Harrington, *CEO*
Chuck Harvey, *CEO*
Michelle Bouchard, *COO*
Monica Colondres, *Executive*
EMP: 105
SALES: 102MM **Privately Held**
SIC: 4111 Local railway passenger opera-

(P-3698)
REDDING AERO ENTERPRISES INC
Also Called: Redding Jet Center
3775 Flight Ave Ste 100, Redding
(96002-9376)
PHONE.................................530 224-2300
Jack Kilpatrick, *President*
Steve Hoppes, *Corp Secy*
Victor Clarke, *Vice Pres*
EMP: 60
SQ FT: 31,000
SALES (est): 6.4MM **Privately Held**
WEB: www.reddingjet.com
SIC: 4111 4581 Airport transportation
services, regular route; aircraft servicing
& repairing

(P-3699)
RIVERSIDE TRANSIT AGENCY (PA)
Also Called: R T A
1825 3rd St, Riverside (92507-3484)
P.O. Box 59968 (92517-1968)
PHONE.................................951 565-5000
Larry Rubio, *CEO*
Tammi Ford, *Executive Asst*
Sharyn Alexander, *Administration*
Darlees Brogdon, *Administration*
Leif Lovegren, *Planning*
EMP: 350
SQ FT: 10,400
SALES: 10.3MM **Privately Held**
WEB: www.riversidetransit.com
SIC: 4111 Bus transportation

(P-3700)
SACRAMENTO REGIONAL TRNST DIST (PA)
1400 29th St, Sacramento (95816-6406)
P.O. Box 2110 (95812-2110)
PHONE.................................916 726-2877
Mike Wiley, *CEO*
Katie Lichty, *Marketing Staff*
Wendy Williams, *Director*
EMP: 700
SQ FT: 10,000
SALES: 28MM **Privately Held**
WEB: www.sacrt.com
SIC: 4111 Bus line operations; commuter
rail passenger operation

(P-3701)
SACRAMENTO REGIONAL TRNST DIST
Transit System Development
1400 29th St, Sacramento (95816-6406)
P.O. Box 2110 (95812-2110)
PHONE.................................916 321-2800
Beverly Scott, *Manager*
Laura Ham, *Vice Pres*
Camille Tyler, *Admin Asst*
Maria Whitworth, *Admin Asst*
Bonnie Andrade, *Technician*
EMP: 118
SALES (corp-wide): 28MM **Privately
Held**
SIC: 4111 Bus line operations
PA: Sacramento Regional Transit Dist.
1400 29th St
Sacramento CA 95816
916 726-2877

(P-3702)
SAN DIEGO METRO TRNST SYS
1255 Imperial Ave # 1000, San Diego
(92101-7490)
PHONE.................................619 231-1466
Paul Jadlonski, *CEO*
Stan Abrams, *CEO*
Sergio Iniguez, *Officer*
Julia Tuer, *Executive Asst*
Socky Grabowski, *Admin Asst*
EMP: 1600
SQ FT: 40,000

SALES: 113.5MM **Privately Held**
WEB: www.sdtc.sdmts.com
SIC: 4111 Bus line operations

(P-3703)
SAN DIEGO TRANSIT CORPORATION (PA)
100 16th St, San Diego (92101-7694)
PHONE.................................619 238-0100
Langley Powell, *President*
Bill Spraul, *COO*
Tom Lee, *Executive Asst*
Thomas Frantz, *Admin Sec*
Ernesto Garcia, *Engineer*
EMP: 650
SQ FT: 20,000
SALES (est): 58.3MM **Privately Held**
WEB: www.sdcommute.com
SIC: 4111 Commuter bus operation; bus
line operations

(P-3704)
SAN DIEGO TRANSIT CORPORATION
100 16th St, San Diego (92101-7694)
PHONE.................................619 238-0100
Cliff Telfer, *Branch Mgr*
EMP: 350
SALES (corp-wide): 58.3MM **Privately
Held**
WEB: www.sdcommute.com
SIC: 4111 Commuter bus operation
PA: San Diego Transit Corporation
100 16th St
San Diego CA 92101
619 238-0100

(P-3705)
SAN DIEGO TROLLEY INC
1341 Commercial St, San Diego
(92113-1021)
PHONE.................................619 595-4933
Bill Brown, *Branch Mgr*
EMP: 370
SALES (corp-wide): 28.6MM **Privately
Held**
WEB: www.sdrotary.org
SIC: 4111 Trolley operation
PA: San Diego Trolley Inc
1255 Imperial Ave Ste 900
San Diego CA 92101
619 595-4949

(P-3706)
SAN FRANCISCO BAY AREA RAPID
Also Called: 1st Interstate Bank Building
1330 Broadway, Oakland (94612-2503)
PHONE.................................510 464-6000
Thomas Margro, *Manager*
EMP: 50
SALES (corp-wide): 545.8MM **Privately
Held**
SIC: 4111 Local railway passenger opera-
tion
PA: San Francisco Bay Area Rapid Transit
District
300 Lakeside Dr
Oakland CA 94604
510 464-6000

(P-3707)
SAN FRANCISCO BAY AREA RAPID
Also Called: Operations Control Center
800 Madison St, Oakland (94607-4730)
PHONE.................................510 834-1297
Rudy Crespo, *Manager*
Paula Eubanks-Major, *Buyer*
EMP: 100
SALES (corp-wide): 545.8MM **Privately
Held**
SIC: 4111 Local railway passenger opera-
tion
PA: San Francisco Bay Area Rapid Transit
District
300 Lakeside Dr
Oakland CA 94604
510 464-6000

(P-3708)
SAN FRANCISCO BAY AREA RAPID
Also Called: Records Center/Storage
300 Lakeside Dr 23, Oakland
(94612-3534)
PHONE.................................510 464-6126
Tom Margaro, *Branch Mgr*
EMP: 103
SALES (corp-wide): 545.8MM **Privately
Held**
SIC: 4111 Local railway passenger opera-
tion
PA: San Francisco Bay Area Rapid Transit
District
300 Lakeside Dr
Oakland CA 94604
510 464-6000

(P-3709)
SAN FRANCISCO BAY AREA RAPID
Also Called: Richmond Repair Shop
1101 13th St, Richmond (94801-2302)
PHONE.................................510 233-6848
Sean Steel, *Branch Mgr*
EMP: 150
SALES (corp-wide): 545.8MM **Privately
Held**
SIC: 4111 Local railway passenger opera-
tion
PA: San Francisco Bay Area Rapid Transit
District
300 Lakeside Dr
Oakland CA 94604
510 464-6000

(P-3710)
SAN FRANCISCO BAY AREA RAPID (PA)
Also Called: Bart
300 Lakeside Dr, Oakland (94604)
P.O. Box 12688 (94604-2688)
PHONE.................................510 464-6000
Grace Crunican, *General Mgr*
Louise Holsten, *CFO*
Scott Schroeder, *Treasurer*
Roy Aguilera, *Officer*
Jim Allison, *Officer*
EMP: 400
SQ FT: 150,000
SALES: 545.8MM **Privately Held**
SIC: 4111 Local railway passenger opera-
tion

(P-3711)
SAN FRANCISCO BAY AREA RAPID
Also Called: Richmond Yard Tower
1101 13th St, Richmond (94801-2302)
PHONE.................................510 233-7444
Steve Brigham, *Branch Mgr*
EMP: 100
SALES (corp-wide): 545.8MM **Privately
Held**
SIC: 4111 Local & suburban transit
PA: San Francisco Bay Area Rapid Transit
District
300 Lakeside Dr
Oakland CA 94604
510 464-6000

(P-3712)
SAN FRANCISCO BAY AREA RAPID
Also Called: Oakland Shops/Annex
601 E 8th St, Oakland (94606-3606)
PHONE.................................510 286-2893
Tom Delaney, *Superintendent*
Theresa Stuart, *Technician*
EMP: 2000
SALES (corp-wide): 545.8MM **Privately
Held**
SIC: 4111 Local railway passenger opera-
tion
PA: San Francisco Bay Area Rapid Transit
District
300 Lakeside Dr
Oakland CA 94604
510 464-6000

(P-3713)
SAN FRANCISCO BAY AREA RAPID
Also Called: Police Department
800 Madison St, Oakland (94607-4730)
P.O. Box 12668 (94604)
PHONE.................................510 464-7000
Kenton Rainey, *Chief*
Bruno Peguese, *Officer*
Elsie Shea, *Vice Pres*
James Pak, *Buyer*
Lewis Williams, *Manager*
EMP: 99
SALES (corp-wide): 545.8MM **Privately
Held**
SIC: 4111 Local railway passenger opera-
tion
PA: San Francisco Bay Area Rapid Transit
District
300 Lakeside Dr
Oakland CA 94604
510 464-6000

(P-3714)
SAN FRANCISCO BAY AREA RAPID
Also Called: Madison Square Building
300 Lakeside Dr Fl 17, Oakland
(94612-3534)
PHONE.................................510 464-6000
Thomas Margro, *Manager*
EMP: 103
SALES (corp-wide): 545.8MM **Privately
Held**
SIC: 4111 Local railway passenger opera-
tion
PA: San Francisco Bay Area Rapid Transit
District
300 Lakeside Dr
Oakland CA 94604
510 464-6000

(P-3715)
SAN GABRIEL TRANSIT INC (PA)
Also Called: San Gabriel Valley Cab Co
3650 Rockwell Ave, El Monte (91731-2322)
PHONE.................................626 258-1310
Timmy Mardirossian, *President*
Eda Aghajanian, *Treasurer*
Keshishian Petros, *Vice Pres*
Luisa Sun, *General Mgr*
Sedik Mardirossian, *Admin Sec*
EMP: 220
SQ FT: 8,000
SALES (est): 21.5MM **Privately Held**
WEB: www.sgtransit.com
SIC: 4111 Local & suburban transit

(P-3716)
SAN JOAQUIN REGIONAL TRNST DST
421 E Weber Ave, Stockton (95202-3024)
P.O. Box 201010 (95201-9010)
PHONE.................................209 948-5566
Donna Demartino, *CEO*
Gloria Salazar, *CFO*
Donna Kelsay, *General Mgr*
EMP: 201
SQ FT: 29,100
SALES (est): 13.4MM **Privately Held**
WEB: www.sanjoaquinrtd.com
SIC: 4111 Bus line operations

(P-3717)
SAN LUIS OBISPO REGIONAL
Also Called: Slorta
179 Cross St Ste A, San Luis Obispo
(93401-7597)
PHONE.................................805 781-4465
Omar McPherson, *Principal*
Tania Arnold, *CFO*
Geoff Straw, *Director*
EMP: 90
SALES (est): 5MM **Privately Held**
WEB: www.caltip.org
SIC: 4111 Local & suburban transit

(P-3718)
SAN MATEO COUNTY TRANSIT DST (PA)
1250 San Carlos Ave, San Carlos
(94070-2468)
P.O. Box 3006 (94070-1306)
PHONE.................................650 508-6200

Mike Scanlon, *CEO*
Jerry Deal, *Vice Chairman*
Jim Kellner, *President*
Bill Likens, *President*
Ch Harvey, *COO*
EMP: 250
SQ FT: 20,000
SALES: 17MM **Privately Held**
WEB: www.samtrans.com
SIC: 4111 Bus line operations

(P-3719)
SAN MATEO COUNTY TRANSIT DST
Also Called: Sam Trans
301 N Access Rd, South San Francisco (94080-6901)
PHONE.............................650 588-4860
John Gerbo, *Branch Mgr*
Elliot Rivas, *Maint Spvr*
EMP: 300
SQ FT: 2,000
SALES (corp-wide): 17MM **Privately Held**
SIC: 4111 Bus line operations
PA: San Mateo County Transit District
1250 San Carlos Ave
San Carlos CA 94070
650 508-6200

(P-3720)
SANTA BARBARA METRO TRNST DST (PA)
Also Called: M T D
550 Olive St, Santa Barbara (93101-1610)
PHONE.............................805 963-3364
David Davis, *Chairman*
John Britton, *Ch of Bd*
Chuck McQuary, *Vice Chairman*
Richard Weinberg, *Exec Dir*
Bill Shelor, *Admin Sec*
EMP: 66
SQ FT: 8,500
SALES (est): 16.4MM **Privately Held**
WEB: www.sbmtd.gov
SIC: 4111 Bus line operations

(P-3721)
SANTA CLARA VALLEY TRNSP AUTH (PA)
3331 N 1st St, San Jose (95134-1906)
PHONE.............................408 321-2300
Michael Burns, *General Mgr*
Steve Turner, *Comms Mgr*
Harvinder Saini, *Principal*
Valerie Tucker, *Admin Sec*
Keisha Carnahan, *Administration*
▲ **EMP:** 2053
SQ FT: 217,000
SALES: 16.6MM **Privately Held**
SIC: 4111 Local & suburban transit

(P-3722)
SANTA CLARA VALLEY TRNSP AUTH
Document Control-Central File
3331 N 1st St Bldg B, San Jose (95134-1906)
PHONE.............................408 321-5559
Michael Burns, *Manager*
EMP: 120
SALES (est): 2.1MM
SALES (corp-wide): 16.6MM **Privately Held**
SIC: 4111 9621 Local & suburban transit; subway operation;
PA: Santa Clara Valley Transportation Authority
3331 N 1st St
San Jose CA 95134
408 321-2300

(P-3723)
SANTA CRUZ METRO
135 Aviation Way Ste 2, Watsonville (95076-2046)
PHONE.............................831 426-6080
Lesley White, *Manager*
Angela Aitken, *COO*
Isaac Holly, *Administration*
Debbie Kinslow, *Administration*
Alex Strudley, *Purch Agent*
EMP: 300
SALES (est): 9.8MM **Privately Held**
SIC: 4111 Local & suburban transit

(P-3724)
SFO AIRPORTER INC (PA)
Also Called: Compass Transportation Charter
160 S Linden Ave Ste 300, South Francisco (94080-6436)
PHONE.............................650 246-2734
Nicholas C Leonoudakis, *Ch of Bd*
Jeffrey G Leonoudakis, *President*
Michael McLean, *President*
Stephan C Leonoudakis, *Exec VP*
Timothy K Leonoudakis, *Vice Pres*
EMP: 100
SALES (est): 26.3MM **Privately Held**
SIC: 4111 4141 4131 Airport transportation; local bus charter service; intercity bus line

(P-3725)
SFO AIRPORTER INC
325 5th St, San Francisco (94107-1040)
PHONE.............................415 495-3909
Gordis Esposto, *Branch Mgr*
EMP: 100
SALES (corp-wide): 26.3MM **Privately Held**
SIC: 4111 4141 4131 Airport transportation; local bus charter service; intercity bus line
PA: Sfo Airporter, Inc.
160 S Linden Ave Ste 300
South San Francisco CA 94080
650 246-2734

(P-3726)
SFO SHUTTLE BUS INC
San Francisco Intl Arprt, San Francisco (94128)
PHONE.............................650 877-0430
Jeffrey Leonoudakis, *President*
Tim Leonoudakis, *Vice Pres*
EMP: 197
SQ FT: 20,000
SALES: 7.2MM **Privately Held**
SIC: 4111 Airport transportation services, regular route

(P-3727)
SMS TRANSPORTATION SVCS INC
865 S Figueroa St # 2750, Los Angeles (90017-2627)
PHONE.............................213 489-5367
John Harris, *CEO*
Delilah Lanoix, *President*
Jennifer Wiltz, *COO*
Danielle Wiltz, *CFO*
EMP: 150
SQ FT: 3,000
SALES: 10MM **Privately Held**
SIC: 4111 Airport transportation

(P-3728)
SONOMA COUNTY AIRPORT EX INC
5807 Old Redwood Hwy, Santa Rosa (95403-1167)
PHONE.............................707 837-8700
Howard Emigh, *President*
Tony Geraldi, *Treasurer*
Janet Emigh, *Vice Pres*
EMP: 80
SQ FT: 5,500
SALES: 5.5MM
SALES (corp-wide): 37.1MM **Privately Held**
WEB: www.airportexpressinc.com
SIC: 4111 4141 Airport transportation services, regular route; local bus charter service
PA: Groome Transportation, Incorporated
2289 Dabney Rd
Richmond VA 23230
804 222-7226

(P-3729)
SOUTH BAY AIRPORT SHUTTLE
Also Called: East Bay Airport Shuttle
14420 Union Ave, San Jose (95124-2815)
P.O. Box 219, Campbell (95009-0219)
PHONE.............................408 225-4444
Behzad Fatemi, *President*
Donia Fatemi, *Treasurer*
EMP: 95
SQ FT: 2,000

SALES: 15MM **Privately Held**
WEB: www.southbayairportshuttle.com
SIC: 4111 Airport transportation services, regular route

(P-3730)
SOUTHERN CAL RGIONAL RAIL AUTH
Also Called: Metrolink
900 Wilshire Blvd # 1500, Los Angeles (90017-4701)
P.O. Box 812060 (90081-0018)
PHONE.............................213 452-0200
Arthur T Leahy, *CEO*
Elissa Konove, *CEO*
Gary Lettengarver, *COO*
Ronnie Campbell, *CFO*
Paul Anninos, *Admin Asst*
EMP: 275
SALES (est): 45.2MM **Privately Held**
WEB: www.metrolinktrains.com
SIC: 4111 Commuter rail passenger operation

(P-3731)
STORER TRANSPORTATION
1909 S Argonaut St, Stockton (95206-1826)
PHONE.............................209 644-5100
Donald Storer, *Owner*
EMP: 80
SALES (est): 1.7MM **Privately Held**
WEB: www.storerbus.com
SIC: 4111 Bus transportation

(P-3732)
SUPERSHUTTLE INTERNATIONAL INC
9559 Center Ave Ste F, Rancho Cucamonga (91730-5815)
PHONE.............................909 944-2606
Margaret Nathan, *Principal*
Michael Branon, *Opers Mgr*
Jennifer Streeter, *Director*
EMP: 150 **Privately Held**
SIC: 4111 Airport transportation
HQ: Supershuttle International, Inc.
14500 N Northsight Blvd # 329
Scottsdale AZ 85260
480 609-3000

(P-3733)
SUPERSHUTTLE INTERNATIONAL INC
Also Called: Supershuttle Sacramento
3100 Northgate Blvd, Sacramento (95833-1349)
PHONE.............................916 648-2500
Igor Avanto, *General Mgr*
EMP: 65
SQ FT: 1,600 **Privately Held**
WEB: www.execucar.com
SIC: 4111 Airport transportation services, regular route
HQ: Supershuttle International, Inc.
14500 N Northsight Blvd # 329
Scottsdale AZ 85260
480 609-3000

(P-3734)
SUPERSHUTTLE LOS ANGELES INC
531 Van Ness Ave, Torrance (90501-6233)
PHONE.............................310 222-5500
Gene Hauk, *President*
R Brian Wier, *CEO*
Thomas C Lavoy, *CFO*
Johanna Miranda, *Clerk*
EMP: 165
SQ FT: 15,000
SALES (est): 4.8MM **Privately Held**
WEB: www.execucar.com
SIC: 4111 Local & suburban transit
HQ: Supershuttle International, Inc.
14500 N Northsight Blvd # 329
Scottsdale AZ 85260
480 609-3000

(P-3735)
SUPERSHUTTLE ORANGE COUNTY INC
531 Van Ness Ave, Torrance (90501-6233)
PHONE.............................310 222-5500
Steven Allan, *President*
EMP: 300

SQ FT: 12,000
SALES (est): 5.1MM **Privately Held**
WEB: www.execucar.com
SIC: 4111 Airport transportation
HQ: Supershuttle International, Inc.
14500 N Northsight Blvd # 329
Scottsdale AZ 85260
480 609-3000

(P-3736)
TRANSPORTATION CONCEPT INC
Also Called: T C I
1521 Kingsdale Ave, Redondo Beach (90278-3939)
PHONE.............................323 268-2202
Brian Connell, *Office Mgr*
EMP: 70
SALES (est): 2.2MM **Privately Held**
SIC: 4111 Bus transportation

(P-3737)
TWO HARBORS ENTERPRISES INC
150 Metropole Ave, Avalon (90704)
P.O. Box 5086 (90704-5086)
PHONE.............................310 510-2000
Kathy Thompson, *Vice Pres*
EMP: 75
SALES (est): 4.7MM **Privately Held**
SIC: 4111 Bus transportation

(P-3738)
WEST COUNTY TRNSP AGCY
367 W Robles Ave, Santa Rosa (95407-8126)
PHONE.............................707 206-9988
Chad Barksdale, *Exec Dir*
Michael REA, *Principal*
Dee Khaleck, *Tech/Comp Coord*
Janice Siebert, *Manager*
EMP: 177
SQ FT: 125,017
SALES (est): 7.1MM **Privately Held**
SIC: 4111 Local & suburban transit

> **4119 Local Passenger Transportation: NEC**

(P-3739)
A-PARA TRANSIT CORP
Also Called: Yefllow Shttle Vtrans Sdan Svc
1400 Doolittle Dr, San Leandro (94577-2226)
PHONE.............................510 562-5500
Shiv D Kumar, *President*
EMP: 110
SQ FT: 2,200
SALES (est): 6.4MM **Privately Held**
SIC: 4119 Limousine rental, with driver

(P-3740)
ADVANTAGE GROUND TRNSP CORP
Also Called: Advantage Ground Trnsp
2960 Airway Ave Ste B102, Costa Mesa (92626-6001)
PHONE.............................714 557-2465
Vo Van Vu, *President*
Joseph Dullulo, *Vice Pres*
EMP: 80
SQ FT: 3,200
SALES (est): 4MM **Privately Held**
WEB: www.agtcorp.com
SIC: 4119 Limousine rental, with driver

(P-3741)
AEGIS AMBULANCE SERVICE INC (PA)
1059 E Bedmar St, Carson (90746-3601)
PHONE.............................626 685-9410
Paul Richart, *President*
Jonathan Raya, *Opers Spvr*
Michael Lagrosas, *Manager*
EMP: 62
SALES (est): 1.6MM **Privately Held**
WEB: www.aegisambulance.com
SIC: 4119 Ambulance service

PRODUCTS & SVCS

(P-3742)
ALLIED MEDICAL SERVICE OF CAL
2570 Bush St, San Francisco (94115-3002)
PHONE..................415 931-1400
Josette Mani, *President*
Leif Engman, *President*
Glen Millar, *CFO*
EMP: 50
SQ FT: 6,000
SALES (est): 1.9MM **Privately Held**
WEB: www.kingamerican.com
SIC: 4119 6411 Ambulance service; insurance agents, brokers & service

(P-3743)
AMATO INDUSTRIES INCORPORATED
Also Called: Gateway Limousine
1550 Gilbreth Rd, Burlingame (94010-1605)
PHONE..................650 697-5548
Sam A Mato, *CEO*
Joel Amato, *Vice Pres*
Karen Amato, *Vice Pres*
Gerri Jacinto, *Human Res Mgr*
John Debenedetto, *Sales Staff*
EMP: 75
SQ FT: 9,500
SALES (est): 6.1MM **Privately Held**
WEB: www.gatewaylimousine.com
SIC: 4119 Limousine rental, with driver

(P-3744)
AMBULNZ HEALTH LLC
12531 Vanowen St, North Hollywood (91605-5321)
PHONE..................877 311-5555
EMP: 294
SALES (corp-wide): 15.5MM **Privately Held**
SIC: 4119 Ambulance service
PA: Ambulnz Health, Llc
1059 E Bedmar St
Carson CA 90746
877 311-5555

(P-3745)
AMERICAN MED
Also Called: Redlands Division
600 Iowa St, Redlands (92373-8047)
PHONE..................909 793-7676
James Price, *Director*
EMP: 250
SALES (corp-wide): 643.1MM **Privately Held**
WEB: www.amr-inc.com
SIC: 4119 Ambulance service
HQ: American Medical Response, Inc.
6363 S Fiddlers Green Cir # 1400
Greenwood Village CO 80111

(P-3746)
AMERICAN MED
Also Called: A M R
5257 Vincent Ave, Irwindale (91706-2042)
PHONE..................626 633-4600
Art McKierman, *Branch Mgr*
EMP: 260
SALES (corp-wide): 643.1MM **Privately Held**
SIC: 4119 Ambulance service
HQ: American Medical Response, Inc.
6363 S Fiddlers Green Cir # 1400
Greenwood Village CO 80111

(P-3747)
AMERICAN MED
1510 Rollins Rd, Burlingame (94010-2306)
PHONE..................650 235-1333
John Odle, *Principal*
Lily Farmer, *Branch Mgr*
EMP: 106
SALES (corp-wide): 643.1MM **Privately Held**
WEB: www.amr-inc.com
SIC: 4119 Ambulance service
HQ: American Medical Response, Inc.
6363 S Fiddlers Green Cir # 1400
Greenwood Village CO 80111

(P-3748)
AMERICAN MED
7575 Southfront Rd, Livermore (94551-8226)
PHONE..................510 895-7600
Brad Cooper, *CFO*
EMP: 106
SALES (corp-wide): 643.1MM **Privately Held**
SIC: 4119 Ambulance service
HQ: American Medical Response, Inc.
6363 S Fiddlers Green Cir # 1400
Greenwood Village CO 80111

(P-3749)
AMERICAN MED
7925 Center Ave, Rancho Cucamonga (91730-3007)
PHONE..................909 948-1714
Rene Polarossa, *General Mgr*
EMP: 106
SALES (corp-wide): 643.1MM **Privately Held**
WEB: www.amr-inc.com
SIC: 4119 Ambulance service
HQ: American Medical Response, Inc.
6363 S Fiddlers Green Cir # 1400
Greenwood Village CO 80111

(P-3750)
AMERICAN MED RESP AMBLNC SVC
Also Called: Sonoma Life Support
930 S A St, Santa Rosa (95404-5439)
PHONE..................707 536-0400
Lori Price, *Director*
EMP: 70
SALES (corp-wide): 643.1MM **Privately Held**
WEB: www.amr-inc.com
SIC: 4119 Ambulance service
HQ: American Medical Response, Inc.
6363 S Fiddlers Green Cir # 1400
Greenwood Village CO 80111

(P-3751)
AMERICAN MED RSPNSE STHERN CAL
1055 W Avenue J, Lancaster (93534-3328)
PHONE..................661 945-9310
Louis Meyer, *President*
Don Harvey, *COO*
Randel Owen, *CFO*
Todd Zimmerman, *Exec VP*
Tim Dorn, *Vice Pres*
EMP: 2806 EST: 2000
SALES (est): 18.9MM
SALES (corp-wide): 643.1MM **Privately Held**
SIC: 4119 Ambulance service
HQ: American Medical Response, Inc.
6363 S Fiddlers Green Cir # 1400
Greenwood Village CO 80111

(P-3752)
AMERICAN MEDICAL RESPONSE
2400 Bisso Ln, Concord (94520-4832)
PHONE..................925 454-6000
Mike Esslinger, *Director*
EMP: 180
SALES (corp-wide): 643.1MM **Privately Held**
SIC: 4119 Ambulance service
HQ: American Medical Response
879 Marlborough Ave
Riverside CA 92507

(P-3753)
AMERICAN MEDICAL RESPONSE
1041 Fee Dr, Sacramento (95815-3908)
PHONE..................916 563-0600
Doug Petric, *Director*
EMP: 400
SALES (corp-wide): 643.1MM **Privately Held**
SIC: 4119 Ambulance service

HQ: American Medical Response
879 Marlborough Ave
Riverside CA 92507

(P-3754)
AMERICAN MEDICAL RESPONSE
1300 Illinois St, San Francisco (94107-3107)
PHONE..................415 922-9400
James Salvante, *Manager*
EMP: 75
SALES (corp-wide): 643.1MM **Privately Held**
SIC: 4119 Ambulance service
HQ: American Medical Response
879 Marlborough Ave
Riverside CA 92507

(P-3755)
AMERICAN MEDICAL RESPONSE
116 Hubbard St, Santa Cruz (95060-2938)
PHONE..................831 423-7030
David Zenker, *Manager*
EMP: 57
SALES (corp-wide): 643.1MM **Privately Held**
SIC: 4119 Ambulance service
HQ: American Medical Response
879 Marlborough Ave
Riverside CA 92507

(P-3756)
AMERICAN MEDICAL RESPONSE (DH)
879 Marlborough Ave, Riverside (92507-2133)
PHONE..................951 782-5200
Bill Fanger, *President*
EMP: 80
SQ FT: 24,000
SALES (est): 36.6MM
SALES (corp-wide): 643.1MM **Privately Held**
SIC: 4119 Ambulance service

(P-3757)
AMERICAN MEDICAL RESPONSE
1510 Rollins Rd, Burlingame (94010-2306)
PHONE..................650 235-1333
Lily Farmer, *Branch Mgr*
EMP: 100
SALES (corp-wide): 643.1MM **Privately Held**
SIC: 4119 Ambulance service
HQ: American Medical Response
879 Marlborough Ave
Riverside CA 92507

(P-3758)
AMERICAN MEDICAL RESPONSE INC
2400 Bisso Ln, Concord (94520-4832)
PHONE..................925 602-1300
EMP: 106
SALES (corp-wide): 643.1MM **Privately Held**
SIC: 4119 Ambulance service
HQ: American Medical Response, Inc.
6363 S Fiddlers Green Cir # 1400
Greenwood Village CO 80111

(P-3759)
AMERICAN MEDICAL RESPONSE INC
1420 Lander Ave, Turlock (95380-6202)
PHONE..................209 567-4030
Cindy Woolston, *Manager*
EMP: 106
SALES (corp-wide): 643.1MM **Privately Held**
SIC: 4119 Ambulance service
HQ: American Medical Response, Inc.
6363 S Fiddlers Green Cir # 1400
Greenwood Village CO 80111

(P-3760)
AMERICAN MEDICAL RESPONSE INC
208 E Devonshire Ave A, Hemet (92543-2985)
PHONE..................951 658-2826
Jack Hanson, *Branch Mgr*
EMP: 113
SALES (corp-wide): 643.1MM **Privately Held**
SIC: 4119 Ambulance service
HQ: American Medical Response, Inc.
6363 S Fiddlers Green Cir # 1400
Greenwood Village CO 80111

(P-3761)
AMERICAN MEDICAL RESPONSE INC
3465 Camino Del Rio S # 410, San Diego (92108-3909)
PHONE..................858 492-3500
Rich Ahrendt, *Vice Pres*
EMP: 250
SALES (corp-wide): 643.1MM **Privately Held**
WEB: www.amr-inc.com
SIC: 4119 Ambulance service
HQ: American Medical Response, Inc.
6363 S Fiddlers Green Cir # 1400
Greenwood Village CO 80111

(P-3762)
AMERICAN MEDICAL RESPONSE INC
3465 Camino Del Rio S # 410, San Diego (92108-3909)
PHONE..................858 492-8111
Edward Van Horne, *CEO*
EMP: 1200
SALES (corp-wide): 643.1MM **Privately Held**
SIC: 4119 Ambulance service
HQ: American Medical Response, Inc.
6363 S Fiddlers Green Cir # 1400
Greenwood Village CO 80111

(P-3763)
AMERICAN MEDICAL RESPONSE INC
Mobile Life Support
240 E Highway 246 Ste 300, Buellton (93427-9648)
PHONE..................805 688-6550
John H Eaglesham, *Branch Mgr*
EMP: 125
SQ FT: 2,000
SALES (corp-wide): 643.1MM **Privately Held**
WEB: www.amr-inc.com
SIC: 4119 Ambulance service
HQ: American Medical Response, Inc.
6363 S Fiddlers Green Cir # 1400
Greenwood Village CO 80111

(P-3764)
AMERICAN MEDICAL RESPONSE INC
1111 Montalvo Way, Palm Springs (92262-5440)
PHONE..................760 883-5000
Wayne Dennis, *Principal*
EMP: 160
SALES (corp-wide): 643.1MM **Privately Held**
SIC: 4119 8099 Ambulance service; medical rescue squad
HQ: American Medical Response, Inc.
6363 S Fiddlers Green Cir # 1400
Greenwood Village CO 80111

(P-3765)
AMERICAN MEDICAL RESPONSE INC
4548 A St, Marina (93933)
PHONE..................831 718-9555
Chris Weinress, *Manager*
EMP: 175

SALES (corp-wide): 643.1MM **Privately Held**
WEB: www.amr-inc.com
SIC: 4119 Ambulance service
HQ: American Medical Response, Inc.
6363 S Fiddlers Green Cir # 1400
Greenwood Village CO 80111
-

(P-3766)
AMERICAN MEDICAL RESPONSE INC
Also Called: Hemet Valley Ambulance
208 E Devonshire Ave A, Hemet
(92543-2985)
PHONE.....................951 765-3900
Jack Hansen, *Branch Mgr*
EMP: 106
SALES (corp-wide): 643.1MM **Privately Held**
SIC: 4119 Ambulance service
HQ: American Medical Response, Inc.
6363 S Fiddlers Green Cir # 1400
Greenwood Village CO 80111
-

(P-3767)
AMERICAN MEDICAL RESPONSE INC
1870 Hillcrest Rd, Hollister (95023-5204)
PHONE.....................831 636-9391
Edward Van Horne, *Branch Mgr*
EMP: 107
SALES (corp-wide): 643.1MM **Privately Held**
SIC: 4119 Ambulance service
HQ: American Medical Response, Inc.
6363 S Fiddlers Green Cir # 1400
Greenwood Village CO 80111
-

(P-3768)
AMERICAN MEDICAL RESPONSE INC
13146 Lincoln Way, Auburn (95603-4114)
PHONE.....................530 887-9440
Michael Mendenhall, *Manager*
EMP: 50
SALES (corp-wide): 643.1MM **Privately Held**
WEB: www.amr-inc.com
SIC: 4119 Ambulance service
HQ: American Medical Response, Inc.
6363 S Fiddlers Green Cir # 1400
Greenwood Village CO 80111
-

(P-3769)
AMERICAN MEDICAL RESPONSE INC
13992 Catalina St, San Leandro
(94577-5506)
PHONE.....................415 794-9204
Thomas Wagner, *CEO*
EMP: 250 EST: 1992
SALES (est): 1.6MM
SALES (corp-wide): 643.1MM **Privately Held**
SIC: 4119 7372 Ambulance service; application computer software
HQ: Envision Healthcare Corporation
1a Burton Hills Blvd
Nashville TN 37215
615 665-1283

(P-3770)
AMERICAN MEDICAL RESPONSE WEST
Also Called: San Joaquin County Operations
3755 West Ln, Stockton (95204-2431)
PHONE.....................209 948-5136
Barry Elzig, *Regional Dir*
EMP: 320
SALES (corp-wide): 643.1MM **Privately Held**
SIC: 4119 Ambulance service
HQ: American Medical Response West
6363 S Fiddlers Green Cir # 1400
Greenwood Village CO 80111

(P-3771)
AMERICAN PROF AMBULANCE CORP
16945 Sherman Way, Van Nuys
(91406-3614)
P.O. Box 7263 (91409-7263)
PHONE.....................818 996-2200
Lyubov Popok, *President*
Wanda Mayfield, *General Mgr*
EMP: 175
SALES (est): 5.5MM **Privately Held**
SIC: 4119 Ambulance service

(P-3772)
AMERICARE MEDSERVICES INC (PA)
Also Called: Americare Ambulance Service
6524 Fremont Cir, Huntington Beach
(92648-6637)
PHONE.....................310 632-1141
Michael Summers, *President*
Mark Ewing, *Manager*
EMP: 155
SQ FT: 10,000
SALES (est): 5.6MM **Privately Held**
WEB: www.americare.org
SIC: 4119 Ambulance service

(P-3773)
ATLANTIC EXPRESS TRNSP
Also Called: Atlantic Express of California
2450 Long Beach Blvd, Long Beach
(90806-3125)
PHONE.....................562 997-6868
Darinda Garnett, *Manager*
EMP: 120
SALES (corp-wide): 288.3MM **Privately Held**
SIC: 4119 8748 4151 Local passenger transportation; traffic consultant; school buses
HQ: Atlantic Express Transportation Corp
7 North St
Staten Island NY 10302
-

(P-3774)
BAUERS INTELLIGENT TRNSP INC (PA)
50 Pier, San Francisco (94158-2193)
PHONE.....................415 522-1212
Gary Bauer, *CEO*
Dennis Jackson, *COO*
Gary Schwartz, *CFO*
Mike Harshfield MBA, *Senior VP*
Carmen Hays, *Executive Asst*
EMP: 250
SQ FT: 125,000
SALES: 48.3MM **Privately Held**
WEB: www.bauersIT.com
SIC: 4119 Limousine rental, with driver

(P-3775)
BAY MEDIC TRANSPORTATION INC
959 Detroit Ave, Concord (94518-2501)
PHONE.....................800 689-9511
Nesar Abdiani, *CEO*
Ali Abdani, *President*
EMP: 56
SQ FT: 1,600
SALES (est): 2.1MM **Privately Held**
WEB: www.baymedic.com
SIC: 4119 Ambulance service

(P-3776)
BAYSHORE AMBULANCE INC (PA)
370 Hatch Dr, Foster City (94404-1106)
P.O. Box 4622 (94404-0622)
PHONE.....................650 525-9700
William Bockholt, *President*
David Bockholt, *Treasurer*
EMP: 45
SQ FT: 5,000
SALES (est): 5.9MM **Privately Held**
WEB: www.bayshoreambulance.com
SIC: 4119 Ambulance service

(P-3777)
BI-COUNTY AMBULANCE SERVICE
1700 Poole Blvd, Yuba City (95993-2610)
P.O. Box 3130 (95992-3130)
PHONE.....................530 674-2780
Kelly W Bumpus, *President*
EMP: 50
SQ FT: 1,600
SALES (est): 1.9MM **Privately Held**
WEB: www.bicountyambulance.com
SIC: 4119 Ambulance service

(P-3778)
BLACK TIE TRANSPORTATION LLC
7080 Commerce Dr, Pleasanton
(94588-8021)
PHONE.....................925 847-0747
Bill Wheeler, *Mng Member*
Debbie Moore,
Jennifer Wheeler,
EMP: 130
SQ FT: 18,000
SALES (est): 6.7MM **Privately Held**
WEB: www.blacktietrans.com
SIC: 4119 4724 Limousine rental, with driver; travel agencies

(P-3779)
BLS LMSINE SVC LOS ANGELES INC (PA)
Also Called: B L S Limousine Service
2860 Fletcher Dr, Los Angeles
(90039-2452)
PHONE.....................323 644-7166
Jay D Okon, *President*
Phyllis Okon, *Corp Secy*
William Kain, *Manager*
EMP: 350
SQ FT: 20,000
SALES (est): 9.3MM **Privately Held**
SIC: 4119 Limousine rental, with driver

(P-3780)
BOWERS COMPANIES INC (HQ)
Also Called: Bowers Ambulance Service
5257 Vincent Ave, Baldwin Park
(91706-2042)
PHONE.....................562 988-6460
Michael P Dimino, *CEO*
Brian Cates, *President*
Raymond S Iskander, *Vice Pres*
EMP: 83
SQ FT: 32,000
SALES (est): 6MM
SALES (corp-wide): 16.9MM **Privately Held**
SIC: 4119 Ambulance service
PA: Rural/Metro Of Northern California, Inc.
2400 Bisso Ln A
Concord CA 94520
619 726-6495

(P-3781)
C O T S INC (PA)
Also Called: Continental Trnsp Svcs
6242 Cherry Ave, Long Beach
(90805-3205)
P.O. Box 4742, Irvine (92616-4742)
PHONE.....................714 751-5466
Anne Stachel Garkani, *President*
MO Garkani, *Controller*
EMP: 53
SALES (est): 1.6MM **Privately Held**
SIC: 4119 Limousine rental, with driver

(P-3782)
CALIFORNIA LIMOUSINES
23016 Lake Forest Dr A, Laguna Hills
(92653-1324)
PHONE.....................949 581-7531
Joseph Magnano, *President*
Frank J Duvall, *Senior VP*
EMP: 55
SQ FT: 5,600
SALES (est): 3MM **Privately Held**
SIC: 4119 Limousine rental, with driver

(P-3783)
CALIFORNIA MED RESPONSE INC
Also Called: Cal-Med Ambulance
1557 Santa Anita Ave, South El Monte
(91733-3313)
PHONE.....................562 968-1818
Ronald A Marks, *President*
Linda Marks, *Treasurer*
Tyler Marks, *Officer*
EMP: 70
SALES (est): 2.5MM **Privately Held**
SIC: 4119 Ambulance service

(P-3784)
CAV INC
Also Called: Care A Van Transport
5411 Avenida Encinas # 210, Carlsbad
(92008-4409)
PHONE.....................760 729-5199
Richard Dripps, *President*
Bob Newkirk, *Director*
Robert Sneedon, *Director*
Deana Mason, *Manager*
EMP: 75
SQ FT: 1,200
SALES (est): 4.4MM **Privately Held**
SIC: 4119 Ambulance service

(P-3785)
CLS TRNSPRTTION LOS ANGLES LLC (HQ)
Also Called: Empire Cls Worldwide
600 S Allied Way, El Segundo
(90245-4727)
PHONE.....................310 414-8189
David Singler, *Mng Member*
William Minich, *CFO*
Joel Stein, *General Mgr*
EMP: 150
SALES (est): 17MM **Privately Held**
WEB: www.clslimo.com
SIC: 4119 Limousine rental, with driver

(P-3786)
COLS INC
1611 S Melrose Dr 253&278, Vista
(92081-5407)
PHONE.....................714 720-6100
MO Garkani, *President*
EMP: 150 EST: 2008
SALES: 12MM **Privately Held**
SIC: 4119 Limousine rental, with driver

(P-3787)
CROWN TRANSPORTATION INC
Also Called: Crown Limousine L.A.
12300 W Washington Blvd, Los Angeles
(90066-5510)
PHONE.....................310 737-0888
David Navon, *President*
Memphis Jasper, *Admin Asst*
EMP: 51
SQ FT: 1,000
SALES (est): 3.5MM **Privately Held**
WEB: www.crownlimola.com
SIC: 4119 Limousine rental, with driver

(P-3788)
EAST SAN GBRIEL VLY CONSORTIUM
Also Called: La Works
5200 Irwindale Ave # 210, Irwindale
(91706-2097)
PHONE.....................626 960-3964
Salvador Velasquez, *President*
Kevin Stapleston, *Chairman*
EMP: 60
SQ FT: 28,000
SALES (est): 2.6MM **Privately Held**
SIC: 4119 8331 Local passenger transportation; job training services

(P-3789)
EASTWESTPROTO INC
Also Called: Lifeline Ambulance
1120 S Maple Ave Ste 200, Montebello
(90640-6043)
PHONE.....................888 535-5728
Genady Gorin, *CEO*
Genia Gorin, *President*
Matthew Sundquist, *Office Mgr*
Dan Santillan, *Opers Staff*
Cesar Gil, *Director*
EMP: 120

SQ FT: 10,000
SALES (est): 6MM **Privately Held**
SIC: 4119 Ambulance service

(P-3790)
EMERGENCY AMBULANCE SERVICE
3200 E Birch St Ste A, Brea (92821-6287)
PHONE........................714 990-1331
Phillip E Davis, *President*
Scott Pipkin, *CFO*
Randy Wolmart, *Exec Dir*
Terri Davis, *Finance*
Cory Osburn, *Controller*
EMP: 80
SALES (est): 4.5MM **Privately Held**
WEB: www.emergencyambulance.com
SIC: 4119 Ambulance service

(P-3791)
EMPIRE ENTERPRISES INC
Also Called: Empire Parking
8800 Park St, Bellflower (90706-5529)
PHONE........................562 529-2676
Mike Oliver, *President*
EMP: 145
SQ FT: 1,700
SALES (est): 3.7MM **Privately Held**
SIC: 4119 7521 4725 4142 Local rental transportation; automobile parking; tour operators; bus charter service, except local; local bus charter service

(P-3792)
EXECUTIVE NETWORK ENTPS INC
1224 21st St Apt E, Santa Monica (90404-1390)
PHONE........................310 457-8822
Patricia Stephenson, *Manager*
EMP: 60 **Privately Held**
WEB: www.ezeclimo.com
SIC: 4119 Limousine rental, with driver
PA: Executive Network Enterprises, Inc.
13440 Beach Ave
Marina Del Rey CA 90292

(P-3793)
EXECUTIVE NETWORK ENTPS INC (PA)
Also Called: Malibu Limousine Service
13440 Beach Ave, Marina Del Rey (90292-5624)
PHONE........................310 447-2759
Patricia Stephenson, *President*
Trish Rudd, *CFO*
Stori Stephenson, *Vice Pres*
EMP: 80
SQ FT: 5,000
SALES (est): 22.8MM **Privately Held**
WEB: www.ezeclimo.com
SIC: 4119 Limousine rental, with driver

(P-3794)
FILYN CORPORATION
Also Called: Lynch Ambulance Service
2950 E La Jolla St, Anaheim (92806-1307)
PHONE........................714 632-0225
Walter John Lynch, *CEO*
Nancy Lynch, *CEO*
Eric Somers, *Info Tech Mgr*
Jacob Wagoner, *Opers Mgr*
Robert Banuelos, *Manager*
EMP: 200
SALES (est): 9.7MM **Privately Held**
WEB: www.lynchambulance.com
SIC: 4119 Ambulance service

(P-3795)
FIRST RESPONDER EMS INC
10161 Croydon Way Ste 1, Sacramento (95827-2107)
P.O. Box 24, Chico (95927-0024)
PHONE........................916 381-3780
Byron Parsons, *CEO*
Thomas Arjil, *President*
EMP: 114
SALES (est): 3.3MM **Privately Held**
SIC: 4119 Ambulance service

(P-3796)
FIRST RESPONDER EMS INC
Also Called: Paradise Ambulance Service
333 Huss Dr Ste 100, Chico (95928-8242)
PHONE........................530 897-6345
Byron Parsons, *President*
Bob Hall, *General Mgr*
EMP: 80
SALES (est): 1.3MM **Privately Held**
SIC: 4119 Ambulance service

(P-3797)
FIRST RSPONDER EMRGNCY MED SVC
Also Called: Chico Paramedic Rescue
333 Huss Dr Ste 300, Chico (95928-8242)
PHONE........................530 891-4357
Byron Parsons, *President*
Bob Hall, *General Mgr*
Louwayne Parsons, *Admin Sec*
EMP: 106
SALES (est): 3.8MM **Privately Held**
SIC: 4119 4522 Ambulance service; air transportation, nonscheduled

(P-3798)
FRANCISCAN LINES INC
Also Called: San Francisco Sightseeing
41 Pier, San Francisco (94133-1009)
PHONE........................415 642-9400
Michael Waters, *Vice Pres*
Jim Casey, *General Mgr*
Renee Torres, *Adv Mgr*
EMP: 130
SQ FT: 50,000
SALES (est): 3.6MM **Privately Held**
WEB: www.graylinesanfrancisco.com
SIC: 4119 Sightseeing bus

(P-3799)
GARY CARDIFF ENTERPRISES INC
Also Called: Cardiff Transportation
75255 Sheryl Ave, Palm Desert (92211-5129)
PHONE........................760 568-1403
Gary Cardiff, *CEO*
Sharon Cardiff, *Admin Sec*
Cathy Smith, *Human Res Dir*
Rodney Betsargon, *Manager*
EMP: 89
SQ FT: 10,000
SALES (est): 5.7MM **Privately Held**
WEB: www.cardifflimo.com
SIC: 4119 Limousine rental, with driver

(P-3800)
GENTLECARE TRANSPORT INC
Also Called: Gcti
3539 Casitas Ave, Los Angeles (90039-1903)
PHONE........................323 662-8777
Mike Panassian, *CEO*
Eddie Avakian, *CFO*
EMP: 75
SQ FT: 8,000
SALES (est): 3MM **Privately Held**
SIC: 4119 Ambulance service

(P-3801)
GERBER AMBULANCE COMPANY INC
Also Called: Gerber Ambulance Service
19801 Mariner Ave, Torrance (90503-1651)
P.O. Box 3487 (90510-3487)
PHONE........................310 542-6464
Robert Gerber, *President*
Rebecca Gerber, *Vice Pres*
EMP: 110
SQ FT: 2,400
SALES (est): 3.8MM **Privately Held**
SIC: 4119 Ambulance service

(P-3802)
GLOBAL EMERGENCY ROAD SVC LLC
9908 San Fernando Rd, Pacoima (91331-2605)
PHONE........................818 518-1166
Max Krumer, *Mng Member*
EMP: 50
SQ FT: 1,000
SALES (est): 2MM **Privately Held**
SIC: 4119 Local passenger transportation

(P-3803)
GLOBAL PARATRANSIT INC
400 W Compton Blvd, Gardena (90248-1700)
PHONE........................310 715-7550
Reza Nasrollahy, *President*
Luis Garcia, *General Mgr*
Karina Abrica, *Project Mgr*
Sam Grinberg, *Controller*
Victor Garate, *Pub Rel Mgr*
EMP: 300 EST: 2000
SQ FT: 17,000
SALES (est): 13.7MM **Privately Held**
SIC: 4119 Ambulance service

(P-3804)
GM CRUISE LLC (HQ)
1201 Bryant St, San Francisco (94103-4306)
PHONE........................415 335-4097
Kyle Vogt, *Mng Member*
EMP: 75
SALES (est): 63.5MM **Publicly Held**
SIC: 4119 Automobile rental, with driver

(P-3805)
GREYBOR MEDICAL TRANSPORTATION
119 Belmont Ave Ste 107, Los Angeles (90026-5708)
P.O. Box 17239, Beverly Hills (90209-3239)
PHONE........................213 250-4444
Gregory Plotkin, *Ch of Bd*
Boris Shpirt, *President*
EMP: 50
SQ FT: 1,000
SALES (est): 1MM **Privately Held**
SIC: 4119 5999 Ambulance service; technical aids for the handicapped

(P-3806)
HALL AMBULANCE SERVICE INC
2001 O St O, Bakersfield (93301-4724)
PHONE........................661 322-8741
Harvy Hall, *President*
EMP: 55
SALES (corp-wide): 25.1MM **Privately Held**
WEB: www.hallamb.com
SIC: 4119 Ambulance service
PA: Hall Ambulance Service, Inc.
1001 21st St
Bakersfield CA 93301
661 322-8741

(P-3807)
HALL AMBULANCE SERVICE INC (PA)
1001 21st St, Bakersfield (93301-4792)
PHONE........................661 322-8741
Harvey L Hall, *President*
Mary Kenny, *CFO*
John Surface, *Vice Pres*
Jeff Bunn, *Technology*
Tracy Burnside, *Technology*
EMP: 60
SQ FT: 4,000
SALES (est): 25.1MM **Privately Held**
WEB: www.hallamb.com
SIC: 4119 4729 4789 Ambulance service; transportation ticket offices; cargo loading & unloading services

(P-3808)
HERREN ENTERPRISES INC
Also Called: Doctors Ambulance Services
23091 Terra Dr, Laguna Hills (92653-1320)
PHONE........................949 951-1666
Bruce W Herren, *President*
Michael Herren, *Vice Pres*
EMP: 56
SQ FT: 4,000
SALES (est): 1.9MM
SALES (corp-wide): 643.1MM **Privately Held**
WEB: www.doctorsambulance.com
SIC: 4119 Ambulance service
HQ: Envision Healthcare Corporation
1a Burton Hills Blvd
Nashville TN 37215
615 665-1283

(P-3809)
INTEGRATED TRNSP SVCS INC
9740 W Pico Blvd, Los Angeles (90035-4711)
P.O. Box 6960, Beverly Hills (90212-6960)
PHONE........................310 553-6060
Albert E Sabroff, *President*
Jonna Sabroff, *Vice Pres*
Beverly Jones, *Director*
EMP: 75
SQ FT: 3,000
SALES (est): 5.5MM **Privately Held**
WEB: www.itslimo.com
SIC: 4119 Limousine rental, with driver

(P-3810)
JASON PROCTOR TRNSP CO
2375 Dairy Ave, Corcoran (93212-3503)
P.O. Box 623 (93212-0623)
PHONE........................559 992-1767
Jason Proctor, *Owner*
EMP: 50
SALES (est): 1.1MM **Privately Held**
SIC: 4119 Automobile rental, with driver

(P-3811)
JP MOTORSPORTS INC
11582 Sheldon St, Sun Valley (91352-1501)
PHONE........................818 381-8313
Ovsep Sukunyan, *CEO*
George Sukunyan, *President*
EMP: 54 EST: 2009
SQ FT: 18,000
SALES (est): 3.2MM **Privately Held**
SIC: 4119 Automobile rental, with driver

(P-3812)
K W P H ENTERPRISES
Also Called: American Ambulance
2911 E Tulare St, Fresno (93721-1502)
PHONE........................559 443-5900
James Kaufman, *President*
Todd R Valeri, *CEO*
Edgar Escobedo, *Business Dir*
Erik Peterson, *Info Tech Dir*
Donna Hankins, *Info Tech Mgr*
EMP: 500
SQ FT: 22,000
SALES (est): 27.6MM **Privately Held**
WEB: www.americanambulance.com
SIC: 4119 Ambulance service

(P-3813)
KEOLIS TRANSIT AMERICA INC (DH)
6053 W Century Blvd # 900, Los Angeles (90045-6400)
PHONE........................310 981-9500
Steve Shaw, *President*
Joseph Cardoso, *CFO*
Kevin Adams, *Exec VP*
Michael Ake, *Senior VP*
Stephen Helriegel, *Senior VP*
EMP: 50
SQ FT: 25,000
SALES (est): 201MM **Privately Held**
WEB: www.tectransinc.com
SIC: 4119 Local passenger transportation
HQ: Keolis America Inc.
3003 Washington Blvd
Arlington VA 22201
301 251-5612

(P-3814)
KMA EMERGENCY SERVICES INC
Also Called: West Medions
14275 Wicks Blvd, San Leandro (94577-5613)
PHONE........................510 614-1420
Erik Mandler, *President*
EMP: 100
SALES (est): 2.9MM **Privately Held**
SIC: 4119 Ambulance service

(P-3815)
LA COSTA LIMOUSINE (PA)
2770 Loker Ave W, Carlsbad (92010-6610)
PHONE........................760 438-4455
Rick Brown, *Partner*
Dale Theriot, *Partner*
EMP: 95
SQ FT: 11,000

SALES (est): 4.9MM **Privately Held**
WEB: www.lacostalimo.com
SIC: **4119** Limousine rental, with driver

(P-3816)
LEADER INDUSTRIES INC
Also Called: Leader Emergency Vehicles
10941 Weaver Ave, South El Monte
(91733-2752)
PHONE..........................626 575-0880
Gary Hunter, *Principal*
Boyd Barlett, *Controller*
EMP: 160
SALES (est): 8.3MM **Privately Held**
WEB: www.leader-ambulance.com
SIC: **4119** 5046 3711 Ambulance service;
commercial equipment; motor vehicles &
car bodies

(P-3817)
LEGRANDE AFFAIRE INC
651 Aldo Ave, Santa Clara (95054-2208)
PHONE..........................408 988-4884
James Brown, *CEO*
Phil Restivo, *President*
EMP: 120
SQ FT: 25,000
SALES (est): 3.6MM **Privately Held**
WEB: www.lagrandeaffaire.com
SIC: **4119** 4724 Limousine rental, with
driver; travel agencies

(P-3818)
LIBERTY AMBULANCE LLC
9441 Washburn Rd, Downey (90242-2912)
PHONE..........................562 741-6230
Kelvin Carlisle,
Frank Heyman, *Managing Dir*
Josh Clark, *Traffic Dir*
Joshua Effle-Hoy, *Opers Spvr*
Louie Arreola, *Supervisor*
EMP: 68
SALES (est): 2.9MM **Privately Held**
SIC: **4119** Ambulance service

(P-3819)
LYFT INC (PA)
185 Berry St Ste 5000, San Francisco
(94107-2503)
PHONE..........................415 230-2905
Logan Green, *CEO*
Danilae Smith, *Partner*
John Zimmer, *President*
Jon McNeill, *COO*
David Estrada, *Vice Pres*
EMP: 257
SALES (est): 136.5MM **Privately Held**
SIC: **4119** Local rental transportation; auto-
mobile rental, with driver

(P-3820)
MED-LIFE AMBULANCE
SERVICES
4304 Alger St, Los Angeles (90039-1206)
P.O. Box 4525, Glendale (91222-0525)
PHONE..........................818 242-1785
EMP: 94
SQ FT: 3,000
SALES (est): 2.5MM **Privately Held**
SIC: **4119**

(P-3821)
MEDIC AMBULANCE SERVICE
INC (PA)
506 Couch St, Vallejo (94590-2408)
P.O. Box 4467 (94590-0459)
PHONE..........................707 644-1761
Rodolfo Manfredi, *President*
Helen Pierson, *CFO*
Marissa Luchini, *Vice Pres*
Kristi Kendall, *Finance*
EMP: 130
SQ FT: 7,000
SALES (est): 15.3MM **Privately Held**
SIC: **4119** Ambulance service

(P-3822)
MEDSTAR LLC
20 Busneca Pk Way Ste 100, Sacramento
(95828)
P.O. Box 292007 (95829-2007)
PHONE..........................916 669-0550
Adam C Ruggles,
Adrianna Gonzalez, *Human Res Dir*
Alison Lugo, *Opers Mgr*
Todd J Ruggles,

Todd Ruggles,
EMP: 65
SQ FT: 2,000
SALES (est): 2.9MM **Privately Held**
SIC: **4119** Ambulance service

(P-3823)
MISSION AMBULANCE INC
1055 E 3rd St, Corona (92879-1606)
P.O. Box 3111 (92878-3111)
PHONE..........................951 272-2300
Daniel Gold, *President*
EMP: 81
SALES (est): 4.7MM **Privately Held**
WEB: www.missionambulance.com
SIC: **4119** Ambulance service

(P-3824)
MV TRANSPORTATION INC
1944 Williams St, San Leandro
(94577-2304)
PHONE..........................510 351-1603
Jay Jeter, *Branch Mgr*
EMP: 180
SALES (corp-wide): 1.7B **Privately Held**
WEB: www.mvtransit.com
SIC: **4119** Local passenger transportation
PA: Mv Transportation, Inc.
2711 N Haskell Ave
Dallas TX 75204
214 265-3400

(P-3825)
NIPOMO DIAL A RIDE
179 Cross St, San Luis Obispo
(93401-7597)
PHONE..........................805 929-2881
Catherine Wynn, *Manager*
EMP: 80
SALES (est): 977.6K **Privately Held**
SIC: **4119** Local passenger transportation

(P-3826)
NORTH STAR EMERGENCY
SVCS INC
Also Called: Norcal Ambulance Services
2537 Willow St, Oakland (94607-1723)
P.O. Box 12347, Pleasanton (94588-2347)
PHONE..........................510 452-3400
David Plaza, *COO*
Barry Sutherland, *CEO*
Makenzie Kelly, *CFO*
Karla Nazareno, *Administration*
EMP: 52
SALES: 2.1MM **Privately Held**
WEB: www.norcalambulance.com
SIC: **4119** Ambulance service

(P-3827)
OJAI AMBULANCE INC
Also Called: Lifeline Medical Transport
632 E Thompson Blvd, Ventura
(93001-2829)
P.O. Box 1089 (93002-1089)
PHONE..........................805 653-9111
Stephen Frank, *President*
Karen Frank, *Vice Pres*
Wynne Schumacher, *Director*
EMP: 50
SALES: 7MM **Privately Held**
WEB: www.lifelineems.net
SIC: **4119** Ambulance service

(P-3828)
PARATRANSIT INCORPORATED
(PA)
2501 Florin Rd, Sacramento (95822-4467)
P.O. Box 231100 (95823-0401)
PHONE..........................916 429-2009
Linda Jean Deavens, *CEO*
Ninh Dao-Dickinson, *COO*
Steve Robinson-Burmester, *CFO*
Sue Ash, *Admin Mgr*
Sean Powers, *Sr Consultant*
EMP: 220
SQ FT: 250,000
SALES: 31.5MM **Privately Held**
SIC: **4119** 7539 Ambulance service; auto-
motive repair shops

(P-3829)
PARATRANSIT INCORPORATED
3300 Tully Rd, Modesto (95350-0836)
PHONE..........................209 522-2300
Andrea Anderson, *Branch Mgr*
EMP: 149

SALES (corp-wide): 31.5MM **Privately
Held**
SIC: **4119** Ambulance service
PA: Paratransit, Incorporated
2501 Florin Rd
Sacramento CA 95822
916 429-2009

(P-3830)
PREMIER MEDICAL TRNSP INC
575 Maple Ct Ste A, Colton (92324-3209)
P.O. Box 690 (92324-0690)
PHONE..........................909 433-3939
Antonio Myrell, *CEO*
Rick Card, *Vice Pres*
Richmond Taylor, *Vice Pres*
Susana Garcia, *Human Resources*
Rosemary Dudevoir, *Opers Staff*
EMP: 65
SALES (est): 4.8MM **Privately Held**
WEB:
www.premiermedicaltransportation.com
SIC: **4119** Ambulance service

(P-3831)
PRIORITY ONE MED TRNSPT
INC (PA)
9327 Fairway View Pl # 300, Rancho Cuca-
monga (91730-0968)
PHONE..........................909 948-4400
Michael Parker, *President*
EMP: 70
SQ FT: 7,000
SALES (est): 10.8MM **Privately Held**
WEB: www.prioritylink.com
SIC: **4119** Ambulance service

(P-3832)
PRN AMBULANCE LLC
8928 Sepulveda Blvd, North Hills
(91343-4306)
PHONE..........................818 810-3600
Mike Sechrist, *CEO*
Avo Avetisyan, *President*
Elena Whorton, *President*
Michael Gorman, *COO*
Kevin Gorman, *CFO*
EMP: 300
SQ FT: 3,000
SALES (est): 12.9MM
SALES (corp-wide): 38.5MM **Privately
Held**
WEB: www.prnambulance.com
SIC: **4119** Ambulance service
PA: Protransport-1, Llc
720 Portal St
Cotati CA 94931
707 975-2386

(P-3833)
PURE LUXURY LIMOUSINE
SERVICE
Also Called: Pure Luxury Worldwide Trnsp
4246 Petaluma Blvd N, Petaluma
(94952-1240)
P.O. Box 910, Penngrove (94951-0910)
PHONE..........................800 626-5466
Gary L Buffo Jr, *CEO*
Kristina Maxwell, *Executive Asst*
Antoinette Allison, *Business Mgr*
Linda Reinecke, *Business Mgr*
Debbie Hawkins, *Human Resources*
EMP: 111
SQ FT: 35,000
SALES (est): 8.5MM **Privately Held**
WEB: www.pureluxury.com
SIC: **4119** Limousine rental, with driver

(P-3834)
RENTY LLC
8025 Clairemont Mesa Blvd, San Diego
(92111-1634)
PHONE..........................858 560-0066
Shariar Delalat, *Mng Member*
EMP: 50
SQ FT: 45,000
SALES: 5MM **Privately Held**
SIC: **4119** Limousine rental, with driver

(P-3835)
RESTIVO ENTERPRISES
Also Called: Legrande Affaire
2590 Lafayette St, Santa Clara
(95050-2602)
PHONE..........................408 988-4884
Phil Restivo, *General Mgr*

EMP: 100
SQ FT: 22,120
SALES (est): 2.5MM **Privately Held**
SIC: **4119** Limousine rental, with driver

(P-3836)
ROYAL AMBULANCE INC
14472 Wicks Blvd, San Leandro
(94577-6712)
PHONE..........................510 568-6161
Steve Grau, *President*
Leon Botoshansky, *CFO*
Hasieb Lemar, *Vice Pres*
Ana David, *Human Res Mgr*
Eve Grau, *Human Res Mgr*
EMP: 120
SQ FT: 5,000
SALES (est): 9.1MM **Privately Held**
WEB: www.royalambulance.com
SIC: **4119** Ambulance service

(P-3837)
RURAL/METRO CORPORATION
2364 W Winton Ave, Hayward
(94545-1102)
PHONE..........................510 266-0885
EMP: 111
SALES (corp-wide): 3.7B **Publicly Held**
SIC: **4119**
HQ: Rural/Metro Corporation
8465 N Pima Rd
Scottsdale AZ 85258
480 606-3886

(P-3838)
RURAL/METRO CORPORATION
1345 Vander Way, San Jose (95112-2809)
PHONE..........................888 876-0740
Scott Bartos, *Branch Mgr*
EMP: 111
SALES (corp-wide): 643.1MM **Privately
Held**
SIC: **4119** Ambulance service
HQ: Rural/Metro Corporation
8465 N Pima Rd
Scottsdale AZ 85258
480 606-3886

(P-3839)
RURAL/METRO SAN DIEGO INC
10405 San Diego Mission R, San Diego
(92108-2174)
PHONE..........................619 280-6060
Michael P Dimino, *CEO*
EMP: 99
SALES (est): 3.4MM
SALES (corp-wide): 643.1MM **Privately
Held**
SIC: **4119**
HQ: Rural/Metro Of California, Inc.
1345 Vander Way
San Jose CA 95112

(P-3840)
SAN DIEGO MED SVCS ENTP
LLC
10405 Sn Diego Mn Rd 20, San Diego
(92108)
PHONE..........................619 280-6060
Michael P Dimino,
Rural Metro Corporation,
EMP: 375
SALES (est): 6.5MM
SALES (corp-wide): 643.1MM **Privately
Held**
SIC: **4119** Ambulance service
HQ: Envision Healthcare Corporation
1a Burton Hills Blvd
Nashville TN 37215
615 665-1283

(P-3841)
SAN LUIS AMBULANCE
SERVICE INC
3546 S Higuera St, San Luis Obispo
(93401-7352)
P.O. Box 954 (93406-0954)
PHONE..........................805 543-2626
Frank I Kelton, *President*
Betsy Kelton, *Corp Secy*
Jody Soule, *Office Mgr*
EMP: 124 EST: 1967
SQ FT: 7,500

PRODUCTS & SVCS

SALES: 14.3MM **Privately Held**
WEB: www.sanluisambulance.com
SIC: 4119 Ambulance service

(P-3842)
SANTA BARBARA AIRBUS
750 Technology Dr, Goleta (93117-3839)
PHONE..................................805 964-7759
Eric Onnen, *President*
Kelly Onnen, *Corp Secy*
Mark Klopstein, *Vice Pres*
Margaret Clemency, *Admin Mgr*
Samantha Onnen, *Cust Mgr*
EMP: 60
SQ FT: 10,000
SALES: 5MM **Privately Held**
WEB: www.sbairbus.com
SIC: 4119 4724 Limousine rental, with
   driver; travel agencies

(P-3843)
SCHAEFER AMBULANCE SERVICE INC (PA)
Also Called: Gold Cross Ambulance
4627 Beverly Blvd, Los Angeles
(90004-3101)
P.O. Box 74609 (90004-0609)
PHONE..................................323 469-1473
James McNeal II, *CEO*
Louella McNeal, *President*
Leslie McNeal, *Treasurer*
Samir Yanni, *Vice Pres*
Marlene McNeal, *Principal*
EMP: 100
SQ FT: 45,000
SALES (est): 41.4MM **Privately Held**
WEB: www.schaeferamb.com
SIC: 4119 Ambulance service

(P-3844)
SCHAEFER AMBULANCE SERVICE INC
Gold Cross Ambulance Service
905 S Imperial Ave, El Centro
(92243-3721)
P.O. Box 1834 (92244-1834)
PHONE..................................760 353-3380
John Goodall, *Branch Mgr*
EMP: 50
SALES (corp-wide): 41.4MM **Privately
Held**
WEB: www.schaeferamb.com
SIC: 4119 Ambulance service
PA: Schaefer Ambulance Service, Inc.
   4627 Beverly Blvd
   Los Angeles CA 90004
   323 469-1473

(P-3845)
SCHAEFER AMBULANCE SERVICE INC
Also Called: Cole-Schaefer Ambulance Svc
324 N Towne Ave, Pomona (91767-5648)
PHONE..................................626 333-4533
Manny Galvez, *Manager*
EMP: 100
SALES (corp-wide): 41.4MM **Privately
Held**
WEB: www.schaeferamb.com
SIC: 4119 Ambulance service
PA: Schaefer Ambulance Service, Inc.
   4627 Beverly Blvd
   Los Angeles CA 90004
   323 469-1473

(P-3846)
SECURE TRANSPORTATION CO INC (PA)
Also Called: Secure Limousine
13111 Meyer Rd, Whittier (90605-3555)
PHONE..................................562 941-0107
Steve Dobbs, *President*
David Kurtz, *CFO*
Michael Espinoza, *Vice Pres*
Gerard Linsmeier, *Vice Pres*
Anne Marin, *Vice Pres*
▲ **EMP:** 230
SQ FT: 5,200
SALES (est): 17.5MM **Privately Held**
WEB: www.securetransportation.com
SIC: 4119 Limousine rental, with driver

(P-3847)
SECURE TRANSPORTATION COMPANY
12785 Magnolia Ave # 102, Riverside
(92503-4686)
PHONE..................................951 737-7300
EMP: 71
SALES (corp-wide): 48.2MM **Privately
Held**
SIC: 4119
PA: Secure Transportation Company, Inc.
   13111 Meyer Rd
   Whittier CA 90605
   562 941-0107

(P-3848)
SOL TRANSPORTATION INC
2525 Ramona Dr, Vista (92084-1632)
PHONE..................................760 720-4327
Arturo Ayala, *President*
EMP: 50
SALES: 426K **Privately Held**
SIC: 4119 Ambulance service

(P-3849)
SOUTHLAND TRANSIT INC (PA)
3650 Rockwell Ave, El Monte (91731-2322)
PHONE..................................626 258-1310
Timmy Mardirossian, *CEO*
Dave Daley, *President*
Jaime Lopez, *General Mgr*
Siquia Harris, *Office Mgr*
Sergio Urbina, *Maintenance Dir*
EMP: 200
SALES (est): 8.4MM **Privately Held**
WEB: www.southlandtransit.com
SIC: 4119 Local rental transportation

(P-3850)
SPRINGS AMBULANCE SERVICE INC
Also Called: American Medical Response
1111 Montalvo Way, Palm Springs
(92262-5440)
PHONE..................................760 883-5000
Edward Vanhorne, *President*
Timothy Dorn, *CFO*
EMP: 99
SALES (est): 839.2K
SALES (corp-wide): 643.1MM **Privately
Held**
SIC: 4119 Ambulance service
HQ: Envision Healthcare Corporation
   1a Burton Hills Blvd
   Nashville TN 37215
   615 665-1283

(P-3851)
STUDENT TRNSP AMER INC
Also Called: Student Transportation America
1540 S 7th St, San Jose (95112-5929)
PHONE..................................408 998-8275
Evie Galdraith, *Manager*
John Carey, *President*
Paul Fichner, *Vice Pres*
Ronald Ferek, *General Mgr*
Brian Hemenway, *General Mgr*
EMP: 100
SALES (corp-wide): 1.8B **Privately Held**
SIC: 4119 4151 Local passenger trans-
   portation; school buses
PA: Student Transportation Of America, Inc.
   3349 Hwy 138
   Wall Township NJ 07719
   732 280-4200

(P-3852)
SUNLINE TRANSIT AGENCY
790 Vine Ave, Coachella (92236-1736)
PHONE..................................760 972-4059
EMP: 119
SALES (corp-wide): 22.1MM **Privately
Held**
SIC: 4119 Local passenger transportation
PA: Sunline Transit Agency
   32505 Harry Oliver Trl
   Thousand Palms CA 92276
   760 343-3456

(P-3853)
TRANSDEV SERVICES INC
5640 Peck Rd, Arcadia (91006-5850)
PHONE..................................626 357-7912
EMP: 251 **Privately Held**

SIC: 4119 4121 Local passenger transportation; taxicabs
HQ: Transdev Services, Inc.
   720 E Bttrfield Rd Ste 300
   Lombard IL 60148
   630 571-7070

(P-3854)
TRIPLE R TRANSPORTATION INC
978 Rd 192, Delano (93215)
P.O. Box 38 (93216-0038)
PHONE..................................661 725-6494
Joe Rodriguez, *President*
Kent Ikeler, *General Mgr*
EMP: 80
SALES (est): 3.2MM **Privately Held**
SIC: 4119 Local rental transportation

(P-3855)
UNIVERSAL LIMOUSINE & TRNSP CO
9944 Mills Station Rd C, Sacramento
(95827-2202)
PHONE..................................916 361-5466
Marc Sievers, *CEO*
EMP: 70
SQ FT: 10,000
SALES (est): 2.2MM **Privately Held**
SIC: 4119 Limousine rental, with driver

(P-3856)
VALLEY MEDICAL TRNSP LLC
43612 Jackson St Ste 4, Indio
(92201-2567)
P.O. Box 1327 (92202-1327)
PHONE..................................760 501-8929
Jose Efren Padilla,
EMP: 60
SALES (est): 1.3MM **Privately Held**
SIC: 4119 Ambulance service

(P-3857)
VIRGIN FISH INC (PA)
Also Called: Avalon Transportation Co
1000 Corporate Pointe # 150, Culver City
(90230-7690)
PHONE..................................310 391-6161
Jeff Brush, *Principal*
David Dinwiddie, *Vice Pres*
Luis Rosario, *General Mgr*
EMP: 150
SQ FT: 3,000
SALES (est): 30.5MM **Privately Held**
WEB: www.avalontrans.com
SIC: 4119 Limousine rental, with driver

(P-3858)
WEST COAST AMBULANCE CORP
Also Called: Wca
6739 S Victoria Ave, Los Angeles
(90043-4617)
P.O. Box 8721 (90008-0721)
PHONE..................................310 435-1862
Olga Binman, *President*
EMP: 135
SALES (est): 3.9MM **Privately Held**
SIC: 4119 Ambulance service

(P-3859)
WESTMED AMBULANCE
14275 Wicks Blvd, San Leandro
(94577-5613)
PHONE..................................510 401-5420
Alan Cress, *Director*
Andrew Thomas, *Admin Mgr*
Kathy Whelan, *Marketing Staff*
Joe Chiedley, *Director*
EMP: 88
SALES (est): 3.2MM **Privately Held**
WEB: www.westmedambulance.com
SIC: 4119 Ambulance service

(P-3860)
WESTMED AMBULANCE INC
3872 Las Flores Canyon Rd, Malibu
(90265-5264)
PHONE..................................310 456-3830
EMP: 165
SALES (corp-wide): 37MM **Privately
Held**
SIC: 4119 Ambulance service

PA: Westmed Ambulance, Inc
   13933 Crenshaw Blvd
   Hawthorne CA 90250
   510 614-1420

(P-3861)
WESTMED AMBULANCE INC
2537 Old San Pasqual Rd, Escondido
(92027-4753)
PHONE..................................310 219-1779
Allen Cress, *Principal*
EMP: 254
SALES (corp-wide): 37MM **Privately
Held**
SIC: 4119 Ambulance service
PA: Westmed Ambulance, Inc
   13933 Crenshaw Blvd
   Hawthorne CA 90250
   510 614-1420

(P-3862)
WORLDWIDE GROUND TRANSPORTATIO
Also Called: El Paseo Limousine
651 Aldo Ave, Santa Clara (95054-2208)
PHONE..................................408 727-0000
James Brown, *President*
EMP: 75
SQ FT: 8,900
SALES (est): 3.3MM **Privately Held**
SIC: 4119 4131 Limousine rental, with
   driver; intercity bus line

4121 Taxi Cabs

(P-3863)
A WHITE AND YELLOW CAB INC
Also Called: A Taxi Cab
2082 Se Bristol St # 212, Newport Beach
(92660-1740)
PHONE..................................714 258-1000
Hossein Nabati, *President*
EMP: 180
SALES (est): 9.8MM **Privately Held**
SIC: 4121 Taxicabs

(P-3864)
ADMINISTRATIVE SERVICES SD
Also Called: Yellow Radio Service
3473 Kurtz St, San Diego (92110-4430)
PHONE..................................619 398-2314
Anthony Palmeri, *Principal*
Sharon Geraty,
EMP: 50
SALES (est): 950K **Privately Held**
SIC: 4121 Taxicabs

(P-3865)
CHECKER CAB CO
Also Called: La Checker Cab Co
14943 Califa St, Van Nuys (91411-3002)
PHONE..................................818 488-5088
Eugene Smolyar, *President*
EMP: 52
SALES (est): 3.2MM **Privately Held**
SIC: 4121 Taxicabs

(P-3866)
LUXOR CABS INC
2230 Jerrold Ave, San Francisco
(94124-1012)
PHONE..................................415 282-4141
John Lazar, *CEO*
William Falcon, *Corp Secy*
Dolores Parlomenko, *Vice Pres*
EMP: 51 **EST:** 1946
SQ FT: 7,000
SALES (est): 3.9MM **Privately Held**
WEB: www.luxorcab.com
SIC: 4121 7521 Taxicabs; parking lots

(P-3867)
NEESE INC
Also Called: Georges Yellow Taxi Cab Co
588 Roseland Ave, Santa Rosa
(95407-6837)
PHONE..................................707 544-4444
Ray Neese, *President*
EMP: 50
SQ FT: 1,500
SALES: 1.6MM **Privately Held**
SIC: 4121 Taxicabs

(P-3868)
SAN GABRIEL TRANSIT INC
Also Called: Southland Transit Co
14913 Ramona Blvd, Baldwin Park
(91706-3421)
PHONE..............................626 430-3650
EMP: 78
SALES (corp-wide): 20.3MM **Privately Held**
SIC: 4121
PA: San Gabriel Transit, Inc.
3650 Rockwell Ave
El Monte CA 91731
626 258-1310

(P-3869)
SAN GABRIEL TRANSIT INC
7955 San Fernando Rd, Sun Valley
(91352-4614)
PHONE..............................818 771-0374
Debbie Waters, *Manager*
EMP: 75
SALES (est): 1.9MM
SALES (corp-wide): 21.6MM **Privately Held**
WEB: www.sgtransit.com
SIC: 4121 4119 Taxicabs; local passenger transportation
PA: San Gabriel Transit, Inc.
3650 Rockwell Ave
El Monte CA 91731
626 258-1310

(P-3870)
SITOA
6900 Airport Blvd, Sacramento (95837)
PHONE..............................916 444-0008
Kuldip Dosanjh, *Owner*
EMP: 98 EST: 2015
SALES (est): 1.1MM **Privately Held**
SIC: 4121 Taxicabs

(P-3871)
UNITED IND TAXI DRIVERS (PA)
Also Called: United Taxi San Fernando Vly
900 N Alvarado St, Los Angeles
(90026-3105)
PHONE..............................323 462-1088
Andrey Primushko, *CEO*
Martin Shatakhyan, *President*
Neil Evans, *Representative*
EMP: 60
SQ FT: 3,500
SALES (est): 3.6MM **Privately Held**
SIC: 4121 Taxicabs

(P-3872)
UNITED INDEPENDENT TAXI CO
900 N Alvarado St, Los Angeles
(90026-3105)
PHONE..............................213 385-2227
Andrey Primushko, *President*
Mohammad Pourrsegar, *Vice Pres*
Felix Knyazher, *Admin Sec*
EMP: 50 EST: 1977
SALES (est): 1.5MM **Privately Held**
SIC: 4121 Taxicabs

(P-3873)
WESTERN TRANSIT SYSTEMS INC
13591 Harbor Blvd, Garden Grove
(92843-3818)
PHONE..............................949 515-0188
Michael Griffus, *President*
Francis G Homan, *CFO*
EMP: 65
SQ FT: 6,000
SALES (est): 2.2MM **Privately Held**
WEB: www.tectransinc.com
SIC: 4121 Taxicabs
HQ: Keolis Transit America, Inc.
6053 W Century Blvd # 900
Los Angeles CA 90045

(P-3874)
YELLOW CAB COMPANY PENNINSULA
Also Called: Yellow Cabs
7013 Realm Dr Ste A, San Jose
(95119-1354)
PHONE..............................408 739-1234
Vikramjeet Singh, *President*
EMP: 150 EST: 1948

SQ FT: 5,000
SALES: 1.2MM **Privately Held**
WEB: www.yellowcabpeninsula.com
SIC: 4121 Taxicabs

(P-3875)
YELLOW CAB COOPERATIVE INC
Also Called: All Taxi Electronics
55 New Montgomery St # 208, San Francisco (94105-3421)
PHONE..............................415 333-3333
Richard Wiener, *CEO*
Harlan Mellegard, *Exec VP*
Jim Gillespie, *General Mgr*
Sheldon Miller, *Admin Sec*
Pam Martinez, *Controller*
EMP: 90
SQ FT: 150,000
SALES (est): 10MM **Privately Held**
SIC: 4121 Taxicabs

4131 Intercity & Rural Bus Transportation

(P-3876)
CITY OF NAPA
Also Called: Vine Transit
1151 Pearl St, NAPA (94559-2528)
PHONE..............................707 255-7631
Rick Levitt, *General Mgr*
EMP: 50 **Privately Held**
WEB: www.naparcd.org
SIC: 4131 9111 Intercity & rural bus transportation; mayors' offices
PA: City Of Napa
955 School St
Napa CA 94559
707 257-9516

(P-3877)
EASTERN SIERRA TRANSIT AUTH
703 Airport Rd, Bishop (93514-3603)
P.O. Box 1357 (93515-1357)
PHONE..............................760 872-1901
Brad Koehn, *Principal*
John Helm, *Principal*
Jonathan Robertson, *Opers Spvr*
EMP: 50
SALES (est): 2.2MM **Privately Held**
SIC: 4131 Intercity & rural bus transportation

(P-3878)
GREYHOUND LINES INC
1033 Broadway St, Fresno (93721-2535)
PHONE..............................559 268-1829
Tom Fries, *Manager*
EMP: 118
SALES (corp-wide): 8.9B **Privately Held**
WEB: www.greyhound.com
SIC: 4131 Intercity & rural bus transportation
HQ: Greyhound Lines, Inc.
350 N Saint Paul St # 300
Dallas TX 75201
214 849-8000

(P-3879)
LINCOLN SCHOOL BUS TRNSP
6749 Harrisburg Pl, Stockton (95207)
PHONE..............................209 953-8596
George Anzo, *Director*
Ted Bestolarides, *Bd of Directors*
Saragon Yousef, *Principal*
Dwight Fanning, *Director*
EMP: 65
SALES (est): 1.3MM **Privately Held**
WEB: www.lusd.net
SIC: 4131 Intercity & rural bus transportation

(P-3880)
MARIN AIRPORTER INC
1455 N Hamilton Pkwy, Novato
(94949-8205)
PHONE..............................415 884-2878
Guy Murta, *Branch Mgr*
Lawrence Forrest, *Project Mgr*
EMP: 63

SALES (corp-wide): 3.6MM **Privately Held**
WEB: www.marinairporter.com
SIC: 4131 Intercity & rural bus transportation
PA: Marin Airporter, Inc
8 Lovell Ave
San Rafael CA 94901
415 256-8830

(P-3881)
MONTEREY-SALINAS TRANSIT CORP
1375 Burton Ave, Salinas (93901-4403)
PHONE..............................831 754-2804
Carl Sedoryk, *Branch Mgr*
EMP: 140
SALES (corp-wide): 17.9MM **Privately Held**
SIC: 4131 Intercity & rural bus transportation
PA: Monterey-Salinas Transit Corporation
19 Upper Ragsdale Dr # 200
Monterey CA 93940
888 678-2871

(P-3882)
SANTA CLARA VALLEY TRNSP AUTH
3331 N 1st St, San Jose (95134-1906)
PHONE..............................408 321-5555
Michael Burns, *Manager*
EMP: 500
SALES (est): 8.1MM
SALES (corp-wide): 16.6MM **Privately Held**
SIC: 4131 9111 Intercity bus line; county supervisors' & executives' offices
PA: Santa Clara Valley Transportation Authority
3331 N 1st St
San Jose CA 95134
408 321-2300

(P-3883)
SANTA CLARITA CITY OF
Also Called: Bus Company
28250 Constellation Rd, Santa Clarita
(91355-5000)
PHONE..............................661 294-1287
Mike Hynes, *Director*
EMP: 300 **Privately Held**
WEB: www.golfsantaclarita.com
SIC: 4131 9111 Intercity & rural bus transportation; mayors' offices
PA: Santa Clarita, City Of
23920 Valencia Blvd # 300
Santa Clarita CA 91355
661 259-2489

(P-3884)
SANTA CRUZ METRO TRNST DST
Also Called: Fleet Maintenance Dept
110 Vernon St Ste B, Santa Cruz
(95060-2130)
PHONE..............................831 469-1954
Tom Stickel, *Manager*
EMP: 54
SALES (corp-wide): 9.7MM **Privately Held**
WEB: www.scmtd.com
SIC: 4131 Intercity bus line
PA: Santa Cruz Metropolitan Transit District
110 Vernon St
Santa Cruz CA 95060
831 426-6143

(P-3885)
SANTA MONICA CITY OF
Santa Monica Big Blue Bus
1334 5th St, Santa Monica (90401)
PHONE..............................310 451-5444
Edward King, *Manager*
John Catoe, *Director*
EMP: 325 **Privately Held**
SIC: 4131 Intercity & rural bus transportation
PA: City Of Santa Monica
1685 Main St
Santa Monica CA 90401
310 458-8411

(P-3886)
SUNLINE TRANSIT AGENCY (PA)
Also Called: STA
32505 Harry Oliver Trl, Thousand Palms
(92276-3501)
PHONE..............................760 343-3456
Glenn Miller, *Chairman*
Peter Gregor, *Officer*
Vanessa Mora, *Officer*
Greg Pettis, *Principal*
Caroline Rude, *Admin Sec*
EMP: 160 EST: 1977
SQ FT: 19,006
SALES (est): 22.1MM **Privately Held**
WEB: www.sunline.org
SIC: 4131 Intercity bus line

4141 Local Bus Charter Svc

(P-3887)
AMADOR STAGE LINES INC
Also Called: Allen Transportation Co
1331 C St, Sacramento (95814-0913)
P.O. Box 15707 (95852-0707)
PHONE..............................916 444-7880
W R Allen, *CEO*
Alex B Allen, *President*
William R Allen, *Treasurer*
R E Allen, *Vice Pres*
Debbie Perryman, *Accounting Mgr*
EMP: 80
SQ FT: 2,000
SALES (est): 7.3MM **Privately Held**
SIC: 4141 Local bus charter service

(P-3888)
EMPIRE TRANSPORTATION
8800 Park St, Bellflower (90706-5529)
PHONE..............................562 529-2676
Miguel Oliver, *CEO*
Bertha Aguirre, *President*
Monica Escorza Oliver, *CFO*
EMP: 425
SQ FT: 25,000
SALES (est): 30.2MM **Privately Held**
SIC: 4141 7521 4111 Local bus charter service; indoor parking services; bus transportation

(P-3889)
MAJESTIC TERMINAL SERVICES INC
2300 E Airport Dr, Ontario (91761-2139)
PHONE..............................909 937-2580
Brian Cella Jr, *Director*
EMP: 86
SALES (corp-wide): 1.2MM **Privately Held**
SIC: 4141 Local bus charter service
PA: Majestic Terminal Services, Inc.
15127 Main St E Ste 104p
Sumner WA 98390
253 862-1269

(P-3890)
MCCLINTOCK ENTERPRISES INC
Also Called: Goldfield Stage Company
777 Gable Way, El Cajon (92020-1908)
PHONE..............................619 579-5300
Kevin McClintock, *President*
Brianna McClintock, *COO*
Dalyce McClintock, *Admin Sec*
Randy Lohrenz, *Sales Mgr*
Daisy Padaon, *Sales Mgr*
EMP: 60
SQ FT: 1,000
SALES (est): 6.7MM **Privately Held**
WEB: www.goldfieldstage.com
SIC: 4141 Local bus charter service

(P-3891)
MICHAELS TRNSP SVC INC
140 Yolano Dr, Vallejo (94589-2251)
PHONE..............................707 674-6013
Michael Brown, *President*
Carl Mosebach, *General Mgr*
Keith Judkins, *Recruiter*
Greg Robertson, *Recruiter*
Corby Harvey, *Director*
EMP: 95
SQ FT: 26,000

SALES (est): 9.3MM **Privately Held**
WEB: www.bustransportation.com
SIC: **4141** 7363 8331 4111 Local bus charter service; employee leasing service; job training services; bus transportation; school buses

(P-3892)
STORER TRANSPORTATION SERVICE (PA)
Also Called: Storer Travel Service
3519 Mcdonald Ave, Modesto (95358-9771)
PHONE....................209 521-8250
Donald Storer, *CEO*
Warren Storer, *CEO*
Jim Hsia, *CFO*
Steven Fernandes, *Sls & Mktg Exec*
Theresa Waters, *Sales Staff*
EMP: 275
SQ FT: 6,000
SALES (est): 43.4MM **Privately Held**
WEB: www.storercoachways.com
SIC: **4141** 4725 4724 4151 Local bus charter service; tours, conducted; travel agencies; school buses; bus charter service, except local

---

4142 Bus Charter Service, Except Local

(P-3893)
ALL WEST COACHLINES INC
Also Called: A Coach USA Company
7701 Wilbur Way, Sacramento (95828-4994)
PHONE....................916 423-4000
Dan Eisentrager, *President*
EMP: 65
SALES (est): 2.4MM
SALES (corp-wide): 4.5B **Privately Held**
WEB: www.allwestcoachlines.com
SIC: **4142** Bus charter service, except local
PA: Stagecoach Group Plc
    10 Dunkeld Road
    Perth PH1 5
    173 844-2111

(P-3894)
CUSA FL LLC
Also Called: Coach Bus Lines
41 Pier, San Francisco (94133-1009)
PHONE....................415 642-9400
Michael Waters,
Craig Lentzch,
EMP: 150
SALES (est): 3.6MM **Privately Held**
WEB: www.cusa.org
SIC: **4142** Bus charter service, except local

(P-3895)
EL PAS-LOS ANGELES LMSNE EX INC
Also Called: Los Angeles Terminal
260 E 6th St, Los Angeles (90014-2117)
PHONE....................213 623-2323
Marisela Gonzalez, *Branch Mgr*
EMP: 50
SQ FT: 5,680
SALES (corp-wide): 21.4MM **Privately Held**
SIC: **4142** Bus charter service, except local
PA: El Paso-Los Angeles Limousine Express, Inc.
    720 S Oregon St
    El Paso TX 79901
    915 778-3337

(P-3896)
FAST DEER BUS CHRTR INCRPRTION
8105 Slauson Ave, Montebello (90640-6621)
PHONE....................323 201-8988
Eddie Wong, *President*
Carmina Delacruz, *General Mgr*
EMP: 57
SQ FT: 65,000
SALES (est): 2.3MM **Privately Held**
WEB: www.fastdeerbus.com
SIC: **4142** Bus charter service, except local

(P-3897)
FIRST STUDENT INC
2477 Arnold Indus Way, Concord (94520-5327)
PHONE....................925 676-1976
Mary Walker, *Manager*
EMP: 90
SALES (corp-wide): 8.9B **Privately Held**
WEB: www.leag.com
SIC: **4142** Bus charter service, except local
HQ: First Student, Inc.
    600 Vine St Ste 1400
    Cincinnati OH 45202

(P-3898)
GREEN TORTOISE ADVENTURE TRVL
494 Broadway, San Francisco (94133-4515)
PHONE....................415 834-1000
Gardner L Kent, *President*
James Barbush, *Vice Pres*
EMP: 65
SALES (est): 2.8MM **Privately Held**
WEB: www.greyrabbit.com
SIC: **4142** Bus charter service, except local

(P-3899)
HOT DOGGER TOURS INC
Also Called: Gold Coast Tours
223 Imperial Hwy Ste 165, Fullerton (92835-1060)
PHONE....................714 988-4088
John Hartley, *President*
Mark Wilkerson, *Vice Pres*
EMP: 120
SQ FT: 955
SALES (est): 11.7MM **Privately Held**
WEB: www.goldcoasttours.com
SIC: **4142** 4725 4141 Bus charter service, except local; tours, conducted; local bus charter service

(P-3900)
ORANGE BELT STAGES (PA)
Also Called: Orange Belt Adventures
2134 E Mineral King Ave, Visalia (93292-6905)
P.O. Box 949 (93279-0949)
PHONE....................559 733-4408
Michael Haworth, *President*
Bryan A Haworth Trust, *Shareholder*
Margaret V Haworth Trust, *Shareholder*
Bruce Lynn, *President*
EMP: 65
SQ FT: 10,000
SALES (est): 15.1MM **Privately Held**
WEB: www.orangebelt.com
SIC: **4142** 4141 Bus charter service, except local; local bus charter service

(P-3901)
ROYAL COACH TOURS (PA)
630 Stockton Ave, San Jose (95126-2433)
PHONE....................408 279-4801
Sandra Allen, *CEO*
Joanne Smith Christian, *Shareholder*
Daniel Smith, *Vice Pres*
Diana Yuan, *Finance*
Earl Reed, *Manager*
EMP: 110
SQ FT: 2,500
SALES: 13MM **Privately Held**
WEB: www.royal-coach.com
SIC: **4142** Bus charter service, except local

(P-3902)
RYANS EXPRESS TRNSP SVCS INC (PA)
19500 Mariner Ave, Torrance (90503-1644)
PHONE....................310 219-2960
John Busskohl, *CEO*
George Cohen, *CFO*
Alexander E Hansen, *CFO*
Chris Sanchez, *Vice Pres*
Jessie Alcocer, *General Mgr*
EMP: 80
SQ FT: 20,000
SALES (est): 20.5MM **Privately Held**
SIC: **4142** Bus charter service, except local

(P-3903)
SURERIDE CHARTER INC
Also Called: Sun Diego Charter
522 W 8th St, National City (91950-1004)
PHONE....................619 336-9200
Richard Illes, *President*
Lisa Alton, *Controller*
Carolina Urista, *Human Res Mgr*
Andrew Freer, *Sales Mgr*
Hector Cuatepotzo, *Manager*
EMP: 120
SQ FT: 60,000
SALES (est): 8.3MM **Privately Held**
WEB: www.sundiegocharter.com
SIC: **4142** Bus charter service, except local

(P-3904)
THE GRAY-LINE TOURS COMPANY
6541 Hollywood Blvd, Los Angeles (90028-6256)
PHONE....................323 463-3333
Vahid Sapir, *President*
EMP: 200
SQ FT: 10,000
SALES (est): 6MM **Privately Held**
SIC: **4142** Bus charter service, except local

(P-3905)
TRANSPORTATION CHRTR SVCS INC
1931 N Batavia St, Orange (92865-4107)
PHONE....................714 396-0346
Terry Fischer, *President*
Kathryn Mayer, *Vice Pres*
Dave Jeffers, *Principal*
Candice Martinez, *Controller*
Teresa Harshfield, *Sales Staff*
EMP: 50
SALES: 9.7MM **Privately Held**
WEB: www.tcsbus.com
SIC: **4142** Bus charter service, except local

(P-3906)
VIA ADVENTURES INC (PA)
Also Called: Via Charter Lines
300 Grogan Ave, Merced (95341-6446)
PHONE....................209 384-1315
Curtis A Riggs, *President*
Gaye Riggs, *Corp Secy*
EMP: 50
SALES (est): 8.6MM **Privately Held**
WEB: www.via-adventures.com
SIC: **4142** 4724 4725 Bus charter service, except local; travel agencies; sightseeing tour companies

---

4151 School Buses

(P-3907)
ANTELOPE VLY SCHL TRNSP AGCY
670 W Avenue L8, Lancaster (93534-7100)
PHONE....................661 945-3621
Jene Jansen, *CEO*
Morris Fuselier III, *CEO*
Jeff Foster, *Executive*
Kathy Phillips, *Info Tech Mgr*
Joanne Downen, *Accountant*
EMP: 190
SALES: 12.5MM **Privately Held**
WEB: www.avsta.com
SIC: **4151** School buses

(P-3908)
BEAUMONT UNIFIED SCHOOL DST
1001 Cougar Way, Beaumont (92223-5124)
P.O. Box 187 (92223-0187)
PHONE....................951 845-3010
Robin Dailey, *Director*
EMP: 2755
SALES (corp-wide): 114.4MM **Privately Held**
SIC: **4151** School buses
PA: Beaumont Unified School District Public Facilities Corporation
    350 W Brookside Ave
    Cherry Valley CA 92223
    951 845-1631

(P-3909)
BERKELEY UNIFIED SCHOOL DST
Also Called: Transportation Department
1314 7th St, Berkeley (94710-1465)
PHONE....................510 644-6182
Bernadette Cormier, *Manager*
Josh Church, *Athletic Dir*
EMP: 50
SALES (corp-wide): 175.2MM **Privately Held**
WEB: www.latms.berkeley.k12.ca.us
SIC: **4151** School buses
PA: Berkeley Unified School District
    2020 Bonar St Rm 202
    Berkeley CA 94702
    510 644-4500

(P-3910)
CATHOLIC CHRTS CYO ARCHDIOCS
Also Called: CATHOLIC YOUTH ORGANIZATION
699 Serramonte Blvd 210, Daly City (94015-4132)
PHONE....................650 757-2110
Bill Avalos, *Manager*
Daniel Gallagher, *Director*
EMP: 50
SALES (corp-wide): 39.6MM **Privately Held**
SIC: **4151** 8322 School buses; individual & family services
PA: Catholic Charities Cyo Of The Archdiocese Of San Francisco
    990 Eddy St
    San Francisco CA 94109
    415 972-1200

(P-3911)
CERTIFIED TRNSP SVCS INC
1038 N Custer St, Santa Ana (92701-3915)
PHONE....................714 835-8676
David Gregory, *CEO*
EMP: 70
SQ FT: 3,000
SALES (est): 5.6MM **Privately Held**
WEB: www.ctsbus.com
SIC: **4151** School buses

(P-3912)
COUNTY OF LOS ANGELES
Also Called: Pupil Transportation
9402 Greenleaf Ave, Whittier (90605)
PHONE....................562 945-2581
Dan Ibarra, *Director*
Carina Lazcano, *Opers Mgr*
EMP: 110 **Privately Held**
WEB: www.co.la.ca.us
SIC: **4151** 9621 School buses; regulation, administration of transportation;
PA: County Of Los Angeles
    500 W Temple St Ste 437
    Los Angeles CA 90012
    213 974-1101

(P-3913)
DURHAM SCHOOL SERVICES
Also Called: Perterman
3001 Ross Ave Ste 11, San Jose (95124-2358)
PHONE....................408 448-0740
Ron Mahler, *Branch Mgr*
EMP: 80 **Privately Held**
SIC: **4151** School buses
HQ: Durham School Services
    506 Se 15th St
    Oak Grove MO 64075
    816 690-3813

(P-3914)
DURHAM SCHOOL SERVICES L P
16627 Avalon Blvd Ste B, Carson (90746-1051)
PHONE....................310 767-5820
Raphael Balonos, *Manager*
Alma Lawrence, *Human Res Dir*
EMP: 250 **Privately Held**
SIC: **4151** School buses
HQ: Durham School Services, L. P.
    2601 Navistar Dr
    Lisle IL 60532
    630 836-0292

(P-3915)
DURHAM SCHOOL SERVICES L P

1506 White Oaks Rd, Campbell
(95008-6724)
PHONE..................408 377-6655
EMP: 105 Privately Held
SIC: 4151 School buses
HQ: Durham School Services, L. P.
2601 Navistar Dr
Lisle IL 60532
630 836-0292

(P-3916)
DURHAM SCHOOL SERVICES L P

365 E Avnda De Los Alvare, Thousand
Oaks (91360)
PHONE..................805 495-8338
Terry Walker, *Branch Mgr*
Terry L Walker, *Manager*
EMP: 55 Privately Held
SIC: 4151 4142 4141 School buses; bus
charter service, except local; local bus
charter service
HQ: Durham School Services, L. P.
2601 Navistar Dr
Lisle IL 60532
630 836-0292

(P-3917)
DURHAM SCHOOL SERVICES L P

27577 Industrial Blvd A, Hayward
(94545-4044)
PHONE..................510 887-6005
Chris Stone, *Principal*
EMP: 190
SQ FT: 1,200 Privately Held
SIC: 4151
HQ: Durham School Services, L. P.
2601 Navistar Dr
Lisle IL 60532
630 836-0292

(P-3918)
DURHAM SCHOOL SERVICES L P

10701 E Bennett Rd, Grass Valley
(95945-9361)
PHONE..................530 273-7282
Paula Davidson, *General Mgr*
EMP: 70 Privately Held
SIC: 4151 4119 4111 School buses; local
passenger transportation; local & subur-
ban transit
HQ: Durham School Services, L. P.
2601 Navistar Dr
Lisle IL 60532
630 836-0292

(P-3919)
DURHAM SCHOOL SERVICES L P

2121 Piedmont Way, Pittsburg
(94565-5017)
PHONE..................925 686-3391
Joe Cobillas, *Branch Mgr*
EMP: 120 Privately Held
SIC: 4151 School buses
HQ: Durham School Services, L. P.
2601 Navistar Dr
Lisle IL 60532
630 836-0292

(P-3920)
DURHAM SCHOOL SERVICES L P

2713 River Ave, Rosemead (91770-3303)
PHONE..................626 573-3769
David Gonzales, *General Mgr*
EMP: 150 Privately Held
SIC: 4151 School buses
HQ: Durham School Services, L. P.
2601 Navistar Dr
Lisle IL 60532
630 836-0292

(P-3921)
ELK GROVE UNIFIED SCHOOL DST

Also Called: Transportation Department
8421 Gerber Rd, Sacramento
(95828-3711)
PHONE..................916 686-7733
Jill Gayaldo, *Branch Mgr*
EMP: 200
SALES (corp-wide): 741.9MM Privately Held
SIC: 4151 School buses
PA: Grove Elk Unified School District
9510 Elk Grove Florin Rd
Elk Grove CA 95624
916 686-5085

(P-3922)
FACILITIES OPERATION AND TRNSP

Also Called: Los Banos School District
2657 E Pacheco Blvd, Los Banos
(93635-9417)
PHONE..................209 826-1936
Tom Worthy, *Director*
EMP: 100
SALES (est): 2.3MM Privately Held
SIC: 4151 School buses

(P-3923)
FIRST STUDENT INC

436 Parr Blvd, Richmond (94801-1123)
PHONE..................510 237-6677
Brian Rutford, *Principal*
EMP: 79
SALES (corp-wide): 8.9B Privately Held
SIC: 4151 School buses
HQ: First Student, Inc.
600 Vine St Ste 1400
Cincinnati OH 45202

(P-3924)
FIRST STUDENT INC

991 E Poplar Ave, San Mateo
(94401-1479)
PHONE..................650 685-8245
EMP: 83
SALES (corp-wide): 8.9B Privately Held
SIC: 4151 School buses
HQ: First Student, Inc.
600 Vine St Ste 1400
Cincinnati OH 45202

(P-3925)
FIRST STUDENT INC

234 S I St, San Bernardino (92410-2408)
PHONE..................909 383-1640
Cheryl Seifert, *Manager*
EMP: 100
SALES (corp-wide): 8.9B Privately Held
WEB: www.leag.com
SIC: 4151 School buses
HQ: First Student, Inc.
600 Vine St Ste 1400
Cincinnati OH 45202

(P-3926)
FIRST STUDENT INC

Also Called: Laidlaw Educational Services
5006 E Calle San Raphael, Palm Springs
(92264-3452)
PHONE..................760 320-4659
Mike Robertson, *Manager*
EMP: 75
SALES (corp-wide): 8.9B Privately Held
WEB: www.leag.com
SIC: 4151 School buses
HQ: First Student, Inc.
600 Vine St Ste 1400
Cincinnati OH 45202

(P-3927)
FIRST STUDENT INC

2005 Navy Dr, Stockton (95206-1142)
PHONE..................209 466-7737
Drigden Summers, *Manager*
EMP: 200
SALES (corp-wide): 8.9B Privately Held
WEB: www.leag.com
SIC: 4151 School buses

HQ: First Student, Inc.
600 Vine St Ste 1400
Cincinnati OH 45202

(P-3928)
FIRST STUDENT INC

Also Called: Laidlaw Education Services
844 E 9th St, San Bernardino
(92410-4012)
PHONE..................909 383-7104
Norm Foisy, *Manager*
EMP: 65
SQ FT: 2,500
SALES (corp-wide): 8.9B Privately Held
WEB: www.leag.com
SIC: 4151 School buses
HQ: First Student, Inc.
600 Vine St Ste 1400
Cincinnati OH 45202

(P-3929)
FIRST STUDENT INC

14800 S Avalon Blvd, Gardena
(90248-2012)
PHONE..................310 715-6122
Mike Sherrill, *Branch Mgr*
EMP: 250
SALES (corp-wide): 8.9B Privately Held
WEB: www.leag.com
SIC: 4151 4141 School buses; local bus
charter service
HQ: First Student, Inc.
600 Vine St Ste 1400
Cincinnati OH 45202

(P-3930)
FIRST STUDENT INC

2270 Jerrold Ave, San Francisco
(94124-1012)
PHONE..................415 647-9012
Bob Gonzales, *Manager*
EMP: 285
SALES (corp-wide): 8.9B Privately Held
WEB: www.leag.com
SIC: 4151 School buses
HQ: First Student, Inc.
600 Vine St Ste 1400
Cincinnati OH 45202

(P-3931)
FIRST STUDENT INC

436 Parr Blvd, Richmond (94801-1123)
PHONE..................510 237-6365
Brian Rudford, *Branch Mgr*
EMP: 100
SQ FT: 6,488
SALES (corp-wide): 8.9B Privately Held
WEB: www.firststudentinc.com
SIC: 4151 School buses
HQ: First Student, Inc.
600 Vine St Ste 1400
Cincinnati OH 45202

(P-3932)
FIRST STUDENT INC

5320 Derry Ave Ste O, Agoura Hills
(91301-5029)
PHONE..................818 707-2082
EMP: 79
SALES (corp-wide): 9.2B Privately Held
SIC: 4151
HQ: First Student, Inc.
600 Vine St Ste 1400
Cincinnati OH 45202
513 241-2200

(P-3933)
FIRST STUDENT INC

Also Called: Laidlaw Education Services
3401 W Castor St, Santa Ana
(92704-3909)
PHONE..................714 850-7578
Debi Manley, *Manager*
EMP: 100
SALES (corp-wide): 8.9B Privately Held
WEB: www.leag.com
SIC: 4151 School buses
HQ: First Student, Inc.
600 Vine St Ste 1400
Cincinnati OH 45202

(P-3934)
FIRST STUDENT INC

11233 San Fernando Rd, San Fernando
(91340-3409)
PHONE..................818 896-0333
Sue Wagnon, *Branch Mgr*
EMP: 135
SALES (corp-wide): 8.9B Privately Held
WEB: www.leag.com
SIC: 4151 School buses
HQ: First Student, Inc.
600 Vine St Ste 1400
Cincinnati OH 45202

(P-3935)
FIRST STUDENT INC

Also Called: Laidlaw Transit Services
123 N E St Ste 102, Madera (93638-3286)
PHONE..................559 661-7433
Roberta Collins, *Branch Mgr*
EMP: 126
SALES (corp-wide): 8.9B Privately Held
WEB: www.leag.com
SIC: 4151 School buses
HQ: First Student, Inc.
600 Vine St Ste 1400
Cincinnati OH 45202

(P-3936)
FIRST STUDENT INC

Also Called: Cardinal Transportation
14800 S Avalon Blvd, Gardena
(90248-2012)
PHONE..................310 769-2400
Ray Borales, *President*
Roy J Weber, *President*
EMP: 220
SQ FT: 18,000
SALES (est): 6.1MM
SALES (corp-wide): 8.9B Privately Held
WEB: www.cardinaltransportationltd.com
SIC: 4151 School buses
HQ: Firstgroup America, Inc.
600 Vine St Ste 1400
Cincinnati OH 45202
513 241-2200

(P-3937)
FRESNO CNTY SPRNTNDENT SCHOOLS

Also Called: Southwest Transportation Agcy
16644 S Elm Ave, Caruthers (93609-9757)
P.O. Box 785, Riverdale (93656-0785)
PHONE..................559 644-1000
Tony Mendes, *Branch Mgr*
Lynn Hill, *Admin Asst*
Greg Durrenberger, *Technology*
Maricela Ordonez, *Finance*
Jerry Thomas, *Maint Spvr*
EMP: 75
SALES (corp-wide): 84.3MM Privately Held
WEB: www.southwestjpa.org
SIC: 4151 School buses
PA: Fresno County Superintendent Of
Schools
1111 Van Ness Ave
Fresno CA 93721
559 265-3000

(P-3938)
IRVINE UNIFIED SCHOOL DISTICT

Also Called: Maintenance & Trnsp Fcilty
100 Nightmist, Irvine (92618-1710)
PHONE..................949 936-5300
Rose Clegg, *Director*
EMP: 100
SALES (corp-wide): 380.9MM Privately Held
WEB: www.gvarvas.com
SIC: 4151 7349 School buses; building
maintenance services
PA: Irvine Unified School Distict
5050 Barranca Pkwy
Irvine CA 92604
949 936-5000

(P-3939)
LAKE ELSINORE UNIFIED SCHL DST
Also Called: Lake Elsn SC Trans
21641 Bundy Canyon Rd, Wildomar (92595-8778)
PHONE..........................951 253-7830
Silvia Schwing, *Director*
EMP: 100
SALES (corp-wide): 255.2MM **Privately Held**
WEB: www.leusd.k12.ca.us
SIC: 4151 School buses
PA: Lake Elsinore Unified School District
545 Chaney St
Lake Elsinore CA 92530
951 253-7000

(P-3940)
LODI UNIFIED SCHOOL DISTRICT
Also Called: Transportation
820 S Cuff Ave, Lodi (95240)
PHONE..........................209 331-7169
Carlos Garcia, *Director*
EMP: 120
SALES (corp-wide): 360.5MM **Privately Held**
WEB: www.lodiusd.net
SIC: 4151 School buses
PA: Lodi Unified School District
1305 E Vine St
Lodi CA 95240
209 331-7000

(P-3941)
LONG BEACH UNIFIED SCHOOL DST
Also Called: Transportation Department
2700 Pine Ave, Long Beach (90806-2617)
PHONE..........................562 426-6176
Paul Bailey, *Director*
Susan Ginder, *Officer*
Amy Smith, *Exec Dir*
Matt Woods, *Exec Dir*
Les Leahy, *Admin Asst*
EMP: 100
SALES (corp-wide): 867.6MM **Privately Held**
WEB: www.lbusd.k12.ca.us
SIC: 4151 School buses
PA: Long Beach Unified School District
1515 Hughes Way
Long Beach CA 90810
562 997-8000

(P-3942)
MERCED TRANSPORTATION COMPANY
300 Grogan Ave, Merced (95341-6446)
PHONE..........................209 384-2575
Curtis Riggs, *President*
Gaye Riggs, *CFO*
EMP: 100
SQ FT: 8,000
SALES (est): 7.2MM **Privately Held**
SIC: 4151 School buses

(P-3943)
MONTEBELLO SCHOOL TRANSPORTION
505 S Greenwood Ave, Montebello (90640-5109)
PHONE..........................323 887-7900
Kennedy E Benedetta, *Principal*
Lea Yeng, *Admin Sec*
Daniel Ibarra, *Director*
EMP: 55
SALES (est): 1.2MM **Privately Held**
SIC: 4151 School buses

(P-3944)
SANTA BARBARA TRNSP CORP (HQ)
6414 Hollister Ave, Goleta (93117-3145)
PHONE..........................805 681-8355
Denis J Hallagher, *CEO*
Patrick Walker, *CFO*
Dennis McGurk, *Director*
EMP: 90
SQ FT: 15,000

SALES (est): 59.6MM
SALES (corp-wide): 1.8B **Privately Held**
WEB: www.sta-ips.com
SIC: 4151 4141 School buses; local bus charter service
PA: Student Transportation Of America, Inc.
3349 Hwy 138
Wall Township NJ 07719
732 280-4200

(P-3945)
SANTA BARBARA TRNSP CORP
Also Called: Student Transportation America
1331 Jason Way, Santa Maria (93455-1000)
PHONE..........................805 928-0402
Paula Sauvadon, *Vice Pres*
EMP: 75
SALES (corp-wide): 1.8B **Privately Held**
WEB: www.sta-ips.com
SIC: 4151 4121 School buses; taxicabs
HQ: Santa Barbara Transportation Corporation
6414 Hollister Ave
Goleta CA 93117
805 681-8355

(P-3946)
TEMECULA VALLEY UNIFIED SCHOOL
40516 Roripaugh Rd, Temecula (92591-4563)
PHONE..........................951 695-7110
Thomas Forrest, *Branch Mgr*
EMP: 364
SALES (corp-wide): 305.6MM **Privately Held**
SIC: 4151 School buses
PA: Temecula Valley Unified School District School Facilities Corporation
31350 Rancho Vista Rd
Temecula CA 92592
951 676-2661

(P-3947)
UKIAH SC TRANSPORTATION
710 Maple Ave, Ukiah (95482-3743)
PHONE..........................707 463-5234
Dave Turner, *Director*
EMP: 55
SALES (est): 823.5K **Privately Held**
SIC: 4151 School buses

(P-3948)
WOODLAND JINT UNIFIED SCHL DST
25 Matmor Rd, Woodland (95776-6008)
PHONE..........................530 662-0201
John Houston, *Manager*
EMP: 50
SALES (corp-wide): 121.9MM **Privately Held**
WEB: www.leejhs.wjusd.k12.ca.us
SIC: 4151 School buses
PA: Woodland Joint Unified School District
435 6th St
Woodland CA 95695
530 662-0201

4173 Bus Terminal & Svc Facilities

(P-3949)
ALAMEDA-CONTRA COSTA TRNST DST
A C Transit
10626 International Blvd, Oakland (94603-3806)
PHONE..........................510 577-8816
Glen Andrade, *Manager*
EMP: 130
SALES (corp-wide): 67.6MM **Privately Held**
WEB: www.actransit.org
SIC: 4173 Maintenance facilities for motor vehicle passenger transport
PA: Alameda-Contra Costa Transit District
1600 Franklin St
Oakland CA 94612
510 891-4777

(P-3950)
CITY OF LOS ANGELES
Also Called: Port of Los Angeles
500 Pier A Pl, Wilmington (90744-6210)
PHONE..........................310 732-3550
Joannie Mukai, *Branch Mgr*
EMP: 500 **Privately Held**
WEB: www.lacity.org
SIC: 4173 9621 Maintenance facilities for motor vehicle passenger transport; regulation, administration of transportation;
PA: City Of Los Angeles
200 N Spring St Ste 303
Los Angeles CA 90012
213 978-0600

(P-3951)
CITY OF LOS ANGELES
Also Called: General Services
2513 E 24th St, Vernon (90058-1205)
PHONE..........................213 485-4981
John Ferris, *Superintendent*
Jacque Lorraine, *Supervisor*
EMP: 100 **Privately Held**
WEB: www.lacity.org
SIC: 4173 9621 Maintenance facilities for motor vehicle passenger transport; regulation, administration of transportation;
PA: City Of Los Angeles
200 N Spring St Ste 303
Los Angeles CA 90012
213 978-0600

(P-3952)
DURHAM SCHOOL SERVICES L P
2818 W 5th St, Santa Ana (92703-1824)
PHONE..........................714 542-8989
Debbie Williams, *Manager*
Rafaela Rodriguez, *Human Res Mgr*
EMP: 200
SQ FT: 4,843 **Privately Held**
SIC: 4173 4151 Maintenance facilities for motor vehicle passenger transport; school buses
HQ: Durham School Services, L. P.
2601 Navistar Dr
Lisle IL 60532
630 836-0292

(P-3953)
FIRST STUDENT INC
300 S Buena Vista Ave, Corona (92882-1937)
PHONE..........................951 736-3234
Jackie Mansperger, *Manager*
EMP: 101
SALES (corp-wide): 8.9B **Privately Held**
WEB: www.leag.com
SIC: 4173 4151 Maintenance facilities, buses; school buses
HQ: First Student, Inc.
600 Vine St Ste 1400
Cincinnati OH 45202

(P-3954)
GREYHOUND LINES INC
1716 E 7th St, Los Angeles (90021-1202)
PHONE..........................213 629-8400
Mark Jacobson, *Principal*
EMP: 400
SQ FT: 100,000
SALES (corp-wide): 8.9B **Privately Held**
WEB: www.greyhound.com
SIC: 4173 Bus terminal operation
HQ: Greyhound Lines, Inc.
350 N Saint Paul St # 300
Dallas TX 75201
214 849-8000

(P-3955)
SACRAMENTO REGIONAL TRNST DIST
Also Called: Light Rail
2700 Academy Way, Sacramento (95815-2362)
PHONE..........................916 869-8611
Gabriel Avila, *Director*
EMP: 200

SALES (corp-wide): 28MM **Privately Held**
WEB: www.sacrt.com
SIC: 4173 4111 Maintenance facilities for motor vehicle passenger transport; local & suburban transit
PA: Sacramento Regional Transit Dist.
1400 29th St
Sacramento CA 95816
916 726-2877

(P-3956)
SAN MATEO COUNTY TRANSIT DST
Also Called: Sam Trans
501 Pico Blvd, San Carlos (94070-2706)
PHONE..........................650 508-6412
Ed Proctor, *Manager*
Tom Blalock, *Administration*
EMP: 175
SALES (corp-wide): 17MM **Privately Held**
SIC: 4173 4111 Maintenance facilities, buses; local & suburban transit
PA: San Mateo County Transit District
1250 San Carlos Ave
San Carlos CA 94070
650 508-6200

4212 Local Trucking Without Storage

(P-3957)
A & D HAULING SERVICES INC
13337 South St, Cerritos (90703-7308)
PHONE..........................310 514-8969
Lillian Wang, *Exec Dir*
Andrew Wang, *General Mgr*
Grace Wang, *General Mgr*
EMP: 60
SQ FT: 75,000
SALES (est): 5.2MM **Privately Held**
WEB: www.adhls.net
SIC: 4212 Light haulage & cartage, local

(P-3958)
A & I TRUCKING INC (PA)
Also Called: A & I Transportation
123 Lee Rd Ste E, Watsonville (95076-9422)
P.O. Box 1270 (95077-1270)
PHONE..........................831 763-7805
Albert Tadevosyan, *CEO*
EMP: 50
SQ FT: 1,000
SALES (est): 11.6MM **Privately Held**
SIC: 4212 Local trucking, without storage

(P-3959)
A A A PACKING AND SHIPPING INC
2000 E 49th St, Vernon (90058-2802)
PHONE..........................626 310-7787
Bruce Nebens, *President*
Frank Hallberg, *COO*
EMP: 50
SQ FT: 80,000
SALES (est): 5.3MM **Privately Held**
WEB: www.aaapack.com
SIC: 4212 4213 4783 Local trucking, without storage; trucking, except local; packing goods for shipping

(P-3960)
A G HACIENDA INCORPORATED
32794 Sherwood Ave, Mc Farland (93250-9626)
P.O. Box 367 (93250-0367)
PHONE..........................661 792-2418
Xochilht Gonzalez, *President*
EMP: 400
SALES (est): 28.4MM **Privately Held**
SIC: 4212 0761 4214 Local trucking, without storage; farm labor contractors; local trucking with storage

(P-3961)
A J R TRUCKING INC
915 Monterey Rd, Glendale (91206-2518)
PHONE..........................562 989-9555
Khachatur Khudikyan, *President*
Jehan Reyes, *Shareholder*
Hakop Khudikyan, *CFO*
Angel Reyes, *Director*

EMP: 84
SQ FT: 12,000
SALES (est): 9.9MM **Privately Held**
SIC: 4212 Mail carriers, contract

(P-3962)
A-1 DELIVERY CO
1777 S Vintage Ave, Ontario (91761-3659)
PHONE...................909 444-1220
Joe Romine, *President*
William Turner, *Corp Secy*
Johnny Romine, *Vice Pres*
EMP: 75
SQ FT: 10,000
SALES (est): 8.5MM **Privately Held**
WEB: www.jromine.com
SIC: 4212 Delivery service, vehicular

(P-3963)
A-1 EXPRESS DELIVERY SERVICE (PA)
4520 S Maywood Ave, Vernon (90058-2611)
PHONE...................323 585-4440
John Georgino, *CEO*
John Buss, *Vice Pres*
Lynda Curatalo, *Vice Pres*
EMP: 50 EST: 1971
SQ FT: 50,000
SALES (est): 5.2MM **Privately Held**
SIC: 4212 Delivery service, vehicular

(P-3964)
ACCURATE COURIER SERVICES INC
11022 Santa Monica Blvd # 360, Los Angeles (90025-7513)
P.O. Box 252061 (90025-8939)
PHONE...................310 481-3937
Joseph Yemini, *President*
Miguel Meza, *Director*
EMP: 92
SALES (est): 7.7MM **Privately Held**
SIC: 4212 Delivery service, vehicular

(P-3965)
ACCURATE DELIVERY SYSTEMS INC
Also Called: ADS
173 Resource Dr, Bloomington (92316-3540)
P.O. Box 1620, Chino (91708-1620)
PHONE...................951 823-8870
Mahmoud Maraach, *President*
EMP: 55
SQ FT: 10,000
SALES (est): 8.5MM **Privately Held**
SIC: 4212 Delivery service, vehicular

(P-3966)
ACE RELOCATION SYSTEMS INC (PA)
5608 Eastgate Dr, San Diego (92121-2816)
PHONE...................858 677-5500
Lawrence R Lammers, *President*
Laura Marion, *Treasurer*
Richard Clarke, *Senior VP*
Daniel J Lammers, *Vice Pres*
Phyllis Cain, *Executive Asst*
▲ **EMP:** 69
SQ FT: 48,000
SALES: 67.2MM **Privately Held**
WEB: www.acerelocation.com
SIC: 4212 Moving services

(P-3967)
ACE RELOCATION SYSTEMS INC
189 W Victoria St, Long Beach (90805-2162)
PHONE...................310 632-2800
Kevin Casey, *Branch Mgr*
EMP: 50
SALES (corp-wide): 67.2MM **Privately Held**
WEB: www.acerelocation.com
SIC: 4212 4213 Moving services; trucking, except local
PA: Ace Relocation Systems, Inc.
5608 Eastgate Dr
San Diego CA 92121
858 677-5500

(P-3968)
ADVANCED ENVIRONMENTAL INC
Also Called: Advanced Resources
13579 Whittram Ave, Fontana (92335-2950)
PHONE...................909 356-9025
Bruce De Menno, *President*
EMP: 50
SALES (est): 3.5MM
SALES (corp-wide): 198.5MM **Privately Held**
SIC: 4212 8742 Hazardous waste transport; management consulting services
HQ: De Menno-Kerdoon Trading Company
2000 N Alameda St
Compton CA 90222

(P-3969)
AGRI-MIX TRANSPORT INC
1400 S Union Ave Ste 110, Bakersfield (93307-4179)
P.O. Box 327, Lamont (93241-0327)
PHONE...................661 833-6280
Cesar Juarez, *President*
Gonzalo Juarez, *Treasurer*
Walter Juarez, *Vice Pres*
Ramon Juarez, *Admin Sec*
EMP: 150
SQ FT: 435,600
SALES: 30MM **Privately Held**
SIC: 4212 Local trucking, without storage

(P-3970)
AJR TRUCKING INC
2700 Rose Ave Ste A, Signal Hill (90755-1929)
P.O. Box 10129, Glendale (91209-3129)
PHONE...................562 989-9555
Jack Khudikyan, *Vice Pres*
EMP: 140
SALES (est): 10.5MM **Privately Held**
SIC: 4212 Delivery service, vehicular

(P-3971)
ANDERSNCTTONWOOD DISPOSAL SVCS
Also Called: Waste Managment
3281 State Highway 99w S, Corning (96021-9736)
P.O. Box 496 (96021-0496)
PHONE...................530 824-4700
Bill Manneo, *Manager*
EMP: 51
SALES (corp-wide): 4.9MM **Privately Held**
SIC: 4212 Garbage collection & transport, no disposal
PA: Andersoncottonwood Disposal Services Inc
8592 Commercial Way
Redding CA 96002
530 221-6510

(P-3972)
ANTONINI FREIGHT EXPRESS INC (PA)
287 N Cardinal Ave, Stockton (95215-4001)
P.O. Box 8468 (95208-0468)
PHONE...................209 466-4900
Joseph Antonini, *President*
Karen Wuellner, *Vice Pres*
Jim Givens, *Branch Mgr*
Andy Wuellner, *Information Mgr*
Mary Laughin, *Hum Res Coord*
EMP: 101
SQ FT: 4,000
SALES (est): 10.6MM **Privately Held**
WEB: www.antoniniusa.com
SIC: 4212 Delivery service, vehicular

(P-3973)
ARAKELIAN ENTERPRISES INC
Also Called: Athens Services
11121 Pendleton St, Sun Valley (91352-1513)
PHONE...................818 768-1492
Ron Arakelian Jr, *CEO*
EMP: 164
SALES (corp-wide): 150MM **Privately Held**
SIC: 4212 Garbage collection & transport, no disposal

PA: Arakelian Enterprises, Inc.
14048 Valley Blvd
City Of Industry CA 91746
626 336-3636

(P-3974)
ARMADA TRUCKING GROUP INC
225 Hermosa Ave Unit 202, Long Beach (90802-3970)
PHONE...................800 620-8592
Zoran Maric, *President*
Boris Stricevic, *Vice Pres*
EMP: 74 EST: 2014
SQ FT: 972
SALES: 2.9MM **Privately Held**
SIC: 4212 Delivery service, vehicular

(P-3975)
ASBURY ENVIRONMENTAL SERVICES (PA)
1300 S Santa Fe Ave, Compton (90221-4916)
PHONE...................310 886-3400
Steve Kerdoon, *CEO*
Chris Mahoney, *CFO*
Anne Asbury, *Treasurer*
Bruce De Menno, *Vice Pres*
EMP: 75
SQ FT: 22,000
SALES (est): 68.2MM **Privately Held**
WEB: www.asburyenv.com
SIC: 4212 Local trucking, without storage

(P-3976)
ATCHESONS EXPRESS INC
1590 S Archibald Ave, Ontario (91761-7629)
PHONE...................714 808-9199
Brad Atcheson, *President*
Gail Atcheson, *CFO*
Mark Atcheson, *Vice Pres*
Jennifer Bowles, *General Mgr*
Evelyn Abel, *Accounts Exec*
EMP: 50
SQ FT: 10,000
SALES (est): 6.5MM **Privately Held**
WEB: www.atchesonexpress.com
SIC: 4212 4731 Local trucking, without storage; freight transportation arrangement

(P-3977)
B & G DELIVERY SYSTEM INC
2549 Harris Ave, Sacramento (95838-3128)
PHONE...................916 921-4401
Bruce Allgier, *President*
Vicky Allgier, *CFO*
John Margetich, *General Mgr*
Rebecca Allgier, *Admin Sec*
Amanda Davidson, *Administration*
EMP: 125
SQ FT: 20,000
SALES (est): 25.8MM **Privately Held**
WEB: www.bgdelivery.com
SIC: 4212 4215 Delivery service, vehicular; courier services, except by air

(P-3978)
BEST OVERNITE EXPRESS INC (PA)
Also Called: Best Overnight Express
406 Live Oak Ave, Irwindale (91706-1314)
P.O. Box 90816, City of Industry (91715-0816)
PHONE...................626 256-6340
William K Applebee, *President*
Mike Salcedo, *COO*
Mike White, *CFO*
Mike Saucedo, *Vice Pres*
Jeff Siri, *Branch Mgr*
EMP: 160
SQ FT: 25,000
SALES (est): 32.3MM **Privately Held**
SIC: 4212 Delivery service, vehicular

(P-3979)
BLUE EAGLE CONTRACTING INC
2059 Nev Cy Hwy Ste 204, Grass Valley (95945)
PHONE...................530 272-0287
Daniel L Rackley, *President*
Marvin L Rackley, *Ch of Bd*

Ray Rackley, *Vice Pres*
EMP: 53
SQ FT: 700
SALES (est): 6.9MM **Privately Held**
SIC: 4212 Mail carriers, contract

(P-3980)
BOB HUBBARD HORSE TRNSP INC (PA)
3730 S Riverside Ave, Colton (92324-3329)
PHONE...................951 369-3770
Bob Hubbard, *CEO*
Tom Hubbard, *President*
Pat Hubbard, *Vice Pres*
Patricia Hubbard, *Vice Pres*
Kathy Copeland, *CIO*
EMP: 50
SQ FT: 9,375
SALES (est): 12.7MM **Privately Held**
WEB: www.bobhubbardhorsetrans.com
SIC: 4212 4213 4789 Animal transport; trucking, except local; cargo loading & unloading services

(P-3981)
BUDS & SON TRUCKING INC
12570 Highway 67, Lakeside (92040-1159)
P.O. Box 1521 (92040-0912)
PHONE...................619 443-4200
Marvin J Struiksma, *President*
Robert Struiksma, *Corp Secy*
John Struiksma, *Vice Pres*
Michael Willingham, *Admin Sec*
EMP: 85 EST: 1942
SQ FT: 10,800
SALES (est): 5MM **Privately Held**
SIC: 4212 4213 Local trucking, without storage; trucking, except local

(P-3982)
BURNS AND SONS TRUCKING INC
Also Called: Dependable Disposal and Recycl
9210 Olive Dr, Spring Valley (91977-2305)
P.O. Box 1640 (91979-1640)
PHONE...................619 460-5394
Eva N Burns, *CEO*
Jack Burns Sr, *President*
Tom McFarlane, *CFO*
Jim Burns, *Vice Pres*
Sonia Serrano, *Accounts Mgr*
EMP: 85
SQ FT: 6,000
SALES (est): 16.7MM **Privately Held**
WEB: www.burnsandsonstrucking.com
SIC: 4212 4214 Local trucking, without storage; local trucking with storage

(P-3983)
BURRTEC WASTE GROUP INC
2340 W Main St, Barstow (92311-3612)
PHONE...................760 256-2730
EMP: 84
SALES (corp-wide): 309.8MM **Privately Held**
SIC: 4212 Garbage collection & transport, no disposal
PA: Burrtec Waste Group, Inc.
9890 Cherry Ave
Fontana CA 92335
909 429-4200

(P-3984)
C P S EXPRESS (HQ)
3401 Etiwanda Ave B, Mira Loma (91752-1128)
P.O. Box 248 (91752-0248)
PHONE...................951 685-1041
William Smerber, *CEO*
Kirt Allen, *Corp Secy*
James E Ford, *Vice Pres*
EMP: 100
SQ FT: 7,000
SALES (est): 13.3MM
SALES (corp-wide): 42.2MM **Privately Held**
SIC: 4212 4213 4214 Local trucking, without storage; trucking, except local; local trucking with storage
PA: Haddy, J G Sales Co, Inc
3401 Etiwanda Ave
Mira Loma CA 91752
951 685-4100

(P-3985)
C S TRANSPORT INC
Also Called: Southern California Carriers
425 E Heber Rd Ste 200, Heber
(92249-9660)
PHONE....................760 666-5661
Samuel Colin, *President*
EMP: 64
SQ FT: 700
SALES: 9MM **Privately Held**
SIC: 4212 4731 Local trucking, without
storage; transportation agents & brokers

(P-3986)
CALIFORNIA MATERIALS INC
Also Called: Cmat
3736 S Highway 99, Stockton
(95215-8028)
P.O. Box 32314 (95213-2314)
PHONE....................209 472-7422
Earl Rogers, *President*
Renee Limon, *Traffic Dir*
EMP: 50 EST: 2008
SALES (est): 7MM **Privately Held**
SIC: 4212 Dump truck haulage

(P-3987)
CEMAK TRUCKING INC (PA)
4621 Teller Ave Ste 130, Newport Beach
(92660-2165)
PHONE....................949 253-2800
Kurt Callier, *President*
Randy Callier, *Vice Pres*
EMP: 70
SQ FT: 8,000
SALES (est): 7MM **Privately Held**
SIC: 4212 Local trucking, without storage

(P-3988)
CENTRAL COURIER LLC
1957 Eastman Ave Ste C, Ventura
(93003-6491)
PHONE....................805 654-1145
Nkosi Khumalo, *President*
EMP: 55
SQ FT: 3,038
SALES (est): 3MM **Privately Held**
SIC: 4212 Light haulage & cartage, local;
delivery service, vehicular

(P-3989)
CENTRAL FREIGHT LINES INC
4575 S Chestnut Ave, Fresno
(93725-9211)
PHONE....................559 233-5559
Robert Ibarra, *Manager*
Brandon McKeehan, *Manager*
Will Young, *Manager*
EMP: 53
SQ FT: 5,790
SALES (corp-wide): 1.7B **Privately Held**
WEB: www.centralfreight.com
SIC: 4212 4213 Local trucking, without
storage; trucking, except local
HQ: Central Freight Lines, Inc.
5601 W Waco Dr
Waco TX 76710
254 772-2120

(P-3990)
CENTRAL VALLEY CONCRETE INC (PA)
Also Called: Central Valley Trucking
3823 N State Highway 59, Merced
(95348-9370)
PHONE....................209 723-8846
Scott Neal, *CEO*
Brandon Williams, *General Mgr*
EMP: 150
SQ FT: 2,000
SALES (est): 33.3MM **Privately Held**
WEB: www.centralvalleyconcrete.com
SIC: 4212 3273 Local trucking, without
storage; ready-mixed concrete

(P-3991)
CLAY MIRANDA TRUCKING INC
3220 W Belmont Ave, Fresno
(93722-5905)
P.O. Box 11983 (93776-1983)
PHONE....................559 275-6250
Debbie Cooper, *Vice Pres*
Mike Miranda, *President*
EMP: 53
SQ FT: 9,600

SALES (est): 6.1MM **Privately Held**
SIC: 4212 5032 Dump truck haulage; asphalt mixture; gravel; sand, construction; stone, crushed or broken

(P-3992)
CLEM-TRANS INC
213 W Valley Blvd, Rialto (92376-7713)
P.O. Box 3124, San Dimas (91773-7124)
PHONE....................909 877-4450
Glory M Clemons, *President*
EMP: 50 EST: 1965
SQ FT: 3,500
SALES (est): 4.3MM **Privately Held**
SIC: 4212 4213 Mail carriers, contract;
contract haulers

(P-3993)
COASTAL TRANSPORT CO INC
9950 San Diego Mission Rd F, San Diego
(92108-1705)
PHONE....................619 584-1055
Brian Martin, *Manager*
EMP: 52
SALES (corp-wide): 90.1MM **Privately Held**
SIC: 4212 4213 Liquid haulage, local; liquid petroleum transport, non-local
PA: Coastal Transport Co., Inc.
1603 Ackerman Rd
San Antonio TX 78219
210 661-4287

(P-3994)
COMMAND DELIVERY SYSTEMS INC (PA)
20935 Currier Rd, Walnut (91789-3020)
P.O. Box 190, Los Alamitos (90720-0190)
PHONE....................909 444-1475
Gregory Selmanson, *President*
EMP: 65
SQ FT: 14,000
SALES: 8.8MM **Privately Held**
SIC: 4212 4213 Delivery service, vehicular; trucking, except local

(P-3995)
COMPLETE LOGISTICS COMPANY
13831 Slover Ave, Fontana (92337-7037)
PHONE....................909 427-9800
Tim Telbsio, *Manager*
Richard Wheeler, *VP Opers*
EMP: 150
SALES (corp-wide): 70.7MM **Privately Held**
SIC: 4212 Local trucking, without storage
PA: The Complete Logistics Company
1670 Etiwanda Ave Ste A
Ontario CA 91761
909 544-5040

(P-3996)
COORDNTED DLVRY INSTLLTION INC
905 E Katella Ave, Anaheim (92805-6616)
PHONE....................714 501-4040
Flynn A Olsen, *CEO*
Jimmie D Mc Gee, *President*
EMP: 60
SQ FT: 35,000
SALES (est): 3.8MM **Privately Held**
WEB: www.coordinateddelivery.com
SIC: 4212 Delivery service, vehicular

(P-3997)
DALTON TRUCKING INC (PA)
13560 Whittram Ave, Fontana
(92335-2951)
P.O. Box 5025 (92334-5025)
PHONE....................909 823-0663
Terry Klenske, *CEO*
Mathew Klenske, *Vice Pres*
Eleanor Klenske, *Admin Sec*
EMP: 215
SQ FT: 11,000
SALES: 23.9MM **Privately Held**
SIC: 4212 Local trucking, without storage

(P-3998)
DAVID W GOLEN ✪
Also Called: Dw Logistix
20253 Gifford St, Winnetka (91306-3210)
PHONE....................213 716-0706
David W Golen, *Owner*

EMP: 80 EST: 2018
SALES (est): 1.1MM **Privately Held**
SIC: 4212 7389 Local trucking, without
storage; business services

(P-3999)
DAVIS TRUCKING LLC (PA)
7345 Mission Gorge Rd H, San Diego
(92120-1268)
PHONE....................619 229-9997
Gary Davis, *President*
Maria Da, *CFO*
Brandon Davis, *Vice Pres*
Troy Gonzalez, *Business Mgr*
Jim Ortega, *Traffic Dir*
EMP: 100
SQ FT: 40,000
SALES (est): 7.6MM **Privately Held**
WEB: www.davistrucking.com
SIC: 4212 4213 Local trucking, without
storage; less-than-truckload (LTL) transport

(P-4000)
DEDICATED FLEET SYSTEMS INC (PA)
1350 Philadelphia St, Pomona
(91766-5563)
P.O. Box 2829 (91769-2829)
PHONE....................909 590-8209
Anthony Osterkamp Jr, *Ch of Bd*
Gene Segrist, *Vice Pres*
Shelley Fajardo, *Admin Sec*
EMP: 59 EST: 1970
SALES (est): 4.9MM **Privately Held**
WEB: www.dedicatedfleetsystems.com
SIC: 4212 Local trucking, without storage

(P-4001)
DELUXE AUTO CARRIERS INC
Also Called: Excel Auto Transporting Towing
4788 Brookhollow Cir, Jurupa Valley
(92509-3072)
PHONE....................909 746-0900
Jesus Holguin, *President*
Raul Silva, *Vice Pres*
EMP: 60
SALES (est): 12.6MM **Privately Held**
SIC: 4212 Local trucking, without storage

(P-4002)
DEMENNO-KERDOON
1300 S Santa Fe Ave, Compton
(90221-4916)
PHONE....................310 898-3848
Steve Kerdoon, *President*
EMP: 500
SALES (est): 19.9MM **Privately Held**
SIC: 4212 Hazardous waste transport

(P-4003)
DEPENDABLE HIGHWAY EXPRESS INC
830 E St, West Sacramento (95605-2309)
PHONE....................916 374-0782
Tim Wallmark, *Branch Mgr*
Mike La Porte, *Manager*
EMP: 50
SALES (corp-wide): 283MM **Privately Held**
WEB: www.godependable.com
SIC: 4212 4213 Local trucking, without
storage; trucking, except local
PA: Dependable Highway Express, Inc.
2555 E Olympic Blvd
Los Angeles CA 90023
323 526-2200

(P-4004)
DESMOND MAIL DELIVERY SERVICE
4600 Worth St, Los Angeles (90063-1623)
P.O. Box 4836, Anaheim (92803-4836)
PHONE....................323 262-1085
Fax: 323 262-6440
EMP: 75
SQ FT: 3,000
SALES (est): 2.6MM
SALES (corp-wide): 33.1MM **Privately Held**
SIC: 4212
PA: Norco Delivery Service, Inc.
1560 N Missile Way
Anaheim CA 92801
714 520-8600

(P-4005)
DOUBLE D TRANSPORTATION CO
22991 Clawiter Rd, Hayward (94545-1316)
P.O. Box 2999, Dublin (94568-0999)
PHONE....................510 783-2335
Kathryn De Silva, *President*
EMP: 55
SQ FT: 1,000
SALES (est): 6.1MM **Privately Held**
SIC: 4212 Dump truck haulage

(P-4006)
DOUGLAS L MYOVICH TRUCKING INC
1895 W Jefferson Ave, Fresno
(93706-9732)
PHONE....................559 233-8242
Douglas Myovich, *President*
Cynthia Myovich, *Admin Sec*
EMP: 60
SALES (est): 4.6MM **Privately Held**
SIC: 4212 Liquid haulage, local

(P-4007)
DSC LOGISTICS INC
12350 Philadelphia Ave, Eastvale
(91752-3228)
PHONE....................909 605-7233
Adrian Potgieter, *Manager*
Mark Diaz, *General Mgr*
Chris Boughey, *Opers Mgr*
Rodriguez Grace, *Manager*
Rigo Mendoza, *Manager*
EMP: 56
SALES (corp-wide): 355MM **Privately Held**
SIC: 4212 4213 4225 4731 Local trucking, without storage; trucking, except local; general warehousing & storage; freight consolidation
PA: Dsc Logistics, Inc.
1750 S Wolf Rd
Des Plaines IL 60018
847 390-6800

(P-4008)
DTI INC
1628 S Sportsman Dr, Compton
(90221-4714)
P.O. Box 1739, Paramount (90723-1739)
PHONE....................310 635-9002
Gary Cross, *Partner*
Geoff Cross, *Partner*
EMP: 57 EST: 1975
SQ FT: 90,000
SALES (est): 5.5MM **Privately Held**
SIC: 4212 Liquid haulage, local

(P-4009)
EDS WEST LLC
6666 E Washington Blvd, Commerce
(90040-1814)
PHONE....................323 887-7367
Ronnie Moyal,
EMP: 75
SALES (est): 5.2MM **Privately Held**
SIC: 4212 Local trucking, without storage

(P-4010)
EMERALD TRANS LOS ANGELES LLC
5756 Alba St, Los Angeles (90058-3808)
PHONE....................323 277-2500
Al Harrell, *Manager*
Eric Zimmer, *Senior VP*
Mark Zimmerman, *Senior VP*
Clyde Phillips, *Vice Pres*
Alex Richard, *Vice Pres*
EMP: 50
SQ FT: 23,350
SALES (corp-wide): 127.1MM **Privately Held**
SIC: 4212 Hazardous waste transport
HQ: Emerald Transformer Los Angeles Llc
9820 Westpoint Dr Ste 300
Indianapolis IN 46256
972 841-7690

▲ = Import ▼=Export
◆ =Import/Export

(P-4011)
EMPIRE CHAUFFEUR SERVICE LTD
Also Called: Empire International
600 S Allied Way, El Segundo
(90245-4727)
PHONE..................310 414-8189
David Seelinger, *President*
EMP: 80
SALES (est): 5.4MM **Privately Held**
SIC: 4212 Local trucking, without storage

(P-4012)
FEDERAL EXPRESS CORPORATION
Also Called: Fedex
1600 63rd St, Emeryville (94608-2033)
PHONE..................800 463-3339
Mark Morris, *General Mgr*
Marc Morris, *General Mgr*
EMP: 120
SALES (corp-wide): 65.4B **Publicly Held**
WEB: www.federalexpress.com
SIC: 4212 4513 Local trucking, without storage; air courier services
HQ: Federal Express Corporation
3610 Hacks Cross Rd
Memphis TN 38125
901 369-3600

(P-4013)
FEDEX FREIGHT CORPORATION
3255 Victor St, Santa Clara (95054-2318)
PHONE..................408 988-2111
Mike Lujan, *Manager*
George Ortiz, *Opers Mgr*
EMP: 50
SQ FT: 18,200
SALES (corp-wide): 65.4B **Publicly Held**
SIC: 4212 4213 Local trucking, without storage; trucking, except local
HQ: Fedex Freight Corporation
1715 Aaron Brenner Dr
Memphis TN 38120
-

(P-4014)
FOOD EXPRESS INC
5127 Maywood Ave, Maywood (90270-2009)
PHONE..................323 589-1417
Mike Hess, *Manager*
EMP: 50
SALES (corp-wide): 37.1MM **Privately Held**
WEB: www.foodexp.com
SIC: 4212 5411 4214 Local trucking, without storage; grocery stores; local trucking with storage
PA: Food Express Inc.
521 N 1st Ave
Arcadia CA 91006
626 574-9094

(P-4015)
FRANK GHIGLIONE INC (PA)
Also Called: Rodgers Trucking Co
14327 Washington Ave, San Leandro (94578-3418)
P.O. Box 923 (94577-0445)
PHONE..................510 483-7000
Frank Ghiglione, *President*
Alan Osofsky, *Vice Pres*
Winifred Ghiglione, *Admin Sec*
Steve Strom, *Personnel*
EMP: 160
SQ FT: 8,000
SALES (est): 17.6MM **Privately Held**
WEB: www.rodgerstrucking.com
SIC: 4212 Delivery service, vehicular

(P-4016)
FRANK GHIGLIONE INC
Also Called: Rogers Trucking
2972 Alvarado St Ste H, San Leandro (94577-5732)
PHONE..................510 483-2063
Frank Ghiglione, *Manager*
EMP: 100
SALES (est): 2.3MM
SALES (corp-wide): 17.6MM **Privately Held**
WEB: www.rodgerstrucking.com
SIC: 4212 4214 Delivery service, vehicular; local trucking with storage

PA: Frank Ghiglione, Inc.
14327 Washington Ave
San Leandro CA 94578
510 483-7000

(P-4017)
FRONTIER CALIFORNIA INC
Also Called: Verizon
9000 Hellman Ave, Rancho Cucamonga (91730-4425)
PHONE..................909 941-4068
Richard Perry, *Manager*
EMP: 70
SALES (corp-wide): 9.1B **Publicly Held**
SIC: 4212 Local trucking, without storage
HQ: Frontier California Inc.
140 West St
New York NY 10007
212 395-1000

(P-4018)
HANKS INC
Also Called: Sun Express
13866 Slover Ave, Fontana (92337-7037)
PHONE..................909 350-8365
Brian Bachar, *President*
Shirley Bachar, *Vice Pres*
Brenda Cash, *Controller*
Maira M Mack, *Opers Mgr*
EMP: 68
SQ FT: 24,000
SALES (est): 11.5MM **Privately Held**
WEB: www.shipsun.com
SIC: 4212 4213 Local trucking, without storage; trucking, except local

(P-4019)
HARTWICK & HAND INC (PA)
Also Called: H & H Truck Terminal
16953 N D St, Victorville (92394-1417)
P.O. Box 1595 (92393-1595)
PHONE..................760 245-1666
Stacy L Hand, *CEO*
Edward Perreria, *President*
EMP: 73
SQ FT: 8,800
SALES (est): 14MM **Privately Held**
SIC: 4212 Local trucking, without storage

(P-4020)
HD SUPPLY INC
101 Rverview Pkwy Ste 100, Santee (92071)
P.O. Box 2273, Orlando FL (32802-2273)
PHONE..................800 431-3000
David Kahn, *Vice Pres*
Matthew Duoos, *Executive*
Douglas Wahlert, *Executive*
Louie Kusa, *Branch Mgr*
Mark Wilson, *Branch Mgr*
EMP: 63 **Publicly Held**
SIC: 4212 Delivery service, vehicular
HQ: Hd Supply, Inc.
3100 Cumberland Blvd Se # 1700
Atlanta GA 30339
770 852-9000

(P-4021)
HEAVY LOAD TRANSFER LLC
18735 S Ferris Pl, Rancho Dominguez (90220-6405)
P.O. Box 750, San Pedro (90733-0750)
PHONE..................310 816-0260
Victor Larosa,
EMP: 75 EST: 2016
SALES (est): 2.3MM **Privately Held**
SIC: 4212 Local trucking, without storage

(P-4022)
HUB GROUP TRUCKING INC
13867 Valley Blvd, Fontana (92335-5230)
PHONE..................909 770-8950
Roy Sheredon, *Branch Mgr*
EMP: 500
SALES (corp-wide): 4B **Publicly Held**
SIC: 4212 Local trucking, without storage
HQ: Hub Group Trucking, Inc.
2000 Clearwater Dr
Oak Brook IL 60523
630 271-3600

(P-4023)
HUB GROUP TRUCKING INC
Also Called: Hgt
3801 E Guasti Rd, Ontario (91761-1575)
PHONE..................951 693-9813

EMP: 174
SALES (corp-wide): 4B **Publicly Held**
SIC: 4212
HQ: Hub Group Trucking, Inc.
2000 Clearwater Dr
Oak Brook IL 60523
630 271-3600

(P-4024)
ICE DELIVERY SYSTEMS INC
Also Called: Inner-City Express
6920 Santa Teresa Blvd # 206, San Jose (95119-1344)
PHONE..................408 640-4625
Michael S Hubert, *President*
Lizette P Hubert, *Principal*
EMP: 130
SQ FT: 30,000
SALES (est): 11.7MM **Privately Held**
SIC: 4212 7389 4215 Delivery service, vehicular; courier or messenger service; courier services, except by air

(P-4025)
J D L MOTOR EXPRESS
1250 Delevan Dr, San Diego (92102-2437)
PHONE..................619 232-6136
John Lenore, *President*
Dorothy Lenore, *Treasurer*
Harold Gursky, *Vice Pres*
EMP: 75
SALES (est): 3.3MM
SALES (corp-wide): 173.8MM **Privately Held**
WEB: www.johnlenore.com
SIC: 4212 4213 Local trucking, without storage; automobiles, transport & delivery
PA: Lenore John & Co
1250 Delevan Dr
San Diego CA 92102
619 232-6136

(P-4026)
JACK JONES TRUCKING INC
1090 E Belmont St, Ontario (91761-4501)
PHONE..................909 456-2500
Valerie Liese, *President*
Erin Craig, *Exec VP*
Mike Brooks, *Vice Pres*
Robert Liese, *Vice Pres*
Bob Liese, *General Mgr*
EMP: 100
SQ FT: 3,000
SALES (est): 14.6MM **Privately Held**
WEB: www.jjtinc.com
SIC: 4212 Local trucking, without storage

(P-4027)
JACOBS FARM/DEL CABO INC
144 Holm Rd Spc 42, Watsonville (95076-2428)
PHONE..................831 460-3500
Paul Rabadan, *Branch Mgr*
EMP: 180
SALES (corp-wide): 68.2MM **Privately Held**
WEB: www.delcabo.com
SIC: 4212 5148 Farm to market haulage, local; fresh fruits & vegetables
PA: Jacobs Farm/Del Cabo, Inc.
2450 Stage Rd
Pescadero CA 94060
650 879-0580

(P-4028)
JEREMIAH PHILLIPS LLC
Also Called: Airline Coach Service
863 Malcolm Rd, Burlingame (94010-1406)
P.O. Box 4427 (94011-4427)
PHONE..................650 697-7733
Alex Morrison, *Mng Member*
Charles Morrison,
EMP: 105
SQ FT: 10,000
SALES: 6.3MM **Privately Held**
SIC: 4212 Local trucking, without storage

(P-4029)
JIM AARTMAN INC (PA)
Also Called: Jim Aartman Milk Transport
805 S Locust Ave, Ripon (95366-2789)
PHONE..................209 599-5066
Adrian Aartman, *President*
Kathryn Aartman, *Corp Secy*
James Aartman, *Vice Pres*
EMP: 120

SQ FT: 40,000
SALES (est): 13.6MM **Privately Held**
SIC: 4212 Liquid haulage, local

(P-4030)
JOHN AGUILAR & COMPANY INC
Also Called: Vernon Transportation Company
1505 Navy Dr, Stockton (95206-4104)
P.O. Box 31450 (95213-1450)
PHONE..................209 546-0171
Gregg Wilson, *President*
Joe Lacey, *CFO*
Tony Ketner, *Vice Pres*
Dennis Carey, *General Mgr*
Dave Wilson, *Admin Sec*
EMP: 85
SQ FT: 5,600
SALES (est): 20.3MM **Privately Held**
WEB: www.sugartrux.com
SIC: 4212 Liquid haulage, local

(P-4031)
JS HOMEN TRUCKING INC
4224 Turlock Rd, Snelling (95369-9729)
P.O. Box 382 (95369-0382)
PHONE..................209 723-9559
Joe Homen, *President*
Margaret Homen, *Corp Secy*
EMP: 65
SQ FT: 2,484
SALES (est): 1.8MM **Privately Held**
SIC: 4212 Local trucking, without storage

(P-4032)
K W K TRUCKING INC
6131 Manorfield Dr, Huntington Beach (92648-1066)
PHONE..................714 791-7928
Kirt W Keller, *President*
Gina Keller, *Corp Secy*
EMP: 137
SALES (est): 6MM **Privately Held**
SIC: 4212 Local trucking, without storage

(P-4033)
KEENEY TRUCK LINES INC
3500 Fruitland Ave, Maywood (90270-2008)
PHONE..................323 589-3231
Dan Hubbard, *President*
Carol Alsip, *Corp Secy*
EMP: 50
SALES (est): 8MM **Privately Held**
WEB: www.keeneytruck.com
SIC: 4212 4731 Local trucking, without storage; freight transportation arrangement

(P-4034)
KELVIN HILDEBRAND INC
6 Lewis Rd, Royal Oaks (95076-5303)
PHONE..................831 768-9104
Kelvin Hildebrand, *President*
EMP: 50
SALES (est): 1.2MM **Privately Held**
SIC: 4212 Local trucking, without storage

(P-4035)
KFCO INC
Also Called: Labite
12100 W Washington Blvd, Los Angeles (90066-5502)
PHONE..................310 441-2483
Kenneth Fischer, *President*
EMP: 117 EST: 2014
SQ FT: 300
SALES (est): 3.5MM **Privately Held**
SIC: 4212 5812 Delivery service, vehicular; carry-out only (except pizza) restaurant

(P-4036)
LEE JENNINGS TARGET EX INC (PA)
1465 E Franklin Ave, Pomona (91766-5453)
PHONE..................909 868-1040
L Lee Jennings, *CEO*
Grant Campbell, *Human Res Dir*
Brent Campbell, *Director*
EMP: 123
SALES (est): 19.4MM **Privately Held**
SIC: 4212 4213 Delivery service, vehicular; trucking, except local

(PA)=Parent Co (HQ)=Headquarters (DH)=Div Headquarters
♻ = New Business established in last 2 years

2019 Directory of California
Wholesalers and Services Companies

173

PRODUCTS & SVCS

(P-4037)
MAD DOG EXPRESS INC (PA)
299 Lawrence Ave, South San Francisco
(94080-6818)
P.O. Box 281585, San Francisco (94128-
1585)
PHONE..............................650 588-1900
Steve Harth, *President*
John Coleman, *Vice Pres*
EMP: 70
SQ FT: 18,500
SALES (est): 3.7MM **Privately Held**
WEB: www.maddogexpress.com
SIC: 4212 Local trucking, without storage

(P-4038)
MASSOLO TRUCKING LLC (PA)
18765 Gould Rd, Salinas (93908-9703)
PHONE..............................831 424-7205
Joseph Massolo, *President*
Steve Massolo, *Vice Pres*
EMP: 50
SQ FT: 5,997
SALES (est): 5.2MM **Privately Held**
SIC: 4212 Local trucking, without storage

(P-4039)
MAT PARCEL EXPRESS INC (PA)
Also Called: Mat Express
2719 Kurtz St Ste C, San Diego
(92110-3117)
PHONE..............................619 849-9600
Thomas A Eggert, *President*
Diane Eggert, *Vice Pres*
Matthew Eggert, *Vice Pres*
Alan Eggert, *General Mgr*
Steve Gonzaba, *General Mgr*
EMP: 100
SQ FT: 28,000
SALES (est): 25.6MM **Privately Held**
SIC: 4212 Delivery service, vehicular

(P-4040)
MAYOR WEST COAST LLC
335 E Albertoni St 200-867, Carson
(90746-1425)
PHONE..............................424 221-5229
Michael Mayor,
EMP: 50
SALES (est): 805.3K **Privately Held**
SIC: 4212 Local trucking, without storage

(P-4041)
MISSION TRAIL WSTE SYSTEMS INC
Also Called: Recycle Waste
1060 Richard Ave, Santa Clara
(95050-2816)
PHONE..............................408 727-5365
Louie Pellegrini, *President*
William Dobert, *CFO*
Robert Molinaro, *Vice Pres*
Douglas Button, *Admin Sec*
EMP: 75 **EST:** 1960
SALES (est): 17.2MM **Privately Held**
SIC: 4212 4953 Garbage collection &
transport, no disposal; recycling, waste
materials

(P-4042)
MORE TRUCK LINES INC
1776 All American Way, Corona
(92879-2070)
P.O. Box 2229 (92878-2229)
PHONE..............................951 371-6673
Daniel D Sisemore, *President*
Thomas Toscas, *Corp Secy*
Bill Anselm, *Manager*
EMP: 80 **EST:** 1952
SQ FT: 800
SALES (est): 5.2MM **Privately Held**
WEB: www.moretrucklines.com
SIC: 4212 Local trucking, without storage

(P-4043)
MULECHAIN INC
2901 W Coast Hwy Ste 200, Newport
Beach (92663-4045)
PHONE..............................888 456-8881
Ralph Liu, *CEO*
EMP: 56
SALES: 1MM **Privately Held**
SIC: 4212 7372 Delivery service, vehicu-
lar; application computer software

(P-4044)
NEAL TRUCKING INC
9749 Bellegrave Ave, Riverside
(92509-2642)
PHONE..............................951 685-5048
Dianne Neal, *CEO*
Corey Gouthro, *Executive*
Randy Neal, *Principal*
EMP: 65
SQ FT: 1,500
SALES (est): 8.8MM **Privately Held**
SIC: 4212 Dump truck haulage

(P-4045)
NIPPON EX NEC LGSTICS AMER INC
18615 S Ferris Pl, Rancho Dominguez
(90220-6452)
PHONE..............................310 604-6100
Kazuhiko Takahashi, *CEO*
Hidehito Tachikawa, *CEO*
Gerald Sabino, *Director*
EMP: 75
SQ FT: 353,000
SALES (est): 16.6MM
SALES (corp-wide): 26.7B **Privately Held**
WEB: www.necam.com
SIC: 4212 4213 4225 Local trucking, with-
out storage; trucking, except local; gen-
eral warehousing & storage
HQ: Nec Corporation Of America
3929 W John Carpenter Fwy
Irving TX 75063
214 262-6000

(P-4046)
NR 2 GROUP INC
1561 Chapin Unit C, Baldwin Park (91706)
PHONE..............................626 251-6681
CHI On Wong, *CEO*
EMP: 50
SQ FT: 100,000
SALES: 2.5MM **Privately Held**
SIC: 4212 Local trucking, without storage

(P-4047)
OCEAN BLUE ENVMTL SVCS INC (PA)
925 W Esther St, Long Beach
(90813-1423)
PHONE..............................562 624-4120
Maria C Lee, *CEO*
Ron Dare, *President*
Moonho C Lee, *CFO*
Cherisse Patterson, *Admin Asst*
Wendy Mejia, *Administration*
EMP: 63
SQ FT: 5,000
SALES (est): 11.9MM **Privately Held**
WEB: www.ocean-blue.com
SIC: 4212 8734 Hazardous waste trans-
port; hazardous waste testing

(P-4048)
OLDENKAMP TRUCKING INC (PA)
13535 S Union Ave, Bakersfield
(93307-9124)
PHONE..............................661 833-3400
Harold Oldenkamp, *CEO*
Dana Oldenkamp, *CFO*
Monica Espinoza, *Production*
EMP: 62
SALES (est): 7.8MM **Privately Held**
SIC: 4212 Light haulage & cartage, local

(P-4049)
PACIFIC WINE DISTRIBUTORS INC
15751 Tapia St, Irwindale (91706-2177)
PHONE..............................626 471-9997
Gino Pacella, *President*
Diane Dancel, *Office Admin*
Eyvonne Nong, *Human Res Mgr*
EMP: 85
SQ FT: 46,546
SALES: 6MM **Privately Held**
SIC: 4212 4225 4213 Local trucking, with-
out storage; general warehousing & stor-
age; trucking, except local

(P-4050)
PROPANE TRANSPORT SERVICE INC
903 W Center St Ste 7, Manteca
(95337-7315)
PHONE..............................209 823-8005
John Paul, *President*
Jack Penzes, *Vice Pres*
Jan Peterson, *Vice Pres*
EMP: 170
SALES (est): 8.2MM **Privately Held**
WEB: www.economytransport.com
SIC: 4212 Petroleum haulage, local
PA: Kamps Propane, Inc.
1262 Dupont Ct
Manteca CA 95336
-

(P-4051)
PSC INDUSTRIAL OUTSOURCING LP
Also Called: Hydrochempsc
62117 Railroad Ave, San Ardo (93450)
PHONE..............................831 627-2595
Paul Dewitt, *Principal*
Joe Hamby, *General Mgr*
Elaine Talerico, *Human Res Mgr*
EMP: 55
SALES (corp-wide): 750MM **Privately
Held**
WEB: www.tscnow.com
SIC: 4212 Hazardous waste transport
PA: Psc Industrial Outsourcing, Lp
900 Georgia Ave
Deer Park TX 77536
713 393-5600

(P-4052)
PT LOGISTICS INC
144 W Lake Ave Ste B, Watsonville
(95076-4554)
PHONE..............................831 728-4535
Rainderpau S Tut, *President*
EMP: 50
SALES (est): 1.8MM **Privately Held**
SIC: 4212 Light haulage & cartage, local

(P-4053)
RADFORD ALEXANDER CORPORATION
Also Called: Chemtrans
14700 S Avalon Blvd, Gardena
(90248-2010)
PHONE..............................310 523-2555
Reginald Lathan, *CEO*
Nancy Lathan, *Vice Pres*
Reid Lathan, *Manager*
EMP: 55 **EST:** 1973
SQ FT: 4,000
SALES (est): 9.5MM **Privately Held**
WEB: www.chemtrans.com
SIC: 4212 Light haulage & cartage, local

(P-4054)
RAIL DELIVERY SERVICES INC
8600 Banana Ave, Fontana (92335-3033)
PHONE..............................909 355-4100
Judi Girard, *Ch of Bd*
Sharon Brooks, *President*
Greg Stefflre, *CEO*
EMP: 68
SQ FT: 50,000
SALES (est): 11.1MM **Privately Held**
WEB: www.raildelivery.com
SIC: 4212 Moving services

(P-4055)
RHINO READY MIX TRUCKING INC (PA)
3701 Pegasus Dr Ste 126, Bakersfield
(93308-6843)
P.O. Box 80297 (93380-0297)
PHONE..............................661 679-3643
Freddy Amaya, *President*
Marco Arambula, *Vice Pres*
EMP: 50
SALES: 8MM **Privately Held**
SIC: 4212

(P-4056)
ROADSTAR TRUCKING INC
30527 San Antonio St, Hayward
(94544-7101)
PHONE..............................510 487-2404
Charles Ramorino, *Chairman*

Robert Ramorino, *President*
EMP: 55
SQ FT: 43,000
SALES (est): 9.8MM **Privately Held**
SIC: 4212 Local trucking, without storage

(P-4057)
ROLO TRANSPORTATION COMPANY
Also Called: Rolo Logistics
9935 Beverly Blvd, Pico Rivera
(90660-1812)
P.O. Box 4157, Long Beach (90804-0157)
PHONE..............................562 463-1440
D Antonio Roman, *President*
Margarita Roman, *Vice Pres*
EMP: 60
SQ FT: 91,000
SALES (est): 5.5MM **Privately Held**
SIC: 4212 Local trucking, without storage

(P-4058)
ROY MILLER FREIGHT LINES LLC (PA)
3165 E Coronado St, Anaheim
(92806-1915)
P.O. Box 18419 (92817-8419)
PHONE..............................714 632-5511
Danny Miller, *CEO*
Wiley R Miller Jr, *Mng Member*
EMP: 100 **EST:** 1942
SALES (est): 29.5MM **Privately Held**
WEB: www.roymiller.com
SIC: 4212 Local trucking, without storage

(P-4059)
RUAN
830 W Glenwood Ave, Turlock
(95380-5751)
PHONE..............................209 634-4928
Bill Hagney, *Manager*
EMP: 85
SALES (corp-wide): 5.4MM **Privately
Held**
SIC: 4212 Local trucking, without storage
PA: Ruan
1354 S Blackstone St
Tulare CA 93274
559 688-0591

(P-4060)
SANTA MONICA EXPRESS INC
11150 W Olympic Blvd # 150, Los Angeles
(90064-1831)
P.O. Box 7457, Santa Monica (90406-
7457)
PHONE..............................310 458-6000
Muhammed Mahmodi, *President*
Janet Barahona, *Admin Asst*
EMP: 65
SQ FT: 3,500
SALES: 3MM **Privately Held**
WEB: www.smexpress.com
SIC: 4212 7389 Delivery service, vehicu-
lar; mailing & messenger services

(P-4061)
SHIPBYCOM LLC
218 Machlin Ct, Walnut (91789-3048)
PHONE..............................626 271-9800
Jeff Wu, *Branch Mgr*
EMP: 75
SALES (corp-wide): 8.2MM **Privately
Held**
SIC: 4212 Local trucking, without storage
PA: Shipby.Com, Llc
900 Turnbull Canyon Rd
City Of Industry CA 91745
626 271-9800

(P-4062)
SHUSTERS TRANSPORTATION INC
750 E Valley St, Willits (95490-9749)
PHONE..............................707 459-4131
Phillip L Shuster, *President*
Marvin Lawrence, *Corp Secy*
Steve Shuster, *Vice Pres*
EMP: 100
SQ FT: 3,000
SALES (est): 7MM **Privately Held**
SIC: 4212 Local trucking, without storage

▲ = Import ▼=Export
◆ =Import/Export

(P-4063)
SIERRA TRANSPORT INC
12856 Old River Rd, Bakersfield
(93311-9707)
PHONE.................................661 836-3166
Roy Lutrel, *President*
Mark Lutrel, *Vice Pres*
Gayle Lutrel, *Admin Sec*
EMP: 53
SALES (est): 5.9MM **Privately Held**
WEB: www.sierratransport.com
SIC: 4212 Local trucking, without storage

(P-4064)
SILVA TRUCKING INC
36 W Mathews Rd, French Camp
(95231-9684)
P.O. Box 1449 (95231-1449)
PHONE.................................209 982-1114
David Silva, *President*
EMP: 50 EST: 1943
SQ FT: 4,000
SALES (est): 8.1MM **Privately Held**
SIC: 4212 Dump truck haulage

(P-4065)
SOLID WASTES OF WILLITS INC (PA)
Also Called: WILLITS SOLID WASTES
351 Franklin Ave, Willits (95490-5109)
P.O. Box 1425 (95490-1425)
PHONE.................................707 459-4845
Gerald Wayne Ward, *President*
Julie Martin, *Vice Pres*
Kim Pavich, *Office Mgr*
Sandra Ward, *Admin Sec*
EMP: 56
SALES: 14.3MM **Privately Held**
WEB: www.solidwasteservices.net
SIC: 4212 4953 Garbage collection &
transport, no disposal; recycling, waste
materials

(P-4066)
SOUTHWEST EXPRESS LLC
1720 E Garry Ave Ste 107, Santa Ana
(92705-5831)
PHONE.................................949 474-5038
Bill Ruxby,
William Roxby, *Financial Exec*
Coy Garcia,
Ron Lind,
Charles McDonald,
EMP: 60
SQ FT: 1,000
SALES: 1.2MM **Privately Held**
WEB: www.southwestexpress.net
SIC: 4212 4731 Delivery service, vehicu-
lar; freight transportation arrangement

(P-4067)
SUGAR TRANSPORT OF THE NW
5463 Cherokee Rd, Stockton (95215-1128)
PHONE.................................209 931-3587
Gary Scannavino, *President*
Leanne Scannavino, *Corp Secy*
Jack Riella, *Vice Pres*
EMP: 100
SQ FT: 1,000
SALES (est): 6.7MM **Privately Held**
SIC: 4212 Farm to market haulage, local

(P-4068)
TALLEY TRANSPORTATION
12325 Road 29, Madera (93638-8401)
P.O. Box 568 (93639-0568)
PHONE.................................559 673-9013
Martin Talley, *CEO*
Kenneth Talley, *Vice Pres*
EMP: 57
SQ FT: 5,500
SALES (est): 6.8MM **Privately Held**
WEB: www.talleytrans.com
SIC: 4212 Local trucking, without storage

(P-4069)
TRAIL LINES INC
9415 Sorensen Ave, Santa Fe Springs
(90670-2648)
P.O. Box 3567 (90670-1567)
PHONE.................................562 758-6980
Ofer Shitrit, *CEO*
Reuven Spivak, *Vice Pres*
Adriana Ortega, *Manager*

EMP: 75
SALES (est): 16.4MM **Privately Held**
SIC: 4212 4789 Local trucking, without
storage; pipeline terminal facilities, independently operated

(P-4070)
TRANSPORTATION MANAGEMENT LLC
880 Apollo St Ste 235, El Segundo
(90245-4752)
PHONE.................................310 524-1555
Eric Reese,
Dan Reed, *Vice Pres*
Chris Carey,
EMP: 50
SQ FT: 14,000
SALES (est): 5.4MM **Privately Held**
SIC: 4212 4513 Delivery service, vehicu-
lar; air courier services

(P-4071)
TRANSPRTTION BRKG SPCLISTS INC
Also Called: Tbs
3151 Airway Ave Ste F208, Costa Mesa
(92626-4621)
PHONE.................................714 754-4230
Ben Haeri, *CEO*
Steve Kennedy, *Managing Prtnr*
Fred Khac, *Managing Prtnr*
Mike Owens, *COO*
Lee Mayer, *Vice Pres*
EMP: 450
SQ FT: 3,000
SALES: 25MM **Privately Held**
SIC: 4212 Local trucking, without storage

(P-4072)
TRIPLE E TRUCKING
1215 E White Ln, Bakersfield (93307-5061)
PHONE.................................661 834-0071
Mike Ehoff, *Partner*
Jim Ehoff, *Partner*
Loretta Ehoff, *Partner*
EMP: 50
SALES (est): 5.7MM **Privately Held**
SIC: 4212 Local trucking, without storage

(P-4073)
TST INC
Also Called: Timco
11601 Etiwanda Ave, Fontana
(92337-6929)
P.O. Box 1563, Wildomar (92595-1563)
PHONE.................................310 835-0115
Andrew G Stein, *CEO*
EMP: 100
SALES (corp-wide): 67.6MM **Privately
Held**
SIC: 4212 Local trucking, without storage
PA: Tst, Inc.
13428 Benson Ave
Chino CA 91710
951 685-2155

(P-4074)
UNION ASPHALT INC
1625 E Donovan Rd, Santa Maria
(93454-2500)
PHONE.................................805 922-3551
George Hamill, *President*
Andy Hermreck, *Admin Sec*
EMP: 60
SQ FT: 4,000
SALES (est): 2.6MM **Privately Held**
SIC: 4212 Dump truck haulage

(P-4075)
UNITED PUMPING SERVICE INC
14000 Valley Blvd, City of Industry
(91746-2801)
PHONE.................................626 961-9326
Eduardo T Perry Jr, *President*
Eduardo Perry Jr, *Corp Secy*
Daniel C Perry, *Vice Pres*
Margaret Perry, *Vice Pres*
Rayda Deato, *General Mgr*
EMP: 95
SQ FT: 25,000
SALES (est): 30.7MM **Privately Held**
WEB: www.unitedpumping.com
SIC: 4212 Hazardous waste transport

(P-4076)
UNIVERSAL MAIL DELIVERY SVC (PA)
Also Called: Universal Custom Courier
501 S Brand Blvd Ste 4, San Fernando
(91340-4931)
P.O. Box 60250, Los Angeles (90060-0250)
PHONE.................................818 997-7531
Robert M Reznick, *CEO*
Barbara Reznick, *Shareholder*
Saddie Reznick, *Shareholder*
Bernard Reznick, *CEO*
EMP: 95
SQ FT: 1,000
SALES (est): 11.4MM **Privately Held**
WEB: www.umds.biz
SIC: 4212 Delivery service, vehicular

(P-4077)
USA WASTE OF CALIFORNIA INC
Also Called: Sac Val Waste Disposal
8761 Younger Creek Dr, Sacramento
(95828-1023)
PHONE.................................916 379-2611
Alex Oseguerra, *General Mgr*
EMP: 115
SALES (corp-wide): 14.4B **Publicly Held**
SIC: 4212 4953 Garbage collection &
transport, no disposal; refuse systems
HQ: Usa Waste Of California, Inc.
11931 Foundation Pl # 200
Gold River CA 95670
916 387-1400

(P-4078)
USA WASTE OF CALIFORNIA INC
Also Called: Carmel Marina
11240 Commercial Pkwy, Castroville
(95012-3206)
P.O. Box 1306 (95012-1306)
PHONE.................................831 384-4860
George Reddom, *President*
EMP: 120
SALES (est): 5.6MM **Privately Held**
SIC: 4212 Local trucking, without storage

(P-4079)
USA WASTE OF CALIFORNIA INC
Also Called: Stockton Scavengers Assn
1240 Navy Dr, Stockton (95206-1167)
PHONE.................................209 946-5721
Frank Jarvis, *Branch Mgr*
EMP: 50
SALES (corp-wide): 14.4B **Publicly Held**
SIC: 4212 Garbage collection & transport,
no disposal
HQ: Usa Waste Of California, Inc.
11931 Foundation Pl # 200
Gold River CA 95670
916 387-1400

(P-4080)
USA WASTE OF CALIFORNIA INC
Also Called: Waste Management Nevada
County
13083 Grass Valley Ave, Grass Valley
(95945-9325)
PHONE.................................530 274-3090
Art Rassmussen, *Principal*
EMP: 50
SQ FT: 8,000
SALES (corp-wide): 14.4B **Publicly Held**
SIC: 4212 8748 4953 Garbage collection
& transport, no disposal; business con-
sulting; refuse systems
HQ: Usa Waste Of California, Inc.
11931 Foundation Pl # 200
Gold River CA 95670
916 387-1400

(P-4081)
VALLEY AGGREGATE TRANSPORT INC
753 N George Wash Blvd, Yuba City
(95993-9065)
PHONE.................................530 821-2600
Kevin Cotter, *CEO*
EMP: 65

SALES (est): 4.2MM **Privately Held**
WEB: www.valleyaggregate.com
SIC: 4212 4213 Local trucking, without
storage; trucking, except local

(P-4082)
VALLEY COURIERS INC (PA)
646 N San Fernando Rd, Los Angeles
(90065-1031)
P.O. Box 8036, Calabasas (91372-8036)
PHONE.................................818 591-2212
Nasrollah Alamdari, *President*
Hassan Alamadari, *Vice Pres*
Asdullah Alamdari, *Vice Pres*
EMP: 65
SQ FT: 8,000
SALES (est): 12.3MM **Privately Held**
SIC: 4212 Delivery service, vehicular

(P-4083)
VALLEY TRANSPORTATION INC (PA)
2837 S East Ave, Fresno (93725-1943)
P.O. Box 12663 (93778-2663)
PHONE.................................559 266-6674
Deborah B Simpson, *President*
Rodney D Heintz, *COO*
EMP: 58
SQ FT: 6,000
SALES (est): 9.1MM **Privately Held**
SIC: 4212 Delivery service, vehicular

(P-4084)
VAN DYK TANK LINES INC
Also Called: Cool Transport
1800 S Riverside Ave, Colton
(92324-3349)
P.O. Box 341, Bloomington (92316-0341)
PHONE.................................951 682-5000
Ronald Nuckles, *President*
EMP: 50
SALES (est): 4.7MM **Privately Held**
SIC: 4212 4213 Local trucking, without
storage; trucking, except local

(P-4085)
VAN KING & STORAGE INC (PA)
Also Called: KING RELOCATION SERVICES
13535 Larwin Cir, Santa Fe Springs
(90670-5032)
PHONE.................................562 921-0555
Steve Komorous, *President*
Edwin Nabal, *CFO*
Keith Hindsley, *Senior VP*
Don Blackwell, *Vice Pres*
Martin Delaney, *Vice Pres*
EMP: 75
SQ FT: 60,000
SALES: 16.5MM **Privately Held**
WEB: www.kingrelocation.com
SIC: 4212 4225 Moving services; general
warehousing & storage

(P-4086)
WASTE MGT COLLECTN & RECYCL
2658 N Main St, Walnut Creek
(94597-2729)
PHONE.................................925 935-8900
Ronald J Proto, *Manager*
EMP: 170
SALES (corp-wide): 14.4B **Publicly Held**
SIC: 4212 4953 Garbage collection &
transport, no disposal; refuse systems
HQ: Waste Management Collection And
Recycling, Inc.
1001 Fannin St Ste 4000
Houston TX 77002

(P-4087)
WESTERN MESSENGER SERVICE INC
75 Columbia Sq, San Francisco
(94103-4099)
PHONE.................................415 487-4229
Dennis Golladay, *President*
Joe McManus, *President*
Patty Sokolecki, *Admin Sec*
Raymond Crosetti, *Assistant VP*
EMP: 115
SQ FT: 11,000
SALES (est): 10.2MM **Privately Held**
WEB: www.westernmessenger.com
SIC: 4212 Delivery service, vehicular

4213 Trucking, Except Local

(P-4088)
A C FREIGHT SYSTEMS INC (PA)
850 Service St, San Jose (95112-1360)
P.O. Box 90816, City of Industry (91715-0816)
PHONE.................................408 392-8900
Blair Johnson, *President*
EMP: 180
SQ FT: 20,000
SALES (est): 9.6MM **Privately Held**
SIC: 4213 Trucking, except local

(P-4089)
ABF FREIGHT SYSTEM INC
2135 Otoole Ave, San Jose (95131-1314)
PHONE.................................408 435-8550
Penny Podio, *Manager*
Aaron Gold, *General Mgr*
EMP: 50
SALES (corp-wide): 2.8B **Publicly Held**
WEB: www.abfs.com
SIC: 4213 Contract haulers
HQ: Abf Freight System, Inc.
3801 Old Greenwood Rd
Fort Smith AR 72903
479 785-8700

(P-4090)
ABF FREIGHT SYSTEM INC
8001 Telegraph Rd, Pico Rivera (90660-4822)
PHONE.................................323 773-2580
Kelly Underwood, *Manager*
Jacob Hall, *General Mgr*
EMP: 50
SALES (corp-wide): 2.8B **Publicly Held**
WEB: www.abfs.com
SIC: 4213 Contract haulers
HQ: Abf Freight System, Inc.
3801 Old Greenwood Rd
Fort Smith AR 72903
479 785-8700

(P-4091)
ABF FREIGHT SYSTEM INC
4575 Tidewater Ave, Oakland (94601-3917)
PHONE.................................510 533-8575
Josh Eversville, *Manager*
Doug Thiel, *Branch Mgr*
Kraig Gratiot, *Opers Mgr*
EMP: 70
SQ FT: 10,000
SALES (corp-wide): 2.8B **Publicly Held**
WEB: www.abfs.com
SIC: 4213 Contract haulers
HQ: Abf Freight System, Inc.
3801 Old Greenwood Rd
Fort Smith AR 72903
479 785-8700

(P-4092)
ABF FREIGHT SYSTEM INC
1601 N Batavia St, Orange (92867-3508)
PHONE.................................714 974-2485
Jerry Wright, *Manager*
EMP: 50
SQ FT: 13,326
SALES (corp-wide): 2.8B **Publicly Held**
WEB: www.abfs.com
SIC: 4213 Contract haulers
HQ: Abf Freight System, Inc.
3801 Old Greenwood Rd
Fort Smith AR 72903
479 785-8700

(P-4093)
ABF FREIGHT SYSTEM INC
3250 47th Ave, Sacramento (95824-2441)
PHONE.................................916 428-3531
David Fox, *General Mgr*
Keith Blum, *Branch Mgr*
Jeremy Sands, *General Mgr*
EMP: 65
SALES (corp-wide): 2.8B **Publicly Held**
WEB: www.abfs.com
SIC: 4213 Contract haulers

HQ: Abf Freight System, Inc.
3801 Old Greenwood Rd
Fort Smith AR 72903
479 785-8700

(P-4094)
ABF FREIGHT SYSTEM INC
10744 Almond Ave, Fontana (92337-7153)
PHONE.................................909 355-9805
Matt Trirta, *Manager*
John Demary, *Branch Mgr*
Jason Apple, *Opers Mgr*
Gutensohn Gary, *Supervisor*
Gary Gutensohn, *Supervisor*
EMP: 200
SQ FT: 30,248
SALES (corp-wide): 2.8B **Publicly Held**
WEB: www.abfs.com
SIC: 4213 Contract haulers
HQ: Abf Freight System, Inc.
3801 Old Greenwood Rd
Fort Smith AR 72903
479 785-8700

(P-4095)
ADVANCED LOGISTICS MGT INC
Also Called: Advanced Trans Grp
19067 S Reyes Ave, Compton (90221-5813)
PHONE.................................310 638-0715
Rene Edmunds, *President*
Gerald R Edmunds, *Vice Pres*
EMP: 50
SQ FT: 100,000
SALES (est): 8.2MM **Privately Held**
SIC: 4213 Trucking, except local

(P-4096)
AMAR TRANSPORTATION INC (PA)
Also Called: Paul Trucking
144 W Lake Ave Ste C, Watsonville (95076-4554)
P.O. Box 39 (95077-0039)
PHONE.................................831 728-8209
Amarjit S Tut, *President*
Surjit S Tut, *Treasurer*
Paritan S Tut, *Vice Pres*
Ranjit S Tut, *Vice Pres*
EMP: 130
SQ FT: 4,872
SALES (est): 9.9MM **Privately Held**
SIC: 4213 4212 Trucking, except local; local trucking, without storage

(P-4097)
AMERICAN FREIGHTWAYS LP
10845 Rancho Bernardo Rd # 100, San Diego (92127-2107)
PHONE.................................866 326-5902
Kirk Carmichael, *General Ptnr*
Mark Goodacre, *General Ptnr*
Renee Goodacre, *Accountant*
EMP: 62
SQ FT: 10,000
SALES (est): 19.5MM **Privately Held**
SIC: 4213 Trucking, except local

(P-4098)
AMERICAN WEST
511 Zaca Ln Ste 120, San Luis Obispo (93401)
PHONE.................................805 926-2800
Josh Brown, *CEO*
EMP: 50 EST: 2014
SALES (est): 2.7MM **Privately Held**
SIC: 4213 Heavy hauling

(P-4099)
AMGEN DISTRIBUTION INC
1244 Valley View Rd # 119, Glendale (91202-1752)
PHONE.................................760 989-4424
EMP: 73
SQ FT: 3,900
SALES (est): 4.8MM **Privately Held**
SIC: 4213

(P-4100)
ARDWIN INC
Also Called: Ardwin Freight
2940 N Hollywood Way, Burbank (91505-1024)
P.O. Box 1609 (91507-1609)
PHONE.................................818 767-7777
Edwin Sahakian, *President*

Richard Breault, *Info Tech Mgr*
Julio Rios, *Human Resources*
Tom Salzmann, *Sales Executive*
David Holland, *Cust Mgr*
EMP: 130
SQ FT: 10,000
SALES (est): 28.9MM **Privately Held**
WEB: www.ardwin.com
SIC: 4213 Contract haulers

(P-4101)
ASBURY TRANSPORTATION CO
2144 Mohawk St, Bakersfield (93308-6001)
PHONE.................................661 327-2271
Richard Boyer, *CEO*
Bruce Haupt, *Vice Pres*
Rolando Ramos, *Traffic Dir*
EMP: 52
SQ FT: 2,100
SALES (est): 10.9MM **Privately Held**
WEB: www.asburytrans.com
SIC: 4213 Contract haulers

(P-4102)
ATECH WAREHOUSING & DIST INC (PA)
7 College Ave, Santa Rosa (95401-4702)
P.O. Box 6836 (95406-0836)
PHONE.................................707 526-1910
Jesse E Amaral, *President*
Geri Amaral, *Vice Pres*
Isaias Santos, *Opers Mgr*
EMP: 60
SQ FT: 35,000
SALES (est): 14.4MM **Privately Held**
WEB: www.atechdist.com
SIC: 4213 Less-than-truckload (LTL) transport

(P-4103)
BERT E JESSUP TRANSPORTATION
641 Old Gilroy St, Gilroy (95020-6233)
PHONE.................................408 848-3390
Leonard Milanowski, *CEO*
Len Milanowski, *CFO*
Robin Jessup, *Admin Sec*
EMP: 85
SQ FT: 10,000
SALES (est): 15.8MM **Privately Held**
WEB: www.jessup.net
SIC: 4213 Trucking, except local

(P-4104)
BETTENDORF ENTERPRISES INC
Also Called: Bettendorf Trucking
20943 Bettendorf Way, Anderson (96007-8721)
PHONE.................................530 365-1937
Mike Tully, *Branch Mgr*
Josh Youngman, *Human Res Mgr*
EMP: 60
SALES (corp-wide): 35.1MM **Privately Held**
WEB: www.bettendorftrucking.com
SIC: 4213 Contract haulers
PA: Bettendorf Enterprises, Inc.
4545 West End Rd
Arcata CA 95521
707 822-0173

(P-4105)
BHANDAL BROS INC
2490 San Juan Rd, Hollister (95023-9107)
P.O. Box 190 (95024-0190)
PHONE.................................831 728-2691
Maninder Singh, *President*
EMP: 50 EST: 2012
SALES (est): 8MM **Privately Held**
SIC: 4213 Trucking, except local

(P-4106)
BHANDAL BROS TRUCKING INC
2490 San Juan Rd, Hollister (95023-9107)
P.O. Box 1900 (95024-1900)
PHONE.................................831 728-2691
Mangal S Bhandal, *President*
EMP: 55
SQ FT: 4,000
SALES (est): 12.6MM **Privately Held**
WEB: www.bhandalbrotherstrucking.com
SIC: 4213 Refrigerated products transport

(P-4107)
BIAGI BROS INC
Also Called: F & G Biagi Transportation
3655 E Airport Dr, Ontario (91761-1562)
PHONE.................................909 390-6910
John Boggus, *Branch Mgr*
EMP: 200
SALES (corp-wide): 140.9MM **Privately Held**
WEB: www.biagibros.com
SIC: 4213 Trucking, except local
PA: Biagi Bros., Inc.
787 Airpark Rd
Napa CA 94558
707 745-8115

(P-4108)
BIAGI BROS INC
Also Called: Biagi Brothers Bezzerides Co
650 Stone Rd, Benicia (94510-1140)
PHONE.................................707 745-8115
Tom Tunt, *Branch Mgr*
EMP: 80
SALES (corp-wide): 140.9MM **Privately Held**
WEB: www.biagibros.com
SIC: 4213 Trucking, except local
PA: Biagi Bros., Inc.
787 Airpark Rd
Napa CA 94558
707 745-8115

(P-4109)
BJJ COMPANY LLC (PA)
Also Called: Westland Trailer Mfg
1040 W Kettleman Ln, Lodi (95240-6056)
PHONE.................................209 941-8361
Fax: 209 941-0476
EMP: 70
SQ FT: 4,000
SALES (est): 12.1MM **Privately Held**
SIC: 4213

(P-4110)
BLUE CHIP MOVING AND STOR INC
Also Called: Blue Chip Mayflower
13525 Crenshaw Blvd, Hawthorne (90250-7811)
PHONE.................................323 463-6888
Dennis Doody, *CEO*
Jack Doody, *Vice Pres*
EMP: 55 EST: 1963
SQ FT: 30,000
SALES (est): 8.7MM **Privately Held**
SIC: 4213 4214 Household goods transport; contract haulers; local trucking with storage

(P-4111)
BUDWAY ENTERPRISES INC (PA)
Also Called: Budway Trucking & Warehousing
13600 Napa St, Fontana (92335-2944)
PHONE.................................909 463-0500
Vincent McLeod, *CEO*
Jim Barbour, *CFO*
Daniel Heykoop, *Exec VP*
Marcy McKenzie, *Vice Pres*
Alex Nicholas, *Vice Pres*
EMP: 55 EST: 1974
SQ FT: 120,000
SALES (est): 20.9MM **Privately Held**
SIC: 4213 Contract haulers

(P-4112)
BULK TRANSPORTATION (PA)
415 S Lemon Ave, Walnut (91789-2911)
P.O. Box 390 (91788-0390)
PHONE.................................909 594-2855
Brett Richardson, *President*
Gary K Cross, *President*
George G Cross, *CEO*
Frank Cutter, *Vice Pres*
Jeff Machado, *Vice Pres*
EMP: 60
SQ FT: 3,500
SALES: 38.4MM **Privately Held**
WEB: www.bulk-dti.com
SIC: 4213 4789 Contract haulers; cargo loading & unloading services

(P-4113)
BUTTON TRANSPORTATION INC
7000 Button Ln, Dixon (95620-9116)
PHONE..................................707 678-1983
Robert Button, *President*
Anthony Iten, *President*
Christine C Button, *Vice Pres*
EMP: 175
SQ FT: 5,000
SALES (est): 35.4MM Privately Held
SIC: 4213 Contract haulers; liquid petroleum transport, non-local

(P-4114)
CALIFRNIA INTERMODAL ASSOC INC (PA)
6666 E Washington Blvd, Commerce (90040-1814)
PHONE..................................323 562-7788
Gabriel Chaul, *CEO*
Ron Mejia, *Manager*
Stephani Mejia, *Supervisor*
EMP: 60
SALES (est): 7.2MM Privately Held
WEB: www.ciatrucking.com
SIC: 4213 Trucking, except local

(P-4115)
CENTRAL FREIGHT LINES INC
1621 Main Ave, Sacramento (95838-2427)
PHONE..................................800 782-5036
Jack Buckley, *Manager*
EMP: 100
SALES (corp-wide): 1.7B Privately Held
WEB: www.centralfreight.com
SIC: 4213 Trucking, except local
HQ: Central Freight Lines, Inc.
5601 W Waco Dr
Waco TX 76710
254 772-2120

(P-4116)
CERTIFIED FRT LOGISTICS INC (PA)
1344 White Ct, Santa Maria (93458-3732)
P.O. Box 5668 (93456-5668)
PHONE..................................805 925-9900
James O Nelson, *President*
Scott Cramer, *COO*
Jon Cramer, *Vice Pres*
Edwin F Nelson Jr, *Vice Pres*
Chuck Alloway, *Info Tech Mgr*
EMP: 150
SQ FT: 40,000
SALES: 39.4MM Privately Held
WEB: www.cfl-usa.com
SIC: 4213 Refrigerated products transport

(P-4117)
CHIPMAN CORPORATION
Also Called: Unitd Van Lines Agnt
1555 Zephyr Ave, Hayward (94544-7835)
PHONE..................................510 748-8787
John Chipman Jr, *Branch Mgr*
Pamela Welsh, *Vice Pres*
Tom Byron, *Business Dir*
EMP: 60
SALES (corp-wide): 33.1MM Privately Held
WEB: www.chipmancorp.com
SIC: 4213 4212 Household goods transport; moving services
PA: Chipman Corporation
1040 Marina Village Pkwy # 100
Alameda CA 94501
510 748-8700

(P-4118)
CONTRACTORS CARGO COMPANY (PA)
Also Called: Contractors Rigging & Erectors
500 S Alameda St, Compton (90221-3801)
P.O. Box 5290 (90224-5290)
PHONE..................................310 609-1957
Carla Ann Wheeler, *CEO*
Gerald D Wheeler, *President*
Kimberly Dorio, *Corp Secy*
Steve Cummins, *Natl Sales Mgr*
Keoni Rabaino, *Sales Staff*
EMP: 120
SQ FT: 25,000

SALES (est): 51.9MM Privately Held
WEB: www.contractorscargo.com
SIC: 4213 4731 1623 4741 Contract haulers; freight transportation arrangement; water, sewer & utility lines; rental of railroad cars; cargo loading & unloading services; boiler maintenance contractor

(P-4119)
CRST INTERNATIONAL INC
10641 Calabash Ave, Fontana (92337-7011)
PHONE..................................909 829-1313
EMP: 149
SALES (corp-wide): 2B Privately Held
SIC: 4213
PA: Crst International, Inc.
3930 16th Ave Sw
Cedar Rapids IA 52401
319 396-4400

(P-4120)
CUNHA DRAYING INC
1500 Madruga Rd, Lathrop (95330-9779)
PHONE..................................209 858-1400
Paul Buttini, *President*
Peggy Deforest, *Vice Pres*
EMP: 65
SQ FT: 10,000
SALES (est): 9.9MM Privately Held
WEB: www.cunhadraying.com
SIC: 4213 Contract haulers

(P-4121)
D E F EXPRESS CORPORATION
2626 S Railroad Ave, Fresno (93725-1925)
P.O. Box 12427 (93777-2427)
PHONE..................................559 264-0500
Mike Shuemake, *President*
EMP: 100
SQ FT: 20,000
SALES (est): 6.8MM Privately Held
SIC: 4213 Trucking, except local

(P-4122)
DAYLIGHT TRANSPORT LLC (PA)
1501 Hughes Way Ste 200, Long Beach (90810-1879)
P.O. Box 93155 (90809-3155)
PHONE..................................310 507-8200
Richard S Breen, *CEO*
Jim Mc Carthy, *CFO*
Edward Marsh, *Vice Pres*
EMP: 100 EST: 1997
SQ FT: 3,000
SALES (est): 50.8MM Privately Held
WEB: www.dylt.com
SIC: 4213 Contract haulers

(P-4123)
DC TRANSPORT INC
5411 Raley Blvd, Sacramento (95838-1726)
PHONE..................................916 438-0888
Andrew Romanov, *President*
Mike Deford, *CFO*
Sergey Romanov, *Vice Pres*
Evelina R Popovich, *Admin Sec*
Evelina Popovich, *Admin Sec*
EMP: 55
SQ FT: 21,000
SALES (est): 18.9MM Privately Held
WEB: www.dctransport.com
SIC: 4213 Trucking, except local

(P-4124)
DEPENDABLE HIGHWAY EXPRESS INC
Also Called: Dhe
1351 S Campus Ave, Ontario (91761-4352)
PHONE..................................909 923-0065
Bob Bianchi, *Branch Mgr*
EMP: 60
SALES (corp-wide): 283MM Privately Held
WEB: www.godependable.com
SIC: 4213 Contract haulers
PA: Dependable Highway Express, Inc.
2555 E Olympic Blvd
Los Angeles CA 90023
323 526-2200

(P-4125)
DEPENDABLE HIGHWAY EXPRESS INC
1343 Lone Palm Ave, Modesto (95351-1536)
PHONE..................................209 342-0184
Don Hillman, *President*
EMP: 218
SALES (corp-wide): 283MM Privately Held
SIC: 4213 Trucking, except local
PA: Dependable Highway Express, Inc.
2555 E Olympic Blvd
Los Angeles CA 90023
323 526-2200

(P-4126)
DEPENDABLE HIGHWAY EXPRESS INC (PA)
2555 E Olympic Blvd, Los Angeles (90023-2605)
P.O. Box 58047 (90058-0047)
PHONE..................................323 526-2200
Ronald Massman, *President*
Nicole Felix, *Partner*
Blanca Reyes, *Partner*
Karen Shaw, *Partner*
Michael Dougan, *CFO*
EMP: 300
SQ FT: 1,680,000
SALES (est): 283MM Privately Held
WEB: www.godependable.com
SIC: 4213 4225 Contract haulers; general warehousing & storage

(P-4127)
DEPENDABLE HIGHWAY EXPRESS INC
Also Called: Dhe
3199 Alvarado St, San Leandro (94577-5709)
PHONE..................................510 357-2223
Georgia Briggs, *Branch Mgr*
EMP: 82
SALES (corp-wide): 283MM Privately Held
WEB: www.godependable.com
SIC: 4213 4225 Trucking, except local; general warehousing & storage
PA: Dependable Highway Express, Inc.
2555 E Olympic Blvd
Los Angeles CA 90023
323 526-2200

(P-4128)
DESERT COASTAL TRANSPORT INC (PA)
Also Called: Dct
10686 Banana Ave, Fontana (92337-7002)
PHONE..................................909 357-3395
Tim Wyant, *President*
Timothy A Wyant, *CEO*
Chuck Wyant, *Admin Sec*
EMP: 55
SQ FT: 6,000
SALES: 29.2MM Privately Held
WEB: www.desertcoastal.com
SIC: 4213 Trucking, except local

(P-4129)
DOT-LINE TRANSPORTATION INC
4366 E 26th St, Vernon (90058-4301)
P.O. Box 8739, Fountain Valley (92728-8739)
PHONE..................................877 900-7768
Dennis Watson, *President*
Dottie Watson, *Corp Secy*
EMP: 55
SALES (est): 4.8MM Privately Held
SIC: 4213 Trucking, except local

(P-4130)
DOUBLE EAGLE TRNSP CORP
12135 Scarbrough Ct, Oak Hills (92344-9200)
PHONE..................................760 956-3770
Gerald E Butcher, *President*
EMP: 140
SQ FT: 10,125
SALES: 16MM Privately Held
SIC: 4213 4212 Contract haulers; local trucking, without storage

(P-4131)
DOUDELL TRUCKING COMPANY (PA)
1505 N 4th St, San Jose (95112-4607)
P.O. Box 5879 (95150-5879)
PHONE..................................408 263-7300
Armand Kunde, *President*
John Kunde, *CFO*
Al Kunde, *General Mgr*
EMP: 180
SQ FT: 20,000
SALES (est): 12.9MM Privately Held
SIC: 4213 4214 4212 Contract haulers; local trucking with storage; local trucking, without storage

(P-4132)
DSC LOGISTICS INC
1895 Marigold Ave, Redlands (92374-5028)
PHONE..................................909 363-4354
Greg Hart, *General Ptnr*
EMP: 68
SALES (corp-wide): 355MM Privately Held
SIC: 4213 4212 Trucking, except local; local trucking, without storage
PA: Dsc Logistics, Inc.
1750 S Wolf Rd
Des Plaines IL 60018
847 390-6800

(P-4133)
EAGLE SYSTEMS INC
Also Called: Eagle Intermodel Services
395 N Mount Vernon Ave, San Bernardino (92411-2673)
PHONE..................................909 386-4343
Al Thompson, *Branch Mgr*
EMP: 250 Privately Held
WEB: www.eagleis.com
SIC: 4213 Contract haulers
HQ: Eagle Systems, Inc.
230 Grant Rd Ste A1
East Wenatchee WA 98802
509 884-7575

(P-4134)
EARLY TRANSPORTATION SERVICES
Also Called: Bay Area Garment
30796 San Clemente St, Hayward (94544-7131)
PHONE..................................510 324-1119
Earl I Ramer Sr, *President*
EMP: 100
SALES (est): 5.7MM Privately Held
SIC: 4213 Trucking, except local

(P-4135)
ED ROCHA LIVESTOCK TRNSP INC
Also Called: Rocha Transportation
2400 Nickerson Dr, Modesto (95358-9409)
P.O. Box 40, Ceres (95307-0040)
PHONE..................................209 538-1302
Henry Dirksen, *President*
Zach Dirksen, *Treasurer*
Zachary Dirksen, *Treasurer*
Corrie M Toste, *Admin Sec*
Grant Hannink, *Opers Mgr*
EMP: 70
SQ FT: 5,500
SALES (est): 11.3MM Privately Held
WEB: www.rochatrans.com
SIC: 4213 Contract haulers

(P-4136)
ERRAMA TRUCKING COMPANY INC
Also Called: Tough2beat Auto Sales
11336 Montgomery Ave, Granada Hills (91344-3841)
PHONE..................................818 381-3341
Souhayl Errama, *President*
Alejandro Pacheco, *Vice Pres*
Taha Aerrama, *Director*
EMP: 50
SQ FT: 15,000
SALES (est): 3MM Privately Held
SIC: 4213 5511 Household goods transport; automobiles, new & used

(P-4137)
ESPARZA ENTERPRISES INC
500 Workman St, Bakersfield (93307-6871)
PHONE.....................................661 631-0347
EMP: 1360
SALES (corp-wide): 90.9MM Privately
Held
SIC: 4213 Trucking, except local
PA: Esparza Enterprises, Inc.
3851 Fruitvale Ave
Bakersfield CA 93308
661 831-0002

(P-4138)
ESTES EXPRESS LINES INC
14727 Alondra Blvd, La Mirada
(90638-5617)
PHONE.....................................714 994-3770
Benjamin J Torman, Branch Mgr
EMP: 121
SALES (corp-wide): 2.7B Privately Held
SIC: 4213 Trucking, except local
PA: Estes Express Lines, Inc.
3901 W Broad St
Richmond VA 23230
804 353-1900

(P-4139)
ESTES EXPRESS LINES INC
10736 Cherry Ave, Fontana (92337-7196)
PHONE.....................................909 427-9850
Mark Brown, Manager
Joel Cherry, Opers Mgr
Brad Arison, Sales Mgr
EMP: 58
SALES (corp-wide): 2.7B Privately Held
WEB: www.estes-express.com
SIC: 4213 4212 Less-than-truckload (LTL)
transport; local trucking, without storage
PA: Estes Express Lines, Inc.
3901 W Broad St
Richmond VA 23230
804 353-1900

(P-4140)
ESTES EXPRESS LINES INC
13327 Temple Ave, City of Industry
(91746-1513)
PHONE.....................................626 333-9090
Kieran O'Carroll, Manager
Kieren Okcarol, Executive
Greg Atkins, Manager
Martin Sakamoto, Accounts Mgr
EMP: 67
SQ FT: 6,156
SALES (corp-wide): 2.7B Privately Held
WEB: www.estes-express.com
SIC: 4213 4212 Less-than-truckload (LTL)
transport; local trucking, without storage
PA: Estes Express Lines, Inc.
3901 W Broad St
Richmond VA 23230
804 353-1900

(P-4141)
ESTES EXPRESS LINES INC
1634 S 7th St, San Jose (95112-5931)
PHONE.....................................408 286-3894
John Martin, Branch Mgr
Mary Edmonson, Manager
EMP: 50
SALES (corp-wide): 2.7B Privately Held
WEB: www.estes-express.com
SIC: 4213 Contract haulers
PA: Estes Express Lines, Inc.
3901 W Broad St
Richmond VA 23230
804 353-1900

(P-4142)
ESTES EXPRESS LINES INC
1750 Adams Ave, San Leandro
(94577-1002)
PHONE.....................................510 635-0165
Bill Wardell, Manager
EMP: 58
SALES (corp-wide): 2.7B Privately Held
WEB: www.estes-express.com
SIC: 4213 Contract haulers
PA: Estes Express Lines, Inc.
3901 W Broad St
Richmond VA 23230
804 353-1900

(P-4143)
ESTES EXPRESS LINES INC
9120 San Fernando Rd, Sun Valley
(91352-1413)
PHONE.....................................818 504-4155
Eric Reyes, Manager
EMP: 58
SALES (corp-wide): 2.7B Privately Held
WEB: www.estes-express.com
SIC: 4213 Contract haulers
PA: Estes Express Lines, Inc.
3901 W Broad St
Richmond VA 23230
804 353-1900

(P-4144)
ESTES EXPRESS LINES INC
7611 S Airport Way, Stockton (95206-3918)
PHONE.....................................209 982-1841
Mark Hancock, Branch Mgr
EMP: 58
SALES (corp-wide): 2.7B Privately Held
WEB: www.estes-express.com
SIC: 4213 Trucking, except local
PA: Estes Express Lines, Inc.
3901 W Broad St
Richmond VA 23230
804 353-1900

(P-4145)
ESTES EXPRESS LINES INC
1531 Blinn Ave, Wilmington (90744-1601)
PHONE.....................................310 549-7306
Rob Clagg, Manager
EMP: 58
SALES (corp-wide): 2.7B Privately Held
WEB: www.estes-express.com
SIC: 4213 Contract haulers
PA: Estes Express Lines, Inc.
3901 W Broad St
Richmond VA 23230
804 353-1900

(P-4146)
ESTES EXPRESS LINES INC
14727 Alondra Blvd, La Mirada
(90638-5617)
PHONE.....................................714 523-1122
William Reid, President
Marty Whitacre, Info Tech Mgr
EMP: 58
SALES (corp-wide): 2.7B Privately Held
WEB: www.estes-express.com
SIC: 4213 Trucking, except local
PA: Estes Express Lines, Inc.
3901 W Broad St
Richmond VA 23230
804 353-1900

(P-4147)
**EVANS DEDICATED SYSTEMS
INC (PA)**
6001 E Wash Blvd Ste 200, Commerce
(90040-2455)
PHONE.....................................323 725-2928
William H Culbertson, CEO
Thomas Forrest, CFO
Robert Forrest, Principal
Stephen Meleen, Principal
EMP: 170
SQ FT: 7,500
SALES (est): 37MM Privately Held
SIC: 4213 Liquid petroleum transport, non-
local

(P-4148)
**FAST LANE TRANSPORTATION
INC (PA)**
Also Called: Fast Lane Container Services
2400 E Pacific Coast Hwy, Wilmington
(90744-2921)
PHONE.....................................562 435-3000
Patrick L Wilson, President
Christine Henry, Corp Secy
James Henry, Exec VP
Chris Henry, Info Tech Mgr
Eric Martin, Manager
EMP: 70
SQ FT: 36,000
SALES (est): 9.9MM Privately Held
WEB: www.fastlanetrans.com
SIC: 4213 4214 Trailer or container on flat
car (TOFC/COFC); local trucking with
storage

(P-4149)
FAULKNER TRUCKING INC
3645 S K St, Tulare (93274-7178)
PHONE.....................................559 684-9298
Ronald D Faulkner, President
Wade Magden, Safety Dir
Mike Servillo, Facilities Mgr
Sally Faulkner, Clerk
EMP: 58
SQ FT: 3,600
SALES (est): 14.3MM Privately Held
WEB: www.faulknertrucking.com
SIC: 4213 Contract haulers

(P-4150)
**FEDERAL EXPRESS
CORPORATION**
Also Called: Fedex
3333 S Grand Ave, Los Angeles
(90007-4116)
PHONE.....................................800 463-3339
Dave Vint, Branch Mgr
EMP: 100
SALES (corp-wide): 65.4B Publicly Held
WEB: www.federalexpress.com
SIC: 4213 Contract haulers
HQ: Federal Express Corporation
3610 Hacks Cross Rd
Memphis TN 38125
901 369-3600

(P-4151)
FEDEX FREIGHT CORPORATION
4500 Bandini Blvd, Vernon (90058-5409)
PHONE.....................................323 269-9800
Matt Lowe, Sales/Mktg Mgr
Tore Richardson, IT/INT Sup
EMP: 200
SQ FT: 20,000
SALES (corp-wide): 65.4B Publicly Held
WEB: www.watkins.com
SIC: 4213 4231 Contract haulers; trucking
terminal facilities
HQ: Fedex Freight Corporation
1715 Aaron Brenner Dr
Memphis TN 38120

(P-4152)
FEDEX FREIGHT CORPORATION
1379 N Miller St, Anaheim (92806-1412)
PHONE.....................................714 996-8720
Brad Housner, Manager
Mike Hutton, General Mgr
Cruz Mendoza, Warehouse Mgr
EMP: 160
SQ FT: 20,802
SALES (corp-wide): 65.4B Publicly Held
SIC: 4213 4212 7538 Trucking, except
local; delivery service, vehicular; general
automotive repair shops
HQ: Fedex Freight Corporation
1715 Aaron Brenner Dr
Memphis TN 38120

(P-4153)
FEDEX FREIGHT CORPORATION
7250 Cajon Blvd, San Bernardino
(92407-1887)
PHONE.....................................909 887-3970
EMP: 185
SALES (corp-wide): 65.4B Publicly Held
SIC: 4213 7513 Less-than-truckload (LTL)
transport; truck leasing, without drivers
HQ: Fedex Freight Corporation
1715 Aaron Brenner Dr
Memphis TN 38120

(P-4154)
FEDEX FREIGHT CORPORATION
193 Willow St, Bishop (93514-2750)
PHONE.....................................760 873-8655
EMP: 53
SALES (corp-wide): 65.4B Publicly Held
SIC: 4213 Less-than-truckload (LTL) trans-
port
HQ: Fedex Freight Corporation
1715 Aaron Brenner Dr
Memphis TN 38120

(P-4155)
FEDEX FREIGHT CORPORATION
2250 Airway Ln, San Diego (92154-6205)
PHONE.....................................619 710-0268
Willie Macias, Branch Mgr
EMP: 76
SALES (corp-wide): 65.4B Publicly Held
SIC: 4213 Trucking, except local
HQ: Fedex Freight Corporation
1715 Aaron Brenner Dr
Memphis TN 38120

(P-4156)
FEDEX FREIGHT CORPORATION
15200 S Main St, Gardena (90248-1957)
PHONE.....................................310 323-5230
Chaug Rios, Manager
EMP: 280
SALES (corp-wide): 65.4B Publicly Held
SIC: 4213 4215 4731 Trucking, except
local; courier services, except by air;
freight forwarding
HQ: Fedex Freight Corporation
1715 Aaron Brenner Dr
Memphis TN 38120

(P-4157)
FEDEX FREIGHT CORPORATION
29001 Hopkins St, Hayward (94545-5003)
PHONE.....................................510 895-0440
Mike Farrell, Manager
EMP: 350
SALES (corp-wide): 65.4B Publicly Held
SIC: 4213 4231 4212 4731 Trucking, ex-
cept local; trucking terminal facilities; local
trucking, without storage; freight forward-
ing; airports, flying fields & services
HQ: Fedex Freight Corporation
1715 Aaron Brenner Dr
Memphis TN 38120

(P-4158)
FEDEX FREIGHT CORPORATION
11911 Branford St, Sun Valley
(91352-1026)
PHONE.....................................818 899-1141
Greg Sullivan, Manager
Roxanne Talman, Human Res Dir
Simon Yeung, Purch Agent
EMP: 75
SALES (corp-wide): 65.4B Publicly Held
SIC: 4213 Less-than-truckload (LTL) trans-
port
HQ: Fedex Freight Corporation
1715 Aaron Brenner Dr
Memphis TN 38120

(P-4159)
FEDEX FREIGHT CORPORATION
4520 S Highway 99, Stockton
(95215-8235)
PHONE.....................................209 466-7726
Carlos Gonzales, Manager
EMP: 200
SALES (corp-wide): 65.4B Publicly Held
SIC: 4213 Trucking, except local
HQ: Fedex Freight Corporation
1715 Aaron Brenner Dr
Memphis TN 38120

(P-4160)
FEDEX FREIGHT CORPORATION
56 Fairbanks, Irvine (92618-1602)
PHONE.....................................800 706-1687
Mike Sendayhoff, Manager
EMP: 76
SALES (corp-wide): 65.4B Publicly Held
SIC: 4213 4731 Trucking, except local;
freight forwarding
HQ: Fedex Freight Corporation
1715 Aaron Brenner Dr
Memphis TN 38120

(P-4161)
FEDEX FREIGHT WEST INC
3050 Teagarden St, San Leandro
(94577-5721)
PHONE.....................................650 244-9522
EMP: 89

SALES (corp-wide): 47.4B **Publicly Held**
SIC: 4213
HQ: Fedex Freight West, Inc.
6411 Guadalupe Mines Rd
San Jose CA 95120
775 356-7600

(P-4162)
FEDEX FREIGHT WEST INC
4570 S Maple Ave, Fresno (93725-9358)
PHONE.................................559 266-0732
EMP: 125
SALES (corp-wide): 47.4B **Publicly Held**
SIC: 4213 4231 4214
HQ: Fedex Freight West, Inc.
6411 Guadalupe Mines Rd
San Jose CA 95120
775 356-7600

(P-4163)
FEDEX FREIGHT WEST INC
11153 Mulberry Ave, Fontana
(92337-7030)
PHONE.................................909 357-3555
EMP: 355
SQ FT: 79,735
SALES (corp-wide): 47.4B **Publicly Held**
SIC: 4213 4731 4212
HQ: Fedex Freight West, Inc.
6411 Guadalupe Mines Rd
San Jose CA 95120
775 356-7600

(P-4164)
FEDEX FREIGHT WEST INC
1230 N Mcdowell Blvd, Petaluma
(94954-1113)
PHONE.................................707 778-3191
EMP: 50
SQ FT: 13,920
SALES (corp-wide): 47.4B **Publicly Held**
SIC: 4213
HQ: Fedex Freight West, Inc.
6411 Guadalupe Mines Rd
San Jose CA 95120
775 356-7600

(P-4165)
FEDEX GROUND PACKAGE SYS INC
1497 George Dr Ste G, Redding
(96003-1472)
PHONE.................................800 463-3339
Troy Manns, *Branch Mgr*
EMP: 50
SALES (corp-wide): 65.4B **Publicly Held**
SIC: 4213 Contract haulers
HQ: Fedex Ground Package System, Inc.
1000 Fed Ex Dr
Coraopolis PA 15108
412 269-1000

(P-4166)
FEDEX GROUND PACKAGE SYS INC
590 E Orangethorpe Ave, Anaheim
(92801-1021)
PHONE.................................800 463-3339
Martin Daza, *Manager*
Sean Davis, *Manager*
EMP: 250
SALES (corp-wide): 65.4B **Publicly Held**
SIC: 4213 4215 Contract haulers; courier
services, except by air
HQ: Fedex Ground Package System, Inc.
1000 Fed Ex Dr
Coraopolis PA 15108
412 269-1000

(P-4167)
FEDEX GROUND PACKAGE SYS INC
1844 S Haster St, Anaheim (92802-3737)
PHONE.................................800 463-3339
Lester Huffmire, *Principal*
EMP: 88
SALES (corp-wide): 65.4B **Publicly Held**
SIC: 4213 Contract haulers
HQ: Fedex Ground Package System, Inc.
1000 Fed Ex Dr
Coraopolis PA 15108
412 269-1000

(P-4168)
FEDEX GROUND PACKAGE SYS INC
1 Carousel Ln Unit B, Ukiah (95482-9509)
PHONE.................................800 463-3339
EMP: 87
SALES (corp-wide): 65.4B **Publicly Held**
SIC: 4213 Contract haulers
HQ: Fedex Ground Package System, Inc.
1000 Fed Ex Dr
Coraopolis PA 15108
412 269-1000

(P-4169)
FEDEX GROUND PACKAGE SYS INC
101 Book Farm Rd, Durham (95938-9521)
PHONE.................................800 463-3339
EMP: 146
SALES (corp-wide): 65.4B **Publicly Held**
SIC: 4213 Contract haulers
HQ: Fedex Ground Package System, Inc.
1000 Fed Ex Dr
Coraopolis PA 15108
412 269-1000

(P-4170)
FEDEX GROUND PACKAGE SYS INC
1725 Charles Willard St, Carson
(90746-4031)
PHONE.................................800 463-3339
EMP: 146
SALES (corp-wide): 65.4B **Publicly Held**
SIC: 4213 Contract haulers
HQ: Fedex Ground Package System, Inc.
1000 Fed Ex Dr
Coraopolis PA 15108
412 269-1000

(P-4171)
FEDEX GROUND PACKAGE SYS INC
311 Otterson Dr, Chico (95928-8236)
PHONE.................................800 463-3339
EMP: 146
SALES (corp-wide): 65.4B **Publicly Held**
SIC: 4213 Contract haulers
HQ: Fedex Ground Package System, Inc.
1000 Fed Ex Dr
Coraopolis PA 15108
412 269-1000

(P-4172)
FEDEX GROUND PACKAGE SYS INC
375 Airport Rd, Bishop (93514-3614)
PHONE.................................800 463-3339
EMP: 146
SALES (corp-wide): 65.4B **Publicly Held**
SIC: 4213 Contract haulers
HQ: Fedex Ground Package System, Inc.
1000 Fed Ex Dr
Coraopolis PA 15108
412 269-1000

(P-4173)
FEDEX GROUND PACKAGE SYS INC
500 Caletti Ave, Windsor (95492-6822)
PHONE.................................800 463-3339
EMP: 146
SALES (corp-wide): 65.4B **Publicly Held**
SIC: 4213 Contract haulers
HQ: Fedex Ground Package System, Inc.
1000 Fed Ex Dr
Coraopolis PA 15108
412 269-1000

(P-4174)
FEDEX GROUND PACKAGE SYS INC
Also Called: Fedex Home Delivery
1500 E Wooley Rd Ste B, Oxnard
(93030-7381)
PHONE.................................800 463-3339
EMP: 88
SALES (corp-wide): 65.4B **Publicly Held**
SIC: 4213 Contract haulers
HQ: Fedex Ground Package System, Inc.
1000 Fed Ex Dr
Coraopolis PA 15108
412 269-1000

(P-4175)
FEDEX GROUND PACKAGE SYS INC
696 E Trimble Rd Ste 10, San Jose
(95131-1236)
PHONE.................................800 463-3339
Steve Brenner, *Principal*
EMP: 300
SALES (corp-wide): 65.4B **Publicly Held**
SIC: 4213 Contract haulers
HQ: Fedex Ground Package System, Inc.
1000 Fed Ex Dr
Coraopolis PA 15108
412 269-1000

(P-4176)
FEDEX GROUND PACKAGE SYS INC
300 Manabe Ow Rd, Watsonville
(95076-7200)
PHONE.................................800 463-3339
EMP: 88
SALES (corp-wide): 65.4B **Publicly Held**
SIC: 4213 Contract haulers
HQ: Fedex Ground Package System, Inc.
1000 Fed Ex Dr
Coraopolis PA 15108
412 269-1000

(P-4177)
FEDEX GROUND PACKAGE SYS INC
9175 San Fernando Rd, Sun Valley
(91352-1414)
PHONE.................................800 463-3339
Kevin Dixon, *Manager*
EMP: 90
SALES (corp-wide): 65.4B **Publicly Held**
SIC: 4213 Contract haulers
HQ: Fedex Ground Package System, Inc.
1000 Fed Ex Dr
Coraopolis PA 15108
412 269-1000

(P-4178)
FLASH TRANSPORT INC
14796 Washington Dr, Fontana
(92335-6263)
P.O. Box 4712, Diamond Bar (91765-0712)
PHONE.................................909 829-1369
William Faulkner, *President*
EMP: 75
SQ FT: 2,000
SALES (est): 6.4MM **Privately Held**
SIC: 4213 4212 Trucking, except local;
local trucking, without storage

(P-4179)
FRANK C ALEGRE TRUCKING INC (PA)
5100 W Highway 12, Lodi (95242-9529)
P.O. Box 1508 (95241-1508)
PHONE.................................209 334-2112
Anthony J Alegre, *President*
Michelle Schultz, *General Mgr*
EMP: 230
SQ FT: 34,200
SALES (est): 44.5MM **Privately Held**
SIC: 4213 4212 Contract haulers; dump
truck haulage

(P-4180)
FREDERICKSEN TANK LINES INC (PA)
Also Called: Nevada Truck & Trailer Repair
840 Delta Ln, West Sacramento
(95691-2801)
P.O. Box 235 (95691-0235)
PHONE.................................916 371-4960
Leonard D Robinson, *CEO*
Jeanne Haskell, *President*
Larry Kenobbie, *Vice Pres*
EMP: 93
SQ FT: 8,000
SALES (est): 6.9MM **Privately Held**
SIC: 4213 4212 Liquid petroleum trans-
port, non-local; petroleum haulage, local

(P-4181)
FRIENDS GROUP EXPRESS INC
14520 Village Dr Apt 1013, Fontana
(92337-2501)
P.O. Box 310488 (92331-0488)
PHONE.................................909 346-6814

Parmjit Singh Grewal, *Principal*
EMP: 78 EST: 2014
SQ FT: 700
SALES: 194K **Privately Held**
SIC: 4213 4212 Trucking, except local;
local trucking, without storage

(P-4182)
FUEL DELIVERY SERVICES INC
4895 S Airport Way, Stockton
(95206-3915)
P.O. Box 1369 (95201-1369)
PHONE.................................209 751-2185
Ronald M Vandepol, *CEO*
David Atwater, *Shareholder*
Mike Boswart, *Shareholder*
Tom V Depol, *Shareholder*
David Robinson, *Manager*
EMP: 94
SQ FT: 2,000
SALES (est): 15.2MM **Privately Held**
SIC: 4213 Liquid petroleum transport, non-
local

(P-4183)
GARDNER TRUCKING INC
Also Called: Gardner Logistics
9032 Merrill Ave, Chino (91708)
P.O. Box 747 (91708-0747)
PHONE.................................909 563-5606
Ron Lanting, *Vice Pres*
Sam Bailey, *District Mgr*
Sohn Tippetts, *Admin Asst*
Mariela Diaz, *Administration*
Salina Herrera, *Administration*
EMP: 53
SALES (corp-wide): 2.1B **Privately Held**
SIC: 4213 Contract haulers
HQ: Gardner Trucking, Inc.
1219 E Elm St
Ontario CA 91761

(P-4184)
GARDNER TRUCKING INC (HQ)
1219 E Elm St, Ontario (91761-4585)
P.O. Box 747, Chino (91708-0747)
PHONE.................................909 563-5606
Thomas J Lanting, *President*
Cory Peters, *Vice Pres*
Raymond Huerta, *Admin Asst*
Leonard Lebarre, *Sales Staff*
Dee Eakes, *Manager*
EMP: 490
SQ FT: 3,000
SALES (est): 96.9MM
SALES (corp-wide): 2.1B **Privately Held**
SIC: 4213 4212 Trucking, except local;
local trucking, without storage
PA: Crst International, Inc.
201 1st St Se
Cedar Rapids IA 52401
319 396-4400

(P-4185)
GCU TRUCKING INC
7819 Crane Rd, Oakdale (95361-8114)
P.O. Box 1423 (95361-1423)
PHONE.................................209 845-2117
Leo Arcos Jr, *CEO*
EMP: 52
SQ FT: 7,000
SALES (est): 9.1MM **Privately Held**
SIC: 4213 5032 Contract haulers; brick,
stone & related material

(P-4186)
GILL TRANSPORT LLC
1051 Pacific Ave, Oxnard (93030-7254)
PHONE.................................805 240-1979
Steven H Gill, *Mng Member*
David L Gill, *Mng Member*
EMP: 400
SALES (est): 22.2MM **Privately Held**
SIC: 4213 Trucking, except local

(P-4187)
GOLDEN EAGLE MOVING SVCS INC
1450 N Benson Ave Unit B, Upland
(91786-2127)
PHONE.................................909 946-7655
Robert Johnson, *President*
Thomas Johnson Jr, *CFO*
Constance Johnson, *Vice Pres*
Constance A Johnson, *Vice Pres*

EMP: 55
SQ FT: 50,000
SALES: 6.2MM **Privately Held**
WEB: www.goldeneaglemoving.com
SIC: 4213 4214 Household goods transport; household goods moving & storage, local

(P-4188)
H & H TRANSPORTATION LLC
300 El Sobrante Rd, Corona (92879-5757)
P.O. Box 77697 (92877-0123)
PHONE....................................951 817-2300
Tim Hyde,
EMP: 60
SALES (est): 6.6MM **Privately Held**
SIC: 4213 4212 Trucking, except local; local trucking, without storage

(P-4189)
H F COX INC (PA)
Also Called: Cox Petroleum Transport
118 Cox Transport Way, Bakersfield (93307)
PHONE....................................661 366-3236
Dainiel L Mairs, *President*
Larry Oconnell, *COO*
Gwen Mairs, *Treasurer*
Teri Gonzalez, *Vice Pres*
Bruce McKinnon, *Vice Pres*
EMP: 60
SQ FT: 5,000
SALES: 683.2K **Privately Held**
WEB: www.coxpetroleum.com
SIC: 4213 4212 Trucking, except local; petroleum haulage, local

(P-4190)
HANSEN ADKINS AUTO TRNSPT INC (PA)
3552 Green Ave, Los Alamitos (90720-3243)
PHONE....................................562 430-4100
Louie R Adkins, *CEO*
Steve Hansen, *Vice Pres*
Mark Rumfola, *Vice Pres*
Barry Williams, *Vice Pres*
Bob Roehrig, *Director*
EMP: 511
SQ FT: 4,000
SALES (est): 91.1MM **Privately Held**
WEB: www.hansenadkins.com
SIC: 4213 Automobiles, transport & delivery

(P-4191)
HAWK TRANSPORTATION INC
15238 Arrow Blvd, Fontana (92335-3250)
PHONE....................................800 709-4295
Manprit K Sandhu, *CEO*
Jagtar Sandhu, *President*
Harry Bhangu, *Manager*
EMP: 60
SQ FT: 1,300
SALES (est): 13.1MM **Privately Held**
WEB: www.hawktrans.com
SIC: 4213 Trucking, except local

(P-4192)
HEARTLAND EXPRESS INC IOWA
10131 Redwood Ave, Fontana (92335-6236)
PHONE....................................319 626-3600
Matthew Gonzalez, *Supervisor*
EMP: 50
SALES (corp-wide): 607.3MM **Publicly Held**
WEB: www.intd.com
SIC: 4213 Trucking, except local
HQ: Heartland Express, Inc. Of Iowa
901 N Kansas Ave
North Liberty IA 52317
319 626-3600

(P-4193)
HENDRICKSON TRUCK LINES INC
7080 Florin Perkins Rd, Sacramento (95828-2609)
P.O. Box 277806 (95827-7806)
PHONE....................................916 387-9614
William Hendrickson, *Chairman*
Ward Hendrickson, *CEO*
Alban Lang, *CFO*

EMP: 148
SALES: 23MM **Privately Held**
SIC: 4213 Trucking, except local

(P-4194)
HENDRICKSON TRUCKING INC
7080 Florin Perkins Rd, Sacramento (95828-2609)
P.O. Box 292219 (95829-2219)
PHONE....................................916 387-9614
William Hendrickson, *CEO*
Ward Hendrickson, *President*
Carmen Flack, *Sales Associate*
EMP: 280
SQ FT: 5,480
SALES (est): 70.2MM **Privately Held**
WEB: www.hendricksontrucking.com
SIC: 4213 Trucking, except local

(P-4195)
INDIAN RIVER TRANSPORT CO
8444 W Doe Ave, Visalia (93291-9261)
PHONE....................................209 664-0456
John J Harned Jr, *Branch Mgr*
EMP: 290
SALES (corp-wide): 104.5MM **Privately Held**
SIC: 4213 Contract haulers
PA: Indian River Transport Co.
2580 Executive Rd
Winter Haven FL 33884
863 324-2430

(P-4196)
INLAND STAR DIST CTRS INC (PA)
3146 S Chestnut Ave, Fresno (93725-2606)
P.O. Box 2396 (93745-2396)
PHONE....................................559 237-2052
Michael K Kelton, *CEO*
Kim Shirkey, *Vice Pres*
John Neale, *Comms Dir*
Daniel Alvarado, *General Mgr*
Jason Williamson, *General Mgr*
◆ **EMP:** 60 EST: 1985
SQ FT: 550,000
SALES (est): 39.1MM **Privately Held**
WEB: www.inlandstar.com
SIC: 4213 4225 Trucking, except local; general warehousing

(P-4197)
J B HUNT TRANSPORT INC
11559 Jersey Blvd, Rancho Cucamonga (91730-4924)
PHONE....................................909 466-5361
EMP: 167
SALES (corp-wide): 6.1B **Publicly Held**
SIC: 4213
HQ: J. B. Hunt Transport, Inc.
615 J B Hunt Corporate Dr
Lowell AR 72745
479 820-0000

(P-4198)
JE WILLIAMS TRUCKING INC
1875 Century Park E # 600, Los Angeles (90067-2337)
PHONE....................................406 248-7397
Bobby L Williams, *President*
EMP: 50 EST: 1969
SALES (est): 8.8MM **Privately Held**
WEB: www.jewilliamstrucking.com
SIC: 4213 Contract haulers

(P-4199)
JOE L COELHO INC
18637 E Bradbury Rd, Turlock (95380)
P.O. Box 3640 (95381-3640)
PHONE....................................209 667-2676
Dominic Coelho, *President*
Mary Kelly, *Admin Sec*
EMP: 50
SQ FT: 3,100
SALES: 5.4MM **Privately Held**
SIC: 4213 5191 Trucking, except local; hay

(P-4200)
K K W TRUCKING INC (PA)
3100 Pomona Blvd, Pomona (91768-3230)
P.O. Box 2960 (91769-2960)
PHONE....................................909 869-1200
Dennis W Firestone, *CEO*
Lynnette Brown, *CFO*

Susan Dancel, *Office Mgr*
Heather Hess, *Asst Controller*
Mark Knickerbocker, *Opers Mgr*
EMP: 350
SQ FT: 150,000
SALES (est): 91.1MM **Privately Held**
SIC: 4213 4231 4226 4214 Contract haulers; trucking terminal facilities; special warehousing & storage; local trucking with storage

(P-4201)
KENAN ADVANTAGE GROUP INC
2709 E 37th St, Vernon (90058-1706)
PHONE....................................323 582-3778
Tom Franz, *Manager*
EMP: 70
SALES (corp-wide): 2.6B **Privately Held**
SIC: 4213 Trucking, except local
PA: The Kenan Advantage Group Inc
4366 Mount Pleasant St Nw
North Canton OH 44720
800 969-5419

(P-4202)
KINGDOM EXPRESS INC
18640 Crenshaw Blvd, Torrance (90504-5032)
P.O. Box 622, Newbury Park (91319-0622)
PHONE....................................310 258-0900
Larry King, *President*
Brenda King, *Shareholder*
Greg King, *Vice Pres*
Jim Stone, *Vice Pres*
Lisa Martinez, *Manager*
EMP: 65
SQ FT: 40,000
SALES (est): 7.4MM **Privately Held**
WEB: www.kingdomexpress.com
SIC: 4213 Trucking, except local

(P-4203)
KINGS COUNTY TRUCK LINES (HQ)
754 S Blackstone St, Tulare (93274-5757)
P.O. Box 1016 (93275-1016)
PHONE....................................559 686-2857
Mark Tisdale, *Vice Pres*
EMP: 162 EST: 1940
SQ FT: 45,000
SALES (est): 16.5MM
SALES (corp-wide): 1.7B **Privately Held**
WEB: www.kctl.com
SIC: 4213 Refrigerated products transport
PA: Ruan Transportation Management Systems, Inc.
666 Grand Ave Ste 3100
Des Moines IA 50309
515 245-2500

(P-4204)
KLX INC
3645 S K St, Tulare (93274-7178)
P.O. Box 4438, Visalia (93278-4438)
PHONE....................................559 684-1037
Ron Greenberg, *President*
Jeff Peterson, *Corp Secy*
Pamela Titus, *Benefits Mgr*
Percy Greenberg, *Director*
EMP: 65
SQ FT: 12,000
SALES (est): 9MM **Privately Held**
WEB: www.klx.net
SIC: 4213 Trucking, except local

(P-4205)
KNIGHT TRANSPORTATION INC
Also Called: Knight Port Services
2960 E Victoria St, Compton (90221-5615)
PHONE....................................888 549-7802
EMP: 130
SALES (corp-wide): 2.4B **Publicly Held**
SIC: 4213 Trucking, except local
HQ: Knight Transportation, Inc.
20002 N 19th Ave
Phoenix AZ 85027
602 269-2000

(P-4206)
KNIGHT-SWIFT TRNSP HLDINGS INC
901 Darcy Pkwy, Lathrop (95330-8764)
PHONE....................................209 858-1630
Kevin Vadnal, *Branch Mgr*

Vivian Navarro, *Executive*
EMP: 100
SALES (corp-wide): 2.4B **Publicly Held**
SIC: 4213 Contract haulers
PA: Knight-Swift Transportation Holdings Inc.
2200 S 75th Ave
Phoenix AZ 85043
602 269-9700

(P-4207)
KNIGHT-SWIFT TRNSP HLDINGS INC
2797 S Orange Ave, Fresno (93725-1919)
PHONE....................................559 441-0340
Mark Peed, *Manager*
EMP: 56
SALES (corp-wide): 2.4B **Publicly Held**
SIC: 4213 Trucking, except local
PA: Knight-Swift Transportation Holdings Inc.
2200 S 75th Ave
Phoenix AZ 85043
602 269-9700

(P-4208)
KNIGHT-SWIFT TRNSP HLDINGS INC
11888 Mission Blvd, Mira Loma (91752-1003)
PHONE....................................951 360-0130
Renaldo Gonzales, *Manager*
EMP: 56
SALES (corp-wide): 2.4B **Publicly Held**
SIC: 4213 Contract haulers
PA: Knight-Swift Transportation Holdings Inc.
2200 S 75th Ave
Phoenix AZ 85043
602 269-9700

(P-4209)
KNIGHT-SWIFT TRNSP HLDINGS INC
6933 Calle De Linea, Chula Vista (91911)
PHONE....................................619 671-0588
Dennis Brown, *Branch Mgr*
EMP: 56
SALES (corp-wide): 2.4B **Publicly Held**
SIC: 4213 Trucking, except local
PA: Knight-Swift Transportation Holdings Inc.
2200 S 75th Ave
Phoenix AZ 85043
602 269-9700

(P-4210)
L A S TRANSPORTATION INC
Also Called: Produces Dairy
250 E Belmont Ave, Fresno (93701-1405)
PHONE....................................559 264-6583
Richard Shehady, *President*
Lawrence Shehady, *Chairman*
Dewayne Scott, *Purch Agent*
Marc Antonetti, *Sales Staff*
EMP: 300
SQ FT: 30,000
SALES (est): 26.6MM **Privately Held**
SIC: 4213 Refrigerated products transport

(P-4211)
L J TRUCKING USA
120 S Anderson St, Los Angeles (90033-3220)
PHONE....................................323 469-9663
John Stewart, *President*
Carlin Ferro, *Vice Pres*
EMP: 80
SALES (est): 7.5MM **Privately Held**
SIC: 4213 Trucking, except local

(P-4212)
LANDFORCE EXPRESS CORPORATION
17201 N D St, Victorville (92394-1401)
PHONE....................................760 843-7839
Rajinder Bhangu, *CEO*
EMP: 120
SALES (est): 30.8MM **Privately Held**
SIC: 4213 Trucking, except local

(P-4213)
LAS VEGAS / LA EXPRESS INC (PA)
1000 S Cucamonga Ave, Ontario
(91761-3461)
PHONE...........................909 972-3100
Ronald Cain Jr, *CEO*
Beverly A Adley, *Vice Pres*
Michael P Adley, *Admin Sec*
Michael Adley, *Admin Sec*
EMP: 170
SQ FT: 163,000
SALES (est): 53.1MM **Privately Held**
WEB: www.lvla.com
SIC: 4213 Trucking, except local

(P-4214)
LAZTRANS INC
5200 District Blvd, Bakersfield
(93313-2330)
P.O. Box 9517 (93389-9517)
PHONE...........................661 833-3783
Bill Lazzerini Jr, *President*
Mary Huser, *Shareholder*
Maria Pisar, *Shareholder*
Anthony Lazzerini, *Vice Pres*
EMP: 50
SQ FT: 52,000
SALES (est): 5.4MM **Privately Held**
WEB: www.laztrans.com
SIC: 4213 Heavy hauling

(P-4215)
LEMORE TRANSPORTATION INC (PA)
Also Called: Royal Trucking
1420 Royal Industrial Way, Concord
(94520-4914)
P.O. Box 6085 (94524-1085)
PHONE...........................925 689-6444
Barbara Querio, *CEO*
Roy Querio, *President*
Heidi Becker, *Vice Pres*
Jeremy Hunt, *Administration*
Dan Sander, *Controller*
EMP: 73
SQ FT: 6,000
SALES (est): 8.9MM **Privately Held**
WEB: www.royaltruckingco.com
SIC: 4213 Contract haulers

(P-4216)
LEXMAR DISTRIBUTION INC
200 Erie St, Pomona (91768-3327)
PHONE...........................909 620-7001
Alex Kole, *President*
Alex Kolesnikov, *Vice Pres*
Apollo Reyes, *Information Mgr*
Tony Kole, *Human Res Mgr*
Marlon Brover, *Opers Dir*
EMP: 170
SQ FT: 10,000
SALES (est): 24.7MM **Privately Held**
WEB: www.lexmardistribution.com
SIC: 4213 Trucking, except local

(P-4217)
LORETTA LIMA TRNSP CORP
240 S 6th Ave, City of Industry
(91746-2915)
P.O. Box 3984 (91744-0984)
PHONE...........................626 330-5517
Michael Lima, *CEO*
Cherlyn Converse, *CFO*
Loretta Lima, *Vice Pres*
EMP: 65
SALES (est): 8.7MM **Privately Held**
SIC: 4213 Trucking, except local

(P-4218)
MAJOR TRANSPORTATION SVCS INC
3342 N Weber Ave, Fresno (93722-4909)
PHONE...........................559 485-5949
Gill Baljinder, *President*
Bhupinde Gill, *Vice Pres*
Joe Garcia, *Principal*
EMP: 50
SALES (est): 7.3MM **Privately Held**
SIC: 4213 Trucking, except local

(P-4219)
MARK CLEMONS
Also Called: Mtc Transportation
4584 Adobe Rd, Twentynine Palms
(92277-1671)
P.O. Box 148 (92277-0148)
PHONE...........................760 361-1531
Mark Clemons, *Owner*
Rebecca Hewson Hubbard, *Office Mgr*
Genevieve Clemons, *Manager*
EMP: 200
SALES: 21MM **Privately Held**
SIC: 4213 4212 4513 4522 Heavy machinery transport; local trucking, without storage; mail carriers, contract; air courier services; air transportation, nonscheduled

(P-4220)
MASHBURN TRNSP SVCS INC
1423 Kern St, Taft (93268-4607)
P.O. Box 66 (93268-8066)
PHONE...........................661 763-5724
Denise Mashburn, *President*
Michael Mashburn, *Vice Pres*
EMP: 120
SQ FT: 2,000
SALES: 15.1MM **Privately Held**
SIC: 4213 4212 Contract haulers; local trucking, without storage

(P-4221)
MATHESON FAST FREIGHT INC
9785 Goethe Rd, Sacramento
(95827-3559)
PHONE...........................209 342-0184
Mark Matheson, *Branch Mgr*
EMP: 70
SALES (corp-wide): 412.8MM **Privately Held**
SIC: 4213 Less-than-truckload (LTL) transport
HQ: Matheson Fast Freight, Inc.
9780 Dino Dr
Elk Grove CA 95624
916 686-4600

(P-4222)
MATHESON FAST FREIGHT INC (HQ)
9780 Dino Dr, Elk Grove (95624-9477)
PHONE...........................916 686-4600
Robert B Matheson, *Ch of Bd*
Mark B Matheson, *President*
Laurie Johnson, *Corp Secy*
Carole L Matheson, *Exec VP*
Donald G Brocca, *Vice Pres*
EMP: 70
SQ FT: 7,200
SALES (est): 25.6MM
SALES (corp-wide): 412.8MM **Privately Held**
SIC: 4213 Less-than-truckload (LTL) transport
PA: Matheson Trucking, Inc.
9785 Goethe Rd
Sacramento CA 95827
916 685-2330

(P-4223)
MATHESON TRUCKING INC (PA)
9785 Goethe Rd, Sacramento
(95827-3559)
PHONE...........................916 685-2330
Mark Matheson, *President*
Patricia Kepner, *CEO*
Tamrya Ford, *CFO*
Charles J Mellor, *Officer*
Carole L Matheson, *Exec VP*
EMP: 50
SQ FT: 3,000
SALES (est): 412.8MM **Privately Held**
SIC: 4213 4731 Contract haulers; less-than-truckload (LTL) transport; freight transportation arrangement

(P-4224)
MEATHEAD MOVERS
101 W Canon Perdido St, Santa Maria
(93454)
PHONE...........................805 349-8000
Aaron Steed, *Branch Mgr*
EMP: 70
SALES (corp-wide): 16.9MM **Privately Held**
SIC: 4213 4789 Household goods transport; cargo loading & unloading services

PA: Meathead Movers, Inc.
3600 S Higuera St
San Luis Obispo CA 93401
805 544-6328

(P-4225)
MEATHEAD MOVERS INC
300 Rolling Oaks Dr, Thousand Oaks
(91361-1269)
PHONE...........................805 496-1416
EMP: 70
SALES (corp-wide): 16.9MM **Privately Held**
SIC: 4213 4212 Household goods transport; moving services
PA: Meathead Movers, Inc.
3600 S Higuera St
San Luis Obispo CA 93401
805 544-6328

(P-4226)
MEATHEAD MOVERS INC
3600 S Higuera St, San Luis Obispo
(93401-7306)
PHONE...........................805 541-4285
Aaron B Steed, *President*
EMP: 70
SALES (corp-wide): 16.9MM **Privately Held**
WEB: www.meatheadmovers.com
SIC: 4213 Household goods transport
PA: Meathead Movers, Inc.
3600 S Higuera St
San Luis Obispo CA 93401
805 544-6328

(P-4227)
MEATHEAD MOVERS INC (PA)
3600 S Higuera St, San Luis Obispo
(93401-7306)
PHONE...........................805 544-6328
Evan Steed, *COO*
Aaron B Steed, *CEO*
Angela Aleen, *General Mgr*
Kendra Mason, *Admin Asst*
Erin Steed, *Controller*
EMP: 68
SQ FT: 1,700
SALES (est): 16.9MM **Privately Held**
WEB: www.meatheadmovers.com
SIC: 4213 Household goods transport

(P-4228)
MEATHEAD MOVERS INC
412 Calle San Pablo, Camarillo
(93012-8502)
PHONE...........................805 437-5100
Aaron Steed, *Branch Mgr*
Erin Norton, *Opers Mgr*
Cody Johnston, *Manager*
EMP: 70
SALES (corp-wide): 16.9MM **Privately Held**
SIC: 4213 4212 Household goods transport; moving services
PA: Meathead Movers, Inc.
3600 S Higuera St
San Luis Obispo CA 93401
805 544-6328

(P-4229)
MEATHEAD MOVERS INC
1524 State St, Santa Barbara
(93101-2514)
PHONE...........................805 966-6328
EMP: 70
SALES (corp-wide): 16.9MM **Privately Held**
SIC: 4213 4212 Household goods transport; moving services
PA: Meathead Movers, Inc.
3600 S Higuera St
San Luis Obispo CA 93401
805 544-6328

(P-4230)
MICHAEL DUSI TRUCKING INC
3230 Rverside Ave Ste 220, Paso Robles
(93446)
P.O. Box 2339 (93447-2339)
PHONE...........................805 237-9499
Michael Dusi, *President*
Matt Dusi, *CFO*
Sharon Lawson, *Manager*
EMP: 68

(P-4231)
MOUNTAIN VALLEY EXPRESS CO INC (PA)
6750 Longe St Ste 100, Stockton
(95206-4938)
P.O. Box 2569, Manteca (95336-1167)
PHONE...........................209 823-2168
James Scott Blevins, *President*
Jackie Torres, *Executive*
Penny Regelman, *Office Mgr*
Ryan V Veen, *Info Tech Mgr*
Mary Warrick, *Human Res Mgr*
EMP: 100
SALES (est): 52MM **Privately Held**
WEB: www.mountainvalleyexpress.com
SIC: 4213 Contract haulers

(P-4232)
MULTIMODAL ESQUER INC
8856 Siempre Viva Rd, San Diego
(92154-6272)
PHONE...........................619 710-0477
Alfonsa Esquer, *CEO*
Federico Esquer, *Treasurer*
Jose Esquer, *Admin Sec*
EMP: 56
SQ FT: 2,100
SALES (est): 8.2MM **Privately Held**
WEB: www.fletesesquer.com
SIC: 4213 Trucking, except local

(P-4233)
NATIONAL RETAIL TRNSP INC
355 W Carob St, Compton (90220-5212)
PHONE...........................310 605-3777
Manuel Villasenor, *Branch Mgr*
EMP: 100
SALES (corp-wide): 264MM **Privately Held**
WEB: www.nrsonline.com
SIC: 4213 Trucking, except local
HQ: National Retail Transportation, Inc.
2820 16th St
North Bergen NJ 07047
201 866-0462

(P-4234)
NELSON MOVING & STORAGE INC
Also Called: Nelson North American
25742 Atlantic Ocean Dr, Lake Forest
(92630-8854)
PHONE...........................949 582-0380
Gust Nelson, *President*
Rosean Maricondo, *Office Mgr*
EMP: 50
SQ FT: 24,000
SALES (est): 5.4MM **Privately Held**
WEB: www.nelsonmoving.com
SIC: 4213 4731 4214 Household goods transport; freight transportation arrangement; household goods moving & storage, local

(P-4235)
NEW LEGEND INC
Also Called: Legend Transpotation
1235 Oswald Rd, Yuba City (95991-9719)
PHONE...........................530 674-3100
Baveljit Singh Samara, *CEO*
EMP: 108 **Privately Held**
SIC: 4213 4212 Trucking, except local; local trucking, without storage
PA: New Legend, Inc.
3617 W Cmbridge Ave Ste B
Phoenix AZ 85009

(P-4236)
NORTHERN RFRIGERATED TRNSP INC (PA)
2700 W Main St, Turlock (95380-9537)
PHONE...........................209 664-3800
Richard Mello, *CEO*
Judi Mello, *Treasurer*
John Doidge, *Vice Pres*
EMP: 120
SQ FT: 25,000
SALES (est): 40.6MM **Privately Held**
WEB: www.northernrefrigerated.com
SIC: 4213 Refrigerated products transport

SALES (est): 19.4MM **Privately Held**
WEB: www.michaeldusitrucking.com
SIC: 4213 Trucking, except local

PA: Meathead Movers, Inc.
3600 S Higuera St
San Luis Obispo CA 93401
805 544-6328

(P-4237)
NY TRANSPORT INC
14998 Washington Dr, Fontana
(92335-6268)
PHONE..................909 355-9832
Nazario Yanez, *CEO*
Nazario Y Perez, *President*
Jose Conrado, *Controller*
EMP: 65
SQ FT: 1,000
SALES: 16MM **Privately Held**
SIC: 4213 Trucking, except local

(P-4238)
OAK HARBOR FREIGHT LINES INC
6700 Smith Ave, Newark (94560-4222)
PHONE..................510 608-8841
Toll Free:..................888 -
Dennis Weishaar, *Manager*
Andrew Jonsson, *Opers Mgr*
EMP: 75
SALES (corp-wide): 200.6MM **Privately Held**
WEB: www.oakh.com
SIC: 4213 Contract haulers
PA: Oak Harbor Freight Lines, Inc
1339 W Valley Hwy N
Auburn WA 98001
206 246-2600

(P-4239)
OAK HARBOR FREIGHT LINES INC
832 F St, West Sacramento (95605-2314)
PHONE..................916 371-3960
Greg Gommenginger, *Manager*
EMP: 80
SALES (corp-wide): 200.6MM **Privately Held**
WEB: www.oakh.com
SIC: 4213 4212 Contract haulers; local trucking, without storage
PA: Oak Harbor Freight Lines, Inc
1339 W Valley Hwy N
Auburn WA 98001
206 246-2600

(P-4240)
OLD DOMINION FREIGHT LINE INC
1225 Washington Blvd, Montebello
(90640-6013)
PHONE..................323 725-3400
Marc Meskin, *CFO*
EMP: 200
SQ FT: 4,000
SALES (corp-wide): 3.3B **Publicly Held**
WEB: www.odfl.com
SIC: 4213 4212 Contract haulers; local trucking, without storage
PA: Old Dominion Freight Line Inc
500 Old Dominion Way
Thomasville NC 27360
336 889-5000

(P-4241)
PAN PACIFIC PETROLEUM CO INC (PA)
9302 Garfield Ave, South Gate
(90280-3805)
P.O. Box 1966 (90280-1966)
PHONE..................562 928-0100
Robert Roth, *CEO*
Dale Snyder, *Exec VP*
Steven Roth, *Vice Pres*
Scott McGowan, *Agent*
EMP: 300
SQ FT: 600
SALES (est): 664.6K **Privately Held**
SIC: 4213 5172 Liquid petroleum transport, non-local; petroleum brokers

(P-4242)
PAN PACIFIC PETROLEUM CO INC
Also Called: Truck Terminal
1850 Coffee Rd, Bakersfield (93308-5746)
PHONE..................661 589-3200
Dave Palmer, *Manager*
EMP: 100
SALES (corp-wide): 664.6K **Privately Held**
SIC: 4213 Liquid petroleum transport, non-local

PA: Pan Pacific Petroleum Company, Inc.
9302 Garfield Ave
South Gate CA 90280
562 928-0100

(P-4243)
PENSKE LOGISTICS LLC
2090 Etiwanda Ave, Ontario (91761-2803)
PHONE..................800 529-6531
EMP: 60
SALES (corp-wide): 2.7B **Privately Held**
WEB: www.penskelogistics.com
SIC: 4213 4212 Trucking, except local; furniture moving, local: without storage
HQ: Penske Logistics Llc
2675 Morgantown Rd
Reading PA 19607
610 775-6000

(P-4244)
PIEDMONT TRANSFER & STORAGE
1555 S 7th St Ste A, San Jose
(95112-5926)
PHONE..................408 288-5600
David R Bartels, *President*
EMP: 50
SQ FT: 100,000
SALES (est): 4.7MM **Privately Held**
WEB: www.piedmontmoving.com
SIC: 4213 4214 Household goods transport; local trucking with storage

(P-4245)
POPPY STATE EXPRESS INC
2700 W Main St, Turlock (95380-9537)
PHONE..................209 664-3950
Richard D Mello, *President*
Daniel N Watson, *CFO*
Judy Mello, *Treasurer*
John Doidge, *Vice Pres*
Claudia Doidge, *Admin Sec*
EMP: 80
SQ FT: 30,000
SALES (est): 5.9MM **Privately Held**
WEB: www.poppystate.com
SIC: 4213 Refrigerated products transport

(P-4246)
PRODUCTION DELIVERY SVCS INC
Also Called: Production Transport
12133 Greenstone Ave, Santa Fe Springs
(90670-4728)
PHONE..................562 777-0060
James Harkins, *President*
Michelle Harkins, *Corp Secy*
EMP: 55
SALES (est): 7MM **Privately Held**
SIC: 4213 Trucking, except local

(P-4247)
PYRAMID LOGISTICS SERVICES INC (PA)
14650 Hoover St, Westminster
(92683-5346)
PHONE..................714 903-2600
Timothy J Winningham, *CEO*
Jeannie Rivera, *Executive*
Michael Connolly, *Principal*
Robert Dissman, *Admin Sec*
Michelle Thomas, *Accounting Mgr*
EMP: 57
SQ FT: 59,000
SALES (est): 13.6MM **Privately Held**
SIC: 4213 4731 4225 Heavy hauling; contract haulers; foreign freight forwarding; general warehousing & storage

(P-4248)
QUALITY CARRIERS INC
Also Called: Montgomery Tank Lines
5042 Cecelia St, South Gate (90280-3511)
PHONE..................800 282-2031
George Heinze, *Manager*
EMP: 70
SALES (corp-wide): 974.1MM **Privately Held**
WEB: www.qualitycarriers.com
SIC: 4213 Contract haulers
HQ: Quality Carriers, Inc.
1208 E Kennedy Blvd
Tampa FL 33602
800 282-2031

(P-4249)
REEVE TRUCKING COMPANY INC (PA)
5050 Carpenter Rd, Stockton
(95215-8105)
P.O. Box 5126 (95205-0126)
PHONE..................209 948-4061
Lori J Reeve, *President*
Don Reeve, *Vice Pres*
Donald E Reeve, *Vice Pres*
Donald J Reeve Aka Spike, *Vice Pres*
Bob Costanza, *Executive*
EMP: 70
SQ FT: 100,000
SALES (est): 35.6MM **Privately Held**
WEB: www.reevetrucking.com
SIC: 4213 Contract haulers; heavy machinery transport

(P-4250)
RELIABLE CARRIERS INC
Also Called: Relibale Carries
9122 Glenoaks Blvd, Sun Valley
(91352-2611)
PHONE..................818 252-6400
Tom Abraham, *Branch Mgr*
EMP: 50
SALES (corp-wide): 30.3MM **Privately Held**
SIC: 4213 Automobiles, transport & delivery
PA: Reliable Carriers, Inc.
41555 Koppernick Rd
Canton MI 48187
734 453-6677

(P-4251)
RENN TRANSPORTATION INC
8845 Forest St, Gilroy (95020-3651)
PHONE..................408 842-3545
Brad E Renn, *President*
Robert Renn, *Vice Pres*
Patricia Renn, *Admin Sec*
Richard Renn, *Maintence Staff*
EMP: 100
SQ FT: 9,609
SALES (est): 21.2MM **Privately Held**
WEB: www.renntransportation.com
SIC: 4213 Trucking, except local

(P-4252)
RICK STUDER
Also Called: Nordstrom
2610 Wisconsin Ave, South Gate
(90280-5598)
P.O. Box 471 (90280-0471)
PHONE..................323 357-1720
Rick Studer, *Owner*
EMP: 50
SALES (est): 5.4MM **Privately Held**
SIC: 4213 Trucking, except local

(P-4253)
RPM TRANSPORTATION INC (HQ)
11660 Arroyo Ave, Santa Ana
(92705-3057)
PHONE..................714 388-3500
Shawn Duke, *President*
Andrew Lewes, *CFO*
Linda Dickey, *Human Res Dir*
Cheryl Hill, *Natl Sales Mgr*
Robert Ogdon, *Manager*
EMP: 110
SQ FT: 175,000
SALES (est): 22.7MM
SALES (corp-wide): 63.5MM **Privately Held**
SIC: 4213 4225 4214 Trailer or container on flat car (TOFC/COFC); general warehousing; local trucking with storage
PA: Rpm Consolidated Services, Inc.
1901 Raymer Ave
Fullerton CA 92833
714 388-3500

(P-4254)
S & M MOVING SYSTEMS
Also Called: SM International
48551 Warm Springs Blvd, Fremont
(94539-7765)
PHONE..................510 497-2300
Gerald P Stadler, *Principal*
John Stadler, *Vice Pres*
Christal Davis, *Accounting Dir*

EMP: 60
SQ FT: 38,000
SALES (est): 13.7MM
SALES (corp-wide): 111MM **Privately Held**
WEB: www.sandmoving.com
SIC: 4213 4214 Household goods transport; local trucking with storage
PA: Torrance Van & Storage Company
12128 Burke St
Santa Fe Springs CA 90670
562 567-2100

(P-4255)
SAIA INC
Also Called: Saia S Reno Barbara K
1508 Wyant Way, Sacramento
(95864-2642)
PHONE..................916 483-8331
EMP: 115
SALES (corp-wide): 1.3B **Publicly Held**
SIC: 4213 Trucking, except local
PA: Saia, Inc.
11465 Johns Creek Pkwy # 400
Johns Creek GA 30097
770 232-5067

(P-4256)
SAIA MOTOR FREIGHT LINE LLC
9119 Elkmont Dr, Elk Grove (95624-9706)
PHONE..................916 690-8417
Joe Meyer, *Branch Mgr*
EMP: 50
SALES (corp-wide): 1.3B **Publicly Held**
WEB: www.saia.com
SIC: 4213 Contract haulers
HQ: Saia Motor Freight Line, Llc
11465 Johns Creek Pkwy # 400
Duluth GA 30097
770 232-5067

(P-4257)
SAIA MOTOR FREIGHT LINE LLC
2550 E 28th St, Vernon (90058-1430)
PHONE..................323 277-2880
Gerard Francois, *Branch Mgr*
EMP: 100
SALES (corp-wide): 1.3B **Publicly Held**
WEB: www.saia.com
SIC: 4213 Contract haulers
HQ: Saia Motor Freight Line, Llc
11465 Johns Creek Pkwy # 400
Duluth GA 30097
770 232-5067

(P-4258)
SAIA MOTOR FREIGHT LINE LLC
1755 Aurora Dr, San Leandro
(94577-3103)
PHONE..................510 347-6890
John Dentony, *Manager*
EMP: 51
SALES (corp-wide): 1.3B **Publicly Held**
WEB: www.saia.com
SIC: 4213 4212 Contract haulers; local trucking, without storage
HQ: Saia Motor Freight Line, Llc
11465 Johns Creek Pkwy # 400
Duluth GA 30097
770 232-5067

(P-4259)
SCAN-VINO LLC (PA)
Also Called: Cherokee Freight Lines
5463 Cherokee Rd, Stockton (95215-1128)
PHONE..................209 931-3570
Leanne Scannavino, *Principal*
EMP: 100 EST: 1965
SQ FT: 1,000
SALES (est): 23MM **Privately Held**
WEB: www.gocfl.com
SIC: 4213 Contract haulers

(P-4260)
SCHNEIDER NATIONAL INC
4193 Industrial Pkwy Dr, Lebec
(93243-9719)
PHONE..................661 858-1031
Mark Griffin, *Branch Mgr*
EMP: 205
SALES (corp-wide): 4.3B **Publicly Held**
SIC: 4213 Trucking, except local

▲ = Import ▼=Export
◆ =Import/Export

PA: Schneider National, Inc.
3101 Packerland Dr
Green Bay WI 54313
920 592-2000

(P-4261)
SEA-LOGIX LLC
1425 Maritime St, Oakland (94607-1022)
PHONE..........................510 271-1400
Mary Brown, *Superintendent*
EMP: 60
SALES (corp-wide): 234.4MM **Privately Held**
SIC: 4213 Trucking, except local
HQ: Sea-Logix, Llc
4040 Civic Center Dr # 350
San Rafael CA 94903
415 927-6400

(P-4262)
SEA-LOGIX LLC (DH)
4040 Civic Center Dr # 350, San Rafael
(94903-4150)
PHONE.........................415 927-6400
Peter McLoughlin,
George Pasha IV, *Ch of Bd*
James Britton, *CFO*
Amy Sherburne Manning,
EMP: 60
SALES (est): 8.9MM
SALES (corp-wide): 234.4MM **Privately Held**
SIC: 4213 Trucking, except local

(P-4263)
SEASIDE RFRIGERATED TRNSPT INC (PA)
7041 Las Positas Rd Ste H, Livermore
(94551-5124)
PHONE.........................510 732-0472
Lynn Johnson, *President*
Beverly Johnson, *Vice Pres*
Dianna Johnson, *Human Res Dir*
EMP: 50
SQ FT: 9,000
SALES (est): 7.9MM **Privately Held**
WEB: www.seasidetransport.com
SIC: 4213 Refrigerated products transport

(P-4264)
SIRVA INC
2010 Crow Canyon Pl, San Ramon
(94583-4634)
PHONE.........................925 824-3109
EMP: 130
SALES (corp-wide): 2.2B **Privately Held**
SIC: 4213 Household goods transport
PA: Sirva, Inc.
1 Parkview Plz
Oakbrook Terrace IL 60181
630 570-3047

(P-4265)
SNOOZIE SHAVINGS INC (PA)
525 Elk Valley Rd, Crescent City
(95531-9460)
PHONE.........................707 464-6186
Dwayne C Reichlin, *President*
Robert Matthess, *Treasurer*
Jay M Freeman, *Vice Pres*
Charlie F Compton, *Admin Sec*
EMP: 51
SQ FT: 18,000
SALES (est): 2.5MM **Privately Held**
WEB: www.ssitrucking.com
SIC: 4213 5099 Trucking, except local;
shavings, wood; wood & wood by-products

(P-4266)
SPECIAL DISPATCH CAL INC
8328 Central Ave, Newark (94560-3432)
PHONE.........................510 713-0300
Keith Donahue, *Manager*
Martin Mantilla, *President*
EMP: 60
SALES (corp-wide): 24.6MM **Privately Held**
SIC: 4213 Trucking, except local
PA: Special Dispatch Of California, Inc.
16330 Phoebe Ave
La Mirada CA 90638
714 521-8200

(P-4267)
SS HERT TRUCKING INC (PA)
33924 Old Woman Sprng Rd, Lucerne Valley (92356-8869)
P.O. Box 590 (92356-0590)
PHONE.........................760 248-9327
Scott Hert, *President*
Katherine Hert, *Corp Secy*
EMP: 50
SQ FT: 726
SALES: 8.9MM **Privately Held**
SIC: 4213 Trucking, except local

(P-4268)
SUDDATH RELO SYS OF NO CA
2055 S 7th St, San Jose (95112-6141)
PHONE.........................408 288-3030
Gene Kopecky, *President*
Dan Lambers, *Controller*
Keith Rocha, *Marketing Staff*
EMP: 51
SALES (est): 7.9MM
SALES (corp-wide): 456.3MM **Privately Held**
SIC: 4213 4731 4214 Household goods transport; freight forwarding; household goods moving & storage, local
HQ: Suddath Van Lines Inc
815 S Main St Ste 400
Jacksonville FL 32207
904 390-7100

(P-4269)
SUDDATH RELOCATION SYSTEMS OF
2020 S 10th St, San Jose (95112-4112)
PHONE.........................904 858-1273
Jacob Moreno, *President*
EMP: 50
SALES (est): 1MM **Privately Held**
SIC: 4213 Household goods transport

(P-4270)
SULLIVAN MOVING & STORAGE (HQ)
Also Called: United Van Lines
5704 Copley Dr, San Diego (92111-7905)
PHONE.........................858 874-2600
Rick Smith, *CEO*
Mark Fischer, *President*
Pat Reid, *CFO*
Mark Keiper, *Vice Pres*
EMP: 50 EST: 1988
SQ FT: 60,000
SALES: 16MM **Privately Held**
WEB: www.sullivanunited.com
SIC: 4213 4214 Household goods transport; local trucking with storage
PA: Corporate Moving Systems, Inc.
21620 88th Pl S
Kent WA 98031
253 395-5432

(P-4271)
SUPERIOR TRUCK LINES INC
527 F St, Lemoore (93245-2601)
PHONE.........................559 924-6418
Calvin Fagundes, *Manager*
EMP: 50
SALES (est): 2.2MM
SALES (corp-wide): 12.4MM **Privately Held**
WEB: www.stlinc.org
SIC: 4213 Contract haulers
PA: Superior Truck Lines, Inc.
1457 Main St Ste A
Newman CA 95360
209 862-9430

(P-4272)
SUPERIOR TRUCK LINES INC (PA)
1457 Main St Ste A, Newman
(95360-1342)
P.O. Box 307, Gustine (95322-0307)
PHONE.........................209 862-9430
Frank R Amaral III, *President*
Deanie Azevedo, *Corp Secy*
Frank R Amaral Jr, *Vice Pres*
EMP: 75
SQ FT: 1,238
SALES (est): 12.4MM **Privately Held**
WEB: www.stlinc.org
SIC: 4213 Contract haulers

(P-4273)
SWIFT WORLDWIDE INC (PA)
Also Called: Swift Courier Service
1390 Willow Pass Rd # 420, Concord
(94520-5200)
PHONE.........................510 351-7949
Qaiser A Chaudhery, *CEO*
Zia Chaudhery, *President*
Shawn Chaudhery, *Vice Pres*
EMP: 150
SQ FT: 120,000
SALES: 35MM **Privately Held**
SIC: 4213 4215 Trucking, except local; courier services, except by air

(P-4274)
T & T TRUCKING INC (PA)
11396 N Hwy 99, Lodi (95240-6899)
PHONE.........................800 692-3457
Terry M Tarditi, *President*
John King, *Treasurer*
Mary Lou Tarditi, *Admin Sec*
Dan Badger, *Traffic Mgr*
Lisa Garcia, *Manager*
EMP: 107
SQ FT: 25,000
SALES (est): 23MM **Privately Held**
WEB: www.tttrucking.com
SIC: 4213 Contract haulers

(P-4275)
TAMO INC
8545 Pecan Ave, Rancho Cucamonga
(91739-9621)
P.O. Box 4469 (91729-4469)
PHONE.........................909 803-1030
Nick Coffey, *President*
Shivaji Shankar, *Vice Pres*
EMP: 50 EST: 1979
SQ FT: 12,000
SALES (est): 3.3MM **Privately Held**
WEB: www.tamoinc.com
SIC: 4213 Trucking, except local

(P-4276)
TERESI TRUCKING LLC (PA)
900 1/2 E Victor Rd, Lodi (95240-0722)
P.O. Box 1270 (95241-1270)
PHONE.........................209 368-2472
John M Teresi, *Mng Member*
Anthony T Teresi,
Varene Teresi,
EMP: 65
SQ FT: 20,000
SALES: 9.7MM **Privately Held**
WEB: www.teresitrucking.com
SIC: 4213 Contract haulers

(P-4277)
TIGER LINES LLC (HQ)
927 Black Diamond Way, Lodi
(95240-0738)
P.O. Box 1120 (95241-1120)
PHONE.........................209 334-4100
Dennis Altnow, *CEO*
Emil Canlas, *Human Res Dir*
Jason Henry, *Purch Agent*
Donald Altnow, *Mng Member*
Greg Gray, *Manager*
EMP: 75 EST: 1935
SQ FT: 20,000
SALES: 35.5MM
SALES (corp-wide): 2.2MM **Privately Held**
SIC: 4213 4214 4212 Contract haulers; local trucking with storage; local trucking, without storage
PA: Lts Rentals, Llc
927 Black Diamond Way
Lodi CA 95240
209 334-4100

(P-4278)
TIMMERMAN STARLITE TRCKG INC
3955 Starlite Dr, Ceres (95307-9733)
P.O. Box 2710 (95307-7710)
PHONE.........................209 538-1706
Colby Bell, *CEO*
Agnes Timmerman, *Corp Secy*
Geneveve Timmerman, *Vice Pres*
EMP: 65 EST: 1976
SALES: 9.7MM **Privately Held**
SIC: 4213 4212 Trucking, except local; farm to market haulage, local

(P-4279)
TMT INDUSTRIES INC
8978 Haven Ave, Rancho Cucamonga
(91730-5401)
PHONE.........................909 493-3441
Antonio Y Martinez, *CEO*
Tony Martinez Sr, *President*
Evelyn Martinez, *Corp Secy*
Tony Martinez Jr, *Vice Pres*
Debbie Rush, *Office Mgr*
EMP: 63
SQ FT: 3,000
SALES (est): 20.4MM **Privately Held**
SIC: 4213 4212 Trucking, except local; local trucking, without storage

(P-4280)
TONYS EXPRESS INC (PA)
10613 Jasmine St, Fontana (92337-8241)
PHONE.........................909 427-8700
George Raluy, *President*
Lorraine Khair, *Corp Secy*
Tony Raluy, *Exec VP*
Ken Fasola, *Vice Pres*
Anthony Raluy, *Vice Pres*
EMP: 127
SQ FT: 180,000
SALES (est): 21.3MM **Privately Held**
SIC: 4213 4214 4212 Less-than-truckload (LTL) transport; local trucking with storage; local trucking, without storage

(P-4281)
TOTAL TRNSP LOGISTICS INC
4325 Etiwanda Ave Ste A, Mira Loma
(91752-3720)
PHONE.........................951 360-9521
Robert E Hicks, *President*
Michael Doliveira, *CFO*
Mike Stadler, *CFO*
Steve Todare, *Vice Pres*
Loriann Aberle, *Executive*
EMP: 75
SQ FT: 125,000
SALES (est): 24.1MM **Privately Held**
WEB: www.ttllogistics.com
SIC: 4213 Contract haulers

(P-4282)
TRIPLE-E MACHINERY MOVING INC
3301 Gilman Rd, El Monte (91732-3225)
PHONE.........................626 444-1137
Steve Englebrecht, *CEO*
Joe Englbrecht, *Vice Pres*
EMP: 60
SQ FT: 12,000
SALES (est): 7.7MM **Privately Held**
WEB: www.trpleemachinery.com
SIC: 4213 Heavy machinery transport

(P-4283)
U C L INCORPORATED (PA)
Also Called: United Cargo Logistics
620 S Hacienda Blvd, City of Industry
(91745-1126)
PHONE.........................323 235-0099
Byung Y Chang, *CEO*
Chris Chang, *President*
Jenny Kim, *Department Mgr*
Yong Ku, *General Mgr*
James Chung, *Controller*
EMP: 100
SQ FT: 16,000
SALES (est): 81.5MM **Privately Held**
WEB: www.uclinc.com
SIC: 4213 Trucking, except local

(P-4284)
U S XPRESS INC
363 Nina Lee Rd, Calexico (92231-9527)
PHONE.........................760 768-6707
EMP: 124 **Publicly Held**
SIC: 4213 Trucking, except local
HQ: U. S. Xpress, Inc.
4080 Jenkins Rd
Chattanooga TN 37421
866 266-7270

(P-4285)
UPS FREIGHT SERVICES INC
2650 S Willow Ave, Bloomington
(92316-3257)
PHONE.........................909 879-7400
Criss Sowers, *Manager*
EMP: 73

PRODUCTS & SVCS

SALES (corp-wide): 65.8B Publicly Held
SIC: 4213 Contract haulers
HQ: Ups Freight Services, Inc.
1000 Semmes Ave
Richmond VA 23224
804 231-8000

(P-4286)
UPS GROUND FREIGHT INC
Also Called: Martrac
4587 S Chestnut Ave, Fresno
(93725-9211)
PHONE..................................559 445-9010
Steve Sutton, Manager
EMP: 56
SALES (corp-wide): 65.8B Publicly Held
SIC: 4213 Contract haulers
HQ: Ups Ground Freight, Inc.
1000 Semmes Ave
Richmond VA 23224
866 372-5619

(P-4287)
UPS GROUND FREIGHT INC
600 Williams St, Bakersfield (93305-5438)
PHONE..................................661 395-9500
Fax: 661 395-9510
EMP: 95
SALES (corp-wide): 58.2B Publicly Held
SIC: 4213
HQ: Ups Ground Freight, Inc.
1000 Semmes Ave
Richmond VA 23224
804 231-8000

(P-4288)
UPS GROUND FREIGHT INC
1444 Lathrop Rd, Lathrop (95330-9771)
PHONE..................................209 858-5095
Bill Rose, Branch Mgr
EMP: 98
SALES (corp-wide): 65.8B Publicly Held
SIC: 4213 Contract haulers
HQ: Ups Ground Freight, Inc.
1000 Semmes Ave
Richmond VA 23224
866 372-5619

(P-4289)
UPS GROUND FREIGHT INC
12455 Harvest Dr, Eastvale (91752-1025)
PHONE..................................951 361-1300
Andre Campbell, Manager
EMP: 95
SALES (corp-wide): 65.8B Publicly Held
WEB: www.overnite.com
SIC: 4213 Contract haulers
HQ: Ups Ground Freight, Inc.
1000 Semmes Ave
Richmond VA 23224
866 372-5619

(P-4290)
UPS GROUND FREIGHT INC
7 College Ave, Santa Rosa (95401-4702)
P.O. Box 6836 (95406-0836)
PHONE..................................707 526-1910
Jesse Amarel, Manager
EMP: 95
SALES (corp-wide): 65.8B Publicly Held
WEB: www.overnite.com
SIC: 4213 Contract haulers
HQ: Ups Ground Freight, Inc.
1000 Semmes Ave
Richmond VA 23224
866 372-5619

(P-4291)
UPS GROUND FREIGHT INC
925 Morse Ave, Sunnyvale (94089-1601)
PHONE..................................408 400-0595
EMP: 95
SALES (corp-wide): 58.2B Publicly Held
SIC: 4213
HQ: Ups Ground Freight, Inc.
1000 Semmes Ave
Richmond VA 23224
804 231-8000

(P-4292)
UPS GROUND FREIGHT INC
20760 Spence Rd, Salinas (93908-9511)
PHONE..................................831 751-0262
Pam Keller, Branch Mgr
EMP: 95

SALES (corp-wide): 65.8B Publicly Held
WEB: www.overnite.com
SIC: 4213 Contract haulers
HQ: Ups Ground Freight, Inc.
1000 Semmes Ave
Richmond VA 23224
866 372-5619

(P-4293)
UPS GROUND FREIGHT INC
Also Called: UPS Freight
7754 Paramount Blvd, Pico Rivera
(90660-4309)
PHONE..................................562 801-1300
Cliff Sowers, Branch Mgr
EMP: 95
SALES (corp-wide): 65.8B Publicly Held
WEB: www.overnite.com
SIC: 4213 Contract haulers
HQ: Ups Ground Freight, Inc.
1000 Semmes Ave
Richmond VA 23224
866 372-5619

(P-4294)
UPS GROUND FREIGHT INC
900 E St, West Sacramento (95605-2310)
PHONE..................................916 371-9101
EMP: 60
SALES (corp-wide): 58.2B Publicly Held
SIC: 4213
HQ: Ups Ground Freight, Inc.
1000 Semmes Ave
Richmond VA 23224
804 231-8000

(P-4295)
UPS GROUND FREIGHT INC
650 S Acacia Ave, Fullerton (92831-5107)
PHONE..................................866 372-5619
Arthur Morales, General Mgr
EMP: 80
SALES (corp-wide): 65.8B Publicly Held
WEB: www.overnite.com
SIC: 4213 Automobiles, transport & delivery
HQ: Ups Ground Freight, Inc.
1000 Semmes Ave
Richmond VA 23224
866 372-5619

(P-4296)
USA TRUCK INC
5861 Pine Ave Ste A-2, Chino Hills
(91709-6540)
PHONE..................................909 334-1406
EMP: 67
SALES (corp-wide): 446.5MM Publicly Held
SIC: 4213 Trucking, except local
PA: Usa Truck, Inc.
3200 Industrial Park Rd
Van Buren AR 72956
479 471-2500

(P-4297)
USF REDDAWAY INC
11937 Regentview Ave, Downey
(90241-5515)
PHONE..................................562 923-0648
Sal Leal, Manager
EMP: 150
SQ FT: 28,300
SALES (corp-wide): 4.8B Publicly Held
SIC: 4213 Less-than-truckload (LTL) transport
HQ: Usf Reddaway Inc.
7720 Sw Mohawk St Bldg H
Tualatin OR 97062
503 650-1286

(P-4298)
VALLEY BULK INC
17649 Turner Rd, Victorville (92394-8716)
P.O. Box 1100 (92393-1100)
PHONE..................................760 843-0574
Jeff W Golson, President
EMP: 85
SALES (est): 14.2MM Privately Held
WEB: www.valleybulk.com
SIC: 4213 Contract haulers

(P-4299)
VENTURA TRANSFER COMPANY
(PA)
2418 E 223rd St, Long Beach
(90810-1697)
PHONE..................................310 549-1660
Randall J Clifford, CEO
Ian Hart, CFO
Galen Clifford, Vice Pres
Greg Clifford, Vice Pres
Steven F Clifford, Vice Pres
EMP: 75 EST: 1927
SQ FT: 10,000
SALES (est): 18.5MM Privately Held
WEB: www.venturatransfercompany.com
SIC: 4213 4212 4214 Contract haulers;
local trucking, without storage; local truck-
ing with storage

(P-4300)
VIP TRANSPORT INC
2703 Wardlow Rd, Corona (92882-2869)
PHONE..................................951 272-3700
Brittany Johnson, CEO
Laurie Griffiths, Treasurer
Laurie L Griffiths, Treasurer
Brittany Griffiths, Admin Sec
Josh Toth, Opers Mgr
EMP: 50 EST: 1982
SQ FT: 127,000
SALES (est): 10.4MM Privately Held
WEB: www.viptransport.com
SIC: 4213 4214 4731 Trucking, except
local; local trucking with storage; foreign
freight forwarding

(P-4301)
WAGGONERS TRUCKING
801 Mcwane Blvd, Port Hueneme
(93043-0001)
PHONE..................................800 999-9097
Rick Salazar, Manager
EMP: 60
SALES (corp-wide): 234.9MM Privately
Held
SIC: 4213 Contract haulers
PA: The Waggoners Trucking
5220 Midland Rd
Billings MT 59101
406 248-1919

(P-4302)
WERNER ENTERPRISES INC
10251 Calabash Ave, Fontana
(92335-5275)
PHONE..................................909 823-5803
John Bidaurri, Branch Mgr
EMP: 50
SQ FT: 1,316
SALES (corp-wide): 2.1B Publicly Held
WEB: www.werner.com
SIC: 4213 4731 Contract haulers; freight
consolidation
PA: Werner Enterprises, Inc
14507 Frontier Rd
Omaha NE 68138
402 895-6640

(P-4303)
WESTERN STAR TRNSP LLC
1065 E Walnut St, Carson (90746-1346)
PHONE..................................310 605-1300
Lee Cadwallader,
Kelly Cadwallader, VP Sales
Warren Cadwallader,
Norm Fritz,
Gail Werner,
EMP: 240
SQ FT: 80,000
SALES (est): 720.5K Privately Held
WEB: www.westernstartransportation.com
SIC: 4213 Less-than-truckload (LTL) trans-
port

(P-4304)
WILDWOOD EXPRESS
12416 Swanson Ave, Kingsburg
(93631-9516)
P.O. Box 397 (93631-0397)
PHONE..................................559 805-3237
Mark Anthony Woods, President
Matthew Woods, Treasurer
Sue Woods, Vice Pres
EMP: 50
SQ FT: 3,500

SALES (est): 11.9MM Privately Held
SIC: 4213 Contract haulers

(P-4305)
WILLIAMS TANK LINES (PA)
1477 Tillie Lewis Dr, Stockton
(95206-1130)
PHONE..................................209 944-5613
Michael I Williams, CEO
Marlys A Williams, Admin Sec
Eli Vasquez, Foreman/Supr
Garth Williams, Maintence Staff
Megan Uribe, Transportation
EMP: 90 EST: 1978
SQ FT: 15,000
SALES (est): 62.9MM Privately Held
SIC: 4213 Liquid petroleum transport, non-
local

(P-4306)
WOLFE TRUCKING INC
7131 Valjean Ave, Van Nuys (91406-3917)
PHONE..................................818 376-6960
Jack Wolfe, President
EMP: 107
SQ FT: 7,200
SALES (est): 10.7MM Privately Held
SIC: 4213 Trucking, except local

(P-4307)
WRAG-TIME AIR FREIGHT INC
(PA)
Also Called: Vision Express/Wrag-Time Trnsp
596 W 135th St, Gardena (90248-1506)
PHONE..................................800 586-9701
Leonard C Emrick, President
Nick Brooks, Admin Sec
Patrick Diehl, Administration
EMP: 265
SQ FT: 200,000
SALES (est): 45.6MM Privately Held
SIC: 4213 4731 Trucking, except local;
freight forwarding

(P-4308)
XPO ENTERPRISE SERVICES
INC
Also Called: Con-Way
3810 Hill Rd, Lakeport (95453-7015)
PHONE..................................916 399-8291
EMP: 120
SALES (corp-wide): 7.6B Publicly Held
SIC: 4213
HQ: Xpo Enterprise Services, Inc.
2211 Old Earhart Rd # 100
Ann Arbor MI 48105
734 998-4200

(P-4309)
XPO LOGISTICS FREIGHT INC
5475 S Airport Way, Stockton
(95206-3918)
PHONE..................................209 983-8285
Rudy Romo, Manager
EMP: 60
SQ FT: 1,000
SALES (corp-wide): 15.3B Publicly Held
WEB: www.con-way.com
SIC: 4213 Contract haulers
HQ: Xpo Logistics Freight, Inc.
2211 Old Earhart Rd # 100
Ann Arbor MI 48105
734 998-4200

(P-4310)
XPO LOGISTICS FREIGHT INC
2171 Otoole Ave, San Jose (95131-1314)
PHONE..................................408 435-3876
Jon Sullivan, Branch Mgr
EMP: 60
SQ FT: 8,834
SALES (corp-wide): 15.3B Publicly Held
WEB: www.con-way.com
SIC: 4213 Contract haulers
HQ: Xpo Logistics Freight, Inc.
2211 Old Earhart Rd # 100
Ann Arbor MI 48105
734 998-4200

(P-4311)
XPO LOGISTICS FREIGHT INC
4965 Convoy St, San Diego (92111-1600)
PHONE..................................858 569-8921
Tim Tuerk, Manager
Manuel Landeros, Safety Dir
EMP: 50

▲ = Import ▼=Export
◆ =Import/Export

SQ FT: 20,344
SALES (corp-wide): 15.3B **Publicly Held**
WEB: www.con-way.com
SIC: 4213 Contract haulers
HQ: Xpo Logistics Freight, Inc.
2211 Old Earhart Rd # 100
Ann Arbor MI 48105
734 998-4200

(P-4312)
XPO LOGISTICS FREIGHT INC
4195 E Central Ave, Fresno (93725-9026)
PHONE..................559 485-1164
Bud Whitney, *Principal*
John Dervishian, *Human Res Mgr*
EMP: 62
SQ FT: 39,620
SALES (corp-wide): 15.3B **Publicly Held**
WEB: www.con-way.com
SIC: 4213 Contract haulers
HQ: Xpo Logistics Freight, Inc.
2211 Old Earhart Rd # 100
Ann Arbor MI 48105
734 998-4200

(P-4313)
XPO LOGISTICS FREIGHT INC
787 Airport Blvd, Salinas (93901-4509)
PHONE..................831 758-8874
Nick Fletcher, *Sales/Mktg Mgr*
Ted Garcia, *Manager*
EMP: 62
SALES (corp-wide): 15.3B **Publicly Held**
WEB: www.con-way.com
SIC: 4213 Contract haulers
HQ: Xpo Logistics Freight, Inc.
2211 Old Earhart Rd # 100
Ann Arbor MI 48105
734 998-4200

(P-4314)
XPO LOGISTICS FREIGHT INC
12466 Montague St, Pacoima
(91331-2121)
PHONE..................818 890-2095
Paul Styers, *Manager*
EMP: 200
SQ FT: 20,187
SALES (corp-wide): 15.3B **Publicly Held**
WEB: www.con-way.com
SIC: 4213 4214 Contract haulers; local
trucking with storage
HQ: Xpo Logistics Freight, Inc.
2211 Old Earhart Rd # 100
Ann Arbor MI 48105
734 998-4200

(P-4315)
XPO LOGISTICS FREIGHT INC
2102 N Batavia St, Orange (92865-3104)
PHONE..................714 282-7717
Tim Worner, *Manager*
Neil Smith, *VP Opers*
EMP: 100
SALES (corp-wide): 15.3B **Publicly Held**
WEB: www.con-way.com
SIC: 4213 Contract haulers
HQ: Xpo Logistics Freight, Inc.
2211 Old Earhart Rd # 100
Ann Arbor MI 48105
734 998-4200

(P-4316)
XPO LOGISTICS FREIGHT INC
3516 Kiessig Ave, Sacramento
(95823-1036)
PHONE..................916 399-8291
John Sullivan, *Branch Mgr*
Tim Myles, *Human Res Dir*
EMP: 120
SALES (corp-wide): 15.3B **Publicly Held**
WEB: www.con-way.com
SIC: 4213 Contract haulers
HQ: Xpo Logistics Freight, Inc.
2211 Old Earhart Rd # 100
Ann Arbor MI 48105
734 998-4200

(P-4317)
XPO LOGISTICS FREIGHT INC
20697 Prism Pl, Lake Forest (92630-7803)
PHONE..................949 581-9030
Joseph Tickford, *Branch Mgr*
EMP: 60
SQ FT: 13,890

SALES (corp-wide): 15.3B **Publicly Held**
WEB: www.con-way.com
SIC: 4213 Less-than-truckload (LTL) trans-
port
HQ: Xpo Logistics Freight, Inc.
2211 Old Earhart Rd # 100
Ann Arbor MI 48105
734 998-4200

(P-4318)
XPO LOGISTICS FREIGHT INC
1955 E Washington Blvd, Los Angeles
(90021-3206)
PHONE..................213 744-0664
Todd Liverman, *Branch Mgr*
EMP: 120
SQ FT: 39,842
SALES (corp-wide): 15.3B **Publicly Held**
WEB: www.con-way.com
SIC: 4213 4212 4731 Contract haulers;
local trucking, without storage; freight for-
warding
HQ: Xpo Logistics Freight, Inc.
2211 Old Earhart Rd # 100
Ann Arbor MI 48105
734 998-4200

(P-4319)
XPO LOGISTICS FREIGHT INC
Also Called: Con-Way
12555 Mesa Dr, Blythe (92225-3363)
PHONE..................760 922-8538
Butch Russell, *General Mgr*
EMP: 62
SALES (corp-wide): 15.3B **Publicly Held**
WEB: www.con-way.com
SIC: 4213 Contract haulers
HQ: Xpo Logistics Freight, Inc.
2211 Old Earhart Rd # 100
Ann Arbor MI 48105
734 998-4200

(P-4320)
XPO LOGISTICS FREIGHT INC
Also Called: Con-Way
4095 S Moorland Ave, Santa Rosa
(95407-8110)
PHONE..................707 584-0211
Rich Gonzales, *Manager*
EMP: 62
SALES (corp-wide): 15.3B **Publicly Held**
WEB: www.con-way.com
SIC: 4213 Contract haulers
HQ: Xpo Logistics Freight, Inc.
2211 Old Earhart Rd # 100
Ann Arbor MI 48105
734 998-4200

(P-4321)
XPO LOGISTICS FREIGHT INC
2200 Claremont Ct, Hayward (94545-5002)
PHONE..................510 785-6920
Terry Smith, *Manager*
Edward Boe, *Safety Mgr*
EMP: 200
SQ FT: 28,704
SALES (corp-wide): 15.3B **Publicly Held**
WEB: www.con-way.com
SIC: 4213 4212 4731 Contract haulers;
local trucking, without storage; freight
transportation arrangement
HQ: Xpo Logistics Freight, Inc.
2211 Old Earhart Rd # 100
Ann Arbor MI 48105
734 998-4200

(P-4322)
XPO LOGISTICS FREIGHT INC
13364 Marlay Ave, Fontana (92337-6919)
PHONE..................951 685-1244
Mark Logan, *General Mgr*
EMP: 200
SALES (corp-wide): 15.3B **Publicly Held**
SIC: 4213 Contract haulers
HQ: Xpo Logistics Freight, Inc.
2211 Old Earhart Rd # 100
Ann Arbor MI 48105
734 998-4200

(P-4323)
XPO LOGISTICS FREIGHT INC
12903 Lakeland Rd, Santa Fe Springs
(90670-4516)
PHONE..................562 946-8331
Jim Lutze, *Manager*
EMP: 200

SALES (corp-wide): 15.3B **Publicly Held**
WEB: www.con-way.com
SIC: 4213 Contract haulers
HQ: Xpo Logistics Freight, Inc.
2211 Old Earhart Rd # 100
Ann Arbor MI 48105
734 998-4200

(P-4324)
YRC INC
Also Called: Yellow Transportation
25555 Clawiter Rd, Hayward (94545-2740)
PHONE..................510 783-7010
Pete Kell, *Manager*
Robert Correia, *General Mgr*
Kriss Nokiangthong, *Project Engr*
EMP: 100
SQ FT: 33,872
SALES (corp-wide): 4.8B **Publicly Held**
WEB: www.roadway.com
SIC: 4213 4231 Contract haulers; trucking
terminal facilities
HQ: Yrc Inc.
10990 Roe Ave
Overland Park KS 66211
913 696-6100

(P-4325)
YRC INC
Also Called: Yellow Transportation
15400 S Main St, Gardena (90248-2215)
PHONE..................310 404-2221
Tony Edmondson, *Manager*
EMP: 200
SQ FT: 56,821
SALES (corp-wide): 4.8B **Publicly Held**
WEB: www.roadway.com
SIC: 4213 Trucking, except local
HQ: Yrc Inc.
10990 Roe Ave
Overland Park KS 66211
913 696-6100

(P-4326)
YRC INC
3210 52nd Ave, Sacramento (95823-1024)
PHONE..................916 371-4555
Scott Kamman, *Owner*
Denise Hummer, *Admin Sec*
EMP: 99
SALES (corp-wide): 4.8B **Publicly Held**
SIC: 4213 Contract haulers
HQ: Yrc Inc.
10990 Roe Ave
Overland Park KS 66211
913 696-6100

(P-4327)
YRC WORLDWIDE INC
201 Haskins Way, South San Francisco
(94080-6215)
PHONE..................650 952-1112
Mike Sighn, *Principal*
Brad Stevens, *Manager*
EMP: 100
SALES (corp-wide): 4.8B **Publicly Held**
SIC: 4213 Contract haulers
PA: Yrc Worldwide Inc.
10990 Roe Ave
Overland Park KS 66211
913 696-6100

4214 Local Trucking With Storage

(P-4328)
AMERICAN RLCTION LOGISTICS INC
13565 Larwin Cir, Santa Fe Springs
(90670-5032)
PHONE..................562 229-3600
Lawrence D Whittet, *CEO*
James Hooper, *President*
Bob Lechich, *CFO*
Robert Lechich, *CFO*
Tina Madrigal, *Sales Mgr*
EMP: 86
SQ FT: 120,000
SALES (est): 15.7MM **Privately Held**
WEB: www.american-moving.com
SIC: 4214 4213 4212 Household goods
moving & storage, local; trucking, except
local; household goods transport; moving
services

(P-4329)
AMERICAN WEST WORLDWIDE EX INC (PA)
51 Zaca Ln Ste 120, San Luis Obispo
(93401-7353)
PHONE..................800 788-4534
Josh Brown, *CEO*
Cathie Brown, *President*
EMP: 68
SALES (est): 38MM **Privately Held**
SIC: 4214 4213 4225 Local trucking with
storage; trucking, except local; general
warehousing

(P-4330)
AMS RELOCATION INCORPORATED
Also Called: AMS Bekins Van Lines
1873 Rollins Rd, Burlingame (94010-2209)
PHONE..................650 697-3530
Mike Foster, *General Mgr*
Gary P Wolfe, *President*
Bill Evans, *Sales Staff*
EMP: 55
SQ FT: 45,000
SALES (est): 6.2MM **Privately Held**
SIC: 4214 Household goods moving &
storage, local

(P-4331)
BAKERSFIELD MOVING & STORAGE
Also Called: Reliable Moving & Storage
3820 Herring Rd, Arvin (93203-9661)
P.O. Box 13128 (93203)
PHONE..................661 397-4521
Steve Gutierrez, *President*
Martha Gutierrez, *Vice Pres*
EMP: 50
SALES (est): 5.5MM **Privately Held**
WEB: www.reliablemove.com
SIC: 4214 4213 4212 Household goods
moving & storage, local; household goods
transport; moving services

(P-4332)
BEAR TRUCKING INC
Also Called: Gate City Beverage Bear Trckg
19768 Kendall Dr, San Bernardino
(92407-1633)
P.O. Box 9158 (92427-0158)
PHONE..................909 799-1616
Leona Aronoff, *President*
Summer McManaway, *Controller*
EMP: 100
SQ FT: 10,000
SALES (est): 18.9MM **Privately Held**
SIC: 4214 Local trucking with storage

(P-4333)
BEKINS MOVING SOLUTIONS INC (PA)
Also Called: Bekins Moving & Storage
12610 Shoemaker Ave, Santa Fe Springs
(90670-6344)
PHONE..................562 356-9460
David Caruso, *President*
Doug Nichols, *Opers Mgr*
EMP: 71
SALES (est): 18.5MM **Privately Held**
SIC: 4214 4213 Local trucking with stor-
age; trucking, except local

(P-4334)
C & M TRANSFER SAN DIEGO INC
Also Called: C&M Relocation Systems
8787 Olive Ln, Santee (92071-4137)
P.O. Box 2184, Ramona (92065-0937)
PHONE..................619 562-6111
Mick Mahaffey, *President*
EMP: 60
SALES (est): 6.4MM **Privately Held**
WEB: www.cmtransfer.com
SIC: 4214 Local trucking with storage

(P-4335)
CALKO TRANSPORT COMPANY INC
Also Called: Redman Container
720 E Watson Center Rd, Carson
(90745-4108)
PHONE..................310 816-0602
Chong Suh, *President*

Simon Chung, *Vice Pres*
Tim Suh, *Manager*
Sophia Song, *Supervisor*
EMP: 58
SQ FT: 24,000
SALES (est): 6.7MM **Privately Held**
WEB: www.calko.com
SIC: 4214 4225 Local trucking with storage; general warehousing

(P-4336)
CHIPMAN CORPORATION (PA)
Also Called: Caton Moving & Storage
1040 Marina Village Pkwy # 100, Alameda (94501-6478)
PHONE....................510 748-8700
Tom Chipman, *CEO*
Justin Chipman, *President*
John H Chipman Sr, *Chairman*
Thomas Chipman, *Exec VP*
Greg Dolan, *Senior VP*
EMP: 50
SQ FT: 400,000
SALES (est): 33.1MM **Privately Held**
WEB: www.chipmancorp.com
SIC: 4214 4213 4731 Household goods moving & storage, local; household goods transport; foreign freight forwarding

(P-4337)
COMPLETE RELOCATION SVCS INC
7361 Doig Dr, Garden Grove (92841-1806)
PHONE....................714 901-7411
Marc Kranz, *President*
EMP: 99 **EST:** 2007
SALES (est): 4.6MM **Privately Held**
SIC: 4214 Local trucking with storage

(P-4338)
COROVAN CORPORATION (PA)
12302 Kerran St, Poway (92064-6884)
PHONE....................858 762-8100
Richard R Schmitz, *CEO*
Robert J Schmitz, *Ch of Bd*
Thomas A Schmitz, *Admin Sec*
Jim Goff, *Technician*
BJ Kaske, *Sales Associate*
EMP: 175
SQ FT: 80,000
SALES (est): 80.8MM **Privately Held**
SIC: 4214 Furniture moving & storage, local

(P-4339)
COROVAN MOVING & STORAGE CO (HQ)
12302 Kerran St, Poway (92064-6884)
PHONE....................858 748-1100
Richard R Schmitz, *President*
Jerry P Brothers, *CFO*
Robert J Schmitz, *Co-President*
David Drach, *Executive*
Thomas A Schmitz, *Admin Sec*
EMP: 100
SQ FT: 600,000
SALES (est): 34.5MM **Privately Held**
SIC: 4214 4213 Household goods moving & storage, local; household goods transport

(P-4340)
CRUZ MODULAR INC (PA)
Also Called: Systechs
249 W Baywood Ave Ste B, Orange (92865-2604)
PHONE....................714 283-2890
Linda Galleran, *CEO*
Vince Schlachter, *President*
Malcolm Craycroft, *Vice Pres*
EMP: 56
SALES (est): 11.6MM **Privately Held**
WEB: www.systechs.com
SIC: 4214 7641 4226 1799 Furniture moving & storage, local; reupholstery & furniture repair; special warehousing & storage; office furniture installation

(P-4341)
DARRELL L GREEN INC
Also Called: Green Trucking
12652 Avenue 240, Tulare (93274-9531)
PHONE....................559 688-0686
Phyllis Green, *President*
Darrell L Green, *Corp Secy*
EMP: 67 **EST:** 1973

SQ FT: 4,000
SALES: 12MM **Privately Held**
WEB: www.greentrucking.com
SIC: 4214 Local trucking with storage

(P-4342)
DART INTERNATIONAL A CORP (HQ)
Also Called: Dart Entities
1430 S Eastman Ave, Commerce (90023-4006)
P.O. Box 23944, Los Angeles (90023-0944)
PHONE....................323 264-8746
Terence Dedeaux, *CEO*
Paul Martin, *President*
William J Smollen, *Corp Secy*
Lorena Paredes, *Administration*
Joseph M Medlin, *Sales Staff*
EMP: 110
SQ FT: 50,000
SALES (est): 25.2MM
SALES (corp-wide): 101.2MM **Privately Held**
SIC: 4214 Local trucking with storage
PA: Dart Transportation Service, A Corporation
1430 S Eastman Ave Ste 1
Commerce CA 90023
323 981-8205

(P-4343)
DGA SERVICES INC (PA)
Also Called: J I T Transportation
1075 Montague Expy, Milpitas (95035-6828)
P.O. Box 41372, San Jose (95160-1372)
PHONE....................408 232-4800
Deborah S Ashley, *CEO*
Gene Ashley, *President*
David Butcher, *Executive*
Ross Williams, *Info Tech Mgr*
Russ Watkins, *Opers Mgr*
EMP: 54
SQ FT: 125,000
SALES (est): 13.2MM **Privately Held**
WEB: www.jittransportation.com
SIC: 4214 4213 Local trucking with storage; trucking, except local

(P-4344)
DOUBLE DAY OFFICE SERVICES INC
340 Shaw Rd, South San Francisco (94080-6606)
P.O. Box 591405, San Francisco (94159-1405)
PHONE....................650 872-6600
Cheryl Ringelmann, *President*
EMP: 50
SQ FT: 45,000
SALES: 4.5MM **Privately Held**
WEB: www.doubleday-corprelo.com
SIC: 4214 7389 Local trucking with storage; relocation service

(P-4345)
DURKEE DRAYAGE COMPANY
539 Stone Rd, Benicia (94510-1113)
PHONE....................510 970-7550
Jeffrey J Fenton, *President*
Cathy Lashin, *Vice Pres*
EMP: 80 **EST:** 1933
SQ FT: 80,000
SALES (est): 7.3MM **Privately Held**
WEB: www.durkeedrayage.com
SIC: 4214 Local trucking with storage

(P-4346)
EXCEL MOVING SERVICES
30047 Ahern Ave, Union City (94587-1234)
PHONE....................800 392-3596
Bruce D Owashi, *President*
Vyvyanne S Owashi, *Shareholder*
Robert Friederang, *Vice Pres*
EMP: 60
SQ FT: 23,400
SALES (est): 3.9MM **Privately Held**
SIC: 4214 Household goods moving & storage, local

(P-4347)
GILBERT SERVICE CORP
Also Called: Gilbert West
6725 Kimball Ave, Chino (91708-9177)
PHONE....................909 393-7575
Ken Gross, *President*

Richard Gilbert, *Vice Pres*
EMP: 125
SALES (est): 13.2MM **Privately Held**
SIC: 4214 4225 Local trucking with storage; general warehousing

(P-4348)
GSC LOGISTICS INC (PA)
530 Water St Fl 5, Oakland (94607-3532)
PHONE....................510 844-3700
Scott E Taylor, *CEO*
Marc Jensen, *CFO*
Joel Lesser, *CFO*
Garcia Andres, *Vice Pres*
EMP: 120
SQ FT: 8,000
SALES (est): 17.9MM **Privately Held**
SIC: 4214 4225 4213 Local trucking with storage; general warehousing; trucking, except local

(P-4349)
HALBERT BROTHERS INC
17400 Chestnut St, City of Industry (91748-1013)
PHONE....................626 913-1800
John W Miller, *CEO*
James R Miller, *Treasurer*
Jim Miller, *Vice Pres*
EMP: 60
SQ FT: 110,000
SALES (est): 7.2MM **Privately Held**
WEB: www.halbertbrothersinc.com
SIC: 4214 1796 Local trucking with storage; machine moving & rigging

(P-4350)
HARRISON NICHOLS CO LTD
501 W Foothill Blvd, Azusa (91702-2345)
PHONE....................626 337-5020
Kenneth Harrison, *CEO*
Randall P Harrison, *President*
EMP: 133
SQ FT: 12,000
SALES (est): 15.6MM **Privately Held**
SIC: 4214 4212 Local trucking with storage; local trucking, without storage

(P-4351)
HIDDEN VALLEY MVG & STOR INC (PA)
1218 Pacific Oaks Pl, Escondido (92029-2900)
PHONE....................602 252-7800
Robert L Berti, *CEO*
David Boeller, *CFO*
EMP: 100
SQ FT: 55,000
SALES (est): 11.7MM **Privately Held**
SIC: 4214 4213 Household goods moving & storage, local; contract haulers

(P-4352)
JAMES B BRANCH INC (PA)
Also Called: Gemini Moving Specialists
4367 Clyburn Ave, Toluca Lake (91602-2906)
PHONE....................818 765-3521
Eugene W Luni, *President*
Mark A Luni, *Corp Secy*
Louise W Luni, *Vice Pres*
EMP: 50
SQ FT: 35,000
SALES (est): 5.9MM **Privately Held**
SIC: 4214 Furniture moving & storage, local

(P-4353)
JAVELIN LOGISTICS CORPORATION (PA)
7447 Morton Ave Ste A, Newark (94560-4208)
PHONE....................510 795-7287
Malcolm George Winspear, *CEO*
Jeff Hoover, *Vice Pres*
Mary White, *Admin Mgr*
Mike Sacrey, *General Mgr*
Celeste Steele, *Data Proc Staff*
EMP: 50
SQ FT: 100,000
SALES (est): 44MM **Privately Held**
SIC: 4214 4731 4225 Local trucking with storage; freight transportation arrangement; general warehousing

(P-4354)
LDI TRANSPORTATION INC
200 Erie St, Pomona (91768-3327)
PHONE....................909 620-7001
Alex Kolesnikov, *President*
EMP: 100
SQ FT: 2,500
SALES: 3.5MM **Privately Held**
SIC: 4214 Local trucking with storage

(P-4355)
LEGACY TRANSPORTATION SVCS INC (PA)
Also Called: Legacy Global Logistics Svcs
935 Mclaughlin Ave, San Jose (95122-2612)
PHONE....................408 294-9800
John Migliozzi, *President*
Kerry Carlson, *President*
Charles McClure, *President*
Michael Quinn, *Exec VP*
Shelly Gipson, *Senior VP*
EMP: 140
SQ FT: 200,000
SALES (est): 54.3MM **Privately Held**
SIC: 4214 4213 Local trucking with storage; trucking, except local

(P-4356)
LINEAGE LOGISTICS HOLDINGS LLC
1 Park Plz Ste 550, Irvine (92614-2594)
PHONE....................909 433-3100
Bill Hendricksen, *CEO*
EMP: 800
SALES (corp-wide): 1.2B **Privately Held**
SIC: 4214 4213 4222 Household goods moving & storage, local; household goods transport; warehousing, cold storage or refrigerated
PA: Lineage Logistics Holdings, Llc
1 Park Plz Ste 550
Irvine CA 92614
800 678-7271

(P-4357)
LINEAGE LOGISTICS HOLDINGS LLC
Also Called: Inland Cold Storage
2551 S Lilac Ave, Bloomington (92316-3209)
PHONE....................909 874-1200
Bill Hendricksen, *CEO*
EMP: 800
SALES (corp-wide): 1.2B **Privately Held**
SIC: 4214 4222 Household goods moving & storage, local; warehousing, cold storage or refrigerated
PA: Lineage Logistics Holdings, Llc
1 Park Plz Ste 550
Irvine CA 92614
800 678-7271

(P-4358)
MASA TRUCKING CO
231 W 135th St, Los Angeles (90061-1625)
PHONE....................310 329-1567
Mauro A Arce, *CEO*
Paula Morales, *Admin Sec*
EMP: 50
SQ FT: 40,000
SALES: 9MM **Privately Held**
SIC: 4214 Local trucking with storage

(P-4359)
MCCOLLISTERS TRNSP GROUP INC
Also Called: United Van Lines
10672 Jasmine St, Fontana (92337-8242)
PHONE....................909 428-5700
Chris Ciofreddi, *Branch Mgr*
EMP: 55
SALES (corp-wide): 187.6MM **Privately Held**
SIC: 4214 Local trucking with storage
PA: Mccollister's Transportation Group, Inc.
1800 N Route 130
Burlington NJ 08016
609 386-0600

(P-4360)
MOVING SOLUTIONS INC
Also Called: North American Van Lines
7093 Central Ave, Newark (94560-4201)
PHONE....................408 920-0110

Rick S Philpott, *CEO*
Janet Philpott, *Vice Pres*
EMP: 150
SQ FT: 200,000
SALES (est): 15.5MM **Privately Held**
WEB: www.movingsolutionsinc.com
SIC: 4214 8742 7376 1799 Household goods moving & storage, local; construction project management consultant; computer facilities management; office furniture installation

(P-4361)
NOR-CAL MOVING SERVICES (PA)
Also Called: Allied Intl San Franisco
3129 Corporate Pl, Hayward (94545-3915)
PHONE................................510 371-4942
Peter Mazzetti Jr, *CEO*
Dennis D Goza, *President*
John Mizera, *CFO*
Dave Konecny, *Exec VP*
Louis Marchiorlatti, *Admin Sec*
EMP: 125
SQ FT: 200,000
SALES (est): 20MM **Privately Held**
WEB: www.nor-calmoving.com
SIC: 4214 4213 Household goods moving & storage, local; furniture moving & storage, local; household goods transport

(P-4362)
NOR-CAL MOVING SERVICES
560 E Trimble Rd, San Jose (95131-1221)
PHONE................................408 954-1175
Karen Aparton, *Branch Mgr*
EMP: 100
SALES (corp-wide): 20MM **Privately Held**
WEB: www.nor-calmoving.com
SIC: 4214 4213 Household goods moving & storage, local; trucking, except local
PA: Nor-Cal Moving Services
3129 Corporate Pl
Hayward CA 94545
510 371-4942

(P-4363)
OFFICE MOVERS INC
4020 Nelson Ave Ste 200, Concord (94520-8526)
PHONE................................408 254-5010
James Robinson, *President*
EMP: 50
SALES (est): 2.2MM **Privately Held**
SIC: 4214 Household goods moving & storage, local

(P-4364)
PACK & CRATE SERVICES INC
238 N Quince St, Escondido (92025-2518)
P.O. Box 2964 (92033-2964)
PHONE................................760 737-6893
Robert H Shepard, *President*
EMP: 50
SQ FT: 35,000
SALES (est): 4.8MM **Privately Held**
SIC: 4214

(P-4365)
PEETERS TRANSPORTATION CO
Also Called: Peeters/Mayflower
451 Eccles Ave, South San Francisco (94080-1902)
P.O. Box 2724 (94083-2724)
PHONE................................800 356-5877
Robert Peeters, *President*
Frederick D Peeters, *CEO*
Shirley Peeters, *Corp Secy*
De Loss Wood, *Vice Pres*
EMP: 50 EST: 1915
SALES (est): 4.5MM **Privately Held**
SIC: 4214 Household goods moving & storage, local

(P-4366)
PORT LOGISTICS GROUP INC
19801 S Santa Fe Ave, Compton (90221-5915)
PHONE................................310 669-2551
Timothy Page, *Principal*
Maria Corona, *Supervisor*
EMP: 120 **Privately Held**
SIC: 4214 Local trucking with storage

PA: Port Logistics Group, Inc.
288 S Mayo Ave
City Of Industry CA 91789

(P-4367)
PORT LOGISTICS GROUP INC
501 Cheryl Ln Bldg 10, City of Industry (91789-3031)
PHONE................................909 839-5901
Julio Gonzelos, *Principal*
EMP: 64 **Privately Held**
SIC: 4214 Local trucking with storage
PA: Port Logistics Group, Inc.
288 S Mayo Ave
City Of Industry CA 91789

(P-4368)
PRECISION RELOCATION INC
16055 Heron Ave Ste B, La Mirada (90638-5514)
PHONE................................714 690-9344
Kirk O O'Gilvy, *CEO*
Douglas Piersant, *President*
Patsy Ogilvy, *Controller*
Jose Navarro, *Manager*
EMP: 120
SQ FT: 60,000
SALES (est): 7.8MM **Privately Held**
WEB: www.precisionrelocation.com
SIC: 4214 Local trucking with storage

(P-4369)
ROYAL EXPRESS INC (PA)
3545 E Date Ave, Fresno (93725-1933)
PHONE................................559 272-3500
Kirpal S Shiota, *CEO*
EMP: 111
SQ FT: 435,600
SALES (est): 29.3MM **Privately Held**
WEB: www.royalexp.com
SIC: 4214 Local trucking with storage

(P-4370)
SAMUEL J PIAZZA & SON INC (PA)
Also Called: Piazza Trucking
9001 Rayo Ave, South Gate (90280-3606)
PHONE................................323 357-1999
Michael Piazza, *CEO*
Basil Piazza, *President*
Robert Piazza, *Vice Pres*
William Piazza, *Vice Pres*
Beth Elkins, *Regional Mgr*
EMP: 70
SQ FT: 20,000
SALES (est): 21.7MM **Privately Held**
WEB: www.piazzatrucking.com
SIC: 4214 4213 Local trucking with storage; trucking, except local

(P-4371)
SCHICK MOVING & STORAGE CO (PA)
2721 Michelle Dr, Tustin (92780-7018)
P.O. Box 3627 (92781-3627)
PHONE................................714 731-5500
Gordon C Schick, *President*
Lynn Larson, *CFO*
Lynne M Larson, *Treasurer*
Arthur C Schick Jr, *Vice Pres*
Beverly C Schick, *Vice Pres*
EMP: 104 EST: 1956
SQ FT: 113,000
SALES: 7MM **Privately Held**
WEB: www.schickusa.com
SIC: 4214 Household goods moving & storage, local

(P-4372)
SERVICE TRANSPORT INC
29991 Cyn Hls Rd Ste 137, Lake Elsinore (92532-2578)
PHONE................................951 403-3464
Robert Kausman, *CEO*
EMP: 65
SQ FT: 2,500
SALES: 4MM **Privately Held**
SIC: 4214 Local trucking with storage

(P-4373)
SOUTH COAST LOGISTICS
Also Called: North American Van Lines
4160 Temescal Canyon Rd # 311, Corona (92883-4629)
PHONE................................714 894-4744
Craig Schueller, *President*
EMP: 50
SALES (est): 6.7MM **Privately Held**
WEB: www.southcoastlogistics.com
SIC: 4214 Local trucking with storage

(P-4374)
SPECIAL DISPATCH CAL INC (PA)
16330 Phoebe Ave, La Mirada (90638-5612)
P.O. Box 3838, Cerritos (90703-3838)
PHONE................................714 521-8200
John Edward Dearing, *CEO*
Thomas Dearing, *Vice Pres*
Veronica Belmonte, *Office Mgr*
Ty Clarno, *Opers Mgr*
Shane Maxwell, *Opers Staff*
EMP: 60
SQ FT: 120,000
SALES (est): 24.6MM **Privately Held**
SIC: 4214 4212 Local trucking with storage; delivery service, vehicular

(P-4375)
SPIREON INC (PA)
Also Called: Goldstar
16802 Aston, Irvine (92606-4835)
PHONE................................800 557-1449
Kevin Weiss, *CEO*
Tim Welch, *COO*
Rita Parvaneh, *CFO*
Carla Fitzgerald, *Chief Mktg Ofcr*
Jason Penkethman, *Opers Staff*
EMP: 175
SALES (est): 123.3MM **Privately Held**
WEB: www.procon.net
SIC: 4214 8741 Local trucking with storage; business management

(P-4376)
SS SKIKOS INCORPORATED
1289 Sebastopol Rd, Santa Rosa (95407-6834)
PHONE................................707 575-3000
Shad Skikos, *CEO*
Pete Skikos, *President*
EMP: 80
SALES (est): 8.5MM **Privately Held**
SIC: 4214 Local trucking with storage

(P-4377)
STUDENT MOVERS INC
Also Called: College Movers
825 Chalcedony St, San Diego (92109-2560)
PHONE................................303 296-0600
Steve Linane, *President*
Gloria Linane, *Chairman*
▲ **EMP:** 80
SQ FT: 65,000
SALES: 4.5MM **Privately Held**
WEB: www.studentmovers.com
SIC: 4214 Furniture moving & storage, local

(P-4378)
TOTAL TRNSP & DIST INC
1551 E Victoria St, Carson (90746-2861)
PHONE................................310 603-0467
Ruben Dominguez, *President*
Lauri Salazar, *Controller*
EMP: 75
SQ FT: 100,010
SALES (est): 12.7MM **Privately Held**
SIC: 4214 Local trucking with storage

(P-4379)
TRANSPORT EXPRESS INC
19801 S Santa Fe Ave, Compton (90221-5915)
PHONE................................310 898-2000
Robert L Stull, *CEO*
Steven Senecal, *President*
William Meroth, *Vice Pres*
Patricia Senecal, *Admin Sec*
EMP: 55
SQ FT: 230,000

SALES (est): 8.6MM **Privately Held**
SIC: 4214 4225 4731 Local trucking with storage; general warehousing; brokers, shipping

(P-4380)
TRANSWEST SAN DIEGO LLC
Also Called: Miramar Truck Center
6066 Miramar Rd, San Diego (92121-2542)
PHONE................................858 450-0707
Brad Fauvre, *President*
EMP: 500
SALES (est): 21.1MM **Privately Held**
SIC: 4214 Local trucking with storage

(P-4381)
TRI-MODAL DIST SVCS INC (PA)
Also Called: City Distribution Services
2011 E Carson St, Carson (90810-1223)
PHONE................................310 522-5506
Joshua Owen, *President*
Bill Owen, *COO*
Ron Gill, *Vice Pres*
Michael Kelso, *Vice Pres*
Tim Mullaney, *Vice Pres*
EMP: 200
SQ FT: 170,000
SALES (est): 19.5MM **Privately Held**
WEB: www.trimodal.com
SIC: 4214 Local trucking with storage

(P-4382)
TRIWAYS INC
Also Called: Warehouse and Distribution
11201 Iberia St Ste B, Mira Loma (91752-3280)
P.O. Box 9342, Ontario (91762-9342)
PHONE................................951 361-4840
Juan M Jauregui, *President*
Fredy R Jimenez, *CFO*
Bob Schwenig, *Vice Pres*
Maria Paez, *Administration*
Jo Anderson, *Human Resources*
EMP: 65
SQ FT: 228,000
SALES (est): 14.4MM **Privately Held**
WEB: www.triways.net
SIC: 4214 Local trucking with storage

(P-4383)
URIBE TRUCKING INC
Also Called: Alex Moving & Storage
542 Flynn Rd, Camarillo (93012-8027)
PHONE................................805 483-1125
Alejandro Uribe, *President*
Christine Uribe, *Corp Secy*
Mike Kachmar, *Manager*
EMP: 130
SQ FT: 60,000
SALES (est): 10.4MM **Privately Held**
SIC: 4214 4731 4225 Local trucking with storage; freight forwarding; warehousing; self-storage

(P-4384)
USA TRANSPORT INC
12191 Violet Rd, Adelanto (92301-2713)
PHONE................................559 783-3563
Gary Leslie, *President*
EMP: 50
SQ FT: 5,000
SALES (est): 2.8MM **Privately Held**
SIC: 4214 4213 Local trucking with storage; trucking, except local

(P-4385)
VALLEY RELOCATION AND STORAGE (PA)
Also Called: Valley Northamerican
5000 Marsh Dr, Concord (94520-5322)
PHONE................................925 230-2025
James Robson, *President*
John A Burks, *CEO*
Mark Robson, *General Mgr*
EMP: 200
SQ FT: 58,000
SALES (est): 27.9MM **Privately Held**
SIC: 4214 Local trucking with storage

(P-4386)
VAN TORRANCE & STORAGE COMPANY (PA)
Also Called: S & M Moving Systems
12128 Burke St, Santa Fe Springs
(90670-2678)
PHONE..............................562 567-2100
Steven Todare, *President*
Martin Stadler, *Vice Pres*
Daniel Clark, *Administration*
EMP: 100
SQ FT: 95,000
SALES (est): 111MM **Privately Held**
WEB: www.sandmoving.com
SIC: 4214 4213 Local trucking with storage; trucking, except local

(P-4387)
VERNON CENTRAL WAREHOUSE INC
Also Called: Vernon Warehouse Co
2050 E 38th St, Vernon (90058-1615)
P.O. Box 58426 (90058-0426)
PHONE..............................323 234-2200
Joseph E Tack, *CEO*
Joe Tack, *President*
Jim Boltinghouse, *Corp Secy*
Tom Rodd, *Vice Pres*
Steve Shanklin, *Vice Pres*
EMP: 125
SQ FT: 100,000
SALES (est): 26.8MM **Privately Held**
WEB: www.vernonwarehouse.com
SIC: 4214 5149 Local trucking with storage; natural & organic foods

(P-4388)
W WHY W ENTERPRISES INC
Also Called: Atlas/Eastern Van Lines
2671 Pomona Blvd, Pomona (91768-3221)
PHONE..............................626 969-4292
William Coffman, *President*
Yvonne Coffman, *Vice Pres*
EMP: 60
SALES (est): 6.4MM **Privately Held**
SIC: 4214 4213 Local trucking with storage; household goods transport

(P-4389)
WATERS MOVING & STORAGE INC
37 Bridgehead Rd, Martinez (94553-1300)
P.O. Box 1029 (94553-0102)
PHONE..............................925 372-0914
Ken Waters, *CEO*
Paulette Waters, *CFO*
EMP: 75
SQ FT: 50,000
SALES (est): 6.2MM **Privately Held**
SIC: 4214 Furniture moving & storage, local

(P-4390)
WETZEL & SONS MOVING AND STOR
Also Called: Wetzel Trucking
12400 Osborne St, Pacoima (91331-2002)
PHONE..............................818 890-0992
Donald C Wetzel, *President*
Daniel S Wetzel, *Vice Pres*
EMP: 70 EST: 1976
SQ FT: 146,000
SALES (est): 5.4MM **Privately Held**
WEB: www.wetzelmovingandstorage.com
SIC: 4214 Furniture moving & storage, local; household goods moving & storage, local

(P-4391)
ZIKKO INC
6345 Auburn Blvd Ste C, Citrus Heights (95621-5277)
PHONE..............................916 949-8989
Vladimir Skots, *CEO*
EMP: 200
SALES (est): 192.5K **Privately Held**
SIC: 4214 Local trucking with storage

4215 Courier Svcs, Except Air

(P-4392)
ALL COUNTIES COURIER INC
14811 Myford Rd, Tustin (92780-7227)
PHONE..............................949 224-0900
Patricia Cochran, *President*
Dean Steward, *Senior VP*
Jack Lipczynski, *General Mgr*
Liliana Cordova, *Receptionist*
EMP: 200
SALES (est): 22.8MM **Privately Held**
SIC: 4215 Package delivery, vehicular

(P-4393)
APOLLO COURIERS INC (PA)
1039 W Hillcrest Blvd, Inglewood (90301-2023)
PHONE..............................310 337-0377
Frank Ghamari, *President*
Fred Ghamarifard, *President*
Payman Khosravi, *CFO*
EMP: 70
SQ FT: 2,200
SALES (est): 9.3MM **Privately Held**
WEB: www.apollocouriers.com
SIC: 4215 Package delivery, vehicular

(P-4394)
CEA-PACK SERVICES INC
Also Called: Cea-Pack Logistics
12607 Hiddencreek Way, Cerritos (90703-2146)
P.O. Box 3777 (90703-3777)
PHONE..............................562 407-0660
Robert Ceja-Simpson, *President*
EMP: 235
SQ FT: 2,730
SALES (est): 16.6MM **Privately Held**
SIC: 4215 Parcel delivery, vehicular

(P-4395)
CLASSIC COURIERS INC (PA)
Also Called: A A A Couriers
1601 N El Centro Ave, Los Angeles (90028-6412)
P.O. Box 1069 (90078-1069)
PHONE..............................323 461-3741
Jose J Perez, *President*
Mario Alaniz, *CFO*
Eddie Perez, *Vice Pres*
Carol Lynn, *MIS Staff*
Chris Karapetyan, *Technology*
EMP: 65
SQ FT: 2,500
SALES (est): 8.1MM **Privately Held**
WEB: www.classic-couriers.com
SIC: 4215 Courier services, except by air

(P-4396)
COMPREMEX LLC
14849 Firestone Blvd, La Mirada (90638-6017)
P.O. Box 778030, Henderson NV (89077-8030)
PHONE..............................714 739-1348
Mike Catapano,
EMP: 200
SQ FT: 8,000
SALES (est): 9.7MM **Privately Held**
SIC: 4215 Courier services, except by air

(P-4397)
DYNAMEX INC
4790 Frontier Way Ste A, Stockton (95215-9424)
PHONE..............................209 464-7008
EMP: 60
SALES (corp-wide): 3.2B **Privately Held**
SIC: 4215
HQ: Dynamex Inc.
　5429 L B Johnson Fwy 90 Ste 900
　Dallas TX 75240
　214 560-9000

(P-4398)
DYNAMEX OPERATIONS WEST INC
16900 Valley View Ave, La Mirada (90638-5825)
PHONE..............................714 994-1615
Scott Levrage, *Manager*
EMP: 50

SALES (corp-wide): 3.7B **Privately Held**
SIC: 4215 Courier services, except by air
HQ: Dynamex Operations West, Inc
　1870 Crown Dr
　Dallas TX 75234

(P-4399)
EXECUTIVE EXPRESS INC (PA)
Also Called: Executive Ex Mssngr-Air Curier
2007 Quail St, Newport Beach (92660-2222)
P.O. Box 8382 (92658-8382)
PHONE..............................949 852-0450
James A Myers Jr, *President*
EMP: 65
SQ FT: 3,600
SALES (est): 4MM **Privately Held**
SIC: 4215 Parcel delivery, vehicular

(P-4400)
EXPRESS MESSENGER SYSTEMS INC
5829 Smithway St, Commerce (90040-1605)
PHONE..............................323 725-2100
Kim Kugel, *Branch Mgr*
EMP: 68 **Privately Held**
SIC: 4215 Courier services, except by air
PA: Express Messenger Systems, Inc.
　2501 S Price Rd Ste 201
　Chandler AZ 85286

(P-4401)
EXPRESS MESSENGER SYSTEMS INC
1627 Industrial Dr, Stockton (95206-4984)
PHONE..............................209 234-8255
EMP: 68 **Privately Held**
SIC: 4215 Courier services, except by air
PA: Express Messenger Systems, Inc.
　2501 S Price Rd Ste 201
　Chandler AZ 85286

(P-4402)
EXPRESS MESSENGER SYSTEMS INC
Also Called: California Overnight
555 Zephyr St, Stockton (95206-4209)
PHONE..............................209 234-8255
EMP: 64 **Privately Held**
SIC: 4215 Package delivery, vehicular
PA: Express Messenger Systems, Inc.
　2501 S Price Rd Ste 201
　Chandler AZ 85286

(P-4403)
EXPRESS MESSENGER SYSTEMS INC
Also Called: California Overnight
1240 S Allec St, Anaheim (92805-6301)
PHONE..............................949 235-1400
Dave Denholm, *Manager*
EMP: 70 **Privately Held**
WEB: www.calover.com
SIC: 4215 7389 Courier services, except by air; courier or messenger service
PA: Express Messenger Systems, Inc.
　2501 S Price Rd Ste 201
　Chandler AZ 85286

(P-4404)
EXPRESS MESSENGER SYSTEMS INC
Also Called: Ontrac
914 W Boone St, Santa Maria (93458-5450)
PHONE..............................800 488-2829
Polo Cabello, *Branch Mgr*
EMP: 70 **Privately Held**
SIC: 4215 Courier services, except by air
PA: Express Messenger Systems, Inc.
　2501 S Price Rd Ste 201
　Chandler AZ 85286

(P-4405)
EXPRESS MESSENGER SYSTEMS INC
Ontrac
11085 Olinda St, Sun Valley (91352-3302)
PHONE..............................818 504-9043
Christa Bognet, *Engineer*
Michael Harris, *Engineer*
Audra Ferguson, *Manager*
Larry Hardie, *Manager*
EMP: 119 **Privately Held**
SIC: 4215 Courier services, except by air
PA: Express Messenger Systems, Inc.
　2501 S Price Rd Ste 201
　Chandler AZ 85286

(P-4406)
EXPRESS MESSENGER SYSTEMS INC
Also Called: Ontrac
375 W Apra St, Compton (90220-5528)
PHONE..............................800 359-2959
Michael Kerper, *Principal*
EMP: 59 **Privately Held**
SIC: 4215 Package delivery, vehicular
PA: Express Messenger Systems, Inc.
　2501 S Price Rd Ste 201
　Chandler AZ 85286

(P-4407)
EXPRESS MESSENGER SYSTEMS INC
Also Called: Ontrac
250 Utah Ave, South San Francisco (94080-6801)
PHONE..............................650 553-4001
EMP: 59 **Privately Held**
SIC: 4215 Courier services, except by air
PA: Express Messenger Systems, Inc.
　2501 S Price Rd Ste 201
　Chandler AZ 85286

(P-4408)
EXPRESS MESSENGER SYSTEMS INC
Also Called: California Overnight
1635 Main Ave Ste 3, Sacramento (95838-2452)
PHONE..............................916 921-6016
Ian Burton, *Manager*
EMP: 60 **Privately Held**
WEB: www.calover.com
SIC: 4215 Package delivery, vehicular
PA: Express Messenger Systems, Inc.
　2501 S Price Rd Ste 201
　Chandler AZ 85286

(P-4409)
EXPRESS MESSENGER SYSTEMS INC
Also Called: Ontrac
4603 N Brawley Ave # 103, Fresno (93722-3960)
PHONE..............................559 277-4910
EMP: 56 **Privately Held**
SIC: 4215
PA: Express Messenger Systems, Inc.
　2501 S Price Rd Ste 201
　Chandler AZ 85286

(P-4410)
EXPRESS MESSENGER SYSTEMS INC
Also Called: California Overnight
101 Spear St Ste A1, San Francisco (94105-1557)
PHONE..............................415 495-7300
Fax: 415 495-7420
EMP: 63 **Privately Held**
SIC: 4215
PA: Express Messenger Systems, Inc.
　2501 S Price Rd Ste 201
　Chandler AZ 85286

▲ = Import ▼=Export
◆ =Import/Export

(P-4411)
FEDERAL EXPRESS CORPORATION
Also Called: Fedex
2660 Research Park Dr, Soquel (95073-2087)
PHONE..................................800 463-3339
David Rugherford, *Manager*
EMP: 56
SALES (corp-wide): 65.4B **Publicly Held**
SIC: 4215 Package delivery, vehicular
HQ: Federal Express Corporation
3610 Hacks Cross Rd
Memphis TN 38125
901 369-3600

(P-4412)
FEDERAL EXPRESS CORPORATION
Also Called: Fedex
1081 Fullerton Rd, City of Industry (91748-1234)
PHONE..................................800 463-3339
Raquel Moreno, *Manager*
Rick Sanqui, *Project Engr*
EMP: 200
SALES (corp-wide): 65.4B **Publicly Held**
WEB: www.federalexpress.com
SIC: 4215 4513 Package delivery, vehicular; package delivery, private air
HQ: Federal Express Corporation
3610 Hacks Cross Rd
Memphis TN 38125
901 369-3600

(P-4413)
FEDERAL EXPRESS CORPORATION
Also Called: Fedex
710 Dado St, San Jose (95131-1225)
PHONE..................................800 463-3339
Ruben Maines, *Manager*
Josh Lens, *Manager*
EMP: 150
SALES (corp-wide): 65.4B **Publicly Held**
WEB: www.federalexpress.com
SIC: 4215 4512 Package delivery, vehicular; air cargo carrier, scheduled
HQ: Federal Express Corporation
3610 Hacks Cross Rd
Memphis TN 38125
901 369-3600

(P-4414)
FEDERAL EXPRESS CORPORATION
Also Called: Fedex
9190 Edes Ave, Oakland (94603-1116)
PHONE..................................510 382-2344
EMP: 300
SALES (corp-wide): 47.4B **Publicly Held**
SIC: 4215 4513
HQ: Federal Express Corporation
3610 Hacks Cross Rd
Memphis TN 38125
901 369-3600

(P-4415)
FEDEX GROUND PACKAGE SYS INC
10132 Airway Rd, San Diego (92154-7901)
PHONE..................................800 463-3339
EMP: 104
SALES (corp-wide): 65.4B **Publicly Held**
SIC: 4215 Parcel delivery, vehicular
HQ: Fedex Ground Package System, Inc.
1000 Fed Ex Dr
Coraopolis PA 15108
412 269-1000

(P-4416)
FEDEX GROUND PACKAGE SYS INC
1070 San Mateo Ave, South San Francisco (94080-6601)
PHONE..................................800 463-3339
James Faris, *Manager*
Chad Allen, *Manager*
Dorothy Gorman, *Accounts Exec*
EMP: 50
SALES (corp-wide): 65.4B **Publicly Held**
SIC: 4215 Package delivery, vehicular

HQ: Fedex Ground Package System, Inc.
1000 Fed Ex Dr
Coraopolis PA 15108
412 269-1000

(P-4417)
FEDEX GROUND PACKAGE SYS INC
601 Stone Rd, Benicia (94510-1141)
PHONE..................................800 463-3339
Jeffrey Carowley, *Branch Mgr*
EMP: 89
SALES (corp-wide): 65.4B **Publicly Held**
SIC: 4215 Parcel delivery, vehicular
HQ: Fedex Ground Package System, Inc.
1000 Fed Ex Dr
Coraopolis PA 15108
412 269-1000

(P-4418)
FEDEX OFFICE & PRINT SVCS INC
8642 Whittier Blvd, Pico Rivera (90660-2655)
PHONE..................................562 942-1953
EMP: 100
SALES (corp-wide): 47.4B **Publicly Held**
SIC: 4215 5999 7221 7389
HQ: Fedex Office And Print Services, Inc.
7900 Legacy Dr
Dallas TX 75024
214 550-7000

(P-4419)
FEDEX SMARTPOST INC
5560 Ferguson Dr, Commerce (90022-5140)
PHONE..................................323 888-8879
EMP: 85
SALES (corp-wide): 47.4B **Publicly Held**
SIC: 4215
HQ: Fedex Smartpost, Inc.
16555 W Rogers Dr
New Berlin WI 53151
262 796-6800

(P-4420)
INTEGRATED PARCEL NETWORK
1706 W Orangethorpe Ave, Fullerton (92833-4538)
PHONE..................................714 278-6100
Nadia Youssef, *CEO*
EMP: 275
SQ FT: 30,000
SALES (est): 21MM **Privately Held**
WEB: www.pacific-couriers.com
SIC: 4215 4214 7389 Package delivery, vehicular; local trucking with storage; courier or messenger service

(P-4421)
JET DELIVERY INC (PA)
2169 Wright Ave, La Verne (91750-5835)
PHONE..................................800 716-7177
Michael Barbata, *President*
Mark Sur, *Vice Pres*
Jason Barbata, *CIO*
Shannon Cermak, *Controller*
Joseph Parra, *Accounts Exec*
EMP: 90
SQ FT: 34,000
SALES (est): 22.6MM **Privately Held**
WEB: www.jetdelivery.com
SIC: 4215 4231 4212 4213 Package delivery, vehicular; trucking terminal facilities; local trucking, without storage; trucking, except local

(P-4422)
MEDICAL COURIERS INC
176 Otto Cir, Sacramento (95822-3817)
PHONE..................................916 452-5700
Steve Reiff, *Vice Pres*
EMP: 85
SALES (est): 1.4MM **Privately Held**
SIC: 4215 Courier services, except by air

(P-4423)
MEDICAL COURIERS INC
1611 Neptune Dr, San Leandro (94577-3162)
PHONE..................................650 872-1144
Stephen Reiff, *President*
Richard Reiff, *Vice Pres*

EMP: 60
SQ FT: 5,000
SALES (est): 4.4MM **Privately Held**
SIC: 4215 Courier services, except by air

(P-4424)
MESSENGER EXPRESS (PA)
5435 Cahuenga Blvd Ste C, North Hollywood (91601-2948)
PHONE..................................213 614-0475
Gilbert Kort, *President*
EMP: 143
SALES (est): 5.4MM **Privately Held**
WEB: www.messengerexpress.net
SIC: 4215 7389 4212 Package delivery, vehicular; courier or messenger service; delivery service, vehicular

(P-4425)
MESSENGER EXPRESS
10671 Roselle St Ste 200, San Diego (92121-1525)
P.O. Box 12424 (92112-3424)
PHONE..................................858 550-1400
Greg King, *Manager*
EMP: 85
SALES (corp-wide): 5.4MM **Privately Held**
WEB: www.messengerexpress.net
SIC: 4215 Package delivery, vehicular
PA: Messenger Express
5435 Cahuenga Blvd Ste C
North Hollywood CA 91601
213 614-0475

(P-4426)
PEACH INC
Also Called: Action Messenger Service
1311 N Highland Ave, Los Angeles (90028-7608)
P.O. Box 69673 (90069-0673)
PHONE..................................323 654-2333
Arthur P Ruben, *President*
EMP: 125
SQ FT: 3,500
SALES: 5MM **Privately Held**
WEB: www.actionmessenger.com
SIC: 4215 7389 Courier services, except by air; courier or messenger service

(P-4427)
PRIORITY DISPATCH SERVICE INC
309 Laurelwood Rd Ste 10, Santa Clara (95054-2313)
PHONE..................................408 400-3860
Walter Strobel, *CEO*
EMP: 60 **EST**: 2009
SALES: 950K **Privately Held**
SIC: 4215 Courier services, except by air

(P-4428)
RAPPI INC
353 Mission St Fl 14, San Francisco (94105)
PHONE..................................347 740-4824
Sebastian Mejia, *Founder*
EMP: 497 **EST**: 2016
SALES (est): 5.3MM **Privately Held**
SIC: 4215 Courier services, except by air

(P-4429)
SAN DIEGO MESSENGER INC
Also Called: The Messenger Company
4848 Ronson Ct Ste G, San Diego (92111-1809)
PHONE..................................858 514-8866
Richard Villalodos, *President*
Rick Smith, *Vice Pres*
EMP: 50 **EST**: 2000
SQ FT: 3,000
SALES: 1.3MM **Privately Held**
SIC: 4215 Courier services, except by air

(P-4430)
SUNRISE DELIVERY SERVICE INC
13351 Riverside Dr 672d, Sherman Oaks (91423-2542)
PHONE..................................323 464-5121
Charles R Audia, *President*
EMP: 60
SQ FT: 3,000
SALES (est): 4.5MM **Privately Held**
SIC: 4215 Courier services, except by air

(P-4431)
SYNCTRUCK LLC
415 Darrell Rd, Hillsborough (94010-6709)
PHONE..................................415 425-0447
Luis Toledo, *Principal*
EMP: 116
SALES (est): 4.2MM **Privately Held**
SIC: 4215 Package delivery, vehicular
PA: Synctruck Llc
510 Eccles Ave
South San Francisco CA 94080
650 239-6231

(P-4432)
TELE-CAR COURIERS INC
Also Called: Tele-Car Courier Service
4035 Eagle Rock Blvd, Los Angeles (90065-3607)
PHONE..................................877 910-1313
Shagen Galstanyan, *Principal*
EMP: 75
SALES: 2.8MM **Privately Held**
SIC: 4215 Courier services, except by air

(P-4433)
TF COURIER INC
8331 Demetre Ave, Sacramento (95828-0920)
PHONE..................................916 379-0708
Ed Feliciano, *Manager*
Gabriel Santos, *Opers Mgr*
Terrence Johnson, *Supervisor*
EMP: 60
SALES (corp-wide): 3.7B **Privately Held**
SIC: 4215 Courier services, except by air
HQ: Tf Courier, Inc.
5429 Lyndon B Johnson Fwy
Dallas TX 75240

(P-4434)
TF COURIER INC
7130 Miramar Rd Ste 400, San Diego (92121-2340)
PHONE..................................888 541-2965
John Mc Loughlin, *Manager*
Steve Merriweather, *Opers Mgr*
EMP: 60
SALES (corp-wide): 3.7B **Privately Held**
SIC: 4215 Courier services, except by air
HQ: Tf Courier, Inc.
5429 Lyndon B Johnson Fwy
Dallas TX 75240

(P-4435)
TF COURIER INC
2051 Raymer Ave Ste A, Fullerton (92833-2678)
PHONE..................................714 888-1452
Scott Leveridge, *Manager*
EMP: 70
SALES (corp-wide): 3.7B **Privately Held**
SIC: 4215 Courier services, except by air
HQ: Tf Courier, Inc.
5429 Lyndon B Johnson Fwy
Dallas TX 75240

(P-4436)
TF COURIER INC
21760 Garcia Ln, City of Industry (91789-0940)
PHONE..................................214 560-9000
EMP: 60
SALES (corp-wide): 3.7B **Privately Held**
SIC: 4215 Courier services, except by air
HQ: Tf Courier, Inc.
5429 Lyndon B Johnson Fwy
Dallas TX 75240

(P-4437)
TOP PRIORITY COURIERS INC (PA)
1257 Columbia Ave Ste D1, Riverside (92507-2124)
P.O. Box 20376 (92516-0376)
PHONE..................................951 781-1000
Siroos Zakikhani, *President*
Rick Johnson, *Exec VP*
EMP: 60
SQ FT: 6,000

PRODUCTS & SVCS

SALES (est): 10.8MM **Privately Held**
WEB: www.topprioritycouriers.com
SIC: 4215 Package delivery, vehicular

(P-4438)
TRICOR AMERICA INC
1465 N Brasher St, Anaheim (92807-2048)
PHONE..................................714 701-9880
David Solis, *Branch Mgr*
EMP: 60
SALES (corp-wide): 92.9MM **Privately Held**
WEB: www.tricor.com
SIC: 4215 Parcel delivery, vehicular; package delivery, vehicular
PA: Tricor America, Inc.
　　717 Airport Blvd
　　South San Francisco CA 94080
　　650 877-3650

(P-4439)
TRICOR AMERICA INC
Also Called: Tricor California
1690 Cebrian St, West Sacramento (95691-3802)
PHONE..................................916 371-1704
Fred Kamper, *Branch Mgr*
EMP: 125
SALES (corp-wide): 92.9MM **Privately Held**
WEB: www.tricor.com
SIC: 4215 4212 Courier services, except by air; delivery service, vehicular
PA: Tricor America, Inc.
　　717 Airport Blvd
　　South San Francisco CA 94080
　　650 877-3650

(P-4440)
ULTRAEX LLC
2633 Barrington Ct, Hayward (94545-1100)
PHONE..................................510 723-3760
William Carlson,
Alfredo Flores,
Ernesto Holbrook,
EMP: 75 **EST:** 2014
SALES (est): 3.1MM **Privately Held**
SIC: 4215 4513 4225 Courier services, except by air; air courier services; general warehousing & storage

(P-4441)
UNITED PARCEL SERVICE INC
Also Called: UPS
12745 Arroyo St, Sylmar (91342-5332)
PHONE..................................800 742-5877
EMP: 86
SALES (corp-wide): 65.8B **Publicly Held**
SIC: 4215 4513 4522 Package delivery, vehicular; parcel delivery, vehicular; letter delivery, private air; package delivery, private air; parcel delivery, private air; flying charter service
PA: United Parcel Service, Inc.
　　55 Glenlake Pkwy
　　Atlanta GA 30328
　　404 828-6000

(P-4442)
UNITED PARCEL SERVICE INC
Also Called: UPS
657 Forbes Blvd, South San Francisco (94080-2059)
PHONE..................................650 737-3737
Timothy Huxtable, *Branch Mgr*
Brian Wasem, *Area Mgr*
EMP: 159
SALES (corp-wide): 65.8B **Publicly Held**
WEB: www.martrac.com
SIC: 4215 Parcel delivery, vehicular
PA: United Parcel Service, Inc.
　　55 Glenlake Pkwy
　　Atlanta GA 30328
　　404 828-6000

(P-4443)
UNITED PARCEL SERVICE INC
OH
Also Called: UPS
160 W Main St, El Centro (92243-2513)
PHONE..................................858 541-2336
Edgar Zaragoza, *Manager*
EMP: 85

SALES (corp-wide): 65.8B **Publicly Held**
WEB: www.upsscs.com
SIC: 4215 4513 Parcel delivery, vehicular; parcel delivery, private air
HQ: United Parcel Service, Inc. (Oh)
　　55 Glenlake Pkwy
　　Atlanta GA 30328
　　404 828-6000

(P-4444)
UNITED PARCEL SERVICE INC
OH
Also Called: UPS
650 N Commercial Rd, Palm Springs (92262-6299)
PHONE..................................760 325-1762
Doug Nelson, *Manager*
Rick Vanden Bossche, *Business Mgr*
Richard Day, *Manager*
Rick Vandenbossche, *Manager*
EMP: 500
SALES (corp-wide): 65.8B **Publicly Held**
WEB: www.upsscs.com
SIC: 4215 4513 Parcel delivery, vehicular; air courier services
HQ: United Parcel Service, Inc. (Oh)
　　55 Glenlake Pkwy
　　Atlanta GA 30328
　　404 828-6000

(P-4445)
UNITED PARCEL SERVICE INC
OH
Also Called: UPS
1601 Atlas Rd, Richmond (94806-1101)
PHONE..................................510 262-2338
Jim Kelly, *President*
EMP: 152
SALES (corp-wide): 65.8B **Publicly Held**
WEB: www.upsscs.com
SIC: 4215 4513 Parcel delivery, vehicular; air courier services
HQ: United Parcel Service, Inc. (Oh)
　　55 Glenlake Pkwy
　　Atlanta GA 30328
　　404 828-6000

(P-4446)
UNITED PARCEL SERVICE INC
OH
Also Called: UPS
1139 Madison Ln, Salinas (93907-1817)
PHONE..................................831 758-9112
EMP: 158
SQ FT: 3,000
SALES (corp-wide): 65.8B **Publicly Held**
SIC: 4215 Parcel delivery, vehicular
HQ: United Parcel Service, Inc. (Oh)
　　55 Glenlake Pkwy
　　Atlanta GA 30328
　　404 828-6000

(P-4447)
UNITED PARCEL SERVICE INC
OH
Also Called: UPS
2800 W 227th St, Torrance (90505-2912)
PHONE..................................800 742-5877
EMP: 80
SALES (corp-wide): 65.8B **Publicly Held**
WEB: www.upsscs.com
SIC: 4215 Package delivery, vehicular
HQ: United Parcel Service, Inc. (Oh)
　　55 Glenlake Pkwy
　　Atlanta GA 30328
　　404 828-6000

(P-4448)
UNITED PARCEL SERVICE INC
OH
Also Called: UPS
6845 Eastside Rd, Anderson (96007-9406)
PHONE..................................530 365-7850
Lauren Lnd, *Manager*
EMP: 100
SALES (corp-wide): 65.8B **Publicly Held**
WEB: www.upsscs.com
SIC: 4215 4213 Parcel delivery, vehicular; trucking, except local
HQ: United Parcel Service, Inc. (Oh)
　　55 Glenlake Pkwy
　　Atlanta GA 30328
　　404 828-6000

(P-4449)
UNITED PARCEL SERVICE INC
OH
Also Called: UPS
2915 N Sierra Hwy, Bishop (93514-7633)
PHONE..................................760 872-7661
EMP: 158
SALES (corp-wide): 65.8B **Publicly Held**
WEB: www.upsscs.com
SIC: 4215 Parcel delivery, vehicular
HQ: United Parcel Service, Inc. (Oh)
　　55 Glenlake Pkwy
　　Atlanta GA 30328
　　404 828-6000

(P-4450)
UNITED PARCEL SERVICE INC
OH
Also Called: UPS
5000 W Cordelia Rd, Fairfield (94534-1628)
PHONE..................................707 864-8200
EMP: 158
SALES (corp-wide): 65.8B **Publicly Held**
SIC: 4215 Parcel delivery, vehicular
HQ: United Parcel Service, Inc. (Oh)
　　55 Glenlake Pkwy
　　Atlanta GA 30328
　　404 828-6000

(P-4451)
UNITED PARCEL SERVICE INC
OH
Also Called: UPS
1400 Hil Mor Dr, Ceres (95307-9292)
PHONE..................................800 742-5877
Dave Walker, *Principal*
EMP: 200
SALES (corp-wide): 65.8B **Publicly Held**
WEB: www.upsscs.com
SIC: 4215 Parcel delivery, vehicular
HQ: United Parcel Service, Inc. (Oh)
　　55 Glenlake Pkwy
　　Atlanta GA 30328
　　404 828-6000

(P-4452)
UNITED PARCEL SERVICE INC
OH
Also Called: UPS
1380 Shore St, West Sacramento (95691-3522)
PHONE..................................916 373-4076
Tom Karls, *Manager*
EMP: 200
SALES (corp-wide): 65.8B **Publicly Held**
WEB: www.upsscs.com
SIC: 4215 Parcel delivery, vehicular
HQ: United Parcel Service, Inc. (Oh)
　　55 Glenlake Pkwy
　　Atlanta GA 30328
　　404 828-6000

(P-4453)
UNITED PARCEL SERVICE INC
OH
Also Called: UPS
2531 Napa Valley Corp Dr, NAPA (94558)
PHONE..................................707 224-1205
Josh Young, *Principal*
EMP: 158
SALES (corp-wide): 65.8B **Publicly Held**
SIC: 4215 Package delivery, vehicular
HQ: United Parcel Service, Inc. (Oh)
　　55 Glenlake Pkwy
　　Atlanta GA 30328
　　404 828-6000

(P-4454)
UNITED PARCEL SERVICE INC
OH
Also Called: UPS
128 Shore St, Sacramento (95829)
PHONE..................................916 373-4089
Chris Wagner, *Manager*
EMP: 70
SALES (corp-wide): 65.8B **Publicly Held**
WEB: www.upsscs.com
SIC: 4215 Parcel delivery, vehicular
HQ: United Parcel Service, Inc. (Oh)
　　55 Glenlake Pkwy
　　Atlanta GA 30328
　　404 828-6000

(P-4455)
UNITED PARCEL SERVICE INC
OH
Also Called: UPS
17115 S Western Ave, Gardena (90247-5299)
PHONE..................................310 217-2646
Randy Hulhellt, *Manager*
Rick Garcia, *General Mgr*
Roger Flores, *Opers Mgr*
EMP: 500
SALES (corp-wide): 65.8B **Publicly Held**
WEB: www.upsscs.com
SIC: 4215 4513 Parcel delivery, vehicular; air courier services
HQ: United Parcel Service, Inc. (Oh)
　　55 Glenlake Pkwy
　　Atlanta GA 30328
　　404 828-6000

(P-4456)
UNITED PARCEL SERVICE INC
OH
Also Called: UPS
1999 S 7th St, San Jose (95112-6009)
PHONE..................................408 291-2942
Frank Cademarti, *Manager*
Peter Kolotouros, *Director*
EMP: 300
SALES (corp-wide): 65.8B **Publicly Held**
WEB: www.upsscs.com
SIC: 4215 Parcel delivery, vehicular
HQ: United Parcel Service, Inc. (Oh)
　　55 Glenlake Pkwy
　　Atlanta GA 30328
　　404 828-6000

(P-4457)
UNITED PARCEL SERVICE INC
OH
UPS
2222 17th St, San Francisco (94103-5015)
PHONE..................................415 252-4564
Tom Dalto, *Manager*
EMP: 152
SALES (corp-wide): 65.8B **Publicly Held**
WEB: www.upsscs.com
SIC: 4215 4513 Parcel delivery, vehicular; air courier services
HQ: United Parcel Service, Inc. (Oh)
　　55 Glenlake Pkwy
　　Atlanta GA 30328
　　404 828-6000

(P-4458)
UNITED PARCEL SERVICE INC
OH
Also Called: UPS
1012 Sterling St, Vallejo (94591-8686)
PHONE..................................707 252-4560
EMP: 165
SALES (corp-wide): 65.8B **Publicly Held**
WEB: www.upsscs.com
SIC: 4215 Parcel delivery, vehicular
HQ: United Parcel Service, Inc. (Oh)
　　55 Glenlake Pkwy
　　Atlanta GA 30328
　　404 828-6000

(P-4459)
UNITED PARCEL SERVICE INC
OH
Also Called: UPS
6060 Cornerstone Ct W, San Diego (92121-3712)
PHONE..................................858 455-8800
Donald Higginson, *Vice Pres*
Jay Patel, *General Mgr*
Andrew White, *Business Mgr*
Tiffany Drumm, *Director*
Shruti Bhalla, *Manager*
EMP: 158
SALES (corp-wide): 65.8B **Publicly Held**
SIC: 4215 Parcel delivery, vehicular
HQ: United Parcel Service, Inc. (Oh)
　　55 Glenlake Pkwy
　　Atlanta GA 30328
　　404 828-6000

(P-4460)

UNITED PARCEL SERVICE INC
OH
Also Called: UPS
10690 Santa Monica Blvd, Los Angeles
(90025-4838)
PHONE...................310 474-0019
EMP: 158
SALES (corp-wide): 65.8B **Publicly Held**
SIC: 4215 Parcel delivery, vehicular
HQ: United Parcel Service, Inc. (Oh)
55 Glenlake Pkwy
Atlanta GA 30328
404 828-6000

(P-4461)

UNITED PARCEL SERVICE INC
OH
Also Called: UPS
22 Brookline, Aliso Viejo (92656-1461)
PHONE...................949 643-6595
Carolyn Macneil, *Branch Mgr*
EMP: 152
SALES (corp-wide): 65.8B **Publicly Held**
SIC: 4215 Parcel delivery, vehicular
HQ: United Parcel Service, Inc. (Oh)
55 Glenlake Pkwy
Atlanta GA 30328
404 828-6000

(P-4462)

UNITED PARCEL SERVICE INC
OH
Also Called: UPS
22 Brookline, Aliso Viejo (92656-1461)
PHONE...................951 377-8253
Scott Corrigan, *Manager*
EMP: 60
SQ FT: 10,000
SALES (corp-wide): 65.8B **Publicly Held**
WEB: www.upsscs.com
SIC: 4215 Parcel delivery, vehicular
HQ: United Parcel Service, Inc. (Oh)
55 Glenlake Pkwy
Atlanta GA 30328
404 828-6000

(P-4463)

UNITED PARCEL SERVICE INC
OH
Also Called: UPS
290 W Avenue L, Lancaster (93534-7109)
PHONE...................800 828-8264
James Adams, *Principal*
EMP: 150
SALES (corp-wide): 65.8B **Publicly Held**
WEB: www.upsscs.com
SIC: 4215 Parcel delivery, vehicular
HQ: United Parcel Service, Inc. (Oh)
55 Glenlake Pkwy
Atlanta GA 30328
404 828-6000

(P-4464)

UNITED PARCEL SERVICE INC
OH
Also Called: UPS
16000 Arminta St, Van Nuys (91406-1895)
PHONE...................404 828-6000
EMP: 158
SALES (corp-wide): 65.8B **Publicly Held**
SIC: 4215 Parcel delivery, vehicular
HQ: United Parcel Service, Inc. (Oh)
55 Glenlake Pkwy
Atlanta GA 30328
404 828-6000

(P-4465)

UNITED PARCEL SERVICE INC
OH
Also Called: UPS
7925 Ronson Rd, San Diego (92111-1997)
PHONE...................909 279-5111
Keith Hughes, *Marketing Mgr*
Jeff Walsingham, *Marketing Mgr*
EMP: 158
SALES (corp-wide): 65.8B **Publicly Held**
SIC: 4215 Parcel delivery, vehicular
HQ: United Parcel Service, Inc. (Oh)
55 Glenlake Pkwy
Atlanta GA 30328
404 828-6000

(P-4466)

UNITED PARCEL SERVICE INC
OH
Also Called: UPS
8400 Pardee Dr, Oakland (94621-1456)
PHONE...................510 813-5662
Denise Padilla, *Sales Mgr*
EMP: 158
SALES (corp-wide): 65.8B **Publicly Held**
SIC: 4215 Parcel delivery, vehicular
HQ: United Parcel Service, Inc. (Oh)
55 Glenlake Pkwy
Atlanta GA 30328
404 828-6000

(P-4467)

UNITED PARCEL SERVICE INC
OH
Also Called: UPS
13233 Moore St, Cerritos (90703-2276)
PHONE...................562 404-3236
Gary Mieredos, *Manager*
EMP: 152
SALES (corp-wide): 65.8B **Publicly Held**
WEB: www.upsscs.com
SIC: 4215 Parcel delivery, vehicular
HQ: United Parcel Service, Inc. (Oh)
55 Glenlake Pkwy
Atlanta GA 30328
404 828-6000

(P-4468)

UNITED PARCEL SERVICE INC
OH
Also Called: UPS
259 Cherry St, Ukiah (95482-5804)
PHONE...................707 468-5481
EMP: 158
SALES (corp-wide): 65.8B **Publicly Held**
WEB: www.upsscs.com
SIC: 4215 Parcel delivery, vehicular
HQ: United Parcel Service, Inc. (Oh)
55 Glenlake Pkwy
Atlanta GA 30328
404 828-6000

(P-4469)

UNITED PARCEL SERVICE INC
OH
Also Called: UPS
6 Upper Ragsdale Dr, Monterey
(93940-5730)
PHONE...................831 757-6294
EMP: 158
SALES (corp-wide): 65.8B **Publicly Held**
SIC: 4215 Courier services, except by air
HQ: United Parcel Service, Inc. (Oh)
55 Glenlake Pkwy
Atlanta GA 30328
404 828-6000

(P-4470)

UNITED PARCEL SERVICE INC
OH
Also Called: UPS
3601 Sacramento Dr, San Luis Obispo
(93401-7115)
PHONE...................801 973-3400
EMP: 158
SALES (corp-wide): 65.8B **Publicly Held**
SIC: 4215 Parcel delivery, vehicular
HQ: United Parcel Service, Inc. (Oh)
55 Glenlake Pkwy
Atlanta GA 30328
404 828-6000

(P-4471)

UNITED PARCEL SERVICE INC
OH
Also Called: UPS
3860 Cypress Dr, Petaluma (94954-5613)
PHONE...................650 952-5200
Richard Catton, *Supervisor*
EMP: 158
SALES (corp-wide): 65.8B **Publicly Held**
SIC: 4215 Parcel delivery, vehicular
HQ: United Parcel Service, Inc. (Oh)
55 Glenlake Pkwy
Atlanta GA 30328
404 828-6000

(P-4472)

UNITED PARCEL SERVICE INC
OH
Also Called: UPS
1970 Olivera Rd, Concord (94520-5425)
PHONE...................925 689-6584
EMP: 158
SALES (corp-wide): 65.8B **Publicly Held**
SIC: 4215 Parcel delivery, vehicular
HQ: United Parcel Service, Inc. (Oh)
55 Glenlake Pkwy
Atlanta GA 30328
404 828-6000

(P-4473)

UNITED PARCEL SERVICE INC
OH
Also Called: UPS
505 Pine Ave, Goleta (93117-3707)
PHONE...................805 964-7848
Jason Chang, *Manager*
EMP: 112
SALES (corp-wide): 65.8B **Publicly Held**
WEB: www.upsscs.com
SIC: 4215 Parcel delivery, vehicular
HQ: United Parcel Service, Inc. (Oh)
55 Glenlake Pkwy
Atlanta GA 30328
404 828-6000

(P-4474)

UNITED PARCEL SERVICE INC
OH
Also Called: UPS
309 Cooley Ln, Santa Maria (93455-1218)
PHONE...................805 922-7851
Michael King, *Manager*
EMP: 140
SALES (corp-wide): 65.8B **Publicly Held**
WEB: www.upsscs.com
SIC: 4215 Parcel delivery, vehicular
HQ: United Parcel Service, Inc. (Oh)
55 Glenlake Pkwy
Atlanta GA 30328
404 828-6000

(P-4475)

UNITED PARCEL SERVICE INC
OH
Also Called: UPS
2342 Gun Club Rd, Angels Camp (95222)
PHONE...................209 736-0878
EMP: 158
SALES (corp-wide): 65.8B **Publicly Held**
SIC: 4215 Parcel delivery, vehicular
HQ: United Parcel Service, Inc. (Oh)
55 Glenlake Pkwy
Atlanta GA 30328
404 828-6000

(P-4476)

UNITED PARCEL SERVICE INC
OH
Also Called: UPS
1501 Rancho Conejo Blvd, Newbury Park
(91320-1410)
PHONE...................805 375-1832
Grant Nissan, *Branch Mgr*
EMP: 200
SALES (corp-wide): 65.8B **Publicly Held**
WEB: www.upsscs.com
SIC: 4215 Parcel delivery, vehicular
HQ: United Parcel Service, Inc. (Oh)
55 Glenlake Pkwy
Atlanta GA 30328
404 828-6000

(P-4477)

UNITED PARCEL SERVICE INC
OH
Also Called: UPS
1355 Adams Ct, Menlo Park (94025-1443)
PHONE...................650 952-5200
Kathy Spivey, *Branch Mgr*
EMP: 152
SALES (corp-wide): 65.8B **Publicly Held**
WEB: www.upsscs.com
SIC: 4215 Parcel delivery, vehicular
HQ: United Parcel Service, Inc. (Oh)
55 Glenlake Pkwy
Atlanta GA 30328
404 828-6000

(P-4478)

UNITED PARCEL SERVICE INC
OH
Also Called: UPS
3000 E Washington Blvd, Los Angeles
(90023-4220)
PHONE...................323 729-6762
Art Nakamoto, *Branch Mgr*
EMP: 800
SALES (corp-wide): 65.8B **Publicly Held**
WEB: www.upsscs.com
SIC: 4215 Parcel delivery, vehicular
HQ: United Parcel Service, Inc. (Oh)
55 Glenlake Pkwy
Atlanta GA 30328
404 828-6000

(P-4479)

UNITED PARCEL SERVICE INC
OH
Also Called: UPS
2300 Boswell Ct, Chula Vista (91914-3520)
PHONE...................619 482-8119
Erik Archambault, *Director*
EMP: 158
SALES (corp-wide): 65.8B **Publicly Held**
SIC: 4215 Parcel delivery, vehicular
HQ: United Parcel Service, Inc. (Oh)
55 Glenlake Pkwy
Atlanta GA 30328
404 828-6000

(P-4480)

UNITED PARCEL SERVICE INC
OH
Also Called: UPS
7401 W Sunnyview Ave, Visalia
(93291-9601)
PHONE...................559 651-7690
Dave Hill, *Manager*
EMP: 100
SALES (corp-wide): 65.8B **Publicly Held**
WEB: www.upsscs.com
SIC: 4215 7322 Parcel delivery, vehicular;
adjustment & collection services
HQ: United Parcel Service, Inc. (Oh)
55 Glenlake Pkwy
Atlanta GA 30328
404 828-6000

(P-4481)

UNITED PARCEL SERVICE INC
OH
Also Called: UPS
251 Sylvania Ave, Santa Cruz
(95060-2161)
PHONE...................831 425-1054
EMP: 158
SALES (corp-wide): 65.8B **Publicly Held**
WEB: www.upsscs.com
SIC: 4215 Courier services, except by air
HQ: United Parcel Service, Inc. (Oh)
55 Glenlake Pkwy
Atlanta GA 30328
404 828-6000

(P-4482)

UNITED PARCEL SERVICE INC
OH
Also Called: UPS
3140 Jurupa St, Ontario (91761-2902)
PHONE...................909 974-7000
Brenda Hiza, *Branch Mgr*
EMP: 80
SALES (corp-wide): 65.8B **Publicly Held**
WEB: www.upsscs.com
SIC: 4215 Package delivery, vehicular; par-
cel delivery, vehicular
HQ: United Parcel Service, Inc. (Oh)
55 Glenlake Pkwy
Atlanta GA 30328
404 828-6000

(P-4483)

UNITED PARCEL SERVICE INC
OH
Also Called: UPS
4500 Norris Canyon Rd, San Ramon
(94583-1369)
PHONE...................800 833-9943
EMP: 164
SALES (corp-wide): 65.8B **Publicly Held**
WEB: www.upsscs.com
SIC: 4215 Courier services, except by air

PRODUCTS & SVCS

HQ: United Parcel Service, Inc. (Oh)
55 Glenlake Pkwy
Atlanta GA 30328
404 828-6000

(P-4484)
UNITED PARCEL SERVICE INC
OH
Also Called: UPS
2559 Palma Dr, Ventura (93003-5733)
PHONE.................................805 642-6784
EMP: 158
SALES (corp-wide): 65.8B Publicly Held
WEB: www.upsscs.com
SIC: 4215 Courier services, except by air
HQ: United Parcel Service, Inc. (Oh)
55 Glenlake Pkwy
Atlanta GA 30328
404 828-6000

(P-4485)
UNITED PARCEL SERVICE INC
OH
Also Called: UPS
1100 Baldwin Park Blvd, Baldwin Park
(91706-5895)
PHONE.................................626 814-6216
Lero Stamply, Manager
EMP: 200
SALES (corp-wide): 65.8B Publicly Held
WEB: www.upsscs.com
SIC: 4215 4513 Parcel delivery, vehicular;
air courier services
HQ: United Parcel Service, Inc. (Oh)
55 Glenlake Pkwy
Atlanta GA 30328
404 828-6000

(P-4486)
UNITED PARCEL SERVICE INC
OH
Also Called: UPS
3930 Kristi Ct, Sacramento (95827-9716)
PHONE.................................916 857-0311
EMP: 152
SALES (corp-wide): 65.8B Publicly Held
SIC: 4215 Parcel delivery, vehicular
HQ: United Parcel Service, Inc. (Oh)
55 Glenlake Pkwy
Atlanta GA 30328
404 828-6000

(P-4487)
UNITY COURIER SERVICE INC
(PA)
3231 Fletcher Dr, Los Angeles
(90065-2919)
PHONE.................................323 255-9800
Ali Sharifi, President
Larry Lum, CEO
Eric Cook, IT/INT Sup
Louis Lipson, Controller
Corina Martinez, Human Res Mgr
EMP: 700
SQ FT: 11,000
SALES (est): 64.3MM Privately Held
WEB: www.unitycourier.com
SIC: 4215 Package delivery, vehicular

4221 Farm Product
Warehousing & Storage

(P-4488)
BUTTE-YB-STTER WTR QLTY
CLTION
625 Cooper Ave, Yuba City (95991-3864)
P.O. Box 729 (95992-0729)
PHONE.................................530 673-5131
Stephen F Danna, Chairman
Claudia Street, General Mgr
EMP: 75
SALES: 428.7K Privately Held
SIC: 4221 Farm product warehousing &
storage

(P-4489)
HONEYVILLE INC
11600 Dayton Dr, Rancho Cucamonga
(91730-5525)
PHONE.................................909 980-9500
Johnny Ferry, President
Edgar Hinojosa, Research
Devin Bergquist, Human Res Mgr

Manuel Barrera, Sales Staff
Enrique Erazo, Manager
EMP: 85
SALES (corp-wide): 181.2MM Privately
Held
WEB: www.honeyvillegrain.com
SIC: 4221 5153 2045 2041 Grain eleva-
tor, storage only; grains; prepared flour
mixes & doughs; flour & other grain mill
products
PA: Honeyville, Inc.
1040 W 600 N
Ogden UT 84404
435 494-4193

(P-4490)
PURATOS CORPORATION
Also Called: Puratos Bakery Supply
11167 White Birch Dr, Rancho Cucamonga
(91730-3820)
PHONE.................................909 484-1312
Ron Bouter, General Mgr
EMP: 100 Privately Held
WEB: www.puratos.com
SIC: 4221 2041 Farm product warehous-
ing & storage; flour
HQ: Puratos Corporation
1660 Suckle Hwy
Pennsauken NJ 08110

(P-4491)
VEG-LAND INC
Also Called: J B J Distributing
1518 E Valencia Dr, Fullerton (92831-4734)
P.O. Box 1287 (92836-8287)
PHONE.................................714 871-6712
James E Matiasevich, President
John P Matiasevich, Corp Secy
EMP: 50 EST: 1976
SQ FT: 70,000
SALES (est): 6.3MM
SALES (corp-wide): 24MM Privately
Held
SIC: 4221 Farm product warehousing &
storage
PA: Veg Land Sales Inc
1518 E Valencia Dr
Fullerton CA 92831
714 871-6712

4222 Refrigerated
Warehousing & Storage

(P-4492)
AMERICOLD LOGISTICS LLC
Also Called: (P&O COLD LOGISTICS, LLC)
2750 Orbiter St, Brea (92821-6256)
PHONE.................................714 993-3533
Brent Sugden,
Randy Benish, Regional VP
Rich Kappmeier, Regional VP
Hal Leddy, Regional VP
Richard Bastianelli, Senior VP
EMP: 1230 EST: 1952
SQ FT: 194,000
SALES (est): 899.2K
SALES (corp-wide): 1.5B Privately Held
SIC: 4222 Warehousing, cold storage or
refrigerated
HQ: Versacold U.S. Inc
19840 S Rancho Way
Compton CA 90220
310 632-6265

(P-4493)
AMERICOLD LOGISTICS LLC
1415 N Raymond Ave, Anaheim
(92801-1111)
PHONE.................................678 441-1468
Tony Esquivel, Branch Mgr
Kevin Alderson, General Mgr
Montes Armondo, Manager
EMP: 60
SALES (corp-wide): 1.5B Privately Held
SIC: 4222 4213 Warehousing, cold stor-
age or refrigerated; refrigerated products
transport
HQ: Americold Logistics, Llc
10 Glenlake Pkwy Ste 324
Atlanta GA 30328
678 441-1400

(P-4494)
AMERICOLD LOGISTICS LLC
950 S Sanborn Rd, Salinas (93901-4530)
P.O. Box 1548 (93902-1548)
PHONE.................................831 424-1537
Pat Zimmerman, General Mgr
EMP: 50
SALES (corp-wide): 1.5B Privately Held
SIC: 4222 Warehousing, cold storage or
refrigerated
HQ: Americold Logistics, Llc
10 Glenlake Pkwy Ste 324
Atlanta GA 30328
678 441-1400

(P-4495)
AMERICOLD LOGISTICS LLC
Also Called: Americold Realty
700 Malaga St, Ontario (91761-8627)
PHONE.................................909 390-4950
Jeff Canfield, Manager
Anthony Espinoza, General Mgr
Bonne Martin, Admin Asst
Jose Juarez, Opers Mgr
EMP: 50
SALES (corp-wide): 1.5B Privately Held
WEB: www.americoldlogistics.com
SIC: 4222 Warehousing, cold storage or
refrigerated
HQ: Americold Logistics, Llc
10 Glenlake Pkwy Ste 324
Atlanta GA 30328
678 441-1400

(P-4496)
AMERICOLD LOGISTICS LLC
3420 E Vernon Ave, Vernon (90058-1812)
PHONE.................................323 581-0025
Ian McGagh, Branch Mgr
Mike Cardenas, Opers Mgr
EMP: 78
SALES (corp-wide): 1.5B Privately Held
SIC: 4222 Warehousing, cold storage or
refrigerated
HQ: Americold Logistics, Llc
10 Glenlake Pkwy Ste 324
Atlanta GA 30328
678 441-1400

(P-4497)
CAL PACKING & STORAGE LP
Also Called: Bravante Produce
1356 S Buttonwillow Ave, Reedley
(93654-9333)
PHONE.................................559 638-2929
George Bravante, Managing Prtnr
Ken Collins, Manager
Steve Spaulding, Manager
Richard Sullivan, Manager
EMP: 70
SQ FT: 100,000
SALES (est): 12.1MM Privately Held
SIC: 4222 7389 5148 Warehousing, cold
storage or refrigerated; packaging & la-
beling services; fresh fruits & vegetables

(P-4498)
CENTRAL COAST COOLING
LLC
1107 Merrill St, Salinas (93901-4430)
P.O. Box 1527 (93902-1527)
PHONE.................................831 422-7265
Mike Storm, President
Denny Bertlesman, Vice Pres
EMP: 90
SQ FT: 30,000
SALES (est): 15MM Privately Held
WEB: www.centralcoastcooling.com
SIC: 4222 Warehousing, cold storage or
refrigerated

(P-4499)
DELMART COLD STORAGE CO
INC
1401 19th St, Bakersfield (93301-4453)
PHONE.................................661 849-8608
Robert Vignolo, Principal
EMP: 85
SALES (corp-wide): 8.5MM Privately
Held
SIC: 4222 Warehousing, cold storage or
refrigerated

PA: Delmart Cold Storage Co Inc
30988 Riverside Ave
Shafter CA 93263
661 746-2148

(P-4500)
E STREET COLD LOGISTICS
LLC (PA)
901 E E St, Wilmington (90744-6144)
PHONE.................................310 233-7300
Richard Burke, Mng Member
G Brent Larson, Exec VP
EMP: 50
SQ FT: 150,000
SALES (est): 4.9MM Privately Held
SIC: 4222 Warehousing, cold storage or
refrigerated

(P-4501)
EXEL N AMERCN LOGISTICS
INC
Freeze Point Cold Storage Div
3735 Imperial Way, Stockton (95215-9691)
PHONE.................................209 942-0102
Mike Hernandez, Manager
Chris Lares, Opers Mgr
EMP: 100
SALES (corp-wide): 71.2B Privately Held
SIC: 4222 Storage, frozen or refrigerated
goods
HQ: Exel North American Logistics, Inc.
570 Players Pkwy
Westerville OH 43081
800 272-1052

(P-4502)
EXEL N AMERCN LOGISTICS
INC
Also Called: Power Logistics
4512 Frontier Way, Stockton (95215-9676)
PHONE.................................209 932-2400
Charles McElwain, Manager
EMP: 100
SALES (corp-wide): 71.2B Privately Held
SIC: 4222 5149 Storage, frozen or refrig-
erated goods; groceries & related prod-
ucts
HQ: Exel North American Logistics, Inc.
570 Players Pkwy
Westerville OH 43081
800 272-1052

(P-4503)
EXETER PACKERS INC
Also Called: Sun Pacific Cold Storage
33374 Lerdo Hwy, Bakersfield
(93308-9782)
PHONE.................................661 399-0416
Richard Peters, Manager
EMP: 220
SALES (est): 5.8MM
SALES (corp-wide): 57.6MM Privately
Held
SIC: 4222 0172 Warehousing, cold stor-
age or refrigerated; grapes
PA: Exeter Packers, Inc.
1250 E Myer Ave
Exeter CA 93221
559 592-5168

(P-4504)
KONOIKE-PACIFIC CALIFORNIA
INC (HQ)
Also Called: Kpac
1420 Coil Ave, Wilmington (90744-2205)
PHONE.................................310 518-1000
Bob Smola, President
Ulises Sam, CFO
Wayne Lamb, Vice Pres
Yutaka Kane Urabe, Vice Pres
Jeffrey Waite, Vice Pres
EMP: 68
SQ FT: 784,080
SALES (est): 29.7MM
SALES (corp-wide): 2.6B Privately Held
SIC: 4222 Warehousing, cold storage or
refrigerated
PA: Konoike Transport Co.,Ltd.
4-3-9, Fushimimachi, Chuo-Ku
Osaka OSK 541-0
662 274-600

(P-4505)
LINEAGE LOGISTICS LLC
2045 E Vernon Ave, Vernon (90058-1612)
PHONE...................................323 583-3163
Ralph Newton, *Manager*
EMP: 150
SALES (corp-wide): 1.2B **Privately Held**
WEB: www.usgrowers.com
SIC: 4222 Warehousing, cold storage or refrigerated
HQ: Lineage Logistics, Llc
   46500 Humboldt Dr
   Novi MI 48377
   248 863-4400

(P-4506)
LINEAGE LOGISTICS LLC
3251 De Forest Cir Ste C, Mira Loma (91752-3277)
PHONE...................................951 360-7970
Reginald Burke, *General Mgr*
EMP: 50
SALES (corp-wide): 1.2B **Privately Held**
SIC: 4222 Warehousing, cold storage or refrigerated
HQ: Lineage Logistics, Llc
   46500 Humboldt Dr
   Novi MI 48377
   248 863-4400

(P-4507)
LINEAGE LOGISTICS HOLDINGS LLC (PA)
1 Park Plz Ste 550, Irvine (92614-2594)
PHONE...................................800 678-7271
Greg Lehmkuhl, *President*
Timothy Dayton, *President*
Paul Hendricksen, *President*
Mike McClendon, *President*
Bill Hendricksen, *CEO*
EMP: 146
SALES (est): 1.2B **Privately Held**
SIC: 4222 Warehousing, cold storage or refrigerated

(P-4508)
LINEAGE LOGISTICS ICM LLC
1 Park Plz Ste 550, Irvine (92614-2594)
PHONE...................................972 462-0042
Bill Hendricksen, *CEO*
Paul Hendricksen, *President*
EMP: 120
SALES (est): 837.1K
SALES (corp-wide): 1.2B **Privately Held**
SIC: 4222 Warehousing, cold storage or refrigerated
HQ: Lineage Logistics, Llc
   46500 Humboldt Dr
   Novi MI 48377
   248 863-4400

(P-4509)
MIKE CAMPBELL & ASSOCIATES LTD
Also Called: Mike Campbell Assoc Logistics
10907 Downey Ave Ste 203, Downey (90241-3737)
PHONE...................................626 369-3981
Vickie J Campbell, *CEO*
James Heermans, *President*
Paul Trump, *President*
Andrea Arce, *Administration*
EMP: 1000
SALES (est): 91.1MM **Privately Held**
SIC: 4222 4225 4214 4213 Storage, frozen or refrigerated goods; general warehousing & storage; local trucking with storage; trucking, except local

(P-4510)
STANDARD-SOUTHERN CORPORATION
Also Called: Los Angeles Cold Storage Co
400 S Central Ave, Los Angeles (90013-1712)
P.O. Box 54244 (90054-0244)
PHONE...................................213 624-1831
Larry Rauch, *Manager*
Renee Ross, *Technology*
EMP: 80
SALES (corp-wide): 36.5MM **Privately Held**
WEB: www.lacold.com
SIC: 4222 Warehousing, cold storage or refrigerated

PA: Standard-Southern Corporation
   4635 Suthwest Fwy Ste 910
   Houston TX 77027
   713 627-1700

(P-4511)
STANDARD-SOUTHERN CORPORATION
Also Called: L.A. Cold Storage
440 S Central Ave, Los Angeles (90013-1712)
PHONE...................................213 624-1831
Larry Rauch, *President*
John Scherer, *Engineer*
Chuck Gunther, *Chief Engr*
Terry Miller, *Warehouse Mgr*
EMP: 130
SALES (corp-wide): 36.5MM **Privately Held**
SIC: 4222 Warehousing, cold storage or refrigerated
PA: Standard-Southern Corporation
   4635 Suthwest Fwy Ste 910
   Houston TX 77027
   713 627-1700

(P-4512)
STANDARD-SOUTHERN CORPORATION
Also Called: Los Angeles Cold Storage
715 E 4th St, Los Angeles (90013-1727)
PHONE...................................213 624-1831
Thom Thomas, *Branch Mgr*
EMP: 90
SALES (corp-wide): 36.5MM **Privately Held**
WEB: www.lacold.com
SIC: 4222 Warehousing, cold storage or refrigerated
PA: Standard-Southern Corporation
   4635 Suthwest Fwy Ste 910
   Houston TX 77027
   713 627-1700

(P-4513)
UNITED STATES COLD STORAGE INC
Also Called: United States Cold Storage Cal
6501 District Blvd, Bakersfield (93313-2000)
P.O. Box 45001 (93384-5001)
PHONE...................................661 832-2653
Randall Dorrell, *Manager*
Randy Dorrell, *General Mgr*
Rick Solano, *Maintence Staff*
EMP: 75
SALES (corp-wide): 13.8B **Privately Held**
WEB: www.uscold.com
SIC: 4222 Warehousing, cold storage or refrigerated
HQ: United States Cold Storage, Inc.
   2 Aquarium Dr Ste 400
   Camden NJ 08103
   856 354-8181

(P-4514)
UNITED STATES COLD STORAGE INC
810 E Continental Ave, Tulare (93274-6816)
PHONE...................................559 686-1110
Brian Ford, *Opers-Prdtn-Mfg*
Chris Harrington, *General Mgr*
EMP: 50
SALES (corp-wide): 13.8B **Privately Held**
WEB: www.uscold.com
SIC: 4222 Warehousing, cold storage or refrigerated
HQ: United States Cold Storage, Inc.
   2 Aquarium Dr Ste 400
   Camden NJ 08103
   856 354-8181

(P-4515)
UNITED STATES COLD STORAGE INC
2003 S Cherry Ave, Fresno (93721-3300)
PHONE...................................559 237-6145
John Bodden, *Manager*
EMP: 50
SQ FT: 87,184
SALES (corp-wide): 13.8B **Privately Held**
WEB: www.uscold.com
SIC: 4222 Warehousing, cold storage or refrigerated

(P-4516)
HQ: United States Cold Storage, Inc.
   2 Aquarium Dr Ste 400
   Camden NJ 08103
   856 354-8181

(P-4516)
UNITED STATES COLD STORAGE INC
1400 N Macarthur Dr Ste A, Tracy (95376-2829)
PHONE...................................209 835-2653
Stanley Moya, *Manager*
EMP: 50
SALES (corp-wide): 13.8B **Privately Held**
WEB: www.uscold.com
SIC: 4222 Warehousing, cold storage or refrigerated
HQ: United States Cold Storage, Inc.
   2 Aquarium Dr Ste 400
   Camden NJ 08103
   856 354-8181

(P-4517)
VALLEY SWEET LLC
222 N Garden St Ste 400, Visalia (93291-6328)
PHONE...................................559 686-3381
F C Farming,
Steven Blizzard, *General Mgr*
EMP: 100
SQ FT: 163,000
SALES (est): 5.1MM **Privately Held**
SIC: 4222 0723 Warehousing, cold storage or refrigerated; fruit (fresh) packing services

(P-4518)
WEBER DISTRIBUTION LLC (PA)
Also Called: Weber Logistics
13530 Rosecrans Ave, Santa Fe Springs (90670-5087)
PHONE...................................855 469-3237
Harry Drajpuch, *President*
Connie Anderson, *Senior VP*
Jim Emmerling, *Senior VP*
Marc Levin, *Senior VP*
Michael Accomando, *Vice Pres*
EMP: 382
SALES (est): 52.7MM **Privately Held**
SIC: 4222 4225 4213 4212 Refrigerated warehousing & storage; general warehousing & storage; trucking, except local; local trucking, without storage; local trucking with storage

(P-4519)
YOSEMITE MEAT COMPANY INC
601 Zeff Rd, Modesto (95351-3942)
P.O. Box 580008 (95358-0001)
PHONE...................................209 524-5117
Johnnie F Lau, *President*
Gay Lau, *Vice Pres*
EMP: 100
SQ FT: 3,600
SALES (est): 29.6MM **Privately Held**
WEB: www.yosemitemeat.com
SIC: 4222 5421 5147 5142 Storage, frozen or refrigerated goods; meat markets, including freezer provisioners; meats, fresh; packaged frozen goods

---

4225 General Warehousing & Storage

(P-4520)
3M COMPANY
5151 E Philadelphia St, Ontario (91761-2801)
P.O. Box 51459 (91761-1049)
PHONE...................................909 974-3004
Richard Campbell, *Manager*
EMP: 150
SALES (corp-wide): 31.6B **Publicly Held**
WEB: www.mmm.com
SIC: 4225 General warehousing
PA: 3m Company
   3m Center
   Saint Paul MN 55144
   651 733-1110

(P-4521)
ACT FULFILLMENT INC
3155 Universe Dr, Mira Loma (91752-3252)
PHONE...................................909 930-9083
Randolph Cox, *President*
Lydiann Cox, *CFO*
Richard Maya, *Vice Pres*
Brennan Haines, *Info Tech Mgr*
Ryan Cox, *Technology*
EMP: 220
SALES (est): 25.2MM **Privately Held**
WEB: www.allcartage.com
SIC: 4225 General warehousing

(P-4522)
ACTIVISION BLIZZARD INC
653 W Fallbrook Ave # 104, Fresno (93711-5503)
PHONE...................................310 431-4000
Tony Suarez, *Branch Mgr*
EMP: 200
SALES (corp-wide): 7B **Publicly Held**
WEB: www.blizzard.com
SIC: 4225 General warehousing & storage
PA: Activision Blizzard, Inc.
   3100 Ocean Park Blvd
   Santa Monica CA 90405
   310 255-2000

(P-4523)
ADIR INTERNATIONAL LLC
4444-46 Ayers Ave, Los Angeles (90023)
PHONE...................................213 386-4412
Russell Yeager, *Manager*
EMP: 77
SALES (corp-wide): 500.7MM **Privately Held**
WEB: www.lacuracao.com
SIC: 4225 Warehousing, self-storage
PA: Adir International, Llc
   1605 W Olympic Blvd # 405
   Los Angeles CA 90015
   213 639-2100

(P-4524)
ADVANCED STERLIZATION
13135 Napa St, Fontana (92335-2961)
PHONE...................................909 350-6987
Ted Snavely, *Manager*
EMP: 100
SALES (corp-wide): 76.4B **Publicly Held**
SIC: 4225 General warehousing & storage
HQ: Advanced Sterlization Products Services Inc.
   33 Technology Dr
   Irvine CA 92618

(P-4525)
ADVANTAGE MEDIA SERVICES INC
Also Called: AMS Fulfillment
28220 Industry Dr, Valencia (91355-4105)
PHONE...................................661 705-7588
John Bevacqua, *Vice Pres*
EMP: 71
SALES (corp-wide): 62MM **Privately Held**
SIC: 4225 General warehousing
PA: Advantage Media Services, Inc.
   29010 Commerce Center Dr
   Valencia CA 91355
   661 775-0611

(P-4526)
ALBERTSONS LLC
Also Called: Albertsons Dist Ctr 8795
700 Crocker Dr, Vacaville (95688-8707)
PHONE...................................707 446-5922
Kirk Hansen, *Manager*
EMP: 350
SALES (corp-wide): 59.9B **Privately Held**
WEB: www.albertsons.com
SIC: 4225 General warehousing & storage
HQ: Albertson's Llc
   250 E Parkcenter Blvd
   Boise ID 83706
   208 395-6200

(P-4527)
ALBERTSONS LLC
Also Called: Albertsons Dist Ctr 8760
777 S Harbor Blvd, La Habra (90631-6800)
PHONE...................................714 578-4670
Tony Vasquez, *Manager*

EMP: 100
SALES (corp-wide): 59.9B **Privately Held**
SIC: 4225 General warehousing & storage
HQ: Albertson's Llc
250 E Parkcenter Blvd
Boise ID 83706
208 395-6200

(P-4528)
ALBERTSONS LLC
Also Called: Albertsons Brea Dist Ctr
200 N Puente St, Brea (92821-3841)
PHONE..........................714 990-8200
Mike Ketcham, *Branch Mgr*
Roy Almond, *Maintence Staff*
EMP: 1000
SALES (corp-wide): 59.9B **Privately Held**
SIC: 4225 General warehousing & storage
HQ: Albertson's Llc
250 E Parkcenter Blvd
Boise ID 83706
208 395-6200

(P-4529)
AMERIFREIGHT INC
Also Called: Logistics Team
218 Machlin Ct, Walnut (91789-3048)
PHONE..........................909 839-2600
Alan Mao Yang, *President*
Joe Dabbs, *Vice Pres*
Isabel Hernandez, *Office Spvr*
Robert Chung, *VP Opers*
Mark Lojo, *Accounts Mgr*
EMP: 675
SALES (est): 55.6MM **Privately Held**
SIC: 4225 4731 General warehousing;
freight transportation arrangement

(P-4530)
ARB INC
Also Called: Northern Division
1875 Loveridge Rd, Pittsburg (94565-4110)
P.O. Box 8189 (94565-8189)
PHONE..........................925 432-3649
Donnie Brown, *Branch Mgr*
EMP: 50
SALES (corp-wide): 2.3B **Publicly Held**
WEB: www.arbinc.com
SIC: 4225 1623 3444 General warehous-
ing & storage; pipeline construction; sheet
metalwork
HQ: Arb, Inc.
26000 Commercentre Dr
Lake Forest CA 92630
949 598-9242

(P-4531)
ARDEN-MAYFAIR INC
Arden Group
6191 Peachtree St, Commerce
(90040-4064)
PHONE..........................310 638-2842
Jim Baron, *Manager*
Jim Lowe, *Buyer*
Robert Langley, *Opers Staff*
EMP: 50
SALES (corp-wide): 317MM **Privately Held**
SIC: 4225 General warehousing
HQ: Arden-Mayfair, Inc.
13833 Freeway Dr
Santa Fe Springs CA 90670
310 638-2842

(P-4532)
BACO REALTY CORPORATION
2071 Camino Ramon, San Ramon
(94583-1378)
PHONE..........................925 275-0100
George Bamburg, *Principal*
EMP: 86
SQ FT: 48,000
SALES (corp-wide): 37.1MM **Privately Held**
SIC: 4225 Warehousing, self-storage
PA: Baco Realty Corporation
51 Federal St Ste 202
San Francisco CA 94107
415 281-3700

(P-4533)
BIAGI BROS INC
1200 Green Island Rd, American Canyon
(94503-9639)
PHONE..........................707 642-4412
EMP: 74

SALES (corp-wide): 140.9MM **Privately Held**
SIC: 4225 General warehousing
PA: Biagi Bros., Inc.
787 Airpark Rd
Napa CA 94558
707 745-8115

(P-4534)
C & B DELIVERY SERVICES
Also Called: Temco
230 Diamond St, Laguna Beach
(92651-3610)
PHONE..........................909 623-4708
Virginia Templeton, *President*
EMP: 85
SQ FT: 91,000
SALES (est): 9.2MM **Privately Held**
SIC: 4225 General warehousing & storage

(P-4535)
C & S WHOLESALE GROCERS INC
8301 Fruitridge Rd, Sacramento
(95826-4806)
PHONE..........................916 383-5275
Ric Clark, *General Mgr*
Frank Costa, *Manager*
EMP: 285
SALES (corp-wide): 28.2B **Privately Held**
SIC: 4225 General warehousing
PA: C&S Wholesale Grocers, Inc.
7 Corporate Dr
Keene NH 03431
603 354-7000

(P-4536)
CALIFORNIA SUPER MARKET
Also Called: California Mayoreo-Y-Menudeo
363 W 2nd St, Calexico (92231-2114)
PHONE..........................760 357-3065
Alex Loo Jr, *Manager*
Rita Guzman, *Bookkeeper*
Carlos Cuevas, *Opers-Prdtn-Mfg*
EMP: 61
SALES (corp-wide): 19.9MM **Privately Held**
SIC: 4225 General warehousing & storage
PA: California Super Market
601 S Imperial Ave
Calexico CA 92231
760 357-6888

(P-4537)
CASAS INTERNATIONAL BRKG INC (PA)
9355 Airway Rd Ste 4, San Diego
(92154-7931)
PHONE..........................619 661-6162
Sylvia Casas, *President*
Martha Casas, *Vice Pres*
John Jolliffe, *Vice Pres*
Alberto Ortega, *Info Tech Mgr*
Karla Casas, *Human Res Mgr*
EMP: 100
SQ FT: 120,000
SALES (est): 15.7MM **Privately Held**
WEB: www.casasinternational.com
SIC: 4225 4731 General warehousing;
customhouse brokers; freight forwarding

(P-4538)
CASCADE LOGISTICS LLC
857 Stonebridge Dr, Tracy (95376-2852)
P.O. Box 1157, Brattleboro VT (05302-1157)
PHONE..........................209 832-4205
James Bringham,
Brian Shaver, *Software Engr*
EMP: 51
SALES (est): 2.2MM
SALES (corp-wide): 28.2B **Privately Held**
WEB: www.es3.com
SIC: 4225 General warehousing & storage
HQ: Es3, Llc
6 Optical Ave
Keene NH 03431
603 354-6100

(P-4539)
CAT LOGISTICS INC
Also Called: Caterpillar
5491 E Francis St, Ontario (91761-3604)
PHONE..........................909 390-1920
James Ralston, *Manager*
EMP: 69

SALES (corp-wide): 45.4B **Publicly Held**
SIC: 4225 General warehousing
HQ: C.A.T. Logistics Inc.
500 N Morton Ave
Morton IL 61550
309 675-1000

(P-4540)
CHINO-PACIFIC WAREHOUSE CORP (PA)
Also Called: Pcwc
3601 Jurupa St, Ontario (91761-2905)
PHONE..........................909 545-8100
Jim Marcoly, *President*
David Boras, *CFO*
George Ramirez, *Vice Pres*
David Strawn, *Vice Pres*
Adrian Limon, *General Mgr*
EMP: 100
SQ FT: 975,000
SALES (est): 17.2MM **Privately Held**
WEB: www.pcwc.com
SIC: 4225 General warehousing

(P-4541)
CITY FIBERS INC
2525 E 25th St, Vernon (90058)
PHONE..........................323 583-1013
David Jones, *Manager*
EMP: 60
SALES (corp-wide): 35.9MM **Privately Held**
SIC: 4225 General warehousing & storage
PA: City Fibers, Inc.
2500 S Santa Fe Ave
Vernon CA 90058
323 583-1013

(P-4542)
CONCORDE BATTERY CORPORATION
1125 N Azusa Canyon Rd, West Covina
(91790-1002)
PHONE..........................626 962-4006
Donald Godberg, *Principal*
EMP: 115
SALES (corp-wide): 23MM **Privately Held**
WEB: www.concordebattery.com
SIC: 4225 General warehousing & storage
PA: Concorde Battery Corp
2009 W San Bernardino Rd
West Covina CA 91790
626 813-1234

(P-4543)
CUSTOM GOODS LLC (PA)
1035 E Watson Center Rd, Carson
(90745-4203)
PHONE..........................310 241-6700
Tony Gregory,
James Fox, *CFO*
Alan Oto, *General Mgr*
Billy Cathcart,
Marie Olivarez, *Accounts Mgr*
EMP: 50
SQ FT: 240,000
SALES: 62MM **Privately Held**
WEB: www.custom-goods.com
SIC: 4225 General warehousing

(P-4544)
DEPENDABLE HIGHWAY EXPRESS INC
3012 Alvarado St, San Leandro
(94587-5735)
PHONE..........................510 357-2223
Trevor Schirmer, *Manager*
EMP: 50
SALES (corp-wide): 283MM **Privately Held**
SIC: 4225 General warehousing & storage
PA: Dependable Highway Express, Inc.
2555 E Olympic Blvd
Los Angeles CA 90023
323 526-2200

(P-4545)
DHL SUPPLY CHAIN (USA)
9211 Kaiser Way, Fontana (92335-2600)
PHONE..........................909 350-6976
John Haley, *Branch Mgr*
EMP: 50
SALES (corp-wide): 71.2B **Privately Held**
SIC: 4225 General warehousing

HQ: Exel Inc.
570 Polaris Pkwy
Westerville OH 43082
614 865-8500

(P-4546)
DHL SUPPLY CHAIN (USA)
2391 W Winton Ave, Hayward
(94545-1101)
PHONE..........................510 784-7360
Mario Lombardi, *Branch Mgr*
EMP: 55
SALES (corp-wide): 71.2B **Privately Held**
WEB: www.exel-logistics.com
SIC: 4225 General warehousing
HQ: Exel Inc.
570 Polaris Pkwy
Westerville OH 43082
614 865-8500

(P-4547)
DHL SUPPLY CHAIN (USA)
5576 Ontario Mills Pkwy, Ontario
(91764-5101)
PHONE..........................623 907-2338
Kraig Foreman, *Branch Mgr*
Freda Williams, *Assistant*
EMP: 70
SALES (corp-wide): 71.2B **Privately Held**
WEB: www.exel-logistics.com
SIC: 4225 General warehousing
HQ: Exel Inc.
570 Polaris Pkwy
Westerville OH 43082
614 865-8500

(P-4548)
DIGNITY HEALTH
Regional Distribution Center
3400 Data Dr, Rancho Cordova
(95670-7956)
PHONE..........................916 851-3800
Bob Rodda, *Dir Ops-Prd-Mfg*
EMP: 50
SALES (corp-wide): 6.7B **Privately Held**
WEB: www.mercycare.net
SIC: 4225 General warehousing & storage
PA: Dignity Health
185 Berry St Ste 300
San Francisco CA 94107
415 438-5500

(P-4549)
DISTRIBUTION ALTERNATIVES INC
Also Called: Scholls
17820 Slover Ave, Bloomington
(92316-2333)
PHONE..........................909 673-1000
Mark Chase, *Manager*
EMP: 109
SALES (corp-wide): 89.3MM **Privately Held**
SIC: 4225 7319 General warehousing &
storage; distribution of advertising mate-
rial or sample services
PA: Distribution Alternatives, Inc.
435 Park Ct
Lino Lakes MN 55014
651 636-9167

(P-4550)
DIVERSIFIED TRANSPORT SYSTEMS
3150 S Willow Ave, Fresno (93725-9349)
P.O. Box 2879 (93745-2879)
PHONE..........................559 268-2760
Michael Gambos, *Owner*
EMP: 50
SALES (est): 2.1MM **Privately Held**
SIC: 4225 General warehousing & storage

(P-4551)
DOT PRINTER INC
Also Called: DOT Printer Warehouse
1801 S Standard Ave, Santa Ana
(92707-2465)
PHONE..........................949 752-7730
Jeff Shattuck, *General Mgr*
Anne Thompson, *Executive*
EMP: 50
SALES (corp-wide): 51.4MM **Privately Held**
WEB: www.dotprinter.com
SIC: 4225 General warehousing

PA: The Dot Printer Inc
2424 Mcgaw Ave
Irvine CA 92614
949 474-1100

(P-4552)
DSC LOGISTICS INC
1565 N Macarthur Dr, Tracy (95376-2839)
PHONE.................................209 362-2232
Bob Justice, *Manager*
Kent Sparks, *Opers Mgr*
Laila Belmonte, *Director*
EMP: 60
SALES (corp-wide): 355MM **Privately Held**
SIC: 4225 General warehousing & storage
PA: Dsc Logistics, Inc.
1750 S Wolf Rd
Des Plaines IL 60018
847 390-6800

(P-4553)
EPSON AMERICA INC
Also Called: Epson West
1650 Glenn Curtiss St, Carson (90746-4013)
PHONE.................................562 290-5855
Dan Wolsey, *Branch Mgr*
Karrie Thompson, *Admin Asst*
Alan Rupert, *Engineer*
Rick Brookshire, *Senior Mgr*
Jason Meyer, *Manager*
EMP: 140
SALES (corp-wide): 10.3B **Privately Held**
WEB: www.presentersonline.com
SIC: 4225 5045 5044 General warehousing & storage; computers, peripherals & software; office equipment
HQ: Epson America Inc
3840 Kilroy Airport Way
Long Beach CA 90806
800 463-7766

(P-4554)
ES3 LLC
Also Called: Cascade Logistics
857 Stonebridge Dr, Tracy (95376-2852)
PHONE.................................209 832-4205
James Bringham, *Manager*
EMP: 50
SALES (corp-wide): 28.2B **Privately Held**
WEB: www.es3.com
SIC: 4225 General warehousing & storage
HQ: Es3, Llc
6 Optical Ave
Keene NH 03431
603 354-6100

(P-4555)
F R T INTERNATIONAL INC (PA)
Also Called: Frontier Logistics Services
1700 N Alameda St, Compton (90222-4128)
PHONE.................................310 604-8208
Brian Chung, *CEO*
Joyce Chung, *Admin Sec*
◆ EMP: 227
SQ FT: 200,000
SALES: 27.6MM **Privately Held**
WEB: www.frontier-logistics.com
SIC: 4225 4731 4412 4214 General warehousing; customhouse brokers; deep sea foreign transportation of freight; local trucking with storage

(P-4556)
FARO SERVICES INC
Also Called: Faro Logistics
15625 Shoemaker Ave, Norwalk (90650-6862)
PHONE.................................562 483-7799
Tim Thomas, *Branch Mgr*
EMP: 102
SALES (est): 5MM **Privately Held**
SIC: 4225 General warehousing & storage
PA: Faro Services, Inc.
7070 Pontius Rd
Groveport OH 43125

(P-4557)
FEDEX SUPPLY CHAIN
Also Called: Genco
1670 Champagne Ave, Ontario (91761-3612)
PHONE.................................909 605-9210

Larry Schoeneberger, *Manager*
EMP: 50
SALES (corp-wide): 65.4B **Publicly Held**
SIC: 4225 General warehousing & storage
HQ: Fedex Supply Chain Distribution System, Inc.
700 Cranberry Woods Dr
Cranberry Township PA 16066

(P-4558)
FORD MOTOR COMPANY
812 Union St, Montebello (90640-6523)
PHONE.................................323 267-6121
Helmut Nittman, *Manager*
EMP: 225
SALES (corp-wide): 156.7B **Publicly Held**
WEB: www.ford.com
SIC: 4225 General warehousing & storage
PA: Ford Motor Company
1 American Rd
Dearborn MI 48126
313 322-3000

(P-4559)
FTDI WEST INC
3375 Enterprise Dr, Bloomington (92316-3539)
PHONE.................................909 473-1111
Alan Baum, *President*
Steve Rocha, *Vice Pres*
EMP: 80
SALES: 11MM **Privately Held**
SIC: 4225 Warehousing, self-storage

(P-4560)
GENERAL MOTORS LLC
9150 Hermosa Ave, Rancho Cucamonga (91730-5304)
PHONE.................................800 521-7300
Mark Smith, *Branch Mgr*
Chris Farmer, *Manager*
EMP: 141 **Publicly Held**
SIC: 4225 General warehousing & storage
HQ: General Motors Llc
300 Renaissance Ctr L1
Detroit MI 48243

(P-4561)
GENERAL MOTORS LLC
11900 Cabernet Dr Dr1, Fontana (92337-7707)
PHONE.................................951 361-6302
EMP: 80 **Publicly Held**
SIC: 4225
HQ: General Motors Llc
300 Renaissance Ctr L1
Detroit MI 48243
-

(P-4562)
GENESIS LOGISTICS INC
4013 Whipple Rd, Union City (94587-1521)
PHONE.................................510 476-0790
Scott Mullins, *General Mgr*
Aran Kahn, *Executive*
EMP: 70
SQ FT: 37,000
SALES (est): 6.7MM
SALES (corp-wide): 71.2B **Privately Held**
WEB: www.genesislogistics.net
SIC: 4225 General warehousing & storage
HQ: Exel Inc.
570 Polaris Pkwy
Westerville OH 43082
614 865-8500

(P-4563)
GEODIS LOGISTICS LLC
301 W Walnut St, Compton (90220-5219)
PHONE.................................310 604-8185
Robert Sanders, *Branch Mgr*
EMP: 88 **Privately Held**
SIC: 4225 General warehousing & storage
HQ: Geodis Logistics Llc
7101 Executive Center Dr # 333
Brentwood TN 37027
615 401-6400

(P-4564)
GEODIS LOGISTICS LLC
Also Called: Ohl
2301 W San Bernardino Ave, Redlands (92374-5007)
PHONE.................................909 801-3145
Jim Moynihan, *Branch Mgr*
EMP: 83 **Privately Held**
SIC: 4225 General warehousing
HQ: Geodis Logistics Llc
7101 Executive Center Dr # 333
Brentwood TN 37027
615 401-6400

(P-4565)
GEODIS LOGISTICS LLC
1710 W Base Line Rd, Rialto (92376-3015)
PHONE.................................909 240-6298
EMP: 90 **Privately Held**
SIC: 4225 General warehousing & storage
HQ: Geodis Logistics Llc
7101 Executive Center Dr # 333
Brentwood TN 37027
615 401-6400

(P-4566)
GEODIS LOGISTICS LLC
Also Called: Stila Styles
3285 De Forest Cir, Mira Loma (91752-3239)
PHONE.................................951 571-2481
Ozburn Hholdin, *Branch Mgr*
Jane Jones, *General Mgr*
EMP: 60 **Privately Held**
SIC: 4225 General warehousing & storage
HQ: Geodis Logistics Llc
7101 Executive Center Dr # 333
Brentwood TN 37027
615 401-6400

(P-4567)
GOODWIN AMMONIA COMPANY
Also Called: The Goodwin Company
12361 Monarch St, Garden Grove (92841-2908)
PHONE.................................714 894-0531
Tom Goodwin, *President*
EMP: 100
SALES (corp-wide): 31.9MM **Privately Held**
SIC: 4225 General warehousing & storage
PA: The Goodwin Ammonia Company
12102 Industry St
Garden Grove CA 92841
714 894-0531

(P-4568)
GRIFOLS BIOLOGICALS LLC
2410 Lillyvale Ave, Los Angeles (90032-3514)
PHONE.................................323 255-2221
Edward Colton, *CEO*
Samuel O'Callaghan, *Engineer*
EMP: 350
SALES (corp-wide): 696.8MM **Privately Held**
WEB: www.alphather.com
SIC: 4225 8731 3085 2836 General warehousing & storage; commercial physical research; plastics bottles; biological products, except diagnostic
HQ: Grifols Biologicals Llc
2410 Lillyvale Ave
Los Angeles CA 90032
323 225-2221

(P-4569)
GRUPE PROPERTIES CO
Also Called: Executive Living Apartments
2944 W Swain Rd, Stockton (95219-3917)
P.O. Box 7576 (95267-0576)
PHONE.................................209 956-7885
Michael V Clark, *President*
EMP: 50
SQ FT: 1,000
SALES (est): 2.2MM
SALES (corp-wide): 87.6MM **Privately Held**
WEB: www.grupe.com
SIC: 4225 Warehousing, self-storage
PA: The Grupe Company
3255 W March Ln Ste 400
Stockton CA 95219
209 473-6000

(P-4570)
H RAUVEL INC (PA)
Also Called: Nova Container Freight Station
1710 E Sepulveda Blvd, Carson (90745-6142)
PHONE.................................310 604-0060
Hector R Velasco, *President*
Vicky Ruste, *Manager*
EMP: 70
SQ FT: 258,000
SALES (est): 33.8MM **Privately Held**
WEB: www.novafreight.net
SIC: 4225 4731 General warehousing; agents, shipping; brokers, shipping; freight consolidation; railroad freight agency

(P-4571)
HARTE HANKS INC
2337 W Commonwealth Ave, Fullerton (92833-2997)
PHONE.................................210 829-9000
Maria Koebel, *Manager*
EMP: 100
SALES (corp-wide): 383.9MM **Publicly Held**
SIC: 4225 7389 7374 General warehousing; telemarketing services; calculating service (computer)
PA: Harte Hanks, Inc.
9601 Mcallister Fwy # 610
San Antonio TX 78216
210 829-9000

(P-4572)
HAULAWAY STORAGE CNTRS INC
11292 Western Ave, Stanton (90680-2912)
P.O. Box 125 (90680-0125)
PHONE.................................800 826-9040
Clifford Robert Ronnenberg, *CEO*
Daniel Letto, *President*
Joyce Amato, *CFO*
Benjamin Davenport, *District Mgr*
EMP: 929
SALES (est): 7.9MM
SALES (corp-wide): 121MM **Privately Held**
SIC: 4225 General warehousing & storage
PA: Cr&R Incorporated
11292 Western Ave
Stanton CA 90680
714 826-9049

(P-4573)
HAYWARD AREA RECREATION PKDIST
Also Called: Corporate Yard
1099 E St Rear, Hayward (94541-5210)
PHONE.................................510 881-6750
Eric Willyerd, *Superintendent*
EMP: 65
SALES (corp-wide): 34.9MM **Privately Held**
SIC: 4225 General warehousing & storage
PA: Hayward Area Recreation & Pk.Dist
1099 E St
Hayward CA 94541
510 670-1665

(P-4574)
HOME DEPOT USA INC
Also Called: Home Depot, The
1400 E Pescadero Ave, Tracy (95304-8523)
PHONE.................................209 835-5133
Gerry Balagtas, *Branch Mgr*
EMP: 72
SALES (corp-wide): 100.9B **Publicly Held**
WEB: www.homerentalsdepot.com
SIC: 4225 General warehousing & storage
HQ: Home Depot U.S.A., Inc.
2455 Paces Ferry Rd Se
Atlanta GA 30339

(P-4575)
HOUDINI INC
6311 Knott Ave, Buena Park (90620-1021)
PHONE.................................714 228-4406
Timothy J Dean, *President*
Melanie Palmer, *Graphic Designe*
EMP: 125

SALES (corp-wide): 71.8MM **Privately Held**
WEB: www.houdiniinc.com
SIC: **4225**
PA: Houdini, Inc.
4225 N Palm St
Fullerton CA 92835
714 525-0325

(P-4576)
HOWARDS APPLIANCES INC
Also Called: Howards Warehouse & Svc Ctr
5102 Industry Ave, Pico Rivera
(90660-2504)
PHONE..................................626 288-4010
Rudy Rodriquez, *Branch Mgr*
EMP: 69
SQ FT: 173,100
SALES (corp-wide): 41.3MM **Privately Held**
SIC: **4225** 5722 General warehousing; electric household appliances, major
PA: Howard's Appliances, Inc.
901 E Imperial Hwy
La Habra CA 90631
714 871-2700

(P-4577)
HSN LLC
13423 Santa Ana Ave, Fontana
(92337-8209)
PHONE..................................909 349-2600
Robert Goodwin, *Manager*
Chris Stewart, *Chief Engr*
EMP: 120 **Publicly Held**
WEB: www.hsn.com
SIC: **4225** General warehousing & storage
HQ: Hsn, Llc
1 Hsn Dr
Saint Petersburg FL 33729
727 872-1000

(P-4578)
INFONET SERVICES CORPORATION
Also Called: Warehouse
1320 E Franklin Ave, El Segundo
(90245-4306)
PHONE..................................310 335-2600
Jose A Collazo, *President*
EMP: 572
SALES (corp-wide): 33.2B **Privately Held**
WEB: www.infonet.com
SIC: **4225** General warehousing & storage
HQ: Infonet Services Corporation
2160 E Grand Ave
El Segundo CA 90245
310 335-2859

(P-4579)
J T R COMPANY INC
Also Called: Area Distributing Company
1102 S 3rd St, San Jose (95112-5918)
P.O. Box 8589 (95155-8589)
PHONE..................................408 293-3272
Josephine Ryan, *Manager*
EMP: 50
SALES (corp-wide): 41.9MM **Privately Held**
WEB: www.jtrsport.com
SIC: **4225** General warehousing & storage
PA: J. T. R. Company, Inc.
1102 S 3rd St
San Jose CA 95112
408 975-7733

(P-4580)
JAM INDUSTRIES INC
Also Called: Jam Warehouse
2101 E Via Arado, Compton (90220-6113)
PHONE..................................310 254-0300
Mautiscio Enriques, *Manager*
EMP: 80
SALES (corp-wide): 19.4MM **Privately Held**
WEB: www.jamwarehouse.com
SIC: **4225** General warehousing & storage
PA: J.A.M. Industries, Inc.
13605 Cimarron Ave
Gardena CA
310 532-4526

(P-4581)
JAVELIN LOGISTICS COMPANY INC
7447 Morton Ave Ste A, Newark
(94560-4208)
PHONE..................................800 577-1060
Malcolm Winspear, *President*
Michael Sacrey, *General Mgr*
EMP: 225
SQ FT: 94,000
SALES (est): 2.5MM **Privately Held**
SIC: **4225** General warehousing & storage

(P-4582)
JC PENNEY CORPORATION INC
Also Called: JC Penney
6800 Valley View St, Buena Park
(90620-1162)
PHONE..................................714 523-6558
Paul Langone, *Manager*
EMP: 200
SALES (corp-wide): 12.5B **Publicly Held**
SIC: **4225** General warehousing
HQ: J. C. Penney Corporation, Inc.
6501 Legacy Dr
Plano TX 75024
972 431-1000

(P-4583)
KUEHNE + NAGEL INC
2660 W Winton Ave, Hayward
(94545-1108)
PHONE..................................510 785-0555
Arlene Van Meter, *Manager*
EMP: 57
SALES (corp-wide): 18.8B **Privately Held**
WEB: www.kuehnenagel.com
SIC: **4225** General warehousing
HQ: Kuehne + Nagel Inc.
10 Exchange Pl Fl 19
Jersey City NJ 07302
201 413-5500

(P-4584)
KUEHNE + NAGEL INC
9425 Nevada St, Redlands (92374-5106)
PHONE..................................909 574-2300
Paul Schmidt, *Branch Mgr*
Paul Schmitt, *Opers Mgr*
EMP: 52
SALES (corp-wide): 18.8B **Privately Held**
WEB: www.kuehnenagel.com
SIC: **4225** General warehousing & storage
HQ: Kuehne + Nagel Inc.
10 Exchange Pl Fl 19
Jersey City NJ 07302
201 413-5500

(P-4585)
LINDA PLACENTIA-YORBA
Also Called: District Warehouse
1301 E Orangethorpe Ave, Placentia
(92870-5302)
PHONE..................................714 985-8775
Gregory Thomson, *Administration*
EMP: 69
SALES (corp-wide): 313.8MM **Privately Held**
SIC: **4225** General warehousing
PA: Placentia-Yorba Linda Unified School District
1301 E Orangethorpe Ave
Placentia CA 92870
714 986-7000

(P-4586)
LISI AEROSPACE NORTH AMER INC (DH)
2602 Skypark Dr, Torrance (90505-5314)
PHONE..................................310 326-8110
Christian Darville, *CEO*
Patrick Hutchins, *Vice Pres*
◆ EMP: 900 EST: 2009
SALES: 100MM **Privately Held**
SIC: **4225** General warehousing & storage
HQ: Hi-Shear Corporation
2600 Skypark Dr
Torrance CA 90505
310 784-4025

(P-4587)
LONG BEACH CMNTY COLLEGE DST
Also Called: Long Beach City College Whse
1855 Walnut Ave, Long Beach
(90806-5724)
PHONE..................................562 938-4291
John Peterson, *Branch Mgr*
EMP: 1855
SALES (corp-wide): 213.9MM **Privately Held**
SIC: **4225** 8222 General warehousing & storage; community college
PA: Long Beach Community College District
4901 E Carson St
Long Beach CA 90808
562 938-5020

(P-4588)
M BLOCK & SONS INC
26875 Pioneer Ave, Redlands
(92374-2026)
PHONE..................................909 335-6684
Ken Oliveira, *Branch Mgr*
EMP: 200
SALES (corp-wide): 286.6MM **Privately Held**
SIC: **4225** General warehousing
PA: M. Block & Sons, Inc.
5020 W 73rd St
Bedford Park IL 60638
708 728-8400

(P-4589)
M&G DURAVENT INC
877 Cotting Ct, Vacaville (95688-9354)
PHONE..................................800 835-4429
Jeff Cowan, *Manager*
Ed Stegall, *Research*
Todd Lampey, *Purch Agent*
Nicki Harris, *Director*
EMP: 375 **Privately Held**
SIC: **4225** 3564 3444 General warehousing; blowers & fans; sheet metalwork
HQ: M&G Duravent, Inc.
877 Cotting Ct
Vacaville CA 95688
707 446-1786

(P-4590)
MAGNELL ASSOCIATE INC
Also Called: ABS Computer Technologies
9997 Rose Hills Rd, Whittier (90601-1701)
PHONE..................................626 271-1420
Brian Cheng, *Branch Mgr*
EMP: 200
SALES (corp-wide): 1.8B **Privately Held**
SIC: **4225** General warehousing
HQ: Magnell Associate, Inc.
17560 Rowland St
City Of Industry CA 91748
626 271-9700

(P-4591)
MARUCHAN INC
15800 Laguna Canyon Rd, Irvine
(92618-3103)
PHONE..................................949 789-2300
Tom Yoshimora, *General Mgr*
EMP: 100
SQ FT: 90,200
SALES (corp-wide): 3.6B **Privately Held**
WEB: www.maruchaninc.com
SIC: **4225** General warehousing & storage
HQ: Maruchan, Inc.
15800 Laguna Canyon Rd
Irvine CA 92618
949 789-2300

(P-4592)
MCR PRINTING AND PACKG CORP
8830 Siempre Viva Rd, San Diego
(92154-6272)
PHONE..................................619 488-3012
Edgar Perez, *Human Resources*
EMP: 170
SALES (corp-wide): 26.7MM **Privately Held**
SIC: **4225** General warehousing
PA: Mcr Printing And Packaging, Corp.
15630 Timberidge Ln
Chino Hills CA 91709
619 488-3169

(P-4593)
MEIKO AMERICA INC
Also Called: American Honda
12300 Riverside Dr, Eastvale (91752-1006)
PHONE..................................951 360-0281
Mike Sole, *Branch Mgr*
Sergio Cardenas, *Manager*
EMP: 63
SALES (corp-wide): 606.5MM **Privately Held**
WEB: www.meikoamerica.com
SIC: **4225** General warehousing
HQ: Meiko America, Inc.
19600 Magellan Dr
Torrance CA 90502
310 483-7400

(P-4594)
MIDAS EXPRESS LOS ANGELES INC
11854 Alameda St, Lynwood (90262-4019)
PHONE..................................310 609-0366
Jack Wu, *President*
Jacky Strong, *Shareholder*
▲ EMP: 200
SQ FT: 90,000
SALES (est): 18.4MM **Privately Held**
WEB: www.midasexpress.com
SIC: **4225** 4731 4226 General warehousing & storage; freight forwarding; textile warehousing

(P-4595)
MITSUBISHI WAREHOUSE CAL CORP
3040 E Victoria St, Compton (90221-5617)
PHONE..................................310 886-5500
Soichiro Sam Orihara, *President*
EMP: 100
SQ FT: 750,000
SALES (est): 10.4MM
SALES (corp-wide): 2B **Privately Held**
WEB: www.mwc-corp.com
SIC: **4225** General warehousing
PA: Mitsubishi Logistics Corporation
1-19-1, Nihombashi
Chuo-Ku TKY 103-0
332 786-611

(P-4596)
MSBLOUS LLC
11671 Dayton Dr, Rancho Cucamonga
(91730-5526)
PHONE..................................909 929-9689
Jiayi CU, *Manager*
EMP: 96
SALES (corp-wide): 400K **Privately Held**
SIC: **4225** General warehousing & storage
PA: Msblous Llc
8 The Grn Ste 7360
Dover DE 19901
909 908-1889

(P-4597)
NATIONAL DISTRIBUTION AGCY INC (HQ)
Also Called: Pacific Coast Warehouse Co
7025 Central Ave, Newark (94560-4201)
PHONE..................................510 487-6226
Sheryl Sadler, *President*
EMP: 62
SQ FT: 305,000
SALES (est): 3.3MM
SALES (corp-wide): 15.4MM **Privately Held**
SIC: **4225** General warehousing
PA: Public Investment Corporation
1207 W Magnolia Blvd C
Burbank CA 91506
310 451-5227

(P-4598)
NAVY EXCHANGE SERVICE COMMAND
4250 Eucalyptus Ave, Chino (91710-9704)
PHONE..................................909 517-2640
Ron Patel, *Manager*
EMP: 155 **Publicly Held**
WEB: www.navy-nex.com
SIC: **4225** 9711 General warehousing & storage; Navy;
HQ: Navy Exchange Service Command
3280 Virginia Beach Blvd
Virginia Beach VA 23452
757 631-3696

▲ = Import ▼=Export
◆ =Import/Export

(P-4599)
NISSAN NORTH AMERICA INC
3939 N Freeway Blvd, Sacramento
(95834-1217)
PHONE..................................916 920-4712
Mariano Loria, *General Mgr*
EMP: 51
SALES (corp-wide): 112.1B **Privately
Held**
WEB: www.nissan-na.com
SIC: 4225 General warehousing
HQ: Nissan North America Inc
1 Nissan Way
Franklin TN 37067
615 725-1000

(P-4600)
NORDSTROM INC
1600 S Milliken Ave, Ontario (91761-2301)
PHONE..................................909 390-1040
Pat Smith, *Manager*
EMP: 300
SALES (corp-wide): 15.4B **Publicly Held**
WEB: www.nordstrom.com
SIC: 4225 4226 General warehousing &
storage; special warehousing & storage
PA: Nordstrom, Inc.
1617 6th Ave
Seattle WA 98101
206 628-2111

(P-4601)
**NORTH BAY DISTRIBUTION INC
(PA)**
2050 Cessna Dr, Vacaville (95688-8712)
PHONE..................................707 452-9984
Lee Perry, *President*
Ray George, *Technology*
Phoebe Nguyen, *Controller*
Greg Cioffi, *VP Opers*
Steven Christianson, *Opers Staff*
EMP: 100
SQ FT: 220,000
SALES: 40MM **Privately Held**
WEB: www.northbaydistribution.net
SIC: 4225 General warehousing

(P-4602)
NUGGET MARKET INC
Also Called: Nugget Mkts Pharmacy
157 Main St, Woodland (95695-3163)
PHONE..................................530 662-5479
Ray Munoz, *Manager*
EMP: 120
SALES (corp-wide): 306.8MM **Privately
Held**
WEB: www.nuggetmarket.com
SIC: 4225 5411 5912 5461 General
warehousing; grocery stores; drug stores
& proprietary stores; bakeries
PA: Nugget Market Inc.
168 Court St
Woodland CA 95695
530 669-3300

(P-4603)
OFFICEMAX INCORPORATED
7300 Chapman Ave, Garden Grove
(92841-2105)
PHONE..................................951 485-9353
Harry Goodman, *Admin Sec*
Nicole Rasic, *Business Dir*
Ted Walter, *Opers Mgr*
Julie Cade, *Manager*
Jane Neubert, *Manager*
EMP: 82
SALES (corp-wide): 10.2B **Publicly Held**
SIC: 4225 5112 5021 General warehous-
ing & storage; stationery & office supplies;
furniture
HQ: Officemax Incorporated
6600 N Military Trl
Boca Raton FL 33496
630 438-7800

(P-4604)
PACIFIC CYCLE INC
Also Called: Pacific Cycle P Finished Goods
9282 Pittsburgh Ave, Rancho Cucamonga
(91730-5516)
PHONE..................................909 481-5613
Rich Jordan, *Branch Mgr*
EMP: 50
SALES (corp-wide): 2.5B **Privately Held**
WEB: www.pacific-cycle.com
SIC: 4225 General warehousing & storage

HQ: Pacific Cycle Inc.
4902 Hammersley Rd
Madison WI 53711
608 268-2468

(P-4605)
**PANAMA-BUENA VISTA UN
SCHL DST**
Also Called: Purchasing & Warehouse
4200 Ashe Rd, Bakersfield (93313-2029)
PHONE..................................661 831-7879
Kip Hearron, *Manager*
EMP: 100
SALES (corp-wide): 203.4MM **Privately
Held**
SIC: 4225 7389 General warehousing;
purchasing service
PA: Panama-Buena Vista Union School
District
4200 Ashe Rd
Bakersfield CA 93313
661 831-8331

(P-4606)
PATINA FREIGHT INC
Also Called: Dura Freight Lines
525 S Lemon Ave, Walnut (91789-2912)
PHONE..................................909 444-1025
Clint Schaffer, *Manager*
EMP: 147
SALES (corp-wide): 40.5MM **Privately
Held**
SIC: 4225 General warehousing
PA: Patina Freight, Inc.
20405 Business Pkwy
Walnut CA 91789
909 595-8100

(P-4607)
**PEPSI-COLA METRO BTLG CO
INC**
200 River Rd, Modesto (95351-3912)
PHONE..................................209 557-5100
Jake Aigen, *Sales/Mktg Mgr*
EMP: 150
SQ FT: 5,000
SALES (corp-wide): 63.5B **Publicly Held**
WEB: www.joy-of-cola.com
SIC: 4225 5962 5149 2086 General
warehousing & storage; merchandising
machine operators; soft drinks; bottled &
canned soft drinks
HQ: Pepsi-Cola Metropolitan Bottling Com-
pany, Inc.
1111 Westchester Ave
White Plains NY 10604
914 767-6000

(P-4608)
**PEPSI-COLA METRO BTLG CO
INC**
4701 Park Rd, Benicia (94510-1125)
PHONE..................................707 746-5404
Neal Sturrock, *Owner*
EMP: 125
SQ FT: 5,000
SALES (corp-wide): 63.5B **Publicly Held**
WEB: www.joy-of-cola.com
SIC: 4225 5149 General warehousing &
storage; groceries & related products
HQ: Pepsi-Cola Metropolitan Bottling Com-
pany, Inc.
1111 Westchester Ave
White Plains NY 10604
914 767-6000

(P-4609)
**PERFORMANCE TEAM FRT SYS
INC**
Also Called: PERFORMANCE TEAM
FREIGHT SYSTEM, INC.
12816 Shoemaker Ave, Santa Fe Springs
(90670-6346)
PHONE..................................562 741-1300
Bob Kaplan, *Branch Mgr*
Brian Briggs, *Opers Dir*
Art Chavarin, *Opers Dir*
Sonya Medlin, *Opers Dir*
EMP: 55
SALES (corp-wide): 372MM **Privately
Held**
SIC: 4225 4731 4213 General warehous-
ing; freight transportation arrangement;
trucking, except local

PA: Performance Team Llc
2240 E Maple Ave
El Segundo CA 90245
562 345-2200

(P-4610)
**PERFORMANCE TEAM FRT SYS
INC**
Also Called: Gale/Triangle
401 Westmont Dr, San Pedro (90731-1011)
PHONE..................................310 241-4100
Scott Pearigan, *Manager*
EMP: 120
SALES (corp-wide): 372MM **Privately
Held**
WEB: www.ptgt.net
SIC: 4225 General warehousing
PA: Performance Team Llc
2240 E Maple Ave
El Segundo CA 90245
562 345-2200

(P-4611)
**PHYSICAL DISTRIBUTION SVC
INC (PA)**
16000 Heron Ave, La Mirada (90638-5513)
P.O. Box 60622, Los Angeles (90060-0622)
PHONE..................................323 881-0886
Trygve W Lodrup Jr, *President*
Greg Lodrupp Sr, *General Mgr*
Amy Chavez, *Sales Executive*
Steven Wheeldon, *Warehouse Mgr*
EMP: 65 EST: 1969
SQ FT: 120,000
SALES (est): 9.4MM **Privately Held**
SIC: 4225 4214 General warehousing;
local trucking with storage

(P-4612)
PRECISE DISTRIBUTION INC
12215 Holly St, Riverside (92509-2315)
PHONE..................................951 367-1037
Debra Catherine Martinez, *CEO*
Levone Myro, *Vice Pres*
Ricardo Cazessus, *Admin Sec*
Gilbert Cazessus, *Info Tech Mgr*
EMP: 50
SQ FT: 350,000
SALES (est): 9.3MM **Privately Held**
SIC: 4225 General warehousing & storage

(P-4613)
**PRIORITY 1 WAREHOUSING INC
(PA)**
2577 W Yosemite Ave, Manteca
(95337-9641)
PHONE..................................209 824-8876
Ron Lanting, *Owner*
James D Van Otterloo, *CFO*
Emma Dirksen, *Admin Sec*
EMP: 65 EST: 1997
SQ FT: 350,000
SALES (est): 5MM **Privately Held**
SIC: 4225 General warehousing

(P-4614)
PS PARTNERS III LTD
701 Western Ave Ste 200, Glendale
(91201-2349)
PHONE..................................818 244-8080
B Wayne Hughes, *General Ptnr*
EMP: 114
SALES (est): 4.8MM **Privately Held**
SIC: 4225 Miniwarehouse, warehousing

(P-4615)
**PUBLIC STORAGE PRPTS IV
LTD**
701 Western Ave, Glendale (91201-2349)
PHONE..................................818 244-8080
Ronald L Havner Jr, *President*
Mark C Good, *COO*
John Reyes, *CFO*
Candace N Krol, *Senior VP*
EMP: 54
SALES: 12.9MM **Privately Held**
SIC: 4225 Warehousing, self-storage

(P-4616)
**PUBLIC STORAGE PRPTS XVIII
INC**
701 Western Ave Ste 200, Glendale
(91201-2349)
PHONE..................................818 244-8080
B Wayne Hughes, *Ch of Bd*

Harvey Lenkin, *President*
Orben B Gerich, *CFO*
Ronald L Havner Jr, *Vice Pres*
Hugh W Horne, *Vice Pres*
EMP: 100
SALES (est): 3.3MM **Privately Held**
SIC: 4225 Warehousing, self-storage

(P-4617)
QUAKER OATS COMPANY
2501 E Orangethorpe Ave, Fullerton
(92831-5333)
PHONE..................................714 526-8800
EMP: 50
SALES (corp-wide): 66.4B **Publicly Held**
SIC: 4225 5149
HQ: The Quaker Oats Company
555 W Monroe St Fl 1
Chicago IL 60661
312 821-1000

(P-4618)
RALPHS GROCERY COMPANY
Also Called: Ralphs 00134
211 N Glendale Ave, Glendale
(91206-4455)
PHONE..................................818 549-0035
Peggy Lizarraga, *Branch Mgr*
Nicole Sabeh, *Store Mgr*
Michael Fatigate, *Sales Staff*
EMP: 164
SALES (corp-wide): 122.6B **Publicly
Held**
WEB: www.ralphs.com
SIC: 4225 General warehousing & storage
HQ: Ralphs Grocery Company
1100 W Artesia Blvd
Compton CA 90220

(P-4619)
RALPHS GROCERY COMPANY
4841-45 San Fernando W, Los Angeles
(90039)
PHONE..................................310 637-1101
Larry Cooper, *Vice Pres*
EMP: 700
SQ FT: 275,000
SALES (corp-wide): 122.6B **Publicly
Held**
SIC: 4225 General warehousing & storage
HQ: Ralphs Grocery Company
1100 W Artesia Blvd
Compton CA 90220

(P-4620)
RALPHS GROCERY COMPANY
Also Called: Food 4 Less
13525 Lakewood Blvd, Downey
(90242-5229)
PHONE..................................562 633-0830
Dave Dopson, *Director*
EMP: 75
SALES (corp-wide): 122.6B **Publicly
Held**
WEB: www.ralphs.com
SIC: 4225 4212 General warehousing &
storage; local trucking, without storage
HQ: Ralphs Grocery Company
1100 W Artesia Blvd
Compton CA 90220

(P-4621)
RALPHS GROCERY COMPANY
Also Called: Ralphs 6
17840 Ventura Blvd, Encino (91316-3615)
PHONE..................................818 345-6882
Jim Sanders, *Manager*
EMP: 135
SQ FT: 37,059
SALES (corp-wide): 122.6B **Publicly
Held**
WEB: www.ralphs.com
SIC: 4225 General warehousing & storage
HQ: Ralphs Grocery Company
1100 W Artesia Blvd
Compton CA 90220

PRODUCTS & SVCS

(P-4622)
RALPHS GROCERY COMPANY
Also Called: Ralphs 00173
9200 Lakewood Blvd, Downey
(90240-2909)
PHONE.....................562 869-2042
Fernando Ortiz, *Manager*
EMP: 62
SALES (corp-wide): 122.6B **Publicly Held**
WEB: www.ralphs.com
SIC: 4225 General warehousing & storage
HQ: Ralphs Grocery Company
1100 W Artesia Blvd
Compton CA 90220
-

(P-4623)
RALPHS GROCERY COMPANY
Also Called: Ralphs 96
160 N Lake Ave, Pasadena (91101-1836)
PHONE.....................626 793-7480
Chuck Hamman, *Manager*
EMP: 100
SALES (corp-wide): 122.6B **Publicly Held**
WEB: www.ralphs.com
SIC: 4225 General warehousing & storage
HQ: Ralphs Grocery Company
1100 W Artesia Blvd
Compton CA 90220

(P-4624)
RAS MANAGEMENT INC (PA)
Also Called: Aaaaa Rent-A-Space
4545 Crow Canyon Pl, Castro Valley
(94552-4803)
P.O. Box 20385 (94546-8385)
PHONE.....................510 727-1800
H James Knuppe, *President*
Barbara Knuppe, *Corp Secy*
David O' Brien, *Manager*
Mike Rizzo, *Consultant*
EMP: 50
SQ FT: 6,000
SALES (est): 16MM **Privately Held**
SIC: 4225 Warehousing, self-storage

(P-4625)
REDWOOD VALLEY INDUSTRIAL PARK
8800 West Rd, Redwood Valley
(95470-6199)
PHONE.....................707 485-8766
Orin Burgess, *President*
EMP: 65
SALES (est): 1.8MM **Privately Held**
SIC: 4225 General warehousing

(P-4626)
ROMARK LOGISTICS OF CALIFORNIA
13521 Santa Ana Ave Ste A, Fontana
(92337-8243)
PHONE.....................909 356-5600
Michael O Conner, *President*
EMP: 75
SQ FT: 320,000
SALES (est): 4.7MM **Privately Held**
SIC: 4225 General warehousing & storage

(P-4627)
RPM CONSOLIDATED SERVICES INC (PA)
1901 Raymer Ave, Fullerton (92833-2512)
PHONE.....................714 388-3500
Shawn K Duke, *CEO*
Emily James, *COO*
Dan Laporte, *Vice Pres*
Jimmy Barkley, *Regional Mgr*
Ian Smith, *Admin Asst*
EMP: 100
SQ FT: 15,000
SALES: 63.5MM **Privately Held**
WEB: www.rpmcsi.com
SIC: 4225 4214 General warehousing & storage; local trucking with storage

(P-4628)
SAFEWAY STORES INCORPORATED
16900 W Schulte Rd, Tracy (95377-8985)
PHONE.....................209 833-4700
Mike Kindy, *Branch Mgr*

EMP: 315
SALES (corp-wide): 59.9B **Privately Held**
WEB: www.safeway.com
SIC: 4225 General warehousing & storage
HQ: Safeway Stores, Incorporated
5918 Stoneridge Mall Rd
Pleasanton CA 94588
925 467-3000

(P-4629)
SCHAFER BROS TRNSF PANO MOVERS (PA)
Also Called: Schafer Logistics
1981 E 213th St, Carson (90810-1202)
PHONE.....................310 835-7231
Gary A Schafer, *President*
Richard W Schafer, *Vice Pres*
Patricia A McMahon, *Accounts Mgr*
EMP: 55
SQ FT: 402,000
SALES: 10.4MM **Privately Held**
WEB: www.schaferbros.com
SIC: 4225 4214 4213 General warehousing; local trucking with storage; heavy hauling

(P-4630)
SCHNEIDER ELECTRIC USA INC
Also Called: Pelco By Schneider Electric
14725 Monte Vista Ave, Chino
(91710-5732)
PHONE.....................909 438-2295
Jessie Ortega, *Director*
EMP: 100
SALES (corp-wide): 200.4K **Privately Held**
SIC: 4225 General warehousing & storage
HQ: Schneider Electric Usa, Inc.
800 Federal St
Andover MA 01810
978 975-9600

(P-4631)
SKY CHEFS INC
1845 Rollins Rd, Burlingame (94010-2209)
PHONE.....................650 652-7886
Dan Joseph, *Branch Mgr*
EMP: 106
SALES (corp-wide): 41.9B **Privately Held**
SIC: 4225 General warehousing
HQ: Sky Chefs, Inc.
6191 N State Highway 161 # 100
Irving TX 75038
972 793-9000

(P-4632)
SOLUTION ONE INDUSTRIES INC
Ave G St Bldg 934, Fort Irwin (92310)
PHONE.....................254 702-7329
Bettie McLaurin, *CEO*
Tyrone McLaurin, *COO*
Daniel Bartlett, *Manager*
EMP: 99
SALES (est): 1.6MM **Privately Held**
SIC: 4225 General warehousing

(P-4633)
SPACE SYSTEMS/LORAL LLC
1140 Hamilton Ct, Menlo Park
(94025-1425)
PHONE.....................650 852-4000
Pat Downey, *Branch Mgr*
EMP: 200
SALES (corp-wide): 581.1MM **Publicly Held**
SIC: 4225 General warehousing
HQ: Space Systems/Loral, Llc
3825 Fabian Way
Palo Alto CA 94303
650 852-7320

(P-4634)
SPROUTS FARMERS MARKET INC
280 De Berry St, Colton (92324-4404)
PHONE.....................888 577-7688
EMP: 190
SALES (corp-wide): 4.6B **Publicly Held**
SIC: 4225 5411 General warehousing & storage; grocery stores
PA: Sprouts Farmers Market, Inc.
5455 E High St Ste 111
Phoenix AZ 85054
480 814-8016

(P-4635)
ST GEORGE WHSNG TRCKG CAL INC (DH)
Also Called: St. George Logistics
1650 S Central Ave, Compton
(90220-5317)
PHONE.....................310 764-4395
Anthony Fortunato, *CEO*
Linda Kuper, *President*
Henry Gothier, *Admin Sec*
Elva Perea, *Finance Mgr*
Shaun Nakhost, *Terminal Mgr*
EMP: 58
SALES (est): 60.7MM
SALES (corp-wide): 1.5B **Privately Held**
SIC: 4225 4731 4214 General warehousing; freight transportation arrangement; local trucking with storage

(P-4636)
STATES LOGISTICS SERVICES INC (PA)
5650 Dolly Ave, Buena Park (90621-1872)
PHONE.....................714 521-6520
Daniel Monson, *CEO*
William Donovan, *President*
Kirk Hellofs, *Vice Pres*
Jennifer Monson, *Admin Sec*
Tim Richards, *Manager*
EMP: 140
SQ FT: 900,000
SALES (est): 74MM **Privately Held**
WEB: www.stateslogistics.com
SIC: 4225 General warehousing & storage

(P-4637)
STORQUEST SELF STORAGE (HQ)
201 Wilshire Blvd Ste 102, Santa Monica
(90401-1220)
P.O. Box 2034 (90406-2034)
PHONE.....................310 451-2130
William Hobin, *Principal*
Tracey Powell, *Store Mgr*
Bridgett Domingo, *Property Mgr*
Maria Valverde, *Property Mgr*
EMP: 51
SALES (est): 23.7MM
SALES (corp-wide): 29.3MM **Privately Held**
SIC: 4225 Warehousing, self-storage
PA: The William Warren Group Inc
201 Wilshire Blvd Ste 102
Santa Monica CA 90401
310 451-2130

(P-4638)
SYNNEX CORPORATION
Also Called: Ontario-Don
3655 E Philadelphia St, Ontario
(91761-2959)
PHONE.....................909 923-8900
Edgar Mendez, *Branch Mgr*
EMP: 52
SALES (corp-wide): 17B **Publicly Held**
SIC: 4225 General warehousing
PA: Synnex Corporation
44201 Nobel Dr
Fremont CA 94538
510 656-3333

(P-4639)
TACTICAL LGISTIC SOLUTIONS INC
13799 Monte Vista Ave, Chino
(91710-5562)
PHONE.....................909 464-2813
Abraham Ausch, *Branch Mgr*
Keith Parks, *Opers Staff*
EMP: 65
SALES (corp-wide): 9.7MM **Privately Held**
SIC: 4225 General warehousing
PA: Tactical Logistic Solutions Inc.
1000 Jefferson Ave
Elizabeth NJ 07201
201 809-1222

(P-4640)
TANIMURA & ANTLE INC
761 Commercial Ave, Oxnard
(93030-7233)
PHONE.....................805 483-2358
Sergio Romero, *Manager*
EMP: 100

SALES (corp-wide): 682.4MM **Privately Held**
WEB: www.taproduce.com
SIC: 4225 Warehousing, self-storage
PA: Tanimura & Antle Fresh Foods, Inc.
1 Harris Rd
Salinas CA 93908
831 455-2950

(P-4641)
TAYLORED SERVICES LLC (DH)
1495 E Locust St, Ontario (91761-4570)
PHONE.....................909 510-4800
Jim Deveau, *CEO*
Mark Chamberlain, *Controller*
Steven Aceves, *Opers Spvr*
EMP: 80
SQ FT: 330,000
SALES (est): 27MM
SALES (corp-wide): 30MM **Privately Held**
WEB: www.tpservices.com
SIC: 4225 4731 General warehousing & storage; agents, shipping
HQ: Taylored Services Holdings, Llc
1495 E Locust St
Ontario CA 91761
909 510-4800

(P-4642)
UNIS LLC
19914 S Via Baron, Rancho Dominguez
(90220-6104)
PHONE.....................310 747-7388
Omar Garcia, *Branch Mgr*
EMP: 90
SALES (corp-wide): 47.9MM **Privately Held**
SIC: 4225 General warehousing & storage
PA: Unis, Llc
218 Machlin Ct
Walnut CA 91789
909 839-2600

(P-4643)
UNITED FACILITIES INC
25451 Mountain House Pkwy, Tracy
(95377-8903)
PHONE.....................209 839-8051
Rich Turner, *Branch Mgr*
EMP: 50
SALES (corp-wide): 74.7MM **Privately Held**
WEB: www.unifac.com
SIC: 4225 General warehousing
PA: United Facilities, Inc.
603 N Main St
East Peoria IL 61611
309 699-7271

(P-4644)
UNITED FACILITIES INC
11618 Mulberry Ave, Fontana
(92337-7618)
P.O. Box 559, Peoria IL (61651-0559)
PHONE.....................951 685-7030
Kevin Alderson, *Manager*
EMP: 50
SALES (corp-wide): 74.7MM **Privately Held**
WEB: www.unifac.com
SIC: 4225 General warehousing
PA: United Facilities, Inc.
603 N Main St
East Peoria IL 61611
309 699-7271

(P-4645)
UNITED MATERIAL HANDLING INC
1190 Harley Knox Blvd, Perris
(92571-7599)
PHONE.....................951 657-4900
Ryan Bartlett, *President*
Brook Bartlett, *Vice Pres*
EMP: 61 EST: 2011
SQ FT: 74,000
SALES (est): 4.6MM **Privately Held**
SIC: 4225 General warehousing & storage

(P-4646)
UNIVERSAL PACKG SYSTEMS INC
Also Called: Paklab
14570 Monte Vista Ave, Chino
(91710-5743)
PHONE....................909 517-2442
EMP: 125
SALES (corp-wide): 423.8MM **Privately Held**
SIC: 4225 General warehousing
PA: Universal Packaging Systems, Inc.
380 Townline Rd Ste 130
Hauppauge NY 11788
631 543-2277

(P-4647)
UNIVERSAL SELF STORAGE
25980 Barton Rd, Loma Linda
(92354-3869)
P.O. Box 8008, Newport Beach (92658-8008)
PHONE....................951 206-5263
Rene Jacober, *Managing Prtnr*
EMP: 50
SALES (est): 2.4MM **Privately Held**
SIC: 4225 Warehousing, self-storage

(P-4648)
UNIVERSITY CAL SAN FRANCISCO
Materiel Management
616 Forbes Blvd, South San Francisco
(94080-2009)
PHONE....................510 987-0700
Diana Hopper, *Principal*
Lori Issler, *Prgrmr*
Charles Murphy, *Med Doctor*
Guy Shochat, *Med Doctor*
EMP: 100 **Privately Held**
SIC: 4225 8221 9411 General warehousing & storage; university; administration of educational programs;
HQ: University Cal San Francisco
500 Parnassus Ave
San Francisco CA 94143

(P-4649)
UPS SUPPLY CHAIN SOLUTIONS INC
601 Van Neca Ave Ste E, San Francisco
(94102)
PHONE....................415 775-6644
Debbie Wong, *Manager*
EMP: 50
SALES (corp-wide): 65.8B **Publicly Held**
SIC: 4225 General warehousing & storage
HQ: Ups Supply Chain Solutions, Inc.
12380 Morris Rd
Alpharetta GA 30005
800 742-5727

(P-4650)
US ELOGISTICS SERVICE CORP
1521 E Francis St, Ontario (91761-8326)
PHONE....................732 357-6665
Hang Feng Wu, *CEO*
EMP: 62
SALES (corp-wide): 47.9MM **Privately Held**
SIC: 4225 General warehousing & storage
PA: Us Elogistics Service Corp
1100 Cranbury S River Rd
Monroe NJ 08831
732 881-6606

(P-4651)
US ELOGISTICS SERVICE CORP
13725 Pipeline Ave, Chino (91710-5417)
PHONE....................732 881-6606
EMP: 62
SALES (corp-wide): 47.9MM **Privately Held**
SIC: 4225 General warehousing & storage
PA: Us Elogistics Service Corp
1100 Cranbury S River Rd
Monroe NJ 08831
732 881-6606

(P-4652)
VAN KING & STORAGE INC
Also Called: King Relocation Services
13535 Larwin Cir, Santa Fe Springs
(90670-5032)
PHONE....................562 921-0555
Steve Komorous, *President*
EMP: 50
SALES (corp-wide): 16.5MM **Privately Held**
WEB: www.kingrelocation.com
SIC: 4225 Warehousing, self-storage
PA: Van King & Storage Inc
13535 Larwin Cir
Santa Fe Springs CA 90670
562 921-0555

(P-4653)
VANGUARD LGISTICS SVCS USA INC
2665 E Del Amo Blvd, Compton
(90221-6003)
PHONE....................310 637-3700
Owen Glenn, *Manager*
EMP: 100
SALES (corp-wide): 232.2MM **Privately Held**
SIC: 4225 4731 General warehousing & storage; freight transportation arrangement
HQ: Vanguard Logistics Services (Usa), Inc.
5000 Arprt Plz Dr Ste 200
Long Beach CA 90815
310 847-3000

(P-4654)
VERIFONE INC
1401 Aviation Blvd, Lincoln (95648-9312)
PHONE....................916 408-4900
Darrin Richards, *Manager*
EMP: 100
SALES (corp-wide): 1.8B **Publicly Held**
SIC: 4225 Warehousing, self-storage
HQ: Verifone, Inc.
88 W Plumeria Dr
San Jose CA 95134
408 232-7800

(P-4655)
VITRAN LOGISTICS INC
1000 S Cucamonga Ave, Ontario
(91761-3461)
PHONE....................909 972-3100
Rick Gaetz, *CEO*
Mike Glodziak, *President*
Joanna Pencak, *Admin Sec*
Jody McGuire, *Manager*
EMP: 78 EST: 2009
SALES (est): 6.5MM **Privately Held**
SIC: 4225 General warehousing

(P-4656)
WALT DISNEY COMPANY
1313 S Harbor Blvd, Anaheim
(92802-2309)
PHONE....................714 781-4532
Paul Margdia, *Manager*
EMP: 500 **Publicly Held**
SIC: 4225 7699 General warehousing & storage; engine repair & replacement, non-automotive
PA: The Walt Disney Company
500 S Buena Vista St
Burbank CA 91521

(P-4657)
WEBER DISTRIBUTION WAREHOUSES
Also Called: Weber Distribution Cwo
9345 Santa Anita Ave B, Rancho Cucamonga (91730-6126)
PHONE....................909 481-1600
John Nutt, *Vice Pres*
EMP: 50
SALES (corp-wide): 117.1MM **Privately Held**
WEB: www.weberdist.com
SIC: 4225 4214 General warehousing; local trucking with storage
PA: Weber Distribution Warehouses
13530 Rosecrans Ave
Santa Fe Springs CA 90670
562 356-6300

(P-4658)
WEBER DISTRIBUTION WAREHOUSES
15301 Shoemaker Ave, Norwalk
(90650-6859)
PHONE....................562 404-9996
John Nutt, *Vice Pres*
EMP: 50
SALES (corp-wide): 117.1MM **Privately Held**
WEB: www.weberdist.com
SIC: 4225 4214 General warehousing; local trucking with storage
PA: Weber Distribution Warehouses
13530 Rosecrans Ave
Santa Fe Springs CA 90670
562 356-6300

(P-4659)
WESTCOAST WAREHOUSING LLC
100 W Manville St, Rancho Dominguez
(90220-5612)
PHONE....................310 537-9958
Jay Patel, *President*
EMP: 50 EST: 2002
SQ FT: 61,440
SALES: 6MM **Privately Held**
SIC: 4225 General warehousing

(P-4660)
WESTERN WINE SERVICES INC (PA)
880 Hanna Dr, American Canyon
(94503-9605)
PHONE....................800 999-8463
Michael W Hodes, *President*
Bruce Cohen, *Senior VP*
Marc Cohen, *Vice Pres*
Tad Franzman, *Vice Pres*
EMP: 100
SALES (est): 13.6MM **Privately Held**
SIC: 4225 General warehousing & storage

(P-4661)
WORLD CLASS DISTRIBUTION INC
2121 Boeing Way, Stockton (95206-4934)
PHONE....................909 574-4140
Michael Campbell, *Principal*
EMP: 151 **Privately Held**
SIC: 4225 General warehousing & storage
PA: World Class Distribution Inc.
10288 Calabash Ave
Fontana CA 92335

(P-4662)
WORLD CLASS DISTRIBUTION INC
800 S Shamrock Ave, Monrovia
(91016-6346)
PHONE....................909 574-4140
Charles Pilliter, *Branch Mgr*
EMP: 189 **Privately Held**
SIC: 4225 General warehousing & storage
PA: World Class Distribution Inc.
10288 Calabash Ave
Fontana CA 92335

(P-4663)
WWL VEHICLE SVCS AMERICAS INC
500 E Water St, Wilmington (90744-6517)
PHONE....................310 835-8806
Martin Richards, *Branch Mgr*
EMP: 163
SALES (corp-wide): 3B **Privately Held**
SIC: 4225 5531 7549 General warehousing & storage; automotive accessories; automotive maintenance services
HQ: Wwl Vehicle Services Americas, Inc.
300 Interpace Pkwy Ste A
Parsippany NJ 07054
201 505-5100

4226 Special Warehousing & Storage, NEC

(P-4664)
ACCESS INFO MGT SHRED SVCS LLC
4501 Pell Dr, Sacramento (95838-2172)
PHONE....................925 461-5352
Susan Gee, *Branch Mgr*
EMP: 76 **Privately Held**
SIC: 4226 Document & office records storage
PA: Access Information Management Shared Services, Llc
500 Unicorn Park Dr # 503
Woburn MA 01801

(P-4665)
AZ/CFS WEST INC
Also Called: AZ West
250 W Manville St, Compton (90220-5600)
PHONE....................310 898-2090
Richard Lombardi, *President*
EMP: 60
SQ FT: 175,000
SALES (est): 15.9MM
SALES (corp-wide): 1.5B **Privately Held**
SIC: 4226 Storage of goods at foreign trade zones
HQ: Az Container Freight Station, Inc.
2001 Lower Rd
Linden NJ 07036
908 374-2250

(P-4666)
CAPACITY LLC
19852 Business Pkwy, Walnut
(91789-2838)
PHONE....................732 745-7770
Anthony P Ruiz, *Branch Mgr*
Anthony Ruiz, *Branch Mgr*
EMP: 171 **Privately Held**
SIC: 4226 Special warehousing & storage
PA: Capacity Llc
1112 Corporate Rd
North Brunswick NJ 08902

(P-4667)
CCC2931 LLC
2401 E Pacific Coast Hwy, Wilmington
(90744-2920)
PHONE....................562 590-8591
Pete Jacpin, *General Mgr*
David Garcia, *General Mgr*
Martin Verma, *General Mgr*
Lon Kettering, *Safety Mgr*
Freddy Rivera, *Facilities Mgr*
EMP: 70
SALES (corp-wide): 2.7B **Privately Held**
SIC: 4226 4225 Storage of goods at foreign trade zones; general warehousing & storage
HQ: Ccc2931, Llc
2931 Redondo Ave
Long Beach CA 90806
888 537-1432

(P-4668)
CEVA LOGISTICS US INC
11290 Cntu Gllano Rnch Rd, Mira Loma
(91752-1448)
PHONE....................951 332-3202
Greg Hart, *Branch Mgr*
EMP: 50
SQ FT: 400,000
SALES (corp-wide): 6.9B **Privately Held**
SIC: 4226 Automobile dead storage
HQ: Ceva Logistics U.S., Inc.
15350 Vickery Dr
Houston TX 77032
281 618-3100

(P-4669)
CONGLOBAL INDUSTRIES LLC
1711 Alameda St, Wilmington
(90744-1700)
P.O. Box 1617 (90748-1617)
PHONE....................310 518-2850
Tom Dielman, *Branch Mgr*
EMP: 73

SALES (corp-wide): 183.7MM **Privately Held**
WEB: www.cgini.com
SIC: 4226 Special warehousing & storage
HQ: Conglobal Industries, Llc
8200 185th St Ste A
Tinley Park IL 60487

(P-4670)
CORODATA CORPORATION (PA)
12375 Kerran St, Poway (92064-6801)
PHONE...............................858 748-1100
Robert J Schmitz, *President*
Jerry Brothers, *CFO*
Richard R Schmitz, *Principal*
Thomas A Schmitz, *Admin Sec*
Bob Grosbeck, *Opers Mgr*
EMP: 59
SQ FT: 600,000
SALES (est): 33.8MM **Privately Held**
SIC: 4226 Document & office records storage

(P-4671)
DATASAFE INC (PA)
574 Eccles Ave, South San Francisco
(94080-1905)
P.O. Box 7794, San Francisco (94120-7794)
PHONE...............................650 875-3800
Robert S Reis, *Ch of Bd*
Thomas S Reis, *CEO*
Debra Pierce, *Vice Pres*
Ronald P Reis, *Vice Pres*
Arnold Cabrera, *Info Tech Mgr*
EMP: 50
SQ FT: 375,000
SALES (est): 10.8MM **Privately Held**
WEB: www.datasafe.com
SIC: 4226 Document & office records storage

(P-4672)
DATASAFE INC
3160 W Bayshore Rd, Palo Alto
(94303-4042)
P.O. Box 7794, San Francisco (94120-7794)
PHONE...............................650 875-3800
Tom Reis, *CEO*
EMP: 50
SALES (corp-wide): 10.8MM **Privately Held**
WEB: www.datasafe.com
SIC: 4226 4225 Document & office records storage; general warehousing & storage
PA: Datasafe, Inc.
574 Eccles Ave
South San Francisco CA 94080
650 875-3800

(P-4673)
DNOW LP
Also Called: Wilson Supply
1111 W Artesia Blvd, Compton
(90220-5107)
PHONE...............................310 900-3900
Nick Leute, *Branch Mgr*
EMP: 53
SALES (corp-wide): 2.6B **Publicly Held**
WEB: www.iwilson.com
SIC: 4226 Special warehousing & storage
HQ: Dnow L.P.
7402 N Eldridge Pkwy
Houston TX 77041
281 823-4700

(P-4674)
DOMINOS PIZZA LLC
301 S Rockefeller Ave, Ontario
(91761-7865)
PHONE...............................909 390-1990
Sal Melgoza, *General Mgr*
EMP: 120
SALES (corp-wide): 2.7B **Publicly Held**
SIC: 4226 4222 Special warehousing & storage; refrigerated warehousing & storage
HQ: Domino's Pizza Llc
30 Frank Lloyd Wright Dr
Ann Arbor MI 48105
734 930-3030

(P-4675)
EXPRESS IMAGING SERVICES INC
1805 W 208th St Ste 202, Torrance
(90501-1808)
PHONE...............................888 846-8804
Paul Terry, *President*
Kenny Ly, *Vice Pres*
Tan Ly, *CIO*
Anh Le, *Opers Mgr*
Anni Ly, *Manager*
EMP: 100
SQ FT: 10,000
SALES: 13MM **Privately Held**
SIC: 4226 Document & office records storage

(P-4676)
IMPERIAL CFS INC
1000 Francisco St, Torrance (90502-1216)
PHONE...............................310 768-8188
Tong Hsing Hsu, *CEO*
Kathy Hsu, *CFO*
Penny Hsing, *General Mgr*
I-Hsin Chen, *Admin Sec*
Gladys Corona, *Technology*
EMP: 50
SQ FT: 200,000
SALES (est): 14.9MM **Privately Held**
WEB: www.imperialcfs.com
SIC: 4226 Document & office records storage

(P-4677)
IRON MOUNTAIN INCORPORATED
28751 Witherspoon Pkwy, Valencia
(91355-5415)
PHONE...............................661 775-9008
EMP: 51
SALES (corp-wide): 3.8B **Publicly Held**
SIC: 4226 Document & office records storage
PA: Iron Mountain Incorporated
1 Federal St Fl 7
Boston MA 02110
617 535-4766

(P-4678)
IRON MOUNTAIN INCORPORATED
P.O. Box 7877 (92658-7877)
PHONE...............................562 345-6900
EMP: 51
SALES (corp-wide): 3.8B **Publicly Held**
SIC: 4226 Document & office records storage
PA: Iron Mountain Incorporated
1 Federal St Fl 7
Boston MA 02110
617 535-4766

(P-4679)
IRON MOUNTAIN INFO MGT LLC
12958 Midway Pl, Cerritos (90703-2119)
PHONE...............................714 526-0916
Richard Melrose, *Manager*
EMP: 60
SALES (corp-wide): 3.8B **Publicly Held**
SIC: 4226 Special warehousing & storage
HQ: Iron Mountain Information Management, Llc
1 Federal St
Boston MA 02110
800 899-4766

(P-4680)
KINDER MRGAN ENRGY PARTNERS LP
2000 E Sepulveda Blvd, Carson
(90810-1937)
P.O. Box 9007, Long Beach (90810-0007)
PHONE...............................310 518-7700
Randy Hartle, *Branch Mgr*
EMP: 50 **Publicly Held**
SIC: 4226 Oil & gasoline storage caverns for hire
HQ: Kinder Morgan Energy Partners, L.P.
1001 La St Ste 1000
Houston TX 77002
713 369-9000

(P-4681)
KINDER MRGAN LQDS TRMINALS LLC
950 Tunnel Ave, Brisbane (94005-1100)
PHONE...............................415 467-8107
Mike Rounds, *Branch Mgr*
EMP: 62 **Publicly Held**
SIC: 4226 Special warehousing & storage
HQ: Kinder Morgan Liquids Terminals Llc
1001 La St Ste 1000
Houston TX 77002
713 369-9000

(P-4682)
KINDER MRGAN LQDS TRMINALS LLC
2150 Kruse Dr, San Jose (95131-1213)
PHONE...............................408 435-7399
Kelly Johnson, *Manager*
EMP: 62 **Publicly Held**
SIC: 4226 Special warehousing & storage
HQ: Kinder Morgan Liquids Terminals Llc
1001 La St Ste 1000
Houston TX 77002
713 369-9000

(P-4683)
KW INTERNATIONAL INC
18724 S Broadwick St, Rancho Dominguez
(90220-6426)
PHONE...............................213 703-6914
Allen Lee, *Branch Mgr*
EMP: 339 **Privately Held**
SIC: 4226 8744 4731 Special warehousing & storage; facilities support services; freight forwarding
PA: Kw International, Inc.
18655 Bishop Ave
Carson CA 90746

(P-4684)
MACYS INC
6200 Franklin Blvd, Sacramento
(95824-3400)
PHONE...............................916 373-0333
Craig O'Connor, *Manager*
EMP: 80
SALES (corp-wide): 24.8B **Publicly Held**
SIC: 4226 4225 Special warehousing & storage; general warehousing & storage
PA: Macy's, Inc.
7 W 7th St
Cincinnati OH 45202
513 579-7000

(P-4685)
PACIFIC CHEMICAL DIST CORP (HQ)
6250 Caballero Blvd, Buena Park
(90620-1124)
PHONE...............................714 521-7161
James N Tausz, *President*
Rhonda Tausz, *Corp Secy*
James Banister, *Vice Pres*
EMP: 100 EST: 1978
SQ FT: 144,000
SALES (est): 9.2MM
SALES (corp-wide): 290.2MM **Privately Held**
SIC: 4226 Special warehousing & storage
PA: A&R Logistics, Inc.
600 N Hurstbourne Pkwy # 110
Louisville KY 40222
815 941-5200

(P-4686)
PRIDE INDUSTRIES (PA)
10030 Foothills Blvd, Roseville
(95747-7102)
P.O. Box 1200, Rocklin (95677-7200)
PHONE...............................916 788-2100
Michael Ziegler, *CEO*
Jeff Dern, *President*
Steve Twitchell, *President*
Peter Berghuis, *COO*
Leslie King, *COO*
EMP: 250 EST: 1966
SQ FT: 177,000
SALES: 290.6MM **Privately Held**
WEB: www.prideindustries.com/
SIC: 4226 7349 3679 Special warehousing & storage; building maintenance services; electronic circuits

(P-4687)
TARGET CORPORATION
Also Called: T.com Ontario Fc T-9479
1505 S Haven Ave, Ontario (91761-2928)
PHONE...............................909 937-5500
Jacqueline Yee, *Owner*
EMP: 177
SALES (corp-wide): 71.8B **Publicly Held**
SIC: 4226 Special warehousing & storage
PA: Target Corporation
1000 Nicollet Mall
Minneapolis MN 55403
612 304-6073

(P-4688)
TARGET CORPORATION
2050 E Beamer St, Woodland
(95776-6213)
PHONE...............................530 666-3705
Dave Sartin, *Manager*
EMP: 400
SALES (corp-wide): 71.8B **Publicly Held**
WEB: www.target.com
SIC: 4226 Special warehousing & storage
PA: Target Corporation
1000 Nicollet Mall
Minneapolis MN 55403
612 304-6073

(P-4689)
TARGET CORPORATION
7600 N Blackstone Ave, Fresno
(93720-4300)
PHONE...............................559 431-0104
Ralph Watkins, *Manager*
EMP: 200
SALES (corp-wide): 71.8B **Publicly Held**
WEB: www.target.com
SIC: 4226 Special warehousing & storage
PA: Target Corporation
1000 Nicollet Mall
Minneapolis MN 55403
612 304-6073

(P-4690)
VINTRUST INC
38 Keyes Ave Ste 200, San Francisco
(94129-1769)
PHONE...............................877 846-8787
Barry Waitte, *CEO*
Ozzie Ayscue, *CFO*
Andr De Baubigny, *Chairman*
EMP: 50
SALES (est): 3.7MM **Privately Held**
WEB: www.vintrust.com
SIC: 4226 Whiskey warehousing

4231 Terminal & Joint Terminal Maint Facilities

(P-4691)
FEDEX FREIGHT CORPORATION
310 W Grove Ave, Orange (92865-3206)
PHONE...............................714 637-9346
Jim O'Conner, *Manager*
EMP: 50
SQ FT: 18,195
SALES (corp-wide): 65.4B **Publicly Held**
WEB: www.watkins.com
SIC: 4231 Trucking terminal facilities
HQ: Fedex Freight Corporation
1715 Aaron Brenner Dr
Memphis TN 38120

(P-4692)
FEDEX FREIGHT CORPORATION
3200 Workman Mill Rd, Whittier
(90601-1550)
PHONE...............................800 288-0743
Darrin Van Wagenen, *Manager*
EMP: 500
SQ FT: 38,090
SALES (corp-wide): 65.4B **Publicly Held**
SIC: 4231 4785 4213 Trucking terminal facilities; inspection & fixed facilities; trucking, except local
HQ: Fedex Freight Corporation
1715 Aaron Brenner Dr
Memphis TN 38120

(P-4693)
INTRADE INDUSTRIES INC (PA)
2559 S East Ave, Fresno (93706-5104)
PHONE.................................559 274-9877
Tejinder S Mehta, CEO
Baljinder Kaur, Vice Pres
Ravi Cheema, Accounting Mgr
Sandi Azua, Manager
EMP: 84
SALES (est): 18.4MM Privately Held
SIC: 4231 Trucking terminal facilities

(P-4694)
YRC INC
Also Called: Yrc Freight
17401 Adelanto Rd, Adelanto
(92301-2701)
PHONE.................................760 246-0031
Randy Perez, Branch Mgr
EMP: 54
SALES (corp-wide): 4.8B Publicly Held
SIC: 4231 Trucking terminal facilities
HQ: Yrc Inc.
10990 Roe Ave
Overland Park KS 66211
913 696-6100

4412 Deep Sea Foreign Transportation Of Freight

(P-4695)
APL LOGISTICS LTD
180 E Ocean Blvd Ste 800, Long Beach
(90802-4720)
PHONE.................................310 548-8700
Gale Bull, Branch Mgr
EMP: 200
SALES (corp-wide): 5.1B Privately Held
WEB: www.apl.com
SIC: 4412 Deep sea foreign transportation
of freight
HQ: Apl Logistics, Ltd.
17600 N Perimeter Dr # 150
Scottsdale AZ 85255
602 357-9100

(P-4696)
FOSS MARITIME COMPANY
1316 Canal Blvd, Richmond (94804-3556)
PHONE.................................510 307-4271
Bob Gregory, Manager
EMP: 100
SALES (corp-wide): 2B Privately Held
WEB: www.foss-maritime.com
SIC: 4412 4492 Deep sea foreign trans-
portation of freight; tugboat service
HQ: Foss Maritime Company
450 Alaskan Way S
Seattle WA 98104
206 281-3800

(P-4697)
FOSS MARITIME COMPANY
Also Called: Pacific Southwest
Berth 35 Pier D, Long Beach (90801)
PHONE.................................562 435-0171
Bob Gregory, Manager
EMP: 200
SALES (corp-wide): 2B Privately Held
WEB: www.foss-maritime.com
SIC: 4412 4492 Deep sea foreign trans-
portation of freight; towing & tugboat serv-
ice
HQ: Foss Maritime Company
450 Alaskan Way S
Seattle WA 98104
206 281-3800

(P-4698)
K LINE AMERICA INC
950 S Coast Dr Ste 178, Costa Mesa
(92626-7731)
PHONE.................................714 861-5000
Michelle Boden, Manager
Michelle Savage, Human Resources
Melissa Spata, Manager
EMP: 50
SALES (corp-wide): 10.9B Privately Held
SIC: 4412 4212 Deep sea foreign trans-
portation of freight; local trucking, without
storage

HQ: K Line America, Inc.
4860 Cox Rd Ste 300
Glen Allen VA 23060
804 762-6600

(P-4699)
PATRIOT CONTRACT SERVICES LLC
Also Called: P C S
1320 Willow Pass Rd # 485, Concord
(94520-5232)
PHONE.................................925 296-2000
Jordan Truchan, CEO
Judy Collins, CFO
Frank Angelacci, Vice Pres
Timothy M Gill,
EMP: 400
SQ FT: 7,800
SALES (est): 28.5MM Privately Held
SIC: 4412 4424 4449 4481 Deep sea for-
eign transportation of freight; deep sea
domestic transportation of freight; canal &
intracoastal freight transportation; deep
sea passenger transportation, except
ferry; ferries; marine surveyors

4424 Deep Sea Domestic Transportation Of Freight

(P-4700)
MATSON NAVIGATION COMPANY INC (HQ)
555 12th St Fl 7, Oakland (94607-4046)
PHONE.................................510 628-4000
Matthew J Cox, President
Ronald J Forest, President
Joel M Wine, CFO
Ben Bowler, Treasurer
Benedict J Bowler, Treasurer
EMP: 200 EST: 1882
SQ FT: 105,000
SALES (est): 711.4MM
SALES (corp-wide): 2B Publicly Held
WEB: www.matson.com
SIC: 4424 4491 4492 Deep sea domestic
transportation of freight; marine cargo
handling; stevedoring; marine terminals;
tugboat service
PA: Matson, Inc.
1411 Sand Island Pkwy
Honolulu HI 96819
808 848-1211

(P-4701)
PASHA HAWAII TRNSPT LINES LLC
1425 Maritime St, Oakland (94607-1022)
PHONE.................................510 271-1400
Mary Brown, Office Mgr
EMP: 100
SALES (est): 2.2MM
SALES (corp-wide): 13.8MM Privately
Held
WEB: www.horizonlines.net
SIC: 4424 4783 Deep sea domestic trans-
portation of freight; containerization of
goods for shipping
PA: Pasha Hawaii Transport Lines Llc
4040 Civic Center Dr # 350
San Rafael CA 94903
415 927-6400

(P-4702)
PASHA STEVEDORING TERMINALS LP
802 S Fries Ave, Wilmington (90744-6415)
PHONE.................................415 927-6353
Jeff Burgin, Senior VP
Jackie Bailey, Treasurer
Braxton Craghill, Controller
EMP: 50
SALES (est): 7.2MM
SALES (corp-wide): 234.4MM Privately
Held
WEB: www.psterminals.com
SIC: 4424 4412 Deep sea domestic trans-
portation of freight; deep sea foreign
transportation of freight

PA: The Pasha Group
4040 Civic Center Dr # 350
San Rafael CA 94903
415 927-6400

(P-4703)
POLAR TANKERS INC (DH)
300 Oceangate, Long Beach (90802-6801)
PHONE.................................562 388-1400
John R Hennon, President
George McShea, Vice Pres
John L Sullivan, Vice Pres
EMP: 75
SALES (est): 22MM
SALES (corp-wide): 32.5B Publicly Held
WEB: www.polartankers.com
SIC: 4424 4412 Deep sea domestic trans-
portation of freight; deep sea foreign
transportation of freight
HQ: Conocophillips Company
600 N Dairy Ashford Rd
Houston TX 77079
281 293-1000

4449 Water Transportation Of Freight, NEC

(P-4704)
DEVINE & SON TRUCKING CO INC (PA)
Also Called: Devine Intermodal
3870 Channel Dr, West Sacramento
(95691-3466)
P.O. Box 980160 (95798-0160)
PHONE.................................559 486-7440
John Frederick Drewes, CEO
Richard Coyle, President
Melissa Bruns, Asst Controller
Amanda Nichols, Cust Mgr
EMP: 200
SQ FT: 6,000
SALES (est): 36.9MM Privately Held
WEB: www.devineintermodal.com
SIC: 4449 4213 Canal & intracoastal
freight transportation; trucking, except
local

(P-4705)
FINN HOLDING CORPORATION (PA)
Also Called: Platinum Equity
360 N Crescent Dr, Beverly Hills
(90210-4874)
PHONE.................................310 712-1850
Tom Gores, Ch of Bd
Mary Ann Sigler, CFO
Eva M Kalawski, Vice Pres
EMP: 2575
SALES (est): 1B Privately Held
SIC: 4449 3731 4491 Canal barge opera-
tions; barges, building & repairing; marine
terminals

(P-4706)
PASHA HAWAII TRNSPT LINES LLC (PA)
Also Called: Phtl
4040 Civic Center Dr # 350, San Rafael
(94903-4187)
PHONE.................................415 927-6400
Steve Hunter,
EMP: 102
SALES (est): 13.8MM Privately Held
WEB: www.pashahawaii.com
SIC: 4449 Transportation (freight) on bays
& sounds of the ocean

4481 Deep Sea Transportation Of

(P-4707)
CRYSTAL CRUISES LLC (DH)
11755 Wilshire Blvd # 900, Los Angeles
(90025-1506)
PHONE.................................310 785-9300
Tom Wolber, President
Angela Composto, Vice Pres
Michael Dolan, Vice Pres
Bertha Espinosa, Vice Pres
Walter Littlejohn, Vice Pres
EMP: 150
SQ FT: 50,000

SALES (est): 76.8MM Privately Held
WEB: www.crystalcruises.com
SIC: 4481 4724 Deep sea passenger
transportation, except ferry; travel agen-
cies
HQ: Genting Hong Kong Limited
Rm 1501 Ocean Ctr
Tsim Sha Tsui KLN
237 820-00

(P-4708)
PRINCESS CRUISE LINES LTD (HQ)
Also Called: Princess Cruises
24305 Town Center Dr, Santa Clarita
(91355-1307)
PHONE.................................661 753-0000
Jan Swartz, CEO
Nina Kass, President
Don O'Neal, Officer
Mary Horwath, Exec VP
Mario Siebaldi, Senior VP
◆ EMP: 2000
SALES (est): 2.4B
SALES (corp-wide): 7.6B Privately Held
WEB: www.princess.com
SIC: 4481 4725 7011 Deep sea passen-
ger transportation, except ferry; tour oper-
ators; hotels
PA: Carnival Plc
Carnival House
Southampton HANTS SO15
238 065-6653

4489 Water Transport Of Passengers, NEC

(P-4709)
BAHIA STERNWHEELERS INC
998 W Mission Bay Dr, San Diego
(92109-7803)
PHONE.................................858 539-7720
William L Evans, Ch of Bd
Grace Cershore, President
Nancy Evans-Kyzer, Treasurer
Anne Evans-Quinn, Vice Pres
Margaret Evans, Admin Sec
EMP: 50
SQ FT: 5,000
SALES (est): 3.4MM Privately Held
WEB: www.bahiahotel.com
SIC: 4489 7299 4499 Excursion boat op-
erators; banquet hall facilities; chartering
of commercial boats

(P-4710)
BLUE AND GOLD FLEET
Also Called: Pier Restaurant
Marine Terminal Pier 41 St Pier, San Fran-
cisco (94133)
PHONE.................................415 705-8200
Ron Duckhorn, Owner
Molly South, Treasurer
Robert Moore, Admin Sec
EMP: 70 EST: 1979
SALES (est): 13.3MM
SALES (corp-wide): 40MM Privately
Held
WEB: www.blueandgoldfleet.com
SIC: 4489 4724 Excursion boat operators;
travel agencies
PA: Pier 39 Limited Partnership
Beach Embarcadero Level 3
San Francisco CA 94133
415 705-5500

(P-4711)
BOMBARD MAR & RESORT MGT SVCS (PA)
95 Berth, San Pedro (90731-3384)
PHONE.................................310 519-7971
Greg Bombard, Shareholder
Tim Bombard, Shareholder
Wendy Adams Bombard, Shareholder
EMP: 375
SALES (est): 9.3MM Privately Held
SIC: 4489 Excursion boat operators

(P-4712)
CATALINA CHANNEL EXPRESS INC (HQ)
Also Called: Catalina Express Cruises
385 E Swinford St, San Pedro
(90731-1002)
PHONE..................310 519-7971
Greg Bombard, *President*
Douglas Bombard, *Ch of Bd*
EMP: 375
SQ FT: 20,000
SALES (est): 55.6MM
SALES (corp-wide): 9.3MM **Privately Held**
WEB: www.catalinaexpress.com
SIC: 4489 Excursion boat operators
PA: Bombard Marine And Resort Management Services Inc
95 Berth
San Pedro CA 90731
310 519-7971

(P-4713)
CATALINA CHANNEL EXPRESS INC
Also Called: Catalina Express
1046 Queens Hwy, Long Beach
(90802-6329)
PHONE..................562 495-3565
Greg Bombard, *Manager*
EMP: 200
SALES (est): 7.1MM
SALES (corp-wide): 9.3MM **Privately Held**
WEB: www.catalinaexpress.com
SIC: 4489 4481 Excursion boat operators; deep sea passenger transportation, except ferry
HQ: Catalina Channel Express, Inc.
385 E Swinford St
San Pedro CA 90731
310 519-7971

(P-4714)
CATALINA GLASSBOTTOM BOAT INC
1 Cabrillo Mole, Avalon (90704)
PHONE..................310 510-2888
Jeff Stickler, *CEO*
Steve Smith, *Vice Pres*
EMP: 65
SALES: 6MM **Privately Held**
SIC: 4489 Sightseeing boats

(P-4715)
EAGLE RAFTING
13226 Sierra Way, Kernville (93238-9712)
P.O. Box 2013 (93238-2013)
PHONE..................760 376-3648
Loxie Chesney, *Owner*
EMP: 250
SALES (est): 5MM **Privately Held**
WEB: www.eaglerafting.com
SIC: 4489 Excursion boat operators

(P-4716)
GOLDEN GATE SCNIC STMSHIP CORP
Also Called: Red and White Fleet
Shed C Pier 45 St Pier, San Francisco
(94133)
PHONE..................415 901-5249
Thomas E Escher, *President*
EMP: 50
SALES: 10MM **Privately Held**
SIC: 4489 4482 Sightseeing boats; ferries

(P-4717)
HORNBLOWER YACHTS INC
Also Called: Hornblower Cruises & Events
2825 5th Ave, San Diego (92103-6326)
PHONE..................619 686-8700
Jim Unger, *Branch Mgr*
Kathryn Wells, *Sales Dir*
Bill Lovens, *Manager*
EMP: 160
SALES (corp-wide): 126.6MM **Privately Held**
WEB: www.hornbloweryachts.com
SIC: 4489 7299 4499 Excursion boat operators; banquet hall facilities; chartering of commercial boats

PA: Hornblower Yachts, Llc
On The Embarcadero Pier 3 St Pier
San Francisco CA 94111
415 788-8866

(P-4718)
HORNBLOWER YACHTS LLC
200 Marina Blvd, Berkeley (94710-1608)
PHONE..................916 446-1185
Daniel Montoya, *Manager*
Cameron Clark, *Vice Pres*
Mike Whitman, *Director*
EMP: 90
SALES (corp-wide): 126.6MM **Privately Held**
SIC: 4489 Excursion boat operators
PA: Hornblower Yachts, Llc
On The Embarcadero Pier 3 St Pier
San Francisco CA 94111
415 788-8866

(P-4719)
HORNBLOWER YACHTS LLC (PA)
Also Called: Hornblower Cruises & Event
On The Embarcadero Pier 3 St Pier, San
Francisco (94111)
PHONE..................415 788-8866
Terry Macrae, *CEO*
Estelle Miller, *Business Mgr*
Lisa Medulun, *Human Res Dir*
Aaron Warren, *Opers Staff*
Hilary Popeck, *Sales Mgr*
EMP: 250
SALES (est): 126.6MM **Privately Held**
WEB: www.hornbloweryachts.com
SIC: 4489 Excursion boat operators

(P-4720)
SO CAL SHIP SERVICES
971 S Seaside Ave, San Pedro
(90731-7331)
PHONE..................310 519-8411
Michael A Lanham, *President*
Mark Wrobel, *General Mgr*
Doug Malin, *Manager*
EMP: 85
SQ FT: 10,000
SALES (est): 13.6MM **Privately Held**
WEB: www.ship-services.com
SIC: 4489 Water taxis

(P-4721)
STAR & CRESCENT BOAT COMPANY (PA)
Also Called: San Diego Harbor Excursion
1311 1st St, Coronado (92118-1502)
P.O. Box 120751, San Diego (92112-0751)
PHONE..................619 234-4111
Arthur E Engel, *CEO*
George Palermo, *President*
David Engel, *Vice Pres*
Herbert Engel, *Vice Pres*
William Johnston, *Vice Pres*
EMP: 50 **EST:** 1905
SALES (est): 16.3MM **Privately Held**
WEB: www.sdhe.com
SIC: 4489 4482 5812 5947 Excursion boat operators; sightseeing boats; ferries operating across rivers or within harbors; cafe; gift shop

(P-4722)
USG ENTERPRISES INC
Also Called: Fantasea Yacht Charters
4325 Glencoe Ave, Marina Del Rey
(90292-6444)
PHONE..................310 827-2220
Uri S Ginzburg, *President*
Daniel Ginzburg, *President*
Maureen Ness, *Vice Pres*
Jasmine Lee, *General Mgr*
Stephanie Ginzburg, *Director*
▲ **EMP:** 55
SQ FT: 13,000
SALES (est): 7.1MM **Privately Held**
WEB: www.fantaseayachts.com
SIC: 4489 7299 Excursion boat operators; banquet hall facilities

---

4491 Marine Cargo Handling

(P-4723)
APM TERMINALS PACIFIC LLC (DH)
2500 Navy Way, San Pedro (90731-7554)
PHONE..................704 571-2768
Steven Trombley, *CEO*
John Loepprich, *Treasurer*
EMP: 104
SQ FT: 33,000
SALES (est): 56.1MM **Privately Held**
SIC: 4491 Stevedoring
HQ: Apm Terminals North America, Inc.
9300 Arrowpoint Blvd
Charlotte NC 28273
704 571-2768

(P-4724)
AVIATION PORT SERVICES LLC
Also Called: Aviation Port Services LLC
2081 Adams Ave, San Leandro
(94577-1007)
PHONE..................510 636-8790
EMP: 79 **Privately Held**
SIC: 4491 Unloading vessels
PA: Aviation Port Services L.L.C
5814 Graham Ave Ste 205
Sumner WA 98390
-

(P-4725)
CATALINA CHANNEL EXPRESS INC
Also Called: Catalina Express
320 Golden Shore Lbby, Long Beach
(90802-4200)
PHONE..................562 435-8686
Rachel Lane, *Branch Mgr*
EMP: 125
SALES (corp-wide): 9.3MM **Privately Held**
WEB: www.catalinaexpress.com
SIC: 4491 Docks, piers & terminals
HQ: Catalina Channel Express, Inc.
385 E Swinford St
San Pedro CA 90731
310 519-7971

(P-4726)
CITY OF LOS ANGELES
Also Called: Harbor Department
425 S Palos Verdes St, San Pedro
(90731-3309)
PHONE..................310 732-7681
Geraldine Knatz, *Branch Mgr*
EMP: 250 **Privately Held**
WEB: www.lacity.org
SIC: 4491 9199 Marine cargo handling; general government administration;
PA: City Of Los Angeles
200 N Spring St Ste 303
Los Angeles CA 90012
213 978-0600

(P-4727)
INTERNATIONAL TRNSP SVC (HQ)
Also Called: I T S
1281 Pier G Way, Long Beach
(90802-6353)
P.O. Box 22704 (90801-5704)
PHONE..................562 435-7781
Sho Ishitobi, *President*
Yuji Yamamoto, *Corp Secy*
John Miller, *Exec VP*
Michael Shanks, *Vice Pres*
Ken Southerland, *Director*
EMP: 220
SQ FT: 10,000
SALES (est): 69.1MM
SALES (corp-wide): 10.9B **Privately Held**
WEB: www.itsasafety.org
SIC: 4491 Marine loading & unloading services
PA: Kawasaki Kisen Kaisha, Ltd.
2-1-1, Uchisaiwaicho
Chiyoda-Ku TKY 100-0
335 955-000

(P-4728)
LEVIN-RICHMOND TERMINAL CORP
402 Wright Ave, Richmond (94804-3532)
PHONE..................510 232-4422
Gary Levin, *President*
Sylvia San Andres, *Admin Asst*
Nenita Magpayo, *Technology*
Pat O'Driscoll, *Opers Mgr*
Joe Rotter, *Opers Mgr*
EMP: 60
SALES (est): 8.3MM
SALES (corp-wide): 9.7MM **Privately Held**
WEB: www.levinterminal.com
SIC: 4491 Marine cargo handling
PA: Levin Enterprises Inc
112 Wshington Ave Ste 250
Richmond CA 94801
510 215-1515

(P-4729)
M T C HOLDINGS (DH)
3 Embarcadero Ctr Ste 550, San Francisco
(94111-4048)
PHONE..................912 651-4000
Michael Hassing, *President*
Gail Parris, *CFO*
Christopher Redlich Jr, *Chairman*
Mikaela Lopez, *Supervisor*
EMP: 50
SALES (est): 44.6MM
SALES (corp-wide): 49.5B **Publicly Held**
SIC: 4491 Stevedoring; marine terminals; loading vessels; unloading vessels
HQ: Ports America, Inc.
525 Washington Blvd
Jersey City NJ 07310
732 635-3899

(P-4730)
PASHA STEVEDORING TERMINALS LP
802 S Fries Ave, Wilmington (90744-6415)
PHONE..................310 233-2006
EMP: 50
SALES (est): 1.6MM **Privately Held**
SIC: 4491

(P-4731)
PORT DEPT CITY OF OAKLAND (PA)
Also Called: Port of Oakland
530 Water St Fl 3, Oakland (94607-3525)
P.O. Box 2064 (94604-2064)
PHONE..................510 627-1100
Veteran Chris Lytle, *Exec Dir*
Laurice Henry-Ross, *President*
Fred Rickert, *CFO*
Earl Hamlin, *Vice Pres*
Michael Zampa, *Comms Dir*
EMP: 350
SQ FT: 285,600
SALES (est): 65.3MM **Privately Held**
WEB: www.portofoakland.com
SIC: 4491 4581 Marine cargo handling; airport leasing, if operating airport

(P-4732)
PORTS AMERICA INC
1601 Harbor Bay Pkwy # 150, Alameda
(94502-3029)
PHONE..................510 749-7400
Michael Hassing, *President*
Naftali Lyandres, *QA Dir*
Ho Lam, *Technology*
Aleksandr Latman, *Med Doctor*
Irina Sheykh-Zade, *Manager*
EMP: 80
SALES (corp-wide): 49.5B **Publicly Held**
SIC: 4491 Stevedoring; marine terminals
HQ: Ports America, Inc.
525 Washington Blvd
Jersey City NJ 07310
732 635-3899

(P-4733)
SACRAMENTO-YOLO PORT DISTRICT
Also Called: Port of Sacramento
1110 W Capitol Ave, West Sacramento
(95691-2717)
PHONE..................916 371-8000
Mike Luken, *Principal*
John Sulpizio, *Exec Dir*

Polly Harris, *Admin Sec*
EMP: 125 **EST:** 1963
SALES (est): 8.6MM **Privately Held**
WEB: www.portofsacramento.com
SIC: 4491 Marine terminals

(P-4734)
SAN DIEGO UNIFIED PORT DST
1400 Tidelands Ave, National City
(91950-4224)
PHONE..................................619 686-6200
Wendy Ong, *Program Mgr*
Gabby Livingston, *Admin Asst*
Kenneth Umbarger, *Technology*
Vanessa Padilla, *Analyst*
Maria Sarchi, *Analyst*
EMP: 106
SALES (corp-wide): 170.3MM **Privately Held**
SIC: 4491 Marine cargo handling
PA: San Diego Unified Port District
3165 Pacific Hwy
San Diego CA 92101
619 686-6200

(P-4735)
SAN DIEGO UNIFIED PORT DST
Also Called: San Diego Unified Hbr Police
3380 N Harbor Dr, San Diego
(92101-1023)
PHONE..................................619 686-6585
Betty Kelepecz, *Branch Mgr*
EMP: 120
SALES (corp-wide): 170.3MM **Privately Held**
WEB: www.thebigbay.com
SIC: 4491 Marine cargo handling
PA: San Diego Unified Port District
3165 Pacific Hwy
San Diego CA 92101
619 686-6200

(P-4736)
SAN DIEGO UNIFIED PORT DST (PA)
Also Called: PORT OF SAN DIEGO
3165 Pacific Hwy, San Diego (92101-1128)
P.O. Box 120488 (92112-0488)
PHONE..................................619 686-6200
John Bolduc, *CEO*
Dan Malcolm, *Vice Chairman*
Robert Deangelis, *CFO*
Mike Bishop, *Officer*
Tanya Castaneda, *Officer*
EMP: 240 **EST:** 1962
SQ FT: 120,000
SALES: 170.3MM **Privately Held**
WEB: www.thebigbay.com
SIC: 4491 Marine cargo handling

(P-4737)
SSA CONTAINERS INC
1521 Pier J Ave, Long Beach (90802-6327)
P.O. Box 24868, Seattle WA (98124-0868)
PHONE..................................206 623-0304
Knud Stubkjaer, *CEO*
John Aldaya, *CFO*
Jaime Neal, *Senior VP*
Theresa Bicknell, *Vice Pres*
Kyle Lukins, *Admin Sec*
EMP: 99
SALES (est): 5MM
SALES (corp-wide): 2B **Privately Held**
SIC: 4491 Stevedoring
HQ: Ssa Marine, Inc.
1131 Sw Klickitat Way
Seattle WA 98134
206 623-0304

(P-4738)
SSA MARINE INC
1521 Pier J Ave, Long Beach (90802-6327)
PHONE..................................562 983-1001
Sal Ferrigno, *Manager*
Jason Brouttier, *Manager*
EMP: 50
SALES (corp-wide): 2B **Privately Held**
WEB: www.ssamarine.com
SIC: 4491 Stevedoring
HQ: Ssa Marine, Inc.
1131 Sw Klickitat Way
Seattle WA 98134
206 623-0304

(P-4739)
SSA PACIFIC INC
2895 Industrial Blvd # 100, West Sacramento (95691-3804)
P.O. Box 24868, Seattle WA (98124-0868)
PHONE..................................916 374-1866
Mark Knudsen, *President*
Theresa Bicknell, *Vice Pres*
Kyle Lukins, *Admin Sec*
EMP: 99 **EST:** 2004
SALES (est): 2.6MM **Privately Held**
SIC: 4491 Stevedoring

(P-4740)
SSA PACIFIC INC
Outer Harbor Berth 54 55, San Pedro
(90731)
PHONE..................................310 833-9606
Mark Knudsen, *President*
Kyle Lukins, *Corp Secy*
Theresa Bicknell, *Vice Pres*
Chad Pittman, *Vice Pres*
EMP: 99
SALES (est): 10.2MM **Privately Held**
SIC: 4491 Stevedoring; marine terminals; waterfront terminal operation

(P-4741)
STOCKTON PORT DISTRICT
Also Called: PORT OF STOCKTON
2201 W Washington St # 13, Stockton
(95203-2991)
P.O. Box 2089 (95201-2089)
PHONE..................................209 946-0246
Richard Aschieris, *Director*
Elise Hermesky, *Admin Asst*
Tricia Rosenow, *Technology*
Timothy Deerinck, *Engineer*
Michelle Bowling, *Controller*
EMP: 100
SQ FT: 18,000
SALES: 51.7MM **Privately Held**
WEB: www.stocktonport.com
SIC: 4491 4225 Waterfront terminal operation; warehousing, self-storage

(P-4742)
TOTAL INTERMODAL SERVICES INC (PA)
2396 E Sepulveda Blvd, Long Beach
(90810-1943)
PHONE..................................562 427-6300
Amador Sanchez Jr, *President*
EMP: 50
SALES (est): 6.1MM **Privately Held**
WEB: www.totalintermodal.com
SIC: 4491 4213 7534 4731 Marine cargo handling; trucking, except local; tire retreading & repair shops; freight forwarding

(P-4743)
TRAPAC LLC (HQ)
630 W Harry Bridges Blvd, Wilmington
(90744-5733)
P.O. Box 1178 (90748-1178)
PHONE..................................310 513-1572
Yoshiharu Hirakawa, *CEO*
K Kurahara, *CFO*
Robert Owens, *Vice Pres*
Frank Pisano, *Vice Pres*
Jerome Marshall, *Info Tech Mgr*
EMP: 50
SQ FT: 50,000
SALES (est): 21.2MM
SALES (corp-wide): 15.5B **Privately Held**
WEB: www.trapac.com
SIC: 4491 Waterfront terminal operation
PA: Mitsui O.S.K. Lines, Ltd.
2-1-1, Toranomon
Minato-Ku TKY 105-0
335 877-017

(P-4744)
YUSEN TERMINALS LLC (DH)
Also Called: Yti
701 New Dock St, San Pedro
(90731-7535)
PHONE..................................310 548-8000
Patrick Burgoyne, *CEO*
Betsy Christie, *CFO*
Phillip Healey, *Planning Mgr*
Sean Marron, *Safety Dir*
Carl Lovio, *Cust Mgr*
EMP: 63

SALES (est): 13.5MM
SALES (corp-wide): 20.4B **Privately Held**
WEB: www.yti.com
SIC: 4491 Marine terminals

4492 Towing & Tugboat

(P-4745)
CROSS LINK INC
Also Called: Westar Marine Services
Bldg C Pier 50, San Francisco (94158)
P.O. Box 78100 (94107-8100)
PHONE..................................415 495-3191
Mary C McMillan, *CEO*
Wendy Heffron-Morrow, *Vice Pres*
Sarah Morrow, *Personnel Assit*
Bill Capasso, *Sls & Mktg Exec*
Dennis Oconnor, *Manager*
EMP: 65
SQ FT: 16,000
SALES (est): 9.3MM **Privately Held**
SIC: 4492 Marine towing services

(P-4746)
FOSS MARITIME CO INC
Also Called: Pacific Towboat & Salvage Co
Berth 35 Pier D, Long Beach (90802)
PHONE..................................562 435-0171
Steve Scalzo, *President*
EMP: 85
SQ FT: 50,000
SALES (est): 4.5MM
SALES (corp-wide): 2B **Privately Held**
WEB: www.foss-maritime.com
SIC: 4492 Marine towing services
HQ: Foss Maritime Company
450 Alaskan Way S
Seattle WA 98104
206 281-3800

(P-4747)
OFFICIAL POLICE GARAGE ASSN OF
67 W Boulder Creek Rd, Simi Valley
(93065-7362)
PHONE..................................805 624-0572
Eric Rose, *Exec Dir*
EMP: 800
SALES (est): 20MM **Privately Held**
SIC: 4492 Towing & tugboat service

4493 Marinas

(P-4748)
CALIFORNIA YACHT MARINA INC (PA)
Also Called: Port Royal Marina
22905 Lockness Ave, Torrance
(90501-5118)
PHONE..................................310 534-8436
Gerald Thomas, *Vice Pres*
Kathie Sitton, *CFO*
William Thomas, *Treasurer*
EMP: 50
SQ FT: 3,000
SALES (est): 5.1MM **Privately Held**
SIC: 4493 4225 5551 Marine basins; miniwarehouse, warehousing; marine supplies

(P-4749)
HARBOR FUEL DOCK
1 Johnson Pier, Half Moon Bay
(94019-4000)
P.O. Box 158 (94019-0158)
PHONE..................................650 726-4419
Keith Nerhan, *Owner*
EMP: 100
SALES (est): 2.6MM **Privately Held**
SIC: 4493 Marinas

(P-4750)
OAKLAND MRTIME SPPORT SVCS INC
11 Burma Rd, Oakland (94607)
PHONE..................................510 868-1005
William Aboudi, *President*
Nishant Sharma, *CFO*
EMP: 50
SALES (est): 2.1MM **Privately Held**
SIC: 4493 Marinas

(P-4751)
SHELTER POINTE LLC
Also Called: Shelter Pointe Hotel & Marina
1551 Shelter Island Dr, San Diego
(92106-3102)
PHONE..................................619 221-8000
Jeff Foster, *Mng Member*
EMP: 200
SALES (est): 14.4MM
SALES (corp-wide): 147.6MM **Privately Held**
WEB: www.shelterpointe.com
SIC: 4493 7011 7997 5812 Marinas; resort hotel; country club, membership; American restaurant; drinking places
HQ: Pacifica Hotel Company
39 Argonaut
Aliso Viejo CA 92656
805 957-0095

(P-4752)
WESTREC MARINA MANAGEMENT INC
Also Called: Tower Park Marina
14900 W Highway 12 Frnt, Lodi
(95242-9514)
PHONE..................................209 369-1041
Jeff Lewis, *Manager*
EMP: 60
SALES (corp-wide): 30.9MM **Privately Held**
WEB: www.martinez-marina.com
SIC: 4493 7299 Marine basins; banquet hall facilities
HQ: Westrec Marina Management Inc
16633 Ventura Blvd Fl 6
Encino CA 91436

4499 Water Transportation Svcs, NEC

(P-4753)
C & C BOATS INC
1861 Baja Vista Way, Camarillo
(93010-9273)
P.O. Box 2359 (93011-2359)
PHONE..................................805 445-9456
Tom Croft, *President*
EMP: 50
SALES (est): 2.3MM **Privately Held**
SIC: 4499 Chartering of commercial boats

(P-4754)
HANJIN SHIPPING CO LTD
301 Hanjin Rd, Long Beach (90802-6216)
PHONE..................................201 291-4600
Taisoo Suk, *Exec Dir*
EMP: 691
SALES (est): 91.1MM **Privately Held**
WEB: www.cyberlogitec.com
SIC: 4499 Steamship leasing

(P-4755)
WESTSTAR MARINE SERVICES INC
50 Pier, San Francisco (94158-2193)
PHONE..................................415 495-3191
Mary McMillan, *President*
Wendy Morrow, *Vice Pres*
Janis Smith, *Mktg Coord*
Ken Friman, *Director*
EMP: 160
SALES (est): 9.1MM **Privately Held**
SIC: 4499 7359 Boat & ship rental & leasing, except pleasure; equipment rental & leasing

---
4512 Air Transportation, Scheduled

(P-4756)
AEROFLOT RUSSIAN AIRLINES
Also Called: Aeroflot Rssina Internatl Arln
8383 Wilshire Blvd # 648, Beverly Hills
(90211-2444)
PHONE..................................323 272-4861
Olga Alexeva, *Manager*
Yuriy Gregorev, *Manager*
EMP: 75 **Privately Held**
WEB: www.aeroflot.ru

P R O D U C T S & S V C S

SIC: 4512 Air passenger carrier, scheduled
HQ: Aeroflot, Pao
10 Ul. Arbat
Moscow 11900
495 258-0684

(P-4757)

AEROTRANSPORTE DE CARGE UNION
Also Called: Aerounion
5625 W Imperial Hwy, Los Angeles (90045-6316)
PHONE..................310 649-0069
Luis Ramo, *Partner*
Steven Connolly, *Partner*
EMP: 400
SALES (est): 21.9MM **Privately Held**
SIC: 4512 Air cargo carrier, scheduled

(P-4758)

AIR FRANCE (AIR NATIONALE)
San Francisco Intl A, San Francisco (94125)
PHONE..................415 877-0179
Percy Bouloux, *Branch Mgr*
EMP: 51
SALES (corp-wide): 47.1MM **Privately Held**
WEB: www.airfrance.com
SIC: 4512 Air transportation, scheduled
PA: Air France - Klm
2 Rue Robert Esnault Pelterie
Paris 75007
142 612-377

(P-4759)

AIR NEW ZEALAND LIMITED
222 N Pacific Coast Hwy # 900, El Segundo (90245-5648)
PHONE..................310 648-7000
Roger Poulton, *Vice Pres*
Diane Stripsky, *Officer*
Albert Suh, *Info Tech Mgr*
Kelly White, *Technology*
Chrystal Peters, *Human Res Mgr*
EMP: 100 **Privately Held**
SIC: 4512 Air transportation, scheduled
PA: Air New Zealand Limited
185 Fanshawe Street
Auckland 1010

(P-4760)

ALASKA AIRLINES INC
1800 W Airport Dr Han Hangar, Ontario (91761)
PHONE..................800 426-0333
John Kelly, *President*
EMP: 75
SALES (corp-wide): 7.9B **Publicly Held**
WEB: www.alaskaair.com
SIC: 4512 Air passenger carrier, scheduled
HQ: Alaska Airlines, Inc
19300 International Blvd
Seatac WA 98188
206 433-3200

(P-4761)

ALASKA AIRLINES INC
600 World Way, Los Angeles (90045-5897)
PHONE..................310 925-2409
Linn Sloper, *Manager*
EMP: 150
SALES (corp-wide): 7.9B **Publicly Held**
WEB: www.alaskaair.com
SIC: 4512 Air cargo carrier, scheduled; air passenger carrier, scheduled
HQ: Alaska Airlines, Inc
19300 International Blvd
Seatac WA 98188
206 433-3200

(P-4762)

ALASKA AIRLINES INC
2357 Airlane Rd Ste D, San Diego (92101-1060)
PHONE..................619 238-2042
Danny Flores, *Manager*
EMP: 50
SALES (corp-wide): 7.9B **Publicly Held**
WEB: www.alaskaair.com
SIC: 4512 Air cargo carrier, scheduled; air passenger carrier, scheduled

HQ: Alaska Airlines, Inc
19300 International Blvd
Seatac WA 98188
206 433-3200

(P-4763)

ALASKA AIRLINES INC
1 Alan Shepard Way, Oakland (94621)
PHONE..................510 577-5813
Kathy Denkar, *General Mgr*
EMP: 64
SALES (corp-wide): 7.9B **Publicly Held**
WEB: www.alaskaair.com
SIC: 4512 4729 Air cargo carrier, scheduled; air passenger carrier, scheduled; airline ticket offices
HQ: Alaska Airlines, Inc
19300 International Blvd
Seatac WA 98188
206 433-3200

(P-4764)

AMERICA WEST AIRLINES INC
3835 N Harbor Dr Ste 128, San Diego (92101-1081)
PHONE..................619 231-7340
Murray Bauer, *Manager*
EMP: 150
SALES (corp-wide): 42.2B **Publicly Held**
WEB: www.americawest.com
SIC: 4512 Air passenger carrier, scheduled
HQ: America West Airlines, Inc.
4000 E Sky Harbor Blvd
Phoenix AZ 85034
480 693-0800

(P-4765)

AMERICA WEST AIRLINES INC
18601 Airport Way Ste 238, Santa Ana (92707-5204)
PHONE..................949 852-5471
Paul Berns, *Manager*
EMP: 80
SALES (corp-wide): 42.2B **Publicly Held**
WEB: www.americawest.com
SIC: 4512
HQ: America West Airlines, Inc.
4000 E Sky Harbor Blvd
Phoenix AZ 85034
480 693-0800

(P-4766)

AMERICAN AIRLINES INC
2077 Airport Blvd Ste 103, San Jose (95110-1219)
PHONE..................408 291-3800
Lee Sims, *General Mgr*
EMP: 80
SALES (corp-wide): 42.2B **Publicly Held**
WEB: www.aa.com
SIC: 4512 Air passenger carrier, scheduled
HQ: American Airlines, Inc.
4333 Amon Carter Blvd
Fort Worth TX 76155
817 963-1234

(P-4767)

AMERICAN AIRLINES INC
International Airport, San Francisco (94128)
P.O. Box 8277 (94128-8277)
PHONE..................650 877-6000
Phillip Bock, *Manager*
EMP: 450
SQ FT: 4,000
SALES (corp-wide): 42.2B **Publicly Held**
WEB: www.aa.com
SIC: 4512 Air passenger carrier, scheduled
HQ: American Airlines, Inc.
4333 Amon Carter Blvd
Fort Worth TX 76155
817 963-1234

(P-4768)

AMERICAN AIRLINES INC
Also Called: AMR
5950 W Avion Dr, Los Angeles (90045-5682)
PHONE..................310 215-7054
Gerard Arpey, *CEO*
EMP: 228
SALES (corp-wide): 42.2B **Publicly Held**
WEB: www.aa.com
SIC: 4512 Air cargo carrier, scheduled; air passenger carrier, scheduled

HQ: American Airlines, Inc.
4333 Amon Carter Blvd
Fort Worth TX 76155
817 963-1234

(P-4769)

AMERICAN AIRLINES INC
18601 Airport Way Ste 213, Santa Ana (92707-5219)
PHONE..................949 852-5470
Catherine Connolly, *Branch Mgr*
EMP: 250
SALES (corp-wide): 42.2B **Publicly Held**
WEB: www.aa.com
SIC: 4512 Air passenger carrier, scheduled
HQ: American Airlines, Inc.
4333 Amon Carter Blvd
Fort Worth TX 76155
817 963-1234

(P-4770)

AMERICAN AIRLINES INC
7000 World Way W, Los Angeles (90045-7503)
PHONE..................213 935-6045
EMP: 150
SALES (corp-wide): 42.2B **Publicly Held**
SIC: 4512
HQ: American Airlines, Inc.
4333 Amon Carter Blvd
Fort Worth TX 76155
817 963-1234

(P-4771)

AMERICAN AIRLINES INC
Also Called: US Airways
100 World Way Ste D, Los Angeles (90045-5854)
PHONE..................310 646-0093
Mike Cilani, *Branch Mgr*
EMP: 325
SALES (corp-wide): 42.2B **Publicly Held**
WEB: www.usair.com
SIC: 4512 Air passenger carrier, scheduled
HQ: American Airlines, Inc.
4333 Amon Carter Blvd
Fort Worth TX 76155
817 963-1234

(P-4772)

AMERICAN AIRLINES INC
Also Called: US Airways
3707 N Harbor Dr Ste 103, San Diego (92101-1068)
PHONE..................619 574-0615
Lynn Silva, *Manager*
Letty Villamarin, *Human Resources*
EMP: 50
SALES (corp-wide): 42.2B **Publicly Held**
WEB: www.usair.com
SIC: 4512 Air passenger carrier, scheduled
HQ: American Airlines, Inc.
4333 Amon Carter Blvd
Fort Worth TX 76155
817 963-1234

(P-4773)

AMERICAN AIRLINES INC
Also Called: US Airways
7183 World Way W, Los Angeles (90045-5824)
PHONE..................310 646-3013
George Knoblock, *Branch Mgr*
EMP: 175
SALES (corp-wide): 42.2B **Publicly Held**
WEB: www.usair.com
SIC: 4512 Air passenger carrier, scheduled
HQ: American Airlines, Inc.
4333 Amon Carter Blvd
Fort Worth TX 76155
817 963-1234

(P-4774)

AMERICAN AIRLINES INC
3100 Wright Rd, Camarillo (93010-8307)
PHONE..................805 988-0407
Wilma Barkley, *Branch Mgr*
EMP: 75
SALES (corp-wide): 42.2B **Publicly Held**
WEB: www.aa.com
SIC: 4512 Air passenger carrier, scheduled
HQ: American Airlines, Inc.
4333 Amon Carter Blvd
Fort Worth TX 76155
817 963-1234

(P-4775)

AMERICAN AIRLINES GROUP INC
3543 Carlisle St, Perris (92571-7303)
PHONE..................310 251-9184
Susie Kimball, *Principal*
EMP: 658
SALES (corp-wide): 42.2B **Publicly Held**
SIC: 4512 Air passenger carrier, scheduled
PA: American Airlines Group Inc.
4333 Amon Carter Blvd
Fort Worth TX 76155
817 963-1234

(P-4776)

AMERIFLIGHT LLC
21889 Skywest Dr, Hayward (94541-7021)
PHONE..................510 569-6000
EMP: 57
SALES (corp-wide): 183.1MM **Privately Held**
SIC: 4512
PA: Ameriflight, Llc
4700 W Empire Ave
Burbank CA 75261
818 847-0000

(P-4777)

CALIFORNIA AIR CARTAGE INC (PA)
Also Called: Shaker Express
2357 Airlane Rd Ste B, San Diego (92101-1060)
P.O. Box 122430 (92112-2430)
PHONE..................619 291-8544
Ralph A Wilson, *President*
EMP: 96 **EST:** 1959
SQ FT: 11,000
SALES (est): 6.9MM **Privately Held**
SIC: 4512 4513 Air cargo carrier, scheduled; parcel delivery, private air

(P-4778)

CHINA AIRLINES LTD (HQ)
11201 Aviation Blvd, Los Angeles (90045-6100)
PHONE..................310 646-4233
Huang Hsiang Sun, *President*
Gerard Castillo, *Officer*
Yu-Kuang Yu, *Human Res Mgr*
David Tang, *Opers Mgr*
Jiajie Chen, *Marketing Staff*
EMP: 118
SALES (est): 29.4MM
SALES (corp-wide): 5.1B **Privately Held**
SIC: 4512 Air transportation, scheduled
PA: China Airlines Ltd.
1, Hangqin S. Rd.,
Taoyuan City TAY 33758
339 988-88

(P-4779)

DELTA AIR LINES INC
Also Called: Delta Airlines
500 World Way, Los Angeles (90045-5891)
P.O. Box 90676 (90009-0676)
PHONE..................323 417-7374
Dick Cassella, *Manager*
EMP: 64
SALES (corp-wide): 41.2B **Publicly Held**
WEB: www.delta.com
SIC: 4512 Air transportation, scheduled
PA: Delta Air Lines, Inc.
1030 Delta Blvd
Atlanta GA 30354
404 715-2600

(P-4780)

FEDERAL EXPRESS CORPORATION
Also Called: Fedex
11340 Sherman Way, Sun Valley (91352-4944)
PHONE..................800 463-3339
Rus Bronson, *Manager*
EMP: 135
SALES (corp-wide): 65.4B **Publicly Held**
WEB: www.federalexpress.com
SIC: 4512 4513 4215 Air transportation, scheduled; air courier services; courier services, except by air
HQ: Federal Express Corporation
3610 Hacks Cross Rd
Memphis TN 38125
901 369-3600

(P-4781)
FEDERAL EXPRESS CORPORATION
Also Called: Fedex
1500 Nichols Dr, Rocklin (95765-1310)
PHONE..................................800 463-3339
Nick Drikas, *Manager*
EMP: 122
SALES (corp-wide): 65.4B **Publicly Held**
WEB: www.federalexpress.com
SIC: 4512 Air cargo carrier, scheduled
HQ: Federal Express Corporation
3610 Hacks Cross Rd
Memphis TN 38125
901 369-3600

(P-4782)
FEDERAL EXPRESS CORPORATION
Also Called: Fedex
1111 Bird Center Dr, Palm Springs
(92262-8000)
PHONE..................................800 463-3339
EMP: 122
SALES (corp-wide): 65.4B **Publicly Held**
WEB: www.federalexpress.com
SIC: 4512 Air cargo carrier, scheduled
HQ: Federal Express Corporation
3610 Hacks Cross Rd
Memphis TN 38125
901 369-3600

(P-4783)
FEDERAL EXPRESS CORPORATION
Also Called: Fedex
2601 Main St Ste 1000, Irvine
(92614-4233)
PHONE..................................949 862-4500
EMP: 120
SALES (corp-wide): 47.4B **Publicly Held**
SIC: 4512 4513
HQ: Federal Express Corporation
3610 Hacks Cross Rd
Memphis TN 38125
901 369-3600

(P-4784)
HAWAIIAN AIRLINES INC
200 World Way Ste 9, Los Angeles
(90045-5844)
PHONE..................................310 417-1677
Lisa Jones, *General Mgr*
EMP: 55
SALES (corp-wide): 2.7B **Publicly Held**
WEB: www.hawaiianair.com
SIC: 4512 Air passenger carrier, scheduled
HQ: Hawaiian Airlines, Inc.
3375 Koapaka St Ste G350
Honolulu HI 96819
808 835-3700

(P-4785)
JET AIRWAYS OF INDIA INC
111 Anza Blvd Ste 300, Burlingame
(94010-1917)
PHONE..................................650 762-2345
Victoriano P Dungca, *President*
Gordana Onica, *Supervisor*
EMP: 70
SALES (est): 4.3MM **Privately Held**
SIC: 4512 Air passenger carrier, scheduled

(P-4786)
JETBLUE AIRWAYS CORPORATION
Also Called: Burbank Bob Hope Airport
2627 N Hollywood Way, Burbank
(91505-1062)
PHONE..................................718 286-7900
Tom Greer, *Branch Mgr*
Jillian Ruffino, *Admin Asst*
Jennifer Hood, *Analyst*
Abad Ortega, *Analyst*
Richard Davies, *Accountant*
EMP: 77
SALES (corp-wide): 7B **Publicly Held**
SIC: 4512 Air passenger carrier, scheduled
PA: Jetblue Airways Corporation
2701 Queens Plz N
Long Island City NY 11101
718 286-7900

(P-4787)
JETBLUE AIRWAYS CORPORATION
130 Alan Shepard Way M, Oakland
(94621-4501)
PHONE..................................510 381-1369
EMP: 81
SALES (corp-wide): 7B **Publicly Held**
PA: Jetblue Airways Corporation
2701 Queens Plz N
Long Island City NY 11101
718 286-7900

(P-4788)
JETBLUE AIRWAYS CORPORATION
3835 N Harbor Dr Ste 108, San Diego
(92101-1059)
PHONE..................................619 725-0807
EMP: 81
SALES (corp-wide): 7B **Publicly Held**
SIC: 4512 Air passenger carrier, scheduled
PA: Jetblue Airways Corporation
2701 Queens Plz N
Long Island City NY 11101
718 286-7900

(P-4789)
KOREAN AIR LINES CO LTD
380 World Way Ste S4, Los Angeles
(90045-5847)
PHONE..................................310 646-4866
EMP: 175
SALES (corp-wide): 10.8B **Privately Held**
WEB: www.laxda.koreanair.com
SIC: 4512 Air transportation, scheduled
PA: Korean Air Lines Co., Ltd.
260 Haneul-Gil, Gangseo-Gu
Seoul 07505
825 197-0579

(P-4790)
KOREAN AIRLINES
380 World Way, Los Angeles (90045-5800)
PHONE..................................310 417-5294
Tom Bradley, *Manager*
EMP: 175
SALES (corp-wide): 10.8B **Privately Held**
WEB: www.laxda.koreanair.com
SIC: 4512 Air transportation, scheduled
PA: Korean Air Lines Co., Ltd.
260 Haneul-Gil, Gangseo-Gu
Seoul 07505
825 197-0579

(P-4791)
KOREAN AIRLINES CO LTD
Also Called: Korean Arln Crgo Reservations
6101 W Imperial Hwy, Los Angeles
(90045-6305)
PHONE..................................310 410-2000
Jinkul Lee, *President*
Jong Myung Park, *Treasurer*
Sung Kim, *General Mgr*
Steven Kang, *Technology*
Gilles Hurtaud, *Manager*
EMP: 250
SALES (corp-wide): 10.8B **Privately Held**
WEB: www.laxda.koreanair.com
SIC: 4512 4513 Air transportation, scheduled; package delivery, private air
PA: Korean Air Lines Co., Ltd.
260 Haneul-Gil, Gangseo-Gu
Seoul 07505
825 197-0579

(P-4792)
LUFTHNSA CRGO AKTNGESELLSCHAFT
5721 W Imperial Hwy, Los Angeles
(90045-6301)
PHONE..................................310 242-2590
Veli Polat, *President*
EMP: 150
SALES (corp-wide): 41.9B **Privately Held**
SIC: 4512 Air passenger carrier, scheduled
HQ: Lufthansa Cargo Ag
Flughafen Frankfurt Am Main
Frankfurt Am Main 60549
696 960-

(P-4793)
LUKENBILL ENTERPRISES
Also Called: Sky King
3600 Power Inn Rd Ste H, Sacramento
(95826-3826)
PHONE..................................916 454-2400
Greg Lukenbill, *Partner*
EMP: 100
SQ FT: 12,000
SALES (est): 7.6MM **Privately Held**
SIC: 4512 6531 Air transportation, scheduled; real estate agents & managers

(P-4794)
PHILIPPINE AIRLINES
11001 Aviation Blvd, Los Angeles
(90045-6123)
PHONE..................................310 646-1981
CHI Marquec, *Branch Mgr*
EMP: 65
SALES (corp-wide): 38.3MM **Privately Held**
WEB: www.pal.com
SIC: 4512 Air passenger carrier, scheduled
HQ: Philippine Airlines, Inc.
8th Floor Pnb Financial Centre
Pasay 1307
277 748-00

(P-4795)
PHILIPPINE AIRLINES INC
447 Sutter St Ste 200, San Francisco
(94108-4636)
PHONE..................................415 217-3100
Rodolfo Llora, *Branch Mgr*
EMP: 150
SALES (corp-wide): 38.3MM **Privately Held**
WEB: www.pal.com
SIC: 4512 8741 4513 Air passenger carrier, scheduled; management services; package delivery, private air
HQ: Philippine Airlines, Inc.
8th Floor Pnb Financial Centre
Pasay 1307
277 748-00

(P-4796)
SINGAPORE AIRLINES CARGO PTE
710 Mcdonald Rd, San Francisco (94128)
P.O. Box 280746 (94128-0746)
PHONE..................................650 876-7363
Lee Liik Hsin, *CEO*
EMP: 60
SQ FT: 60,000
SALES (est): 6.8MM **Privately Held**
SIC: 4512 Air cargo carrier, scheduled

(P-4797)
SINGAPORE AIRLINES LIMITED
222 N Pacific Coast Hwy # 1600, El Segundo (90245-5615)
PHONE..................................310 647-1922
Tee Hooi Teoh, *Manager*
Loh Meng See Meng See, *Senior VP*
Yau Seng Chin, *Vice Pres*
Kok Wah Chow, *Vice Pres*
Kah Kheng Goh, *Vice Pres*
EMP: 135 **Privately Held**
WEB: www.singaporeair.com
SIC: 4512 Air passenger carrier, scheduled
HQ: Singapore Airlines Limited
25 Airline Road
Singapore 81982
678 981-88

(P-4798)
SKYWEST AIRLINES INC
32128 Chagall Ct, Winchester
(92596-9024)
PHONE..................................951 926-9511
EMP: 75
SALES (corp-wide): 3.5B **Publicly Held**
SIC: 4512
HQ: Skywest Airlines, Inc.
444 S River Rd
St George UT 84790
435 634-3000

(P-4799)
SKYWEST AIRLINES INC
26818 Bahama Way, Murrieta
(92563-2553)
PHONE..................................951 600-9181
EMP: 75

(P-4800)
SOUTHWEST AIRLINES CO
1 Airport Dr Ste 25, Oakland (94621-1432)
PHONE..................................510 563-1000
Teddy Rowell, *Manager*
EMP: 75
SALES (corp-wide): 21.1B **Publicly Held**
WEB: www.southwest.com
SIC: 4512 Air passenger carrier, scheduled
PA: Southwest Airlines Co.
2702 Love Field Dr
Dallas TX 75235
214 792-4000

(P-4801)
SOUTHWEST AIRLINES CO
3665 N Harbor Dr Ste 216, San Diego
(92101-1038)
PHONE..................................619 231-7345
Cheryl Black, *Branch Mgr*
EMP: 255
SQ FT: 11,137
SALES (corp-wide): 21.1B **Publicly Held**
WEB: www.southwest.com
SIC: 4512 Air passenger carrier, scheduled
PA: Southwest Airlines Co.
2702 Love Field Dr
Dallas TX 75235
214 792-4000

(P-4802)
SOUTHWEST AIRLINES CO
100 World Way Ste 328, Los Angeles
(90045-5854)
PHONE..................................310 665-5700
Fax: 310 670-0723
EMP: 70
SALES (corp-wide): 21.1B **Publicly Held**
SIC: 4512 4581
PA: Southwest Airlines Co.
2702 Love Field Dr
Dallas TX 75235
214 792-4000

(P-4803)
SOUTHWEST AIRLINES CO
10 Alan Shepard Way, Oakland
(94621-4501)
PHONE..................................510 563-1234
John Mactherson, *Manager*
EMP: 105
SALES (corp-wide): 21.1B **Publicly Held**
WEB: www.southwest.com
SIC: 4512 Air passenger carrier, scheduled
PA: Southwest Airlines Co.
2702 Love Field Dr
Dallas TX 75235
214 792-4000

(P-4804)
UNITED AIRLINES INC
United Airlines Mnt Optnb, San Francisco
(94128)
PHONE..................................650 634-4209
Bill Norman, *Vice Pres*
Bernard Corbins, *Engineer*
Haosheng Wu, *Engineer*
EMP: 102
SALES (corp-wide): 37.7B **Publicly Held**
WEB: www.united.com
SIC: 4512 Air passenger carrier, scheduled
HQ: United Airlines, Inc.
233 S Wacker Dr Ste 710
Chicago IL 60606
872 825-4000

(P-4805)
UNITED AIRLINES INC
2435 Whitman Way, San Bruno
(94066-3852)
PHONE..................................650 634-2468
Lon Wildurin, *Manager*
EMP: 101
SALES (corp-wide): 37.7B **Publicly Held**
WEB: www.united.com
SIC: 4512 Air passenger carrier, scheduled

PRODUCTS & SVCS

HQ: United Airlines, Inc.
233 S Wacker Dr Ste 710
Chicago IL 60606
872 825-4000

(P-4806)
UNITED AIRLINES INC
6018 Avion Dr, Los Angeles (90045-5679)
PHONE..................310 342-8086
Don Nelson, *Office Mgr*
EMP: 102
SALES (corp-wide): 37.7B **Publicly Held**
SIC: 4512 Air passenger carrier, scheduled
HQ: United Airlines, Inc.
233 S Wacker Dr Ste 710
Chicago IL 60606
872 825-4000

(P-4807)
UNITED AIRLINES INC
Maintenance Operation Ctr, San Francisco
(94124)
PHONE..................650 634-7800
D K Loo, *Director*
EMP: 60
SALES (corp-wide): 37.7B **Publicly Held**
WEB: www.united.com
SIC: 4512 Air passenger carrier, scheduled
HQ: United Airlines, Inc.
233 S Wacker Dr Ste 710
Chicago IL 60606
872 825-4000

(P-4808)
UNITED AIRLINES INC
3835 N Harbor Dr Ste 115, San Diego
(92101-1081)
PHONE..................619 692-3310
Al Turner, *Manager*
EMP: 140
SQ FT: 80,705
SALES (corp-wide): 37.7B **Publicly Held**
WEB: www.united.com
SIC: 4512 Air passenger carrier, scheduled
HQ: United Airlines, Inc.
233 S Wacker Dr Ste 710
Chicago IL 60606
872 825-4000

(P-4809)
UNITED AIRLINES INC
Also Called: Continental Airlines
7300 World Way W Rm 144, Los Angeles
(90045-5829)
PHONE..................310 258-3319
Ken Jaminson, *Manager*
EMP: 275
SALES (corp-wide): 37.7B **Publicly Held**
WEB: www.continental.com
SIC: 4512 Air passenger carrier, scheduled
HQ: United Airlines, Inc.
233 S Wacker Dr Ste 710
Chicago IL 60606
872 825-4000

(P-4810)
UNITED AIRLINES INC
San Francisco Intl Arprt, San Francisco
(94128)
PHONE..................650 634-4469
Daniel Cummins, *Manager*
Gil Shaw, *Manager*
EMP: 102
SALES (corp-wide): 37.7B **Publicly Held**
WEB: www.united.com
SIC: 4512 Air passenger carrier, scheduled
HQ: United Airlines, Inc.
233 S Wacker Dr Ste 710
Chicago IL 60606
872 825-4000

(P-4811)
UNITED AIRLINES INC
3400 E Tahquitz Cyn 17, Palm Springs
(92262-6920)
PHONE..................760 778-5690
Peg James, *Manager*
EMP: 57
SALES (corp-wide): 37.7B **Publicly Held**
WEB: www.united.com
SIC: 4512 Air passenger carrier, scheduled
HQ: United Airlines, Inc.
233 S Wacker Dr Ste 710
Chicago IL 60606
872 825-4000

(P-4812)
UNITED AIRLINES INC
545 Mcdonald Rd 68305, San Francisco
(94128)
PHONE..................650 634-2772
DK Loo, *Branch Mgr*
EMP: 101
SALES (corp-wide): 37.7B **Publicly Held**
SIC: 4512 Air passenger carrier, scheduled
HQ: United Airlines, Inc.
233 S Wacker Dr Ste 710
Chicago IL 60606
872 825-4000

(P-4813)
UNITED COURIERS INC (DH)
Also Called: U C I Distribution Plus
3280 E Foothill Blvd, Pasadena
(91107-3103)
PHONE..................213 383-3611
Stephan Cretier, *CEO*
Richard R Irvin, *President*
Robert G Irvin, *Treasurer*
EMP: 200
SQ FT: 25,000
SALES (est): 34.7MM **Privately Held**
WEB: www.unitedcouriers.net
SIC: 4512 4215 4212 7381 Air cargo car-
rier, scheduled; courier services, except
by air; local trucking, without storage; ar-
mored car services; freight forwarding
HQ: Ati Systems International, Inc.
2000 Nw Corp Blvd Ste 101
Boca Raton FL 33431
561 939-7000

(P-4814)
VIRGIN AMERICA INC (HQ)
555 Airport Blvd, Burlingame (94010-2000)
PHONE..................877 359-8474
Benito Minicucci, *CEO*
Donald J Carty, *Ch of Bd*
Stephen A Forte, *COO*
Peter D Hunt, *CFO*
Samuel K Skinner, *Vice Ch Bd*
EMP: 198
SQ FT: 85,674
SALES: 1.5B
SALES (corp-wide): 7.9B **Publicly Held**
WEB: www.virginamerica.com
SIC: 4512 Air passenger carrier, scheduled
PA: Alaska Air Group, Inc
19300 International Blvd
Seatac WA 98188
206 392-5040

(P-4815)
WORLDWIDE FLIGHT SERVICES INC
Also Called: Wfs
5758 W Century Blvd, Los Angeles
(90045-5613)
P.O. Box 90220 (90009-0220)
PHONE..................310 342-7830
John OH, *Branch Mgr*
EMP: 120
SALES (corp-wide): 2.7B **Privately Held**
SIC: 4512 Air cargo carrier, scheduled
PA: Worldwide Flight Services, Inc.
E Hangar Rd Bldg 151
Jamaica NY 11430
718 244-0900

4513 Air Courier Svcs

(P-4816)
DHL EXPRESS (USA) INC
401 23rd St, San Francisco (94107-3102)
PHONE..................415 826-7338
Jeffrey Funk, *Manager*
Warfield Thornton, *General Mgr*
Marsten Tullius, *Manager*
EMP: 70
SALES (corp-wide): 71.2B **Privately Held**
SIC: 4513 Air courier services
HQ: Dhl Express (Usa), Inc.
1210 S Pine Island Rd
Plantation FL 33324
954 888-7000

(P-4817)
FEDERAL EXPRESS CORPORATION
Also Called: Fedex
3541 Regional Pkwy, Petaluma (94954)
PHONE..................800 463-3339
EMP: 80
SALES (corp-wide): 47.4B **Publicly Held**
SIC: 4513
HQ: Federal Express Corporation
3610 Hacks Cross Rd
Memphis TN 38125
901 369-3600

(P-4818)
FEDERAL EXPRESS CORPORATION
Also Called: Fedex
1650 47th St, San Diego (92102-2508)
PHONE..................800 463-3339
John Staback, *Manager*
EMP: 225
SALES (corp-wide): 65.4B **Publicly Held**
WEB: www.federalexpress.com
SIC: 4513 Air courier services
HQ: Federal Express Corporation
3610 Hacks Cross Rd
Memphis TN 38125
901 369-3600

(P-4819)
FEDERAL EXPRESS CORPORATION
Also Called: Fedex
1330 Fortress St, Chico (95973-9031)
PHONE..................800 463-3339
EMP: 109
SALES (corp-wide): 65.4B **Publicly Held**
SIC: 4513 Air courier services
HQ: Federal Express Corporation
3610 Hacks Cross Rd
Memphis TN 38125
901 369-3600

(P-4820)
FEDERAL EXPRESS CORPORATION
Also Called: Fedex
1286 Lawrence Station Rd, Sunnyvale
(94089-2220)
PHONE..................800 463-3339
Gail Caldwell, *Branch Mgr*
EMP: 100
SALES (corp-wide): 65.4B **Publicly Held**
WEB: www.federalexpress.com
SIC: 4513 4215 Letter delivery, private air;
package delivery, private air; parcel deliv-
ery, private air; courier services, except
by air
HQ: Federal Express Corporation
3610 Hacks Cross Rd
Memphis TN 38125
901 369-3600

(P-4821)
FEDERAL EXPRESS CORPORATION
Also Called: Fedex
12600 Prairie Ave, Hawthorne
(90250-4685)
PHONE..................800 463-3339
Ted Strong, *Branch Mgr*
EMP: 200
SALES (corp-wide): 65.4B **Publicly Held**
WEB: www.federalexpress.com
SIC: 4513 4215 Air courier services;
courier services, except by air
HQ: Federal Express Corporation
3610 Hacks Cross Rd
Memphis TN 38125
901 369-3600

(P-4822)
FEDERAL EXPRESS CORPORATION
Also Called: Fedex
1601 Aurora Dr, San Leandro
(94577-3101)
PHONE..................510 347-2430
EMP: 130
SALES (corp-wide): 47.4B **Publicly Held**
SIC: 4513 4215

HQ: Federal Express Corporation
3610 Hacks Cross Rd
Memphis TN 38125
901 369-3600

(P-4823)
FEDERAL EXPRESS CORPORATION
Also Called: Fedex
1650 Sunflower Ave, Costa Mesa
(92626-1513)
PHONE..................800 463-3339
Mike Stanley, *Manager*
EMP: 53
SQ FT: 75,000
SALES (corp-wide): 65.4B **Publicly Held**
WEB: www.federalexpress.com
SIC: 4513 Air courier services
HQ: Federal Express Corporation
3610 Hacks Cross Rd
Memphis TN 38125
901 369-3600

(P-4824)
FEDERAL EXPRESS CORPORATION
Also Called: Fedex
1 Lower Ragsdale Dr # 4, Monterey
(93940-5757)
PHONE..................800 463-3339
Mike Luders, *Manager*
Don Bailey, *General Mgr*
EMP: 60
SALES (corp-wide): 65.4B **Publicly Held**
WEB: www.federalexpress.com
SIC: 4513 Package delivery, private air
HQ: Federal Express Corporation
3610 Hacks Cross Rd
Memphis TN 38125
901 369-3600

(P-4825)
FEDERAL EXPRESS CORPORATION
Also Called: Fedex
500 12th St Ste 139, Oakland
(94607-4010)
PHONE..................510 465-5209
EMP: 107
SALES (corp-wide): 47.4B **Publicly Held**
SIC: 4513
HQ: Federal Express Corporation
3610 Hacks Cross Rd
Memphis TN 38125
901 369-3600

(P-4826)
FEDERAL EXPRESS CORPORATION
Also Called: Fedex
8455 Pardee Dr, Oakland (94621-1411)
PHONE..................800 463-3339
Ron Fraser, *Manager*
EMP: 100
SALES (corp-wide): 65.4B **Publicly Held**
WEB: www.federalexpress.com
SIC: 4513 4215 Letter delivery, private air;
package delivery, private air; parcel deliv-
ery, private air; courier services, except
by air
HQ: Federal Express Corporation
3610 Hacks Cross Rd
Memphis TN 38125
901 369-3600

(P-4827)
FEDERAL EXPRESS CORPORATION
Also Called: Fedex
6775 Woodrum Cir, Redding (96002-9386)
PHONE..................800 463-3339
Craig McLaughlin, *Manager*
EMP: 150
SALES (corp-wide): 65.4B **Publicly Held**
WEB: www.federalexpress.com
SIC: 4513 4215 Letter delivery, private air;
package delivery, private air; parcel deliv-
ery, private air; package delivery, vehicu-
lar
HQ: Federal Express Corporation
3610 Hacks Cross Rd
Memphis TN 38125
901 369-3600

(P-4828)
FEDERAL EXPRESS CORPORATION
Also Called: Fedex
935 Performance Dr, Stockton
(95206-4930)
PHONE..................................800 463-3339
Val Thomas, *Principal*
EMP: 50
SALES (corp-wide): 65.4B **Publicly Held**
SIC: 4513 Package delivery, private air; letter delivery, private air
HQ: Federal Express Corporation
3610 Hacks Cross Rd
Memphis TN 38125
901 369-3600

(P-4829)
FEDERAL EXPRESS CORPORATION
Also Called: Fedex
9339 Ann St, Santa Fe Springs
(90670-2655)
PHONE..................................800 463-3339
Doug Sander, *Branch Mgr*
EMP: 100
SALES (corp-wide): 65.4B **Publicly Held**
WEB: www.federalexpress.com
SIC: 4513 Package delivery, private air; letter delivery, private air
HQ: Federal Express Corporation
3610 Hacks Cross Rd
Memphis TN 38125
901 369-3600

(P-4830)
FEDERAL EXPRESS CORPORATION
Also Called: Fedex
9510 W Airport Dr, Visalia (93277-9501)
PHONE..................................800 463-3339
Richard Keeling, *Branch Mgr*
EMP: 150
SALES (corp-wide): 65.4B **Publicly Held**
WEB: www.federalexpress.com
SIC: 4513 Package delivery, private air; letter delivery, private air
HQ: Federal Express Corporation
3610 Hacks Cross Rd
Memphis TN 38125
901 369-3600

(P-4831)
FEDERAL EXPRESS CORPORATION
Also Called: Fedex
2060 S Wineville Ave B, Ontario
(91761-3633)
PHONE..................................909 390-3237
EMP: 60
SALES (corp-wide): 47.4B **Publicly Held**
SIC: 4513
HQ: Federal Express Corporation
3610 Hacks Cross Rd
Memphis TN 38125
901 369-3600

(P-4832)
FEDERAL EXPRESS CORPORATION
Also Called: Fedex
2500 Kimberly Ave, Fullerton (92831-5142)
PHONE..................................800 463-3339
Kim Cooper, *Branch Mgr*
Lynn Garcia, *Safety Mgr*
EMP: 130
SALES (corp-wide): 65.4B **Publicly Held**
WEB: www.federalexpress.com
SIC: 4513 Letter delivery, private air; package delivery, private air; parcel delivery, private air
HQ: Federal Express Corporation
3610 Hacks Cross Rd
Memphis TN 38125
901 369-3600

(P-4833)
FEDERAL EXPRESS CORPORATION
Also Called: Fedex
3150 Paseo Mercado, Oxnard
(93036-8918)
PHONE..................................800 463-3339
Bert Hawkins, *Director*

David Teems, *Manager*
EMP: 70
SALES (corp-wide): 65.4B **Publicly Held**
WEB: www.federalexpress.com
SIC: 4513 Letter delivery, private air; package delivery, private air; parcel delivery, private air
HQ: Federal Express Corporation
3610 Hacks Cross Rd
Memphis TN 38125
901 369-3600

(P-4834)
FEDERAL EXPRESS CORPORATION
Also Called: Fedex
8950 Cal Center Dr # 370, Sacramento
(95826-3262)
PHONE..................................916 361-5500
EMP: 100
SALES (corp-wide): 47.4B **Publicly Held**
SIC: 4513 4512 4212 4213
HQ: Federal Express Corporation
3610 Hacks Cross Rd
Memphis TN 38125
901 369-3600

(P-4835)
FEDERAL EXPRESS CORPORATION
Also Called: Fedex
1875 Marin St, San Francisco
(94124-1139)
PHONE..................................800 463-3339
EMP: 109
SALES (corp-wide): 65.4B **Publicly Held**
WEB: www.federalexpress.com
SIC: 4513 4512 4522 4213 Letter delivery, private air; air transportation, scheduled; air transportation, nonscheduled; trucking, except local
HQ: Federal Express Corporation
3610 Hacks Cross Rd
Memphis TN 38125
901 369-3600

(P-4836)
FEDERAL EXPRESS CORPORATION
Also Called: Fedex
2451 N Palm Dr, Long Beach
(90755-4006)
PHONE..................................800 463-3339
EMP: 150
SALES (corp-wide): 47.4B **Publicly Held**
SIC: 4513
HQ: Federal Express Corporation
3610 Hacks Cross Rd
Memphis TN 38125
901 369-3600

(P-4837)
FEDERAL EXPRESS CORPORATION
Also Called: Fedex
1 World Trade Ctr Ste 191, Long Beach
(90831-0191)
PHONE..................................562 522-4014
EMP: 150
SALES (corp-wide): 45.5B **Publicly Held**
SIC: 4513
HQ: Federal Express Corporation
3610 Hacks Cross Rd
Memphis TN 38125
901 369-3600

(P-4838)
FEDEX GROUND PACKAGE SYS INC
9999 Olson Dr Ste 100, San Diego
(92121-2837)
PHONE..................................800 463-3339
EMP: 107
SALES (corp-wide): 65.4B **Publicly Held**
SIC: 4513 Package delivery, private air
HQ: Fedex Ground Package System, Inc.
1000 Fed Ex Dr
Coraopolis PA 15108
412 269-1000

(P-4839)
FEDEX GROUND PACKAGE SYS INC
330 Resource Dr, Bloomington
(92316-3528)
PHONE..................................800 463-3339
Richard Greene, *Manager*
EMP: 800
SALES (corp-wide): 65.4B **Publicly Held**
SIC: 4513 Air courier services
HQ: Fedex Ground Package System, Inc.
1000 Fed Ex Dr
Coraopolis PA 15108
412 269-1000

(P-4840)
GREYHOUND LINES INC
121 S Center St, Stockton (95202-2817)
PHONE..................................209 466-3568
Jackie Wilson, *Manager*
EMP: 50
SALES (corp-wide): 8.9B **Privately Held**
WEB: www.greyhound.com
SIC: 4513 Package delivery, private air
HQ: Greyhound Lines, Inc.
350 N Saint Paul St # 300
Dallas TX 75201
214 849-8000

(P-4841)
LBC MUNDIAL CORPORATION (HQ)
Also Called: LBC North America
3563 Inv Blvd Ste 3, Hayward (94545)
PHONE..................................650 873-0750
Hugo Bonilla, *President*
Carlos Araneta, *Ch of Bd*
Fely Ruiz, *Corp Secy*
Patricia Garcia, *Adv Mgr*
James Taylor, *Warehouse Mgr*
EMP: 60
SQ FT: 25,000
SALES (est): 61MM **Privately Held**
SIC: 4513 4215 6099 6221 Air courier services; courier services, except by air; foreign currency exchange; commodity contracts brokers, dealers

(P-4842)
MEJICO EXPRESS INC (PA)
Also Called: Grupoex
14849 Firestone Blvd Fl 1, La Mirada
(90638)
PHONE..................................714 690-8300
Jose Leon, *President*
EMP: 150
SALES (est): 23.3MM **Privately Held**
SIC: 4513 Letter delivery, private air

(P-4843)
MIDNITE AIR CORP
8801 Bellanca Ave, Los Angeles
(90045-4705)
PHONE..................................310 330-2300
Tom Belmont, *Branch Mgr*
EMP: 50
SALES (corp-wide): 370.8MM **Privately Held**
SIC: 4513 Air courier services
HQ: Midnite Air Corp.
5001 Arprt Plz Dr Ste 250
Long Beach CA 90815
310 910-9199

(P-4844)
MIDNITE AIR CORP (HQ)
Also Called: MNX
5001 Arprt Plz Dr Ste 250, Long Beach
(90815)
PHONE..................................310 910-9199
Paul J Martins, *President*
Thomas Belmont, *COO*
Fred Deleeuw, *CFO*
Nathan Gesse, *Exec VP*
Paul Hickey, *Exec VP*
EMP: 55
SQ FT: 10,000
SALES (est): 97.1MM
SALES (corp-wide): 370.8MM **Privately Held**
WEB: www.mnx.com
SIC: 4513 Air courier services

PA: Audax Private Equity Fund Ii, L.P.
101 Huntington Ave
Boston MA 02199
617 859-1500

(P-4845)
NETWORK GLOBAL LOGISTICS LLC
Also Called: NGL
13479 Valley Blvd, Fontana (92335-5245)
PHONE..................................888 285-7447
EMP: 139
SALES (corp-wide): 233.6MM **Privately Held**
SIC: 4513 4214 4225 Air courier services; local trucking with storage; general warehousing & storage
PA: Network Global Logistics, Llc
320 Interlocken Pkwy # 100
Broomfield CO 80021
866 938-1870

(P-4846)
TNT USA INC
Also Called: TNT Express Worldwide
8500 Osage Ave, Los Angeles
(90045-4421)
PHONE..................................310 242-9700
David Giannelli, *Branch Mgr*
EMP: 70
SALES (corp-wide): 65.4B **Publicly Held**
WEB: www.tnt.com
SIC: 4513 Air courier services
HQ: Tnt Usa Inc.
510 Stewart Ave
Garden City NY 11530
631 712-6700

(P-4847)
TRICOR AMERICA INC
3149 Diablo Ave, Hayward (94545-2701)
PHONE..................................510 293-3960
Mike Chung, *Branch Mgr*
EMP: 150
SALES (corp-wide): 92.9MM **Privately Held**
WEB: www.tricor.com
SIC: 4513 4215 Package delivery, private air; courier services, except by air
PA: Tricor America, Inc.
717 Airport Blvd
South San Francisco CA 94080
650 877-3650

(P-4848)
ULTRAEX INC
2633 Barrington Ct, Hayward (94545-1100)
PHONE..................................800 882-1000
Ernest Holbrook, *President*
Patrick Larouche, *Technology*
Shirley Sun, *Technology*
William Carlson, *Business Mgr*
Alfredo Flores,
EMP: 100
SQ FT: 10,000
SALES (est): 10.1MM **Privately Held**
WEB: www.ultraex.com
SIC: 4513 4214 4215 Air courier services; local trucking with storage; package delivery, vehicular

(P-4849)
UNITED PARCEL SERVICE INC OH
Also Called: UPS
3333 S Downey Rd, Vernon (90058-4116)
PHONE..................................323 260-8957
Tony Peralta, *Manager*
Debbie Bateman, *Manager*
EMP: 350
SALES (corp-wide): 65.8B **Publicly Held**
WEB: www.upsscs.com
SIC: 4513 4215 Air courier services; courier services, except by air
HQ: United Parcel Service, Inc. (Oh)
55 Glenlake Pkwy
Atlanta GA 30328
404 828-6000

PRODUCTS & SVCS

(P-4850)
UNITED PARCEL SERVICE INC OH
Also Called: UPS
25283 Sherman Rd, Sun City
(92585-9352)
PHONE....................951 928-5221
Sean Nichols, *Branch Mgr*
EMP: 208
SALES (corp-wide): 65.8B **Publicly Held**
SIC: 4513 Parcel delivery, private air
HQ: United Parcel Service, Inc. (Oh)
55 Glenlake Pkwy
Atlanta GA 30328
404 828-6000

(P-4851)
UNITED PARCEL SERVICE INC OH
Also Called: UPS
1724 Wawona St, Manteca (95337-9437)
PHONE....................209 944-5932
EMP: 208
SALES (corp-wide): 65.8B **Publicly Held**
WEB: www.upsscs.com
SIC: 4513 Parcel delivery, private air
HQ: United Parcel Service, Inc. (Oh)
55 Glenlake Pkwy
Atlanta GA 30328
404 828-6000

(P-4852)
UNITED PARCEL SERVICE INC OH
Also Called: UPS
Ontario Airport, Ontario (91758)
PHONE....................909 974-7190
Steve Welsh, *Manager*
EMP: 208
SALES (corp-wide): 65.8B **Publicly Held**
WEB: www.upsscs.com
SIC: 4513 Parcel delivery, private air
HQ: United Parcel Service, Inc. (Oh)
55 Glenlake Pkwy
Atlanta GA 30328
404 828-6000

(P-4853)
WEST AIR INC
5005 E Andersen Ave, Fresno
(93727-1502)
PHONE....................559 454-7843
Lawrence W Olson, *Ch of Bd*
Timothy Flynn, *Shareholder*
Maurice Gallagher, *Shareholder*
Beth Wood, *President*
Pauline E Wood, *President*
EMP: 70
SQ FT: 10,000
SALES: 7.5MM **Privately Held**
WEB: www.westair.net
SIC: 4513 Package delivery, private air

(P-4854)
WING AVIATION LLC
100 Mayfield Ave, Mountain View
(94043-4122)
PHONE....................650 260-8170
James Burgess, *CEO*
Adam Woodworth, *CTO*
Divya Chandra, *Controller*
EMP: 100
SALES (est): 2MM
SALES (corp-wide): 110.8B **Publicly Held**
SIC: 4513 Package delivery, private air
PA: Alphabet Inc.
1600 Amphitheatre Pkwy
Mountain View CA 94043
650 253-0000

4522 Air Transportation, Nonscheduled

(P-4855)
ADVANCED AIR LLC
Also Called: Jet Center Los Angeles
12101 Crenshaw Blvd Ste 1, Hawthorne
(90250-3369)
PHONE....................310 676-4673
Levi Stockton, *Mng Member*
Donny Sandusky, *General Mgr*
Erika Gonzalez, *Admin Asst*

Ryan Emslie, *Train & Dev Mgr*
EMP: 88
SALES (est): 2MM
SALES (corp-wide): 15.8MM **Privately Held**
SIC: 4522 Flying charter service
PA: Wedgewood Inc.
2015 Manhattan Beach Blvd # 100
Redondo Beach CA 90278
310 640-3070

(P-4856)
BOUTIQUE AIR INC
5 3rd St Ste 925, San Francisco
(94103-3220)
PHONE....................415 449-0505
Shawn Simpson, *President*
Brian Murphy, *COO*
Cameron Campbell, *Officer*
Curtis McKerrow, *Officer*
Tyler Dietz, *Project Mgr*
EMP: 450
SALES (est): 2.4MM **Privately Held**
SIC: 4522 4512 Flying charter service; air passenger carrier, scheduled

(P-4857)
CALIFRNIA SHOCK TRUMA A RESCUE (PA)
Also Called: Calstar
4933 Bailey Loop, McClellan (95652-2516)
PHONE....................916 921-4000
Lynn Malmstrom, *President*
Tom Pandola, *Comms Dir*
Sonja Vargas, *Admin Asst*
David Osuna, *Director*
EMP: 63
SQ FT: 44,000
SALES: 52.9MM **Privately Held**
WEB: www.calstar.org
SIC: 4522 Ambulance services, air

(P-4858)
ELITE AVIATION LLC
7501 Hayvenhurst Pl, Van Nuys
(91406-2851)
PHONE....................818 988-5387
Kacani Shina, *Mng Member*
EMP: 100
SQ FT: 54,000
SALES (est): 16.4MM **Privately Held**
WEB: www.eliteaviation.com
SIC: 4522 4581 Flying charter service; aircraft maintenance & repair services

(P-4859)
FAYAKA AIRWAYS LLC
659 Macarthur Blvd, San Leandro
(94577-2115)
PHONE....................800 771-5489
Yannick Kamate, *CEO*
EMP: 200
SALES: 1MM **Privately Held**
SIC: 4522 Air transportation, nonscheduled

(P-4860)
JET EDGE INTERNATIONAL LLC
16700 Roscoe Blvd Hngr C, Van Nuys
(91406-1102)
PHONE....................818 442-0096
Richard Bard, *CEO*
William Papariella, *President*
David Erich, *COO*
Jim Hansen, *Exec VP*
Geoff Makely, *Senior VP*
EMP: 100 EST: 2011
SALES (corp-wide): 13.2MM **Privately Held**
SIC: 4522 Air transportation, nonscheduled

(P-4861)
JETSUITE INC (PA)
18952 Macarthur Blvd # 200, Irvine
(92612-1401)
PHONE....................949 892-4300
Alex Wilcox, *CEO*
Stephanie Chung, *President*
Michael Bata, *COO*
Keith Rabin, *CFO*
Jordan Lamotte, *Officer*
EMP: 170
SQ FT: 7,641
SALES (est): 48.7MM **Privately Held**
SIC: 4522 Flying charter service

(P-4862)
JONAIR SERVICES LLC
9800 S Sepulveda Blvd, Los Angeles
(90045-5208)
PHONE....................310 529-5482
David Jones, *CEO*
EMP: 99
SQ FT: 110,000
SALES (est): 2.3MM **Privately Held**
SIC: 4522 Air transportation, nonscheduled

(P-4863)
MAGUIRE AVIATION GROUP LLC
7155 Valjean Ave, Van Nuys (91406-3917)
PHONE....................818 989-2300
Alec Maguire, *President*
EMP: 50
SALES (est): 5.8MM **Privately Held**
SIC: 4522 Flying charter service

(P-4864)
MERCY AIR TRI-COUNTY LLC
1670 Miro Way, Rialto (92376-8629)
P.O. Box 2532, Fontana (92334-2532)
PHONE....................909 829-1051
David Dolstein, *Mng Member*
Aaron Todd,
EMP: 250
SQ FT: 11,288
SALES (est): 9.2MM
SALES (corp-wide): 1.1B **Privately Held**
SIC: 4522 4119 7623 7359 Ambulance services, air; local passenger transportation; air conditioning repair; aircraft & industrial truck rental services; helicopters
HQ: Air Methods Corporation
5500 S Quebec St Ste 310
Greenwood Village CO 80111
303 792-7400

(P-4865)
MERLIN GLOBAL SERVICES LLC
380 Stevens Ave Ste 305, Solana Beach
(92075-2069)
PHONE....................904 305-9559
Conner Searcy, *President*
Brian Raduenz, *CEO*
David Scott, *COO*
J Wayne Miller, *Vice Pres*
David Stinnett, *Admin Sec*
EMP: 110
SALES (est): 13.2MM **Privately Held**
WEB: www.merlinramco.com
SIC: 4522 8711 8731 8748 Air transportation, nonscheduled; engineering services; commercial physical research; test development & evaluation service; educational services

(P-4866)
SUTTER CENTRAL VLY HOSPITALS
Also Called: Medi-Flight Northern Cal
1700 Coffee Rd, Modesto (95355-2803)
PHONE....................209 526-4500
Terry Sweeney, *Director*
EMP: 50
SALES (corp-wide): 12.4B **Privately Held**
WEB: www.memorialmedicalcenter.org
SIC: 4522 Air transportation, nonscheduled
HQ: Sutter Central Valley Hospitals
1700 Coffee Rd
Modesto CA 95355
209 526-4500

4581 Airports, Flying Fields & Terminal Svcs

(P-4867)
ABM AVIATION INC
601 Gateway Blvd Ste 1145, South San Francisco (94080-7413)
PHONE....................650 872-5400
Doug Kreuckamp, *Vice Pres*
EMP: 400
SALES (corp-wide): 5.4B **Publicly Held**
SIC: 4581 Airport
HQ: Abm Aviation, Inc.
3399 Peachtree Rd Ne
Atlanta GA 30326
404 926-4200

(P-4868)
AEROGROUND INC (DH)
Also Called: Air Cargo Handling Service
270 Lawrence Ave, South San Francisco
(94080-6817)
PHONE....................650 266-6965
Anthony Bonino, *CEO*
EMP: 800
SQ FT: 175,000
SALES (est): 86.3MM
SALES (corp-wide): 3.2B **Privately Held**
SIC: 4581 4213 Air freight handling at airports; trucking, except local

(P-4869)
AIRPORT COMMISIONS
Also Called: Business of Finance
San Francisco Intl Arprt, San Francisco
(94128)
PHONE....................650 821-5000
John L Martin, *Director*
EMP: 1121
SALES (est): 30MM **Privately Held**
SIC: 4581 Airports, flying fields & services
PA: City & County Of San Francisco
1 Dr Carlton B Goodlett P
San Francisco CA 94102
415 554-7500

(P-4870)
ALLIANCE GROUND INTL LLC
6181 W Imperial Hwy, Los Angeles
(90045-6305)
PHONE....................310 646-2446
EMP: 73
SALES (corp-wide): 120.5MM **Privately Held**
SIC: 4581 Airfreight loading & unloading services
PA: Alliance Ground International, Llc
2 Datran Ctr
Miami FL 33156
305 740-3252

(P-4871)
ALLIANCE GROUND INTL LLC
648 Rest Field Rd, San Francisco (94128)
PHONE....................650 821-0855
Peter Ferrantelli, *General Mgr*
Isaac Donkor, *Opers Mgr*
Alberto Guerrero, *Opers Staff*
Miles Mosca, *Director*
Mark Pitts, *Manager*
EMP: 73
SALES (corp-wide): 120.5MM **Privately Held**
SIC: 4581 Airfreight loading & unloading services
PA: Alliance Ground International, Llc
2 Datran Ctr
Miami FL 33156
305 740-3252

(P-4872)
ARINWINE ARCFT MAINT SVCS LLC
Also Called: F&E Aircraft Maintenance
1720 E Holly Ave, El Segundo
(90245-4404)
PHONE....................310 338-0063
Lisa Arinwine, *COO*
EMP: 63
SQ FT: 10,000
SALES (est): 1.9MM **Privately Held**
SIC: 4581 Aircraft maintenance & repair services; aircraft servicing & repairing

(P-4873)
ATLANTIC AVIATION SVC
1250 Aviation Ave Hngr E2, San Jose
(95110-1142)
PHONE....................408 297-7552
Dan Ryan, *President*
Harold Deguzman, *CFO*
Jim Blair, *Treasurer*
Jim Rutherford, *Exec VP*
Barry Fernald, *Admin Sec*
EMP: 50
SQ FT: 196,000
SALES (est): 4.8MM **Privately Held**
WEB: www.sjjc.com
SIC: 4581 Aircraft maintenance & repair services; hangars & other aircraft storage facilities

(P-4874)
AVIATION & DEFENSE INC
Also Called: ADI
255 S Leland Norton Way, San Bernardino
(92408-0103)
PHONE.....................909 382-3487
Daniel M Scanlon, *CEO*
Hector Guerrero, *Ch of Bd*
Mike Scanlon, *President*
Ben Flores, *CFO*
Dan Scanlon, *Vice Pres*
EMP: 180
SQ FT: 180,000
SALES (est): 24.4MM **Privately Held**
SIC: 4581 Aircraft maintenance & repair
   services

(P-4875)
BOEING COMPANY
Slc 2 Bldg 1628, San Luis Obispo (93401)
P.O. Box 5219, Lompoc (93437-0219)
PHONE.....................805 606-6340
Rich Niederhauser, *Manager*
EMP: 80
SALES (corp-wide): 93.3B **Publicly Held**
SIC: 4581 3761 3721 Airports & flying
   fields; guided missiles & space vehicles;
   aircraft
   PA: The Boeing Company
      100 N Riverside Plz
      Chicago IL 60606
      312 544-2000

(P-4876)
CERTIFIED AVIATION SVCS LLC
5720 Avion Dr, Los Angeles (90045-5620)
PHONE.....................310 338-1224
Henry Havash, *Manager*
EMP: 66
SALES (corp-wide): 54.7MM **Privately
   Held**
SIC: 4581 Aircraft maintenance & repair
   services
   PA: Certified Aviation Services Llc
      6201 W Imperial Hwy
      Los Angeles CA 90045
      909 605-0380

(P-4877)
CITY OF LONG BEACH
Also Called: Long Beach Airport
4100 E Don Douglas Dr Fl Flr 2, Long
Beach (90808)
PHONE.....................562 570-2600
Chris Kunze, *Manager*
EMP: 65 **Privately Held**
WEB: www.polb.com
SIC: 4581 9111 Airport; mayors' offices
   PA: City Of Long Beach
      333 W Ocean Blvd Fl 10
      Long Beach CA 90802
      562 570-6450

(P-4878)
CITY OF LOS ANGELES
Also Called: Van Nuys Airport
16461 Sherman Way Ste 210, Van Nuys
(91406-3841)
PHONE.....................818 908-5950
Selena Birk, *Manager*
Danielle Stewart, *Sales Executive*
EMP: 100 **Privately Held**
WEB: www.lacity.org
SIC: 4581 9621 6531 Airport; regulation,
   administration of transportation; ; real es-
   tate managers
   PA: City Of Los Angeles
      200 N Spring St Ste 303
      Los Angeles CA 90012
      213 978-0600

(P-4879)
CITY OF PALM SPRINGS
3400 E Tahquitz Canyon Wa, Palm Springs
(92262-6966)
P.O. Box 2743 (92263-2743)
PHONE.....................760 318-3800
Thomas Nolan, *Director*
EMP: 58 **Privately Held**
WEB: www.psfire.com
SIC: 4581 Airport
   PA: City Of Palm Springs
      3200 E Tahquitz Cyn Way
      Palm Springs CA 92262
      760 322-8362

(P-4880)
CITY OF SAN JOSE
Also Called: Mineta San Jose Intl Arprt
1701 Arprt Blvd Ste B1130, San Jose
(95110)
PHONE.....................408 392-3600
William Sherry, *Director*
EMP: 310
SQ FT: 30,000 **Privately Held**
WEB: www.csjfinance.org
SIC: 4581 9199 Airport;
   PA: City Of San Jose
      200 E Santa Clara St
      San Jose CA 95113
      408 535-3500

(P-4881)
CLAY LACY AVIATION INC (PA)
Also Called: C L A
7435 Valjean Ave, Van Nuys (91406-2977)
PHONE.....................818 989-2900
Brian Kirkdoffer, *President*
Jimmy Dailey, *COO*
Hershel Clay Lacy, *Founder*
Scott Cutshall, *Vice Pres*
David Lamb, *Vice Pres*
EMP: 350
SQ FT: 18,000
SALES (est): 63.1MM **Privately Held**
WEB: www.claylacy.com
SIC: 4581 Airport terminal services

(P-4882)
**COMAV TECHNICAL SERVICES
LLC**
Also Called: S C A
18438 Readiness St, Victorville
(92394-7945)
PHONE.....................760 530-2400
Craig Garrick, *CEO*
Jon Day, *CFO*
▲ EMP: 155
SQ FT: 47,625
SALES (est): 26.7MM
SALES (corp-wide): 154.8MM **Privately
   Held**
WEB: www.scaviation.com
SIC: 4581 Aircraft servicing & repairing
   PA: Comav, Llc
      18499 Phantom St Ste 17
      Victorville CA 92394
      760 523-5100

(P-4883)
COUNTY OF MENDOCINO
Also Called: Department of Transportation
340 Lake Mendocino Dr, Ukiah
(95482-9432)
PHONE.....................707 463-4363
Howard Dashiell, *Branch Mgr*
EMP: 96 **Privately Held**
WEB: www.mcdss.org
SIC: 4581 Airport
   PA: County Of Mendocino
      501 Low Gap Rd Rm 1010
      Ukiah CA 95482
      707 463-4441

(P-4884)
COUNTY OF ORANGE
Also Called: John Wayne Airport
3160 Airway Ave, Costa Mesa
(92626-4608)
PHONE.....................949 252-5006
Loan Leblow, *Branch Mgr*
Barry Rondinella, *General Mgr*
Charles Meyersdecisionm, *Info Tech Mgr*
Jeff Oviedo, *Project Mgr*
Leo Tang, *Project Mgr*
EMP: 135 **Privately Held**
SIC: 4581 9621 Airport; aircraft regulating
   agencies;
   PA: County Of Orange
      333 W Santa Ana Blvd 3f
      Santa Ana CA 92701
      714 834-6200

(P-4885)
DSD TRUCKING INC (PA)
2411 Santa Fe Ave, Redondo Beach
(90278-1125)
PHONE.....................310 338-3395
Dan Cuevas, *President*
Jovita Reyes, *Office Mgr*
Kalonde Gilbert, *CTO*
Wendy Silva, *Human Res Mgr*

Carlos Guerra, *Facilities Mgr*
EMP: 100
SQ FT: 300,000
SALES (est): 17.2MM **Privately Held**
SIC: 4581 Air freight handling at airports

(P-4886)
DYNAMO AVIATION INC
16760 Schoenborn St, North Hills
(91343-6108)
P.O. Box 14040, Van Nuys (91409-4040)
PHONE.....................818 785-9561
Masoud S Rabadi, *CEO*
Robin C Scott, *CFO*
Lary Hockens,
George Qatto, *General Mgr*
Young Lee, *Info Tech Mgr*
EMP: 75
SALES (est): 41.3MM **Privately Held**
WEB: www.dynamoaviation.com
SIC: 4581 3444 3679 5063 Aircraft serv-
   icing & repairing; sheet metalwork; har-
   ness assemblies for electronic use: wire
   or cable; storage batteries, industrial

(P-4887)
DYNCORP INTERNATIONAL LLC
Also Called: Logcap IV - Task Order 7
896 Langford Lake Rd, Fort Irwin (92310)
P.O. Box 105033 (92310-5033)
PHONE.....................817 224-8200
Steve Gassney, *Branch Mgr*
EMP: 53
SALES (corp-wide): 31.2B **Privately Held**
SIC: 4581 Aircraft maintenance & repair
   services
   HQ: Dyncorp International Llc
      1700 Old Meadow Rd
      Mc Lean VA 22102
      571 722-0210

(P-4888)
ENVOY AIR INC
Also Called: AMR Eagle
3707 N Harbor Dr Ste 124, San Diego
(92101-1080)
PHONE.....................619 260-9069
Steve Terry, *Branch Mgr*
EMP: 50
SALES (corp-wide): 42.2B **Publicly Held**
WEB: www.americanair.com
SIC: 4581 Airports, flying fields & services
   HQ: Envoy Air Inc.
      4301 Regent Blvd
      Irving TX 75063
      972 374-5200

(P-4889)
F KORBEL & BROS
Korbel Flight Department
4384 Becker Blvd, Santa Rosa
(95403-8283)
PHONE.....................707 525-1875
Gary Krambs, *Branch Mgr*
EMP: 129
SALES (corp-wide): 93.2MM **Privately
   Held**
SIC: 4581 Airport
   PA: F. Korbel & Bros.
      13250 River Rd
      Guerneville CA 95446
      707 824-7000

(P-4890)
**F&E AIRCRAFT MAINTENANCE
(PA)**
531 Main St, El Segundo (90245-3060)
PHONE.....................310 338-0063
Everett R Arinwine,
Keiney Mosley, *Manager*
EMP: 350
SALES (est): 23.7MM **Privately Held**
SIC: 4581 7699 Aircraft servicing & repair-
   ing; aircraft & heavy equipment repair
   services

(P-4891)
**GAT - ARLN GROUND SUPPORT
INC**
6701 Lindbergh Dr, Sacramento
(95837-1138)
PHONE.....................916 923-2349
EMP: 304

SALES (corp-wide): 116MM **Privately
   Held**
SIC: 4581 Aircraft maintenance & repair
   services; airfreight loading & unloading
   services
   PA: Gat - Airline Ground Support, Inc.
      246 City Cir
      Peachtree City GA 30269
      251 633-3888

(P-4892)
GE AVIATION SYSTEMS LLC
295 N Wolfe Ave Bldg 3810, Edwards Afb
(93524-6003)
PHONE.....................661 277-7308
EMP: 193
SALES (corp-wide): 122B **Publicly Held**
SIC: 4581 Airports, flying fields & services
   HQ: Ge Aviation Systems Llc
      1 Neumann Way
      Cincinnati OH 45215
      937 898-9600

(P-4893)
**HUNTLEIGH USA
CORPORATION**
3707 N Harbor Dr A-110, San Diego
(92101-1096)
PHONE.....................619 231-8111
Richard Madison, *Branch Mgr*
EMP: 75
SALES (corp-wide): 255.5MM **Privately
   Held**
SIC: 4581 Airports, flying fields & services
   HQ: Huntleigh Usa Corporation
      545 E John Carpenter Fwy
      Irving TX
      -

(P-4894)
**ICARUS FUEL SERVICES US
CORP**
7251 World Way W, Los Angeles
(90045-5826)
PHONE.....................310 417-0124
David C Matthew, *CEO*
EMP: 65
SALES (est): 5.5MM **Privately Held**
SIC: 4581 Aircraft servicing & repairing

(P-4895)
**INTERNTNAL AROSPC
COATINGS INC**
13640 Phantom St, Victorville
(92394-7900)
PHONE.....................760 246-1651
Niall Cunningham, *Manager*
EMP: 183 **Privately Held**
SIC: 4581 Aircraft maintenance & repair
   services; aircraft painting
   PA: International Aerospace Coatings, Inc.
      5709 W Sunset Hwy Ste 205
      Spokane WA 99224

(P-4896)
JET SOURCE INC
2056 Palomar Airport Rd, Carlsbad
(92011-4463)
PHONE.....................760 438-0877
Vivianne B McWilliam, *CEO*
Jay Brentzel, *President*
Ian Ewing, *Vice Pres*
EMP: 80
SALES (est): 11.5MM **Privately Held**
SIC: 4581 Airports, flying fields & services

(P-4897)
**JETT PRO LINE MAINTENANCE
INC (PA)**
2910 Inland Empire Blvd # 102, Ontario
(91764-4896)
P.O. Box 3190 (91761-0919)
PHONE.....................909 980-0552
Sam Nugud, *CEO*
Willie Nugud, *President*
Al Nugud, *CFO*
EMP: 54
SQ FT: 1,500
SALES (est): 10.8MM **Privately Held**
SIC: 4581 Aircraft maintenance & repair
   services

(P-4898)
LOS ANGELES WORLD AIRPORTS (PA)
6320 W 96th St, Los Angeles (90045-5233)
P.O. Box 92216 (90009-2216)
PHONE..................310 646-7911
Arif Alikhan, *Director*
Robert L Gilbert, *Officer*
Michael Cummings, *Principal*
EMP: 158 **EST:** 2010
SALES (est): 78.6MM **Privately Held**
SIC: 4581 Airport

(P-4899)
LOS ANGELES WORLD AIRPORTS
1230 Tower St, Ontario (91761-2400)
PHONE..................909 544-5490
Dan Meier, *Foreman/Supr*
EMP: 54
SALES (est): 2.4MM **Privately Held**
SIC: 4581 Airports, flying fields & services

(P-4900)
MATHER AVIATION LLC (PA)
10360 Macready Ave, Mather (95655-4109)
PHONE..................916 364-4711
Victor Cushing, *President*
Anita Cushing, *Vice Pres*
Eric Negendank, *Info Tech Dir*
Frank Shaver, *Technician*
Brenda Pena, *Technology*
EMP: 63
SQ FT: 95,000
SALES (est): 13.5MM **Privately Held**
WEB: www.matheraviationllc.com
SIC: 4581 7699 Airport hangar rental; aircraft maintenance & repair services; aircraft & heavy equipment repair services

(P-4901)
MENZIES AVIATION (TEXAS) INC
Also Called: Asig
1049 S Vineyard Ave, Ontario (91761-8029)
P.O. Box 4178 (91761-1011)
PHONE..................909 937-3998
Debbie Martin, *Manager*
EMP: 63
SALES (corp-wide): 3.2B **Privately Held**
WEB: www.asig.com
SIC: 4581 Airport
HQ: Menzies Aviation (Texas), Inc.
4900 Diplomacy Rd
Fort Worth TX 76155
469 281-8200

(P-4902)
MERCURY AIR CARGO INC (HQ)
Also Called: Mercury World Cargo
6040 Avion Dr Ste 200, Los Angeles (90045-5654)
PHONE..................310 258-6100
Joseph A Czyzyk, *CEO*
John Peery, *COO*
Lawrence Samuels, *CFO*
Dan K Barnard, *Treasurer*
Clive Langeveldt, *Exec VP*
▲ **EMP:** 180
SQ FT: 206,000
SALES (est): 50MM
SALES (corp-wide): 445.8MM **Privately Held**
WEB: www.mercuryaircargo.com
SIC: 4581 4512 4522 Airports, flying fields & services; air cargo carrier, scheduled; air cargo carriers, nonscheduled
PA: Mercury Air Group, Inc.
2780 Skypark Dr Ste 300
Torrance CA 90505
310 602-3770

(P-4903)
PACIFIC AVIATION CORPORATION (PA)
380 World Way Ste S31, Los Angeles (90045-5898)
PHONE..................310 646-4015
Phil Shah, *President*
Victor Mena, *Corp Secy*
Preethi Cheriyan, *Human Res Mgr*
Teresa Morales, *Cust Mgr*
Eddie Castillo, *Manager*

EMP: 200
SQ FT: 3,500
SALES: 13.8MM **Privately Held**
WEB: www.pacificaviation.com
SIC: 4581 Airport terminal services

(P-4904)
PHS / MWA (HQ)
Also Called: Phs/Mwa Aviation Services
42355 Rio Nedo, Temecula (92590-3701)
PHONE..................950 695-1008
Mary Bale, *CEO*
Bill Voetsch, *President*
Scott Stanton, *Business Dir*
Didier Vansteenberghe, *Business Dir*
Adam Wells, *Business Dir*
EMP: 50
SQ FT: 30,000
SALES (est): 38.2MM
SALES (corp-wide): 467.7MM **Privately Held**
WEB: www.phsmwa.com
SIC: 4581 3492 7629 Aircraft servicing & repairing; control valves, aircraft: hydraulic & pneumatic; electrical repair shops
PA: Wencor Group, Llc
416 Dividend Dr
Peachtree City GA 30269
678 490-0140

(P-4905)
PORT DEPT CITY OF OAKLAND
Also Called: Metroplitan Oakland Intl Arprt
1 Airport Dr Ste 45, Oakland (94621-1476)
PHONE..................510 563-3300
Bill Wade, *Manager*
EMP: 250
SALES (corp-wide): 65.3MM **Privately Held**
WEB: www.portofoakland.com
SIC: 4581 Airport
PA: Port Department Of The City Of Oakland
530 Water St Fl 3
Oakland CA 94607
510 627-1100

(P-4906)
ROTORCRAFT SUPPORT INC
16425 Hart St, Van Nuys (91406-4640)
PHONE..................818 997-7667
Phillip G Difiore, *President*
Teri Neville, *Vice Pres*
Jeffrey Teubner, *Vice Pres*
Matt Roach, *Sales Staff*
Jason Thompson, *Asst Director*
EMP: 63
SQ FT: 10,000
SALES: 24MM **Privately Held**
SIC: 4581 5088 5599 Aircraft maintenance & repair services; helicopter parts; aircraft instruments, equipment or parts

(P-4907)
SAN DEGO CNTY RGNAL ARPRT AUTH (PA)
Also Called: Sdcraa
3225 N Harbor Dr Fl 3, San Diego (92101-1045)
P.O. Box 82776 (92138-2776)
PHONE..................619 400-2400
Thella F Bowens, *CEO*
Paul Robinson, *Vice Chairman*
Maria Quiroz, *Vice Pres*
Keith Wilschetz, *Plan/Corp Dev D*
Rita Ohaya, *Program Mgr*
EMP: 90
SALES (est): 56.7MM **Privately Held**
SIC: 4581 Airport; air freight handling at airports

(P-4908)
SAN DEGO CNTY RGNAL ARPRT AUTH
2320 Stillwater Rd, San Diego (92101-1016)
PHONE..................619 400-2404
EMP: 143
SALES (corp-wide): 56.7MM **Privately Held**
SIC: 4581 Airport

PA: San Diego County Regional Airport Authority
3225 N Harbor Dr Fl 3
San Diego CA 92101
619 400-2400

(P-4909)
SIGNATURE FLIGHT SUPPORT CORP
3050 N Winery Ave, Fresno (93703-1616)
PHONE..................559 981-2490
Justin Zaklan, *Manager*
EMP: 74
SALES (corp-wide): 2.3B **Privately Held**
SIC: 4581 Aircraft maintenance & repair services
HQ: Signature Flight Support Corporation
201 S Orange Ave Ste 1100
Orlando FL 32801

(P-4910)
SIGNATURE FLIGHT SUPPORT CORP
1052 N Access Rd, San Francisco (94128-3120)
PHONE..................650 877-6800
Ken Setser, *Manager*
EMP: 76
SALES (corp-wide): 2.3B **Privately Held**
SIC: 4581 Airports, flying fields & services
HQ: Signature Flight Support Corporation
201 S Orange Ave Ste 1100
Orlando FL 32801

(P-4911)
SIGNATURE FLIGHT SUPPORT CORP
7240 Hayvenhurst Ave, Van Nuys (91406)
PHONE..................818 464-9500
Stephen W Lee, *Vice Pres*
EMP: 74
SALES (corp-wide): 2.3B **Privately Held**
SIC: 4581 Airports, flying fields & services
HQ: Signature Flight Support Corporation
201 S Orange Ave Ste 1100
Orlando FL 32801

(P-4912)
SIGNATURE FLIGHT SUPPORT CORP
3333 E Spring St Ste 205, Long Beach (90806-2446)
PHONE..................562 997-0700
Eric Hill, *Branch Mgr*
EMP: 74
SALES (corp-wide): 2.3B **Privately Held**
SIC: 4581 Aircraft servicing & repairing
HQ: Signature Flight Support Corporation
201 S Orange Ave Ste 1100
Orlando FL 32801

(P-4913)
SUNSET AVIATION LLC (PA)
Also Called: Solairus Aviation
201 1st St Ste 307, Petaluma (94952-4290)
PHONE..................707 775-2786
Daniel Drohan, *CEO*
John King, *President*
Greg Petersen, *COO*
Mark Dennen, *CFO*
Bob Marinace, *Exec VP*
EMP: 50
SALES (est): 80.7MM **Privately Held**
SIC: 4581 Airports, flying fields & services

(P-4914)
SWISSPORT CARGO SERVICES LP
Also Called: Cargo Service Center
11001 Aviation Blvd, Los Angeles (90045-6123)
PHONE..................310 910-9541
Mark Wood, *General Mgr*
EMP: 562 **Privately Held**
SIC: 4581 Air freight handling at airports
HQ: Swissport Cargo Services, L.P.
23723 Air Frt Ln Bldg 5
Dulles VA 20166
703 742-4300

(P-4915)
SWISSPORT USA INC
San Francisco Intl Arprt, San Francisco (94128)
PHONE..................650 821-6220
Cecilia Guillen, *Station Mgr*
EMP: 220 **Privately Held**
WEB: www.swissport-sfo.com
SIC: 4581 Airport terminal services
HQ: Swissport Usa, Inc.
45025 Aviation Dr Ste 350
Dulles VA 20166

(P-4916)
SWISSPORT USA INC
Also Called: Employment Intake Training Ctr
7025 W Imperial Hwy, Los Angeles (90045-6313)
PHONE..................310 345-1986
Jerry Harris, *General Mgr*
EMP: 400 **Privately Held**
SIC: 4581 Air freight handling at airports
HQ: Swissport Usa, Inc.
45025 Aviation Dr Ste 350
Dulles VA 20166

(P-4917)
SWISSPORT USA INC
Delta Cargo Bldg 612, San Francisco (94128)
PHONE..................571 214-7068
Joe Phelan, *Exec VP*
EMP: 216 **Privately Held**
SIC: 4581 Airports, flying fields & services
HQ: Swissport Usa, Inc.
45025 Aviation Dr Ste 350
Dulles VA 20166

(P-4918)
SWISSPORT USA INC
11001 Aviation Blvd, Los Angeles (90045-6123)
PHONE..................310 910-9560
Dion Fatafehi, *Manager*
EMP: 453 **Privately Held**
WEB: www.swissport-sfo.com
SIC: 4581 Airport terminal services
HQ: Swissport Usa, Inc.
45025 Aviation Dr Ste 350
Dulles VA 20166

(P-4919)
TEXTRON AVIATION INC
Also Called: Cessna Scrmnto Ctation Svc Ctr
5850 Citation Way, Sacramento (95837-1105)
PHONE..................916 929-5656
Thomas Defoe, *Sales/Mktg Mgr*
Jeff Bakker, *Manager*
EMP: 85
SALES (corp-wide): 14.2B **Publicly Held**
WEB: www.cessna.com
SIC: 4581 Aircraft maintenance & repair services
HQ: Textron Aviation Inc.
1 Cessna Blvd
Wichita KS 67215
316 517-6000

(P-4920)
THRESHOLD TECHNOLOGIES INC
8352 Kimball Ave Bldg F35, Chino (91708-9267)
PHONE..................909 606-1666
Mark Dilullo, *CEO*
Lisa Dilullo, *President*
Chris Ladeau, *Info Tech Mgr*
Jerry Perez, *Director*
EMP: 55
SQ FT: 10,000
SALES (est): 8MM **Privately Held**
WEB: www.flytti.com
SIC: 4581 Aircraft storage at airports; airport hangar rental; aircraft cleaning & janitorial service; aircraft servicing & repairing

(P-4921)
TOTAL AIRPORT SERVICES LLC
3537 Branson Dr, San Mateo (94403-2901)
PHONE..................650 358-0144
Ralph Eichenbaum, *Branch Mgr*

EMP: 65
SALES (corp-wide): 168.2MM **Privately Held**
SIC: 4581 Aircraft maintenance & repair services
PA: Total Airport Services, Llc
28420 Hardy Toll Rd # 220
Spring TX 77373
832 592-0048

(P-4922)
WORLD SERVICE WEST
Also Called: L A Inflight Service Company
1812 W 135th St, Gardena (90249-2520)
PHONE.....................................310 538-7000
Byung Yoon, *Owner*
Mall Yoon,
EMP: 170
SQ FT: 13,572
SALES (est): 8.8MM **Privately Held**
SIC: 4581 Aircraft maintenance & repair services; aircraft cleaning & janitorial service; aircraft servicing & repairing

(P-4923)
WORLDWIDE FLIGHT SERVICES INC
5908 Avion Dr, Los Angeles (90045-5622)
P.O. Box 90220 (90009-0220)
PHONE.....................................310 646-7510
Dennis Hudson, *Manager*
EMP: 250
SALES (corp-wide): 2.7B **Privately Held**
SIC: 4581 Aircraft upholstery repair
PA: Worldwide Flight Services, Inc.
E Hangar Rd Bldg 151
Jamaica NY 11430
718 244-0900

(P-4924)
XOJET INC (PA)
2000 Sierra Point Pkwy # 200, Brisbane (94005-1846)
PHONE.....................................650 594-6300
Bradley Stewart, *CEO*
David N Siegel, *Ch of Bd*
Paul Touw, *Ch of Bd*
Benjamin Murray, *President*
Eilif Serck-Hanssen, *President*
EMP: 54
SALES (est): 48.7MM **Privately Held**
WEB: www.xojet.com
SIC: 4581 Aircraft servicing & repairing

4613 Refined Petroleum Pipelines

(P-4925)
SFPP LP (DH)
1100 W Town And Country R, Orange (92868-4647)
PHONE.....................................714 560-4400
Park Shaper, *General Ptnr*
Richard D Kinder, *General Ptnr*
Stephen Seibly, *Financial Analy*
EMP: 150
SQ FT: 75,000
SALES: 302MM **Publicly Held**
SIC: 4613 Gasoline pipelines (common carriers)
HQ: Kinder Morgan Energy Partners, L.P.
1001 La St Ste 1000
Houston TX 77002
713 369-9000

4619 Pipelines, NEC

(P-4926)
KINDER MRGAN ENRGY PARTNERS LP
Also Called: Santa Fe Pacific Pipeline
2319 S Riverside Ave, Bloomington (92316-2931)
PHONE.....................................909 873-5100
Ron Moranes, *Manager*
EMP: 50 **Publicly Held**
WEB: www.kindermorgan.com
SIC: 4619 1623 Coal pipeline operation; pipeline construction

HQ: Kinder Morgan Energy Partners, L.P.
1001 La St Ste 1000
Houston TX 77002
713 369-9000

(P-4927)
UNITED STATES PIPE FNDRY LLC
1295 Whipple Rd, Union City (94587-2036)
P.O. Box 707 (94587-0707)
PHONE.....................................510 441-5810
Jim Kelly, *General Mgr*
EMP: 115
SALES (corp-wide): 1.5B **Publicly Held**
SIC: 4619 Coal pipeline operation
HQ: United States Pipe And Foundry Company Llc
2 Chase Corporate Dr # 200
Hoover AL 35244
205 263-8540

4724 Travel Agencies

(P-4928)
ALTOUR INTERNATIONAL INC
Also Called: Altour Travel Master
12100 W Olympic Blvd # 300, Los Angeles (90064-1051)
PHONE.....................................310 571-6000
Julie Valentine, *Branch Mgr*
EMP: 130
SALES (corp-wide): 73.6MM **Privately Held**
WEB: www.altourtravelmaster.com
SIC: 4724 Travel agencies
PA: Altour International, Inc.
1270 Avenue Of The Flr 15
New York NY 10020
212 897-5000

(P-4929)
ALTOUR INTERNATIONAL INC (PA)
12100 W Olympic Blvd # 300, Los Angeles (90064-1051)
PHONE.....................................310 571-6000
Alexander Chemla, *President*
David Sefton, *Senior VP*
Nancy Lambrechts, *Store Mgr*
Andy Acosta, *Purch Mgr*
Scott Davis, *Director*
EMP: 80
SQ FT: 8,000
SALES: 1.6MM **Privately Held**
SIC: 4724 Travel agencies

(P-4930)
AMERICAN EXPRESS TRAVEL
15353 Barranca Pkwy, Irvine (92618-2216)
PHONE.....................................949 453-7123
Linda Duffy, *Director*
EMP: 100
SALES (corp-wide): 35.5B **Publicly Held**
WEB: www.astoriasoftware.com
SIC: 4724 Travel agencies
HQ: American Express Travel Related Services Company, Inc.,
200 Vesey St
New York NY 10285
212 640-2000

(P-4931)
AMERICAN TRAVEL SOLUTIONS LLC
Also Called: Amtrav
26707 Agoura Rd Ste 204, Calabasas (91302-3831)
PHONE.....................................818 359-6514
Jeff Klee, *CEO*
Ted Perlstein, *Vice Pres*
Wayne Hustis, *CIO*
Rebecca Gavin, *Opers Staff*
Cassie Sclafani, *Marketing Staff*
EMP: 65
SQ FT: 4,000
SALES (est): 12.3MM **Privately Held**
SIC: 4724 4729 Tourist agency arranging transport, lodging & car rental; airline ticket offices

(P-4932)
B T & T TRAVEL INC
Also Called: Best Tours & Travel
2609 E Mckinley Ave Ste N, Fresno (93703-3028)
PHONE.....................................559 237-9410
Nick W Sayah, *President*
Margaret Sayah, *Treasurer*
Jasmine Sayah, *Opers Mgr*
EMP: 56 **EST:** 1980
SQ FT: 4,200
SALES (est): 14.1MM **Privately Held**
WEB: www.besttoursandtravel.com
SIC: 4724 4725 Travel agencies; tours, conducted

(P-4933)
CARIBBEAN SOUTH AMERCN COUNCIL
Also Called: Internationl TV Media Wireless
12 Ambrose Ave, Bay Point (94565-3106)
PHONE.....................................925 709-3433
Dalchand Singhbhairo, *President*
EMP: 50 **EST:** 1984
SALES (est): 4MM **Privately Held**
SIC: 4724 8748 Travel agencies; telecommunications consultant

(P-4934)
CARNIVAL CORPORATION
231 Windsor Way, Long Beach (90802-6350)
PHONE.....................................562 843-5569
EMP: 5006
SALES (corp-wide): 17.5B **Publicly Held**
SIC: 4724 Travel agencies
PA: Carnival Corporation
3655 Nw 87th Ave
Doral FL 33178
305 599-2600

(P-4935)
CARNIVAL CORPORATION
231 Windsor Way, Long Beach (90802-6350)
PHONE.....................................562 901-3232
Hector Patino, *Principal*
EMP: 4999
SALES (corp-wide): 17.5B **Publicly Held**
SIC: 4724 Travel agencies
PA: Carnival Corporation
3655 Nw 87th Ave
Doral FL 33178
305 599-2600

(P-4936)
GEOGRAPHIC EXPEDITIONS INC
Also Called: Innerasia Travel Group
1008 General Kennedy Ave # 3, San Francisco (94129-1731)
P.O. Box 29902 (94129-0902)
PHONE.....................................415 922-0448
George Doubleday, *Ch of Bd*
Lisa Parker, *Admin Sec*
Sara Barbieri, *Director*
Amanda McKee, *Senior Editor*
EMP: 54
SALES (est): 21.8MM **Privately Held**
WEB: www.geoex.com
SIC: 4724 Travel agencies

(P-4937)
GOWAY TRAVEL INC
Also Called: Global Network Travel
505 N Brand Blvd Ste 810, Glendale (91203-4723)
PHONE.....................................800 810-3687
Bruce Hodge, *CEO*
Peter Lacy, *CFO*
Ben Stasiuk, *General Mgr*
Soran Prasad, *Business Mgr*
Steve Spurlock, *Business Mgr*
EMP: 95
SQ FT: 1,200
SALES (est): 11.9MM **Privately Held**
WEB: www.goway.com
SIC: 4724 Tourist agency arranging transport, lodging & car rental

(P-4938)
HELLOWORLD TRAVEL SVCS USA INC
Also Called: Qantas Vctons Nwmans Vacations
6171 W Century Blvd # 160, Los Angeles (90045-5335)
PHONE.....................................310 535-1000
Ross Webster, *President*
Gary Goeldner, *CEO*
Andre Eubanks, *Finance Mgr*
Lynn Walker, *Opers Mgr*
Jackie Fontanez, *Director*
EMP: 100
SQ FT: 18,000
SALES (est): 19.5MM **Privately Held**
WEB: www.jetaboutfijivacations.com
SIC: 4724 Tourist agency arranging transport, lodging & car rental
PA: Helloworld Travel Limited
L13 80 Pacific Hwy
North Sydney NSW 2060
-

(P-4939)
IDEA TRAVEL COMPANY
13145 Byrd Ln Ste 101, Los Altos Hills (94022-3211)
PHONE.....................................650 948-0207
Michael Schoendorf, *CEO*
Ram Bodapati, *CTO*
Beverly Hoh, *Software Dev*
EMP: 1100
SALES: 453.4MM **Privately Held**
WEB: www.ideatravel.com
SIC: 4724 Tourist agency arranging transport, lodging & car rental

(P-4940)
IDS INC
20335 Ventura Blvd # 210, Woodland Hills (91364-2451)
PHONE.....................................855 997-7437
Nathan Morad, *CEO*
Alberto Gamez, *Chief Mktg Ofcr*
Teres Mamann, *Vice Pres*
John Ledo, *CTO*
Gary Kurtz, *Legal Staff*
EMP: 52
SQ FT: 9,000
SALES: 65MM **Privately Held**
SIC: 4724 7372 Travel agencies; business oriented computer software

(P-4941)
JAPAN AIRLINES CO LTD
300 Continental Blvd # 620, El Segundo (90245-5047)
PHONE.....................................310 607-2305
Hiroyuki Hioka, *CEO*
Kenji Nakahashi, *Partner*
Paul Moore, *Officer*
Yasuhiro Nakamura, *Senior VP*
Yusuke Araki, *Vice Pres*
EMP: 90
SALES (corp-wide): 12.9B **Privately Held**
WEB: www.jal.co.jp
SIC: 4724 8741 4581 4512 Tourist agency arranging transport, lodging & car rental; management services; airports, flying fields & services; air transportation, scheduled
PA: Japan Airlines Co.,Ltd.
2-4-11, Higashishinagawa
Shinagawa-Ku TKY 140-0
354 603-121

(P-4942)
JTB AMERICAS LTD (HQ)
19700 Mariner Ave, Torrance (90503-1648)
PHONE.....................................310 303-3750
Tsuneo Irita, *President*
EMP: 100
SALES (est): 245.3MM
SALES (corp-wide): 12.4B **Privately Held**
SIC: 4724 Travel agencies
PA: Jtb Corp.
2-3-11, Higashishinagawa
Shinagawa-Ku TKY 140-0
354 792-211

PRODUCTS & SVCS

(P-4943)
L B C HOLDINGS U S A CORP (PA)
362 E Grand Ave, South San Francisco (94080-6210)
PHONE..................650 873-0750
Carlos Araneta, Ch of Bd
Mylene Larsen, Officer
EMP: 164
SQ FT: 25,000
SALES (est): 56MM Privately Held
SIC: 4724 4513 4412 Travel agencies; air courier services; deep sea foreign transportation of freight

(P-4944)
NIPPON TRAVEL AGENCY AMER INC
Also Called: Nta America
1411 W 190th St Ste 650, Gardena (90248-4369)
PHONE..................310 768-1817
Tadashi Wakayama, President
Tsutomu Ochiai, Senior Mgr
Romeo Dublin, Asst Mgr
Miyuki Holihan, Consultant
Noriko Paulsen, Consultant
EMP: 70 EST: 1999
SQ FT: 8,000
SALES (est): 14.1MM
SALES (corp-wide): 14B Privately Held
WEB: www.ntasfb.com
SIC: 4724 Tourist agency arranging transport, lodging & car rental
HQ: Nippon Travel Agency Pacific, Inc.
1025 W 190th St Ste 300
Gardena CA 90248
310 768-0017

(P-4945)
NIPPON TRAVEL AGENCY PCF INC (DH)
Also Called: Nta Pacific
1025 W 190th St Ste 300, Gardena (90248-4332)
PHONE..................310 768-0017
Tadashi Wakayama, President
Akio Tsuna, CFO
EMP: 80
SQ FT: 20,000
SALES (est): 33.5MM
SALES (corp-wide): 14B Privately Held
SIC: 4724 Tourist agency arranging transport, lodging & car rental
HQ: Nippon Travel Agency Co., Ltd.
1-19-1, Nihombashi
Chuo-Ku TKY 103-0
368 957-800

(P-4946)
PENINSULA WORLD TRAVEL LLC (PA)
Also Called: Meridian World Travel
825 Santa Cruz Ave, Menlo Park (94025-4609)
PHONE..................650 328-2030
Don Freeman, Principal
Barbara Freeman,
EMP: 50
SALES (est): 5.6MM Privately Held
WEB: www.summittravelgroup.com
SIC: 4724 Travel agencies

(P-4947)
PINNACLE TRAVEL SERVICES LLC
390 N Pacific Coast Hwy, El Segundo (90245-4475)
PHONE..................310 414-1787
Robert G Singh, CEO
Kathy Underwood, Human Res Dir
Shelley Boothby, Manager
Lora Mayfield, Supervisor
Cynthia Rigsby, Supervisor
EMP: 151
SQ FT: 15,000
SALES: 10MM Privately Held
WEB: www.ptsla.com
SIC: 4724 Tourist agency arranging transport, lodging & car rental

(P-4948)
PRINCESS CRUISE LINES LTD
Also Called: Princess Cruises
P.O. Box 966 (91380-9066)
PHONE..................661 753-2291
Princess Cruise, Principal
EMP: 1114
SALES (corp-wide): 7.6B Privately Held
SIC: 4724 Travel agencies
HQ: Princess Cruise Lines, Ltd.
24305 Town Center Dr
Santa Clarita CA 91355
661 753-0000

(P-4949)
PRINCESS CRUISES AND TOURS INC (HQ)
24305 Town Center Dr # 200, Valencia (91355-4999)
PHONE..................206 336-6000
Will Wenholz, Principal
EMP: 5027
SALES (est): 91.1MM
SALES (corp-wide): 17.5B Publicly Held
SIC: 4724 Travel agencies
PA: Carnival Corporation
3655 Nw 87th Ave
Doral FL 33178
305 599-2600

(P-4950)
PROTRAVEL INTERNATIONAL LLC
9171 Wilshire Blvd # 428, Beverly Hills (90210-5516)
PHONE..................310 271-9566
Sara Sessa, Branch Mgr
EMP: 100
SALES (corp-wide): 66.7MM Privately Held
WEB: www.protravelinternational.com
SIC: 4724 Travel agencies
PA: Protravel International Llc
515 Madison Ave Fl 10
New York NY 10022
212 755-4550

(P-4951)
REVEL TRAVEL SERVICE INC
Also Called: Revel Travel At Altour
449 S Beverly Dr Ste 101, Beverly Hills (90212-4463)
PHONE..................310 553-5555
Jack Revel, President
EMP: 65
SALES (est): 1MM Privately Held
SIC: 4724 Travel agencies
PA: Altour International Inc.
12100 W Olympic Blvd # 300
Los Angeles CA 90064

(P-4952)
STUDENT GOVERNMENT ASSOCIAT
Also Called: Associated Students Uc Irvine
D200 Student Center, Irvine (92697-0001)
PHONE..................949 824-5547
Dennis Hampton, Exec Dir
EMP: 155
SQ FT: 6,000
SALES: 4.2MM Privately Held
SIC: 4724 5813 5947 4481 Travel agencies; drinking places; gifts & novelties; deep sea passenger transportation, except ferry; women's accessory & specialty stores

(P-4953)
TRAVEL STORE
633 S Brea Blvd, Brea (92821-5308)
PHONE..................714 529-1947
Eva Bailon, Manager
EMP: 72
SALES (est): 5.1MM
SALES (corp-wide): 37.5MM Privately Held
SIC: 4724 Tourist agency arranging transport, lodging & car rental
PA: Travel Store
11601 Wilshire Blvd
Los Angeles CA 90025
310 575-5540

(P-4954)
TRAVEL STORE (PA)
Also Called: Travelstore
11601 Wilshire Blvd, Los Angeles (90025-0509)
PHONE..................310 575-5540
Wido Schaefer, President
Osvaldo Ramos, CFO
Dan Ilves, Vice Pres
Melody Francis, Technical Mgr
Jim Wright, Sales Executive
EMP: 70
SQ FT: 7,000
SALES (est): 37.5MM Privately Held
WEB: www.travel-store.com
SIC: 4724 Tourist agency arranging transport, lodging & car rental

(P-4955)
TRAVEL SYNDICATE
350 S Beverly Dr Ste 170, Beverly Hills (90212-4818)
PHONE..................818 297-9979
Arline Fiorto, Partner
Roger Lipkis, Partner
EMP: 60
SQ FT: 9,800
SALES (est): 6.8MM Privately Held
WEB: www.travelsyndicate.com
SIC: 4724 Travel agencies

(P-4956)
TRAVELMASTERS INC
Also Called: Goldrush Getaways
8350 Auburn Blvd Ste 200, Citrus Heights (95610-0396)
PHONE..................916 722-1648
Brian A Carr, President
John Oestreich, Marketing Staff
Cynthia Langhof, Manager
EMP: 50
SALES (est): 8MM Privately Held
WEB: www.goldrushgetaways.com
SIC: 4724 Tourist agency arranging transport, lodging & car rental

(P-4957)
UNIGLOBE TRAVEL WEST INC (PA)
Also Called: Uniglobe Travel Planner
18662 Macarthur Blvd # 100, Irvine (92612-1205)
PHONE..................949 623-9000
Gary Charlewood, President
Raymond Townsend, Ch of Bd
EMP: 60
SQ FT: 5,920
SALES (est): 7.9MM Privately Held
SIC: 4724 Tourist agency arranging transport, lodging & car rental

(P-4958)
VIKING RIVER CRUISES INC (HQ)
Also Called: Viking Ocean Cruises
5700 Canoga Ave Ste 200, Woodland Hills (91367-6569)
PHONE..................818 227-1234
Milton Hugh, CEO
Cheri Allen, Vice Pres
Karine Hagen, Vice Pres
Pete Levine, Vice Pres
Joost Ouendag, Vice Pres
EMP: 63
SALES (est): 32.2MM Privately Held
WEB: www.vikingrivercruises.com
SIC: 4724 Tourist agency arranging transport, lodging & car rental
PA: Viking River Cruises Ag
Schaferweg 18
Basel BS
616 386-011

4725 Tour Operators

(P-4959)
AAT KINGS TOURS USA INC
801 E Katella Ave Fl 3, Anaheim (92805-6614)
PHONE..................714 456-0505
Richard Launder, President
Bob Housepenny, Director
EMP: 75

SALES (est): 6.9MM Privately Held
SIC: 4725 Tours, conducted

(P-4960)
ALCATRAZ CRUISES LLC
Hornb Alcat Landi Pier 33 St Pier, San Francisco (94111)
PHONE..................415 981-7625
Terry A Macrae,
Ann Levine, Human Res Dir
Yukiko Watanabe, Payroll Mgr
Bobby Martinez, Purch Mgr
Christopher Shock, Food Svc Dir
EMP: 120
SALES (est): 14.5MM Privately Held
SIC: 4725 Arrangement of travel tour packages, wholesale

(P-4961)
AMERICANTOURS INTL LLC (HQ)
6053 W Century Blvd, Los Angeles (90045-6430)
PHONE..................310 641-9953
Noel Irwin-Hentschel,
Michael Fitzpatrick,
EMP: 105
SQ FT: 20,000
SALES (est): 33.5MM Privately Held
SIC: 4725 4724 Tour operators; travel agencies
PA: Americantours International Inc
6053 W Century Blvd Ste 7
Los Angeles CA 90045
310 641-9953

(P-4962)
APPELLATION TOURS INC
Also Called: Beau Wine Tours
21707 8th St E, Sonoma (95476-9781)
PHONE..................707 938-9390
Thomas Buck, President
EMP: 50
SQ FT: 21,000
SALES (est): 8.4MM Privately Held
WEB: www.appellationtours.com
SIC: 4725 4111 4141 Tours, conducted; airport limousine, scheduled service; local bus charter service

(P-4963)
BACKROADS (PA)
801 Cedar St, Berkeley (94710-1800)
PHONE..................510 527-1555
Tom Hale, CEO
Karen Bennett, Info Tech Dir
Jerry Delozier, Technical Staff
Mike Louvau, Human Res Dir
Louie Orleans, Sales Staff
EMP: 400
SQ FT: 10,000
SALES (est): 51.1MM Privately Held
WEB: www.walkingvacation.com
SIC: 4725 4724 Sightseeing tour companies; travel agencies

(P-4964)
BRENDAN TOURS (PA)
Also Called: Brendan Worldwide Vacations
801 E Katella Ave, Anaheim (92805-6614)
PHONE..................818 428-6000
James J Murphy, CEO
Gary J Murphy, President
Larry McCloned, Info Tech Mgr
Jonathan Melendez, Data Proc Staff
Melody Tauchman, Technology
EMP: 140
SQ FT: 26,000
SALES (est): 14MM Privately Held
SIC: 4725 Arrangement of travel tour packages, wholesale

(P-4965)
CLASSIC CUSTOM VACATIONS INC
5893 Rue Ferrari, San Jose (95138-1857)
PHONE..................800 221-3949
Timothy Scott Macdonald, CEO
Gregge Brockway, President
Robert Burja, Administration
Thomas Van Dorn, Business Mgr
EMP: 250
SQ FT: 31,000

SALES (est): 1.7MM
SALES (corp-wide): 10B **Publicly Held**
WEB: www.classicvacations.com
SIC: 4725 Arrangement of travel tour packages, wholesale
PA: Expedia Group, Inc.
333 108th Ave Ne
Bellevue WA 98004
425 679-7200

(P-4966)
CLASSIC VACATIONS LLC
Also Called: Classic Custom Vacations
5893 Rue Ferrari, San Jose (95138-1857)
PHONE..............................800 221-3949
David Hu, *President*
Ronald M Letterman, *Vice Chairman*
Susan Anderson, *Vice Pres*
Eddie Sanchez, *Vice Pres*
Lea Nelson, *Admin Asst*
EMP: 149
SALES (est): 18.1MM
SALES (corp-wide): 10B **Publicly Held**
WEB: www.expedia.com
SIC: 4725 Arrangement of travel tour packages, wholesale
PA: Expedia Group, Inc.
333 108th Ave Ne
Bellevue WA 98004
425 679-7200

(P-4967)
COACH USA INC
Also Called: Pacific Cast Sightseeing Tours
2001 S Manchester Ave, Anaheim (92802-3803)
PHONE..........................714 978-8855
Darlene Cochran, *Branch Mgr*
EMP: 200
SALES (corp-wide): 4.5B **Privately Held**
SIC: 4725 Tours, conducted
HQ: Coach Usa, Inc.
160 S Route 17 N
Paramus NJ 07652

(P-4968)
CONTIKI US HOLDINGS INC
Also Called: Contiki Holidays
801 E Katella Ave Frnt, Anaheim (92805-6614)
PHONE..........................714 935-0808
Frank Marini, *President*
Michael Kidd, *CFO*
Amanda Kelly, *Info Tech Mgr*
Brianna McCarthy, *Opers Spvr*
Kelly Pitre, *Opers Staff*
EMP: 60
SALES (est): 10.9MM **Privately Held**
SIC: 4725 4724 Tours, conducted; tourist agency arranging transport, lodging & car rental

(P-4969)
CUSA GCBS LLC
Also Called: Goodall's Charter Bus Company
3888 Beech St, San Diego (92105-5905)
PHONE..........................619 266-7365
Craig Lentzsch, *Mng Member*
John Busskohl, *Mng Member*
EMP: 100
SALES (est): 7.4MM **Privately Held**
SIC: 4725 Arrangement of travel tour packages, wholesale; sightseeing tour companies

(P-4970)
GO WEST TOURS INC (PA)
790 Eddy St, San Francisco (94109-7806)
PHONE..........................415 837-0154
Stephan Forget, *President*
Julia Matheson, *Vice Pres*
Florence Solal, *Vice Pres*
Benoit Demonsant, *General Mgr*
Emmanuelle Legoff, *General Mgr*
EMP: 50
SQ FT: 2,858
SALES: 61.2MM **Privately Held**
WEB: www.gowesttours.com
SIC: 4725 Tours, conducted

(P-4971)
JOGURU INC
2600 El Camino Real Ste 4, Palo Alto (94306-1705)
PHONE..........................855 526-4332

Praveen Kumar, *CEO*
Saket Newaskar, *Director*
EMP: 75
SQ FT: 2,500
SALES: 500K **Privately Held**
SIC: 4725 Arrangement of travel tour packages, wholesale

(P-4972)
MARITZCX RESEARCH LLC
20285 S Wstn Ave Ste 101, Torrance (90501)
PHONE..........................310 783-4300
Joe Sarquiz, *Principal*
Ron Steinkamp, *President*
Phillip Schmidt, *Prdtn Mgr*
Bradley Craig, *Producer*
Bill Higgins, *Accounts Mgr*
EMP: 61
SALES (corp-wide): 1.2B **Privately Held**
SIC: 4725 8748 8732 4899 Arrangement of travel tour packages, wholesale; employee programs administration; market analysis or research; data communication services; advertising consultant
HQ: Maritzcx Research Llc
1355 N Highway Dr
Fenton MO 63026
636 827-4000

(P-4973)
OKABE INTERNATIONAL INC (PA)
Also Called: Pacific Leisure Management
1739 Buchanan St Ste B, San Francisco (94115-3208)
PHONE..........................415 921-0808
Mitsufumi Okabe, *President*
Rumi Okabe, *Corp Secy*
EMP: 50 **EST:** 1973
SQ FT: 3,600
SALES (est): 2.6MM **Privately Held**
SIC: 4725 4833 5941 Tour operators; television broadcasting stations; sporting goods & bicycle shops; tennis goods & equipment; golf goods & equipment

(P-4974)
OLD TOWN TRLLEY TURS SAN DIEGO
Also Called: Historic Tours of America
2115 Kurtz St, San Diego (92110-2016)
PHONE..........................619 298-8687
Chris Belland, *CEO*
Edwin O Swift, *President*
Gerald Mosher, *Vice Pres*
Lorin Stewart, *General Mgr*
EMP: 60
SQ FT: 22,000
SALES (est): 8.8MM
SALES (corp-wide): 61.3MM **Privately Held**
WEB: www.conchtourtrain.com
SIC: 4725 Sightseeing tour companies
HQ: Conch Tour Trains Inc
1805 Staples Ave Ste 101
Key West FL 33040
305 294-5161

(P-4975)
PACIFIC COAST SIGHTSEEING TOUR
2001 S Manchester Ave, Anaheim (92802-3803)
PHONE..........................714 507-1157
Kristin Martinez, *Vice Pres*
Luis Silva, *Controller*
EMP: 230
SALES: 23MM
SALES (corp-wide): 4.5B **Privately Held**
SIC: 4725 4173 Arrangement of travel tour packages, wholesale; sightseeing tour companies; bus terminal operation
HQ: Coach Usa, Inc.
160 S Route 17 N
Paramus NJ 07652

(P-4976)
PLEASANT HOLIDAYS LLC (HQ)
Also Called: Pleasant Hawaiian Holiday
2404 Townsgate Rd, Westlake Village (91361-2505)
PHONE..........................818 991-3390
Jack E Richards, *CEO*
Gary Hunn, *Partner*

Bruce Rosenberg, *Senior VP*
Kimberly Daley, *Vice Pres*
Mark Klaschka, *Vice Pres*
EMP: 300
SQ FT: 55,000
SALES (est): 104.7MM
SALES (corp-wide): 7.2B **Privately Held**
WEB: www.pleasantactivities.com
SIC: 4725 Tour operators
PA: Automobile Club Of Southern California
2601 S Figueroa St
Los Angeles CA 90007
213 741-3686

(P-4977)
ROYALTY TOURS
630 Stockton Ave, San Jose (95126-2433)
PHONE..........................408 279-4801
Sandra S Allen, *President*
EMP: 50
SQ FT: 3,000
SALES (est): 4.2MM
SALES (corp-wide): 13MM **Privately Held**
WEB: www.royal-coach.com
SIC: 4725 Arrangement of travel tour packages, wholesale; sightseeing tour companies
PA: Royal Coach Tours
630 Stockton Ave
San Jose CA 95126
408 279-4801

(P-4978)
SANTA BARBARA CITY OF
Also Called: Courthuse Tours-Docent Council
1100 Anacapa St Dept 3, Santa Barbara (93101-6013)
PHONE..........................805 962-6464
Lori Bevon, *President*
EMP: 60 **Privately Held**
SIC: 4725 Tour operators
PA: City Of Santa Barbara
735 Anacapa St
Santa Barbara CA 93101
805 564-5334

(P-4979)
SANTA CATALINA ISLAND COMPANY (PA)
Also Called: Scico
150 Metropole Ave, Avalon (90704)
P.O. Box 737 (90704-0737)
PHONE..........................310 510-2000
Randall Herrel Sr, *CEO*
Paxson H Offield, *Ch of Bd*
John T Dravinski, *COO*
Ronald C Doutt, *Treasurer*
Dave Stevenson, *Vice Pres*
EMP: 71 **EST:** 1959
SALES (est): 36.5MM **Privately Held**
WEB: www.scico.com
SIC: 4725 Sightseeing tour companies

(P-4980)
SCREAMLINE INVESTMENT CORP (PA)
Also Called: Tourcoach Transportation
2130 S Tubeway Ave, Commerce (90040-1614)
PHONE..........................323 201-0114
Kamrouz Farhadi, *CEO*
Vahid Sapir, *President*
Shoeleh Sapir, *Treasurer*
Farima Akopians, *VP Sales*
EMP: 120
SQ FT: 8,000
SALES (est): 22.6MM **Privately Held**
WEB: www.tourcoach.com
SIC: 4725 Sightseeing tour companies; tours, conducted

(P-4981)
STARLINE TOURS HOLLYWOOD INC
2130 S Tubeway Ave, Commerce (90040-1614)
PHONE..........................323 262-1114
Tony Cordon, *Manager*
EMP: 60
SALES (est): 5MM **Privately Held**
WEB: www.starlinetours.com
SIC: 4725 Tours, conducted

PA: Starline Tours Of Hollywood, Inc.
6801 Hollywood Blvd # 221
Los Angeles CA 90028

(P-4982)
STARLINE TOURS HOLLYWOOD INC (PA)
6801 Hollywood Blvd # 221, Los Angeles (90028-6142)
PHONE..........................323 463-3333
Kamrouz Farhadi, *CEO*
Noonoosh Farhadi, *Vice Pres*
Galina Kirkilevich, *Controller*
EMP: 71
SALES (est): 15.9MM **Privately Held**
WEB: www.starlinetours.com
SIC: 4725 Tours, conducted

(P-4983)
UNIWORLD RIVER CRUISES INC
Also Called: Uniworld Boutique River Cruise
17323 Ventura Blvd # 300, Encino (91316-3964)
PHONE..........................818 382-2322
Guy A Young, *President*
David Thomas, *Senior VP*
Kristian Anderson, *Vice Pres*
Kathryn Beadle, *Managing Dir*
Silva Reyes, *Office Mgr*
EMP: 110
SALES (est): 19.1MM **Privately Held**
SIC: 4725 Tour operators
PA: Uniworld River Cruises Sa
Rue Guillaume Kroll 5
Luxembourg

(P-4984)
VIP TOURS OF CALIFORNIA INC
9830 Bellanca Ave, Los Angeles (90045-5608)
PHONE..........................310 216-7507
Marco Khorasani, *President*
Nicole J Khorasani, *Vice Pres*
EMP: 70
SALES (est): 11.2MM **Privately Held**
WEB: www.viptoursandcharters.com
SIC: 4725 Tours, conducted

(P-4985)
YOUR MAN TOURS INC (DH)
Also Called: Jet Advertising
100 N Pacific Coast Hwy # 1700, El Segundo (90245-5662)
PHONE..........................310 649-3820
William Price, *President*
Frank Chanell, *Vice Pres*
James Gallas, *Vice Pres*
Eileen Amagna, *Controller*
EMP: 80
SQ FT: 20,000
SALES (est): 16.9MM
SALES (corp-wide): 21.8B **Privately Held**
WEB: www.ymtvacations.com
SIC: 4725 Tour operators

4729 Passenger Transportation

(P-4986)
CATHAY PACIFIC AIRWAYS LIMITED
1960 E Grand Ave Ste 540, El Segundo (90245-5092)
PHONE..........................310 615-1113
Jake Olver, *Branch Mgr*
James Barrington, *Marketing Staff*
EMP: 100
SALES (corp-wide): 12.4B **Privately Held**
WEB: www.cathaypacific.com
SIC: 4729 4512 Airline ticket offices; air transportation, scheduled
PA: Cathay Pacific Airways Limited
33/F One Pacific Place
Admiralty HK
274 752-10

(P-4987)
CUSTOM TOURS INC
Also Called: Kushner & Associates
24003 Ventura Blvd 100a, Calabasas (91302-2542)
PHONE..........................310 274-8819

PRODUCTS & SVCS

Susan Kushner, *CEO*
Kayleen Hicks, *Managing Dir*
Jonathon Dekarr, *Program Mgr*
Val Hamann, *Info Tech Mgr*
Leanne Anell, *Director*
EMP: 85
SQ FT: 3,000
SALES (est): 10.1MM **Privately Held**
WEB: www.kushnerdmc.com
SIC: 4729 Carpool/vanpool arrangement

(P-4988)
EL AL ISRAEL AIRLINES LTD
6404 Wilshire Blvd # 1250, Los Angeles
(90048-5501)
PHONE................................323 852-1252
Rami Fischer, *Branch Mgr*
EMP: 150
SALES (corp-wide): 2.1B **Privately Held**
WEB: www.elal.co.il
SIC: 4729 4512 Ticket offices, transportation; air transportation, scheduled
PA: El Al Israel Airlines Ltd
    Lod Airport
    Lod Airport 70100
    397 162-02

(P-4989)
ELITE AIRWAYS LLC
4607 Lakeview Canyon Rd, Westlake Village (91361-4028)
PHONE................................805 496-3334
Robert Lyle, *Exec VP*
Jackie Smock, *Accountant*
EMP: 145
SQ FT: 5,000
SALES (est): 13.6MM **Privately Held**
SIC: 4729 Airline ticket offices

(P-4990)
FIVE STAR TRANSPORTATION INC
8703 La Tijera Blvd # 102, Los Angeles
(90045-3900)
PHONE................................310 348-0820
George Reyes, *President*
Linda Reyes, *Vice Pres*
Demetri Ross, *Exec Dir*
EMP: 50
SALES (est): 6MM **Privately Held**
SIC: 4729 Airline ticket offices

(P-4991)
GAT - ARLN GROUND SUPPORT INC
2627 N Hollywood Way, Burbank
(91505-1062)
PHONE................................818 847-9127
EMP: 243
SALES (corp-wide): 116MM **Privately Held**
SIC: 4729 Airline ticket offices
PA: Gat - Airline Ground Support, Inc.
    246 City Cir
    Peachtree City GA 30269
    251 633-3888

(P-4992)
HONK TECHNOLOGIES INC
2251 Barry Ave, Los Angeles (90064-1401)
PHONE................................800 979-3162
Corey Brundage, *CEO*
EMP: 85
SQ FT: 8,000
SALES (est): 24MM **Privately Held**
SIC: 4729 7374 Bus ticket offices; data processing & preparation

(P-4993)
MATRIX AVIATION SERVICES INC
6171 W Century Blvd Ste 1, Los Angeles
(90045-5300)
PHONE................................310 337-3037
Ramez Reno, *CEO*
Borseen Oushana, *Officer*
EMP: 175 **EST:** 2008
SQ FT: 3,000
SALES (est): 15.4MM **Privately Held**
SIC: 4729 Airline ticket offices

(P-4994)
UNITED AIRLINES INC
6850 Airport Blvd Ste 34, Sacramento
(95837-1126)
PHONE................................916 877-3002
Ken Brown, *Manager*
EMP: 150
SALES (corp-wide): 37.7B **Publicly Held**
WEB: www.united.com
SIC: 4729 4512 Airline ticket offices; air transportation, scheduled
HQ: United Airlines, Inc.
    233 S Wacker Dr Ste 710
    Chicago IL 60606
    872 825-4000

4731 Freight Forwarding & Arrangement

(P-4995)
ADVANTAGE LOGISTICS INC
Also Called: CTS Advantage Logistics
2071 Ringwood Ave Ste D, San Jose
(95131-1760)
P.O. Box 612438 (95161-2438)
PHONE................................408 943-6300
Steve L Haney, *President*
Donna Haney, *CFO*
EMP: 185
SQ FT: 183,000
SALES (est): 23.3MM **Privately Held**
SIC: 4731 Freight transportation arrangement

(P-4996)
AGILITY HOLDINGS INC (DH)
Also Called: Agility Logistics
310 Commerce Ste 250, Irvine
(92602-1399)
PHONE................................714 617-6300
Essa Al-Saleh, *President*
John Iacouzzi, *President*
Jamie Robertson, *President*
Mark Soubry, *CEO*
James Fredholm, *CFO*
EMP: 80
SALES (est): 394.6MM
SALES (corp-wide): 4.6B **Privately Held**
WEB: www.agilitylogistics.com
SIC: 4731 4213 4214 Domestic freight forwarding; foreign freight forwarding; transportation agents & brokers; household goods transport; heavy machinery transport; household goods moving & storage, local
HQ: Agility Logistics International B.V.
    Fokkerweg 300 Gebouw 2a
    Oude Meer
    205 214-777

(P-4997)
AGILITY LOGISTICS CORP
21906 Arnold Center Rd, Carson
(90810-1646)
PHONE................................310 507-6700
Kia Kittscher, *Manager*
EMP: 65
SALES (corp-wide): 4.6B **Privately Held**
SIC: 4731 Freight forwarding
HQ: Agility Logistics Corp.
    310 Commerce Ste 250
    Irvine CA 92602
    714 617-6300

(P-4998)
AGRIHOLDING INC (PA)
Also Called: Fts Global
3330 S Fairway St, Visalia (93277-8109)
P.O. Box 334, Pebble Beach (93953-0334)
PHONE................................559 738-5880
Charles Schimmel, *President*
Robert Igleheart, *Ch of Bd*
EMP: 70
SALES (est): 9.6MM **Privately Held**
SIC: 4731 Truck transportation brokers

(P-4999)
AIR TIGER EXPRESS (USA) INC
17000 Gale Ave, City of Industry
(91745-1807)
PHONE................................626 965-8647
Sean Lee, *Manager*
Matt Tran, *Sales Executive*
EMP: 50 **Privately Held**

WEB: www.airtiger.com
SIC: 4731 Freight forwarding
PA: Air Tiger Express (Usa), Inc.
    14909 183rd St Ste 2
    Springfield Gardens NY 11413

(P-5000)
AIR-SEA FORWARDERS INC (PA)
9009 S La Cienega Blvd, Inglewood
(90301-4459)
P.O. Box 90637, Los Angeles (90009-0637)
PHONE................................310 216-1616
Todd Hinkley, *CEO*
Paul Talley, *COO*
Monica Villavicencio, *CFO*
Hans Leuenberger, *Vice Pres*
Luisa Nakamura, *Vice Pres*
EMP: 60
SQ FT: 42,000
SALES (est): 18.3MM **Privately Held**
WEB: www.airseainc.com
SIC: 4731 Foreign freight forwarding; customhouse brokers

(P-5001)
AIT WORLDWIDE LOGISTICS INC
19901 Hamilton Ave Ste D, Torrance
(90502-1364)
PHONE................................310 538-4383
Ty Bradford, *Manager*
Sam Cortez, *Manager*
EMP: 100
SALES (corp-wide): 381.5MM **Privately Held**
WEB: www.aitworldwide.com
SIC: 4731 Domestic freight forwarding
PA: Ait Worldwide Logistics, Inc.
    701 N Rohlwing Rd
    Itasca IL 60143
    630 766-0711

(P-5002)
ALLEN LUND COMPANY LLC (HQ)
4529 Angeles Crest Hwy # 300, La Canada Flintridge (91011-3247)
P.O. Box 1369, La Canada (91012-5369)
PHONE................................818 790-1110
Allen Lund, *Mng Member*
Steve Doerfler, *CFO*
David F Lund, *Vice Pres*
Edward V Lund, *Vice Pres*
Kathleen M Lund, *Vice Pres*
EMP: 70 **EST:** 1976
SQ FT: 16,000
SALES: 515.9MM **Privately Held**
WEB: www.allenlund.com
SIC: 4731 Truck transportation brokers

(P-5003)
ALLEN LUND COMPANY LLC
1825 S Grant St Ste 320, San Mateo
(94402-2660)
PHONE................................650 358-9454
Bob Rose, *Branch Mgr*
EMP: 60 **Privately Held**
SIC: 4731 Truck transportation brokers
HQ: Allen Lund Company, Llc
    4529 Angeles Crest Hwy # 300
    La Canada Flintridge CA 91011
    818 790-1110

(P-5004)
ALLEN LUND CORPORATION (PA)
4529 Angeles Crest Hwy, La Canada Flintridge (91011-3247)
P.O. Box 1369, La Canada (91012-5369)
PHONE................................818 790-8412
David Allen Lund, *President*
Steve Doerfler, *CFO*
David F Lund, *Vice Pres*
Ed Lund, *Vice Pres*
Edward V Lund, *Vice Pres*
EMP: 50
SQ FT: 18,000
SALES (est): 515.9MM **Privately Held**
SIC: 4731 Truck transportation brokers

(P-5005)
ALLPRO INDUSTRY SOLUTIONS LLC
7850 White Ln, Bakersfield (93309-7698)
PHONE................................661 854-3613
Joshua R Kimball, *President*
Josh Kimball, *President*
EMP: 50
SALES (est): 4.2MM **Privately Held**
SIC: 4731 4212 3537 3523 Freight transportation arrangement; local trucking, without storage; platforms, stands, tables, pallets & similar equipment; crop storage bins; grain storage bins

(P-5006)
AMERICAN PRESIDENT LINES LLC
1579 Middle Harbor Rd, Oakland
(94607-1808)
PHONE................................510 272-3990
Paul Clouse, *Manager*
EMP: 80 **Privately Held**
SIC: 4731 Foreign freight forwarding
HQ: American President Lines, Llc
    1667 K St Nw Ste 400
    Washington DC 20006
    602 586-4894

(P-5007)
ANDREWS AIR CORPORATION
Also Called: Main Freight Sfo
50 Tanforan Ave, South San Francisco
(94080-6608)
PHONE................................650 871-4747
Jay Bellin, *CEO*
EMP: 110
SQ FT: 35,000
SALES (est): 12.5MM **Privately Held**
SIC: 4731 Freight forwarding

(P-5008)
AO FREIGHT CORPORATION (PA)
419 N Oak St, Inglewood (90302-3314)
PHONE................................310 419-8833
Alex Chan, *President*
Cherry Chan, *Partner*
William Liang, *Partner*
Margaret LI, *Partner*
Spencer Ho, *Vice Pres*
EMP: 50
SQ FT: 3,000
SALES (est): 13.5MM **Privately Held**
SIC: 4731 4412 Foreign freight forwarding; domestic freight forwarding; deep sea foreign transportation of freight

(P-5009)
AP EXPRESS LLC
Also Called: A P Express Worldwide
8500 Rex Rd, Pico Rivera (90660-3779)
PHONE................................562 236-2250
Jeffery D Pont, *Manager*
Keith Davis, *Exec VP*
Silvia Martinez, *Human Res Mgr*
Danielle Braden, *Manager*
Desiree Reyes, *Accounts Exec*
EMP: 75
SQ FT: 170,000
SALES (est): 22MM **Privately Held**
WEB: www.apexpress.com
SIC: 4731 Freight forwarding

(P-5010)
APEX LOGISTICS INTL INC (PA)
17511 S Susana Rd, Compton
(90221-5405)
PHONE................................310 665-0288
Minjiang Song, *President*
▲ **EMP:** 58
SALES: 175.9MM **Privately Held**
SIC: 4731 Freight forwarding

(P-5011)
APM TERMINALS PACIFIC LLC
Also Called: Mearsk
2500 Navy Way Pier 400, San Pedro
(90731-7554)
PHONE................................310 221-4000
Milan Do, *Branch Mgr*
Dan Carnahan, *Administration*
EMP: 50 **Privately Held**
SIC: 4731 Agents, shipping

HQ: Apm Terminals Pacific Llc
2500 Navy Way
San Pedro CA 90731
704 571-2768

(P-5012)
APM TERMINALS PACIFIC LTD
5801 Christie Ave, Emeryville
(94608-1964)
PHONE....................510 992-6430
EMP: 350
SALES (corp-wide): 38.6B **Privately Held**
SIC: 4731
HQ: Apm Terminals Pacific Ltd.
9300 Arrowpoint Blvd
Charlotte NC 90731
704 571-2768

(P-5013)
ATECH LOGISTICS INC
7 College Ave, Santa Rosa (95401-4702)
P.O. Box 6836 (95406-0836)
PHONE....................707 526-1910
Jesse E Amaral, *President*
Geri Amaral, *Vice Pres*
Kristian Knox, *Opers Mgr*
Travis Amaral, *Manager*
EMP: 130
SQ FT: 35,000
SALES (est): 42.3MM **Privately Held**
WEB: www.atechlogistics.com
SIC: 4731 Freight forwarding

(P-5014)
AUTO STRAP TRANSPORT LLC (PA)
15252 Slover Ave, Fontana (92337-7297)
P.O. Box 310375 (92331-0375)
PHONE....................909 795-4088
Richard Rudder,
Benito Rudder,
EMP: 109
SALES (est): 35.4MM **Privately Held**
SIC: 4731 Freight transportation arrangement

(P-5015)
BAJA FREIGHT FORWARDERS INC (PA)
8662 Siempre Viva Rd, San Diego
(92154-6211)
PHONE....................619 671-3100
Miguel Perez, *CEO*
Ana Diaz, *CFO*
Sergio Rodriguez, *General Mgr*
EMP: 55
SQ FT: 50,000
SALES (est): 14.5MM **Privately Held**
WEB: www.bajafreight.com
SIC: 4731 Foreign freight forwarding;
freight forwarding

(P-5016)
BINEX LINE CORP (PA)
19515 S Vermont Ave, Torrance
(90502-1121)
PHONE....................310 416-8600
David Paek, *President*
Hyun K Cho, *CFO*
Tim Park, *Vice Pres*
◆ EMP: 70
SQ FT: 32,000
SALES (est): 72.4MM **Privately Held**
SIC: 4731 4513 Freight forwarding; air
courier services

(P-5017)
BLACKROCK LOGISTICS INC
7031 Koll Center Pkwy # 250, Pleasanton
(94566-3134)
PHONE....................925 523-3878
Larry T James, *President*
Jeff R Mitchell, *CFO*
Mark J Polland, *Vice Pres*
Nora Schild, *Administration*
Rebecca Scheer, *Asst Controller*
EMP: 177
SALES: 211.9MM **Privately Held**
SIC: 4731 Freight forwarding

(P-5018)
BLUE SKY SERVICES INC
Also Called: Blue Freight
5530 Corbin Ave Ste 220, Tarzana
(91356-6020)
P.O. Box 571085 (91357-1085)
PHONE....................818 609-8779
Barry Keller, *President*
Brian Friedman, *Regl Sales Mgr*
EMP: 100
SQ FT: 1,500
SALES: 2.8MM **Privately Held**
SIC: 4731 Freight forwarding

(P-5019)
BLUE-GRACE LOGISTICS LLC
8765 Aero Dr Ste 133, San Diego
(92123-1767)
PHONE....................858 427-5093
Eric Bouvin, *President*
EMP: 52
SALES (corp-wide): 113MM **Privately Held**
SIC: 4731 Freight transportation arrangement
PA: Blue-Grace Logistics Llc
2846 S Falkenburg Rd
Riverview FL 33578
813 641-0357

(P-5020)
BROCK LLC (PA)
Also Called: Brock Transportation
333 N Canyons Pkwy # 221, Livermore
(94551-7700)
PHONE....................925 371-2184
Christopher R Obrien, *Mng Member*
Patricia Paolini, *Info Tech Mgr*
Gabriel Patton, *Opers Mgr*
William T Obrien, *Mng Member*
William O'Brien, *Manager*
EMP: 65
SQ FT: 3,000
SALES (est): 40.1MM **Privately Held**
WEB: www.brockweb.com
SIC: 4731 4789 4212 Brokers, shipping;
pipeline terminal facilities, independently
operated; local trucking, without storage

(P-5021)
BROKERAGE LGSTICS SLUTIONS INC
Also Called: JD Group
1659 Gailes Blvd Ste 101, San Diego
(92154-8230)
PHONE....................619 671-0276
Jorge Diaz Jr, *President*
Ricardo Rebeil, *Vice Pres*
Laura Diego, *Executive*
Alexandra Ramos, *Financial Exec*
Bertha Carrera, *Sales Dir*
EMP: 55 EST: 2001
SQ FT: 50,000
SALES (est): 14.8MM **Privately Held**
WEB: www.agenciajorgediaz.com
SIC: 4731 Domestic freight forwarding

(P-5022)
C H ROBINSON INTL INC
Also Called: Robinson Fresh
680 Knox St Ste 210, Torrance
(90502-1325)
PHONE....................310 763-6080
John Vestal, *Manager*
EMP: 100
SALES (corp-wide): 14.8B **Publicly Held**
SIC: 4731 Foreign freight forwarding
HQ: C. H. Robinson International, Inc.
14701 Charlson Rd
Eden Prairie MN 55347

(P-5023)
C-AIR INTERNATIONAL INC
9841 Arprt Blvd Ste 1400, Los Angeles
(90045)
PHONE....................310 695-3400
Guss Antico, *President*
Eric Jones, *Executive*
EMP: 55
SQ FT: 7,000
SALES (est): 15.5MM **Privately Held**
WEB: www.cairla.com
SIC: 4731 Customhouse brokers; domestic
freight forwarding

(P-5024)
CALIFORNIA SIERRA EXPRESS INC
2975 Oates St Ste 30, West Sacramento
(95691-6401)
PHONE....................916 375-7070
Jeff Phillips, *Manager*
EMP: 144
SALES (corp-wide): 20MM **Privately Held**
WEB: www.calsierraexpress.com
SIC: 4731 4212 Agents, shipping; delivery
service, vehicular
PA: California Sierra Express, Inc.
4965 Joule St
Reno NV 89502
775 856-8008

(P-5025)
CARMICHAEL INTERNATIONAL SVC (DH)
Also Called: C I Container Line
533 Glendale Blvd Ste 102, Los Angeles
(90026-5097)
PHONE....................213 353-0800
John Salvo, *President*
Vince Salvo, *President*
Jim Ryan, *CFO*
Daniel Meylor, *Officer*
Sandra Mendoza, *Administration*
EMP: 100
SQ FT: 19,000
SALES: 24MM
SALES (corp-wide): 5.1B **Privately Held**
WEB: www.carmnet.com
SIC: 4731 Customhouse brokers
HQ: Apl Logistics Americas, Ltd.
17600 N Perimeter Dr # 150
Scottsdale AZ 85255
602 586-4800

(P-5026)
CASESTACK INC (PA)
3000 Ocean Park Blvd, Santa Monica
(90405-3020)
PHONE....................310 473-8885
Daniel A Sanker, *President*
Keith Carvin, *CFO*
David Isaksen, *Finance Dir*
Craig Long, *VP Sales*
Chelsea Johnson, *Manager*
▲ EMP: 65
SQ FT: 10,000
SALES (est): 65.8MM **Privately Held**
WEB: www.casestack.com
SIC: 4731 4225 General warehousing &
storage; freight transportation arrangement

(P-5027)
CEVA FREIGHT LLC
Also Called: Ceva Ocean Line
19600 S Western Ave, Torrance
(90501-1117)
PHONE....................310 972-5500
Randy Mondello, *Vice Pres*
EMP: 80
SALES (corp-wide): 6.9B **Privately Held**
WEB: www.tntlogistics.com
SIC: 4731 Freight forwarding
HQ: Ceva Freight, Llc
15350 Vickery Dr
Houston TX 77032

(P-5028)
CEVA FREIGHT LLC
Also Called: Ceva Ocean Line
8670 Younger Creek Dr, Sacramento
(95828-1043)
PHONE....................916 379-6000
Scott Mann, *Branch Mgr*
EMP: 150
SALES (corp-wide): 6.9B **Privately Held**
WEB: www.tntlogistics.com
SIC: 4731 Domestic freight forwarding
HQ: Ceva Freight, Llc
15350 Vickery Dr
Houston TX 77032

(P-5029)
CEVA LOGISTICS LLC
19600 S Western Ave, Torrance
(90501-1117)
PHONE....................310 223-6500
Marvin O Schlanger, *Manager*
EMP: 300
SALES (corp-wide): 6.9B **Privately Held**
SIC: 4731 Domestic freight forwarding; foreign freight forwarding
HQ: Ceva Logistics, Llc
15350 Vickery Dr
Houston TX 77032
281 618-3100

(P-5030)
CFR RINKENS LLC (PA)
15501 Texaco Ave, Paramount
(90723-3921)
PHONE....................310 639-7725
Maximiliaan Hoes, *Mng Member*
Ivo Lindner, *Info Tech Mgr*
Dennys Deniz, *Systs Prg Mgr*
Mayra Sanchez, *Human Res Mgr*
Gino Bermeo, *Export Mgr*
EMP: 93
SALES (est): 17MM **Privately Held**
SIC: 4731 Freight forwarding

(P-5031)
CH ROBINSON FREIGHT SVCS LTD
Also Called: Phoenix International
680 Knox St Ste 210, Torrance
(90502-1325)
PHONE....................310 515-7755
Pat Nelms, *Branch Mgr*
Amy K Elliott, *Marketing Staff*
Craig S Carter, *Warehouse Mgr*
John Bestal, *Manager*
Viet Nguyen, *Supervisor*
EMP: 50
SALES (corp-wide): 14.8B **Publicly Held**
SIC: 4731 4225 Freight forwarding; customhouse brokers; general warehousing
HQ: C.H. Robinson Freight Services, Ltd.
1501 N Mittel Blvd Ste A
Wood Dale IL 60191
630 766-4445

(P-5032)
CHEEMA FREIGHTLINES LLC
Also Called: Cheema Logistics
223 W 5th St, Ripon (95366-2771)
P.O. Box 2234, Sumner WA (98390-0490)
PHONE....................209 599-0777
Harman Cheema, *Mng Member*
Mandy Reed, *Accountant*
Jessica Henry, *Manager*
EMP: 53
SQ FT: 1,900
SALES: 28.8MM **Privately Held**
SIC: 4731 Transportation agents & brokers
PA: Cheema Freightlines, Llc
4504 East Valley Hwy E # 102
Sumner WA 98390
253 733-5718

(P-5033)
CITY FASHION EXPRESS INC
Also Called: C F X
2888 E El Presidio St, Carson
(90810-1119)
PHONE....................310 223-1010
Walter John Malishka, *CEO*
Cammie Leroy, *Technology*
EMP: 58
SALES (est): 14.3MM **Privately Held**
WEB: www.cityx.com
SIC: 4731 Freight forwarding

(P-5034)
CNS LOGISTICS INC
108 W Walnut St Ste 270, Gardena
(90248-3102)
PHONE....................562 229-1133
Kevin Kim, *COO*
Jae Lee, *CFO*
EMP: 84
SALES (est): 13.7MM **Privately Held**
SIC: 4731 Foreign freight forwarding

(P-5035)
COMMODITY FORWARDERS INC (DH)
Also Called: C F I
11101 S La Cienega Blvd, Los Angeles (90045-6111)
PHONE..................................310 348-8855
Alfred P Kuehlewind, CEO
Christopher A Connell, President
Jennifer Martin, Admin Sec
Willy Paredes, Information Mgr
Jenny Mendez, Accounting Mgr
EMP: 60
SQ FT: 30,000
SALES (est): 116.8MM
SALES (corp-wide): 18.8B Privately Held
WEB: www.cfi-lax.com
SIC: 4731 Foreign freight forwarding; freight forwarding
HQ: Kuhne + Nagel International Ag
Dorfstrasse 50
Schindellegi SZ
447 869-511

(P-5036)
CONTINENTAL AGENCY INC (PA)
1768 W 2nd St, Pomona (91766-1206)
PHONE..................................909 595-8884
Jimmy Jiang, CEO
Beverly Jiang, President
EMP: 64
SQ FT: 105,000
SALES (est): 150.6MM Privately Held
WEB: www.continentalagency.com
SIC: 4731 Customhouse brokers

(P-5037)
COSCO AGENCIES (LOS ANGELES) (DH)
588 Harbor Scenic Way, Long Beach (90802-6317)
PHONE..................................213 689-6700
Jin Guoqiang, President
Tom Somma, Exec VP
Betty Brown, Executive
Zhang Xiaolan, General Mgr
Yang Yong, General Mgr
EMP: 56
SQ FT: 11,000
SALES (est): 6.3MM Privately Held
SIC: 4731 Agents, shipping
HQ: Cosco Shipping Lines (North America) Inc.
100 Lighting Way Fl 3
Secaucus NJ 07094
201 422-0500

(P-5038)
CSC AUTO SALV DISMANTLING INC
12207 Branford St, Sun Valley (91352-1010)
PHONE..................................818 532-4624
Scott Sakajian, President
Garrett Brady, Admin Sec
EMP: 54
SALES: 8MM Privately Held
SIC: 4731 4953 Freight transportation arrangement; refuse systems

(P-5039)
CUSTOM COMPANIES INC
13012 Molette St, Santa Fe Springs (90670-5522)
PHONE..................................310 672-8800
Mark Inman, Manager
EMP: 70
SALES (corp-wide): 122.6MM Privately Held
SIC: 4731 4214 Transportation agents & brokers; freight forwarding; local trucking with storage
PA: The Custom Companies Inc
317 W Lake St
Northlake IL 60164
708 344-5555

(P-5040)
DEFENDERS TRNSP SVCS INC
Also Called: Sam Kholi Transport
14562 Slover Ave, Fontana (92337-7148)
PHONE..................................909 854-7000
Christopher T Kato, CEO
EMP: 110 EST: 2010

SQ FT: 10,000
SALES: 10MM Privately Held
SIC: 4731 Agents, shipping

(P-5041)
DELTA AIR LINES INC
Also Called: Delta Airlines
5625 W Imperial Hwy, Los Angeles (90045-6316)
PHONE..................................310 646-9614
Kelvin Wimbish, Branch Mgr
EMP: 72
SALES (corp-wide): 41.2B Publicly Held
WEB: www.delta.com
SIC: 4731 4581 4512 Freight forwarding; airports, flying fields & services; air transportation, scheduled
PA: Delta Air Lines, Inc.
1030 Delta Blvd
Atlanta GA 30354
404 715-2600

(P-5042)
DEPENDABLE AIRCARGO EX INC
19201 S Susana Rd, Compton (90221-5710)
PHONE..................................310 537-2000
Bradley Dechter, President
EMP: 150
SALES (est): 14.4MM Privately Held
SIC: 4731 Transportation agents & brokers

(P-5043)
DFDS INTERNATIONAL CORPORATION
Also Called: Dfds Transport US
898 N Pacific Coast Hwy # 6, El Segundo (90245-2705)
PHONE..................................310 414-1516
Tina Larsen, General Mgr
EMP: 80
SALES (corp-wide): 2.2B Privately Held
WEB: www.us.dsv.com
SIC: 4731 Foreign freight forwarding
HQ: Dfds International Corporation
100 Walnut Ave Ste 405
Clark NJ 07066

(P-5044)
DHL SUPPLY CHAIN (USA)
Also Called: Msas Cargo International
485 Valley Dr, Brisbane (94005-1209)
PHONE..................................415 531-0596
Kevin Duson, General Mgr
EMP: 125
SALES (corp-wide): 71.2B Privately Held
SIC: 4731 Freight forwarding
HQ: Exel Inc.
570 Polaris Pkwy
Westerville OH 43082
614 865-8500

(P-5045)
DHX-DEPENDABLE HAWAIIAN EX INC
2375 Davis St, San Leandro (94577-2205)
PHONE..................................510 686-2600
EMP: 134
SALES (corp-wide): 90.9MM Privately Held
SIC: 4731 Freight forwarding
PA: Dhx-Dependable Hawaiian Express, Inc.
19201 S Susana Rd
Compton CA 90221
310 537-2000

(P-5046)
DHX-DEPENDABLE HAWAIIAN EX INC (PA)
19201 S Susana Rd, Compton (90221-5710)
PHONE..................................310 537-2000
Ronald Massman, Chairman
Gerard Crisostomo, President
Cammie Laster, President
Denise Jackson, Officer
Anthony Culpepper, Vice Pres
EMP: 150
SQ FT: 106,000
SALES (est): 90.9MM Privately Held
SIC: 4731 Foreign freight forwarding; freight forwarding

(P-5047)
DISPATCH TRUCKING LLC (PA)
14032 Santa Ana Ave, Fontana (92337-7035)
PHONE..................................909 355-5531
Bruce L Degler, CEO
Jalayne Pugmire, Vice Pres
EMP: 70 EST: 1991
SQ FT: 600
SALES (est): 9.2MM Privately Held
WEB: www.dispatchtrans.com
SIC: 4731 Truck transportation brokers

(P-5048)
DSC LOGISTICS INC
5690 Industrial Pkwy, San Bernardino (92407-1885)
PHONE..................................540 377-2302
EMP: 423
SALES (corp-wide): 355MM Privately Held
SIC: 4731 Freight transportation arrangement
PA: Dsc Logistics, Inc.
1750 S Wolf Rd
Des Plaines IL 60018
847 390-6800

(P-5049)
DTM SERVICES INC (PA)
Also Called: Diversified Trnsp Svcs
19829 Hamilton Ave, Torrance (90502-1341)
PHONE..................................310 521-1200
Marc Meskin, CEO
Robbie Thone, Senior VP
Michael Doyle, Vice Pres
Steve Singer, Executive
Tami Potvin, Financial Exec
EMP: 54
SQ FT: 7,000
SALES (est): 12.5MM Privately Held
WEB: www.dtsone.com
SIC: 4731 Truck transportation brokers

(P-5050)
DW MORGAN LLC
4185 Blackhawk, Danville (94506)
PHONE..................................925 460-2700
David W Morgan, CEO
EMP: 63 EST: 2013
SALES (est): 4.5MM Privately Held
SIC: 4731 4212 4789 Domestic freight forwarding; local trucking, without storage; cargo loading & unloading services

(P-5051)
ECO FLOW TRANSPORTATION LLC
18735 S Ferris Pl, Rancho Dominguez (90220-6405)
PHONE..................................310 816-0260
Bill Allen, President
EMP: 60
SALES (est): 2.3MM Privately Held
SIC: 4731 Freight transportation arrangement

(P-5052)
ELITE ANYWHERE CORP
82585 Showcase Pkwy, Indio (92203-9811)
PHONE..................................917 860-9247
Robert Sabo, CEO
EMP: 70
SQ FT: 50,000
SALES: 2MM Privately Held
SIC: 4731 4225 Freight transportation arrangement; general warehousing & storage

(P-5053)
ENTHUSIAST NETWORK INC (PA)
Also Called: Ten
2221 Rosecrans Ave # 195, El Segundo (90245-4931)
PHONE..................................310 531-9900
Scott Dickey, CEO
Scott Bailey, President
Bill Sutman, CFO
Eric Schwab, Ch Credit Ofcr
Jonathan Anastas, Chief Mktg Ofcr
◆ EMP: 300

SALES (est): 781MM Privately Held
WEB: www.sourceinterlink.com
SIC: 4731 Transportation agents & brokers

(P-5054)
ERIC JONES CUSTOMS BROKERAGE
9841 Arprt Blvd Ste 1400, Los Angeles (90045)
PHONE..................................310 348-3777
Eric Jones, Vice Pres
EMP: 50
SALES (est): 3.3MM Privately Held
SIC: 4731 Customhouse brokers

(P-5055)
EXPEDITORS INTL WASH INC
Also Called: Sfo-3 - San Francisco Full Svc
425 Valley Dr, Brisbane (94005-1209)
PHONE..................................415 657-3600
Kevin Niduaza, General Mgr
EMP: 50
SALES (corp-wide): 6.9B Publicly Held
WEB: www.expd.com
SIC: 4731 Freight forwarding
PA: Expeditors International Of Washington, Inc.
1015 3rd Ave Fl 12
Seattle WA 98104
206 674-3400

(P-5056)
EXPEDITORS INTL WASH INC
578 Eccles Ave, South San Francisco (94080-1905)
PHONE..................................919 489-7431
Jeff Musser, Manager
EMP: 131
SALES (corp-wide): 6.9B Publicly Held
WEB: www.expd.com
SIC: 4731 Freight forwarding; foreign freight forwarding; domestic freight forwarding
PA: Expeditors International Of Washington, Inc.
1015 3rd Ave Fl 12
Seattle WA 98104
206 674-3400

(P-5057)
EXPEDITORS INTL WASH INC
5757 W Century Blvd, Los Angeles (90045-6401)
PHONE..................................310 343-6200
EMP: 64
SALES (corp-wide): 6.9B Publicly Held
SIC: 4731 Foreign freight forwarding
PA: Expeditors International Of Washington, Inc.
1015 3rd Ave Fl 12
Seattle WA 98104
206 674-3400

(P-5058)
EXPEDITORS INTL WASH INC
5757 W Century Blvd, Los Angeles (90045-6401)
PHONE..................................310 343-6200
Karl Francisco, Branch Mgr
Angelica Sanchez, Sales Executive
Sara Fielder, Sales Staff
Felecia Dufauchard, Manager
Pepito Holandez, Supervisor
EMP: 125
SALES (corp-wide): 6.9B Publicly Held
WEB: www.expd.com
SIC: 4731 Foreign freight forwarding
PA: Expeditors International Of Washington, Inc.
1015 3rd Ave Fl 12
Seattle WA 98104
206 674-3400

(P-5059)
EXPEDITORS INTL WASH INC
1470 Expo Way Ste 110, San Diego (92154)
PHONE..................................619 710-1900
Trevor Moulton, Manager
EMP: 60
SALES (corp-wide): 6.9B Publicly Held
WEB: www.expd.com
SIC: 4731 Freight forwarding

▲ = Import ▼=Export
◆ =Import/Export

PA: Expeditors International Of Washington, Inc.
1015 3rd Ave Fl 12
Seattle WA 98104
206 674-3400

(P-5060)
EXPRESS SYSTEM INTERMODAL INC
2633 Camino Ramon Ste 400, San Ramon (94583-2176)
PHONE..........................801 302-6625
Peter Leng, *President*
EMP: 150
SALES (est): 16.5MM **Privately Held**
WEB: www.esi-intermodal.com
SIC: 4731 Freight transportation arrangement
HQ: Oocl (Usa) Inc.
10913 S River Front Pkwy # 200
South Jordan UT 84095
801 302-6625

(P-5061)
EXTRA EXPRESS (CERRITOS) INC
20405 Business Pkwy, Walnut (91789-2939)
P.O. Box 5100, Cerritos (90703-5100)
PHONE..........................714 985-6000
Kirk Baerwaldt, *President*
Kevin Westberg, *CFO*
Robert Bell, *Vice Pres*
Mike Thomas, *Software Engr*
Joe Kent, *Sales Executive*
EMP: 50
SALES (est): 9.5MM
SALES (corp-wide): 21MM **Privately Held**
WEB: www.extraexpress.com
SIC: 4731 Freight transportation arrangement
HQ: Dicom West Llc
676 N Michigan Ave # 3700
Chicago IL 60611
312 255-4800

(P-5062)
F R T INTERNATIONAL INC
Also Called: Frontier Logistics Services
2825 Jurupa St, Ontario (91761-2903)
PHONE..........................909 390-4892
Steven Hall, *Branch Mgr*
EMP: 123
SALES (corp-wide): 27.6MM **Privately Held**
SIC: 4731 Customhouse brokers
PA: F. R. T. International, Inc.
1700 N Alameda St
Compton CA 90222
310 604-8208

(P-5063)
FEDERAL EXPRESS CORPORATION
Also Called: Fedex
2221 W Washington St, San Diego (92110-2037)
PHONE..........................800 463-3339
Doug Eacros, *Manager*
EMP: 140
SALES (corp-wide): 65.4B **Publicly Held**
WEB: www.federalexpress.com
SIC: 4731 Agents, shipping
HQ: Federal Express Corporation
3610 Hacks Cross Rd
Memphis TN 38125
901 369-3600

(P-5064)
FNS INC (PA)
1545 Francisco St, Torrance (90501-1330)
PHONE..........................661 615-2300
Bennett B Koo, *CEO*
Jason Kwon, *Branch Mgr*
Wook Jin Choi, *Admin Sec*
Wendy Chang, *Accountant*
Gerald Kim, *Accountant*
EMP: 100
SQ FT: 100,000
SALES (est): 85.6MM **Privately Held**
WEB: www.fnsusa.com
SIC: 4731 Freight forwarding

(P-5065)
FNS CUSTOMS BROKERS INC
18301 S Broadwick St, Compton (90220-6442)
PHONE..........................310 667-4880
Bennett Koo, *CEO*
Wookjin Choi, *CFO*
EMP: 50
SQ FT: 2,000
SALES (est): 7.7MM **Privately Held**
SIC: 4731 Customhouse brokers

(P-5066)
FORWARD AIR INC
30108 Eigenbrodt Way # 100, Union City (94587-1225)
PHONE..........................415 570-6040
Fax: 650 794-9923
EMP: 50
SALES (corp-wide): 1.1B **Publicly Held**
SIC: 4731
HQ: Forward Air, Inc.
430 Airport Rd
Greeneville TN 37745
423 639-7196

(P-5067)
FURNITURE TRNSP SYSTEMS
3100 Pomona Blvd, Pomona (91768-3230)
P.O. Box 2960 (91769-2960)
PHONE..........................909 869-1200
Dennis Firestone, *President*
Lynnette Genereux, *Corp Secy*
John Naughton, *Vice Pres*
EMP: 65
SQ FT: 100,000
SALES (est): 12.5MM
SALES (corp-wide): 91.1MM **Privately Held**
SIC: 4731 4212 Freight consolidation; local trucking, without storage
PA: K. K. W. Trucking, Inc.
3100 Pomona Blvd
Pomona CA 91768
909 869-1200

(P-5068)
G KATEN PARTNERS LTD LBLTY CO
Also Called: My Express Freight
9903 Santa Monica Blvd, Beverly Hills (90212-1671)
PHONE..........................424 354-3241
Gerald Katen,
EMP: 550
SALES (est): 41.6MM **Privately Held**
SIC: 4731 Freight forwarding

(P-5069)
G3 ENTERPRISES INC (PA)
502 E Whitmore Ave, Modesto (95358-9411)
P.O. Box 624 (95353-0624)
PHONE..........................209 341-5115
Robert Lubeck, *President*
Stephanie Hardy, *Partner*
Michael Ellis, *CFO*
Steve Anderson, *Vice Pres*
Thomas Gallo, *Vice Pres*
EMP: 160 EST: 1961
SQ FT: 10,000
SALES (est): 128.2MM **Privately Held**
SIC: 4731 Transportation agents & brokers

(P-5070)
G3 ENTERPRISES INC
G3 Enterprises Mineral Div
1300 Camino Diablo Rd, Byron (94514)
P.O. Box 216 (94514-0216)
PHONE..........................209 341-3441
EMP: 103
SALES (corp-wide): 128.2MM **Privately Held**
SIC: 4731 Truck transportation brokers
PA: G3 Enterprises, Inc.
502 E Whitmore Ave
Modesto CA 95358
209 341-7515

(P-5071)
G3 ENTERPRISES INC
G3 Enterprises Closure Div
500 S Santa Rosa Ave, Modesto (95354-3717)
PHONE..........................209 341-4045
EMP: 69

(P-5072)
GELS LOGISTICS INC
20275 Business Pkwy, City of Industry (91789-2950)
PHONE..........................909 610-2277
Xindi Hu, *CEO*
Ling Wang, *CFO*
Liangna Zhong, *General Mgr*
EMP: 60
SALES (est): 915.9K **Privately Held**
SIC: 4731 Transportation agents & brokers

(P-5073)
GEODIS WILSON USA INC
229 Littlefield Ave Ste 1, South Francisco (94080-6926)
PHONE..........................650 692-9850
Jimmy Huang, *Branch Mgr*
EMP: 125 **Privately Held**
SIC: 4731 Freight forwarding
HQ: Geodis Wilson Usa, Inc.
75a Northfield Ave
Edison NJ 08837
732 362-0600

(P-5074)
GLOBAL MAIL INC
921 W Artesia Blvd, Compton (90220-5105)
PHONE..........................310 735-0800
Eric Ricardo, *Branch Mgr*
EMP: 200
SALES (corp-wide): 71.2B **Privately Held**
SIC: 4731 Freight transportation arrangement
HQ: Global Mail, Inc.
2700 S Comm Pkwy Ste 300
Weston FL 33331
800 805-9306

(P-5075)
GLOVIS AMERICA INC (HQ)
17305 Von Karman Ave # 200, Irvine (92614-6674)
PHONE..........................714 435-2960
Kyung B Kim, *President*
Glenn Clift, *COO*
Sandra V BSN, *Bd of Directors*
Sonia V Aprn, *Vice Pres*
Sharon Choi, *Supervisor*
EMP: 80
SQ FT: 34,700
SALES (est): 52.6MM
SALES (corp-wide): 11.8B **Privately Held**
WEB: www.glovisusa.com
SIC: 4731 Freight forwarding
PA: Hyundai Glovis Co., Ltd.
301 Teheran-Ro, Gangnam-Gu
Seoul 06152
822 619-1911

(P-5076)
GOLDEN BRIDGE INTL GROUP
727 9th Ave, City of Industry (91745-1416)
PHONE..........................626 968-8229
EMP: 97
SALES (est): 19.3MM **Privately Held**
SIC: 4731 Freight forwarding

(P-5077)
GOLDEN HOUR DATA SYSTEMS INC
10052 Mesa Ridge Ct # 200, San Diego (92121-2971)
PHONE..........................858 768-2500
Kevin Hutton, *President*
Tom Whalen, *COO*
Charles Haczewski, *Vice Pres*
EMP: 120 EST: 1997
SQ FT: 14,000
SALES (est): 34.7MM **Privately Held**
WEB: www.goldenhour.com
SIC: 4731 Transportation agents & brokers

(P-5078)
GONZALEZ BARBA ENTERPRISES
1575 E 46th St, Los Angeles (90011-4315)
PHONE..........................323 233-7995
Elizabeth Gonzalez, *Principal*
EMP: 50
SALES (est): 3.8MM **Privately Held**
SIC: 4731 Transportation agents & brokers

(P-5079)
GREATWIDE LOGISTICS SVCS LLC
Also Called: Greatwide Dedicated Transport
4310 Bandini Blvd, Vernon (90058-4308)
PHONE..........................323 268-7100
Angela Remling, *Branch Mgr*
William Ross, *Opers Spvr*
Christopher Russell, *Opers Mgr*
Bill Smith, *Plant Mgr*
Michael Clarke, *Prdtn Mgr*
EMP: 75
SALES (corp-wide): 2.5B **Privately Held**
SIC: 4731 Truck transportation brokers
HQ: Greatwide Logistics Services, Llc.
12404 Park Central Dr # 300
Dallas TX 75251

(P-5080)
HANJIN TRANSPORTATION CO LTD
Also Called: Hanjin Global Logistics
1111 E Watson Center Rd A, Carson (90745-4217)
PHONE..........................310 522-5030
Bryce Dalziel, *President*
J B Park, *Admin Sec*
EMP: 90
SQ FT: 28,000
SALES (est): 36.4MM **Privately Held**
SIC: 4731 Transportation agents & brokers
PA: Hanjin Corporation Co., Ltd
137 Hongdo-Dong, Tong-Gu
Daejeon
824 262-5474

(P-5081)
HANSOL GOLDPOINT LLC
12792 Valley View St # 211, Garden Grove (92845-2510)
PHONE..........................714 594-5073
Min Ho Inn, *Branch Mgr*
EMP: 84
SALES (corp-wide): 4.5MM **Privately Held**
SIC: 4731 Freight forwarding
PA: Hansol Goldpoint Llc
2396 E Pacifica Pl # 290
Rancho Dominguez CA 90220
619 710-1728

(P-5082)
HAPAG-LLOYD (AMERICA) LLC
180 Grand Ave Ste 1535, Oakland (94612-3702)
PHONE..........................510 251-8405
Manfred Braun, *Manager*
Darin Wright, *Marketing Mgr*
EMP: 50
SQ FT: 16,639
SALES (corp-wide): 11.7B **Privately Held**
SIC: 4731 Agents, shipping
HQ: Hapag-Lloyd (America) Llc
399 Hoes Ln Ste 101
Piscataway NJ 08854
732 562-1800

(P-5083)
HARRY GROUP INC
Also Called: J M K C Express
2839 E El Presidio St, Carson (90810-1120)
PHONE..........................310 631-9646
Tom Villardi, *President*
Georganna Villardi, *Corp Secy*
EMP: 100
SQ FT: 65,000
SALES (est): 13.8MM **Privately Held**
SIC: 4731 Freight transportation arrangement

P R O D U C T S & S V C S

(P-5084)
HAVEN ENGINEERING INC
25 Kearny St Ste 304, San Francisco
(94108-5515)
PHONE..................888 838-3868
Matt Tillman, *Director*
Jeff Wehner, *Director*
EMP: 50 **EST:** 2014
SALES (est): 3.7MM **Privately Held**
SIC: 4731 Freight transportation arrangement

(P-5085)
**HELLMANN WRLDWIDE
LGISTICS INC**
2270 E 220th St, Long Beach
(90810-1638)
PHONE..................310 847-4600
Jonas Welch, *Branch Mgr*
Jacqueline Flores, *Executive*
Maureen Lapiz, *Executive*
Esperanza Campos, *Manager*
Steve Kim, *Manager*
EMP: 60
SALES (corp-wide): 2.4B **Privately Held**
SIC: 4731 Freight forwarding
HQ: Hellmann Worldwide Logistics Inc.
10450 Doral Blvd
Doral FL 33178
305 406-4500

(P-5086)
**HELLMANN WRLDWIDE
LGISTICS INC**
2270 E 220th St, Carson (90810-1638)
PHONE..................310 847-4600
Roger Haeussler, *President*
EMP: 50
SALES (corp-wide): 2.4B **Privately Held**
WEB: www.hellmann.net
SIC: 4731 Freight forwarding
HQ: Hellmann Worldwide Logistics Inc.
10450 Doral Blvd
Doral FL 33178
305 406-4500

(P-5087)
**HES TRANSPORTATION SVCS
INC**
3623 Munster St, Hayward (94545-1646)
P.O. Box 57136 (94545-7136)
PHONE..................510 783-6100
Jeff Graham, *President*
Joyce C Schaul, *Vice Pres*
Galen Kitamura, *Manager*
EMP: 50
SQ FT: 38,000
SALES (est): 5.9MM **Privately Held**
SIC: 4731 Freight forwarding

(P-5088)
**HOME EXPRESS DELIVERY SVC
LLC**
Also Called: Temco Logistics
230 Diamond St, Laguna Beach
(92651-3610)
PHONE..................949 715-9844
Lance Templeton,
Virginia Templeton,
EMP: 1000
SALES: 35MM **Privately Held**
SIC: 4731 Freight transportation arrangement

(P-5089)
**HONOLULU FREIGHT SERVICE
(PA)**
1400 Date St, Montebello (90640-6323)
PHONE..................323 887-6777
Michael Biedleman, *President*
Dorene Beidleman, *CFO*
Thomas Biedleman, *Vice Pres*
Patrick Toves, *General Mgr*
Christopher Toye, *Administration*
EMP: 50 **EST:** 1945
SQ FT: 1,500
SALES (est): 20.9MM **Privately Held**
WEB: www.hfsnet.com
SIC: 4731 Foreign freight forwarding; domestic freight forwarding

(P-5090)
ICAT LOGISTICS INC
11 Wandering Rill, Irvine (92603-3430)
PHONE..................310 884-5923
EMP: 93 **Privately Held**
SIC: 4731 Freight transportation arrangement
PA: Icat Logistics, Inc.
6805 Douglas Legum Dr # 3
Elkridge MD 21075
-

(P-5091)
INNOVEL SOLUTIONS INC
Also Called: Sears
521 Stone Rd, Benicia (94510-1113)
PHONE..................707 748-1940
Dixie Shaw, *Manager*
EMP: 99
SALES (corp-wide): 16.7B **Publicly Held**
WEB: www.slslogistics.com+%22sears+logistics+servi
SIC: 4731 Agents, shipping
HQ: Innovel Solutions, Inc.
3333 Beverly Rd
Hoffman Estates IL 60179
847 286-2500

(P-5092)
INNOVEL SOLUTIONS INC
Also Called: Sears
1700 Schuster Rd, Delano (93215-9572)
PHONE..................661 721-5910
Mike Velton, *General Mgr*
EMP: 600
SALES (corp-wide): 16.7B **Publicly Held**
WEB: www.slslogistics.com+%22sears+logistics+servi
SIC: 4731 Agents, shipping
HQ: Innovel Solutions, Inc.
3333 Beverly Rd
Hoffman Estates IL 60179
847 286-2500

(P-5093)
**JS INTERNATIONAL SHIPG
CORP (PA)**
Also Called: Jsi Shipping
1535 Rollins Rd Ste B, Burlingame
(94010-2305)
P.O. Box 4267 (94011-4267)
PHONE..................650 697-3963
James G Cullen, *CEO*
Scott French, *Vice Pres*
Will Waller, *Vice Pres*
Jeff Beck, *Branch Mgr*
Richard Bryant, *General Mgr*
EMP: 70
SQ FT: 50,000
SALES (est): 259.2MM **Privately Held**
WEB: www.jsishipping.com
SIC: 4731 Freight forwarding; customhouse brokers

(P-5094)
KLS AIR EXPRESS INC (PA)
Also Called: Freight Solution Providers
2870 Gold Tailings Ct, Rancho Cordova
(95670-6106)
PHONE..................916 857-6305
Lielanie Steers, *CEO*
Kenneth Steers, *President*
Elizabeth Adair, *Exec VP*
Jeff Adams, *Vice Pres*
Kaitlin Ryder, *Program Mgr*
EMP: 60
SQ FT: 9,700
SALES (est): 22.5MM **Privately Held**
WEB: www.shipfsp.com
SIC: 4731 Freight forwarding

(P-5095)
KOJENOV ARKADI NILOVICH
5335 Hackberry Ln, Sacramento
(95841-3268)
PHONE..................916 718-1790
Arkadi Kojenov, *Owner*
EMP: 50 **EST:** 1997
SQ FT: 2,000
SALES: 5MM **Privately Held**
SIC: 4731 Freight transportation arrangement

(P-5096)
KSI CORP (PA)
839 Mitten Rd, San Bruno (94066)
P.O. Box 2182, South San Francisco
(94083-2182)
PHONE..................650 952-0815
Carl Bellante, *CEO*
Dennis Siu, *CFO*
Michael Ford, *Senior VP*
Chris Ramos, *Vice Pres*
EMP: 64
SQ FT: 13,000
SALES (est): 8.1MM **Privately Held**
WEB: www.ksicorp.com
SIC: 4731 8741 Customhouse brokers;
management services

(P-5097)
KSI CORP
839 Mitten Rd Ste 200, Burlingame
(94010-1331)
PHONE..................650 952-0815
Carl Bellante, *CEO*
Dennis Siu, *CFO*
Michael Ford, *Senior VP*
Chris Ramos, *Vice Pres*
EMP: 60
SALES (est): 6MM **Privately Held**
SIC: 4731 Freight transportation arrangement

(P-5098)
KUEHNE + NAGEL INC
150 W Hill Pl, Brisbane (94005-1216)
PHONE..................415 656-4100
Christian Herwig, *Branch Mgr*
Matthew Hamilton, *Branch Mgr*
Diana Tang, *Export Mgr*
Olaf Greifenhagen, *Director*
Joerg Lehmann, *Manager*
EMP: 50
SALES (corp-wide): 18.8B **Privately Held**
WEB: www.kuehnenagel.com
SIC: 4731 Freight forwarding
HQ: Kuehne + Nagel Inc.
10 Exchange Pl Fl 19
Jersey City NJ 07302
201 413-5500

(P-5099)
KW INTERNATIONAL INC
18511 S Broadwick St, Rancho Dominguez
(90220-6440)
PHONE..................310 747-1380
Dj Kim, *Manager*
EMP: 70 **Privately Held**
SIC: 4731 Freight forwarding
PA: Kw International, Inc.
18655 Bishop Ave
Carson CA 90746

(P-5100)
L E COPPERSMITH INC (PA)
Also Called: Coppersmith Global Logistics
525 S Douglas St Ste 100, El Segundo
(90245-4828)
PHONE..................310 607-8000
Jeffrey Craig Coppersmith, *President*
Doug Walkley, *CFO*
Douglas S Walkley, *CFO*
Lew Coppersmith Jr, *Vice Pres*
L E Coppersmith, *Admin Sec*
EMP: 80
SQ FT: 40,000
SALES: 20MM **Privately Held**
SIC: 4731 4789 Customhouse brokers;
cargo loading & unloading services

(P-5101)
L E COPPERSMITH INC
525 S Douglas St, El Segundo
(90245-4826)
PHONE..................310 607-8000
D Walkley, *Branch Mgr*
EMP: 80
SALES (corp-wide): 20MM **Privately
Held**
SIC: 4731 Freight forwarding
PA: L. E. Coppersmith, Inc.
525 S Douglas St Ste 100
El Segundo CA 90245
310 607-8000

(P-5102)
LOUP LOGISTICS COMPANY
Also Called: Union Pacific
2121 S Browning Rd, Delano (93215-9298)
PHONE..................661 370-4341
Kim Sakata, *Branch Mgr*
EMP: 135
SALES (corp-wide): 21.2B **Publicly Held**
WEB: www.railex.net
SIC: 4731 Railroad freight agency
HQ: Loup Logistics Company
1400 Douglas St Stop 1230
Omaha NE 68179
402 544-7094

(P-5103)
LUTREL TRUCKING INC
12856 Old River Rd, Bakersfield
(93311-9707)
PHONE..................661 397-9756
Roy G Lutrel, *President*
Gail Lutrel, *Treasurer*
Mark Lutrel, *Vice Pres*
EMP: 65 **EST:** 1973
SALES (est): 12.2MM **Privately Held**
WEB: www.lutreltrucking.com
SIC: 4731 Customs clearance of freight;
freight forwarding

(P-5104)
MAERSK INC
Also Called: Maersk Line
555 Anton Blvd Ste 300, Costa Mesa
(92626-7667)
PHONE..................714 428-5500
Celia Miller, *Branch Mgr*
EMP: 80 **Privately Held**
WEB: www.maersksealand.com
SIC: 4731 Agents, shipping
HQ: Maersk Inc.
180 Park Ave Ste 105
Florham Park NJ 07932
973 514-5000

(P-5105)
MAINFREIGHT INC (HQ)
1400 Glenn Curtiss St, Carson
(90746-4030)
PHONE..................310 900-1974
John Hepworth, *President*
Christopher Coppersmith, *CEO*
John Eshuis, *Vice Pres*
EMP: 90
SQ FT: 100,000
SALES (est): 227.3MM
SALES (corp-wide): 1.9B **Privately Held**
WEB: www.mainfreightusa.com
SIC: 4731 Domestic freight forwarding; foreign freight forwarding
PA: Mainfreight Limited
2 Railway Lane
Auckland 1062
925 955-00

(P-5106)
**MAP CARGO GLOBAL
LOGISTICS (PA)**
2501 Santa Fe Ave, Redondo Beach
(90278-1117)
PHONE..................310 297-8300
Marek Adam Panasewicz, *President*
EMP: 74
SQ FT: 20,000
SALES (est): 27.2MM **Privately Held**
WEB: www.mapcargo.com
SIC: 4731 2448 Domestic freight forwarding; cargo containers, wood & wood with metal

(P-5107)
MATUS INTERNATIONAL INC
1120 De Forest Ave, Long Beach
(90813-2824)
PHONE..................562 435-5200
Luis Matus, *Principal*
EMP: 155 **EST:** 2014
SALES (est): 30.8MM **Privately Held**
SIC: 4731 Freight forwarding

(P-5108)
MENDOCINO RAILWAY
Also Called: Skunk Train, The
100 W Laurel St, Fort Bragg (95437-3410)
PHONE..................707 964-6371
David Magaw, *President*
Ed Ring, *Treasurer*

Chris Hart, *Vice Pres*
Torgny Nilsson, *Admin Sec*
EMP: 101
SALES (est): 169.2K **Privately Held**
SIC: 4731 4011 Railroad freight agency;
railroads, line-haul operating
PA: Sierra Railroad Company
341 Industrial Way
Woodland CA 95776

(P-5109)
MERIT LOGISTICS LLC
Also Called: Drop Lot Services
33332 Valle Rd Ste 100, San Juan Capis-
trano (92675-4856)
PHONE..........................949 481-0685
Mike Bletko, *Principal*
Krishae Baldwin, *Human Res Mgr*
Bob Shade, *Marketing Staff*
Jim Henricksen, *Manager*
Mary-Jane Mormile, *Clerk*
EMP: 1100 **EST:** 2013
SALES: 60MM **Privately Held**
SIC: 4731 Cargo loading & unloading serv-
ices; general warehousing & storage

(P-5110)
MHX LLC
22707 Wilmington Ave, Carson
(90745-4321)
PHONE..........................800 234-2098
Rick McLeod, *President*
Conrad Hardin,
Vincent McLeod,
EMP: 75 **EST:** 2016
SALES (est): 6.7MM **Privately Held**
SIC: 4731 Domestic freight forwarding

(P-5111)
**MILLENNIUM TRANSPORTATION
INC**
3164 E La Palma Ave Ste D, Anaheim
(92806-2811)
PHONE..........................714 956-7882
Reuban Bedi, *President*
EMP: 99
SALES (est): 11.6MM **Privately Held**
SIC: 4731 Truck transportation brokers

(P-5112)
**MIRAMAR TRANSPORTATION
INC**
Also Called: Pilot Freight Services
9340 Cabot Dr Ste I, San Diego
(92126-4397)
PHONE..........................858 693-0071
Richard Evan Fore, *President*
Robert Mirenda, *Vice Pres*
Bob Mirinda, *Vice Pres*
Liz Beck, *District Mgr*
Fred Mackay, *District Mgr*
EMP: 100
SALES (est): 31.6MM **Privately Held**
SIC: 4731 Freight forwarding

(P-5113)
**MOUNTAIN VALLEY EXPRESS
CO INC**
7701 Rosecrans Ave, Paramount
(90723-2534)
P.O. Box 152, Manteca (95336-1122)
PHONE..........................562 630-5500
Robert Baker, *Branch Mgr*
EMP: 130
SALES (corp-wide): 52MM **Privately
Held**
WEB: www.mountainvalleyexpress.com
SIC: 4731 4212 Freight transportation
arrangement; local trucking, without stor-
age
PA: Mountain Valley Express Co. , Inc.
6750 Longe St Ste 100
Stockton CA 95206
209 823-2168

(P-5114)
NATIONAL AIR CARGO INC
222 N Sepulveda Blvd # 2000, El Segundo
(90245-5648)
PHONE..........................310 662-4766
Ray Macchlowski, *Manager*
EMP: 80 **Privately Held**
SIC: 4731 Freight forwarding

HQ: National Air Cargo Inc
350 Windward Dr
Orchard Park NY 14127

(P-5115)
**NATIONAL DISTRIBUTION
CENTERS**
Also Called: Ontario Distribution Center
5140 Santa Ana St, Ontario (91761-8632)
PHONE..........................909 390-5696
Andy Traupman, *General Mgr*
EMP: 76 **EST:** 2012
SALES (est): 5.4MM **Privately Held**
SIC: 4731 Freight transportation arrange-
ment

(P-5116)
NATIONWIDE TRANS INC (PA)
1633 S Campus Ave, Ontario (91761-4335)
P.O. Box 4207 (91761-8907)
PHONE..........................909 355-3211
Kong Lee, *President*
EMP: 100
SALES (est): 17.8MM **Privately Held**
SIC: 4731 Freight transportation arrange-
ment

(P-5117)
NEOVIA LOGISTICS DIST LP
600 Live Oak Ave, Irwindale (91706-1344)
PHONE..........................626 359-4500
Hector Legaspi, *Branch Mgr*
EMP: 106
SALES (corp-wide): 63.5MM **Privately
Held**
SIC: 4731 Truck transportation brokers
HQ: Neovia Logistics Distribution, Lp
6363 N State Highway # 700
Irving TX 75038

(P-5118)
NIPPON EXPRESS USA INC
970 Francisco St, Torrance (90502-1201)
PHONE..........................310 532-6300
Yozo Komiya, *Vice Pres*
EMP: 50
SALES (corp-wide): 18.7B **Privately Held**
SIC: 4731 4412 4491 Freight forwarding;
deep sea foreign transportation of freight;
marine cargo handling
HQ: Nippon Express U.S.A., Inc.
2401 44th Rd Fl 14
Long Island City NY 11101
212 758-6100

(P-5119)
NIPPON EXPRESS USA INC
300 Westmont Dr, San Pedro
(90731-1000)
PHONE..........................310 532-6300
Y Totani, *Manager*
EMP: 62
SALES (corp-wide): 18.7B **Privately Held**
SIC: 4731 4424 Freight forwarding; deep
sea domestic transportation of freight
HQ: Nippon Express U.S.A., Inc.
2401 44th Rd Fl 14
Long Island City NY 11101
212 758-6100

(P-5120)
NIPPON EXPRESS USA INC
2233 E Grand Ave, El Segundo
(90245-2837)
PHONE..........................310 535-7200
Yozo Komiya, *Manager*
EMP: 56
SALES (corp-wide): 18.7B **Privately Held**
SIC: 4731 Foreign freight forwarding; do-
mestic freight forwarding; customhouse
brokers
HQ: Nippon Express U.S.A., Inc.
2401 44th Rd Fl 14
Long Island City NY 11101
212 758-6100

(P-5121)
**NISSIN INTL TRNSPT USA INC
(HQ)**
1540 W 190th St, Torrance (90501-1121)
PHONE..........................310 222-8500
Yasushi Ihara, *CEO*
Mitsugu Matsusaka, *CFO*
Hirokazu Ikuta, *Vice Pres*

Andrew Sclafani, *Vice Pres*
David Thompson, *Vice Pres*
EMP: 50
SQ FT: 98,000
SALES (est): 206.2MM
SALES (corp-wide): 2B **Privately Held**
WEB: www.nitusa.com
SIC: 4731 Domestic freight forwarding;
customhouse brokers
PA: Nissin Corporation
6-81, Onoecho, Naka-Ku
Yokohama KNG 231-0
456 716-111

(P-5122)
**NNR GLOBAL LOGISTICS USA
INC**
Also Called: N N R
21023 Main St Ste D, Carson
(90745-1246)
PHONE..........................310 357-2100
Natomi Yamata, *Branch Mgr*
William Chancy, *Supervisor*
EMP: 110
SQ FT: 23,650
SALES (corp-wide): 3.5B **Privately Held**
WEB: www.northportlandwellness.com
SIC: 4731 Foreign freight forwarding
HQ: Nnr Global Logistics Usa Inc.
450 E Devon Ave Ste 260
Itasca IL 60143
630 773-1490

(P-5123)
NRI USA LLC (PA)
Also Called: Nri Distribution
13200 S Broadway, Los Angeles
(90061-1124)
PHONE..........................323 345-6456
Chris Maydaniuk,
EMP: 100 **EST:** 2011
SQ FT: 65,000
SALES (est): 27.1MM **Privately Held**
SIC: 4731 Freight forwarding

(P-5124)
NRI USA LLC
227 E Compton Blvd, Gardena
(90248-1909)
PHONE..........................323 345-6456
EMP: 57
SALES (corp-wide): 27.1MM **Privately
Held**
SIC: 4731 Freight transportation arrange-
ment
PA: Nri Usa, Llc
13200 S Broadway
Los Angeles CA 90061
323 345-6456

(P-5125)
O E C SHIPG LOS ANGELES INC
Also Called: Oec Group
13100 Alondra Blvd # 100, Cerritos
(90703-2278)
PHONE..........................562 926-7186
Robert Han, *President*
John Su, *President*
EMP: 50
SALES (est): 27.7MM **Privately Held**
SIC: 4731 Foreign freight forwarding

(P-5126)
OCEAN KNIGHT SHIPPING INC
19516 S Susana Rd # 101, Compton
(90221-5714)
PHONE..........................310 885-3388
Henry Chu, *President*
EMP: 200
SALES: 3.1MM **Privately Held**
WEB: www.okshipping.com
SIC: 4731 Freight forwarding

(P-5127)
OOCL (USA) INC
2700 Zanker Rd Ste 200, San Jose
(95134-2140)
PHONE..........................408 576-6543
Karen Heller, *Branch Mgr*
Nieto Andreas, *General Mgr*
Elisabeth Erickson, *General Mgr*
Jim Stewart, *CPA*
Warren MA, *Manager*
EMP: 64 **Privately Held**
SIC: 4731 Freight transportation arrange-
ment

HQ: Oocl (Usa) Inc.
10913 S River Front Pkwy # 200
South Jordan UT 84095
801 302-6625

(P-5128)
OOCL (USA) INC
111 W Ocean Blvd Ste 1800, Long Beach
(90802-7936)
PHONE..........................562 499-2600
Chris Favro, *Human Res Mgr*
Michael Toomey, *Opers Staff*
EMP: 56 **Privately Held**
WEB: www.esi-intermodal.com
SIC: 4731 4729 Agents, shipping;
steamship ticket offices
HQ: Oocl (Usa) Inc.
10913 S River Front Pkwy # 200
South Jordan UT 84095
801 302-6625

(P-5129)
OOCL (USA) INC
17777 Center Court Dr N # 500, Cerritos
(90703-9320)
PHONE..........................562 499-2600
Paul Conolly, *Principal*
Peter Liu, *Admin Sec*
James Lester, *Manager*
EMP: 65 **Privately Held**
WEB: www.esi-intermodal.com
SIC: 4731 Freight forwarding
HQ: Oocl (Usa) Inc.
10913 S River Front Pkwy # 200
South Jordan UT 84095
801 302-6625

(P-5130)
P& JP BROKERAGE LLC
15301 Ventura Blvd Ste P2, Sherman Oaks
(91403-5882)
PHONE..........................310 801-9707
Paul Mantea,
EMP: 50
SQ FT: 15,000
SALES (est): 3.9MM **Privately Held**
SIC: 4731 Brokers, shipping

(P-5131)
PACIFIC LOGISTICS CORP (PA)
Also Called: Paclo
7255 Rosemead Blvd, Pico Rivera
(90660-4047)
PHONE..........................562 478-4700
Douglas E Hockersmith, *President*
Timothy K Hewey, *COO*
Mark Nakamura, *CFO*
Timothy Hewey, *Officer*
Clare Witt, *Executive Asst*
EMP: 208
SQ FT: 206,000
SALES (est): 115.5MM **Privately Held**
WEB: www.pacific-logistics.com
SIC: 4731 Freight forwarding

(P-5132)
PANALPINA INC
401 E Grand Ave, South San Francisco
(94080-6208)
P.O. Box 1850 (94083)
PHONE..........................650 825-3036
Tommy Lau, *Branch Mgr*
EMP: 50
SALES (corp-wide): 5.6B **Privately Held**
WEB: www.panalpina.com
SIC: 4731 Freight forwarding
HQ: Panalpina, Inc.
703 Waterford Way Ste 890
Miami FL 33126
305 894-1300

(P-5133)
PANALPINA INC
19900 S Vermont Ave Ste A, Torrance
(90502-1147)
PHONE..........................310 819-4060
Maurice Joseph, *Branch Mgr*
EMP: 60
SALES (corp-wide): 5.6B **Privately Held**
WEB: www.panalpina.com
SIC: 4731 Freight forwarding
HQ: Panalpina, Inc.
703 Waterford Way Ste 890
Miami FL 33126
305 894-1300

(P-5134)
PARAMOUNT TRNSP SYSTEMS INC (PA)
1350 Grand Ave, San Marcos
(92078-2404)
PHONE..................760 510-7979
Mike Keller, *CEO*
Grace Bishar, *CFO*
Brian Goates, *Vice Pres*
Robert Vespa, *Vice Pres*
John Miranda, *Branch Mgr*
EMP: 50
SQ FT: 32,000
SALES (est) 93.1MM **Privately Held**
WEB: www.pts-ca.com
SIC: 4731 Brokers, shipping

(P-5135)
PASHA DISTRIBUTION SVCS LLC
3010 Old Ranch Pkwy # 220, Seal Beach
(90740-2750)
PHONE..................714 889-2460
George W Pasha IV, *Branch Mgr*
EMP: 60 **Privately Held**
SIC: 4731 Freight transportation arrangement
PA: Pasha Distribution Services Llc
500 W Elm St
Lebanon MO 65536

(P-5136)
PASHA GROUP (PA)
Also Called: Pasha Freight
4040 Civic Center Dr # 350, San Rafael
(94903-4187)
PHONE..................415 927-6400
George W Pasha III, *Ch of Bd*
James Britton, *CFO*
Steve Hunter, *Treasurer*
Jeff Burgin, *Senior VP*
Amy Sherburne, *Vice Pres*
EMP: 400
SQ FT: 18,000
SALES (est) 234.4MM **Privately Held**
WEB: www.pashagroup.com
SIC: 4731 Freight forwarding

(P-5137)
PASHA GROUP
19020 S Dminguez Hills Dr, Compton
(90220-6404)
PHONE..................310 735-0952
EMP: 103
SALES (corp-wide): 234.4MM **Privately Held**
SIC: 4731 Freight forwarding
PA: The Pasha Group
4040 Civic Center Dr # 350
San Rafael CA 94903
415 927-6400

(P-5138)
PATRIOT BROKERAGE INC
7840 Foothill Blvd Ste H, Sunland
(91040-2907)
PHONE..................910 227-4142
Ross Tsarukyan, *Mng Member*
Liyan Tsarukyan,
EMP: 84
SQ FT: 13,000
SALES: 13MM **Privately Held**
SIC: 4731 Freight forwarding

(P-5139)
PEGASUS MARITIME INC
535 N Brand Blvd Ste 400, Glendale
(91203-3907)
PHONE..................714 728-8565
Khurram Mahmood, *President*
Moazam Mahmood, *CEO*
Mookie Mahmood, *Exec VP*
Syed M Ali, *Vice Pres*
Harry Yang, *Broker*
EMP: 75
SQ FT: 10,000
SALES (est) 13.9MM **Privately Held**
SIC: 4731 Freight forwarding

(P-5140)
PERFORMANCE TEAM FRT SYS INC
1331 Torrance Blvd, Torrance
(90501-2351)
PHONE..................562 345-2200
Craig Kaplan, *CEO*
EMP: 86
SALES (corp-wide): 372MM **Privately Held**
SIC: 4731 Customs clearance of freight
PA: Performance Team Llc
2240 E Maple Ave
El Segundo CA 90245
562 345-2200

(P-5141)
PERFORMANCE TEAM FRT SYS INC
1651 California St, Redlands (92374-2904)
PHONE..................424 358-6943
EMP: 108
SALES (corp-wide): 372MM **Privately Held**
SIC: 4731 Freight forwarding
PA: Performance Team Llc
2240 E Maple Ave
El Segundo CA 90245
562 345-2200

(P-5142)
PERFORMANCE TEAM LLC (PA)
2240 E Maple Ave, El Segundo
(90245-6507)
PHONE..................562 345-2200
Craig Kaplan,
Jim Snodgrass, *President*
Marc Koenig, *Senior VP*
Fred Gilbert, *Vice Pres*
Tom Wilkinson, *Vice Pres*
EMP: 200
SQ FT: 80,000
SALES (est) 372MM **Privately Held**
WEB: www.ptgt.net
SIC: 4731 4225 4213 Freight forwarding; general warehousing & storage; trucking, except local

(P-5143)
POINTDIRECT TRANSPORT INC
10858 Almond Ave, Fontana (92337-7103)
PHONE..................909 371-0837
Adolfo De La Herran, *President*
Adolfo D La Herran, *President*
EMP: 100
SQ FT: 2,500
SALES: 500K **Privately Held**
SIC: 4731 Freight forwarding

(P-5144)
PORT LOGISTICS GROUP INC
15530 Salt Lake Ave, City of Industry
(91745-1113)
PHONE..................626 330-1300
Louis P Gram, *Principal*
Cristina Wilson, *Human Res Mgr*
Noemi Cabanilla, *Warehouse Mgr*
Todd Larson, *Warehouse Mgr*
EMP: 350 **Privately Held**
SIC: 4731 4225 Agents, shipping; general warehousing
PA: Port Logistics Group, Inc.
288 S Mayo Ave
City Of Industry CA 91789

(P-5145)
PREMIER MEDICAL TRANSPORT INC
260 N Palm St 200, Brea (92821-2870)
PHONE..................888 353-9556
David Johnson, *President*
EMP: 90
SALES (est) 15MM **Privately Held**
SIC: 4731 Freight transportation arrangement

(P-5146)
PREMIUM TRNSP SVCS INC (PA)
Also Called: Ttsi
18735 S Ferris Pl, Rancho Dominguez
(90220-6405)
PHONE..................310 816-0260
Victor Larosa, *CEO*
Victor La Rosa, *CEO*

Sam Joumblat, *CFO*
Bill Allen, *Exec VP*
EMP: 170
SQ FT: 10,000
SALES: 45MM **Privately Held**
SIC: 4731 5399 4212 Freight forwarding; warehouse club stores; local trucking, without storage

(P-5147)
PRIMARY FREIGHT SERVICES INC (PA)
6545 Caballero Blvd, Buena Park
(90620-1133)
PHONE..................310 635-3000
John Brown, *CEO*
Ernie Donner, *CFO*
Karen Liu, *Vice Pres*
Michael Squadrille, *Vice Pres*
Renee Yepez, *Vice Pres*
EMP: 65 **EST:** 1998
SQ FT: 87,900
SALES: 32.3MM **Privately Held**
SIC: 4731 4212 4789 Customs clearance of freight; baggage transfer; pipeline terminal facilities, independently operated

(P-5148)
PRIME GLOBAL SOLUTIONS INC (PA)
Also Called: PGS 360
15801 E Valley Blvd, City of Industry
(91744-3929)
P.O. Box 1669, Walnut (91788-1669)
PHONE..................800 424-7746
Michael Katyal, *CEO*
Garrett Fisher, *CFO*
Jess Khorana, *Vice Pres*
Javier Adame, *Accounts Mgr*
EMP: 60
SQ FT: 125,000
SALES: 9.2MM **Privately Held**
WEB: www.primeamerica.biz
SIC: 4731 4225 Domestic freight forwarding; general warehousing & storage

(P-5149)
PRO LOADERS INC (PA)
14032 Santa Ana Ave, Fontana
(92337-7035)
PHONE..................909 355-5531
Bruce Degler, *President*
Christopher Ebert, *CFO*
Kim Pugmire, *Vice Pres*
EMP: 200
SQ FT: 600
SALES (est) 28MM **Privately Held**
SIC: 4731 1629 7359 7519 Truck transportation brokers; earthmoving contractor; equipment rental & leasing; trailer rental

(P-5150)
PUROLATOR INTERNATIONAL INC
775 W Manville St, Compton (90220-5505)
PHONE..................650 871-7075
EMP: 59
SALES (corp-wide): 213.4B **Privately Held**
SIC: 4731
HQ: Purolator International, Inc.
2 Jericho Plz Ste 204
Jericho NY 11753
888 511-4811

(P-5151)
QUARTZ LOGISTICS INC
780 Nogales St Ste D, City of Industry
(91748-1306)
PHONE..................626 606-2001
Tai Ruenn Wang, *CEO*
Sandy Chen, *Admin Sec*
EMP: 60
SQ FT: 12,000
SALES: 4.3MM **Privately Held**
SIC: 4731 Freight forwarding

(P-5152)
QUIK PICK EXPRESS LLC
1021 E 233rd St, Carson (90745-6206)
P.O. Box 1129, Lakewood (90714-1129)
PHONE..................310 763-3000
George Boyle, *CEO*
Mirian Zuniga, *Admin Asst*
Patricia Andrade, *Technology*

Christine Walters-Reyes, *Director*
Chinedu Okonkwo, *Manager*
EMP: 150
SQ FT: 500,000
SALES (est) 29.9MM **Privately Held**
WEB: www.quikpickexpress.com
SIC: 4731 4214 Freight transportation arrangement; local trucking with storage

(P-5153)
R L JONES-SAN DIEGO INC (PA)
1778 Zinetta Rd Ste A, Calexico
(92231-9511)
P.O. Box 472 (92232-0472)
PHONE..................760 357-3177
Russell L Jones, *President*
Earl Roberts, *Vice Pres*
Lucy Topete, *Info Tech Dir*
Baltazar Espinoza, *Info Tech Mgr*
Jarr Baltazar, *Web Dvlpr*
EMP: 100
SALES (est) 35.1MM **Privately Held**
WEB: www.rljones.com
SIC: 4731 4225 Customhouse brokers; freight forwarding; general warehousing & storage

(P-5154)
R L JONES-SAN DIEGO INC
1778 Zinetta Rd Ste A1, Calexico
(92231-9510)
PHONE..................760 357-0140
Russell L Jones, *Branch Mgr*
EMP: 63
SALES (corp-wide): 35.1MM **Privately Held**
SIC: 4731 4225 Customhouse brokers; general warehousing & storage
PA: R. L. Jones-San Diego, Inc.
1778 Zinetta Rd Ste A
Calexico CA 92231
760 357-3177

(P-5155)
RESOURCE MANAGEMENT GROUP INC (PA)
Also Called: Rmg Recycling
4686 Mercury St, San Diego (92111-2428)
PHONE..................858 677-0884
Armen Derderian, *President*
Robert Garcia, *COO*
Josie Pantangco, *CFO*
John Lentz, *Vice Pres*
Steve Joseph, *Managing Dir*
▲ **EMP:** 70
SQ FT: 3,000
SALES (est) 18.3MM **Privately Held**
WEB: www.rmgrecycling.com
SIC: 4731 Freight transportation arrangement

(P-5156)
RITE WAY ENTERPRISES
7131 Valjean Ave, Van Nuys (91406-3917)
PHONE..................818 376-6960
Helen Wolfe, *President*
EMP: 50
SQ FT: 18,000
SALES (est) 8.1MM **Privately Held**
SIC: 4731 Truck transportation brokers

(P-5157)
RK LOGISTICS GROUP INC (PA)
41707 Christy St, Fremont (94538-4195)
P.O. Box 610670, San Jose (95161-0670)
PHONE..................408 942-8107
Rodney F Kalune, *President*
Rock Magnan, *Vice Pres*
Victoria Jones, *Finance*
Hope Conci, *Human Res Mgr*
Ramon Garcia, *Opers Spvr*
EMP: 80 **EST:** 1983
SQ FT: 180,000
SALES: 29MM **Privately Held**
WEB: www.rkgllc.com
SIC: 4731 8742 4214 4225 Freight forwarding; transportation consultant; local trucking with storage; general warehousing & storage

(P-5158)
ROADEX AMERICA INC
1515 W 178th St, Gardena (90248-3203)
PHONE..................310 878-9800
Nicholas Sim, *President*
Russle Loh, *Vice Pres*

▲ = Import ▼=Export
◆ =Import/Export

Johnny Kwan, *Principal*
Kamischke Chad, *Regional Mgr*
Derek Wong, *Project Mgr*
EMP: 100
SALES (est): 25.6MM **Privately Held**
WEB: www.roadexamerica.com
SIC: 4731 5113 4789 Domestic freight
forwarding; industrial & personal service
paper; cargo loading & unloading services

(P-5159)
ROCK-IT CARGO USA LLC
120 N Topanga Canyon Blvd # 215,
Topanga (90290-3851)
PHONE.....................310 455-1900
Sasha Goodman, *Branch Mgr*
EMP: 60 **Privately Held**
SIC: 4731 Freight forwarding
PA: Rock-It Cargo Usa Llc
201 Rock Lititz Blvd # 90
Lititz PA 17543
-

(P-5160)
ROCK-IT CARGO USA LLC
5343 W Imperial Hwy # 900, Los Angeles
(90045-6262)
PHONE.....................310 410-0935
Jordan Lenhoff, *Administration*
Barry Becker, *Opers Mgr*
Michelle Hayflich, *Opers Mgr*
EMP: 199 **Privately Held**
SIC: 4731 Freight forwarding
PA: Rock-It Cargo Usa Llc
201 Rock Lititz Blvd # 90
Lititz PA 17543
-

(P-5161)
SCHENKER INC
380 Littlefield Ave, South San Francisco
(94080-6103)
PHONE.....................650 745-3000
Tammy Breen, *Manager*
EMP: 61
SQ FT: 60,000 **Privately Held**
SIC: 4731 Foreign freight forwarding
HQ: Schenker, Inc.
41 Pinelawn Rd 110
Melville NY 11747
757 821-3400

(P-5162)
SCHNEIDER NATIONAL INC
14392 Valley Blvd, Fontana (92335-5240)
PHONE.....................909 574-2165
Ray Eastwood, *Manager*
EMP: 140
SALES (corp-wide): 4.3B **Publicly Held**
SIC: 4731 Freight transportation arrange-
ment
PA: Schneider National, Inc.
3101 Packerland Dr
Green Bay WI 54313
920 592-2000

(P-5163)
**SCHUMACHER CARGO
LOGISTICS INC (PA)**
Also Called: S C L
550 W 135th St, Gardena (90248-1506)
PHONE.....................562 408-6677
Martin D Baker, *CEO*
EMP: 59
SQ FT: 200,000
SALES (est): 14.4MM **Privately Held**
WEB: www.schumachercargo.com
SIC: 4731 Foreign freight forwarding;
freight forwarding

(P-5164)
SEA-AIR INTERNATIONAL INC
11222 S La Cienega Blvd # 100, Inglewood
(90304-1109)
PHONE.....................310 338-0778
Milton Heid, *President*
Eric Jones, *Vice Pres*
EMP: 52
SALES (est): 4.1MM **Privately Held**
SIC: 4731 Customhouse brokers

(P-5165)
SEAPASSION LOGISTICS INC
20450 E Walnut Dr N, Walnut
(91789-2921)
PHONE.....................562 907-4300

Jun Zhang, *President*
Alex Zhong, *CFO*
EMP: 60
SALES (est): 4MM **Privately Held**
SIC: 4731 Freight forwarding

(P-5166)
**SEAWORLD GLOBAL
LOGISTICS**
1421 Barry Ave Apt 5, Los Angeles
(90025-2309)
PHONE.....................310 208-9488
Dhakshitha Gabriel, *President*
EMP: 385 **EST:** 2017
SALES (est): 6.3MM **Privately Held**
SIC: 4731 Foreign freight forwarding

(P-5167)
SHIPCO TRANSPORT INC
100 W Victoria St, Long Beach
(90805-2147)
PHONE.....................562 295-2900
Gary Osterbach, *Principal*
Jacob Niemiec, *Accounts Exec*
EMP: 65
SALES (corp-wide): 650.3MM **Privately
Held**
SIC: 4731 Freight forwarding
HQ: Shipco Transport Inc.
127 Main St
Chatham NJ 07928
973 457-3300

(P-5168)
**SHO-AIR INTERNATIONAL INC
(PA)**
5401 Argosy Ave Ste 102, Huntington
Beach (92649-1038)
PHONE.....................949 476-9111
James Nicoll, *Ch of Bd*
R Scott Tedro, *President*
Jessica Elende, *CFO*
Gregg Thomas, *Vice Pres*
Rory Mason, *General Mgr*
EMP: 50
SQ FT: 18,000
SALES (est): 17.1MM **Privately Held**
WEB: www.shoair.com
SIC: 4731 Domestic freight forwarding

(P-5169)
SIMPLER POSTAGE INC (PA)
Also Called: Easypost
1 Montgomery St Ste 400, San Francisco
(94104-4533)
PHONE.....................408 915-0063
Jarrett Lee Streebin, *CEO*
Ron Harel, *Officer*
Kathryn Berry, *Office Mgr*
April Rosenberg, *IT/INT Sup*
Sarbari Mukherjee, *Human Res Mgr*
EMP: 100
SALES (est): 22.9MM **Privately Held**
SIC: 4731 Brokers, shipping

(P-5170)
SMARTWAY EXPRESS INC
2660 S Railroad Ave, Fresno (93725-1925)
PHONE.....................559 272-3500
Kirpal S Sihota, *CEO*
Tarlochan Singh, *President*
EMP: 120
SALES (est): 14.5MM **Privately Held**
SIC: 4731 Freight transportation arrange-
ment

(P-5171)
SMD LOGISTICS INC
26710 Encinal Rd, Salinas (93908-9763)
PHONE.....................831 758-5300
Steve Scaroni, *President*
EMP: 155
SALES (corp-wide): 20.2MM **Privately
Held**
SIC: 4731 Freight transportation arrange-
ment
PA: Smd Logistics, Inc.
101 E Main St
Heber CA 92249
760 352-3194

(P-5172)
**SOURCE LOGISTICS CENTER
CORP**
812 Union St, Montebello (90640-6523)
PHONE.....................323 887-3884
Marcelo Sada, *President*
Wendy Escobedo, *Vice Pres*
Raul Villarreal, *Vice Pres*
Fernando Ramirez, *Admin Sec*
EMP: 75
SQ FT: 300,000
SALES (est): 501.9K **Privately Held**
SIC: 4731 Freight transportation arrange-
ment

(P-5173)
**SOUTH BAY FREIGHT SYSTEM
LLC (PA)**
Also Called: South Bay Group
900 Turnbull Canyon Rd, City of Industry
(91745-1404)
PHONE.....................626 271-9800
James Lin, *Mng Member*
Alan Yang, *Marketing Staff*
Nichole Zamorano, *Manager*
Denice Garcia, *Accounts Exec*
EMP: 100
SALES (est): 28.7MM **Privately Held**
SIC: 4731 Freight forwarding

(P-5174)
**STATES LOGISTICS SERVICES
INC**
7221 Cate Dr, Buena Park (90621-1883)
PHONE.....................714 523-1276
Cathy J Monson, *Branch Mgr*
EMP: 200
SALES (corp-wide): 74MM **Privately
Held**
SIC: 4731 Truck transportation brokers
PA: States Logistics Services, Inc.
5650 Dolly Ave
Buena Park CA 90621
714 521-6520

(P-5175)
**STEVENS GLOBAL LOGISTICS
INC (PA)**
Also Called: Steven Global Freight Services
3700 Redondo Beach Ave, Redondo Beach
(90278-1108)
P.O. Box 729, Lawndale (90260-0729)
PHONE.....................310 216-5645
Thomas J Petrizzio, *CEO*
Gary Hooper, *CFO*
Karl Chambers, *Vice Pres*
Tim O'Neill, *Regional Mgr*
Lisley Davenport-Go, *Executive Asst*
EMP: 95
SQ FT: 48,000
SALES (est): 37.9MM **Privately Held**
WEB: www.stevensglobal.com
SIC: 4731 Freight forwarding

(P-5176)
SURETY WEST LOGISTICS INC
Also Called: Surety West Transportation
980 9th St Fl 16, Sacramento
(95814-2736)
PHONE.....................800 761-2551
Barry Henning, *President*
EMP: 77
SALES (est): 3.2MM **Privately Held**
SIC: 4731 Truck transportation brokers

(P-5177)
**TAYLORED SERVICES
HOLDINGS LLC (HQ)**
1495 E Locust St, Ontario (91761-4570)
PHONE.....................909 510-4800
Bill Butler, *CEO*
Michael Yusko, *CFO*
Brandon Nakamura, *Administration*
Andrea Dente, *Technology*
John Franco, *VP Opers*
EMP: 80
SQ FT: 330,000
SALES (est): 27MM
SALES (corp-wide): 30MM **Privately
Held**
SIC: 4731 Agents, shipping
PA: Taylored Services Parent Co. Inc.
1495 E Locust St
Ontario CA 91761
909 510-4800

(P-5178)
**TAYLORED SVCS PARENT CO
INC (PA)**
1495 E Locust St, Ontario (91761-4570)
PHONE.....................909 510-4800
Bill Butler, *CEO*
Michael Yusko, *CFO*
EMP: 80 **EST:** 2012
SQ FT: 330,000
SALES (est): 30MM **Privately Held**
SIC: 4731 Agents, shipping

(P-5179)
**THREE WAY LOGISTICS INC
(PA)**
42505 Christy St, Fremont (94538-3993)
P.O. Box 1806 (94538-0032)
PHONE.....................408 748-3929
Anthony J Bonino, *CEO*
Kevin Scherer, *President*
Philipp Scherer, *CFO*
Stan Aikman, *Vice Pres*
Michael Bonino, *Vice Pres*
EMP: 60
SQ FT: 135,000
SALES (est): 43.3MM **Privately Held**
WEB: www.threeway.com
SIC: 4731 Freight transportation arrange-
ment

(P-5180)
**TOLL GLOBAL FWDG SCS USA
INC**
3355 Dulles Dr, Mira Loma (91752-3244)
PHONE.....................951 360-8310
Bryan Howber, *Senior VP*
EMP: 100
SALES (corp-wide): 121.2B **Privately
Held**
SIC: 4731 Freight forwarding
HQ: Toll Global Forwarding Scs (Usa) Inc.
800 Federal Blvd Ste 2
Carteret NJ 07008
732 750-9000

(P-5181)
**TOPOCEAN CONSOLIDATION
SERVICE (PA)**
2727 Workman Mill Rd, City of Industry
(90601-1452)
PHONE.....................562 908-1688
Robert Wang, *President*
Andy Wang, *Vice Pres*
Cameron Brown, *Natl Sales Mgr*
Kim Ho, *Manager*
◆ **EMP:** 145
SQ FT: 350,000
SALES (est): 38MM **Privately Held**
WEB: www.topocean.com
SIC: 4731 Foreign freight forwarding;
freight forwarding

(P-5182)
TRAFFIC TECH INC
910 Hale Pl Ste 100, Chula Vista
(91914-3598)
PHONE.....................800 396-2531
Paul Johnson, *President*
Karl Godbout, *Vice Pres*
Eleanor Merritt, *Sales Mgr*
Liliana Passarini, *Sales Staff*
EMP: 155 **Privately Held**
SIC: 4731 Brokers, shipping
HQ: Traffic Tech, Inc.
180 N Michigan Ave # 700
Chicago IL 60601
877 383-1167

(P-5183)
TRANSIT AIR CARGO INC
2204 E 4th St, Santa Ana (92705-3868)
PHONE.....................714 571-0393
Gulnawaz Khodayar, *CEO*
Christy Colton, *Vice Pres*
Tania Khodayar, *Vice Pres*
Michelle Nguyen, *Vice Pres*
Kimberly Hill, *Opers Staff*
EMP: 75
SQ FT: 10,000
SALES (est): 30.7MM **Privately Held**
WEB: www.transitair.com
SIC: 4731 Foreign freight forwarding

(P-5184)
TRI-TECH LOGISTICS LLC
3230 E Imperial Hwy # 140, Brea
(92821-6721)
PHONE..................................855 373-7049
Kuldip Singh Dhaliwal,
Gurdeep Singh Dhaliwal,
Jeremy Engstrom, *Manager*
EMP: 210
SALES (est): 261.9K **Privately Held**
SIC: 4731 Freight transportation arrangement
ment
PA: Tri-Tech Logistics Ltd
17660 65a Ave Unit 208
Surrey BC V3S 5
604 415-9898

(P-5185)
TRICOR AMERICA INC
12441 Eucalyptus Ave 7, Hawthorne
(90250-4208)
PHONE..................................310 676-0800
Fax: 310 973-1565
EMP: 100
SALES (corp-wide): 102.7MM **Privately Held**
SIC: 4731
PA: Tricor America, Inc.
717 Airport Blvd
South San Francisco CA 94080
650 877-3650

(P-5186)
TRICOR INTERNATIONAL
717 Airport Blvd, South San Francisco
(94080-1815)
P.O. Box 8100, San Francisco (94128-8100)
PHONE..................................650 877-3678
Chee B Louie, *President*
Christina Louie, *Vice Pres*
John Hoard, *Controller*
EMP: 100
SQ FT: 20,000
SALES (est): 10.8MM **Privately Held**
SIC: 4731 4581 4424 Freight forwarding;
airports, flying fields & services; deep sea
domestic transportation of freight

(P-5187)
TRIPLE B FORWARDERS INC
(PA)
Also Called: Triple B Forwarders
1511 Glenn Curtiss St, Carson
(90746-4035)
PHONE..................................310 604-5840
Richard Beliveau, *CEO*
Connie Ladin, *Treasurer*
Sal Lacagnina, *Business Mgr*
Bob Mathieu, *Export Mgr*
Heidi O'Neill, *Opers Mgr*
EMP: 110
SQ FT: 37,800
SALES (est): 20MM **Privately Held**
WEB: www.pmlfreight.com
SIC: 4731 4783 Domestic freight forwarding; foreign freight forwarding; packing
goods for shipping

(P-5188)
TRITON LOGISTICS
CORPORATION
706 Steffy Rd, Ramona (92065-3533)
PHONE..................................619 822-8832
Jason Lawrence Foyer, *Principal*
EMP: 71
SALES (corp-wide): 4.9MM **Privately Held**
SIC: 4731 Foreign freight forwarding
PA: Triton Logistics, Corporation
6780 Miramar Rd Ste 200b
San Diego CA 92121
619 822-8832

(P-5189)
TRIUS TRUCKING INC
4692 E Lincoln Ave, Fowler (93625-9685)
P.O. Box 2700, Fresno (93745-2700)
PHONE..................................559 834-4000
Tehal Singh Thandi, *CEO*
EMP: 87
SQ FT: 3,900
SALES (est): 31.1MM **Privately Held**
SIC: 4731 Freight transportation arrangement
ment

(P-5190)
UNIS LLC (PA)
Also Called: United Network Info Svcs
218 Machlin Ct, Walnut (91789-3048)
PHONE..................................909 839-2600
James Lin, *President*
Gracie Leung, *CFO*
Stephen Tsao, *Info Tech Mgr*
EMP: 200
SALES (est): 47.9MM **Privately Held**
SIC: 4731 Freight forwarding

(P-5191)
UNITED STTES INTRMDAL SVCS
LLC
Also Called: G3 Enterprises
502 E Whitmore Ave, Modesto
(95358-9411)
PHONE..................................209 341-4045
John R Gallo,
Gregory J Coleman,
EMP: 75
SQ FT: 10,000
SALES (est): 16.8MM **Privately Held**
SIC: 4731 5182 Truck transportation brokers; bottling wines & liquors

(P-5192)
UPS SUPPLY CHAIN SOLUTIONS
INC
550-3 Eccles Ave, San Francisco (94101)
PHONE..................................650 635-2693
EMP: 9000
SALES (corp-wide): 65.8B **Publicly Held**
SIC: 4731 Freight transportation arrangement
ment
HQ: Ups Supply Chain Solutions, Inc.
12380 Morris Rd
Alpharetta GA 30005
800 742-5727

(P-5193)
UPS SUPPLY CHAIN SOLUTIONS
INC
U P S
19701 Hamilton Ave # 250, Torrance
(90502-1316)
PHONE..................................310 404-2719
Homayoun Kandari, *Branch Mgr*
EMP: 200
SALES (corp-wide): 65.8B **Publicly Held**
SIC: 4731 Freight forwarding
HQ: Ups Supply Chain Solutions, Inc.
12380 Morris Rd
Alpharetta GA 30005
800 742-5727

(P-5194)
UPS SUPPLY CHAIN SOLUTIONS
INC
455 Forbes Blvd, South San Francisco
(94080-2017)
PHONE..................................650 875-8300
Randy Nelson, *Manager*
Randy Nelsen, *Manager*
EMP: 50
SQ FT: 14,000
SALES (corp-wide): 65.8B **Publicly Held**
SIC: 4731 Freight transportation arrangement
ment
HQ: Ups Supply Chain Solutions, Inc.
12380 Morris Rd
Alpharetta GA 30005
800 742-5727

(P-5195)
UPS WORLDWIDE LOGISTICS
INC
3600 W Century Blvd, Inglewood
(90303-1139)
PHONE..................................310 673-7661
Tom Bliss, *Branch Mgr*
Pietro Barone, *Manager*
EMP: 200
SALES (corp-wide): 65.8B **Publicly Held**
SIC: 4731 Freight transportation arrangement
ment
HQ: Ups Worldwide Logistics Inc
12380 Morris Rd
Alpharetta GA 30005
-

(P-5196)
USAS EXPRESS
INTERNATIONAL
420 Hindry Ave Ste G, Inglewood
(90301-2062)
PHONE..................................310 645-2313
Young I Choi, *President*
EMP: 56
SALES (est): 8.4MM **Privately Held**
WEB: www.usasexpress.com
SIC: 4731 Freight transportation arrangement
ment

(P-5197)
VANGUARD LGISTICS SVCS
USA INC (HQ)
5000 Arprt Plz Dr Ste 200, Long Beach
(90815)
PHONE..................................310 847-3000
Charles Brennan, *Chairman*
James Julian, *President*
J Thurso Barendse, *CFO*
Scott Shellow, *Treasurer*
Therese Groff, *Vice Pres*
EMP: 100
SALES (est): 156.4MM
SALES (corp-wide): 232.2MM **Privately Held**
SIC: 4731 Freight consolidation
PA: Naca Holdings, Inc.
5000 Arprt Plz Dr Ste 200
Long Beach CA 90815
650 872-0800

(P-5198)
WESTERN FREIGHT CARRIER
INC
13819 Slover Ave, Fontana (92337-7037)
PHONE..................................909 357-1011
Tony Kim, *Owner*
EMP: 52
SALES (corp-wide): 15MM **Privately Held**
SIC: 4731 Transportation agents & brokers
PA: Western Freight Carrier, Inc.
321 E Gardena Blvd
Gardena CA 90248
310 767-1042

(P-5199)
WESTERN OVERSEAS
CORPORATION (PA)
10731 Walker St Ste B, Cypress
(90630-4757)
P.O. Box 90099, Long Beach (90809-0099)
PHONE..................................562 985-0616
Michael F Dugan, *President*
Carlo Deatougia, *Vice Pres*
Fred Bebee, *Admin Sec*
Richard Simpson, *Director*
EMP: 50
SQ FT: 40,000
SALES: 11MM **Privately Held**
SIC: 4731 Customhouse brokers; foreign
freight forwarding

(P-5200)
WESTRUX INTERNATIONAL INC
2200 E Steel Rd, Colton (92324-4509)
PHONE..................................909 825-5121
Don Kenney, *CFO*
Jody Johnson, *Manager*
EMP: 60
SALES (corp-wide): 118.4MM **Privately Held**
SIC: 4731 Truck transportation brokers
PA: Westrux International, Inc.
15555 Valley View Ave
Santa Fe Springs CA 90670
562 404-1020

(P-5201)
XPO LOGISTICS SUPPLY CHAIN
INC
3825 S Willow Ave, Fresno (93725-9025)
PHONE..................................559 408-7951
EMP: 109
SALES (corp-wide): 15.3B **Publicly Held**
SIC: 4731 Freight forwarding
HQ: Xpo Logistics Supply Chain, Inc.
4035 Piedmont Pkwy
High Point NC 27265
336 232-4100

(P-5202)
XPO LOGISTICS SUPPLY CHAIN
INC
5200a E Airport Dr, Ontario (91761-8601)
PHONE..................................909 975-6300
Steve Mackintosh, *Branch Mgr*
EMP: 124
SALES (corp-wide): 15.3B **Publicly Held**
SIC: 4731 Freight forwarding
HQ: Xpo Logistics Supply Chain, Inc.
4035 Piedmont Pkwy
High Point NC 27265
336 232-4100

(P-5203)
YANG MING AMERICA
CORPORATION
181 W Huntington Dr # 202, Monrovia
(91016-8406)
PHONE..................................626 782-9797
Frank Chao, *Branch Mgr*
EMP: 55
SALES (corp-wide): 4.3B **Privately Held**
SIC: 4731 Agents, shipping
HQ: Ming Yang America Corporation
1085 Raymond Blvd Fl 9 Flr 9
Newark NJ 07102
201 222-8899

(P-5204)
YUSEN LOGISTICS AMERICAS
INC
2417 E Carson St Ste 100, Carson
(90810-1252)
PHONE..................................310 518-3008
P Smith, *Branch Mgr*
Steve Frasco, *Opers Staff*
Karen Quintana, *Director*
EMP: 200
SALES (corp-wide): 20.4B **Privately Held**
SIC: 4731 Freight forwarding
HQ: Yusen Logistics (Americas) Inc.
300 Lighting Way Ste 600
Secaucus NJ 07094
201 553-3800

4783 Packing & Crating
Svcs

(P-5205)
AMAWATERWAYS LLC (PA)
26010 Mureau Rd, Calabasas
(91302-3130)
PHONE..................................800 626-0126
Rudi Schreiner, *Mng Member*
Ron Santangelo, *President*
Denise M Kelly, *Business Mgr*
INA Vainio, *Business Mgr*
Sachin Shah, *Marketing Staff*
EMP: 250
SALES: 6.2MM **Privately Held**
SIC: 4783 Packing goods for shipping

(P-5206)
CALAVO GROWERS INC
Also Called: Calavo Foods
15765 W Telegraph Rd, Santa Paula
(93060-3041)
P.O. Box 751 (93061-0751)
PHONE..................................805 525-5511
George Hatfield, *Plant Mgr*
Gary Gunther, *Opers Mgr*
EMP: 80
SALES (corp-wide): 1B **Publicly Held**
WEB: www.calavo.com
SIC: 4783
PA: Calavo Growers, Inc.
1141 Cummings Rd Ste A
Santa Paula CA 93060
805 525-1245

(P-5207)
CENTRA FREIGHT SERVICES
INC (PA)
279 Lawrence Ave, South San Francisco
(94080-6818)
PHONE..................................650 873-8147
Jonathan Wang, *CEO*
Stanley Wang, *President*
Goldine Wang, *Vice Pres*
Winnie Lo, *General Mgr*
Julie Wang, *Admin Sec*
EMP: 53 **EST:** 1980

SQ FT: 11,500
SALES (est): 18MM **Privately Held**
SIC: **4783** 4731 Containerization of goods for shipping; domestic freight forwarding

(P-5208)
GLASS PAK INC
5825 Old School Rd, Pleasanton (94588-9407)
PHONE...............................707 207-0400
Marc Silvani, *President*
Rick Silvani, *Vice Pres*
Dallas Nelson, *General Mgr*
EMP: 70
SQ FT: 90,000
SALES (est): 7.8MM **Privately Held**
WEB: www.glasspak.com
SIC: **4783** Packing goods for shipping

(P-5209)
INTEGRATED PKG & CRATING SVCS
Also Called: Inovative Packaging
38505 Cherry St, Newark (94560-4700)
PHONE...............................510 745-8180
Ben F Polando, *CEO*
Donna Fernandez, *HR Admin*
EMP: 50
SQ FT: 90,000
SALES (est): 7.2MM **Privately Held**
SIC: **4783** Packing & crating

(P-5210)
SUNTREAT PKG SHIPG A LTD PRTNR
391 Oxford Ave, Lindsay (93247-2208)
P.O. Box 850 (93247-0850)
PHONE...............................559 562-4991
Dennis A Griffith, *Managing Prtnr*
Dwight J Griffith, *Partner*
EMP: 200
SQ FT: 75,000
SALES (est): 28.2MM **Privately Held**
WEB: www.suntreat.net
SIC: **4783** 8742 Packing goods for shipping; management consulting services

(P-5211)
TRANSPAK INC
8710 Avenida De La Fuente, San Diego (92154-6243)
PHONE...............................858 292-9094
Jennifer Kay, *Branch Mgr*
Arlene Inch, *CEO*
EMP: 51
SALES (corp-wide): 187.9MM **Privately Held**
SIC: **4783** 2449 3081 3086 Packing & crating; wood containers; packing materials, plastic sheet; packaging & shipping materials, foamed plastic; corrugated & solid fiber boxes; nailed wood boxes & shook
PA: Transpak, Inc.
   520 Marburg Way
   San Jose CA 95133
   408 254-0500

(P-5212)
UNIFIED AIRCRAFT SERVICES INC (PA)
1571 S Lilac Ave, Bloomington (92316-2141)
P.O. Box 401060, Las Vegas NV (89140-1060)
PHONE...............................909 877-0535
Ben C Warren, *President*
Venida L Warren, *Corp Secy*
Benjamin T Warren, *Vice Pres*
EMP: 65
SQ FT: 14,500
SALES (est): 15.4MM **Privately Held**
WEB: www.uasnet.com
SIC: **4783** Packing goods for shipping; containerization of goods for shipping

(P-5213)
VENIDA PACKING COMPANY
19823 Avenue 300, Exeter (93221-9771)
P.O. Box 212 (93221-0212)
PHONE...............................559 592-2816
Verne Crookshanks, *CEO*
Michael Murray, *Treasurer*
George Tantua, *Admin Sec*
EMP: 125

SQ FT: 50,000
SALES (est): 17.5MM **Privately Held**
SIC: **4783** Packing goods for shipping

4785 Fixed Facilities, Inspection, Weighing Svcs Transptn

(P-5214)
CALIFORNIA PRIVATE TRNSP CO LP
Also Called: C P T C
180 N Rverview Dr Ste 200, Anaheim (92808)
PHONE...............................714 637-9191
Greg Hulsizer, *General Mgr*
EMP: 75
SQ FT: 5,000
SALES (est): 3MM **Privately Held**
SIC: **4785** Toll road operation

(P-5215)
COFIROUTE USA LLC
200 Spectrum Center Dr # 1650, Irvine (92618-5012)
PHONE...............................949 754-0198
Gary Hausdorfer, *CEO*
Darla Casby, *VP Finance*
Michelle Ebbert, *Director*
EMP: 112
SQ FT: 9,000
SALES: 18MM
SALES (corp-wide): 14.1MM **Privately Held**
WEB: www.cofiroutegm.com
SIC: **4785** Toll road operation
HQ: Vinci Concessions
   12 14
   Rueil Malmaison
   147 164-477

(P-5216)
GOLDEN GATE
Also Called: Golden Gate Ferry
101 E Sir Francis Drake, Larkspur (94939-1803)
PHONE...............................415 455-2000
David Clark, *Manager*
Alfonso Beasley, *Marketing Staff*
EMP: 84
SALES (corp-wide): 19.3MM **Privately Held**
WEB: www.goldengatetransit.org
SIC: **4785** 4482 Toll bridge operation; ferries operating across rivers or within harbors
PA: Golden Gate Bridge Highway & Transportation District
   Toll Plz
   San Francisco CA 94129
   415 921-5858

(P-5217)
GOLDEN GATE BRDG HWY & TRANSPO (PA)
Toll Plz, San Francisco (94129)
PHONE...............................415 921-5858
James C Eddie, *President*
Jeffrey Sylvester, *COO*
Kellee Hopper, *Chief Mktg Ofcr*
Mona Babauta, *General Mgr*
Denis J Mulligan, *General Mgr*
EMP: 250
SQ FT: 20,000
SALES (est): 19.3MM **Privately Held**
WEB: www.goldengatetransit.org
SIC: **4785** 4131 4482 4111 Toll bridge operation; interstate bus line; ferries operating across rivers or within harbors; bus transportation

(P-5218)
GOLDEN GATE BRIDGE HIGH
Also Called: Golden Gate Transit
1011 Andersen Dr, San Rafael (94901-5318)
PHONE...............................415 457-3110
Susan Chiaroni, *Manager*
Aida Caputo, *Officer*
William Stafford, *Risk Mgmt Dir*
Marcus Lo, *Admin Asst*
Susan Spencer, *Admin Asst*

EMP: 535
SQ FT: 50,000
SALES (corp-wide): 19.3MM **Privately Held**
WEB: www.goldengatetransit.org
SIC: **4785** 4111 Toll bridge operation; airport transportation services, regular route
PA: Golden Gate Bridge Highway & Transportation District
   Toll Plz
   San Francisco CA 94129
   415 921-5858

4789 Transportation Svcs, NEC

(P-5219)
ANS WORLD SERVICE INC
2751 E Chapman Ave # 204, Fullerton (92831-3752)
P.O. Box 784, Placentia (92871-0784)
PHONE...............................714 441-2400
Charles S An, *President*
EMP: 100
SQ FT: 600
SALES (est): 3.2MM **Privately Held**
SIC: **4789** 4212 Cargo loading & unloading services; local trucking, without storage

(P-5220)
AP EXPRESS INTERNATIONAL LLC
Also Called: Champion Transportation Svcs
8500 Rex Rd, Pico Rivera (90660-3779)
PHONE...............................562 236-2250
Jeff Pont, *President*
Mike Choi, *Vice Pres*
EMP: 75
SQ FT: 50,000
SALES: 14.5MM **Privately Held**
WEB: www.championtransportation.com
SIC: **4789** Freight car loading & unloading

(P-5221)
COMPREHENSIVE DIST SVCS INC
18726 S Wstn Ave Ste 300, Gardena (90248)
PHONE...............................310 523-1546
Sam Lee, *President*
EMP: 150
SALES (est): 1.9MM **Privately Held**
SIC: **4789** Freight car loading & unloading

(P-5222)
COUNTY OF LOS ANGELES
Also Called: Transportation Bureau
441 Bauchet St, Los Angeles (90012-2906)
PHONE...............................213 974-4561
EMP: 250 **Privately Held**
SIC: **4789** 9621
PA: County Of Los Angeles
   500 W Temple St Ste 375
   Los Angeles CA 90012
   213 974-1101

(P-5223)
DSV SOLUTIONS LLC
3454 E Miraloma Ave, Anaheim (92806-2101)
PHONE...............................714 630-0110
EMP: 74
SALES (corp-wide): 11.8B **Privately Held**
SIC: **4789** Pipeline terminal facilities, independently operated
HQ: Dsv Solutions, Llc
   1100 Laval Blvd Ste 100
   Lawrenceville GA 30043
   678 381-0553

(P-5224)
EASY RIDE TRANSPORTATION
1820 W Carson St Ste 202, Torrance (90501-2885)
PHONE...............................424 999-8830
Said Dabas, *President*
EMP: 100 EST: 2014
SALES (est): 2.1MM **Privately Held**
SIC: **4789** Transportation services

(P-5225)
FLEXPORT INC (PA)
760 Market St Fl 8, San Francisco (94102-2300)
PHONE...............................415 231-5252
Ryan Petersen, *CEO*
Sanne Manders, *COO*
Sandy Manders, *CFO*
Paige Delacey,
Ben Braverman, *Officer*
EMP: 68
SALES (est): 133.8MM **Privately Held**
SIC: **4789** 4731 Pipeline terminal facilities, independently operated; freight transportation arrangement

(P-5226)
GATX CORPORATION
Also Called: G A T X Rail
20878 Slover St, Colton (92324-7300)
PHONE...............................909 825-3043
James Allen, *Manager*
Barbara Hanes, *Executive*
EMP: 60
SALES (corp-wide): 1.3B **Publicly Held**
WEB: www.gatx.com
SIC: **4789** Railroad car repair
PA: Gatx Corporation
   222 W Adams St
   Chicago IL 60606
   312 621-6200

(P-5227)
HEALTH LINK MEDI VAN
Also Called: Medi-Van Ambulette
6053 W Century Blvd # 900, Los Angeles (90045-6430)
PHONE...............................310 981-9500
Greg Linsmeier, *General Mgr*
EMP: 100
SALES (est): 6.5MM **Privately Held**
SIC: **4789** Freight car loading & unloading

(P-5228)
HYPERLOOP TECHNOLOGIES INC
Also Called: Hyperloop One
2159 Bay St, Los Angeles (90021-1707)
PHONE...............................213 800-3270
Jay Walder, *CEO*
Sultan Ahmed Bin Sulayem, *Ch of Bd*
Brent Callinicos, *COO*
William Mulholland, *Exec VP*
Josh Giegel, *Vice Pres*
EMP: 200
SALES (est): 22MM **Privately Held**
SIC: **4789** Pipeline terminal facilities, independently operated

(P-5229)
INTER-RAIL TRNSPT NSHVILLE LLC
861 Wharf St, Richmond (94804-3557)
PHONE...............................510 231-2744
Francisco Oliver, *Manager*
EMP: 52
SALES (corp-wide): 31.4MM **Privately Held**
WEB: www.interrail-transport.com
SIC: **4789** Freight car loading & unloading
PA: Inter-Rail Transport, Inc
   115 Lawyers Row Ste 3
   Centreville MD 21617
   410 758-2893

(P-5230)
INTER-RAIL TRNSPT NSHVILLE LLC
3800 Industrial Way, Benicia (94510-1200)
PHONE...............................707 746-1695
Luis Michel, *Manager*
EMP: 60
SALES (corp-wide): 31.4MM **Privately Held**
WEB: www.interrail-transport.com
SIC: **4789** 4213 Freight car loading & unloading; automobiles, transport & delivery
PA: Inter-Rail Transport, Inc
   115 Lawyers Row Ste 3
   Centreville MD 21617
   410 758-2893

(P-5231)
ITS TECHNOLOGIES LOGISTICS LLC
6540 Austin Rd, Stockton (95215-9662)
PHONE..................................209 460-6023
Dave Carlock, *Branch Mgr*
EMP: 60
SALES (corp-wide): 204.1MM **Privately Held**
SIC: 4789 Cargo loading & unloading services
HQ: Its Technologies & Logistics, Llc
8205 Cass Ave Ste 115
Darien IL 60561
708 225-2400

(P-5232)
J B HUNT TRANSPORT SVCS INC
Also Called: Jbhunt Transport
1620 5th Ave, San Diego (92101-2703)
PHONE..................................619 230-0054
EMP: 473
SALES (corp-wide): 7.1B **Publicly Held**
SIC: 4789 Cargo loading & unloading services
PA: J. B. Hunt Transport Services, Inc.
615 Jb Hunt Corp Dr
Lowell AR 72745
479 820-0000

(P-5233)
JESSE ALEXANDER TRANSPORT
9338 Azurite Ave, Hesperia (92344-4611)
PHONE..................................760 669-0379
Jesus Gomez, *Mng Member*
EMP: 60 EST: 2014
SALES (est): 164.7K **Privately Held**
SIC: 4789 Transportation services

(P-5234)
LOCATION SERVICES LLC (PA)
Also Called: Pathfinder Services
2365 Iron Point Rd # 160, Folsom
(95630-8713)
PHONE..................................800 588-0097
Lee McCarty, *CEO*
Erik Grotte, *CFO*
EMP: 90 EST: 2014
SQ FT: 15,000
SALES (est): 21.4MM **Privately Held**
SIC: 4789 Car loading

(P-5235)
M V TRANSPORTATION
1375 Britain Ave, Salinas (93901)
PHONE..................................831 373-1395
Lance Atencio, *Branch Mgr*
EMP: 200
SALES (corp-wide): 18.3MM **Privately Held**
SIC: 4789 Pipeline terminal facilities, independently operated
PA: M V Transportation
16738 Stagg St
Van Nuys CA 91406
818 374-9145

(P-5236)
M V TRANSPORTATION
1612 State St, Barstow (92311-4107)
PHONE..................................760 255-3330
Tom Conlon, *Manager*
EMP: 200
SALES (corp-wide): 16.4MM **Privately Held**
SIC: 4789 Pipeline terminal facilities, independently operated
PA: M V Transportation
16738 Stagg St
Van Nuys CA 91406
818 374-9145

(P-5237)
MV TRANSPORTATION INC
7231 Rosecrans Ave, Paramount
(90723-2501)
PHONE..................................562 790-8642
EMP: 78
SALES (corp-wide): 1.7B **Privately Held**
SIC: 4789 Pipeline terminal facilities, independently operated

PA: Mv Transportation, Inc.
2711 N Haskell Ave
Dallas TX 75204
214 265-3400

(P-5238)
PACIFIC COAST CONTAINER INC (PA)
Also Called: PCC Northwest
432 Estudillo Ave Ste 1, San Leandro
(94577-4908)
PHONE..................................510 346-6100
Michael Mc Donnell, *CEO*
Abdel Zaharan, *Officer*
EMP: 113
SQ FT: 12,000
SALES (est): 74.6MM **Privately Held**
WEB: www.pccfs.com
SIC: 4789 4225 4222 Cargo loading & unloading services; general warehousing; warehousing, cold storage or refrigerated

(P-5239)
PACIFIC COAST TRNSP SVCS INC
Also Called: Material Transport
7500 San Joaquin St, Sacramento
(95820-2141)
PHONE..................................916 266-5300
Tom Allgaier, *Manager*
EMP: 50
SALES (corp-wide): 1.7B **Privately Held**
SIC: 4789 Cargo loading & unloading services
HQ: Pacific Coast Transportation Services, Inc.
10600 White Rock Rd Ste 1
Rancho Cordova CA 95670
916 631-6500

(P-5240)
PARSEC INC
4940 Sheila St, Commerce (90040-1112)
PHONE..................................323 268-5011
Jose Huerta, *Manager*
Hildur Vera, *Admin Asst*
EMP: 600
SALES (corp-wide): 171.3MM **Privately Held**
WEB: www.parsecinc.com
SIC: 4789 1629 Cargo loading & unloading services; railroad & subway construction
PA: Parsec Inc.
1100 Gest St
Cincinnati OH 45203
513 621-6111

(P-5241)
PARSEC INC
750 Lamar St, Los Angeles (90031-2515)
PHONE..................................323 276-3116
Tony Madrigar, *Manager*
EMP: 54
SALES (corp-wide): 171.3MM **Privately Held**
WEB: www.parsecinc.com
SIC: 4789 Cargo loading & unloading services
PA: Parsec Inc.
1100 Gest St
Cincinnati OH 45203
513 621-6111

(P-5242)
POSTMATES INC (PA)
201 3rd St Fl 2, San Francisco
(94103-3153)
PHONE..................................800 882-6106
Bastian Lehmann, *CEO*
Sean Plaice, *Chief Engr*
Ashlie Gudmundsen, *Manager*
EMP: 230
SQ FT: 2,400
SALES (est): 13.6MM **Privately Held**
SIC: 4789 Cargo loading & unloading services

(P-5243)
RIOLO TRANSPORTATION INC
2725 Jefferson St Ste 2d, Carlsbad
(92008-1705)
PHONE..................................760 729-4405
Gail Phipps, *Branch Mgr*
Ricky Lohse, *Manager*
EMP: 216

SALES (corp-wide): 63.7MM **Privately Held**
SIC: 4789 Pipeline terminal facilities, independently operated
PA: Riolo Transportation, Inc.
759 N Vulcan Ave
Encinitas CA 92024
760 635-8500

(P-5244)
SALSON LOGISTICS INC
1331 Torrance Blvd, Torrance
(90501-2351)
PHONE..................................310 328-6800
Fax: 310 328-6897
EMP: 145
SALES (corp-wide): 237.1MM **Privately Held**
SIC: 4789
PA: Salson Logistics, Inc.
888 Doremus Ave
Newark NJ 07114
973 986-0200

(P-5245)
SECURE TRANSPORTATION CO INC
9557 Candida St, San Diego (92126-4539)
PHONE..................................858 790-3958
Shawana Walters, *Manager*
EMP: 95
SALES (corp-wide): 17.5MM **Privately Held**
SIC: 4789 Pipeline terminal facilities, independently operated
PA: Secure Transportation Company, Inc.
13111 Meyer Rd
Whittier CA 90605
562 941-0107

(P-5246)
SIERRA WASTE TRANSPORT INC
6956 Florin Perkins Rd, Sacramento
(95828-2607)
PHONE..................................916 386-9937
Sunil Dutt, *CEO*
EMP: 50
SALES: 3.5MM **Privately Held**
SIC: 4789 Cargo loading & unloading services

(P-5247)
SOUTHERN CALIFORNIA CAR TRANSF
11139 Roxboro Rd, San Diego
(92131-3655)
PHONE..................................858 586-0006
Mike Magnett, *President*
EMP: 100 EST: 1994
SALES (est): 3.6MM **Privately Held**
SIC: 4789 Cargo loading & unloading services

(P-5248)
TRANSMONTAIGNE PDT SVCS LLC
Also Called: Morgan Stanley
555 California St # 2100, San Francisco
(94104-1503)
PHONE..................................415 576-2000
Susan Clampsey, *Branch Mgr*
John Marren, *Principal*
EMP: 300 **Privately Held**
SIC: 4789 Pipeline terminal facilities, independently operated
HQ: Transmontaigne Product Services Llc
1670 Broadway Ste 3100
Denver CO 80202
303 626-8200

(P-5249)
TTX COMPANY
Calpro Division
10800 San Sevaine Way, Mira Loma
(91752-1116)
PHONE..................................951 685-0158
Tom Peterson, *Principal*
EMP: 290
SALES (corp-wide): 542.4MM **Privately Held**
WEB: www.ttx.com
SIC: 4789 Railroad car repair

PA: Ttx Company
101 N Wacker Dr
Chicago IL 60606
312 853-3223

(P-5250)
TW SERVICES INC
2751 E Chapman Ave # 204, Fullerton
(92831-3758)
PHONE..................................714 441-2400
Charles An, *President*
Thomas Hwang, *Controller*
EMP: 300
SALES (est): 20MM **Privately Held**
SIC: 4789 Freight car loading & unloading

(P-5251)
VIRGIN GALACTIC LLC (DH)
16555 Spcship Landing Way, Mojave
(93501-1534)
PHONE..................................562 384-4400
George Whitesides, *CEO*
Jonathan Firth, *Exec VP*
Michael P Moses Sr, *Senior VP*
Will Pomerantz, *Vice Pres*
Mike Cosenza, *Info Tech Dir*
EMP: 83
SALES (est): 94.3MM **Privately Held**
WEB: www.virgingalactic.com/overview/
SIC: 4789 Space flight operations, except government
HQ: Virgin Management Limited
The Battleship Building
London
207 313-2000

(P-5252)
VITAL EXPRESS INC
4000 Macarthur Blvd Ste 6, Newport Beach
(92660-2558)
PHONE..................................330 777-5450
Steve Janssen, *President*
Dan Boaz, *President*
Lisa Boaz, *CEO*
EMP: 50
SQ FT: 10,000
SALES (est): 5.5MM **Privately Held**
SIC: 4789 4212 Pipeline terminal facilities, independently operated; delivery service, vehicular

(P-5253)
WHO DAT NATION TRNSP LLC
13186 Rincon Rd, Apple Valley
(92308-6214)
PHONE..................................760 403-7237
Ricky D Jones, *Mng Member*
EMP: 73 EST: 2017
SALES (est): 1.1MM **Privately Held**
SIC: 4789 Cargo loading & unloading services

(P-5254)
YRC INC
Also Called: Yellow Transportation
1535 E Pescadero Ave, Tracy
(95304-8501)
PHONE..................................209 833-1300
Maynard Skarka, *Manager*
Kevin Anderson, *Manager*
Kevin Shoemaker, *Manager*
EMP: 217
SALES (corp-wide): 4.8B **Publicly Held**
WEB: www.roadway.com
SIC: 4789 Cargo loading & unloading services
HQ: Yrc Inc.
10990 Roe Ave
Overland Park KS 66211
913 696-6100

4812 Radiotelephone Communications

(P-5255)
4G WIRELESS INC (PA)
Also Called: Verizon Wireless
8871 Research Dr, Irvine (92618-4236)
PHONE..................................949 748-6100
Mohammad Honarkar, *President*
EMP: 163
SQ FT: 5,000
SALES (est): 353.1MM **Privately Held**
SIC: 4812 Cellular telephone services

(P-5256)
ABC PHONES NORTH CAROLINA INC
Also Called: Verizon Wireless
3935 E Castro Valley Blvd, Castro Valley
(94552-4810)
PHONE..................510 314-0981
Chris Kim, *Branch Mgr*
EMP: 55
SALES (corp-wide): 172.8MM **Privately Held**
SIC: **4812** Cellular telephone services
PA: Abc Phones Of North Carolina, Inc.
8510 Colonnade Center Dr
Raleigh NC 27615
252 317-0388

(P-5257)
ABC PHONES NORTH CAROLINA INC
Also Called: Verizon Wireless
2230 Lake Tahoe Blvd # 130, South Lake Tahoe (96150-7102)
PHONE..................530 541-9500
EMP: 71
SALES (corp-wide): 172.8MM **Privately Held**
SIC: **4812** Cellular telephone services
PA: Abc Phones Of North Carolina, Inc.
8510 Colonnade Center Dr
Raleigh NC 27615
252 317-0388

(P-5258)
AERONAUTICAL RADIO INC
6011 Industrial Way, Livermore
(94551-9755)
PHONE..................925 294-8400
Mike Ostapiej, *Manager*
EMP: 80
SQ FT: 27,781 **Publicly Held**
SIC: **4812** Radio telephone communication
HQ: Aeronautical Radio, Inc.
2551 Riva Rd
Annapolis MD 21401
410 266-4000

(P-5259)
AMERICAN VOICE MAIL INC (PA)
11150 W Olympic Blvd # 975, Los Angeles
(90064-1850)
PHONE..................310 478-4949
Mark Gordon, *President*
Sam Gordon, *Treasurer*
Robert Gordon, *Admin Sec*
EMP: 50
SQ FT: 7,800
SALES (est): 2.7MM **Privately Held**
WEB: www.americanvoicemail.com
SIC: **4812** 7389 Radio pager (beeper) communication services; telephone services

(P-5260)
AT&T CORP
10035 Adams Ave, Huntington Beach
(92646-4940)
PHONE..................714 965-4685
Nora Facenda, *Branch Mgr*
EMP: 69
SALES (corp-wide): 160.5B **Publicly Held**
WEB: www.att.com
SIC: **4812** Cellular telephone services
HQ: At&T Corp.
1 At&T Way
Bedminster NJ 07921
800 403-3302

(P-5261)
AT&T CORP
2390 Monument Blvd, Pleasant Hill
(94523-3983)
PHONE..................925 603-9476
Nichol McCroy, *Branch Mgr*
EMP: 69
SALES (corp-wide): 160.5B **Publicly Held**
SIC: **4812** Cellular telephone services
HQ: At&T Corp.
1 At&T Way
Bedminster NJ 07921
800 403-3302

(P-5262)
AT&T CORP
2410 Mission St, San Francisco
(94110-2415)
PHONE..................415 970-8520
EMP: 69
SALES (corp-wide): 160.5B **Publicly Held**
SIC: **4812** Cellular telephone services
HQ: At&T Corp.
1 At&T Way
Bedminster NJ 07921
800 403-3302

(P-5263)
AT&T CORP
50 Town Center Pkwy, Santee
(92071-5806)
PHONE..................619 448-1798
EMP: 69
SALES (corp-wide): 160.5B **Publicly Held**
WEB: www.sbc.com
SIC: **4812** Cellular telephone services
HQ: At&T Corp.
1 At&T Way
Bedminster NJ 07921
800 403-3302

(P-5264)
AT&T CORP
2219 Park Ave Ste 8a, Tustin (92782-2701)
PHONE..................714 258-8290
Russel Martinez, *Branch Mgr*
Kelly Berg, *Persnl Dir*
Anthony Nguyen, *Manager*
Marcus Stewart, *Manager*
EMP: 69
SALES (corp-wide): 160.5B **Publicly Held**
WEB: www.sbc.com
SIC: **4812** Cellular telephone services
HQ: At&T Corp.
1 At&T Way
Bedminster NJ 07921
800 403-3302

(P-5265)
AT&T CORP
12379 S Mainstreet, Rancho Cucamonga
(91739-8810)
PHONE..................909 646-9644
EMP: 69
SALES (corp-wide): 160.5B **Publicly Held**
WEB: www.sbc.com
SIC: **4812** Cellular telephone services
HQ: At&T Corp.
1 At&T Way
Bedminster NJ 07921
800 403-3302

(P-5266)
AT&T CORP
2508 S Grove Ave, Ontario (91761-6253)
PHONE..................909 930-6508
Lorenzo Mejia, *Branch Mgr*
EMP: 97
SALES (corp-wide): 160.5B **Publicly Held**
SIC: **4812** Radio telephone communication
HQ: At&T Corp.
1 At&T Way
Bedminster NJ 07921
800 403-3302

(P-5267)
AT&T CORP
830 W Arrow Hwy, San Dimas
(91773-2498)
PHONE..................626 912-0600
Carolyn Wilder, *Manager*
EMP: 97
SALES (corp-wide): 160.5B **Publicly Held**
WEB: www.cingular.com
SIC: **4812** Cellular telephone services
HQ: At&T Corp.
1 At&T Way
Bedminster NJ 07921
800 403-3302

(P-5268)
AT&T CORP
20810 Avalon Blvd, Carson (90746-3316)
PHONE..................310 225-3028

Carolyn Wilder, *Manager*
EMP: 69
SALES (corp-wide): 160.5B **Publicly Held**
SIC: **4812** Cellular telephone services
HQ: At&T Corp.
1 At&T Way
Bedminster NJ 07921
800 403-3302

(P-5269)
AT&T CORP
27762 Antonio Pkwy Ste L3, Ladera Ranch
(92694-1141)
PHONE..................949 364-4052
Denny Tsai, *Branch Mgr*
EMP: 69
SALES (corp-wide): 160.5B **Publicly Held**
WEB: www.att.com
SIC: **4812** Cellular telephone services
HQ: At&T Corp.
1 At&T Way
Bedminster NJ 07921
800 403-3302

(P-5270)
AT&T CORP
1100 Pacific Coast Hwy # 5, Hermosa Beach (90254-3951)
PHONE..................310 303-3888
Dennis Graber, *Branch Mgr*
EMP: 97
SALES (corp-wide): 160.5B **Publicly Held**
WEB: www.cingular.com
SIC: **4812** Radio telephone communication
HQ: At&T Corp.
1 At&T Way
Bedminster NJ 07921
800 403-3302

(P-5271)
AT&T CORP
6833 Pacific Blvd, Huntington Park
(90255-4111)
PHONE..................323 589-7045
Frankie Valenzuela, *Manager*
EMP: 97
SALES (corp-wide): 160.5B **Publicly Held**
WEB: www.cingular.com
SIC: **4812** Cellular telephone services
HQ: At&T Corp.
1 At&T Way
Bedminster NJ 07921
800 403-3302

(P-5272)
AT&T CORP
6328 Irvine Blvd, Irvine (92620-2102)
PHONE..................949 559-1457
Linda Fisher, *Owner*
EMP: 97
SALES (corp-wide): 160.5B **Publicly Held**
WEB: www.att.com
SIC: **4812** Cellular telephone services
HQ: At&T Corp.
1 At&T Way
Bedminster NJ 07921
800 403-3302

(P-5273)
AT&T CORP
2333 S Sepulveda Blvd, Los Angeles
(90064-1910)
PHONE..................310 473-3649
Carolyn Wilder, *Manager*
EMP: 97
SALES (corp-wide): 160.5B **Publicly Held**
WEB: www.att.com
SIC: **4812** Cellular telephone services
HQ: At&T Corp.
1 At&T Way
Bedminster NJ 07921
800 403-3302

(P-5274)
AT&T CORP
83 E Colorado Blvd, Pasadena
(91105-1916)
PHONE..................626 396-0100
Martin Choe, *Branch Mgr*
EMP: 69

(P-5275)
AT&T CORP
7060 Market Place Dr, Goleta
(93117-5902)
PHONE..................805 562-0121
Nicole Jurzenski, *Manager*
EMP: 97
SALES (corp-wide): 160.5B **Publicly Held**
WEB: www.cingular.com
SIC: **4812** Cellular telephone services
HQ: At&T Corp.
1 At&T Way
Bedminster NJ 07921
800 403-3302

(P-5276)
AT&T CORP
980 N Western Ave Ste H, San Pedro
(90732-2451)
PHONE..................310 547-0400
Jack Aiello, *Manager*
EMP: 69
SALES (corp-wide): 160.5B **Publicly Held**
WEB: www.att.com
SIC: **4812** Cellular telephone services
HQ: At&T Corp.
1 At&T Way
Bedminster NJ 07921
800 403-3302

(P-5277)
AT&T CORP
26453 Bouquet Canyon Rd, Santa Clarita
(91350-2396)
PHONE..................661 297-1720
Carolyn Wilder, *Owner*
EMP: 69
SALES (corp-wide): 160.5B **Publicly Held**
WEB: www.att.com
SIC: **4812** Cellular telephone services
HQ: At&T Corp.
1 At&T Way
Bedminster NJ 07921
800 403-3302

(P-5278)
AT&T CORP
217 N Lemon St Rm 205, Anaheim
(92805-2943)
PHONE..................714 284-3818
Chris Nguyen, *Technical Mgr*
EMP: 95
SALES (corp-wide): 160.5B **Publicly Held**
SIC: **4812** Cellular telephone services
HQ: At&T Corp.
1 At&T Way
Bedminster NJ 07921
800 403-3302

(P-5279)
AT&T CORP
24935 Pico Canyon Rd, Stevenson Ranch
(91381-1708)
PHONE..................661 799-0800
Chris Lopez, *Branch Mgr*
EMP: 69
SALES (corp-wide): 160.5B **Publicly Held**
WEB: www.att.com
SIC: **4812** Cellular telephone services
HQ: At&T Corp.
1 At&T Way
Bedminster NJ 07921
800 403-3302

(P-5280)
AT&T CORP
3977 Chicago Ave, Riverside (92507-5338)
PHONE..................951 275-8801
Gil Leon, *Branch Mgr*
EMP: 69

SALES (corp-wide): 160.5B **Publicly Held**
SIC: 4812 Cellular telephone services
HQ: At&T Corp.
1 At&T Way
Bedminster NJ 07921
800 403-3302

(P-5281)
AT&T CORP
3750 Morrow Ln, Chico (95928-8865)
PHONE..................530 891-2025
Bill Rose, *Branch Mgr*
EMP: 96
SALES (corp-wide): 160.5B **Publicly Held**
SIC: 4812 Cellular telephone services
HQ: At&T Corp.
1 At&T Way
Bedminster NJ 07921
800 403-3302

(P-5282)
AT&T CORP
1955 E Daily Dr, Camarillo (93010-6300)
PHONE..................805 445-6562
EMP: 82
SALES (corp-wide): 160.5B **Publicly Held**
SIC: 4812 Cellular telephone services
HQ: At&T Corp.
1 At&T Way
Bedminster NJ 07921
800 403-3302

(P-5283)
AT&T CORP
1054 Harter Pkwy Ste 9, Yuba City
(95993-2653)
PHONE..................530 822-2700
Raj Sharma, *Branch Mgr*
EMP: 69
SALES (corp-wide): 160.5B **Publicly Held**
SIC: 4812 Cellular telephone services
HQ: At&T Corp.
1 At&T Way
Bedminster NJ 07921
800 403-3302

(P-5284)
AT&T CORP
133 S Las Posas Rd # 141, San Marcos
(92078-2468)
PHONE..................760 752-3273
Ron Manley, *Branch Mgr*
EMP: 69
SALES (corp-wide): 160.5B **Publicly Held**
WEB: www.att.com
SIC: 4812 Cellular telephone services
HQ: At&T Corp.
1 At&T Way
Bedminster NJ 07921
800 403-3302

(P-5285)
AT&T CORP
835 4th St, San Rafael (94901-3260)
PHONE..................415 721-1470
Don Klein, *Branch Mgr*
EMP: 97
SALES (corp-wide): 160.5B **Publicly Held**
SIC: 4812 Cellular telephone services
HQ: At&T Corp.
1 At&T Way
Bedminster NJ 07921
800 403-3302

(P-5286)
AT&T CORP
1855 41st Ave, Capitola (95010-2511)
PHONE..................831 465-6771
Amel Dunanes, *Principal*
EMP: 97
SALES (corp-wide): 160.5B **Publicly Held**
SIC: 4812 Cellular telephone services
HQ: At&T Corp.
1 At&T Way
Bedminster NJ 07921
800 403-3302

(P-5287)
AT&T CORP
1263 Simi Town Center Way, Simi Valley
(93065-8406)
PHONE..................805 583-9483
Kim Erwin, *Branch Mgr*
EMP: 97
SALES (corp-wide): 160.5B **Publicly Held**
SIC: 4812 Cellular telephone services
HQ: At&T Corp.
1 At&T Way
Bedminster NJ 07921
800 403-3302

(P-5288)
AT&T CORP
8225 Mira Mesa Blvd, San Diego
(92126-2603)
PHONE..................858 693-0815
Matt Holderness, *Branch Mgr*
Bill Troup, *Manager*
EMP: 69
SALES (corp-wide): 160.5B **Publicly Held**
WEB: www.att.com
SIC: 4812 Cellular telephone services
HQ: At&T Corp.
1 At&T Way
Bedminster NJ 07921
800 403-3302

(P-5289)
AT&T CORP
1810 E Main St, Woodland (95776-6234)
PHONE..................530 661-7724
EMP: 97
SALES (corp-wide): 160.5B **Publicly Held**
SIC: 4812 Cellular telephone services
HQ: At&T Corp.
1 At&T Way
Bedminster NJ 07921
800 403-3302

(P-5290)
AT&T CORP
7100 Santa Monica Blvd # 125, West Hollywood (90046-5896)
PHONE..................323 874-7000
EMP: 95
SALES (corp-wide): 160.5B **Publicly Held**
SIC: 4812 Cellular telephone services
HQ: At&T Corp.
1 At&T Way
Bedminster NJ 07921
800 403-3302

(P-5291)
AT&T CORP
134 Sunset Dr, San Ramon (94583-2340)
PHONE..................925 327-7100
Carolyn Wilder, *Owner*
EMP: 95
SALES (corp-wide): 160.5B **Publicly Held**
SIC: 4812 Cellular telephone services
HQ: At&T Corp.
1 At&T Way
Bedminster NJ 07921
800 403-3302

(P-5292)
AT&T CORP
1705 Story Rd, San Jose (95122-1935)
PHONE..................408 729-8400
EMP: 68
SALES (corp-wide): 160.5B **Publicly Held**
SIC: 4812 Cellular telephone services
HQ: At&T Corp.
1 At&T Way
Bedminster NJ 07921
800 403-3302

(P-5293)
AT&T CORP
1546 Saratoga Ave, San Jose
(95129-4961)
PHONE..................408 871-3870
Ben Hosseini, *Manager*
EMP: 69
SALES (corp-wide): 160.5B **Publicly Held**
SIC: 4812 Cellular telephone services

HQ: At&T Corp.
1 At&T Way
Bedminster NJ 07921
800 403-3302

(P-5294)
AT&T CORP
17675 Harvard Ave Ste B, Irvine
(92614-3527)
PHONE..................949 622-8240
Travis Stanford, *Branch Mgr*
EMP: 69
SALES (corp-wide): 160.5B **Publicly Held**
SIC: 4812 Cellular telephone services
HQ: At&T Corp.
1 At&T Way
Bedminster NJ 07921
800 403-3302

(P-5295)
AT&T CORP
6000 Lankershim Blvd, North Hollywood
(91606-4806)
PHONE..................818 506-9118
Ashur Paul, *Sales Associate*
Rricha Kale, *Manager*
Steve Spiller, *Assistant VP*
EMP: 69
SALES (corp-wide): 160.5B **Publicly Held**
SIC: 4812 Cellular telephone services
HQ: At&T Corp.
1 At&T Way
Bedminster NJ 07921
800 403-3302

(P-5296)
AT&T CORP
998 S Robertson Blvd # 103, Los Angeles
(90035-1637)
PHONE..................310 659-7600
Sia Bardi, *Branch Mgr*
EMP: 94
SALES (corp-wide): 160.5B **Publicly Held**
SIC: 4812
HQ: At&T Corp.
1 At&T Way
Bedminster NJ 07921
800 403-3302

(P-5297)
AT&T CORP
400 Del Monte Ctr, Monterey (93940-6159)
PHONE..................831 642-0100
Mike Godina, *Branch Mgr*
EMP: 97
SALES (corp-wide): 160.5B **Publicly Held**
WEB: www.att.com
SIC: 4812 Cellular telephone services
HQ: At&T Corp.
1 At&T Way
Bedminster NJ 07921
800 403-3302

(P-5298)
AT&T CORP
8420 Firestone Blvd, Downey
(90241-3844)
PHONE..................562 923-3032
Carolyn Wilder, *Branch Mgr*
EMP: 69
SALES (corp-wide): 160.5B **Publicly Held**
WEB: www.att.com
SIC: 4812 Cellular telephone services
HQ: At&T Corp.
1 At&T Way
Bedminster NJ 07921
800 403-3302

(P-5299)
B-PER ELECTRONIC INC
Also Called: My Wireless
1600 N Brwy, Santa Ana (92706)
PHONE..................626 912-0600
Shawn Yeh, *CEO*
EMP: 100
SALES (est): 10.4MM **Privately Held**
SIC: 4812 Cellular telephone services

(P-5300)
BLACK DOT WIRELESS LLC
27271 Las Ramblas Ste 300, Mission Viejo
(92691-8042)
PHONE..................949 502-3800
Marc Anthony, *CEO*
Gary Arnett, *President*
Jason Forgey, *Vice Pres*
Christopher Gianni, *Vice Pres*
Joseph Winkler, *Vice Pres*
EMP: 85
SQ FT: 22,000
SALES (est): 12.2MM **Privately Held**
SIC: 4812 Cellular telephone services

(P-5301)
BRAVO TECH INC
Also Called: Bti Wireless
14600 Industry Cir, La Mirada
(90638-5815)
PHONE..................714 230-8333
Bailey Zheng, *CEO*
Jason Lu, *Engineer*
▲ **EMP:** 50
SALES (est): 5.3MM **Privately Held**
WEB: www.bravotechinc.com
SIC: 4812 Cellular telephone services

(P-5302)
CALIFORNIA WIRELESS SOLUTIONS
4095 Evergrn Vlg S 200, Milpitas (95035)
PHONE..................408 771-1249
Zaid Hamed, *President*
EMP: 80
SALES (est): 1.3MM **Privately Held**
SIC: 4812 Cellular telephone services

(P-5303)
CELL SITE MANAGEMENT GROUP LLC
25109 Jefferson Ave, Murrieta
(92562-8116)
PHONE..................800 906-9778
Jack W Hawley, *Mng Member*
EMP: 50
SQ FT: 3,000
SALES (est): 3.5MM **Privately Held**
SIC: 4812 Cellular telephone services

(P-5304)
CELLCO PARTNERSHIP
Also Called: Verizon Wireless
1484 E Second St, Beaumont
(92223-3161)
PHONE..................951 769-0985
EMP: 71
SALES (corp-wide): 126B **Publicly Held**
SIC: 4812 4813 Cellular telephone services; telephone communication, except radio
HQ: Cellco Partnership
1 Verizon Way
Basking Ridge NJ 07920

(P-5305)
CELLCO PARTNERSHIP
Also Called: Verizon Wireless
26480 Ynez Rd, Temecula (92591-5628)
PHONE..................951 296-3499
Mike Remily, *Branch Mgr*
EMP: 71
SALES (corp-wide): 126B **Publicly Held**
SIC: 4812 Cellular telephone services
HQ: Cellco Partnership
1 Verizon Way
Basking Ridge NJ 07920

(P-5306)
CELLCO PARTNERSHIP
Also Called: Verizon
24329 Crenshaw Blvd Ste D, Torrance
(90505-5338)
PHONE..................310 891-6991
Norma Torqueza, *Manager*
EMP: 71
SALES (corp-wide): 126B **Publicly Held**
SIC: 4812 5999 5065 Cellular telephone services; mobile telephones & equipment; mobile telephone equipment

HQ: Cellco Partnership
1 Verizon Way
Basking Ridge NJ 07920
-

(P-5307)
CELLCO PARTNERSHIP
Also Called: Verizon
2428 Las Positas Rd, Livermore
(94551-8838)
PHONE....................925 245-0494
Gary Larsen, *Manager*
EMP: 71
SALES (corp-wide): 126B **Publicly Held**
SIC: 4812 Cellular telephone services
HQ: Cellco Partnership
1 Verizon Way
Basking Ridge NJ 07920
-

(P-5308)
CELLCO PARTNERSHIP
Also Called: Verizon Wireless
1680 Del Monte Ctr, Monterey
(93940-6169)
PHONE....................831 644-0858
EMP: 71
SALES (corp-wide): 126B **Publicly Held**
SIC: 4812 Cellular telephone services
HQ: Cellco Partnership
1 Verizon Way
Basking Ridge NJ 07920
-

(P-5309)
CELLCO PARTNERSHIP
Also Called: Verizon Wireless
1500 E Village Way # 2205, Orange
(92865-3616)
PHONE....................714 921-5130
EMP: 76
SALES (corp-wide): 126B **Publicly Held**
SIC: 4812 Cellular telephone services
HQ: Cellco Partnership
1 Verizon Way
Basking Ridge NJ 07920
-

(P-5310)
CELLCO PARTNERSHIP
Also Called: Verizon Wireless
6471 Lone Tree Way, Brentwood
(94513-5265)
PHONE....................925 626-3480
EMP: 71
SALES (corp-wide): 126B **Publicly Held**
SIC: 4812 Cellular telephone services
HQ: Cellco Partnership
1 Verizon Way
Basking Ridge NJ 07920
-

(P-5311)
CELLCO PARTNERSHIP
Also Called: Verizon Wireless
2851 Canyon Springs Pkwy, Riverside
(92507-0935)
PHONE....................951 697-3035
EMP: 76
SALES (corp-wide): 126B **Publicly Held**
SIC: 4812 Cellular telephone services
HQ: Cellco Partnership
1 Verizon Way
Basking Ridge NJ 07920
-

(P-5312)
CELLCO PARTNERSHIP
2535 W Hillcrest Dr, Thousand Oaks
(91320-2457)
PHONE....................805 376-8917
EMP: 71
SALES (corp-wide): 126B **Publicly Held**
SIC: 4812 Cellular telephone services
HQ: Cellco Partnership
1 Verizon Way
Basking Ridge NJ 07920
-

(P-5313)
CELLCO PARTNERSHIP
255 Parkshore Dr, Folsom (95630-4716)
P.O. Box 2167 (95763-2167)
PHONE....................212 395-1000
EMP: 71

SALES (corp-wide): 126B **Publicly Held**
SIC: 4812 Cellular telephone services
HQ: Cellco Partnership
1 Verizon Way
Basking Ridge NJ 07920

(P-5314)
CELLCO PARTNERSHIP
1101 Los Olivos Ave, Los Osos
(93402-3232)
PHONE....................805 596-2300
EMP: 71
SALES (corp-wide): 126B **Publicly Held**
SIC: 4812 Cellular telephone services
HQ: Cellco Partnership
1 Verizon Way
Basking Ridge NJ 07920
-

(P-5315)
CELLCO PARTNERSHIP
Also Called: Verizon Wireless
550 S Clovis Ave Ste 105, Fresno
(93727-4513)
PHONE....................559 454-0803
Joe Gomez, *Branch Mgr*
EMP: 71
SALES (corp-wide): 126B **Publicly Held**
SIC: 4812 Cellular telephone services
HQ: Cellco Partnership
1 Verizon Way
Basking Ridge NJ 07920
-

(P-5316)
CELLCO PARTNERSHIP
Also Called: Verizon
901 S Coast Dr Ste K120, Costa Mesa
(92626-7710)
PHONE....................714 427-0733
David Mendoza, *Manager*
EMP: 71
SALES (corp-wide): 126B **Publicly Held**
SIC: 4812 5999 Cellular telephone services; telephone equipment & systems
HQ: Cellco Partnership
1 Verizon Way
Basking Ridge NJ 07920
-

(P-5317)
CELLCO PARTNERSHIP
Also Called: Verizon Wireless
12459 Limonite Ave C-2, Eastvale
(91752-2458)
PHONE....................951 361-1850
Joseph Chappa, *Asst Mgr*
EMP: 71
SALES (corp-wide): 126B **Publicly Held**
SIC: 4812 Cellular telephone services
HQ: Cellco Partnership
1 Verizon Way
Basking Ridge NJ 07920
-

(P-5318)
CELLCO PARTNERSHIP
Also Called: Verizon
1900 Douglas Blvd Ste D, Roseville
(95661-3823)
PHONE....................916 786-6151
Rapheal Jones, *Branch Mgr*
EMP: 71
SALES (corp-wide): 126B **Publicly Held**
SIC: 4812 Cellular telephone services
HQ: Cellco Partnership
1 Verizon Way
Basking Ridge NJ 07920
-

(P-5319)
CELLCO PARTNERSHIP
Also Called: Verizon
15505 Sand Canyon Ave, Irvine
(92618-3114)
PHONE....................949 286-7000
Margaret Holzmann, *Administration*
Larry Bell, *Exec Dir*
Chintan Sheth, *Sr Software Eng*
Reynaldo Pagtakhan, *Software Dev*
Sheena Joseph, *Technology*
EMP: 2000
SALES (corp-wide): 126B **Publicly Held**
SIC: 4812 Cellular telephone services

HQ: Cellco Partnership
1 Verizon Way
Basking Ridge NJ 07920
-

(P-5320)
CELLCO PARTNERSHIP
Also Called: Verizon Wireless
1051 S Green Valley Rd, Watsonville
(95076-4164)
PHONE....................831 786-0267
EMP: 71
SALES (corp-wide): 126B **Publicly Held**
SIC: 4812 Cellular telephone services
HQ: Cellco Partnership
1 Verizon Way
Basking Ridge NJ 07920
-

(P-5321)
CELLCO PARTNERSHIP
Also Called: Verizon Wireless
1401 W Imperial Hwy Ste C, La Habra
(90631-6996)
PHONE....................562 694-8630
David Mendova, *Principal*
EMP: 71
SALES (corp-wide): 126B **Publicly Held**
SIC: 4812 Cellular telephone services
HQ: Cellco Partnership
1 Verizon Way
Basking Ridge NJ 07920
-

(P-5322)
CELLCO PARTNERSHIP
Also Called: Verizon Wireless
691 S Main St Ste 80, Orange
(92868-5619)
PHONE....................714 564-0050
EMP: 71
SALES (corp-wide): 126B **Publicly Held**
SIC: 4812 Cellular telephone services
HQ: Cellco Partnership
1 Verizon Way
Basking Ridge NJ 07920
-

(P-5323)
CELLCO PARTNERSHIP
Also Called: Verizon Wireless
711 Center Dr Ste 6a, San Marcos
(92069-3500)
PHONE....................760 738-0088
EMP: 71
SALES (corp-wide): 126B **Publicly Held**
SIC: 4812 Cellular telephone services
HQ: Cellco Partnership
1 Verizon Way
Basking Ridge NJ 07920
-

(P-5324)
CELLCO PARTNERSHIP
Also Called: Verizon
1440 41st Ave Ste B, Capitola
(95010-2940)
PHONE....................831 475-3100
Jeff Dehaven, *Manager*
EMP: 71
SALES (corp-wide): 126B **Publicly Held**
SIC: 4812 Cellular telephone services
HQ: Cellco Partnership
1 Verizon Way
Basking Ridge NJ 07920
-

(P-5325)
CELLCO PARTNERSHIP
Also Called: Verizon
2701 Ming Ave Spc 100a, Bakersfield
(93304-4451)
PHONE....................661 827-8728
Tricia Brown, *Branch Mgr*
Howard Chapman, *General Mgr*
EMP: 71
SALES (corp-wide): 126B **Publicly Held**
SIC: 4812 5999 Cellular telephone services; mobile telephones & equipment
HQ: Cellco Partnership
1 Verizon Way
Basking Ridge NJ 07920
-

(P-5326)
CELLCO PARTNERSHIP
Also Called: Verizon
1846 Marron Rd, Carlsbad (92008-1172)
PHONE....................760 720-8400
Arlene Strametz, *Principal*
Jeff Cummins, *Accounts Exec*
EMP: 71
SALES (corp-wide): 126B **Publicly Held**
SIC: 4812 Cellular telephone services; telephone equipment & systems
HQ: Cellco Partnership
1 Verizon Way
Basking Ridge NJ 07920
-

(P-5327)
CELLCO PARTNERSHIP
Also Called: Verizon
125 Corte Madera Town Ctr, Corte Madera
(94925-1209)
PHONE....................415 924-9084
Lonnie Tuck, *Principal*
EMP: 71
SALES (corp-wide): 126B **Publicly Held**
SIC: 4812 Cellular telephone services
HQ: Cellco Partnership
1 Verizon Way
Basking Ridge NJ 07920
-

(P-5328)
CELLCO PARTNERSHIP
Also Called: Verizon
1571 N Magnolia Ave # 212, El Cajon
(92020-1208)
PHONE....................619 596-7201
Larry Shuller, *Principal*
EMP: 71
SALES (corp-wide): 126B **Publicly Held**
SIC: 4812 Cellular telephone services
HQ: Cellco Partnership
1 Verizon Way
Basking Ridge NJ 07920
-

(P-5329)
CELLCO PARTNERSHIP
Also Called: Verizon
7723 N Blackstone Ave # 102, Fresno
(93720-4311)
PHONE....................559 451-0556
Holly O Brien, *Manager*
EMP: 71
SALES (corp-wide): 126B **Publicly Held**
SIC: 4812 Cellular telephone services
HQ: Cellco Partnership
1 Verizon Way
Basking Ridge NJ 07920
-

(P-5330)
CELLCO PARTNERSHIP
Also Called: Verizon
12607 Artesia Blvd, Cerritos (90703-8501)
PHONE....................562 809-5650
Bill Seager, *Manager*
EMP: 71
SALES (corp-wide): 126B **Publicly Held**
SIC: 4812 5999 Cellular telephone services; mobile telephones & equipment
HQ: Cellco Partnership
1 Verizon Way
Basking Ridge NJ 07920
-

(P-5331)
CELLCO PARTNERSHIP
Also Called: Verizon
1950 E 20th St Ste 803, Chico
(95928-7330)
PHONE....................530 892-6900
Erik Zuniga, *Branch Mgr*
EMP: 71
SALES (corp-wide): 126B **Publicly Held**
SIC: 4812 Cellular telephone services
HQ: Cellco Partnership
1 Verizon Way
Basking Ridge NJ 07920
-

(P-5332)
CELLCO PARTNERSHIP
Also Called: Verizon
2210 Griffin Way Ste 101, Corona
(92879-6532)
PHONE....................951 549-6400
Kyung OH, *Manager*
EMP: 71
SALES (corp-wide): 126B **Publicly Held**
SIC: 4812 5999 Cellular telephone serv-
ices; mobile telephones & equipment
HQ: Cellco Partnership
1 Verizon Way
Basking Ridge NJ 07920

(P-5333)
CELLCO PARTNERSHIP
Also Called: Verizon Wireless
39050 Argonaut Way, Fremont
(94538-1302)
PHONE....................510 490-3800
Dolores Joy, *Manager*
EMP: 71
SALES (corp-wide): 126B **Publicly Held**
SIC: 4812 Cellular telephone services
HQ: Cellco Partnership
1 Verizon Way
Basking Ridge NJ 07920

(P-5334)
CELLCO PARTNERSHIP
Also Called: Verizon
2500 E Imperial Hwy # 178, Brea
(92821-6122)
PHONE....................714 256-6015
Greg Schuler, *Manager*
Miosha Cuadra, *Asst Mgr*
EMP: 71
SALES (corp-wide): 126B **Publicly Held**
SIC: 4812 Cellular telephone services
HQ: Cellco Partnership
1 Verizon Way
Basking Ridge NJ 07920

(P-5335)
CELLCO PARTNERSHIP
1023 E Colorado St, Glendale
(91205-4542)
PHONE....................818 500-7779
EMP: 71
SALES (corp-wide): 126B **Publicly Held**
SIC: 4812
HQ: Cellco Partnership
1 Verizon Way
Basking Ridge NJ 07920

(P-5336)
CELLCO PARTNERSHIP
10525 Vista Sorrento Pkwy # 150, San
Diego (92121-2745)
PHONE....................858 625-7751
Stan Parker, *Opers Staff*
EMP: 71
SALES (corp-wide): 126B **Publicly Held**
SIC: 4812 Cellular telephone services
HQ: Cellco Partnership
1 Verizon Way
Basking Ridge NJ 07920

(P-5337)
CELLCO PARTNERSHIP
Also Called: Verizon Wireless
8300 Van Nuys Blvd, Panorama City
(91402-3608)
PHONE....................818 920-4848
EMP: 71
SALES (corp-wide): 126B **Publicly Held**
SIC: 4812 Cellular telephone services
HQ: Cellco Partnership
1 Verizon Way
Basking Ridge NJ 07920

(P-5338)
CELLCO PARTNERSHIP
Also Called: Verizon Wireless
488 S Mills Rd, Ventura (93003-3498)
PHONE....................805 650-0410
EMP: 71
SALES (corp-wide): 126B **Publicly Held**
SIC: 4812 Cellular telephone services

HQ: Cellco Partnership
1 Verizon Way
Basking Ridge NJ 07920

(P-5339)
CELLCO PARTNERSHIP
205 Oak Hill Rd, Paso Robles
(93446-5438)
PHONE....................805 237-8200
Maria Navarro, *Manager*
EMP: 71
SALES (corp-wide): 126B **Publicly Held**
SIC: 4812 Cellular telephone services
HQ: Cellco Partnership
1 Verizon Way
Basking Ridge NJ 07920

(P-5340)
CELLCO PARTNERSHIP
Also Called: Verizon Wireless
258 N El Cmino Real Ste A, Encinitas
(92024)
PHONE....................760 642-0430
EMP: 71
SALES (corp-wide): 126B **Publicly Held**
SIC: 4812 Cellular telephone services
HQ: Cellco Partnership
1 Verizon Way
Basking Ridge NJ 07920

(P-5341)
CELLCO PARTNERSHIP
Also Called: Verizon Wireless
2540 Tuscany St, Corona (92881-4649)
PHONE....................951 898-0980
EMP: 71
SALES (corp-wide): 126B **Publicly Held**
SIC: 4812 Cellular telephone services
HQ: Cellco Partnership
1 Verizon Way
Basking Ridge NJ 07920

(P-5342)
CELLCO PARTNERSHIP
125 Cyber Ct, Rocklin (95765-1205)
PHONE....................916 408-7958
EMP: 71
SALES (corp-wide): 126B **Publicly Held**
SIC: 4812 Cellular telephone services
HQ: Cellco Partnership
1 Verizon Way
Basking Ridge NJ 07920

(P-5343)
CELLCO PARTNERSHIP
Also Called: Verizon Wireless
1729 N Victory Pl, Burbank (91502-1646)
PHONE....................818 842-2722
Abe Osman, *Principal*
EMP: 71
SALES (corp-wide): 126B **Publicly Held**
SIC: 4812 Cellular telephone services
HQ: Cellco Partnership
1 Verizon Way
Basking Ridge NJ 07920

(P-5344)
CELLCO PARTNERSHIP
Also Called: Verizon Wireless
14510 Baldwn Prk Town Ctr, Baldwin Park
(91706-5549)
PHONE....................626 472-6196
EMP: 76
SALES (corp-wide): 126B **Publicly Held**
SIC: 4812 Cellular telephone services
HQ: Cellco Partnership
1 Verizon Way
Basking Ridge NJ 07920

(P-5345)
CELLCO PARTNERSHIP
Also Called: Verizon Wireless
6965 Camino Arroyo Ste 60, Gilroy
(95020-7343)
PHONE....................408 846-5170
Ignacio Solorio, *Principal*
EMP: 71
SALES (corp-wide): 126B **Publicly Held**
SIC: 4812 Cellular telephone services

HQ: Cellco Partnership
1 Verizon Way
Basking Ridge NJ 07920

(P-5346)
CELLCO PARTNERSHIP
Also Called: Verizon Wireless
368 S Lake Ave, Pasadena (91101-3508)
PHONE....................626 395-0956
EMP: 71
SALES (corp-wide): 126B **Publicly Held**
SIC: 4812 Cellular telephone services
HQ: Cellco Partnership
1 Verizon Way
Basking Ridge NJ 07920

(P-5347)
CELLCO PARTNERSHIP
Also Called: Verizon Wireless
5051 Auburn Blvd, Sacramento
(95841-2661)
PHONE....................916 331-6833
Walter Gallo, *Principal*
EMP: 71
SALES (corp-wide): 126B **Publicly Held**
SIC: 4812 Cellular telephone services
HQ: Cellco Partnership
1 Verizon Way
Basking Ridge NJ 07920

(P-5348)
CELLCO PARTNERSHIP
Also Called: Verizon Wireless
71800 Highway 111 A110, Rancho Mirage
(92270-4492)
PHONE....................760 568-5542
Hicks Duana, *Principal*
EMP: 71
SALES (corp-wide): 126B **Publicly Held**
SIC: 4812 Cellular telephone services
HQ: Cellco Partnership
1 Verizon Way
Basking Ridge NJ 07920

(P-5349)
CELLCO PARTNERSHIP
Also Called: Verizon Wireless
172 Ranch Dr, Milpitas (95035-5101)
PHONE....................408 263-1960
Paul Gutierrez, *Principal*
Michael Rojas, *Asst Mgr*
EMP: 71
SALES (corp-wide): 126B **Publicly Held**
SIC: 4812 Cellular telephone services
HQ: Cellco Partnership
1 Verizon Way
Basking Ridge NJ 07920

(P-5350)
CELLCO PARTNERSHIP
Also Called: Verizon Wireless
23718 El Toro Rd Ste A, Lake Forest
(92630-8908)
PHONE....................949 472-0700
Tracie Kemper, *Branch Mgr*
EMP: 71
SALES (corp-wide): 126B **Publicly Held**
SIC: 4812 Cellular telephone services
HQ: Cellco Partnership
1 Verizon Way
Basking Ridge NJ 07920

(P-5351)
CELLCO PARTNERSHIP
Also Called: Verizon Wireless
768 Market St, San Francisco
(94102-2514)
PHONE....................415 402-0640
Bob Wall, *Principal*
Daniel Estelita, *Sales Staff*
Daniel Wingo, *Manager*
EMP: 71
SALES (corp-wide): 126B **Publicly Held**
SIC: 4812 Cellular telephone services
HQ: Cellco Partnership
1 Verizon Way
Basking Ridge NJ 07920

(P-5352)
CELLCO PARTNERSHIP
Also Called: Verizon Wireless
3202 W Monte Vista Ave, Turlock
(95380-8412)
PHONE....................209 668-9579
Irene Alvarez, *Principal*
EMP: 71
SALES (corp-wide): 126B **Publicly Held**
SIC: 4812 Cellular telephone services
HQ: Cellco Partnership
1 Verizon Way
Basking Ridge NJ 07920

(P-5353)
CELLCO PARTNERSHIP
18012 Bollinger Canyon Rd, San Ramon
(94583-1502)
PHONE....................925 743-9327
EMP: 74
SALES (corp-wide): 127B **Publicly Held**
SIC: 4812
HQ: Cellco Partnership
1 Verizon Way
Basking Ridge NJ 07920

(P-5354)
CELLCO PARTNERSHIP
Also Called: Verizon Wireless
17237 Ventura Blvd, Encino (91316-4058)
PHONE....................818 990-4610
EMP: 71
SALES (corp-wide): 126B **Publicly Held**
SIC: 4812 Cellular telephone services
HQ: Cellco Partnership
1 Verizon Way
Basking Ridge NJ 07920

(P-5355)
CELLCO PARTNERSHIP
Also Called: Verizon Wireless
2015 Birch Rd Ste 1805, Chula Vista
(91915-2014)
PHONE....................619 216-5840
EMP: 71
SALES (corp-wide): 126B **Publicly Held**
SIC: 4812 Cellular telephone services
HQ: Cellco Partnership
1 Verizon Way
Basking Ridge NJ 07920

(P-5356)
CELLCO PARTNERSHIP
Also Called: Verizon Wireless
3264 Lakeshore Ave, Oakland
(94610-2720)
PHONE....................510 267-0731
EMP: 71
SALES (corp-wide): 126B **Publicly Held**
SIC: 4812 Cellular telephone services
HQ: Cellco Partnership
1 Verizon Way
Basking Ridge NJ 07920

(P-5357)
CELLCO PARTNERSHIP
333 Biscayne Dr, San Rafael (94901-1577)
PHONE....................415 258-8404
EMP: 71
SALES (corp-wide): 126B **Publicly Held**
SIC: 4812 Cellular telephone services
HQ: Cellco Partnership
1 Verizon Way
Basking Ridge NJ 07920

(P-5358)
CELLCO PARTNERSHIP
Also Called: Verizon Wireless
3635 N Freeway Blvd, Sacramento
(95834-2926)
PHONE....................916 419-6200
Dennis Strigl, *Principal*
EMP: 71
SALES (corp-wide): 126B **Publicly Held**
SIC: 4812 Cellular telephone services
HQ: Cellco Partnership
1 Verizon Way
Basking Ridge NJ 07920

(P-5359)
CELLCO PARTNERSHIP
11265 Ventura Blvd, Studio City
(91604-3136)
PHONE..............................818 980-4200
EMP: 71
SALES (corp-wide): 126B **Publicly Held**
SIC: 4812 Cellular telephone services
HQ: Cellco Partnership
1 Verizon Way
Basking Ridge NJ 07920

(P-5360)
CELLCO PARTNERSHIP
1199 Dunsyre Dr, Lafayette (94549-3217)
PHONE..............................925 472-0487
EMP: 74
SALES (corp-wide): 126B **Publicly Held**
SIC: 4812 Cellular telephone services
HQ: Cellco Partnership
1 Verizon Way
Basking Ridge NJ 07920

(P-5361)
CELLCO PARTNERSHIP
Also Called: Verizon Wireless
12006 Lakewood Blvd, Downey
(90242-2661)
PHONE..............................562 401-1045
Ronnie Mendoza, *Branch Mgr*
EMP: 71
SALES (corp-wide): 126B **Publicly Held**
SIC: 4812 Cellular telephone services
HQ: Cellco Partnership
1 Verizon Way
Basking Ridge NJ 07920

(P-5362)
CELLCO PARTNERSHIP
Also Called: Verizon Wireless
12821 Main St, Hesperia (92345-9126)
PHONE..............................760 662-5914
EMP: 71
SALES (corp-wide): 126B **Publicly Held**
SIC: 4812 Cellular telephone services
HQ: Cellco Partnership
1 Verizon Way
Basking Ridge NJ 07920

(P-5363)
CELLCO PARTNERSHIP
Also Called: Verizon Wireless
1398 Shaw Ave, Clovis (93612-3977)
PHONE..............................559 325-1420
EMP: 71
SALES (corp-wide): 126B **Publicly Held**
SIC: 4812 Cellular telephone services
HQ: Cellco Partnership
1 Verizon Way
Basking Ridge NJ 07920

(P-5364)
CELLCO PARTNERSHIP
Also Called: Verizon Wireless
39575 Trade Center Dr, Palmdale
(93551-3783)
PHONE..............................661 274-2112
Andy Taylor, *Principal*
EMP: 71
SALES (corp-wide): 126B **Publicly Held**
SIC: 4812 Cellular telephone services
HQ: Cellco Partnership
1 Verizon Way
Basking Ridge NJ 07920

(P-5365)
CELLCO PARTNERSHIP
Also Called: Verizon Wireless
16120 Beach Blvd, Huntington Beach
(92647-3805)
PHONE..............................714 847-8799
Thomas Johnson, *Branch Mgr*
EMP: 71
SALES (corp-wide): 126B **Publicly Held**
SIC: 4812 Cellular telephone services
HQ: Cellco Partnership
1 Verizon Way
Basking Ridge NJ 07920

(P-5366)
CELLCO PARTNERSHIP
Also Called: Verizon Wireless
100 N La Cienega Blvd # 233, Los Angeles
(90048-1938)
PHONE..............................310 659-0775
Tony Chu, *Principal*
EMP: 71
SALES (corp-wide): 126B **Publicly Held**
SIC: 4812 Cellular telephone services
HQ: Cellco Partnership
1 Verizon Way
Basking Ridge NJ 07920

(P-5367)
CELLCO PARTNERSHIP
Also Called: Verizon
255 Parkshore Dr Bldg B, Folsom
(95630-4716)
PHONE..............................916 357-1000
C Lee Cox, *CEO*
Brad Keller, *Associate Dir*
Robert Elmore, *Senior Engr*
Chris Rock, *Manager*
EMP: 400
SALES (corp-wide): 126B **Publicly Held**
SIC: 4812 Cellular telephone services
HQ: Cellco Partnership
1 Verizon Way
Basking Ridge NJ 07920

(P-5368)
CELLCO PARTNERSHIP
Also Called: Verizon Wireless
3801 Pelandale Ave Ste B3, Modesto
(95356-8308)
PHONE..............................209 543-6500
EMP: 76
SALES (corp-wide): 126B **Publicly Held**
SIC: 4812 Cellular telephone services
HQ: Cellco Partnership
1 Verizon Way
Basking Ridge NJ 07920

(P-5369)
CELLCO PARTNERSHIP
Also Called: Verizon Wireless
3785 Wilshire Blvd, Los Angeles
(90010-2889)
PHONE..............................213 738-9771
Mindy Reibman, *Sales Staff*
EMP: 76
SALES (corp-wide): 126B **Publicly Held**
SIC: 4812 Cellular telephone services
HQ: Cellco Partnership
1 Verizon Way
Basking Ridge NJ 07920

(P-5370)
CELLCO PARTNERSHIP
Also Called: Verizon Wireless
20820 Avalon Blvd, Carson (90746-3300)
PHONE..............................310 329-9325
EMP: 76
SALES (corp-wide): 126B **Publicly Held**
SIC: 4812 Cellular telephone services
HQ: Cellco Partnership
1 Verizon Way
Basking Ridge NJ 07920

(P-5371)
CELLCO PARTNERSHIP
Also Called: Verizon Wireless
1503 Vine St, Hollywood (90028-7304)
PHONE..............................323 465-0640
EMP: 76
SALES (corp-wide): 126B **Publicly Held**
SIC: 4812 Cellular telephone services
HQ: Cellco Partnership
1 Verizon Way
Basking Ridge NJ 07920

(P-5372)
CELLCO PARTNERSHIP
Also Called: Verizon Wireless
7100 Santa Monica Blvd, West Hollywood
(90046-5896)
PHONE..............................323 603-0369
EMP: 76

(P-5373)
CELLCO PARTNERSHIP
Also Called: Verizon Wireless
2654 Mission St, San Francisco
(94110-3102)
PHONE..............................415 695-8400
EMP: 76
SALES (corp-wide): 126B **Publicly Held**
SIC: 4812 Cellular telephone services
HQ: Cellco Partnership
1 Verizon Way
Basking Ridge NJ 07920

(P-5374)
CELLCO PARTNERSHIP
Also Called: Verizon Wireless
30935 Courthouse Dr Spc 1, Union City
(94587-1716)
PHONE..............................510 324-5740
EMP: 76
SALES (corp-wide): 126B **Publicly Held**
SIC: 4812 Cellular telephone services
HQ: Cellco Partnership
1 Verizon Way
Basking Ridge NJ 07920

(P-5375)
CELLCO PARTNERSHIP
Also Called: Verizon Wireless
24201 Valencia Blvd, Valencia
(91355-1861)
PHONE..............................661 286-2399
EMP: 76
SALES (corp-wide): 126B **Publicly Held**
SIC: 4812 Cellular telephone services
HQ: Cellco Partnership
1 Verizon Way
Basking Ridge NJ 07920

(P-5376)
CELLCO PARTNERSHIP
Also Called: Verizon Wireless
6856 Katella Ave, Cypress (90630-5108)
PHONE..............................714 899-4690
EMP: 76
SALES (corp-wide): 126B **Publicly Held**
SIC: 4812 Cellular telephone services
HQ: Cellco Partnership
1 Verizon Way
Basking Ridge NJ 07920

(P-5377)
CELLCO PARTNERSHIP
Also Called: Verizon Wireless
880 N Imperial Ave, El Centro
(92243-1916)
PHONE..............................760 337-5508
EMP: 76
SALES (corp-wide): 126B **Publicly Held**
SIC: 4812 Cellular telephone services
HQ: Cellco Partnership
1 Verizon Way
Basking Ridge NJ 07920

(P-5378)
CELLCO PARTNERSHIP
Also Called: Verizon Wireless
1555 Simi Town Center Way, Simi Valley
(93065-0518)
PHONE..............................805 955-9035
EMP: 76
SALES (corp-wide): 126B **Publicly Held**
SIC: 4812 Cellular telephone services
HQ: Cellco Partnership
1 Verizon Way
Basking Ridge NJ 07920

(P-5379)
CELLCO PARTNERSHIP
Also Called: Verizon Wireless
6600 Topanga Canyon Blvd, Canoga Park
(91303-2609)
PHONE..............................818 715-9143

(P-5380)
CELLCO PARTNERSHIP
Also Called: Verizon Wireless
110 Cooper St Ste A, Santa Cruz
(95060-4566)
PHONE..............................831 421-0753
EMP: 76
SALES (corp-wide): 126B **Publicly Held**
SIC: 4812 Cellular telephone services
HQ: Cellco Partnership
1 Verizon Way
Basking Ridge NJ 07920

(P-5381)
CELLCO PARTNERSHIP
Also Called: Verizon Wireless
500 Inland Center Dr # 459, San
Bernardino (92408-1912)
PHONE..............................909 381-0576
EMP: 76
SALES (corp-wide): 126B **Publicly Held**
SIC: 4812 Cellular telephone services
HQ: Cellco Partnership
1 Verizon Way
Basking Ridge NJ 07920

(P-5382)
CELLCO PARTNERSHIP
Also Called: Verizon Wireless
6065 Sunrise Blvd, Citrus Heights
(95610-6833)
PHONE..............................916 536-0440
EMP: 76
SALES (corp-wide): 126B **Publicly Held**
SIC: 4812 Cellular telephone services
HQ: Cellco Partnership
1 Verizon Way
Basking Ridge NJ 07920

(P-5383)
CELLCO PARTNERSHIP
Also Called: Verizon
1 Daniel Burnham Ct Bsmt, San Francisco
(94109-5474)
PHONE..............................415 351-1700
Minh Luong, *Manager*
Kaleem Anwar, *Engineer*
EMP: 76
SALES (corp-wide): 126B **Publicly Held**
SIC: 4812 5999 Cellular telephone serv-
ices; mobile telephones & equipment
HQ: Cellco Partnership
1 Verizon Way
Basking Ridge NJ 07920

(P-5384)
CELLCO PARTNERSHIP
Also Called: Verizon
12376 Washington Blvd A, Whittier
(90606-3810)
PHONE..............................562 789-0911
Victor Cardenes, *Manager*
EMP: 71
SALES (corp-wide): 126B **Publicly Held**
SIC: 4812 Cellular telephone services
HQ: Cellco Partnership
1 Verizon Way
Basking Ridge NJ 07920

(P-5385)
CELLCO PARTNERSHIP
Also Called: Verizon Wireless
7061 Clairemont Mesa Blvd, San Diego
(92111-1041)
PHONE..............................858 614-0011
EMP: 71
SALES (corp-wide): 126B **Publicly Held**
SIC: 4812 Cellular telephone services
HQ: Cellco Partnership
1 Verizon Way
Basking Ridge NJ 07920

PRODUCTS & SVCS

(P-5386)
CELLCO PARTNERSHIP
Also Called: Verizon Wireless
3825 Grand Ave, Chino (91710-5448)
PHONE..............................909 591-9740
Myung Choi, *Asst Mgr*
EMP: 71
SALES (corp-wide): 126B **Publicly Held**
SIC: 4812 Cellular telephone services
HQ: Cellco Partnership
1 Verizon Way
Basking Ridge NJ 07920

(P-5387)
CELLCO PARTNERSHIP
Also Called: Verizon Wireless
1145 Colusa Ave Ste A, Yuba City
(95991-3630)
PHONE..............................530 674-8007
EMP: 76
SALES (corp-wide): 126B **Publicly Held**
SIC: 4812 Cellular telephone services
HQ: Cellco Partnership
1 Verizon Way
Basking Ridge NJ 07920

(P-5388)
CELLCO PARTNERSHIP
Also Called: Verizon
27040 Alicia Pkwy Ste E, Laguna Niguel
(92677-3408)
PHONE..............................949 831-3955
Lawrence Lee, *Manager*
EMP: 71
SALES (corp-wide): 126B **Publicly Held**
SIC: 4812 Cellular telephone services
HQ: Cellco Partnership
1 Verizon Way
Basking Ridge NJ 07920

(P-5389)
CELLCO PARTNERSHIP
Also Called: Verizon Wireless
2980 State St, Santa Barbara
(93105-3445)
PHONE..............................805 569-2525
Kevin Warren, *Principal*
EMP: 71
SALES (corp-wide): 126B **Publicly Held**
SIC: 4812 Cellular telephone services
HQ: Cellco Partnership
1 Verizon Way
Basking Ridge NJ 07920

(P-5390)
CELLCO PARTNERSHIP
Also Called: Verizon Wireless
844 4th St, Santa Rosa (95404-4505)
PHONE..............................707 525-5010
Crystal Willis, *Program Mgr*
EMP: 71
SALES (corp-wide): 126B **Publicly Held**
SIC: 4812 Cellular telephone services
HQ: Cellco Partnership
1 Verizon Way
Basking Ridge NJ 07920

(P-5391)
CELLCO PARTNERSHIP
503 N State College Blvd, Fullerton
(92831-3545)
PHONE..............................714 449-0715
EMP: 71
SALES (corp-wide): 126B **Publicly Held**
SIC: 4812 Cellular telephone services
HQ: Cellco Partnership
1 Verizon Way
Basking Ridge NJ 07920

(P-5392)
CELLCO PARTNERSHIP
Also Called: Verizon Wireless
219 University Ave, Palo Alto (94301-1712)
PHONE..............................650 323-6127
Ian Yahya, *Manager*
EMP: 71
SALES (corp-wide): 126B **Publicly Held**
SIC: 4812 5065 5999 Cellular telephone
services; telephone & telegraphic equip-
ment; mobile telephones & equipment

HQ: Cellco Partnership
1 Verizon Way
Basking Ridge NJ 07920

(P-5393)
CELLCO PARTNERSHIP
Also Called: Verizon
994 Mill St Ste 100, San Luis Obispo
(93401-2777)
PHONE..............................805 549-6260
Robin Okoneski, *Branch Mgr*
Austin Otagburuagu, *Manager*
EMP: 71
SALES (corp-wide): 126B **Publicly Held**
SIC: 4812 Cellular telephone services
HQ: Cellco Partnership
1 Verizon Way
Basking Ridge NJ 07920

(P-5394)
CELLCO PARTNERSHIP
Also Called: Verizon Wireless
3770 W Mcfadden Ave Ste H, Santa Ana
(92704-1395)
PHONE..............................714 775-0600
EMP: 76
SALES (corp-wide): 126B **Publicly Held**
SIC: 4812 Cellular telephone services
HQ: Cellco Partnership
1 Verizon Way
Basking Ridge NJ 07920

(P-5395)
CELLCO PARTNERSHIP
Also Called: Verizon Wireless
11134 Rancho Carmel Dr # 101, San Diego
(92128-4671)
PHONE..............................858 618-2100
Joann Hartmann, *Branch Mgr*
EMP: 153
SALES (corp-wide): 126B **Publicly Held**
SIC: 4812 Cellular telephone services
HQ: Cellco Partnership
1 Verizon Way
Basking Ridge NJ 07920

(P-5396)
CELLCO PARTNERSHIP
Also Called: Verizon Wireless
43458 10th St W Ste C, Lancaster
(93534-6417)
PHONE..............................661 726-4762
EMP: 71
SALES (corp-wide): 126B **Publicly Held**
SIC: 4812 Cellular telephone services
HQ: Cellco Partnership
1 Verizon Way
Basking Ridge NJ 07920

(P-5397)
CELLCO PARTNERSHIP
638 Camino De Ls Mrs H140, San
Clemente (92673)
PHONE..............................949 488-9990
Aj Bezer, *Branch Mgr*
EMP: 71
SALES (corp-wide): 126B **Publicly Held**
SIC: 4812 Cellular telephone services
HQ: Cellco Partnership
1 Verizon Way
Basking Ridge NJ 07920

(P-5398)
CELLCO PARTNERSHIP
Also Called: Verizon Wireless
5438 Whittier Blvd, Commerce
(90022-4113)
PHONE..............................323 725-9750
Kristina King, *Branch Mgr*
EMP: 71
SALES (corp-wide): 126B **Publicly Held**
SIC: 4812 Cellular telephone services
HQ: Cellco Partnership
1 Verizon Way
Basking Ridge NJ 07920

(P-5399)
CELLCO PARTNERSHIP
Also Called: Verizon Wireless
8724 Washington Blvd, Pico Rivera
(90660-3791)
PHONE..............................562 942-8527
EMP: 71
SALES (corp-wide): 126B **Publicly Held**
SIC: 4812 Cellular telephone services
HQ: Cellco Partnership
1 Verizon Way
Basking Ridge NJ 07920

(P-5400)
COMCAST OF
CALIFORNIA/COLO
3055 Comcast Pl, Livermore (94551-7594)
PHONE..............................925 424-0273
Stephen B Burke, *President*
Garrett Owens, *Administration*
Elaine Barden, *VP Mktg*
Marc Miguel, *Senior Mgr*
Daniel Pryor, *Director*
EMP: 69
SALES (est): 654.2K
SALES (corp-wide): 84.5B **Publicly Held**
SIC: 4812 4841 Radio telephone commu-
nication; cable television services
PA: Comcast Corporation
1701 Jfk Blvd
Philadelphia PA 19103
215 286-1700

(P-5401)
CORTEL INC
14621 Arroyo Hondo, San Diego
(92127-3641)
PHONE..............................650 703-7217
Michael Jackson, *President*
John Barker, *CFO*
Michael Miller, *Admin Sec*
EMP: 52
SALES (est): 3.6MM **Privately Held**
SIC: 4812 Cellular telephone services

(P-5402)
CRICKET COMMUNICATIONS
LLC (DH)
Also Called: Cricket Wireless
7337 Trade St, San Diego (92121-2423)
PHONE..............................858 882-6000
S Douglas Hutcheson, *CEO*
Nitu Arora, *President*
David Davis, *President*
Glen Flowers, *President*
Annette Jacobs, *President*
EMP: 65
SALES (est): 623.1MM
SALES (corp-wide): 160.5B **Publicly
Held**
WEB: www.cricketcommunications.com
SIC: 4812 Cellular telephone services
HQ: Leap Wireless International, Inc.
7337 Trade St
San Diego CA 92121
858 882-6000

(P-5403)
CRICKET INDIANA PROPERTY
CO
10307 Pacific Center Ct, San Diego
(92121-4340)
PHONE..............................858 587-2648
EMP: 86
SALES (est): 1.8MM
SALES (corp-wide): 160.5B **Publicly
Held**
WEB: www.leapwireless.com
SIC: 4812 Radio telephone communication
HQ: Leap Wireless International, Inc.
7337 Trade St
San Diego CA 92121
858 882-6000

(P-5404)
DIGITAL COMMUNICATIONS
NETWORK (PA)
Also Called: D C N Wireless
6300 Canoga Ave Ste 1625, Woodland Hills
(91367-8045)
PHONE..............................818 227-3333
Robert H Mogadam, *President*
Margrit Dorgelo, *Vice Pres*
Terry Gilson, *Info Tech Mgr*

Robert Mogadam, *CPA*
EMP: 54
SALES (est): 6.6MM **Privately Held**
WEB: www.digitalcomnet.com
SIC: 4812 5999 Cellular telephone serv-
ices; telephone & communication equip-
ment

(P-5405)
DOWNTOWN METRO
1030 6th St Ste 16, Coachella
(92236-1710)
PHONE..............................760 398-3310
H Yun, *Owner*
EMP: 50
SALES (est): 717.9K **Privately Held**
SIC: 4812 Cellular telephone services

(P-5406)
DUST NETWORKS INC
32990 Alvrdo Niles Rd # 910, Union City
(94587-8106)
PHONE..............................510 400-2900
Joy Weiss, *President*
Eva Chen, *Vice Pres*
Brenda Glaze, *Vice Pres*
Dave Lynch, *Vice Pres*
Sharon Kuhn, *Manager*
EMP: 51
SQ FT: 15,000
SALES (est): 3.8MM
SALES (corp-wide): 5.1B **Publicly Held**
WEB: www.dust-inc.com
SIC: 4812 Cellular telephone services
HQ: Linear Technology Llc
1630 Mccarthy Blvd
Milpitas CA 95035
408 432-1900

(P-5407)
EA MOBILE INC
5510 Lincoln Blvd, Los Angeles
(90094-2034)
PHONE..............................310 754-7125
Mitch Lasky, *Ch of Bd*
Scott Lahman, *President*
Craig Gatarz, *COO*
Michael Marchetti, *CFO*
Minard Hamilton, *Exec VP*
EMP: 400
SQ FT: 23,000
SALES (est): 14.3MM
SALES (corp-wide): 5.1B **Publicly Held**
SIC: 4812 Cellular telephone services
PA: Electronic Arts Inc.
209 Redwood Shores Pkwy
Redwood City CA 94065
650 628-1500

(P-5408)
FRONTIER CALIFORNIA INC
Also Called: Verizon
5195 N Blackstone Ave, Fresno
(93710-6701)
PHONE..............................559 224-9222
Randall Petty-John, *Manager*
EMP: 60
SALES (corp-wide): 9.1B **Publicly Held**
SIC: 4812 Cellular telephone services
HQ: Frontier California Inc.
140 West St
New York NY 10007
212 395-1000

(P-5409)
IMOBILE LLC
2613 Naglee Rd, Tracy (95304-7317)
PHONE..............................209 833-6757
Armando Baltazar, *President*
EMP: 266 **Privately Held**
SIC: 4812 Cellular telephone services
PA: Imobile Llc
207 Terminal Dr
Plainview NY 11803

(P-5410)
J5 INFRASTRUCTURE
PARTNERS LLC
2030 Main St Ste 200, Irvine (92614-8223)
PHONE..............................949 299-5258
Jerry Elliott, *CEO*
Brian Kennell, *Exec VP*
EMP: 58
SALES (est): 1.8MM **Privately Held**
SIC: 4812 Cellular telephone services

▲ = Import ▼=Export
◆ =Import/Export

(P-5411)
NEW CINGULAR WIRELESS SVCS INC
Also Called: AT&T Wireless
9830 Norwalk Blvd Ste 100, Santa Fe Springs (90670-2987)
PHONE..................562 941-6422
Yong Kim, *Branch Mgr*
EMP: 100
SALES (corp-wide): 160.5B **Publicly Held**
WEB: www.attws.com
SIC: **4812** Cellular telephone services
HQ: New Cingular Wireless Services, Inc.
7277 164th Ave Ne
Redmond WA 98052
425 827-4500

(P-5412)
NEXTEL COMMUNICATIONS INC
1810 W Slauson Ave Ste G, Los Angeles (90047-1133)
PHONE..................323 290-2400
Ivan Arvizu, *Principal*
EMP: 60
SALES (corp-wide): 85.9B **Publicly Held**
SIC: **4812** Cellular telephone services
HQ: Nextel Communications, Inc.
12502 Sunrise Valley Dr
Reston VA 20191
703 433-4000

(P-5413)
NEXTEL COMMUNICATIONS INC
272 Sun Valley Mall, Concord (94520-5808)
PHONE..................925 682-2355
Sean Fanopulous, *Manager*
EMP: 60
SALES (corp-wide): 85.9B **Publicly Held**
WEB: www.nextel.com
SIC: **4812** 5999 Radio telephone communication; mobile telephones & equipment
HQ: Nextel Communications, Inc.
12502 Sunrise Valley Dr
Reston VA 20191
703 433-4000

(P-5414)
OFFICE OF THE LEGISLATIVE COUN
Also Called: Legislative Data Center
1100 J St Fl 7, Sacramento (95814-2826)
PHONE..................916 341-8708
Nancy Pabst, *IT/INT Sup*
Diana Waldo, *Technology*
Bill Eubanks, *Deputy Dir*
EMP: 330 **Privately Held**
SIC: **4812** Radio telephone communication
HQ: Office Of The Legislative Counsel
State Cpitol Bldg Rm 3021
Sacramento CA 95814
-

(P-5415)
SIERRA WIRELESS AMERICA INC (HQ)
2738 Loker Ave W Ste A, Carlsbad (92010-6629)
PHONE..................760 444-5650
Jason W Cohenour, *CEO*
EMP: 82
SALES (est): 10.2MM
SALES (corp-wide): 692MM **Privately Held**
PA: Sierra Wireless, Inc.
13811 Wireless Way
Richmond BC V6V 3
604 231-1100

(P-5416)
SPRINT CORPORATION
6591 Irvine Center Dr # 100, Irvine (92618-2130)
PHONE..................949 748-3353
Mohammed Nasser, *Exec Dir*
EMP: 400
SALES (corp-wide): 85.9B **Publicly Held**
SIC: **4812** Cellular telephone services
HQ: Sprint Corporation
6200 Sprint Pkwy
Overland Park KS 66251
877 564-3166

(P-5417)
STX WIRELESS OPERATIONS LLC
Also Called: Cricket Stx
5887 Copley Dr, San Diego (92111-7906)
PHONE..................858 882-6000
Douglas Hutcheson, *President*
Jerry Elliot, *CFO*
Kristie Randall, *Executive*
Jeff Wagner, *Site Mgr*
Firas Alahmad, *Marketing Mgr*
EMP: 4000
SALES (est): 410.7MM **Privately Held**
SIC: **4812** Cellular telephone services

(P-5418)
T-MOBILE USA INC
Also Called: Metropcs-Fremont
4095 Mowry Ave, Fremont (94538-1339)
PHONE..................510 797-8290
EMP: 170
SALES (corp-wide): 88.3B **Publicly Held**
SIC: **4812 4813** Cellular telephone services; telephone communication, except radio; wire telephone
HQ: T-Mobile Usa, Inc.
12920 Se 38th St
Bellevue WA 98006
425 378-4000

(P-5419)
T-MOBILE USA INC
Also Called: Metropcs-Modesto
2225 Plaza Pkwy Ste I1b, Modesto (95350-6220)
PHONE..................209 529-0539
EMP: 170
SALES (corp-wide): 88.3B **Publicly Held**
SIC: **4812 4813**
HQ: T-Mobile Usa, Inc.
12920 Se 38th St
Bellevue WA 98006
425 378-4000

(P-5420)
T-MOBILE USA INC
Also Called: Metropcs-Van Ness
900 Van Ness Ave Ste 1, San Francisco (94109-6970)
PHONE..................415 440-5370
EMP: 153
SALES (corp-wide): 88.3B **Publicly Held**
SIC: **4812 4813** Cellular telephone services; telephone communication, except radio; wire telephone
HQ: T-Mobile Usa, Inc.
12920 Se 38th St
Bellevue WA 98006
425 378-4000

(P-5421)
TEXTPLUS INC
Also Called: Gogii
13160 Mindanao Way # 217, Marina Del Rey (90292-6358)
PHONE..................424 272-0296
Nanea Reeves, *President*
Zachary Norman, *President*
Chandra Hill, *Vice Pres*
Cory Radcliff, *Vice Pres*
Alex Scissors, *Project Mgr*
EMP: 65
SALES (est): 8.2MM **Privately Held**
SIC: **4812** Cellular telephone services

(P-5422)
TRELLISWARE TECHNOLOGIES INC
16516 Via Esprillo # 300, San Diego (92127-1728)
PHONE..................858 753-1600
Thomas Carter, *CEO*
Steven Fisher, *CFO*
Michael Smith, *Officer*
Metin Bayram, *Vice Pres*
Jim Morse, *Vice Pres*
EMP: 90
SQ FT: 46,000
SALES (est): 23.3MM **Privately Held**
WEB: www.trellisware.com
SIC: **4812 4813 3663** Radio telephone communication; local & long distance telephone communications; airborne radio communications equipment

(P-5423)
TWILIO INC (PA)
375 Beale St Ste 300, San Francisco (94105-2177)
PHONE..................415 390-2337
Jeff Lawson, *Ch of Bd*
George Hu, *COO*
Lee Kirkpatrick, *CFO*
Scott Raney, *Bd of Directors*
Genevieve Haldeman, *Vice Pres*
EMP: 167
SQ FT: 90,000
SALES: 399MM **Publicly Held**
SIC: **4812 7372** Cellular telephone services; business oriented computer software

(P-5424)
U S MBILE WRLESS CMMUNICATIONS (PA)
Also Called: Day Wireless Systems
8300 Juniper Creek Ln # 100, San Diego (92126-1072)
PHONE..................858 537-0709
Stanley A Decosmo, *Ch of Bd*
Gordon Day, *President*
Edward Carey, *Vice Pres*
Mike Miller, *Technician*
Amador Macias, *Project Mgr*
EMP: 75
SQ FT: 18,000
SALES: 5.5MM **Privately Held**
SIC: **4812** Cellular telephone services

(P-5425)
UST DEVELOPMENT INC
Also Called: UST Telecom
2001 Elm Ct, Ontario (91761-7619)
P.O. Box 3790 (91761-0977)
PHONE..................626 205-1123
David William Bell, *CEO*
EMP: 127
SALES (est): 6.9MM **Privately Held**
SIC: **4812** Radio telephone communication

(P-5426)
VERIZON WIRELESS INC
15 Montebello Way, Los Gatos (95030-6808)
PHONE..................408 354-6374
Joseph Edens, *Branch Mgr*
EMP: 122
SALES (corp-wide): 126B **Publicly Held**
WEB: www.verizonwireless.com
SIC: **4812** Cellular telephone services
HQ: Verizon Wireless, Inc.
1 Verizon Way
Basking Ridge NJ 07920
-

(P-5427)
WM WIRELESS INC
6723 N Paramount Blvd, Long Beach (90805-1901)
PHONE..................562 633-9288
Ferdinand L Aguinaldo, *President*
EMP: 50
SALES (est): 6.9MM **Privately Held**
SIC: **4812** Cellular telephone services

4813 Telephone Communications, Except

(P-5428)
11 MAIN INC
527 Flume St, Chico (95928-5608)
PHONE..................530 892-9191
Jeff Schlicht, *CEO*
Mike Effle, *President*
Ray Kaminski, *Vice Pres*
Christina Liu, *Vice Pres*
Amber Minson, *Vice Pres*
EMP: 105
SALES (est): 18.7MM **Privately Held**
SIC: **4813**
HQ: Alibaba.Com Inc
400 S El Camino Real # 400
San Mateo CA 94402
408 785-5580

(P-5429)
2WIRE INC (DH)
2450 Walsh Ave, Santa Clara (95051-1303)
PHONE..................408 235-5500
Tim O'Loughlin, *CEO*
Pasquale Romano, *President*
Tom Bohan, *Admin Sec*
▲ EMP: 138
SQ FT: 82,000
SALES (est): 113.8MM
SALES (corp-wide): 6.6B **Privately Held**
WEB: www.2wire.com
SIC: **4813**
HQ: Ruckus Wireless, Inc.
350 W Java Dr
Sunnyvale CA 94089
650 265-4200

(P-5430)
4G WIRELESS INC
Also Called: Verizon Wreless Authorized Ret
7220 Eastern Ave, Bell (90201-4505)
PHONE..................562 928-2972
EMP: 55 **Privately Held**
SIC: **4813 4812** Telephone communication, except radio; cellular telephone services
PA: 4g Wireless, Inc.
8871 Research Dr
Irvine CA 92618

(P-5431)
4G WIRELESS INC
Also Called: Verizon Wreless Authorized Ret
4620 Tassajara Rd, Dublin (94568-4607)
PHONE..................925 307-8990
EMP: 55 **Privately Held**
SIC: **4813 4812** Telephone communication, except radio; cellular telephone services
PA: 4g Wireless, Inc.
8871 Research Dr
Irvine CA 92618

(P-5432)
4G WIRELESS INC
Also Called: Verizon Wreless Authorized Ret
8342 Lincoln Blvd, Los Angeles (90045-2414)
PHONE..................310 429-9048
EMP: 55 **Privately Held**
SIC: **4813 4812** Telephone communication, except radio; cellular telephone services
PA: 4g Wireless, Inc.
8871 Research Dr
Irvine CA 92618

(P-5433)
4G WIRELESS INC
Also Called: Verizon Wreless Authorized Ret
4925 Eagle Rock Blvd, Los Angeles (90041-1906)
PHONE..................323 679-9991
EMP: 55 **Privately Held**
SIC: **4813 4812** Telephone communication, except radio; cellular telephone services
PA: 4g Wireless, Inc.
8871 Research Dr
Irvine CA 92618

(P-5434)
4G WIRELESS INC
Also Called: Verizon Wreless Authorized Ret
501 W Felicita Ave # 104, Escondido (92025-5638)
PHONE..................760 705-7133
EMP: 55 **Privately Held**
SIC: **4813 4812** Telephone communication, except radio; cellular telephone services
PA: 4g Wireless, Inc.
8871 Research Dr
Irvine CA 92618

(P-5435)
4G WIRELESS INC
Also Called: Verizon Wireless Premium Ret
2635 Gateway Rd Ste 103, Carlsbad
(92009-1753)
PHONE...................760 828-2543
Ameen Elashqar, *Branch Mgr*
EMP: 55 **Privately Held**
SIC: 4813 4812 4833 Telephone communication, except radio; cellular telephone services; television broadcasting stations
PA: 4g Wireless, Inc.
8871 Research Dr
Irvine CA 92618

(P-5436)
4G WIRELESS INC
Also Called: Verizon Wreless Authorized Ret
2560 N Perris Blvd Ste G8, Perris
(92571-3253)
PHONE...................951 210-7980
EMP: 55 **Privately Held**
SIC: 4813 4812 Telephone communication, except radio; cellular telephone services
PA: 4g Wireless, Inc.
8871 Research Dr
Irvine CA 92618

(P-5437)
4G WIRELESS INC
Also Called: Verizon Wreless Authorized Ret
407 N Pacific Coast Hwy # 101, Redondo
Beach (90277-2872)
PHONE...................310 376-2299
EMP: 55 **Privately Held**
SIC: 4813 4812 Telephone communication, except radio; cellular telephone services
PA: 4g Wireless, Inc.
8871 Research Dr
Irvine CA 92618

(P-5438)
4G WIRELESS INC
Also Called: Verizon Wreless Authorized Ret
285 E 5th St, Long Beach (90802-2484)
PHONE...................562 432-7744
EMP: 55 **Privately Held**
SIC: 4813 4812 Telephone communication, except radio; cellular telephone services
PA: 4g Wireless, Inc.
8871 Research Dr
Irvine CA 92618

(P-5439)
8X8 INC (PA)
2125 Onel Dr, San Jose (95131-2032)
PHONE...................408 727-1885
Vikram Verma, *CEO*
Bryan R Martin, *Ch of Bd*
Mary Ellen Genovese, *CFO*
Rani Hublou, *Chief Mktg Ofcr*
Dejan Deklich,
EMP: 129
SQ FT: 140,831
SALES: 296.5MM **Publicly Held**
WEB: www.bryanandlisa.com
SIC: 4813 7372 ; ; prepackaged software

(P-5440)
AAMCOM LLC
800 N Pacific Coast Hwy, Redondo Beach
(90277-2148)
PHONE...................310 318-8100
Steve Diels, *Mng Member*
Jose Carrera, *Info Tech Dir*
Norma Soto, *Business Mgr*
Elisabeth Diels,
Carlton Bonner, *Director*
EMP: 50 EST: 2009
SQ FT: 4,000
SALES: 2.6MM **Privately Held**
SIC: 4813 Telephone communication, except radio

(P-5441)
AB CELLULAR HOLDING LLC
Also Called: At & T Wireless Service
1452 Edinger Ave, Tustin (92780-6246)
PHONE...................562 468-6846

Glen Lurie,
Robert Dingman, *Engineer*
EMP: 2100
SALES (est): 229.3MM
SALES (corp-wide): 160.5B **Publicly Held**
WEB: www.cingular.com
SIC: 4813 Local & long distance telephone communications; local telephone communications; long distance telephone communications
HQ: At&T Mobility Llc
1025 Lenox Park Blvd Ne
Brookhaven GA 30319
800 331-0500

(P-5442)
ADAPTIVE SPECTRUM AND SIGNAL A
333 Twin Dolphin Dr # 300, Redwood City
(94065-1449)
PHONE...................650 264-2667
John M Cioffi, *CEO*
Barry Gray, *Senior VP*
Chris Fisher, *Vice Pres*
David Stevenson, *Risk Mgmt Dir*
David Fligor, *Admin Sec*
EMP: 60
SALES (est): 3.2MM
SALES (corp-wide): 4.2MM **Privately Held**
SIC: 4813
PA: Assia Ela Sl.
Calle Claudio Coello, 24 - Piso 4 A 2
Madrid 28001
917 815-130

(P-5443)
ADICIO INC
5993 Avenida Encinas # 100, Carlsbad
(92008-4459)
PHONE...................760 602-9502
Richard Miller, *President*
Richette Lock, *COO*
Paul Jarrad, *CFO*
Bob Miller, *Officer*
Mike Cavallo, *Exec VP*
EMP: 90
SQ FT: 15,000
SALES: 15MM **Privately Held**
WEB: www.adicio.com
SIC: 4813

(P-5444)
AERIS COMMUNICATIONS INC (PA)
1745 Tech Dr Ste 700, San Jose (95110)
PHONE...................408 557-1900
Marc Jones, *CEO*
John Molise, *CFO*
Mark Cratsenburg, *Vice Pres*
Nancy Lai, *Vice Pres*
Harry Plant, *Vice Pres*
EMP: 52
SQ FT: 30,000
SALES (est): 17.6MM **Privately Held**
WEB: www.aeris.net
SIC: 4813 4812 Local & long distance telephone communications; cellular telephone services

(P-5445)
AIRESPRING INC
Also Called: Global Fibernet
7800 Woodley Ave, Van Nuys
(91406-1722)
PHONE...................818 786-8990
AVI Lonstein, *CEO*
Daniel Lonstein, *COO*
Arno Vigen, *CFO*
Ron McNab, *Senior VP*
Wendell Nelson, *Senior VP*
▲ EMP: 100 EST: 2001
SQ FT: 12,500
SALES (est): 44.2MM **Privately Held**
SIC: 4813

(P-5446)
ALTABA INC
Also Called: Geocities
3420 Central Expy, Santa Clara
(95051-0703)
PHONE...................408 349-5080
Terry Semel, *Principal*
Patrick Bennett, *President*
Chuck Haas, *President*

P Hanley, *President*
Charlie Hoffman, *Sr Corp Ofcr*
EMP: 200 **Publicly Held**
WEB: www.yahoo.com
SIC: 4813 7375 ; information retrieval services
PA: Altaba Inc.
140 E 45th St Ste 15a
New York NY 10017

(P-5447)
AMERICAN MESSAGING SVCS LLC
Also Called: Verizon
2181 W Winton Ave, Hayward
(94545-1209)
PHONE...................510 889-2300
Scott Falconer, *Branch Mgr*
Dave Andersen, *COO*
EMP: 70
SALES (corp-wide): 490MM **Privately Held**
SIC: 4813 Telephone communication, except radio
PA: American Messaging Services, Llc
1720 Lakepointe Dr # 100
Lewisville TX 75057
888 699-9014

(P-5448)
ASIAINFO-LINKAGE INC
5201 Great America Pkwy # 356, Santa
Clara (95054-1122)
PHONE...................408 970-9788
Steve Zhang, *CEO*
Ying Han, *CFO*
Michael Wu, *CFO*
Yadong Jin, *Exec VP*
Jie LI, *Vice Pres*
EMP: 1500
SALES: 481MM **Privately Held**
SIC: 4813
HQ: Asiainfo Technology (China) Co., Ltd.
Asiainfo Plaza East Area, No. 10
Xibeiwang East Road Haidian Dis
Beijing 10019
108 216-6905

(P-5449)
AT&T CORP
795 Folsom St, San Francisco
(94107-1243)
PHONE...................415 442-2600
K McNeely, *Principal*
Raymond Choon, *Sales Staff*
Walter Hagge, *Manager*
Marka Phiglera, *Accounts Mgr*
EMP: 575
SALES (corp-wide): 160.5B **Publicly Held**
WEB: www.att.com
SIC: 4813 4812 Long distance telephone communications; radio telephone communication
HQ: At&T Corp.
1 At&T Way
Bedminster NJ 07921
800 403-3302

(P-5450)
AT&T CORP
4332 Tweedy Blvd, South Gate
(90280-6220)
PHONE...................323 568-2006
Carolyn Wilder, *Branch Mgr*
EMP: 69
SALES (corp-wide): 160.5B **Publicly Held**
WEB: www.att.com
SIC: 4813 Local & long distance telephone communications
HQ: At&T Corp.
1 At&T Way
Bedminster NJ 07921
800 403-3302

(P-5451)
AT&T CORP
2745 Cloverdale Ave, Concord
(94518-2402)
PHONE...................925 356-6204
Hugh Johnston, *Branch Mgr*
Marty Martinez, *Manager*
EMP: 69

SALES (corp-wide): 160.5B **Publicly Held**
SIC: 4813 Telephone communication, except radio
HQ: At&T Corp.
1 At&T Way
Bedminster NJ 07921
800 403-3302

(P-5452)
AT&T CORP
624 S Grand Ave Ste 2940, Los Angeles
(90017-3872)
PHONE...................213 787-0055
Arnold Larson, *Branch Mgr*
EMP: 69
SALES (corp-wide): 160.5B **Publicly Held**
WEB: www.att.com
SIC: 4813 Telephone communication, except radio
HQ: At&T Corp.
1 At&T Way
Bedminster NJ 07921
800 403-3302

(P-5453)
AT&T CORP
1610 W Yosemite Ave Ste 2, Manteca
(95337-5189)
PHONE...................209 956-8324
Brian McCart, *Manager*
EMP: 69
SALES (corp-wide): 160.5B **Publicly Held**
WEB: www.att.com
SIC: 4813 Telephone communication, except radio
HQ: At&T Corp.
1 At&T Way
Bedminster NJ 07921
800 403-3302

(P-5454)
AT&T CORP
6920 Van Nuys Blvd Rm 100, Van Nuys
(91405-3986)
PHONE...................818 374-6458
Randy Paquette, *Manager*
EMP: 100
SALES (corp-wide): 160.5B **Publicly Held**
WEB: www.swbell.com
SIC: 4813 Local & long distance telephone communications
HQ: At&T Corp.
1 At&T Way
Bedminster NJ 07921
800 403-3302

(P-5455)
AT&T CORP
14709 Vanoan St, Van Nuys (91405)
PHONE...................818 373-6896
EMP: 69
SALES (corp-wide): 160.5B **Publicly Held**
SIC: 4813 Telephone communication, except radio
HQ: At&T Corp.
1 At&T Way
Bedminster NJ 07921
800 403-3302

(P-5456)
AT&T CORP
1121 Jefferson Ave Rm 222, Redwood City
(94063-1814)
PHONE...................650 780-1005
EMP: 69
SALES (corp-wide): 160.5B **Publicly Held**
SIC: 4813 Telephone communication, except radio
HQ: At&T Corp.
1 At&T Way
Bedminster NJ 07921
800 403-3302

(P-5457)
AT&T CORP
2600 Camino Ramon, San Ramon
(94583-5000)
PHONE...................415 394-3000
Marianne Strobel, *Manager*
Kelly King, *Vice Pres*

Herb Patten, *Vice Pres*
Angie Wiskocil, *Vice Pres*
Imre Solymosi, *Associate Dir*
EMP: 200
SALES (corp-wide): 160.5B **Publicly Held**
WEB: www.swbell.com
SIC: 4813 7375 Local telephone communications; information retrieval services
HQ: At&T Corp.
1 At&T Way
Bedminster NJ 07921
800 403-3302

(P-5458)
AT&T CORP
2600 Camino Ramon, San Ramon
(94583-5000)
PHONE..................925 275-8048
Kathleen Randazo, *Manager*
Deborah Mendonca, *Administration*
Gerald Blount, *Finance*
Greg Toretta, *Sales Staff*
Sherri Khan, *Director*
EMP: 69
SALES (corp-wide): 160.5B **Publicly Held**
WEB: www.swbell.com
SIC: 4813 Telephone communication, except radio
HQ: At&T Corp.
1 At&T Way
Bedminster NJ 07921
800 403-3302

(P-5459)
AT&T CORP
2600 Camino Ramon 2w856, San Ramon
(94583-5000)
PHONE..................925 823-5388
Debbie Johnson, *Manager*
Scott Matkin, *Comp Spec*
EMP: 7650
SALES (corp-wide): 160.5B **Publicly Held**
WEB: www.att.com
SIC: 4813 Telephone communication, except radio
HQ: At&T Corp.
1 At&T Way
Bedminster NJ 07921
800 403-3302

(P-5460)
AT&T CORP
3925 E Coronado St, Anaheim
(92807-1608)
PHONE..................714 666-5504
EMP: 69
SALES (corp-wide): 160.5B **Publicly Held**
WEB: www.swbell.com
SIC: 4813 Local & long distance telephone communications
HQ: At&T Corp.
1 At&T Way
Bedminster NJ 07921
800 403-3302

(P-5461)
AT&T CORP
4130 S Market Ct, Sacramento
(95834-1222)
PHONE..................916 830-5000
Welty P Espine, *Manager*
EMP: 400
SALES (corp-wide): 160.5B **Publicly Held**
WEB: www.att.com
SIC: 4813 Local telephone communications
HQ: At&T Corp.
1 At&T Way
Bedminster NJ 07921
800 403-3302

(P-5462)
AT&T CORP
3375 Peach Ave, Clovis (93612-5617)
PHONE..................559 294-5431
EMP: 69
SALES (corp-wide): 160.5B **Publicly Held**
SIC: 4813 Telephone communication, except radio

(P-5463)
AT&T CORP
455 W 2nd St, San Bernardino
(92401-1525)
PHONE..................909 381-7729
Ken Fenton, *Manager*
John Bradley, *Manager*
EMP: 69
SALES (corp-wide): 160.5B **Publicly Held**
WEB: www.att.com
SIC: 4813 Telephone communication, except radio
HQ: At&T Corp.
1 At&T Way
Bedminster NJ 07921
800 403-3302

(P-5464)
AT&T CORP
3025 Raymond St, Santa Clara
(95054-3431)
PHONE..................408 980-2004
EMP: 69
SALES (corp-wide): 160.5B **Publicly Held**
SIC: 4813 Telephone communication, except radio
HQ: At&T Corp.
1 At&T Way
Bedminster NJ 07921
800 403-3302

(P-5465)
AT&T CORP
2105 Macdonald Ave, Richmond
(94801-3310)
PHONE..................510 965-9714
EMP: 69
SALES (corp-wide): 160.5B **Publicly Held**
WEB: www.att.com
SIC: 4813 Local & long distance telephone communications
HQ: At&T Corp.
1 At&T Way
Bedminster NJ 07921
800 403-3302

(P-5466)
AT&T CORP
625 Ellis St Ste 205, Mountain View
(94043-2223)
PHONE..................415 276-0039
Ed Trumbull, *Branch Mgr*
EMP: 69
SALES (corp-wide): 160.5B **Publicly Held**
WEB: www.att.com
SIC: 4813 Telephone communication, except radio
HQ: At&T Corp.
1 At&T Way
Bedminster NJ 07921
800 403-3302

(P-5467)
AT&T CORP
700 S Flower St Ste 810, Los Angeles
(90017-4121)
PHONE..................213 787-0055
Robert Annunziata, *President*
EMP: 80
SALES (corp-wide): 160.5B **Publicly Held**
WEB: www.att.com
SIC: 4813 Telephone communication, except radio
HQ: At&T Corp.
1 At&T Way
Bedminster NJ 07921
800 403-3302

(P-5468)
AT&T CORP
2701 Verne Roberts Cir, Antioch
(94509-7913)
PHONE..................925 776-1200
Chris Wiggin, *President*
EMP: 70

SALES (corp-wide): 160.5B **Publicly Held**
SIC: 4813 Telephone communication, except radio
HQ: At&T Corp.
1 At&T Way
Bedminster NJ 07921
800 403-3302

(P-5469)
AT&T DATACOMM LLC
16755 Von Karman Ave # 120, Irvine
(92606-4930)
PHONE..................714 675-9752
Kent Kofai, *Manager*
EMP: 50
SALES (corp-wide): 160.5B **Publicly Held**
SIC: 4813 Telephone communication, except radio
HQ: At&T Datacomm, Llc
175 E Houston St Ste 100
San Antonio TX 78205
210 821-4105

(P-5470)
AT&T SERVICES
Also Called: SBC
2 Circle E Ranch Pl, San Ramon
(94583-9134)
PHONE..................925 901-9318
William Dyer, *Branch Mgr*
EMP: 97
SALES (corp-wide): 160.5B **Publicly Held**
WEB: www.dsdllc.com
SIC: 4813 Telephone communication, except radio
HQ: At&T Services, Inc.
208 S Akard St Ste 110
Dallas TX 75202
210 821-4105

(P-5471)
AT&T SERVICES INC
Also Called: SBC
101 Broadway, San Diego (92101-5001)
PHONE..................619 515-5100
Daena Mason, *Principal*
EMP: 168
SALES (corp-wide): 160.5B **Publicly Held**
WEB: www.dsdllc.com
SIC: 4813 Telephone communication, except radio
HQ: At&T Services, Inc.
208 S Akard St Ste 110
Dallas TX 75202
210 821-4105

(P-5472)
AT&T SERVICES INC
4300 Ming Ave, Bakersfield (93309-4802)
PHONE..................661 398-2000
Charles Moe, *Branch Mgr*
EMP: 168
SALES (corp-wide): 160.5B **Publicly Held**
WEB: www.dsdllc.com
SIC: 4813 Local & long distance telephone communications
HQ: At&T Services, Inc.
208 S Akard St Ste 110
Dallas TX 75202
210 821-4105

(P-5473)
AT&T SERVICES INC
Also Called: SBC
161 Calle Del Oaks, Monterey
(93940-5701)
PHONE..................831 394-2690
Rodney Graves, *Manager*
EMP: 63
SALES (corp-wide): 160.5B **Publicly Held**
WEB: www.dsdllc.com
SIC: 4813 Telephone communication, except radio
HQ: At&T Services, Inc.
208 S Akard St Ste 110
Dallas TX 75202
210 821-4105

(P-5474)
AT&T SERVICES INC
610 Brannan St, San Francisco
(94107-1512)
PHONE..................415 545-9051
EMP: 187
SALES (corp-wide): 146.8B **Publicly Held**
SIC: 4813
HQ: At&T Services, Inc.
208 S Akard St Ste 110
Dallas TX 75202
210 821-4105

(P-5475)
AT&T SERVICES INC
Also Called: SBC
303 Church St, Jackson (95642-2103)
PHONE..................209 223-0012
Dan Adam, *Manager*
EMP: 168
SALES (corp-wide): 160.5B **Publicly Held**
WEB: www.dsdllc.com
SIC: 4813 Local telephone communications
HQ: At&T Services, Inc.
208 S Akard St Ste 110
Dallas TX 75202
210 821-4105

(P-5476)
AT&T SERVICES INC
Also Called: S B C
5555 E Olive Ave Ste A315, Fresno
(93727-2559)
PHONE..................559 454-3579
Greg Toeman, *Manager*
EMP: 270
SALES (corp-wide): 160.5B **Publicly Held**
WEB: www.dsdllc.com
SIC: 4813 Telephone communication, except radio
HQ: At&T Services, Inc.
208 S Akard St Ste 110
Dallas TX 75202
210 821-4105

(P-5477)
AT&T SERVICES INC
50101 Office Park Dr, Bakersfield (93304)
PHONE..................661 327-6030
Janice Bernette, *Manager*
EMP: 270
SALES (corp-wide): 160.5B **Publicly Held**
WEB: www.dsdllc.com
SIC: 4813 4812 Local telephone communications; radio telephone communication
HQ: At&T Services, Inc.
208 S Akard St Ste 110
Dallas TX 75202
210 821-4105

(P-5478)
AT&T SERVICES INC
Also Called: SBC
200 W Center Street Prome, Anaheim
(92805-3960)
PHONE..................210 886-4922
Heewon Lee, *Exec Dir*
Aleck Galuska, *Technical Staff*
George Warf, *Sr Project Mgr*
EMP: 168
SALES (corp-wide): 160.5B **Publicly Held**
WEB: www.dsdllc.com
SIC: 4813 Telephone communication, except radio
HQ: At&T Services, Inc.
208 S Akard St Ste 110
Dallas TX 75202
210 821-4105

(P-5479)
AT&T SERVICES INC
Also Called: SBC
7337 Trade St Rm 3600, San Diego
(92121-2423)
PHONE..................858 886-2762
John Nelson, *Manager*
Kellie Scroggins, *Info Tech Mgr*
Doug Emery, *Project Mgr*
James Jansma, *Director*
Doug Shimansky, *Director*

PRODUCTS & SVCS

EMP: 168
SALES (corp-wide): 160.5B Publicly Held
WEB: www.dsdllc.com
SIC: 4813 Telephone communication, except radio
HQ: At&T Services, Inc.
208 S Akard St Ste 110
Dallas TX 75202
210 821-4105

(P-5480)
AT&T SERVICES INC
1834 W Victoria Ave, Anaheim
(92804-2537)
P.O. Box 3644, Tustin (92781-3644)
PHONE......................714 259-4441
Glyns Falls, Manager
EMP: 168
SALES (corp-wide): 160.5B Publicly Held
WEB: www.dsdllc.com
SIC: 4813 Telephone communication, except radio
HQ: At&T Services, Inc.
208 S Akard St Ste 110
Dallas TX 75202
210 821-4105

(P-5481)
AT&T SERVICES INC
Also Called: SBC
908 28th St, Paso Robles (93446-1250)
PHONE......................805 237-9503
EMP: 168
SALES (corp-wide): 160.5B Publicly Held
WEB: www.dsdllc.com
SIC: 4813 Telephone communication, except radio
HQ: At&T Services, Inc.
208 S Akard St Ste 110
Dallas TX 75202
210 821-4105

(P-5482)
AT&T SERVICES INC
Also Called: SBC
3580 Warm St, Riverside (92501)
PHONE......................951 369-2282
EMP: 168
SALES (corp-wide): 160.5B Publicly Held
WEB: www.dsdllc.com
SIC: 4813 Telephone communication, except radio
HQ: At&T Services, Inc.
208 S Akard St Ste 110
Dallas TX 75202
210 821-4105

(P-5483)
AT&T SERVICES INC
Also Called: S B C
787 Munras Ave, Monterey (93940-3128)
PHONE......................831 649-2029
Carlime Plummer, General Mgr
Klyde Aipoalani, Manager
EMP: 66
SALES (corp-wide): 160.5B Publicly Held
WEB: www.dsdllc.com
SIC: 4813 Local telephone communications
HQ: At&T Services, Inc.
208 S Akard St Ste 110
Dallas TX 75202
210 821-4105

(P-5484)
AT&T SERVICES INC
Also Called: SBC
360 Pioneer Way, Mountain View
(94041-1506)
PHONE......................650 960-2255
Nancy Cruz, Manager
EMP: 153
SALES (corp-wide): 160.5B Publicly Held
WEB: www.dsdllc.com
SIC: 4813 Telephone communication, except radio
HQ: At&T Services, Inc.
208 S Akard St Ste 110
Dallas TX 75202
210 821-4105

(P-5485)
AT&T SERVICES INC
3464 El Camino Ave, Sacramento
(95821-6310)
P.O. Box 15038 (95851-0038)
PHONE......................916 972-2248
Ed Widker, Manager
EMP: 168
SALES (corp-wide): 160.5B Publicly Held
WEB: www.dsdllc.com
SIC: 4813 Telephone communication, except radio
HQ: At&T Services, Inc.
208 S Akard St Ste 110
Dallas TX 75202
210 821-4105

(P-5486)
AT&T SERVICES INC
Also Called: SBC
3280 E Foothill Blvd, Pasadena
(91107-3103)
PHONE......................626 578-4168
Steve Kawa, Manager
Melissa Miranda, Manager
EMP: 90
SALES (corp-wide): 160.5B Publicly Held
WEB: www.dsdllc.com
SIC: 4813 6512 Long distance telephone communications; bank building operation
HQ: At&T Services, Inc.
208 S Akard St Ste 110
Dallas TX 75202
210 821-4105

(P-5487)
AT&T SERVICES INC
Also Called: SBC
1010 Wilshire Blvd, Los Angeles
(90017-5662)
PHONE......................213 975-4089
Cathy Bazieto, Branch Mgr
John Concklin, Program Mgr
EMP: 720
SALES (corp-wide): 160.5B Publicly Held
WEB: www.dsdllc.com
SIC: 4813 2741 7331 4812 Local & long distance telephone communications; local telephone communications; directories, telephone: publishing only, not printed on site; direct mail advertising services; radio telephone communication
HQ: At&T Services, Inc.
208 S Akard St Ste 110
Dallas TX 75202
210 821-4105

(P-5488)
AT&T SERVICES INC
2600 Camino Ramon 2e750ll, San Ramon
(94583-5000)
PHONE......................925 823-1443
Mark Fishler, Branch Mgr
EMP: 2700
SALES (corp-wide): 160.5B Publicly Held
WEB: www.dsdllc.com
SIC: 4813 Telephone communication, except radio
HQ: At&T Services, Inc.
208 S Akard St Ste 110
Dallas TX 75202
210 821-4105

(P-5489)
AT&T SERVICES INC
666 Folsom St Rm 1132, San Francisco
(94107-1397)
PHONE......................415 545-9058
EMP: 90
SALES (corp-wide): 160.5B Publicly Held
SIC: 4813 4812
HQ: At&T Services, Inc.
208 S Akard St Ste 110
Dallas TX 75202
210 821-4105

(P-5490)
AT&T SERVICES INC
1270 Arroyo Way, Walnut Creek
(94596-4216)
PHONE......................510 836-6889

Bill Blase, Manager
Robert C Wiles, Analyst
Robert Bailey, Consultant
EMP: 270
SALES (corp-wide): 160.5B Publicly Held
WEB: www.dsdllc.com
SIC: 4813 7375 4812 Telephone communication, except radio; information retrieval services; radio telephone communication
HQ: At&T Services, Inc.
208 S Akard St Ste 110
Dallas TX 75202
210 821-4105

(P-5491)
AT&T SERVICES INC
Also Called: SBC Communications
2615 Mercantile Dr, Rancho Cordova
(95742-6521)
PHONE......................916 638-6096
Scott Heiser, Manager
EMP: 180
SALES (corp-wide): 160.5B Publicly Held
WEB: www.dsdllc.com
SIC: 4813 1542 Telephone communication, except radio; nonresidential construction
HQ: At&T Services, Inc.
208 S Akard St Ste 110
Dallas TX 75202
210 821-4105

(P-5492)
AT&T SERVICES INC
Also Called: SBC
2125 Occidental Rd, Santa Rosa
(95401-9034)
PHONE......................707 545-5000
Curtis Cavin, Manager
Dale Graves, Consultant
EMP: 180
SALES (corp-wide): 160.5B Publicly Held
WEB: www.dsdllc.com
SIC: 4813 4812 Local telephone communications; radio telephone communication
HQ: At&T Services, Inc.
208 S Akard St Ste 110
Dallas TX 75202
210 821-4105

(P-5493)
AT&T SERVICES INC
1480 Burlingame Ave, Burlingame
(94010-4111)
PHONE......................650 579-5266
Sally Calvert, Branch Mgr
EMP: 168
SALES (corp-wide): 160.5B Publicly Held
WEB: www.dsdllc.com
SIC: 4813 Local telephone communications
HQ: At&T Services, Inc.
208 S Akard St Ste 110
Dallas TX 75202
210 821-4105

(P-5494)
AT&T SERVICES INC
1122 Western St, Fairfield (94533-2459)
PHONE......................707 428-2512
Carl Alexander, Branch Mgr
EMP: 450
SALES (corp-wide): 160.5B Publicly Held
WEB: www.dsdllc.com
SIC: 4813 Local telephone communications
HQ: At&T Services, Inc.
208 S Akard St Ste 110
Dallas TX 75202
210 821-4105

(P-5495)
AT&T SERVICES INC
Also Called: SBC
1900 S Grand Ave Rm 100, Los Angeles
(90007-1436)
PHONE......................213 741-3111
Al Hernandez, Branch Mgr
EMP: 50

SALES (corp-wide): 160.5B Publicly Held
WEB: www.dsdllc.com
SIC: 4813 Local telephone communications
HQ: At&T Services, Inc.
208 S Akard St Ste 110
Dallas TX 75202
210 821-4105

(P-5496)
AT&T SERVICES INC
Also Called: SBC
485 S Monroe St 13a, San Jose (95128)
PHONE......................408 554-3335
EMP: 168
SALES (corp-wide): 160.5B Publicly Held
SIC: 4813
HQ: At&T Services, Inc.
208 S Akard St Ste 110
Dallas TX 75202
210 821-4105

(P-5497)
AT&T SERVICES INC
Also Called: SBC
140 New Montgomery St, San Francisco
(94105-3705)
PHONE......................415 394-3000
Ed Mueller, President
Michael J Fitzpatrick, President
L N Causby,
Steven P Coger,
Ruth Dev,
EMP: 270
SALES (corp-wide): 160.5B Publicly Held
WEB: www.dsdllc.com
SIC: 4813 2741 Local & long distance telephone communications; directories, telephone: publishing only, not printed on site
HQ: At&T Services, Inc.
208 S Akard St Ste 110
Dallas TX 75202
210 821-4105

(P-5498)
AT&T SERVICES INC
Also Called: SBC
44900 Industrial Dr, Fremont (94538-6435)
PHONE......................510 791-6605
Bob Alex, General Mgr
EMP: 54
SALES (corp-wide): 160.5B Publicly Held
WEB: www.dsdllc.com
SIC: 4813 Local telephone communications
HQ: At&T Services, Inc.
208 S Akard St Ste 110
Dallas TX 75202
210 821-4105

(P-5499)
AT&T SERVICES INC
146 S Broadway, Escondido (92025-4239)
PHONE......................760 489-3519
EMP: 168
SALES (corp-wide): 160.5B Publicly Held
WEB: www.dsdllc.com
SIC: 4813 Local telephone communications
HQ: At&T Services, Inc.
208 S Akard St Ste 110
Dallas TX 75202
210 821-4105

(P-5500)
AT&T SERVICES INC
Also Called: SBC
8925 Orangethorpe Ave, Buena Park
(90621-3716)
PHONE......................714 992-3359
Pat Gonzalez, Systems Analyst
Mike Matrese, Systems Analyst
EMP: 89

▲ = Import ▼=Export
◆ =Import/Export

SALES (corp-wide): 160.5B **Publicly Held**
WEB: www.dsdllc.com
SIC: 4813 2741 4822 7331 Local & long distance telephone communications; local telephone communications; voice telephone communications; data telephone communications; directories, telephone: publishing only, not printed on site; telegraph & other communications; electronic mail; direct mail advertising services; radio telephone communication
HQ: At&T Services, Inc.
208 S Akard St Ste 110
Dallas TX 75202
210 821-4105

(P-5501)
AT&T SERVICES INC
Also Called: SBC
1714 Colfax St Ste 300, Concord
(94520-2134)
PHONE.....................925 671-1902
Jennifer Sullivan, *Manager*
EMP: 90
SALES (corp-wide): 160.5B **Publicly Held**
WEB: www.dsdllc.com
SIC: 4813 4812 Local telephone communications; radio telephone communication
HQ: At&T Services, Inc.
208 S Akard St Ste 110
Dallas TX 75202
210 821-4105

(P-5502)
AT&T SERVICES INC
2345 Pine St, San Francisco (94115-2714)
PHONE.....................415 774-1957
Robert L Miller, *Branch Mgr*
EMP: 168
SALES (corp-wide): 160.5B **Publicly Held**
WEB: www.dsdllc.com
SIC: 4813 Local telephone communications
HQ: At&T Services, Inc.
208 S Akard St Ste 110
Dallas TX 75202
210 821-4105

(P-5503)
AT&T SERVICES INC
7701 Artesia Blvd, Buena Park
(90621-2313)
PHONE.....................510 732-0830
Scott Shelly, *Director*
EMP: 168
SALES (corp-wide): 160.5B **Publicly Held**
WEB: www.dsdllc.com
SIC: 4813 Local & long distance telephone communications
HQ: At&T Services, Inc.
208 S Akard St Ste 110
Dallas TX 75202
210 821-4105

(P-5504)
AT&T SERVICES INC
Also Called: SBC
1821 24th St Rm 122, Sacramento
(95816-7208)
PHONE.....................916 453-6267
Steven Solis, *Principal*
EMP: 69
SALES (corp-wide): 160.5B **Publicly Held**
WEB: www.dsdllc.com
SIC: 4813 Local & long distance telephone communications
HQ: At&T Services, Inc.
208 S Akard St Ste 110
Dallas TX 75202
210 821-4105

(P-5505)
AT&T SERVICES INC
Also Called: SBC
2727 Oceanside Blvd, Oceanside
(92054-4542)
PHONE.....................760 722-7261
Daniel Menendez, *Manager*
EMP: 168

SALES (corp-wide): 160.5B **Publicly Held**
WEB: www.dsdllc.com
SIC: 4813 Local telephone communications
HQ: At&T Services, Inc.
208 S Akard St Ste 110
Dallas TX 75202
210 821-4105

(P-5506)
AT&T SERVICES INC
Also Called: SBC
3707 Kings Way, Sacramento
(95821-6405)
PHONE.....................916 972-2423
Hector Lenaos, *Manager*
Jonathan Yee, *Sr Project Mgr*
EMP: 114
SALES (corp-wide): 160.5B **Publicly Held**
WEB: www.dsdllc.com
SIC: 4813 4812 Telephone communication, except radio; radio telephone communication
HQ: At&T Services, Inc.
208 S Akard St Ste 110
Dallas TX 75202
210 821-4105

(P-5507)
AT&T SERVICES INC
Also Called: SBC
1033 Shary Cir Ste A, Concord
(94518-2469)
PHONE.....................925 671-1059
EMP: 450
SQ FT: 15,600
SALES (corp-wide): 160.5B **Publicly Held**
WEB: www.dsdllc.com
SIC: 4813 4812 Local & long distance telephone communications; radio telephone communication
HQ: At&T Services, Inc.
208 S Akard St Ste 110
Dallas TX 75202
210 821-4105

(P-5508)
AT&T SERVICES INC
Also Called: SBC
7650 Convoy Ct Ste 106, San Diego
(92111-1104)
PHONE.....................858 495-3907
Pattie St Clair, *Branch Mgr*
EMP: 450
SALES (corp-wide): 160.5B **Publicly Held**
WEB: www.dsdllc.com
SIC: 4813 4812 Local & long distance telephone communications; local telephone communications; radio telephone communication
HQ: At&T Services, Inc.
208 S Akard St Ste 110
Dallas TX 75202
210 821-4105

(P-5509)
AT&T SERVICES INC
Also Called: SBC
950 W Washington Ave, Escondido
(92025-1637)
PHONE.....................760 489-3187
George Rivera, *Principal*
EMP: 450
SALES (corp-wide): 160.5B **Publicly Held**
WEB: www.dsdllc.com
SIC: 4813 2741 4822 7331 Local & long distance telephone communications; local telephone communications; voice telephone communications; data telephone communications; directories, telephone: publishing only, not printed on site; telegraph & other communications; electronic mail; direct mail advertising services; radio telephone communication
HQ: At&T Services, Inc.
208 S Akard St Ste 110
Dallas TX 75202
210 821-4105

(P-5510)
AT&T SERVICES INC
1755 Locust St Fl 2, Walnut Creek
(94596-4120)
PHONE.....................925 943-4383
Timothy Bayliss, *Manager*
EMP: 450
SALES (corp-wide): 160.5B **Publicly Held**
WEB: www.dsdllc.com
SIC: 4813 Telephone communication, except radio
HQ: At&T Services, Inc.
208 S Akard St Ste 110
Dallas TX 75202
210 821-4105

(P-5511)
AT&T SERVICES INC
1429 N Gower St, Los Angeles
(90028-8317)
PHONE.....................323 468-6813
Dovon Green, *Branch Mgr*
EMP: 450
SALES (corp-wide): 160.5B **Publicly Held**
WEB: www.dsdllc.com
SIC: 4813 Local telephone communications
HQ: At&T Services, Inc.
208 S Akard St Ste 110
Dallas TX 75202
210 821-4105

(P-5512)
AT&T SERVICES INC
Also Called: SBC
501 S Marengo Ave, Alhambra
(91803-1640)
PHONE.....................626 308-8582
Ed Mueller, *CEO*
EMP: 450
SALES (corp-wide): 160.5B **Publicly Held**
WEB: www.dsdllc.com
SIC: 4813 4812 Local telephone communications; radio telephone communication
HQ: At&T Services, Inc.
208 S Akard St Ste 110
Dallas TX 75202
210 821-4105

(P-5513)
AT&T SERVICES INC
2600 Camino Ramon Rm 1-E, San Ramon
(94583-5000)
PHONE.....................415 823-0993
Greg Torretta, *Exec Dir*
Sophia Chang,
EMP: 168
SALES (corp-wide): 160.5B **Publicly Held**
WEB: www.dsdllc.com
SIC: 4813 Local telephone communications
HQ: At&T Services, Inc.
208 S Akard St Ste 110
Dallas TX 75202
210 821-4105

(P-5514)
AT&T SERVICES INC
504 C 1550, Oakland (94612)
PHONE.....................510 645-7684
Paul Burke, *Branch Mgr*
EMP: 168
SALES (corp-wide): 160.5B **Publicly Held**
WEB: www.dsdllc.com
SIC: 4813 Local telephone communications
HQ: At&T Services, Inc.
208 S Akard St Ste 110
Dallas TX 75202
210 821-4105

(P-5515)
AT&T SERVICES INC
Also Called: SBC
5285 Doyle Rd Rm 3, San Jose
(95129-4230)
PHONE.....................408 973-7504
Art Sebantis, *Manager*
EMP: 168

SALES (corp-wide): 160.5B **Publicly Held**
WEB: www.dsdllc.com
SIC: 4813 Telephone communication, except radio
HQ: At&T Services, Inc.
208 S Akard St Ste 110
Dallas TX 75202
210 821-4105

(P-5516)
AT&T SERVICES INC
Also Called: SBC
1587 Franklin St Rm 1353, Oakland
(94612-2803)
PHONE.....................510 645-4507
Scott Dial, *Manager*
EMP: 168
SALES (corp-wide): 160.5B **Publicly Held**
WEB: www.dsdllc.com
SIC: 4813 Local telephone communications
HQ: At&T Services, Inc.
208 S Akard St Ste 110
Dallas TX 75202
210 821-4105

(P-5517)
AT&T SERVICES INC
3900 Channel Dr, West Sacramento
(95691-3432)
PHONE.....................916 376-2006
Richard Cronan, *Branch Mgr*
Will Venlos, *Business Mgr*
EMP: 168
SALES (corp-wide): 160.5B **Publicly Held**
WEB: www.dsdllc.com
SIC: 4813 Telephone communication, except radio
HQ: At&T Services, Inc.
208 S Akard St Ste 110
Dallas TX 75202
210 821-4105

(P-5518)
AUTOMATTIC INC
60 29th St Ste 343, San Francisco
(94110-4929)
PHONE.....................877 273-3049
Mattew Mullenweg, *CEO*
Stuart West, *CFO*
Paul Maiorana, *Vice Pres*
MO Carter, *Executive*
Toni Schneider, *Admin Sec*
EMP: 62
SALES (est): 16.8MM **Privately Held**
SIC: 4813 7375   ; information retrieval services; data base information retrieval; on-line data base information retrieval

(P-5519)
AVAYA INC
18201 Von Karman Ave # 600, Irvine
(92612-1176)
PHONE.....................949 225-5678
Marci Mobely, *Principal*
Brandon Reed, *Software Engr*
EMP: 111 **Publicly Held**
WEB: www.avaya.com
SIC: 4813
HQ: Avaya Inc.
4655 Great America Pkwy
Santa Clara CA 95054
908 953-6000

(P-5520)
AXAIO INDUSTRIES LLC
538 S Oxford Ave Apt 302, Los Angeles
(90020-4288)
PHONE.....................323 504-1074
An Arafat Abir,
EMP: 50
SALES (est): 555.1K **Privately Held**
SIC: 4813

(P-5521)
BAID VIVEK
Also Called: Bizringer.com
2335 Irvine Ave, Newport Beach
(92660-3410)
PHONE.....................888 550-8553
Vivek Baid, *Owner*
EMP: 75 **EST:** 2013

SALES (est): 1.7MM **Privately Held**
SIC: 4813 7389 Telephone communication, except radio;

(P-5522)
BLUE CASA COMMUNICATIONS INC
114 E Haley St Ste A, Santa Barbara (93101-2347)
PHONE..............................805 966-1669
Donald N Oas, *CEO*
Brian Plackischeng, *CFO*
Nancy Ford, *Accounting Mgr*
EMP: 50
SALES (est): 5.2MM **Privately Held**
WEB: www.bluecasa.com
SIC: 4813 Telephone communications broker

(P-5523)
BRIGHTERTECH INCORPORATED
510 Strtford Ct Unit 204a, Del Mar (92014)
PHONE..............................310 909-4940
Thomas Gonzales, *President*
EMP: 50
SALES (est): 351K **Privately Held**
SIC: 4813

(P-5524)
BROADSPIRE INC
19425 Soled Canyo Rd Ste, Santa Clarita (91351)
PHONE..............................213 785-8043
Suresh Srinivasan, *CEO*
Arun Srinivasan, *COO*
Matt Hughes, *Manager*
EMP: 65 **EST:** 2000
SALES (est): 4.7MM **Privately Held**
WEB: www.broadspire.com
SIC: 4813
PA: Platinum Equity, Llc
360 N Crescent Dr Bldg S
Beverly Hills CA 90210

(P-5525)
CAL CONSOLDATED COMMUNICATIONS
211 Lincoln St, Roseville (95678-2614)
PHONE..............................916 786-6141
Bob Udell, *CEO*
EMP: 78 **EST:** 1914
SQ FT: 21,500
SALES (est): 7.6MM
SALES (corp-wide): 1B **Publicly Held**
SIC: 4813 Local telephone communications; long distance telephone communications
HQ: Surewest Communications
211 Lincoln St
Roseville CA 95678
916 786-6141

(P-5526)
CALIFRNIA RGIONAL INTRANET INC
Also Called: Carinet
8929 Complex Dr Ste A, San Diego (92123-1454)
PHONE..............................858 974-5080
Tim Caulfield, *CEO*
Michael C Robert, *CFO*
Joe McMillen, *Principal*
EMP: 85
SQ FT: 40,000
SALES (est): 16.8MM **Privately Held**
WEB: www.cari.net
SIC: 4813

(P-5527)
CAMPUS EXPLORER INC
2850 Ocean Park Blvd # 310, Santa Monica (90405-6208)
PHONE..............................310 574-2243
Jerry Slavonia, *CEO*
Stephen Caldwell, *Vice Pres*
Brian Hartnack, *Vice Pres*
Nick Roberts, *Vice Pres*
John Van Fleet, *Vice Pres*
EMP: 54
SQ FT: 8,000
SALES (est): 11.3MM **Privately Held**
WEB: www.campusexplorer.com
SIC: 4813

(P-5528)
CBS MAXPREPS INC
4364 Town Center Blvd # 320, El Dorado Hills (95762-7127)
PHONE..............................530 676-6440
Andy Beal, *President*
Deborah Finneran, *Office Mgr*
Bryce Escobar, *Project Mgr*
Todd Shurtleff, *Director*
Michelle Gaudy, *Assistant*
EMP: 50
SQ FT: 9,000
SALES (est): 8.5MM
SALES (corp-wide): 13.7B **Publicly Held**
WEB: www.maxpreps.com
SIC: 4813
HQ: Cbs Corporation
51 W 52nd St Bsmt 1
New York NY 10019
212 975-4321

(P-5529)
CDNETWORKS INC (DH)
1919 S Bascom Ave Ste 600, Campbell (95008-2220)
PHONE..............................408 228-3379
Jongchan Kim, *CEO*
John J Kang, *President*
Samuyeol Ko, *President*
EMP: 55
SALES (est): 19.9MM
SALES (corp-wide): 810.8MM **Privately Held**
SIC: 4813
HQ: Cdnetworks Co., Ltd.
37 Teheran-Ro 8-Gil, Gangnam-Gu
Seoul 06239
822 344-1040

(P-5530)
CHANNEL INTELLIGENCE INC (DH)
1600 Amphitheatre Pkwy, Mountain View (94043-1351)
PHONE..............................321 939-5600
Doug Alexander, *CEO*
Robert Wight, *Ch of Bd*
Michael Evanoff, *CFO*
Frank Lane, *Officer*
EMP: 90
SALES (est): 23.2MM
SALES (corp-wide): 110.8B **Publicly Held**
WEB: www.channelintelligence.com
SIC: 4813 ; ; ;
HQ: Google Llc
1600 Amphitheatre Pkwy
Mountain View CA 94043
650 253-0000

(P-5531)
CLEAR WORLD COMMUNICATIONS
3100 S Harbor Blvd # 300, Santa Ana (92704-6823)
PHONE..............................714 445-3900
Mike Mancuso, *President*
James Mancuso, *Admin Sec*
EMP: 450
SQ FT: 10,000
SALES (est): 27.7MM **Privately Held**
SIC: 4813

(P-5532)
CLEARCAPTIONS LLC
3001 Lava Ridge Ct # 100, Roseville (95661-2837)
PHONE..............................866 868-8695
Robert Rae, *President*
Corrine Perritano, *COO*
Rita Beier Braman, *Vice Pres*
Gordon L Ellis, *Vice Pres*
Blaine Reeve, *CTO*
EMP: 50 **EST:** 2015
SALES (est): 2.8MM
SALES (corp-wide): 216.8MM **Privately Held**
SIC: 4813 ; telephone/video communications
PA: Purple Communications, Inc.
595 Menlo Dr
Rocklin CA 95765
888 600-4780

(P-5533)
CLOVER NETWORK INC
415 N Mathilda Ave, Sunnyvale (94085-4222)
PHONE..............................650 210-7888
Leonard Speiser, *CEO*
Zan Aronowitz, *COO*
John Beatty, *Vice Pres*
Vincent Durieux, *Vice Pres*
Ronnie Mongon, *Vice Pres*
EMP: 65
SQ FT: 8,200
SALES (est): 9.8MM **Privately Held**
WEB: www.clover.com
SIC: 4813

(P-5534)
COFA MEDIA GROUP LLC
5650 El Camino Real, Carlsbad (92008-7124)
PHONE..............................877 293-2007
Edwin Lap, *CEO*
EMP: 86 **EST:** 2009
SALES (est): 224K
SALES (corp-wide): 71.7MM **Privately Held**
SIC: 4813
PA: Geary Lsf Group, Inc.
332 Pine St Ste 600
San Francisco CA 94104
877 616-8226

(P-5535)
COMPUTER CONSULTING (PA)
600 Corporate Pointe # 1010, Culver City (90230-7677)
PHONE..............................310 568-5000
Brian Hardy, *President*
Shirley Franklin, *Vice Pres*
EMP: 2000
SQ FT: 20,000
SALES (est): 338.3MM **Privately Held**
WEB: www.ccops.com
SIC: 4813 4899 5045 7378 Telephone communication, except radio; data communication services; computers, peripherals & software; computer maintenance & repair

(P-5536)
CONDUIT INC
180 Sansome St 18, San Francisco (94104-3713)
PHONE..............................650 340-1550
Ronen Shilo, *CEO*
Adam Boyden, *President*
Gaby Bilczyk, *COO*
Roy Gen, *CFO*
Dror Erez, *CTO*
EMP: 200
SALES (est): 9.3MM **Privately Held**
SIC: 4813

(P-5537)
CONNEXITY INC (HQ)
Also Called: Shopzilla.com
2120 Colorado Ave Ste 400, Santa Monica (90404-3563)
PHONE..............................310 571-1235
William Glass, *CEO*
Aaron Young, *CFO*
Blythe Holden, *Senior VP*
Lonna Bell Rimestad, *Senior VP*
Niladri Batabyal, *Vice Pres*
EMP: 203
SALES (est): 123.9MM
SALES (corp-wide): 569.5MM **Privately Held**
WEB: www.shopzilla.com
SIC: 4813 7383 7331 ; news syndicates; direct mail advertising services
PA: Symphony Technology Group, L.L.C.
428 University Ave
Palo Alto CA 94301
650 935-9500

(P-5538)
CONTENT GURU INC
1901 S Bascom Ave # 1100, Campbell (95008-2215)
PHONE..............................408 559-3988
Madeleine Keenan, *President*
EMP: 60
SALES (est): 905K **Privately Held**
SIC: 4813 Telephone communication, except radio

(P-5539)
COX CALIFORNIA TELCOM LLC
43 Peninsula Ctr, Rllng HLS Est (90274-3583)
PHONE..............................310 377-1800
Paul Fornelli, *Branch Mgr*
Katherine Paezle Harris, *Manager*
EMP: 85
SALES (corp-wide): 32.8B **Privately Held**
SIC: 4813 Telephone communication, except radio
HQ: Cox California Telcom, L.L.C.
6205-B Pchtree Dnwoody Rd
Atlanta GA 30328

(P-5540)
COX COMMUNICATIONS INC
26181 Avenida Aeropuerto, San Juan Capistrano (92675-4821)
PHONE..............................949 240-1212
Leo Brennan, *Branch Mgr*
EMP: 250
SALES (corp-wide): 32.8B **Privately Held**
SIC: 4813 Telephone communication, except radio
HQ: Cox Communications, Inc.
6205 B Pchtree Dunwody Ne
Atlanta GA 30328

(P-5541)
CREDO MOBILE INC
Also Called: Working Assets Long Distance
101 Market St Ste 700, San Francisco (94105-1533)
P.O. Box 7015 (94120-7015)
PHONE..............................415 369-2000
Michael Hall Kieschnick, *CEO*
Janice Crump, *CFO*
Douglas Moore, *CFO*
Stephen Gunn, *Vice Pres*
Haruko Kurata, *Vice Pres*
EMP: 100
SQ FT: 21,000
SALES (est): 24.9MM **Privately Held**
WEB: www.giveforchange.com
SIC: 4813 Long distance telephone communications

(P-5542)
CURATEL LLC
1605 W Olympic Blvd # 600, Los Angeles (90015-3808)
PHONE..............................213 427-7411
Ron Sahar Azarkman,
Jerry Azarkman,
EMP: 300
SALES (est): 13.5MM **Privately Held**
WEB: www.curatel.com
SIC: 4813 Local & long distance telephone communications

(P-5543)
DANGER INC
3101 Park Blvd, Palo Alto (94306-2233)
PHONE..............................650 323-9700
Hank Nothhaft, *Ch of Bd*
Andy Rubin, *President*
Nancy Hilker, *CFO*
Joe Britt, *Senior VP*
Les Hamilton, *Senior VP*
▲ **EMP:** 135
SALES (est): 7.8MM
SALES (corp-wide): 110.3B **Publicly Held**
WEB: www.danger.com
SIC: 4813 Telephone communication, except radio
PA: Microsoft Corporation
1 Microsoft Way
Redmond WA 98052
425 882-8080

(P-5544)
DAVIS ZIFF PUBLISHING INC
235 2nd St, San Francisco (94105-3124)
PHONE..............................415 551-4800
Kenneth Evans, *Principal*
EMP: 150
SALES (corp-wide): 1.1B **Publicly Held**
WEB: www.zdnet.com
SIC: 4813

▲ = Import ▼=Export
◆ =Import/Export

HQ: Ziff Davis Publishing, Llc
28 E 28th St Fl 10
New York NY 10016

(P-5545)
DEVXCOM INC
Also Called: Development Exchange
310 Villa St, Mountain View (94041-1321)
PHONE...............................650 390-6553
James E Fawcette, *President*
Peter Horan, *CEO*
Jim Cook, *COO*
Greg Stern, *Vice Pres*
EMP: 50
SALES (est): 1.7MM **Privately Held**
SIC: 4813

(P-5546)
DIGEX INC
2950 Zanker Rd, San Jose (95134-2113)
PHONE...............................408 468-5000
Benjamin Yang, *Principal*
EMP: 50
SALES (corp-wide): 126B **Publicly Held**
WEB: www.digex.com
SIC: 4813
HQ: Digex, Incorporated
14400 Sweitzer Ln
Laurel MD 20707

(P-5547)
DIGITAL PATH INC
1065 Marauder St, Chico (95973-9039)
PHONE...............................800 676-7284
James A Higgins, *President*
Erica Higgins, *CFO*
Brock Eastman, *VP Engrg*
▲ EMP: 50
SALES (est): 20.1MM **Privately Held**
WEB: www.digitalpath.net
SIC: 4813 5045 ; ; computers, peripherals
& software

(P-5548)
DIGITALMOJO INC (PA)
3111 Camino Del Rio N # 400, San Diego
(92108-5724)
PHONE...............................800 413-5916
Martin Smith, *CEO*
Martin Caverly, *CFO*
Jerry Papazian, *CFO*
Omar Cruz, *Vice Pres*
Michael Hart, *Vice Pres*
EMP: 75
SQ FT: 800
SALES (est): 3.9MM **Privately Held**
WEB: www.gobroadband.com
SIC: 4813 8742 ; marketing consulting
services

(P-5549)
DIVERSFIED CMMNCTIONS SVCS INC
Also Called: D C S
1260 Pioneer St, Brea (92821-3725)
PHONE...............................562 696-9660
Ken Doll, *President*
Steven Hurley, *Vice Pres*
Bill Shields, *Vice Pres*
▲ EMP: 63 EST: 1972
SQ FT: 19,000
SALES (est): 20.1MM **Privately Held**
WEB: www.diversified.net
SIC: 4813 Telephone communications bro-
ker

(P-5550)
DOCIRCLE INC
Also Called: Trumpia
2544 W Woodland Dr, Anaheim
(92801-2636)
PHONE...............................415 484-4221
Kyung Hoon Rhie, *CEO*
Tim Nguyen, *Sales Staff*
Kevin Yan, *Manager*
EMP: 50
SALES: 8MM **Privately Held**
SIC: 4813

(P-5551)
DROPCAR INC
521 Railroad Ave, Suisun City
(94585-4244)
PHONE...............................707 421-1300

EMP: 62
SALES (corp-wide): 22.4MM **Publicly
Held**
SIC: 4813 Telephone communication, ex-
cept radio
PA: Dropcar, Inc.
1412 Broadway Ste 2105
New York NY 10018
646 342-1595

(P-5552)
ECOMPANIES LLC
2120 Colorado Ave Fl 3, Santa Monica
(90404-5510)
PHONE...............................310 586-4000
Jake Winebaum,
Sky Dayton,
EMP: 50
SALES: 38.2K **Privately Held**
WEB: www.ecompanies.com
SIC: 4813

(P-5553)
EDGEWATER NETWORKS INC
5225 Hellyer Ave Ste 100, San Jose
(95138-1021)
PHONE...............................408 351-7200
David G Norman, *CEO*
Steve Pattison, *COO*
John Macario, *Senior VP*
Rumus Sakya, *Senior VP*
▲ EMP: 75
SALES (est): 17.9MM
SALES (corp-wide): 612.7MM **Publicly
Held**
WEB: www.edgewaternetworks.com
SIC: 4813 Telephone/video communica-
tions
PA: Ribbon Communications Inc.
4 Technology Park Dr
Westford MA 01886
978 614-8100

(P-5554)
ENVIVIO INC
535 Mission St Fl 27, San Francisco
(94105-3224)
PHONE...............................650 243-2700
Julien Signes, *President*
Terry D Kramer, *Ch of Bd*
Erik E Miller, *CFO*
Jean-Pierre Henot, *CTO*
EMP: 163
SALES (est): 41.5MM
SALES (corp-wide): 23.8B **Privately Held**
WEB: www.envivio.com
SIC: 4813 Telephone/video communica-
tions
HQ: Ericsson Inc.
6300 Legacy Dr
Plano TX 75024
972 583-0000

(P-5555)
ERICSSON INC
2755 Augustine Dr, Santa Clara
(95054-2919)
PHONE...............................408 750-5000
Kevin A Denuccio, *Manager*
EMP: 1100
SALES (corp-wide): 23.8B **Privately Held**
WEB: www.redbacknetworks.com
SIC: 4813 Telephone communication, ex-
cept radio
HQ: Ericsson Inc.
6300 Legacy Dr
Plano TX 75024
972 583-0000

(P-5556)
EVERETT BASHAM
Also Called: Labrent.com
3567 Benton St Ste 300, Santa Clara
(95051-4404)
PHONE...............................408 261-3000
Everett Basham, *Owner*
Joe Reid, *CFO*
EMP: 99
SQ FT: 4,060
SALES (est): 2.1MM **Privately Held**
SIC: 4813 Telephone communication, ex-
cept radio

(P-5557)
EVERNOTE CORPORATION (PA)
Also Called: Skitch
305 Walnut St, Redwood City
(94063-1731)
PHONE...............................650 216-7700
Chris O'Neill, *CEO*
Norman Happ, *Partner*
Linda Kozlowski, *COO*
Jeff Shotts, *CFO*
Hitoshi Hokamura, *Chairman*
▲ EMP: 63 EST: 2004
SALES (est): 151.3MM **Privately Held**
SIC: 4813

(P-5558)
EXTREME TELECOM INC
9221 Corbin Ave Ste 260, Northridge
(91324-1625)
PHONE...............................818 902-4821
ARI Ramezani, *CEO*
James Murphy, *President*
EMP: 113 EST: 1997
SQ FT: 12,000
SALES (est): 5.4MM **Privately Held**
SIC: 4813

(P-5559)
FLEXTRONICS INTL USA INC
Also Called: Flextronics Global Services
890 Yosemite Dr Bldg 14, Milpitas
(95035-5437)
PHONE...............................408 576-6769
Mike McNamara, *Principal*
EMP: 170
SALES (corp-wide): 23.8B **Privately Held**
SIC: 4813 Telephone communication, ex-
cept radio
HQ: Flextronics International Usa, Inc.
6201 America Center Dr
San Jose CA 95002

(P-5560)
FREE CONFERENCING CORPORATION
Also Called: Freeconferencecall.com
4300 E Pacific Coast Hwy, Long Beach
(90804-2114)
P.O. Box 41069 (90853-1069)
PHONE...............................562 437-1411
David Erickson, *CEO*
Josh Lowenthal, *COO*
Scott Southron, *CFO*
Robert Wise, *Exec VP*
Jeff Erickson, *Vice Pres*
EMP: 116
SQ FT: 10,000
SALES: 65MM **Privately Held**
SIC: 4813 7389 ; Voice telephone commu-
nications;

(P-5561)
FRONTIER CALIFORNIA INC
Also Called: Verizon
83793 Dr Carreon Blvd, Indio
(92201-7035)
PHONE...............................760 342-0500
EMP: 64
SALES (corp-wide): 9.1B **Publicly Held**
SIC: 4813 Local & long distance telephone
communications
HQ: Frontier California Inc.
140 West St
New York NY 10007
212 395-1000

(P-5562)
FRONTIER CALIFORNIA INC
Also Called: Verizon
200 W Church St, Santa Maria
(93458-5005)
PHONE...............................805 925-0000
Carrie Ramsey, *Manager*
EMP: 64
SALES (corp-wide): 9.1B **Publicly Held**
SIC: 4813 Long distance telephone com-
munications
HQ: Frontier California Inc.
140 West St
New York NY 10007
212 395-1000

(P-5563)
FRONTIER CALIFORNIA INC
Also Called: Verizon
135 Cozy Ln, Barstow (92311-2238)
PHONE...............................760 256-3511
Frank Herrera, *Branch Mgr*
EMP: 55
SALES (corp-wide): 9.1B **Publicly Held**
SIC: 4813 Telephone communication, ex-
cept radio
HQ: Frontier California Inc.
140 West St
New York NY 10007
212 395-1000

(P-5564)
FRONTIER CALIFORNIA INC
Also Called: Verizon
510 Park Ave, San Fernando (91340-2527)
PHONE...............................818 365-0542
Gloria Caudill, *Branch Mgr*
EMP: 150
SALES (corp-wide): 9.1B **Publicly Held**
SIC: 4813 Telephone communication, ex-
cept radio
HQ: Frontier California Inc.
140 West St
New York NY 10007
212 395-1000

(P-5565)
FRONTIER CALIFORNIA INC
Also Called: Verizon
525 E Yosemite Ave, Manteca
(95336-5806)
P.O. Box 992 (95336-1139)
PHONE...............................209 239-4128
Luanne Weldon, *Branch Mgr*
EMP: 180
SALES (corp-wide): 9.1B **Publicly Held**
SIC: 4813 4812 Local telephone commu-
nications; radio telephone communication
HQ: Frontier California Inc.
140 West St
New York NY 10007
212 395-1000

(P-5566)
FRONTIER CALIFORNIA INC
Also Called: Verizon
1 Wellpoint Way, Westlake Village
(91362-3893)
PHONE...............................805 372-6000
Alex Stadler, *Principal*
John Dixon,
EMP: 64
SALES (corp-wide): 9.1B **Publicly Held**
SIC: 4813 Telephone communication, ex-
cept radio
HQ: Frontier California Inc.
140 West St
New York NY 10007
212 395-1000

(P-5567)
FRONTIER CALIFORNIA INC
Also Called: Verizon
200 W Firebaugh Ave, Exeter
(93221-1653)
PHONE...............................559 592-2100
Steve Bryant, *Branch Mgr*
EMP: 64
SALES (corp-wide): 9.1B **Publicly Held**
SIC: 4813 Local telephone communica-
tions
HQ: Frontier California Inc.
140 West St
New York NY 10007
212 395-1000

(P-5568)
FRONTIIR CORPORATION
1586 Parkview Ave Apt 3, San Jose
(95130-1042)
PHONE...............................510 996-2071
Godfrey Tan, *CEO*
EMP: 250
SALES: 3MM **Privately Held**
SIC: 4813 7389 ;

(P-5569)
GAIA INTERACTIVE INC
Also Called: Gaia Online
2540 N 1st St Ste 101, San Jose
(95131-1016)
PHONE...............................408 573-8800

Gary A Schofield, *CEO*
Elaine Kitagawa, *CFO*
James Butler, *Administration*
Cole Dudley, *Director*
▲ EMP: 105
SALES (est): 16.7MM **Privately Held**
SIC: 4813

(P-5570)
GLOBAL DOMAINS INTERNATIONAL
Also Called: Worldsite.ws
701 Palomar Airport Rd # 300, Carlsbad (92011-1027)
PHONE.................................760 602-3000
Michael S Starr, *President*
Allen Ezier, *Vice Pres*
EMP: 50
SQ FT: 5,000
SALES: 14MM **Privately Held**
WEB: www.globaldomainsinternational.com
SIC: 4813

(P-5571)
GLOBALENGLISH CORPORATION (PA)
2000 Sierra Point Pkwy # 300, Brisbane (94005-1857)
PHONE.................................425 868-0271
Karine Allouche Salanon, *CEO*
Tom Kahl, *President*
Roger Piskulick, *CFO*
Julien Salanon, *CFO*
Daniel Rasmus, *Chief Mktg Ofcr*
▲ EMP: 105
SQ FT: 46,000
SALES (est): 34.5MM **Privately Held**
WEB: www.globalenglish.net
SIC: 4813 7375 ; information retrieval services

(P-5572)
GOOGLE FIBER INC (DH)
1600 Amphitheatre Pkwy, Mountain View (94043-1351)
PHONE.................................650 253-0000
Milo Medin, *Vice Pres*
EMP: 74 **EST:** 2010
SALES (est): 31.3MM
SALES (corp-wide): 110.8B **Publicly Held**
SIC: 4813
HQ: Google Llc
1600 Amphitheatre Pkwy
Mountain View CA 94043
650 253-0000

(P-5573)
GOOGLE INTERNATIONAL LLC (DH)
1600 Amphitheatre Pkwy, Mountain View (94043-1351)
PHONE.................................650 253-0000
Eric Schmidt, *Ch of Bd*
Larry Page, *CEO*
David C Drummond, *Senior VP*
Rob Clifton, *Info Tech Mgr*
Jesse Rosenstock, *Software Engr*
▼ EMP: 74
SALES (est): 1.2B
SALES (corp-wide): 110.8B **Publicly Held**
SIC: 4813 7375 ; ; information retrieval services
HQ: Google Llc
1600 Amphitheatre Pkwy
Mountain View CA 94043
650 253-0000

(P-5574)
GT NEXUS INC (DH)
1111 Broadway 5f, Oakland (94607-4139)
PHONE.................................510 808-2222
Sean Feeney, *CEO*
Jamie O'Halloran, *Partner*
Guy Rey-Herme, *COO*
Andreas Stinnes, *Exec VP*
John Urban, *Exec VP*
EMP: 54
SALES (est): 34.2MM
SALES (corp-wide): 3.1B **Privately Held**
WEB: www.gtnexus.com
SIC: 4813 Telephone communication, except radio

HQ: Infor, Inc.
641 Ave Of The Americas # 4
New York NY 10011
646 336-1700

(P-5575)
GTT COMMUNICATIONS (MP) INC (DH)
Also Called: Megapath
6700 Koll Center Pkwy, Pleasanton (94566-7060)
PHONE.................................925 201-2500
Craig Young, *CEO*
Sean Mitchell, *Partner*
Paul Milley, *CFO*
Kurt Hoffman, *Co-President*
Steve Chisholm, *Senior VP*
EMP: 150
SQ FT: 12,000
SALES (est): 95.3MM **Publicly Held**
WEB: www.megapath.net
SIC: 4813 7375 ; information retrieval services
HQ: Gtt Americas, Llc
7900 Tysons One Pl
Mc Lean VA 22102
703 442-5500

(P-5576)
HERE MEDIA INC (PA)
10990 Wilshire Blvd Fl 18, Los Angeles (90024-3927)
PHONE.................................310 806-4288
Paul Colichman, *CEO*
Tony Shyngle, *CFO*
Stephen Jarchow, *Chairman*
EMP: 66
SQ FT: 12,000
SALES (est): 41.1MM **Privately Held**
WEB: www.heremedia.com
SIC: 4813 2721 ; periodicals: publishing only; magazines: publishing only, not printed on site

(P-5577)
HIVE TECH GURUS INCORPORATED
510 Strtford Ct Unit 204a, Del Mar (92014)
PHONE.................................323 445-1770
Adrian Escobar, *President*
EMP: 50 **EST:** 2017
SALES (est): 351K **Privately Held**
SIC: 4813

(P-5578)
HORNITOS TELEPHONE CO
Also Called: TDS
2896 Bear Vly, Hornitos (95325)
PHONE.................................608 831-1000
David Wittwer, *President*
Mike Gasser, *Principal*
EMP: 99
SQ FT: 4,000
SALES: 950K
SALES (corp-wide): 5B **Publicly Held**
SIC: 4813 Telephone communication, except radio
HQ: Tds Telecommunications Corporation
525 Junction Rd Ste 1000
Madison WI 53717
608 664-4000

(P-5579)
HOTWIRE INC
114 Sansome St Ste 400, San Francisco (94104-3810)
PHONE.................................415 645-7350
Dara Khosrowshahi, *CEO*
Margarita Mikhaltchouk, *Partner*
Clem Bason, *President*
Gabriela Contreras, *Executive Asst*
Hung Nguyen, *Admin Asst*
EMP: 175
SALES (est): 37.4MM
SALES (corp-wide): 10B **Publicly Held**
WEB: www.hotwire.com
SIC: 4813
PA: Expedia Group, Inc.
333 108th Ave Ne
Bellevue WA 98004
425 679-7200

(P-5580)
HUAWEI ENTERPRISE USA INC
20400 Stevens Creek Blvd, Cupertino (95014-2217)
PHONE.................................408 394-4295
EMP: 80
SALES (est): 6.4MM **Privately Held**
SIC: 4813
PA: Huawei Investment & Holding Co., Ltd.
Bantian Huawei Base, Longgang District
Shenzhen 51812

(P-5581)
HULU LLC
12312 W Olympic Boulev, Los Angeles (90064)
PHONE.................................888 631-4858
Mike Hopkins, *CEO*
EMP: 890 **Privately Held**
SIC: 4813 4833 ; television translator station
PA: Hulu, Llc
2500 Broadway Ste 200
Santa Monica CA 90404

(P-5582)
IAC PUBLISHING LLC
555 12th St Ste 300, Oakland (94607-3698)
PHONE.................................510 985-7400
Adam Roston, *CEO*
Jeffrey Spitzer, *Vice Pres*
EMP: 100
SQ FT: 47,679
SALES (est): 574.3K **Privately Held**
SIC: 4813

(P-5583)
ICALLFIRST
18141 Beach Blvd Ste 290, Huntington Beach (92648-8602)
PHONE.................................808 557-9299
Charlie Waters, *Partner*
EMP: 99
SALES (est): 2.1MM **Privately Held**
SIC: 4813 Telephone communication, except radio

(P-5584)
IMOBILE LLC
875 W Arrow Hwy, San Dimas (91773-2406)
PHONE.................................909 599-8822
Nahrain Simonov, *Branch Mgr*
EMP: 426 **Privately Held**
SIC: 4813 Local & long distance telephone communications
PA: Imobile Llc
207 Terminal Dr
Plainview NY 11803

(P-5585)
INFONET SERVICES CORPORATION (DH)
Also Called: BT Infonet
2160 E Grand Ave, El Segundo (90245-5024)
PHONE.................................310 335-2859
David Andrew, *CEO*
Jose A Collazo, *President*
Pete Sweers, *COO*
Akbar H Firdosy, *CFO*
John C Hoffman, *Exec VP*
▲ EMP: 600
SQ FT: 150,000
SALES (est): 272.6MM
SALES (corp-wide): 33.2B **Privately Held**
WEB: www.infonet.com
SIC: 4813 7373 7375 Data telephone communications; computer integrated systems design; information retrieval services
HQ: British Telecommunications Public Limited Company
Bt Centre
London EC1A
207 356-5000

(P-5586)
INGENIO INC
182 Howard St 826, San Francisco (94105-1611)
PHONE.................................415 248-4000
Warren Heffelfinger, *CEO*
Mark Britto, *CEO*
EMP: 120
SQ FT: 25,000
SALES (est): 49MM
SALES (corp-wide): 160.5B **Publicly Held**
SIC: 4813
PA: At&T Inc.
208 S Akard St
Dallas TX 75202
210 821-4105

(P-5587)
INREACH INTERNET LLC (HQ)
4635 Georgetown Pl, Stockton (95207-6203)
P.O. Box 312, West Enfield ME (04493-0312)
PHONE.................................888 467-3224
EMP: 57
SQ FT: 5,075
SALES (est): 7.5MM
SALES (corp-wide): 16.4MM **Privately Held**
SIC: 4813
PA: Mobilepro Corp.
6100 Oak Tree Blvd # 200
Independence OH 44131
216 986-2745

(P-5588)
INTELPEER CLOUD CMMNCTIONS LLC
155 Bovet Rd Ste 405, San Mateo (94402-3137)
PHONE.................................650 525-9200
Frank Fawzi, *President*
Andre Simone, *CFO*
Rob Clarke, *Ch Credit Ofcr*
Luis Mago, *Officer*
Phil Bronsdon, *Senior VP*
EMP: 106
SQ FT: 6,000
SALES (est): 26.1MM **Privately Held**
WEB: www.intelepeer.com
SIC: 4813 Data telephone communications; telephone/video communications

(P-5589)
IPASS INC (PA)
3800 Bridge Pkwy, Redwood City (94065-1171)
PHONE.................................650 232-4100
Gary A Griffiths, *President*
Michael Tedesco, *Ch of Bd*
Patricia R Hume, *Ch Credit Ofcr*
Michael Chang, *Bd of Directors*
David Panos, *Bd of Directors*
EMP: 70
SQ FT: 25,000
SALES: 54.4MM **Publicly Held**
SIC: 4813 7374 ; ; data processing & preparation

(P-5590)
JAMCRACKER INC
4677 Old Ironsides Dr # 450, Santa Clara (95054-1845)
PHONE.................................408 496-5500
K B Chandrasekhar, *Ch of Bd*
Todd Johnson, *President*
Harold Chen, *CFO*
Jay Gokul, *Architect*
EMP: 50
SALES (est): 9.2MM **Privately Held**
WEB: www.jamcracker.com
SIC: 4813 7375 ; information retrieval services

(P-5591)
KERMAN TELEPHONE CO
Also Called: Sebastian
811 S Madera Ave, Kerman (93630-1740)
PHONE.................................559 846-4954
William S Barcus, *President*
Ruth Barcus, *Vice Pres*
Mitch Drake, *Vice Pres*
Susan Moran, *Admin Sec*
EMP: 52 **EST:** 1911
SQ FT: 36,000

SALES: 12.7MM
SALES (corp-wide): 51.4MM **Privately Held**
WEB: www.kermantel.net
SIC: 4813 Local telephone communications
PA: Sebastian Enterprises, Inc.
　811 S Madera Ave
　Kerman CA 93630
　559 946-4954

(P-5592)
KERMANTELNET INTERNET SERVICE
811 S Madera Ave, Kerman (93630-1740)
PHONE..........................559 842-2223
Bill Sebastian, *Owner*
EMP: 60
SALES (est): 1.2MM **Privately Held**
WEB: www.kertelweb.com
SIC: 4813

(P-5593)
LAUNCH MEDIA INC (HQ)
Also Called: Tourdates.com
25 Taylor St, San Francisco (94102-3916)
PHONE..........................310 593-6152
David Goldberg, *Ch of Bd*
Robert Roback, *President*
Jeff Mickeal, *CFO*
EMP: 120
SQ FT: 21,375
SALES (est): 28.8MM **Publicly Held**
SIC: 4813

(P-5594)
LUXAR TECH INC
42840 Christy St Ste 231, Fremont (94538-3194)
PHONE..........................408 835-2551
Tongqing Wang, *CEO*
Kapany Raj, *Advisor*
EMP: 130 **EST:** 2014
SQ FT: 4,000
SALES: 16MM **Privately Held**
SIC: 4813 Data telephone communications

(P-5595)
MCI COMMUNICATIONS SVCS INC
Also Called: Verizon Business
700 S Flower St Ste 1600, Los Angeles (90017-4203)
PHONE..........................213 625-1005
Ron Garretson, *Manager*
EMP: 200
SALES (corp-wide): 126B **Publicly Held**
WEB: www.mci.com
SIC: 4813 4812 Long distance telephone communications; radio telephone communication
HQ: Mci Communications Services, Inc.
　22001 Loudoun County Pkwy
　Ashburn VA 20147
　703 886-5600

(P-5596)
MEDIA TEMPLE INC
6060 Center Dr Fl 5, Los Angeles (90045-1596)
PHONE..........................877 578-4000
Russell P Reeder, *CEO*
Marc Dumont, *Ch of Bd*
Rod Stoddard, *President*
John Carey, *CFO*
Albert Lopez, *CTO*
EMP: 203
SQ FT: 33,000
SALES (est): 41.6MM
SALES (corp-wide): 2.2B **Publicly Held**
WEB: www.mediatemple.net
SIC: 4813 7371 ; computer software development & applications
HQ: Godaddy.Com, Llc
　14455 N Hayden Rd Ste 219
　Scottsdale AZ 85260

(P-5597)
MEGAPATH CLOUD COMPANY LLC (PA)
6800 Koll Center Pkwy, Pleasanton (94566-7045)
PHONE..........................925 201-2500
Donald Craig Young, *CEO*

Paul Milley, *CFO*
Derek Heins, *Vice Pres*
EMP: 56
SALES (est): 338.7MM **Privately Held**
SIC: 4813 Data telephone communications

(P-5598)
MEGAPATH GROUP INC (HQ)
2510 Zanker Rd, San Jose (95131-1127)
PHONE..........................408 952-6400
D Craig Young, *CEO*
Brett Flinchum, *COO*
Jeffrey Bailey, *CFO*
Douglas A Carlen, *Senior VP*
Jennis Narayan, *Manager*
▲ **EMP:** 125
SQ FT: 133,310
SALES (est): 313.5MM
SALES (corp-wide): 338.7MM **Privately Held**
WEB: www.covad.com
SIC: 4813 Voice telephone communications; data telephone communications;
PA: Megapath Cloud Company, Llc
　6800 Koll Center Pkwy
　Pleasanton CA 94566
　925 201-2500

(P-5599)
MEGAPATH GROUP INC
Also Called: Covad Communications
2510 Zanker Rd, San Jose (95131-1127)
PHONE..........................408 324-1353
Robetr Knowling Jr, *Principal*
EMP: 203
SALES (corp-wide): 338.7MM **Privately Held**
WEB: www.covad.com
SIC: 4813 Data telephone communications
HQ: Megapath Group, Inc.
　2510 Zanker Rd
　San Jose CA 95131
　408 952-6400

(P-5600)
MEGAPATH INC (PA)
6800 Koll Center Pkwy # 200, Pleasanton (94566-7045)
PHONE..........................877 611-6342
D Craig Young, *Ch of Bd*
Stephanie Thurman, *Partner*
Dan Foster, *President*
Mark Senda, *COO*
Paul Milley, *CFO*
EMP: 60
SALES (est): 258.1MM **Privately Held**
WEB: www.megapath.com
SIC: 4813

(P-5601)
MIS SCIENCES CORP
2550 N Hollywood Way, Burbank (91505-1055)
PHONE..........................818 847-0213
Lauren Ross, *President*
Jeff Willis, *CFO*
Ricky Torre, *General Mgr*
Ricardo De La Torre, *Engineer*
EMP: 125
SQ FT: 7,500
SALES (est): 16MM **Privately Held**
WEB: www.misssciences.com
SIC: 4813 8748 7376 8742 ; ; systems engineering consultant, ex. computer or professional; computer facilities management; management information systems consultant; custom computer programming services

(P-5602)
MOBILITIE INVESTMENTS III LLC
2955 Red Hill Ave Ste 200, Costa Mesa (92626-1205)
PHONE..........................877 999-7070
Gary Jabara, *Chairman*
Christos Karmis, *CEO*
Dana Tardelli, *COO*
Dissy Saraboing, *CFO*
EMP: 125
SALES: 50MM
SALES (corp-wide): 408.1MM **Privately Held**
SIC: 4813 Local telephone communications

PA: Mobilitie Management, Llc
　660 Nwport Ctr Dr Ste 200
　Newport Beach CA 92660
　877 999-7070

(P-5603)
MOBILITIE SERVICES LLC
660 Newport Center Dr, Newport Beach (92660-6401)
PHONE..........................877 999-7070
Gary Jabara, *Chairman*
Christos Karmis, *CEO*
Dana Tardelli, *COO*
Dissy Sarabosing, *CFO*
EMP: 500
SALES: 350MM
SALES (corp-wide): 408.1MM **Privately Held**
SIC: 4813 Local telephone communications
PA: Mobilitie Management, Llc
　660 Nwport Ctr Dr Ste 200
　Newport Beach CA 92660
　877 999-7070

(P-5604)
MOBITV INC
1900 Powell St Ste 900, Emeryville (94608-1885)
PHONE..........................510 981-1303
Charlie Nooney, *Ch of Bd*
Stephen Coney, *President*
Paul Scanlan, *President*
Anders Norstr M, *COO*
Anders Norstrom, *COO*
EMP: 100 **EST:** 2000
SQ FT: 3,200
SALES (est): 18.9MM **Privately Held**
WEB: www.mobitv.com
SIC: 4813 4899 ; data communication services

(P-5605)
MONS VIRIDIS LLC
960 Jackson St, San Francisco (94133-4809)
PHONE..........................415 297-6765
Trung Vu, *CFO*
EMP: 95
SALES: 800K **Privately Held**
SIC: 4813

(P-5606)
MPOWER COMMUNICATIONS CORP (DH)
515 S Flower St, Los Angeles (90071-2201)
PHONE..........................866 699-8242
Rolla P Huff, *Ch of Bd*
Joseph M Wetzel, *President*
S Gregory Clevenger, *CFO*
Michael J Tschiderer, *Treasurer*
Russell I Zuckerman, *Senior VP*
▲ **EMP:** 75
SQ FT: 20,000
SALES (est): 110.2MM **Privately Held**
WEB: www.mpowercom.com
SIC: 4813 Telephone communication, except radio
HQ: Mpower Holding Corporation
　515 S Flower St Fl 36
　Los Angeles CA 90071
　866 699-8242

(P-5607)
MYINTERNETSERVICESCOM LLC
Also Called: Fairfight
1010 E Union St Ste 125, Pasadena (91106-1793)
PHONE..........................213 256-0575
Greg Howard, *CEO*
Trenton Hill, *COO*
Edmar Mendizabal, *Director*
EMP: 100
SQ FT: 2,000
SALES (est): 1MM **Privately Held**
WEB: www.myinternetservices.com
SIC: 4813

(P-5608)
NAVISITE LLC
2805 Lafayette St, Santa Clara (95050-2639)
PHONE..........................408 965-9000
Lorie Tolley, *Branch Mgr*

Mike Davis, *Technology*
EMP: 50
SALES (corp-wide): 41.5B **Publicly Held**
WEB: www.navisite.com
SIC: 4813
HQ: Navisite Llc
　400 Minuteman Rd
　Andover MA 01810

(P-5609)
NEOPETS INC
412 W Broadway Ste 303, Glendale (91204-4117)
PHONE..........................818 551-4338
Doug Dohring, *President*
Patty Lutton, *CFO*
Kyra E Reppen, *Senior VP*
Peter Green, *Vice Pres*
Debra Pierson, *Vice Pres*
EMP: 50
SALES (est): 2.1MM
SALES (corp-wide): 13.2B **Publicly Held**
WEB: www.neopets.com
SIC: 4813
HQ: Viacom International Inc.
　1515 Broadway
　New York NY 10036

(P-5610)
NETNOW
41 Heritage Village Ln, Campbell (95008-2036)
PHONE..........................408 370-0425
Daniel Bryant, *Owner*
Peggy Patwardhan, *Vice Pres*
EMP: 300
SALES: 15MM **Privately Held**
WEB: www.netnow.com
SIC: 4813

(P-5611)
NEW CINGULAR WIRELESS SVCS INC
Also Called: AT&T
P.O. Box 68055
PHONE..........................562 924-0000
Hank Bonde, *Branch Mgr*
EMP: 99
SALES (corp-wide): 160.5B **Publicly Held**
WEB: www.attws.com
SIC: 4813 Local & long distance telephone communications
HQ: New Cingular Wireless Services, Inc.
　7277 164th Ave Ne
　Redmond WA 98052
　425 827-4500

(P-5612)
NEW DREAM NETWORK LLC (PA)
Also Called: Dreamhost.com
135 S State College Blvd, Brea (92821-5823)
PHONE..........................626 644-9466
Simon Anderson, *Mng Member*
Patrick Lane, *Vice Pres*
Dallas Bethune,
Joseph Jones,
Michael Rodriguez,
EMP: 60
SQ FT: 16,380
SALES (est): 56.6MM **Privately Held**
WEB: www.newdream.net
SIC: 4813

(P-5613)
NEW DREAM NETWORK LLC
Also Called: Dreamhost.com
707 Wilshire Blvd # 5050, Los Angeles (90017-3607)
PHONE..........................323 375-3842
Art Elivarov, *Manager*
EMP: 74
SALES (corp-wide): 56.6MM **Privately Held**
SIC: 4813
PA: New Dream Network, Llc
　135 S State College Blvd
　Brea CA 92821
　626 644-9466

PRODUCTS & SVCS

(P-5614)
NEXTPOINT INC (PA)
Also Called: Break Media
8750 Wilshire Blvd 300e, Beverly Hills
(90211-2700)
PHONE..........................310 360-5904
Keith Richman, *President*
Andrew Doyle, *CFO*
David Subar, *CTO*
Christina Capone, *Human Resources*
EMP: 80
SALES (est): 28MM **Privately Held**
SIC: 4813

(P-5615)
O1 COMMUNICATIONS INC
4359 Town Center Blvd # 217, El Dorado
Hills (95762-7113)
PHONE..........................888 444-1111
Bradley Jenkins, *CEO*
Jim Beausoleil, *CFO*
Max Seely, *Senior VP*
EMP: 89 EST: 1998
SQ FT: 20,000
SALES (est): 29MM **Privately Held**
WEB: www.o1tel.com
SIC: 4813 Data telephone communications

(P-5616)
ODYSSEY TELECORP INC
550 Lytton Ave Fl 2, Palo Alto
(94301-1577)
PHONE..........................650 470-7550
Sean Doherty, *CEO*
Joe Stockwell, *COO*
Mike Woods, *Senior VP*
Karl O Forsman, *Software Engr*
EMP: 131
SALES (est): 5.8MM **Privately Held**
WEB: www.odysseytel.com
SIC: 4813 Telephone communication, except radio

(P-5617)
OOMA INC (PA)
525 Almanor Ave Ste 200, Sunnyvale
(94085-3542)
PHONE..........................650 566-6600
Eric B Stang, *Ch of Bd*
Pushpa Wijewardena, *Partner*
Ravi Narula, *CFO*
Susan Butenhoff, *Bd of Directors*
Alison Davis, *Bd of Directors*
▲ EMP: 101
SQ FT: 18,000
SALES (est): 114.4MM **Publicly Held**
WEB: www.ooma.com
SIC: 4813 7374 ; data processing & preparation

(P-5618)
OPEX COMMUNICATIONS INC
3777 Long Beach Blvd # 400, Long Beach
(90807-3341)
P.O. Box 9270, Uniondale NY (11555-9270)
PHONE..........................562 968-5420
Mark Leafstedt, *CEO*
Sean Trepeta, *President*
John Wonak, *CFO*
Lucy Sung, *Principal*
Robert Yap, *Admin Sec*
EMP: 50 EST: 1998
SQ FT: 14,400
SALES (est): 7.1MM **Privately Held**
WEB: www.opexld.com
SIC: 4813 Local telephone communications
PA: Premiercom Management Company
6 Jacqueline Ln
Fox River Grove IL

(P-5619)
PACIFIC BELL TELEPHONE COMPANY (HQ)
Also Called: Pacbell
430 Bush St Fl 3, San Francisco
(94108-3735)
PHONE..........................415 542-9000
Kenneth P McNeely, *CEO*
Ray Wilkins Jr, *President*
Heather Hayse, *Technical Staff*
Lois Jones, *Technical Staff*
Howard Duff, *Engineer*
▲ EMP: 2000

SQ FT: 500,000
SALES (est): 18.9B
SALES (corp-wide): 160.5B **Publicly Held**
WEB: www.pacbell.com
SIC: 4813 2741 4822 Local & long distance telephone communications; local telephone communications; voice telephone communications; data telephone communications; directories, telephone: publishing only, not printed on site; telegraph & other communications; electronic mail
PA: At&T Inc.
208 S Akard St
Dallas TX 75202
210 821-4105

(P-5620)
PACIFIC CENTREX SERVICES INC
Also Called: Pcs1
114 E Haley St Ste A, Santa Barbara
(93101-2347)
PHONE..........................818 623-2300
M Devin Semler, *President*
EMP: 52
SALES (est): 5.3MM **Privately Held**
WEB: www.pcs1.net
SIC: 4813 5999 ; telephone equipment & systems

(P-5621)
PARETO NETWORKS INC
1183 Bordeaux Dr Ste 22, Sunnyvale
(94089-1201)
PHONE..........................877 727-8020
Daniel Ryan, *CEO*
EMP: 219
SALES (est): 4.9MM **Publicly Held**
SIC: 4813
PA: Aerohive Networks, Inc.
1011 Mccarthy Blvd
Milpitas CA 95035

(P-5622)
PAYCHEX BENEFIT TECH INC
Also Called: Benetrac
2385 Northside Dr Ste 100, San Diego
(92108-2716)
PHONE..........................800 322-7292
Martin Mucci, *CEO*
B Thomas Golisano, *Ch of Bd*
John B Gibson, *Senior VP*
Jan Hawthorne, *Vice Pres*
Susan Short, *Vice Pres*
EMP: 110
SALES (est): 14.1MM
SALES (corp-wide): 3.3B **Publicly Held**
WEB: www.benetrac.com
SIC: 4813
PA: Paychex, Inc.
911 Panorama Trl S
Rochester NY 14625
585 385-6666

(P-5623)
PAYCYCLE INC
210 Portage Ave, Palo Alto (94306-2242)
P.O. Box 397850, Mountain View (94039-7850)
PHONE..........................866 729-2925
Jim Heeger, *CEO*
John Eichhorn, *CFO*
Martin Gates, *CTO*
Susan Dunn, *General Counsel*
EMP: 75
SQ FT: 15,000
SALES (est): 4.7MM
SALES (corp-wide): 5.9B **Publicly Held**
WEB: www.paycycle.com
SIC: 4813 8721 ; accounting, auditing & bookkeeping
PA: Intuit Inc.
2700 Coast Ave
Mountain View CA 94043
650 944-6000

(P-5624)
PAYPAL INC (HQ)
2211 N 1st Ave, San Jose (95131-2021)
PHONE..........................877 981-2163
Daniel H Schulman, *President*
David Carter, *Partner*
Christoph Scheuermann, *Partner*

Daniel Schulman, *President*
Jonathan Auerbach, *Vice Pres*
EMP: 170
SALES (est): 4.3B
SALES (corp-wide): 13B **Publicly Held**
WEB: www.paypal.com
SIC: 4813 7374 6099 ; data processing & preparation; data processing service; electronic funds transfer network, including switching
PA: Paypal Holdings, Inc.
2211 N 1st St
San Jose CA 95131
408 967-1000

(P-5625)
PAYPAL HOLDINGS INC (PA)
2211 N 1st St, San Jose (95131-2021)
PHONE..........................408 967-1000
Daniel H Schulman, *President*
John J Donahoe, *Ch of Bd*
William J Ready, *COO*
John D Rainey, *CFO*
Rodney Adkins, *Bd of Directors*
EMP: 118
SQ FT: 700,000
SALES: 13B **Publicly Held**
SIC: 4813 7374 ; data processing & preparation; data processing service

(P-5626)
PC WORLD CORP (PA)
Also Called: Sap, Oracle, Service Provider
2017 Merkley Ave, West Sacramento
(95691-3119)
PHONE..........................240 855-8988
Mohammad Naz, *President*
EMP: 250
SALES (est): 9MM **Privately Held**
SIC: 4813

(P-5627)
PCS MOBILE SOLUTIONS LLC
3534 Tweedy Blvd, South Gate
(90280-6026)
PHONE..........................323 567-2490
EMP: 73
SALES (corp-wide): 33.9MM **Privately Held**
SIC: 4813 4812 Local & long distance telephone communications; cellular telephone services
PA: Pcs Mobile Solutions, Llc
32000 Northwestern Hwy # 279
Farmington Hills MI 48334
248 539-2221

(P-5628)
PLANETOUT INC (HQ)
795 Folsom St Fl 1, San Francisco
(94107-4226)
PHONE..........................415 834-6500
Daniel E Steimle, *CEO*
Karen Magee, *CEO*
EMP: 50
SQ FT: 56,000
SALES (est): 15.1MM **Privately Held**
WEB: www.planetoutinc.com
SIC: 4813

(P-5629)
PLIVO INC (PA)
Also Called: Plivo US
201 Mission St Ste 230, San Francisco
(94105-1883)
PHONE..........................415 758-3659
Venkatesh Balasubramanian, *President*
Michael Lauricella, *Vice Pres*
Michael Ricordeau, *Principal*
Ramya Raghu, *Engineer*
Abhijit More, *Marketing Staff*
EMP: 72
SQ FT: 2,500
SALES: 14.7MM **Privately Held**
SIC: 4813 Data telephone communications

(P-5630)
PRIME COMMUNICATIONS LP
29273 Central Ave, Lake Elsinore
(92532-2254)
PHONE..........................951 253-3304
EMP: 69
SALES (corp-wide): 280MM **Privately Held**
SIC: 4813 Telephone communication, except radio

PA: Prime Communications, L.P.
12550 Reed Rd Ste 100
Sugar Land TX 77478
281 240-7800

(P-5631)
PUBLIC COMMUNICATIONS SVCS INC
11859 Wilshire Blvd # 600, Los Angeles
(90025-6616)
P.O. Box 2868, Mobile AL (36652-2868)
PHONE..........................310 231-1000
Paul Jennings, *CEO*
Tommie Joe, *President*
Dennis Komai, *CFO*
EMP: 150
SQ FT: 15,000
SALES (est): 15.8MM **Privately Held**
WEB: www.pcstelcom.com
SIC: 4813 Local & long distance telephone communications

(P-5632)
QWEST CORPORATION
1350 Treat Blvd Ste 200, Walnut Creek
(94597-2150)
PHONE..........................925 974-4908
Trish Stuber, *Branch Mgr*
EMP: 59
SALES (corp-wide): 17.6B **Publicly Held**
SIC: 4813 Telephone communication, except radio
HQ: Qwest Corporation
100 Centurylink Dr
Monroe LA 71203
318 388-9000

(P-5633)
RED POCKET INC
Also Called: Red Pocket Mobile
2060d E Avenida De Los, Thousand Oaks
(91362)
PHONE..........................888 993-3888
Joshua Gordon, *President*
Steve Bowman, *CFO*
EMP: 75 EST: 2005
SALES (est): 2.9MM **Privately Held**
SIC: 4813 Telephone communication, except radio

(P-5634)
RENTJUICE CORPORATION
225 Bush St Ste 1100, San Francisco
(94104-4250)
PHONE..........................415 376-0369
David Vivero, *CEO*
Kunal Shah, *CTO*
EMP: 92
SALES (est): 5.5MM
SALES (corp-wide): 1B **Publicly Held**
SIC: 4813
HQ: Zillow, Inc.
1301 2nd Ave Fl 31
Seattle WA 98101
206 470-7000

(P-5635)
RHYTHMONE LLC (HQ)
601 Montgomery St Fl 16, San Francisco
(94111-2620)
PHONE..........................415 655-1450
Mark Bonney, *President*
Ed Reginelli, *CFO*
Amy Rothstein, *Officer*
EMP: 62
SALES (est): 60.3MM **Privately Held**
WEB: www.blinkx.com
SIC: 4813 2741 7319 ; ; display advertising service

(P-5636)
RIVIO INC
2500 Augustine Dr Ste 100, Santa Clara
(95054-3020)
PHONE..........................408 653-4400
Navin Chaddha, *President*
Pradip Madan, *COO*
James Walker, *Exec VP*
Craig Douchy, *Admin Sec*
EMP: 50
SALES (est): 1.6MM
SALES (corp-wide): 244.6MM **Privately Held**
WEB: www.cpa2biz.com
SIC: 4813

HQ: Cpa.Com
1211 Ave Of The Americas
New York NY 10036
212 596-6230

(P-5637)
RUCKUS WIRELESS INC (HQ)
350 W Java Dr, Sunnyvale (94089-1026)
PHONE....................................650 265-4200
Ken Cheng, *CEO*
Jean Furter, *CFO*
Bart Giordano, *Senior VP*
Larry Birnbaum, *Vice Pres*
Louis Au Kwok-Leung, *Vice Pres*
▲ **EMP:** 110
SQ FT: 95,000
SALES (est): 1.3B
SALES (corp-wide): 6.6B **Privately Held**
WEB: www.ruckuswireless.com
SIC: 4813
PA: Arris International Plc
Victoria Road Saltaire,
Shipley BD18
127 453-2000

(P-5638)
SALESFORCECOM FOUNDATION
The Landmark One St The Landma, San
Francisco (94105)
PHONE....................................800 667-6389
Marc Benioff, *CEO*
Keith Block, *President*
Suzanne Dibianca, *President*
Rob Acker, *COO*
Kurt Hagen, *CFO*
EMP: 150
SALES (est): 8.6MM **Privately Held**
SIC: 4813

(P-5639)
SEBASTIAN ENTERPRISES INC (PA)
811 S Madera Ave, Kerman (93630-1740)
PHONE....................................559 946-4954
Ruth Barcus, *President*
William Barcus, *Vice Pres*
Susan Moran, *Admin Sec*
Jeff McClure, *Info Tech Dir*
Ashley Lozano, *Technician*
EMP: 157
SQ FT: 70,775
SALES: 51.4MM **Privately Held**
SIC: 4813 1731 Local telephone commu-
nications; telephone & telephone equip-
ment installation; general electrical
contractor

(P-5640)
SENDMAIL INC (HQ)
892 Ross Dr, Sunnyvale (94089-1443)
PHONE....................................510 594-5400
Gary Steele, *CEO*
Sandy Abbott, *CFO*
Paul Auvil, *CFO*
Kimberly Getgem Bargero, *Vice Pres*
Stephanie Nevin, *Vice Pres*
EMP: 75
SQ FT: 30,000
SALES (est): 20.1MM
SALES (corp-wide): 515.2MM **Publicly Held**
WEB: www.sendmail.com
SIC: 4813 7371 7372 7373 ; computer
software development; prepackaged soft-
ware; computer integrated systems de-
sign
PA: Proofpoint, Inc.
892 Ross Dr
Sunnyvale CA 94089
408 517-4710

(P-5641)
SENDME INC
Also Called: Sendmemobile.com
150 Spear St Ste 1400, San Francisco
(94105-1540)
P.O. Box 190878 (94119-0878)
PHONE....................................415 978-9504
Russell Klein, *CEO*
John Witchel, *CTO*
EMP: 60
SQ FT: 8,400
SALES (est): 6.7MM **Privately Held**
SIC: 4813 Data telephone communications

(P-5642)
SIERRA TEL CMMUNICATIONS GROUP
Also Called: Sierra Tel Business Systems
40044 Highway 49 Ste C2, Oakhurst
(93644-8875)
P.O. Box 160 (93644-0160)
PHONE....................................559 683-7777
Mike Cary, *Manager*
EMP: 80
SALES (corp-wide): 111.6MM **Privately Held**
WEB: www.sierratelephone.com
SIC: 4813 Local telephone communica-
tions
PA: Sierra Tel Communications Group
49150 Road 426
Oakhurst CA 93644
559 683-4611

(P-5643)
SIERRA TEL CMMUNICATIONS GROUP (PA)
Also Called: Sierra Telephone
49150 Road 426, Oakhurst (93644-8702)
P.O. Box 219 (93644-0219)
PHONE....................................559 683-4611
John H Baker, *CEO*
Harry H Baker, *Ch of Bd*
Linda Oldfield, *HR Admin*
Karen Kirk, *Purch Mgr*
Lee Lambert, *Purchasing*
EMP: 54
SQ FT: 12,000
SALES (est): 111.6MM **Privately Held**
WEB: www.sierratelephone.com
SIC: 4813 Local telephone communica-
tions; long distance telephone communi-
cations;

(P-5644)
SIERRA TELEPHONE COMPANY INC
49150 Crane Valley Rd 426, Oakhurst
(93644)
P.O. Box 219 (93644-0219)
PHONE....................................559 683-4611
Harry H Baker, *President*
John H Baker, *Vice Pres*
Heidi D Baker, *Admin Sec*
Judi Thomas, *Info Tech Mgr*
Eva Busto, *Business Anlyst*
EMP: 190
SALES (est): 37.6MM
SALES (corp-wide): 111.6MM **Privately Held**
WEB: www.stcg.net
SIC: 4813 Local telephone communica-
tions; long distance telephone communi-
cations
PA: Sierra Tel Communications Group
49150 Road 426
Oakhurst CA 93644
559 683-4611

(P-5645)
SIGMA NETWORKS INC
2191 Zanker Rd, San Jose (95131-2109)
PHONE....................................408 876-4002
John K Peters, *President*
Michael A Depatie, *CFO*
Robert Decker, *Vice Pres*
Lonny Orona, *Vice Pres*
Scott Young, *Vice Pres*
EMP: 120
SALES (est): 4.2MM **Privately Held**
SIC: 4813 Local telephone communica-
tions

(P-5646)
SKYPE INC
1 Microsoft Way Redmond, Palo Alto
(94304)
PHONE....................................650 493-7900
Donald Albert, *President*
Tony Bates, *CEO*
Laura Shesgreen, *Vice Pres*
Shauna Kline, *Controller*
▲ **EMP:** 70
SQ FT: 90,698
SALES (est): 11.8MM
SALES (corp-wide): 110.3B **Publicly Held**
SIC: 4813 ;

PA: Microsoft Corporation
1 Microsoft Way
Redmond WA 98052
425 882-8080

(P-5647)
SOUTHERN CALIFORNIA TELE CO (PA)
Also Called: Southern Cal Tele & Enrgy
27515 Enterprise Cir W, Temecula
(92590-4864)
PHONE....................................951 693-1880
Greg Michaels, *President*
Kristine Michaels, *CFO*
Kevin Reno, *Vice Pres*
Ryan McGuire, *Executive Asst*
Stephanie Moreau, *Executive Asst*
EMP: 60
SQ FT: 10,000
SALES (est): 10.2MM **Privately Held**
SIC: 4813 Local & long distance telephone
communications

(P-5648)
SPRINT COMMUNICATIONS CO LP
111 Universal Hollywood Dr, Universal City
(91608-1054)
PHONE....................................818 755-7100
Bill Henry, *Manager*
EMP: 50
SALES (corp-wide): 85.9B **Publicly Held**
SIC: 4813 4812 Long distance telephone
communications; radio telephone commu-
nication
HQ: Sprint Communications Company L.P.
6391 Sprint Pkwy
Overland Park KS 66251
800 829-0965

(P-5649)
SPRINT COMMUNICATIONS CO LP
1505 E Enterprise Dr, San Bernardino
(92408-0159)
PHONE....................................909 382-6030
Bill Neece, *Manager*
EMP: 100
SALES (corp-wide): 85.9B **Publicly Held**
SIC: 4813 4812 Long distance telephone
communications; radio telephone commu-
nication
HQ: Sprint Communications Company L.P.
6391 Sprint Pkwy
Overland Park KS 66251
800 829-0965

(P-5650)
TACHYON INC
9339 Carroll Park Dr # 150, San Diego
(92121-3278)
PHONE....................................858 882-8108
EMP: 50
SALES (est): 5.4MM **Privately Held**
SIC: 4813

(P-5651)
TACTIVOS INC
Also Called: Mural
303 2nd St Ste S200, San Francisco
(94107-1328)
PHONE....................................415 687-2501
Mariano Suarez Battan, *CEO*
Pato Jutard, *CTO*
EMP: 52
SALES (est): 263.2K **Privately Held**
SIC: 4813 ;

(P-5652)
TEKWORKS INC
12742 Knott St, Garden Grove
(92841-3904)
PHONE....................................877 835-9675
William E Bourgeois, *CEO*
Scott Wiedrick, *Engineer*
Joshua Montana, *Sales Staff*
EMP: 70
SALES (corp-wide): 44.7MM **Privately Held**
SIC: 4813 1731 Telephone communica-
tion, except radio; communications spe-
cialization

PA: Tekworks Inc.
13000 Gregg St Ste B
Poway CA 92064
858 668-1705

(P-5653)
TELISIMO INTERNATIONAL CORP
2330 Shelter Island Dr 210a, San Diego
(92106-3126)
PHONE....................................619 325-1593
Linda G Noda Hobbs, *President*
Mark D Wooster, *CFO*
EMP: 400
SQ FT: 15,000
SALES (est): 19.6MM **Privately Held**
SIC: 4813 Telephone communication, ex-
cept radio

(P-5654)
TNCI OPERATING COMPANY LLC (HQ)
114 E Haley St Ste I, Santa Barbara
(93101-5323)
PHONE....................................800 800-8400
Brian McClintock, *COO*
Erin Loughlin, *Sales Mgr*
Scott Chun, *Manager*
EMP: 85 **EST:** 2013
SQ FT: 5,000
SALES (est): 27.4MM **Privately Held**
SIC: 4813 Telephone communication, ex-
cept radio

(P-5655)
TOPICA INC
1 Post St Ste 875, San Francisco
(94104-5262)
P.O. Box 34280 (94134-0280)
PHONE....................................415 344-0800
Ariel Poler, *CEO*
Anna Zornosa, *President*
Roy Maynard, *CFO*
Roberto Mameli, *Vice Pres*
Glenn Marcus, *CTO*
EMP: 93
SALES (est): 7.1MM **Privately Held**
WEB: www.topica.com
SIC: 4813 7375 ; information retrieval
services

(P-5656)
TRUCONNECT COMMUNICATIONS INC (PA)
Also Called: Telescape
1149 S Hill St Ste 400, Los Angeles
(90015-2894)
PHONE....................................800 430-0443
Mathew Johnson, *CEO*
Robert A Yap, *President*
Nathan Johnson, *CEO*
Juan Carlos Davila, *Senior VP*
Rusty Wolf, *Info Tech Mgr*
EMP: 201
SALES: 22.9MM **Privately Held**
WEB: www.telscape.net
SIC: 4813

(P-5657)
TWITCH INTERACTIVE INC
225 Bush St Ste 900, San Francisco
(94104-4218)
PHONE....................................415 919-5000
Emmett Shear, *CEO*
Kevin Lin, *COO*
John Sutton, *CFO*
Jonathan Simpson-Bint, *Risk Mgmt Dir*
Colin Carrier, *Security Dir*
EMP: 1146 **EST:** 2006
SALES (est): 18.9MM **Publicly Held**
SIC: 4813
PA: Amazon.Com, Inc.
410 Terry Ave N
Seattle WA 98109

(P-5658)
US INTERSTATE DISTRG INC
Also Called: Allstate Communications ASC
21621 Nordhoff St, Chatsworth
(91311-5825)
PHONE....................................818 678-4592
Russel Leventhal, *President*
Frank Montelione, *Vice Pres*
EMP: 150

PRODUCTS & SVCS

SALES (est): 11.9MM **Privately Held**
SIC: 4813 Telephone communication, except radio

(P-5659)
US TELEPACIFIC CORP (HQ)
Also Called: Tpx Communications
515 S Flower St Ste 4500, Los Angeles
(90071-2237)
PHONE..................866 699-8242
Richard A Jalkut, *President*
David Glickman, *Ch of Bd*
Timothy Medina, *CFO*
Ken Bisnoff, *Senior VP*
Erich Everbach, *Senior VP*
◆ **EMP:** 50
SQ FT: 75,000
SALES (est): 437.6MM **Privately Held**
WEB: www.telepacific.com
SIC: 4813 Local & long distance telephone communications

(P-5660)
USTREAM INC
410 Townsend St Fl 4, San Francisco
(94107-1581)
PHONE..................415 489-9400
John Ham, *CEO*
Brad Hunstable, *President*
EMP: 65
SALES (est): 10.3MM
SALES (corp-wide): 79.1B **Publicly Held**
SIC: 4813
PA: International Business Machines Corporation
1 New Orchard Rd Ste 1 # 1
Armonk NY 10504
914 499-1900

(P-5661)
VERIZON BUS NETWRK SVCS INC
11080 White Rock Rd # 100, Rancho Cordova (95670-6299)
PHONE..................916 779-5600
Bert C Roberts, *Branch Mgr*
EMP: 225
SALES (corp-wide): 126B **Publicly Held**
WEB: www.gtl.net
SIC: 4813 Long distance telephone communications
HQ: Verizon Business Network Services Inc.
1 Verizon Way
Basking Ridge NJ 07920
908 559-2000

(P-5662)
VERIZON BUS NETWRK SVCS INC
1740 Creekside Oaks 200, Sacramento
(95833)
PHONE..................916 569-5999
Suresh Madala, *Principal*
EMP: 119
SALES (corp-wide): 126B **Publicly Held**
WEB: www.gtl.net
SIC: 4813 Long distance telephone communications
HQ: Verizon Business Network Services Inc.
1 Verizon Way
Basking Ridge NJ 07920
908 559-2000

(P-5663)
VERIZON BUSINESS GLOBAL LLC
1516 Stillwell Rd Apt F, San Francisco
(94129-1054)
PHONE..................415 606-3621
Scott Smallsreed, *Principal*
EMP: 79
SALES (corp-wide): 126B **Publicly Held**
SIC: 4813 Local & long distance telephone communications
HQ: Verizon Business Global Llc
22001 Loudoun County Pkwy
Ashburn VA 20147
703 886-5600

(P-5664)
VERIZON BUSINESS GLOBAL LLC
800 W 6th St Ste 1150, Los Angeles
(90017-2714)
PHONE..................909 466-5633
Mark Levy, *Branch Mgr*
EMP: 60
SALES (corp-wide): 126B **Publicly Held**
WEB: www.mccmt.com
SIC: 4813 Local & long distance telephone communications
HQ: Verizon Business Global Llc
22001 Loudoun County Pkwy
Ashburn VA 20147
703 886-5600

(P-5665)
VERIZON COMMUNICATIONS INC
5077 E Lew Davis St, Long Beach
(90808-1714)
PHONE..................562 496-0288
Jerry Milton, *Manager*
EMP: 250
SALES (corp-wide): 126B **Publicly Held**
WEB: www.verizon.com
SIC: 4813 4812 Local & long distance telephone communications; radio telephone communications
PA: Verizon Communications Inc.
1095 Ave Of The Americas
New York NY 10036
212 395-1000

(P-5666)
VERIZON COMMUNICATIONS INC
16461 Mojave Dr, Victorville (92395-3800)
PHONE..................760 245-0409
Susan Rowe, *Branch Mgr*
EMP: 113
SALES (corp-wide): 126B **Publicly Held**
WEB: www.verizon.com
SIC: 4813 Local telephone communications
PA: Verizon Communications Inc.
1095 Ave Of The Americas
New York NY 10036
212 395-1000

(P-5667)
VERIZON COMMUNICATIONS INC
1625 E Dinuba Ave, Reedley (93654-9327)
PHONE..................559 637-0204
EMP: 143
SALES (corp-wide): 126B **Publicly Held**
WEB: www.gte.com
SIC: 4813 Telephone communication, except radio
PA: Verizon Communications Inc.
1095 Ave Of The Americas
New York NY 10036
212 395-1000

(P-5668)
VERIZON COMMUNICATIONS INC
994 Mill St, San Luis Obispo (93401-2788)
PHONE..................805 441-4001
EMP: 143
SALES (corp-wide): 126B **Publicly Held**
WEB: www.gte.com
SIC: 4813 Telephone communication, except radio
PA: Verizon Communications Inc.
1095 Ave Of The Americas
New York NY 10036
212 395-1000

(P-5669)
VERIZON COMMUNICATIONS INC
1220 Oak St Ste M, Bakersfield
(93304-1072)
PHONE..................661 328-2226
Mike Minord, *Principal*
Alice Thetford, *Executive*
Ryan Monnastes, *Site Mgr*
Deborah Harris, *Accounts Exec*
EMP: 50

SALES (corp-wide): 126B **Publicly Held**
WEB: www.gte.com
SIC: 4813 Telephone communication, except radio
PA: Verizon Communications Inc.
1095 Ave Of The Americas
New York NY 10036
212 395-1000

(P-5670)
VERIZON COMMUNICATIONS INC
Also Called: GTE
2943 Exposition Blvd, Santa Monica
(90404-5024)
PHONE..................310 319-6148
Steve Campanion, *Manager*
EMP: 300
SALES (corp-wide): 126B **Publicly Held**
WEB: www.gte.com
SIC: 4813 4812 Local & long distance telephone communications; radio telephone communication
PA: Verizon Communications Inc.
1095 Ave Of The Americas
New York NY 10036
212 395-1000

(P-5671)
VERIZON COMMUNICATIONS INC
21306 Superior St, Chatsworth
(91311-4312)
PHONE..................818 388-8549
EMP: 113
SALES (corp-wide): 126B **Publicly Held**
SIC: 4813 Local & long distance telephone communications
PA: Verizon Communications Inc.
1095 Ave Of The Americas
New York NY 10036
212 395-1000

(P-5672)
VERIZON NETWORK INTEGRATION
12905 Los Nietos Rd, Santa Fe Springs
(90670-3011)
PHONE..................562 903-7953
Mark Ryan, *Manager*
EMP: 250
SALES (corp-wide): 126B **Publicly Held**
WEB: www.ba-dsg.com
SIC: 4813 Telephone communication, except radio
HQ: Verizon Network Integration Corp
1050 Virginia Dr 3
Fort Washington PA 19034

(P-5673)
VERIZON SOUTH INC
424 S Patterson Ave, Goleta (93111-2404)
PHONE..................805 681-8527
Dennis Candini, *Manager*
EMP: 75
SALES (corp-wide): 126B **Publicly Held**
SIC: 4813 Local & long distance telephone communications
HQ: Verizon South Inc
600 Hidden Rdg
Irving TX 75038

(P-5674)
VOLCANO COMMUNICATIONS COMPANY (PA)
Also Called: Volcano Telephone Company
20000 State Highway 88, Pine Grove
(95665-9512)
P.O. Box 1070 (95665-1070)
PHONE..................209 296-7502
Sharon J Lundgren, *President*
Elizabeth Lundgren, *Treasurer*
John M Lundgren, *Vice Pres*
Delia P Dede Harder, *Admin Sec*
David Dobbie, *Opers Staff*
EMP: 100
SQ FT: 19,600
SALES (est): 21.2MM **Privately Held**
WEB: www.volcanovti.com
SIC: 4813 4841 Local telephone communications; cable television services

(P-5675)
VSS MONITORING INC (HQ)
178 E Tasman Dr, San Jose (95134-1619)
PHONE..................408 585-6800
Terrence M Breslin, *President*
James McNicholas, *CFO*
Dave Butler, *Vice Pres*
Andrew R Harding, *Vice Pres*
Jeffrey B Jones, *Vice Pres*
EMP: 160
SQ FT: 10,000
SALES (est): 30.5MM
SALES (corp-wide): 986.7MM **Publicly Held**
WEB: www.vssmonitoring.com
SIC: 4813
PA: Netscout Systems, Inc.
310 Littleton Rd
Westford MA 01886
978 614-4000

(P-5676)
WEBPASS INC
267 8th St, San Francisco (94103-3910)
PHONE..................415 233-4100
Charles Barr, *President*
Blake Drager, *President*
Jennifer Gayden, *Executive*
Bob Pompa, *General Mgr*
Paul Giordano, *Administration*
EMP: 100
SQ FT: 8,000
SALES (est): 13.7MM **Privately Held**
SIC: 4813

(P-5677)
WHOLESALE AIR-TIME INC
27515 Enterprise Cir W, Temecula
(92590-4864)
PHONE..................951 693-1880
Greg Michaels, *President*
Kevin Reno, *Vice Pres*
Wendy L Walker, *Admin Sec*
EMP: 50
SQ FT: 9,000
SALES (est): 6.2MM **Privately Held**
SIC: 4813 Local & long distance telephone communications

(P-5678)
WILINE NETWORKS INC (PA)
1164 Triton Dr, Foster City (94404-1240)
PHONE..................888 494-5463
John McGuire, *CEO*
David Hertgen, *President*
Thomas W Reilly, *Executive*
Michael Reusch, *Sr Software Eng*
Bryton Tang, *Opers Staff*
▲ **EMP:** 50
SALES (est): 20.1MM **Privately Held**
WEB: www.wiline.com
SIC: 4813

(P-5679)
XOBEE NETWORKS INC
7910 N Ingram Ave Ste 101, Fresno
(93711-5828)
PHONE..................559 579-1300
Eric Raw, *President*
Mario Ariaz, *Vice Pres*
Bryan Smith, *Vice Pres*
Edie Roach, *Executive Asst*
Sierra Hongthamaly, *Admin Asst*
EMP: 53
SQ FT: 5,500
SALES: 5MM **Privately Held**
SIC: 4813 7379 8741 8748 ; computer related consulting services; management services; telecommunications consultant

(P-5680)
YOUR PRACTICE ONLINE LLC
4590 Macarthur Blvd # 500, Newport Beach
(92660-2030)
PHONE..................877 388-8569
Prem Lobo, *Practice Mgr*
Holly Edmonds, *Vice Pres*
Holly Olds, *Marketing Staff*
Mark Ryan, *Marketing Staff*
EMP: 110
SALES: 1.8MM **Privately Held**
SIC: 4813

(P-5681)
ZADAONET
685 Scofield Ave Apt 22, East Palo Alto
(94303-2350)
PHONE..................................650 556-6377
Wenda Zhao, *President*
EMP: 60
SALES (est): 399.6K **Privately Held**
SIC: 4813

(P-5682)
ZOOSK INC (PA)
989 Market St Fl 5, San Francisco
(94103-1741)
PHONE..................................415 728-9543
Mike Hodges, *CEO*
Behzad Behrouzi, *Vice Pres*
Carol Mahoney, *Vice Pres*
Doug Wehmeier, *Vice Pres*
Diane Dietz, *Principal*
EMP: 52
SALES (est): 24.8MM **Privately Held**
SIC: 4813 7299 ; dating service

(P-5683)
ZYXEL COMMUNICATIONS INC
1130 N Miller St, Anaheim (92806-2001)
PHONE..................................714 632-0882
Howie Chu, *President*
Robert Mackinnon, *Manager*
◆ EMP: 80
SQ FT: 32,000
SALES: 100MM
SALES (corp-wide): 635.9MM **Privately Held**
WEB: www.zyxel.com.tw
SIC: 4813
HQ: Zyxel Communications Corporation
    11f, 223, Pei Hsin Rd., Sec. 3,
    New Taipei City 23143
    227 399-889

4822 Telegraph & Other Message Communications

(P-5684)
J2 CLOUD SERVICES LLC (HQ)
Also Called: J2 Cloud Services, Inc.
6922 Hollywood Blvd # 500, Los Angeles
(90028-6117)
PHONE..................................323 860-9200
Nehemia Zucker, *CEO*
Laura Hinson, *President*
Vince Niedzielski, *President*
Ken Truesdale, *President*
R Scott Turicchi, *President*
EMP: 57
SQ FT: 40,000
SALES (est): 746.2MM
SALES (corp-wide): 1.1B **Publicly Held**
WEB: www.efaxcorporate.com
SIC: 4822 Telegraph & other communications
PA: J2 Global, Inc.
    6922 Hollywood Blvd # 500
    Los Angeles CA 90028
    323 860-9200

(P-5685)
J2 GLOBAL INC (PA)
6922 Hollywood Blvd # 500, Los Angeles
(90028-6125)
PHONE..................................323 860-9200
Chul Min Chun, *CEO*
Richard S Ressler, *Ch of Bd*
Hector Escardo, *President*
Steve Horowitz, *President*
Harmeet Singh, *President*
EMP: 149
SQ FT: 40,000
SALES: 1.1B **Publicly Held**
SIC: 4822 Telegraph & other communications

(P-5686)
NIGAL INC (PA)
Also Called: Express Financial
561 E San Ysidro Blvd A, San Ysidro
(92173-3130)
PHONE..................................619 428-5051
Nesim Adato, *President*
Morse Adato, *Shareholder*
Israel Adato, *Vice Pres*
EMP: 91

SQ FT: 900
SALES (est): 4.5MM **Privately Held**
WEB: www.nigal.com
SIC: 4822 6099 6331 Telegraph services; telegram services; check cashing agencies; automobile insurance

(P-5687)
WEST INTERACTIVE SERVICES CORP
100 Enterprise Way, Scotts Valley
(95066-3248)
PHONE..................................888 527-5225
EMP: 89
SALES (corp-wide): 2.2B **Privately Held**
SIC: 4822 Nonvocal message communications
HQ: West Interactive Services Corporation
    11808 Miracle Hills Dr
    Omaha NE 68154

4832 Radio Broadcasting Stations

(P-5688)
ABC CABLE NETWORKS GROUP (DH)
500 S Buena Vista St, Burbank
(91521-0007)
PHONE..................................818 460-7477
John F Cooke, *President*
Anne M Sweeney, *President*
Patrick Lopker, *Senior VP*
▲ EMP: 200
SALES (est): 280.8MM **Publicly Held**
WEB: www.breakbar.com
SIC: 4832 4833 Radio broadcasting stations; television broadcasting stations
HQ: Disney Enterprises, Inc.
    500 S Buena Vista St
    Burbank CA 91521
    818 560-1000

(P-5689)
ABC CABLE NETWORKS GROUP
Also Called: Jimmy Kimmel Live
6834 Hollywood Blvd, Los Angeles
(90028-6116)
PHONE..................................323 860-5900
Jill Leiderman, *Principal*
EMP: 200 **Publicly Held**
SIC: 4832 4833 Radio broadcasting stations; television broadcasting stations
HQ: Abc Cable Networks Group
    500 S Buena Vista St
    Burbank CA 91521
    818 460-7477

(P-5690)
ABE ENTERCOM HOLDINGS LLC
Also Called: Kbzt Broadcasting
1615 Murray Canyon Rd # 710, San Diego
(92108-4314)
PHONE..................................619 291-9797
Bob Boliger, *Vice Pres*
Fay Von Herzen, *Data Proc Exec*
Kevin Callahan, *Director*
EMP: 75
SALES (corp-wide): 592.8MM **Publicly Held**
WEB: www.jpc.com
SIC: 4832 Radio broadcasting stations
HQ: Abe Entercom Holdings Llc
    401 E City Ave Ste 809
    Bala Cynwyd PA 19004
    404 239-7211

(P-5691)
AMATURO SONOMA MEDIA GROUP LLC
1410 Neotomas Ave Ste 200, Santa Rosa
(95405-7533)
PHONE..................................707 543-0126
Michael Williams, *President*
Danny Wright, *Program Dir*
Jennifer Routh, *Director*
Cathy Slack, *Manager*
Victoria Mann, *Supervisor*
EMP: 67

SALES: 5.5MM **Privately Held**
SIC: 4832 Radio broadcasting stations

(P-5692)
BONNEVILLE INTERNATIONAL CORP
Also Called: Kswb
5900 Wilshire Blvd # 1900, Los Angeles
(90036-5020)
PHONE..................................323 634-1800
Peter Durton, *Branch Mgr*
EMP: 50
SALES (corp-wide): 3.9B **Privately Held**
SIC: 4832 Radio broadcasting stations
HQ: Bonneville International Corporation
    55 N 300 W Ste 315
    Salt Lake City UT 84101
    303 321-0950

(P-5693)
BONNEVILLE INTERNATIONAL CORP
Also Called: Kdfcfm Radio
2013rd St Ste 1200, San Francisco
(94103)
PHONE..................................415 764-1021
Chuck Tweedle, *Manager*
EMP: 100
SALES (corp-wide): 3.9B **Privately Held**
WEB: www.boncom.com
SIC: 4832 Radio broadcasting stations
HQ: Bonneville International Corporation
    55 N 300 W Ste 315
    Salt Lake City UT 84101
    303 321-0950

(P-5694)
BONNEVILLE INTERNATIONAL CORP
Also Called: Koit
201 3rd St Fl 12, San Francisco
(94103-3133)
PHONE..................................415 777-0965
Chuck Tweedle, *General Mgr*
EMP: 50
SALES (corp-wide): 3.9B **Privately Held**
SIC: 4832 7313 Radio broadcasting stations, music format; radio advertising representative
HQ: Bonneville International Corporation
    55 N 300 W Ste 315
    Salt Lake City UT 84101
    303 321-0950

(P-5695)
BROADCAST CO OF AMERICAS LLC (PA)
6160 Cornerstone Ct E, San Diego
(92121-3720)
PHONE..................................858 453-0658
Larry Patrick, *CEO*
John T Lynch, *President*
EMP: 62
SALES (est): 4MM **Privately Held**
SIC: 4832 Radio broadcasting stations

(P-5696)
CAPITAL PUBLIC RADIO INC
7055 Folsom Blvd, Sacramento
(95826-2625)
PHONE..................................916 278-8900
Rick Eytcheson, *President*
EMP: 50
SQ FT: 19,838
SALES: 74.4K **Privately Held**
WEB: www.capradio.net
SIC: 4832 Radio broadcasting stations

(P-5697)
CBS BROADCASTING INC
A65 Bettery St, San Francisco (94111)
PHONE..................................415 765-4097
Doug Harvill, *CEO*
EMP: 100
SALES (corp-wide): 13.7B **Publicly Held**
WEB: www.cbs4.com
SIC: 4832 Radio broadcasting stations
HQ: Cbs Broadcasting Inc.
    51 W 52nd St
    New York NY 10019
    212 975-4321

(P-5698)
CBS CORPORATION
865 Battery St Fl 2/3, San Francisco
(94111-1503)
PHONE..................................415 765-4000
Doug Harvill, *General Mgr*
EMP: 84
SALES (corp-wide): 13.7B **Publicly Held**
SIC: 4832 Radio broadcasting stations
HQ: Cbs Corporation
    51 W 52nd St Bsmt 1
    New York NY 10019
    212 975-4321

(P-5699)
CBS RADIO INC
1071 W Shaw Ave, Fresno (93711-3702)
PHONE..................................559 490-0106
El Smith, *Manager*
EMP: 195
SQ FT: 5,938
SALES (corp-wide): 592.8MM **Publicly Held**
WEB: www.infinityradio.com
SIC: 4832 Radio broadcasting stations, music format
HQ: Cbs Radio Inc.
    345 Hudson St Fl 10
    New York NY 10014
    212 314-9200

(P-5700)
CBS RADIO INC
865 Battery St Fl 3, San Francisco
(94111-1503)
PHONE..................................415 765-4097
EMP: 100
SALES (corp-wide): 592.8MM **Publicly Held**
SIC: 4832 Radio broadcasting stations, music format
HQ: Cbs Radio Inc.
    345 Hudson St Fl 10
    New York NY 10014
    212 314-9200

(P-5701)
CBS RADIO INC
5670 Wilshire Blvd # 200, Los Angeles
(90036-5657)
PHONE..................................323 525-0980
Sials Marshall, *Branch Mgr*
EMP: 200
SALES (corp-wide): 592.8MM **Publicly Held**
SIC: 4832 Radio broadcasting stations, music format
HQ: Cbs Radio Inc.
    345 Hudson St Fl 10
    New York NY 10014
    212 314-9200

(P-5702)
CBS RADIO INC
900 E Washington St # 315, Colton
(92324-8182)
PHONE..................................909 825-9525
Kevin Murphy, *General Mgr*
EMP: 65
SALES (corp-wide): 592.8MM **Publicly Held**
WEB: www.infinityradio.com
SIC: 4832 Radio broadcasting stations
HQ: Cbs Radio Inc.
    345 Hudson St Fl 10
    New York NY 10014
    212 314-9200

(P-5703)
CBS RADIO INC
5901 Venice Blvd, Los Angeles
(90034-1708)
PHONE..................................323 930-1067
Kevin Weatherly, *Manager*
Trevor Shand, *Producer*
Sherry Hanover, *Accounts Exec*
EMP: 100
SALES (corp-wide): 592.8MM **Publicly Held**
WEB: www.infinityradio.com
SIC: 4832 News
HQ: Cbs Radio Inc.
    345 Hudson St Fl 10
    New York NY 10014
    212 314-9200

PRODUCTS & SVCS

(PA)=Parent Co (HQ)=Headquarters (DH)=Div Headquarters

✪ = New Business established in last 2 years

(P-5704)
CBS RADIO INC
5901 Venice Blvd, Los Angeles
(90034-1708)
PHONE................................323 930-7580
Ed Krampf, *Manager*
EMP: 150
SALES (corp-wide): 592.8MM **Publicly Held**
WEB: www.infinityradio.com
SIC: 4832 Radio broadcasting stations
HQ: Cbs Radio Inc.
345 Hudson St Fl 10
New York NY 10014
212 314-9200

(P-5705)
CBS RADIO INC
280 Commerce Cir, Sacramento
(95815-4212)
PHONE................................916 923-6800
Micheal Hornetto, *Manager*
Steve Cottingim, *General Mgr*
EMP: 100
SALES (corp-wide): 592.8MM **Publicly Held**
WEB: www.infinityradio.com
SIC: 4832 Radio broadcasting stations, music format
HQ: Cbs Radio Inc.
345 Hudson St Fl 10
New York NY 10014
212 314-9200

(P-5706)
CM WIND DOWN TOPCO INC
Also Called: Cumulus Media
750 Battery St Ste 300, San Francisco
(94111-1525)
PHONE................................415 995-6800
Mary G Berner, *President*
EMP: 93
SALES (corp-wide): 1.1B **Publicly Held**
SIC: 4832 Radio broadcasting stations
PA: Cm Wind Down Topco Inc.
3280 Peachtree Rd Ne Ne2300
Atlanta GA 30305
404 949-0700

(P-5707)
CUMULUS INTRMDATE HOLDINGS INC
Also Called: Kabc 790 Talk Radio
3321 S La Cienega Blvd, Los Angeles
(90016-3114)
PHONE................................310 840-4900
Octavio Gallardo, *Principal*
EMP: 74
SALES (corp-wide): 1.1B **Publicly Held**
SIC: 4832 Radio broadcasting stations
HQ: Cumulus Intermediate Holdings Inc.
3280 Peachtree Rd Ne # 2300
Atlanta GA 30305

(P-5708)
CUMULUS INTRMDATE HOLDINGS INC
Also Called: Khop
3136 Boeing Way 125, Stockton
(95206-4989)
PHONE................................209 766-5103
Roy Williams, *General Mgr*
EMP: 125
SALES (corp-wide): 1.1B **Publicly Held**
WEB: www.citadelradio.com
SIC: 4832 Radio broadcasting stations
HQ: Cumulus Intermediate Holdings Inc.
3280 Peachtree Rd Ne # 2300
Atlanta GA 30305

(P-5709)
EDUCATIONAL MEDIA FOUNDATION (PA)
Also Called: K-Love Radio Network
5700 West Oaks Blvd, Rocklin
(95765-3719)
PHONE................................916 251-1600
Darrell Chambliss, *Ch of Bd*
Richard Jenkins, *President*
Mike Novak, *CEO*
Jon Taylor, *CFO*
David Atkinson, *Vice Pres*
EMP: 325

SQ FT: 55,000
SALES: 167.4MM **Privately Held**
SIC: 4832 Radio broadcasting stations

(P-5710)
EMMIS COMMUNICATIONS CORP
Emmis Marketting Group
2600 W Olive Ave Fl 8, Burbank
(91505-4553)
PHONE................................818 238-6705
Val Maki, *Branch Mgr*
EMP: 175
SALES (corp-wide): 148.4MM **Publicly Held**
WEB: www.emmis.com
SIC: 4832 Radio broadcasting stations
PA: Emmis Communications Corp
40 Monument Cir Ste 700
Indianapolis IN 46204
317 266-0100

(P-5711)
EMMIS COMMUNICATIONS CORP
790 E Colorado Blvd Fl 9, Pasadena
(91101-2193)
PHONE................................626 484-4440
EMP: 123
SALES (corp-wide): 148.4MM **Publicly Held**
SIC: 4832 Radio broadcasting stations
PA: Emmis Communications Corp
40 Monument Cir Ste 700
Indianapolis IN 46204
317 266-0100

(P-5712)
ENTERCOM COMMUNICATIONS CORP
Also Called: Kseg-FM
5345 Madison Ave, Sacramento
(95841-3141)
PHONE................................916 766-5000
John Geary, *Manager*
Jim Fox, *Vice Pres*
Derrick Dodson, *Info Tech Mgr*
Brian Lopez, *Director*
EMP: 120
SALES (corp-wide): 592.8MM **Publicly Held**
WEB: www.entercom.com
SIC: 4832 7929 Radio broadcasting stations, music format; entertainers & entertainment groups
PA: Entercom Communications Corp.
401 E City Ave Ste 809
Bala Cynwyd PA 19004
610 660-5610

(P-5713)
ENTERCOM COMMUNICATIONS CORP
201 3rd St Fl 12, San Francisco
(94103-3133)
PHONE................................610 660-5610
Betsy O'Connor, *Branch Mgr*
Carolyn Shaw, *Software Dev*
EMP: 109
SALES (corp-wide): 592.8MM **Publicly Held**
WEB: www.entercom.com
SIC: 4832 Radio broadcasting stations
PA: Entercom Communications Corp.
401 E City Ave Ste 809
Bala Cynwyd PA 19004
610 660-5610

(P-5714)
ENTERCOM COMMUNICATIONS CORP
Also Called: K S S J Radio-101.9 FM City
5345 Madison Ave Ste 100, Sacramento
(95841-3141)
PHONE................................916 334-7777
John Geary, *Vice Pres*
EMP: 120
SALES (corp-wide): 592.8MM **Publicly Held**
WEB: www.entercom.com
SIC: 4832 7929 Radio broadcasting stations; entertainers & entertainment groups

PA: Entercom Communications Corp.
401 E City Ave Ste 809
Bala Cynwyd PA 19004
610 660-5610

(P-5715)
ENTRAVSION COMMUNICATIONS CORP
Also Called: Krcx 99 9 FM Tricolor
1436 Auburn Blvd, Sacramento
(95815-2745)
PHONE................................916 646-4000
Angie Balderas, *Manager*
EMP: 50 **Publicly Held**
SIC: 4832 Radio broadcasting stations
PA: Entravision Communications Corporation
2425 Olympic Blvd Ste 600
Santa Monica CA 90404

(P-5716)
FAMILY STATIONS INC (PA)
Also Called: Family Radio
1350 S Loop Rd, Alameda (94502-7095)
PHONE................................510 568-6200
Harold Camping, *President*
Gary Cook, *CFO*
Bill Thornton, *Treasurer*
EMP: 130 EST: 1958
SQ FT: 3,000
SALES: 7.4MM **Privately Held**
WEB: www.familyradio.com
SIC: 4832 Radio broadcasting stations

(P-5717)
FAR EAST BROADCASTING CO INC
Also Called: RADIO STATION KFBS
15700 Imperial Hwy, La Mirada
(90638-2598)
P.O. Box 1 (90637-0001)
PHONE................................562 947-4651
Gregg Harris, *President*
Robert Bartz, *COO*
Charles Blake, *CFO*
Wayne Shepherd, *Bd of Directors*
Lihung Cheng, *Vice Pres*
▲ EMP: 52 EST: 1945
SQ FT: 20,000
SALES: 9.4MM **Privately Held**
SIC: 4832 Radio broadcasting stations

(P-5718)
FM SEOUL BANG SONG INC
Also Called: Kfox
4525 Wilshire Blvd Fl 3, Los Angeles
(90010-3845)
PHONE................................323 525-1650
Seong Hwan Jun, *President*
EMP: 50
SALES (est): 2.8MM
SALES (corp-wide): 83.9MM **Privately Held**
WEB: www.koreatimeshawaii.com
SIC: 4832 Radio broadcasting stations
PA: The Korea Times Los Angeles Inc
3731 Wilshire Blvd
Los Angeles CA 90010
323 692-2000

(P-5719)
FOOTH-DE ANZA COMMUN COLLEG DI
Also Called: Kfjc FM
12345 S El Monte Rd # 6202, Los Altos Hills (94022-4504)
PHONE................................650 949-7260
Eric Johnson, *General Mgr*
EMP: 70
SALES (corp-wide): 128.3MM **Privately Held**
WEB: www.fhda.edu
SIC: 4832 Radio broadcasting stations, music format
PA: Foothill-De Anza Community College District Financing Corporation
12345 S El Monte Rd
Los Altos Hills CA 94022
650 949-6100

(P-5720)
HENRY BROADCASTING CO
2277 Jerrold Ave, San Francisco
(94124-1011)
PHONE................................415 285-1133
C H Buckley, *President*
EMP: 50 EST: 1996
SALES (est): 1.8MM
SALES (corp-wide): 592.8MM **Publicly Held**
SIC: 4832 Radio broadcasting stations
HQ: Cbs Radio Inc.
83 Leo M Birmingham Pkwy
Boston MA 02135

(P-5721)
IHEARTCOMMUNICATIONS INC
Also Called: K Y L D
340 Townsend St Fl 4, San Francisco
(94107-1633)
PHONE................................415 975-5555
Kim Bryant, *Manager*
EMP: 300 **Publicly Held**
SIC: 4832 7313 Radio broadcasting stations; radio advertising representative
HQ: Iheartcommunications, Inc.
20880 Stone Oak Pkwy
San Antonio TX 78258
210 822-2828

(P-5722)
IHEARTCOMMUNICATIONS INC
Also Called: Clear Channel Riverside
2030 Iowa Ave Ste A, Riverside
(92507-7415)
PHONE................................951 684-1992
Bob Ridzak, *General Mgr*
EMP: 61 **Publicly Held**
SIC: 4832 Radio broadcasting stations
HQ: Iheartcommunications, Inc.
20880 Stone Oak Pkwy
San Antonio TX 78258
210 822-2828

(P-5723)
IHEARTCOMMUNICATIONS INC
Also Called: Krzr 103 7 FM
83 E Shaw Ave Ste 150, Fresno
(93710-7622)
PHONE................................559 230-4300
Jeff Negrete, *Branch Mgr*
EMP: 75 **Publicly Held**
SIC: 4832 Radio broadcasting stations
HQ: Iheartcommunications, Inc.
20880 Stone Oak Pkwy
San Antonio TX 78258
210 822-2828

(P-5724)
IHEARTCOMMUNICATIONS INC
Also Called: Kogoam
9660 Gran Rdge Dr Ste 100, San Diego
(92123)
PHONE................................858 522-5547
Dave Schroeder, *Manager*
EMP: 280 **Publicly Held**
SIC: 4832 Radio broadcasting stations
HQ: Iheartcommunications, Inc.
20880 Stone Oak Pkwy
San Antonio TX 78258
210 822-2828

(P-5725)
IHEARTCOMMUNICATIONS INC
Also Called: Kogoam
9660 Gran Rdge Dr Ste 200, San Diego
(92123)
PHONE................................858 292-2000
Dave Schroeder, *Controller*
EMP: 61 **Publicly Held**
SIC: 4832 Radio broadcasting stations
HQ: Iheartcommunications, Inc.
20880 Stone Oak Pkwy
San Antonio TX 78258
210 822-2828

(P-5726)
IHEARTCOMMUNICATIONS INC
3400 W Olive Ave Ste 550, Burbank
(91505-5544)
PHONE................................818 846-0029
Greg Ashlock, *Executive*
EMP: 81 **Publicly Held**
WEB: www.kget.com
SIC: 4832 Radio broadcasting stations

HQ: Iheartcommunications, Inc.
20880 Stone Oak Pkwy
San Antonio TX 78258
210 822-2828

(P-5727)
IHEARTCOMMUNICATIONS INC
1545 River Park Dr # 500, Sacramento
(95815-4616)
PHONE......................................916 929-5325
Sarah McClure, *General Mgr*
EMP: 120 **Publicly Held**
SIC: 4832 Radio broadcasting stations
HQ: Iheartcommunications, Inc.
20880 Stone Oak Pkwy
San Antonio TX 78258
210 822-2828

(P-5728)
IHEARTCOMMUNICATIONS INC
352 E Avenue K4, Lancaster (93535-4505)
PHONE......................................661 942-1268
EMP: 61
SALES (corp-wide): 6.2B **Publicly Held**
SIC: 4832
HQ: Iheartcommunications, Inc.
200 E Basse Rd
San Antonio TX 78258
210 822-2828

(P-5729)
IHEARTCOMMUNICATIONS INC
1440 Ethan Way, Sacramento
(95825-2225)
PHONE......................................916 929-5325
EMP: 61 **Publicly Held**
SIC: 4832 Radio broadcasting stations
HQ: Iheartcommunications, Inc.
20880 Stone Oak Pkwy
San Antonio TX 78258
210 822-2828

(P-5730)
INFINITY BROADCASTING CORP CAL
Also Called: Krth Radio 101 FM
5670 Wilshire Blvd # 200, Los Angeles
(90036-5679)
PHONE......................................323 936-5784
John Sykes, *President*
Maureen Lesourd, *Vice Pres*
EMP: 60 EST: 2001
SALES (est): 2.6MM
SALES (corp-wide): 13.7B **Publicly Held**
SIC: 4832 Radio broadcasting stations
HQ: Cbs Corporation
51 W 52nd St Bsmt 1
New York NY 10019
212 975-4321

(P-5731)
K G O T V NEWS BUREAU
520 3rd St Ste 200, Oakland (94607-3505)
PHONE......................................510 451-4772
Ed Kosowski, *Principal*
EMP: 100
SALES (est): 87.4K
SALES (corp-wide): 1.1B **Publicly Held**
SIC: 4832 Radio broadcasting stations
HQ: San Francisco Radio Assets Llc
750 Battery St Fl 2
San Francisco CA 94111

(P-5732)
KCBS NEWS RADIO 74
865 Battery St, San Francisco
(94111-1554)
PHONE......................................415 765-4112
Doug Harvill, *Manager*
Douglas Sterne, *General Mgr*
Michael Smith, *Engineer*
Ed Cavagnaro, *Director*
EMP: 90
SALES (est): 4.3MM **Privately Held**
SIC: 4832 Radio broadcasting stations

(P-5733)
KIFM SMOOTH JAZZ 981 INC
1615 Murray Canyon Rd, San Diego
(92108-4314)
PHONE......................................619 297-3698
Mike Stafford, *President*
EMP: 110
SQ FT: 12,000

SALES (est): 1.9MM
SALES (corp-wide): 592.8MM **Publicly Held**
SIC: 4832 Radio broadcasting stations
HQ: Abe Entercom Holdings Llc
401 E City Ave Ste 809
Bala Cynwyd PA 19004
404 239-7211

(P-5734)
KKZZ 1590
Also Called: Gold Coast Broadcasting
2284 S Victoria Ave 2g, Ventura
(93003-6641)
PHONE......................................805 289-1400
Chip Ehrhardt, *Partner*
John Hearne, *Partner*
Chriss Cutter, *Accounts Exec*
EMP: 50
SALES (est): 1.3MM **Privately Held**
SIC: 4832 Radio broadcasting stations

(P-5735)
KOXR SPANISH RADIO
Also Called: K O X R
200 S A St Ste 400, Oxnard (93030-5723)
PHONE......................................805 487-0444
Alfredo Placencia, *Owner*
Vicky Orozco, *Sales Mgr*
Maria Foster, *Accounts Exec*
EMP: 50
SALES (est): 1.5MM **Privately Held**
SIC: 4832 Radio broadcasting stations

(P-5736)
KPWR INC
Also Called: Kpwr Power 106
2600 W Olive Ave Ste 850, Burbank
(91505-4568)
PHONE......................................818 953-4200
Jeffrey Smulyan, *CEO*
Doyle Rose, *President*
Candice Del Villar, *Executive*
Terri Dourian, *Human Res Dir*
Ashley Dingess, *Manager*
EMP: 88
SQ FT: 1,700
SALES (est): 21MM
SALES (corp-wide): 148.4MM **Publicly Held**
WEB: www.power106la.com
SIC: 4832 Radio broadcasting stations
PA: Emmis Communications Corp
40 Monument Cir Ste 700
Indianapolis IN 46204
317 266-0100

(P-5737)
KRTY LTD A CAL LTD PARTNR
750 Story Rd, San Jose (95122-2604)
PHONE......................................408 293-8030
Robert S Kieve, *Partner*
EMP: 50
SALES (est): 3.2MM **Privately Held**
WEB: www.krty.com
SIC: 4832 Radio broadcasting stations

(P-5738)
KUIC INC
Also Called: Kuic-Fm
555 Mason St Ste 245, Vacaville
(95688-4640)
PHONE......................................707 446-0200
James Levitt, *Ch of Bd*
John F Levitt, *President*
Barbara Hoover,
Cindy Sacca, *Manager*
Maria Brana, *Accounts Exec*
EMP: 60
SQ FT: 4,200
SALES (est): 2.1MM
SALES (corp-wide): 27MM **Privately Held**
WEB: www.kuic.com
SIC: 4832 2711 Radio broadcasting stations; newspapers
PA: Coast Radio Company Inc
555 Mason St Ste 245
Vacaville CA 95688
707 446-0200

(P-5739)
KUSC RADIO
1149 S Hill St Ste H100, Los Angeles
(90015-4804)
PHONE......................................213 225-7400

Christopher Mendez, *Director*
EMP: 50
SQ FT: 12,000
SALES (est): 1.4MM **Privately Held**
SIC: 4832 Radio broadcasting stations

(P-5740)
LBI MEDIA INC
1845 W Empire Ave, Burbank
(91504-3402)
PHONE......................................818 729-5316
Mike Todd, *Chief Engr*
Pat Cabello, *VP Human Res*
Cristian Garcia, *Manager*
Richard Salgado, *Manager*
EMP: 355
SALES (est): 318.2K
SALES (corp-wide): 236.1MM **Privately Held**
SIC: 4832 Radio broadcasting stations
HQ: Lbi Media Holdings, Inc.
1845 W Empire Ave
Burbank CA 91504

(P-5741)
LELAND STANFORD JUNIOR UNIV
Also Called: Kzsu 90.1 FM
551 Srra Mall Mem Adtrium Memorial Auditorium, Stanford (94305)
PHONE......................................650 725-4868
Mark Lawrence, *Principal*
EMP: 100
SALES (corp-wide): 5.6B **Privately Held**
SIC: 4832 Radio broadcasting stations
PA: Leland Stanford Junior University
450 Serra Mall
Stanford CA 94305
650 723-2300

(P-5742)
LIBERMAN BROADCASTING INC (PA)
1845 W Empire Ave, Burbank
(91504-3402)
PHONE......................................818 729-5300
Lenard D Liberman, *CEO*
Jose Liberman, *President*
Frederic T Boyer, *CFO*
Winter Horton, *Vice Pres*
Eduardo Leon, *Vice Pres*
EMP: 83
SALES (est): 236.1MM **Privately Held**
SIC: 4832 Radio broadcasting stations

(P-5743)
LOCAL MEDIA SAN DIEGO LLC
Also Called: Magic 92.5
6160 Cornerstone Ct E # 150, San Diego
(92121-3720)
PHONE......................................858 888-7000
John Lynch, *CEO*
Norman McKee, *CFO*
Chuck Scriven, *Accounts Mgr*
EMP: 100
SALES (est): 5.8MM **Privately Held**
SIC: 4832 Radio broadcasting stations, music format

(P-5744)
LOTUS COMMUNICATIONS CORP (PA)
3301 Barham Blvd Ste 200, Los Angeles
(90068-1358)
PHONE......................................323 512-2225
Howard Kalmenson, *President*
William H Shriftman, *Treasurer*
Jim Kalmenson, *Senior VP*
Jerry Roy, *Senior VP*
Jasmin Dorismond, *Vice Pres*
EMP: 60 EST: 1959
SQ FT: 25,848
SALES (est): 92.9MM **Privately Held**
WEB: www.lotuscorp.com
SIC: 4832 Radio broadcasting stations

(P-5745)
LOYOLA MARYMOUNT UNIVERSITY
Also Called: Radio Station
1 Lmu Dr Ste 100, Los Angeles
(90045-2677)
PHONE......................................310 338-2866
Lily O'Brien, *General Mgr*

EMP: 120
SALES (corp-wide): 393.2MM **Privately Held**
WEB: www.lmu.edu
SIC: 4832 8221 Radio broadcasting stations; university
PA: Loyola Marymount University
1 Lmu Dr Uhall Ste 4900
Los Angeles CA 90045
310 338-2700

(P-5746)
PACIFIC SPANISH NETWORK INC
296 H St Ste 300, Chula Vista
(91910-4753)
PHONE......................................619 427-6323
Jaime Bonilla Valdez, *President*
EMP: 69
SQ FT: 5,000
SALES (est): 2.7MM **Privately Held**
SIC: 4832 Radio broadcasting stations

(P-5747)
PANDORA MEDIA INC
3000 Ocean Park Blvd # 3050, Santa Monica (90405-3020)
PHONE......................................424 653-6803
EMP: 425
SALES (corp-wide): 1.4B **Publicly Held**
SIC: 4832 Radio broadcasting stations
PA: Pandora Media, Inc.
2101 Webster St Ste 1650
Oakland CA 94612
510 451-4100

(P-5748)
PANDORA MEDIA INC (PA)
2101 Webster St Ste 1650, Oakland
(94612-3015)
PHONE......................................510 451-4100
Naveen Chopra, *CEO*
Alia Calhoun, *Partner*
Sid Keswani, *President*
Etienne Handman, *COO*
Aimee Lapic, *Chief Mktg Ofcr*
EMP: 131
SQ FT: 233,094
SALES: 1.4B **Publicly Held**
WEB: www.pandora.com
SIC: 4832 Radio broadcasting stations

(P-5749)
POWER 106 RADIO
2600 W Olive Ave Fl 8, Burbank
(91505-4553)
PHONE......................................818 953-4200
Pat Thomas, *Manager*
Val Maki, *General Mgr*
Aimee Bittourna, *Director*
David Criscitelli, *Director*
Terry McGovern, *Director*
EMP: 90
SALES (est): 3.4MM **Privately Held**
WEB: www.power106radio.com
SIC: 4832 Radio broadcasting stations

(P-5750)
SALEM MEDIA GROUP INC (PA)
4880 Santa Rosa Rd, Camarillo
(93012-5190)
PHONE......................................805 987-0400
Stuart W Epperson, *Ch of Bd*
Edward G Atsinger III, *CEO*
Evan D Masyr, *CFO*
Helen Matter, *CFO*
Roland S Hinz, *Bd of Directors*
EMP: 115
SQ FT: 46,000
SALES: 263.7MM **Publicly Held**
WEB: www.srnradio.com
SIC: 4832 2731 4813 Radio broadcasting stations; book publishing;

(P-5751)
SALEM MEDIA GROUP INC
Also Called: Krlh-AM 590-AM
701 N Brand Blvd Ste 550, Glendale
(91203-1235)
P.O. Box 29023 (91209-9023)
PHONE......................................818 956-5254
Terry Sahy, *Manager*
Richard Blythe, *Opers-Prdtn-Mfg*
Joshua Jacobs, *Producer*
EMP: 100

P R O D U C T S & S V C S

SALES (corp-wide): 263.7MM **Publicly Held**
WEB: www.srnradio.com
SIC: 4832 Radio broadcasting stations
PA: Salem Media Group, Inc.
4880 Santa Rosa Rd
Camarillo CA 93012
805 987-0400

(P-5752)
SAN DIEGO STATE UNIVERSITY
Also Called: Kpbs Tv
5200 Campanile Dr, San Diego
(92182-1901)
PHONE..............................619 594-1515
Doug Myrland, *General Mgr*
EMP: 100 **Privately Held**
SIC: 4832 4833 8221 9411 Radio broadcasting stations; television broadcasting stations; university; administration of educational programs;
HQ: San Diego State University
5500 Campanile Dr
San Diego CA 92182
-

(P-5753)
SAN FRANCISCO RADIO ASSETS LLC (DH)
Also Called: Kgo 810am
750 Battery St Fl 2, San Francisco
(94111-1523)
PHONE..............................415 216-1300
Deidrea Lieberman,
EMP: 150
SQ FT: 51,000
SALES (est): 32MM
SALES (corp-wide): 1.1B **Publicly Held**
SIC: 4832 Radio broadcasting stations

(P-5754)
TOAD 1350
2030 Iowa Ave Ste A, Riverside
(92507-7415)
PHONE..............................951 369-1350
Bob Ridzak, *Administration*
EMP: 50
SALES (est): 703.1K **Privately Held**
SIC: 4832 Radio broadcasting stations

(P-5755)
TRIAD BROADCASTING COMPANY (PA)
2511 Garden Rd Ste A104, Monterey
(93940-5376)
P.O. Box 7539, Carmel By The Sea
(93921-7539)
PHONE..............................831 655-6350
David J Benjamin, *President*
Steve Feder, *Vice Pres*
EMP: 140
SALES (est): 30.9MM **Privately Held**
SIC: 4832 Radio broadcasting stations

(P-5756)
TRITON MEDIA GROUP LLC (PA)
15303 Ventura Blvd # 1500, Sherman Oaks
(91403-3137)
PHONE..............................323 290-6900
Nathaniel Parker Hudnut, *CEO*
Sean Moriarty, *Ch of Bd*
Patrick Reynolds, *President*
EMP: 1500
SALES (est): 54.9MM **Privately Held**
SIC: 4832 Radio broadcasting stations, music format

(P-5757)
TRITON MEDIA GROUP LLC
Also Called: Dial Global Digital
8935 Lindblade St, Culver City
(90232-2438)
PHONE..............................661 294-9000
Phil Barry, *Branch Mgr*
EMP: 75 **Privately Held**
SIC: 4832 Radio broadcasting stations, music format
PA: Triton Media Group, Llc
15303 Ventura Blvd # 1500
Sherman Oaks CA 91403

(P-5758)
TUNEIN INC
Also Called: Radio Time
210 King St Fl 3, San Francisco
(94107-1702)
PHONE..............................650 319-7100
John Donham, *CEO*
Jason Hable, *President*
Holly Lim, *CFO*
Juliette Morris, *Officer*
Geoff Dowd, *Vice Pres*
EMP: 200
SALES (est): 18.8MM **Privately Held**
SIC: 4832 Radio broadcasting stations

(P-5759)
TURNER BROADCASTING SYSTEM INC
1888 Century Park E # 1200, Los Angeles
(90067-1715)
PHONE..............................310 788-6767
Frank Merauto, *Principal*
Nadia Zia, *Accounts Exec*
EMP: 70
SALES (corp-wide): 160.5B **Publicly Held**
WEB: www.turner.com
SIC: 4832 Radio broadcasting stations
HQ: Turner Broadcasting System, Inc.
1 Cnn Ctr Nw 14sw
Atlanta GA 30303
404 575-7250

(P-5760)
UNIVISION COMMUNICATIONS INC
655 N Central Ave # 2500, Glendale
(91203-1422)
PHONE..............................818 484-7399
Thomas McSweeney, *Branch Mgr*
EMP: 140 **Privately Held**
WEB: www.univision.com
SIC: 4832 Radio broadcasting stations
HQ: Univision Communications Inc.
114 5th Ave
New York NY 10011
212 455-5200

(P-5761)
UNIVISION RADIO INC
601 W Univision Plz, Fresno (93704-1092)
PHONE..............................559 430-8500
Angela Navarrete, *Branch Mgr*
EMP: 50 **Privately Held**
WEB: www.heftel.com
SIC: 4832 Radio broadcasting stations
HQ: Univision Radio, Inc.
2323 Bryan St Ste 1900
Dallas TX 75201
-

(P-5762)
WALT DISNEY COMPANY
Also Called: Kiid
8265 Sierra College Blvd # 21, Roseville
(95661-9403)
PHONE..............................916 780-1470
EMP: 53 **Publicly Held**
SIC: 4832
PA: The Walt Disney Company
500 S Buena Vista St
Burbank CA 91521
-

```
4833 Television
Broadcasting Stations
```

(P-5763)
ABC INC
500 Circle Seven Dr, Glendale
(91201-2331)
PHONE..............................818 863-7801
Arnold J Kleiner, *Director*
EMP: 500 **Publicly Held**
WEB: www.abc.com
SIC: 4833 Television broadcasting stations
HQ: Abc, Inc.
77 W 66th St Rm 100
New York NY 10023
212 456-7777

(P-5764)
ABC CABLE NETWORKS GROUP
900 Front St, San Francisco (94111-1427)
PHONE..............................415 954-7911
Lynn Dooley, *Branch Mgr*
EMP: 200 **Publicly Held**
WEB: www.breakbar.com
SIC: 4833 Television broadcasting stations
HQ: Abc Cable Networks Group
500 S Buena Vista St
Burbank CA 91521
818 460-7477

(P-5765)
ACCESS HOLLYWOOD
Also Called: Channel 4-NBC 4 Television
3000 W Alameda Ave, Burbank
(91523-0001)
PHONE..............................818 840-4444
Jeff Zaker, *CEO*
EMP: 170
SALES (est): 6.1MM **Privately Held**
SIC: 4833 Television broadcasting stations

(P-5766)
ACME TELEVISION HOLDINGS LLC
4790 Irvine Blvd Ste 105, Irvine
(92620-1998)
PHONE..............................714 245-9499
Doug Gealy,
Tom Allen,
EMP: 300
SALES (est): 2.8MM **Privately Held**
SIC: 4833 Television broadcasting stations

(P-5767)
AMERICAN MULTIMEDIA TV USA
Also Called: Amtv USA
530 S Lake Ave Unit 368, Pasadena
(91101-3515)
PHONE..............................626 466-1038
Jason Quin, *President*
EMP: 67
SALES: 357K **Privately Held**
SIC: 4833 7372 Television broadcasting stations; application computer software

(P-5768)
BAY CITY TELEVISION INC (PA)
8253 Ronson Rd, San Diego (92111-2004)
P.O. Box 712109 (92171-2109)
PHONE..............................858 279-6666
Jose Antonio Baston Patino, *CEO*
Robert Taylor, *President*
Rodrigo Salazar, *Vice Pres*
Lupe Zavala, *Executive Asst*
Mark Jacobs, *Research*
EMP: 100
SQ FT: 12,000
SALES (est): 38.5MM **Privately Held**
SIC: 4833 7311 Television broadcasting stations; advertising agencies

(P-5769)
BURBANK TELEVISION ENTPS LLC
4000 Warner Blvd, Burbank (91522-0001)
PHONE..............................818 954-6000
Barry M Meyer, *CEO*
EMP: 200
SALES (est): 2.9MM
SALES (corp-wide): 160.5B **Publicly Held**
SIC: 4833 Television broadcasting stations
HQ: Warner Bros. Entertainment Inc.
4000 Warner Blvd
Burbank CA 91522
818 954-6000

(P-5770)
BUZZTIME INC
2231 Rutherford Rd # 210, Carlsbad
(92008-8811)
PHONE..............................760 476-1976
Dario Santana, *CEO*
EMP: 120 EST: 2000
SALES (est): 5.2MM **Privately Held**
WEB: www.buzztime.com
SIC: 4833 Television broadcasting stations

(P-5771)
CALIFORNIA OREGON BROADCASTING (HQ)
Also Called: Krcr Tv
755 Auditorium Dr, Redding (96001-0920)
PHONE..............................530 243-7777
Sarah Smith, *General Mgr*
EMP: 70 EST: 1963
SQ FT: 14,000
SALES (est): 5.4MM
SALES (corp-wide): 29.9MM **Privately Held**
WEB: www.krcrtv.com
SIC: 4833 Television broadcasting stations
PA: Appalachian Broadcasting Corp
101 Lee St
Bristol VA
276 645-1555

(P-5772)
CATAMOUNT BROADCASTING OF CHIC (PA)
Also Called: Khsl Tv
3460 Silverbell Rd, Chico (95973-0388)
PHONE..............................530 893-2424
Raymond Johns, *President*
EMP: 104
SQ FT: 18,000
SALES (est): 13.6MM **Privately Held**
WEB: www.knvn.com
SIC: 4833 Television broadcasting stations

(P-5773)
CBS BROADCASTING INC
855 Battery St, San Francisco
(94111-1503)
PHONE..............................415 765-0928
Bruno Cohen, *Manager*
Dan Rosenheim, *Vice Pres*
Jeanette Pavini, *Research*
Don Sharp, *Opers Staff*
Thatiana Cruz, *Production*
EMP: 300
SALES (corp-wide): 13.7B **Publicly Held**
WEB: www.cbs4.com
SIC: 4833 Television translator station
HQ: Cbs Broadcasting Inc.
51 W 52nd St
New York NY 10019
212 975-4321

(P-5774)
CBS BROADCASTING INC
4200 Radford Ave, Studio City
(91604-2189)
PHONE..............................818 655-2000
Steve Mauldin, *General Mgr*
Jason Faust, *Vice Pres*
Eric Kern, *Sales Staff*
Pat Leong, *Manager*
EMP: 500
SALES (corp-wide): 13.7B **Publicly Held**
WEB: www.cbs4.com
SIC: 4833 Television broadcasting stations
HQ: Cbs Broadcasting Inc.
51 W 52nd St
New York NY 10019
212 975-4321

(P-5775)
CBS CORPORATION
7800 Beverly Blvd, Los Angeles
(90036-2112)
PHONE..............................323 575-2345
Jonathan Anshell, *Branch Mgr*
Jeff Shultz, *President*
Marc Rayfield, *Senior VP*
Rob Gelick, *Vice Pres*
Matt Skrobalak, *Vice Pres*
EMP: 72
SALES (corp-wide): 13.7B **Publicly Held**
SIC: 4833 Television broadcasting stations
HQ: Cbs Corporation
51 W 52nd St Bsmt 1
New York NY 10019
212 975-4321

(P-5776)
CBS CORPORATION
31276 Dunham Way, Thousand Palms
(92276-3310)
PHONE..............................760 343-5700
Mike Stutz, *Office Mgr*
EMP: 64

▲ = Import ▼=Export
◆ =Import/Export

SALES (corp-wide): 13.7B **Publicly Held**
SIC: **4833** Television broadcasting stations
HQ: Cbs Corporation
51 W 52nd St Bsmt 1
New York NY 10019
212 975-4321

(P-5777)
CHANNEL 40 INC
Also Called: Ktxl-Fox 40
4655 Fruitridge Rd, Sacramento
(95820-5201)
PHONE..................................916 454-4422
Jerry Del Core, *Vice Pres*
EMP: 105
SQ FT: 25,000
SALES (est): 9.4MM
SALES (corp-wide): 1.8B **Publicly Held**
WEB: www.tribune.com
SIC: **4833** Television translator station
PA: Tribune Media Company
515 N State St Ste 2400
Chicago IL 60654
312 222-3394

(P-5778)
CHRONICLE BROADCASTING CO
Also Called: Kron-TV
900 Front St, San Francisco (94111-1427)
PHONE..................................415 561-8000
Francis A Martin III, *President*
Glen E Pickell, *Treasurer*
Ronald Ingram, *Vice Pres*
Robert M Raymer, *Admin Sec*
EMP: 400
SQ FT: 90,000
SALES (est): 17.6MM
SALES (corp-wide): 6.6B **Privately Held**
SIC: **4833** Television broadcasting stations
HQ: Hearst Communications, Inc.
300 W 57th St
New York NY 10019
212 649-2000

(P-5779)
COLLINS AVENUE LLC
5410 Wilshire Blvd # 800, Los Angeles
(90036-4267)
PHONE..................................323 930-6633
Jeff Collins, *President*
Michael Hammond, *Senior VP*
Melanie Moreau, *Senior VP*
John Bradley, *Vice Pres*
Sandi Johnson, *Vice Pres*
EMP: 50
SALES (est): 4.7MM **Privately Held**
SIC: **4833** Television broadcasting stations

(P-5780)
COWLES CALIFORNIA MEDIA CO
Also Called: Kcba Fox TV 35
1550 Moffett St, Salinas (93905-3342)
PHONE..................................831 422-3500
Paul Daghi, *President*
EMP: 70 **Privately Held**
WEB: www.kion46.com
SIC: **4833** Television broadcasting stations
PA: Cowles California Media Company
1550 Moffett St
Salinas CA 93905

(P-5781)
CW NETWORK LLC (PA)
Also Called: Cwtv
3300 W Olive Ave Fl 3, Burbank
(91505-4640)
PHONE..................................818 977-2500
John Maatta,
Lance Alexander, *Partner*
Russell Myerson, *Exec VP*
Thomas Sherman, *Exec VP*
Craig Adams, *Vice Pres*
EMP: 210
SALES (est): 26.9MM **Privately Held**
WEB: www.cwtv.com
SIC: **4833** Television broadcasting stations

(P-5782)
DESERT TELEVISION LLC
Also Called: U-Dub Productions
73185 Highway 111 Ste D, Palm Desert
(92260-3929)
P.O. Box 13917 (92255-3917)
PHONE..................................760 343-5700
Jacqueline L Houston,
James R Houston,
Coleen Call, *Accounts Exec*
EMP: 85
SQ FT: 6,500
SALES (est): 5.3MM **Privately Held**
WEB: www.deserttelevision.com
SIC: **4833** Television broadcasting stations

(P-5783)
ENTERTAINMENT & SPORTS TODAY
Also Called: Rakstar Production
2966 Wilshire Blvd Ste C, Los Angeles
(90010-1128)
PHONE..................................213 388-9050
William Sturges, *CEO*
Frank Rakovic, *Vice Pres*
Martin Altonaga, *Director*
Katz Ueno, *Editor*
EMP: 100
SALES (est): 22MM **Privately Held**
SIC: **4833** **7812** Television broadcasting
stations; video production

(P-5784)
ENTRAVSION COMMUNICATIONS CORP
Also Called: Univision 67
67 Garden Ct, Monterey (93940-5302)
PHONE..................................831 333-9736
Aaron Scoby, *Manager*
EMP: 50 **Publicly Held**
SIC: **4833** Television translator station
PA: Entravsion Communications Corporation
2425 Olympic Blvd Ste 600
Santa Monica CA 90404

(P-5785)
ENTRAVSION COMMUNICATIONS CORP
Also Called: K S S C - F M
5700 Wilshire Blvd # 250, Los Angeles
(90036-3659)
PHONE..................................323 900-6100
Jeff Liberman, *President*
EMP: 100 **Publicly Held**
SIC: **4833** **4832** Television broadcasting
stations; radio broadcasting stations
PA: Entravsion Communications Corporation
2425 Olympic Blvd Ste 600
Santa Monica CA 90404

(P-5786)
ENTRAVSION COMMUNICATIONS CORP
Also Called: Kmir-Tv6
72920 Parkview Dr, Palm Desert
(92260-9357)
PHONE..................................760 568-3636
Craig E Marrs, *President*
Gene Steinberg, *Vice Pres*
Sandie Ware, *Natl Sales Mgr*
EMP: 75 **Publicly Held**
WEB: www.journalbroadcastgroup.com
SIC: **4833** Television broadcasting stations
PA: Entravsion Communications Corporation
2425 Olympic Blvd Ste 600
Santa Monica CA 90404

(P-5787)
ENTRAVSION COMMUNICATIONS CORP
Also Called: Entravsion Radio
1436 Auburn Blvd, Sacramento
(95815-2745)
PHONE..................................916 648-6029
Larry Lamansky, *Manager*
EMP: 50 **Publicly Held**
SIC: **4833** **4832** Television broadcasting
stations; radio broadcasting stations

PA: Entravsion Communications Corporation
2425 Olympic Blvd Ste 600
Santa Monica CA 90404

(P-5788)
ENTRAVSION COMMUNICATIONS CORP (PA)
2425 Olympic Blvd Ste 600, Santa Monica
(90404-4030)
PHONE..................................310 447-3870
Walter F Ulloa, *Ch of Bd*
Jeffery A Liberman, *COO*
Christopher T Young, *CFO*
Patricia Dennis, *Bd of Directors*
Martha Diaz, *Bd of Directors*
EMP: 170
SQ FT: 16,000
SALES: 536MM **Publicly Held**
SIC: **4833** **4832** Television broadcasting
stations; radio broadcasting stations

(P-5789)
ESTRELLA COMMUNICATIONS INC
Also Called: Kvea-Tv-Channel 52
3000 W Alameda Ave, Burbank
(91523-0001)
PHONE..................................818 260-5700
EMP: 90
SALES (est): 3.7MM
SALES (corp-wide): 68.7B **Publicly Held**
SIC: **4833**
HQ: Telemundo Communications Group, Inc.
2290 W 8th Ave
Hialeah FL 33010
305 884-8200

(P-5790)
EW SCRIPPS COMPANY
Also Called: Kgtv
4600 Air Way, San Diego (92102-2528)
PHONE..................................619 237-1010
Derek Dalton, *Vice Pres*
EMP: 150
SALES (corp-wide): 864.8MM **Publicly Held**
WEB: www.rtv6radio.com
SIC: **4833** Television broadcasting stations
PA: The E W Scripps Company
312 Walnut St Ste 2800
Cincinnati OH 45202
513 977-3000

(P-5791)
FISHER COMMUNICATIONS INC
Also Called: Kbaktv
1901 Westwind Dr, Bakersfield
(93301-3016)
PHONE..................................661 327-7955
Teresa Burgess, *Manager*
EMP: 85
SALES (corp-wide): 2.7B **Publicly Held**
SIC: **4833** Television broadcasting stations
HQ: Fisher Communications, Inc.
140 4th Ave N Ste 500
Seattle WA 98109
206 404-7000

(P-5792)
FOX INC (DH)
Also Called: Home Entertainment Div
2121 Ave Of The, Los Angeles (90067)
P.O. Box 900, Beverly Hills (90213-0900)
PHONE..................................310 369-1000
K Rupert Murdoch, *Ch of Bd*
Dan Bell, *President*
Mike Dunn, *President*
Robert Fusco, *President*
Jay Itzkowitz, *President*
▲ EMP: 2000
SQ FT: 25,000
SALES (est): 842.9MM
SALES (corp-wide): 30.4B **Publicly Held**
WEB: www.foxhome.com
SIC: **4833** **7812** Television broadcasting
stations; motion picture production & distribution; motion picture production & distribution; television
HQ: 21st Century Fox America, Inc.
1211 Ave Of The Americas
New York NY 10036
212 852-7000

(P-5793)
FOX BROADCASTING COMPANY (DH)
10201 W Pico Blvd, Los Angeles
(90064-2606)
P.O. Box 900, Beverly Hills (90213-0900)
PHONE..................................310 369-1000
David F Devoe Jr, *CEO*
Chris Cerbo, *Partner*
Michael Thorn, *President*
Nancy Utley, *President*
Joe Earley, *COO*
EMP: 200
SQ FT: 41,000
SALES (est): 163.6MM
SALES (corp-wide): 30.4B **Publicly Held**
WEB: www.wghp.com
SIC: **4833** Television broadcasting stations
HQ: Fox Entertainment Group, Llc
1211 Ave Of The Americas
New York NY 10036
212 852-7000

(P-5794)
FOX TELEVISION STATIONS INC (DH)
Also Called: K T T V-Fox 11
1999 S Bundy Dr, Los Angeles
(90025-5203)
PHONE..................................310 584-2000
Jim Burke, *President*
Roger Ailes, *Ch of Bd*
Tom Herwitz, *President*
Dennis Swanson, *President*
Brian Lewis, *Exec VP*
▲ EMP: 300
SALES (est): 494.3MM
SALES (corp-wide): 30.4B **Publicly Held**
WEB: www.foxtv.com
SIC: **4833** **7313** Television broadcasting
stations; radio, television, publisher representatives
HQ: Fox Entertainment Group, Llc
1211 Ave Of The Americas
New York NY 10036
212 852-7000

(P-5795)
FUEL TV
1440 S Sepulveda Blvd, Los Angeles
(90025-3458)
PHONE..................................310 444-8564
John Stouffer, *Director*
George Greenberg, *Vice Pres*
Andrew Miller, *Supervisor*
EMP: 75
SALES (est): 5.5MM **Privately Held**
SIC: **4833** Television broadcasting stations

(P-5796)
GULF- CALIFORNIA BROADCAST CO
Also Called: Kesq Tv
31276 Dunham Way, Thousand Palms
(92276-3310)
PHONE..................................760 773-0342
John Kuenuke, *President*
EMP: 116
SALES (est): 7.1MM
SALES (corp-wide): 242.1MM **Privately Held**
WEB: www.kesq.com
SIC: **4833** **7922** Television translator station; theatrical producers & services
PA: News-Press & Gazette Company Inc
825 Edmond St
Saint Joseph MO 64501
816 271-8500

(P-5797)
HEARST STATIONS INC
Also Called: K S B W- T V
238 John St, Salinas (93901-3339)
P.O. Box 81651 (93912)
PHONE..................................831 758-8888
Joseph W Heston, *President*
Thomas Chavarria, *Creative Dir*
Ray Cleaveland, *Director*
EMP: 80
SQ FT: 31,681
SALES (corp-wide): 6.6B **Privately Held**
WEB: www.wbal.com
SIC: **4833** Television translator station

P R O D U C T S & S V C S

HQ: Hearst Stations Inc.
3 Television Cir
Sacramento CA 95814
916 446-3333

(P-5798)
HERRING BROADCASTING COMPANY
Also Called: Wealthtv
4757 Morena Blvd, San Diego
(92117-3462)
PHONE..................858 270-6900
Robert Herring Sr, President
EMP: 50
SQ FT: 40,000
SALES (est): 6.3MM Privately Held
SIC: 4833 Television broadcasting stations

(P-5799)
HERRING NETWORKS INC
Also Called: Awe
4757 Morena Blvd, San Diego
(92117-3462)
PHONE..................858 270-6900
Charles P Herring, President
Bruce Littman, Exec VP
Dustan Reidinger, Producer
Kevin Morgan, Internal Med
EMP: 130
SALES (est): 5MM Privately Held
SIC: 4833 Television broadcasting stations

(P-5800)
HULU LLC (PA)
2500 Broadway Ste 200, Santa Monica
(90404-3071)
PHONE..................310 571-4700
Mike Hopkins,
Claire Burke, Partner
Rigo Guillen, Partner
Oscar Rohena, Partner
Chadwick Ho, Senior VP
EMP: 138
SALES (est): 435.9MM Privately Held
WEB: www.hulu.com
SIC: 4833 4813 Television translator sta-
tion;

(P-5801)
INTERNATIONAL MEDIA GROUP INC
1990 S Bundy Dr Ste 850, Los Angeles
(90025-5253)
PHONE..................310 478-1818
Peter Mathes, Ch of Bd
EMP: 80
SQ FT: 17,000
SALES (est): 3.5MM
SALES (corp-wide): 9.2MM Privately
Held
SIC: 4833 Television broadcasting stations
PA: Asianmedia Group Llc
1990 S Bundy Dr Ste 850
Los Angeles CA 90025
310 478-1818

(P-5802)
ION MEDIA NETWORKS INC
Also Called: Kpxn-Tv
2531 Nina St, Pasadena (91107-3708)
PHONE..................818 953-7193
Tyra Donatto, Branch Mgr
EMP: 50
SALES (corp-wide): 237.3MM Privately
Held
SIC: 4833 Television broadcasting stations
PA: Ion Media Networks, Inc.
601 Clearwater Park Rd
West Palm Beach FL 33401
561 659-4122

(P-5803)
KAZA AZTECA AMERICA INC
3900 W Alameda Ave # 1200, Burbank
(91505-4317)
PHONE..................818 241-5400
Eduardo Urdiola, President
Germon Santiago, Manager
Alejandra Wachler, Manager
EMP: 140
SALES (est): 7.8MM Privately Held
SIC: 4833 Television translator station

(P-5804)
KBAK TV CHANNEL 29 CBS
Also Called: Westwind Communications
1901 Westwind Dr, Bakersfield
(93301-3016)
PHONE..................661 327-7955
Wayne Lansche, Owner
EMP: 80
SALES (est): 1.9MM Privately Held
SIC: 4833 Television broadcasting stations

(P-5805)
KCETLINK (PA)
Also Called: Community TV Southern Cal
2900 W Alameda Ave # 600, Burbank
(91505-4220)
PHONE..................747 201-5000
Al Jerome, President
Richard Cook, Ch of Bd
Paul Mason, Officer
Marcy Rodriguez, Officer
Julie Allen, Exec Dir
EMP: 150
SQ FT: 50,000
SALES (est): 22.7MM Privately Held
SIC: 4833 Television broadcasting stations

(P-5806)
KFSN TELEVISION LLC
Also Called: ABC 30
1777 G St, Fresno (93706-1688)
PHONE..................559 442-1170
Dan Adams, President
EMP: 117
SQ FT: 26,962
SALES (est): 9.8MM Publicly Held
SIC: 4833 Television broadcasting stations
HQ: Disney Enterprises, Inc.
500 S Buena Vista St
Burbank CA 91521
818 560-1000

(P-5807)
KFTV
601 W Univision Plz, Fresno (93704-1092)
PHONE..................559 222-2121
Jose Elgorriaga, General Mgr
EMP: 85 EST: 2011
SALES (est): 1.1MM Privately Held
SIC: 4833 Television broadcasting stations

(P-5808)
KGO TELEVISION INC
Also Called: Abc7 Broadcast Center
900 Front St, San Francisco (94111-1413)
PHONE..................415 954-7777
Bill Burton, President
EMP: 230
SQ FT: 153,000
SALES (est): 27.6MM Publicly Held
WEB: www.kgoam810.com
SIC: 4833 Television broadcasting stations
HQ: Abc Holding Company Inc.
77 W 66th St Rm 100
New York NY 10023
212 456-7777

(P-5809)
KMPH FOX 26
Also Called: Pappas Telecasting Company
5111 E Mckinley Ave, Fresno (93727-2033)
PHONE..................559 255-2600
Harry Pappas, Principal
EMP: 170
SALES (est): 7.4MM
SALES (corp-wide): 2.7B Publicly Held
WEB: www.kmph.com
SIC: 4833 Television broadcasting stations
PA: Sinclair Broadcast Group, Inc.
10706 Beaver Dam Rd
Hunt Valley MD 21030
410 568-1500

(P-5810)
KNET TV
5757 Wilshire Blvd # 470, Los Angeles
(90036-5810)
PHONE..................323 469-5638
Larry Rogow, Chairman
EMP: 50
SALES (est): 855.1K Privately Held
SIC: 4833 Television broadcasting stations

(P-5811)
KOCE-TV FOUNDATION
Also Called: Pbs Socal
3080 Bristol St Ste 400, Costa Mesa
(92626-7335)
P.O. Box 25113, Santa Ana (92799-5113)
PHONE..................714 241-4100
Mel Rogers, CEO
Denielle Flores, COO
Jamie A Myers, COO
Susan Truesdale, CFO
Gordon Smith, Technical Staff
EMP: 52
SALES: 15.7MM Privately Held
WEB: www.koce.org
SIC: 4833 Television broadcasting stations

(P-5812)
KQED INC (PA)
Also Called: Kqed Public Media
2601 Mariposa St, San Francisco
(94110-1426)
P.O. Box 410865 (94141-0865)
PHONE..................415 864-2000
John Boland, President
Donald W Derheim, COO
Mitzie Kelley, CFO
Jo Anne Wallace, Vice Pres
Monica Healy, Associate Dir
EMP: 258 EST: 1952
SQ FT: 75,000
SALES (est): 174.9MM Privately Held
WEB: www.kqed.net
SIC: 4833 4832 Television broadcasting
stations; radio broadcasting stations

(P-5813)
KRCA TELEVISION LLC
Also Called: Krca Television Inc
1845 W Empire Ave, Burbank
(91504-3402)
PHONE..................818 563-5722
Jose Liberman, President
Wisdom W Lu, CFO
Leonard Liberman, Exec VP
EMP: 130
SQ FT: 50,000
SALES (est): 5.2MM
SALES (corp-wide): 236.1MM Privately
Held
SIC: 4833 7922 Television broadcasting
stations
PA: Liberman Broadcasting, Inc.
1845 W Empire Ave
Burbank CA 91504
818 729-5300

(P-5814)
KSBY COMMUNICATIONS INC
1772 Calle Joaquin, San Luis Obispo
(93405-7210)
PHONE..................805 541-6666
Kathleen Choal, President
Steve Barth, Director
Tony Cipolla, Director
EMP: 80
SALES (est): 6MM Privately Held
WEB: www.ksby.com
SIC: 4833 Television broadcasting stations

(P-5815)
KSWB INC
Also Called: C W 5
7191 Engineer Rd, San Diego
(92111-1406)
PHONE..................858 492-9269
Robert J Ramsey, President
EMP: 56
SQ FT: 30,000
SALES (est): 6.1MM
SALES (corp-wide): 1.8B Publicly Held
WEB: www.tribune.com
SIC: 4833 Television broadcasting stations
PA: Tribune Media Company
515 N State St Ste 2400
Chicago IL 60654
312 222-3394

(P-5816)
KTSF CHANNEL 26
100 Valley Dr, Brisbane (94005-1318)
PHONE..................415 467-6397
Lincoln Howell, CEO
EMP: 50

SALES (est): 5.6MM
SALES (corp-wide): 13.6MM Privately
Held
WEB: www.ktsf.com
SIC: 4833 Television broadcasting stations
PA: Lincoln Broadcasting Company, A Cali-
fornia Limited Partnership
100 Valley Dr
Brisbane CA 94005
415 508-1056

(P-5817)
KTVU PARTNERSHIP INC
Also Called: Ktvu Television Fox 2
2 Jack London Sq, Oakland (94607-3727)
PHONE..................510 834-1212
Murdock Lachlan, CEO
Don Thompson, Manager
◆ EMP: 230
SALES (est): 25.1MM
SALES (corp-wide): 30.4B Publicly Held
SIC: 4833 Television broadcasting stations
HQ: Fox Television Stations, Inc.
1999 S Bundy Dr
Los Angeles CA 90025
310 584-2000

(P-5818)
KVIE INC (PA)
Also Called: Kvie Channel 6
2030 W El Camino Ave # 100, Sacramento
(95833-1867)
P.O. Box 6 (95812-0006)
PHONE..................916 929-5843
David Lowe, CEO
David Hosley, President
Staci Orlando, CFO
Julie Saqueton, CFO
Mike Cappi, Info Tech Dir
EMP: 60 EST: 1955
SQ FT: 69,000
SALES: 11.2MM Privately Held
WEB: www.capitolweek.com
SIC: 4833 Television broadcasting stations

(P-5819)
KXTV INC
Also Called: K X T V Channel 10
400 Broadway, Sacramento (95818-2041)
PHONE..................916 441-2345
Risa Omega, President
EMP: 155
SQ FT: 29,000
SALES (est): 31.6MM
SALES (corp-wide): 1.9B Publicly Held
WEB: www.news10.net
SIC: 4833 Television broadcasting stations
PA: Tegna Inc.
7950 Jones Branch Dr
Mc Lean VA 22102
703 873-6600

(P-5820)
LIFETIME ENTRMT SVCS LLC
Also Called: Lifetime TV Network
2049 Century Park E # 840, Los Angeles
(90067-3101)
PHONE..................310 556-7500
Maryann Harris, General Mgr
EMP: 70
SALES (corp-wide): 560.9MM Privately
Held
WEB: www.lifetimepress.com
SIC: 4833 5942 Television broadcasting
stations; book stores
HQ: Lifetime Entertainment Services, Llc
235 E 45th St
New York NY 10017
212 424-7000

(P-5821)
LINCOLN TELEVISION INC
Also Called: Ktff
100 Valley Dr, Brisbane (94005-1318)
PHONE..................415 468-2626
Lillian Lincoln Howell, President
EMP: 60
SQ FT: 20,800
SALES (est): 2.9MM Privately Held
SIC: 4833 Television broadcasting stations

(P-5822)
M NETWORK TELEVISION INC
6007 Sepulveda Blvd, Van Nuys
(91411-2502)
PHONE..................818 756-5150

▲ = Import ▼=Export
◆ =Import/Export

Jonathan Murray, *President*
EMP: 50
SALES (est): 724.7K **Privately Held**
SIC: 4833 Television broadcasting stations

(P-5823)
MCKINNON BROADCASTING COMPANY (HQ)
Also Called: Kusi TV Channel 51
4575 Viewridge Ave, San Diego
(92123-1623)
P.O. Box 719051 (92171-9051)
PHONE..................................858 571-5151
Michael D McKinnon, *CEO*
Heather Culver, *Manager*
Jim Angel, *Accounts Exec*
EMP: 150
SQ FT: 30,000
SALES (est): 17.2MM
SALES (corp-wide): 13.7MM **Privately Held**
WEB: www.kusi.com
SIC: 4833 Television broadcasting stations
PA: San Diego's Fifty One, Inc.
5002 S Padre Island Dr
Corpus Christi TX 78411
361 986-8300

(P-5824)
MCKINNON PUBLISHING COMPANY
4575 Viewridge Ave, San Diego
(92123-1623)
PHONE..................................858 571-5151
Michael McKinnon, *President*
EMP: 600
SALES (est): 14MM
SALES (corp-wide): 13.7MM **Privately Held**
WEB: www.kusi.com
SIC: 4833 Television broadcasting stations
HQ: Mckinnon Broadcasting Company
4575 Viewridge Ave
San Diego CA 92123
858 571-5151

(P-5825)
NBC SUBSIDIARY (KNBC-TV) LLC
100 Universal City Plz, Universal City
(91608-1002)
PHONE..................................818 684-5746
Steve Carlston, *President*
Pam Putch, *Senior VP*
Jeremy Adell, *Vice Pres*
Kjerstin Beatty, *Vice Pres*
Pauline Bohm, *Vice Pres*
EMP: 250
SALES (est): 5MM **Privately Held**
SIC: 4833 Television broadcasting stations

(P-5826)
NBC UNIVERSAL INC
3000 W Alameda Ave, Burbank
(91523-0002)
PHONE..................................818 260-5746
Greg Robinson, *Manager*
Jack Noyes, *Editor*
Gary Hanfling, *Supervisor*
Jeff Evans, *Associate*
EMP: 250
SALES (corp-wide): 84.5B **Publicly Held**
WEB: www.nbc.com
SIC: 4833 Television broadcasting stations
HQ: Nbcuniversal, Llc
1221 Ave Of The Amer
New York NY 10020
212 664-4444

(P-5827)
NEWPORT TELEVISION LLC
Kget-TV
2120 L St, Bakersfield (93301-2331)
PHONE..................................661 283-1700
Sandy Dipasquale, *President*
EMP: 90
SALES (corp-wide): 51.2MM **Privately Held**
SIC: 4833 Television translator station
PA: Newport Television Llc
460 Nichols Rd Ste 250
Kansas City MO 64112
816 751-0200

(P-5828)
NEXSTAR BROADCASTING INC
Also Called: Ksee
5035 E Mckinley Ave, Fresno (93727-1964)
PHONE..................................559 222-2411
Elena Valles, *Manager*
EMP: 125
SALES (est): 2.4B **Publicly Held**
SIC: 4833 Television broadcasting stations
HQ: Nexstar Broadcasting, Inc.
545 E John Carpenter Fwy # 700
Irving TX 75062
972 373-8800

(P-5829)
NEXSTAR BROADCASTING INC
Also Called: Kron
900 Front St Ste 300, San Francisco
(94111-1445)
P.O. Box 3412 (94109)
PHONE..................................415 441-4444
Angela Fawcett, *Manager*
Amy Mc Combs, *Administration*
EMP: 300
SALES (corp-wide): 2.4B **Publicly Held**
WEB: www.telegram.com
SIC: 4833 Television broadcasting stations
HQ: Nexstar Broadcasting, Inc.
545 E John Carpenter Fwy # 700
Irving TX 75062
972 373-8800

(P-5830)
NTN BUZZTIME INC (PA)
2231 Rutherford Rd # 200, Carlsbad
(92008-8820)
PHONE..................................760 438-7400
Ram Krishnan, *CEO*
Jeff Berg, *Ch of Bd*
Allen Wolff, *CFO*
Steve Mitgang, *Bd of Directors*
Dave Miller, *Senior VP*
▲ **EMP:** 95
SQ FT: 28,000
SALES: 21.2MM **Publicly Held**
WEB: www.ntnwireless.com
SIC: 4833 4841 7372 Television broadcasting stations; direct broadcast satellite services (DBS); prepackaged software

(P-5831)
ODS TECHNOLOGIES LP
Also Called: Television Games Network
6701 Center Dr W Ste 160, Los Angeles
(90045-1558)
PHONE..................................310 242-9400
David Nathanson, *General Ptnr*
Andrew Champagne, *Producer*
Luciana Bach, *Marketing Mgr*
Danny Kovoloff, *Marketing Mgr*
Stillman Kelly, *Senior Mgr*
EMP: 165
SQ FT: 20,000
SALES (est): 20MM **Privately Held**
SIC: 4833 7948 Television broadcasting stations; horses, racing
HQ: Betfair Group Limited
Waterfront
London
208 834-8000

(P-5832)
PARTICIPANT CHANNEL INC
331 Foothill Rd Fl 3, Beverly Hills
(90210-3669)
PHONE..................................310 550-7715
Evan Shapiro, *President*
Robert Murphy, *CFO*
Jeff Ivers, *Senior VP*
Gabriel Brakin, *Admin Sec*
EMP: 63
SALES: 13.8MM **Privately Held**
SIC: 4833 Television broadcasting stations

(P-5833)
REVOLT MEDIA AND TV LLC
1800 N Highland Ave Fl 7, Los Angeles
(90028-4522)
PHONE..................................323 645-3000
Keith Clinkscales,
EMP: 120
SALES (est): 10.4MM **Privately Held**
SIC: 4833 Television broadcasting stations

PA: Bad Boy Entertainment Holdings, Inc.
1710 Broadway Fl 2
New York NY 10019
-

(P-5834)
S F BROADCASTING OF WISCONSIN
2425 Olympic Blvd, Santa Monica
(90404-4030)
PHONE..................................310 586-2410
EMP: 151
SALES (est): 2.9MM
SALES (corp-wide): 3.2B **Publicly Held**
SIC: 4833
PA: Iac/Interactivecorp
555 W 18th St
New York NY 10011
212 314-7300

(P-5835)
SACRAMENTO TELEVISION STNS INC (DH)
Also Called: Kmax TV
2713 Kovr Dr, West Sacramento
(95605-1600)
PHONE..................................916 374-1452
Peter Dunn, *CEO*
EMP: 152
SQ FT: 40,000
SALES (est): 47.9MM
SALES (corp-wide): 13.7B **Publicly Held**
SIC: 4833 Television broadcasting stations
HQ: Cbs Corporation
51 W 52nd St Bsmt 1
New York NY 10019
212 975-4321

(P-5836)
SAN MATEO COUNTY COMMUNITY
Also Called: Kcsm TV & Radio
1700 W Hillsdale Blvd, San Mateo
(94402-3757)
PHONE..................................650 574-6586
Marilyn Lawrence, *Manager*
James Carranza, *Dean*
Sharon Bartels, *Hlthcr Dir*
Bryan Faulds, *Associate*
EMP: 51
SALES (corp-wide): 81.5MM **Privately Held**
WEB: www.smcccd.cc.ca.us
SIC: 4833 4832 Television broadcasting stations; radio broadcasting stations
PA: San Mateo County Community College District
3401 Csm Dr
San Mateo CA 94402
650 358-6795

(P-5837)
SITV INC
Also Called: Nuvo TV
700 N Central Ave Ste 600, Glendale
(91203-3438)
PHONE..................................323 317-9534
Michael Schwimmer, *CEO*
Edward Mateo, *Facilities Mgr*
EMP: 57
SALES (est): 3MM
SALES (corp-wide): 17.1MM **Privately Held**
SIC: 4833 Television broadcasting stations
PA: Fuse Media Inc.
700 N Central Ave Fl 6
Glendale CA 91203
323 256-8900

(P-5838)
SMITH BROADCASTING GROUP INC
Also Called: Keyt Television
730 Miramonte Dr, Santa Barbara
(93109-1417)
P.O. Box 729 (93102-0729)
PHONE..................................805 882-3933
Michael Granados, *General Mgr*
EMP: 85
SALES (corp-wide): 15.2MM **Privately Held**
SIC: 4833 7313 Television broadcasting stations; television & radio time sales

PA: Smith Broadcasting Group, Inc
2315 Red Rose Way
Santa Barbara CA 93109
805 965-0400

(P-5839)
STATION VENTURE OPERATIONS LP
Also Called: NBC 7/Channel 39
9680 Granite Ridge Dr, San Diego
(92123-2673)
PHONE..................................619 231-3939
Dick Kelley, *General Mgr*
Greg Dawson, *Vice Pres*
Jackie Bradford, *General Mgr*
Claudine Contreras, *Producer*
Jim Laslavic, *Director*
▲ **EMP:** 76
SQ FT: 23,000
SALES (est): 6.9MM
SALES (corp-wide): 84.5B **Publicly Held**
WEB: www.nbc.com
SIC: 4833 Television broadcasting stations
HQ: Nbcuniversal, Llc
1221 Ave Of The Amer
New York NY 10020
212 664-4444

(P-5840)
TRINITY BRDCSTG NETWRK INC
Also Called: Trinity Christn Ctr Santa Ana
2442 Michelle Dr, Tustin (92780-7015)
PHONE..................................714 665-3619
Paul F Crouch, *President*
EMP: 150
SALES: 5MM
SALES (corp-wide): 141.2MM **Privately Held**
SIC: 4833 Television broadcasting stations
PA: Trinity Christian Center Of Santa Ana, Inc.
2442 Michelle Dr
Tustin CA 92780
714 665-3619

(P-5841)
TRINITY CHRISTIAN CENTER OF SA (PA)
Also Called: Trinity Broadcasting Network
2442 Michelle Dr, Tustin (92780-7015)
P.O. Box A, Santa Ana (92711-2101)
PHONE..................................714 665-3619
Janice W Crouch, *Principal*
Paul F Crouch, *President*
Jim Mittan, *CFO*
Randall Riley, *Executive*
Linda Cook, *General Mgr*
▲ **EMP:** 200
SQ FT: 20,000
SALES: 141.2MM **Privately Held**
WEB: www.paulcrouch.com
SIC: 4833 7922 Television broadcasting stations; television program, including commercial producers

(P-5842)
TV 36
Also Called: Kicu TV 36
2102 Commerce Dr, San Jose
(95131-1804)
PHONE..................................408 953-3636
Tom Raponi, *General Mgr*
Robert Martinez, *Manager*
EMP: 50
SQ FT: 25,000
SALES (est): 2.8MM **Privately Held**
SIC: 4833 Television broadcasting stations

(P-5843)
TVU NETWORKS CORPORATION (PA)
857 Maude Ave, Mountain View
(94043-4021)
PHONE..................................650 969-6732
Paul Shen, *President*
Kap Shin, *Exec VP*
Dan Lofgren, *Senior VP*
Chris Bell, *Vice Pres*
David Robertson, *Vice Pres*
▲ **EMP:** 74
SALES (est): 8.1MM **Privately Held**
SIC: 4833 Television broadcasting stations

(P-5844)
UNIVISION TELEVISION GROUP INC
601 W Univision Plz, Fresno (93704-1092)
PHONE..........................559 222-2121
Maria Guttierrez, *Branch Mgr*
EMP: 65 Privately Held
WEB: www.univison.net
SIC: 4833 Television broadcasting stations
HQ: Univision Television Group, Inc.
500 Frank W Burr Blvd # 20
Teaneck NJ 07666
201 287-4141

(P-5845)
UNIVISION TELEVISION GROUP INC
Also Called: Kdtv
1940 Zanker Rd, San Jose (95112-4216)
PHONE..........................415 538-8000
Marcela Medina, *Principal*
EMP: 70 Privately Held
WEB: www.univison.net
SIC: 4833 Television broadcasting stations
HQ: Univision Television Group, Inc.
500 Frank W Burr Blvd # 20
Teaneck NJ 07666
201 287-4141

(P-5846)
UNIVISION TELEVISION GROUP INC
5770 Ruffin Rd, San Diego (92123-1013)
PHONE..........................858 576-1919
Philip Wilkinson, *Manager*
EMP: 50 Privately Held
WEB: www.univison.net
SIC: 4833 Television broadcasting stations
HQ: Univision Television Group, Inc.
500 Frank W Burr Blvd # 20
Teaneck NJ 07666
201 287-4141

(P-5847)
WALT DISNEY COMPANY
532 Paula Ave, Glendale (91201-2328)
PHONE..........................818 544-5009
EMP: 331 Publicly Held
SIC: 4833 Television broadcasting stations
PA: The Walt Disney Company
500 S Buena Vista St
Burbank CA 91521

(P-5848)
WALT DISNEY COMPANY
914 N Victory Blvd, Burbank (91502-1632)
PHONE..........................818 295-3134
EMP: 331 Publicly Held
SIC: 4833 4841 7011 7996 Television
broadcasting stations; cable television
services; resort hotel; amusement parks;
motion picture & video production; books:
publishing only
PA: The Walt Disney Company
500 S Buena Vista St
Burbank CA 91521

(P-5849)
WALT DISNEY COMPANY
Also Called: Lighting Department
121 E Buena Vista, Burbank (91521-0001)
PHONE..........................818 560-1268
Anthony Orefice, *Branch Mgr*
EMP: 100 Publicly Held
SIC: 4833 Television broadcasting stations
PA: The Walt Disney Company
500 S Buena Vista St
Burbank CA 91521

(P-5850)
WALT DISNEY COMPANY
500 S Buena Vista St, Burbank
(91521-0007)
PHONE..........................818 460-6655
EMP: 331 Publicly Held
SIC: 4833 4841 7011 7996 Television
broadcasting stations; cable television
services; resort hotel; amusement parks;
motion picture & video production only

PA: The Walt Disney Company
500 S Buena Vista St
Burbank CA 91521

(P-5851)
WALT DISNEY COMPANY
Walt Disney Studios HM Entrmt
500 S Buena Vista St, Burbank
(91521-0007)
PHONE..........................818 560-1000
EMP: 1000 Publicly Held
SIC: 4833 Television broadcasting stations
PA: The Walt Disney Company
500 S Buena Vista St
Burbank CA 91521

(P-5852)
WALT DISNEY COMPANY (PA)
500 S Buena Vista St, Burbank
(91521-0007)
PHONE..........................818 560-1000
Robert A Iger, *Ch of Bd*
Christine M McCarthy, *CFO*
Jayne Parker, *Sr Exec VP*
Paul Andersen, *Vice Pres*
Dorothy Attwood, *Vice Pres*
◆ **EMP: 1884**
SALES: 55.1B Publicly Held
WEB: www.corporate.disney.go.com
SIC: 4833 4841 7011 7996 Television
broadcasting stations; cable television
services; resort hotel; amusement parks;
motion picture & video production; books:
publishing only

(P-5853)
WALT DISNEY COMPANY
Also Called: Walt Disney Studios
350 S Buena Vista St, Burbank
(91521-0004)
PHONE..........................818 560-1000
Walter Parkes, *Owner*
Marko Simic, *President*
Eddie Drake, *Vice Pres*
Kevin Frawley, *Vice Pres*
David Jessen, *Vice Pres*
EMP: 331 Publicly Held
SIC: 4833 4841 7011 7996 Television
broadcasting stations; cable television
services; resort hotel; amusement parks
PA: The Walt Disney Company
500 S Buena Vista St
Burbank CA 91521

(P-5854)
YOUNG BRDCSTG OF SAN FRANCISCO
Also Called: Kron-TV
900 Front St, San Francisco (94111-1427)
PHONE..........................415 441-4444
Deb McDermot, *President*
EMP: 150
SALES (est): 9.1MM
SALES (corp-wide): 2.4B Publicly Held
WEB: www.kron-tv.com
SIC: 4833 Television broadcasting stations
HQ: Young Broadcasting, Llc
599 Lexington Ave
New York NY 10022
517 372-8282

4841 Cable & Other Pay TV Svcs

(P-5855)
A&E TELEVISION NETWORKS LLC
2049 Century Park E # 800, Los Angeles
(90067-3101)
PHONE..........................310 201-6015
Jenny Barmach, *Branch Mgr*
Steven Goore, *Account Dir*
EMP: 208
SALES (corp-wide): 560.9MM Privately Held
SIC: 4841 Cable television services
PA: A&E Television Networks, Llc
235 E 45th St Fl 9
New York NY 10017
212 210-1400

(P-5856)
ABS-CBN INTERNATIONAL (DH)
2001 Junipero Serra Blvd # 200, Daly City
(94014-3886)
PHONE..........................800 527-2820
Eugenio Lopez III, *CEO*
Raul Echivarre, *President*
Olivia De Jesus, *Managing Dir*
Chinky Dejesus, *Managing Dir*
Tina Zamora, *Managing Dir*
▲ **EMP: 140**
SQ FT: 12,000
SALES (est): 67.8MM
SALES (corp-wide): 9.2MM Privately Held
WEB: www.abs-cbni.com
SIC: 4841 7822 Cable & other pay televi-
sion services; television & video tape dis-
tribution
HQ: Abs-Cbn Interactive, Inc.
9th Floor Eugenio Lopez Jr., Commu-
nication Center
Quezon City
241 522-72

(P-5857)
BDR INDUSTRIES INC (PA)
Also Called: R N D Enterprises
820 E Avenue L12, Lancaster
(93535-5403)
PHONE..........................661 940-8554
Scott Riddle, *President*
Edward Donovan, *Vice Pres*
▲ **EMP: 95**
SQ FT: 30,000
SALES (est): 21.7MM Privately Held
WEB: www.rndcable.com
SIC: 4841 Cable television services

(P-5858)
BRIGHT HOUSE NETWORKS LLC
4450 California Ave Ste A, Bakersfield
(93309-1196)
PHONE..........................661 634-2200
Joseph Schoenstein, *Manager*
Jared Orton, *Info Tech Mgr*
Peter Bajwa, *Technical Staff*
EMP: 90
SALES (corp-wide): 41.5B Publicly Held
SIC: 4841 Cable television services
HQ: Bright House Networks, Llc
5823 Widewaters Pkwy # 2
East Syracuse NY 13057
315 438-4100

(P-5859)
CALIFORNIA BROADCAST CTR LLC
3800 Via Oro Ave, Long Beach
(90810-1866)
PHONE..........................310 233-2425
Bruce Churchill, *CEO*
EMP: 200
SALES (est): 7.8MM
SALES (corp-wide): 160.5B Publicly Held
SIC: 4841 Cable & other pay television
services
HQ: Directv Latin America, Llc
1 Rockefeller Plz
New York NY 10020
212 205-0500

(P-5860)
CHARTER CMMNCTONS OPRATING LLC
12180 Ridgecrest Rd # 102, Victorville
(92395-7798)
PHONE..........................760 452-8609
Toll Free:..........................877
Robert Brown, *Branch Mgr*
EMP: 100
SALES (corp-wide): 41.5B Publicly Held
WEB: www.charter.ordercableonline.com
SIC: 4841 Cable television services
HQ: Charter Communications Operating Llc
12405 Powerscourt Dr
Saint Louis MO 63131
314 965-0555

(P-5861)
CHARTER CMMNCTONS OPRATING LLC
4031 Via Oro Ave, Long Beach
(90810-1458)
PHONE..........................310 971-4001
Eric Brown, *Vice Pres*
Ron Petke, *Director*
EMP: 300
SALES (corp-wide): 41.5B Publicly Held
WEB: www.charter.ordercableonline.com
SIC: 4841 7371 Cable television services;
custom computer programming services
HQ: Charter Communications Operating Llc
12405 Powerscourt Dr
Saint Louis MO 63131
314 965-0555

(P-5862)
CHARTER CMMNCTONS OPRATING LLC
5797 Eastside Rd, Redding (96001-4548)
PHONE..........................530 241-7352
Marcie Farmer, *Manager*
EMP: 50
SALES (corp-wide): 41.5B Publicly Held
WEB: www.charter.ordercableonline.com
SIC: 4841 Cable television services
HQ: Charter Communications Operating Llc
12405 Powerscourt Dr
Saint Louis MO 63131
314 965-0555

(P-5863)
CNN AMERICA INC
6430 W Sunset Blvd # 300, Los Angeles
(90028-7901)
PHONE..........................323 993-5000
Suzanne Spurgeon, *Principal*
Jason Hochheimer, *Director*
EMP: 80
SALES (corp-wide): 160.5B Publicly Held
SIC: 4841 Cable television services
HQ: Cnn America Inc
190 Marietta St Nw 12s
Atlanta GA 30303
404 827-1700

(P-5864)
COMCA SPORT NET BAY AREA
360 3rd St Fl 2, San Francisco
(94107-2154)
PHONE..........................415 896-2557
Richard Cotton, *Mng Member*
National Broadcasting, *General Ptnr*
G C Broadc, *Director*
EMP: 150
SALES (est): 6.1MM
SALES (corp-wide): 84.5B Publicly Held
WEB: www.ifc.com
SIC: 4841 Cable television services
HQ: Nbcuniversal Media, Llc
30 Rockefeller Plz Fl 2
New York NY 10112
212 664-4444

(P-5865)
COMCAST CALIFORNIA IX INC
1111 Andersen Dr, San Rafael
(94901-5394)
PHONE..........................215 286-3345
Paul Gibson, *Vice Pres*
Megan Bishop, *Info Tech Mgr*
Gary Wasley, *Producer*
EMP: 99
SALES: 950K
SALES (corp-wide): 84.5B Publicly Held
SIC: 4841 Cable & other pay television
services
HQ: Nbcuniversal Media, Llc
30 Rockefeller Plz Fl 2
New York NY 10112
212 664-4444

(P-5866)
COMCAST CBLE CMMUNICATIONS LLC
6320 Arizona Cir, Los Angeles
(90045-1202)
PHONE..........................310 216-3500
Donna Delaney, *Manager*
Anthony Jimenez, *Manager*
EMP: 50

▲ = Import ▼=Export
◆ =Import/Export

SALES (corp-wide): 84.5B **Publicly Held**
WEB: www.comcastmediacenter.com
SIC: **4841** Cable television services
HQ: Comcast Cable Communications, Llc
1701 John F Kennedy Blvd
Philadelphia PA 19103
-

(P-5867)
**COMCAST CBLE
CMMUNICATIONS LLC**
Also Called: Comcast West Bay Area
1485 Bay Shore Blvd # 125, San Francisco
(94124-3002)
PHONE......................415 715-0524
Darrell Johnson, *Manager*
EMP: 101
SALES (corp-wide): 84.5B **Publicly Held**
WEB: www.comcastmediacenter.com
SIC: **4841** Cable television services
HQ: Comcast Cable Communications, Llc
1701 John F Kennedy Blvd
Philadelphia PA 19103

(P-5868)
**COMCAST CBLE
CMMUNICATIONS LLC**
1031 N Plaza Dr, Visalia (93291-9473)
PHONE......................559 253-4050
Tony Queasada, *Principal*
Jess Resendez, *Director*
EMP: 101
SALES (corp-wide): 84.5B **Publicly Held**
SIC: **4841** Cable television services
HQ: Comcast Cable Communications, Llc
1701 John F Kennedy Blvd
Philadelphia PA 19103
-

(P-5869)
**COMCAST CBLE
CMMUNICATIONS LLC**
6357 Arizona Cir, Los Angeles
(90045-1201)
PHONE......................310 216-3686
Dave Scharrer, *Manager*
EMP: 101
SALES (corp-wide): 84.5B **Publicly Held**
WEB: www.comcastmediacenter.com
SIC: **4841** Cable television services
HQ: Comcast Cable Communications, Llc
1701 John F Kennedy Blvd
Philadelphia PA 19103
-

(P-5870)
COMCAST CORPORATION
2860 Gateway Oaks Dr, Sacramento
(95833-3508)
PHONE......................916 459-2964
Bruce W Quick, *Manager*
EMP: 56
SALES (corp-wide): 84.5B **Publicly Held**
SIC: **4841** Cable television services
PA: Comcast Corporation
1701 Jfk Blvd
Philadelphia PA 19103
215 286-1700

(P-5871)
COMCAST CORPORATION
860 Stanton Rd, Burlingame (94010-1404)
PHONE......................650 689-5392
EMP: 57
SALES (corp-wide): 84.5B **Publicly Held**
SIC: **4841** Cable television services
PA: Comcast Corporation
1701 Jfk Blvd
Philadelphia PA 19103
215 286-1700

(P-5872)
COMCAST CORPORATION
1 La Avanzada St Rm 111, San Francisco
(94131-1124)
PHONE......................415 665-5507
Bob Dichappari, *Branch Mgr*
EMP: 57
SALES (corp-wide): 84.5B **Publicly Held**
WEB: www.comcast.com
SIC: **4841** Cable television services

PA: Comcast Corporation
1701 Jfk Blvd
Philadelphia PA 19103
215 286-1700

(P-5873)
COMCAST CORPORATION
166 Watson Ln, American Canyon
(94503-9632)
PHONE......................707 266-7584
EMP: 57
SALES (corp-wide): 84.5B **Publicly Held**
SIC: **4841** Cable television services
PA: Comcast Corporation
1701 Jfk Blvd
Philadelphia PA 19103
215 286-1700

(P-5874)
COMCAST CORPORATION
Also Called: A Comcast
3801 Pelandale Ave A11, Modesto
(95356-8303)
PHONE......................209 222-3656
EMP: 56
SALES (corp-wide): 84.5B **Publicly Held**
SIC: **4841** Cable television services
PA: Comcast Corporation
1701 Jfk Blvd
Philadelphia PA 19103
215 286-1700

(P-5875)
COMCAST CORPORATION
221 2nd St, Sausalito (94965-2429)
PHONE......................415 367-4153
EMP: 55
SALES (corp-wide): 84.5B **Publicly Held**
SIC: **4841** Cable television services
PA: Comcast Corporation
1701 Jfk Blvd
Philadelphia PA 19103
215 286-1700

(P-5876)
COMCAST CORPORATION
23525 Clawiter Rd, Hayward (94545-1328)
PHONE......................510 266-3200
Neal James, *Chairman*
Tony Fox, *Technician*
Michael Serafin, *Producer*
John Dahlman, *Master*
EMP: 56
SALES (corp-wide): 84.5B **Publicly Held**
SIC: **4841** Cable television services
PA: Comcast Corporation
1701 Jfk Blvd
Philadelphia PA 19103
215 286-1700

(P-5877)
COMCAST CORPORATION
425 Corona Mall, Corona (92879-1419)
PHONE......................951 268-9378
Mark Hooper, *Principal*
EMP: 57
SALES (corp-wide): 84.5B **Publicly Held**
SIC: **4841** Cable television services
PA: Comcast Corporation
1701 Jfk Blvd
Philadelphia PA 19103
215 286-1700

(P-5878)
COMCAST CORPORATION
Also Called: Comcast Cable
203 N 27th St, San Jose (95116-1121)
PHONE......................408 216-2878
EMP: 56
SALES (corp-wide): 84.5B **Publicly Held**
SIC: **4841** Cable television services
PA: Comcast Corporation
1701 Jfk Blvd
Philadelphia PA 19103
215 286-1700

(P-5879)
COMCAST CORPORATION
Also Called: Comcast Cable
1300 W Yosemite Ave, Madera
(93637-6320)
PHONE......................559 474-4194
EMP: 56
SALES (corp-wide): 84.5B **Publicly Held**
SIC: **4841** Cable television services

PA: Comcast Corporation
1701 Jfk Blvd
Philadelphia PA 19103
215 286-1700

(P-5880)
COMCAST CORPORATION
Also Called: Comcast Cable
2414 E Acacia Ave, Fresno (93726-0303)
PHONE......................559 718-9917
EMP: 56
SALES (corp-wide): 84.5B **Publicly Held**
SIC: **4841** Cable television services
PA: Comcast Corporation
1701 Jfk Blvd
Philadelphia PA 19103
215 286-1700

(P-5881)
COMCAST CORPORATION
Also Called: Comcast Cable
810 Randolph St, NAPA (94559-2911)
PHONE......................707 266-7012
Timothy J Thorp, *Technician*
EMP: 56
SALES (corp-wide): 84.5B **Publicly Held**
SIC: **4841** Cable television services
PA: Comcast Corporation
1701 Jfk Blvd
Philadelphia PA 19103
215 286-1700

(P-5882)
COMCAST CORPORATION
Also Called: Advertising Department
5462 E Del Amo Blvd 239, Long Beach
(90808-1122)
PHONE......................800 240-3640
EMP: 57
SALES (corp-wide): 84.5B **Publicly Held**
SIC: **4841** 4813 7812 7996 Cable television services; subscription television services; telephone communication, except
radio; ; ; ; television film production;
theme park, amusement
PA: Comcast Corporation
1701 Jfk Blvd
Philadelphia PA 19103
215 286-1700

(P-5883)
COMCAST CORPORATION
550 Garcia Ave, Pittsburg (94565-4901)
PHONE......................925 432-0500
Dee Trotta, *Principal*
Ron Albright, *Software Dev*
William Crawford, *Supervisor*
EMP: 81
SALES (corp-wide): 84.5B **Publicly Held**
WEB: www.comcast.com
SIC: **4841** Cable television services
PA: Comcast Corporation
1701 Jfk Blvd
Philadelphia PA 19103
215 286-1700

(P-5884)
COMCAST CORPORATION
1750 Creekside Oaks Dr # 100, Sacra-
mento (95833-3647)
PHONE......................916 830-6790
Marty Robinson, *Branch Mgr*
Quintan Taylor, *Engineer*
Dameon Campbell, *Manager*
Shannon Bleeker, *Accounts Exec*
EMP: 300
SALES (corp-wide): 84.5B **Publicly Held**
WEB: www.comcast.com
SIC: **4841** Cable television services
PA: Comcast Corporation
1701 Jfk Blvd
Philadelphia PA 19103
215 286-1700

(P-5885)
COMCAST CORPORATION
50 Francisco St Fl 3, San Francisco
(94133-2134)
PHONE......................415 835-5700
Craig Coane, *General Mgr*
Amanda Babb, *Executive*
Drew Bruno, *Sales Staff*
Julien Cornil, *Manager*
Sundra Simmons, *Manager*
EMP: 100

SALES (corp-wide): 84.5B **Publicly Held**
WEB: www.comcast.com
SIC: **4841** Cable television services
PA: Comcast Corporation
1701 Jfk Blvd
Philadelphia PA 19103
215 286-1700

(P-5886)
COMCAST CORPORATION
6505 Tam O Shanter Dr, Stockton
(95210-3349)
PHONE......................209 955-6521
Eileen Martin, *Manager*
Gonzalo Ruiz, *Supervisor*
EMP: 57
SALES (corp-wide): 84.5B **Publicly Held**
WEB: www.comcast.com
SIC: **4841** Cable television services
PA: Comcast Corporation
1701 Jfk Blvd
Philadelphia PA 19103
215 286-1700

(P-5887)
COMCAST CORPORATION
900 N Cahuenga Blvd, Los Angeles
(90038-2615)
PHONE......................323 993-8000
Paula David, *Principal*
John Fouhy, *Director*
EMP: 57
SALES (corp-wide): 84.5B **Publicly Held**
WEB: www.comcast.com
SIC: **4841** Cable television services
PA: Comcast Corporation
1701 Jfk Blvd
Philadelphia PA 19103
215 286-1700

(P-5888)
COMCAST CORPORATION
2001 Diamond Blvd 150, Concord
(94520-5701)
PHONE......................925 271-9794
EMP: 300
SALES (corp-wide): 84.5B **Publicly Held**
WEB: www.comcast.com
SIC: **4841** Cable television services
PA: Comcast Corporation
1701 Jfk Blvd
Philadelphia PA 19103
215 286-1700

(P-5889)
COMCAST CORPORATION
2455 Henderson Way, Monterey
(93940-5303)
P.O. Box 1711 (93942-1711)
PHONE......................831 657-6095
Bob Haehnel, *Branch Mgr*
Dave Thrailkill, *Supervisor*
EMP: 57
SALES (corp-wide): 84.5B **Publicly Held**
WEB: www.comcast.com
SIC: **4841** Cable television services
PA: Comcast Corporation
1701 Jfk Blvd
Philadelphia PA 19103
215 286-1700

(P-5890)
COX COMMUNICATIONS INC
140 Columbia, Aliso Viejo (92656-1495)
PHONE......................949 716-2020
Michael Hale, *Manager*
EMP: 76
SALES (corp-wide): 32.8B **Privately Held**
SIC: **4841** Cable television services
HQ: Cox Communications, Inc.
6205 B Pchtree Dunwody Ne
Atlanta GA 30328

(P-5891)
COX COMMUNICATIONS INC
1535 Euclid Ave, San Diego (92105-5426)
PHONE......................858 715-4500
Deborah Lawrence, *Director*
EMP: 100
SALES (corp-wide): 32.8B **Privately Held**
SIC: **4841** 4812 1731 Cable television
services; radio telephone communication;
electrical work

(PA)=Parent Co (HQ)=Headquarters (DH)=Div Headquarters
✪ = New Business established in last 2 years

2019 Directory of California
Wholesalers and Services Companies

251

PRODUCTS & SVCS

HQ: Cox Communications, Inc.
6205 B Pchtree Dunwody Ne
Atlanta GA 30328

(P-5892)
COX COMMUNICATIONS INC
3303 State St, Santa Barbara
(93105-2623)
PHONE...............805 681-6600
Janice Cass, *Branch Mgr*
Katherine Paezle Harris, *Manager*
EMP: 85
SALES (corp-wide): 32.8B **Privately Held**
SIC: 4841 Cable television services
HQ: Cox Communications, Inc.
6205 B Pchtree Dunwody Ne
Atlanta GA 30328
-

(P-5893)
COX COMMUNICATIONS INC
6771 Quail Hill Pkwy, Irvine (92603-4233)
PHONE...............949 546-1000
Leone Duffy, *Owner*
EMP: 76
SALES (corp-wide): 32.8B **Privately Held**
SIC: 4841 Cable television services
HQ: Cox Communications, Inc.
6205 B Pchtree Dunwody Ne
Atlanta GA 30328
-

(P-5894)
COX COMMUNICATIONS CAL LLC
1175 N Cuyamaca St, El Cajon
(92020-1805)
PHONE...............619 562-9820
Randall Phillips, *Manager*
EMP: 380
SALES (corp-wide): 32.8B **Privately Held**
SIC: 4841 Cable television services
HQ: Cox Communications California, Llc
6205 Pachtree Dunwoody Rd
Atlanta GA 30328
404 843-5000

(P-5895)
COX COMMUNICATIONS CAL LLC
5159 Federal Blvd, San Diego
(92105-5428)
PHONE...............619 262-1122
James Robbins, *CEO*
Jeff Smith, *Info Tech Mgr*
Martin Jones, *Marketing Staff*
EMP: 380
SALES (corp-wide): 32.8B **Privately Held**
SIC: 4841 Cable television services
HQ: Cox Communications California, Llc
6205 Pachtree Dunwoody Rd
Atlanta GA 30328
404 843-5000

(P-5896)
COX COMMUNICATIONS CAL LLC
581 Telegraph Canyon Rd, Chula Vista
(91910-6436)
PHONE...............619 263-9251
Bill Geppert, *Branch Mgr*
EMP: 380
SQ FT: 3,025
SALES (corp-wide): 32.8B **Privately Held**
SIC: 4841 Cable television services
HQ: Cox Communications California, Llc
6205 Pachtree Dunwoody Rd
Atlanta GA 30328
404 843-5000

(P-5897)
CROWN MEDIA UNITED STATES LLC (DH)
Also Called: Hallmark Channel
12700 Ventura Blvd # 100, Studio City
(91604-2469)
PHONE...............818 755-2400
David Evans,
Cheryl Grimley, *President*
Susanne McAvoy, *President*
Amy Ivan, *COO*
Susanne Smit McAvoy, *Exec VP*
EMP: 95

SALES (est): 23MM
SALES (corp-wide): 6.7B **Privately Held**
SIC: 4841 Cable television services
HQ: Crown Media Holdings, Inc.
12700 Ventura Blvd # 100
Studio City CA 91604
888 390-7474

(P-5898)
DIRECTV INC
2230 E Imperial Hwy, El Segundo
(90245-3504)
P.O. Box 105249, Atlanta GA (30348-5249)
PHONE...............888 388-4249
April Ammeter, *Vice Pres*
Nicholas Crincoli, *Vice Pres*
Dennis B Fleming, *Vice Pres*
Frank A Palase, *Vice Pres*
John Ward, *Vice Pres*
EMP: 501
SALES (est): 45.1MM **Privately Held**
SIC: 4841 Cable & other pay television
services

(P-5899)
DIRECTV LLC
1055 E Francis St, Ontario (91761-5633)
PHONE...............909 509-4790
Don Gillespie, *Branch Mgr*
EMP: 80
SALES (corp-wide): 160.5B **Publicly Held**
SIC: 4841 Direct broadcast satellite services (DBS)
HQ: Directv, Llc
2260 E Imperial Hwy
El Segundo CA 90245
310 964-8384

(P-5900)
DIRECTV ENTERPRISES LLC
2230 E Imperial Hwy, El Segundo
(90245-3504)
PHONE...............310 535-5000
Michael D White, *Site Mgr*
Eddy W Hartenstein, *Ch of Bd*
Odie C Donald, *President*
R L Myers, *CFO*
EMP: 1500
SQ FT: 75,000
SALES (est): 97.8MM
SALES (corp-wide): 160.5B **Publicly Held**
SIC: 4841 Direct broadcast satellite services (DBS)
HQ: Directv Holdings Llc
2230 E Imperial Hwy
El Segundo CA 90245
310 964-5000

(P-5901)
DIRECTV GROUP INC
340 Commerce Ave, Fairfield (94533)
PHONE...............707 452-7409
EMP: 128
SALES (corp-wide): 31.7B **Publicly Held**
SIC: 4841
HQ: The Directv Group Inc
2260 E Imperial Hwy
El Segundo CA 90245
310 964-5000

(P-5902)
DIRECTV GROUP INC
1129 B St, San Lorenzo (94580)
PHONE...............510 481-1324
EMP: 128
SALES (corp-wide): 31.7B **Publicly Held**
SIC: 4841
HQ: The Directv Group Inc
2260 E Imperial Hwy
El Segundo CA 90245
310 964-5000

(P-5903)
DIRECTV GROUP HOLDINGS LLC (HQ)
2260 E Imperial Hwy, El Segundo
(90245-3501)
PHONE...............310 964-5000
Michael White, *President*
Patrick Doyle, *CFO*
Fazal Merchant, *Treasurer*
Joseph Bosch, *Officer*
Larry Hunter, *Exec VP*
▲ **EMP:** 170

SALES (est): 12.9B
SALES (corp-wide): 160.5B **Publicly Held**
SIC: 4841 Direct broadcast satellite services (DBS)
PA: At&T Inc.
208 S Akard St
Dallas TX 75202
210 821-4105

(P-5904)
DIRECTV GROUP INC (DH)
2260 E Imperial Hwy, El Segundo
(90245-3501)
PHONE...............310 964-5000
Michael White, *CEO*
Patrick T Doyle, *CFO*
J William Little, *Treasurer*
Romulo Pontual, *Exec VP*
John F Murphy, *Senior VP*
▲ **EMP:** 128
SALES (est): 6B
SALES (corp-wide): 160.5B **Publicly Held**
WEB: www.hughes.com
SIC: 4841 Direct broadcast satellite services (DBS)

(P-5905)
DIRECTV INTERNATIONAL INC (DH)
2230 E Imperial Hwy Fl 10, El Segundo
(90245-3504)
PHONE...............310 964-6460
Michael D White, *Site Mgr*
Kevin McGrath, *President*
Celso Azevedo, *Senior VP*
EMP: 150
SALES (est): 107.6MM
SALES (corp-wide): 160.5B **Publicly Held**
SIC: 4841 Cable & other pay television
services
HQ: The Directv Group Inc
2260 E Imperial Hwy
El Segundo CA 90245
310 964-5000

(P-5906)
DISH NETWORK CORPORATION
396 Orange Show Ln, San Bernardino
(92408-2012)
PHONE...............909 381-4767
EMP: 52 **Publicly Held**
SIC: 4841 Direct broadcast satellite services (DBS)
PA: Dish Network Corporation
9601 S Meridian Blvd
Englewood CO 80112

(P-5907)
DISH NETWORK CORPORATION
1297 N Verdugo Rd, Glendale
(91206-1508)
PHONE...............818 334-8740
EMP: 50 **Publicly Held**
SIC: 4841 Direct broadcast satellite services (DBS)
PA: Dish Network Corporation
9601 S Meridian Blvd
Englewood CO 80112

(P-5908)
DISH NETWORK CORPORATION
2602 Halladay St, Santa Ana (92705-5601)
PHONE...............714 424-0503
Raul Guidi, *General Mgr*
Dan Hartman, *Manager*
EMP: 50 **Publicly Held**
SIC: 4841 Direct broadcast satellite services (DBS)
PA: Dish Network Corporation
9601 S Meridian Blvd
Englewood CO 80112
-

(P-5909)
DISH NETWORK CORPORATION
5671 Warehouse Way, Sacramento
(95826-4906)
PHONE...............916 381-5084
Jim Spreitcer, *Manager*
Bryan Bonacquisti, *Opers Mgr*
EMP: 50 **Publicly Held**

WEB: www.dishnetwork.com
SIC: 4841 Direct broadcast satellite services (DBS)
PA: Dish Network Corporation
9601 S Meridian Blvd
Englewood CO 80112

(P-5910)
DIVA SYSTEMS CORPORATION
800 Saginaw Dr, Redwood City
(94063-4740)
PHONE...............650 779-3000
Hendrik A Hanselaar, *President*
Paul Cook, *Ch of Bd*
Robert B Snow, *COO*
William M Scharninghausen, *CFO*
Steven Brookstein, *Senior VP*
EMP: 179
SQ FT: 82,000
SALES: 18.4MM **Privately Held**
SIC: 4841 7829 7822 Cable & other pay
television services; motion picture distribution services; motion picture distribution

(P-5911)
ESPN INC
800 W Olympic Blvd, Los Angeles
(90015-1360)
PHONE...............212 456-7439
Steven Bornstein, *Ch of Bd*
Hernani Lantin, *Associate Dir*
Breton Goers, *Sr Software Eng*
Leonardo Lozano, *Software Engr*
Takashi Aoki, *Engineer*
EMP: 300 **Publicly Held**
SIC: 4841 Cable television services
HQ: Espn, Inc.
Espn Plz
Bristol CT 06010
860 766-2000

(P-5912)
ETTV AMERICA CORP
Also Called: B N E U S A
18430 San Jose Ave Ste A, City of Industry
(91748-1263)
PHONE...............626 581-8899
May Chiang, *Exec VP*
Su Kuo, *Manager*
EMP: 80
SQ FT: 300,000
SALES (est): 5.8MM **Privately Held**
SIC: 4841 Cable television services

(P-5913)
EXPRESS CABLE COMMUNICATION
350 S Maple St Ste L, Corona
(92880-6948)
PHONE...............951 272-2029
Sam Kouhkan, *President*
EMP: 60
SALES: 12.1MM **Privately Held**
SIC: 4841 Cable television services

(P-5914)
FOX NETWORKS GROUP INC
Also Called: Nat Geo TV
10201 W Pico Blvd, Los Angeles
(90064-2606)
PHONE...............310 369-5104
Brian Sullivan, *President*
EMP: 135
SALES (corp-wide): 30.4B **Publicly Held**
SIC: 4841 Direct broadcast satellite services (DBS)
HQ: Fox Networks Group, Inc.
10201 W Pico Blvd 101
Los Angeles CA 90064
310 369-9369

(P-5915)
FOX NETWORKS GROUP INC (DH)
Also Called: Fox Network Center
10201 W Pico Blvd 101, Los Angeles
(90064-2606)
PHONE...............310 369-9369
Brian Sullivan, *President*
Raul De Quesada, *Info Tech Dir*
EMP: 57
SALES (est): 53.5MM
SALES (corp-wide): 30.4B **Publicly Held**
SIC: 4841 Direct broadcast satellite services (DBS)

▲ = Import ▼=Export
◆ =Import/Export

HQ: Fox Entertainment Group, Llc
1211 Ave Of The Americas
New York NY 10036
212 852-7000

(P-5916)
FX NETWORKS LLC
10201 W Pico Blvd, Los Angeles
(90064-2606)
P.O. Box 900, Beverly Hills (90213-0900)
PHONE..................................310 369-1000
John Landgraf, *President*
Stephanie Gibbons, *Partner*
Nick Grad, *Exec VP*
Julie Piepenkotter, *Exec VP*
Eric Schrier, *Exec VP*
EMP: 150
SALES (est): 18.1MM
SALES (corp-wide): 30.4B **Publicly Held**
WEB: www.fox.com
SIC: 4841 Cable television services
HQ: Fox Entertainment Group, Llc
1211 Ave Of The Americas
New York NY 10036
212 852-7000

(P-5917)
GAME SHOW NETWORK LLC (DH)
Also Called: G S N
2150 Colorado Ave Ste 100, Santa Monica
(90404-5514)
PHONE..................................310 255-6800
Mark Seldman, *Mng Member*
Steven Brunell, *Exec VP*
Karen Dullea, *Controller*
EMP: 100
SALES (est): 55MM
SALES (corp-wide): 80.1B **Privately Held**
WEB: www.gsn.com
SIC: 4841 Cable television services
HQ: Sony Pictures Entertainment, Inc.
10202 Washington Blvd
Culver City CA 90232
310 244-4000

(P-5918)
GLOBECAST AMERICA INCORPORATED (HQ)
10525 Washington Blvd, Culver City
(90232-3311)
PHONE..................................310 845-3900
Michele Gosetti, *CEO*
Lisa Coelho, *CEO*
Batrice De Lagrevol, *Vice Pres*
Tim Jackson, *Vice Pres*
Didier Mainard, *Vice Pres*
▲ **EMP:** 56
SALES (est): 98.9MM
SALES (corp-wide): 27.3B **Privately Held**
SIC: 4841 Satellite master antenna systems services (SMATV)
PA: Orange
78 84
Paris 75015
153 867-790

(P-5919)
HEARST COMMUNICATIONS INC
Also Called: Western Communications
2323 Teller Rd, Newbury Park
(91320-2219)
PHONE..................................805 375-3121
Dave Laroue, *Branch Mgr*
EMP: 500
SALES (corp-wide): 6.6B **Privately Held**
WEB: www.telegram.com
SIC: 4841 Cable television services
HQ: Hearst Communications, Inc.
300 W 57th St
New York NY 10019
212 649-2000

(P-5920)
HOME BOX OFFICE INC
2500 Broadway Ste 400, Santa Monica
(90404-3176)
PHONE..................................310 382-3000
Chris Albrecht, *Manager*
Oscar Montemayor, *Executive Asst*
Allison Wasserman, *Executive Asst*
Hiral Amin, *Project Mgr*
Julie Bender, *Engineer*
EMP: 95

SALES (corp-wide): 160.5B **Publicly Held**
WEB: www.hbo.com
SIC: 4841 7812 Cable television services; motion picture & video production
HQ: Home Box Office, Inc.
1100 Avenue Of The Americ
New York NY 10036
212 512-1000

(P-5921)
INTEL MEDIA INC
2200 Mission College Blvd, Santa Clara
(95054-1549)
PHONE..................................408 765-0063
Erik Huggers, *President*
EMP: 350
SALES: 33.2K
SALES (corp-wide): 62.7B **Publicly Held**
SIC: 4841 Subscription television services
PA: Intel Corporation
2200 Mission College Blvd
Santa Clara CA 95054
408 765-8080

(P-5922)
INTERNATIONAL FMLY ENTRMT INC (DH)
Also Called: Fox Family Channel
3800 W Alameda Ave, Burbank
(91505-4300)
PHONE..................................818 560-1000
Mel Woods, *President*
EMP: 144
SALES (est): 36.4MM **Publicly Held**
SIC: 4841 7812 7922 7999 Cable television services; television film production; theatrical producers; legitimate live theater producers; television program, including commercial producers; recreation services
HQ: Abc Family Worldwide, Inc.
500 S Buena Vista St
Burbank CA 91521
818 560-1000

(P-5923)
NDS AMERICAS INC (DH)
3500 Hyland Ave, Costa Mesa
(92626-1469)
PHONE..................................714 434-2100
Abe Peled, *President*
Dov Rubin, *Vice Pres*
Alex Gersh, *Admin Sec*
Jason Mercier, *Info Tech Mgr*
Vien Dang, *Network Mgr*
EMP: 90
SALES (est): 76.1MM **Privately Held**
WEB: www.ndsuk.com
SIC: 4841 Cable & other pay television services
HQ: Nds Group Limited
One London Road
Staines MIDDX TW18
208 824-1000

(P-5924)
OC COMMUNICATIONS INC (PA)
2204 Kausen Dr Ste 100, Elk Grove
(95758-7176)
PHONE..................................916 686-3700
Forrest C Freeman, *CEO*
Craig Freeman, *President*
Larry Wray, *COO*
Peter Tataryn, *CFO*
Steve Fazio, *Vice Pres*
EMP: 115
SQ FT: 7,335
SALES (est): 184MM **Privately Held**
WEB: www.occommunications.com
SIC: 4841 Cable & other pay television services

(P-5925)
OWN LLC
Also Called: Oprah Winfrey Network
1041 N Formosa Ave, West Hollywood
(90046-6703)
PHONE..................................323 602-5500
Oprah Winfrey, *Officer*
Erik Logan, *Co-President*
Sheri Salata, *Co-President*
Yujin CHI, *Vice Pres*
Jill Dickerson, *Vice Pres*
EMP: 140
SQ FT: 50,000

SALES (est): 16.8MM
SALES (corp-wide): 6.2MM **Privately Held**
SIC: 4841 Cable television services
PA: Discovery Communications, Inc.
10100 Santa Monica Blvd
Los Angeles CA 90067
310 975-5906

(P-5926)
PETES CONNECTION INC
407 Ranger Rd, Fallbrook (92028-8482)
P.O. Box 2080 (92088-2080)
PHONE..................................760 723-1972
Peter Cavaretta, *President*
Ann Cavaretta, *Vice Pres*
EMP: 50
SALES (est): 2.4MM **Privately Held**
SIC: 4841 Direct broadcast satellite services (DBS)

(P-5927)
PHOENIX AMERICAN INCORPORATED (PA)
2401 Kerner Blvd, San Rafael
(94901-5569)
PHONE..................................415 485-4500
Gus Constantin, *Ch of Bd*
Andrew N Gregson, *CFO*
Gary W Martinez, *Exec VP*
Alfred Armenteros, *Vice Pres*
Muna A Hobaika, *Vice Pres*
EMP: 100
SQ FT: 60,000
SALES (est): 36.4MM **Privately Held**
SIC: 4841 7377 Cable television services; computer rental & leasing

(P-5928)
PHOENIX SATELLITE TV US INC
3810 Durbin St, Baldwin Park
(91706-6800)
PHONE..................................626 388-1188
Xiaoyong Wu, *CEO*
Shing Ping, *CEO*
Victor Liang, *General Mgr*
Karin Hsu, *Manager*
▲ **EMP:** 50
SQ FT: 18,000
SALES (est): 5.1MM **Privately Held**
WEB: www.pstv-us.net
SIC: 4841 Cable television services
HQ: Phoenix Media Investment (Holdings) Limited (Formerly Known As ?phoenix Satellite Televisi
Tai Po Industrial Estate
Tai Po NT

(P-5929)
ROKU INC (PA)
150 Winchester Cir, Los Gatos
(95032-1812)
PHONE..................................408 556-9040
Anthony Wood, *Ch of Bd*
Seth Walters, *Partner*
Steve Louden, *CFO*
Matthew Anderson, *Chief Mktg Ofcr*
Stephen Kay, *Senior VP*
▲ **EMP:** 360
SQ FT: 156,000
SALES: 512.7MM **Publicly Held**
WEB: www.roku.com
SIC: 4841 Cable & other pay television services

(P-5930)
SKY SCAN SATELITE SYSTEMS
9994 Willowbrook Rd, Riverside
(92509-8827)
PHONE..................................909 322-1393
Mike Khan, *Owner*
EMP: 68
SALES (est): 1.5MM **Privately Held**
SIC: 4841 Satellite master antenna systems services (SMATV)

(P-5931)
SONIFI SOLUTIONS INC
1065 E Hillsdale Blvd # 228, Foster City
(94404-1614)
PHONE..................................650 752-1980
Sean Minnit, *Branch Mgr*
EMP: 109

SALES (corp-wide): 95.7MM **Privately Held**
SIC: 4841 Subscription television services
PA: Sonifi Solutions, Inc.
3900 W Innovation St
Sioux Falls SD 57107
605 988-1000

(P-5932)
SPECTRUM MGT HOLDG CO LLC
Also Called: Time Warner Media Sales
6021 Katella Ave Ste 100, Cypress
(90630-5250)
PHONE..................................714 657-1040
Rich Ambrose, *Vice Pres*
EMP: 83
SALES (corp-wide): 41.5B **Publicly Held**
SIC: 4841 Cable television services
HQ: Spectrum Management Holding Company, Llc
400 Atlantic St
Stamford CT 06901
203 905-7801

(P-5933)
SPECTRUM MGT HOLDG CO LLC
4077 W Stetson Ave, Hemet (92545-9704)
PHONE..................................951 260-3143
Andre Mora, *Manager*
EMP: 83
SALES (corp-wide): 41.5B **Publicly Held**
SIC: 4841 Cable television services
HQ: Spectrum Management Holding Company, Llc
400 Atlantic St
Stamford CT 06901
203 905-7801

(P-5934)
SPECTRUM MGT HOLDG CO LLC
1041 E Route 66, Glendora (91740-6357)
PHONE..................................626 857-1075
Erwin Tando, *Branch Mgr*
EMP: 86
SALES (corp-wide): 41.5B **Publicly Held**
SIC: 4841 Cable television services
HQ: Spectrum Management Holding Company, Llc
400 Atlantic St
Stamford CT 06901
203 905-7801

(P-5935)
SPECTRUM MGT HOLDG CO LLC
Also Called: Time Warner
27555 Ynez Rd Ste 203, Temecula
(92591-4677)
PHONE..................................951 587-8660
Doug Walker, *Branch Mgr*
EMP: 83
SALES (corp-wide): 41.5B **Publicly Held**
SIC: 4841 Cable television services
HQ: Spectrum Management Holding Company, Llc
400 Atlantic St
Stamford CT 06901
203 905-7801

(P-5936)
SPECTRUM MGT HOLDG CO LLC
Also Called: Time Warner
1078 E Hospitality Ln D, San Bernardino
(92408-2878)
PHONE..................................909 918-6972
Kathleen Ouilette, *Branch Mgr*
EMP: 83
SALES (corp-wide): 41.5B **Publicly Held**
SIC: 4841 Cable television services; subscription television services
HQ: Spectrum Management Holding Company, Llc
400 Atlantic St
Stamford CT 06901
203 905-7801

PRODUCTS & SVCS

(P-5937)
SPECTRUM MGT HOLDG CO LLC
17777 Center Court Dr N, Cerritos (90703-9320)
PHONE..............................562 677-0228
Hector Carmona, *Accounts Exec*
EMP: 84
SALES (corp-wide): 41.5B **Publicly Held**
SIC: 4841 Cable television services
HQ: Spectrum Management Holding Company, Llc
400 Atlantic St
Stamford CT 06901
203 905-7801

(P-5938)
SPECTRUM MGT HOLDG CO LLC
Also Called: Adelphia
1565 S Harbor Blvd, Fullerton (92832-3402)
PHONE..............................714 871-2643
Rick Rivas, *Branch Mgr*
EMP: 84
SALES (corp-wide): 41.5B **Publicly Held**
SIC: 4841 Cable television services
HQ: Spectrum Management Holding Company, Llc
400 Atlantic St
Stamford CT 06901
203 905-7801

(P-5939)
SPECTRUM MGT HOLDG CO LLC
350 Stonewood St, Downey (90241-3909)
PHONE..............................562 372-4008
EMP: 83
SALES (corp-wide): 41.5B **Publicly Held**
SIC: 4841 Cable television services
HQ: Spectrum Management Holding Company, Llc
400 Atlantic St
Stamford CT 06901
203 905-7801

(P-5940)
SPECTRUM MGT HOLDG CO LLC
9260 Topanga Canyon Blvd, Chatsworth (91311-5726)
PHONE..............................818 700-6126
Michael Snider, *Branch Mgr*
Cynthia Haywood, *Supervisor*
EMP: 86
SALES (corp-wide): 41.5B **Publicly Held**
SIC: 4841 Cable television services
HQ: Spectrum Management Holding Company, Llc
400 Atlantic St
Stamford CT 06901
203 905-7801

(P-5941)
SPECTRUM MGT HOLDG CO LLC
Also Called: Time Warner
6021 Katella Ave Ste 100, Cypress (90630-5250)
PHONE..............................714 657-1060
EMP: 120
SALES (corp-wide): 29B **Publicly Held**
SIC: 4841
HQ: Spectrum Management Holding Company, Llc
400 Atlantic St
Stamford CT 06901
203 905-7801

(P-5942)
SPECTRUM MGT HOLDG CO LLC
Also Called: Time Warner
12040 Western Ave, Garden Grove (92841-2913)
PHONE..............................714 903-4000
Tad Yo, *Manager*
Dale Bowles, *Engineer*
Janice Manuel, *Manager*
EMP: 83
SALES (corp-wide): 41.5B **Publicly Held**
SIC: 4841 Cable television services

HQ: Spectrum Management Holding Company, Llc
400 Atlantic St
Stamford CT 06901
203 905-7801

(P-5943)
SPECTRUM MGT HOLDG CO LLC
Also Called: Time Warner
550 Continental Blvd # 250, El Segundo (90245-5049)
PHONE..............................310 647-3000
Debi Picciolo, *Branch Mgr*
Kathryn St John, *Vice Pres*
Lisa Simon, *Senior Mgr*
EMP: 83
SALES (corp-wide): 41.5B **Publicly Held**
SIC: 4841 Cable television services
HQ: Spectrum Management Holding Company, Llc
400 Atlantic St
Stamford CT 06901
203 905-7801

(P-5944)
SPECTRUM MGT HOLDG CO LLC
Time Warner
41725 Cook St, Palm Desert (92211-5100)
PHONE..............................760 340-2225
Juan Ochoa, *Principal*
EMP: 200
SALES (corp-wide): 41.5B **Publicly Held**
SIC: 4841 Cable television services
HQ: Spectrum Management Holding Company, Llc
400 Atlantic St
Stamford CT 06901
203 905-7801

(P-5945)
SPECTRUM MGT HOLDG CO LLC
1500 Auto Center Dr, Ontario (91761-2243)
PHONE..............................909 821-8159
Brian Ha, *Manager*
EMP: 83
SALES (corp-wide): 41.5B **Publicly Held**
SIC: 4841 Cable television services
HQ: Spectrum Management Holding Company, Llc
400 Atlantic St
Stamford CT 06901
203 905-7801

(P-5946)
SPECTRUM MGT HOLDG CO LLC
Also Called: Time Warner
3430 E Miraloma Ave, Anaheim (92806-2101)
PHONE..............................714 414-1431
Preston Hayslette, *Branch Mgr*
EMP: 83
SALES (corp-wide): 41.5B **Publicly Held**
SIC: 4841 Cable television services
HQ: Spectrum Management Holding Company, Llc
400 Atlantic St
Stamford CT 06901
203 905-7801

(P-5947)
SPECTRUM MGT HOLDG CO LLC
12625 Frederick St F10, Moreno Valley (92553-5216)
PHONE..............................951 571-8738
Steve Naber, *Branch Mgr*
EMP: 83
SALES (corp-wide): 41.5B **Publicly Held**
SIC: 4841 Cable television services
HQ: Spectrum Management Holding Company, Llc
400 Atlantic St
Stamford CT 06901
203 905-7801

(P-5948)
TIME WARNER CABLE ENTPS LLC
1438 N Gower St, Los Angeles (90028-8383)
PHONE..............................323 993-7076

Richard Battaglia, *President*
EMP: 120
SALES (corp-wide): 41.5B **Publicly Held**
SIC: 4841 Cable television services
HQ: Time Warner Cable Enterprises Llc
400 Atlantic St Ste 6
Stamford CT 06901
-

(P-5949)
TIME WARNER CABLE ENTPS LLC
550 Continental Blvd # 250, El Segundo (90245-5049)
PHONE..............................469 665-7735
Debi Picciolo, *Principal*
EMP: 2500
SALES (corp-wide): 41.5B **Publicly Held**
SIC: 4841 Cable television services
HQ: Time Warner Cable Enterprises Llc
400 Atlantic St Ste 6
Stamford CT 06901
-

(P-5950)
TIME WARNER CABLE ENTPS LLC
3300 Warner Blvd, Burbank (91505-4632)
PHONE..............................818 953-3283
Tom Whalley, *Branch Mgr*
EMP: 200
SALES (corp-wide): 41.5B **Publicly Held**
SIC: 4841 Cable television services
HQ: Time Warner Cable Enterprises Llc
400 Atlantic St Ste 6
Stamford CT 06901
-

(P-5951)
TIME WARNER CABLE INC
3051 Clairemont Dr, San Diego (92117-6802)
PHONE..............................619 346-4573
Margie Herrera, *Branch Mgr*
EMP: 76
SALES (corp-wide): 41.5B **Publicly Held**
SIC: 4841 Cable television services
HQ: Spectrum Management Holding Company, Llc
400 Atlantic St
Stamford CT 06901
203 905-7801

(P-5952)
TIME WARNER CABLE INC
118 N 8th St, Santa Paula (93060-2710)
PHONE..............................888 892-2253
Warner Cable, *Owner*
EMP: 86
SALES (corp-wide): 41.5B **Publicly Held**
SIC: 4841 Cable television services
HQ: Spectrum Management Holding Company, Llc
400 Atlantic St
Stamford CT 06901
203 905-7801

(P-5953)
TIME WARNER CABLE INC
2323 Teller Rd, Newbury Park (91320-2219)
PHONE..............................805 214-1353
David Bultman, *Branch Mgr*
EMP: 83
SALES (corp-wide): 41.5B **Publicly Held**
SIC: 4841 Cable television services
HQ: Spectrum Management Holding Company, Llc
400 Atlantic St
Stamford CT 06901
203 905-7801

(P-5954)
TIME WARNER CABLE INC
10450 Pacific Center Ct, San Diego (92121-4338)
PHONE..............................858 695-3220
Jim Fellhauer, *President*
EMP: 410
SQ FT: 25,500
SALES (corp-wide): 41.5B **Publicly Held**
SIC: 4841 Cable television services

HQ: Spectrum Management Holding Company, Llc
400 Atlantic St
Stamford CT 06901
203 905-7801

(P-5955)
TIME WARNER CABLE INC
660 W Acacia Ave, Hemet (92543-4073)
PHONE..............................951 306-3117
EMP: 84
SALES (corp-wide): 41.5B **Publicly Held**
SIC: 4841 Cable television services
HQ: Spectrum Management Holding Company, Llc
400 Atlantic St
Stamford CT 06901
203 905-7801

(P-5956)
TIME WARNER CABLE INC
500 Lakewood Center Mall, Lakewood (90712-2407)
PHONE..............................424 529-6011
EMP: 170
SALES (corp-wide): 41.5B **Publicly Held**
SIC: 4841 Cable television services
HQ: Spectrum Management Holding Company, Llc
400 Atlantic St
Stamford CT 06901
203 905-7801

(P-5957)
TIME WARNER CABLE INC
15255 Salt Lake Ave, City of Industry (91745-1130)
PHONE..............................626 705-7482
Kurt Taylor, *Manager*
EMP: 95
SALES (corp-wide): 41.5B **Publicly Held**
SIC: 4841 Cable television services
HQ: Spectrum Management Holding Company, Llc
400 Atlantic St
Stamford CT 06901
203 905-7801

(P-5958)
TIME WARNER CABLE INC
1881 W Main St, Barstow (92311-3715)
PHONE..............................760 256-3526
Chuck Gibson, *Branch Mgr*
EMP: 83
SALES (corp-wide): 41.5B **Publicly Held**
SIC: 4841 Cable television services
HQ: Spectrum Management Holding Company, Llc
400 Atlantic St
Stamford CT 06901
203 905-7801

(P-5959)
TIME WARNER CABLE INC
900 N Cahuenga Blvd, Los Angeles (90038-2615)
PHONE..............................323 993-8000
Debbie Picciolo, *Branch Mgr*
EMP: 300
SALES (corp-wide): 41.5B **Publicly Held**
SIC: 4841 Cable television services
HQ: Spectrum Management Holding Company, Llc
400 Atlantic St
Stamford CT 06901
203 905-7801

(P-5960)
TIME WARNER CABLE INC
8949 Ware Ct, San Diego (92121-2222)
PHONE..............................858 695-3110
Lisa Simon, *Branch Mgr*
EMP: 300
SALES (corp-wide): 41.5B **Publicly Held**
SIC: 4841 Cable television services; subscription television services
HQ: Spectrum Management Holding Company, Llc
400 Atlantic St
Stamford CT 06901
203 905-7801

(P-5961)
TIME WARNER CABLE INC
313 N 8th St, El Centro (92243-2303)
PHONE..............................760 335-4800

EMP: 83
SALES (corp-wide): 41.5B **Publicly Held**
SIC: 4841
HQ: Spectrum Management Holding Company, Llc
400 Atlantic St
Stamford CT 06901
203 905-7801

(P-5962)
TVB (USA) INC (DH)
15411 Blackburn Ave, Norwalk
(90650-6844)
PHONE....................562 345-9871
Philip Tam, *President*
Melissa Wang, *Vice Pres*
▲ **EMP:** 50
SQ FT: 25,000
SALES (est): 7.9MM
SALES (corp-wide): 555.1MM **Privately Held**
SIC: 4841 Cable television services
HQ: Tvb Holdings (Usa) Inc
15411 Blackburn Ave
Norwalk CA 90650
562 802-8868

(P-5963)
VERIZON BUSINESS GLOBAL LLC
6177 River Crest Dr Ste B, Riverside
(92507-0786)
P.O. Box 635, Jackson MS (39205-0635)
PHONE....................951 653-4482
Gar Gatia, *Manager*
EMP: 50
SALES (corp-wide): 126B **Publicly Held**
WEB: www.mccmt.com
SIC: 4841 Cable television services
HQ: Verizon Business Global Llc
22001 Loudoun County Pkwy
Ashburn VA 20147
703 886-5600

(P-5964)
VOLCANO VISION INC
Also Called: Volcano Telephone Co.
20000 State Highway 88, Pine Grove
(95665-9512)
P.O. Box 1070 (95665-1070)
PHONE....................209 296-2288
Toll Free:....................888 -
Sharon J Lundgren, *President*
John M Lundgren, *Vice Pres*
Deilia P Harder, *Human Resources*
EMP: 115
SQ FT: 1,000
SALES (est): 2.6MM **Privately Held**
SIC: 4841 Cable television services

(P-5965)
VUBIQUITY HOLDINGS INC (PA)
15301 Ventura Blvd # 3000, Sherman Oaks
(91403-5837)
PHONE....................818 526-5000
Darcy Antonellis, *CEO*
Doug Sylvester, *President*
William G Arendt, *CFO*
James P Riley, *Officer*
Anupam Gupta, *Exec VP*
EMP: 185
SALES (est): 196.8MM **Privately Held**
SIC: 4841 Cable & other pay television services

(P-5966)
WARNER MEDIA LLC
Also Called: Time Warner
2014 W Avenue K, Lancaster (93536-5229)
PHONE....................661 344-1546
EMP: 76
SALES (corp-wide): 160.5B **Publicly Held**
SIC: 4841 Cable television services
HQ: Warner Media, Llc
1 Time Warner Ctr Bsmt B
New York NY 10019

(P-5967)
WARNER MEDIA LLC
Also Called: Time Warner
2650 Tapo Canyon Rd, Simi Valley
(93063-2308)
PHONE....................805 421-4467
EMP: 76

SALES (corp-wide): 160.5B **Publicly Held**
SIC: 4841 Cable television services
HQ: Warner Media, Llc
1 Time Warner Ctr Bsmt B
New York NY 10019

4899 Communication Svcs, NEC

(P-5968)
1105 MEDIA INC
4 Venture Ste 150, Irvine (92618-7442)
PHONE....................949 265-1520
Richard Vitale, *Owner*
EMP: 175
SALES (corp-wide): 136.4MM **Privately Held**
SIC: 4899 Data communication services
PA: 1105 Media, Inc.
6300 Canoga Ave Ste 1150
Woodland Hills CA 91367
818 814-5200

(P-5969)
BELLA TERRA TECHNOLOGIES INC
1600 Amphitheatre Pkwy, Mountain View
(94043-1351)
PHONE....................650 316-6660
Tom Ingersoll, *CEO*
Dan Berkenstock,
Dirk Robinson, *Director*
EMP: 54
SALES (est): 3.3MM
SALES (corp-wide): 110.8B **Publicly Held**
SIC: 4899 Satellite earth stations
HQ: Google Llc
1600 Amphitheatre Pkwy
Mountain View CA 94043
650 253-0000

(P-5970)
BLUE JEANS NETWORK INC (PA)
516 Clyde Ave, Mountain View
(94043-2212)
PHONE....................408 550-2828
Quentin Gallivan, *CEO*
Robert Park, *CFO*
Krish Ramakrishnan, *Chairman*
Rosanne Saccone, *Chief Mktg Ofcr*
Lori Wright, *Chief Mktg Ofcr*
EMP: 66
SALES (est): 15.4MM **Privately Held**
SIC: 4899 Data communication services

(P-5971)
BYTEMOBILE INC
Also Called: Byte Mobile
2860 De La Cruz Blvd # 200, Santa Clara
(95050-2635)
PHONE....................408 327-7700
Hatim Tyabji, *CEO*
Adrian Hall, *COO*
Thomas Hubbs, *CFO*
Tom Proquent, *CFO*
JD Howard, *Vice Pres*
▲ **EMP:** 260
SQ FT: 30,000
SALES (est): 8.5MM
SALES (corp-wide): 55.3K **Privately Held**
SIC: 4899 7361 Communication signal enhancement network system; employment agencies
HQ: Citrix Systems International Gmbh
Rheinweg 9
Schaffhausen SH
526 357-700

(P-5972)
CAMBIUM NETWORKS INC
2010 N 1st St, San Jose (95131-2018)
PHONE....................847 640-3809
EMP: 159
SALES (corp-wide): 62.1MM **Privately Held**
SIC: 4899 Data communication services
PA: Cambium Networks, Inc.
3800 Golf Rd Ste 360
Rolling Meadows IL 60008
888 863-5250

(P-5973)
CELLCO PARTNERSHIP
5508 Young St, Bakersfield (93311-9648)
PHONE....................661 663-9451
EMP: 57
SALES (corp-wide): 126B **Publicly Held**
SIC: 4899 Data communication services
HQ: Cellco Partnership
1 Verizon Way
Basking Ridge NJ 07920

(P-5974)
CELLCO PARTNERSHIP
Also Called: Verizon Wireless
6400 Pacific Blvd, Huntington Park
(90255-4104)
PHONE....................323 826-9880
Louis Armendariz, *Principal*
EMP: 57
SALES (corp-wide): 126B **Publicly Held**
SIC: 4899 Data communication services
HQ: Cellco Partnership
1 Verizon Way
Basking Ridge NJ 07920

(P-5975)
COMMUNICATIONS SUPPLY CORP
6251 Knott Ave, Buena Park (90620-1010)
PHONE....................714 670-7711
Michael Davis, *General Mgr*
Miryam Lopez, *Sales Associate*
EMP: 70 **Publicly Held**
WEB: www.gocsc.com
SIC: 4899 1731 3577 3357 Data communication services; communications specialization; computer peripheral equipment; nonferrous wiredrawing & insulating
HQ: Communications Supply Corp
200 E Lies Rd
Carol Stream IL 60188
630 221-6400

(P-5976)
CONVO COMMUNICATIONS LLC
6601 Owens Dr Ste 155, Pleasanton
(94588-3356)
PHONE....................925 227-5500
Wayne G Betts, *Principal*
Joshua Shaffner, *President*
Evan Winegard, *Officer*
Daniel Millikin, *Software Dev*
Isidore Niyongabo, *Human Res Mgr*
EMP: 241
SALES (est): 1.2MM **Privately Held**
SIC: 4899 Data communication services

(P-5977)
COX CALIFORNIA TELCOM LLC
1922 Avenida Del Oro, Oceanside
(92056-5803)
PHONE....................760 966-0447
Jeff Trotter, *Manager*
Katherine Paezle Harris, *Manager*
EMP: 190
SALES (corp-wide): 32.8B **Privately Held**
SIC: 4899 Data communication services
HQ: Cox California Telcom, L.L.C.
6205-B Pchtree Dnwoody Rd
Atlanta GA 30328

(P-5978)
DANG QUINTEN
Also Called: T2d Media
11272 Frankmont Ct, El Monte
(91732-2152)
PHONE....................626 429-6332
Quinten Dang, *Owner*
EMP: 60
SALES (est): 499.7K **Privately Held**
SIC: 4899 Communication services

(P-5979)
DIGITAL MAP PRODUCTS INC
5201 California Ave # 200, Irvine
(92617-3098)
PHONE....................949 333-5111
James Skurzynski, *CEO*
James S Skurzynski, *CEO*
Thomas R Patterson Jr, *CFO*
Annie Schwab, *Vice Pres*
Steve Stautzenbach, *Vice Pres*

EMP: 51
SQ FT: 8,000
SALES (est): 8.4MM **Privately Held**
WEB: www.digmap.com
SIC: 4899 Data communication services

(P-5980)
DISCOVERY COMMUNICATIONS INC (PA)
10100 Santa Monica Blvd, Los Angeles
(90067-4003)
PHONE....................310 975-5906
David Zazlov, *CEO*
Jorge Hernandez, *Sr Software Eng*
EMP: 400
SALES (est): 6.2MM **Privately Held**
SIC: 4899 Data communication services

(P-5981)
EQUINIX (US) ENTERPRISES INC (HQ)
1 Lagoon Dr, Redwood City (94065-1562)
PHONE....................650 598-6363
Donald Campbell, *CFO*
EMP: 99 **EST:** 2005
SALES (est): 6.2MM
SALES (corp-wide): 4.3B **Publicly Held**
SIC: 4899 Communication signal enhancement network system
PA: Equinix, Inc.
1 Lagoon Dr Ste 400
Redwood City CA 94065
650 598-6000

(P-5982)
FOUR MEDICA INC
13160 Mindanao Way # 280, Marina Del
Rey (90292-6358)
PHONE....................310 348-4100
Oleg Bess, *Principal*
EMP: 74
SALES (est): 9MM **Privately Held**
SIC: 4899 Data communication services

(P-5983)
INTELSAT US LLC
Also Called: Intell Set
1600 Forbes Way, Long Beach
(90810-1830)
PHONE....................310 525-5500
Tom Nassis, *Vice Pres*
EMP: 150 **Privately Held**
SIC: 4899 Satellite earth stations; data communication services
HQ: Intelsat Us Llc
7900 Tysons One Pl
Mc Lean VA 22102

(P-5984)
IPS GROUP INC (PA)
7737 Kenamar Ct, San Diego
(92121-2425)
PHONE....................858 404-0607
David W King, *CEO*
Chad Randal, *COO*
Dario Paduano, *CFO*
Amir Sedadi, *Vice Pres*
Alexander M Schwarz, *CTO*
▲ **EMP:** 53
SALES (est): 24MM **Privately Held**
WEB: www.ipsgroupinc.com
SIC: 4899 3824 Communication signal enhancement network system; parking meters

(P-5985)
ITRON NETWORKED SOLUTIONS INC (HQ)
230 W Tasman Dr, San Jose (95134-1714)
PHONE....................669 770-4000
Thomas L Deitrich, *President*
Robert Farrow, *Treasurer*
Catriona M Fallon, *Senior VP*
Scott Blackburn, *Executive*
Howell Leung, *Program Mgr*
▲ **EMP:** 400
SQ FT: 191,800
SALES: 311MM
SALES (corp-wide): 2B **Publicly Held**
WEB: www.silverspringnetworks.com
SIC: 4899 7372 Communication signal enhancement network system; prepackaged software

PA: Itron, Inc.
2111 N Molter Rd
Liberty Lake WA 99019
509 924-9900

(P-5986)
KBRWYLE TECH SOLUTIONS LLC
Also Called: Honeywell
Vanonbrg Air Frc Bldg 660, Lompoc (93438)
PHONE..................805 734-2982
T A Yancey, *Manager*
EMP: 277 **Publicly Held**
WEB: www.honeywell-tsi.com
SIC: 4899 Missile tracking by telemetry & photography
HQ: Kbrwyle Technology Solutions, Llc
7000 Columbia Gateway Dr # 100
Columbia MD 21046
410 964-7000

(P-5987)
L3 TECHNOLOGIES INC
10770 Wtridge Cir Ste 200, San Diego (92121)
PHONE..................858 623-6513
Michelle Petty, *Branch Mgr*
EMP: 100
SALES (corp-wide): 9.5B **Publicly Held**
SIC: 4899 Data communication services
PA: L3 Technologies, Inc.
600 3rd Ave Fl 34
New York NY 10016
212 697-1111

(P-5988)
LUXN INC
580 Maude Ct, Sunnyvale (94085-2822)
PHONE..................408 213-7437
Thomas Alexander, *President*
Lee Zipin, *Ch of Bd*
Agnes Emory, *Vice Pres*
Paul Strudwick, *Vice Pres*
EMP: 53 EST: 1998
SALES (est): 1.5MM
SALES (corp-wide): 27.2MM **Publicly Held**
WEB: www.luxn.com
SIC: 4899 Data communication services
HQ: Sorrento Networks Corporation
7195 Oakport St
Oakland CA 94621
510 577-1400

(P-5989)
NPHASE LLC
6195 Lusk Blvd Ste 200, San Diego (92121-3723)
PHONE..................312 577-1650
EMP: 75
SQ FT: 20,000
SALES (est): 4.3MM **Privately Held**
WEB: www.nphasem2m.com
SIC: 4899

(P-5990)
OPLINK COMMUNICATIONS INC (DH)
46360 Fremont Blvd, Fremont (94538-6406)
PHONE..................510 933-7200
Joseph Y Liu, *CEO*
Peter Lee, *President*
Shirley Yin, *CFO*
River Gong, *Exec VP*
Stephen M Welles, *Senior VP*
▲ EMP: 59
SQ FT: 51,000
SALES (est): 824.3MM
SALES (corp-wide): 42.9B **Privately Held**
WEB: www.oplink.com
SIC: 4899 3661 Communication signal enhancement network system; data communication services; fiber optics communications equipment
HQ: Molex, Llc
2222 Wellington Ct
Lisle IL 60532
630 969-4550

(P-5991)
PAGERDUTY INC (PA)
600 Townsend St Ste 200e, San Francisco (94103-5690)
PHONE..................650 989-2965

Jennifer Tejada, *CEO*
Steven Gatoff, *CFO*
Howard Wilson, *Officer*
Tim Armandpour, *Vice Pres*
Sophie Kitson, *Vice Pres*
EMP: 74
SALES (est): 102.3MM **Privately Held**
WEB: www.pagerduty.com
SIC: 4899 Data communication services

(P-5992)
PROSOFT TECHNOLOGY INC (HQ)
9201 Camino Media Ste 200, Bakersfield (93311-1362)
PHONE..................661 716-5100
Thomas Crone, *President*
Chris Williams, *Vice Pres*
Stephen Wojtowicz, *Business Dir*
Sergio D Arias, *Regional Mgr*
Chris Hines, *Technical Mgr*
EMP: 64
SALES (est): 47.6MM
SALES (corp-wide): 2.3B **Publicly Held**
WEB: www.psft.com
SIC: 4899 Data communication services
PA: Belden Inc.
1 N Brentwood Blvd Fl 15
Saint Louis MO 63105
314 854-8000

(P-5993)
SCHOOLWIRES INC
645 S Barranca St, West Covina (91791-2943)
PHONE..................626 974-7600
Kris Kemp, *Principal*
EMP: 56
SALES (est): 557.9K **Privately Held**
SIC: 4899 Communication services

(P-5994)
SEFNCO COMMUNICATIONS INC
9714 Tanqueray Ct Ste A, Redding (96003-6893)
PHONE..................530 338-2460
EMP: 68
SALES (corp-wide): 163.6MM **Privately Held**
SIC: 4899 Data communication services
PA: Sefnco Communications, Inc.
4610 Tacoma Ave
Sumner WA 98390
877 385-2903

(P-5995)
SOUTH BAY RGONAL PUB COMM AUTH
Also Called: S B Communications
4440 W Broadway, Hawthorne (90250-3802)
PHONE..................310 973-1802
Ralph Mailloux, *Director*
Agnes Walker, *Finance Mgr*
EMP: 50
SQ FT: 1,632
SALES: 10.3MM **Privately Held**
SIC: 4899 Communication signal enhancement network system

(P-5996)
SPACE SYSTEMS/LORAL LLC (DH)
Also Called: Ssl
3825 Fabian Way, Palo Alto (94303-4604)
P.O. Box 51551 (94303-0709)
PHONE..................650 852-7320
John Celli, *President*
Barbara Ellis, *President*
Ed McFarlane, *President*
Ron Haley, *CFO*
Michael Santoro, *CFO*
◆ EMP: 75
SALES (est): 425.5MM
SALES (corp-wide): 581.1MM **Publicly Held**
SIC: 4899 3663 Satellite earth stations; satellites, communications
HQ: Maxar Technologies Ltd
200 Burrard St Suite 1570
Vancouver BC V6C 3
604 974-5275

(P-5997)
SPIDERCLOUD WIRELESS INC (HQ)
475 Sycamore Dr, Milpitas (95035-7428)
PHONE..................408 567-9165
Michael Gallagher, *CEO*
Thomas Scott, *CFO*
Chris Evarts, *Vice Pres*
Mike Finlayson, *Vice Pres*
Kieren Ashlee, *Technical Staff*
▲ EMP: 51
SALES (est): 24.2MM
SALES (corp-wide): 10.1B **Publicly Held**
SIC: 4899 Communication signal enhancement network system
PA: Corning Incorporated
1 Riverfront Plz
Corning NY 14831
607 974-9000

(P-5998)
SS8 NETWORKS INC (PA)
Also Called: S S 8
750 Tasman Dr, Milpitas (95035-7456)
PHONE..................408 894-8400
Dennis Haar, *CEO*
Faizel Lakhani, *President*
Kam Wong, *CFO*
Cemal Dikmen, *Principal*
EMP: 161
SQ FT: 83,000
SALES (est): 29.1MM **Privately Held**
WEB: www.ss8.com
SIC: 4899 7381 Communication signal enhancement network system; detective services

(P-5999)
TELETRAC INC (HQ)
Also Called: Fleet Mangement Solutions
7391 Lincoln Way, Garden Grove (92841-1428)
PHONE..................714 897-0877
Tj Chung, *President*
Tim Van Cleve, *COO*
Lisa Lane, *Executive*
Julie Poelking, *Executive*
Hoang Pham, *Sr Software Eng*
▲ EMP: 96
SQ FT: 40,000
SALES (est): 87.9MM
SALES (corp-wide): 6.6B **Publicly Held**
WEB: www.teletrac.net
SIC: 4899 Data communication services
PA: Fortive Corporation
6920 Seaway Blvd
Everett WA 98203
425 446-5000

(P-6000)
TERABURST NETWORKS INC
1289 Anvilwood Ave, Sunnyvale (94089-2204)
PHONE..................408 400-4100
Ashok Jain, *CEO*
EMP: 50
SALES (est): 3.5MM **Privately Held**
WEB: www.teraburst.com
SIC: 4899 Communication signal enhancement network system

(P-6001)
THINKOM SOLUTIONS INC
4881 W 145th St, Hawthorne (90250-6701)
PHONE..................310 371-5486
Mark Silk, *CEO*
Michael Burke, *President*
Stuart Coppedge, *CFO*
Matthew Turk, *CFO*
William W Milroy, *Principal*
EMP: 116
SQ FT: 74,000
SALES (est): 14.8MM **Privately Held**
WEB: www.thin-kom.com
SIC: 4899 Satellite earth stations; television antenna construction & rental

(P-6002)
TRI-POWER GROUP INC
617 N Mary Ave, Sunnyvale (94085-2907)
PHONE..................925 583-8200
Seth Buechley, *CEO*
Chip Laughton, *President*
Bryan Kemper, *COO*
Barry Bruce, *CFO*
▲ EMP: 60

SQ FT: 13,000
SALES (est): 5.4MM **Privately Held**
WEB: www.tripowergroup.com
SIC: 4899 Data communication services

(P-6003)
UPROXX MEDIA GROUP INC (PA)
Also Called: Redwood
10381 Jefferson Blvd, Culver City (90232-3511)
PHONE..................310 424-2080
Benjamin Blank, *CEO*
Jarret Myer, *Founder*
Julie Butler, *Vice Pres*
Jeremy Kenik, *Vice Pres*
Michael Le, *Vice Pres*
EMP: 90
SQ FT: 12,000
SALES (est): 20.7MM **Privately Held**
SIC: 4899 Data communication services; entertainment service

(P-6004)
US DEPT OF THE AIR FORCE
Also Called: 95cs/Scxc Comp
35 N Wolfe Ave, Edwards (93524-6701)
PHONE..................661 277-3030
EMP: 250 **Publicly Held**
WEB: www.af.mil
SIC: 4899 9711 Communication signal enhancement network system; Air Force;
HQ: United States Department Of The Air Force
1000 Air Force Pentagon
Washington DC 20330

(P-6005)
VERIZON COMMUNICATIONS INC
9900 Flower St, Bellflower (90706-5411)
PHONE..................562 804-0354
EMP: 165
SALES (corp-wide): 126B **Publicly Held**
WEB: www.verizon.com
SIC: 4899 Data communication services
PA: Verizon Communications Inc.
1095 Ave Of The Americas
New York NY 10036
212 395-1000

(P-6006)
VIDEO VICE DATA COMMUNICATIONS
Also Called: Vvd Comuunications
12681 Pala Dr, Garden Grove (92841-3926)
P.O. Box 91421, Long Beach (90809-1421)
PHONE..................714 897-6300
Bantofin Montoya, *President*
EMP: 396 EST: 2002
SALES: 9.7MM **Privately Held**
SIC: 4899 1731 Data communication services; electrical work; cable television installation; fiber optic cable installation; voice, data & video wiring contractor

(P-6007)
WIRELESS STORE INC
2217 10th St, Sacramento (95818-1315)
PHONE..................916 206-3600
Fadi Rashed, *CEO*
EMP: 250 EST: 2005
SQ FT: 5,000
SALES: 60MM **Privately Held**
SIC: 4899 4812 Data communication services; cellular telephone services

4911 Electric Svcs

(P-6008)
AES ALAMITOS LLC
690 N Studebaker Rd, Long Beach (90803-2221)
PHONE..................562 493-7891
Weikko Wirta, *Mng Member*
Sid Phan, *Engineer*
Jim Beach, *Maintence Staff*
EMP: 90
SALES: 200MM
SALES (corp-wide): 10.5B **Publicly Held**
SIC: 4911 Electric services

PA: The Aes Corporation
4300 Wilson Blvd Ste 1100
Arlington VA 22203
703 522-1315

(P-6009)
AES HUNTINGTON BEACH LLC
21730 Newland St, Huntington Beach
(92646-7612)
PHONE..................714 374-1476
Eric Pendergraft,
Jason Molina, *Buyer*
Minh Hoang,
Stephen O'Kane, *Mng Member*
EMP: 50
SALES (est): 33MM
SALES (corp-wide): 10.5B **Publicly Held**
WEB: www.aescorp.com
SIC: 4911 Generation, electric power
PA: The Aes Corporation
4300 Wilson Blvd Ste 1100
Arlington VA 22203
703 522-1315

(P-6010)
AES SOUTHLAND LLC
690 N Studebaker Rd, Long Beach
(90803-2221)
PHONE..................562 430-8685
Jeff Evans, *Mng Member*
EMP: 89 EST: 1998
SALES (est): 20.2MM
SALES (corp-wide): 10.5B **Publicly Held**
WEB: www.aescorp.com
SIC: 4911 Generation, electric power
PA: The Aes Corporation
4300 Wilson Blvd Ste 1100
Arlington VA 22203
703 522-1315

(P-6011)
ALAMEDA BUREAU ELEC
IMPRV CORP (HQ)
Also Called: Alameda Municipal Power
2000 Grand St, Alameda (94501-1228)
P.O. Box H (94501-0263)
PHONE..................510 748-3902
Edwin Dankworth, *CEO*
Gregory Hamm, *President*
Dean Batchelor, *COO*
Peter Holmes, *Vice Pres*
Margie Sherratt, *Vice Pres*
▲ EMP: 85
SALES (est): 79.1MM **Privately Held**
WEB: www.alamedapt.com
SIC: 4911 Distribution, electric power;
transmission, electric power
PA: City Of Alameda
2263 Santa Clara Ave
Alameda CA 94501
510 747-7400

(P-6012)
ALTAMONT INFRASTRUCTURE
CO
6185 Industrial Way, Livermore
(94551-9750)
PHONE..................925 245-5500
Tom Kelly, *Principal*
Green Ridge LLC, *Mng Member*
EMP: 60
SQ FT: 8,000
SALES: 30MM **Privately Held**
SIC: 4911 Generation, electric power

(P-6013)
CALIFRNIA IND SYS OPRATOR
CORP (PA)
Also Called: CALIFORNIA ISO
250 Outcropping Way, Folsom
(95630-8773)
P.O. Box 639014 (95763-9014)
PHONE..................916 351-4400
Stephen Berberich, *President*
Bob Foster, *Ch of Bd*
William J Regan, *CFO*
Andrew Ulmer, *Bd of Directors*
Ryan Seghesio, *Officer*
EMP: 530
SQ FT: 79,000
SALES: 220.6MM **Privately Held**
WEB: www.caiso.com
SIC: 4911 Distribution, electric power;
transmission, electric power

(P-6014)
CALPINE CORPORATION
5029 S Township Rd, Yuba City
(95993-9748)
PHONE..................530 821-2075
Scott Reynolds, *Branch Mgr*
EMP: 50
SALES (corp-wide): 8.7B **Privately Held**
WEB: www.calpine.com
SIC: 4911 Generation, electric power;
HQ: Calpine Corporation
717 Texas St Ste 1000
Houston TX 77002
713 830-2000

(P-6015)
CATALINA SOLAR 2 LLC
15445 Innovation Dr, San Diego
(92128-3432)
PHONE..................888 903-6926
Tristan Grimbert, *President*
Ryan Pfaff, *Vice Pres*
Robert Miller, *Admin Sec*
EMP: 826
SQ FT: 70,000
SALES (est): 299.2MM **Privately Held**
SIC: 4911 Generation, electric power

(P-6016)
CATALINA SOLAR LESSEE LLC
11585 Willow Springs Rd, Rosamond
(93560)
PHONE..................888 903-6926
Tristan Grimbert, *President*
Robert Miller, *Admin Sec*
EMP: 826 EST: 2014
SQ FT: 70,000
SALES (est): 213.4MM
SALES (corp-wide): 569.6MM **Privately Held**
SIC: 4911 Electric services
PA: Edf Renewables, Inc.
15445 Innovation Dr
San Diego CA 92128
858 521-3300

(P-6017)
CITY OF GLENDALE
Also Called: Glendale Water & Power
141 N Glendale Ave Fl 2, Glendale
(91206-4975)
PHONE..................818 548-3300
John Dolan, *Manager*
EMP: 300 **Privately Held**
WEB: www.glendaleca.com
SIC: 4911 Electric services
PA: City Of Glendale
141 N Glendale Ave Fl 2
Glendale CA 91206
818 548-2085

(P-6018)
CITY OF GLENDALE
Also Called: Power Plant
634 Bekins Way, Glendale (91201-3013)
PHONE..................818 548-3980
Larry Moorehouse, *Superintendent*
EMP: 50 **Privately Held**
WEB: www.glendaleca.com
SIC: 4911 Generation, electric power
PA: City Of Glendale
141 N Glendale Ave Fl 2
Glendale CA 91206
818 548-2085

(P-6019)
CITY OF SANTA CLARA
Also Called: Silicon Valley Power
1500 Warburton Ave, Santa Clara
(95050-3796)
PHONE..................408 615-2300
John Roukema, *Director*
Erik Nichols, *Technical Staff*
EMP: 50 **Privately Held**
SIC: 4911 Electric services
PA: City Of Santa Clara
1500 Warburton Ave
Santa Clara CA 95050
408 615-2200

(P-6020)
CITY OF SANTA CLARA
Also Called: Electric Department
1705 Martin Ave, Santa Clara
(95050-2557)
PHONE..................408 615-2046

Chris Cervelli, *Principal*
EMP: 125
SQ FT: 15,000 **Privately Held**
SIC: 4911
PA: City Of Santa Clara
1500 Warburton Ave
Santa Clara CA 95050
408 615-2200

(P-6021)
COMBUSTION ASSOCIATES INC
Also Called: Cai
555 Monica Cir, Corona (92880-5447)
PHONE..................951 272-6999
Mukund Kavia, *President*
Kusum Kavia, *Vice Pres*
Prajesh Kavia, *Admin Sec*
Bharat Kavia, *Administration*
Mark Bernal, *Design Engr*
▲ EMP: 50
SQ FT: 40,000
SALES (est): 85.3MM **Privately Held**
WEB: www.cai3.com
SIC: 4911 3443 ; boiler & boiler shop
work

(P-6022)
CONSTELLATION NEWENERGY
INC
350 S Grand Ave Ste 3800, Los Angeles
(90071-3479)
PHONE..................213 576-6001
Michael Peevey, *Branch Mgr*
EMP: 70
SALES (corp-wide): 33.5B **Publicly Held**
SIC: 4911 Generation, electric power
HQ: Constellation Newenergy, Inc.
1310 Point St Fl 4
Baltimore MD 21231
-

(P-6023)
COSO OPERATING COMPANY
LLC
2 Gill Station Coso Rd, Little Lake (93542)
P.O. Box 1690, Inyokern (93527-1690)
PHONE..................760 764-1300
Jim Pagano, *CEO*
Joseph Greco, *Senior VP*
Chris Ellis, *Manager*
Jeff Harding, *Supervisor*
▲ EMP: 90
SALES (est): 61.1MM **Privately Held**
SIC: 4911 Generation, electric power
PA: Terra-Gen Power, Llc
437 Madison Ave Fl 22
New York NY 10022

(P-6024)
COVANTA DELANO INC
Also Called: Delano Energy
31500 Pond Rd, Delano (93215)
P.O. Box 39, Mariposa (95338-0039)
PHONE..................661 792-3067
Anthony J Orlando, *CEO*
▲ EMP: 50
SALES (est): 22.4MM
SALES (corp-wide): 1.7B **Publicly Held**
WEB: www.aescorp.com
SIC: 4911 Generation, electric power
PA: Covanta Holding Corporation
445 South St
Morristown NJ 07960
862 345-5000

(P-6025)
CPN WILD HORSE
GEOTHERMAL LLC
10350 Socrates Mine Rd, Middletown
(95461-9732)
PHONE..................707 431-6229
Alison Mannwieler, *President*
EMP: 300
SQ FT: 4,000
SALES: 1.8MM
SALES (corp-wide): 8.7B **Privately Held**
SIC: 4911 Generation, electric power;
HQ: Calpine Corporation
717 Texas St Ste 1000
Houston TX 77002
713 830-2000

(P-6026)
CYPRESS CREEK HOLDINGS
LLC
3250 Ocean Park Blvd # 355, Santa Monica
(90405-3206)
PHONE..................310 581-6299
Ben Van De Bunt, *Chairman*
Michael Cohen, *President*
Matthew McGovern, *CEO*
EMP: 100
SALES (est): 20.5MM **Privately Held**
SIC: 4911

(P-6027)
DUKE ENERGY CORPORATION
8001 Irvine Center Dr, Irvine (92618-2938)
PHONE..................949 727-7434
EMP: 170
SALES (corp-wide): 23.4B **Publicly Held**
SIC: 4911 4924
PA: Duke Energy Corporation
550 S Tryon St
Charlotte NC 28202
704 382-3853

(P-6028)
DYNEGY MOSS LANDING LLC
Also Called: Moss Landing Power Plant
7301 Highway 1, Moss Landing (95039)
P.O. Box 690 (95039-0690)
PHONE..................831 633-6618
Robert C Flexon, *CEO*
David Gillespie, *Vice Pres*
Kent Nelson, *Engineer*
Janet Bowen, *Train & Dev Mgr*
▲ EMP: 75
SALES (est): 750K
SALES (corp-wide): 5.4B **Publicly Held**
WEB: www.dynegy.com
SIC: 4911 Electric services
PA: Vistra Energy Corp.
6555 Sierra Dr
Irving TX 75039
214 812-4600

(P-6029)
EDF MSSCHSTTS SPNSOR
MMBER LLC
15445 Innovation Dr, San Diego
(92128-3432)
PHONE..................888 903-6926
Tristan Grimber, *President*
Kara Vongphakdy, *Treasurer*
Larry Barr, *Exec VP*
Robert Miller, *Exec VP*
Ryan Pfaff, *Exec VP*
EMP: 827 EST: 2014
SQ FT: 70,000
SALES (est): 248.1K
SALES (corp-wide): 569.6MM **Privately Held**
SIC: 4911 Electric services
PA: Edf Renewables, Inc.
15445 Innovation Dr
San Diego CA 92128
858 521-3300

(P-6030)
EDF RNWBLES ASSET
HOLDINGS INC
15445 Innovation Dr, San Diego
(92128-3432)
PHONE..................888 903-6926
Tristan Grimbert, *President*
Richard Jigarjian, *Vice Pres*
Robert Miller, *Admin Sec*
EMP: 826 EST: 2009
SQ FT: 70,000
SALES (est): 302.5MM **Privately Held**
SIC: 4911 Generation, electric power

(P-6031)
EDISON CAPITAL (DH)
18101 Von Karman Ave, Irvine
(92612-1012)
PHONE..................909 594-3789
Thomas Mc Daniel, *President*
Oded Rhone, *President*
Phillip Dandridge, *CFO*
Steve Dandridge, *CFO*
Jim Phillipsen, *Treasurer*
EMP: 92
SQ FT: 12,000

SALES (est): 30.7MM
SALES (corp-wide): 12.3B **Publicly Held**
WEB: www.edisoncapital.com
SIC: 4911 Electric services
HQ: Edison Mission Group Inc.
2244 Walnut Grove Ave
Rosemead CA 91770
626 302-2222

(P-6032)
EDISON INTERNATIONAL (PA)
2244 Walnut Grove Ave, Rosemead
(91770-3714)
P.O. Box 976 (91770-0976)
PHONE....................626 302-2222
Theodore F Craver Jr, *Ch of Bd*
Pedro J Pizarro, *President*
Robert Voss, *President*
W James Scilacci, *CFO*
Ronald L Litzinger, *Exec VP*
EMP: 52
SALES: 12.3B **Publicly Held**
WEB: www.edisonx.com
SIC: 4911 Electric services; distribution,
electric power; generation, electric power;
transmission, electric power

(P-6033)
EDISON MISSION ENERGY (DH)
2244 Walnut Grove Ave, Rosemead
(91770-3714)
PHONE....................626 302-5778
Pedro J Pizarro, *President*
Andrew J Hertneky, *Senior VP*
Paul Jacob, *Senior VP*
John C Kennedy, *Senior VP*
S Daniel Melita, *Senior VP*
▲ **EMP:** 50
SQ FT: 71,000
SALES (est): 1.4B **Publicly Held**
SIC: 4911 Electric services
HQ: Nrg Energy Holdings Inc.
849 Eastwood Dr
Golden CO 80401
609 524-4500

(P-6034)
EDISON MSSION MIDWEST HOLDINGS
2244 Walnut Grove Ave, Rosemead
(91770-3714)
PHONE....................626 302-2222
Guy F Gorney, *President*
Oded Rhone, *Vice Pres*
Johanna Pyles, *Manager*
EMP: 2483
SALES (est): 3.2B
SALES (corp-wide): 12.3B **Publicly Held**
SIC: 4911 Electric services
HQ: Edison Mission Group Inc.
2244 Walnut Grove Ave
Rosemead CA 91770
626 302-2222

(P-6035)
ELK HILLS POWER LLC
101 Ash St, San Diego (92101-3017)
PHONE....................661 763-2730
EMP: 126
SALES (est): 2MM
SALES (corp-wide): 2B **Publicly Held**
SIC: 4911 Electric services
PA: California Resources Corporation
9200 Oakdale Ave Ste 900
Chatsworth CA 91311
888 848-4754

(P-6036)
ENPOWER MANAGEMENT CORP
2420 Camino Ramon Ste 101, San Ramon
(94583-4207)
PHONE....................925 244-1100
Edward Tomeo, *President*
Alex Sugaoka, *Vice Pres*
EMP: 50
SQ FT: 3,500
SALES (est): 10.9MM
SALES (corp-wide): 59.4MM **Privately Held**
WEB: www.enpowercorp.com
SIC: 4911 Generation, electric power; dis-
tribution, electric power

PA: Enpower Corp.
2420 Camino Ramon Ste 101
San Ramon CA 94583
925 244-1100

(P-6037)
GENERAL ELECTRIC COMPANY
288 Campus Dr Bldg 14105, Stanford
(94305-4109)
PHONE....................650 725-0516
Ron Dahlin, *Manager*
EMP: 217
SALES (corp-wide): 122B **Publicly Held**
SIC: 4911 Generation, electric power
PA: General Electric Company
41 Farnsworth St
Boston MA 02210
617 443-3000

(P-6038)
GOLDEN STATE WATER COMPANY
Bear Valley Electric
42020 Garstin Dr, Big Bear Lake
(92315-1580)
P.O. Box 1547 (92315-1547)
PHONE....................909 866-4678
Roger Kropke, *Manager*
EMP: 50
SALES (corp-wide): 440.6MM **Publicly Held**
WEB: www.gswater.com
SIC: 4911 Distribution, electric power
HQ: Golden State Water Company
630 E Foothill Blvd
San Dimas CA 91773
909 394-3600

(P-6039)
GREAT WESTERN WIND ENERGY LLC
15445 Innovation Dr, San Diego
(92128-3432)
PHONE....................888 903-6926
Tristan Grimbert, *President*
Ryan Pfaff, *Vice Pres*
EMP: 99
SALES (est): 2.7MM **Privately Held**
SIC: 4911

(P-6040)
GREEN RIDGE SERVICES LLC
6185 Industrial Way, Livermore
(94551-9750)
PHONE....................925 245-5500
Tom Kelly,
EMP: 60
SQ FT: 30,000
SALES (est): 23.8MM **Privately Held**
SIC: 4911 Electric services

(P-6041)
HANERGY HOLDING AMERICA INC
1350 Bayshore Hwy Ste 825, Burlingame
(94010-1848)
PHONE....................650 288-3722
Yi Wu, *Ch of Bd*
Jeff Zhou, *President*
Richard Gaertner, *COO*
Edward Yu, *General Mgr*
Abraham Liu, *Technology*
EMP: 360
SQ FT: 7,000
SALES (est): 227.3MM **Privately Held**
SIC: 4911 6719 Generation, electric
power; investment holding companies,
except banks
PA: Hanergy Holding Group Limited
No.0-A, Anli Road, Chaoyang Dist.
Beijing
108 391-4567

(P-6042)
HIGH RIDGE WIND LLC
15445 Innovation Dr, San Diego
(92128-3432)
PHONE....................888 903-6926
Tristan Grimbert, *President*
Ryan Pfaff, *Vice Pres*
Robert Miller, *Admin Sec*
EMP: 826 EST: 2013
SQ FT: 70,000
SALES (est): 258.5MM **Privately Held**
SIC: 4911 Electric services

(P-6043)
HUDSON RANCH POWER I LLC
12250 El Camino Real # 280, San Diego
(92130-2226)
P.O. Box 67, Calipatria (92233-0067)
PHONE....................858 509-0150
Eric L Spomer, *Mng Member*
George Donlou, *Treasurer*
Carol A Thimot, *Asst Treas*
David K Watson,
EMP: 55
SALES (est): 42.2MM **Privately Held**
SIC: 4911 Generation, electric power

(P-6044)
IMPERIAL IRRIGATION DISTRICT (PA)
Also Called: I I D
333 E Barioni Blvd, Imperial (92251-1773)
P.O. Box 937 (92251-0937)
PHONE....................800 303-7756
Stephen Benson, *President*
Anthony Sanchez, *President*
Keven Kelly, *CEO*
Raquel Lopez, *Officer*
Mike Abatti, *Vice Pres*
▲ **EMP:** 700
SQ FT: 10,000
SALES (est): 634.6MM **Privately Held**
WEB: www.iidwater.com
SIC: 4911 4971 4931 ; water distribution
or supply systems for irrigation; electric &
other services combined

(P-6045)
JETMORE WIND LLC
15445 Innovation Dr, San Diego
(92128-3432)
PHONE....................888 903-6926
Tristan Grimbert, *President*
Ryan Pfaff, *Vice Pres*
Robert Miller, *Admin Sec*
EMP: 826
SQ FT: 70,000
SALES (est): 180.6MM **Privately Held**
SIC: 4911 Electric services

(P-6046)
KERN RIVER CO GENERATION CO
Sw China Grade Loop, Bakersfield (93308)
PHONE....................661 392-2663
Neil Bridges, *Exec Dir*
Gaylord Edward, *Treasurer*
EMP: 65
SALES (est): 30.8MM **Publicly Held**
SIC: 4911 4961 ; steam supply systems,
including geothermal
HQ: Southern Sierra Energy Company
18101 Von Karman Ave
Irvine CA 92612

(P-6047)
KJC OPERATING COMPANY
41100 Us Highway 395, Boron
(93516-2109)
PHONE....................760 762-5562
Chris Kelleher, *Chairman*
Janet Doyle, *President*
Scott Frier, *COO*
EMP: 117
SQ FT: 10,000
SALES (est): 30.8MM **Privately Held**
WEB: www.kjcsolar.com
SIC: 4911 Electric services

(P-6048)
LEEMAH ELECTRONICS INC
Also Called: (415 LOCATION)
1080 Sansome St, San Francisco (94111)
PHONE....................415 394-1288
Jack Wang, *Manager*
EMP: 120
SALES (corp-wide): 101MM **Privately Held**
SIC: 4911 3672 3669 3571 Electric serv-
ices; printed circuit boards; intercommuni-
cation systems, electric; electronic
computers
HQ: Leemah Electronics, Inc.
155 S Hill Dr
Brisbane CA 94005
415 394-1288

(P-6049)
LIBERTY UTLTIES CLPECO ELC LLC
Also Called: Liberty Energy
933 Eloise Ave, South Lake Tahoe
(96150-6470)
PHONE....................800 782-2506
Ian Robertson, *Mng Member*
Mike Smart, *President*
Jan Bagnall, *Vice Pres*
Chico Dafonte, *Vice Pres*
Darrel Lytle, *Program Mgr*
EMP: 60
SQ FT: 10,000
SALES (est): 36.1MM **Privately Held**
SIC: 4911 Distribution, electric power

(P-6050)
LOS ANGELES DEPT WTR & PWR
Also Called: Ladwp
111 N Hope St, Los Angeles (90012-2607)
P.O. Box 51111 (90051-5700)
PHONE....................213 367-4211
Ronald Nichols, *Branch Mgr*
Silvia Denis, *Executive Asst*
Walter Ramirez, *Administration*
Sunil Dharmarathne, *Info Tech Mgr*
Minh Le, *Info Tech Mgr*
EMP: 99
SALES (corp-wide): 1.1B **Privately Held**
SIC: 4911 4941 Generation, electric
power; water supply
PA: Los Angeles Department Of Water And
Power
111 N Hope St
Los Angeles CA 90012
213 367-4211

(P-6051)
MARIN CLEAN ENERGY
Also Called: McE
1125 Tamalpais Ave, San Rafael
(94901-3221)
PHONE....................415 464-6028
Dawn Weisz, *CEO*
Alice Stover, *Program Mgr*
Allen Chiu, *Business Mgr*
Chris Kubik, *Business Mgr*
David McNeil, *Finance Mgr*
EMP: 75
SQ FT: 10,000
SALES (est): 151.6MM **Privately Held**
SIC: 4911 Distribution, electric power

(P-6052)
MERCED IRRIGATION DISTRICT (PA)
744 W 20th St, Merced (95340-3601)
P.O. Box 2288 (95344-0288)
PHONE....................209 722-5761
Tim Pellissier, *President*
Andre Urquidez, *Treasurer*
Dave Long, *Vice Pres*
EMP: 50 EST: 1919
SQ FT: 20,000
SALES: 89MM **Privately Held**
WEB: www.mercedid.org
SIC: 4911 4971 Generation, electric
power; water distribution or supply sys-
tems for irrigation

(P-6053)
MILO WIND PROJECT LLC
Also Called: Edf Renewable Energy
15445 Innovation Dr, San Diego
(92128-3432)
PHONE....................888 903-6926
EMP: 82
SQ FT: 70,000
SALES (est): 6.8MM **Privately Held**
SIC: 4911

(P-6054)
MODESTO IRRIGATION DISTRICT
1231 11th St, Modesto (95354-0701)
P.O. Box 4060 (95352-4060)
PHONE....................209 526-7563
Don Durman, *Treasurer*
EMP: 400
SALES (corp-wide): 384.3MM **Privately Held**
SIC: 4911 4941 ; water supply

PA: Modesto Irrigation District (Inc)
1231 11th St
Modesto CA 95354
209 526-7337

(P-6055)
MODESTO IRRIGATION DISTRICT (PA)
1231 11th St, Modesto (95354-0701)
P.O. Box 4060 (95352-4060)
PHONE.............................209 526-7337
Allen Short, *President*
Jeffrey Fairbanks, *Officer*
Scott Vuren, *Risk Mgmt Dir*
Roger Van Hoy, *General Mgr*
Barbara Solarez, *Admin Sec*
EMP: 175
SQ FT: 90,000
SALES: 384.3MM **Privately Held**
SIC: 4911 4971 ; water distribution or supply systems for irrigation

(P-6056)
MODESTO IRRIGATION DISTRICT
929 Woodland Ave, Modesto (95351-1553)
P.O. Box 4060 (95352-4060)
PHONE.............................209 526-7373
Ellen Short, *General Mgr*
Jason Roysdon, *Technology*
EMP: 400
SALES (corp-wide): 384.3MM **Privately Held**
SIC: 4911 4971 Distribution, electric power; irrigation systems
PA: Modesto Irrigation District (Inc)
1231 11th St
Modesto CA 95354
209 526-7337

(P-6057)
NORTHERN CALIFORNIA POWER AGCY (PA)
Also Called: Ncpa
651 Commerce Dr, Roseville (95678-6411)
PHONE.............................916 781-3636
Rui Dai, *Risk Mgmt Dir*
Randy Howard, *General Mgr*
John Koos, *Manager*
EMP: 65 **EST:** 1968
SQ FT: 17,400
SALES (est): 113.4MM **Privately Held**
WEB: www.NCPA.com
SIC: 4911 Transmission, electric power; generation, electric power

(P-6058)
NORTHERN CALIFORNIA POWER AGCY
Also Called: Ncpa- Plant 1
12000 Ridge Rd, Middletown (95461-9585)
P.O. Box 663 (95461-0663)
PHONE.............................707 987-2381
Murry Grande, *Opers-Prdtn-Mfg*
EMP: 56
SALES (est): 9.8MM
SALES (corp-wide): 113.4MM **Privately Held**
SIC: 4911 Generation, electric power
PA: Northern California Power Agency
651 Commerce Dr
Roseville CA 95678
916 781-3636

(P-6059)
NRG CALIFORNIA SOUTH LP
Also Called: Etiwanda Power Plant
8996 Etiwanda Ave, Rancho Cucamonga (91739-9662)
PHONE.............................909 899-7241
Lee Moore, *Branch Mgr*
Gary Ackerman, *Exec Dir*
Vince Munoz, *Analyst*
EMP: 55 **Publicly Held**
SIC: 4911 Generation, electric power
HQ: Nrg California South Lp
804 Carnegie Ctr
Princeton NJ 08540

(P-6060)
NRG CLEAN POWER INC
7012 Owensmouth Ave, Canoga Park (91303-2005)
PHONE.............................818 444-2020

Oren Tamir, *CEO*
EMP: 50 **EST:** 2016
SALES (est): 1.1MM **Privately Held**
SIC: 4911

(P-6061)
NRG EL SEGUNDO OPERATIONS INC
301 Vista Del Mar, El Segundo (90245-3650)
PHONE.............................310 615-6344
John Ragan, *President*
▲ **EMP:** 65
SALES (est): 20.9MM **Publicly Held**
SIC: 4911 Electric services
PA: Nrg Energy, Inc.
804 Carnegie Ctr
Princeton NJ 08540
-

(P-6062)
NRG ENERGY INC
455 Golden Gate Ave, San Francisco (94102-3660)
PHONE.............................415 255-8105
EMP: 65 **Publicly Held**
SIC: 4911 Generation, electric power
PA: Nrg Energy, Inc.
804 Carnegie Ctr
Princeton NJ 08540
-

(P-6063)
NRG ENERGY INC
3201 Wilbur Ave, Antioch (94509-8546)
PHONE.............................913 689-3904
EMP: 55 **Publicly Held**
SIC: 4911 Generation, electric power
PA: Nrg Energy, Inc.
804 Carnegie Ctr
Princeton NJ 08540

(P-6064)
OASIS REPOWER LLC
15445 Innovation Dr, San Diego (92128-3432)
PHONE.............................888 903-6926
Tristan Grimbert, *President*
Ryan Pfaff, *Vice Pres*
Robert Miller, *Admin Sec*
EMP: 826
SQ FT: 70,000
SALES (est): 283.6MM **Privately Held**
SIC: 4911 Electric services

(P-6065)
OLYMPUS POWER LLC
34759 Lencioni Ave, Bakersfield (93308-9797)
PHONE.............................661 393-6885
Todd Witwer, *Manager*
EMP: 147 **Privately Held**
WEB: www.deltapower.com
SIC: 4911 Generation, electric power
HQ: Olympus Power, Llc
67 E Park Pl Ste 4
Morristown NJ 07960
973 889-9100

(P-6066)
ORMESA LLC
3300 E Evan Hewes Hwy, Holtville (92250-9429)
P.O. Box 86 (92250-0086)
PHONE.............................760 356-3020
Lucien Brunicki,
▲ **EMP:** 55
SALES (est): 14.4MM **Publicly Held**
WEB: www.ormesa.com
SIC: 4911
PA: Ormat Technologies, Inc.
6225 Neil Rd Ste 300
Reno NV 89511

(P-6067)
PACIFIC GAS AND ELECTRIC CO
Also Called: PG&e
425 Beck Ave, Fairfield (94533-6808)
PHONE.............................415 973-7000
Dana McKiddin, *Principal*
EMP: 100 **Publicly Held**
WEB: www.pge.com
SIC: 4911 Transmission, electric power

HQ: Pacific Gas And Electric Company
77 Beale St
San Francisco CA 94105
415 973-7000

(P-6068)
PACIFIC GAS AND ELECTRIC CO (HQ)
Also Called: PG&E
77 Beale St, San Francisco (94105-1814)
P.O. Box 770000 (94177-0001)
PHONE.............................415 973-7000
Nickolas Stavropoulos, *President*
Forrest E Miller, *Ch of Bd*
David S Thomason, *CFO*
Loraine M Giammona, *Ch Credit Ofcr*
Karen A Austin, *Senior VP*
▲ **EMP:** 3000 **EST:** 1905
SQ FT: 160,000
SALES: 17.1B **Publicly Held**
WEB: www.pge.com
SIC: 4911 4924 Generation, electric power; transmission, electric power; distribution, electric power; natural gas distribution

(P-6069)
PACIFIC GAS AND ELECTRIC CO
Also Called: PG&e
885 Embarcadero Dr, West Sacramento (95605-1503)
PHONE.............................916 375-5005
Richard Yamacuchi, *Branch Mgr*
EMP: 130 **Publicly Held**
WEB: www.pge.com
SIC: 4911 Transmission, electric power
HQ: Pacific Gas And Electric Company
77 Beale St
San Francisco CA 94105
415 973-7000

(P-6070)
PACIFIC GAS AND ELECTRIC CO
Also Called: PG&e
530 E St, Marysville (95901-5530)
P.O. Box 671 (95901-0018)
PHONE.............................530 742-3251
Dennis Grilione, *Branch Mgr*
EMP: 450 **Publicly Held**
WEB: www.pge.com
SIC: 4911 4924 Distribution, electric power; natural gas distribution
HQ: Pacific Gas And Electric Company
77 Beale St
San Francisco CA 94105
415 973-7000

(P-6071)
PACIFIC GAS AND ELECTRIC CO
PG&e
4525 Hollis St, Oakland (94608-2911)
PHONE.............................510 450-5744
G L Fairbanks, *Branch Mgr*
EMP: 90 **Publicly Held**
WEB: www.pge.com
SIC: 4911 Transmission, electric power
HQ: Pacific Gas And Electric Company
77 Beale St
San Francisco CA 94105
415 973-7000

(P-6072)
PACIFIC GAS AND ELECTRIC CO
Also Called: PG&e
650 O St, Fresno (93721-2708)
PHONE.............................559 268-2868
C R Martin, *Branch Mgr*
Ryan Durant, *Manager*
EMP: 450 **Publicly Held**
WEB: www.pge.com
SIC: 4911 4922 Generation, electric power; natural gas transmission
HQ: Pacific Gas And Electric Company
77 Beale St
San Francisco CA 94105
415 973-7000

(P-6073)
PACIFIC GAS AND ELECTRIC CO
Also Called: PG&e
210 Corona Rd, Petaluma (94954-1319)
PHONE.............................707 765-5118
Tom Reimer, *Manager*
EMP: 50
SQ FT: 168,577 **Publicly Held**
WEB: www.pge.com

SIC: 4911 Transmission, electric power
HQ: Pacific Gas And Electric Company
77 Beale St
San Francisco CA 94105
415 973-7000

(P-6074)
PACIFIC GAS AND ELECTRIC CO
Also Called: PG&e
788 Taylorville Rd, Grass Valley (95949-7713)
PHONE.............................530 477-3245
Art Bartolome, *Manager*
EMP: 200 **Publicly Held**
WEB: www.pge.com
SIC: 4911 4922 Generation, electric power; natural gas transmission
HQ: Pacific Gas And Electric Company
77 Beale St
San Francisco CA 94105
415 973-7000

(P-6075)
PACIFIC GAS AND ELECTRIC CO
PG&e
111 Stony Cir, Santa Rosa (95401-9599)
PHONE.............................800 756-7243
Gary F Heitz, *Principal*
EMP: 240
SQ FT: 100,000 **Publicly Held**
WEB: www.pge.com
SIC: 4911 Transmission, electric power
HQ: Pacific Gas And Electric Company
77 Beale St
San Francisco CA 94105
415 973-7000

(P-6076)
PACIFIC GAS AND ELECTRIC CO
Also Called: PG&e
4690 Evora Rd, Concord (94520-1004)
PHONE.............................925 676-0948
John Glenn, *Branch Mgr*
EMP: 65 **Publicly Held**
WEB: www.pge.com
SIC: 4911 Transmission, electric power
HQ: Pacific Gas And Electric Company
77 Beale St
San Francisco CA 94105
415 973-7000

(P-6077)
PACIFIC GAS AND ELECTRIC CO
Also Called: PG&e
4636 Missouri Flat Rd, Placerville (95667-6823)
PHONE.............................530 621-7237
Gordon Smith, *Branch Mgr*
EMP: 50 **Publicly Held**
WEB: www.pge.com
SIC: 4911 Transmission, electric power
HQ: Pacific Gas And Electric Company
77 Beale St
San Francisco CA 94105
415 973-7000

(P-6078)
PACIFIC GAS AND ELECTRIC CO
Also Called: PG&e
9 Mi Nw Of Avila Bch, Avila Beach (93424)
PHONE.............................805 506-5280
David Oatley, *Branch Mgr*
Karen Brower, *Executive*
Richard Van Der Linden, *Sr Project Mgr*
EMP: 1400 **Publicly Held**
WEB: www.pge.com
SIC: 4911 Generation, electric power
HQ: Pacific Gas And Electric Company
77 Beale St
San Francisco CA 94105
415 973-7000

(P-6079)
PACIFIC GAS AND ELECTRIC CO
Also Called: PG&e
3600 Meadow View Dr, Redding (96002-9701)
PHONE.............................530 365-7672
John Duncan, *Manager*
EMP: 109 **Publicly Held**
WEB: www.pge.com
SIC: 4911 Transmission, electric power
HQ: Pacific Gas And Electric Company
77 Beale St
San Francisco CA 94105
415 973-7000

PRODUCTS & SVCS

(P-6080)
PACIFIC GAS AND ELECTRIC CO
Also Called: PG&e
12840 Bill Clark Way, Auburn (95602-9527)
PHONE..............................530 889-3102
Steve Pennett, *Manager*
EMP: 50 **Publicly Held**
WEB: www.pge.com
SIC: 4911 Transmission, electric power
HQ: Pacific Gas And Electric Company
77 Beale St
San Francisco CA 94105
415 973-7000

(P-6081)
PACIFIC GAS AND ELECTRIC CO
Also Called: PG&e
1850 Gateway Blvd Ste 800, Concord
(94520-8473)
PHONE..............................925 674-6305
Kim Lawson, *Branch Mgr*
EMP: 65 **Publicly Held**
WEB: www.pge.com
SIC: 4911
HQ: Pacific Gas And Electric Company
77 Beale St
San Francisco CA 94105
415 973-7000

(P-6082)
PACIFIC GAS AND ELECTRIC CO
Also Called: PG&e
2311 Garden Rd, Monterey (93940-5325)
PHONE..............................831 648-3231
Richard Brent, *Branch Mgr*
EMP: 50 **Publicly Held**
WEB: www.pge.com
SIC: 4911 Transmission, electric power
HQ: Pacific Gas And Electric Company
77 Beale St
San Francisco CA 94105
415 973-7000

(P-6083)
PACIFIC GAS AND ELECTRIC CO
Also Called: PG&e
42105 Boyce Rd, Fremont (94538)
PHONE..............................510 770-2025
Gary Commick, *Principal*
EMP: 150 **Publicly Held**
WEB: www.pge.com
SIC: 4911 Transmission, electric power
HQ: Pacific Gas And Electric Company
77 Beale St
San Francisco CA 94105
415 973-7000

(P-6084)
PACIFIC GAS AND ELECTRIC CO
Also Called: PG&e
1000 King Salmon Ave, Eureka
(95503-6859)
PHONE..............................707 444-0700
Roy Willis, *Manager*
EMP: 100 **Publicly Held**
WEB: www.pge.com
SIC: 4911 Generation, electric power
HQ: Pacific Gas And Electric Company
77 Beale St
San Francisco CA 94105
415 973-7000

(P-6085)
PACIFIC GAS AND ELECTRIC CO
Also Called: PG&e
33755 Old Mill Rd, Auberry (93602-9655)
P.O. Box 425 (93602-0425)
PHONE..............................559 855-6112
John Moore, *General Mgr*
EMP: 50 **Publicly Held**
WEB: www.pge.com
SIC: 4911 ; generation, electric power
HQ: Pacific Gas And Electric Company
77 Beale St
San Francisco CA 94105
415 973-7000

(P-6086)
PACIFIC GAS AND ELECTRIC CO
Also Called: PG&e
450 Eastmoor Ave, Daly City (94015-2041)
PHONE..............................650 755-1236
Len Jackson, *Branch Mgr*
EMP: 150 **Publicly Held**
WEB: www.pge.com
SIC: 4911 Transmission, electric power

HQ: Pacific Gas And Electric Company
77 Beale St
San Francisco CA 94105
415 973-7000

(P-6087)
PACIFIC GAS AND ELECTRIC CO
Also Called: PG&e
1524 N Carpenter Rd, Modesto
(95351-1110)
PHONE..............................209 576-6636
Sheila Radford, *Branch Mgr*
Kevin Chacon, *Manager*
EMP: 50 **Publicly Held**
WEB: www.pge.com
SIC: 4911 4923 4932 Transmission, electric power; gas transmission & distribution; gas & other services combined
HQ: Pacific Gas And Electric Company
77 Beale St
San Francisco CA 94105
415 973-7000

(P-6088)
PACIFIC GAS AND ELECTRIC CO
Also Called: PG&e
3136 Boeing Way, Stockton (95206-4989)
PHONE..............................209 942-1787
Robert Eggert, *Branch Mgr*
EMP: 54
SQ FT: 138,000 **Publicly Held**
WEB: www.pge.com
SIC: 4911 4922 Generation, electric power; natural gas transmission
HQ: Pacific Gas And Electric Company
77 Beale St
San Francisco CA 94105
415 973-7000

(P-6089)
PACIFIC GAS AND ELECTRIC CO
Also Called: PG&e
800 Price Canyon Rd, Pismo Beach
(93449-2722)
PHONE..............................805 773-6109
Don Boatman, *Branch Mgr*
EMP: 65 **Publicly Held**
WEB: www.pge.com
SIC: 4911
HQ: Pacific Gas And Electric Company
77 Beale St
San Francisco CA 94105
415 973-7000

(P-6090)
PACIFIC GAS AND ELECTRIC CO
Also Called: PG&e
3797 1st St, Livermore (94551-4905)
PHONE..............................925 373-2623
Kermit Pol, *Branch Mgr*
EMP: 120 **Publicly Held**
WEB: www.pge.com
SIC: 4911 Transmission, electric power
HQ: Pacific Gas And Electric Company
77 Beale St
San Francisco CA 94105
415 973-7000

(P-6091)
PACIFIC GAS AND ELECTRIC CO
Also Called: PG&e
316 L St, Davis (95616-4231)
PHONE..............................530 757-5803
Gail Sanchez, *Manager*
EMP: 300 **Publicly Held**
WEB: www.pge.com
SIC: 4911 Transmission, electric power
HQ: Pacific Gas And Electric Company
77 Beale St
San Francisco CA 94105
415 973-7000

(P-6092)
PACIFIC GAS AND ELECTRIC CO
Also Called: PG&e
2180 Harrison St, San Francisco
(94110-1300)
PHONE..............................415 695-3513
Dave Bradley, *Branch Mgr*
EMP: 300 **Publicly Held**
WEB: www.pge.com

SIC: 4911 4922 4924 1311 Generation, electric power; transmission, electric power; distribution, electric power; pipelines, natural gas; natural gas distribution; natural gas production; crude petroleum production; land subdividers & developers, residential; land subdividers & developers, commercial; power plant construction
HQ: Pacific Gas And Electric Company
77 Beale St
San Francisco CA 94105
415 973-7000

(P-6093)
PACIFIC GAS AND ELECTRIC CO
Also Called: PG&e
66 Ranch Dr, Milpitas (95035-5103)
PHONE..............................408 945-6215
Jeff Klotz, *Branch Mgr*
EMP: 65 **Publicly Held**
WEB: www.pge.com
SIC: 4911 Transmission, electric power
HQ: Pacific Gas And Electric Company
77 Beale St
San Francisco CA 94105
415 973-7000

(P-6094)
PACIFIC GAS AND ELECTRIC CO
Also Called: PG&e
28570 Tiger Creek Rd, Pioneer
(95666-9646)
PHONE..............................209 295-2651
EMP: 65 **Publicly Held**
WEB: www.pge.com
SIC: 4911 Transmission, electric power
HQ: Pacific Gas And Electric Company
77 Beale St
San Francisco CA 94105
415 973-7000

(P-6095)
PACIFIC GAS AND ELECTRIC CO
Also Called: PG&e
4201 Arrow St, Bakersfield (93308-4938)
PHONE..............................661 398-5918
Don Hacks, *Manager*
EMP: 65 **Publicly Held**
WEB: www.pge.com
SIC: 4911 Transmission, electric power
HQ: Pacific Gas And Electric Company
77 Beale St
San Francisco CA 94105
415 973-7000

(P-6096)
PACIFIC GAS AND ELECTRIC CO
Also Called: PG&e
160 Cow Meadow Pl, Templeton (93465)
PHONE..............................805 434-4418
Bob Burroughs, *Branch Mgr*
EMP: 60 **Publicly Held**
WEB: www.pge.com
SIC: 4911 Transmission, electric power
HQ: Pacific Gas And Electric Company
77 Beale St
San Francisco CA 94105
415 973-7000

(P-6097)
PATTERN ENERGY GROUP LP (PA)
Bay 3 Pier 1, San Francisco (94111)
PHONE..............................415 283-4000
Michael Garland, *CEO*
Alan Batkin, *Partner*
Robert Boak, *Facilities Mgr*
Karen Luk, *Senior Mgr*
Patrick Pyle, *Director*
EMP: 85
SALES (est) 94.9MM **Privately Held**
SIC: 4911 Transmission, electric power

(P-6098)
PLACER COUNTY WATER AGENCY (PA)
144 Ferguson Rd, Auburn (95603-3231)
P.O. Box 6570 (95604-6570)
PHONE..............................530 823-4850
David Breninger, *General Mgr*
Greg Young, *Admin Asst*
Brent Smith, *Info Tech Dir*
Stephan Raper, *Technician*
Ross Hooper, *Project Mgr*
EMP: 173

SQ FT: 22,750
SALES: 70.7MM **Privately Held**
WEB: www.pcwa.net
SIC: 4911 4941 4971 Electric services; water supply; irrigation systems

(P-6099)
RE BARREN RIDGE 1 LLC
300 California St Fl 7, San Francisco
(94104-1415)
PHONE..............................415 675-1500
Greg Wilson,
EMP: 130
SQ FT: 10,000
SALES (est): 19.2MM **Privately Held**
SIC: 4911

(P-6100)
RIDGETOP ENERGY LLC
7021 Oak Creek Rd, Mojave (93501-7723)
PHONE..............................661 822-2400
Dale L Smith,
EMP: 50 **EST:** 1998
SALES (est): 19.7MM **Privately Held**
SIC: 4911 Generation, electric power

(P-6101)
ROCKLIN POWER INVESTORS LP
Also Called: Rio Bravo Rocklin
3100 Thunder Valley Ct, Lincoln
(95648-9579)
PHONE..............................916 645-3383
Stephen B Gross, *CFO*
EMP: 60
SALES (est): 45.2MM **Privately Held**
SIC: 4911 Generation, electric power

(P-6102)
SACRAMENTO MUNICPL UTILITY DST (PA)
Also Called: S M U D
6201 S St, Sacramento (95817-1818)
P.O. Box 15830 (95852-0830)
PHONE..............................916 452-3211
Arlen Orchard, *CEO*
Jim Tracy, *CFO*
Noreen Roche-Carter, *Treasurer*
James Kendall, *Officer*
Lisa Mackie, *Admin Sec*
▲ **EMP:** 710
SQ FT: 118,000
SALES: 1.5B **Privately Held**
WEB: www.smud.org
SIC: 4911 Generation, electric power

(P-6103)
SACRAMENTO MUNICPL UTILITY DST
6201 S St, Sacramento (95817-1818)
PHONE..............................916 452-3211
Carlos Diaz, *Branch Mgr*
EMP: 1000
SALES (corp-wide): 1.5B **Privately Held**
SIC: 4911 Generation, electric power
PA: Sacramento Municipal Utility District
6201 S St
Sacramento CA 95817
916 452-3211

(P-6104)
SACRAMENTO MUNICPL UTILITY DST
Also Called: Smud Energy Services
6301 S St, Sacramento (95817)
P.O. Box 15830 (95852-0830)
PHONE..............................916 732-5155
Jan Schori, *Manager*
John Aliotti, *Program Mgr*
Janis Erickson, *Project Mgr*
Ann Graef, *Project Mgr*
Dwight Maccurdy, *Project Mgr*
EMP: 88
SALES (corp-wide): 1.5B **Privately Held**
SIC: 4911 Generation, electric power
PA: Sacramento Municipal Utility District
6201 S St
Sacramento CA 95817
916 452-3211

(P-6105)
SACRAMENTO MUNICPL UTILITY DST
Also Called: Supply Change Services
6201 S St, Sacramento (95817-1818)
P.O. Box 15830 (95852-0830)
PHONE..................916 732-5616
Frankie McDermott, *Manager*
EMP: 300
SALES (corp-wide): 1.5B **Privately Held**
SIC: **4911** ; generation, electric power
PA: Sacramento Municipal Utility District
6201 S St
Sacramento CA 95817
916 452-3211

(P-6106)
SCE EASTERN HYDRO DIVISION
4000 Bishop Creek Rd, Bishop
(93514-7026)
PHONE..................760 873-0767
John Bryson, *Principal*
Susie Davis, *Principal*
EMP: 99
SALES (est): 7.6MM **Privately Held**
SIC: **4911** Electric services

(P-6107)
SEMPRA ENERGY
9305 Lightwave Ave, San Diego
(92123-6463)
PHONE..................619 696-2000
Sean Luko, *Branch Mgr*
Marissa Colburn, *Manager*
EMP: 1000
SALES (corp-wide): 11.2B **Publicly Held**
SIC: **4911** 4923 Distribution, electric
power; gas transmission & distribution
PA: Sempra Energy
488 8th Ave
San Diego CA 92101
619 696-2000

(P-6108)
SEMPRA ENERGY INTERNATIONAL (HQ)
Also Called: Sempra Energy Utilities
101 Ash St, San Diego (92101-3017)
PHONE..................619 696-2000
Luis Eduardo Pawluszek, *CEO*
Randall Clark, *President*
Tania Ortiz, *President*
Mark A Snell, *President*
Donald E Felsinger, *Chairman*
EMP: 800
SALES (est): 421MM
SALES (corp-wide): 11.2B **Publicly Held**
SIC: **4911** Electric services
PA: Sempra Energy
488 8th Ave
San Diego CA 92101
619 696-2000

(P-6109)
SILVERADO ENERGY COMPANY
18101 Von Karman Ave, Irvine
(92612-1012)
PHONE..................949 752-5588
Thomas McDaniel, *Principal*
Alan Fohrer, *President*
EMP: 300
SALES (est): 59MM **Publicly Held**
SIC: **4911** Generation, electric power
HQ: Edison Mission Energy
2244 Walnut Grove Ave
Rosemead CA 91770
626 302-5778

(P-6110)
SLATE CREEK WIND PROJECT LLC
15445 Innovation Dr, San Diego
(92128-3432)
PHONE..................888 903-6926
Tristan Grimbert, *President*
Kara Vongphakdy, *Treasurer*
Ryan Pfaff, *Vice Pres*
Robert Miller, *Admin Sec*
EMP: 826 EST: 2013
SQ FT: 70,000
SALES (est): 339.3MM **Privately Held**
SIC: **4911** Generation, electric power

(P-6111)
SMART SYSTEMS TECHNOLOGIES (PA)
9 Goodyear, Irvine (92618-2001)
PHONE..................949 367-9375
Craig Steven Curran, *CEO*
Peter Scolara, *CFO*
Melissa Ramos, *Office Mgr*
Christina Hanna, *Admin Asst*
Gregory Valdovinos, *Controller*
EMP: 64
SQ FT: 7,000
SALES (est): 31MM **Privately Held**
WEB: www.smartsystemstechnologies.com
SIC: **4911** Electric services

(P-6112)
SOLARRESERVE INC
520 Broadway Fl 6, Santa Monica
(90401-2420)
PHONE..................310 315-2200
Kevin B Smith, *CEO*
Tim Connor, *President*
Stephen Mullennix, *CFO*
Sumeet Bidani, *Vice Pres*
Mary Grikas, *Vice Pres*
EMP: 99
SQ FT: 20,000
SALES: 18.1MM **Privately Held**
SIC: **4911** Distribution, electric power

(P-6113)
SOUTHERN CALIFORNIA EDISON CO (HQ)
Also Called: SCE
2244 Walnut Grove Ave, Rosemead
(91770-3714)
P.O. Box 976 (91770-0976)
PHONE..................626 302-1212
Kevin M Payne, *CEO*
Ronald O Nichols, *President*
William M Petmecky III, *CFO*
Caroline Choi, *Senior VP*
Janet T Clayton, *Senior VP*
EMP: 1200
SALES: 12.2B
SALES (corp-wide): 12.3B **Publicly Held**
WEB: www.sce.com
SIC: **4911** Generation, electric power;
transmission, electric power; distribution,
electric power
PA: Edison International
2244 Walnut Grove Ave
Rosemead CA 91770
626 302-2222

(P-6114)
SOUTHERN CALIFORNIA EDISON CO
4900 Rivergrade Rd 2b1, Irwindale
(91706-1401)
PHONE..................626 543-8081
Peter Quon, *Branch Mgr*
Elizabeth Wallenius, *Manager*
EMP: 155
SALES (corp-wide): 12.3B **Publicly Held**
SIC: **4911** Generation, electric power
HQ: Southern California Edison Company
2244 Walnut Grove Ave
Rosemead CA 91770
626 302-1212

(P-6115)
SOUTHERN CALIFORNIA EDISON CO
Also Called: Northern Hydro
54205 Mt Poplar Ave, Big Creek (93605)
PHONE..................559 893-3611
David Dormire, *Manager*
Bryan Troll, *Human Res Mgr*
EMP: 160
SALES (corp-wide): 12.3B **Publicly Held**
SIC: **4911** Electric services
HQ: Southern California Edison Company
2244 Walnut Grove Ave
Rosemead CA 91770
626 302-1212

(P-6116)
SOUTHERN CALIFORNIA EDISON CO
Also Called: Monrovia Service Center
1440 S California Ave, Monrovia
(91016-4211)
PHONE..................626 303-8480

Robert Robinson, *Principal*
EMP: 97
SQ FT: 31,603
SALES (corp-wide): 12.3B **Publicly Held**
WEB: www.sce.com
SIC: **4911** Electric services
HQ: Southern California Edison Company
2244 Walnut Grove Ave
Rosemead CA 91770
626 302-1212

(P-6117)
SOUTHERN CALIFORNIA EDISON CO
4000 Bishop Creek Rd, Bishop
(93514-7026)
PHONE..................760 873-0715
EMP: 155
SALES (corp-wide): 12.3B **Publicly Held**
SIC: **4911** Generation, electric power
HQ: Southern California Edison Company
2244 Walnut Grove Ave
Rosemead CA 91770
626 302-1212

(P-6118)
SOUTHERN CALIFORNIA EDISON CO
14799 Chestnut St, Westminster
(92683-5240)
PHONE..................714 934-0838
Frank Salomone, *CEO*
Maribel Gonzalez, *Admin Asst*
Josh Mauzey, *Planning*
Aaron Renfro, *Project Mgr*
My Hong, *Electrical Engi*
EMP: 176
SALES (corp-wide): 12.3B **Publicly Held**
SIC: **4911** Generation, electric power
HQ: Southern California Edison Company
2244 Walnut Grove Ave
Rosemead CA 91770
626 302-1212

(P-6119)
SOUTHERN CALIFORNIA EDISON CO
55481 Mt Poplar, Big Creek (93605)
P.O. Box 130 (93605-0130)
PHONE..................559 893-2037
Southern Edison, *Branch Mgr*
EMP: 155
SALES (corp-wide): 12.3B **Publicly Held**
SIC: **4911** Distribution, electric power;
transmission, electric power
HQ: Southern California Edison Company
2244 Walnut Grove Ave
Rosemead CA 91770
626 302-1212

(P-6120)
SOUTHERN CALIFORNIA EDISON CO
8380 Klingerman St, Rosemead (91770)
PHONE..................626 302-5101
Arthur Guerra, *Principal*
EMP: 176
SALES (corp-wide): 12.3B **Publicly Held**
SIC: **4911** Generation, electric power
HQ: Southern California Edison Company
2244 Walnut Grove Ave
Rosemead CA 91770
626 302-1212

(P-6121)
SOUTHERN CALIFORNIA EDISON CO
4900 Rivergrade Rd, Baldwin Park
(91706-1401)
PHONE..................626 543-6093
Linda Gilleland, *Principal*
Paul Caldarone, *Manager*
EMP: 149
SALES (corp-wide): 12.3B **Publicly Held**
SIC: **4911** Generation, electric power
HQ: Southern California Edison Company
2244 Walnut Grove Ave
Rosemead CA 91770
626 302-1212

(P-6122)
SOUTHERN CALIFORNIA EDISON CO
Also Called: North Orange County Svc Ctr
1851 W Valencia Dr, Fullerton
(92833-3215)
PHONE..................714 870-3225
David Kama, *District Mgr*
James Thaxter, *Clerk*
EMP: 70
SALES (corp-wide): 12.3B **Publicly Held**
WEB: www.sce.com
SIC: **4911** Distribution, electric power
HQ: Southern California Edison Company
2244 Walnut Grove Ave
Rosemead CA 91770
626 302-1212

(P-6123)
SOUTHERN CALIFORNIA EDISON CO
Also Called: San Onfre Nclear Gnerating Stn
14300 Mesa Rd, San Clemente (92672)
PHONE..................949 368-2881
R W Kreiger, *Vice Pres*
Kelli Gallion, *Manager*
EMP: 1998
SALES (corp-wide): 12.3B **Publicly Held**
SIC: **4911** Generation, electric power
HQ: Southern California Edison Company
2244 Walnut Grove Ave
Rosemead CA 91770
626 302-1212

(P-6124)
SOUTHERN CALIFORNIA EDISON CO
Also Called: Southern Clfrn Edsn - Prvt CHR
2131 Walnut Grove Ave, Rosemead
(91770-3769)
PHONE..................626 302-1212
Grant Thomas, *Branch Mgr*
Chris Pahl, *Program Mgr*
Doreen Mendoza, *Executive Asst*
Richard Fujikawa, *Business Analyst*
Albert Melikian, *Design Engr*
EMP: 155
SALES (corp-wide): 12.3B **Publicly Held**
SIC: **4911** Distribution, electric power; gen-
eration, electric power; transmission,
electric power
HQ: Southern California Edison Company
2244 Walnut Grove Ave
Rosemead CA 91770
626 302-1212

(P-6125)
SOUTHERN CALIFORNIA EDISON CO
Also Called: Central Orange County Svc Ctr
1241 S Grand Ave, Santa Ana
(92705-4404)
PHONE..................714 973-5481
Percy Haralson, *Principal*
Cindy Leejulien, *Engineer*
Mike Lantz, *Supervisor*
EMP: 216
SALES (corp-wide): 12.3B **Publicly Held**
WEB: www.sce.com
SIC: **4911** Electric services
HQ: Southern California Edison Company
2244 Walnut Grove Ave
Rosemead CA 91770
626 302-1212

(P-6126)
SOUTHERN CALIFORNIA EDISON CO
Also Called: Thousand Oaks Service Center
3589 Foothill Dr, Thousand Oaks
(91361-2475)
PHONE..................818 999-1880
Jerry Willaferd, *Branch Mgr*
EMP: 122
SALES (corp-wide): 12.3B **Publicly Held**
WEB: www.sce.com
SIC: **4911** 8741 Electric services; busi-
ness management
HQ: Southern California Edison Company
2244 Walnut Grove Ave
Rosemead CA 91770
626 302-1212

PRODUCTS & SVCS

(P-6127)
**SOUTHERN CALIFORNIA
EDISON CO**
Also Called: Irwindale 6000
6000 N Irwindale Ave A, Irwindale
(91702-3200)
PHONE..............................626 815-7296
Ray Maese, *Branch Mgr*
Ken Reichley, *Manager*
EMP: 50
SALES (corp-wide): 12.3B **Publicly Held**
WEB: www.sce.com
SIC: 4911 Electric services
HQ: Southern California Edison Company
2244 Walnut Grove Ave
Rosemead CA 91770
626 302-1212

(P-6128)
**SOUTHERN CALIFORNIA
EDISON CO**
265 N East End Ave, Pomona
(91767-5803)
PHONE..............................909 469-0251
John Risen, *Branch Mgr*
Javier Garcia, *Technical Staff*
Diego Hinojosa, *Engineer*
Robert Werth, *Engineer*
Ben Badal, *Purchasing*
EMP: 65
SALES (corp-wide): 12.3B **Publicly Held**
WEB: www.sce.com
SIC: 4911 Electric services
HQ: Southern California Edison Company
2244 Walnut Grove Ave
Rosemead CA 91770
626 302-1212

(P-6129)
**SOUTHERN CALIFORNIA
EDISON CO**
Also Called: San Dimas Bushnell Building
1515 Walnut Grove Ave, Rosemead
(91770-3710)
PHONE..............................714 895-0488
Helen Ronando, *Manager*
Maricela Carlos, *Program Mgr*
Greg Buchler, *Project Mgr*
Venus Jenkins, *Project Mgr*
Louise Tang, *Project Mgr*
EMP: 67
SALES (corp-wide): 12.3B **Publicly Held**
WEB: www.sce.com
SIC: 4911 Electric services
HQ: Southern California Edison Company
2244 Walnut Grove Ave
Rosemead CA 91770
626 302-1212

(P-6130)
**SOUTHERN CALIFORNIA
EDISON CO**
Also Called: Compton Service Center
1924 E Cashdan St, Compton
(90220-6403)
PHONE..............................310 608-5029
Floyd Rich, *Branch Mgr*
Nelson Herrera, *Engineer*
Henry Darnell, *Finance Mgr*
Richard Richard Clarke, *Manager*
Susan Musick, *Manager*
EMP: 180
SALES (corp-wide): 12.3B **Publicly Held**
WEB: www.sce.com
SIC: 4911 Electric services
HQ: Southern California Edison Company
2244 Walnut Grove Ave
Rosemead CA 91770
626 302-1212

(P-6131)
**SOUTHERN CALIFORNIA
EDISON CO**
Also Called: Santa Barbara Service Center
103 Love Pl, Goleta (93117-3200)
PHONE..............................805 683-5291
Brian Adair, *Manager*
Randy Yanez, *Manager*
EMP: 60
SALES (corp-wide): 12.3B **Publicly Held**
WEB: www.sce.com
SIC: 4911 Generation, electric power

HQ: Southern California Edison Company
2244 Walnut Grove Ave
Rosemead CA 91770
626 302-1212

(P-6132)
**SOUTHERN CALIFORNIA
EDISON CO**
Also Called: Southeastern Westminster
7300 Fenwick Ln, Westminster
(92683-5238)
PHONE..............................714 895-0420
Dee Pak Nanda, *Vice Pres*
Catherine Melton, *Program Mgr*
Lauren Simpson, *Business Anlyst*
Charles Rihbany, *Technology*
Lamar Cunningham, *Technical Staff*
EMP: 320
SALES (corp-wide): 12.3B **Publicly Held**
WEB: www.sce.com
SIC: 4911 Electric services
HQ: Southern California Edison Company
2244 Walnut Grove Ave
Rosemead CA 91770
626 302-1212

(P-6133)
**SOUTHERN CALIFORNIA
EDISON CO**
Also Called: Saddleback Valley Service Ctr
14155 Bake Pkwy, Irvine (92618-1818)
PHONE..............................949 587-5416
Robert Torres, *Manager*
Edgardo Cruz, *Supervisor*
EMP: 143
SALES (corp-wide): 12.3B **Publicly Held**
WEB: www.sce.com
SIC: 4911 Electric services
HQ: Southern California Edison Company
2244 Walnut Grove Ave
Rosemead CA 91770
626 302-1212

(P-6134)
**SOUTHERN CALIFORNIA
EDISON CO**
6042a N Irwindale Ave, Irwindale
(91702-3207)
PHONE..............................626 633-3070
Jami McDonald, *Branch Mgr*
Teren Abear, *Project Mgr*
Yun Han, *Project Mgr*
Genevieve Feng, *Technology*
Martell Washington, *Engineer*
EMP: 147
SALES (corp-wide): 12.3B **Publicly Held**
WEB: www.sce.com
SIC: 4911 Generation, electric power
HQ: Southern California Edison Company
2244 Walnut Grove Ave
Rosemead CA 91770
626 302-1212

(P-6135)
**SOUTHERN CALIFORNIA
EDISON CO**
Also Called: Orange Coast Service Center
7333 Bolsa Ave, Westminster
(92683-5210)
PHONE..............................714 895-0163
Jeff Lebow, *Branch Mgr*
EMP: 133
SALES (corp-wide): 12.3B **Publicly Held**
WEB: www.sce.com
SIC: 4911 Electric services
HQ: Southern California Edison Company
2244 Walnut Grove Ave
Rosemead CA 91770
626 302-1212

(P-6136)
**SOUTHERN CALIFORNIA
EDISON CO**
13025 Los Angeles St, Irwindale
(91706-2241)
PHONE..............................626 814-4212
Ed Entillon, *Branch Mgr*
EMP: 53
SQ FT: 21,000
SALES (corp-wide): 12.3B **Publicly Held**
WEB: www.sce.com
SIC: 4911 Electric services

HQ: Southern California Edison Company
2244 Walnut Grove Ave
Rosemead CA 91770
626 302-1212

(P-6137)
**SOUTHERN CALIFORNIA
EDISON CO**
Also Called: Covina Service Center
800 W Cienega Ave, San Dimas
(91773-2490)
PHONE..............................909 592-3757
Gary Martinez, *Branch Mgr*
James Creason, *Supervisor*
EMP: 210
SALES (corp-wide): 12.3B **Publicly Held**
WEB: www.sce.com
SIC: 4911 Electric services
HQ: Southern California Edison Company
2244 Walnut Grove Ave
Rosemead CA 91770
626 302-1212

(P-6138)
**SOUTHERN CALIFORNIA
EDISON CO**
Also Called: Whittier Service Center
9901 Geary Ave, Santa Fe Springs
(90670-3251)
PHONE..............................562 903-3191
Fred Swearingen, *Principal*
Inkyoo Chang, *Supervisor*
EMP: 60
SALES (corp-wide): 12.3B **Publicly Held**
WEB: www.sce.com
SIC: 4911 Electric services
HQ: Southern California Edison Company
2244 Walnut Grove Ave
Rosemead CA 91770
626 302-1212

(P-6139)
**SOUTHERN CALIFORNIA
EDISON CO**
Also Called: Western Division Regional Off
125 Elm Ave, Long Beach (90802-4918)
PHONE..............................562 491-3803
Lorene Miller, *Manager*
EMP: 310
SALES (corp-wide): 12.3B **Publicly Held**
WEB: www.sce.com
SIC: 4911 Electric services
HQ: Southern California Edison Company
2244 Walnut Grove Ave
Rosemead CA 91770
626 302-1212

(P-6140)
**SOUTHERN CALIFORNIA
EDISON CO**
Also Called: High Desert
12353 Hesperia Rd, Victorville
(92395-4797)
PHONE..............................760 951-3242
EMP: 200
SALES (corp-wide): 12.3B **Publicly Held**
SIC: 4911
HQ: Southern California Edison Company
2244 Walnut Grove Ave
Rosemead CA 91770
626 302-1212

(P-6141)
**SOUTHERN CALIFORNIA
EDISON CO**
Also Called: So CA Edison
1515 Walnut Grove Ave, Rosemead
(91770-3710)
PHONE..............................626 302-0530
Helen Ronando, *Manager*
Ronnie Fierro, *Officer*
Robert Palutzke, *Project Mgr*
Lois Pitterbruce, *Manager*
EMP: 149
SALES (corp-wide): 12.3B **Publicly Held**
SIC: 4911 Electric services
HQ: Southern California Edison Company
2244 Walnut Grove Ave
Rosemead CA 91770
626 302-1212

(P-6142)
**SPINNING SPUR WIND THREE
LLC**
15445 Innovation Dr, San Diego
(92128-3432)
PHONE..............................858 521-3319
Tristan Grimbert, *President*
Kara Vongphakdy, *Treasurer*
Larry Barr, *Exec VP*
Robert Miller, *Exec VP*
Ryan Pfaff, *Exec VP*
EMP: 827 EST: 2014
SQ FT: 70,000
SALES (est): 1.5MM
SALES (corp-wide): 569.6MM **Privately
Held**
SIC: 4911 Electric services
PA: Edf Renewables, Inc.
15445 Innovation Dr
San Diego CA 92128
858 521-3300

(P-6143)
**SYCAMORE COGENERATION
CO (PA)**
1546 China Grade Loop, Bakersfield
(93308-9700)
P.O. Box 81438 (93380-1438)
PHONE..............................661 615-4630
Neal Burgess, *Exec Dir*
▲ EMP: 57
SQ FT: 10,000
SALES (est): 41.9MM **Privately Held**
SIC: 4911 4961 Distribution, electric
power; steam supply systems, including
geothermal

(P-6144)
**TRUCKEE DONNER PUB UTLY
DIST F**
Also Called: TRUCKEE DONNER PUD
11570 Donner Pass Rd, Truckee
(96161-4947)
PHONE..............................530 587-3896
Michael D Holley, *General Mgr*
EMP: 68
SQ FT: 48,000
SALES: 38.3MM **Privately Held**
WEB: www.tdpud.org
SIC: 4911 4941 Distribution, electric
power; water supply

(P-6145)
TWIN OAKS POWER LP (HQ)
101 Ash St Hq10b, San Diego
(92101-3017)
PHONE..............................619 696-2034
Mike Niggli, *Managing Dir*
Regina Grimes, *Manager*
EMP: 100
SALES (est): 54.3MM
SALES (corp-wide): 11.2B **Publicly Held**
SIC: 4911 4924 Generation, electric
power; transmission, electric power; distri-
bution, electric power; natural gas distri-
bution
PA: Sempra Energy
488 8th Ave
San Diego CA 92101
619 696-2000

(P-6146)
**TYLER BLUFF WIND PROJECT
LLC**
15445 Innovation Dr, San Diego
(92128-3432)
PHONE..............................888 903-6926
Tristan Grimbert, *President*
Kara Vongphakdy, *Treasurer*
Larry Barr, *Exec VP*
Robert Miller, *Exec VP*
Ryan Pfaff, *Exec VP*
EMP: 827
SQ FT: 70,000
SALES (est): 103.4MM
SALES (corp-wide): 569.6MM **Privately
Held**
SIC: 4911 Electric services
PA: Edf Renewables, Inc.
15445 Innovation Dr
San Diego CA 92128
858 521-3300

(P-6147)
VEXILLUM INC
Also Called: EZ Electric
10636 Industrial Ave, Roseville
(95678-5902)
PHONE..................916 218-3815
Scott Zachman, *President*
EMP: 175
SALES (corp-wide): 20.5MM **Privately Held**
WEB: www.ez-electric.com
SIC: 4911 Electric services
PA: Vexillum, Inc.
1250 Birchwood Dr
Sunnyvale CA 94089
408 541-4245

(P-6148)
WATSON COGENERATION CO INC
22850 Wilmington Ave, Carson
(90745-5021)
P.O. Box 6203 (90749-6203)
PHONE..................310 816-8100
Paul L Foster, *Ch of Bd*
Joshua Valdez, *Exec Dir*
EMP: 63
SQ FT: 1,000
SALES (est): 40MM **Publicly Held**
SIC: 4911 Generation, electric power
HQ: Western Refining, Inc.
212 N Clark Dr
El Paso TX 79905
915 775-3300

(P-6149)
WELLHEAD ELECTRIC COMPANY INC
650 Bercut Dr Ste C, Sacramento
(95811-0100)
PHONE..................916 447-5171
Harold Dittner, *President*
Paul Cummins, *Vice Pres*
EMP: 50
SALES (est): 30.7MM **Privately Held**
SIC: 4911 Generation, electric power

(P-6150)
WHEATLAND WIND PROJECT LLC
15445 Innovation Dr, San Diego
(92128-3432)
PHONE..................888 903-6926
Tristan Grimbert, *President*
Ryan Pfaff, *Vice Pres*
Robert Miller, *Admin Sec*
EMP: 826 EST: 2013
SQ FT: 70,000
SALES (est): 206.6MM **Privately Held**
SIC: 4911 Generation, electric power

4922 Natural Gas Transmission

(P-6151)
KINDER MRGAN LQDS TRMINALS LLC
9950 San Diego Mission Rd, San Diego
(92108-1705)
PHONE..................619 283-6511
Craig Bishop, *Branch Mgr*
EMP: 62 **Publicly Held**
SIC: 4922 Natural gas transmission
HQ: Kinder Morgan Liquids Terminals Llc
1001 La St Ste 1000
Houston TX 77002
713 369-9000

(P-6152)
SAN DIEGO GAS & ELECTRIC CO
Also Called: South Bay Power Plant
990 Bay Blvd, Chula Vista (91911-1651)
PHONE..................800 411-7343
Carl Creelman, *Branch Mgr*
EMP: 120
SALES (corp-wide): 11.2B **Publicly Held**
SIC: 4922 4911 Natural gas transmission; generation, electric power
HQ: San Diego Gas & Electric Company
8326 Century Park Ct
San Diego CA 92123
619 696-2000

(P-6153)
SOUTHERN CALIFORNIA GAS CO
9400 Oakdale Ave, Chatsworth
(91311-6511)
P.O. Box 2300 (91313-2300)
PHONE..................818 701-2592
Cathy Maguire, *Branch Mgr*
EMP: 300
SALES (corp-wide): 11.2B **Publicly Held**
WEB: www.gasselect.com
SIC: 4922 4923 Pipelines, natural gas; gas transmission & distribution
HQ: Southern California Gas Company
555 W 5th St
Los Angeles CA 90013
213 244-1200

(P-6154)
WILD GOOSE STORAGE INC
2780 W Liberty Rd, Gridley (95948-9335)
P.O. Box 8 (95948-0008)
PHONE..................530 846-7350
David Pope, *President*
EMP: 70
SALES (est): 9.3MM **Privately Held**
SIC: 4922 Storage, natural gas

4923 Natural Gas Transmission & Distribution

(P-6155)
PACIFIC TANK LINES INC
5230 Wilson St Ste A, Riverside
(92509-2435)
PHONE..................951 680-1900
Ted Honcharik, *CEO*
Gregory Batten, *President*
▲ EMP: 68
SALES (est): 19.5MM **Privately Held**
WEB: www.pacifictanklines.com
SIC: 4923 Gas transmission & distribution

(P-6156)
SOUTHERN CALIFORNIA GAS CO
1050 Overland Ct, San Dimas
(91773-1704)
PHONE..................909 305-8297
Janet Yee, *Manager*
EMP: 600
SQ FT: 39,344
SALES (corp-wide): 11.2B **Publicly Held**
WEB: www.gasselect.com
SIC: 4923 Gas transmission & distribution
HQ: Southern California Gas Company
555 W 5th St
Los Angeles CA 90013
213 244-1200

4924 Natural Gas Distribution

(P-6157)
CLEAN ENERGY
4675 Macarthur Ct Ste 800, Newport Beach
(92660-1895)
PHONE..................949 437-1000
Andrew Littlefair, *President*
Marty Swartz, *President*
Mitchell Pratt, *COO*
Robert Vreeland, *CFO*
Kenneth M Socha, *Bd of Directors*
EMP: 832
SALES (est): 341.6MM **Publicly Held**
SIC: 4924 Natural gas distribution
PA: Clean Energy Fuels Corp.
4675 Macarthur Ct Ste 800
Newport Beach CA 92660
949 437-1000

(P-6158)
PACIFIC ENERGY FUELS COMPANY
Also Called: PG&e
77 Beale St Ste 100, San Francisco
(94105-1814)
PHONE..................415 973-8200
Gordon R Smith, *President*
Bob Buhrer, *Technology*
EMP: 999

SALES (est): 30.4MM **Publicly Held**
WEB: www.pge.com
SIC: 4924 Natural gas distribution
HQ: Pacific Gas And Electric Company
77 Beale St
San Francisco CA 94105
415 973-7000

(P-6159)
PACIFIC GAS AND ELECTRIC CO
Also Called: PG&e
24300 Clawiter Rd, Hayward (94545-2218)
PHONE..................510 784-3253
Tom Webb, *Branch Mgr*
EMP: 409 **Publicly Held**
WEB: www.pge.com
SIC: 4924 4911 Natural gas distribution; distribution, electric power
HQ: Pacific Gas And Electric Company
77 Beale St
San Francisco CA 94105
415 973-7000

(P-6160)
PACIFIC GAS AND ELECTRIC CO
Also Called: PG&e
460 Rio Lindo Ave, Chico (95926-1815)
PHONE..................530 894-4739
Todd Stewart, *Manager*
EMP: 110 **Publicly Held**
WEB: www.pge.com
SIC: 4924 4911 4923 Natural gas distribution; electric services; gas transmission & distribution
HQ: Pacific Gas And Electric Company
77 Beale St
San Francisco CA 94105
415 973-7000

(P-6161)
PACIFIC GAS AND ELECTRIC CO
Also Called: PG&e
245 Market St Ste 104, San Francisco
(94105-1708)
PHONE..................415 973-8089
EMP: 65 **Publicly Held**
SIC: 4924 4911 Natural gas distribution; generation, electric power
HQ: Pacific Gas And Electric Company
77 Beale St
San Francisco CA 94105
415 973-7000

(P-6162)
SEMPRA ENERGY GLOBAL ENTPS
101 Ash St, San Diego (92101-3017)
PHONE..................619 696-2000
Mark Snell, *President*
Michael Allman, *CFO*
Mark Fisher, *Vice Pres*
EMP: 1000
SQ FT: 10,000
SALES (est): 362.4MM
SALES (corp-wide): 11.2B **Publicly Held**
SIC: 4924 4911 Natural gas distribution; generation, electric power
PA: Sempra Energy
488 8th Ave
San Diego CA 92101
619 696-2000

(P-6163)
SOUTHERN CALIFORNIA GAS CO (DH)
Also Called: GAS COMPANY, THE
555 W 5th St, Los Angeles (90013-1010)
PHONE..................213 244-1200
Debra L Reed, *CEO*
Mark A Snell, *President*
Steven D Davis, *Exec VP*
Joseph A Householder, *Exec VP*
Justin C Bird, *Vice Pres*
EMP: 170
SALES: 3.7B
SALES (corp-wide): 11.2B **Publicly Held**
WEB: www.gasselect.com
SIC: 4924 4922 4932 Natural gas distribution; natural gas transmission; gas & other services combined
HQ: Pacific Enterprises
101 Ash St
San Diego CA 92101
619 696-2020

(P-6164)
SOUTHERN CALIFORNIA GAS CO
1 Liberty, Aliso Viejo (92656-3830)
PHONE..................714 634-7221
Bill Jameson, *Branch Mgr*
EMP: 54
SALES (corp-wide): 11.2B **Publicly Held**
SIC: 4924 Natural gas distribution
HQ: Southern California Gas Company
555 W 5th St
Los Angeles CA 90013
213 244-1200

(P-6165)
SOUTHERN CALIFORNIA GAS CO
Also Called: Northern Reg. Sub Base
1510 N Chester Ave, Bakersfield
(93308-2559)
PHONE..................661 399-4431
James Pina, *Manager*
EMP: 50
SALES (corp-wide): 11.2B **Publicly Held**
WEB: www.gasselect.com
SIC: 4924 Natural gas distribution
HQ: Southern California Gas Company
555 W 5th St
Los Angeles CA 90013
213 244-1200

(P-6166)
SOUTHERN CALIFORNIA GAS CO
1801 S Atlantic Blvd, Monterey Park
(91754-5207)
PHONE..................213 244-1200
W J Torres, *Branch Mgr*
Warren Mitchell, *President*
Jim Nguyen, *Info Tech Dir*
Anthony Orta, *Manager*
EMP: 293
SALES (corp-wide): 11.2B **Publicly Held**
WEB: www.gasselect.com
SIC: 4924 Natural gas distribution
HQ: Southern California Gas Company
555 W 5th St
Los Angeles CA 90013
213 244-1200

(P-6167)
SOUTHERN CALIFORNIA GAS CO
Also Called: Regional Office
1981 W Lugonia Ave, Redlands
(92374-9796)
P.O. Box 3003 (92373-0306)
PHONE..................909 335-7802
James Boland, *Manager*
Robert E Quiroz, *Supervisor*
EMP: 383
SALES (corp-wide): 11.2B **Publicly Held**
WEB: www.gasselect.com
SIC: 4924 Natural gas distribution
HQ: Southern California Gas Company
555 W 5th St
Los Angeles CA 90013
213 244-1200

(P-6168)
SOUTHERN CALIFORNIA GAS CO
Also Called: Industry Station
920 S Stimson Ave, City of Industry
(91745-1640)
PHONE..................213 244-1200
EMP: 69
SALES (corp-wide): 11.2B **Publicly Held**
SIC: 4924 Natural gas distribution
HQ: Southern California Gas Company
555 W 5th St
Los Angeles CA 90013
213 244-1200

(P-6169)
SOUTHERN CALIFORNIA GAS CO
25200 Trumble Rd, Romoland
(92585-9664)
PHONE..................213 244-1200
EMP: 69
SALES (corp-wide): 11.2B **Publicly Held**
SIC: 4924 Natural gas distribution

HQ: Southern California Gas Company
555 W 5th St
Los Angeles CA 90013
213 244-1200

(P-6170)
SOUTHERN CALIFORNIA GAS CO
333 E Main St Ste J, Alhambra
(91801-3914)
PHONE................323 881-3587
G H Chavez, *Branch Mgr*
EMP: 72
SALES (corp-wide): 11.2B **Publicly Held**
WEB: www.gasselect.com
SIC: 4924 Natural gas distribution
HQ: Southern California Gas Company
555 W 5th St
Los Angeles CA 90013
213 244-1200

(P-6171)
SOUTHERN CALIFORNIA GAS CO
6738 Bright Ave, Whittier (90601-4306)
PHONE................562 803-3341
Richard Duran, *Branch Mgr*
EMP: 69
SALES (corp-wide): 11.2B **Publicly Held**
WEB: www.gasselect.com
SIC: 4924 Natural gas distribution
HQ: Southern California Gas Company
555 W 5th St
Los Angeles CA 90013
213 244-1200

(P-6172)
SOUTHERN CALIFORNIA GAS CO
8141 Gulana Ave, Venice (90293-7930)
PHONE................310 823-7945
James Wine, *Manager*
EMP: 67
SALES (corp-wide): 11.2B **Publicly Held**
WEB: www.gasselect.com
SIC: 4924 Natural gas distribution
HQ: Southern California Gas Company
555 W 5th St
Los Angeles CA 90013
213 244-1200

(P-6173)
SOUTHERN CALIFORNIA GAS CO
155 S G St, San Bernardino (92410-3317)
PHONE................909 335-7941
Al Garcia, *Branch Mgr*
EMP: 117
SALES (corp-wide): 11.2B **Publicly Held**
WEB: www.gasselect.com
SIC: 4924 Natural gas distribution
HQ: Southern California Gas Company
555 W 5th St
Los Angeles CA 90013
213 244-1200

(P-6174)
SOUTHERN CALIFORNIA GAS CO
1600 Corporate Center Dr, Monterey Park
(91754-7626)
P.O. Box C (91756-0001)
PHONE................213 244-1200
Joe M Rivera, *Regional Mgr*
EMP: 223
SALES (corp-wide): 11.2B **Publicly Held**
WEB: www.gasselect.com
SIC: 4924 Natural gas distribution
HQ: Southern California Gas Company
555 W 5th St
Los Angeles CA 90013
213 244-1200

(P-6175)
SOUTHERN CALIFORNIA GAS CO
Also Called: Energy Resource Center
9240 Firestone Blvd, Downey
(90241-5388)
PHONE................562 803-7453
Carlos Ruiz, *Manager*
EMP: 50
SALES (corp-wide): 11.2B **Publicly Held**
WEB: www.gasselect.com
SIC: 4924 Natural gas distribution

HQ: Southern California Gas Company
555 W 5th St
Los Angeles CA 90013
213 244-1200

(P-6176)
SOUTHERN CALIFORNIA GAS CO
Also Called: Honor Rancho Station
23130 Valencia Blvd, Valencia
(91355-1716)
PHONE................800 427-2200
Dan Skope, *Vice Pres*
EMP: 64
SALES (corp-wide): 11.2B **Publicly Held**
WEB: www.gasselect.com
SIC: 4924 Natural gas distribution
HQ: Southern California Gas Company
555 W 5th St
Los Angeles CA 90013
213 244-1200

(P-6177)
SOUTHERN CALIFORNIA GAS TOWER
555 W 5th St, Los Angeles (90013-1010)
PHONE................213 244-1200
Ed Guiles, *President*
EMP: 400
SALES (est): 133.1MM
SALES (corp-wide): 11.2B **Publicly Held**
SIC: 4924 Natural gas distribution
HQ: Southern California Gas Company
555 W 5th St
Los Angeles CA 90013
213 244-1200

(P-6178)
SOUTHWEST GAS CORPORATION
S W Gas Southern California
13471 Mariposa Rd, Victorville
(92395-5396)
P.O. Box 1498 (92393-1498)
PHONE................760 951-4000
Joan Rowell, *Manager*
Michael Clausell, *Engineer*
Phillis Neumayer, *Human Resources*
Jason Hall, *Supervisor*
EMP: 100
SALES (corp-wide): 2.5B **Publicly Held**
SIC: 4924 4923 Natural gas distribution;
gas transmission & distribution
HQ: Southwest Gas Corporation
5241 Spring Mountain Rd
Las Vegas NV 89150
702 876-7237

(P-6179)
STEELRIVER INFRASTRUCTURE FUND (HQ)
1 Letterman Dr Bldg C, San Francisco
(94129-2402)
PHONE................415 291-2200
Chris Kinney, *Partner*
John Anderson, *Partner*
Dennis Mahoney, *Partner*
EMP: 200
SALES (est): 208.3MM **Privately Held**
SIC: 4924 Natural gas distribution

4931 Electric & Other Svcs Combined

(P-6180)
CALPINE ENERGY SOLUTIONS LLC (DH)
Also Called: Noble Americas Enrgy Solutions
401 W A St Ste 500, San Diego
(92101-7991)
PHONE................877 273-6772
Jim Wood, *President*
Kirsten Alvarez, *Sales Dir*
EMP: 98
SALES (est): 393.4MM
SALES (corp-wide): 8.7B **Privately Held**
WEB: www.noblesolutions.com
SIC: 4931 4932 Electric & other services
combined; gas & other services combined
HQ: Calpine Corporation
717 Texas St Ste 1000
Houston TX 77002
713 830-2000

(P-6181)
CITY OF BURBANK
Also Called: Burbank Water & Power
164 W Magnolia Blvd, Burbank
(91502-1772)
PHONE................818 238-3550
Ronald E Davis, *Branch Mgr*
EMP: 315 **Privately Held**
SIC: 4931 4941 4911 7389 Electric &
other services combined; water supply;
electric services; interior design services
PA: City Of Burbank
275 E Olive Ave
Burbank CA 91502
818 238-5800

(P-6182)
CITY OF CORONADO
Also Called: Public Services
101 B Ave, Coronado (92118-1510)
PHONE................619 522-7380
Scott Huth, *Director*
EMP: 55 **Privately Held**
WEB: www.coronadoplayhouse.com
SIC: 4931 9111 Electric & other services
combined; mayors' offices
PA: City Of Coronado
1825 Strand Way
Coronado CA 92118
619 522-7300

(P-6183)
IMPERIAL IRRIGATION DISTRICT
2151 W Adams Ave, El Centro
(92243-9457)
P.O. Box 937, Imperial (92251-0937)
PHONE................760 339-9800
Frank Montoya, *Branch Mgr*
Brian Brady, *General Mgr*
EMP: 75
SALES (corp-wide): 634.6MM **Privately Held**
WEB: www.iidwater.com
SIC: 4931 Electric & other services combined
PA: Imperial Irrigation District
333 E Barioni Blvd
Imperial CA 92251
800 303-7756

(P-6184)
MEKWUS SOLAR ENERGY
20283 Santa Maria Ave # 2103, Castro Valley (94546-5005)
PHONE................510 731-4134
De Anna Mekwunye, *Partner*
Elijah Mekwunye, *Partner*
EMP: 99
SQ FT: 1,200
SALES (est): 1.2MM **Privately Held**
SIC: 4931

(P-6185)
PG&E CORPORATION (PA)
77 Beale St, San Francisco (94105-1814)
P.O. Box 770000 (94177-0001)
PHONE................415 973-1000
Anthony F Earley Jr, *Ch of Bd*
Nickolas Stavropoulos, *President*
Geisha J Williams, *President*
Jason P Wells, *CFO*
Eric Mullins, *Bd of Directors*
▲ EMP: 166
SQ FT: 42,000
SALES: 17.1B **Publicly Held**
WEB: www.pgecorp.com
SIC: 4931 4923 Electric & other services
combined; gas transmission & distribution

(P-6186)
SAN DIEGO GAS & ELECTRIC CO (DH)
Also Called: SDG&E
8326 Century Park Ct, San Diego
(92123-1530)
PHONE................619 696-2000
J Walker Martin, *CEO*
Jessie J Knight Jr, *Ch of Bd*
Steven D Davis, *President*
Scott D Drury, *President*
Robert M Schlax, *CFO*
◆ EMP: 170

SALES: 4.4B
SALES (corp-wide): 11.2B **Publicly Held**
SIC: 4931 4911 4924 Electric & other
services combined; generation, electric
power; transmission, electric power; distribution, electric power; natural gas distribution

(P-6187)
SAN DIEGO GAS & ELECTRIC CO
Also Called: Orange County Service Center
662 Camino De Los Mares, San Clemente
(92673-2827)
PHONE................949 361-8090
James Valentine, *Branch Mgr*
EMP: 50
SALES (corp-wide): 11.2B **Publicly Held**
SIC: 4931 4911 Electric & other services
combined; electric services
HQ: San Diego Gas & Electric Company
8326 Century Park Ct
San Diego CA 92123
619 696-2000

(P-6188)
UNDERGROUND CNSTR CO INC
5145 Industrial Way, Benicia (94510-1042)
PHONE................707 746-8800
Christopher Ronco, *President*
Jeff Tinsley, *CFO*
George R Bradshaw, *Exec VP*
Loren Hudson, *Vice Pres*
Giff Ludwigsen, *Vice Pres*
EMP: 250 EST: 1936
SQ FT: 32,946
SALES (est): 95.6MM
SALES (corp-wide): 9.4B **Publicly Held**
WEB: www.undergmd.com
SIC: 4931 5172 4923 Electric & other
services combined; aircraft fueling serv-
ices; gas transmission & distribution
PA: Quanta Services, Inc.
2800 Post Oak Blvd # 2600
Houston TX 77056
713 629-7600

4932 Gas & Other Svcs Combined

(P-6189)
CITY OF LONG BEACH
City of Long Beach Gas & Oil
2400 E Spring St, Long Beach
(90806-2203)
PHONE................562 570-2000
Christopher J Garner, *Manager*
EMP: 204 **Privately Held**
WEB: www.polb.com
SIC: 4932 9111 4924 Gas & other serv-
ices combined; mayors' offices; natural
gas distribution
PA: City Of Long Beach
333 W Ocean Blvd Fl 10
Long Beach CA 90802
562 570-6450

(P-6190)
CLEAN ENERGY FUELS CORP (PA)
4675 Macarthur Ct Ste 800, Newport Beach
(92660-1895)
PHONE................949 437-1000
Warren I Mitchell, *Ch of Bd*
Stephen A Scully, *Ch of Bd*
Andrew J Littlefair, *President*
Mitchell W Pratt, *COO*
Robert M Vreeland, *CFO*
▲ EMP: 148
SQ FT: 48,000
SALES: 341.6MM **Publicly Held**
SIC: 4932 4924 4922 Gas & other serv-
ices combined; natural gas distribution;
natural gas transmission

(P-6191)
FIELDSERVER TECHNOLOGIES
1991 Tarob Ct, Milpitas (95035-6825)
PHONE................408 262-2299
Loree Calderon, *President*
EMP: 50

SALES (est): 2.8MM
SALES (corp-wide): 19.7MM **Publicly
Held**
WEB: www.fieldserver.com
SIC: 4932 Gas & other services combined
PA: Sierra Monitor Corporation
1991 Tarob Ct
Milpitas CA 95035
408 262-6611

(P-6192)
MAXGEN ENERGY SERVICES CORP
1690 Scenic Ave, Costa Mesa
(92626-1410)
PHONE..................................714 908-5266
Mark McLanahan, *CEO*
Ilan Tordjaman, *CFO*
Michael Eyman, *VP Bus Dvlpt*
James Tillman, *Business Dir*
Thomas Mak, *Info Tech Mgr*
EMP: 376
SALES (est): 63.2MM **Publicly Held**
SIC: 4932 Gas & other services combined
HQ: Oaktree Capital Management, L.P.
333 S Grand Ave Ste 2800
Los Angeles CA 90071

(P-6193)
SEMPRA ENERGY (PA)
488 8th Ave, San Diego (92101-7123)
PHONE..................................619 696-2000
Jeffrey W Martin, *CEO*
Frank Urtasun, *Partner*
Debra L Reed, *Ch of Bd*
Steven D Davis, *President*
Joseph A Householder, *President*
EMP: 1000
SALES: 11.2B **Publicly Held**
WEB: www.sempra.com
SIC: 4932 4911 5172 4922 Gas & other
services combined; electric services; distribution, electric power; generation, electric power; transmission, electric power; petroleum products; natural gas transmission; pipelines, natural gas; storage, natural gas

4939 Combination Utilities, NEC

(P-6194)
AGILE SOURCING PARTNERS INC
2385 Railroad St, Corona (92880-5411)
PHONE..................................951 279-4154
Maria Thompson, *President*
Mitchell Diehl, *President*
Courtney Gaik, *Vice Pres*
Sherry Neu, *Program Mgr*
Sean Dempsey, *Business Anlyst*
EMP: 180
SQ FT: 2,300
SALES: 222.5MM **Privately Held**
SIC: 4939 Combination utilities

(P-6195)
CHESTER PUBLIC UTILITY DST
251 Chester Airport Rd, Chester (96020)
P.O. Box 177 (96020-0177)
PHONE..................................530 258-2171
William D Turner, *Manager*
▲ EMP: 70
SALES (est): 3.9MM **Privately Held**
SIC: 4939 Combination utilities

(P-6196)
CITY OF CORONA
Also Called: Public Works
400 S Vicentia Ave # 210, Corona
(92882-2187)
PHONE..................................951 736-2266
Kip D Field, *Manager*
EMP: 99 **Privately Held**
WEB: www.coronautilities.com
SIC: 4939 Combination utilities
PA: City Of Corona
400 S Vicentia Ave
Corona CA 92882
951 736-2372

(P-6197)
IMPERIAL IRRIGATION DISTRICT
81600 58th Ave, La Quinta (92253-7663)
P.O. Box 1080 (92247-1080)
PHONE..................................760 398-5811
Charles Haskin, *General Mgr*
Oscar Jauregui, *Info Tech Mgr*
Cedric Stephens, *Technology*
Dan Devoy, *Human Res Mgr*
Luis Garcia, *Marketing Staff*
EMP: 150
SALES (corp-wide): 634.6MM **Privately
Held**
WEB: www.iidwater.com
SIC: 4939 4911 Combination utilities; electric services
PA: Imperial Irrigation District
333 E Barioni Blvd
Imperial CA 92251
800 303-7756

(P-6198)
LA DEPARTMENT WATER AND POWER
17031 State Highway 14, Mojave
(93501-1230)
PHONE..................................661 824-7900
Mike Gratt, *Superintendent*
◆ EMP: 54
SALES (est): 3.1MM **Privately Held**
SIC: 4939 Combination utilities

(P-6199)
LOS ANGELES DEPT WTR & PWR
Also Called: Scattergood Generation Plant
12700 Vista Del Mar, Playa Del Rey
(90293-8502)
PHONE..................................310 524-8500
Nazih Batarseh, *Branch Mgr*
EMP: 100
SALES (corp-wide): 1.1B **Privately Held**
SIC: 4939 Combination utilities
PA: Los Angeles Department Of Water And
Power
111 N Hope St
Los Angeles CA 90012
213 367-4211

(P-6200)
ORMAT NEVADA INC
947 Dogwood Rd, Heber (92249-9762)
PHONE..................................760 353-8200
Celia Velasco, *Admin Mgr*
EMP: 50 **Publicly Held**
SIC: 4939 Combination utilities
HQ: Ormat Nevada, Inc.
6225 Neil Rd
Reno NV 89511

(P-6201)
SAN DIEGO GAS & ELECTRIC CO
North Coast O & M Center
5016 Carlsbad Blvd, Carlsbad
(92008-4303)
PHONE..................................760 438-6200
Jim Boland, *Director*
EMP: 120
SALES (corp-wide): 11.2B **Publicly Held**
SIC: 4939 4924 4911 Combination utilities; natural gas distribution; electric services
HQ: San Diego Gas & Electric Company
8326 Century Park Ct
San Diego CA 92123
619 696-2000

(P-6202)
SAN DIEGO GAS & ELECTRIC CO
Also Called: Northern Cnstr & Operations
571 Enterprise St, Escondido
(92029-1244)
PHONE..................................760 432-5885
Victor Gonzales, *Manager*
Ed Caudillo, *QA Dir*
Vicky Serrano, *Opers Mgr*
EMP: 400
SQ FT: 1,660
SALES (corp-wide): 11.2B **Publicly Held**
SIC: 4939 Combination utilities

HQ: San Diego Gas & Electric Company
8326 Century Park Ct
San Diego CA 92123
619 696-2000

(P-6203)
SAN DIEGO GAS & ELECTRIC CO
Project Construction Metro
701 33rd St, San Diego (92102-3341)
PHONE..................................619 699-1018
Scott Furgerson, *Manager*
EMP: 200
SALES (corp-wide): 11.2B **Publicly Held**
SIC: 4939 Combination utilities
HQ: San Diego Gas & Electric Company
8326 Century Park Ct
San Diego CA 92123
619 696-2000

(P-6204)
TRIUNFO PUBLIC FACILITIES CORP
1001 Partridge Dr, Ventura (93003-5562)
PHONE..................................805 658-4605
Vickie Dragan, *Principal*
EMP: 70 EST: 2010
SALES (est): 884.1K **Privately Held**
SIC: 4939 Combination utilities

4941 Water Sply

(P-6205)
AAB WATER COMPANY INC
Also Called: Yosemite Waters
226 S Avenue 54, Los Angeles
(90042-4512)
PHONE..................................559 497-2700
Mike Larue, *President*
EMP: 75
SALES: 10K **Privately Held**
SIC: 4941 Water supply

(P-6206)
ALAMEDA COUNTY WATER DISTRICT (PA)
Also Called: ACWD
43885 S Grimmer Blvd, Fremont
(94538-6375)
P.O. Box 5110 (94537-5110)
PHONE..................................510 668-4200
Walt Wadlow, *General Mgr*
Julie Taylor, *Officer*
Paul Piraino, *General Mgr*
Robert Shaver, *General Mgr*
Gina Markou, *Executive Asst*
EMP: 217
SQ FT: 60,000
SALES: 115.6MM **Privately Held**
WEB: www.acwd.org
SIC: 4941 Water supply

(P-6207)
AMADOR WATER AGENCY
12800 Ridge Rd, Sutter Creek
(95685-9630)
PHONE..................................209 223-3018
Jim Abercrombie, *District Mgr*
Terance W Moore, *President*
John P Swift, *Vice Pres*
Karen Gish, *General Mgr*
Linda Nafus, *Admin Asst*
EMP: 52
SQ FT: 2,000
SALES: 8.9MM **Privately Held**
WEB: www.amadorwa.com
SIC: 4941 4952 Water supply; sewerage systems

(P-6208)
AMERICAN WATER WORKS CO INC
4701 Beloit Dr, Sacramento (95838-2434)
P.O. Box 15468 (95851-0468)
PHONE..................................916 568-4236
Rob Roscoe, *Engineer*
Catherine Bowie, *Pub Rel Mgr*
EMP: 80
SALES (corp-wide): 3.3B **Publicly Held**
WEB: www.amwater.com
SIC: 4941 Water supply

PA: American Water Works Company, Inc.
1025 Laurel Oak Rd
Voorhees NJ 08043
856 346-8200

(P-6209)
ANDERSON PUMP COMPANY
Also Called: Dragon Engineering
24719 Robertson Blvd, Chowchilla
(93610-9090)
P.O. Box 906 (93610-0906)
PHONE..................................559 665-4477
Daniel Skeen, *President*
Imogene Anderson, *Treasurer*
Leon Anderson, *Vice Pres*
Jim Smith, *Vice Pres*
Edgar Sauceda, *Purch Mgr*
EMP: 55
SQ FT: 10,000
SALES (est): 20.1MM **Privately Held**
WEB: www.andersonpumpcompany.com
SIC: 4941 4971 Water supply; irrigation systems

(P-6210)
CALAVERAS COUNTY WATER DST
120 Toma Ct, San Andreas (95249)
P.O. Box 846 (95249-9002)
PHONE..................................209 754-3543
Scott Ratterman, *President*
Jeff Davidson, *Vice Pres*
David Eggerton, *General Mgr*
Jeffrey Meyer, *General Mgr*
Joel Metzger, *Manager*
EMP: 66
SQ FT: 5,000
SALES (est): 20.5MM **Privately Held**
WEB: www.ccwd.org
SIC: 4941 Water supply

(P-6211)
CALIFORNIA AMERICAN WATER CO (HQ)
655 W Broadway Ste 1410, San Diego
(92101-8491)
PHONE..................................619 409-7703
Kent Turner, *President*
Judith Almond, *COO*
Anthony J Cerasuolo, *Vice Pres*
EMP: 57
SQ FT: 16,500
SALES (est): 79.8MM
SALES (corp-wide): 3.3B **Publicly Held**
SIC: 4941 Water supply
PA: American Water Works Company, Inc.
1025 Laurel Oak Rd
Voorhees NJ 08043
856 346-8200

(P-6212)
CALIFORNIA AMERICAN WATER CO
880 Kuhn Dr, Chula Vista (91914-3514)
PHONE..................................619 656-2400
Kent Turner, *Controller*
EMP: 70
SALES (corp-wide): 3.3B **Publicly Held**
SIC: 4941 Water supply
HQ: California American Water Co.
655 W Broadway Ste 1410
San Diego CA 92101
619 409-7703

(P-6213)
CALIFORNIA AMERICAN WATER CO
4787 Old Redwood Hwy, Santa Rosa
(95403-1485)
PHONE..................................707 542-1717
Tony Lindstrom, *Manager*
EMP: 50
SALES (corp-wide): 3.3B **Publicly Held**
SIC: 4941 4953 Water supply; refuse systems
HQ: California American Water Co.
655 W Broadway Ste 1410
San Diego CA 92101
619 409-7703

(P-6214)
CALIFORNIA AMERICAN WATER CO
4701 Beloit Dr, Sacramento (95838-2434)
PHONE..................................916 568-4216

Robert Bloor, *CFO*
Melinda Weinrich, *Manager*
EMP: 50
SALES (corp-wide): 3.3B **Publicly Held**
SIC: 4941 4953 Water supply; refuse systems
HQ: California American Water Co.
655 W Broadway Ste 1410
San Diego CA 92101
619 409-7703

(P-6215)
CALIFORNIA WATER SERVICE CO (HQ)
1720 N 1st St, San Jose (95112-4598)
PHONE..................408 367-8200
Martin A Kropelnicki, *CEO*
Michael P Ireland, *President*
Helen Del Grosso, *Vice Pres*
Francis S Ferraro, *Vice Pres*
Robert R Guzzetta, *Vice Pres*
EMP: 160 **EST:** 1926
SQ FT: 43,000
SALES (est): 550.2MM
SALES (corp-wide): 666.8MM **Publicly Held**
SIC: 4941 Water supply
PA: California Water Service Group
1720 N 1st St
San Jose CA 95112
408 367-8200

(P-6216)
CALIFORNIA WATER SERVICE CO
3725 S H St, Bakersfield (93304-6535)
PHONE..................661 396-2400
Tim Terloar, *Manager*
EMP: 77
SALES (corp-wide): 666.8MM **Publicly Held**
SIC: 4941 Water supply
HQ: California Water Service Company
1720 N 1st St
San Jose CA 95112
408 367-8200

(P-6217)
CALIFORNIA WATER SERVICE CO
1505 E Sonora St, Stockton (95205-6112)
PHONE..................209 547-7900
Henry Wind, *Manager*
EMP: 51
SALES (corp-wide): 666.8MM **Publicly Held**
SIC: 4941 Water supply
HQ: California Water Service Company
1720 N 1st St
San Jose CA 95112
408 367-8200

(P-6218)
CALLEGUAS MUNICIPAL WATER DICT
2100 E Olsen Rd, Thousand Oaks (91360-6800)
PHONE..................805 526-9323
Thomas Slosson, *President*
Andy Waters, *Admin Sec*
Candace Cooper, *Admin Asst*
Dan Smith, *Finance Mgr*
Bruce Fischer, *Human Res Dir*
EMP: 62
SQ FT: 8,000
SALES: 120MM **Privately Held**
WEB: www.calleguas.com
SIC: 4941 Water supply

(P-6219)
CARLSBAD MUNICIPAL WATER DST
5950 El Camino Real, Carlsbad (92008-8802)
PHONE..................760 438-2722
Robert Greaney, *Manager*
EMP: 50
SQ FT: 12,000
SALES (est): 6.8MM **Privately Held**
SIC: 4941 Water supply
PA: City Of Carlsbad
1635 Faraday Ave
Carlsbad CA 92008
760 602-2490

(P-6220)
CASTAIC LK WTR AGCY FING CORP (PA)
27234 Bouquet Canyon Rd, Santa Clarita (91350-2102)
PHONE..................661 259-2737
Tom Campbell, *CEO*
Ronald J Kelly, *President*
Dan Masnada, *Treasurer*
Bill Cooper, *Vice Pres*
William Cooper, *Vice Pres*
EMP: 120
SQ FT: 1,000
SALES (est): 38MM **Privately Held**
WEB: www.clwa.org
SIC: 4941 Water supply

(P-6221)
CITY & COUNTY OF SAN FRANCISCO
525 Golden Gate Ave, San Francisco (94102-3220)
PHONE..................415 551-3000
Barbara Hale, *Manager*
Manuel Rodriguez, *Electrical Engi*
Sergio Barraza, *Engineer*
Sanda Thaik, *Manager*
EMP: 900 **Privately Held**
SIC: 4941 9631 Water supply;
PA: City & County Of San Francisco
1 Dr Carlton B Goodlett P
San Francisco CA 94102
415 554-7500

(P-6222)
CITY OF FRESNO
Also Called: Water Division
1910 E University Ave, Fresno (93703-2927)
PHONE..................559 621-5300
Lon Martin, *Manager*
Elizabeth Jones, *Officer*
Martin McIntyre, *Manager*
EMP: 165 **Privately Held**
WEB: www.fresnocitizencorps.org
SIC: 4941 Water supply
PA: City Of Fresno
2600 Fresno St
Fresno CA 93721
559 621-7001

(P-6223)
CITY OF GLENDALE
Also Called: Public Service Yard
800 Air Way, Glendale (91201-3012)
PHONE..................818 548-2011
Pat Reily, *Manager*
EMP: 150 **Privately Held**
WEB: www.glendaleca.com
SIC: 4941 Water supply
PA: City Of Glendale
141 N Glendale Ave Fl 2
Glendale CA 91206
818 548-2085

(P-6224)
CITY OF LOMITA
Also Called: Publis Works
24373 Walnut St, Lomita (90717-1259)
PHONE..................310 325-9830
Vince Demasse, *Manager*
EMP: 50
SQ FT: 59,893 **Privately Held**
WEB: www.lomita.com
SIC: 4941 9111 Water supply; mayors' offices
PA: City Of Lomita
24300 Narbonne Ave
Lomita CA 90717
310 325-7110

(P-6225)
CITY OF LONG BEACH
Also Called: Water Emergency Dispatch
1800 E Wardlow Rd, Long Beach (90807-4931)
PHONE..................562 570-2390
Kevin Wattier, *General Mgr*
Robert Cole, *President*
EMP: 100 **Privately Held**
WEB: www.polb.com
SIC: 4941 9511 Water supply; air, water & solid waste management;

PA: City Of Long Beach
333 W Ocean Blvd Fl 10
Long Beach CA 90802
562 570-6450

(P-6226)
CITY OF NORCO
Parks and Recreation Dept
2870 Clark Ave, Norco (92860-1903)
PHONE..................951 270-5632
Brian Petree, *Director*
EMP: 75 **Privately Held**
WEB: www.ci.norco.ca.us
SIC: 4941 4953 Water supply; refuse systems
PA: City Of Norco
2870 Clark Ave
Norco CA 92860
951 270-5617

(P-6227)
CITY OF ORLAND (PA)
Also Called: Accounting Department
815 4th St, Orland (95963-1714)
PHONE..................530 865-1610
Peter Arr, *Finance*
Daryl Brock, *Finance Dir*
Paul Poczobut, *Manager*
Janet Wackerman, *Accounts Mgr*
EMP: 50 **EST:** 1909
SALES (est): 6.9MM **Privately Held**
WEB: www.cityoforland.com
SIC: 4941 Water supply

(P-6228)
CITY OF OXNARD
Also Called: Water Svcs Operations & Repr
251 S Hayes Ave, Oxnard (93030-6058)
PHONE..................805 385-8136
Anthony Emmert, *Superintendent*
EMP: 60 **Privately Held**
WEB: www.oxnardtourism.com
SIC: 4941 9111 Water supply; mayors' offices
PA: City Of Oxnard
300 W 3rd St Uppr Fl4
Oxnard CA 93030
805 385-7803

(P-6229)
COACHELLA VALLEY WATER DST (PA)
Also Called: C V Water District
85995 Avenue 52, Coachella (92236-2568)
P.O. Box 1058 (92236-1058)
PHONE..................760 398-2651
Toll Free:..................888 -
Steve Robbins, *General Mgr*
Jim Barrett, *General Mgr*
Robert Cheng, *General Mgr*
Isabel Luna, *Executive Asst*
Amy Ammons, *Finance Dir*
▲ **EMP:** 225
SALES: 159.3MM **Privately Held**
SIC: 4941 4971 4952 7389 Water supply; water distribution or supply systems for irrigation; sewerage systems; water softener service

(P-6230)
COACHELLA VALLEY WATER DST
75515 Hovley Ln E, Palm Desert (92211-5104)
PHONE..................760 398-2651
Steve Robbins, *Branch Mgr*
EMP: 226
SALES (corp-wide): 159.3MM **Privately Held**
SIC: 4941 4952 4971 Water supply; sewerage systems; water distribution or supply systems for irrigation
PA: Coachella Valley Water District
85995 Avenue 52
Coachella CA 92236
760 398-2651

(P-6231)
COACHELLA VALLEY WATER DST
75 525 Hovley Ln, Palm Desert (92260)
PHONE..................760 398-2651
Steve Robbins, *Branch Mgr*
EMP: 226

SALES (corp-wide): 159.3MM **Privately Held**
SIC: 4941 4952 4971 Water supply; sewerage systems; irrigation systems
PA: Coachella Valley Water District
85995 Avenue 52
Coachella CA 92236
760 398-2651

(P-6232)
CONTRA COSTA WATER DISTRICT (PA)
1331 Concord Ave, Concord (94520-4907)
PHONE..................925 688-8000
Lisa Borba, *President*
Ron Jacobsma, *Assistant*
▲ **EMP:** 225
SQ FT: 22,000
SALES: 3.8MM **Privately Held**
WEB: www.ccwater.com
SIC: 4941 Water supply

(P-6233)
COUNTY OF LOS ANGELES
Also Called: Water & Power Department
6801 E 2nd St, Long Beach (90803-4324)
PHONE..................213 367-3176
Victor Barra, *Director*
EMP: 160 **Privately Held**
WEB: www.co.la.ca.us
SIC: 4941 9511 9631 4939 Water supply; air, water & solid waste management; ; regulation, administration of utilities; combination utilities
PA: County Of Los Angeles
500 W Temple St Ste 437
Los Angeles CA 90012
213 974-1101

(P-6234)
COUNTY OF LOS ANGELES
Also Called: Department of Public Works
900 S Fremont Ave, Alhambra (91803-1331)
P.O. Box 1460 (91802-2460)
PHONE..................626 458-4000
Gail Farber, *Director*
Jeff Orlin, *IT/INT Sup*
Patrick Holland, *Research*
Patricia Wood, *Research*
Ken Farris, *Technology*
EMP: 300 **Privately Held**
WEB: www.co.la.ca.us
SIC: 4941 9511 4971 Water supply; air, water & solid waste management; irrigation systems
PA: County Of Los Angeles
500 W Temple St Ste 437
Los Angeles CA 90012
213 974-1101

(P-6235)
COUNTY OF LOS ANGELES
Also Called: Community Facilities Dst No 6
500 W Temple St Ste 525, Los Angeles (90012-3873)
PHONE..................213 974-8301
Bruce Huthmacher, *MIS Mgr*
EMP: 172 **Privately Held**
SIC: 4941 Water supply
PA: County Of Los Angeles
500 W Temple St Ste 437
Los Angeles CA 90012
213 974-1101

(P-6236)
COUNTY OF SOLANO
Also Called: Water Supply
810 Vaca Valley Pkwy # 203, Vacaville (95688-8835)
PHONE..................707 451-6090
David Okita, *Manager*
EMP: 100 **Privately Held**
SIC: 4941 8641 Water supply; civic social & fraternal associations
PA: County Of Solano
675 Texas St Ste 2600
Fairfield CA 94533
707 784-6706

(P-6237)
CUCAMONGA VALLEY WATER DST
10440 Ashford St, Rancho Cucamonga (91730-3057)
P.O. Box 638 (91729-0638)
PHONE..........................909 987-2591
Martin Zvirbulis, *CEO*
Diane Schumacher, *Senior Partner*
Kathleen Tiegs, *President*
John Bosler, *COO*
Chad Brantley, *Officer*
EMP: 100 **EST:** 1955
SQ FT: 15,000
SALES: 84.5MM **Privately Held**
WEB: www.ccwdwater.com
SIC: 4941 Water supply

(P-6238)
DESERT WATER AGENCY FING CORP
Also Called: DWA
1200 S Gene Autry Trl, Palm Springs (92264-3533)
P.O. Box 1710 (92263-1710)
PHONE..........................760 323-4971
Patricia G Oyga, *CEO*
Joseph Stuart, *Vice Pres*
John Tessman, *Administration*
Mario Ballesteros, *Info Tech Dir*
Kory Knox, *Info Tech Mgr*
EMP: 72
SQ FT: 38,000
SALES: 29MM **Privately Held**
WEB: www.dwa.org
SIC: 4941 Water supply

(P-6239)
DUBLIN SAN RAMON SERVICES DST (PA)
7051 Dublin Blvd, Dublin (94568-3018)
PHONE..........................925 875-2276
Bert Michalczyk, *CEO*
Lori Rose, *Treasurer*
▲ **EMP:** 110 **EST:** 1953
SQ FT: 19,400
SALES: 59.6MM **Privately Held**
WEB: www.dsrsd.com
SIC: 4941 Water supply

(P-6240)
DUBLIN SAN RAMON SERVICES DST
7399 Johnson Dr, Pleasanton (94588-3862)
PHONE..........................925 846-4565
Bert Michalczyk, *General Mgr*
EMP: 100
SALES (corp-wide): 59.6MM **Privately Held**
WEB: www.dsrsd.com
SIC: 4941 Water supply
PA: Dublin San Ramon Services District
7051 Dublin Blvd
Dublin CA 94568
925 875-2276

(P-6241)
EAST BAY MUNICIPAL UTILITY DST
Also Called: Ebmud - Construction and Maint
2149 Union St, Oakland (94607)
PHONE..........................866 403-2683
Alexander Coate, *General Mgr*
William Patterson, *Vice Pres*
Michael Hartlaub, *Engineer*
Andy Katz, *Director*
EMP: 54
SALES (est): 6.2MM **Privately Held**
SIC: 4941 9441 Water supply; administration of social & manpower programs

(P-6242)
EAST BAY MUNICIPL UTILTY DISTR
Also Called: Ebmud
1100 21st St, Oakland (94607-2887)
PHONE..........................866 403-2683
Dennis Dimer, *Branch Mgr*
EMP: 55
SALES (corp-wide): 534MM **Privately Held**
SIC: 4941 Water supply

PA: East Bay Municipal Utility District, Water System
375 11th St
Oakland CA 94607
866 403-2683

(P-6243)
EAST BAY MUNICIPL UTILTY DISTR
Also Called: Ebmud
3999 Lakeside Dr, Richmond (94806-1964)
PHONE..........................866 403-2683
Karl Gillson, *Branch Mgr*
EMP: 110
SALES (corp-wide): 534MM **Privately Held**
WEB: www.ebmud.com
SIC: 4941 Water supply
PA: East Bay Municipal Utility District, Water System
375 11th St
Oakland CA 94607
866 403-2683

(P-6244)
EAST BAY MUNICIPL UTILTY DISTR
Also Called: East Area Office
2551 N Main St, Walnut Creek (94597-3122)
P.O. Box 1000, Oakland (94649-0001)
PHONE..........................866 403-2683
Alexander Coate, *Manager*
EMP: 55
SALES (corp-wide): 534MM **Privately Held**
SIC: 4941 Water supply
PA: East Bay Municipal Utility District, Water System
375 11th St
Oakland CA 94607
866 403-2683

(P-6245)
EAST BAY MUNICIPL UTILTY DISTR (PA)
Also Called: EBMUD
375 11th St, Oakland (94607-4246)
P.O. Box 24055 (94623-1055)
PHONE..........................866 403-2683
Alexander Coate, *General Mgr*
Sophia Skoda, *Treasurer*
Polly Villarreal, *Vice Pres*
Dave Fulk, *General Mgr*
Dawn Benson, *Executive Asst*
EMP: 629
SQ FT: 264,427
SALES: 534MM **Privately Held**
WEB: www.ebmud.com
SIC: 4941 Water supply

(P-6246)
EAST BAY MUNICIPL UTILTY DISTR
Also Called: Ebmud
375 11th St, Oakland (94607-4246)
PHONE..........................510 287-0760
Alexander Coate, *General Mgr*
Elizabeth Grassetti, *Senior VP*
Wanda Prevost, *Technician*
Paresh Gandhi, *Electrical Engi*
Edward Chang, *Engineer*
EMP: 64
SALES (corp-wide): 534MM **Privately Held**
SIC: 4941 Water supply
PA: East Bay Municipal Utility District, Water System
375 11th St
Oakland CA 94607
866 403-2683

(P-6247)
EAST VALLEY WATER DISTRICT
31111 Greenspot Rd, Highland (92346-4427)
P.O. Box 3427, San Bernardino (92413-3427)
PHONE..........................909 889-9501
John Mura, *CEO*
Matt Levesque, *President*
Brian W Tompkins, *CFO*
Kip E Sturgeon, *Vice Pres*
Donald D Goodin, *Director*
EMP: 61

SALES: 37.4MM **Privately Held**
WEB: www.eastvalley.org
SIC: 4941 8734 Water supply; water testing laboratory

(P-6248)
EASTERN MUNICIPAL WATER DST (PA)
2270 Trumble Rd, Perris (92572)
P.O. Box 8300 (92572-8300)
PHONE..........................951 928-3777
Paul D Jones II, *CEO*
Joe Hansen, *Info Tech Dir*
Brian Agner, *Manager*
Tamela White, *Assistant*
▲ **EMP:** 420
SQ FT: 160,000
SALES: 221.2MM **Privately Held**
SIC: 4941 4952 Water supply; sewerage systems

(P-6249)
EL DORADO HILLS COUNTY WTR DST
Also Called: El Dorado Hills Fire Dept
1050 Wilson Blvd, El Dorado Hills (95762-7263)
PHONE..........................916 933-6623
John Hidahl, *President*
James O'Camb, *COO*
Christina Burroughs, *Admin Asst*
Christopher Landry, *Engineer*
Jessica Braddock, *Finance*
EMP: 51
SALES (est): 6.9MM **Privately Held**
WEB: www.edhfire.com
SIC: 4941 Water supply

(P-6250)
EL DORADO IRRIGATION DISTRICT
2890 Mosquito Rd, Placerville (95667-4700)
PHONE..........................530 622-4513
George Osborne, *President*
Jim Abercrombie, *General Mgr*
Ane Deister, *General Mgr*
Elizabeth Wells, *General Mgr*
Pat Johnson, *Executive Asst*
EMP: 300
SQ FT: 27,000
SALES: 67MM **Privately Held**
SIC: 4941 4952 8741 4971 Water supply; sewerage systems; management services; irrigation systems

(P-6251)
EL DORADO WATER & SHOWER SVC
5821 Mother Lode Dr, Placerville (95667-8227)
P.O. Box 944 (95667-0944)
PHONE..........................530 622-8995
Robert V Williams, *President*
Mellisa Peterson, *Principal*
EMP: 50
SQ FT: 816
SALES (est): 2MM **Privately Held**
SIC: 4941 Water supply

(P-6252)
EL TORO WATER DISTR PUBLIC FAC (PA)
24251 Los Alisos Blvd, Lake Forest (92630-5246)
P.O. Box 4000, Laguna Hills (92654-4000)
PHONE..........................949 837-1662
Robert R Hill, *Admin Sec*
Jose Vergara, *Treasurer*
Bob Hazzard, *Bd of Directors*
Dominic Bergin, *Admin Asst*
Michael Miazga, *Technology*
EMP: 54 **EST:** 1960
SQ FT: 7,200
SALES: 23.1MM **Privately Held**
WEB: www.etwd.com
SIC: 4941 4959 Water supply; sanitary services

(P-6253)
ELSINORE VLY MUNICPL WTR DST (PA)
31315 Chaney St, Lake Elsinore (92530-2743)
P.O. Box 3000 (92531-3000)
PHONE..........................951 674-3146
Harvey R Ryan, *President*
Andy Morris, *Treasurer*
Phil Williams, *Vice Pres*
Ronald Young, *Vice Pres*
Margie Armstrong, *Executive*
EMP: 65
SQ FT: 4,000
SALES: 67.4MM **Privately Held**
WEB: www.evmwd.com
SIC: 4941 4971 4952 Water supply; water distribution or supply systems for irrigation; sewerage systems

(P-6254)
FALLBROOK PUBLIC UTILITY DST
990 E Mission Rd, Fallbrook (92028-2232)
P.O. Box 2290 (92088-2290)
PHONE..........................760 728-1125
Nick Hoskot, *President*
Marcie Eilers, *Treasurer*
Mary McNeil, *Vice Pres*
Ruth Resch, *Admin Sec*
Larry Ragsdale, *Administration*
EMP: 67
SQ FT: 12,000
SALES: 25.3MM **Privately Held**
WEB: www.fpud.com
SIC: 4941 Water supply

(P-6255)
FRIANT WATER AUTHORITY (PA)
854 N Harvard Ave, Lindsay (93247-1715)
PHONE..........................559 562-6305
Jason Phillips, *CEO*
Ron Jacobsma, *General Mgr*
Nina Hurtado, *Purch Agent*
EMP: 50
SALES: 2.5MM **Privately Held**
SIC: 4941 Water supply

(P-6256)
FRIANT WATER USERS ASSOCIATION
Also Called: Friant Water Users Authority
854 N Harvard Ave, Lindsay (93247-1715)
PHONE..........................559 562-6305
Marvin Huss, *Chairman*
Doug Deflitch, *COO*
Kathy Bennett, *General Mgr*
Gary Perez, *Opers Spvr*
Jeff Payne, *Opers Staff*
EMP: 53
SQ FT: 4,000
SALES (est): 6.3MM **Privately Held**
SIC: 4941 Water supply

(P-6257)
GOLDEN STATE WATER COMPANY
1920 W Corporate Way, Anaheim (92801-5373)
PHONE..........................714 535-7711
Randall Vogel, *Vice Pres*
Claudia Di-Majo, *Office Admin*
Toby Moore, *Manager*
EMP: 70
SALES (corp-wide): 440.6MM **Publicly Held**
WEB: www.gswater.com
SIC: 4941 4911 Water supply; distribution, electric power
HQ: Golden State Water Company
630 E Foothill Blvd
San Dimas CA 91773
909 394-3600

(P-6258)
GOLDEN STATE WATER COMPANY (HQ)
Also Called: AWR
630 E Foothill Blvd, San Dimas (91773-1212)
PHONE..........................909 394-3600
Robert J Sprowls, *President*
Eva G Tang, *CFO*
Eva Tang, *Treasurer*
Gladys Farrow, *Vice Pres*

Bill Gedney, *Vice Pres*
EMP: 170
SALES: 340.3MM
SALES (corp-wide): 440.6MM **Publicly Held**
WEB: www.gswater.com
SIC: 4941　4911　Water supply; distribution, electric power
PA: American States Water Company
　　630 E Foothill Blvd
　　San Dimas CA 91773
　　909 394-3600

(P-6259)
GOLDEN STATE WATER COMPANY
Also Called: American State Water Company
630 E Foothill Blvd, San Dimas (91773-1212)
PHONE.......................909 394-3600
Floydee Wibks, *CEO*
EMP: 100
SALES (corp-wide): 440.6MM **Publicly Held**
WEB: www.gswater.com
SIC: 4941　Water supply
HQ: Golden State Water Company
　　630 E Foothill Blvd
　　San Dimas CA 91773
　　909 394-3600

(P-6260)
GOLDEN STATE WATER COMPANY
Also Called: Sanitation
600 W Los Angeles Ave, Simi Valley (93065-1642)
PHONE.......................805 583-6400
Jim Buell, *Manager*
EMP: 50
SALES (corp-wide): 440.6MM **Publicly Held**
WEB: www.gswater.com
SIC: 4941　Water supply
HQ: Golden State Water Company
　　630 E Foothill Blvd
　　San Dimas CA 91773
　　909 394-3600

(P-6261)
HELIX WATER DISTRICT (PA)
7811 University Ave, La Mesa (91942-0427)
PHONE.......................619 466-0585
Deana R Verbeke, *President*
Lisa Irvine, *Treasurer*
Sandy Janzen, *Bd of Directors*
John Linden, *Vice Pres*
Patricia Rutan, *Info Tech Mgr*
EMP: 126
SQ FT: 15,000
SALES: 92.7MM **Privately Held**
WEB: www.hwd.com
SIC: 4941　Water supply

(P-6262)
HELIX WATER DISTRICT
Also Called: Nat L Eggert Operations Center
1233 Vernon Way, El Cajon (92020-1838)
PHONE.......................619 596-3860
Doug Emery, *Branch Mgr*
Mark Weston, *Branch Mgr*
Rita Mooney, *Admin Asst*
Joe Garuba, *Facilities Mgr*
Paul Lafalce, *Supervisor*
EMP: 55
SALES (est): 3.7MM
SALES (corp-wide): 92.7MM **Privately Held**
WEB: www.hwd.com
SIC: 4941　Water supply
PA: Helix Water District
　　7811 University Ave
　　La Mesa CA 91942
　　619 466-0585

(P-6263)
INLAND EMPIRE UTILITIES AGENCY
12811 6th St, Rancho Cucamonga (91739-9222)
PHONE.......................909 993-1755
Dan Foley, *Branch Mgr*
Tina Cheng, *Officer*
Martha Davis, *Executive*
Terry Catlin, *Manager*

EMP: 71
SALES (corp-wide): 119.6MM **Privately Held**
SIC: 4941　Water supply
PA: Inland Empire Utilities Agency A Municipal Water District (Inc)
　　6075 Kimball Ave
　　Chino CA 91708
　　909 993-1600

(P-6264)
INLAND EMPIRE UTILITIES AGENCY (PA)
6075 Kimball Ave, Chino (91708-9174)
P.O. Box 9020, Chino Hills (91709-0902)
PHONE.......................909 993-1600
Terry Catlin, *President*
John Anderson, *President*
Jon Florio, *COO*
Michael Camacho, *Treasurer*
Ging Cookman, *Corp Secy*
EMP: 92
SQ FT: 60,000
SALES: 119.6MM **Privately Held**
SIC: 4941　Water supply

(P-6265)
INLAND EMPIRE UTILITIES AGENCY
9400 Cherry Ave, Fontana (92335-5359)
PHONE.......................909 993-1600
Cameron Langner, *Branch Mgr*
EMP: 71
SALES (corp-wide): 119.6MM **Privately Held**
SIC: 4941　Water supply
PA: Inland Empire Utilities Agency A Municipal Water District (Inc)
　　6075 Kimball Ave
　　Chino CA 91708
　　909 993-1600

(P-6266)
IRVINE RANCH WATER DISTRICT (PA)
15600 Sand Canyon Ave, Irvine (92618-3102)
P.O. Box 57000 (92619-7000)
PHONE.......................949 453-5300
Paul Jones, *General Mgr*
Robert Jacobson, *Treasurer*
Kristine Swan, *Admin Asst*
John Fabris, *Manager*
Sergio De La Torre, *Supervisor*
EMP: 110
SQ FT: 52,000
SALES: 144.3MM **Privately Held**
SIC: 4941　4952　Water supply; sewerage systems

(P-6267)
IRVINE RANCH WATER DISTRICT
3512 Michelson Dr, Irvine (92612-1757)
P.O. Box 14128 (92623-4128)
PHONE.......................949 453-5300
Carl Ballard, *Director*
EMP: 170
SALES (est): 13.5MM
SALES (corp-wide): 144.3MM **Privately Held**
SIC: 4941　4952　Water supply; sewerage systems
PA: Irvine Ranch Water District Inc
　　15600 Sand Canyon Ave
　　Irvine CA 92618
　　949 453-5300

(P-6268)
KERN COUNTY WATER AGENCY
811 Nadine Ln, Bakersfield (93308)
P.O. Box 58 (93302-0058)
PHONE.......................661 634-1512
James M Beck, *District Mgr*
EMP: 63
SALES (corp-wide): 34MM **Privately Held**
SIC: 4941　Water supply
PA: Kern County Water Agency
　　3200 Rio Mirada Dr
　　Bakersfield CA 93308
　　661 634-1400

(P-6269)
LAKE HEMET MUNICIPAL WTR DST (PA)
26385 Fairview Ave, Hemet (92544-6607)
P.O. Box 5039 (92544-0039)
PHONE.......................951 927-1816
Tom Wagoner, *General Mgr*
Noah Bischof, *Officer*
Vince Leone, *Officer*
Jeff Wall, *Technology*
Jason Venable, *Engineer*
EMP: 58
SQ FT: 4,900
SALES: 16.7MM **Privately Held**
WEB: www.lhmwd.org
SIC: 4941　4971　Water supply; water distribution or supply systems for irrigation

(P-6270)
LAS VIRGENES MUNICIPAL WTR DST
4232 Las Virgenes Rd Lbby, Calabasas (91302-3594)
PHONE.......................818 251-2100
Glen Peterson, *President*
Jay Lewitt, *Treasurer*
Lee Renger, *Vice Pres*
Harold Matthews, *MIS Dir*
Angela Saccareccia, *Finance Mgr*
EMP: 125
SQ FT: 10,000
SALES: 61.9MM **Privately Held**
WEB: www.lvmwd.com
SIC: 4941　Water supply

(P-6271)
LIBERTY UTILITIES PK WTR CORP (DH)
9750 Washburn Rd, Downey (90241-5625)
PHONE.......................562 923-0711
Greg Sorensen, *President*
Chris Alario, *CFO*
Jeanne Marie Bruno, *Senior VP*
Jeanne-Marie Bruno, *General Mgr*
Lisa Mendum, *Admin Asst*
EMP: 68
SQ FT: 15,000
SALES (est): 81.8MM
SALES (corp-wide): 1.5B **Privately Held**
SIC: 4941　Water supply
HQ: Liberty Utilities (Canada) Corp
　　354 Davis Rd
　　Oakville ON L6J 0
　　905 465-4500

(P-6272)
LINDA YORBA WATER DISTRICT (PA)
1717 E Miraloma Ave, Placentia (92870-6785)
P.O. Box 309, Yorba Linda (92885-0309)
PHONE.......................714 701-3000
Ken Vecchiarelli, *General Mgr*
Cindy Mejia-Ylwd, *President*
Marc Marcantonio, *General Mgr*
Ariel Bacani, *Technician*
Bryan Hong, *Engineer*
▲ **EMP:** 76
SQ FT: 7,900
SALES: 32.4MM **Privately Held**
WEB: www.ylwd.com
SIC: 4941　4952　Water supply; sewerage systems

(P-6273)
LOS ANGELES DEPT WTR & PWR
4030 Crenshaw Blvd, Los Angeles (90008-2533)
P.O. Box 51211 (90051-5511)
PHONE.......................323 256-8079
Becky Ng, *Administration*
EMP: 4472
SALES (corp-wide): 1.1B **Privately Held**
SIC: 4941　4911　Water supply; electric services
PA: Los Angeles Department Of Water And Power
　　111 N Hope St
　　Los Angeles CA 90012
　　213 367-4211

(P-6274)
LOS ANGELES DEPT WTR & PWR
11801 Sheldon St, Sun Valley (91352-1508)
PHONE.......................213 367-1342
Kirk Bergland, *Branch Mgr*
Thieu Doan, *Electrical Engi*
Rick Garcia, *Training Super*
Olivia Morales, *Security Mgr*
Roberto Sedano, *Chief*
EMP: 932
SALES (corp-wide): 1.1B **Privately Held**
SIC: 4941　Water supply
PA: Los Angeles Department Of Water And Power
　　111 N Hope St
　　Los Angeles CA 90012
　　213 367-4211

(P-6275)
LOS ANGELES DEPT WTR & PWR
Also Called: Ladwp
201 S Webster St, Independence (93526-1769)
PHONE.......................760 878-2156
Steve Howe, *Supervisor*
EMP: 2050
SALES (corp-wide): 1.1B **Privately Held**
SIC: 4941　Water supply
PA: Los Angeles Department Of Water And Power
　　111 N Hope St
　　Los Angeles CA 90012
　　213 367-4211

(P-6276)
LOS ANGELES DEPT WTR & PWR (PA)
Also Called: Ladwp
111 N Hope St, Los Angeles (90012-2607)
P.O. Box 51111 (90051-5700)
PHONE.......................213 367-4211
David H Wright, *General Mgr*
Martin L Adams, *COO*
Ann M Santilli, *CFO*
Donna I Stevener, *Officer*
Nancy Sutley, *Officer*
EMP: 170
SALES: 1.1B **Privately Held**
WEB: www.lacity.org
SIC: 4941　4911　Water supply; electric services

(P-6277)
LOS ANGELES DEPT WTR & PWR
1141 W 2nd St Bldg D, Los Angeles (90012-2007)
PHONE.......................213 367-5706
Carol Tharp, *Branch Mgr*
Rafik Alsawalhy, *Project Mgr*
Vladimir Kapisarov, *Electrical Engi*
Erika Hill, *Analyst*
Chris Repp, *Agent*
EMP: 932
SALES (corp-wide): 1.1B **Privately Held**
SIC: 4941　Water supply
PA: Los Angeles Department Of Water And Power
　　111 N Hope St
　　Los Angeles CA 90012
　　213 367-4211

(P-6278)
MARIN MUNICIPAL WATER DISTRICT (PA)
220 Nellen Ave, Corte Madera (94925-1169)
PHONE.......................415 945-1455
Krishna Kumar, *General Mgr*
Libby Pischel, *Executive*
Grabow Larry, *Lab Dir*
Oreen Delgado, *Division Mgr*
Paul Helliker, *General Mgr*
EMP: 220
SQ FT: 32,000
SALES: 68.5MM **Privately Held**
SIC: 4941　4971　Water supply; irrigation systems

▲ = Import ▼=Export
◆ =Import/Export

(P-6279)
MESA CNSLD WTR DST IMPRV CORP (PA)
Also Called: Mesa Water District
1965 Placentia Ave, Costa Mesa
(92627-3420)
PHONE....................949 631-1200
Lee Pearl, *Director*
James R Fisler, *President*
Shawn Dewane, *Vice Pres*
Coleen L Monteleone, *Admin Sec*
EMP: 53
SQ FT: 26,000
SALES: 29.2MM **Privately Held**
WEB: www.mesawater.org
SIC: 4941 Water supply

(P-6280)
METROPOLITAN WATER DISTRICT
1820 Commercenter Cir, San Bernardino
(92408-3430)
PHONE....................909 890-3776
Ron Gastelum, *Principal*
EMP: 50
SALES (corp-wide): 1.3B **Privately Held**
WEB: www.mwdh2o.com
SIC: 4941 Water supply
PA: The Metropolitan Water District Of
Southern California
700 N Alameda St
Los Angeles CA 90012
213 217-6000

(P-6281)
METROPOLITAN WATER DISTRICT
18250 La Sierra Ave, Riverside
(92503-6531)
PHONE....................951 688-5672
Al Ubrun, *Manager*
EMP: 50
SALES (corp-wide): 1.3B **Privately Held**
WEB: www.mwdh2o.com
SIC: 4941 1711 Water supply; septic system construction
PA: The Metropolitan Water District Of
Southern California
700 N Alameda St
Los Angeles CA 90012
213 217-6000

(P-6282)
METROPOLITAN WATER DISTRICT
33740 Borel Rd, Winchester (92596-9625)
P.O. Box 38, Parker Dam (92267-0038)
PHONE....................760 663-4911
Greg Ensminger, *Branch Mgr*
EMP: 150
SALES (corp-wide): 1.3B **Privately Held**
WEB: www.mwdh2o.com
SIC: 4941 Water supply
PA: The Metropolitan Water District Of
Southern California
700 N Alameda St
Los Angeles CA 90012
213 217-6000

(P-6283)
METROPOLITAN WATER DISTRICT
Also Called: Joseph Jensen Filtration Plant
13100 Balboa Blvd, Granada Hills
(91344-1199)
PHONE....................818 368-3731
Ezell Culver, *Manager*
EMP: 72
SALES (corp-wide): 1.3B **Privately Held**
WEB: www.mwdh2o.com
SIC: 4941 Water supply
PA: The Metropolitan Water District Of
Southern California
700 N Alameda St
Los Angeles CA 90012
213 217-6000

(P-6284)
METROPOLITAN WATER DISTRICT
Also Called: Metropolitan Water Lavern
700 Moreno Ave, La Verne (91750-3399)
P.O. Box 54153, Los Angeles (90054-0153)
PHONE....................909 593-7474
Wendell Williams, *Branch Mgr*
EMP: 370
SALES (corp-wide): 1.3B **Privately Held**
WEB: www.mwdh2o.com
SIC: 4941 Water supply
PA: The Metropolitan Water District Of
Southern California
700 N Alameda St
Los Angeles CA 90012
213 217-6000

(P-6285)
METROPOLITAN WATER DISTRICT
33752 Newport Rd, Winchester
(92596-9475)
PHONE....................951 926-7095
Marty Hundley, *Manager*
EMP: 66
SALES (corp-wide): 1.3B **Privately Held**
WEB: www.mwdh2o.com
SIC: 4941 Water supply
PA: The Metropolitan Water District Of
Southern California
700 N Alameda St
Los Angeles CA 90012
213 217-6000

(P-6286)
METROPOLITAN WATER DISTRICT
550 E Alessandro Blvd, Riverside
(92508-2400)
PHONE....................951 780-1511
Richard Green, *Branch Mgr*
EMP: 75
SALES (corp-wide): 1.3B **Privately Held**
WEB: www.mwdh2o.com
SIC: 4941 Water supply
PA: The Metropolitan Water District Of
Southern California
700 N Alameda St
Los Angeles CA 90012
213 217-6000

(P-6287)
METROPOLITAN WATER DISTRICT
2300 Palos Verdes Dr N, Rllng HLS Est
(90274-4222)
PHONE....................310 832-6106
Dave Rendon, *Manager*
EMP: 2000
SALES (corp-wide): 1.3B **Privately Held**
WEB: www.mwdh2o.com
SIC: 4941 Water supply
PA: The Metropolitan Water District Of
Southern California
700 N Alameda St
Los Angeles CA 90012
213 217-6000

(P-6288)
METROPOLITAN WATER DISTRICT
Also Called: Robert Sknner Filtration Plant
33740 Borel Rd, Winchester (92596-9625)
PHONE....................951 926-1501
Fax: 951 926-3531
EMP: 80
SALES (corp-wide): 1.5B **Privately Held**
SIC: 4941
PA: The Metropolitan Water District Of
Southern California
700 N Alameda St
Los Angeles CA 90012
213 217-6000

(P-6289)
MOULTON NIGUEL WATER (PA)
27500 La Paz Rd, Laguna Niguel
(92677-3402)
P.O. Box 30203 (92607-0203)
PHONE....................949 831-2500
Richard Fiore, *President*
David Cain, *Treasurer*
John V Foley, *General Mgr*
Joone Lopez, *General Mgr*
Drew Atwater, *Planning*
EMP: 97 EST: 1960
SQ FT: 9,000
SALES: 57.7MM **Privately Held**
WEB: www.mnwd.com
SIC: 4941 4959 Water supply; sanitary services

(P-6290)
NORTH MARIN WATER DISTRICT (PA)
Also Called: Nmwd
999 Rush Creek Pl, Novato (94945-7716)
P.O. Box 146 (94948-0146)
PHONE....................415 897-4133
Chris Degabriele, *Principal*
Carmela Chandrasekera, *Engineer*
David Jackson, *Engineer*
Drew McIntyre, *Chief Engr*
Dan Garrett, *Foreman/Supr*
EMP: 50
SQ FT: 7,200
SALES: 17.4MM **Privately Held**
WEB: www.nmwd.com
SIC: 4941 Water supply

(P-6291)
OAKDALE IRRGTION DST FING CORP
1205 E F St, Oakdale (95361-4112)
PHONE....................209 847-0341
Alfred Bairos, *President*
Kathy Cook, *CFO*
Steve Knell, *Exec Dir*
▲ EMP: 69 EST: 1909
SQ FT: 5,000
SALES: 2.7MM **Privately Held**
WEB: www.oakdaleirrigation.com
SIC: 4941 Water supply

(P-6292)
OLIVENHAIN MUNICIPAL WATER DST
1966 Olivenhain Rd, Encinitas
(92024-5676)
PHONE....................760 753-6466
Edmund Sprague, *President*
Mark A Muir, *Treasurer*
Robert F Topolavac, *Vice Pres*
Ken Thorner, *General Mgr*
Kimberly A Thorner, *General Mgr*
EMP: 79
SQ FT: 11,000
SALES: 52.1MM **Privately Held**
SIC: 4941 4971 Water supply; impounding reservoir, irrigation

(P-6293)
OTAY WATER DISTRICT
2554 Swetwater Sprng Blvd, Spring Valley
(91978-2096)
PHONE....................619 670-2222
Gary Croucher, *President*
Jose Lopez, *President*
Joe Beachem, *CFO*
Joseph R Beachem, *CFO*
David Gonzalez, *Vice Pres*
EMP: 170 EST: 1956
SQ FT: 6,000
SALES: 88.4MM **Privately Held**
WEB: www.otaywater.gov
SIC: 4941 1623 Water supply; water, sewer & utility lines

(P-6294)
PADRE DAM MUNICIPAL WATER DST (PA)
9300 Fanita Pkwy, Santee (92071-7906)
P.O. Box 719003 (92072-9003)
PHONE....................619 258-4617
Allen Carlisle, *CEO*
William Pommering, *President*
Karen Jassoy, *CFO*
Doug Wilson, *Treasurer*
August Caires, *Vice Pres*
EMP: 63
SQ FT: 10,000
SALES: 67.3MM **Privately Held**
WEB: www.padredam.org
SIC: 4941 4952 7033 Water supply; sewerage systems; campgrounds

(P-6295)
PALMDALE WATER DISTRICT
2029 E Avenue Q, Palmdale (93550-4050)
PHONE....................661 947-4111
Michael Williams, *CFO*
EMP: 93
SALES: 22.5MM **Privately Held**
SIC: 4941 Water supply

(P-6296)
RAINBOW MUNICIPAL WATER DST
3707 Old Highway 395, Fallbrook
(92028-9372)
PHONE....................760 728-1178
Dave Seymour, *General Mgr*
Tom Kennedy, *General Mgr*
EMP: 50
SALES: 22MM **Privately Held**
SIC: 4941 Water supply

(P-6297)
RANCHO CALIFORNIA WATER DST (PA)
Also Called: Rcwd
42135 Winchester Rd, Temecula
(92590-4800)
P.O. Box 9017 (92589-9017)
PHONE....................951 296-6900
William E Plummer, *Vice Pres*
Stephen J Corona, *President*
Ralph Daily, *President*
Bennet Drake, *President*
Jeff Armstrong, *CFO*
EMP: 145
SQ FT: 71,000
SALES: 69MM **Privately Held**
WEB: www.ranchowater.com
SIC: 4941 Water supply

(P-6298)
SACRAMENTO COUNTY WATER AGENCY
Also Called: Scwa
827 7th St Ste 301, Sacramento
(95814-2406)
PHONE....................916 874-6851
Susan Purdin, *Principal*
William Konigsmark, *Principal*
EMP: 99
SALES (est): 5.4MM **Privately Held**
SIC: 4941 Water supply
PA: County Of Sacramento
700 H St Ste 7650
Sacramento CA 95814
916 874-5544

(P-6299)
SACRAMENTO SUBURBAN WATER DST
3701 Marconi Ave Ste 100, Sacramento
(95821-5346)
PHONE....................916 972-7171
Robert Roscoe, *General Mgr*
Annette Oleary, *Principal*
Jerry Ness, *Personnel*
EMP: 60 EST: 1958
SQ FT: 13,500
SALES: 44.1MM **Privately Held**
SIC: 4941 Water supply

(P-6300)
SACRAMENTO SUBURBAN WATER DST
3701 Marconi Ave Ste 100, Sacramento
(95821-5346)
PHONE....................916 972-7171
Robert Rosco, *General Mgr*
Roy Kimura, *Principal*
Robert Roscoe, *General Mgr*
Ken Gebert, *Technology*
Wayne Scherffius, *Technology*
EMP: 52
SALES: 41.8MM **Privately Held**
WEB: www.sswd.org
SIC: 4941 Water supply

(P-6301)
SAN DIEGO COUNTY WATER AUTH (PA)
4677 Overland Ave, San Diego
(92123-1233)
PHONE....................858 522-6600
Maureen Stapleton, *General Mgr*
Eric Sandler, *CFO*
Mark Muir, *Chairman*
Mike Lee, *Officer*
Stephen Lee, *Officer*
▲ EMP: 280
SQ FT: 26,000
SALES (est): 44.4MM **Privately Held**
SIC: 4941 Water supply

PRODUCTS & SVCS

(P-6302)
SAN DIEGO COUNTY WATER AUTH
610 W 5th Ave, Escondido (92025-4093)
PHONE..............................760 480-1991
Brendan Sheehan, *President*
EMP: 70
SALES (corp-wide): 44.4MM **Privately Held**
SIC: 4941 Water supply
PA: San Diego County Water Authority
4677 Overland Ave
San Diego CA 92123
858 522-6600

(P-6303)
SAN GABRIEL VALLEY WATER ASSN
725 N Azusa Ave, Azusa (91702-2528)
PHONE..............................626 815-1305
Carol Williams, *Principal*
EMP: 100
SALES: 181.7K **Privately Held**
SIC: 4941 Water supply

(P-6304)
SAN GABRIEL VALLEY WATER CO (PA)
Also Called: Fontana Water Company
11142 Garvey Ave, El Monte (91733-2498)
P.O. Box 6010 (91734-2010)
PHONE..............................626 448-6183
R H Nicholson Jr, *Ch of Bd*
Michael L Whitehead, *President*
David Batt, *Treasurer*
Robert Diprimio, *Senior VP*
Frank A Lo Guidice, *Vice Pres*
EMP: 125 **EST:** 1936
SQ FT: 30,000
SALES (est): 133.3MM **Privately Held**
WEB: www.fontanawater.com
SIC: 4941 Water supply

(P-6305)
SAN GABRIEL VALLEY WATER CO
8440 Nuevo Ave, Fontana (92335-3824)
P.O. Box 987 (92334-0987)
PHONE..............................909 822-2201
Mike McGraw, *Manager*
EMP: 76
SQ FT: 2,727
SALES (corp-wide): 133.3MM **Privately Held**
WEB: www.fontanawater.com
SIC: 4941 Water supply
PA: San Gabriel Valley Water Co.
11142 Garvey Ave
El Monte CA 91733
626 448-6183

(P-6306)
SAN JOSE WATER COMPANY (HQ)
Also Called: S J W
110 W Taylor St, San Jose (95110-2131)
PHONE..............................408 288-5314
W Richard Roth, *CEO*
Charles Toeniskoetter, *Ch of Bd*
Angela Yip, *CFO*
Sandy Freeman, *Officer*
Richard Balocco, *Vice Pres*
EMP: 140
SQ FT: 5,000
SALES: 366.8MM
SALES (corp-wide): 389.2MM **Publicly Held**
SIC: 4941 Water supply
PA: Sjw Group
110 W Taylor St
San Jose CA 95110
408 279-7800

(P-6307)
SAN JOSE WATER COMPANY
1221 S Bascom Ave, San Jose (95128-3514)
PHONE..............................408 298-0364
Paul Schreiber, *Manager*
EMP: 180
SALES (corp-wide): 389.2MM **Publicly Held**
SIC: 4941 Water supply

HQ: San Jose Water Company
110 W Taylor St
San Jose CA 95110
408 288-5314

(P-6308)
SANTA CLARA VALLEY WATER (PA)
5750 Almaden Expy, San Jose (95118-3614)
P.O. Box 20670 (95160-0670)
PHONE..............................408 265-2600
Beau Goldie, *CEO*
Norma Camacho, *COO*
Katherine Oven, *Officer*
Melanie Richardson, *Officer*
Meenakshi Ganjoo, *Executive*
▲ **EMP:** 850 **EST:** 1951
SQ FT: 40,780
SALES: 144.6MM **Privately Held**
WEB: www.valleywater.org
SIC: 4941 Water supply

(P-6309)
SANTA CLARA VALLEY WATER
400 More Ave, Los Gatos (95032-1111)
PHONE..............................408 395-8121
Greg Gibson, *Branch Mgr*
EMP: 70
SALES (corp-wide): 144.6MM **Privately Held**
WEB: www.valleywater.org
SIC: 4941 Water supply
PA: Santa Clara Valley Water District Public Facilities Financing Corporation
5750 Almaden Expy
San Jose CA 95118
408 265-2600

(P-6310)
SANTA MARGARITA WATER DISTRICT (PA)
26111 Antonio Pkwy, Rcho STA Marg (92688-5596)
P.O. Box 7005, Mission Viejo (92690-7005)
PHONE..............................949 459-6400
Daniel R Ferons, *Manager*
Cindy Lane, *Admin Asst*
Dustin Navarro, *Info Tech Mgr*
Pilar Yager, *Technician*
Joann Morishita, *Accountant*
EMP: 70 **EST:** 1964
SQ FT: 5,600
SALES: 60MM **Privately Held**
WEB: www.smwd.com
SIC: 4941 4952 Water supply; sewerage systems

(P-6311)
SANTA MARGARITA WATER DISTRICT
26101 Antonio Pkwy, Rcho STA Marg (92688-5505)
P.O. Box 7005, Mission Viejo (92690-7005)
PHONE..............................949 459-6400
Daniel Ferns, *Manager*
Kelly Radvansky, *Chief Engr*
Jim Leach, *Director*
Nicole Stanfield, *Manager*
EMP: 135
SALES (corp-wide): 60MM **Privately Held**
WEB: www.smwd.com
SIC: 4941 4952 Water supply; sewerage systems
PA: Santa Margarita Water District
26111 Antonio Pkwy
Rcho Sta Marg CA 92688
949 459-6400

(P-6312)
SJW GROUP (PA)
110 W Taylor St, San Jose (95110-2131)
PHONE..............................408 279-7800
Eric W Thornburg, *Ch of Bd*
James P Lynch, *CFO*
Suzy Papazian, *Admin Sec*
Wendy Avila-Walker, *Controller*
EMP: 357
SALES: 389.2MM **Publicly Held**
WEB: www.sjwater.com
SIC: 4941 6531 Water supply; real estate agent, commercial

(P-6313)
SONOMA COUNTY WATER AGENCY
404 Aviation Blvd Ste 0, Santa Rosa (95403-9019)
PHONE..............................707 526-5370
Grant Davis, *General Mgr*
Ann Dubay, *Executive*
George Lincoln, *Project Mgr*
James Jasperse, *Enginr/R&D Mgr*
Kyle Evans, *Engineer*
EMP: 200 **EST:** 1950
SQ FT: 57,000
SALES: 40.4MM **Privately Held**
SIC: 4941 Water supply

(P-6314)
SOUTH COAST WATER DISTRICT (PA)
Also Called: SCWD
31592 West St, Laguna Beach (92651-6907)
P.O. Box 30205, Laguna Niguel (92607-0205)
PHONE..............................949 499-4555
Wayne Rayfield, *President*
Michele Collins, *Officer*
Rober Moore, *Vice Pres*
Andrew Brunhart, *General Mgr*
Betty Burnett, *General Mgr*
EMP: 100
SQ FT: 8,400
SALES: 28.4MM **Privately Held**
WEB: www.scwd.org
SIC: 4941 1629 Water supply; waste water & sewage treatment plant construction

(P-6315)
SWEETWATER AUTHORITY (PA)
505 Garrett Ave, Chula Vista (91910-5584)
P.O. Box 2328 (91912-2328)
PHONE..............................619 422-8395
Mark Rogers, *Exec Dir*
Margaret C Welsh, *President*
Andrew Reitzel, *Treasurer*
Ron Morrison, *Vice Pres*
W D Pocklington, *Vice Pres*
EMP: 132
SQ FT: 11,000
SALES: 53.4MM **Privately Held**
SIC: 4941 Water supply

(P-6316)
TUOLUMNE UTILITIES DISTRICT
Also Called: T U D
18885 Nugget Blvd, Sonora (95370-9284)
PHONE..............................209 532-5536
Pet Kampa, *General Mgr*
Erik Johnson, *Engineer*
Glen Nunnelley, *Engineer*
Steve Sheffield, *Finance Dir*
Elaine Wolfgang, *Finance*
EMP: 80
SQ FT: 6,000
SALES (est): 18MM **Privately Held**
WEB: www.tuolumneutilities.com
SIC: 4941 4952 Water supply; sewerage systems

(P-6317)
VALLEY CENTER MUNICIPAL
29300 Valley Center Rd, Valley Center (92082-6207)
P.O. Box 67 (92082-0067)
PHONE..............................760 735-4500
Gary Broomell, *President*
Bill Jeffrey, *CFO*
Robert A Polito, *Vice Pres*
Gary Arant, *General Mgr*
Kathy Stetson, *Admin Sec*
EMP: 69
SQ FT: 40,000
SALES (est): 19.3MM **Privately Held**
SIC: 4941 Water supply

(P-6318)
WALNUT VALLEY WATER DISTRICT
271 Brea Canyon Rd, Walnut (91789-3002)
P.O. Box 508 (91788-0508)
PHONE..............................909 595-7554
Theodore Ebenkamp, *President*
Scarlet Kwong, *Vice Pres*

Edwin Hilden, *Principal*
Michael Holmes, *General Mgr*
Barbara Herrara, *Director*
EMP: 55
SQ FT: 7,900
SALES: 34.9MM **Privately Held**
WEB: www.wvwd.com
SIC: 4941 Water supply

(P-6319)
YUCAIPA VALLEY WATER DISTRICT (PA)
12770 2nd St, Yucaipa (92399-5670)
P.O. Box 730 (92399-0730)
PHONE..............................909 797-5117
Bruce Granlund, *President*
Joan Cadiz, *Purch Agent*
Bob Wall, *Opers Mgr*
EMP: 56
SQ FT: 2,500
SALES: 20.4MM **Privately Held**
SIC: 4941 Water supply

4952 Sewerage Systems

(P-6320)
BIG BEAR CITY CMNTY SVCS DST (PA)
Also Called: Bbccsd
139 E Big Bear Blvd, Big Bear City (92314-9130)
P.O. Box 558 (92314-0558)
PHONE..............................909 585-2565
Scott Heule, *General Mgr*
EMP: 63
SQ FT: 7,000
SALES (est): 9.4MM **Privately Held**
WEB: www.bbccsd.org
SIC: 4952 4941 4953 Sewerage systems; water supply; garbage: collecting, destroying & processing

(P-6321)
CENTRAL CONTRA COSTA SANIT
5019 Imhoff Pl, Martinez (94553-4316)
PHONE..............................925 228-9500
Roger Bailey, *General Mgr*
Roy Ll, *IT/INT Sup*
John Phillips, *Network Analyst*
William Grant, *Engineer*
Nathan Hodges, *Engineer*
EMP: 99
SQ FT: 40,000
SALES (est): 26.6MM **Privately Held**
SIC: 4952 Sewerage systems

(P-6322)
ENCINA WASTEWATER AUTHORITY
Also Called: Encina Water Pollution Control
6200 Avenida Encinas, Carlsbad (92011-1009)
PHONE..............................760 438-3941
Kevinmhardy, *Principal*
Donald Little, *Vice Pres*
Kevin Hardy, *General Mgr*
Michael Steinlicht, *General Mgr*
Paula Clowar, *Executive Asst*
EMP: 52
SQ FT: 30,000
SALES (est): 19.3MM **Privately Held**
WEB: www.encinajpa.com
SIC: 4952 Sewerage systems

(P-6323)
MONTEREY ONE WATER (PA)
Also Called: Mrwpca
5 Harris Ct Bldg D, Monterey (93940-5756)
PHONE..............................831 372-3367
Keith Israel, *General Mgr*
EMP: 80
SQ FT: 9,000
SALES: 26.7MM **Privately Held**
WEB: www.mrwpca.org
SIC: 4952 Sewerage systems

(P-6324)
NAPA SANITATION DISTRICT
1515 Soscol Ferry Rd, NAPA (94558-6247)
P.O. Box 2480 (94558-0522)
PHONE..............................707 254-9231
Tim Healy, *General Mgr*

Jeffery Tucker, *General Mgr*
Elsa Seal, *Admin Asst*
Gamble Holley, *Project Mgr*
Andrew Damron, *Engineer*
EMP: 50 **EST:** 1945
SQ FT: 3,600
SALES: 28.9MM **Privately Held**
WEB: www.napasanitationdistrict.com
SIC: 4952 Sewerage systems

(P-6325)
OCCIDENTAL CNTY SANITATION DST
404 Aviation Blvd, Santa Rosa
(95403-1069)
PHONE.....................707 547-1900
Grant Davis, *General Mgr*
Eric Wilhelm, *Info Tech Mgr*
Lynne Rosselli, *Accounts Mgr*
EMP: 99
SALES: 562.8K **Privately Held**
SIC: 4952 Sewerage systems

(P-6326)
ORANGE COUNTY SANITATION
22212 Brookhurst St, Huntington Beach
(92646-8406)
PHONE.....................714 962-2411
Blake Anderson, *Manager*
EMP: 200
SALES (est): 6.3MM
SALES (corp-wide): 315.4MM **Privately Held**
WEB: www.ocsd.com
SIC: 4952 Sewerage systems
PA: Orange County Sanitation District Financing Corporation
10844 Ellis Ave
Fountain Valley CA 92708
714 962-2411

(P-6327)
SACRAMENTO REG CO SANIT DIST
Sacramento Regional Waste
8521 Laguna Station Rd, Elk Grove
(95758-9550)
PHONE.....................916 875-9000
Ruben Robles, *Manager*
Jodie Sites, *Technician*
Chris Heikkila, *Technology*
Dean Wyley, *Engineer*
Verna Cimperman, *Human Res Mgr*
EMP: 500
SALES (est): 37.5MM
SALES (corp-wide): 95.9MM **Privately Held**
SIC: 4952 Sewerage systems
PA: Sacramento Regional County Sanitation District
10060 Goethe Rd
Sacramento CA 95827
916 876-6000

(P-6328)
SILICON VALLEY CLEAN WATER
Also Called: SBSA
1400 Radio Rd, Redwood City
(94065-1220)
PHONE.....................650 591-7121
Ronald W Shepherd, *Principal*
Daniel T Child, *Manager*
EMP: 79 **EST:** 1975
SQ FT: 180,000
SALES: 38.3MM **Privately Held**
WEB: www.sbsa.org
SIC: 4952 Sewerage systems

(P-6329)
SONOMA VLY CNTY SANITATION DST
404 Aviation Blvd, Santa Rosa
(95403-1069)
PHONE.....................707 547-1900
Grant Davis, *General Mgr*
Lynne Rosselli, *Accounting Mgr*
David Rabbitt, *Supervisor*
EMP: 200
SALES: 14.5MM **Privately Held**
SIC: 4952 Sewerage systems

(P-6330)
SOUTH TAHOE PUBLIC UTILITY DST
1275 Meadow Crest Dr, South Lake Tahoe
(96150-7401)
PHONE.....................530 544-6474
Richard Solbrig, *General Mgr*
Paul Hughes, *CFO*
Paul Sciuto, *Principal*
EMP: 113
SALES: 26.2MM **Privately Held**
WEB: www.stpud.dst.ca.us
SIC: 4952 4941 Sewerage systems; water supply

(P-6331)
STREET AND SEWER YARD CORP
Also Called: Public Work Dept
1361 N Carolan Ave, Burlingame
(94010-2401)
PHONE.....................650 696-7260
Rob Mallick, *Principal*
EMP: 50
SALES (est): 650.4K **Privately Held**
SIC: 4952 Sewerage systems

(P-6332)
TAHOE-TRUCKEE SANITATION AGCY
Also Called: TTSA
13720 Butterfield Dr, Truckee
(96161-3316)
PHONE.....................530 587-2525
Marcia Beals, *General Mgr*
Michael Peak, *Vice Pres*
Laura Mader, *Lab Dir*
Larue Griffin, *General Mgr*
Robert Gray, *Info Tech Mgr*
▲ **EMP:** 59 **EST:** 1972
SQ FT: 500,083
SALES: 12.4MM **Privately Held**
WEB: www.ttsa.net
SIC: 4952 Sewerage systems

(P-6333)
UNION SANITARY DISTRICT
Also Called: Usd
5072 Benson Rd, Union City (94587-2508)
P.O. Box 5050 (94587-8528)
PHONE.....................510 477-7500
Paul Eldredge, *Principal*
Manny Fernandez,
Tom Handley,
Pat Kite,
Anjali Lathi,
▲ **EMP:** 130
SALES: 51.9MM **Privately Held**
WEB: www.unionsanitary.com
SIC: 4952 Sewerage systems

(P-6334)
VALLEY CENTER MUNICPL WTR DST
29300 Valley Center Rd, Valley Center
(92082-6207)
PHONE.....................760 735-4500
Gary Broomell, *President*
Gary Arant, *General Mgr*
Wally Grabbe, *Engineer*
Jim Pugh, *Finance*
EMP: 64
SQ FT: 5,000
SALES (est): 492.5K **Privately Held**
SIC: 4952 4941 Sewerage systems; water supply

4953 Refuse Systems

(P-6335)
AER ELECTRONICS INC (PA)
Also Called: Aerelectronics
42744 Boscell Rd, Fremont (94538-5132)
PHONE.....................510 300-0500
Andre Weiglein, *President*
William Schoening, *CFO*
John Dickenson, *Vice Pres*
Janet Rianda, *Vice Pres*
James Quintal, *Admin Sec*
▲ **EMP:** 55
SQ FT: 75,000

SALES (est): 42.7MM **Privately Held**
WEB: www.aerworldwide.com
SIC: 4953 5093 Recycling, waste materials; scrap & waste materials

(P-6336)
ALAMEDA COUNTY INDUSTRIES INC
610 Aladdin Ave, San Leandro
(94577-4302)
PHONE.....................510 357-7282
Louis Pellegrini, *Exec VP*
Robert Molinaro, *CEO*
Kent Kenney, *CFO*
Mary Vigil, *Human Resources*
Teresa Montgomery, *Pub Rel Mgr*
EMP: 50
SQ FT: 39,648
SALES (est): 9.7MM **Privately Held**
WEB: www.alamedacountyindustries.com
SIC: 4953 Rubbish collection & disposal

(P-6337)
ALEMEDA COUNTY INDUSTRIES LLC
610 Aladdin Ave, San Leandro
(94577-4302)
PHONE.....................510 357-7282
Robert Molinaro,
EMP: 70 **EST:** 1999
SQ FT: 5,400
SALES (est): 5.7MM **Privately Held**
SIC: 4953 Refuse systems

(P-6338)
APPLIANCE RECYCLING CTRS AMER
Also Called: Arca Los Angeles
1920 S Acacia Ave, Compton (90220-4945)
PHONE.....................310 223-2800
Edward Cameron, *President*
EMP: 64
SQ FT: 40,000
SALES (est): 8.5MM
SALES (corp-wide): 41.5MM **Publicly Held**
WEB: www.arcainc.com
SIC: 4953 Recycling, waste materials
PA: Appliance Recycling Centers Of America, Inc.
175 Jackson Ave N Ste 102
Hopkins MN 55343
952 930-9000

(P-6339)
ARACO ENTERPRISES LLC
Also Called: Athens Environmental Services
9189 De Garmo Ave, Sun Valley
(91352-2609)
PHONE.....................818 767-0675
Ronald Krall,
Michael R Arakelian,
EMP: 400 **EST:** 2017
SALES (est): 2.5MM **Privately Held**
SIC: 4953 Garbage: collecting, destroying & processing

(P-6340)
ARAKELIAN ENTERPRISES INC
11121 Pendleton St, Sun Valley
(91352-1513)
PHONE.....................818 768-0689
Godjamanian Mego, *Branch Mgr*
EMP: 126
SQ FT: 4,904
SALES (corp-wide): 150MM **Privately Held**
SIC: 4953 Rubbish collection & disposal
PA: Arakelian Enterprises, Inc.
14048 Valley Blvd
City Of Industry CA 91746
626 336-3636

(P-6341)
ARAKELIAN ENTERPRISES INC
Also Called: Athens Services
15045 Salt Lake Ave, City of Industry
(91746-3315)
PHONE.....................626 336-3636
Ron Arakelian Jr, *Owner*
Steven Estrada, *Sales Staff*
David Miramontes, *Supervisor*
EMP: 314

SALES (corp-wide): 150MM **Privately Held**
SIC: 4953 Rubbish collection & disposal; street refuse systems
PA: Arakelian Enterprises, Inc.
14048 Valley Blvd
City Of Industry CA 91746
626 336-3636

(P-6342)
ARAKELIAN ENTERPRISES INC
687 Iowa Ave, Riverside (92507-1610)
PHONE.....................951 342-3300
Sal Orozco, *Manager*
EMP: 157
SALES (corp-wide): 150MM **Privately Held**
SIC: 4953 Recycling, waste materials; hazardous waste collection & disposal
PA: Arakelian Enterprises, Inc.
14048 Valley Blvd
City Of Industry CA 91746
626 336-3636

(P-6343)
ARAKELIAN ENTERPRISES INC
14048 Valley Blvd, La Puente
(91746-2801)
PHONE.....................818 768-1477
EMP: 94
SALES (corp-wide): 150MM **Privately Held**
SIC: 4953 Refuse systems
PA: Arakelian Enterprises, Inc.
14048 Valley Blvd
City Of Industry CA 91746
626 336-3636

(P-6344)
ARAKELIAN ENTERPRISES INC (PA)
Also Called: Athens Services
14048 Valley Blvd, City of Industry
(91746-2801)
P.O. Box 60009 (91716-0009)
PHONE.....................626 336-3636
Ron Arakelian Jr, *CEO*
Michael Arakelian, *CEO*
Gary Clifford, *COO*
Kevin Hanifin, *CFO*
Dennis Chiappetta, *Exec VP*
EMP: 121
SQ FT: 10,000
SALES (est): 150MM **Privately Held**
WEB: www.athensservices.com
SIC: 4953 Rubbish collection & disposal; street refuse systems

(P-6345)
ARROW DISPOSAL SERVICES INC
14332 Valley Blvd, La Puente
(91746-2931)
P.O. Box 2917 (91746-0917)
PHONE.....................626 336-2255
Kirk Tahmizian, *President*
EMP: 50
SQ FT: 40,000
SALES: 10MM **Privately Held**
SIC: 4953 Garbage: collecting, destroying & processing

(P-6346)
ASCON RECYCLE COMPANY
6500 E Avenue T, Littlerock (93543-1722)
PHONE.....................661 533-0154
Chris Giampietro, *Manager*
EMP: 50
SALES (est): 756.6K **Privately Held**
SIC: 4953 Recycling, waste materials

(P-6347)
ASCON RECYCLING CO
17671 Bear Valley Rd, Hesperia
(92345-4902)
PHONE.....................760 948-1538
John Hove, *President*
EMP: 250
SALES (est): 5.3MM **Privately Held**
SIC: 4953 Recycling, waste materials

PRODUCTS & SVCS

(P-6348)
ATHENS DISPOSAL COMPANY INC (PA)
14048 Valley Blvd, La Puente (91746-2801)
P.O. Box 60009, City of Industry (91716-0009)
PHONE...................626 336-3636
Ron Arakelian Sr, *President*
Ron Arakelian Jr, *Vice Pres*
David Patterson, *CIO*
Evelyn Cornejo, *Cust Mgr*
EMP: 350
SALES (est): 261.4MM **Privately Held**
SIC: 4953 Rubbish collection & disposal

(P-6349)
ATLAS DISPOSAL INDUSTRIES LLC
3000 Power Inn Rd, Sacramento (95826-3801)
PHONE...................916 455-2800
Dave Sikich, *CEO*
Nick Sikich, *COO*
Steven Bruce, *Vice Pres*
Sean Moen, *General Mgr*
Natalie Peebles, *Info Tech Mgr*
EMP: 70
SALES (est): 18.7MM **Privately Held**
WEB: www.atlasdisposal.com
SIC: 4953 Garbage: collecting, destroying & processing; refuse collection & disposal services

(P-6350)
AUBURN PLACER DISPOSAL SERVICE
Also Called: Auburn-Placer Recycling Center
12305 Shale Ridge Ln, Auburn (95602-8879)
P.O. Box 6566 (95604-6566)
PHONE...................530 885-3735
Michael Sangiacomo, *President*
Mark Lomele, *Vice Pres*
EMP: 80
SQ FT: 2,200
SALES (est): 7.4MM
SALES (corp-wide): 1.3B **Privately Held**
WEB: www.auburnplacer.com
SIC: 4953 Recycling, waste materials
PA: Recology Inc.
　50 California St Ste 2400
　San Francisco CA 94111
　415 875-1000

(P-6351)
BAY COUNTIES WASTE SVCS INC
Also Called: Specialty Solid Waste & Recycl
3355 Thomas Rd, Santa Clara (95054-2060)
PHONE...................408 565-9900
Robert J Molinaro, *CEO*
William Dobert, *CFO*
Douglas Button, *Treasurer*
Jerry Nabhan, *Admin Sec*
▲ EMP: 80 EST: 1930
SQ FT: 2,000
SALES (est): 19.5MM **Privately Held**
WEB: www.sswr.com
SIC: 4953 Rubbish collection & disposal

(P-6352)
BERTOLOTTIS CERES DISPOSAL
231 Flamingo Rd, Ceres (95307)
P.O. Box 127 (95307-0127)
PHONE...................209 537-8000
Bert Bertolotti, *President*
Steve Holloway, *General Mgr*
EMP: 74
SALES (est): 7.3MM **Privately Held**
SIC: 4953 Refuse collection & disposal services

(P-6353)
BEST WAY DISPOSAL CO INC
Also Called: Advance Disposal Company
17105 Mesa St, Hesperia (92345-5155)
P.O. Box 400997 (92340-0997)
PHONE...................760 244-9773
Robert Bath, *Ch of Bd*
Sheila Bath, *President*
Annie Hopkins, *Controller*
EMP: 56

SALES (est): 15.2MM **Privately Held**
WEB: www.advancedisposal.com
SIC: 4953 Rubbish collection & disposal

(P-6354)
BFI WASTE SERVICES LLC
5501 N Golden State Blvd, Fresno (93722-5021)
PHONE...................559 275-1551
Keith Hester, *General Mgr*
EMP: 70
SALES (corp-wide): 10B **Publicly Held**
WEB: www.sunsetwaste.com
SIC: 4953 Refuse systems
HQ: Bfi Waste Services, Llc
　18500 N Allied Way # 100
　Phoenix AZ 85054
　480 627-2700

(P-6355)
BFI WASTE SYSTEMS N AMER INC
Also Called: Site 910
800 Cacique St, Santa Barbara (93103-3622)
P.O. Box 4010 (93140-4010)
PHONE...................805 965-5248
Darryl Reno, *General Mgr*
EMP: 82
SALES (corp-wide): 10B **Publicly Held**
WEB: www.mjes.com
SIC: 4953 Garbage: collecting, destroying & processing; street refuse systems
HQ: Bfi Waste Systems Of North America, Inc.
　2394 E Camelback Rd
　Phoenix AZ 85016

(P-6356)
BFI WASTE SYSTEMS N AMER INC
Also Called: Republic Services
271 Rianda St, Salinas (93901-3725)
PHONE...................831 775-3850
Doug Kenyon, *Manager*
EMP: 54
SALES (corp-wide): 10B **Publicly Held**
WEB: www.mjes.com
SIC: 4953 Garbage: collecting, destroying & processing
HQ: Bfi Waste Systems Of North America, Inc.
　2394 E Camelback Rd
　Phoenix AZ 85016

(P-6357)
BFI WASTE SYSTEMS N AMER INC
Also Called: Site 916
42600 Boyce Rd, Fremont (94538-3131)
P.O. Box 5013 (94537-5013)
PHONE...................510 657-1350
Fred Penning, *Manager*
Pam Enriquez, *General Mgr*
EMP: 95
SALES (corp-wide): 10B **Publicly Held**
WEB: www.mjes.com
SIC: 4953 4212 Refuse collection & disposal services; local trucking, without storage
HQ: Bfi Waste Systems Of North America, Inc.
　2394 E Camelback Rd
　Phoenix AZ 85016

(P-6358)
BISHOP WASTE DISPOSAL INC
100 Snland Reservation Rd, Bishop (93514)
PHONE...................760 872-6561
George Kelley, *President*
EMP: 50
SQ FT: 7,300
SALES (est): 3.7MM **Privately Held**
SIC: 4953 4952 Garbage: collecting, destroying & processing; sewerage systems

(P-6359)
BKK CORPORATION (PA)
2210 S Azusa Ave, West Covina (91792-1510)
PHONE...................626 965-0911

Fax: 626 965-9569
EMP: 57
SALES (est): 22.2MM **Privately Held**
SIC: 4953 Sanitary landfill operation

(P-6360)
BROWNING-FERRIS INDUSTRIES INC
Solid Waste Division
9200 Glenoaks Blvd, Sun Valley (91352-2613)
PHONE...................818 790-5410
Pat Gavin, *Manager*
EMP: 140
SALES (corp-wide): 10B **Publicly Held**
SIC: 4953 Rubbish collection & disposal
HQ: Browning-Ferris Industries, Llc
　18500 N Allied Way # 100
　Phoenix AZ 85054
　480 627-2700

(P-6361)
BROWNING-FERRIS INDUSTRIES LLC
Also Called: Site R45
1601 Dixon Landing Rd, Milpitas (95035-8100)
PHONE...................408 262-1401
Gil Cheso, *Manager*
EMP: 65
SALES (corp-wide): 10B **Publicly Held**
WEB: www.alliedwaste.com
SIC: 4953 Refuse collection & disposal services
HQ: Browning-Ferris Industries, Llc
　18500 N Allied Way # 100
　Phoenix AZ 85054
　480 627-2700

(P-6362)
BURRTEC WASTE INDUSTRIES INC (HQ)
9890 Cherry Ave, Fontana (92335-5298)
PHONE...................909 429-4200
Cole Burr, *President*
Eric Herbert, *Vice Pres*
Trevor Scrogins, *Vice Pres*
Nick Burciaga, *Division Mgr*
Michael Rhodes, *Division Mgr*
▲ EMP: 150
SQ FT: 10,000
SALES (est): 305.6MM
SALES (corp-wide): 309.8MM **Privately Held**
WEB: www.burrtec.com
SIC: 4953 4212 Rubbish collection & disposal; recycling, waste materials; local trucking, without storage
PA: Burrtec Waste Group, Inc.
　9890 Cherry Ave
　Fontana CA 92335
　909 429-4200

(P-6363)
CACTUS RECYCLING INC (PA)
8710 Avenida Fuente, San Diego (92154)
PHONE...................619 661-1283
Edward M Fitch III, *President*
Richard Russell, *Vice Pres*
Steve Russell, *Vice Pres*
Steven Russell, *Vice Pres*
Luis Prado, *Accountant*
EMP: 125
SQ FT: 4,000
SALES (est): 13.8MM **Privately Held**
WEB: www.cactusrecycling.com
SIC: 4953 Recycling, waste materials

(P-6364)
CALIFORNIA MARINE CLEANING INC (PA)
2049 Main St, San Diego (92113-2216)
P.O. Box 13653 (92170-3653)
PHONE...................619 231-8788
Matthew R Carr, *President*
Hazel Carr, *CFO*
Kristen Sosa, *Purchasing*
EMP: 160
SQ FT: 10,000
SALES (est): 25.7MM **Privately Held**
WEB: www.calmarineinc.com
SIC: 4953 Hazardous waste collection & disposal

(P-6365)
CALIFORNIA WASTE SERVICES LLC
621 W 152nd St, Gardena (90247-2732)
PHONE...................310 538-5998
Eric Casper, *President*
Oscar Cruel, *Accounting Mgr*
Ricardo Vallejo, *Human Resources*
Giovanni Lopez, *Opers Mgr*
EMP: 120
SQ FT: 20,000
SALES (est): 27.5MM **Privately Held**
WEB: www.californiawasteservices.com
SIC: 4953 Refuse collection & disposal services

(P-6366)
CALIFORNIA WASTE SOLUTIONS INC
1820 10th St, Oakland (94607-1450)
PHONE...................408 292-0830
David Duong, *President*
EMP: 75 **Privately Held**
WEB: www.calwaste.com
SIC: 4953 Garbage: collecting, destroying & processing
PA: California Waste Solutions Inc.
　1005 Timothy Dr
　San Jose CA 95133

(P-6367)
CALIFORNIA WASTE SOLUTIONS INC (PA)
1005 Timothy Dr, San Jose (95133-1043)
PHONE...................510 832-8111
David Duong, *CEO*
Victor Duong, *Vice Pres*
Kristina Duong, *Exec Dir*
Linda Duong, *Admin Sec*
Sherri Ornelas, *Admin Asst*
◆ EMP: 87
SQ FT: 120,000
SALES (est): 33.7MM **Privately Held**
WEB: www.calwaste.com
SIC: 4953 Garbage: collecting, destroying & processing

(P-6368)
CALMET INC (PA)
Also Called: Metropolitan Waste Disposal
7202 Petterson Ln, Paramount (90723-2022)
PHONE...................323 721-8120
Thomas K Blackman, *President*
Gary Kazarian, *Treasurer*
William Kalpakoff, *Vice Pres*
Art Kazarian, *Vice Pres*
Kris Kazarian, *Admin Sec*
EMP: 180
SQ FT: 38,000
SALES (est): 44.8MM **Privately Held**
WEB: www.calmet.com
SIC: 4953 4212 Rubbish collection & disposal; recycling, waste materials; local trucking, without storage

(P-6369)
CARAUSTAR INDUSTRIES INC
Newark Recovery & Recycling
2800 W March Ln Ste 480, Stockton (95219-8220)
PHONE...................209 476-7710
Crawford Carpenter, *Manager*
EMP: 120
SALES (corp-wide): 1.7B **Privately Held**
SIC: 4953 Recycling, waste materials
PA: Caraustar Industries, Inc.
　5000 Astell Pwdr Sprng Rd
　Austell GA 30106
　770 948-3101

(P-6370)
CASTLE & COOKE CALIFORNIA INC
10000 Stockdale Hwy # 300, Bakersfield (93311-3604)
P.O. Box 11165 (93389-1165)
PHONE...................661 664-6500
Bruce Freeman, *President*
Edward C Roohan, *Treasurer*
Bruce Davis, *Vice Pres*
Takashi Fujii, *Vice Pres*
Robert W Hibbs, *Vice Pres*
EMP: 50

SALES (est): 6.6MM
SALES (corp-wide): 911.7MM Privately Held
WEB: www.sevenoaksrealestate.com
SIC: 4953 Sanitary landfill operation
PA: Castle & Cooke, Inc.
1 Dole Dr
Westlake Village CA 91362
310 374-3952

(P-6371)
CEDARWOOD-YOUNG COMPANY (PA)
Also Called: Allan Company
14620 Joanbridge St, Baldwin Park (91706-1750)
PHONE...........................626 962-4047
Jason Young, *President*
Michael Ochniak, *CFO*
Stephen Young, *Chairman*
Francisco Del Rincon, *Vice Pres*
Yun Koo, *Vice Pres*
◆ EMP: 175
SQ FT: 4,350
SALES: 299.9MM Privately Held
WEB: www.allancompany.com
SIC: 4953 Recycling, waste materials

(P-6372)
CHEMICAL WASTE MANAGEMENT INC
35251 Old Skyline Rd, Kettleman City (93239)
PHONE...........................559 386-9711
Robert Henry, *Manager*
EMP: 80
SQ FT: 5,000
SALES (corp-wide): 14.4B Publicly Held
WEB: www.wastemanagement.com
SIC: 4953 Non-hazardous waste disposal sites
HQ: Chemical Waste Management, Inc.
1001 Fannin St Ste 4000
Houston TX 77002
713 512-6200

(P-6373)
CHINO VALLEY SAWDUST INC
Also Called: Chino Valley Rock
13434 S Ontario Ave, Ontario (91761-7956)
PHONE...........................909 947-5983
Brigiette Delaura, *President*
Mary W Hebb, *Treasurer*
EMP: 75
SALES (est): 3.5MM Privately Held
SIC: 4953 Recycling, waste materials

(P-6374)
CITY OF INDUSTRY DISPOSAL CO
17445 Railroad St, City of Industry (91748-1026)
PHONE...........................626 336-5439
Manuel Perez, *Partner*
Chris Perez, *Manager*
EMP: 50
SALES (est): 2.1MM Privately Held
SIC: 4953 Recycling, waste materials

(P-6375)
CITY OF LEMOORE
Also Called: Refuse Department
711 W Cinnamon Dr, Lemoore (93245-9142)
PHONE...........................559 924-6744
David Wlaschin, *Director*
EMP: 50 Privately Held
SIC: 4953 Refuse systems
PA: City Of Lemoore
119 Fox St
Lemoore CA 93245
559 924-6700

(P-6376)
CITY OF POMONA
Also Called: Pomona City Refuse Collection
636 W Monterey Ave, Pomona (91768-3527)
PHONE...........................909 620-2361
Henry Pepper, *Manager*
EMP: 132 Privately Held
SIC: 4953 Refuse collection & disposal services

PA: Pomona, City Of (Inc)
585 E Holt Ave
Pomona CA 91767
909 620-2051

(P-6377)
CITY OF REDLANDS
Also Called: Purchasing Department
35 Cajon St, Redlands (92373-4746)
PHONE...........................909 798-7525
Gary Vendorst, *Manager*
EMP: 50 Privately Held
WEB: www.akspl.org
SIC: 4953 Refuse collection & disposal services
PA: City Of Redlands
35 Cajon St
Redlands CA 92373
909 798-7531

(P-6378)
CITY OF TULARE
3981 S K St, Tulare (93274-7189)
PHONE...........................559 684-4200
Kevin Northcraft, *Manager*
EMP: 60 Privately Held
WEB: www.ci.tulare.ca.us
SIC: 4953 Refuse collection & disposal services
PA: City Of Tulare
411 E Kern Ave
Tulare CA 93274
559 685-2300

(P-6379)
CIVICORPS
6315 San Leandro St, Oakland (94621-3727)
PHONE...........................510 992-7800
Bill Zenoni, *Branch Mgr*
EMP: 184
SALES (corp-wide): 7.8MM Privately Held
SIC: 4953 Recycling, waste materials
PA: Civicorps
101 Myrtle St
Oakland CA 94607
510 992-7800

(P-6380)
CLEAN HARBORS ENVMTL SVCS INC
4101 Industrial Way, Benicia (94510-1211)
PHONE...........................707 747-6699
Kevin Carnahan, *President*
EMP: 100
SALES (corp-wide): 2.9B Publicly Held
SIC: 4953 Hazardous waste collection & disposal
HQ: Clean Harbors Environmental Services, Inc.
42 Longwater Dr
Norwell MA 02061
781 792-5000

(P-6381)
COAST WASTE MANAGEMENT
5960 El Camino Real, Carlsbad (92008-8802)
P.O. Box 947 (92018-0947)
PHONE...........................760 753-9412
Arie De Jong, *Director*
Conrad B Pawelski, *President*
Margaret Bierd, *Admin Sec*
Arie D Jong, *Director*
EMP: 180
SQ FT: 3,000
SALES (est): 62.9MM
SALES (corp-wide): 14.4B Publicly Held
SIC: 4953 Rubbish collection & disposal
PA: Waste Management, Inc.
1001 Fannin St Ste 4000
Houston TX 77002
713 512-6200

(P-6382)
CONTAIN-A-WAY INC
Also Called: 20/20 Recycle Centers
25837 Bus Ctr Dr Ste F, Redlands (92374)
PHONE...........................909 796-2860
Keith Harradence, *CEO*
John Ferrari, *Senior VP*
Jackie Brinlee, *Finance Dir*
EMP: 450
SQ FT: 30,000

SALES (est): 19.8MM Privately Held
WEB: www.nexcycle.com
SIC: 4953 4212 Recycling, waste materials; local trucking, without storage
PA: Nexcycle, Inc.
5221 N O Connor Blvd # 850
Irving TX 75039

(P-6383)
CORRIDOR RECYCLING INC
22500 S Alameda St, Long Beach (90810-1905)
PHONE...........................310 835-3849
Gilbert Dodson, *President*
Steve Young, *Vice Pres*
Mark Tranckino, *CPA*
▲ EMP: 52
SQ FT: 13,594
SALES (est): 10.1MM Privately Held
WEB: www.corridorrecycling.com
SIC: 4953 5941 5093 Recycling, waste materials; sporting goods & bicycle shops; metal scrap & waste materials

(P-6384)
COUNTY OF EL DORADO
Also Called: Waste Connections
3940 Hwy 49, Diamond Springs (95619)
PHONE...........................530 626-4141
Sue Farris, *Manager*
EMP: 93 Privately Held
WEB: www.filmtahoe.com
SIC: 4953 Garbage: collecting, destroying & processing
PA: County Of El Dorado
330 Fair Ln
Placerville CA 95667
530 621-5830

(P-6385)
COUNTY OF ORANGE
Also Called: Oc Waste & Recycling
300 N Sunflower Ste 400, Santa Ana (92703)
PHONE...........................714 834-4000
Mike Giancola, *Manager*
EMP: 350 Privately Held
SIC: 4953 Recycling, waste materials
PA: County Of Orange
333 W Santa Ana Blvd 3f
Santa Ana CA 92701
714 834-6200

(P-6386)
COUNTY SANTTN DIST 2 OF LA CO
Also Called: Puente Hills Landfill
2800 Workman Mill Rd, Whittier (90601-1548)
P.O. Box 4998 (90607-4998)
PHONE...........................562 699-5204
Grace Han, *Chief*
Loraine De La Torre, *Admin Sec*
Pete Corral, *Technician*
Howard Wolfer, *Technical Staff*
Gary Henson, *Manager*
EMP: 100
SALES (corp-wide): 1.1B Privately Held
SIC: 4953 9511 Sanitary landfill operation;
PA: County Sanitation District No. 2 Of Los Angeles County
1955 Workman Mill Rd
Whittier CA 90601
562 699-7411

(P-6387)
CROWN DISPOSAL COMPANY INC
Also Called: Coastal Rubbish
9189 De Garmo Ave, Sun Valley (91352-2609)
P.O. Box 1063 (91353-1063)
PHONE...........................818 767-0675
Thomas H Fry, *CEO*
John Richardson, *Treasurer*
EMP: 200
SQ FT: 12,000
SALES (est): 42.3MM Privately Held
WEB: www.crowndisposal.com
SIC: 4953 Rubbish collection & disposal

(P-6388)
DESERT RECYCLING INC
17105 Mesa St, Hesperia (92345-5155)
P.O. Box 400725 (92340-0725)
PHONE...........................760 948-3122
Sheila Bath, *President*
EMP: 50
SALES (est): 2MM Privately Held
SIC: 4953 5093 Recycling, waste materials; metal scrap & waste materials

(P-6389)
E J HARRISON & SONS INC
Also Called: Harrison, E J & Sons Recycling
1589 Lirio Ave, Ventura (93004-3227)
PHONE...........................805 647-1414
Ken Keys, *General Mgr*
David Tripp, *Data Proc Staff*
Fred Lopez, *Marketing Staff*
EMP: 175
SALES (est): 4.8MM
SALES (corp-wide): 82.4MM Privately Held
WEB: www.ejharrison.com
SIC: 4953 2611 Rubbish collection & disposal; pulp mills
PA: E. J. Harrison & Sons, Inc.
5275 Colt St
Ventura CA 93003
805 647-1414

(P-6390)
EARTH TECHNOLOGY CORP USA
1999 Avenue Of, Los Angeles (90067)
PHONE...........................213 593-8000
Michael S Burke, *Ch of Bd*
Phil Watts, *Vice Pres*
EMP: 4655
SALES (est): 673K
SALES (corp-wide): 20.1B Publicly Held
SIC: 4953 8748 8742 8711 Refuse systems; environmental consultant; management consulting services; engineering services
PA: Aecom
1999 Avenue Of The Stars # 2600
Los Angeles CA 90067
213 593-8000

(P-6391)
EAST BAY MUNICIPL UTILTY DISTR
Also Called: Ebmud
2020 Wake Ave, Oakland (94607-5100)
PHONE...........................866 403-2683
Alexander Coate, *General Mgr*
EMP: 87
SALES (corp-wide): 534MM Privately Held
SIC: 4953 9511 ;
PA: East Bay Municipal Utility District, Water System
375 11th St
Oakland CA 94607
866 403-2683

(P-6392)
ECULLET INC
1 Vintage Ct, Woodside (94062-2560)
PHONE...........................650 493-7300
Craig J London, *CEO*
Mark D Muenchow, *CFO*
Farook Afsari, *Chairman*
Dr Yue Min Wong, *Director*
EMP: 100 EST: 1999
SALES (est): 2.5MM Privately Held
SIC: 4953 Recycling, waste materials

(P-6393)
EDCO DISPOSAL CORPORATION INC (PA)
Also Called: La Mesa Disposal
2755 California Ave, Signal Hill (90755-3304)
PHONE...........................619 287-7555
Steve South, *CEO*
Edward Burr, *President*
Sandra Burr, *Vice Pres*
Yvette Snyder, *Comms Dir*
Don Harris, *Exec Dir*
EMP: 250 EST: 1967
SQ FT: 8,000

SALES (est): 391.5MM **Privately Held**
SIC: 4953 Garbage: collecting, destroying & processing

(P-6394)
EDCO DISPOSAL CORPORATION INC
Also Called: Park Disposal Service
6762 Stanton Ave, Buena Park (90621-3611)
P.O. Box 398 (90621-0398)
PHONE..................................714 522-3577
Efrain Ramirez, *Vice Pres*
Mark Billings, *Marketing Staff*
EMP: 70
SALES (corp-wide): 391.5MM **Privately Held**
SIC: 4953 Rubbish collection & disposal
PA: Edco Disposal Corporation Inc.
2755 California Ave
Signal Hill CA 90755
619 287-7555

(P-6395)
EDCO WASTE & RECYCL SVCS INC (HQ)
Also Called: Solid Waste Services
224 S Las Posas Rd, San Marcos (92078-2421)
PHONE..................................760 744-2700
Steve South, *CEO*
Edward Burr, *President*
Alan Walsh, *CFO*
Sandra Burr, *Corp Secy*
Jeffrey Ritchie, *Vice Pres*
EMP: 74 **EST:** 1954
SQ FT: 37,000
SALES (est): 126.2MM
SALES (corp-wide): 391.5MM **Privately Held**
SIC: 4953 4212 Rubbish collection & disposal; garbage: collecting, destroying & processing; local trucking, without storage
PA: Edco Disposal Corporation Inc.
2755 California Ave
Signal Hill CA 90755
619 287-7555

(P-6396)
ELECTRONIC RECYCLERS
7815 N Palm Ave Ste 140, Fresno (93711-5531)
PHONE..................................253 736-2627
John Shegerian, *President*
Tammy Shegerian, *Treasurer*
Linda Ramos, *Admin Sec*
EMP: 99
SALES (est): 5.6MM
SALES (corp-wide): 499.9MM **Privately Held**
SIC: 4953 Non-hazardous waste disposal sites
PA: Electronic Recyclers International Inc.
7815 N Palm Ave Ste 140
Fresno CA 93711
800 374-3473

(P-6397)
ELECTRONIC RECYCLERS INTL INC (PA)
Also Called: Electronic Recyclers America
7815 N Palm Ave Ste 140, Fresno (93711-5531)
PHONE..................................800 374-3473
John S Shegerian, *CEO*
Dann V Angeloff, *President*
Kelly Thomas, *COO*
James Kim, *CFO*
Rich Calzada, *Officer*
▲ **EMP:** 101
SQ FT: 75,000
SALES (est): 499.9MM **Privately Held**
SIC: 4953 Recycling, waste materials

(P-6398)
EMPIRE DISPOSAL LLC
Also Called: Curran's Disposal
5455 Industrial Pkwy, San Bernardino (92407-1803)
PHONE..................................909 797-9125
Cole Burr,
Lou Estrella, *Manager*
EMP: 50 **EST:** 1995

SALES (est): 1.8MM
SALES (corp-wide): 309.8MM **Privately Held**
SIC: 4953 4212 Garbage: collecting, destroying & processing; local trucking, without storage
PA: Burrtec Waste Group, Inc.
9890 Cherry Ave
Fontana CA 92335
909 429-4200

(P-6399)
FAIRFIELD-SUISUN SEWER DST
1010 Chadbourne Rd, Fairfield (94534-9700)
PHONE..................................707 429-8930
Richard F Luthy Jr, *General Mgr*
EMP: 65
SQ FT: 15,000
SALES: 24.9MM **Privately Held**
WEB: www.fssd.com
SIC: 4953 Refuse collection & disposal services

(P-6400)
FILTER RECYCLING SERVICES INC (PA)
180 W Monte Ave, Rialto (92376)
PHONE..................................909 873-4141
Jon L Bennett Jr, *President*
Jim Arnold, *Treasurer*
Jim Goyich, *Vice Pres*
Dianna Vepeda, *Admin Sec*
▲ **EMP:** 63
SQ FT: 33,000
SALES (est): 59.6MM **Privately Held**
WEB: www.filterrecycling.com
SIC: 4953 Hazardous waste collection & disposal

(P-6401)
FOOTHILL WASTE RECLAMATION INC
12221 Lopez Canyon Rd, Sylmar (91342-5730)
P.O. Box 923637 (91392-3637)
PHONE..................................818 897-5099
Kevork Sarkisian, *President*
Dick Sarkisian, *Vice Pres*
EMP: 55
SQ FT: 2,500
SALES (est): 3.3MM **Privately Held**
SIC: 4953 Refuse systems

(P-6402)
GI INDUSTRIES
195 W Los Angeles Ave, Simi Valley (93065-1651)
P.O. Box 940430 (93094-0430)
PHONE..................................805 522-2150
Michael Smith, *Senior VP*
EMP: 100
SQ FT: 7,000
SALES (est): 34.9MM
SALES (corp-wide): 14.4B **Publicly Held**
WEB: www.wm.com
SIC: 4953 4212 Garbage: collecting, destroying & processing; recycling, waste materials; local trucking, without storage
PA: Waste Management, Inc.
1001 Fannin St Ste 4000
Houston TX 77002
713 512-6200

(P-6403)
GILTON RESOURCE RECOVERY
755 S Yosemite Ave, Oakdale (95361-4039)
PHONE..................................209 527-3781
Richard Gilton, *President*
Tedford Gilton, *Vice Pres*
Karen Gilton Hardister, *Vice Pres*
Donna Love, *Vice Pres*
EMP: 55
SALES (est): 5.5MM **Privately Held**
SIC: 4953 Recycling, waste materials

(P-6404)
GILTON SOLID WASTE MGT INC
755 S Yosemite Ave, Oakdale (95361-4991)
PHONE..................................209 527-3781
Richard Gilton, *President*
Tedford Gilton, *Vice Pres*
Karen Gilton Hardister, *Vice Pres*
Donna Gilton Love, *Vice Pres*

Mike Pereira, *Foreman/Supr*
EMP: 136
SQ FT: 3,000
SALES (est): 41.4MM **Privately Held**
WEB: www.gilton.com
SIC: 4953 Rubbish collection & disposal; recycling, waste materials

(P-6405)
GREENWASTE RECOVERY INC
565 Charles St, San Jose (95112-1402)
PHONE..................................408 283-4804
Chris Almeida, *Manager*
EMP: 50
SQ FT: 7,050
SALES (est): 1.3MM **Privately Held**
SIC: 4953 Garbage: collecting, destroying & processing
PA: Greenwaste Recovery, Inc.
625 Charles St
San Jose CA 95112

(P-6406)
GREENWASTE RECOVERY INC (PA)
625 Charles St, San Jose (95112-1402)
PHONE..................................408 283-4800
Richard Christina, *President*
Frank Weigel, *COO*
Don Dean, *CFO*
Dave Tilton, *CFO*
Jesse Weigel, *Corp Secy*
EMP: 93
SQ FT: 115,000
SALES (est): 124.1MM **Privately Held**
SIC: 4953 Rubbish collection & disposal; waste materials, disposal at sea

(P-6407)
IMS RECYCLING SERVICES INC (PA)
2697 Main St, San Diego (92113-3612)
P.O. Box 13666 (92170-3666)
PHONE..................................619 231-2521
Robert M Davis, *CEO*
Theodora Davis Inman, *CFO*
Ruth Davis, *Chairman*
Deborah Odle, *Vice Pres*
Karla Diaz, *Admin Asst*
▼ **EMP:** 70
SQ FT: 25,000
SALES (est): 113.6MM **Privately Held**
WEB: www.imsrecyclingservices.com
SIC: 4953 Recycling, waste materials

(P-6408)
INTERNTIONAL DISPOSAL CORP CAL
Also Called: Site L69
1601 Dixon Landing Rd, Milpitas (95035-8100)
PHONE..................................408 945-2802
Bruce Ranck, *President*
EMP: 75
SQ FT: 1,613
SALES (est): 4.3MM
SALES (corp-wide): 10B **Publicly Held**
WEB: www.alliedwaste.com
SIC: 4953 Sanitary landfill operation
HQ: Browning-Ferris Industries, Llc
18500 N Allied Way # 100
Phoenix AZ 85054
480 627-2700

(P-6409)
JOES SWEEPING INC
Also Called: Nationwide Environmental Svcs
11914 Front St, Norwalk (90650-2911)
PHONE..................................562 929-4344
Never Samuelian, *President*
Joe Samuelian, *Vice Pres*
Ani Samuelian, *Admin Sec*
EMP: 65
SQ FT: 10,500
SALES (est): 18MM **Privately Held**
WEB: www.nes-sweeping.com
SIC: 4953 Street refuse systems

(P-6410)
LOONEY BINS INC (PA)
12153 Montague St, Pacoima (91331-2210)
PHONE..................................818 485-8200
Myan Spaccarelli, *President*

Jerry Lucera, *CFO*
Phyllis Shukiar, *Admin Sec*
EMP: 70
SQ FT: 1,000
SALES (est): 20.4MM **Privately Held**
WEB: www.looneybins.com
SIC: 4953 Garbage: collecting, destroying & processing

(P-6411)
LOPEZ CANYON LANDFILL
11950 Lopez Canyon Rd, Sylmar (91342-6036)
PHONE..................................818 834-5122
James Kurz, *Superintendent*
Paul Blount, *Manager*
EMP: 110
SALES (est): 2.7MM **Privately Held**
SIC: 4953 Sanitary landfill operation

(P-6412)
M P VACUUM TRUCK SERVICE (PA)
Also Called: M P Environmental Services
3400 Manor St, Bakersfield (93308-1451)
PHONE..................................661 393-1151
Dawn Calderwood, *President*
EMP: 175
SQ FT: 2,500
SALES (est): 5.5MM **Privately Held**
SIC: 4953 Hazardous waste collection & disposal

(P-6413)
MADISON MATERIALS
1035 E 4th St, Santa Ana (92701-4750)
PHONE..................................714 664-0159
Judith Ware, *President*
Ben Ware, *Vice Pres*
Jay Ware, *General Mgr*
EMP: 70
SQ FT: 10,400
SALES (est): 7.7MM **Privately Held**
SIC: 4953 Recycling, waste materials

(P-6414)
MAIN STREET FIBERS INC
608 E Main St, Ontario (91761-1711)
P.O. Box 51491 (91761-0091)
PHONE..................................909 986-6310
Gregory S Young, *CEO*
Wayne Young, *President*
Steve Young, *Corp Secy*
EMP: 60
SQ FT: 25,000
SALES: 46MM **Privately Held**
WEB: www.mainstreetfibers.com
SIC: 4953 Recycling, waste materials

(P-6415)
MARBORG INDUSTRIES (PA)
728 E Yanonali St, Santa Barbara (93103-3233)
P.O. Box 4127 (93140-4127)
PHONE..................................805 963-1852
Mario Borgatello Jr, *President*
David Borgatello, *CFO*
Alan Coulter, *Risk Mgmt Dir*
Anthony Borgatello, *General Mgr*
Roberto Medina, *Office Mgr*
EMP: 250
SALES (est): 138.8MM **Privately Held**
WEB: www.marborg.com
SIC: 4953 7359 7699 4212 Rubbish collection & disposal; portable toilet rental; septic tank cleaning service; local trucking, without storage

(P-6416)
MARIN SANITARY SERVICE (PA)
Also Called: Marin Resource Recovery Center
1050 Andersen Dr, San Rafael (94901-5316)
P.O. Box 10067 (94912-0067)
PHONE..................................415 456-2601
Patricia Garbarino, *CEO*
Kathy Wall, *COO*
John Oranje, *Vice Pres*
Ron Piombo, *Vice Pres*
Steve Rosa, *Vice Pres*
EMP: 85

SALES (est): 82.3MM **Privately Held**
WEB: www.marinsanitary.com
SIC: 4953 5099 4212 Garbage: collecting, destroying & processing; recycling,
waste materials; wood chips; local trucking, without storage

(P-6417)
MASTER DISPOSAL CO
1980 S Reservoir St, Pomona
(91766-5543)
PHONE..................626 444-6789
Dave Samarin, *President*
Bill Nazaroff Sr, *Vice Pres*
Bill Nazaroff Jr, *Admin Sec*
EMP: 50
SALES (est): 3.7MM **Privately Held**
SIC: 4953 Recycling, waste materials

(P-6418)
MILL VALLEY REFUSE SERVICE INC
112 Front St, San Rafael (94901-4011)
P.O. Box 3557 (94912-3557)
PHONE..................415 457-2287
Dave Biggio, *President*
James Iavarone, *Treasurer*
Dave Dellazoppa, *Vice Pres*
Jennifer Dami, *VP Admin*
Lynda Mendoza, *Sales Mgr*
EMP: 57
SQ FT: 52,000
SALES (est): 13.5MM **Privately Held**
WEB: www.millvalleyrefuse.com
SIC: 4953 Rubbish collection & disposal;
recycling, waste materials

(P-6419)
MODESTO WSTEWATER TRTMNT PLANT
1221 Sutter Ave, Modesto (95351-3603)
PHONE..................209 577-5300
Dan Wilkowsky, *Director*
EMP: 70
SALES (est): 2.6MM **Privately Held**
SIC: 4953

(P-6420)
MOLECULAR BIOPRODUCTS INC (DH)
9389 Waples St, San Diego (92121-3903)
PHONE..................858 453-7551
Seth H Hoogasian, *CEO*
Verner Andersen, *Vice Pres*
Gary J Marmontello, *Admin Sec*
Chris Le, *Project Engr*
John Buono, *Asst Treas*
◆ EMP: 110 EST: 1978
SQ FT: 45,000
SALES (est): 285.7MM
SALES (corp-wide): 20.9B **Publicly Held**
WEB: www.mbpinc.com
SIC: 4953 Medical waste disposal
HQ: Fisher Scientific International Llc
81 Wyman St
Waltham MA 02451
781 622-1000

(P-6421)
MONTEREY RGIONAL WASTE MGT DST
14201 Del Monte Blvd, Marina (93933)
P.O. Box 1670 (93933-1670)
PHONE..................831 384-5313
William Merry, *President*
Charles Rees, *CFO*
Leo Laska, *Chairman*
EMP: 120 EST: 1951
SQ FT: 5,500
SALES (est): 26.4MM **Privately Held**
WEB: www.mrwmd.org
SIC: 4953 4911 4931 Sanitary landfill op-
eration; recycling, waste materials; gener-
ation, electric power; electric & other
services combined

(P-6422)
MP ENVIRONMENTAL SERVICES INC (PA)
3400 Manor St, Bakersfield (93308-1451)
P.O. Box 80358 (93380-0358)
PHONE..................800 458-3036
Dawn Calderwood, *President*
Greg Brandom, *Project Mgr*
Matt Hoffman, *Project Mgr*

Laren Kaufman, *Project Mgr*
Doug Killian, *Project Mgr*
▲ EMP: 117
SQ FT: 8,000
SALES (est): 111.9MM **Privately Held**
WEB: www.mpenviro.com
SIC: 4953 4213 8748 7699 Hazardous
waste collection & disposal; radioactive
waste materials, disposal; trucking, ex-
cept local; environmental consultant; tank
repair & cleaning services

(P-6423)
NORTECH WASTE LLC
3033 Fiddyment Rd, Roseville
(95747-9705)
PHONE..................916 645-5230
Paul Szura, *Mng Member*
Arthur A Daniels,
Donald M Moriel,
Michael J Sangiacomo,
Jerry Jackson, *Mng Member*
EMP: 120
SQ FT: 9,000
SALES (est): 34.7MM **Privately Held**
WEB: www.nortechwaste.com
SIC: 4953 3341 3312 3231 Sanitary
landfill operation; secondary nonferrous
metals; blast furnaces & steel mills; prod-
ucts of purchased glass; pulp mills

(P-6424)
NRC ENVIRONMENTAL SERVICES INC
3777 Long Beach Blvd, Long Beach
(90807-3325)
PHONE..................562 432-1304
Todd Roloff, *Branch Mgr*
EMP: 60 **Privately Held**
WEB: www.nrces.com
SIC: 4953 Hazardous waste collection &
disposal
HQ: Nrc Environmental Services, Inc.
1605 Ferry Pt
Alameda CA 94501

(P-6425)
ORANGE COUNTY SANITATION (PA)
10844 Ellis Ave, Fountain Valley
(92708-7018)
P.O. Box 8127 (92728-8127)
PHONE..................714 962-2411
James Herberg, *General Mgr*
James Ruth, *General Mgr*
▲ EMP: 626
SALES: 315.4MM **Privately Held**
WEB: www.ocsd.com
SIC: 4953 Waste materials, disposal at sea

(P-6426)
PALM SPRINGS DISPOSAL SERVICES
4690 E Mesquite Ave, Palm Springs
(92264-3510)
P.O. Box 2711 (92263-2711)
PHONE..................760 327-1351
Frederic Wade, *CEO*
James Cunningham, *President*
Mike Jaycox, *Treasurer*
Ray Wade, *Vice Pres*
Rick Wade, *General Mgr*
EMP: 82
SQ FT: 2,000
SALES (est): 21.4MM **Privately Held**
WEB: www.palmspringsdisposal.com
SIC: 4953 Rubbish collection & disposal

(P-6427)
PENAS DISPOSAL INC
Also Called: Pena's Recycling Center
12094 Avenue 408, Cutler (93615-2055)
PHONE..................559 528-3909
Gabriel Pena, *President*
Arthur Pena, *Vice Pres*
Maria Pena, *Admin Sec*
Sherri Pena, *Marketing Staff*
Yvette Botello, *Manager*
EMP: 91 EST: 1968
SQ FT: 1,000
SALES (est): 16.5MM **Privately Held**
WEB: www.penasdisposal.com
SIC: 4953 Garbage: collecting, destroying
& processing

(P-6428)
PJBS HOLDINGS INC (PA)
Also Called: Benz - One Complete Operation
1401 Goodrick Dr, Tehachapi (93561-1532)
P.O. Box 1750 (93581-1750)
PHONE..................661 822-5273
Paul Benz, *CEO*
Joan Benz, *Corp Secy*
Louis Visco, *Vice Pres*
Harry Morse, *General Mgr*
Julie Sanchez, *Human Resources*
EMP: 75
SQ FT: 4,500
SALES (est): 61.9MM **Privately Held**
SIC: 4953 4212 Refuse collection & dis-
posal services; petroleum haulage, local

(P-6429)
PLEASANT HL BYSHORE DSPSAL INC
Also Called: Site 210
441 N Buchanan Cir, Pacheco
(94553-5119)
PHONE..................925 685-4711
J Frederick Snyder, *CEO*
Tim Argenti, *General Mgr*
EMP: 200
SQ FT: 4,000
SALES (est): 12.3MM
SALES (corp-wide): 10B **Publicly Held**
WEB:
www.pleasanthillbayshoredisposal.com
SIC: 4953 Refuse collection & disposal
services
HQ: Allied Waste Industries, Llc
18500 N Allied Way # 100
Phoenix AZ 85054
480 627-2700

(P-6430)
POTENTIAL INDUSTRIES INC (PA)
922 E E St, Wilmington (90744-6145)
P.O. Box 293 (90748-0293)
PHONE..................310 807-4466
Anthony J Fan, *President*
Simon Chen, *President*
Tony Fan, *President*
Henry J Chen, *CEO*
Jessie Chen, *Corp Secy*
◆ EMP: 149
SQ FT: 45,000
SALES (est): 242.8MM **Privately Held**
SIC: 4953 5093 Recycling, waste materi-
als; scrap & waste materials

(P-6431)
PSC INDUSTRIAL OUTSOURCING LP
Also Called: Philip West Industrial Service
1661 E 32nd St, Long Beach (90807-5233)
PHONE..................562 997-6000
Bill Hearley, *Manager*
EMP: 99
SALES (corp-wide): 750MM **Privately Held**
SIC: 4953 4959 5093 Hazardous waste
collection & disposal; environmental
cleanup services; ferrous metal scrap &
waste
PA: Psc Industrial Outsourcing, Lp
900 Georgia Ave
Deer Park TX 77536
713 393-5600

(P-6432)
RAINBOW DISPOSAL CO INC (HQ)
Also Called: Rainbow Refuse Recycling
17121 Nichols Ln, Huntington Beach
(92647-5719)
P.O. Box 1026 (92647-1026)
PHONE..................714 847-3581
Jerry Moffatt, *CEO*
Stan Tkaczyck, *President*
Fernando Duque, *Database Admin*
Leo Deleon, *Asst Controller*
EMP: 115 EST: 1956
SQ FT: 6,000
SALES (est): 102.2MM
SALES (corp-wide): 10B **Publicly Held**
WEB: www.rainbowdisposal.com
SIC: 4953 Garbage: collecting, destroying
& processing; recycling, waste materials

PA: Republic Services, Inc.
18500 N Allied Way # 100
Phoenix AZ 85054
480 627-2700

(P-6433)
RAINBOW TRANSFER RECYCLING
17121 Nichols Ln, Huntington Beach
(92647-5719)
P.O. Box 1026 (92647-1026)
PHONE..................714 847-5818
Jim Brownell, *Principal*
Stan Tkaczyk, *President*
Bruce Shuman, *CFO*
EMP: 165
SQ FT: 10,000
SALES (est): 7.5MM
SALES (corp-wide): 10B **Publicly Held**
WEB: www.rainbowdisposal.com
SIC: 4953 Rubbish collection & disposal
HQ: Rainbow Disposal Co. Inc.
17121 Nichols Ln
Huntington Beach CA 92647
714 847-3581

(P-6434)
RECOLOGY INC (PA)
50 California St Ste 2400, San Francisco
(94111-4796)
PHONE..................415 875-1000
Michael J Sangiacomo, *President*
George P McGrath, *COO*
Mark R Lomele, *CFO*
Dennis Wu, *Chairman*
Julie Bertani-Kiser, *Vice Pres*
EMP: 60 EST: 1988
SQ FT: 25,000
SALES (est): 1.3B **Privately Held**
WEB: www.norcalwastesystemsofbutte-
county.com
SIC: 4953 Garbage: collecting, destroying
& processing; recycling, waste materials

(P-6435)
RECOLOGY INC
Tunnel Ave And Beatty Rd, San Francisco
(94134)
PHONE..................415 330-1300
Mike Sangiacomo, *Branch Mgr*
EMP: 64
SALES (corp-wide): 1.3B **Privately Held**
WEB: www.norcalwastesystemsofbutte-
county.com
SIC: 4953 Recycling, waste materials
PA: Recology Inc.
50 California St Ste 2400
San Francisco CA 94111
415 875-1000

(P-6436)
RECOLOGY INC
245 N 1st St, Dixon (95620-3027)
PHONE..................916 379-3300
EMP: 63
SALES (corp-wide): 1.3B **Privately Held**
SIC: 4953 Garbage: collecting, destroying
& processing
PA: Recology Inc.
50 California St Ste 2400
San Francisco CA 94111
415 875-1000

(P-6437)
RECOLOGY INC
Also Called: Recology Sustainable Crushing
100 Cargo Way, San Francisco
(94124-1734)
PHONE..................415 970-1582
EMP: 56
SALES (corp-wide): 1.3B **Privately Held**
SIC: 4953 Garbage: collecting, destroying
& processing
PA: Recology Inc.
50 California St Ste 2400
San Francisco CA 94111
415 875-1000

(P-6438)
RECOLOGY INC
2720 S 5th Ave, Oroville (95965-5826)
P.O. Box 1512 (95965-1512)
PHONE..................530 533-5868
Joe Matz, *Manager*
EMP: 76
SQ FT: 9,086

PRODUCTS & SVCS

SALES (corp-wide): 1.3B **Privately Held**
WEB: www.norcalwastesystemsofbutte-county.com
SIC: 4953 Garbage: collecting, destroying & processing
PA: Recology Inc.
50 California St Ste 2400
San Francisco CA 94111
415 875-1000

(P-6439)
RECOLOGY INC
Also Called: Sanitary Fill
501 Tunnel Ave, San Francisco
(94134-2940)
PHONE..........................415 330-1400
John Legnitto, *Branch Mgr*
EMP: 150
SALES (corp-wide): 1.3B **Privately Held**
WEB: www.norcalwastesystemsofbutte-county.com
SIC: 4953 8611 Recycling, waste materials; business associations
PA: Recology Inc.
50 California St Ste 2400
San Francisco CA 94111
415 875-1000

(P-6440)
RECOLOGY LOS ALTOS
Also Called: Rocology South Bay
650 Martin Ave, Santa Clara (95050-2914)
PHONE..........................650 961-8044
Michael Sangiacomo, *President*
EMP: 89 **EST:** 1923
SALES (est): 6.5MM
SALES (corp-wide): 1.3B **Privately Held**
WEB: www.losaltosgarbage.com
SIC: 4953 Garbage: collecting, destroying & processing; recycling, waste materials
PA: Recology Inc.
50 California St Ste 2400
San Francisco CA 94111
415 875-1000

(P-6441)
RECOLOGY SAN FRANCISCO
501 Tunnel Ave, San Francisco (94134-2940)
PHONE..........................415 468-1752
Michael Sangiacomo, *President*
Robert Coyle, *COO*
EMP: 167
SQ FT: 3,800
SALES (est): 20MM
SALES (corp-wide): 1.3B **Privately Held**
WEB: www.sfrecyclinganddisposal.com
SIC: 4953 Garbage: collecting, destroying & processing
PA: Recology Inc.
50 California St Ste 2400
San Francisco CA 94111
415 875-1000

(P-6442)
RECOLOGY SAN MATEO COUNTY
225 Shoreway Rd, San Carlos (94070-2712)
PHONE..........................650 595-3900
Michael J Sangiacomo, *CEO*
Paul Dougherty, *Manager*
EMP: 99
SALES: 950K **Privately Held**
SIC: 4953 Garbage: collecting, destroying & processing

(P-6443)
RECOLOGY SOUTH VALLEY (HQ)
1351 Pacheco Pass Hwy, Gilroy (95020-9579)
PHONE..........................408 842-3358
Robert Coyle, *President*
Mike Sanjiacomo, *Vice Pres*
Monica Estrada, *General Mgr*
EMP: 65 **EST:** 1949
SQ FT: 6,000
SALES (est): 20.5MM
SALES (corp-wide): 1.3B **Privately Held**
SIC: 4953 Garbage: collecting, destroying & processing; recycling, waste materials; sanitary landfill operation

PA: Recology Inc.
50 California St Ste 2400
San Francisco CA 94111
415 875-1000

(P-6444)
RECOLOGY VACAVILLE SOLANO
1 Town Sq Ste 200, Vacaville (95688-3928)
PHONE..........................707 448-2945
Michael Sangiacomo, *President*
EMP: 75
SQ FT: 10,000
SALES (est): 9.3MM
SALES (corp-wide): 1.3B **Privately Held**
WEB: www.norcalwastesystemsofbutte-county.com
SIC: 4953 Garbage: collecting, destroying & processing; recycling, waste materials
PA: Recology Inc.
50 California St Ste 2400
San Francisco CA 94111
415 875-1000

(P-6445)
RECOLOGY VALLEJO (HQ)
Also Called: Vallejo Garbage & Recycling
2021 Broadway St, Vallejo (94589-1701)
PHONE..........................707 552-3110
Ed Farewell, *General Mgr*
EMP: 115
SQ FT: 40,000
SALES: 16MM
SALES (corp-wide): 1.3B **Privately Held**
WEB: www.vallejogarbage.com
SIC: 4953 Garbage: collecting, destroying & processing
PA: Recology Inc.
50 California St Ste 2400
San Francisco CA 94111
415 875-1000

(P-6446)
RECOLOGY YUBA-SUTTER
3001 N Levee Rd, Marysville (95901-3600)
P.O. Box G (95901-0062)
PHONE..........................530 743-6933
Michael Sangiacomo, *President*
Robert Coyle, *COO*
EMP: 90 **EST:** 1974
SQ FT: 7,000
SALES (est): 12.7MM
SALES (corp-wide): 1.3B **Privately Held**
WEB: www.ysdi.com
SIC: 4953 4212 Garbage: collecting, destroying & processing; recycling, waste materials; hazardous waste collection & disposal; hazardous waste transport
PA: Recology Inc.
50 California St Ste 2400
San Francisco CA 94111
415 875-1000

(P-6447)
RECYCLERS I ELECTRONIC
7815 N Palm Ave Ste 140, Fresno (93711-5531)
PHONE..........................317 522-1414
John S Shegerian, *President*
Tammy L Shegerian, *Treasurer*
Linda L Ramos, *Admin Sec*
▼ **EMP:** 99
SALES (est): 14.3MM
SALES (corp-wide): 499.9MM **Privately Held**
SIC: 4953 Recycling, waste materials
PA: Electronic Recyclers International Inc.
7815 N Palm Ave Ste 140
Fresno CA 93711
800 374-3473

(P-6448)
RECYCLING INDUSTRIES INC
4741 Watt Ave, North Highlands (95660-5526)
PHONE..........................916 452-3961
Scott Kuhnen, *President*
David Kuhnen, *CFO*
Mike Rexroad, *Maintence Staff*
Jeff Donlevy, *Manager*
David Flores, *Manager*
EMP: 75
SQ FT: 155,000
SALES (est): 19.7MM **Privately Held**
WEB: www.recyclingindustries.com
SIC: 4953 Recycling, waste materials

(P-6449)
REDWOOD EMPIR
3400 Standish Ave, Santa Rosa (95407-8112)
PHONE..........................707 586-5533
James Rappo, *President*
EMP: 70
SALES (est): 5MM **Privately Held**
SIC: 4953 Refuse systems

(P-6450)
REPLANET LLC
Also Called: Tomra Recycling Network
9910 6th St, Rancho Cucamonga (91730-5715)
PHONE..........................909 980-1203
Ralph Alcantar, *Manager*
EMP: 55
SALES (corp-wide): 901.9MM **Privately Held**
SIC: 4953 8741 5093 Recycling, waste materials; management services; metal scrap & waste materials
HQ: Replanet, Llc
800 N Haven Ave Ste 120
Ontario CA 91764
951 520-1700

(P-6451)
REPUBLIC SERVICES INC
2059 E Steel Rd, Colton (92324-4008)
PHONE..........................909 370-3377
Peter Sperenberg, *Manager*
EMP: 50
SQ FT: 3,200
SALES (corp-wide): 10B **Publicly Held**
SIC: 4953 Garbage: collecting, destroying & processing
PA: Republic Services, Inc.
18500 N Allied Way # 100
Phoenix AZ 85054
480 627-2700

(P-6452)
REPUBLIC SERVICES INC
1449 W Rosecrans Ave, Gardena (90249-2639)
PHONE..........................310 527-6980
Lewis Glynn, *President*
EMP: 100
SQ FT: 39,755
SALES (corp-wide): 10B **Publicly Held**
WEB: www.republicservices.com
SIC: 4953 Medical waste disposal
PA: Republic Services, Inc.
18500 N Allied Way # 100
Phoenix AZ 85054
480 627-2700

(P-6453)
REPUBLIC SERVICES INC
111 S Del Norte Blvd, Oxnard (93030-7915)
PHONE..........................805 385-8060
Anthony Bertrand, *Branch Mgr*
EMP: 58
SALES (corp-wide): 10B **Publicly Held**
WEB: www.republicservices.com
SIC: 4953 Recycling, waste materials
PA: Republic Services, Inc.
18500 N Allied Way # 100
Phoenix AZ 85054
480 627-2700

(P-6454)
RUUHWA DANN AND ASSOCIATES INC
Also Called: Cal Micro
1541 Brooks St, Ontario (91762-3619)
PHONE..........................909 467-4800
Ruuhwa Dann, *CEO*
Harry Saliba, *President*
Jess Panopio, *Project Mgr*
◆ **EMP:** 77
SQ FT: 88,000
SALES (est): 19.9MM **Privately Held**
SIC: 4953 Recycling, waste materials

(P-6455)
SA RECYCLING LLC
3055 Commercial St, San Diego (92113-1412)
PHONE..........................619 238-6740
Mark Sweetman, *Manager*
EMP: 68 **Privately Held**
SIC: 4953 Recycling, waste materials

PA: Sa Recycling Llc
2411 N Glassell St
Orange CA 92865

(P-6456)
SA RECYCLING LLC
10313 S Alameda St, Los Angeles (90002-3838)
PHONE..........................323 564-5601
Carlos Escamilla, *Manager*
EMP: 68 **Privately Held**
SIC: 4953 Recycling, waste materials
PA: Sa Recycling Llc
2411 N Glassell St
Orange CA 92865

(P-6457)
SA RECYCLING LLC
780 E Easy St, Simi Valley (93065-1810)
PHONE..........................805 483-0512
EMP: 68 **Privately Held**
SIC: 4953 5093 Recycling, waste materials; scrap & waste materials; ferrous metal scrap & waste; nonferrous metals scrap
PA: Sa Recycling Llc
2411 N Glassell St
Orange CA 92865

(P-6458)
SA RECYCLING LLC
2006 W 5th St, Santa Ana (92703-2806)
PHONE..........................714 667-7898
EMP: 68 **Privately Held**
SIC: 4953 5093 Recycling, waste materials; scrap & waste materials; ferrous metal scrap & waste; nonferrous metals scrap
PA: Sa Recycling Llc
2411 N Glassell St
Orange CA 92865

(P-6459)
SA RECYCLING LLC
9754 San Fernando Rd, Sun Valley (91352-1424)
PHONE..........................323 875-2520
Steve Rios, *Branch Mgr*
EMP: 68 **Privately Held**
SIC: 4953 Recycling, waste materials
PA: Sa Recycling Llc
2411 N Glassell St
Orange CA 92865

(P-6460)
SA RECYCLING LLC
2525 S K St, Tulare (93274-6875)
PHONE..........................559 688-0271
Brandon Dye, *General Mgr*
EMP: 68 **Privately Held**
SIC: 4953 Recycling, waste materials
PA: Sa Recycling Llc
2411 N Glassell St
Orange CA 92865

(P-6461)
SA RECYCLING LLC
521 N Rice Ave, Oxnard (93030-8924)
PHONE..........................805 486-7525
Matt Essler, *Branch Mgr*
EMP: 68 **Privately Held**
SIC: 4953 5093 Recycling, waste materials; scrap & waste materials
PA: Sa Recycling Llc
2411 N Glassell St
Orange CA 92865

(P-6462)
SA RECYCLING LLC
2495 Buena Vista St, Duarte (91010-3330)
PHONE..........................626 359-5815
Carlos Rodriguez, *Manager*
EMP: 68 **Privately Held**
SIC: 4953 5093 Recycling, waste materials; scrap & waste materials; ferrous metal scrap & waste; nonferrous metals scrap

PA: Sa Recycling Llc
2411 N Glassell St
Orange CA 92865
-

(P-6463)
SA RECYCLING LLC
1540 S Greenwood Ave, Montebello
(90640-6536)
PHONE..........................323 723-8327
James Adams, *Branch Mgr*
EMP: 68 **Privately Held**
SIC: 4953 5093 Recycling, waste materials; scrap & waste materials; ferrous metal scrap & waste; nonferrous metals scrap
PA: Sa Recycling Llc
2411 N Glassell St
Orange CA 92865
-

(P-6464)
SA RECYCLING LLC
3489 S Chestnut Ave, Fresno
(93725-2610)
PHONE..........................559 237-6677
Mark Leizer, *Branch Mgr*
EMP: 64 **Privately Held**
SIC: 4953 Recycling, waste materials
PA: Sa Recycling Llc
2411 N Glassell St
Orange CA 92865
-

(P-6465)
SA RECYCLING LLC
48100 Harrison St, Coachella
(92236-1214)
PHONE..........................760 391-5591
Ben Wilcox, *Branch Mgr*
EMP: 68 **Privately Held**
SIC: 4953 Recycling, waste materials
PA: Sa Recycling Llc
2411 N Glassell St
Orange CA 92865
-

(P-6466)
SA RECYCLING LLC
12301 Valley Blvd, El Monte (91732-3603)
PHONE..........................626 444-9530
Carlos Escamilla, *Branch Mgr*
EMP: 64 **Privately Held**
SIC: 4953 Recycling, waste materials
PA: Sa Recycling Llc
2411 N Glassell St
Orange CA 92865
-

(P-6467)
SA RECYCLING LLC
2000 E Brundage Ln, Bakersfield
(93307-2734)
PHONE..........................661 327-3559
Brandon Dye, *Manager*
EMP: 65 **Privately Held**
SIC: 4953 Recycling, waste materials
PA: Sa Recycling Llc
2411 N Glassell St
Orange CA 92865
-

(P-6468)
SA RECYCLING LLC
11614 Eastend Ave, Chino (91710-1557)
PHONE..........................909 622-3337
EMP: 68
SALES (corp-wide): 49.7MM **Privately Held**
SIC: 4953 5093
PA: Sa Recycling Llc
2411 N Glassell St
Orange CA 92865
714 632-2000

(P-6469)
SA RECYCLING LLC
42353 8th St E, Lancaster (93535-5439)
PHONE..........................661 723-1383
EMP: 68
SALES (corp-wide): 49.7MM **Privately Held**
SIC: 4953

PA: Sa Recycling Llc
2411 N Glassell St
Orange CA 92865
714 632-2000

(P-6470)
SA RECYCLING LLC
790 E M St, Colton (92324-3910)
PHONE..........................909 825-1662
Alex Arriaga, *Branch Mgr*
EMP: 68 **Privately Held**
SIC: 4953 Recycling, waste materials
PA: Sa Recycling Llc
2411 N Glassell St
Orange CA 92865
-

(P-6471)
SA RECYCLING LLC
3202 Main St, San Diego (92113-3719)
PHONE..........................714 632-2000
EMP: 68 **Privately Held**
SIC: 4953 Recycling, waste materials
PA: Sa Recycling Llc
2411 N Glassell St
Orange CA 92865
-

(P-6472)
SACRAMENTO AREA SEWER DISTRICT (PA)
10060 Goethe Rd, Sacramento
(95827-3553)
PHONE..........................916 876-6000
Joseph Maestretti, *CFO*
Rodger Kuchik, *Officer*
Prabhaker Somavarapu, *Principal*
Steven Delozier, *Exec Dir*
Glen Iwamura, *Info Tech Mgr*
EMP: 300
SALES (est): 270.4MM **Privately Held**
SIC: 4953 Rubbish collection & disposal

(P-6473)
SAN DIEGO RECYLING INC
6670 Federal Blvd, Lemon Grove
(91945-1312)
PHONE..........................619 287-7555
Edward Burr, *President*
EMP: 300
SALES (est): 9.5MM **Privately Held**
SIC: 4953 Recycling, waste materials

(P-6474)
SANITATION DISTRICTS
1955 Workman Mill Rd, Whittier
(90601-1415)
P.O. Box 4998 (90607-4998)
PHONE..........................562 908-4288
Steve McGuin, *Manager*
Phil Markle, *Bd of Directors*
Grace Robinson Chan, *General Mgr*
Denise Springer, *Admin Sec*
Elizabeth Weiland, *Admin Sec*
EMP: 1698
SALES: 576MM **Privately Held**
SIC: 4953 Sanitary landfill operation; rubbish collection & disposal

(P-6475)
SELF SERVE AUTO DISMANTLERS (PA)
Also Called: Adams Steel
3200 E Frontera St, Anaheim (92806-2822)
P.O. Box 6258 (92816-0258)
PHONE..........................714 630-8901
George Adams Jr, *President*
Wendy Adams, *CFO*
Mike Adams, *Exec VP*
Thomas Knippel, *Vice Pres*
Jed Holley, *General Mgr*
◆ **EMP:** 215
SQ FT: 41,000
SALES (est): 28.2MM **Privately Held**
WEB: www.remedyenvironmental.com
SIC: 4953 Recycling, waste materials

(P-6476)
SOLAG INCORPORATED
Also Called: Solag Disposal Co
31641 Ortega Hwy, San Juan Capistrano
(92675)
PHONE..........................949 728-1206
Clifford Ronnenberg, *Ch of Bd*
Patricia Leyes, *Vice Pres*
EMP: 58

SALES (est): 3.6MM
SALES (corp-wide): 121MM **Privately Held**
WEB: www.crrincorporated.com
SIC: 4953 4212 Rubbish collection & disposal; local trucking, without storage
PA: Cr&R Incorporated
11292 Western Ave
Stanton CA 90680
714 826-9049

(P-6477)
SOLANO GARBAGE COMPANY INC
2901 Industrial Ct, Fairfield (94533-6500)
P.O. Box B (94533-0601)
PHONE..........................707 437-8900
Richard Granzella, *President*
Dennis Varni, *CFO*
Joe Della Zoppa, *Exec VP*
Pina Barbieri, *Admin Sec*
EMP: 55 **EST:** 1978
SQ FT: 2,000
SALES: 11MM **Privately Held**
WEB: www.solanorecycles.com
SIC: 4953 Garbage: collecting, destroying & processing

(P-6478)
SOUTH TAHOE REFUSE CO
Also Called: Sierra Disposal Service
2140 Ruth Ave, South Lake Tahoe
(96150-4357)
PHONE..........................530 541-5105
Jeffrey Tillman, *President*
Gloria Lehman, *Treasurer*
John Tillman, *Vice Pres*
John De Marchini, *Admin Sec*
Leslie Breisch, *Info Tech Dir*
EMP: 100
SQ FT: 5,000
SALES (est): 17.2MM **Privately Held**
WEB: www.southtahoerefuse.com
SIC: 4953 Garbage: collecting, destroying & processing

(P-6479)
STAR SCRAP METAL COMPANY INC
1509 S Bluff Rd, Montebello (90640-6601)
PHONE..........................562 921-5045
Rose Starow Stein, *President*
Allen Stein, *Vice Pres*
Zack Stein, *Manager*
▼ **EMP:** 70 **EST:** 1974
SQ FT: 600
SALES (est): 12.6MM **Privately Held**
SIC: 4953 Recycling, waste materials

(P-6480)
SUNSET SCAVENGER COMPANY
Also Called: Recology Sunset Scavenger
250 Executive Park Blvd # 2100, San Francisco (94134-3306)
PHONE..........................415 330-1300
Archie Humphrey, *COO*
Gary Kirk, *Administration*
John Legnitto, *Manager*
EMP: 420 **EST:** 1920
SQ FT: 3,800
SALES (est): 31.3MM
SALES (corp-wide): 1.3B **Privately Held**
WEB: www.norcalwastesystemsofbutte-county.com
SIC: 4953 Recycling, waste materials
PA: Recology Inc.
50 California St Ste 2400
San Francisco CA 94111
415 875-1000

(P-6481)
TALCO PLASTICS INC (PA)
1000 W Rincon St, Corona (92880-9228)
PHONE..........................951 531-2000
John L Shedd Sr, *Chairman*
John L Shedd Jr, *President*
William O'Grady, *Vice Pres*
Ron Petty, *Vice Pres*
Bob Shedd, *Vice Pres*
EMP: 85
SQ FT: 110,000
SALES (est): 90.5MM **Privately Held**
WEB: www.talcoplastics.com
SIC: 4953 2821 Recycling, waste materials; plastics materials & resins

(P-6482)
TEMARRY RECYCLING INC
476 Tecate Rd, Tecate (91980)
PHONE..........................619 270-9453
Matt Songer, *CEO*
Teresa Songer, *Vice Pres*
Larry Burton, *Business Dir*
EMP: 63 **EST:** 2004
SALES (est): 4.4MM **Privately Held**
SIC: 4953 Recycling, waste materials

(P-6483)
TRACY DLTA SOLID WASTE MGT INC
Also Called: Delta Disposal Service Co
30703 S Macarthur Dr, Tracy (95377-9170)
P.O. Box 274 (95378-0274)
PHONE..........................209 835-0601
Michael Repetto, *President*
Carl Repetto, *Vice Pres*
Anna Lovecchio, *CPA*
Gina Baker, *Controller*
Susan Hudson, *Controller*
EMP: 61
SQ FT: 1,000
SALES (est): 12MM **Privately Held**
SIC: 4953 Garbage: collecting, destroying & processing; recycling, waste materials

(P-6484)
TRI-CITY ECONOMIC DEV CORP
Also Called: Tri Ced Community Recycling
33377 Western Ave, Union City
(94587-2210)
PHONE..........................510 429-8030
Richard Valle, *Principal*
Mangee Austria, *Opers Staff*
Wong Mangee, *Mktg Dir*
Geoffrey Fisher, *Manager*
EMP: 59
SQ FT: 74,055
SALES: 9.6MM **Privately Held**
SIC: 4953 Recycling, waste materials

(P-6485)
UNITED PACIFIC WASTE
4334 San Gbriel Rver Pkwy, Pico Rivera
(90660-1837)
P.O. Box 908 (90660-0908)
PHONE..........................562 699-7600
Michael Kandilian, *President*
Mike Kandilian, *Exec VP*
Shawna Kandilian, *Admin Sec*
EMP: 70
SQ FT: 3,500
SALES: 12MM **Privately Held**
SIC: 4953 4213 Garbage: collecting, destroying & processing; rubbish collection & disposal; contract haulers

(P-6486)
UNITED SITE SERVICES CAL INC
1 Oak Rd, Benicia (94510-2910)
PHONE..........................707 747-2810
Debbi Thornton, *Manager*
EMP: 50
SALES (corp-wide): 3.9MM **Privately Held**
WEB: www.americanclassicsanitation.com
SIC: 4953 4959 5082 7359 Refuse systems; sanitary services; construction & mining machinery; equipment rental & leasing
PA: United Site Services Of California, Inc.
242 Live Oak Ave
Irwindale CA 91706
626 462-9110

(P-6487)
USA WASTE OF CALIFORNIA INC
Also Called: Waste Management
26951 Road 140, Visalia (93292-9454)
P.O. Box 78251, Phoenix AZ (85062-8251)
PHONE..........................559 741-1766
Kurt Nielson, *Manager*
Tom Patron, *Manager*
EMP: 75
SALES (corp-wide): 14.4B **Publicly Held**
WEB: www.wastebusinessjournal.com
SIC: 4953 Ashes, collection & disposal
HQ: Usa Waste Of California, Inc.
11931 Foundation Pl # 200
Gold River CA 95670
916 387-1400

PRODUCTS & SVCS

(P-6488)

USA WASTE OF CALIFORNIA INC

8491 Fruitridge Rd, Sacramento
(95826-4807)
PHONE..................................916 379-0500
Alex Oseguera, *Manager*
EMP: 93
SALES (corp-wide): 14.4B **Publicly Held**
SIC: 4953 Refuse collection & disposal
services
HQ: Usa Waste Of California, Inc.
11931 Foundation Pl # 200
Gold River CA 95670
916 387-1400

(P-6489)

USA WASTE OF CALIFORNIA INC

Also Called: Los Angeles City Hauling
9081 Tujunga Ave, Sun Valley
(91352-1516)
P.O. Box 541, Los Angeles (90078-0541)
PHONE..................................818 252-3112
Jim Fish, *CEO*
EMP: 100
SALES (corp-wide): 14.4B **Publicly Held**
SIC: 4953 Recycling, waste materials
HQ: Usa Waste Of California, Inc.
11931 Foundation Pl # 200
Gold River CA 95670
916 387-1400

(P-6490)

USA WASTE OF CALIFORNIA INC (HQ)

Also Called: Waste Management
11931 Foundation Pl # 200, Gold River
(95670-4540)
PHONE..................................916 387-1400
Barry S Skolnick, *CEO*
Mike Witt, *CEO*
Earl E Defrates, *Treasurer*
Ed Aurand, *Ch Credit Ofcr*
Alex Oseguera, *General Mgr*
EMP: 147
SQ FT: 3,200
SALES (est): 52.4MM
SALES (corp-wide): 14.4B **Publicly Held**
WEB: www.wm.com
SIC: 4953 Refuse collection & disposal
services
PA: Waste Management, Inc.
1001 Fannin St Ste 4000
Houston TX 77002
713 512-6200

(P-6491)

USA WASTE OF CALIFORNIA INC

Also Called: Inland Empire Hauling
800 S Temescal St, Corona (92879-2058)
PHONE..................................800 423-9986
EMP: 100
SALES (corp-wide): 14.4B **Publicly Held**
SIC: 4953 Refuse systems
HQ: Usa Waste Of California, Inc.
11931 Foundation Pl # 200
Gold River CA 95670
916 387-1400

(P-6492)

USA WASTE OF CALIFORNIA INC

Also Called: San Gabriel-Pomona Valley Hlg
13970 Live Oak Ave, Baldwin Park (91706)
PHONE..................................626 856-1285
Richard Schackel, *Director*
Kevin Franco, *Opers Mgr*
Sylvia Granillo, *Opers Mgr*
Darrel Kato, *Opers Mgr*
EMP: 100
SALES (corp-wide): 14.4B **Publicly Held**
SIC: 4953 Garbage: collecting, destroying
& processing
HQ: Usa Waste Of California, Inc.
11931 Foundation Pl # 200
Gold River CA 95670
916 387-1400

(P-6493)

USA WASTE OF CALIFORNIA INC

Also Called: Waste Management
8740 Pueblo Ave Ste B, Atascadero
(93422-4605)
PHONE..................................805 466-3636
Randi Rebhan, *Branch Mgr*
Tina Arvin, *Supervisor*
EMP: 100
SALES (corp-wide): 14.4B **Publicly Held**
SIC: 4953 Refuse collection & disposal
services
HQ: Usa Waste Of California, Inc.
11931 Foundation Pl # 200
Gold River CA 95670
916 387-1400

(P-6494)

USA WASTE OF CALIFORNIA INC

Also Called: Waste Management
1001 W Bradley Ave, El Cajon
(92020-1501)
PHONE..................................619 596-5117
Paul Pistono, *Vice Pres*
EMP: 100
SALES (corp-wide): 14.4B **Publicly Held**
SIC: 4953 Refuse systems
HQ: Usa Waste Of California, Inc.
11931 Foundation Pl # 200
Gold River CA 95670
916 387-1400

(P-6495)

USA WASTE OF CALIFORNIA INC

Also Called: Waste Management
13793 Redwood St, Chino (91710-5506)
PHONE..................................909 590-1793
Steve Kanow, *Director*
EMP: 100
SALES (corp-wide): 14.4B **Publicly Held**
SIC: 4953 Refuse systems
HQ: Usa Waste Of California, Inc.
11931 Foundation Pl # 200
Gold River CA 95670
916 387-1400

(P-6496)

USA WASTE OF CALIFORNIA INC

Also Called: Fresno Hauling
4333 E Jefferson Ave, Fresno
(93725-9707)
PHONE..................................559 834-9151
Paul Pistono, *Vice Pres*
EMP: 100
SALES (corp-wide): 14.4B **Publicly Held**
SIC: 4953 Refuse collection & disposal
services
HQ: Usa Waste Of California, Inc.
11931 Foundation Pl # 200
Gold River CA 95670
916 387-1400

(P-6497)

USA WASTE OF CALIFORNIA INC

Also Called: La Metro Hauling
1970 E 213th St, Long Beach
(90810-1201)
PHONE..................................310 830-7100
Ed King, *Manager*
Maria Diaz, *Human Resources*
EMP: 100
SALES (corp-wide): 14.4B **Publicly Held**
SIC: 4953 Recycling, waste materials
HQ: Usa Waste Of California, Inc.
11931 Foundation Pl # 200
Gold River CA 95670
916 387-1400

(P-6498)

USA WASTE OF CALIFORNIA INC

Also Called: Compton Hauling
407 E El Segundo Blvd, Compton
(90222-2316)
PHONE..................................310 763-8500
Hovseb Shadarevian, *Branch Mgr*
EMP: 100
SALES (corp-wide): 14.4B **Publicly Held**
SIC: 4953 Refuse systems

HQ: Usa Waste Of California, Inc.
11931 Foundation Pl # 200
Gold River CA 95670
916 387-1400

(P-6499)

USA WASTE OF CALIFORNIA INC

Also Called: Paradise Solid Waste
951 American Way, Paradise (95969-6315)
PHONE..................................530 877-2777
Bill Mannel, *General Mgr*
Doug Speicher, *General Mgr*
Ron Law, *Controller*
Lee Hicks, *Contract Law*
EMP: 100
SALES (corp-wide): 14.4B **Publicly Held**
SIC: 4953 Refuse systems
HQ: Usa Waste Of California, Inc.
11931 Foundation Pl # 200
Gold River CA 95670
916 387-1400

(P-6500)

USA WASTE OF CALIFORNIA INC

Also Called: Salinas Disposal Service
1120 Madison Ln, Salinas (93907-1818)
PHONE..................................831 754-2500
Jan McCombs, *Branch Mgr*
EMP: 93
SALES (corp-wide): 14.4B **Publicly Held**
SIC: 4953 Refuse systems
HQ: Usa Waste Of California, Inc.
11931 Foundation Pl # 200
Gold River CA 95670
916 387-1400

(P-6501)

USA WASTE OF CALIFORNIA INC

Also Called: Fresno Hauling
10725 W Goshen Ave, Visalia
(93291-9496)
P.O. Box 541065, Los Angeles (90054-
1065)
PHONE..................................559 834-4070
Kurt Nielson, *Branch Mgr*
EMP: 100
SALES (corp-wide): 14.4B **Publicly Held**
SIC: 4953 Refuse systems
HQ: Usa Waste Of California, Inc.
11931 Foundation Pl # 200
Gold River CA 95670
916 387-1400

(P-6502)

USA WASTE OF CALIFORNIA INC

Also Called: Santa Clarita Hauling/Blue
25772 Springbrook Ave, Santa Clarita
(91350-2563)
PHONE..................................661 259-2398
Larry Rinkenberger, *Manager*
EMP: 100
SALES (corp-wide): 14.4B **Publicly Held**
SIC: 4953 Refuse systems
HQ: Usa Waste Of California, Inc.
11931 Foundation Pl # 200
Gold River CA 95670
916 387-1400

(P-6503)

USA WASTE OF CALIFORNIA INC

Also Called: Waste Management Orange
County
1800 S Grand Ave, Santa Ana
(92705-4800)
PHONE..................................714 637-3010
Jeremiah Gilliam, *Accounts Mgr*
EMP: 74
SALES (corp-wide): 14.4B **Publicly Held**
SIC: 4953 Refuse systems
HQ: Usa Waste Of California, Inc.
11931 Foundation Pl # 200
Gold River CA 95670
916 387-1400

(P-6504)

USA WASTE OF CALIFORNIA INC

Also Called: Salinas Disposal Service
29331 Pacific St, Hayward (94544-6017)
PHONE..................................831 384-5000

Paul Pistono, *Branch Mgr*
EMP: 100
SALES (corp-wide): 14.4B **Publicly Held**
SIC: 4953 Refuse systems
HQ: Usa Waste Of California, Inc.
11931 Foundation Pl # 200
Gold River CA 95670
916 387-1400

(P-6505)

VALLEY GARBAGE RUBBISH CO INC

Also Called: Heallth Sanitation Services
1850 W Betteravia Rd, Santa Maria
(93455-1065)
PHONE..................................805 614-1131
Keith Ramsey, *Principal*
Becky Gipson, *Executive*
Ginger Kaladas, *Credit Staff*
Peder Lauridsen, *Maint Spvr*
Lee Hicks, *Contract Law*
EMP: 70
SQ FT: 3,000
SALES (est): 24.4MM
SALES (corp-wide): 14.4B **Publicly Held**
WEB: www.wm.com
SIC: 4953 Rubbish collection & disposal
PA: Waste Management, Inc.
1001 Fannin St Ste 4000
Houston TX 77002
713 512-6200

(P-6506)

VEOLIA ES WASTE-TO-ENERGY INC

Also Called: Montenay Pacific Power
100 Pier S Ave, Long Beach (90802-1039)
PHONE..................................562 436-0636
Francois Screve, *Branch Mgr*
EMP: 70
SALES (corp-wide): 156.6MM **Privately
Held**
SIC: 4953 Refuse collection & disposal
services
PA: Veolia Es Waste-To-Energy, Inc.
1 Penn Plz Ste 4401
New York NY 10119
212 947-5824

(P-6507)

WARE DISPOSAL INC

1451 Manhattan Ave, Fullerton
(92831-5221)
PHONE..................................714 834-0234
Judith Helaine Ware, *CEO*
Michael Shaffer, *CFO*
Ben Ware, *Vice Pres*
Jay Ware, *General Mgr*
Jason Rush, *Info Tech Dir*
EMP: 120
SQ FT: 48,900
SALES (est): 25.7MM **Privately Held**
WEB: www.waredisposal.com
SIC: 4953 Refuse collection & disposal
services

(P-6508)

WASTE CONNECTIONS CAL INC

301 Carl Rd, Sunnyvale (94089-1012)
PHONE..................................408 752-8530
Todd Storti, *Manager*
EMP: 110
SALES (corp-wide): 3.3B **Privately Held**
WEB: www.greenteam.com
SIC: 4953 Garbage: collecting, destroying
& processing
HQ: Waste Connections Of California, Inc.
1333 Oakland Rd
San Jose CA 95112
408 282-4400

(P-6509)

WASTE CONNECTIONS CAL INC (DH)

Also Called: Greenteam of San Jose
1333 Oakland Rd, San Jose (95112-1364)
PHONE..................................408 282-4400
Paul Nelson, *Vice Pres*
Ron Mittelstaedt, *CEO*
Pual Nelson, *Vice Pres*
Michael Harlan,
Kobi Brown, *Accounts Mgr*
EMP: 150
SQ FT: 6,000

SALES (est): 538.2K
SALES (corp-wide): 3.3B **Privately Held**
WEB: www.greenteam.com
SIC: **4953** Garbage: collecting, destroying & processing

(P-6510)
WASTE MANAGEMENT CAL INC (HQ)
9081 Tujunga Ave, Sun Valley (91352-1516)
PHONE..............................877 836-6526
Larry Metter, *Vice Pres*
Scott Slighting, *District Mgr*
Ken Maxey, *General Mgr*
Rebecca Zayatz, *Engineer*
Glynis Pope, *Buyer*
EMP: 230 EST: 1953
SQ FT: 35,000
SALES (est): 420.6MM
SALES (corp-wide): 14.4B **Publicly Held**
SIC: **4953** Garbage: collecting, destroying & processing; recycling, waste materials
PA: Waste Management, Inc.
   1001 Fannin St Ste 4000
   Houston TX 77002
   713 512-6200

(P-6511)
WASTE MANAGEMENT CAL INC
1001 W Bradley Ave, El Cajon (92020-1501)
PHONE..............................619 596-5100
Rex Buck, *Principal*
EMP: 68
SQ FT: 2,000
SALES (corp-wide): 14.4B **Publicly Held**
WEB: www.wastebusinessjournal
SIC: **4953** Rubbish collection & disposal
HQ: Waste Management Of California, Inc.
   9081 Tujunga Ave
   Sun Valley CA 91352
   877 836-6526

(P-6512)
WASTE MANAGEMENT CAL INC
1200 W City Ranch Rd, Palmdale (93551-4456)
PHONE..............................661 947-7197
Carl McCarthy, *Manager*
EMP: 54
SALES (corp-wide): 14.4B **Publicly Held**
WEB: www.wastebusinessjournal.com
SIC: **4953** Rubbish collection & disposal
HQ: Waste Management Of California, Inc.
   9081 Tujunga Ave
   Sun Valley CA 91352
   877 836-6526

(P-6513)
WASTE MANAGEMENT CAL INC
2141 Oceanside Blvd, Oceanside (92054-4405)
PHONE..............................760 439-2824
John Lusignan, *Manager*
Michael Leigh, *Opers Mgr*
David Curnow, *Facilities Mgr*
EMP: 95
SQ FT: 4,500
SALES (corp-wide): 14.4B **Publicly Held**
SIC: **4953 4212** Garbage: collecting, destroying & processing; local trucking, without storage
HQ: Waste Management Of California, Inc.
   9081 Tujunga Ave
   Sun Valley CA 91352
   877 836-6526

(P-6514)
WASTE MGT COLLECTN & RECYCL
17700 Indian St, Moreno Valley (92551-9511)
PHONE..............................951 242-0421
Scott Jenkins, *Manager*
Carson Brown, *Manager*
EMP: 200
SALES (corp-wide): 14.4B **Publicly Held**
WEB: www.wastemanagement.com
SIC: **4953** Refuse systems
HQ: Waste Management Collection And Recycling, Inc.
   1001 Fannin St Ste 4000
   Houston TX 77002

(P-6515)
WASTE MGT COLLECTN & RECYCL
5701 S Eastrn Ave Ste 300, Commerce (90040)
PHONE..............................626 960-7551
Rick Decaiva, *Manager*
Ryan Burgess, *Accounts Mgr*
EMP: 245
SALES (corp-wide): 14.4B **Publicly Held**
SIC: **4953 4212** Rubbish collection & disposal; local trucking, without storage
HQ: Waste Management Collection And Recycling, Inc.
   1001 Fannin St Ste 4000
   Houston TX 77002

(P-6516)
WASTE MGT COLLECTN & RECYCL
1340 W Beach St, Watsonville (95076-5122)
P.O. Box 2347 (95077-2347)
PHONE..............................831 768-9505
James Moresco, *Branch Mgr*
Rini Van Every, *Info Tech Dir*
EMP: 93
SALES (corp-wide): 14.4B **Publicly Held**
SIC: **4953** Refuse collection & disposal services
HQ: Waste Management Collection And Recycling, Inc.
   1001 Fannin St Ste 4000
   Houston TX 77002

(P-6517)
WASTE MGT COLLECTN & RECYCL
219 Pudding Creek Rd, Fort Bragg (95437-8136)
PHONE..............................707 462-0210
Kaladas Ginger, *Branch Mgr*
EMP: 93
SALES (corp-wide): 14.4B **Publicly Held**
SIC: **4953** Refuse systems
HQ: Waste Management Collection And Recycling, Inc.
   1001 Fannin St Ste 4000
   Houston TX 77002

(P-6518)
WASTE MGT COLLECTN & RECYCL
17700 Indian St, Moreno Valley (92551-9511)
PHONE..............................909 242-0421
EMP: 93
SALES (corp-wide): 14.4B **Publicly Held**
SIC: **4953** Refuse systems
HQ: Waste Management Collection And Recycling, Inc.
   1001 Fannin St Ste 4000
   Houston TX 77002

(P-6519)
WASTE MGT COLLECTN & RECYCL
450 Orr Springs Rd, Ukiah (95482-3131)
PHONE..............................707 462-0210
Lee Hicks, *Branch Mgr*
EMP: 93
SALES (corp-wide): 14.4B **Publicly Held**
SIC: **4953** Refuse systems
HQ: Waste Management Collection And Recycling, Inc.
   1001 Fannin St Ste 4000
   Houston TX 77002

(P-6520)
WASTE MGT COLLECTN RECYCL INC
16122 Construction Cir E, Irvine (92606-4498)
PHONE..............................949 451-2600
Fidel Gutierrez, *Branch Mgr*
David Steiner, *CEO*
Joel Robledo, *Project Mgr*
Jose Loaiza, *Maintence Staff*
EMP: 93

SALES (corp-wide): 14.4B **Publicly Held**
SIC: **4953 4212** Recycling, waste materials; garbage collection & transport, no disposal
HQ: Waste Management Collection And Recycling, Inc.
   1001 Fannin St Ste 4000
   Houston TX 77002

(P-6521)
WASTE MGT OF ALAMEDA CNTY (HQ)
172 98th Ave, Oakland (94603-1004)
PHONE..............................510 613-8710
Barry S Skolnick, *CEO*
James C Fish Jr, *Exec VP*
James E Trevathan, *Exec VP*
Angel Gallardo, *Info Tech Mgr*
Greg Ong, *Analyst*
EMP: 550
SALES (est): 297.2MM
SALES (corp-wide): 14.4B **Publicly Held**
WEB: www.wastebusinessjournal.com
SIC: **4953** Rubbish collection & disposal
PA: Waste Management, Inc.
   1001 Fannin St Ste 4000
   Houston TX 77002
   713 512-6200

(P-6522)
WASTE MGT OF ALAMEDA CNTY
2615 Davis St, San Leandro (94577-2211)
PHONE..............................510 638-2303
Jack Isloa, *Manager*
Devon Ward, *Safety Mgr*
Erika-Alexand Solis, *Opers Staff*
Edgardo Jauregui, *Manager*
EMP: 100
SALES (corp-wide): 14.4B **Publicly Held**
WEB: www.wastebusinessjournal.com
SIC: **4953 5093** Dumps, operation of; scrap & waste materials
HQ: Waste Management Of Alameda County, Inc
   172 98th Ave
   Oakland CA 94603
   510 613-8710

(P-6523)
WEST COUNTY RESOURCE RECOVERY
101 Pittsburg Ave, Richmond (94801-1201)
PHONE..............................510 231-4200
Richard Granzella, *President*
Peter Nuti, *General Mgr*
EMP: 50
SALES: 12.8MM
SALES (corp-wide): 10B **Publicly Held**
WEB: www.recyclemore.com
SIC: **4953** Non-hazardous waste disposal sites
HQ: Richmond Sanitary Service, Inc.
   3260 Blume Dr Ste 100
   Richmond CA 94806
   510 262-7100

(P-6524)
WEST VALLEY MANUFACTURING LLC
Also Called: West Valley M R F
13373 Napa St, Fontana (92335-2930)
PHONE..............................909 899-5501
Richard Crockett, *General Mgr*
Kaiser Recycling Corporation,
West Valley Recycling Transf,
EMP: 120 EST: 1997
SQ FT: 65,000
SALES (est): 6MM **Privately Held**
SIC: **4953 4212** Refuse collection & disposal services; recycling, waste materials; local trucking, without storage

(P-6525)
WM HEALTHCARE SOLUTIONS INC
4280 Bandini Blvd, Vernon (90058-4207)
PHONE..............................713 328-7350
David Steiner, *President*
EMP: 99
SALES (est): 4.5MM **Privately Held**
SIC: **4953** Refuse systems

(P-6526)
WM RECYCLE AMERICA LLC
Waste Management
8405 Loch Lomond Dr, Pico Rivera (90660-2508)
PHONE..............................562 948-3888
Gary Lane, *Branch Mgr*
EMP: 90
SALES (corp-wide): 14.4B **Publicly Held**
WEB: www.wm.com
SIC: **4953** Recycling, waste materials
HQ: Wm Recycle America, L.L.C.
   1001 Fannin St Ste 4000
   Houston TX 77002
   713 512-6200

(P-6527)
ZANKER ROAD RESOURCE MGT LTD
Also Called: Zanker Road Landfill
675 Los Esteros Rd, San Jose (95134-1004)
PHONE..............................408 457-1189
Scott Beal, *Manager*
Kellie Lopez, *Admin Asst*
William Lineberry, *Engineer*
Danny Naranjo, *Manager*
EMP: 90
SALES (corp-wide): 57.2MM **Privately Held**
WEB: www.greenwaste.com
SIC: **4953** Rubbish collection & disposal
PA: Zanker Road Resource Management, Ltd.
   705 Los Esteros Rd
   San Jose CA 95134
   408 263-2385

(P-6528)
ZEREP MANAGEMENT CORPORATION
17445 Railroad St, City of Industry (91748-1026)
PHONE..............................626 961-6291
Manuel Perez, *CEO*
Jesse Quintana, *Controller*
EMP: 100
SQ FT: 4,000
SALES (est): 24.6MM **Privately Held**
SIC: **4953 4212** Refuse systems; local trucking, without storage

4959 Sanitary Svcs, NEC

(P-6529)
AMPCO CONTRACTING INC
1420 S Allec St, Anaheim (92805-6305)
PHONE..............................949 955-2255
Andrew Pennor, *President*
Matthew Suiter, *President*
Joe Ha, *Vice Pres*
Trung Joe Q Ha, *Vice Pres*
Michael King, *Vice Pres*
EMP: 220
SALES (est): 105.5MM **Privately Held**
SIC: **4959 1795 1794** Environmental cleanup services; wrecking & demolition work; excavation & grading, building construction

(P-6530)
CITY OF ANTIOCH
Also Called: Dept of Maintenance
1201 W 4th St, Antioch (94509-1005)
P.O. Box 5007 (94531-5007)
PHONE..............................925 779-6950
Pat Scott, *Director*
Ron Bernal, *Director*
EMP: 100 **Privately Held**
WEB: www.ci.antioch.ca.us
SIC: **4959 9111** Sanitary services; mayors' offices
PA: City Of Antioch
   200 H St
   Antioch CA 94509
   925 779-7055

(P-6531)
CITY OF CHINO
Also Called: Street Sidewalks St Tree Maint
5050 Schaefer Ave, Chino (91710-5549)
PHONE..............................909 591-9843
Ed Nylund, *Principal*
EMP: 66

SALES (est): 1.9MM **Privately Held**
WEB: www.chinopd.org
SIC: 4959 Sweeping service: road, airport, parking lot, etc.
PA: City Of Chino
13220 Central Ave
Chino CA 91710
909 591-9824

(P-6532)
CITY OF LONG BEACH
Also Called: City Long Bch Prkg Enforcement
2929 E Willow St, Long Beach (90806-2303)
PHONE..................................562 570-2890
James Kuhl, *Manager*
EMP: 250 **Privately Held**
WEB: www.polb.com
SIC: 4959 Sweeping service: road, airport, parking lot, etc.
PA: City Of Long Beach
333 W Ocean Blvd Fl 10
Long Beach CA 90802
562 570-6450

(P-6533)
CLEANSTREET
1937 W 169th St, Gardena (90247-5253)
PHONE..................................310 329-3078
Jere Costello, *CEO*
Claudia Cervantes, *Executive*
Richard Anderson, *General Mgr*
Jennie Gamboa, *Admin Sec*
Angie Cruz, *Administration*
EMP: 137
SQ FT: 15,000
SALES (est): 35MM **Privately Held**
WEB: www.cleanstreet.com
SIC: 4959 Sweeping service: road, airport, parking lot, etc.

(P-6534)
COUNTY OF STANISLAUS
Also Called: Public Works Operations
1716 Morgan Rd, Modesto (95358-5805)
PHONE..................................209 525-4130
Dave Nordell, *General Mgr*
EMP: 115 **Privately Held**
WEB: www.co.stanislaus.ca.us
SIC: 4959 Road, airport & parking lot maintenance services
PA: County Of Stanislaus
1010 10th St Ste 5100
Modesto CA 95354
209 525-6398

(P-6535)
COUNTY SANTTN DIST 2 OF LA CO (PA)
Also Called: L.A.cO.
1955 Workman Mill Rd, Whittier (90601-1415)
P.O. Box 4998 (90607-4998)
PHONE..................................562 699-7411
Stephen Maguin, *General Mgr*
Rechelle Asperin, *Bd of Directors*
Kristen Ruffell, *Vice Pres*
Sam Perdoza, *General Mgr*
Kim Compton, *Admin Sec*
EMP: 850
SALES (est): 1.1B **Privately Held**
SIC: 4959 Sanitary services

(P-6536)
COUNTY SANTTN DIST 2 OF LA CO
24501 Figueroa St, Carson (90745-6311)
PHONE..................................310 830-2400
Ken Redemacher, *Manager*
Amado Urtis, *Administration*
David Walbeck, *Project Engr*
Joe McCaffrey, *Safety Mgr*
Ken Rademacher, *Plant Mgr*
EMP: 500
SALES (corp-wide): 1.1B **Privately Held**
SIC: 4959 Sanitary services
PA: County Sanitation District No. 2 Of Los Angeles County
1955 Workman Mill Rd
Whittier CA 90601
562 699-7411

(P-6537)
COUNTY SANTTN DIST 2 OF LA CO
920 S Alameda St, Compton (90221-4807)
PHONE..................................310 638-1161
Samuel Espinoza, *Manager*
EMP: 100
SALES (corp-wide): 1.1B **Privately Held**
SIC: 4959 9511 Sanitary services; sanitary engineering agency, government;
PA: County Sanitation District No. 2 Of Los Angeles County
1955 Workman Mill Rd
Whittier CA 90601
562 699-7411

(P-6538)
ECOLOGY CONTROL INDUSTRIES
255 Parr Blvd, Richmond (94801-1119)
PHONE..................................510 235-1393
Curtis Lindskog, *Manager*
EMP: 100 **Privately Held**
SIC: 4959 4953 4212 Environmental cleanup services; hazardous waste collection & disposal; hazardous waste transport
PA: Ecology Control Industries, Inc
15707 S Main St
Gardena CA 90248

(P-6539)
ENGINEERING/REMDTN RSRCS GRP (PA)
Also Called: Errg
4585 Pacheco Blvd Ste 200, Martinez (94553-2228)
PHONE..................................925 839-2200
Cynthia A Liu, *CEO*
Todd Katz, *CFO*
EMP: 70 **EST:** 1997
SQ FT: 31,000
SALES: 42MM **Privately Held**
WEB: www.errg.com
SIC: 4959 8744 Environmental cleanup services;

(P-6540)
ENVIRONMENTAL PROTECTION AGCY
Also Called: E P A
1001 I St Ste 19b, Sacramento (95814-2828)
PHONE..................................916 324-7572
Joan Denton, *Director*
Deborah L O'Jones, *Manager*
EMP: 55 **Publicly Held**
WEB: www.epa.gov
SIC: 4959 Toxic or hazardous waste cleanup
HQ: Environmental Protection Agency
1200 Pennsylvania Ave Nw
Washington DC 20460
202 564-4700

(P-6541)
GARYS CONSTRUCTION INC
2517 Dos Lomas, Fallbrook (92028-9159)
P.O. Box 189, Bonsall (92003-0189)
PHONE..................................760 639-4456
Gary Albery, *President*
Tammy Albery, *Admin Sec*
EMP: 120
SQ FT: 1,200
SALES (est): 9.9MM **Privately Held**
SIC: 4959 1799 0782 Sweeping service: road, airport, parking lot, etc.; construction site cleanup; lawn & garden services

(P-6542)
JONSET CORPORATION
Also Called: Sunset Property Services
16251 Construction Cir W, Irvine (92606-4412)
PHONE..................................949 551-5151
John Howhannesian, *President*
Carmen Howhannesian, *Admin Sec*
Andrea Howhannesian, *Info Tech Mgr*
Angie Ramos, *Manager*
EMP: 96
SQ FT: 6,000

SALES (est): 14.6MM **Privately Held**
WEB: www.sunsetpropertyservices.com
SIC: 4959 7349 Sweeping service: road, airport, parking lot, etc.; janitorial service, contract basis

(P-6543)
NRC ENVIRONMENTAL SERVICES INC (HQ)
1605 Ferry Pt, Alameda (94501)
PHONE..................................510 749-1390
Steven Candito, *President*
Neil Challis, *Senior VP*
Mike Reese, *Senior VP*
Todd Roloff, *Senior VP*
Sal Sacco, *Senior VP*
▲ **EMP:** 80
SQ FT: 18,000
SALES (est): 48.2MM **Privately Held**
WEB: www.nrces.com
SIC: 4959 Toxic or hazardous waste cleanup; oil spill cleanup; environmental cleanup services

(P-6544)
PACIFIC PARKING & VALET LLC
Also Called: National Parking & Valet
2560 Garden Rd Ste 109, Monterey (93940-5395)
PHONE..................................831 646-0426
Steven Summers, *President*
EMP: 130
SQ FT: 900
SALES: 1.3MM **Privately Held**
SIC: 4959 1799 7521 Road, airport & parking lot maintenance services; parking facility equipment & maintenance; parking garage

(P-6545)
PSC INDUSTRIAL OUTSOURCING LP
Also Called: Hydrochempsc
5780 Obata Way Ste A, Gilroy (95020-7092)
PHONE..................................831 635-0220
William Fiedler, *Manager*
EMP: 60
SALES (corp-wide): 750MM **Privately Held**
SIC: 4959 Environmental cleanup services
PA: Psc Industrial Outsourcing, Lp
900 Georgia Ave
Deer Park TX 77536
713 393-5600

(P-6546)
RHO CHEM LLC (DH)
425 Isis Ave, Inglewood (90301-2076)
PHONE..................................323 776-6234
Ramon Robles, *CEO*
▲ **EMP:** 50
SALES (est): 17.3MM
SALES (corp-wide): 3.5B **Publicly Held**
SIC: 4959 Sanitary services
HQ: Nortru, Llc
515 Lycaste St
Detroit MI 48214
313 824-5840

(P-6547)
RICHMOND SANITARY SERVICE INC (HQ)
Also Called: Crockett Garbage Service
3260 Blume Dr Ste 100, Richmond (94806-1960)
P.O. Box 4100 (94804-0100)
PHONE..................................510 262-7100
Richard Granzella, *President*
Dennis Varni, *CFO*
Mario Acquilino, *Vice Pres*
Pina Barbiere, *Principal*
Loyd Bonfante, *Principal*
▲ **EMP:** 200
SALES (est): 78MM
SALES (corp-wide): 10B **Publicly Held**
SIC: 4959 Sanitary services
PA: Republic Services, Inc.
18500 N Allied Way # 100
Phoenix AZ 85054
480 627-2700

(P-6548)
SACRAMENTO REG CO SANIT DIST (PA)
Also Called: Srcsd
10060 Goethe Rd, Sacramento (95827-3553)
PHONE..................................916 876-6000
Prabhakar Somavarapu, *Director*
Joe Maestretti, *CFO*
Phil Serna, *Principal*
Anna Johnson, *Research*
Pedro Ceja, *Technology*
EMP: 700 **EST:** 1973
SQ FT: 136,000
SALES (est): 95.9MM **Privately Held**
SIC: 4959 Sanitary services

(P-6549)
SACRAMENTO YOLO CNTY MOSQUITO
8631 Bond Rd, Elk Grove (95624-1477)
PHONE..................................916 685-1022
Raul Deanda, *President*
Vern Bruhn, *Vice Pres*
Paula Macedo, *Lab Dir*
Janna McLeod, *Admin Mgr*
Marcia Reed, *Admin Mgr*
EMP: 51
SALES (est): 7.7MM **Privately Held**
WEB: www.sac-yolomvcd.com
SIC: 4959 Mosquito eradication

(P-6550)
SULLINOVO
2750 Womble Rd Ste 100, San Diego (92106-6114)
PHONE..................................619 260-1432
Steven Sullivan, *Partner*
Scott Blount, *Partner*
Steven Bonde, *Partner*
EMP: 206
SALES (est): 5.7MM **Privately Held**
SIC: 4959 8744 Toxic or hazardous waste cleanup;

4961 Steam & Air Conditioning Sply

(P-6551)
CGP HOLDINGS LLC
2 Gill Station Coastal Rd, Little Lake (93542)
PHONE..................................760 764-1300
EMP: 82
SALES (est): 439.9K **Privately Held**
SIC: 4961

(P-6552)
TRI-STATE AG INC
Also Called: Priority Cooling
47375 W Dakota Ave, Firebaugh (93622-9516)
PHONE..................................209 364-6185
James M Hammonds, *President*
Mary H Hicks, *Treasurer*
William E Hammond, *Vice Pres*
William E Hammonds, *Vice Pres*
EMP: 82
SALES (est): 4.5MM **Privately Held**
SIC: 4961 Cooled air supplier

4971 Irrigation Systems

(P-6553)
ARVIN-EDISON WATER STORAGE DST (PA)
20401 E Bear Mtn Blvd, Arvin (93203-9475)
P.O. Box 175 (93203-0175)
PHONE..................................661 854-5573
Howard Frick, *President*
John C Moore, *Corp Secy*
Salvadore Giumarra, *Vice Pres*
Christy Kong, *Accountant*
EMP: 50
SQ FT: 5,000
SALES: 17.7MM **Privately Held**
SIC: 4971 Water distribution or supply systems for irrigation

(P-6554)
FRESNO IRRIGATION DISTRICT
2907 S Maple Ave, Fresno (93725-2218)
PHONE..........................559 233-7161
Gary R Serrato, *General Mgr*
Deann Hailey, *CFO*
Julio Padilla, *Engineer*
Laurence Kimura, *Manager*
EMP: 83
SQ FT: 18,000
SALES: 17.8MM **Privately Held**
WEB: www.fresnoirrigation.com
SIC: 4971 Water distribution or supply systems for irrigation

(P-6555)
GLENN-COLUSA IRRIGATION DST (PA)
344 E Laurel St, Willows (95988-3114)
P.O. Box 150 (95988-0150)
PHONE..........................530 934-8881
Donald Bransford, *President*
Dennis Michum, *Treasurer*
EMP: 75
SQ FT: 5,000
SALES: 12.7MM **Privately Held**
WEB: www.gcid.net
SIC: 4971 Water distribution or supply systems for irrigation

(P-6556)
IMPERIAL IRRIGATION DISTRICT
Also Called: Imperial Irrgtion Dst Wtr Dept
333 E Barioni Blvd, Imperial (92251-1773)
P.O. Box 937 (92251-0937)
PHONE..........................760 339-9220
Robert McCullough, *Branch Mgr*
EMP: 400
SQ FT: 10,000
SALES (corp-wide): 634.6MM **Privately Held**
WEB: www.iidwater.com
SIC: 4971 Water distribution or supply systems for irrigation
PA: Imperial Irrigation District
333 E Barioni Blvd
Imperial CA 92251
800 303-7756

(P-6557)
MERCED IRRIGATION DISTRICT
3321 Franklin Rd, Merced (95348-9345)
PHONE..........................209 722-2719
Jarith Krause, *Manager*
EMP: 160
SALES (corp-wide): 89MM **Privately Held**
WEB: www.mercedid.org
SIC: 4971 Water distribution or supply systems for irrigation
PA: Merced Irrigation District
744 W 20th St
Merced CA 95340
209 722-5761

(P-6558)
METROPOLITAN WATER DISTRICT
700 N Alameda St Ste 1, Los Angeles (90012-3353)
PHONE..........................213 217-6667
Ronald Gastelum, *CEO*
EMP: 1000
SALES (corp-wide): 1.3B **Privately Held**
WEB: www.mwdh2o.com
SIC: 4971 Water distribution or supply systems for irrigation
PA: The Metropolitan Water District Of Southern California
700 N Alameda St
Los Angeles CA 90012
213 217-6000

(P-6559)
NEVADA IRRIGATION DISTRICT (PA)
Also Called: N I D
1036 W Main St, Grass Valley (95945-5424)
PHONE..........................530 273-6185
Remleh Scherzinger, *General Mgr*
John H Drew, *President*
Keane Sommers, *CEO*
Marie Owens, *Treasurer*
Doug Roderick, *Vice Pres*

▲ EMP: 160
SQ FT: 11,050
SALES: 48.7MM **Privately Held**
SIC: 4971 4911 Water distribution or supply systems for irrigation; generation, electric power

(P-6560)
OAK SPRINGS NURSERY INC
13761 Eldridge Ave, Sylmar (91342-1764)
P.O. Box 922906 (91392-2906)
PHONE..........................818 367-5832
Manuel Cacho, *President*
Fred Siegler, *Contractor*
EMP: 90
SALES (est): 10.3MM **Privately Held**
SIC: 4971 0781 Irrigation systems; landscape services

(P-6561)
PALO VERDE IRRIGATION DISTRICT
180 W 14th Ave, Blythe (92225-2714)
PHONE..........................760 922-3144
Ed Smith, *General Mgr*
Janice Love, *Treasurer*
EMP: 85 EST: 1923
SQ FT: 8,125
SALES (est): 14MM **Privately Held**
WEB: www.pvid.org
SIC: 4971 Water distribution or supply systems for irrigation

(P-6562)
PANOCHE WATER DISTRICT
52027 W Althea Ave, Firebaugh (93622-9401)
PHONE..........................209 364-6136
ARA Azhderian, *General Mgr*
John Bennet, *President*
Sue Redfern, *Vice Pres*
Michael Linneman, *Director*
Mike Sterns, *Director*
EMP: 50
SQ FT: 1,200
SALES (est): 4.1MM **Privately Held**
WEB: www.panochewd.org
SIC: 4971 Water distribution or supply systems for irrigation

(P-6563)
RAIN BIRD CORPORATION
2475-A Paseo De Las Ameri, San Diego (92154-7255)
PHONE..........................619 661-4493
Catherine Wade, *Branch Mgr*
EMP: 64
SALES (corp-wide): 98.2MM **Privately Held**
WEB: www.rainbird.com
SIC: 4971 Irrigation systems
PA: Rain Bird Corporation
970 W Sierra Madre Ave
Azusa CA 91702
626 812-3400

(P-6564)
SAN LUIS DLTA-MENDOTA WTR AUTH
15990 Kelso Rd, Byron (94514-1916)
PHONE..........................209 835-2593
Frances Mizuno, *Principal*
Dan Nelson, *Exec Dir*
Jim Lenhardt, *Planning*
Jeff Belwood, *Engineer*
EMP: 80
SALES (corp-wide): 34.4MM **Privately Held**
SIC: 4971 8611 Water distribution or supply systems for irrigation; public utility association
PA: San Luis & Delta-Mendota Water Authority
842 6th St
Los Banos CA 93635
209 826-9696

(P-6565)
SOLANO IRRIGATION DISTRICT
810 Vaca Valley Pkwy # 201, Vacaville (95688-8835)
PHONE..........................707 448-6847
Robert Hansen, *President*
Guido E Colla, *Vice Pres*
Cary Keaten, *General Mgr*
Charles Mueller, *Admin Asst*

Victor Nava, *Admin Asst*
EMP: 99
SQ FT: 8,500
SALES: 12.9MM **Privately Held**
WEB: www.sidwater.org
SIC: 4971 Irrigation systems

(P-6566)
SOUTH FEATHER WATER & PWR AGCY (PA)
2310 Oro Quincy Hwy, Oroville (95966-5226)
PHONE..........................530 533-4578
James Edward, *Director*
Lou Lodigiani, *President*
Steve Wong, *CFO*
Patricia A Sands, *Treasurer*
Michael Glaze, *General Mgr*
EMP: 57
SQ FT: 5,000
SALES (est): 12.3MM **Privately Held**
WEB: www.southfeather.com
SIC: 4971 Water distribution or supply systems for irrigation

(P-6567)
SOUTH SAN JQUIN IRRIGATION DST
Also Called: Ssjid
11011 E Highway 120, Manteca (95336-9751)
P.O. Box 747, Ripon (95366-0747)
PHONE..........................209 249-4600
Betty Garcia, *Exec Sec*
Walt Luihn, *Officer*
Julie Jeleti, *Division Mgr*
Lee Rice, *Division Mgr*
Shawn Ussery, *Division Mgr*
EMP: 93
SQ FT: 8,500
SALES: 9.6MM **Privately Held**
WEB: www.ssjid.com
SIC: 4971 Water distribution or supply systems for irrigation

(P-6568)
TURLOCK IRRIGATION DISTRICT
Also Called: T I D
901 N Broadway, Turlock (95380-3012)
P.O. Box 949 (95381-0949)
PHONE..........................209 883-8300
Larry Weis, *Branch Mgr*
Jeff Leal, *IT/INT Sup*
Jessica Vieths, *Technician*
Peggy Harding, *Engineer*
Mark Jones, *Opers Staff*
EMP: 400
SQ FT: 1,554
SALES (corp-wide): 52.2MM **Privately Held**
WEB: www.tid.com
SIC: 4971 Impounding reservoir, irrigation; water distribution or supply systems for irrigation
PA: Turlock Irrigation District
333 E Canal Dr
Turlock CA 95380
209 883-8222

(P-6569)
VISTA IRRIGATION DISTRICT
Also Called: Vid
1391 Engineer St, Vista (92081-8836)
PHONE..........................760 597-3100
John Amodeo, *General Mgr*
Brett Hodgkiss, *Admin Mgr*
Roy Coox, *General Mgr*
Chris Craghead, *Engineer*
Al Ducusin, *Engineer*
EMP: 99
SQ FT: 2,500
SALES: 43.1MM **Privately Held**
WEB: www.vid-h2o.org
SIC: 4971 Water distribution or supply systems for irrigation

---

5012 Automobiles & Other Motor Vehicles Wholesale

(P-6570)
A-Z BUS SALES INC (PA)
Also Called: John Deere Authorized Dealer
1900 S Riverside Ave, Colton (92324-3344)
PHONE..........................951 781-7188
Edwin John Landherr, *CEO*
James Reynolds, *President*
Brian Hunt, *Sales Staff*
Jerry Locken, *Sales Staff*
Dave Reynolds, *Manager*
▼ EMP: 90
SQ FT: 20,000
SALES: 3.9MM **Privately Held**
WEB: www.a-zbus.com
SIC: 5012 5082 Buses; construction & mining machinery

(P-6571)
ABC BUS INC
1485 Dale Way, Costa Mesa (92626-3918)
PHONE..........................714 444-5888
Dane Cornell, *CEO*
EMP: 57
SALES (corp-wide): 160.9MM **Privately Held**
SIC: 5012 4173 Buses; bus terminal & service facilities
HQ: Abc Bus, Inc.
1506 30th St Nw
Faribault MN 55021
507 334-1871

(P-6572)
ABC BUS INC
3508 Haven Ave, Redwood City (94063-4603)
PHONE..........................650 368-3364
Mike Lawrence, *Manager*
EMP: 57
SALES (corp-wide): 164.9MM **Privately Held**
SIC: 5012 4173 Buses; bus terminal & service facilities
HQ: Abc Bus, Inc.
1506 30th St Nw
Faribault MN 55021
507 334-1871

(P-6573)
ADESA CORPORATION LLC
Also Called: Adesa Auction
8649 Kiefer Blvd, Sacramento (95826-3907)
PHONE..........................916 388-8899
Jim Sale, *Branch Mgr*
Raymond Klingaman, *General Mgr*
Raymond Killingaman, *Info Tech Mgr*
EMP: 115 **Publicly Held**
WEB: www.adesa.com
SIC: 5012 Automobile auction
HQ: Adesa Corporation, Llc
13085 Hamilton Crossing B
Carmel IN 46032

(P-6574)
ADESA CORPORATION LLC
11625 Nino Way, Mira Loma (91752-1437)
PHONE..........................951 361-9400
Scott Spalder, *Manager*
Jill Almeter, *Office Mgr*
Stephen Spinola, *Network Enginr*
Lora Rivera, *Human Res Dir*
Jeff Hyde, *Manager*
EMP: 50 **Publicly Held**
WEB: www.adesa.com
SIC: 5012 7549 Automobile auction; automotive maintenance services
HQ: Adesa Corporation, Llc
13085 Hamilton Crossing B
Carmel IN 46032

(P-6575)
ADESA CORPORATION LLC
2175 Cactus Rd, San Diego (92154-8002)
PHONE..........................619 661-5565
Dale McIlroy, *Manager*

(PA)=Parent Co (HQ)=Headquarters (DH)=Div Headquarters
✿ = New Business established in last 2 years
2019 Directory of California
Wholesalers and Services Companies
281

P R O D U C T S & S V C S

Barry Fabricant, *General Mgr*
Jose Hyoro, *Mktg Dir*
Dale Mc Ilroy, *Manager*
EMP: 120 **Publicly Held**
WEB: www.adesa.com
SIC: 5012 5521 Automobile auction; used car dealers
HQ: Adesa Corporation, Llc
13085 Hamilton Crossing B
Carmel IN 46032

(P-6576)
AICHINGER INTERNATIONAL INC
5423 Littlebow Rd, Pls Vrds Pnsl
(90275-2364)
PHONE..................................310 375-1533
Hans Aichinger, *President*
EMP: 70
SALES (est): 2.9MM **Privately Held**
SIC: 5012 Automobiles

(P-6577)
AMERICAN HONDA MOTOR CO INC (HQ)
1919 Torrance Blvd, Torrance
(90501-2722)
P.O. Box 2200 (90509-2200)
PHONE..................................310 783-2000
Takuji Yamada, *CEO*
Takanobu Ito, *President*
Hiroyuki Suganuma, *CFO*
H Okada, *Treasurer*
Thomas G Elliott, *Exec VP*
◆ **EMP:** 2375 **EST:** 1959
SALES (est): 11B
SALES (corp-wide): 144.1B **Privately Held**
WEB: www.honda.com
SIC: 5012 3732 Automobiles; jet skis
PA: Honda Motor Co., Ltd.
2-1-1, Minamiaoyama
Minato-Ku TKY 107-0
334 231-111

(P-6578)
AQUIRECORPS NORWALK AUTO AUCTN
12405 Rosecrans Ave, Norwalk
(90650-5056)
PHONE..................................562 864-7464
Rj Romero, *Ch of Bd*
Lou Rudich, *COO*
Steve Fleurant, *CFO*
Chuck Doskow, *Admin Sec*
David Aker, *Controller*
EMP: 125 **EST:** 1979
SQ FT: 55,000
SALES (est): 23.8MM **Privately Held**
WEB: www.norwalkautoauction.com
SIC: 5012 Automobile auction

(P-6579)
AUTO BUYLINE SYSTEMS INC (PA)
Also Called: A B S Auto Auctions
341 Corporate Terrace Cir, Corona
(92879-6028)
PHONE..................................909 881-7828
Thomas Harmon, *President*
Steve Boyes, *District Mgr*
George Chickering, *District Mgr*
Vince Pytel, *District Mgr*
Annette Harmon, *Admin Sec*
EMP: 50
SALES (est): 31.9MM **Privately Held**
WEB: www.absbidsales.com
SIC: 5012 Automobile auction

(P-6580)
CALIFRNIA AUTO DALERS EXCH LLC
Also Called: Riverside Auto Auction
1320 N Tustin Ave, Anaheim (92807-1619)
PHONE..................................714 996-2400
Tim Van Dam, *General Mgr*
EMP: 400
SALES (est): 78.6MM
SALES (corp-wide): 32.8B **Privately Held**
WEB: www.riversideautoauction.com
SIC: 5012 Automobile auction

HQ: Manheim Investments, Inc.
6205 Pachtree Dunwoody Rd
Atlanta GA 30328
866 626-4346

(P-6581)
CARSON CAPITAL CORP (PA)
42882 Ivy St, Murrieta (92562-7218)
PHONE..................................951 684-9585
Dale E Carson, *President*
Terri L Carson, *Corp Secy*
Dean Wm Carson, *Senior VP*
EMP: 51
SQ FT: 5,000
SALES (est): 11.8MM **Privately Held**
WEB: www.carsoncapital.com
SIC: 5012 5511 4111 Buses; new & used car dealers; commuter bus operation

(P-6582)
COAST COUNTIES TRUCK & EQP CO
Also Called: Coast Counties Peterbilt
260 Doolittle Dr, San Leandro
(94577-1014)
PHONE..................................510 568-6933
Jon Wacker, *Branch Mgr*
EMP: 52
SALES (corp-wide): 79.9MM **Privately Held**
WEB: www.coastcounties.com
SIC: 5012 Trucks, commercial
PA: Coast Counties Truck & Equipment Company
1740 N 4th St
San Jose CA 95112
408 453-5510

(P-6583)
COPART
5251 Business Center Dr, Fairfield
(94534-1951)
PHONE..................................707 863-0297
Brad Richman, *Principal*
Sriram Vaidyanathan, *Info Tech Dir*
Paula Holland, *Engineer*
Rick Davis, *Manager*
EMP: 50
SALES (est): 5.9MM **Privately Held**
SIC: 5012 Automobile auction

(P-6584)
COX AUTOMOTIVE INC
Also Called: Los Angeles Auto Auction
8001 Garvey Ave, Rosemead
(91770-2420)
PHONE..................................626 573-8001
Ed Pullen, *General Mgr*
EMP: 200
SALES (corp-wide): 32.8B **Privately Held**
WEB: www.manheim.com
SIC: 5012 5521 7389 Automobile auction; used car dealers; auctioneers, fee basis
HQ: Cox Automotive, Inc.
6205-A Pchtree Dnwoody Rd
Atlanta GA 30328
404 843-5000

(P-6585)
COX AUTOMOTIVE INC
10700 Beech Ave, Fontana (92337-7205)
PHONE..................................404 843-5000
Russ Norrish, *Manager*
Glenn Terrell, *Manager*
EMP: 600
SALES (corp-wide): 32.8B **Privately Held**
WEB: www.manheim.com
SIC: 5012 5521 5531 Automobile auction; used car dealers; automotive accessories
HQ: Cox Automotive, Inc.
6205-A Pchtree Dnwoody Rd
Atlanta GA 30328
404 843-5000

(P-6586)
COX AUTOMOTIVE INC
29900 Auction Ct, Hayward (94544-6914)
PHONE..................................510 786-4500
Tina Novoa, *General Mgr*
Lisa Simon, *Controller*
EMP: 500
SQ FT: 150,000
SALES (corp-wide): 32.8B **Privately Held**
WEB: www.manheim.com
SIC: 5012 Automobiles & other motor vehicles

HQ: Cox Automotive, Inc.
6205-A Pchtree Dnwoody Rd
Atlanta GA 30328
404 843-5000

(P-6587)
COX AUTOMOTIVE INC
Also Called: Manheim Riverside Auto Auction
6446 Fremont St, Riverside (92504-1437)
PHONE..................................951 689-6000
Scott Hurst, *Manager*
Allia Haque, *Manager*
EMP: 440
SALES (corp-wide): 32.8B **Privately Held**
WEB: www.manheim.com
SIC: 5012 7389 5531 5521 Automobile auction; auctioneers, fee basis; automotive accessories; automobiles, used cars only
HQ: Cox Automotive, Inc.
6205-A Pchtree Dnwoody Rd
Atlanta GA 30328
404 843-5000

(P-6588)
COX AUTOMOTIVE INC
Also Called: Manheim San Diego
691 Calle Joven, Oceanside (92057)
PHONE..................................760 754-3600
Jill Scott, *Branch Mgr*
EMP: 290
SALES (corp-wide): 32.8B **Privately Held**
WEB: www.manheim.com
SIC: 5012 Automobile auction
HQ: Cox Automotive, Inc.
6205-A Pchtree Dnwoody Rd
Atlanta GA 30328
404 843-5000

(P-6589)
DEALIX CORPORATION
720 Bay Rd Ste 200, Redwood City
(94063-2480)
PHONE..................................650 599-5500
Lee J Brunz, *CEO*
Samara Jaffe, *VP Opers*
Daleen Martinez, *Manager*
Jay Halloran, *Accounts Mgr*
EMP: 135
SQ FT: 31,000
SALES (est): 18.8MM **Publicly Held**
WEB: www.dealix.com
SIC: 5012 Automotive brokers
PA: Autoweb, Inc.
18872 Macarthur Blvd
Irvine CA 92612

(P-6590)
DESERT VIEW AUTO AUCTIONS INC (PA)
14280 Danielson St A, Poway
(92064-8819)
PHONE..................................760 788-6955
Joseph Mulcahy Jr, *President*
Sean Mulcahy, *Vice Pres*
EMP: 105
SQ FT: 3,000
SALES (est): 12.3MM **Privately Held**
SIC: 5012 Automobiles

(P-6591)
E M THARP INC (PA)
Also Called: Golden Peterbilt
15243 Road 192, Porterville (93257-8967)
PHONE..................................559 782-5800
Morris Tharp, *President*
Morris A Tharp, *President*
Jim Angle, *Foreman/Supr*
Randy Ray, *Sales Staff*
Charlie Simpson, *Manager*
EMP: 96
SALES (est): 34.3MM **Privately Held**
SIC: 5012 5013 5511 5531 Trucks, commercial; truck parts & accessories; trucks, tractors & trailers: new & used; truck equipment & parts; recreational vehicle repairs

(P-6592)
FRESNO AUTO DEALERS AUCTION
278 N Marks Ave, Fresno (93706-1136)
PHONE..................................559 268-8051
Darryl Ceccolil, *President*
▼ **EMP:** 107

SQ FT: 15,000
SALES (est): 10.6MM
SALES (corp-wide): 32.8B **Privately Held**
SIC: 5012 Automobile auction
HQ: Manheim Investments, Inc.
6205 Pachtree Dunwoody Rd
Atlanta GA 30328
866 626-4346

(P-6593)
FRESNO TRUCK CENTER
2727 E Central Ave, Fresno (93725-2425)
P.O. Box 12346 (93777-2346)
PHONE..................................559 486-4310
Randy Moore, *Manager*
Michael Belles, *Principal*
EMP: 80
SQ FT: 40,000
SALES (corp-wide): 161.5MM **Privately Held**
WEB: www.fresnotruckcenter.com
SIC: 5012 5511 7538 5531 Truck tractors; trucks, tractors & trailers: new & used; general truck repair; truck equipment & parts; truck tires & tubes
PA: Fresno Truck Center
2727 E Central Ave
Fresno CA 93725
559 486-4310

(P-6594)
FRESNO TRUCK CENTER
Also Called: Delta Truck Center
10182 S Harlan Rd, French Camp
(95231-9647)
P.O. Box 20 (95231-0020)
PHONE..................................209 983-2400
John Gannon, *Manager*
EMP: 125
SALES (est): 14.4MM
SALES (corp-wide): 161.5MM **Privately Held**
WEB: www.fresnotruckcenter.com
SIC: 5012 5013 7538 5531 Trucks, commercial; automotive supplies & parts; general automotive repair shops; truck equipment & parts; pickups, new & used; engines & parts, diesel
PA: Fresno Truck Center
2727 E Central Ave
Fresno CA 93725
559 486-4310

(P-6595)
GATEWAY AUTO SALES & LSG INC
Also Called: Gateway Auto Auction Group
3260 E Annadale Ave, Fresno
(93725-1903)
PHONE..................................800 921-4336
Larry B Champagne, *President*
EMP: 52
SQ FT: 4,000
SALES (est): 18.7MM **Privately Held**
WEB: www.champagnecars.com
SIC: 5012 Automobile auction

(P-6596)
HAAKER EQUIPMENT COMPANY (PA)
Also Called: TOTAL CLEAN
2070 N White Ave, La Verne (91750-5679)
PHONE..................................909 542-0800
Edward R Blackman, *CEO*
Randy Blackman, *President*
Edward C Haaker, *CFO*
Michelle Haaker, *Executive*
Wilson Shyu, *General Mgr*
▼ **EMP:** 76
SQ FT: 50,000
SALES: 56.2MM **Privately Held**
SIC: 5012 5087 5999 Ambulances; cleaning & maintenance equipment & supplies; cleaning equipment & supplies

(P-6597)
INLAND KENWORTH (US) INC (HQ)
9730 Cherry Ave, Fontana (92335-5257)
PHONE..................................909 823-9955
Leigh Parker, *Chairman*
Jim Beidrwieden, *President*
William Currie, *CEO*
Les Ziegler, *CFO*
▼ **EMP:** 105 **EST:** 1934
SQ FT: 60,000

▲ = Import ▼=Export
◆ =Import/Export

SALES (est): 141.2MM **Privately Held**
WEB: www.inland-group.com
SIC: **5012** 7538 5013 7513 Trucks, commercial; diesel engine repair: automotive; truck parts & accessories; truck rental & leasing, no drivers
PA: Inland Industries Ltd
    2482 Douglas Rd
    Burnaby BC V5C 6
    604 291-6021

(P-6598)
INSURANCE AUTO AUCTIONS INC
7245 Laurel Canyon Blvd # 5, North Hollywood (91605-3718)
PHONE..................................818 487-2222
Charles Sanders, *Manager*
Heath Gridley, *Sales Mgr*
EMP: 59 **Publicly Held**
SIC: **5012** 5531 5093 Automobile auction; automobiles; automotive accessories; automotive wrecking for scrap
HQ: Insurance Auto Auctions, Inc.
    2 Westbrook Corporate Ctr # 1000
    Westchester IL 60154
    708 492-7000

(P-6599)
INTERSTATE TRUCK CENTER LLC (PA)
Also Called: Valley Peterbilt
2110 S Sinclair Ave, Stockton (95215-7556)
PHONE..................................209 944-5821
David T Morganson, *Mng Member*
Rick Coslett, *CFO*
Don Hoffman, *Info Tech Mgr*
Radawna Hanson, *Asst Controller*
Mark Wells, *Mktg Dir*
EMP: 100
SQ FT: 22,000
SALES (est): 66.8MM **Privately Held**
WEB: www.itctrucks.com
SIC: **5012** 7513 Trucks, commercial; truck rental, without drivers

(P-6600)
JETWORLD INC
Also Called: Jetmore International
2656 Chico Ave, South El Monte (91733-1617)
PHONE..................................626 448-0150
Leo Lea Young Lee, *President*
Chen Li-Fun Lee, *Corp Secy*
◆ EMP: 110
SQ FT: 5,000
SALES: 11.1MM **Privately Held**
WEB: www.jetworld.com
SIC: **5012** 5065 5063 5999 Automobiles & other motor vehicles; security control equipment & systems; flashlights; alarm signal systems; automotive supplies & parts

(P-6601)
KAWASAKI MOTORS CORP USA (HQ)
26972 Burbank, Foothill Ranch (92610-2506)
P.O. Box 25252, Santa Ana (92799-5252)
PHONE..................................949 837-4683
Masatoshi Tsurutani, *President*
Richard N Beattie, *Officer*
Bill Jenkins, *Senior VP*
Terunori Kitajima, *Executive*
Jesse Koeller, *District Mgr*
◆ EMP: 400
SQ FT: 40,000
SALES (est): 231.9MM
SALES (corp-wide): 14.7B **Privately Held**
SIC: **5012** 5013 5084 5091 Motorcycles; motorcycle parts; engines; gasoline; boats, canoes, watercrafts & equipment
PA: Kawasaki Heavy Industries, Ltd.
    1-1-3, Higashikawasakicho, Chuo-Ku
    Kobe HYO 650-0
    783 719-530

(P-6602)
LOS ANGELES TRUCK CENTERS LLC
Also Called: Los Angeles Freightliner
13800 Valley Blvd, Fontana (92335-5216)
PHONE..................................909 510-4000

Ricardo Flores, *Manager*
Scott Zeppenfeldt, *General Mgr*
Billie Davis, *Technology*
Reyna Espinoza, *Technology*
Priscilla Segala, *Technology*
EMP: 200
SALES (corp-wide): 113.3MM **Privately Held**
WEB: www.laflr.com
SIC: **5012** 7538 5531 5511 Trucks, commercial; general automotive repair shops; automotive & home supply stores; new & used car dealers
PA: Los Angeles Truck Centers, Llc
    2429 Peck Rd
    Whittier CA 90601
    562 447-1200

(P-6603)
MARATHON INDUSTRIES INC
Also Called: Marathon Truck Bodies
25597 Springbrook Ave, Santa Clarita (91350-2427)
P.O. Box 800279 (91380-0279)
PHONE..................................661 286-1520
Chad Hess, *President*
Roger K Hess, *Chairman*
Tom Garcia, *VP Sales*
EMP: 145
SQ FT: 75,000
SALES (est): 25MM **Privately Held**
WEB: www.marathontruckbody.com
SIC: **5012** 3713 Automobiles & other motor vehicles; truck & bus bodies

(P-6604)
MIRAMAR FORD TRUCK SALES INC
Also Called: NationaLease
6066 Miramar Rd, San Diego (92121-2591)
PHONE..................................619 272-5340
Michael Buscher, *President*
Michael Maury, *Corp Secy*
Richard Harrigan, *Vice Pres*
Mike Maury, *Human Res Dir*
Justin Brown, *Purch Mgr*
EMP: 74 EST: 1982
SQ FT: 22,000
SALES: 15.8MM **Privately Held**
WEB: www.miramartruck.com
SIC: **5012** 5013 7513 Trucks, commercial; trucks, noncommercial; truck parts & accessories; truck rental & leasing, no drivers

(P-6605)
MOBIS PARTS AMERICA LLC (HQ)
10550 Talbert Ave Fl 4, Fountain Valley (92708-6031)
PHONE..................................786 515-1101
Yun Dong Park, *Mng Member*
Joyce Choi, *Executive Asst*
Sharon Lee, *Executive Asst*
Latoya Gordon, *Admin Asst*
Joyce Nakamura, *Analyst*
▲ EMP: 90
SALES (est): 182.9MM
SALES (corp-wide): 17.7B **Privately Held**
SIC: **5012** Automobiles & other motor vehicles
PA: Hyundai Mobis Co., Ltd.
    203 Teheran-Ro, Gangnam-Gu
    Seoul 06141
    822 201-8528

(P-6606)
NORMANDIN AUTO BROKERS
900 Cptl Expy Aut Mall, San Jose (95136-1102)
PHONE..................................408 266-2824
Louis Normandin, *Owner*
EMP: 80
SALES (est): 4.3MM **Privately Held**
SIC: **5012** Automobiles & other motor vehicles

(P-6607)
SHIFT TECHNOLOGIES INC
2500 Market St, San Francisco (94114-1915)
PHONE..................................415 800-2038
George Arison, *CEO*
I Arison Areshidze, *President*
Joel Washington, *CFO*

Katie Horne, *Principal*
Michael Lintz, *Software Engr*
EMP: 60
SQ FT: 1,500
SALES (est): 19.8MM **Privately Held**
SIC: **5012** 5511 Automotive brokers; automobiles, new & used

(P-6608)
SOUTH BAY AUTO AUCTION
13210 S Normandie Ave, Gardena (90249-2208)
PHONE..................................310 719-2000
Rod Rentfrow, *Manager*
Tony Callaway, *Vice Pres*
Blanca Chavez, *Office Mgr*
Samir Hessami, *Administration*
Blanca Carrasco, *Accounting Mgr*
EMP: 60
SALES (est): 9.9MM **Privately Held**
SIC: **5012** Automobile auction

(P-6609)
SSMB PACIFIC HOLDING CO INC (HQ)
Also Called: Bay Area Kenworth
1755 Adams Ave, San Leandro (94577-1001)
PHONE..................................510 836-6100
Harry Mamizuka, *President*
Tom Bertolino, *Vice Pres*
Xavier Martinez, *Sales Executive*
▼ EMP: 55 EST: 1942
SQ FT: 35,000
SALES (est): 132.3MM
SALES (corp-wide): 19.4B **Publicly Held**
WEB: www.bayareakenworth.com
SIC: **5012** 7699 Trucks, commercial; industrial truck repair
PA: Paccar Inc
    777 106th Ave Ne
    Bellevue WA 98004
    425 468-7400

(P-6610)
SSMB PACIFIC HOLDING CO INC
20769 Industry Rd, Anderson (96007-8703)
PHONE..................................530 222-1212
Glenn Reed, *Branch Mgr*
EMP: 52
SALES (corp-wide): 19.4B **Publicly Held**
SIC: **5012** Trucks, commercial
HQ: Ssmb Pacific Holding Co Inc
    1755 Adams Ave
    San Leandro CA 94577
    510 836-6100

(P-6611)
SSMB PACIFIC HOLDING CO INC
Also Called: Sacramento Kenworth
707 Display Way, Sacramento (95838-3386)
PHONE..................................916 371-3372
Tom Bertilino, *Branch Mgr*
EMP: 52
SALES (corp-wide): 19.4B **Publicly Held**
WEB: www.bayareakenworth.com
SIC: **5012** 7538 5531 5511 Trucks, commercial; general truck repair; truck equipment & parts; pickups, new & used
HQ: Ssmb Pacific Holding Co Inc
    1755 Adams Ave
    San Leandro CA 94577
    510 836-6100

(P-6612)
UTILITY TRAILER SALES OF S CA (PA)
15567 Valley Blvd, Fontana (92335-6351)
PHONE..................................877 275-4887
Paul F Bennett,
Walter Figueroa, *Administration*
Daniel Anchia, *Inv Control Mgr*
Bobby Garcia, *Marketing Staff*
Eduardo Martos, *Sales Staff*
EMP: 100
SALES: 88.1MM **Privately Held**
SIC: **5012** 5013 5531 5561 Trailers for passenger vehicles; automotive supplies & parts; automobile & truck equipment & parts; travel trailers: automobile, new & used

(P-6613)
WAH HUNG INTL MCHY INC
800 Monterey Pass Rd, Monterey Park (91754-3609)
PHONE..................................323 263-3513
Raymond Ng, *Manager*
EMP: 69 **Privately Held**
SIC: **5012** 5521 Automobiles; automobiles, used cars only
PA: Wah Hung International Machinery, Inc.
    1000 E Garvey Ave
    Monterey Park CA 91755

(P-6614)
WIND RIVER ENTERPRISES INC
Also Called: North Bay Auto Auction
250 Dittmer Rd, Fairfield (94534-1621)
PHONE..................................707 864-1040
Don Morrow, *President*
Maureen Green, *Corp Secy*
EMP: 95
SQ FT: 20,000
SALES: 14.3MM **Privately Held**
WEB: www.nbauto.com
SIC: **5012** Automobile auction

(P-6615)
ZERO MOTORCYCLES INC
380 El Pueblo Rd, Scotts Valley (95066-4212)
PHONE..................................831 438-3500
Richard Michael Walker, *CEO*
Karl Wharton, *COO*
John Boroska, *CFO*
Curt Sacks, *CFO*
Jay Friedland, *Vice Pres*
◆ EMP: 95
SQ FT: 34,000
SALES (est): 90.1MM **Privately Held**
WEB: www.zeromotorcycles.com
SIC: **5012** Motorcycles

5013 Motor Vehicle Splys & New Parts Wholesale

(P-6616)
1-800 RADIATOR & A/C (PA)
Also Called: 1-800-Radiator
4401 Park Rd, Benicia (94510-1124)
PHONE..................................707 747-7400
Mike Rippey, *Ch of Bd*
Joe Rippey, *President*
David Gruner, *Officer*
Kurtis Keala, *Vice Pres*
Joseph Bierer, *Program Mgr*
◆ EMP: 100
SALES (est): 46.5MM **Privately Held**
WEB: www.radiater.com
SIC: **5013** Radiators

(P-6617)
ALL STAR AUTOMOTIVE PRODUCTS
4257 Auction Ave Ste N, Baldwin Park (91706)
PHONE..................................626 960-5164
Fritz Ehlers, *President*
▲ EMP: 80
SQ FT: 28,000
SALES (est): 9.3MM **Privately Held**
WEB: www.allstarproducts.com
SIC: **5013** 3714 3694 Automotive supplies & parts; clutches, motor vehicle; engine electrical equipment

(P-6618)
ANTHONY LAMBE
Also Called: Fashion Wheel
1521 W Nielsen Ave Ste 69, Fresno (93706-1309)
PHONE..................................559 268-0709
Anthony Lambe, *Manager*
Jack Glos, *Owner*
EMP: 66
SQ FT: 25,000
SALES (est): 4.2MM **Privately Held**
WEB: www.steelband.com
SIC: **5013** Wheels, motor vehicle

(P-6619)
APU INC (PA)
14939 Oxnard St, Van Nuys (91411-2611)
PHONE..................................661 948-2880

John Christy Jr, *President*
EMP: 60
SQ FT: 20,000
SALES (est): 18.3MM **Privately Held**
WEB: www.apu.com
SIC: 5013 5531 Automotive supplies &
parts; automotive parts

(P-6620)
APW INTERNATIONAL INC
1073 E Artesia Blvd, Carson (90746-1601)
PHONE..................................310 884-5003
Jae W Chang, *President*
Young Suhr, *Exec VP*
Natalie Medina, *Asst Director*
▲ EMP: 140
SALES (est): 10.7MM **Privately Held**
SIC: 5013 Automotive supplies & parts

(P-6621)
**APW KNOX-SEEMAN
WAREHOUSE INC (HQ)**
1073 E Artesia Blvd, Carson (90746-1601)
PHONE..................................310 604-4373
Tong Y Suhr, *CEO*
Susan Suhr, *Admin Sec*
Charles Yu, *Info Tech Dir*
Jorge Hidalgo, *Purch Agent*
Anabell Maradiaga, *Purch Agent*
▲ EMP: 98 EST: 1972
SQ FT: 32,000
SALES (est): 56.9MM
SALES (corp-wide): 72.2MM **Privately
Held**
WEB: www.apwks.com
SIC: 5013 5531 Automotive supplies &
parts; automotive parts
PA: Auto Parts Warehouse, Inc.
16941 Keegan Ave
Carson CA 90746
800 913-6119

(P-6622)
AUTO EXPRESSIONS LLC
505 E Euclid Ave, Compton (90222-2811)
PHONE..................................310 639-0666
Lawrence McIsaac, *President*
Blake Barnett, *CFO*
John Fiumefreddo, *Senior VP*
Steve Lazzara, *Senior VP*
▲ EMP: 100 EST: 2010
SALES (est): 22.4MM
SALES (corp-wide): 71.8MM **Privately
Held**
SIC: 5013 Alternators
PA: Kraco Enterprises, Llc
505 E Euclid Ave
Compton CA 90222
310 639-0666

(P-6623)
**AUTO PARTS WAREHOUSE INC
(PA)**
16941 Keegan Ave, Carson (90746-1307)
PHONE..................................800 913-6119
Tong Young Suhr, *Principal*
Jim Hastie, *President*
Sarah Gustafson, *Vice Pres*
Sleung Ja Suhr, *Vice Pres*
Byung Joon Lee, *Admin Sec*
▼ EMP: 50
SQ FT: 40,000
SALES (est): 72.2MM **Privately Held**
SIC: 5013 Automotive supplies & parts

(P-6624)
**AUTOMOTIVE SUP CO
SOUTHERN CAL (PA)**
Also Called: Asco
10580 Mulberry Ave, Fontana
(92337-7024)
PHONE..................................909 428-9072
Chai Pong, *President*
▲ EMP: 65
SQ FT: 46,900
SALES (est): 19.9MM **Privately Held**
SIC: 5013 Automotive supplies & parts

(P-6625)
AZIMC INVESTMENTS INC (HQ)
8901 Canoga Ave, Canoga Park
(91304-1512)
P.O. Box 3939, Chatsworth (91313-3939)
PHONE..................................818 678-6571
◆ EMP: 200 EST: 1962

SALES (est): 199MM
SALES (corp-wide): 11.2B **Publicly Held**
WEB: www.imcparts.com
SIC: 5013 5599 Automotive supplies &
parts; dunebuggies
PA: Autozone, Inc.
123 S Front St
Memphis TN 38103
901 495-6500

(P-6626)
BBK PERFORMANCE INC
Also Called: Gripp
27440 Bostik Ct, Temecula (92590-3698)
PHONE..................................951 296-1771
Brian Murphy, *President*
Ken Murphy, *Treasurer*
EMP: 75
SQ FT: 40,000
SALES (est): 12.1MM **Privately Held**
WEB: www.bbkperformance.com
SIC: 5013 5531 Automotive supplies &
parts; automotive parts

(P-6627)
BMW DESIGNWORKS
2201 Corporate Center Dr, Newbury Park
(91320-1421)
PHONE..................................503 614-3403
Laurenz Schaffer, *President*
Neil Brooker, *Vice Pres*
Felix Nagelin, *Creative Dir*
Elke Weisbarth, *Creative Dir*
Jirawat Jeamvigite, *Design Engr*
EMP: 200
SALES (est): 2.4MM **Privately Held**
SIC: 5013 5531 7549 Body repair or paint
shop supplies, automotive;
automotive accessories; automotive maintenance
services

(P-6628)
BST ENTERPRISES INC
Also Called: Saddlemen
17801 S Susana Rd, Compton
(90221-5411)
PHONE..................................310 638-1222
Thomas W Seymour, *CEO*
David Echert, *Treasurer*
John Baricevic, *Vice Pres*
Kelly Rowe, *Accounting Dir*
▲ EMP: 65
SQ FT: 20,000
SALES (est): 19.4MM **Privately Held**
WEB: www.saddlemen.com
SIC: 5013 3751 Motorcycle parts; motor-
cycle accessories

(P-6629)
**CAL-STATE AUTO PARTS INC
(PA)**
Also Called: Auto Pride
1361 N Red Gum St, Anaheim
(92806-1318)
PHONE..................................714 630-5954
Richard J Deblasi, *CEO*
John McMillin, *CFO*
Steven Brooker, *Vice Pres*
Max Madagril, *Info Tech Mgr*
Douglas Mayes, *Info Tech Mgr*
▲ EMP: 105
SQ FT: 76,000
SALES (est): 69MM **Privately Held**
WEB: www.csautoparts.com
SIC: 5013 Automotive supplies & parts

(P-6630)
**CLUB ASSIST NORTH AMERICA
INC (PA)**
888 W 6th St Ste 300, Los Angeles
(90017-2729)
PHONE..................................213 388-4333
Brett Davies, *CEO*
Scott Davies, *COO*
Alex Leombruni, *CFO*
Candace Enman, *Treasurer*
Stuart Davies, *Admin Sec*
▲ EMP: 64
SALES (est): 91.2MM **Privately Held**
SIC: 5013 Automotive batteries

(P-6631)
CLUB ASSIST US LLC
Also Called: Battery Assist
888 W 6th St Ste 300, Los Angeles
(90017-2729)
PHONE..................................213 388-4333
John Tutt, *President*
Alex Leombruni, *Treasurer*
Peter Aguilar, *General Mgr*
Jack Rahner, *CTO*
Scott Davies,
▲ EMP: 250
SQ FT: 6,382
SALES (est): 91.2MM **Privately Held**
SIC: 5013 Automotive batteries
PA: Club Assist North America Inc.
888 W 6th St Ste 300
Los Angeles CA 90017
213 388-4333

(P-6632)
DAE-IL USA INC
Also Called: Custom Crome
7227 W Sunnyview Ave, Visalia
(93291-9639)
PHONE..................................559 651-5170
Robert Russell, *Director*
EMP: 69
SALES (corp-wide): 332.7MM **Privately
Held**
SIC: 5013
HQ: Dae-Il Usa, Inc.
155 E Main Ave Ste 150
Morgan Hill CA 95037

(P-6633)
**DENSO PDTS & SVCS
AMERICAS INC (DH)**
Also Called: Dsca
3900 Via Oro Ave, Long Beach
(90810-1868)
PHONE..................................310 834-6352
Yoshihiko Yamada, *CEO*
Hisashi Matsunobu, *President*
Roy Nakaue, *Exec VP*
Peter Clotz, *Vice Pres*
Fran Labun, *Vice Pres*
◆ EMP: 153
SQ FT: 235,000
SALES (est): 229.8MM
SALES (corp-wide): 47.9B **Privately Held**
WEB: www.densorobots.com
SIC: 5013 7361 5075 3714 Automotive
supplies & parts; employment agencies;
warm air heating & air conditioning; motor
vehicle parts & accessories
HQ: Denso International America, Inc.
24777 Denso Dr
Southfield MI 48033
248 350-7500

(P-6634)
**DIVERSFIED ENVMTL CTALYSTS
INC (PA)**
14645 Keswick St, Van Nuys (91405-1204)
PHONE..................................818 994-1908
Robert J Perret Jr, *President*
Cristina Zarubin, *Info Tech Mgr*
▲ EMP: 500
SALES (est): 63MM **Privately Held**
SIC: 5013 Automotive supplies & parts

(P-6635)
DNA SPECIALTY INC
200 W Artesia Blvd, Compton
(90220-5500)
PHONE..................................310 767-4070
James Choi, *President*
Sun Choi, *Admin Sec*
▲ EMP: 90
SQ FT: 80,000
SALES (est): 24.4MM **Privately Held**
SIC: 5013 3714 Wheels, motor vehicle;
wheels, motor vehicle

(P-6636)
**DRIVEN PERFORMANCE
BRANDS INC (PA)**
Also Called: B & M Racing
100 Stony Point Rd # 125, Santa Rosa
(95401-4117)
PHONE..................................707 544-4761
Brian Applegate, *President*
Steve Potter, *CFO*

Jonathan Miller, *Principal*
▲ EMP: 71 EST: 2000
SALES (est): 139.7MM **Privately Held**
WEB: www.bmracing.com
SIC: 5013 Automotive engines & engine
parts; automotive supplies & parts

(P-6637)
ELLIOTT AUTO SUPPLY CO INC
Also Called: Factory Motor Parts
448 W Katella Ave, Orange (92867-4604)
PHONE..................................800 278-6394
Mike Cote, *Manager*
EMP: 50
SALES (corp-wide): 700.6MM **Privately
Held**
SIC: 5013 5015 Automotive supplies &
parts; automotive parts & supplies, used
PA: Elliott Auto Supply Co., Inc.
1380 Corporate Center Cur
Eagan MN 55121
651 454-4100

(P-6638)
ELLIOTT AUTO SUPPLY CO INC
Factory Motor Parts
1600 E Orangethorpe Ave, Fullerton
(92831-5231)
PHONE..................................310 527-2500
Rich Carol, *Principal*
EMP: 65
SALES (corp-wide): 700.6MM **Privately
Held**
SIC: 5013 Automotive supplies & parts
PA: Elliott Auto Supply Co., Inc.
1380 Corporate Center Cur
Eagan MN 55121
651 454-4100

(P-6639)
FAST PRO INC
Also Called: Fast Undercar
2555 Lafayette St Ste 103, Santa Clara
(95050-2644)
PHONE..................................408 566-0200
Brian Smits, *President*
Ken Luchswich, *Sales Executive*
Rob Matuzek, *Manager*
EMP: 60
SQ FT: 13,000
SALES (est): 12.6MM **Privately Held**
SIC: 5013 Automotive supplies; automotive
supplies & parts

(P-6640)
FORD MOTOR COMPANY
1269 Phoenix Dr, Manteca (95336-6006)
P.O. Box 1666, Richmond (94802-0666)
PHONE..................................209 824-6600
William Stewart, *Manager*
Rachel Varias, *Analyst*
EMP: 220
SALES (corp-wide): 156.7B **Publicly
Held**
WEB: www.ford.com
SIC: 5013 5531 Automotive supplies &
parts; automotive parts
PA: Ford Motor Company
1 American Rd
Dearborn MI 48126
313 322-3000

(P-6641)
FOX FACTORY HOLDING CORP
750 Vernon Way Ste 101, El Cajon
(92020-1979)
PHONE..................................619 768-1800
John Marking, *Branch Mgr*
EMP: 655
SALES (corp-wide): 475.6MM **Publicly
Held**
SIC: 5013 Springs, shock absorbers &
struts
PA: Fox Factory Holding Corp.
915 Disc Dr
Scotts Valley CA 95066
831 274-6500

(P-6642)
**GENUINE PARTS
DISTRIBUTORS**
Also Called: Tracy Industries
3200 E Guasti Rd Ste 100, Ontario
(91761-8661)
PHONE..................................562 692-9034
Tim Engball, *CEO*

David M Rosenberger, *Admin Sec*
Lisa Schumacher, *Info Tech Dir*
Kim Edwards, *Human Res Mgr*
EMP: 75
SALES (est): 6.2MM
SALES (corp-wide): 30.5MM **Privately Held**
SIC: 5013 Automotive engines & engine parts
PA: Fred Jones Enterprises, L.L.C.
6200 Sw 29th St
Oklahoma City OK 73179
800 927-7845

(P-6643)
GOODRIDGE USA INC (DH)
529 Van Ness Ave, Torrance (90501-1424)
PHONE.................................310 533-1924
Celso Pierre, *CEO*
Mark Hansen, *Engineer*
Daniel Fung, *Purchasing*
Jack Hastings, *Director*
▲ **EMP:** 55
SQ FT: 15,000
SALES (est): 27.1MM
SALES (corp-wide): 571K **Privately Held**
WEB: www.goodridge.net
SIC: 5013 Automotive supplies
HQ: Goodridge Limited
Dart Building
Exeter EX1 3
139 236-9090

(P-6644)
HANSON DISTRIBUTING COMPANY (PA)
975 W 8th St, Azusa (91702-2246)
PHONE.................................626 224-9800
Daniel L Hanson, *CEO*
Steven A Cox, *COO*
Jake Boggs, *Vice Pres*
Dan Hanson, *Vice Pres*
Daniel L Hanson II, *Vice Pres*
EMP: 115
SQ FT: 160,000
SALES (est): 77.2MM **Privately Held**
WEB: www.HansonDistributing.com
SIC: 5013 Automotive supplies & parts

(P-6645)
HANSON DISTRIBUTING COMPANY
975 W 8th St, Azusa (91702-2246)
PHONE.................................626 357-5241
Daniel L Hanson, *President*
EMP: 145
SALES (corp-wide): 77.2MM **Privately Held**
SIC: 5013 Automotive supplies & parts
PA: Hanson Distributing Company
975 W 8th St
Azusa CA 91702
626 224-9800

(P-6646)
HINO MOTORS MFG USA INC
4550 Wineville Ave, Mira Loma (91752-3723)
PHONE.................................951 727-0286
Debra Martinas, *Branch Mgr*
EMP: 159
SALES (corp-wide): 275.7B **Privately Held**
WEB: www.hinointl.com
SIC: 5013 Truck parts & accessories
HQ: Hino Motors Manufacturing U.S.A., Inc.
45501 W 12 Mile Rd
Novi MI 48377

(P-6647)
IAP WEST INC
20036 S Via Baron, Rancho Dominguez (90220-6105)
PHONE.................................310 667-9720
Michel Berg, *CEO*
Louis L Berg, *President*
John Kelley, *CFO*
Sharon Berg, *Admin Sec*
Leon Leong, *Technology*
◆ **EMP:** 54
SQ FT: 80,000
SALES (est): 16.5MM **Privately Held**
SIC: 5013 Automotive engines & engine parts

(P-6648)
INTERSTATE BTRY SAN DIEGO INC
9345 Cabot Dr, San Diego (92126-4310)
PHONE.................................858 790-8244
Ron Cummings, *President*
EMP: 50
SQ FT: 20,000
SALES (est): 21MM **Privately Held**
WEB: www.battery.com
SIC: 5013 5531 Automotive batteries; batteries, automotive & truck

(P-6649)
JAMM MANAGEMENT LLC
Also Called: Fast Undercar Stockton
2447 Stanford Way, Antioch (94531-8249)
PHONE.................................510 437-5200
Jose R Montilla,
Francisco Mendoza,
John Cabello, *Manager*
EMP: 50
SQ FT: 4,100
SALES (est): 5.4MM **Privately Held**
WEB: www.jammentgraphics.net
SIC: 5013 Automotive engines & engine parts

(P-6650)
K AUTOMOTIVE DISTRIBUTORS (PA)
Also Called: Automotive Expediters
14650 Calvert St, Van Nuys (91411-2807)
PHONE.................................818 988-1550
Jonah Kardish, *President*
Annette Kardish, *Vice Pres*
EMP: 57
SALES (est): 3.5MM **Privately Held**
SIC: 5013 5531 Automotive supplies & parts; automotive parts

(P-6651)
KATANA RACING INC (PA)
Also Called: Katana Racing Whl & Tire Distr
14407 Alondra Blvd, La Mirada (90638-5504)
PHONE.................................562 977-8565
ARA Tchaghlassian, *President*
Patrick Karapetian, *CFO*
▲ **EMP:** 105
SALES (est): 70.5MM **Privately Held**
SIC: 5013 5014 Wheels, motor vehicle; automobile tires & tubes; truck tires & tubes

(P-6652)
KEYSTONE AUTOMOTIVE INDS INC
2530 Lindsey Privado Dr C, Ontario (91761-3459)
PHONE.................................909 986-4586
Jim Francis, *Branch Mgr*
EMP: 75
SALES (corp-wide): 9.7B **Publicly Held**
WEB: www.kool-vue.com
SIC: 5013 Automotive supplies & parts
HQ: Keystone Automotive Industries, Inc.
655 Grassmere Park
Nashville TN 37211
615 781-5200

(P-6653)
KNIESELS AUTO COLLISION CENTER
4680 Pacific St, Rocklin (95677-2406)
PHONE.................................916 315-8888
Tom Kniesel, *Owner*
EMP: 50
SALES (est): 3MM **Privately Held**
SIC: 5013 Body repair or paint shop supplies, automotive

(P-6654)
LAX WHEEL REFINISHING INC
1520 Spence St, Los Angeles (90023-3920)
PHONE.................................323 269-1484
Jesus Sanchez, *President*
EMP: 60
SALES (est): 4.7MM **Privately Held**
SIC: 5013 Wheels, motor vehicle

(P-6655)
LEXANI WHEEL CORPORATION
2380 Railroad St Ste 101, Corona (92880-5471)
PHONE.................................951 808-4220
Frank Hodges, *CEO*
Michael Kim, *General Mgr*
Kim Pemberton, *Sales Dir*
Carlos Parrott, *Marketing Mgr*
John Wallace, *Sales Mgr*
▲ **EMP:** 120
SQ FT: 35,000
SALES (est): 35MM **Privately Held**
SIC: 5013 Wheels, motor vehicle

(P-6656)
MAXZONE VEHICLE LIGHTING CORP (HQ)
Also Called: Depo Auto Parts
15889 Slover Ave Unit A, Fontana (92337-7299)
PHONE.................................909 822-3288
Polo Hsu, *President*
Shu Sheng Hsu, *Principal*
Hojin Lee, *Sales Executive*
David Sanchez, *Sales Executive*
Tina Hsieh, *Mktg Coord*
◆ **EMP:** 50
SQ FT: 32,000
SALES (est): 40.8MM
SALES (corp-wide): 535.3MM **Privately Held**
SIC: 5013 3714 Automotive supplies & parts; motor vehicle electrical equipment
PA: Depo Auto Parts Ind. Co., Ltd.
20-3, Nanshi Lane,
Lukang Chen CHA 50564
477 223-11

(P-6657)
MERIDIAN RACK & PINION INC
6740 Cobra Way Ste 200, San Diego (92121-4102)
PHONE.................................858 587-8777
Dara Greaney, *CEO*
Matt Glauber, *President*
Chris Struempler, *CFO*
▼ **EMP:** 130
SQ FT: 55,000
SALES (est): 69.8MM **Privately Held**
WEB: www.meridianautoparts.com
SIC: 5013 5961 Automotive supplies & parts; mail order house, order taking office only

(P-6658)
MIKUNI AMERICAN CORPORATION (HQ)
Also Called: M A C
8910 Mikuni Ave, Northridge (91324-3403)
PHONE.................................310 676-0522
Satoshi Fujimori, *President*
Hirokazu Masahashi, *CFO*
Masaki Ikuta, *Chairman*
Shigeru Ikuta, *Vice Pres*
Yutaka Fujita, *Admin Sec*
▲ **EMP:** 64
SQ FT: 50,000
SALES (est): 99MM
SALES (corp-wide): 974MM **Privately Held**
WEB: www.mikuni.com
SIC: 5013 5088 Automotive hardware; aircraft engines & engine parts; aircraft & parts
PA: Mikuni Corporation
6-13-11, Sotokanda
Chiyoda-Ku TKY 101-0
338 330-392

(P-6659)
MYERS TIRE SUPPLY DIST INC
Also Called: Myers Tire Supply Division
107 Exchange Pl, Pomona (91768-4307)
PHONE.................................602 233-1037
Joel Schotz, *Branch Mgr*
John Orr, *CEO*
EMP: 99
SALES (corp-wide): 547MM **Publicly Held**
WEB: www.myerstiresupply.com
SIC: 5013 Automotive supplies & parts
HQ: Myers Tire Supply Distribution, Inc.
1293 S Main St
Akron OH 44301
330 253-5592

(P-6660)
MYGRANT GLASS COMPANY INC (PA)
3271 Arden Rd, Hayward (94545-3901)
PHONE.................................510 785-4360
Michael Mygrant, *CEO*
Kathy Mygrant, *Treasurer*
Carol Rivano, *Admin Asst*
Junior Rivas, *Administration*
Daniel Parkinson, *Info Tech Dir*
◆ **EMP:** 50
SQ FT: 128,222
SALES (est): 178.4MM **Privately Held**
SIC: 5013 Automobile glass

(P-6661)
NSV INTERNATIONAL CORP
1250 E 29th St, Signal Hill (90755-1800)
P.O. Box 14660, Long Beach (90853-4660)
PHONE.................................562 438-3836
Stephan Humphries, *CEO*
Isabel Palafox, *COO*
EMP: 100
SQ FT: 1,200
SALES: 1.1MM **Privately Held**
SIC: 5013 Automotive supplies

(P-6662)
PACIFIC COAST TRUCK AND WHSE (PA)
692 Anita St, Chula Vista (91911-4620)
P.O. Box 13400, San Diego (92170-3400)
PHONE.................................619 661-5451
Mark Secord, *President*
Jennifer Secord, *Admin Sec*
▲ **EMP:** 50
SALES (est): 7.2MM **Privately Held**
WEB: www.e-pacificcoast.com
SIC: 5013 Truck parts & accessories

(P-6663)
PARAMOUNT RESTYLING AUTO INC (PA)
1410 E Holt Blvd, Ontario (91761-2103)
PHONE.................................909 781-6492
Mingfa Yang, *President*
Qiong LI, *Admin Sec*
Anh Hua, *Controller*
Kim Burnsworth, *Sales Dir*
Mario Gonzalez, *Warehouse Mgr*
EMP: 55
SQ FT: 100,000
SALES: 13MM **Privately Held**
SIC: 5013 5531 Automotive supplies; automotive parts

(P-6664)
PARTSCHANNEL INC
8905 Rex Rd, Pico Rivera (90660-3799)
PHONE.................................562 654-3400
Alex Marquez, *Manager*
EMP: 50
SALES (corp-wide): 9.7B **Publicly Held**
SIC: 5013 Body repair or paint shop supplies, automotive
HQ: Partschannel, Inc.
4003 Grand Lakes Way # 200
Grand Prairie TX 75050
214 688-0018

(P-6665)
PERFORMANCE WAREHOUSE CO
901 Arden Way, Sacramento (95815-3201)
PHONE.................................916 920-2221
Gary Petit, *Branch Mgr*
EMP: 85
SALES (corp-wide): 85.8MM **Privately Held**
SIC: 5013 5531 Automotive supplies & parts; automotive & home supply stores
PA: Performance Warehouse Co.
9440 N Whitaker Rd
Portland OR 97217
503 417-5302

(P-6666)
PRESTIGE AUTOTECH CORPORATION
Also Called: Panther Custom Wheels
4975 Edison Ave, Chino (91710-5714)
PHONE.................................909 627-6411
Fenton Liffick, *President*
▲ **EMP:** 50

SQ FT: 150,000
SALES (est): 9.3MM Privately Held
WEB: www.akuza.com
SIC: 5013 Wheels, motor vehicle

(P-6667)
QUALITY PLUS AUTO PARTS INC
1333 30th St Ste C, San Diego
(92154-3486)
PHONE..................................619 424-9991
Roger Yang, *President*
Jeffrey Shong Lowe, *Admin Sec*
Fernando Torres, *Buyer*
▲ EMP: 50
SQ FT: 17,000
SALES (est): 8.5MM Privately Held
WEB: www.qualityplusauto.com
SIC: 5013 5531 Automotive supplies &
parts; automotive parts

(P-6668)
RAMCAR BATTERIES INC
2700 Carrier Ave, Commerce (90040-2572)
PHONE..................................323 726-1212
Clifford J Crowe, *President*
▲ EMP: 50
SQ FT: 90,000
SALES (est): 17.8MM Privately Held
SIC: 5013 3691 Automotive batteries; lead
acid batteries (storage batteries)

(P-6669)
RECYCLER CORE COMPANY INC
2727 Kansas Ave, Riverside (92507-2638)
PHONE..................................951 276-1687
Ken Meier, *President*
Gisela Meier, *Corp Secy*
Bob Palmer, *Vice Pres*
Robert Palmer, *Executive*
Simona Johnson, *Office Mgr*
◆ EMP: 100
SQ FT: 280,000
SALES (est): 38.6MM Privately Held
WEB: www.rccauto.com
SIC: 5013 Automotive supplies & parts

(P-6670)
RICHARD HUETTER INC
Also Called: Pacific Parts International
21050 Osborne St, Canoga Park
(91304-1744)
PHONE..................................818 700-8001
Richard Huetter, *CEO*
Maria L Huetter, *Treasurer*
▲ EMP: 70
SQ FT: 30,000
SALES (est): 12.8MM Privately Held
SIC: 5013 Automotive supplies & parts

(P-6671)
S F AUTO PARTS WHSE INC
Also Called: Mac Kenzie Warehouse
6000 3rd St, San Francisco (94124-3106)
PHONE..................................415 255-0115
M Mackenzie Menendez, *President*
Michelle Mackenzie Menendez, *President*
Anna-Maria Mac Kenzie, *Treasurer*
Eduardo Menendez, *Exec VP*
EMP: 56 EST: 1951
SQ FT: 53,000
SALES (est): 17.5MM Privately Held
WEB: www.mackenziewarehouse.com
SIC: 5013 Automotive supplies &
parts

(P-6672)
SCAT ENTERPRISES INC
1400 Kingsdale Ave, Redondo Beach
(90278-3983)
PHONE..................................310 370-5501
Philip T Lieb, *President*
Craig Schenasi, *CFO*
Travis Kennedy, *Engineer*
Thomas Mendoza, *Accounting Mgr*
Matthew Hajimomen, *Sales Associate*
◆ EMP: 65
SQ FT: 42,000
SALES (est): 21MM Privately Held
WEB: www.scatenterprises.com
SIC: 5013 3714 Automotive supplies &
parts; automotive supplies; motor vehicle
parts & accessories

(P-6673)
SERRATO-MCDERMOTT INC
Also Called: Allied Auto Store
43815 S Grimmer Blvd, Fremont
(94538-6348)
PHONE..................................510 656-6233
Bill Bailey, *CEO*
Anthony Barnes, *Sales Staff*
EMP: 55
SQ FT: 17,000
SALES (est): 21.7MM Privately Held
SIC: 5013 5531 Automotive supplies &
parts; automotive parts

(P-6674)
SILLA AUTOMOTIVE LLC
1901 Mineral Ct Ste C, Bakersfield
(93308-6819)
PHONE..................................661 392-8880
EMP: 52
SALES (corp-wide): 73.4MM Privately
Held
SIC: 5013
PA: Silla Automotive, Llc
1217 W Artesia Blvd
Compton CA 90220
310 323-0001

(P-6675)
SPECTRA PREMIUM (USA) CORP
2220 Almond Ave, Redlands (92374-2073)
PHONE..................................951 653-0640
Sergio Zapata, *Branch Mgr*
EMP: 58
SALES (corp-wide): 381MM Privately
Held
SIC: 5013 Automotive supplies & parts
HQ: Spectra Premium (Usa) Corp.
3052 N Distribution Way
Greenfield IN 46140
317 891-1700

(P-6676)
SSF IMPORTED AUTO PARTS LLC
21175 Main St Ste A, Carson (90745-1500)
PHONE..................................310 782-8859
Bruce Brown, *Manager*
EMP: 60
SALES (corp-wide): 1.7B Privately Held
WEB: www.ssfautoparts.com
SIC: 5013 4225 Automotive supplies &
parts; general warehousing & storage
HQ: Ssf Imported Auto Parts Llc
466 Forbes Blvd
South San Francisco CA 94080
800 203-9287

(P-6677)
SSF IMPORTED AUTO PARTS LLC (DH)
Also Called: S S F
466 Forbes Blvd, South San Francisco
(94080-2015)
PHONE..................................800 203-9287
Thomas Beer, *Mng Member*
Leticia Parraz, *Administration*
Nerissa Wong, *Programmer Anys*
Mark Gunson, *Graphic Designe*
David Debolt, *Purch Mgr*
▲ EMP: 100
SALES (est): 124MM
SALES (corp-wide): 1.7B Privately Held
WEB: www.ssfautoparts.com
SIC: 5013 Automotive supplies & parts
HQ: Wm Se
Pagenstecherstr. 121
Osnabruck 49090
541 998-90

(P-6678)
TAP OPERATING CO LLC
400 W Artesia Blvd, Compton
(90220-5501)
PHONE..................................310 900-5500
EMP: 1200
SALES (est): 87.2MM Privately Held
SIC: 5013 Truck parts & accessories

(P-6679)
TAP WORLDWIDE LLC (PA)
Also Called: 4 Wheel Parts Performance Ctrs
400 W Artesia Blvd, Compton
(90220-5501)
PHONE..................................310 900-5500
Greg Adler, *President*
Tim Mongi, *COO*
Mark Lane, *CFO*
Greg Bolton, *Opers Mgr*
Darren Marcus Salvin,
◆ EMP: 1200
SALES (est): 221.8MM Privately Held
SIC: 5013 Motor vehicle supplies & new
parts

(P-6680)
TRANSTAR INDUSTRIES INC
Also Called: Transtar Automotive
15010 Calvert St, Van Nuys (91411-2605)
PHONE..................................818 785-2000
David Pianannamore, *Manager*
EMP: 50 Privately Held
WEB: www.transtarindustries.com
SIC: 5013 Automotive supplies & parts
HQ: Transtar Industries, Inc.
7350 Young Dr
Cleveland OH 44146
440 232-5100

(P-6681)
UQUALITY AUTOMOTIVE PDTS CORP (PA)
16411 Shoemaker Ave, Cerritos
(90703-2217)
PHONE..................................562 282-2888
Zhongren Meng, *CEO*
Tom Chen, *CFO*
John Aniunas, *Vice Pres*
Rich Sanderson, *Vice Pres*
Mike Droullard, *VP Sales*
▲ EMP: 50
SQ FT: 70,000
SALES (est): 16MM Privately Held
WEB: www.uquality.com
SIC: 5013 Motor vehicle supplies & new
parts

(P-6682)
VEHICLE ACCESSORY CENTER LLC
10863 Jersey Blvd # 101, Rancho Cuca-
monga (91730-5113)
PHONE..................................909 987-8237
Russell Hoyt, *Mng Member*
Ana McDonald, *Office Mgr*
Keith Sawyer, *Mng Member*
EMP: 53
SQ FT: 100,000
SALES (est): 7.2MM
SALES (corp-wide): 81.8MM Privately
Held
WEB: www.vehicleaccessorycenter.com
SIC: 5013 Automotive supplies & parts
PA: Mark Christopher Chevrolet Inc
2131 E Convention Ctr Way
Ontario CA 91764
909 390-2900

(P-6683)
VETRONIX SALES CORPORATION
Also Called: Vetronix Crpration/Bosch Group
2030 Alameda Padre Serra, Santa Barbara
(93103-1716)
PHONE..................................805 966-2000
James Zaleski, *President*
Larry James, *Manager*
EMP: 68
SQ FT: 26,000
SALES: 8.9MM
SALES (corp-wide): 3MM Privately Held
WEB: www.vetronix.com
SIC: 5013 Testing equipment, electrical:
automotive
PA: Bosch Automotive Service Solutions
Inc.
2030 Alameda Padre Serra
Santa Barbara CA 93103
805 966-2000

(P-6684)
WAGAN CORPORATION
31088 San Clemente St, Hayward
(94544-7811)
PHONE..................................510 471-9221
Alex Hsu, *CEO*
John Hsu, *Ch of Bd*
Po-Jung Hsu, *CEO*
Mamie Hsu, *CFO*
Bryan Kawaye, *Engineer*
◆ EMP: 50
SQ FT: 30,000
SALES (est): 13.4MM Privately Held
WEB: www.wagan.com
SIC: 5013 Automotive supplies & parts

(P-6685)
WARREN DISTRIBUTING INC (PA)
Also Called: Wdi
8737 Dice Rd, Santa Fe Springs
(90670-2513)
PHONE..................................562 789-3360
Brian Weiss, *President*
Linnea Herndon, *CFO*
Jake Boggs, *Vice Pres*
Dave Erlenbach, *Vice Pres*
Gary Jacobson, *Vice Pres*
◆ EMP: 55
SQ FT: 68,000
SALES (est): 77.2MM Privately Held
WEB: www.warrendist.com
SIC: 5013 Automotive supplies

(P-6686)
WEBASTO CHARGING SYSTEMS INC (DH) ✪
800 Royal Oaks Dr Ste 210, Monrovia
(91016-6364)
PHONE..................................626 415-4000
John Thomas, *CEO*
Doug McElroy, *CFO*
EMP: 100 EST: 2018
SALES (est): 29K
SALES (corp-wide): 411.9K Privately
Held
SIC: 5013 Automobile service station
equipment
HQ: Webasto Roof Systems Inc.
1757 Northfield Dr
Rochester Hills MI 48309
248 997-5100

(P-6687)
WORLDPAC INC (DH)
37137 Hickory St, Newark (94560-3340)
P.O. Box 5022 (94560-5522)
PHONE..................................510 742-8900
Bob Cushing, *CEO*
Roy Geddie, *President*
Darius Kondaki, *President*
David Heine, *Exec VP*
Michael Hellweg, *Exec VP*
◆ EMP: 200
SQ FT: 256,000
SALES (est): 799.1MM
SALES (corp-wide): 9.3B Publicly Held
WEB: www.worldpac.com
SIC: 5013 5531 Automotive supplies &
parts; automotive parts
HQ: General Parts International, Inc.
2635 E Millbrook Rd
Raleigh NC 27604
919 573-3000

(P-6688)
YOSHIMURA RESEARCH & DEV AMER
5420 Daniels St Ste A, Chino (91710-9012)
PHONE..................................909 628-4722
Fujio Yoshimura, *President*
Suehiro Watanabe, *CFO*
Don Sakakura, *Senior VP*
▲ EMP: 100
SQ FT: 12,000
SALES (est): 34.9MM Privately Held
WEB: www.yoshimura-rd.com
SIC: 5013 Motorcycle parts

5014 Tires & Tubes Wholesale

(P-6689)
AMERICAN TIRE DISTRIBUTORS
645 Dado St, San Jose (95131-1209)
PHONE..............................408 435-3340
Bob Goularte, *Manager*
Dave Barry, *Vice Pres*
EMP: 50
SALES (corp-wide): 5B **Privately Held**
WEB: www.heafnertire.com
SIC: 5014 Tires & tubes
HQ: American Tire Distributors Inc.
12200 Herbert Wayne Ct # 150
Huntersville NC 28078
704 992-2000

(P-6690)
FALKEN TIRE HOLDINGS INC
Also Called: Falken Tires
8656 Haven Ave, Rancho Cucamonga (91730-9103)
PHONE..............................800 723-2553
Richard Smallwood, *President*
Hideo Honda, *President*
Joyce Ho, *Executive Asst*
Leeann Martinez, *Admin Asst*
Ken Masaoka, *Planning*
▲ EMP: 80
SALES (est): 22.8MM
SALES (corp-wide): 7.8B **Privately Held**
WEB: www.sri.dunlop.co.jp
SIC: 5014 Automobile tires & tubes
PA: Sumitomo Rubber Industries, Ltd.
3-6-9, Wakinohamacho, Chuo-Ku
Kobe HYO 651-0
782 653-000

(P-6691)
GITI TIRE (USA) LTD (DH)
10404 6th St, Rancho Cucamonga (91730-5831)
PHONE..............................909 527-8800
Enki Tan, *CEO*
Sylvia Soerijadi, *CFO*
Armand Allaire, *Exec VP*
Julianto Djajadi, *Exec VP*
John Aben, *Vice Pres*
▲ EMP: 55
SALES (est): 52.3MM **Privately Held**
SIC: 5014 Tires & tubes

(P-6692)
GREENBALL CORP (PA)
Also Called: Towmaster Tire & Wheel
222 S Harbor Blvd Ste 700, Anaheim (92805-3730)
PHONE..............................714 782-3060
Chris S H Tsai, *CEO*
Jenny Tsai, *Vice Pres*
Ray Hou, *Buyer*
Walt Kaufman, *Sales Staff*
Phil Browning, *Warehouse Mgr*
◆ EMP: 50
SQ FT: 80,000
SALES (est): 51.8MM **Privately Held**
WEB: www.greenball.com
SIC: 5014 5013 3999 Automobile tires & tubes; wheels, motor vehicle; atomizers, toiletry

(P-6693)
LAKIN TIRE WEST INCORPORATED (PA)
Also Called: Lakin Tire of Calif
15305 Spring Ave, Santa Fe Springs (90670-5645)
PHONE..............................562 802-2752
Robert Lakin, *CEO*
Marco Jimenez, *Vice Pres*
David Lakin, *Vice Pres*
Sean Lakin, *Vice Pres*
Yuly Moreno, *Administration*
▼ EMP: 81
SQ FT: 50,000
SALES (est): 85.5MM **Privately Held**
WEB: www.lakintire.com
SIC: 5014 5531 Tires, used; automotive & home supply stores

(P-6694)
SEALANT SYSTEMS INTERNATIONAL
Also Called: Ssi
125 Venture Dr Ste 210, San Luis Obispo (93401-9105)
PHONE..............................805 489-0490
Chris Auerbach, *President*
EMP: 67
SALES: 6.5MM **Privately Held**
SIC: 5014 Tires & tubes

(P-6695)
SUMITOMO RUBBER NORTH AMER INC (HQ)
Also Called: Falken Tire
8656 Haven Ave, Rancho Cucamonga (91730-9103)
PHONE..............................909 466-1116
Richard Smallwood, *CEO*
Fumikazu Yamashita, *Vice Pres*
Rick Brennan, *Exec Dir*
Monica Fuqua, *Executive Asst*
Robert Escobar, *Admin Asst*
◆ EMP: 75
SQ FT: 190,000
SALES (est): 125.3MM
SALES (corp-wide): 7.8B **Privately Held**
WEB: www.falkentire.com
SIC: 5014 Automobile tires & tubes
PA: Sumitomo Rubber Industries, Ltd.
3-6-9, Wakinohamacho, Chuo-Ku
Kobe HYO 651-0
782 653-000

(P-6696)
TIRE & WHEEL MASTER INC
3745 Petersen Rd, Stockton (95215-7945)
PHONE..............................209 465-9000
Ammad Hussain, *CEO*
Rashad Hussain, *President*
Ana Becerril, *Manager*
◆ EMP: 52
SQ FT: 72,000
SALES (est): 32MM **Privately Held**
SIC: 5014 Tires & tubes

(P-6697)
TIRE CENTERS WEST LLC
10516 Commerce Way # 875, Fontana (92337-8236)
PHONE..............................909 854-1200
J D Cassa, *General Mgr*
EMP: 135
SQ FT: 83,470
SALES (corp-wide): 803.2MM **Privately Held**
WEB: www.tirecenters.com
SIC: 5014 5531 7534 Automobile tires & tubes; automotive tires; rebuilding & retreading tires
HQ: Tire Centers West, Llc
1 Parkway S
Greenville SC 29615
864 458-5000

(P-6698)
TIRECO INC (PA)
500 W 190th St Ste 100, Gardena (90248-4270)
PHONE..............................310 767-7990
Robert W Liu, *CEO*
John Chen, *CFO*
Chris Holbert, *Vice Pres*
Fiona Wang, *Executive Asst*
Alfred Cariaga, *Administration*
▲ EMP: 150
SALES (est): 151MM **Privately Held**
WEB: www.tireco.com
SIC: 5014 5013 5051 Tires, used; wheels, motor vehicle; tubing, metal

(P-6699)
TOYO TIRE USA CORP
2151 S Vintage Ave, Ontario (91761-2824)
PHONE..............................562 431-6502
Steve Morgan, *Manager*
EMP: 50
SALES (corp-wide): 3.6B **Privately Held**
SIC: 5014 Automobile tires & tubes
HQ: Toyo Tire U.S.A. Corp.
5665 Plaza Dr Ste 300
Cypress CA 90630
714 236-2080

(P-6700)
TURBO WHOLESALE TIRES INC (PA)
Also Called: Turbo Tires
5793 Martin Rd, Irwindale (91706-6211)
PHONE..............................626 856-1400
Sarkis Paul Sepetjian, *CEO*
Sepetjian Nune, *CFO*
Nune Sepetjian, *CFO*
Jorge Lopez, *Marketing Staff*
Darren Tannehill, *Sales Staff*
▲ EMP: 700
SQ FT: 290,000
SALES (est): 46.7MM **Privately Held**
WEB: www.turbotires.net
SIC: 5014 Automobile tires & tubes

5015 Motor Vehicle Parts, Used Wholesale

(P-6701)
AMERICAN CORPORATION
315 N Doheny Dr, Beverly Hills (90211-1621)
PHONE..............................310 274-1800
David Morad, *President*
Eli Yadegar, *Vice Pres*
EMP: 80
SQ FT: 300,000
SALES (est): 22.5MM **Privately Held**
SIC: 5015 Automotive supplies, used

(P-6702)
CADNCHEV INC
Also Called: Lakenor Auto Salvage
13603 Foster Rd, Santa Fe Springs (90670-4834)
PHONE..............................562 944-6422
Donald Flynn, *Ch of Bd*
Thomas Raterman, *CFO*
Frank Erlain, *Vice Pres*
EMP: 60
SQ FT: 10,000
SALES (est): 11.1MM
SALES (corp-wide): 9.7B **Publicly Held**
WEB: www.lkqcorp.com
SIC: 5015 5531 Automotive parts & supplies, used; automotive parts
PA: Lkq Corporation
500 W Madison St Ste 2800
Chicago IL 60661
312 621-1950

(P-6703)
PICK PULL AUTO DISMANTLING INC (HQ)
Also Called: Auto Parts Group
10850 Gold Center Dr # 325, Rancho Cordova (95670-6177)
PHONE..............................916 689-2000
Thomas Klauer, *President*
John Hebert, *COO*
Glenn Soden, *Administration*
Mike Brinkley, *VP Opers*
Jeramiah Nelson, *Site Mgr*
EMP: 50
SQ FT: 9,000
SALES (est): 266.2MM
SALES (corp-wide): 2.3B **Publicly Held**
WEB: www.picknpull.com
SIC: 5015 Automotive parts & supplies, used
PA: Schnitzer Steel Industries, Inc.
299 Sw Clay St Ste 350
Portland OR 97201
503 224-9900

(P-6704)
TEAM TRUCK DISMANTLING INC
Also Called: Hillside Auto Salvage
3760 Pyrite St, Riverside (92509-1103)
PHONE..............................951 685-6744
Ted Smith, *President*
Jerry Jaeckles, *Corp Secy*
Tom Hutton, *Vice Pres*
EMP: 70
SQ FT: 1,500
SALES (est): 9.2MM **Privately Held**
WEB: www.hillsideautosalvage.com
SIC: 5015 Automotive parts & supplies, used

5021 Furniture Wholesale

(P-6705)
ABBYSON LIVING CORP
26500 W Agrra Rd 102-87, Calabasas (91302)
PHONE..............................805 465-5500
Yavar A Rafieha, *President*
Doddy Rafieha, *COO*
Dana Andrew, *Principal*
Mike Pollard, *Principal*
Vida Azizi, *Manager*
▲ EMP: 325
SQ FT: 156,000
SALES (est): 88.2MM **Privately Held**
WEB: www.abbysonliving.com
SIC: 5021 Household furniture

(P-6706)
ACME FURNITURE INDUSTRY INC (PA)
Also Called: Acme Trading
18895 Arenth Ave, City of Industry (91748-1304)
PHONE..............................626 964-3456
George Chen, *CEO*
CHI-Chu Chen, *President*
Tomy Chen, *Treasurer*
James Chen, *Vice Pres*
Jean Chen, *Vice Pres*
◆ EMP: 85
SQ FT: 330,000
SALES (est): 47.6MM **Privately Held**
SIC: 5021 Furniture

(P-6707)
ADM FURNITURE INC
11680 Wright Rd, Lynwood (90262-3945)
PHONE..............................310 762-2800
Alfonso Ayon, *President*
▲ EMP: 55
SALES (est): 8.6MM **Privately Held**
SIC: 5021 2511 Household furniture; wood household furniture

(P-6708)
ALTON IRVINE INC
Also Called: Millwork Holdings
2052 Alton Pkwy, Irvine (92606-4905)
PHONE..............................949 428-4141
Alan True, *CEO*
Dan Tacheny, *President*
Tom Pierce, *Info Tech Dir*
Jesse Greenhalgh, *Opers Mgr*
▲ EMP: 53
SQ FT: 45,000
SALES (est): 21.6MM **Privately Held**
WEB: www.trueseating.com
SIC: 5021 Office furniture

(P-6709)
AMINI INNOVATION CORP
Also Called: Aico
8725 Rex Rd, Pico Rivera (90660-6703)
PHONE..............................562 222-2500
Michael Amini, *CEO*
Martin Ploy, *Exec VP*
Jeff Santanello, *Vice Pres*
Darla Lester, *Executive Asst*
James Fang, *Info Tech Dir*
◆ EMP: 110
SQ FT: 320,000
SALES (est): 64.7MM **Privately Held**
WEB: www.amini.com
SIC: 5021 Office furniture

(P-6710)
ASPECTS FURNITURE MFG INC
15830 El Prado Rd Ste A, Chino (91708-9127)
PHONE..............................909 606-5806
Amy Sivixay, *President*
Amy A Sivixay, *Vice Pres*
Jay Sivixay, *Info Tech Mgr*
Lisa Lew, *Controller*
▲ EMP: 170
SQ FT: 12,900
SALES (est): 25.3MM **Privately Held**
WEB: www.aspectsfurniture.com
SIC: 5021 Office furniture

(P-6711)
BENETTIS ITALIA INC
3037 E Maria St, Compton (90221-5803)
PHONE.....................................310 537-8036
Mohammad A Ahmadinia, *CEO*
Sarah Ahmadinia, *CFO*
◆ **EMP:** 56
SQ FT: 120,000
SALES (est): 11.4MM **Privately Held**
SIC: 5021 2426 Office furniture; furniture
stock & parts, hardwood

(P-6712)
BLUMENTHAL DISTRIBUTING
INC (PA)
Also Called: Office Star Products
1901 S Archibald Ave, Ontario
(91761-8548)
P.O. Box 3520 (91761-0952)
PHONE.....................................909 930-2000
Richard Blumenthal, *President*
Rose Blumenthal, *Shareholder*
Jennifer Blumenthal, *Corp Secy*
Robin Tenpas, *Vice Pres*
Austin Engle, *Info Tech Mgr*
◆ **EMP:** 150
SQ FT: 200,000
SALES (est): 70.7MM **Privately Held**
WEB: www.officestar.net
SIC: 5021 2522 Office furniture; chairs, of-
fice: padded or plain, except wood

(P-6713)
BOYD FLOTATION INC
7551 Cherry Ave, Fontana (92336-4276)
PHONE.....................................909 357-6400
Alfred Mayen, *Manager*
EMP: 73
SALES (corp-wide): 55MM **Privately**
Held
WEB: www.boydflotation.com
SIC: 5021 2515 Mattresses; household
furniture; mattresses & bedsprings
PA: Boyd Flotation, Inc.
2440 Adie Rd
Maryland Heights MO 63043
314 997-5222

(P-6714)
BUSINESS FURN SOLUTIONS
INC (PA)
Also Called: Vanguard Legato Group
2150 N 1st St Ste 100, San Jose
(95131-2045)
P.O. Box 641417 (95164-1417)
PHONE.....................................408 325-3100
Jeff Tuttle, *CEO*
Dwight A Jackson, *President*
Tim Thomas, *CFO*
Joe Azzolina, *Vice Pres*
Mike Clow, *Vice Pres*
EMP: 60
SALES (est): 38.2MM **Privately Held**
SIC: 5021 Office furniture

(P-6715)
CALIFORNIA CREATIONS INC
1100 S Vail Ave, Montebello (90640-6021)
PHONE.....................................323 722-9832
Cuong Huynh, *President*
Julie Nguyen, *Treasurer*
Kim Huynh, *Vice Pres*
EMP: 50
SQ FT: 20,000
SALES (est): 9.2MM **Privately Held**
WEB: www.calcreations.com
SIC: 5021 Furniture

(P-6716)
CAMBIUM BUSINESS GROUP
INC (PA)
Also Called: Fairmont Designs
6950 Noritsu Ave, Buena Park
(90620-1311)
PHONE.....................................714 670-1171
George Tsai, *Chairman*
Kevin Fitzgerald, *President*
Jason Liu, *CEO*
David Campbell, *CFO*
Mark Klingensmith, *Vice Pres*
▲ **EMP:** 120
SQ FT: 200,000

SALES (est): 53.4MM **Privately Held**
WEB: www.fairmontdesigns.com
SIC: 5021 2511 Household furniture; dining room furniture; tables, occasional;
beds; wood household furniture

(P-6717)
COA INC (PA)
Also Called: Coaster Company of America
12928 Sandoval St, Santa Fe Springs
(90670-4061)
PHONE.....................................562 944-7899
Michael Yeh, *President*
Marc Alters, *Vice Pres*
Larry Furiani, *Vice Pres*
Crystal Nguyen, *Vice Pres*
Lisa KAO, *Admin Sec*
◆ **EMP:** 200
SQ FT: 210,000
SALES (est): 260.3MM **Privately Held**
WEB: www.coa.net
SIC: 5021 Household furniture; dining
room furniture; beds & bedding; shelving

(P-6718)
COMPLETE OFFICE
CALIFORNIA INC
12724 Moore St, Cerritos (90703-2121)
PHONE.....................................714 880-1222
Edward B Walter, *CEO*
Andy Cohn, *Exec VP*
Tim Arnzen, *Executive*
Sean Bradley, *Executive*
Rick Israel, *Principal*
EMP: 62
SQ FT: 28,000
SALES (est): 14MM
SALES (corp-wide): 10.2B **Publicly Held**
WEB: www.completeofficeca.com
SIC: 5021 5112 Office furniture; office sup-
plies
PA: Office Depot, Inc.
6600 N Military Trl
Boca Raton FL 33496
561 438-4800

(P-6719)
COPPEL CORPORATION
503 Scaroni Ave, Calexico (92231-9791)
PHONE.....................................760 357-3707
Olegario Gomez, *CFO*
◆ **EMP:** 80
SQ FT: 70,000
SALES: 329.5MM **Privately Held**
SIC: 5021 5137 5136 Household furni-
ture; women's & children's clothing; men's
& boys' clothing
HQ: Coppel, S.A. De C.V.
Republica Poniente No. 2855
Culiacan SIN. 80105

(P-6720)
EC GROUP INC (PA)
Also Called: Dennis & Leen
5960 Bowcroft St, Los Angeles
(90016-4302)
PHONE.....................................310 815-2700
Richard Hallberg, *President*
Daniel Cuevas, *Vice Pres*
Barbara Wiseley, *Admin Sec*
▲ **EMP:** 80
SQ FT: 18,000
SALES (est): 34.1MM **Privately Held**
SIC: 5021 Furniture

(P-6721)
ERGOMOTION INC
6790 Navigator Way, Goleta (93117-3656)
P.O. Box 8330 (93118-8330)
PHONE.....................................805 979-9400
Wenbiao Hou, *CEO*
Guohai Tang, *CEO*
Damien Clenet, *Creative Dir*
Gui Peres, *Managing Dir*
Emily Hanson, *Purchasing*
▲ **EMP:** 70
SALES (est): 27.8MM **Privately Held**
SIC: 5021 Beds & bedding

(P-6722)
FURNITURE AMERICA CAL INC
(PA)
Also Called: Furniture America California
19605 E Walnut Dr N, City of Industry
(91789-2815)
PHONE.....................................909 718-7276
George Wells, *CEO*
Rocky Yang, *Vice Pres*
Aki Furutani, *Superintendent*
◆ **EMP:** 71
SQ FT: 200,000
SALES (est): 34.9MM **Privately Held**
WEB: www.importdirectinc.com
SIC: 5021 2512 Furniture; upholstered
household furniture

(P-6723)
GOFORTH & MARTI (PA)
Also Called: G/M Business Interiors
110 W A St Ste 140, San Diego
(92101-3702)
PHONE.....................................951 684-0870
Stephen L Easley, *President*
Mike Akin, *Vice Pres*
William F Easley, *Vice Pres*
Bill Easley, *Executive*
Steve Easley, *Executive*
▲ **EMP:** 90
SQ FT: 38,000
SALES (est): 98.2MM **Privately Held**
WEB: www.gmbi.net
SIC: 5021 Office furniture

(P-6724)
HAWORTH INC
931 Cadillac Ct, Milpitas (95035-3053)
PHONE.....................................408 262-6400
Agnes Allen, *Branch Mgr*
EMP: 75
SALES (corp-wide): 1.9B **Privately Held**
WEB: www.haworth-furn.com
SIC: 5021 Office furniture
HQ: Haworth, Inc.
1 Haworth Ctr
Holland MI 49423
616 393-3000

(P-6725)
HOMELEGANCE INC
Also Called: A G A
48200 Fremont Blvd, Fremont
(94538-6509)
PHONE.....................................510 933-6888
Puhsien C Chao, *CEO*
Rosa Chao, *President*
Hutch Chao, *Vice Pres*
Chrissy Chang, *General Mgr*
◆ **EMP:** 90
SQ FT: 800,000
SALES (est): 31.8MM **Privately Held**
SIC: 5021 Household furniture

(P-6726)
HUMAN TOUCH LLC
4600 E Conant St, Long Beach
(90808-1874)
PHONE.....................................562 426-8700
Andrew Cohen, *President*
David Wood, *CEO*
Bruce Maccallum, *CFO*
Chang Han, *Principal*
Ralph Obregon, *Technical Mgr*
◆ **EMP:** 80
SQ FT: 98,500
SALES (est): 43.2MM **Privately Held**
SIC: 5021 Chairs

(P-6727)
INSIDE SOURCE INC (PA)
Also Called: Inside Source/Young
985 Industrial Rd Ste 101, San Carlos
(94070-4157)
PHONE.....................................650 508-9101
David Denny, *President*
Kristen Haren, *COO*
Gary Young, *Senior VP*
Tina Fong, *Vice Pres*
Nancy Kusich, *Vice Pres*
EMP: 75
SQ FT: 50,000
SALES (est): 109.1MM **Privately Held**
WEB: www.insidesource.com
SIC: 5021 Office furniture

(P-6728)
INTEX RECREATION CORP
4001 Via Oro Ave Ste 210, Long Beach
(90810-1400)
PHONE.....................................310 549-1846
Tien P Zee, *CEO*
Jim Lai, *President*
Bill Smith, *Vice Pres*
Bob Howe, *Asst Treas*
◆ **EMP:** 100 **EST:** 1966
SQ FT: 330,000
SALES (est): 19.3MM
SALES (corp-wide): 171.8MM **Privately**
Held
WEB: www.intexcorp.com
SIC: 5021 5092 5091 5162 Waterbeds;
toys; watersports equipment & supplies;
plastics materials & basic shapes
PA: Intex Recreation Corp
4001 Via Oro Ave Ste 210
Long Beach CA 90810
310 549-5400

(P-6729)
JANUS ET CIE (PA)
12310 Greenstone Ave, Santa Fe Springs
(90670-4737)
PHONE.....................................310 601-2908
Janice K Feldman, *CEO*
Cindy Wolf, *President*
Paul Warren, *COO*
Greg Buscher, *CFO*
Danya Lane, *Vice Pres*
◆ **EMP:** 110
SQ FT: 154,000
SALES (est): 57.9MM **Privately Held**
WEB: www.janusetcie.com
SIC: 5021 5712 Outdoor & lawn furniture;
household furniture; furniture stores

(P-6730)
K&I INTERNATIONAL TRADE INC
3592 Rosemead Blvd # 220, Rosemead
(91770-2053)
PHONE.....................................312 766-1848
Jinhong Lin, *CEO*
EMP: 50
SALES (est): 2.2MM **Privately Held**
SIC: 5021 Furniture

(P-6731)
MODANI LOS ANGELES LLC
Also Called: Modani Furniture
8873 W Sunset Blvd, West Hollywood
(90069-2107)
PHONE.....................................310 652-2323
John Momo, *Manager*
▲ **EMP:** 50
SALES (est): 6.7MM **Privately Held**
SIC: 5021 Furniture

(P-6732)
OMNIA ITALIAN DESIGN INC
4900 Edison Ave, Chino (91710-5713)
PHONE.....................................909 393-4400
Peter Zolferino, *President*
Luie Nastri, *Vice Pres*
Randy Gleckman, *Natl Sales Mgr*
David Santos, *Cust Mgr*
◆ **EMP:** 200
SQ FT: 110,000
SALES (est): 63.2MM **Privately Held**
SIC: 5021 Household furniture

(P-6733)
ONE WORKPLACE L FERRARI
LLC
Also Called: One Workplace L Ferrari
475 Brannan St, San Francisco
(94107-5418)
PHONE.....................................415 357-2200
Brian Wilson, *Mng Member*
EMP: 50
SALES (est): 7.7MM
SALES (corp-wide): 225.6MM **Privately**
Held
SIC: 5021 Filing units; office furniture
PA: One Workplace L. Ferrari, Llc
2500 De La Cruz Blvd
Santa Clara CA 95050
669 800-2500

(P-6734)
PALECEK IMPORTS INC (PA)
601 Parr Blvd, Richmond (94801-1316)
PHONE.....................................510 236-7730

Allan Palecek, *President*
Andrew T Palecek, *Vice Pres*
Pat Sexson, *General Mgr*
Charles Reisbol, *Administration*
Annabelle Whitney, *Financial Analy*
◆ EMP: 61
SQ FT: 250,000
SALES (est): 39.2MM **Privately Held**
WEB: www.palecek.com
SIC: 5021 5023 Household furniture; home furnishings

(P-6735)
POUNDEX ASSOCIATES CORPORATION
21490 Baker Pkwy, City of Industry (91789-5239)
PHONE..................................909 444-5878
Lionel Chen, *President*
Kimberly Flores, *Asst Mgr*
◆ EMP: 100
SQ FT: 55,000
SALES (est): 39.9MM **Privately Held**
SIC: 5021 Household furniture; dining room furniture; tables, occasional

(P-6736)
PRIVILEGE INTERNATIONAL INC
2323 Firestone Blvd, South Gate (90280-2684)
PHONE..................................323 585-0777
Eddy Sarraf, *President*
Mark Darwish, *Senior VP*
Richard Darwish, *Vice Pres*
Christine Alvarado, *Cust Mgr*
Luis Saldana, *Manager*
▲ EMP: 75
SQ FT: 350,000
SALES (est): 22.2MM **Privately Held**
WEB: www.privilegeinc.com
SIC: 5021 Furniture

(P-6737)
SITONIT SEATING INC
6415 Katella Ave, Cypress (90630-5245)
PHONE..................................714 995-4800
Paul Devries, *CEO*
EMP: 200
SALES (est): 34.1MM **Privately Held**
SIC: 5021 Office furniture
PA: Exemplis Llc
6415 Katella Ave
Cypress CA 90630

(P-6738)
UNISOURCE SOLUTIONS INC (PA)
8350 Rex Rd, Pico Rivera (90660-3785)
PHONE..................................562 654-3500
James Kastner, *CEO*
Marc Flax, *President*
Ken Kastner, *President*
Clem Nieto, *CFO*
Jim Kastner, *Chairman*
▲ EMP: 105
SQ FT: 186,000
SALES (est): 67.6MM **Privately Held**
WEB: www.unisourceit.com
SIC: 5021 Office furniture

(P-6739)
VAN SARK INC
Also Called: Dependable Furniture Mfrs
1255 Battery St Ste 200, San Francisco (94111-1164)
PHONE..................................415 362-5888
Edwin Essary, *Officer*
Felipe Castillo, *Project Mgr*
Jack Crane, *Consultant*
EMP: 75
SALES (corp-wide): 13.4MM **Privately Held**
SIC: 5021 Furniture
PA: Van Sark, Inc.
888 Doolittle Dr
San Leandro CA 94577
510 635-1111

(P-6740)
VANGUARD LEGATO A CAL CORP
Also Called: Vanguard Legato
2121 Williams St, San Leandro (94577-3224)
PHONE..................................510 351-3333
Darlene Patch, *Director*
EMP: 68
SQ FT: 20,000
SALES (est): 9.3MM **Privately Held**
WEB: www.brg.com
SIC: 5021 5112 5023 Furniture; office supplies; home furnishings

(P-6741)
VERSA PRODUCTS INC (PA)
Also Called: Versatables.com
14105 Avalon Blvd, Los Angeles (90061-2637)
PHONE..................................310 353-7100
Christopher Laudadio, *CEO*
Chris Stormer, *General Mgr*
Frank Jamison, *Contract Mgr*
Martha Wilson, *HR Admin*
Fernando Fregoso, *Purch Mgr*
▲ EMP: 82 EST: 2000
SQ FT: 35,000
SALES: 22MM **Privately Held**
WEB: www.versatables.com
SIC: 5021 2512 Office furniture; couches, sofas & davenports: upholstered on wood frames

(P-6742)
VIRCO INC (HQ)
2027 Harpers Way, Torrance (90501-1524)
PHONE..................................310 533-0474
Robert Virtue, *CEO*
Robert Lind, *Bd of Directors*
Scotty Bell, *Vice Pres*
Robert Dose, *Vice Pres*
James Johnson, *Vice Pres*
▼ EMP: 56
SQ FT: 560,000
SALES (est): 124.1MM
SALES (corp-wide): 189.2MM **Publicly Held**
WEB: www.virco.com
SIC: 5021 Furniture
PA: Virco Mfg. Corporation
2027 Harpers Way
Torrance CA 90501
310 533-0474

(P-6743)
WATERHILL LTD
140 N Orange Ave, City of Industry (91744-3431)
PHONE..................................626 369-6828
Brian Yip, *President*
Carol Yip, *Admin Sec*
▲ EMP: 50
SQ FT: 125,000
SALES (est): 6.6MM **Privately Held**
WEB: www.waterhill.com
SIC: 5021 Dining room furniture

(P-6744)
WINNERS ONLY INC
1365 Park Center Dr, Vista (92081-8338)
PHONE..................................760 599-0300
Alex Shu, *Chairman*
Sheue-Wen Lee, *CEO*
Fred Dizon, *President*
Marco Salinas, *HR Admin*
▲ EMP: 200
SALES (est): 81.3MM **Privately Held**
WEB: www.winnersonly.com
SIC: 5021 Office furniture; dining room furniture

(P-6745)
WMK OFFICE SAN DIEGO LLC (PA)
Also Called: BKM Officeworks
4780 Estgate Mall Ste 100, San Diego (92121)
PHONE..................................858 569-4700
William Kuhnert, *CEO*
Jim Skidmore, *COO*
Shelly Miller, *General Mgr*
Dan Martinez, *Project Mgr*
Troy McLaughlin, *Project Mgr*
EMP: 70

SQ FT: 100,000
SALES (est): 79.6MM **Privately Held**
WEB: www.bkmofficeworks.com
SIC: 5021 Office furniture

5023 Home Furnishings Wholesale

(P-6746)
ALPINE INTERIORS CORPORATION (PA)
Also Called: Alpine Carpets
3961 Sepulveda Blvd # 205, Culver City (90230-4600)
PHONE..................................310 390-7639
Johannes Van Ierland, *CEO*
Klaus Friederic, *President*
EMP: 90
SQ FT: 21,000
SALES (est): 17.6MM **Privately Held**
SIC: 5023 5713 Floor coverings; carpets; carpets

(P-6747)
AMERICAN FAUCET COATINGS CORP
3280 Corporate Vw, Vista (92081-8528)
PHONE..................................760 598-5895
Susan E Butler, *President*
▲ EMP: 50
SALES (est): 23.3MM **Privately Held**
WEB: www.sigmafaucet.com
SIC: 5023 3432 Home furnishings; plumbing fixture fittings & trim

(P-6748)
B R FUNSTEN & CO
Also Called: BR Funsten
105 Lndustrial Park, Manteca (95337)
PHONE..................................209 825-5375
Rod Tilson, *Branch Mgr*
EMP: 60
SALES (corp-wide): 107.6MM **Privately Held**
WEB: www.brfunsten.com
SIC: 5023 5713 Resilient floor coverings: tile or sheet; floor covering stores
PA: B. R. Funsten & Co.
5200 Watt Ct Ste B
Fairfield CA 94534
209 825-5375

(P-6749)
B R FUNSTEN & CO
Tom Duffy Company Division
5200 Watt Ct Ste B, Fairfield (94534-4209)
PHONE..................................707 863-8300
Don Jackson, *Manager*
EMP: 100
SALES (corp-wide): 107.6MM **Privately Held**
WEB: www.brfunsten.com
SIC: 5023 Carpets
PA: B. R. Funsten & Co.
5200 Watt Ct Ste B
Fairfield CA 94534
209 825-5375

(P-6750)
BENZARA INC
8600 Mercury Ln, Pico Rivera (90660-3797)
PHONE..................................562 633-7612
Arvind Singh, *CEO*
▲ EMP: 65
SALES (est): 13.2MM **Privately Held**
SIC: 5023 Decorative home furnishings & supplies

(P-6751)
BP INDUSTRIES INCORPORATED
5300 E Concours St, Ontario (91764)
PHONE..................................909 481-0227
Dong Koo Kim, *President*
Jim Clark, *Vice Pres*
Kathy Choi, *Administration*
Maria Hon, *Controller*
Charles Wang, *Controller*
◆ EMP: 57
SQ FT: 140,000

SALES (est): 26.9MM **Privately Held**
WEB: www.bpindustries.com
SIC: 5023 Mirrors & pictures, framed & un-framed

(P-6752)
BRADSHAW INTERNATIONAL INC (HQ)
Also Called: Bradshaw Home
9409 Buffalo Ave, Rancho Cucamonga (91730-6012)
PHONE..................................909 476-3884
Michael Rodrigue, *CEO*
Thomas Barber, *President*
Brett R Bradshaw, *President*
Julie Hayes, *President*
Sandip Grewald, *CFO*
◆ EMP: 280
SQ FT: 750,000
SALES (est): 467.9MM **Privately Held**
WEB: www.goodcook.com
SIC: 5023 Kitchenware
PA: Oncap Ii L.P.
161 Bay St 47 & 49 Flr
Toronto ON M5J 2
416 214-4300

(P-6753)
BREVILLE USA INC
19400 S Western Ave, Torrance (90501-1119)
PHONE..................................310 755-3000
Damian Baden Court, *CEO*
Simon Schober, *CFO*
◆ EMP: 50
SQ FT: 135,000
SALES (est): 31.3MM **Privately Held**
SIC: 5023 5064 Home furnishings; appliance parts, household
HQ: Breville Holdings Pty Limited
G Se 2 170 Bourke Rd
Alexandria NSW
293 848-100

(P-6754)
BYTHEWAYS MANUFACTURING INC
Also Called: B T W
2080 Enterprise Blvd, West Sacramento (95691-5051)
PHONE..................................916 453-1212
Mervin Bytheway Jr, *President*
Jann Bytheway, *Corp Secy*
EMP: 300
SALES (est): 20MM **Privately Held**
SIC: 5023 Window furnishings
HQ: Hunter Douglas N.V.
Piekstraat 2
Rotterdam 3071
104 869-911

(P-6755)
CONRAD IMPORTS INC
540 Barneveld Ave Ste H, San Francisco (94124-1805)
PHONE..................................415 626-3303
Ruth M Holland, *President*
Timothy Moran, *CFO*
Janice Holland, *Vice Pres*
Buck Irwin, *Vice Pres*
Ed Fernandez, *Info Tech Dir*
EMP: 93 EST: 1956
SALES (est): 25.2MM **Privately Held**
WEB: www.conradshades.com
SIC: 5023 Window furnishings

(P-6756)
CONTRACTORS FLRG SVC CAL INC
300 E Dyer Rd, Santa Ana (92707-3740)
P.O. Box 15106 (92735-0106)
PHONE..................................714 556-6100
Joseph J Ott, *President*
EMP: 110
SQ FT: 10,000
SALES: 16.6MM **Privately Held**
WEB: www.conflorsvcofca.com
SIC: 5023 Floor coverings

(P-6757)
E & E CO LTD
Also Called: Jla Home
2222 E Beamer St, Woodland (95776-6226)
PHONE..................................530 669-5991

EMP: 157 **Privately Held**
SIC: 5023 Home furnishings
PA: E & E Co., Ltd.
45875 Northport Loop E
Fremont CA 94538

(P-6758)
E & E CO LTD (PA)
Also Called: Jla Home
45875 Northport Loop E, Fremont
(94538-6414)
PHONE..................510 490-9788
Edmund Jin, *CEO*
Rusty Ortiz, *COO*
Nancy Hattersley, *Chairman*
Hellen Xu, *Exec VP*
Winnie Cheung, *Vice Pres*
◆ EMP: 180
SQ FT: 60,000
SALES (est): 236MM **Privately Held**
WEB: WWW.ESHEER.COM
SIC: 5023 Sheets, textile

(P-6759)
ELEGANCE WOOD PRODUCTS INC
Also Called: Elegance Exotic Wood Flooring
7351 Mcguire Ave, Fontana (92336-1668)
PHONE..................909 484-7676
Jean Tong, *CEO*
Michael Liu, *Accountant*
▲ EMP: 60
SQ FT: 500,000
SALES (est): 12.7MM **Privately Held**
SIC: 5023 Wood flooring

(P-6760)
EV RAY INC
6400 Variel Ave, Woodland Hills
(91367-2577)
PHONE..................818 346-5381
Lee Brown, *President*
Helen Kim, *Finance Mgr*
Beatrice Gomes, *Manager*
EMP: 50
SQ FT: 22,000
SALES (est): 6.5MM **Privately Held**
WEB: www.rayev.com
SIC: 5023 2211 2591 2391 Draperies; draperies & drapery fabrics, cotton; drapery hardware & blinds & shades; curtains & draperies

(P-6761)
EVRIHOLDER PRODUCTS LLC (HQ)
1500 S Lewis St, Anaheim (92805-6423)
PHONE..................714 490-7878
Ivan Stein, *CEO*
Scott Neamand, *CFO*
▲ EMP: 50
SQ FT: 45,000
SALES (est): 34MM
SALES (corp-wide): 68.4MM **Privately Held**
WEB: www.evriholder.com
SIC: 5023 5085 5087 Kitchenware; bins & containers, storage; cleaning & maintenance equipment & supplies
PA: Clearlight Partners, Llc
100 Bayview Cir Ste 5000
Newport Beach CA 92660
949 725-6616

(P-6762)
GALLEHER LLC (PA)
9303 Greenleaf Ave, Santa Fe Springs
(90670-3029)
PHONE..................562 944-8885
Jeff Hamar, *CEO*
Ray Iodice, *CFO*
Rick Coates, *Senior VP*
Todd Hamar, *Senior VP*
Mike Parkhurst, *Division Mgr*
EMP: 110 EST: 1937
SQ FT: 100,000
SALES (est): 141.7MM **Privately Held**
WEB: www.galleher.com
SIC: 5023 Wood flooring

(P-6763)
GATE FIVE GROUP LLC
Also Called: Roost
200 Gate 5 Rd Ste 116, Sausalito
(94965-1456)
PHONE..................415 339-9500
Scott Donnellan,
Nick Shorten, *Design Engr*
Sarah Lukenbill, *Human Res Dir*
Kevin Freswick, *Opers Staff*
Lisa Grundy, *Director*
▲ EMP: 50
SQ FT: 1,500
SALES (est): 17.7MM **Privately Held**
SIC: 5023 Decorative home furnishings & supplies

(P-6764)
GIBSON OVERSEAS INC
Also Called: Gibson Outlet
2410 Yates Ave, Commerce (90040-1918)
PHONE..................323 832-8900
Sohail Gabbay, *CEO*
Darioush Gabbay, *COO*
Soloman Gabbay, *CFO*
Ken Cook, *Vice Pres*
Syed Haneef, *Vice Pres*
◆ EMP: 510
SQ FT: 850,000
SALES (est): 220.5MM **Privately Held**
WEB: www.gibsonusa.com
SIC: 5023 Glassware; china; kitchen tools & utensils

(P-6765)
GINA B LTD INC
Also Called: Gina B Showroom
1601 W 134th St, Gardena (90249-2013)
PHONE..................310 366-7926
Rolf Berschneider, *President*
Gina Berschneider, *Vice Pres*
EMP: 62 EST: 1968
SALES (est): 5.7MM **Privately Held**
SIC: 5023 2599 2542 2273 Home furnishings; factory furniture & fixtures; partitions & fixtures, except wood; carpets & rugs

(P-6766)
GLOBAL ACCENTS INC
19808 Normandie Ave, Torrance
(90502-1112)
PHONE..................310 639-2600
Danny Partielli, *President*
▲ EMP: 110
SQ FT: 50,000
SALES (est): 10.6MM **Privately Held**
SIC: 5023 Rugs; bedspreads

(P-6767)
HORNER-HALLEHER HOLDING CO (PA)
9303 Greenleaf Ave, Santa Fe Springs
(90670-3029)
PHONE..................562 944-8885
Rick Coates, *Senior VP*
Michelle Credit, *Analyst*
Jonathan Leon, *Buyer*
David Goodman, *Post Master*
EMP: 149
SQ FT: 100,000
SALES (est): 10.4MM **Privately Held**
SIC: 5023 Floor coverings

(P-6768)
INTERNTONAL WIN TREATMENTS INC (PA)
Also Called: Custom Craft Company
12301 Hawkins St, Santa Fe Springs
(90670-3366)
PHONE..................562 236-2120
Tsong Shih, *President*
Hsawn Shih, *Shareholder*
◆ EMP: 100
SQ FT: 30,000
SALES (est): 16.7MM **Privately Held**
SIC: 5023 Venetian blinds

(P-6769)
K T W PRODUCTIONS INC
6303 E Cedarbrooks Rd, Orange
(92867-2491)
PHONE..................714 685-0428
Lola Wang, *President*
Rex Wang, *Vice Pres*

▲ EMP: 800
SALES (est): 64.7MM **Privately Held**
SIC: 5023 Home furnishings

(P-6770)
KEECO LLC (PA)
30736 Wiegman Rd, Hayward
(94544-7819)
PHONE..................510 324-8800
Christopher Grassi, *CEO*
Greg Wyman, *Mktg Dir*
Martin Berry,
Kristine Igoe,
Ben Steingl,
◆ EMP: 70
SQ FT: 500,000
SALES (est): 256.5K **Privately Held**
WEB: www.lkeeco.com
SIC: 5023 Linens & towels; linens, table

(P-6771)
KINCAID & DECKER INC (PA)
Also Called: Woodmart Window Coverings
15800 Straden St, Van Nuys (91406)
PHONE..................818 785-1528
Richard M Decker, *President*
Robert Kincaid, *Vice Pres*
▲ EMP: 70 EST: 1995
SQ FT: 40,000
SALES (est): 5.5MM **Privately Held**
WEB: www.woodmart.com
SIC: 5023 Window covering parts & accessories

(P-6772)
LE CROCHET BY SARO INC (PA)
3333 W Pacific Ave, Burbank (91505-1553)
PHONE..................818 846-3314
Kevork Kalenderian, *President*
◆ EMP: 50
SQ FT: 6,000
SALES (est): 13MM **Privately Held**
SIC: 5023 5131 Linens & towels; linen piece goods, woven

(P-6773)
LEDRA BRANDS INC
Also Called: Bruck Lighting Systems
15774 Gateway Cir, Tustin (92780-6469)
PHONE..................714 259-9959
Alex Ladjevardi, *President*
Farah Emami, *COO*
Jade Turney, *Vice Pres*
Jason Luckenbill, *Graphic Designe*
Cinthia Ojeda, *Accounting Mgr*
▲ EMP: 55 EST: 1993
SQ FT: 30,000
SALES (est): 23.1MM **Privately Held**
WEB: www.brucklightingsystems.com
SIC: 5023 Lamps: floor, boudoir, desk

(P-6774)
LONGUST DISTRIBUTING LLC
1206 N Miller St Unit A, Anaheim
(92806-1960)
PHONE..................480 820-6244
John Trujillo, *Branch Mgr*
Ron Herrmann, *Manager*
Debbie McGrath, *Manager*
EMP: 50
SALES (corp-wide): 60MM **Privately Held**
SIC: 5023 Floor coverings; resilient floor coverings: tile or sheet; carpets; wood flooring
PA: Longust Distributing, Llc
2432 W Birchwood Ave
Mesa AZ 85202
480 820-6244

(P-6775)
MARIAK INDUSTRIES INC
Also Called: Mariak Window Fashion
575 W Manville St, Rancho Dominguez
(90220-5509)
PHONE..................310 661-4400
Leo Elinson, *CEO*
▲ EMP: 380
SQ FT: 80,000
SALES (est): 122.3MM
SALES (corp-wide): 2.6B **Privately Held**
SIC: 5023 2591 Vertical blinds; blinds vertical

HQ: Springs Window Fashions, Llc
7549 Graber Rd
Middleton WI 53562
608 836-1011

(P-6776)
MEYER CORPORATION US
Also Called: Faberware Div
2001 Meyer Way, Fairfield (94533-6802)
PHONE..................707 399-2100
Stuart Levine, *Manager*
EMP: 100 **Privately Held**
WEB: www.meyer.com
SIC: 5023 3469 1541 5046 Kitchenware; cooking ware, except porcelain enamelled; industrial buildings & warehouses; commercial equipment; pressed & blown glass
HQ: Meyer Corporation, U.S.
1 Meyer Plz
Vallejo CA 94590
707 551-2800

(P-6777)
NEUBERG NUBERG IMPORTERS GROUP
Also Called: Framing Fabrics
6001 Santa Monica Blvd, Los Angeles
(90038-1807)
PHONE..................800 832-2742
Larry Neuberg, *President*
▲ EMP: 50
SQ FT: 15,000
SALES (est): 5.7MM **Privately Held**
SIC: 5023 Frames & framing, picture & mirror

(P-6778)
NORMAN INTERNATIONAL INC
Also Called: Norman Charter
12301 Hawkins St, Santa Fe Springs
(90670-3366)
PHONE..................562 946-0420
Ranjan Mada, *CEO*
Ricky Wang, *Info Tech Dir*
James Wang, *Info Tech Mgr*
Susan Huang, *Business Mgr*
Renee Lee, *Human Res Mgr*
◆ EMP: 70
SALES (est): 53.5MM **Privately Held**
WEB: www.normanintlusa.com
SIC: 5023 Home furnishings

(P-6779)
OLDE THOMPSON INC
3250 Camino Del Sol, Oxnard
(93030-8998)
PHONE..................800 827-1565
Jeffrey M Shumway, *CEO*
Scott Ash, *CFO*
Bill Harris, *Vice Pres*
Heidi Slocumb, *Vice Pres*
Larry Valenzuela, *General Mgr*
◆ EMP: 150 EST: 1917
SQ FT: 88,000
SALES (est): 88.2MM **Privately Held**
WEB: www.oldethompson.com
SIC: 5023 2631 5149 Kitchenware; container, packaging & boxboard; spices & seasonings

(P-6780)
OMEGA MOULDING WEST LLC
5500 Lindbergh Ln, Bell (90201-6410)
PHONE..................323 261-3510
Bernard Portnoy, *Mng Member*
David Merzin,
Anastasia Portnoy,
Peter Shulman, *Director*
◆ EMP: 130
SQ FT: 130,000
SALES (est): 18.2MM **Privately Held**
WEB: www.omegamoulding.com
SIC: 5023 Frames & framing, picture & mirror

(P-6781)
PAVIGYM AMERICA CORP
1902 Wright Pl Fl 2, Carlsbad
(92008-6583)
PHONE..................858 414-8624
Marcos Requena Penat, *CEO*
EMP: 100
SALES (est): 12.5MM **Privately Held**
SIC: 5023 Floor coverings

(P-6782)
PEKING HANDICRAFT INC (PA)
Also Called: P H I
1388 San Mateo Ave, South San Francisco
(94080-6501)
PHONE..................................650 871-3788
Derrick Lo, *CEO*
Clinton Chien, *COO*
▲ EMP: 120
SQ FT: 150,000
SALES: 113.4MM **Privately Held**
WEB: www.pkhc.com
SIC: 5023 Linens & towels; bedspreads;
sheets, textile; decorative home furnishings & supplies

(P-6783)
PSI3G INC
2979 Promenade St Ste 100, West Sacramento (95691-6410)
PHONE..................................916 803-2879
Shawn Still, *Branch Mgr*
EMP: 58
SALES (corp-wide): 16.8MM **Privately Held**
SIC: 5023 5713 Floor coverings; floor covering stores
PA: Psi3g, Inc.
505 San Marin Dr Ste A120
Novato CA 94945
415 493-3854

(P-6784)
R&S CARPET SERVICES INC
Also Called: R & S Floor Covering
1485 Spruce St Ste C106, Riverside
(92507-2445)
PHONE..................................909 740-6645
Roy Paswaters, *President*
Steven Birito, *Vice Pres*
Marcos Carrasco, *Vice Pres*
EMP: 61
SQ FT: 9,000
SALES (est): 7MM **Privately Held**
SIC: 5023 1752 Carpets; carpet laying

(P-6785)
RONCO INVENTIONS LLC (PA)
21344 Superior St, Chatsworth
(91311-4312)
PHONE..................................800 486-1806
Ronald Popeil,
EMP: 150 EST: 1989
SALES (est): 17MM **Privately Held**
SIC: 5023 5719 3634 3556 Kitchenware;
kitchenware; electric housewares & fans;
food products machinery

(P-6786)
SIERRA LIVING CONCEPTS INC
46560 Fremont Blvd # 414, Fremont
(94538-6491)
PHONE..................................510 402-4906
Chetna Nathawat, *President*
Raj Nathawat, *Director*
▲ EMP: 55
SALES (est): 1MM **Privately Held**
SIC: 5023 Decorative home furnishings &
supplies

(P-6787)
SIMPLEHUMAN LLC (PA)
19850 Magellan Dr, Torrance (90502-1106)
PHONE..................................310 436-2250
Frank Yang, *Mng Member*
Jackson Yang,
Julie Yang,
◆ EMP: 55
SQ FT: 55,000
SALES (est): 44.5MM **Privately Held**
WEB: www.simplehuman.net
SIC: 5023 Kitchenware

(P-6788)
SOTO PROVISION INC
Also Called: Soto Food Service
488 Parriott Pl W, Hacienda Heights
(91745-1015)
PHONE..................................626 458-4600
John R Renna Sr, *President*
Bonnie Lea, *Officer*
John R Renna Jr, *Vice Pres*
EMP: 70
SQ FT: 35,000

SALES (est): 64.5MM **Privately Held**
WEB: www.sotofoodservice.com
SIC: 5023 5046 Kitchen tools & utensils;
kitchenware; commercial cooking & food
service equipment

(P-6789)
SUNDAY BAZAAR INC
Also Called: Lunares
495 Barneveld Ave, San Francisco
(94124-1501)
PHONE..................................415 621-0764
Nimerta Oberoi, *President*
Sunena Balain, *Marketing Staff*
▲ EMP: 87
SQ FT: 4,000
SALES (est): 13.6MM **Privately Held**
WEB: www.lunares.com
SIC: 5023 5199 Decorative home furnishings & supplies; gifts & novelties

(P-6790)
TABLETOPS UNLIMITED INC (PA)
23000 Avalon Blvd, Carson (90745-5017)
PHONE..................................310 549-6000
Javad Asgari, *CEO*
Mohsen Asgari, *President*
Hamid Ebrahimi, *President*
Daryoush Molayem, *Vice Pres*
Masod Tehrani, *Admin Sec*
◆ EMP: 64
SQ FT: 350,000
SALES (est): 39.5MM **Privately Held**
WEB: www.tabletopsunltd.com
SIC: 5023 China; glassware; stainless
steel flatware

(P-6791)
TEST-RITE PRODUCTS CORP (DH)
1900 Burgundy Pl, Ontario (91761-2308)
PHONE..................................909 605-9899
Jack Ho, *Treasurer*
Diana Quezada, *Receptionist*
▲ EMP: 80
SQ FT: 400,000
SALES (corp-wide): 1.2B **Privately Held**
SIC: 5023 Home furnishings

(P-6792)
THUNDER GROUP INC (PA)
780 Nogales St Ste C, City of Industry
(91748-1380)
PHONE..................................626 935-1605
Eddie Liu, *CEO*
Chun Chieh Liu, *President*
Ralph Liu, *Vice Pres*
Lin CHI Liu, *Admin Sec*
Cindy Tung, *Technology*
◆ EMP: 50
SQ FT: 340,000
SALES (est): 27.2MM **Privately Held**
SIC: 5023 Kitchenware

(P-6793)
TIFFANY DALE INC (PA)
14765 Industry Cir, La Mirada
(90638-5818)
PHONE..................................714 739-2700
Ye H Chung, *CEO*
Garbiel Chung, *Vice Pres*
Connie Chung, *Admin Sec*
Serina Chung, *Administration*
Jonathan Kim, *Info Tech Mgr*
▲ EMP: 83
SQ FT: 88,480
SALES (est): 13.1MM **Privately Held**
SIC: 5023 Lamps: floor, boudoir, desk

(P-6794)
TOM RAY INDUSTRIES INC
Also Called: Thefloorstore/Flor Stor
23182 Alcalde Dr Ste G, Laguna Hills
(92653-1450)
PHONE..................................949 380-8333
Thomas Ray, *President*
EMP: 100
SQ FT: 700,000

SALES (est): 15.5MM **Privately Held**
WEB: www.florstor.com
SIC: 5023 5211 1752 5713 Floor coverings; flooring, wood; wood floor installation & refinishing; floor tile; specialty cleaning & sanitation preparations; interior decorating

(P-6795)
TRI - STAR WIN COVERINGS INC
Also Called: Carpet Care By Tri-Star
19555 Prairie St, Northridge (91324-2424)
PHONE..................................818 718-3188
Bernard Warshauer, *CEO*
Bernard Warshauser, *Chief Mktg Ofcr*
Deborah Newhouse, *Controller*
EMP: 50
SQ FT: 22,000
SALES (est): 27.1MM **Privately Held**
WEB: www.tsinteriors.com
SIC: 5023 5719 Floor coverings; window furnishings; window furnishings

(P-6796)
TRI-WEST LTD (PA)
12005 Pike St, Santa Fe Springs
(90670-6100)
PHONE..................................562 692-9166
Allen Gage, *Partner*
Randy Sims, *CFO*
Bob Taylor, *Executive*
Laura Robledo, *Administration*
Allison Copeland, *Credit Mgr*
▲ EMP: 200 EST: 1981
SQ FT: 300,000
SALES: 182.6MM **Privately Held**
WEB: www.triwestltd.com
SIC: 5023 Floor coverings; resilient floor coverings: tile or sheet; wood flooring

(P-6797)
UMA ENTERPRISES INC (PA)
350 W Apra St, Compton (90220-5529)
PHONE..................................310 631-1166
James Buch, *CEO*
Larry Woods, *CFO*
Ravi Gandhi, *Database Admin*
Kamal Arody, *Opers Mgr*
Charles Graham, *Opers Staff*
◆ EMP: 140
SQ FT: 460,000
SALES (est): 76.3MM **Privately Held**
WEB: www.umainc.com
SIC: 5023 Decorative home furnishings & supplies

(P-6798)
UNIQUE CARPETS LTD
7360 Jurupa Ave, Riverside (92504-1025)
PHONE..................................951 352-8125
Bill D Graves, *President*
Robert L Binford, *Exec VP*
Martin Lopez, *Vice Pres*
R Arce, *Technology*
Christina Murray, *Production*
▲ EMP: 55
SALES (est): 16.8MM **Privately Held**
WEB: www.uniquecarpets.com
SIC: 5023 2273 Carpets; carpets & rugs

(P-6799)
UNIVERSAL WOOD MOULDING INC (PA)
Also Called: Universal Framing Products
21139 Centre Pointe Pkwy, Santa Clarita
(91350-2994)
PHONE..................................661 362-6262
Jon M Bromberg, *CEO*
AVI Feibenlatt, *Ch of Bd*
Mark Gottlieb, *President*
Cliff Uytingco, *Engineer*
Michelle Bryant, *Human Res Mgr*
▲ EMP: 50
SALES (est): 25MM **Privately Held**
WEB: www.universalframing.com
SIC: 5023 3999 Frames & framing, picture
& mirror; atomizers; toiletry; advertising
curtains

(P-6800)
VALLEY WHOLESALE SUPPLY CORP (PA)
Also Called: Valley Molding & Frame
10708 Vanowen St, North Hollywood
(91605-6401)
PHONE..................................818 769-5656

Charles Aaron, *Ch of Bd*
Michelle Merritt, *Shareholder*
David A Labowitz, *President*
Suzanne Ehrmann, *Vice Pres*
▲ EMP: 57
SQ FT: 30,000
SALES (est): 21.9MM **Privately Held**
WEB: www.valleymoulding.com
SIC: 5023 5031 Frames & framing, picture
& mirror; decorating supplies; molding, all
materials

(P-6801)
VALYRIA LLC (HQ)
Also Called: Transpac
1050 Aviator Dr, Vacaville (95688-8900)
PHONE..................................707 452-0600
Laurie Gilner, *President*
Craig Mackley, *Vice Pres*
Lori Benedetti, *Executive*
Courtney Guerino, *Executive*
Jose Gomez, *Technology*
▲ EMP: 60 EST: 2016
SQ FT: 175,000
SALES (est): 7.7MM
SALES (corp-wide): 47.5MM **Privately Held**
SIC: 5023 Decorative home furnishings &
supplies
PA: C & F Enterprises, Inc.
819 Bluecrab Rd
Newport News VA 23606
757 310-6100

(P-6802)
VENUS GROUP INC
Also Called: Venus Textiles
25861 Wright, Foothill Ranch (92610-3504)
PHONE..................................949 609-1299
Kirit D Patel, *CEO*
Rajni D Patel, *Vice Pres*
Ryen Masters, *Project Mgr*
Dennis Jackson, *VP Prdtn*
Mike Sager, *Manager*
◆ EMP: 85
SALES (est): 65.1MM **Privately Held**
WEB: www.venusgroup.com
SIC: 5023 2392 5719 Towels; towels, fabric & nonwoven: made from purchased
materials; towels

(P-6803)
W DIAMOND SUPPLY CO (DH)
Also Called: Diamond W Floorcovering
19321 E Walnut Dr N, City of Industry
(91748-1436)
PHONE..................................909 859-8939
Louis J Bettitta, *CEO*
Mike Klingele, *President*
Kandi Anderson, *COO*
Daniel Erickson, *CFO*
Becky Aguilar, *Human Res Mgr*
▲ EMP: 60
SQ FT: 106,000
SALES (est): 20.2MM
SALES (corp-wide): 528.7K **Privately Held**
WEB: www.diamondw.com
SIC: 5023 Floor coverings
HQ: Tarkett, Inc.
30000 Aurora Rd
Solon OH 44139
800 899-8916

(P-6804)
ZODAX LP (PA)
14040 Arminta St, Panorama City
(91402-6080)
PHONE..................................818 785-5626
Philip Cohanim, *Managing Prtnr*
Edward Cohanim, *Partner*
Ginalin Tan, *COO*
Eddie Kohan, *Vice Pres*
Carmela Donato Pineda, *Accountant*
▲ EMP: 75
SQ FT: 100,000
SALES (est): 2.2MM **Privately Held**
SIC: 5023 Decorative home furnishings &
supplies

5031 Lumber, Plywood & Millwork Wholesale

(P-6805)
ALLIED BUILDING PRODUCTS CORP
Also Called: AMS
456 Industrial Rd, San Bernardino (92408-3716)
PHONE..................909 796-6926
Paul Lynd, *Manager*
Nancy Wetzel, *Project Mgr*
Josh Bejarano, *Traffic Dir*
Kami Gonzalez, *Sales Associate*
Irene Hernandez, *Asst Mgr*
EMP: 50
SQ FT: 25,000
SALES (corp-wide): 4.3B **Publicly Held**
WEB: www.a-m-s.com
SIC: 5031 Building materials, exterior
HQ: Allied Building Products Corp.
   15 E Union Ave
   East Rutherford NJ 07073
   201 507-8400

(P-6806)
AMERICAN BUILDING SUPPLY INC (HQ)
Also Called: Abs-American Building Supply
8360 Elder Creek Rd, Sacramento (95828-1705)
P.O. Box 293030 (95829-3030)
PHONE..................916 503-4100
Mark Ballantyne, *CEO*
Dave Baker, *President*
Son Winn, *President*
Jan Leonard, *Vice Pres*
John Logan, *Vice Pres*
▲ EMP: 250
SQ FT: 230,000
SALES (est): 333.4MM **Publicly Held**
WEB: www.infinitydoor.com
SIC: 5031 3231 Doors; door frames, all materials; doors, glass: made from purchased glass

(P-6807)
AMERICAN BUILDING SUPPLY INC
1488 Tillie Lewis Dr, Stockton (95206-1131)
PHONE..................209 941-8852
Randy Neto, *Branch Mgr*
Alan Terry, *Maintence Staff*
EMP: 100 **Publicly Held**
WEB: www.infinitydoor.com
SIC: 5031 Doors
HQ: American Building Supply, Inc.
   8360 Elder Creek Rd
   Sacramento CA 95828
   916 503-4100

(P-6808)
ANFINSON LUMBER SALES INC (PA)
13041 Union Ave, Fontana (92337-6952)
PHONE..................951 681-4707
Richard Anfinson, *President*
Patricia J Anfinson, *Admin Sec*
EMP: 60
SQ FT: 48,000
SALES (est): 11.2MM **Privately Held**
WEB: www.anfinson.com
SIC: 5031 Lumber: rough, dressed & finished

(P-6809)
B B & T MANAGEMENT CORP
Also Called: Blomberg Window
1453 Blair Ave, Sacramento (95822-3410)
P.O. Box 22485 (95822-0485)
PHONE..................916 428-8060
J Philip Collier, *President*
Ralph S Blomberg, *Vice Pres*
EMP: 200
SALES (est): 21.4MM **Privately Held**
SIC: 5031 Windows

(P-6810)
BUILDERS FIRSTSOURCE INC
1262 E Main St, El Cajon (92021-7250)
PHONE..................619 440-7711
Tom Iannacone, *Executive*

Brian Hall, *Site Mgr*
EMP: 50
SALES (corp-wide): 7B **Publicly Held**
WEB: www.hopelumber.com
SIC: 5031 5072 Lumber: rough, dressed & finished; hardware
PA: Builders Firstsource, Inc.
   2001 Bryan St Ste 1600
   Dallas TX 75201
   214 880-3500

(P-6811)
BUILDERS FIRSTSOURCE INC
3450 Highland Ave, National City (91950-7420)
PHONE..................619 425-6660
Ted Teran, *Manager*
EMP: 50
SALES (corp-wide): 7B **Publicly Held**
WEB: www.hopelumber.com
SIC: 5031 Lumber, plywood & millwork
PA: Builders Firstsource, Inc.
   2001 Bryan St Ste 1600
   Dallas TX 75201
   214 880-3500

(P-6812)
BUILDERS FIRSTSOURCE INC
663 Lomas Santa Fe Dr, Solana Beach (92075-1412)
PHONE..................858 755-0246
Sergio Paz, *Branch Mgr*
Annie Peck, *Buyer*
EMP: 66
SALES (corp-wide): 7B **Publicly Held**
WEB: www.hopelumber.com
SIC: 5031 Lumber: rough, dressed & finished
PA: Builders Firstsource, Inc.
   2001 Bryan St Ste 1600
   Dallas TX 75201
   214 880-3500

(P-6813)
BUILDING MATERIAL DISTRS INC (PA)
Also Called: B M D
225 Elm Ave, Galt (95632-1558)
P.O. Box 606 (95632-0606)
PHONE..................209 745-3001
Mike Garrison, *Chairman*
Jeff Gore, *President*
Cynthia Thompson, *CFO*
Steven Ellinwood, *Chairman*
▲ EMP: 170
SQ FT: 100,000
SALES (est): 169.4MM **Privately Held**
WEB: www.bmdusa.com
SIC: 5031 Building materials, exterior; building materials, interior; window frames, all materials; door frames, all materials

(P-6814)
CERTAINTEED GYPSUM INC
27442 Portola Pkwy # 100, El Toro (92610-2823)
PHONE..................949 282-5300
Jeff Dushack, *Manager*
EMP: 50
SALES (corp-wide): 213.5MM **Privately Held**
WEB: www.bpb-na.com
SIC: 5031 Wallboard
HQ: Certainteed Gypsum, Inc.
   20 Moores Rd
   Malvern PA 19355

(P-6815)
CHA-DOR REALTY
Also Called: Meek's
4243 Dominguez Rd, Rocklin (95677-2101)
P.O. Box 1688 (95677-7688)
PHONE..................916 624-0627
Creig Miller, *Manager*
Heidi Scardina, *Sales Staff*
EMP: 52
SQ FT: 30,842
SALES (corp-wide): 47.2MM **Privately Held**
SIC: 5031 5211 Lumber, plywood & millwork; lumber & other building materials

PA: Cha-Dor Realty
   1651 Response Rd Ste 200
   Sacramento CA 95815
   916 565-1586

(P-6816)
COLLIER WAREHOUSE INC
Also Called: Cwi
90 Dorman Ave, San Francisco (94124-1807)
PHONE..................415 920-9720
Paul C Akin, *CEO*
David C Freer, *President*
Christy Akin, *Admin Sec*
▼ EMP: 50
SQ FT: 8,000
SALES (est): 34.1MM **Privately Held**
WEB: www.collier-sf.com
SIC: 5031 Windows; doors; skylights, all materials; window & door (prefabricated) installation

(P-6817)
COMMERCIAL LBR & PALLET CO INC
135 Long Ln, City of Industry (91746-2633)
PHONE..................626 968-0631
Catheline Detrick, *Manager*
EMP: 150
SALES (corp-wide): 87.2MM **Privately Held**
SIC: 5031 Lumber: rough, dressed & finished
PA: Commercial Lumber & Pallet Co., Inc.
   135 Long Ln
   City Of Industry CA 91746
   626 968-0631

(P-6818)
COMPLETE MILLWORK SERVICES INC
405 Aldo Ave, Santa Clara (95054-2302)
PHONE..................408 567-9664
Isaiah Clapp, *Project Mgr*
EMP: 75
SALES (corp-wide): 74.7MM **Privately Held**
SIC: 5031 Millwork
PA: Complete Millwork Services, Inc.
   4909 Goni Rd Ste A
   Carson City NV 89706
   775 246-0485

(P-6819)
COUNTY BUILDING MATERIALS INC
Also Called: Payless Patio & Rockery
2927 S King Rd, San Jose (95122-1597)
PHONE..................408 274-4920
Jay Robert Williams Jr, *CEO*
Jay R William Sr, *President*
Harry Glaze, *Vice Pres*
▲ EMP: 60
SQ FT: 26,000
SALES (est): 10.9MM **Privately Held**
SIC: 5031 5032 5261 5193 Building materials, exterior; building materials, interior; brick, stone & related material; nursery stock, seeds & bulbs; nursery stock; masonry materials & supplies

(P-6820)
DISCOUNT BUILDERS SUPPLY
1695 Mission St, San Francisco (94103-2432)
PHONE..................415 285-2800
Charles Goodman, *President*
▲ EMP: 69
SQ FT: 40,000
SALES (est): 29.9MM **Privately Held**
SIC: 5031 5211 Building materials, exterior; lumber & other building materials

(P-6821)
EL & EL WOOD PRODUCTS CORP (PA)
6011 Schaefer Ave, Chino (91710-7043)
P.O. Box 5105 (91708-5105)
PHONE..................909 591-0339
Cathy Vidas, *President*
Paul Conley, *Vice Pres*
Flavia Silva, *Accounting Mgr*
Michelle Levotch, *Controller*
Martha Valadez, *Human Resources*
▲ EMP: 116 EST: 1963

SQ FT: 72,000
SALES (est): 65.2MM **Privately Held**
WEB: www.elandelwoodproducts.com
SIC: 5031 Millwork

(P-6822)
EMPIRE COMPANY LLC
31 Heron Ln, Riverside (92507-1243)
PHONE..................951 742-5273
Scott Price, *Branch Mgr*
EMP: 82
SALES (corp-wide): 238.4MM **Privately Held**
SIC: 5031 Lumber, plywood & millwork
HQ: The Empire Company Llc
   8181 Logistics Dr
   Zeeland MI 49464
   800 253-9000

(P-6823)
FOREST PRODUCTS DISTRS INC
1090 W Waterfront Dr, Eureka (95501-0169)
P.O. Box 8088, Rapid City SD (57709-8088)
PHONE..................707 443-7024
Carroll Korb, *President*
Jeff Plooster, *Controller*
EMP: 65
SALES (est): 950K **Privately Held**
SIC: 5031 Lumber, plywood & millwork

(P-6824)
GOLDEN STATE LUMBER INC
3033 S Airport Way, Stockton (95206)
P.O. Box 31810 (95213-1810)
PHONE..................209 234-7700
Ralph Panttaja, *Branch Mgr*
Renae Gunkel, *Credit Mgr*
Mike Romano, *Sales Staff*
Keith Zehm, *Sales Staff*
EMP: 200
SALES (corp-wide): 235MM **Privately Held**
WEB: www.goldenstatelumber.com
SIC: 5031 5211 Lumber: rough, dressed & finished; lumber & other building materials
PA: Golden State Lumber, Inc.
   855 Lakeville St Ste 200
   Petaluma CA 94952
   707 206-4100

(P-6825)
GROVE LUMBER & BLDG SUPS INC (PA)
1300 S Campus Ave, Ontario (91761-4378)
PHONE..................909 947-0277
Raymond G Croll Jr, *CEO*
Jim Armas, *Store Mgr*
Ron Hillman, *Technology*
EMP: 240 EST: 1979
SQ FT: 3,000
SALES (est): 132.1MM **Privately Held**
SIC: 5031 5211 Lumber: rough, dressed & finished; lumber products

(P-6826)
HARDY WINDOW COMPANY (PA)
1639 E Miraloma Ave, Placentia (92870-6623)
PHONE..................714 996-1807
Chance P Hardy, *President*
Diana Gonzalez, *Human Resources*
Jim Lavin,
EMP: 141
SQ FT: 14,000
SALES: 30.5MM **Privately Held**
WEB: www.hardywindows.com
SIC: 5031 Windows

(P-6827)
HEPPNER HARDWOODS INC
555 W Danlee St, Azusa (91702-2342)
PHONE..................626 969-7983
Lorraine Heppner, *President*
Brent Heppner, *COO*
Jack Bogle, *CFO*
Brian Giertz, *Executive Asst*
Christine Byrd, *Credit Mgr*
▲ EMP: 60
SQ FT: 217,800
SALES (est): 31.7MM **Privately Held**
WEB: www.heppnerhardwoods.com
SIC: 5031 Lumber: rough, dressed & finished

(P-6828)

HERITAGE 1 WINDOW AND BUILDING

4300 Jetway Ct, North Highlands (95660-5702)
P.O. Box 214609, Sacramento (95821-0609)
PHONE.....................916 481-5030
Charles Gardemeyer, *CEO*
Stephen Beckham, *COO*
Geoff Hughes, *CFO*
John Ballou, *Sales Mgr*
Tyler Randolth, *Manager*
EMP: 171
SQ FT: 80,000
SALES: 24MM
SALES (corp-wide): 89.5MM **Privately Held**
SIC: 5031 Doors & windows
PA: Heritage Interests, Llc
4300 Jetway Ct
North Highlands CA 95660
916 481-5030

(P-6829)

HERITAGE ONE CARPENTRY INC

2107 Forest Ave Ste 100, Chico (95928-7696)
PHONE.....................530 345-6622
Charles Gardemeyer, *President*
Stephen Beckham, *COO*
Geoffrey Hughes, *CFO*
EMP: 162 **EST:** 2012
SQ FT: 3,000
SALES: 33.9MM
SALES (corp-wide): 89.5MM **Privately Held**
SIC: 5031 1751 Lumber, plywood & millwork; cabinet & finish carpentry
PA: Heritage Interests, Llc
4300 Jetway Ct
North Highlands CA 95660
916 481-5030

(P-6830)

HERITAGE ONE DOOR AND BUILDING

4300 Jetway Ct, North Highlands (95660-5702)
P.O. Box 214609, Sacramento (95821-0609)
PHONE.....................916 481-5030
Charles Gardemeyer, *Mng Member*
Stephen Beckham, *COO*
John Dutter, *COO*
Geoff Hughes, *CFO*
John Ballou, *Sales Mgr*
EMP: 86
SQ FT: 80,000
SALES: 31.6MM
SALES (corp-wide): 89.5MM **Privately Held**
SIC: 5031 2431 Doors & windows; windows & window parts & trim, wood
PA: Heritage Interests, Llc
4300 Jetway Ct
North Highlands CA 95660
916 481-5030

(P-6831)

HIGH COUNTRY LUMBER INC (PA)

Also Called: Ace Hardware
444 S Main St, Bishop (93514-3421)
PHONE.....................760 873-5874
Steven Joseph, *President*
Scott Piercey, *Treasurer*
EMP: 50
SQ FT: 10,000
SALES (est): 29.4MM **Privately Held**
SIC: 5031 5211 Lumber, plywood & millwork; lumber & other building materials

(P-6832)

HIGHLAND LUMBER SALES INC

300 E Santa Ana St, Anaheim (92805-3953)
PHONE.....................714 778-2293
Ken Lobue, *President*
Richard Phillips, *President*
Richard J Phillips, *CEO*
Alan Arbiso, *Relg Ldr*
▲ **EMP:** 60
SQ FT: 2,000

SALES (est): 24MM **Privately Held**
SIC: 5031 2493 2431 5211 Lumber: rough, dressed & finished; reconstituted wood products; millwork; lumber products

(P-6833)

HUMBOLDT REDWOOD COMPANY LLC (HQ)

125 Main St, Scotia (95565)
P.O. Box 712 (95565-0712)
PHONE.....................707 764-4472
Bob Mertz,
Mike Jani,
Marty Olhiser,
EMP: 300
SALES (est): 103MM
SALES (corp-wide): 75.1MM **Privately Held**
SIC: 5031 Lumber: rough, dressed & finished
PA: Mendocino Redwood Company, Llc
850 Kunzler Ranch Rd
Ukiah CA 95482
707 463-5110

(P-6834)

HUTTIG BUILDING PRODUCTS INC

Also Called: Huttig Sash & Door Co
8120 Pwr Rdge Rd Bldg 100, Sacramento (95826)
PHONE.....................916 383-3721
Doug Brian, *General Mgr*
EMP: 60
SALES (corp-wide): 753.2MM **Publicly Held**
WEB: www.huttig.com
SIC: 5031 Building materials, exterior
PA: Huttig Building Products, Inc.
555 Maryville University
Saint Louis MO 63141
314 216-2600

(P-6835)

JAMES HARDIE BUILDING PDTS INC (DH)

Also Called: Jameshardie
26300 La Alameda Ste 400, Mission Viejo (92691-8372)
PHONE.....................949 348-1800
Louis Gries, *CEO*
Matthew Marsh, *CFO*
Ginger Lester, *Treasurer*
Mark Fisher, *Exec VP*
Ryan Sullivan, *Exec VP*
◆ **EMP:** 200
SQ FT: 10,000
SALES (est): 531.2MM **Privately Held**
SIC: 5031 Building materials, exterior; building materials, interior
HQ: James Hardie Transition Co., Inc.
26300 La Alameda Ste 400
Mission Viejo CA 92691
949 348-1800

(P-6836)

JAMES HARDIE BUILDING PDTS INC

10901 Elm Ave, Fontana (92337-7327)
PHONE.....................909 355-6500
Bob Mussleman, *Branch Mgr*
Steven Terzian, *Technical Mgr*
EMP: 190 **Privately Held**
SIC: 5031 3272 Building materials, exterior; areaways, basement window: concrete
HQ: James Hardie Building Products Inc.
26300 La Alameda Ste 400
Mission Viejo CA 92691
949 348-1800

(P-6837)

JELD-WEN INC

Also Called: Jeld-Wen Windows
2760 Progress St Ste B, Vista (92081-8449)
PHONE.....................760 597-4201
Clint Honeycutt, *Vice Pres*
Bill Maschmeier, *General Mgr*
Will Elchrick, *Technology*
Craig Nath, *Manager*
EMP: 300 **Publicly Held**
SIC: 5031 Doors & windows

HQ: Jeld-Wen, Inc.
2645 Silver Crescent Dr
Charlotte NC 28273
800 535-3936

(P-6838)

JONES LUMBER COMPANY INC

10711 Alameda St, Lynwood (90262-1753)
P.O. Box 40 (90262-0040)
PHONE.....................323 564-6656
Roderick M Jones, *CEO*
John M Cencak, *President*
Rick H Jones, *Vice Pres*
Alisha Ferguson, *Admin Sec*
EMP: 71
SQ FT: 800,000
SALES: 35.6MM **Privately Held**
WEB: www.joneslumber.com
SIC: 5031 Lumber: rough, dressed & finished

(P-6839)

MENDOCINO FOREST PDTS CO LLC

Also Called: Sawmill
850 Kunzler Ranch Rd, Ukiah (95482-7294)
P.O. Box 996 (95482-0996)
PHONE.....................707 468-1431
Dean Kerstetter, *Exec VP*
EMP: 200
SALES (est): 13.7MM
SALES (corp-wide): 134.9MM **Privately Held**
SIC: 5031 2421 2499 Lumber: rough, dressed & finished; fencing, wood; sawmills & planing mills, general; fencing, docks & other outdoor wood structural products
PA: Mendocino Forest Products Company Llc
3700 Old Redwood Hwy # 200
Santa Rosa CA 95403
707 620-2961

(P-6840)

MENDOCINO FOREST PDTS CO LLC (PA)

3700 Old Redwood Hwy # 200, Santa Rosa (95403-5739)
P.O. Box 390, Calpella (95418-0390)
PHONE.....................707 620-2961
Sandy Dean, *CEO*
John Russell, *President*
Bob Mertz, *CEO*
Jim Pelkey, *CFO*
EMP: 400
SQ FT: 5,000
SALES (est): 134.9MM **Privately Held**
SIC: 5031 2421 Lumber: rough, dressed & finished; sawmills & planing mills, general

(P-6841)

MENDOCINO FOREST PDTS CO LLC

Also Called: Calpella Distribution Center
6375 N State St, Calpella (95418)
P.O. Box 336 (95418-0336)
PHONE.....................707 485-6800
Mike Benetti, *Branch Mgr*
EMP: 94
SALES (est): 6.7MM
SALES (corp-wide): 134.9MM **Privately Held**
SIC: 5031 2421 Lumber: rough, dressed & finished; sawmills & planing mills, general
PA: Mendocino Forest Products Company Llc
3700 Old Redwood Hwy # 200
Santa Rosa CA 95403
707 620-2961

(P-6842)

NICHOLS LUMBER & HARDWARE CO

13470 Dalewood St, Baldwin Park (91706-5883)
PHONE.....................626 960-4802
Judith A Nichols, *President*
Rick Dean, *Vice Pres*
Judy Nichols, *Executive*
Charles Nichols, *Admin Sec*
Derek Chang, *Sales Associate*
EMP: 75

SALES (est): 46.5MM **Privately Held**
SIC: 5031 5251 2421 Lumber: rough, dressed & finished; hardware; sawmills & planing mills, general

(P-6843)

OAKLAND PALLET COMPANY INC (PA)

2500 Grant Ave, San Lorenzo (94580-1810)
PHONE.....................510 278-1291
Jose G Padilla, *President*
Javier Padilla, *Corp Secy*
Carlos Padilla, *Vice Pres*
Graciela Padilla, *Sales Staff*
Manuel Padilla, *Sales Staff*
EMP: 130
SALES (est): 50.2MM **Privately Held**
SIC: 5031 7699 Pallets, wood; pallet repair

(P-6844)

OREGON PCF BLDG PDTS CALIF INC

Also Called: Orepac Building Products
8185 Signal Ct Ste A, Sacramento (95824-2354)
PHONE.....................916 381-8051
John Dutter, *Manager*
Mark Statham, *Sales Staff*
Cesar Moreno, *Manager*
EMP: 87
SALES (corp-wide): 610.7MM **Privately Held**
SIC: 5031 Building materials, exterior; building materials, interior; lumber: rough, dressed & finished; millwork
HQ: Oregon Pacific Building Products (Calif.), Inc.
30170 Sw Ore Pac Ave
Wilsonville OR 97070
503 685-5499

(P-6845)

OREGON PCF BLDG PDTS MAPLE INC

Also Called: Orepac Millwork Products
2401 E Philadelphia St, Ontario (91761-7743)
PHONE.....................909 627-4043
Douglas Hart, *President*
Alex Miranda, *Sales Associate*
▲ **EMP:** 125
SALES (est): 27.8MM
SALES (corp-wide): 610.7MM **Privately Held**
SIC: 5031 5032 Lumber, plywood & millwork; brick, stone & related material
PA: Orepac Holding Company
30170 Sw Orepac Ave
Wilsonville OR 97070
503 682-5050

(P-6846)

PACIFIC COAST SUPPLY LLC

Also Called: Weyrick Pacific
626 N Main St, Templeton (93465-9010)
PHONE.....................805 434-4800
Colin Weyrick, *Branch Mgr*
EMP: 81
SALES (corp-wide): 1.7B **Privately Held**
SIC: 5031 Lumber, plywood & millwork
HQ: Pacific Coast Supply, Llc
4290 Roseville Rd
North Highlands CA 95660
916 971-2301

(P-6847)

PACIFIC COAST SUPPLY LLC

Also Called: Anderson Lumber
4290 Roseville Rd, North Highlands (95660-5710)
PHONE.....................916 481-2220
Chris Lucchetti, *Branch Mgr*
EMP: 150
SALES (corp-wide): 1.7B **Privately Held**
SIC: 5031 5211 Lumber, plywood & millwork; lumber & other building materials
HQ: Pacific Coast Supply, Llc
4290 Roseville Rd
North Highlands CA 95660
916 971-2301

PRODUCTS & SVCS

(P-6848)
PACIFIC COAST SUPPLY LLC (HQ)
4290 Roseville Rd, North Highlands (95660-5710)
PHONE...............916 971-2301
Curt Gomes, *President*
Robert Ramos, *COO*
Lisa Goeppner, *CFO*
Walter Payne, *Bd of Directors*
Joe Gower, *Vice Pres*
EMP: 151
SALES (est): 443.6MM
SALES (corp-wide): 1.7B **Privately Held**
WEB: www.paccoast.com
SIC: 5031 Lumber, plywood & millwork
PA: Pacific Coast Building Products, Inc.
10600 White Rock Rd # 100
Rancho Cordova CA 95670
916 631-6500

(P-6849)
PACIFIC STATES INDUSTRIES INC
Also Called: Redwood Empire Division
31401 Mccray Rd, Cloverdale (95425)
P.O. Box 156 (95425-0156)
PHONE...............707 894-4242
Nolan Schweikl, *General Mgr*
Troy Turner, *Marketing Staff*
EMP: 250
SALES (corp-wide): 191.1MM **Privately Held**
SIC: 5031 Lumber: rough, dressed & finished
PA: Pacific States Industries, Incorporated
10 Madrone Ave
Morgan Hill CA 95037
408 779-7354

(P-6850)
PACIFIC STATES INDUSTRIES INC
Also Called: Redwood Empire Whl Lbr Pdts
10 Madrone Ave, Morgan Hill (95037-9227)
P.O. Box 1300 (95038-1300)
PHONE...............408 779-7354
Cindy Hernandez, *Manager*
EMP: 60
SALES (corp-wide): 191.1MM **Privately Held**
SIC: 5031 5211 Lumber: rough, dressed & finished; lumber products
PA: Pacific States Industries, Incorporated
10 Madrone Ave
Morgan Hill CA 95037
408 779-7354

(P-6851)
PHILLIPS PLYWOOD CO INC
Also Called: Quality Laminating
13599 Desmond St, Pacoima (91331-2300)
P.O. Box 51396, Los Angeles (90051-5696)
PHONE...............818 897-7736
Douglas F Madsen, *CEO*
Shawn Carlisle, *President*
Lynne Corwin, *VP Finance*
Jeanne Wilson, *Personnel*
Robert Perez, *Mktg Dir*
EMP: 55 EST: 1986
SQ FT: 100,000
SALES (est): 29.7MM **Privately Held**
WEB: www.phillipsplywood.com
SIC: 5031 Plywood

(P-6852)
PINE TREE LUMBER COMPANY LP (PA)
707 N Andreasen Dr, Escondido (92029-1497)
PHONE...............760 745-0411
Jacob Brouwer, *Partner*
Betty Lipton, *Controller*
Gail Psqueda, *Human Res Mgr*
Marvin Newton, *Sales Staff*
Clay Rosman, *Sales Staff*
EMP: 56
SQ FT: 45,000
SALES (est): 43.2MM **Privately Held**
WEB: www.pinetreelumber.com
SIC: 5031 5211 Building materials, interior; building materials, exterior; lumber & other building materials

(P-6853)
PJS LUMBER INC
Also Called: P J'S Construction Supplies
45055 Fremont Blvd, Fremont (94538-6318)
PHONE...............510 743-5300
Shane McMillan, *CEO*
Carlton J McMillan, *President*
Terry W Protto, *CEO*
Jeff Veilleux, *Vice Pres*
EMP: 145
SQ FT: 2,000
SALES (est): 112.6MM **Privately Held**
SIC: 5031 5051 Lumber: rough, dressed & finished; steel

(P-6854)
PLY GEM PACIFIC WINDOWS CORP
235 Radio Rd, Corona (92879-1725)
PHONE...............951 272-1300
Randy Dasalla, *Branch Mgr*
EMP: 100
SALES (corp-wide): 218.4MM **Privately Held**
SIC: 5031 Windows
HQ: Ply Gem Pacific Windows Corporation
2600 Grand Blvd Ste 900
Kansas City MO 64108
816 426-8200

(P-6855)
POTTER ROEMER LLC (HQ)
17451 Hurley St, City of Industry (91744-5106)
P.O. Box 3527 (91744-0527)
PHONE...............626 855-4890
Donald E Morris, *Mng Member*
Jeff Herne, *Regional Mgr*
George Brown, *VP Mktg*
Jim Henry, *Regl Sales Mgr*
Katherine Song, *Sales Staff*
▲ EMP: 95
SQ FT: 110,000
SALES: 26.2MM
SALES (corp-wide): 85MM **Privately Held**
WEB: www.potterroemer.com
SIC: 5031 3569 2542 Skylights, all materials; firefighting apparatus & related equipment; partitions & fixtures, except wood
PA: Acorn Engineering Company
15125 Proctor Ave
City Of Industry CA 91746
800 488-8999

(P-6856)
REDWOOD PRODUCTS CHINO INC
Also Called: Rancho Wholesale
9301 Remington Ave, Chino (91710-9346)
P.O. Box 2662, Corona (92878-2662)
PHONE...............909 923-5656
Jaime Carlos, *President*
Maricela Rodriguez, *Vice Pres*
EMP: 60 EST: 2000
SALES (est): 23.1MM **Privately Held**
WEB: www.redwoodproductschino.com
SIC: 5031 Lumber: rough, dressed & finished

(P-6857)
RELIABLE WHOLESALE LUMBER INC (PA)
7600 Redondo Cir, Huntington Beach (92648-1303)
P.O. Box 191 (92648-0191)
PHONE...............714 848-8222
Jerome M Higman, *President*
Will Higman, *COO*
David Higman, *CFO*
EMP: 90
SQ FT: 4,500
SALES (est): 159.3MM **Privately Held**
WEB: www.rwli.net
SIC: 5031 2421 Lumber: rough, dressed & finished; sawmills & planing mills, general

(P-6858)
ROBERTS LUMBER SALES INC
Also Called: Robert's Lumber
2661 S Lilac Ave, Bloomington (92316-3211)
PHONE...............909 350-9164
Robert Cantero Jr, *CEO*
Lori Cantero, *Principal*
EMP: 57 EST: 1997
SALES (est): 15.1MM **Privately Held**
SIC: 5031 2448 Lumber: rough, dressed & finished; wood pallets & skids

(P-6859)
ROSEBURG FOREST PRODUCTS CO
98 Mill St, Weed (96094-2251)
PHONE...............530 938-2721
Tom Didgs, *Manager*
Robin Styers, *Opers Staff*
EMP: 161
SQ FT: 180,000
SALES (corp-wide): 1B **Privately Held**
WEB: www.rfpco.com
SIC: 5031 Lumber: rough, dressed & finished
HQ: Roseburg Forest Products Co
3660 Gateway St Ste A
Springfield OR 97477
541 391-3364

(P-6860)
ROYAL PLYWOOD COMPANY LLC
6003 88th St Ste 100, Sacramento (95828-1143)
P.O. Box 728, La Mirada (90637-0728)
PHONE...............916 386-9873
EMP: 78
SALES (corp-wide): 74.6MM **Privately Held**
SIC: 5031
PA: Royal Plywood Company, Llc
14171 Park Pl
Cerritos CA 90703
562 404-2989

(P-6861)
ROYAL PLYWOOD COMPANY LLC (PA)
14171 Park Pl, Cerritos (90703-2463)
P.O. Box 728, La Mirada (90637-0728)
PHONE...............562 404-2989
Gabriel N Marshi,
Elaine Weston, *Sales Staff*
Stephen Fuller,
▲ EMP: 78
SQ FT: 120,000
SALES (est): 67.9MM **Privately Held**
WEB: www.royalplywood.com
SIC: 5031 Building materials, exterior

(P-6862)
SAROYAN LUMBER COMPANY INC (PA)
Also Called: Saroyan Lumber and Moulding Co
6230 S Alameda St, Huntington Park (90255-3503)
PHONE...............800 624-9309
Richard Saroyan, *President*
Dorothy A Robinson, *Shareholder*
Maryline Nahery, *CFO*
John Saroyan, *Corp Secy*
Robert Lemke, *Vice Pres*
▲ EMP: 66
SQ FT: 144,000
SALES (est): 36.9MM **Privately Held**
WEB: www.saroyanlumber.com
SIC: 5031 Lumber: rough, dressed & finished; millwork

(P-6863)
SHAPP INTERNATIONAL TRDG INC
Also Called: Shapp Internatioonal
6000 Reseda Blvd, Tarzana (91356-1500)
P.O. Box 893, Woodland Hills (91365-0893)
PHONE...............818 348-3000
Allan Shapiro, *President*
Louis Justin, *Treasurer*
EMP: 118
SQ FT: 8,000
SALES (est): 33.2MM **Privately Held**
SIC: 5031 5064 5112 5021 Lumber, plywood & millwork; electrical appliances, major; stationery & office supplies; furniture

(P-6864)
SIERRA FOREST PRODUCTS
9000 Road 234, Terra Bella (93270-9560)
P.O. Box 10060 (93270-0060)
PHONE...............559 535-4893
Kent Duysen, *CEO*
Glenn Duysen, *Treasurer*
EMP: 110
SQ FT: 3,000
SALES (est): 29.8MM **Privately Held**
SIC: 5031 Lumber, plywood & millwork

(P-6865)
SINGLEY ENTERPRISES (PA)
Also Called: Garage Door Specialists
121 Main Ave, Sacramento (95838-2041)
P.O. Box 572, West Sacramento (95691-0572)
PHONE...............866 890-1776
Gary B Singley, *CEO*
Charlene Singley, *Treasurer*
Gerald Weirton, *Foreman/Supr*
▲ EMP: 50
SQ FT: 14,400
SALES (est): 22.3MM **Privately Held**
SIC: 5031 Doors, garage

(P-6866)
STATES DRAWER BOX SPC LLC
1482 N Batavia St, Orange (92867-3505)
PHONE...............714 744-4247
Cathy Blankenship, *President*
EMP: 60
SALES (est): 15.6MM **Privately Held**
WEB: www.dbsdrawers.com
SIC: 5031 Lumber: rough, dressed & finished
PA: States Industries, Llc
29545 E Enid Rd
Eugene OR 97402

(P-6867)
SUNSET MOULDING CO
2200 Paseo Rd, Live Oak (95953-9721)
PHONE...............530 695-3379
Jim Perigo, *Branch Mgr*
Howard Little, *Branch Mgr*
EMP: 60
SALES (corp-wide): 24.3MM **Privately Held**
WEB: www.sunsetmoulding.com
SIC: 5031 Lumber, plywood & millwork
PA: Sunset Moulding Co.
2231 Paseo Rd
Live Oak CA 95953
530 790-2700

(P-6868)
T M COBB COMPANY
Also Called: Tom Ray
8490 Rovana Cir, Sacramento (95828-2529)
PHONE...............916 381-7330
Steve Grambush, *Manager*
EMP: 70
SQ FT: 40,000
SALES (corp-wide): 92.5MM **Privately Held**
WEB: www.tmcobbco.com
SIC: 5031 5032 2431 Doors; door frames, all materials; masons' materials; millwork
PA: T. M. Cobb Company
500 Palmyrita Ave
Riverside CA 92507
951 248-2400

(P-6869)
TABER COMPANY INC
1442 Ritchey St, Santa Ana (92705-4717)
PHONE...............714 543-7100
Brian Taber, *President*
EMP: 65
SQ FT: 11,000
SALES (est): 27.8MM **Privately Held**
WEB: www.taberco.net
SIC: 5031 Building materials, interior

(P-6870)
TRIM TECH INDUSTRIES INC
1724 Ringwood Ave, San Jose (95131-1711)
PHONE...............408 573-4514
Ellen Medeiros, *President*
Andy Medeiros, *Project Mgr*
Shinoa Refuerzo, *Accountant*

▲ = Import ▼=Export
◆ =Import/Export

Jon Gibson, *Human Resources*
Cyndy Thomas, *Purch Mgr*
EMP: 50 **EST:** 1992
SALES (est): 8.9MM **Privately Held**
SIC: 5031 Doors, combination, screen-storm

(P-6871)
USG INTERIORS LLC
2575 Loomis Rd, Stockton (95205-8045)
PHONE.....................209 466-4636
Sandy Hirzel, *Manager*
John Wesley, *Plant Mgr*
EMP: 70
SALES (corp-wide): 3.2B **Publicly Held**
SIC: 5031 Building materials, exterior
HQ: Usg Interiors, Llc
125 S Franklin St
Chicago IL 60606
800 874-4968

(P-6872)
VIRGINIA HARDWOOD COMPANY (PA)
1000 W Foothill Blvd, Azusa (91702-2840)
PHONE.....................626 815-0540
David V Ferrari, *Chairman*
Gary Henzie, *President*
Robin Ezzo, *Corp Secy*
Jeannette Ferrari, *Vice Pres*
Mike Ferrari, *Vice Pres*
▲ **EMP:** 56 **EST:** 1946
SQ FT: 60,000
SALES (est): 27.2MM **Privately Held**
WEB: www.virginiahardwood.com
SIC: 5031 Hardboard

(P-6873)
WEYERHAEUSER COMPANY
Also Called: Marketing Sales & Dist Div
17400 Slover Ave, Fontana (92337-8004)
P.O. Box 487 (92334-0487)
PHONE.....................909 877-6100
Mark Davis, *Branch Mgr*
EMP: 65
SQ FT: 85,000
SALES (corp-wide): 7.2B **Publicly Held**
SIC: 5031 Lumber: rough, dressed & finished
PA: Weyerhaeuser Company
220 Occidental Ave S
Seattle WA 98104
206 539-3000

5032 Brick, Stone & Related Construction Mtrls Wholesale

(P-6874)
A TEICHERT & SON INC (HQ)
Also Called: Teichert Construction
3500 American River Dr, Sacramento (95864-5893)
P.O. Box 15002 (95851-0002)
PHONE.....................916 484-3011
Judson T Riggs, *President*
Dana M Davis, *President*
Kenneth A Kayser, *President*
Narendra M Pathipati, *CFO*
Terri A Bakken, *Vice Pres*
▼ **EMP:** 131
SALES (est): 775.9MM
SALES (corp-wide): 784MM **Privately Held**
SIC: 5032 3273 1611 1442 Brick, stone & related material; ready-mixed concrete; highway & street construction; construction sand & gravel; single-family housing construction
PA: Teichert, Inc.
3500 American River Dr
Sacramento CA 95864
916 484-3011

(P-6875)
ARIZONA TILE LLC
1620 S Lewis St, Anaheim (92805-6436)
PHONE.....................714 978-6403
EMP: 100
SALES (corp-wide): 322.1MM **Privately Held**
SIC: 5032

PA: Arizona Tile, L.L.C.
8829 S Priest Dr
Tempe AZ 85284
480 893-9393

(P-6876)
ARRIAGA USA INC (PA)
Also Called: Stoneland
12000 Sherman Way, North Hollywood (91605-3727)
PHONE.....................818 982-9559
Shalom Rubin, *President*
◆ **EMP:** 135
SALES (est): 24.8MM **Privately Held**
SIC: 5032 Marble building stone

(P-6877)
ATLAS CONSTRUCTION SUPPLY INC (PA)
4640 Brinnell St, San Diego (92111-2302)
PHONE.....................858 277-2100
Brian Quinn, *President*
James E Wright, *Treasurer*
Tom Vargas, *Exec VP*
Tammy Rossman, *General Mgr*
Siegfried Barthel, *Project Mgr*
▲ **EMP:** 75
SQ FT: 30,000
SALES (est): 85.2MM **Privately Held**
WEB: www.atlasform.com
SIC: 5032 Concrete building products

(P-6878)
CARRARA MARBLE CO AMER INC (PA)
15939 Phoenix Dr, City of Industry (91745-1624)
PHONE.....................626 961-6010
William Cordova, *President*
James Hogan, *Senior VP*
Dirk Wietstock, *Vice Pres*
Eloise Paz, *Controller*
Steve Barron, *Opers Staff*
▲ **EMP:** 70
SQ FT: 30,000
SALES (est): 30.7MM **Privately Held**
SIC: 5032 1743 1741 Ceramic wall & floor tile; marble installation, interior; masonry & other stonework

(P-6879)
CEMEX CEMENT INC
1201 W Gladstone St, Azusa (91702-5142)
P.O. Box 575 (91702-0575)
PHONE.....................626 969-1747
Steve Hayes, *Manager*
EMP: 200 **Privately Held**
SIC: 5032 3273 3251 1411 Concrete mixtures; ready-mixed concrete; brick & structural clay tile; dimension stone
HQ: Cemex Cement, Inc.
10100 Katy Fwy Ste 300
Houston TX 77043
713 650-6200

(P-6880)
CEMEX CNSTR MTLS PCF LLC
Also Called: Cem - Victorville River Plant
16888 E St, Victorville (92394-2999)
PHONE.....................760 381-7600
Don Kelly, *Manager*
EMP: 234
SQ FT: 2,684 **Privately Held**
SIC: 5032 Cement
HQ: Cemex Construction Materials Pacific, Llc
1501 Belvedere Rd
West Palm Beach FL 33406
561 833-5555

(P-6881)
CLASSIC TILE & MOSAIC INC (PA)
Also Called: Ctm
14463 S Broadway, Gardena (90248-1807)
PHONE.....................310 538-9605
Vincent Cullinan, *CEO*
Bonnie Daland, *Vice Pres*
Ana Gilliam, *Controller*
▲ **EMP:** 60
SALES (est): 27.8MM **Privately Held**
WEB: www.classictileandmosaic.com
SIC: 5032 5211 Tile, clay or other ceramic, excluding refractory; tile, ceramic

(P-6882)
CONCRETE TIE INDUSTRIES INC (PA)
130 E Oris St, Compton (90222-2714)
P.O. Box 5406 (90224-5406)
PHONE.....................310 886-1000
Paul J Schoendienst, *President*
Jerry Croce, *Vice Pres*
Marty Schoendienst, *Vice Pres*
Steve Sim, *Admin Sec*
Steve Sims, *Controller*
EMP: 70
SQ FT: 280,000
SALES (est): 27.8MM **Privately Held**
WEB: www.concretetie.com
SIC: 5032 3452 Concrete & cinder building products; bolts, nuts, rivets & washers

(P-6883)
COUNTRY FLOORS AMERICA LLC (PA)
8735 Melrose Ave, Vernon (90058)
PHONE.....................310 657-0510
Munir Turumc,
▲ **EMP:** 75
SALES (est): 7MM **Privately Held**
WEB: www.countryfloors.com
SIC: 5032 5713 Tile, clay or other ceramic, excluding refractory; terra cotta; floor tile

(P-6884)
CPC SERVICES INC
2025 E Fincl Way Ste 200, Glendora (91741)
PHONE.....................626 852-6200
James Repman, *President*
Marcus Eminhizer, *Vice Pres*
David Hatcher, *Admin Asst*
Edward Harrison, *Engineer*
Alice Maupin, *Engineer*
EMP: 75
SALES (est): 3MM **Privately Held**
SIC: 5032 Brick, stone & related material

(P-6885)
DAL-TILE CORPORATION
1132 Duryea Ave, Irvine (92614-5520)
PHONE.....................949 260-0488
Terri M Girr, *Branch Mgr*
EMP: 68
SALES (corp-wide): 9.4B **Publicly Held**
WEB: www.mohawk.com
SIC: 5032 Ceramic wall & floor tile
HQ: Dal-Tile Corporation
7834 C F Hawn Fwy
Dallas TX 75217
214 398-1411

(P-6886)
DAL-TILE CORPORATION
7484 Raytheon Rd Ste A, San Diego (92111-1551)
PHONE.....................858 571-0283
Gregg Hudson, *Office Mgr*
EMP: 68
SALES (corp-wide): 9.4B **Publicly Held**
SIC: 5032 Ceramic wall & floor tile
HQ: Dal-Tile Corporation
7834 C F Hawn Fwy
Dallas TX 75217
214 398-1411

(P-6887)
DAL-TILE CORPORATION
2303 Merced St, San Leandro (94577-4208)
PHONE.....................510 357-6197
Kevin Murphy, *Principal*
EMP: 68
SALES (corp-wide): 9.4B **Publicly Held**
SIC: 5032 Ceramic wall & floor tile
HQ: Dal-Tile Corporation
7834 C F Hawn Fwy
Dallas TX 75217
214 398-1411

(P-6888)
DAL-TILE CORPORATION
3625 Jurupa St, Ontario (91761-2905)
PHONE.....................909 390-7000
Liz Haendiges, *President*
EMP: 68

SALES (corp-wide): 9.4B **Publicly Held**
WEB: www.mohawk.com
SIC: 5032 Ceramic wall & floor tile
HQ: Dal-Tile Corporation
7834 C F Hawn Fwy
Dallas TX 75217
214 398-1411

(P-6889)
DAL-TILE CORPORATION
4201 Technology Dr, Modesto (95356-9493)
PHONE.....................209 543-0924
Gwen Kemple, *Manager*
EMP: 68
SALES (corp-wide): 9.4B **Publicly Held**
WEB: www.mohawk.com
SIC: 5032 Ceramic wall & floor tile
HQ: Dal-Tile Corporation
7834 C F Hawn Fwy
Dallas TX 75217
214 398-1411

(P-6890)
ELEGANT SURFACES
3640 Amrcn Rver Dr 150, Sacramento (95864)
P.O. Box 705, Byron (94514-0705)
PHONE.....................209 823-9388
John Polimeno, *CEO*
Dan Thompson, *President*
Kristie Polimeno, *Vice Pres*
▲ **EMP:** 100 **EST:** 1967
SQ FT: 48,000
SALES (est): 15.5MM **Privately Held**
WEB: www.elegantsurfaces.com
SIC: 5032 3281 Brick, stone & related material; marble, building: cut & shaped

(P-6891)
EMSER INTERNATIONAL LLC (PA)
8431 Santa Monica Blvd, Los Angeles (90069-4294)
PHONE.....................323 650-2000
Sam Ghodsian, *Mng Member*
Cindy Dalessio, *Branch Mgr*
Mary A Yoen, *CIO*
Lori Olena, *Sales Staff*
Ehsan Ghodsian,
▲ **EMP:** 70
SQ FT: 50,000
SALES (est): 116.5MM **Privately Held**
SIC: 5032 Ceramic wall & floor tile

(P-6892)
FRANK SCIARRINO MARBLE G
7505 Trade St, San Diego (92121-2411)
P.O. Box 600265 (92160-0265)
PHONE.....................858 695-8030
Frank Sciarrino, *President*
Anna Maria, *Vice Pres*
▲ **EMP:** 80
SQ FT: 20,000
SALES (est): 8MM **Privately Held**
WEB: www.fsmarble.com
SIC: 5032 5211 1799 1743 Marble building stone; cabinets, kitchen; counter top installation; tile installation, ceramic

(P-6893)
FST SAND & GRAVEL INC
21780 Temescal Canyon Rd, Corona (92883-5669)
P.O. Box 2798 (92878-2798)
PHONE.....................951 277-8440
Frank Smith, *President*
Jennifer Reece, *Office Mgr*
Dave Sanchez, *Sales Associate*
Frances Martinez, *Sales Staff*
EMP: 50
SQ FT: 1,078
SALES (est): 29.3MM **Privately Held**
WEB: www.fstsand.com
SIC: 5032 Sand, construction; gravel

(P-6894)
GBI TILE & STONE INC (PA)
Also Called: Quarry Collection
5900 Skylab Rd Ste 150, Huntington Beach (92647-2075)
PHONE.....................949 567-1880
Jeff Jonas, *Principal*
Dan Foy, *CFO*
Marco A Gonzalez, *Vice Pres*
Eric Eichstaedt, *Business Anlyst*

PRODUCTS & SVCS

Cy Donaldson, *Sales Staff*
◆ EMP: 50
SALES (est): 18.4MM **Privately Held**
SIC: 5032 Brick, stone & related material

(P-6895)
GOLDEN STATE PLASTERING
7082 N Harrison Ave, Fresno (93650-1008)
P.O. Box 3452 (93650-3452)
PHONE....................559 439-3920
Monty Bound, *Supervisor*
EMP: 90
SQ FT: 4,920
SALES (est): 4.5MM **Privately Held**
SIC: 5032 Stucco

(P-6896)
GRANITE ROCK CO
Also Called: A R Wilson Quarry & Asp Plant
End Of Quarry Rd, Aromas (95004)
P.O. Box 699 (95004-0699)
PHONE....................831 392-3780
Bruce Woolpert, *President*
EMP: 200
SALES (corp-wide): 1.1B **Privately Held**
WEB: www.graniterock.com
SIC: 5032 Brick, stone & related material
PA: Granite Rock Co.
350 Technology Dr
Watsonville CA 95076
831 768-2000

(P-6897)
HOLLIDAY ROCK CO INC (PA)
1401 N Benson Ave, Upland (91786-2166)
PHONE....................909 982-1553
Penny Holliday, *CEO*
Ethel Holliday, *President*
Fredrick N Holliday, *Vice Pres*
John Holliday, *Vice Pres*
Gabe Shenk, *Regional Mgr*
EMP: 54
SQ FT: 2,000
SALES (est): 49.1MM **Privately Held**
WEB: www.hollidayrock.com
SIC: 5032 Asphalt mixture; concrete mixtures; stone, crushed or broken; sand, construction

(P-6898)
L & W SUPPLY CORPORATION
Also Called: Calply
7750 Convoy Ct, San Diego (92111-1106)
PHONE....................858 627-0811
Donald Smith, *Manager*
EMP: 50
SALES (corp-wide): 4.1B **Privately Held**
WEB: www.calply.com
SIC: 5032 Drywall materials
HQ: L & W Supply Corporation
300 S Riverside Plz # 200
Chicago IL 60606
312 606-4000

(P-6899)
L & W SUPPLY CORPORATION
Also Called: Calply
31625 Hayman St, Hayward (94544-7121)
PHONE....................510 429-8003
K W McKinney, *Manager*
Paulos Tilahun, *Admin Asst*
EMP: 70
SALES (corp-wide): 4.1B **Privately Held**
WEB: www.calply.com
SIC: 5032 5031 Drywall materials; lumber, plywood & millwork
HQ: L & W Supply Corporation
300 S Riverside Plz # 200
Chicago IL 60606
312 606-4000

(P-6900)
LYNGSO GARDEN MATERIALS INC
345 Shoreway Rd, San Carlos (94070-2708)
PHONE....................650 364-1730
Theresa Lyngso, *President*
Linda K Lyngso, *Vice Pres*
Pamela Parkinson, *Admin Sec*
Mike Gillen, *Safety Mgr*
Steve Powers, *Manager*
▲ EMP: 50

SALES (est): 24.6MM **Privately Held**
WEB: www.lyngso.net
SIC: 5032 5261 5211 5191 Brick, stone & related material; nurseries & garden centers; lumber & other building materials; greenhouse equipment & supplies

(P-6901)
M S INTERNATIONAL INC (PA)
Also Called: MSI
2095 N Batavia St, Orange (92865-3101)
PHONE....................714 685-7500
Manahar Shah, *CEO*
Rajesh Shah, *President*
Chandrika Shah, *Corp Secy*
Marlene Ramirez, *Officer*
Phillip Caudillo, *Vice Pres*
◆ EMP: 300
SQ FT: 500,000
SALES (est): 580.2MM **Privately Held**
WEB: www.msistone.com
SIC: 5032 Granite building stone

(P-6902)
PACIFIC CLAY PRODUCTS INC
14741 Lake St, Lake Elsinore (92530-1610)
PHONE....................661 857-1401
Barry Coley, *President*
Kai Chin, *Vice Pres*
Dale Kline, *Vice Pres*
Christopher West, *Info Tech Mgr*
Brenna De Paris, *HR Admin*
▲ EMP: 160 **EST:** 1930
SQ FT: 200,000
SALES (est): 46.7MM **Privately Held**
WEB: www.pacificclay.com
SIC: 5032 3251 Tile & clay products; paving brick, clay

(P-6903)
PARAGON INDUSTRIES INC
Also Called: Bedrosian's Tile & Marble
1235 S State College Blvd, Anaheim (92806-5145)
PHONE....................714 778-8453
Lonnie Martinez, *Branch Mgr*
EMP: 60
SALES (corp-wide): 294.7MM **Privately Held**
SIC: 5032 5211 Tile, clay or other ceramic, excluding refractory; tile, ceramic
PA: Paragon Industries Inc.
4285 N Golden State Blvd
Fresno CA 93722
559 275-5000

(P-6904)
PATRICK INDUSTRIES INC
Also Called: Custom Vinyls
13414 Slover Ave, Fontana (92337-6977)
PHONE....................909 350-4440
Vince Fergan, *Branch Mgr*
EMP: 150
SALES (corp-wide): 1.6B **Publicly Held**
WEB: www.patrickind.com
SIC: 5032 1799 2435 3083 Brick, stone & related material; building site preparation; hardwood veneer & plywood; laminated plastics plate & sheet
PA: Patrick Industries, Inc.
107 W Franklin St
Elkhart IN 46516
574 294-7511

(P-6905)
PLAYMAR INC
2502 Channing Ave, San Jose (95131-1004)
PHONE....................408 324-1930
EMP: 70
SALES (est): 1.1MM **Privately Held**
SIC: 5032 Granite building stone

(P-6906)
RAILWAY DISTRIBUTING INC (PA)
Also Called: Foundation Building Material
675 Emory St, San Jose (95110-1824)
PHONE....................408 280-7625
Joe Salvador, *President*
Narda Salvador, *Vice Pres*
EMP: 50
SQ FT: 2,000

SALES (est): 7.6MM **Privately Held**
SIC: 5032 5033 Drywall materials; insulation, thermal

(P-6907)
SYAR INDUSTRIES INC
13666 Healdsburg Ave, Healdsburg (95448-9234)
P.O. Box 325 (95448-0325)
PHONE....................707 433-3366
Dick Love, *Manager*
EMP: 65
SALES (corp-wide): 100.2MM **Privately Held**
WEB: www.syar.com
SIC: 5032 Gravel; sand, construction; stone, crushed or broken
PA: Syar Industries, Inc.
2301 Napa Vallejo Hwy
Napa CA 94558
707 252-8711

(P-6908)
THOMPSON BUILDING MTLS INC
6618 Federal Blvd, Lemon Grove (91945-1312)
PHONE....................619 287-9410
Kenneth R Thompson, *President*
Tracy Pelchat, *Office Mgr*
EMP: 50
SQ FT: 15,000
SALES (est): 12.1MM
SALES (corp-wide): 77.9MM **Privately Held**
SIC: 5032 5211 Plastering materials; lime & plaster
PA: Opal Service, Inc.
282 S Anita Dr
Orange CA 92868
714 935-0900

(P-6909)
UGM CITATAH INC (PA)
Also Called: Ugmc
13220 Cambridge St, Santa Fe Springs (90670-4902)
PHONE....................562 921-9549
Viken Dave Yaghjian, *President*
Bruce Feaster, *Exec VP*
Irmen Yaghjian, *Admin Sec*
▲ EMP: 125
SQ FT: 46,000
SALES (est): 31.4MM **Privately Held**
WEB: www.ugmcstone.com
SIC: 5032 1741 1743 Marble building stone; stone masonry; terrazzo, tile, marble, mosaic work

(P-6910)
UNITED MARBLE & GRANITE INC
2163 Martin Ave, Santa Clara (95050-2701)
PHONE....................408 347-3300
Manuel De Oliveira, *President*
Velma De Oliveira, *Executive*
Greg Thompkins, *Division Mgr*
Connie Silveira, *Office Admin*
▲ EMP: 80
SALES (est): 254.7K **Privately Held**
WEB: www.umgslabs.com
SIC: 5032 Marble building stone

(P-6911)
VALORI SAND & GRAVEL COMPANY (PA)
Also Called: Thompson Building Materials
141 W Taft Ave, Orange (92865-4217)
PHONE....................714 637-0104
Kenneth R Thompson, *President*
▲ EMP: 100
SALES (est): 49.5MM **Privately Held**
SIC: 5032 Sand, construction

(P-6912)
VALORI SAND & GRAVEL COMPANY
Also Called: Thompson Building Materials
11027 Cherry Ave, Fontana (92337-7118)
P.O. Box 950 (92334-0950)
PHONE....................909 350-3000
Tom Rievley, *Branch Mgr*
Jeremy Rievley, *Sales Staff*
EMP: 150

SALES (corp-wide): 49.5MM **Privately Held**
SIC: 5032 5211 Brick, stone & related material; cement
PA: Valori Sand & Gravel Company Inc
141 W Taft Ave
Orange CA 92865
714 637-0104

(P-6913)
WALKER & ZANGER INC (PA)
16719 Schoenborn St, North Hills (91343-6115)
PHONE....................818 280-8300
Jonathan Zanger, *CEO*
Pat Petrocelli, *COO*
Jim Nikolopoulos, *Opers Mgr*
Kim Bernard, *Director*
Coleen Wright, *Director*
◆ EMP: 60
SQ FT: 30,000
SALES (est): 69.4MM **Privately Held**
SIC: 5032 Marble building stone; ceramic wall & floor tile

(P-6914)
WEST COAST SAND AND GRAVEL INC (PA)
Also Called: West Coast Materials
7282 Orangethorpe Ave, Buena Park (90621-3331)
P.O. Box 5067 (90622-5067)
PHONE....................714 522-0282
Daniel C Reyneveld, *CEO*
Marvin J Struiksma, *President*
John Struiksma, *Vice Pres*
James Slater, *General Mgr*
Bob Struiksma, *Admin Sec*
EMP: 71
SQ FT: 4,200
SALES (est): 38.2MM **Privately Held**
WEB: www.wcsg.com
SIC: 5032 Sand, construction; gravel

(P-6915)
WESTERN PACIFIC DISTRG LLC
Also Called: Westpac Materials
341 W Meats Ave, Orange (92865-2623)
PHONE....................714 974-6837
Mark Hamilton, *General Mgr*
Leslie Dickson, *Manager*
EMP: 150
SALES (est): 34.7MM **Privately Held**
WEB: www.westernpacificdistributing.com
SIC: 5032 Drywall materials

5033 Roofing, Siding & Insulation Mtrls Wholesale

(P-6916)
ALLIED BUILDING PRODUCTS CORP
1201 E Mcfadden Ave, Santa Ana (92705-4101)
PHONE....................714 647-9792
Stephen Rhorer, *Manager*
EMP: 50
SALES (corp-wide): 4.3B **Publicly Held**
WEB: www.alliedbuilding.com
SIC: 5033 Roofing, asphalt & sheet metal
HQ: Allied Building Products Corp.
15 E Union Ave
East Rutherford NJ 07073
201 507-8400

(P-6917)
ALLIED BUILDING PRODUCTS CORP
4159 Santa Rosa Ave, Santa Rosa (95407-8276)
PHONE....................707 584-7599
Jim Brenton, *Manager*
John Ording, *Asst Mgr*
EMP: 50
SALES (corp-wide): 4.3B **Publicly Held**
WEB: www.alliedbuilding.com
SIC: 5033 5211 Roofing & siding materials; roofing material

HQ: Allied Building Products Corp.
15 E Union Ave
East Rutherford NJ 07073
201 507-8400

(P-6918)
ALLIED BUILDING PRODUCTS CORP
Also Called: AMS
1620 S Maple Ave, Montebello
(90640-6510)
PHONE...................................323 721-9011
Bill Wick, *Branch Mgr*
Oj Dutcher, *Sales Staff*
Jeff Fedderson, *Sales Staff*
Julie Hoey, *Sales Staff*
Chris Kleven, *Sales Staff*
EMP: 100
SALES (corp-wide): 4.3B **Publicly Held**
WEB: www.a-m-s.com
SIC: 5033 Roofing, siding & insulation
HQ: Allied Building Products Corp.
15 E Union Ave
East Rutherford NJ 07073
201 507-8400

(P-6919)
BEACON ROOFING SUPPLY INC
200 San Jose Ave, San Jose (95125-1008)
PHONE...................................408 293-5947
EMP: 99
SALES (corp-wide): 4.3B **Publicly Held**
SIC: 5033 Roofing & siding materials
PA: Beacon Roofing Supply, Inc.
505 Huntmar Park Dr # 300
Herndon VA 20170
571 323-3939

(P-6920)
BEACON SALES ACQUISITION INC
Also Called: Pacific Supply
1201 E Mcfadden Ave, Santa Ana
(92705-4101)
PHONE...................................714 288-1974
Gina Cashner, *Branch Mgr*
Zach Paine, *Branch Mgr*
Matt Pouliot, *Sales Mgr*
EMP: 110
SALES (corp-wide): 4.3B **Publicly Held**
SIC: 5033 5211 Roofing, asphalt & sheet metal; roofing material
HQ: Beacon Sales Acquisition, Inc.
50 Webster Ave
Somerville MA 02143
877 645-7663

(P-6921)
BURLINGAME INDUSTRIES INC
Also Called: Eagle Roofing Products
4555 Mckinley Ave, Stockton (95206-4008)
PHONE...................................209 464-9001
Hersch Beahm, *Purchasing*
Robert Villa, *Maintence Staff*
EMP: 100
SALES (corp-wide): 81.5MM **Privately Held**
SIC: 5033 Roofing, siding & insulation
PA: Burlingame Industries, Incorporated
3546 N Riverside Ave
Rialto CA 92377
909 355-7000

(P-6922)
CARLISLE CONSTRUCTION MTLS INC
Also Called: Western Insulfoam
5635 Schaefer Ave, Chino (91710-9048)
PHONE...................................909 591-7425
Tom Tartaglione, *Manager*
EMP: 100
SQ FT: 45,464
SALES (corp-wide): 4B **Publicly Held**
WEB: www.insulfoam.com
SIC: 5033 3086 Insulation materials; cups & plates, foamed plastic
HQ: Carlisle Construction Materials, Llc
1285 Ritner Hwy
Carlisle PA 17013

(P-6923)
CARLISLE CONSTRUCTION MTLS INC
Also Called: Insulfoam
1155 Business Park Dr, Dixon
(95620-4303)
PHONE...................................707 678-6900
Rick Canady, *Manager*
EMP: 55
SALES (corp-wide): 4B **Publicly Held**
WEB: www.insulfoam.com
SIC: 5033 3086 Insulation materials; plastics foam products
HQ: Carlisle Construction Materials, Llc
1285 Ritner Hwy
Carlisle PA 17013

(P-6924)
EXTERIOR SOLUTIONS INC
25752 Simpson Pl, Calabasas
(91302-3154)
PHONE...................................310 400-3510
Craig Carson, *CEO*
EMP: 70
SALES (est): 11.2MM **Privately Held**
SIC: 5033 Roofing, siding & insulation

(P-6925)
OWENS CORNING SALES LLC
960 Central Expy, Santa Clara
(95050-2665)
PHONE...................................408 235-1351
Chris Rukman, *Branch Mgr*
EMP: 400 **Publicly Held**
WEB: www.owenscorning.com
SIC: 5033 3296 Fiberglass building materials; mineral wool
HQ: Owens Corning Sales, Llc
1 Owens Corning Pkwy
Toledo OH 43659
419 248-8000

(P-6926)
REVCHEM COMPOSITES INC (PA)
Also Called: Revchem Plastics
2720 S Willow Ave B, Bloomington
(92316-3259)
P.O. Box 333 (92316-0333)
PHONE...................................909 877-8477
Douglas L Dennis, *CEO*
Gina L Dennis, *Principal*
▲ **EMP:** 60
SALES (est): 30.7MM **Privately Held**
WEB: www.revchem.com
SIC: 5033 Fiberglass building materials

(P-6927)
ROOFING SUPPLY GROUP LLC
14128 Kornblum Ave, Hawthorne
(90250-8114)
PHONE...................................424 269-7330
Richard Oliva, *Branch Mgr*
EMP: 68
SALES (corp-wide): 4.3B **Publicly Held**
SIC: 5033 Roofing & siding materials
HQ: Roofing Supply Group, Llc
505 Huntmar Park Dr # 300
Herndon VA 20170

(P-6928)
ROOFING WHOLESALE CO INC
8674 Jamacha Rd, Spring Valley
(91977-4034)
PHONE...................................619 287-7600
Mike Nicholson, *Opers-Prdtn-Mfg*
EMP: 50
SALES (corp-wide): 143.8MM **Privately Held**
WEB: www.rwc.org
SIC: 5033 Roofing & siding materials
PA: Roofing Wholesale Co., Inc.
1918 W Grant St
Phoenix AZ 85009
602 258-3794

(P-6929)
ROOFING WHOLESALE CO INC
118 Commercial Rd, San Bernardino
(92408-4148)
PHONE...................................909 825-8440
Rick Knudsen, *Branch Mgr*
Pat Paszternak, *Manager*

EMP: 60
SALES (corp-wide): 143.8MM **Privately Held**
WEB: www.rwc.org
SIC: 5033 Roofing, asphalt & sheet metal
PA: Roofing Wholesale Co., Inc.
1918 W Grant St
Phoenix AZ 85009
602 258-3794

(P-6930)
STANDARD INDUSTRIES INC
Also Called: GAF Materials
3301 Navone Rd, Stockton (95215-9312)
PHONE...................................209 242-5000
David Kirkham, *Director*
EMP: 50
SQ FT: 30,000
SALES (corp-wide): 2.7B **Privately Held**
SIC: 5033 Roofing & siding materials
HQ: Standard Industries Inc.
1 Campus Dr
Parsippany NJ 07054

(P-6931)
STANDARD INDUSTRIES INC
Also Called: GAF Materials
6505 S Zerker Rd, Shafter (93263-9614)
PHONE...................................661 387-1110
Phil Halpin, *General Mgr*
EMP: 100
SALES (corp-wide): 2.7B **Privately Held**
SIC: 5033 Roofing & siding materials
HQ: Standard Industries Inc.
1 Campus Dr
Parsippany NJ 07054

(P-6932)
TRI-VALLEY SUPPLY INC (PA)
Also Called: Tri Valley Wholesale
1705 Enterprise Dr, Fairfield (94533-5801)
PHONE...................................707 469-7470
James P Petersen, *President*
Joe Dean, *Vice Pres*
David Van Beek, *Vice Pres*
▲ **EMP:** 85 **EST:** 1993
SQ FT: 15,000
SALES (est): 39.6MM **Privately Held**
WEB: www.trivalleysupply.com
SIC: 5033 Roofing & siding materials

5039 Construction Materials, NEC Wholesale

(P-6933)
JENSEN ENTERPRISES INC
Also Called: Jensen Precast
5400 Raley Blvd, Sacramento
(95838-1700)
PHONE...................................916 992-8301
Mark Voiselle, *General Mgr*
Miles Bennett, *President*
David Shacklett, *General Mgr*
Michael Bedard, *Human Res Mgr*
Brian Burton, *Sales Associate*
EMP: 70
SALES (corp-wide): 154.1MM **Privately Held**
SIC: 5039 5211 Septic tanks; masonry materials & supplies
PA: Jensen Enterprises, Inc.
825 Steneri Way
Sparks NV 89431
775 352-2700

(P-6934)
LA CANTINA DOORS INC
1875 Ord Way, Oceanside (92056-3589)
PHONE...................................888 221-0141
Matthew Power, *CEO*
Toby Jones, *Vice Pres*
Sandra Michelson, *Purch Mgr*
Benjamin Woo, *Marketing Mgr*
Josh Manuto, *Sales Associate*
◆ **EMP:** 50
SALES (est): 39.5MM **Privately Held**
WEB: www.lacantinadoors.com
SIC: 5039 Doors, sliding

(P-6935)
LSF9 CYPRESS HOLDINGS LLC
2741 Walnut Ave Ste 200, Tustin
(92780-7063)
PHONE...................................714 380-3127
Ruben Mendoza, *President*
EMP: 3398 **EST:** 2015
SALES (est): 25.7MM
SALES (corp-wide): 2B **Publicly Held**
SIC: 5039 5031 5033 Ceiling systems & products; wallboard; insulation materials
HQ: Lsf9 Cypress Parent, Llc
2741 Walnut Ave Ste 200
Tustin CA 92780
714 380-3127

(P-6936)
SECURITY CONTRACTOR SVCS INC (PA)
Also Called: S C S
5339 Jackson St, North Highlands
(95660-5004)
PHONE...................................916 338-4200
Barry J Marrs, *CEO*
Ron Kyewski, *CFO*
Steve Mann, *Branch Mgr*
Tim Miller, *Data Proc Staff*
Laurie Sullivan, *Credit Staff*
EMP: 60 **EST:** 1961
SQ FT: 50,000
SALES (est): 37.6MM **Privately Held**
WEB: www.scsfence.com
SIC: 5039 7359 3315 Wire fence, gates & accessories; equipment rental & leasing; steel wire & related products

(P-6937)
SOUTHGATE GLASS & SCREEN INC (PA)
6852 Franklin Blvd, Sacramento
(95823-1810)
PHONE...................................916 476-8396
Scott Davis, *President*
Tim Wolhart, *Division Mgr*
Dave Megarry, *General Mgr*
Jim Boller, *Project Mgr*
Tony Muljat, *Project Mgr*
EMP: 50
SQ FT: 5,000
SALES: 10MM **Privately Held**
SIC: 5039 5231 Glass construction materials; glass

(P-6938)
SOUTHGATE GLASS & SCREEN INC
6199 Warehouse Way, Sacramento
(95826-4907)
PHONE...................................916 476-8396
Dave Megeary, *Branch Mgr*
EMP: 50
SALES (corp-wide): 10MM **Privately Held**
SIC: 5039 5231 Glass construction materials; glass
PA: Southgate Glass & Screen, Inc.
6852 Franklin Blvd
Sacramento CA 95823
916 476-8396

5043 Photographic Eqpt & Splys Wholesale

(P-6939)
ADOLPH GASSER INC
Also Called: Adolph Gasser Photography
4340 Redwood Hwy Ste 227, San Rafael
(94903-2104)
PHONE...................................415 495-3852
John Gasser, *President*
EMP: 137 **EST:** 1960
SALES (est): 765.2K **Privately Held**
WEB: www.adolphgasser.com
SIC: 5043 5946 7359 5731 Photographic cameras, projectors, equipment & supplies; cameras; photographic supplies; audio-visual equipment & supply rental; video cameras & accessories

(P-6940)
CANON USA INC
15955 Alton Pkwy, Irvine (92618-3731)
PHONE...................................949 753-4000

PRODUCTS & SVCS

Glen Takahashi, *Manager*
David Mah, *Executive*
Javier Michel, *Technician*
Bajo Allison, *Engineer*
Benedict Del Rosario, *Purch Mgr*
EMP: 350
SALES (corp-wide): 36.4B **Privately Held**
WEB: www.usa.canon.com
SIC: 5043 5044 5045 8741 Photographic cameras, projectors, equipment & supplies; office equipment; computers; management services
HQ: Canon U.S.A., Inc.
1 Canon Park
Melville NY 11747
516 328-5000

(P-6941)
CHRISTIE DGTAL SYSTEMS USA INC (DH)
10550 Camden Dr, Cypress (90630-4600)
PHONE................714 527-7056
Jack Kline, *President*
▲ **EMP:** 71
SQ FT: 85,000
SALES (est): 123.8MM
SALES (corp-wide): 1.6B **Privately Held**
SIC: 5043 Projection apparatus, motion picture & slide
HQ: Christie Digital Systems, Inc.
10550 Camden Dr
Cypress CA 90630
714 236-8610

(P-6942)
FUJIFILM NORTH AMERICA CORP
Also Called: Fuji Photo Film
6200 Phyllis Dr, Cypress (90630-5239)
PHONE................714 372-4200
Bobby Bruce, *Manager*
George Gush, *Technical Staff*
George Bouchard, *Business Mgr*
Nathan Mayes, *Credit Staff*
Jeff Ash, *VP Mktg*
EMP: 150
SALES (corp-wide): 22.8B **Privately Held**
SIC: 5043 Photographic equipment & supplies
HQ: Fujifilm North America Corporation
200 Summit Lake Dr Fl 2
Valhalla NY 10595
914 789-8100

(P-6943)
GELSHMAL ENTERPRISES LLC
Also Called: Imageologist
945 W Hyde Park Blvd, Inglewood (90302-3307)
P.O. Box 4668 (90309-4668)
PHONE................310 672-9090
David Golshirazi, *CEO*
Doug Pircher, *General Mgr*
Erik Bartelt, *Info Tech Dir*
Harry Baltazar, *Human Res Dir*
Michael Tabor, *Art Dir*
▲ **EMP:** 50
SALES (est): 10.7MM **Privately Held**
WEB: www.orientalphotousa.com
SIC: 5043 Photographic equipment & supplies

(P-6944)
JK IMAGING LTD
17239 S Main St, Gardena (90248-3129)
PHONE................310 755-6848
Joe Atick, *CEO*
Shu-Ping Wu, *CFO*
Mike Feng, *Admin Sec*
▲ **EMP:** 100
SQ FT: 6,000
SALES (est): 100MM **Privately Held**
SIC: 5043 Cameras & photographic equipment

(P-6945)
KYOCERA INTERNATIONAL INC
222 N Pacific Coast Hwy, El Segundo (90245-5648)
PHONE................310 647-2805
Steve Clark, *Manager*
EMP: 60
SALES (corp-wide): 14.8B **Publicly Held**
SIC: 5043 Cameras & photographic equipment

HQ: Kyocera International, Inc.
8611 Balboa Ave
San Diego CA 92123
858 492-1456

(P-6946)
NORITSU AMERICA CORPORATION (HQ)
6900 Noritsu Ave, Buena Park (90620-1372)
P.O. Box 5039 (90622-5039)
PHONE................714 521-9040
Michiro Niikura, *CEO*
Kanichi Nishimoto, *Ch of Bd*
Rick Voutour, *President*
Frank Morrow, *Vice Pres*
Patrik Norrby, *Vice Pres*
◆ **EMP:** 115 **EST:** 1978
SQ FT: 27,500
SALES (est): 66.8MM
SALES (corp-wide): 440.3MM **Privately Held**
WEB: www.noritsu.com
SIC: 5043 Photographic processing equipment
PA: Noritsu Koki Co., Ltd.
1-10-10, Azabujuban
Minato-Ku TKY 106-0
335 055-053

(P-6947)
PILGRIM OPERATIONS LLC
Also Called: Tailbroom Media Grop
12020 Chanl Blvd Ste 200, North Hollywood (91607)
PHONE................818 478-4500
Douglas Liechty, *Mng Member*
Rita Doumar, *Vice Pres*
Matthew Ducey, *Personnel*
James Voda, *Production*
Miguel Camargo, *Editor*
EMP: 400
SALES (est): 319.5K **Privately Held**
SIC: 5043 Motion picture studio & theater equipment

5044 Office Eqpt Wholesale

(P-6948)
ACM TECHNOLOGIES INC (PA)
Also Called: Allstate
2535 Research Dr, Corona (92882-7607)
PHONE................951 738-9898
Stan Shue Lin, *CEO*
Sharon Lee, *COO*
Monica Lin, *Corp Secy*
Joseph Wayne, *Executive*
Tim Purugganan, *Business Mgr*
◆ **EMP:** 89
SALES (est): 35.1MM **Privately Held**
WEB: www.acmtech.com
SIC: 5044 Copying equipment; photocopy machines

(P-6949)
ALLSTATE IMAGING INC (PA)
21621 Nordhoff St, Chatsworth (91311-5825)
PHONE................818 678-4550
Alan Jurick, *President*
Russel Leventhal, *CEO*
Richard Shapiro, *CFO*
EMP: 80
SALES (est): 42.5MM **Privately Held**
SIC: 5044 Office equipment

(P-6950)
BANKCARD USA MERCHANT SRVC
5701 Lindero Canyon Rd, Westlake Village (91362-4060)
PHONE................818 597-7000
Shawn Skelton, *President*
Alan Griefer, *Exec VP*
Chris Jimenez, *VP Sales*
Ryan Zone, *Sales Dir*
Dina Moss, *Manager*
EMP: 85
SQ FT: 20,000
SALES (est): 16.4MM **Privately Held**
WEB: www.busams.com
SIC: 5044 Check writing, signing & endorsing machines

(P-6951)
CANON BUS SOLUTIONS-WEST INC
110 W Walnut St, Gardena (90248-3100)
P.O. Box 51075, Los Angeles (90074-1075)
PHONE................310 217-3000
Bill Joseph, *President*
Keiko Brockel, *Vice Pres*
Stephen Meyer, *Engineer*
John Murphy, *Director*
EMP: 450
SQ FT: 100,000
SALES (est): 34.4MM
SALES (corp-wide): 36.4B **Privately Held**
WEB: www.usa.canon.com
SIC: 5044 Office equipment
HQ: Canon U.S.A., Inc.
1 Canon Park
Melville NY 11747
516 328-5000

(P-6952)
CANON SOLUTIONS AMERICA INC
203 S Waterman Ave, El Centro (92243-2228)
PHONE................800 323-4827
EMP: 80
SALES (corp-wide): 36.4B **Privately Held**
SIC: 5044 Office equipment
HQ: Canon Solutions America, Inc.
1 Canon Park
Melville NY 11747
631 330-5000

(P-6953)
CANON SOLUTIONS AMERICA INC
3237 E Guasti Rd Ste 200, Ontario (91761-1243)
PHONE................909 390-7400
Larry Candejas, *Branch Mgr*
EMP: 65
SALES (corp-wide): 36.4B **Privately Held**
SIC: 5044 Office equipment
HQ: Canon Solutions America, Inc.
1 Canon Park
Melville NY 11747
631 330-5000

(P-6954)
CANON SOLUTIONS AMERICA INC
201 California St Ste 100, San Francisco (94111-5003)
PHONE................415 743-7300
Kim Haydel, *Branch Mgr*
Marc Faichtyger, *Executive*
Wesley Kidd, *Executive*
Quintus Vaughn, *Info Tech Mgr*
Jeff Le, *Software Dev*
EMP: 51
SALES (corp-wide): 36.4B **Privately Held**
SIC: 5044 Copying equipment
HQ: Canon Solutions America, Inc.
1 Canon Park
Melville NY 11747
631 330-5000

(P-6955)
CANON SOLUTIONS AMERICA INC
123 Paularino Ave, Costa Mesa (92626-3311)
PHONE................949 753-4200
Mark Hix, *Branch Mgr*
Alex Bruk, *Director*
Chuck Arnold, *Accounts Exec*
Anita Martinez, *Accounts Exec*
Blake Poole, *Accounts Exec*
EMP: 80
SALES (corp-wide): 36.4B **Privately Held**
SIC: 5044 Photocopy machines
HQ: Canon Solutions America, Inc.
1 Canon Park
Melville NY 11747
631 330-5000

(P-6956)
COAST TO COAST BUS EQP INC (PA)
8 Vanderbilt Ste 200, Irvine (92618-2080)
PHONE................949 457-7300
Paul M Faus, *President*

Julie Davis, *Treasurer*
Zach Reeves, *Director*
Vince Eastin, *Manager*
Gilbert Gastelum, *Manager*
EMP: 55
SQ FT: 20,100
SALES (est): 13.7MM **Privately Held**
WEB: www.ctcbe.com
SIC: 5044 5065 Photocopy machines; teletype equipment

(P-6957)
COPIER SOURCE INC (PA)
Also Called: Image Source
650 E Hospitality Ln # 500, San Bernardino (92408-3535)
PHONE................909 890-4040
David Bradley Craft, *CEO*
Jill Craft, *Treasurer*
EMP: 65
SALES (est): 49MM **Privately Held**
SIC: 5044 Office equipment

(P-6958)
CUSTOM BUSINESS SOLUTIONS INC (PA)
Also Called: Northstar
12 Morgan, Irvine (92618-2003)
PHONE................949 380-7674
Art Julian, *CEO*
Colleen Julian, *President*
Rom Krupp, *President*
Michael Block, *CFO*
Joseph Castillo, *Vice Pres*
◆ **EMP:** 68
SQ FT: 21,000
SALES (est): 64.4MM **Privately Held**
WEB: www.cbs-posi.com
SIC: 5044 Cash registers

(P-6959)
DUPLO USA CORPORATION (PA)
3050 Daimler St, Santa Ana (92705-5813)
PHONE................949 752-8222
Peter Tu, *President*
Jim Peffer, *COO*
Joyce Crocker, *Administration*
Eric Von Schimpf, *Info Tech Dir*
Eric Schimpf, *Data Proc Staff*
◆ **EMP:** 80
SQ FT: 30,000
SALES (est): 33.6MM **Privately Held**
WEB: www.duplousa.com
SIC: 5044 Duplicating machines

(P-6960)
IMAGE IV SYSTEMS INC (PA)
512 S Varney St, Burbank (91502-2196)
PHONE................323 849-3049
Ronald Warren, *President*
Darryl Lee, *Partner*
Sue Warren, *Vice Pres*
Josh Smith, *Executive*
Armando Castellanos, *Department Mgr*
EMP: 79
SQ FT: 4,000
SALES (est): 23.8MM **Privately Held**
WEB: www.imageiv.com
SIC: 5044 Photocopy machines; copying equipment

(P-6961)
INTEGRATED OFFICE TECH LLC (PA)
Also Called: Iotec
12150 Mora Dr Ste 2, Santa Fe Springs (90670-3700)
PHONE................562 236-9200
Robert Zieman,
Doug Lu,
Dana Ruf,
EMP: 70
SQ FT: 30,000
SALES: 20MM **Privately Held**
WEB: www.iotecdigital.com
SIC: 5044 7371 7379 Copying equipment; computer software systems analysis & design, custom; computer related maintenance services

(P-6962)
INTEGRUS LLC
Also Called: Advanced Office
1430 Village Way Ste K, Santa Ana (92705-4760)
PHONE................714 547-9500

Mike Dixon, *CEO*
Richard Van Dyke, *President*
Tim Wickers, *Vice Pres*
James Formby, *Opers Mgr*
EMP: 100 **EST:** 2011
SQ FT: 14,000
SALES: 18MM **Privately Held**
SIC: 5044 Office equipment

(P-6963)
INTERNATIONAL BUS MCHS CORP
Also Called: IBM
425 Market St, San Francisco
(94105-2532)
PHONE....................415 545-4747
Wirt Cook, *CEO*
Jeffrey Spicer, *Vice Pres*
Robert Hahn, *Executive*
James Reget, *Executive*
Hunter Medney, *Software Dev*
EMP: 208
SALES (corp-wide): 79.1B **Publicly Held**
WEB: www.ibm.com
SIC: 5044 5045 3571 Office equipment; computers, peripherals & software; electronic computers
PA: International Business Machines Corporation
1 New Orchard Rd Ste 1 # 1
Armonk NY 10504
914 499-1900

(P-6964)
INTERNATIONAL BUS MCHS CORP
Also Called: IBM
2077 Gateway Pl, San Jose (95110-1090)
P.O. Box 49015 (95161)
PHONE....................408 452-4800
Barry Gafner, *Principal*
EMP: 200
SALES (corp-wide): 79.1B **Publicly Held**
WEB: www.ibm.com
SIC: 5044 5045 Office equipment; computers, peripherals & software
PA: International Business Machines Corporation
1 New Orchard Rd Ste 1 # 1
Armonk NY 10504
914 499-1900

(P-6965)
INTERNATIONAL LITIGATION SVCS
65 Enterprise, Aliso Viejo (92656-2705)
PHONE....................888 313-4457
Joseph Thorpe, *CEO*
Ketan Parekh, *COO*
Mark Liekkio, *Senior VP*
Elizabeth Koenig, *Consultant*
EMP: 50
SQ FT: 7,000
SALES (est): 10.3MM **Privately Held**
SIC: 5044 Office equipment

(P-6966)
KONICA MINOLTA BUSINESS SOLUTI
1831 Commercenter W, San Bernardino
(92408-3303)
PHONE....................909 824-2000
Linda F Turner, *Manager*
EMP: 69
SQ FT: 13,000
SALES (corp-wide): 9.6B **Privately Held**
WEB: www.konicabt.com
SIC: 5044 5065 5943 Photocopy machines; facsimile equipment; office forms & supplies
HQ: Konica Minolta Business Solutions U.S.A., Inc.
100 Williams Dr
Ramsey NJ 07446
201 825-4000

(P-6967)
KONICA MINOLTA BUSINESS SOLUTI
Also Called: Minolta Business Systems
879 W 190th St Ste 200, Gardena
(90248-4223)
PHONE....................310 214-6696
Brian Shaw, *General Mgr*
EMP: 50

SALES (corp-wide): 9.6B **Privately Held**
WEB: www.konicabt.com
SIC: 5044 Office equipment
HQ: Konica Minolta Business Solutions U.S.A., Inc.
100 Williams Dr
Ramsey NJ 07446
201 825-4000

(P-6968)
KYOCERA DCMENT SLTONS AMER INC
Also Called: Kyocera Technology Development
1855 Gateway Blvd Ste 400, Concord
(94520-3289)
PHONE....................925 849-3300
Atsushi Yuki, *Manager*
EMP: 70
SALES (corp-wide): 14.8B **Publicly Held**
SIC: 5044 Photocopy machines
HQ: Kyocera Document Solutions America, Inc.
225 Sand Rd
Fairfield NJ 07004
973 808-8444

(P-6969)
MICROTEK LAB INC (HQ)
13337 South St, Cerritos (90703-7308)
PHONE....................310 687-5823
Clark Hsu, *President*
Stewart Chow, *President*
▲ **EMP:** 110 **EST:** 1980
SQ FT: 126,000
SALES (est): 27.5MM
SALES (corp-wide): 21.4MM **Privately Held**
WEB: www.microtek.com
PA: Microtek International Inc.
6., Ind. E. 3rd Rd.,
Hsinchu City 30075
357 721-55

(P-6970)
MR COPY INC (DH)
Also Called: Mrc, Smart Tech Solutions
5657 Copley Dr, San Diego (92111-7903)
PHONE....................858 573-6300
Bob Leone, *President*
EMP: 75
SQ FT: 18,000
SALES (est): 140.1MM
SALES (corp-wide): 10.2B **Publicly Held**
SIC: 5044 Copying equipment; photocopy machines

(P-6971)
NATIONAL LINK INCORPORATED
2235 Auto Centre Dr, Glendora
(91740-6721)
PHONE....................909 670-1900
Sam Kandah, *President*
Jim Scott, *CFO*
Carol Kandah, *Admin Sec*
Rafael De La Garza, *Marketing Staff*
Mark Wasilow, *Director*
EMP: 68
SQ FT: 5,000
SALES (est): 24.8MM **Privately Held**
SIC: 5044 7389 7359 Bank automatic teller machines; credit card service; electronic equipment rental, except computers

(P-6972)
OFFICE DEPOT INC
4720 Northgate Blvd, Sacramento
(95834-1101)
PHONE....................916 927-0171
Dennise Moran, *Principal*
EMP: 100
SALES (corp-wide): 10.2B **Publicly Held**
WEB: www.officedepot.com
SIC: 5044 5045 5112 Office equipment; computers, peripherals & software; computers; office supplies
PA: Office Depot, Inc.
6600 N Military Trl
Boca Raton FL 33496
561 438-4800

(P-6973)
PINNACLE DOCUMENT SYSTEMS (PA)
470 Boulder Ct Ste 100, Pleasanton
(94566-8315)
PHONE....................925 417-8400
Toll Free:....................877 -
Todd Court, *Ch of Bd*
Samuel Pulino, *President*
EMP: 60 **EST:** 1998
SQ FT: 30,000
SALES (est): 13.2MM **Privately Held**
WEB: www.pinnacleds.com
SIC: 5044 Office equipment

(P-6974)
RICOH USA INC
Also Called: Data-Image Systems
3046 Prospect Park Dr # 100, Rancho Cordova (95670-6356)
PHONE....................916 638-3333
Merlin Shoemaker, *CEO*
Jack Fisher, *General Mgr*
EMP: 75
SALES (corp-wide): 19.3B **Privately Held**
WEB: www.ikon.com
SIC: 5044 Office equipment
HQ: Ricoh Usa, Inc.
70 Valley Stream Pkwy
Malvern PA 19355
610 296-8000

(P-6975)
RICOH USA INC
333 Bush St Ste 2500, San Francisco
(94104-2862)
PHONE....................415 733-5600
Joan Meyer, *Manager*
EMP: 68
SALES (corp-wide): 19.3B **Privately Held**
WEB: www.ikon.com
SIC: 5044 Photocopy machines
HQ: Ricoh Usa, Inc.
70 Valley Stream Pkwy
Malvern PA 19355
610 296-8000

(P-6976)
RICOH USA INC
9430 Topanga Canyon Blvd # 100,
Chatsworth (91311-5765)
PHONE....................818 294-8601
Daniel Walsh, *Manager*
EMP: 50
SALES (corp-wide): 19.3B **Privately Held**
SIC: 5044 Photocopy machines
HQ: Ricoh Usa, Inc.
70 Valley Stream Pkwy
Malvern PA 19355
610 296-8000

(P-6977)
RICOH USA INC
Also Called: Ricoh Business Solutions
17011 Beach Blvd Ste 1000, Huntington
Beach (92647-7402)
PHONE....................714 396-0568
Tracy Wood, *Manager*
Mike McNamee, *Production*
EMP: 50
SALES (corp-wide): 19.3B **Privately Held**
SIC: 5044 5112 3861 3661 Copying equipment; photocopying supplies; photographic equipment & supplies; telephone & telegraph apparatus
HQ: Ricoh Usa, Inc.
70 Valley Stream Pkwy
Malvern PA 19355
610 296-8000

(P-6978)
RICOH USA INC
6330 Variel Ave, Woodland Hills
(91367-2543)
PHONE....................213 629-1838
Steve Smith, *Exec VP*
EMP: 100
SALES (corp-wide): 19.3B **Privately Held**
WEB: www.ikon.com
SIC: 5044 Photocopy machines
HQ: Ricoh Usa, Inc.
70 Valley Stream Pkwy
Malvern PA 19355
610 296-8000

(P-6979)
RICOH USA INC
Also Called: Nightrider Overnite Copy Svc
333 Bush St Ste 2500, San Francisco
(94104-2862)
PHONE....................415 392-6850
John Wilkinson, *Manager*
EMP: 60
SALES (corp-wide): 19.3B **Privately Held**
WEB: www.ikon.com
SIC: 5044 Photocopy machines
HQ: Ricoh Usa, Inc.
70 Valley Stream Pkwy
Malvern PA 19355
610 296-8000

(P-6980)
RICOH USA INC
21820 Burbank Blvd # 229, Woodland Hills
(91367-6476)
PHONE....................818 703-0265
David Burton, *Manager*
Bryce Decastro, *Accounts Exec*
EMP: 50
SALES (corp-wide): 19.3B **Privately Held**
SIC: 5044 Photocopy machines
HQ: Ricoh Usa, Inc.
70 Valley Stream Pkwy
Malvern PA 19355
610 296-8000

(P-6981)
RICOH USA INC
Also Called: Nightrider Overnite Copy Svc
1300 Clay St Ste 165, Oakland
(94612-1421)
PHONE....................510 839-6399
Charles Dickinson, *Manager*
EMP: 50
SALES (corp-wide): 19.3B **Privately Held**
WEB: www.ikon.com
SIC: 5044 Office equipment
HQ: Ricoh Usa, Inc.
70 Valley Stream Pkwy
Malvern PA 19355
610 296-8000

(P-6982)
RICOH USA INC
1320 Willow Pass Rd, Concord
(94520-5232)
PHONE....................925 988-4000
Renee Faxton, *Branch Mgr*
EMP: 150
SALES (corp-wide): 19.3B **Privately Held**
WEB: www.ikon.com
SIC: 5044 5065 7629 7359 Photocopy machines; typewriters; facsimile equipment; electronic equipment repair; office machine rental, except computers; stationery stores; computer rental & leasing
HQ: Ricoh Usa, Inc.
70 Valley Stream Pkwy
Malvern PA 19355
610 296-8000

(P-6983)
RICOH USA INC
16969 Von Karman Ave, Irvine
(92606-4948)
PHONE....................949 225-2300
Steve Bastien, *Manager*
Laura Russell, *Manager*
EMP: 75
SALES (corp-wide): 19.3B **Privately Held**
WEB: www.ikon.com
SIC: 5044 Photocopy machines
HQ: Ricoh Usa, Inc.
70 Valley Stream Pkwy
Malvern PA 19355
610 296-8000

(P-6984)
TOSHIBA AMER BUS SOLUTIONS INC (DH)
25530 Commercentre Dr, Lake Forest
(92630-8855)
PHONE....................949 462-6000
Scott Maccabe, *CEO*
Matt Barnes, *President*
Mark Mathews, *President*
Desmond Allen, *CFO*
Larry White, *Officer*
◆ **EMP:** 350 **EST:** 1999
SQ FT: 90,000

PRODUCTS & SVCS

SALES (est): 1.7B
SALES (corp-wide): 37B **Privately Held**
WEB: www.levenstein.com
SIC: 5044 Copying equipment
HQ: Toshiba Tec Corporation
    1-11-1, Osaki
    Shinagawa-Ku TKY 141-0
    368 309-100

(P-6985)
ULTREX MANAGEMENT SERVICES (PA)
712 Fiero Ln Ste 33, San Luis Obispo (93401-7979)
PHONE..................805 783-1234
Rolf W Berkfeld, *CEO*
Caroline Berkfeld, *Admin Sec*
Karoline Berkseld, *Human Res Dir*
Greg Berkefeld, *Sales Staff*
EMP: 60
SALES (est): 15.8MM **Privately Held**
WEB: www.ultrex.net
SIC: 5044 Copying equipment

(P-6986)
UNITED MERCHANT SVCS CAL INC
Also Called: Ums Banking
750 Fairmont Ave Ste 201, Glendale (91203-1074)
PHONE..................818 246-6767
Joyce Gaines, *President*
Lynda Neuman, *CFO*
Jorge Torres, *Treasurer*
Jacki Cass, *Exec VP*
Bruce Ferguson, *Exec VP*
EMP: 72
SQ FT: 8,580
SALES (est): 33.2MM **Privately Held**
WEB: www.umsbanking.com
SIC: 5044 5065 7629 Office equipment; electronic parts & equipment; electronic equipment repair

(P-6987)
UNITED RIBBON COMPANY INC
Also Called: United Imaging
21201 Oxnard St, Woodland Hills (91367-5015)
PHONE..................818 716-1515
Michael Cohen, *President*
Yigal Avrahamy, *Vice Pres*
Antonio Flores, *Sales Staff*
Tyler Kendrick, *Accounts Exec*
EMP: 85
SQ FT: 22,000
SALES (est): 57.7MM **Privately Held**
WEB: www.unitedimaging.com
SIC: 5044 5943 5021 7699 Office equipment; office forms & supplies; office & public building furniture; office equipment & accessory customizing; computer & photocopying supplies

(P-6988)
XEROX CORPORATION
2118 Wilshire Blvd, Santa Monica (90403-5704)
PHONE..................310 526-3940
Kalika Marina, *Principal*
EMP: 84
SALES (corp-wide): 10.2B **Publicly Held**
SIC: 5044 Office equipment
PA: Xerox Corporation
    201 Merritt 7
    Norwalk CT 06851
    203 968-3000

(P-6989)
XEROX CORPORATION
478 Ferne Ave, Palo Alto (94306-4620)
PHONE..................650 813-6787
Rich Hyde, *Principal*
EMP: 80
SALES (corp-wide): 10.2B **Publicly Held**
SIC: 5044 Office equipment
PA: Xerox Corporation
    201 Merritt 7
    Norwalk CT 06851
    203 968-3000

(P-6990)
XEROX CORPORATION
560 J St 300, Sacramento (95814-2343)
PHONE..................916 444-8100
Anne Pitt, *Branch Mgr*

EMP: 65
SALES (corp-wide): 10.2B **Publicly Held**
WEB: www.xerox.com
SIC: 5044 Photocopy machines
PA: Xerox Corporation
    201 Merritt 7
    Norwalk CT 06851
    203 968-3000

(P-6991)
XEROX CORPORATION
3333 Coyote Hill Rd, Palo Alto (94304-1314)
PHONE..................650 813-7138
David Smith, *Vice Pres*
Rob McHenry, *Vice Pres*
Lisa Andreasen, *Admin Sec*
Christopher Chua, *Research*
Yutaka Yamauchi, *Research*
EMP: 150
SALES (corp-wide): 10.2B **Publicly Held**
WEB: www.xerox.com
SIC: 5044 Office equipment
PA: Xerox Corporation
    201 Merritt 7
    Norwalk CT 06851
    203 968-3000

(P-6992)
XEROX CORPORATION
1851 E 1st St Ste 200, Santa Ana (92705-4072)
PHONE..................714 565-1100
Hunt Gammel, *District Mgr*
April Morgan-Leonetti, *Marketing Staff*
EMP: 400
SALES (corp-wide): 10.2B **Publicly Held**
WEB: www.xerox.com
SIC: 5044 5045 5065 5112 Photocopy machines; typewriters; computers, peripherals & software; printers, computer; facsimile equipment; computer & photocopying supplies
PA: Xerox Corporation
    201 Merritt 7
    Norwalk CT 06851
    203 968-3000

(P-6993)
XEROX EDUCATION SERVICES LLC (DH)
2277 E 220th St, Long Beach (90810-1639)
PHONE..................310 830-9847
J M Peffer, *Mng Member*
Bill Krouss, *Vice Pres*
Jerry Gordon, *Administration*
Gennady Mamzhi, *Business Anlyst*
Gil Guzman, *Human Res Mgr*
EMP: 90 EST: 1970
SALES (est): 272.9MM
SALES (corp-wide): 6B **Publicly Held**
WEB: www.acseducationservices.com
SIC: 5044 Office equipment
HQ: Conduent Business Services, Llc
    100 Campus Dr Ste 200
    Florham Park NJ 07932
    973 261-7100

(P-6994)
YOUNG SYSTEMS CORPORATION
Also Called: Nuworld Business Systems
13125 Midway Pl, Cerritos (90703-2232)
PHONE..................562 921-2256
Young H Lee, *President*
June S Lee, *Admin Sec*
Lian Nguyen, *Admin Asst*
Anna Rodriguez, *Administration*
Chris Chang, *Info Tech Dir*
◆ **EMP:** 53
SQ FT: 46,000
SALES: 24.5MM **Privately Held**
WEB: www.nuworldinc.com
SIC: 5044 5999 Photocopy machines; business machines & equipment

---

5045 Computers & Peripheral Eqpt & Software Wholesale

(P-6995)
ACCEL NORTH AMERICA INC
4633 Old Ironsides Dr # 400, Santa Clara (95054-1846)
PHONE..................408 514-5199
David Kumar, *CEO*
Goda Kumar, *Vice Pres*
Aju Kuriakose, *Vice Pres*
Ken Morris, *Vice Pres*
Steve Oldenburg, *Vice Pres*
EMP: 217
SQ FT: 4,000
SALES (est): 19.4MM
SALES (corp-wide): 125K **Privately Held**
WEB: www.accelna.com
SIC: 5045 Computer software
PA: Accel Limited
    Accel House, 3rd Floor,
    Chennai TN
    442 822-2262

(P-6996)
ACROSS SYSTEMS INC
100 N Brand Blvd Ste 100, Glendale (91203-2636)
PHONE..................877 922-7677
Daniel Nackovski, *President*
EMP: 70
SALES (est): 5.7MM **Privately Held**
SIC: 5045 Computer software

(P-6997)
ADESSO INC
Also Called: ADS Techonlogy
160 Commerce Way, Walnut (91789-2714)
PHONE..................909 839-2929
Allen Ku, *President*
Ray Shih, *Sales Staff*
▲ **EMP:** 200
SQ FT: 31,000
SALES (est): 10.5MM **Privately Held**
WEB: www.adesso.com
SIC: 5045 Computer peripheral equipment

(P-6998)
ADVANCED INDUSTRIAL CMPT INC (PA)
Also Called: Aic Inc USA
21808 Garcia Ln, City of Industry (91789-0941)
PHONE..................909 895-8989
Michael Liang, *Ch of Bd*
Shun Ying Liang, *CEO*
Belle Wang, *CFO*
Kit Chui, *Vice Pres*
Sophia Tsai, *Program Mgr*
▲ **EMP:** 57
SQ FT: 65,000
SALES (est): 24.4MM **Privately Held**
WEB: www.aicipc.com
SIC: 5045 Mainframe computers

(P-6999)
ADVANTECH CORPORATION (HQ)
380 Fairview Way, Milpitas (95035-3062)
P.O. Box 45895, San Francisco (94145-0895)
PHONE..................408 519-3800
Ke-Cheng Liu, *CEO*
Chaney Ho, *President*
Eric Chen, *Vice Pres*
Kenny Deng, *Vice Pres*
Deryu Yin, *Vice Pres*
▲ **EMP:** 70
SQ FT: 100,000
SALES: 355MM
SALES (corp-wide): 1.4B **Privately Held**
SIC: 5045 7379 Computers, peripherals & software; computer hardware requirements analysis
PA: Advantech Co., Ltd.
    1, Alley 20, Lane 26, Jui Kuang Rd.,
    Taipei City TAP 11491
    227 927-818

(P-7000)
AGILYSYS INC
5383 Hollister Ave # 120, Santa Barbara (93111-2304)
PHONE..................805 692-6339
Michael Hinojosa, *Principal*
Nancy Naretto, *Marketing Staff*
EMP: 108
SALES (corp-wide): 127.3MM **Publicly Held**
WEB: www.pios.com
SIC: 5045 Computer software
PA: Agilysys, Inc.
    1000 Windward Concourse # 250
    Alpharetta GA 30005
    770 810-7800

(P-7001)
AGILYSYS INC
1900 Powell St Ste 230, Emeryville (94608-1837)
PHONE..................702 759-4879
Christian Fisher, *Manager*
EMP: 50
SALES (corp-wide): 127.3MM **Publicly Held**
WEB: www.pios.com
SIC: 5045 7371 Computer software; computer software development & applications
PA: Agilysys, Inc.
    1000 Windward Concourse # 250
    Alpharetta GA 30005
    770 810-7800

(P-7002)
ALTAMETRICS LLC
3191 Red Hill Ave Ste 100, Costa Mesa (92626-3451)
PHONE..................800 676-1281
Mitesh Gala, *President*
Anand Gala, *CFO*
Kimberly Lebish, *Administration*
Ajay Shiv, *CIO*
Chase Ascari, *Sales Staff*
EMP: 140
SQ FT: 6,000
SALES (est): 31.7MM **Privately Held**
WEB: www.altametrics.com
SIC: 5045 Computer software

(P-7003)
AMAX ENGINEERING CORPORATION (PA)
Also Called: Amax Computer
1565 Reliance Way, Fremont (94539-6103)
PHONE..................510 651-8886
Jerry Kc Shih, *CEO*
CHI-Lei Ni, *Vice Pres*
Jean Shih, *Vice Pres*
Thomas Zhu, *Technology*
Tino Chang, *Engineer*
▲ **EMP:** 150
SQ FT: 110,000
SALES (est): 212.8MM **Privately Held**
WEB: www.amaxit.com
SIC: 5045 Computer peripheral equipment; computer software

(P-7004)
AMBERFIN LIMITED
7590 N Glenoaks Blvd # 101, Burbank (91504-1011)
PHONE..................818 768-8948
Jeremy Mh Deaner, *President*
Simon Adler, *Vice Pres*
EMP: 50
SALES (est): 2.3MM **Privately Held**
SIC: 5045 Computers, peripherals & software

(P-7005)
AMERICAN FUTURE TECH CORP
Also Called: Ibuypower
529 Baldwin Park Blvd, City of Industry (91746-1419)
PHONE..................888 462-3899
Alex Hou, *CEO*
Darren Su, *Vice Pres*
▲ **EMP:** 120
SQ FT: 25,000
SALES (est): 104.8MM **Privately Held**
WEB: www.aftcorp.com
SIC: 5045 Computer peripheral equipment

(P-7006)
AMERICAN PORTWELL TECH INC (PA)
Also Called: AP Tech
44200 Christy St, Fremont (94538-3179)
PHONE.................................510 403-3399
Allen Lee, *CEO*
Shineyang Shih, *Vice Pres*
Jacob Siu, *Info Tech Mgr*
Danny Chuang, *Design Engr*
Matthew Wu, *Project Mgr*
▲ EMP: 60
SQ FT: 42,515
SALES: 82.3MM **Privately Held**
WEB: www.portwell.com
SIC: 5045 Computer peripheral equipment

(P-7007)
AOPEN AMERICA INCORPORATED
2150 N 1st St Ste 300, San Jose
(95131-2044)
PHONE.................................408 586-1200
Dale Tsai, *President*
James Huang, *Vice Pres*
Erik Siera, *Business Mgr*
Brett McCarthy, *Natl Sales Mgr*
▲ EMP: 70 EST: 1997
SQ FT: 50,000
SALES: 13MM
SALES (corp-wide): 45MM **Privately Held**
SIC: 5045 Computer software
PA: Aopen Incorporated
5f, 15, Lane 128, Sinhu 1st Rd.,
Taipei City TAP 11494
277 101-195

(P-7008)
ARBITECH LLC
64 Fairbanks, Irvine (92618-1602)
PHONE.................................949 376-6650
Francisco Llaca, *President*
David Walker, *CFO*
Jimmy Whalen, *Exec VP*
Doug Kari, *Principal*
Jason McCarty, *Data Proc Dir*
▲ EMP: 74
SQ FT: 40,000
SALES: 116.1MM **Privately Held**
WEB: www.arbitech.com
SIC: 5045 Computer peripheral equipment

(P-7009)
ASI COMPUTER TECHNOLOGIES INC (PA)
Also Called: A S I
48289 Fremont Blvd, Fremont
(94538-6510)
PHONE.................................510 226-8000
Christine Liang, *President*
Marcel Liang, *CEO*
Steve Vangellow, *General Mgr*
Kelvin Smith, *Administration*
Allan Kam, *Info Tech Mgr*
▲ EMP: 200
SQ FT: 155,000
SALES (est): 591.4MM **Privately Held**
WEB: www.asipartner.com
SIC: 5045 3577 Disk drives; keying equipment; printers, computer; terminals, computer; computer output to microfilm units

(P-7010)
ASUS COMPUTER INTERNATIONAL
48720 Kato Rd, Fremont (94538-7312)
PHONE.................................510 739-3777
Steve Chang, *CEO*
Ivan Hoe, *President*
Raymond Chen, *Vice Pres*
Alan Hsieh, *Vice Pres*
William Sheu, *Vice Pres*
▲ EMP: 130
SQ FT: 13,000
SALES (est): 139.7MM
SALES (corp-wide): 14.4B **Privately Held**
WEB: www.asus.com
SIC: 5045 3577 Computer peripheral equipment; computer peripheral equipment
PA: Asustek Computer Incorporation
15, Lide Rd.,
Taipei City TAP 11259
228 943-447

(P-7011)
ATEN TECHNOLOGY INC
Also Called: Iogear
15365 Barranca Pkwy, Irvine (92618-2216)
PHONE.................................949 428-1111
Kevin Sun-Chung Chen, *President*
Holly Garcia, *Vice Pres*
Olivia KAO, *Info Tech Mgr*
Rick Levesque, *Info Tech Mgr*
Brandon Orth, *Web Dvlpr*
▲ EMP: 80
SALES (est): 54.8MM
SALES (corp-wide): 164.3MM **Privately Held**
SIC: 5045 Computers & accessories, personal & home entertainment
PA: Aten International Co., Ltd.
3f, 125, Ta Tung Rd., Sec. 2,
New Taipei City 22183
286 926-789

(P-7012)
AUTOMATION ANYWHERE INC (PA)
633 River Oaks Pkwy, San Jose
(95134-1907)
P.O. Box 640007 (95164-0007)
PHONE.................................888 484-3535
Mihir Shukla, *CEO*
Sridhar Gunapu, *President*
Richard French, *COO*
Ankur Kothari, *CFO*
Mark Fletcher, *Vice Pres*
EMP: 65
SQ FT: 14,000
SALES (est): 197.1MM **Privately Held**
WEB: www.tethyssolutions.com
SIC: 5045 7371 Computer software; computer software writing services

(P-7013)
AVER INFORMATION INC
668 Mission Ct, Fremont (94539-8206)
PHONE.................................408 263-3828
Arthur S Pait, *President*
Sinar Pait, *CEO*
Jeff McNall, *Business Mgr*
▲ EMP: 50
SQ FT: 15,000
SALES (est): 17.4MM
SALES (corp-wide): 64.9MM **Privately Held**
SIC: 5045 7382 5099 Computer software; computers & accessories, personal & home entertainment; security systems services; confinement surveillance systems maintenance & monitoring; video & audio equipment
PA: Aver Information Inc.
8f, 157, Ta An Rd,
New Taipei City 23673
222 698-535

(P-7014)
AXIOM MEMORY SOLUTIONS INC
15 Chrysler, Irvine (92618-2009)
PHONE.................................949 581-1450
Keith Carpenter, *President*
Josue Tarin, *Partner*
Laura Ward, *CFO*
Eric Devaney, *Vice Pres*
Greg Piligian, *Executive*
EMP: 75 EST: 1995
SALES: 26MM **Privately Held**
WEB: www.axiommemory.com
SIC: 5045 Computer peripheral equipment

(P-7015)
BACKWEB TECHNOLOGIES INC
2727 Walsh Ave Ste 102, Santa Clara
(95051-0956)
PHONE.................................408 933-1700
Eli Barkat, *Ch of Bd*
Daniel Platzker, *Vice Pres*
EMP: 50
SQ FT: 16,000
SALES (est): 4.4MM **Privately Held**
WEB: www.backweb.com
SIC: 5045 Computer software

(P-7016)
BAYNOTE INC
75 E Santa Clara St # 600, San Jose
(95113-1826)
PHONE.................................866 921-0919
Bill Hustad, *President*
Dario Calia, *Engineer*
Dan Darnell, *Marketing Staff*
EMP: 55
SALES (est): 8.4MM
SALES (corp-wide): 59.8MM **Privately Held**
SIC: 5045 Computer software
PA: Kibo Software, Inc.
717 N Harwood St Ste 1800
Dallas TX 75201
707 780-1600

(P-7017)
BENQ AMERICA CORP (HQ)
3200 Park Center Dr # 150, Costa Mesa
(92626-7163)
PHONE.................................714 559-4900
KY Lee, *Chairman*
Lars Yoder, *President*
Ellin Lee, *CFO*
Anna Castagnaro, *Officer*
Mia Videman, *Administration*
◆ EMP: 65 EST: 1997
SALES (est): 40.2MM
SALES (corp-wide): 4.5B **Privately Held**
SIC: 5045 Computer peripheral equipment
PA: Qisda Corporation
159, 157, Shan Ying Rd.,
Taoyuan City TAY 33341
335 988-00

(P-7018)
BIZCOM ELECTRONICS INC (HQ)
1171 Montague Expy, Milpitas
(95035-6845)
PHONE.................................408 262-7877
Ray Chen, *CEO*
Duan Wang, *President*
Gary Lu, *CFO*
Mina Chen, *Vice Pres*
Heman Liou, *Info Tech Mgr*
▲ EMP: 140
SQ FT: 50,000
SALES (est): 36.3MM
SALES (corp-wide): 29.4B **Privately Held**
WEB: www.bizcom-us.com
SIC: 5045 7629 7378 Computers; telecommunication equipment repair (except telephones); computer maintenance & repair
PA: Compal Electronics, Inc.
No. 581, 581-1, Ruiguang Rd.,
Taipei City TAP 11492
287 978-588

(P-7019)
BRAMASOL INC
3979 Freedom Cir Ste 620, Santa Clara
(95054-1262)
PHONE.................................408 831-0046
Dave Fellers, *CEO*
Jonathan Bell, *CFO*
EMP: 80
SQ FT: 2,000
SALES (est): 22.4MM **Privately Held**
WEB: www.bramasol.com
SIC: 5045 Computer software

(P-7020)
BROADWAY TYPEWRITER CO INC
Also Called: AREY JONES EDUCATIONAL SOLUTIO
1055 6th Ave Ste 101, San Diego
(92101-5229)
PHONE.................................800 998-9199
Michael Scarpella, *President*
David Scarpella, *CFO*
Peter Scarpella, *Vice Pres*
Margaret Scarpella, *Admin Sec*
Erik Pitti, *Technology*
EMP: 80 EST: 1968
SQ FT: 40,000
SALES: 101.1MM **Privately Held**
SIC: 5045 7378 Computers, peripherals & software; computer maintenance & repair

(P-7021)
C9 EDGE INC
177 Bovet Rd Ste 520, San Mateo
(94402-3144)
PHONE.................................650 561-7855
Michael Howard, *CEO*
Stephen Lucas, *CFO*
David Thompson, *Vice Pres*
Andy Twigg, *CTO*
Justin Shriber, *VP Prdtn*
EMP: 60
SQ FT: 10,000
SALES (est): 7.3MM **Privately Held**
SIC: 5045 Computer software

(P-7022)
CACI NSS INC
Also Called: Enganering and Technical Svcs
3201 Airpark Dr Ste 109, Santa Maria
(93455-1834)
PHONE.................................703 841-7800
Brad Bush, *Senior VP*
Deanna Cole, *Admin Asst*
Brenda Jordan, *Admin Asst*
Dave Haralson, *Project Engr*
Leita Ford, *QC Mgr*
EMP: 150
SALES (corp-wide): 4.4B **Publicly Held**
SIC: 5045 3663 Computers, peripherals & software; radio & TV communications equipment
HQ: Caci Nss, Inc.
11955 Freedom Dr Fl 2
Reston VA 20190
703 434-4000

(P-7023)
CASEWISE SYSTEMS INC (DH)
9465 Wilshire Blvd # 300, Beverly Hills
(90212-2612)
PHONE.................................424 284-4101
Alexandre Wentzo, *CEO*
Michael R Hodes, *CFO*
EMP: 85
SQ FT: 5,000
SALES: 9.7MM **Privately Held**
WEB: www.casewise.com
SIC: 5045 8742 7372 Computer software; management consulting services; business oriented computer software
HQ: Casewise Systems Limited
25 Grosvenor Street
London W1K 4
203 758-7250

(P-7024)
COMMERCIAL INDUS DESIGN CO INC
Also Called: C I Design
20372 N Sea Cir, Lake Forest
(92630-8806)
PHONE.................................949 273-6199
Jeff Wu, *CEO*
Kae J Lee, *President*
Matthew Martel, *Sales Staff*
▲ EMP: 60
SALES (est): 12.5MM **Privately Held**
WEB: www.cidesign.com
SIC: 5045 Computer peripheral equipment

(P-7025)
CONTEC MICROELECTRONICS USA
Also Called: Contec USA
17811 Gillette Ave Fl 1, Irvine
(92614-6501)
PHONE.................................949 250-4025
Fax: 408 400-9115
▲ EMP: 52
SQ FT: 4,500
SALES: 3.2MM **Privately Held**
SIC: 5045

(P-7026)
CREATIVE LABS INC (DH)
1901 Mccarthy Blvd, Milpitas (95035-7427)
PHONE.................................408 428-6600
Keh Long Ng, *CEO*
Russ Swerdon, *Owner*
Craig McHugh, *President*
Robert Gilsdorf, *Program Mgr*
Danielle Dunlap, *Executive Asst*
▲ EMP: 200
SQ FT: 57,000

SALES (est): 81.7MM
SALES (corp-wide): 69.9MM **Privately Held**
WEB: www.creativelabs.com
SIC: 5045 5734 3577 Computer peripheral equipment; computer & software stores; computer peripheral equipment

(P-7027)
CURVATURE LLC (DH)
6500 Hollister Ave # 210, Santa Barbara (93117-3011)
PHONE..............................800 230-6638
Peter Weber, *CEO*
Douglas Weinstein, *Partner*
Sanford Tassel, *CFO*
Sachi Thompson, *Exec VP*
Michael W Lodato, *Vice Pres*
◆ **EMP:** 300
SQ FT: 59,000
SALES (est): 311.1MM
SALES (corp-wide): 349MM **Privately Held**
WEB: www.networkhardware.com
SIC: 5045 7379 Computer peripheral equipment; computer related maintenance services
HQ: Nhr Newco Holdings Llc
6500 Hollister Ave # 210
Santa Barbara CA 93117
805 964-9975

(P-7028)
CYARA SOLUTIONS CORP
999 Main St Ste 101, Redwood City (94063-1903)
PHONE..............................650 549-8522
Alok Kulkarni, *CEO*
Phil Dur, *Partner*
James Isaacs, *President*
Mark Verbeck, *CFO*
Martin Doettling, *Chief Mktg Ofcr*
EMP: 143
SQ FT: 2,875
SALES (est): 4.7MM **Privately Held**
SIC: 5045 Computer software

(P-7029)
CYBERCSI INC
3511 Thomas Rd Ste 5, Santa Clara (95054-2039)
PHONE..............................408 727-2900
Dave Sanders, *CEO*
Darrell Miller, *CTO*
Bryan Bennett, *Software Dev*
Chris Herring, *Software Dev*
Tim Markos, *Technology*
EMP: 95
SQ FT: 11,000
SALES (est): 39.5MM **Privately Held**
SIC: 5045 7378 Computers, peripherals & software; computer maintenance & repair

(P-7030)
CYBERPOWER INC
730 Baldwin Park Blvd, City of Industry (91746-1503)
PHONE..............................626 813-7730
Stanley Kwong Ho, *CEO*
Eric Cheung, *President*
Judy Chen, *CFO*
Andy Kwok, *Business Dir*
Tjandra Afandi, *Information Mgr*
▲ **EMP:** 91
SQ FT: 100,000
SALES (est): 100MM **Privately Held**
WEB: www.cyberpowerpc.com
SIC: 5045 Computer peripheral equipment

(P-7031)
CYPHORT INC
1133 Innovation Way, Sunnyvale (94089-1228)
PHONE..............................408 841-4665
Manoj B Leelanivas, *CEO*
Gord Boyce, *Officer*
Fengmin Gong, *Officer*
Denis Eversen, *Vice Pres*
Anthony James, *Vice Pres*
EMP: 50
SQ FT: 10,000
SALES (est): 13.7MM **Privately Held**
SIC: 5045 Computer software

(P-7032)
D-LINK SYSTEMS INCORPORATED
Also Called: D - Link
17595 Mount Herrmann St, Fountain Valley (92708-4160)
PHONE..............................714 885-6000
Steven Joe, *President*
Carlos Casassus Fontecilla, *President*
A J Wang, *President*
Lou Reda, *Vice Pres*
April Richardson, *Executive*
▲ **EMP:** 164
SQ FT: 120,000
SALES: 122MM
SALES (corp-wide): 641.7MM **Privately Held**
WEB: www.dlink.com
SIC: 5045 3577 Computers; computer peripheral equipment
PA: D-Link Corporation
289, Sinhu 3rd Rd.,
Taipei City TAP 11494
266 000-123

(P-7033)
DATA EXCHANGE CORPORATION (PA)
Also Called: D E X
3600 Via Pescador, Camarillo (93012-5035)
PHONE..............................805 388-1711
Sheldon Malchicoff, *CEO*
Shawn Howie, *CFO*
Paul Gettings, *Exec VP*
▲ **EMP:** 300
SQ FT: 100,000
SALES (est): 132.4MM **Privately Held**
SIC: 5045 7378 Computers, peripherals & software; computer & data processing equipment repair/maintenance; computer peripheral equipment repair & maintenance

(P-7034)
DATALLEGRO INC
85 Enterprise Ste 200, Aliso Viejo (92656-2614)
PHONE..............................949 680-3000
Stuart Frost, *Ch of Bd*
Mark Theissen, *Vice Pres*
EMP: 100
SQ FT: 16,000
SALES (est): 10MM
SALES (corp-wide): 110.3B **Publicly Held**
WEB: www.datallegro.com
SIC: 5045 Computer software
PA: Microsoft Corporation
1 Microsoft Way
Redmond WA 98052
425 882-8080

(P-7035)
DEMAND CHAIN INC
Also Called: Homerun.com
301 Howard St Fl 20, San Francisco (94105-6670)
PHONE..............................800 466-3786
Brad Brodigan, *CEO*
EMP: 127
SALES (est): 13.4MM
SALES (corp-wide): 80.7MM **Privately Held**
SIC: 5045 Computer software
PA: Deem, Inc.
642 Harrison St Fl 2
San Francisco CA 94107
415 590-8300

(P-7036)
DFI TECHNOLOGIES LLC
1065 National Dr Ste 1, Sacramento (95834-2037)
P.O. Box 340759 (95834-0759)
PHONE..............................916 568-1234
David Lu, *President*
▲ **EMP:** 58
SQ FT: 50,000
SALES (est): 10.2MM
SALES (corp-wide): 123.5MM **Privately Held**
WEB: www.dfitech.com
SIC: 5045 Computers, peripherals & software

PA: Dfi Inc.
10f, 97, Xintai 5th Rd., Sec. 1,
New Taipei City 22175
226 972-986

(P-7037)
DIGIQUEST CORP
989 Talcey Ter, Riverside (92506-7517)
PHONE..............................951 776-4344
K B Reddy, *President*
EMP: 50
SALES (est): 3.5MM **Privately Held**
WEB: www.digiquestindia.com
SIC: 5045 7379 Computer peripheral equipment; computer related consulting services

(P-7038)
ELECTRIC CLOUD INC (PA)
125 S Market St Ste 400, San Jose (95113-2241)
PHONE..............................408 419-4300
Carmine Napolitano, *CEO*
John Ousterhout, *Ch of Bd*
Anders Wallgren, *President*
Steven Vattuone, *CFO*
Jim Ensell, *Chief Mktg Ofcr*
EMP: 55
SQ FT: 10,000
SALES (est): 29.8MM **Privately Held**
WEB: www.electric-cloud.com
SIC: 5045 Computer software

(P-7039)
ELITEGROUP CMPT SYSTEMS INC
6851 Mowry Ave, Newark (94560-4925)
PHONE..............................510 226-7333
Ray Lin, *CEO*
Lena Ruan, *Corp Secy*
See See Lo, *Principal*
Brenda Riveros, *Sales Executive*
▲ **EMP:** 200
SQ FT: 60,000
SALES (est): 50.2MM
SALES (corp-wide): 26.1MM **Privately Held**
SIC: 5045 Computer peripheral equipment
HQ: Elitegroup Computer Systems Holding Company (Inc)
6851 Mowry Ave
Newark CA 94560
510 794-2952

(P-7040)
ELO TOUCH SOLUTIONS INC (HQ)
670 N Mccarthy Blvd # 100, Milpitas (95035-5119)
PHONE..............................408 597-8000
Craig A Witsoe, *CEO*
Michael Duong, *Partner*
Dan Ludwick, *President*
Roxi Wen, *CFO*
John Lamb, *Chief Mktg Ofcr*
◆ **EMP:** 124
SQ FT: 75,000
SALES (est): 196.4MM
SALES (corp-wide): 4.5B **Privately Held**
SIC: 5045 Computers, peripherals & software
PA: The Gores Group Llc
9800 Wilshire Blvd
Beverly Hills CA 90212
310 209-3010

(P-7041)
EN POINTE TECHNOLOGIES SLS LLC
1940 E Mariposa Ave, El Segundo (90245-3457)
PHONE..............................310 337-6151
Frank Khulusi, *CEO*
Robert Miley, *President*
Brandon Laverne, *CFO*
EMP: 200
SQ FT: 29,032
SALES (est): 18.4MM
SALES (corp-wide): 2.1B **Publicly Held**
SIC: 5045 Computer peripheral equipment; computers
PA: Pcm, Inc.
1940 E Mariposa Ave
El Segundo CA 90245
310 354-5600

(P-7042)
ENDORSE CORP
60 E 3rd Ave, San Mateo (94401-4030)
PHONE..............................617 470-8332
Steven Carpenter, *CEO*
EMP: 752
SALES (est): 245.9K **Publicly Held**
SIC: 5045 Computer software
PA: Dropbox, Inc.
333 Brannan St
San Francisco CA 94107

(P-7043)
ENVIRONMENTAL SYSTEMS RESEARCH
1600 K St Ste 4c, Sacramento (95814-4022)
PHONE..............................916 448-2412
EMP: 76
SALES (corp-wide): 1B **Privately Held**
SIC: 5045 Computer software
PA: Environmental Systems Research Institute, Inc.
380 New York St
Redlands CA 92373
909 793-2853

(P-7044)
EON REALITY INC (PA)
39 Parker Ste 100, Irvine (92618-1605)
PHONE..............................949 460-2000
Dan I Lejerskar, *Chairman*
Mats Johansson, *President*
Sridhar Sunkad, *President*
Tyler Spring, *CFO*
Yann Froger, *Managing Dir*
EMP: 50
SQ FT: 16,000
SALES (est): 19.2MM **Privately Held**
WEB: www.eonreality.com
SIC: 5045 5734 Computer software; computer software & accessories

(P-7045)
EPHESOFT INC (PA)
8707 Research Dr, Irvine (92618-4217)
PHONE..............................949 335-5335
Ike Kavas, *CEO*
Naren Goel, *CFO*
Marco Zuffanelli, *Officer*
Richard Bosworth, *Senior VP*
David Talarico, *Vice Pres*
▼ **EMP:** 71
SQ FT: 3,600
SALES (est): 12.1MM **Privately Held**
SIC: 5045 Computer software

(P-7046)
ESET LLC (HQ)
Also Called: Eset North America
610 W Ash St Ste 1700, San Diego (92101-3373)
PHONE..............................619 876-5400
Anton Zajac, *President*
Kristina Hodge, *Partner*
Charlie Hurd, *Partner*
Warren Kamealoha, *Partner*
Sean Moran, *Partner*
EMP: 69
SQ FT: 57,000
SALES: 75.2MM
SALES (corp-wide): 554.3MM **Privately Held**
WEB: www.nod32.com
SIC: 5045 Computer software
PA: Eset, Spol. S R.O.
Einsteinova 24
Bratislava 85101
232 244-111

(P-7047)
EWORKPLACE SOLUTIONS INC
Also Called: Batchmaster Software
9861 Irvine Center Dr, Irvine (92618-4307)
PHONE..............................949 583-1646
Sahib Dudani, *President*
Bryan Forte, *Program Mgr*
Maria Figueroa, *Office Mgr*
Suraj Chouhan, *Sr Software Eng*
Amit Goyal, *Sr Software Eng*
EMP: 200
SQ FT: 5,000
SALES (est): 72.6MM **Privately Held**
WEB: www.batchmaster.com
SIC: 5045 Computer software

(P-7048)
F-SECURE INC
470 Ramona St, Palo Alto (94301-1707)
PHONE........................888 432-8233
Risto Siilasmaa, *Ch of Bd*
Mikko Peltola, *President*
Ilkka Starck, *Exec VP*
Janne Jarvinen, *Vice Pres*
Sean Obrey, *Vice Pres*
EMP: 50
SALES (est): 13.4MM
SALES (corp-wide): 200.1MM **Privately Held**
WEB: www.f-secure.com
SIC: 5045 Computer software
PA: F-Secure Oyj
    Tammasaarenkatu 7
    Helsinki 00180
    925 200-700

(P-7049)
FRYS ELECTRONICS INC
3600 N Sepulveda Blvd, Manhattan Beach (90266-3633)
PHONE........................310 364-3797
Joel Byer, *Manager*
EMP: 200
SALES (corp-wide): 21.8MM **Privately Held**
WEB: www.frys.com
SIC: 5045 5731 Computers, peripherals & software; radio, television & electronic stores
PA: Fry's Electronics, Inc.
    600 E Brokaw Rd
    San Jose CA 95112
    408 487-4500

(P-7050)
FUJITSU COMPUTER PDTS AMER INC (HQ)
1250 E Arques Ave, Sunnyvale (94085-5401)
PHONE........................408 746-7000
Etsuro Sato, *President*
Victor Kan, *COO*
Motoyasu Matsuzaki, *CFO*
Carlos Huang, *Accountant*
Dan Dalton, *Director*
▲ EMP: 340
SQ FT: 75,335
SALES (est): 93MM
SALES (corp-wide): 38.4B **Privately Held**
WEB: www.fcpa.com
SIC: 5045 Computer peripheral equipment
PA: Fujitsu Limited
    1-5-2, Higashishimbashi
    Minato-Ku TKY 105-0
    362 522-220

(P-7051)
GAR ENTERPRISES (PA)
Also Called: K G S Electronics
418 E Live Oak Ave, Arcadia (91006-5619)
PHONE........................626 574-1175
Nathan Sugimoto, *CEO*
Kazuo G Sugimoto, *Pastor*
EMP: 100 EST: 1960
SQ FT: 17,000
SALES (est): 34.4MM **Privately Held**
WEB: www.kgselectronics.com
SIC: 5045 3728 Anti-static equipment & devices; aircraft assemblies, subassemblies & parts

(P-7052)
GBT INC
Also Called: Gigabyte Technology
17358 Railroad St, City of Industry (91748-1023)
PHONE........................626 854-9338
Eric C Lu, *President*
James Liao, *Principal*
Olga Veko, *Marketing Mgr*
▲ EMP: 80
SQ FT: 35,000
SALES (est): 30.6MM
SALES (corp-wide): 1.9B **Privately Held**
WEB: www.giga-byte.com
SIC: 5045 Computers & accessories, personal & home entertainment
PA: Giga-Byte Technology Co., Ltd.
    5f, 6, Baoqiao Rd.,
    New Taipei City 23144
    289 124-000

(P-7053)
GENERAL DYNMICS MSSION SYSTEMS
250 S Milpitas Blvd, Milpitas (95035-5420)
PHONE........................954 846-3400
EMP: 208
SALES (corp-wide): 30.9B **Publicly Held**
SIC: 5045 7371 Computers, peripherals & software; custom computer programming services
HQ: General Dynamics Mission Systems, Inc.
    12450 Fair Lakes Cir # 200
    Fairfax VA 22033
    703 263-2800

(P-7054)
GENERAL PROCUREMENT INC (PA)
Also Called: Connect Computers
2601 Walnut Ave, Tustin (92780-7005)
PHONE........................949 679-7960
Imad Boukai, *President*
Sam Boukai, *Vice Pres*
▲ EMP: 50
SQ FT: 2,800
SALES (est): 101MM **Privately Held**
WEB: www.connect-computers.com
SIC: 5045 Computers, peripherals & software

(P-7055)
GENTEK MEDIA INC
13900 Sycamore Way, Chino (91710-7016)
PHONE........................909 476-3818
Gene Seto, *CEO*
▲ EMP: 50
SALES (est): 9.4MM **Privately Held**
WEB: www.gentekmedia.com
SIC: 5045 Computers, peripherals & software

(P-7056)
HITACHI VANTARA CORPORATION
15231 Ave Of Science # 100, San Diego (92128-3449)
PHONE........................858 537-3000
Hicham Abdessanad, *Vice Pres*
EMP: 200
SALES (corp-wide): 87.9B **Privately Held**
WEB: www.hds.com
SIC: 5045 7378 Computers; computer maintenance & repair
HQ: Hitachi Vantara Corporation
    2845 Lafayette St
    Santa Clara CA 95050
    408 970-1000

(P-7057)
HON HAI PRECISION INDUST LTD
500 S Kraemer Blvd # 100, Brea (92821-6763)
PHONE........................714 988-9388
Vincent Ho, *Manager*
EMP: 70
SALES (corp-wide): 60.3B **Privately Held**
SIC: 5045 Computers & accessories, personal & home entertainment
PA: Hon Hai Precision Industry Co., Ltd.
    66, Zhongshan Rd.,
    New Taipei City 23680
    222 683-477

(P-7058)
HONEYWELL INTERNATIONAL INC
1099 Sneath Ln, San Bruno (94066-2311)
PHONE........................650 918-3229
Cathy Ward, *Regional Mgr*
EMP: 60
SQ FT: 16,400
SALES (corp-wide): 40.5B **Publicly Held**
WEB: www.honeywell.com
SIC: 5045 7382 7381 Computer peripheral equipment; security systems services; detective & armored car services
PA: Honeywell International Inc.
    115 Tabor Rd
    Morris Plains NJ 07950
    973 455-2000

(P-7059)
HORIZON TECHNOLOGIES INC
Also Called: Horizon Systems
1270 Oakmead Pkwy Ste 115, Sunnyvale (94085-4031)
PHONE........................408 733-1530
Santosh Addagulla, *President*
EMP: 213
SALES (est): 27.1MM **Privately Held**
WEB: www.horizontechnol.com
SIC: 5045 Computers, peripherals & software

(P-7060)
I2C INC
1300 Island Dr Ste 105, Redwood City (94065-5170)
PHONE........................650 480-5222
Amir Wain, *CEO*
Ted Dargan, *Partner*
Christy Padilla, *President*
Scott Salmon, *President*
Charlie Noreen, *CFO*
EMP: 400 EST: 2000
SQ FT: 7,000
SALES (est): 146.5MM **Privately Held**
WEB: www.i2cinc.com
SIC: 5045 Computer software

(P-7061)
IMAGESTAT CORPORATION
2950 28th St, Santa Monica (90405)
PHONE........................310 392-1100
Robert G Milne III, *President*
EMP: 120
SQ FT: 8,000
SALES (est): 11.5MM **Privately Held**
WEB: www.imagestat.com
SIC: 5045 7334 Computers, peripherals & software; photocopying & duplicating services

(P-7062)
INFRASCALE INC
Also Called: SOS Hosting
999 N Pacific Coast Hwy # 100, El Segundo (90245-2719)
PHONE........................310 878-2621
Ken Shaw Jr, *Principal*
Michael Bell, *President*
Kenneth Shaw, *CEO*
Hardy Parungao, *CFO*
Bill Falk, *Risk Mgmt Dir*
EMP: 140
SQ FT: 8,000
SALES: 14MM **Privately Held**
SIC: 5045 7372 Computers, peripherals & software; computer software; business oriented computer software

(P-7063)
INGRAM MICRO INC (HQ)
3351 Michelson Dr Ste 100, Irvine (92612-0697)
PHONE........................714 566-1000
Alain Monie, *CEO*
Gina Mastantuono, *CFO*
Ramesh Nair, *CFO*
Augusto P Aragone, *Exec VP*
Paul Bay, *Exec VP*
◆ EMP: 4000 EST: 1979
SALES: 43B
SALES (corp-wide): 47.6B **Privately Held**
WEB: www.ingrammicro.com
SIC: 5045 Computer software
PA: Hna Technology Co., Ltd.
    Rm 2801, Tianjin Center, No.219,
    Nanjing Road, Heping District
    Tianjin 30005
    225 867-9088

(P-7064)
INSIDEVIEW TECHNOLOGIES INC
444 De Haro St Ste 210, San Francisco (94107-2398)
PHONE........................415 728-9309
Umberto Milletti, *CEO*
Janice Bowen, *Partner*
Tracy Eiler, *Chief Mktg Ofcr*
Gordon Anderson, *Vice Pres*
Lisa Bailey, *Vice Pres*
EMP: 150
SALES (est): 72.3MM **Privately Held**
SIC: 5045 Computer software

(P-7065)
IXOS SOFTWARE INC (PA)
8717 Research Dr, Irvine (92618-4200)
PHONE........................949 784-8000
Mark Smith, *CFO*
EMP: 100
SQ FT: 30,000
SALES (est): 40.1MM **Privately Held**
WEB: www.ixos.com
SIC: 5045 Computer software

(P-7066)
JAG SOFTWARE INC
2235 Skyline Dr, Milpitas (95035-6682)
PHONE........................408 262-0572
Suresh Kottappalli, *President*
EMP: 69
SQ FT: 2,400
SALES (est): 7.1MM **Privately Held**
WEB: www.jagsoftware.com
SIC: 5045 Computer software

(P-7067)
JAGUAR COMPUTER SYSTEMS INC
4135 Indus Way, Riverside (92503-4848)
PHONE........................951 273-7950
Joan E Hoanzl, *President*
George Hoanzl, *Vice Pres*
EMP: 50
SQ FT: 17,000
SALES (est): 6.6MM **Privately Held**
WEB: www.jaguarcomputersystems.com
SIC: 5045 8742 7378 Computer peripheral equipment; marketing consulting services; computer maintenance & repair

(P-7068)
K-MICRO INC
Also Called: Corpinfo Services
1618 Stanford St, Santa Monica (90404-4114)
PHONE........................310 442-3200
Michael Sabourian, *President*
Ahmad Gramian, *Vice Pres*
EMP: 96
SQ FT: 25,000
SALES: 16.6MM **Privately Held**
SIC: 5045 7378 7373 7371 Computers & accessories, personal & home entertainment; computer maintenance & repair; computer integrated systems design; custom computer programming services

(P-7069)
LASERTECH COMPUTER DISTR INC
139 N Sunset Ave, City of Industry (91744-1850)
PHONE........................626 435-2800
Tony Ho, *President*
Annie Ho, *Admin Sec*
Kitty Lam, *Controller*
▲ EMP: 70
SQ FT: 28,000
SALES (est): 9.1MM **Privately Held**
WEB: www.ltcom.com
SIC: 5045 5734 Computer peripheral equipment; computer & software stores

(P-7070)
LD PRODUCTS INC
Also Called: 4inkjets.com
3700 Cover St, Long Beach (90808-1782)
PHONE........................562 986-6940
Aaron Leon, *CEO*
Patrick Devane, *Senior VP*
Frank Farina, *Marketing Staff*
◆ EMP: 150
SQ FT: 25,000
SALES (est): 119.3MM **Privately Held**
WEB: www.ldproducts.com
SIC: 5045 2621 Printers, computer; stationery, envelope & tablet papers

(P-7071)
LITE-ON SALES AND DIST INC
726 S Hillview Dr, Milpitas (95035-5455)
PHONE........................510 687-1800
Ren-Wu Gong, *President*
Lando Lin, *CEO*
Chin-Sou Tsai Hong, *CFO*
June Ly, *Administration*
Norlis Amaya, *Engineer*
▲ EMP: 100

SQ FT: 8,100
SALES (est): 13.7MM
SALES (corp-wide): 7.1B **Privately Held**
SIC: 5045 Computer peripheral equipment
PA: Lite-On Technology Corporation
　22f, 392, Ruey Kuang Rd.,
　Taipei City TAP 11492
　287 982-888

(P-7072)
LIVESCRIBE INC
930 Roosevelt, Irvine (92620-3664)
PHONE..................503 290-4029
Gilles Bouchard, *CEO*
Ken Cucarola, *CFO*
Paul Machle, *CFO*
Brett Halle, *Senior VP*
Sherri Schultz, *Administration*
▲ EMP: 50
SQ FT: 24,000
SALES (est): 22.2MM
SALES (corp-wide): 20.5MM **Privately Held**
WEB: www.livescribe.com
SIC: 5045 Computer software
PA: Anoto Group Ab
　Traktorvagen 11
　Lund 226 6
　465 401-200

(P-7073)
MAGNELL ASSOCIATE INC (DH)
Also Called: A B S
17560 Rowland St, City of Industry
(91748-1114)
PHONE..................626 271-9700
James Wu, *CEO*
Craig Hayes, *Vice Pres*
Elizabeth Rojo, *Administration*
Albert Chong, *Info Tech Mgr*
Daniel Hu, *Manager*
◆ EMP: 130
SALES (est): 2B
SALES (corp-wide): 1.8B **Privately Held**
SIC: 5045 Computers & accessories, personal & home entertainment
HQ: Newegg Inc.
　17560 Rowland St
　City Of Industry CA 91748
　626 271-9700

(P-7074)
MAGNELL ASSOCIATE INC
Also Called: ABS Computer Technologies
18045 Rowland St, City of Industry
(91748-1205)
PHONE..................626 271-1580
Fred Chang, *President*
EMP: 100
SALES (corp-wide): 1.8B **Privately Held**
SIC: 5045 Computers & accessories, personal & home entertainment
HQ: Magnell Associate, Inc.
　17560 Rowland St
　City Of Industry CA 91748
　626 271-9700

(P-7075)
MARIADB USA INC
350 Bay St Ste 100-319, San Francisco
(94133-1966)
PHONE..................847 562-9000
Michael Howard, *CEO*
Juha Aropaltio, *Controller*
EMP: 100
SALES: 34MM **Privately Held**
SIC: 5045 Computer software

(P-7076)
MAX GROUP CORPORATION (PA)
17011 Green Dr, City of Industry
(91745-1800)
PHONE..................626 935-0050
Su-Tzu Tsai, *CEO*
Chung-Jen Tsai, *President*
◆ EMP: 65
SQ FT: 120,000
SALES (est): 87.9MM **Privately Held**
WEB: www.maxgroup.com
SIC: 5045 Computer peripheral equipment; disk drives; keying equipment; printers; computer

(P-7077)
MBH ENTERPRISES INC
1430 Franklin St Ste 201, Oakland
(94612-3209)
PHONE..................510 302-6680
Michael B Hudson, *CEO*
David Rubin, *Exec VP*
EMP: 55
SALES (est): 3.7MM **Privately Held**
SIC: 5045 Computers, peripherals & software

(P-7078)
MEMORY TO GO
10801 National Blvd # 101, Los Angeles
(90064-4139)
PHONE..................310 446-0111
Isaac Faliz, *President*
EMP: 100
SALES (est): 11.3MM **Privately Held**
WEB: www.memorytogo.com
SIC: 5045 Computers, peripherals & software

(P-7079)
MICRO-TECHNOLOGY CONCEPTS INC
Also Called: M T C
17837 Rowland St, City of Industry
(91748-1122)
PHONE..................626 839-6800
Roy Han, *President*
Richard Shyu, *Senior VP*
Alan D'Jen, *Mktg Dir*
Alan Djen, *Mktg Dir*
Faye Teng, *Sales Associate*
▲ EMP: 85
SQ FT: 42,500
SALES (est): 59.7MM
SALES (corp-wide): 16.3MM **Privately Held**
WEB: www.mtcusa.com
SIC: 5045 Computer peripheral equipment
PA: Mtc Direct, Inc.
　17837 Rowland St
　City Of Industry CA 91748
　626 839-6800

(P-7080)
MITSUBA CORPORATION
2509 Reata Pl, Diamond Bar (91765-3661)
PHONE..................909 374-2631
Jen Jon Chen, *President*
Monica Chen, *Corp Secy*
EMP: 75
SQ FT: 40,000
SALES (est): 6.7MM **Privately Held**
SIC: 5045 Computer peripheral equipment; computers; computer software

(P-7081)
MSI COMPUTER CORP (HQ)
901 Canada Ct, City of Industry
(91748-1136)
PHONE..................626 913-0828
Andy Tung, *CEO*
Connie Chang, *CFO*
David Wu, *Vice Pres*
Renee Gastellum, *Office Mgr*
Tommy MO, *Technical Staff*
◆ EMP: 90
SQ FT: 77,500
SALES (est): 31.8MM
SALES (corp-wide): 3.5B **Privately Held**
WEB: www.msicomputer.com
SIC: 5045 Computer peripheral equipment
PA: Micro-Star International Co., Ltd.
　69, Li Te St.,
　New Taipei City 23584
　232 345-599

(P-7082)
MTC DIRECT INC (PA)
17837 Rowland St, City of Industry
(91748-1122)
PHONE..................626 839-6800
Roy Han, *CEO*
Helena Cheung, *Credit Mgr*
Brian Wang, *VP Sales*
▲ EMP: 106
SQ FT: 41,000
SALES (est): 16.3MM **Privately Held**
SIC: 5045 Computer peripheral equipment

(P-7083)
MTC WORLDWIDE CORP
17837 Rowland St, City of Industry
(91748-1122)
PHONE..................626 839-6800
Roy Han, *Principal*
▲ EMP: 79
SQ FT: 42,500
SALES (est): 29.5MM
SALES (corp-wide): 16.3MM **Privately Held**
WEB: www.mtcdirect.com
SIC: 5045 3577 Computer peripheral equipment; computer peripheral equipment
PA: Mtc Direct, Inc.
　17837 Rowland St
　City Of Industry CA 91748
　626 839-6800

(P-7084)
NEXINFO SOLUTIONS INC
8502 E Chapman Ave # 364, Orange
(92869-2461)
PHONE..................714 368-1452
Arun Cavale, *President*
Sahil Gupta, *Technical Staff*
Wilma Flanagan, *Director*
Moises Oropeza, *Assistant*
Mahesh Naalla, *Consultant*
EMP: 50
SALES: 5MM **Privately Held**
SIC: 5045 8742 Computer software; management consulting services

(P-7085)
NHR NEWCO HOLDINGS LLC (HQ)
6500 Hollister Ave # 210, Santa Barbara
(93117-3011)
PHONE..................805 964-9975
Peter Weber, *CEO*
Genichi Ishii, *President*
Sachi Thompson, *COO*
Sanford Tassel, *CFO*
Betty Silva, *Officer*
EMP: 101
SALES (est): 311.1MM
SALES (corp-wide): 349MM **Privately Held**
SIC: 5045 Computers, peripherals & software
PA: Curvature, Inc.
　2810 Coliseum Centre Dr
　Charlotte NC 28217
　704 921-1620

(P-7086)
ORACLE AMERICA INC
500 Oracle Pkwy, Redwood City
(94065-1677)
PHONE..................800 633-0584
EMP: 58
SALES (corp-wide): 39.8B **Publicly Held**
SIC: 5045 8731 Computer software; computer (hardware) development
HQ: Oracle America, Inc.
　500 Oracle Pkwy
　Redwood City CA 94065
　650 506-7000

(P-7087)
PARASOFT CORPORATION (PA)
101 E Huntington Dr Fl 2, Monrovia
(91016-3496)
PHONE..................626 256-3680
Elzbieta Kolawa, *President*
Erika Delgado, *Marketing Staff*
Jim Clune, *Director*
EMP: 50
SALES (est): 28MM **Privately Held**
WEB: www.foodmagic.com
SIC: 5045 7371 8748 Computers; computer software development; systems engineering consultant, ex. computer or professional

(P-7088)
PAYDARFAR INDUSTRIES INC
Also Called: Saratech
26054 Acero, Mission Viejo (92691-2768)
PHONE..................949 481-3267
Saeed Paydarfar PHD, *CEO*
Caden Reiman, *Info Tech Mgr*
Daniel Nadeau, *Technology*
Daniel Rubio, *Engineer*
Jason West, *Engineer*
EMP: 60
SQ FT: 5,930
SALES (est): 39.4MM **Privately Held**
SIC: 5045 8711 7372 7373 Computer software; engineering services; prepackaged software; value-added resellers; computer systems; computer-aided design (CAD) systems service; computer-aided engineering (CAE) systems service

(P-7089)
PCM SALES INC (HQ)
Also Called: Micro P Technologies
1940 E Mariposa Ave, El Segundo
(90245-3457)
PHONE..................310 354-5600
Joseph Hayek, *CEO*
Mike M Mogavero, *President*
Kristin Rogers, *President*
Peter Freix, *CEO*
Greg Richey, *CEO*
▼ EMP: 153
SALES (est): 1.4B
SALES (corp-wide): 2.1B **Publicly Held**
WEB: www.pcmall.com
SIC: 5045 Computers, peripherals & software
PA: Pcm, Inc.
　1940 E Mariposa Ave
　El Segundo CA 90245
　310 354-5600

(P-7090)
PENGUIN COMPUTING INC (DH)
45800 Northport Loop W, Fremont
(94538-6413)
PHONE..................415 954-2800
Tom Coull, *President*
Lisa Cummins, *CFO*
Ford Jacobs, *Officer*
Daniel Dowling, *Vice Pres*
Barbara Fernandez, *Executive Asst*
▲ EMP: 85
SQ FT: 86,000
SALES: 166.5MM
SALES (corp-wide): 1.2B **Publicly Held**
WEB: www.penguincomputing.com
SIC: 5045 7371 7379 Computer software; custom computer programming services; computer related maintenance services

(P-7091)
PHIHONG USA CORP (HQ)
47800 Fremont Blvd, Fremont
(94538-6551)
PHONE..................510 445-0100
Fei Hung Alex Lin, *President*
Emily Tsai, *Finance*
▲ EMP: 58
SQ FT: 33,000
SALES (est): 118.8MM
SALES (corp-wide): 374.9MM **Privately Held**
WEB: www.phihong.com
SIC: 5045 3572 Computer peripheral equipment; computer disk & drum drives & components
PA: Phihong Technology Co., Ltd.
　568, Fusing 3rd Rd.,
　Taoyuan City TAY 33383
　332 772-88

(P-7092)
POWER FACTORS LLC
80 E Sir Francis Drake Bl, Larkspur
(94939-1709)
PHONE..................415 299-7448
Steve Scales, *Mng Member*
Charlie Driscoll, *Administration*
Will Troppe, *Senior Engr*
Jeremy Baxter, *Manager*
EMP: 55
SALES (est): 3.8MM **Privately Held**
SIC: 5045 Computer software

(P-7093)
PRIVATE LABEL PC LLC
748 Epperson Dr Ste B, City of Industry
(91748-1336)
PHONE..................626 965-8686
Rachel Luke, *Mng Member*
Chris Luke, *Treasurer*
Blake Nagle, *Business Mgr*
Frank Wang, *Manager*
Jonathan Wang, *Manager*

▲ EMP: 120
SALES (est): 57.9MM **Privately Held**
WEB: www.vistapc.com
SIC: 5045 Computer peripheral equipment

(P-7094)
PROFICIO INC (PA)
3264 Grey Hawk Ct, Carlsbad
(92010-6651)
PHONE...................................800 779-5042
Brad Taylor, *President*
Tim McElwee, *COO*
Dustin Ritter, *Chief Mktg Ofcr*
Dickon Smart-Gill, *Senior VP*
Paul Hennebury, *Vice Pres*
EMP: 50
SQ FT: 5,000
SALES (est): 29.3MM **Privately Held**
SIC: 5045 Computer software

(P-7095)
PROMISE TECHNOLOGY INC
580 Cottonwood Dr, Milpitas (95035-7403)
PHONE...................................408 228-1400
Tung-Hsu Lin, *CEO*
James Lee, *President*
Edward Lin, *CFO*
Corrina Villalovos, *Administration*
Esteban Guzman Ptu, *Technician*
▲ EMP: 80
SQ FT: 40,000
SALES (est): 60.2MM
SALES (corp-wide): 60.8MM **Privately Held**
WEB: www.promise.com
SIC: 5045 7379 Computers, peripherals &
   software; data processing consultant
PA: Promise Technology Inc.
   2f, 30, Industry E. 9th Rd., Hsinchu
   Science-Based Ind. Park
   Paoshan Hsiang HSI 30075
   357 823-95

(P-7096)
QUADRANT COMPONENTS INC
46567 Fremont Blvd, Fremont
(94538-6409)
PHONE...................................510 656-9988
Chad Yau, *Ch of Bd*
Wenli Yau, *CFO*
▲ EMP: 80
SQ FT: 30,000
SALES (est): 9MM **Privately Held**
WEB: www.quadrant.com
SIC: 5045 3679 Computers, peripherals &
   software; electronic circuits

(P-7097)
RAVIG INC
Also Called: Salient Global Technologies
510 Garcia Ave Ste E, Pittsburg
(94565-7405)
PHONE...................................925 526-1234
Ravikanth Ganapavarapu, *CEO*
Ravi Ganapa, *General Mgr*
William Lee, *Director*
EMP: 60
SQ FT: 34,000
SALES (est): 2.7MM **Privately Held**
SIC: 5045 7373 3571 Computers, periph-
   erals & software; systems software devel-
   opment services; electronic computers

(P-7098)
ROLAND DGA CORPORATION (HQ)
15363 Barranca Pkwy, Irvine (92618-2216)
PHONE...................................949 727-2100
David Goward, *President*
Andrew Oransky, *President*
Bruce Lauper, *CFO*
Arturo Alvarado, *Admin Asst*
Nick Potawsky, *Administration*
◆ EMP: 105
SQ FT: 53,000
SALES: 119.4MM
SALES (corp-wide): 388.8MM **Privately Held**
WEB: www.rolanddga.com
SIC: 5045 8741 Computer peripheral
   equipment; management services
PA: Roland Dg Corporation
   1-6-4, Shimmiyakoda, Kita-Ku
   Hamamatsu SZO 431-2
   534 841-200

(P-7099)
SALESTAR LLC (PA)
300 Lakeside Dr Fl 11, Oakland
(94612-3534)
PHONE...................................510 637-4700
David Joseph-Lacagnina, *President*
EMP: 60
SQ FT: 11,000
SALES (est): 5.9MM **Privately Held**
SIC: 5045 7372 Computer software;
   prepackaged software

(P-7100)
SANYO DENKI AMERICA INC (HQ)
468 Amapola Ave, Torrance (90501-1474)
PHONE...................................310 783-5400
Stan Kato, *CEO*
Rieko Suzuki, *Executive*
June Fujii, *Human Resources*
Zhiping Yu, *Regl Sales Mgr*
Joshua Green, *Sales Associate*
▲ EMP: 52
SQ FT: 45,000
SALES (est): 30MM
SALES (corp-wide): 658.1MM **Privately Held**
WEB: www.sanyo-denki.com
SIC: 5045 7373 Computers & acces-
   sories, personal & home entertainment;
   computer-aided system services
PA: Sanyo Denki Co.,Ltd.
   3-33-1, Minamiotsuka
   Toshima-Ku TKY 170-0
   359 271-020

(P-7101)
SEGA OF AMERICA INC
350 Rhode Island St # 400, San Francisco
(94103-5188)
PHONE...................................415 701-6000
Mike Hayes, *CEO*
Masanao Maeda, *President*
John Cheng, *CFO*
Naoya Tsurumi, *Chairman*
Irene Gregorio, *Info Tech Mgr*
EMP: 165
SQ FT: 70,000
SALES (est): 94.3MM
SALES (corp-wide): 3B **Privately Held**
SIC: 5045 5092 Computers & acces-
   sories, personal & home entertainment;
   video games
HQ: Sega Of America, Inc.
   6400 Oak Cyn Ste 100
   Irvine CA 92618
   415 806-0169

(P-7102)
SIGMANET INC (HQ)
4290 E Brickell St, Ontario (91761-1524)
PHONE...................................909 230-7500
Ahmed Al Khatib, *CEO*
Neil Wada, *President*
Apo Hagopian, *Senior VP*
Laura Avila, *Admin Asst*
Daniel Omeh, *Network Enginr*
EMP: 153
SQ FT: 100,000
SALES (est): 296.6MM **Privately Held**
WEB: www.sigmanet.com
SIC: 5045 7373 Computers, peripherals &
   software; computer integrated systems
   design

(P-7103)
SK HYNIX AMERICA INC (HQ)
3101 N 1st St, San Jose (95134-1934)
PHONE...................................408 232-8000
Kun Chul Suh, *CEO*
Jae H Park, *President*
Richard H Chin, *Chief Mktg Ofcr*
Lisa Schmidt, *Vice Pres*
David Yoo, *Vice Pres*
▲ EMP: 80
SQ FT: 190,000
SALES (est): 301.9MM
SALES (corp-wide): 27.1B **Privately Held**
SIC: 5045 5065 Computer peripheral
   equipment; semiconductor devices
PA: Sk Hynix Inc.
   2091 Gyeongchung-Daero, Bubal-Eup
   Icheon 17336
   823 163-0411

(P-7104)
SMC NETWORKS INC (HQ)
20 Mason, Irvine (92618-2706)
PHONE...................................949 679-8029
Alex Kim, *CEO*
Inho Kim, *President*
Frank Kuo, *President*
Lane Ruoff, *CFO*
▲ EMP: 80 EST: 1971
SQ FT: 22,650
SALES (est): 25.3MM
SALES (corp-wide): 1.2B **Privately Held**
WEB: www.smc.com
SIC: 5045 Computer peripheral equipment
PA: Accton Technology Corporation
   1, Creation 3rd Rd.., Science-Based In-
   dustrial Park,
   Hsinchu City 30077
   357 702-70

(P-7105)
SOLVER INC
10780 Santa Monica Blvd # 370, Los Ange-
les (90025-4779)
PHONE...................................310 691-5300
Nils Rasmussen, *President*
Corey Barak, *COO*
Hadrian Knotz, *CIO*
Michael Applegate, *CTO*
EMP: 50
SQ FT: 5,000
SALES: 10.5MM **Privately Held**
WEB: www.solverusa.com
SIC: 5045 7379 7374 Computer software;
   computer related consulting services;
   data processing & preparation

(P-7106)
SOMANSA TECHNOLOGIES INC
3003 N 1st St 301, San Jose (95134-2004)
PHONE...................................408 297-1234
Suk Won Kwon, *CEO*
EMP: 60
SALES (est): 1.5MM **Privately Held**
SIC: 5045 Computers, peripherals & soft-
   ware

(P-7107)
SOUTHLAND TECHNOLOGY INC
8053 Vickers St, San Diego (92111-1917)
PHONE...................................858 694-0932
Grace Pedigo, *CEO*
Robert Pedigo, *President*
Brandon Collins, *Design Engr*
Darrin Lee, *Design Engr*
Evan Young, *Project Mgr*
EMP: 65
SQ FT: 16,000
SALES (est): 60.1MM **Privately Held**
WEB: www.southlandtechnology.com
SIC: 5045 8748 7373 7379 Computer
   peripheral equipment; systems engineer-
   ing consultant, ex. computer or profes-
   sional; computer integrated systems
   design; computer related maintenance
   services; home entertainment computer
   software

(P-7108)
SPACE AGE METAL PRODUCTS INC
23605 Telo Ave, Torrance (90505-4028)
PHONE...................................310 539-5500
Arnold Klein, *CEO*
Emma Klein, *Corp Secy*
EMP: 200
SQ FT: 20,000
SALES (est): 16.4MM **Privately Held**
SIC: 5045 Computer peripheral equipment

(P-7109)
SPOTCUES INC
Also Called: Smartcues Inc
1975 W El Cmno Real 301, Mountain View
(94040)
PHONE...................................408 435-2700
Jay Pullur, *President*
Vijay Pullur, *President*
K V Prasad, *Vice Pres*
Dimple Pandya, *Executive*
Narasimha Gadepalli, *Info Tech Dir*
EMP: 700 EST: 2001

SALES: 6MM **Privately Held**
WEB: www.pramati.com
SIC: 5045 Computer peripheral equipment
PA: Pramati Technologies Private Limited
   No-301, Block-1 White House
   Hyderabad TS
   -

(P-7110)
SQUARE ENIX INC
999 N Pacific Coast Hwy # 3, El Segundo
(90245-2731)
PHONE...................................310 846-0400
Mike Fischer, *President*
Clinton Foy, *COO*
Kazuharu Watanabe, *CFO*
Michihiro Sasaki, *Officer*
Phil Rogers, *Principal*
▲ EMP: 110
SALES (est): 60.5MM
SALES (corp-wide): 2.3B **Privately Held**
SIC: 5045 7372 Computer software; pub-
   lishers' computer software
HQ: Square Enix Of America Holdings, Inc.
   999 N Pacific Coast Hwy # 3
   El Segundo CA 90245

(P-7111)
SUPER TALENT TECHNOLOGY CORP
2077 N Capitol Ave, San Jose
(95132-1009)
PHONE...................................408 957-8133
Abraham MA, *President*
◆ EMP: 670
SALES (est): 91MM **Privately Held**
WEB: www.superlightwave.com
SIC: 5045 Computer peripheral equipment

(P-7112)
SWANN COMMUNICATIONS USA INC
12636 Clark St, Santa Fe Springs
(90670-3950)
PHONE...................................562 777-2551
Keith Oldridge, *President*
Jeffrey Lew, *Chairman*
Dennis McTighe, *Vice Pres*
Guy Pithie, *Vice Pres*
Kane Chan, *Manager*
◆ EMP: 87
SQ FT: 45,000
SALES (est): 120MM **Privately Held**
WEB: www.swann.com
SIC: 5045 7382 Computers, peripherals &
   software; security systems services

(P-7113)
SWITCHFLY INC (PA)
601 Montgomery St Fl 17, San Francisco
(94111-2621)
PHONE...................................415 541-9100
Daniel Farrar, *CEO*
Jared Wright, *Administration*
Graham Blankenbaker, *CTO*
Kerry Griffin, *Manager*
EMP: 100
SALES (est): 38MM **Privately Held**
SIC: 5045 Computer software

(P-7114)
SYSPRO IMPACT SOFTWARE INC
959 S Coast Dr Ste 100, Costa Mesa
(92626-1786)
PHONE...................................714 437-1000
Brian Stein, *CEO*
Joey Benadretti, *President*
Dawna Olsen, *Chief Mktg Ofcr*
Kristin Valentyn, *Risk Mgmt Dir*
Keith Sponseller, *Info Tech Mgr*
EMP: 200
SALES (est): 78.1MM **Privately Held**
WEB: www.syspro.com
SIC: 5045 7372 7371 Computer software;
   prepackaged software; custom computer
   programming services

PRODUCTS & SVCS

(P-7115)
THOMAS GALLAWAY CORPORATION (PA)
Also Called: Technologent
100 Spectrum Center Dr # 700, Irvine (92618-4962)
PHONE..................................949 716-9500
Lezlie L Gallaway, CEO
Dori Stuchinsky, Partner
Marco Mohajer, President
Tom Gallaway, Chairman
Jim Bevis, Vice Pres
EMP: 70
SQ FT: 4,500
SALES (est): 391.6MM Privately Held
WEB: www.technologent.com
SIC: 5045 Computers, peripherals & software

(P-7116)
TIDEBREAK INC
958 San Leandro Ave # 500, Mountain View (94043-1995)
P.O. Box 855, Palo Alto (94302-0855)
PHONE..................................650 289-9869
Andrew J Milne, CEO
Brad Johanson, CTO
EMP: 80
SALES (est): 6.6MM Privately Held
SIC: 5045 Computers, peripherals & software

(P-7117)
TONER SUPPLY USA INC
Also Called: Tsu Corporate Services
8055 Lankershim Blvd # 11, North Hollywood (91605-1628)
PHONE..................................818 504-6540
Omar Bian, President
Gus Obregon, Vice Pres
▲ EMP: 50
SQ FT: 120,000
SALES (est): 7.6MM Privately Held
SIC: 5045 7378 Computer peripheral equipment; computer peripheral equipment repair & maintenance

(P-7118)
TRANQUILMONEY INC
5823 Ruddy Duck Ct, Stockton (95207-4518)
PHONE..................................800 979-6739
EMP: 75
SALES (corp-wide): 10.9MM Privately Held
SIC: 5045 Computers, peripherals & software
PA: Tranquilmoney Inc.
461 Vose Ave
South Orange NJ 07079
212 494-0383

(P-7119)
TREND MICRO INCORPORATED
10101 N De Anza Blvd, Cupertino (95014-2264)
PHONE..................................408 257-1500
Anrew Lai, Branch Mgr
EMP: 67
SALES (corp-wide): 1.3B Privately Held
SIC: 5045 7382 7372 Computer software; security systems services; prepackaged software
HQ: Trend Micro Incorporated
225 E John Carpenter Fwy # 1500
Irving TX 75062
408 257-1500

(P-7120)
TRENDNET INC (PA)
20675 Manhattan Pl, Torrance (90501-1827)
PHONE..................................310 961-5500
Pei Cheng Huang, President
Peggy Huang, CFO
Jaime Castro, General Mgr
Steve Kuo, Technology
Eddie Shih, Accounting Mgr
◆ EMP: 80
SQ FT: 90,000
SALES (est): 22.1MM Privately Held
WEB: www.trendware.com
SIC: 5045 Computer peripheral equipment

(P-7121)
TRIVAD INC
1350 Bayshore Hwy Ste 450, Burlingame (94010-1833)
PHONE..................................650 286-1086
Jenna Lim, CEO
William Allen, Vice Pres
Dave Thompson, Vice Pres
Hans Lim, General Mgr
Margaret Lee, Purch Mgr
EMP: 150
SQ FT: 6,000
SALES (est): 67.2MM Privately Held
WEB: www.trivad.com
SIC: 5045 7373 5734 3721 Computers, peripherals & software; computer integrated systems design; computer & software stores; airplanes, fixed or rotary wing; airborne radio communications equipment; search & navigation equipment; aircraft control systems, electronic; navigational systems & instruments

(P-7122)
TW SECURITY CORP (DH)
5 Park Plz Ste 400, Irvine (92614-8524)
PHONE..................................949 932-1000
John Vigouroux, CEO
Bruce Green, COO
Rodney S Miller, CFO
William Kilmer, Chief Mktg Ofcr
Paul D Myer, Senior VP
EMP: 120
SQ FT: 28,000
SALES (est): 32.7MM
SALES (corp-wide): 13.3B Privately Held
WEB: www.marhsa18e6.com
SIC: 5045 Computer software
HQ: Trustwave Holdings, Inc.
70 W Madison St Ste 600
Chicago IL 60602
312 750-0950

(P-7123)
TYAN COMPUTER CORPORATION
3288 Laurelview Ct, Fremont (94538-6535)
PHONE..................................510 651-8868
Jhi-Wu Ho, CEO
James Sytwu, Exec VP
Eric Cho, Senior VP
Danny Hsu, Vice Pres
George Koivun, Vice Pres
◆ EMP: 85
SALES (est): 23.6MM
SALES (corp-wide): 1.6B Privately Held
WEB: www.tyan.com
SIC: 5045 Computers, peripherals & software
HQ: Mitac Computing Technology Corporation
3f, No. 1, Yanfa 2nd Rd., Hsinchu Science Industrial Park
Hsinchu City
357 790-88

(P-7124)
UNICAL ENTERPRISES INC
Also Called: Northwestern Bell Telephones
16960 Gale Ave, City of Industry (91745-1805)
PHONE..................................626 965-5588
Frank Liu, President
Rebecca Tsui, Vice Pres
▲ EMP: 65
SQ FT: 72,000
SALES (est): 8.5MM Privately Held
WEB: www.unical-usa.com
SIC: 5045 5065 Terminals, computer; telephone & telegraphic equipment

(P-7125)
UPGRADEDETECT INC (PA)
Also Called: Goldenram
3303 Harbor Blvd Ste D7, Costa Mesa (92626-1519)
PHONE..................................949 460-9000
Christ Zomaya, CEO
Karen Zomaya, Vice Pres
Joey Zomaya, Natl Sales Mgr
EMP: 75
SALES (est): 16.5MM Privately Held
SIC: 5045 Computer peripheral equipment

(P-7126)
VALGENESIS INC
395 Oyster Point Blvd # 228, South San Francisco (94080-1930)
PHONE..................................510 445-0505
Siva Samy, President
Shanti Mulyadi, Manager
▼ EMP: 50
SQ FT: 1,000
SALES (est): 7.5MM Privately Held
SIC: 5045 7371 Computer software; computer software development & applications

(P-7127)
VIEWSONIC CORPORATION (PA)
10 Pointe Dr Ste 200, Brea (92821-7620)
PHONE..................................909 444-8888
James Chu, Ch of Bd
Jeff Volpe, President
Sung Yi, CFO
Brian Igoe, Vice Pres
Caroline Lin, Vice Pres
◆ EMP: 140
SQ FT: 298,050
SALES (est): 500MM Privately Held
WEB: www.viewsonic.com
SIC: 5045 Computer peripheral equipment

(P-7128)
VISCIRA LLC
200 Vallejo St, San Francisco (94111-1512)
PHONE..................................415 848-8010
Dave Gulezian, President
Rick Barker, COO
Hagop Kane Kaneboughazian, Vice Pres
EMP: 100
SQ FT: 10,000
SALES (est): 36.6MM
SALES (corp-wide): 20.1B Privately Held
SIC: 5045 7371 Computer software; computer software development & applications
HQ: Sudler & Hennessey, Llc
230 Park Ave S
New York NY 10003
212 614-4100

(P-7129)
WONDERWARE CORPORATION (DH)
26561 Rancho Pkwy S, Lake Forest (92630-8301)
PHONE..................................949 727-3200
Rick Bullotta, Vice Pres
Brian Dibenedetto, Senior VP
Karen Hamilton, Senior VP
Peter Kent, Senior VP
Dave Pickett, Senior VP
EMP: 300
SQ FT: 32,000
SALES (est): 68.1MM
SALES (corp-wide): 200.4K Privately Held
WEB: www.wonderware.com
SIC: 5045 Computer software

(P-7130)
WORLD WIDE TECHNOLOGY INC
1165 W Walnut St, Compton (90220-5113)
PHONE..................................310 537-8335
Rob Macphee, Manager
Sevan Yeghiazarian, Network Enginr
Peter Chen, Project Mgr
Christopher Auxier, Sr Project Mgr
Jaime-Christi Garrett, Sr Project Mgr
EMP: 50
SALES (corp-wide): 7.4B Privately Held
SIC: 5045 5065 Computers, peripherals & software; communication equipment
HQ: World Wide Technology, Llc
60 Weldon Pkwy
Maryland Heights MO 63146
314 569-7000

(P-7131)
XTRAPLUS CORPORATION
Also Called: Zipzoomfly
39889 Eureka Dr, Newark (94560-4811)
PHONE..................................510 897-1890
MEI F Chan, President
▲ EMP: 90

SALES (est): 9.9MM Privately Held
WEB: www.zipzoomfly.com
SIC: 5045 3577 Computer peripheral equipment; computer peripheral equipment

---

5046 Commercial Eqpt, NEC Wholesale

(P-7132)
BUYEFFICIENT LLC
903 Calle Amanecer # 200, San Clemente (92673-6251)
PHONE..................................949 382-3129
Dennis Baker, President
EMP: 76
SALES (est): 7.7MM Publicly Held
SIC: 5046 Hotel equipment & supplies
HQ: Avendra, Llc
540 Gaither Rd Ste 200
Rockville MD 20850
301 825-0500

(P-7133)
CLIPPER CORPORATION (PA)
21124 Figueroa St, Carson (90745-1938)
PHONE..................................310 533-8585
Lina Hu, CEO
Nancy Hejran, CFO
Jason Ledbetter, Sales Dir
Eddie Miyamoto, Cust Mgr
Craig Hagedorn, Director
◆ EMP: 50 EST: 1994
SQ FT: 59,810
SALES (est): 43.4MM Privately Held
WEB: www.clipper-corp.com
SIC: 5046 Restaurant equipment & supplies; cooking equipment, commercial

(P-7134)
EQUATOR COFFEES LLC
115 Jordan St, San Rafael (94901-3919)
PHONE..................................415 485-2213
Helen Russell, CEO
EMP: 90
SALES (est): 1.4MM Privately Held
SIC: 5046 Commercial equipment

(P-7135)
HANNAM CHAIN USA INC (PA)
Also Called: Hannam Chain Super 1 Market
2740 W Olympic Blvd, Los Angeles (90006-2633)
PHONE..................................213 382-2922
Kee W Ha, CEO
Perry King, General Mgr
▲ EMP: 105
SQ FT: 22,000
SALES (est): 72MM Privately Held
SIC: 5046 5411 Restaurant equipment & supplies; supermarkets, independent

(P-7136)
HARPER MECHANICAL CONTRS LLC
1011 Camino Del Rio S, San Diego (92108-3531)
PHONE..................................619 543-1296
Jeffrey A Harper, Mng Member
Ronald D Harper,
EMP: 80
SALES (est): 33.9MM Privately Held
SIC: 5046 1611 Commercial equipment; grading

(P-7137)
INTERSTATE ELECTRIC CO INC (PA)
Also Called: IEC
2240 Yates Ave, Commerce (90040-1914)
PHONE..................................323 724-0420
Edward Urlik, President
Hortensia Gomez, CFO
Arnie Binter, Branch Mgr
Ed Brent, Branch Mgr
Dan Carson, General Mgr
▲ EMP: 94
SQ FT: 72,000
SALES (est): 70.5MM Privately Held
WEB: www.interstateelectric.com
SIC: 5046 Signs, electrical

(P-7138)
JC FOODSERVICE INC (PA)
Also Called: Action Sales
415 S Atlantic Blvd, Monterey Park
(91754-3209)
PHONE..........................626 299-3800
Joel Chang, *President*
Jack Chang, *Vice Pres*
Eva Lau, *Accountant*
Johnson Yeh, *Marketing Staff*
James Deng, *Sales Staff*
◆ EMP: 55
SQ FT: 25,000
SALES (est): 47.3MM **Privately Held**
WEB: www.actionsales.com
SIC: 5046 Restaurant equipment & supplies

(P-7139)
JETRO HOLDINGS LLC
7466 Carroll Rd Ste 100, San Diego
(92121-2356)
PHONE..........................858 564-0466
Dan Camacho, *Branch Mgr*
EMP: 135 **Privately Held**
SIC: 5046 Restaurant equipment & supplies
PA: Jetro Holdings, Llc
1506 132nd St
College Point NY 11356

(P-7140)
JETRO HOLDINGS LLC
1611 E Washington Blvd, Los Angeles
(90021-3133)
PHONE..........................213 516-0301
Javier Gomez, *Branch Mgr*
EMP: 170 **Privately Held**
SIC: 5046 Commercial cooking & food
service equipment
PA: Jetro Holdings, Llc
1506 132nd St
College Point NY 11356

(P-7141)
JONES SIGN CO INC
Also Called: Ultrasigns Electrical Advg
9025 Balboa Ave Ste 150, San Diego
(92123-1522)
PHONE..........................858 569-1400
John Mortensen, *President*
Beth Olmstead, *Vice Pres*
Mary Jo Wenzel, *Controller*
EMP: 120
SALES (corp-wide): 60.3MM **Privately
Held**
SIC: 5046 Signs, electrical
PA: Jones Sign Co., Inc.
1711 Scheuring Rd
De Pere WI 54115
920 983-6700

(P-7142)
**JUSTMAN PACKAGING &
DISPLAY**
5819 Telegraph Rd, Commerce
(90040-1515)
PHONE..........................323 728-8888
Morley Justman, *President*
Barbara Cabaret, *CFO*
Russell Justman, *Vice Pres*
▲ EMP: 70
SQ FT: 125,000
SALES (est): 64.8MM **Privately Held**
WEB: www.justman.com
SIC: 5046 5113 2752 Display equipment,
except refrigerated; corrugated & solid
fiber boxes; commercial printing, lithographic

(P-7143)
OPTEC DISPLAYS INC
1700 S De Soto Pl Ste A, Ontario
(91761-8060)
PHONE..........................626 369-7188
Shu Hwa Wu, *President*
David Pratt, *Exec Dir*
Wenny Tsay, *General Mgr*
George Lain, *Info Tech Dir*
Yifeng Liang, *Software Dev*
▲ EMP: 64
SALES (est): 29MM **Privately Held**
WEB: www.optecdisplays.com
SIC: 5046 Signs, electrical

(P-7144)
**PBI-BIRKENWALD MARKET EQP
INC (PA)**
Also Called: P B I
2667 Gundry Ave, Long Beach
(90755-1808)
P.O. Box 6097 (90806-0097)
PHONE..........................562 595-4785
Thomas L Everson, *President*
Kim Everson, *COO*
Jim Ennis, *CFO*
Laurie Stone, *Senior VP*
Erik Everson, *Vice Pres*
▲ EMP: 50 EST: 1949
SQ FT: 85,000
SALES (est): 25.1MM **Privately Held**
WEB: www.pbimarketing.com
SIC: 5046 Store equipment; scales, except
laboratory; shelving, commercial & industrial; cooking equipment, commercial

(P-7145)
SHOPPER INC
3987 Heritage Oak Ct, Simi Valley
(93063-6711)
PHONE..........................805 527-6700
Bill Bieda, *CEO*
Elliot Bieda, *Vice Pres*
Eta Bieda, *Admin Sec*
Michelle Nadler, *Controller*
Jon Benson, *Opers Mgr*
◆ EMP: 300
SQ FT: 80,000
SALES (est): 74.7MM **Privately Held**
WEB: www.shopperinc.com
SIC: 5046 Store fixtures & display equipment

(P-7146)
STEUBER CORPORATION (PA)
Also Called: Foodcraft Cof Refreshment Svcs
20425 S Susana Rd, Long Beach
(90810-1136)
PHONE..........................310 632-8255
Robert A Steuber, *President*
Cathy H Steuber, *Corp Secy*
Stuart Harris, *Vice Pres*
Philip Steuber, *Vice Pres*
EMP: 85
SQ FT: 18,000
SALES (est): 23.9MM **Privately Held**
SIC: 5046 5963 5149 5411 Coffee brewing equipment & supplies; direct selling
establishments; groceries & related products; convenience stores; medicine cabinet sundries

---

**5047 Medical, Dental &
Hospital Eqpt & Splys
Wholesale**

(P-7147)
AAXIS PHARMACEUTICALS INC
Also Called: Aaxis Pacific
1835 262nd St, Lomita (90717-3346)
PHONE..........................424 263-5294
Soa Sher, *CEO*
EMP: 101
SALES (est): 1.8MM **Privately Held**
SIC: 5047 7389 Medical equipment & supplies;

(P-7148)
ACON LABORATORIES INC (PA)
10125 Mesa Rim Rd, San Diego
(92121-2915)
PHONE..........................858 875-8000
Jinn-Nan Lin, *President*
Mary Long, *Vice Pres*
Leigh Thorup, *Info Tech Mgr*
Jasmine Dare, *Purchasing*
Claudio Cordeiro, *Sales Mgr*
▲ EMP: 65
SQ FT: 36,000
SALES (est): 16.3MM **Privately Held**
WEB: www.aconlabs.com
SIC: 5047 Medical equipment & supplies

(P-7149)
**ADVANCED REHABILITATION
TECH**
7950 Dunbrook Rd, San Diego
(92126-4371)
P.O. Box 915, Cardiff By The Sea (92007-0915)
PHONE..........................858 621-5959
Richard M Harris, *President*
Jack Bailey, *Shareholder*
Darrel Blomberg, *Shareholder*
Stan Dunlap, *Vice Pres*
Chet Teklinski, *Vice Pres*
EMP: 57
SQ FT: 12,000
SALES (est): 11MM **Privately Held**
SIC: 5047 Medical & hospital equipment

(P-7150)
**AFTER MARKET GROUP INC
(HQ)**
10173 Croydon Way Ste 1, Sacramento
(95827-2108)
PHONE..........................916 361-1687
Gerald Blouch, *Ch of Bd*
A Malachi Mixon III, *President*
Joseph Richey II, *Vice Pres*
▲ EMP: 75
SALES (est): 11.1MM
SALES (corp-wide): 966.5MM **Publicly
Held**
SIC: 5047 Medical & hospital equipment
PA: Invacare Corporation
1 Invacare Way
Elyria OH 44035
440 329-6000

(P-7151)
AMERICAN MEDICAL TECH INC
Also Called: Gordian Medical
17595 Cartwright Rd, Irvine (92614-5847)
PHONE..........................949 553-0359
Jean Signore, *President*
Jerry Signore, *Vice Pres*
EMP: 100
SALES (est): 22.2MM **Privately Held**
SIC: 5047 Medical equipment & supplies

(P-7152)
AMPRONIX INC
15 Whatney, Irvine (92618-2808)
PHONE..........................949 273-8000
Nausser Fathollahi, *President*
Aladdin Doroudi, *CFO*
Courtney Goydos, *Admin Asst*
Evelyn Navarro, *Admin Asst*
Adrian Cirpean, *Info Tech Mgr*
▲ EMP: 78 EST: 1982
SQ FT: 58,000
SALES (est): 49.9MM **Privately Held**
WEB: www.ampronix.com
SIC: 5047 Diagnostic equipment, medical

(P-7153)
ANGIOSCORE INC
5055 Brandin Ct, Fremont (94538-3140)
PHONE..........................510 933-7900
Thomas R Trotter, *President*
EMP: 140
SQ FT: 44,000
SALES (est): 45.2MM
SALES (corp-wide): 20.9B **Privately Held**
SIC: 5047 Medical equipment & supplies
HQ: Spectranetics Corporation
9965 Federal Dr Ste 100
Colorado Springs CO 80921
719 447-2000

(P-7154)
APRIA HEALTHCARE LLC
480 Carlton Ct, South San Francisco
(94080-2012)
PHONE..........................650 588-9744
Geronimo Jimenez, *Manager*
EMP: 56 **Privately Held**
WEB: www.apria.com
SIC: 5047 7352 5999 Hospital equipment
& furniture; dental equipment & supplies;
medical equipment & supplies; medical
equipment rental; medical apparatus &
supplies
HQ: Apria Healthcare Llc
26220 Enterprise Ct
Lake Forest CA 92630
949 639-2163

(P-7155)
APRIA HEALTHCARE LLC
1450 Expo Pkwy, Sacramento
(95815-4231)
PHONE..........................530 677-2713
Jim Hay, *Branch Mgr*
EMP: 192 **Privately Held**
WEB: www.apria.com
SIC: 5047 Hospital equipment & furniture
HQ: Apria Healthcare Llc
26220 Enterprise Ct
Lake Forest CA 92630
949 639-2163

(P-7156)
APRIA HEALTHCARE LLC (DH)
26220 Enterprise Ct, Lake Forest
(92630-8405)
P.O. Box 610 (92609-0610)
PHONE..........................949 639-2163
Daniel J Starck, *CEO*
Donna Blake, *President*
Matt Gallagher, *President*
Debra Morris, *Treasurer*
Nicolette Laurie, *Vice Pres*
◆ EMP: 400
SALES (est): 1.1B **Privately Held**
WEB: www.apria.com
SIC: 5047 7352 5999 Hospital equipment
& furniture; dental equipment & supplies;
medical equipment & supplies; medical
equipment rental; medical apparatus &
supplies

(P-7157)
APRIA HEALTHCARE LLC
2510 Dean Lesher Dr Ste D, Concord
(94520-1368)
PHONE..........................925 827-8800
Dencio Chua, *Manager*
EMP: 63
SQ FT: 2,400 **Privately Held**
WEB: www.apria.com
SIC: 5047 7352 Hospital equipment & furniture; medical equipment rental
HQ: Apria Healthcare Llc
26220 Enterprise Ct
Lake Forest CA 92630
949 639-2163

(P-7158)
AVITA MEDICAL AMERICAS LLC
28159 Ave Stnford Ste 220, Valencia
(91355)
PHONE..........................661 367-9170
Michael S Perry, *Mng Member*
Timothy Rooney,
EMP: 71
SQ FT: 23,000
SALES (est): 3.3MM
SALES (corp-wide): 1.2MM **Publicly Held**
SIC: 5047 Medical & hospital equipment
PA: Avita Medical Ltd
Se G01 68 South Tce
South Perth WA 6151
894 747-738

(P-7159)
BACKPROJECT CORPORATION
170 N Wolfe Rd, Sunnyvale (94086-5211)
PHONE..........................408 730-1111
Steve Hoffman, *President*
◆ EMP: 66
SQ FT: 18,000
SALES (est): 7.6MM **Privately Held**
WEB: www.backproject.com
SIC: 5047 Medical equipment & supplies

(P-7160)
**BECTON DICKINSON AND
COMPANY**
Also Called: Bdc Distribution Center
2200 W San Bernardino Ave, Redlands
(92374-5008)
PHONE..........................909 748-7300
Ricardo Frias, *Branch Mgr*
EMP: 100
SALES (corp-wide): 12B **Publicly Held**
SIC: 5047 Medical equipment & supplies
PA: Becton, Dickinson And Company
1 Becton Dr
Franklin Lakes NJ 07417
201 847-6800

(P-7161)
BENCO DENTAL SUPPLY CO
3590 Harbor Gtwy N, Costa Mesa
(92626-1425)
PHONE..............................714 424-0977
EMP: 98
SALES (corp-wide): 565.1MM **Privately Held**
SIC: 5047 Dental equipment & supplies
PA: Benco Dental Supply Co.
    295 Centerpoint Blvd
    Pittston PA 18640
    570 602-7781

(P-7162)
BINDING SITE INC (PA)
6730 Mesa Ridge Rd Ste B, San Diego
(92121-2951)
PHONE..............................858 453-9177
Doug Kurth, *President*
Doug Anderson, *Exec VP*
▲ EMP: 62
SQ FT: 23,000
SALES (est): 24.6MM **Privately Held**
WEB: www.thebindingsite.com
SIC: 5047 Diagnostic equipment, medical

(P-7163)
BIOMARIN INC
7250 Redwood Blvd Ste 300, Novato
(94945-3269)
PHONE..............................415 761-8600
Alison Chaney, *President*
Douglas Clark, *Vice Pres*
Michael Yin, *Manager*
EMP: 102
SALES: 37MM **Privately Held**
SIC: 5047 Medical equipment & supplies

(P-7164)
BIOMEDICAL LIFE SYSTEMS INC
2448 Cades Way, Vista (92081-7830)
P.O. Box 1360 (92085-1360)
PHONE..............................760 727-5600
Richard Saxon, *President*
Vladimir Archipov, *Mfg Staff*
Hans Reiss, *Marketing Mgr*
Ray Paclebar, *Sales Staff*
Kevin Swystun, *Sales Staff*
▲ EMP: 65
SALES (est): 14.3MM **Privately Held**
WEB: www.bmls.com
SIC: 5047 Medical & hospital equipment

(P-7165)
BIOSITE INC
9975 Summers Ridge Rd, San Diego
(92121-2997)
PHONE..............................510 683-9063
Yonkin John, *President*
Andrew Dang, *Administration*
Albert Ruiz, *Administration*
Gillian Parker, *Info Tech Mgr*
Colleen Santana, *Project Mgr*
EMP: 62 EST: 2011
SALES (est): 17.2MM **Privately Held**
SIC: 5047 Medical equipment & supplies

(P-7166)
BONGMI INC
68 Harriet St Unit 3, San Francisco
(94103-4094)
PHONE..............................415 823-8595
Snow LI, *Director*
EMP: 50
SALES: 20K **Privately Held**
SIC: 5047 7389 Medical equipment & supplies;

(P-7167)
BRADEN PARTNERS LP A CALIF
7500 District Blvd, Bakersfield
(93313-4832)
PHONE..............................661 632-1979
Patrick Sullivan, *Manager*
EMP: 87
SALES (corp-wide): 68.9MM **Privately Held**
SIC: 5047 Medical equipment & supplies
HQ: Braden Partners, L.P., A California Limited Partnership
    1304 Sthpint Blvd Ste 130
    Petaluma CA 94954

(P-7168)
BRENTWOOD MEDICAL TECH CORP
Also Called: Midmark Diagnostics Group
1125 W 190th St, Gardena (90248-4303)
PHONE..............................800 624-8950
Rebecca Mabry, *President*
EMP: 60
SQ FT: 27,000
SALES (est): 8.1MM
SALES (corp-wide): 322.2MM **Privately Held**
WEB: www.midmarkdiagnostics.com
SIC: 5047 Medical & hospital equipment
PA: Midmark Corporation
    1700 S Patterson Blvd # 400
    Kettering OH 45409
    937 526-3662

(P-7169)
BURBANK DENTAL LABORATORY INC
2101 Floyd St, Burbank (91504-3411)
PHONE..............................818 841-2256
Anatony Sedler, *CEO*
Tony Sedler, *President*
Bob Vartanian, *Exec VP*
David French, *Vice Pres*
Robert Vartanian, *Vice Pres*
▲ EMP: 175
SALES (est): 38.5MM **Privately Held**
SIC: 5047 Dentists' professional supplies

(P-7170)
CANON MEDICAL SYSTEMS USA INC (DH)
Also Called: Toshiba Medical Systems
2441 Michelle Dr, Tustin (92780-7047)
P.O. Box 2068 (92781-2068)
PHONE..............................714 730-5000
Shuzo Yamamoto, *President*
John Patterson, *CFO*
Peter N S Annand, *Senior VP*
Steve Casella, *Vice Pres*
Calum G Cunningham, *Vice Pres*
◆ EMP: 300
SQ FT: 135,000
SALES (est): 5.6MM
SALES (corp-wide): 36.4B **Privately Held**
WEB: www.tams.com
SIC: 5047 X-ray machines & tubes; medical equipment & supplies
HQ: Canon Medeical Systemsco.,Ltd.
    1385, Shimoishigami
    Otawara TCG 324-0
    287 266-211

(P-7171)
CARDINAL HEALTH INC
1100 Bird Center Dr, Palm Springs
(92262-8000)
PHONE..............................951 360-2199
EMP: 52
SALES (corp-wide): 102.5B **Publicly Held**
SIC: 5047
PA: Cardinal Health, Inc.
    7000 Cardinal Pl
    Dublin OH 43017
    614 757-5000

(P-7172)
CARDINAL HEALTH 200 LLC
3750 Torrey View Ct, San Diego
(92130-2622)
PHONE..............................951 686-8900
Michael McMahon, *Manager*
Geoffrey Healthcare, *Engineer*
Donna O'Connor, *Mktg Dir*
EMP: 210
SQ FT: 28,000
SALES (corp-wide): 136.8B **Publicly Held**
WEB: www.allegiancehealth.com
SIC: 5047 3845 3672 Medical & hospital equipment; electromedical equipment; printed circuit boards
HQ: Cardinal Health 200, Llc
    3651 Birchwood Dr
    Waukegan IL 60085

(P-7173)
CAREFUSION SOLUTIONS LLC (DH)
3750 Torrey View Ct, San Diego
(92130-2622)
PHONE..............................858 617-2100
Keiran Gallahue, *CEO*
Tom Leonard, *President*
James Hinrichs, *CFO*
Don Abbey, *Exec VP*
Scott Bostick, *Senior VP*
EMP: 600
SALES (est): 330.5MM
SALES (corp-wide): 12B **Publicly Held**
SIC: 5047 Medical equipment & supplies

(P-7174)
CHEN DVID MD DGNSTC MED GROUP
Also Called: Diagnstic Med Group Sthern Cal
25 N Santa Anita Ave, Arcadia
(91006-3111)
PHONE..............................626 566-3900
EMP: 101 **Privately Held**
SIC: 5047 Medical & hospital equipment
PA: Chen, David Md Diagnostic Medical Group Inc
    1129 S San Gabriel Blvd
    San Gabriel CA 91776

(P-7175)
CHINA YNGXIN PHRMCEUTICALS INC
927 Canada Ct, City of Industry
(91748-1136)
PHONE..............................626 581-9098
Yongxin Liu, *Ch of Bd*
Ning Liu, *President*
Harry Zhang, *CFO*
EMP: 673
SALES: 47.5MM **Privately Held**
SIC: 5047 Medical equipment & supplies

(P-7176)
CONSENSUS ORTHOPEDICS INC
1115 Windfield Way # 100, El Dorado Hills
(95762-9835)
PHONE..............................916 355-7110
Collen Gray, *President*
Curt Wiedenhoefer, *President*
Gail V Dalen, *Exec VP*
Thomas Killian, *Exec VP*
Carolyn Hayes, *Vice Pres*
EMP: 85
SQ FT: 25,000
SALES (est): 39MM **Privately Held**
WEB: www.hayesmed.com
SIC: 5047 Medical equipment & supplies; surgical & medical instruments

(P-7177)
CUSTOM MEDICAL PRODUCTS INC
9680 Alto Dr, La Mesa (91941-4446)
PHONE..............................619 461-2068
Thomas D Petersen, *Principal*
EMP: 167
SALES (est): 4.3MM
SALES (corp-wide): 100B **Publicly Held**
WEB: www.custometical.com
SIC: 5047 Medical equipment & supplies
HQ: Express Scripts, Inc.
    1 Express Way
    Saint Louis MO 63121
    314 996-0900

(P-7178)
EDGE SYSTEMS LLC (PA)
Also Called: Hydrafacial Company, The
2165 E Spring St, Long Beach
(90806-2114)
PHONE..............................800 603-4996
Clint Carnell, *CEO*
Jeff Nardoci, *COO*
Randy Sieve, *CFO*
◆ EMP: 170
SQ FT: 22,515
SALES (est): 99MM **Privately Held**
WEB: www.edgesystem.net
SIC: 5047 Medical equipment & supplies

(P-7179)
FEATHER RIVER HOSPITAL
Also Called: Feather River Hospital HM Oxgn
1295 Bille Rd, Paradise (95969-3443)
PHONE..............................530 876-7216
Christine Venard, *Branch Mgr*
EMP: 123
SQ FT: 2,685
SALES (corp-wide): 207MM **Privately Held**
SIC: 5047 Medical equipment & supplies; oxygen therapy equipment
PA: Feather River Hospital
    5974 Pentz Rd
    Paradise CA 95969
    530 877-9361

(P-7180)
FISHER & PAYKEL HEALTHCARE INC
173 Technology Dr Ste 100, Irvine
(92618-2489)
PHONE..............................949 453-4000
Justin Callahan, *President*
Tony Barclay, *CFO*
Bryan Goudzwaard, *Vice Pres*
Paul Shearer, *Director*
Win Miller, *Accounts Mgr*
▲ EMP: 150
SQ FT: 5,000
SALES (est): 79.9MM **Privately Held**
SIC: 5047 Medical equipment & supplies
PA: Fisher & Paykel Healthcare Corporation Limited
    15 Maurice Paykel Place
    Auckland 1061

(P-7181)
GENERAL HOME MEDICAL SUP INC
4607 Lakeview Canyon Rd # 584, Westlake
Village (91361-4028)
PHONE..............................805 449-1559
Kambiz Yadidi, *CEO*
▲ EMP: 88 EST: 1998
SQ FT: 5,700
SALES (est): 7.8MM **Privately Held**
WEB: www.sinusdynamics.com
SIC: 5047 Medical equipment & supplies

(P-7182)
GORDIAN MEDICAL INC
Also Called: American Medical Technologies
17595 Cartwright Rd, Irvine (92614-5847)
PHONE..............................714 556-0200
Joseph Del Signore, *President*
Gerald Del Signore, *CEO*
David Simon, *Vice Pres*
EMP: 290
SALES (est): 86.7MM **Privately Held**
SIC: 5047 Medical equipment & supplies

(P-7183)
HARDY DIAGNOSTICS (PA)
1430 W Mccoy Ln, Santa Maria
(93455-1005)
P.O. Box 645264, Cincinnati OH (45264-5264)
PHONE..............................805 346-2766
Jay R Hardy, *President*
Darla Prevish, *CFO*
Sue Pruett, *QA Dir*
Nathan Bowersock,
Anthony Mendoza, *IT/INT Sup*
◆ EMP: 300
SQ FT: 75,000
SALES: 45MM **Privately Held**
WEB: www.hardydiagnostics.com
SIC: 5047 2836 Medical equipment & supplies; agar culture media

(P-7184)
HONEY LAKE HOSPICE INC
60 S Lassen St, Susanville (96130-4363)
P.O. Box 1166 (96130-1166)
PHONE..............................530 257-3137
Andria Cuypers, *Coordinator*
EMP: 60
SALES (est): 4.2MM **Privately Held**
SIC: 5047 Medical equipment & supplies

(P-7185)
JB DENTAL SUPPLY CO INC (PA)
17000 Kingsview Ave, Carson (90746-1230)
PHONE.................................310 202-8855
Joseph Berman, *President*
Manny Chada, *Vice Pres*
EMP: 120 EST: 1973
SQ FT: 26,000
SALES (est): 36.3MM **Privately Held**
SIC: 5047 Dental equipment & supplies

(P-7186)
JOERNS LLC (HQ)
19748 Dearborn St, Chatsworth (91311-6509)
PHONE.................................800 966-6662
Mark Ludwig, *Mng Member*
Mark Urbania, *CFO*
EMP: 150
SQ FT: 28,000
SALES (est): 54.3MM
SALES (corp-wide): 163MM **Privately Held**
WEB: www.trilinemedical.com
SIC: 5047 Hospital equipment & furniture
PA: Quad-C Jh Holdings Inc.
2430 Whitehall Park Dr
Charlotte NC 28273
800 826-0270

(P-7187)
KLM ORTHOTIC LABORATORIES INC
28280 Alta Vista Ave, Valencia (91355-0958)
PHONE.................................661 295-2600
Kirk Marshall, *President*
Scott Marshall, *Corp Secy*
Kent Marshall, *Vice Pres*
EMP: 100
SQ FT: 35,000
SALES (est): 24.3MM **Privately Held**
SIC: 5047 3842 Medical laboratory equipment; foot appliances, orthopedic

(P-7188)
MARDX DIAGNOSTICS INC
5919 Farnsworth Ct, Carlsbad (92008-7303)
P.O. Box 1059, Jamestown NY (14702-1059)
PHONE.................................760 929-0500
Ian Woodwards, *CEO*
EMP: 53
SQ FT: 21,500
SALES (est): 9.2MM **Privately Held**
SIC: 5047 Diagnostic equipment, medical
HQ: Trinity Biotech, Inc.
2823 Girts Rd
Jamestown NY 14701
800 325-3424

(P-7189)
MCKESSON MEDICAL-SURGICAL INC
16043 El Prado Rd, Chino (91708-9144)
PHONE.................................800 767-6339
Stanton McComb, *Branch Mgr*
EMP: 78
SALES (corp-wide): 208.3B **Publicly Held**
SIC: 5047 Medical equipment & supplies
HQ: Mckesson Medical-Surgical Inc.
9954 Mayland Dr Ste 4000
Richmond VA 23233
804 264-7500

(P-7190)
MCKESSON MEDICAL-SURGICAL INC
1525 Rnch Conejo Blvd # 104, Newbury Park (91320-1441)
PHONE.................................805 375-8800
Mike Douglas, *Branch Mgr*
Cheryl Wilson, *Opers Staff*
Garrett Muramoto, *Senior Mgr*
EMP: 54
SALES (corp-wide): 208.3B **Publicly Held**
WEB: www.gmholdings.com
SIC: 5047 Medical equipment & supplies

HQ: Mckesson Medical-Surgical Inc.
9954 Mayland Dr Ste 4000
Richmond VA 23233
804 264-7500

(P-7191)
MENTOR WORLDWIDE LLC
5425 Hollister Ave, Santa Barbara (93111-3341)
PHONE.................................805 681-6000
Diane Becker, *Manager*
EMP: 500
SALES (corp-wide): 76.4B **Publicly Held**
WEB: www.mentordirect.com
SIC: 5047 Medical & hospital equipment
HQ: Mentor Worldwide Llc
33 Technology Dr
Irvine CA 92618
800 636-8678

(P-7192)
MERRY X-RAY CHEMICAL CORP (PA)
Also Called: M X R
4909 Murphy Canyon Rd # 120, San Diego (92123-4300)
PHONE.................................858 565-4472
Ted Sloan, *CEO*
Bernard Amato, *CFO*
Cheryl Gray, *Executive*
Sondra Beith, *Admin Sec*
Pam Hicks, *Opers Mgr*
EMP: 151 EST: 1958
SQ FT: 10,000
SALES (est): 120MM **Privately Held**
SIC: 5047 X-ray machines & tubes; X-ray film & supplies

(P-7193)
MILTENYI BIOTEC INC (HQ)
2303 Lindbergh St, Auburn (95602-9562)
PHONE.................................530 745-2800
Stefan Miltenyi, *President*
Fred Koller, *President*
Adam Stevens, *Technician*
Barbara Malerstein, *Research*
Katherine Hoffman, *Technical Staff*
▲ EMP: 66
SQ FT: 20,000
SALES (est): 37.5MM
SALES (corp-wide): 259.5MM **Privately Held**
WEB: www.miltenyibiotec.com
SIC: 5047 8731 Medical & hospital equipment; biotechnical research, commercial
PA: Miltenyi Biotec Gmbh
Friedrich-Ebert-Str. 68
Bergisch Gladbach 51429
220 483-060

(P-7194)
MORIGON TECHNOLOGIES LLC
Also Called: Medstop Medical
7615 Fulton Ave, North Hollywood (91605-1805)
PHONE.................................818 764-8880
Amaury J Agoncillo, *CEO*
EMP: 50
SQ FT: 8,000
SALES (est): 2.6MM **Privately Held**
SIC: 5047 Medical equipment & supplies

(P-7195)
NDS SURGICAL IMAGING LLC
5750 Hellyer Ave, San Jose (95138-1000)
PHONE.................................408 776-0085
Karim Khadr, *President*
Sam Brown, *CFO*
Dave Cantin, *Vice Pres*
Rainer Scholl, *Vice Pres*
Darko Spoljaric, *Vice Pres*
◆ EMP: 215
SQ FT: 73,000
SALES (est): 69.2MM **Publicly Held**
WEB: www.ndssi.com
SIC: 5047 Patient monitoring equipment
HQ: Novanta Corporation
125 Middlesex Tpke
Bedford MA 01730
781 266-5700

(P-7196)
NIHON KOHDEN AMERICA INC (HQ)
15353 Barranca Pkwy, Irvine (92618-2216)
PHONE.................................949 580-1555

Fumio Izumida, *CEO*
Mark Cieplinski, *President*
Barry Klegerman, *President*
Josh Lewis, *President*
Eiichi Tanaka, *President*
▲ EMP: 60
SQ FT: 35,000
SALES (est): 72.4MM
SALES (corp-wide): 1.6B **Privately Held**
WEB: www.nkusa.com
SIC: 5047 Electro-medical equipment
PA: Nihon Kohden Corporation
1-31-4, Nishiochiai
Shinjuku-Ku TKY 161-0
359 968-000

(P-7197)
NOVA ORTHO-MED INC (PA)
1470 Beachey Pl, Carson (90746-4002)
PHONE.................................310 352-3600
Sue Chen, *Principal*
Ronald Gaudiano, *Vice Pres*
▲ EMP: 50
SQ FT: 5,500
SALES (est): 19.6MM **Privately Held**
WEB: www.novaorthomed.com
SIC: 5047 Medical equipment & supplies

(P-7198)
NUVI GLOBAL
518 W Henderson Ave Apt 9, Porterville (93257-1769)
P.O. Box 2568 (93258-2568)
PHONE.................................559 306-2646
Herlinda Ruelas, *Owner*
EMP: 600
SALES (est): 16.4MM **Privately Held**
SIC: 5047 Incontinent care products & supplies

(P-7199)
OLYMPUS AMERICA INC
Also Called: OLYMPUS AMERICA INC.
23342 Madero, Mission Viejo (92691-2796)
PHONE.................................949 466-3548
EMP: 110
SALES (corp-wide): 7.3B **Privately Held**
SIC: 5047 Medical equipment & supplies; diagnostic equipment, medical
HQ: Olympus America Inc
3500 Corporate Pkwy
Center Valley PA 18034
484 896-5000

(P-7200)
ORCHID MPS
3233 W Harvard St, Santa Ana (92704-3917)
PHONE.................................714 549-9203
Mark Deischter, *Vice Pres*
EMP: 100
SALES (est): 12.6MM **Privately Held**
SIC: 5047 Medical equipment & supplies

(P-7201)
OTISMED CORPORATION
1600 Harbor Bay Pkwy # 200, Alameda (94502-3085)
PHONE.................................510 786-3171
Charlie CHI, *President*
Ilwhan Park, *Vice Pres*
EMP: 63
SALES (est): 10.4MM
SALES (corp-wide): 12.4B **Publicly Held**
SIC: 5047 Medical equipment & supplies
PA: Stryker Corporation
2825 Airview Blvd
Portage MI 49002
269 385-2600

(P-7202)
OWENS & MINOR INC
5125 Ontario Mills Pkwy, Ontario (91764-5103)
PHONE.................................909 944-2100
Tom Kelly, *Branch Mgr*
EMP: 57 **Publicly Held**
WEB: www.owens-minor.com
SIC: 5047 Medical equipment & supplies
PA: Owens & Minor, Inc.
9120 Lockwood Blvd
Mechanicsville VA 23116

(P-7203)
OWENS & MINOR INC
18520 Stanford Rd, Tracy (95377-9708)
PHONE.................................209 833-4600
Jim Bierman, *President*
EMP: 57 **Publicly Held**
SIC: 5047 Medical equipment & supplies
PA: Owens & Minor, Inc.
9120 Lockwood Blvd
Mechanicsville VA 23116

(P-7204)
PATTERSON DENTAL SUPPLY INC
Also Called: Patterson Dental 426
185 S Douglas St Ste 100, El Segundo (90245-4673)
PHONE.................................310 426-3100
Ken Sartin, *Manager*
EMP: 75
SALES (corp-wide): 5.4B **Publicly Held**
WEB: www.pattersondentalsupply.com
SIC: 5047 Dental equipment & supplies
HQ: Patterson Dental Supply, Inc.
1031 Mendota Heights Rd
Saint Paul MN 55120
651 686-1600

(P-7205)
PATTERSON DENTAL SUPPLY INC
Also Called: Patterson Dental 454
1030 Winding Creek Rd # 150, Roseville (95678-7045)
PHONE.................................916 780-5100
James Ryan, *Manager*
EMP: 69
SALES (corp-wide): 5.4B **Publicly Held**
WEB: www.pattersondentalsupply.com
SIC: 5047 Dental equipment & supplies
HQ: Patterson Dental Supply, Inc.
1031 Mendota Heights Rd
Saint Paul MN 55120
651 686-1600

(P-7206)
PATTERSON DENTAL SUPPLY INC
Also Called: Patterson Dental 590
800 Monte Vista Dr, Dinuba (93618-9117)
PHONE.................................559 595-1450
Ceasar Lopez, *Manager*
EMP: 58
SALES (corp-wide): 5.4B **Publicly Held**
WEB: www.pattersondentalsupply.com
SIC: 5047 Dental equipment & supplies
HQ: Patterson Dental Supply, Inc.
1031 Mendota Heights Rd
Saint Paul MN 55120
651 686-1600

(P-7207)
PEARSON DENTAL SUPPLIES INC (PA)
Also Called: Pearson Surgical Supply Co
13161 Telfair Ave, Sylmar (91342-3574)
PHONE.................................818 362-2600
Keyhan Kashfian, *President*
Nader Kashfian, *Treasurer*
Parviz Kashfian, *Vice Pres*
Patricia Castrellon, *Technology*
Mat Dyson, *Analyst*
◆ EMP: 105 EST: 1983
SQ FT: 88,000
SALES (est): 70.8MM **Privately Held**
WEB: www.pearsondental.com
SIC: 5047 Dental equipment & supplies

(P-7208)
PHILIPS MEDICAL SYSTEMS CLEVEL
1 Marconi, Irvine (92618-2520)
PHONE.................................949 699-2300
David Carter, *Branch Mgr*
EMP: 100
SALES (corp-wide): 20.9B **Privately Held**
SIC: 5047 X-ray machines & tubes; diagnostic equipment, medical; X-ray film & supplies
HQ: Philips Medical Systems (Cleveland), Inc.
595 Miner Rd
Cleveland OH 44143
440 247-2652

(P-7209)
POLESTAR LABS INC
1223 Pacific Oaks Pl # 102, Escondido
(92029-2913)
P.O. Box 460249 (92046-0249)
PHONE.....................................760 480-2600
Michael Dunaway, CEO
Charles Chuck Fabijanic, Senior VP
Trudy Dunaway, Admin Sec
EMP: 70
SALES: 5MM Privately Held
SIC: 5047 5999 7699 7363 Medical labo-
ratory equipment; medical apparatus &
supplies; laboratory instrument repair;
medical help service; management serv-
ices

(P-7210)
PORTERVILLE SHELTERED
WORKSHOP
1853 E Cross Ave, Tulare (93274-7388)
PHONE.....................................559 684-9168
EMP: 59
SALES (corp-wide): 10.4MM Privately
Held
SIC: 5047
PA: Porterville Sheltered Workshop
194 W Poplar Ave
Porterville CA 93257
559 784-7187

(P-7211)
PRACTICE WARES INC
Also Called: Practicewares Dental Supply
2377 Gold Meadow Way, Gold River
(95670-4405)
PHONE.....................................916 526-2674
EMP: 50
SALES (corp-wide): 12.5MM Privately
Held
SIC: 5047
PA: Practice Wares, Inc
3400 E Mcdowell Rd
Phoenix AZ
602 225-9090

(P-7212)
PRI MEDICAL TECHNOLOGIES
INC (DH)
Also Called: UHS Surgical Services
10939 Pendleton St, Sun Valley
(91352-1522)
PHONE.....................................818 394-2800
Bradley Jacobsen, CEO
Louis Buther, President
William M McKay, Treasurer
Lee Pulju, Treasurer
Gary Blackford, Director
EMP: 55
SQ FT: 14,500
SALES (est): 18.6MM Privately Held
SIC: 5047 7352 8741 Instruments, surgi-
cal & medical; medical equipment rental;
administrative management; financial
management for business; personnel
management
HQ: Universal Hospital Services, Inc.
6625 W 78th St Ste 300
Minneapolis MN 55439
952 893-3200

(P-7213)
PROFESSIONAL HOSPITAL SUP
INC (HQ)
42500 Winchester Rd, Temecula
(92590-2570)
PHONE.....................................951 699-5000
Jenise Luttgens, CEO
John Augustine, CFO
Doug Hoffee, Exec VP
Shawn Huber, QA Dir
Linda Langhans, QA Dir
▲ EMP: 1200
SQ FT: 300,000
SALES (est): 612.5MM
SALES (corp-wide): 5.6B Privately Held
WEB: www.phsyes.com
SIC: 5047 Medical equipment & supplies
PA: Medline Industries, Inc.
3 Lakes Dr
Northfield IL 60093
847 949-5500

(P-7214)
RADIOMETER AMERICA INC
(HQ)
250 S Kraemer Blvd Ms, Brea
(92821-6232)
PHONE.....................................800 736-0600
Torben Neilson, President
Frank T McFaden, Treasurer
Cathy Yang, Vice Pres
Loren Cochrun, Engineer
Kamran Kaboli, Engineer
▲ EMP: 114
SQ FT: 35,000
SALES (est): 64.1MM
SALES (corp-wide): 18.3B Publicly Held
WEB: www.radiometeramerica.com
SIC: 5047 Medical equipment & supplies
PA: Danaher Corporation
2200 Penn Ave Nw Ste 800w
Washington DC 20037
202 828-0850

(P-7215)
SAKURA FINETEK USA INC
(HQ)
1750 W 214th St, Torrance (90501-2857)
PHONE.....................................310 972-7800
Takashi Tsuzuki, Ch of Bd
Anthony C Marotti, President
Kenichi Matsumoto, Chm Emeritus
Kam Patel, Corp Secy
Leonel Medina, Technician
◆ EMP: 109
SQ FT: 68,000
SALES (est): 60.6MM Privately Held
WEB: www.sakura-americas.com
SIC: 5047 Medical laboratory equipment;
diagnostic equipment, medical
PA: Sakura Global Holding Co., Ltd.
3-1-9, Nihombashihoncho
Chuo-Ku TKY
332 701-666

(P-7216)
SAN JOSE SURGICAL SUPPLY
INC (PA)
902 S Bascom Ave, San Jose
(95128-3599)
PHONE.....................................408 293-9033
Dennis J Collins, President
Leann Troutman, Accounting Mgr
Kim Smith, Purch Dir
Greg Guio, Sales Mgr
Bob Reggiani, Accounts Exec
▲ EMP: 50
SQ FT: 15,000
SALES (est): 18.6MM Privately Held
WEB: www.sjsurgical.com
SIC: 5047 5122 Surgical equipment &
supplies; pharmaceuticals

(P-7217)
SHIMADZU PRECISION INSTRS
INC
Shimadzu Medical Systems
20101 S Vermont Ave, Torrance
(90502-1328)
PHONE.....................................310 217-8855
Akinori Yamaguchi, President
Wendy Decastro, Admin Asst
Jim Mekker, Manager
EMP: 80
SALES (corp-wide): 3.5B Privately Held
WEB: www.spi-inc.com
SIC: 5047 Medical equipment & supplies
HQ: Shimadzu Precision Instruments, Inc.
3645 N Lakewood Blvd
Long Beach CA 90808
562 420-6226

(P-7218)
SIEMENS MED SOLUTIONS USA
INC
Ultra Sound Division
685 E Middlefield Rd, Mountain View
(94043-4045)
P.O. Box 7393 (94039-7393)
PHONE.....................................650 694-5747
Franz Wiehler, CFO
Hitomi Smith, Finance Dir
EMP: 300
SQ FT: 373,000
SALES (corp-wide): 97.7B Privately Held
WEB: www.siemensmedical.com
SIC: 5047 Diagnostic equipment, medical

HQ: Siemens Medical Solutions Usa, Inc.
40 Liberty Blvd
Malvern PA 19355
888 826-9702

(P-7219)
SOUND TECHNOLOGIES INC
Also Called: Sound-Eklin
5810 Van Allen Way, Carlsbad
(92008-7300)
PHONE.....................................760 918-9626
Kevin Wilson, President
Jon Maynard, Info Tech Dir
Patrick Batchelder, Technology
Maureen Dresch, Buyer
George Black, Opers Staff
▼ EMP: 52
SQ FT: 11,933
SALES (est): 50.3MM
SALES (corp-wide): 2.5B Privately Held
WEB: www.soundvet.com
SIC: 5047 Veterinarians' equipment & sup-
plies
HQ: Vca Inc.
12401 W Olympic Blvd
Los Angeles CA 90064
310 571-6500

(P-7220)
SUPER CARE INC
12176 Industrial Blvd, Victorville
(92395-5879)
PHONE.....................................760 245-2034
EMP: 82
SALES (corp-wide): 64MM Privately
Held
SIC: 5047 Instruments, surgical & medical
PA: Super Care, Inc.
8345 Firestone Blvd # 210
Downey CA 90241
800 206-4880

(P-7221)
TEAM MAKENA LLC (PA)
Also Called: Restore Motion
27051 Towne Centre Dr # 180, Foothill
Ranch (92610-2819)
PHONE.....................................949 474-1753
Mark Tymchenko, Sales Staff
Jim Schuerger,
EMP: 53
SALES: 14.6MM Privately Held
SIC: 5047 Hospital equipment & supplies

(P-7222)
TEAM POST-OP INC (DH)
17256 Red Hill Ave, Irvine (92614-5628)
P.O. Box 650846, Dallas TX (75265-0846)
PHONE.....................................949 253-5500
Jeffrey Salamon, President
Lisa Salamon, Admin Sec
EMP: 60
SQ FT: 1,400
SALES (est): 14MM
SALES (corp-wide): 1B Publicly Held
SIC: 5047 Orthopedic equipment & sup-
plies
HQ: Hanger Prosthetics & Orthotics, Inc.
10910 Domain Dr Ste 300
Austin TX 78758
512 777-3800

(P-7223)
THERAPAK LLC (DH)
651 Wharton Dr, Claremont (91711-4819)
PHONE.....................................909 267-2000
Todd Gates, President
▲ EMP: 70
SQ FT: 24,000
SALES (est): 296.1MM Privately Held
WEB: www.therapak.com
SIC: 5047 Medical equipment & supplies;
diagnostic equipment, medical
HQ: Vwr Corporation
Radnor Corp Ctr 1 200
Radnor PA 19087
610 386-1700

(P-7224)
TOSOH BIOSCIENCE INC
Also Called: Tosoh USA
6000 Shoreline Ct Ste 101, South San
Francisco (94080-7606)
PHONE.....................................650 615-4970
Max Yamata, President
David White, General Mgr

Todd Brill, Info Tech Mgr
Gregory Mitchell, Engineer
▲ EMP: 75
SQ FT: 13,917
SALES (est): 16.5MM
SALES (corp-wide): 7.7B Privately Held
WEB: www.tosohbioscience.com
SIC: 5047 Diagnostic equipment, medical
HQ: Tosoh America, Inc.
3600 Gantz Rd
Grove City OH 43123
614 539-8622

(P-7225)
TRADECOM MED
TRANSCRIPTION INC
363 Piercy Rd, San Jose (95138-1403)
PHONE.....................................408 225-9200
Samit Shah, President
Dhaval Patel, CFO
Ram Mankad, Vice Pres
Deval Nanavati, Vice Pres
EMP: 110 EST: 1997
SQ FT: 1,500
SALES: 850K Privately Held
WEB: www.tradecomusa.com
SIC: 5047 X-ray machines & tubes; diag-
nostic equipment, medical

(P-7226)
TWIN MED LLC (PA)
11333 Greenstone Ave, Santa Fe Springs
(90670-4618)
PHONE.....................................323 582-9900
David Blonder,
David Klarner,
EMP: 65
SALES (est): 179.5MM Privately Held
SIC: 5047 8082 8093 Medical & hospital
equipment; home health care services;
specialty outpatient clinics

(P-7227)
ULTRA SOLUTIONS LLC
1137 E Philadelphia St, Ontario
(91761-5611)
PHONE.....................................909 628-1778
Sterling Peloso, CEO
Tommy Ly, Vice Pres
Alice Stewart, Vice Pres
Brian Gorman, General Mgr
Felix Hoang, Engineer
▲ EMP: 50
SQ FT: 7,500
SALES (est): 19.8MM Privately Held
SIC: 5047 Diagnostic equipment, medical;
medical equipment & supplies

(P-7228)
VETERINARY SERVICE INC
935 Palmyrita Ave, Riverside (92507-1819)
PHONE.....................................951 328-4900
Colin Anderson, Branch Mgr
EMP: 57
SALES (corp-wide): 180.1MM Privately
Held
WEB: www.vsi.cc
SIC: 5047 5199 5083 Veterinarians'
equipment & supplies; pet supplies; poul-
try equipment
PA: Veterinary Service, Inc.
4100 Bangs Ave
Modesto CA 95356
209 545-5100

(P-7229)
VIDENT
Also Called: Vita North America
22705 Savi Ranch Pkwy # 100, Yorba Linda
(92887-4604)
PHONE.....................................714 221-6700
Emanuel Rauter, CEO
Nhi Nguyen, General Mgr
Janette Gorman, VP Finance
Tim Thompson, VP Opers
Andy Klein, Mktg Dir
▲ EMP: 70
SQ FT: 43,000
SALES (est): 24.6MM
SALES (corp-wide): 115.4MM Privately
Held
WEB: www.vident.com
SIC: 5047 Dental equipment & supplies

HQ: Vita - Zahnfabrik H. Rauter
Gesellschaft Mit Beschrankter Haftung
& Co Kg
Spitalgasse 3
Bad Sackingen 79713
776 156-20

(P-7230)
VIEWRAY TECHNOLOGIES INC
815 E Middlefield Rd, Mountain View
(94043-4025)
PHONE...............................650 252-0920
EMP: 75
SALES (corp-wide): 2.2MM Privately
Held
SIC: 5047 Medical & hospital equipment
PA: Vieyray Technologies, Inc.
2 Thermo Fisher Way
Oakwood Village OH 44146
440 703-3210

5048 Ophthalmic Goods Wholesale

(P-7231)
ABB/CON-CISE OPTICAL GROUP LLC
Also Called: Primary Eyecare Network
1750 N Loop Rd Ste 150, Alameda
(94502-8013)
PHONE...............................800 852-8089
EMP: 80
SALES (corp-wide): 1.3B Privately Held
SIC: 5048 5044
HQ: Abb/Con-Cise Optical Group Llc
12301 Nw 39th St
Coral Springs FL 33065
800 852-8089

(P-7232)
ABB/CON-CISE OPTICAL GROUP LLC
Also Called: ABB Optical Group
1750 N Loop Rd Ste 150, Alameda
(94502-8013)
PHONE...............................510 483-9400
Angel Alvarez, CEO
Hannah Cleveringa, Manager
EMP: 80
SALES (corp-wide): 345.4MM Privately
Held
SIC: 5048 5049 Ophthalmic goods; optical
goods
HQ: Abb/Con-Cise Optical Group Llc
12301 Nw 39th St
Coral Springs FL 33065

(P-7233)
ATLANTIC OPTICAL CO INC
Also Called: Ltd Eyewear
20801 Nordhoff St, Chatsworth
(91311-5925)
P.O. Box 3519 (91313-3519)
PHONE...............................818 407-1890
Sheldon H Lehrer, President
Chett Lehrer, Corp Secy
Keith Lehrer, Vice Pres
Rob Blatt, Regl Sales Mgr
Stuart Winefsky, Sales Staff
▲ EMP: 80 EST: 1950
SQ FT: 40,000
SALES (est): 13.2MM Privately Held
SIC: 5048 Frames, ophthalmic

(P-7234)
ESSILOR LABORATORIES AMER INC
Also Called: Bartley Optical
1300 W Optical Dr, Irwindale (91702-3282)
PHONE...............................626 969-6181
Robert Babcock, Manager
Anthony Gonzales, General Mgr
EMP: 70 Privately Held
WEB: www.crizal.com
SIC: 5048 3851 Frames, ophthalmic;
lenses, ophthalmic; ophthalmic goods
HQ: Essilor Laboratories Of America, Inc.
13515 N Stemmons Fwy
Dallas TX 75234
972 241-4141

(P-7235)
HOYA CORPORATION
Also Called: Hoya San Diego
4255 Ruffin Rd, San Diego (92123-1232)
PHONE...............................858 309-6050
Charlie Pendrell, Principal
Elsa Demetrioff, Human Res Mgr
EMP: 200
SALES (corp-wide): 5B Privately Held
SIC: 5048 Ophthalmic goods
HQ: Hoya Corporation
651 E Corporate Dr
Lewisville TX 75057
972 221-4141

(P-7236)
MARCOLIN USA INC
Also Called: Viva International
6 Janet Way Apt 116, Belvedere Tiburon
(94920-2164)
PHONE...............................415 383-6348
EMP: 66 Privately Held
SIC: 5048 5099
HQ: Marcolin U.S.A., Inc.
3140 Us Highway 22
Branchburg NJ 08876
800 345-8482

(P-7237)
NEOSTYLE EYEWEAR CORPORATION
2651 La Mirada Dr Ste 150, Vista
(92081-8435)
PHONE...............................760 305-4004
Helmuth Igel, President
Helga Igel, Corp Secy
EMP: 70
SQ FT: 17,000
SALES (est): 9.4MM Privately Held
WEB: www.neostyle.com
SIC: 5048 Frames, ophthalmic

(P-7238)
NIDEK INCORPORATED
47651 Westinghouse Dr, Fremont
(94539-7474)
PHONE...............................510 226-5700
Motoki Ozawa, CEO
Hideo Ozawa, Ch of Bd
Jun Iwata, COO
Gary Mikaelian, Research
Faye Custodio, Technology
▲ EMP: 50
SQ FT: 18,700
SALES (est): 17.2MM
SALES (corp-wide): 391.7MM Privately
Held
SIC: 5048 8011 3845 3841 Optometric
equipment & supplies; offices & clinics of
medical doctors; electromedical equip-
ment; surgical & medical instruments;
electrical equipment & supplies
PA: Nidek Co.,Ltd.
34-14, Maehama, Hiroishicho
Gamagori AIC 443-0
533 676-611

5049 Professional Eqpt & Splys, NEC Wholesale

(P-7239)
ABC SCHOOL EQUIPMENT INC
Also Called: Platinum Visual Systems
1451 E 6th St, Corona (92879-1715)
PHONE...............................951 817-2200
Gary P Stell Jr, CEO
Thomas Mendez, CFO
Tom Mendez, Controller
EMP: 70
SQ FT: 35,000
SALES (est): 29.7MM Privately Held
WEB: www.abcschoolequipment.com
SIC: 5049 3861 2531 School supplies;
photographic equipment & supplies; pub-
lic building & related furniture

(P-7240)
CPI INTERNATIONAL
5580 Skylane Blvd, Santa Rosa
(95403-1030)
PHONE...............................707 521-6327
Ryan Vice, CEO
Joseph Phillips, CFO
Chris Woodruff, Vice Pres

▲ EMP: 70
SQ FT: 20,000
SALES (est): 20.5MM Privately Held
WEB: www.colitag.com
SIC: 5049 3826 Analytical instruments;
analytical instruments

(P-7241)
E JORDAN BROOKES CO INC (PA)
Also Called: E Jordan Brookes Co.
10634 Shoemaker Ave, Santa Fe Springs
(90670-4038)
P.O. Box 2220 (90670-0220)
PHONE...............................562 968-2100
Robert Brooke, CEO
R J Brookes Jr, President
Robert J Brookes Jr, President
Valentine Brookes, Corp Secy
Stephen Johnson, Business Mgr
▲ EMP: 69
SQ FT: 75,000
SALES (est): 39.3MM Privately Held
WEB: www.ejbco.com
SIC: 5049 Engineers' equipment & sup-
plies

(P-7242)
FACTORY R D
23192 Verdugo Dr, Laguna Hills
(92653-1377)
PHONE...............................949 900-3460
Tom Swanecamp, Owner
EMP: 60
SALES (est): 1.7MM Privately Held
SIC: 5049 Engineers' equipment & sup-
plies

(P-7243)
FISHER SCIENTIFIC COMPANY LLC
6722 Bickmore Ave, Chino (91708-9101)
PHONE...............................909 393-2100
John Pouk, Vice Pres
Renard Hoffman, Opers Staff
EMP: 100
SALES (corp-wide): 20.9B Publicly Held
WEB: www.fishersci.com
SIC: 5049 Laboratory equipment, except
medical or dental
HQ: Fisher Scientific Company Llc
300 Industry Dr
Pittsburgh PA 15275
724 517-1500

(P-7244)
INTERLAB INC
636 Broadway Ste 322, San Diego
(92101-5410)
PHONE...............................619 302-3095
Alexander Vedemin, President
Boris Urslts, Admin Sec
▼ EMP: 50
SALES (est): 18MM Privately Held
SIC: 5049 Laboratory equipment, except
medical or dental

(P-7245)
MOLECULAR BIOPRODUCTS INC
2200 S Mcdowell Blvd Ext, Petaluma
(94954-5659)
PHONE...............................707 762-6689
Warner Johnson, Director
EMP: 220
SALES (corp-wide): 20.9B Publicly Held
WEB: www.mbpinc.com
SIC: 5049 Scientific recording equipment
HQ: Molecular Bioproducts, Inc.
9389 Waples St
San Diego CA 92121
858 453-7551

(P-7246)
R C I ENTERPRISES INC
Also Called: R C I Image Systems
3848 Del Amo Blvd Ste 301, Torrance
(90503-7711)
PHONE...............................310 370-5900
Richard Corrales, President
Lynda Deibner, Corp Secy
Lyla Corrales, Vice Pres
Eric Gungab, Info Tech Mgr
Vickie Corrales, VP Sls/Mktg
EMP: 50

SQ FT: 12,000
SALES (est): 7.8MM Privately Held
SIC: 5049 7389 Optical goods; microfilm
recording & developing service

(P-7247)
REM OPTICAL COMPANY INC
Also Called: REM Eye Wear
10941 La Tuna Canyon Rd, Sun Valley
(91352-2012)
PHONE...............................818 504-3950
Michael L Hundert, CEO
Steve Horowitz, President
Donna Gindy, COO
Gerry Hundert, Chairman
Mike Hundert, Officer
▲ EMP: 100
SQ FT: 42,000
SALES (est): 40.9MM Privately Held
WEB: www.remeyewear.com
SIC: 5049 Optical goods

(P-7248)
SOCIAL STUDIES SCHOOL SERVICE
Also Called: Writing Company
10200 Jefferson Blvd, Culver City
(90232-3524)
P.O. Box 802 (90232-0802)
PHONE...............................310 839-2436
David M Weigner, CEO
Irwin Ledin, President
Sanford Weiner, President
Matthew Kraus, Opers Mgr
Aaron Willis, Marketing Mgr
▲ EMP: 65 EST: 1967
SALES (est): 34.2MM Privately Held
WEB: www.socialstudies.com
SIC: 5049 School supplies

(P-7249)
TECAN SP INC
14180 Live Oak Ave, Baldwin Park
(91706-1350)
P.O. Box 1608 (91706-7608)
PHONE...............................626 962-0010
Philip A Dimson, CEO
Christian Herr, CFO
Nancy Dimson, Vice Pres
Misty McFarren, Office Mgr
John Laycock, Info Tech Dir
▲ EMP: 84
SALES (est): 2.2MM
SALES (corp-wide): 554.6MM Privately
Held
WEB: www.speware.com
SIC: 5049 Laboratory equipment, except
medical or dental
PA: Tecan Group Ag
Seestrasse 103
MAnnedorf ZH 8708
449 228-888

(P-7250)
VWR INTERNATIONAL LLC
Also Called: VWR Scientific
6609 Mount Whitney Dr, Buena Park
(90620-4237)
PHONE...............................714 220-2615
Jenny Nelson, Branch Mgr
Yvonne Ng, Officer
David Lawless, Executive
Chris Cardoza, Office Mgr
Alan Sullivan, Administration
EMP: 50 Privately Held
WEB: www.vwrsp.com
SIC: 5049 5169 Laboratory equipment,
except medical or dental; chemicals & al-
lied products
HQ: Vwr International, Llc
100 W Matsonford Rd # 1
Radnor PA 19087
610 386-1700

5051 Metals Service Centers

(P-7251)
ACME METALS LLC
Also Called: Acme Metals & Steel Supply Inc
14930 S San Pedro St, Gardena
(90248-2036)
PHONE...............................310 329-2263
Howard Brand, CEO

Jack Goldberg, *Chairman*
Avelino Garcia, *General Mgr*
Cristina Martinez, *Controller*
◆ EMP: 60
SQ FT: 265,000
SALES: 32MM **Privately Held**
SIC: **5051** Steel

(P-7252)
AJ OSTER WEST LLC
Also Called: Ajo
22833 La Palma Ave, Yorba Linda
(92887-4767)
PHONE..................714 692-1000
Aaron Baldridge, *General Mgr*
Marc R Bacon, *CFO*
Robert M James, *Vice Pres*
Joseph T Woo, *Vice Pres*
Bob Judge, *Plant Mgr*
EMP: 57
SQ FT: 55,000
SALES (est): 29.5MM **Publicly Held**
WEB: www.olinbrass.com
SIC: **5051** Metals service centers & offices
HQ: A.J. Oster, Llc
301 Metro Center Blvd # 204
Warwick RI 02886
401 736-2600

(P-7253)
ALPERT & ALPERT IRON & MET INC
2350 W 16th St, Long Beach (90813-1044)
PHONE..................562 624-8833
George Soto, *Branch Mgr*
EMP: 50
SALES (corp-wide): 51.1MM **Privately Held**
SIC: **5051** Iron & steel (ferrous) products; miscellaneous nonferrous products
PA: Alpert & Alpert Iron & Metal, Inc.
1815 S Soto St
Los Angeles CA 90023
323 265-4040

(P-7254)
ALUMINUM PRECISION PDTS INC (PA)
3333 W Warner Ave, Santa Ana (92704-5898)
PHONE..................714 546-8125
Gregory S Keeler, *President*
Roark Keeler, *CFO*
Simona Manoiu, *CFO*
David P Silva, *Vice Pres*
Terry Seibert, *VP Bus Dvlpt*
▲ EMP: 550 EST: 1965
SALES (est): 213.4MM **Privately Held**
WEB: www.aluminumprecision.com
SIC: **5051** Metals service centers & offices

(P-7255)
AM PRODUCTS INC
1661 Palm St, Santa Ana (92701-5189)
PHONE..................714 662-4454
Tim Van Mechelen, *President*
Case Van Mechelen, *CEO*
EMP: 50
SALES (est): 6.6MM **Privately Held**
WEB: www.amproducts.net
SIC: **5051** 5072 Sheets, metal; structural shapes, iron or steel; power tools & accessories

(P-7256)
AMERICAN METALS CORPORATION (HQ)
1499 Parkway Blvd, West Sacramento (95691-5019)
P.O. Box 980100 (95798-0100)
PHONE..................916 371-7700
Nicole Heater, *CEO*
Chris Montgomery, *Sales Staff*
Ann McMicking, *Receptionist*
▲ EMP: 105
SALES (est): 94.7MM
SALES (corp-wide): 9.7B **Publicly Held**
WEB: www.rsac.com
SIC: **5051** Iron or steel flat products; castings, rough: iron or steel; steel; aluminum bars, rods, ingots, sheets, pipes, plates, etc.
PA: Reliance Steel & Aluminum Co.
350 S Grand Ave Ste 5100
Los Angeles CA 90071
213 687-7700

(P-7257)
AOC TECHNOLOGIES INC
5960 Inglewood Dr, Pleasanton (94588-8610)
PHONE..................925 875-0808
Gordon Gu, *President*
▲ EMP: 315
SALES (est): 124.4MM **Privately Held**
WEB: www.aoctech.com
SIC: **5051** 3357 Metal wires, ties, cables & screening; fiber optic cable (insulated)

(P-7258)
ARCHITECTURAL GL & ALUM CO INC (PA)
6400 Brisa St, Livermore (94550-2550)
PHONE..................925 583-2460
Joseph Brescia, *CEO*
John Buckley, *President*
William Coll Jr, *Vice Pres*
William Coll Sr, *Admin Sec*
▲ EMP: 155 EST: 1970
SQ FT: 33,000
SALES (est): 145.6MM **Privately Held**
SIC: **5051** 1793 1791 3442 Aluminum bars, rods, ingots, sheets, pipes, plates, etc.; glass & glazing work; exterior wall system installation; sash, door or window: metal

(P-7259)
ASC PROFILES LLC (DH)
Also Called: ASC Building Products
2110 Enterprise Blvd, West Sacramento (95691-3428)
PHONE..................916 372-6851
John Cross, *President*
Mike Wire, *CFO*
Michele Cabral, *Info Tech Dir*
Shane Smith, *Info Tech Mgr*
Susan Nahlen, *Accountant*
EMP: 85 EST: 1972
SQ FT: 87,120
SALES (est): 94MM **Privately Held**
WEB: www.ascpacific.com
SIC: **5051** Steel

(P-7260)
B & B SURPLUS INC (PA)
Also Called: B & B Specialty Metals
7020 Rosedale Hwy, Bakersfield (93308-5842)
PHONE..................661 589-0381
Donice Boylan, *President*
Mike Georgino, *Vice Pres*
Dominick Pisano, *General Mgr*
Allen Arrington, *Admin Sec*
Michael Arrington, *Credit Mgr*
▲ EMP: 65
SQ FT: 20,000
SALES (est): 48.8MM **Privately Held**
SIC: **5051** Pipe & tubing, steel; steel

(P-7261)
BLUE CHIP STAMPS
301 E Colo Blvd Ste 300, Pasadena (91101)
PHONE..................626 585-6700
Robert H Bird, *CEO*
Charles T Munger, *CEO*
Jeffrey L Jacobson, *CFO*
Kenneth E Wittmeyer, *Vice Pres*
EMP: 3074
SQ FT: 123,732
SALES (est): 221.8MM
SALES (corp-wide): 242.1B **Publicly Held**
WEB: www.bluechipstamps.com
SIC: **5051** Steel
PA: Berkshire Hathaway Inc.
3555 Farnam St Ste 1140
Omaha NE 68131
402 346-1400

(P-7262)
BORRMANN METAL CENTER (PA)
110 W Olive Ave, Burbank (91502-1822)
PHONE..................818 846-7171
Robert Wedeen, *President*
Bob Persson, *President*
Jane Borrmann, *CEO*
William L Todd, *Corp Secy*
Michelle Pitini, *Office Mgr*
▲ EMP: 60

SQ FT: 75,000
SALES: 43MM **Privately Held**
WEB: www.borrmannmetalcenter.com
SIC: **5051** Steel

(P-7263)
BPS SUPPLY GROUP (PA)
Also Called: Imperial Pipe & Supply
3301 Zachary Ave, Shafter (93263-9424)
P.O. Box 639, Bakersfield (93302-0639)
PHONE..................661 589-9141
Dwight Byrum, *Chairman*
Dan Byrum, *President*
John Byrum, *COO*
Cary Evans, *CFO*
Dwight Byrumm, *Chairman*
▲ EMP: 60 EST: 1968
SQ FT: 20,000
SALES (est): 150.6MM **Privately Held**
SIC: **5051** 5085 Pipe & tubing, steel; valves & fittings

(P-7264)
CALPIPE INDUSTRIES LLC (HQ)
Also Called: Calbond
19440 S Dminguez Hills Dr, Rancho Dominguez (90220-6417)
PHONE..................562 803-4388
Daniel J Markus, *CEO*
Fred Arjani, *CFO*
Sheri Caine-Markus, *Admin Sec*
▲ EMP: 150
SQ FT: 60,000
SALES (est): 79.8MM **Publicly Held**
SIC: **5051** 3498 Metals service centers & offices; fabricated pipe & fittings; tube fabricating (contract bending & shaping)

(P-7265)
CLEMENT SUPPORT SERVICES INC
1001 Yosemite Dr, Milpitas (95035-5409)
PHONE..................408 227-1171
Anthony Clement, *CEO*
John White, *CFO*
Michelle Clement, *Vice Pres*
Mike Golini, *Vice Pres*
EMP: 54
SQ FT: 36,000
SALES (est): 36.7MM **Privately Held**
WEB: www.clementsupport.com
SIC: **5051** Nonferrous metal sheets, bars, rods, etc.

(P-7266)
COAST ALUM & ARCHITECTURAL INC (PA)
10628 Fulton Wells Ave, Santa Fe Springs (90670-3740)
P.O. Box 2144 (90670-0440)
PHONE..................562 946-6061
Thomas C Clark, *President*
Bonnie Clark, *Shareholder*
Julio Marrero, *COO*
Charley Holton, *Branch Mgr*
Karen Smith, *General Mgr*
▲ EMP: 125
SQ FT: 112,000
SALES (est): 198.4MM **Privately Held**
SIC: **5051** Miscellaneous nonferrous products; nonferrous metal sheets, bars, rods, etc.

(P-7267)
CREST STEEL CORPORATION
6580 General Rd, Riverside (92509-0103)
PHONE..................310 830-2651
James D Hoffman, *CEO*
Kris Farris, *President*
David Vercuche, *CFO*
Dave Zertuche, *CFO*
Mike Gilbert, *Branch Mgr*
▲ EMP: 90
SQ FT: 12,000
SALES (est): 118.8MM
SALES (corp-wide): 9.7B **Publicly Held**
SIC: **5051** Steel
PA: Reliance Steel & Aluminum Co.
350 S Grand Ave Ste 5100
Los Angeles CA 90071
213 687-7700

(P-7268)
DANIEL GERARD WORLDWIDE INC
Also Called: City Wire Cloth
13055 Jurupa Ave, Fontana (92337-6982)
PHONE..................951 361-1111
Todd Snelbaker, *Manager*
Jackie Puga, *Sales Mgr*
EMP: 71
SQ FT: 50,000
SALES (corp-wide): 91.8MM **Privately Held**
WEB: www.gerarddaniels.com
SIC: **5051** 3496 3356 3315 Wire; mesh, made from purchased wire; nonferrous rolling & drawing; steel wire & related products
PA: Daniel Gerard Worldwide Inc
34 Barnhart Dr
Hanover PA 17331
800 232-3332

(P-7269)
DIX METALS INC
14801 Able Ln Ste 101, Huntington Beach (92647-2059)
PHONE..................714 677-0777
Donald Carr, *Vice Pres*
Bob Dix Sr, *Vice Pres*
Kimberly Schear, *Human Resources*
Jon Nutter, *Sales Associate*
Jenny Bermudez, *Sales Staff*
▲ EMP: 59
SQ FT: 111,000
SALES (est): 28.9MM **Privately Held**
WEB: www.dixmetals.com
SIC: **5051** Ferrous metals; nonferrous metal sheets, bars, rods, etc.

(P-7270)
DOUGLAS STEEL SUPPLY INC (PA)
Also Called: Douglas Steel Supply Co.
4804 Laurel Canyon Blvd, Valley Village (91607-3717)
PHONE..................323 587-7676
Douglas Stein, *CEO*
Don Hecht, *Vice Pres*
Donal Hecht, *Vice Pres*
Michael King, *Vice Pres*
Don Beier, *Controller*
EMP: 57
SQ FT: 100,000
SALES (est): 41.4MM **Privately Held**
WEB: www.douglassteelsupply.com
SIC: **5051** Steel; sheets

(P-7271)
EARLE M JORGENSEN COMPANY
Also Called: EMJ Hayward
31100 Wiegman Rd, Hayward (94544-7850)
PHONE..................510 487-2700
Barbara Nemeth, *Branch Mgr*
Richard Kotalik, *Sales Associate*
EMP: 54
SQ FT: 91,982
SALES (corp-wide): 9.7B **Publicly Held**
WEB: www.emjmetals.com
SIC: **5051** Steel
HQ: Earle M. Jorgensen Company
10650 Alameda St
Lynwood CA 90262
323 567-1122

(P-7272)
EARLE M JORGENSEN COMPANY
350 S Grand Ave Ste 5100, Los Angeles (90071-3421)
PHONE..................323 567-1122
Janice Day, *Info Tech Dir*
EMP: 54
SALES (corp-wide): 9.7B **Publicly Held**
SIC: **5051** Steel
HQ: Earle M. Jorgensen Company
10650 Alameda St
Lynwood CA 90262
323 567-1122

(P-7273)
FALLON LAND COMPANY INC
Also Called: Southland Steel
4 Corporate Plaza Dr # 210, Newport
Beach (92660-7906)
P.O. Box 1755 (92659-0755)
PHONE..........................213 880-1279
Robert Fallon, *President*
EMP: 50
SQ FT: 48,000
SALES (est): 9.9MM **Privately Held**
SIC: 5051 Metals service centers & offices

(P-7274)
GEORG FISCHER LLC (DH)
Also Called: Georg Fischer Piping
9271 Jeronimo Rd, Irvine (92618-1906)
PHONE..........................714 731-8800
James Jackson,
Heidi Defazio, *Chief Mktg Ofcr*
Oshaben Daniel, *Exec VP*
Thomas Sixsmith, *Vice Pres*
Brett Hicks, *Area Mgr*
▲ EMP: 70
SQ FT: 55,000
SALES (est): 77MM
SALES (corp-wide): 4.2B **Privately Held**
WEB: www.us.piping.georgefischer.com
SIC: 5051 5085 Pipe & tubing, steel;
valves & fittings
HQ: George Fischer, Inc.
3401 Aero Jet Ave
El Monte CA 91731
626 571-2770

(P-7275)
GERDAU REINFORCING STEEL
5425 Industrial Pkwy, San Bernardino
(92407-1803)
PHONE..........................909 713-1130
Lee Albright, *Manager*
EMP: 65 **Privately Held**
SIC: 5051 Steel
HQ: Gerdau Reinforcing Steel
3880 Murphy Canyon Rd # 100
San Diego CA 92123

(P-7276)
GLOBAL STAINLESS SUPPLY
17006 S Figueroa St, Gardena
(90248-3019)
PHONE..........................310 525-1865
Art Shelton, *President*
Michelle Brunlehler, *Exec Sec*
▲ EMP: 300
SALES (est): 19.8MM **Privately Held**
SIC: 5051 Steel

(P-7277)
GVS ITALY
8616 La Tijera Blvd, Los Angeles
(90045-3944)
PHONE..........................424 382-4343
Bruno Montesano, *Manager*
EMP: 100
SALES: 30MM **Privately Held**
SIC: 5051 Aluminum bars, rods, ingots,
sheets, pipes, plates, etc.

(P-7278)
HARBOR PIPE AND STEEL INC
Also Called: James Metals
1495 Columbia Ave Bldg 10, Riverside
(92507-2074)
PHONE..........................951 369-3990
Joseph W Beattie, *President*
Martha Fournier, *Corp Secy*
Joe Beattie, *Principal*
Tom Liljegren, *Principal*
P Jay Peterson, *Principal*
▲ EMP: 150 EST: 1962
SALES (est): 134.5MM **Privately Held**
SIC: 5051 Steel

(P-7279)
HARTMAN INDUSTRIES
Also Called: Commercial Casting Co
14933 Whittram Ave, Fontana
(92335-3186)
PHONE..........................909 428-0114
Brad J Hartman, *CEO*
Brett Hartman, *Vice Pres*
Sean Hartman, *Vice Pres*
▲ EMP: 60
SQ FT: 73,000

SALES: 8MM **Privately Held**
WEB: www.cmeworkholding.com
SIC: 5051 Castings, rough: iron or steel

(P-7280)
HUBBARD IRON DOORS INC
7407 Telegraph Rd, Montebello
(90640-6515)
PHONE..........................323 724-6500
Ron Hubbard, *President*
EMP: 50
SQ FT: 20,000
SALES (est): 12MM **Privately Held**
WEB: www.hubbardirondoors.com
SIC: 5051 Iron or steel semifinished products

(P-7281)
INFINITY METALS INC
600 E Lambert Rd, La Habra (90631-6141)
PHONE..........................562 697-8826
Kevin Ufholtz, *President*
Joellyn Bowker, *Finance Mgr*
EMP: 50
SQ FT: 2,000
SALES (est): 35MM **Privately Held**
SIC: 5051 Steel

(P-7282)
JACK RUBIN & SONS INC (PA)
13103 S Alameda St, Compton
(90222-2898)
P.O. Box 3005 (90223-3005)
PHONE..........................310 635-5407
Bruce Rubin, *CEO*
Michael Rubin, *Vice Pres*
Phillip Mandel, *Admin Sec*
▲ EMP: 50
SQ FT: 30,000
SALES (est): 10MM **Privately Held**
WEB: www.wirerope.net
SIC: 5051 3496 3999 Rope, wire (not insulated); woven wire products; atomizers,
toiletry

(P-7283)
JFE SHOJI TRADE AMERICA INC
(DH)
301 E Ocean Blvd Ste 1750, Long Beach
(90802-4879)
PHONE..........................562 637-3500
Toshihiro Kabasawa, *Exec VP*
Hidehiko Ogawa, *Exec VP*
▲ EMP: 85
SQ FT: 7,500
SALES (est): 326.8MM
SALES (corp-wide): 34.5B **Privately Held**
SIC: 5051 Steel
HQ: Jfe Shoji Trade Corporation
1-9-5, Otemachi
Chiyoda-Ku TKY 100-0
352 035-055

(P-7284)
JIMS SUPPLY CO INC (PA)
3530 Buck Owens Blvd, Bakersfield
(93308-4920)
P.O. Box 668 (93302-0668)
PHONE..........................661 324-6514
Doreen M Boylan, *CEO*
Bryan Boylan, *CFO*
Jon Thomas, *CFO*
Jennifer Drake, *Corp Secy*
Greg Boylan, *Vice Pres*
▲ EMP: 85
SQ FT: 25,300
SALES (est): 94.9MM **Privately Held**
WEB: www.jimssupply.com
SIC: 5051 Steel

(P-7285)
JOSEPH T RYERSON & SON
INC
4310 Bandini Blvd, Vernon (90058-4308)
P.O. Box 513817, Los Angeles (90051-1817)
PHONE..........................323 267-6000
Steve Bosway, *Branch Mgr*
Edward J Lehner, *CEO*
Rod Newcombe, *Facilities Mgr*
David Logan, *Manager*
EMP: 80 **Publicly Held**

SIC: 5051 5162 5085 Aluminum bars,
rods, ingots, sheets, pipes, plates, etc.;
iron & steel (ferrous) products; plastics
materials & basic shapes; industrial supplies
HQ: Joseph T. Ryerson & Son, Inc.
227 W Monroe St Fl 27
Chicago IL 60606
312 292-5000

(P-7286)
KLOECKNER METALS
CORPORATION
Also Called: Gary Steel Division
9804 Norwalk Blvd Ste 8, Santa Fe Springs
(90670-2936)
PHONE..........................562 906-2020
Bob Tripp, *Vice Pres*
Said Armanious, *Sales Mgr*
EMP: 75
SALES (corp-wide): 7.4B **Privately Held**
SIC: 5051 Steel
HQ: Kloeckner Metals Corporation
500 Colonial Center Pkwy # 500
Roswell GA 30076

(P-7287)
KLOECKNER METALS
CORPORATION
9804 Norwalk Blvd Bldg A, Santa Fe
Springs (90670-2936)
PHONE..........................562 906-2020
Marshall Katz, *General Mgr*
EMP: 50
SALES (corp-wide): 7.4B **Privately Held**
WEB: www.macsteelusa.com
SIC: 5051 Steel
HQ: Kloeckner Metals Corporation
500 Colonial Center Pkwy # 500
Roswell GA 30076

(P-7288)
KLOECKNER METALS
CORPORATION
2000 S O St, Tulare (93274-6852)
PHONE..........................559 688-7980
Bob Kyle, *Branch Mgr*
Gary Hinchey, *Purch Agent*
EMP: 52
SALES (corp-wide): 7.4B **Privately Held**
SIC: 5051 Steel
HQ: Kloeckner Metals Corporation
500 Colonial Center Pkwy # 500
Roswell GA 30076

(P-7289)
MAXX METALS INC
355 Quarry Rd, San Carlos (94070-6217)
P.O. Box 10963, Pleasanton (94588-0963)
PHONE..........................650 654-1500
Paul A Wallace, *President*
Debra L Wallace, *CFO*
EMP: 68
SQ FT: 13,000
SALES (est): 5.2MM **Privately Held**
SIC: 5051 Steel

(P-7290)
MITSUI & CO (USA) INC
Also Called: Mitsui USA
601 S Figueroa St # 1900, Los Angeles
(90017-5704)
PHONE..........................213 896-1100
Shozaburo Marayama, *Manager*
EMP: 52
SALES (corp-wide): 45.9B **Privately Held**
WEB: www.mitsui.com
SIC: 5051 5094 Steel; bullion, precious
metals
HQ: Mitsui & Co. (U.S.A.), Inc.
200 Park Ave Fl 36
New York NY 10166
212 878-4000

(P-7291)
MONICO ALLOYS INC (PA)
3039 E Ana St, Compton (90221-5604)
PHONE..........................310 928-0168
Jason Zenk, *President*
Jason D Zenk, *President*
Saul Zenk, *CFO*
Ken Larson, *Senior VP*

Bruce Botansky, *Vice Pres*
◆ EMP: 98
SQ FT: 60,000
SALES (est): 56.8MM **Privately Held**
WEB: www.monicoalloys.com
SIC: 5051 Metals service centers & offices

(P-7292)
MWS PRECISION WIRE INDS INC
Also Called: Mws Wire Industries
31200 Cedar Valley Dr, Westlake Village
(91362-4035)
PHONE..........................818 991-8553
Toll Free:..........................888 -
Darrell H Friedman, *President*
Alan Friedman, *President*
Lois J Friedman, *Admin Sec*
Tomm Carlson, *Info Tech Mgr*
Denis Goss, *Controller*
EMP: 52
SQ FT: 32,000
SALES (est): 48.1MM **Privately Held**
WEB: www.mwswire.com
SIC: 5051 3351 3357 Copper sheets,
plates, bars, rods, pipes, etc.; wire, copper & copper alloy; nonferrous wiredrawing & insulating

(P-7293)
NORMAN INDUSTRIAL MTLS INC
(PA)
Also Called: Industrial Metal Supply Co
8300 San Fernando Rd, Sun Valley
(91352-3222)
PHONE..........................818 729-3333
Eric Steinhauer, *CEO*
David Pace, *President*
Dave Cohen, *COO*
David Berkey, *CFO*
Jack Costella, *General Mgr*
▲ EMP: 300
SQ FT: 70,000
SALES (est): 221.8MM **Privately Held**
WEB: www.industrialmetalsupply.com
SIC: 5051 3441 3449 Metals service centers & offices; fabricated structural metal;
miscellaneous metalwork

(P-7294)
NORMAN INDUSTRIAL MTLS INC
Also Called: Industrial Metal Supply Co Eba
7550 Ronson Rd, San Diego (92111-1500)
PHONE..........................858 277-8200
Wesley Sykes, *Manager*
Damon Bonaccorso, *Safety Mgr*
Art Villafana, *Safety Mgr*
EMP: 50
SALES (est): 6.1MM
SALES (corp-wide): 221.8MM **Privately
Held**
WEB: www.industrialmetalsupply.com
SIC: 5051 5211 Steel; lumber & other
building materials
PA: Norman Industrial Materials, Inc.
8300 San Fernando Rd
Sun Valley CA 91352
818 729-3333

(P-7295)
PACIFIC STEEL CASTING CO
LLC
1333 2nd St, Berkeley (94710-1375)
PHONE..........................510 558-2283
Jeff Stone, *CEO*
Mike Emmerichs, *President*
Krishnan Venkatesan, *COO*
Barry G Scott, *Vice Pres*
Katie Delsol, *Exec Dir*
▲ EMP: 430
SQ FT: 400,000
SALES: 80MM **Privately Held**
SIC: 5051 Metals service centers & offices

(P-7296)
PATTON SALES CORP (PA)
Also Called: Patton's Steel
1095 E California St, Ontario (91761-1909)
P.O. Box 273 (91762-8273)
PHONE..........................909 988-0661
Jonathan Novack, *CEO*
Matt Taylor, *Branch Mgr*
Rebecca Peters, *Credit Mgr*
Dani Novack, *Advt Staff*
David Wheaton, *Sales Staff*
◆ EMP: 120
SQ FT: 16,000

SALES (est): 136.8MM **Privately Held**
WEB: www.pattonscorp.com
SIC: 5051 5084 5712 5211 Steel; industrial machinery & equipment; office furniture; lumber & other building materials

(P-7297)
PDM STEEL SERVICE CENTERS
3500 Bassett St, Santa Clara (95054-2704)
PHONE.................................408 988-3000
John Norman, *General Mgr*
Debbie Lamica, *Purchasing*
Andrew Sanchez, *Warehouse Mgr*
EMP: 65
SQ FT: 46,080
SALES (corp-wide): 9.7B **Publicly Held**
WEB: www.pdmsteel.com
SIC: 5051 3444 3272 Steel; sheet metalwork; concrete products
HQ: Pdm Steel Service Centers, Inc
3535 E Myrtle St
Stockton CA 95205
209 943-0555

(P-7298)
PDM STEEL SERVICE CENTERS
4005 E Church Ave, Fresno (93725-1415)
P.O. Box 11188 (93772-1188)
PHONE.................................559 442-1410
Mike Hill, *Branch Mgr*
Paul Lowe, *Sales Dir*
Brendon Olson, *Warehouse Mgr*
Alan Ware, *Manager*
EMP: 50
SALES (corp-wide): 9.7B **Publicly Held**
WEB: www.pdmsteel.com
SIC: 5051 Steel
HQ: Pdm Steel Service Centers, Inc
3535 E Myrtle St
Stockton CA 95205
209 943-0555

(P-7299)
PDM STEEL SERVICE CENTERS (HQ)
Also Called: Specialty Steel Service
3535 E Myrtle St, Stockton (95205-4721)
P.O. Box 310 (95201-0310)
PHONE.................................209 943-0555
Derick Halecky, *President*
Joseph Anderson, *Vice Pres*
Brad Blickle, *Vice Pres*
Randy H Kearns, *Vice Pres*
William Nixon, *Vice Pres*
▲ **EMP:** 100 **EST:** 1954
SALES (est): 243MM
SALES (corp-wide): 9.7B **Publicly Held**
WEB: www.pdmsteel.com
SIC: 5051 Steel
PA: Reliance Steel & Aluminum Co.
350 S Grand Ave Ste 5100
Los Angeles CA 90071
213 687-7700

(P-7300)
PDM STEEL SERVICE CENTERS
Also Called: Feralloy PDM Steel Service
936 Performance Dr, Stockton
(95206-4930)
PHONE.................................209 234-0548
Frances Espinosa, *Branch Mgr*
EMP: 60
SALES (corp-wide): 9.7B **Publicly Held**
WEB: www.feralloy.com
SIC: 5051 Steel
HQ: Pdm Steel Service Centers, Inc
3535 E Myrtle St
Stockton CA 95205
209 943-0555

(P-7301)
PHILLIPS STEEL COMPANY
1368 W Anaheim St, Long Beach
(90813-2779)
PHONE.................................562 435-7571
Daryl S Phillips, *President*
Greg Phillips, *Vice Pres*
Paul Phillips, *Principal*
Sandy Phillips, *Principal*
Todd Phillips, *Principal*
▲ **EMP:** 50
SQ FT: 25,000
SALES (est): 67.7MM **Privately Held**
WEB: www.phillipssteel.com
SIC: 5051 Steel; aluminum bars, rods, ingots, sheets, pipes, plates, etc.; copper

(P-7302)
PRIMUS PIPE AND TUBE INC (DH)
5855 Obispo Ave, Long Beach
(90805-3715)
PHONE.................................562 808-8000
Tommy Grahn, *President*
Scott Templeton, *Exec VP*
Karl Almond, *Vice Pres*
Domenick Di Giallonardo, *Vice Pres*
Roy Harrison, *Vice Pres*
▲ **EMP:** 100
SQ FT: 120,000
SALES (est): 43.8MM
SALES (corp-wide): 2.1B **Privately Held**
SIC: 5051 Metals service centers & offices
HQ: Ta Chen International, Inc.
5855 Obispo Ave
Long Beach CA 90805
562 808-8000

(P-7303)
RAMCAST ORNAMENTAL SUP CO INC (PA)
2201 Firestone Blvd, Los Angeles
(90002-1547)
PHONE.................................323 585-1625
Rosalba R Warschaw, *CEO*
Ismael Ramirez, *President*
Hector Ramirez, *Treasurer*
Juan Ramirez, *Vice Pres*
Ricardo Ramirez, *Director*
▲ **EMP:** 105
SQ FT: 30,000
SALES: 47.9MM **Privately Held**
WEB: www.ramcast.net
SIC: 5051 Steel

(P-7304)
RELIANCE STEEL & ALUMINUM CO (PA)
350 S Grand Ave Ste 5100, Los Angeles
(90071-3421)
PHONE.................................213 687-7700
Gregg J Mollins, *President*
Mark V Kaminski, *Ch of Bd*
James D Hoffman, *COO*
Karla R Lewis, *CFO*
John Figueroa, *Bd of Directors*
◆ **EMP:** 82 **EST:** 1939
SALES: 9.7B **Publicly Held**
WEB: www.rsac.com
SIC: 5051 Structural shapes, iron or steel

(P-7305)
RELIANCE STEEL & ALUMINUM CO
Reliance Metal Center
33201 Western Ave, Union City
(94587-2208)
PHONE.................................510 476-4400
Dave Buchanan, *Manager*
Briana Cash, *Administration*
Joe Tulley, *Administration*
Bud Stevens, *Human Res Mgr*
EMP: 90
SQ FT: 137,757
SALES (corp-wide): 9.7B **Publicly Held**
WEB: www.rsac.com
SIC: 5051 Steel; aluminum bars, rods, ingots, sheets, pipes, plates, etc.; bars, metal; copper
PA: Reliance Steel & Aluminum Co.
350 S Grand Ave Ste 5100
Los Angeles CA 90071
213 687-7700

(P-7306)
RELIANCE STEEL & ALUMINUM CO
Tube Service
9351 Norwalk Blvd, Santa Fe Springs
(90670-2925)
P.O. Box 2728 (90670-0728)
PHONE.................................562 695-0467
Jan Hollar, *Branch Mgr*
Dorothy Kinsey, *Executive*
Doug McGowen, *Division Mgr*
John Rede, *Purch Mgr*
Klauss Van Beers, *Safety Mgr*
EMP: 58
SQ FT: 40,000
SALES (corp-wide): 9.7B **Publicly Held**
WEB: www.rsac.com
SIC: 5051 Steel

PA: Reliance Steel & Aluminum Co.
350 S Grand Ave Ste 5100
Los Angeles CA 90071
213 687-7700

(P-7307)
RELIANCE STEEL & ALUMINUM CO
Bralco Metals
15090 Northam St, La Mirada
(90638-5757)
PHONE.................................714 736-4800
Michael Hubbart, *Branch Mgr*
Shashi Bagai, *General Mgr*
Tim Deputy, *General Mgr*
Mike Hubbart, *General Mgr*
Ben Terry, *Administration*
EMP: 118
SALES (corp-wide): 9.7B **Publicly Held**
WEB: www.rsac.com
SIC: 5051 Steel; ferrous metals
PA: Reliance Steel & Aluminum Co.
350 S Grand Ave Ste 5100
Los Angeles CA 90071
213 687-7700

(P-7308)
RELIANCE STEEL & ALUMINUM CO
Also Called: Reliance Steel Company
2537 E 27th St, Vernon (90058-1284)
PHONE.................................323 583-6111
John Becknell, *Branch Mgr*
EMP: 200
SALES (corp-wide): 9.7B **Publicly Held**
WEB: www.rsac.com
SIC: 5051 Steel
PA: Reliance Steel & Aluminum Co.
350 S Grand Ave Ste 5100
Los Angeles CA 90071
213 687-7700

(P-7309)
RELIANCE STEEL & ALUMINUM CO
Metalcenter
12034 Greenstone Ave, Santa Fe Springs
(90670-4727)
P.O. Box 2101 (90670-0013)
PHONE.................................562 944-3322
Jay Rose, *Branch Mgr*
Al Cawley, *Opers Mgr*
EMP: 80
SQ FT: 142,000
SALES (corp-wide): 9.7B **Publicly Held**
WEB: www.rsac.com
SIC: 5051 Steel
PA: Reliance Steel & Aluminum Co.
350 S Grand Ave Ste 5100
Los Angeles CA 90071
213 687-7700

(P-7310)
ROLLED STEEL PRODUCTS CORP (PA)
Also Called: R S P
2187 Garfield Ave, Commerce
(90040-1855)
PHONE.................................323 723-8836
Robert Alperson, *Ch of Bd*
Steven Alperson, *President*
Lonnie Alperson, *CFO*
Dennis Moslenko, *MIS Dir*
Nellie Romanu, *Controller*
EMP: 68
SQ FT: 125,000
SALES (est): 27.8MM **Privately Held**
WEB: www.rolledsteel.com
SIC: 5051 3316 Steel; cold finishing of steel shapes

(P-7311)
ROSSIN STEEL INC
2660 Cactus Rd, San Diego (92154-8022)
PHONE.................................619 656-9200
Ted F Rossin, *CEO*
Jeffrey Clinkscleas, *Vice Pres*
EMP: 110
SALES: 30MM **Privately Held**
WEB: www.rossinsteel.com
SIC: 5051 Steel

(P-7312)
SAC INTERNATIONAL STEEL INC (PA)
6130 Avalon Blvd, Los Angeles
(90003-1633)
PHONE.................................323 232-2467
Shaukat A Chohan, *President*
Shaukaj Ali Chohan, *President*
Omar Chohan, *Vice Pres*
Mahmooda Chohan, *Admin Sec*
◆ **EMP:** 74
SQ FT: 100,000
SALES (est): 20.4MM **Privately Held**
WEB: www.sacintl.com
SIC: 5051 Sheets, metal

(P-7313)
SIMPSON STRONG-TIE INTL INC
Simpson Strong-Tie Anchor Syst
5956 W Las Positas Blvd, Pleasanton
(94588-8540)
PHONE.................................925 560-9000
Undetermin BR, *Manager*
EMP: 100
SALES (corp-wide): 977MM **Publicly Held**
SIC: 5051 Forms, concrete construction (steel)
HQ: Simpson Strong-Tie International, Inc.
5956 W Las Positas Blvd
Pleasanton CA 94588

(P-7314)
SLAKEY BROTHERS INC
1001 Oates Ct, Modesto (95358-5818)
P.O. Box 4099 (95352-4099)
PHONE.................................209 556-1100
Bob Wirowek, *Manager*
EMP: 50
SALES (corp-wide): 197MM **Privately Held**
WEB: www.slakey.com
SIC: 5051 5084 5078 5064 Sheets, metal; industrial machine parts; fixtures, refrigerated; air conditioning room units, self-contained; heating & air conditioning contractors; heating equipment (hydronic)
PA: Slakey Brothers, Inc.
2215 Kausen Dr Ste 1
Elk Grove CA 95758
916 478-2000

(P-7315)
SPECIALTY STEEL SERVICE CO INC (HQ)
3300 Douglas Blvd Ste 128, Roseville
(95661-3897)
PHONE.................................916 771-4737
Fax: 916 771-8658
▲ **EMP:** 70
SQ FT: 3,000
SALES (est): 24.4MM
SALES (corp-wide): 10.4B **Publicly Held**
WEB: www.specialtysteel.net
SIC: 5051
PA: Reliance Steel & Aluminum Co.
350 S Grand Ave Ste 5100
Los Angeles CA 90071
213 687-7700

(P-7316)
STATE PIPE & SUPPLY INC
Westcoast Pipe Lining Division
2180 N Locust Ave, Rialto (92377-4166)
PHONE.................................909 356-5670
Kenneth Walker, *Manager*
Laurie Dodson, *Engineer*
EMP: 50
SALES (corp-wide): 1.5B **Privately Held**
WEB: www.statepipe.com
SIC: 5051 Pipe & tubing, steel
HQ: State Pipe & Supply, Inc.
183 S Cedar Ave
Rialto CA 92376
909 877-9999

(P-7317)
STATE PIPE & SUPPLY INC (DH)
183 S Cedar Ave, Rialto (92376-9011)
PHONE.................................909 877-9999
Byung Joon Lee, *CEO*
Honggie Kim, *President*
Gary Knoroski, *Vice Pres*
Howard W Lee, *Admin Sec*

Erik Estrada, *Marketing Staff*
EMP: 55
SQ FT: 20,000
SALES (est): 47.7MM
SALES (corp-wide): 1.5B **Privately Held**
WEB: www.statepipe.com
SIC: 5051 5085 Pipe & tubing, steel; industrial supplies
HQ: Seah Steel California, Llc
2100 Main St Ste 100
Irvine CA 92614
949 655-8000

(P-7318)
TA CHEN INTERNATIONAL INC (HQ)
Also Called: SUNLAND SHUTTERS
5855 Obispo Ave, Long Beach (90805-3715)
PHONE.............................562 808-8000
Johnny Hsieh, *CEO*
Andrew Chang, *CFO*
James Chang, *Vice Pres*
John Hellighausen, *Vice Pres*
◆ **EMP:** 172
SQ FT: 200,000
SALES: 1.2B
SALES (corp-wide): 2.1B **Privately Held**
WEB: www.tachen.com
SIC: 5051 5085 5023 Pipe & tubing, steel; steel; valves & fittings; window covering parts & accessories
PA: Ta Chen Stainless Pipe Co., Ltd.
125, Hsin Tien 2nd St.,
Tainan City 71752
627 017-56

(P-7319)
TCI ALUMINUM/NORTH INC
2353 Davis Ave, Hayward (94545-1111)
PHONE.............................510 786-3750
Jeff Bordalampe, *President*
Jim Clifton, *Vice Pres*
EMP: 60
SQ FT: 60,000
SALES (est): 40.3MM **Privately Held**
WEB: www.tcialuminum.com
SIC: 5051 Aluminum bars, rods, ingots, sheets, pipes, plates, etc.

(P-7320)
TELL STEEL INC
2345 W 17th St, Long Beach (90813-1097)
PHONE.............................562 435-4826
Greg More, *President*
Pete V Trigt, *Admin Sec*
Valerie Varchil, *Finance*
Donna Hansen, *Human Res Dir*
Kevin McClister, *Sales Executive*
▲ **EMP:** 60
SQ FT: 100,000
SALES (est): 65.2MM
SALES (corp-wide): 68.2MM **Privately Held**
WEB: www.tellsteel.com
SIC: 5051 Steel; aluminum bars, rods, ingots, sheets, pipes, plates, etc.
PA: Tuffli Company Incorporated
2780 Skypark Dr Ste 460
Torrance CA 90505
310 326-5500

(P-7321)
TOTTEN TUBES INC (PA)
500 W Danlee St, Azusa (91702-2341)
PHONE.............................626 812-0220
Tracy N Totten, *CEO*
Linda Furse, *CFO*
David Totten, *Chairman*
Jeffrey Totten, *Treasurer*
Laura Morick, *Vice Pres*
EMP: 60
SQ FT: 73,000
SALES (est): 51.9MM **Privately Held**
WEB: www.tottentubes.com
SIC: 5051 Pipe & tubing, steel; steel

(P-7322)
VER SALES INC (PA)
2509 N Naomi St, Burbank (91504-3236)
PHONE.............................818 567-3000
Gloria Ryan, *CEO*
James J Ryan, *CEO*
Craig Ryan, *Vice Pres*
Patrick Ryan, *Vice Pres*
Paul Ryan, *Vice Pres*

▲ **EMP:** 54
SQ FT: 30,000
SALES (est): 22.9MM **Privately Held**
WEB: www.versales.com
SIC: 5051 5099 3357 Metal wires, ties, cables & screening; safety equipment & supplies; nonferrous wiredrawing & insulating

5052 Coal & Other Minerals & Ores Wholesale

(P-7323)
MORRISON LANDSCAPING INC
Also Called: Earthco
1225 E Wakeham Ave, Santa Ana (92705-4145)
PHONE.............................714 571-0455
Robert Morrison, *President*
Denise Morrison, *Vice Pres*
Kyle Morrison, *Opers Mgr*
Dan Morrison, *Manager*
EMP: 50
SALES: 4.4MM **Privately Held**
SIC: 5052 Coal & other minerals & ores

5063 Electrl Apparatus, Eqpt, Wiring Splys Wholesale

(P-7324)
ACT LIGHTING INC
2313 N Valley St, Burbank (91505-1114)
PHONE.............................818 707-0884
Mario Collazo, *Vice Pres*
Andrew Beck, *General Mgr*
David MA, *Business Anlyst*
Rick Dobbie, *Opers Staff*
Joe Goshert, *Sales Staff*
EMP: 560
SALES (corp-wide): 59MM **Privately Held**
WEB: www.aclighting.com
SIC: 5063 Lighting fixtures
PA: A.C.T. Lighting Inc.
122 John St
Hackensack NJ 07601
844 996-0884

(P-7325)
ADJ PRODUCTS LLC (PA)
6122 S Eastern Ave, Commerce (90040-3402)
PHONE.............................323 582-2650
Charles J Davies, *CEO*
Toby Velasquez, *President*
EMP: 120 **EST** 2012
SALES (est): 38MM **Privately Held**
SIC: 5063 Lighting fixtures

(P-7326)
ADVANCED LIGHTING CONCEPTS INC
Also Called: Environmental Lights
11235 W Bernardo Ct # 102, San Diego (92127-1628)
PHONE.............................858 521-0233
Gregory D Thorson, *CEO*
Anne M Thorson, *Vice Pres*
Scott Drever, *Engineer*
Candice Garcia, *Engineer*
Eric Goveia, *Engineer*
▲ **EMP:** 50
SQ FT: 30,000
SALES (est): 11MM **Privately Held**
WEB: www.environmentallights.com
SIC: 5063 Light bulbs & related supplies

(P-7327)
ALLIED ELECTRIC MOTOR SVC INC (PA)
4690 E Jensen Ave, Fresno (93725-1698)
PHONE.............................559 486-4222
Salvatore Rome, *Ch of Bd*
Gail Mandal, *President*
Joyce Barnes, *Corp Secy*
Henry Mandal, *Senior VP*
Richard Johnson, *Vice Pres*
EMP: 65
SQ FT: 100,000

SALES (est): 43.9MM **Privately Held**
WEB: www.alliedelectric.net
SIC: 5063 7694 Electrical supplies; electric motor repair

(P-7328)
AMERICAN DE ROSA LAMPARTS LLC (PA)
Also Called: Luminance
1945 S Tubeway Ave, Commerce (90040-1611)
PHONE.............................800 777-4440
Christopher M Larocca, *CEO*
Andy Marosi, *CIO*
Lacey Baker, *Graphic Designe*
Tiffany Tran, *Controller*
Lilli Rodriguez, *Human Res Dir*
◆ **EMP:** 77
SQ FT: 155,000
SALES (est): 78.7MM **Privately Held**
SIC: 5063 3364 3229 Lighting fixtures; light bulbs & related supplies; lighting fittings & accessories; brass & bronze die-castings; bulbs for electric lights

(P-7329)
AMERICAN ELECTRIC SUPPLY INC (PA)
361 S Maple St, Corona (92880-6907)
P.O. Box 2710 (92878-2710)
PHONE.............................951 734-7910
Michael Pratt, *CEO*
Jerry Empson, *Treasurer*
Barry Van Fossan, *Vice Pres*
Kevin Klinzing, *Admin Sec*
David Gutierrez, *Project Mgr*
▲ **EMP:** 99
SQ FT: 13,086
SALES (est): 118.9MM **Privately Held**
WEB: www.amelect.com
SIC: 5063 Electrical supplies; wire & cable; lighting fixtures

(P-7330)
ANIXTER INC
855 National Dr Ste 103, Sacramento (95834-1195)
PHONE.............................916 563-7560
Rich Westphal, *Manager*
William Evans, *Branch Mgr*
EMP: 100
SALES (corp-wide): 7.9B **Publicly Held**
SIC: 5063 Electrical apparatus & equipment
HQ: Anixter Inc.
2301 Patriot Blvd
Glenview IL 60026
800 323-8167

(P-7331)
ANIXTER INC
7140 Opportunity Rd, San Diego (92111-2202)
PHONE.............................858 571-6571
Tina O'Donnell, *Manager*
EMP: 50
SALES (corp-wide): 7.9B **Publicly Held**
WEB: www.clarksecurity.com
SIC: 5063 Electrical apparatus & equipment
HQ: Anixter Inc.
2301 Patriot Blvd
Glenview IL 60026
800 323-8167

(P-7332)
ANIXTER INC
30061 Ahern Ave, Union City (94587-1234)
PHONE.............................510 477-2400
Willie Rivera, *Principal*
EMP: 60
SALES (corp-wide): 7.9B **Publicly Held**
SIC: 5063 Wire & cable
HQ: Anixter Inc.
2301 Patriot Blvd
Glenview IL 60026
800 323-8167

(P-7333)
ANIXTER INC
5000 Franklin Dr 200, Pleasanton (94588-3354)
PHONE.............................925 469-8500
Sabrina Vasquez, *Manager*
EMP: 50

SALES (corp-wide): 7.9B **Publicly Held**
SIC: 5063 Wire & cable
HQ: Anixter Inc.
2301 Patriot Blvd
Glenview IL 60026
800 323-8167

(P-7334)
ARROW WIRE & CABLE INC (PA)
13911 Yorba Ave, Chino (91710-5521)
PHONE.............................909 282-1940
Zahid Karim, *President*
Cathy Riley, *Corp Secy*
Jim Morales, *Vice Pres*
Steve Sandys, *Opers Mgr*
Alexis Holland, *Marketing Mgr*
▲ **EMP:** 50
SQ FT: 26,000
SALES (est): 34.2MM **Privately Held**
WEB: www.arrow-wc.com
SIC: 5063 Electronic wire & cable; wire & cable

(P-7335)
B & K ELECTRIC WHOLESALE (PA)
1225 S Johnson Dr, City of Industry (91745-2409)
P.O. Box 3080 (91744-0080)
PHONE.............................626 965-5040
Robert T Brown, *CEO*
Kenneth W Kindrick, *Ch of Bd*
Kathleen Ellison, *President*
Mike Blanchard, *Vice Pres*
Todd Brown, *Vice Pres*
EMP: 90
SQ FT: 26,000
SALES (est): 93MM **Privately Held**
SIC: 5063 5211 Electrical supplies; electrical construction materials; electrical construction materials

(P-7336)
BARTCO LIGHTING INC
5761 Research Dr, Huntington Beach (92649-1616)
PHONE.............................714 230-3200
Robert Barton, *CEO*
Daniel Barton, *Exec VP*
Dana B McKe, *Exec VP*
Brian Labbe, *Vice Pres*
Rob Barton, *CTO*
▲ **EMP:** 70
SALES: 20MM **Privately Held**
WEB: www.bartcolighting.com
SIC: 5063 3648 Lighting fixtures, commercial & industrial; lighting fixtures; airport lighting fixtures: runway approach, taxi or ramp

(P-7337)
BAY CITY EQUIPMENT INDS INC
Also Called: John Deere Authorized Dealer
13625 Danielson St, Poway (92064-6829)
PHONE.............................619 938-8200
Mark Loftin, *CEO*
Rodney Lee, *President*
Charles Loftin, *Corp Secy*
Patricia Alarcon, *Administration*
EMP: 100
SQ FT: 20,000
SALES: 32.8MM **Privately Held**
WEB: www.bcew.com
SIC: 5063 5082 Generators; motors, electric; construction & mining machinery

(P-7338)
BEL AIR LIGHTING INC (PA)
Also Called: Trans Globe Lighting
28104 Witherspoon Pkwy, Valencia (91355-4175)
PHONE.............................818 768-5511
Eli Haber, *CEO*
Cary Haber, *President*
Nazanine Amiri, *CFO*
David Ziv, *Exec VP*
Guy Zvi, *Opers Staff*
◆ **EMP:** 102
SQ FT: 200,000
SALES (est): 51.2MM **Privately Held**
WEB: www.tglighting.com
SIC: 5063 Lighting fixtures

(P-7339)
BML INDUSTRIES INC
Also Called: American International Inds
1040 Avenida Acaso, Camarillo
(93012-8712)
PHONE..............................805 388-6800
David Eisenstein, *President*
▲ EMP: 65
SQ FT: 50,000
SALES (est): 9.7MM
SALES (corp-wide): 34.1MM **Privately Held**
WEB: www.aius.net
SIC: 5063 Electrical apparatus & equipment
PA: Aamp Of Florida, Inc.
   15500 Lightwave Dr # 202
   Clearwater FL 33760
   727 572-9255

(P-7340)
BRITHINEE ELECTRIC
620 S Rancho Ave, Colton (92324-3296)
PHONE..............................909 825-7971
Wallace P Brithinee, *President*
Donald P Brithinee, *Vice Pres*
Wallace Brithinee, *Info Tech Dir*
Carlos Mazariegos, *Design Engr*
Frank Storck, *Draft/Design*
EMP: 57
SALES (est): 33.2MM **Privately Held**
WEB: www.brithinee.com
SIC: 5063 7694 Motors, electric; electric
   motor repair

(P-7341)
CABLECONN INDUSTRIES INC
7198 Convoy Ct, San Diego (92111-1019)
PHONE..............................858 571-7111
Lisa Coffman, *President*
Rod Coffman, *Vice Pres*
Roger Newman, *Vice Pres*
Kimm Bronk, *Purch Mgr*
Aaron Yip, *Prdtn Mgr*
EMP: 65
SQ FT: 20,000
SALES (est): 9.1MM **Privately Held**
WEB: www.cableconn-sd.com
SIC: 5063 3678 3643 Building wire &
   cable; electronic connectors; current-car-
   rying wiring devices

(P-7342)
CAL SOUTHERN ILLUMINATION
240 Commerce, Irvine (92602-5004)
PHONE..............................949 622-3000
Thomas Thompson, *President*
Steve Leszuk, *Vice Pres*
Susanna Hammond, *Admin Asst*
Edward Blackford, *Project Mgr*
Kammie Derringer, *Project Mgr*
EMP: 50
SALES: 18.4MM **Privately Held**
WEB: www.scilights.com
SIC: 5063 Lighting fixtures

(P-7343)
**CALIFORNIA LIGHTING SALES
INC (PA)**
4900 Rivergrade Rd D110, Baldwin Park
(91706-1459)
PHONE..............................626 775-6000
Roger David, *President*
Marcus Cone, *CFO*
Ned Maccahan, *Project Mgr*
Matthew Ghobadi, *Sales Staff*
Barry Hurwitz, *Sales Staff*
EMP: 59
SQ FT: 16,000
SALES (est): 9.6MM **Privately Held**
WEB: www.californialightingsales.com
SIC: 5063 Lighting fixtures, commercial &
   industrial; lighting fixtures

(P-7344)
**CENTURY COMMERCIAL
SERVICE**
12820 Earhart Ave, Auburn (95602-9027)
P.O. Box 6793 (95604-6793)
PHONE..............................530 823-1004
Keith Estes, *President*
Brent Estes, *Vice Pres*
Brian Kolitsch, *Division Mgr*
Jason Smith, *Division Mgr*
Aly Vogel, *Admin Asst*

EMP: 50
SQ FT: 6,500
SALES (est): 31.9MM **Privately Held**
WEB: www.centurylighting.com
SIC: 5063 1731 8748 Light bulbs & re-
   lated supplies; lighting contractor; energy
   conservation consultant

(P-7345)
**CHESTER C LEHMANN CO INC
(PA)**
Also Called: Electrical Distributors Co
1135 Auzerais Ave, San Jose (95126-3402)
P.O. Box 26830 (95159-6830)
PHONE..............................408 293-5818
Chester C Lehmann III, *CEO*
Scott Lehmann, *President*
Teresa T Nielsen, *Project Mgr*
Steve Soliz, *Train & Dev Mgr*
Darlene McEvoy, *Marketing Mgr*
▼ EMP: 65
SQ FT: 80,000
SALES (est): 164.7MM **Privately Held**
WEB: www.electdist.com
SIC: 5063 Electrical supplies

(P-7346)
CIRCLE W ENTERPRISES INC
Also Called: Wirenetics Co
27737 Avenue Hopkins, Valencia
(91355-1223)
PHONE..............................661 257-2400
Howard Weiss, *CEO*
Michael Weiss, *President*
Phyllis G Weiss, *CEO*
Mark Lee, *Vice Pres*
▲ EMP: 50
SQ FT: 65,000
SALES (est): 26.2MM
SALES (corp-wide): 32MM **Privately Held**
WEB: www.wireandcable.com
SIC: 5063 Wire & cable
PA: Whitmor Plastic Wire And Cable Corp.
   27737 Avenue Hopkins
   Santa Clarita CA 91355
   661 257-2400

(P-7347)
**COASTAL TRAFFIC SYSTEMS
INC**
9391 Power Dr, Huntington Beach
(92646-7236)
PHONE..............................714 641-3744
Steven Beiber, *President*
Paul Beiber, *Treasurer*
EMP: 58
SALES (est): 8.1MM **Privately Held**
SIC: 5063 Signaling equipment, electrical

(P-7348)
**COMMERCIAL LIGHTING INDS
INC**
Also Called: Cli
81161 Indio Blvd, Indio (92201-1931)
PHONE..............................800 755-0155
Frank Halcovich, *CEO*
Jennifer Johnson, *Manager*
▼ EMP: 74
SQ FT: 81,000
SALES (est): 46.1MM **Privately Held**
WEB: www.commercial-lighting.net
SIC: 5063 Light bulbs & related supplies;
   lighting fixtures

(P-7349)
**CONSOLIDATED ELEC DISTRS
INC**
5457 Ruffin Rd, San Diego (92123-1312)
PHONE..............................858 268-1020
Scott Branstetter, *Manager*
Valerie Rubalcaba, *Project Mgr*
Daniel Holland, *Purchasing*
Aj Egoian, *Opers Mgr*
Joel Garcia, *Opers-Prdtn-Mfg*
EMP: 51
SQ FT: 30,000
SALES (corp-wide): 2.7B **Privately Held**
SIC: 5063 Electrical supplies
PA: Consolidated Electrical Distributors,
   Inc.
   1920 Westridge Dr
   Irving TX 75038
   972 582-5300

(P-7350)
**CONSOLIDATED ELEC DISTRS
INC**
Also Called: All-Phase Electric Supply
3020 W Empire Ave, Burbank
(91504-3109)
PHONE..............................626 345-0000
Ed Carney, *Branch Mgr*
Robert Feller, *Principal*
Carol Stiekaley, *Principal*
Glenn Kriske, *Branch Mgr*
Jose Contreras, *Purch Mgr*
EMP: 53
SALES (corp-wide): 2.7B **Privately Held**
SIC: 5063 Electrical supplies
PA: Consolidated Electrical Distributors,
   Inc.
   1920 Westridge Dr
   Irving TX 75038
   972 582-5300

(P-7351)
CORDELIA LIGHTING INC
20101 S Santa Fe Ave, Compton
(90221-5917)
PHONE..............................310 886-3490
James Keng, *President*
James Madden, *Vice Pres*
Jay Spowart, *Vice Pres*
Li-WEI Wang, *Vice Pres*
Singh Chang, *Data Proc Staff*
▲ EMP: 106
SQ FT: 200,000
SALES (est): 28.2MM **Privately Held**
WEB: www.cordelia.com
SIC: 5063 Lighting fixtures

(P-7352)
**COUNTY WHL ELC CO LOS
ANGELES**
Also Called: C E D
560 N Main St, Orange (92868-1102)
PHONE..............................714 633-3801
Joe Mihelich, *Principal*
Fernando Yazon, *Purchasing*
Dan Caballero, *Sales Mgr*
Jose Merino, *Sales Staff*
David Wallace, *Manager*
EMP: 76 EST: 1986
SALES (est): 24.8MM
SALES (corp-wide): 2.7B **Privately Held**
SIC: 5063 Electrical supplies
PA: Consolidated Electrical Distributors,
   Inc.
   1920 Westridge Dr
   Irving TX 75038
   972 582-5300

(P-7353)
DAHL-BECK ELECTRIC CO
2775 Goodrick Ave, Richmond
(94801-1109)
PHONE..............................510 237-2325
Roger Beck, *CEO*
William R Beck, *President*
James Ross, *Corp Secy*
Gerald Vaio, *Vice Pres*
▲ EMP: 65 EST: 1932
SQ FT: 75,000
SALES (est): 24.3MM **Privately Held**
WEB: www.dahl-beck.com
SIC: 5063 1731 Electrical supplies; gen-
   eral electrical contractor

(P-7354)
DMF INC
Also Called: Dmf Lighting
1118 E 223rd St, Carson (90745-4210)
PHONE..............................323 934-7779
Morteza Danesh, *CEO*
Ian Ibbitson, *COO*
Fariba Danesh, *Vice Pres*
Michael Danesh, *Vice Pres*
Andrew Wakefield, *Vice Pres*
▲ EMP: 80
SQ FT: 8,000
SALES: 103MM **Privately Held**
WEB: www.dmflighting.com
SIC: 5063 Lighting fixtures, commercial &
   industrial

(P-7355)
EATON CORPORATION
Eaton Aerospace
4690 Colorado Blvd, Los Angeles
(90039-1106)
PHONE..............................818 409-0200
Stephanie Stewart, *Manager*
Cindy Gordon, *Executive*
Steve Thornock, *Technician*
Arthur Gryszkiewicz, *Design Engr*
Hai Nguyen, *Design Engr*
EMP: 376
SQ FT: 41,117 **Privately Held**
WEB: www.eaton.com
SIC: 5063 Electrical apparatus & equip-
   ment
HQ: Eaton Corporation
   1000 Eaton Blvd
   Cleveland OH 44122
   440 523-5000

(P-7356)
**EDGES ELECTRICAL GROUP
LLC (HQ)**
1135 Auzerais Ave, San Jose (95126-3402)
P.O. Box 26830 (95159-6830)
PHONE..............................408 293-5818
Mark Arndt, *CFO*
Cale Dodd, *Branch Mgr*
Jason Marci, *Branch Mgr*
Wayne Redmond, *Branch Mgr*
Leah Dillard, *Project Mgr*
EMP: 60
SALES (est): 164.7MM **Privately Held**
SIC: 5063 Electrical supplies
PA: Chester C. Lehmann Co., Inc.
   1135 Auzerais Ave
   San Jose CA 95126
   408 293-5818

(P-7357)
ELECTRIC MOTOR SHOP
Also Called: Electric Motor & Supply Co.
250 Broadway St, Fresno (93721-3103)
P.O. Box 446 (93709-0446)
PHONE..............................559 233-1153
Dicks Caglia, *President*
EMP: 80
SQ FT: 1,296
SALES (est): 6.5MM
SALES (corp-wide): 127.8MM **Privately Held**
WEB: www.electricmotorshop.com
SIC: 5063 Electrical supplies
PA: Electric Motor Shop
   253 Fulton St
   Fresno CA 93721
   559 233-1153

(P-7358)
ELECTRIC SALES UNLIMITED
9023 Norwalk Blvd, Santa Fe Springs
(90670-2531)
PHONE..............................562 463-8300
John J Defazio, *President*
Chuck Beadle, *Vice Pres*
John J Defazio Jr, *Vice Pres*
Teresa Fackiner, *Vice Pres*
Cindy Arce, *Sales Associate*
▲ EMP: 50
SQ FT: 75,000
SALES (est): 17.5MM **Privately Held**
WEB: www.esu.com
SIC: 5063 Electrical supplies

(P-7359)
**EMERGENCY TECHNOLOGIES
INC**
Also Called: American Two-Way
7345 Varna Ave, North Hollywood
(91605-4009)
PHONE..............................818 765-4421
Christopher Baskin, *CEO*
Verny Grajeda, *Info Tech Mgr*
EMP: 72 EST: 1995
SQ FT: 13,000
SALES (est): 15.7MM **Privately Held**
WEB: www.americantwoway.com
SIC: 5063 Alarm systems

(P-7360)

ERS SEC ALARM SYSTEMS INC

Also Called: Emergency Reporting Systems
4538 Santa Anita Ave, El Monte
(91731-1318)
PHONE..............................626 579-2525
David Chao, *President*
Kevin Tsao, *Exec VP*
Winnie Siu, *Controller*
EMP: 53
SQ FT: 15,000
SALES (est): 18.8MM **Privately Held**
WEB: www.erssecurity.com
SIC: 5063 1731 Burglar alarm systems;
fire detection & burglar alarm systems
specialization

(P-7361)

FACILITY SOLUTIONS GROUP INC

801 Richfield Rd, Placentia (92870-6731)
PHONE..............................714 993-3966
Jeff Johnson, *District Mgr*
Craig Carlson, *Natl Sales Mgr*
EMP: 64
SALES (corp-wide): 961.6MM **Privately Held**
WEB: www.americanlight.com
SIC: 5063 1731 Lighting fixtures, commercial & industrial; light bulbs & related supplies; electrical work; lighting contractor
PA: Facility Solutions Group, Inc.
4401 West Gate Blvd # 310
Austin TX 78745
512 440-7985

(P-7362)

GRAYBAR ELECTRIC COMPANY INC

1370 Valley Vista Dr # 100, Diamond Bar
(91765-3921)
PHONE..............................909 451-4300
Bruce Spencer, *Engr R&D*
Vanessa Razo, *Finance Mgr*
Sean Singleton, *Sales Mgr*
Stephen Cray, *Sales Staff*
Raul Parra, *Sales Staff*
EMP: 153
SALES (corp-wide): 6.6B **Privately Held**
WEB: www.graybar.com
SIC: 5063 5065 Electrical supplies; telephone equipment
PA: Graybar Electric Company, Inc.
34 N Meramec Ave
Saint Louis MO 63105
314 573-9200

(P-7363)

GRAYBAR ELECTRIC COMPANY INC

3089 Whipple Rd, Union City (94587-1236)
PHONE..............................925 557-3000
Eric Ortega, *Branch Mgr*
David Maxwell, *Vice Pres*
EMP: 74
SQ FT: 117,648
SALES (corp-wide): 6.6B **Privately Held**
WEB: www.graybar.com
SIC: 5063 5065 Electrical supplies; telephone equipment
PA: Graybar Electric Company, Inc.
34 N Meramec Ave
Saint Louis MO 63105
314 573-9200

(P-7364)

HOCHIKI AMERICA CORPORATION

7051 Village Dr Ste 100, Buena Park
(90621-2268)
P.O. Box 514689, Los Angeles (90051-4689)
PHONE..............................714 522-2246
Hisham Harake, *CEO*
Hiroshi Kamei, *CFO*
Hideyuki Umehara, *CFO*
Rick Boisclair, *Vice Pres*
Jeffrey Rotondo, *Vice Pres*
▲ EMP: 104
SQ FT: 30,000

SALES (est): 79.1MM
SALES (corp-wide): 712.9MM **Privately Held**
WEB: www.hochiki.com
SIC: 5063 3669 Fire alarm systems; fire detection systems, electric
PA: Hochiki Corporation
2-10-43, Kamiosaki
Shinagawa-Ku TKY 141-0
334 444-111

(P-7365)

HONEYWELL INTERNATIONAL INC

1635 N Batavia St, Orange (92867-3508)
PHONE..............................714 283-0110
Mary Peterson, *Manager*
EMP: 50
SALES (corp-wide): 40.5B **Publicly Held**
WEB: www.adilink.com
SIC: 5063 Alarm systems
PA: Honeywell International Inc.
115 Tabor Rd
Morris Plains NJ 07950
973 455-2000

(P-7366)

INDEPENDENT ELECTRIC SUP INC (DH)

2001 Marina Blvd, San Leandro
(94577-3204)
PHONE..............................510 877-9850
David Jones, *President*
Roy Thornton, *Regional Mgr*
Kris Beauchman, *Branch Mgr*
Rick Crew, *Branch Mgr*
Brett Massip, *Branch Mgr*
EMP: 153 EST: 1973
SALES: 600MM
SALES (corp-wide): 12.2MM **Privately Held**
WEB: www.iesupply.com
SIC: 5063 Electrical supplies; wiring devices; electrical construction materials; cable conduit
HQ: Sonepar Management Us, Inc.
510 Walnut St Ste 400
Philadelphia PA 19106
215 399-5900

(P-7367)

JELIGHT COMPANY INC

2 Mason, Irvine (92618-2513)
PHONE..............................949 380-8774
Marinko Jelic, *President*
Renata Jelic, *Admin Sec*
▲ EMP: 65
SQ FT: 27,000
SALES (est): 25MM **Privately Held**
WEB: www.jelight.com
SIC: 5063 Electrical apparatus & equipment

(P-7368)

JME INC (PA)

Also Called: T M B
527 Prk Ave San Fernando, San Fernando
(91340)
PHONE..............................201 896-8600
Colin R Waters, *CEO*
Thomas M Bissett, *President*
Luis V De Dios, *Administration*
▲ EMP: 80
SQ FT: 34,000
SALES (est): 67.3MM **Privately Held**
WEB: www.tmb.com
SIC: 5063 Lighting fittings & accessories

(P-7369)

JOHN SHANNON MC GEE CO INC

Also Called: McGee Company
8190 Byron Rd, Whittier (90606-2616)
PHONE..............................562 789-1777
Glenn Hitomi, *President*
Desiree Contreras, *COO*
Tracey Miller, *CFO*
Lee Hatcher, *Vice Pres*
Ken Porter, *Vice Pres*
▲ EMP: 50 EST: 1963
SQ FT: 74,000
SALES (est): 7.9MM **Privately Held**
WEB: www.mcgeeco.com
SIC: 5063 Electrical apparatus & equipment

(P-7370)

KOFFLER ELEC MECH APPRTS REPAI

527 Whitney St, San Leandro (94577-1113)
PHONE..............................510 567-0630
Lari Koffler, *President*
Michael Bucedi, *Treasurer*
Charles H Koffler, *Vice Pres*
Kerry Koffler, *Admin Sec*
Wayne Berner, *Controller*
▲ EMP: 80
SQ FT: 77,548
SALES (est): 21.4MM **Privately Held**
WEB: www.koffler.com
SIC: 5063 7694 Motors, electric; electric motor repair

(P-7371)

LGE ELECTRICAL SALES INC

7866 Convoy Ct, San Diego (92111-1210)
PHONE..............................408 379-8568
Gregory Adrian, *CFO*
EMP: 293
SALES (corp-wide): 12.2MM **Privately Held**
SIC: 5063 Electrical supplies
HQ: Lge Electrical Sales, Inc.
650 University Ave # 218
Sacramento CA 95825
916 563-2737

(P-7372)

LOS ANGELES RUBBER COMPANY (PA)

Also Called: Mechanical Drives and Belting
2915 E Washington Blvd, Los Angeles
(90023-4218)
P.O. Box 23910 (90023-0910)
PHONE..............................323 263-4131
Carol A Durst, *CEO*
David Durst, *Vice Pres*
Michael Durst, *Vice Pres*
Wayne Roberts, *Vice Pres*
▲ EMP: 55
SQ FT: 31,000
SALES (est): 37.3MM **Privately Held**
SIC: 5063 Power transmission equipment, electric

(P-7373)

LUMENS LLC (HQ)

2020 L St Ste Ll10, Sacramento
(95811-4260)
PHONE..............................916 444-5585
Ken Plumlee, *President*
Peter Weight, *Admin Sec*
Brian Del Vecchio, *Sr Software Eng*
◆ EMP: 52
SQ FT: 5,700
SALES (est): 31.7MM **Privately Held**
SIC: 5063 5712 Lighting fixtures; furniture stores

(P-7374)

MAGNETIKA INC (PA)

2041 W 139th St, Gardena (90249-2409)
PHONE..............................310 527-8100
Francis Ishida, *President*
Basil P Caloyeras, *CEO*
Ieng Liu, *Info Tech Mgr*
Brenda Vieyra, *Production*
Tom Chew, *Sales Dir*
EMP: 80
SQ FT: 40,000
SALES (est): 40.4MM **Privately Held**
SIC: 5063 3612 Transformers, electric; power transmission equipment, electric; ballasts for lighting fixtures; power transformers, electric

(P-7375)

MAIN ELECTRIC SUPPLY CO LLC (PA)

3600 W Segerstrom Ave, Santa Ana
(92704-6408)
P.O. Box 25750 (92799-5750)
PHONE..............................949 833-3052
Scott R Germann, *President*
Paul Vowels, *COO*
Karen Morris, *CFO*
Josh Lajoie, *Branch Mgr*
Maurice Orozco, *Branch Mgr*
▲ EMP: 69
SQ FT: 35,000

SALES (est): 385.9MM **Privately Held**
WEB: www.mainelectricsupply.com
SIC: 5063 Electrical supplies

(P-7376)

MAIN ELECTRIC SUPPLY CO LLC

461 Main St, Riverside (92501-1029)
PHONE..............................951 784-2900
Rich Ramirez, *Sales Staff*
EMP: 78
SALES (corp-wide): 385.9MM **Privately Held**
SIC: 5063 Electrical supplies
PA: Main Electric Supply Company Llc
3600 W Segerstrom Ave
Santa Ana CA 92704
949 833-3052

(P-7377)

MINKA LIGHTING INC (PA)

Also Called: Minka Group
1151 Bradford Cir, Corona (92882-7166)
PHONE..............................951 735-9220
Marian Tang, *CEO*
Kurt Schulzman, *Principal*
Andrea Vasquez, *Administration*
John Terazona, *Controller*
Paul Tabeek, *Natl Sales Mgr*
▲ EMP: 70
SQ FT: 350,000
SALES (est): 92MM **Privately Held**
WEB: www.minka.com
SIC: 5063 Lighting fixtures

(P-7378)

MOTIVE ENERGY INC (PA)

125 E Coml St Bldg B, Anaheim (92801)
PHONE..............................714 888-2525
Robert J Istwan, *President*
▼ EMP: 85
SQ FT: 35,000
SALES (est): 89MM **Privately Held**
SIC: 5063 Storage batteries, industrial

(P-7379)

MULTIQUIP INC (DH)

Also Called: Mq Power
18910 Wilmington Ave, Carson
(90746-2820)
PHONE..............................310 537-3700
Tom Yasuda, *Ch of Bd*
Bob Graydon, *CEO*
Jim Henehan, *CFO*
◆ EMP: 300
SQ FT: 190,000
SALES (est): 271.4MM
SALES (corp-wide): 51.7B **Privately Held**
WEB: www.multiquip.com
SIC: 5063 5082 3645 Generators; general construction machinery & equipment; garden, patio, walkway & yard lighting fixtures: electric
HQ: Itochu International Inc.
1251 Avenue Of The Americ
New York NY 10020
212 818-8000

(P-7380)

MYERS POWER PRODUCTS INC (PA)

Also Called: Myers FSI
2950 E Philadelphia St, Ontario
(91761-8545)
PHONE..............................909 923-1800
Diana Grootonk, *CEO*
Jose Cudal, *CFO*
Robert Hodous, *Planning Mgr*
Juan Amador, *Design Engr*
Ricardo Morfin, *Engineer*
◆ EMP: 130
SQ FT: 40,000
SALES (est): 178.2MM **Privately Held**
WEB: www.myerspower.com
SIC: 5063 Electrical apparatus & equipment

(P-7381)

NELSON & ASSOCIATES INC

12816 Leffingwell Ave, Santa Fe Springs
(90670-6343)
PHONE..............................562 921-4423
Todd James Nelson, *CEO*
Brian Haupt, *Exec VP*
Kurt Nelson, *Principal*
▲ EMP: 75

P
R
O
D
U
C
T
S

&

S
V
C
S

SQ FT: 120,000
SALES (est): 32.2MM **Privately Held**
WEB: www.nelsonreps.com
SIC: 5063 Electrical supplies; telephone & telegraph wire & cable

(P-7382)
NORA LIGHTING INC
6505 Gayhart St, Commerce (90040-2507)
PHONE..................800 686-6672
Fred Farzan, *CEO*
Jill Farzan, *Exec VP*
David Muzzy, *Vice Pres*
▲ **EMP:** 72
SQ FT: 150,000
SALES (est): 59.1MM **Privately Held**
WEB: www.noralighting.com
SIC: 5063 3648 5719 Lighting fixtures; lighting fixtures, except electric: residential; lighting fixtures

(P-7383)
ORIENTAL MOTOR USA CORPORATION (DH)
570 Alaska Ave, Torrance (90503-3904)
PHONE..................310 715-3300
Ryan Kanemura, *President*
Kulie Fintak, *President*
Greg Johnston, *Exec VP*
Pete Derose, *Vice Pres*
Jake Kitayama, *Principal*
◆ **EMP:** 60
SQ FT: 31,600
SALES (est): 50.7MM
SALES (corp-wide): 8MM **Privately Held**
SIC: 5063 Motors, electric
HQ: Oriental Motor Co., Ltd.
4-8-1, Higashiueno
Taito-Ku TKY 110-0
367 440-411

(P-7384)
PACIFIC LIGHTING MFR INC
Also Called: Utopia Lighting
2329 E Pacifica Pl, Compton (90220-6210)
PHONE..................310 327-7711
▲ **EMP:** 62
SQ FT: 100,000
SALES: 12.5MM **Privately Held**
SIC: 5063

(P-7385)
PACIFIC LIGHTING MFR INC
Also Called: Utopia Lighting
2329 E Pacifica Pl, Rancho Dominguez (90220-6210)
PHONE..................310 327-7711
Soon Goo Hong, *CEO*
David Kim, *President*
Bohi Hong, *Admin Sec*
EMP: 56
SALES: 14.1MM **Privately Held**
SIC: 5063 Lighting fixtures

(P-7386)
POWER PLUS LLC
1210 N Red Gum St, Anaheim (92806-1820)
PHONE..................714 507-1881
Steven Bray,
EMP: 70
SALES (est): 10.5MM **Privately Held**
SIC: 5063 Generators

(P-7387)
Q L P INC
2285 Ward Ave, Simi Valley (93065-1863)
PHONE..................805 579-0440
Andy Sreden, *President*
Milton Edwards, *Supervisor*
▲ **EMP:** 50
SQ FT: 15,000
SALES (est): 22MM **Privately Held**
SIC: 5063 Light bulbs & related supplies; lighting fixtures

(P-7388)
REGENCY ENTERPRISES INC (PA)
Also Called: Regency Lighting
9261 Jordan Ave, Chatsworth (91311-5739)
PHONE..................818 901-0255
Ron Regenstreif, *CEO*
Scott Anderson, *President*
Isaac Regenstreif, *President*

Judah Regenstreif, *President*
Michael Goldstone, *COO*
◆ **EMP:** 272
SALES: 150MM **Privately Held**
WEB: www.regencylighting.com
SIC: 5063 Light bulbs & related supplies; lighting fixtures

(P-7389)
ROKSTAD POWER CORP
8825 Aero Dr Ste 305, San Diego (92123-2270)
PHONE..................888 310-8830
Adam Day, *Branch Mgr*
EMP: 50 **Privately Held**
SIC: 5063 Wiring devices
PA: Rokstad Power Corporation
80 Golden Dr
Coquitlam BC V3K 6
604 553-1810

(P-7390)
ROMACH LLC
2956 Sparrow Dr, Fullerton (92835-2322)
PHONE..................805 378-1174
Alexander Ghibu,
John Pierce,
▲ **EMP:** 65
SALES (est): 4.1MM **Privately Held**
WEB: www.romach.com
SIC: 5063 Motors, electric

(P-7391)
SCHNEIDER ELECTRIC USA INC
Also Called: Schneider Electric 600
6160 Stoneridge Mall Rd # 200, Pleasanton (94588-3285)
PHONE..................925 462-0986
Scott Day, *Manager*
Rick McKay, *Sales Mgr*
EMP: 55
SALES (corp-wide): 200.4K **Privately Held**
WEB: www.squared.com
SIC: 5063 Electrical apparatus & equipment
HQ: Schneider Electric Usa, Inc.
800 Federal St
Andover MA 01810
978 975-9600

(P-7392)
SCHNEIDER ELECTRIC USA INC
Also Called: Schneider Electric 650
21680 Gateway Center Dr # 300, Diamond Bar (91765-2453)
PHONE..................909 612-5400
Scott Forry, *Manager*
Edison Nguyen, *Engineer*
Rick Hendrix, *Manager*
EMP: 51
SALES (corp-wide): 200.4K **Privately Held**
WEB: www.squared.com
SIC: 5063 Electrical apparatus & equipment
HQ: Schneider Electric Usa, Inc.
800 Federal St
Andover MA 01810
978 975-9600

(P-7393)
SELECTA PRODUCTS INC (PA)
Also Called: Selecta Switch
1200 E Tehachapi Blvd, Tehachapi (93561-8129)
P.O. Box 888 (93581-0888)
PHONE..................661 823-7050
John Kenyon, *President*
Charles Kenyon, *Ch of Bd*
James Kenyon, *President*
Dorothy Kenyon, *Vice Pres*
Charlotte Tathwell, *Vice Pres*
▼ **EMP:** 60
SQ FT: 20,000
SALES (est): 36.4MM **Privately Held**
WEB: www.selectaproductsinc.com
SIC: 5063 5065 Electrical supplies; electronic parts

(P-7394)
SIEMENS INDUSTRY INC
25821 Industrial Blvd # 300, Hayward (94545-2919)
PHONE..................510 783-6000
John P Nichols, *Manager*

Darryl Barbata, *Opers Spvr*
Dale McGrath, *Marketing Staff*
EMP: 300
SALES (corp-wide): 97.7B **Privately Held**
SIC: 5063 Electrical apparatus & equipment
HQ: Siemens Industry, Inc.
100 Technology Dr
Alpharetta GA 30005
770 740-3000

(P-7395)
SIEMENS INDUSTRY INC
2420 S Reservoir St, Pomona (91766-6412)
PHONE..................909 627-6141
Gary Rowe, *Branch Mgr*
EMP: 60
SALES (corp-wide): 97.7B **Privately Held**
WEB: www.sea.siemens.com
SIC: 5063 Electrical apparatus & equipment
HQ: Siemens Industry, Inc.
100 Technology Dr
Alpharetta GA 30005
770 740-3000

(P-7396)
SIEMENS INDUSTRY INC
6141 Katella Ave, Cypress (90630-5202)
PHONE..................714 761-2200
Eric Ackerman, *General Mgr*
Joseph Wurzelbacher, *Pharmacy Dir*
Diana Young, *Office Mgr*
Stephen Chlopecki, *Technology*
Asif Shaikh, *Purchasing*
EMP: 122
SALES (corp-wide): 97.7B **Privately Held**
WEB: www.sibt.com
SIC: 5063 Electrical apparatus & equipment
HQ: Siemens Industry, Inc.
100 Technology Dr
Alpharetta GA 30005
770 740-3000

(P-7397)
SILICONSYSTEMS INC
26840 Aliso Viejo Pkwy # 1, Aliso Viejo (92656-2624)
PHONE..................949 900-9400
Michael Hajeck, *CEO*
Andrew Talbot, *CFO*
David Merry, *CTO*
▲ **EMP:** 85
SALES (est): 11.1MM
SALES (corp-wide): 20.6B **Publicly Held**
WEB: www.siliconsystems.com
SIC: 5063 Electrical apparatus & equipment
PA: Western Digital Corporation
5601 Great Oaks Pkwy
San Jose CA 95119
408 717-6000

(P-7398)
SOLAREDGE TECHNOLOGIES INC
2225 E Bayshore Rd, Palo Alto (94303-3220)
PHONE..................650 320-7695
Guy Sella, *Principal*
Jessica Singh, *Accounting Mgr*
Shimon Kringel, *VP Opers*
EMP: 347
SALES (corp-wide): 97.4MM **Privately Held**
SIC: 5063 Electrical apparatus & equipment
PA: Solaredge Technologies, Inc.
47505 Seabridge Dr
Fremont CA 94538
510 498-3200

(P-7399)
SOUTHWIRE COMPANY LLC
Southwire Master Service Ctr
9199 Cleveland Ave # 100, Rancho Cucamonga (91730-8559)
PHONE..................909 989-2888
David Jordan, *Branch Mgr*
Freddy Hernandez, *Supervisor*
EMP: 60
SALES (corp-wide): 2.4B **Privately Held**
WEB: www.southwire.com
SIC: 5063 Wire & cable

PA: Southwire Company, Llc
1 Southwire Dr
Carrollton GA 30119
770 832-4242

(P-7400)
USHIO AMERICA INC (HQ)
5440 Cerritos Ave, Cypress (90630-4567)
PHONE..................714 236-8600
Shinji Kameda, *President*
Yuichi Asaka, *CFO*
C Asato, *Marketing Mgr*
Keith Cordero, *Director*
Jing MO, *Director*
◆ **EMP:** 90
SQ FT: 70,000
SALES (est): 69.6MM
SALES (corp-wide): 1.6B **Privately Held**
WEB: www.ushio.com
SIC: 5063 Lighting fixtures, commercial & industrial
PA: Ushio Inc.
1-6-5, Marunouchi
Chiyoda-Ku TKY 100-0
356 571-000

(P-7401)
WALTERS WHOLESALE ELECTRIC CO (HQ)
2825 Temple Ave, Signal Hill (90755-2212)
PHONE..................562 988-3100
John L Walter, *CEO*
Bill Durkee, *President*
Roland Wood, *CFO*
Jeff Maggio, *Branch Mgr*
Nancy Nielsen, *Admin Sec*
▼ **EMP:** 50
SQ FT: 10,000
SALES (est): 474.1MM
SALES (corp-wide): 2.7B **Privately Held**
WEB: www.walterswholesale.com
SIC: 5063 3699 1731 Wire & cable; electrical equipment & supplies; lighting contractor
PA: Consolidated Electrical Distributors, Inc.
1920 Westridge Dr
Irving TX 75038
972 582-5300

(P-7402)
WALTERS WHOLESALE ELECTRIC CO
200 N Berry St, Brea (92821-3903)
PHONE..................714 784-1900
Ron Byrd, *Branch Mgr*
EMP: 140
SALES (corp-wide): 2.7B **Privately Held**
WEB: www.walterswholesale.com
SIC: 5063 Electrical supplies
HQ: Walters Wholesale Electric Co.
2825 Temple Ave
Signal Hill CA 90755
562 988-3100

(P-7403)
WW GRAINGER INC
Also Called: Grainger 732
2261 Ringwood Ave, San Jose (95131-1792)
PHONE..................408 432-8200
Alicia Bugos, *Manager*
EMP: 120
SQ FT: 38,082
SALES (corp-wide): 10.4B **Publicly Held**
WEB: www.grainger.com
SIC: 5063 5084 5075 5078 Motors, electric; motor controls, starters & relays: electric; power transmission equipment, electric; generators; fans, industrial; pumps & pumping equipment; compressors, except air conditioning; pneumatic tools & equipment; warm air heating equipment & supplies; air conditioning equipment, except room units; refrigeration equipment & supplies; electric tools; power tools & accessories; hand tools
PA: W.W. Grainger, Inc.
100 Grainger Pkwy
Lake Forest IL 60045
847 535-1000

(P-7404)
YDESIGN GROUP LLC (PA)
Also Called: Yliving
1850 Mt Diablo Blvd # 510, Walnut Creek
(94596-4428)
PHONE.............................866 842-6209
Graham C Weaver,
Sean Callahan,
EMP: 50
SALES (est): 34.9MM Privately Held
SIC: 5063 5031 Lighting fixtures; lighting
fittings & accessories; lighting fixtures,
commercial & industrial; lighting fixtures,
residential; building materials, interior

(P-7405)
ZIPPY USA INC
Also Called: Kpower Sup McRswitch Inverters
1 Morgan, Irvine (92618-1917)
PHONE.............................949 366-9525
Chin W Chou, President
Chin S Tsai, Treasurer
Frank Lee, Admin Mgr
Bijender Kumar, Project Mgr
Jonathan Wang, Project Mgr
▲ EMP: 54 EST: 1996
SQ FT: 19,000
SALES (est): 11MM
SALES (corp-wide): 97.2MM Privately
Held
WEB: www.zippyusa.com
SIC: 5063 Motor controls, starters & relays:
electric
PA: Zippy Technology Corp.
10f, 50, Min Chuan Rd.
New Taipei City 23141
229 188-512

(P-7406)
ZSPACE INC
490 De Guigne Dr Ste 200, Sunnyvale
(94085-3903)
PHONE.............................408 498-4050
Paul Kellenberger, CEO
Joseph Powers, CFO
EMP: 100
SALES (est): 51.9MM Privately Held
SIC: 5063 Transformers, electric

**5064 Electrical Appliances,
TV & Radios Wholesale**

(P-7407)
**ALPINE ELECTRONICS
AMERICA INC**
2012 Abalone Ave Ste D, Torrance
(90501-3726)
PHONE.............................310 783-7391
James Doboe, Branch Mgr
EMP: 102
SALES (corp-wide): 2.5B Privately Held
SIC: 5064 Radios, motor vehicle
HQ: Alpine Electronics Of America, Inc.
19145 Gramercy Pl
Torrance CA 90501
310 326-8000

(P-7408)
**ALPINE ELECTRONICS
AMERICA INC (HQ)**
19145 Gramercy Pl, Torrance
(90501-1162)
P.O. Box 2859 (90509-2859)
PHONE.............................310 326-8000
Toshinori Kobayashi, CEO
Isao Nagasako, President
Masanobu Takagi, CFO
Jim Walter, Program Mgr
Jean Pumilia, Admin Asst
▲ EMP: 200 EST: 1978
SQ FT: 120,000
SALES (est): 375.2MM
SALES (corp-wide): 2.5B Privately Held
WEB: www.alpine-usa.com
SIC: 5064 3651 3679 Radios, motor vehi-
cle; household audio & video equipment;
harness assemblies for electronic use:
wire or cable

(P-7409)
AVA ENTERPRISES INC
Also Called: Boss Audio Systems
3451 Lunar Ct, Oxnard (93030-8976)
PHONE.............................805 988-0192
Soheil Rabbani, President
Kam Mobini, Shareholder
Sheila Rabbani, Vice Pres
Rebecca Webber, Manager
▲ EMP: 50
SQ FT: 70,000
SALES (est): 22.2MM Privately Held
WEB: www.bossaudio.com
SIC: 5064 Radios, motor vehicle

(P-7410)
**CLARION CORPORATION
AMERICA (DH)**
6200 Gateway Dr, Cypress (90630-4842)
PHONE.............................310 327-9100
Paul Lachner, President
Chris Honma, Exec VP
▲ EMP: 77 EST: 1964
SQ FT: 53,208
SALES (est): 470.7MM
SALES (corp-wide): 87.9B Privately Held
SIC: 5064 Radios, motor vehicle
HQ: Clarion Co., Ltd.
7-2, Shintoshin, Chuo-Ku
Saitama STM 330-0
486 013-700

(P-7411)
CONCEPT ENTERPRISES INC
152 S Brent Cir, Walnut (91789-3050)
PHONE.............................626 968-8827
Edward Liu, CEO
Calvin Liu, Exec VP
Willie Liu, Vice Pres
▲ EMP: 60 EST: 1976
SALES (est): 14.3MM Privately Held
SIC: 5064 Electrical entertainment equip-
ment; radios, motor vehicle

(P-7412)
**E & S INTERNATIONAL ENTPS
INC (PA)**
Also Called: Import Direct
7801 Hayvenhurst Ave, Van Nuys
(91406-1712)
PHONE.............................818 887-0700
Philip Asherian, CEO
Farshad Asherian, President
Mike RAD, COO
Mark W Barron, CFO
Steve Dodge, Vice Pres
◆ EMP: 136
SQ FT: 60,000
SALES (est): 174.6MM Privately Held
WEB: www.esintl.com
SIC: 5064 Electrical appliances, television
& radio

(P-7413)
**ELECTROLUX HOME
PRODUCTS INC**
701 Malaga St, Ontario (91761-8627)
PHONE.............................909 605-9448
Jeff Bee Cont, Branch Mgr
EMP: 64
SALES (corp-wide): 14.4B Privately Held
WEB: www.eureka.com
SIC: 5064 Electric household appliances
HQ: Electrolux Home Products, Inc.
10200 David Taylor Dr
Charlotte NC 28262

(P-7414)
EXPRESCOM LLC
Also Called: Exprescom S.A. De C.V.
10145 Via De La Amistad, San Diego
(92154-5216)
PHONE.............................619 271-0531
EMP: 58
SALES (corp-wide): 4.1MM Privately
Held
SIC: 5064 5065

PA: Alpine Electronics, Inc.
1-7, Yukigayaotsukamachi
Ota-Ku TKY 145-0
354 998-111

(P-7415)
**F O C ELECTRONICS
CORPORATION**
Also Called: Crazy Gideons
830 Traction Ave, Los Angeles
(90013-1816)
PHONE.............................213 625-5775
Gideon Kotzer, President
Leonie Kotzer, Corp Secy
EMP: 50
SQ FT: 50,000
SALES (est): 6.1MM Privately Held
WEB: www.crazygideons.com
SIC: 5064 5731 Electrical entertainment
equipment; television sets; video cassette
recorders & accessories; radios; radio,
television & electronic stores

(P-7416)
FLW INC
5672 Bolsa Ave, Huntington Beach
(92649-1113)
PHONE.............................714 751-7512
Andrew Peek, President
Andy Peek, Vice Pres
Matthew Peek, Controller
Ginny Ainsworth, Human Res Dir
Doug Falunkner, Manager
EMP: 55
SALES (est): 2.5MM Privately Held
SIC: 5064 Electrical appliances, major

(P-7417)
**FUJITSU TEN CORP OF
AMERICA**
19600 S Vermont Ave, Torrance
(90502-1140)
PHONE.............................310 327-2151
Masami Yamamoto, President
Adriana Somarriba, Human Resources
Alden Salazar, Manager
EMP: 120
SALES (corp-wide): 47.9B Privately Held
SIC: 5064 7539 Radios, motor vehicle; ra-
dios; automotive repair shops
HQ: Denso Ten Limited
1-2-28, Goshodori, Hyogo-Ku
Kobe HYO 652-0
786 715-081

(P-7418)
HOMELAND HOUSEWARES LLC
Also Called: Magic Bullet
11601 Wilshire Blvd Fl 23, Los Angeles
(90025-1759)
PHONE.............................310 996-7200
Rich Krause, CEO
▲ EMP: 80
SALES (est): 37MM
SALES (corp-wide): 7.8MM Privately
Held
SIC: 5064 5963 Electrical appliances,
major; appliance sales, house-to-house
HQ: Capital Brands, Llc
11601 Wilshire Blvd Fl 23
Los Angeles CA 90025

(P-7419)
**JVCKENWOOD USA
CORPORATION (HQ)**
2201 E Dominguez St, Long Beach
(90810-1009)
P.O. Box 22745 (90801-5745)
PHONE.............................310 639-9000
Kuhiro Aigami, President
Kazuhiro Aigami, President
Joseph Glassett, CEO
Dilip Patki, CFO
Craig Geiger, Exec VP
◆ EMP: 160
SQ FT: 238,000
SALES (est): 88.9MM
SALES (corp-wide): 2.8B Privately Held
WEB: www.kenwoodusa.com
SIC: 5064 High fidelity equipment
PA: Jvc Kenwood Corporation
3-12, Moriyacho, Kanagawa-Ku
Yokohama KNG 221-0
454 445-232

(P-7420)
MEMOREX PRODUCTS INC
17777 Center Court Dr N S, Cerritos
(90703-9320)
P.O. Box 64742, Saint Paul MN (55164-
0742)
PHONE.............................562 653-2800
Michael Golacinski, President
Allan Yap, Ch of Bd
Kevin McDonnell, CFO
Mae Higa, Admin Sec
▲ EMP: 159
SQ FT: 212,000
SALES (est): 6.6MM Publicly Held
WEB: www.memorex.com
SIC: 5064 5065 5045 3652 Electrical en-
tertainment equipment; radio & television
equipment & parts; computer peripheral
equipment; pre-recorded records & tapes;
household audio & video equipment
PA: Glassbridge Enterprises, Inc.
1099 Helmo Ave N Ste 250
Oakdale MN 55128

(P-7421)
PANASONIC
26160 Enterprise Way, Lake Forest
(92630-8403)
PHONE.............................949 581-0661
Susan Hall, President
Rob Lindquist, Officer
Rippon Simpson, Officer
Al McGowan, Business Dir
Thomas Bubernak, Program Mgr
EMP: 137
SALES (est): 21.6MM Privately Held
SIC: 5064 Electrical appliances, television
& radio

(P-7422)
**PANASONIC CORP NORTH
AMERICA**
Also Called: Panasonic Broadcast TV Sys-
tems
3330 Chnga Blvd W Ste 505, Los Angeles
(90068-1355)
PHONE.............................323 436-3500
Russ Walker, Manager
EMP: 125
SALES (corp-wide): 74.9B Privately Held
WEB: www.panasonic.com
SIC: 5064 Electrical appliances, television
& radio
HQ: Panasonic Corporation Of North Amer-
ica
2 Riverfront Plz Ste 200
Newark NJ 07102
201 348-7000

(P-7423)
**PANASONIC CORP NORTH
AMERICA**
Also Called: TV Group
2055 Sanyo Ave, San Diego (92154-6234)
P.O. Box 2000, Forrest City AR (72336-
2000)
PHONE.............................619 661-1134
Joji Sewa, Branch Mgr
EMP: 50
SALES (corp-wide): 74.9B Privately Held
WEB: www.sanyoctv.com
SIC: 5064 Electrical appliances, television
& radio
HQ: Panasonic Corporation Of North Amer-
ica
2 Riverfront Plz Ste 200
Newark NJ 07102
201 348-7000

(P-7424)
**PANASONIC CORP NORTH
AMERICA**
2033 Gateway Pl Ste 200, San Jose
(95110-3714)
PHONE.............................201 348-7000
Shauna Peterson, Director
EMP: 54
SALES (corp-wide): 74.9B Privately Held
WEB: www.panasonic.com
SIC: 5064 Electrical appliances, television
& radio

PRODUCTS & SVCS

HQ: Panasonic Corporation Of North America
2 Riverfront Plz Ste 200
Newark NJ 07102
201 348-7000

(P-7425)
PANASONIC CORP NORTH AMERICA
Panasonic Avc Networks Company
2055 Sanyo Ave, San Diego (92154-6234)
PHONE..................................619 661-1134
EMP: 54
SALES (corp-wide): 74.9B Privately Held
SIC: 5064 Television sets
HQ: Panasonic Corporation Of North America
2 Riverfront Plz Ste 200
Newark NJ 07102
201 348-7000

(P-7426)
R & B WHOLESALE DISTRS INC (PA)
2350 S Milliken Ave, Ontario (91761-2332)
PHONE..................................909 230-5400
Robert O Burggraf, President
Shamsul Hyder, CFO
Robert Burggrat, Treasurer
Masako Burggraf, Vice Pres
Romeo Roque, Vice Pres
▲ EMP: 135
SQ FT: 72,000
SALES (est): 96.4MM Privately Held
WEB: www.rbdist.com
SIC: 5064 Electrical appliances, major;
electrical entertainment equipment

(P-7427)
REPUBLIC SVCS VSCO RD LANDFILL
4001 N Vasco Rd, Livermore (94551-9766)
PHONE..................................925 447-0491
Kevin Finn, President
Eric Horton, General Mgr
H Wayne Huizenga,
EMP: 50
SQ FT: 600
SALES (est): 5.9MM
SALES (corp-wide): 10B Publicly Held
WEB: www.republicservices.com
SIC: 5064 Garbage disposals
PA: Republic Services, Inc.
18500 N Allied Way # 100
Phoenix AZ 85054
480 627-2700

(P-7428)
SAMSUNG ELECTRONICS AMER INC
18600 S Broadwick St, Rancho Dominguez
(90220-6434)
PHONE..................................310 537-7000
K Hilm, General Mgr
Tae Kim, Purchasing
James MO, Sales Staff
EMP: 100
SALES (corp-wide): 148.1B Privately Held
WEB: www.samsung.com
SIC: 5064 5065 Electrical appliances, television & radio; communication equipment
HQ: Samsung Electronics America, Inc.
85 Challenger Rd Fl 7
Ridgefield Park NJ 07660
201 229-4000

(P-7429)
SONY ELECTRONICS INC
Also Called: Sony Logistics
2201 E Carson St, Carson (90810-1227)
PHONE..................................310 835-6121
Alan Schwab, Manager
EMP: 127
SALES (corp-wide): 80.1B Privately Held
SIC: 5064 5065 Electrical appliances, television & radio; electronic parts & equipment
HQ: Sony Electronics Inc.
16535 Via Esprillo Bldg 1
San Diego CA 92127
858 942-2400

(P-7430)
TV GUIDE ENTRMT GROUP LLC
2700 Colorado Ave Ste 200, Santa Monica
(90404-5502)
PHONE..................................310 360-1441
EMP: 57
SALES: 78.4MM
SALES (corp-wide): 13.7B Publicly Held
SIC: 5064 Electrical entertainment equipment
HQ: Cbs Interactive Inc.
235 2nd St
San Francisco CA 94105

(P-7431)
WATER HEATERS ONLY INC
3620 Haven Ave, Redwood City
(94063-4640)
PHONE..................................650 368-9998
Tom Crabtree, President
Michelle Dean, Admin Asst
Tony Edwards, Technician
Bill Lee, Sales Associate
Yana Carpenter, Marketing Staff
EMP: 90
SALES (est): 8.2MM Privately Held
SIC: 5064 5999 1711 Water heaters, electric; plumbing & heating supplies; heating systems repair & maintenance

---

5065 Electronic Parts & Eqpt Wholesale

(P-7432)
7DAYS INC
3503 Jack Northrop Ave, Hawthorne
(90250-4433)
PHONE..................................424 255-5872
Shiu Hou Sing, President
Hong Xia LI, Manager
EMP: 200
SALES: 13MM Privately Held
SIC: 5065 Electronic parts & equipment

(P-7433)
ABX ENGINEERING INC
875 Stanton Rd, Burlingame (94010-1403)
PHONE..................................650 552-2300
Paul Leininger II, CEO
Brian Helm, Vice Pres
Silvia De Leon-Lind, Purch Mgr
Michele Giguere, Purch Mgr
Peter Krapivkin, Senior Buyer
EMP: 100
SQ FT: 16,000
SALES (est): 54MM Privately Held
WEB: www.abxengr.com
SIC: 5065 7373 3672 Electronic parts;
turnkey vendors, computer systems;
printed circuit boards

(P-7434)
ADVANCED MP TECHNOLOGY INC (PA)
1010 Calle Sombra, San Clemente
(92673-6227)
PHONE..................................949 492-6589
Homayoun Shorooghi, President
Kamran Malek, Vice Pres
Mehdi Taghiei, Vice Pres
Alexander Romaniolis, Executive
Amir Sabei, Software Dev
◆ EMP: 126
SQ FT: 86,000
SALES: 120MM Privately Held
WEB: www.advancedmp.com
SIC: 5065 Electronic parts

(P-7435)
ALTURA COMM SOLUTIONS LLC (DH)
Also Called: Altura Communication Systems
1335 S Acacia Ave, Fullerton (92831-5315)
PHONE..................................714 948-8400
Robert Blazek, CEO
Tim Henion, President
David Key, CFO
EMP: 55
SQ FT: 25,000
SALES (est): 72.5MM Privately Held
WEB: www.alturacs.com
SIC: 5065 Electronic parts & equipment

(P-7436)
ALVARION INC (HQ)
555 N Mathilda Ave # 210, Sunnyvale
(94085-3503)
PHONE..................................650 314-2500
Zvi Slonimsky, President
Amir Rosenzweg, President
▲ EMP: 50
SQ FT: 16,000
SALES (est): 8.5MM Privately Held
WEB: www.alvarion-usa.com
SIC: 5065 Communication equipment
PA: Alvarion Ltd
21 Habarzel
Tel Aviv-Jaffa
364 562-62

(P-7437)
AMERICAN ZETTLER INC (HQ)
75 Columbia, Aliso Viejo (92656-4115)
PHONE..................................949 360-5830
Michael P Morgan, President
Rainer Moegling, CFO
Scott Peavey, Vice Pres
▲ EMP: 60
SQ FT: 63,000
SALES (est): 22.2MM Privately Held
WEB: www.azettler.com
SIC: 5065 Communication equipment

(P-7438)
AP GLOBAL INC
Also Called: Accessory Power
31352 Via Colinas Ste 101, Westlake Village (91362-6810)
PHONE..................................818 707-3167
Robert Breines, President
Gail Breines, Vice Pres
EMP: 60 EST: 2013
SALES (est): 31.5MM Privately Held
SIC: 5065 Electronic parts & equipment

(P-7439)
APUMAC LLC
Also Called: Apumac.com
6404 Wilshire Blvd # 106, Los Angeles
(90048-5501)
PHONE..................................888 248-7775
Lilyane Bensimon,
EMP: 214
SQ FT: 1,500
SALES (est): 21.7MM Privately Held
SIC: 5065 Mobile telephone equipment

(P-7440)
ARCONIX/USA INC
Also Called: Arconix USA
880 Avenida Acaso Ste 100, Camarillo
(93012-8721)
PHONE..................................805 388-2525
Allen Kay, President
Mark G Harris, Vice Pres
Cameron Hill, Vice Pres
John R Danzi, Controller
EMP: 52 EST: 1948
SALES: 5.5MM
SALES (corp-wide): 483.7MM Privately Held
WEB: www.penn-eng.com
SIC: 5065 Electronic parts & equipment
HQ: Penn Engineering & Manufacturing Corp.
5190 Old Easton Rd
Danboro PA 18916
215 766-8853

(P-7441)
ARROW ELECTRONICS INC
Also Called: Arrow Alliance Group
3000 Bowers Ave, Santa Clara
(95051-0942)
PHONE..................................631 847-2918
Glen Moore, Principal
EMP: 160
SALES (corp-wide): 26.8B Publicly Held
WEB: www.arrow.com
SIC: 5065 Electronic parts
PA: Arrow Electronics, Inc.
9201 E Dry Creek Rd
Centennial CO 80112
303 824-4000

(P-7442)
ARROW ELECTRONICS INC
Also Called: Arrow Bell
20935 Warner Center Ln A, Woodland Hills
(91367-6581)
PHONE..................................818 932-1022
Mike Jerworski, General Mgr
Jacqueline Counter, Marketing Staff
EMP: 85
SALES (corp-wide): 26.8B Publicly Held
WEB: www.arrow.com
SIC: 5065 Electronic parts
PA: Arrow Electronics, Inc.
9201 E Dry Creek Rd
Centennial CO 80112
303 824-4000

(P-7443)
AUDIOBAHN INC
114 S Berry St, Brea (92821-4826)
PHONE..................................714 988-0400
Nasser A Abdo, President
Saad Abou Abdo, COO
▲ EMP: 60
SQ FT: 130,000
SALES: 35MM Privately Held
SIC: 5065 Electronic parts & equipment

(P-7444)
AVI SYSTEMS INC
44150 S Grimmer Blvd, Fremont
(94538-6310)
PHONE..................................415 915-2070
EMP: 195
SALES (corp-wide): 219.6MM Privately Held
SIC: 5065 Sound equipment, electronic
PA: Avi Systems, Inc.
9675 W 76th St Ste 200
Eden Prairie MN 55344
952 949-3700

(P-7445)
AVNET INC
Also Called: Avnet Computers
220 Commerce Ste 100, Irvine
(92602-1346)
PHONE..................................949 789-4100
Tony Coletto, Branch Mgr
Brian Stroud, Technical Staff
Liza Polin, Human Res Dir
Sandy Rey, Accounts Mgr
EMP: 75
SALES (corp-wide): 17.4B Publicly Held
WEB: www.avnet.com
SIC: 5065 Semiconductor devices; electronic parts
PA: Avnet, Inc.
2211 S 47th St
Phoenix AZ 85034
480 643-2000

(P-7446)
AVNET INC
Also Called: Avnet Computers
20951 Burbank Blvd Ste A, Woodland Hills
(91367-6696)
PHONE..................................818 594-8310
James Williams, Manager
Mehrdad Bradaran, Accounts Mgr
EMP: 60
SALES (corp-wide): 17.4B Publicly Held
WEB: www.avnet.com
SIC: 5065 Electronic parts
PA: Avnet, Inc.
2211 S 47th St
Phoenix AZ 85034
480 643-2000

(P-7447)
AVNET INC
Also Called: Avnet Computers
2110 Zanker Rd, San Jose (95131-2111)
PHONE..................................408 501-3925
Dan Weiss, Director
Eric Winter, Production
EMP: 86
SALES (corp-wide): 17.4B Publicly Held
SIC: 5065 Semiconductor devices
PA: Avnet, Inc.
2211 S 47th St
Phoenix AZ 85034
480 643-2000

(P-7448)
AVNET INC
Electronics Div.
1400 Montefino Ave # 100, Diamond Bar
(91765-5501)
PHONE.....................760 946-5030
Beth Boedeke, *Branch Mgr*
EMP: 270
SALES (corp-wide): 19B **Publicly Held**
WEB: www.avnet.com
SIC: 5065 Electronic parts
PA: Avnet, Inc.
2211 S 47th St
Phoenix AZ 85034
480 643-2000

(P-7449)
AVNET INC
Also Called: Avnet Computers
15231 Avenue Of Science # 150, San
Diego (92128-3450)
PHONE.....................858 385-7500
Mark Goodding, *Branch Mgr*
EMP: 400
SALES (corp-wide): 17.4B **Publicly Held**
SIC: 5065 5045 7379 Semiconductor de-
vices; computers, peripherals & software;
computer related consulting services
PA: Avnet, Inc.
2211 S 47th St
Phoenix AZ 85034
480 643-2000

(P-7450)
BELKIN INTERNATIONAL INC
(DH)
Also Called: Belkin Components
12045 Waterfront Dr, Playa Vista
(90094-2999)
PHONE.....................310 751-5100
Chester J Pipkin, *President*
George C Platisa, *CFO*
Janice Pipkin, *Treasurer*
Kieran Hannon, *Chief Mktg Ofcr*
D Thomas Triggs,
◆ EMP: 450 EST: 1983
SQ FT: 218,000
SALES (est): 419.4MM
SALES (corp-wide): 60.3B **Privately Held**
WEB: www.belkin.com
SIC: 5065 5045 Intercommunication
equipment, electronic; communication
equipment; computers & accessories,
personal & home entertainment

(P-7451)
BRIX GROUP INC (PA)
Also Called: Pana-Pacific
838 N Laverne Ave, Fresno (93727-6868)
PHONE.....................559 457-4700
Harrison Brix, *CEO*
Kristina Reed, *President*
John Trenberth, *President*
Dennis Pastirik, *CFO*
Charlie Nguyen, *Admin Mgr*
▲ EMP: 80 EST: 1973
SQ FT: 35,000
SALES (est): 143.4MM **Privately Held**
WEB: www.brixcom.com
SIC: 5065 5013 Mobile telephone equip-
ment; paging & signaling equipment;
motor vehicle supplies & new parts

(P-7452)
BT AMERICAS INC
2160 E Grand Ave, El Segundo
(90245-5024)
PHONE.....................646 487-7400
Kristen Verderame, *Manager*
EMP: 100
SALES (corp-wide): 33.2B **Privately Held**
WEB: www.b-t.com
SIC: 5065
HQ: Bt Americas Inc.
8951 Cypress Waters Blvd # 200
Coppell TX 75019
877 272-0832

(P-7453)
BUYERS CONSULTATION SVC
INC (PA)
Also Called: B C S
8735 Remmet Ave, Canoga Park
(91304-1519)
P.O. Box 8427, Calabasas (91372-8427)
PHONE.....................818 341-4820
Jo Manhan, *President*
▲ EMP: 75
SQ FT: 40,000
SALES (est): 57.9MM **Privately Held**
SIC: 5065 7389 5093 4953 Electronic
parts & equipment; auctioneers, fee
basis; metal scrap & waste materials; re-
cycling, waste materials

(P-7454)
C P DOCUMENT
TECHNOLOGIES LLC (PA)
Also Called: Copypage
800 W 6th St Ste 1400, Los Angeles
(90017-2718)
PHONE.....................213 617-4040
Zorast Driver,
EMP: 70
SQ FT: 8,350
SALES (est): 26.3MM **Privately Held**
WEB: www.copypage.com
SIC: 5065 7334 7374 Electronic parts;
photocopying & duplicating services; opti-
cal scanning data service

(P-7455)
CAL SOUTHERN SOUND IMAGE
INC (PA)
2425 Auto Park Way, Escondido
(92029-1222)
PHONE.....................760 737-3900
David R Shadoan, *CEO*
Ross Ritto, *Partner*
Ralph Wagner, *CFO*
Larry Itatlia, *Vice Pres*
Henry Lafaille, *Executive*
EMP: 65
SQ FT: 28,000
SALES (est): 56.9MM **Privately Held**
SIC: 5065 3651 5064 Sound equipment,
electronic; speaker systems; electrical ap-
pliances, television & radio

(P-7456)
CALIFORNIA EASTERN LABS
INC (PA)
4590 Patrick Henry Dr, Santa Clara
(95054-1817)
PHONE.....................408 919-2500
Jerry A Arden, *Ch of Bd*
Paul A S Minton, *President*
Mark A Sargent, *CFO*
Kevin Beber, *Vice Pres*
Masaru Kaneko, *Vice Pres*
▲ EMP: 80
SQ FT: 42,000
SALES (est): 27.5MM **Privately Held**
WEB: www.cel.com
SIC: 5065 Semiconductor devices

(P-7457)
CAVENDISH KINETICS INC
2960 N 1st St, San Jose (95134-2021)
PHONE.....................408 627-4504
Paul Dal Santo, *CEO*
Patrick Murray, *CFO*
Dan Smith, *Exec VP*
Atul P Shingal, *Vice Pres*
Rose Reilly, *Admin Mgr*
EMP: 50
SALES: 1MM **Privately Held**
SIC: 5065 Semiconductor devices

(P-7458)
CBOL CORPORATION
19850 Plummer St, Chatsworth
(91311-5652)
PHONE.....................818 704-8200
Howard Nam, *COO*
Spencer H Kim, *CEO*
Kenneth Cheung, *CFO*
Lynn Turk, *Admin Sec*
Elizabeth Ahn, *Project Mgr*
▲ EMP: 131
SQ FT: 69,820

SALES (est): 178.2MM **Privately Held**
WEB: www.cbolcorp.com
SIC: 5065 5072 5013 5088 Electronic
parts & equipment; hardware; staples;
motor vehicle supplies & new parts; transportation equipment & supplies; industrial
machinery & equipment; plastics materials & basic shapes

(P-7459)
CELESTICA LLC
895 S Rockefeller Ave # 102, Ontario
(91761-8182)
PHONE.....................909 418-6986
James Rodriguez, *Branch Mgr*
EMP: 400
SALES (corp-wide): 24.5B **Privately Held**
SIC: 5065 7629 Electronic parts & equip-
ment; electronic equipment repair
HQ: Celestica Llc
11 Continental Blvd # 103
Merrimack NH 03054

(P-7460)
CELLULAR PALACE INC
Also Called: Wireless Lines
10435 Santa Monica Blvd F, Los Angeles
(90025-6936)
PHONE.....................310 278-2007
Rahim Bobby Malmed, *President*
Shahram Javidzad, *Officer*
▲ EMP: 89
SALES (est): 11.4MM **Privately Held**
SIC: 5065 5064 5999 5731 Telephone &
telegraphic equipment; paging & signaling
equipment; high fidelity equipment; alarm
signal systems; telephone & communication equipment; high fidelity stereo equipment; radios, two-way, citizens' band;
weather, short-wave, etc.

(P-7461)
CELLUPHONE LLC
6119 E Washington Blvd, Commerce
(90040-2436)
PHONE.....................323 727-9131
EMP: 110
SALES (est): 9.1MM **Privately Held**
SIC: 5065 5999 Electronic parts & equip-
ment; telephone equipment & systems

(P-7462)
CNET TECHNOLOGY
CORPORATION (HQ)
26291 Prod Ave Ste 205, Hayward (94545)
PHONE.....................408 392-9966
Simon J Chang, *President*
▲ EMP: 179
SQ FT: 50,000
SALES (est): 30MM
SALES (corp-wide): 167.8MM **Privately
Held**
WEB: www.cnetusa.com
SIC: 5065 3661 3577 Communication
equipment; modems, computer; tele-
phone & telegraph apparatus; computer
peripheral equipment
PA: Kmc (Kuei Meng) International Inc.
8f-5, 425, Jhong Hua Rd.,
Tainan City 71079
630 371-11

(P-7463)
CORNER PRODUCTS COMPANY
Also Called: CP Technologies
17110 Armstrong Ave, Irvine (92614-5718)
PHONE.....................800 876-8889
Chao-Jen Lin, *CEO*
Rick Hsu, *CEO*
Michael Hsu, *Principal*
▲ EMP: 55
SQ FT: 17,000
SALES (est): 12.9MM **Privately Held**
SIC: 5065 5045 Telephone equipment;
computer peripheral equipment

(P-7464)
DAVID LEVY CO INC
Also Called: Dlc
12753 Moore St, Cerritos (90703-2136)
PHONE.....................562 404-9998
David Levy, *CEO*
John Latino, *Vice Pres*
Gordon Schaer, *Admin Sec*
Alex Blanco, *Marketing Mgr*

Dale Lincoln, *Sales Staff*
▲ EMP: 50 EST: 1978
SQ FT: 25,000
SALES (est): 16.3MM **Privately Held**
WEB: www.cybertraklocate.com
SIC: 5065 Electronic parts

(P-7465)
DECISION SCIENCES INTL
CORP
12345 First American Way # 100, Poway
(92064-6828)
PHONE.....................858 571-1900
Dwight Johnson, *President*
Brian Gallagher, *President*
Mike Goll, *CFO*
Jerry Ackerman, *Software Dev*
James Weibel, *Software Dev*
▼ EMP: 60 EST: 1993
SALES (est): 19.6MM **Privately Held**
SIC: 5065 Radar detectors

(P-7466)
DELTA AMERICA LTD (HQ)
Also Called: Delta Products
46101 Fremont Blvd, Fremont
(94538-6468)
PHONE.....................510 668-5100
Ming H Huang, *President*
Yao Chou, *Admin Sec*
Eunice Lin, *Manager*
◆ EMP: 130
SALES (est): 250.5MM
SALES (corp-wide): 7.4B **Privately Held**
SIC: 5065 3679 8731 Electronic parts &
equipment; switches, stepping; power
supplies, all types: static; electronic re-
search
PA: Delta Electronics, Inc.
186, Ruiguang Rd.,
Taipei City TAP 11491
287 972-088

(P-7467)
DELTA ELECTRONICS
AMERICAS LTD (DH)
46101 Fremont Blvd, Fremont
(94538-6468)
PHONE.....................510 668-5100
Ming H Huang, *President*
Sheryl Chen, *CFO*
Simon Product, *Director*
◆ EMP: 100
SALES (est): 250.5MM
SALES (corp-wide): 7.4B **Privately Held**
WEB: www.delta-corp.com
SIC: 5065 5045 8741 5063 Electronic
parts & equipment; computer peripheral
equipment; management services; electri-
cal apparatus & equipment; computer pe-
ripheral equipment
HQ: Delta America Ltd
46101 Fremont Blvd
Fremont CA 94538
510 668-5100

(P-7468)
DIALOG SEMICONDUCTOR INC
1515 Wyatt Dr, Santa Clara (95054-1586)
PHONE.....................408 327-8800
EMP: 235
SALES (corp-wide): 1.3B **Privately Held**
SIC: 5065 Semiconductor devices
HQ: Dialog Semiconductor, Inc.
2560 Mission College Blvd # 110
Santa Clara CA 95054
408 845-8500

(P-7469)
EDGEWISE MEDIA SERVICES
INC (PA)
Also Called: Comtel Pro Media
4518 W Vanowen St, Burbank
(91505-1135)
PHONE.....................714 919-2020
David Cohen, *President*
▲ EMP: 84
SQ FT: 33,000
SALES (est): 11.4MM **Privately Held**
SIC: 5065 Tapes, audio & video recording

PRODUCTS & SVCS

(P-7470)
EFORCITY CORP - NFM
Also Called: Ascend Distribution
18525 Railroad St, City of Industry
(91748-1316)
PHONE..................................626 442-3168
Michael Wong, *Warehouse Mgr*
Jack Sheng, *CEO*
Eugene Wong, *CFO*
Bolan You, *Info Tech Dir*
Bao Jean, *Engineer*
▲ EMP: 60
SQ FT: 100,000
SALES (est): 48.4MM **Privately Held**
WEB: www.eforcity.com
SIC: 5065 Telephone equipment

(P-7471)
ELMA ELECTRONIC INC
17700 Shideler Pkwy, Lathrop
(95330-9356)
PHONE..................................209 858-2411
Badri Rajan, *VP Mfg*
David Meyer, *Regl Sales Mgr*
Marc Gallant, *Manager*
EMP: 50
SALES (corp-wide): 145.6MM **Privately Held**
SIC: 5065 Electronic parts & equipment
HQ: Elma Electronic Inc.
44350 S Grimmer Blvd
Fremont CA 94538

(P-7472)
ELROB INC
Also Called: El-Com Cabletek
12691 Monarch St, Garden Grove
(92841-3918)
PHONE..................................714 230-6100
Elie Vrobel, *CEO*
Arik Vrobel, *President*
Dan Balentine, *Vice Pres*
Kevin Malstrom, *Info Tech Dir*
Ken Chau, *Purch Agent*
▲ EMP: 54 EST: 1960
SQ FT: 38,500
SALES (est): 47.6MM **Privately Held**
WEB: www.elcomcabletek.com
SIC: 5065 3679 3613 3643 Electronic parts; harness assemblies for electronic use: wire or cable; switchgear & switchboard apparatus; current-carrying wiring devices

(P-7473)
EURASIA POWER LLC
4022 Cmino Ranchero Ste D, Camarillo
(93012)
PHONE..................................805 383-1234
Marilou Erb,
Dan Erb,
▲ EMP: 50
SALES (est): 14.7MM **Privately Held**
WEB: www.eurasiapower.com
SIC: 5065 Electronic parts & equipment

(P-7474)
EVER WIN INTERNATIONAL CORP
17579 Railroad St, City of Industry
(91748-1125)
PHONE..................................626 810-8218
Charles Chen, *CEO*
Henry Chen, *President*
Mae Hsu, *Exec VP*
Brian Firestone, *Vice Pres*
Jim Obrien, *Vice Pres*
▲ EMP: 50
SQ FT: 90,000
SALES (est): 39.9MM **Privately Held**
WEB: www.everwin.com
SIC: 5065 Telephone & telegraphic equipment

(P-7475)
EWING-FOLEY INC (PA)
10061 Bubb Rd Ste 100, Cupertino
(95014-4162)
PHONE..................................408 342-1201
Richard Foley, *Ch of Bd*
Gary Lessing, *President*
Robert Lessing, *Corp Secy*
Doug Likens, *Vice Pres*
Cathy Coement, *Executive*
EMP: 50 EST: 1964

SQ FT: 13,000
SALES (est): 16.7MM **Privately Held**
WEB: www.ewingfoley.com
SIC: 5065 Electronic parts

(P-7476)
EXIS INC
1570 The Alameda Ste 150, San Jose
(95126-2331)
PHONE..................................408 944-4600
Jim Bailey, *President*
Carmen Haney, *Assistant*
EMP: 50
SQ FT: 22,000
SALES (est): 7.4MM **Privately Held**
WEB: www.exisinc.com
SIC: 5065 Electronic parts

(P-7477)
FIBERTRON CORPORATION
6400 Artesia Blvd, Buena Park
(90620-1006)
P.O. Box 5220 (90622-5220)
PHONE..................................714 670-7711
Marlene Spiegel, *President*
Eileen Cohen, *Treasurer*
Henry J Cohen, *Finance Other*
▼ EMP: 75
SQ FT: 104,000
SALES (est): 34MM **Privately Held**
SIC: 5065 Communication equipment

(P-7478)
FLIR COMMERCIAL SYSTEMS INC (HQ)
6769 Hollister Ave # 100, Goleta
(93117-5572)
PHONE..................................805 964-9797
James J Cannon, *President*
Carol P Lowe, *CFO*
Darren Haley, *Manager*
▲ EMP: 350
SALES (est): 419.7MM
SALES (corp-wide): 1.8B **Publicly Held**
SIC: 5065 3699 Security control equipment & systems; security devices
PA: Flir Systems, Inc.
27700 Sw Parkway Ave
Wilsonville OR 97070
503 498-3547

(P-7479)
FRONTIER CALIFORNIA INC
112 S Lakeview Canyon Rd, Westlake Village (91362-3925)
PHONE..................................805 372-6000
Deb Anders, *President*
EMP: 650
SALES (corp-wide): 9.1B **Publicly Held**
SIC: 5065 4813 4812 Telephone equipment; telephone communication, except radio; radio telephone communication
HQ: Frontier California Inc.
140 West St
New York NY 10007
212 395-1000

(P-7480)
FULL CIRCLE WIRELESS INC
8900 Research Dr, Irvine (92618-4245)
PHONE..................................949 783-7979
Shelton Basham, *CEO*
EMP: 50
SALES (est): 7MM **Privately Held**
WEB: www.fullcirclewireless.com
SIC: 5065 Mobile telephone equipment

(P-7481)
FUMAI INDUSTRIAL INC
735 W Duarte Rd, Arcadia (91007-7522)
PHONE..................................626 272-1788
John Whang, *Branch Mgr*
EMP: 75
SALES (corp-wide): 7.5MM **Privately Held**
SIC: 5065 Communication equipment
PA: Shanghai Pudong Fumei Industry & Trade Co., Ltd.
No.5, Xinchun Road, Xinchun Village, Huanglou, Chuansha Town, Pu
Shanghai 20120
215 894-4666

(P-7482)
GCT SEMICONDUCTOR INC (PA)
2121 Ringwood Ave Ste A, San Jose
(95131-1741)
PHONE..................................408 434-6040
John Schlaefer, *CEO*
Kyeong Ho Lee, *Ch of Bd*
Gene Kulzer, *CFO*
Jay Jang, *Vice Pres*
David Yoon, *Vice Pres*
EMP: 210 EST: 2001
SQ FT: 15,000
SALES (est): 24.6MM **Privately Held**
WEB: www.gctsemi.com
SIC: 5065 Semiconductor devices

(P-7483)
GGEC AMERICA INC
20450 Stevens Creek Blvd # 220, Cupertino (95014-6812)
PHONE..................................714 750-2280
Dave Cox, *President*
Jiaxi Huang, *President*
Kobe Zhang, *Vice Pres*
▲ EMP: 72
SQ FT: 2,700
SALES (est): 11.4MM
SALES (corp-wide): 611MM **Privately Held**
WEB: www.gabrielkoneta.com
SIC: 5065 Electronic parts
PA: Guoguang Electric Limited
No.8, Jinghu Ave., Xinya Street, Huadu District
Guangzhou 51080
202 860-9988

(P-7484)
GRIFFIN TECHNOLOGY LLC (HQ)
6001 Oak Cyn, Irvine (92618-5200)
PHONE..................................615 399-7000
Dean Shortland, *Business Mgr*
Brian Swartz, *Manager*
▲ EMP: 70
SALES (est): 53.2MM
SALES (corp-wide): 71.4MM **Privately Held**
WEB: www.griffintechnology.com
SIC: 5065 Communication equipment
PA: Incipio Technologies, Inc.
3347 Michelson Dr Ste 100
Irvine CA 92612
949 250-4929

(P-7485)
H M ELECTRONICS INC (PA)
Also Called: H M E
2848 Whiptail Loop, Carlsbad
(92010-6708)
PHONE..................................858 535-6000
Harrison Y Miyahira, *Ch of Bd*
Charles Miyahira, *CEO*
Paul Foley, *Vice Pres*
Scott Weldner, *Vice Pres*
Ricci Fretz, *Exec Dir*
◆ EMP: 315 EST: 1971
SQ FT: 73,000
SALES (est): 515.5MM **Privately Held**
WEB: www.hme.com
SIC: 5065 Electronic parts & equipment

(P-7486)
HEILIND ELECTRONICS INC
Also Called: Force Electronics
700 N Plaza Dr, Visalia (93291-9327)
PHONE..................................559 651-0168
Mark Adams, *Manager*
EMP: 55
SALES (corp-wide): 740.7MM **Privately Held**
WEB: www.heilind.com
SIC: 5065 Electronic parts
PA: Heilind Electronics, Inc
58 Jonspin Rd
Wilmington MA 01887
978 657-4870

(P-7487)
HIRSCH ELECTRONICS LLC
1900 Carnegie Ave Ste B, Santa Ana
(92705-5557)
PHONE..................................949 250-8888
John Picc, *Mng Member*
Brian Culhane, *General Mgr*
Joe Melendez, *Info Tech Mgr*

Diana Midland, *Info Tech Mgr*
Vouy Yeng, *Technology*
EMP: 85 EST: 1981
SQ FT: 34,600
SALES (est): 12.1MM **Publicly Held**
WEB: www.hirschelectronics.com
SIC: 5065 Security control equipment & systems
PA: Identiv, Inc.
2201 Walnut Ave Ste 100
Fremont CA 94538

(P-7488)
HITACHI HIGH TECH AMER INC
5960 Inglewood Dr Ste 200, Pleasanton
(94588-8611)
PHONE..................................925 218-2800
Bob Gordon, *Manager*
Tom Heiser, *Vice Pres*
John Giudicessi, *Executive*
Donna Armanino, *Managing Dir*
Doug Kraneman, *Department Mgr*
EMP: 70
SALES (corp-wide): 87.9B **Privately Held**
WEB: www.hitachi-hhta.com
SIC: 5065 Electronic parts
HQ: Hitachi High Technologies America, Inc.
10 N Martingale Rd # 500
Schaumburg IL 60173
847 273-4141

(P-7489)
HONEYWELL INTERNATIONAL INC
1349 Moffett Park Dr, Sunnyvale
(94089-1134)
PHONE..................................408 962-2000
Barry Russell, *Manager*
EMP: 50
SALES (corp-wide): 40.5B **Publicly Held**
WEB: www.honeywell.com
SIC: 5065 3674 Electronic parts; semiconductors & related devices
PA: Honeywell International Inc.
115 Tabor Rd
Morris Plains NJ 07950
973 455-2000

(P-7490)
HONEYWELL INTERNATIONAL INC
487 Mathew St, Santa Clara (95050-3105)
PHONE..................................408 986-8200
Dave Nash, *Owner*
EMP: 57
SALES (corp-wide): 40.5B **Publicly Held**
SIC: 5065 Security control equipment & systems
PA: Honeywell International Inc.
115 Tabor Rd
Morris Plains NJ 07950
973 455-2000

(P-7491)
I C CLASS COMPONENTS CORP (PA)
Also Called: Classic
23605 Telo Ave, Torrance (90505-4028)
PHONE..................................310 539-5500
Jeffrey Klein, *President*
Chris Klein, *COO*
Kris Klein, *COO*
Emma Klein, *Corp Secy*
Perry Klein, *Vice Pres*
▲ EMP: 100
SQ FT: 53,000
SALES (est): 87MM **Privately Held**
WEB: www.connxx.com
SIC: 5065 Electronic parts

(P-7492)
IDEC CORPORATION (HQ)
1175 Elko Dr, Sunnyvale (94089-2209)
PHONE..................................408 747-0550
Toshiyuki Funaki, *CEO*
Mikio Funaki, *President*
Donald L Scrivner, *CFO*
Juan Moreno, *Chief Mktg Ofcr*
Sumie Fukano, *Executive Asst*
▲ EMP: 89
SQ FT: 84,000

SALES (est): 45.2MM
SALES (corp-wide): 561.1MM **Privately
Held**
WEB: www.idec.com
SIC: **5065** Electronic parts
PA: Idec Corporation
2-6-64, Nishimiyahara, Yodogawa-Ku
Osaka OSK 532-0
663 982-500

(P-7493)
INDUCTORS INC
Also Called: Central Technologies
140 Technology Dr Ste 500, Irvine
(92618-2427)
PHONE....................................949 623-2460
Judy Macdonald, CEO
Angie Pham, Marketing Staff
▲ EMP: 50
SQ FT: 24,600
SALES (est): 21.8MM **Privately Held**
WEB: www.inductor.com
SIC: **5065** Electronic parts

(P-7494)
INSULECTRO (PA)
20362 Windrow Dr Ste 100, Lake Forest
(92630-8140)
PHONE....................................949 587-3200
Timothy P Redfern, CEO
Patrick Redfern, President
Brad Biddle, CFO
Chris Hunrath, Vice Pres
John Lee, Vice Pres
▲ EMP: 70
SQ FT: 40,000
SALES (est): 126.8MM **Privately Held**
WEB: www.cac-inc.com
SIC: **5065** Electronic parts

(P-7495)
JIT CORPORATION
Also Called: J I T Supply
2790 Valley View Ave, Norco (92860-2349)
PHONE....................................805 238-5000
Brent Smith, President
Sharon Smith, Corp Secy
Rick Box, CIO
Tom Earl, Engineer
Frank Huggins, QC Mgr
EMP: 60
SQ FT: 30,000
SALES (est): 55.7MM **Privately Held**
WEB: www.jitmfg.com
SIC: **5065** Electronic parts

(P-7496)
JOHNSON CONTROLS INC
1757 Tapo Canyon Rd # 120, Simi Valley
(93063-3390)
PHONE....................................805 522-5555
Patrick Young, Regional Mgr
EMP: 60 **Privately Held**
SIC: **5065** Security control equipment &
systems
HQ: Johnson Controls, Inc.
5757 N Green Bay Ave
Milwaukee WI 53209
414 524-1200

(P-7497)
JRI INC
Also Called: J R Industries
31280 La Baya Dr, Westlake Village
(91362-4005)
PHONE....................................818 706-2424
Kathy Becker, President
Gary Becker, Corp Secy
▲ EMP: 50
SQ FT: 20,000
SALES (est): 25.8MM **Privately Held**
WEB: www.jri.com
SIC: **5065** 3679 Electronic parts; harness
assemblies for electronic use: wire or
cable

(P-7498)
KYOCERA INTERNATIONAL INC
3565 Cadillac Ave, Costa Mesa
(92626-1401)
PHONE....................................714 428-3600
EMP: 50

SALES (corp-wide): 14.8B **Publicly Held**
SIC: **5065** 5013 5085 Electronic parts;
connectors, electronic; semiconductor devices; heaters, motor vehicle; industrial
tools
HQ: Kyocera International, Inc.
8611 Balboa Ave
San Diego CA 92123
858 492-1456

(P-7499)
LEGACY FRAMES
11220 Wright Rd, Lynwood (90262-3124)
PHONE....................................310 537-4210
Angelica Serrano, CEO
EMP: 54
SALES: 5MM **Privately Held**
SIC: **5065** Mobile telephone equipment

(P-7500)
LEMO USA INC
635 Park Ct, Rohnert Park (94928-7940)
P.O. Box 2408 (94927-2408)
PHONE....................................707 206-3700
Dinshaw Pohwala, CEO
Michael Grieco, COO
Win Baerthel, General Mgr
Marian Johnson, Administration
Joe De Sena, Technician
EMP: 100
SQ FT: 55,000
SALES (est): 70MM **Privately Held**
WEB: www.lemousa.com
SIC: **5065** 3678 Connectors, electronic;
electronic connectors
HQ: Interlemo U.S.A. Inc.
635 Park Ct
Rohnert Park CA 94928
707 578-8811

(P-7501)
LG DISPLAY AMERICA INC
2791 Loker Ave W, Carlsbad (92010-6601)
PHONE....................................760 692-0900
Byungdo Park, Branch Mgr
Michael Kim, President
Dawit Kim, Administration
Jiyung Lee, Human Res Mgr
Kim Chanelle, Human Resources
EMP: 50
SALES (corp-wide): 23.4B **Privately Held**
SIC: **5065** Modems, computer
HQ: Lg Display America, Inc.
2540 N 1st St Ste 400
San Jose CA 95131
408 350-0190

(P-7502)
LG DISPLAY AMERICA INC (HQ)
2540 N 1st St Ste 400, San Jose
(95131-1016)
PHONE....................................408 350-0190
Chris Min, President
Davis Lee, President
James Jeong, CFO
Yong Kee Huang, Senior VP
Cheol D Ong Jeong, Principal
▲ EMP: 70
SQ FT: 1,000
SALES (est): 46.7MM
SALES (corp-wide): 23.4B **Privately Held**
SIC: **5065** Modems, computer
PA: Lg Display Co., Ltd.
128 Yeoui-Daero, Yeongdeungpo-Gu
Seoul 07336
822 377-7248

(P-7503)
LINKSYS LLC
12045 Waterfront Dr, Playa Vista
(90094-2999)
PHONE....................................310 751-5100
Chet Pipkin, Branch Mgr
EMP: 110
SALES (corp-wide): 60.3B **Privately Held**
SIC: **5065** Electronic parts & equipment
HQ: Linksys Llc
131 Theory
Irvine CA 92617
949 270-8500

(P-7504)
LINKSYS LLC (DH)
131 Theory, Irvine (92617-3045)
P.O. Box 91830, Los Angeles (90009-1830)
PHONE....................................949 270-8500

Chet Pipkin, Mng Member
▲ EMP: 275
SQ FT: 20,000
SALES (est): 388.1MM
SALES (corp-wide): 60.3B **Privately Held**
WEB: www.cisco.com
SIC: **5065** Communication equipment
HQ: Belkin International, Inc.
12045 Waterfront Dr
Playa Vista CA 90094
310 751-5100

(P-7505)
LITE-ON INC (HQ)
Also Called: Lite-On U S A
720 S Hillview Dr, Milpitas (95035-5455)
PHONE....................................408 946-4873
Sonny Hsuen-Ching Chao, President
Tammy Ho, Treasurer
Jerry Basham, Vice Pres
Jing Shao, Sr Software Eng
Nancy Chow, CTO
▲ EMP: 50
SQ FT: 25,000
SALES (est): 17.7MM
SALES (corp-wide): 7.1B **Privately Held**
WEB: www.liteonus.com
SIC: **5065** Semiconductor devices
PA: Lite-On Technology Corporation
22f, 392, Ruey Kuang Rd.,
Taipei City TAP 11492
287 982-888

(P-7506)
MACRONIX AMERICA INC (HQ)
Also Called: Mxic
680 N Mccarthy Blvd # 200, Milpitas
(95035-5120)
PHONE....................................408 262-8887
Arthur Yang, CEO
John J Wong, President
Alan Portnoy, COO
Wilvin Lee, Engineer
Tina Lin, Controller
EMP: 53
SQ FT: 20,000
SALES (est): 18.9MM
SALES (corp-wide): 1.1B **Privately Held**
WEB: www.macronix.com
SIC: **5065** 3674 Semiconductor devices;
semiconductors & related devices
PA: Macronix International Co., Ltd.
16, Li Hsin Rd., Science-Based Indus-
trial Park,
Hsinchu City 30078
357 866-88

(P-7507)
**METRIC EQUIPMENT SALES
INC**
Also Called: Microlease
25841 Industrial Blvd # 200, Hayward
(94545-2991)
PHONE....................................510 264-0887
Nigel Brown, CEO
Mike Clark, CEO
Nathan Hurst, CFO
David Sherve, Senior VP
Gordon Curwen, Vice Pres
EMP: 70
SQ FT: 25,000
SALES (est): 57.7MM
SALES (corp-wide): 142MM **Privately
Held**
WEB: www.metrictest.com
SIC: **5065** 5084 7359 3825 Electronic
parts; measuring & testing equipment,
electrical; electronic equipment rental, ex-
cept computers; instruments to measure
electricity
HQ: Microlease Inc.
6060 Sepulveda Blvd
Van Nuys CA 91411
866 520-0200

(P-7508)
MICRO-MECHANICS INC
465 Woodview Ave, Morgan Hill
(95037-2800)
PHONE....................................408 779-2927
Christopher R Borch, President
Marco Ramirez, QA Dir
Michael Maguire, Engineer
Kathleen Edmiston, Finance
Thom Wojno, Mfg Staff
EMP: 50

SQ FT: 42,000
SALES (est): 24.7MM **Privately Held**
WEB: www.micromechanics.com
SIC: **5065** 3674 Semiconductor devices;
semiconductors & related devices
PA: Micro-Mechanics (Holdings) Ltd.
31 Kaki Bukit Place
Singapore 41620

(P-7509)
MITSUBISHI ELECTRIC US INC
7345 Orangewood Ave, Garden Grove
(92841-1411)
PHONE....................................714 934-5300
EMP: 60
SALES (corp-wide): 36.3B **Privately Held**
SIC: **5065** 5045
HQ: Mitsubishi Electric Us, Inc.
5900 Katella Ave Ste A
Cypress CA 90630
714 220-2500

(P-7510)
MOBILYGEN CORPORATION
160 Rio Robles, San Jose (95134-1813)
PHONE....................................408 601-1000
Joseph Perl, Ch of Bd
Chris Day, President
EMP: 60
SQ FT: 13,000
SALES (est): 6.2MM
SALES (corp-wide): 2.4B **Publicly Held**
WEB: www.mobilygen.com
SIC: **5065** Semiconductor devices
PA: Maxim Integrated Products, Inc.
160 Rio Robles
San Jose CA 95134
408 601-1000

(P-7511)
**MOSCHIP SEMICONDUCTOR
TECH USA**
840 N Hillview Dr, Milpitas (95035-4544)
PHONE....................................408 737-7141
Ram K Reddey, CEO
Shiri Kadambi, President
Ashok Kumar, Vice Pres
Dayakar Reddy, Managing Dir
Sam Sanyal, Marketing Staff
EMP: 120
SQ FT: 4,000
SALES (est): 16.2MM **Privately Held**
WEB: www.moschip.com
SIC: **5065** Semiconductor devices
PA: Moschip Semiconductor Technology
Limited
Plot No. 83 & 84, 2nd Floor,
Hyderabad TS 50003

(P-7512)
MOTOROLA MOBILITY LLC
6450 Sequence Dr, San Diego
(92121-4376)
PHONE....................................858 455-1500
Rick Neal, Branch Mgr
Mark Schmidl, Vice Pres
Arsalan Khan, Software Engr
Hai Lin, Manager
Tanya Scott, Manager
EMP: 80
SQ FT: 30,000
SALES (corp-wide): 43B **Privately Held**
WEB: www.motorola-labs.com
SIC: **5065** 3663 Communication equip-
ment; radio & TV communications equip-
ment
HQ: Motorola Mobility Llc
222 Merchandise Mart Plz # 1800
Chicago IL 60654

(P-7513)
NALLATECH INC
741 Flynn Rd, Camarillo (93012-8056)
PHONE....................................805 383-8997
Colin Rutherford, Chairman
Allan Cantle, President
William P Miller, CEO
Ed Hennessy, Vice Pres
Chelsea Palmer, Manager
EMP: 64

SALES (est): 24.3MM
SALES (corp-wide): 42.9B **Privately Held**
WEB: www.nallatech.com
SIC: 5065 Electronic parts & equipment
HQ: Interconnect Systems, Inc.
741 Flynn Rd
Camarillo CA 93012
805 482-2870

(P-7514)
NEST LABS INC (DH)
3400 Hillview Ave, Palo Alto (94304-1346)
PHONE..................650 331-1127
Tony Fadell, *CEO*
Matthew Rogers, *Owner*
Ray Vieweg, *Lab Dir*
Andy Baynes, *Business Dir*
Scott Fisher, *Program Mgr*
◆ **EMP:** 58
SALES (est): 71MM
SALES (corp-wide): 110.8B **Publicly Held**
SIC: 5065 Electronic parts & equipment
HQ: Google Llc
1600 Amphitheatre Pkwy
Mountain View CA 94043
650 253-0000

(P-7515)
NU HORIZONS ELECTRONICS CORP
890 N Mccarthy Blvd, San Jose (95131)
PHONE..................408 946-4154
EMP: 50
SALES (corp-wide): 23.2B **Publicly Held**
SIC: 5065
HQ: Nu Horizons Electronics Corp.
70 Maxess Rd
Melville NY 11747
631 396-5000

(P-7516)
NUCOURSE DISTRIBUTION INC
22342 Avenida Empresa # 200, Rcho STA Marg (92688-2148)
PHONE..................866 655-4366
Nicholas Troy Seedorf, *CEO*
Brandon Seedorf, *Vice Pres*
Ian Shiry, *Finance*
Jeff Eisses, *Director*
EMP: 55
SALES: 89MM **Privately Held**
SIC: 5065 Electronic parts & equipment

(P-7517)
NUVOTON TECHNOLOGY CORP AMER
2727 N 1st St, San Jose (95134-2029)
PHONE..................408 544-1718
Arthur Yu-Cheng Chiao, *Chairman*
Robert Hsu, *President*
Mark Hemming, *Chief Mktg Ofcr*
Stephen Rei-Min Huang, *Vice Pres*
Bor-Yuan Hwang, *Vice Pres*
EMP: 60
SALES (est): 24.3MM
SALES (corp-wide): 1.5B **Privately Held**
SIC: 5065 Semiconductor devices
HQ: Nuvoton Technology Corporation
4, Creation 3rd Rd.,
Hsinchu City 30077
357 700-66

(P-7518)
ODU-USA INC (HQ)
300 Camarillo Ranch Rd A, Camarillo (93012-5208)
PHONE..................805 484-0540
Michael Savage, *CEO*
Joseph Cisi, *President*
Kurt Woelfl, *CEO*
Joe Vigil, *Business Mgr*
▲ **EMP:** 60
SQ FT: 20,000
SALES (est): 36.7MM
SALES (corp-wide): 110.5MM **Privately Held**
WEB: www.odu-usa.com
SIC: 5065 Connectors, electronic
PA: Odu Gmbh & Co. Kg
Pregelstr. 11
Muhldorf A. Inn 84453
863 161-560

(P-7519)
OPTIMUS VENTURES LLC
143 Selby Ln, Atherton (94027-3951)
PHONE..................888 881-5969
Meera Koul, *Mng Member*
EMP: 50
SALES (est): 1.6MM **Privately Held**
SIC: 5065 Mobile telephone equipment

(P-7520)
ORGANIC AFFINITY LLC
3980 Hopevale Dr, Sherman Oaks (91403-4414)
PHONE..................801 870-7433
David Surber, *Mng Member*
EMP: 65
SALES (est): 2.6MM **Privately Held**
SIC: 5065 Electronic parts & equipment

(P-7521)
OSRAM OPTO SEMICONDUCTORS INC
1150 Kifer Rd Ste 100, Sunnyvale (94086-5302)
PHONE..................408 588-3800
Tom Shottes, *Manager*
EMP: 52
SALES (corp-wide): 4.8B **Privately Held**
WEB: www.osram-os.com
SIC: 5065 Semiconductor devices
HQ: Osram Opto Semiconductors Inc.
1150 Kifer Rd Ste 100
Sunnyvale CA 94086

(P-7522)
OSRAM OPTO SEMICONDUCTORS INC (HQ)
1150 Kifer Rd Ste 100, Sunnyvale (94086-5302)
PHONE..................408 962-3736
Thomas Shottes, *CEO*
Ron Terry, *CFO*
▲ **EMP:** 50
SALES (est): 29.9MM
SALES (corp-wide): 4.8B **Privately Held**
WEB: www.osram-os.com
SIC: 5065 Semiconductor devices
PA: Osram Licht Ag
Marcel-Breuer-Str. 6
Munchen 80807
896 213-0

(P-7523)
PARTSEARCH TECHNOLOGIES INC
Also Called: Andrews Electronics
25158 Avenue Stanford, Santa Clarita (91355-1226)
PHONE..................661 257-7700
John Zeitlin, *Manager*
EMP: 50
SALES (corp-wide): 42.1B **Publicly Held**
SIC: 5065 3679 Electronic parts; commutators, electronic
HQ: Partsearch Technologies Inc.
27460 Avenue Scott D
Valencia CA 91355
800 289-0300

(P-7524)
PERILLO INDUSTRIES INC
Also Called: Century Electronics
2150 Anchor Ct Ste A, Newbury Park (91320-1609)
PHONE..................805 498-9838
Mary Perillo, *President*
Perry Boeck, *Engineer*
Grace Abaya, *Human Resources*
EMP: 50 **EST:** 1973
SQ FT: 20,000
SALES (est): 26.2MM **Privately Held**
SIC: 5065 Electronic parts & equipment

(P-7525)
PRESIDIO COMPONENTS INC
7169 Construction Ct, San Diego (92121-2615)
PHONE..................858 578-9390
Violet Devoe, *President*
Alan Devoe, *Vice Pres*
Daniel Devoe, *Vice Pres*
Lambert Devoe, *Vice Pres*
▲ **EMP:** 120 **EST:** 1980
SQ FT: 35,000

SALES (est): 60.9MM **Privately Held**
WEB: www.presidiocomponents.com
SIC: 5065 Electronic parts & equipment

(P-7526)
PRISM ELECTRONICS CORP (PA)
900 Lightpost Way 100, Morgan Hill (95037-2869)
PHONE..................408 778-7050
John Jules Mauro, *CEO*
John Mauro, *CFO*
Chris Eversole, *General Mgr*
Sofia Fedotova, *Admin Sec*
◆ **EMP:** 50
SQ FT: 21,373
SALES (est): 12.3MM **Privately Held**
SIC: 5065 Electronic parts

(P-7527)
QMADIX INC
14350 Arminta St, Panorama City (91402-6869)
PHONE..................818 988-4300
Ezra Soumekh, *CEO*
David Khalepari, *President*
Richard Mertz, *COO*
▲ **EMP:** 51
SQ FT: 30,000
SALES (est): 15.5MM **Privately Held**
WEB: www.paramountwireless.com
SIC: 5065 Mobile telephone equipment

(P-7528)
QNG INC
2809 Whipple Rd, Union City (94587-1233)
PHONE..................480 330-3804
William Guo, *Owner*
EMP: 67
SQ FT: 6,750
SALES (est): 1.3MM **Privately Held**
SIC: 5065 Electronic parts & equipment

(P-7529)
QUEST COMPONENTS INC
14711 Clark Ave, City of Industry (91745-1307)
PHONE..................626 333-5858
Dave A Hozen, *CEO*
Andre A Hozen, *Treasurer*
Liz Claridge, *Executive Asst*
Connie Celaya, *Sales Staff*
Linda Olivas, *Sales Staff*
▲ **EMP:** 50
SQ FT: 32,000
SALES (est): 29MM **Privately Held**
WEB: www.quest-comp.com
SIC: 5065 Electronic parts

(P-7530)
QUINSTAR TECHNOLOGY INC
24085 Garnier St, Torrance (90505-5319)
PHONE..................310 320-1111
Leo Fong, *President*
Naresh Deo, *President*
John Kuno, *Exec VP*
Hj Kuno, *Vice Pres*
Robert Ying, *Program Mgr*
▲ **EMP:** 72
SALES (est): 37.8MM **Privately Held**
WEB: www.quinstar.com
SIC: 5065 Electronic parts & equipment

(P-7531)
R&M USA INC
Also Called: Realm
840 Yosemite Way, Milpitas (95035-6360)
PHONE..................408 945-6626
Markus Huber, *President*
Kimberly Horowitz, *Treasurer*
Agnes Edusada, *Accounting Mgr*
Kim Horowitz, *Finance*
Debbie Alvarez, *Buyer*
▲ **EMP:** 85
SQ FT: 34,865
SALES: 7.8MM **Privately Held**
WEB: www.rcgoptic.com
SIC: 5065 Communication equipment
HQ: Reichle & De-Massari Ag
Binzstrasse 32
Wetzikon ZH
449 338-111

(P-7532)
RAKON AMERICA LLC
7600 Dublin Blvd Ste 220, Dublin (94568-2944)
PHONE..................847 930-5100
Dean Ransom,
EMP: 600
SALES (est): 42.4MM
SALES (corp-wide): 74.5MM **Privately Held**
WEB: www.rakon.com
SIC: 5065 Electronic parts & equipment
PA: Rakon Limited
8 Sylvia Park Road
Auckland 1060
957 355-54

(P-7533)
RAND TECHNOLOGY LLC (PA)
15225 Alton Pkwy Unit 100, Irvine (92618-2351)
PHONE..................949 255-5700
Andrea Klein, *President*
Paul Bockstedt, *President*
Tawnie Bassett-Parkins, *CFO*
Sean Sloan, *CFO*
Trang Nguyen, *Vice Pres*
EMP: 67
SQ FT: 25,000
SALES (est): 66.6MM **Privately Held**
WEB: www.randtech.com
SIC: 5065 Semiconductor devices

(P-7534)
RAYTHEON COMMAND AND CONTROL
2000 E El Segundo Blvd, El Segundo (90245-4501)
PHONE..................714 446-3232
Ron Levesque, *Branch Mgr*
EMP: 50
SALES (corp-wide): 25.3B **Publicly Held**
SIC: 5065 Security control equipment & systems
HQ: Raytheon Command And Control Solutions Llc
1801 Hughes Dr
Fullerton CA 92833

(P-7535)
RAYTHEON COMMAND AND CONTROL (HQ)
1801 Hughes Dr, Fullerton (92833-2200)
P.O. Box 34055 (92834-9455)
PHONE..................714 446-3118
Peter W Chiarelli,
Alex Cresswell,
Don Johnson,
▲ **EMP:** 700
SALES (est): 295MM
SALES (corp-wide): 25.3B **Publicly Held**
SIC: 5065 Security control equipment & systems
PA: Raytheon Company
870 Winter St
Waltham MA 02451
781 522-3000

(P-7536)
SAMSUNG ELECTRONICS AMER INC
665 Clyde Ave, Mountain View (94043-2235)
PHONE..................650 210-1000
Evan Maxei, *Director*
Anshul Khandelwal, *Sr Software Eng*
Adeet Shah, *Sr Software Eng*
Jesus Gallegos, *Engineer*
Sam Kim, *Engineer*
EMP: 1000
SQ FT: 395
SALES (corp-wide): 148.1B **Privately Held**
WEB: www.samsung.com
SIC: 5065 Electronic parts & equipment
HQ: Samsung Electronics America, Inc.
85 Challenger Rd Fl 7
Ridgefield Park NJ 07660
201 229-4000

(P-7537)
SAMSUNG INTERNATIONAL INC (DH)
333 H St Ste 6000, Chula Vista
(91910-5565)
PHONE....................619 671-6859
Jong Hyun Won, *CEO*
Hyunsik Lee, *Senior Mgr*
Steve Hong, *Manager*
David Jang, *Manager*
Pravin Sharma, *Asst Mgr*
◆ EMP: 50
SALES (est): 144.3MM
SALES (corp-wide): 148.1B Privately Held
SIC: 5065 Electronic parts & equipment
HQ: Samsung Electronics America, Inc.
85 Challenger Rd Fl 7
Ridgefield Park NJ 07660
201 229-4000

(P-7538)
SAMSUNG SEMICONDUCTOR INC (DH)
3655 N 1st St, San Jose (95134-1707)
PHONE....................408 544-4000
Young Chang Bae, *President*
Damian Huh, *CFO*
Tom Quinn, *Senior VP*
Yoon Ha, *Exec Dir*
Brijesh Chauhan, *Planning Mgr*
▼ EMP: 216
SQ FT: 206,816
SALES (est): 966.8MM
SALES (corp-wide): 148.1B Privately Held
SIC: 5065 5045 Semiconductor devices; computers, peripherals & software
HQ: Samsung Electronics America, Inc.
85 Challenger Rd Fl 7
Ridgefield Park NJ 07660
201 229-4000

(P-7539)
SARCO INC
Also Called: 123ewireless
30412 Esperanza, Rcho STA Marg
(92688-2144)
PHONE....................949 888-5548
Kristina D Sar, *CEO*
Ali Sar, *President*
Megan Flower, *Exec VP*
Derren Versoza, *Engineer*
Claudia Hernandez, *Accounting Mgr*
▲ EMP: 50
SQ FT: 30,000
SALES (est): 17.4MM Privately Held
WEB: www.123edistribution.com
SIC: 5065 Electronic parts & equipment

(P-7540)
SCREEN SPE USA LLC (DH)
Also Called: Dns Electronics
820 Kifer Rd Ste B, Sunnyvale
(94086-5200)
PHONE....................408 523-9140
Tadahiro Suhara, *CEO*
James Beard, *President*
Scott C Galler, *CFO*
Kirk Kitaguchi, *Senior VP*
George Petricich, *Vice Pres*
▲ EMP: 177
SQ FT: 28,400
SALES (est): 68MM
SALES (corp-wide): 3.1B Privately Held
WEB: www.dnse.com
SIC: 5065 7629 Electronic parts; electrical repair shops
HQ: Screen North America Holdings, Inc.
5110 Tollview Dr
Rolling Meadows IL 60008
847 870-7400

(P-7541)
SILICONWARE USA INC (DH)
1735 Tech Dr Ste 300 Fl 3, San Jose
(95110)
PHONE....................408 573-5500
Bough Lin, *Ch of Bd*
Randy Hsiao Yu Lo, *President*
Yi Hsin Lin, *CFO*
Willie Henson, *Accounting Mgr*
EMP: 50 EST: 1996
SQ FT: 8,000
SALES: 13.2MM Privately Held
WEB: www.spilca.com
SIC: 5065 Semiconductor devices
HQ: Siliconware Precision Industries Co., Ltd.
123, Sec. 3, Dafeng Rd.,
Taichung City 42749
425 341-525

(P-7542)
SMA SOLAR TECHNOLOGY AMER LLC (HQ)
Also Called: SMA America
6020 West Oaks Blvd, Rocklin
(95765-5472)
PHONE....................916 625-0870
Jurgen Krehnke,
Charles Morrill, *President*
Marko Wittich, *President*
Martina Cole, *Executive Asst*
Michael Dawson, *Project Mgr*
◆ EMP: 74 EST: 2000
SQ FT: 25,000
SALES (est): 245.1MM
SALES (corp-wide): 1B Privately Held
WEB: www.sma-america.com
SIC: 5065 Electronic parts
PA: Sma Solar Technology Ag
Sonnenallee 1
Niestetal 34266
561 952-20

(P-7543)
SOLIGENT DISTRIBUTION LLC (HQ)
1400 N Mcdowell Blvd # 201, Petaluma
(94954-6553)
PHONE....................707 992-3100
Jonathan Doochin, *CEO*
Thomas Enzendorfer, *President*
Justin Davidson, *Vice Pres*
Corey Geiger, *Vice Pres*
Brandon Guichard, *Executive*
▼ EMP: 57 EST: 2013
SALES (est): 122.8MM
SALES (corp-wide): 154.6MM Privately Held
SIC: 5065 8711 Electronic parts & equipment; engineering services
PA: Soligent Holdings Inc.
1500 Valley House Dr
Rohnert Park CA 94928
707 992-3100

(P-7544)
STELLAR MICROELECTRONICS INC
28454 Livingston Ave, Valencia
(91355-4172)
PHONE....................661 775-3500
Sudesh Arora, *President*
Rolf Linden, *Engineer*
V U Ngyen, *Engineer*
Silvana Avina, *Buyer*
Julius Davis, *Facilities Mgr*
EMP: 239
SQ FT: 140,000
SALES (est): 146.7MM
SALES (corp-wide): 1.2B Privately Held
WEB: www.stellarmicro.com
SIC: 5065 Semiconductor devices
PA: Natel Engineering Company Inc
9340 Owensmouth Ave
Chatsworth CA 91311
818 734-6523

(P-7545)
STEREN ELECTRONICS INTL LLC (PA)
Also Called: Steren Shop
6920 Carroll Rd Ste 100, San Diego
(92121-2211)
PHONE....................800 266-3333
Leon Shteremberg Ttee,
David Shteremberg,
Vick Soffer,
Jose Zyman,
▲ EMP: 100
SQ FT: 75,000
SALES (est): 43.8MM Privately Held
WEB: www.steren.com
SIC: 5065 Connectors, electronic

(P-7546)
STMICROELECTRONICS INC
2755 Great America Way, Santa Clara
(95054-1166)
PHONE....................408 452-8585
EMP: 140
SALES (corp-wide): 8.3B Privately Held
SIC: 5065
HQ: Stmicroelectronics, Inc
750 Canyon Dr Ste 300
Coppell TX 75019
972 466-6000

(P-7547)
SUMITOMO ELECTRIC DEVICE INNOV
2355 Zanker Rd, San Jose (95131-1109)
PHONE....................408 232-9500
Mike Nishiguchi, *CEO*
Frank Sanada, *President*
Manabu Yoshimura, *President*
John Wyatt, *CFO*
Eddie Tsumura, *Vice Pres*
▲ EMP: 80
SQ FT: 52,600
SALES (est): 28.6MM
SALES (corp-wide): 28.9B Privately Held
WEB: www.sei-device.com
SIC: 5065 Electronic parts
PA: Sumitomo Electric Industries, Ltd.
4-5-33, Kitahama, Chuo-Ku
Osaka OSK 541-0
662 204-141

(P-7548)
SUPERIOR COMMUNICATIONS INC (PA)
Also Called: Puregear
5027 Irwindale Ave # 900, Irwindale
(91706-2187)
PHONE....................877 522-4727
Solomon Chen, *Ch of Bd*
Michael Cavanah, *Shareholder*
Jeffrey Banks, *President*
Mike Cavah, *President*
Mike Cost, *COO*
▲ EMP: 248
SQ FT: 11,000
SALES (est): 746.4MM Privately Held
WEB: www.scp4me.com
SIC: 5065 Communication equipment

(P-7549)
SURVEILLANCE SYSTEMS
Also Called: Ssi
4465 Granite Dr Ste 700, Rocklin
(95677-2143)
PHONE....................800 508-6981
Michael T Flowers, *CEO*
Jon Ward, *President*
Mark Haney, *Chairman*
Tim Mulligan, *Controller*
Candy Barry, *Human Resources*
EMP: 50
SQ FT: 15,000
SALES (est): 20MM Privately Held
WEB: www.ssicctv.com
SIC: 5065 Video equipment, electronic; security control equipment & systems

(P-7550)
TABULA INC
1100 La Avenida St Ste A, Mountain View
(94043-1453)
PHONE....................408 986-9140
Dennis Segers, *CEO*
Steven Teig, *President*
EMP: 100
SALES (est): 57.3MM Privately Held
WEB: www.tabula.com
SIC: 5065 Semiconductor devices

(P-7551)
TALLEY INC (PA)
Also Called: Talley & Associates
12976 Sandoval St, Santa Fe Springs
(90670-4061)
P.O. Box 3123 (90670-0123)
PHONE....................562 906-8000
John R Talley, *CEO*
Mark D Talley, *President*
George R Hulbert, *CFO*
Karen Frankenberg, *Officer*
Elizabeth J Talley, *Exec VP*
◆ EMP: 110

SQ FT: 80,000
SALES (est): 116MM Privately Held
WEB: www.talleycom.com
SIC: 5065 Communication equipment; amateur radio communications equipment

(P-7552)
TECH SYSTEMS INC
7372 Walnut Ave Ste J, Buena Park
(90620-1718)
PHONE....................714 523-5404
Raymond Downs, *Manager*
EMP: 120
SALES (corp-wide): 23.4MM Privately Held
SIC: 5065 Closed circuit television
PA: Tech Systems, Inc.
4942 Summer Oak Dr
Buford GA 30518
770 495-8700

(P-7553)
TECOM INDUSTRIES INCORPORATED
375 Conejo Ridge Ave, Thousand Oaks
(91361-4928)
PHONE....................805 267-0100
Arsen Melconian, *CEO*
Martin Cox, *President*
Gene Joles, *President*
Kal Kapur, *Program Mgr*
Greg Lackmeyer, *CTO*
◆ EMP: 160 EST: 1971
SQ FT: 67,000
SALES (est): 24.9MM
SALES (corp-wide): 4.1B Privately Held
WEB: www.tecom-ind.com
SIC: 5065 Electronic parts
HQ: Trak Microwave Corporation
4726 Eisenhower Blvd
Tampa FL 33634
813 901-7200

(P-7554)
TOSHIBA MEMORY AMERICA INC (DH)
Also Called: Toshiba Amer Elctrnic Cmpnents
2610 Orchard Pkwy, San Jose
(95134-2020)
PHONE....................408 526-2400
Takanori Nakazawa, *CFO*
EMP: 200
SQ FT: 60,000
SALES: 3B
SALES (corp-wide): 37B Privately Held
SIC: 5065 Semiconductor devices
HQ: Toshiba America Electronic Components Inc
5231 California Ave
Irvine CA 92617
949 462-7700

(P-7555)
U-2 HOME ENTERTAINMENT INC
Also Called: Tai Seng Entertainment
170 S Spruce Ave Ste 200, South San Francisco (94080-4557)
P.O. Box 818, San Bruno (94066-0818)
PHONE....................650 871-8118
▲ EMP: 50
SALES (est): 10.2MM Privately Held
SIC: 5065

(P-7556)
UNIFIED TELDATA INC
Also Called: Utdi
126 Neider Ln, Mill Valley (94941-2474)
PHONE....................415 888-8940
Toll Free:....................888 -
Lyhn Haller, *President*
EMP: 52
SQ FT: 3,500
SALES (est): 7MM Privately Held
WEB: www.utdi.com
SIC: 5065 Telephone equipment; communication equipment; intercommunication equipment, electronic

(P-7557)
UNION TECHNOLOGY CORP (PA)
718 Monterey Pass Rd, Monterey Park
(91754-3607)
PHONE....................323 266-6871

David I Chu, *CEO*
John Yang, *Shareholder*
▲ **EMP:** 50
SQ FT: 21,800
SALES (est): 11.3MM **Privately Held**
WEB: www.uniontechcorp.com
SIC: 5065 3675 Electronic parts; electronic capacitors

(P-7558)
US MERCHANT SYSTEMS LLC
48073 Fremont Blvd, Fremont
(94538-6541)
P.O. Box 6018 (94538-0618)
PHONE...................877 432-8871
Stuart Rosenbaum, *CEO*
Richard L Fenn II, *COO*
Jeff Gardiner, *CFO*
Lisa Super, *Controller*
EMP: 52
SALES (est): 21MM **Privately Held**
SIC: 5065 Electronic parts & equipment

(P-7559)
VERIZON NEW YORK INC
961 N Milliken Ave # 101, Ontario
(91764-5021)
PHONE...................909 481-7897
Terry L Lukens, *Principal*
Terri Berry, *Asst Mgr*
EMP: 100
SALES (corp-wide): 126B **Publicly Held**
SIC: 5065 Telephone equipment
HQ: Verizon New York Inc.
140 West St
New York NY 10007
212 395-1000

(P-7560)
VIA TECHNOLOGIES INC
Also Called: Via Embedded Store
940 Mission Ct, Fremont (94539-8202)
PHONE...................510 683-3300
Wenchi Chen, *President*
Cher Wang, *CFO*
Tzumu Lin, *Senior VP*
Robert Wang, *Admin Sec*
Fan Lu, *Project Mgr*
▲ **EMP:** 130
SQ FT: 55,000
SALES (est): 49.3MM **Privately Held**
WEB: www.via.com.tw
SIC: 5065 Electronic parts
PA: Via Usa Inc
940 Mission Ct
Fremont CA 94539
510 683-3300

(P-7561)
WDPT FILM DISTRIBUTION LLC
500 S Buena Vista St, Burbank
(91521-0001)
PHONE...................818 560-1000
Walt Disney Pictures, *Mng Member*
EMP: 176
SALES (est): 94.1MM **Privately Held**
SIC: 5065 Video equipment, electronic

(P-7562)
WENZLAU ENGINEERING INC
2950 E Harcourt St, Compton
(90221-5502)
PHONE...................310 604-3400
William D Wenzlau Jr, *CEO*
▲ **EMP:** 64
SQ FT: 40,000
SALES (est): 20MM **Privately Held**
WEB: www.wenzlau.com
SIC: 5065 8711 5511 Electronic parts & equipment; consulting engineer; trucks, tractors & trailers: new & used

(P-7563)
WESTAK INTERNATIONAL SALES INC (HQ)
1116 Elko Dr, Sunnyvale (94089-2207)
PHONE...................408 734-8686
Louise Crisham, *President*
▲ **EMP:** 130
SQ FT: 20,000
SALES (est): 25.7MM
SALES (corp-wide): 64.1MM **Privately Held**
SIC: 5065 Electronic parts

PA: Westak, Inc
1116 Elko Dr
Sunnyvale CA 94089
408 734-8686

(P-7564)
WINBOND ELECTRONICS CORP AMER
2727 N 1st St, San Jose (95134-2029)
PHONE...................408 943-6666
Yuan Mou Shu, *Principal*
Yung Chin, *Treasurer*
Anil Gupta, *Executive*
Ming-Huei Shieh, *Executive*
Johnny Chan, *Design Engr Mgr*
▲ **EMP:** 60
SQ FT: 50,000
SALES (est): 23.9MM
SALES (corp-wide): 1.5B **Privately Held**
WEB: www.winbond-usa.com
SIC: 5065 8731 3674 Electronic parts; commercial physical research; semiconductors & related devices
PA: Winbond Electronics Corp.
8, Keya 1st Rd.,
Taichung City 42881
425 218-168

(P-7565)
WURLDTECH SECURITY TECH LTD
2623 Camino Ramon, San Ramon
(94583-9130)
PHONE...................604 669-6674
William Ruh, *CEO*
Connie Higgins, *Director*
EMP: 75 **EST:** 2016
SALES: 26MM **Privately Held**
SIC: 5065 Security control equipment & systems

(P-7566)
XCERRA CORPORATION
Also Called: Western Region
880 N Mccarthy Blvd # 100, Milpitas
(95035-5126)
PHONE...................408 635-4300
Ken Daub, *Branch Mgr*
Stephen Wigley, *Executive*
Ben Brown, *VP Engrg*
Timothy Wrye, *Sales Staff*
Chris Stambaugh, *Director*
EMP: 200
SALES (corp-wide): 352.7MM **Publicly Held**
WEB: www.ltx.com
SIC: 5065 Semiconductor devices
HQ: Xcerra Corporation
825 University Ave
Norwood MA 02062
781 461-1000

(P-7567)
XP POWER LLC
Also Called: Emco High Voltage
11383 Prospect Dr, Jackson (95642-9311)
PHONE...................209 267-1630
Michael Doherty, *Vice Pres*
EMP: 60 **Privately Held**
SIC: 5065 Electronic parts & equipment
HQ: Xp Power Llc
990 Benecia Ave
Sunnyvale CA 94085
408 732-7777

(P-7568)
YUNEEC USA INC
2275 Sampson Ave Ste 200, Corona
(92879-3402)
PHONE...................855 284-8888
Mike Kahn, *CEO*
Ryan Borders, *COO*
Larry Liu, *CFO*
Min Fu, *Controller*
▲ **EMP:** 70 **EST:** 2013
SQ FT: 37,000
SALES: 54MM **Privately Held**
SIC: 5065 7629 Video equipment, electronic; electrical equipment repair services
PA: Yuneec International Co., Limited
Rm 2301 23/F
Kwun Tong KLN
361 660-71

(P-7569)
ZETTLER COMPONENTS INC (PA)
75 Columbia, Orange (92868)
PHONE...................949 831-5000
Kurt Rexius, *General Mgr*
▲ **EMP:** 250
SQ FT: 27,000
SALES (est): 35.8MM **Privately Held**
WEB: www.zettlercomponents.com
SIC: 5065 3669 5087 Intercommunication equipment, electronic; intercommunication systems, electric; firefighting equipment

(P-7570)
ZMODO TECHNOLOGY CORP LTD
17870 Castleton St # 200, City of Industry
(91748-1755)
PHONE...................217 903-5673
Kejia Wan, *President*
EMP: 700
SALES (est): 47.5MM **Privately Held**
SIC: 5065 Mobile telephone equipment

5072 Hardware Wholesale

(P-7571)
ACF COMPONENTS & FASTENERS INC
Also Called: A C F
742 Arrow Grand Cir, Covina (91722-2147)
PHONE...................949 833-0506
Jill Alvarez, *Manager*
Tanya Moore, *Credit Staff*
Lin Baluyut, *Controller*
EMP: 55
SQ FT: 20,000
SALES (est): 5.1MM
SALES (corp-wide): 26.3MM **Privately Held**
WEB: www.acfcom.com
SIC: 5072 5065 5085 Miscellaneous fasteners; electronic parts; fasteners, industrial: nuts, bolts, screws, etc.
PA: Acf Components & Fasteners, Inc.
31012 Huntwood Ave
Hayward CA 94544
510 487-2100

(P-7572)
ALLTRADE TOOLS LLC
6122 Katella Ave, Cypress (90630-5203)
PHONE...................310 522-9008
Dennis Hale, *Principal*
Robert Ellis, *CFO*
Don Hart, *Vice Pres*
Golden Huang, *Info Tech Dir*
David Tarashandegan, *Engineer*
◆ **EMP:** 50
SQ FT: 140,000
SALES (est): 29.4MM **Privately Held**
SIC: 5072 Hand tools

(P-7573)
AMERICAN BOLT & SCREW MFG CORP (PA)
14650 Miller Ave Ste 200, Fontana
(92336-1694)
P.O. Box 548 (92334-0548)
PHONE...................909 390-0522
Jimmie W Hooper, *President*
Cynthia Alvarez, *Vice Pres*
Josh Hutton, *Purch Mgr*
Melissa Pittenger, *Purchasing*
Tony Fulmer, *Purch Agent*
▲ **EMP:** 52 **EST:** 1970
SQ FT: 110,000
SALES: 52.4MM **Privately Held**
SIC: 5072 Bolts, nuts & screws

(P-7574)
AMERICAN KAL ENTERPRISES INC (PA)
Also Called: Pro America Premium Tools
4265 Puente Ave, Baldwin Park
(91706-3420)
PHONE...................626 338-7308
John Toshima, *President*
Mila Bierotte, *Admin Sec*
▲ **EMP:** 90
SQ FT: 32,000

SALES (est): 23MM **Privately Held**
SIC: 5072 3546 3463 3462 Hand tools; power-driven handtools; nonferrous forgings; iron & steel forgings; hand & edge tools

(P-7575)
AMERIWEST INDUSTRIES INC
Also Called: Tenpo Hardware
2910 S Archibald Ave A, Ontario
(91761-7323)
PHONE...................909 930-1898
Weidan Wu, *CEO*
▲ **EMP:** 50 **EST:** 2001
SQ FT: 112,000
SALES (est): 10.1MM **Privately Held**
WEB: www.ameriwestindustries.com
SIC: 5072 Hardware

(P-7576)
ARCONIC GLOBAL FAS & RINGS INC
Also Called: Arconic Fstening Systems Rings
1925 N Macarthur Dr # 200, Tracy
(95376-2835)
PHONE...................209 839-3005
Rod Alavi, *Director*
EMP: 60
SALES (corp-wide): 12.9B **Publicly Held**
WEB: www.alcoafasteners.com
SIC: 5072 Hardware
HQ: Arconic Global Fasteners & Rings, Inc.
3990a Heritage Oak Ct
Simi Valley CA 93063
805 527-3600

(P-7577)
ARROW TOOLS FAS & SAW INC
7635 Burnet Ave, Van Nuys (91405-1006)
PHONE...................818 780-1464
Jeffrey S Silverman, *CEO*
Stewart Epstein, *President*
Susan Epstein, *Corp Secy*
Jeff Burch, *Branch Mgr*
Mike Glazier, *Project Mgr*
EMP: 50
SQ FT: 25,000
SALES (est): 55MM **Privately Held**
WEB: www.arrowtools.com
SIC: 5072 Hand tools

(P-7578)
ASSA ABLOY RSDENTIAL GROUP INC
600 Balwin Park Blvd, City of Industry
(91746)
PHONE...................626 369-4718
Birk Sorennsen, *Manager*
Frank Verduzco, *Technology*
EMP: 400
SALES (corp-wide): 9B **Privately Held**
WEB: www.emtek.com
SIC: 5072 Hardware
HQ: Assa Abloy Residential Group, Inc.
15250 Stafford St
City Of Industry CA 91744
626 961-0413

(P-7579)
B & B SPECIALTIES INC
G S Aerospace Division
4321 E La Palma Ave, Anaheim
(92807-1887)
PHONE...................714 985-3075
Tom Rutan, *Manager*
EMP: 100
SALES (est): 3.9MM
SALES (corp-wide): 40.3MM **Privately Held**
WEB: www.bbspecialties.com
SIC: 5072 3429 Miscellaneous fasteners; manufactured hardware (general)
PA: B & B Specialties, Inc.
4321 E La Palma Ave
Anaheim CA 92807
714 985-3000

(P-7580)
BAY STANDARD MANUFACTURING INC (PA)
Also Called: Bsmi
24485 Marsh Creek Rd, Brentwood
(94513-4319)
P.O. Box 801 (94513-0801)
PHONE...................925 634-1181

Gary W Landgraf, *CEO*
Gregory Iverson, *President*
Karen Landgraf, *Vice Pres*
Paige Shamblin, *Purch Agent*
Mark Heaney, *Sales Mgr*
▲ EMP: 50
SQ FT: 25,000
SALES (est): 25.3MM **Privately Held**
WEB: www.baystandard.com
SIC: 5072 3452 Bolts; bolts, metal

(P-7581)
CAMSTAR INTERNATIONAL INC
939 W 9th St, Upland (91786-4543)
PHONE..................................909 931-2540
Bingqing LI, *President*
Eric De, *Sales Executive*
Eric De La Cruz, *Sales Executive*
Monica Wise, *Manager*
Jessica Michel, *Accounts Mgr*
▲ EMP: 75
SQ FT: 1,500
SALES (est): 12.5MM
SALES (corp-wide): 134.9K **Privately Held**
SIC: 5072 Security devices, locks
PA: Yuxin Technology Company
Dayao Village
Weifang
536 784-8108

(P-7582)
CENTRAL INDIANA HDWR CO INC (PA)
Also Called: Schricker
3512 Seagate Way Ste 190, Oceanside
(92056-2689)
P.O. Box 501850, Indianapolis IN (46250-6850)
PHONE..................................317 558-5700
Ron Couch, *President*
Norman L Bristley, *Ch of Bd*
Rondal Couch, *President*
Gary Wilson, *Senior VP*
◆ EMP: 118
SQ FT: 129,000
SALES (est): 45.4MM **Privately Held**
WEB: www.cih-indy.com
SIC: 5072 5031 5211 Builders' hardware; metal doors, sash & trim; door frames, all materials; doors; lumber & other building materials

(P-7583)
CHARLES MCMURRAY CO (PA)
2520 N Argyle Ave, Fresno (93727-1399)
P.O. Box 569 (93709-0569)
PHONE..................................559 292-5751
Louis Mc Murray, *President*
Cassie Mc Murray, *Admin Sec*
▲ EMP: 62
SQ FT: 58,000
SALES (est): 49.8MM **Privately Held**
SIC: 5072 Builders' hardware

(P-7584)
CORONA CLIPPER INC
22440 Temescal Canyon Rd # 102, Corona
(92883-4200)
PHONE..................................951 737-6515
Stephen J Erickson, *CEO*
Al Schulten, *CFO*
John Reisveck, *Exec VP*
Armando Del Valle, *Marketing Staff*
◆ EMP: 70
SQ FT: 85,000
SALES (est): 40.8MM
SALES (corp-wide): 26.9MM **Privately Held**
WEB: www.coronaclipper.com
SIC: 5072 3524 Hand tools; lawn & garden equipment
PA: Natt Tools Group Inc
460 Sherman Ave N
Hamilton ON L8L 8
905 549-7433

(P-7585)
CPO COMMERCE LLC
120 W Bellevue Dr Ste 300, Pasadena
(91105-2579)
PHONE..................................626 585-3600
Robert H Tolleson, *President*
Girisha Chandraraj, *COO*
Todd A Shelton, *CFO*
Robert J Kelderhouse, *Treasurer*

Eric A Blanchard, *Senior VP*
▼ EMP: 81
SALES (est): 97.9MM
SALES (corp-wide): 5B **Publicly Held**
SIC: 5072 Power tools & accessories
HQ: Essendant Co.
1 Parkway North Blvd # 100
Deerfield IL 60015
847 627-7000

(P-7586)
CROWN HARDWARE INC
745 S Coast Highway 101 # 104, Encinitas
(92024-4450)
PHONE..................................760 334-0300
Glenn Maguire, *Branch Mgr*
EMP: 141
SALES (corp-wide): 52.8MM **Privately Held**
SIC: 5072 Hardware
PA: Crown Hardware, Inc.
9045 Adams Ave
Huntington Beach CA 92646
714 962-4160

(P-7587)
EXCELTA CORPORATION (PA)
60 Easy St Ste F, Buellton (93427-9560)
PHONE..................................805 686-4686
Lynn Bonzer, *President*
Joan Dalseme, *CEO*
Greg Johnson, *Vice Pres*
Janis Papiro, *Admin Sec*
Wendy Mack, *Controller*
EMP: 94
SQ FT: 6,300
SALES (est): 33.4MM **Privately Held**
WEB: www.excelta.com
SIC: 5072 Hand tools

(P-7588)
G K TOOL CORP
Also Called: Kal Tool Co
4265 Puente Ave, Baldwin Park
(91706-3420)
PHONE..................................626 338-7300
EMP: 90
SQ FT: 32,000
SALES (est): 8.6MM
SALES (corp-wide): 24.9MM **Privately Held**
SIC: 5072
PA: American Kal Enterprises, Inc.
4265 Puente Ave
Baldwin Park CA 91706
626 338-7308

(P-7589)
HAMPTON PRODUCTS INTL CORP (PA)
50 Icon, Foothill Ranch (92610-3000)
PHONE..................................949 472-4256
Hayward K Kelley III, *President*
Bobbie Thompson, *Admin Asst*
Randy Voss, *Director*
▲ EMP: 100
SQ FT: 160,000
SALES (est): 141.8MM **Privately Held**
WEB: www.hamptonproducts.com
SIC: 5072 Builders' hardware

(P-7590)
HD SUPPLY CONSTRUCTION SUPPLY
Also Called: White Cap 24
1995 W Cordelia Rd, Fairfield
(94534-1661)
PHONE..................................707 863-8282
Marcelus Joanes, *Principal*
EMP: 53 **Publicly Held**
SIC: 5072 Hardware
HQ: Hd Supply Construction Supply, Ltd (Lp)
3100 Cumberland Blvd Se
Atlanta GA 30339
770 852-9000

(P-7591)
HD SUPPLY CONSTRUCTION SUPPLY
Also Called: White Cap 35
595 Brennan St, San Jose (95131-1202)
P.O. Box 610640 (95161-0640)
PHONE..................................408 428-2000
Larry Holloway, *Manager*

Mark Charon, *Branch Mgr*
EMP: 50 **Publicly Held**
SIC: 5072 Hardware
HQ: Hd Supply Construction Supply, Ltd (Lp)
3100 Cumberland Blvd Se
Atlanta GA 30339
770 852-9000

(P-7592)
JACKSONS HARDWARE INC
Also Called: Marin Industrial Distributors
435 Du Bois St, San Rafael (94901-3910)
P.O. Box 10247 (94912-0247)
PHONE..................................415 870-4083
Matthew R Olson, *President*
Anna Buss, *Treasurer*
EMP: 61
SQ FT: 50,000
SALES (est): 24.9MM **Privately Held**
WEB: www.jacksonshardware.com
SIC: 5072 5251 Hardware; hardware

(P-7593)
LEIGHT SALES CO INC
1611 S Catalina Ave L45, Redondo Beach
(90277-5255)
PHONE..................................310 223-1000
Bryan Moskowitz, *CEO*
Helene Moskowitz, *Corp Secy*
Alan Moskowitz, *Principal*
▲ EMP: 75
SQ FT: 60,000
SALES (est): 50.9MM **Privately Held**
WEB: www.leightsales.com
SIC: 5072 Miscellaneous fasteners; hand tools

(P-7594)
LIBERTY HARDWARE MFG CORP
5555 Jurupa St, Ontario (91761-3606)
PHONE..................................909 605-2300
Kevin Buckner, *Branch Mgr*
EMP: 51
SALES (corp-wide): 7.6B **Publicly Held**
WEB: www.libertyhardware.com
SIC: 5072 Hardware
HQ: Liberty Hardware Mfg. Corp.
140 Business Park Dr
Winston Salem NC 27107
336 769-4077

(P-7595)
LONG-LOK FASTENERS CORPORATION
20501 Belshaw Ave, Carson (90746-3505)
PHONE..................................310 667-4200
Robert M Bennett, *CEO*
Barcia Glenn, *Purchasing*
Deanne Spawton, *Cust Mgr*
EMP: 50
SALES (est): 5.4MM **Privately Held**
SIC: 5072 Miscellaneous fasteners

(P-7596)
LOUIS WURTH AND COMPANY (DH)
895 Columbia St, Brea (92821-2917)
P.O. Box 2253 (92822-2253)
PHONE..................................714 529-1771
Vito Mancini, *President*
Tom Mauss, *President*
Ed McGraw, *CFO*
Todd Beckstrand, *Regional Mgr*
Steven Branham, *Regional Mgr*
▲ EMP: 90
SQ FT: 116,000
SALES (est): 95.4MM
SALES (corp-wide): 15B **Privately Held**
WEB: www.louisandcompany.com
SIC: 5072 5198 Furniture hardware; stain
HQ: Wurth Group Of North America Inc.
93 Grant St
Ramsey NJ 07446
201 818-8877

(P-7597)
MAKITA USA INC (HQ)
14930 Northam St, La Mirada
(90638-5753)
PHONE..................................714 522-8088
Hiroshi Tsujimura, *CEO*
Richszrd Chapman, *Senior VP*
Randy D Caillier, *Vice Pres*

Rich Chapman, *Vice Pres*
Eunice Han, *Vice Pres*
▲ EMP: 160
SQ FT: 130,000
SALES (est): 227.5MM
SALES (corp-wide): 4.4B **Privately Held**
WEB: www.makita.com
SIC: 5072 Power handtools; power tools & accessories
PA: Makita Corporation
3-11-8, Sumiyoshicho
Anjo AIC 446-0
566 981-711

(P-7598)
MILSPEC INDUSTRIES INC (DH)
5825 Greenwood Ave, Commerce
(90040-3846)
P.O. Box 60887, Los Angeles (90060-0887)
PHONE..................................213 680-9690
David Lifschitz, *CEO*
Galen Ho'o, *President*
Saleem Baakza, *Vice Pres*
Anthony Batista, *Vice Pres*
Dan Arnold, *Executive*
▼ EMP: 70
SALES (est): 21.9MM
SALES (corp-wide): 92.6MM **Privately Held**
WEB: www.milspecind.com
SIC: 5072 5085 Hardware; industrial supplies
HQ: Gehr Industries, Inc.
7400 E Slauson Ave
Commerce CA 90040
323 728-5558

(P-7599)
PORTEOUS ENTERPRISES INC
12801 Leffingwell Ave, Santa Fe Springs
(90670-6339)
PHONE..................................310 549-9180
John B Porteous, *Principal*
EMP: 200
SALES (corp-wide): 375.1MM **Privately Held**
WEB: www.porteousfastener.com
SIC: 5072 Nuts (hardware); bolts; screws; washers (hardware)
HQ: Porteous Enterprises, Inc.
12801 Leffingwell Ave
Santa Fe Springs CA 90670
310 549-9180

(P-7600)
PRIME-LINE PRODUCTS COMPANY (PA)
Also Called: Slide Go
26950 San Bernardino Ave, Redlands
(92374-5022)
PHONE..................................909 887-8118
Ronald F Turk, *President*
Bryan Aernan, *Vice Pres*
Paul Entwisele, *Vice Pres*
Jeff Grande, *Vice Pres*
Howard Kauffman, *Vice Pres*
◆ EMP: 375
SQ FT: 100,000
SALES (est): 221.8MM **Privately Held**
WEB: www.prime-line-products.com
SIC: 5072 Builders' hardware

(P-7601)
SEREC ENTERTAINMENT LLC
1671 N Rocky Rd, Upland (91784-2500)
PHONE..................................626 893-0600
Steven A Ferraiuolo,
EMP: 50
SALES (est): 5MM **Privately Held**
SIC: 5072 7389 Hardware;

(P-7602)
SHAMROCK SUPPLY COMPANY INC (PA)
Also Called: Shamrock Companies, The
3366 E La Palma Ave, Anaheim
(92806-2814)
PHONE..................................714 575-1800
John J O'Connor, *Ch of Bd*
Michael O'Connor, *President*
John O'Conner, *Vice Pres*
Juan Ossa, *Info Tech Dir*
Fanny McShane, *Info Tech Mgr*
▲ EMP: 52
SQ FT: 45,000

P R O D U C T S & S V C S

SALES (est): 82.7MM **Privately Held**
WEB: www.shamrocksupply.com
SIC: 5072 5084 3842 Hand tools; industrial machinery & equipment; personal safety equipment

(P-7603)
SNAP-ON INCORPORATED
Also Called: Snap-On Tools
19220 San Jose Ave, City of Industry (91748-1417)
PHONE..............................626 965-0668
Michael King, *Branch Mgr*
Vivian Lee, *General Mgr*
Dwayne Thompson, *CTO*
Duane Vallejos, *Training Spec*
Patricia Garcia, *Sales Mgr*
EMP: 95
SALES (corp-wide): 3.6B **Publicly Held**
WEB: www.snapon.com
SIC: 5072 Hand tools
PA: Snap-On Incorporated
2801 80th St
Kenosha WI 53143
262 656-5200

(P-7604)
SOFFIETTI CO
236 W Orange Show, San Bernardino (92408)
PHONE..............................909 907-2277
EMP: 65 **EST:** 2009
SQ FT: 2,700
SALES (est): 200K **Privately Held**
SIC: 5072 5084 5511

(P-7605)
SUNKIST ENTERPRISES
1308 Rollins Rd, Burlingame (94010-2410)
PHONE..............................650 347-3900
Ali Husain, *Owner*
EMP: 75
SQ FT: 6,000
SALES (est): 6.9MM **Privately Held**
WEB: www.sunkistenterprises.com
SIC: 5072 5031 Hardware; lumber, plywood & millwork

(P-7606)
TOMARCO CONTRACTOR SPC INC (PA)
Also Called: Tomarco Fastening Systems
14848 Northam St, La Mirada (90638-5747)
PHONE..............................714 523-1771
William Thompson, *CEO*
Keith Watkins, *President*
▲ **EMP:** 60
SQ FT: 33,000
SALES (est): 66MM **Privately Held**
WEB: www.tomarco.com
SIC: 5072 Hand tools; power handtools; builders' hardware

(P-7607)
VENTURE PACIFIC TOOLS INC
17152 Daimler St, Irvine (92614-5509)
PHONE..............................949 475-5505
Daniel Congellieri, *President*
▲ **EMP:** 61
SALES (est): 2.3MM **Privately Held**
SIC: 5072 Power tools & accessories

(P-7608)
VIAWORLD ADVANCED PRODUCTS
920 Saratoga Ave Ste 103, San Jose (95129-3445)
PHONE..............................408 597-7051
John Xingqiang Wu, *President*
EMP: 56
SALES: 5MM **Privately Held**
WEB: www.viaworld.com
SIC: 5072 Power tools & accessories

(P-7609)
WILDENRADT-MCMURRAY INC
Also Called: Macmurray Pacific
568 7th St, San Francisco (94103-4710)
PHONE..............................510 835-5500
Eric Wildenradt, *CEO*
Theodore Wildenradt, *President*
Vernelle Wildenradt, *Corp Secy*
Lorenzo Longheito, *Sales Staff*
Adrian Restauro, *Sales Staff*
▲ **EMP:** 70

SQ FT: 25,000
SALES (est): 31.5MM **Privately Held**
WEB: www.macmurraypacific.com
SIC: 5072 Builders' hardware

5074 Plumbing & Heating Splys Wholesale

(P-7610)
ATLAS INTERNATIONAL INC
Also Called: Aii Group
500 W Warner Ave Ste A, Santa Ana (92707-3345)
PHONE..............................714 622-1550
Son Nguyen, *President*
▲ **EMP:** 50
SALES (est): 7.2MM **Privately Held**
SIC: 5074 Sanitary ware, china or enameled iron; pipes & fittings, plastic; plumbers' brass goods & fittings

(P-7611)
BRITA PRODUCTS COMPANY
1221 Broadway Ste 290, Oakland (94612-1838)
P.O. Box 24305 (94623-1305)
PHONE..............................510 271-7000
Greg Frank, *President*
EMP: 85
SALES (est): 42.2MM
SALES (corp-wide): 6.1B **Publicly Held**
WEB: www.brita.com
SIC: 5074 Water purification equipment
PA: The Clorox Company
1221 Broadway Ste 1300
Oakland CA 94612
510 271-7000

(P-7612)
BUILDCOM INC
Also Called: Faucetdirect.com
402 Otterson Dr Ste 100, Chico (95928-8247)
PHONE..............................800 375-3403
Christian B Friedland, *President*
Erik Lukasek, *President*
Danielle Porto Mohn, *Chief Mktg Ofcr*
Ryan Brewer, *Vice Pres*
Lindsay Fee, *Vice Pres*
▼ **EMP:** 380
SQ FT: 22,100
SALES (est): 240.5K
SALES (corp-wide): 19.2B **Privately Held**
WEB: www.improvementdirect.com
SIC: 5074 5999 Plumbing fittings & supplies; plumbing & heating supplies
HQ: Ferguson Enterprises, Inc.
12500 Jefferson Ave
Newport News VA 23602
757 874-7795

(P-7613)
ELMCO SALES INC (PA)
15070 Proctor Ave, City of Industry (91746-3305)
P.O. Box 3787 (91744-0787)
PHONE..............................626 855-4831
Donald E Morris, *Ch of Bd*
Kristin E Kahle, *Corp Secy*
EMP: 90
SQ FT: 49,650
SALES (est): 34.5MM **Privately Held**
SIC: 5074 Plumbing fittings & supplies

(P-7614)
ELMCO/DUDDY INC (HQ)
15070 Proctor Ave, City of Industry (91746-3305)
P.O. Box 3787 (91744-0787)
PHONE..............................626 333-9942
Donald E Morris, *CEO*
Thomas Duddy, *President*
John Plowman, *Controller*
Brendon St Claire, *Sales Associate*
EMP: 50
SQ FT: 49,650
SALES (est): 32.8MM
SALES (corp-wide): 34.5MM **Privately Held**
WEB: www.elmcoduddy.com
SIC: 5074 Plumbers' brass goods & fittings

PA: Elmco Sales Inc.
15070 Proctor Ave
City Of Industry CA 91746
626 855-4831

(P-7615)
EPS CORPORATE HOLDINGS INC
1235 S Lewis St, Anaheim (92805-6429)
PHONE..............................714 635-3131
Greg Boiko, *Manager*
EMP: 60 **Privately Held**
SIC: 5074 1711 Plumbing & hydronic heating supplies; plumbing contractors
HQ: Eps Corporate Holdings, Inc.
3100 Donald Douglas
Santa Monica CA 90405

(P-7616)
EVERSOFT INC (PA)
Also Called: Eversoft Products
707 W 16th St, Long Beach (90813-1410)
P.O. Box 92769 (90809-2769)
PHONE..............................562 495-7766
Scott Burrows, *President*
Bruce Burrows, *Vice Pres*
Matt Burrows, *Research*
Mike York, *Engineer*
Tony Cox, *Sales Staff*
EMP: 52
SQ FT: 12,585
SALES (est): 21.7MM **Privately Held**
WEB: www.eversoftwater.net
SIC: 5074 Water purification equipment

(P-7617)
FERGUSON ENTERPRISES INC
Also Called: Cal-Steam
777 Mariposa St, San Francisco (94107-2516)
PHONE..............................408 441-7276
Stew Corbin, *Manager*
EMP: 75
SALES (corp-wide): 19.2B **Privately Held**
SIC: 5074 Plumbing & hydronic heating supplies
HQ: Ferguson Enterprises, Inc.
12500 Jefferson Ave
Newport News VA 23602
757 874-7795

(P-7618)
FERGUSON ENTERPRISES INC
Also Called: Lincoln Products
18825 San Jose Ave, City of Industry (91748-1326)
PHONE..............................626 965-0724
Michael Aucoin, *Branch Mgr*
Lou Razza, *General Mgr*
Dee Thorne, *Human Res Mgr*
Brad Blakeley, *Opers Mgr*
Kevin Taylor, *Manager*
EMP: 80
SALES (corp-wide): 19.2B **Privately Held**
WEB: www.ferguson.com
SIC: 5074 Plumbing fittings & supplies
HQ: Ferguson Enterprises, Inc.
12500 Jefferson Ave
Newport News VA 23602
757 874-7795

(P-7619)
FERGUSON ENTERPRISES INC
704 N Laverne Ave, Fresno (93727-6850)
PHONE..............................559 253-2900
Greg Lourente, *Branch Mgr*
Greg Lourence, *General Mgr*
EMP: 50
SALES (corp-wide): 19.2B **Privately Held**
SIC: 5074 Plumbing fittings & supplies
HQ: Ferguson Enterprises, Inc.
12500 Jefferson Ave
Newport News VA 23602
757 874-7795

(P-7620)
FERGUSON ENTERPRISES INC
Also Called: Ferguson 667
3280 Market St, San Diego (92102-3334)
PHONE..............................619 515-0300
Louie Armstrong, *Branch Mgr*
Maricel Duque, *Human Res Dir*
Veronica Crawford, *Marketing Mgr*
Larry Howerton, *Manager*
Tom H Lazet, *Accounts Mgr*

EMP: 70
SQ FT: 45,000
SALES (corp-wide): 19.2B **Privately Held**
WEB: www.ferguson.com
SIC: 5074 Plumbing fittings & supplies
HQ: Ferguson Enterprises, Inc.
12500 Jefferson Ave
Newport News VA 23602
757 874-7795

(P-7621)
FERGUSON ENTERPRISES INC
9750 S Town Ave, Pomona (91766)
PHONE..............................909 364-8700
Brian Hohn, *Manager*
EMP: 115
SALES (corp-wide): 19.2B **Privately Held**
WEB: www.ferguson.com
SIC: 5074 Plumbing fittings & supplies
HQ: Ferguson Enterprises, Inc.
12500 Jefferson Ave
Newport News VA 23602
757 874-7795

(P-7622)
FERGUSON ENTERPRISES INC
Also Called: Ferguson 677
6421 Industry Way, Westminster (92683-3696)
PHONE..............................714 893-1936
Matthew Moore, *Manager*
Tom Raleigh, *General Mgr*
Dan Poppen, *Manager*
EMP: 250
SALES (corp-wide): 19.2B **Privately Held**
WEB: www.ferguson.com
SIC: 5074 Plumbing fittings & supplies
HQ: Ferguson Enterprises, Inc.
12500 Jefferson Ave
Newport News VA 23602
757 874-7795

(P-7623)
FERGUSON ENTERPRISES INC
Also Called: Ferguson 601
7651 Woodman Ave, Van Nuys (91402-6536)
PHONE..............................818 786-9720
Fred Raviol, *Branch Mgr*
Jeff Van Wagesen, *Vice Pres*
Tabitha Nieto, *Human Res Dir*
Jon Balano, *Opers Mgr*
Chris Souza, *Sls & Mktg Exec*
EMP: 50
SALES (corp-wide): 19.2B **Privately Held**
WEB: www.ferguson.com
SIC: 5074 Plumbing fittings & supplies
HQ: Ferguson Enterprises, Inc.
12500 Jefferson Ave
Newport News VA 23602
757 874-7795

(P-7624)
FERGUSON FIRE FABRICATION INC (DH)
Also Called: Pacific Fire Safety
2750 S Towne Ave, Pomona (91766-6205)
PHONE..............................909 517-3085
Leo J Klien, *President*
Leo J Klein, *President*
Dave Keltner, *CFO*
Dave Richey, *Export Mgr*
▲ **EMP:** 100
SQ FT: 120,000
SALES (est): 379.8K
SALES (corp-wide): 19.2B **Privately Held**
WEB: www.sierracraft.com
SIC: 5074 5099 Plumbing fittings & supplies; safety equipment & supplies; fire extinguishers
HQ: Ferguson Enterprises, Inc.
12500 Jefferson Ave
Newport News VA 23602
757 874-7795

(P-7625)
GCO INC (PA)
27750 Industrial Blvd, Hayward (94545-4043)
PHONE..............................510 786-3333
Michael H Groeniger, *Ch of Bd*
Beverly J Groeniger, *Treasurer*
Richard Alexander, *Exec VP*
Richard Old, *Vice Pres*
James Wunsche, *Vice Pres*
EMP: 50

SQ FT: 15,000
SALES (est): 118.9MM **Privately Held**
WEB: www.groeniger.com
SIC: **5074** 5087 Pipe & boiler covering; pipes & fittings, plastic; plumbing & heating valves; firefighting equipment; sprinkler systems

(P-7626)
GREEN CONVERGENCE (PA)
Also Called: Sunpower By Green Convergence
28490 Wstnghuse Pl Ste 16, Valencia (91355)
PHONE..............................661 491-5111
Mark Clinton Figearo, *CEO*
Donald Schramm, *President*
Stacy Hitt, *CFO*
Kelsey Lynd, *Administration*
Connor Robbins, *Analyst*
EMP: 57 EST: 2008
SQ FT: 6,000
SALES: 1MM **Privately Held**
SIC: **5074** 1711 Heating equipment & panels, solar; solar energy contractor

(P-7627)
HARRINGTON INDUSTRIAL PLAS LLC (HQ)
14480 Yorba Ave, Chino (91710-5766)
P.O. Box 5128 (91708-5128)
PHONE..............................909 597-8641
James W Swanson, *Mng Member*
James Swanson, *President*
Jay Rooney, *CFO*
Doug Hodge, *Managing Dir*
Craig Giles, *Area Mgr*
◆ EMP: 85
SQ FT: 50,000
SALES: 210MM **Privately Held**
WEB: www.harringtonplastics.com
SIC: **5074** Pipes & fittings, plastic; plumbing & heating valves
PA: Aliaxis Sa
Avenue Arnaud Fraiteur 1523
Bruxelles
277 550-50

(P-7628)
LARSEN SUPPLY CO (PA)
Also Called: Lasco
12055 Slauson Ave, Santa Fe Springs (90670-2601)
P.O. Box 4388 (90670-1400)
PHONE..............................562 698-0731
Richard Larsen, *Ch of Bd*
Ruth Larsen, *Shareholder*
Alan Holderness, *CFO*
Rella Bodinus, *Vice Pres*
Danny Pro, *Technology*
▲ EMP: 100
SQ FT: 60,000
SALES (est): 34.6MM **Privately Held**
WEB: www.lasco.net
SIC: **5074** 5075 Plumbing fittings & supplies; warm air heating & air conditioning

(P-7629)
MERIDIAN HOLDINGS
2580 El Camino Real, Atascadero (93422-1916)
PHONE..............................805 539-2752
Jason Devries, *President*
EMP: 55
SALES (est): 16.6MM **Privately Held**
SIC: **5074** Plumbing & hydronic heating supplies

(P-7630)
MMA RENEWABLE VENTURES LLC
44 Montgomery St Ste 2200, San Francisco (94104-4709)
PHONE..............................415 229-8817
Matthew Cheney,
EMP: 100
SALES (est): 49.5MM
SALES (corp-wide): 36.8MM **Publicly Held**
WEB: www.munimae.com
SIC: **5074** Heating equipment & panels, solar
PA: Mma Capital Management, Llc
3600 Odonnell St Ste 600
Baltimore MD 21224
443 263-2900

(P-7631)
OATEY SUPPLY CHAIN SVCS INC
6600 Smith Ave, Newark (94560-4220)
PHONE..............................510 797-4677
Armando Romo, *Manager*
EMP: 50
SALES (corp-wide): 470MM **Privately Held**
SIC: **5074** Plumbing & hydronic heating supplies
HQ: Oatey Supply Chain Services, Inc.
20600 Emerald Pkwy
Cleveland OH 44135
216 267-7100

(P-7632)
PACE SUPPLY CORP (PA)
6000 State Farm Dr # 200, Rohnert Park (94928-2226)
P.O. Box 6407 (94927-6407)
PHONE..............................707 755-2499
Ron Bohannon, *President*
Ted M Green, *Ch of Bd*
Albert Bacci, *Admin Sec*
Gene Gorman, *Info Tech Dir*
Lynette Sisemore, *Accounting Mgr*
EMP: 80
SQ FT: 10,000
SALES (est): 188.4MM **Privately Held**
WEB: www.pacesupply.com
SIC: **5074** Plumbing fittings & supplies

(P-7633)
PURCELL-MURRAY COMPANY INC (PA)
999 Skyway Rd Ste 100, San Carlos (94070-2722)
PHONE..............................415 468-6620
Timothy J Murray, *President*
Laurence D Purcell, *Vice Pres*
Brigitte Castillo, *Administration*
Brigitte Polianos, *Administration*
Mildred Sierra, *Administration*
▲ EMP: 67
SQ FT: 40,000
SALES (est): 56MM **Privately Held**
SIC: **5074** 5064 Plumbing fittings & supplies; electrical appliances, major

(P-7634)
PURONICS WATER SYSTEMS INC
5775 Las Positas Rd, Livermore (94551-7819)
PHONE..............................925 456-7000
Scott Batiste, *CEO*
Mark H Cosmez II, *CFO*
Mark Cosmez, *CFO*
Arnie D Harmon, *VP Sales*
◆ EMP: 60
SQ FT: 25,000
SALES (est): 19.4MM **Privately Held**
WEB: www.ionicsfidelity.com
SIC: **5074** Water purification equipment

(P-7635)
RYAN HERCO PRODUCTS CORP (DH)
Also Called: Ryan Herco Flow Solutions
3010 N San Fernando Blvd, Burbank (91504-2524)
PHONE..............................818 841-1141
Randy Beckwith, *CEO*
Sue Nickol, *General Mgr*
Natalee Pucher, *Technology*
John Tornetta, *Technical Staff*
Gregg Lao, *Finance Mgr*
◆ EMP: 60 EST: 1948
SQ FT: 48,000
SALES (est): 172.6MM **Privately Held**
WEB: www.ryanherco.com
SIC: **5074** 5162 Pipes & fittings, plastic; plastics materials & basic shapes

(P-7636)
SLAKEY BROTHERS INC
1480 Nicora Ave, San Jose (95133-1639)
PHONE..............................408 494-0460
Tom Trapani, *Sales/Mktg Mgr*
Diane Blythe, *Financial Exec*
Luis Carrillo, *Sales Staff*
Ken Varnes, *Manager*
EMP: 50

SALES (corp-wide): 197MM **Privately Held**
WEB: www.slakey.com
SIC: **5074** Plumbing & hydronic heating supplies
PA: Slakey Brothers, Inc.
2215 Kausen Dr Ste 1
Elk Grove CA 95758
916 478-2000

(P-7637)
SOUTH WEST SUN SOLAR INC
13752 Harbor Blvd, Garden Grove (92843-4009)
PHONE..............................714 582-3909
Hieu Nguyen, *CEO*
Mimi Ngo, *President*
Trang Pham, *Regional Mgr*
EMP: 50
SALES (est): 7.1MM **Privately Held**
SIC: **5074** Heating equipment & panels, solar

(P-7638)
SUEZ WTS SYSTEMS USA INC
Also Called: Apollo Div Ionics Ultrapure
5900 Silvercreek Vly Rd, San Jose (95138-1083)
PHONE..............................408 360-5900
Tim Addleman, *Manager*
Mike Cone, *General Mgr*
EMP: 80
SALES (corp-wide): 51.4MM **Privately Held**
WEB: www.ionics.com
SIC: **5074** Plumbing & hydronic heating supplies
HQ: Suez Wts Systems Usa, Inc.
4636 Somerton Rd
Trevose PA 19053
781 359-7000

(P-7639)
SUNERGY CALIFORNIA LLC
4741 Urbani Ave, McClellan (95652-2016)
PHONE..............................916 550-5370
EMP: 50 EST: 2017
SALES (est): 74.8K **Privately Held**
SIC: **5074** Heating equipment & panels, solar

(P-7640)
TA INDUSTRIES INC (PA)
Also Called: Truaire
11335 Greenstone Ave, Santa Fe Springs (90670-4618)
P.O. Box 4448 (90670-1460)
PHONE..............................562 466-1000
Yongki Yi, *Principal*
Janice Kim, *CFO*
Elizabeth Yi, *Vice Pres*
Jamie Kwon, *Accounting Mgr*
Alex Yi, *VP Opers*
▲ EMP: 57
SQ FT: 86,000
SALES (est): 30.2MM **Privately Held**
WEB: www.truaire.com
SIC: **5074** 5075 3567 Heating equipment (hydronic); air conditioning & ventilation equipment & supplies; heating units & devices, industrial: electric

(P-7641)
WESTERN NEVADA SUPPLY CO
10990 Industrial Way A, Truckee (96161-0257)
PHONE..............................530 582-5009
Theodore Reviglio, *Branch Mgr*
EMP: 237
SALES (corp-wide): 284.8MM **Privately Held**
SIC: **5074** Plumbing fittings & supplies
PA: Western Nevada Supply Co.
950 S Rock Blvd
Sparks NV 89431
775 359-5800

(P-7642)
AIR TREATMENT CORPORATION (PA)
640 N Puente St, Brea (92821-2830)
PHONE..............................909 869-7975
Mark Hartman, *President*
Deborah Hudson, *CFO*
Greg Blackfelner, *Vice Pres*
Craig Domagala, *Vice Pres*
Tim Thomas, *Vice Pres*
▲ EMP: 65
SQ FT: 12,238
SALES (est): 114.8MM **Privately Held**
SIC: **5075** Electrical heating equipment; air conditioning equipment, except room units

(P-7643)
ALLIED REFRIGERATION INC
3650 Holdrege Ave, Los Angeles (90016-4304)
PHONE..............................310 202-2220
Chinnavy Lyman, *President*
Robert Nichols, *President*
Scott Melton, *Branch Mgr*
EMP: 99 EST: 2016
SALES (est): 3.9MM **Privately Held**
SIC: **5075** Air conditioning & ventilation equipment & supplies

(P-7644)
BAKER DISTRIBUTING COMPANY LLC
241 Market Pl, Escondido (92029-1301)
P.O. Box 848459, Dallas TX (75284-8459)
PHONE..............................760 708-4201
Rhonda Waag, *Branch Mgr*
EMP: 99
SQ FT: 12,000
SALES (corp-wide): 4.3B **Publicly Held**
SIC: **5075** Warm air heating & air conditioning
HQ: Baker Distributing Company Llc
14610 Breakers Dr Ste 100
Jacksonville FL 32258
904 407-4500

(P-7645)
CALIFORNIA HYDRONICS CORP (PA)
Also Called: Columbia Hydronics Co.
2293 Tripaldi Way, Hayward (94545-5024)
P.O. Box 5049 (94540-5049)
PHONE..............................510 293-1993
David Attard, *President*
John Arthur, *CFO*
Kevin McCloud, *Treasurer*
James A Attard, *Vice Pres*
Mark Copeland, *Executive*
EMP: 85
SQ FT: 50,000
SALES (est): 77.2MM **Privately Held**
WEB: www.calhydro.com
SIC: **5075** 3585 Warm air heating equipment & supplies; refrigeration & heating equipment

(P-7646)
EDWARD B WARD & COMPANY INC (DH)
Also Called: Ward, E B
99 S Hill Dr Ste B, Brisbane (94005-1282)
PHONE..............................415 330-6600
James Lazor, *President*
John Ward, *Ch of Bd*
Robert McDonough, *CEO*
Edward B Ward, *COO*
Paul Caputi, *Vice Pres*
▲ EMP: 50
SQ FT: 45,000
SALES (est): 12.8MM
SALES (corp-wide): 59.8B **Publicly Held**
WEB: www.valair.com
SIC: **5075** Air conditioning equipment, except room units

(PA)=Parent Co (HQ)=Headquarters (DH)=Div Headquarters
✿ = New Business established in last 2 years

2019 Directory of California
Wholesalers and Services Companies

329

P R O D U C T S & S V C S

HQ: Carrier Corporation
13995 Pasteur Blvd
Palm Beach Gardens FL 33418
800 379-6484

(P-7647)
EL CAJON PLUMBING & HTG SUP CO
1655 N Magnolia Ave, El Cajon (92020-1297)
PHONE....................619 449-7300
Morton B Hirshman, *CEO*
Naomi Hirshman, *Vice Pres*
Shelly Olsher, *Principal*
Kathy Esposito, *Director*
EMP: 50
SQ FT: 13,000
SALES (est): 13.9MM **Privately Held**
WEB: www.elcajonplumbing.com
SIC: 5075 5074 Dust collecting equipment; plumbing & hydronic heating supplies

(P-7648)
FLORENCE FILTER CORPORATION
530 W Manville St, Compton (90220-5587)
PHONE....................310 637-1137
Adrian M Anhood, *CEO*
Erika A Anhood, *President*
Floriana A Anhood, *CEO*
Karen Lopez, *Manager*
▲ EMP: 60
SQ FT: 55,000
SALES (est): 20.7MM **Privately Held**
WEB: www.florencefilter.com
SIC: 5075 3564 5211 Air filters; filters, air: furnaces, air conditioning equipment, etc.; lumber & other building materials

(P-7649)
GOODMAN MANUFACTURING CO LP
41670 Reagan Way, Murrieta (92562-6930)
PHONE....................951 304-7402
EMP: 292
SALES (corp-wide): 21.5B **Privately Held**
WEB: www.goodmanmfg.com
SIC: 5075 Warm air heating & air conditioning
HQ: Goodman Manufacturing Company, Lp
5151 San Felipe St # 500
Houston TX 77056
877 254-4729

(P-7650)
GOODMAN MANUFACTURING CO LP
3562 Ruffin Rd, San Diego (92123-2596)
PHONE....................858 569-1715
Steve Thoreson, *Manager*
EMP: 266
SALES (corp-wide): 21.5B **Privately Held**
SIC: 5075 Warm air heating & air conditioning
HQ: Goodman Manufacturing Company, Lp
5151 San Felipe St # 500
Houston TX 77056
877 254-4729

(P-7651)
HKF INC (PA)
Also Called: Therm Pacific
5983 Smithway St, Commerce (90040-1607)
PHONE....................323 225-1318
James P Hartfield, *President*
▲ EMP: 450
SALES (est): 116.6MM **Privately Held**
SIC: 5075 3873 5064 3567 Warm air heating & air conditioning; watches, clocks, watchcases & parts; electrical appliances, television & radio; industrial furnaces & ovens; current-carrying wiring devices

(P-7652)
HONEYWELL INTERNATIONAL INC
514 S Lyon St, Santa Ana (92701-6362)
PHONE....................714 796-7500
Emily McCue, *Manager*
EMP: 115

SALES (corp-wide): 40.5B **Publicly Held**
WEB: www.honeywell.com
SIC: 5075 8748 7382 Warm air heating & air conditioning; business consulting; security systems services
PA: Honeywell International Inc.
115 Tabor Rd
Morris Plains NJ 07950
973 455-2000

(P-7653)
LENNOX INDUSTRIES INC
19801 Nordhoff Pl Ste 109, Chatsworth (91311-6612)
PHONE....................818 739-1616
EMP: 140
SALES (corp-wide): 3.8B **Publicly Held**
SIC: 5075 Warm air heating & air conditioning
HQ: Lennox Industries Inc.
2100 Lake Park Blvd
Richardson TX 75080
972 497-5000

(P-7654)
NORITZ AMERICA CORPORATION (HQ)
11160 Grace Ave, Fountain Valley (92708-5436)
PHONE....................714 433-2905
Hisashi Uryu, *CEO*
Toshiyuki Otaki, *CEO*
▲ EMP: 56
SALES (est): 33MM
SALES (corp-wide): 1.9B **Privately Held**
SIC: 5075 Warm air heating equipment & supplies
PA: Noritz Corporation
93, Edomachi, Chuo-Ku
Kobe HYO 650-0
783 913-361

(P-7655)
NORMAN S WRIGHT MECH EQP CORP (PA)
99 S Hill Dr Ste A, Brisbane (94005-1282)
PHONE....................415 467-7600
Richard F Leao, *President*
Robert L Beyer, *Exec VP*
Salvatore M Giglio, *Exec VP*
EMP: 62
SQ FT: 50,000
SALES (est): 169.7MM **Privately Held**
WEB: www.norman-wright.com
SIC: 5075 Warm air heating equipment & supplies; air conditioning & ventilation equipment & supplies

(P-7656)
SIERRA PCF HM & COMFORT INC
Also Called: Sierra Pacific Htg & Air-Solar
2550 Mercantile Dr Ste D, Rancho Cordova (95742-8202)
PHONE....................916 638-0543
Jason Hanson, *President*
Mike Loer, *Vice Pres*
Lynne Bertolino, *Accounting Mgr*
Lyn Lockwood, *Controller*
Shannon King, *Marketing Mgr*
EMP: 75
SALES (est): 48.2MM **Privately Held**
WEB: www.sierrapacifichome.com
SIC: 5075 5074 Warm air heating & air conditioning; heating equipment & panels, solar

(P-7657)
TRANE US INC
4145 Delmar Ave Ste 2, Rocklin (95677-4041)
PHONE....................916 577-1100
Tyler Clemmer, *Manager*
Eric Svensson, *Engineer*
EMP: 90 **Privately Held**
SIC: 5075 Air conditioning & ventilation equipment & supplies
HQ: Trane U.S. Inc.
3600 Pammel Creek Rd
La Crosse WI 54601
608 787-2000

(P-7658)
TUCKER DISTRIBUTORS
Also Called: Tucker Sheet Metal Distr
5380 E Hunter Ave, Anaheim (92807-2053)
PHONE....................714 970-5742
Tom Tucker, *Partner*
Sue Tucker, *Partner*
EMP: 50
SQ FT: 16,000
SALES: 12.6MM **Privately Held**
SIC: 5075 5051 5084 Ventilating equipment & supplies; tin & tin base metals, shapes, forms, etc.; metalworking machinery

(P-7659)
ULTRAVIOLET DEVICES INC
26145 Technology Dr, Valencia (91355-1138)
PHONE....................661 295-8140
Peter Veloz, *CEO*
David Veloz, *Shareholder*
Richard Hayes, *Vice Pres*
Ashish Mathur, *Vice Pres*
Lev Rotkop, *Vice Pres*
▲ EMP: 53
SQ FT: 45,000
SALES (est): 34.7MM **Privately Held**
WEB: www.uvdi.com
SIC: 5075 5074 Air filters; water purification equipment

(P-7660)
US AIR CONDITIONING DISTRS LLC
16900 Chestnut St, City of Industry (91748-1012)
PHONE....................626 854-0429
John Staples, *CEO*
John Scarsi, *Vice Pres*
Brodstreet Ned, *Controller*
Alvaro Madrid, *Sales Engr*
Bruce Fuhrmann, *Sales Staff*
EMP: 70
SALES (est): 42.7MM **Privately Held**
SIC: 5075 Warm air heating & air conditioning

5078 Refrigeration Eqpt & Splys Wholesale

(P-7661)
ALLIED BEVERAGE LLC
13235 Golden State Rd, Sylmar (91342-1129)
PHONE....................818 493-6400
Mark Smith, *CEO*
Kimberly Clift, *CFO*
EMP: 500
SALES (est): 27.3MM **Privately Held**
SIC: 5078 Beverage coolers

(P-7662)
CUSTOM COOLER INC
420 E Arrow Hwy, San Dimas (91773-3340)
PHONE....................909 592-1111
Sangyup Steve Lee, *President*
Young G Kim, *Vice Pres*
Ray Tolcher, *Vice Pres*
Dennis Bjerk, *Sales Mgr*
▲ EMP: 80
SALES (est): 47MM **Privately Held**
SIC: 5078 Refrigeration equipment & supplies

(P-7663)
OMNITEAM INC
9300 Hall Rd, Downey (90241-5309)
PHONE....................562 923-9660
Kans Haasis Jr, *CEO*
Robert Davis, *Vice Pres*
Don Hyatt Sr, *Vice Pres*
Dick Hendershot, *Finance*
EMP: 125
SQ FT: 100,000
SALES (est): 49.9MM **Privately Held**
WEB: www.omniteam.com
SIC: 5078 Commercial refrigeration equipment

(P-7664)
PEPSI-COLA METRO BTLG CO INC
6659 Sycamore Canyon Blvd, Riverside (92507-0733)
PHONE....................951 697-3200
Jerry Sime, *Manager*
EMP: 500
SALES (corp-wide): 63.5B **Publicly Held**
WEB: www.joy-of-cola.com
SIC: 5078 2086 5149 Refrigerated beverage dispensers; bottled & canned soft drinks; soft drinks
HQ: Pepsi-Cola Metropolitan Bottling Company, Inc.
1111 Westchester Ave
White Plains NY 10604
914 767-6000

(P-7665)
REFRIGERATION HDWR SUP CORP
9021 Norris Ave, Sun Valley (91352-2618)
PHONE....................818 768-3636
Pamela Sylvester, *Branch Mgr*
Pamela Sylvestre, *Sales Executive*
EMP: 50
SALES (corp-wide): 27.9MM **Privately Held**
SIC: 5078 5722 3585 7699 Refrigeration equipment & supplies; household appliance stores; refrigeration & heating equipment; restaurant equipment repair
PA: Refrigeration Hardware Supply Corporation
632 Foresight Cir
Grand Junction CO 81505
970 241-2800

(P-7666)
STELLAR GROUP INCORPORATED
1035 Reno Ave, Modesto (95351-1165)
PHONE....................209 549-0899
Christine Clark, *Branch Mgr*
Mark Turner, *Sales Staff*
EMP: 52 **Privately Held**
SIC: 5078 Refrigeration equipment & supplies
HQ: Stellar Group, Incorporated
2900 Hartley Rd
Jacksonville FL 32257
904 260-2044

(P-7667)
UNITED REFRIGERATION INC
3573a Hayden Ave, Culver City (90232-2412)
PHONE....................310 204-2500
John Nunez, *President*
EMP: 99
SQ FT: 2,000
SALES (corp-wide): 50MM **Privately Held**
SIC: 5078 Refrigeration equipment & supplies
PA: United Refrigeration, Inc.
11401 Roosevelt Blvd
Philadelphia PA 19154
215 698-9100

5082 Construction & Mining Mach & Eqpt Wholesale

(P-7668)
BIG CITY ACCESS INC (PA)
3131 52nd Ave, West Sacramento (95691)
PHONE....................916 428-4090
Linda McCurdy, *CEO*
Barbara Roberts, *President*
Michael McCurdy, *CFO*
EMP: 69
SALES (est): 19.2MM **Privately Held**
SIC: 5082 Scaffolding

(P-7669)
BRAND SERVICES INC
Also Called: Brand Services of California
535 Watt Dr, Fairfield (94534-1790)
PHONE....................707 603-3400
Paul Wood, *President*

EMP: 50
SALES (est): 16MM **Privately Held**
SIC: 5082 Scaffolding

(P-7670)
CALIFORNIA CONTRS SUPS INC
7729 Burnet Ave, Van Nuys (91405-1008)
PHONE..................................818 785-8823
David Rogal, *CEO*
Phil Kaufmann, *President*
Al Lester, *Corp Secy*
EMP: 55
SQ FT: 16,000
SALES (est): 12.8MM **Privately Held**
SIC: 5082 Contractors' materials; general construction machinery & equipment

(P-7671)
CAMERON WEST COAST INC
Also Called: Cameron Surface Systems
4316 Yeager Way, Bakersfield (93313)
PHONE..................................661 837-4980
Stefan Radwanski, *Principal*
▲ EMP: 90 EST: 1992
SQ FT: 48,000
SALES (est): 42.1MM **Publicly Held**
SIC: 5082 1389 7353 Oil field equipment; oil field services; oil field equipment, rental or leasing
HQ: Cameron International Corporation
4646 W Sam Houston Pkwy N
Houston TX 77041

(P-7672)
CASE DEALER HOLDING CO LLC
1751 Bell Ave, Sacramento (95838-2862)
PHONE..................................916 649-0096
Trevor Ward, *Mng Member*
EMP: 150
SALES (est): 524K
SALES (corp-wide): 27.9B **Privately Held**
SIC: 5082 General construction machinery & equipment
HQ: Cnh Industrial America Llc
700 State St
Racine WI 53404
262 636-6011

(P-7673)
CNH INDUSTRIAL AMERICA LLC
1919 Williams St, San Leandro (94577-2303)
PHONE..................................510 351-2015
Norma Smith, *Manager*
EMP: 50
SALES (corp-wide): 27.9B **Privately Held**
SIC: 5082 General construction machinery & equipment
HQ: Cnh Industrial America Llc
700 State St
Racine WI 53404
262 636-6011

(P-7674)
EMPIRE SOUTHWEST LLC
Also Called: Caterpillar Authorized Dealer
3393 Us Highway 86, Imperial (92251-9527)
PHONE..................................760 545-6200
Diane Madrigal, *Manager*
EMP: 300
SALES (corp-wide): 881.9MM **Privately Held**
WEB: www.empire-cat.com
SIC: 5082 General construction machinery & equipment
PA: Empire Southwest, Llc
1725 S Country Club Dr
Mesa AZ 85210
480 633-4000

(P-7675)
FLUOR ENTERPRISES INC
3 Polaris Way, Aliso Viejo (92656-5338)
PHONE..................................949 349-2000
Ronald Albright, *Branch Mgr*
EMP: 200
SALES (corp-wide): 19.5B **Publicly Held**
SIC: 5082 Construction & mining machinery
HQ: Fluor Enterprises, Inc.
6700 Las Colinas Blvd
Irving TX 75039
469 398-7000

(P-7676)
GAMA CONTRACTING SERVICES INC
1835 Floradale Ave, South El Monte (91733-3605)
PHONE..................................626 442-7200
Jose Sergio Duenas, *President*
EMP: 140
SALES (est): 8.5MM **Privately Held**
SIC: 5082 1795 8744 General construction machinery & equipment; wrecking & demolition work;

(P-7677)
HAWTHORNE MACHINERY CO
Also Called: Caterpillar Authorized Dealer
8050 Othello Ave, San Diego (92111-3714)
PHONE..................................858 974-6800
Bob Price, *Manager*
EMP: 100
SALES (corp-wide): 195.6MM **Privately Held**
SIC: 5082 General construction machinery & equipment
PA: Hawthorne Machinery Co.
16945 Camino San Bernardo
San Diego CA 92127
858 674-7000

(P-7678)
HERCA TELECOMM SERVICES INC
Also Called: Herca Construction Services
18610 Beck St, Perris (92570-9185)
PHONE..................................951 940-5941
Hector R Castellon, *President*
Tracy Hertel, *Officer*
Raul Castellon, *Opers Staff*
Alfonso Castellon, *Director*
Alfredo Castellon, *Director*
EMP: 56
SQ FT: 67,900
SALES: 16.2MM **Privately Held**
WEB: www.hercatelecomm.com
SIC: 5082 1623 1731 3663 General construction machinery & equipment; communication line & transmission tower construction; general electrical contractor; antennas, transmitting & communications

(P-7679)
HOLT OF CALIFORNIA (HQ)
Also Called: Holt CA
7310 Pacific Ave, Pleasant Grove (95668-9708)
PHONE..................................916 991-8200
Victor Wykoff Jr, *Ch of Bd*
Kenneth Monroe, *President*
Daniel Johns, *CFO*
Gordon Beatie, *Vice Ch Bd*
Ronald Monroe, *Exec VP*
▲ EMP: 155
SQ FT: 160,000
SALES (est): 369.9MM **Privately Held**
WEB: www.holtcausedparts.com
SIC: 5082 5084 5083 7359 General construction machinery & equipment; tractors, construction; materials handling machinery; agricultural machinery; equipment rental & leasing
PA: Hoc Holdings, Inc.
7310 Pacific Ave
Pleasant Grove CA 95668
916 921-8950

(P-7680)
HOLT OF CALIFORNIA
Also Called: Caterpillar Authorized Dealer
3850 Channel Dr, West Sacramento (95691-3466)
PHONE..................................916 373-4100
Toll Free:.............................888   -
Carry Roulet, *Manager*
Mike Cottrell, *Mktg Dir*
Dave Dobberteen, *Accounts Mgr*
EMP: 150
SALES (corp-wide): 369.9MM **Privately Held**
WEB: www.holtcausedparts.com
SIC: 5082 5083 5084 General construction machinery & equipment; agricultural machinery & equipment; materials handling machinery

HQ: Holt Of California
7310 Pacific Ave
Pleasant Grove CA 95668
916 991-8200

(P-7681)
HOLT OF CALIFORNIA
1234 W Charter Way, Stockton (95206-1109)
PHONE..................................209 462-3660
Ken Monroe, *Owner*
EMP: 108
SALES (corp-wide): 369.9MM **Privately Held**
SIC: 5082 Tractors, construction
HQ: Holt Of California
7310 Pacific Ave
Pleasant Grove CA 95668
916 991-8200

(P-7682)
HUB CONSTRUCTION SPC INC
1856 S Bon View Ave, Ontario (91761-5501)
PHONE..................................909 947-4669
Tim Robuck, *Manager*
EMP: 50
SALES (corp-wide): 48.1MM **Privately Held**
SIC: 5082 3444 Concrete processing equipment; concrete forms, sheet metal
PA: Hub Construction Specialties, Inc.
379 S I St
San Bernardino CA 92410
909 889-0161

(P-7683)
J M EQUIPMENT COMPANY INC
3751 E Calwa Ave, Fresno (93725-2002)
P.O. Box 2400 (93745-2400)
PHONE..................................559 233-0187
Scott Anderson, *Manager*
Rod Kiser, *Materials Mgr*
Mike Koop, *Manager*
EMP: 50
SQ FT: 900
SALES (corp-wide): 38.3MM **Privately Held**
WEB: www.jmequipment.com
SIC: 5082 7353 5084 General construction machinery & equipment; heavy construction equipment rental; materials handling machinery
PA: J. M. Equipment Company, Inc.
321 Spreckels Ave
Manteca CA 95336
209 522-3271

(P-7684)
JOHNSON MACHINERY CO (PA)
Also Called: Caterpillar Authorized Dealer
800 E La Cadena Dr, Riverside (92507-8715)
P.O. Box 351 (92502-0351)
PHONE..................................951 686-4560
William Johnson Jr, *President*
Kevin Kelly, *Exec VP*
Matt Merickel, *Exec VP*
Bryn Glover, *CTO*
Rob Millerd, *Network Mgr*
◆ EMP: 175
SQ FT: 70,000
SALES (est): 205.9MM **Privately Held**
WEB: www.johnson-machinery.com
SIC: 5082 General construction machinery & equipment

(P-7685)
PAPE MACHINERY INC
Also Called: John Deere Authorized Dealer
2850 El Centro Rd, Sacramento (95833-9602)
P.O. Box 15017 (95851-0017)
PHONE..................................916 922-7181
Josh Juenger, *Branch Mgr*
Jordan Pape, *CEO*
Mike Pilat, *Sales Mgr*
EMP: 82
SALES (corp-wide): 587.9MM **Privately Held**
WEB: www.papemh.com
SIC: 5082 General construction machinery & equipment

HQ: Pape' Machinery, Inc.
355 Goodpasture Island Rd
Eugene OR 97401
541 683-5073

(P-7686)
QUINN COMPANY
13275 Golden State Rd, Sylmar (91342-1129)
PHONE..................................818 767-7171
EMP: 61
SALES (corp-wide): 455MM **Privately Held**
SIC: 5082 General construction machinery & equipment
HQ: Quinn Company
10006 Rose Hills Rd
City Of Industry CA 90601
562 463-4000

(P-7687)
QUINN COMPANY
Also Called: Caterpillar Authorized Dealer
2200 Pegasus Dr, Bakersfield (93308-6801)
PHONE..................................661 393-5800
Steve Eucce, *Branch Mgr*
Nick Tafolla, *Sales Staff*
EMP: 62
SALES (corp-wide): 455MM **Privately Held**
WEB: www.quinngroup.net
SIC: 5082 5083 5084 7353 General construction machinery & equipment; farm & garden machinery; industrial machinery & equipment; heavy construction equipment rental
HQ: Quinn Company
10006 Rose Hills Rd
City Of Industry CA 90601
562 463-4000

(P-7688)
QUINN COMPANY
Also Called: Caterpillar Authorized Dealer
801 Del Norte Blvd, Oxnard (93030-8966)
PHONE..................................805 485-2171
Jay Ervine, *Branch Mgr*
Tree Ferrell, *Sales Staff*
EMP: 62
SALES (corp-wide): 455MM **Privately Held**
WEB: www.quinngroup.net
SIC: 5082 5083 5084 7353 General construction machinery & equipment; farm & garden machinery; industrial machinery & equipment; heavy construction equipment rental
HQ: Quinn Company
10006 Rose Hills Rd
City Of Industry CA 90601
562 463-4000

(P-7689)
QUINN COMPANY
Also Called: Caterpillar Authorized Dealer
1655 Carlotti Dr, Santa Maria (93454-1503)
PHONE..................................805 925-8611
Dan Hunt, *Manager*
EMP: 62
SALES (corp-wide): 455MM **Privately Held**
WEB: www.quinngroup.net
SIC: 5082 5083 5084 7353 General construction machinery & equipment; farm & garden machinery; industrial machinery & equipment; heavy construction equipment rental
HQ: Quinn Company
10006 Rose Hills Rd
City Of Industry CA 90601
562 463-4000

(P-7690)
QUINN GROUP INC
Also Called: Caterpillar Authorized Dealer
1300 Abbott St, Salinas (93901-4507)
PHONE..................................831 758-8461
Kelly Francis, *Store Mgr*
Jesse Sandoval, *Manager*
EMP: 1000
SALES (corp-wide): 455MM **Privately Held**
WEB: www.quinnengines.com
SIC: 5082 General construction machinery & equipment

PA: Quinn Group, Inc.
10006 Rose Hills Rd
City Of Industry CA 90601
562 463-4000

(P-7691)
QUINN SHEPHERD MACHINERY
Also Called: Caterpillar Authorized Dealer
10006 Rose Hills Rd, City of Industry
(90601-1702)
P.O. Box 226789, Los Angeles (90022-6789)
PHONE......................562 463-6000
Blake Quinn, *President*
▲ **EMP:** 287
SQ FT: 163,000
SALES (est): 99.9MM
SALES (corp-wide): 455MM **Privately Held**
SIC: 5082 5084 General construction machinery & equipment; excavating machinery & equipment; mining machinery & equipment, except petroleum; industrial machinery & equipment
PA: Quinn Group, Inc.
10006 Rose Hills Rd
City Of Industry CA 90601
562 463-4000

(P-7692)
RDO VERMEER LLC
Also Called: Vermeer Pacific
3980 Research Dr, Sacramento
(95838-3257)
PHONE......................916 643-0999
Christi Offutt,
Michael Oberbillig, *Regl Sales Mgr*
EMP: 99
SALES (est): 8.4MM **Privately Held**
SIC: 5082 Contractors' materials

(P-7693)
SAFWAY SERVICES LP
1660 Gilbreth Rd, Burlingame
(94010-1408)
PHONE......................650 652-9255
Fax: 650 652-9255
EMP: 50
SALES (corp-wide): 1.7B **Privately Held**
SIC: 5082
HQ: Safway Services, L.P.
N19w24200 Riverwood Dr # 200
Waukesha WI 53188
262 523-6500

(P-7694)
SAFWAY SERVICES LP
4072b Teal Ct, Benicia (94510-1238)
PHONE......................707 745-2000
Sully Cittadino, *Manager*
Kathy Perotti, *Executive*
EMP: 50
SALES (corp-wide): 1.2B **Privately Held**
WEB: www.safway.com
SIC: 5082 Scaffolding
HQ: Safway Services, L.P.
N19w24200 Riverwood Dr # 200
Waukesha WI 53188
262 523-6500

(P-7695)
SOUND-CRETE CONTRACTING
530 Opper St Ste A, Escondido
(92029-1034)
PHONE......................760 291-1240
Louis Fisher, *President*
Terry Russo, *Vice Pres*
Jim Dorsey, *Manager*
EMP: 65
SALES (est): 6.7MM **Privately Held**
SIC: 5082 General construction machinery & equipment

(P-7696)
SOUTHWEST GENERAL CONTRS INC
912 S Andreasen Dr # 101, Escondido
(92029-1900)
PHONE......................760 480-8747
Dane Crown, *President*
EMP: 50
SQ FT: 4,500
SALES (est): 10.4MM **Privately Held**
SIC: 5082 General construction machinery & equipment

(P-7697)
TOM MALLOY CORPORATION (PA)
Also Called: Trench Shoring Company
636 E Rosecrans Ave, Los Angeles
(90059-3507)
PHONE......................310 327-5554
Thomas E Malloy, *CEO*
Kevin Malloy, *President*
Bridgett Baril, *Vice Pres*
John Baril, *Branch Mgr*
Dave Medbery, *Branch Mgr*
▲ **EMP:** 50 **EST:** 1973
SALES (est): 54MM **Privately Held**
SIC: 5082 7353 Construction & mining machinery; heavy construction equipment rental

(P-7698)
WHITE CAP CONSTRUCTION SUPPLY
1815 Ritchey St, Santa Ana (92705-5127)
PHONE......................949 794-5300
Jack Karg, *Principal*
Kevin Burns, *Branch Mgr*
Brad Jones, *District Mgr*
Erin McCabe, *Project Mgr*
Jim Dierker, *VP Finance*
EMP: 1129
SALES (est): 20.6MM **Publicly Held**
SIC: 5082 Construction & mining machinery
HQ: White Cap Construction Supply, Inc.
3100 Cumberland Blvd Se # 1700
Atlanta GA 30339
404 879-7740

5083 Farm & Garden Mach & Eqpt Wholesale

(P-7699)
ALSCO - GEYER IRRIGATION INC
700 5th St, Arbuckle (95912-9550)
P.O. Box 111 (95912-0111)
PHONE......................530 476-2253
Charles Geyer, *President*
Marjoria Martinez, *Admin Sec*
Andrew Geyer, *Sales Staff*
Rocio Hernandez, *Cashier*
EMP: 90
SQ FT: 3,000
SALES (est): 64.5MM **Privately Held**
WEB: www.alscogeyer.com
SIC: 5083 Irrigation equipment

(P-7700)
ATI MACHINERY INC
Also Called: NAPA West
21436 S Lassen Ave, Five Points (93624)
P.O. Box 445 (93624-0445)
PHONE......................559 884-2471
Toll Free:......................888 -
Leo A Marihart, *Ch of Bd*
Mark Moorhead, *President*
Richard Demler, *Admin Sec*
EMP: 50
SQ FT: 22,000
SALES (est): 17.3MM **Privately Held**
WEB: www.atimachinery.com
SIC: 5083 7699 7359 Farm equipment parts & supplies; farm machinery repair; equipment rental & leasing

(P-7701)
BIANCHI AG SERVICES INC (PA)
1210 Richvale Hwy, Richvale (95974)
P.O. Box 1216, Durham (95938-1216)
PHONE......................530 882-4575
Jim Bianchi, *CEO*
Moe Dean, *CFO*
EMP: 120
SALES (est): 41.1MM **Privately Held**
SIC: 5083 Agricultural machinery & equipment

(P-7702)
EURODRIP USA INC
1850 W Almond Ave, Madera (93637-5214)
PHONE......................559 674-2670
Rowland Wilkinson, *CEO*
◆ **EMP:** 80
SQ FT: 33,180

SALES: 76MM **Privately Held**
WEB: www.eurodripusa.com
SIC: 5083 3084 Irrigation equipment; plastics pipe
HQ: Eurodrip S.A.
Athinon - Lamias National Rd (55th Km), P.O. Box 34
Oinofyta 32011
226 205-4800

(P-7703)
GREEN ACRES NURSERY & SUP LLC
604 Sutter St, Folsom (95630-2575)
PHONE......................916 782-2273
Mark Gill,
Kellie Natoli, *Corp Comm Staff*
▲ **EMP:** 90
SALES (est): 52.3MM **Privately Held**
SIC: 5083 5261 Irrigation equipment; nursery stock, seeds & bulbs

(P-7704)
KRC EQUIPMENT LLC
700 N Twin Oaks Valley Rd, San Marcos
(92069-1714)
P.O. Box 729 (92079-0729)
PHONE......................760 744-1036
Gerald Sebby, *President*
Nina Snyder, *Purchasing*
Cathy Sebby,
EMP: 58 **EST:** 1998
SALES (est): 5.2MM **Privately Held**
SIC: 5083 Landscaping equipment

(P-7705)
LAWRENCE TRACTOR COINC (PA)
Also Called: John Deere Authorized Dealer
2436 E Valley Oaks Dr, Visalia
(93292-6713)
PHONE......................559 734-7406
Mark Lawrence, *President*
Angie Lawrence, *Shareholder*
Richard Nunes, *Corp Secy*
Steven Lawrence, *Vice Pres*
Neil Walden, *Foreman/Supr*
▲ **EMP:** 98
SQ FT: 72,000
SALES (est): 51.6MM **Privately Held**
WEB: www.lawrencetractor.com
SIC: 5083 7699 Agricultural machinery; farm implements; farm equipment parts & supplies; farm machinery repair

(P-7706)
MAYFIELD EQUIPMENT COMPANY (PA)
Also Called: Rainbow Agricultural Services
235 E Perkins St, Ukiah (95482-4401)
PHONE......................707 462-2404
James Mayfield, *President*
Mark Wedegaertner, *CFO*
John Mayfield Jr, *Chairman*
Ted Mayfield, *Vice Pres*
Keith Shields, *Branch Mgr*
▲ **EMP:** 88
SQ FT: 15,000
SALES (est): 39.8MM **Privately Held**
WEB: www.rainbowag.com
SIC: 5083 5191 5211 Irrigation equipment; farm implements; agricultural machinery; farm equipment parts & supplies; farm supplies; animal feeds; lumber & other building materials

(P-7707)
NETAFIM IRRIGATION INC (HQ)
5470 E Home Ave, Fresno (93727-2107)
PHONE......................559 453-6800
Igal Aisenberg, *President*
Eli Bensimon, *President*
Mahesh Kalmane, *COO*
Lauri Hanover, *CFO*
Naty Barak, *Officer*
▲ **EMP:** 110 **EST:** 1965
SQ FT: 100,000
SALES (est): 91.1MM **Privately Held**
WEB: www.netafimusa.com
SIC: 5083 3523 Irrigation equipment; irrigation equipment, self-propelled
PA: Netafim Ltd
10 Hashalom Rd.
Tel Aviv-Jaffa
864 747-47

(P-7708)
QUINN GROUP INC
Also Called: Caterpillar Authorized Dealer
801 Del Norte Blvd, Oxnard (93030-8966)
PHONE......................805 485-2171
Jim Barr, *Manager*
EMP: 80
SQ FT: 5,000
SALES (corp-wide): 455MM **Privately Held**
WEB: www.catpower.com
SIC: 5083 5082 5084 Agricultural machinery & equipment; construction & mining machinery; industrial machinery & equipment
PA: Quinn Group, Inc.
10006 Rose Hills Rd
City Of Industry CA 90601
562 463-4000

(P-7709)
QUINN GROUP INC
2200 Pegasus Dr, Bakersfield
(93308-6801)
PHONE......................661 393-5800
Mike Ford, *Branch Mgr*
Robin Camp, *Sales Staff*
EMP: 110
SALES (corp-wide): 455MM **Privately Held**
WEB: www.catpower.com
SIC: 5083 5084 7359 Tractors, agricultural; tractors, industrial; industrial truck rental
PA: Quinn Group, Inc.
10006 Rose Hills Rd
City Of Industry CA 90601
562 463-4000

(P-7710)
RDO CONSTRUCTION EQUIPMENT CO
Also Called: John Deere Authorized Dealer
20 Iowa Ave, Riverside (92507-1028)
PHONE......................951 778-3700
Greg Burgman, *General Mgr*
EMP: 50
SALES (corp-wide): 1.7B **Privately Held**
SIC: 5083 Farm & garden machinery
HQ: Rdo Construction Equipment Co.
2000 Industrial Dr
Bismarck ND 58501
701 223-5798

(P-7711)
S A CAMP COMPANIES (PA)
17876 Zerker Rd, Bakersfield
(93308-9221)
PHONE......................661 399-4451
James S Camp, *President*
D M Hart, *Vice Pres*
EMP: 50
SQ FT: 10,000
SALES (est): 18.1MM **Privately Held**
WEB: www.sacamp.net
SIC: 5083 0191 6552 Agricultural machinery; general farms, primarily crop; subdividers & developers

(P-7712)
SEABOARD PRODUCE DISTRS INC
Also Called: Del Norte Distribution
710 Del Norte Blvd, Oxnard (93030-8963)
PHONE......................805 981-8001
J Woodford Hansen, *President*
James Sullivan, *General Mgr*
Heather Wise, *Controller*
EMP: 64
SALES (corp-wide): 28.1MM **Privately Held**
SIC: 5083 Irrigation equipment
PA: Seaboard Produce Distributors, Inc.
601 Mountain View Ave
Oxnard CA 93030
805 486-4773

(P-7713)
SPEARS MANUFACTURING CO (PA)
15853 Olden St, Sylmar (91342-1293)
P.O. Box 9203 (91392-9203)
PHONE......................818 364-1611
Robert W Spears, *CEO*
Wayne Spears, *President*

Ken Ruggles, *Corp Secy*
Paul Eng, *Vice Pres*
Michael Valasquez, *Vice Pres*
◆ **EMP:** 134
SQ FT: 119,088
SALES (est): 1.6B **Privately Held**
WEB: www.spearsmfg.com
SIC: 5083 3494 Irrigation equipment;
valves & pipe fittings

(P-7714)
THOMASON TRACTOR CO CALIFORNIA
Also Called: John Deere Authorized Dealer
985 12th St, Firebaugh (93622)
P.O. Box 97 (93622-0097)
PHONE..................................559 659-2039
Audrey Thomason, *President*
Rodney Thomason, *Vice Pres*
Jessica Diaz, *Office Admin*
Don York Jr, *Sales Mgr*
Nathan Chang, *Sales Staff*
EMP: 50 **EST:** 1967
SQ FT: 33,000
SALES (est): 29MM **Privately Held**
WEB: www.thomasontractor.com
SIC: 5083 Agricultural machinery & equipment

(P-7715)
TURF STAR INC
Also Called: Turfstar
79253 Country Club Dr, Bermuda Dunes
(92203-1229)
PHONE..................................760 772-3575
Leonard Gregory, *President*
EMP: 100
SALES (corp-wide): 60.3MM **Privately Held**
WEB: www.turfstar.com
SIC: 5083 Garden machinery & equipment;
lawn machinery & equipment; irrigation equipment
PA: Turf Star, Inc.
2438 Radley Ct
Hayward CA 94545
800 585-8001

(P-7716)
TURLOCK DAIRY & RFRGN INC
Also Called: T D R
1819 S Walnut Rd, Turlock (95380-9219)
P.O. Box 1530 (95381-1530)
PHONE..................................209 667-6455
Mathew Anthony Bruno, *CEO*
Tony Bruno, *President*
John Penton, *Info Tech Mgr*
Jonathan Risley, *Financial Analy*
Jeanette Sanders, *Controller*
EMP: 100 **EST:** 1972
SQ FT: 10,000
SALES (est): 86.3MM **Privately Held**
WEB: www.turlockdairy.com
SIC: 5083 7699 1542 Dairy machinery & equipment; industrial equipment services;
nonresidential construction

(P-7717)
VUCOVICH INC (PA)
Also Called: John Deere Authorized Dealer
4288 S Bagley Ave, Fresno (93725-9014)
P.O. Box 2513 (93745-2513)
PHONE..................................559 486-8020
Marsha Vucovich, *President*
Dave Mouw, *Sales Staff*
Brian Montgomery, *Manager*
EMP: 60
SQ FT: 42,800
SALES: 50MM **Privately Held**
WEB: www.fresnoequipment.com
SIC: 5083 Farm equipment parts & supplies; agricultural machinery & equipment

---

5084 Industrial Mach & Eqpt Wholesale

(P-7718)
A MEISSNERS HHLD & INDUS SVC
2417 Cormorant Way, Sacramento
(95815-2714)
PHONE..................................916 920-2121
Jim Meissners, *Owner*
EMP: 57 **EST:** 2001

SALES (est): 2.8MM **Privately Held**
SIC: 5084 Sewing machines, industrial

(P-7719)
AIRGAS INC
653 N Market St, Redding (96003-3609)
PHONE..................................530 241-1544
John Sabo, *Branch Mgr*
EMP: 281
SALES (corp-wide): 164.2MM **Privately Held**
SIC: 5084 Welding machinery & equipment
HQ: Airgas, Inc.
259 N Radnor Chester Rd # 100
Radnor PA 19087
610 687-5253

(P-7720)
AIRGAS INC
9010 Clairemont Mesa Blvd, San Diego
(92123-1208)
PHONE..................................858 279-8200
Leigh Hart, *Branch Mgr*
Dan Bloch, *Manager*
EMP: 110
SALES (corp-wide): 164.2MM **Privately Held**
WEB: www.airgas.com
SIC: 5084 Welding machinery & equipment
HQ: Airgas, Inc.
259 N Radnor Chester Rd # 100
Radnor PA 19087
610 687-5253

(P-7721)
AIRGAS SAFETY INC
2355 Workman Mill Rd, City of Industry
(90601-1459)
PHONE..................................562 699-5239
Olaya Rivera, *Branch Mgr*
Mary Larson, *Technology*
Mauricio Gonzalez, *Manager*
Renee Laird, *Manager*
Darryl Langdon, *Accounts Mgr*
EMP: 80
SALES (corp-wide): 164.2MM **Privately Held**
WEB: www.airgassafety.com
SIC: 5084 5085 3561 3841 Safety equipment; welding supplies; cylinders, pump;
surgical & medical instruments
HQ: Airgas Safety, Inc.
2501 Green Ln
Levittown PA 19057

(P-7722)
AIRGAS USA LLC
11711 S Alameda St, Los Angeles
(90059-2130)
PHONE..................................323 568-2244
Dennis Beukelmau, *Branch Mgr*
EMP: 58
SALES (corp-wide): 164.2MM **Privately Held**
WEB: www.airgaswest.com
SIC: 5084 Welding machinery & equipment
HQ: Airgas Usa, Llc
259 N Radnor Chester Rd # 100
Radnor PA 19087
610 687-5253

(P-7723)
AIRGAS USA LLC
441 Hobson St, San Jose (95110-2016)
PHONE..................................408 998-6380
Al Shull, *Manager*
Max Hooper, *President*
Peter McCausland, *CEO*
EMP: 65
SQ FT: 7,200
SALES (corp-wide): 164.2MM **Privately Held**
SIC: 5084 5169 Welding machinery & equipment; industrial gases
HQ: Airgas Usa, Llc
259 N Radnor Chester Rd # 100
Radnor PA 19087
610 687-5253

(P-7724)
ALLTEK COMPANY U S A INC
18281 Gothard St Ste 102, Huntington
Beach (92648-1205)
PHONE..................................714 375-9785
Weishui W Zhang, *President*

Joline Yin, *Vice Pres*
John Zhang, *Vice Pres*
Linda Zhu, *Vice Pres*
Wesley Zhang, *Info Tech Mgr*
EMP: 50
SQ FT: 2,000
SALES (est): 16.9MM **Privately Held**
WEB: www.alltekusa.com
SIC: 5084 5065 Industrial machinery & equipment; semiconductor devices

(P-7725)
AMADA AMERICA INC (HQ)
7025 Firestone Blvd, Buena Park
(90621-1869)
PHONE..................................714 739-2111
Mike Guarin, *CEO*
KOA Nakata, *CFO*
Pablo Cervantes, *Senior VP*
Charles Wittig, *Exec Dir*
Themis Alexopoulos, *Regional Mgr*
◆ **EMP:** 75
SQ FT: 103,000
SALES (est): 191.2MM
SALES (corp-wide): 2.8B **Privately Held**
SIC: 5084 6159 Metalworking machinery;
metalworking tools (such as drills, taps,
dies, files); machinery & equipment finance leasing
PA: Amada Holdings Co., Ltd.
200, Ishida
Isehara KNG 259-1
463 961-111

(P-7726)
ANA TRADING CORP USA (DH)
3625 Del Amo Blvd Ste 300, Torrance
(90503-1693)
PHONE..................................310 542-2500
Hideto Osada, *President*
Hisato Teruyama, *Exec VP*
Takashi Kinoshita, *Vice Pres*
Noriyuki Shibata, *Vice Pres*
Masatsugu Kakitani, *Accounting Mgr*
◆ **EMP:** 54
SQ FT: 11,000
SALES (est): 21.3MM
SALES (corp-wide): 18.5B **Privately Held**
SIC: 5084 5088 0179 Industrial machine
parts; aircraft & parts; banana grove
HQ: All Nippon Airways Trading Co., Ltd.
1-5-2, Higashishimbashi
Minato-Ku TKY 105-0
367 355-011

(P-7727)
ANHEUSER-BUSCH LLC
3101 Busch Dr, Fairfield (94534-9726)
PHONE..................................707 429-7595
Kevin Finger, *Manager*
Corry Smith, *Area Mgr*
Emily Hubert, *General Mgr*
Sean Williams, *Engineer*
Steven Biasca, *Opers Mgr*
EMP: 450
SALES (corp-wide): 1.9B **Privately Held**
WEB: www.hispanicbud.com
SIC: 5084 Brewery products manufacturing
machinery, commercial
HQ: Anheuser-Busch, Llc
1 Busch Pl
Saint Louis MO 63118
314 632-6777

(P-7728)
B C RENTALS INC
Also Called: Bc Traffic Specialists
638 W Southern Ave, Orange
(92865-3219)
PHONE..................................714 974-1190
Robert Carson, *President*
Rick Webb, *General Mgr*
Sally Carson, *Admin Sec*
Carol Rodriguez, *Payroll Mgr*
John Peters, *Sales Staff*
▲ **EMP:** 75
SQ FT: 3,000
SALES: 15MM **Privately Held**
SIC: 5084 5999 7359 Safety equipment;
safety supplies & equipment; equipment
rental & leasing

(P-7729)
BAY ADVANCED TECHNOLOGIES LLC
Also Called: Bay Advanced Tech 0045
8100 Central Ave, Newark (94560-3449)
PHONE..................................510 857-0900
Mike Stimson, *Branch Mgr*
EMP: 88
SALES (est): 3B **Publicly Held**
SIC: 5084 Pneumatic tools & equipment
HQ: Bay Advanced Technologies, Llc
8100 Central Ave
Newark CA 94560
510 857-0900

(P-7730)
BEJAC CORPORATION (PA)
569 S Van Buren St, Placentia
(92870-6613)
PHONE..................................714 528-6224
Ron Barlet, *President*
Kim Smith-Grime, *CFO*
Peggy Barlet, *Treasurer*
Paline Lok, *Administration*
Adrian Vega, *Technician*
▼ **EMP:** 66 **EST:** 1953
SQ FT: 2,000
SALES (est): 41.9MM **Privately Held**
WEB: www.bejac.com
SIC: 5084 7353 Industrial machinery &
equipment; heavy construction equipment
rental

(P-7731)
BIG JOE CALIFORNIA NORTH INC (PA)
Also Called: Big Joe Handling Systems
25932 Eden Landing Rd, Hayward
(94545-3816)
PHONE..................................510 785-6900
Boyd J Kiefus, *CEO*
Rod D Kiefus, *CFO*
EMP: 125
SQ FT: 52,000
SALES (est): 95.1MM **Privately Held**
SIC: 5084 5999 7359 8331 Lift trucks &
parts; business machines & equipment;
equipment rental & leasing; job training
services

(P-7732)
BLAKE H BROWN INC (DH)
Also Called: John Tillman Company
1300 W Artesia Blvd, Compton
(90220-5307)
P.O. Box 6257 (90224-6257)
PHONE..................................310 764-0110
Blake H Brown, *CEO*
▲ **EMP:** 100
SQ FT: 25,000
SALES (est): 37.9MM
SALES (corp-wide): 11.3B **Privately Held**
WEB: www.jtillman.com
SIC: 5084 3842 3548 Safety equipment;
personal safety equipment; welding apparatus

(P-7733)
BORETECH RESRCE RECOVRY ENGINE
Also Called: Boretech Rsource Recovery
Engrg
1820 Industrial Dr, Stockton (95206-4975)
PHONE..................................209 373-2588
Jo Hua Lee, *President*
Alice KAO, *Vice Pres*
▲ **EMP:** 50
SQ FT: 68,000
SALES: 24MM **Privately Held**
SIC: 5084 2611 Recycling machinery &
equipment; pulp manufactured from
waste or recycled paper

(P-7734)
BUCKEYE FIRE EQUIPMENT COMPANY
2416 Teagarden St, San Leandro
(94577-4336)
PHONE..................................510 483-1815
Mark Libardos, *Principal*
EMP: 291
SALES (corp-wide): 99.2MM **Privately Held**
SIC: 5084 Industrial machinery & equipment

PA: Buckeye Fire Equipment Company
110 Kings Rd
Kings Mountain NC 28086
704 739-7415

(P-7735)
BUCKLES-SMITH ELECTRIC COMPANY (PA)
540 Martin Ave, Santa Clara (95050-2954)
PHONE..........................408 280-7777
Art Cook, *CEO*
Pat Berry, *Vice Pres*
Roger Stanger, *Vice Pres*
Ron Zimmerman, *Admin Sec*
Laurie Smith, *Sales Associate*
EMP: 55
SALES (est): 123.1MM **Privately Held**
WEB: www.geindustrial.com
SIC: 5084 5063 Industrial machinery & equipment; electrical supplies

(P-7736)
CAL-LIFT INC
13027 Crossroads Pkwy S, La Puente (91746-3406)
PHONE..........................562 566-1400
Mark T Maechling, *CEO*
Robert Bey, *VP Sales*
EMP: 55
SQ FT: 40,000
SALES (est): 34.6MM **Privately Held**
SIC: 5084 7699 7359 Materials handling machinery; industrial equipment services; industrial machinery & equipment repair; equipment rental & leasing

(P-7737)
CANON SOLUTIONS AMERICA INC
Also Called: Ona
15975 Alton Pkwy, Irvine (92618-3731)
PHONE..........................800 333-6395
Richard Adinolsi, *Branch Mgr*
EMP: 60
SALES (corp-wide): 36.4B **Privately Held**
WEB: www.dgs.oceusa.com
SIC: 5084 5044 Printing trades machinery, equipment & supplies; copying equipment
HQ: Canon Solutions America, Inc.
1 Canon Park
Melville NY 11747
631 330-5000

(P-7738)
CARRIER TOTALINE (PA)
205 S Puente St, Brea (92821-3828)
PHONE..........................714 578-5200
Steve Gardsmoe, *Regional Mgr*
EMP: 75
SALES (est): 10.8MM **Privately Held**
SIC: 5084 Engines & parts, air-cooled

(P-7739)
CDS MOVING EQUIPMENT INC (PA)
375 W Manville St, Rancho Dominguez (90220-5617)
PHONE..........................310 631-1100
Allen J Sidor, *President*
▲ EMP: 80
SQ FT: 100,000
SALES (est): 53.3MM **Privately Held**
WEB: www.cds-usa.com
SIC: 5084 Materials handling machinery

(P-7740)
CLARKLIFT LOS ANGELES INC
8314 Slauson Ave, Pico Rivera (90660-4323)
PHONE..........................562 949-1006
Homan C Moore, *CEO*
Tim Cleary, *President*
Homan C Moore, *CEO*
Tom Labrador, *Vice Pres*
EMP: 160
SALES (est): 13.4MM **Privately Held**
SIC: 5084 Conveyor systems; cranes, industrial; lift trucks & parts

(P-7741)
CLARKLIFT-WEST INC
Also Called: Team Power Forklift
4750 Illinois Ave, Fair Oaks (95628-6313)
PHONE..........................916 381-5674
Joe Hensler, *President*

Pete Thomas, *Vice Pres*
Dean Walker, *Vice Pres*
▲ EMP: 121
SQ FT: 50,000
SALES (est): 22.1MM **Privately Held**
WEB: www.teampowerforklift.com
SIC: 5084 7699 7359 Lift trucks & parts; materials handling machinery; industrial truck repair; industrial machinery & equipment repair; industrial truck rental

(P-7742)
CLAUDE LAVAL CORPORATION
Also Called: Lakos
1365 N Clovis Ave, Fresno (93727-2295)
P.O. Box 6119 (93703-6119)
PHONE..........................559 255-1601
Scott Marion, *CEO*
Brian Ketcham, *CFO*
Eric Arneson, *Admin Sec*
Michael Thekkumthottam, *Engineer*
Allyn Troisi, *Engineer*
◆ EMP: 90
SQ FT: 100,000
SALES (est): 74.8MM
SALES (corp-wide): 4.4MM **Privately Held**
WEB: www.lakos.com
SIC: 5084 Industrial machinery & equipment
PA: Lakos Acquisition Holdco, Llc
1365 N Clovis Ave
Fresno CA 93727
559 255-1601

(P-7743)
CONTROLCO (PA)
Also Called: Johnson Contrls Authorized Dlr
3451 Vincent Rd Ste C, Pleasant Hill (94523-7317)
PHONE..........................800 800-7126
Terry L Turner, *President*
Chip Cummins, *Vice Pres*
Jason Dewar, *Vice Pres*
Bridgette Ann T Davies, *Principal*
Mark Alexander, *Regional Mgr*
EMP: 75 EST: 1962
SQ FT: 10,000
SALES (est): 198.9MM **Privately Held**
WEB: www.controlco.com
SIC: 5084 8742 5074 Controlling instruments & accessories; automation & robotics consultant; plumbing & hydronic heating supplies

(P-7744)
CUMMINS PACIFIC LLC
14775 Wicks Blvd, San Leandro (94577-6717)
PHONE..........................510 351-6101
EMP: 270
SALES (corp-wide): 20.4B **Publicly Held**
SIC: 5084 Engines & parts, diesel
HQ: Cummins Pacific, Llc
1939 Deere Ave
Irvine CA 92606

(P-7745)
CUSTOM BILT HOLDINGS LLC
15133 Sierra Bonita Ln, Chino (91710-8904)
PHONE..........................909 664-1587
Neil Goldstein, *Manager*
EMP: 90
SALES (corp-wide): 40MM **Privately Held**
SIC: 5084 1761 Metalworking machinery; roofing contractor
PA: Custom Bilt Holdings, Llc
3001 Skyway Cir N Ste 160
Irving TX 75038
214 699-4876

(P-7746)
E & M ELECTRIC AND MCHY INC (PA)
Also Called: E&M
126 Mill St, Healdsburg (95448-4438)
PHONE..........................707 433-5578
Steven Edgar Deas, *CEO*
Scott Townsend, *Info Tech Mgr*
Daniel Nicholas, *Technical Staff*
Gabe Chamberlain, *Purchasing*
Jennifer Carroll, *Purch Agent*
▲ EMP: 50

SQ FT: 25,000
SALES (est): 75.4MM **Privately Held**
WEB: www.enm.com
SIC: 5084 5999 5063 7694 Instruments & control equipment; motors, electric; motors, electric; electric motor repair

(P-7747)
EAST BAY CLARKLIFT INC
4646 E Jensen Ave, Fresno (93725-1603)
P.O. Box 2808 (93745-2808)
PHONE..........................559 268-6621
Kerry Perez, *General Mgr*
EMP: 73
SALES (corp-wide): 40.2MM **Privately Held**
SIC: 5084 7359 7699 Materials handling machinery; equipment rental & leasing; industrial equipment services
PA: East Bay Clarklift, Inc.
4701 Oakport St
Oakland CA 94601
510 534-6566

(P-7748)
ELLISON MACHINERY CO (DH)
Also Called: Ellison Technologies
9912 Pioneer Blvd, Santa Fe Springs (90670-3257)
PHONE..........................562 949-8311
W J Ellison, *President*
Donald Bendix, *Corp Secy*
Leonard C Atkins, *Vice Pres*
Klaus Rindt, *Vice Pres*
Gary Heineman, *Area Mgr*
EMP: 75
SQ FT: 45,000
SALES (est): 76.8MM
SALES (corp-wide): 45.9B **Privately Held**
WEB: www.ellisontechnologies.com
SIC: 5084 Metalworking machinery
HQ: Ellison Technologies, Inc.
9912 Pioneer Blvd
Santa Fe Springs CA 90670
562 949-8311

(P-7749)
ELLISON TECHNOLOGIES INC
9912 Pioneer Blvd, Santa Fe Springs (90670-3250)
PHONE..........................562 949-8311
Melanie Rodriguez, *Human Res Mgr*
Howard Smith, *Manager*
EMP: 61
SALES (corp-wide): 45.9B **Privately Held**
SIC: 5084 Metalworking machinery
HQ: Ellison Technologies, Inc.
9912 Pioneer Blvd
Santa Fe Springs CA 90670
562 949-8311

(P-7750)
ESYS ENERGY CONTROL COMPANY
4520 Stine Rd Ste 7, Bakersfield (93313-2372)
PHONE..........................661 833-1902
Fabio Russoniello, *President*
Andrew Landwehr, *Design Engr*
Casey Lessley, *Project Mgr*
Koshy Varghese, *Engineer*
Andrea Prise, *Auditor*
EMP: 60
SQ FT: 12,000
SALES (est): 47MM **Privately Held**
WEB: www.esys-tecc.com
SIC: 5084 1731 Controlling instruments & accessories; electronic controls installation

(P-7751)
FARM PUMP & IRRIGATION CO INC (PA)
Also Called: F P I
535 N Shafter Ave, Shafter (93263-1900)
P.O. Box 1477 (93263-1477)
PHONE..........................661 589-6901
John Gargan, *CEO*
Kathy Gargan, *Corp Secy*
Amy Gargan, *Manager*
EMP: 60
SQ FT: 4,000
SALES (est): 22.9MM **Privately Held**
WEB: www.fpi-co.com
SIC: 5084 5083 Pumps & pumping equipment; irrigation equipment

(P-7752)
FUELING AND SERVICE TECH INC
Also Called: Fastech
7050 Village Dr Ste D, Buena Park (90621-2281)
PHONE..........................714 523-0194
M Dan McGill, *CEO*
Christine Hawley, *Vice Pres*
Glen Ragle, *Program Mgr*
Bill Dickey, *Technician*
Mark Peale, *Technician*
EMP: 75
SQ FT: 15,000
SALES (est): 59.7MM **Privately Held**
SIC: 5084 Petroleum industry machinery

(P-7753)
GENMARK AUTOMATION (DH)
46723 Lakeview Blvd, Fremont (94538-6528)
PHONE..........................510 897-3400
Yuji Shioga, *CEO*
▼ EMP: 98
SQ FT: 86,000
SALES (est): 31.6MM
SALES (corp-wide): 13.9B **Privately Held**
WEB: www.genmarkautomation.com
SIC: 5084 3674 Industrial machinery & equipment; wafers (semiconductor devices)
HQ: Nidec Sankyo Corporation
5329, Shimosuwa-Machi
Suwa-Gun NAG 393-0
266 273-111

(P-7754)
GLOBAL GROUND AUTOMATION INC
1051 E Hillsdale Blvd, Foster City (94404-1640)
PHONE..........................201 293-4900
EMP: 76
SALES (est): 1.9MM
SALES (corp-wide): 80.7MM **Privately Held**
SIC: 5084 Industrial machinery & equipment
PA: Deem, Inc.
642 Harrison St Fl 2
San Francisco CA 94107
415 590-8300

(P-7755)
HARBOR DIESEL AND EQP INC
Also Called: Diesel Parts and Service
537 W Anaheim St, Long Beach (90813-2895)
P.O. Box 21399 (90801-4399)
PHONE..........................562 591-5665
James V Zupanovich, *Ch of Bd*
Mike Zupanovich, *President*
David Hively, *CFO*
▲ EMP: 51 EST: 1971
SALES: 26.7MM **Privately Held**
WEB: www.harbordiesel.com
SIC: 5084 5531 7538 Engines & parts, diesel; truck equipment & parts; diesel engine repair: automotive

(P-7756)
INDUSTRIAL PARTS DEPOT LLC (HQ)
Also Called: Ipd
23231 Normandie Ave, Torrance (90501-5096)
PHONE..........................310 530-1900
Russell Kneipp, *President*
Mark Tu, *Information Mgr*
Dave Simpson, *Engineer*
Henry Wandrie, *Engineer*
Bruno Lucidarme, *Asst Controller*
◆ EMP: 70
SQ FT: 40,000
SALES (est): 40.1MM
SALES (corp-wide): 76MM **Privately Held**
WEB: www.ipdparts.com
SIC: 5084 3519 Engines & parts, diesel; parts & accessories, internal combustion engines
PA: Storm Industries, Inc.
23223 Normandie Ave
Torrance CA 90501
310 534-5232

▲ = Import ▼=Export
◆ =Import/Export

(P-7757)
INOXPA USA INC
3721 Santa Rosa Ave B4, Santa Rosa
(95407-8240)
PHONE.....................707 585-3900
Candi Granes Campasol, *President*
▲ **EMP:** 300
SQ FT: 1,600
SALES (est): 29.8MM **Privately Held**
SIC: 5084 Pumps & pumping equipment

(P-7758)
INTERNATIONAL THERMOPRODUCTS
11015 Mission Park Ct, Santee
(92071-5601)
PHONE.....................619 562-7001
Randall Newcomb, *Owner*
EMP: 50
SALES (est): 3.7MM **Privately Held**
SIC: 5084 3567 Heat exchange equipment, industrial; electrical furnaces, ovens & heating devices, exc. induction

(P-7759)
JA AUTOMATION & CONTROL LLC
6965 Cmino Mqladora Ste H, San Diego
(92154)
PHONE.....................619 661-2591
Jose A Fernandez, *Mng Member*
EMP: 50
SALES (est): 6.4MM **Privately Held**
SIC: 5084 Industrial machinery & equipment

(P-7760)
KENTMASTER MFG CO INC (PA)
1801 S Mountain Ave, Monrovia
(91016-4270)
PHONE.....................626 359-8888
Ralph Karubian, *CEO*
▲ **EMP:** 50
SQ FT: 50,000
SALES (est): 24.2MM **Privately Held**
WEB: www.kentmaster.com
SIC: 5084 Industrial machinery & equipment

(P-7761)
LABORATORY SPECIALTY GASES
Also Called: Westair Gas and Equipment
2506 Market St, San Diego (92102-3010)
PHONE.....................619 234-6060
Steve Castiglione, *President*
EMP: 110
SALES (est): 13.1MM **Privately Held**
SIC: 5084 Welding machinery & equipment

(P-7762)
LINDSAY TRANSPORTATION
Also Called: Lindsay Trnsp Solutions
180 River Rd, Rio Vista (94571-1208)
PHONE.....................707 374-6800
Bill Cooley, *President*
Kristel Flores,
EMP: 250
SALES (est): 30.1MM
SALES (corp-wide): 547.7MM **Publicly Held**
SIC: 5084 Safety equipment
HQ: Lindsay Transportation Solutions, Inc.
180 River Rd
Rio Vista CA 94571
707 374-6800

(P-7763)
LMC WEST INC
5300 Claus Rd, Riverbank (95367)
P.O. Box 325 (95367-0325)
PHONE.....................209 869-0144
Fax: 209 869-0258
EMP: 50
SQ FT: 50,000
SALES (est): 10.3MM
SALES (corp-wide): 2.3B **Publicly Held**
SIC: 5084
PA: Donaldson Company, Inc.
1400 W 94th St
Minneapolis MN 55431
952 887-3131

(P-7764)
LORING SMART ROAST INC
3200 Dutton Ave Ste 413, Santa Rosa
(95407-5736)
PHONE.....................707 526-7215
Mark Ludwig, *Founder*
Scott Robinson, *Mfg Dir*
Duncan Elcombe, *Sales Staff*
EMP: 54
SQ FT: 19,000
SALES (est): 12MM **Privately Held**
SIC: 5084 Food industry machinery

(P-7765)
LUFKIN INDUSTRIES LLC
31127 Coberly Rd, Shafter (93263-9702)
PHONE.....................661 746-0030
Mel Trubey, *Sales/Mktg Mgr*
EMP: 85
SALES (corp-wide): 122B **Publicly Held**
WEB: www.lufkin.com
SIC: 5084 Industrial machinery & equipment
HQ: Lufkin Industries, Llc
601 S Raguet St
Lufkin TX 75904
936 634-2211

(P-7766)
MACHINING TIME SAVERS INC
Also Called: Haas Factory Outlet
1338 S State College Pkwy, Anaheim
(92806-5241)
PHONE.....................714 635-7373
Donald Martin, *President*
EMP: 53
SQ FT: 10,000
SALES (est): 22.5MM **Privately Held**
WEB: www.mtscnc.com
SIC: 5084 7699 Machine tools & accessories; metalworking machinery; industrial machinery & equipment repair

(P-7767)
MASON-WEST INC
3910 Chapman St Ste D, San Diego
(92110-5644)
PHONE.....................619 226-8253
Joe Hastings, *Manager*
EMP: 50
SALES (corp-wide): 22MM **Privately Held**
SIC: 5084 Controlling instruments & accessories
PA: Mason-West, Inc.
1601 E Miraloma Ave
Placentia CA 92870
714 630-0701

(P-7768)
MATERIAL HANDLING SUPPLY INC (HQ)
12900 Firestone Blvd, Santa Fe Springs
(90670-5405)
PHONE.....................562 921-7715
Alexander Stephen Lynn, *CEO*
Donn C Lynn Jr, *Ch of Bd*
John Hanson, *Corp Secy*
Robert Hewitt, *Buyer*
Brian Challoner, *Manager*
EMP: 80 **EST:** 1962
SQ FT: 85,000
SALES (est): 33.8MM
SALES (corp-wide): 8MM **Privately Held**
SIC: 5084 7629 5046 Food industry machinery; engines & transportation equipment; materials handling machinery; electrical repair shops; commercial equipment
PA: Envicor
12900 Firestone Blvd
Santa Fe Springs CA 90670
562 921-7715

(P-7769)
MAXON LIFT CORPORATION
11921 Slauson Ave, Santa Fe Springs
(90670-2221)
PHONE.....................562 464-0099
Casey Lugash, *President*
Brenda Leung, *CFO*
Bill Moore, *Vice Pres*
Raymundo Sidon, *Vice Pres*
Lawrence Jones, *Administration*
▲ **EMP:** 110
SQ FT: 30,000

SALES (est): 179.7MM **Privately Held**
WEB: www.maxonlift.com
SIC: 5084 3537 3534 Lift trucks & parts; industrial trucks & tractors; elevators & moving stairways

(P-7770)
MCCAIN INC (DH)
2365 Oak Ridge Way, Vista (92081-8348)
PHONE.....................760 727-8100
Michael Schuch, *CEO*
Carl McCollum, *CFO*
Mike Trevino, *Buyer*
▲ **EMP:** 250
SQ FT: 6,700
SALES (est): 157.6MM **Privately Held**
WEB: www.mccaintraffic.com
SIC: 5084 3444 3669 Industrial machinery & equipment; sheet metalwork; traffic signals, electric
HQ: Swarco Ag
Blattenwaldweg 8
Wattens 6112
522 458-770

(P-7771)
MCGRATH RENTCORP
Also Called: Mobile Modular
5700 Las Positas Rd, Livermore
(94551-7806)
PHONE.....................877 221-2813
Kristina Vantrease, *Vice Pres*
Tom Wagoner, *Vice Pres*
Saul Kasiulionis, *Branch Mgr*
Karina Olvera, *Administration*
Mark Rowell, *Info Tech Dir*
EMP: 102
SALES (corp-wide): 462MM **Publicly Held**
SIC: 5084 7359 Measuring & testing equipment, electrical; electronic equipment rental, except computers
PA: Mcgrath Rentcorp
5700 Las Positas Rd
Livermore CA 94551
925 606-9200

(P-7772)
MCGRATH RENTCORP (PA)
5700 Las Positas Rd, Livermore
(94551-7806)
PHONE.....................925 606-9200
Joseph F Hanna, *President*
Ronald H Zech, *Ch of Bd*
Keith E Pratt, *CFO*
Randle F Rose, *Officer*
Joe Hanna, *Vice Pres*
EMP: 153 **EST:** 1979
SQ FT: 26,160
SALES: 462MM **Publicly Held**
SIC: 5084 7359 Measuring & testing equipment, electrical; electronic equipment rental, except computers

(P-7773)
MCKINLEY EQUIPMENT CORPORATION (PA)
17611 Armstrong Ave, Irvine (92614-5760)
PHONE.....................800 770-6094
W Michael Mc Kinley, *President*
Kevin Rusin, *CFO*
William White Mc Kinley, *Vice Pres*
McKinley Mark, *General Mgr*
Stephanie Porter, *Project Mgr*
▲ **EMP:** 67
SQ FT: 12,000
SALES (est): 58.4MM **Privately Held**
WEB: www.mckinleyequipment.com
SIC: 5084 Materials handling machinery

(P-7774)
MIGHTY ENTERPRISES INC
Also Called: Mighty USA
19706 Normandie Ave, Torrance
(90502-1111)
PHONE.....................310 516-7478
Peter Th Tsai, *President*
Daniel Huang, *Vice Pres*
Gloria Zuniga, *Admin Sec*
Karen Chen, *Technology*
Alana Tsai, *Human Res Mgr*
▲ **EMP:** 55
SQ FT: 18,000
SALES (est): 35.7MM **Privately Held**
SIC: 5084 Machine tools & accessories

(P-7775)
NAGRA USA INC
485 Clyde Ave, Mountain View
(94043-2245)
PHONE.....................310 335-5225
Yves Pitton, *Branch Mgr*
Henry Fang, *Engineer*
EMP: 50
SALES (corp-wide): 1B **Privately Held**
SIC: 5084 Safety equipment
HQ: Nagra Usa, Inc.
841 Apollo St Ste 300
El Segundo CA 90245

(P-7776)
NAGRA USA INC (HQ)
841 Apollo St Ste 300, El Segundo
(90245-4769)
PHONE.....................310 335-5225
Virginio Trevisan, *President*
Mark Beariault, *Admin Sec*
Paula Ward, *Admin Asst*
EMP: 85
SQ FT: 1,100
SALES (est): 57.8MM
SALES (corp-wide): 1B **Privately Held**
WEB: www.nagra.com
SIC: 5084 Safety equipment
PA: Kudelski S.A.
Route De Geneve 22-24
Cheseaux-Sur-Lausanne VD 1033
217 320-311

(P-7777)
NAN FANG DIST GROUP INC
2100 Williams St, San Leandro
(94577-3225)
PHONE.....................510 297-5382
Ze Pan, *CEO*
Zhen Poon, *Vice Pres*
▲ **EMP:** 100
SALES (est): 32.3MM **Privately Held**
SIC: 5084 Engines & parts, diesel

(P-7778)
NAUMANN/HOBBS MATERIAL
Also Called: Hawthorne Lift Systems
8575 Cherry Ave, Fontana (92335-3029)
PHONE.....................909 427-0125
Ed Gen, *Manager*
EMP: 105
SALES (corp-wide): 90MM **Privately Held**
SIC: 5084 Materials handling machinery
PA: Naumann/Hobbs Material Handling Corporation Ii, Inc.
4335 E Wood St
Phoenix AZ 85040
602 437-1331

(P-7779)
NAUMANN/HOBBS MATERIAL
Also Called: Hawthorne Lift Systems
1600 E Mission Rd, San Marcos
(92069-4564)
PHONE.....................858 207-6274
Jim Ventors, *Branch Mgr*
Maria Armendariz, *COO*
Jim Venters, *Branch Mgr*
Kelly Arneman, *Administration*
Dan Kennedy, *Technician*
EMP: 105
SALES (corp-wide): 90MM **Privately Held**
SIC: 5084 Materials handling machinery
PA: Naumann/Hobbs Material Handling Corporation Ii, Inc.
4335 E Wood St
Phoenix AZ 85040
602 437-1331

(P-7780)
NIKON PRECISION INC (DH)
1399 Shoreway Rd, Belmont (94002-4107)
PHONE.....................650 508-4674
Toyohiro Takamine, *CEO*
Takao Naito, *President*
Hamid Zarringhalam, *Exec VP*
Bill Cole, *Associate Dir*
David Mahan, *Comp Lab Dir*
▲ **EMP:** 250
SQ FT: 30,000

SALES (est): 212.5MM
SALES (corp-wide): 6.7B **Privately Held**
WEB: www.nikonprecision.com
SIC: 5084 5065 Industrial machinery & equipment; electronic parts & equipment

(P-7781)
ONLINE ENERGY LLC
Also Called: Online Energy Uv Systems
20885 Redwood Rd Unit 405, Castro Valley (94546-5915)
PHONE......................510 583-0091
Craig Blair, *Mng Member*
Bill Hoagland, *Principal*
EMP: 50
SALES (est): 12MM **Privately Held**
SIC: 5084 8711 Industrial machinery & equipment; consulting engineer

(P-7782)
OTIS ELEVATOR COMPANY
2701 Media Center Dr # 2, Los Angeles (90065-1700)
PHONE......................323 342-4500
Marcus Burten, *Manager*
EMP: 50
SALES (corp-wide): 59.8B **Publicly Held**
WEB: www.otis.com
SIC: 5084 Elevators
HQ: Otis Elevator Company
1 Carrier Pl
Farmington CT 06032
860 674-3000

(P-7783)
PAPE MATERIAL HANDLING INC
47132 Kato Rd, Fremont (94538-7333)
PHONE......................510 659-4100
Ken Mader, *Branch Mgr*
Chris Wetle, *President*
Jordan Pape, *CEO*
EMP: 80
SQ FT: 37,536
SALES (corp-wide): 626.5MM **Privately Held**
SIC: 5084 8743 7359 5082 Materials handling machinery; sales promotion; stores & yards equipment rental; contractors' materials
HQ: Pape' Material Handling, Inc.
355 Goodpasture Island Rd
Eugene OR 97401
541 683-5073

(P-7784)
POWELL WORKS INC
17807 Maclaren St Ste B, La Puente (91744-5700)
PHONE......................909 861-6699
Jerry Wang, *President*
▲ **EMP:** 256
SQ FT: 2,500
SALES (est): 18.8MM **Privately Held**
SIC: 5084 Compressors, except air conditioning

(P-7785)
POWER GENERATION ENTPS INC
11411 Cumpston St Ste 104, North Hollywood (91601-2674)
PHONE......................818 484-8550
Vartan Seropian, *CEO*
Victor Seropian, *Sales Staff*
EMP: 110
SALES (est): 23.2MM **Privately Held**
SIC: 5084 Industrial machinery & equipment

(P-7786)
PRAXAIR INC
2677 Signal Pkwy, Long Beach (90755-2260)
PHONE......................562 427-0099
Mike Alives, *Manager*
Roy Beattie, *VP Sales*
EMP: 60
SALES (corp-wide): 11.4B **Privately Held**
SIC: 5084 Welding machinery & equipment
PA: Praxair, Inc.
10 Riverview Dr
Danbury CT 06810
203 837-2000

(P-7787)
PROGAUGE TECHNOLOGIES INC
2331 Cepheus Ct, Bakersfield (93308-6944)
P.O. Box 1312 (93302-1312)
PHONE......................661 392-9600
Donald C Nelson, *CEO*
Danny B Henderson, *Admin Sec*
EMP: 50
SQ FT: 9,000
SALES (est): 16MM **Privately Held**
SIC: 5084 Industrial machinery & equipment

(P-7788)
PROVOAST AUTOMATION CONTROLS (PA)
12635 Danielson Ct # 205, Poway (92064-8806)
PHONE......................858 748-2237
Mitch Provoast, *President*
Kathy Provoast, *Treasurer*
Ron Mayhew, *Vice Pres*
EMP: 100
SQ FT: 5,000
SALES (est): 33MM **Privately Held**
WEB: www.proautocon.com
SIC: 5084 5085 Industrial machinery & equipment; valves & fittings

(P-7789)
QUINN LIFT INC
Also Called: Caterpillar Authorized Dealer
1300 Abbott St, Salinas (93901-4507)
P.O. Box 1908 (93902-1908)
PHONE......................831 758-4086
Mike Gularte, *Manager*
EMP: 68
SALES (corp-wide): 455MM **Privately Held**
WEB: www.altalift.net
SIC: 5084 Industrial machinery & equipment
HQ: Quinn Lift, Inc.
10273 S Golden State Blvd
Selma CA 93662

(P-7790)
R B INTERNATIONAL INC (PA)
Also Called: Rbi Bearings
13450 Brooks Dr Ste B, Baldwin Park (91706-2202)
PHONE......................626 357-7652
Rubien Hao Chen, *CEO*
Mike Kenney, *Vice Pres*
James Watkins, *VP Mktg*
Tina Tucci, *Manager*
▲ **EMP:** 50
SQ FT: 30,000
SALES (est): 12.1MM **Privately Held**
SIC: 5084 5085 Industrial machine parts; bearings

(P-7791)
R F MACDONALD CO (PA)
25920 Eden Landing Rd, Hayward (94545-3816)
PHONE......................510 784-0110
Michael D Macdonald, *Co-President*
James T Macdonald, *President*
Don Patten, *Vice Pres*
Chris Sentner, *Vice Pres*
Robert Sygiel, *Vice Pres*
EMP: 153
SQ FT: 25,000
SALES (est): 103MM **Privately Held**
SIC: 5084 7699 5074 Pumps & pumping equipment; industrial machinery & equipment repair; boilers, power (industrial)

(P-7792)
RAYMOND HANDLING SOLUTIONS INC (DH)
9939 Norwalk Blvd, Santa Fe Springs (90670-3321)
P.O. Box 3683 (90670-1683)
PHONE......................562 944-8067
James Wilcox, *CEO*
Adrian Castelan, *District Mgr*
Mike Slater, *District Mgr*
James Thomas, *District Mgr*
Edwin Funes, *Admin Asst*
EMP: 111

SQ FT: 5,000
SALES (est): 124.5MM
SALES (corp-wide): 18.8B **Privately Held**
SIC: 5084 7699 7359 Materials handling machinery; industrial machinery & equipment repair; industrial truck rental
HQ: The Raymond Corporation
22 S Canal St
Greene NY 13778
607 656-2311

(P-7793)
RAYMOND HANDLING SOLUTIONS INC
4602 E Brickell St, Ontario (91761-1573)
PHONE......................909 930-9399
James Wilcox, *President*
EMP: 83
SALES (corp-wide): 18.8B **Privately Held**
SIC: 5084 Materials handling machinery
HQ: Raymond Handling Solutions, Inc.
9939 Norwalk Blvd
Santa Fe Springs CA 90670
562 944-8067

(P-7794)
RJMS CORPORATION (PA)
Also Called: Toyota Material Hdlg Nthrn Cal
6999 Southfront Rd, Livermore (94551-8221)
PHONE......................510 675-0500
Richard Andres, *CEO*
Mark Andres, *Vice Pres*
Stephen Andres, *Vice Pres*
Gregg Robinson, *Branch Mgr*
Timo Soeganda, *Administration*
▲ **EMP:** 100
SQ FT: 45,000
SALES (est): 120.9MM **Privately Held**
WEB: www.tmhnc.com
SIC: 5084 5085 7699 Materials handling machinery; industrial supplies; industrial machinery & equipment repair

(P-7795)
RKI INSTRUMENTS INC (PA)
Also Called: R K I
33248 Central Ave, Union City (94587-2010)
PHONE......................510 441-5656
Robert Pellissier, *President*
Sandra Gallagher, *Vice Pres*
Leanne Walden, *Admin Asst*
Steve Peluffo, *Technical Mgr*
Michael Jeter, *Technology*
◆ **EMP:** 55
SQ FT: 10,000
SALES (est): 26.3MM **Privately Held**
WEB: www.rkiinstruments.com
SIC: 5084 3823 Industrial machinery & equipment; on-stream gas/liquid analysis instruments, industrial

(P-7796)
SIEMENS INDUSTRY INC
25821 Industrial Blvd # 300, Hayward (94545-2919)
PHONE......................510 783-6000
John P Nichols, *Manager*
EMP: 150
SALES (corp-wide): 97.7B **Privately Held**
WEB: www.sibt.com
SIC: 5084 Instruments & control equipment
HQ: Siemens Industry, Inc.
100 Technology Dr
Alpharetta GA 30005
770 740-3000

(P-7797)
SIEMENS INDUSTRY INC
9835 Carroll Ctre Rd 10, San Diego (92126)
PHONE......................858 693-8711
Majd Khleis, *Manager*
Dietsch Michael, *Sales Executive*
Richard Slubowski, *Accounts Exec*
EMP: 75
SQ FT: 3,300

SALES (corp-wide): 97.7B **Privately Held**
WEB: www.sibt.com
SIC: 5084 1711 3822 3825 Pneumatic tools & equipment; mechanical contractor; auto controls regulating residntl & coml environmt & applncs; instruments to measure electricity; industrial instrmnts msrmnt display/control process variable
HQ: Siemens Industry, Inc.
100 Technology Dr
Alpharetta GA 30005
770 740-3000

(P-7798)
SIGNODE INDUSTRIAL GROUP LLC
Also Called: Down River
3901 Navone Rd, Stockton (95215-9311)
PHONE......................209 931-0917
E Scott Santi, *Branch Mgr*
EMP: 92
SALES (corp-wide): 8.7B **Publicly Held**
SIC: 5084 Packaging machinery & equipment
HQ: Signode Industrial Group Llc
3650 W Lake Ave
Glenview IL 60026
847 724-7500

(P-7799)
SMC CORPORATION OF AMERICA
2841 Junction Ave Ste 110, San Jose (95134-1921)
PHONE......................408 943-9600
Joe Hanna, *Manager*
Jason Cristobal, *Sales Mgr*
Kathryn Prater, *Sales Mgr*
EMP: 50
SALES (corp-wide): 5.5B **Privately Held**
WEB: www.smcusa.com
SIC: 5084 Pneumatic tools & equipment
HQ: Smc Corporation Of America
10100 Smc Blvd
Noblesville IN 46060
317 899-4440

(P-7800)
SOUTHERN CALIFORNIA MTL HDLG
Also Called: Southern Calif Mtl Hdlg Co
19755 Bahama St, Northridge (91324-3304)
PHONE......................805 650-6000
Toni Edgar, *Manager*
EMP: 65
SALES (corp-wide): 38.5B **Privately Held**
WEB: www.scmh.com
SIC: 5084 Materials handling machinery
HQ: Southern California Material Handling Inc
12393 Slauson Ave
Whittier CA 90606
562 949-1006

(P-7801)
SOUTHERN CALIFORNIA MTL HDLG
8124 Deering Ave, Canoga Park (91304-5013)
PHONE......................818 349-1220
S Handling, *Branch Mgr*
EMP: 61
SALES (corp-wide): 38.5B **Privately Held**
SIC: 5084 Conveyor systems
HQ: Southern California Material Handling Inc
12393 Slauson Ave
Whittier CA 90606
562 949-1006

(P-7802)
SOUTHERN CALIFORNIA MTL HDLG (DH)
Also Called: Scmh
12393 Slauson Ave, Whittier (90606-2824)
P.O. Box 80770, San Marino (91118-8770)
PHONE......................562 949-1006
Tim Cleary, *President*
Mike Wolfe, *COO*
Alfred Gallegos, *General Mgr*
Margaret Antonelli, *Admin Asst*
Cindy Bautista, *Controller*
▲ **EMP:** 140

SALES (est): 51.2MM
SALES (corp-wide): 38.5B **Privately Held**
WEB: www.scmh.com
SIC: **5084** Conveyor systems; materials handling machinery

(P-7803)
SOUTHWEST MATERIAL HDLG INC (PA)
Also Called: Southwest Toyota Lift
3725 Nobel Ct, Mira Loma (91752-3267)
P.O. Box 1070 (91752-8070)
PHONE.............................951 727-0477
Kirt Little, *CEO*
Joseph G Little, *President*
▲ EMP: 115
SQ FT: 10,000
SALES (est): 47.8MM **Privately Held**
SIC: **5084** 7389 7699 7359 Lift trucks & parts; design, commercial & industrial; industrial machinery & equipment repair; equipment rental & leasing; building site preparation

(P-7804)
SSTMAS Y ARANDA EQPOS HDRLICOS
280 Campillo St Ste L, Calexico (92231-3200)
PHONE.............................619 245-4502
Armando Aranda, *President*
Carlos Verdugo, *Principal*
Roberto Pena, *Director*
EMP: 50
SALES: 15MM **Privately Held**
SIC: **5084** Hydraulic systems equipment & supplies
PA: Aranda Sistemas Y Equipos Hidraulicos, S. De R.L. De C.V.
Blvd. Lazaro Cardenas No. 1159
Mexicali B.C. 21190

(P-7805)
STAINLESS STL FABRICATORS INC
Also Called: Cook King
15120 Desman Rd, La Mirada (90638-5737)
PHONE.............................714 739-9904
Craig Miller, *President*
Glenna Miller, *CFO*
Dave Hart, *Vice Pres*
EMP: 60
SQ FT: 11,204
SALES (est): 23.4MM **Privately Held**
SIC: **5084** 3444 Industrial machinery & equipment; restaurant sheet metalwork

(P-7806)
SUPERIOR MACHINING MFG CO INC
322 Oak Pl, Brea (92821-4135)
PHONE.............................714 529-6000
Hussein Suheimat, *CEO*
EMP: 100
SALES (est): 10.2MM **Privately Held**
SIC: **5084** Industrial machinery & equipment

(P-7807)
SUPPLYPRO INC (PA)
Also Called: Supply Pro
9401 Waples St Ste 150, San Diego (92121-3919)
PHONE.............................858 587-6400
Floyd Miller, *CEO*
Michael Reynolds, *Officer*
Justin Dass, *Vice Pres*
Stan Signman, *Vice Pres*
◆ EMP: 60
SQ FT: 28,000
SALES (est): 48.5MM **Privately Held**
SIC: **5084** Industrial machinery & equipment

(P-7808)
SURFACE PUMPS INC (PA)
3301 Unicorn Rd, Bakersfield (93308-6852)
P.O. Box 5757 (93388-5757)
PHONE.............................661 393-1545
Steven J Durrett, *President*
Marty Rushing, *Corp Secy*
David Cook, *Vice Pres*

Carly Collins, *Human Resources*
Dennis Wren, *Sales Staff*
EMP: 51
SQ FT: 14,000
SALES (est): 57MM **Privately Held**
SIC: **5084** 7699 8711 3519 Pumps & pumping equipment; pumps & pumping equipment repair; engineering services; parts & accessories, internal combustion engines

(P-7809)
THYSSENKRUPP ELEVATOR CORP
14400 Catalina St, San Leandro (94577-5516)
PHONE.............................510 476-1900
Ed Persico, *Manager*
EMP: 100
SALES (corp-wide): 48.7B **Privately Held**
WEB: www.thyssenkruppelevator.com
SIC: **5084** 1796 3534 Elevators; elevator installation & conversion; elevators & moving stairways
HQ: Thyssenkrupp Elevator Corporation
11605 Haynes Bridge Rd # 650
Alpharetta GA 30009
678 319-3240

(P-7810)
THYSSENKRUPP ELEVATOR CORP
30984 Santana St, Hayward (94544-7058)
PHONE.............................510 476-1900
Homer Guerra, *Principal*
EMP: 50
SALES (corp-wide): 48.7B **Privately Held**
SIC: **5084** Elevators
HQ: Thyssenkrupp Elevator Corporation
11605 Haynes Bridge Rd # 650
Alpharetta GA 30009
678 319-3240

(P-7811)
THYSSENKRUPP ELEVATOR CORP
2850 N California St, Burbank (91504-2560)
PHONE.............................818 847-2568
Christina Siebold, *Manager*
EMP: 58
SALES (corp-wide): 48.7B **Privately Held**
WEB: www.tyssenkrupp.com
SIC: **5084** Elevators
HQ: Thyssenkrupp Elevator Corporation
11605 Haynes Bridge Rd # 650
Alpharetta GA 30009
678 319-3240

(P-7812)
TOYOTALIFT INC (PA)
1850 John Towers Ave, El Cajon (92020-1134)
P.O. Box 710280, Santee (92072-0280)
PHONE.............................619 562-5438
Garland Pierce, *CEO*
Sheila Sison, *General Mgr*
Alice Pierce, *Admin Sec*
Norma Caro, *Human Resources*
Armando Hernandez, *Sales Mgr*
▲ EMP: 50 EST: 1976
SALES (est): 38.8MM **Privately Held**
WEB: www.toyotaliftinc.com
SIC: **5084** 7359 Materials handling machinery; equipment rental & leasing

(P-7813)
TRI TOOL INC (PA)
3041 Sunrise Blvd, Rancho Cordova (95742-6502)
PHONE.............................916 288-6100
George J Wernette III, *CEO*
George J Wernette, *President*
Chris Soriano, *CFO*
Thomas Emmerling, *Regional Mgr*
Greg Fontes, *Regional Mgr*
▲ EMP: 163 EST: 1972
SQ FT: 125,000
SALES (est): 99.2MM **Privately Held**
WEB: www.tritool.com
SIC: **5084** 3548 3541 Industrial machinery & equipment; welding apparatus; pipe cutting & threading machines

(P-7814)
UNICO MECHANICAL CORP
1209 Polk St, Benicia (94510-2906)
P.O. Box 847 (94510-0847)
PHONE.............................707 745-4540
Michael Potter, *President*
Randy Potter, *President*
Michael Guthrie, *CFO*
Tom Clougher, *Info Tech Mgr*
Amy Sterry, *Controller*
▲ EMP: 80
SQ FT: 80,000
SALES (est): 49.9MM **Privately Held**
WEB: www.unicomechanical.com
SIC: **5084** 7699 Industrial machinery & equipment; industrial machinery & equipment repair

(P-7815)
UTILITY TRLR SLS OF CENTL CAL
2680 S East Ave, Fresno (93706-5400)
P.O. Box 11845 (93775-1845)
PHONE.............................559 237-2001
Michael Sutherland, *Manager*
EMP: 50
SALES (corp-wide): 35.5MM **Privately Held**
WEB: www.utilitycc.com
SIC: **5084** Trailers, industrial
PA: Utility Trailer Sales Of Central California, Inc
2680 S East Ave
Lathrop CA 95330
209 444-8800

(P-7816)
VALIN CORPORATION (PA)
1941 Ringwood Ave, San Jose (95131-1721)
PHONE.............................408 730-9850
Joseph C Nettemeyer, *CEO*
John Pregenzer, *COO*
David Hefler, *CFO*
Ray Herrera, *Vice Pres*
Dan Colletto, *VP Bus Dvlpt*
◆ EMP: 96
SQ FT: 66,850
SALES (est): 3.5MM **Privately Held**
WEB: www.valinonline.com
SIC: **5084** Materials handling machinery; processing & packaging equipment

(P-7817)
VALLEY POWER SYSTEMS INC
Also Called: Valley Detriot Diesel
4000 Rosedale Hwy, Bakersfield (93308-6131)
PHONE.............................661 325-9001
Ken Relyea, *Branch Mgr*
EMP: 50
SALES (corp-wide): 181.2MM **Privately Held**
WEB: www.valleypowersystems.com
SIC: **5084** Engines & parts, diesel
PA: Valley Power Systems, Inc.
425 S Hacienda Blvd
City Of Industry CA 91745
626 333-1243

(P-7818)
VERITIV OPERATING COMPANY
Also Called: International Paper
7337 Las Positas Rd, Livermore (94551-5110)
PHONE.............................925 245-6075
EMP: 151
SALES (corp-wide): 8.3B **Publicly Held**
SIC: **5084** Processing & packaging equipment; printing trades machinery, equipment & supplies
HQ: Veritiv Operating Company
1000 Abernathy Rd
Atlanta GA 30328
770 391-8200

(P-7819)
WASSER FILTRATION INC
Also Called: Force Measurement Systems
1215 N Fee Ana St, Anaheim (92807-1804)
PHONE.............................714 525-0630
Greg Stewart, *Vice Pres*
EMP: 70

SALES (corp-wide): 18.4MM **Privately Held**
WEB: www.pacpress.com
SIC: **5084** Industrial machinery & equipment
PA: Wasser Filtration, Inc.
1215 N Fee Ana St
Anaheim CA 92807
714 982-5600

(P-7820)
WESTAIR GASES & EQUIPMENT INC
2300 Haffley Ave, National City (91950-6419)
PHONE.............................619 474-0079
Pat Dalton, *Branch Mgr*
EMP: 60
SALES (corp-wide): 69.2MM **Privately Held**
WEB: www.westairgases.com
SIC: **5084** Welding machinery & equipment
PA: Westair Gases & Equipment, Inc.
2506 Market St
San Diego CA 92102
866 937-8247

(P-7821)
WESTAIR GASES & EQUIPMENT INC (PA)
Also Called: San Diego Welders Supply
2506 Market St, San Diego (92102-3010)
P.O. Box 131902 (92170-1902)
PHONE.............................866 937-8247
Andrew J Castiglione, *CEO*
Steve Castiglione, *President*
Tim Van Linge, *CFO*
Sue Castiglione, *Corp Secy*
Mike Fuette, *Vice Pres*
EMP: 50 EST: 1970
SQ FT: 10,000
SALES (est): 69.2MM **Privately Held**
WEB: www.westairgases.com
SIC: **5084** Welding machinery & equipment

(P-7822)
YALE/CHASE EQP & SVCS INC (PA)
2615 Pellissier Pl, City of Industry (90601-1508)
P.O. Box 1231, La Puente (91749-1231)
PHONE.............................562 463-8000
Roger Ketelsleger, *President*
James Douglas Graven, *CFO*
Teresa Abando, *Officer*
Michael Ketelsleger, *Vice Pres*
Jana Ketelsleger, *Administration*
◆ EMP: 116
SQ FT: 33,000
SALES: 94.9MM **Privately Held**
WEB: www.yalechase.com
SIC: **5084** 7699 7359 Lift trucks & parts; industrial machinery & equipment repair; industrial truck rental

(P-7823)
ZEMARC CORPORATION (PA)
6431 Flotilla St, Commerce (90040-1597)
PHONE.............................323 721-5598
Viren Patel, *CEO*
Dave Manzi, *President*
Abdul Zeke Zahid, *Founder*
Irma K Zahid, *Vice Pres*
Irma Zahid, *Vice Pres*
EMP: 50
SQ FT: 50,000
SALES (est): 30.7MM **Privately Held**
SIC: **5084** Hydraulic systems equipment & supplies; pneumatic tools & equipment

---

5085 Industrial Splys Wholesale

(P-7824)
ACHEM INDUSTRY AMERICA INC (PA)
13226 Alondra Blvd, Cerritos (90703-2237)
PHONE.............................562 802-0998
Joseph Lin, *CEO*
Shin Pai Kuei, *President*
Bob Kuminski, *Natl Sales Mgr*
Serena Lu, *Sales Dir*
Edgar Contreras, *Regl Sales Mgr*

▲ **EMP:** 50
SQ FT: 48,000
SALES (est): 31.6MM **Privately Held**
WEB: www.achem.com
SIC: 5085 Industrial supplies

(P-7825)
ADCO CONTAINER COMPANY
9959 Canoga Ave, Chatsworth
(91311-3090)
PHONE..................818 998-2565
Fax: 818 998-3648
EMP: 50
SQ FT: 24,000
SALES (est): 12.2MM **Privately Held**
WEB: www.adcocontainer.com
SIC: 5085 7336

(P-7826)
ALLIED HIGH TECH PRODUCTS INC
2376 E Pacifica Pl, Rancho Dominguez
(90220-6214)
P.O. Box 4608, Compton (90224-4608)
PHONE..................310 635-2466
Robert C Smith, *Ch of Bd*
Clayton A Smith, *President*
Shirley A Smith, *Corp Secy*
Eddie Padilla, *General Mgr*
Betsy Oconnell, *Human Res Mgr*
▲ **EMP:** 70
SQ FT: 34,000
SALES (est): 71.2MM **Privately Held**
WEB: www.alliedhightech.com
SIC: 5085 Abrasives

(P-7827)
AMERICAN INDUSTRIAL SUPPLY
9817 Variel Ave, Chatsworth (91311-4317)
PHONE..................818 841-7788
Robert Nadler, *President*
Thelma Nadler, *Admin Sec*
EMP: 53
SQ FT: 15,000
SALES (est): 13MM **Privately Held**
SIC: 5085 Industrial supplies

(P-7828)
ARC FASTENER SUPPLY & MFG
Also Called: A R C Fastener Supply
2104 Wembley Ln, Corona (92881-7441)
PHONE..................909 481-8171
Joseph Myers, *President*
Christie Rockwood, *Controller*
▲ **EMP:** 78
SQ FT: 70,000
SALES (est): 13.4MM **Privately Held**
WEB: www.arcfasteners.com
SIC: 5085 5072 Fasteners, industrial:
nuts, bolts, screws, etc.; hardware

(P-7829)
ARCONIC GLOBAL FAS & RINGS INC
Also Called: Arconic Fstening Systems Rings
135 N Unruh Ave, City of Industry
(91744-4427)
PHONE..................626 968-3831
Hatty Ao, *Director*
Kelly Liao, *Engineer*
Morgan Gantt, *Maintence Staff*
George Cameron, *Manager*
Steve Martin, *Manager*
EMP: 350
SQ FT: 58,400
SALES (corp-wide): 12.9B **Publicly Held**
WEB: www.alcoafasteners.com
SIC: 5085 Fasteners & fastening equipment
HQ: Arconic Global Fasteners & Rings, Inc.
3990a Heritage Oak Ct
Simi Valley CA 93063
805 527-3600

(P-7830)
ARCONIC GLOBAL FAS & RINGS INC
Also Called: Arconic Fstening Systems Rings
3000 Lomita Blvd, Torrance (90505-5103)
PHONE..................310 784-0700
Kenneth Paine, *Manager*
Roberto Christensen, *Engineer*
Karen Harlan, *Human Res Mgr*
Gwen Moore, *Human Res Mgr*

David Lawton, *Maintence Staff*
EMP: 60
SALES (corp-wide): 12.9B **Publicly Held**
WEB: www.alcoafasteners.com
SIC: 5085 Fasteners & fastening equipment
HQ: Arconic Global Fasteners & Rings, Inc.
3990a Heritage Oak Ct
Simi Valley CA 93063
805 527-3600

(P-7831)
ARCONIC GLOBAL FAS & RINGS INC
Also Called: Arconic Fstening Systems Rings
3014 Lomita Blvd, Torrance (90505-5103)
PHONE..................310 530-2220
Oliver Jarraolt, *President*
EMP: 500
SALES (corp-wide): 12.9B **Publicly Held**
WEB: www.alcoafasteners.com
SIC: 5085 Industrial supplies
HQ: Arconic Global Fasteners & Rings, Inc.
3990a Heritage Oak Ct
Simi Valley CA 93063
805 527-3600

(P-7832)
ARCONIC GLOBAL FAS & RINGS INC (HQ)
Also Called: Arconic Fastening Systems
3990a Heritage Oak Ct, Simi Valley
(93063-6715)
PHONE..................805 527-3600
Olivier Jarrault, *President*
▲ **EMP:** 120
SQ FT: 37,000
SALES (est): 1.6B
SALES (corp-wide): 12.9B **Publicly Held**
WEB: www.alcoafasteners.com
SIC: 5085 5072 5065 Fasteners & fastening equipment; hardware; electronic parts & equipment
PA: Arconic Inc.
390 Park Ave Fl 12
New York NY 10022
212 836-2758

(P-7833)
ARCONIC GLOBAL FAS & RINGS INC
Also Called: Arconic Fstening Systems Rings
800 S State College Blvd, Fullerton
(92831-5334)
PHONE..................714 871-1550
Craig Brown, *Manager*
Joe Crumpler, *Info Tech Mgr*
Mario Barrientos, *Engineer*
Virginia Camarillo, *Engineer*
Michael Caton, *Engineer*
EMP: 100
SQ FT: 153,604
SALES (corp-wide): 12.9B **Publicly Held**
WEB: www.alcoafasteners.com
SIC: 5085 Fasteners & fastening equipment
HQ: Arconic Global Fasteners & Rings, Inc.
3990a Heritage Oak Ct
Simi Valley CA 93063
805 527-3600

(P-7834)
ARCONIC GLOBAL FAS & RINGS INC
Also Called: Arconic Fstening Systems Rings
3000 Lomita Blvd, Torrance (90505-5103)
PHONE..................310 530-2220
William Hart, *Director*
EMP: 50
SALES (corp-wide): 12.9B **Publicly Held**
SIC: 5085 Industrial supplies
HQ: Arconic Global Fasteners & Rings, Inc.
3990a Heritage Oak Ct
Simi Valley CA 93063
805 527-3600

(P-7835)
ARCONIC GLOBAL FAS & RINGS INC
Also Called: Arconic Fstening Systems Rings
3018 Lomita Blvd, Torrance (90505-5103)
PHONE..................310 530-2220
Melanie Brooks, *Branch Mgr*
EMP: 1000

SALES (corp-wide): 12.9B **Publicly Held**
WEB: www.alcoafasteners.com
SIC: 5085 Fasteners & fastening equipment
HQ: Arconic Global Fasteners & Rings, Inc.
3990a Heritage Oak Ct
Simi Valley CA 93063
805 527-3600

(P-7836)
ARIES FILTERWORKS
13850 Van Ness Ave, Gardena
(90249-2476)
PHONE..................323 262-1600
Jeffrey Gottlieb, *President*
▲ **EMP:** 50
SQ FT: 20,000
SALES (est): 4MM **Privately Held**
SIC: 5085 Filters, industrial

(P-7837)
BAY STANDARD INC
24485 Marsh Creek Rd, Brentwood
(94513-4319)
P.O. Box 801 (94513-0801)
PHONE..................925 634-1181
Gary W Landgraf, *President*
Karen Landgraf, *Corp Secy*
Tom Landgraf, *Vice Pres*
▲ **EMP:** 100
SALES (est): 13MM **Privately Held**
SIC: 5085 3965 Fasteners & fastening equipment; fasteners

(P-7838)
BEACON ROOFING SUPPLY INC
8501 Telfair Ave, Sun Valley (91352-3928)
PHONE..................818 768-4661
EMP: 60
SALES (corp-wide): 4.3B **Publicly Held**
SIC: 5085 5169 Industrial supplies; sealants
PA: Beacon Roofing Supply, Inc.
505 Huntmar Park Dr # 300
Herndon VA 20170
571 323-3939

(P-7839)
BEARING ENGINEERS INC (PA)
Also Called: Motion Solutions
27 Argonaut, Aliso Viejo (92656-1423)
PHONE..................949 586-7442
Harold Lee Katz, *President*
Harold Lee Lee, *CEO*
Henry Kim, *Vice Pres*
Wallis Logan, *Vice Pres*
▲ **EMP:** 57
SQ FT: 22,000
SALES (est): 32MM **Privately Held**
WEB: www.bearingengineers.com
SIC: 5085 Bearings

(P-7840)
BELL PIPE & SUPPLY CO
215 E Ball Rd, Anaheim (92805-6394)
P.O. Box 151 (92815-0151)
PHONE..................714 772-3200
Franklin M Bell III, *CEO*
Kristin C Bell, *Corp Secy*
Ariel Vigo, *Admin Asst*
Jeff Hightower, *Purchasing*
Larry Harper, *Sales Associate*
▲ **EMP:** 50 **EST:** 1956
SQ FT: 35,000
SALES (est): 58.4MM **Privately Held**
WEB: www.bellpipe.com
SIC: 5085 Valves & fittings

(P-7841)
BOSSARD NORTH AMERICA INC
2000 Chabot Ct, Tracy (95304-8841)
PHONE..................562 906-2003
Brent Wright, *Branch Mgr*
EMP: 68 **Privately Held**
SIC: 5085 Fasteners, industrial: nuts, bolts, screws, etc.; tools
HQ: Bossard North America, Inc.
6521 Production Dr
Cedar Falls IA 50613
319 277-5520

(P-7842)
BOYD CORPORATION
Also Called: Specialty Sealing
4990 E Hunter Ave, Anaheim (92807-2057)
PHONE..................714 777-5995
Mitch Aiello, *Manager*
EMP: 144
SALES (corp-wide): 12.2MM **Privately Held**
SIC: 5085 Seals, industrial
PA: The Boyd Corporation
5832 Ohio St
Yorba Linda CA 92886
714 533-2375

(P-7843)
CENTRAL PURCHASING LLC (PA)
Also Called: Harbor Freight Tools
26541 Agoura Rd, Calabasas
(91302-2093)
P.O. Box 6010, Camarillo (93011-6010)
PHONE..................805 388-1000
Eric L Smidt, *CEO*
Robert Rene, *COO*
Christopher Gurtcheff, *Vice Pres*
Donovan Johnson, *Area Mgr*
Rodrigo Munoz, *Area Mgr*
▼ **EMP:** 500
SQ FT: 277,000
SALES (est): 2.6B **Privately Held**
WEB: www.harborfreight.com
SIC: 5085 5961 5251 Tools; tools & hardware; mail order; tools

(P-7844)
CRANE CO
3201 Walnut Ave, Long Beach
(90755-5225)
PHONE..................562 426-2531
Kevin McKown, *Manager*
Ajay Nayyar, *Manager*
EMP: 110
SALES (corp-wide): 2.7B **Publicly Held**
WEB: www.craneco.com
SIC: 5085 Valves & fittings
PA: Crane Co.
100 1st Stamford Pl # 300
Stamford CT 06902
203 363-7300

(P-7845)
DAILY SAW SERVICE INC
4481 Firestone Blvd, South Gate
(90280-3320)
P.O. Box 3458, Fullerton (92834-3458)
PHONE..................323 564-1791
Robert Daily, *President*
Greg R Daily, *CEO*
▲ **EMP:** 50
SQ FT: 65,000
SALES (est): 23.5MM **Privately Held**
SIC: 5085 7699 3546 Knives, industrial; industrial machinery & equipment repair; saws & sawing equipment

(P-7846)
DB ROBERTS INC
880 Avenida Acaso Ste 100, Camarillo
(93012-8721)
PHONE..................805 988-4882
Mark Harris, *Vice Pres*
EMP: 52
SALES (corp-wide): 84.8MM **Privately Held**
WEB: www.dbroberts.com
SIC: 5085 Fasteners, industrial: nuts, bolts, screws, etc.
PA: D.B. Roberts, Inc.
30 Upton Dr Ste 3
Wilmington MA 01887
978 988-5777

(P-7847)
DHV INDUSTRIES INC
3451 Pegasus Dr, Bakersfield
(93308-6827)
PHONE..................661 392-8948
Tingchun Huang, *President*
Ross Dillon, *Sr Exec VP*
Eric Lingle, *Vice Pres*
Sonny Simmons, *Vice Pres*
Sam Lingle, *Sales Staff*
◆ **EMP:** 52
SQ FT: 180,000

SALES (est): 15MM **Privately Held**
WEB: www.dhvindustries.com
SIC: **5085** 3491 Valves & fittings; industrial valves

(P-7848)
G W MAINTENANCE INC (PA)
Also Called: Petroquip
1101 E 6th St, Santa Ana (92701-4912)
PHONE.....................714 541-2211
Kami Keshmiri, *President*
Barry F Branin, *Ch of Bd*
Vivian Branin, *Treasurer*
EMP: 59
SQ FT: 24,000
SALES (est): 7.4MM **Privately Held**
WEB: www.gwmaintenance.com
SIC: **5085** 5084 Valves & fittings; gas equipment, parts & supplies; instruments & control equipment; hoists; pumps & pumping equipment

(P-7849)
GENERAL TOOL INC
Also Called: Gt Diamond
2025 Alton Pkwy, Irvine (92606-4904)
PHONE.....................949 261-2322
Jae Woo Kim, *CEO*
Jae Kim, *Engineer*
Juan Montejano, *Regl Sales Mgr*
Steve Rimmer, *Regl Sales Mgr*
▲ EMP: 90
SQ FT: 40,000
SALES (est): 26.8MM **Privately Held**
WEB: www.gtdiamond.com
SIC: **5085** Diamonds, industrial: natural, crude

(P-7850)
GRISWOLD INDUSTRIES
Also Called: Griswald Industries
24100 Water Ave, Perris (92570-6738)
PHONE.....................951 657-1718
Fred Zimmer, *Manager*
EMP: 55
SQ FT: 25,000
SALES (corp-wide): 115MM **Privately Held**
SIC: **5085** 3494 Valves & fittings; valves & pipe fittings
PA: Griswold Industries
    1701 Placentia Ave
    Costa Mesa CA 92627
    949 722-4800

(P-7851)
INDUSTRIAL CONTAINER SERVICES
Also Called: Ics-CA North
749 Galleria Blvd, Roseville (95678-1331)
PHONE.....................916 781-2775
Charles Veniez, *CEO*
Gerald Butler,
Alain G Magnan,
Kay Rykowski,
Calvin G Lee, *Mng Member*
EMP: 52
SQ FT: 10,000
SALES: 15.3MM
SALES (corp-wide): 1.1B **Privately Held**
WEB: www.capitaldrum.com
SIC: **5085** 2655 Commercial containers; fiber cans, drums & similar products
HQ: Industrial Container Services Llc
    2600 Mtland Ctr Pkwy 20 # 200
    Maitland FL 32751
    407 930-4182

(P-7852)
INDUSTRIAL VALCO INC (PA)
3135 E Ana St, Compton (90221-5606)
PHONE.....................310 635-0711
Rob C Raban, *President*
Eddie Lujan, *Branch Mgr*
Annette Rodriguez, *Administration*
Lisa Preston, *Accounting Mgr*
Michael Kasper, *Sales Associate*
▲ EMP: 50
SQ FT: 62,000
SALES (est): 37MM **Privately Held**
WEB: www.industrialvalco.com
SIC: **5085** 3498 Valves & fittings; pipe fittings, fabricated from purchased pipe

(P-7853)
KAMAN INDUSTRIAL TECH CORP
910 S Wanamaker Ave, Ontario (91761-8151)
PHONE.....................909 390-7919
Tom Serafin, *Branch Mgr*
Mick Horne, *Manager*
EMP: 50
SALES (corp-wide): 1.8B **Publicly Held**
SIC: **5085** Bearings
HQ: Kaman Industrial Technologies Corporation
    1 Vision Way
    Bloomfield CT 06002
    860 687-5000

(P-7854)
KIRKHILL RUBBER COMPANY
2500 E Thompson St, Long Beach (90805-1836)
PHONE.....................562 803-1117
David Schlothauer, *President*
Edward Reker, *President*
EMP: 99
SALES (est): 7.5MM
SALES (corp-wide): 1.4B **Privately Held**
SIC: **5085** Rubber goods, mechanical
HQ: Hexpol Holding Inc.
    14330 Kinsman Rd
    Burton OH 44021
    440 834-4644

(P-7855)
LEWIS-GOETZ AND COMPANY INC
Also Called: Valley Rubber & Gasket
10182 Croydon Way, Sacramento (95827-2102)
PHONE.....................916 366-9340
Les A Shively, *CEO*
Debbie Herbers, *Technology*
Brian Vigil, *Mktg Dir*
Todd Brenneman, *Sales Staff*
EMP: 98 **Privately Held**
SIC: **5085** 3053 3052 Hose, belting & packing; gaskets & seals; gaskets, packing & sealing devices; rubber & plastics hose & beltings
HQ: Eriks North America, Inc.
    650 Washington Rd Ste 500
    Pittsburgh PA 15228
    800 937-9070

(P-7856)
LINEAR INDUSTRIES LTD (PA)
1850 Enterprise Way, Monrovia (91016-4271)
PHONE.....................626 303-1130
Anthony Dell Angelica, *President*
Jean Cade, *Manager*
Savonia Angelica, *Vice Pres*
▲ EMP: 62
SQ FT: 45,000
SALES (est): 30MM **Privately Held**
WEB: www.linearindustries.com
SIC: **5085** 3625 5065 5072 Bearings; positioning controls, electric; electronic parts; hardware; power transmission equipment; machine tool accessories

(P-7857)
LONESTAR SIERRA LLC
1820 W Orangewood Ave, Orange (92868-2043)
PHONE.....................866 575-5680
David Wood,
EMP: 225
SALES: 15MM **Privately Held**
SIC: **5085** Refractory material

(P-7858)
MECHANICAL DRIVES CO (PA)
Also Called: L A Rubber Co
2915 E Washington Blvd, Los Angeles (90023-4218)
P.O. Box 23910 (90023-0910)
PHONE.....................323 263-4131
Michael Durst, *CEO*
T Wayne Gehan, *CEO*
David Durst, *Vice Pres*
EMP: 54
SQ FT: 33,000

SALES (est): 27MM **Privately Held**
SIC: **5085** Bearings; gears; power transmission equipment & apparatus

(P-7859)
MILLENNIA STAINLESS INC
10016 Romandel Ave, Santa Fe Springs (90670-3424)
PHONE.....................562 946-3545
Ching-PO LI, *CEO*
Lisa Chen, *Accounting Mgr*
▲ EMP: 75
SQ FT: 10,500
SALES (est): 26.2MM
SALES (corp-wide): 573.4MM **Privately Held**
SIC: **5085** 5065 5051 Industrial supplies; coils, electronic; steel
PA: Chain Chon Industrial Co., Ltd.
    178, Ta Guan Rd.,
    Taoyuan City TAY 33753
    338 569-85

(P-7860)
MITSUBISHI MATERIALS USA CORP (HQ)
11250 Slater Ave, Fountain Valley (92708-5421)
PHONE.....................714 352-6100
Motoharu Yamamoto, *CEO*
Niro Odani, *Corp Secy*
Kevin Caldwell, *District Mgr*
Kent Deisher, *District Mgr*
Doug Feldt, *District Mgr*
◆ EMP: 50
SQ FT: 55,000
SALES (est): 63.7MM
SALES (corp-wide): 15B **Privately Held**
SIC: **5085** 5084 Industrial tools; machine tools & accessories
PA: Mitsubishi Materials Corporation
    1-3-2, Otemachi
    Chiyoda-Ku TKY 100-0
    352 525-200

(P-7861)
MT SUPPLY INC (DH)
Also Called: Machine Tools Supply
3505 Cadillac Ave Ste K2, Costa Mesa (92626-1432)
PHONE.....................800 938-6658
George H Ponce Jr, *CEO*
Joseph Custer, *Principal*
Steve Gurley, *Principal*
Steve Pixley, *Principal*
George Ponce, *General Mgr*
EMP: 163
SALES (est): 195.9MM
SALES (corp-wide): 2.6B **Publicly Held**
SIC: **5085** 5084 Industrial supplies; materials handling machinery
HQ: Dnow L.P.
    7402 N Eldridge Pkwy
    Houston TX 77041
    281 823-4700

(P-7862)
PACIFIC COAST DRUM COMPANY
Also Called: Gene's Cooperage
2200 Rosemead Blvd 2204, El Monte (91733-1520)
P.O. Box 3593 (91733-0593)
PHONE.....................626 443-3096
Darryl Bartolotti, *President*
Gene Bartolotti, *Ch of Bd*
EMP: 80 EST: 1961
SQ FT: 50,000
SALES: 11.5MM **Privately Held**
SIC: **5085** Drums, new or reconditioned

(P-7863)
PACIFIC ECHO INC
23540 Telo Ave, Torrance (90505-4098)
PHONE.....................310 539-1822
Yasuo Ogami, *CEO*
▲ EMP: 90
SQ FT: 110,000
SALES (est): 36.1MM
SALES (corp-wide): 2.4MM **Privately Held**
WEB: www.pacificecho.com
SIC: **5085** Hose, belting & packing

HQ: Kakuichi Co., Ltd.
    1415, Midoricho, Tsuruga
    Nagano NAG 380-0
    262 346-111

(P-7864)
PRH PRO INC
13089 Peyton Dr Ste C362, Chino Hills (91709-6018)
PHONE.....................714 510-7226
Wayman Bill Peng, *President*
EMP: 161
SQ FT: 2,000
SALES: 100MM **Privately Held**
SIC: **5085** Cooperage stock

(P-7865)
PRINTING TECHNOLOGY INC
Also Called: Pti
21001 Nordhoff St, Chatsworth (91311-5911)
PHONE.....................818 576-9220
Peter De Salay, *President*
Julian Desalay, *Vice Pres*
Tim Purugganan, *Vice Pres*
Claudia Cruz, *Cust Mgr*
▲ EMP: 160
SQ FT: 89,000
SALES (est): 39.3MM **Privately Held**
WEB: www.ptiimaging.com
SIC: **5085** 5111 Ink, printers'; printing trades machinery, equipment & supplies; printing paper

(P-7866)
PROGRESSIVE TRNSP SVCS INC
19500 S Alameda St, Compton (90221-6204)
PHONE.....................510 268-3776
Edgar Tafolla, *Branch Mgr*
EMP: 56 **Privately Held**
SIC: **5085** Commercial containers
PA: Progressive Transportation Services, Llc
    1360 W Pacific Coast Hwy
    Long Beach CA 90810
    -

(P-7867)
ROPE PARTNER INC
125 Mcpherson St Ste B, Santa Cruz (95060-5883)
PHONE.....................831 460-9448
Eric Stanfield, *President*
Chris Bley, *Founder*
Grant Deitchman, *Technician*
Alberto Mancera, *Project Mgr*
Aliyah Nance, *Controller*
EMP: 65
SQ FT: 1,900
SALES: 950K **Privately Held**
WEB: www.ropepartner.com
SIC: **5085** Rope, cord & thread

(P-7868)
RUTLAND TOOL & SUPPLY CO (HQ)
Also Called: MSC Metalworking
2225 Workman Mill Rd, City of Industry (90601-1437)
PHONE.....................562 566-5000
Thomas J Neri, *CEO*
Andrew Verey, *President*
▲ EMP: 140
SALES (est): 27.6MM **Publicly Held**
SIC: **5085** 5251 Industrial supplies; tools

(P-7869)
S & S TOOL & SUPPLY INC (PA)
Also Called: S and S Supplies and Solutions
2700 Maxwell Way, Fairfield (94534-9708)
P.O. Box 1111, Martinez (94553-0111)
PHONE.....................925 313-0360
Tracy Tomkovicz, *CEO*
Tanya Powell, *CFO*
Charles Fromm, *QA Dir*
Phil Jones, *Info Tech Mgr*
Jarred Henry, *Technology*
▲ EMP: 100
SQ FT: 90,000

SALES: 153.2MM **Privately Held**
WEB: www.sns-tool.com
SIC: 5085 7699 5072 7359 Industrial tools; industrial equipment services; tool repair services; hand tools; power handtools; equipment rental & leasing; tool rental

(P-7870)
SEGUIN MREAU NAPA COPERAGE INC
Also Called: Fine Northern Oak
151 Camino Dorado, NAPA (94558-6213)
PHONE..........................707 252-3408
Nicolas Mahler-Besse, *Principal*
◆ **EMP:** 57
SQ FT: 40,000
SALES (est): 15.5MM **Privately Held**
SIC: 5085 2449 Barrels, new or reconditioned; barrels, wood: coopered
PA: Seguin Moreau Holdings Inc
151 Camino Dorado
Napa CA 94558
-

(P-7871)
SO CAL SANDBAGS INC
12620 Bosley Ln, Corona (92883-6358)
PHONE..........................951 277-3404
Peter Rasinski, *President*
Dennis Feidner, *General Mgr*
Wanda Chavez, *Controller*
Lynn Hamblin, *Manager*
EMP: 100
SALES (est): 54.1MM **Privately Held**
WEB: www.socalsandbags.com
SIC: 5085 5999 Industrial supplies; safety supplies & equipment

(P-7872)
SOLAR LINK INTERNATIONAL INC
4652 E Brickell St Ste A, Ontario (91761-1593)
P.O. Box 56, San Dimas (91773-0056)
PHONE..........................909 605-7789
Johnny Tsai, *Vice Pres*
▲ **EMP:** 218 **EST:** 1998
SALES (est): 55.5MM **Privately Held**
SIC: 5085 Industrial supplies

(P-7873)
STEVEN ENGINEERING INC
230 Ryan Way, South San Francisco (94080-6370)
PHONE..........................650 588-9200
Bonnie A Walter, *CEO*
Kenneth D Walter, *President*
Bryan J Woifgram, *Exec VP*
Bryan Wolfgram, *Exec VP*
Paul E Burk III, *Vice Pres*
◆ **EMP:** 110
SQ FT: 66,000
SALES (est): 145.6MM **Privately Held**
WEB: www.stevenengineering.com
SIC: 5085 Industrial supplies

(P-7874)
SUNNYVALE FLUID SYS TECH INC
Also Called: Swagelok Northern California
3393 W Warren Ave, Fremont (94538-6424)
P.O. Box 14470 (94539-1170)
PHONE..........................510 933-2500
Rod Fallow, *CEO*
Ian Lahaye, *Executive*
Alan Barker, *Purchasing*
Victor Jung, *Cust Mgr*
Morgan Zealear, *Manager*
EMP: 50
SQ FT: 14,000
SALES (est): 24.3MM **Privately Held**
WEB: www.sunnyvale.swagelok.com
SIC: 5085 3492 Valves & fittings; fluid power valves & hose fittings

(P-7875)
TCT CIRCUIT SUPPLY INC
560 S Melrose St, Placentia (92870-6327)
PHONE..........................714 644-9700
Ian Hemmings, *President*
Kathy Chen, *Principal*
Amie Chien Chien, *Principal*
EMP: 55

SALES (est): 1.8MM **Privately Held**
SIC: 5085 Tools

(P-7876)
VAT INCORPORATED (DH)
655 River Oaks Pkwy, San Jose (95134-1907)
PHONE..........................781 935-1446
Andrew Witken, *President*
Robert Campbell, *President*
Simon Mansbridge, *President*
Brian J Darcy, *Treasurer*
Sean Gentry, *Vice Pres*
▲ **EMP:** 50
SALES (est): 13.2MM
SALES (corp-wide): 700.3MM **Privately Held**
WEB: www.vat.com
SIC: 5085 7699 3491 Valves & fittings; valve repair, industrial; industrial valves
HQ: Vat Holding Ag
Seelistrasse 1
Haag (Rheintal) SG
817 716-161

(P-7877)
WEST-SPEC PARTNERS
20525 Nordhoff St Ste 42, Chatsworth (91311-6135)
PHONE..........................818 725-7000
Dave Kukanek, *Partner*
EMP: 50
SALES (est): 4.8MM **Privately Held**
WEB: www.vertexdistribution.com
SIC: 5085 Fasteners & fastening equipment

(P-7878)
WW GRAINGER INC
4700 Hamner Ave, Eastvale (91752-1018)
PHONE..........................951 727-2300
Brian Williams, *Opers-Prdtn-Mfg*
EMP: 220
SQ FT: 20,000
SALES (corp-wide): 10.4B **Publicly Held**
WEB: www.grainger.com
SIC: 5085 Industrial supplies
PA: W.W. Grainger, Inc.
100 Grainger Pkwy
Lake Forest IL 60045
847 535-1000

5087 Service Establishment Eqpt & Splys Wholesale

(P-7879)
AMERICAN SANITARY SUPPLY INC
Also Called: American Chemical & Sanitary
592 Explorer St, Brea (92821-3108)
P.O. Box 6436, Anaheim (92816-0436)
PHONE..........................714 632-3010
Luis Salazar, *CEO*
Silvia Salazar, *Vice Pres*
▲ **EMP:** 50
SQ FT: 20,000
SALES: 15MM **Privately Held**
SIC: 5087 Cleaning & maintenance equipment & supplies

(P-7880)
ANIXTER INC
7140 Opportunity Rd, San Diego (92111-2202)
PHONE..........................800 854-2088
Marshall Merrifield, *Branch Mgr*
EMP: 76
SALES (corp-wide): 7.9B **Publicly Held**
WEB: www.clarksecurity.com
SIC: 5087 Locksmith equipment & supplies
HQ: Anixter Inc.
2301 Patriot Blvd
Glenview IL 60026
800 323-8167

(P-7881)
ARROW USA
1105 Highland Ct, Beaumont (92223-7091)
PHONE..........................951 845-6144
Sam Chang, *President*
Zuhair Klenzi, *President*
Wen Zhang, *Treasurer*

S Kalanzeh, *Vice Pres*
Susan Chen, *Director*
EMP: 75
SQ FT: 3,000
SALES: 500MM **Privately Held**
SIC: 5087 Beauty salon & barber shop equipment & supplies

(P-7882)
BEAUTITUDES BEAUTY SUPPLY LLC
7850 White Ln Ste E, Bakersfield (93309-7699)
PHONE..........................800 830-6076
Jaime Hecht, *President*
EMP: 51 **EST:** 2015
SQ FT: 1,500
SALES (est): 3.7MM **Privately Held**
SIC: 5087 Beauty salon & barber shop equipment & supplies

(P-7883)
BENEX LLC
169 Saxony Rd Ste 111, Encinitas (92024-6779)
PHONE..........................310 675-6200
Vim Dutt,
EMP: 62
SALES (est): 996.5K **Privately Held**
SIC: 5087

(P-7884)
CHIRO INC (PA)
Also Called: Mr Clean Maintenance Systems
2260 S Vista Ave, Bloomington (92316-2908)
P.O. Box 31, Colton (92324-0031)
PHONE..........................909 879-1160
Arthur Rose, *President*
Timothy Russell, *Vice Pres*
Jenni Fischer, *Office Mgr*
Denise Peters, *Human Res Dir*
Duane Chandler, *Sales Mgr*
EMP: 68
SQ FT: 10,000
SALES (est): 79.2MM **Privately Held**
WEB: www.mrcleansystems.com
SIC: 5087 7349 5169 Cleaning & maintenance equipment & supplies; cleaning service, industrial or commercial; chemicals & allied products

(P-7885)
CSE HOLDINGS INC (DH)
650 Brennan St, San Jose (95131-1204)
PHONE..........................408 436-1907
Gary Fredkin, *President*
Marvin Wenger, *COO*
Ronaldo Erazo, *Accounts Mgr*
▲ **EMP:** 100
SQ FT: 64,000
SALES (est): 140.9MM
SALES (corp-wide): 100.9B **Publicly Held**
WEB: www.cleansource.com
SIC: 5087 5084 7699 5113 Janitors' supplies; cleaning equipment, high pressure, sand or steam; industrial machinery & equipment repair; industrial & personal service paper; packaging materials; office supplies
HQ: Interline Brands, Inc.
701 San Marco Blvd
Jacksonville FL 32207
904 421-1400

(P-7886)
FISHMAN SUPPLY COMPANY
1345 Industrial Ave, Petaluma (94952-6500)
P.O. Box 750279 (94975-0279)
PHONE..........................707 763-8161
Leland Fishman, *President*
Valerie Gossage, *Corp Secy*
Andrew Fishman, *Vice Pres*
Julie Fishman, *Vice Pres*
John Tully, *General Mgr*
EMP: 52
SQ FT: 26,000
SALES (est): 12.9MM **Privately Held**
WEB: www.fishmansupply.com
SIC: 5087 5113 5112 Janitors' supplies; shipping supplies; office filing supplies

(P-7887)
HYDRO TEK SYSTEMS INC
2353 Almond Ave, Redlands (92374-2035)
PHONE..........................909 799-9222
John S Koen, *President*
Andrea S Koen, *Admin Sec*
◆ **EMP:** 63
SQ FT: 45,000
SALES (est): 14MM
SALES (corp-wide): 1.2B **Privately Held**
WEB: www.hydroteksystems.com
SIC: 5087 3589 5084 Service establishment equipment; commercial cleaning equipment; industrial machinery & equipment
HQ: Nilfisk A/S
Kornmarksvej 1
BRondby 2605
721 821-20

(P-7888)
JWDANGELO COMPANY INC
601 S Harbor Blvd, La Habra (90631-6187)
P.O. Box 3744 (90632-3744)
PHONE..........................562 690-1000
John W D Angelo, *CEO*
Jack Giguere, *Vice Pres*
Cathy Lite, *Vice Pres*
Shannon Smith, *Admin Asst*
Rodney Gifford, *Info Tech Mgr*
EMP: 50
SQ FT: 35,000
SALES (est): 17.3MM **Privately Held**
WEB: www.jwdangelo.com
SIC: 5087 Firefighting equipment

(P-7889)
LN CURTIS AND SONS (PA)
1800 Peralta St, Oakland (94607-1609)
P.O. Box 60000, San Francisco (94160-0001)
PHONE..........................510 839-5111
Paul F Curtis, *CFO*
John Viboch, *Treasurer*
Jeff Curtis, *Vice Pres*
Tim Henderson, *Vice Pres*
Troy Garside, *Branch Mgr*
▲ **EMP:** 65
SQ FT: 25,000
SALES (est): 70.1MM **Privately Held**
SIC: 5087 5099 Firefighting equipment; safety equipment & supplies

(P-7890)
NAIL EMPORIUM
Also Called: Nail Emporium Beauty Supply
1221 N Lakeview Ave, Anaheim (92807-1830)
PHONE..........................714 779-9889
James George, *Owner*
EMP: 50
SQ FT: 41,000
SALES (est): 2.5MM **Privately Held**
SIC: 5087 5122 Beauty parlor equipment & supplies; cosmetics, perfumes & hair products

(P-7891)
NIKKEN GLOBAL INC (HQ)
2 Corporate Park Ste 100, Irvine (92606-5103)
PHONE..........................949 789-2000
Tom Toshizo Watanabe, *Ch of Bd*
Kendall Cho, *President*
Ruth Ann Bellino, *Accountant*
▲ **EMP:** 155
SQ FT: 213,000
SALES (est): 35.4MM
SALES (corp-wide): 57.1MM **Privately Held**
SIC: 5087 5023 5013 5122 Stress reducing equipment, electric; bedspreads; seat covers; vitamins & minerals; long distance telephone communications
PA: Nikken International, Inc.
2 Corporate Park Ste 200
Irvine CA 92606
949 789-2000

(P-7892)
O P I PRODUCTS INC (HQ)
13034 Saticoy St, North Hollywood (91605-3510)
PHONE..........................818 759-8688
Jules Kaufman, *CEO*
John Heffner, *President*

Eric Schwartz, *COO*
William Halfacre, *Exec VP*
Susan Weiss-Fischmann, *Exec VP*
◆ **EMP:** 500
SQ FT: 250,000
SALES (est): 321.4MM **Publicly Held**
SIC: 5087 2844 Beauty parlor equipment & supplies; toilet preparations

(P-7893)
PAGE FRONT CATERING
Also Called: Pacific Dining Food Svc MGT
34793 Ardentech Ct, Fremont (94555-3657)
P.O. Box 32761, San Jose (95152-2761)
PHONE.....................408 406-8487
Richard McMahon, *Owner*
EMP: 57
SALES (est): 4.6MM **Privately Held**
SIC: 5087 5812 7389 Vending machines & supplies; caterers; coffee service

(P-7894)
PUREBEAUTY INC
Also Called: Pure Beauty-A Freeman Company
32920 Alvarado Niles Rd # 220, Union City (94587-8102)
PHONE.....................510 477-7950
Jeno Reynoso, *General Mgr*
EMP: 50 **Privately Held**
WEB: www.embarcaderoshop.com
SIC: 5087 Beauty parlor equipment & supplies
HQ: Purebeauty, Inc.
10610 E 26th Cir N
Wichita KS 67226
888 232-8891

(P-7895)
PWS INC (PA)
12020 Garfield Ave, South Gate (90280-7823)
PHONE.....................323 721-8832
Morton E Pollack, *Chairman*
Brad Pollack, *President*
Eric Steinberg, *CEO*
▲ **EMP:** 51
SQ FT: 50,000
SALES (est): 51.8MM **Privately Held**
WEB: www.pwslaundry.com
SIC: 5087 Laundry equipment & supplies

(P-7896)
PWS HOLDINGS LLC
6500 Flotilla St, Commerce (90040-1714)
PHONE.....................323 721-8832
Morton Pollack, *Mng Member*
Victoria Vela, *Vice Pres*
Galen Buckley, *Info Tech Mgr*
Eric Steinberg, *CEO*
EMP: 125
SALES (est): 10.4MM **Privately Held**
WEB: www.pwsholdings.com
SIC: 5087 Laundry equipment & supplies

(P-7897)
RASHMAN CORPORATION
Also Called: Uniform Accessories
8600 Wilbur Ave, Northridge (91324-4438)
PHONE.....................818 993-3030
Richard Rashman, *CEO*
Roger Rashman, *Vice Pres*
Brian Spangenberg, *Executive*
Catalina Parocua, *Purch Agent*
Cathi Eicher, *Director*
▲ **EMP:** 65 **EST:** 1969
SQ FT: 50,000
SALES (est): 17.6MM **Privately Held**
WEB: www.neve.com
SIC: 5087 Service establishment equipment

(P-7898)
SPILO WORLDWIDE INC
233 Wilshire Blvd Ste 400, Santa Monica (90401-1214)
PHONE.....................213 687-8600
Ann Spilo, *CEO*
Marc Spilo, *Owner*
▲ **EMP:** 100
SQ FT: 24,000
SALES (est): 31.1MM **Privately Held**
SIC: 5087 Beauty parlor equipment & supplies; barber shop equipment & supplies

(P-7899)
SWEIS INC (PA)
23760 Hawthorne Blvd, Torrance (90505-5906)
PHONE.....................310 375-0558
Karl Sweis, *President*
Theresa Sweis, *Vice Pres*
Tanya Del Pozzo, *Consultant*
EMP: 125
SQ FT: 4,200
SALES (est): 23.3MM **Privately Held**
WEB: www.sweisinc.com
SIC: 5087 2844 Beauty parlor equipment & supplies; hair preparations, including shampoos

(P-7900)
UNITED FABRICARE SUPPLY INC (PA)
1237 W Walnut St, Compton (90220-5009)
P.O. Box 1796, Los Angeles (90001-0796)
PHONE.....................310 886-3790
Steve S Hong, *CEO*
Hae S Hong, *Corp Secy*
Mike Fahar, *Exec VP*
Kirby Schnebly, *Exec VP*
W David Weimer, *Exec VP*
▲ **EMP:** 75
SQ FT: 50,000
SALES (est): 43.5MM **Privately Held**
WEB: www.unitedfabricaresupply.com
SIC: 5087 Laundry & dry cleaning equipment & supplies

(P-7901)
WAXIES ENTERPRISES INC
905 Wineville Ave, Ontario (91764-5595)
P.O. Box 5926, San Bernardino (92412)
PHONE.....................909 942-3100
Jeff Roberts, *General Mgr*
Duke Ordaz, *COO*
EMP: 115
SALES (corp-wide): 322.3MM **Privately Held**
WEB: www.waxie.com
SIC: 5087 Janitors' supplies
PA: Waxie's Enterprises, Inc.
9353 Waxie Way
San Diego CA 92123
800 995-4466

(P-7902)
WAXIES ENTERPRISES INC
901 N Canyon Pkwy, Livermore (94551)
PHONE.....................925 454-2900
John Bielenberg, *General Mgr*
Matt Lacivita, *Opers Mgr*
Tiffany McLaughlin, *Consultant*
EMP: 50
SALES (corp-wide): 322.3MM **Privately Held**
WEB: www.waxie.com
SIC: 5087 Janitors' supplies
PA: Waxie's Enterprises, Inc.
9353 Waxie Way
San Diego CA 92123
800 995-4466

(P-7903)
WINCO INDUSTRIES COMPANY
Also Called: Winco Dwl Industries Co
14950 Valley View Ave, La Mirada (90638-5224)
PHONE.....................562 926-5600
David LI, *President*
Lilly Song, *Purch Mgr*
Angela Black, *Traffic Mgr*
Bob Burzin, *Natl Sales Mgr*
Lucy Martinez,
▲ **EMP:** 50 **EST:** 2008
SALES (est): 9.2MM **Privately Held**
SIC: 5087 Restaurant supplies

(P-7904)
WORLDWIDE INTGRTED RSURCES INC
7171 Telegraph Rd, Montebello (90640-6511)
PHONE.....................323 838-8938
Fred Morad, *President*
Sina Salamat, *CFO*
Susan Morad, *Admin Sec*
◆ **EMP:** 60
SQ FT: 20,000

SALES (est): 9.7MM **Privately Held**
WEB: www.wwir.com
SIC: 5087 Cleaning & maintenance equipment & supplies

5088 Transportation Eqpt & Splys, Except Motor Vehicles Wholesale

(P-7905)
AIREY ENTERPRISES LLC
Also Called: A Transportation
5530 Corbin Ave Ste 325, Tarzana (91356-6037)
P.O. Box 17328, Encino (91416-7328)
PHONE.....................818 530-3362
Latasha George, *Owner*
EMP: 50
SALES (est): 4.5MM **Privately Held**
SIC: 5088 5147 7361 Transportation equipment & supplies; meats & meat products; labor contractors (employment agency)

(P-7906)
APICAL INDUSTRIES INC
Also Called: Dart Aerospace
3030 Enterprise Ct Ste A, Vista (92081-8358)
PHONE.....................760 724-5300
Alain Madore, *CEO*
Daniela Delarosa, *Office Mgr*
Lisa Mansfield, *Project Mgr*
Steve Montgomery, *Engineer*
David Barker, *Senior Engr*
EMP: 100
SQ FT: 30,000
SALES (est): 46.3MM **Privately Held**
WEB: www.apicalindustries.com
SIC: 5088 3728 Helicopter parts; aircraft landing assemblies & brakes
HQ: Dart Aerospace Ltd
1270 Aberdeen St
Hawkesbury ON K6A 1
613 632-5200

(P-7907)
KIRKHILL AIRCRAFT PARTS CO (PA)
Also Called: Proponent
3120 Enterprise St, Brea (92821-6236)
PHONE.....................714 223-5400
Andrew Todhunter, *President*
Scott Joynt, *President*
Steven Frields, *CFO*
Rita Mould, *Vice Pres*
Stephen Scott, *Program Mgr*
▲ **EMP:** 175
SQ FT: 177,000
SALES (est): 182MM **Privately Held**
WEB: www.kapcovaltec.com
SIC: 5088 3728 Aircraft & parts; aircraft parts & equipment

(P-7908)
KIRKHILL AIRCRAFT PARTS CO
3101 Enterprise St, Brea (92821-6237)
PHONE.....................714 223-5400
EMP: 67
SALES (corp-wide): 182MM **Privately Held**
SIC: 5088 Aircraft & parts
PA: Kirkhill Aircraft Parts Co.
3120 Enterprise St
Brea CA 92821
714 223-5400

(P-7909)
KLX INC
Also Called: Klx Aerospace Solutions
1351 Charles Willard St, Carson (90746-4023)
PHONE.....................310 900-1300
Chris Caudana, *Branch Mgr*
Sherry Hancock, *Sales Dir*
EMP: 246
SALES (corp-wide): 93.3B **Publicly Held**
SIC: 5088 Aircraft equipment & supplies
HQ: Klx Inc.
1300 Corp Ctr Way Ste 200
Wellington FL 33414
561 383-5100

(P-7910)
LJ WALCH CO INC
6600 Preston Ave, Livermore (94551-5132)
P.O. Box 2798 (94551-2798)
PHONE.....................925 449-9252
Ron Luty, *CEO*
Tony Ippolito, *President*
Mark Nelson, *Senior VP*
Bill Luty, *Vice Pres*
Tom Walch, *Vice Pres*
▲ **EMP:** 60
SQ FT: 38,500
SALES (est): 24.5MM **Privately Held**
WEB: www.ljwalch.com
SIC: 5088 7629 Aircraft & parts; aircraft electrical equipment repair

(P-7911)
LOGISTICAL SUPPORT LLC
Also Called: RTC Aerospace
20409 Prairie St, Chatsworth (91311-6029)
PHONE.....................818 341-3344
Joseph Lucan,
William Hart, *Vice Pres*
Jerry Hill, *Vice Pres*
EMP: 120
SQ FT: 14,600
SALES (est): 9.7MM
SALES (corp-wide): 2.2MM **Privately Held**
WEB: www.logisticalsupport.com
SIC: 5088 Aircraft & parts
PA: Rtc Aerospace Llc
7215 45th Street Ct E
Fife WA 98424
918 407-0291

(P-7912)
ONTIC ENGINEERING AND MFG INC (HQ)
20400 Plummer St, Chatsworth (91311-5372)
P.O. Box 2424 (91313-2424)
PHONE.....................818 678-6555
Greth Hall, *CEO*
Peg Billson, *President*
Nicole Perez, *Program Mgr*
Bryan Kalfus, *Office Mgr*
Jesilin Hoffmann, *Admin Asst*
EMP: 269
SQ FT: 54,000
SALES (est): 143.6MM
SALES (corp-wide): 2.3B **Privately Held**
SIC: 5088 3728 3812 Aircraft equipment & supplies; aircraft parts & equipment; search & navigation equipment
PA: Bba Aviation Plc
105 Wigmore Street
London W1U 1
207 514-3999

(P-7913)
PACIFIC CONTOURS CORPORATION (PA)
5340 E Hunter Ave, Anaheim (92807-2053)
PHONE.....................714 693-1260
Michael Rapacz, *CEO*
Tim Anderson, *CFO*
EMP: 60
SQ FT: 32,000
SALES: 18MM **Privately Held**
WEB: www.pacificcontours.com
SIC: 5088 3728 Aircraft & parts; aircraft assemblies, subassemblies & parts

(P-7914)
SHIMADZU PRECISION INSTRS INC (DH)
Also Called: Shimadzu Medical Systems USA
3645 N Lakewood Blvd, Long Beach (90808-1797)
PHONE.....................562 420-6226
Yutaka Nakamura, *CEO*
Koki Aoyama, *President*
Atsushi Nishizaki, *President*
Akira Watanabe, *President*
▲ **EMP:** 70
SQ FT: 60,000
SALES (est): 167.9MM
SALES (corp-wide): 3.5B **Privately Held**
WEB: www.spi-inc.com
SIC: 5088 5047 5084 Aircraft equipment & supplies; medical equipment & supplies; industrial machinery & equipment

(P-7915)
STRECH PLASTICS INCORPORATED
900 John St Ste J, Banning (92220-6204)
PHONE..................951 922-2224
James M Strech, *CEO*
James Strech, *CEO*
Jim Underwood, *Info Tech Dir*
Ray Strech, *Analyst*
Sherrie Shaw, *Accountant*
▲ EMP: 50
SQ FT: 52,000
SALES (est): 22.8MM **Privately Held**
WEB: www.strechplastics.com
SIC: 5088 3949 Golf carts; sporting & athletic goods

(P-7916)
TPS AVIATION INC (PA)
1515 Crocker Ave, Hayward (94544-7038)
PHONE..................510 475-1010
George Sozaburo Kujiraoka, *CEO*
Chris Ybarra, *Info Tech Mgr*
Jane Milanes, *Controller*
David Lim, *Purch Mgr*
Kevin Suyeyasu, *Purch Mgr*
◆ EMP: 107
SQ FT: 58,700
SALES (est): 85.3MM **Privately Held**
WEB: www.tpsaviation.com
SIC: 5088 5065 3728 Aircraft & parts; aircraft engines & engine parts; aircraft equipment & supplies; guided missiles & space vehicles; electronic parts; aircraft parts & equipment

(P-7917)
UNICAL AVIATION INC (PA)
680 S Lemon Ave, City of Industry (91789-2934)
PHONE..................909 348-1700
Han Tan, *President*
Fred Goetschel, *President*
Mercy Tan, *CFO*
Leonard Karsana, *Exec VP*
Phil Arroyo, *Vice Pres*
▲ EMP: 190
SQ FT: 480,000
SALES (est): 144.6MM **Privately Held**
WEB: www.unical.com
SIC: 5088 Aircraft & parts

(P-7918)
WESCO AIRCRAFT HARDWARE CORP (HQ)
24911 Avenue Stanford, Valencia (91355-1281)
PHONE..................661 775-7200
Dave Currence, *CIO*
Alex Murray, *COO*
Richard Weller, *CFO*
Todd Renehan, *Ch Credit Ofcr*
John Holland,
▲ EMP: 370 EST: 1953
SALES (est): 374.4MM **Publicly Held**
SIC: 5088 3728 Aircraft & parts; research & dev by manuf., aircraft parts & auxiliary equip

(P-7919)
WESCO AIRCRAFT HARDWARE CORP
27727 Avenue Scott, Valencia (91355-3909)
PHONE..................661 775-7200
Steve Halford, *Opers Mgr*
EMP: 400 **Publicly Held**
SIC: 5088 Aircraft & parts
HQ: Wesco Aircraft Hardware Corp.
24911 Avenue Stanford
Valencia CA 91355
661 775-7200

(P-7920)
WILLIAM F KELLOGG CORPORATION
Also Called: Airmotive Carburetor Co
475 W Riverside Dr 479dr, Burbank (91506-3256)
PHONE..................818 845-7455
Elaine Hubbell, *CEO*
Dennis Wright, *President*
EMP: 100 EST: 1947
SQ FT: 7,400

SALES: 2MM **Privately Held**
SIC: 5088 7699 Aircraft engines & engine parts; engine repair & replacement, non-automotive

(P-7921)
YAMAHA MOTOR CORPORATION USA (HQ)
6555 Katella Ave, Cypress (90630-5101)
PHONE..................714 761-7300
Toshi Kato, *CEO*
Phil Dyskow, *President*
Jeff Young, *President*
Takuwy Watanabe, *Corp Secy*
Claude Von Plate, *Division Mgr*
◆ EMP: 400
SQ FT: 200,000
SALES (est): 1.3B
SALES (corp-wide): 14.9B **Privately Held**
WEB: www.yamaha-motor.com
SIC: 5088 5013 5091 5012 Marine crafts & supplies; golf carts; motor vehicle supplies & new parts; boats, canoes, watercrafts & equipment; motorcycles; snowmobiles; motor scooters; recreation vehicles, all-terrain
PA: Yamaha Motor Co., Ltd.
2500, Shingai
Iwata SZO 438-0
538 321-115

┌─────────────────────────┐
│ **5091 Sporting &** │
│ **Recreational Goods & Splys** │
│ **Wholesale** │
└─────────────────────────┘

(P-7922)
BARRYS BOOTCAMP HOLDINGS LLC (PA)
7373 Beverly Blvd, Los Angeles (90036-2502)
PHONE..................270 535-5005
Joseph Gonzalez,
John Mumford,
Rachelle Mumford,
Barry Stitch,
EMP: 500
SALES: 30MM **Privately Held**
SIC: 5091 7999 Fitness equipment & supplies; physical fitness instruction

(P-7923)
BAUER HOCKEY INC
Also Called: Easton Hockey
3500 Willow Ln, Thousand Oaks (91361-4921)
PHONE..................818 782-6445
Bernard McDonell, *Ch of Bd*
EMP: 423
SALES (corp-wide): 166.2MM **Privately Held**
SIC: 5091 Sporting & recreation goods
PA: Old Bh Inc.
100 Domain Dr
Exeter NH 03833
603 430-2111

(P-7924)
CALLAWAY GOLF BALL OPRTONS INC
2180 Rutherford Rd, Carlsbad (92008-7328)
PHONE..................760 931-1771
Chip Brewer, *CEO*
EMP: 1700 EST: 2003
SALES (est): 577.5K
SALES (corp-wide): 1B **Publicly Held**
SIC: 5091 Golf equipment
PA: Callaway Golf Company
2180 Rutherford Rd
Carlsbad CA 92008
760 931-1771

(P-7925)
CHEM QUIP INC
Also Called: White House Sales
2551 Land Ave, Sacramento (95815-2363)
PHONE..................800 821-1678
Don Aston, *CEO*
Greg Durkee, *President*
Steve Hubbard, *CFO*
Jim Morrison, *Vice Pres*
Brain Long, *Admin Sec*

EMP: 62
SQ FT: 20,000
SALES: 24MM **Privately Held**
WEB: www.chemquip.com
SIC: 5091 5169 Swimming pools, equipment & supplies; chlorine

(P-7926)
DAIWA CORPORATION
Also Called: Daiwa Golf Company Division
11137 Warland Dr, Cypress (90630-5034)
P.O. Box 6600 (90630-0066)
PHONE..................562 375-6800
Tomoaki Komatsu, *CEO*
Tad Suzuki, *President*
William Steiner, *Vice Pres*
Cynthia Young, *Vice Pres*
◆ EMP: 58
SALES (est): 20.1MM
SALES (corp-wide): 805.1MM **Privately Held**
WEB: www.daiwa.com
SIC: 5091 3949 Fishing tackle; golf equipment
PA: Globeride, Inc.
3-14-16, Maesawa
Higashi Kurume TKY 203-0
424 752-111

(P-7927)
EVIKECOM INC
2801 W Mission Rd, Alhambra (91803-1223)
PHONE..................626 286-0360
Evike Change, *CEO*
Julie Chang, *COO*
▲ EMP: 70
SALES (est): 24MM **Privately Held**
SIC: 5091 5941 Sporting & recreation goods; sporting goods & bicycle shops

(P-7928)
FESTIVAL FUN PARKS LLC
Also Called: Raging Waters San Dimas 703
111 Raging Waters Dr, San Dimas (91773-3928)
PHONE..................909 802-2200
Robert Zues, *General Mgr*
EMP: 700 **Privately Held**
SIC: 5091 Water slides (recreation park)
HQ: Festival Fun Parks, Llc
4590 Macarthur Blvd # 400
Newport Beach CA 92660
949 261-0404

(P-7929)
GENERAL POOL & SPA SUPPLY INC (PA)
11285 Sunco Dr, Rancho Cordova (95742-6517)
PHONE..................916 853-2401
Philip Gelhaus, *President*
Patty Gelhaus, *Corp Secy*
Mark Yomogida, *Vice Pres*
▼ EMP: 55
SQ FT: 25,000
SALES (est): 27.4MM **Privately Held**
WEB: www.gpspool.com
SIC: 5091 Swimming pools, equipment & supplies; spa equipment & supplies

(P-7930)
GIANT BICYCLE INC (DH)
3587 Old Conejo Rd, Newbury Park (91320-2122)
PHONE..................805 267-4600
Elysa Walk, *Principal*
Dave Karneboge, *Vice Pres*
Timothy Johnson, *Executive*
Coree Chen, *Info Tech Dir*
Jean Scott, *Technology*
◆ EMP: 55
SQ FT: 75,000
SALES (est): 34.7MM
SALES (corp-wide): 1.8B **Privately Held**
SIC: 5091 Bicycles
HQ: Gaiwin B.V.
Pascallaan 66
Lelystad 8218
320 296-296

(P-7931)
INTER VALLEY POOL SUPPLY INC
Also Called: Intervalley Pools
1415 E 3rd St, Pomona (91766-2241)
PHONE..................626 969-5657
John A Fry, *President*
EMP: 60
SQ FT: 23,000
SALES (est): 9.7MM
SALES (corp-wide): 65.7MM **Privately Held**
SIC: 5091 5963 Swimming pools, equipment & supplies; bottled water delivery
PA: Hasa, Inc.
23119 Drayton St
Santa Clarita CA 91350
661 259-5848

(P-7932)
INTEX RECREATION CORP (PA)
4001 Via Oro Ave Ste 210, Long Beach (90810-1400)
PHONE..................310 549-5400
Tien P Zee, *President*
William Smith, *Vice Pres*
Fatima Echavez, *Admin Asst*
Wayne Farmer, *Info Tech Dir*
Ally Nomura, *Graphic Designe*
◆ EMP: 58
SQ FT: 80,000
SALES (est): 171.8MM **Privately Held**
WEB: www.intexcorp.net
SIC: 5091 5092 5021 3081 Watersports equipment & supplies; toys; waterbeds; vinyl film & sheet; polyethylene film

(P-7933)
MANDUKA LLC (HQ)
2121 Park Pl Ste 250, El Segundo (90245)
PHONE..................310 426-1495
Sky Meltzer, *CEO*
Beau Swenson, *CFO*
Joanne Sessler, *Vice Pres*
Heather Williams, *Mktg Dir*
Victoria Walls, *Sales Staff*
◆ EMP: 50
SALES (est): 32.2MM
SALES (corp-wide): 48.3MM **Privately Held**
SIC: 5091 5941 5699 Sporting & recreation goods; specialty sport supplies; golf, tennis & ski shops; sports apparel
PA: Valor Equity Partner Holdings, Llc
875 N Michigan Ave # 3214
Chicago IL 60611
312 683-1900

(P-7934)
NATIONAL LIQUIDATORS
2715 W Coast Hwy, Newport Beach (92663-4723)
PHONE..................949 631-6715
Robert G Tony, *Director*
Robert Tony, *President*
Charlene Girardey, *Supervisor*
EMP: 50
SALES (est): 3.3MM **Privately Held**
WEB: www.yachtauctions.com
SIC: 5091 Boats, canoes, watercrafts & equipment

(P-7935)
NEW CENTURY SCIENCE & TECH
18031 Cortney Ct, City of Industry (91748-1203)
PHONE..................626 581-5500
Carson Cheng, *President*
EMP: 60
SALES: 5MM **Privately Held**
SIC: 5091 Sporting & recreation goods

(P-7936)
RAZOR USA LLC (PA)
12723 166th St, Cerritos (90703-2102)
P.O. Box 3610 (90703-3610)
PHONE..................562 345-6000
Carlton Calvin, *Mng Member*
Ryan McLean, *COO*
Paul Chan, *Info Tech Dir*
Dong Lam, *Technician*
Tracy Bui, *Accountant*
◆ EMP: 70
SQ FT: 50,000

SALES (est): 36.9MM **Privately Held**
WEB: www.razor.com
SIC: 5091 Sporting & recreation goods

(P-7937)
REC CENTER
501 Stanyan St, San Francisco
(94117-1898)
PHONE..................................415 831-6818
Elizabeth Goldstein, *Director*
Richard Allen, *Officer*
Peter Silva, *Officer*
Patricia Walsh, *Admin Sec*
Erin Anderson, *Admin Asst*
EMP: 144 **EST:** 2011
SALES (est): 7.1MM **Privately Held**
SIC: 5091 Water slides (recreation park)

(P-7938)
SHIMANO NORTH AMER HOLDG INC (HQ)
1 Holland, Irvine (92618-2506)
PHONE..................................949 951-5003
David Pfeiffer, *President*
Dave Pfeiffer, *COO*
Jim Lafrance, *CFO*
Chiam Teng, *Vice Pres*
Bob Mahoney, *Executive*
▲ **EMP:** 150
SQ FT: 122,000
SALES (est): 72.8MM
SALES (corp-wide): 3B **Privately Held**
SIC: 5091 Bicycle parts & accessories;
   fishing equipment & supplies
PA: Shimano Inc.
   3-77, Oimatsucho, Sakai-Ku
   Sakai OSK 590-0
   722 233-210

(P-7939)
TROXEL CYCLING & FITNESS LLC
6222 Ferris Sq Ste A, San Diego
(92121-3205)
PHONE..................................858 587-7720
Richard M Timms, *Mng Member*
Steve Norton, *Accounting Mgr*
Tim Tran, *Accountant*
Jorge Garcia, *VP Opers*
Monique Sullivan,
▲ **EMP:** 160 **EST:** 1948
SALES (est): 8.7MM **Privately Held**
WEB: www.troxelhelmets.com
SIC: 5091 Sporting & recreation goods

(P-7940)
TROY LEE DESIGNS LLC (PA)
155 E Rincon St, Corona (92879-1328)
PHONE..................................951 371-5219
Dave Bertran, *CEO*
Troy Michael Lee, *President*
Ricardo Gonzalez, *Vice Pres*
Maki Ushiroyama, *Creative Dir*
Jessica Hernandez, *Executive Asst*
▲ **EMP:** 79
SQ FT: 6,000
SALES (est): 26.3MM **Privately Held**
WEB: www.troyleedesigns.com
SIC: 5091 7336 Sporting & recreation
   goods; graphic arts & related design

(P-7941)
TUM YETO INC
Also Called: Foundation Super Skateboard
2001 Commercial St, San Diego
(92113-1109)
PHONE..................................619 232-7523
Tod Swank, *CEO*
Tara Lewis, *Controller*
▲ **EMP:** 50
SQ FT: 29,000
SALES (est): 10.3MM **Privately Held**
WEB: www.tumyeto.com
SIC: 5091 5137 Sporting & recreation
   goods; sportswear, women's & children's

(P-7942)
WARRIOR CUSTOM GOLF INC (PA)
Also Called: Warrior Golf
15 Mason, Irvine (92618-2707)
PHONE..................................949 699-2499
Brendan M Flaherty, *CEO*
Jorge Festini, *Vice Pres*
Pete Wheelahan, *Vice Pres*

Pedro Villanueva, *General Mgr*
Monica Palacios, *Admin Asst*
▲ **EMP:** 146
SQ FT: 20,000
SALES (est): 52.6MM **Privately Held**
WEB: www.warriorcustomgolf.com
SIC: 5091 5941 Golf equipment; sporting
   goods & bicycle shops

5092 Toys & Hobby Goods & Splys Wholesale

(P-7943)
A L S INDUSTRIES INC (PA)
1942 Artesia Blvd, Torrance (90504-3599)
PHONE..................................310 532-9262
Richard D Smith, *President*
David Albert, *Vice Pres*
▲ **EMP:** 50 **EST:** 1970
SQ FT: 70,000
SALES (est): 10.8MM **Privately Held**
SIC: 5092 Video games

(P-7944)
AURORA WORLD INC
8820 Mercury Ln, Pico Rivera
(90660-6706)
PHONE..................................562 205-1222
Heui-Yul Noh, *CEO*
Kee Sun Hong, *Exec VP*
Daniel Rah, *CIO*
Melissa Neal, *Graphic Designe*
Maline Sip, *Credit Staff*
◆ **EMP:** 110
SQ FT: 100,000
SALES (est): 68.4MM
SALES (corp-wide): 101.3MM **Privately Held**
WEB: www.auroragift.com
SIC: 5092 Toys
PA: Aurora World Corporation
   624 Teheran-Ro, Gangnam-Gu
   Seoul 06175
   822 342-0411

(P-7945)
AZUBU NORTH AMERICA INC
15303 Ventura Blvd # 900, Sherman Oaks
(91403-3199)
PHONE..................................310 759-9529
Ian Sharpe, *CEO*
Jason Katz, *COO*
Abe Gottesman, *Vice Pres*
Andrew Greaves, *Vice Pres*
EMP: 50
SALES (est): 10.2MM **Privately Held**
SIC: 5092 5734 Video games; software,
   computer games

(P-7946)
BANDAI NAMCO ENTRMT AMER INC
Also Called: Ndga
2051 Mission College Blvd, Santa Clara
(95054-1519)
PHONE..................................408 235-2000
Kenji Hisatsune, *CEO*
Masaaki Tsuji, *President*
Hide Irie, *COO*
Shuji Nakata, *CFO*
Robert Stevenson, *Vice Pres*
▲ **EMP:** 200
SQ FT: 51,118
SALES (est): 147.8MM
SALES (corp-wide): 6.3B **Privately Held**
WEB: www.namcobandaigames.com
SIC: 5092 Video games
HQ: Bandai Namco Holdings Usa Inc.
   2120 Park Pl Ste 120
   El Segundo CA 90245

(P-7947)
BLUE BOX OPCO LLC (PA)
Also Called: Infantino
10025 Mesa Rim Rd, San Diego
(92121-2913)
PHONE..................................800 840-4916
Alex Chan,
Alicia Barone, *Executive*
Gail Smith, *VP Mktg*
Sophia Le, *Sales Staff*
▲ **EMP:** 97 **EST:** 2014

SALES (est): 35.5MM **Privately Held**
SIC: 5092 Toys & hobby goods & supplies

(P-7948)
CAPCOM ENTERTAINMENT INC
Also Called: Capcom U.S.a
185 Berry St Ste 1200, San Francisco
(94107-1794)
PHONE..................................650 350-6500
Kazuhiro Abe, *CEO*
Hiroshi Tobisawa, *President*
Mark Beaumont, *COO*
Jason Mueller, *Senior VP*
Kirk Black, *Vice Pres*
▲ **EMP:** 80
SALES (est): 25.1MM
SALES (corp-wide): 887.1MM **Privately Held**
SIC: 5092 Video games
HQ: Capcom U.S.A. Inc
   185 Berry St Ste 1200
   San Francisco CA 94107
   650 350-6500

(P-7949)
CAPCOM U S A INC (HQ)
185 Berry St Ste 1200, San Francisco
(94107-1794)
PHONE..................................650 350-6500
Koko Ishikawa, *President*
Rob Dyer, *COO*
Chao Peterson, *Administration*
Aki Nishiyama, *Financial Analy*
Bao Le, *Manager*
▲ **EMP:** 180
SALES (est): 51.9MM
SALES (corp-wide): 887.1MM **Privately Held**
SIC: 5092 7993 7372 Video games; ar-
   cades; prepackaged software
PA: Capcom Co., Ltd.
   3-1-3, Uchihiranomachi, Chuo-Ku
   Osaka OSK 540-0
   669 203-600

(P-7950)
DELTA CREATIVE INC
2690 Pellissier Pl, City of Industry
(90601-1507)
PHONE..................................800 423-4135
William B George, *President*
Martina Mueller, *CEO*
Alexander Ritchie, *Vice Pres*
▲ **EMP:** 105 **EST:** 1974
SQ FT: 112,000
SALES (est): 13.3MM
SALES (corp-wide): 11.1B **Privately Held**
WEB: www.deltacreative.com
SIC: 5092 5198 Arts & crafts equipment &
   supplies; paints
HQ: Dk Household Brands Holding Ag
   Muhlebachstrasse 20
   ZUrich ZH 8008

(P-7951)
FAO ROC HOLDINGS LLC
Also Called: Fao Schwarz
15 Cushing, Irvine (92618-4220)
PHONE..................................949 900-6501
David Conn, *CEO*
David Niggli, *Chief Mktg Ofcr*
Robert Tuscano, *VP Opers*
EMP: 170
SALES (est): 41.7K **Privately Held**
SIC: 5092 7371 Toys & hobby goods &
   supplies; computer software development
   & applications

(P-7952)
INTERNATIONAL TOY INC
17682 Cowan Ste 100, Irvine (92614-1609)
PHONE..................................949 333-3777
Steve Asher, *President*
EMP: 50
SQ FT: 2,500
SALES (est): 17.5MM **Privately Held**
SIC: 5092 Toys & hobby goods & supplies

(P-7953)
JAKKS SALES CORPORATION
2951 28th St Ste 51, Santa Monica
(90405-2961)
PHONE..................................424 268-9444
Jack Friedman, *Ch of Bd*
Stephen Berman, *President*

Joel Bennett, *CFO*
Joel M Bennett, *Exec VP*
EMP: 50
SALES (est): 5.8MM **Publicly Held**
SIC: 5092 Toys
PA: Jakks Pacific, Inc.
   2951 28th St Ste 51
   Santa Monica CA 90405

(P-7954)
JINX INC
Also Called: Jinx Hackwear/Jinx.com
13465 Gregg St, Poway (92064-7135)
PHONE..................................888 546-9266
Sean Gailey, *CEO*
Tim Norris, *COO*
Billy Baggins, *Vice Pres*
Chris Hope, *Creative Dir*
Jorge Tirado, *Creative Dir*
◆ **EMP:** 57
SALES (est): 36.4MM **Privately Held**
WEB: www.jinx.com
SIC: 5092 5136 5137 Video games;
   men's & boys' clothing; women's & chil-
   dren's clothing

(P-7955)
KELLYTOY WORLDWIDE INC
4811 S Alameda St, Vernon (90058-2805)
PHONE..................................323 923-1300
Jonathan Kelly, *President*
▲ **EMP:** 70
SALES (est): 8.7MM
SALES (corp-wide): 72.4MM **Privately Held**
SIC: 5092 Toys
PA: Kellytoy (Usa), Inc.
   4811 S Alameda St
   Vernon CA 90058
   323 588-8697

(P-7956)
MATTEL TOY COMPANY
333 Continental Blvd, El Segundo
(90245-5032)
PHONE..................................310 252-2357
Robert Eckert, *CEO*
▼ **EMP:** 1900
SALES (est): 221.8MM
SALES (corp-wide): 4.8B **Publicly Held**
SIC: 5092 Toys & games
PA: Mattel, Inc.
   333 Continental Blvd
   El Segundo CA 90245
   310 252-2000

(P-7957)
MERCHSOURCE LLC
Also Called: Threesixty Group
7755 Irvine Center Dr, Irvine (92618-2906)
PHONE..................................800 374-2744
Johann Clapp, *Mng Member*
Jolene Myers, *CFO*
Carrie Blodgett, *Marketing Staff*
Jenny Wang, *General Counsel*
Kirk McLean,
◆ **EMP:** 80
SALES (est): 310MM **Privately Held**
WEB: www.merchsource.com
SIC: 5092 Toys & hobby goods & supplies

(P-7958)
MGA ENTERTAINMENT INC (PA)
16300 Roscoe Blvd Ste 150, Van Nuys
(91406-1257)
PHONE..................................818 894-2525
Isaac Larian, *President*
AME Cameron, *VP Mktg*
◆ **EMP:** 300 **EST:** 1980
SQ FT: 50,000
SALES (est): 464.1MM **Privately Held**
WEB: www.mgae.com
SIC: 5092 Toys; toys & games

(P-7959)
PERFORMANCE DESIGNED PDTS LLC (HQ)
2300 W Empire Ave # 600, Burbank
(91504-3341)
PHONE..................................323 234-9911
Chris Richards,
Kathryn Browne, *President*
Storm Orion, *President*
Shawn Kinninger, *Vice Pres*
Todd Koniares, *Vice Pres*

◆ **EMP:** 64
SQ FT: 18,000
SALES (est): 136.1MM
SALES (corp-wide): 4.1B **Privately Held**
WEB: www.pelicanacc.com
SIC: 5092 Toys & games; video games
PA: Patriarch Partners, Llc
  1 Liberty Plz Rm 3500
  New York NY 10006
  212 825-0550

(P-7960)
RADICA ENTERPRISES LTD
Also Called: Radica USA
333 Continental Blvd, El Segundo
(90245-5032)
PHONE....................310 252-2000
Patrick Feely, *CEO*
◆ **EMP:** 57
SQ FT: 24,000
SALES (est): 3.6MM
SALES (corp-wide): 4.8B **Publicly Held**
SIC: 5092 Toy novelties & amusements
HQ: Radica Games Limited
  C/O Appleby Spurling Hunter
  Hamilton
  -

(P-7961)
SOLUTIONS 2 GO LLC
20091 Ellipse, Foothill Ranch
(92610-3001)
PHONE....................949 825-7700
Nima Taghavi, *Mng Member*
Wayne Yodzio, *President*
Michael Maas,
▲ **EMP:** 56
SQ FT: 14,000
SALES (est): 270MM **Privately Held**
SIC: 5092 Toys & hobby goods & supplies

(P-7962)
STK INTERNATIONAL INC
6160 Peach Tree St, Compton (90220)
PHONE....................310 720-1277
Stuart Kole, *President*
◆ **EMP:** 70
SQ FT: 120,000
SALES: 12MM **Privately Held**
WEB: www.stkinternational.com
SIC: 5092 5072 5023 Toys; hand tools;
  power tools & accessories; home furnish-
  ings; kitchenware

(P-7963)
WHAM-O INC
6301 Owensmouth Ave # 700, Woodland
Hills (91367-2265)
PHONE....................818 963-4200
Raylin Hsieh, *CEO*
Blake Wong, *CFO*
Jeff Hsieh, *Chairman*
Thomas Lindahl, *Sales Staff*
◆ **EMP:** 59
SALES (est): 16.3MM **Privately Held**
WEB: www.wham-o.com
SIC: 5092 5091 3944 3949 Toys &
  games; surfing equipment & supplies; toy
  trains, airplanes & automobiles; sporting
  & athletic goods

**5093 Scrap & Waste
Materials Wholesale**

(P-7964)
**AADLEN BROTHERS AUTO
WRECKING (PA)**
11590 Tuxford St, Sun Valley (91352-3112)
PHONE....................323 875-1400
Sam Adlen, *President*
Samuel Lewinstein, *Corp Secy*
Jorge Trujillo, *Creative Dir*
EMP: 79 **EST:** 1951
SALES (est): 19.5MM **Privately Held**
WEB: www.aadlenbros.com
SIC: 5093 Metal scrap & waste materials

(P-7965)
ALCO IRON & METAL CO (PA)
2140 Davis St, San Leandro (94577-1062)
PHONE....................510 562-1107
Kem Kantor, *President*
Michael Bercovich, *COO*
Kevin Kantor, *Exec VP*

Keith Kantor, *Vice Pres*
Tony Nam, *Vice Pres*
◆ **EMP:** 100
SQ FT: 35,000
SALES (est): 82.1MM **Privately Held**
SIC: 5093 5051 Metal scrap & waste ma-
  terials; steel

(P-7966)
**AMERICA CHUNG NAM (GROUP)
(PA)**
1163 Fairway Dr, City of Industry
(91789-2846)
PHONE....................909 839-8383
Teresa Cheung, *CEO*
Sam Liu, *COO*
Kevin Zhao, *CFO*
Ken Liu, *Vice Pres*
John Wong, *Vice Pres*
▼ **EMP:** 125
SQ FT: 30,000
SALES (est): 222.8MM **Privately Held**
WEB: www.acni.net
SIC: 5093 Waste paper

(P-7967)
AMERICA CHUNG NAM LLC (HQ)
Also Called: A C N
1163 Fairway Dr Fl 3, City of Industry
(91789-2851)
PHONE....................909 839-8383
Teresa Cheung, *CEO*
Yan Cheung, *Shareholder*
Ming Chung Liu, *Shareholder*
Sam Liu, *COO*
Xue Bai, *CFO*
◆ **EMP:** 200
SALES (est): 221.8MM
SALES (corp-wide): 222.8MM **Privately
Held**
SIC: 5093 Waste paper
PA: America Chung Nam (Group) Holdings
  Llc
  1163 Fairway Dr
  City Of Industry CA 91789
  909 839-8383

(P-7968)
AMERICAN METAL & IRON INC
2377 Tulip Rd, San Jose (95128-1141)
P.O. Box 610 (95106-0610)
PHONE....................408 452-0777
Howard Misle, *President*
Debra L Ginestra, *Principal*
◆ **EMP:** 55
SQ FT: 10,000
SALES (est): 5.8MM **Privately Held**
WEB: www.amerimetals.com
SIC: 5093 Metal scrap & waste materials

(P-7969)
**ANGELUS WESTERN PPR
FIBERS INC**
2474 Porter St, Los Angeles (90021-2511)
PHONE....................213 623-9221
Greg Rouchon, *President*
Steve Young, *Treasurer*
Tom Rouchon, *Vice Pres*
David Jones, *Admin Sec*
EMP: 51 **EST:** 1977
SQ FT: 10,000
SALES (est): 25MM **Privately Held**
SIC: 5093 Waste paper

(P-7970)
**B & B PLASTICS RECYCLERS
INC (PA)**
3040 N Locust Ave, Rialto (92377-3706)
PHONE....................909 829-3606
Baltasar Mejia, *President*
Bacilio Mejia, *Vice Pres*
Christy Dawson, *Human Resources*
Alex Mejia, *Marketing Staff*
Eddie Sigala, *Representative*
EMP: 65
SQ FT: 100,000
SALES (est): 117.2MM **Privately Held**
SIC: 5093 2673 Plastics scrap; bags: plas-
  tic, laminated & coated

(P-7971)
**BESTWAY RECYCLING
COMPANY INC (PA)**
2268 Firestone Blvd, Los Angeles
(90002-1546)
P.O. Box 109, South Gate (90280-0109)
PHONE....................323 588-8157
Edward Young Kim, *President*
David Cho, *CFO*
Nam Sook Kim, *Corp Secy*
Dong Kim, *Opers Mgr*
▼ **EMP:** 52 **EST:** 1963
SQ FT: 165,000
SALES (est): 18.3MM **Privately Held**
SIC: 5093 Waste paper; nonferrous metals
  scrap; bottles, waste; plastics scrap

(P-7972)
CASS INC (PA)
2730 Peralta St, Oakland (94607-1707)
P.O. Box 24222 (94623-1222)
PHONE....................510 893-6476
Edward B Kangeter IV, *CEO*
Chal Sulprizio, *President*
Carmen Zeng, *CFO*
◆ **EMP:** 120
SQ FT: 20,000
SALES (est): 56.5MM **Privately Held**
SIC: 5093 Nonferrous metals scrap

(P-7973)
**CEDARWOOD-YOUNG
COMPANY**
Also Called: Allan Company
14618 Arrow Hwy, Baldwin Park
(91706-1733)
PHONE....................626 962-4047
Ernesto Lopez, *Branch Mgr*
David Romberg, *Vice Pres*
EMP: 55
SQ FT: 10,664
SALES (corp-wide): 299.9MM **Privately
Held**
WEB: www.allancompany.com
SIC: 5093 2611 Waste paper; pulp mills
PA: Cedarwood-Young Company
  14620 Joanbridge St
  Baldwin Park CA 91706
  626 962-4047

(P-7974)
CITY FIBERS INC (PA)
2500 S Santa Fe Ave, Vernon
(90058-1116)
P.O. Box 58646, Los Angeles (90058-0646)
PHONE....................323 583-1013
David T Jones, *President*
Kipp Jones, *Vice Pres*
Scott Jones, *Info Tech Mgr*
Maria Quiane, *Asst Mgr*
Vanessa Acosta, *Advisor*
EMP: 100
SQ FT: 55,000
SALES (est): 35.9MM **Privately Held**
SIC: 5093 4953 Waste paper; recycling,
  waste materials

(P-7975)
**COMMODITY RESOURCE
ENVMTL INC (PA)**
Also Called: Cre
116 E Prospect Ave, Burbank
(91502-2035)
PHONE....................818 843-2811
Larry J Dewitt, *President*
Don Buckles, *Vice Pres*
Alexsandra Jaric, *Technology*
Natasa Zeljkovic-Karab, *Human Res Mgr*
Chuck Yohn, *VP Sales*
▲ **EMP:** 55
SQ FT: 10,000
SALES (est): 13.7MM **Privately Held**
SIC: 5093 Scrap & waste materials

(P-7976)
**CUSTOM ALLOY SCRAP SALES
INC (HQ)**
2730 Peralta St, Oakland (94607-1707)
P.O. Box 24222 (94623-1222)
PHONE....................510 893-6476
Chal Sulprizio, *President*
Dan Gellepes, *Auditor*
Martha Bisso, *Buyer*
Anne Lee, *Mktg Dir*
Chad Mueller, *Marketing Staff*

EMP: 50
SQ FT: 1,000
SALES (est): 7.3MM
SALES (corp-wide): 56.5MM **Privately
Held**
SIC: 5093 Metal scrap & waste materials;
  nonferrous metals scrap
PA: Cass, Inc.
  2730 Peralta St
  Oakland CA 94607
  510 893-6476

(P-7977)
GEORGIA-PACIFIC LLC
15500 Valley View Ave, La Mirada
(90638-5230)
PHONE....................562 926-8888
Jeff McCranie, *Manager*
Kelley Hill, *Human Res Mgr*
John Taylor, *Plant Mgr*
EMP: 81
SALES (corp-wide): 42.9B **Privately Held**
SIC: 5093 Waste paper
HQ: Georgia-Pacific Llc
  133 Peachtree St Nw
  Atlanta GA 30303
  404 652-4000

(P-7978)
GLOBAL PLASTICS INC
145 Malbert St, Perris (92570-8624)
PHONE....................951 657-5466
Nadim Salim Bahou, *President*
Patti Gilmour, *CFO*
▲ **EMP:** 120
SQ FT: 55,000
SALES (est): 25MM **Privately Held**
WEB: www.globalpet.com
SIC: 5093 4953 3053 Plastics scrap; re-
  cycling, waste materials; packing materi-
  als

(P-7979)
GREEN PLANET 21 INC (PA)
336 Adeline St, Oakland (94607-2520)
PHONE....................510 873-8777
Stephen Sutta, *President*
▲ **EMP:** 50
SQ FT: 10,000
SALES (est): 15.7MM **Privately Held**
SIC: 5093 Waste paper

(P-7980)
**GREENPATH RECOVERY WEST
INC**
Also Called: Greenpath Recovery Recycl
Svcs
330 W Citrus St Ste 250, Colton
(92324-1422)
PHONE....................909 954-0686
Joe Castro, *President*
Rebecca Somerville, *Opers Staff*
EMP: 60
SQ FT: 90,000
SALES (est): 34.6MM **Privately Held**
SIC: 5093 3089 2821 Scrap & waste ma-
  terials; plastic processing; injection mold-
  ing of plastics; plastics materials & resins;
  molding compounds, plastics

(P-7981)
JACK ENGLE & CO (PA)
8440 S Alameda St, Los Angeles
(90001-4112)
P.O. Box 1705 (90001-0705)
PHONE....................323 589-8111
Alan M Engle, *CEO*
Jack Engle, *CEO*
Jason Engle, *Vice Pres*
Julius Miller, *General Mgr*
Karina Moreno, *Office Mgr*
◆ **EMP:** 55 **EST:** 1965
SQ FT: 25,000
SALES (est): 33.9MM **Privately Held**
WEB: www.jackengleco.com
SIC: 5093 Ferrous metal scrap & waste;
  metal scrap & waste materials

(P-7982)
**KINSBURSKY BROS SUPPLY
INC (PA)**
Also Called: K B I
125 E Commercial St Ste A, Anaheim
(92801-1214)
PHONE....................714 738-8516
Steven Kinsbursky, *President*

Aaron Zisman, *CFO*
Scott Kinsbursky, *Vice Pres*
Todd Coy, *Admin Sec*
Akshay Mangale, *Engineer*
▲ **EMP:** 75
SQ FT: 35,000
SALES (est): 37MM **Privately Held**
WEB: www.kinsbursky.com
SIC: 5093 Metal scrap & waste materials

(P-7983)
MIDNIGHT AUTO RECYCLING LLC
434 E 6th St, San Bernardino (92410-4507)
P.O. Box 24003 (92406-0503)
PHONE..........................909 884-5308
Ted Smith, *Administration*
EMP: 50 **EST:** 1998
SALES (est): 6.3MM **Privately Held**
SIC: 5093 Automotive wrecking for scrap

(P-7984)
NEW NGC INC
Also Called: Gold Bond Building Products
1040 Canal Blvd, Richmond (94804-3550)
PHONE..........................510 234-6745
John Phillips, *Principal*
JD Cohen, *Marketing Staff*
EMP: 50
SALES (corp-wide): 685.8MM **Privately Held**
WEB: www.natgyp.com
SIC: 5093 3275 Scrap & waste materials; gypsum products
HQ: New Ngc, Inc.
2001 Rexford Rd
Charlotte NC 28211

(P-7985)
NEWPORT CH INTERNATIONAL LLC (PA)
1100 W Town And Country R, Orange (92868-4662)
PHONE..........................714 572-8881
Clark Hahne,
Mike Milby, *CFO*
Jim Fagelson, *Vice Pres*
Becky Spradley, *Human Resources*
Norma Vargas, *Purchasing*
◆ **EMP:** 58
SQ FT: 8,300
SALES (est): 230MM **Privately Held**
WEB: www.newportchintl.com
SIC: 5093 Waste paper; plastics scrap

(P-7986)
PAVEMENT RECYCLING SYSTEMS INC (PA)
Also Called: Prsi
10240 San Sevaine Way, Jurupa Valley (91752-1100)
PHONE..........................951 682-1091
Richard W Gove, *President*
Stephen Concannon, *President*
Nathan Beyler, *CFO*
Doug Ford, *Vice Pres*
Trisha V Sluis, *Executive*
▲ **EMP:** 125
SQ FT: 40,000
SALES (est): 126.7MM **Privately Held**
SIC: 5093 1611 Scrap & waste materials; surfacing & paving; concrete construction: roads, highways, sidewalks, etc.; resurfacing contractor

(P-7987)
PICK-A-PART AUTO WRECKING
9445 Cambridge St, Cypress (90630-2705)
PHONE..........................559 485-3071
Christopher L McElroy, *CEO*
EMP: 70
SQ FT: 1,200
SALES (est): 16.2MM
SALES (corp-wide): 9.7B **Publicly Held**
WEB: www.pickapart.com
SIC: 5093 5531 5015 Automotive wrecking for scrap; automotive parts; automotive parts & supplies, used
HQ: Pick-Your-Part Auto Wrecking
1235 S Beach Blvd
Anaheim CA 92804
800 962-2277

(P-7988)
RALISON INTERNATIONAL INC
15328 Central Ave, Chino (91710-7658)
PHONE..........................909 393-0008
Jihong Luo, *President*
Byron Luo, *Vice Pres*
Ross LI, *Managing Dir*
Joyce Chan, *Purch Mgr*
Albert Chiu, *Manager*
▼ **EMP:** 50
SQ FT: 6,000
SALES (est): 27.5MM **Privately Held**
SIC: 5093 Waste paper

(P-7989)
RIVERSIDE SCRAP IR & MET CORP (PA)
Also Called: Redlands Recycling
2993 6th St, Riverside (92507-4131)
P.O. Box 5288 (92517-5288)
PHONE..........................951 686-2120
Samuel Frankel, *Ch of Bd*
Daniel Jay Frankel, *President*
Raj Gandhi, *Exec VP*
Muriel K Frankel, *Vice Pres*
EMP: 50
SQ FT: 22,275
SALES (est): 17.2MM **Privately Held**
SIC: 5093 Nonferrous metals scrap; waste paper; bottles, waste; plastics scrap

(P-7990)
SA RECYCLING LLC (PA)
2411 N Glassell St, Orange (92865-2717)
PHONE..........................714 632-2000
George Adams, *Mng Member*
Cristi Rossi, *Vice Pres*
David Garmon, *General Mgr*
Francisco Mendoza, *General Mgr*
Steve Rios, *General Mgr*
◆ **EMP:** 160
SQ FT: 40,000
SALES (est): 807.4MM **Privately Held**
SIC: 5093 Ferrous metal scrap & waste

(P-7991)
SCHNITZER STEEL INDUSTRIES INC
1101 Embarcadero W, Oakland (94607-2536)
P.O. Box 747 (94604-0747)
PHONE..........................510 444-3919
Gary Schnitzer, *Vice Pres*
EMP: 100
SALES (corp-wide): 2.3B **Publicly Held**
WEB: www.schn.com
SIC: 5093 Ferrous metal scrap & waste
PA: Schnitzer Steel Industries, Inc.
299 Sw Clay St Ste 350
Portland OR 97201
503 224-9900

(P-7992)
SIERRA INTERNATIONAL MCHY LLC
1620 E Brundage Ln Frnt, Bakersfield (93307-2756)
P.O. Box 1340 (93302-1340)
PHONE..........................661 327-7073
Phillip Sacco, *Mng Member*
Len Lawrence, *Sales Mgr*
Jessica Driggers, *Sales Staff*
Brian Mihm, *Sales Staff*
Ben Sacco,
◆ **EMP:** 65
SQ FT: 15,000
SALES (est): 51.1MM **Privately Held**
SIC: 5093 5084 Nonferrous metals scrap; ferrous metal scrap & waste; industrial machinery & equipment

(P-7993)
SIMS GROUP USA CORPORATION
Also Called: Sims/LMC Recyclers
1900 Monterey Hwy, San Jose (95112-6100)
PHONE..........................408 494-4242
Tom Sorci, *Manager*
EMP: 100 **Privately Held**
SIC: 5093 4953 3231 Ferrous metal scrap & waste; refuse systems; products of purchased glass

HQ: Sims Group Usa Corporation
600 S 4th St
Richmond CA 94804
510 412-5300

(P-7994)
SIMS GROUP USA CORPORATION (DH)
Also Called: Simsmetal America
600 S 4th St, Richmond (94804-3504)
PHONE..........................510 412-5300
Galdino Claro, *CEO*
Bob Kelman, *President*
Myles Partridge, *CFO*
Jimmie Buckland, *Exec VP*
John Crabb, *Principal*
◆ **EMP:** 100
SQ FT: 4,000
SALES (est): 157.9MM **Privately Held**
SIC: 5093 4953 Ferrous metal scrap & waste; nonferrous metals scrap; recycling, waste materials
HQ: Sims Group Usa Holdings Corp
16 W 22nd St Fl 10
New York NY 10010
212 604-0710

(P-7995)
SIMS GROUP USA CORPORATION
Simsmtals America-Richmond Div
600 S 4th St, Richmond (94804-3504)
PHONE..........................510 236-0606
Jimmie Buckland, *Vice Pres*
EMP: 75 **Privately Held**
SIC: 5093 Ferrous metal scrap & waste
HQ: Sims Group Usa Corporation
600 S 4th St
Richmond CA 94804
510 412-5300

(P-7996)
SOLARIS PAPER INC
13415 Carmenita Rd, Santa Fe Springs (90670-4906)
PHONE..........................562 653-1680
Andre Soetjahja, *President*
Funadi Wongso, *CFO*
Peter Brown, *Vice Pres*
James Rice, *Vice Pres*
Corey Rodriguez, *Vice Pres*
◆ **EMP:** 231
SQ FT: 200,000
SALES (est): 159.9MM **Privately Held**
SIC: 5093 Waste paper

(P-7997)
SOS METALS INC (DH)
201 E Gardena Blvd, Gardena (90248-2813)
PHONE..........................310 217-8848
Kenneth Buck, *CEO*
◆ **EMP:** 165
SQ FT: 115,000
SALES (est): 90.3MM
SALES (corp-wide): 242.1B **Publicly Held**
WEB: www.sosmetals.com
SIC: 5093 5051 Ferrous metal scrap & waste; ferroalloys
HQ: Precision Castparts Corp.
4650 Sw Mcdam Ave Ste 300
Portland OR 97239
503 946-4800

(P-7998)
STANDARD IRON & METALS CO
4525 San Leandro St, Oakland (94601-4449)
PHONE..........................510 535-0222
Jason Allen, *Principal*
Lloyd Weinstein, *Corp Secy*
▼ **EMP:** 50
SQ FT: 20,000
SALES (est): 22.5MM **Privately Held**
WEB: www.standardiron.net
SIC: 5093 Ferrous metal scrap & waste; nonferrous metals scrap

(P-7999)
TST INC
Tandem Division
11601 Etiwanda Ave, Fontana (92337-6929)
PHONE..........................909 590-1098
Andrew G Stein, *CEO*

EMP: 75
SALES (corp-wide): 67.6MM **Privately Held**
SIC: 5093 Metal scrap & waste materials
PA: Tst, Inc.
13428 Benson Ave
Chino CA 91710
951 685-2155

5094 Jewelry, Watches, Precious Stones Wholesale

(P-8000)
A-MARK PRECIOUS METALS INC (PA)
2121 Rosecrans Ave # 6300, El Segundo (90245-7528)
PHONE..........................310 587-1477
Gregory N Roberts, *CEO*
Jeffrey D Benjamin, *Ch of Bd*
Thor G Gjerdrum, *President*
Cary Dickson, *CFO*
Carol Meltzer, *Exec VP*
▲ **EMP:** 50
SQ FT: 9,000
SALES: 7.6B **Publicly Held**
SIC: 5094 Jewelry; precious metals

(P-8001)
ARTS ELEGANCE INC (PA)
Also Called: Liberty Investments Exchange
739 E Walnut St Ste 200, Pasadena (91101-1656)
P.O. Box 307, La Canada (91012-0307)
PHONE..........................626 405-1522
Art Mikaelian, *President*
Karen Mikaelian, *Vice Pres*
Sima Mikaelian, *Vice Pres*
Robert Kedikian, *Supervisor*
EMP: 60
SALES (est): 13.4MM **Privately Held**
SIC: 5094 Jewelry

(P-8002)
BASK JEWELRY INC
2607 S Main St, Soquel (95073-2409)
PHONE..........................831 479-8849
Steve Battelle, *President*
▼ **EMP:** 100
SQ FT: 2,400
SALES (est): 9.9MM **Privately Held**
WEB: www.bask.com
SIC: 5094 Jewelry & precious stones

(P-8003)
BJS RESTAURANTS INC
3401 Dale Rd Ste 840, Modesto (95356-0549)
PHONE..........................209 526-8850
Brandon Mynear, *Principal*
EMP: 192
SALES (corp-wide): 1B **Publicly Held**
SIC: 5094 Jewelry
PA: Bj's Restaurants, Inc.
7755 Center Ave Ste 300
Huntington Beach CA 92647
714 500-2400

(P-8004)
BUNGALOW 16 ENTERTAINMENT LLC
8113 Melrose Ave, Los Angeles (90046-7011)
PHONE..........................310 226-7870
▲ **EMP:** 50
SQ FT: 2,000
SALES (est): 4.2MM **Privately Held**
SIC: 5094

(P-8005)
C&C JEWELRY MFG INC
323 W 8th St Fl 4, Los Angeles (90014-3109)
PHONE..........................213 623-6800
Mikhail Chekhman, *President*
Robert Connolly, *Vice Pres*
▲ **EMP:** 56
SQ FT: 3,000
SALES: 28.3MM **Privately Held**
SIC: 5094 3911 Jewelry & precious stones; jewelry, precious metal

PRODUCTS & SVCS

(P-8006)
CHATHAM INC
300 Rancheros Dr Ste 360, San Marcos
(92069-2970)
PHONE.................................800 222-2002
Harry Stubbert, *CEO*
EMP: 50
SALES (est): 2.1MM **Privately Held**
SIC: 5094 Jewelry & precious stones

(P-8007)
CPI LUXURY GROUP
Also Called: China Pearl
10220 Norris Ave, Pacoima (91331-2217)
PHONE.................................818 249-9888
Harold Jabarian, *CEO*
Kevork Hasbanian, *Vice Pres*
▲ EMP: 54
SQ FT: 15,000
SALES: 23MM **Privately Held**
WEB: www.chinapearl-usa.com
SIC: 5094 Pearls

(P-8008)
CW WELDING SERVICE INC
761 Majors Ct, Bakersfield (93308-9436)
PHONE.................................661 399-5422
Ellis Firatt, *Branch Mgr*
EMP: 51 **Privately Held**
SIC: 5094 5051 1761 Precious stones &
metals; metals service centers & offices;
sheet metalwork
PA: C.W. Welding Service, Inc.
1735 Santa Fe Ave
Long Beach CA 90813

(P-8009)
EMMI INC
Also Called: Emmi Universal Fine Jeweller
631 S Olive St Ste 302, Los Angeles
(90014-3656)
PHONE.................................213 622-7234
Edward Zohrabian, *President*
Isabel Zohrabian, *Treasurer*
▲ EMP: 60
SQ FT: 20,000
SALES (est): 12.2MM **Privately Held**
SIC: 5094 Jewelry & precious stones

(P-8010)
MEL BERNIE AND COMPANY INC (PA)
Also Called: 1928 Jewelry Company
3000 W Empire Ave, Burbank
(91504-3109)
PHONE.................................818 841-1928
Melvyn Bernie, *CEO*
▲ EMP: 250 EST: 1968
SQ FT: 65,000
SALES (est): 55.6MM **Privately Held**
WEB: www.1928.com
SIC: 5094 Jewelry

(P-8011)
NER PRECIOUS METALS INC
10660 Wilshire Blvd, Los Angeles
(90024-4522)
PHONE.................................213 489-1549
Pedram Shamekh, *CEO*
▲ EMP: 60
SALES: 5MM **Privately Held**
SIC: 5094 5131 5085 Precious metals;
piece goods & other fabrics; industrial
supplies

(P-8012)
NIXON INC (PA)
Also Called: Nixon Watches
701 S Coast Highway 101, Encinitas
(92024-4441)
PHONE.................................760 944-0900
Nicholas Stowe, *CEO*
Andrus Laats, *President*
Brian White, *Vice Pres*
Chad Dinenna, *Admin Sec*
Jorden Fontenot, *Credit Mgr*
▲ EMP: 120
SQ FT: 3,000
SALES (est): 56.3MM **Privately Held**
WEB: www.nixonnow.com
SIC: 5094 5611 5136 Watches & parts;
clothing accessories: men's & boys';
leather & sheep lined clothing, men's &
boys'

(P-8013)
SWEDA COMPANY LLC
17411 E Valley Blvd, City of Industry
(91744-5159)
PHONE.................................626 357-9999
Jim Hagan, *CEO*
Kellie Claudio, *Vice Pres*
Scott Pearson, *Vice Pres*
Cindy Qin, *Vice Pres*
Paul Beck, *CFO*
▲ EMP: 200
SQ FT: 350,000
SALES (est): 121.4MM **Privately Held**
WEB: www.sweda.com
SIC: 5094 5044 Watches & parts; clocks;
calcvlators, electronic

(P-8014)
TACORI ENTERPRISES
1736 Gardena Ave, Glendale (91204-2907)
PHONE.................................818 863-1536
Haig Tacorian, *CEO*
Alred Margousian, *CFO*
Gilda Tacorian, *Vice Pres*
Teddy Lapina, *Analyst*
Alfred Margousian, *Accountant*
▲ EMP: 58
SQ FT: 16,000
SALES: 65MM **Privately Held**
WEB: www.tacori.com
SIC: 5094 Jewelry

(P-8015)
TOUCAN INC (PA)
Also Called: Tomas Jewelry
824 L St Unit 6, Arcata (95521-5766)
P.O. Box 4808 (95518-4808)
PHONE.................................707 822-6662
Thomas S Perrett, *President*
Chris Albright, *Vice Pres*
Karen Lu, *Manager*
▲ EMP: 80
SQ FT: 25,000
SALES (est): 20.5MM **Privately Held**
WEB: www.tomasjewelry.com
SIC: 5094 Jewelry; precious metals

5099 Durable Goods: NEC Wholesale

(P-8016)
AGRITEC INTERNATIONAL LTD
Also Called: Cleantech Environmental
5820 Martin Rd, Irwindale (91706-6213)
PHONE.................................626 812-7200
Robert Eldon Brown III, *President*
Loretta Ventura, *Office Mgr*
EMP: 50
SQ FT: 5,000
SALES (est): 24MM **Privately Held**
WEB: www.cleantechenv.com
SIC: 5099 Safety equipment & supplies

(P-8017)
ALPHA SYSTEMS FIRE PROTECTION
7356 Fulton Ave, North Hollywood
(91605-4113)
PHONE.................................323 227-0700
Jerry Pivnik, *President*
Jill Pivnik, *Principal*
EMP: 50
SQ FT: 2,776
SALES: 5MM **Privately Held**
SIC: 5099 Fire extinguishers

(P-8018)
ARTISAN PICTURES INC
Also Called: Live International
2700 Colorado Ave Fl 2, Santa Monica
(90404-5502)
PHONE.................................310 449-9200
Jon Feltheimer, *CEO*
Anthony J Scotti, *Ch of Bd*
Steve Beeks, *President*
Amir Malin, *President*
Ronald B Cushey, *CFO*
EMP: 150
SALES (est): 26.9MM
SALES (corp-wide): 3.2B **Privately Held**
SIC: 5099 Video cassettes, accessories &
supplies

HQ: Lions Gate Entertainment Inc.
2700 Colorado Ave Ste 200
Santa Monica CA 90404
310 449-9200

(P-8019)
BAY MARINE & INDUS SUP LLC
2900 Main St, Alameda (94501-7522)
PHONE.................................510 337-9122
Bill Elliott, *Principal*
James Whitman, *Principal*
EMP: 50
SALES (est): 4.8MM **Privately Held**
SIC: 5099 Durable goods

(P-8020)
BRETHREN INC
Also Called: Fire Safety First
1170 E Fruit St, Santa Ana (92701-4205)
PHONE.................................714 836-4800
Al Saia, *CEO*
Mike Saia, *Vice Pres*
Peggy Saia, *Admin Sec*
EMP: 50 EST: 1984
SQ FT: 4,000
SALES (est): 18.2MM **Privately Held**
WEB: www.firesafetyfirst.com
SIC: 5099 7389 Fire extinguishers; fire ex-
tinguisher servicing

(P-8021)
BURGETT INCORPORATED
Also Called: Piano Disc
4111a N Freeway Blvd, Sacramento
(95834-1209)
PHONE.................................916 567-9999
Gary Burgett, *CEO*
Stephanie Johnston, *President*
Kirk Burgett, *Vice Pres*
Jan Kiser, *Executive*
David Honeywell, *Engineer*
▲ EMP: 70
SQ FT: 48,000
SALES (est): 16MM **Privately Held**
WEB: www.pianodisc.com
SIC: 5099 3429 3931 3651 Pianos; piano
hardware; musical instruments; house-
hold audio & video equipment

(P-8022)
CELLMARK INC (DH)
Also Called: United International
88 Rowland Way Ste 300, Novato
(94945-5049)
PHONE.................................415 927-1700
Fredrik Anderson, *CEO*
Michael J Cussen, *CFO*
Thomas Hedberg, *Principal*
Nancy Cohen, *Accountant*
John Agel, *Sales Staff*
◆ EMP: 65
SQ FT: 13,000
SALES (est): 154.7MM
SALES (corp-wide): 2.8B **Privately Held**
SIC: 5099 5093 5111 Pulpwood; waste
paper; fine paper
HQ: Cellmark Ab
Lilla Bommen 3c
Goteborg 411 0
311 003-00

(P-8023)
CENTERLINE WOOD PRODUCTS
10007 Yucca Rd, Adelanto (92301-2242)
PHONE.................................760 246-4530
Michael Rodriguez, *President*
EMP: 99
SALES (est): 2.5MM **Privately Held**
SIC: 5099 Wood & wood by-products

(P-8024)
D J AMERICAN SUPPLY INC
Also Called: American Dj Group of Compa-
nies
6122 S Eastern Ave, Commerce
(90040-3402)
PHONE.................................323 582-2650
Charles Davies, *President*
Alfred Gonzales, *President*
Toby Velazquez, *President*
Brian Dowdle, *Telecom Exec*
Gabriel Trujillo, *Graphic Designe*
◆ EMP: 126
SQ FT: 100,000

SALES (est): 52.1MM **Privately Held**
SIC: 5099 5719 5999 Firearms & ammunition, except sporting; lighting fixtures;
theatrical equipment & supplies

(P-8025)
DAMAO LUGGAGE INTL INC
Also Called: Chariot Travelware
1909 S Vineyard Ave, Ontario
(91761-7747)
PHONE.................................909 923-6531
Moon Woo, *President*
Wendy Fan, *CFO*
Abby Kee, *Director*
Jian Kee, *Director*
Wilson Xu, *Director*
▲ EMP: 3014
SQ FT: 60,000
SALES (est): 161.4MM **Privately Held**
SIC: 5099 3161 Luggage; luggage

(P-8026)
DAW INDUSTRIES INC
6610 Nncy Rdge Dr Ste 100, San Diego
(92121)
PHONE.................................858 622-4955
Hugo Belzidsky, *President*
Stuart Marquette, *Vice Pres*
Lisa Miller, *Graphic Designe*
Nick Burrow, *Human Res Mgr*
Craig Johnson, *Sales Mgr*
▲ EMP: 50
SALES (est): 9.4MM **Privately Held**
WEB: www.daw-usa.com
SIC: 5099 Safety equipment & supplies;
fire extinguishers

(P-8027)
DENNIS FOLAND INC
Also Called: Logo Expressions
1500 S Hellman Ave, Ontario (91761-7634)
PHONE.................................909 930-9900
Dennis Foland, *CEO*
Beverly Foland, *Corp Secy*
Miguel Tugas, *Info Tech Mgr*
Ervin Millanes, *Purch Agent*
Darren Foland, *VP Opers*
▲ EMP: 100
SQ FT: 140,000
SALES (est): 51.2MM **Privately Held**
SIC: 5099 3944 Souvenirs; games, toys &
children's vehicles

(P-8028)
DZ TRADING LTD
12492 Feather Dr, Eastvale (91752-1483)
PHONE.................................951 479-5700
Berenice Monay, *Manager*
EMP: 152
SALES (corp-wide): 48.7MM **Privately
Held**
SIC: 5099 Brass goods
PA: Dz Trading, Ltd.
58 W 40th St Fl 8
New York NY 10018
212 869-3939

(P-8029)
EASTMAN MUSIC COMPANY (PA)
Also Called: Eastmans Guitars
2158 Pomona Blvd, Pomona (91768-3332)
PHONE.................................909 868-1777
Saul Friedgood, *CEO*
Qian Ni, *CEO*
Jay Schreiber, *Accounts Mgr*
▲ EMP: 51 EST: 2001
SALES (est): 18.6MM **Privately Held**
WEB: www.eastmanstrings.com
SIC: 5099 3931 Musical instruments; ac-
cordions & parts

(P-8030)
FOX LUGGAGE INC
5353 E Slauson Ave, Commerce
(90040-2916)
PHONE.................................323 588-1688
Wayne Wang, *CEO*
Sherrishan H Lee, *President*
Skip She, *Manager*
▲ EMP: 65
SQ FT: 80,000
SALES (est): 10.6MM **Privately Held**
WEB: www.foxluggage.com
SIC: 5099 Luggage

(P-8031)
FRESH PICK PRODUCE
195 San Pedro Ave Ste D, Morgan Hill
(95037-5142)
PHONE..................................408 315-4612
Stephanie Tsigaris,
EMP: 50
SALES (est): 777.2K **Privately Held**
SIC: 5099 Durable goods

(P-8032)
GENIUS PRODUCTS INC
3301 Expo Blvd Ste 100, Santa Monica
(90404)
PHONE..................................310 453-1222
Trevor Drinkwater, *President*
Stephen K Bannon, *Ch of Bd*
Edward J Byrnes, *CFO*
▲ **EMP:** 222
SQ FT: 40,520
SALES (est): 132.2K **Privately Held**
SIC: 5099 3652 7819 Video & audio
equipment; pre-recorded records & tapes;
video tape or disk reproduction

(P-8033)
**GOLDEN STATE MEDICAL
SUPPLY**
5247 Camino Ruiz, Camarillo
(93012-8602)
PHONE..................................805 477-8966
Benjamin Hall, *CEO*
Thomas Weaver, *CFO*
EMP: 99
SALES (est): 1.4MM **Privately Held**
SIC: 5099 Durable goods

(P-8034)
**GOLDEN WEST CUSTOM WD
SHUTTERS**
20561 Pascal Way, Lake Forest
(92630-8119)
PHONE..................................949 951-0600
Fax: 949 595-0363
EMP: 50
SALES (est): 3.4MM **Privately Held**
SIC: 5099

(P-8035)
GUTHY-RENKER LLC (PA)
Also Called: Proactiv
100 N Pacific Coast Hwy # 1600, El Se-
gundo (90245-4359)
P.O. Box 13670, Palm Desert (92255-
3670)
PHONE..................................760 773-9022
Greg Renker, *President*
Kimber Maderazzo, *Exec VP*
Bill Guthy, *Vice Pres*
Doo Lee, *Vice Pres*
Laura Lum, *Vice Pres*
▲ **EMP:** 60
SQ FT: 15,000
SALES (est): 370.7MM **Privately Held**
WEB: www.sheercover.com
SIC: 5099 7812 5999 7389 Tapes & cas-
settes, prerecorded; commercials, televi-
sion: tape or film; cosmetics;
telemarketing services

(P-8036)
GUTHY-RENKER LLC
Also Called: Guthy-Renker Direct
3340 Ocean Park Blvd Fl 2, Santa Monica
(90405-3204)
PHONE..................................310 581-6250
Bill Guthy, *President*
Cameron Dougan, *Marketing Mgr*
Jena Hui, *Marketing Mgr*
Michael Mrozowski, *Marketing Staff*
Scott Wilson, *Director*
EMP: 80
SALES (corp-wide): 370.7MM **Privately
Held**
WEB: www.sheercover.com
SIC: 5099 7812 5999 Tapes & cassettes,
prerecorded; commercials, television:
tape or film; cosmetics
PA: Guthy-Renker Llc
100 N Pacific Coast Hwy # 1600
El Segundo CA 90245
760 773-9022

(P-8037)
GYPSUM DRY WALL SUPPLY CO
2049 Senter Rd, San Jose (95112-2600)
PHONE..................................408 993-9710
Denise Willis, *Manager*
EMP: 50
SALES (est): 195.5K **Privately Held**
SIC: 5099 Firearms & ammunition, except
sporting

(P-8038)
H AND H DRUG STORES INC
Also Called: Western Drug Medical Supply
4692 E Waterloo Rd, Stockton
(95215-2309)
PHONE..................................209 931-5200
Haig J Youredjian, *Principal*
EMP: 89
SALES (corp-wide): 42.3MM **Privately
Held**
SIC: 5099 Brass goods
PA: H And H Drug Stores, Inc.
3604 San Fernando Rd
Glendale CA 91204
818 956-6691

(P-8039)
JIMS STEEL SUPPLY LLC
3530 Buck Owens Blvd, Bakersfield
(93308-4920)
P.O. Box 191 (93302-0191)
PHONE..................................661 324-6514
Greg Boylan,
Gregory Boylan, *Principal*
EMP: 50 **EST:** 2017
SALES (est): 15MM **Privately Held**
SIC: 5099 Durable goods

(P-8040)
JORGENSEN & SONS INC (PA)
Also Called: Jorgensen & Co
2467 Foundry Park Ave, Fresno
(93706-4531)
PHONE..................................559 268-6241
Darrell Hefley, *CEO*
Donald Jorgensen, *Ch of Bd*
Leon Young, *President*
Jim Rushing, *Treasurer*
Al V Jorgensen, *Vice Ch Bd*
EMP: 55
SQ FT: 28,000
SALES (est): 30.4MM **Privately Held**
SIC: 5099 1731 Safety equipment & sup-
plies; fire detection & burglar alarm sys-
tems specialization

(P-8041)
**KAWAI AMERICA CORPORATION
(HQ)**
2055 E University Dr, Compton
(90220-6411)
PHONE..................................310 631-1771
Hirotaka Kawai, *President*
Naoki Mori, *President*
Yoshiro Kataoka, *Admin Sec*
Gene Yanagi, *Info Tech Mgr*
Joel Bonifacio, *Manager*
◆ **EMP:** 50
SQ FT: 73,000
SALES (est): 25.4MM
SALES (corp-wide): 664.4MM **Privately
Held**
SIC: 5099 Pianos
PA: Kawai Musical Instruments Manufactur-
ing Co., Ltd.
200, Terajimacho, Naka-Ku
Hamamatsu SZO 430-0
534 571-213

(P-8042)
LIBERTY GLOVE INC (PA)
Also Called: Liberty Glove & Safety Co
433 Cheryl Ln, City of Industry
(91789-3023)
PHONE..................................909 595-2992
Michael Young, *President*
Vicki Lin, *CFO*
Oscar Mejia, *Branch Mgr*
Carmen Leung, *Accounting Mgr*
Lucy Luo, *Buyer*
▲ **EMP:** 50
SALES (est): 42.3MM **Privately Held**
WEB: www.libertyglove.com
SIC: 5099 Safety equipment & supplies

(P-8043)
**MENDOCINO FOREST PDTS CO
LLC**
6500 Durable Mill Rd, Calpella (95418)
PHONE..................................707 620-2961
Jon Roi, *Branch Mgr*
EMP: 52
SALES (corp-wide): 134.9MM **Privately
Held**
SIC: 5099 Wood & wood by-products
PA: Mendocino Forest Products Company
Llc
3700 Old Redwood Hwy # 200
Santa Rosa CA 95403
707 620-2961

(P-8044)
MONOPRICE INC (HQ)
Also Called: Monoprice.com
1 Pointe Dr Ste 400, Brea (92821-7626)
PHONE..................................909 989-6887
Bernard Luthi, *CEO*
Eric Krause, *Regl Sales Mgr*
◆ **EMP:** 109
SQ FT: 30,000
SALES (est): 144.7MM
SALES (corp-wide): 392.6MM **Privately
Held**
SIC: 5099 Video & audio equipment
PA: Yfc-Boneagle Electric Co., Ltd.
No. 12-9, Ln. 130, Sec. 2, Zhongshan
E. Rd.,
Taoyuan City TAY 32741
347 788-46

(P-8045)
MONSTER INC (PA)
Also Called: Monster Products
601 Gateway Blvd Ste 900, South San
Francisco (94080-7070)
P.O. Box 435, Brisbane (94005-0435)
PHONE..................................415 840-2000
Noel Lee, *President*
Irene Baron, *Vice Pres*
Emma Barton, *Recruiter*
David Haines, *Manager*
Stephanie Kuntz, *Manager*
▲ **EMP:** 330
SQ FT: 50,000
SALES (est): 255.2MM **Privately Held**
WEB: www.monstercable.com
SIC: 5099 4841 3679 Video & audio
equipment; cable & other pay television
services; headphones, radio

(P-8046)
MSC CHATSWORTH
9324 Corbin Ave, Northridge (91324-2405)
PHONE..................................818 718-7696
Wendy Araiza, *Principal*
EMP: 89
SALES (est): 11.5MM **Privately Held**
SIC: 5099 Durable goods

(P-8047)
**NATIONAL DISTRIBUTION
SERVICES**
340 N Grant Ave, Corona (92882-1828)
PHONE..................................951 739-2400
Gregor Gekghyan, *President*
EMP: 52
SALES (est): 25.9MM **Privately Held**
SIC: 5099 Firearms & ammunition, except
sporting

(P-8048)
NEW CENTURY MEDIA CORP
2727 Pellissier Pl, City of Industry
(90601-1510)
PHONE..................................562 695-1000
Carson Yu, *President*
Andy Forman, *Vice Pres*
Jennifer Yu, *Vice Pres*
Eva Gonzalez, *Office Mgr*
▲ **EMP:** 50
SQ FT: 21,000
SALES (est): 17.8MM **Privately Held**
WEB: www.newcenturymediausa.com
SIC: 5099 Video cassettes, accessories &
supplies

(P-8049)
**OLIVET INTERNATIONAL INC
(PA)**
11015 Hopkins St, Mira Loma
(91752-3248)
PHONE..................................951 681-8888
Lydia Hsu, *President*
Andrew Bomes, *President*
David Yu, *CFO*
Jeanelle Harris, *Vice Pres*
Neal Weinstein, *Vice Pres*
▲ **EMP:** 200
SQ FT: 456,000
SALES (est): 164MM **Privately Held**
WEB: www.olivetintl.com
SIC: 5099 Luggage

(P-8050)
**PRAJIN 1 STOP DISTRIBUTORS
INC (PA)**
Also Called: Prajin Discount Distributors
5701 Pacific Blvd 5711, Huntington Park
(90255-2615)
PHONE..................................323 395-5302
Antonio Prajin, *President*
Maria Gina Prajin, *Shareholder*
George Prajin, *Corp Secy*
Anthony Prajin Jr, *Vice Pres*
Peter Prajin, *General Mgr*
EMP: 50
SQ FT: 1,000
SALES (est): 14.1MM **Privately Held**
WEB: www.prajin1stop.com
SIC: 5099 5735 Compact discs; compact
discs

(P-8051)
QUEST GROUP (PA)
Also Called: Audioquest
2621 White Rd, Irvine (92614-6247)
PHONE..................................949 585-0111
William E Low, *CEO*
Joe Anzenberger, *Vice Pres*
Brian Long, *General Mgr*
Adri Meesters, *Office Mgr*
Carmen Wilcox, *Office Mgr*
▲ **EMP:** 67
SQ FT: 45,000
SALES (est): 24.2MM **Privately Held**
WEB: www.audioquest.com
SIC: 5099 Video & audio equipment

(P-8052)
READY AMERICA INC (PA)
Also Called: Quakehold
1399 Specialty Dr, Vista (92081-8521)
PHONE..................................760 295-0234
Dean H Reese, *CEO*
▲ **EMP:** 53
SALES (est): 14.5MM **Privately Held**
WEB: www.marlyco.com
SIC: 5099 Safety equipment & supplies

(P-8053)
RGGD INC (PA)
Also Called: Crystal Art of Florida
4950 S Santa Fe Ave, Vernon
(90058-2106)
PHONE..................................323 581-6617
Randy Greenberg, *CEO*
Douglas Song, *President*
Glenn Knecht, *Admin Sec*
▲ **EMP:** 80
SQ FT: 120,000
SALES (est): 31.6MM **Privately Held**
SIC: 5099 3441 Wood & wood by-prod-
ucts; fabricated structural metal

(P-8054)
**ROLAND CORPORATION US
(HQ)**
5100 S Eastern Ave, Los Angeles
(90040-2938)
P.O. Box 910921 (90091-0921)
PHONE..................................323 890-3700
Christopher Bristol, *CEO*
Roland Apps, *Partner*
Fumie Wolff, *President*
Dennis M Houlihan, *Vice Pres*
Mark S Malbon, *Vice Pres*
◆ **EMP:** 165
SQ FT: 50,000

SALES (est): 80.1MM
SALES (corp-wide): 384.5MM **Privately Held**
SIC: 5099 5045 3931 Musical instruments; computer peripheral equipment; organs, all types: pipe, reed, hand, electronic, etc.
PA: Roland Corporation
2036-1, Nakagawa, Hosoecho, Kita-Ku
Hamamatsu SZO 431-1
535 230-230

(P-8055)
ROSEN ELECTRONICS LLC
1120 California Ave, Corona (92881-3324)
PHONE..........................951 898-9808
W Thomas Clements, *President*
Greg Perez, *Regl Sales Mgr*
▲ **EMP:** 75
SQ FT: 48,000
SALES (est): 17MM
SALES (corp-wide): 34.1MM **Privately Held**
WEB: www.rosenentertainment.com
SIC: 5099 3679 Video & audio equipment; liquid crystal displays (LCD)
PA: Aamp Of Florida, Inc.
15500 Lightwave Dr # 202
Clearwater FL 33760
727 572-9255

(P-8056)
RWP TRANSFER INC
Also Called: Recycled Wood Products
1313 E Phillips Blvd, Pomona (91766-5431)
PHONE..........................909 868-6882
Chris Kiralla, *President*
EMP: 50
SQ FT: 1,100
SALES (est): 14.1MM **Privately Held**
SIC: 5099 5083 Wood & wood by-products; landscaping equipment

(P-8057)
SAN DIMAS LUGGAGE COMPANY
2095 S Archibald Ave, Ontario (91761-8579)
PHONE..........................909 510-8820
Laurent Kabbabe, *Controller*
Vovoama Castro, *Human Res Mgr*
EMP: 60 **EST:** 1977
SALES (est): 12.8MM **Privately Held**
SIC: 5099 Luggage

(P-8058)
SCOPE SEVEN LLC
2201 Park Pl Ste 100, El Segundo (90245-4909)
PHONE..........................310 220-3939
Gordon Doran, *Mng Member*
EMP: 62
SALES (est): 6.8MM **Privately Held**
SIC: 5099 Compact discs

(P-8059)
SONY MUSIC ENTERTAINMENT INC
Also Called: Sony Publishers
9830 Wilshire Blvd, Beverly Hills (90212-1804)
PHONE..........................310 272-2555
EMP: 250
SALES (corp-wide): 80.1B **Privately Held**
WEB: www.sonymusic.com
SIC: 5099 Phonograph records
HQ: Sony Music Entertainment
25 Madison Ave Fl 19
New York NY 10010

(P-8060)
SUN COAST MERCHANDISE CORP
6315 Bandini Blvd, Commerce (90040-3115)
PHONE..........................323 720-9700
Kumar C Bhavnani, *President*
Walter Rubin, *Chief Mktg Ofcr*
Dilip Bhavnani, *Vice Pres*
Vidya Bhavnani, *Admin Sec*
Vinay Arora, *CIO*
◆ **EMP:** 250

SQ FT: 120,000
SALES (est): 79.5MM **Privately Held**
SIC: 5099 Brass goods

(P-8061)
SUNSCAPE EYEWEAR INC
17526 Von Karman Ave A, Irvine (92614-4258)
PHONE..........................949 553-0590
Ali Adam Rizza, *President*
Adam Rizza, *CFO*
Wally Rizza, *Vice Pres*
▲ **EMP:** 78
SQ FT: 10,500
SALES (est): 9.8MM **Privately Held**
WEB: www.isunscape.com
SIC: 5099 Sunglasses

(P-8062)
TRAVELERS CLUB LUGGAGE INC
5911 Fresca Dr, La Palma (90623-1056)
PHONE..........................714 523-8808
Peter D Yu, *CEO*
Sam Hur, *Marketing Staff*
◆ **EMP:** 54
SQ FT: 120,000
SALES (est): 21.7MM **Privately Held**
WEB: www.travelersclub.com
SIC: 5099 Luggage

(P-8063)
TREEFROG DEVELOPMENTS INC
Also Called: Lifeproof
15110 Ave Of Science, San Diego (92128-3440)
PHONE..........................619 324-7755
Gary Rayner, *CEO*
Kevin Morse, *CFO*
Dan Koziol, *Vice Pres*
▲ **EMP:** 75 **EST:** 2009
SQ FT: 20,000
SALES (est): 35.8MM
SALES (corp-wide): 228MM **Privately Held**
SIC: 5099 Cases, carrying
PA: Otter Products, Llc
209 S Meldrum St
Fort Collins CO 80521
855 688-7269

(P-8064)
TRENDSETTAH USA INC
1420 S Highland Ave L203, Fullerton (92832-3514)
PHONE..........................888 775-4881
Akrum Alrahib, *CEO*
Sal Kureh, *CFO*
Ramzy Rahib, *Treasurer*
Bill Schoep, *Senior VP*
Mousa Rahib, *Admin Sec*
▼ **EMP:** 63
SQ FT: 40,000
SALES (est): 15.5MM **Privately Held**
SIC: 5099 Novelties, durable

(P-8065)
TUMI INC
333 Santana Row Apt 230, San Jose (95128-2007)
PHONE..........................408 244-6512
Laurence Franklin, *President*
EMP: 70 **Privately Held**
SIC: 5099 Luggage
HQ: Tumi, Inc.
499 Thornall St Ste 10
Edison NJ 08837
908 756-4400

(P-8066)
UNIVERSAL MUS GROUP HLDNGS INC
21301 Burbank Blvd # 100, Woodland Hills (91367-6679)
PHONE..........................317 871-0319
Steven Margeotes, *Vice Pres*
EMP: 600
SALES (corp-wide): 78.4MM **Privately Held**
SIC: 5099 Video & audio equipment
HQ: Universal Music Group Holdings, Inc.
1755 Broadway Fl 6
New York NY 10019
212 333-8000

(P-8067)
YALEY ENTERPRISES INC
7664 Avianca Dr, Redding (96002-9703)
PHONE..........................530 365-5252
Patricia J Yaley, *CEO*
Thomas O'Rourke, *Corp Secy*
Thomas J Yaley, *Vice Pres*
Barbara Sletner, *Manager*
EMP: 50
SQ FT: 30,000
SALES (est): 11MM **Privately Held**
SIC: 5099 3544 Brass goods; special dies, tools, jigs & fixtures

(P-8068)
YAMAHA CORPORATION OF AMERICA (HQ)
Also Called: Yamaha Music Corporation U S A
6600 Orangethorpe Ave, Buena Park (90620-1396)
PHONE..........................714 522-9011
Hitoshi Fukutome, *CEO*
Terry Lewis, *Senior VP*
Brian Jemelian, *Administration*
Jerry Andreas, *CIO*
David Dexter, *Manager*
◆ **EMP:** 300
SALES (est): 276.5MM
SALES (corp-wide): 4B **Privately Held**
WEB: www.yamaha.com
SIC: 5099 5065 5091 3931 Musical instruments; pianos; sound equipment, electronic; sporting & recreation goods; golf equipment; musical instruments
PA: Yamaha Corporation
10-1, Nakazawacho, Naka-Ku
Hamamatsu SZO 430-0
534 601-111

5111 Printing & Writing Paper Wholesale

(P-8069)
DOT LEASING COMPANY
2424 Mcgaw Ave, Irvine (92614-5834)
PHONE..........................949 474-1100
Bruce Carson, *Managing Prtnr*
William Clark, *Partner*
Charles Massingill, *Partner*
Eric Pepys, *Partner*
Melissa May, *IT/INT Sup*
EMP: 151
SQ FT: 40,000
SALES (est): 9.5MM **Privately Held**
SIC: 5111 Printing & writing paper

(P-8070)
KELLY PAPER COMPANY (HQ)
288 Brea Canyon Rd, Walnut (91789-3087)
PHONE..........................909 859-8200
Janice Gottesman, *President*
Theron Alford, *Branch Mgr*
Gary Edwards, *Branch Mgr*
Danny Hernandez, *Branch Mgr*
Paul Mason, *Branch Mgr*
▲ **EMP:** 50 **EST:** 1936
SALES (est): 306.9MM
SALES (corp-wide): 4.1B **Privately Held**
WEB: www.kellypaper.com
SIC: 5111 5943 Printing paper; office forms & supplies
PA: Central National Gottesman Inc.
3 Manhattanville Rd # 301
Purchase NY 10577
914 696-9000

(P-8071)
SPICERS PAPER INC (HQ)
12310 Slauson Ave, Santa Fe Springs (90670-2629)
PHONE..........................562 698-1199
Janice L Gottesman, *CEO*
Rick Anderson, *Vice Pres*
George Seymour, *Regional Mgr*
Kathy Markley, *Admin Mgr*
Sergio Grajales, *General Mgr*
◆ **EMP:** 180
SQ FT: 365,000

SALES (est): 527.4MM
SALES (corp-wide): 4.1B **Privately Held**
WEB: www.spicers.com
SIC: 5111 Fine paper; printing paper; writing paper
PA: Central National Gottesman Inc.
3 Manhattanville Rd # 301
Purchase NY 10577
914 696-9000

5112 Stationery & Office Splys Wholesale

(P-8072)
5 DAY BUSINESS FORMS MFG INC (PA)
2910 E La Cresta Ave, Anaheim (92806-1818)
P.O. Box 6269 (92816-0269)
PHONE..........................213 623-3577
Leslie Messick, *President*
Walter Messick, *Shareholder*
Bob Bemmer, *Purchasing*
EMP: 54 **EST:** 1976
SQ FT: 22,500
SALES (est): 11.8MM **Privately Held**
WEB: 5daybf.com
SIC: 5112 Business forms

(P-8073)
5 DAY BUSINESS FORMS MFG INC
2921 E La Cresta Ave, Anaheim (92806-1873)
PHONE..........................714 632-8674
Lesley Messick, *Branch Mgr*
Norman Hamamoto, *Chief Mktg Ofcr*
Wendy Schul, *Human Res Mgr*
Scott Kirschner, *Purch Agent*
Lisa Sandell, *Sales Staff*
EMP: 62
SALES (corp-wide): 11.8MM **Privately Held**
SIC: 5112 Business forms
PA: 5 Day Business Forms Mfg., Inc.
2910 E La Cresta Ave
Anaheim CA 92806
213 623-3577

(P-8074)
A YAFA PEN COMPANY
21306 Gault St, Canoga Park (91303-2123)
PHONE..........................818 704-8888
Yair Greenberg, *CEO*
Niv Avidan, *Exec VP*
Ken Jones, *Vice Pres*
Anita Sebetic, *General Mgr*
Eddie Olague, *Webmaster*
▲ **EMP:** 50 **EST:** 1978
SQ FT: 25,000
SALES (est): 14.6MM **Privately Held**
WEB: www.aldodomani.com
SIC: 5112 5199 Office supplies; advertising specialties

(P-8075)
ALL PHASE BUSINESS SUPPLIES
1920 E Gladwick St, Compton (90220-6201)
PHONE..........................310 631-1900
Jeffrey Kraus, *President*
EMP: 50
SQ FT: 10,000
SALES (est): 4.8MM **Privately Held**
SIC: 5112 5943 Office supplies; office forms & supplies

(P-8076)
BANGKIT (USA) INC
Also Called: Bazic Product
10511 Valley Blvd, El Monte (91731-2403)
PHONE..........................626 672-0888
Handy Hioe, *CEO*
Eric Concepcion, *Vice Pres*
Daniel Graham, *Vice Pres*
Anita Handojo, *Vice Pres*
Lysa Hioe, *Vice Pres*
◆ **EMP:** 80
SQ FT: 195,000
SALES: 49.6MM **Privately Held**
SIC: 5112 Office supplies

(P-8077)
CARTRIDGE FAMILY INC
Also Called: Cartridge Family Ink
1940 Union St Ste 29, Oakland
(94607-2352)
PHONE..................................510 658-0400
Nate Laskin, *CEO*
EMP: 148
SQ FT: 2,750
SALES (est): 15.5MM **Privately Held**
WEB: www.cartridgefamily.com
SIC: 5112 5065 5044 7389 Laserjet supplies; facsimile equipment; copying equipment; printers' services: folding, collating

(P-8078)
DIETRICH POST CO INC
945 Bryant St, San Francisco
(94103-4523)
PHONE..................................510 596-0080
EMP: 50
SALES (est): 4.1MM **Privately Held**
SIC: 5112

(P-8079)
ESSENDANT CO
Also Called: United Stationers
918 S Stimson Ave, City of Industry
(91745-1640)
PHONE..................................626 961-0011
Terry Deines, *Manager*
Bill Sutter, *MIS Dir*
EMP: 230
SALES (corp-wide): 5B **Publicly Held**
WEB: www.ussco.com
SIC: 5112 5044 5021 5943 Office supplies; office equipment; furniture; office forms & supplies
HQ: Essendant Co.
1 Parkway North Blvd # 100
Deerfield IL 60015
847 627-7000

(P-8080)
ESSENDANT CO
5440 Stationers Way, Sacramento
(95842-1900)
PHONE..................................916 344-6707
Greg Birdsall, *Branch Mgr*
Sheryl Weber, *Safety Mgr*
Ted Pinnow, *Facilities Mgr*
David Belcher, *Manager*
EMP: 200
SALES (corp-wide): 5B **Publicly Held**
WEB: www.ussco.com
SIC: 5112 Office supplies
HQ: Essendant Co.
1 Parkway North Blvd # 100
Deerfield IL 60015
847 627-7000

(P-8081)
GIVE SOMETHING BACK INC (PA)
Also Called: Give Something Back Off Sups
7730 Pardee Ln Ste A, Oakland
(94621-1555)
PHONE..................................800 261-2619
Toll Free:.............................888 -
Sean Marx, *CEO*
Mike Hannigan, *President*
Dan Kelley, *Accounts Exec*
▲ EMP: 58
SQ FT: 19,800
SALES (est): 106.2MM **Privately Held**
WEB: www.givesomethingback.com
SIC: 5112 Office supplies

(P-8082)
IMAGING TECHNOLOGIES GROUP LLC
Also Called: Itd Print Solutions
5220 Pacific Concourse Dr, Los Angeles
(90045-6277)
PHONE..................................310 638-2500
Benjamin Alexander,
David Mullen, *Sales Staff*
▼ EMP: 50 EST: 1980
SQ FT: 7,000
SALES (est): 11.1MM **Privately Held**
WEB: www.rhinotek.com
SIC: 5112 Computer & photocopying supplies

(P-8083)
JOHN A MAIDA ENTERPRISES
Also Called: Maida Specialties Co
P.O. Box 6144 (95150-6144)
PHONE..................................408 254-3100
Neil Callahan, *President*
Sandra Callahan, *Vice Pres*
EMP: 50 EST: 1968
SQ FT: 17,000
SALES (est): 7.7MM **Privately Held**
SIC: 5112 5199 5099 Greeting cards; party favors, balloons, hats, etc.; sunglasses

(P-8084)
NAT SIM CORP
Also Called: U S Office & Industry Supply
7405 Woodley Ave, Van Nuys
(91406-2924)
P.O. Box 10540, Canoga Park (91309-1540)
PHONE..................................818 705-3131
Yzes Yallouz, *President*
EMP: 53
SQ FT: 3,000
SALES (est): 6.3MM **Privately Held**
SIC: 5112 5085 Office supplies; industrial tools

(P-8085)
PENTEL OF AMERICA LTD (HQ)
2715 Columbia St, Torrance (90503-3861)
PHONE..................................310 320-3831
Chotaro Koumi, *President*
Norikazu Hasegama, *CFO*
Nobuo Aihara, *Chief Mktg Ofcr*
Minoru Mike Osada, *Exec VP*
Toshiro Hemmi, *Vice Pres*
▲ EMP: 132 EST: 1966
SQ FT: 46,000
SALES (est): 105MM
SALES (corp-wide): 225.4MM **Privately Held**
WEB: www.pentel.com
SIC: 5112 3951 5199 3952 Pens &/or pencils; pens & mechanical pencils; artists' materials; artists' materials, except pencils & leads
PA: Pentel Co., Ltd.
7-2, Nihombashikoamicho
Chuo-Ku TKY 103-0
336 673-333

(P-8086)
PENTEL OF AMERICA LTD
4000 E Airport Dr Ste C, Ontario
(91761-1592)
PHONE..................................909 975-2200
Steve Mukai, *Manager*
Michael Storie, *Manager*
EMP: 50
SALES (corp-wide): 225.4MM **Privately Held**
SIC: 5112 Pens &/or pencils
HQ: Pentel Of America, Ltd.
2715 Columbia St
Torrance CA 90503
310 320-3831

(P-8087)
PUNCH STUDIO LLC (PA)
6025 W Slauson Ave, Culver City
(90230-6507)
P.O. Box 3663 (90231-3663)
PHONE..................................310 390-9900
Todd Kirshner, *Mng Member*
Nathalie Carrer, *CFO*
◆ EMP: 292
SQ FT: 106,000
SALES: 55MM **Privately Held**
WEB: www.punchstudio.com
SIC: 5112 Greeting cards

(P-8088)
RR DONNELLEY & SONS COMPANY
Also Called: Moore Business Forms
40610 County Center Dr, Temecula
(92591-6019)
PHONE..................................951 296-2890
Rick Budge, *Manager*
EMP: 100
SALES (corp-wide): 6.9B **Publicly Held**
WEB: www.moore.com
SIC: 5112 2761 2752 Business forms; manifold business forms; color lithography
PA: R. R. Donnelley & Sons Company
35 W Wacker Dr Ste 3650
Chicago IL 60601
312 326-8000

(P-8089)
S P RICHARDS COMPANY
Also Called: S.p Richards
10235 San Sevaine Way # 120, Mira Loma
(91752-1153)
PHONE..................................951 681-3114
Jay Brooks, *Branch Mgr*
Jeremy Murphy, *Plant Mgr*
EMP: 100
SALES (corp-wide): 16.3B **Publicly Held**
WEB: www.sprichards.com
SIC: 5112 5021 Stationery & office supplies; office furniture
HQ: S. P. Richards Company
6300 Highlands Pkwy Se
Smyrna GA 30082
770 434-4571

(P-8090)
SAFEGUARD BUSINESS SYSTEMS INC
414 N A St, Oxnard (93030)
PHONE..................................805 486-9769
Greg Cook, *Branch Mgr*
EMP: 110
SALES (corp-wide): 1.9B **Publicly Held**
WEB: www.gosafeguard.com
SIC: 5112 Business forms
HQ: Safeguard Business Systems, Inc.
8585 N Stemmons Fwy 600n
Dallas TX 75247
800 523-2422

(P-8091)
TROWBRIDGE ENTERPRISES (PA)
Also Called: Palace Business Solutions
2606 Chanticleer Ave, Santa Cruz
(95065-1810)
PHONE..................................831 476-3815
Toll Free:.............................888 -
Roy M Trowbridge, *CEO*
Frank H Trowbridge III, *CFO*
Margaret Trowbridge, *Corp Secy*
Neal Heckman, *Vice Pres*
Tom Urbani, *Area Mgr*
EMP: 80
SQ FT: 11,000
SALES (est): 31.1MM **Privately Held**
WEB: www.gopalace.com
SIC: 5112 5943 5999 Office supplies; stationery stores; artists' supplies & materials

(P-8092)
VIKING OFFICE PRODUCTS INC (HQ)
3366 E Willow St, Signal Hill (90755-2311)
PHONE..................................562 490-1000
M Bruce Nelson, *President*
Ronald W Weissman, *Senior VP*
Mark R Brown, *Vice Pres*
▲ EMP: 292
SQ FT: 187,000
SALES (est): 729.7MM
SALES (corp-wide): 10.2B **Publicly Held**
SIC: 5112 5021 5045 5087 Office supplies; business forms; stationery; office furniture; computers, peripherals & software; janitors' supplies; photographic equipment & supplies; catalog & mail-order houses
PA: Office Depot, Inc.
6600 N Military Trl
Boca Raton FL 33496
561 438-4800

5113 Indl & Personal Svc Paper Wholesale

(P-8093)
AMERICAN PAPER & PLASTICS INC
Also Called: American Paper & Provisions
550 S 7th Ave, City of Industry
(91746-3120)
PHONE..................................626 444-0000
Daniel Emrani, *CEO*
Rod Lynch, *Vice Pres*
Jacob Handy, *Executive*
Chris Tellez, *Adv Board Mem*
Angel Herandez, *Admin Sec*
EMP: 119
SQ FT: 300,000
SALES (est): 130.1MM **Privately Held**
WEB: www.appinc.com
SIC: 5113 Bags, paper & disposable plastic

(P-8094)
ANDWIN CORPORATION (PA)
Also Called: Andwin Scientific
6636 Variel Ave, Woodland Hills
(91303-2808)
P.O. Box 689 (91365-0689)
PHONE..................................818 999-2828
Natalie Sarraf, *CEO*
Abner Levy, *President*
Andrew Fox, *Vice Pres*
Marla Goldberg, *Purch Mgr*
Sandy Rosenblum, *Purchasing*
▲ EMP: 110
SQ FT: 45,000
SALES (est): 67.7MM **Privately Held**
WEB: www.andwin.com
SIC: 5113 3842 5199 5087 Industrial & personal service paper; surgical appliances & supplies; packaging materials; janitors' supplies; hospital equipment & furniture; in vitro & in vivo diagnostic substances

(P-8095)
BUNZL DISTRIBUTION CAL LLC (DH)
3310 E Miraloma Ave, Anaheim
(92806-1911)
PHONE..................................714 688-1900
Patrick L Larmon, *President*
Scot Gregory, *General Mgr*
Derek R Goodin,
◆ EMP: 98
SQ FT: 150,000
SALES (est): 126MM
SALES (corp-wide): 11.3B **Privately Held**
SIC: 5113 Paper & products, wrapping or coarse
HQ: Bunzl Distribution Usa, Llc
1 Cityplace Dr Ste 200
Saint Louis MO 63141
314 997-5959

(P-8096)
BUNZL RETAIL SERVICES LLC
8449 Milliken Ave Ste 102, Rancho Cucamonga (91730-5540)
PHONE..................................909 476-2457
EMP: 87
SALES (corp-wide): 11.3B **Privately Held**
SIC: 5113 Paper & products, wrapping or coarse
HQ: Bunzl Retail Services, Llc
8338 Austin Ave
Morton Grove IL 60053
847 966-2550

(P-8097)
BUNZL USA INC
Also Called: Papercraft Los Angeles
15959 Piuma Ave, Cerritos (90703-1526)
PHONE..................................314 997-5959
Jeff McElroy, *Principal*
EMP: 66
SALES (corp-wide): 11.3B **Privately Held**
SIC: 5113 Industrial & personal service paper
HQ: Bunzl Usa, Inc.
1 Cityplace Dr Ste 200
Saint Louis MO 63141
314 997-5959

P R O D U C T S & S V C S

(P-8098)
CALIFORNIA SUPPLY INC (PA)
491 E Compton Blvd, Gardena
(90248-2078)
P.O. Box 3906 (90247-7598)
PHONE..........................310 532-2500
Mark Weinstein, *CEO*
Art Gaford, *CFO*
Michael Rosson, *Exec VP*
Mike McMillen, *Vice Pres*
Dan Bartlett, *Purch Dir*
▲ **EMP:** 69 **EST:** 1975
SQ FT: 75,000
SALES (est): 70.4MM **Privately Held**
WEB: www.calsupply.com
SIC: 5113 5087 Industrial & personal service paper; janitors' supplies

(P-8099)
CALPINE CONTAINERS INC
42779 Road 80, Dinuba (93618-9342)
PHONE..........................559 591-6555
Roger Bell, *Branch Mgr*
Keith Oden, *Opers Mgr*
EMP: 100
SQ FT: 35,780
SALES (corp-wide): 138.1MM **Privately Held**
WEB: www.calpineinc.com
SIC: 5113 5085 2441 2448 Corrugated & solid fiber boxes; boxes, paperboard & disposable plastic; box shooks; boxes, crates, etc., other than paper; boxes, wood; pallets, wood; corrugated & solid fiber boxes
PA: Calpine Containers, Inc.
380 W Spruce Ave
Clovis CA 93611
559 519-7199

(P-8100)
CALVEY INCORPORATED
Also Called: Ernest Packaging Solutions
8670 Fruitridge Rd # 300, Sacramento
(95826-9735)
PHONE..........................916 681-4800
A Charles Wilson, *Chairman*
Tim Wilson, *President*
▲ **EMP:** 60
SQ FT: 155,000
SALES (est): 36.1MM
SALES (corp-wide): 240.9MM **Privately Held**
SIC: 5113 Boxes, paperboard & disposable plastic; corrugated & solid fiber boxes
PA: Ernest Packaging
5777 Smithway St
Commerce CA 90040
800 233-7788

(P-8101)
ELKAY PLASTICS CO INC (PA)
6000 Sheila St, Commerce (90040-2405)
P.O. Box 910968, Los Angeles (90091-0931)
PHONE..........................323 722-7073
Louis Chertkow, *President*
Geoff Pankau, *CFO*
Geoffrey Pankau, *CFO*
Mariana Mendez, *Admin Asst*
Vickie Gosnell, *Info Tech Mgr*
▲ **EMP:** 100
SQ FT: 175,000
SALES (est): 103.4MM **Privately Held**
WEB: www.elkayplastics.com
SIC: 5113 Bags, paper & disposable plastic

(P-8102)
FRICK PAPER COMPANY
Also Called: Paper Mart Indus & Ret Packg
2164 N Batavia St, Orange (92865-3104)
PHONE..........................323 726-8200
John Frick, *Partner*
Thomas Frick, *Partner*
Tom Frick, *Partner*
Carlos Sandoval, *Database Admin*
Sally Salvador, *Purchasing*
▲ **EMP:** 106
SQ FT: 210,000
SALES (est): 61.1MM **Privately Held**
WEB: www.papermart.com
SIC: 5113 Paper & products, wrapping or coarse

(P-8103)
GAHVEJIAN ENTERPRISES INC
Also Called: Mid Valley Packaging & Sup Co
2004 S Temperance Ave, Fowler
(93625-9759)
P.O. Box 96 (93625-0096)
PHONE..........................559 834-5956
Carrie L Gahvejian, *President*
John Gahvejian, *President*
Lorrie Gahvejian, *Corp Secy*
Erik Creede, *President*
Dwayne Harris, *Controller*
◆ **EMP:** 50
SQ FT: 150,000
SALES (est): 54.9MM **Privately Held**
SIC: 5113 Bags, paper & disposable plastic; boxes, paperboard & disposable plastic; folding paperboard boxes

(P-8104)
GEORGIA-PACIFIC LLC
9525 W Nicholas Ct, Visalia (93291-9468)
PHONE..........................559 651-5500
Barbera Fox, *Branch Mgr*
EMP: 150
SALES (corp-wide): 42.9B **Privately Held**
WEB: www.gp.com
SIC: 5113 Corrugated & solid fiber boxes
HQ: Georgia-Pacific Llc
133 Peachtree St Nw
Atlanta GA 30303
404 652-4000

(P-8105)
GEORGIA-PACIFIC LLC
Also Called: Reliable Container
9206 Santa Fe Springs Rd, Santa Fe
Springs (90670-2618)
PHONE..........................562 861-6226
EMP: 275
SALES (corp-wide): 42.9B **Privately Held**
SIC: 5113 2653 Corrugated & solid fiber boxes; bags, paper & disposable plastic; boxes, corrugated: made from purchased materials; display items, corrugated: made from purchased materials
HQ: Georgia-Pacific Llc
133 Peachtree St Nw
Atlanta GA 30303
404 652-4000

(P-8106)
GHAZAL & SONS INC (PA)
Also Called: All American Plastic & Packg
3020 Hoover Ave, National City
(91950-7220)
PHONE..........................619 474-6677
Munther Ghazal, *President*
Duraid Ghazal, *Treasurer*
Betool Y Elia, *Vice Pres*
Mike Ghazal, *Vice Pres*
Norman M Ghazal, *Admin Sec*
▼ **EMP:** 87
SQ FT: 50,000
SALES: 5MM **Privately Held**
WEB: www.aaplastic.com
SIC: 5113 Bags, paper & disposable plastic

(P-8107)
GREENLEAF PAPER PRODUCTS
Also Called: Moor Products
26431 Crown Valley Pkwy # 150, Mission
Viejo (92691-7201)
PHONE..........................949 348-0048
Greg Mosby, *President*
EMP: 60
SALES (est): 245.7K **Privately Held**
SIC: 5113 Industrial & personal service paper

(P-8108)
MAXCO SUPPLY INC (PA)
605 S Zediker Ave, Parlier (93648-2033)
P.O. Box 814 (93648-0814)
PHONE..........................559 646-8449
Max Flaming, *President*
David Bryant, *COO*
Robert Grote, *VP Mfg*
Roy Ortega, *Manager*
▲ **EMP:** 200 **EST:** 1972
SQ FT: 8,500
SALES (est): 151.4MM **Privately Held**
SIC: 5113 2436 3554 Shipping supplies; softwood veneer & plywood; box making machines, paper

(P-8109)
MAXCO SUPPLY INC
8419 Di Giorgio Rd, Lamont (93241-2547)
PHONE..........................559 646-6700
Steve Grote, *Principal*
EMP: 83
SALES (corp-wide): 151.4MM **Privately Held**
SIC: 5113 Bags, paper & disposable plastic
PA: Maxco Supply, Inc.
605 S Zediker Ave
Parlier CA 93648
559 646-8449

(P-8110)
MICHAEL MADDEN CO INC
Also Called: Paper Company, The
2815 Warner Ave, Irvine (92606-4443)
P.O. Box 17807 (92623-7807)
PHONE..........................800 834-6248
Michael L Madden, *President*
Julie Scheibe, *CFO*
Jody Madden, *Vice Pres*
Julie K Scheide, *Vice Pres*
Omar Dandan, *Executive*
◆ **EMP:** 70
SQ FT: 75,000
SALES (est): 57.5MM **Privately Held**
SIC: 5113 Industrial & personal service paper

(P-8111)
NEWAY PACKAGING CORP (PA)
1973 E Via Arado, Rancho Dominguez
(90220-6102)
PHONE..........................602 454-9000
Russell E Freebury, *President*
Sarah D Giles-Bell, *Vice Pres*
Carole Freebury, *Controller*
Robert Hayward, *Sales Executive*
◆ **EMP:** 60
SQ FT: 36,000
SALES (est): 79.7MM **Privately Held**
WEB: www.newaypackaging.com
SIC: 5113 5084 Shipping supplies; packaging machinery & equipment

(P-8112)
OAK PAPER PRODUCTS CO INC (PA)
Also Called: Oak Distribution
3686 E Olympic Blvd, Los Angeles
(90023-3146)
P.O. Box 23965 (90023-0965)
PHONE..........................323 268-0507
Max Weissberg, *President*
Richard Seff, *Ch of Bd*
David Weissberg, *CEO*
David Karr, *COO*
Dick Seff, *Chairman*
▲ **EMP:** 174
SQ FT: 250,000
SALES (est): 141.8MM **Privately Held**
WEB: www.oakdistribution.com
SIC: 5113 5199 5087 2653 Shipping supplies; packaging materials; janitors' supplies; corrugated & solid fiber boxes

(P-8113)
OASIS BRANDS INC
6700 Artesia Blvd, Buena Park
(90620-1014)
PHONE..........................540 658-2830
Lee Shuchun, *Director*
Winnie Tung, *Marketing Staff*
▼ **EMP:** 75
SALES (est): 156MM **Privately Held**
SIC: 5113 Napkins, paper

(P-8114)
ORORA NORTH AMERICA
Also Called: Mpp San Diego Div 6064
664 N Twin Oaks Valley Rd, San Marcos
(92069-1712)
PHONE..........................760 510-7170
Scott Romagnoli, *Manager*
Amy Brown, *Human Res Dir*
Geraldine Saalfeld, *Purchasing*
Gayle Baker, *Cust Mgr*
Roque Garcia, *Manager*
EMP: 63 **Privately Held**
SIC: 5113 2653 Paper & products, wrapping or coarse; boxes, corrugated: made from purchased materials

HQ: Orora Packaging Solutions
6600 Valley View St
Buena Park CA 90620
714 562-6000

(P-8115)
ORORA NORTH AMERICA
Mpp Los Angeles Div 6060
3201 W Mission Rd, Alhambra
(91803-1113)
PHONE..........................626 284-9524
Marc Fenster, *Manager*
EMP: 140 **Privately Held**
SIC: 5113 2653 Paper & products, wrapping or coarse; boxes, corrugated: made from purchased materials
HQ: Orora Packaging Solutions
6600 Valley View St
Buena Park CA 90620
714 562-6000

(P-8116)
ORORA NORTH AMERICA
Also Called: Landsberg San Diego Div 1007
664 N Twin Oaks Valley Rd, San Marcos
(92069-1712)
PHONE..........................760 510-7000
Brian Reynolds, *Branch Mgr*
EMP: 62
SQ FT: 5,000
SALES (corp-wide): 3B **Privately Held**
SIC: 5113 2653 Paper & products, wrapping or coarse; boxes, corrugated: made from purchased materials
HQ: Orora Packaging Solutions
6600 Valley View St
Buena Park CA 90620
714 562-6000

(P-8117)
ORORA NORTH AMERICA
Also Called: Corru Kraft Buena Pk Div 5058
6200 Caballero Blvd, Buena Park
(90620-1124)
PHONE..........................714 562-6002
Jim Wilczek, *Branch Mgr*
Geoff O'Shannassy, *Opers Staff*
John Homolak, *Manager*
Sergio Ortega, *Manager*
EMP: 149 **Privately Held**
SIC: 5113 2653 Paper & products, wrapping or coarse; boxes, corrugated: made from purchased materials
HQ: Orora Packaging Solutions
6600 Valley View St
Buena Park CA 90620
714 562-6000

(P-8118)
ORORA PACKAGING SOLUTIONS (HQ)
Also Called: Landsberg Orora
6600 Valley View St, Buena Park
(90620-1145)
PHONE..........................714 562-6000
Bernardino Salvatore, *President*
Bernardino Salvatorre, *President*
David Conley, *CFO*
Ray Huelskamp, *Vice Pres*
Preston Geeting, *VP Bus Dvlpt*
▲ **EMP:** 100 **EST:** 1951
SQ FT: 300,000
SALES (est): 2.4B **Privately Held**
WEB: www.amcor.com
SIC: 5113 2653 Paper & products, wrapping or coarse; sanitary food containers; boxes, corrugated: made from purchased materials

(P-8119)
ORORA PACKAGING SOLUTIONS
Also Called: Mpp Brea Div 6079
3200 Enterprise St, Brea (92821-6238)
PHONE..........................714 984-2300
Carol Hortick, *Manager*
EMP: 84 **Privately Held**
SIC: 5113 2653 Paper & products, wrapping or coarse; boxes, corrugated: made from purchased materials
HQ: Orora Packaging Solutions
6600 Valley View St
Buena Park CA 90620
714 562-6000

(P-8120)
ORORA PACKAGING SOLUTIONS
Mpp Union City Div 6062
33463 Western Ave, Union City
(94587-3201)
P.O. Box 60000, San Francisco (94160-0001)
PHONE..................................510 487-1211
Nafiz Korustan, *Manager*
EMP: 95 **Privately Held**
SIC: 5113 2653 Paper & products, wrapping or coarse; boxes, corrugated: made from purchased materials
HQ: Orora Packaging Solutions
6600 Valley View St
Buena Park CA 90620
714 562-6000

(P-8121)
ORORA PACKAGING SOLUTIONS
Also Called: Landsberg Los Angeles Div 1001
1640 S Greenwood Ave, Montebello
(90640-6538)
PHONE..................................323 832-2000
Jed Wockenfuss, *Manager*
David Graney, *Finance*
Lynette Goodrich, *Human Res Mgr*
Debra Duran, *Safety Mgr*
Mike Hallstrom, *Sales Staff*
EMP: 168 **Privately Held**
SIC: 5113 2653 Paper & products, wrapping or coarse; boxes, corrugated: made from purchased materials
HQ: Orora Packaging Solutions
6600 Valley View St
Buena Park CA 90620
714 562-6000

(P-8122)
ORORA PACKAGING SOLUTIONS
Also Called: Mpp Fullerton Div 6061
1901 E Rosslynn Ave, Fullerton
(92831-5141)
PHONE..................................714 278-6000
Carol Hortick, *Branch Mgr*
Anthony Visciotti, *Mfg Staff*
EMP: 101 **Privately Held**
SIC: 5113 2653 Paper & products, wrapping or coarse; boxes, corrugated: made from purchased materials
HQ: Orora Packaging Solutions
6600 Valley View St
Buena Park CA 90620
714 562-6000

(P-8123)
ORORA PACKAGING SOLUTIONS
Also Called: Corru Kraft Fullerton Div 5068
1911 E Rosslynn Ave, Fullerton
(92831-5141)
PHONE..................................714 773-0124
Ron Crawford, *Manager*
EMP: 85
SALES (corp-wide): 3B **Privately Held**
SIC: 5113 2653 Paper & products, wrapping or coarse; boxes, corrugated: made from purchased materials
HQ: Orora Packaging Solutions
6600 Valley View St
Buena Park CA 90620
714 562-6000

(P-8124)
P & R PAPER SUPPLY CO INC (PA)
1898 E Colton Ave, Redlands
(92374-9798)
P.O. Box 590 (92373-0201)
PHONE..................................909 389-1811
Mark S Maiberger, *CEO*
Joe Maiberger, *CFO*
Luke Maiberger, *Vice Pres*
Amanda Stromsheim, *Branch Mgr*
Renee Berry, *Executive Asst*
▲ **EMP:** 103
SQ FT: 75,000

SALES (est): 102.2MM **Privately Held**
WEB: www.prpaper.com
SIC: 5113 5169 5149 5072 Paper & products, wrapping or coarse; chemicals & allied products; groceries & related products; hardware; commercial equipment

(P-8125)
PACIFIC PAPER CONVERTING INC (PA)
Also Called: Paper Cutters
6023 Bandini Blvd, Los Angeles
(90040-2904)
PHONE..................................323 888-1330
Susan Feinstein, *President*
Beth Feinstein Thurber, *Vice Pres*
EMP: 70
SQ FT: 150,000
SALES (est): 20.1MM **Privately Held**
SIC: 5113 Industrial & personal service paper

(P-8126)
PACKAGING INNOVATORS LLC
6650 National Dr, Livermore (94550-8802)
P.O. Box 1110 (94551-1110)
PHONE..................................925 371-2000
William E Mazzocco, *President*
Beverly J Flynt, *Corp Secy*
Mark Andrew Mazzocco, *Vice Pres*
Mike Mazzocco, *Vice Pres*
Jenny McLaughlin, *Human Resources*
▲ **EMP:** 90
SQ FT: 114,000
SALES (est): 59.2MM
SALES (corp-wide): 20.5MM **Privately Held**
WEB: www.callpic.com
SIC: 5113 2653 3993 Shipping supplies; corrugated & solid fiber boxes; display items, solid fiber: made from purchased materials; signs & advertising specialties
PA: Golden West Packaging Group Llc
8333 24th Ave
Sacramento CA 95826
404 345-8365

(P-8127)
ROYAL PAPER CORP (PA)
Also Called: Royal Supply Midwest
10232 Palm Dr, Santa Fe Springs
(90670-3368)
PHONE..................................562 903-9030
Michael Rashtchi, *CEO*
George ABI-Aad, *President*
Marianne Abiaad, *Exec VP*
Marianne ABI-Aad, *Exec VP*
Johnathan Soon, *Vice Pres*
▲ **EMP:** 60
SQ FT: 65,000
SALES (est): 53.2MM **Privately Held**
WEB: www.royal-paper.com
SIC: 5113 5087 Containers, paper & disposable plastic; paper & products, wrapping or coarse; cleaning & maintenance equipment & supplies

(P-8128)
UNISOURCE PACKAGING INC
4225 Hacienda Dr Ste A, Pleasanton
(94588-2720)
P.O. Box 8803 (94588)
PHONE..................................925 227-6000
Allan Dragone, *CEO*
▲ **EMP:** 112
SALES (est): 21.8MM
SALES (corp-wide): 8.3B **Publicly Held**
WEB: www.unisourcelink.com
SIC: 5113 Shipping supplies
HQ: Veritiv Operating Company
1000 Abernathy Rd
Atlanta GA 30328
770 391-8200

(P-8129)
VERITIV OPERATING COMPANY
Northern California Mkt Area
4395 S Minnewawa Ave # 101, Fresno
(93725-9479)
P.O. Box 11368 (93773-1368)
PHONE..................................559 268-0467
Fax: 559 233-9136
EMP: 90
SALES (corp-wide): 8.3B **Publicly Held**
SIC: 5113

HQ: Veritiv Operating Company
1000 Abernathy Rd
Atlanta GA 30328
770 391-8200

(P-8130)
VERITIV OPERATING COMPANY
Also Called: International Paper
15005 Northam St, La Mirada
(90638-5759)
PHONE..................................714 690-4000
Dale Alby, *Manager*
EMP: 100
SALES (corp-wide): 8.3B **Publicly Held**
WEB: www.internationalpaper.com
SIC: 5113 1101 Industrial & personal service paper; printing & writing paper
HQ: Veritiv Operating Company
1000 Abernathy Rd
Atlanta GA 30328
770 391-8200

(P-8131)
VERITIV OPERATING COMPANY
Also Called: Northern California Mkt Area
1701 National Dr Ste 110, Sacramento
(95834-2915)
PHONE..................................916 283-2160
Rich Griffin, *Manager*
EMP: 100
SALES (corp-wide): 8.3B **Publicly Held**
WEB: www.unisourcelink.com
SIC: 5113 Industrial & personal service paper
HQ: Veritiv Operating Company
1000 Abernathy Rd
Atlanta GA 30328
770 391-8200

(P-8132)
VERITIV OPERATING COMPANY
International Paper
345 Schwerin St, San Francisco
(94134-3246)
PHONE..................................415 586-9160
Jim Teahan, *Manager*
EMP: 63
SALES (corp-wide): 8.3B **Publicly Held**
WEB: www.internationalpaper.com
SIC: 5113 Industrial & personal service paper
HQ: Veritiv Operating Company
1000 Abernathy Rd
Atlanta GA 30328
770 391-8200

(P-8133)
VERITIV OPERATING COMPANY
Also Called: Southern California Mkt Area
13217 S Figueroa St, Los Angeles
(90061-1139)
PHONE..................................310 527-3000
Chris Hendrix, *Manager*
EMP: 200
SQ FT: 13,000
SALES (corp-wide): 8.3B **Publicly Held**
WEB: www.unisourcelink.com
SIC: 5113 Industrial & personal service paper
HQ: Veritiv Operating Company
1000 Abernathy Rd
Atlanta GA 30328
770 391-8200

(P-8134)
VERITIV OPERATING COMPANY
Also Called: Southern California Mkt Area
2600 Commerce Way, Commerce
(90040-1413)
P.O. Box 910907, Los Angeles (90091-0907)
PHONE..................................323 725-3700
Garryl Lasayette, *Manager*
Marc Edwards, *Sales Associate*
Kevin Kunda, *Sales Associate*
EMP: 200
SALES (corp-wide): 8.3B **Publicly Held**
WEB: www.unisourcelink.com
SIC: 5113 Industrial & personal service paper
HQ: Veritiv Operating Company
1000 Abernathy Rd
Atlanta GA 30328
770 391-8200

HQ: Veritiv Operating Company
1000 Abernathy Rd
Atlanta GA 30328
770 391-8200

(P-8135)
VERITIV OPERATING COMPANY
Also Called: Unisource Maint Sup Systems
20 Centerpointe Dr # 130, La Palma
(90623-2505)
PHONE..................................714 690-6600
Jim Speights, *Manager*
EMP: 300
SALES (corp-wide): 8.3B **Publicly Held**
WEB: www.unisourcelink.com
SIC: 5113 Industrial & personal service paper
HQ: Veritiv Operating Company
1000 Abernathy Rd
Atlanta GA 30328
770 391-8200

(P-8136)
VITCO DISTRIBUTORS INC
Also Called: Vitco Food Service
715 E California St, Ontario (91761-1814)
PHONE..................................909 355-1300
Kostas Vitakis, *President*
Emmanuel Vitakis, *Treasurer*
Dee Combs, *Vice Pres*
Terry Morvan, *Vice Pres*
Scott Seward, *Purch Mgr*
EMP: 60
SQ FT: 20,000
SALES (est): 65.4MM **Privately Held**
SIC: 5113 Disposable plates, cups, napkins & eating utensils

5122 Drugs, Drug Proprietaries & Sundries Wholesale

(P-8137)
ACCESS BIOLOGICALS LLC
995 Park Center Dr, Vista (92081-8312)
PHONE..................................760 597-9749
Barry Plost, *Mng Member*
Mark Ferreira, *Exec VP*
Susan Mills, *Accounting Dir*
Christopher Hunsucker, *VP Opers*
Heather Newsom, *Sales Associate*
EMP: 71
SQ FT: 1,000
SALES (est): 34.4MM **Privately Held**
SIC: 5122 2836 Biologicals & allied products; biological products, except diagnostic

(P-8138)
AGILENT TECHNOLOGIES INC
6392 Via Real, Carpinteria (93013-2921)
PHONE..................................805 566-6655
EMP: 225
SALES (corp-wide): 4.4B **Publicly Held**
SIC: 5122 3841 Biologicals & allied products; diagnostic apparatus, medical
PA: Agilent Technologies, Inc.
5301 Stevens Creek Blvd
Santa Clara CA 95051
408 345-8886

(P-8139)
ALLERGAN SALES LLC (DH)
2525 Dupont Dr 14th, Irvine (92612-1599)
P.O. Box 19534 (92623-9534)
PHONE..................................862 261-7000
David E I Pyott, *Ch of Bd*
Raymond H Diradoorian, *Exec VP*
Scott D Sherman, *Exec VP*
Scott M Whitcup, *Exec VP*
Julian S Gangolli, *Vice Pres*
▲ **EMP:** 600
SQ FT: 10,000
SALES (est): 758.5MM **Privately Held**
WEB: www.myallerganbenefits.com
SIC: 5122 Pharmaceuticals
HQ: Allergan, Inc.
5 Giralda Farms
Madison NJ 07940
862 261-7000

(P-8140)
AMERISOURCEBERGEN CORPORATION
215 Deininger Cir, Corona (92880-1707)
PHONE..................................951 493-2339
EMP: 122

SALES (corp-wide): 153.1B **Publicly Held**
SIC: 5122 Drugs & drug proprietaries
PA: Amerisourcebergen Corporation
1300 Morris Dr Ste 100
Chesterbrook PA 19087
610 727-7000

(P-8141)
AMERISOURCEBERGEN DRUG CORP
Also Called: ABC Valencia
24903 Avenue Kearny, Valencia
(91355-1252)
PHONE..................661 257-6400
Ron Green, *Division Mgr*
Henry McGee, *Bd of Directors*
Dan Cauffiel, *Data Proc Staff*
James Georges, *Engineer*
Gina Universal, *Human Res Dir*
EMP: 150
SALES (corp-wide): 153.1B **Publicly Held**
WEB: www.amerisourcebergen.net
SIC: 5122 Pharmaceuticals
HQ: Amerisourcebergen Drug Corporation
1300 Morris Dr Ste 100
Chesterbrook PA 19087
610 727-7000

(P-8142)
AMERISOURCEBERGEN DRUG CORP
Also Called: ABC Sacramento Striker
1325 Striker Ave, Sacramento
(95834-1164)
PHONE..................916 830-4500
Bruce Bennett, *Branch Mgr*
Randy Howery, *Research*
Jeff Lester, *Technology*
Ida Henson, *Technical Staff*
Sean Martin, *Accounts Mgr*
EMP: 102
SALES (corp-wide): 153.1B **Publicly Held**
WEB: www.amerisourcebergen.net
SIC: 5122 Pharmaceuticals
HQ: Amerisourcebergen Drug Corporation
1300 Morris Dr Ste 100
Chesterbrook PA 19087
610 727-7000

(P-8143)
AMERISOURCEBERGEN DRUG CORP
Also Called: ABC Corona
1851 California Ave, Corona (92881-6477)
PHONE..................951 371-2000
Joe Cheney, *Manager*
Lori Bunton, *Technology*
Jerilynn King, *Sales Staff*
John Stavich, *Manager*
EMP: 200
SALES (corp-wide): 153.1B **Publicly Held**
WEB: www.amerisourcebergen.net
SIC: 5122 Pharmaceuticals
HQ: Amerisourcebergen Drug Corporation
1300 Morris Dr Ste 100
Chesterbrook PA 19087
610 727-7000

(P-8144)
BAXCO PHARMACEUTICAL INC
2393 Bateman Ave, Duarte (91010-3313)
PHONE..................909 595-0826
Dennis Wong, *President*
Manuel Amaya, *Sales Mgr*
Lorraine Johnson, *Manager*
▲ **EMP:** 120
SALES (est): 73.4MM **Privately Held**
WEB: www.baxcoinc.com
SIC: 5122 Pharmaceuticals

(P-8145)
BAXTER HEALTHCARE CORPORATION
1 Baxter Way Ste 100, Westlake Village
(91362-3813)
PHONE..................805 372-3000
John Bacich, *President*
Barry Deutsch, *President*
Bill Krosky, *Manager*
EMP: 1000

SALES (corp-wide): 10.5B **Publicly Held**
SIC: 5122 2834 2836 5047 Drugs, proprietaries & sundries; solutions, pharmaceutical; biological products, except diagnostic; medical equipment & supplies
HQ: Baxter Healthcare Corporation
1 Baxter Pkwy
Deerfield IL 60015
224 948-2000

(P-8146)
BEAUTY 21 COSMETICS INC
Also Called: L A Girl
2021 S Archibald Ave, Ontario
(91761-8535)
PHONE..................909 945-2220
Lan Jack Yu, *CEO*
Mahon Yu, *Vice Pres*
Kim Hamilton, *Marketing Staff*
Dione Montes, *Sales Staff*
◆ **EMP:** 105
SQ FT: 250,000
SALES (est): 83MM **Privately Held**
WEB: www.lagirlusa.com
SIC: 5122 2844 Cosmetics; toilet preparations

(P-8147)
BERGEN BRUNSWIG DRUG COMPANY
4000 W Metropolitan Dr # 200, Orange
(92868-3503)
PHONE..................714 385-4000
Brent Martini, *President*
John H Mc Alpine, *CFO*
Doug Batezel,
EMP: 2845
SALES (est): 177.9MM **Privately Held**
SIC: 5122 Pharmaceuticals

(P-8148)
BRIGHT PHARMACEUTICAL SERVICES
4570 Van Nuys Blvd, Sherman Oaks
(91403-2913)
PHONE..................818 981-9100
Alison Macpherson, *President*
Kadam Freeman, *Managing Prtnr*
Susie Szembek, *Manager*
Aperna Mital, *Consultant*
EMP: 55
SQ FT: 2,500
SALES (est): 12.7MM **Privately Held**
WEB: www.brightps.com
SIC: 5122 Pharmaceuticals

(P-8149)
BRYANT RANCH PREPACK
1919 N Victory Pl, Burbank (91504-3425)
PHONE..................818 764-7225
Sanjay Anand, *President*
EMP: 50
SALES (est): 20.7MM **Privately Held**
SIC: 5122 Pharmaceuticals

(P-8150)
CALIFORNIA SUNCARE INC
Also Called: California Tan
12777 W Jefferson Blvd, Los Angeles
(90066-7048)
PHONE..................310 578-4400
Duncan Robins, *CEO*
Sandy Kagan, *CFO*
EMP: 77
SALES (est): 7.1MM **Privately Held**
WEB: www.californiatan.com
SIC: 5122 5199 Cosmetics, perfumes & hair products; pet supplies

(P-8151)
CARDINAL HEALTH INC
793 Via Lata, Colton (92324-3930)
PHONE..................909 824-1820
Dennis Kephert, *Manager*
Noel Figueroa, *Pharmacist*
EMP: 74
SALES (corp-wide): 136.8B **Publicly Held**
SIC: 5122 Pharmaceuticals
PA: Cardinal Health, Inc.
7000 Cardinal Pl
Dublin OH 43017
614 757-5000

(P-8152)
CARDINAL HEALTH INC
3238 Dwight Rd, Elk Grove (95758-6439)
PHONE..................916 372-9880
Trey Almonza, *Manager*
Dan Brechbill, *Technician*
EMP: 200
SALES (corp-wide): 136.8B **Publicly Held**
SIC: 5122 Pharmaceuticals
PA: Cardinal Health, Inc.
7000 Cardinal Pl
Dublin OH 43017
614 757-5000

(P-8153)
CARDINAL HEALTH INC
700 Vaughn Rd, Dixon (95620-9226)
PHONE..................530 406-3600
Dan Evert, *Branch Mgr*
Rhonda Elliott, *Sales Staff*
Romeyn Webb, *Supervisor*
EMP: 230
SALES (corp-wide): 136.8B **Publicly Held**
SIC: 5122 Drugs, proprietaries & sundries
PA: Cardinal Health, Inc.
7000 Cardinal Pl
Dublin OH 43017
614 757-5000

(P-8154)
CARDINAL HEALTH INC
1007 Canal Blvd, Richmond (94804-3549)
PHONE..................510 232-2030
Alan Kim, *Branch Mgr*
Shannon Byrne, *Administration*
EMP: 74
SALES (corp-wide): 136.8B **Publicly Held**
SIC: 5122 Pharmaceuticals
PA: Cardinal Health, Inc.
7000 Cardinal Pl
Dublin OH 43017
614 757-5000

(P-8155)
CARDINAL HEALTH INC
7330 N Palm Ave Ste 104, Fresno
(93711-5768)
PHONE..................559 448-0788
Mark Stassen, *Branch Mgr*
Laurel Bejeckian, *Vice Pres*
Martin Jeffries, *Associate*
EMP: 74
SALES (corp-wide): 136.8B **Publicly Held**
SIC: 5122 Pharmaceuticals
PA: Cardinal Health, Inc.
7000 Cardinal Pl
Dublin OH 43017
614 757-5000

(P-8156)
CARDINAL HEALTH INC
1935 Pine St, Redding (96001-1921)
PHONE..................530 225-8735
Kurt Dunphy, *Branch Mgr*
EMP: 74
SALES (corp-wide): 136.8B **Publicly Held**
SIC: 5122 Pharmaceuticals
PA: Cardinal Health, Inc.
7000 Cardinal Pl
Dublin OH 43017
614 757-5000

(P-8157)
CARDINAL HEALTH INC
4551 E Philadelphia St, Ontario
(91761-2316)
PHONE..................909 605-0900
Mark Summers, *Manager*
Krista Gallagher, *Human Res Dir*
Robin Lockwood, *Human Res Mgr*
Jeremy Fortune, *Opers Mgr*
Brian Merrill, *Warehouse Mgr*
EMP: 73
SALES (corp-wide): 136.8B **Publicly Held**
SIC: 5122 Pharmaceuticals
PA: Cardinal Health, Inc.
7000 Cardinal Pl
Dublin OH 43017
614 757-5000

(P-8158)
CARDINAL HEALTH INC
Also Called: Whitmire Distribution
27680 Avenue Mentry, Valencia
(91355-1200)
PHONE..................661 295-6100
Stewert Levin, *Manager*
Chris Gong, *Manager*
EMP: 120
SALES (corp-wide): 136.8B **Publicly Held**
SIC: 5122 Pharmaceuticals
PA: Cardinal Health, Inc.
7000 Cardinal Pl
Dublin OH 43017
614 757-5000

(P-8159)
CC WELLNESS LLC (HQ)
Also Called: United Consortium
29000 Hancock Pkwy, Valencia
(91355-1007)
PHONE..................661 295-1700
Marek Jan Olszewski, *CEO*
Joe Walls, *COO*
Octavio Cervantes, *Prdtn Mgr*
Janette Bewley, *Mktg Dir*
Philip Miller, *Regl Sales Mgr*
▲ **EMP:** 55 **EST:** 1999
SQ FT: 38,000
SALES (est): 15MM **Privately Held**
SIC: 5122 Pharmaceuticals
PA: Cc Wellness Acquisition Llc
29000 Hancock Pkwy
Valencia CA 91355
661 295-1700

(P-8160)
CELGENE CORPORATION
Also Called: Celgene Signal Research
10300 Campus Point Dr # 100, San Diego
(92121-1504)
PHONE..................858 677-0034
EMP: 134
SALES (corp-wide): 11.2B **Publicly Held**
SIC: 5122
PA: Celgene Corporation
86 Morris Ave
Summit NJ 07901
908 673-9000

(P-8161)
CELL DESIGN LABS INC
5858 Horton St Ste 240, Emeryville
(94608-2018)
PHONE..................510 398-0501
Brian Atwood, *CEO*
Peter Emtage, *Officer*
Roger Sidhu, *Officer*
Daphne Wilkerson, *Admin Mgr*
EMP: 50
SQ FT: 19,000
SALES: 1MM **Privately Held**
SIC: 5122 Biotherapeutics

(P-8162)
CENTRAL REFILL PHARMACEUTICALS
Also Called: Central Retail Pharmaceuticals
9521 Dalen St, Downey (90242-4847)
PHONE..................562 401-4214
Benjamin Chu, *Owner*
EMP: 100 **EST:** 2008
SALES (est): 5.3MM **Privately Held**
SIC: 5122 Pharmaceuticals

(P-8163)
COLORESCIENCE INC
2141 Palomar Airport Rd R, Carlsbad
(92011-1423)
PHONE..................866 426-5673
Mary Fisher, *CEO*
Steve P Loomis, *CFO*
Josie Juncal, *Ch Credit Ofcr*
Ted Ebel, *Officer*
David Crist, *Exec Dir*
▲ **EMP:** 111
SQ FT: 15,000
SALES (est): 1.7MM **Privately Held**
WEB: www.colorescience.com
SIC: 5122 2844 Cosmetics; cosmetic preparations

▲ = Import ▼=Export
◆ =Import/Export

(P-8164)

COUNTER BRANDS LLC (PA)
Also Called: Beautycounter
2803 Colorado Ave, Santa Monica
(90404-3613)
PHONE.............................310 828-0111
Gregg Renfrew, *CEO*
Linda Simon, *Officer*
Meaghan Curcio, *Vice Pres*
Lindsay Dahl, *Vice Pres*
Bree Pastalaniec, *Vice Pres*
◆ **EMP:** 57
SQ FT: 9,700
SALES (est): 90.7MM **Privately Held**
SIC: 5122 Cosmetics

(P-8165)

COUNTY OF LOS ANGELES
Also Called: Health Services, Dept of
1000 W Crson St Bsmnt 404 Basement,
Torrance (90502)
PHONE.............................310 222-2357
Wes Kamikawa, *Director*
Jennie Ung, *Supervisor*
EMP: 95 **Privately Held**
WEB: www.co.la.ca.us
SIC: 5122 9431 Pharmaceuticals; admin-
istration of public health programs;
PA: County Of Los Angeles
500 W Temple St Ste 437
Los Angeles CA 90012
213 974-1101

(P-8166)

DR FRESH LLC
Also Called: High Ridge Brands
6 Centerpointe Dr Ste 640, La Palma
(90623-2587)
PHONE.............................714 690-1573
Doug Corbett, *CEO*
Natalie Pineda, *Admin Asst*
Nikhil Jindal, *Manager*
◆ **EMP:** 100 **EST:** 2012
SQ FT: 55,000
SALES (est): 89.3MM
SALES (corp-wide): 8.1B **Privately Held**
SIC: 5122 Toothbrushes, except electric
HQ: High Ridge Brands Co.
333 Ludlow St Ste 2
Stamford CT 06902

(P-8167)

FENTY BEAUTY LLC
425 Market St Fl 19, San Francisco
(94105-2425)
PHONE.............................818 973-2709
David Suliteanu, *Mng Member*
Kristin Walcott,
EMP: 200
SALES (est): 10.7MM **Privately Held**
SIC: 5122 Cosmetics

(P-8168)

FFF ENTERPRISES INC (PA)
44000 Winchester Rd, Temecula
(92590-2578)
PHONE.............................951 296-2500
Patrick M Schmidt, *CEO*
Chris Ground, *COO*
Bradley Cooper, *CFO*
Bob Coates, *Vice Pres*
Nancy Creadon, *Vice Pres*
EMP: 380
SQ FT: 162,000
SALES (est): 1.4B **Privately Held**
WEB: www.fffenterprises.com
SIC: 5122 Pharmaceuticals

(P-8169)

GALE LINA INC
230 S 9th Ave, City of Industry
(91746-3309)
PHONE.............................909 595-8898
John Chen, *CEO*
Lina Chen, *CFO*
▲ **EMP:** 100 **EST:** 1991
SALES (est): 49MM **Privately Held**
SIC: 5122 Cosmetics

(P-8170)

GLAMOUR INDUSTRIES CO
Also Called: American International Inds
2220 Gaspar Ave, Commerce
(90040-1516)
PHONE.............................323 728-2999

Zvi Ryzman, *President*
Theresa Cooper, *Exec VP*
Betty Ryzman, *Admin Sec*
EMP: 300
SQ FT: 224,000
SALES (est): 49.3MM **Privately Held**
SIC: 5122 Cosmetics

(P-8171)

GLAXOSMITHKLINE LLC
3366 N Torrey Pines Ct, La Jolla
(92037-1025)
PHONE.............................858 260-5900
EMP: 50
SALES (corp-wide): 39.8B **Privately Held**
SIC: 5122 2834 Toothbrushes, except
electric; pharmaceutical preparations
HQ: Glaxosmithkline Llc
5 Crescent Dr
Philadelphia PA 19112
215 751-4000

(P-8172)

**GOLDEN N-LIFE DIAMITE INTL
INC (PA)**
3500 Gateway Blvd, Fremont
(94538-6584)
PHONE.............................510 651-0405
Roget Uys, *CEO*
Daniel L Lewis, *COO*
Robert Galano, *Vice Pres*
▲ **EMP:** 80
SQ FT: 66,000
SALES (est): 40.5MM **Privately Held**
WEB: www.us.gnld.com
SIC: 5122 Cosmetics, perfumes & hair
products

(P-8173)

**GREEN WAVE INGREDIENTS
INC**
Also Called: Ingredients Online
14821 Northam St, La Mirada
(90638-5748)
PHONE.............................562 207-9770
Sherry Wang, *President*
Danielle Backus, *Executive*
Steven Cornejo, *Executive*
Frank Gieseke, *Executive*
Wilson Yiu, *Info Tech Mgr*
▲ **EMP:** 50
SQ FT: 50,000
SALES: 16MM **Privately Held**
SIC: 5122 Vitamins & minerals

(P-8174)

**GRIFOLS SHARED SVCS N
AMER INC (HQ)**
2410 Lillyvale Ave, Los Angeles
(90032-3514)
PHONE.............................323 225-2221
Gregory Rich, *CEO*
Max Debrouwer, *CFO*
Thomas Glanzmann, *Chairman*
David Bell, *Vice Pres*
Juan Diaz, *Vice Pres*
▲ **EMP:** 153
SALES (est): 4B
SALES (corp-wide): 696.8MM **Privately
Held**
WEB: www.grifolsusa.com
SIC: 5122 2834 Drugs, proprietaries &
sundries; druggists' preparations (phar-
maceuticals)
PA: Grifols Sa
Calle Jesus I Maria 6
Barcelona 08022
935 710-196

(P-8175)

H D SMITH LLC
1370 E Victoria St, Carson (90746-7501)
P.O. Box 6231 (90749-6231)
PHONE.............................310 641-1885
Bob Schwartz, *Manager*
EMP: 100
SALES (corp-wide): 153.1B **Publicly
Held**
WEB: www.hdsmith.com
SIC: 5122 5047 Drugs & drug propri-
etaries; medical & hospital equipment
HQ: H. D. Smith, Llc
3063 Fiat Ave
Springfield IL 62703
866 232-1222

(P-8176)

**HATCHBEAUTY PRODUCTS
LLC (PA)**
10951 W Pico Blvd Ste 300, Los Angeles
(90064-2188)
P.O. Box 641415 (90064-6415)
PHONE.............................310 396-7070
Ben Bennett, *Managing Prtnr*
Benjamin Bennett, *Partner*
Tracy Holland, *Managing Prtnr*
◆ **EMP:** 83 **EST:** 2010
SQ FT: 1,500
SALES (est): 82.9MM **Privately Held**
SIC: 5122 Cosmetics, perfumes & hair
products

(P-8177)

HERBALIFE INTL AMER INC (DH)
800 W Olympic Blvd # 406, Los Angeles
(90015-1360)
PHONE.............................213 745-0500
Richard Goudis, *CEO*
John Agwunobi, *Co-President*
John Desimone, *Co-President*
Eric Zepeda, *Senior VP*
Dan Moran, *Info Tech Mgr*
◆ **EMP:** 500
SQ FT: 115,000
SALES (est): 1B **Privately Held**
WEB: www.herbalifefamily.com
SIC: 5122 Vitamins & minerals
HQ: Herbalife International, Inc.
800 W Olympic Blvd # 406
Los Angeles CA 90015
310 410-9600

(P-8178)

HOYU AMERICA CO
Also Called: Samy Co
6265 Phyllis Dr, Cypress (90630-5240)
PHONE.............................714 230-3000
Yoshihiro Sasaki, *President*
Minoru Tsuda, *Senior VP*
▲ **EMP:** 58
SALES (est): 35MM **Privately Held**
SIC: 5122 5999 Cosmetics, perfumes &
hair products; hair care products
HQ: Hoyu Co.,Ltd.
1-501, Tokugawa, Higashi-Ku
Nagoya AIC 461-0
529 359-556

(P-8179)

IRWIN NATURALS
5310 Beethoven St, Los Angeles
(90066-7015)
PHONE.............................310 306-3636
Marc Washington, *CEO*
Klee Irwin, *President*
Mark Green, *CFO*
Jeffrey Sugawara, *Senior VP*
Mark Greene, *Creative Dir*
▼ **EMP:** 80
SQ FT: 52,000
SALES (est): 53.2MM **Privately Held**
SIC: 5122 Vitamins & minerals

(P-8180)

J T R COMPANY INC (PA)
Also Called: Area Distributing Co
1102 S 3rd St, San Jose (95112-5918)
P.O. Box 8589 (95155-8589)
PHONE.............................408 975-7733
Josy T Ryan, *President*
Louis Ryan, *Corp Secy*
Kelly Ryan, *Vice Pres*
Kevin Ryan, *Vice Pres*
Gary G Smith, *Vice Pres*
EMP: 80
SQ FT: 130,000
SALES (est): 41.9MM **Privately Held**
WEB: www.jtrsport.com
SIC: 5122 5199 5113 Toilet articles; pack-
aging materials; towels, paper

(P-8181)

**JAN MARINI SKIN RESEARCH
INC**
5883 Rue Ferrari Ste 175, San Jose
(95138-1863)
PHONE.............................408 620-3600
John Connors, *CEO*
Jan Marini, *Ch of Bd*
Bob James, *CFO*
Robert James, *CFO*

Reed Anderson, *Vice Pres*
◆ **EMP:** 80
SQ FT: 5,000
SALES (est): 52.2MM **Privately Held**
WEB: www.janmarini.com
SIC: 5122 Cosmetics

(P-8182)

JARROW FORMULAS INC (PA)
1824 S Robertson Blvd, Los Angeles
(90035-4317)
PHONE.............................310 204-6936
Ben Khowong, *CEO*
Jarrow L Rogovin, *President*
Clayton Dubose, *Treasurer*
Peilin Guo, *Exec VP*
Michael Jacobs, *Vice Pres*
◆ **EMP:** 90
SQ FT: 37,000
SALES (est): 106MM **Privately Held**
SIC: 5122 Vitamins & minerals

(P-8183)

JESSICA COSMETICS INTL INC
Also Called: Jessica's Cosmetics
13209 Saticoy St, North Hollywood
(91605-3405)
PHONE.............................818 759-1050
Jessica Vartoughian, *President*
Peter Sarkissian, *Marketing Staff*
◆ **EMP:** 60 **EST:** 1968
SALES (est): 24MM **Privately Held**
SIC: 5122 7231 Cosmetics; beauty shops

(P-8184)

**JORDANA COSMETICS
CORPORATION**
2035 E 49th St, Vernon (90058-2801)
P.O. Box 8382, Los Angeles (90008-0382)
PHONE.............................323 589-5625
Laurie Minc, *President*
Ralph Bijou, *COO*
Gina Hagen, *CFO*
Lisa De La Flor, *Export Mgr*
Ericka Molina, *Manager*
◆ **EMP:** 65
SQ FT: 30,000
SALES (est): 42.2MM **Privately Held**
WEB: www.jordanacosmetics.com
SIC: 5122 Cosmetics

(P-8185)

**KATE SOMERVILLE HOLDINGS
LLC (HQ)**
144 S Beverly Dr Ste 500, Beverly Hills
(90212-3023)
PHONE.............................323 655-4170
Kate Somerville, *Mng Member*
Sarah Skinner, *Director*
▲ **EMP:** 51 **EST:** 2007
SALES (est): 22.9MM
SALES (corp-wide): 63B **Privately Held**
SIC: 5122 Toiletries; cosmetics; perfumes
PA: Unilever Plc
Unilever House
London EC4Y
207 822-5252

(P-8186)

KINSALE HOLDINGS INC
Also Called: Validant
475 Sansome St Ste 570, San Francisco
(94111-3136)
PHONE.............................415 400-2600
Brian Burns, *CEO*
Bob Rhoades, *Managing Prtnr*
Michael Beatrice, *President*
Purvi Chekuri, *Vice Pres*
Tanya Klaslo, *Vice Pres*
EMP: 250
SQ FT: 10,000
SALES (est): 97MM **Privately Held**
SIC: 5122 Pharmaceuticals

(P-8187)

LIFETECH RESOURCES LLC
700 Science Dr, Moorpark (93021-2012)
PHONE.............................818 885-1199
Mc Alcine, *Branch Mgr*
EMP: 50
SALES (corp-wide): 109.4MM **Privately
Held**
SIC: 5122 Cosmetics

PA: Lifetech Resources Llc
700 Science Dr
Moorpark CA 93021
818 885-1199

(P-8188)
LOREAL USA INC
1848 4th St, Berkeley (94710-1911)
PHONE..................510 548-0130
Doug Vangoerkan, *Manager*
EMP: 227
SALES (corp-wide): 4.2B **Privately Held**
SIC: 5122 Cosmetics
HQ: L'oreal Usa, Inc.
10 Hudson Yards Fl 30
New York NY 10001
212 818-1500

(P-8189)
M P O INC (HQ)
3760 Kilroy Airport Way # 5, Long Beach
(90806-2443)
PHONE..................562 628-1007
Al Hummel, *President*
Preston Romm, *CFO*
Laurence Dryer, *Exec VP*
David Goldstein, *Exec VP*
Albert F Hummel, *Principal*
EMP: 72
SQ FT: 16,000
SALES (est): 31.7MM **Privately Held**
WEB: www.obagi.com
SIC: 5122 Cosmetics

(P-8190)
MARKWINS BEAUTY PRODUCTS INC
22067 Ferrero, City of Industry
(91789-5214)
PHONE..................909 595-8898
Eric Chen, *President*
Stefano Curti, *President*
Michael Shaw, *COO*
Shawn Haynes, *Senior VP*
James Koeppl, *Senior VP*
▲ **EMP:** 66
SQ FT: 200,000
SALES (est): 40.3MM
SALES (corp-wide): 240.1MM **Privately Held**
WEB: www.markwins.com
SIC: 5122 Cosmetics
PA: Markwins International Corp
22067 Ferrero
Walnut CA 91789
909 595-8898

(P-8191)
MCKESSON CORPORATION
6969 Brockton Ave Ste B, Riverside
(92506-3813)
PHONE..................951 686-3575
Robert Bourne, *Branch Mgr*
Lucy Hu, *Software Dev*
Marissa Tamayo, *Human Resources*
EMP: 65
SALES (corp-wide): 208.3B **Publicly Held**
WEB: www.imckesson.com
SIC: 5122 5047 5199 7372 Pharmaceuticals; proprietary (patent) medicines; toiletries; druggists' sundries; medical equipment & supplies; first aid supplies; general merchandise, non-durable; prepackaged software
PA: Mckesson Corporation
1 Post St Fl 18
San Francisco CA 94104
415 983-8300

(P-8192)
MCKESSON CORPORATION
3000 Colby St, Berkeley (94705-2083)
PHONE..................510 666-0854
Micah Wakamatsu, *Branch Mgr*
EMP: 66
SALES (corp-wide): 208.3B **Publicly Held**
SIC: 5122 Pharmaceuticals
PA: Mckesson Corporation
1 Post St Fl 18
San Francisco CA 94104
415 983-8300

(P-8193)
MCKESSON CORPORATION
Also Called: McKesson Drug
9501 Norwalk Blvd, Santa Fe Springs
(90670-2929)
P.O. Box 2116 (90670-0116)
PHONE..................562 463-2100
Todd Kleinow, *Vice Pres*
Marcus Mandagie, *Facilities Mgr*
EMP: 120
SALES (corp-wide): 208.3B **Publicly Held**
WEB: www.imckesson.com
SIC: 5122 Pharmaceuticals
PA: Mckesson Corporation
1 Post St Fl 18
San Francisco CA 94104
415 983-8300

(P-8194)
MCKESSON CORPORATION
Also Called: Drohan Trade Center
11000 Trade Center Dr, Rancho Cordova
(95670-6153)
PHONE..................916 636-8700
Donna Draher, *Branch Mgr*
Michael Lenox, *Administration*
Jeffrey Frankel, *Sr Ntwrk Engine*
Mark Rissing, *Information Mgr*
John Keeling, *Technology*
EMP: 51
SQ FT: 3,000
SALES (corp-wide): 208.3B **Publicly Held**
WEB: www.imckesson.com
SIC: 5122 Pharmaceuticals
PA: Mckesson Corporation
1 Post St Fl 18
San Francisco CA 94104
415 983-8300

(P-8195)
MCKESSON CORPORATION
Also Called: McKesson Drug
3775 Seaport Blvd, West Sacramento
(95691-3558)
P.O. Box 15858, Sacramento (95852-0858)
PHONE..................916 372-3655
Larry Honley, *Sales/Mktg Mgr*
EMP: 150
SALES (corp-wide): 208.3B **Publicly Held**
WEB: www.imckesson.com
SIC: 5122 Pharmaceuticals
PA: Mckesson Corporation
1 Post St Fl 18
San Francisco CA 94104
415 983-8300

(P-8196)
MCKESSON CORPORATION (PA)
1 Post St Fl 18, San Francisco
(94104-5284)
PHONE..................415 983-8300
John H Hammergren, *Ch of Bd*
Brian S Tyler, *President*
Britt Vitalone, *CFO*
Lori A Schechter, *Ch Credit Ofcr*
Jorge L Figueredo, *Exec VP*
◆ **EMP:** 755
SALES: 208.3B **Publicly Held**
WEB: www.imckesson.com
SIC: 5122 5047 5199 7372 Pharmaceuticals; proprietary (patent) medicines; druggists' sundries; medical equipment & supplies; first aid supplies; general merchandise, non-durable; prepackaged software

(P-8197)
METAGENICS INC (DH)
25 Enterprise Ste 200, Aliso Viejo
(92656-2713)
PHONE..................949 366-0818
Brent Eck, *President*
Jean M Bellin, *President*
Dave Tuit, *CFO*
Sara Gottfried, *Chief Mktg Ofcr*
John Troup, *Officer*
◆ **EMP:** 150
SQ FT: 88,000
SALES (est): 223.9MM
SALES (corp-wide): 8.7B **Privately Held**
WEB: www.ethicalnutrients.com
SIC: 5122 Vitamins & minerals; medicinals & botanicals

HQ: Alticor Inc.
7575 Fulton St E
Ada MI 49355
616 787-1000

(P-8198)
METAGENICS INC
100 Avenida La Pata, San Clemente
(92673-6305)
PHONE..................800 692-9400
Carol Perkovich, *Manager*
EMP: 100
SALES (corp-wide): 8.7B **Privately Held**
WEB: www.ethicalnutrients.com
SIC: 5122 5047 Vitamins & minerals; physician equipment & supplies
HQ: Metagenics, Inc.
25 Enterprise Ste 200
Aliso Viejo CA 92656
949 366-0818

(P-8199)
N QIAGEN AMERCN HOLDINGS INC (HQ)
27220 Turnberry Ln # 200, Valencia
(91355-1018)
PHONE..................800 426-8157
Peer Schatz, *President*
Melissa Van Dorn, *Marketing Staff*
EMP: 250
SALES (est): 205.5MM
SALES (corp-wide): 1.4B **Privately Held**
SIC: 5122 Biologicals & allied products
PA: Qiagen N.V.
Hulsterweg 82
Venlo 5912
773 556-600

(P-8200)
OMNICARE INC
20967 Cabot Blvd, Hayward (94545-1155)
PHONE..................510 293-9663
EMP: 99
SALES (corp-wide): 184.7B **Publicly Held**
SIC: 5122 Pharmaceuticals
HQ: Omnicare, Inc.
900 Omnicare Ctr 201e4t
Cincinnati OH 45202
513 719-2600

(P-8201)
PACIFIC PHARMA INC
18600 Von Karman Ave, Irvine
(92612-1513)
PHONE..................714 246-4600
EMP: 2000
SALES (est): 108.7MM **Privately Held**
SIC: 5122
HQ: Allergan, Inc.
400 Interpace Pkwy
Parsippany NJ 07940
862 261-7000

(P-8202)
PACIRA PHARMACEUTICALS INC
Also Called: Research & Dev & Mfg Site
10578 Science Center Dr, San Diego
(92121-1143)
PHONE..................858 625-2424
EMP: 366 **Publicly Held**
SIC: 5122 Pharmaceuticals
PA: Pacira Pharmaceuticals, Inc.
5 Sylvan Way Ste 300
Parsippany NJ 07054

(P-8203)
PAUL MITCHELL JOHN SYSTEMS (PA)
20705 Centre Pointe Pkwy, Santa Clarita
(91350-2967)
P.O. Box 10597, Beverly Hills (90213-3597)
PHONE..................310 248-3888
John P Dejoria, *CEO*
Rick Battaglini, *Officer*
Julia Provost, *Vice Pres*
Briana Wolfe, *Administration*
Jim Reilly, *Info Tech Dir*
◆ **EMP:** 80
SQ FT: 90,000
SALES (est): 136.7MM **Privately Held**
SIC: 5122 Hair preparations

(P-8204)
PHARMERICA LONG-TERM CARE LLC
Also Called: Ltc Pharmacy
8930 Activity Rd Ste K, San Diego
(92126-4457)
PHONE..................858 537-9374
Todd Reames, *Manager*
Marijen Lao, *Pharmacist*
EMP: 140
SALES (corp-wide): 129MM **Privately Held**
WEB: www.pharmerica.com
SIC: 5122 Pharmaceuticals
HQ: Pharmerica Long-Term Care, Llc
3625 Queen Palm Dr
Tampa FL 33619
877 975-2273

(P-8205)
PHARMERICA LONG-TERM CARE LLC
Also Called: Ltc Pharmacy
1130 Palmyrita Ave # 350, Riverside
(92507-1742)
PHONE..................951 784-1616
Kim Young, *Branch Mgr*
EMP: 60
SALES (corp-wide): 129MM **Privately Held**
WEB: www.pharmerica.com
SIC: 5122 Pharmaceuticals
HQ: Pharmerica Long-Term Care, Llc
3625 Queen Palm Dr
Tampa FL 33619
877 975-2273

(P-8206)
PPHM INC
14282 Franklin Ave, Tustin (92780-7009)
PHONE..................714 508-6100
Steve King, *CEO*
Paul Lytle, *CFO*
Tracy L Kinjerski, *Vice Pres*
Jeffrey Masten, *Vice Pres*
EMP: 100
SALES (est): 50.5MM
SALES (corp-wide): 53.6MM **Publicly Held**
WEB: www.avidbioservices.com
SIC: 5122 Pharmaceuticals
PA: Avid Bioservices, Inc.
2642 Michelle Dr Ste 200
Tustin CA 92780
714 508-6000

(P-8207)
PRIMAL ELEMENTS INC
18062 Redondo Cir, Huntington Beach
(92648-1326)
PHONE..................714 899-0757
Faith Freeman, *CEO*
Scott Freeman, *President*
▲ **EMP:** 99
SQ FT: 56,500
SALES (est): 38.1MM **Privately Held**
WEB: www.primalelements.com
SIC: 5122 Cosmetics

(P-8208)
RUGBY LABORATORIES INC (DH)
311 Bonnie Cir, Corona (92880-2882)
PHONE..................951 270-1400
David C Hsia PHD, *President*
Michael E Boser, *CFO*
Michel J Feldman, *Officer*
Frederick Wilkinson, *Vice Pres*
Chato Abad, *VP Finance*
EMP: 90
SALES (est): 20.8MM
SALES (corp-wide): 136.8B **Publicly Held**
WEB: www.watsonpharm.com
SIC: 5122 2834 Pharmaceuticals; pharmaceutical preparations
HQ: The Harvard Drug Group L L C
17177 N Laurel Park Dr # 233
Livonia MI 48152
734 525-8700

(P-8209)
SGII INC
Also Called: Senegence International
19651 Alter, Foothill Ranch (92610-2507)
PHONE..............................949 521-6161
Joni Rogers Kante, *CEO*
Philippe Guerreau, *President*
Steve Jarvi, *COO*
Ben Kante, *COO*
James Roh, *Officer*
▲ EMP: 250
SQ FT: 49,415
SALES (est): 20.8MM **Privately Held**
WEB: www.senegence.com
SIC: 5122 Cosmetics; vitamins & minerals

(P-8210)
SIGNAL PHARMACEUTICALS LLC
10300 Campus Point Dr # 100, San Diego
(92121-1504)
PHONE..............................858 795-4700
Alan J Lewis PHD, *President*
R Michael Gendreau, *Chief Mktg Ofcr*
Shripad Bhagwat, *Vice Pres*
David R Webb, *Vice Pres*
Kara West, *Accounts Mgr*
EMP: 134
SQ FT: 78,202
SALES (est): 37.2MM
SALES (corp-wide): 13B **Publicly Held**
SIC: 5122 Pharmaceuticals
PA: Celgene Corporation
86 Morris Ave
Summit NJ 07901
908 673-9000

(P-8211)
STAR NAIL PRODUCTS INC
Also Called: Star Nail International
29120 Avenue Paine, Valencia
(91355-5402)
PHONE..............................661 257-3376
Tony Cuccio, *CEO*
Anthony Cuccio, *President*
Roberta Cuccio, *Vice Pres*
Elaine Watson, *Vice Pres*
Shelley Cassulo, *Marketing Staff*
◆ EMP: 55
SQ FT: 14,000
SALES (est): 28.2MM **Privately Held**
WEB: www.allseasonnails.com
SIC: 5122 2844 7231 Cosmetics; toilet
preparations; beauty shops

(P-8212)
STARLIGHT INTERNATIONAL LTD LP
38 Saint Joseph Ave, Long Beach
(90803-3156)
PHONE..............................562 439-5740
Pat Ellington, *Agent*
EMP: 52 **Privately Held**
WEB: www.starlightint.com
SIC: 5122 Vitamins & minerals
PA: Starlight International, Ltd. Lp
80 Garden Ct Ste 100
Monterey CA 93940

(P-8213)
SUPERBALIFE INTERNATIONAL LLC
Also Called: Prostavar Rx
1171 S Robertson Blvd # 525, Los Angeles
(90035-1403)
PHONE..............................310 553-7400
Fred Buckley, *President*
Corrine Buckley, *Mng Member*
EMP: 62
SALES (est): 22MM **Privately Held**
SIC: 5122 Vitamins & minerals

(P-8214)
SUTTER HEALTH
Also Called: Peralta Pharmacy
3300 Webster St Ste 101, Oakland
(94609-3106)
PHONE..............................510 869-8835
Charles Prosper, *President*
EMP: 159
SALES (corp-wide): 12.4B **Privately Held**
SIC: 5122 Pharmaceuticals

PA: Sutter Health
2200 River Plaza Dr
Sacramento CA 95833
916 733-8800

(P-8215)
UNITE EUROTHERAPY INC
2870 Whiptail Loop, Carlsbad
(92010-6709)
PHONE..............................760 585-1800
Andrew Dale, *President*
Jerry Trombetta, *President*
Chris Hlavaty, *CFO*
Brenda Buenaflor, *Accounts Exec*
Danielle Durfee, *Accounts Exec*
▲ EMP: 80
SALES (est): 23MM **Privately Held**
SIC: 5122 Hair preparations

(P-8216)
VALLEY OF SUN COSMETICS LLC
Also Called: Valley of The Sun Labs
535 Patrice Pl, Gardena (90248-4232)
PHONE..............................310 327-9062
Jimmy Ajmal,
Ajmal Shehzad,
◆ EMP: 156
SQ FT: 10,000
SALES (est): 48.5MM **Privately Held**
WEB: www.cosmeticusa.com
SIC: 5122 Cosmetics

(P-8217)
VALLEY WHOLESALE DRUG CO LLC
1401 W Fremont St, Stockton
(95203-2627)
P.O. Box 2065 (95201-2065)
PHONE..............................209 466-0131
Henry Dale Smith, *CEO*
Dan Matteoli, *Vice Pres*
Angelo Grande, *Principal*
EMP: 75 EST: 1948
SQ FT: 10,000
SALES (est): 64.9MM
SALES (corp-wide): 153.1B **Publicly Held**
SIC: 5122 Pharmaceuticals; cosmetics;
druggists' sundries
HQ: H. D. Smith, Llc
3063 Fiat Ave
Springfield IL 62703
866 232-1222

(P-8218)
VETERINARY PHARMACEUTICALS INC
13159 Hanford Armona Rd, Hanford
(93230)
PHONE..............................559 582-6800
Harold Des Jardins, *CEO*
Alice Desjardins, *Vice Pres*
Alice Des Jardins, *Vice Pres*
Marilyn K Bracy, *Director*
▲ EMP: 52
SALES (est): 18.9MM **Privately Held**
SIC: 5122 Pharmaceuticals

(P-8219)
VICTORY PHARMA INC
11682 El Camino Real # 250, San Diego
(92130-2092)
PHONE..............................858 720-4500
James W Newman, *Ch of Bd*
Matthew Heck, *President*
Daniel Stokely, *COO*
David Parker, *CFO*
EMP: 150
SALES (est): 17.4MM **Privately Held**
WEB: www.victorypharma.com
SIC: 5122 Pharmaceuticals

(P-8220)
VIVA LIFE SCIENCE INC
350 Paularino Ave, Costa Mesa
(92626-4616)
PHONE..............................949 645-6100
David Fan, *President*
On Seng, *General Mgr*
Ning Hong, *Research*
Millie Hardi, *Purchasing*
Nasim Moradai, *Mktg Dir*
EMP: 100
SQ FT: 60,000

SALES (est): 14.6MM **Privately Held**
SIC: 5122 2833 Vitamins & minerals; cosmetics; medicinals & botanicals

(P-8221)
WAKUNAGA OF AMERICA CO LTD (HQ)
Also Called: KYOLIC
23501 Madero, Mission Viejo (92691-2744)
PHONE..............................949 855-2776
Kazuhiko Nomura, *CEO*
Kenro Nakamura, *President*
Albert Dahbour, *Officer*
Hiyoshi Sakai, *Vice Pres*
Kathy Comstock, *Admin Asst*
◆ EMP: 64
SQ FT: 36,000
SALES: 30.9MM
SALES (corp-wide): 72.9MM **Privately Held**
WEB: www.kyolic.com
SIC: 5122 Pharmaceuticals
PA: Wakunaga Pharmaceutical Co., Ltd.
4-5-36, Miyahara, Yodogawa-Ku
Osaka OSK 532-0
663 503-555

(P-8222)
WITHROW PHRM & HLTH SPC LAB
2235 Via Puerta Unit A, Laguna Woods
(92637-8114)
PHONE..............................323 721-4281
Sergio Quinones, *President*
Selma Quinones, *Controller*
EMP: 100 EST: 1928
SALES (est): 9.9MM **Privately Held**
WEB: www.withrow-pharm.com
SIC: 5122 7231 Pharmaceuticals; beauty
shops

5131 Piece Goods, Notions & Dry Goods Wholesale

(P-8223)
CHARMING TRIM & PACKAGING
28 Brookside Ct, Novato (94947-3847)
PHONE..............................415 302-7021
Richard Ringeisen, *President*
Barry Chan, *Exec Dir*
EMP: 1000
SALES (est): 53.6MM **Privately Held**
SIC: 5131 3111 Trimmings; apparel; gar-
ment leather

(P-8224)
DAZIAN LLC
Also Called: Dazian's
10671 Lorne St, Sun Valley (91352-4642)
PHONE..............................818 287-3800
Chris Diaz, *Branch Mgr*
EMP: 60
SALES (est): 7.4MM
SALES (corp-wide): 61.8MM **Privately Held**
WEB: www.dazian.com
SIC: 5131 Piece goods & other fabrics
PA: Dazian, Llc
18 Central Blvd
South Hackensack NJ 07606
877 232-9426

(P-8225)
DESIGN COLLECTION INC
Also Called: Global Garments
2209 S Santa Fe Ave, Los Angeles
(90058-1109)
PHONE..............................323 277-9200
Simon Barlava, *CEO*
Sohail Hussain, *CFO*
Sohaila Hussaini, *CFO*
Morris Barlava, *Vice Pres*
Nasser Barlava, *Admin Sec*
▲ EMP: 60
SQ FT: 67,000
SALES (est): 23.1MM **Privately Held**
WEB: www.designcollection.com
SIC: 5131 5023 Trimmings; apparel;
sheets; textile

(P-8226)
FABRIC BARN
3123 E Anaheim St, Long Beach
(90804-3862)
PHONE..............................562 494-3450
Jay Keegan, *Partner*
Linda Hanna, *Partner*
Betsy Greenstein, *Human Res Dir*
▲ EMP: 230
SQ FT: 8,000
SALES (est): 18.8MM **Privately Held**
SIC: 5131 5092 Lace fabrics; ribbons; toys
& hobby goods & supplies

(P-8227)
INNOVO AZTECA APPAREL INC
5901 S Eastern Ave 104, Commerce
(90040-4003)
PHONE..............................323 837-3700
Marc Crossman, *President*
Hamish Sandhu, *CFO*
▲ EMP: 80
SALES (est): 31.1MM
SALES (corp-wide): 164MM **Publicly Held**
WEB: www.innovogroup.com
SIC: 5131 Trimmings, apparel
PA: Centric Brands Inc.
350 5th Ave Lbby 6
New York NY 10118
323 890-1800

(P-8228)
J ROBERT SCOTT INC (PA)
500 N Oak St, Inglewood (90302-2942)
PHONE..............................310 659-4910
Andrew Frumovitz, *CEO*
Sally Lewis, *President*
Nancy Preller, *Admin Sec*
Carol Weiss, *Sales Staff*
▲ EMP: 120 EST: 1972
SQ FT: 110,000
SALES (est): 47.4MM **Privately Held**
WEB: www.jrobertscott.com
SIC: 5131 2512 2511 Textiles, woven; up-
holstered household furniture; wood
household furniture

(P-8229)
L & R DISTRIBUTORS INC
9292 9th St, Rancho Cucamonga
(91730-4407)
PHONE..............................909 980-3807
EMP: 275
SALES (corp-wide): 949.8MM **Privately Held**
SIC: 5131 Notions
PA: L. & R. Distributors, Inc.
88 35th St Ste 5
Brooklyn NY 11232
718 272-2100

(P-8230)
LAFAYETTE TEXTILE INDS LLC
2051 E 55th St, Vernon (90058-3441)
PHONE..............................323 264-2212
Ali Reza Zahedi, *CEO*
Ali Dehbahani, *COO*
Moshan Dibaei, *CFO*
Carol Ueng, *Accounting Mgr*
Hermineh Megeredchian, *Manager*
▲ EMP: 85
SQ FT: 68,000
SALES (est): 24.1MM **Privately Held**
WEB: www.lafayettetextiles.com
SIC: 5131 Piece goods & notions

(P-8231)
M M FAB INC
Also Called: South Seas Imports
2300 E Gladwick St, Compton
(90220-6208)
PHONE..............................310 763-3800
Richard Friedman, *Principal*
Albert Mass, *VP Finance*
Samuel Alvarado, *Warehouse Mgr*
▲ EMP: 85
SQ FT: 110,000
SALES (est): 23.5MM **Privately Held**
SIC: 5131 Textiles, woven

(P-8232)
MERIDIAN TEXTILES INC (PA)
6415 Canning St, Commerce (90040-3121)
PHONE..............................323 869-5700
Howard Deutchman, *President*

▲ **EMP:** 74
SQ FT: 36,000
SALES (est): 39.8MM **Privately Held**
WEB: www.markfabrics.com
SIC: 5131 Textile converters

(P-8233)
MODERN BUTTON COMPANY OF CAL
3957 S Hill St, Los Angeles (90037-1313)
PHONE..................213 747-7431
Alan Failo, *President*
EMP: 50
SQ FT: 4,400
SALES (est): 4.8MM **Privately Held**
SIC: 5131 Buttons

(P-8234)
MORGAN FABRICS CORPORATION (PA)
Also Called: Michael Jon Designs
4265 Exchange Ave, Vernon (90058-2604)
P.O. Box 58523, Los Angeles (90058-0523)
PHONE..................323 583-9981
Arnold Gittelson, *Chairman*
Michael Gittelson, *President*
Ken Yang, *CFO*
Robert Gittelson, *Vice Pres*
Steve Gittelson, *Vice Pres*
▲ **EMP:** 94 **EST:** 1956
SQ FT: 50,000
SALES (est): 47MM **Privately Held**
WEB: www.morganfabrics.com
SIC: 5131 Textiles, woven; upholstery fabrics, woven

(P-8235)
PHOENIX TEXTILE INC (PA)
Also Called: Level 99
14600 S Broadway, Gardena (90248-1812)
PHONE..................310 715-7090
Dominic Poon, *President*
Joseph TSE, *Treasurer*
Charlton Wang, *Info Tech Mgr*
Nancy Pedroley, *Financial Analy*
Robert Jones, *Regl Sales Mgr*
▲ **EMP:** 100
SQ FT: 39,000
SALES (est): 29.4MM **Privately Held**
SIC: 5131 7389 Textiles, woven; sewing contractor; textile designers

(P-8236)
PINDLER & PINDLER INC (PA)
11910 Poindexter Ave, Moorpark (93021-1748)
P.O. Box 8007 (93020-8007)
PHONE..................805 531-9090
Curt R Pindler, *President*
S L Crawford Jr, *Exec VP*
Barbara Bick, *Admin Sec*
Sarah Bacon, *Design Engr*
Kelley Gleghorn, *Opers Mgr*
▼ **EMP:** 95 **EST:** 1939
SQ FT: 75,000
SALES (est): 117.9MM **Privately Held**
WEB: www.pindler.com
SIC: 5131 Drapery material, woven; upholstery fabrics, woven

(P-8237)
RADIX TEXTILE INC
750 E Jefferson Blvd, Los Angeles (90011-2435)
PHONE..................323 234-1667
Arad Shemirani, *CEO*
▲ **EMP:** 99 **EST:** 2007
SQ FT: 6,000
SALES (est): 5MM **Privately Held**
SIC: 5131 2211 Piece goods & other fabrics; broadwoven fabric mills, cotton

(P-8238)
ROBERT KAUFMAN CO INC (PA)
Also Called: Robert Kaufman Fabrics
129 W 132nd St, Los Angeles (90061-1619)
P.O. Box 59266 (90059-0266)
PHONE..................310 538-3482
Kenneth Kaufman, *CEO*
Joseph Kaufman, *CFO*
Alvin Kaufman, *Admin Sec*
Jerrold Stein, *Technology*
Reva Carroll, *Credit Mgr*

◆ **EMP:** 114
SQ FT: 24,000
SALES (est): 61.4MM **Privately Held**
WEB: www.robertkaufman.com
SIC: 5131 Piece goods & other fabrics

(P-8239)
ROBERT KAUFMAN CO INC
135 W 132nd St, Los Angeles (90061-1682)
P.O. Box 59266 (90059-0266)
PHONE..................310 538-3482
Eric Thompson, *Manager*
Jessica Meza, *Technology*
Evie Ashworth, *Director*
EMP: 50
SALES (corp-wide): 61.4MM **Privately Held**
WEB: www.robertkaufman.com
SIC: 5131 Piece goods & other fabrics
PA: Robert Kaufman Co., Inc.
129 W 132nd St
Los Angeles CA 90061
310 538-3482

(P-8240)
ROMEX TEXTILES INC (PA)
785 E 14th Pl, Los Angeles (90021-2117)
PHONE..................213 749-9090
Shahab Binafard, *CEO*
Soleyman Binafard, *Admin Sec*
Grethelle Simon, *Opers Mgr*
▲ **EMP:** 50
SQ FT: 10,000
SALES (est): 18MM **Privately Held**
SIC: 5131 2211 Textiles, woven; apparel & outerwear fabrics, cotton

(P-8241)
SAM JUNG USA INC
Also Called: S & J
843 E 31st St, Los Angeles (90011-2006)
PHONE..................323 231-0811
Joung Ha Lee, *President*
▲ **EMP:** 60
SQ FT: 50,000
SALES (est): 8.6MM **Privately Held**
SIC: 5131 Piece goods & notions

(P-8242)
SEXY HAIR CONCEPTS
9232 Eton Ave, Chatsworth (91311-5807)
PHONE..................800 848-3383
Carl Heinzsch, *President*
◆ **EMP:** 100
SALES (est): 13.6MM **Privately Held**
SIC: 5131 Hair accessories

(P-8243)
SHASON INC (PA)
Also Called: Dream River
4940 Triggs St Ste B, Commerce (90022-4805)
PHONE..................323 269-6666
Barok Shahery, *President*
Henry Shahery, *Vice Pres*
Sevada Nazzarian, *Director*
Vic Japson, *Manager*
▲ **EMP:** 55
SQ FT: 120,000
SALES (est): 15.5MM **Privately Held**
WEB: www.shasoninc.com
SIC: 5131 Textiles, woven

(P-8244)
SPECIALTY TEXTILE SERVICES LLC
1333 30th St Ste A, San Diego (92154-3484)
PHONE..................619 476-8750
Mark Wilstine, *Manager*
Dora Ramirez, *Admin Asst*
Todd Jenks, *Sales Executive*
EMP: 72 **Privately Held**
SIC: 5131 Textiles, woven
PA: Specialty Textile Services Llc
737 W Buchanan St
Phoenix AZ 85007

(P-8245)
STAR FABRICS INC (PA)
1440 Walnut St, Los Angeles (90011-1351)
PHONE..................213 688-2871
Elias Haroni, *President*
Soussan Heroni, *Vice Pres*

Debra Grauten, *Sales Executive*
Marylou Manzo, *Sales Mgr*
▲ **EMP:** 70
SQ FT: 100,000
SALES (est): 11MM **Privately Held**
SIC: 5131 Textiles, woven

(P-8246)
TALON INTERNATIONAL INC (PA)
21900 Burbank Blvd # 270, Woodland Hills (91367-7461)
PHONE..................818 444-4100
Larry Dyne, *CEO*
Mark Dyne, *Ch of Bd*
James Reeder, *COO*
Jamey Johns, *Officer*
Gary Dyne, *Exec VP*
EMP: 58
SALES: 48.2MM **Publicly Held**
SIC: 5131 3965 Sewing supplies & notions; zipper

(P-8247)
UNITED FABRICS INTL INC
Also Called: U F I
1723 S Central Ave, Los Angeles (90021-3030)
PHONE..................213 749-8200
Shahariar S Simantob, *President*
Ramin Simantob, *Vice Pres*
Arbi Rostami, *Technology*
Robert Shostack, *Sales Staff*
▲ **EMP:** 51
SQ FT: 35,000
SALES (est): 17.2MM **Privately Held**
WEB: www.unitedfabric.com
SIC: 5131 5949 Piece goods & other fabrics; fabric stores piece goods

(P-8248)
ZABIN INDUSTRIES INC (PA)
3957 S Hill St Ste A, Los Angeles (90037-1343)
P.O. Box 15218 (90015-0218)
PHONE..................213 749-1215
Alan Faiola, *President*
Virginia Acosta, *Vice Pres*
Johnny Pelayo, *Info Tech Mgr*
Manolo Alvaro, *Human Res Mgr*
Fernando F Garcia, *Manager*
▲ **EMP:** 70
SQ FT: 43,000
SALES (est): 25.6MM **Privately Held**
WEB: www.zabin.com
SIC: 5131 Zippers; textile converters; buttons; net goods

5136 Men's & Boys' Clothing & Furnishings Wholesale

(P-8249)
ARTWEAR INC
13621 S Main St, Los Angeles (90061-2163)
PHONE..................310 217-1393
Ora Ketpongsuda, *President*
Paul Ketpongsuda, *Vice Pres*
Janchay Bhongjan, *Controller*
▲ **EMP:** 50
SQ FT: 48,000
SALES (est): 12.4MM **Privately Held**
WEB: www.lesliejordan.com
SIC: 5136 5137 2396 2331 Shirts, men's & boys'; women's & children's sportswear & swimsuits; automotive & apparel trimmings; women's & misses' blouses & shirts; men's & boys' furnishings; finishing plants, cotton

(P-8250)
BRAD RAMBO & ASSOCIATES INC (PA)
Also Called: Independent Trading Company
1341 Calle Avanzado, San Clemente (92673-6351)
PHONE..................949 366-9911
Brad Rambo, *President*
Brandon Rambo, *Principal*
Dena Marques, *Info Tech Dir*
Ian Swanson, *Graphic Designe*

Alia Ahmed, *Human Res Mgr*
▲ **EMP:** 55
SQ FT: 20,500
SALES (est): 25.7MM **Privately Held**
WEB: www.independenttradingco.com
SIC: 5136 Shirts, men's & boys'

(P-8251)
BRODER BROS CO
3443 E Central Ave, Fresno (93725-2542)
PHONE..................559 233-9900
Keith Hamilton, *Manager*
Tom Doran, *Credit Staff*
EMP: 59
SALES (corp-wide): 3.9B **Privately Held**
WEB: www.broderbros.com
SIC: 5137 Sportswear, men's & boys'; sportswear, women's & children's
PA: Broder Bros., Co.
6 Neshaminy Interplex Dr
Trevose PA 19053
215 291-0300

(P-8252)
CHEF WORKS INC (PA)
12325 Kerran St, Poway (92064-6801)
PHONE..................858 643-5600
Dale Gross, *CEO*
Dave Roth, *COO*
David Forster, *CFO*
Diane Harnly, *Exec VP*
Marc Batten, *Vice Pres*
◆ **EMP:** 139
SQ FT: 50,000
SALES (est): 110.3MM **Privately Held**
WEB: www.chefwork.com
SIC: 5136 5137 Uniforms, men's & boys'; uniforms, women's & children's

(P-8253)
COLOSSEUM ATHLETICS CORP
2400 S Wilmington Ave, Compton (90220-5403)
PHONE..................310 667-8341
Stuart Whang, *CEO*
Sean Lee, *CFO*
Jeff Jung, *General Mgr*
Yuri Choi, *Graphic Designe*
Chae Kim, *Graphic Designe*
▲ **EMP:** 85
SQ FT: 64,227
SALES (est): 44MM **Privately Held**
SIC: 5136 5137 Sportswear, men's & boys'; sportswear, women's & children's

(P-8254)
DECKY CO INC (PA)
2121 S Wilmington Ave, Compton (90220-5447)
PHONE..................310 608-2726
John Whang, *President*
Sun Wook Whang, *Shareholder*
Felicia Guardado, *Sales Mgr*
▲ **EMP:** 55
SQ FT: 20,000
SALES (est): 9.3MM **Privately Held**
WEB: www.decky.com
SIC: 5136 Sportswear, men's & boys'; hats, men's & boys'

(P-8255)
DORFMAN-PACIFIC CO (HQ)
Also Called: Dorfman Pacific
2615 Boeing Way, Stockton (95206-3984)
P.O. Box 213005 (95213-9005)
PHONE..................209 982-1400
Douglas Highsmith, *CEO*
Debra Highsmith, *Admin Sec*
Bakul Patel, *VP Finance*
Kirk Fallgatter, *Manager*
◆ **EMP:** 140
SQ FT: 278,000
SALES (est): 74.3MM
SALES (corp-wide): 10.8MM **Privately Held**
WEB: www.dorfman-pacific.com
SIC: 5136 5137 Caps, men's & boys'; hats, men's & boys'; men's & boys' outerwear; caps & gowns; hats: women's, children's & infants'; women's & children's outerwear
PA: Young An Hat Co., Ltd.
215 Ojeong-Ro
Bucheon 14442
823 267-1711

(P-8256)
DREAM LOUNGE INC
11271 Ventura Blvd 456, Studio City
(91604-3136)
PHONE.................................213 688-7888
John Vorzimer, *CEO*
EMP: 2210 **EST:** 2011
SALES (est): 225MM **Privately Held**
SIC: 5136 5137 Hosiery, men's & boys';
hosiery: women's, children's & infants'

(P-8257)
EISENBERG INTERNATIONAL
CORP (PA)
9128 Jordan Ave, Chatsworth
(91311-5707)
PHONE.................................818 365-8161
Joel Eisenberg, *President*
Lynn Eisenberg, *Corp Secy*
Richard Eisenberg, *Vice Pres*
▲ **EMP:** 55
SQ FT: 36,000
SALES (est): 13.4MM **Privately Held**
WEB: www.eisenbergintl.com
SIC: 5136 Coats, men's & boys'; sports-
wear, men's & boys'; suits, men's & boys';
trousers, men's & boys'

(P-8258)
FAM LLC
Also Called: Fam Brands
5553 Bandini Blvd Ste B, Bell
(90201-6421)
PHONE.................................323 888-7755
Frank Zarabi, *Mng Member*
Carrie Henley, *President*
Rich Campanelli, *COO*
Patrick Chow, *CFO*
Norah Emamjomeh, *Senior VP*
▲ **EMP:** 75
SQ FT: 75,000
SALES (est): 53.8MM **Privately Held**
WEB: www.fambrands.com
SIC: 5136 5137 Sportswear, men's &
boys'; women's & children's sportswear &
swimsuits

(P-8259)
FAMMA GROUP INC (PA)
4510 Loma Vista Ave, Vernon
(90058-2602)
PHONE.................................323 826-9600
Don X Ho, *CEO*
Joe Kamari, *President*
Jack Luk, *Controller*
Vickie Rodriguez, *Manager*
EMP: 100
SQ FT: 30,288
SALES (est): 53.1MM **Privately Held**
SIC: 5136 Men's & boys' clothing

(P-8260)
FORIA INTERNATIONAL INC
(PA)
18689 Arenth Ave, City of Industry
(91748-1302)
PHONE.................................626 912-8836
Teddy Mang, *CEO*
Danny K Wang, *President*
Lyanna Liang, *Vice Pres*
Joe Wang, *Vice Pres*
Timothy Wu, *Vice Pres*
▲ **EMP:** 111
SQ FT: 120,000
SALES (est): 24.4MM **Privately Held**
WEB: www.foria.com
SIC: 5136 Men's & boys' clothing

(P-8261)
FOX HEAD INC (PA)
Also Called: Fox Racing
16752 Armstrong Ave, Irvine (92606-4912)
PHONE.................................888 369-7223
Peter Fox, *Chairman*
Pete Fox, *President*
Paul E Harrington, *CEO*
Geoffrey T Fox, *Vice Pres*
Gregory Fox, *Vice Pres*
◆ **EMP:** 153 **EST:** 1975
SALES (est): 283.2MM **Privately Held**
WEB: www.foxbmx.com
SIC: 5136 5137 5961 Sportswear, men's
& boys'; sportswear, women's & chil-
dren's; mail order house

(P-8262)
GONZALES ENTERPRISES INC
Also Called: Aztlan Graphics
495 Ryan Ave, Chico (95973-8846)
PHONE.................................530 343-8725
Daniel Gonzales, *CEO*
Dawn Gonzales, *Treasurer*
BJ Larossa, *Vice Pres*
Michael Treacy, *Software Dev*
Heather Wilhelm, *Associate*
▲ **EMP:** 174
SQ FT: 26,000
SALES (est): 147.3MM **Privately Held**
WEB: www.5sun.com
SIC: 5136 Shirts, men's & boys'

(P-8263)
HELMET HOUSE INC (PA)
Also Called: Tour Master
26855 Malibu Hills Rd, Calabasas Hills
(91301-5100)
PHONE.................................800 421-7247
Robert M Miller, *CEO*
Randy Hutchings, *CFO*
Philip Bellomy, *Vice Pres*
Helen Ivener, *Admin Asst*
Robert Miller, *CTO*
▲ **EMP:** 73
SQ FT: 80,000
SALES (est): 73.6MM **Privately Held**
WEB: www.helmethouse.com
SIC: 5136 3949 Men's & boys' clothing;
helmets, athletic

(P-8264)
HYBRID PROMOTIONS LLC (PA)
10711 Walker St, Cypress (90630-4720)
PHONE.................................714 952-3866
Jarrod Dogan,
David Lederman, *COO*
Rick Saenz, *Exec VP*
James Wolfe, *Exec VP*
Terry Glynn, *Vice Pres*
▲ **EMP:** 134
SQ FT: 100,000
SALES (est): 685.7MM **Privately Held**
WEB: www.hybridtees.com
SIC: 5136 5137 5611 Sportswear, men's
& boys'; women's & children's clothing;
men's & boys' clothing stores

(P-8265)
KELLWOOD COMPANY LLC
Also Called: Xoxo
1307 E Temple Ave, City of Industry
(91746)
PHONE.................................626 934-4133
Arthur K Gordon, *Branch Mgr*
Jim Odonnell, *CFO*
EMP: 120
SALES (corp-wide): 350.8MM **Privately**
Held
WEB: www.kellwoodco.com
SIC: 5136 5137 Men's & boys' clothing;
women's & children's clothing
PA: Kellwood Company, Llc
600 Kellwood Pkwy Ste 200
Chesterfield MO 63017
314 576-3100

(P-8266)
L A CSTM AP & PROMOTIONS
INC (PA)
2680 Temple Ave, Long Beach
(90806-2209)
PHONE.................................562 595-1770
Chris Roybal, *President*
Luis Hernandez, *General Mgr*
EMP: 56
SQ FT: 10,000
SALES (est): 14.5MM **Privately Held**
WEB: www.lacustomapparel.com
SIC: 5136 Men's & boys' clothing

(P-8267)
LANDMARK PROTECTION INC
675 N 1st St Ste 620, San Jose
(95112-5145)
PHONE.................................408 293-6300
Daniel Miranda, *President*
EMP: 300
SQ FT: 6,000

SALES: 10MM **Privately Held**
WEB: www.landmarkprotection.com
SIC: 5136 5099 7381 Uniforms, men's &
boys'; safety equipment & supplies; guard
services; security guard service

(P-8268)
LIQUIDITY SERVICES INC
Str
741 E Ball Rd Ste 200, Anaheim
(92805-5952)
PHONE.................................714 738-6446
Carl Jones, *Branch Mgr*
EMP: 100 **Publicly Held**
WEB: www.liquidation.com
SIC: 5136 5137 5139 5611 Men's &
boys' clothing; women's & children's
clothing; footwear; men's & boys' clothing
stores; radio, television & electronic
stores; salvaging of damaged merchan-
dise, service only
PA: Liquidity Services, Inc.
6931 Arlington Rd Ste 200
Bethesda MD 20814

(P-8269)
M & S TRADING INC
Also Called: 7 Diamonds Clothing
15778 Gateway Cir, Tustin (92780-6469)
PHONE.................................714 241-7190
Sami Khalil, *CEO*
Christopher Vicente, *Graphic Designe*
▲ **EMP:** 71
SQ FT: 36,000
SALES (est): 14MM **Privately Held**
WEB: www.7diamonds.com
SIC: 5136 5137 Sportswear, men's &
boys'; women's & children's clothing

(P-8270)
MOUNTAIN GEAR
CORPORATION
Also Called: Tri-Mountain
4889 4th St, Irwindale (91706-2194)
PHONE.................................626 851-2488
Daniel Tsai, *CEO*
Sandy Treagus, *CFO*
Jennifer Tsai, *Vice Pres*
Rosie Tsai, *Vice Pres*
Olga Duran, *CTO*
▲ **EMP:** 125
SQ FT: 300,000
SALES (est): 48.3MM **Privately Held**
WEB: www.trimountain.com
SIC: 5136 Sportswear, men's & boys'

(P-8271)
NORTH BAY DISTRIBUTION INC
2029 E Monte Vista Ave, Vacaville
(95688-3100)
PHONE.................................707 450-1219
Lee Perry, *Branch Mgr*
EMP: 70
SQ FT: 250,000
SALES (corp-wide): 40MM **Privately**
Held
SIC: 5136 Men's & boys' clothing
PA: North Bay Distribution, Inc.
2050 Cessna Dr
Vacaville CA 95688
707 452-9984

(P-8272)
OTTO INTERNATIONAL INC (PA)
Also Called: Otto Cap
3550 Jurupa St Ste A, Ontario
(91761-2946)
PHONE.................................909 937-1998
Razgo Lee, *President*
Frank Jou, *CFO*
Heidi Soria, *Sales Associate*
Christine Villamor, *Sales Staff*
◆ **EMP:** 50
SQ FT: 136,000
SALES (est): 41.4MM **Privately Held**
WEB: www.ottocap.com
SIC: 5136 Caps, men's & boys'

(P-8273)
PIEGE CO (PA)
Also Called: Felina Lingerie
20120 Plummer St, Chatsworth
(91311-5448)
PHONE.................................818 727-9100
Kambiz Zarabi, *President*

Morad Zarabi, *Ch of Bd*
Michael Zarabi, *Exec VP*
Kass Daeeme, *Info Tech Mgr*
Paul Edwards, *Technology*
▲ **EMP:** 195
SQ FT: 48,000
SALES (est): 78.4MM **Privately Held**
WEB: www.felinausa.com
SIC: 5136 5137 Men's & boys' suits &
trousers; lingerie

(P-8274)
PRANA LIVING LLC (HQ)
3209 Lionshead Ave, Carlsbad
(92010-4710)
PHONE.................................866 915-6457
Scott Kerslake, *CEO*
Larry Callette, *CFO*
Nancy Dynan, *Vice Pres*
Arnould T'Kint, *Vice Pres*
Jessica Mahoney, *Vice Pres*
▲ **EMP:** 90
SALES (est): 50.2MM
SALES (corp-wide): 2.4B **Publicly Held**
SIC: 5136 5137 Men's & boys' clothing;
women's & children's clothing
PA: Columbia Sportswear Company
14375 Nw Science Park Dr
Portland OR 97229
503 985-4000

(P-8275)
QUAKE CITY CASUALS INC
Also Called: Quake City Caps
1800 S Flower St, Los Angeles
(90015-3424)
PHONE.................................213 746-0540
John Glucksman, *CEO*
Steve De Mars, *President*
Soledad Wong, *Chief Mktg Ofcr*
Hilda Yantz, *Purchasing*
Isabella Chan, *Natl Sales Mgr*
▲ **EMP:** 125
SQ FT: 11,500
SALES (est): 23.6MM **Privately Held**
WEB: www.capstoneheadwear.com
SIC: 5136 Men's & boys' clothing

(P-8276)
RICK SOLOMON ENTERPRISES
INC (PA)
Also Called: Axis
8460 Higuera St, Culver City (90232-2520)
P.O. Box 266, Los Angeles (90078-0266)
PHONE.................................310 280-3700
Richard Solomon, *President*
Barbara Baskin, *CFO*
Tony Andreu, *Accountant*
▲ **EMP:** 70
SQ FT: 14,058
SALES (est): 12.9MM **Privately Held**
WEB: www.axisclothing.com
SIC: 5136 Sportswear, men's & boys'

(P-8277)
SOEX WEST USA LLC
Also Called: Soex Group
3294 E 26th St, Vernon (90058-8008)
PHONE.................................323 264-8300
Roubik Aftandilians,
Nursis Ohanian,
◆ **EMP:** 300
SQ FT: 120,000
SALES (est): 91.8MM **Privately Held**
WEB: www.soexgroup.com
SIC: 5136 Men's & boys' clothing

(P-8278)
STUSSY INC
17426 Daimler St, Irvine (92614-5514)
PHONE.................................949 474-9255
Frank Sinatra, *CEO*
Andy Tirpstra, *General Mgr*
Mindy Cook, *Admin Sec*
Desiree Hardy, *Admin Asst*
Cameron Deeds, *Administration*
▲ **EMP:** 90
SQ FT: 30,000
SALES (est): 40MM **Privately Held**
SIC: 5136 Men's & boys' clothing

PRODUCTS & SVCS

(P-8279)
T M P INC
Also Called: Pro TEC Manufacturing
21051 Osborne St, Canoga Park
(91304-1744)
PHONE..................818 718-1222
Humberto Carlos, *CEO*
▲ EMP: 100
SQ FT: 16,000
SALES (est): 21MM **Privately Held**
SIC: 5136 5137 2329 Uniforms, men's &
boys'; uniforms, women's & children's;
knickers, dress (separate): men's & boys'

(P-8280)
TOPWIN CORPORATION (PA)
Also Called: People's Place
1808 Abalone Ave, Torrance (90501-3703)
PHONE..................310 325-2255
Tomokazu Yoshimura, *CEO*
Kacey Abe, *Manager*
Takeshi Yogi, *Manager*
Tamami Murata, *Asst Mgr*
▲ EMP: 60
SQ FT: 22,000
SALES (est): 32.6MM **Privately Held**
WEB: www.topwin.com
SIC: 5136 5137 5611 5621 Men's &
boys' clothing; women's & children's
clothing; men's & boys' clothing stores;
women's clothing stores; mannequins

(P-8281)
UNI HOSIERY CO INC (PA)
1911 E Olympic Blvd, Los Angeles
(90021-2421)
PHONE..................213 228-0100
Harry Chung, *CEO*
Byong Lee, *Branch Mgr*
Ryan Park, *Purch Mgr*
Richard Kim, *Sales Mgr*
Michelle Choi, *Sales Associate*
◆ EMP: 120
SQ FT: 500,000
SALES (est): 45.3MM **Privately Held**
WEB: www.unihosiery.com
SIC: 5136 5137 Hosiery, men's & boys';
hosiery: women's, children's & infants';
lingerie

(P-8282)
VOLCOM LLC
1725 Monrovia Ave, Costa Mesa
(92627-4401)
PHONE..................949 646-2175
Richard R Woolcott, *Branch Mgr*
Jeff Arnold, *Director*
EMP: 200
SALES (corp-wide): 212.2MM **Privately Held**
SIC: 5136 Men's & boys' clothing
HQ: Volcom, Llc
1740 Monrovia Ave
Costa Mesa CA 92627

(P-8283)
WOR INTERNATIONAL INC
Also Called: Nick and MO
15612 1st St, Irwindale (91706-6220)
P.O. Box 1631, Walnut (91788-1631)
PHONE..................626 812-8888
Hsu WEI Wang, *President*
Roger Liang, *Vice Pres*
▼ EMP: 50
SQ FT: 30,000
SALES: 13.2MM **Privately Held**
WEB: www.worusa.com
SIC: 5136 Men's & boys' clothing

5137 Women's, Children's & Infants Clothing Wholesale

(P-8284)
2253 APPAREL INC (PA)
Also Called: Celebrity Pink USA
1708 Aeros Way, Montebello (90640-6504)
PHONE..................323 837-9800
Doron Kadosh, *President*
Holly Arnesen-Sileo, *Exec VP*
Benny Goldstein, *Admin Sec*
Sharona Zikry, *Controller*

David Kadosh,
▲ EMP: 80
SQ FT: 50,000
SALES: 100MM **Privately Held**
WEB: www.2253apparel.com
SIC: 5137 Women's & children's clothing

(P-8285)
B BOSTON & ASSOCIATES INC (PA)
Also Called: Western Connection, Carol Rose
4871 S Santa Fe Ave, Vernon
(90058-2103)
PHONE..................323 264-3915
Benjamin Boston, *CEO*
Ram Kundani, *President*
Jenifer Bitran, *Manager*
▲ EMP: 128
SQ FT: 100,000
SALES (est): 45.7MM **Privately Held**
SIC: 5137 7389 Sweaters, women's &
children's; women's & children's outer-
wear; personal service agents, brokers &
bureaus

(P-8286)
BCBG MAX AZRIA GROUP LLC
2761 Fruitland Ave, Vernon (90058-3607)
PHONE..................323 589-2224
EMP: 69 EST: 2014
SALES (est): 1.1MM
SALES (corp-wide): 1.5B **Privately Held**
SIC: 5137 5621 2335
PA: Guggenheim Partners, Llc
330 Madison Ave Rm 201
New York NY 10017
212 739-0700

(P-8287)
BCBG MAX AZRIA GROUP LLC (HQ)
2761 Fruitland Ave, Vernon (90058-3607)
PHONE..................323 589-2224
Max Azria,
Brian Fleming, *CFO*
Bernd Kroeber, *Exec VP*
Martine Melloul, *Exec VP*
Richard Ito, *Info Tech Dir*
◆ EMP: 252
SQ FT: 500,000
SALES (est): 1B **Privately Held**
WEB: www.bcbg.com
SIC: 5137 5621 2335 Women's & chil-
dren's clothing; women's clothing stores;
women's, juniors' & misses' dresses
PA: Marquee Brands Llc
50 W 57th St
New York NY 10019
212 203-8135

(P-8288)
BCTC CORPORATION
5500 E Olympic Blvd Ste B, Commerce
(90022-5130)
PHONE..................323 888-9388
Shirley Bao, *Chairman*
Even Chew, *President*
Sally Bao, *Vice Pres*
Edward Hu, *Vice Pres*
Alex Kang, *Finance*
▲ EMP: 80 EST: 1973
SQ FT: 75,000
SALES: 18.9MM **Privately Held**
WEB: www.bctccorp.com
SIC: 5137 Women's & children's clothing

(P-8289)
BLUE PLANET INTERNATIONAL INC
Also Called: Boom-Boom Jeans
2945 E 12th St, Los Angeles (90023-3623)
PHONE..................323 526-9999
Simon Parsakar, *President*
Ezra Parsakar, *Vice Pres*
Rodel Pamintuan, *Human Resources*
Shawn Kay, *Mktg Dir*
▲ EMP: 50
SQ FT: 30,000
SALES (est): 50MM **Privately Held**
WEB: www.boomboomjeans.com
SIC: 5137 Women's & children's clothing

(P-8290)
BRUML MANAGEMENT LLC
Also Called: Techstyles Sportswear
2051 Alpine Way, Hayward (94545-1703)
PHONE..................800 733-3629
Jonathan Bruml, *Mng Member*
Lisa Bruml,
EMP: 50
SQ FT: 20,000
SALES (est): 12MM **Privately Held**
SIC: 5137 5136 Women's & children's
clothing; men's & boys' clothing

(P-8291)
CALIFORNIA RAIN COMPANY INC
1213 E 14th St, Los Angeles (90021-2215)
PHONE..................213 623-6061
Jack Jhy C Jang, *President*
▲ EMP: 90
SQ FT: 8,600
SALES (est): 30.1MM **Privately Held**
WEB: www.californiarainla.com
SIC: 5137 5136 5699 Sportswear,
women's & children's; sportswear, men's
& boys'; customized clothing & apparel

(P-8292)
CECICO INC
Also Called: Cecico Town
1016 Towne Ave Unit 110, Los Angeles
(90021-2078)
PHONE..................323 269-7000
Kelly Kyung Lie Ahn, *Principal*
▲ EMP: 55
SALES (est): 8.7MM **Privately Held**
SIC: 5137 2339 Women's & children's
clothing; women's & misses' accessories

(P-8293)
CHANCE GROUP LLC
911 E 106th St, Los Angeles (90002-3442)
PHONE..................310 343-3766
Shaunt Khandamian, *CEO*
EMP: 50
SALES: 15MM **Privately Held**
SIC: 5137 Women's & children's dresses,
suits, skirts & blouses

(P-8294)
CHILDRENS BTQ AT STEVENS HOPE
Also Called: Childrens Botique, The
10730 Fthill Blvd Ste 170, Rancho Cuca-
monga (91730)
PHONE..................909 256-0100
Tony Campbell, *Owner*
EMP: 50
SALES (est): 2.4MM **Privately Held**
SIC: 5137 3949 8699 Women's & chil-
dren's clothing; sporting & athletic goods;
charitable organization

(P-8295)
CLAUDIA RICHARD INC
4871 S Santa Fe Ave, Vernon
(90058-2103)
PHONE..................323 264-3915
Benjamin Boston, *President*
Ram Kundani, *Vice Pres*
◆ EMP: 59
SALES (est): 15.9MM **Privately Held**
SIC: 5137 Women's & children's clothing

(P-8296)
COLLECTED GROUP COMPANY LLC
Also Called: Joie
5300 S Santa Fe Ave, Vernon
(90058-3520)
PHONE..................323 277-3900
Serge Azria, *Branch Mgr*
EMP: 50
SALES (corp-wide): 187.2MM **Privately Held**
SIC: 5137 Women's & children's clothing
HQ: Dutch, Llc
5301 S Santa Fe Ave
Vernon CA 90058
323 277-3900

(P-8297)
COMAK TRADING INC A CAL CORP
2550 S Soto St, Vernon (90058-8013)
PHONE..................323 261-3404
EMP: 100
SALES (est): 12.6MM **Privately Held**
SIC: 5137 5136 5139

(P-8298)
DELTA GALIL USA INC
Also Called: Loomworks Apparel
16912 Von Karman Ave, Irvine
(92606-4972)
PHONE..................949 296-0380
EMP: 54
SALES (corp-wide): 1.3B **Privately Held**
SIC: 5137 Women's & children's lingerie &
undergarments
HQ: Delta Galil Usa Inc.
1 Harmon Plz Fl 5
Secaucus NJ 07094
201 902-0055

(P-8299)
DUTCH LLC (DH)
Also Called: Joie
5301 S Santa Fe Ave, Vernon
(90058-3519)
PHONE..................323 277-3900
Serge K Azria, *Mng Member*
Morgan Dreyer, *Executive Asst*
Florence Azria,
◆ EMP: 102
SQ FT: 40,000
SALES (est): 187.2MM
SALES (corp-wide): 187.2MM **Privately Held**
SIC: 5137 Women's & children's clothing
HQ: The Collected Group Llc
5301 S Santa Fe Ave
Vernon CA 90058
323 277-3900

(P-8300)
EDGEMINE INC
Also Called: Mine Fashion
1801 E 50th St, Los Angeles (90058-1940)
PHONE..................323 267-8222
Kevin Chang Kang, *President*
▲ EMP: 120 EST: 1994
SQ FT: 45,000
SALES (est): 630.8K **Privately Held**
SIC: 5137 Women's & children's clothing

(P-8301)
EIGHTY ONE ENTERPRISE INC
9401 Whitmore St, El Monte (91731-2821)
PHONE..................626 371-1980
May Sayphraraj, *President*
Darren Sayphraraj, *Treasurer*
◆ EMP: 50 EST: 2012
SQ FT: 60,000
SALES (est): 18MM **Privately Held**
SIC: 5137 Lingerie

(P-8302)
ESP GROUP LTD
2397 Bateman Ave, Duarte (91010-3313)
PHONE..................626 301-0280
Yan Wang, *CEO*
David Ouyang, *President*
William Yue, *CFO*
◆ EMP: 68
SQ FT: 150,000
SALES (est): 28.7MM **Privately Held**
SIC: 5137 Women's & children's clothing

(P-8303)
FACTORY 2-U IMPORT EXPORT INC
Also Called: Oren's Replay
13034 Delano St, Van Nuys (91401-3209)
PHONE..................323 587-9900
Liat Madar, *CEO*
EMP: 60
SALES (est): 2.1MM **Privately Held**
WEB: www.youimport.com
SIC: 5137 5136 Women's & children's
clothing; men's & boys' clothing

(P-8304)
GURU DENIM LLC (DH)
Also Called: True Religion Brand Jeans
1888 Rosecrans Ave # 1000, Manhattan Beach (90266-3712)
PHONE.................................323 266-3072
John Ermatinger, *Mng Member*
Alan Weiss, *Controller*
▲ EMP: 150
SQ FT: 19,300
SALES (est): 449.8MM
SALES (corp-wide): 350MM **Privately Held**
WEB: www.gurudenim.com
SIC: 5137 5611 Women's & children's clothing; clothing accessories: men's & boys'
HQ: True Religion Apparel, Inc.
1888 Rosecrans Ave # 1000
Manhattan Beach CA 90266
323 266-3072

(P-8305)
HARVEYS INDUSTRIES INC
Also Called: Original Seatbeltbag , The
724 N Poinsettia St, Santa Ana (92701-3941)
PHONE.................................714 247-4700
Dana Harvey, *CEO*
Melanie Harvey, *Admin Sec*
Sabrina Montes, *Bookkeeper*
Jessica McNew, *Human Res Mgr*
Jessica Rice, *Human Res Mgr*
▲ EMP: 55
SQ FT: 12,000
SALES (est): 22.2MM **Privately Held**
WEB: www.harveysboutique.com
SIC: 5137 5632 Handbags; women's accessory & specialty stores

(P-8306)
HIBSHMAN TRADING CORPORATION
Also Called: Mattress Liqidation
9843 6th St Ste 103, Rancho Cucamonga (91730-5741)
PHONE.................................909 581-1800
Erik D Hibshman, *President*
EMP: 60
SQ FT: 65,000
SALES (est): 7.5MM **Privately Held**
SIC: 5137 5136 5021 Women's & children's clothing; men's & boys' clothing; mattresses

(P-8307)
HOUSTON SALEM INC
Also Called: Chaser
217 E 157th St, Gardena (90248-2510)
PHONE.................................310 719-7004
Stephen Martin Kayne, *CEO*
Ramsey Salem, *COO*
Jackie Sique Molina, *Controller*
▲ EMP: 50
SQ FT: 70,000
SALES (est): 21.6MM **Privately Held**
WEB: www.bhcompany.com
SIC: 5137 5136 Women's & children's clothing; men's & boys' clothing

(P-8308)
ISABEL GARRETON INC (PA)
770 Miraflores, San Pedro (90731-1437)
PHONE.................................310 833-7768
Isabel Garreton, *President*
Gonzalo Garreton, *Treasurer*
Julia Montes, *Vice Pres*
Erika Whitham, *Marketing Staff*
Alexandra Garreton, *Agent*
EMP: 125
SALES (est): 15.3MM **Privately Held**
WEB: www.isabelgarreton.com
SIC: 5137 Women's & children's clothing

(P-8309)
JEAN MART INC
6700 Avalon Blvd, Los Angeles (90003-1920)
PHONE.................................323 752-7775
Arnold Yu, *Principal*
Helen C Yi, *President*
▲ EMP: 100
SQ FT: 5,000
SALES (est): 50.3MM **Privately Held**
SIC: 5137 7389 Women's & children's clothing; sewing contractor

(P-8310)
KASH APPAREL LLC
1437 E 20th St, Los Angeles (90011-1301)
PHONE.................................213 747-8885
Stephanie Kleinjan, *Mng Member*
Adir Haroni,
▲ EMP: 68
SQ FT: 10,000
SALES (est): 20.8MM **Privately Held**
SIC: 5137 Women's & children's accessories

(P-8311)
KBL GROUP INTERNATIONAL LTD
Also Called: Kbl International
9142 9150 Norwalk Blvd, Santa Fe Springs (90670)
PHONE.................................562 699-9995
Thomas Ko, *Branch Mgr*
EMP: 50
SALES (corp-wide): 47.2MM **Privately Held**
WEB: www.crystalk.com
SIC: 5137 Sportswear, women's & children's
PA: Kbl Group International Ltd.
1441 Broadway Fl 17th
New York NY 10018
212 391-1551

(P-8312)
KELLWOOD COMPANY LLC
Also Called: Xoxo
13085 Temple Ave, City of Industry (91746-1418)
PHONE.................................626 934-4155
Sherri Akers, *Branch Mgr*
EMP: 150
SALES (corp-wide): 350.8MM **Privately Held**
SIC: 5137 Women's & children's clothing
PA: Kellwood Company, Llc
600 Kellwood Pkwy Ste 200
Chesterfield MO 63017
314 576-3100

(P-8313)
KOS-USA
3434 S Broadway, Los Angeles (90007-4409)
PHONE.................................213 747-2591
Donna Shin, *President*
Charlie Shin, *Vice Pres*
EMP: 60
SALES (est): 7.7MM **Privately Held**
WEB: www.kosusa.com
SIC: 5137 Women's & children's clothing

(P-8314)
LDLA CLOTHING LLC
Also Called: Living Doll
13071 Temple Ave, La Puente (91746-1418)
PHONE.................................323 312-2805
Amy Powers, *Owner*
Richard Swartz, *CFO*
EMP: 60
SALES (est): 50MM **Privately Held**
SIC: 5137 Women's & children's clothing

(P-8315)
LEIGH JERRY CALIFORNIA INC (PA)
Also Called: Jerry Leigh Entertainment AP
7860 Nelson Rd, Panorama City (91402-6044)
PHONE.................................818 909-6200
Andrew Leigh, *President*
Samira Jammal, *Vice Pres*
Pamela Wong, *Vice Pres*
Carlos Mejia, *Comp Tech*
Nick Carrillo, *Graphic Designe*
◆ EMP: 550 EST: 1977
SQ FT: 40,000
SALES (est): 221.8MM **Privately Held**
SIC: 5137 2361 Sportswear, women's & children's; girls' & children's dresses, blouses & shirts; girls' & children's blouses & shirts

(P-8316)
LYMI INC (PA)
Also Called: Reformation, The
2263 E Vernon Ave, Vernon (90058-1631)
PHONE.................................213 434-2772
Yael Aflalo, *CEO*
Katie Leneghan, *Partner*
Jennifer Loo, *CFO*
Stuart Leung, *Vice Pres*
Tessa Hanna, *Executive Asst*
▲ EMP: 100
SQ FT: 120,000
SALES (est): 288.7MM **Privately Held**
SIC: 5137 Women's & children's clothing

(P-8317)
MAD DOGG ATHLETICS INC (PA)
Also Called: Spinning
2111 Narcissus Ct, Venice (90291-4818)
PHONE.................................310 823-7008
John R Baudhuin, *President*
Aerin Shaw, *COO*
Jonathan Goldberg, *Admin Sec*
▲ EMP: 120
SALES (est): 60.4MM **Privately Held**
WEB: www.spinning.com
SIC: 5137 5122 7812 Sportswear, women's & children's; vitamins & minerals; video tape production

(P-8318)
MALIBU DESIGN GROUP
Also Called: Ocean Dream
5445 Jillson St, Commerce (90040-2117)
PHONE.................................323 271-1700
Mollie Cha, *CEO*
Mary Chung, *Admin Sec*
◆ EMP: 50
SQ FT: 60,000
SALES (est): 23.5MM **Privately Held**
SIC: 5137 Swimsuits: women's, children's & infants'

(P-8319)
MARIKA GROUP INC
Also Called: Shiva-Shakthi
8960 Carroll Way, San Diego (92121-2429)
PHONE.................................858 537-5300
Donald Schumacher, *Vice Pres*
Scott Kalman, *President*
Lew Corpuz, *Vice Pres*
Zaira Chavez, *Production*
▲ EMP: 60
SQ FT: 60,000
SALES (est): 11.4MM **Privately Held**
SIC: 5137 2339 Sportswear, women's & children's; women's & misses' outerwear

(P-8320)
MEL BERNIE AND COMPANY INC
Edgar Berebi A Div 1928 Jwly
3000 W Empire Ave, Burbank (91504-3109)
PHONE.................................818 841-1928
Mel Bernie, *Branch Mgr*
EMP: 150
SALES (corp-wide): 55.6MM **Privately Held**
WEB: www.1928.com
SIC: 5137 Women's & children's accessories
PA: Mel Bernie And Company, Inc.
3000 W Empire Ave
Burbank CA 91504
818 841-1928

(P-8321)
MIAS FASHION MFG CO INC
Also Called: California Basic
12623 Cisneros Ln, Santa Fe Springs (90670-3373)
PHONE.................................562 906-1060
Peter D Anh, *President*
Brian Song, *CFO*
◆ EMP: 252
SALES: 163MM **Privately Held**
WEB: www.mfmcoinc.com
SIC: 5137 Women's & children's clothing

(P-8322)
MIKEN SALES INC (PA)
Also Called: Miken Clothing
7230 Oxford Way, Commerce (90040-3643)
PHONE.................................323 266-2560
Michael Bobbitt, *CEO*
Kenny Landy, *Vice Pres*
Jonathan Namm, *VP Opers*
Kathryn Higa, *Manager*
▲ EMP: 53
SQ FT: 23,000
SALES (est): 19.8MM **Privately Held**
SIC: 5137 Women's & children's clothing

(P-8323)
MOLA INC
2957 E 46th St, Vernon (90058-2423)
PHONE.................................323 582-0088
▲ EMP: 150
SALES (est): 45.2MM **Privately Held**
SIC: 5137

(P-8324)
MS BUBBLES INC (PA)
Also Called: Eighty Eight
2731 S Alameda St, Los Angeles (90058-1311)
PHONE.................................323 544-0300
Aneeta Chopra, *CEO*
Sanjiv Chopra, *Treasurer*
Lisa Eitelberg, *Bd of Directors*
Renu Chopra, *Vice Pres*
Rajeshwar Chopra, *Admin Sec*
▲ EMP: 75
SQ FT: 50,000
SALES (est): 29.4MM **Privately Held**
WEB: www.msbubbles.com
SIC: 5137 Women's & children's clothing

(P-8325)
MYSTIC INC (PA)
2444 Porter St, Los Angeles (90021-2511)
PHONE.................................213 746-8538
Haejin Han, *President*
Hae Han, *CEO*
Daniel Priano, *COO*
Andy Kim, *Buyer*
Adrian Vazquez, *Sales Dir*
▲ EMP: 64
SQ FT: 45,000
SALES: 15.3MM **Privately Held**
SIC: 5137 2339 Women's & children's clothing; athletic clothing: women's, misses' & juniors'

(P-8326)
NEWPORT APPAREL CORPORATION (PA)
Also Called: I N G
1215 W Walnut St, Compton (90220-5009)
PHONE.................................310 605-1900
James Kim, *President*
Kimberly Kim, *CFO*
James K Kim, *Executive*
Yong Chung, *General Mgr*
Esther Kim, *Info Tech Mgr*
▲ EMP: 62
SQ FT: 38,500
SALES (est): 27.7MM **Privately Held**
WEB: www.newporting.com
SIC: 5137 Sportswear, women's & children's

(P-8327)
NYDJ APPAREL LLC
Also Called: Not Your Daughters Jeans
5401 S Soto St, Vernon (90058-3618)
PHONE.................................323 581-9040
Lisa Collier,
Kate Foster, *Treasurer*
Mila Carril, *Opers Mgr*
Steve Brink,
Robert C Skinner Jr,
▲ EMP: 200
SQ FT: 6,000
SALES (est): 153.6MM **Privately Held**
WEB: www.lls.com
SIC: 5137 Women's & children's clothing

(P-8328)
NYGARD INC
Also Called: Tan Jay-Nygard Outlet Store
14401 S San Pedro St, Gardena (90248-2026)
PHONE.................................310 776-8900

PRODUCTS & SVCS

Murray Batte, *President*
Katrina Cortez, *Manager*
EMP: 63 **Privately Held**
SIC: 5137 Women's & children's clothing
HQ: Nygard Inc.
  1435 Broadway
  New York NY 10018
  646 520-2000

(P-8329)
ONE 3 TWO INC
Also Called: Obey Clothing
17353 Derian Ave, Irvine (92614-5801)
PHONE.............................949 596-8400
Regan Don Juncal, *CEO*
Don Junkal, *President*
Steve Melgren, *CFO*
Chris Broder, *Vice Pres*
◆ **EMP:** 106 **EST:** 2000
SALES (est): 46.2MM **Privately Held**
WEB: www.obey.com
SIC: 5137 Women's & children's clothing

(P-8330)
PARAGON TEXTILES INC
Also Called: Samiyatex
13003 S Figueroa St, Los Angeles
(90061-1136)
PHONE.............................310 323-7500
Murtaza Haji, *President*
Farhana Haji, *Treasurer*
▼ **EMP:** 75
SQ FT: 42,500
SALES (est): 29.6MM **Privately Held**
WEB: www.samiyatex.com
SIC: 5137 Women's & children's clothing

(P-8331)
ROBIN K
4731 Fruitland Ave, Vernon (90058-2721)
PHONE.............................323 235-5152
EMP: 60 **EST:** 2010
SALES (est): 7.9MM **Privately Held**
SIC: 5137 5611 Apparel belts, women's &
  children's; blouses; sportswear, women's
  & children's; nightwear: women's, children's & infants'; clothing accessories:
  men's & boys'; clothing, men's & boys':
  everyday, except suits & sportswear;
  suits, men's; tie shops

(P-8332)
SAME SWIM LLC
2333 E 49th St, Vernon (90058-2820)
PHONE.............................323 582-2588
Shea Petranovic,
Ryan Horne,
EMP: 90
SALES (est): 110.7K **Privately Held**
SIC: 5137 Women's & children's sports-
  wear & swimsuits

(P-8333)
SECRET CHARM LLC (PA)
1433 Walnut St, Los Angeles (90011-1314)
PHONE.............................213 742-7744
Adir Haroni, *Mng Member*
Eran Haroni, *President*
Janette Edwards, *CFO*
Elias Haroni,
Soussan Haroni,
▲ **EMP:** 300
SALES (est): 104.5MM **Privately Held**
SIC: 5137 Children's goods

(P-8334)
SEVEN LICENSING COMPANY LLC
Also Called: Seven7 Brands
801 S Figueroa St # 2500, Los Angeles
(90017-5504)
PHONE.............................323 881-0308
Jacqueline Rose Guez, *Mng Member*
Gerald Guez,
▲ **EMP:** 80
SQ FT: 10,000
SALES (est): 29.4MM **Privately Held**
SIC: 5137 Women's & children's acces-
  sories
PA: Sunrise Brands, Llc
  801 S Figueroa St # 2500
  Los Angeles CA 90017

(P-8335)
SEYMOUR GALE & ASSOCIATES
4501 Cedros Ave Unit 118, Sherman Oaks
(91403-2839)
PHONE.............................213 622-5361
Seymour Gale, *Owner*
EMP: 50
SQ FT: 1,500
SALES (est): 12.1MM **Privately Held**
SIC: 5137 Women's & children's clothing

(P-8336)
SUNRISE BRANDS LLC (PA)
801 S Figueroa St # 2500, Los Angeles
(90017-5504)
PHONE.............................323 780-8250
Gerard Guez, *CEO*
Don Waldman, *COO*
Peter Akaragian, *CFO*
Donald Waldman, *CFO*
Cynthia Bedgood, *Executive Asst*
EMP: 50
SALES (est): 87.5MM **Privately Held**
SIC: 5137 5136 Women's & children's
  clothing; men's & boys' clothing

(P-8337)
SWATFAME INC (PA)
Also Called: Kut From The Kloth
16425 Gale Ave, City of Industry
(91745-1722)
PHONE.............................626 961-7928
Bruce Stern, *Ch of Bd*
Jonathan Greenberg, *President*
Mitchell Quaranta, *CEO*
J P Wolk, *CFO*
JP Wolk, *CFO*
▲ **EMP:** 290
SQ FT: 233,000
SALES (est): 188.8MM **Privately Held**
WEB: www.swatfame.com
SIC: 5137 2211 2339 Dresses; sports-
  wear, women's & children's; denims;
  women's & misses' outerwear

(P-8338)
TARRANT APPAREL GROUP
Also Called: Fashion Resources
801 S Figueroa St # 2500, Los Angeles
(90017-5504)
PHONE.............................323 780-8250
Gerard Guez, *Ch of Bd*
Peter Akaradian, *CFO*
Todd Kay, *Vice Ch Bd*
▲ **EMP:** 250
SALES (est): 57.3MM **Privately Held**
SIC: 5137 Women's & children's clothing
PA: Sunrise Brands, Llc
  801 S Figueroa St # 2500
  Los Angeles CA 90017

(P-8339)
TOPSON DOWNS CALIFORNIA INC (PA)
3840 Watseka Ave, Culver City
(90232-2633)
PHONE.............................310 558-0300
John Poyer, *President*
Kristopher Scott, *CFO*
Joe Wirht, *Admin Sec*
Robert L Handler,
▲ **EMP:** 250
SQ FT: 42,000
SALES (est): 238.7MM **Privately Held**
WEB: www.topsondowns.com
SIC: 5137 Women's & children's clothing

(P-8340)
TYR SPORT INC
Also Called: T Y R
1790 Apollo Ct, Seal Beach (90740-5617)
P.O. Box 1930, Huntington Beach (92647-
1930)
PHONE.............................562 430-1380
Matthew Dilorenzo, *CEO*
Steven Locke, *COO*
Ed Eskew, *Vice Pres*
David Melendez, *Info Tech Mgr*
Daniel Terry, *Graphic Designe*
◆ **EMP:** 60
SQ FT: 80,000

SALES (est): 28.8MM
SALES (corp-wide): 52MM **Privately Held**
WEB: www.tyr.com
SIC: 5137 5136 5091 2329 Sportswear,
  women's & children's; swimsuits:
  women's, children's & infants'; women's
  & children's accessories; beachwear,
  men's & boys'; sporting & recreation
  goods; bathing suits & swimwear: men's
  & boys'; basketball uniforms: men's,
  youths' & boys'
PA: Swimwear Anywhere, Inc.
  85 Sherwood Ave
  Farmingdale NY 11735
  631 420-1400

(P-8341)
YOUNG BAE FASHIONS INC
4811 Hampton St, Vernon (90058-2135)
P.O. Box 58187, Los Angeles (90058-0187)
PHONE.............................323 583-8684
Young Bae, *President*
Chung Bae, *Admin Sec*
▲ **EMP:** 75 **EST:** 1976
SQ FT: 40,000
SALES (est): 12MM **Privately Held**
SIC: 5137 Women's & children's clothing

5139 Footwear Wholesale

(P-8342)
ACI INTERNATIONAL (PA)
844 Moraga Dr, Los Angeles (90049-1632)
PHONE.............................310 889-3400
Steve Jackson, *CEO*
Jay Jackson, *President*
David Mankowitz, *CFO*
Muriel Jackson, *Treasurer*
Anna Liau, *Exec VP*
▲ **EMP:** 79
SQ FT: 40,000
SALES (est): 39.2MM **Privately Held**
WEB: www.aciint.com
SIC: 5139 Shoes; slippers, house

(P-8343)
ASICS AMERICA CORPORATION (HQ)
Also Called: Asics Tiger
80 Technology Dr, Irvine (92618-2301)
PHONE.............................949 453-8888
Kevin Wulff, *CEO*
Seiho Gohashi, *Ch of Bd*
Richard Bourne, *President*
Craig Gillan, *Vice Pres*
Brian Wehner, *Vice Pres*
▲ **EMP:** 109 **EST:** 1973
SQ FT: 45,000
SALES (est): 237.3MM
SALES (corp-wide): 3.5B **Privately Held**
WEB: www.onitsukatiger.com
SIC: 5139 5136 5137 2369 Footwear,
  athletic; sportswear, men's & boys'; men's
  & boys' furnishings; sportswear, women's
  & children's; women's & children's acces-
  sories; girls' & children's outerwear;
  women's & misses' outerwear; men's &
  boys' furnishings
PA: Asics Corporation
  7-1-1, Minatojimanakamachi, Chuo-Ku
  Kobe HYO 650-0
  783 032-231

(P-8344)
AYLESVA INC
14537 Garfield Ave, Paramount
(90723-3425)
PHONE.............................562 688-0592
Jose Luis Solorcano, *President*
EMP: 120
SALES (est): 24MM **Privately Held**
SIC: 5139 5661 5651 5137 Shoes; shoe
  stores; family clothing stores; coordinate
  sets: women's, children's & infants'

(P-8345)
BIRKENSTOCK USA LP (DH)
8171 Redwood Blvd, Novato (94945-1403)
PHONE.............................415 884-3200
Stephan Birkenstock, *Partner*
Bernd Hillen, *Partner*
Annie Lawler, *Mktg Coord*
Nancy E Moock, *Manager*

▲ **EMP:** 62
SQ FT: 15,000
SALES (est): 30.6MM
SALES (corp-wide): 570.2MM **Privately Held**
WEB: www.birkenstockusa.com
SIC: 5139 Footwear

(P-8346)
BUFFALO DISTRIBUTION
Also Called: Keen Account
1624 Pacific St, Union City (94587-2028)
PHONE.............................510 475-9810
Lee Perry, *President*
▲ **EMP:** 50
SALES (est): 6MM **Privately Held**
WEB: www.buffalodistribution.com
SIC: 5139 Footwear

(P-8347)
CELS ENTERPRISES INC (PA)
Also Called: Chinese Laundry Shoes
3485 S La Cienega Blvd A, Los Angeles
(90016-4497)
PHONE.............................310 838-0280
Robert Goldman, *CEO*
Derek Bordeaux, *Vice Pres*
Monte Duncan, *Vice Pres*
Miryan Nogueira, *Vice Pres*
Ellen Schiff, *Vice Pres*
◆ **EMP:** 62
SQ FT: 72,000
SALES (est): 44MM **Privately Held**
WEB: www.chineselaundry.com
SIC: 5139 Shoes

(P-8348)
CHAMBERS BELT COMPANY
5840 El Camino Real Ste 1, Carlsbad
(92008-8851)
PHONE.............................760 602-9688
Scott Sporrer, *CEO*
EMP: 99
SALES: 950K **Privately Held**
SIC: 5139 Footwear

(P-8349)
CHINESE LAUNDRY INC
Also Called: Chinese Laundry Shoes
3485 S La Cienega Blvd, Los Angeles
(90016-4497)
PHONE.............................310 945-3299
Robert Goldman, *President*
Christine Sung, *Vice Pres*
Kyler Jafari, *Buyer*
Jim Barnier, *Sales Staff*
Carlos Chayeb, *Librarian*
EMP: 50 **EST:** 1985
SQ FT: 72,000
SALES (est): 20MM **Privately Held**
SIC: 5139 Shoes

(P-8350)
CONVERSE INC
838 Market St, San Francisco
(94102-3001)
PHONE.............................415 433-1174
Adrian Newman, *President*
EMP: 95
SALES (corp-wide): 36.4B **Publicly Held**
SIC: 5139 Footwear
HQ: Converse Inc.
  1 Lovejoy Wharf
  Boston MA 02114
  978 983-3300

(P-8351)
CONVERSE INC
2150 E Montclair Plaza Ln, Montclair
(91763-1535)
PHONE.............................909 625-6655
EMP: 90
SALES (corp-wide): 36.4B **Publicly Held**
SIC: 5139 Footwear, athletic
HQ: Converse Inc.
  1 Lovejoy Wharf
  Boston MA 02114
  978 983-3300

(P-8352)
CONVERSE INC
1437-39 3rd St Promenade, Santa Monica
(90401)
PHONE.............................310 451-0314
EMP: 89

360   2019 Directory of California
Wholesalers and Services Companies   ▲ = Import ▼=Export
◆ =Import/Export

SALES (corp-wide): 36.4B **Publicly Held**
SIC: 5139 5661 Footwear, athletic;
footwear, athletic
HQ: Converse Inc.
1 Lovejoy Wharf
Boston MA 02114
978 983-3300

(P-8353)
CONVERSE INC
Also Called: Distrirution Center
4450 E Lowell St, Ontario (91761-2220)
PHONE..............................909 974-5695
Samone Carrollin, *Manager*
Enzo Caminotti, *Manager*
EMP: 90
SALES (corp-wide): 36.4B **Publicly Held**
SIC: 5139 Footwear
HQ: Converse Inc.
1 Lovejoy Wharf
Boston MA 02114
978 983-3300

(P-8354)
E M S TRADING INC
Also Called: Michael-Antonio Studio
5161 Richton St, Montclair (91763-1310)
PHONE..............................909 581-7800
Michael C Su, *CEO*
Ruby Su, *CFO*
Roy Nakabayashi, *Exec VP*
Alice Su, *Vice Pres*
Jack Su, *Admin Sec*
◆ **EMP:** 50
SQ FT: 150,000
SALES (est): 14MM **Privately Held**
SIC: 5139 Shoes

(P-8355)
EAST LION CORPORATION
Also Called: Qupid Shoe
318 Brea Canyon Rd, Walnut
(91789-3093)
PHONE..............................626 912-1818
Ben Yi Kuo, *CEO*
Julie Kuo, *Vice Pres*
Connie Kuo, *Creative Dir*
Hanson Zhao, *Info Tech Mgr*
Julia Cho, *CPA*
◆ **EMP:** 50
SQ FT: 62,000
SALES (est): 26.3MM **Privately Held**
WEB: www.eastlioncorp.com
SIC: 5139 Shoes

(P-8356)
FOREVER LINK INTERNATIONAL INC
455 Brea Canyon Rd, Walnut
(91789-3058)
PHONE..............................877 839-9899
Charles Hailongcui, *CEO*
Nicole Chen, *Purchasing*
Jason Lee, *Sales Associate*
Ivy Yang, *Manager*
◆ **EMP:** 50
SALES (est): 6.8MM **Privately Held**
SIC: 5139 Shoes

(P-8357)
FORTUNE DYNAMIC INC
21923 Ferrero, City of Industry
(91789-5210)
PHONE..............................909 979-8318
Carol Lee, *President*
James Lee, *Vice Pres*
◆ **EMP:** 90
SQ FT: 150,000
SALES (est): 46.9MM **Privately Held**
WEB: www.fortunedynamic.com
SIC: 5139 Shoes

(P-8358)
HI-TEC SPORTS USA INC (DH)
Also Called: Magnum USA
5990 Sepulvda Blvd # 600, Van Nuys
(91411-2523)
PHONE..............................209 545-1111
Simon Bonham, *CEO*
Ed Van Wezel, *CEO*
William Berta, *CEO*
Frank Van Wezel, *Chairman*
Brad Gebhard, *Principal*
▲ **EMP:** 57 **EST:** 1978
SQ FT: 120,000

SALES (est): 30.3MM
SALES (corp-wide): 29.3MM **Publicly Held**
WEB: www.magnumboots.com
SIC: 5139 Footwear, athletic; boots
HQ: Hi-Tec Sports Public Limited Company
Aviation Way
Southend-On-Sea SS2 6
170 254-1741

(P-8359)
J P ORIGINAL CORP (PA)
Also Called: Doll House Footwear
19101 E Walnut Dr N, City of Industry
(91748-1429)
PHONE..............................626 839-4300
C H Hsueh, *Ch of Bd*
Si-Tuo Hsu, *President*
Christen Ho, *Human Resources*
Nina Hsu, *Purch Mgr*
◆ **EMP:** 60
SQ FT: 67,000
SALES (est): 27.6MM **Privately Held**
WEB: www.jpo.com
SIC: 5139 Shoes

(P-8360)
KOMMONWEALTH INC
Also Called: Creative Recreation
6420 Wilshire Blvd, Los Angeles
(90048-5502)
PHONE..............................310 278-7328
Robert Nand, *CEO*
▲ **EMP:** 50
SALES (est): 12.9MM **Privately Held**
SIC: 5139 Shoes

(P-8361)
L & L LOGIC AND LOGISTICS LP
6 Hamilton Landing # 250, Novato
(94949-8264)
PHONE..............................707 795-2475
▲ **EMP:** 50
SALES (est): 3.9MM **Privately Held**
WEB: www.ll-logistics.com
SIC: 5139

(P-8362)
MILLENNIAL BRANDS LLC (PA)
Also Called: Rocket Dog Brands
2000 Crow Canyon Pl # 300, San Ramon
(94583-4633)
PHONE..............................866 938-4806
Scott Briskie, *Mng Member*
Carly Marie, *Vice Pres*
Yoni Feliciano, *Office Mgr*
Sue Tillotson, *Sales Staff*
John Peorink,
▲ **EMP:** 90
SQ FT: 20,000
SALES (est): 30.8MM **Privately Held**
SIC: 5139 Footwear

(P-8363)
NIKEWOMAN
447 Great Mall Dr, Milpitas (95035-8041)
PHONE..............................408 942-6457
Jason Cablag, *Manager*
EMP: 50
SALES (est): 1.9MM **Privately Held**
SIC: 5139 Shoes

(P-8364)
OSATA ENTERPRISES INC
Also Called: Globe Shoes
225 S Aviation Blvd, El Segundo
(90245-4604)
PHONE..............................310 297-1550
Matthew Hill, *Principal*
Gary Valentine, *Principal*
▲ **EMP:** 100
SQ FT: 30,000
SALES (est): 32.3MM **Privately Held**
WEB: www.globeshoes.com
SIC: 5139 Shoes

(P-8365)
PRIMA ROYALE ENTERPRISES LTD
Also Called: Prima Royale
150 S Los Robles Ave # 100, Pasadena
(91101-2456)
PHONE..............................626 960-8388
Ing Nan Yu, *CEO*
Harry K T Chow, *President*
Judy Chow, *COO*

Bobby Bruce Levy, *Vice Pres*
Peter Hayden, *Program Mgr*
▲ **EMP:** 55
SQ FT: 55,000
SALES (est): 9MM **Privately Held**
WEB: www.primaroyale.com
SIC: 5139 3143 Shoes; men's footwear, except athletic

(P-8366)
RAINBOW SANDALS INC
900 Calle Negocio, San Clemente
(92673-6201)
PHONE..............................949 276-4431
Jay Longley Jr, *President*
Tony Bordeaux, *Technology*
Amy S Phr, *Human Res Mgr*
Pat Huber, *Mktg Dir*
Chad Fahring,
▲ **EMP:** 50
SQ FT: 5,000
SALES (est): 14.4MM **Privately Held**
WEB: www.rainbowsandals.com
SIC: 5139 Shoes

(P-8367)
REALLY LIKEABLE PEOPLE INC
2251 Las Palmas Dr, Carlsbad
(92011-1527)
P.O. Box 131750 (92013-1750)
PHONE..............................760 431-5577
Jon W Humphrey, *President*
Diana Crawford, *CFO*
EMP: 50
SQ FT: 15,000
SALES (est): 8.6MM **Privately Held**
SIC: 5139 Footwear

(P-8368)
SOUTH CONE INC
Also Called: Reef
5935 Darwin Ct, Carlsbad (92008-7302)
PHONE..............................760 431-2300
Roger Spatz, *CEO*
◆ **EMP:** 120
SQ FT: 37,583
SALES (est): 34.4MM
SALES (corp-wide): 17.9MM **Privately Held**
WEB: www.vfc.com
SIC: 5139 3144 3143 Women's footwear, except athletic; men's footwear, except athletic; shoes
PA: The Rockport Company Llc
1220 Washington St
Boston MA 02118
617 619-5400

5141 Groceries, General Line Wholesale

(P-8369)
ABACUS BUSINESS CAPITAL INC ✪
Also Called: Island Pacific Supermarket
738 Epperson Dr, City of Industry
(91748-1336)
PHONE..............................909 594-8080
Chengbiao Xue, *CEO*
Mina Hong, *General Mgr*
EMP: 50 **EST:** 2018
SALES (est): 1.2MM **Privately Held**
SIC: 5141 Groceries, general line

(P-8370)
ACOSTA INC
Also Called: Acosta Sales & Marketing
915 W Imperial Hwy # 200, Brea
(92821-3851)
PHONE..............................714 988-1500
Rick Nist, *Branch Mgr*
Jon Fagan, *Business Mgr*
Davis La Verne, *Business Mgr*
Dan Pinsky, *Sales Associate*
Kathy Wallis, *Manager*
EMP: 150
SALES (corp-wide): 7B **Privately Held**
WEB: www.acosta.com
SIC: 5141 Food brokers
PA: Acosta Inc.
6600 Corporate Ctr Pkwy
Jacksonville FL 32216
904 332-7986

(P-8371)
ACOSTA INC
Acosta Sales & Marketing
5735 W Las Positas Blvd # 300, Pleasanton
(94588-4002)
P.O. Box 9039 (94566-9039)
PHONE..............................925 600-3500
Tony Mello, *Director*
Ashley Bringham, *Business Mgr*
Rick Mallmans, *Business Mgr*
Mae Estrada, *Receptionist*
EMP: 85
SQ FT: 10,000
SALES (corp-wide): 7B **Privately Held**
WEB: www.acosta.com
SIC: 5141 Food brokers
PA: Acosta Inc.
6600 Corporate Ctr Pkwy
Jacksonville FL 32216
904 332-7986

(P-8372)
ADVANTAGE SALES & MARKETING
5064 Franklin Dr, Pleasanton (94588-3354)
P.O. Box 9135 (94566-9135)
PHONE..............................925 463-5600
Clyde Le Baron, *President*
Steve Derking, *Exec VP*
Cynthia McCann, *Admin Sec*
EMP: 250
SQ FT: 27,000
SALES (est): 24.5MM **Privately Held**
SIC: 5141 5142 5122 Food brokers; packaged frozen goods; druggists' sundries

(P-8373)
ADVANTAGE SALES & MKTG INC
200 N Pacific Coast Hwy # 1000, El Segundo (90245-5606)
PHONE..............................310 321-6869
S D Dorfman, *Branch Mgr*
EMP: 123
SALES (corp-wide): 8.4B **Privately Held**
SIC: 5141 Food brokers
PA: Advantage Sales & Marketing Inc.
18100 Von Karman Ave # 900
Irvine CA 92612
949 797-2900

(P-8374)
ADVANTAGE SALES & MKTG INC (PA)
Also Called: Advantage Solutions
18100 Von Karman Ave # 900, Irvine
(92612-7195)
PHONE..............................949 797-2900
Sonny King, *Chairman*
Chris Cuello, *President*
Dave Thurman, *President*
Tanya Domier, *CEO*
Brian Stevens, *COO*
▲ **EMP:** 250
SQ FT: 48,000
SALES (est): 8.4B **Privately Held**
WEB: www.asmnet.com
SIC: 5141 Food brokers

(P-8375)
ADVANTAGE SALES & MKTG LLC
6700 Koll Center Pkwy # 300, Pleasanton
(94566-7060)
PHONE..............................925 463-5600
Barry Johnson, *President*
EMP: 72
SALES (corp-wide): 8.4B **Privately Held**
SIC: 5141 5142 Food brokers; packaged frozen goods
HQ: Advantage Sales & Marketing Llc
18100 Von Karman Ave # 900
Irvine CA 92612
949 797-2900

(P-8376)
ADVANTAGE WAYPOINT LLC
2642 Michelle Dr, Tustin (92780-7019)
PHONE..............................717 424-4973
Angelica Harris, *Admin Mgr*
Martin Evans, *President*
Kim Hoffman, *Administration*
Sandy McClelland,
Valerie Cole, *Accounts Exec*

EMP: 81
SALES (corp-wide): 200MM **Privately Held**
SIC: 5141 Food brokers
PA: Advantage Waypoint Llc
13521 Prestige Pl
Tampa FL 33635
813 358-5900

(P-8377)
ADVANTAGE-CROWN SLS & MKTG LLC (DH)
1400 S Douglass Rd # 200, Anaheim (92806-6904)
P.O. Box 66010 (92816-6010)
PHONE..................714 780-3000
Sonny King, *CEO*
Bob Vesley, *CFO*
Pat Reilly, *Vice Pres*
Evan Carter, *Department Mgr*
Aj Stukenborg, *General Mgr*
▲ EMP: 1100
SALES (est): 379.3MM
SALES (corp-wide): 8.4B **Privately Held**
SIC: 5141 Food brokers
HQ: Advantage Sales & Marketing Llc
18100 Von Karman Ave # 900
Irvine CA 92612
949 797-2900

(P-8378)
AFC DISTRIBUTION CORP
19205 S Laurel Park Rd, Rancho Dominguez (90220-6032)
PHONE..................310 604-3630
Ryuji Ishii, *President*
Jeffery Seiler, *Vice Pres*
EMP: 50 EST: 2016
SALES (est): 1.5MM
SALES (corp-wide): 34MM **Privately Held**
SIC: 5141 Groceries, general line
PA: Advanced Fresh Concepts Corp.
19205 S Laurel Park Rd
Rancho Dominguez CA 90220
310 604-3630

(P-8379)
AMERICAN ACE INTERNATIONAL CO
Also Called: American Ace Intl Trdg Co
313 Newquist Pl Ste A, City of Industry (91745-1091)
PHONE..................626 937-6116
Jimmy S T Young, *Vice Pres*
Walter Kang Young, *President*
EMP: 55
SALES (est): 7.9MM **Privately Held**
SIC: 5141 5012 5064 Groceries, general line; automobiles; television sets; video cassette recorders & accessories

(P-8380)
AMK FOODSERVICES INC
Also Called: Kaney Foods
830 Capitolio Way, San Luis Obispo (93401-7122)
P.O. Box 1188 (93406-1188)
PHONE..................805 544-7600
John P Kaney, *CEO*
EMP: 130
SQ FT: 35,000
SALES (est): 37.3MM **Privately Held**
SIC: 5141 Food brokers

(P-8381)
ANSAR GALLERY
2505 El Camino Rd, Tustin (92782)
PHONE..................949 220-0000
Ali Akbar Feroozesh, *Principal*
Hussein Saadat, *President*
Andrew Sadat, *General Mgr*
▲ EMP: 200 EST: 2013
SQ FT: 120,000
SALES (est): 72.5MM **Privately Held**
SIC: 5141 Food brokers
PA: Ansar Mall
P.O. Box 38880
Sharjah
653 133-39

(P-8382)
ARKO FOODS INTERNATIONAL INC (PA)
Also Called: Asian Commodities Company
3410 N San Fernando Rd # 1, Los Angeles (90065-1442)
PHONE..................323 257-1888
Paul Chua, *President*
Angelina Serrano, *Shareholder*
Susie Fung, *CFO*
William Chua, *Vice Pres*
Gene Chua, *Director*
◆ EMP: 75
SALES (est): 25.8MM **Privately Held**
SIC: 5141 5411 Food brokers; grocery stores

(P-8383)
BAY BROKERAGE INC
17 Woodleaf Ave, Redwood City (94061-1823)
PHONE..................650 413-1721
Richard Hoadley, *President*
Kevin Pope, *CFO*
Robert Crane, *Vice Pres*
Michael Fouch, *Vice Pres*
EMP: 50 EST: 1978
SQ FT: 8,000
SALES (est): 11MM **Privately Held**
WEB: www.baybrokerage.com
SIC: 5141 Food brokers

(P-8384)
BERNARD PERRIN SUPOWITZ INC
Also Called: Fergadis Enterprises
5496 Lindbergh Ln, Bell (90201-6409)
PHONE..................323 981-2800
Steve Supowitz, *President*
Heide Palikan, *Executive Asst*
Steven Silver, *Business Mgr*
Wanah Velo, *Controller*
Evelyn Zhao, *HR Admin*
EMP: 50
SQ FT: 175,000
SALES (est): 97.2MM **Privately Held**
WEB: www.fergadis.com
SIC: 5141 Groceries, general line

(P-8385)
BI-RITE RESTAURANT SUP CO INC
Also Called: Bi-Rite Foodservice Distrs
123 S Hill Dr, Brisbane (94005-1203)
PHONE..................415 656-0187
William Barulich, *CEO*
Steve Barulich, *President*
Zachary Barulich, *CFO*
Zack Barulich, *CFO*
Tom Whiteside, *Exec VP*
◆ EMP: 300
SQ FT: 220,000
SALES: 314.7MM **Privately Held**
WEB: www.biritefoodservice.com
SIC: 5141 5147 5148 5023 Groceries, general line; meats & meat products; fresh fruits & vegetables; kitchenware; linens, table; towels; commercial equipment; direct selling establishments

(P-8386)
C&S WHOLESALE GROCERS INC
2797 S Orange Ave, Fresno (93725-1919)
P.O. Box 11097 (93771-1097)
PHONE..................559 442-4700
Randy Wood, *Branch Mgr*
Tom Riley, *COO*
Venkata Sreepada, *Executive*
EMP: 475
SALES (corp-wide): 28.2B **Privately Held**
SIC: 5141 Groceries, general line
PA: C&S Wholesale Grocers, Inc.
7 Corporate Dr
Keene NH 03431
603 354-7000

(P-8387)
CANTON FOOD CO INC
750 S Alameda St, Los Angeles (90021-1624)
PHONE..................213 688-7707
Shiu Lit Kwan, *CEO*
Cho W Kwan, *President*
Shui Lit Kwan, *CEO*
Cho Kwan, *Vice Pres*
Wai Kam Kwan, *Vice Pres*
▲ EMP: 106
SQ FT: 96,000
SALES (est): 90.2MM **Privately Held**
WEB: www.cantonfoodco.com
SIC: 5141 5146 5411 5421 Food brokers; seafoods; grocery stores; seafood markets; groceries & related products; refrigerated warehousing & storage

(P-8388)
CERENZIA FOODS INC
8585 White Oak Ave, Rancho Cucamonga (91730-5146)
P.O. Box 3719 (91729-3719)
PHONE..................909 989-4000
Joseph F Annunziato, *CEO*
Chris Annunziato, *Technology*
Laura Deyoung, *Controller*
Erik Zamora, *Buyer*
Armando Curiel, *Sales Staff*
▲ EMP: 60
SQ FT: 75,000
SALES (est): 70.3MM **Privately Held**
WEB: www.cerenziafoods.com
SIC: 5141 Food brokers

(P-8389)
CHEFS WAREHOUSE WESTCOAST LLC (HQ)
16633 Gale Ave, City of Industry (91745-1802)
PHONE..................626 465-4200
Chris Pappas, *President*
Tom Burghardt, *Finance*
Ken Clark, *Mng Member*
John Pappas, *Mng Member*
▲ EMP: 59
SALES (est): 44.1MM **Publicly Held**
WEB: www.chefswarehouse.com
SIC: 5141 Food brokers

(P-8390)
COASTAL PACIFIC FD DISTRS INC (PA)
1015 Performance Dr, Stockton (95206-4925)
P.O. Box 30910 (95213-0910)
PHONE..................909 947-2066
Terrence Wood, *CEO*
Jeff King, *COO*
Matthew Payne, *CFO*
John Payne, *Treasurer*
Edmond Jared, *Vice Pres*
▼ EMP: 220
SQ FT: 500,000
SALES: 1.2B **Privately Held**
WEB: www.cpfd.com
SIC: 5141 4225 7519 4222 Groceries, general line; general warehousing & storage; trailer rental; refrigerated warehousing & storage

(P-8391)
COASTAL PACIFIC FD DISTRS INC
Also Called: Coastal Pacific Foods
1520 E Mission Blvd Ste B, Ontario (91761-2124)
PHONE..................909 947-2066
David Jared, *President*
EMP: 150
SALES (corp-wide): 1.2B **Privately Held**
WEB: www.cpfd.com
SIC: 5141 Groceries, general line
PA: Coastal Pacific Food Distributors, Inc.
1015 Performance Dr
Stockton CA 95206
909 947-2066

(P-8392)
CONCORD FOODS INC (PA)
4601 E Guasti Rd, Ontario (91761-8105)
PHONE..................909 975-2000
Nick J Sciortino Jr, *President*
Roy Sciortino, *CFO*
John Sciortino, *Vice Pres*
Christy Santiago, *Credit Mgr*
John Bernieri, *Purch Mgr*
EMP: 72
SQ FT: 67,000
SALES (est): 90.5MM **Privately Held**
WEB: www.concordfoodsinc.com
SIC: 5141 Food brokers

(P-8393)
CORE-MARK CORONA 2
1550 Magnolia Ave, Corona (92879-2094)
PHONE..................800 622-1206
Thomas Perkins, *President*
Christopher Miller, *CFO*
EMP: 50
SQ FT: 60,000
SALES (est): 1.2MM **Privately Held**
SIC: 5141 Groceries, general line

(P-8394)
CORE-MARK HOLDING COMPANY INC (PA)
395 Oyster Point Blvd # 415, South San Francisco (94080-1932)
P.O. Box 64945, Saint Paul MN (55164-0945)
PHONE..................650 589-9445
Thomas B Perkins, *CEO*
Randolph I Thornton, *Ch of Bd*
Scott McPherson, *President*
Eric J Rolheiser, *President*
Christopher M Miller, *CFO*
EMP: 55
SQ FT: 31,800
SALES: 15.6B **Publicly Held**
WEB: www.coremark.com
SIC: 5141 5194 5145 5122 Food brokers; tobacco & tobacco products; cigarettes; confectionery; druggists' sundries; general merchandise, non-durable; groceries & related products

(P-8395)
CORE-MARK INTERNATIONAL INC (HQ)
395 Oyster Point Blvd # 415, South San Francisco (94080-1955)
PHONE..................650 589-9445
Thomas Perkins, *CEO*
Eric Rolheiser, *President*
Stacy Loretz, *CFO*
Scott McPherson, *Senior VP*
Gerald J Bolduc, *Vice Pres*
EMP: 100
SQ FT: 26,000
SALES (est): 4.2B
SALES (corp-wide): 15.6B **Publicly Held**
WEB: www.core-mark.com
SIC: 5141 5194 Groceries, general line; cigarettes
PA: Core-Mark Holding Company, Inc.
395 Oyster Point Blvd # 415
South San Francisco CA 94080
650 589-9445

(P-8396)
CORE-MARK SACRAMENTO 2
2959 Thomas Pl Ste 150, West Sacramento (95691-5751)
PHONE..................866 791-4210
Thomas Perkins, *President*
Christopher Miller, *CFO*
EMP: 50
SQ FT: 79,000
SALES (est): 1.3MM **Privately Held**
SIC: 5141 Groceries, general line

(P-8397)
CROSSMARK INC
2401 E Katella Ave # 625, Anaheim (92806-5939)
PHONE..................714 464-6318
Cambria Fetherston, *Cust Mgr*
EMP: 57 **Privately Held**
SIC: 5141 Groceries, general line
PA: Crossmark, Inc.
5100 Legacy Dr
Plano TX 75024

(P-8398)
CROSSMARK INC
Also Called: Crossmark Sales & Marketing
3875 Hopyard Rd Ste 250, Pleasanton (94588-2784)
PHONE..................925 463-3555
Jeff Nanna, *Director*
EMP: 300 **Privately Held**
WEB: www.crossmark.com
SIC: 5141 Food brokers

PA: Crossmark, Inc.
5100 Legacy Dr
Plano TX 75024
-

(P-8399)
D&A ENTERPRISES INC
34943 Newark Blvd, Newark (94560-1215)
PHONE..........................510 445-1600
Afit Vyas, *President*
EMP: 300
SALES (est): 29.6MM **Privately Held**
SIC: 5141 Food brokers

(P-8400)
DEL MONACO SPECIALTY FOODS INC
18675 Madrone Pkwy # 150, Morgan Hill (95037-2868)
PHONE..........................408 500-4100
Ernestine Del Monaco, *Ch of Bd*
Vic Del Monaco, *CEO*
Tony Del Monaco, *Vice Pres*
Stephanie Del Monaco, *Research*
EMP: 88
SQ FT: 18,000
SALES (est): 28.3MM
SALES (corp-wide): 105MM **Privately Held**
WEB: www.delmonacofoods.com
SIC: 5141 Food brokers
PA: Kettle Cuisine, Llc
330 Lynnway
Lynn MA 01901
617 409-1100

(P-8401)
DOT FOODS INC
2200 Nickerson Dr, Modesto (95358-9489)
PHONE..........................209 581-9090
Fax: 209 581-9082
EMP: 134
SALES (corp-wide): 5.4B **Privately Held**
SIC: 5141
PA: Dot Foods, Inc.
1 Dot Way
Mount Sterling IL 62353
217 773-4411

(P-8402)
DPI SPECIALTY FOODS WEST INC (DH)
601 S Rockefeller Ave, Ontario (91761-7871)
PHONE..........................909 975-1019
John Jordan, *CEO*
James De Keyser, *President*
Donna Robbins, *President*
Francis Haren, *COO*
Conor Crowley, *CFO*
◆ EMP: 101
SQ FT: 250,000
SALES (est): 490MM
SALES (corp-wide): 1B **Privately Held**
WEB: www.dpi-west.com
SIC: 5141 Food brokers
HQ: Dpi Specialty Foods, Inc.
601 S Rockefeller Ave
Ontario CA 91761
909 390-0892

(P-8403)
E G AYERS DISTRIBUTING INC
5819 S Broadway St, Eureka (95503-6906)
PHONE..........................707 445-2077
Paul A Ayers, *CEO*
Phillip Ayers, *Treasurer*
Pat Gillmore, *Transptn Dir*
EMP: 50
SQ FT: 15,000
SALES (est): 22.4MM **Privately Held**
WEB: www.ayersdistributing.com
SIC: 5141 5149 Food brokers; beverages, except coffee & tea

(P-8404)
EXANDAL CORPORATION
Also Called: Colorexa
17620 Sherman Way Ste 207, Van Nuys (91406-3527)
PHONE..........................818 705-9497
Carlos Alvaro, *President*
Andrea Alvaro, *Director*
▲ EMP: 150

SALES (est): 27.7MM **Privately Held**
WEB: www.exandal.com
SIC: 5141 Food brokers
PA: Exandal S.A.
Av. Los Alamos Mz. I Lt. 8
Lima LM 22
-

(P-8405)
FOOD SALES WEST INC (PA)
235 Baker St, Costa Mesa (92626-4521)
P.O. Box 19738, Irvine (92623-9738)
PHONE..........................714 966-2900
David Lyons, *CEO*
Carl Scharffenberger, *President*
Mary Ellen Scharffenberger, *Corp Secy*
Michael Berkson, *Vice Pres*
Robert Watkins, *Vice Pres*
EMP: 85
SQ FT: 12,000
SALES (est): 16.1MM **Privately Held**
WEB: www.foodsaleswest.com
SIC: 5141 Food brokers

(P-8406)
FOOTHILL PACKING INC
2255 S Broadway, Santa Maria (93454-7871)
PHONE..........................805 925-7900
Jorge Rivera, *President*
EMP: 489
SALES (corp-wide): 43.7MM **Privately Held**
SIC: 5141 Groceries, general line
PA: Foothill Packing, Inc.
1582 Moffett St
Salinas CA 93905
831 784-1453

(P-8407)
FORTUNE AVENUE FOODS INC
2117 Pointe Ave, Ontario (91761-8529)
PHONE..........................909 930-5989
Daniel C Yang, *CEO*
Fula Yang, *Vice Pres*
Harrison Chu, *Marketing Staff*
▲ EMP: 55
SQ FT: 27,000
SALES (est): 23.2MM **Privately Held**
WEB: www.fortuneavenuefoods.com
SIC: 5141 Food brokers

(P-8408)
GOODMAN FOOD PRODUCTS INC (PA)
Also Called: Don Lee Farms
200 E Beach Ave Fl 1, Inglewood (90302-3404)
PHONE..........................310 674-3180
Donald Goodman, *CEO*
Jean Harris, *Senior VP*
Suzanne Bootross, *Technology*
Marcos Lopez, *Accountant*
Jameela Sanchez, *Purch Mgr*
▲ EMP: 250 EST: 1982
SQ FT: 55,000
SALES (est): 185.2MM **Privately Held**
WEB: www.donleefarms.com
SIC: 5141 Groceries, general line

(P-8409)
GOURMET FOODS
Also Called: H.U.G. Company
2557 Barrington Ct, Hayward (94545-1174)
PHONE..........................510 887-0340
Uwe Henze, *President*
EMP: 90
SALES (est): 27.5MM
SALES (corp-wide): 100.3MM **Privately Held**
SIC: 5141 Food brokers
PA: Gourmet Foods, Inc.
2910 E Harcourt St
Compton CA 90221
310 632-3300

(P-8410)
GOURMET FOODS INC (PA)
2910 E Harcourt St, Compton (90221-5502)
PHONE..........................310 632-3300
Heinz Naef, *President*
Gary David, *CFO*
Ursina Naef, *Corp Secy*
Chris Johnson, *Branch Mgr*
Karen McCullough, *CIO*

◆ EMP: 83
SQ FT: 35,000
SALES (est): 100.3MM **Privately Held**
WEB: www.gourmetfoodsinc.com
SIC: 5141 5812 2099 Food brokers; eating places; food preparations

(P-8411)
GRAND SUPERCENTER INC
8550 Chetle Ave Ste B, Whittier (90606-2662)
PHONE..........................562 318-3451
Ilyeon Kwon, *CEO*
EMP: 70
SALES (corp-wide): 15.8MM **Privately Held**
SIC: 5141 5499 Groceries, general line; juices, fruit or vegetable
HQ: Grand Supercenter Inc.
300 Chubb Ave
Lyndhurst NJ 07071
201 507-9900

(P-8412)
GROCERS SPECIALTY COMPANY (DH)
Also Called: G S C Ball
5200 Sheila St, Commerce (90040-3906)
P.O. Box 513396, Los Angeles (90051-1396)
PHONE..........................323 264-5200
Joe Falvey, *President*
Rich Martin, *CFO*
Christine Neal, *Treasurer*
Bob Ling, *Admin Sec*
▲ EMP: 50 EST: 1981
SQ FT: 106,000
SALES (est): 124.9MM **Publicly Held**
SIC: 5141 Groceries, general line
HQ: Unified Grocers, Inc.
5200 Sheila St
Commerce CA 90040
323 264-5200

(P-8413)
HOMEGROWN NATURAL FOODS INC
Also Called: Consorzio
1610 5th St, Berkeley (94710-1715)
PHONE..........................510 558-7500
John Foraker, *President*
Marc Van Valen, *Controller*
EMP: 75
SQ FT: 10,000
SALES (est): 16.8MM
SALES (corp-wide): 15.7B **Publicly Held**
SIC: 5141 5149 Groceries, general line; natural & organic foods
HQ: Annie's, Inc.
1610 5th St
Berkeley CA 94710
-

(P-8414)
HOUWELING NURSERIES OXNARD INC
Also Called: Houweling's Tomatoes
645 Laguna Rd, Camarillo (93012-8523)
PHONE..........................805 488-8832
Casey Houweling, *Chairman*
Kevin Doran, *President*
Chris Brocklesby, *CFO*
Christopher Brocklesby, *CFO*
Richard Vanderburg, *Project Mgr*
▲ EMP: 450
SALES (est): 221.8MM **Privately Held**
WEB: www.houwelings.com
SIC: 5141 Groceries, general line

(P-8415)
ICPK CORPORATION
Also Called: Hpp Food Services
1130 W C St, Wilmington (90744-5102)
PHONE..........................310 830-8020
EMP: 70
SALES (corp-wide): 4MM **Privately Held**
SIC: 5141 Groceries, general line
PA: Icpk Corporation
4380 Cerritos Ave
Los Alamitos CA 90720
714 321-7025

(P-8416)
IMPACT GROUP LLC
Also Called: Co-Sales
7133 Koll Center Pkwy, Pleasanton (94566-3300)
PHONE..........................925 327-7322
Kathy Jean McOmber, *Administration*
Sharon Clennell, *Office Mgr*
Jane Bordalo, *Business Mgr*
Julie Ivers, *Business Mgr*
EMP: 59
SALES (corp-wide): 27.9MM **Privately Held**
SIC: 5141 Food brokers
PA: Impact Group, Llc
950 W Bannock St Ste 850
Boise ID 83702
208 343-5800

(P-8417)
IMPOSSIBLE FOODS INC (PA)
400 Saginaw Dr, Redwood City (94063-4749)
PHONE..........................650 461-4385
Patrick Brown, *CEO*
Dan Wagner,
Marcella Butler,
Nick Halla, *Officer*
David J Lipman, *Security Dir*
▲ EMP: 60
SALES (est): 84.4MM **Privately Held**
SIC: 5141 Food brokers

(P-8418)
JETRO CASH AND CARRY ENTPS LLC
Also Called: Restaurant Depot
1275 Vine St, Sacramento (95811-0427)
PHONE..........................916 492-2305
MI Thao, *Controller*
EMP: 95 **Privately Held**
SIC: 5141 5046 Groceries, general line; restaurant equipment & supplies
HQ: Jetro Cash And Carry Enterprises, Llc
1524 132nd St
College Point NY 11356
718 939-6400

(P-8419)
LASSEN CANYON NURSERY INC (PA)
1300 Salmon Creek Rd, Redding (96003-9641)
P.O. Box 992400 (96099-2400)
PHONE..........................530 223-1075
Elizabeth Elwood Ponce, *CEO*
Kenneth Elwood Jr, *President*
Mel Fernandez, *Marketing Staff*
Curt Gaines, *Manager*
▼ EMP: 125
SQ FT: 3,000
SALES (est): 93.1MM **Privately Held**
WEB: www.lassencanyonnursery.com
SIC: 5141 5191 0171 Groceries, general line; hay; raspberry farm

(P-8420)
LAX-C INC
1100 N Main St, Los Angeles (90012-1832)
PHONE..........................323 343-9000
Suprata Bovornsivamon, *President*
▲ EMP: 50
SALES (est): 24.9MM **Privately Held**
WEB: www.lax-c.com
SIC: 5141 Groceries, general line

(P-8421)
LEE BROS FOODSERVICES INC (PA)
Also Called: Lee Industrial Catering
660 E Gish Rd, San Jose (95112-2707)
PHONE..........................408 275-0700
Chieu Van Le, *CEO*
Huong Le, *Vice Pres*
Jimmy Lee, *Vice Pres*
Diem Truong, *General Mgr*
Vivian Tran, *Purchasing*
◆ EMP: 150
SQ FT: 15,000
SALES (est): 93MM **Privately Held**
SIC: 5141 5142 Food brokers; packaged frozen goods

PRODUCTS & SVCS

(P-8422)
MARKET SMART INC
6900 Koll Center Pkwy # 406, Pleasanton
(94566-3148)
PHONE..........................925 846-6237
Bill Oconnel, *President*
EMP: 59
SALES (est): 3.5MM **Privately Held**
WEB: www.marketsmart.com
SIC: 5141 Groceries, general line

(P-8423)
MARQUEZ BROTHERS ENTPS INC
15480 Valley Blvd, City of Industry
(91746-3325)
PHONE..........................626 330-3310
Gustavo Marquez, *President*
Jaime Marquez, *Vice Pres*
Juan Marquez, *Vice Pres*
◆ EMP: 200
SQ FT: 200,000
SALES (est): 84.3MM **Privately Held**
SIC: 5141 Food brokers

(P-8424)
MARQUEZ BROTHERS INTL INC (PA)
Also Called: M B
5801 Rue Ferrari, San Jose (95138-1857)
PHONE..........................408 960-2700
Gustavo Marquez, *CEO*
Jaime Marquez, *Exec VP*
Yolanda Angulo, *Human Res Dir*
Maria Zamudio, *Clerk*
▲ EMP: 150
SQ FT: 160,000
SALES (est): 329.4MM **Privately Held**
WEB: www.elmexicano.net
SIC: 5141 Groceries, general line

(P-8425)
MARQUEZ BROTHERS INTL INC
Also Called: El Mexicano
1329 W Olympic Blvd, Montebello
(90640-5010)
PHONE..........................323 722-8103
Sal Alcaraz, *Manager*
EMP: 58
SALES (corp-wide): 329.4MM **Privately Held**
WEB: www.elmexicano.net
SIC: 5141 Food brokers
PA: Marquez Brothers International, Inc.
5801 Rue Ferrari
San Jose CA 95138
408 960-2700

(P-8426)
MARQUEZ BROTHERS INTL INC
Also Called: Cheese Plant
179 S 11th Ave, Hanford (93230-5056)
PHONE..........................559 584-8000
Jaun Marquez, *Vice Pres*
EMP: 152
SALES (corp-wide): 329.4MM **Privately Held**
WEB: www.elmexicano.net
SIC: 5141 2022 Groceries, general line; natural cheese
PA: Marquez Brothers International, Inc.
5801 Rue Ferrari
San Jose CA 95138
408 960-2700

(P-8427)
MARTIN-BROWER COMPANY LLC
4704 Fite Ct, Stockton (95215-8308)
P.O. Box 547, Sheridan OR (97378-0547)
PHONE..........................209 466-2980
Mark Peterson, *Principal*
EMP: 138 **Privately Held**
SIC: 5141 Food brokers
HQ: The Martin-Brower Company L L C
6250 N River Rd Ste 9000
Rosemont IL 60018
847 227-6500

(P-8428)
MCLANE COMPANY INC
800 E Pescadero Ave, Tracy (95304-9799)
PHONE..........................209 221-7500
Bruce Bravo, *Manager*
EMP: 217

SALES (corp-wide): 242.1B **Publicly Held**
SIC: 5141 Groceries, general line
HQ: Mclane Company, Inc.
4747 Mclane Pkwy
Temple TX 76504
254 771-7500

(P-8429)
MCLANE/PACIFIC INC
3876 E Childs Ave, Merced (95341-9520)
P.O. Box 2107 (95344-0107)
PHONE..........................209 725-2500
William G Rosier, *CEO*
Mike Youngblood, *President*
Kevin Koch, *Treasurer*
Jim Kent, *Exec VP*
Ramiro Bautista, *Manager*
▲ EMP: 498
SQ FT: 220,000
SALES (est): 158.9MM
SALES (corp-wide): 242.1B **Publicly Held**
WEB: www.mclaneco.com
SIC: 5141 Groceries, general line
HQ: Mclane Company, Inc.
4747 Mclane Pkwy
Temple TX 76504
254 771-7500

(P-8430)
MERCADO LATINO INC (PA)
245 Baldwin Park Blvd, City of Industry
(91746-1404)
P.O. Box 6168, El Monte (91734-6168)
PHONE..........................626 333-6862
Graciliano Rodriguez, *President*
George Rodriguez, *CFO*
Richard Rodriguez, *Senior VP*
Kirk Zehnder, *VP Bus Dvlpt*
Angelita Rodriguez, *Admin Sec*
▲ EMP: 100 EST: 1963
SQ FT: 105,000
SALES (est): 252.9MM **Privately Held**
WEB: www.mercadolatinoinc.com
SIC: 5141 5148 Food brokers; fresh fruits & vegetables

(P-8431)
MERCADO LATINO INC
33430 Western Ave, Union City
(94587-3202)
PHONE..........................510 475-5500
Robert Rodriguez, *Principal*
EMP: 50
SALES (corp-wide): 252.9MM **Privately Held**
WEB: www.mercadolatinoinc.com
SIC: 5141 Food brokers
PA: Mercado Latino, Inc.
245 Baldwin Park Blvd
City Of Industry CA 91746
626 333-6862

(P-8432)
MISHIMA FOODS USA INC (PA)
2340 Plaza Del Amo # 105, Torrance
(90501-3445)
PHONE..........................310 787-1533
Yutaka Mishima, *President*
Tsukasa Hatsukade, *Vice Pres*
Yuho Quintero, *Marketing Staff*
▲ EMP: 80
SALES (est): 12.2MM **Privately Held**
SIC: 5141 Food brokers

(P-8433)
NAFTA DISTRIBUTORS
5120 Santa Ana St, Ontario (91761-8632)
PHONE..........................909 605-7515
Samuel Madikians, *CEO*
▲ EMP: 50
SQ FT: 12,000
SALES (est): 32.8MM **Privately Held**
WEB: www.naftadist.com
SIC: 5141 Food brokers

(P-8434)
NASSER COMPANY INC (PA)
Also Called: Nasser Company of Arizona
22720 Savi Ranch Pkwy, Yorba Linda
(92887-4614)
PHONE..........................714 279-2100
Burhan Nasser, *President*
Bill Arink, *President*
Mary Beth Nasser, *Corp Secy*

Dean Sandello, *Vice Pres*
Becky Salazar, *VP Admin*
EMP: 60
SQ FT: 17,445
SALES (est): 133.7MM **Privately Held**
SIC: 5141 Food brokers

(P-8435)
NONGSHIM AMERICA INC (HQ)
12155 6th St, Rancho Cucamonga
(91730-6115)
PHONE..........................909 481-3698
Dong Y Shin, *CEO*
Kevin Chang, *CFO*
Chris Gepford, *Principal*
Hector Tejeda, *Branch Mgr*
Daniel Morales, *Admin Asst*
◆ EMP: 250
SALES (est): 232.1MM
SALES (corp-wide): 1.7B **Privately Held**
WEB: www.nongshim.us
SIC: 5141 2098 Groceries, general line; noodles (e.g. egg, plain & water), dry
PA: Nong-Shim Co., Ltd.
112 Yeouidaebang-Ro, Dongjak-Gu
Seoul 07057
822 820-7225

(P-8436)
NZG SPECIALTIES INC (PA)
Also Called: Gourmet Trading Company
2580 Santa Fe Ave, Redondo Beach
(90278-1116)
P.O. Box 88432, Los Angeles (90009-8432)
PHONE..........................310 216-7575
Peter Lineen, *President*
Trent Grose, *CFO*
Marisala Morlett, *Admin Sec*
Julia Richardson, *Manager*
◆ EMP: 57
SQ FT: 55,000
SALES (est): 145.8MM **Privately Held**
WEB: www.gourmettrading.net
SIC: 5141 Food brokers

(P-8437)
OAKHURST INDUSTRIES INC
Also Called: Freund Baking Co
3265 Investment Blvd, Hayward
(94545-3806)
PHONE..........................510 265-2400
Jim Freund, *Principal*
Rankin Wood, *Chief Engr*
EMP: 80
SQ FT: 67,896
SALES (corp-wide): 98.3MM **Privately Held**
WEB: www.oakhurstproperties.com
SIC: 5141 2051 Groceries, general line; bread, cake & related products
PA: Oakhurst Industries, Inc.
2050 S Tubeway Ave
Commerce CA 90040
323 724-3000

(P-8438)
OTASTY FOODS INC
160 S Hacienda Blvd, City of Industry
(91745-1101)
PHONE..........................626 330-1229
Ming Chao Huang, *President*
Ken Chen, *Vice Pres*
◆ EMP: 91
SQ FT: 58,000
SALES (est): 41.1MM **Privately Held**
WEB: www.otasty.com
SIC: 5141 Food brokers

(P-8439)
PALISADES RANCH INC
Also Called: Goldberg and Solovy Foods Inc
5925 Alcoa Ave, Vernon (90058-3920)
PHONE..........................323 581-6161
Paul Paget, *CEO*
Earl Goldberg, *President*
EMP: 285 EST: 1974
SQ FT: 70,000
SALES (est): 130MM
SALES (corp-wide): 58.7B **Publicly Held**
WEB: www.gsfoods.com
SIC: 5141 5149 5046 5169 Food brokers; groceries & related products; restaurant equipment & supplies; chemicals & allied products

PA: Sysco Corporation
1390 Enclave Pkwy
Houston TX 77077
281 584-1390

(P-8440)
PALO ALTO EGG AND FOOD SVC CO
Also Called: Palo Alto Food Company
6691 Clark Ave, Newark (94560-3925)
P.O. Box 327 (94560-0327)
PHONE..........................510 456-2420
Eric Jensen, *CEO*
Paul Jensen, *Vice Pres*
Evelyn Vidona, *Accounting Mgr*
Karen Billmaier, *Sales Staff*
Kelly Smith, *Sales Staff*
EMP: 50
SQ FT: 15,000
SALES (est): 20.8MM **Privately Held**
WEB: www.paloaltoegg.com
SIC: 5141 Food brokers

(P-8441)
PERFORMANCE FOOD GROUP INC
Also Called: Performance Roma Southern Cal
16639 Gale Ave, City of Industry
(91745-1802)
P.O. Box 5146, Denver CO (80217-5146)
PHONE..........................800 697-7662
Doug Freitas, *Branch Mgr*
Kenneth Diaz, *Marketing Staff*
EMP: 65
SALES (corp-wide): 17.6B **Publicly Held**
WEB: www.romafood.com
SIC: 5141 Food brokers
HQ: Performance Food Group, Inc.
12500 West Creek Pkwy
Richmond VA 23238
804 484-7700

(P-8442)
PERFORMANCE FOOD GROUP INC
Also Called: Performnce Foodservice-Led-yard
1047 17th Ave, Santa Cruz (95062-3033)
PHONE..........................831 462-4400
Steve Rebottaro, *Branch Mgr*
Richard Fontana, *Sr Corp Ofcr*
Alec Napolitano, *District Mgr*
Cody Walz, *General Mgr*
Debby Haskin, *Personnel Exec*
EMP: 101
SALES (corp-wide): 17.6B **Publicly Held**
SIC: 5141 5046 5087 Food brokers; restaurant equipment & supplies; janitors' supplies
HQ: Performance Food Group, Inc.
12500 West Creek Pkwy
Richmond VA 23238
804 484-7700

(P-8443)
PITTSBURG WHOLESALE GROC INC
1670 Overland Ct, West Sacramento
(95691-3490)
PHONE..........................916 372-7772
Farzam Hariri, *Manager*
EMP: 65
SALES (est): 7.6MM **Privately Held**
WEB: www.pitcofoods.com
SIC: 5141 Food brokers
PA: Pittsburg Wholesale Grocers, Inc.
567 Cinnabar St
San Jose CA 95110
-

(P-8444)
PITTSBURG WHOLESALE GROC INC (PA)
Also Called: Pitco Foods
567 Cinnabar St, San Jose (95110-2306)
PHONE..........................916 372-7772
Pericles Navab, *CEO*
David Luttway, *President*
Carl Carlson, *Marketing Staff*
Michael Perry, *Sales Staff*
▼ EMP: 190
SQ FT: 160,000

▲ = Import ▼=Export
◆ =Import/Export

SALES (est): 181.5MM **Privately Held**
WEB: www.pitcofoods.com
SIC: 5141 Food brokers

(P-8445)
PIVEG INC
10455 Sorrento Valley Rd # 101, San Diego
(92121-1621)
PHONE....................................858 436-3070
Roberto L Espinoza, *CEO*
Ruben Angulo, *Sales Staff*
▲ EMP: 220 EST: 2004
SALES: 57.3MM **Privately Held**
SIC: 5141 Food brokers

(P-8446)
RELIANCE INTERMODAL INC
1919 Martin Luther King, Stockton (95210)
P.O. Box 31238 (95213-1238)
PHONE....................................209 946-0200
Lakhbir S Deol, *CEO*
EMP: 65
SALES: 9.7MM **Privately Held**
SIC: 5141 Groceries, general line

(P-8447)
RESTAURANT DEPOT
17332 Gothard St, Huntington Beach
(92647-6203)
PHONE....................................714 378-3535
Stanley Fleishman, *President*
Richard Kirshner, *Vice Pres*
Samuel Rubanenko, *Vice Pres*
Kely Woodcock, *Manager*
EMP: 50
SQ FT: 42,000
SALES (est): 8.5MM **Privately Held**
SIC: 5141 Groceries, general line

(P-8448)
RIO VISTA VENTURES LLC (PA)
Also Called: Giumarra Companies
15651 Old Milky Way, Escondido
(92027-7104)
P.O. Box 861449, Los Angeles (90086-
1449)
PHONE....................................760 480-8502
Don Corsaro, *Chairman*
Timothy Riley, *President*
Bruce Dowhan, *Vice Pres*
▲ EMP: 50
SALES (est): 92.6MM **Privately Held**
SIC: 5141 Food brokers

(P-8449)
RIO VISTA VENTURES LLC
Also Called: Giumarra Company, The
3646 Avenue 416, Reedley (93654-9111)
PHONE....................................559 897-6730
Donald Corsaro, *President*
EMP: 50
SALES (corp-wide): 92.6MM **Privately
Held**
SIC: 5141 Food brokers
PA: Rio Vista Ventures Llc
15651 Old Milky Way
Escondido CA 92027
760 480-8502

(P-8450)
ROBERT KINSELLA INC
15375 Barranca Pkwy G107, Irvine
(92618-2217)
PHONE....................................949 453-9533
Robert Kinsella, *Owner*
EMP: 77
SALES (corp-wide): 14.3MM **Privately
Held**
WEB: www.premierbakers.com
SIC: 5141 Food brokers
PA: Robert Kinsella, Inc.
535 S Nolen Dr Ste 100
Southlake TX 76092
214 260-8670

(P-8451)
SALADINOS INC (PA)
3325 W Figarden Dr, Fresno (93711-3909)
P.O. Box 12266 (93777-2266)
PHONE....................................559 271-3700
Craig A Saladino, *CEO*
Owen Escola, *President*
Patrick Peters, *COO*
Don Saladino, *Chairman*
John Muro, *Vice Pres*
EMP: 113

SQ FT: 40,000
SALES (est): 326.6MM **Privately Held**
WEB: www.saladinos.com
SIC: 5141 2099 Food brokers; food prepa-
rations

(P-8452)
SHOEI FOODS USA INC
1900 Feather River Blvd, Olivehurst
(95961-9627)
PHONE....................................530 742-7866
Don Soetaert, *CEO*
Sumio Kawanabe, *President*
Tall Matsushima, *President*
Richard Alcantar, *Opers Mgr*
◆ EMP: 100
SQ FT: 68,000
SALES (est): 88.3MM
SALES (corp-wide): 929.1MM **Privately
Held**
SIC: 5141 Food brokers
PA: Shoei Foods Corporation
5-7, Akihabara
Taito-Ku TKY 110-0
332 531-211

(P-8453)
**SMART & FINAL STORES INC
(PA)**
600 Citadel Dr, Commerce (90040-1562)
PHONE....................................323 869-7500
David G Hirz, *President*
David B Kaplan, *Ch of Bd*
Richard N Phegley, *CFO*
Leland P Smith, *Senior VP*
Edward Wong, *Senior VP*
EMP: 447 EST: 2012
SQ FT: 81,000
SALES: 4.5B **Publicly Held**
SIC: 5141 Groceries, general line

(P-8454)
SMART & FINAL STORES INC
303 E Foothill Blvd, Azusa (91702-2516)
PHONE....................................626 334-5189
EMP: 4182
SALES (corp-wide): 4.5B **Publicly Held**
SIC: 5141 Groceries, general line
PA: Smart & Final Stores, Inc.
600 Citadel Dr
Commerce CA 90040
323 869-7500

(P-8455)
SMART & FINAL STORES LLC
4439 Genesee Ave, San Diego
(92117-3005)
PHONE....................................858 268-2400
Denis Clyde, *Manager*
EMP: 70
SALES (corp-wide): 4.5B **Publicly Held**
SIC: 5141 Groceries, general line
HQ: Smart & Final Stores Llc
600 Citadel Dr
Commerce CA 90040
323 869-7500

(P-8456)
SMART & FINAL STORES LLC
1260 Garnet Ave, San Diego (92109-2912)
PHONE....................................858 270-8200
David Schrock, *Manager*
EMP: 80
SALES (corp-wide): 4.5B **Publicly Held**
SIC: 5141 Groceries, general line
HQ: Smart & Final Stores Llc
600 Citadel Dr
Commerce CA 90040
323 869-7500

(P-8457)
SMART & FINAL STORES LLC
3315 Rosecrans St Ste B, San Diego
(92110-4224)
PHONE....................................619 523-3640
Kevin King, *Director*
EMP: 70
SALES (corp-wide): 4.5B **Publicly Held**
SIC: 5141 Groceries, general line
HQ: Smart & Final Stores Llc
600 Citadel Dr
Commerce CA 90040
323 869-7500

(P-8458)
SMART & FINAL STORES LLC
471 College Blvd, Oceanside (92057-5435)
PHONE....................................760 726-7274
Jordan Kelly, *Director*
EMP: 60
SALES (corp-wide): 4.5B **Publicly Held**
SIC: 5141 Groceries, general line
HQ: Smart & Final Stores Llc
600 Citadel Dr
Commerce CA 90040
323 869-7500

(P-8459)
SMART & FINAL STORES LLC
4175 Park Blvd, San Diego (92103-2510)
PHONE....................................619 291-8287
Dennis Gross, *Manager*
EMP: 80
SALES (corp-wide): 4.5B **Publicly Held**
SIC: 5141 Groceries, general line
HQ: Smart & Final Stores Llc
600 Citadel Dr
Commerce CA 90040
323 869-7500

(P-8460)
SMART & FINAL STORES LLC
659 Lomas Santa Fe Dr, Solana Beach
(92075-1412)
PHONE....................................858 350-7900
Davis Sparano, *Manager*
EMP: 100
SALES (corp-wide): 4.5B **Publicly Held**
SIC: 5141 Groceries, general line
HQ: Smart & Final Stores Llc
600 Citadel Dr
Commerce CA 90040
323 869-7500

(P-8461)
**SOUTHWEST TRADERS
INCORPORATED**
4747 Frontier Way, Stockton (95215-9671)
PHONE....................................209 462-1607
Jerry Alestra, *Branch Mgr*
EMP: 91
SALES (corp-wide): 443.1MM **Privately
Held**
SIC: 5141 Food brokers
PA: Southwest Traders Incorporated
27565 Diaz Rd
Temecula CA 92590
951 699-7800

(P-8462)
**SOUTHWEST TRADERS
INCORPORATED (PA)**
Also Called: Swt Stockton
27565 Diaz Rd, Temecula (92590-3411)
PHONE....................................951 699-7800
Ken Smith, *CEO*
Lynne Bredemeier, *CFO*
Tim Shandro, *Exec VP*
Ruben Suarez, *Office Mgr*
Daniel Ruckel, *Info Tech Mgr*
▲ EMP: 180
SQ FT: 130,000
SALES (est): 443.1MM **Privately Held**
SIC: 5141 Food brokers

(P-8463)
SUNFOODS LLC (HQ)
Also Called: Hinode
1620 E Kentucky Ave, Woodland
(95776-6110)
P.O. Box 8729 (95776-8729)
PHONE....................................530 661-1923
Matt Alonso, *CEO*
Chris Willetts, *CFO*
Jacqueline Hartshorn,
John Koury,
Clyde Uchida,
◆ EMP: 70
SQ FT: 1,600
SALES: 22MM **Privately Held**
SIC: 5141 Food brokers

(P-8464)
SYGMA NETWORK INC
3741 Gold River Ln, Stockton
(95215-9669)
PHONE....................................209 932-5300
John Rivers, *Vice Pres*
Valerie Jones, *Human Res Mgr*

Jeff Regan, *Foreman/Supr*
EMP: 125
SALES (corp-wide): 58.7B **Publicly Held**
WEB: www.sygmanetwork.com
SIC: 5141 Food brokers
HQ: The Sygma Network Inc
5550 Blazer Pkwy Ste 300
Dublin OH 43017

(P-8465)
**SYSCO CENTRAL CALIFORNIA
INC**
136 Mariposa Rd, Modesto (95354-4122)
P.O. Box 729 (95353-0729)
PHONE....................................209 527-7700
Elizabeth Aspray, *President*
Robin Kawashima, *CFO*
Pamela Cullors, *Officer*
Patrick Kissee, *Senior VP*
Simon To, *Vice Pres*
▲ EMP: 312
SQ FT: 177,000
SALES (corp-wide): 58.7B **Publicly Held**
SIC: 5141 5142 5046 5148 Food bro-
kers; meat, frozen: packaged; vegetables,
frozen; restaurant equipment & supplies;
fruits, fresh; vegetables, fresh
PA: Sysco Corporation
1390 Enclave Pkwy
Houston TX 77077
281 584-1390

(P-8466)
SYSCO LOS ANGELES INC
20701 Currier Rd, Walnut (91789-2904)
PHONE....................................909 595-9595
Daniel S Haag, *CEO*
Sal Adelberg, *Exec VP*
Saul Adelsberg, *Exec VP*
John KAO, *Senior VP*
Mary Brumbugh, *Vice Pres*
◆ EMP: 1000
SALES (est): 221.8MM
SALES (corp-wide): 58.7B **Publicly Held**
WEB: www.syscola.com
SIC: 5141 5084 Groceries, general line;
food industry machinery
PA: Sysco Corporation
1390 Enclave Pkwy
Houston TX 77077
281 584-1390

(P-8467)
SYSCO RIVERSIDE INC
15750 Meridian Pkwy, Riverside
(92518-3001)
PHONE....................................951 601-5300
Saul Adelsberg, *CEO*
Nancy Drake, *Credit Staff*
EMP: 375
SALES (est): 205.7MM
SALES (corp-wide): 58.7B **Publicly Held**
SIC: 5141 5142 5143 5144 Food bro-
kers; packaged frozen goods; dairy prod-
ucts, except dried or canned; poultry &
poultry products; confectionery; fish &
seafoods
PA: Sysco Corporation
1390 Enclave Pkwy
Houston TX 77077
281 584-1390

(P-8468)
SYSCO SACRAMENTO INC
7062 Pacific Ave, Pleasant Grove
(95668-9731)
P.O. Box 138007, Sacramento (95813-
8007)
PHONE....................................916 275-2714
Jackie L Ward, *Ch of Bd*
Bill Delaney, *President*
Delmer Schnuelle, *President*
Tom Bene, *Exec VP*
Brian Beach, *Senior VP*
▲ EMP: 393
SQ FT: 350,000
SALES (est): 221.8MM
SALES (corp-wide): 58.7B **Publicly Held**
WEB: www.sac.sysco.com
SIC: 5141 5142 Food brokers; packaged
frozen goods
PA: Sysco Corporation
1390 Enclave Pkwy
Houston TX 77077
281 584-1390

PRODUCTS & SVCS

(P-8469)
SYSCO SAN DIEGO INC
12180 Kirkham Rd, Poway (92064-6879)
PHONE..................................858 513-7300
Kevin Mangan, *CEO*
Howard Poole, *President*
Richard Friedlen, *COO*
Debra Morey, *Vice Pres*
Jaime Maldonado, *Buyer*
◆ **EMP:** 370
SQ FT: 250,000
SALES (est): 221.8MM
SALES (corp-wide): 58.7B **Publicly Held**
SIC: 5141 5147 5142 5148 Food bro-
kers; packaged frozen goods; meats &
meat products; fresh fruits & vegetables;
food industry machinery
PA: Sysco Corporation
1390 Enclave Pkwy
Houston TX 77077
281 584-1390

(P-8470)
SYSCO SAN FRANCISCO INC
(HQ)
5900 Stewart Ave, Fremont (94538-3147)
P.O. Box 697 (94537-0697)
PHONE..................................510 226-3000
James Ehlers, *President*
Paul Winterhalder, *Officer*
Bruce Luong, *Vice Pres*
Margaret Snow, *Opers Staff*
▲ **EMP:** 596 **EST:** 1939
SQ FT: 470,000
SALES (est): 347.7MM
SALES (corp-wide): 58.7B **Publicly Held**
WEB: www.syscosf.com
SIC: 5141 5147 5142 Groceries, general
line; meats, fresh; packaged frozen goods
PA: Sysco Corporation
1390 Enclave Pkwy
Houston TX 77077
281 584-1390

(P-8471)
SYSCO SAN FRANCISCO INC
1622 Moffett St, Salinas (93905-3353)
PHONE..................................831 771-5000
Tom Wason, *Vice Pres*
Carolyn Madden, *Manager*
EMP: 205
SALES (corp-wide): 58.7B **Publicly Held**
WEB: www.syscosf.com
SIC: 5141 Groceries, general line
HQ: Sysco San Francisco, Inc.
5900 Stewart Ave
Fremont CA 94538
510 226-3000

(P-8472)
SYSCO VENTURA INC
3100 Sturgis Rd, Oxnard (93030-7276)
PHONE..................................805 205-7000
Jerry L Barash, *President*
Manny Fernandez, *Ch of Bd*
Bill Delaney, *President*
William Mastrosimone, *CFO*
Brian Beach, *Vice Pres*
EMP: 300
SQ FT: 370,000
SALES (est): 183.1MM
SALES (corp-wide): 58.7B **Publicly Held**
SIC: 5141 Food brokers
PA: Sysco Corporation
1390 Enclave Pkwy
Houston TX 77077
281 584-1390

(P-8473)
TAPIA ENTERPRISES INC (PA)
Also Called: Tapia Brothers Co
6067 District Blvd, Maywood (90270-3560)
PHONE..................................323 560-7415
Raul Tapia, *CEO*
Francisco Tapia, *Treasurer*
Graciela Tapia, *General Mgr*
Ramon Tapia, *Admin Sec*
Ramiro Rubalcava, *Marketing Staff*
▲ **EMP:** 95
SQ FT: 40,000
SALES (est): 266.4MM **Privately Held**
WEB: www.tapiabrothers.com
SIC: 5141 Groceries, general line

(P-8474)
UNIFIED GROCERS INC (DH)
Also Called: Supervalu
5200 Sheila St, Commerce (90040-3906)
P.O. Box 513396, Los Angeles (90051-
1396)
PHONE..................................323 264-5200
Karla C Robertson, *President*
Bruce H Besanko, *CFO*
Daniel J Murphy, *Vice Pres*
Peter Hejny, *Exec Dir*
Marnie Ahtye, *Executive Asst*
◆ **EMP:** 550
SQ FT: 344,203
SALES (est): 3.7B **Publicly Held**
SIC: 5141 6331 Food brokers; fire, marine
& casualty insurance; workers' compen-
sation insurance
HQ: Supervalu Inc.
11840 Valley View Rd
Eden Prairie MN 55344
952 828-4000

(P-8475)
UNIFIED GROCERS INC
Also Called: U W G Northern California Div
1990 Piccoli Rd, Stockton (95215-2324)
PHONE..................................209 931-1990
Glenn King, *Administration*
EMP: 238 **Publicly Held**
SIC: 5141 5149 4222 Food brokers; gro-
ceries & related products; refrigerated
warehousing & storage
HQ: Unified Grocers, Inc.
5200 Sheila St
Commerce CA 90040
323 264-5200

(P-8476)
UNIFIED GROCERS INC
Also Called: Market Centre
455 N Canyons Pkwy, Livermore
(94551-7681)
PHONE..................................323 264-5200
Joe Falvey, *Exec VP*
EMP: 100 **EST:** 2015
SALES (est): 3.4MM **Publicly Held**
SIC: 5141 Groceries, general line
HQ: Unified Grocers, Inc.
5200 Sheila St
Commerce CA 90040
323 264-5200

(P-8477)
UNION SUPPLY GROUP INC
(PA)
Also Called: Union Supply Company
2301 E Pacifica Pl, Rancho Dominguez
(90220-6210)
P.O. Box 7006 (90224-7006)
PHONE..................................310 603-8899
Tom Thomas, *CEO*
Scott Schaldenbrand, *CFO*
Lyndel Hay, *Exec VP*
John Son, *Vice Pres*
Ashley Lear, *Program Mgr*
▲ **EMP:** 115
SQ FT: 24,000
SALES (est): 117.3MM **Privately Held**
SIC: 5141 5139 5136 Groceries, general
line; footwear; men's & boys' clothing

(P-8478)
US FOODS INC
1283 Sherborn St Ste 102, Corona
(92879-5003)
PHONE..................................951 256-2400
Brad Bastyr, *Branch Mgr*
EMP: 155 **Publicly Held**
SIC: 5141 Food brokers
HQ: Us Foods, Inc.
9399 W Higgins Rd Ste 500
Rosemont IL 60018

(P-8479)
US FOODS INC
300 Lawrence Dr Frnt, Livermore
(94551-5139)
PHONE..................................925 606-3525
Phil Collins, *Branch Mgr*
EMP: 500 **Publicly Held**
WEB: www.usfoodservice.com
SIC: 5141 Food brokers

HQ: Us Foods, Inc.
9399 W Higgins Rd Ste 500
Rosemont IL 60018

(P-8480)
US FOODS INC
15155 Northam St, La Mirada
(90638-5754)
P.O. Box 29283, Phoenix AZ (85038-9283)
PHONE..................................714 670-3500
David Patterson, *Branch Mgr*
EMP: 172 **Publicly Held**
WEB: www.usfoodservice.com
SIC: 5141 5046 3556 2099 Food bro-
kers; commercial equipment; food prod-
ucts machinery; food preparations;
restaurant equipment repair
HQ: Us Foods, Inc.
9399 W Higgins Rd Ste 500
Rosemont IL 60018

(P-8481)
US FOODS INC
Also Called: U S Foods
15155 Northam St, La Mirada
(90638-5754)
PHONE..................................714 670-3500
Gene McHugh, *General Mgr*
EMP: 50 **Publicly Held**
WEB: www.usfoodservice.com
SIC: 5141 5142 Food brokers; packaged
frozen goods
HQ: Us Foods, Inc.
9399 W Higgins Rd Ste 500
Rosemont IL 60018

(P-8482)
US FOODS INTERNATIONAL
LLC
500 W 140th St Fl 2, Gardena
(90248-1510)
PHONE..................................310 515-2189
Gary Place, *Mng Member*
Chris Lee,
Brian Yoo,
Erick Yoo,
▲ **EMP:** 100
SALES (est): 14.8MM **Privately Held**
SIC: 5141 Food brokers

(P-8483)
USFI INC
110 W Walnut St 221, Gardena
(90248-3100)
PHONE..................................310 768-1937
Gary Place, *President*
William Baek, *CFO*
Steven Choi, *Vice Pres*
Byung Hak Erick Yoo, *Director*
▲ **EMP:** 75
SQ FT: 4,000
SALES (est): 47.5MM **Privately Held**
WEB: www.usfiinc.com
SIC: 5141 5149 Food brokers; groceries &
related products

(P-8484)
USTOV INC
Also Called: U.S. Trading Company
21118 Cabot Blvd, Hayward (94545-1130)
PHONE..................................510 781-1818
Paul M Tov, *CEO*
Joseph Cho, *General Mgr*
◆ **EMP:** 50
SQ FT: 132,000
SALES (est): 29MM **Privately Held**
SIC: 5141 Food brokers

(P-8485)
VEG LAND SALES INC (PA)
1518 E Valencia Dr, Fullerton (92831-4734)
P.O. Box 1267 (92836-8267)
PHONE..................................714 871-6712
John Matiasevich, *President*
James Matiasevich, *Corp Secy*
Thomas White, *Controller*
EMP: 100
SQ FT: 65,000
SALES (est): 24MM **Privately Held**
SIC: 5141 5193 4221 Food brokers; flow-
ers, fresh; farm product warehousing &
storage

(P-8486)
VIELE & SONS INC
Also Called: Viele & Sons Instnl Groc
1820 E Valencia Dr, Fullerton (92831-4847)
PHONE..................................714 447-3663
Anthony J Viele, *President*
Jim Viele, *Shareholder*
Nancy Montez Viele, *Shareholder*
Joseph Viele, *Treasurer*
Anthony Viele Jr, *Vice Pres*
EMP: 90
SQ FT: 95,000
SALES (est): 111MM **Privately Held**
WEB: www.vieleandsons.com
SIC: 5141 Groceries, general line

(P-8487)
WEST PICO DISTRIBUTORS
LLC
5201 S Downey Rd, Vernon (90058-3703)
P.O. Box 58107 (90058-0107)
PHONE..................................323 586-9050
Mordy Herzog,
David Kagan,
Elias Naghi, *Director*
EMP: 55
SALES (est): 2.1MM **Privately Held**
SIC: 5141 Food brokers

(P-8488)
WISMETTAC ASIAN FOODS INC
(DH)
Also Called: Wismettac Fresh Fish
13409 Orden Dr, Santa Fe Springs
(90670-6336)
PHONE..................................562 802-1900
Takayuki Kanai, *CEO*
Tom Kawaguchi, *CFO*
Teijiro Sho, *Officer*
Toshiyoki Nishikawa, *Vice Pres*
Yuji Sasa, *Vice Pres*
◆ **EMP:** 200
SQ FT: 225,000
SALES (est): 587.2MM
SALES (corp-wide): 2.6MM **Privately
Held**
WEB: www.nishimototrading.com
SIC: 5141 Groceries, general line
HQ: Nishimoto Co., Ltd.
3-10-5, Nihombashi
Chuo-Ku TKY 103-0
368 702-015

```
5142 Packaged Frozen
Foods Wholesale
```

(P-8489)
CALBEE NORTH AMERICA LLC
2600 Maxwell Way, Fairfield (94534-1915)
PHONE..................................707 427-2500
Gene Jensen, *Branch Mgr*
EMP: 50
SALES (corp-wide): 2.3B **Privately Held**
SIC: 5142 5145 2038 Packaged frozen
goods; snack foods; snacks, including
onion rings, cheese sticks, etc.
HQ: Calbee North America, Llc
72600 Lewis & Clark Dr
Boardman OR 97818

(P-8490)
GOLD STAR FOODS INC (PA)
3781 E Airport Dr, Ontario (91761-1558)
P.O. Box 4328 (91761-8828)
PHONE..................................909 843-9600
Sean Leer, *CEO*
Marc Jimenez, *President*
Les Wong, *COO*
Greg Johnson, *CFO*
Mahvash Howell, *Senior VP*
▲ **EMP:** 113
SQ FT: 38,000
SALES (est): 406.4MM **Privately Held**
WEB: www.goldstarfoods.com
SIC: 5142 Packaged frozen goods

(P-8491)
INTERSTATE MEAT &
PROVISION
Also Called: Sterling Pacific Meat Company
6114 Scott Way, Commerce (90040-3518)
PHONE..................................323 838-9400

Jim Asher, *CEO*
Roya Galindo, *Director*
▲ **EMP:** 100
SQ FT: 25,038
SALES (est): 85.9MM **Privately Held**
SIC: 5142 5147 Packaged frozen goods; meat brokers

(P-8492)
J AND J WALL BAKING CO INC
8806 Fruitridge Rd, Sacramento (95826-9708)
PHONE..............................916 381-1410
John Wall, *CEO*
EMP: 55
SQ FT: 50,000
SALES (est): 16.2MM **Privately Held**
SIC: 5142 Bakery products, frozen

(P-8493)
JETRO CASH AND CARRY ENTPS LLC
1265 N Kraemer Blvd, Anaheim (92806-1921)
PHONE..............................714 666-8211
Stanley Fleishman,
Pat Rosica, *President*
EMP: 130 **Privately Held**
SIC: 5142 5046 5181 5147 Packaged frozen goods; restaurant equipment & supplies; beer & other fermented malt liquors; meats, fresh; grocery stores
HQ: Jetro Cash And Carry Enterprises, Llc
1524 132nd St
College Point NY 11356
718 939-6400

(P-8494)
L & T MEAT CO
3050 E 11th St, Los Angeles (90023-3606)
PHONE..............................323 262-2815
Chak Por Tea, *President*
Bobby Lu, *Vice Pres*
EMP: 80
SQ FT: 20,000
SALES (est): 30.8MM **Privately Held**
WEB: www.ltmeat.com
SIC: 5142 Frozen fish, meat & poultry

(P-8495)
MARIE CLLENDER WHOLESALERS INC
170 E Rincon St, Corona (92879-1327)
PHONE..............................951 737-6760
Phillip Ratner, *President*
Gerald Tanaka, *Senior VP*
Kurt Schweickhart, *Vice Pres*
EMP: 65
SQ FT: 28,000
SALES (est): 22.3MM
SALES (corp-wide): 985.1MM **Privately Held**
WEB: www.castleharlan.com
SIC: 5142 Bakery products, frozen
HQ: Castle Harlan Partners Iii Lp
150 E 58th St Fl 38
New York NY 10155
212 644-8600

(P-8496)
MEADOWBROOK MEAT COMPANY INC
Also Called: M B M
5675 Sunol Blvd, Pleasanton (94566-7765)
PHONE..............................252 985-7200
Al Monceaux, *Manager*
EMP: 65
SALES (corp-wide): 242.1B **Publicly Held**
WEB: www.mbmlc.com
SIC: 5142 Packaged frozen goods
HQ: Meadowbrook Meat Company, Inc.
2641 Meadowbrook Rd
Rocky Mount NC 27801
252 985-7200

(P-8497)
PACIFIC FRESH SEA FOOD COMPANY (HQ)
Also Called: Pacific Seafood Sacramento
1420 National Dr, Sacramento (95834-1967)
PHONE..............................916 419-5500
Frank Dominic Dulcich, *President*
Tim Horgan, *COO*

◆ **EMP:** 178
SQ FT: 50,000
SALES (est): 94.8MM
SALES (corp-wide): 565.9MM **Privately Held**
SIC: 5142 5146 Fish, frozen: packaged; fish, fresh
PA: Dulcich, Inc.
16797 Se 130th Ave
Clackamas OR 97015
503 226-2200

(P-8498)
PRODUCERS DAIRY FOODS INC (PA)
250 E Belmont Ave, Fresno (93701-1405)
PHONE..............................559 264-6583
Lawrence A Shehadey, *Ch of Bd*
Richard Shehadey, *CEO*
Nick Kelble, *COO*
Scott Shehadey, *Vice Pres*
Ted Enea, *Branch Mgr*
▲ **EMP:** 200
SALES (est): 181.6MM **Privately Held**
WEB: www.producersdairy.com
SIC: 5142 5143 Fruit juices, frozen; dairy products, except dried or canned

(P-8499)
RESTAURANT DEPOT LLC
520 Brennan St, San Jose (95131-1201)
PHONE..............................408 344-0107
Ron McGill, *Branch Mgr*
EMP: 150 **Privately Held**
WEB: www.jrdtuning.com
SIC: 5142 5147 5141 5181 Packaged frozen goods; meats, fresh; groceries, general line; beer & other fermented malt liquors; tobacco & tobacco products
HQ: Restaurant Depot, Llc
1524 132nd St
College Point NY 11356

(P-8500)
RESTAURANT DEPOT LLC
180 N San Gabriel Blvd, Pasadena (91107-3426)
PHONE..............................626 744-0204
Dan Mihal, *Manager*
EMP: 150 **Privately Held**
WEB: www.jrdtuning.com
SIC: 5142 5141 5194 5181 Packaged frozen goods; groceries, general line; tobacco & tobacco products; beer & other fermented malt liquors; meats, fresh
HQ: Restaurant Depot, Llc
1524 132nd St
College Point NY 11356

(P-8501)
RESTAURANT DEPOT LLC
400 High St, Oakland (94601-3904)
PHONE..............................510 628-0600
John Derosa, *Branch Mgr*
EMP: 150 **Privately Held**
WEB: www.jrdtuning.com
SIC: 5142 5147 5141 5181 Packaged frozen goods; meats, fresh; groceries, general line; beer & other fermented malt liquors; tobacco & tobacco products
HQ: Restaurant Depot, Llc
1524 132nd St
College Point NY 11356

(P-8502)
RESTAURANT DEPOT LLC
17332 Gothard St, Huntington Beach (92647-6203)
PHONE..............................714 378-3535
Alan Cummins, *Manager*
EMP: 150 **Privately Held**
WEB: www.jrdtuning.com
SIC: 5142 5194 5147 5181 Packaged frozen goods; tobacco & tobacco products; meats, fresh; beer & other fermented malt liquors; groceries, general line
HQ: Restaurant Depot, Llc
1524 132nd St
College Point NY 11356

(P-8503)
RESTAURANT DEPOT LLC
2300 E 68th St, Long Beach (90805-1728)
PHONE..............................562 634-6771
Adrian Padilla, *Branch Mgr*
EMP: 92 **Privately Held**
WEB: www.jrdtuning.com
SIC: 5142 5147 5141 5181 Packaged frozen goods; meats, fresh; groceries, general line; beer & other fermented malt liquors; tobacco & tobacco products
HQ: Restaurant Depot, Llc
1524 132nd St
College Point NY 11356

(P-8504)
S J S LINK INTERNATIONAL INC (PA)
468 N Camden Dr Ste 311, Beverly Hills (90210-4507)
PHONE..............................310 860-7666
Shiraz Mamedov, *CEO*
Olga Sedova, *CFO*
Alex Zimmer, *Treasurer*
▼ **EMP:** 50
SALES (est): 8.5MM **Privately Held**
WEB: www.sjsusa.com
SIC: 5142 Frozen fish, meat & poultry

(P-8505)
SJ DISTRIBUTORS INC (PA)
625 Vista Way, Milpitas (95035-5433)
P.O. Box 1202, Santa Clara (95052-1202)
PHONE..............................888 988-2328
Scott Chun Ho Suen, *CEO*
Jerry Yeung, *CFO*
Jenny Lin, *Admin Sec*
EMP: 71
SQ FT: 60,000
SALES (est): 149.6MM **Privately Held**
SIC: 5142 5149 5146 Meat, frozen: packaged; canned goods: fruit, vegetables, seafood, meats, etc.; fresh fruits & vegetables; seafoods

(P-8506)
SUPERIOR FOODS INC
Also Called: Superior Foods Companies, The
275 Westgate Dr, Watsonville (95076-2470)
PHONE..............................831 728-3691
David E Moore, *Ch of Bd*
Mateo Lettunich, *President*
R Neil Happee, *CEO*
Neil Happee, *COO*
H Monroe Howser III, *CFO*
◆ **EMP:** 100
SQ FT: 10,782
SALES (est): 101MM **Privately Held**
SIC: 5142 Fruits, frozen; vegetables, frozen; fruit juices, frozen

(P-8507)
VPS COMPANIES INC (PA)
310 Walker St, Watsonville (95076-4525)
P.O. Box 118 (95077-0118)
PHONE..............................831 724-7551
Jack Randle, *Ch of Bd*
Byron Johnson, *President*
Ronald Marker, *CFO*
Fred J Haas, *Corp Secy*
▲ **EMP:** 50
SQ FT: 10,000
SALES (est): 349.1MM **Privately Held**
WEB: www.us-foods.com
SIC: 5142 0723 4731 Fruits, frozen; vegetables, frozen; crop preparation services for market; freight transportation arrangement

(P-8508)
VPS COMPANIES INC
Also Called: Central Cold Storage
13526 Blackie Rd, Castroville (95012-3212)
P.O. Box 610 (95012-0610)
PHONE..............................831 633-4011
Jonathon Thorton, *President*
EMP: 50
SALES (corp-wide): 349.1MM **Privately Held**
WEB: www.us-foods.com
SIC: 5142 Fruits, frozen

PA: The Vps Companies Inc
310 Walker St
Watsonville CA 95076
831 724-7551

(P-8509)
WEI-CHUAN USA INC (PA)
6655 Garfield Ave, Bell Gardens (90201-1807)
PHONE..............................323 587-2101
Steve Lin, *President*
Eric Shih, *COO*
William Huang, *Treasurer*
Robert Huang, *Bd of Directors*
Chienminanth Liu, *Branch Mgr*
◆ **EMP:** 120
SQ FT: 38,000
SALES (est): 98.3MM **Privately Held**
SIC: 5142 2038 Packaged frozen goods; dinners, frozen & packaged; ethnic foods, frozen

(P-8510)
WEST PICO FOODS INC
5201 S Downey Rd, Vernon (90058-3703)
P.O. Box 58107 (90058-0107)
PHONE..............................323 586-9050
Elias Naghi, *President*
Don Lubitz, *Treasurer*
Evelyn Cruz, *Executive*
Steve Kubota, *Purchasing*
Jason Schultz, *Buyer*
▲ **EMP:** 125
SQ FT: 42,000
SALES (est): 101.9MM **Privately Held**
WEB: www.westpicofoods.com
SIC: 5142 5144 Packaged frozen goods; poultry: live, dressed or frozen (unpackaged)

5143 Dairy Prdts, Except Dried Or Canned Wholesale

(P-8511)
ALTA-DENA CERTIFIED DAIRY LLC
4656 Cardin St, San Diego (92111-1419)
PHONE..............................858 292-6930
Frank Reimhard, *General Mgr*
EMP: 75 **Publicly Held**
WEB: www.altadenadairy.com
SIC: 5143 Dairy depot
HQ: Alta-Dena Certified Dairy, Llc
17637 E Valley Blvd
City Of Industry CA 91744
626 964-6401

(P-8512)
ARYA ICE CREAM DISTRG CO INC
914 E 31st St, Los Angeles (90011-2502)
P.O. Box 456, Harbor City (90710-0456)
PHONE..............................323 234-2994
Ali Pakravan, *CEO*
Mansour Azizian, *Shareholder*
Farhad Karamati, *Shareholder*
Mansour Sahabi, *Shareholder*
Hossein Sahabi, *Vice Pres*
▲ **EMP:** 60
SQ FT: 46,000
SALES (est): 70.2MM **Privately Held**
WEB: www.aryaicecream.com
SIC: 5143 Ice cream & ices

(P-8513)
BERKELEY FARMS LLC (DH)
25500 Clawiter Rd, Hayward (94545-2739)
P.O. Box 4616 (94540-4616)
PHONE..............................510 265-8600
Terry Dana,
Jim Butler, *Chief Engr*
David Smydra, *Maintence Staff*
▲ **EMP:** 300
SQ FT: 220,000
SALES (est): 362.8MM **Publicly Held**
WEB: www.berkeleyfarms.com
SIC: 5143 2026 0241 Fluid milk; dairy farms; butter

PRODUCTS & SVCS

(P-8514)
CACIQUE INC
14923 Proctor Ave, La Puente
(91746-3206)
P.O. Box 1047, Monrovia (91017-1047)
PHONE.................................626 961-3399
Mac Moore, *Director*
EMP: 240
SALES (corp-wide): 88.6MM **Privately Held**
SIC: 5143 Cheese
PA: Cacique, Inc.
   800 Royal Oaks Dr Ste 200
   Monrovia CA 91016
   626 961-3399

(P-8515)
CENTRAL VALLEY CHEESE INC
115 S Kilroy Rd, Turlock (95380-9531)
PHONE.................................209 664-1080
Antranik Baghdassarian, *CEO*
EMP: 70
SALES (est): 62.5MM **Privately Held**
WEB: www.karouncheese.com
SIC: 5143 Cheese
PA: Karoun Dairies, Inc.
   13023 Arroyo St
   San Fernando CA 91340

(P-8516)
CHALLENGE DAIRY PRODUCTS INC
5741 Smithway St, Commerce
(90040-1507)
PHONE.................................323 724-3130
Dan Bollinger, *Principal*
EMP: 50
SALES (corp-wide): 265.8MM **Privately Held**
WEB: www.challengedairy.com
SIC: 5143 2023 2021 Dairy depot; dry,
   condensed, evaporated dairy products;
   creamery butter
HQ: Challenge Dairy Products, Inc
   6701 Donlon Way
   Dublin CA 94568
   925 828-6160

(P-8517)
CHALLENGE DAIRY PRODUCTS INC (HQ)
6701 Donlon Way, Dublin (94568-2850)
P.O. Box 2369 (94568-0706)
PHONE.................................925 828-6160
Irvin Holmes, *President*
Jason Morris, *President*
Stanford Alan Maag, *CFO*
Tom Ditto, *Vice Pres*
Mew Ling Fong, *Executive Asst*
▲ EMP: 57
SQ FT: 8,500
SALES (est): 192.9MM
SALES (corp-wide): 265.8MM **Privately Held**
WEB: www.challengedairy.com
SIC: 5143 5149 Butter; milk, canned or dried
PA: California Dairies, Inc.
   2000 N Plaza Dr
   Visalia CA 93291
   559 625-2200

(P-8518)
DAIRYAMERICA INC (PA)
7815 N Palm Ave Ste 250, Fresno
(93711-5528)
PHONE.................................559 251-0992
Hoyt Huffman, *CEO*
Craig Alexander, *Treasurer*
Bill Schreiber, *Admin Sec*
Chris Pritchard, *Credit Mgr*
▲ EMP: 51
SQ FT: 4,600
SALES: 1.6B **Privately Held**
WEB: www.dairyamerica.com
SIC: 5143 Milk

(P-8519)
DEAN SOCAL LLC
Also Called: Swiss Dairy
17637 E Valley Blvd, City of Industry
(91744-5731)
PHONE.................................951 734-3950
Nick Van Hoogmoed, *Mng Member*

Gregg L Engles, *Ch of Bd*
Steve James, *President*
Cletus Beshears, *Vice Pres*
John Maddon, *Vice Pres*
EMP: 140
SQ FT: 25,000
SALES (est): 45.7MM **Publicly Held**
WEB: www.deanfoods.com
SIC: 5143 Dairy products, except dried or canned
PA: Dean Foods Company
   2711 N Haskell Ave
   Dallas TX 75204

(P-8520)
DREYERS GRAND ICE CREAM HOLD (DH)
5929 College Ave, Oakland (94618-1325)
PHONE.................................510 652-8187
Michael T Mitchell, *CEO*
Steve Barbour, *CFO*
Suzanne Saltzman, *Principal*
◆ EMP: 230
SQ FT: 64,000
SALES (est): 612MM
SALES (corp-wide): 90.8B **Privately Held**
SIC: 5143 5451 2024 Frozen dairy
   desserts; ice cream & ices; ice cream
   (packaged); ice cream & frozen desserts;
   ice cream, packaged: molded, on sticks,
   etc.; ice cream, bulk; yogurt desserts,
   frozen
HQ: Nestle Prepared Foods Company
   30003 Bainbridge Rd
   Solon OH 44139
   440 248-3600

(P-8521)
FOSTER DAIRY FARMS
3440 Enterprise Ave, Hayward
(94545-3219)
PHONE.................................510 783-1270
Ann Bartlett, *Manager*
Jon Swadley, *Mktg Dir*
EMP: 50
SALES (corp-wide): 320.5MM **Privately Held**
SIC: 5143 Dairy products, except dried or canned
PA: Foster Dairy Farms
   529 Kansas Ave
   Modesto CA 95351
   209 576-3400

(P-8522)
FOSTER DAIRY PRODUCTS DISTRG (PA)
529 Kansas Ave, Modesto (95351-1515)
PHONE.................................209 576-3400
Jeff Foster, *President*
EMP: 620
SALES (est): 91MM **Privately Held**
SIC: 5143 2026 Dairy products, except
   dried or canned; fluid milk

(P-8523)
KLM MANAGEMENT COMPANY
Also Called: Amcom Food Service
14120 Valley Blvd, City of Industry
(91746-2802)
PHONE.................................626 330-3479
Ted Degroot, *President*
Curtis Degroot, *Admin Sec*
▼ EMP: 70
SQ FT: 91,000
SALES (est): 45.4MM **Privately Held**
SIC: 5143 Dairy products, except dried or canned

(P-8524)
LOS ALTOS FOOD PRODUCTS INC
450 Baldwin Park Blvd, City of Industry
(91746-1407)
PHONE.................................626 330-6555
Raul Andrade, *President*
Alin Andrade, *Vice Pres*
Gloria Andrade, *Vice Pres*
Alfredo Montealegre, *Manager*
EMP: 105
SQ FT: 38,000
SALES (est): 102MM **Privately Held**
WEB: www.losaltosfoods.com
SIC: 5143 Cheese

(P-8525)
NESTLE DREYERS ICE CREAM CO
Also Called: Dreyer's Grand Ice Cream
351 Cheryl Ln, Walnut (91789-3003)
PHONE.................................909 595-0677
Mike Stamper, *Manager*
EMP: 175
SALES (corp-wide): 90.8B **Privately Held**
WEB: www.dreyersinc.com
SIC: 5143 2024 4222 Ice cream & ices;
   ice cream & frozen desserts; refrigerated
   warehousing & storage
HQ: Nestle Dreyer's Ice Cream Company
   5929 College Ave
   Oakland CA 94618
   510 594-9466

(P-8526)
NESTLE ICE CREAM COMPANY
7301 District Blvd, Bakersfield
(93313-2042)
PHONE.................................661 398-3500
James L Dintaman, *CEO*
▲ EMP: 1920
SALES (est): 221.8MM
SALES (corp-wide): 90.8B **Privately Held**
WEB: www.haagendazsrewards.com
SIC: 5143 5451 Ice cream & ices; ice
   cream (packaged)
HQ: Dreyer's Grand Ice Cream Holdings,
   Inc.
   5929 College Ave
   Oakland CA 94618
   510 652-8187

(P-8527)
NESTLE USA INC
6205 Engel Way, Gilroy (95020-7016)
PHONE.................................408 846-6892
Chris Pedro, *Branch Mgr*
EMP: 135
SALES (corp-wide): 90.8B **Privately Held**
SIC: 5143 Ice cream & ices
HQ: Nestle Usa, Inc.
   1812 N Moore St
   Rosslyn VA 22209
   818 549-6000

(P-8528)
PACIFIC CHEESE CO INC (PA)
21090 Cabot Blvd, Hayward (94545-1110)
P.O. Box 56598 (94545-6598)
PHONE.................................510 784-8800
Stephen B Gaddis, *President*
June M Gaddis, *Corp Secy*
Bob Leonard, *Vice Pres*
Jeri Hilley, *QC Mgr*
▲ EMP: 153
SQ FT: 107,000
SALES: 800MM **Privately Held**
WEB: www.pacific-cheese.com
SIC: 5143 Cheese

(P-8529)
SVD INC
Also Called: Sun Valley Dairy
8088 San Fernando Rd, Sun Valley
(91352-4001)
PHONE.................................818 504-1775
Jack Galadjian, *CEO*
ARA Kozanian, *President*
▲ EMP: 55
SQ FT: 40,000
SALES (est): 43.4MM **Privately Held**
WEB: www.voskos.com
SIC: 5143 Yogurt

(P-8530)
UNIFIED GROCERS INC
Also Called: U W G Southern California Div
457 E Martin Luther King, Los Angeles
(90011-5650)
PHONE.................................323 232-6124
Maurice Ochua, *Branch Mgr*
EMP: 74 **Publicly Held**
SIC: 5143 8742 2051 Dairy products, except dried or canned; marketing consulting services; bread; cake & related
   products
HQ: Unified Grocers, Inc.
   5200 Sheila St
   Commerce CA 90040
   323 264-5200

5144 Poultry & Poultry Prdts Wholesale

(P-8531)
GOOD EGGS INC
901 Rankin St, San Francisco
(94124-1626)
PHONE.................................415 483-7344
Rob Spiro, *Chairman*
Alon Salant, *CTO*
EMP: 50
SALES (est): 24.8MM **Privately Held**
SIC: 5144 2099 Eggs; ready-to-eat meals,
   salads & sandwiches

(P-8532)
HIDDEN VILLA RANCH PRODUCE INC
310 N Harbor Blvd Ste 205, Fullerton
(92832-1954)
P.O. Box 34001 (92834-9411)
PHONE.................................714 680-3447
Tim E Luberski, *President*
Don Lawson, *CFO*
Robert J Kelly, *Exec VP*
Greg Schneider, *Exec VP*
Michael Sencer, *Exec VP*
◆ EMP: 270
SQ FT: 21,619
SALES: 410MM
SALES (corp-wide): 350MM **Privately Held**
WEB: www.hiddenvillaranch.com
SIC: 5144 Eggs
PA: Luberski, Inc.
   310 N Harbor Blvd Ste 205
   Fullerton CA 92832
   714 680-3447

(P-8533)
INTERSTATE FOODS INC
310 S Long Beach Blvd, Compton
(90221-3448)
PHONE.................................310 635-0426
Carlos Velasco, *CEO*
EMP: 145 EST: 2000
SQ FT: 13,000
SALES (est): 38.7MM **Privately Held**
SIC: 5144 Poultry products

(P-8534)
LEHAR SALES CO
150 Chestnut St, Oakland (94607-2511)
P.O. Box 24211 (94623-1211)
PHONE.................................510 465-3255
Harold J De Luca, *CEO*
Rick Charles, *President*
Hariette Young, *Treasurer*
Tarry Winfrey, *Vice Pres*
Claire Venturini, *Admin Sec*
EMP: 55
SQ FT: 35,000
SALES (est): 7.6MM
SALES (corp-wide): 71.8MM **Privately Held**
WEB: www.pacagri.com
SIC: 5144 Poultry: live, dressed or frozen
   (unpackaged); poultry products
PA: Pacific Agri-Products, Inc.
   477 Forbes Blvd
   South San Francisco CA 94080
   650 873-0440

(P-8535)
LUBERSKI INC
Also Called: Hidden Villa Ranch
1811 Mountain Ave, Norco (92860-2863)
PHONE.................................951 271-3866
Tim Luberski, *Branch Mgr*
EMP: 70
SALES (corp-wide): 350MM **Privately Held**
WEB: www.calsunshine.com
SIC: 5144 Eggs
PA: Luberski, Inc.
   310 N Harbor Blvd Ste 205
   Fullerton CA 92832
   714 680-3447

(P-8536)
NEW STOCKTON POULTRY INC
302 S San Joaquin St, Stockton
(95203-3536)
P.O. Box 2129 (95201-2129)
PHONE....................209 466-1952
William P K Chan, *CEO*
John Luu, *President*
Ming Luu, *Vice Pres*
▲ EMP: 50
SALES (est): 7.7MM **Privately Held**
SIC: 5144 5499 2015 5421 Poultry: live,
dressed or frozen (unpackaged); eggs &
poultry; poultry, processed: fresh; meat &
fish markets

(P-8537)
NULAID FOODS INC (PA)
200 W 5th St, Ripon (95366-2793)
PHONE....................209 599-2121
David K Crockett, *President*
Scott Hennecke, *CFO*
Amy Parsons, *Accounting Mgr*
Sonja Murray, *QC Dir*
Dustin Barnett, *Manager*
EMP: 76
SQ FT: 5,000
SALES (est): 43.2MM **Privately Held**
WEB: www.nulaid.com
SIC: 5144 2047 2015 2023 Eggs; eggs:
cleaning, oil treating, packing & grading;
dog food; egg processing; cream substi-
tutes

(P-8538)
RACE STREET FOODS INC (PA)
Also Called: Race Street Fish & Poultry
967 W Hedding St, San Jose (95126-1257)
PHONE....................408 294-6161
Gino Barsanti, *Chairman*
Mike Barsanti, *Treasurer*
Michael Barsanti, *Corp Secy*
Dan Barsanti, *Vice Pres*
David Riparbelli, *Vice Pres*
EMP: 80
SQ FT: 63,000
SALES (est): 21.1MM **Privately Held**
WEB: www.racestreetfoods.com
SIC: 5144 5146 5147 5142 Poultry &
poultry products; fish & seafoods; meats
& meat products; packaged frozen goods;
frozen fish, meat & poultry

(P-8539)
ROGERS POULTRY CO (PA)
2020 E 67th St, Los Angeles (90001-2169)
PHONE....................323 585-0802
George V Saffarrans, *CEO*
John C Butler, *COO*
Ken Hayashi, *CFO*
Wen Hai Hong, *Exec VP*
Koen Hennon, *Executive*
EMP: 135
SQ FT: 15,000
SALES: 56.7MM **Privately Held**
WEB: www.rogerspoultry.com
SIC: 5144 Poultry products

(P-8540)
SQUAB PRODUCERS CALIF INC
409 Primo Way, Modesto (95358-5721)
PHONE....................209 537-4744
Robert Shipley, *President*
EMP: 55
SQ FT: 11,000
SALES (est): 8.4MM **Privately Held**
WEB: www.squab.com
SIC: 5144 2015 Poultry: live, dressed or
frozen (unpackaged); poultry slaughtering
& processing

(P-8541)
SUNRISE FARMS LLC
395 Liberty Rd, Petaluma (94952-8104)
PHONE....................707 778-6450
James Carlson, *Manager*
Larry Johnson,
Al Nissen,
Arnold Riebli,
Richard Weber,
▲ EMP: 65
SQ FT: 10,000
SALES (est): 14.7MM **Privately Held**
SIC: 5144 2015 Eggs: cleaning, oil treat-
ing, packing & grading; poultry slaughter-
ing & processing

**5145 Confectionery
Wholesale**

(P-8542)
A & R WHOLESALE DISTRS INC
1765 W Penhall Way, Anaheim
(92801-6728)
PHONE....................714 777-7742
Martin R Alsobrooks, *CEO*
Ron Paz, *President*
Jeff Kuriel, *CEO*
EMP: 60
SALES (est): 45.4MM
SALES (corp-wide): 406.4MM **Privately
Held**
SIC: 5145 Snack foods
PA: Gold Star Foods, Inc.
3781 E Airport Dr
Ontario CA 91761
909 843-9600

(P-8543)
**B B G MANAGEMENT GROUP
(PA)**
Also Called: Granlund Candies
12164 California St, Yucaipa (92399-4333)
PHONE....................909 797-9581
R Scott Burkle, *President*
Margie Rogan, *Vice Pres*
EMP: 58
SQ FT: 10,000
SALES (est): 7.1MM **Privately Held**
SIC: 5145 2064 Candy; candy & other
confectionery products

(P-8544)
**CANTEEN VENDING - SAN
DIEGO**
Also Called: Rainbow Vending & Distributing
5515 Market St, San Diego (92114-2218)
PHONE....................619 527-1900
Greg Karron, *President*
Greg Carron, *President*
Don Martin, *CFO*
EMP: 53 EST: 1968
SQ FT: 10,300
SALES (est): 16MM
SALES (corp-wide): 28.9B **Privately Held**
WEB: www.rainbowvending.com
SIC: 5145 5149 5962 Snack foods; soft
drinks; candy & snack food vending ma-
chines
HQ: Compass Group Usa, Inc.
2400 Yorkmont Rd
Charlotte NC 28217
704 328-4000

(P-8545)
**FRITO-LAY NORTH AMERICA
INC**
401 Burns Dr, Yuba City (95991-7233)
PHONE....................530 671-7854
Randy Meyers, *Branch Mgr*
Tyler Adams, *Manager*
EMP: 164
SALES (corp-wide): 63.5B **Publicly Held**
SIC: 5145 Snack foods
HQ: Frito-Lay North America, Inc.
7701 Legacy Dr
Plano TX 75024

(P-8546)
**FRITO-LAY NORTH AMERICA
INC**
26672 Towne Centre Dr, Foothill Ranch
(92610-2818)
PHONE....................925 734-3100
Cory Frederick, *Principal*
EMP: 164
SALES (corp-wide): 63.5B **Publicly Held**
SIC: 5145 Snack foods
HQ: Frito-Lay North America, Inc.
7701 Legacy Dr
Plano TX 75024

(P-8547)
**FRITO-LAY NORTH AMERICA
INC**
14600 Proctor Ave, City of Industry
(91746-3249)
PHONE....................626 855-1300
Marty McFadden, *Principal*
EMP: 400
SQ FT: 54,844
SALES (corp-wide): 63.5B **Publicly Held**
WEB: www.fritolay.com
SIC: 5145 Snack foods
HQ: Frito-Lay North America, Inc.
7701 Legacy Dr
Plano TX 75024

(P-8548)
**FRITO-LAY NORTH AMERICA
INC**
9535 Archibald Ave, Rancho Cucamonga
(91730-5737)
PHONE....................909 941-6214
Brian Birrell, *Manager*
Faiyaz Nathoo, *Manager*
EMP: 500
SALES (corp-wide): 63.5B **Publicly Held**
WEB: www.fritolay.com
SIC: 5145 Snack foods
HQ: Frito-Lay North America, Inc.
7701 Legacy Dr
Plano TX 75024

(P-8549)
**FRITO-LAY NORTH AMERICA
INC**
28801 Highway 58, Bakersfield
(93314-9000)
PHONE....................661 328-6034
Jason Audler, *Manager*
EMP: 188
SALES (corp-wide): 63.5B **Publicly Held**
SIC: 5145 Snack foods
HQ: Frito-Lay North America, Inc.
7701 Legacy Dr
Plano TX 75024
-

(P-8550)
**FRITO-LAY NORTH AMERICA
INC**
3630 N Hazel Ave, Fresno (93722-4594)
PHONE....................559 226-8153
Cregg Jerri, *Branch Mgr*
EMP: 150
SALES (corp-wide): 63.5B **Publicly Held**
WEB: www.fritolay.com
SIC: 5145 5149 2096 Snack foods; gro-
ceries & related products; potato chips &
similar snacks
HQ: Frito-Lay North America, Inc.
7701 Legacy Dr
Plano TX 75024

(P-8551)
**FRITO-LAY NORTH AMERICA
INC**
751 W Avenue L8, Lancaster (93534-7103)
PHONE....................661 951-1399
Glenn Kliewer, *General Mgr*
EMP: 65
SALES (corp-wide): 63.5B **Publicly Held**
WEB: www.fritolay.com
SIC: 5145 Snack foods
HQ: Frito-Lay North America, Inc.
7701 Legacy Dr
Plano TX 75024
-

(P-8552)
**FRITO-LAY NORTH AMERICA
INC**
1774 Automation Pkwy, San Jose
(95131-1873)
PHONE....................559 312-8553
EMP: 80
SQ FT: 48,250
SALES (corp-wide): 63.5B **Publicly Held**
WEB: www.fritolay.com
SIC: 5145 Snack foods

HQ: Frito-Lay North America, Inc.
7701 Legacy Dr
Plano TX 75024

(P-8553)
**FRITO-LAY NORTH AMERICA
INC**
151 W Hill Pl, Brisbane (94005-1221)
PHONE....................415 467-1860
Luis Andrade, *Manager*
EMP: 85
SALES (corp-wide): 63.5B **Publicly Held**
WEB: www.fritolay.com
SIC: 5145 5149 Snack foods; groceries &
related products
HQ: Frito-Lay North America, Inc.
7701 Legacy Dr
Plano TX 75024

(P-8554)
**FRITO-LAY NORTH AMERICA
INC**
3810 Seaport Blvd, West Sacramento
(95691-3449)
PHONE....................916 372-5400
Troy Shea, *Manager*
EMP: 150
SALES (corp-wide): 63.5B **Publicly Held**
WEB: www.fritolay.com
SIC: 5145 5149 Snack foods; groceries &
related products
HQ: Frito-Lay North America, Inc.
7701 Legacy Dr
Plano TX 75024

(P-8555)
**FRITO-LAY NORTH AMERICA
INC**
6320 District Blvd, Bakersfield
(93313-2142)
PHONE....................661 835-0347
Tim King, *Manager*
EMP: 50
SQ FT: 18,000
SALES (corp-wide): 63.5B **Publicly Held**
WEB: www.fritolay.com
SIC: 5145 5149 Snack foods; groceries &
related products
HQ: Frito-Lay North America, Inc.
7701 Legacy Dr
Plano TX 75024

(P-8556)
**FRITO-LAY NORTH AMERICA
INC**
1450 S Loop Rd, Alameda (94502-2702)
PHONE....................510 769-5000
Steve Pahara, *Principal*
EMP: 62
SALES (corp-wide): 63.5B **Publicly Held**
WEB: www.fritolay.com
SIC: 5145 Snack foods
HQ: Frito-Lay North America, Inc.
7701 Legacy Dr
Plano TX 75024

(P-8557)
**FRITO-LAY NORTH AMERICA
INC**
1390 Vantage Ct, Vista (92081-8524)
PHONE....................760 727-6022
Fred Schmidt, *Manager*
EMP: 100
SQ FT: 19,836
SALES (corp-wide): 63.5B **Publicly Held**
WEB: www.fritolay.com
SIC: 5145 5149 Snack foods; groceries &
related products
HQ: Frito-Lay North America, Inc.
7701 Legacy Dr
Plano TX 75024

(P-8558)
**FRITO-LAY NORTH AMERICA
INC**
26962 Vista Ter, El Toro (92630-8123)
PHONE....................949 586-4644
Tyrone Suruta, *Manager*
EMP: 75

SQ FT: 14,356
SALES (corp-wide): 63.5B **Publicly Held**
WEB: www.fritolay.com
SIC: 5145 Snack foods
HQ: Frito-Lay North America, Inc.
7701 Legacy Dr
Plano TX 75024

(P-8559)
FRITO-LAY NORTH AMERICA INC
8316 W Elowin Ct, Visalia (93291-9262)
PHONE..............................559 651-1334
Jim Johnson, *Manager*
EMP: 70
SQ FT: 19,800
SALES (corp-wide): 63.5B **Publicly Held**
WEB: www.fritolay.com
SIC: 5145 Snack foods
HQ: Frito-Lay North America, Inc.
7701 Legacy Dr
Plano TX 75024

(P-8560)
FRITO-LAY NORTH AMERICA INC
4029 Leckron Rd, Modesto (95357-0516)
PHONE..............................209 544-5424
EMP: 187
SALES (corp-wide): 63.5B **Publicly Held**
SIC: 5145 Snack foods
HQ: Frito-Lay North America, Inc.
7701 Legacy Dr
Plano TX 75024

(P-8561)
FRITO-LAY NORTH AMERICA INC
1924 E Maple Ave, El Segundo
(90245-3411)
PHONE..............................310 322-5001
Ed Castro, *Branch Mgr*
EMP: 50
SALES (corp-wide): 63.5B **Publicly Held**
WEB: www.fritolay.com
SIC: 5145 Snack foods
HQ: Frito-Lay North America, Inc.
7701 Legacy Dr
Plano TX 75024

(P-8562)
GICO MANAGEMENT
23073 S Frederick Rd, Ripon (95366-9616)
PHONE..............................209 599-7131
Steve Gikas, *Owner*
▲ **EMP:** 75
SQ FT: 100,000
SALES (est): 20.3MM **Privately Held**
SIC: 5145 Confectionery

(P-8563)
INNER CIRCLE ENTERTAINMENT
Also Called: Ruby Sky
464 Monterey Ave Ste A, Los Gatos
(95030-5326)
PHONE..............................415 693-0777
George Karpaty, *President*
Frank Finelli, *Principal*
Dina Jacobsen, *Accountant*
Matt Whitlock, *Director*
EMP: 60
SQ FT: 17,500
SALES (est): 12.8MM **Privately Held**
SIC: 5145 Snack foods

(P-8564)
MONTPELIER NUT COMPANY INC (PA)
1518 K St, Modesto (95354-1108)
PHONE..............................209 566-9084
Kenfield Alldrin, *CEO*
Steve Zeff, *CFO*
▼ **EMP:** 55
SALES (est): 15.8MM **Privately Held**
SIC: 5145 Nuts, salted or roasted

(P-8565)
PEPSICO INC
4416 Azusa Canyon Rd, Baldwin Park
(91706-2740)
PHONE..............................626 338-5531
Kip Zaughan, *Manager*
Louanne Wallace, *Senior Mgr*
Sven Pirkl, *Director*
EMP: 200
SALES (corp-wide): 63.5B **Publicly Held**
WEB: www.pepsico.com
SIC: 5145 2086 Confectionery; carbon-
ated beverages, nonalcoholic: bottled &
canned
PA: Pepsico, Inc.
700 Anderson Hill Rd
Purchase NY 10577
914 253-2000

(P-8566)
R W GARCIA CO INC (PA)
100 Enterprise Way, Scotts Valley
(95066-3248)
P.O. Box 8290, San Jose (95155-8290)
PHONE..............................408 287-4616
Robert W Garcia, *President*
Margaret Garcia, *Vice Pres*
Janette Rosales, *Office Mgr*
John Justice, *VP Opers*
Allan Perkins, *Plant Mgr*
◆ **EMP:** 50
SQ FT: 30,000
SALES (est): 105.1MM **Privately Held**
WEB: www.rwgarcia.com
SIC: 5145 2096 2099 Snack foods; tortilla
chips; food preparations

(P-8567)
S&E GOURMET CUTS INC
Also Called: Country Archer Jerky
379 Industrial Rd, San Bernardino
(92408-3713)
PHONE..............................909 370-0155
Eugene Kang, *CEO*
Susan Kang, *Vice Pres*
EMP: 150
SALES (est): 20MM **Privately Held**
SIC: 5145 Snack foods

5146 Fish & Seafood Wholesale

(P-8568)
ANOVA FOOD LLC
280 10th Ave, San Diego (92101-7406)
PHONE..............................858 715-4000
Christopher Lischewski, *CEO*
◆ **EMP:** 100
SALES (est): 3.8MM **Privately Held**
SIC: 5146 Seafoods
HQ: Bee Bumble Foods Llc
280 10th Ave
San Diego CA 92101
858 715-4000

(P-8569)
ANTHONYS FISH GROTTO
Also Called: Ghio Seafood Products
9530 Murray Dr, La Mesa (91942-3924)
PHONE..............................619 713-1853
Anthony A Ghio, *Partner*
Cottardo Ghio, *Partner*
Adele Weber, *Partner*
Dan Shehan, *Controller*
EMP: 60 **EST:** 1946
SQ FT: 11,000
SALES (est): 6.9MM **Privately Held**
SIC: 5146 5141 Seafoods; groceries, gen-
eral line

(P-8570)
ATLANTA SEAFOODS LLC
Also Called: Sea Catch Seafoods
10501 Valley Blvd # 1820, El Monte
(91731-2461)
PHONE..............................626 626-4900
Wayne Berman, *Mng Member*
▲ **EMP:** 65
SQ FT: 48,000
SALES (est): 32.1MM **Privately Held**
SIC: 5146 Fish & seafoods

(P-8571)
BLUE RIVER SEAFOOD INC
Also Called: Joe Pucci & Sons Seafoods
25447 Industrial Blvd, Hayward
(94545-2931)
PHONE..............................510 300-6800
Chris Lam, *President*
Lam Nguyen, *Executive*
Sean Nguyen, *General Mgr*
Merry Xiao, *Engineer*
Myrla Best, *Controller*
▲ **EMP:** 50
SQ FT: 53,000
SALES (est): 30.5MM **Privately Held**
SIC: 5146 2092 Fish, fresh; fish, frozen,
unpackaged; fresh or frozen packaged
fish

(P-8572)
BSM UNI
712 Ceres Ave, Los Angeles (90021-1516)
PHONE..............................213 626-2557
Shigeru Matsushita, *President*
Darlene Matsushita, *Vice Pres*
EMP: 50
SQ FT: 8,000
SALES (est): 7.3MM **Privately Held**
WEB: www.smuni.com
SIC: 5146 Seafoods

(P-8573)
CAITO FISHERIES INC (PA)
19400 Harbor Ave, Fort Bragg
(95437-5615)
P.O. Box 1370 (95437-1370)
PHONE..............................707 964-6368
Joseph A Caito, *CEO*
James G Caito, *Vice Pres*
EMP: 100 **EST:** 1975
SQ FT: 10,000
SALES (est): 23.6MM **Privately Held**
WEB: www.caitofisheries.com
SIC: 5146 Fish & seafoods

(P-8574)
CALIFORNIA SHELLFISH CO INC
Point St George Fisheries
1280 Columbus Ave 300r, San Francisco
(94133-1302)
P.O. Box 1386, Santa Rosa (95402-1386)
PHONE..............................707 542-9490
Tony Delima, *Branch Mgr*
EMP: 350
SALES (corp-wide): 105.4MM **Privately
Held**
SIC: 5146 Fish, fresh; fish, frozen, unpack-
aged
PA: California Shellfish Company, Inc.
818 E Broadway C
San Gabriel CA 91776
415 923-7400

(P-8575)
DEL MAR SEAFOODS INC
1449 Spinnaker Dr, Ventura (93001-4355)
PHONE..............................805 850-0421
EMP: 185
SALES (corp-wide): 38.3MM **Privately
Held**
SIC: 5146 Seafoods
PA: Del Mar Seafoods, Inc.
331 Ford St
Watsonville CA 95076
831 763-3000

(P-8576)
H & N FOODS INTERNATIONAL INC (HQ)
Also Called: H & N Fish Company
5580 S Alameda St, Vernon (90058-3426)
P.O. Box 58626, Los Angeles (90058-0626)
PHONE..............................323 586-9300
Hua Thanh Ngo, *President*
Bobby Ngo, *Vice Pres*
Christine Ngo, *Vice Pres*
Dat Trieu, *Vice Pres*
Mario Guardado, *General Mgr*
◆ **EMP:** 125
SQ FT: 45,000
SALES (est): 78.4MM
SALES (corp-wide): 155.1MM **Privately
Held**
SIC: 5146 Fish, fresh; fish, frozen, unpack-
aged

PA: H & N Group, Inc.
5580 S Alameda St
Vernon CA 90058
323 586-9388

(P-8577)
IMP FOODS INC
1650 Delta Ct, Hayward (94544-7043)
PHONE..............................510 429-4600
Masamitsu Furuta, *President*
Glen Sakata, *Vice Pres*
▲ **EMP:** 60
SQ FT: 48,000
SALES (est): 8.3MM **Privately Held**
SIC: 5146 Fish, frozen, unpackaged; fish,
fresh

(P-8578)
INTERNATIONAL MARINE PDTS INC (HQ)
Also Called: Imp
500 E 7th St, Los Angeles (90014-2410)
PHONE..............................213 893-6123
James Ho, *CEO*
Yoshihiro Momose, *President*
Clifford Uota, *Manager*
▲ **EMP:** 50
SQ FT: 10,000
SALES (est): 34.6MM **Privately Held**
WEB: www.intmarine.com
SIC: 5146 Fish, fresh; fish, frozen, unpack-
aged

(P-8579)
KINGS SEAFOOD COMPANY LLC
Also Called: NGS Fish House
12427 N Mainstreet, Rancho Cucamonga
(91739-8887)
PHONE..............................909 803-1280
Bunny Bennett, *Manager*
EMP: 100
SALES (corp-wide): 77MM **Privately
Held**
SIC: 5146 Seafoods
PA: King's Seafood Company, Llc
3185 Airway Ave Ste J
Costa Mesa CA 92626
310 451-4595

(P-8580)
KINGS SEAFOOD COMPANY LLC
7691 Edinger Ave, Huntington Beach
(92647-3604)
PHONE..............................714 793-1177
Malia Cappuccio, *Branch Mgr*
EMP: 100
SALES (corp-wide): 77MM **Privately
Held**
SIC: 5146 Seafoods
PA: King's Seafood Company, Llc
3185 Airway Ave Ste J
Costa Mesa CA 92626
310 451-4595

(P-8581)
KINGS SEAFOOD COMPANY LLC
1521 W Katella Ave, Orange (92867-3410)
PHONE..............................714 771-6655
Fred Belez, *Branch Mgr*
EMP: 100
SALES (corp-wide): 77MM **Privately
Held**
SIC: 5146 Seafoods
PA: King's Seafood Company, Llc
3185 Airway Ave Ste J
Costa Mesa CA 92626
310 451-4595

(P-8582)
LUSAMERICA FOODS INC (PA)
16480 Railroad Ave, Morgan Hill
(95037-5210)
PHONE..............................408 294-6622
Fernando Luis Frederico, *CEO*
Ana Frederico, *CFO*
Anna Frederico, *Vice Pres*
Nicole Silva, *Executive*
Jacob Salas, *IT/INT Sup*
▲ **EMP:** 85
SQ FT: 40,000

▲ = Import ▼=Export
◆ =Import/Export

SALES (est): 87.1MM **Privately Held**
WEB: www.lusamericafish.com
SIC: **5146** 5142 Fish, fresh; fish, frozen, unpackaged; packaged frozen goods

(P-8583)
M & J SEAFOOD COMPANY INC
6859 Walthall Way, Paramount
(90723-2028)
PHONE..................................562 529-2786
J Jesus Rodriguez, *CEO*
Wendy McDonalds, *COO*
EMP: 55
SALES: 75MM **Privately Held**
SIC: **5146** 5147 Seafoods; meats & meat products

(P-8584)
NORTH COAST FISHERIES LLC
Also Called: Alca Trax Sea Foods
2255 Challenger Way # 101, Santa Rosa
(95407-5423)
PHONE..................................707 579-0679
Michael Lucas, *Mng Member*
EMP: 65
SQ FT: 10,000
SALES (est): 32.3MM **Privately Held**
WEB: www.northcoastfisheries.com
SIC: **5146** 2091 Seafoods; fish, cured; fish, fresh; fish, frozen, unpackaged; canned & cured fish & seafoods

(P-8585)
NORTH PACIFIC RESOURCES INC
333 S Grand Ave Ste 4200, Los Angeles
(90071-1567)
PHONE..................................206 676-3828
Shozo Tsuru, *President*
EMP: 53 EST: 1991
SALES (est): 5.9MM **Privately Held**
SIC: **5146** Seafoods

(P-8586)
OCEAN GROUP INC (PA)
Also Called: Ocean Fresh Fish Seafood Mktg
1100 S Santa Fe Ave, Los Angeles
(90021-1743)
PHONE..................................213 622-3677
Young Won Kim, *President*
Hyojin Ahn, *CFO*
Ikki Fujij, *Branch Mgr*
Tae S Kim, *Admin Sec*
Kurt Kim, *Human Resources*
▲ EMP: 60
SQ FT: 20,000
SALES (est): 40MM **Privately Held**
SIC: **5146** Seafoods

(P-8587)
OCEAN QUEEN 87 INC
4511 Everett Ave, Vernon (90058-2621)
PHONE..................................323 585-1200
Yuho Nagata, *President*
Justin Genochio, *Opers Mgr*
EMP: 50
SQ FT: 3,700
SALES (est): 13.1MM **Privately Held**
SIC: **5146** Seafoods

(P-8588)
ORE-CAL CORP (PA)
Also Called: Harvest of The Sea
634 Crocker St, Los Angeles (90021-1002)
P.O. Box 21832 (90021-0832)
PHONE..................................213 623-8493
Mark Shinbane, *President*
Sandra Shinbane, *Corp Secy*
Charlie Molinelli, *Vice Pres*
Debra Edgemon, *Regional Mgr*
David Rovner, *Info Tech Dir*
◆ EMP: 55
SQ FT: 80,000
SALES (est): 260MM **Privately Held**
SIC: **5146** 5142 Fish & seafoods; packaged frozen goods

(P-8589)
ORIENT FISHERIES INC
Also Called: Ofi Markesa International
1912 E Vernon Ave Ste 110, Vernon
(90058-1611)
PHONE..................................323 588-4185
Ming Shin Kou, *President*
David L Prince,
▲ EMP: 52

SQ FT: 3,000
SALES (est): 9.6MM **Privately Held**
SIC: **5146** Seafoods

(P-8590)
PACIFIC AMERICAN FISH CO INC (PA)
Also Called: Pafco
5525 S Santa Fe Ave, Vernon
(90058-3523)
PHONE..................................323 319-1551
Peter Huh, *CEO*
Paul Huh, *Exec VP*
Nancy Armas, *Facilities Mgr*
Danae Lucas, *Manager*
▲ EMP: 300
SQ FT: 100,000
SALES (est): 166.8MM **Privately Held**
WEB: www.pafco.net
SIC: **5146** 2091 Fish, fresh; fish, frozen, unpackaged; seafoods; fish, filleted (boneless)

(P-8591)
PACIFIC CHOICE SEAFOOD COMPANY
1 Commercial St, Eureka (95501-0241)
PHONE..................................707 442-2981
Rick Harris, *Manager*
Chuck Corcoran, *QC Dir*
EMP: 300
SALES (corp-wide): 565.9MM **Privately Held**
SIC: **5146** Fish & seafoods
HQ: Pacific Choice Seafood Company
3220 Sw 1st Ave
Portland OR 97239
503 226-2200

(P-8592)
PACIFIC SEA FOOD CO INC
Also Called: Jakes Crawfish & Seafood
1420 National Dr, Sacramento
(95834-1967)
PHONE..................................916 419-5500
Barb Pacella, *Branch Mgr*
George Pisano, *Purch Agent*
Mark Gordon, *Sales Mgr*
EMP: 100
SALES (corp-wide): 565.9MM **Privately Held**
WEB: www.pacificseafoodco.com
SIC: **5146** 5142 5143 Fish, fresh; fish, frozen, unpackaged; seafoods; fish, frozen: packaged; meat, frozen: packaged; poultry, frozen: packaged; cheese
HQ: Pacific Sea Food Co. Inc.
16797 Se 130th Ave
Clackamas OR 97015
503 905-4500

(P-8593)
PACIFIC SEA FOOD CO INC
Also Called: Pacific Fresh Seafood Company
605 Flint Ave, Wilmington (90744-6110)
PHONE..................................310 835-4343
James Lanter, *General Mgr*
EMP: 50
SALES (corp-wide): 565.9MM **Privately Held**
WEB: www.pacificseafoodco.com
SIC: **5146** Fish & seafoods
HQ: Pacific Sea Food Co. Inc.
16797 Se 130th Ave
Clackamas OR 97015
503 905-4500

(P-8594)
PLD ENTERPRISES INC
Also Called: Superior Seafood Co
440 Stanford Ave, Los Angeles
(90013-2121)
PHONE..................................213 626-4444
Chip Mezin, *General Mgr*
EMP: 61
SALES (est): 5.8MM **Privately Held**
SIC: **5146** Fish & seafoods
PA: P.L.D. Enterprises, Inc.
1621 W 25th St Ste 228
San Pedro CA 90732

(P-8595)
PLD ENTERPRISES INC (PA)
Also Called: Superior Seafood Co
1621 W 25th St Ste 228, San Pedro
(90732-4301)
PHONE..................................310 547-3366
Paul Di Girolamo, *CEO*
Dannesh Alam, *Sales Mgr*
▲ EMP: 72
SQ FT: 10,000
SALES (est): 37.5MM **Privately Held**
SIC: **5146** Fish & seafoods

(P-8596)
PROSPECT ENTERPRISES INC (PA)
Also Called: American Fish and Seafood
625 Kohler St, Los Angeles (90021-1023)
PHONE..................................213 599-5700
Ernest Y Doizaki, *Ch of Bd*
Jack King, *President*
Paula Eberhardt, *CFO*
James Lanter, *General Mgr*
Shawn Sisler, *Info Tech Mgr*
▲ EMP: 160
SQ FT: 20,000
SALES (est): 239.8MM **Privately Held**
WEB: www.americanfish.com
SIC: **5146** 2092 Fish, fresh; fish, frozen, unpackaged; seafoods; fresh or frozen packaged fish

(P-8597)
RED CHAMBER CO (PA)
1912 E Vernon Ave, Vernon (90058-1611)
PHONE..................................323 234-9000
Shan Chun Kou, *Ch of Bd*
Shu Kin Kou, *Ch of Bd*
Ming Bin Kou, *CEO*
◆ EMP: 341
SQ FT: 15,000
SALES (est): 339.2MM **Privately Held**
WEB: www.redchamber.com
SIC: **5146** 4222 Seafoods; warehousing, cold storage or refrigerated

(P-8598)
SANTA MONICA SEAFOOD COMPANY
1000 Wilshire Blvd, Santa Monica
(90401-1907)
PHONE..................................310 393-5244
Vince Cigiliano, *Director*
EMP: 203
SALES (corp-wide): 121.7MM **Privately Held**
SIC: **5146** Seafoods
PA: Santa Monica Seafood Company
18531 S Broadwick St
Rancho Dominguez CA 90220
310 886-7900

(P-8599)
SEA WIN INC
526 Stanford Ave, Los Angeles
(90013-2123)
PHONE..................................213 688-2899
Nam Tran, *CEO*
Frances Tran, *Admin Sec*
◆ EMP: 50
SQ FT: 29,000
SALES (est): 24.7MM **Privately Held**
SIC: **5146** Fish, fresh; fish, frozen, unpackaged

(P-8600)
SHOWA MARINE INC (PA)
668 S Alameda St Ste A, Los Angeles
(90021-1270)
PHONE..................................213 627-4091
Taro John Ikeda, *CEO*
Goro Ikeda, *President*
Dennis Kimoshita, *Corp Secy*
Kumiko Ikeda, *Vice Pres*
Caz Kitani, *Principal*
▲ EMP: 60
SQ FT: 100,000
SALES (est): 25.7MM **Privately Held**
SIC: **5146** 5149 Seafoods; specialty food items

(P-8601)
SLADE GORTON & CO INC
1 Centerpointe Dr Ste 311, La Palma
(90623-2512)
PHONE..................................714 676-4200
EMP: 66 **Privately Held**
SIC: **5146**
HQ: Gorton Slade & Co Inc
225 Southampton St
Boston MA 02118
617 442-5800

(P-8602)
SOUTHWIND FOODS LLC (PA)
Also Called: Great Amercn Seafood Import Co
20644 S Fordyce Ave, Carson
(90810-1018)
P.O. Box 86021, Los Angeles (90086-0021)
PHONE..................................323 262-8222
Buddy Galletti, *President*
Sam Galletti, *CEO*
Jim Lee, *CFO*
Jim Elie, *Vice Pres*
Paul Galletti, *Vice Pres*
▲ EMP: 100
SQ FT: 80,000
SALES (est): 202.2MM **Privately Held**
SIC: **5146** 5147 Seafoods; meats & meat products

(P-8603)
STAGNARO BROTHERS SEAFOOD INC
320 Washington St, Santa Cruz
(95060-4929)
PHONE..................................831 423-1188
Giovanni Stagnaro, *Ch of Bd*
Robert Tara, *President*
Virginia Stagnaro, *Treasurer*
Ernest M Stagnaro, *Vice Ch Bd*
Robert Mc Pherson, *Vice Pres*
EMP: 73
SQ FT: 12,000
SALES (est): 19.7MM **Privately Held**
WEB: www.stagnarobros.com
SIC: **5146** 5812 5421 Seafoods; seafood restaurants; seafood markets

(P-8604)
STAR FISHERIES
Also Called: Seaport Fish Company
841 Watson Ave, Wilmington (90744-3732)
PHONE..................................310 549-4992
Anthony Di Maggio, *President*
EMP: 55
SALES (est): 3.5MM
SALES (corp-wide): 56.5MM **Privately Held**
SIC: **5146** Seafoods
PA: Star Fisheries
222 W 6th St Ste 500
San Pedro CA 90731
310 832-8395

(P-8605)
STAR FISHERIES (PA)
222 W 6th St Ste 500, San Pedro
(90731-3646)
P.O. Box 1150 (90733-1150)
PHONE..................................310 832-8395
Jolene Dimagrio, *President*
Anthony Di Maggio, *President*
Louie J Bozanich, *Vice Pres*
Deanne Inman, *Director*
▲ EMP: 90
SQ FT: 8,000
SALES (est): 56.5MM **Privately Held**
WEB: www.starfisheries.com
SIC: **5146** Seafoods

(P-8606)
TRADEWIND SEAFOOD INC
1505 Mountain View Ave, Oxnard
(93030-5107)
PHONE..................................805 483-8555
Mack Demachi, *President*
Hiromi Demachi, *Vice Pres*
EMP: 50
SQ FT: 5,000
SALES (est): 9.4MM **Privately Held**
SIC: **5146** Seafoods

PRODUCTS & SVCS

(P-8607)
TRI-MARINE FISH COMPANY LLC
220 Cannery St, San Pedro (90731-7308)
PHONE.................................310 547-1144
Vince Torre, *Mng Member*
Benny Caserma, *Prdtn Mgr*
◆ **EMP:** 75
SQ FT: 30,000
SALES (est): 25.1MM **Privately Held**
SIC: 5146 Seafoods

(P-8608)
TRI-UNION SEAFOODS LLC (DH)
Also Called: Chicken of Sea International
2150 E Grand Ave, El Segundo (90245-5024)
P.O. Box 85568, San Diego (92186-5568)
PHONE.................................858 558-9662
Shue Wing Chan, *President*
David E Roszmann, *COO*
Jim Cox, *Senior VP*
Christie Fleming, *Senior VP*
Ignatius Dharma, *Vice Pres*
◆ **EMP:** 69
SQ FT: 24,000
SALES (est): 74MM
SALES (corp-wide): 4.1B **Privately Held**
SIC: 5146 2091 Seafoods; tuna fish: packaged in cans, jars, etc.; salmon: packaged in cans, jars, etc.
HQ: Thai Union International, Inc.
9330 Scranton Rd Ste 500
San Diego CA 92121
858 558-9662

(P-8609)
TRUE WRLD FODS LOS ANGELES LLC
4200 S Alameda St, Vernon (90058-1602)
PHONE.................................323 846-3300
Jang Hoee Kim, *President*
▲ **EMP:** 55
SQ FT: 55,000
SALES (est): 22.7MM
SALES (corp-wide): 582.7MM **Privately Held**
SIC: 5146 Fish, frozen, unpackaged; fish, fresh
HQ: True World Foods New York Llc
32-34 Papetti Plz
Elizabeth NJ 07206
908 351-9090

(P-8610)
TRUE WRLD FODS SAN FRNCSCO LLC
1815 Williams St, San Leandro (94577-2301)
PHONE.................................510 352-8140
Shinryo Shimada, *Mng Member*
Makoto Kikuchi,
David Miller,
◆ **EMP:** 62 **EST:** 1978
SQ FT: 27,000
SALES (est): 21.1MM
SALES (corp-wide): 582.7MM **Privately Held**
SIC: 5146 Fish & seafoods
HQ: True World Holdings Llc
24 Link Dr Unit D
Rockleigh NJ 07647
201 750-0024

5147 Meats & Meat Prdts Wholesale

(P-8611)
BICARA LTD
318 Avenue I Ste 65, Redondo Beach (90277-5601)
PHONE.................................310 316-6222
William Jeffrey Hughes, *CEO*
William D Hughes, *President*
Raymond Rosenthal, *Vice Pres*
◆ **EMP:** 300
SQ FT: 105,000
SALES (est): 64.5MM **Privately Held**
WEB: www.bicara.net
SIC: 5147 5146 5141 Meats & meat products; seafoods; groceries, general line

(P-8612)
BRIDGFORD MARKETING COMPANY (DH)
1308 N Patt St, Anaheim (92801-2551)
P.O. Box 3773 (92803-3773)
PHONE.................................714 526-5533
Allan L Bridgford, *Chairman*
John Simmons, *President*
Ray Lancey, *CFO*
William L Bridgford, *Chairman*
David Rowe, *Manager*
EMP: 89
SQ FT: 100,000
SALES (est): 40.1MM
SALES (corp-wide): 167.2MM **Publicly Held**
SIC: 5147 5149 Meats & meat products; bakery products
HQ: Bridgford Foods Corporation
1308 N Patt St
Anaheim CA 92801
714 526-5533

(P-8613)
CALIFORNIA FARMS MEAT CO INC
4401 S Downey Rd, Vernon (90058-2518)
PHONE.................................323 581-3663
Erik Litmanovich, *CEO*
EMP: 61 **EST:** 2013
SALES (est): 1.6MM
SALES (corp-wide): 18.8MM **Privately Held**
SIC: 5147 Meats & meat products
PA: Golden West Food Group, Inc.
4401 S Downey Rd
Vernon CA 90058
888 807-3663

(P-8614)
DANIELS WESTERN MT PACKERS INC
5217 Industry Ave, Pico Rivera (90660-2505)
PHONE.................................562 948-2254
Alfred Santos, *CEO*
▲ **EMP:** 80
SQ FT: 12,000
SALES (est): 44.6MM **Privately Held**
WEB: www.danielswesternmeatpackers.com
SIC: 5147 Meats, fresh

(P-8615)
DEL MAR HOLDING LLC
1022 Bay Marina Dr 10, National City (91950-6398)
PHONE.................................313 659-7300
Leon Bergmann, *CEO*
Joel Jorgensen, *CFO*
EMP: 1600
SQ FT: 9,700
SALES: 3.5B **Privately Held**
SIC: 5147 Meats & meat products

(P-8616)
GOLDEN WEST TRADING INC
Also Called: Royal Poultry
4401 S Downey Rd, Vernon (90058-2518)
P.O. Box 58161 (90058-0161)
PHONE.................................323 581-3663
Erik Litmanovich, *CEO*
Levi Litmanovich, *Ch of Bd*
Tony Cimolino, *President*
David Karp, *President*
Josh Solovy, *President*
▲ **EMP:** 180
SQ FT: 40,000
SALES (est): 221.8MM **Privately Held**
WEB: www.gwtinc.com
SIC: 5147 5142 Meats & meat products; meat, frozen: packaged

(P-8617)
HARVEST MEAT COMPANY INC (HQ)
Also Called: Harvest Food Distributors
1022 Bay Marina Dr # 106, National City (91950-6327)
PHONE.................................619 477-0185
John J Leavy, *CEO*
Kevin Leavy, *President*
Eric Doan, *CFO*
Dennis Kevin, *Principal*
Jennifer Sitz, *Personnel Assit*

◆ **EMP:** 80
SQ FT: 60,000
SALES (est): 223.5MM
SALES (corp-wide): 302.4MM **Privately Held**
WEB: www.harvestmeat.com
SIC: 5147 Meats & meat products
PA: Sand Dollar Holdings, Inc.
1022 Bay Marina Dr # 106
National City CA 91950
619 477-0185

(P-8618)
HEARTLAND MEAT COMPANY INC
Also Called: H M C
3461 Main St, Chula Vista (91911-5828)
PHONE.................................619 407-3668
Joseph E Stidman, *CEO*
Stephanie Stidman, *Corp Secy*
James Methey, *Vice Pres*
Ranae West, *Accountant*
Blanca Lowery, *Human Res Mgr*
EMP: 70
SQ FT: 49,000
SALES (est): 34.2MM **Privately Held**
WEB: www.heartlandmeat.com
SIC: 5147 2013 Meats, fresh; sausages & other prepared meats

(P-8619)
HOLIDAY MEAT & PROVISION CORP
405 Centinela Ave, Inglewood (90302-3294)
PHONE.................................310 674-0541
Nat Rocker, *President*
Sue Rocker, *Admin Sec*
EMP: 200
SQ FT: 14,000
SALES: 60MM **Privately Held**
SIC: 5147 5144 5146 Meats, fresh; poultry products; seafoods

(P-8620)
JETRO CASH AND CARRY ENTPS LLC
Also Called: Restaurant Depot
2045 Evans Ave, San Francisco (94124-1022)
PHONE.................................415 920-2888
Bob Britton, *Branch Mgr*
EMP: 100 **Privately Held**
WEB: www.jetro.com
SIC: 5147 5141 5142 5181 Meats, fresh; groceries, general line; packaged frozen goods; beer & other fermented malt liquors; tobacco & tobacco products
HQ: Jetro Cash And Carry Enterprises, Llc
1524 132nd St
College Point NY 11356
718 939-6400

(P-8621)
MACSEI INDUSTRIES CORPORATION
1784 E Vernon Ave, Vernon (90058-1526)
PHONE.................................323 233-7864
Seiichi Shibata, *President*
◆ **EMP:** 52
SQ FT: 8,913
SALES (est): 8.6MM **Privately Held**
SIC: 5147 Meat brokers

(P-8622)
NEWPORT MEAT SOUTHERN CAL INC
Also Called: Newport Meat Company
16691 Hale Ave, Irvine (92606-5025)
PHONE.................................949 399-4200
Timothy K Hussman, *CEO*
Denise Van Voorhis, *CFO*
EMP: 227 **EST:** 1976
SQ FT: 92,000
SALES (est): 134.4MM
SALES (corp-wide): 58.7B **Publicly Held**
WEB: www.newportmeat.com
SIC: 5147 5142 Meats, fresh; packaged frozen goods
PA: Sysco Corporation
1390 Enclave Pkwy
Houston TX 77077
281 584-1390

(P-8623)
ORITZ CORPORATION (PA)
1555 Old Bayshore Hwy # 400, Burlingame (94010-1617)
P.O. Box 4646 (94011-4646)
PHONE.................................650 692-8000
Vladimir R Grave, *President*
Janet Tang, *Accounts Mgr*
◆ **EMP:** 103
SQ FT: 45,000
SALES (est): 48.6MM **Privately Held**
WEB: www.oritz.com
SIC: 5147 Meats & meat products

(P-8624)
PNC INC
Also Called: SEAPORT MEAT COMPANY
2533 Folex Way, Spring Valley (91978-2038)
P.O. Box 1159 (91979-1159)
PHONE.................................619 713-2278
Nancy Camarda, *CEO*
Pete Camarda, *Admin Sec*
EMP: 51
SQ FT: 17,995
SALES: 23.9MM **Privately Held**
SIC: 5147 Meats, fresh

(P-8625)
R W ZANT CO (PA)
1470 E 4th St, Los Angeles (90033-4288)
PHONE.................................323 980-5457
Robert W Zant, *President*
William Zant, *Principal*
Mary Zant, *Admin Sec*
Ibrahim El-Helou, *Info Tech Dir*
Tereza Messer, *Controller*
▲ **EMP:** 90
SQ FT: 42,000
SALES: 301MM **Privately Held**
SIC: 5147 5146 5144 4222 Meats, fresh; fish & seafoods; poultry & poultry products; cheese warehouse

(P-8626)
RANCHO FOODS INC
2528 E 37th St, Vernon (90058-1725)
P.O. Box 58504, Los Angeles (90058-0504)
PHONE.................................323 585-0503
Annette Mac Donald, *President*
John Mac Donald, *Vice Pres*
EMP: 100
SQ FT: 26,000
SALES (est): 90.3MM **Privately Held**
WEB: www.ranchofoods.com
SIC: 5147 2013 Meats, fresh; sausages & other prepared meats

(P-8627)
RICHMOND WHOLESALE MEAT CO
Also Called: Richmond Peak Quality
2920 Regatta Blvd, Richmond (94804-4528)
PHONE.................................510 233-5111
Richard Doellstedt, *President*
Alan Bell, *CFO*
Carl Doellstedt, *Vice Pres*
John Doellstedt, *Principal*
◆ **EMP:** 85
SQ FT: 100,000
SALES: 100MM **Privately Held**
WEB: www.rwm.biz
SIC: 5147 Meats, fresh

(P-8628)
RITE-WAY MEAT PACKERS INC
5151 Alcoa Ave, Vernon (90058-3715)
PHONE.................................323 826-2144
Irwin Miller, *President*
Carol Miller, *Corp Secy*
▲ **EMP:** 69
SQ FT: 64,000
SALES (est): 33.1MM **Privately Held**
SIC: 5147 Meats, fresh

(P-8629)
RONGCHENG TRADING LLC
Also Called: Always Best
19319 Arenth Ave, City of Industry (91748-1401)
PHONE.................................626 338-1090
MEI Lan Liang, *Mng Member*
Fannie Yang, *COO*
Angie Lee, *CFO*
Tim Chen, *Buyer*

Xiao Mou Zhang, *Mng Member*
▲ EMP: 50
SQ FT: 80,000
SALES (est): 42.3MM **Privately Held**
SIC: 5147 Meats, fresh

(P-8630)
SAND DOLLAR HOLDINGS INC
(PA)
1022 Bay Marina Dr # 106, National City
(91950-6398)
PHONE..................................619 477-0185
John Leavy, *President*
Eric Doan, *CFO*
Kevin Leavy, *Vice Pres*
▲ EMP: 80
SALES (est): 302.4MM **Privately Held**
SIC: 5147 Meats, fresh

(P-8631)
THREE SONS INC
Also Called: American Companies
5201 Industry Ave, Pico Rivera
(90660-2505)
P.O. Box 6 (90660-0006)
PHONE..................................562 801-4100
Michael Shannon Day, *CEO*
David Day, *Shareholder*
Mariellen Day, *Shareholder*
Michael Day, *Shareholder*
John Brenan, *Vice Pres*
▲ EMP: 87
SQ FT: 40,000
SALES (est): 47MM **Privately Held**
WEB: www.threesons.com
SIC: 5147 2013 2011 Meats, cured or
smoked; meats, fresh; sausages & other
prepared meats; meat packing plants

(P-8632)
TONYS FINE FOODS (HQ)
3575 Reed Ave, West Sacramento
(95605-1628)
P.O. Box 1501, Broderick (95605-0698)
PHONE..................................916 374-4000
Karl Berger, *President*
▲ EMP: 390
SQ FT: 143,000
SALES (est): 2.5MM **Publicly Held**
WEB: www.tonysfinefoods.com
SIC: 5147 5143 5149 Meats, cured or
smoked; cheese; groceries & related
products

(P-8633)
WAYNE PROVISION CO INC (PA)
Also Called: Premier Meat Company
5030 Gifford Ave, Vernon (90058-2726)
P.O. Box 58183, Los Angeles (90058-0183)
PHONE..................................323 277-5888
Naftali Greenberg, *CEO*
Terry Hanks, *Shareholder*
Eldad Hadar, *Vice Pres*
▼ EMP: 70
SQ FT: 7,822
SALES (est): 53.1MM **Privately Held**
WEB: www.premiermeats.com
SIC: 5147 5144 Meats, fresh; poultry &
poultry products

(P-8634)
WEBERS QUALITY MEATS INC
Also Called: Butcher's Brand
990 Carden St, San Leandro (94577-1164)
PHONE..................................510 635-9892
Stefan Weber, *President*
Linda Weber, *Corp Secy*
EMP: 60
SQ FT: 10,000
SALES (est): 34.6MM **Privately Held**
WEB: www.webersqualitymeats.com
SIC: 5147 5142 Meats, fresh; meat,
frozen: packaged

(P-8635)
WEST COAST PRIME MEATS
LLC
344 Cliffwood Park St, Brea (92821-4103)
PHONE..................................714 255-8560
William H Hustedt, *Mng Member*
Amy Nickoloff, *Managing Prtnr*
Samuel Rachal, *QA Dir*
Nathan Bennett, *VP Finance*
Justin Schulze, *Accounting Mgr*
EMP: 120

SALES (est): 71.9MM **Privately Held**
SIC: 5147 Meats, fresh

5148 Fresh Fruits &
Vegetables Wholesale

(P-8636)
4 EARTH FARMS INC (PA)
5555 E Olympic Blvd, Commerce
(90022-5129)
PHONE..................................323 201-5800
David Lake, *CEO*
Robert Lake, *COO*
Mark Munger, *Vice Pres*
Kevin Whiteman, *Executive*
Ben Bowden, *Info Tech Dir*
▼ EMP: 79
SQ FT: 165,000
SALES: 230.3MM **Privately Held**
WEB: www.mclproduce.com
SIC: 5148 Fresh fruits & vegetables

(P-8637)
ABP LIQUIDATING CORP
299 Lawrence Ave, South San Francisco
(94080-6818)
PHONE..................................650 871-7689
Brett Besser, *CEO*
Ardynne Besser, *Principal*
Paula Amaya, *Buyer*
Oscar Martin, *Sales Dir*
EMP: 50 EST: 1971
SQ FT: 11,000
SALES (est): 12.8MM **Privately Held**
WEB: www.abproduce.com
SIC: 5148 5144 Fruits, fresh; vegetables,
fresh; eggs

(P-8638)
ADVANTAGE PRODUCE INC
1511 Bay St, Los Angeles (90021-1634)
P.O. Box 86388 (90086-0388)
PHONE..................................213 627-2777
Steven A Beck, *President*
Don Beck, *Vice Pres*
EMP: 50
SQ FT: 27,000
SALES: 40MM **Privately Held**
SIC: 5148 Fruits; vegetables

(P-8639)
AMS - EXOTIC LLC
720 S Alameda St, Los Angeles
(90021-1616)
PHONE..................................213 612-5888
Sinera Chau-Pech, *Mng Member*
Sig Cube, *Controller*
Donna Hazelton, *Regl Sales Mgr*
Thierry Delappe,
Martin Seymour,
◆ EMP: 55
SQ FT: 14,000
SALES: 20MM **Privately Held**
WEB: www.ams-exotic.com
SIC: 5148 Fruits

(P-8640)
ANDREW AND WILLIAMSON
SALES CO (PA)
Also Called: Andrew Williamson Fresh Prod
9940 Marconi Dr, San Diego (92154-7270)
PHONE..................................619 661-6000
Fred M Williamson, *CEO*
Ira Gershow, *CFO*
Gershow Ira, *CFO*
John King, *Vice Pres*
Mitch Williamson, *Vice Pres*
▲ EMP: 60
SQ FT: 20,000
SALES (est): 65.6MM **Privately Held**
WEB: www.andrew-williamson.com
SIC: 5148 Fruits, fresh; vegetables

(P-8641)
BETTER LIFE PRODUCE INC
Also Called: Better Life Organic Produce
2020 E 7th Pl, Los Angeles (90021-1702)
P.O. Box 2841, Fullerton (92837-0841)
PHONE..................................213 623-0640
German Ruiz, *President*
William McCoy, *CFO*
Dawn McCoy, *Admin Sec*
EMP: 50
SQ FT: 22,500

SALES (est): 19.3MM **Privately Held**
SIC: 5148 Fresh fruits & vegetables

(P-8642)
BLAZER WILKINSON LP
19040 Portola Dr, Salinas (93908-1213)
P.O. Box 7428, Spreckels (93962-7428)
PHONE..................................831 455-3700
John Wilkinson, *General Ptnr*
Scott Blazer, *Partner*
Kiana Amaral, *Controller*
Jeff Wilkinson, *Sales Staff*
EMP: 300
SQ FT: 25,000
SALES (est): 88MM **Privately Held**
SIC: 5148 Fresh fruits & vegetables

(P-8643)
BONTADELLI INC
2611 Mission St, Santa Cruz (95060-5702)
P.O. Box 879 (95061-0879)
PHONE..................................831 423-8572
Ernest J Bontadelli, *President*
Steven Bontadelli, *Vice Pres*
EMP: 60 EST: 1971
SALES (est): 10.7MM **Privately Held**
SIC: 5148 Vegetables, fresh

(P-8644)
BUY FRESH PRODUCE INC
6636 E 26th St, Commerce (90040-3216)
PHONE..................................323 796-0127
Ted Kasnetsis, *President*
Traci Kasnetsis, *CFO*
Wayde Nichols, *General Mgr*
Marlene Mendoza, *Manager*
EMP: 80
SQ FT: 23,500
SALES (est): 1.8MM **Privately Held**
WEB: www.buyfreshproduceinc.com
SIC: 5148 Fruits, fresh

(P-8645)
CAL FRESCO LLC
6850 Artesia Blvd, Buena Park
(90620-1015)
PHONE..................................714 690-7700
Fernando Vargas, *President*
Greg Hess, *Sales Staff*
John Timossi, *Sales Staff*
Jean Gallegos, *Manager*
Alex Vargas, *Manager*
▼ EMP: 112
SQ FT: 75,000
SALES: 116.2MM **Privately Held**
WEB: www.calfresco.com
SIC: 5148 Fruits, fresh

(P-8646)
CALAVO GROWERS INC (PA)
1141 Cummings Rd Ste A, Santa Paula
(93060-9118)
PHONE..................................805 525-1245
Lecil E Cole, *Ch of Bd*
James E Gibson, *President*
B John Lindeman, *CFO*
Ronald A Araiza, *Vice Pres*
Michael A Browne, *Vice Pres*
◆ EMP: 153 EST: 1924
SALES: 1B **Publicly Held**
WEB: www.calavo.com
SIC: 5148 5142 5149 Fruits, fresh; fruits,
frozen; groceries & related products

(P-8647)
CALAVO GROWERS INC
28410 Vincent Moraga Dr, Temecula
(92590-3654)
PHONE..................................951 676-7331
Gerry Watts, *Vice Pres*
EMP: 50
SALES (corp-wide): 1B **Publicly Held**
WEB: www.calavo.com
SIC: 5148 5142 Fruits, fresh; frozen veg-
etables & fruit products
PA: Calavo Growers, Inc.
1141 Cummings Rd Ste A
Santa Paula CA 93060
805 525-1245

(P-8648)
CALIFORNIA FRUIT EXCHANGE
LLC (PA)
Also Called: Golden State Fruit
6011 E Pine St, Lodi (95240-0815)
P.O. Box 1264 (95241-1264)
PHONE..................................209 365-2340
Paul Marchand,
Suzanne Hernandez, *Mktg Dir*
▲ EMP: 150
SQ FT: 47,200
SALES (est): 190.8MM **Privately Held**
SIC: 5148 5499 Fruits; food gift baskets

(P-8649)
CALIFORNIA PRODUCE
WHOLSALERS
6818 Watcher St, Commerce (90040-3715)
PHONE..................................562 776-5770
Alex Pappas, *CEO*
Harry Pappas, *Treasurer*
EMP: 50
SQ FT: 18,000
SALES (est): 33.3MM **Privately Held**
SIC: 5148 Fruits, fresh; vegetables, fresh

(P-8650)
CALIFORNIA VEGETABLE SPC
INC
Also Called: California Endive Farm
15 Poppy House Rd, Rio Vista
(94571-1201)
P.O. Box 638 (94571-0638)
PHONE..................................707 374-2111
Alexandre Pierron-Darbonne, *CEO*
Richard Collins, *President*
Luc Darbonne, *CEO*
Jose Arias, *Vice Pres*
▲ EMP: 70
SQ FT: 11,000
SALES: 8MM **Privately Held**
WEB: www.endive.com
SIC: 5148 Fresh fruits & vegetables

(P-8651)
CAPURRO MARKETING LLC
Also Called: Capurro Farms
2250 Highway 1, Moss Landing
(95039-9631)
P.O. Box 450 (95039-0450)
PHONE..................................831 728-1767
Frank L Capurro,
Kristofer Capurro,
John Manfre,
Michael Manfre,
EMP: 60
SQ FT: 70,000
SALES (est): 15.7MM **Privately Held**
WEB: www.capurromkt.com
SIC: 5148 Vegetables

(P-8652)
CHARLIES ENTERPRISES
Also Called: OK Produce
1888 S East Ave, Fresno (93721-3231)
P.O. Box 12838 (93779-2838)
PHONE..................................559 445-8600
Matty Matoian, *President*
Angel Burnett, *Partner*
Pam Ruiz, *Admin Mgr*
Jennifer Wright, *Project Mgr*
Charlotte Showers, *Financial Exec*
EMP: 200
SQ FT: 70,000
SALES (est): 139MM **Privately Held**
WEB: www.okproduce.com
SIC: 5148 Fruits, fresh; vegetables, fresh

(P-8653)
CHICO PRODUCE INC (PA)
Also Called: Pro Pacific Fresh
70 Pepsi Way, Durham (95938-9798)
P.O. Box 1069 (95938-1069)
PHONE..................................530 893-0596
Terry Richardson, *CEO*
Bruce Parks, *Ch of Bd*
Martin Sanchez, *Info Tech Mgr*
Dave Deuel, *Technology*
Angela Garcia, *Finance Mgr*
▼ EMP: 141
SQ FT: 70,000
SALES (est): 60MM **Privately Held**
WEB: www.propacificfresh.com
SIC: 5148 5149 Fruits, fresh; dried or
canned foods

(P-8654)
CHIQUITA BRANDS INTL INC
746 Market Ct, Los Angeles (90021-1103)
PHONE..............................213 488-0925
Jay Jebbia, *President*
EMP: 60
SALES (corp-wide): 3B **Privately Held**
WEB: www.chiquita.com
SIC: 5148 Fruits, fresh
HQ: Chiquita Brands International, Inc.
1855 Griffin Rd Ste C436
Dania FL 33004
954 453-1201

(P-8655)
CHRISTOPHER RANCH LLC
Also Called: California Produce
1690 Freitas Rd, San Juan Bautista
(95045-9530)
PHONE..............................831 636-8722
Steve Moss, *Manager*
EMP: 65
SALES (est): 5.6MM
SALES (corp-wide): 103.5MM **Privately Held**
WEB: www.christopher-ranch.com
SIC: 5148 Fresh fruits & vegetables
PA: Christopher Ranch, Llc
305 Bloomfield Ave
Gilroy CA 95020
408 847-1100

(P-8656)
CHURCH BROTHERS LLC (PA)
19065 Portola Dr Ste C, Salinas
(93908-1250)
P.O. Box 509 (93902-0509)
PHONE..............................831 796-1000
Tom Church,
Jay Brown, *CFO*
Drew McDonald, *Vice Pres*
Paula Crabtree, *Executive*
Lisa Dennis, *Sales Mgr*
EMP: 85
SQ FT: 1,000
SALES (est): 104.5MM **Privately Held**
SIC: 5148 Fresh fruits & vegetables

(P-8657)
COAST CITRUS DISTRIBUTORS (PA)
Also Called: Coast Tropical
7597 Bristow Ct, San Diego (92154-7419)
P.O. Box 530369 (92153-0369)
PHONE..............................619 661-7950
James M Alvarez, *Ch of Bd*
Nick Alvarez, *Officer*
Margarita Alvarez, *Admin Sec*
Erica Alvarez, *Administration*
Pattie Arias, *Credit Mgr*
▲ EMP: 100
SQ FT: 80,000
SALES: 293.3MM **Privately Held**
WEB: www.coastcitrus.com
SIC: 5148 Fruits, fresh

(P-8658)
COAST CITRUS DISTRIBUTORS
Also Called: Olympic Frt & Vegatable Distr
1601 E Olympic Blvd, Los Angeles
(90021-1936)
PHONE..............................213 955-3444
Tom Hall, *Vice Pres*
EMP: 150
SALES (corp-wide): 293.3MM **Privately Held**
WEB: www.coastcitrus.com
SIC: 5148 Fruits, fresh
PA: Coast Citrus Distributors
7597 Bristow Ct
San Diego CA 92154
619 661-7950

(P-8659)
COAST CITRUS DISTRIBUTORS
Also Called: Coast Tropical
131 Terminal Ct 13, South San Francisco
(94080-6526)
P.O. Box 2884 (94083)
PHONE..............................650 588-0707
Patrick Graham, *Manager*
EMP: 50
SALES (corp-wide): 293.3MM **Privately Held**
WEB: www.coastcitrus.com
SIC: 5148 Fruits, fresh

PA: Coast Citrus Distributors
7597 Bristow Ct
San Diego CA 92154
619 661-7950

(P-8660)
COAST PRODUCE COMPANY (PA)
1791 Bay St, Los Angeles (90021-1655)
P.O. Box 86468 (90086-0468)
PHONE..............................213 955-4900
Mike Ito, *CEO*
Rick Uyeno, *CFO*
John K Dunn, *Principal*
Rafael Elizalde, *Buyer*
▲ EMP: 165
SQ FT: 80,000
SALES (est): 73MM **Privately Held**
WEB: www.coastpro.com
SIC: 5148 Fruits, fresh

(P-8661)
COHN WHOLESALE FRUIT & GROCERY (PA)
3511 Camino Del Rio S # 306, San Diego
(92108-4020)
PHONE..............................619 528-1113
Phillip L Cohn, *President*
Alice Cohn, *Treasurer*
Aaron Cohn, *Vice Pres*
EMP: 201
SALES (est): 32.3MM **Privately Held**
WEB: www.cohngrocery.com
SIC: 5148 Fruits

(P-8662)
D & D WHOLESALE DISTRS INC
777 Baldwin Park Blvd, City of Industry
(91746-1504)
PHONE..............................626 333-2111
Joe Dupree, *President*
Pamela Dupree, *Corp Secy*
Jean D Dupre, *Vice Pres*
John Fracasso, *Accounting Mgr*
EMP: 90
SQ FT: 20,000
SALES (est): 58.8MM **Privately Held**
SIC: 5148 5143 Fruits, fresh; dairy products, except dried or canned

(P-8663)
DAVALAN SALES INC
Also Called: Davalan Fresh
1601 E Olympic Blvd # 325, Los Angeles
(90021-1957)
PHONE..............................213 623-2500
Alan Frick, *President*
Dave Bouton, *CEO*
Bob Morse, *Sales Staff*
▲ EMP: 200
SQ FT: 15,000
SALES (est): 107.1MM **Privately Held**
SIC: 5148 Fruits; vegetables

(P-8664)
DAYLIGHT FOODS INC
660 Vista Way, Milpitas (95035-5456)
PHONE..............................408 284-7300
Chris Vlahopouliotis, *President*
Paul Jennings, *Vice Pres*
▲ EMP: 120
SQ FT: 20,000
SALES: 49.5MM **Privately Held**
SIC: 5148 Fruits, fresh; vegetables, fresh

(P-8665)
DEARDORFF-JACKSON CO
Also Called: Deardorff Family Farm
400 Lombard St, Oxnard (93030-5100)
P.O. Box 1188 (93032-1188)
PHONE..............................805 487-7801
Tom Deardorff Jr, *President*
Scott Deardorff, *Admin Sec*
Juana Gonzalez, *Personnel*
Geremy Olsen, *Director*
Edgar Cruz, *Supervisor*
EMP: 50 EST: 1954
SQ FT: 115,000
SALES (est): 44MM **Privately Held**
WEB: www.deardorffjackson.com
SIC: 5148 Fresh fruits & vegetables

(P-8666)
DIMARE FRESH
4050 Pell Cir, Sacramento (95838-2527)
P.O. Box 340188 (95834-0188)
PHONE..............................916 921-6302
Jerry Just, *General Mgr*
Bob Canisso, *Manager*
John Jarin, *Manager*
EMP: 300
SALES (est): 64.4MM **Privately Held**
SIC: 5148 Fruits, fresh

(P-8667)
DOLE FRESH FRUIT COMPANY (DH)
1 Dole Dr, Westlake Village (91362-7300)
P.O. Box 5700, Thousand Oaks (91359-5700)
PHONE..............................818 874-4000
Johan Linden, *President*
John Trummel, *President*
Johan L Malmqvist, *Treasurer*
Ronald D Bouchard, *Vice Pres*
David Bright, *Vice Pres*
◆ EMP: 460
SQ FT: 57,000
SALES (est): 875.5MM
SALES (corp-wide): 11.7B **Privately Held**
SIC: 5148 Fruits, fresh; banana ripening
HQ: Dole Food Company, Inc.
1 Dole Dr
Westlake Village CA 91362
818 874-4000

(P-8668)
DOLE FRESH VEGETABLES INC
32655 Camphora Rd, Soledad
(93960-9600)
PHONE..............................831 678-5030
Sheila Lee, *Manager*
Kim Cruz, *Buyer*
Mario Martinez, *Maint Spvr*
EMP: 210
SQ FT: 1,664
SALES (corp-wide): 11.7B **Privately Held**
SIC: 5148 Fresh fruits & vegetables
HQ: Dole Fresh Vegetables, Inc.
2959 Salinas Hwy
Monterey CA 93940
831 422-8871

(P-8669)
DOLE HOLDINGS INC (PA)
1 Dole Dr, Westlake Village (91362-7300)
PHONE..............................818 879-6600
David Delorenzo, *President*
Amanda France, *Technology*
Roxana Gonzalez, *Analyst*
Christina Kessler, *QC Mgr*
David Cairns, *Director*
◆ EMP: 51
SALES (est): 11.4MM **Privately Held**
SIC: 5148 0161 0174 0175 Fresh fruits & vegetables; vegetables & melons; citrus fruits; deciduous tree fruits; canned fruits & specialties

(P-8670)
DRISCOLLS INC (PA)
345 Westridge Dr, Watsonville
(95076-4169)
P.O. Box 50045 (95077-5045)
PHONE..............................831 424-0506
Miles Reiter, *CEO*
Joseph Miles Reiter, *Ch of Bd*
Sean Martin, *CFO*
Elly Hoever, *Treasurer*
Kevin Murphy, *Senior VP*
◆ EMP: 60
SQ FT: 19,932
SALES (est): 427MM **Privately Held**
WEB: www.driscolls.com
SIC: 5148 5431 Fruits, fresh; fruit & vegetable markets

(P-8671)
DRISCOLLS INC
150 Westridge Dr, Watsonville
(95076-6602)
PHONE..............................800 871-3333
Paul Cracknell, *Vice Pres*
Beverlee Parker, *Vice Pres*
Manuel Rosas, *Vice Pres*
Lisa Edmunds, *Admin Sec*
Chithra Mohanavelu, *Software Dev*
EMP: 75

SALES (corp-wide): 427MM **Privately Held**
SIC: 5148 Fruits, fresh
PA: Driscoll's, Inc.
345 Westridge Dr
Watsonville CA 95076
831 424-0506

(P-8672)
DRISCOLLS INC
1750 San Juan Rd, Aromas (95004-9027)
P.O. Box 50045, Watsonville (95077-5045)
PHONE..............................831 763-5100
Rick Reyes, *Branch Mgr*
Brian McElroy, *Sales Mgr*
EMP: 50
SALES (corp-wide): 427MM **Privately Held**
WEB: www.driscolls.com
SIC: 5148 Fruits, fresh
PA: Driscoll's, Inc.
345 Westridge Dr
Watsonville CA 95076
831 424-0506

(P-8673)
EARLS ORGANIC
Also Called: Earl's Organic Produce
2101 Jerrold Ave Ste 100, San Francisco
(94124-1009)
PHONE..............................415 824-7419
Earl Herrick, *Principal*
Vianney Trujillo, *Admin Asst*
Michele Smith-Jefferies, *Accounting Dir*
Robert Lichtenberg, *Purchasing*
Rodrigo Velasquez, *Buyer*
▲ EMP: 78
SALES: 50MM **Privately Held**
SIC: 5148 Fresh fruits & vegetables

(P-8674)
ECO FARMS SALES INC (PA)
28790 Las Haciendas St, Temecula
(92590-2614)
PHONE..............................951 694-3013
Steve Taft, *President*
Norman Traner, *Corp Secy*
▲ EMP: 100
SQ FT: 20,000
SALES (est): 24.6MM **Privately Held**
SIC: 5148 Fresh fruits & vegetables

(P-8675)
EVOLUTION FRESH INC (HQ)
Also Called: Evolution Juice
11655 Jersey Blvd, Rancho Cucamonga
(91730-4903)
PHONE..............................800 794-9986
Chris Bruzzo, *CEO*
James Rosenberg, *Ch of Bd*
Ricki Reves, *CFO*
▲ EMP: 65
SQ FT: 70,000
SALES (est): 250.9MM
SALES (corp-wide): 22.3B **Publicly Held**
SIC: 5148 2037 Fruits; vegetables, fresh; frozen fruits & vegetables
PA: Starbucks Corporation
2401 Utah Ave S
Seattle WA 98134
206 447-1575

(P-8676)
FAMILY TREE PRODUCE INC
5510 E La Palma Ave, Anaheim
(92807-2108)
PHONE..............................714 693-5688
Fidel Guzman, *President*
Christy Guzman, *Corp Secy*
Carlos Villa, *Accounts Exec*
EMP: 115
SQ FT: 33,000
SALES: 38.3MM **Privately Held**
WEB: www.ftproduce.com
SIC: 5148 Fruits, fresh; potatoes, fresh; vegetables, fresh

(P-8677)
FIELD FRESH FARMS LLC
320 Industrial Rd, Watsonville
(95076-5116)
P.O. Box 2731 (95077-2731)
PHONE..............................831 722-1422
Anthony Casnacci,
Cary Lee, *Opers Staff*
Michael Oliverio, *Sales Staff*

▲ = Import ▼=Export
◆ =Import/Export

Mike Dobler,
Robert Rossi,
EMP: 80
SQ FT: 66,000
SALES (est): 23.7MM **Privately Held**
SIC: 5148 Vegetables, fresh

(P-8678)
FRESHKO PRODUCE SERVICES INC
2155 E Muscat Ave, Fresno (93725-2326)
P.O. Box 11097 (93771-1097)
PHONE.............................559 497-7000
Manny Robles, *Principal*
Randall Shepherd, *Principal*
Manuel Robles,
EMP: 142
SQ FT: 47,000
SALES (est): 56.7MM
SALES (corp-wide): 28.2B **Privately Held**
WEB: www.freshkoproduce.com
SIC: 5148 5499 Fruits, fresh; juices, fruit or vegetable
PA: C&S Wholesale Grocers, Inc.
  7 Corporate Dr
  Keene NH 03431
  603 354-7000

(P-8679)
FRESHPOINT INC
30336 Whipple Rd, Union City (94587-1525)
PHONE.............................510 476-5900
Robert Gordon, *Branch Mgr*
EMP: 135
SALES (corp-wide): 58.7B **Publicly Held**
SIC: 5148 Fresh fruits & vegetables
HQ: Freshpoint, Inc.
  1390 Enclave Pkwy
  Houston TX 77077
-

(P-8680)
FRESHPOINT INC
Also Called: Freshpoint Las Vegas
155 N Orange Ave, City of Industry (91744-3432)
PHONE.............................626 855-1400
Terry Owen, *President*
Nathain Raymond, *Info Tech Dir*
Chris Sheilke, *Manager*
EMP: 136
SALES (corp-wide): 58.7B **Publicly Held**
SIC: 5148 Fresh fruits & vegetables
HQ: Freshpoint, Inc.
  1390 Enclave Pkwy
  Houston TX 77077

(P-8681)
FRESHPOINT CENTRAL CALIFORNIA
5900 N Golden State Blvd, Turlock (95382-9671)
PHONE.............................209 216-0200
Brian M Sturgeon, *President*
Jeffrey A Sacchini, *CEO*
Melissa Gaffaney, *Purchasing*
Bob McKelvey, *Transportation*
EMP: 150
SQ FT: 54,000
SALES (est): 53.4MM
SALES (corp-wide): 58.7B **Publicly Held**
WEB: www.piranhaproduce.com
SIC: 5148 Fresh fruits & vegetables
HQ: Freshpoint, Inc.
  1390 Enclave Pkwy
  Houston TX 77077

(P-8682)
FRESHPOINT SOUTHERN CAL INC
Also Called: Freshpoint Southern California
155 N Orange Ave, City of Industry (91744-3432)
PHONE.............................626 855-1400
Verne L Lusby Jr, *CEO*
Jeff Ronk, *Exec VP*
Jon Greco, *Vice Pres*
Luis Garcia, *Sales Executive*
Joel Barker, *Director*
EMP: 208 **EST:** 1921
SQ FT: 97,000

SALES (est): 98.8MM
SALES (corp-wide): 58.7B **Publicly Held**
WEB: www.theproducehunter.com
SIC: 5148 Fruits, vegetables, fresh; packaged frozen goods
PA: Sysco Corporation
  1390 Enclave Pkwy
  Houston TX 77077
  281 584-1390

(P-8683)
FRIEDAS INC
Also Called: Friedas Specialty Produce
4465 Corporate Center Dr, Los Alamitos (90720-2561)
PHONE.............................714 733-7655
Karen Caplan, *President*
Jackie Caplan Wiggins, *COO*
Tom Kieran, *Executive*
Linda Frankel, *Executive Asst*
Brittany Laukat, *Human Res Mgr*
▲ **EMP:** 80
SQ FT: 81,306
SALES (est): 62.4MM **Privately Held**
WEB: www.friedas.com
SIC: 5148 Vegetables, fresh; fruits, fresh

(P-8684)
FRUIT GUYS
4465 Corporate Center Dr, Los Alamitos (90720-2540)
PHONE.............................714 826-2993
Nicole Joseph, *General Mgr*
EMP: 60 **EST:** 2014
SALES (est): 3.7MM **Privately Held**
SIC: 5148 Fruits

(P-8685)
FRUIT PATCH SALES LLC
38773 Road 48, Dinuba (93618-9718)
PHONE.............................559 591-1170
Dennis Bergquist, *Mng Member*
Doug Reader, *Treasurer*
William L Byers,
Jim Gallagher,
Scott Wallace,
▼ **EMP:** 500
SQ FT: 3,000
SALES (est): 162.5MM **Privately Held**
SIC: 5148 Fruits

(P-8686)
GALLI PRODUCE COMPANY
1650 Old Bayshore Hwy, San Jose (95112-4304)
P.O. Box 612620 (95161-2620)
PHONE.............................408 436-6100
Gerald Pieracci, *President*
Kristin Killin, *Corp Secy*
Jeff Pieracci, *Vice Pres*
Dennis Tinucci, *Vice Pres*
Joseph Vanni, *Vice Pres*
EMP: 60
SQ FT: 10,000
SALES (est): 22.3MM **Privately Held**
WEB: www.galliproduce.com
SIC: 5148 5142 Fruits, fresh; vegetables, fresh; fruits, frozen; vegetables, frozen

(P-8687)
GENERAL PROD A CAL LTD PARTNR (PA)
1330 N B St, Sacramento (95811-0605)
P.O. Box 308 (95812-0308)
PHONE.............................916 441-6431
Tom Chan, *CEO*
Dan Chan, *President*
Don Weersing, *Vice Pres*
Sheryl Weichert, *Vice Pres*
▼ **EMP:** 200 **EST:** 1933
SQ FT: 110,000
SALES (est): 99.9MM **Privately Held**
WEB: www.generalproduce.com
SIC: 5148 Fruits, fresh; vegetables, fresh

(P-8688)
GILLS ONIONS LLC
1051 Pacific Ave, Oxnard (93030-7254)
PHONE.............................805 240-1983
Steve Gill, *Mng Member*
Jaime Cota, *Purchasing*
Arturo Coronado, *Plant Mgr*
Teri Trost, *Regl Sales Mgr*
Oscar Guzman, *Sales Mgr*
▲ **EMP:** 55

SALES (est): 34MM **Privately Held**
WEB: www.gillsonions.com
SIC: 5148 Fresh fruits & vegetables

(P-8689)
GIUMARRA BROS FRUIT CO INC (PA)
Also Called: Giumarra International Berry
1601 E Olympic Blvd # 408, Los Angeles (90021-1943)
P.O. Box 861449 (90086-1449)
PHONE.............................213 627-2900
Donald Corsaro, *CEO*
John Corsaro, *President*
John Giumarra Jr, *Treasurer*
Tom Richardson, *Manager*
◆ **EMP:** 74
SQ FT: 8,000
SALES (est): 67.9MM **Privately Held**
WEB: www.giumarra.com
SIC: 5148 Fresh fruits & vegetables

(P-8690)
GOURMET SPECIALTIES INC
2120 E 25th St, Vernon (90058-1126)
PHONE.............................323 587-1734
Abundio Ruiz, *CEO*
Michelle Medina, *Office Mgr*
EMP: 75
SALES (est): 8.2MM **Privately Held**
SIC: 5148 Fresh fruits & vegetables

(P-8691)
GREEN FARMS INC
Also Called: Worldwide Produce
2652 Long Beach Ave, Los Angeles (90058-1323)
PHONE.............................858 831-7701
Abbas Ghulam, *Branch Mgr*
EMP: 286 **Privately Held**
SIC: 5148 Fresh fruits & vegetables
PA: Green Farms, Inc.
  2652 Long Beach Ave Ste 2
  Los Angeles CA 90058

(P-8692)
GREEN FARMS INC (PA)
Also Called: Worldwide Produce
2652 Long Beach Ave Ste 2, Los Angeles (90058-1323)
P.O. Box 54399 (90054-0399)
PHONE.............................213 747-4411
Stuart Weisfeld, *CEO*
Ghulam Abbas, *President*
Ron Warenkiewicz, *CFO*
Laura Ramos, *General Mgr*
Silvia Macias, *Human Res Mgr*
EMP: 114
SQ FT: 150
SALES (est): 297MM **Privately Held**
WEB: www.worldwideproduce.com
SIC: 5148 Fresh fruits & vegetables

(P-8693)
GREEN THUMB PRODUCE
2648 W Ramsey St, Banning (92220-3716)
P.O. Box 1357 (92220-0010)
PHONE.............................951 849-4711
Lonnie Saverino, *President*
Michael Ingalls, *Vice Pres*
Jeff Young, *Buyer*
Brent Portell, *Sales Staff*
Darrell Scriven, *Supervisor*
EMP: 250
SALES (est): 83.2MM **Privately Held**
SIC: 5148 Fresh fruits & vegetables

(P-8694)
GRIMMWAY ENTERPRISES INC
Also Called: Cal-Organic Farms
12000 Main St, Lamont (93241-2836)
P.O. Box 81498, Bakersfield (93380-1498)
PHONE.............................661 845-3758
Roodzant Steve, *General Mgr*
Rhonda Perez, *Admin Asst*
Maria Quiroz, *Purchasing*
Imelda Vidaurri, *Production*
EMP: 364
SALES (corp-wide): 2.1B **Privately Held**
SIC: 5148 Vegetables, fresh
PA: Grimmway Enterprises, Inc.
  14141 Di Giorgio Rd
  Arvin CA 93203
  800 301-3101

(P-8695)
GROWERS EXPRESS LLC (PA)
150 Main St Ste 210, Salinas (93901-3439)
P.O. Box 948 (93902-0948)
PHONE.............................831 757-9951
David L Gill, *Mng Member*
Chris Pollard, *Manager*
▼ **EMP:** 400
SQ FT: 10,000
SALES (est): 125.2MM **Privately Held**
SIC: 5148 Vegetables

(P-8696)
INDEX FRESH INC (PA)
3880 Lemon St Ste 210, Riverside (92501-3355)
PHONE.............................909 877-0999
Dana L Thomas, *President*
Stephen Miller, *Vice Chairman*
Giovanni Cavaletto, *COO*
Merrill Causey, *CFO*
Lorena Dominguez, *Vice Pres*
◆ **EMP:** 52
SQ FT: 40,000
SALES (est): 199.9MM **Privately Held**
WEB: www.indexfresh.com
SIC: 5148 Fresh fruits & vegetables

(P-8697)
JACK H CALDWELL & SONS INC
Also Called: Choice Pak Products
4035 E 52nd St, Maywood (90270-2205)
PHONE.............................323 589-4008
Harry Caldwell, *President*
Duke Caldwell, *Vice Pres*
Ana Baldridge, *Mktg Dir*
EMP: 60
SQ FT: 5,000
SALES (est): 35.7MM **Privately Held**
SIC: 5148 Vegetables, fresh

(P-8698)
JHP PRODUCE INC
1601 E Olympic Blvd # 200, Los Angeles (90021-1936)
PHONE.............................213 627-1093
Chuck Johnson, *President*
Breccia Hellman, *Shareholder*
Tracy Hellman, *Corp Secy*
Justin Layton, *Sales Staff*
Susan Steinberg, *Manager*
EMP: 55
SQ FT: 21,000
SALES (est): 15.6MM **Privately Held**
SIC: 5148 Vegetables; potatoes, fresh; vegetables, fresh; fruits, fresh

(P-8699)
KINGSBURG APPLE PACKERS INC
Also Called: Kingsburg Orchards
10363 Davis Ave, Kingsburg (93631-9539)
P.O. Box 38 (93631-0038)
PHONE.............................559 897-5132
George H Jackson, *President*
Colleen Jackson, *Treasurer*
Becky Stark, *Controller*
Brian Keavy, *Export Mgr*
Ken Okajima, *Marketing Staff*
◆ **EMP:** 450
SQ FT: 10,000
SALES (est): 137.3MM **Privately Held**
SIC: 5148 Fruits, fresh

(P-8700)
LA SPECIALTY PRODUCE CO (PA)
Also Called: San Fransisco Speciality Prod
13527 Orden Dr, Santa Fe Springs (90670-6338)
P.O. Box 2293 (90670-0293)
PHONE.............................562 741-2200
Michael Glick, *President*
Kathleen Glick, *Vice Pres*
Scotty Matthews, *Vice Pres*
Joycee Del Toro, *Executive*
Hector Lopez, *Controller*
EMP: 475
SQ FT: 188,000
SALES (est): 221.8MM **Privately Held**
WEB: www.laspecialtyproduce.com
SIC: 5148 Fruits, fresh

(P-8701)
LEGACY FARMS LLC
6625 Caballero Blvd, Buena Park
(90620-1131)
PHONE..................714 736-1800
Nick Cancellieri,
Rick Baxter, *Principal*
Vince Mendoza, *Principal*
Ron Shimizu, *Principal*
Wally Sinner, *Principal*
▲ EMP: 120
SQ FT: 95,000
SALES (est): 70.9MM **Privately Held**
SIC: 5148 Fruits, fresh

(P-8702)
**LIBERTY PACKING COMPANY
LLC (PA)**
Also Called: Morning Star Company The
724 Main St, Woodland (95695-3491)
PHONE..................209 826-7100
Chris Rufer,
▲ EMP: 96
SALES (est): 130.3MM **Privately Held**
SIC: 5148 2033 Vegetables; tomato prod-
ucts: packaged in cans, jars, etc.

(P-8703)
LJ DISTRIBUTORS INC
Also Called: Team Tomato
12840 Leyva St, Norwalk (90650-6852)
P.O. Box 610, Bellflower (90707-0610)
PHONE..................562 229-7660
Lute Miyazaki, *President*
Marlene Castro, *Vice Pres*
◆ EMP: 54
SQ FT: 115,000
SALES (est): 13.1MM **Privately Held**
WEB: www.teamtomato.com
SIC: 5148 Fruits; vegetables

(P-8704)
LOEWY ENTERPRISES
Also Called: Sunrise Produce Company
500 Burning Tree Rd, Fullerton
(92833-1400)
PHONE..................323 726-3838
Paul Carone, *President*
EMP: 90
SQ FT: 41,000
SALES (est): 67.8MM **Privately Held**
SIC: 5148 Fruits, fresh

(P-8705)
MISSION PRODUCE INC
3803 Dufau Rd, Oxnard (93033-8296)
P.O. Box 5267 (93031-5267)
PHONE..................805 981-3650
Steven J Barnard, *President*
Stephanie McKeown, *QC Mgr*
David Hall, *Manager*
Olga Hernandez, *Manager*
EMP: 75
SALES (corp-wide): 246.8MM **Privately
Held**
WEB: www.missionpro.com
SIC: 5148 Fruits, fresh
PA: Mission Produce, Inc.
2500 E Vineyard Ave # 300
Oxnard CA 93036
805 981-3650

(P-8706)
MONSANTO COMPANY
37437 State Highway 16, Woodland
(95695-9353)
PHONE..................530 669-6224
Rusty Myer, *Branch Mgr*
Rebeca Benitez, *Research*
Francine Dickie, *Research*
Carl Jones, *Research*
Terry Berke, *Associate*
EMP: 300
SALES (corp-wide): 41.2B **Privately Held**
SIC: 5148 Vegetables
HQ: Monsanto Company
800 N Lindbergh Blvd
Saint Louis MO 63167
314 694-1000

(P-8707)
**MOONLIGHT PACKING
CORPORATION (PA)**
Also Called: Moonlight Companies
17719 E Huntsman Ave, Reedley
(93654-9205)
P.O. Box 846 (93654-0846)
PHONE..................559 638-7799
Russell Tavlan, *President*
Ty Tavlan, *CFO*
Jay Reimer, *Info Tech Dir*
Teresa Jimenez, *Finance*
Leonor Lopez, *Human Resources*
EMP: 185
SQ FT: 80,000
SALES (est): 485.7MM **Privately Held**
WEB: www.moonlightcompanies.com
SIC: 5148 4783 Fruits, fresh; packing &
crating

(P-8708)
NATURES PRODUCE COMPANY
3305 Bandini Blvd, Vernon (90058-4130)
P.O. Box 58366 (90058-0366)
PHONE..................323 235-4343
Rick Polisky, *CEO*
Irene Perez, *Office Mgr*
Jenny Nguyen, *Controller*
Michael Feuerstein, *Sales Dir*
Blake Polisky, *Sales Staff*
▲ EMP: 80
SALES (est): 47.4MM **Privately Held**
WEB: www.naturesproducecompany.com
SIC: 5148 Fruits, fresh

(P-8709)
NOR-CAL PRODUCE INC
2995 Oates St, West Sacramento
(95691-5902)
P.O. Box 980188 (95798-0188)
PHONE..................916 373-0830
Todd Achondo, *CEO*
▼ EMP: 130
SQ FT: 85,000
SALES (est): 57.6MM **Publicly Held**
WEB: www.nor-calproduce.com
SIC: 5148 Fruits, fresh
PA: United Natural Foods, Inc.
313 Iron Horse Way
Providence RI 02908

(P-8710)
NUNES COMPANY INC (PA)
Also Called: Foxy
925 Johnson Ave, Salinas (93901-4327)
P.O. Box 673 (93902-0673)
PHONE..................831 751-7510
Tom P Nunes Jr, *CEO*
Mike Scarr, *CFO*
Enos Barera, *Treasurer*
Mark Crossgrove, *Vice Pres*
Bob Nunes, *Vice Pres*
▼ EMP: 50 EST: 1976
SALES (est): 38.5MM **Privately Held**
WEB: www.foxy.com
SIC: 5148 Vegetables

(P-8711)
**OAKVILLE PRODUCE
PARTNERS LLC**
Also Called: Greenleaf
453 Valley Dr, Brisbane (94005-1209)
PHONE..................415 647-2991
William F Wilkinson, *Mng Member*
Frank Ballentine, *President*
Mark Natividad, *Finance Dir*
Huy Tran, *Credit Mgr*
Rocky Martini, *Sales Staff*
EMP: 150
SQ FT: 32,000
SALES (est): 110.5MM **Privately Held**
WEB: www.greenleafsf.com
SIC: 5148 5451 Fruits, fresh; vegetables,
fresh; dairy products stores

(P-8712)
PACIFIC COAST PRODUCE INC
950 Mountain View Ave # 1, Oxnard
(93030-6201)
PHONE..................805 240-3385
Carlos Marez, *CEO*
Uvence Cortez, *Treasurer*
Maribelle Cortez, *Vice Pres*
EMP: 50

SQ FT: 16,000
SALES (est): 25.5MM **Privately Held**
WEB: www.pacificcoastproduce.com
SIC: 5148 5149 5812 5142 Fruits, fresh;
canned goods: fruit, vegetables, seafood,
meats, etc.; contract food services; frozen
fish, meat & poultry; frozen dairy desserts

(P-8713)
**PACIFIC INTL VGETABLE MKTG
INC (PA)**
Also Called: Pacific International Mktg
740 Airport Blvd, Salinas (93901-4510)
P.O. Box 3737 (93912-3737)
PHONE..................831 422-3745
Dave L Johnson, *CEO*
David Black, *Vice Pres*
Steve Tripp, *Admin Sec*
Veronica Urzua, *Human Res Dir*
Robert Perez, *Human Res Mgr*
◆ EMP: 75
SQ FT: 1,800
SALES: 35.1MM **Privately Held**
WEB: www.purepacificorganic.com
SIC: 5148 Fresh fruits & vegetables

(P-8714)
**PACIFIC TRELLIS FRUIT LLC
(PA)**
Also Called: DULCINEA FARMS
2301 E 7th St Ste C200, Los Angeles
(90023-1041)
PHONE..................323 859-9600
Linda Chen,
David Sullivan,
▲ EMP: 130
SQ FT: 10,000
SALES: 187.8MM **Privately Held**
WEB: www.pacifictrellisfruit.com
SIC: 5148 Fruits, fresh

(P-8715)
PANDOL BROS INC (PA)
33150 Pond Rd, Delano (93215-9804)
PHONE..................661 725-3755
Cheri Diebel, *CEO*
Louis Pandol, *Ch of Bd*
Matt Pandol, *CFO*
Frank Calzo, *Data Proc Dir*
Stewart Shavinsky, *Controller*
◆ EMP: 103
SQ FT: 10,000
SALES: 29.7MM **Privately Held**
WEB: www.pandol.com
SIC: 5148 Fruits, fresh; vegetables, fresh

(P-8716)
**PARAMOUNT EXPORT
COMPANY**
5875 Lamas St, San Diego (92122-3146)
PHONE..................858 452-8101
James Galagan, *Principal*
EMP: 55
SALES (corp-wide): 76.6MM **Privately
Held**
SIC: 5148 5149 Fruits, fresh; specialty
food items
PA: Paramount Export Company
175 Filbert St Ste 201
Oakland CA 94607
510 839-0150

(P-8717)
PREMIER MUSHROOMS LP (PA)
2880 Niagara Ave, Colusa (95932)
PHONE..................530 458-2700
John Ashbaugh, *Partner*
Rex Pugh, *CFO*
▲ EMP: 170
SQ FT: 10,000
SALES (est): 96.3MM **Privately Held**
SIC: 5148 Fresh fruits & vegetables

(P-8718)
**PRIMETIME INTERNATIONAL
INC**
86705 Avenue 54 Ste A, Coachella
(92236-3814)
PHONE..................760 399-4166
Carl Sam Maggio, *CEO*
Mark Nickerson, *Mng Member*
Jeff Taylor, *Mng Member*
Mike Way, *Mng Member*
▲ EMP: 95
SQ FT: 4,000

SALES: 200MM
SALES (corp-wide): 123.9MM **Privately
Held**
WEB: www.primetimeproduce.com
SIC: 5148 4783 Vegetables, fresh; pack-
ing goods for shipping
PA: Sun And Sands Enterprises, Llc
86705 Avenue 54 Ste A
Coachella CA 92236
760 399-4278

(P-8719)
PRO ACT LLC
40 Ragsdale Dr Ste 200, Monterey
(93940-5774)
PHONE..................831 655-4250
Max Yeater, *CEO*
Lloyd Ligier, *President*
Steve Grinstead, *CEO*
Bob Kiehnle, *CFO*
Dave Peterson, *Senior VP*
▲ EMP: 80
SALES (est): 55.4MM **Privately Held**
WEB: www.proactusa.com
SIC: 5148 Vegetables

(P-8720)
PRODUCE COMPANY
Also Called: Finest Produce
16809 Bellflower Blvd # 32, Bellflower
(90706-5901)
PHONE..................310 508-7760
Edward L Puppo, *President*
Steven Morris, *Vice Pres*
EMP: 130
SQ FT: 2,000
SALES: 5.5MM **Privately Held**
SIC: 5148 Fresh fruits & vegetables

(P-8721)
**PRODUCE EXCHANGE
INCORPORATED (DH)**
7407 Southfront Rd, Livermore
(94551-8224)
PHONE..................925 454-8700
Marty Mazzanti, *Manager*
Samuel E Jones Jr, *President*
Carrie Barnes, *Administration*
Anna Melo, *Buyer*
Craig Beecher, *Manager*
▲ EMP: 65
SQ FT: 10,000
SALES (est): 10MM
SALES (corp-wide): 188.2MM **Privately
Held**
WEB: www.tpemail.com
SIC: 5148 Fruits, fresh; vegetables
HQ: Lipman-Texas, Llc
315 New Market Rd E
Immokalee FL 34142
239 657-4421

(P-8722)
PROFESSIONAL PRODUCE
2570 E 25th St, Los Angeles (90058-1211)
P.O. Box 58308 (90058-0308)
PHONE..................323 277-1550
Ted Kaplan, *CEO*
Maribel Reyes, *CFO*
Patricia Gonzalez, *Human Resources*
Michael Gaskins, *Sales Executive*
Kevin Oliphant, *Manager*
◆ EMP: 99
SQ FT: 5,000
SALES (est): 76MM **Privately Held**
WEB: www.profproduce.com
SIC: 5148 Fruits, fresh

(P-8723)
**PROGRESSIVE PRODUCE LLC
(HQ)**
Also Called: Progressive Marketing Group
5790 Peachtree St, Commerce
(90040-4000)
PHONE..................323 890-8100
James K Leimkuhler, *President*
Ralph Heimann, *CFO*
Jack Gyben, *Vice Pres*
Don Hessel, *General Mgr*
Jaclyn Rodgers, *Executive Asst*
▲ EMP: 104
SQ FT: 106,000

SALES (est): 72.9MM **Privately Held**
WEB: www.progressiveproduce.com
SIC: **5148** 4213 7389 Fruits, fresh; vegetables, fresh; refrigerated products transport; packaging & labeling services

(P-8724)
REGATTA TROPICALS LTD (PA)
1742 Manhattan Ave Ste C, Grover Beach (93433-2500)
PHONE.................................805 473-1320
Steven J Matych, *President*
Teresa Barnes-Matych, *Corp Secy*
◆ EMP: 80
SQ FT: 1,000
SALES (est): 57.1MM **Privately Held**
SIC: **5148** Fruits, fresh

(P-8725)
RIVER RANCH FRESH FOODS LLC (HQ)
911 Blanco Cir Ste B, Salinas (93901-4449)
PHONE.................................831 758-1390
Bruce Knobeloch, *CEO*
John Bowman, *President*
Tom Welch, *CFO*
Ped Mills,
Brian Thure,
▲ EMP: 450
SALES (est): 136.7MM **Privately Held**
WEB: www.rrff.com
SIC: **5148** Vegetables, fresh

(P-8726)
SAMBAZON INC (PA)
209 Avenida Fabricante # 200, San Clemente (92672-7544)
PHONE.................................877 726-2296
Ryan Black, *CEO*
Bruce Peasland, *CFO*
Jeremy Black, *Vice Pres*
Ed Nichols, *Vice Pres*
Travis Baumgardner, *Director*
◆ EMP: 60
SQ FT: 10,000
SALES (est): 51.1MM **Privately Held**
WEB: www.sambazon.com
SIC: **5148** 5499 Fruits; juices, fruit or vegetable

(P-8727)
SEASON PRODUCE CO INC
1601 E Olympic Blvd # 315, Los Angeles (90021-1942)
PHONE.................................213 689-0008
Patrick R Horwath, *President*
Daniel Horwath, *Vice Pres*
Timothy R Horwath, *Vice Pres*
EMP: 342
SQ FT: 20,000
SALES (est): 78.1MM
SALES (corp-wide): 78.6MM **Privately Held**
WEB: www.s-hpacking.com
SIC: **5148** Fresh fruits & vegetables
PA: S & H Packing & Sales Co., Inc.
2590 Harriet St
Vernon CA 90058
323 581-7172

(P-8728)
SEQUOIA ENTERPRISES INC
Also Called: Sequoia Orange
150 W Pine St, Exeter (93221-1613)
PHONE.................................559 592-9455
James Wilson, *CEO*
Marvin L Wilson, *President*
▼ EMP: 70 EST: 1975
SQ FT: 5,100
SALES (est): 16.6MM **Privately Held**
SIC: **5148** Fruits, fresh

(P-8729)
SGF PRODUCE HOLDING CORP
701 W Kimberly Ave # 210, Placentia (92870-6342)
PHONE.................................714 630-6292
Ed Haft, *CEO*
Joe McCarthy, *CFO*
EMP: 360 EST: 2008
SALES (est): 56.2MM **Privately Held**
SIC: **5148** 2037 0191 Fruits; vegetables; frozen fruits & vegetables; general farms, primarily crop

(P-8730)
SHAPIRO-GILMAN-SHANDLER CO (PA)
Also Called: S G S Produce
739 Decatur St, Los Angeles (90021-1649)
PHONE.................................213 593-1200
Carol C Shandler, *President*
Muriel Shandler, *Vice Pres*
Morris Shander, *Principal*
▲ EMP: 101
SQ FT: 50,000
SALES (est): 37.9MM **Privately Held**
WEB: www.sgsproduce.com
SIC: **5148** Fruits, fresh; vegetables

(P-8731)
SOUTHERN FRESH PROD PROVS INC
11954 Washington Blvd, Whittier (90606-2608)
PHONE.................................562 236-2784
Daniel Meza, *President*
Daniel Silverman, *CFO*
Naomi Silverman, *Treasurer*
Sanford Deutsch, *Vice Pres*
Tracey Goldstein, *Admin Sec*
EMP: 65
SALES (est): 29.9MM **Privately Held**
SIC: **5148** Fresh fruits & vegetables

(P-8732)
STELLAR DISTRIBUTING INC
21801 Ave Ste 16, Madera (93637)
PHONE.................................559 664-8400
Paul Catania Jr, *President*
Robert Farnam, *CFO*
Connie Gil, *Purchasing*
Nick Cappelluti, *Sales Staff*
Kurt Cappelluti, *Manager*
◆ EMP: 350
SQ FT: 30,000
SALES (est): 61.6MM **Privately Held**
WEB: www.stellardistributing.com
SIC: **5148** Vegetables, fresh; fruits, fresh

(P-8733)
SUN PACIFIC MARKETING COOP INC (PA)
1095 E Green St, Pasadena (91106-2503)
PHONE.................................213 612-9957
Berne H Evans III, *CEO*
Barney Evans, *President*
Adam Smith, *CFO*
Robert Reniers, *Treasurer*
▲ EMP: 1600
SQ FT: 7,000
SALES (est): 221.8MM **Privately Held**
SIC: **5148** Fresh fruits & vegetables

(P-8734)
SUN PACIFIC MARKETING COOP INC
Also Called: Sun Pacific Farming
31452 Old River Rd, Bakersfield (93311-9621)
PHONE.................................661 847-1015
Bob Dipiazza, *Branch Mgr*
Chris Bradley, *Controller*
EMP: 316
SALES (corp-wide): 221.8MM **Privately Held**
SIC: **5148** Fresh fruits & vegetables
PA: Sun Pacific Marketing Cooperative, Inc.
1095 E Green St
Pasadena CA 91106
213 612-9957

(P-8735)
SUNBERRY GROWERS LLC
2224 Westgate Rd, Santa Maria (93455-1028)
PHONE.................................805 922-9888
Carlos Ramirez, *Mng Member*
EMP: 991
SALES (est): 28.1MM
SALES (corp-wide): 85MM **Privately Held**
SIC: **5148** Fresh fruits & vegetables
PA: Ramco Enterprises, L.P.
710 La Guardia St
Salinas CA 93905
831 758-5272

(P-8736)
SUNKIST GROWERS INC (PA)
27770 Entertainment Dr # 120, Valencia (91355-1093)
PHONE.................................661 290-8900
Russell Hanlin II, *President*
Richard G French, *CFO*
Terra Jacobs, *CFO*
Michael Wootton, *Senior VP*
Russell L Hanlin II, *Vice Pres*
◆ EMP: 223 EST: 1893
SQ FT: 50,000
SALES (est): 1.3B **Privately Held**
WEB: www.sunkist.com
SIC: **5148** 2033 2037 2899 Fruits, fresh; fruit juices: packaged in cans, jars, etc.; fruit juice concentrates, frozen; lemon oil (edible); orange oil; grapefruit oil; copyright buying & licensing; display equipment, except refrigerated

(P-8737)
SUNRISE GROWERS INC (HQ)
Also Called: Sunrise Growers-Frozsun Foods
701 W Kimberly Ave # 210, Placentia (92870-6354)
PHONE.................................714 630-2170
Edward Haft, *President*
Joe McCarthy, *CFO*
Maria Gonzalez, *General Mgr*
◆ EMP: 300
SALES (est): 341MM
SALES (corp-wide): 1.2B **Privately Held**
WEB: www.frozsun.com
SIC: **5148** 2037 Fruits, fresh; frozen fruits & vegetables
PA: Sunopta Inc
2233 Argentia Rd Suite 401
Mississauga ON L5N 2
905 821-9669

(P-8738)
TOMATOES EXTRAORDINAIRE INC
Also Called: Specialty Produce
1929 Hancock St Ste 150, San Diego (92110-2062)
P.O. Box 82066 (92138-2066)
PHONE.................................619 295-3172
Robert Harrington, *President*
Richard Harrington, *Vice Pres*
Alan Guevara, *Technology*
Janet Harrington, *Accountant*
David Johnson, *Buyer*
EMP: 150
SQ FT: 26,000
SALES (est): 73.6MM **Privately Held**
SIC: **5148** Fresh fruits & vegetables

(P-8739)
UMINA BROS INC (PA)
1601 E Olympic Blvd # 403, Los Angeles (90021-1943)
P.O. Box 861146 (90086-1146)
PHONE.................................213 622-9206
Richard Flamminio, *President*
Mark Golden, *Vice Pres*
Vic Grosso, *Executive*
Matt Beltran, *General Mgr*
Janice Quan, *Safety Dir*
◆ EMP: 100
SQ FT: 24,800
SALES (est): 54.6MM **Privately Held**
SIC: **5148** Fruits, fresh

(P-8740)
V & L PRODUCE INC
Also Called: General Produce
2550 E 25th St, Vernon (90058-1211)
PHONE.................................323 589-3125
Victor Mendoza, *President*
▲ EMP: 140
SQ FT: 12,000
SALES (est): 61.5MM **Privately Held**
SIC: **5148** Fresh fruits & vegetables

(P-8741)
VAL-PRO INC
Also Called: Continental Sales Co.
1661 Mcgarry St, Los Angeles (90021-3116)
PHONE.................................213 689-0844
Joe Vidal, *Branch Mgr*
EMP: 60

SALES (corp-wide): 202.8MM **Privately Held**
SIC: **5148** Fruits, fresh
PA: Val-Pro, Inc.
1601 E Olympic Blvd # 300
Los Angeles CA 90021
213 627-8736

(P-8742)
VEG-FRESH FARMS LLC
1400 W Rincon St, Corona (92880-9205)
PHONE.................................800 422-5535
Lawrence Cancellieri Jr,
Mark Resnikoff,
Mark C Widder,
EMP: 220
SQ FT: 94,000
SALES (est): 189.6MM **Privately Held**
WEB: www.vegfresh.com
SIC: **5148** Vegetables, fresh; fruits

(P-8743)
VEGIWORKS INC
2101 Jerrold Ave, San Francisco (94124-1009)
PHONE.................................415 643-8686
Shing Ho, *CFO*
Calvin Leong, *Vice Pres*
Phillip Woo, *Admin Sec*
EMP: 65
SQ FT: 16,000
SALES (est): 27.9MM **Privately Held**
WEB: www.vegiworks.com
SIC: **5148** Fresh fruits & vegetables

(P-8744)
VERITABLE VEGETABLE INC
1100 Cesar Chavez, San Francisco (94124-1214)
PHONE.................................415 641-3500
Maryjane Evans, *President*
Gerilyn Botting, *CFO*
Mary J Evans, *General Mgr*
Terina McCraw, *Admin Sec*
Ruth Lalputan, *Administration*
EMP: 57
SQ FT: 8,000
SALES (est): 38.5MM **Privately Held**
WEB: www.veritablevegetable.com
SIC: **5148** Fruits, fresh; vegetables

(P-8745)
WATSONVILLE COAST PRODUCE INC
275 Kearney Ext Frnt, Watsonville (95076-4463)
P.O. Box 490 (95077-0490)
PHONE.................................831 722-3851
Gary L Manfre, *CEO*
Douglas Peterson, *Treasurer*
John Burkett, *Vice Pres*
Frank L Capurro, *Vice Pres*
Sergio Gomez, *Human Res Mgr*
EMP: 105
SQ FT: 40,000
SALES: 31MM **Privately Held**
SIC: **5148** Fresh fruits & vegetables

(P-8746)
WEST CENTRAL PRODUCE INC
Also Called: West Central Food Service
12840 Leyva St, Norwalk (90650-6852)
PHONE.................................213 629-3600
Michael Dodo, *CEO*
Lance Shiring, *COO*
Jamie Purcell, *CFO*
Bryson Igarta, *Mktg Dir*
▲ EMP: 400
SQ FT: 34,000
SALES (est): 171.5MM **Privately Held**
WEB: www.westcentralproduce.com
SIC: **5148** 5147 5149 5146 Fresh fruits & vegetables; meats & meat products; dairy products, dried or canned; seafoods

(P-8747)
WIEMAR DISTRIBUTORS INC
Also Called: M & M Distributors
1953 S Alameda St, Los Angeles (90058-1013)
PHONE.................................213 747-7036
Marco Moreno, *President*
Rosa Moreno, *Vice Pres*
Margarita Orduno, *Controller*
▲ EMP: 65
SQ FT: 31,000

(PA)=Parent Co (HQ)=Headquarters (DH)=Div Headquarters
✪ = New Business established in last 2 years

2019 Directory of California
Wholesalers and Services Companies

PRODUCTS & SVCS

377

SALES: 34.6MM **Privately Held**
WEB: www.mmdistributors.org
SIC: 5148 Fruits, fresh

(P-8748)
WILLIAM BRAMMER
Also Called: Be Wise Ranch
20505 San Pasqual Rd, Escondido
(92025-7821)
PHONE..........................760 746-6006
William Brammer, *Owner*
EMP: 115
SALES (est): 12.5MM **Privately Held**
WEB: www.bewiseranch.com
SIC: 5148 0161 Fresh fruits & vegetables;
vegetables & melons

(P-8749)
WORLD VARIETY PRODUCE INC
Also Called: Melissas World Variety Produce
5325 S Soto St, Vernon (90058-3624)
P.O. Box 514599, Los Angeles (90051-
2599)
PHONE..........................800 588-0151
Anna Raya, *Principal*
Joe V Hernandez, *President*
Sharon Hernandez, *Corp Secy*
Samuel Rodriguez, *Executive*
Matt Bergholz, *Regional Mgr*
▲ EMP: 325
SQ FT: 244,000
SALES (est): 205.9MM **Privately Held**
SIC: 5148 Fruits, fresh

5149 Groceries & Related Prdts, NEC Wholesale

(P-8750)
ALHAMBRA/SIERRA SPRINGS
485 Vista Way, Milpitas (95035-5405)
PHONE..........................408 727-0677
K Dillion Schickli, *Principal*
EMP: 99
SALES: 950K **Privately Held**
SIC: 5149 Groceries & related products

(P-8751)
ALLIED FOOD DISTRIBUTORS INC
1225 California Ave, Pittsburg
(94565-4112)
P.O. Box 1510, Los Altos (94023-1510)
PHONE..........................925 432-1625
James G Scharetg, *President*
Jeffrey Scharetg, *Vice Pres*
▲ EMP: 60 EST: 1973
SQ FT: 80,000
SALES (est): 5.6MM **Privately Held**
SIC: 5149 Canned goods: fruit, vegetables,
seafood, meats, etc.

(P-8752)
ANNIES HOMEGROWN INC
1610 5th St, Berkeley (94710-1715)
PHONE..........................510 558-7500
John Foraker, *CEO*
Stephen Palmer, *Admin Sec*
David Tran, *VP Sales*
Jocy Upton, *VP Sales*
Sandy Cortez, *Manager*
▼ EMP: 75
SQ FT: 10,000
SALES (est): 18.4MM
SALES (corp-wide): 15.7B **Publicly Held**
SIC: 5149 Natural & organic foods
HQ: Annie's, Inc.
1610 5th St
Berkeley CA 94710

(P-8753)
APP WHOLESALE LLC
3686 E Olympic Blvd, Los Angeles
(90023-3146)
PHONE..........................323 980-3746
David Weissberg,
EMP: 500 EST: 2013
SQ FT: 220,000
SALES (est): 217MM **Privately Held**
SIC: 5149 2741 Specialty food items;
business service newsletters: publishing
& printing

(P-8754)
ARCHER-DANIELS-MIDLAND COMPANY
ADM
3390 S Chestnut Ave, Fresno
(93725-2609)
PHONE..........................559 233-6262
Bob Rogers, *Plant Mgr*
Miguel Perez, *Director*
EMP: 80
SQ FT: 25,000
SALES (corp-wide): 60.8B **Publicly Held**
WEB: www.admworld.com
SIC: 5149 2041 Oleomargarine; pancake
batter, frozen or refrigerated
PA: Archer-Daniels-Midland Company
77 W Wacker Dr Ste 4600
Chicago IL 60601
312 634-8100

(P-8755)
ARTISAN BAKERS
21684 8th St E Ste 400, Sonoma
(95476-2816)
PHONE..........................707 939-1765
Bill Dozier, *CEO*
Craig Ponsford, *President*
Elizabeth Ponsford, *Treasurer*
Sharon Ponsford, *Vice Pres*
Chris Jones, *Admin Sec*
EMP: 60
SQ FT: 4,400
SALES (est): 25.8MM **Privately Held**
WEB: www.artisanbakers.com
SIC: 5149 5461 Bakery products; bakeries

(P-8756)
ARYZTA LLC
Also Called: Fresh Start Bakeries
920 Shaw Rd, Stockton (95215-4014)
PHONE..........................209 469-4920
Dan Bailey, *Mng Officer*
Christopher Woo, *Division VP*
Clyde Kawamoto, *Vice Pres*
Steve Mills, *Vice Pres*
Jill Weyhgandt, *Vice Pres*
EMP: 50
SALES (corp-wide): 4.4B **Privately Held**
WEB: www.fsbglobal.net
SIC: 5149 Bakery products
HQ: Aryzta Llc
6080 Center Dr Ste 900
Los Angeles CA 90045
310 417-4700

(P-8757)
ASHBURY MARKET INC
Also Called: Raison D'Etre Bakery
179 Starlite St, South San Francisco
(94080-6313)
PHONE..........................650 952-8889
Arnold E Wong, *President*
Richard Wong, *CEO*
Mary Wong, *CFO*
David Brogan, *Consultant*
EMP: 80
SQ FT: 10,000
SALES (est): 19.1MM **Privately Held**
SIC: 5149 Bakery products

(P-8758)
BAKERY EX SOUTHERN CAL LLC
1910 W Malvern Ave, Fullerton
(92833-2105)
PHONE..........................714 446-9470
Charles Burman,
Ronald Currie, *General Mgr*
EMP: 100
SQ FT: 28,000
SALES (est): 28MM **Privately Held**
SIC: 5149 Bakery products

(P-8759)
BAKKAVOR FOODS USA INC (DH)
18201 Central Ave, Carson (90746-4007)
PHONE..........................704 522-1977
Ivan Clingan, *CEO*
Jolyon Punnett, *CFO*
Joe Alonso, *CIO*
John Aviles, *Accountant*
Jim Collins, *Human Res Dir*
▲ EMP: 300
SQ FT: 100,000

SALES (est): 403.8MM
SALES (corp-wide): 2.4B **Privately Held**
WEB: www.twochefsonaroll.com
SIC: 5149 2051 Bakery products; bread,
cake & related products

(P-8760)
BAY BREAD LLC
Also Called: La Boulange
2325 Pine St, San Francisco (94115-2714)
PHONE..........................415 440-0356
Pascal Rigo, *Mng Member*
Fred Estrada,
Lori Goodman,
EMP: 70
SALES (est): 16MM
SALES (corp-wide): 22.3B **Publicly Held**
SIC: 5149 Breading mixes
PA: Starbucks Corporation
2401 Utah Ave S
Seattle WA 98134
206 447-1575

(P-8761)
BUBBLES DEVINE BAKERIES INC
15215 Keswick St, Van Nuys (91405-1014)
PHONE..........................818 786-1700
Homan Nathan Farahmand, *CEO*
EMP: 95
SALES (est): 1.2MM **Privately Held**
SIC: 5149 Bakery products

(P-8762)
BUENA VISTA FOOD PRODUCTS INC (DH)
823 W 8th St, Azusa (91702-2247)
PHONE..........................626 815-8859
Laura Trujillo, *President*
Silvia Madrid, *Office Mgr*
Philippe Francoz, *VP Opers*
Brian Dedick, *Plant Mgr*
Craig Stanley, *Sales Dir*
EMP: 230
SALES (est): 59.4MM **Privately Held**
WEB: www.dvfoods.com
SIC: 5149 Bakery products
HQ: Sterling Foods, Llc
1075 Arion Pkwy
San Antonio TX 78216
210 490-0607

(P-8763)
CALIFORNIA BAKING COMPANY
Also Called: California Bread Co.
681 Anita St, Chula Vista (91911-4663)
PHONE..........................619 591-8289
Abraham Levy, *President*
EMP: 300
SALES (est): 31.2MM **Privately Held**
SIC: 5149 2051 Bakery products; sponge
goods, bakery: except frozen

(P-8764)
CAMPANILE II LP
Also Called: Campanile Restaurant
13721 Ventura Blvd, Sherman Oaks
(91423-3023)
PHONE..........................323 939-6813
Lawrence E Silverton, *Partner*
EMP: 280
SALES (est): 17.3MM **Privately Held**
SIC: 5149 5812 Bakery products; Ameri-
can restaurant

(P-8765)
CAPAY INCORPORATED (PA)
Also Called: Capay Fruits and Vegetables
3880 Seaport Blvd, West Sacramento
(95691-3449)
PHONE..........................530 796-0730
Thaddeus Barsotti, *CEO*
Noah Barnes, *President*
Javier Vargas, *Vice Pres*
Moyra Barsotti, *Admin Sec*
Chase Teodorson-Vau, *Marketing Staff*
EMP: 99
SALES (est): 69.1MM **Privately Held**
WEB: www.capay.com
SIC: 5149 Natural & organic foods

(P-8766)
CAPITAL BRANDS LLC (HQ)
11601 Wilshire Blvd Fl 23, Los Angeles
(90025-1759)
P.O. Box 4564, Pacoima (91333-4564)
PHONE..........................310 996-7200
Rich Krause, *CEO*
Jeff Klausner, *Officer*
Richard Kam, *Exec VP*
Edward Suarez, *Administration*
Brad Stevenson, *Engineer*
EMP: 72
SALES (est): 65.1MM
SALES (corp-wide): 7.8MM **Privately Held**
SIC: 5149 Groceries & related products
PA: Capital Brands Holdings Inc.
11601 Wilshire Blvd Fl 23
Los Angeles CA 90025
310 996-7200

(P-8767)
CHOOLJIAN BROS PACKING CO INC
3192 S Indianola Ave, Sanger
(93657-9716)
P.O. Box 395 (93657-0395)
PHONE..........................559 875-5501
Michael Chuoolgin, *CEO*
Darrell Smith, *Controller*
◆ EMP: 50
SQ FT: 1,800
SALES (est): 18.9MM **Privately Held**
SIC: 5149 Dried or canned foods

(P-8768)
CJ AMERICA INC (HQ)
Also Called: C J Foods
5700 Wilshire Blvd # 550, Los Angeles
(90036-3790)
PHONE..........................213 427-5566
Jin Won Kim, *President*
Han Jong Kim, *CFO*
Justin Cho, *General Mgr*
Rebecca Cho, *Analyst*
Hoongoo Jung, *Human Res Dir*
◆ EMP: 118
SQ FT: 6,000
SALES (est): 58.7MM
SALES (corp-wide): 4.8B **Privately Held**
SIC: 5149 1541 3556 5169 Groceries &
related products; food products manufac-
turing or packing plant construction; food
products machinery; food additives &
preservatives
PA: Cj Cheiljedang Corporation
330 Dongho-Ro, Jung-Gu
Seoul 04560
822 674-0111

(P-8769)
CLIF BAR & COMPANY (PA)
1451 66th St, Emeryville (94608-1004)
PHONE..........................510 596-6300
Kevin Cleary, *CEO*
Kit Crawform, *Co-COB*
Brian Braden, *Vice Pres*
Randy Erickson, *Vice Pres*
Melissa Wilson, *Admin Asst*
▲ EMP: 153
SQ FT: 120,000
SALES (est): 2.3B **Privately Held**
WEB: www.clifbar.com
SIC: 5149 Specialty food items

(P-8770)
CLOVER-STORNETTA FARMS INC (PA)
Also Called: Clover Sonoma
1800 S Mcdowell Blvd, Petaluma
(94954-6962)
P.O. Box 750369 (94975-0369)
PHONE..........................707 769-3282
Marcus Benedetti, *President*
Dan Benedetti, *Ch of Bd*
Ken Gott, *COO*
Richard Lewis, *Bd of Directors*
Gene Benedetti, *Vice Pres*
EMP: 180
SQ FT: 80,000
SALES (est): 142.3MM **Privately Held**
WEB: www.clo-cow.com
SIC: 5149 5143 2026 Juices; dairy prod-
ucts, except dried or canned; milk &
cream, except fermented, cultured & fla-
vored

▲ = Import ▼=Export
◆ =Import/Export

(P-8771)
COLUSA PRODUCE CORPORATION
1954 Progress Rd, Meridian (95957-9643)
PHONE.....................530 696-0121
Jim Wallace, *President*
Barbara Overton, *Office Mgr*
◆ **EMP:** 78
SQ FT: 5,000
SALES (est): 16.7MM **Privately Held**
SIC: 5149 5159 5148 Spices & seasonings; broomcorn; fresh fruits & vegetables

(P-8772)
COMPLETE FOOD SERVICE INC
3815 Wabash Dr, Mira Loma (91752-1143)
PHONE.....................951 685-8490
Keith Kahn, *President*
Mitchell Kahn, *Vice Pres*
Mark Kahn, *Admin Sec*
EMP: 90
SQ FT: 40,000
SALES (est): 17.5MM **Privately Held**
SIC: 5149 5722 Groceries & related products; sewing machines

(P-8773)
COMPLETELY FRESH FOODS INC
4401 S Downey Rd, Vernon (90058-2518)
P.O. Box 58667, Los Angeles (90058-0667)
PHONE.....................323 722-9136
Josh Solovy, *President*
Eric Litmanovich, *Vice Pres*
Levi Litmanovich, *Vice Pres*
EMP: 200
SQ FT: 15,000
SALES (est): 68.3MM **Privately Held**
SIC: 5149 5046 Specialty food items; commercial equipment; commercial cooking & food service equipment

(P-8774)
CORE NUTRITION LLC
100 N Pacific Coast Hwy # 325, El Segundo (90245-4359)
PHONE.....................310 640-0500
Lance Collins, *Mng Member*
Christina Kim, *Accountant*
Ben Horner, *VP Opers*
Brandon Cervelli, *Regl Sales Mgr*
Zen Mayo, *Sales Staff*
EMP: 82
SALES: 12.9MM **Privately Held**
SIC: 5149 Mineral or spring water bottling

(P-8775)
CORE NUTRITION LLC
1222 E Grand Ave Ste 102, El Segundo (90245-4219)
PHONE.....................310 640-0500
EMP: 50 **EST:** 2014
SALES (est): 4MM **Privately Held**
SIC: 5149 2834

(P-8776)
CORE-MARK INTERNATIONAL INC
200 Coremark Ct, Bakersfield (93307-8402)
P.O. Box 70458 (93387-0458)
PHONE.....................661 366-2673
Caral Parker, *President*
EMP: 107
SALES (corp-wide): 15.6B **Publicly Held**
WEB: www.core-mark.com
SIC: 5149 Groceries & related products
HQ: Core-Mark International, Inc.
395 Oyster Point Blvd # 415
South San Francisco CA 94080
650 589-9445

(P-8777)
CORE-MARK INTERNATIONAL INC
2311 E 48th St, Vernon (90058-2007)
PHONE.....................323 583-6531
Julian Puentes, *Branch Mgr*
EMP: 150
SALES (corp-wide): 15.6B **Publicly Held**
WEB: www.core-mark.com
SIC: 5149 5194 5145 Groceries & related products; tobacco & tobacco products; confectionery

HQ: Core-Mark International, Inc.
395 Oyster Point Blvd # 415
South San Francisco CA 94080
650 589-9445

(P-8778)
CORE-MARK INTERNATIONAL INC
3030 Mulvany Pl, West Sacramento (95691-5745)
PHONE.....................509 535-9768
Christopher Ladesich, *Principal*
EMP: 150
SQ FT: 25,000
SALES (corp-wide): 15.6B **Publicly Held**
WEB: www.core-mark.com
SIC: 5149 5194 5141 Groceries & related products; tobacco & tobacco products; groceries, general line
HQ: Core-Mark International, Inc.
395 Oyster Point Blvd # 415
South San Francisco CA 94080
650 589-9445

(P-8779)
CORE-MARK INTERNATIONAL INC
31300 Medallion Dr, Hayward (94544-7902)
PHONE.....................510 487-3000
Bob Norton, *Manager*
EMP: 150
SALES (corp-wide): 15.6B **Publicly Held**
WEB: www.core-mark.com
SIC: 5149 5194 5145 5141 Groceries & related products; tobacco & tobacco products; confectionery; groceries, general line
HQ: Core-Mark International, Inc.
395 Oyster Point Blvd # 415
South San Francisco CA 94080
650 589-9445

(P-8780)
CORNER BAKERY STORE
1040 W Imperial Hwy Ste A, La Habra (90631-0608)
PHONE.....................714 459-1420
Jim Vinz, *CEO*
EMP: 50
SALES (est): 2MM **Privately Held**
SIC: 5149 Bakery products

(P-8781)
CREATIVE ENERGY FOODS INC
9957 Medford Ave Ste 4, Oakland (94603-2360)
PHONE.....................510 638-8668
Richard C Dwinell, *CEO*
George Jewell, *President*
Marv Bennett, *CFO*
Jacker Wong, *CFO*
Drew Goldberg, *Vice Pres*
▲ **EMP:** 95
SQ FT: 105,000
SALES (est): 56.2MM **Privately Held**
WEB: www.energybar.com
SIC: 5149 2026 Health foods; dips, sour cream based

(P-8782)
CTC FOOD INTERNATIONAL INC (PA)
Also Called: Oriental Trading Co
50 W Ohio Ave, Richmond (94804-2039)
PHONE.....................650 873-7600
Ike Fukmoto, *President*
Yoichi Kadona, *Shareholder*
Morihiro Ogawa, *Shareholder*
Hideki Otani, *Ch of Bd*
Lawrence Tanita, *CFO*
◆ **EMP:** 50
SQ FT: 40,000
SALES (est): 17.4MM **Privately Held**
SIC: 5149 5182 Specialty food items; wine

(P-8783)
CULINARY HISPANIC FOODS INC
Also Called: Productos Chata
805 Bow St, Chula Vista (91914)
PHONE.....................619 955-6101
Jorge Aguilar, *CEO*
Carlos Machado, *Principal*
▲ **EMP:** 1458

SQ FT: 4,000
SALES: 1MM **Privately Held**
SIC: 5149 Canned goods: fruit, vegetables, seafood, meats, etc.

(P-8784)
DS SERVICES OF AMERICA INC
Also Called: Sparkletts
7817 Haskell Ave, Van Nuys (91406-1908)
PHONE.....................818 787-9397
Frank Lubich, *Branch Mgr*
EMP: 70
SQ FT: 5,805
SALES (corp-wide): 2.2B **Privately Held**
WEB: www.suntorywatergroup.com
SIC: 5149 7389 Water, distilled; coffee service
HQ: Ds Services Of America, Inc.
2300 Windy Ridge Pkwy Se 500n
Atlanta GA 30339
770 933-1400

(P-8785)
DS SERVICES OF AMERICA INC
Also Called: Sparkletts
4548 Azusa Canyon Rd, Irwindale (91706-2742)
PHONE.....................626 472-7201
Linda Gonzales, *Manager*
EMP: 200
SQ FT: 67,508
SALES (corp-wide): 2.2B **Privately Held**
WEB: www.suntorywatergroup.com
SIC: 5149 5963 Water, distilled; direct selling establishments
HQ: Ds Services Of America, Inc.
2300 Windy Ridge Pkwy Se 500n
Atlanta GA 30339
770 933-1400

(P-8786)
EL GUAPO SPICES INC (PA)
Also Called: El Guapo Spices and Herbs Pkg
6200 E Slauson Ave, Commerce (90040-3012)
PHONE.....................213 312-1300
Dan Terrazas, *President*
EMP: 100
SALES (est): 11.8MM **Privately Held**
SIC: 5149 Spices & seasonings

(P-8787)
FALCON TRADING COMPANY (PA)
Also Called: Sunridge Farms
423 Salinas Rd, Royal Oaks (95076-5232)
PHONE.....................831 786-7000
Morty Cohen, *CEO*
Rebecca Cohen, *Vice Pres*
Bruce Brinker, *Executive*
Robin Van Soest, *Executive*
Ron Giannini, *General Mgr*
◆ **EMP:** 215 **EST:** 1977
SQ FT: 24,500
SALES (est): 108.7MM **Privately Held**
WEB: www.sunridgefarms.com
SIC: 5149 Natural & organic foods

(P-8788)
FAMOUS RAMONA WATER INC
250 Aqua Ln, Ramona (92065-2024)
P.O. Box 1195 (92065-0860)
PHONE.....................760 789-0174
Julian C Filer, *CEO*
Joe Bruni, *President*
Mark N Filer, *Exec VP*
Mark Filer, *Vice Pres*
Debbie Bruni, *Admin Sec*
EMP: 50
SQ FT: 48,000
SALES (est): 15.6MM **Privately Held**
WEB: www.famousramonawater.com
SIC: 5149 5085 Mineral or spring water bottling; commercial containers

(P-8789)
FIJI WATER COMPANY LLC (HQ)
11444 W Olympic Blvd # 250, Los Angeles (90064-1534)
PHONE.....................310 966-5700
Stewart A Resnick, *Ch of Bd*
Kim Katzenberger, *CFO*
William Foltz, *Senior VP*
Craig Cooper, *Admin Sec*
Tony Ken, *Admin Asst*
◆ **EMP:** 50

SQ FT: 12,000
SALES (est): 43MM **Privately Held**
SALES (corp-wide): 1.5B **Privately Held**
WEB: www.fijiwater.com
SIC: 5149 Mineral or spring water bottling
PA: The Wonderful Company Llc
11444 W Olympic Blvd # 210
Los Angeles CA 90064
310 966-5700

(P-8790)
FRESH GRILL LLC
111 E Garry Ave, Santa Ana (92707-4201)
PHONE.....................714 444-2126
Jeff Heavirland, *Mng Member*
Iris Rodriguez, *Purch Mgr*
Phil Abreo, *Sales Staff*
▲ **EMP:** 200
SQ FT: 27,000
SALES (est): 62.3MM
SALES (corp-wide): 10.8MM **Privately Held**
WEB: www.freshgrillfoods.com
SIC: 5149 8742 Specialty food items; food & beverage consultant
PA: Fb Holding Company, Llc
111 E Garry Ave
Santa Ana CA 92707
714 444-2126

(P-8791)
FRESHOLOGY INC
12400 Wilshire Blvd # 1180, Los Angeles (90025-1058)
PHONE.....................818 847-1888
Todd Demann, *Principal*
▲ **EMP:** 71
SQ FT: 15,500
SALES (est): 15.5MM **Privately Held**
WEB: www.freshology.com/
SIC: 5149 Diet foods

(P-8792)
FUJI FOOD PRODUCTS INC (PA)
14420 Bloomfield Ave, Santa Fe Springs (90670-5410)
PHONE.....................562 404-2590
Farrell Hirsch, *CEO*
Humberto Villagomez, *COO*
Javier Aceves, *CFO*
Philip Schoen, *Regional Mgr*
Wilma Arellano, *Office Mgr*
▲ **EMP:** 100 **EST:** 2010
SQ FT: 90,000
SALES (est): 405.9MM **Privately Held**
WEB: www.fujifood.com
SIC: 5149 Groceries & related products

(P-8793)
FUJI FOOD PRODUCTS INC
8660 Miramar Rd Ste N, San Diego (92126-4362)
PHONE.....................619 268-3118
Kenny Sung, *Branch Mgr*
EMP: 125
SALES (corp-wide): 405.9MM **Privately Held**
WEB: www.fujifood.com
SIC: 5149 Specialty food items
PA: Fuji Food Products, Inc.
14420 Bloomfield Ave
Santa Fe Springs CA 90670
562 404-2590

(P-8794)
GALASSOS BAKERY (PA)
10820 San Sevaine Way, Mira Loma (91752-1116)
PHONE.....................951 360-1211
Jeannette Galasso, *President*
Mark Bailey, *Treasurer*
Rick Vargas, *Vice Pres*
Pearl Denault, *Project Mgr*
EMP: 180
SQ FT: 110,000
SALES (est): 120.6MM **Privately Held**
WEB: www.galassos.com
SIC: 5149 Bakery products

(P-8795)
GANO EXCEL (USA) INC
15439 Dupont Ave, Chino (91710-7605)
P.O. Box 9275, Glendale (91226-0275)
PHONE.....................626 338-8081
Chin Iakooi, *CEO*
Ruben Cardenas, *President*

PRODUCTS & SVCS

Bernard Chua, *President*
Soon Seng Leow, *President*
Chang Ching Lew, *Treasurer*
▲ EMP: 67
SQ FT: 3,216
SALES: 18MM **Privately Held**
SIC: 5149 Coffee, green or roasted; coffee & tea

(P-8796)
GIANNAS BAKING COMPANY
11165 Commercial Pkwy, Castroville (95012-3207)
PHONE...................................831 633-3700
Peter Uli, *President*
EMP: 54
SALES (est): 12.6MM **Privately Held**
WEB: www.giannas.com
SIC: 5149 Bakery products

(P-8797)
GLOBAL BAKERIES INC
13336 Paxton St, Pacoima (91331-2339)
PHONE...................................818 896-0525
Albert Boyajian, *President*
▲ EMP: 60
SQ FT: 44,000
SALES (est): 19.7MM **Privately Held**
WEB: www.globalbakeriesinc.com
SIC: 5149 Bakery products

(P-8798)
GOGLANIAN BAKERIES INC (HQ)
3401 W Segerstrom Ave, Santa Ana (92704-6404)
PHONE...................................714 549-1524
William G Gisel, *CEO*
◆ EMP: 300
SQ FT: 71,500
SALES (est): 366.2MM
SALES (corp-wide): 4B **Privately Held**
WEB: www.goglanian.com
SIC: 5149 Bakery products
PA: Rich Products Corporation
1 Robert Rich Way
Buffalo NY 14213
716 878-8000

(P-8799)
GOLD COAST INGREDIENTS INC
2429 Yates Ave, Commerce (90040-1917)
PHONE...................................323 724-8935
Clarence H Brasher, *CEO*
James A Sgro, *President*
Laurie Goddard, *Vice Pres*
Jon Wellwood, *General Mgr*
Haitao Yu, *Info Tech Mgr*
◆ EMP: 53
SQ FT: 50,000
SALES (est): 37MM **Privately Held**
WEB: www.goldcoastinc.com
SIC: 5149 2087 Baking supplies; flavourings & fragrances; flavoring extracts & syrups

(P-8800)
GOLDA & I CHOCOLATIERS INC
23052 Alicia Pkwy Ste H, Mission Viejo (92692-1661)
PHONE...................................949 660-9581
Golda Imbernino, *President*
Mary Anne Osier, *Owner*
EMP: 55
SQ FT: 3,000
SALES (est): 6.5MM **Privately Held**
WEB: www.crowncityconfections.com
SIC: 5149

(P-8801)
GOURMET INDIA FOOD COMPANY LLC
12220 Rivera Rd Ste A, Whittier (90606-6206)
PHONE...................................562 698-9763
Sam Jeevan,
Saleem Hai,
▲ EMP: 75
SALES (est): 12.8MM **Privately Held**
SIC: 5149 Bakery products

(P-8802)
GOURMETS FRESH PASTA
950 N Fair Oaks Ave, Pasadena (91103-3009)
PHONE...................................626 798-0841

Michael A Yagjian, *President*
William J Cullinane Jr, *Vice Pres*
William Coulvane, *Admin Mgr*
Peggy Flores, *Human Res Mgr*
Jerry Guerrero, *Plant Mgr*
▲ EMP: 65
SQ FT: 30,000
SALES (est): 19.5MM **Privately Held**
WEB: www.gourmetpasta.com
SIC: 5149 5812 Pasta & rice; eating places

(P-8803)
HARRIS FREEMAN & CO INC (PA)
Also Called: Harris Tea Company
3110 E Miraloma Ave, Anaheim (92806-1906)
PHONE...................................714 765-1190
Anil J Shah, *CEO*
Kevin Shah, *President*
Martin Clay, *CFO*
Meena Shah, *Treasurer*
Mark Robinson, *Officer*
◆ EMP: 500
SQ FT: 58,000
SALES (est): 360.7MM **Privately Held**
SIC: 5149 2099 Coffee & tea; spices, including grinding

(P-8804)
HEALTH VALLEY FOODS INC
16007 Cmino De La Cantera, Irwindale (91702)
PHONE...................................626 334-3241
Irwin Simon, *President*
▲ EMP: 300
SALES (est): 13.6MM **Publicly Held**
WEB: www.hain-celestial.com
SIC: 5149 Health foods; natural & organic foods
PA: The Hain Celestial Group Inc
1111 Marcus Ave Ste 100
New Hyde Park NY 11042

(P-8805)
INTERBAKE FOODS LLC
Also Called: Norse Dairy Systems
1910 W Temple St, Los Angeles (90026-4929)
P.O. Box 26338 (90026-0338)
PHONE...................................213 484-8161
Randy Obrien, *Branch Mgr*
Jack Frysvtak, *Plant Mgr*
EMP: 60
SALES (corp-wide): 37.8B **Privately Held**
WEB: www.interbake.com
SIC: 5149 Bakery products
HQ: Interbake Foods Llc
3951 Westerre Pkwy # 200
Henrico VA 23233
804 755-7107

(P-8806)
INTERNATIONAL DELICACIES
2100 Atlas Rd Ste F, Richmond (94806-1100)
PHONE...................................510 669-2444
Hossein Banejad, *CEO*
Ruth Banejad, *CFO*
Dean Wilkinson, *Vice Pres*
Amanda Lee, *Office Mgr*
Abu Taghizadeh, *VP Sales*
▲ EMP: 50
SQ FT: 45,000
SALES: 60MM **Privately Held**
WEB: www.internationaldelicacies.net
SIC: 5149 Pasta & rice; cookies; fruits, dried; cooking oils

(P-8807)
IONICS ALTRPURE WTR CRPARATION
Also Called: Apollo Cpr
7777 Industry Ave, Pico Rivera (90660-4303)
PHONE...................................562 948-2188
Winston Mar, *Vice Pres*
Michael Wilbanks, *Vice Pres*
EMP: 95
SQ FT: 12,000
SALES (est): 7.4MM **Privately Held**
SIC: 5149 5999 Mineral or spring water bottling; water purification equipment

(P-8808)
ITALFOODS INC
205 Shaw Rd, South San Francisco (94080-6605)
P.O. Box 2563 (94083-2563)
PHONE...................................650 873-2640
Georgette Guerra, *CEO*
Don Raphael, *General Mgr*
Rafael Zabaljauregui, *Technology*
Richard De Gaetano, *Purch Mgr*
Lorenzo Chiostri, *Sales Staff*
▲ EMP: 80 EST: 1978
SQ FT: 114,000
SALES (est): 31.6MM **Privately Held**
WEB: www.italfoods.com
SIC: 5149 Specialty food items

(P-8809)
J & D MEAT COMPANY
Also Called: JD Food
4671 E Edgar Ave, Fresno (93725)
P.O. Box 12051 (93776-2051)
PHONE...................................559 445-1123
Mark K Ford, *President*
Robert Maxey, *CFO*
Arman Astrian, *Vice Pres*
Steven Maxey, *Admin Sec*
Steve Lloyd, *Human Res Mgr*
EMP: 115
SQ FT: 51,000
SALES (est): 90.1MM **Privately Held**
WEB: www.jdfoodservice.com
SIC: 5149 5147 5148 5143 Groceries & related products; meats & meat products; fresh fruits & vegetables; dairy products, except dried or canned; packaged frozen goods

(P-8810)
JACMAR DDC LLC
Also Called: Jacmar Food Service Dist
3057 Promenade St, West Sacramento (95691-5941)
PHONE...................................916 372-9795
James A Dalpozzo, *Mng Member*
Esmeralda Endeje, *Executive Asst*
Tracey Donato, *Buyer*
Michael Oliver, *Purch Agent*
Theresa Jordan, *Marketing Staff*
EMP: 55
SQ FT: 100,000
SALES (est): 19.8MM
SALES (corp-wide): 535MM **Privately Held**
WEB: www.jacmar.com
SIC: 5149 Natural & organic foods
PA: The Jacmar Companies
300 Baldwin Park Blvd
City Of Industry CA 91746
800 834-8806

(P-8811)
JAGPREET ENTERPRISES INC
Also Called: Quick-N-Ezee Indian Foods
25823 Clawiter Rd, Hayward (94545-3217)
PHONE...................................510 336-8376
Sukhjeet K Singh, *CEO*
Surinder Singh, *President*
Dalbir Singh, *Director*
▲ EMP: 150
SQ FT: 30,000
SALES (est): 56.4MM **Privately Held**
WEB: www.sukhis.com
SIC: 5149 Groceries & related products

(P-8812)
JFC INTERNATIONAL INC (HQ)
7101 E Slauson Ave, Commerce (90040-3622)
P.O. Box 875349, Los Angeles (90087-0449)
PHONE...................................323 721-6100
Yoshiyuki Ishigaki, *CEO*
Hiroyuki Enomoto, *President*
Masanori Takenaka, *Vice Pres*
Ichiro Komatsubara, *Branch Mgr*
Kiyoshi Tamai, *Branch Mgr*
◆ EMP: 203 EST: 1948
SALES (est): 457.2MM
SALES (corp-wide): 4B **Privately Held**
WEB: www.jfc.com
SIC: 5149 7389 Specialty food items; labeling bottles, cans, cartons, etc.

PA: Kikkoman Corporation
2-1-1, Nishishimbashi
Minato-Ku TKY 105-0
355 215-131

(P-8813)
JFC INTERNATIONAL INC
Also Called: Los Angeles Branch
7101 E Slauson Ave, Commerce (90040-3622)
PHONE...................................323 721-6900
Shoso Ota, *Branch Mgr*
EMP: 165
SALES (corp-wide): 4B **Privately Held**
SIC: 5149 Specialty food items
HQ: Jfc International Inc.
7101 E Slauson Ave
Commerce CA 90040
323 721-6100

(P-8814)
JOHNS DOG FOOD DISTRIBUTING
Also Called: John's Pet Products
1633 Monterey Hwy, San Jose (95112-6111)
PHONE...................................408 275-1943
Johnannes G Rademakers, *Owner*
EMP: 60 EST: 1970
SQ FT: 7,000
SALES (est): 2.8MM **Privately Held**
SIC: 5149 5999 Pet foods; pet supplies

(P-8815)
JOYRIDE COFFEE DISTRS LLC
1485 Yosemite Ave, San Francisco (94124-3321)
PHONE...................................718 841-7206
EMP: 78
SALES (corp-wide): 10MM **Privately Held**
SIC: 5149 Coffee & tea
PA: Joyride Coffee Distributors, Llc
3712 56th St
Woodside NY 11377
917 670-3314

(P-8816)
K T LUCKY CO INC
10925 Schmidt Rd, El Monte (91733-2707)
PHONE...................................626 579-7272
Hang Huynh, *President*
▲ EMP: 70
SQ FT: 12,000
SALES (est): 11.9MM **Privately Held**
SIC: 5149 Macaroni; rice, polished

(P-8817)
KEHE DISTRIBUTORS LLC
6 Pointe Dr Ste 300, Brea (92821-6323)
PHONE...................................714 255-4600
Brandon Barnholt, *President*
EMP: 360
SALES (corp-wide): 4.2B **Privately Held**
SIC: 5149 Health foods
PA: Kehe Distributors, Llc
1245 E Diehl Rd Ste 200
Naperville IL 60563
630 343-0000

(P-8818)
KRADJIAN IMPORTING COMPANY INC (PA)
5018 San Fernando Rd, Glendale (91204-1114)
PHONE...................................818 502-1313
Raffi Kradjian, *President*
Viken Kradjian, *Vice Pres*
Ram Sethuram, *Controller*
Sahag Arabian, *Marketing Staff*
◆ EMP: 61 EST: 1987
SQ FT: 50,000
SALES (est): 32.9MM **Privately Held**
SIC: 5149 Specialty food items

(P-8819)
KRAFT HEINZ FOODS COMPANY
5000 Hopyard Rd Ste 235, Pleasanton (94588-3314)
PHONE...................................925 469-0057
Carroll Wine, *Branch Mgr*
EMP: 500
SALES (corp-wide): 26.2B **Publicly Held**
SIC: 5149 Groceries & related products

HQ: Kraft Heinz Foods Company
1 Ppg Pl Ste 3200
Pittsburgh PA 15222
412 456-5700

(P-8820)
KRAFT HEINZ FOODS COMPANY
1055 E North Ave, Fresno (93725-1914)
PHONE..................................559 499-5300
Tony Lacerva, *General Mgr*
EMP: 50
SALES (corp-wide): 26.2B **Publicly Held**
WEB: www.kraftfoods.com
SIC: 5149 Groceries & related products
HQ: Kraft Heinz Foods Company
1 Ppg Pl Ste 3200
Pittsburgh PA 15222
412 456-5700

(P-8821)
KRONOS FOODS CORP
Also Called: Rain Creek Baking
2401 W Almond Ave, Madera (93637-4807)
PHONE..................................559 674-4445
Michael Austin, *CEO*
EMP: 75
SALES (corp-wide): 120MM **Privately Held**
SIC: 5149 Bakery products
PA: Kronos Foods Corp.
1 Kronos
Glendale Heights IL 60139
224 353-5400

(P-8822)
LA PROVENCE INC
Also Called: La Provence Bakery
1370 W San Marcos Blvd # 130, San Marcos (92078-1601)
PHONE..................................760 736-3299
Philip Dardaine, *CEO*
Karen Dardaine, *Corp Secy*
Thierry Bouchereau, *Vice Pres*
EMP: 95
SQ FT: 6,000
SALES (est): 23.2MM **Privately Held**
SIC: 5149 Bakery products

(P-8823)
LA TORTILLA FACTORY INC (PA)
3300 Westwind Blvd, Santa Rosa
(95403-8273)
PHONE..................................707 586-4000
Samuel Carlos Tamayo, *CEO*
Carlos G Tamayo, *President*
Carlos Tamayo, *President*
Dave Davis, *COO*
David Trogdon, *CFO*
EMP: 280 EST: 1977
SALES (est): 157.8MM **Privately Held**
WEB: www.latortillafactory.com
SIC: 5149 2051 Specialty food items; bakery products; bread, cake & related products

(P-8824)
LENORE JOHN & CO (PA)
1250 Delevan Dr, San Diego (92102-2437)
PHONE..................................619 232-6136
John G Lenore, *CEO*
Jamie Lenore, *President*
Robin Silva, *Administration*
Doris Anthony, *Human Res Dir*
Jose Perez, *Marketing Staff*
◆ EMP: 120
SQ FT: 50,000
SALES (est): 173.8MM **Privately Held**
WEB: www.johnlenore.com
SIC: 5149 5182 5181 Soft drinks; mineral or spring water bottling; wine; liquor; beer & other fermented malt liquors

(P-8825)
MHH HOLDINGS INC
5653 Alton Pkwy, Irvine (92618-4058)
PHONE..................................949 651-9903
Cynthia Espere, *Branch Mgr*
EMP: 177
SALES (corp-wide): 68.2MM **Privately Held**
SIC: 5149 Tea
PA: Mhh Holdings, Inc.
4580 Calle Alto
Camarillo CA 93012
805 484-7924

(P-8826)
MHH HOLDINGS INC
415 S Lake Ave Ste 108, Pasadena
(91101-5047)
PHONE..................................626 744-9370
Xiomara Bellido, *Principal*
EMP: 68
SALES (corp-wide): 68.2MM **Privately Held**
SIC: 5149 Tea
PA: Mhh Holdings, Inc.
4580 Calle Alto
Camarillo CA 93012
805 484-7924

(P-8827)
MIGHTY LEAF TEA
100 Smith Ranch Rd # 120, San Rafael
(94903-1979)
PHONE..................................415 491-2650
Shiela Stanziale, *CEO*
Jill Portman, *President*
Paul Crawley, *CFO*
Tom Smallhorn, *Chief Mktg Ofcr*
Leigh Clark, *Vice Pres*
▲ EMP: 65
SQ FT: 5,000
SALES (est): 32.4MM
SALES (corp-wide): 2.2B **Privately Held**
WEB: www.mightyleaf.com
SIC: 5149 5499 Tea; tea
HQ: Peet's Coffee & Tea, Llc
1400 Park Ave
Emeryville CA 94608
510 594-2100

(P-8828)
MONDELEZ GLOBAL LLC
Also Called: Nabisco
5815 Clark St, Ontario (91761-3676)
PHONE..................................909 605-0140
Botie Magee, *Branch Mgr*
EMP: 70 **Publicly Held**
WEB: www.kraftfoods.com
SIC: 5149 2099 2052 Crackers, cookies & bakery products; food preparations; cookies & crackers
HQ: Mondelez Global Llc
3 N Pkwy Ste 300
Deerfield IL 60015
847 943-4000

(P-8829)
MONSTER ENERGY COMPANY (DH)
1 Monster Way, Corona (92879-7101)
PHONE..................................951 739-6200
Rodney C Sacks, *CEO*
Ray La Rue, *President*
Hilton H Scholsberg, *Vice Ch Bd*
Tom Davis, *Officer*
John Beasley, *Vice Pres*
▼ EMP: 153
SQ FT: 300,000
SALES (est): 1.1B
SALES (corp-wide): 3.3B **Publicly Held**
WEB: www.hansens.com
SIC: 5149 Juices; soft drinks
HQ: Monster Beverage 1990 Corporation
1 Monster Way
Corona CA 92879
951 739-6200

(P-8830)
MORRIS NATIONAL INC (HQ)
Also Called: McGreever and Danlee Very
760 N Mckeever Ave, Azusa (91702-2349)
PHONE..................................626 385-2000
Gerry Morris Zubatoff, *CEO*
Gerald Morris, *President*
David Pistole, *CFO*
Bram Zubatoff, *Admin Sec*
◆ EMP: 56
SQ FT: 125,000
SALES (est): 183.6MM **Privately Held**
WEB: www.morrisnational.com
SIC: 5149 5145 Chocolate; confectionery
PA: Morris National Inc
100 Jacob Keffer Pky
Concord ON L4K 4
905 879-7777

(P-8831)
MUTUAL TRADING CO INC (DH)
Also Called: M T C
431 Crocker St, Los Angeles (90013-2180)
PHONE..................................213 626-9458
Kosei Yamamoto, *CEO*
Noritoshi Kanai, *President*
Seicho Fujikawa, *Vice Pres*
Kotaro Hoshizaki, *Principal*
Keita Yagai, *Info Tech Dir*
◆ EMP: 105
SQ FT: 100,000
SALES (est): 126.1MM
SALES (corp-wide): 2.5B **Privately Held**
WEB: www.lamtc.com
SIC: 5149 5141 5023 Groceries & related products; groceries, general line; home furnishings
HQ: Takara Shuzo Co.,Ltd.
Shijodori-Karasumahigashiiru
Shimogyo-Ku, Kyoto KYO 600-8
752 415-110

(P-8832)
NAVITAS LLC
Also Called: Navitas Naturals
15 Pamaron Way, Novato (94949-6231)
PHONE..................................415 883-8116
Zachary Adelman, *Mng Member*
▲ EMP: 50
SALES (est): 19.2MM **Privately Held**
WEB: www.navitasnaturals.com
SIC: 5149 Health foods

(P-8833)
NESTLE WATERS NORTH AMER INC
Also Called: Arrowhead Water
619 N Main St, Orange (92868-1103)
PHONE..................................714 532-6220
Dan Miller, *Sales/Mktg Mgr*
EMP: 135
SQ FT: 16,312
SALES (corp-wide): 90.8B **Privately Held**
WEB: www.zephyronline.com
SIC: 5149 5499 5963 5078 Water, distilled; water: distilled mineral or spring; bottled water delivery; refrigeration equipment & supplies; plumbing & hydronic heating supplies
HQ: Nestle Waters North America Inc.
900 Long Ridge Rd Bldg 2
Stamford CT 06902

(P-8834)
NESTLE WATERS NORTH AMER INC
Also Called: Arrowhead Mountain Spring Wtr
14020 Elm St, Cabazon (92230-4444)
PHONE..................................951 572-4600
Ron Kane, *Branch Mgr*
EMP: 230
SALES (corp-wide): 90.8B **Privately Held**
WEB: www.zephyronline.com
SIC: 5149 Mineral or spring water bottling
HQ: Nestle Waters North America Inc.
900 Long Ridge Rd Bldg 2
Stamford CT 06902

(P-8835)
NESTLE WATERS NORTH AMER INC
9400 Mason Ave, Chatsworth
(91311-5203)
PHONE..................................818 349-9201
Bob Bride, *Manager*
EMP: 75
SALES (corp-wide): 90.8B **Privately Held**
WEB: www.zephyronline.com
SIC: 5149 Mineral or spring water bottling
HQ: Nestle Waters North America Inc.
900 Long Ridge Rd Bldg 2
Stamford CT 06902

(P-8836)
NESTLE WATERS NORTH AMER INC
7480 Las Positas Rd, Livermore
(94551-5115)
PHONE..................................925 294-7720
Bill Klink, *Branch Mgr*
EMP: 60

SALES (corp-wide): 90.8B **Privately Held**
WEB: www.zephyronline.com
SIC: 5149 Mineral or spring water bottling
HQ: Nestle Waters North America Inc.
900 Long Ridge Rd Bldg 2
Stamford CT 06902

(P-8837)
NEUROBRANDS LLC
Also Called: Neuro Drinks
15303 Ventura Blvd # 675, Sherman Oaks
(91403-6608)
PHONE..................................310 393-6444
Diana Jenkins, *CEO*
Scott Laporta, *President*
Chad Bell, *Area Mgr*
Rigo De Leon, *Area Mgr*
Armando Lassale, *Area Mgr*
▲ EMP: 125
SALES (est): 82.3MM **Privately Held**
SIC: 5149 Soft drinks

(P-8838)
NEW DESSERTS INC
Also Called: Just Desserts
5000 Fulton Dr, Fairfield (94534-1677)
PHONE..................................415 780-6860
Michael Mendes, *CEO*
Leighton Mue, *Vice Pres*
Marc Cabi, *Technology*
Megan Chan, *Accountant*
Tom Margulis, *Human Res Mgr*
EMP: 93
SQ FT: 73,500
SALES (est): 54.8MM **Privately Held**
SIC: 5149 2024 Bakery products; ice cream & frozen desserts

(P-8839)
NGS GROUP INC
4152 W Washington Blvd, Los Angeles
(90018-1054)
PHONE..................................323 735-1700
Steven Ngu, *President*
EMP: 54
SQ FT: 1,500
SALES (est): 5.9MM **Privately Held**
WEB: www.pacificfrenchbakery.com
SIC: 5149 Bakery products

(P-8840)
NICOLA INTERNATIONAL INC
11119 Dora St, Sun Valley (91352-3339)
PHONE..................................818 767-1133
Nicola Khachatoorian, *President*
Adik Khachatoorian, *Corp Secy*
Alice Toomanian, *Exec VP*
▲ EMP: 125
SQ FT: 150,000
SALES (est): 11.1MM **Privately Held**
WEB: www.nicolainternational.com
SIC: 5149 5148 Cooking oils & shortenings; vegetables

(P-8841)
NOWHER PARTNERS LLC
Also Called: Erewhon Natural Foods Market
26767 Agoura Rd Ste A, Calabasas
(91302-1992)
PHONE..................................818 857-3366
Victor Grenner, *Branch Mgr*
EMP: 100
SALES (corp-wide): 19.6MM **Privately Held**
SIC: 5149 Natural & organic foods
PA: Nowher Partners Llc
7600 Beverly Blvd
Los Angeles CA 90036
818 857-3366

(P-8842)
OH MY GREEN INC
1845 Rollins Rd, Burlingame (94010-2209)
PHONE..................................650 989-8181
Michael Heinrich, *CEO*
Jennifer Sassenus, *Executive Asst*
Brian Maloney, *Warehouse Mgr*
Grover Reece, *Warehouse Mgr*
EMP: 80 EST: 2013
SALES (est): 24.6MM **Privately Held**
SIC: 5149 Health foods

P R O D U C T S & S V C S

(P-8843)
ORWICK FRESH FOODS INC
7940 Cherry Ave Ste 203, Fontana
(92336-4021)
PHONE..................................909 985-5604
Richard V Orwick, *President*
EMP: 50 **EST:** 2000
SALES (est): 7.7MM **Privately Held**
SIC: 5149 Groceries & related products

(P-8844)
OSF INTERNATIONAL INC
Also Called: Old Spaghetti Factory, The
71743 Highway 111, Rancho Mirage
(92270-4427)
PHONE..................................760 341-5600
Valerie Pickart, *Manager*
EMP: 66
SALES (corp-wide): 151.2MM **Privately Held**
SIC: 5149 Spaghetti
PA: Osf International, Inc.
0715 Sw Bancroft St
Portland OR 97239
503 222-5375

(P-8845)
PACIFIC FOODS & DIST INC
3431 W Carriage Dr, Santa Ana
(92704-6411)
PHONE..................................714 547-0787
James H Loftus Jr, *President*
Michael Robledo, *Opers Mgr*
Sam Garza, *Sales Mgr*
EMP: 100
SALES (est): 32.1MM **Privately Held**
WEB: www.pacificfoodsdistribution.com
SIC: 5149 Bakery products

(P-8846)
PASADENA BAKING CO
70 W Pal Meto Ave, Pasadena (91105)
PHONE..................................626 796-5093
Armen Shirvanvian, *Partner*
Akis Markoutsis, *Partner*
Julia Montano, *Financial Exec*
Gonzalo Wieler, *Sales Mgr*
Ursula Lopez, *Representative*
EMP: 50
SQ FT: 10,000
SALES (est): 7.9MM **Privately Held**
WEB: www.pasadenabaking.com
SIC: 5149 Bakery products

(P-8847)
PASTA SHOP (PA)
Also Called: Market Hall Foods
5655 College Ave Ste 201, Oakland
(94618-1583)
PHONE..................................510 250-6005
Sara Wilson, *Managing Prtnr*
Anthony Wilson, *Partner*
Peter Wilson, *Partner*
Nel Da Silva, *Executive*
Francisco Lizarraga, *Director*
▲ **EMP:** 80
SQ FT: 4,500
SALES (est): 65.7MM **Privately Held**
WEB: www.rockridgemarkethall.com
SIC: 5149 5411 5812 5431 Pasta & rice;
delicatessens; caterers; fruit & vegetable
markets

(P-8848)
PEPSI-COLA METRO BTLG CO
INC
3029 Coffey Ln, Santa Rosa (95403-2513)
PHONE..................................707 535-4560
Brad Pighin, *General Mgr*
EMP: 80
SQ FT: 32,000
SALES (corp-wide): 63.5B **Publicly Held**
WEB: www.joy-of-cola.com
SIC: 5149 4225 2086 Soft drinks; general
warehousing & storage; bottled & canned
soft drinks
HQ: Pepsi-Cola Metropolitan Bottling Com-
pany, Inc.
1111 Westchester Ave
White Plains NY 10604
914 767-6000

(P-8849)
PEPSI-COLA METRO BTLG CO
INC
4416 Azusa Canyon Rd, Baldwin Park
(91706-2797)
PHONE..................................626 338-5531
Terry Dana, *Manager*
EMP: 200
SQ FT: 65,113
SALES (corp-wide): 63.5B **Publicly Held**
WEB: www.joy-of-cola.com
SIC: 5149 Soft drinks
HQ: Pepsi-Cola Metropolitan Bottling Com-
pany, Inc.
1111 Westchester Ave
White Plains NY 10604
914 767-6000

(P-8850)
PEPSI-COLA METRO BTLG CO
INC
1200 Arroyo St, San Fernando
(91340-1545)
PHONE..................................818 898-3829
Bob Simpson, *Branch Mgr*
Andy Irvin, *Warehouse Mgr*
Chris Bozzo, *Manager*
Paul Cachay, *Manager*
EMP: 207
SALES (corp-wide): 63.5B **Publicly Held**
WEB: www.joy-of-cola.com
SIC: 5149 2086 Soft drinks; bottled &
canned soft drinks
HQ: Pepsi-Cola Metropolitan Bottling Com-
pany, Inc.
1111 Westchester Ave
White Plains NY 10604
914 767-6000

(P-8851)
PEPSI-COLA METRO BTLG CO
INC
200 Jennings St, San Francisco
(94124-1723)
PHONE..................................415 206-7400
Dan Atkins, *Branch Mgr*
Justin Rau, *Opers Mgr*
EMP: 95
SALES (corp-wide): 63.5B **Publicly Held**
WEB: www.joy-of-cola.com
SIC: 5149 5142 Soft drinks; packaged
frozen goods
HQ: Pepsi-Cola Metropolitan Bottling Com-
pany, Inc.
1111 Westchester Ave
White Plains NY 10604
914 767-6000

(P-8852)
PERFECT BAR LLC
Also Called: Perfect Foods
3931 Sorrento Valley Blvd, San Diego
(92121-1402)
PHONE..................................866 628-8548
Bill Keith, *CEO*
Leigh Keith, *Vice Pres*
Christine Fernandez, *QA Dir*
Elizabeth Carter, *VP Finance*
Kristin Silva, *Accountant*
EMP: 95
SQ FT: 16,000
SALES (est): 47.5MM **Privately Held**
SIC: 5149 Health foods

(P-8853)
POMWONDERFUL LLC (DH)
11444 W Olympic Blvd, Los Angeles
(90064-1549)
PHONE..................................310 966-5800
Richard Cottrell, *CEO*
Matt Tupper, *President*
Kurt Vetter, *Vice Pres*
Leon Tin Change, *Controller*
Molly Flynn, *Marketing Staff*
◆ **EMP:** 116
SALES (est): 500.4MM
SALES (corp-wide): 1.5B **Privately Held**
WEB: www.pomwonderful.com
SIC: 5149 5148 5085 Beverage concen-
trates; juices; tea; fruits, fresh; plastic bot-
tles
HQ: Pom Wonderful Holdings Llc
11444 W Olympic Blvd # 210
Los Angeles CA 90064
310 966-5800

(P-8854)
POMWONDERFUL LLC
900 Airport Blvd, Mendota (93640-2441)
PHONE..................................310 966-5800
Larry Isonio, *Branch Mgr*
EMP: 100
SALES (corp-wide): 1.5B **Privately Held**
SIC: 5149 5148 5085 Beverage concen-
trates; fruits, fresh; plastic bottles
HQ: Pomwonderful Llc
11444 W Olympic Blvd
Los Angeles CA 90064
310 966-5800

(P-8855)
POSH BAGEL INC (PA)
445 Nelo St, Santa Clara (95054-2145)
PHONE..................................408 980-8451
Jeff Ottoveggio, *President*
Sergio Donoso, *Vice Pres*
EMP: 75
SQ FT: 15,000
SALES (est): 38.3MM **Privately Held**
WEB: www.theposhbagel.com
SIC: 5149 Bakery products

(P-8856)
POSH BAKERY INC
445 Nelo St, Santa Clara (95054-2145)
PHONE..................................408 980-8451
Cherly Lee, *President*
▼ **EMP:** 120 **EST:** 2008
SALES (est): 20.4MM **Privately Held**
SIC: 5149 Bakery products

(P-8857)
PRESTIGE SALES II LLC
1038 E Bastanchury Rd, Fullerton
(92835-2786)
PHONE..................................714 632-8020
Greg Zail, *Mng Member*
Bernie Barrad,
▲ **EMP:** 75
SQ FT: 27,000
SALES (est): 4.9MM **Privately Held**
WEB: www.psana.com
SIC: 5149 5181 Soft drinks; beer & ale

(P-8858)
REAL GOOD FOOD COMPANY
LLC
A11 N Maryland Ave 201, Glendale
(91206)
PHONE..................................909 744-0073
Josh Schreider,
Mista Asbury,
EMP: 200 **EST:** 2016
SALES (est): 20MM **Privately Held**
SIC: 5149 Specialty food items

(P-8859)
RED BULL DISTRIBUTION CO
INC (HQ)
Also Called: Redbull Distribution Co Colo
1740 Stewart St, Santa Monica
(90404-4022)
PHONE..................................916 515-3501
Selin Chidiak, *CEO*
Peter Kwon, *Admin Sec*
Ryan Snyder, *Manager*
EMP: 84
SALES (est): 103.7MM
SALES (corp-wide): 3.9B **Privately Held**
SIC: 5149 Beverage concentrates
PA: Red Bull Gmbh
Am Brunnen 1
Fuschl Am See 5330
662 658-20

(P-8860)
REYES COCA-COLA BOTTLING
LLC
12925 Bradley Ave, Sylmar (91342-3830)
PHONE..................................818 362-4307
Larry Campbell, *Branch Mgr*
EMP: 75
SALES (corp-wide): 648.9MM **Privately**
Held
SIC: 5149 4225 2086 Soft drinks; general
warehousing; bottled & canned soft drinks
PA: Reyes Coca-Cola Bottling, L.L.C.
3 Park Plz Ste 600
Irvine CA 92614
213 744-8616

(P-8861)
ROCKVIEW DAIRIES INC (PA)
Also Called: Motive Nation
7011 Stewart And Gray Rd, Downey
(90241-4347)
P.O. Box 668 (90241-0668)
PHONE..................................562 927-5511
Egbert Jim Degroot, *CEO*
Valarie Cooke, *President*
Edgar Del Rio, *CFO*
Joe Valadez, *CFO*
Carlos Lopez, *Lab Dir*
◆ **EMP:** 96
SALES (est): 181.7MM **Privately Held**
WEB: www.rockviewfarms.com
SIC: 5149 5143 2026 Dried or canned
foods; milk; fluid milk

(P-8862)
ROMA FOOD ENTERPRISES INC
Also Called: Roma of Northern California
6211 Las Positas Rd, Livermore
(94551-5101)
PHONE..................................800 233-6211
EMP: 90
SALES (corp-wide): 15.2B **Publicly Held**
SIC: 5149 5141
HQ: Roma Food Enterprises, Inc.
1 Roma Blvd
Piscataway NJ 08854
732 463-7662

(P-8863)
ROYAL CROWN ENTERPRISES
INC (PA)
780 Epperson Dr, City of Industry
(91748-1336)
PHONE..................................626 854-8080
Juergen Lotter, *President*
Christiane Lotter, *Vice Pres*
◆ **EMP:** 100
SQ FT: 60,000
SALES (est): 21.4MM **Privately Held**
SIC: 5149 5141 Canned goods: fruit, veg-
etables, seafood, meats, etc.; groceries,
general line

(P-8864)
SADIE ROSE BAKING CO
8926 Ware Ct, San Diego (92121-2222)
PHONE..................................858 831-0290
Jennifer Ann Curran, *CEO*
Michael Lipman, *President*
Ryan Block, *Plant Mgr*
Debra Kapz, *Sales Executive*
Therese Wootton, *Regl Sales Mgr*
◆ **EMP:** 70
SQ FT: 23,000
SALES (est): 21.3MM **Privately Held**
SIC: 5149 Bakery products

(P-8865)
SEMIFREDDIS INC (PA)
Also Called: Semifreddi's Bakery
1980 N Loop Rd, Alameda (94502-3540)
PHONE..................................510 596-9930
Thomas Frainier, *President*
Michael Rose, *Admin Sec*
John Tredgold, *Director*
Ken Simmons, *Manager*
Craig West, *Manager*
EMP: 110
SQ FT: 36,000
SALES (est): 51.4MM **Privately Held**
WEB: www.semifreddis.com
SIC: 5149 5461 Bakery products; bakeries

(P-8866)
SETTON PSTCHIO TERRA
BELLA INC (HQ)
9370 Road 234, Terra Bella (93270-9226)
P.O. Box 11089 (93270-1089)
PHONE..................................559 535-6050
Joshua Setton, *President*
Morris Setton, *Vice Pres*
Kellie Shepard, *Hum Res Coord*
Carl Scruton, *QC Mgr*
▲ **EMP:** 70
SQ FT: 133,000
SALES (est): 69.6MM
SALES (corp-wide): 23.6MM **Privately**
Held
SIC: 5149 5145 0173 2068 Fruits, dried;
nuts, salted or roasted; pistachio grove;
salted & roasted nuts & seeds

PA: Setton's International Foods, Inc.
85 Austin Blvd
Commack NY 11725
631 543-8090

(P-8867)
SHAW BAKERS LLC
320b Shaw Rd Ste B, South San Francisco (94080-6623)
PHONE..................650 273-1440
Darrell Smith, *Mng Member*
EMP: 100
SALES: 10MM **Privately Held**
SIC: 5149 Bakery products

(P-8868)
SIMONS WHOLESALE BAKERY INC
1901 Ritchey St, Santa Ana (92705-5129)
PHONE..................714 259-0855
Simon Meyerowitz, *President*
EMP: 50
SQ FT: 3,700
SALES (est): 8MM **Privately Held**
SIC: 5149 Bakery products

(P-8869)
SMOKEHOUSE PET PRODUCTS INC
11850 Sheldon St, Sun Valley (91352-1507)
PHONE..................818 771-0181
Zelto Mazistorovich, *Owner*
Michelle Majstorich, *Administration*
Chris Cobb, *Sales Mgr*
Lisa Kahn, *Sales Mgr*
Zelko Majstorich, *Director*
EMP: 50
SALES (est): 6.7MM
SALES (corp-wide): 6.2MM **Privately Held**
SIC: 5149 Pet foods
PA: Smokehouse Pet Products, Inc.
17 W Magnolia Blvd
Burbank CA 91502
818 771-0181

(P-8870)
SOOFER CO INC
Also Called: Sadaf Foods
2828 S Alameda St, Vernon (90058-1347)
PHONE..................323 234-6666
Dariush Soofer, *CEO*
Jamshid Soofer, *President*
Behrooz David Soofer, *COO*
David Soofer, *COO*
George Melikian, *Principal*
▲ EMP: 75 EST: 1981
SQ FT: 70,000
SALES (est): 55.3MM **Privately Held**
WEB: www.sadaf.com
SIC: 5149 Spices & seasonings

(P-8871)
STAPLETON - SPENCE PACKING CO (PA)
1900 State Highway 99, Gridley (95948-9401)
P.O. Box 948 (95948-0948)
PHONE..................408 297-8815
Martin Bradley Stapleton, *CEO*
Gavin Heitman, *Admin Sec*
◆ EMP: 114 EST: 1951
SQ FT: 105,000
SALES (est): 40.6MM **Privately Held**
WEB: www.stapleton-spence.com
SIC: 5149 Groceries & related products

(P-8872)
STARWEST BOTANICALS INC (PA)
161 Main Ave, Sacramento (95838-2080)
PHONE..................916 638-8100
Van Joerger, *President*
Melissa Waters, *Mktg Dir*
Megan Strawn, *Accounts Mgr*
◆ EMP: 95 EST: 1975
SQ FT: 68,400
SALES (est): 35.7MM **Privately Held**
WEB: www.starwestherb.com
SIC: 5149 Tea; spices & seasonings

(P-8873)
SUJA LIFE LLC
Also Called: Suja Juice
3841 Ocean Ranch Blvd # 101, Oceanside (92056-2694)
PHONE..................855 879-7852
Jeffrey Church, *CEO*
James Brennan, *President*
▲ EMP: 205
SALES (est): 150.6MM **Privately Held**
SIC: 5149 Fruit peel

(P-8874)
SUN CHLORELLA USA CORP
3305 Kashiwa St, Torrance (90505-4022)
PHONE..................310 891-0600
Futoshi Nakayama, *CEO*
Yoshihito Nishimaki, *President*
Rose Straub, *COO*
Ellen Kubijanto, *CFO*
Nicola Lott, *Admin Asst*
▲ EMP: 54
SQ FT: 20,000
SALES (est): 14.4MM
SALES (corp-wide): 21.5MM **Privately Held**
WEB: www.sunchlorellausa.com
SIC: 5149 Health foods
PA: Sun Chlorella Corp.
369, Osakacho, Karasumadori-Gojosagaru, Shimogyo-Ku
Kyoto KYO 600-8
752 883-000

(P-8875)
SUN TEN LABS LIQUIDATION CO
9250 Jeronimo Rd, Irvine (92618-1905)
PHONE..................949 587-0509
Charleson C Hsu, *CEO*
Jack Yang, *VP Sales*
◆ EMP: 60
SALES (est): 14.2MM **Privately Held**
WEB: www.sunten.com
SIC: 5149 2834 2833 Spices & seasonings; pharmaceutical preparations; medicinals & botanicals

(P-8876)
SUN-MAID GROWERS CALIFORNIA (PA)
13525 S Bethel Ave, Kingsburg (93631-9232)
PHONE..................559 897-6235
Barry F Kriebel, *President*
Braden Bender, *CFO*
Richard Paumen, *Senior VP*
Michael Cassidy, *Vice Pres*
Kayhan Hazrati, *Vice Pres*
◆ EMP: 750
SALES (est): 360.8MM **Privately Held**
SIC: 5149 Groceries & related products

(P-8877)
SUN-MAID GROWERS CALIFORNIA
Also Called: Sun Maid Growers
15628 E Nebraska Ave, Kingsburg (93631-9714)
PHONE..................559 897-8900
EMP: 273
SALES (corp-wide): 360.8MM **Privately Held**
SIC: 5149 Groceries & related products
PA: Sun-Maid Growers Of California
13525 S Bethel Ave
Kingsburg CA 93631
559 897-6235

(P-8878)
SUPER STORE INDUSTRIES
Also Called: Ssi
16888 Mckinley Ave, Lathrop (95330-9705)
P.O. Box 549 (95330-0549)
PHONE..................209 858-3365
Tom Hughes, *Branch Mgr*
Russ Davis, *Chief Mktg Ofcr*
Rod Reiswig, *Info Tech Dir*
Scott Sommerfeld, *Facilities Mgr*
Sarah Goreham, *Director*
EMP: 400

SALES (corp-wide): 279.6MM **Privately Held**
SIC: 5149 5141 4225 Groceries & related products; groceries, general line; general warehousing & storage
PA: Super Store Industries
2800 W March Ln Ste 210
Stockton CA 95219
209 473-8100

(P-8879)
SURVIVALCAVE INC
10620 Treena St Ste 230, San Diego (92131-1140)
PHONE..................800 719-7650
J R Fisher, *President*
EMP: 50 EST: 2010
SALES (est): 7.8MM **Privately Held**
SIC: 5149 Canned goods: fruit, vegetables, seafood, meats, etc.

(P-8880)
SYGMA NETWORK INC
46905 47th St W, Lancaster (93536-8527)
PHONE..................661 723-0405
Mike Wren, *Branch Mgr*
EMP: 200
SALES (corp-wide): 58.7B **Publicly Held**
WEB: www.sygmanetwork.com
SIC: 5149 Specialty food items
HQ: The Sygma Network Inc
5550 Blazer Pkwy Ste 300
Dublin OH 43017

(P-8881)
TADIN INC
Also Called: Tadin Herb & Tea Co.
3345 E Slauson Ave, Vernon (90058-3914)
PHONE..................213 406-8880
Jose M Gonzalez, *President*
Maria Diaz, *Controller*
Alexis Castellanos, *Human Resources*
Luis Cruz, *Purch Mgr*
Arely Campos, *Sales Executive*
▲ EMP: 95
SQ FT: 40,000
SALES: 17.4MM **Privately Held**
SIC: 5149 Tea

(P-8882)
TAMA TRADING COMPANY
1920 E 20th St, Vernon (90058-1076)
PHONE..................213 748-8262
William A Sauro, *CEO*
Sandra Sauro, *Corp Secy*
◆ EMP: 61
SQ FT: 60,000
SALES (est): 24.4MM **Privately Held**
SIC: 5149 5143 5147 5145 Specialty food items; seasonings, sauces & extracts; pasta & rice; cheese; meats & meat products; candy

(P-8883)
TANAKA FARMS
5380 University Dr, Irvine (92612-2944)
PHONE..................949 653-2100
Glenn Tannaka, *Owner*
EMP: 60 EST: 1975
SALES (est): 5.1MM **Privately Held**
WEB: www.tanakafarms.com
SIC: 5149 Groceries & related products

(P-8884)
TAWA SERVICES INC (PA)
6281 Regio Ave Fl 2, Buena Park (90620-1023)
PHONE..................714 521-8899
Jonson Chen, *CEO*
Young You, *CEO*
▼ EMP: 220
SALES (est): 195.5MM **Privately Held**
SIC: 5149 5411 Groceries & related products; grocery stores

(P-8885)
TOO GOOD GOURMET INC (PA)
2380 Grant Ave, San Lorenzo (94580-1806)
PHONE..................510 317-8150
Amie G Watson, *CEO*
Jennifer Finley, *President*
Joe Waldrep, *Business Dir*
John Campbell, *Mktg Dir*
Emily Melo, *Clerk*

▲ EMP: 71
SQ FT: 50,000
SALES (est): 6.6MM **Privately Held**
WEB: www.toogoodgourmet.com
SIC: 5149 5461 2052 Cookies; crackers, cookies & bakery products; cookies; cookies

(P-8886)
TOOT SWEETS LTD (PA)
Also Called: Toot Sweets Fine Desserts
1277 Gilman St, Berkeley (94706-2351)
PHONE..................510 526-0610
Marcy Wheeler, *President*
Robert Kelso, *Admin Sec*
EMP: 50 EST: 1974
SQ FT: 2,000
SALES (est): 12.3MM **Privately Held**
SIC: 5149 Bakery products

(P-8887)
TRAINA DRIED FRUIT INC
Also Called: Traina Foods
337 1/2 Lemon Ave, Patterson (95363-9634)
P.O. Box 157 (95363-0157)
PHONE..................209 892-5472
William Traina, *CEO*
Joseph Traina, *CFO*
Justin A Traina, *Vice Pres*
Josephine Traina, *Admin Sec*
▲ EMP: 240
SQ FT: 5,000
SALES (est): 18.9MM **Privately Held**
WEB: www.trainadriedfruit.com
SIC: 5149 Fruits, dried

(P-8888)
TRINITY FRESH DISTRIBUTION LLC
8200 Berry Ave Ste 140, Sacramento (95828-1612)
PHONE..................916 714-7368
Paul Abess,
EMP: 70
SALES (est): 17.3MM **Privately Held**
SIC: 5149 Dairy products, dried or canned

(P-8889)
UNITED NATURAL FOODS INC
2450 17th Ave Ste 250, Santa Cruz (95062-1987)
PHONE..................831 462-5870
Melody Meyer, *Branch Mgr*
EMP: 133 **Publicly Held**
SIC: 5149 5122 5142 Organic & diet foods; health foods; natural & organic foods; cosmetics, perfumes & hair products; vitamins & minerals; packaged frozen goods
PA: United Natural Foods, Inc.
313 Iron Horse Way
Providence RI 02908

(P-8890)
UNITED NATURAL FOODS INC
Also Called: Unfi
1101 Sunset Blvd, Rocklin (95765-3786)
PHONE..................916 625-4100
Steven L Spinner, *CEO*
◆ EMP: 86 EST: 1994
SALES (est): 37.2MM **Privately Held**
SIC: 5149 5122 5142 Organic & diet foods; cosmetics, perfumes & hair products; packaged frozen goods

(P-8891)
UNITED NATURAL FOODS WEST INC (HQ)
Also Called: Unfi
1101 Sunset Blvd, Rocklin (95765-3786)
PHONE..................401 528-8634
Kurt M Luttecke, *CEO*
Michael S Funk, *Ch of Bd*
Steven L Spinner, *President*
Eric A Dorne, *Senior VP*
Sean F Griffin, *Vice Pres*
▲ EMP: 385 EST: 1976
SQ FT: 150,000
SALES (est): 551.5MM **Publicly Held**
WEB: www.mpwnw.com
SIC: 5149 5141 Groceries & related products; groceries, general line

(P-8892)
US FOODS INC
US Foods Corona
1283 Sherborn St Ste 102, Corona
(92879-5003)
PHONE...................800 888-3147
Graylon Macfall, *Division Pres*
EMP: 250 **Publicly Held**
SIC: 5149 Dried or canned foods
HQ: Us Foods, Inc.
    9399 W Higgins Rd Ste 500
    Rosemont IL 60018

(P-8893)
US FOODS INC
1283 Sherborn St Ste 102, Corona
(92879-5003)
PHONE...................951 582-8500
Patrick Waller, *Manager*
EMP: 150 **Publicly Held**
WEB: www.usfoodservice.com
SIC: 5149 Groceries & related products
HQ: Us Foods, Inc.
    9399 W Higgins Rd Ste 500
    Rosemont IL 60018

(P-8894)
US FOODS INC
Also Called: Mesa Cold Strg 4145
700 S Raymond Ave, Fullerton
(92831-5233)
PHONE...................714 449-9990
Ed Libel, *Branch Mgr*
EMP: 161 **Publicly Held**
SIC: 5149 Dried or canned foods
HQ: Us Foods, Inc.
    9399 W Higgins Rd Ste 500
    Rosemont IL 60018

(P-8895)
US FOODS INC
Also Called: Sierra Pacific 4117
4300 Finch Rd, Modesto (95357-4102)
PHONE...................209 572-2882
EMP: 159 **Publicly Held**
SIC: 5149 Dried or canned foods
HQ: Us Foods, Inc.
    9399 W Higgins Rd Ste 500
    Rosemont IL 60018

(P-8896)
US FOODS INC
Also Called: Csi Cold Storage 4150
1415 N Raymond Ave, Anaheim
(92801-1111)
PHONE...................714 449-2880
EMP: 159 **Publicly Held**
SIC: 5149 Dried or canned foods
HQ: Us Foods, Inc.
    9399 W Higgins Rd Ste 500
    Rosemont IL 60018

(P-8897)
US FOODS INC
Also Called: USF-La Mirada 4150
15155 Northam St, La Mirada
(90638-5754)
PHONE...................714 670-3500
David Patterson, *Branch Mgr*
EMP: 159 **Publicly Held**
SIC: 5149 Dried or canned foods
HQ: Us Foods, Inc.
    9399 W Higgins Rd Ste 500
    Rosemont IL 60018

(P-8898)
US FOODS INC
Also Called: San Diego CLD Stg 4140
1240 W 28th St, National City
(91950-6319)
PHONE...................619 474-6525
EMP: 159 **Publicly Held**
SIC: 5149 Dried or canned foods
HQ: Us Foods, Inc.
    9399 W Higgins Rd Ste 500
    Rosemont IL 60018

(P-8899)
US FOODS INC
Also Called: USF Import FWD Wh 4150
1283 Sherborn St Ste 102, Corona
(92879-5003)
PHONE...................951 256-2400
EMP: 159 **Publicly Held**
SIC: 5149 Dried or canned foods
HQ: Us Foods, Inc.
    9399 W Higgins Rd Ste 500
    Rosemont IL 60018

(P-8900)
VISTA VERDE FARMS
11251 Melcher Rd, Delano (93215-9310)
PHONE...................661 720-9733
Santos Montmayor, *Owner*
EMP: 50
SALES (est): 2.4MM **Privately Held**
SIC: 5149 Groceries & related products

(P-8901)
WALONG MARKETING INC (PA)
Also Called: Foods and Produce
6281 Regio Ave, Buena Park (90620-1023)
PHONE...................714 670-8899
Chang Hua K Chen, *CEO*
Roger Chen, *Ch of Bd*
Chen James, *Officer*
Philip Yang, *Buyer*
Teddy Huang, *Marketing Mgr*
◆ EMP: 100
SALES (est): 79.9MM **Privately Held**
SIC: 5149 5411 Groceries & related products; grocery stores

(P-8902)
YAMAMOTO OF ORIENT INC (HQ)
Also Called: Yamamotoyama of America
122 Voyager St, Pomona (91768-3252)
PHONE...................909 594-7356
Kahei Yamamoto, *Ch of Bd*
Hisayuki Nakagawa, *President*
Daniel Goldstein, *COO*
Kazumi Ikeda, *Treasurer*
Kaichiro Yamamoto, *Admin Sec*
▲ EMP: 130 EST: 1975
SQ FT: 60,000
SALES (est): 62.8MM
SALES (corp-wide): 64.4MM **Privately Held**
WEB: www.yamamotoyama.com
SIC: 5149 6512 5812 Tea; shopping center, property operation only; eating places
PA: Yamamotoyama Co., Ltd.
    1-2-5, Kyobashi
    Chuo-Ku TKY 104-0
    332 713-261

5153 Grain & Field Beans Wholesale

(P-8903)
A L GILBERT COMPANY
Also Called: Berry Seed & Feed
4431 Jessup Rd, Keyes (95328)
P.O. Box 459 (95328-0459)
PHONE...................209 537-0766
Edwin Gallagher, *Branch Mgr*
EMP: 60
SALES (corp-wide): 338.9MM **Privately Held**
SIC: 5153 Grains
PA: A. L. Gilbert Company
    304 N Yosemite Ave
    Oakdale CA 95361
    209 847-1721

(P-8904)
ANDERSON HAY & GRAIN CO INC
915 E Colon St, Wilmington (90744-2101)
PHONE...................310 518-2935
EMP: 105
SALES (corp-wide): 1.7MM **Privately Held**
SIC: 5153 Grains
PA: Anderson Hay & Grain Co., Inc.
    910 Anderson Rd
    Ellensburg WA 98926
    509 925-9818

(P-8905)
CALIFORNIA CEREAL PRODUCTS INC (PA)
1267 14th St, Oakland (94607-2246)
PHONE...................510 452-4500
Robert Sterling Savely, *CEO*
Mark Graham, *President*
Nestor Pajuleras, *Products*
Phil Gunter, *Manager*
Jorge Mendez, *Manager*
◆ EMP: 51
SQ FT: 120,000
SALES (est): 50.5MM **Privately Held**
SIC: 5153 Grain & field beans

(P-8906)
PACIFIC GRAIN & FOODS LLC (PA)
Also Called: Pacific Grain and Foods
4067 W Shaw Ave Ste 116, Fresno
(93722-6214)
P.O. Box 3928, Pinedale (93650-3928)
PHONE...................559 276-2580
Lee Perkins, *President*
Karen Perkins, *Vice Pres*
Jose M Alvarado, *Executive*
Martha Prado, *Executive Asst*
Dan Weggenman, *Sales Mgr*
◆ EMP: 135
SQ FT: 172,000
SALES: 30MM **Privately Held**
WEB: www.pacificgrainfoods.com
SIC: 5153 7389 5149 Grains; packaging & labeling services; spices & seasonings

5154 Livestock Wholesale

(P-8907)
SHASTA LIVESTOCK AUCTION YARD
3917 Main St, Cottonwood (96022)
P.O. Box 558 (96022-0558)
PHONE...................530 347-3793
Ellington Peek, *President*
Beatrice Peek, *Vice Pres*
EMP: 60
SQ FT: 15,000
SALES (est): 9.3MM **Privately Held**
SIC: 5154 Auctioning livestock

(P-8908)
STANDARD CATTLE LLC
729 E Jefferson Rd, El Nido (95317-9707)
PHONE...................559 693-1977
Michael Vander Dussen,
EMP: 131
SALES (est): 490.9K **Privately Held**
SIC: 5154 Cattle

5159 Farm-Prdt Raw Mtrls, NEC Wholesale

(P-8909)
ALTRIA GROUP DISTRIBUTION CO
3500 W Olive Ave Ste 1490, Burbank
(91505-5521)
PHONE...................804 274-2000
Craig A Johnson, *President*
EMP: 104
SALES (corp-wide): 25.5B **Publicly Held**
SIC: 5159 Tobacco distributors & products
HQ: Altria Group Distribution Company
    6601 W Broad St
    Richmond VA 23230

(P-8910)
SELECT HARVEST USA LLC (PA)
Also Called: Spycher Brothers
14827 W Harding Rd, Turlock
(95380-9012)
PHONE...................209 668-2471
Robert L Nunes, *Mng Member*
Juan-Carlos Veraza, *Officer*
Sheryl Wheeler, *Marketing Staff*
◆ EMP: 87 EST: 2008
SQ FT: 100,000

SALES (est): 54MM **Privately Held**
SIC: 5159 0173 Nuts & nut by-products; almond grove

(P-8911)
SOUTH VALLEY ALMOND CO LLC
Also Called: South Valley Farms
15443 Beech Ave, Wasco (93280-7604)
PHONE...................661 391-9000
Paul C Genho, *Mng Member*
Bobbie Sanocki, *Purch Mgr*
Jason Barnum, *Foreman/Supr*
Alex Parsons, *Foreman/Supr*
Daryl Wilkendorf,
▼ EMP: 200
SQ FT: 4,000
SALES (est): 60.8MM **Privately Held**
SIC: 5159 Nuts & nut by-products

5162 Plastics Materials & Basic Shapes Wholesale

(P-8912)
CIRRUS ENTERPRISES LLC
Also Called: E.V. Roberts
18027 Bishop Ave, Carson (90746-4019)
PHONE...................310 204-6159
Ron Cloud, *CEO*
Donna Knapp, *Executive Asst*
Keiko Clark, *Administration*
Kevin Hart, *Technical Staff*
Tracy Robel, *Controller*
▲ EMP: 52
SQ FT: 26,000
SALES (est): 33.5MM **Privately Held**
WEB: www.evroberts.com
SIC: 5162 2821 2891 5198 Plastics products; epoxy resins; adhesives & sealants; paints, varnishes & supplies; chemicals & allied products

(P-8913)
CONSOLIDATED PLASTICS CORP (PA)
Also Called: Paragon Plastics Co Div
14954 La Palma Dr, Chino (91710-9695)
PHONE...................909 393-8222
Jean Bouris, *President*
Gloria Jean Bouris, *CEO*
EMP: 55
SQ FT: 45,000
SALES (est): 14.4MM **Privately Held**
WEB: www.planetplastics.com
SIC: 5162 3599 Plastics sheets & rods; machine shop, jobbing & repair

(P-8914)
DONGALEN ENTERPRISES INC (PA)
Also Called: Interstate Plastics
330 Commerce Cir, Sacramento
(95815-4213)
P.O. Box 130027 (95853-0027)
PHONE...................916 422-3110
Mark Courtright, *President*
Cole Klokkevold, *CFO*
▲ EMP: 165
SQ FT: 33,000
SALES (est): 142.2MM **Privately Held**
WEB: www.interstateplastics.com
SIC: 5162 Plastics products

(P-8915)
VPET USA INC (PA)
12925 Marlay Ave, Fontana (92337-6939)
PHONE...................909 605-1668
Henry Lee, *CEO*
Benson Liu, *Vice Pres*
Penson Liu, *Vice Pres*
Wayne Smith, *Branch Mgr*
Henry Hsieh, *Project Engr*
▲ EMP: 60
SALES (est): 67.6MM **Privately Held**
WEB: www.vpetusa.com
SIC: 5162 Plastics basic shapes

5169 Chemicals & Allied Prdts, NEC Wholesale

(P-8916)
AIRGAS USA LLC
9010 Clairemont Mesa Blvd, San Diego (92123-1208)
P.O. Box 6030, Lakewood (90714-6030)
PHONE....................858 279-8200
Pat Muller, *Vice Pres*
EMP: 110
SALES (corp-wide): 164.2MM **Privately Held**
WEB: www.airgaswest.com
SIC: 5169 5084 5047 5046 Industrial gases; industrial machinery & equipment; medical & hospital equipment; commercial equipment
HQ: Airgas Usa, Llc
259 N Radnor Chester Rd # 100
Radnor PA 19087
610 687-5253

(P-8917)
AQUA-SERV ENGINEERS INC (HQ)
13560 Colombard Ct, Fontana (92337-7702)
PHONE....................951 681-9696
Earl L Harper, *CEO*
Garland Rachels, *President*
Buck Long, *Senior VP*
Sarah Centanni, *Info Tech Mgr*
Cindy Dykstra, *Controller*
EMP: 56 EST: 1958
SQ FT: 63,000
SALES (est): 32.4MM **Privately Held**
WEB: www.aqua-serv.com
SIC: 5169 Chemicals & allied products

(P-8918)
ASHLAND LLC
Also Called: Ashland Performance Materials
20915 S Wilmington Ave, Carson (90810-1039)
PHONE....................310 223-3505
Randy Weld, *Manager*
EMP: 90
SALES (corp-wide): 3.2B **Publicly Held**
WEB: www.ashland.com
SIC: 5169 Alkalines & chlorine
HQ: Ashland Llc
50 E Rivercenter Blvd # 1600
Covington KY 41011
859 815-3333

(P-8919)
ASHLAND LLC
Also Called: Ashland Distribution
6608 E 26th St, Commerce (90040-3216)
P.O. Box 22118, Los Angeles (90022-0118)
PHONE....................323 767-1300
Reid Mork, *Branch Mgr*
Fernando Celaya, *Maintence Staff*
EMP: 60
SQ FT: 45,845
SALES (corp-wide): 3.2B **Publicly Held**
WEB: www.ashland.com
SIC: 5169 Alkalines & chlorine
HQ: Ashland Llc
50 E Rivercenter Blvd # 1600
Covington KY 41011
859 815-3333

(P-8920)
BACHEM AMERICAS INC
1271 Avenida Chelsea, Vista (92081-8315)
PHONE....................760 597-8820
EMP: 86 **Privately Held**
SIC: 5169 2836 Chemicals & allied products; biological products, except diagnostic
HQ: Bachem Americas, Inc.
3132 Kashiwa St
Torrance CA 90505
310 784-4440

(P-8921)
BRENNTAG PACIFIC INC (DH)
10747 Patterson Pl, Santa Fe Springs (90670-4043)
PHONE....................562 903-9626
William A Fidler, *CEO*
Steven Pozzi, *President*

H Edward Boyadjian, *CFO*
Julia Tu, *Controller*
▲ EMP: 153
SALES (est): 436.3MM
SALES (corp-wide): 13.8B **Privately Held**
SIC: 5169 Chemicals, industrial & heavy
HQ: Brenntag North America, Inc.
5083 Pottsville Pike
Reading PA 19605
610 926-6100

(P-8922)
CARGILL INCORPORATED
7220 Central Ave, Newark (94560-4205)
PHONE....................510 797-1820
Warren Staley, *CEO*
EMP: 250
SALES (corp-wide): 51.2B **Privately Held**
WEB: www.cargill.com
SIC: 5169 Chemicals & allied products
PA: Cargill, Incorporated
15407 Mcginty Rd W
Wayzata MN 55391
952 742-7575

(P-8923)
CHEMICAL DEPENDENCY RECOVERY
2829 Watt Ave Ste 150, Sacramento (95821-6245)
PHONE....................916 482-1132
Melissa Rose, *Director*
EMP: 50
SALES (est): 2.3MM **Privately Held**
SIC: 5169 Chemicals & allied products

(P-8924)
CZECH COMMERCE LTD
3063 Larkin Rd, Pebble Beach (93953-2910)
PHONE....................831 649-4633
Jaroslav Stepanek, *President*
Scott Conner, *Vice Pres*
EMP: 53
SQ FT: 450
SALES: 2MM **Privately Held**
SIC: 5169 5031 Alcohols; building materials, exterior

(P-8925)
DESERT STAR CO
23119 Drayton St, Saugus (91350-2547)
PHONE....................661 259-5848
Mary Flynn, *Vice Pres*
EMP: 50
SALES (est): 2.3MM **Privately Held**
WEB: www.desertstar.net
SIC: 5169 Chemicals & allied products

(P-8926)
E T HORN COMPANY (PA)
16050 Canary Ave, La Mirada (90638-5585)
P.O. Box 1238 (90637-1238)
PHONE....................714 523-8050
Jeffrey Martin, *CEO*
Kevin Salerno, *President*
Julie Wubbena, *CFO*
Roger Clemens, *Officer*
Vince Anderson, *Vice Pres*
▲ EMP: 70 EST: 1961
SQ FT: 1,200
SALES (est): 319MM **Privately Held**
SIC: 5169 Industrial chemicals

(P-8927)
ENVIRO TECH CHEMICAL SVCS INC (PA)
500 Winmoore Way, Modesto (95358-5750)
PHONE....................209 581-9576
Michael S Harvey, *President*
Michael B Archibald, *Vice Pres*
◆ EMP: 102
SQ FT: 136,551
SALES: 53.2MM **Privately Held**
WEB: www.amcor.com.au
SIC: 5169 Industrial chemicals

(P-8928)
HILL BROTHERS CHEMICAL COMPANY (PA)
1675 N Main St, Orange (92867-3499)
PHONE....................714 998-8800
Ronald R Hill, *President*

Thomas F James, *CFO*
Kathryn Waters, *Treasurer*
Kathryn J Waters, *Corp Secy*
Matthew Thorne, *Exec VP*
▲ EMP: 153
SALES (est): 110.9MM **Privately Held**
WEB: www.norfox.ws
SIC: 5169 2819 Acids; calcium chloride & hypochlorite; magnesium compounds or salts, inorganic

(P-8929)
JACOB STERN & SONS INC (PA)
Also Called: Acme-Hardesty Co.
1464 E Valley Rd, Santa Barbara (93108-1241)
P.O. Box 50740 (93150-0740)
PHONE....................805 565-4532
Phillip L Bernstein, *President*
Jeff Kenton, *President*
Doug Shreves, *CEO*
Chip Hull, *CFO*
Kerry Arnold, *Vice Pres*
◆ EMP: 100 EST: 1857
SQ FT: 3,000
SALES (est): 97.2MM **Privately Held**
WEB: www.jacobstern.com
SIC: 5169 5191 5199 Industrial chemicals; animal feeds; greases, animal or vegetable

(P-8930)
K R ANDERSON INC (PA)
Also Called: Krayden
18330 Sutter Blvd, Morgan Hill (95037-2841)
PHONE....................408 825-1800
Dennis Wagner, *CEO*
Jim Caviglia, *Treasurer*
Doreen Oroshnik, *Administration*
Johnny Quilenderino, *QC Mgr*
Lindy Swaner, *Sales Staff*
▲ EMP: 60
SQ FT: 60,000
SALES (est): 43.3MM **Privately Held**
WEB: www.andfab.com
SIC: 5169 Synthetic resins, rubber & plastic materials

(P-8931)
MCP INDUSTRIES INC
Also Called: Purosil Division
10039 Norwalk Blvd, Santa Fe Springs (90670-3323)
P.O. Box 2467, Corona (92878-2467)
PHONE....................562 944-5511
Surrender Marwaha, *Manager*
EMP: 100
SALES (corp-wide): 126.4MM **Privately Held**
WEB: www.missionrubber.com
SIC: 5169 Silicon lubricants
PA: Mcp Industries, Inc.
708 S Temescal St Ste 101
Corona CA 92879
951 736-1881

(P-8932)
NALCO COMPANY LLC
1320 Arnold Dr Ste 246, Martinez (94553-6537)
PHONE....................925 957-9720
Bob Smith, *District Mgr*
Matt Del Bonta, *Area Mgr*
EMP: 100
SALES (corp-wide): 13.8B **Publicly Held**
WEB: www.nalco.com
SIC: 5169 Industrial chemicals
HQ: Nalco Company Llc
1601 W Diehl Rd
Naperville IL 77478
630 305-1000

(P-8933)
NORMAN FOX & CO (PA)
14970 Don Julian Rd, City of Industry (91746-3111)
PHONE....................626 581-5600
Stephen Halpin, *CEO*
Anh Hua, *Controller*
Lori Williams, *Manager*
▲ EMP: 63
SQ FT: 5,000

SALES: 6MM **Privately Held**
WEB: www.norfox.ws
SIC: 5169 2841 Chemicals & allied products; soap: granulated, liquid, cake, flaked or chip; detergents, synthetic organic or inorganic alkaline

(P-8934)
PRAXAIR INC
2300 E Pacific Coast Hwy, Wilmington (90744-2919)
P.O. Box 1309 (90748)
PHONE....................562 983-2100
Ted Mayberry, *Branch Mgr*
EMP: 96
SALES (corp-wide): 11.4B **Privately Held**
SIC: 5169 2813 Industrial gases; industrial gases
PA: Praxair, Inc.
10 Riverview Dr
Danbury CT 06810
203 837-2000

(P-8935)
PROCTER & GAMBLE DISTRG LLC
1992 Rockefeller Dr, Ceres (95307-7274)
PHONE....................209 538-3987
Michael Wheatley, *Branch Mgr*
EMP: 273
SALES (corp-wide): 66.8B **Publicly Held**
SIC: 5169 Detergents
HQ: Procter & Gamble Distributing Llc
1 Procter And Gamble Plz
Cincinnati OH 45202
513 983-1100

(P-8936)
PROCTER & GAMBLE DISTRG LLC
2010 Crow Canyon Pl # 230, San Ramon (94583-1344)
PHONE....................925 867-4900
Virginia Cavlin, *Manager*
Michael McDonald, *Wholesale*
EMP: 273
SALES (corp-wide): 66.8B **Publicly Held**
SIC: 5169 5122 5149 5113 Detergents; laundry soap chips & powder; drugs, proprietaries & sundries; groceries & related products; coffee, green or roasted; napkins, paper; towels, paper; dishes, disposable plastic & paper; diapers; service establishment equipment
HQ: Procter & Gamble Distributing Llc
1 Procter And Gamble Plz
Cincinnati OH 45202
513 983-1100

(P-8937)
UNITED PETROCHEMICALS INC
3000 W Macarthur Blvd # 300, Santa Ana (92704-7930)
PHONE....................949 629-8736
Lynne Vanderwall, *CEO*
Zach Smith, *Vice Pres*
EMP: 75
SQ FT: 25,000
SALES (est): 2.8MM **Privately Held**
SIC: 5169 Industrial chemicals

(P-8938)
UNIVAR USA INC
2600 Garfield Ave, Commerce (90040-2608)
P.O. Box 512062 (90040)
PHONE....................323 727-7005
Gary Cramer, *Branch Mgr*
Darren Wong, *Planning*
Mary Lubetski, *Technology*
Jim Foley, *Train & Dev Mgr*
Anna Arnold, *Purchasing*
EMP: 175
SALES (corp-wide): 8.2B **Publicly Held**
SIC: 5169 Industrial chemicals
HQ: Univar Usa Inc.
3075 Highland Pkwy # 200
Downers Grove IL 60515
331 777-6000

(P-8939)
UNIVAR USA INC
2256 Junction Ave, San Jose (95131-1216)
PHONE....................408 435-8649
Dan Manners, *Branch Mgr*
Esperanza Fregoso, *Admin Asst*

P R O D U C T S & S V C S

Kristin Kistler, *Admin Asst*
Carly Richard, *Opers Staff*
John James, *Regl Sales Mgr*
EMP: 80
SALES (corp-wide): 8.2B **Publicly Held**
SIC: 5169 5191 Industrial chemicals; farm
supplies
HQ: Univar Usa Inc.
3075 Highland Pkwy # 200
Downers Grove IL 60515
331 777-6000

(P-8940)
**VALEANT BIOMEDICALS INC
(DH)**
1 Enterprise, Aliso Viejo (92656-2606)
PHONE.............................949 461-6000
Tim Tyson, *President*
Jocelyne Lachapelle, *President*
Joe Morales, *Officer*
Laurie W Little, *Vice Pres*
Charles Perez, *Vice Pres*
EMP: 100
SQ FT: 55,000
SALES (est): 58.2MM
SALES (corp-wide): 8.7B **Privately Held**
SIC: 5169 5047 2835 3826 Chemicals &
allied products; biotechnical research,
commercial; medical equipment & sup-
plies; analytical instruments; liquid testing
apparatus; in vitro & in vivo diagnostic
substances; blood derivative diagnostic
agents
HQ: Bausch Health Companies Inc.
400 Somerset Corp Blvd
Bridgewater NJ 08807
908 927-1400

**5171 Petroleum Bulk
Stations & Terminals**

(P-8941)
**BP WEST COAST PRODUCTS
LLC**
Also Called: BP Products W Coast Refinery
1801 E Sepulveda Blvd, Carson
(90745-6121)
PHONE.............................310 549-6204
George Nicolaides, *Plant Mgr*
EMP: 250
SALES (corp-wide): 240.2B **Privately
Held**
SIC: 5171 Petroleum bulk stations & termi-
nals
HQ: Bp West Coast Products Llc
4519 Grandview Rd
Blaine WA 98230
310 549-6204

(P-8942)
C L BRYANT INC
7401 Del Cielo Way, Modesto
(95356-8874)
PHONE.............................209 566-5000
Toll Free:.............................877
Charles L Bryant Jr, *President*
EMP: 159
SQ FT: 16,164
SALES (est): 32.4MM **Privately Held**
SIC: 5171 5541 Petroleum bulk stations;
filling stations, gasoline

(P-8943)
FLYERS ENERGY LLC
11211 G Ave, Hesperia (92345-5134)
PHONE.............................760 949-3356
Rick Teske, *Branch Mgr*
EMP: 65
SALES (corp-wide): 126.7MM **Privately
Held**
SIC: 5171 Petroleum bulk stations
PA: Flyers Energy, Llc
2360 Lindbergh St
Auburn CA 95602
530 885-0401

(P-8944)
**GENERAL PETROLEUM
CORPORATION**
237 E Whitmore Ave, Modesto
(95358-9411)
PHONE.............................209 537-1056
EMP: 70

SALES (corp-wide): 1.1B **Privately Held**
SIC: 5171
HQ: General Petroleum Corporation
19501 S Santa Fe Ave
Compton CA 90221
562 983-7300

(P-8945)
RAMOS OIL CO INC (PA)
1515 S River Rd, West Sacramento
(95691-2882)
P.O. Box 401 (95691-0401)
PHONE.............................916 371-2570
Kent Ramos, *President*
Kyle Ramos, *President*
William Ramos, *President*
John Bailey, *CFO*
Jan Bard, *CFO*
EMP: 100
SQ FT: 3,200
SALES (est): 123.3MM **Privately Held**
WEB: www.ramosoil.com
SIC: 5171 5172 Petroleum bulk stations;
lubricating oils & greases

(P-8946)
**SOUTHERN COUNTIES OIL CO
(PA)**
Also Called: SC Fuels
1800 W Katella Ave # 400, Orange
(92867-3449)
P.O. Box 4159 (92863-4159)
PHONE.............................714 744-7140
Frank P Greinke, *CEO*
Steve Greinke, *President*
David Larimer, *COO*
Mimi Taylor, *CFO*
Brian Decker, *Bd of Directors*
EMP: 95
SALES (est): 1.2B **Privately Held**
SIC: 5171 5541 5172 Petroleum bulk sta-
tions; gasoline service stations; petroleum
products

(P-8947)
WESTERN ENERGETIX LLC
Also Called: Berry-Hinckley
2360 Lindbergh St, Auburn (95602-9562)
PHONE.............................530 885-0401
Rick Teske, *General Mgr*
EMP: 140
SALES (est): 48.9MM **Privately Held**
SIC: 5171 Petroleum bulk stations

**5172 Petroleum & Petroleum
Prdts Wholesale**

(P-8948)
ALL-POINTS PETROLEUM LLC
640 Noyes Ct, Benicia (94510-1229)
P.O. Box 278 (94510-0278)
PHONE.............................707 745-1116
Ronald Myska,
EMP: 61
SQ FT: 4,000
SALES (est): 49.9MM **Privately Held**
WEB: www.allpointspetroleum.com
SIC: 5172 Gasoline

(P-8949)
AMERIGAS PROPANE LP
11030 White Rock Rd # 100, Rancho Cor-
dova (95670-6011)
PHONE.............................916 852-7400
Fax: 916 631-3180
EMP: 100 **Publicly Held**
SIC: 5172 7374
HQ: Amerigas Propane, L.P.
460 N Gulph Rd Ste 100
King Of Prussia PA 19406

(P-8950)
**BAY AREA/DIABLO PETROLEUM
CO (HQ)**
1340 Arnold Dr Ste 231, Martinez
(94553-4189)
P.O. Box 4450, San Francisco (94144-
0001)
PHONE.............................925 228-2222
Dennis M O'Keefe, *CEO*
Patrick O'Keefe, *Vice Pres*
EMP: 125 **EST:** 1970
SQ FT: 6,000

SALES (est): 102.4MM
SALES (corp-wide): 101.1MM **Privately
Held**
SIC: 5172 Gasoline
PA: Golden Gate Petroleum Co.
1340 Arnold Dr Ste 231
Martinez CA 94553
925 335-3700

(P-8951)
**BAY AREA/DIABLO PETROLEUM
CO**
1800 Sutter St, Concord (94520-2563)
P.O. Box 44550, San Francisco (94144-
0001)
PHONE.............................925 228-2222
Russell Mederios, *Manager*
EMP: 130
SALES (corp-wide): 101.1MM **Privately
Held**
SIC: 5172 Gases, liquefied petroleum
(propane)
HQ: Bay Area/Diablo Petroleum, Co.
1340 Arnold Dr Ste 231
Martinez CA 94553
925 228-2222

(P-8952)
CASEY COMPANY (PA)
180 E Ocean Blvd Ste 1010, Long Beach
(90802-4711)
PHONE.............................562 436-9685
Larry Delpit Sr, *Chairman*
Barbara Odom, *Treasurer*
Betty Jane Blanchette, *Admin Sec*
EMP: 138
SQ FT: 4,000
SALES (est): 53.7MM **Privately Held**
SIC: 5172 Petroleum products

(P-8953)
DASSELS PETROLEUM INC
340 El Camino Real S, Salinas
(93901-4553)
PHONE.............................831 636-5100
Graham Mackie, *Branch Mgr*
EMP: 50
SALES (corp-wide): 33MM **Privately
Held**
WEB: www.dassels.com
SIC: 5172 Gases, liquefied petroleum
(propane)
PA: Dassel's Petroleum, Inc.
31 Wright Rd
Hollister CA 95023
831 636-5100

(P-8954)
DOWNS FUEL TRANSPORT INC
1296 Magnolia Ave, Corona (92879-2027)
PHONE.............................951 256-8286
Michael J Downs, *President*
EMP: 50
SALES (est): 13.3MM **Privately Held**
SIC: 5172 Engine fuels & oils

(P-8955)
**ED STAUB & SONS PETROLEUM
INC**
406 W 8th St, Alturas (96101-3205)
P.O. Box 1684 (96101-1684)
PHONE.............................530 233-2610
Sam Lutz, *Manager*
EMP: 55
SALES (corp-wide): 327.9MM **Privately
Held**
SIC: 5172 Petroleum products
PA: Ed Staub & Sons Petroleum, Inc.
1301 Esplanade Ave
Klamath Falls OR 97601
541 887-8900

(P-8956)
EFUEL LLC
Also Called: Easy Fuel
65 Enterprise Fl 3, Aliso Viejo
(92656-2705)
PHONE.............................949 330-7145
Donald Harper, *CEO*
EMP: 90
SALES (est): 65MM **Privately Held**
SIC: 5172 Petroleum products

(P-8957)
EMPIRE OIL CO
2756 S Riverside Ave, Bloomington
(92316-3500)
PHONE.............................909 877-0226
Richard Alden Sr, *CEO*
Richard Scott Alden Jr, *President*
Donald Welker, *CFO*
EMP: 52
SQ FT: 2,300
SALES (est): 51.8MM **Publicly Held**
WEB: www.empireoil.com
SIC: 5172 Diesel fuel; lubricating oils &
greases
HQ: Northern Tier Energy Lp
1250 W Washington St # 101
Tempe AZ 85281
602 302-5450

(P-8958)
FLYERS ENERGY LLC
4200 Buck Owens Blvd, Bakersfield
(93308-4935)
PHONE.............................661 321-9961
Henry Medina, *President*
EMP: 320
SALES (corp-wide): 126.7MM **Privately
Held**
SIC: 5172 Engine fuels & oils
PA: Flyers Energy, Llc
2360 Lindbergh St
Auburn CA 95602
530 885-0401

(P-8959)
FLYERS ENERGY LLC
571 W Slover Ave, Bloomington
(92316-2454)
PHONE.............................909 877-2441
David Larimer, *Branch Mgr*
EMP: 118
SALES (corp-wide): 126.7MM **Privately
Held**
SIC: 5172 Engine fuels & oils
PA: Flyers Energy, Llc
2360 Lindbergh St
Auburn CA 95602
530 885-0401

(P-8960)
FLYERS ENERGY LLC
444 Yolanda Ave Ste A, Santa Rosa
(95404-8090)
PHONE.............................707 546-0766
EMP: 70
SALES (corp-wide): 126.7MM **Privately
Held**
SIC: 5172 3569 Lubrication equipment, in-
dustrial; lubricating oils & greases
PA: Flyers Energy, Llc
2360 Lindbergh St
Auburn CA 95602
530 885-0401

(P-8961)
**GENERAL PETROLEUM
CORPORATION (DH)**
Also Called: G P Resources
19501 S Santa Fe Ave, Compton
(90221-5913)
PHONE.............................562 983-7300
James A Halsam III, *CEO*
Michael Ruehring, *President*
Charles McDaniel, *Senior VP*
Sean Kha, *Vice Pres*
Mark Mason, *General Mgr*
▲ **EMP:** 150
SQ FT: 5,000
SALES (est): 83.3MM
SALES (corp-wide): 1.2B **Privately Held**
SIC: 5172 Crude oil
HQ: Pecos, Inc.
19501 S Santa Fe Ave
Compton CA 90221
310 356-2300

(P-8962)
INTER-STATE OIL CO (PA)
8221 Alpine Ave, Sacramento
(95826-4708)
PHONE.............................916 457-6572
Brent Andrews, *President*
Terrance W Andrews, *President*
Greg Michael, *CFO*
Laurie Andrews, *Corp Secy*
Glen Jager, *Branch Mgr*

EMP: 65
SQ FT: 20,000
SALES (est): 100.1MM **Privately Held**
WEB: www.interstateoil.com
SIC: 5172 Lubricating oils & greases

(P-8963)
INTERSTATE FUEL SYSTEMS INC
8221 Alpine Ave, Sacramento
(95826-4708)
PHONE.................................916 457-6572
Terrance Andrews, *President*
Laurene Andrews, *Treasurer*
Dan Dalio, *Admin Sec*
EMP: 100
SQ FT: 20,000
SALES (est): 21.5MM **Privately Held**
SIC: 5172 Fuel oil

(P-8964)
IPC (USA) INC (HQ)
4 Hutton Cntre Dr Ste 700, Santa Ana
(92707)
PHONE.................................949 648-5600
Hiroki Okinaga, *CEO*
James Takeuchi, *CFO*
Randy Jones, *Vice Pres*
EMP: 65
SQ FT: 9,450
SALES (est): 191.3MM
SALES (corp-wide): 51.7B **Privately Held**
WEB: www.usipc.com
SIC: 5172 Aircraft fueling services; diesel
    fuel; gasoline
PA: Itochu Corporation
    2-5-1, Kitaaoyama
    Minato-Ku TKY 107-0
    334 972-121

(P-8965)
KAISERAIR INC (PA)
8735 Earhart Rd, Oakland (94621-4547)
P.O. Box 2626 (94614-0626)
PHONE.................................510 569-9622
Ronald J Guerra, *President*
Jim Strickland, *CFO*
Rob Guerra, *Senior VP*
Glenn Barrett, *Vice Pres*
David A Mancebo, *Vice Pres*
EMP: 148 EST: 1979
SQ FT: 970,000
SALES (est): 36.3MM **Privately Held**
WEB: www.kaiserair.com
SIC: 5172 4522 7359 4581 Aircraft fuel-
    ing services; air transportation, nonsched-
    uled; aircraft rental; aircraft maintenance
    & repair services

(P-8966)
M O DION & SONS INC (PA)
1543 W 16th St, Long Beach (90813-1210)
PHONE.................................562 432-3946
Toll Free:..................................888 -
Pat Cullen, *CEO*
Matt Cullen, *President*
Patrick B Cullen, *CEO*
Bill Frank, *CFO*
EMP: 60 EST: 1930
SQ FT: 85,000
SALES (est): 157.2MM **Privately Held**
WEB: www.dionandsons.com
SIC: 5172 Gasoline; diesel fuel; lubricating
    oils & greases

(P-8967)
STURDY OIL COMPANY
721 Vertin Ave, Salinas (93901-4526)
PHONE.................................831 970-9897
EMP: 72
SALES (corp-wide): 77.4MM **Privately Held**
SIC: 5172 Gasoline
PA: Sturdy Oil Company
    1511 Abbott St
    Salinas CA 93901
    831 422-8801

(P-8968)
SWISSPORT FUELING INC
1 Edward White Way, Oakland
(94621-4553)
P.O. Box 6366 (94603-0366)
PHONE.................................510 562-1701
Ken Carlson, *Manager*
James Stucky, *Executive*

Patrick Chan, *Finance Mgr*
EMP: 72
SALES (corp-wide): 175.4MM **Privately Held**
SIC: 5172 4925 Aircraft fueling services;
    gas production and/or distribution
PA: Swissport Fueling, Inc.
    45025 Aviation Dr Ste 350
    Dulles VA 20166
    703 742-4338

(P-8969)
TOWER ENERGY GROUP (PA)
1983 W 190th St Ste 100, Torrance
(90504-6240)
PHONE.................................310 538-8000
John Rogers, *Principal*
Twanna Rogers, *Vice Pres*
Nick Battaglia, *General Mgr*
Siamak Heshmati, *Admin Asst*
Kim Scioli, *Analyst*
EMP: 83
SQ FT: 22,702
SALES (est): 159.3MM **Privately Held**
SIC: 5172 Gasoline

(P-8970)
UNITED EL SEGUNDO INC (PA)
Also Called: United Oil
4130 Cover St, Long Beach (90808-1885)
PHONE.................................310 323-3992
Ronald Appel, *President*
Jeff Appel, *Corp Secy*
Alan Beaudette, *Director*
Kathryn Dalton, *Manager*
EMP: 60
SQ FT: 3,500
SALES (est): 111.2MM **Privately Held**
WEB: www.unitedoil.net
SIC: 5172 6531 Gasoline; real estate leas-
    ing & rentals

(P-8971)
VALLEY PACIFIC PETRO SVCS INC
9521 Enos Ln, Bakersfield (93314-8007)
PHONE.................................661 746-7737
Kat Bowen, *Branch Mgr*
EMP: 103
SALES (corp-wide): 113.6MM **Privately Held**
SIC: 5172 Gasoline
PA: Valley Pacific Petroleum Services, Inc.
    152 Frank West Cir # 100
    Stockton CA 95206
    209 948-9412

(P-8972)
VAN DE POL ENTERPRISES INC (PA)
4895 S Airport Way, Stockton
(95206-3915)
P.O. Box 1107 (95201-1107)
PHONE.................................209 465-3421
Lee Atwater, *Ch of Bd*
Paul Gosal, *Owner*
Ted Wysoki, *Owner*
Ronald M Vandepol, *CEO*
Scott Macewan, *CFO*
EMP: 75
SQ FT: 10,000
SALES (est): 129.1MM **Privately Held**
SIC: 5172 Gasoline

(P-8973)
WARREN E&P INC
Also Called: Warren E & P
400 Oceangate Ste 200, Long Beach
(90802-4306)
PHONE.................................877 587-9494
James A Watt, *CEO*
Mike Mojzisik, *Engineer*
EMP: 67
SQ FT: 7,000
SALES (est): 1.9MM **Publicly Held**
SIC: 5172 Gasoline
PA: Warren Resources, Inc.
    5420 Lbj Fwy Ste 600
    Dallas TX 75240

(P-8974)
WHOLESALE FUELS INC
2200 E Brundage Ln, Bakersfield
(93307-3066)
P.O. Box 82277 (93380-2277)
PHONE.................................661 327-4900
Charles McCan, *Officer*
Brian Bucassa, *CFO*
Tom Jamieson, *Corp Secy*
Jeff Shultz, *General Mgr*
EMP: 63 EST: 1982
SQ FT: 5,000
SALES (est): 46.3MM **Privately Held**
WEB: www.wholesalefuels.com
SIC: 5172 Gasoline

5181 Beer & Ale Wholesale

(P-8975)
ACE BEVERAGE CO
550 S Mission Rd, Los Angeles
(90033-4234)
P.O. Box 33256 (90033-0256)
PHONE.................................323 266-6238
Dan Holland, *Principal*
John Lavarias, *Manager*
EMP: 100
SALES (corp-wide): 391.4MM **Privately Held**
SIC: 5181 Beer & ale
HQ: Ace Beverage Co.
    401 S Anderson St
    Los Angeles CA 90033
    323 264-6001

(P-8976)
ADVANCE BEVERAGE CO INC
5200 District Blvd, Bakersfield
(93313-2330)
P.O. Box 9517 (93389-9517)
PHONE.................................661 833-3783
William K Lazzerini Sr, *Ch of Bd*
William K Lazzerini Jr, *President*
Anthony Lazzerini, *Vice Pres*
▲ EMP: 90
SQ FT: 93,000
SALES (est): 49.6MM **Privately Held**
WEB: www.advancebeverage.com
SIC: 5181 5182 Beer & other fermented
    malt liquors; wine

(P-8977)
ALLIED COMPANY HOLDINGS INC (PA)
Also Called: Best-Way Distributing Co
13235 Golden State Rd, Sylmar
(91342-1129)
PHONE.................................818 493-6400
Kevin Williams, *CEO*
Erin S Gabler, *CFO*
Erin Gabler, *CFO*
William L Larson, *Vice Pres*
Earl J Whitehead, *Admin Sec*
▲ EMP: 420
SQ FT: 240,000
SALES (est): 119.7MM **Privately Held**
WEB: www.alliedbeverages.com
SIC: 5181 Beer & other fermented malt
    liquors

(P-8978)
ANHEUSER-BUSCH LLC
1400 Marlborough Ave, Riverside
(92507-2097)
PHONE.................................951 782-3935
Yo Sanchez, *Manager*
Bruce Larson, *President*
William Bowker, *Info Tech Mgr*
Chris Massie, *Manager*
EMP: 150
SQ FT: 100,000
SALES (corp-wide): 1.9B **Privately Held**
WEB: www.hispanicbud.com
SIC: 5181 Beer & other fermented malt
    liquors
HQ: Anheuser-Busch, Llc
    1 Busch Pl
    Saint Louis MO 63118
    314 632-6777

(P-8979)
ANHEUSER-BUSCH LLC
20499 S Reeves Ave, Carson
(90810-1011)
PHONE.................................310 761-4600
Damian Bonnenfant, *Manager*
Al Gee, *Manager*
EMP: 115
SALES (corp-wide): 1.9B **Privately Held**
WEB: www.hispanicbud.com
SIC: 5181 Beer & other fermented malt
    liquors
HQ: Anheuser-Busch, Llc
    1 Busch Pl
    Saint Louis MO 63118
    314 632-6777

(P-8980)
ANHEUSER-BUSCH LLC
18952 Macarthur Blvd, Irvine (92612-1432)
PHONE.................................949 263-9270
Patrick Waters, *Branch Mgr*
EMP: 111
SALES (corp-wide): 1.9B **Privately Held**
WEB: www.hispanicbud.com
SIC: 5181
HQ: Anheuser-Busch, Llc
    1 Busch Pl
    Saint Louis MO 63118
    314 632-6777

(P-8981)
BAY AREA DISTRIBUTING CO INC
1061 Factory St, Richmond (94801-2161)
PHONE.................................510 232-8554
Kenneth G Sodo, *President*
Jackie Defabio, *Office Admin*
Janice Kwiatkowski, *Admin Asst*
Jeanine Mills, *Human Res Mgr*
Marian Freeman, *Opers Staff*
▲ EMP: 50 EST: 1973
SQ FT: 22,000
SALES (est): 18.3MM **Privately Held**
SIC: 5181 5149 Beer & other fermented
    malt liquors; mineral or spring water bot-
    tling; soft drinks

(P-8982)
BEAUCHAMP DISTRIBUTING COMPANY
1911 S Santa Fe Ave, Compton
(90221-5306)
PHONE.................................310 639-5320
Patrick L Beauchamp, *President*
Peter J Gumpert, *CFO*
Mary S Beauchamp, *Corp Secy*
Stacee L Beauchamp, *Vice Pres*
▲ EMP: 100
SQ FT: 100,000
SALES (est): 62.5MM **Privately Held**
SIC: 5181 5149 Beer & other fermented
    malt liquors; groceries & related products

(P-8983)
BOTTOMLEY DISTRIBUTING CO INC
755 Yosemite Dr, Milpitas (95035-5463)
PHONE.................................408 945-0660
Donald A Bottomley, *President*
Jeremy Smith, *Area Mgr*
Gus Gomez, *Admin Sec*
Craig Shore, *Sales Mgr*
Javier Arevalo, *Sales Associate*
▲ EMP: 90
SQ FT: 96,000
SALES (est): 21.6MM **Privately Held**
SIC: 5181 Beer & other fermented malt
    liquors

(P-8984)
CAPITAL BEVERAGE COMPANY (PA)
2500 Del Monte St, West Sacramento
(95691-3835)
P.O. Box 914 (95691-0914)
PHONE.................................916 371-8164
Kenneth M Adamson, *President*
Charles Moulton, *CFO*
◆ EMP: 110 EST: 1960
SQ FT: 130,000

SALES (est): 28.7MM **Privately Held**
SIC: 5181 5182 5149 Beer & other fermented malt liquors; wine coolers, alcoholic; juices; mineral or spring water bottling

(P-8985)
CENTRAL COAST DISTRIBUTING LLC
815 S Blosser Rd, Santa Maria (93458-4915)
PHONE..........................805 922-2108
Michael Larrabee Jr,
Moises Gomez, *Executive*
Gil Fierros, *Area Mgr*
Brian Hutton, *Area Mgr*
Jacob Main, *Opers Mgr*
▲ **EMP:** 90
SQ FT: 51,651
SALES (est): 40.5MM **Privately Held**
SIC: 5181 Beer & other fermented malt liquors

(P-8986)
CLASSIC DISTRG & BEV GROUP INC
120 Puente Ave, City of Industry (91746-2301)
PHONE..........................626 934-3700
Carlos Joseph Sanchez, *President*
John Thomas, *CFO*
Alex Hernandez, *Manager*
Mike Sanchez, *Manager*
▲ **EMP:** 261
SQ FT: 102,000
SALES (est): 138.9MM **Privately Held**
WEB: www.classicdist.com
SIC: 5181 Beer & other fermented malt liquors

(P-8987)
COUCH DISTRIBUTING COMPANY INC
104 Lee Rd, Watsonville (95076-9448)
P.O. Box 50004 (95077-5004)
PHONE..........................831 724-0649
George W Couch III, *CEO*
Geoffrey A Couch, *Vice Pres*
Rod Crowell, *Vice Pres*
Louie Pieracci, *Vice Pres*
Ken Paulson, *Opers Staff*
▲ **EMP:** 160
SQ FT: 72,000
SALES (est): 75.2MM **Privately Held**
WEB: www.couchdistributing.com
SIC: 5181 Beer & other fermented malt liquors

(P-8988)
CREST BEVERAGE COMPANY INC
3840 Via De La Valle, Del Mar (92014-4268)
P.O. Box 9160, Rancho Santa Fe (92067-4160)
PHONE..........................858 452-2300
Steven S Sourapas Sr, *President*
Dean McMillan, *General Mgr*
▲ **EMP:** 170
SQ FT: 160,000
SALES (est): 57.4MM **Privately Held**
WEB: www.crestbeverage.com
SIC: 5181 5182 5149 Beer & other fermented malt liquors; wine; groceries & related products

(P-8989)
DBI BEVERAGE INC
4140 Brew Master Dr, Ceres (95307-7583)
PHONE..........................209 524-2477
Jeffrey D Skinner, *Branch Mgr*
EMP: 75
SALES (corp-wide): 203.7MM **Privately Held**
SIC: 5181 Beer & other fermented malt liquors
PA: Dbi Beverage Inc.
　2 Ingram Blvd
　La Vergne TN 37089
　615 793-2337

(P-8990)
DBI BEVERAGE SAN FRANCISCO
245 S Spruce Ave Ste 100, South San Francisco (94080-4597)
PHONE..........................415 643-9900
David Ingram, *Ch of Bd*
Bob Stahl, *Co-President*
Sergio Serrano, *District Mgr*
Rick Guida, *General Mgr*
Kyle Baldwin, *Buyer*
▲ **EMP:** 250
SALES (est): 30.7MM
SALES (corp-wide): 203.7MM **Privately Held**
WEB: www.goldenbrands.com
SIC: 5181 5149 Beer & other fermented malt liquors; soft drinks; mineral or spring water bottling
PA: Dbi Beverage Inc.
　2 Ingram Blvd
　La Vergne TN 37089
　615 793-2337

(P-8991)
DBI BEVERAGE SAN JOAQUIN
Also Called: San Joaquin Beverage
4547 Frontier Way, Stockton (95215-9675)
PHONE..........................209 948-9400
David Yoder, *President*
Donnie Daniel, *President*
David Ingram, *Chairman*
John Janosko, *Vice Pres*
Mike Sayler, *General Mgr*
▲ **EMP:** 80
SQ FT: 8,000
SALES (est): 25MM **Privately Held**
SIC: 5181 Beer & other fermented malt liquors

(P-8992)
DELTA BRANDS INC
3700 Finch Rd, Modesto (95357-4152)
PHONE..........................209 522-9044
Donald J Stewart Sr, *Ch of Bd*
Robert Stewart, *President*
Betty Stewart, *Corp Secy*
Donald J Stewart Jr, *Vice Pres*
EMP: 67
SQ FT: 62,000
SALES (est): 12.3MM **Privately Held**
SIC: 5181 Beer & other fermented malt liquors

(P-8993)
DONAGHY SALES INC
2363 S Cedar Ave, Fresno (93725-1078)
PHONE..........................559 486-0901
Edward Donaghy, *CEO*
Janis Donaghy, *Admin Sec*
▲ **EMP:** 150
SQ FT: 75,000
SALES (est): 74.4MM **Privately Held**
SIC: 5181 Beer & other fermented malt liquors

(P-8994)
ELYXIR DISTRIBUTING LLC
270 W Riverside Dr, Watsonville (95076-5106)
PHONE..........................831 761-6400
Paul C Ely III,
Brian Mullaly, *President*
Pau Ely, *COO*
Frederick Martinez, *District Mgr*
Modesto Hernandez, *Sales Mgr*
EMP: 103
SQ FT: 35,000
SALES (est): 58.7MM **Privately Held**
WEB: www.elyxir.com
SIC: 5181 5149 Beer & other fermented malt liquors; beverages, except coffee & tea

(P-8995)
FOOTHILL DISTRIBUTING CO INC
1530 Beltline Rd, Redding (96003-1408)
P.O. Box 492800 (96049-2800)
PHONE..........................530 243-3932
Lance Goble, *President*
Lynn Goble, *Corp Secy*
Gary Burks, *Vice Pres*
Andi Fox, *Office Mgr*
John McShane, *QC Mgr*

▲ **EMP:** 101
SQ FT: 33,000
SALES (est): 39MM **Privately Held**
WEB: www.foothilldistributing.com
SIC: 5181 5182 Beer & other fermented malt liquors; wine

(P-8996)
FRESNO BEVERAGE COMPANY INC
Also Called: Valley Wide Beverage Company
3525 S East Ave, Fresno (93725)
PHONE..........................559 650-1500
Louis J Amendola, *CEO*
Dan Boitano, *Vice Pres*
Brian Kennedy, *VP Admin*
Jeff Beal, *Sales Mgr*
Drew Lamoure, *Manager*
◆ **EMP:** 180
SQ FT: 140,000
SALES (est): 81.9MM **Privately Held**
WEB: www.valleywidebeverage.com
SIC: 5181 Beer & other fermented malt liquors

(P-8997)
GATE CITY BEVERAGE DISTRS (PA)
2505 Steele Rd, San Bernardino (92408-3913)
PHONE..........................909 799-0281
Leona Aronoff, *President*
Barry Aronoff, *CFO*
▲ **EMP:** 294 **EST:** 1940
SQ FT: 280,000
SALES (est): 72.4MM **Privately Held**
WEB: www.gcbev.com
SIC: 5181 5149 5145 Beer & other fermented malt liquors; soft drinks; mineral or spring water bottling; confectionery

(P-8998)
GATE CITY BEVERAGE DISTRS
31315 Plantation Dr, Thousand Palms (92276-6602)
PHONE..........................760 775-5483
Barry J Aronoff, *Owner*
EMP: 294
SQ FT: 10,000
SALES (corp-wide): 72.4MM **Privately Held**
WEB: www.gcbev.com
SIC: 5181 5149 Beer & other fermented malt liquors; water, distilled
PA: Gate City Beverage Distributors
　2505 Steele Rd
　San Bernardino CA 92408
　909 799-0281

(P-8999)
HARALAMBOS BEVERAGE COMPANY
26717 Palmetto Ave, Redlands (92374-1513)
PHONE..........................909 307-1777
Gary Leavitt, *Branch Mgr*
EMP: 157
SALES (corp-wide): 258MM **Privately Held**
WEB: www.haralambos.com
SIC: 5181 Beer & other fermented malt liquors
PA: Haralambos Beverage Company.
　2300 Pellissier Pl
　City Of Industry CA 90601
　562 347-4300

(P-9000)
HARALAMBOS BEVERAGE COMPANY (PA)
2300 Pellissier Pl, City of Industry (90601-1500)
P.O. Box 6005, El Monte (91734-2005)
PHONE..........................562 347-4300
H T Haralambos, *CEO*
Anthony Haralambos, *President*
Thomas Haralambos, *Vice Pres*
Liz Celaya, *Admin Sec*
Sally Haralambos, *Admin Sec*
▲ **EMP:** 143
SQ FT: 270,000

SALES (est): 258MM **Privately Held**
WEB: www.haralambos.com
SIC: 5181 5149 Beer & other fermented malt liquors; beverages, except coffee & tea

(P-9001)
HARBOR DISTRIBUTING LLC (HQ)
5901 Bolsa Ave, Huntington Beach (92647-2053)
PHONE..........................714 933-2400
David K Reyes,
Tim McGuire,
Chris Reyes,
Jude Reyes,
▲ **EMP:** 200
SQ FT: 150,000
SALES (est): 112.2MM **Privately Held**
SIC: 5181 Beer & other fermented malt liquors

(P-9002)
HARBOR DISTRIBUTING LLC
Also Called: Harbor Distributing Co
16407 S Main St, Gardena (90248-2823)
PHONE..........................310 538-5483
David Reyes, *Branch Mgr*
EMP: 300 **Privately Held**
SIC: 5181 Beer & other fermented malt liquors
HQ: Harbor Distributing, Llc
　5901 Bolsa Ave
　Huntington Beach CA 92647
　714 933-2400

(P-9003)
HORIZON BEVERAGE COMPANY
8380 Pardee Dr, Oakland (94621-1481)
P.O. Box 6639 (94603-0639)
PHONE..........................510 465-2212
Ces Butner, *Partner*
Denny Suzuki, *Partner*
EMP: 80
SQ FT: 20,000
SALES (est): 7.8MM **Privately Held**
SIC: 5181 Beer & other fermented malt liquors

(P-9004)
HORIZON BEVERAGE COMPANY LP
8380 Pardee Dr, Oakland (94621-1481)
P.O. Box 6639 (94603-0639)
PHONE..........................510 465-2212
Gary Shinn,
Mike Thomas, *President*
Bonnie Medina, *Manager*
▲ **EMP:** 94
SALES (est): 21.7MM **Privately Held**
SIC: 5181 Beer & other fermented malt liquors

(P-9005)
JETRO CASH AND CARRY ENTPS LLC
5333 W Jefferson Blvd, Los Angeles (90016-3713)
PHONE..........................323 964-1200
Enrique Gallard, *Principal*
EMP: 100 **Privately Held**
WEB: www.jetro.com
SIC: 5181 5142 5194 5147 Beer & other fermented malt liquors; packaged frozen goods; tobacco & tobacco products; meats, fresh; groceries, general line
HQ: Jetro Cash And Carry Enterprises, Llc
　1524 132nd St
　College Point NY 11356
　718 939-6400

(P-9006)
JORDANOS INC (PA)
Also Called: Jordano's Food Service
550 S Patterson Ave, Santa Barbara (93111-2498)
P.O. Box 6803 (93160-6803)
PHONE..........................805 964-0611
Peter Jordano, *CEO*
Michael F Sieckowski, *CFO*
Jeffrey S Jordano, *Exec VP*
▲ **EMP:** 250
SQ FT: 80,000

SALES (est): 432.9MM **Privately Held**
WEB: www.jordanos.com
SIC: **5181** 5182 5149 5141 Beer & other fermented malt liquors; wine; soft drinks; groceries, general line; packaged frozen goods; fresh fruits & vegetables

(P-9007)
LARRABEE BROTHRS DISTRIBTNG CO
815 S Blosser Rd, Santa Maria (93458-4915)
P.O. Box 1850 (93456-1850)
PHONE..............................805 922-2108
Michael Larrabee, *President*
Margaret Larrabee, *Vice Pres*
EMP: 100
SQ FT: 51,651
SALES (est): 11.2MM **Privately Held**
SIC: **5181** Beer & other fermented malt liquors

(P-9008)
LE VECKE CORPORATION (PA)
Also Called: Le Vecke Group
10810 Inland Ave, Mira Loma (91752-3235)
PHONE..............................951 681-8600
Joseph Neil Levecke, *CEO*
Neil Levecke, *President*
Maggie Weaver, *Human Resources*
◆ EMP: 62
SALES (est): 64.6MM **Privately Held**
WEB: www.levecke.com
SIC: **5181** Beer & other fermented malt liquors

(P-9009)
LIQUID INVESTMENTS INC (PA)
3840 Via De La Valle # 300, Del Mar (92014-4268)
PHONE..............................858 509-8510
Ron L Fowler, *CEO*
Mark Herculson, *Exec VP*
Terry L Harris, *VP Finance*
▲ EMP: 170 EST: 1981
SQ FT: 190,000
SALES (est): 202.6MM **Privately Held**
WEB: www.lqdinv.com
SIC: **5181** 5145 5182 Beer & other fermented malt liquors; fountain supplies; wine

(P-9010)
MARKSTEIN BEV CO SACRAMENTO
Also Called: Markstein Beverage Company
60 Main Ave, Sacramento (95838-2034)
P.O. Box 15379 (95851-0379)
PHONE..............................916 920-3911
Hayden Markstein, *CEO*
Richard Markstein, *Ch of Bd*
Steve Markstein, *President*
▲ EMP: 150
SALES (est): 97.6MM **Privately Held**
WEB: www.marksteinbev.com
SIC: **5181** 5149 Beer & other fermented malt liquors; soft drinks; mineral or spring water bottling

(P-9011)
MARKSTEIN BEVERAGE CO
505 S Pacific St, San Marcos (92078-4049)
P.O. Box 6902 (92079-6902)
PHONE..............................760 744-9100
Kenneth W Markstein, *CEO*
Steven Markstein, *Vice Pres*
▲ EMP: 120
SQ FT: 118,000
SALES (est): 61.2MM **Privately Held**
WEB: www.abwholesaler.com
SIC: **5181** Beer & other fermented malt liquors

(P-9012)
MATAGRANO INC
440 Forbes Blvd, South San Francisco (94080-2015)
P.O. Box 2588 (94083-2588)
PHONE..............................650 829-4829
Louis Matagrano, *President*
William Hill, *CFO*
Tom Haas, *Vice Pres*
Frank Matagrano Jr, *Vice Pres*
Gary Nagle, *Division Mgr*

▲ EMP: 175
SQ FT: 100,000
SALES (est): 123.9MM **Privately Held**
WEB: www.matagrano.com
SIC: **5181** 5149 Beer & other fermented malt liquors; mineral or spring water bottling; juices

(P-9013)
ME FOX & COMPANY INC
128 Component Dr, San Jose (95131-1180)
P.O. Box 2336, Saratoga (95070-0336)
PHONE..............................408 435-8510
Michael E Fox Sr, *Ch of Bd*
Terence Fox, *President*
Doug Webenbauer, *CFO*
Catherine Fox, *Treasurer*
Mary Ellen Fox, *Exec VP*
▲ EMP: 100
SQ FT: 126,000
SALES (est): 75.4MM **Privately Held**
SIC: **5181** 5149 Beer & other fermented malt liquors; soft drinks; mineral or spring water bottling; juices

(P-9014)
MESA DISTRIBUTING COINC (HQ)
3840 Via De La Valle # 300, Del Mar (92014-4268)
PHONE..............................858 452-2300
Ronald Fowler, *Ch of Bd*
Ron L Fowler, *Ch of Bd*
Jack F Studebaker, *Admin Sec*
EMP: 225
SQ FT: 190,000
SALES (est): 27.6MM
SALES (corp-wide): 202.6MM **Privately Held**
WEB: www.mesadistributing.com
SIC: **5181** 0182 5182 Beer & other fermented malt liquors; vegetable crops grown under cover; wine & distilled beverages
PA: Liquid Investments, Inc.
3840 Via De La Valle # 300
Del Mar CA 92014
858 509-8510

(P-9015)
MISSION BEVERAGE CO (HQ)
550 S Mission Rd, Los Angeles (90033-4256)
P.O. Box 33256 (90033-0256)
PHONE..............................323 266-6238
John E Anderson Sr, *Ch of Bd*
Don Holland, *President*
Therese D Curtis, *Corp Secy*
▲ EMP: 210
SALES (est): 48.7MM
SALES (corp-wide): 391.4MM **Privately Held**
SIC: **5181** 5149 Beer & other fermented malt liquors; soft drinks
PA: Topa Equities, Ltd.
1800 Ave Of The
Los Angeles CA 90067
310 203-9199

(P-9016)
MORRIS DISTRIBUTING INC
3800a Lakeville Hwy, Petaluma (94954-5673)
P.O. Box 5699 (94955-5699)
PHONE..............................707 769-7294
Ronald L Morris, *CEO*
Joe Netter, *Corp Secy*
▲ EMP: 80
SQ FT: 13,500
SALES (est): 25.7MM **Privately Held**
SIC: **5181** 5149 Beer & other fermented malt liquors; mineral or spring water bottling; juices

(P-9017)
NOR-CAL BEVERAGE CO INC (PA)
2150 Stone Blvd, West Sacramento (95691-4049)
PHONE..............................916 372-0600
Shannon Deary-Bell, *President*
Donald Deary, *Ch of Bd*
Grant Deary, *President*
Tim Deary, *President*
Mike Montroni, *CFO*

◆ EMP: 280
SQ FT: 152,000
SALES (est): 248.5MM **Privately Held**
SIC: **5181** 2086 Beer & other fermented malt liquors; soft drinks; packaged in cans, bottles, etc.; fruit drinks (less than 100% juice); packaged in cans, etc.

(P-9018)
OB USA INC
Also Called: Bws Group Co.
13152 Imperial Hwy, Santa Fe Springs (90670-4817)
PHONE..............................213 465-4876
James Ha, *CEO*
EMP: 120
SALES (est): 23.7MM **Privately Held**
SIC: **5181** Beer & other fermented malt liquors

(P-9019)
RESTAURANT DEPOT LLC
1265 N Kraemer Blvd, Anaheim (92806-1921)
PHONE..............................714 666-9205
Ralph Vasquez, *Manager*
EMP: 150 **Privately Held**
WEB: www.jrdtuning.com
SIC: **5181** 5141 5194 5142 Beer & other fermented malt liquors; groceries, general line; tobacco & tobacco products; packaged frozen goods; meats, fresh
HQ: Restaurant Depot, Llc
1524 132nd St
College Point NY 11356

(P-9020)
RESTAURANT DEPOT LLC
19901 Hamilton Ave Ste A, Torrance (90502-1367)
PHONE..............................310 516-7400
Sue Greene, *Branch Mgr*
EMP: 60 **Privately Held**
WEB: www.jrdtuning.com
SIC: **5181** 5141 5194 5142 Beer & other fermented malt liquors; groceries, general line; tobacco & tobacco products; packaged frozen goods; meats, fresh
HQ: Restaurant Depot, Llc
1524 132nd St
College Point NY 11356

(P-9021)
RESTAURANT DEPOT LLC
2045 Evans Ave, San Francisco (94124-1022)
PHONE..............................415 920-2888
Samuel Cortez, *Branch Mgr*
EMP: 150 **Privately Held**
WEB: www.jrdtuning.com
SIC: **5181** 5141 5194 5142 Beer & other fermented malt liquors; groceries, general line; tobacco & tobacco products; packaged frozen goods; meats, fresh
HQ: Restaurant Depot, Llc
1524 132nd St
College Point NY 11356

(P-9022)
RESTAURANT DEPOT LLC
5333 W Jefferson Blvd, Los Angeles (90016-3713)
PHONE..............................323 964-1220
Enrique Gallard, *Manager*
EMP: 150 **Privately Held**
WEB: www.jrdtuning.com
SIC: **5181** 5194 5147 5142 Beer & other fermented malt liquors; tobacco & tobacco products; meats, fresh; packaged frozen goods; groceries, general line
HQ: Restaurant Depot, Llc
1524 132nd St
College Point NY 11356

(P-9023)
RESTAURANT DEPOT LLC
15853 Strathern St, Van Nuys (91406-1310)
PHONE..............................818 376-7687
Dan Mihal, *Manager*
EMP: 150 **Privately Held**
WEB: www.jrdtuning.com

SIC: **5181** 5147 5141 5142 Beer & other fermented malt liquors; meats, fresh; groceries, general line; packaged frozen goods; tobacco & tobacco products
HQ: Restaurant Depot, Llc
1524 132nd St
College Point NY 11356

(P-9024)
SACCANI DISTRIBUTING COMPANY
2600 5th St, Sacramento (95818-2899)
P.O. Box 1764 (95812-1764)
PHONE..............................916 441-0213
Gary Saccani, *President*
Steven Fishman, *Corp Secy*
Roland Saccani, *Vice Pres*
Rod Bise, *District Mgr*
Mickey Trudelle, *District Mgr*
▲ EMP: 90
SQ FT: 40,000
SALES (est): 37.9MM **Privately Held**
SIC: **5181** 5149 Beer & other fermented malt liquors; soft drinks

(P-9025)
SEQUOIA BEVERAGE COMPANY LP
2122 N Plaza Dr, Visalia (93291-9358)
P.O. Box 5025 (93278-5025)
PHONE..............................559 651-2444
Dan Bueno, *Partner*
Rose Bueno, *Partner*
Joan Carpenter, *Partner*
Lisa Bueno-Loverin, *Executive*
Laurie Zuniga, *Administration*
EMP: 101
SQ FT: 100,000
SALES (est): 77.2MM **Privately Held**
WEB: www.sequoia-beverage.com
SIC: **5181** Beer & other fermented malt liquors

(P-9026)
SIERRA NEVADA BREWING CO
2031 4th St, Berkeley (94710-1912)
PHONE..............................510 647-3439
EMP: 139
SALES (corp-wide): 300MM **Privately Held**
SIC: **5181** Beer & other fermented malt liquors
PA: Sierra Nevada Brewing Co.
1075 E 20th St
Chico CA 95928
530 893-3520

(P-9027)
STRAUB DISTRIBUTING CO LTD (PA)
4633 E La Palma Ave, Anaheim (92807-1909)
PHONE..............................714 779-4000
Michael L Cooper, *General Ptnr*
Robert K Adams, *Partner*
Don Beightol, *Partner*
▲ EMP: 150
SQ FT: 32,000
SALES (est): 136MM **Privately Held**
WEB: www.sdcoc.net
SIC: **5181** Beer & other fermented malt liquors

(P-9028)
T F LOUDERBACK INC (PA)
Also Called: Bay Area Beverage
700 National Ct, Richmond (94804-2008)
PHONE..............................510 965-6120
Thomas J Louderback, *President*
Ron Bishop, *CFO*
Chris Reed, *Division Mgr*
Todd Rovelstad, *General Mgr*
Yik M Wong, *Technology*
▲ EMP: 102
SQ FT: 65,000
SALES (est): 68.2MM **Privately Held**
WEB: www.bayareabev.com
SIC: **5181** 5149 2037 2033 Beer & other fermented malt liquors; beverages, except coffee & tea; juices; frozen fruits & vegetables; canned fruits & specialties

(P-9029)
TRIANGLE DISTRIBUTING CO (PA)
Also Called: Heimark Distributing
12065 Pike St, Santa Fe Springs (90670-2964)
PHONE...........................562 699-3424
Donald Heimark, *Ch of Bd*
Peter H Heimark, *President*
Mike Crow, *Corp Secy*
▲ EMP: 170
SQ FT: 150,000
SALES (est): 86.8MM Privately Held
WEB: www.triangle-dist.com
SIC: 5181 Beer & other fermented malt liquors

(P-9030)
TRIANGLE DISTRIBUTING CO
Also Called: Hallmark Distributing
82851 Avenue 45, Indio (92201-2379)
P.O. Box 3108 (92202-3108)
PHONE...........................760 347-4052
Bill Shiner, *General Mgr*
James B Fleming, *President*
EMP: 55
SALES (corp-wide): 86.8MM Privately Held
WEB: www.triangle-dist.com
SIC: 5181 Beer & other fermented malt liquors
PA: Triangle Distributing Co.
12065 Pike St
Santa Fe Springs CA 90670
562 699-3424

┌─────────────────────────────┐
│ **5182 Wine & Distilled**   │
│ **Alcoholic Beverages**   │
│ **Wholesale**   │
└─────────────────────────────┘

(P-9031)
AV BRANDS INC
Also Called: Aveniu Brands
635 Broadway Ste 2, Sonoma (95476-7004)
PHONE...........................410 884-9463
Andrew Mansinne, *President*
Danielle Bova, *Accounting Mgr*
Beverly Gryder, *Mktg Dir*
Mick Roberts, *Sales Staff*
Laurence Vuelta, *Sales Staff*
◆ EMP: 50
SQ FT: 7,000
SALES (est): 20.6MM Privately Held
WEB: www.avimports.com
SIC: 5182 Wine

(P-9032)
BARREL TEN QUARTER CIRCLE INC
33 Harlow Ct, NAPA (94558-7520)
P.O. Box 3400 (94558-0551)
PHONE...........................707 265-4000
Fred T Franzia, *CEO*
John G Franzia Jr, *Co-President*
Joseph S Franzia, *Co-President*
Daniel Leonard, *Vice Pres*
EMP: 300
SALES (est): 44MM
SALES (corp-wide): 182.4MM Privately Held
SIC: 5182 Bottling wines & liquors
PA: Bronco Wine Company
6342 Bystrum Rd
Ceres CA 95307
209 538-3131

(P-9033)
BAY AREA BEVERAGE CO
700 National Ct, Richmond (94804-2008)
PHONE...........................510 965-6120
Tj Louderback, *President*
Ciaran Byrne, *CFO*
Larry Green, *Vice Pres*
EMP: 205
SALES (est): 49.8MM Privately Held
SIC: 5182 Wine

(P-9034)
BEN MYERSON CANDY CO INC (PA)
Also Called: Wine Warehouse
6550 E Washington Blvd, Commerce (90040-1822)
P.O. Box 910900, Los Angeles (90091-0900)
PHONE...........................800 331-2829
James P Myerson, *President*
Robert Myerson, *Treasurer*
James Myerson, *Corp Secy*
Greg Akins, *Exec VP*
Trevor Thiret, *Exec VP*
▲ EMP: 350
SQ FT: 135,000
SALES (est): 388.2MM Privately Held
SIC: 5182 5023 Wine; glassware

(P-9035)
BEN MYERSON CANDY CO INC
Also Called: Wine Warehouse
3463 Collins Ave, Richmond (94806-2000)
P.O. Box 45616, San Francisco (94145-0616)
PHONE...........................510 236-2233
Michael Cimino, *Manager*
Neil Denin, *CFO*
Jonathan Hartmann, *VP Sales*
Jon Berkland, *Sales Staff*
Liz Ortiz, *Asst Mgr*
EMP: 95
SQ FT: 2,000
SALES (corp-wide): 388.2MM Privately Held
SIC: 5182 5181 Liquor; neutral spirits; beer & ale
PA: Ben Myerson Candy Co., Inc.
6550 E Washington Blvd
Commerce CA 90040
800 331-2829

(P-9036)
DBI BEVERAGE SACRAMENTO (HQ)
3500 Carlin Dr, West Sacramento (95691-5872)
PHONE...........................916 373-5700
Jeff Skinner, *CEO*
Paul Schmitt, *COO*
Ryan Bosch, *Branch Mgr*
Tom Grace, *District Mgr*
Valerie Cavalli, *Administration*
▲ EMP: 55 EST: 2007
SQ FT: 200,000
SALES (est): 85.2MM
SALES (corp-wide): 203.7MM Privately Held
SIC: 5182 5149 Wine & distilled beverages; beverages, except coffee & tea
PA: Dbi Beverage Inc.
2 Ingram Blvd
La Vergne TN 37089
615 793-2337

(P-9037)
DIAGEO NORTH AMERICA INC
21468 8th St E, Sonoma (95476-9767)
PHONE...........................707 939-6200
Claudia Schubert, *Branch Mgr*
EMP: 65
SALES (corp-wide): 16.3B Privately Held
SIC: 5182 Wine
HQ: Diageo North America Inc.
801 Main Ave
Norwalk CT 06851
203 229-2100

(P-9038)
DIAGEO NORTH AMERICA INC
30 Journey, Aliso Viejo (92656-3317)
PHONE...........................949 421-3974
Chris Turbeville, *Branch Mgr*
EMP: 69
SALES (corp-wide): 16.3B Privately Held
SIC: 5182 Wine
HQ: Diageo North America Inc.
801 Main Ave
Norwalk CT 06851
203 229-2100

(P-9039)
DON SEBASTIANI & SONS INTERNAT (PA)
19150 Sonoma Hwy 12, Sonoma (95476)
P.O. Box 1248 (95476-1248)
PHONE...........................707 933-1704
Don Sebastiani, *President*
Tom Hawkins, *COO*
Don V Staaveren, *Vice Pres*
Colleen Gettle, *Business Anlyst*
Dwayne Christensen, *Manager*
▲ EMP: 89
SALES (est): 54.6MM Privately Held
SIC: 5182 Wine

(P-9040)
DRINKS HOLDINGS INC
1125 E Broadway 173, Glendale (91205-1315)
PHONE...........................310 441-8400
EMP: 117
SALES (corp-wide): 93.8MM Privately Held
SIC: 5182 Wine
PA: Drinks Holdings, Inc.
11175 Santa Monica Blvd # 400
Los Angeles CA 90025
310 441-8400

(P-9041)
EPIC VENTURES INC (PA)
Also Called: Epic Wines
200 Concourse Blvd, Santa Rosa (95403-8210)
PHONE...........................831 219-9100
Bill Foley, *President*
Scott Edwards, *President*
Robert W Prough, *CEO*
Sheldon Alexander, *Vice Pres*
Alan Crawford, *Vice Pres*
▲ EMP: 50
SQ FT: 4,000
SALES (est): 28.5MM Privately Held
WEB: www.epicventures.com
SIC: 5182 Wine

(P-9042)
FOLIO WINE COMPANY LLC (PA)
Also Called: Folio Wine Company Imports
550 Gateway Dr Ste 220, NAPA (94558-7578)
PHONE...........................707 254-9885
R Michael Mondavi, *Mng Member*
Jamie Conahan, *Partner*
Holly Delucchi, *Partner*
Jennifer Hornor, *Partner*
Rebecca Hopkins, *President*
▲ EMP: 105
SALES (est): 35.9MM Privately Held
WEB: www.foliowine.com
SIC: 5182 Wine

(P-9043)
FOLIO WINE COMPANY LLC
1285 Dealy Ln, NAPA (94559-9706)
PHONE...........................707 256-2757
Rick Choate, *Branch Mgr*
EMP: 65
SALES (corp-wide): 35.9MM Privately Held
SIC: 5182 Wine
PA: Folio Wine Company, Llc
550 Gateway Dr Ste 220
Napa CA 94558
707 254-9885

(P-9044)
FRANK-LIN DISTILLERS PDTS LTD (PA)
2455 Huntington Dr, Fairfield (94533-9734)
PHONE...........................408 259-8900
Frank J Maestri, *President*
Anthony Demaria, *CFO*
Mark S Pechusick, *Exec VP*
Lindley Maestri, *Vice Pres*
Michael Maestri, *Vice Pres*
◆ EMP: 110 EST: 1966
SQ FT: 54,216
SALES (est): 109.9MM Privately Held
SIC: 5182 2085 Wine; distilled & blended liquors

(P-9045)
FREIXENET USA INC
Also Called: Gloria Ferrer
23555 Arnold Dr, Sonoma (95476-9285)
P.O. Box 1949 (95476-1949)
PHONE...........................707 996-7256
Jose Maria Ferrer, *President*
Eva Bertran, *Exec VP*
David Brown, *VP Mktg*
▲ EMP: 54
SQ FT: 4,000
SALES (est): 33.3MM
SALES (corp-wide): 760.2MM Privately Held
WEB: www.freixenetusa.com
SIC: 5182 Wine
HQ: Freixenet Sa
Plaza Joan Sala 2
Sant Sadurni D Anoia 08770
938 917-000

(P-9046)
GALLO SALES COMPANY INC (DH)
30825 Wiegman Rd, Hayward (94544-7893)
P.O. Box 1266, Union City (94587-6266)
PHONE...........................510 476-5000
Joseph E Gallo, *President*
Andrew Sanchez, *Sales Staff*
EMP: 225
SQ FT: 59,000
SALES (est): 42.1MM
SALES (corp-wide): 2.6B Privately Held
SIC: 5182 Wine
HQ: Gallo Glass Company
605 S Santa Cruz Ave
Modesto CA 95354
209 341-3710

(P-9047)
GUARACHI WINE PARTNERS INC
Also Called: Parker Station
22837 Ventura Blvd # 300, Woodland Hills (91364-1224)
PHONE...........................818 225-5100
Alejandro Guarachi, *CEO*
Daniel Lyons, *President*
Derek Roeder, *Human Resources*
Douglas Ohama, *Manager*
Cindy Randall, *Manager*
▲ EMP: 80
SQ FT: 5,000
SALES (est): 37MM Privately Held
WEB: www.tgicimporters.com
SIC: 5182 Wine

(P-9048)
HALL WINES LLC
401 Saint Helena Hwy S, Saint Helena (94574-2200)
P.O. Box 25, Rutherford (94573-0025)
PHONE...........................707 967-2626
Mike Reynolds,
Natalie Bell, *President*
Whitney Jacobson, *Vice Pres*
Steve Leveque, *Vice Pres*
Wayne Wright, *Vice Pres*
▲ EMP: 50
SQ FT: 20,000
SALES (est): 22.7MM Privately Held
SIC: 5182 0172 Brandy

(P-9049)
HENRY WINE GROUP LLC (HQ)
Also Called: Henry Wine Group of C.A., The
4301 Industrial Way, Benicia (94510-1227)
PHONE...........................707 745-8500
Ed Hogan, *President*
Kent Fitzgerald, *President*
Don Jennings, *COO*
Stephanie O'Brien, *CFO*
Matt Diehm, *Vice Pres*
▲ EMP: 297
SALES (est): 80.2MM
SALES (corp-wide): 709.3MM Privately Held
SIC: 5182 Wine
PA: The Winebow Group Llc
4800 Cox Rd Ste 300
Glen Allen VA 23060
804 752-3670

(P-9050)
JACKSON FAMILY WINES INC
Regal Wine Company, The
1190 Kittyhawk Blvd Ste A, Santa Rosa
(95403-1013)
PHONE..................................415 819-0301
John Grant, *Branch Mgr*
EMP: 150
SQ FT: 20,746
SALES (corp-wide): 350MM **Privately Held**
WEB: www.cambriawines.com
SIC: 5182 Wine
PA: Jackson Family Wines, Inc.
421 And 425 Aviation Blvd
Santa Rosa CA 95403
707 544-4000

(P-9051)
MAGAVE TEQUILA INC
6 Park Pl, Belvedere Tiburon (94920-1048)
PHONE..................................415 515-3536
Michael Patane, *CEO*
▲ EMP: 50
SALES (est): 14.9MM **Privately Held**
SIC: 5182 Wine & distilled beverages

(P-9052)
SOUTHERN GLAZERS WINE
33321 Dowe Ave, Union City (94587-2033)
P.O. Box 5001 (94587-8501)
PHONE..................................510 477-5500
Gary Nedd, *Manager*
Leo Chung, *Technology*
Cherie Collins, *Sales Staff*
John Havens, *Sales Staff*
Jennie De La Rosa,
EMP: 350
SALES (corp-wide): 6.6B **Privately Held**
WEB: www.southernwine.com
SIC: 5182 Wine & distilled beverages
PA: Southern Glazer's Wine And Spirits, Llc
1600 Nw 163rd St
Miami FL 33169
305 625-4171

(P-9053)
SOUTHERN GLAZERS WINE
723 Palmyrita Ave, Riverside (92507-1811)
PHONE..................................951 274-2420
Ryan Okeese, *Manager*
Ivan Rouse, *Manager*
EMP: 50
SALES (corp-wide): 6.6B **Privately Held**
WEB: www.southernwine.com
SIC: 5182 Wine
PA: Southern Glazer's Wine And Spirits, Llc
1600 Nw 163rd St
Miami FL 33169
305 625-4171

(P-9054)
SOUTHERN GLAZERS WINE
10730 Scripps Ranch Blvd, San Diego
(92131-1003)
PHONE..................................858 537-3912
Craig Fontaine, *Manager*
Matthew Gruneisen, *Sales Staff*
EMP: 110
SALES (corp-wide): 6.6B **Privately Held**
WEB: www.southernwine.com
SIC: 5182 Wine
PA: Southern Glazer's Wine And Spirits, Llc
1600 Nw 163rd St
Miami FL 33169
305 625-4171

(P-9055)
SOUTHERN GLAZERS WINE
2320 Kruse Dr, San Jose (95131-1231)
PHONE..................................408 750-3540
Julie Long, *Branch Mgr*
EMP: 75
SALES (corp-wide): 6.6B **Privately Held**
WEB: www.southernwine.com
SIC: 5182 Bottling wines & liquors; wine
PA: Southern Glazer's Wine And Spirits, Llc
1600 Nw 163rd St
Miami FL 33169
305 625-4171

(P-9056)
SOUTHERN GLAZERS WINE
17101 Valley View Ave, Cerritos
(90703-2413)
PHONE..................................562 926-2000

Steve Slader, *Branch Mgr*
Stephen Magliocco, *Vice Pres*
Dane Meza, *Area Mgr*
Scott Niwa, *District Mgr*
Andre Surma, *Purchasing*
EMP: 500
SALES (corp-wide): 6.6B **Privately Held**
WEB: www.southernwine.com
SIC: 5182 5181 Wine; liquor; beer & ale
PA: Southern Glazer's Wine And Spirits, Llc
1600 Nw 163rd St
Miami FL 33169
305 625-4171

(P-9057)
TREASURY WINE ESTATES AMERICAS
555 Gateway Dr, NAPA (94558-6291)
PHONE..................................707 259-4500
Deborah Dubois, *Branch Mgr*
James Casey, *President*
Linnsey Caya, *Officer*
Megghen Driscol, *Vice Pres*
Kory Erickson, *Vice Pres*
EMP: 121 **Privately Held**
SIC: 5182 Wine
HQ: Treasury Wine Estates Americas Company
555 Gateway Dr
Napa CA 94558
707 259-4500

(P-9058)
VINO FARMS LLC
1377 E Lodi Ave, Lodi (95240-0840)
PHONE..................................209 334-6975
James Ledbetter,
John Ledbetter,
EMP: 700
SQ FT: 5,000
SALES (est): 123MM **Privately Held**
SIC: 5182 Wine

(P-9059)
VINTAGE WINE ESTATES INC (PA)
205 Concourse Blvd, Santa Rosa
(95403-8258)
PHONE..................................877 289-9463
Patrick Roney, *CEO*
Terry Wheatley, *President*
Karen L Diepholz, *CFO*
▲ EMP: 118
SALES (est): 102.1MM **Privately Held**
SIC: 5182 Wine

(P-9060)
VINWOOD CELLARS INC
18700 Geyserville Ave, Geyserville
(95441-9526)
P.O. Box 1341, Healdsburg (95448-1341)
PHONE..................................707 857-4011
Alan Hemphill, *President*
EMP: 50
SALES (est): 8MM **Privately Held**
SIC: 5182 2084 Wine & distilled beverages; wines

(P-9061)
WINE GROUP INC
Also Called: Franza Sanger Winery
2916 S Reed Ave, Sanger (93657-9526)
PHONE..................................559 638-3511
Gary Nakagawa, *Manager*
EMP: 95
SALES (corp-wide): 151.9MM **Privately Held**
SIC: 5182 Wine
HQ: The Wine Group Inc
17000 E State Highway 120
Ripon CA 95366
209 599-4111

(P-9062)
WINERY EXCHANGE INC (PA)
Also Called: Wx Brands
500 Redwood Blvd Ste 200, Novato
(94947-6921)
PHONE..................................415 382-6900
Peter Byck, *CEO*
Bryan Moreno, *Vice Pres*
Anne Gustafson, *Creative Dir*
Jon Rickards, *Project Mgr*
Jim Delafuente, *Technology*
▲ EMP: 50
SQ FT: 8,300

SALES (est): 74.9MM **Privately Held**
WEB: www.wineryexchange.com
SIC: 5182 Wine

(P-9063)
WINIARSKI MANAGEMENT INC
5766 Silverado Trl, NAPA (94558-9413)
PHONE..................................707 944-2020
Warren P Winiarski, *President*
EMP: 100
SALES (est): 10MM **Privately Held**
SIC: 5182 0172 Wine; grapes

(P-9064)
YOUNGS HOLDINGS INC (PA)
14402 Franklin Ave, Tustin (92780-7013)
PHONE..................................714 368-4615
Chris Underwood, *CEO*
Vernon Underwood Jr, *Ch of Bd*
Hugh Duncan, *Exec VP*
Claire Carrick, *Vice Pres*
Kevin Fitzsimons, *Vice Pres*
EMP: 100
SALES (est): 1.2B **Privately Held**
SIC: 5182 Wine; neutral spirits

(P-9065)
YOUNGS MARKET COMPANY LLC (HQ)
14402 Franklin Ave, Tustin (92780-7013)
PHONE..................................800 317-6150
Chris Underwood, *CEO*
Dennis Hamann, *CFO*
Kevin Manion, *CFO*
Vern Underwood, *Chairman*
Kevin Perez, *Treasurer*
◆ EMP: 350
SQ FT: 250,000
SALES (est): 955.9MM
SALES (corp-wide): 1.2B **Privately Held**
SIC: 5182 Wine; neutral spirits
PA: Young's Holdings, Inc.
14402 Franklin Ave
Tustin CA 92780
714 368-4615

(P-9066)
YOUNGS MARKET COMPANY LLC
850 Jarvis Dr, Morgan Hill (95037-2846)
PHONE..................................408 782-3121
Ken Feroli, *Manager*
John Benz, *Sales Staff*
David Rose, *Sales Staff*
EMP: 100
SALES (corp-wide): 1.2B **Privately Held**
SIC: 5182 Liquor
HQ: Young's Market Company, Llc
14402 Franklin Ave
Tustin CA 92780
800 317-6150

(P-9067)
YOUNGS MARKET COMPANY LLC
5100 Franklin Dr, Pleasanton (94588-3355)
PHONE..................................510 475-2200
Chris Nicks, *Manager*
Regan Martinez, *Human Res Mgr*
Nicholas Westbrook, *Merchandising*
Lloyd Sgamba, *Sales Staff*
Pat Pittman, *Maintence Staff*
EMP: 400
SQ FT: 20,000
SALES (corp-wide): 1.2B **Privately Held**
SIC: 5182 Wine; liquor
HQ: Young's Market Company, Llc
14402 Franklin Ave
Tustin CA 92780
800 317-6150

(P-9068)
YOUNGS MARKET COMPANY LLC
Also Called: Wine Dept
500 S Central Ave, Los Angeles
(90013-1715)
PHONE..................................213 629-3929
Mark Sneed, *Branch Mgr*
Nick Claitman, *Vice Pres*
Tanya M Griffith, *Vice Pres*
Larry Di, *Program Mgr*
Rachel Tanham, *Office Mgr*
EMP: 450

SALES (corp-wide): 1.2B **Privately Held**
SIC: 5182 Wine
HQ: Young's Market Company, Llc
14402 Franklin Ave
Tustin CA 92780
800 317-6150

(P-9069)
YOUNGS MARKET COMPANY LLC
256 Sutton Pl Ste 106, Santa Rosa
(95407-8163)
PHONE..................................707 584-5170
Mark Delbenny, *Manager*
EMP: 65
SALES (corp-wide): 1.2B **Privately Held**
SIC: 5182 Wine
HQ: Young's Market Company, Llc
14402 Franklin Ave
Tustin CA 92780
800 317-6150

(P-9070)
YOUNGS MARKET COMPANY LLC
3620 Industrial Blvd # 10, West Sacramento
(95691-6518)
PHONE..................................916 617-4402
Jim Morris, *Branch Mgr*
EMP: 50
SALES (corp-wide): 1.2B **Privately Held**
SIC: 5182 Liquor; wine
HQ: Young's Market Company, Llc
14402 Franklin Ave
Tustin CA 92780
800 317-6150

5191 Farm Splys Wholesale

(P-9071)
AG RX (PA)
751 S Rose Ave, Oxnard (93030-5146)
P.O. Box 2008 (93034-2008)
PHONE..................................805 487-0696
Ken Burdullis, *President*
EMP: 92
SQ FT: 45,000
SALES (est): 79.5MM **Privately Held**
WEB: www.agrx.com
SIC: 5191 Fertilizer & fertilizer materials

(P-9072)
ASSOCIATED FEED & SUPPLY CO (PA)
Also Called: Farwest Trading
5213 W Main St, Turlock (95380-9413)
P.O. Box 2367 (95381-2367)
PHONE..................................209 667-2708
Matt Swanson, *President*
Jim Hyer, *Exec VP*
Kurt Hertlein, *Vice Pres*
▲ EMP: 112
SQ FT: 1,800
SALES (est): 120.6MM **Privately Held**
SIC: 5191 Animal feeds

(P-9073)
BIG F COMPANY INC
1445 Jason Way, Santa Maria
(93455-1011)
PHONE..................................805 928-2333
Francisco Contreras, *Principal*
Alicia Contreras, *Vice Pres*
EMP: 54
SQ FT: 1,100
SALES (est): 1.3MM **Privately Held**
SIC: 5191 Straw

(P-9074)
BORDER VALLEY TRADING LTD
604 Mead Rd, Brawley (92227-9748)
P.O. Box 62 (92227-0062)
PHONE..................................760 344-6700
Lucien Bronicki, *General Mgr*
EMP: 56 **Privately Held**
SIC: 5191
PA: Border Valley Trading, Ltd.
14503 W Harding Rd
Turlock CA 95380

PRODUCTS & SVCS

(P-9075)
BORDER VALLEY TRADING LTD (PA)
14503 W Harding Rd, Turlock (95380-9012)
P.O. Box 62, Brawley (92227-0062)
PHONE..............................209 669-6000
Greg Braun, *President*
Paul Cameron, *Corp Secy*
Robert Presley, *Vice Pres*
Denise Smith, *Human Res Mgr*
Jared Brady, *Manager*
◆ **EMP:** 68
SQ FT: 1,200
SALES (est): 65.4MM **Privately Held**
SIC: 5191 Hay

(P-9076)
BRITZ FERTILIZERS INC
Also Called: Bsgs Five Points
21817 S Frsno Coalinga Rd, Five Points (93624)
PHONE..............................559 884-2421
Ken Walls, *Manager*
EMP: 100
SALES (corp-wide): 330.6MM **Privately Held**
WEB: www.britzinc.com
SIC: 5191 Chemicals, agricultural; fertilizer & fertilizer materials
HQ: Britz Fertilizers Inc.
3265 W Figarden Dr
Fresno CA 93711
559 448-8000

(P-9077)
BUTTONWILLOW WAREHOUSE CO INC (HQ)
3430 Unicorn Rd, Bakersfield (93308-6829)
P.O. Box 98, Buttonwillow (93206-0098)
PHONE..............................661 695-6500
Donald Houchin, *President*
Brad Crowder, *COO*
Scott Stanley, *CFO*
Wallace Houchin, *Vice Pres*
Rob Poznoff, *Opers Mgr*
EMP: 75
SALES (est): 80.3MM
SALES (corp-wide): 80.9MM **Privately Held**
SIC: 5191 Fertilizer & fertilizer materials
PA: Tech Agricultural, Inc.
125 Front St
Buttonwillow CA 93206
661 764-5234

(P-9078)
E B STONE & SON INC
Also Called: Greenall
6111 Lambie Rd, Suisun City (94585-9789)
P.O. Box 550 (94585-0550)
PHONE..............................707 426-2500
Bradford G Crandall, *CEO*
Bradford G Crandall Jr, *President*
Lynne Crandall, *Admin Sec*
EMP: 65
SQ FT: 79,000
SALES (est): 42.2MM **Privately Held**
WEB: www.ebstone.org
SIC: 5191 2873 2875 3423 Fertilizer & fertilizer materials; garden supplies; nitrogenous fertilizers; fertilizers, mixing only; hand & edge tools

(P-9079)
FOSTER POULTRY FARMS
4107 Ave 360, Traver (93673)
PHONE..............................559 457-6509
Larry Ficken, *Plant Mgr*
EMP: 929
SALES (corp-wide): 3B **Privately Held**
SIC: 5191 Farm supplies
PA: Foster Poultry Farms
1000 Davis St
Livingston CA 95334
209 394-6914

(P-9080)
JR SIMPLOT COMPANY
Also Called: Simplot Growers Solutions
35836 W Bullard Ave, Firebaugh (93622-9714)
P.O. Box 725 (93622-0725)
PHONE..............................559 659-2033

Johnny Valov, *Branch Mgr*
EMP: 50
SALES (corp-wide): 5.1B **Privately Held**
SIC: 5191 Fertilizer & fertilizer materials
PA: J.R. Simplot Company
1099 W Front St
Boise ID 83702
208 780-3287

(P-9081)
L & L NURSERY SUPPLY INC (PA)
Also Called: Unigro
2552 Shenandoah Way, San Bernardino (92407-1845)
PHONE..............................909 591-0461
Lloyd Swindell, *Ch of Bd*
Harvey Luth, *President*
Tom Medhurst, *President*
Mike Fuson, *Vice Pres*
Larry Tabert, *Info Tech Mgr*
▲ **EMP:** 150 **EST:** 1953
SQ FT: 107,000
SALES (est): 184.4MM **Privately Held**
WEB: www.llnurserysupply.com
SIC: 5191 2875 2449 5193 Insecticides; fertilizer & fertilizer materials; soil, potting & planting; potting soil, mixed; wood containers; flowers & florists' supplies

(P-9082)
L A HEARNE COMPANY (PA)
512 Metz Rd, King City (93930-2503)
PHONE..............................831 385-5441
Francis Giudici, *President*
Dennis Hearne, *Ch of Bd*
Frank Hearne, *Vice Pres*
Mike Hearne, *Vice Pres*
Tim Hearne, *Vice Pres*
▲ **EMP:** 70 **EST:** 1938
SQ FT: 220,000
SALES (est): 75.1MM **Privately Held**
WEB: www.hearneco.com
SIC: 5191 0723 5699 4214 Fertilizers & agricultural chemicals; bean cleaning services; grain drying services; seed cleaning; western apparel; local trucking with storage; livestock feeds; lawn & garden supplies

(P-9083)
LA PALMA FARMS INC
1445 Jason Way, Santa Maria (93455-1011)
PHONE..............................805 928-2333
Jose Alfredo Contreras, *President*
EMP: 60
SALES (est): 1.4MM **Privately Held**
SIC: 5191 Straw

(P-9084)
LANTING HAY DEALER INC
9032 Merrill Ave, Ontario (91762-7234)
P.O. Box 747, Chino (91708-0747)
PHONE..............................909 563-5601
Ronald J Lanting, *President*
Lorraine Lanting, *Corp Secy*
Bradley M Lanting, *Vice Pres*
Curtis J Lanting, *Vice Pres*
Ronald P Lanting, *Vice Pres*
EMP: 75
SQ FT: 40,000
SALES (est): 18.9MM **Privately Held**
SIC: 5191 Hay

(P-9085)
MANN LAKE LTD
500 Santa Anita Dr, Woodland (95776-6117)
PHONE..............................530 662-4061
Eric Foster, *Branch Mgr*
Gabriel Wheeler, *Graphic Designe*
Katie Doyle, *Sales Staff*
Troy Martinson, *Sales Staff*
Ed Waggoner, *Sales Staff*
EMP: 50
SALES (corp-wide): 31.6MM **Privately Held**
SIC: 5191 5149 Beekeeping supplies (non-durable); sugar, refined
HQ: Mann Lake, Ltd.
501 1st St S
Hackensack MN 56452
800 880-7694

(P-9086)
MILHOUS FEED
24077 State Highway 49, Nevada City (95959-8519)
PHONE..............................530 292-3242
Oliver Milhous, *Partner*
Franklin Milhous, *Partner*
Richard Milhous, *Partner*
EMP: 150
SQ FT: 1,280
SALES: 1.5MM **Privately Held**
SIC: 5191 Feed

(P-9087)
NEWCO DISTRIBUTORS INC
9060 Rochester Ave, Rancho Cucamonga (91730-5522)
P.O. Box 1449 (91729-1449)
PHONE..............................909 291-2240
Randall Barb, *CEO*
Kellie Clark, *CFO*
Sarah Watkins, *Vice Pres*
Carlos Elgueta, *Network Enginr*
Jodi Barb, *Technology*
EMP: 60
SQ FT: 60,000
SALES (est): 51.4MM **Privately Held**
WEB: www.newcodistributors.com
SIC: 5191 5149 Animal feeds; pet foods

(P-9088)
NUTRIEN AG SOLUTIONS INC
305 Larsen Rd, Imperial (92251-9757)
P.O. Box 698 (92251-0698)
PHONE..............................760 355-1133
Shane Brady, *Manager*
EMP: 59
SALES (corp-wide): 3.5K **Privately Held**
WEB: www.cropproductionservices.com
SIC: 5191 Fertilizer & fertilizer materials; chemicals, agricultural; herbicides; insecticides
HQ: Nutrien Ag Solutions, Inc.
3005 Rocky Mountain Ave
Loveland CO 80538
970 685-3300

(P-9089)
NUTRIEN AG SOLUTIONS INC
1335 W Main St, Santa Maria (93458-4903)
P.O. Box 669 (93456-0669)
PHONE..............................805 922-5848
Joe Wickham, *Manager*
EMP: 80
SQ FT: 32,165
SALES (corp-wide): 3.5K **Privately Held**
WEB: www.cropproductionservices.com
SIC: 5191 Fertilizer & fertilizer materials; chemicals, agricultural; herbicides; insecticides
HQ: Nutrien Ag Solutions, Inc.
3005 Rocky Mountain Ave
Loveland CO 80538
970 685-3300

(P-9090)
NUTRIEN AG SOLUTIONS INC
21929 S Lassen, Five Points (93624)
P.O. Box 338 (93624-0338)
PHONE..............................559 884-6010
Scott Desmond, *Manager*
EMP: 50
SQ FT: 5,670
SALES (corp-wide): 3.5K **Privately Held**
WEB: www.cropproductionservices.com
SIC: 5191 Fertilizer & fertilizer materials; chemicals, agricultural; herbicides; insecticides
HQ: Nutrien Ag Solutions, Inc.
3005 Rocky Mountain Ave
Loveland CO 80538
970 685-3300

(P-9091)
NUTRIEN AG SOLUTIONS INC
1143 Terven Ave, Salinas (93901-4522)
P.O. Box 657 (93902-0657)
PHONE..............................831 757-5391
John Patinl, *Manager*
Lon Lanini, *Executive*
EMP: 60

SALES (corp-wide): 3.5K **Privately Held**
WEB: www.cropproductionservices.com
SIC: 5191 Fertilizer & fertilizer materials; chemicals, agricultural; herbicides; insecticides
HQ: Nutrien Ag Solutions, Inc.
3005 Rocky Mountain Ave
Loveland CO 80538
970 685-3300

(P-9092)
PLANTERS HAY INC
1295 E St 78, Brawley (92227)
PHONE..............................760 344-0620
Stephen Benson, *CEO*
◆ **EMP:** 52
SALES (est): 15.3MM **Privately Held**
SIC: 5191 7389 Hay; styling of fashions, apparel, furniture, textiles, etc.

(P-9093)
PROFESSIONALS CHOICE SPORT
2025 Gillespie Way # 106, El Cajon (92020-0924)
PHONE..............................619 873-1100
Nina Scott, *CEO*
Michele Scott, *Vice Pres*
Igor Prokopenko, *Technology*
Leah Horstman, *Mfg Staff*
Monty Crist, *Mktg Dir*
▲ **EMP:** 80
SQ FT: 20,000
SALES: 15MM **Privately Held**
WEB: www.profchoice.com
SIC: 5191 Equestrian equipment

(P-9094)
RENTOKIL NORTH AMERICA INC
Also Called: Target Specialty Products
15415 Marquardt Ave, Santa Fe Springs (90670-5711)
PHONE..............................562 802-2238
Bonnie Fallon, *Manager*
Todd Ferguson, *Vice Pres*
Todd Griebe, *Business Dir*
Randy Francis, *Branch Mgr*
Dianna Thongsavanh, *Office Admin*
EMP: 100
SALES (corp-wide): 3.1B **Privately Held**
SIC: 5191 Chemicals, agricultural
HQ: Rentokil North America, Inc.
1125 Berkshire Blvd # 150
Wyomissing PA 19610
610 372-9700

(P-9095)
SAKATA SEED AMERICA INC (HQ)
18095 Serene Dr, Morgan Hill (95037-2833)
P.O. Box 880 (95038-0880)
PHONE..............................408 778-7758
David Armstrong, *CEO*
Koichi Matsunaga, *Vice Pres*
Jeffrey Tajima, *Area Mgr*
Linda Garcia, *Admin Asst*
Ramiro Guel, *Administration*
▲ **EMP:** 90
SQ FT: 48,000
SALES (est): 91.2MM
SALES (corp-wide): 574.3MM **Privately Held**
WEB: www.sakata.com
SIC: 5191 0182 Seeds: field, garden & flower; vegetable crops grown under cover
PA: Sakata Seed Corporation
2-7-1, Nakamachidai, Tsuzuki-Ku
Yokohama KNG 224-0
459 458-800

(P-9096)
SAN LUIS OBISPO CNTY FRM INC (PA)
Also Called: FARM SUPPLY COMPANY
224 Tank Farm Rd, San Luis Obispo (93401-7508)
P.O. Box 111 (93406-0111)
PHONE..............................805 543-3751
James W Brabeck, *President*
Karen Ellsworth, *CFO*
Jon Kelley, *Department Mgr*
Kevin Holmes, *Branch Mgr*

EMP: 102 **EST:** 1950
SQ FT: 15,000
SALES: 25.9MM **Privately Held**
SIC: 5191 5211 Feed; lumber & other
building materials

(P-9097)
SEEDS OF CHANGE INC
Also Called: Sustainable Agriculture
2555 S Dominguez Hills Dr, Rancho
Dominguez (90220-6402)
P.O. Box 4908 (90224-4908)
PHONE....................................310 764-7700
Will Righeimer, *CEO*
◆ **EMP:** 120
SQ FT: 25,411
SALES (est): 46.8MM
SALES (corp-wide): 34.2B **Privately Held**
SIC: 5191 0723 Seeds: field, garden &
flower; crop preparation services for mar-
ket
HQ: Mars Food Us, Llc
   2001 E Cashdan St Ste 201
   Rancho Dominguez CA 90220
   310 933-0670

(P-9098)
SEMINIS VEGETABLE SEEDS INC (DH)
2700 Camino Del Sol, Oxnard
(93030-7967)
PHONE....................................855 733-3834
Michael J Frank, *CEO*
Kerry Preete, *President*
Sergio Becerra, *Analyst*
Angelina Smith, *Auditor*
◆ **EMP:** 600 **EST:** 1962
SQ FT: 370,000
SALES (est): 526.4MM
SALES (corp-wide): 41.2B **Privately Held**
WEB: www.bruinsma.com
SIC: 5191 0723 Seeds: field, garden &
flower; crop preparation services for mar-
ket
HQ: Monsanto Company
   800 N Lindbergh Blvd
   Saint Louis MO 63167
   314 694-1000

(P-9099)
SEMINIS VEGETABLE SEEDS INC
Also Called: Monsanto
37437 State Highway 16, Woodland
(95695-9353)
PHONE....................................530 669-6903
Seminis Vegetable Seeds, *Owner*
Juan Sanchez, *Research*
Susan Vantuyl, *Research*
Brandy Burns, *Human Res Mgr*
Evan Punt, *Buyer*
EMP: 50
SALES (corp-wide): 41.2B **Privately Held**
WEB: www.bruinsma.com
SIC: 5191 Seeds: field, garden & flower
HQ: Seminis Vegetable Seeds, Inc.
   2700 Camino Del Sol
   Oxnard CA 93030
   855 733-3834

(P-9100)
STANISLAUS FARM SUPPLY COMPANY (PA)
Also Called: Stan Farm
624 E Service Rd, Modesto (95358-9451)
PHONE....................................209 538-7070
Nickolas J Biscay, *CEO*
Espiridion Ixta, *CFO*
EMP: 65
SQ FT: 4,000
SALES (est): 90.8MM **Privately Held**
SIC: 5191 Fertilizer & fertilizer materials;
insecticides; seeds: field, garden & flower

(P-9101)
SYNGENTA SEEDS INC
5653 Monterey Frontage Rd, Gilroy
(95020-9588)
PHONE....................................408 847-4242
Ed Merrell, *Branch Mgr*
EMP: 50
SALES (corp-wide): 43.5B **Privately Held**
SIC: 5191 Seeds: field, garden & flower

HQ: Syngenta Seeds, Llc
   11055 Wayzata Blvd
   Hopkins MN 55305
   612 656-8600

(P-9102)
VOLOAGRI INC
3424 Roberto Ct, San Luis Obispo
(93401-7126)
PHONE....................................805 547-9391
Alois Van Vliet, *CEO*
EMP: 150 **EST:** 2012
SALES (est): 24.9MM **Privately Held**
SIC: 5191 Seeds & bulbs

(P-9103)
WESTERN MILLING LLC (HQ)
Also Called: O.H. Kruse Grain and Milling
31120 West St, Goshen (93227)
P.O. Box 1029 (93227-1029)
PHONE....................................559 302-1000
Kevin Kruse, *Mng Member*
Jeremy Wilhelm, *President*
Mark Labounty, *COO*
Chad Pinter, *Exec VP*
Bob Reeves, *Vice Pres*
◆ **EMP:** 243
SALES (est): 553.7MM **Privately Held**
WEB: www.westernmilling.com
SIC: 5191 Animal feeds
PA: Kruse Investment Company, Inc.
   31120 W St
   Goshen CA 93227
   559 302-1000

(P-9104)
WILBUR-ELLIS COMPANY LLC
12550 S Colorado Ave, Helm (93627)
PHONE....................................559 866-5667
Tim Doss, *General Mgr*
EMP: 60
SALES (corp-wide): 3B **Privately Held**
WEB: www.wilbur-ellis.com
SIC: 5191 Fertilizer & fertilizer materials
HQ: Wilbur-Ellis Company Llc
   345 California St Fl 27
   San Francisco CA 94104
   415 772-4000

(P-9105)
WILBUR-ELLIS COMPANY LLC (DH)
345 California St Fl 27, San Francisco
(94104-2644)
PHONE....................................415 772-4000
John P Thacher, *Ch of Bd*
Daniel R Vradenburg, *President*
Michael J Hunter, *CFO*
Alison J Amonette, *Treasurer*
Steven J Dietze, *Vice Pres*
EMP: 423
SALES (est): 2.1B
SALES (corp-wide): 3B **Privately Held**
SIC: 5191 0711 Farm supplies; fertilizer &
fertilizer materials; insecticides; fertilizer
application services
HQ: Wilbur-Ellis Holdings Ii, Inc
   345 California St Fl 27
   San Francisco CA 94104
   415 772-4000

(P-9106)
WILBUR-ELLIS COMPANY LLC
Also Called: Weco - Us.ca. El Centro
45 Danenberg Dr, El Centro (92243-9447)
PHONE....................................760 352-2847
Dan Wray, *Manager*
EMP: 58
SALES (corp-wide): 3B **Privately Held**
WEB: www.wilbur-ellis.com
SIC: 5191 Feed
HQ: Wilbur-Ellis Company Llc
   345 California St Fl 27
   San Francisco CA 94104
   415 772-4000

(P-9107)
WILBUR-ELLIS COMPANY LLC
1427 Abbott St, Salinas (93901-4506)
PHONE....................................831 422-6473
D Sites, *COO*
EMP: 63
SALES (corp-wide): 3B **Privately Held**
SIC: 5191 Chemicals, agricultural

HQ: Wilbur-Ellis Company Llc
   345 California St Fl 27
   San Francisco CA 94104
   415 772-4000

5192 Books, Periodicals & Newspapers Wholesale

(P-9108)
ANDERSON NEWS LLC
15172 Goldenwest Cir, Westminster
(92683-5222)
P.O. Box 8401 (92684-8401)
PHONE....................................714 892-7766
Dave Schultz, *Branch Mgr*
EMP: 74
SALES (corp-wide): 178.9MM **Privately Held**
WEB: www.kadsi.com
SIC: 5192 Magazines
PA: Anderson News, Llc
   265 Brookview Town Ste
   Knoxville TN 37919
   865 584-9765

(P-9109)
BAKER & TAYLOR LLC
10350 Barnes Canyon Rd # 100, San
Diego (92121-2708)
PHONE....................................858 457-2500
James Leidich, *Director*
EMP: 187
SALES (corp-wide): 6.1B **Privately Held**
WEB: www.accupackinc.com
SIC: 5192 5099 5199 5045 Books; tapes
& cassettes, prerecorded; video cas-
settes, accessories & supplies; calendars;
computer software; book stores; audio
tapes, prerecorded; video tapes, prere-
corded
HQ: Baker & Taylor, Llc
   2550 W Tyvola Rd Ste 300
   Charlotte NC 28217
   -

(P-9110)
CLASSIFIED ADVERTISING
715 Anacapa St, Santa Barbara
(93101-2203)
P.O. Box 1359 (93102-1359)
PHONE....................................805 564-5200
Sarah Sinclair, *Manager*
EMP: 85
SALES (est): 403.4K **Privately Held**
SIC: 5192 7311 Newspapers; advertising
agencies

(P-9111)
CONTRA COSTA NEWSPAPERS INC
1650 Cavallo Rd, Antioch (94509-1928)
PHONE....................................925 757-2525
Debbie Mathias, *Manager*
EMP: 50
SQ FT: 24,534
SALES (corp-wide): 4.3B **Privately Held**
WEB: www.contracostatimes.com
SIC: 5192 Newspapers
HQ: Contra Costa Newspapers, Inc.
   175 Lennon Ln Ste 100
   Walnut Creek CA 94598
   925 935-2525

(P-9112)
EL AVISO MAGAZINE
4850 Gage Ave, Bell (90201-1409)
P.O. Box 127, Huntington Park (90255-
0127)
PHONE....................................323 586-9199
Jose Zepeda, *CEO*
Nicolas Ramirez, *Office Mgr*
Maria Reyes, *Office Mgr*
Martha Ramirez, *Office Admin*
Yazmin Gonzalez, *Opers Mgr*
EMP: 300
SALES (est): 31.9MM **Privately Held**
SIC: 5192 Magazines

(P-9113)
EMMIS PUBLISHING CORPORATION
Also Called: Los Angeles Magazine
5900 Wilshire Blvd Fl 10, Los Angeles
(90036-5024)
PHONE....................................323 801-0100
EMP: 55
SALES (corp-wide): 148.4MM **Publicly Held**
SIC: 5192 Magazines
HQ: Emmis Publishing Corporation
   40 Monument Cir Ste 700
   Indianapolis IN 46204
   317 266-0100

(P-9114)
HAY HOUSE INC (PA)
2776 Loker Ave W, Carlsbad (92010-6611)
P.O. Box 5100 (92018-5100)
PHONE....................................760 431-7695
Louise L Hay, *Ch of Bd*
Reid Tracy, *President*
▲ **EMP:** 62
SQ FT: 20,000
SALES (est): 61MM **Privately Held**
WEB: www.hayhouse.com
SIC: 5192 5099 5942 5735 Books; tapes
& cassettes, prerecorded; book stores;
audio tapes, prerecorded

(P-9115)
ICONIC CHRONICLES MAGAZINE LLC
5120 Monetta Ln, Sacramento
(95835-2030)
PHONE....................................707 712-2097
EMP: 57
SALES (est): 62K **Privately Held**
SIC: 5192 Magazines

(P-9116)
INGRAM PUBLISHER SERVICES INC
1700 4th St, Berkeley (94710-1711)
PHONE....................................510 528-1444
Richard C Freese, *President*
Geoffrey V Sutton, *Author*
EMP: 67
SALES (corp-wide): 3.9B **Privately Held**
SIC: 5192 Books, periodicals & newspa-
pers
HQ: Ingram Publisher Services Llc
   1 Ingram Blvd
   La Vergne TN 37086
   615 213-5000

(P-9117)
MADER NEWS INC
913 Ruberta Ave, Glendale (91201-2346)
PHONE....................................818 551-5000
Avan Mader, *President*
Rafael Sotomayor, *Opers Mgr*
Mary Mader, *Director*
EMP: 100
SQ FT: 2,400
SALES (est): 26.1MM **Privately Held**
SIC: 5192 Newspapers

(P-9118)
NEWSWAYS SERVICES INC
Also Called: Newsways Distributors
1324 Cypress Ave, Los Angeles
(90065-1220)
PHONE....................................323 258-6000
John Dorman, *President*
▲ **EMP:** 135
SQ FT: 8,500
SALES (est): 53.6MM **Privately Held**
SIC: 5192 Magazines

(P-9119)
SCHOLASTIC BOOK FAIRS INC
2890 E White Star Ave, Anaheim
(92806-2632)
PHONE....................................714 237-1100
Jim Wind, *Branch Mgr*
Gayathri Sarilla, *QA Dir*
Gina Asprocolas, *Producer*
Dan Shindell, *Producer*
Leslie Hernandez, *Marketing Mgr*
EMP: 75

SALES (corp-wide): 1.6B **Publicly Held**
WEB: www.scholasticbookfairs.com
SIC: 5192 Books, periodicals & newspa-
pers
HQ: Scholastic Book Fairs, Inc.
1080 Greenwood Blvd
Lake Mary FL 32746
407 829-7300

(P-9120)
SCHOLASTIC BOOK FAIRS INC
42001 Christy St, Fremont (94538-3163)
PHONE..................................510 771-1700
Caesey Ryan, *Branch Mgr*
EMP: 100
SALES (corp-wide): 1.6B **Publicly Held**
WEB: www.scholasticbookfairs.com
SIC: 5192 Books
HQ: Scholastic Book Fairs, Inc.
1080 Greenwood Blvd
Lake Mary FL 32746
407 829-7300

(P-9121)
TEN ENTHUSIAST NETWORK LLC
Also Called: TEN ENTHUSIAST NETWORK,
LLC
1821 E Dyer Rd Ste 150, Santa Ana
(92705-5730)
PHONE..................................714 709-9021
Scott Bailey, *Branch Mgr*
EMP: 210
SQ FT: 59,000 **Privately Held**
SIC: 5192 Books, periodicals & newspa-
pers
PA: Ten Publishing Media, Llc
831 S Douglas St Ste 100
El Segundo CA 90245
-

(P-9122)
WHITE DIGITAL MEDIA INC
Also Called: Wdm Group
3394 Carmel Mountain Rd # 250, San
Diego (92121-1072)
PHONE..................................760 827-7800
Brian Smith, *CEO*
Glen White, *President*
Matthew P Melucci, *Officer*
Andy Turner, *Officer*
Keith Amber, *Office Mgr*
EMP: 150
SALES (est): 42.6MM **Privately Held**
SIC: 5192 Magazines

5193 Flowers, Nursery Stock & Florists' Splys Wholesale

(P-9123)
ALTMAN SPECIALTY PLANTS INC (PA)
Also Called: Altman Plants
3742 Blue Bird Canyon Rd, Vista
(92084-7432)
PHONE..................................800 348-4881
Ken Altman, *CEO*
Deena Altman, *Vice Pres*
Erin McCarthy, *Vice Pres*
Kathy Nyquist, *Natl Sales Mgr*
Sherry Schaeffer, *Natl Sales Mgr*
▲ EMP: 800
SQ FT: 4,000
SALES (est): 558.9MM **Privately Held**
WEB: www.altmanplants.com
SIC: 5193 3999 Nursery stock; atomizers,
toiletry

(P-9124)
B & B NURSERIES INC
Also Called: Landscape Center
9505 Cleveland Ave, Riverside
(92503-6241)
P.O. Box 7399 (92513-7399)
PHONE..................................951 352-8383
Mark Barrett, *CEO*
EMP: 109
SQ FT: 2,100
SALES (est): 16.7MM **Privately Held**
SIC: 5193 0781 Flowers & nursery stock;
landscape counseling services

(P-9125)
BAY CITY FLOWER CO (PA)
2265 Cabrillo Hwy S, Half Moon Bay
(94019-2250)
P.O. Box 186 (94019-0186)
PHONE..................................650 726-5535
Harrison Higaki, *Ch of Bd*
Naomi Higaki, *Shareholder*
Sam Hasegawa, *CFO*
Scott Cornwell, *Engineer*
Mayra Gomez, *Human Res Mgr*
▲ EMP: 300
SQ FT: 2,000
SALES (est): 74.5MM **Privately Held**
WEB: www.baycityflower.com
SIC: 5193 Flowers & florists' supplies

(P-9126)
BRAND FLOWER FARMS INC (PA)
Also Called: Farmers W Flowers & Bouquets
5300 Foothill Rd, Carpinteria (93013-3017)
P.O. Box 600 (93014-0600)
PHONE..................................805 684-5531
Wilja Happ, *CEO*
Maximino Santillon, *President*
Monica Preciado, *CFO*
Will Stewart, *Vice Pres*
Fernando Perez, *Marketing Staff*
▲ EMP: 200
SQ FT: 500,000
SALES (est): 18.5MM **Privately Held**
WEB: www.brandflowers.com
SIC: 5193 Flowers, fresh

(P-9127)
BUSHNELL GARDENS
Also Called: Bushnell's Landscape Creations
5255 Douglas Blvd, Granite Bay
(95746-6204)
PHONE..................................916 791-4199
David Bushnell, *Owner*
EMP: 80
SQ FT: 1,040
SALES (est): 6.7MM **Privately Held**
SIC: 5193 0781 0782 5261 Nursery
stock; landscape architects; lawn & gar-
den services; landscape contractors;
nurseries

(P-9128)
CAL COLOR GROWERS LLC
330 Peebles Ave, Morgan Hill
(95037-2712)
P.O. Box 550 (95038-0550)
PHONE..................................408 778-0835
David Vincent, *Mng Member*
Michelle Vincnet,
▲ EMP: 73
SQ FT: 478,000
SALES (est): 6MM **Privately Held**
SIC: 5193 Nursery stock

(P-9129)
CALIFORNIA PAJAROSA FLORAL
133 Hughes Rd, Watsonville (95076-9458)
P.O. Box 684 (95077-0684)
PHONE..................................831 722-6374
John Furman, *President*
Alan Mitchell, *Vice Pres*
EMP: 50
SQ FT: 10,000
SALES (est): 3.4MM **Privately Held**
WEB: www.pajarosa.com
SIC: 5193 Flowers & florists' supplies

(P-9130)
COLOR SPOT NURSERIES INC
321 W Sepulveda Blvd, Carson
(90745-6313)
PHONE..................................310 549-7470
Fax: 310 549-7312
EMP: 98
SALES (corp-wide): 3.2B **Privately Held**
SIC: 5193
HQ: Color Spot Nurseries, Inc.
27368 Via
Temecula CA 92590

(P-9131)
COREY NURSERY CO INC (PA)
1650 Monte Vista Ave, Claremont
(91711-2999)
P.O. Box 609 (91711-0609)
PHONE..................................909 621-6886
Jeffrey E Corey, *CEO*
Brian Corey, *Shareholder*
Ken Corey, *Shareholder*
Gene Corey, *Ch of Bd*
Eugene K Corey, *President*
▲ EMP: 60 EST: 1978
SQ FT: 170,000
SALES (est): 31.9MM **Privately Held**
WEB: www.coreynursery.com
SIC: 5193 Nursery stock

(P-9132)
COUNTRY FLORAL SUPPLY INC (PA)
Also Called: Country Furnishings
3802 Weatherly Cir, Westlake Village
(91361-3821)
PHONE..................................805 520-8026
Mark Reese, *President*
Debbie Reese, *Vice Pres*
▲ EMP: 80
SQ FT: 60,000
SALES (est): 48.5MM **Privately Held**
WEB: www.countryfloralsupply.com
SIC: 5193 5999 Artificial flowers; artificial
flowers

(P-9133)
DELTA FLORAL DISTRIBUTORS INC
6810 West Blvd, Los Angeles
(90043-4668)
PHONE..................................323 751-8116
Foti Defterios, *President*
Heidi Hansen, *Controller*
Colleen McGowan, *Manager*
▲ EMP: 200
SQ FT: 30,000
SALES (est): 23.1MM **Privately Held**
SIC: 5193 Flowers, fresh

(P-9134)
FISHERS NURSERY
24081 S Austin Rd, Ripon (95366-9646)
P.O. Box 657 (95366-0657)
PHONE..................................209 599-3412
Jerry Fisher, *President*
Mary Fisher, *Corp Secy*
▲ EMP: 75 EST: 1968
SQ FT: 450,000
SALES (est): 5.8MM **Privately Held**
WEB: www.fishersnursery.com
SIC: 5193 Nursery stock

(P-9135)
G M FLORAL COMPANY
Also Called: G M Floral Supply
740 Maple Ave, Los Angeles (90014-2261)
PHONE..................................213 489-7055
Mas Yoshida, *Principal*
Mark Mukai, *Controller*
EMP: 50
SALES (corp-wide): 11.2MM **Privately Held**
WEB: www.gmfloral.com
SIC: 5193 Florists' supplies
PA: G M Floral Company
531 E Evelyn Ave
Mountain View CA
-

(P-9136)
GREEN THUMB INTERNATIONAL INC
21812 Sherman Way, Canoga Park
(91303-1940)
PHONE..................................818 340-6400
Del Berquist, *Principal*
EMP: 100
SALES (corp-wide): 60.5MM **Privately Held**
WEB: www.greenthumbinternational.com
SIC: 5193 5261 0782 0181 Nursery
stock; nurseries & garden centers; lawn &
garden services; ornamental nursery
products

PA: Green Thumb International Inc
7105 Jordan Ave
Canoga Park CA 91303
818 340-6400

(P-9137)
GREEN TREE NURSERY
Also Called: Linwood Nursery
23979 Lake Rd, La Grange (95329-9505)
PHONE..................................209 874-9100
Jason Hall, *Partner*
Chris Torres, *Office Mgr*
EMP: 50
SQ FT: 6,000
SALES (est): 3MM **Privately Held**
SIC: 5193 Nursery stock

(P-9138)
GROLINK PLANT COMPANY INC (PA)
4107 W Gonzales Rd, Oxnard
(93036-7783)
P.O. Box 5506 (93031-5506)
PHONE..................................805 984-7958
Anthony Vollering, *CEO*
Harry Van Wingerden, *Shareholder*
Jerry Van Wingerden, *Corp Secy*
Yasmin Jafroodi, *Executive*
Art Gordijin, *Principal*
▲ EMP: 150
SQ FT: 400,000
SALES (est): 21.3MM **Privately Held**
WEB: www.grolink.com
SIC: 5193 0181 Nursery stock; ornamen-
tal nursery products

(P-9139)
HEADSTART NURSERY INC (PA)
4860 Monterey Rd, Gilroy (95020-9511)
PHONE..................................408 842-3030
Steven H Costa, *President*
Don Christopher, *Vice Pres*
Randy Costa, *Vice Pres*
Doug Iten, *General Mgr*
Chris Peck, *General Mgr*
▲ EMP: 85
SQ FT: 3,000
SALES (est): 66.7MM **Privately Held**
WEB: www.headstartnursery.com
SIC: 5193 5261 Plants, potted; nursery
stock; nurseries & garden centers

(P-9140)
HINES HORTICULTURE INC
2500 Rainbow Valley Blvd, Fallbrook
(92028-9778)
PHONE..................................760 723-1500
Jessee Westrup, *Manager*
EMP: 300
SALES (corp-wide): 1.8B **Privately Held**
WEB: www.hineshorticulture.com
SIC: 5193 0181 Nursery stock; ornamen-
tal nursery products
PA: Hines Horticulture, Inc.
12621 Jeffrey Rd
Irvine CA 92620
949 559-4444

(P-9141)
HINES NURSERIES LLC
22941 Mill Creek Dr, Laguna Hills
(92653-1215)
PHONE..................................602 254-2831
Phil Wayne, *Manager*
Lenore Goldberg, *Regional Mgr*
EMP: 100 **Privately Held**
WEB: www.hineshort.com
SIC: 5193 Flowers & florists' supplies
PA: Hines Nurseries Llc
1700 E Putnam Ave Ste 401
Old Greenwich CT

(P-9142)
HOLLAND FLOWER MARKET INC (PA)
755 Wall St Ste 7g, Los Angeles
(90014-2315)
PHONE..................................213 627-9900
Jaap Haverkate, *President*
Arjen Bosma, *General Mgr*
Ginna Hfm, *General Mgr*
▲ EMP: 51
SQ FT: 11,000
SALES (est): 26MM **Privately Held**
SIC: 5193 Flowers, fresh

394   2019 Directory of California
Wholesalers and Services Companies   ▲ = Import ▼=Export
◆ =Import/Export

(P-9143)
KENDAL FLORAL SUPPLY LLC (PA)
Also Called: Kendal North Bouquet Co
1960 Kellogg Ave, Carlsbad (92008-6581)
PHONE.................................760 431-4910
Kenneth X Baca, *President*
▲ **EMP:** 80
SALES (est): 66.6MM **Privately Held**
WEB: www.kendalfloral.com
SIC: 5193 Flowers, fresh

(P-9144)
LOMA VISTA NURSERY
Also Called: Loma Vista Nursery 2
18272 Bastanchury Rd, Yorba Linda
(92886-2447)
PHONE.................................714 779-5583
Norman Van Ginkel, *President*
EMP: 57
SALES (est): 4MM **Privately Held**
SIC: 5193 5261 Nursery stock; nursery
stock, seeds & bulbs

(P-9145)
MAYESH WHOLESALE FLORIST INC (PA)
5401 W 104th St, Los Angeles
(90045-6011)
PHONE.................................310 342-0980
Patrick Dahlson, *CEO*
Cindie Boer, *COO*
Ben Powell, *COO*
Todd Smith, *Branch Mgr*
Isabelle Buckley, *General Mgr*
▲ **EMP:** 50
SQ FT: 20,000
SALES (est): 85.2MM **Privately Held**
WEB: www.mayeshwholesale.com
SIC: 5193 5992 Flowers, fresh; florists

(P-9146)
MB LANDSCAPING & NURSERY INC
20300 Figueroa St, Carson (90745-1005)
PHONE.................................310 965-1923
Federico Martinez, *President*
Maria Martinez, *Corp Secy*
EMP: 57
SALES (est): 7.8MM **Privately Held**
SIC: 5193 Nursery stock

(P-9147)
MELLANO & CO (PA)
Also Called: Mellano Enterprises
766 Wall St, Los Angeles (90014-2316)
P.O. Box 100, San Luis Rey (92068-0100)
PHONE.................................213 622-0796
John Mellano, *President*
Michael Matthew Mellano, *President*
Battista Castellano, *Corp Secy*
Michelle Castellano, *Vice Pres*
Bob Mellano, *Vice Pres*
EMP: 275
SALES (est): 50.9MM **Privately Held**
WEB: www.mellano.com
SIC: 5193 Flowers, fresh

(P-9148)
MELLANO & CO
Also Called: Mellano Enterprises
734 Wilshire Rd, Oceanside (92057-2111)
P.O. Box 100, San Luis Rey (92068-0100)
PHONE.................................760 433-9550
Harry M Mellano, *Owner*
Rosa Mendoza, *Office Mgr*
Ken Taniguchi, *Foreman/Supr*
Ellie Ellsworth, *Sales Associate*
Lily Kocher, *Sales Associate*
EMP: 170
SALES (est): 6.8MM
SALES (corp-wide): 50.9MM **Privately Held**
WEB: www.mellano.com
SIC: 5193 Flowers, fresh
PA: Mellano & Co.
766 Wall St
Los Angeles CA 90014
213 622-0796

(P-9149)
MONTEREY BAY BOUQUET ACQUISIT
481 San Andreas Rd, Watsonville
(95076-9524)
P.O. Box 1778 (95077-1778)
PHONE.................................831 786-2700
Phil Buran, *Mng Member*
EMP: 170
SALES (est): 10.4MM **Privately Held**
SIC: 5193 Flowers & florists' supplies

(P-9150)
NAKASE BROTHERS WHOLESALE NURS (PA)
9441 Krepp Dr, Huntington Beach
(92646-2799)
PHONE.................................949 855-4388
Shigeo Gary Nakase, *Principal*
Jun Turalba, *Executive Asst*
Noreen Nakase, *Accountant*
Joanne Shurlock, *Sales Mgr*
David Boos, *Sales Staff*
▲ **EMP:** 100
SALES (est): 31.5MM **Privately Held**
WEB: www.nakasebros.com
SIC: 5193 Nursery stock

(P-9151)
NAKASE BROTHERS WHOLESALE NURS
20621 Lake Forest Dr, Lake Forest (92630)
PHONE.................................949 855-4388
Joann Shurlock, *Manager*
EMP: 200
SALES (corp-wide): 31.5MM **Privately Held**
WEB: www.nakasebros.com
SIC: 5193 Nursery stock
PA: Nakase Brothers Wholesale Nursery
9441 Krepp Dr
Huntington Beach CA 92646
949 855-4388

(P-9152)
NORMANS NURSERY INC (PA)
8665 Duarte Rd, San Gabriel (91775-1139)
PHONE.................................626 285-9795
Charles Norman, *President*
Caroline Norman, *Treasurer*
▼ **EMP:** 50
SQ FT: 4,000
SALES (est): 177.8MM **Privately Held**
WEB: www.nngrower.com
SIC: 5193 0181 Nursery stock; nursery
stock, growing of

(P-9153)
NORMANS NURSERY INC
6250 N Escalon Bellota Rd, Linden
(95236-9428)
PHONE.................................209 887-2033
Barbara Hayes, *Manager*
EMP: 200
SALES (corp-wide): 177.8MM **Privately Held**
WEB: www.nngrower.com
SIC: 5193 0181 Nursery stock; nursery
stock, growing of
PA: Norman's Nursery, Inc.
8665 Duarte Rd
San Gabriel CA 91775
626 285-9795

(P-9154)
PACIFIC COAST NURSERY INC
2885 E La Cresta Ave, Anaheim
(92806-1817)
PHONE.................................714 630-4868
Richard F Buccola, *President*
Dennis Buccola, *Treasurer*
EMP: 70
SALES (est): 8.5MM **Privately Held**
WEB: www.pacificcoastnursery.com
SIC: 5193 Nursery stock

(P-9155)
PAJARO VALLEY GREENHOUSES (PA)
90 Hecker Pass Rd, Watsonville
(95076-9776)
PHONE.................................831 722-2773
Arne Thirup, *President*
Doris Thirup, *Treasurer*
Karen Thirup-Sambraillo, *Vice Pres*

Sandy Garcia, *Dir Ops-Prd-Mfg*
EMP: 100
SQ FT: 3,000
SALES (est): 37.4MM **Privately Held**
SIC: 5193 Flowers, fresh

(P-9156)
PARDEE TREE NURSERY
30970 Via Puerta Del Sol, Oceanside
(92057)
P.O. Box 240, Bonsall (92003-0240)
PHONE.................................760 630-5400
Lauren Davis, *President*
EMP: 75
SALES (est): 16.3MM **Privately Held**
WEB: www.pardeetree.com
SIC: 5193 Nursery stock

(P-9157)
PLANT SCIENCES INC
234 Juniper Knoll Rd, Macdoel (96058)
P.O. Box 269 (96058-0269)
PHONE.................................530 398-4042
Tom Alvin, *Manager*
EMP: 50
SALES (corp-wide): 35MM **Privately Held**
WEB: www.plantsciences.com
SIC: 5193 Nursery stock
PA: Plant Sciences, Inc.
342 Green Valley Rd
Watsonville CA 95076
831 728-7771

(P-9158)
PLANT SOURCE INC
2029 Sycamore Dr, San Marcos
(92069-9753)
PHONE.................................760 743-7743
Steve Pyle, *CEO*
▲ **EMP:** 50
SALES (est): 19.4MM **Privately Held**
SIC: 5193 Flowers & florists' supplies

(P-9159)
PLANTEL NURSERIES INC
2775 E Clark Ave, Santa Maria
(93455-5813)
PHONE.................................805 349-8952
EMP: 255
SALES (corp-wide): 8MM **Privately Held**
SIC: 5193 Nursery stock
PA: Plantel Nurseries Inc
2775 E Clark Ave
Santa Maria CA 93455
805 349-8952

(P-9160)
PONTO NURSERY INC
2545 Ramona Dr, Vista (92084-1632)
P.O. Box 536 (92085-0536)
PHONE.................................760 724-6003
William Ponto, *President*
Judy Ponto, *Corp Secy*
EMP: 70
SQ FT: 2,000
SALES: 3.5MM **Privately Held**
SIC: 5193 Nursery stock

(P-9161)
RIVERSIDE NURSERY & LDSCP INC
4763 W Spruce Ave Ste 111, Fresno
(93722-3572)
PHONE.................................559 275-1891
Mitchel Hutcheson, *President*
Anglea Hutchenson, *Vice Pres*
James Hutchison, *Vice Pres*
James Hutchinson, *Admin Sec*
EMP: 60
SQ FT: 4,000
SALES (est): 5.5MM **Privately Held**
WEB: www.riversidelandscape.com
SIC: 5193 0781 Nursery stock; landscape
architects

(P-9162)
SONOMA GRAPEVINES INC (PA)
1919 Dennis Ln, Santa Rosa (95403-1520)
P.O. Box 279, Wasco (93280-0279)
PHONE.................................707 542-5521
Richard Kunde, *President*
Saralee McClelland Kunde, *Corp Secy*
EMP: 78 EST: 1972
SQ FT: 100,000

SALES (est): 13.9MM **Privately Held**
WEB: www.saraleesvineyard.com
SIC: 5193 Nursery stock

(P-9163)
SUNCREST NURSERIES INC
400 Casserly Rd, Watsonville
(95076-9700)
PHONE.................................831 728-2595
Stan Iversen, *President*
EMP: 55
SQ FT: 1,000
SALES (est): 6.2MM **Privately Held**
WEB: www.suncrestnurseries.com
SIC: 5193 Nursery stock

(P-9164)
SUNNYSLOPE TREE FARM INC
Also Called: Sunnyslope Trees
1545 N Glassell St, Orange (92867)
PHONE.................................714 532-1440
Todd Flammer, *President*
Jack W Flammer Sr, *Ch of Bd*
EMP: 100
SQ FT: 1,000
SALES (est): 14.8MM **Privately Held**
WEB: www.sunnyslope.net
SIC: 5193 Nursery stock

(P-9165)
SUNSHINE FLORAL INC
4595 Foothill Rd, Carpinteria (93013-3096)
PHONE.................................805 684-1177
Henry Vanwingerden, *President*
Anthony Vollering, *Vice Pres*
Ed Lozano, *General Mgr*
▲ **EMP:** 70
SALES (est): 5.8MM **Privately Held**
SIC: 5193 Flowers, fresh

(P-9166)
SUNSHINE FLORAL LLC
1070 S Rice Ave Ste 1, Oxnard
(93033-2110)
PHONE.................................805 982-8822
Anthony Vollering, *Mng Member*
Adri Durieux, *Prdtn Mgr*
Henry Van Wingerden, *Mng Member*
Ton Vollering, *Mng Member*
▲ **EMP:** 60 EST: 1985
SQ FT: 10,000
SALES (est): 5.6MM **Privately Held**
WEB: www.sunshinefloral.com
SIC: 5193 Flowers, fresh

(P-9167)
SUPER GARDEN CENTERS INC
Also Called: Green Thumb Nursery
7659 Topanga Canyon Blvd, Canoga Park
(91304-5535)
P.O. Box 111 (91305-0111)
PHONE.................................818 348-9266
Nancy Bergquist, *Manager*
EMP: 50
SALES (corp-wide): 28.6MM **Privately Held**
SIC: 5193 5261 Nursery stock; fertilizer;
nursery stock, seeds & bulbs
PA: Super Garden Centers, Inc.
21812 Sherman Way
Canoga Park CA 91303
818 340-6400

(P-9168)
T - Y NURSERY INC
15335 Highway 76, Pauma Valley
(92061-9583)
P.O. Box 424 (92061-0424)
PHONE.................................760 742-2151
Alfonso Ramos, *Manager*
EMP: 200
SALES (corp-wide): 1.2MM **Privately Held**
SIC: 5193 5261 Plants, potted; nurseries
PA: T - Y Nursery, Inc.
5221 Arvada St
Torrance CA 90503
310 370-2561

(P-9169)
TELAFLORA LLC
11444 W Olympic Blvd Fl 4, Los Angeles
(90064-1546)
PHONE.................................310 231-9199
Stewart Resnick,
Lynda Resnick,

EMP: 450
SALES (est): 26.3MM **Privately Held**
SIC: 5193 Flowers & florists' supplies

(P-9170)
TORO NURSERY INC
17585 Crenshaw Blvd, Torrance
(90504-3403)
PHONE..........................310 715-1982
Salvador Sanchez, *President*
Antonio Gomez, *Vice Pres*
EMP: 60
SALES (est): 4.6MM **Privately Held**
SIC: 5193 Nursery stock

(P-9171)
UNITED FLORAL EXCHANGE INC
Also Called: Cal Americas Wholesale Florist
2834 La Mirada Dr Ste B, Vista
(92081-8440)
PHONE..........................760 597-1940
Jim Dionne, *President*
Thayis Dionne, *Vice Pres*
Leticia Ramirez, *Manager*
EMP: 75
SQ FT: 30,000
SALES (est): 4.1MM **Privately Held**
WEB: www.calamericas.com
SIC: 5193 Flowers, fresh

(P-9172)
USA BOUQUET LLC
2834 La Mirada Dr Ste B, Vista
(92081-8440)
PHONE..........................800 878-9909
Edgar Lozano,
EMP: 88
SALES (corp-wide): 319.1MM **Privately Held**
SIC: 5193 Flowers, fresh
HQ: Usa Bouquet Llc
1500 Nw 95th Ave
Doral FL 33172
786 437-6500

(P-9173)
VALLEY FLOWERS INC
3920 Via Real, Carpinteria (93013-1266)
P.O. Box 1279 (93014-1279)
PHONE..........................805 684-6651
Walter Vanwingerden, *President*
John Vanwingerden, *Vice Pres*
▲ **EMP:** 60
SALES (est): 4.1MM **Privately Held**
WEB: www.valleyflowers.com
SIC: 5193 Flowers & nursery stock

(P-9174)
VILLAGE NURSERIES WHL LLC (PA)
1589 N Main St, Orange (92867-3439)
PHONE..........................714 279-3100
David House, *Mng Member*
Rick Rehm, *CFO*
Terri Cook, *Officer*
Dicksey Williams, *Marketing Staff*
Nick Castro, *Sales Staff*
EMP: 50
SQ FT: 12,321
SALES (est): 188.4MM **Privately Held**
SIC: 5193 Nursery stock

(P-9175)
VILLAGE NURSERIES WHL LLC
6901 Bradshaw Rd, Sacramento
(95829-9303)
PHONE..........................916 993-2292
Steve Sawyer, *Branch Mgr*
EMP: 367
SALES (corp-wide): 188.4MM **Privately Held**
SIC: 5193 Nursery stock
PA: Village Nurseries Wholesale, Llc
1589 N Main St
Orange CA 92867
714 279-3100

(P-9176)
VILLAGE NURSERIES WHL LLC
20099 Santa Rosa Mine Rd, Perris
(92570-7774)
PHONE..........................951 657-3940
Joseph Jensen, *Branch Mgr*
Luis Verdoza, *Supervisor*
EMP: 183

SALES (corp-wide): 188.4MM **Privately Held**
SIC: 5193 Nursery stock
PA: Village Nurseries Wholesale, Llc
1589 N Main St
Orange CA 92867
714 279-3100

(P-9177)
W J GRIFFIN INC
Also Called: Por La Mar Nursery
905 S Patterson Ave, Santa Barbara
(93111-2407)
P.O. Box 6354 (93160-6354)
PHONE..........................805 683-5639
Brian Caird, *CEO*
Dan Jauchen, *Vice Pres*
▲ **EMP:** 250
SQ FT: 200,000
SALES (est): 44MM **Privately Held**
WEB: www.miniroses.com
SIC: 5193 Flowers & florists' supplies

(P-9178)
WESTERN STAR NURSERIES LLC
9394 Robson Rd, Galt (95632-8841)
P.O. Box 725 (95632-0725)
PHONE..........................209 744-2552
Robert Painter,
Sally B Painter,
EMP: 50
SALES (est): 1.7MM **Privately Held**
SIC: 5193 Nursery stock

(P-9179)
WESTLAND ORCHIDS INC
Also Called: Westland Floral
1400 Cravens Ln, Carpinteria
(93013-3166)
PHONE..........................805 684-1436
David Van Wingerden, *CEO*
Diana Filippin, *Technology*
Ellie Ramirez, *Human Resources*
Heather Schulenberg, *Marketing Staff*
Kelly Gomez, *Sales Staff*
▲ **EMP:** 50
SALES (est): 12.6MM **Privately Held**
SIC: 5193 Flowers & florists' supplies

(P-9180)
WINWARD INTERNATIONAL INC (PA)
Also Called: Winward Silks
42760 Albrae St, Fremont (94538-3390)
PHONE..........................510 487-8686
Patrick Tai, *President*
Garrison Tai, *President*
▲ **EMP:** 80
SQ FT: 10,000
SALES (est): 12.9MM **Privately Held**
SIC: 5193 5023 Artificial flowers; decorative home furnishings & supplies

---

5194 Tobacco & Tobacco Prdts Wholesale

(P-9181)
ALTRIA GROUP DISTRIBUTION CO
3500 W Olive Ave Ste 1490, Burbank
(91505-5521)
PHONE..........................626 792-2900
Craig A Johnson, *President*
EMP: 70
SALES (corp-wide): 25.5B **Publicly Held**
WEB: www.philipmorrisusa.com
SIC: 5194 Cigarettes
HQ: Altria Group Distribution Company
6601 W Broad St
Richmond VA 23230

(P-9182)
CORE-MARK INTERNATIONAL INC
8333 Edison Hwy, Bakersfield
(93307-9173)
PHONE..........................661 366-2673
Caral Parker, *Principal*
EMP: 121
SALES (corp-wide): 15.6B **Publicly Held**
SIC: 5194 Tobacco & tobacco products

HQ: Core-Mark International, Inc.
395 Oyster Point Blvd # 415
South San Francisco CA 94080
650 589-9445

(P-9183)
CORE-MARK MIDCONTINENT INC (DH)
Also Called: Core-Mark International
395 Oyster Point Blvd # 415, South San
Francisco (94080-1932)
PHONE..........................650 589-9445
J M Walsh, *CEO*
Thomas Perkins, *President*
Gregory P Antholzner, *Corp Secy*
Stacy Loretz Congdon, *Vice Pres*
EMP: 153
SALES (est): 350.8MM
SALES (corp-wide): 15.6B **Publicly Held**
SIC: 5194 5141 Tobacco & tobacco products; groceries, general line
HQ: Core-Mark International, Inc.
395 Oyster Point Blvd # 415
South San Francisco CA 94080
650 589-9445

(P-9184)
KRETEK INTERNATIONAL INC (DH)
5449 Endeavour Ct, Moorpark
(93021-1712)
PHONE..........................805 531-8888
Hugh R Cassar, *CEO*
Sean Cassar, *COO*
Donald Gormley, *CFO*
Lynn K Cassar, *Corp Secy*
Eliot Suied, *VP Sales*
▲ **EMP:** 90
SQ FT: 80,000
SALES (est): 67.5MM
SALES (corp-wide): 1.4B **Privately Held**
WEB: www.kretek.com
SIC: 5194 Cigarettes; smoking tobacco; cigars
HQ: Djarum, Pt
28 Jl. Jend. Achmad Yani
Kudus 59317
291 431-691

(P-9185)
MTC DISTRIBUTING (PA)
4900 Stoddard Rd, Modesto (95356-9389)
P.O. Box 3776 (95352-3776)
PHONE..........................209 523-6449
Todd E Manss, *Principal*
Todd Manss, *CFO*
John Subia, *Executive*
Billy Williams, *Info Tech Dir*
Robert Bettencourt, *Info Tech Mgr*
EMP: 200 **EST:** 1921
SQ FT: 100,000
SALES (est): 144.8MM **Privately Held**
SIC: 5194 5145 5149 Cigarettes; candy; groceries & related products

(P-9186)
PACIFIC GROSERVICE INC
Also Called: Pitco Foods
567 Cinnabar St, San Jose (95110-2306)
PHONE..........................408 727-4826
Pericles Navab, *Ch of Bd*
Azadeh Hariri, *Shareholder*
Frank Hariri, *Shareholder*
Esmael Maboudi, *Shareholder*
Parviz Maboudi, *Shareholder*
▲ **EMP:** 360
SQ FT: 85,000
SALES (est): 198.7MM **Privately Held**
SIC: 5194 5145 5141 5113 Tobacco & tobacco products; candy; groceries, general line; industrial & personal service paper; service establishment equipment

(P-9187)
TREPCO IMPORTS & DIST LTD
Trepco West
11860 Cmnty Rd Ste 150, Poway (92064)
PHONE..........................619 690-7999
Wiam Paulus, *Branch Mgr*
Ginger Giannetti, *Vice Pres*
Raad Audo, *Purch Mgr*
EMP: 50
SALES (corp-wide): 69.8MM **Privately Held**
SIC: 5194 5141 Tobacco & tobacco products; groceries, general line

PA: Trepco Imports & Distribution, Ltd.
1201 E Lincoln Ave
Madison Heights MI 48071
248 546-3661

5198 Paints, Varnishes & Splys Wholesale

(P-9188)
BERG LACQUER CO (PA)
Also Called: Pacific Coast Lacquer
3150 E Pico Blvd, Los Angeles
(90023-3632)
PHONE..........................323 261-8114
Sandra Berg, *President*
Robert O Berg, *Ch of Bd*
Steve Nishi, *CFO*
Donna Berg, *Treasurer*
Debbie Hoover, *Personnel Exec*
▲ **EMP:** 65 **EST:** 1934
SQ FT: 85,000
SALES (est): 59MM **Privately Held**
WEB: www.ellispaint.com
SIC: 5198 2851 Paints, varnishes & supplies; paints & paint additives

(P-9189)
SHILPARK PAINT CORPORATION (PA)
Also Called: Shilpark Paint Automotive
1640 S Vermont Ave, Los Angeles
(90006-4522)
PHONE..........................323 732-7093
Shil Kyoung Park, *CEO*
Mina Park, *Treasurer*
Eloisa Inocencio, *Admin Asst*
Corman Park, *Manager*
Robert Park, *Manager*
EMP: 69
SALES (est): 18.8MM **Privately Held**
SIC: 5198 5231 5013 Paints; paint & painting supplies; body repair or paint shop supplies, automotive

(P-9190)
TCP GLOBAL CORPORATION (PA)
Also Called: Autobody Depot
6695 Rasha St, San Diego (92121-2240)
PHONE..........................858 909-2110
Dean A Faucett, *President*
Dean Faucett, *President*
Rick Faucett, *Vice Pres*
Todd Faucett, *Vice Pres*
Matt Herring, *Store Mgr*
◆ **EMP:** 55
SQ FT: 38,000
SALES (est): 114.5MM **Privately Held**
SIC: 5198 5231 Paints; paint

5199 Nondurable Goods, NEC Wholesale

(P-9191)
ABAD FOAM INC
6560 Caballero Blvd, Buena Park
(90620-1130)
PHONE..........................714 994-2223
Abad Chavez, *President*
Cesar Chavez, *Vice Pres*
Jerry White, *Manager*
▲ **EMP:** 50
SALES (est): 17.6MM **Privately Held**
WEB: www.abadfoam.com
SIC: 5199 Foam rubber

(P-9192)
AJM PACKAGING CORPORATION
1160 Vernon Way, El Cajon (92020-1837)
PHONE..........................619 448-4007
Joe Marcelynas, *Principal*
Juan Franco, *Manager*
EMP: 97
SALES (corp-wide): 351.1MM **Privately Held**
SIC: 5199 Packaging materials
PA: A.J.M. Packaging Corporation
E-4111 Andover Rd
Bloomfield Hills MI 48302
248 901-0040

(P-9193)
ALLAQUARIA LLC
Also Called: Quality Marine
5420 W 104th St, Los Angeles
(90045-6012)
P.O. Box 2439 (90051-0439)
PHONE....................................310 645-1107
G Christopher Bverner, *Mng Member*
Maxine Sulker, *Human Res Mgr*
Mary L Buerner,
Adam Mangino, *Director*
▲ EMP: 60
SQ FT: 45,000
SALES (est): 19.4MM **Privately Held**
SIC: 5199 Tropical fish

(P-9194)
AMD TRADING COMPANY INC
1021 Stockton St, San Francisco
(94108-1109)
PHONE....................................415 391-0601
Amanda Ho, *Principal*
Belinda Locsin, *Accountant*
▲ EMP: 128 EST: 2008
SALES (est): 10.5MM **Privately Held**
SIC: 5199 Nondurable goods

(P-9195)
ARMINAK & ASSOCIATES LLC
4832 Azusa Canyon Rd A, Irwindale
(91706-1904)
P.O. Box 2245, Baldwin Park (91706-1141)
PHONE....................................626 358-4804
Thomas A Amanto, *President*
Gloria Dunlap, *Marketing Staff*
Helga Arminak, *Manager*
Kelvin Giang, *Manager*
▲ EMP: 55
SQ FT: 50,000
SALES (est): 22.7MM
SALES (corp-wide): 817.7MM **Publicly Held**
WEB: www.arminak-associates.com
SIC: 5199 Packaging materials
PA: Trimas Corporation
38505 Woodward Ave # 200
Bloomfield Hills MI 48304
248 631-5450

(P-9196)
ART SUPPLY ENTERPRISES INC (PA)
Also Called: Macpherson's
1375 Ocean Ave, Emeryville (94608-1128)
PHONE....................................510 428-9011
Frank Stapleton, *CEO*
Steve Robinson, *President*
Jim Semitekol, *COO*
Stuart Beattie, *Chairman*
George Bethurem, *Sales Staff*
◆ EMP: 215
SQ FT: 16,000
SALES (est): 150MM **Privately Held**
WEB: www.arts-and-crafts-supplies-whole-sale.a2zyp
SIC: 5199 Artists' materials

(P-9197)
BLOWER-DEMPSAY CORPORATION (PA)
Also Called: Pak West Paper & Packaging
4042 W Garry Ave, Santa Ana
(92704-6300)
PHONE....................................714 481-3800
James F Blower, *President*
Serge Poirier, *CFO*
Linda B Dempsay, *Admin Sec*
▲ EMP: 217
SQ FT: 190,000
SALES (est): 156.9MM **Privately Held**
SIC: 5199 Packaging materials

(P-9198)
BRANDERSCOM INC (PA)
2551 Casey Ave, Mountain View
(94043-1138)
PHONE....................................650 292-2752
Gerald McLaughlin, *President*
▼ EMP: 58 EST: 1999
SQ FT: 19,170
SALES (est): 74.1MM **Privately Held**
WEB: www.branders.com
SIC: 5199 Advertising specialties

(P-9199)
BRANDVIA ALLIANCE INC
2159 Bering Dr, San Jose (95131-2014)
PHONE....................................408 955-0500
James David Childers, *President*
Corrine M Caparros, *Partner*
Diane Garretson, *Partner*
Falle Hutton, *Partner*
Cindy Kahl, *Corp Secy*
▲ EMP: 100
SQ FT: 21,000
SALES (est): 53.5MM **Privately Held**
SIC: 5199 Advertising specialties

(P-9200)
BUBBLA INC
7931 Deering Ave, Canoga Park
(91304-5008)
PHONE....................................818 884-2000
Andrew Cooper, *President*
EMP: 50
SQ FT: 23,500
SALES (est): 4.9MM **Privately Held**
WEB: www.bubbla.com
SIC: 5199 Packaging materials

(P-9201)
CALICO BRANDS INC
Also Called: Scripto
2055 S Haven Ave, Ontario (91761-0736)
PHONE....................................909 930-5000
Felix M Hon, *CEO*
Laurie Hon, *Director*
▲ EMP: 50
SQ FT: 125,000
SALES (est): 13.3MM
SALES (corp-wide): 11.3MM **Privately Held**
SIC: 5199 Lighters, cigarette & cigar
PA: Tokai International Holdings, Inc.
2055 S Haven Ave
Ontario CA 91761
909 930-5000

(P-9202)
CELMOL INC
Also Called: Mark Roberts
1611 E Saint Andrew Pl, Santa Ana
(92705-4932)
PHONE....................................714 259-1000
Mark Rees, *President*
▲ EMP: 60
SQ FT: 36,000
SALES (est): 10.8MM **Privately Held**
WEB: www.xmas-magic.com
SIC: 5199 5193 Christmas novelties; gifts & novelties; flowers, fresh

(P-9203)
CENTRAL GARDEN & PET COMPANY
9235 Activity Rd, San Diego (92126-4440)
PHONE....................................858 695-0743
EMP: 59
SALES (corp-wide): 2B **Publicly Held**
WEB: www.centralgardenandpet.com
SIC: 5199 2048 Pet supplies; prepared feeds
PA: Central Garden & Pet Company
1340 Treat Blvd Ste 600
Walnut Creek CA 94597
925 948-4000

(P-9204)
CENTRAL GARDEN & PET COMPANY
13227 Orden Dr, Santa Fe Springs
(90670-6332)
PHONE....................................562 926-5252
Scott Rath, *Manager*
Joseph Lee, *Manager*
EMP: 115
SQ FT: 70,000
SALES (corp-wide): 2B **Publicly Held**
WEB: www.centralgardenandpet.com
SIC: 5199 Pet supplies
PA: Central Garden & Pet Company
1340 Treat Blvd Ste 600
Walnut Creek CA 94597
925 948-4000

(P-9205)
CENTRAL GARDEN & PET COMPANY
Also Called: Breeders Choice Pet Foods
16321 Arrow Hwy, Irwindale (91706-2018)
PHONE....................................626 334-9301
Jeff Sutherland, *President*
EMP: 80
SALES (corp-wide): 2B **Publicly Held**
SIC: 5199 Pet supplies
PA: Central Garden & Pet Company
1340 Treat Blvd Ste 600
Walnut Creek CA 94597
925 948-4000

(P-9206)
CINTAS CORPORATION NO 2
4320 E Miraloma Ave, Anaheim
(92807-1886)
PHONE....................................714 288-8400
Robert Sklar, *Branch Mgr*
EMP: 88
SALES (corp-wide): 6.4B **Publicly Held**
WEB: www.cintas-corp.com
SIC: 5199 First aid supplies
HQ: Cintas Corporation No. 2
6800 Cintas Blvd
Mason OH 45040

(P-9207)
CLASSIC SOFT TRIM INC
3201 Diablo Ave, Hayward (94545-2701)
PHONE....................................510 782-4911
Steve Robinson, *Manager*
EMP: 75 **Privately Held**
WEB: www.cstdi.com
SIC: 5199 Automobile fabrics
PA: Classic Soft Trim, Inc.
4516 Seton Center Pkwy # 135
Austin TX 78759

(P-9208)
CODE AND THEORY LLC
250 Montgomery St Ste 800, San Francisco
(94104-3423)
PHONE....................................415 839-6455
Michael Martin, *Branch Mgr*
EMP: 100
SALES (corp-wide): 52.7MM **Privately Held**
SIC: 5199 Advertising specialties
PA: Code And Theory Llc
1 World Trade Ctr
New York NY 10007
212 358-0717

(P-9209)
COSTCO WHOLESALE CORPORATION
16505 Sierra Lakes Pkwy, Fontana
(92336-1256)
PHONE....................................909 823-8270
EMP: 196
SALES (corp-wide): 116.2B **Publicly Held**
SIC: 5199
PA: Costco Wholesale Corporation
999 Lake Dr Ste 200
Issaquah WA 98027
425 313-8100

(P-9210)
DEJUNO CORPORATION
6275 Providence Way, Eastvale
(92880-9635)
PHONE....................................909 230-6744
Yuanzhe Gao, *President*
Fei Hong, *Vice Pres*
EMP: 59
SQ FT: 30,000
SALES: 2MM **Privately Held**
SIC: 5199 Leather goods, except footwear, gloves, luggage, belting

(P-9211)
DIAMOND PRODUCTS LLC (PA)
21350 Lassen St, Chatsworth
(91311-4254)
PHONE....................................818 772-0100
EMP: 150
SALES (est): 7.4MM **Privately Held**
SIC: 5199 Gifts & novelties

(P-9212)
DOLPHIN HKG LTD (PA)
Also Called: Dolphin International
1125 W Hillcrest Blvd, Inglewood
(90301-2021)
P.O. Box 91081, Los Angeles (90009-1081)
PHONE....................................310 215-3356
Steven Lundblad, *President*
Helen Lundblad, *Vice Pres*
▲ EMP: 70
SQ FT: 12,000
SALES (est): 41.3MM **Privately Held**
WEB: www.dolphin-int.com
SIC: 5199 Tropical fish

(P-9213)
ECOLOGIC BRANDS INC
550 Carnegie St, Manteca (95337-6141)
P.O. Box 4297 (95337-0005)
PHONE....................................209 239-3600
Stephen Elledge, *Manager*
EMP: 50 **Privately Held**
SIC: 5199 Packaging materials
PA: Eco.Logic Brands Inc.
550 Carnegie St
Manteca CA 95337

(P-9214)
ERLANGER DISTRIBUTION CTR INC
Also Called: Erlanger Sales
797 Palmyrita Ave, Riverside (92507-1811)
PHONE....................................951 784-5147
David Erlanger, *CEO*
Claude M Erlanger, *President*
Doris Erlanger, *Vice Pres*
Steve Erlanger, *Vice Pres*
Larry McFarland, *General Mgr*
▲ EMP: 50 EST: 1946
SQ FT: 160,000
SALES (est): 8.2MM **Privately Held**
WEB: www.erlangerdc.com
SIC: 5199 5192 5099 5137 Leather goods, except footwear, gloves, luggage, belting; books; luggage; handbags

(P-9215)
ERNEST PACKAGING (PA)
Also Called: Ernest Paper
5777 Smithway St, Commerce
(90040-1507)
PHONE....................................800 233-7788
Charles Wilson, *Ch of Bd*
Timothy Wilson, *President*
Rick Browne, *Director*
▲ EMP: 130
SQ FT: 300,000
SALES (est): 240.9MM **Privately Held**
WEB: www.ipdpkg.com
SIC: 5199 7389 5113 Packaging materials; cosmetic kits, assembling & packaging; shipping supplies

(P-9216)
FIGI ACQUISITION COMPANY LLC
3636 Gateway Center Ave, San Diego
(92102-4524)
PHONE....................................800 678-3444
Woody Laforge,
EMP: 200
SQ FT: 216,000
SALES (est): 10.2MM **Privately Held**
SIC: 5199 Gifts & novelties

(P-9217)
FOAM DISTRIBUTORS INCORPORATED
Also Called: Foam Fabrication For Packaging
31009 San Antonio St, Hayward
(94544-7903)
PHONE....................................510 441-8377
Stephanie Wright, *Chairman*
Steve M Doyle, *CEO*
James Doyle, *General Mgr*
David Brown, *CTO*
Fred Wilson, *Marketing Staff*
EMP: 75
SQ FT: 72,000
SALES: 11.6MM **Privately Held**
WEB: www.foamdist.com
SIC: 5199 Packaging materials

PRODUCTS & SVCS

(P-9218)
FREE STREAM MEDIA CORP (PA)
Also Called: Samba TV
123 Townsend St 5, San Francisco (94107-1907)
PHONE..................................415 889-6404
Ashwin Navin, CEO
Dan Ackerman, Officer
Cody Gossett, Vice Pres
Chris Jantz-Sell, Vice Pres
Jay Wolff, Vice Pres
EMP: 80
SQ FT: 11,000
SALES (est): 51.2MM Privately Held
SIC: 5199 Advertising specialties

(P-9219)
GAJU MARKET CORPORATION
450 S Western Ave, Los Angeles (90020-4120)
PHONE..................................213 382-9444
David Rhee, CEO
Charlene Lee, Office Mgr
EMP: 135
SQ FT: 2,000
SALES: 2MM Privately Held
SIC: 5199 General merchandise, non-durable

(P-9220)
GEORGE P JOHNSON COMPANY
999 Skyway Rd Ste 300, San Carlos (94070-2722)
PHONE..................................650 226-0600
Chris Meyer, CEO
Melissa Stevenson, Program Mgr
Mike Arvizu, Foreman/Supr
Elliott Horwitz, Cust Mgr
Jennifer Kasick, Director
EMP: 120
SALES (corp-wide): 273.9MM Privately Held
SIC: 5199 8742 Advertising specialties; marketing consulting services
HQ: George P Johnson Company
3600 Giddings Rd
Auburn Hills MI 48326
248 475-2500

(P-9221)
GRAHAM PACKAGING COMPANY LP
4500 Finch Rd, Modesto (95357-4145)
PHONE..................................209 572-5187
Tom Sponder, Branch Mgr
EMP: 168 Privately Held
SIC: 5199 Packaging materials
HQ: Graham Packaging Company, L.P.
700 Indian Springs Dr # 100
Lancaster PA 17601
717 849-8500

(P-9222)
GRHT INC
Also Called: Foam Co, The
14818 Raymer St, Van Nuys (91405-1219)
PHONE..................................323 873-6393
Gil Rosky, President
Hossein Tehrani, Vice Pres
EMP: 60
SQ FT: 11,000
SALES (est): 11.5MM Privately Held
SIC: 5199 Foam rubber

(P-9223)
HAY KUHN INC
1880 Jeffrey Rd, El Centro (92243-9532)
P.O. Box 338 (92244-0338)
PHONE..................................760 353-0124
Felipe Irigoyen, President
Jim Ohland, General Mgr
Terry Allegranza, Controller
Janet Franklin, Clerk
◆ EMP: 50
SQ FT: 1,500
SALES (est): 12.8MM Privately Held
SIC: 5199 4789 Packaging materials; car loading

(P-9224)
IMPORT COLLECTION (PA)
Also Called: Tic
7885 Nelson Rd, Panorama City (91402-6829)
PHONE..................................818 782-3060
David Mehdyzadeh, CEO
Sina Mehdyzadeh, Corp Secy
Sammy Mehdizadeh, Vice Pres
◆ EMP: 65
SQ FT: 160,000
SALES (est): 33.1MM Privately Held
WEB: www.importcollection.com
SIC: 5199 5023 Gifts & novelties; decorative home furnishings & supplies

(P-9225)
INTERNTIONAL PET SUPS DIST INC
10850 Via Frontera, San Diego (92127-1705)
PHONE..................................858 453-7845
James Myers, CEO
◆ EMP: 100
SQ FT: 70,000
SALES (est): 24.6MM
SALES (corp-wide): 264.1K Privately Held
WEB: www.petco.com
SIC: 5199 Pet supplies
HQ: Petco Animal Supplies, Inc.
10850 Via Frontera
San Diego CA 92127
858 453-7845

(P-9226)
KATZKIN LEATHER INC (PA)
6868 W Acco St, Montebello (90640-5441)
PHONE..................................323 725-1243
Brook Mayberry, President
Jim Roberson, President
▲ EMP: 200
SQ FT: 50,000
SALES (est): 91MM Privately Held
WEB: www.katzkin.com
SIC: 5199 2531 Leather & cut stock; seats, automobile

(P-9227)
KOHLS CORPORATION
890 E Mill St, San Bernardino (92408-1614)
PHONE..................................909 382-4300
EMP: 2785 Publicly Held
SIC: 5199 Advertising specialties
PA: Kohl's Corporation
N56w17000 Ridgewood Dr
Menomonee Falls WI 53051
-

(P-9228)
KOLE IMPORTS
Also Called: Basket Basics
24600 Main St, Carson (90745-6332)
PHONE..................................310 834-0004
Robert Kole, CEO
Jason Kole, President
Fernando Garcia, Exec VP
Alma A Corral, Vice Pres
Dan Kole, Vice Pres
◆ EMP: 84
SQ FT: 150,000
SALES (est): 37.5MM Privately Held
WEB: www.koleimports.com
SIC: 5199 Gifts & novelties; general merchandise, non-durable

(P-9229)
LANE WINPAK INC (HQ)
998 S Sierra Way, San Bernardino (92408-2122)
PHONE..................................909 386-1762
Bruce J Berry, CEO
Ted Torrens, President
M G Johnston, CFO
Olivier Muggli, Vice Pres
Kathy Boynton, Admin Sec
▲ EMP: 52
SQ FT: 45,000
SALES (est): 29.6MM
SALES (corp-wide): 886.7MM Privately Held
WEB: www.wipak.com
SIC: 5199 Packaging materials

PA: Winpak Ltd
100 Saulteaux Cres
Winnipeg MB R3J 3
204 889-1015

(P-9230)
LEE-MAR AQUARIUM & PET SUPS
Also Called: Lee Mar Aquarium & Pet Sups
2459 Dogwood Way, Vista (92081-8421)
PHONE..................................760 727-1300
Terran R Boyd, President
Michael Bruce, Buyer
Jeff Boyd, VP Sales
▲ EMP: 100
SQ FT: 67,000
SALES (est): 25.7MM Privately Held
WEB: www.leemarpet.com
SIC: 5199 3999 Pet supplies; pet supplies

(P-9231)
LIFESTREET CORPORATION
Also Called: Lifestreet Media
981 Industrial Rd Ste F, San Carlos (94070-4150)
PHONE..................................650 508-2220
Mitchell Wiesman, CEO
Patrick McNenny, CFO
EMP: 75 EST: 2008
SALES (est): 17.4MM Privately Held
SIC: 5199 Advertising specialties

(P-9232)
LIVE NATION MERCHANDISE INC (HQ)
Also Called: Signatures Sni
450 Mission St Ste 300, San Francisco (94105-2518)
PHONE..................................415 247-7400
Dell Furano, CEO
Ron Bension, President
Michael Rapino, President
John Reid, President
Arthur Fogel, Chairman
▲ EMP: 50
SQ FT: 27,000
SALES (est): 89.7MM
SALES (corp-wide): 10.3B Publicly Held
WEB: www.signaturesnet.com
SIC: 5199 Advertising specialties
PA: Live Nation Entertainment, Inc.
9348 Civic Center Dr Lbby
Beverly Hills CA 90210
310 867-7000

(P-9233)
LOGOMARK INC
1201 Bell Ave, Tustin (92780-6420)
PHONE..................................714 675-6100
Trevor Gnesin, President
◆ EMP: 250
SQ FT: 200,000
SALES (est): 148.2MM Privately Held
WEB: www.logomark.com
SIC: 5199 Advertising specialties

(P-9234)
MAX LEATHER
8533 Washington Blvd, Culver City (90232-7462)
PHONE..................................310 841-6990
Max Khansefid, President
EMP: 50
SALES (est): 6.6MM Privately Held
WEB: www.maxleatherinc.com
SIC: 5199 Leather & cut stock; leather, leather goods & furs

(P-9235)
MICHAELS STORES INC
Also Called: Warehouse
3501 W Avenue H, Lancaster (93536-8341)
PHONE..................................661 951-3500
John Vilotta, General Mgr
EMP: 200
SALES (corp-wide): 5.3B Publicly Held
WEB: www.michaels.com
SIC: 5199 4225 5945 Art goods; general warehousing & storage; hobby, toy & game shops
HQ: Michaels Stores, Inc.
8000 Bent Branch Dr
Irving TX 75063
972 409-1300

(P-9236)
MIDWAY INTERNATIONAL INC
13131 166th St, Cerritos (90703-2202)
PHONE..................................562 921-2255
Ha Suk Chung, President
◆ EMP: 50
SQ FT: 32,700
SALES (est): 16.6MM Privately Held
SIC: 5199 Wigs

(P-9237)
MISSION PETS INC
986 Mission St Fl 5, San Francisco (94103-2970)
PHONE..................................415 904-9914
Carmine Petruzello, CEO
Jannita Hanson, CFO
Dan Brown, Vice Pres
Michelle Elliot, Vice Pres
Melissa Pera, Vice Pres
▲ EMP: 50
SQ FT: 10,000
SALES (est): 10.2MM Privately Held
SIC: 5199 Pet supplies

(P-9238)
NW PACKAGING LLC (PA)
1201 E Lexington Ave, Pomona (91766-5520)
PHONE..................................909 706-3627
Robert E Sliter, Administration
EMP: 100
SALES (est): 45.3MM Privately Held
SIC: 5199 Packaging materials

(P-9239)
OXGORD INCORPORATED
16325 S Avalon Blvd, Gardena (90248-2909)
PHONE..................................800 221-0718
Akiva Nourollah, President
▲ EMP: 150 EST: 2012
SALES (est): 3.2MM Privately Held
SIC: 5199 General merchandise, non-durable

(P-9240)
P2F HOLDINGS
Also Called: Mulen
1760 Apollo Ct, Seal Beach (90740-5617)
PHONE..................................562 296-1055
Sandra Piontak, President
Leonard Piontak, CEO
Jim Kleban, CFO
Michael Freede, Chairman
Adam Freede, Exec VP
▲ EMP: 75
SQ FT: 64,000
SALES (est): 2.4MM Privately Held
WEB: www.p2fholdings.com
SIC: 5199

(P-9241)
PACIFIC EASTERN INTL PDTS
Also Called: Pacific Eastern Intl Pdts I
12551 Barrett Ln, Santa Ana (92705-1306)
PHONE..................................714 538-3434
Thomas Osbourne, President
Teri Osbourne, Admin Sec
EMP: 90
SALES (est): 4.2MM Privately Held
SIC: 5199 General merchandise, non-durable

(P-9242)
PACIFIC METRO LLC (PA)
Also Called: Thomas Kinkade Company, The
18715 Madrone Pkwy, Morgan Hill (95037-2876)
PHONE..................................408 201-5000
Eric H Halvorson, President
Steve Paszkiewicz, President
Herbert D Montgomery, CFO
Anthony D Thomopoulos, Chairman
Daniel Byrne, Exec VP
▲ EMP: 350
SQ FT: 400,000
SALES (est): 80MM Privately Held
SIC: 5199 Art goods

(P-9243)
PACIFIC ROYAL GROUP
5500 Stewart Ave Ste 113, Fremont (94538-3100)
P.O. Box 3457 (94539-0381)
PHONE..................................510 200-2993

Ronald Ng, *Director*
Kamme Lai, *Vice Pres*
EMP: 120 **EST:** 2013
SQ FT: 1,700
SALES: 5.6MM **Privately Held**
SIC: 5199 Variety store merchandise

(P-9244)
PACIFIC WESTERN SALES (PA)
Also Called: Pbfy Flexible Packaging
2980 Enterprise St Ste A, Brea
(92821-6283)
PHONE....................714 572-6730
Lyndsey William Tidwell, *President*
Jimmy Hou, *President*
Lorraine Clements, *Treasurer*
Jay Johnson, *Vice Pres*
Andrea Pennington, *Vice Pres*
◆ **EMP:** 51
SQ FT: 49,000
SALES: 16MM **Privately Held**
WEB: www.pacificwesternsales.com
SIC: 5199 7336 Packaging materials;
package design

(P-9245)
PACKAGING MANUFACTURING INC
6425 Randolph St, Commerce
(90040-3511)
PHONE....................619 498-9199
Salvatore Anza, *CEO*
Roger Fabricante, *Administration*
EMP: 250 **EST:** 2009
SALES (est): 28MM **Privately Held**
SIC: 5199 Packaging materials

(P-9246)
PACTIV LLC
5370 E Home Ave, Fresno (93727-2104)
PHONE....................559 251-7351
Chris Verard, *General Mgr*
Jim Kisling, *Buyer*
Ricky Bland, *Manager*
EMP: 110
SQ FT: 5,000 **Privately Held**
WEB: www.pactiv.com
SIC: 5199 Packaging materials
HQ: Pactiv Llc
   1900 W Field Ct
   Lake Forest IL 60045
   847 482-2000

(P-9247)
PACTIV LLC
1 Diamond Ave, Red Bluff (96080)
PHONE....................530 529-3340
William Haser, *Branch Mgr*
VI Lindsey, *President*
Jason Nguyen, *Engineer*
V Lindsey, *Human Resources*
Marvin Bagwell, *Manager*
EMP: 100 **Privately Held**
WEB: www.pactiv.com
SIC: 5199 Packaging materials
HQ: Pactiv Llc
   1900 W Field Ct
   Lake Forest IL 60045
   847 482-2000

(P-9248)
PD LIQUIDATION INC
Also Called: Pipe Dream Products
21350 Lassen St, Chatsworth
(91311-4254)
PHONE....................818 772-0100
David Feldman, *CEO*
Robert Feldman, *President*
Brian Flowers, *CFO*
Nicole Braniff, *Executive Asst*
Ana Ortiz, *Admin Asst*
◆ **EMP:** 150
SALES (est): 51MM
SALES (corp-wide): 7.4MM **Privately Held**
WEB: www.pipedreamproducts.com
SIC: 5199 Gifts & novelties
PA: Diamond Products, Llc
   21350 Lassen St
   Chatsworth CA 91311
   818 772-0100

(P-9249)
PHD MARKETING INC
1373 Ridgeway St, Pomona (91768-2701)
PHONE....................909 620-1000

Thaer Ahmad, *President*
John Kamar, *Treasurer*
▲ **EMP:** 60
SQ FT: 20,000
SALES (est): 8.6MM **Privately Held**
SIC: 5199 5399 General merchandise,
non-durable; Army-Navy goods

(P-9250)
POLYVORE INC
701 First Ave, Sunnyvale (94089-1019)
PHONE....................650 968-1195
Jessica Lee, *CEO*
Pasha Sadri, *CTO*
Chihyu Chang, *Software Engr*
Alan Austin, *Engineer*
Chase Chou, *Engineer*
EMP: 60
SALES (est): 9.6MM **Privately Held**
SIC: 5199 Advertising specialties
HQ: Groupe Atallah Inc
   333 Rue Chabanel O Bureau 900
   Montreal QC H2N 2
   514 384-1906

(P-9251)
PREGIS LLC
33340 Central Ave, Union City
(94587-2044)
PHONE....................510 404-1360
Steve Nau, *Manager*
EMP: 65
SALES (corp-wide): 4.7B **Privately Held**
SIC: 5199 Packaging materials
HQ: Pregis Llc
   1650 Lake Cook Rd Ste 400
   Deerfield IL 60015
   847 597-2200

(P-9252)
PRO SPECIALTIES GROUP INC
4863 Shawline St Ste D, San Diego
(92111-1435)
PHONE....................858 541-1100
Cheng Shun LI, *President*
Michael Soberanis, *Executive*
I Chin LI, *Admin Sec*
Jennie Ryan, *Graphic Designe*
Viki Lozano, *Sales Staff*
▲ **EMP:** 70
SQ FT: 23,000
SALES: 35MM **Privately Held**
WEB: www.psginc.com
SIC: 5199 Advertising specialties

(P-9253)
QUAKER PET GROUP INC
160 Mitchell Blvd, San Rafael
(94903-2044)
PHONE....................415 721-7400
Kevin Fick, *CEO*
Mike Trott, *CFO*
▲ **EMP:** 100
SQ FT: 11,000
SALES: 67MM **Privately Held**
SIC: 5199 Pet supplies
HQ: Worldwise, Inc.
   6 Hamilton Landing # 150
   Novato CA 94949

(P-9254)
QUETICO LLC (PA)
5521 Schaefer Ave, Chino (91710-9070)
PHONE....................909 628-6200
Thomas Fenchel, *Mng Member*
Antonio Lopez, *Branch Mgr*
Maria Cantero, *Admin Asst*
Ivan Spiers, *Human Res Mgr*
Janet Guerrero, *Personnel Assit*
◆ **EMP:** 53
SQ FT: 278,500
SALES (est): 458.3MM **Privately Held**
WEB: www.quetico.net
SIC: 5199 7389 General merchandise,
non-durable; packaging & labeling serv-
ices

(P-9255)
R M B PACKAGING CO INC
9667 Canoga Ave, Chatsworth
(91311-4115)
PHONE....................818 998-0658
Paul Thomas, *CEO*
EMP: 50

SALES (est): 6MM **Privately Held**
SIC: 5199 Packaging materials

(P-9256)
REDBARN PET PRODUCTS INC (PA)
Also Called: Redbarn Premium Pet Products
3229 E Spring St Ste 310, Long Beach
(90806-2478)
PHONE....................562 495-7315
Jeff Baikie, *CEO*
Howard Bloxam, *President*
Joe Martinez, *Principal*
Brad Bailey, *Manager*
▼ **EMP:** 123
SQ FT: 50,000
SALES (est): 122MM **Privately Held**
WEB: www.redbarninc.com
SIC: 5199 2047 Pet supplies; dog & cat
food

(P-9257)
ROCKY PACKAGING SOLUTION INC (PA)
13980 Mountain Ave, Chino (91710-9018)
PHONE....................909 591-3331
Fangguo Liu, *CEO*
▲ **EMP:** 50
SQ FT: 100,000
SALES (est): 12.1MM **Privately Held**
SIC: 5199 Packaging materials

(P-9258)
SHIMS BARGAIN INC (PA)
Also Called: J C Sales
2600 S Soto St, Vernon (90058-8015)
PHONE....................323 881-0099
K Kenneth Suh, *President*
BJ Chang, *CFO*
James Shim, *Chairman*
Sena OH, *Bookkeeper*
◆ **EMP:** 100
SQ FT: 420,000
SALES: 177.5MM **Privately Held**
SIC: 5199 General merchandise, non-
durable

(P-9259)
SMART LIVING COMPANY (PA)
Also Called: S M C
4100 Guardian St, Simi Valley
(93063-6717)
PHONE....................805 578-5500
Mark Schelbert, *CEO*
Scott Palladino, *CFO*
Ron Hein, *Exec Dir*
Jeana Berry, *Finance*
Kevin Kiely, *Controller*
▲ **EMP:** 50
SALES (est): 100.8MM **Privately Held**
WEB: www.onlinesmc.com
SIC: 5199 Gifts & novelties

(P-9260)
SMITH PACKING INC
680 S Simas Rd, Santa Maria
(93455-9700)
P.O. Box 1338 (93456-1338)
PHONE....................805 343-0329
Alvaro Quesada, *Principal*
EMP: 130
SALES (corp-wide): 1.1MM **Privately Held**
SIC: 5199 Packaging materials
PA: Smith Packing, Inc.
   111 W Chapel St
   Santa Maria CA 93458
   805 348-1818

(P-9261)
SONORA TRADE COMPANY INC
2127 Olympic Pkwy, Chula Vista
(91915-1359)
PHONE....................619 878-5848
Hanna Shayota, *CEO*
▲ **EMP:** 55
SALES (est): 8.6MM **Privately Held**
SIC: 5199 Art goods & supplies

(P-9262)
TARGUS INTERNATIONAL LLC (PA)
1211 N Miller St, Anaheim (92806-1933)
PHONE....................714 765-5555
Mikel Williams, *CEO*

Bill Oppenlander, *President*
Victor C Streufert, *CFO*
Robert Shortt, *Senior VP*
Allen H Gharapetian, *Vice Pres*
◆ **EMP:** 175
SQ FT: 200,656
SALES (est): 236.2MM **Privately Held**
WEB: www.targus.com
SIC: 5199 Bags, baskets & cases

(P-9263)
TECH PACKAGING INC
9545 Santa Anita Ave A, Rancho Cuca-
monga (91730-6110)
PHONE....................909 243-7047
Steve Andrews, *Manager*
EMP: 80
SALES (corp-wide): 22.1MM **Privately Held**
SIC: 5199 Packaging materials
PA: Tech Packaging, Inc.
   13241 Bartram Park Blvd # 101
   Jacksonville FL 32258
   904 288-6403

(P-9264)
ULINE INC
2950 Jurupa St, Ontario (91761-2936)
PHONE....................909 605-7090
Toll Free:....................877 -
Israel Baluja, *Site Mgr*
EMP: 57
SALES (corp-wide): 3.7B **Privately Held**
WEB: www.uline.com
SIC: 5199 Packaging materials
PA: Uline, Inc.
   12575 Uline Dr
   Pleasant Prairie WI 53158
   262 612-4200

(P-9265)
US FOODS INC
1201 Park Center Dr, Vista (92081-8313)
PHONE....................760 599-6200
Gary Graig, *Branch Mgr*
EMP: 375 **Publicly Held**
WEB: www.usfoodservice.com
SIC: 5199 5147 5144 5142 General mer-
chandise, non-durable; meats & meat
products; poultry & poultry products;
packaged frozen goods; groceries, gen-
eral line
HQ: Us Foods, Inc.
   9399 W Higgins Rd Ste 500
   Rosemont IL 60018

(P-9266)
VEGETABLE GROWERS SUPPLY CO (PA)
Also Called: V G S
1360 Merrill St, Salinas (93901-4432)
P.O. Box 757 (93902-0757)
PHONE....................831 759-4600
Ron Huff, *CEO*
William J Locke III, *President*
Lisa Erling, *CFO*
Susan Gong, *Administration*
Nancy Bauer, *Credit Mgr*
▲ **EMP:** 50
SQ FT: 38,000
SALES (est): 83.1MM **Privately Held**
WEB: www.veggrow.com
SIC: 5199 2449 Packaging materials; rec-
tangular boxes & crates, wood

(P-9267)
VIA TRADING CORPORATION
2520 Industry Way, Lynwood (90262-4015)
PHONE....................877 202-3616
Jacques Stambouli, *CEO*
Alain Stambouli, *President*
Alex Antypas, *COO*
Jose Ramon, *Admin Asst*
Sonia Villagomez, *Administration*
◆ **EMP:** 57
SQ FT: 240,000
SALES: 39.3MM **Privately Held**
WEB: www.viatrading.com
SIC: 5199 General merchandise, non-
durable

(P-9268)
VICTORY FOAM INC (PA)
3 Holland, Irvine (92618-2506)
PHONE....................949 474-0690

PRODUCTS & SVCS

Frank M Comerford, *CEO*
Helen Comerford, *Corp Secy*
Myles Comerford, *Vice Pres*
Shea Oddo, *Technology*
Alejandro Alarcon, *Engineer*
▲ **EMP:** 95
SQ FT: 53,000
SALES (est): 43.7MM **Privately Held**
WEB: www.victoryfoam.com
SIC: 5199 Packaging materials

(P-9269)
VIPSTORE USA CO
13674 Star Ruby Ave, Corona
(92880-5557)
PHONE....................626 934-7880
Hongjie Yang, *President*
EMP: 400
SALES: 12MM **Privately Held**
SIC: 5199 General merchandise, non-durable

(P-9270)
WARREN AUTO DE MEXICO LLC
517 S Cedros Ave, Solana Beach
(92075-1922)
PHONE....................858 794-7947
EMP: 100
SALES (est): 1.3MM **Privately Held**
SIC: 5199

(P-9271)
WEBB SUNRISE INC
3320 Kemper St Ste 201, San Diego
(92110-4905)
PHONE....................619 220-7050
Lawrence R Webb Sr, *President*
Joji Mangubat, *Vice Pres*
Donna Webb, *Vice Pres*
EMP: 50
SQ FT: 10,000
SALES (est): 4.6MM **Privately Held**
SIC: 5199 Advertising specialties

(P-9272)
WONDERTREATS INC
2200 Lapham Dr, Modesto (95354-3911)
PHONE....................209 521-8881
Jocelyn Yu Hall, *CEO*
Greg Hall, *President*
Aileen Ong, *Admin Asst*
Steve Klapak, *Sales Executive*
Don Greenland, *Sales Mgr*
▲ **EMP:** 315
SQ FT: 230,000
SALES (est): 135.8MM **Privately Held**
SIC: 5199 5947 Gift baskets; gift baskets

6011 Federal Reserve Banks

(P-9273)
FEDERAL RSRVE BNK SAN FRNCISCO (HQ)
101 Market St, San Francisco
(94105-1530)
P.O. Box 7702 (94120-7702)
PHONE....................415 974-2000
John C Williams, *President*
Alexander R Mehran, *Ch of Bd*
Patricia E Yarrington, *Ch of Bd*
John F Moore, *COO*
Barry M Meyer, *Chairman*
◆ **EMP:** 1397
SQ FT: 471,543
SALES (est): 4.2MM **Privately Held**
SIC: 6011 Federal reserve banks
PA: Board Of Governors Of The Federal
　　Reserve System
　　20th St Cnsttution Ave Nw
　　Washington DC 20551
　　202 452-3000

(P-9274)
FEDERAL RSRVE BNK SAN FRNCISCO
Also Called: Los Angeles Branch
950 S Grand Ave, Los Angeles
(90015-4202)
P.O. Box 512077 (90051-0077)
PHONE....................213 683-2300
Mark Mullinix, *Manager*
Tony Gin, *Admin Asst*
David Erickson, *Research*
Andres Curtolo, *Senior Mgr*

Anthony Dazzo, *Director*
EMP: 640 **Privately Held**
SIC: 6011 Federal reserve branches
HQ: Federal Reserve Bank Of San Francisco
　　101 Market St
　　San Francisco CA 94105
　　415 974-2000

6021 National Commercial Banks

(P-9275)
AMERICAN PLUS BANK (PA)
630 W Duarte Rd, Arcadia (91007-9205)
PHONE....................626 821-9188
Julian Liu, *Ch Credit Ofcr*
Eric Feder, *Officer*
Sandy Hwang, *General Mgr*
EMP: 50
SALES: 22.5MM **Privately Held**
SIC: 6021 National commercial banks

(P-9276)
BANA HOME LOAN SERVICING
31303 Agoura Rd, Westlake Village
(91361-4635)
PHONE....................213 345-7975
Rachel Fiorillo, *Senior VP*
EMP: 900
SALES (est): 301.6K **Privately Held**
SIC: 6021 National commercial banks

(P-9277)
BANC CALIFORNIA NATIONAL ASSN (HQ)
3 Macarthur Pl, Santa Ana (92707-6067)
PHONE....................877 770-2262
Robert Franko, *President*
George Diaz, *President*
Tigran Karavardanyan, *President*
Jason Marcos, *President*
Sharon Murray, *President*
EMP: 89
SALES: 416.1MM
SALES (corp-wide): 433.8MM **Publicly Held**
SIC: 6021 National commercial banks
PA: Banc Of California, Inc.
　　3 Macarthur Pl Ste 100
　　Santa Ana CA 92707
　　855 361-2262

(P-9278)
BANC CALIFORNIA NATIONAL ASSN
10100 Santa Monica Blvd, Los Angeles
(90067-4003)
PHONE....................310 286-0710
Richard Smith, *President*
George Sacco, *Vice Pres*
EMP: 50
SALES (corp-wide): 433.8MM **Publicly Held**
SIC: 6021 National commercial banks
HQ: Banc Of California, National Association
　　3 Macarthur Pl
　　Santa Ana CA 92707
　　877 770-2262

(P-9279)
BANC OF CALIFORNIA INC (PA)
3 Macarthur Pl Ste 100, Santa Ana
(92707-6068)
P.O. Box 61452, Irvine (92602-6048)
PHONE....................855 361-2262
Robert D Sznewajs, *Ch of Bd*
Douglas H Bowers, *President*
Karen Koepsell, *President*
Jennifer McGaw, *President*
Erin Stuart, *President*
EMP: 120
SALES: 433.8MM **Publicly Held**
SIC: 6021 National commercial banks

(P-9280)
BANK AMERICA NATIONAL ASSN
5292 N Palm Ave, Fresno (93704-2209)
PHONE....................559 445-7731
Kim Garcia, *Manager*
EMP: 80

SALES (corp-wide): 100.2B **Publicly Held**
WEB: www.bofa.com
SIC: 6021 National commercial banks
HQ: Bank Of America, National Association
　　100 S Tryon St
　　Charlotte NC 28202
　　704 386-5681

(P-9281)
BANK AMERICA NATIONAL ASSN
1525 Market St, San Francisco
(94103-1289)
PHONE....................800 432-1000
John Watson, *Branch Mgr*
Duane Miller, *Senior VP*
EMP: 50
SALES (corp-wide): 100.2B **Publicly Held**
WEB: www.bofa.com
SIC: 6021 National commercial banks
HQ: Bank Of America, National Association
　　100 S Tryon St
　　Charlotte NC 28202
　　704 386-5681

(P-9282)
BANK AMERICA NATIONAL ASSN
345 Montgomery St, San Francisco
(94104-1898)
P.O. Box 37000 (94137-0001)
PHONE....................415 913-5891
Thomas Sidon, *Sales/Mktg Mgr*
H Anton Tucher, *Managing Dir*
EMP: 120
SALES (corp-wide): 100.2B **Publicly Held**
WEB: www.bofa.com
SIC: 6021 National commercial banks
HQ: Bank Of America, National Association
　　100 S Tryon St
　　Charlotte NC 28202
　　704 386-5681

(P-9283)
BANK AMERICA NATIONAL ASSN
400 Broadway St, Chico (95928-5323)
P.O. Box 1289 (95927-1289)
PHONE....................530 891-7019
Mark Francis, *Manager*
EMP: 60
SQ FT: 15,763
SALES (corp-wide): 100.2B **Publicly Held**
WEB: www.bofa.com
SIC: 6021 National commercial banks
HQ: Bank Of America, National Association
　　100 S Tryon St
　　Charlotte NC 28202
　　704 386-5681

(P-9284)
BANK AMERICA NATIONAL ASSN
345 N Brand Blvd, Glendale (91203-2368)
PHONE....................800 432-1000
Don Nodell, *Manager*
EMP: 60
SALES (corp-wide): 100.2B **Publicly Held**
WEB: www.bofa.com
SIC: 6021 National commercial banks
HQ: Bank Of America, National Association
　　100 S Tryon St
　　Charlotte NC 28202
　　704 386-5681

(P-9285)
BANK AMERICA NATIONAL ASSN
6351 E Spring St, Long Beach
(90808-4021)
P.O. Box 409 (90801-0409)
PHONE....................562 624-4330
Jennifer Davis, *Branch Mgr*
EMP: 50
SALES (corp-wide): 100.2B **Publicly Held**
WEB: www.bofa.com
SIC: 6021 National commercial banks

HQ: Bank Of America, National Association
　　100 S Tryon St
　　Charlotte NC 28202
　　704 386-5681

(P-9286)
BANK AMERICA NATIONAL ASSN
120 S Brand Blvd, San Fernando
(91340-3377)
PHONE....................818 898-3033
Janice Musgrove, *Branch Mgr*
EMP: 60
SALES (corp-wide): 100.2B **Publicly Held**
WEB: www.bofa.com
SIC: 6021 National commercial banks
HQ: Bank Of America, National Association
　　100 S Tryon St
　　Charlotte NC 28202
　　704 386-5681

(P-9287)
BANK AMERICA NATIONAL ASSN
212 E Main St, Visalia (93291-6356)
P.O. Box 551 (93279-0551)
PHONE....................800 432-1000
Gordon Young, *President*
Wesley Imoto, *Vice Pres*
Bobbie Roth, *Customer Svc Re*
EMP: 50
SALES (corp-wide): 100.2B **Publicly Held**
WEB: www.bofa.com
SIC: 6021 National commercial banks
HQ: Bank Of America, National Association
　　100 S Tryon St
　　Charlotte NC 28202
　　704 386-5681

(P-9288)
BANK AMERICA NATIONAL ASSN
550 S Hill St Ste 101, Los Angeles
(90013-2403)
PHONE....................310 384-4562
Stacy Young, *Manager*
Manohara Maddineni, *Vice Pres*
EMP: 65
SALES (corp-wide): 100.2B **Publicly Held**
WEB: www.bofa.com
SIC: 6021 National commercial banks
HQ: Bank Of America, National Association
　　100 S Tryon St
　　Charlotte NC 28202
　　704 386-5681

(P-9289)
BANK AMERICA NATIONAL ASSN
13220 Harbor Blvd, Garden Grove
(92843-1737)
P.O. Box 758 (92842-0758)
PHONE....................714 973-8495
Rita Castro, *Branch Mgr*
Linda Ropp, *Cust Mgr*
Martha Albert, *Manager*
EMP: 50
SALES (corp-wide): 100.2B **Publicly Held**
WEB: www.bofa.com
SIC: 6021 National commercial banks
HQ: Bank Of America, National Association
　　100 S Tryon St
　　Charlotte NC 28202
　　704 386-5681

(P-9290)
BANK AMERICA NATIONAL ASSN
1687 E Florida Ave, Hemet (92544-8646)
P.O. Box 1406 (92546-1406)
PHONE....................951 929-8614
John Borah, *Branch Mgr*
EMP: 50
SALES (corp-wide): 100.2B **Publicly Held**
WEB: www.bofa.com
SIC: 6021 National commercial banks
HQ: Bank Of America, National Association
　　100 S Tryon St
　　Charlotte NC 28202
　　704 386-5681

▲ = Import ▼=Export
◆ =Import/Export

(P-9291)
BANK AMERICA NATIONAL ASSN
1450 W Redondo Beach Blvd, Gardena (90247-3399)
PHONE.........................800 432-1000
Rosa Caldera, *Branch Mgr*
EMP: 75
SALES (corp-wide): 100.2B **Publicly Held**
WEB: www.bofa.com
SIC: **6021** National commercial banks
HQ: Bank Of America, National Association
100 S Tryon St
Charlotte NC 28202
704 386-5681

(P-9292)
BANK AMERICA NATIONAL ASSN
5901 Canoga Ave, Woodland Hills (91367-5010)
PHONE.........................818 577-2000
Albert Welch, *Sales/Mktg Mgr*
Eric Chen, *Vice Pres*
EMP: 60
SALES (corp-wide): 100.2B **Publicly Held**
WEB: www.bofa.com
SIC: **6021** National commercial banks
HQ: Bank Of America, National Association
100 S Tryon St
Charlotte NC 28202
704 386-5681

(P-9293)
BANK AMERICA NATIONAL ASSN
4100 Chino Hills Pkwy, Chino Hills (91709-2611)
P.O. Box 727, Chino (91708-0727)
PHONE.........................909 393-3002
Kathleen Mossbarger, *Branch Mgr*
EMP: 99
SALES (corp-wide): 100.2B **Publicly Held**
WEB: www.bofa.com
SIC: **6021** National commercial banks
HQ: Bank Of America, National Association
100 S Tryon St
Charlotte NC 28202
704 386-5681

(P-9294)
BANK AMERICA NATIONAL ASSN
27489 Ynez Rd, Temecula (92591-4612)
PHONE.........................951 676-4114
Theresa Fukuda, *Branch Mgr*
EMP: 53
SALES (corp-wide): 100.2B **Publicly Held**
WEB: www.bofa.com
SIC: **6021** National commercial banks
HQ: Bank Of America, National Association
100 S Tryon St
Charlotte NC 28202
704 386-5681

(P-9295)
BANK LEUMI USA
Also Called: Bank Leumi Le
555 W 5th St Fl 33, Los Angeles (90013-1050)
PHONE.........................323 966-4700
Toll Free:.........................877 -
Abraham Maoz, *Exec VP*
Yoav Bentov,
Berta Epelbaum, *Manager*
Chagit Raskin, *Assistant VP*
EMP: 61
SALES (corp-wide): 3.7B **Privately Held**
SIC: **6021** National commercial banks
HQ: Bank Leumi Usa
579 5th Ave Frnt A
New York NY 10017
917 542-2343

(P-9296)
BANK OF HOPE (HQ)
3731 Wilshire Blvd # 400, Los Angeles (90010-2830)
PHONE.........................213 639-1700
Kevin S Kim, *CEO*
Scott Yoon-Suk Whang, *Ch of Bd*

Peter Bae, *President*
Kevin Kim, *President*
Min J Kim, *President*
EMP: 108
SALES (est): 228.5MM
SALES (corp-wide): 638.5MM **Publicly Held**
WEB: www.narabank.com
SIC: **6021** National commercial banks
PA: Hope Bancorp, Inc.
3200 Wilshire Blvd
Los Angeles CA 90010
213 639-1700

(P-9297)
BANK OF SIERRA
Also Called: Bank of Sierra
500 Marsh St, San Luis Obispo (93401-3955)
PHONE.........................805 541-0400
Kevin McPhaill, *Principal*
EMP: 60
SALES (corp-wide): 102.7MM **Publicly Held**
SIC: **6021** National commercial banks
HQ: Bank Of The Sierra
90 N Main St
Porterville CA 93257
559 782-4300

(P-9298)
BANNER BANK
9340 E Stockton Blvd, Elk Grove (95624-1456)
PHONE.........................916 685-6546
Scott A Kisting, *CEO*
Jennifer Gowin, *Opers Mgr*
EMP: 60 **Publicly Held**
WEB: www.premierwestbank.com
SIC: **6021 6029** National commercial banks; commercial banks
HQ: Banner Bank
10 S 1st Ave
Walla Walla WA 99362
800 272-9933

(P-9299)
CALIFORNIA FIRST NAT BANCORP (PA)
28 Executive Park Ste 200, Irvine (92614-4741)
PHONE.........................949 255-0500
Patrick E Paddon, *President*
Glen T Tsuma, *COO*
S Leslie Jewett, *CFO*
Thomas M Duggan, *Senior VP*
EMP: 98
SQ FT: 36,000
SALES: 36.6MM **Publicly Held**
WEB: www.calfirstbancorp.com
SIC: **6021** National commercial banks

(P-9300)
CANADIAN IMPERIAL BANK
620 Newport Center Dr, Newport Beach (92660-6420)
PHONE.........................949 759-4718
Robert Ctvrtlik, *Principal*
EMP: 78
SALES (corp-wide): 11.5B **Privately Held**
WEB: www.cibc.com
SIC: **6021** National commercial banks
PA: Canadian Imperial Bank Of Commerce
199 Bay St Commerce Crt W
Toronto ON M5L 1
416 980-2211

(P-9301)
CARPENTER FUND MANAGER GP LLC
5 Park Plz Ste 950, Irvine (92614-8527)
PHONE.........................949 261-8888
Edward J Carpenter,
Curt Christianssen, *Exec VP*
Arthur Hidalgo, *Exec VP*
Edward Carpenter, *Executive*
Michelle Kaull, *Controller*
EMP: 188
SALES (est): 13.1MM **Privately Held**
SIC: **6021** National commercial banks

(P-9302)
CIT BANK NA
78010 Main St, La Quinta (92253-3408)
PHONE.........................760 771-3498
Robert Kehrberg, *Branch Mgr*

Chauncey Thompson, *Site Mgr*
EMP: 65
SALES (corp-wide): 3.2B **Publicly Held**
SIC: **6021** National commercial banks
HQ: Cit Bank, N.A.
75 N Fair Oaks Ave
Pasadena CA 91103

(P-9303)
CIT BANK NA
1570 Rosecrans Ave, Manhattan Beach (90266-3718)
PHONE.........................310 727-5660
EMP: 63
SALES (corp-wide): 3.2B **Publicly Held**
SIC: **6021** National commercial banks
HQ: Cit Bank, N.A.
75 N Fair Oaks Ave
Pasadena CA 91103

(P-9304)
CIT BANK NA
3410 Grand Ave Ste A, Chino Hills (91709-1473)
PHONE.........................909 631-2560
Jennifer Ferguson, *Branch Mgr*
Fehmida Kumar, *Vice Pres*
EMP: 63
SALES (corp-wide): 3.2B **Publicly Held**
SIC: **6021** National commercial banks
HQ: Cit Bank, N.A.
75 N Fair Oaks Ave Fl 1
Pasadena CA 91103

(P-9305)
CIT BANK NA
2920 N Beverly Glen Cir, Los Angeles (90077-1724)
PHONE.........................310 475-4594
Diane Thomas, *Principal*
EMP: 56
SALES (corp-wide): 3.2B **Publicly Held**
SIC: **6021** National commercial banks
HQ: Cit Bank, N.A.
75 N Fair Oaks Ave Fl 1
Pasadena CA 91103

(P-9306)
CIT BANK NA
1100 Pacific Coast Hwy, Hermosa Beach (90254-3951)
PHONE.........................310 372-8473
Hiran Sumanadasa, *Branch Mgr*
EMP: 56
SALES (corp-wide): 3.2B **Publicly Held**
SIC: **6021** National commercial banks
HQ: Cit Bank, N.A.
75 N Fair Oaks Ave Fl 1
Pasadena CA 91103

(P-9307)
CIT BANK NA
1111 N Brand Blvd Ste A, Glendale (91202-3072)
PHONE.........................818 502-8400
George Lazar, *Principal*
EMP: 59
SALES (corp-wide): 3.2B **Publicly Held**
SIC: **6021** National commercial banks
HQ: Cit Bank, N.A.
75 N Fair Oaks Ave Fl 1
Pasadena CA 91103

(P-9308)
CIT BANK NA
1750 Ocean Park Blvd, Santa Monica (90405-4938)
PHONE.........................310 452-3802
Art Bikidjian, *Branch Mgr*
EMP: 65
SALES (corp-wide): 3.2B **Publicly Held**
SIC: **6021** National commercial banks
HQ: Cit Bank, N.A.
75 N Fair Oaks Ave Fl 1
Pasadena CA 91103

(P-9309)
CIT BANK NA
3500 E 7th St, Long Beach (90804-5137)
PHONE.........................562 433-0972
Nicole Graves, *Branch Mgr*
EMP: 65
SALES (corp-wide): 3.2B **Publicly Held**
SIC: **6021** National commercial banks
HQ: Cit Bank, N.A.
75 N Fair Oaks Ave Fl 1
Pasadena CA 91103

(P-9310)
CIT BANK NA
17050 Ventura Blvd # 100, Encino (91316-4143)
PHONE.........................818 817-5320
Noel Youcefi, *Branch Mgr*
EMP: 63
SALES (corp-wide): 3.2B **Publicly Held**
SIC: **6021** National commercial banks
HQ: Cit Bank, N.A.
75 N Fair Oaks Ave
Pasadena CA 91103

(P-9311)
CIT BANK NA
1727 E Daily Dr, Camarillo (93010-6202)
PHONE.........................805 465-1053
Susan Anderson, *Manager*
EMP: 64
SALES (corp-wide): 3.2B **Publicly Held**
SIC: **6021** National commercial banks
HQ: Cit Bank, N.A.
75 N Fair Oaks Ave
Pasadena CA 91103

(P-9312)
CIT BANK NA
5573 Sepulveda Blvd, Culver City (90230-5513)
PHONE.........................310 390-7745
Millie Davis, *Vice Pres*
EMP: 63
SALES (corp-wide): 3.2B **Publicly Held**
SIC: **6021** National commercial banks
HQ: Cit Bank, N.A.
75 N Fair Oaks Ave Fl 1
Pasadena CA 91103

(P-9313)
CIT BANK NA
Also Called: Onewest Bank
10784 Jefferson Blvd, Culver City (90230-4933)
PHONE.........................310 559-7222
Peter Smith, *Branch Mgr*
EMP: 63
SALES (corp-wide): 3.2B **Publicly Held**
SIC: **6021** National commercial banks
HQ: Cit Bank, N.A.
75 N Fair Oaks Ave
Pasadena CA 91103

(P-9314)
CIT BANK NA
11310 National Blvd, Los Angeles (90064-3727)
PHONE.........................310 477-0546
Delmy Martinez, *Branch Mgr*
EMP: 63
SALES (corp-wide): 3.2B **Publicly Held**
SIC: **6021** National commercial banks
HQ: Cit Bank, N.A.
75 N Fair Oaks Ave
Pasadena CA 91103

(P-9315)
CIT BANK NA
1001 N San Fernando Blvd, Burbank (91504-4303)
PHONE.........................818 525-3760
Luzmarie Nelson, *Site Mgr*
EMP: 64
SALES (corp-wide): 3.2B **Publicly Held**
SIC: **6021** National commercial banks
HQ: Cit Bank, N.A.
75 N Fair Oaks Ave
Pasadena CA 91103

(P-9316)
CIT BANK NA
27620 Marguerite Pkwy B, Mission Viejo
(92692-3607)
PHONE...............................949 347-7014
Dagmar Richter, *Branch Mgr*
EMP: 63
SALES (corp-wide): 3.2B **Publicly Held**
SIC: 6021 National commercial banks
HQ: Cit Bank, N.A.
   75 N Fair Oaks Ave Fl 1
   Pasadena CA 91103
   -

(P-9317)
CIT BANK NA
23072 Alicia Pkwy, Mission Viejo
(92692-1636)
PHONE...............................949 598-9621
Daniel Martin, *Manager*
EMP: 63
SALES (corp-wide): 3.2B **Publicly Held**
SIC: 6021 National commercial banks
HQ: Cit Bank, N.A.
   75 N Fair Oaks Ave
   Pasadena CA 91103

(P-9318)
CIT BANK NA
3700 E Coast Hwy, Corona Del Mar
(92625-2520)
PHONE...............................949 675-2890
Rodney Holder, *Branch Mgr*
EMP: 56
SALES (corp-wide): 3.2B **Publicly Held**
SIC: 6021 National commercial banks
HQ: Cit Bank, N.A.
   75 N Fair Oaks Ave
   Pasadena CA 91103

(P-9319)
CIT BANK NA (HQ)
75 N Fair Oaks Ave Fl 1, Pasadena
(91103-3647)
P.O. Box 7056 (91109-7056)
PHONE...............................626 859-5400
Ellen R Alemany, *Ch of Bd*
James P Broom, *President*
James L Hudak, *President*
C Jeffrey Knittel, *President*
Joseph Otting, *President*
EMP: 80
SALES: 2.4B
SALES (corp-wide): 3.2B **Publicly Held**
WEB: www.loanworks.com
SIC: 6021 National commercial banks
PA: Cit Group Inc.
   11 W 42nd St
   New York NY 10036
   212 461-5200

(P-9320)
CIT BANK NA
199 E Thousand Oaks Blvd, Thousand
Oaks (91360-5710)
PHONE...............................805 379-5520
Tracey Sirkus, *Branch Mgr*
EMP: 56
SALES (corp-wide): 3.2B **Publicly Held**
SIC: 6021 National commercial banks
HQ: Cit Bank, N.A.
   75 N Fair Oaks Ave
   Pasadena CA 91103

(P-9321)
**CIT BANK NATIONAL
ASSOCIATION**
20505 Devonshire St, Chatsworth
(91311-3208)
PHONE...............................818 885-9065
Phyllis Barber, *Branch Mgr*
Wendell Grayson, *Marketing Staff*
EMP: 56
SALES (corp-wide): 3.2B **Publicly Held**
SIC: 6021 National commercial banks
HQ: Cit Bank, N.A.
   75 N Fair Oaks Ave Fl 1
   Pasadena CA 91103

(P-9322)
**CIT BANK NATIONAL
ASSOCIATION**
220 N Hacienda Blvd, City of Industry
(91744-4403)
PHONE...............................626 435-2260
Blanca Deanda, *Manager*
EMP: 64
SALES (corp-wide): 3.2B **Publicly Held**
SIC: 6021 National commercial banks
HQ: Cit Bank, N.A.
   75 N Fair Oaks Ave
   Pasadena CA 91103

(P-9323)
**CIT BANK NATIONAL
ASSOCIATION**
401 Wilshire Blvd, Santa Monica
(90401-1416)
PHONE...............................310 394-1640
Farooq Ganatra, *Branch Mgr*
EMP: 63
SALES (corp-wide): 3.2B **Publicly Held**
SIC: 6021 National commercial banks
HQ: Cit Bank, N.A.
   75 N Fair Oaks Ave
   Pasadena CA 91103
   -

(P-9324)
**CIT BANK NATIONAL
ASSOCIATION**
12401 Wilshire Blvd, Los Angeles
(90025-1085)
PHONE...............................310 820-9650
Leonard Rampulla, *Branch Mgr*
EMP: 56
SALES (corp-wide): 3.2B **Publicly Held**
SIC: 6021 National commercial banks
HQ: Cit Bank, N.A.
   75 N Fair Oaks Ave
   Pasadena CA 91103

(P-9325)
**CIT BANK NATIONAL
ASSOCIATION**
13405 Washington Blvd, Marina Del Rey
(90292-5658)
PHONE...............................310 577-6142
Chris Young, *Branch Mgr*
EMP: 56
SALES (corp-wide): 3.2B **Publicly Held**
SIC: 6021 National commercial banks
HQ: Cit Bank, N.A.
   75 N Fair Oaks Ave
   Pasadena CA 91103

(P-9326)
**CIT BANK NATIONAL
ASSOCIATION**
1630 Montana Ave, Santa Monica
(90403-1808)
PHONE...............................310 829-4477
Euzene Brink, *Manager*
Rory Bliss, *Site Mgr*
EMP: 56
SALES (corp-wide): 3.2B **Publicly Held**
SIC: 6021 National commercial banks
HQ: Cit Bank, N.A.
   75 N Fair Oaks Ave
   Pasadena CA 91103

(P-9327)
**CIT BANK NATIONAL
ASSOCIATION**
5701 S Eastrn Ave Ste 108, Commerce
(90040)
PHONE...............................323 838-6881
Jonathan Silva, *Branch Mgr*
EMP: 56
SALES (corp-wide): 3.2B **Publicly Held**
SIC: 6021 National commercial banks
HQ: Cit Bank, N.A.
   75 N Fair Oaks Ave
   Pasadena CA 91103
   -

(P-9328)
**CIT BANK NATIONAL
ASSOCIATION**
30019 Hawthorne Blvd, Rancho Palos
Verdes (90275-5434)
PHONE...............................310 265-1656
Miguel Gonzalez, *Branch Mgr*
Maria Zalamea, *Branch Mgr*
EMP: 56
SALES (corp-wide): 3.2B **Publicly Held**
SIC: 6021 National commercial banks
HQ: Cit Bank, N.A.
   75 N Fair Oaks Ave Fl 1
   Pasadena CA 91103

(P-9329)
**CITIBANK NATIONAL
ASSOCIATION**
3967 E Thousand Oaks Blvd, Westlake Vil-
lage (91362-3628)
PHONE...............................805 497-7361
EMP: 132
SALES (corp-wide): 71.4B **Publicly Held**
SIC: 6021 National commercial banks
HQ: Citibank, National Association
   701 E 60th St N
   Sioux Falls SD 57104
   605 331-2626

(P-9330)
**CITIBANK NATIONAL
ASSOCIATION**
3580 Tyler St, Riverside (92503-4133)
PHONE...............................800 627-3999
Dawn Latshaw, *Branch Mgr*
EMP: 132
SALES (corp-wide): 71.4B **Publicly Held**
SIC: 6021 National commercial banks
HQ: Citibank, National Association
   701 E 60th St N
   Sioux Falls SD 57104
   605 331-2626

(P-9331)
**CITIBANK NATIONAL
ASSOCIATION**
Also Called: Otay Lakes Road Branch
2240 Otay Lakes Rd 304-3, Chula Vista
(91915-1003)
PHONE...............................619 870-0609
EMP: 211
SALES (corp-wide): 71.4B **Publicly Held**
SIC: 6021 National commercial banks
HQ: Citibank, National Association
   701 E 60th St N
   Sioux Falls SD 57104
   605 331-2626

(P-9332)
**CITIBANK NATIONAL
ASSOCIATION**
Also Called: Sf-Potrero Hill
150 Pennsylvania Ave, San Francisco
(94107-2525)
PHONE...............................415 431-6940
EMP: 211
SALES (corp-wide): 71.4B **Publicly Held**
SIC: 6021 National commercial banks
HQ: Citibank, National Association
   701 E 60th St N
   Sioux Falls SD 57104
   605 331-2626

(P-9333)
CITIGROUP INC
325 E Hillcrest Dr, Thousand Oaks
(91360-5828)
PHONE...............................805 557-0930
Jay Abeywardena, *Vice Pres*
EMP: 65
SALES (corp-wide): 71.4B **Publicly Held**
SIC: 6021 National commercial banks
PA: Citigroup Inc.
   388 Greenwich St
   New York NY 10013
   212 559-1000

(P-9334)
CITIGROUP INC
300 E State St, Redlands (92373-5235)
PHONE...............................909 335-0547
Penny Carroll, *Project Mgr*
EMP: 65

SALES (corp-wide): 71.4B **Publicly Held**
SIC: 6021 National commercial banks
PA: Citigroup Inc.
   388 Greenwich St
   New York NY 10013
   212 559-1000

(P-9335)
CITIGROUP INC
3996 Barranca Pkwy # 130, Irvine
(92606-8239)
PHONE...............................949 726-5124
EMP: 65
SALES (corp-wide): 90.7B **Publicly Held**
SIC: 6021
PA: Citigroup Inc.
   399 Park Ave
   New York NY 10013
   212 559-1000

(P-9336)
CITIGROUP INC
352 H St, Chula Vista (91910-5511)
PHONE...............................619 498-3158
Gustavo Bidart, *Branch Mgr*
EMP: 65
SALES (corp-wide): 71.4B **Publicly Held**
SIC: 6021 National commercial banks
PA: Citigroup Inc.
   388 Greenwich St
   New York NY 10013
   212 559-1000

(P-9337)
CITY NATIONAL BANK (DH)
555 S Flower St Fl 21, Los Angeles
(90071-2303)
PHONE...............................310 888-6000
Russell Goldsmith, *CEO*
Gina Calipes, *President*
Christopher J Warmuth, *President*
Christopher J Carey, *CFO*
John R Randall, *Ch Credit Ofcr*
▲ EMP: 300 EST: 1968
SQ FT: 80,000
SALES: 1.8B **Privately Held**
SIC: 6021 6022 National commercial
   banks; state commercial banks
HQ: Rbc Usa Holdco Corporation
   3 World Financial Ctr
   New York NY 10281
   212 858-7200

(P-9338)
CITY NATIONAL BANK
Also Called: C N B Commercial Banking Ctr
3484 Central Ave, Riverside (92506-2156)
PHONE...............................951 276-8800
Bruce Wachtel, *Manager*
EMP: 50 **Privately Held**
SIC: 6021 National commercial banks
HQ: City National Bank
   555 S Flower St Fl 21
   Los Angeles CA 90071
   310 888-6000

(P-9339)
CITY NATIONAL BANK
Also Called: City National Investments
225 Broadway Ste 500, San Diego
(92101-5029)
PHONE...............................619 645-6100
Michael Nunlee, *Manager*
EMP: 100 **Privately Held**
SIC: 6021 National commercial banks
HQ: City National Bank
   555 S Flower St Fl 21
   Los Angeles CA 90071
   310 888-6000

(P-9340)
CITY NATIONAL BANK
Also Called: Residential Mortgage Ctr 39
2100 Park Pl Ste 150, El Segundo
(90245-4912)
PHONE...............................310 297-6606
J W Lewis, *Senior VP*
EMP: 145 **Privately Held**
SIC: 6021 National commercial banks
HQ: City National Bank
   555 S Flower St Fl 21
   Los Angeles CA 90071
   310 888-6000

(P-9341)
COMERICA BANK
1442 N Main St, Walnut Creek
(94596-4605)
PHONE..................925 941-1900
Christophere Coutelier, *Manager*
Chiristoph Coutelier, *Manager*
EMP: 67
SALES (corp-wide): 3.2B **Publicly Held**
SIC: **6021** National commercial banks
HQ: Comerica Bank
1717 Main St Ste 2100
Dallas TX 75201
214 462-4000

(P-9342)
COMMUNITY WEST BANK
445 Pine Ave, Goleta (93117-3709)
PHONE..................805 692-5821
Toni Genardini, *President*
Will Cunningham, *Officer*
Kimberly Tharpe, *Assoc VP*
Maureen Clark, *Exec VP*
Bill Filippin, *Exec VP*
EMP: 100
SALES (corp-wide): 40.3MM **Publicly Held**
SIC: **6021** National commercial banks
HQ: Community West Bank
5827 Hollister Ave
Goleta CA 93117
805 692-5821

(P-9343)
COMPASS BANK
27851 Bradley Rd Ste 125, Sun City
(92586-2282)
PHONE..................951 672-4829
EMP: 337 **Privately Held**
SIC: **6021** National commercial banks
HQ: Compass Bank
15 20th St S Ste 100
Birmingham AL 35233
205 297-1986

(P-9344)
EXCHANGE BANK
Also Called: Exchange Bank/Loan Service Ctr
440 Aviation Blvd, Santa Rosa
(95403-1069)
P.O. Box 760 (95402-0760)
PHONE..................707 524-3399
Judy Polosuk, *Manager*
EMP: 110
SQ FT: 30,584 **Privately Held**
WEB: www.exchangebank.com
SIC: **6021** National commercial banks
HQ: Exchange Bank
440 Aviation Blvd
Santa Rosa CA 95403
707 524-3000

(P-9345)
FIRST COMMUNITY BANCORP ✪
5900 La Place Ct Ste 200, Carlsbad
(92008-8832)
PHONE..................858 756-3023
Andrew Colker, *Principal*
EMP: 51 EST: 2018
SALES (est): 226.6K
SALES (corp-wide): 1.1B **Publicly Held**
SIC: **6021** National commercial banks
PA: Pacwest Bancorp
9701 Wilshire Blvd # 700
Beverly Hills CA 90212
310 887-8500

(P-9346)
FIRST NATIONAL BANK
6110 El Tordo, Rancho Santa Fe (92067)
PHONE..................858 756-3023
Matthew P Wagner, *CEO*
Robert Borgman, *President*
Vicki Harris, *President*
Rom T Lozares, *President*
Lynn M Hopkins, *CFO*
EMP: 262 EST: 1982
SQ FT: 7,000
SALES (est): 297.5K
SALES (corp-wide): 1.1B **Publicly Held**
SIC: **6021** **6153** National commercial banks; purchasers of accounts receivable & commercial paper; factors of commercial paper

PA: Pacwest Bancorp
9701 Wilshire Blvd # 700
Beverly Hills CA 90212
310 887-8500

(P-9347)
FIRSTFED FINANCIAL CORP
6320 Canoga Ave, Woodland Hills
(91367-2526)
PHONE..................562 618-0573
James Giraldin, *President*
Brian Argrett, *Ch of Bd*
James P Giraldin, *President*
Shannon Millard, *President*
Babette E Heimbuch, *CEO*
EMP: 603
SALES: 439MM **Privately Held**
SIC: **6021** National commercial banks

(P-9348)
JPMORGAN CHASE BANK NAT ASSN
5095 Business Center Dr, Fairfield
(94534-1631)
PHONE..................707 864-4700
Elana Thomas, *Manager*
Jessica Caimol, *Office Mgr*
EMP: 150
SALES (corp-wide): 99.6B **Publicly Held**
SIC: **6021** National commercial banks
HQ: Jpmorgan Chase Bank, National Association
1111 Polaris Pkwy
Columbus OH 43240
614 436-3055

(P-9349)
JPMORGAN CHASE BANK NAT ASSN
860 E Colorado Blvd, Pasadena
(91101-2107)
PHONE..................626 795-5177
Vickie Davinski, *Branch Mgr*
David Chang, *Loan Officer*
EMP: 60
SQ FT: 74,640
SALES (corp-wide): 99.6B **Publicly Held**
SIC: **6021** National commercial banks
HQ: Jpmorgan Chase Bank, National Association
1111 Polaris Pkwy
Columbus OH 43240
614 436-3055

(P-9350)
JPMORGAN CHASE BANK NAT ASSN
Also Called: Washington Mutual
12051 Ventura Blvd, Studio City
(91604-2609)
PHONE..................818 763-7343
Manny Abebi, *Branch Mgr*
EMP: 50
SALES (corp-wide): 99.6B **Publicly Held**
SIC: **6021** National commercial banks
HQ: Jpmorgan Chase Bank, National Association
1111 Polaris Pkwy
Columbus OH 43240
614 436-3055

(P-9351)
JPMORGAN CHASE BANK NAT ASSN
100 S Vincent Ave Fl 1, West Covina
(91790-2902)
PHONE..................626 919-3129
Larry Gomez, *Branch Mgr*
EMP: 89
SALES (corp-wide): 99.6B **Publicly Held**
SIC: **6021** National commercial banks
HQ: Jpmorgan Chase Bank, National Association
1111 Polaris Pkwy
Columbus OH 43240
614 436-3055

(P-9352)
MERCHANTS BANK CALIFORNIA N A
1 Civic Plaza Dr Ste 100, Carson
(90745-7958)
P.O. Box 6008, Long Beach (90806-0008)
PHONE..................310 549-4350
Joyce Yamasaki, *CEO*

Rod Garza, *Exec VP*
Rosario Lopez, *Vice Pres*
Daniel K Roberts, *Principal*
Mike Kruthers, *Administration*
EMP: 75
SQ FT: 5,551
SALES: 6.9MM **Privately Held**
WEB: www.merchantsbankca.com
SIC: **6021** National commercial banks

(P-9353)
MUFG UNION BANK NATIONAL ASSN (DH)
400 California St Fl 14, San Francisco
(94104-1302)
PHONE..................415 705-7000
Norimichi Kanari, *President*
Kyota Omori, *Ch of Bd*
Mark W Midkiff, *Vice Chairman*
Timothy H Wennes, *Vice Chairman*
Patrick Nygren, *President*
▲ EMP: 1000 EST: 1864
SALES: 5.1B
SALES (corp-wide): 56.9B **Privately Held**
SIC: **6021** National commercial banks
HQ: Mufg Americas Holdings Corporation
1251 Ave Of The Americas
New York NY 10020
212 782-6800

(P-9354)
MUFG UNION BANK NATIONAL ASSN
120 S San Pedro St, Los Angeles
(90012-5300)
P.O. Box 3248 (90051-1248)
PHONE..................213 972-5500
Yoshio Morita, *Branch Mgr*
Chris Hernandez, *Assoc VP*
Scott Hammargren, *Managing Dir*
Frankie Yim, *Assistant VP*
EMP: 50
SQ FT: 60,299
SALES (corp-wide): 56.9B **Privately Held**
SIC: **6021** National commercial banks
HQ: Mufg Union Bank, National Association
400 California St Fl 14
San Francisco CA 94104
415 705-7000

(P-9355)
MUFG UNION BANK NATIONAL ASSN
20 E Carrillo St, Santa Barbara
(93101-2707)
PHONE..................805 564-6410
Steve Mihalic, *Vice Pres*
Dave Ristig, *Senior VP*
Penny Sharrett, *Senior VP*
Julia Fox, *Vice Pres*
Joseph Kennedy, *Vice Pres*
EMP: 75
SALES (corp-wide): 56.9B **Privately Held**
WEB: www.pacificcapitalbank.com
SIC: **6021** **6022** National commercial banks; state commercial banks
HQ: Mufg Union Bank, National Association
400 California St Fl 14
San Francisco CA 94104
415 705-7000

(P-9356)
MUFG UNION BANK NATIONAL ASSN
Also Called: U B C 200
9460 Wilshire Blvd # 200, Beverly Hills
(90212-2732)
P.O. Box 1268 (90213-1268)
PHONE..................310 550-6522
G Denton Folkes, *Branch Mgr*
EMP: 80
SALES (corp-wide): 56.9B **Privately Held**
SIC: **6021** National commercial banks
HQ: Mufg Union Bank, National Association
400 California St Fl 14
San Francisco CA 94104
415 705-7000

(P-9357)
MUFG UNION BANK NATIONAL ASSN
1201 5th Ave, San Diego (92101-4214)
PHONE..................619 230-4666
Ralph C Allen, *Branch Mgr*
Abdirahman Ali, *Officer*

Suzuko Burton, *Officer*
Marguerite Boutelle, *Senior VP*
Bruce Breslau, *Vice Pres*
EMP: 62
SALES (corp-wide): 56.9B **Privately Held**
SIC: **6021** National commercial banks
HQ: Mufg Union Bank, National Association
400 California St Fl 14
San Francisco CA 94104
415 705-7000

(P-9358)
MUFG UNION BANK NATIONAL ASSN
900 S Main St, Los Angeles (90015-1730)
P.O. Box 2278 (90051-0278)
PHONE..................213 312-4500
Michael Padula, *Sales/Mktg Mgr*
Alan Previde, *Project Mgr*
EMP: 82
SALES (corp-wide): 56.9B **Privately Held**
SIC: **6021** National commercial banks
HQ: Mufg Union Bank, National Association
400 California St Fl 14
San Francisco CA 94104
415 705-7000

(P-9359)
MUFG UNION BANK NATIONAL ASSN
15800 S Western Ave, Gardena
(90247-3704)
PHONE..................310 354-4700
Takeo Kittaka, *Branch Mgr*
EMP: 50
SALES (corp-wide): 56.9B **Privately Held**
SIC: **6021** National commercial banks
HQ: Mufg Union Bank, National Association
400 California St Fl 14
San Francisco CA 94104
415 705-7000

(P-9360)
MUFG UNION BANK NATIONAL ASSN
460 Hegenberger Rd Fl 3, Oakland
(94621-1423)
PHONE..................510 891-2495
Steve Nicholson, *Business Anlyst*
Charlie Donner, *Business Anlyst*
EMP: 100
SALES (corp-wide): 56.9B **Privately Held**
SIC: **6021** National commercial banks
HQ: Mufg Union Bank, National Association
400 California St Fl 14
San Francisco CA 94104
415 705-7000

(P-9361)
NORTHERN TRUST COMPANY
2049 Century Park E # 3600, Los Angeles
(90067-3210)
PHONE..................310 282-3800
James Dryden, *Branch Mgr*
James Bessolo, *Vice Pres*
Gerald Gallagher, *Vice Pres*
Susie Torres, *Vice Pres*
EMP: 50
SALES (corp-wide): 5.7B **Publicly Held**
SIC: **6021** National commercial banks
HQ: The Northern Trust Company
50 S La Salle St
Chicago IL 60603
312 630-6000

(P-9362)
PACIFIC WESTERN BANK
Also Called: Rancho Santa Fe
6110 El Tordo, Rancho Santa Fe (92067)
PHONE..................858 756-3023
Steen Weber, *Vice Pres*
EMP: 262
SALES (corp-wide): 1.1B **Publicly Held**
SIC: **6021** **6153** National commercial banks; purchasers of accounts receivable & commercial paper; factors of commercial paper
HQ: Pacific Western Bank
9701 Wilshire Blvd # 700
Beverly Hills CA 90212
310 887-8500

PRODUCTS & SVCS

(P-9363)
PACIFIC WESTERN BANK
900 Canterbury Pl Ste 300, Escondido
(92025-3846)
PHONE..................760 432-1350
Bruce Mills, *CFO*
Leticia Trujillo, *Assistant VP*
EMP: 108
SALES (corp-wide): 1.1B **Publicly Held**
WEB: www.pacificwesternbank.com
SIC: 6021 National commercial banks
HQ: Pacific Western Bank
9701 Wilshire Blvd # 700
Beverly Hills CA 90212
310 887-8500

(P-9364)
PACIFIC WESTERN BANK
5900 La Place Ct Ste 200, Carlsbad
(92008-8832)
PHONE..................760 918-2469
Suzanne Brennan, *Manager*
EMP: 52
SALES (corp-wide): 1.1B **Publicly Held**
WEB: www.pacificwesternbank.com
SIC: 6021 National commercial banks
HQ: Pacific Western Bank
9701 Wilshire Blvd # 700
Beverly Hills CA 90212
310 887-8500

(P-9365)
PACIFIC WESTERN BANK
12481 High Bluff Dr # 350, San Diego
(92130-3585)
PHONE..................858 436-3500
Richard Casey, *Branch Mgr*
Carol Dugger, *Administration*
EMP: 53
SALES (corp-wide): 1.1B **Publicly Held**
SIC: 6021 National commercial banks
HQ: Pacific Western Bank
9701 Wilshire Blvd # 700
Beverly Hills CA 90212
310 887-8500

(P-9366)
PACIFIC WESTERN BANK
900 Canterbury Pl Ste 300, Escondido
(92025)
PHONE..................760 432-1100
Michael Perdue, *Branch Mgr*
EMP: 80
SALES (corp-wide): 1.1B **Publicly Held**
WEB: www.pacificwesternbank.com
SIC: 6021 National commercial banks
HQ: Pacific Western Bank
9701 Wilshire Blvd # 700
Beverly Hills CA 90212
310 887-8500

(P-9367)
**PNC BANK NATIONAL
ASSOCIATION**
2 N Lake Ave Ste 440, Pasadena
(91101-4197)
PHONE..................626 432-4500
Thomas Soltz, *Branch Mgr*
EMP: 60
SALES (corp-wide): 18B **Publicly Held**
WEB: www.pncfunds.com
SIC: 6021 National trust companies with
deposits, commercial
HQ: Pnc Bank, National Association
222 Delaware Ave
Wilmington DE 19801
877 762-2000

(P-9368)
**PNC BANK NATIONAL
ASSOCIATION**
465 N Halstead St Ste 160, Pasadena
(91107-6018)
PHONE..................626 351-2211
Dennis Hayashi, *Manager*
Robert Butler, *Manager*
EMP: 76
SALES (corp-wide): 18B **Publicly Held**
WEB: www.pncfunds.com
SIC: 6021 National trust companies with
deposits, commercial
HQ: Pnc Bank, National Association
222 Delaware Ave
Wilmington DE 19801
877 762-2000

(P-9369)
PORREY PINES BANK INC
Also Called: Western Alliance Bank
1951 Webster St, Oakland (94612-2909)
PHONE..................510 899-7500
Larry Fountain, *Manager*
Kiran Rai, *Vice Pres*
Dianne Williams, *Manager*
EMP: 380
SALES (est) 81.4MM
SALES (corp-wide): 890.8MM **Publicly
Held**
WEB: www.altaalliancebank.com
SIC: 6021 National commercial banks
PA: Western Alliance Bancorporation
1 E Wshington St Ste 1400
Phoenix AZ 85004
602 389-3500

(P-9370)
**REDDING BANK OF COMMERCE
(HQ)**
1951 Churn Creek Rd, Redding
(96002-0246)
PHONE..................530 224-7355
Randall S Eslick, *President*
Greg Bambino, *President*
Kendra Groundwater, *President*
Linda J Miles, *CFO*
Patrick J Moty, *Ch Credit Ofcr*
EMP: 80
SQ FT: 10,000
SALES: 50.7MM
SALES (corp-wide): 50.7MM **Publicly
Held**
WEB: www.rosevillebankofcommerce.com
SIC: 6021 National commercial banks
PA: Bank Of Commerce Holdings
1901 Churn Creek Rd
Redding CA 96002
530 722-3952

(P-9371)
SILICON VALLEY BANK
15260 Ventura Blvd # 1800, Sherman Oaks
(91403-5350)
PHONE..................818 382-2600
Mark Turk, *Branch Mgr*
Adam Graham, *Vice Pres*
EMP: 80
SALES (corp-wide): 2B **Publicly Held**
SIC: 6021 National commercial banks
HQ: Silicon Valley Bank
3003 Tasman Dr
Santa Clara CA 95054
408 654-7400

(P-9372)
**SIX RIVERS NATIONAL BANK
(HQ)**
402 F St, Eureka (95501-1008)
PHONE..................707 443-8400
Fax: 707 443-3631
EMP: 51
SALES: 46.3MM
SALES (corp-wide): 206.7MM **Publicly
Held**
SIC: 6021
PA: Trico Bancshares
63 Constitution Dr
Chico CA 95973
530 898-0300

(P-9373)
TRI COUNTIES BANK
975 El Camino Real, South San Francisco
(94080-3203)
PHONE..................650 583-8450
EMP: 184
SALES (corp-wide): 231.4MM **Publicly
Held**
SIC: 6021 National commercial banks
HQ: Tri Counties Bank
63 Constitution Dr
Chico CA 95973
530 898-0300

(P-9374)
UMPQUA BANK
Also Called: Encino Branch
16501 Ventura Blvd, Encino (91436-2007)
PHONE..................818 385-1362
EMP: 62
SALES (corp-wide): 1.2B **Publicly Held**
SIC: 6021 National commercial banks

HQ: Umpqua Bank
445 Se Main St
Roseburg OR 97470
541 440-3961

(P-9375)
**US BANK NATIONAL
ASSOCIATION**
Also Called: US Bank
10021 Bloomfield St, Los Alamitos
(90720-2207)
PHONE..................562 795-7520
Catherine Marker, *Office Mgr*
Kimberly Fedele, *Manager*
EMP: 50
SALES (corp-wide): 24B **Publicly Held**
SIC: 6021 National commercial banks
HQ: U.S. Bank National Association
425 Walnut St Fl 1
Cincinnati OH 45202
513 632-4234

(P-9376)
**US BANK NATIONAL
ASSOCIATION**
Also Called: US Bank
1420 Kettner Blvd Ste 101, San Diego
(92101-2639)
PHONE..................619 744-2140
Murray L Galinson, *Branch Mgr*
EMP: 100
SALES (corp-wide): 24B **Publicly Held**
SIC: 6021 National commercial banks
HQ: U.S. Bank National Association
425 Walnut St Fl 1
Cincinnati OH 45202
513 632-4234

(P-9377)
WACHOVIA A DIVISION WELLS F
420 Montgomery St, San Francisco
(94104-1207)
PHONE..................415 571-2832
John G Stumpf, *Principal*
Kimberly Hanson, *Vice Pres*
Daniel Kravitz, *Vice Pres*
Isaac Washington, *Vice Pres*
EMP: 576 **EST:** 2011
SALES (est) 258.3MM **Privately Held**
SIC: 6021 National commercial banks

(P-9378)
**WELLS FARGO & COMPANY
(PA)**
420 Montgomery St Frnt, San Francisco
(94104-1205)
PHONE..................866 249-3302
Timothy J Sloan, *President*
Mohammed Abuzeineh, *President*
CSM S Armstrong, *President*
Donna K Ashley, *President*
Olga Brahaney, *President*
▲ **EMP:** 233 **EST:** 1929
SALES: 97.7B **Publicly Held**
SIC: 6021 6022 6162 6141 National
commercial banks; state commercial
banks; mortgage bankers; consumer fi-
nance companies; data processing serv-
ice

(P-9379)
WELLS FARGO BANK LTD
333 S Grand Ave Ste 500, Los Angeles
(90071-1569)
PHONE..................213 253-6227
Randy Reyes, *Branch Mgr*
Courtney Cassidy, *Vice Pres*
Daniel MAI, *Vice Pres*
James Shrman, *Vice Pres*
John Brownlee, *Info Tech Mgr*
EMP: 78
SALES: 426.3MM
SALES (corp-wide): 97.7B **Publicly Held**
SIC: 6021 National commercial banks
HQ: Wfc Holdings, Llc
420 Montgomery St
San Francisco CA 94104
415 396-7392

(P-9380)
WELLS FARGO BANK NA
Also Called: Operations
333 S Hope St Ste D100, Los Angeles
(90071-3003)
PHONE..................213 628-2251

Shaffi Poswal, *Branch Mgr*
EMP: 250
SALES (corp-wide): 97.7B **Publicly Held**
WEB: www.wellsfargo.com
SIC: 6021 National commercial banks
HQ: Wells Fargo Bank, National Associa-
tion
101 N Phillips Ave
Sioux Falls SD 57104
605 575-6900

(P-9381)
**WELLS FARGO BANK
NATIONAL ASSN**
10225 Riverside Dr, Toluca Lake
(91602-2501)
PHONE..................818 766-7172
Marita Kesheshyn, *Manager*
EMP: 50
SALES (corp-wide): 97.7B **Publicly Held**
WEB: www.wellsfargo.com
SIC: 6021 National commercial banks
HQ: Wells Fargo Bank, National Associa-
tion
101 N Phillips Ave
Sioux Falls SD 57104
605 575-6900

(P-9382)
**WELLS FARGO BANK
NATIONAL ASSN**
120 Kearny St Ste 1750, San Francisco
(94108-4814)
PHONE..................415 396-6267
Jean Arcos, *Manager*
EMP: 50
SALES (corp-wide): 97.7B **Publicly Held**
WEB: www.wellsfargo.com
SIC: 6021 National commercial banks
HQ: Wells Fargo Bank, National Associa-
tion
101 N Phillips Ave
Sioux Falls SD 57104
605 575-6900

(P-9383)
**WELLS FARGO BANK
NATIONAL ASSN**
1 Montgomery St Ste 200, San Francisco
(94104-4517)
P.O. Box 63005 (94163-0001)
PHONE..................415 396-6161
Bob Besozzi, *Manager*
Simon Fowles, *Vice Pres*
EMP: 60
SQ FT: 4,000
SALES (corp-wide): 97.7B **Publicly Held**
WEB: www.wellsfargo.com
SIC: 6021 National commercial banks
HQ: Wells Fargo Bank, National Associa-
tion
101 N Phillips Ave
Sioux Falls SD 57104
605 575-6900

(P-9384)
**WELLS FARGO BANK
NATIONAL ASSN**
1120 K St, Modesto (95354-2398)
PHONE..................209 578-6810
Robert Moules, *Manager*
EMP: 59
SALES (corp-wide): 97.7B **Publicly Held**
WEB: www.wellsfargo.com
SIC: 6021 National commercial banks
HQ: Wells Fargo Bank, National Associa-
tion
101 N Phillips Ave
Sioux Falls SD 57104
605 575-6900

(P-9385)
**WELLS FARGO BANK
NATIONAL ASSN**
2170 Tully Rd, San Jose (95122-1345)
PHONE..................408 998-3714
Crystal Nguyen, *Manager*
Marlowe Studley, *Site Mgr*
Lisa Vo, *Consultant*
EMP: 50
SALES (corp-wide): 97.7B **Publicly Held**
WEB: www.wellsfargo.com
SIC: 6021 National commercial banks

HQ: Wells Fargo Bank, National Association
101 N Phillips Ave
Sioux Falls SD 57104
605 575-6900

(P-9386)
**WELLS FARGO BANK
NATIONAL ASSN**
4365 Executive Dr Fl 18, San Diego
(92121-2194)
PHONE.................................858 622-6958
James Cimino, *Manager*
Dennis Hall, *President*
Dennis Kim, *President*
Sinan Battah, *Loan Officer*
Alejandro Cervera, *Manager*
EMP: 75
SALES (corp-wide): 97.7B **Publicly Held**
WEB: www.wellsfargo.com
SIC: 6021 National commercial banks
HQ: Wells Fargo Bank, National Association
101 N Phillips Ave
Sioux Falls SD 57104
605 575-6900

(P-9387)
**WELLS FARGO BANK
NATIONAL ASSN**
901 Main St, NAPA (94559-3044)
PHONE.................................707 259-5552
Patty Belt, *Manager*
EMP: 70
SALES (corp-wide): 97.7B **Publicly Held**
WEB: www.wellsfargo.com
SIC: 6021 National commercial banks
HQ: Wells Fargo Bank, National Association
101 N Phillips Ave
Sioux Falls SD 57104
605 575-6900

(P-9388)
**WELLS FARGO BANK
NATIONAL ASSN**
Merchant Paymnt A0347-023
1655 Grant St, Concord (94520-2600)
PHONE.................................925 746-3718
EMP: 60
SQ FT: 57,192
SALES (corp-wide): 97.7B **Publicly Held**
SIC: 6021
HQ: Wells Fargo Bank, National Association
101 N Phillips Ave
Sioux Falls SD 57104
605 575-6900

(P-9389)
**WELLS FARGO BANK
NATIONAL ASSN**
Also Called: Trade Services E2002-031
9000 Flair Dr Fl 3, El Monte (91731-2826)
PHONE.................................626 312-3006
Marilyn Benoit, *Manager*
EMP: 500
SALES (corp-wide): 97.7B **Publicly Held**
WEB: www.wellsfargo.com
SIC: 6021 National commercial banks
HQ: Wells Fargo Bank, National Association
101 N Phillips Ave
Sioux Falls SD 57104
605 575-6900

(P-9390)
**WELLS FARGO BANK
NATIONAL ASSN**
7714 Girard Ave, La Jolla (92037-4483)
PHONE.................................858 454-0362
Ladd Graham, *Manager*
Joseph Caldararo, *Manager*
EMP: 525
SALES (corp-wide): 97.7B **Publicly Held**
WEB: www.wellsfargo.com
SIC: 6021 National commercial banks
HQ: Wells Fargo Bank, National Association
101 N Phillips Ave
Sioux Falls SD 57104
605 575-6900

(P-9391)
**WELLS FARGO BANK
NATIONAL ASSN**
Also Called: Roseville Foothills and Jct
5007 Foothills Blvd, Roseville
(95747-6503)
PHONE.................................916 724-2982
Susan Adams, *Branch Mgr*
EMP: 85
SALES (corp-wide): 97.7B **Publicly Held**
SIC: 6021 National commercial banks
HQ: Wells Fargo Bank, National Association
101 N Phillips Ave
Sioux Falls SD 57104
605 575-6900

(P-9392)
**WELLS FARGO BANK
NATIONAL ASSN**
60 W Hamilton Ave, Campbell
(95008-0505)
PHONE.................................408 378-8155
Titi Vu, *Manager*
EMP: 50
SALES (corp-wide): 97.7B **Publicly Held**
WEB: www.wellsfargo.com
SIC: 6021 National commercial banks
HQ: Wells Fargo Bank, National Association
101 N Phillips Ave
Sioux Falls SD 57104
605 575-6900

(P-9393)
**WELLS FARGO BANK
NATIONAL ASSN**
100 Spear St Ste 100 # 100, San Francisco
(94105-1578)
PHONE.................................415 777-9497
Praneet Chahal, *Principal*
Quynh Nguyen, *Site Mgr*
EMP: 319
SALES (corp-wide): 97.7B **Publicly Held**
SIC: 6021 National commercial banks
HQ: Wells Fargo Bank, National Association
101 N Phillips Ave
Sioux Falls SD 57104
605 575-6900

(P-9394)
**WELLS FARGO BANK
NATIONAL ASSN**
1620 E Roseville Pkwy, Roseville
(95661-3995)
PHONE.................................916 774-2249
Kathie Gedney, *Manager*
Dennis McKey, *Info Tech Dir*
Kelly Garfield, *Info Tech Mgr*
Andrew Osborn, *Info Tech Mgr*
Nichelle Van Rossum, *Manager*
EMP: 300
SALES (corp-wide): 97.7B **Publicly Held**
WEB: www.wellsfargo.com
SIC: 6021 National commercial banks
HQ: Wells Fargo Bank, National Association
101 N Phillips Ave
Sioux Falls SD 57104
605 575-6900

(P-9395)
**WELLS FARGO BANK
NATIONAL ASSN**
3440 Flair Dr, El Monte (91731-2883)
PHONE.................................626 573-1338
Lori Morgan, *Principal*
Carl Herr, *VP Mktg*
EMP: 250
SALES (corp-wide): 97.7B **Publicly Held**
WEB: www.wellsfargo.com
SIC: 6021 National commercial banks
HQ: Wells Fargo Bank, National Association
101 N Phillips Ave
Sioux Falls SD 57104
605 575-6900

(P-9396)
**WELLS FARGO BANK
NATIONAL ASSN**
Also Called: San Lorenzo 0119
16000 Hesperian Blvd, San Lorenzo
(94580-2450)
PHONE.................................510 276-0875
Jan Miller, *Branch Mgr*
EMP: 50
SALES (corp-wide): 97.7B **Publicly Held**
WEB: www.wellsfargo.com
SIC: 6021 National commercial banks
HQ: Wells Fargo Bank, National Association
101 N Phillips Ave
Sioux Falls SD 57104
605 575-6900

(P-9397)
**WELLS FARGO BANK
NATIONAL ASSN**
39265 Paseo Padre Pkwy, Fremont
(94538-1611)
PHONE.................................510 792-3512
George Sezidarias, *Manager*
EMP: 59
SALES (corp-wide): 97.7B **Publicly Held**
WEB: www.wellsfargo.com
SIC: 6021 National commercial banks
HQ: Wells Fargo Bank, National Association
101 N Phillips Ave
Sioux Falls SD 57104
605 575-6900

(P-9398)
**WELLS FARGO BANK
NATIONAL ASSN**
950 Southland Dr, Hayward (94545-1544)
P.O. Box 3367 (94540-3367)
PHONE.................................510 266-0595
Kay Maloy, *Manager*
EMP: 55
SALES (corp-wide): 97.7B **Publicly Held**
WEB: www.wellsfargo.com
SIC: 6021 National commercial banks
HQ: Wells Fargo Bank, National Association
101 N Phillips Ave
Sioux Falls SD 57104
605 575-6900

(P-9399)
**WELLS FARGO BANK
NATIONAL ASSN**
2301 Watt Ave, Sacramento (95825-0666)
PHONE.................................916 440-4570
Scott Caddow, *Manager*
EMP: 50
SALES (corp-wide): 97.7B **Publicly Held**
WEB: www.wellsfargo.com
SIC: 6021 National commercial banks
HQ: Wells Fargo Bank, National Association
101 N Phillips Ave
Sioux Falls SD 57104
605 575-6900

(P-9400)
**WELLS FARGO BANK
NATIONAL ASSN**
5798 Stoneridge Mall Rd, Pleasanton
(94588-2862)
PHONE.................................925 463-1983
Richard Thornton, *Branch Mgr*
EMP: 84
SALES (corp-wide): 97.7B **Publicly Held**
SIC: 6021 National commercial banks
HQ: Wells Fargo Bank, National Association
101 N Phillips Ave
Sioux Falls SD 57104
605 575-6900

(P-9401)
**WELLS FARGO BANK
NATIONAL ASSN**
28350 S Western Ave, Rancho Palos
Verdes (90275-1499)
PHONE.................................310 831-0632
Sandy Walia, *Branch Mgr*
EMP: 60

SALES (corp-wide): 97.7B **Publicly Held**
WEB: www.wellsfargo.com
SIC: 6021 National commercial banks
HQ: Wells Fargo Bank, National Association
101 N Phillips Ave
Sioux Falls SD 57104
605 575-6900

(P-9402)
**WELLS FARGO BANK
NATIONAL ASSN**
455 Market, Fremont (94536)
PHONE.................................415 222-6834
Wyman Yuu, *Manager*
EMP: 250
SALES (corp-wide): 97.7B **Publicly Held**
WEB: www.wellsfargo.com
SIC: 6021 National commercial banks
HQ: Wells Fargo Bank, National Association
101 N Phillips Ave
Sioux Falls SD 57104
605 575-6900

(P-9403)
**WELLS FARGO BANK
NATIONAL ASSN**
665 Marsh St, San Luis Obispo
(93401-3930)
PHONE.................................805 541-0143
Mark Corella, *Branch Mgr*
EMP: 84
SALES (corp-wide): 97.7B **Publicly Held**
WEB: www.wellsfargo.com
SIC: 6021 National commercial banks
HQ: Wells Fargo Bank, National Association
101 N Phillips Ave
Sioux Falls SD 57104
605 575-6900

(P-9404)
**WELLS FARGO BANK
NATIONAL ASSN**
420 Montgomery St Fl 6, San Francisco
(94104-1207)
PHONE.................................415 394-4021
Paul Rettig, *Manager*
EMP: 1000
SALES (corp-wide): 97.7B **Publicly Held**
WEB: www.wellsfargo.com
SIC: 6021 National commercial banks
HQ: Wells Fargo Bank, National Association
101 N Phillips Ave
Sioux Falls SD 57104
605 575-6900

(P-9405)
**WELLS FARGO BANK
NATIONAL ASSN**
2220 Mountain Blvd # 160, Oakland
(94611-2950)
P.O. Box 1559 (94604-1559)
PHONE.................................510 530-3095
Ellen Thomas, *Manager*
EMP: 65
SALES (corp-wide): 97.7B **Publicly Held**
WEB: www.wellsfargo.com
SIC: 6021 National commercial banks
HQ: Wells Fargo Bank, National Association
101 N Phillips Ave
Sioux Falls SD 57104
605 575-6900

(P-9406)
**WELLS FARGO BANK
NATIONAL ASSN**
18712 Gridley Rd, Cerritos (90703-5410)
PHONE.................................562 924-1616
Susan De Lazzer, *Sales/Mktg Mgr*
EMP: 50
SALES (corp-wide): 97.7B **Publicly Held**
WEB: www.wellsfargo.com
SIC: 6021 National commercial banks
HQ: Wells Fargo Bank, National Association
101 N Phillips Ave
Sioux Falls SD 57104
605 575-6900

PRODUCTS & SVCS

(P-9407)
WELLS FARGO BANK
NATIONAL ASSN
3440 Walnut Ave Fl 3, Fremont
(94538-2210)
PHONE..................510 745-5025
Yung Lew, *Division Mgr*
Kirk Cardinotti, *Vice Pres*
EMP: 300
SALES (corp-wide): 97.7B **Publicly Held**
WEB: www.wellsfargo.com
SIC: 6021 National commercial banks
HQ: Wells Fargo Bank, National Association
101 N Phillips Ave
Sioux Falls SD 57104
605 575-6900

(P-9408)
WELLS FARGO BANK
NATIONAL ASSN
Wells Fargo Investments
433 N Camden Dr Ste 1200, Beverly Hills
(90210-4426)
P.O. Box 20160, Long Beach (90801-3160)
PHONE..................310 285-5817
Steve Mann, *Manager*
Kim Mehlman, *Exec VP*
EMP: 200
SALES (corp-wide): 97.7B **Publicly Held**
WEB: www.wellsfargo.com
SIC: 6021 National commercial banks
HQ: Wells Fargo Bank, National Association
101 N Phillips Ave
Sioux Falls SD 57104
605 575-6900

(P-9409)
WELLS FARGO HOME
MORTGAGE INC
3010 Lava Ridge Ct # 150, Roseville
(95661-3075)
PHONE..................916 782-2221
Scott Nutter, *Manager*
Drew Collins, *Vice Pres*
David Skitarelic, *Assistant VP*
EMP: 50
SALES (corp-wide): 97.7B **Publicly Held**
WEB: www.wfhm.com
SIC: 6021 National commercial banks
HQ: Wells Fargo Home Mortgage Inc
1 Home Campus
Des Moines IA 50328
515 324-3707

(P-9410)
WFC HOLDINGS LLC (HQ)
420 Montgomery St, San Francisco
(94104-1207)
PHONE..................415 396-7392
Richard M Kovacevich, *Ch of Bd*
Tami Smith, *Vice Pres*
EMP: 200 **EST:** 1998
SQ FT: 750,000
SALES (est): 1.7B
SALES (corp-wide): 97.7B **Publicly Held**
SIC: 6021 National commercial banks
PA: Wells Fargo & Company
420 Montgomery St Frnt
San Francisco CA 94104
866 249-3302

(P-9411)
ZB NATIONAL ASSOCIATION
California Bank & Trust
11622 El Camino Real, San Diego
(92130-2049)
PHONE..................858 793-7400
Andre Ellis, *President*
Andrew Fain, *President*
Rosemary Larkin, *President*
Sheetal Naidu, *President*
Chris Garton, *Officer*
EMP: 50
SALES (corp-wide): 2.7B **Privately Held**
SIC: 6021 National commercial banks
HQ: Zb, National Association
1 S Main St Fl 11
Salt Lake City UT 84133
801 844-7637

(P-9412)
ZB NATIONAL ASSOCIATION
Also Called: California Bank & Trust
100 Crprate Pinte Ste 110, Culver City
(90230)
PHONE..................310 258-9300
Jeff Watts, *Branch Mgr*
Wayne Ward, *Senior VP*
Kristyn Vessey, *Credit Staff*
EMP: 149
SALES (corp-wide): 2.7B **Privately Held**
WEB: www.calbt.com
SIC: 6021 National commercial banks
HQ: Zb, National Association
1 S Main St Fl 11
Salt Lake City UT 84133
801 844-7637

6022 State Commercial Banks

(P-9413)
BANK OF MARIN
Also Called: Northgate Branch
4460 Redwood Hwy Ste 1, San Rafael
(94903-1952)
PHONE..................415 472-2265
Janet Hayward, *Manager*
EMP: 78 **Publicly Held**
WEB: www.bankofmarin.com
SIC: 6022 State trust companies accepting
deposits, commercial
HQ: Bank Of Marin
504 Redwood Blvd Ste 100
Novato CA 94947
415 763-4520

(P-9414)
BANK OF MARIN BANCORP (PA)
504 Redwood Blvd Ste 100, Novato
(94947-6923)
P.O. Box 2039 (94948-2039)
PHONE..................415 763-4520
Russell A Colombo, *President*
Brian M Sobel, *Ch of Bd*
Megan Garner, *President*
Eddie Roslin, *President*
Carol Trueblood, *President*
EMP: 105
SALES: 84.8MM **Publicly Held**
SIC: 6022 State commercial banks

(P-9415)
BANK OF ORIENT (HQ)
100 Pine St Ste 600, San Francisco
(94111-5108)
P.O. Box 2489 (94126-2489)
PHONE..................415 338-0668
Ernest L Go, *Ch of Bd*
Michael R Delucchi, *COO*
Carl Andersen, *CFO*
John Curtis, *Exec VP*
Mark K McDonald, *Exec VP*
EMP: 137
SQ FT: 20,000
SALES: 30.6MM
SALES (corp-wide): 39.8MM **Privately Held**
SIC: 6022 State trust companies accepting
deposits, commercial
PA: Orient Bancorporation
100 Pine St Ste 600
San Francisco CA 94111
415 567-1554

(P-9416)
BANK OF SIERRA (HQ)
90 N Main St, Porterville (93257-3712)
P.O. Box 1930 (93258-1930)
PHONE..................559 782-4300
Kevin McPhaill, *President*
Morris Tharp, *Ch of Bd*
Karen S Nishimura, *President*
Dustin Oliver, *President*
Albert L Berra, *Bd of Directors*
EMP: 105
SQ FT: 37,000
SALES: 102.1MM
SALES (corp-wide): 102.7MM **Publicly Held**
WEB: www.bankofthesierra.com
SIC: 6022 State commercial banks

PA: Sierra Bancorp
86 N Main St
Porterville CA 93257
559 782-4900

(P-9417)
BANK OF STOCKTON (HQ)
301 E Miner Ave, Stockton (95202-2501)
P.O. Box 1110 (95201-3003)
PHONE..................209 929-1600
Robert M Eberhardt, *President*
Douglass M Eberhardt, *President*
Amy Kieffer, *President*
John Morrison, *President*
Terri Vines, *President*
EMP: 180 **EST:** 1867
SQ FT: 15,000
SALES: 125.6MM
SALES (corp-wide): 81MM **Privately Held**
WEB: www.netbos.com
SIC: 6022 State trust companies accepting
deposits, commercial

(P-9418)
BANK OF THE WEST (HQ)
180 Montgomery St # 1400, San Francisco
(94104-4297)
PHONE..................415 765-4800
J Michael Shepherd, *CEO*
Randy Arnold, *Partner*
Vanessa Midgley, *Shareholder*
Mir Ali, *President*
Nicole Auyang, *President*
EMP: 1000 **EST:** 1874
SQ FT: 30,000
SALES: 3.1B **Publicly Held**
SIC: 6022 State commercial banks
PA: Bnp Paribas
Hello BankU
Paris
140 144-546

(P-9419)
BANNER BANK
1750 Howe Ave Ste 100, Sacramento
(95825-3356)
PHONE..................916 648-2100
William Martin, *Branch Mgr*
EMP: 70 **Publicly Held**
SIC: 6022 State commercial banks
HQ: Banner Bank
10 S 1st Ave
Walla Walla WA 99362
800 272-9933

(P-9420)
BANNER BANK
1350 Rosecrans St, San Diego
(92106-2636)
PHONE..................619 243-7900
Michael R Peters, *Branch Mgr*
Millie McKibbin, *Site Mgr*
EMP: 50 **Publicly Held**
SIC: 6022 State commercial banks
HQ: Banner Bank
10 S 1st Ave
Walla Walla WA 99362
800 272-9933

(P-9421)
BBCN BANK
550 S Western Ave, Los Angeles
(90020-4208)
PHONE..................213 389-5550
EMP: 50
SALES (corp-wide): 638.5MM **Publicly Held**
SIC: 6022 State commercial banks
HQ: Bank Of Hope
3731 Wilshire Blvd # 400
Los Angeles CA 90010
213 639-1700

(P-9422)
BUSA SERVICING INC (DH)
Also Called: Banamex USA
2029 Century Park E # 4200, Los Angeles
(90067-2901)
PHONE..................310 203-3400
Manuel Sanchez Lugo, *Ch of Bd*
Rebecca Macieira-Kaufmann, *CEO*
Roger Johnston, *Ch Credit Ofcr*
Gabriel De La Peza, *Exec VP*
Theodore Michaels, *Exec VP*
EMP: 200

SALES (est): 33.7MM
SALES (corp-wide): 71.4B **Publicly Held**
WEB: www.ccbusa.com
SIC: 6022 State commercial banks
HQ: Banamex Usa Bancorp
2029 Century Park E Fl 42
Los Angeles CA 90067
310 203-3440

(P-9423)
BUSA SERVICING INC
2029 Century Park E # 4200, Los Angeles
(90067-2901)
PHONE..................800 222-1234
EMP: 116
SALES (corp-wide): 71.4B **Publicly Held**
SIC: 6022 State commercial banks
HQ: Busa Servicing, Inc.
2029 Century Park E # 4200
Los Angeles CA 90067
310 203-3400

(P-9424)
CATHAY BANK (HQ)
9650 Flair Dr, El Monte (91731-3005)
PHONE..................626 279-3698
Dunson K Cheng, *Ch of Bd*
Heng W Chen, *CFO*
James R Brewer, *Exec VP*
Edward K Kim, *Exec VP*
Irwin Wong, *Exec VP*
EMP: 125
SALES: 456.2MM
SALES (corp-wide): 612.4MM **Publicly Held**
WEB: www.newasiabk.com
SIC: 6022 State trust companies accepting
deposits, commercial
PA: Cathay General Bancorp
777 N Broadway
Los Angeles CA 90012
213 625-4700

(P-9425)
CATHAY BANK
Also Called: Monterey Park Branch
250 S Atlantic Blvd, Monterey Park
(91754-2778)
PHONE..................626 588-1911
Frank Chen, *Principal*
Joyce Tsao, *Opers Mgr*
EMP: 100
SALES (corp-wide): 612.4MM **Publicly Held**
WEB: www.newasiabk.com
SIC: 6022 6021 State commercial banks;
national commercial banks
HQ: Cathay Bank
9650 Flair Dr
El Monte CA 91731
626 279-3698

(P-9426)
CATHAY BANK
800 W 6th St Ste 200, Los Angeles
(90017-2705)
PHONE..................213 896-0098
Wilson Tang, *Manager*
EMP: 100
SALES (corp-wide): 612.4MM **Publicly Held**
WEB: www.newasiabk.com
SIC: 6022 6082 State commercial banks;
foreign trade & international banking institutions
HQ: Cathay Bank
9650 Flair Dr
El Monte CA 91731
626 279-3698

(P-9427)
CATHAY BANK
General Bank Credit ADM Dept
4128 Temple City Blvd, Rosemead
(91770-1550)
P.O. Box 3302, Los Angeles (90078-3302)
PHONE..................626 452-1582
Domenic Massei, *Manager*
EMP: 120
SALES (corp-wide): 612.4MM **Publicly Held**
WEB: www.newasiabk.com
SIC: 6022 State commercial banks

HQ: Cathay Bank
9650 Flair Dr
El Monte CA 91731
626 279-3698

(P-9428)
CENTRAL VALLEY CMNTY BANCORP (PA)
7100 N Fincl Dr Ste 101, Fresno (93720)
PHONE..................559 298-1775
James M Ford, *President*
Daniel J Doyle, *Ch of Bd*
David A Kinross, *CFO*
Patrick J Carman, *Ch Credit Ofcr*
Gary D Quisenberry, *Exec VP*
EMP: 231 **EST:** 2000
SALES: 68.2MM **Publicly Held**
WEB: www.cvcb.com
SIC: 6022 State commercial banks

(P-9429)
CENTRAL VALLEY COMMUNITY BANK
120 N Floral St, Visalia (93291-6202)
PHONE..................559 625-8733
Tobi Sumida, *COO*
Debbie Monteon, *Assistant VP*
EMP: 75
SALES (corp-wide): 68.2MM **Publicly Held**
SIC: 6022 State commercial banks
HQ: Central Valley Community Bank
600 Pollasky Ave
Clovis CA 93612
559 323-3384

(P-9430)
CENTRAL VALLEY COMMUNITY BANK
Also Called: Folsom Lake Bank
905 Sutter St Ste 100, Folsom (95630-2479)
PHONE..................916 985-8700
Shawna Thibado, *Officer*
Terry Cecchi, *Vice Pres*
David Levin, *Vice Pres*
Sharon Marshall, *Vice Pres*
Sherry Saville, *Vice Pres*
EMP: 50
SALES (corp-wide): 68.2MM **Publicly Held**
SIC: 6022 State commercial banks
HQ: Central Valley Community Bank
600 Pollasky Ave
Clovis CA 93612
559 323-3384

(P-9431)
CENTRAL VALLEY COMMUNITY BANK (HQ)
600 Pollasky Ave, Clovis (93612-1838)
PHONE..................559 323-3384
Daniel J Doyle, *CEO*
James M Ford, *President*
David A Kinross, *CFO*
Thomas L Sommer, *Ch Credit Ofcr*
James Kim, *Exec VP*
EMP: 117
SQ FT: 11,400
SALES: 48MM
SALES (corp-wide): 68.2MM **Publicly Held**
SIC: 6022 State commercial banks
PA: Central Valley Community Bancorp
7100 N Fincl Dr Ste 101
Fresno CA 93720
559 298-1775

(P-9432)
CITIZENS BUSINESS BANK (HQ)
701 N Haven Ste 350, Ontario (91764-4920)
P.O. Box 51000 (91761-1087)
PHONE..................909 980-4030
Toll Free:..................877 -
Christopher D Myers, *President*
D Linn Wiley, *Ch of Bd*
Edward Mosqueda, *President*
Al Vanderploeg, *President*
Edward J Biebrich Jr, *CFO*
EMP: 150
SQ FT: 23,000

SALES: 329MM
SALES (corp-wide): 329.3MM **Publicly Held**
WEB: www.cbbank.com
SIC: 6022 State trust companies accepting deposits, commercial
PA: Cvb Financial Corp.
701 N Haven Ave Ste 350
Ontario CA 91764
909 980-4030

(P-9433)
CITIZENS BUSINESS BANK
1401 Dove St Ste 100, Newport Beach (92660-2425)
PHONE..................949 440-5200
Christopher D Myers, *President*
Kathy Elam, *Vice Pres*
Sandra Velasquez, *Broker*
EMP: 90
SALES (corp-wide): 329.3MM **Publicly Held**
SIC: 6022 State trust companies accepting deposits, commercial
HQ: Citizens Business Bank
701 N Haven Ave Ste 350
Ontario CA 91764
909 980-4030

(P-9434)
CITIZENS BUSINESS BANK
460 Serra Madre Villa Ave, Pasadena (91107-2967)
PHONE..................626 577-1700
EMP: 50
SALES (corp-wide): 329.3MM **Publicly Held**
SIC: 6022 6029 State trust companies accepting deposits, commercial; commercial banks
HQ: Citizens Business Bank
701 N Haven Ave Ste 350
Ontario CA 91764
909 980-4030

(P-9435)
CITIZENS BUSINESS BANK
4100 W Alameda Ave # 101, Burbank (91505-4153)
PHONE..................818 843-0707
Edward J Mylett Jr, *Senior VP*
EMP: 52
SALES (corp-wide): 329.3MM **Publicly Held**
SIC: 6022 State commercial banks
HQ: Citizens Business Bank
701 N Haven Ave Ste 350
Ontario CA 91764
909 980-4030

(P-9436)
CITIZENS BUSINESS BANK
Also Called: Downtown Business Fincl Ctr
1230 17th St, Bakersfield (93301-4609)
PHONE..................661 281-0300
Bart Hill, *Branch Mgr*
Cindy Trejo, *Vice Pres*
Velma Munis, *Controller*
Chris Rhodes, *Mfg Staff*
EMP: 98
SALES (corp-wide): 329.3MM **Publicly Held**
SIC: 6022 State trust companies accepting deposits, commercial
HQ: Citizens Business Bank
701 N Haven Ave Ste 350
Ontario CA 91764
909 980-4030

(P-9437)
COMPASS BANK
201 N Main St, Manteca (95336-4632)
PHONE..................209 239-1381
Grace Henderson, *Branch Mgr*
EMP: 364 **Privately Held**
WEB: www.guarantybank.com
SIC: 6022 State commercial banks
HQ: Compass Bank
15 20th St S Ste 100
Birmingham AL 35233
205 297-1986

(P-9438)
COMPASS BANK
2427 W Hammer Ln, Stockton (95209-2367)
PHONE..................209 473-6925
Gabriel Riley, *Branch Mgr*
EMP: 364 **Privately Held**
WEB: www.guarantybank.com
SIC: 6022 State commercial banks
HQ: Compass Bank
15 20th St S Ste 100
Birmingham AL 35233
205 297-1986

(P-9439)
COMPASS BANK
2562 Pacific Ave, Stockton (95204-4438)
PHONE..................209 939-3288
Brian Stemen, *Branch Mgr*
Hortencia Torres, *Sales Staff*
EMP: 364 **Privately Held**
WEB: www.guarantybank.com
SIC: 6022 State commercial banks
HQ: Compass Bank
15 20th St S Ste 100
Birmingham AL 35233
205 297-1986

(P-9440)
EAST WEST BANK (HQ)
135 N Ls Rbls Ave 100, Pasadena (91101)
PHONE..................626 768-6000
Dominic Ng, *Ch of Bd*
Donald S Chow, *President*
Maureen Finn, *President*
Betty Liu, *President*
Thomas J Tolda, *CFO*
EMP: 300
SQ FT: 18,000
SALES: 1.5B
SALES (corp-wide): 1.5B **Publicly Held**
WEB: www.eastwest.com
SIC: 6022 State commercial banks
PA: East West Bancorp, Inc.
135 N Los Robles Ave Fl 7
Pasadena CA 91101
626 768-6000

(P-9441)
EAST WEST BANK
555 Montgomery St Bsmt, San Francisco (94111-2516)
PHONE..................415 391-8912
Michael Kay, *Branch Mgr*
Ernie Fung, *Vice Pres*
Christian Sporl, *Vice Pres*
Vincent Chan, *Technician*
Abid Rahman, *Technology*
EMP: 200
SALES (corp-wide): 1.5B **Publicly Held**
WEB: www.ibankunited.com
SIC: 6022 State commercial banks
HQ: East West Bank
135 N Ls Rbls Ave 100
Pasadena CA 91101
626 768-6000

(P-9442)
EXCHANGE BANK
2 E Washington St, Petaluma (94952-3197)
PHONE..................707 762-5555
Rick Mossy, *Branch Mgr*
John Meiscahn, *Manager*
EMP: 53 **Privately Held**
WEB: www.exchangebank.com
SIC: 6022 State trust companies accepting deposits, commercial
HQ: Exchange Bank
440 Aviation Blvd
Santa Rosa CA 95403
707 524-3000

(P-9443)
EXCHANGE BANK
6290 Commerce Blvd, Rohnert Park (94928-2166)
P.O. Box 1008 (94927-1008)
PHONE..................707 584-7300
R Marraffino, *Manager*
EMP: 450
SQ FT: 2,500 **Privately Held**
WEB: www.exchangebank.com
SIC: 6022 State commercial banks

HQ: Exchange Bank
440 Aviation Blvd
Santa Rosa CA 95403
707 524-3000

(P-9444)
FARMERS MERCHANTS BNK LONG BCH (HQ)
Also Called: F&M Bank
302 Pine Ave, Long Beach (90802-2326)
P.O. Box 1370 (90801-1370)
PHONE..................562 437-0011
W Henry Walker, *CEO*
Amanda Blanton, *President*
Lamonte Lee, *President*
Larry Prible, *President*
Kenneth G Walker, *President*
EMP: 130
SQ FT: 150,000
SALES: 265.7MM **Privately Held**
WEB: www.fmb.com
SIC: 6022 6029 State trust companies accepting deposits, commercial; commercial banks

(P-9445)
FARMERS MERCHANTS BNK LONG BCH
1695 Adolfo Lopez Dr, Seal Beach (90740-5620)
PHONE..................562 430-4724
Leon Aiossa, *Manager*
EMP: 150 **Privately Held**
WEB: www.fmb.com
SIC: 6022 6029 State trust companies accepting deposits, commercial; commercial banks
HQ: Farmers & Merchants Bank Of Long Beach
302 Pine Ave
Long Beach CA 90802
562 437-0011

(P-9446)
FARMERS MRCHANTS BNK CENTL CAL
8799 Elk Grove Blvd, Elk Grove (95624-1742)
PHONE..................916 394-3200
Patti Ruiz, *Manager*
EMP: 214
SALES (corp-wide): 131.3MM **Publicly Held**
WEB: www.fmbonline.com
SIC: 6022 6021 State commercial banks; national commercial banks
HQ: Farmers & Merchants Bank Of Central California
121 W Pine St
Lodi CA 95240
209 367-2300

(P-9447)
FIRST CHOICE BANK
420 E 3rd St Ste 100, Los Angeles (90013-1645)
PHONE..................213 617-0082
EMP: 65
SALES (corp-wide): 45.8MM **Publicly Held**
SIC: 6022 State commercial banks
HQ: First Choice Bank
17785 Center Court Dr N # 750
Cerritos CA 90703
562 345-9092

(P-9448)
FIRST CHOICE BANK (HQ)
17785 Center Court Dr N # 750, Cerritos (90703-9310)
PHONE..................562 345-9092
Robert Franko, *Principal*
Yvonne Chen, *CFO*
Gene May, *Ch Credit Ofcr*
Homer Chan, *Bd of Directors*
Lorraine Lee, *Officer*
EMP: 73
SQ FT: 6,000
SALES: 36.4MM
SALES (corp-wide): 45.8MM **Publicly Held**
WEB: www.firstchoicebankca.com
SIC: 6022 State trust companies accepting deposits, commercial

PA: First Choice Bancorp
17785 Center Court Dr N # 750
Cerritos CA 90703
562 345-9092

(P-9449)
FIRST NORTHERN BANK OF DIXON (HQ)
Also Called: First Northern Community
195 N 1st St, Dixon (95620-3025)
P.O. Box 547 (95620-0547)
PHONE....................707 678-4422
Owen J Onsum, *President*
Jeremiah Z Smith, *COO*
Louise A Walker, *CFO*
Joe T Danelson, *Ch Credit Ofcr*
T Joe Danelson, *Ch Credit Ofcr*
EMP: 59 EST: 1910
SQ FT: 14,000
SALES: 48.1MM **Publicly Held**
SIC: 6022 State trust companies accepting deposits, commercial

(P-9450)
FIRST REGIONAL BANCORP
1801 Century Park E # 800, Los Angeles (90067-2302)
PHONE....................310 552-1776
H Anthony Gartshore, *President*
Gary M Horgan, *Ch of Bd*
Elizabeth Thompson, *CFO*
Lawrence J Sherman, *Vice Ch Bd*
Thomas E McCullough, *Admin Sec*
EMP: 288
SQ FT: 19,734
SALES (est): 46.1MM **Privately Held**
WEB: www.firstregional.com
SIC: 6022 State commercial banks

(P-9451)
FIRST REPUBLIC BANK
750 Redwood Hwy Frontage # 1218, Mill Valley (94941-2483)
PHONE....................415 389-0880
Vince Franceschi, *Branch Mgr*
Bryce Brownlie, *Branch Mgr*
Ryan Schwarz, *Analyst*
EMP: 162
SALES (corp-wide): 2.9B **Publicly Held**
SIC: 6022 State commercial banks
PA: First Republic Bank
111 Pine St Fl 2
San Francisco CA 94111
415 392-1400

(P-9452)
FIRST REPUBLIC BANK
44 Montgomery St Ste 110, San Francisco (94104-4600)
PHONE....................415 392-3888
Monica Brazil, *Manager*
EMP: 127
SALES (corp-wide): 2.9B **Publicly Held**
WEB: www.firstrepublic.com
SIC: 6022 State commercial banks
PA: First Republic Bank
111 Pine St Fl 2
San Francisco CA 94111
415 392-1400

(P-9453)
FIRST REPUBLIC BANK
2550 Sand Hill Rd Ste 100, Menlo Park (94025-7095)
PHONE....................650 233-8880
Gayle Nickel, *Branch Mgr*
Samir Kaji, *Officer*
Jovee Encinas, *Sales Mgr*
Trish Cashman, *Director*
Jessica Gordon, *Manager*
EMP: 127
SALES (corp-wide): 2.9B **Publicly Held**
SIC: 6022 State commercial banks
PA: First Republic Bank
111 Pine St Fl 2
San Francisco CA 94111
415 392-1400

(P-9454)
FIRST REPUBLIC BANK
888 S Figueroa St Ste 100, Los Angeles (90017-5325)
PHONE....................213 239-8883
Sev Araradian, *Branch Mgr*
EMP: 127

SALES (corp-wide): 2.9B **Publicly Held**
SIC: 6022 State commercial banks
PA: First Republic Bank
111 Pine St Fl 2
San Francisco CA 94111
415 392-1400

(P-9455)
FIRST REPUBLIC BANK
224 Brookwood Rd, Orinda (94563-3015)
PHONE....................925 254-8993
Dina Zapanta, *Branch Mgr*
EMP: 127
SALES (corp-wide): 2.9B **Publicly Held**
SIC: 6022 State commercial banks
PA: First Republic Bank
111 Pine St Fl 2
San Francisco CA 94111
415 392-1400

(P-9456)
FIRST REPUBLIC BANK
1280 4th Ave, San Diego (92101-4294)
PHONE....................619 238-9088
EMP: 122
SALES (corp-wide): 2.9B **Publicly Held**
SIC: 6022 State commercial banks
PA: First Republic Bank
111 Pine St Fl 2
San Francisco CA 94111
415 392-1400

(P-9457)
FIRST REPUBLIC BANK
653 Irving St, San Francisco (94122-2401)
PHONE....................415 564-8881
EMP: 122
SALES (corp-wide): 2.9B **Publicly Held**
SIC: 6022 State commercial banks
PA: First Republic Bank
111 Pine St Fl 2
San Francisco CA 94111
415 392-1400

(P-9458)
FIRST REPUBLIC BANK
1355 Market St Ste 140, San Francisco (94103-1337)
PHONE....................415 487-0888
EMP: 122
SALES (corp-wide): 2.9B **Publicly Held**
SIC: 6022 State commercial banks
PA: First Republic Bank
111 Pine St Fl 2
San Francisco CA 94111
415 392-1400

(P-9459)
FIRST REPUBLIC BANK
405 Howard St Ste 110, San Francisco (94105-2665)
PHONE....................415 975-3877
EMP: 122
SALES (corp-wide): 2.9B **Publicly Held**
SIC: 6022 State commercial banks
PA: First Republic Bank
111 Pine St Fl 2
San Francisco CA 94111
415 392-1400

(P-9460)
FREMONT BANK (HQ)
39150 Fremont Blvd, Fremont (94538-1313)
P.O. Box 5101 (94537-5101)
PHONE....................510 505-5226
Morris Hyman, *Ch of Bd*
Andy Mastorakis, *President*
Bradford L Anderson, *CEO*
Ron Wagner, *CFO*
Michael J Wallace, *Chairman*
EMP: 250
SQ FT: 20,000
SALES: 195.2MM
SALES (corp-wide): 195.5MM **Privately Held**
WEB: www.fremontbank.com
SIC: 6022 State commercial banks
PA: Fremont Bancorporation
39150 Fremont Blvd
Fremont CA 94538
510 792-2300

(P-9461)
GREAT WESTERN BANCORP INC
706 S Hill St, Los Angeles (90014-2711)
PHONE....................213 622-1895
James Tolich, *Branch Mgr*
EMP: 291
SALES (corp-wide): 497.7MM **Publicly Held**
SIC: 6022 State commercial banks
PA: Great Western Bancorp, Inc.
225 S Main Ave
Sioux Falls SD 57104
605 334-2548

(P-9462)
HANMI BANK (HQ)
3660 Wilshire Blvd Ph A, Los Angeles (90010-2387)
PHONE....................213 382-2200
Joon H Lee, *Ch of Bd*
Susan Kim, *President*
Chong Guk Kum, *President*
Vanessa Padilla, *President*
Jenny Park, *President*
EMP: 123 EST: 1981
SQ FT: 35,000
SALES: 242.1MM
SALES (corp-wide): 242.7MM **Publicly Held**
WEB: www.hanmi.com
SIC: 6022 State commercial banks
PA: Hanmi Financial Corporation
3660 Wilshire Blvd Penths
Los Angeles CA 90010
213 382-2200

(P-9463)
HERITAGE BANK OF COMMERCE (HQ)
150 Almaden Blvd Lbby, San Jose (95113-2010)
PHONE....................408 947-6900
Walter Kaczmarek, *CEO*
Keith Wilton, *President*
Michael Ong, *Ch Credit Ofcr*
John Angelesco, *Officer*
Lawrence D McGovern, *Officer*
EMP: 120
SQ FT: 36,000
SALES: 116.4MM
SALES (corp-wide): 116.5MM **Publicly Held**
WEB: www.heritagebankofcommerce.com
SIC: 6022 State trust companies accepting deposits, commercial
PA: Heritage Commerce Corp
150 Almaden Blvd Lbby
San Jose CA 95113
408 947-6900

(P-9464)
ISRAEL DISCOUNT BANK NEW YORK
Also Called: Downtown Los Angeles Branch
888 S Figueroa St Ste 550, Los Angeles (90017-5306)
PHONE....................213 861-6440
Leon Recanati, *Principal*
Lorraine Drasser, *Vice Pres*
EMP: 177
SALES (corp-wide): 2.2B **Privately Held**
SIC: 6022 State commercial banks
HQ: Israel Discount Bank Of New York
511 5th Ave
New York NY 10017
212 551-8500

(P-9465)
LOS ROBLES BANK
33 W Thousand Oaks Blvd, Thousand Oaks (91360-4416)
P.O. Box 1438 (91358-0438)
PHONE....................805 373-6763
Fax: 805 379-2857
EMP: 52
SQ FT: 11,000
SALES (est): 5.3MM
SALES (corp-wide): 5.2B **Privately Held**
SIC: 6022
HQ: Mufg Americas Holdings Corporation
1251 Ave Of The Americas
New York NY 10020
212 782-6800

(P-9466)
MECHANICS BANK
P.O. Box 5610 (94547-5610)
PHONE....................510 741-7545
Carl Clark, *Officer*
Madhuri Anji, *Vice Pres*
Alexey Bulankov, *Vice Pres*
Chad Mallory, *Technology*
Osbaldo Garcia, *Finance Mgr*
EMP: 56
SQ FT: 69,184
SALES (corp-wide): 54.2MM **Privately Held**
SIC: 6022 State commercial banks
HQ: The Mechanics Bank
1111 Civic Dr
Walnut Creek CA 94596
800 797-6324

(P-9467)
MUFG UNION BANK FOUNDATION
445 S Figueroa St Ste 710, Los Angeles (90071-1615)
PHONE....................213 236-5000
Masashi Oka, *President*
John F Harrigan, *Ch of Bd*
Robert Cole, *Officer*
Jose Dizon, *Officer*
Richard Faulkner, *Officer*
EMP: 4200
SALES (est): 399.2MM **Privately Held**
SIC: 6022 State commercial banks

(P-9468)
ONEUNITED BANK
Also Called: Family Savings Bank
3683 Crenshaw Blvd, Los Angeles (90016-4890)
PHONE....................323 295-3381
Kevin Cohee, *Ch of Bd*
John Trotter, *CFO*
Nila Johnson, *Loan Officer*
EMP: 72
SALES (corp-wide): 27.4MM **Privately Held**
SIC: 6022 State commercial banks
PA: Oneunited Bank
100 Franklin St Ste 600
Boston MA 02110
617 457-4400

(P-9469)
OP BANCORP
1000 Wilshire Blvd # 500, Los Angeles (90017-2462)
PHONE....................213 892-9999
Min J Kim, *President*
Brian Choi, *Ch of Bd*
Christine Y OH, *CFO*
EMP: 129 EST: 2016
SQ FT: 15,239
SALES: 49.2MM **Privately Held**
SIC: 6022 State commercial banks

(P-9470)
PACIFIC CAST BNKERS BANCSHARES (PA)
1676 N Calif Blvd Ste 300, Walnut Creek (94596-4185)
PHONE....................415 399-1900
Steven A Brown, *President*
Michael Douhren, *CFO*
Nino Petroni, *Ch Credit Ofcr*
Tracy Holcomb, *Exec VP*
EMP: 65 EST: 1996
SQ FT: 16,000
SALES: 21.1MM **Privately Held**
WEB: www.pcbb.com
SIC: 6022 State commercial banks

(P-9471)
PACIFIC COAST BANKERS BANK
1676 N Calif Blvd Ste 300, Walnut Creek (94596-4185)
PHONE....................415 399-1900
Steve Brown, *President*
Nino Petroni, *COO*
Eric Davis, *Senior VP*
EMP: 60
SALES: 40.7MM
SALES (corp-wide): 21.1MM **Privately Held**
SIC: 6022 State commercial banks

PA: Pacific Coast Bankers' Bancshares
1676 N Calif Blvd Ste 300
Walnut Creek CA 94596
415 399-1900

(P-9472)
PACIFIC MERCANTILE BANK (HQ)
Also Called: PMBC
949 S Coast Dr Ste 300, Costa Mesa
(92626-7733)
PHONE.................................714 438-2500
Steven Buster, *President*
Neil B Kornswiet, *President*
Thomas M Vertin, *President*
Robert E Sjogren, *COO*
Nancy A Gray, *CFO*
EMP: 50
SALES: 53.9MM
SALES (corp-wide): 55.9MM **Publicly Held**
SIC: **6022** 6712 State trust companies accepting deposits, commercial; bank holding companies
PA: Pacific Mercantile Bancorp
949 S Coast Dr Ste 300
Costa Mesa CA 92626
714 438-2500

(P-9473)
PACIFIC PREMIER BANK (HQ)
17901 Von Karman Ave, Irvine
(92614-6297)
PHONE.................................714 431-4000
Steven R Gardner, *President*
Jeff C Jones, *Ch of Bd*
Ronald J Nicolas Jr, *CFO*
Kent Smith, *CFO*
Donn Jakosky, *Ch Credit Ofcr*
EMP: 104
SQ FT: 36,159
SALES: 298.1MM **Publicly Held**
SIC: **6022** State commercial banks

(P-9474)
PACIFIC PREMIER BANK
333 S Grand Ave, Los Angeles
(90071-1504)
PHONE.................................213 626-0085
EMP: 78 **Publicly Held**
SIC: **6022** State trust companies accepting deposits, commercial
HQ: Pacific Premier Bank
17901 Von Karman Ave
Irvine CA 92614
714 431-4000

(P-9475)
PACIFIC WESTERN BANK
818 W 7th St Ste 220, Los Angeles
(90017-3449)
PHONE.................................213 430-7000
EMP: 112
SALES (corp-wide): 1.1B **Publicly Held**
SIC: **6022** State commercial banks
HQ: Pacific Western Bank
9701 Wilshire Blvd # 700
Beverly Hills CA 90212
310 887-8500

(P-9476)
PACIFIC WESTERN BANK
11150 W Olympic Blvd # 100, Los Angeles
(90064-1817)
PHONE.................................310 996-9100
Chris Bower, *Manager*
John Braunschweiger, *Senior VP*
Todd Savitz, *Senior VP*
Soledad Escobedo, *Vice Pres*
EMP: 50
SALES (corp-wide): 1.1B **Publicly Held**
WEB: www.pacificwesternbank.com
SIC: **6022** State commercial banks
HQ: Pacific Western Bank
9701 Wilshire Blvd # 700
Beverly Hills CA 90212
310 887-8500

(P-9477)
PACIFIC WESTERN BANK
9955 Mission Gorge Rd, Santee
(92071-3841)
PHONE.................................619 562-6400
Bruce Ives, *Manager*
EMP: 60

SALES (corp-wide): 1.1B **Publicly Held**
WEB: www.pacificwesternbank.com
SIC: **6022** State trust companies accepting deposits, commercial
HQ: Pacific Western Bank
9701 Wilshire Blvd # 700
Beverly Hills CA 90212
310 887-8500

(P-9478)
PACIFIC WESTERN BANK
Also Called: Los Padres Bank
610 Alamo Pintado Rd, Solvang
(93463-2202)
PHONE.................................805 688-6644
Craig Cerny, *President*
EMP: 189
SALES (corp-wide): 1.1B **Publicly Held**
SIC: **6022** State commercial banks
HQ: Pacific Western Bank
9701 Wilshire Blvd # 700
Beverly Hills CA 90212
310 887-8500

(P-9479)
PREMIER COMMERCIAL BANCORP
2400 E Katella Ave # 125, Anaheim
(92806-5920)
PHONE.................................714 978-2400
Kenneth J Cosgrove, *Ch of Bd*
Ashokkumar Patel, *President*
Viktor R Uehlinger, *CFO*
Stephen W Pihl, *Exec VP*
EMP: 64
SALES: 22.3MM **Privately Held**
SIC: **6022** State commercial banks

(P-9480)
PROVIDENT SAVINGS BANK LLC
Also Called: Provident Bank
3756 Central Ave, Riverside (92506-2469)
PHONE.................................951 686-6060
Craig Blunden, *Mng Member*
Robert G Schrader, *COO*
Donavon P Ternes, *CFO*
Donald L Blanchard, *Senior VP*
Lilian Brunner, *Senior VP*
EMP: 100
SALES: 45.5K **Privately Held**
SIC: **6022** State commercial banks

(P-9481)
RABOBANK NATIONAL ASSOCIATION
301 Main St, Salinas (93901-2700)
PHONE.................................831 422-6642
Ida Chan, *Principal*
Hakan Erdinc, *Vice Pres*
Russell Mills, *Vice Pres*
Lisa Ostarello, *Broker*
Alan Usher, *Director*
EMP: 125
SALES (corp-wide): 16.5B **Privately Held**
WEB: www.community-bnk.com
SIC: **6022** 6163 6029 State commercial banks; loan brokers; commercial banks
HQ: Rabobank, National Association
915 Highland Pointe Dr
Roseville CA 95678
760 352-5000

(P-9482)
RCB CORPORATION (PA)
Also Called: River City Bank
2485 Natomas Park Dr # 100, Sacramento
(95833-2937)
P.O. Box 15247 (95851-0247)
PHONE.................................916 567-2600
Stephen Fleming, *President*
Shawn Devlin, *Ch of Bd*
Anker Christensen, *CFO*
Jon Kelly, *Founder*
Pat McHone, *Ch Credit Ofcr*
EMP: 80
SQ FT: 34,000
SALES (est): 72MM **Privately Held**
SIC: **6022** State commercial banks

(P-9483)
RIVER CITY BANK (HQ)
2485 Natomas Park Dr # 100, Sacramento
(95833-2975)
P.O. Box 15247 (95851-0247)
PHONE.................................916 567-2600
Stephen A Fleming, *President*
Camille Lasky, *President*
Jay Murray, *President*
Anker Christensen, *CFO*
Amii Barnard-Bahn, *Senior VP*
EMP: 80
SQ FT: 15,000
SALES: 71.1MM
SALES (corp-wide): 72MM **Privately Held**
WEB: www.rcbank.com
SIC: **6022** State commercial banks
PA: Rcb Corporation
2485 Natomas Park Dr # 100
Sacramento CA 95833
916 567-2600

(P-9484)
SAEHAN BANK (PA)
3200 Wilshire Blvd # 700, Los Angeles
(90010-1333)
PHONE.................................213 368-7700
Dong IL Kim, *President*
Dong II Kim, *President*
EMP: 50
SQ FT: 12,000
SALES (est): 26.4MM **Privately Held**
SIC: **6022** State trust companies accepting deposits, commercial

(P-9485)
SAVINGS BANK MENDOCINO COUNTY (PA)
Also Called: SBMC
200 N School St, Ukiah (95482-4811)
P.O. Box 3600 (95482-3600)
PHONE.................................707 462-6613
Charles B Mannon, *President*
Scott Yandell, *President*
Bruce Little, *CFO*
Devra Wolf, *Officer*
Dan Gill, *Exec VP*
EMP: 130 EST: 1903
SALES: 41.8MM **Privately Held**
WEB: www.savingsbank.com
SIC: **6022** State commercial banks

(P-9486)
SEACOAST COMMERCE BANK (HQ)
11939 Rancho Bernardo Rd # 200, San Diego (92128-2075)
PHONE.................................858 432-7000
Richard M Sanborn, *CEO*
Allan W Arendsee, *Ch of Bd*
David H Bartram, *COO*
Jay Jung, *Officer*
Ernesto M Arredondo Jr, *Exec VP*
EMP: 60
SALES: 45.3MM **Privately Held**
WEB: www.seacoastcommercebank.com
SIC: **6022** State commercial banks
PA: Seacoast Commerce Banc Holdings
11939 Rancho Bernardo Rd
San Diego CA 92128
858 432-7000

(P-9487)
SIERRA BANCORP
7029 N Ingram Ave Ste 101, Fresno
(93650-1091)
PHONE.................................559 449-8145
Frank Oliver, *Principal*
EMP: 247
SALES (corp-wide): 102.7MM **Publicly Held**
SIC: **6022** State commercial banks
PA: Sierra Bancorp
86 N Main St
Porterville CA 93257
559 782-4900

(P-9488)
STANDARD CHARTERED BANK
601 S Figueroa St # 2775, Los Angeles
(90017-5877)
PHONE.................................626 639-8000
Jim Mc Cabe, *CEO*
EMP: 225

SALES (corp-wide): 21.1B **Privately Held**
SIC: **6022** 6282 6029 State trust companies accepting deposits, commercial; investment advisory service; commercial banks
HQ: Standard Chartered Bank
1 Basinghall Avenue
London EC2V
207 885-8888

(P-9489)
SUNWEST BANK (DH)
2050 Main St Fl 3, Irvine (92614-8255)
P.O. Box 1028, Tustin (92781-1028)
PHONE.................................714 730-4441
Glenn Gray, *President*
Chad Canter, *President*
Carson Lappetito, *President*
Chris Walsh, *President*
Jason Raefski, *CFO*
EMP: 50
SQ FT: 30,000
SALES: 54.6MM **Privately Held**
SIC: **6022** State commercial banks

(P-9490)
SVB FINANCIAL GROUP (PA)
3003 Tasman Dr, Santa Clara
(95054-1191)
PHONE.................................408 654-7400
Roger F Dunbar, *Ch of Bd*
Sulu Mamdani, *Managing Prtnr*
Greg W Becker, *President*
Philip C Cox, *President*
Michael L Dreyer, *COO*
EMP: 67
SQ FT: 213,625
SALES: 2B **Publicly Held**
SIC: **6022** State commercial banks

(P-9491)
TORREY PINES BANK (HQ)
12220 El Camino Real # 200, San Diego
(92130-2091)
PHONE.................................858 523-4600
Fax: 858 755-0875
EMP: 103
SALES (est): 19.1MM
SALES (corp-wide): 554.9MM **Publicly Held**
WEB: www.torreypinesbank.com
SIC: **6022**
PA: Western Alliance Bancorporation
1 E Wshington St Ste 1400
Phoenix AZ 85004
602 389-3500

(P-9492)
UMPQUA BANK
7777 Alvarado Rd Ste 515, La Mesa
(91942-8306)
PHONE.................................619 668-5159
EMP: 81
SALES (corp-wide): 1.2B **Publicly Held**
SIC: **6022**
HQ: Umpqua Bank
445 Se Main St
Roseburg OR 97470
541 440-3961

(P-9493)
VALLEY REPUBLIC BANK
5000 California Ave # 110, Bakersfield
(93309-0711)
PHONE.................................661 371-2000
Bruce Jay, *President*
Cindy Talley, *Officer*
Stephen M Annis, *Exec VP*
Steve Annis, *Exec VP*
Phil McLaughlin, *Exec VP*
EMP: 85
SQ FT: 8,000
SALES: 23.2MM **Privately Held**
SIC: **6022** State commercial banks

(P-9494)
WESTERN ALLIANCE BANK
Also Called: Bridge Bank
55 Almaden Blvd Ste 200, San Jose
(95113-1619)
PHONE.................................408 423-8500
Lee Shodiss, *Vice Pres*
EMP: 70

PRODUCTS & SVCS

SALES (corp-wide): 890.8MM **Publicly Held**
SIC: 6022 8742 State commercial banks; management consulting services
HQ: Western Alliance Bank
1 E Wshington St Ste 1400
Phoenix AZ 85004

6029 Commercial Banks,

(P-9495)
BANK OF TOKYO LTD
Also Called: Union Bank
445 S Figueroa St # 2700, Los Angeles (90071-1602)
PHONE..................213 488-3700
Jiro Ishicaka, *Branch Mgr*
Bevery Henretty, *Vice Pres*
Jeff Orsborn, *Vice Pres*
EMP: 625
SALES (corp-wide): 56.9B **Privately Held**
SIC: 6029 Commercial banks
HQ: Mufg Bank, Ltd.
2-7-1, Marunouchi
Chiyoda-Ku TKY 100-0
332 401-111

(P-9496)
BENEFICIAL STATE BANK (HQ)
Also Called: Onecalifornia Bank
1438 Webster St Ste 100, Oakland (94612-3229)
P.O. Box 400, Ilwaco WA (98624-0400)
PHONE..................510 550-8420
Kat Taylor, *CEO*
Randell Leach, *President*
Thu Ncuyen, *CFO*
Richard Fletcher, *Exec VP*
Cem Bolkan, *Senior VP*
EMP: 57
SALES: 42.7MM **Privately Held**
SIC: 6029 Commercial banks

(P-9497)
CALIFORNIA FIRST NATIONAL BANK
Also Called: UNIVERSITY LEASE
28 Executive Park Ste 200, Irvine (92614-4741)
P.O. Box 2509, Santa Ana (92707-0509)
PHONE..................949 255-0500
S Leslie Jewett, *President*
Glen T Tsuma, *Vice Chairman*
Yvonne Cattell, *CFO*
Darren Higuchi, *Senior VP*
Priscilla Douglas, *Administration*
EMP: 80
SQ FT: 36,000
SALES: 28.5MM
SALES (corp-wide): 36.6MM **Publicly Held**
WEB: www.calfirstbancorp.com
SIC: 6029 Commercial banks
PA: California First National Bancorp
28 Executive Park Ste 200
Irvine CA 92614
949 255-0500

(P-9498)
CENTRAL VALLEY COMMUNITY BANK
Clovis Community Bank RE Div
7100 N Fincl Dr Ste 101, Fresno (93720)
PHONE..................559 298-1775
Jeffrey Pace, *Manager*
Robert Elledge, *Vice Pres*
EMP: 230
SALES (corp-wide): 68.2MM **Publicly Held**
SIC: 6029 Commercial banks
HQ: Central Valley Community Bank
600 Pollasky Ave
Clovis CA 93612
559 323-3384

(P-9499)
CITIZENS BUSINESS BANK
255 E Rincon St Ste 312, Corona (92879-1369)
PHONE..................951 808-8940
Russell Moore, *Manager*
Mike Butler, *Manager*
EMP: 50

SALES (corp-wide): 329.3MM **Publicly Held**
WEB: www.communitybank-ca.com
SIC: 6029 Commercial banks
HQ: Citizens Business Bank
701 N Haven Ave Ste 350
Ontario CA 91764
909 980-4030

(P-9500)
COMMERCIAL FINANCE & L
12626 High Bluff Dr # 370, San Diego (92130-2074)
P.O. Box 2562, Del Mar (92014-1862)
PHONE..................858 866-8525
Vadim Garry Lyulkin, *President*
Dean Lyulkin, *CFO*
Robert Esquivel, *Vice Pres*
ARI Gold, *Vice Pres*
Dean G Lyulkin, *Principal*
EMP: 65
SALES (est): 24.7MM **Privately Held**
WEB: www.bankofcardiff.com
SIC: 6029 Commercial banks

(P-9501)
COMPASS BANK
195 W Ontario Ave, Corona (92882-5276)
PHONE..................951 279-7071
Eileen Blaga, *Branch Mgr*
EMP: 364 **Privately Held**
SIC: 6029 Commercial banks
HQ: Compass Bank
15 20th St S Ste 100
Birmingham AL 35233
205 297-1986

(P-9502)
FIRST REPUBLIC BANK
101 Pine St, San Francisco (94111-5629)
PHONE..................415 392-1400
Brent Chapman, *Vice Pres*
Irene Lim, *Asst Mgr*
EMP: 80
SALES (corp-wide): 2.9B **Publicly Held**
SIC: 6029 Commercial banks
PA: First Republic Bank
111 Pine St Fl 2
San Francisco CA 94111
415 392-1400

(P-9503)
FIRST REPUBLIC BANK
1888 Century Park E # 200, Los Angeles (90067-1706)
PHONE..................310 712-1888
Simon Clark, *Branch Mgr*
Mary Deckebach, *Director*
Mark Sear, *Director*
Robert Skinner, *Director*
EMP: 65
SALES (corp-wide): 2.9B **Publicly Held**
SIC: 6029 Commercial banks
PA: First Republic Bank
111 Pine St Fl 2
San Francisco CA 94111
415 392-1400

(P-9504)
FIRST REPUBLIC BANK (PA)
111 Pine St Fl 2, San Francisco (94111-5606)
PHONE..................415 392-1400
James H Herbert II, *Ch of Bd*
Hafize Gaye Erkan, *President*
Jason C Bender, *COO*
Michael J Roffler, *CFO*
Katherine August-Dewilde, *Vice Ch Bd*
EMP: 332
SALES: 2.9B **Publicly Held**
WEB: www.firstrepublic.com
SIC: 6029 Commercial banks

(P-9505)
FIRST REPUBLIC BANK
1215 El Camino Real, Menlo Park (94025-4208)
PHONE..................650 470-8888
Andrea Jefferson, *Manager*
EMP: 203
SALES (corp-wide): 2.9B **Publicly Held**
SIC: 6029 Commercial banks
PA: First Republic Bank
111 Pine St Fl 2
San Francisco CA 94111
415 392-1400

(P-9506)
HSBC BUSINESS CREDIT (USA)
Also Called: Hsbc Bank USA NA
660 S Figueroa St, Los Angeles (90017-3442)
PHONE..................213 553-8089
Celia Anderson-Hayes, *Manager*
EMP: 85
SQ FT: 4,000
SALES (corp-wide): 79.6B **Privately Held**
SIC: 6029 Commercial banks
HQ: Hsbc Business Credit (Usa) Inc
452 5th Ave Fl 4
New York NY 10018
800 511-1918

(P-9507)
HSBC FINANCE CORPORATION
1420 El Paseo De Saratoga, San Jose (95130-1633)
PHONE..................408 796-3600
Cindy Shen, *Loan Officer*
EMP: 142
SALES (corp-wide): 79.6B **Privately Held**
SIC: 6029 Commercial banks
HQ: Hsbc Finance Corporation
1421 W Shure Dr Ste 100
Arlington Heights IL 60004
224 880-7000

(P-9508)
HSBC FINANCE CORPORATION
725 N Broadway, Los Angeles (90012-2819)
PHONE..................213 628-8167
Clarence Ho, *Branch Mgr*
EMP: 142
SALES (corp-wide): 79.6B **Privately Held**
SIC: 6029 Commercial banks
HQ: Hsbc Finance Corporation
1421 W Shure Dr Ste 100
Arlington Heights IL 60004
224 880-7000

(P-9509)
JPMORGAN CHASE BANK NAT ASSN
Also Called: Financial Division
1100 Palm Ave, Imperial Beach (91932-1619)
PHONE..................619 424-8197
Roger Debock, *Principal*
EMP: 50
SALES (corp-wide): 99.6B **Publicly Held**
SIC: 6029 Commercial banks
HQ: Jpmorgan Chase Bank, National Association
1111 Polaris Pkwy
Columbus OH 43240
614 436-3055

(P-9510)
LUTHER BURBANK CORPORATION
20 Pacifica Ste 600, Irvine (92618-3389)
PHONE..................949 428-8043
EMP: 55 **Publicly Held**
SIC: 6029 Commercial banks
PA: Luther Burbank Corporation
520 3rd St Fl 4
Santa Rosa CA 95401

(P-9511)
MANUFACTURERS BANK (DH)
515 S Figueroa St Fl 4, Los Angeles (90071-3301)
P.O. Box 556000 (90055-1000)
PHONE..................213 489-6200
Mitsugu Serizawa, *CEO*
Luis Gomez, *President*
Koichi Miyata, *President*
Dominic Rosales, *President*
Naresh Sheth, *President*
EMP: 164
SQ FT: 69,206
SALES: 88.9MM
SALES (corp-wide): 54.1B **Privately Held**
WEB: www.manubank.com
SIC: 6029 Commercial banks
HQ: Sumitomo Mitsui Banking Corporation
1-1-2, Marunouchi
Chiyoda-Ku TKY 100-0
332 821-111

(P-9512)
MECHANICS BANK (DH)
1111 Civic Dr, Walnut Creek (94596-3895)
PHONE..................800 797-6324
John Decero, *President*
Carl Webb, *Ch of Bd*
Michael Downer, *Vice Chairman*
Suman Raj, *President*
Nathan Duda, *CFO*
EMP: 110 EST: 1905
SQ FT: 77,000
SALES: 140.9MM
SALES (corp-wide): 54.2MM **Privately Held**
SIC: 6029 Commercial banks
HQ: Eb Acquisition Company Llc
200 Crescent Ct Ste 1350
Dallas TX 75201
214 871-5151

(P-9513)
MUFG BANK LTD
Also Called: Bank of Tokyo
777 S Figueroa St Ste 600, Los Angeles (90017-5806)
PHONE..................213 488-3700
Kim Amada, *Branch Mgr*
EMP: 100
SALES (corp-wide): 56.9B **Privately Held**
SIC: 6029 Commercial banks
HQ: Mufg Bank, Ltd.
1251 Ave Of The Americas
New York NY 10020

(P-9514)
N A TOMATOBANK
901 S Baldwin Ave, Arcadia (91007-6704)
PHONE..................626 759-9200
Charles Fenton, *CEO*
Lichen Herman, *President*
EMP: 57
SALES: 18MM
SALES (corp-wide): 17MM **Privately Held**
SIC: 6029 Commercial banks
PA: Tfc Holding Company
18605 Gale Ave Ste 238
City Of Industry CA 91748
626 363-9708

(P-9515)
OPUS BANK
200 W Commonwealth Ave, Fullerton (92832-1811)
PHONE..................714 578-7500
Stephen H Gordon, *Branch Mgr*
EMP: 110 **Publicly Held**
SIC: 6029 Commercial banks
PA: Opus Bank
19900 Macarthur Blvd # 1200
Irvine CA 92612

(P-9516)
SILICON VALLEY BANK (HQ)
3003 Tasman Dr, Santa Clara (95054-1191)
PHONE..................408 654-7400
Greg Becker, *CEO*
Beau Laskey, *Managing Prtnr*
Michael Dreyer, *COO*
Cecilia Shea, *CFO*
Michael Kruse, *Treasurer*
EMP: 592
SQ FT: 100,000
SALES: 1.8B
SALES (corp-wide): 2B **Publicly Held**
WEB: www.svbsecurities.com
SIC: 6029 Commercial banks
PA: Svb Financial Group
3003 Tasman Dr
Santa Clara CA 95054
408 654-7400

(P-9517)
TRI COUNTIES BANK (HQ)
63 Constitution Dr, Chico (95973-4937)
PHONE..................530 898-0300
William J Casey, *Ch of Bd*
Suzanne Youngs, *Shareholder*
Alex A Vereschagin Jr, *Ch of Bd*
Richard P Smith, *President*
John S Fleshood, *COO*
EMP: 75

SALES: 230.4MM
SALES (corp-wide): 231.4MM **Publicly Held**
WEB: www.tricountiesbank.com
SIC: **6029** 6163 Commercial banks; loan brokers
PA: Trico Bancshares
63 Constitution Dr
Chico CA 95973
530 898-0300

(P-9518)
TRI COUNTIES BANK
305 Railroad Ave Ste 1, Nevada City (95959-2854)
PHONE....................................530 478-6001
Eileen Counts, *Opers Mgr*
EMP: 91
SALES (corp-wide): 231.4MM **Publicly Held**
SIC: **6029** Commercial banks
HQ: Tri Counties Bank
63 Constitution Dr
Chico CA 95973
530 898-0300

(P-9519)
UNITI BANK (PA)
Also Called: UNITIBANK
6301 Beach Blvd Ste 100, Buena Park (90621-4032)
PHONE....................................888 733-2599
Joohak Kim, *President*
Christina Ahn, *Vice Pres*
Ngoc Nguyen, *Vice Pres*
Lawrence Park, *Vice Pres*
Stella Min, *Branch Mgr*
EMP: 59
SQ FT: 7,000
SALES: 16.8MM **Privately Held**
WEB: www.unitibank.com
SIC: **6029** Commercial banks

(P-9520)
WESTERN ALLIANCE BANK
455 Market St Ste 1050, San Francisco (94105-5409)
PHONE....................................415 230-4834
EMP: 70
SALES (corp-wide): 890.8MM **Publicly Held**
SIC: **6029** Commercial banks
HQ: Western Alliance Bank
1 E Wshington St Ste 1400
Phoenix AZ 85004
-

(P-9521)
WESTERN ALLIANCE BANK
7545 Irvine Center Dr # 200, Irvine (92618-2932)
PHONE....................................949 222-0855
EMP: 70
SALES (corp-wide): 890.8MM **Publicly Held**
SIC: **6029** Commercial banks
HQ: Western Alliance Bank
1 E Wshington St Ste 1400
Phoenix AZ 85004

6035 Federal Savings Institutions

(P-9522)
CITIBANK FSB (HQ)
1 Sansome St, San Francisco (94104-4448)
PHONE....................................415 627-6000
David A Brooks, *Ch of Bd*
Jay Compton, *President*
Edgar Ancona, *Treasurer*
Michael McCarthy, *Officer*
EMP: 300 EST: 1921
SQ FT: 20,000
SALES (est): 101.2MM
SALES (corp-wide): 71.4B **Publicly Held**
SIC: **6035** Federal savings banks
PA: Citigroup Inc.
388 Greenwich St
New York NY 10013
212 559-1000

(P-9523)
EL DORADO SAVINGS BANK (PA)
4040 El Dorado Rd, Placerville (95667-5269)
P.O. Box 1208 (95667-1208)
PHONE....................................530 622-1492
Thomas Meuser, *Ch of Bd*
George Cook Jr, *President*
Anne Wilson, *President*
William H Blucher, *CFO*
William Buechler, *CFO*
EMP: 55
SQ FT: 37,779
SALES: 58MM **Privately Held**
WEB: www.eldoradosavingsbank.com
SIC: **6035** Federal savings & loan associations

(P-9524)
JPMORGAN CHASE BANK NAT ASSN
400 E Main St Fl 2, Stockton (95202-3002)
PHONE....................................209 460-2888
Robert T Barnum, *Manager*
EMP: 950
SALES (corp-wide): 99.6B **Publicly Held**
SIC: **6035** 6211 Federal savings banks; security brokers & dealers
HQ: Jpmorgan Chase Bank, National Association
1111 Polaris Pkwy
Columbus OH 43240
614 436-3055

(P-9525)
MALAGA BANK FSB (HQ)
2514 Via Tejon, Palos Verdes Estates (90274-1311)
P.O. Box 908 (90274-0908)
PHONE....................................310 375-9000
Randy Bowers, *President*
Jasna Penich, *CFO*
John Tellenbach, *Ch Credit Ofcr*
Sacha Ohara, *Senior VP*
Mark Smith, *Senior VP*
EMP: 82
SQ FT: 5,000
SALES: 38.2MM
SALES (corp-wide): 8.2MM **Privately Held**
WEB: www.malagabank.com
SIC: **6035** Federal savings banks
PA: Malaga Financial Corporation
2514 Via Tejon
Palos Verdes Estates CA 90274
310 375-9000

(P-9526)
ONEWEST BANK NA
3500 E 7th St, Long Beach (90804-5137)
PHONE....................................562 433-0971
Fax: 562 433-0975
EMP: 56
SALES (corp-wide): 876.3MM **Privately Held**
SIC: **6035**
HQ: Onewest Bank N.A.
888 E Walnut St
Pasadena CA 91103
626 535-4300

(P-9527)
PACIFIC STATE BANCORP
1899 W March Ln, Stockton (95207-6402)
PHONE....................................209 870-3214
Rick D Simas, *President*
Justin R Garner, *CFO*
Gary A Stewart, *Ch Credit Ofcr*
EMP: 89
SALES (est): 564.3K **Privately Held**
WEB: www.pacificstatebank.com
SIC: **6035** Savings institutions, federally chartered

(P-9528)
PAN AMERICAN BANK FSB
18191 Von Karman Ave # 300, Irvine (92612-7106)
PHONE....................................949 224-1917
Jim Vagim, *President*
EMP: 350
SQ FT: 20,000

SALES: 2MM
SALES (corp-wide): 20.5MM **Privately Held**
WEB: www.panamerbank.com
SIC: **6035** Savings institutions, federally chartered
PA: United Panam Financial Corp.
1071 Camelback St Ste 100
Newport Beach CA 92660
949 224-1226

(P-9529)
PROVIDENT SAVINGS BANK (HQ)
6570 Magnolia Ave, Riverside (92506-2410)
P.O. Box 59998 (92517-1998)
PHONE....................................951 782-6177
Craig G Blunden, *Ch of Bd*
Donavon Ternes, *President*
Lee Sunarto, *Treasurer*
David S Weiant,
Richard L Gale, *Senior VP*
EMP: 57
SALES: 68.5MM **Publicly Held**
WEB: www.myprovident.com
SIC: **6035** Federal savings & loan associations

(P-9530)
PROVIDENT SAVINGS BANK
Also Called: Provident Bank
6674 Brockton Ave, Riverside (92506-3020)
PHONE....................................951 686-6060
Pam Cuthbertson, *Manager*
Debra Hill, *VP Human Res*
EMP: 100 **Publicly Held**
SIC: **6035** Federal savings & loan associations
HQ: Provident Savings Bank
6570 Magnolia Ave
Riverside CA 92506
951 782-6177

(P-9531)
TRACY BANCSHARES INC
1003 N Central Ave, Tracy (95376-3914)
PHONE....................................209 836-5111
Janis Mattos, *Branch Mgr*
EMP: 51
SQ FT: 11,500
SALES (est): 4MM **Privately Held**
SIC: **6035** Savings institutions, federally chartered

(P-9532)
UNIVERSAL BANK (PA)
3455 S Nogales St Fl 2, West Covina (91792-5106)
PHONE....................................626 854-2818
Frank Chang, *President*
Dwayne Matsuda, *President*
Edgar Gatchlian, *Vice Pres*
Denise Fletcher, *Human Res Mgr*
Bobbe Sigler, *Director*
EMP: 53
SQ FT: 28,223
SALES: 13.4MM **Privately Held**
WEB: www.universalbank.com
SIC: **6035** Federal savings banks

6036 Savings Institutions, Except Federal

(P-9533)
EAST WEST BANK
228 W Garvey Ave, Monterey Park (91754-1603)
PHONE....................................626 280-1688
John Lee, *Branch Mgr*
Joe Yuan, *Vice Pres*
EMP: 61
SALES (corp-wide): 1.5B **Publicly Held**
WEB: www.eastwest.com
SIC: **6036** Savings & loan associations, not federally chartered
HQ: East West Bank
135 N Ls Rbls Ave 100
Pasadena CA 91101
626 768-6000

(P-9534)
EXCHANGE BANK (HQ)
Also Called: Eb
440 Aviation Blvd, Santa Rosa (95403-1069)
P.O. Box 403 (95402-0403)
PHONE....................................707 524-3000
C William Reinking, *Ch of Bd*
Mary O Beseda, *President*
Kenn Cunningham, *President*
Bill Espindola, *President*
Pam Maslak, *President*
EMP: 135
SQ FT: 50,000
SALES: 106.6MM **Privately Held**
WEB: www.exchangebank.com
SIC: **6036** 8741 6022 State savings banks, not federally chartered; management services; state commercial banks

(P-9535)
LUTHER BURBANK SAVINGS (HQ)
500 3rd St, Santa Rosa (95401-6321)
P.O. Box 1783 (95402-1783)
PHONE....................................707 578-9216
John Biggs, *President*
Victor S Trione, *Ch of Bd*
Donna Baer, *Officer*
Derrick Pitts, *Officer*
Daisy Woskow, *Officer*
EMP: 50
SQ FT: 11,000
SALES: 181.7MM **Publicly Held**
WEB: www.lutherburbanksavings.com
SIC: **6036** 6035 Savings & loan associations, not federally chartered; federal savings & loan associations

(P-9536)
MALAGA FINANCIAL CORPORATION (PA)
2514 Via Tejon, Palos Verdes Estates (90274-1311)
PHONE....................................310 375-9000
Randy C Bowers, *President*
Jerry Donahue, *Ch of Bd*
Jasna Penich, *CFO*
Debbie Richardson, *Vice Pres*
Carmela Carroll, *Assistant VP*
EMP: 88
SALES (est): 8.2MM **Privately Held**
SIC: **6036** State savings banks, not federally chartered

6061 Federal Credit Unions

(P-9537)
1ST UNITED SERVICES CREDIT UN (PA)
5901 Gibraltar Dr, Pleasanton (94588-2718)
P.O. Box 11746 (94588-1746)
PHONE....................................800 649-0193
Victor Quint, *President*
Ed Renteria, *COO*
Shirley Sifuentes, *COO*
Victoria Pipkin, *CFO*
Steve Stone,
EMP: 60
SQ FT: 20,000
SALES: 32.7MM **Privately Held**
SIC: **6061** Federal credit unions

(P-9538)
ALTAONE FEDERAL CREDIT UNION (PA)
Also Called: ALTA ONE FCU
701 S China Lake Blvd, Ridgecrest (93555-5027)
P.O. Box 1209 (93556-1209)
PHONE....................................760 371-7000
Robert M Boland, *President*
George M Haslam, *CFO*
Linda Fisher, *Office Mgr*
Shannen Foreman, *Executive Asst*
Kelly Timmons, *Manager*
EMP: 114
SQ FT: 33,000
SALES: 27.5MM **Privately Held**
WEB: www.altaone.net
SIC: **6061** Federal credit unions

(P-9539)
AMERICAN FIRST CREDIT UNION (PA)
700 N Harbor Blvd, La Habra (90631-4026)
PHONE..................................562 691-1112
Jon Shigematsu, *CFO*
Tam Nguyen, *Vice Pres*
Brian Thompson,
EMP: 96
SQ FT: 10,000
SALES: 21.2MM **Privately Held**
SIC: 6061 Federal credit unions

(P-9540)
ARROWHEAD CENTRAL CREDIT UNION (PA)
8686 Haven Ave, Rancho Cucamonga (91730-9109)
P.O. Box 4100 (91729-4100)
PHONE..................................866 212-4333
Darin Woinarowicz, *CEO*
Raymond Mesler, *CFO*
Marie A Alonzo, *Chairman*
Doug Hallen, *Treasurer*
Tanya Padilla, *Officer*
EMP: 301 **EST:** 1949
SQ FT: 40,000
SALES: 34.1MM **Privately Held**
SIC: 6061 Federal credit unions

(P-9541)
BAY FEDERAL CREDIT UNION (PA)
3333 Clares St, Capitola (95010-2564)
PHONE..................................831 479-6000
Dennis Osmer, *Chairman*
H Duane Smith, *Vice Chairman*
Tiffany Zachmeier, *President*
Michael Leung, *Treasurer*
Tonee Picard, *Exec VP*
EMP: 160
SALES: 29.4MM **Privately Held**
WEB: www.bayfed.com
SIC: 6061 Federal credit unions

(P-9542)
CAL TECH EMPLYEES FDERAL CR UN (PA)
Also Called: Caltech Efcu
528 Foothill Blvd, La Canada Flintridge (91011-3506)
P.O. Box 11001 (91012-6001)
PHONE..................................818 952-4444
Richard Harris, *Principal*
Stephen L Proia, *Ch of Bd*
Richard L Harris, *President*
John Meeker, *CFO*
Willis Chapman, *Vice Ch Bd*
EMP: 64
SALES: 43.1MM **Privately Held**
WEB: www.caltech.edu
SIC: 6061 Federal credit unions

(P-9543)
CALIFORNIA COAST CREDIT UNION
5890 Pcf Ctr Blvd Frnt, San Diego (92121)
PHONE..................................858 495-1600
Alan Carithers, *Branch Mgr*
EMP: 145
SALES (est): 8.8MM
SALES (corp-wide): 67.5MM **Privately Held**
SIC: 6061 Federal credit unions
PA: California Coast Credit Union
9201 Spectrum Center Blvd # 300
San Diego CA 92123
858 495-1600

(P-9544)
CALIFORNIA CREDIT UNION
11331 Camarillo St, North Hollywood (91602-1216)
PHONE..................................818 291-5434
EMP: 91
SALES (corp-wide): 93.6MM **Privately Held**
SIC: 6061 Federal credit unions
PA: The California Credit Union
701 N Brand Blvd Ste 100
Glendale CA 91203
818 291-6700

(P-9545)
CALIFORNIA CREDIT UNION
333 S Beaudry Ave Ste 215, Los Angeles (90017-5141)
PHONE..................................213 975-1254
Harvey Teresa, *Principal*
EMP: 55
SALES (corp-wide): 93.6MM **Privately Held**
SIC: 6061 Federal credit unions
PA: The California Credit Union
701 N Brand Blvd Ste 100
Glendale CA 91203
818 291-6700

(P-9546)
COAST CENTRAL CREDIT UNION (PA)
2650 Harrison Ave, Eureka (95501-3223)
PHONE..................................707 445-8801
Dean Christensen, *President*
Tom Noonan, *Treasurer*
Katie Blair, *Officer*
Robert Taborski, *Officer*
Ed Christians, *Vice Pres*
EMP: 150 **EST:** 1932
SQ FT: 17,000
SALES: 36.8MM **Privately Held**
WEB: www.coastccu.org
SIC: 6061 Federal credit unions

(P-9547)
COMMONWEALTH CENTRAL CREDIT UN (PA)
5890 Silver Creek Vly Rd, San Jose (95138-1027)
P.O. Box 641690 (95164-1690)
PHONE..................................408 531-3100
Craig Weber, *CEO*
EMP: 69
SQ FT: 36,432
SALES: 16.1MM **Privately Held**
WEB: www.commonwealthccu.org
SIC: 6061 Federal credit unions

(P-9548)
CREDIT UNION SOUTHERN CAL (PA)
8028 Greenleaf Ave, Whittier (90602-2109)
P.O. Box 200 (90608-0200)
PHONE..................................562 698-8326
Dave Gunderson, *President*
Ed Fost, *COO*
Peter Putnam, *CFO*
Debbie Childs, *Exec VP*
EMP: 50
SQ FT: 12,000
SALES: 43.5MM **Privately Held**
WEB: www.cusocal.com
SIC: 6061 Federal credit unions

(P-9549)
EDUCATIONAL EMPLOYEES CR UN (PA)
2222 W Shaw Ave, Fresno (93711-3419)
PHONE..................................559 437-7700
Barbara Thomas, *Chairman*
Elizabeth Dooley, *President*
Rick Browning, *Treasurer*
Charles Ciapponi, *Officer*
Julie Mattern, *Exec VP*
EMP: 110 **EST:** 1934
SQ FT: 44,000
SALES: 80.3MM **Privately Held**
SIC: 6061 Federal credit unions

(P-9550)
F & A FEDERAL CREDIT UNION
2625 Corporate Pl, Monterey Park (91754-7645)
P.O. Box 30831, Los Angeles (90030-0831)
PHONE..................................323 268-1226
Richard Andrews, *President*
Rene McLean, *Officer*
Tanya Ruiz, *Officer*
Pam Chick, *Vice Pres*
Dan Rybczyk, *Administration*
EMP: 70 **EST:** 1936
SQ FT: 43,000
SALES: 42.1MM **Privately Held**
WEB: www.fafcu.net
SIC: 6061 Federal credit unions

(P-9551)
FARMERS INSURANCE FED CRED UNI (PA)
4601 Wilshire Blvd # 110, Los Angeles (90010-3880)
P.O. Box 36911 (90036-0911)
PHONE..................................323 209-6000
Mark Herter, *CEO*
Harland Bengs, *CFO*
Laszlo Haredy, *Chairman*
Brian Leonard, *Officer*
Laura Campbell, *Exec VP*
EMP: 132
SQ FT: 12,000
SALES: 39.8MM **Privately Held**
WEB: www.figfederalcu.com
SIC: 6061 Federal credit unions

(P-9552)
FINANCIAL PARTNERS CREDIT UN (PA)
7800 Imperial Hwy, Downey (90242-3457)
P.O. Box 7005 (90241-7005)
PHONE..................................562 904-3000
John Crites, *Ch of Bd*
Nader Moghaddam, *President*
Albert Hernandez, *COO*
Mary Torsney, *CFO*
Michael Sandoval, *Bd of Directors*
EMP: 73
SQ FT: 32,000
SALES: 41.9MM **Privately Held**
WEB: www.fpcu.org
SIC: 6061 Federal credit unions

(P-9553)
FIREFIGHTERS FIRST CREDIT UN (PA)
815 Colorado Blvd, Los Angeles (90041-1720)
PHONE..................................323 254-1700
Dixie Abramian, *CEO*
Ceasar Del Toro, *Officer*
Jessica Armes, *Manager*
David Lillie, *Manager*
EMP: 138
SQ FT: 25,000
SALES: 46.2MM **Privately Held**
WEB: www.lafirecu.org
SIC: 6061 Federal credit unions

(P-9554)
FIRST CITY CREDIT UNION (PA)
717 W Temple St Ste 400, Los Angeles (90012-2632)
P.O. Box 86008 (90086-0008)
PHONE..................................213 482-3477
James D Likens, *Ch of Bd*
Steve Punch, *CEO*
Terry O'Steen, *COO*
Richard Reese, *CFO*
Robert Ciulik, *Treasurer*
EMP: 105
SQ FT: 24,896
SALES: 18.4MM **Privately Held**
SIC: 6061 Federal credit unions

(P-9555)
FIRST ENTERTAINMENT CREDIT UN (PA)
6735 Forest Lawn Dr # 100, Los Angeles (90068-1055)
P.O. Box 100 (90078-0100)
PHONE..................................323 851-3673
Charles A Bruen, *President*
Lucy Wander-Perna, *Ch of Bd*
Lisa Landt, *CFO*
Irwin Jacobson, *Treasurer*
Kasha Reed, *Branch Mgr*
EMP: 80 **EST:** 1998
SQ FT: 57,000
SALES: 44.3MM **Privately Held**
SIC: 6061 Federal credit unions

(P-9556)
FIRST TECHNOLOGY FEDERAL CR UN (PA)
1335 Terra Bella Ave, Mountain View (94043-1835)
PHONE..................................855 855-8805
Greg A Mitchell, *President*
Scott Jenner, *President*
Hank Sigmon, *CFO*
Monique Little,
Keith Conway, *Vice Pres*

EMP: 72
SALES: 352.2MM **Privately Held**
WEB: www.1sttech.com
SIC: 6061 Federal credit unions

(P-9557)
FIRST TECHNOLOGY FEDERAL CR UN (PA)
1011 Sunset Blvd Ste 210, Rocklin (95765-3782)
PHONE..................................855 855-8805
Greg A Mitchell, *CEO*
Naveen Jain, *Director*
EMP: 211
SALES (corp-wide): 352.2MM **Privately Held**
SIC: 6061 Federal credit unions
PA: First Technology Federal Credit Union
1335 Terra Bella Ave
Mountain View CA 94043
855 855-8805

(P-9558)
FIRST US COMMUNITY CREDIT UN (PA)
580 University Ave # 100, Sacramento (95825-6528)
PHONE..................................916 576-5700
Carol Hauck, *CEO*
Richard Cochran, *President*
Brian W Doyle, *Chairman*
Richard D Cochran, *Treasurer*
Richard Bender, *Admin Sec*
EMP: 72
SQ FT: 10,000
SALES: 10.7MM **Privately Held**
SIC: 6061 Federal credit unions

(P-9559)
FOOTHILL FEDERAL CREDIT UNION (PA)
30 S 1st Ave, Arcadia (91006-3604)
P.O. Box 660130 (91066-0130)
PHONE..................................626 445-0950
Brian Hall, *President*
Mike Abata, *Ch of Bd*
Fred Weiss, *Chairman*
Mike Allee, *Treasurer*
Rick Ashley, *Bd of Directors*
EMP: 50
SQ FT: 12,077
SALES: 13.3MM **Privately Held**
WEB: www.foothillfederalcreditunion.com
SIC: 6061 Federal credit unions

(P-9560)
HANIN FEDERAL CREDIT UNION (PA)
3700 Wilshire Blvd # 104, Los Angeles (90010-2902)
PHONE..................................213 368-9000
Howard Ree, *Chairman*
James Lee, *Ch Credit Ofcr*
Kim Michael, *Technology*
EMP: 50
SQ FT: 2,190
SALES: 1.8MM **Privately Held**
WEB: www.haninfcu.org
SIC: 6061 Federal credit unions

(P-9561)
HERITAGE COMMUNITY CREDIT UN (PA)
10399 Old Placerville Rd, Sacramento (95827-2506)
P.O. Box 790, Rancho Cordova (95741-0790)
PHONE..................................916 364-1700
Judy Flores, *CEO*
Matt Harms, *CFO*
Brandon Ivie, *CFO*
Christine Haroldson, *Vice Pres*
Sherry Powers, *IT/INT Sup*
EMP: 75
SALES: 6.1MM **Privately Held**
SIC: 6061 Federal credit unions

(P-9562)
HERITAGE COMMUNITY CREDIT UN
10399 Old Clasaville Rd, Rancho Cordova (95670)
PHONE..................................916 364-1700
Steve Pogemiller, *Branch Mgr*
Diane Walton, *Executive*

▲ = Import ▼=Export
◆ =Import/Export

EMP: 50
SALES (corp-wide): 6.1MM **Privately Held**
SIC: **6061** Federal credit unions
PA: Heritage Community Credit Union
10399 Old Placerville Rd
Sacramento CA 95827
916 364-1700

(P-9563)
KERN FEDERAL CREDIT UNION
1717 Truxtun Ave, Bakersfield
(93301-5102)
PHONE.....................661 327-9461
Brandon Ivie, *CEO*
Brenda O'Doherty, *President*
Shirley Sanchez, *Officer*
Linda Crosby, *Senior VP*
Ashley Morrison,
EMP: 65
SQ FT: 17,000
SALES: 8.3MM **Privately Held**
WEB: www.kernfcu.org
SIC: **6061** 6163 Federal credit unions;
loan brokers

(P-9564)
KERN MEMBER INSURANCE SERVICES
Also Called: Kern Federal Credit Union
1717 Truxtun Ave, Bakersfield
(93301-5102)
PHONE.....................661 327-9461
Deann Straub, *President*
Gloria Scales, *Vice Pres*
Susan Jones, *Principal*
Lauren White, *Admin Asst*
EMP: 50
SALES: 7.8MM **Privately Held**
WEB: www.kernfederalcreditunion.com
SIC: **6061** Federal credit unions

(P-9565)
KERN SCHOOLS FEDERAL CREDIT UN (PA)
Also Called: KSFCU
11500 Bolthouse Dr, Bakersfield
(93311-8822)
P.O. Box 9506 (93389-9506)
PHONE.....................661 833-7900
Stephen P Renock IV, *President*
Neil Marshall, *CFO*
Shelli Anglim, *Admin Sec*
Mallory Kennedy, *Admin Asst*
David R Dubose, *MIS Mgr*
EMP: 60
SQ FT: 18,000
SALES: 47.3MM **Privately Held**
WEB: www.ksfcu.com
SIC: **6061** Federal credit unions

(P-9566)
KINECTA FEDERAL CREDIT UNION (PA)
1440 Rosecrans Ave, Manhattan Beach
(90266-3702)
PHONE.....................310 643-5400
Keith Sultemeier, *CEO*
Randall G Dotemoto, *President*
Douglas C Wicks, *President*
Steve Lumm, *CEO*
Joseph E Whitaker, *COO*
EMP: 250
SQ FT: 80,000
SALES: 147MM **Privately Held**
SIC: **6061** Federal credit unions

(P-9567)
LOGIX FEDERAL CREDIT UNION (PA)
2340 N Hollywood Way, Burbank
(91505-1124)
P.O. Box 10249 (91510-0249)
PHONE.....................888 718-5328
David Styler, *President*
Dave Styler, *COO*
Ana Fonseca, *CFO*
Maria Beltran, *Officer*
Sean Brown, *Officer*
EMP: 210
SQ FT: 75,000
SALES: 202.3MM **Privately Held**
SIC: **6061** Federal credit unions

(P-9568)
LOS ANGELES FEDERAL CREDIT UN (PA)
300 S Glendale Ave # 100, Glendale
(91205-1752)
PHONE.....................818 242-8640
John T DEA, *CEO*
Richard Lie, *CFO*
Anthony Cuevas, *Senior VP*
Leta Cook, *Vice Pres*
Art Sookazian, *Vice Pres*
EMP: 100
SQ FT: 40,000
SALES: 31.2MM **Privately Held**
SIC: **6061** Federal credit unions

(P-9569)
MERCED SCHOOL EMPLOYEES F C U (PA)
Also Called: MSEFCU
1021 Olivewood Dr, Merced (95348-1218)
P.O. Box 1349 (95341-1349)
PHONE.....................209 383-5550
Nancy Deavours, *President*
EMP: 65 EST: 1954
SQ FT: 16,500
SALES: 13.1MM **Privately Held**
WEB: www.mercedschoolcu.org
SIC: **6061** Federal credit unions

(P-9570)
MERIWEST CREDIT UNION (PA)
5615 Chesbro Ave Ste 100, San Jose
(95123-3057)
P.O. Box 530953 (95153-5353)
PHONE.....................408 363-3200
Toll Free:.....................877 -
Julie A Kirsch, *Principal*
Steven G Johnson, *CEO*
Christopher Owen, *CEO*
Brian Hennessey, *CFO*
Hudson Lee, *CFO*
EMP: 230
SQ FT: 61,000
SALES: 45.3MM **Privately Held**
WEB: www.meriwest.com
SIC: **6061** Federal credit unions

(P-9571)
MISSION FEDERAL CREDIT UNION (PA)
5785 Oberlin Dr Ste 312, San Diego
(92121-3752)
PHONE.....................858 546-2184
Debra Schwartz, *CEO*
Jennifer Collins, *President*
Vince Nowicki, *President*
Ron Araujo, *President*
Donna Handwerger, *Treasurer*
EMP: 550
SQ FT: 59,956
SALES: 83.4MM **Privately Held**
SIC: **6061** Federal credit unions

(P-9572)
MISSION FEDERAL SERVICES LLC (PA)
10325 Meanley Dr, San Diego
(92131-3011)
P.O. Box 919023 (92191-9023)
PHONE.....................858 524-2850
Debra Schwartz, *CEO*
Rose Hartley, *COO*
Peter Sainato, *CFO*
Gary M Devan, *Senior VP*
Richard Hartley, *Senior VP*
EMP: 150
SQ FT: 55,000
SALES (est): 83.4MM **Privately Held**
WEB: www.missionfcu.org
SIC: **6061** Federal credit unions

(P-9573)
MOCSE FEDERAL CREDIT UNION
3600 Coffee Rd, Modesto (95355-1164)
PHONE.....................209 572-3600
Tracey Kerr, *President*
Charlie Rodgers, *CFO*
Justin Garcia, *Technical Staff*
EMP: 82
SQ FT: 20,000

SALES: 8MM **Privately Held**
WEB: www.mocse.org
SIC: **6061** 6062 Federal credit unions;
state credit unions

(P-9574)
NAVY FEDERAL CREDIT UNION
2040 Harbison Dr, Vacaville (95687-3906)
PHONE.....................888 842-6328
Patsy Vanouwerkerk, *Branch Mgr*
EMP: 122
SALES (corp-wide): 4.6B **Privately Held**
SIC: **6061** Federal credit unions
PA: Navy Federal Credit Union
820 Follin Ln Se
Vienna VA 22180
703 255-8000

(P-9575)
NOBLE CREDIT UNION (PA)
2580 W Shaw Ln Frnt, Fresno
(93711-2776)
P.O. Box 8027 (93747-8027)
PHONE.....................559 252-5000
Karen B Cobb, *Ch of Bd*
Michelle Connell, *President*
Jeff Bassill, *COO*
Karen Cobb, *CFO*
Doug Papagni, *Chairman*
EMP: 50
SQ FT: 12,000
SALES: 27.1MM **Privately Held**
WEB: www.fresnocfcu.org
SIC: **6061** Federal credit unions

(P-9576)
NUVISION FINCL FEDERAL CR UN (PA)
7812 Edinger Ave Ste 100, Huntington
Beach (92647-3727)
P.O. Box 1220 (92647-1220)
PHONE.....................714 375-8000
Roger Ballard, *CEO*
John Afdem, *CFO*
Brian Hershfield, *CFO*
Robert Geraci, *Treasurer*
Teri Rapp, *Ch Credit Ofcr*
EMP: 137
SALES: 59.1MM **Privately Held**
WEB: www.nuvision.coop
SIC: **6061** Federal credit unions

(P-9577)
ORANGE COUNTYS CREDIT UNION (PA)
1721 E Saint Andrew Pl, Santa Ana
(92705-4934)
P.O. Box 11777 (92711-1777)
PHONE.....................714 755-5900
Shruti S Miyashiro, *Principal*
Amanda Verive, *President*
Dan Dillon, *Chairman*
Art Armas, *Vice Pres*
Donald Carazo, *Vice Pres*
EMP: 157
SALES: 46.3MM **Privately Held**
SIC: **6061** Federal credit unions

(P-9578)
PACIFIC MARINE CREDIT UNION (PA)
1278 Rocky Point Dr, Oceanside
(92056-5867)
PHONE.....................760 430-7511
David L Davis, *CEO*
Michelle Denton, *CFO*
Carrie Foster, *CFO*
Deborah Kennedy, *Vice Pres*
Brad Smith, *Vice Pres*
EMP: 107
SQ FT: 22,000
SALES: 26.7MM **Privately Held**
WEB: www.pmcu.com
SIC: **6061** Federal credit unions

(P-9579)
PACIFIC SERVICE CREDIT UNION (PA)
3000 Clayton Rd, Concord (94519-2731)
P.O. Box 8191, Walnut Creek (94596-8191)
PHONE.....................888 858-6878
Stephen R Punch, *CEO*
Jenna Lampson, *COO*
Lawrence Labonte, *CFO*

David Sena, *Chairman*
Vicki Turano, *Treasurer*
EMP: 76
SQ FT: 23,689
SALES: 30.5MM **Privately Held**
SIC: **6061** Federal credit unions

(P-9580)
PATELCO CREDIT UNION (PA)
5050 Hopyard Rd, Pleasanton
(94588-3353)
P.O. Box 8020 (94588-8601)
PHONE.....................800 358-8228
Erin Mendez, *CEO*
Sue Gruber, *CFO*
Kenn D Darling, *Ch Credit Ofcr*
Richard Wada,
Brent Gifford, *Officer*
EMP: 250
SQ FT: 36,000
SALES: 178.4MM **Privately Held**
WEB: www.patelco.org
SIC: **6061** Federal credit unions

(P-9581)
REDWOOD CREDIT UNION
1129 S Cloverdale Blvd A, Cloverdale
(95425-4482)
PHONE.....................800 479-7928
Cynthia Negri, *Vice Pres*
EMP: 129
SALES (corp-wide): 126.7MM **Privately Held**
SIC: **6061** Federal credit unions
PA: Redwood Credit Union
3033 Cleveland Ave # 100
Santa Rosa CA 95403
707 545-4000

(P-9582)
REDWOOD CREDIT UNION (PA)
3033 Cleveland Ave # 100, Santa Rosa
(95403-2126)
P.O. Box 6104 (95406-0104)
PHONE.....................707 545-4000
Brett Martinez, *President*
Dina Miller, *President*
Daniel Torres, *Officer*
Ron Felder, *Senior VP*
Tony Hildesheim, *Senior VP*
EMP: 190
SQ FT: 20,000
SALES: 126.7MM **Privately Held**
WEB: www.redwoodcu.org
SIC: **6061** Federal credit unions

(P-9583)
SAFE AMERICA CREDIT UNION (PA)
6001 Gibraltar Dr, Pleasanton
(94588-2707)
P.O. Box 11269 (94588-1269)
PHONE.....................925 734-4111
Barry Roach, *CEO*
Chuck Dunbar, *CFO*
Frank Zampella, *Chairman*
Candy Davis, *Vice Pres*
Charles Dunbar, *Vice Pres*
EMP: 70
SQ FT: 27,000
SALES: 12.8MM **Privately Held**
WEB: www.safeamerica.com
SIC: **6061** Federal credit unions

(P-9584)
SAFE CREDIT UNION
Also Called: Financial Transaction
9055 Woodcreek Oaks Blvd # 150, Roseville (95747-5159)
PHONE.....................916 979-7233
Serna Yong, *Branch Mgr*
EMP: 50
SALES (corp-wide): 74.8MM **Privately Held**
SIC: **6061** Federal credit unions
PA: Safe Credit Union
2295 Iron Point Rd # 100
Folsom CA 95630
916 979-7233

(P-9585)
SAG- AFTRA FEDERAL
134 N Kenwood St, Burbank (91505-4201)
P.O. Box 11419 (91510-1419)
PHONE.....................818 562-3400
Randy Kahn, *Chairman*

Roger Runyan, *CEO*
Jose Rodriguez, *CFO*
Phillip Weiss, *Vice Pres*
Edwin Magana, *Technology*
EMP: 52
SQ FT: 5,500
SALES: 7.6MM **Privately Held**
SIC: 6061 Federal credit unions

(P-9586)
SAN FRANCISCO FEDERAL CR UN (PA)
770 Golden Gate Ave Fl 1, San Francisco (94102-3194)
PHONE..............................415 775-5377
William Wolverton, *CEO*
Steve Ho, *COO*
Kyungsook Kim, *Officer*
Rebecca Lytle, *Vice Pres*
Maria Soria, *Branch Mgr*
EMP: 70
SQ FT: 35,500
SALES: 35.4MM **Privately Held**
WEB: www.sffederalcu.org
SIC: 6061 Federal credit unions

(P-9587)
SANTA CLARA CNTY FDERAL CR UN (PA)
1641 N 1st St Ste 245, San Jose (95112-4519)
PHONE..............................408 282-0700
Mike Delmonico, *CEO*
Michael Kadel, *Vice Pres*
Michael Delmonico, *Branch Mgr*
Dominic Serio, *Info Tech Mgr*
Nancy S Cruz, *Manager*
EMP: 112 **EST:** 1950
SQ FT: 42,000
SALES: 22.4MM **Privately Held**
SIC: 6061 Federal credit unions

(P-9588)
SCE FEDERAL CREDIT UNION (PA)
Also Called: SCE FCU
12701 Schabarum Ave, Baldwin Park (91706-6807)
P.O. Box 8017, El Monte (91734-2317)
PHONE..............................626 960-6888
Dennis Huber, *CEO*
George Poitou, *COO*
Daniel Rader, *CFO*
EMP: 134 **EST:** 1952
SQ FT: 30,000
SALES: 28.8MM **Privately Held**
WEB: www.scefcu.org
SIC: 6061 Federal credit unions

(P-9589)
SCHOOLSFIRST FEDERAL CREDIT UN (PA)
2115 N Broadway, Santa Ana (92706-2613)
P.O. Box 11547 (92711-1547)
PHONE..............................714 258-4000
Bill Cheney, *President*
Francisco Nebot, *CFO*
Sandi Brimhall, *Officer*
Adam Jacoby, *Officer*
Martha Monzon, *Exec VP*
EMP: 270
SALES: 413.4MM **Privately Held**
SIC: 6061 Federal credit unions

(P-9590)
SCHOOLSFIRST FEDERAL CREDIT UN
15442 Newport Ave, Tustin (92780-6473)
PHONE..............................714 258-4000
Mark Spencer, *COO*
Alissa Mojica, *Officer*
Daniel Skaggs, *Officer*
Nubia Carrillo, *Vice Pres*
Robert Osterholt, *Vice Pres*
EMP: 118
SALES (corp-wide): 413.4MM **Privately Held**
SIC: 6061 Federal credit unions
PA: Schoolsfirst Federal Credit Union
2115 N Broadway
Santa Ana CA 92706
714 258-4000

(P-9591)
SEA WEST CAST GARD FDRAL CR UN (PA)
8750 Mountain Blvd, Oakland (94605-4500)
P.O. Box 4949 (94605-6949)
PHONE..............................510 568-4100
Tom Doherty, *CEO*
EMP: 56 **EST:** 1959
SQ FT: 12,000
SALES: 8.8MM **Privately Held**
SIC: 6061 Federal credit unions

(P-9592)
SESLOC FEDERAL CREDIT UNION (PA)
3855 Broad St, San Luis Obispo (93401-7109)
P.O. Box 5360 (93403-5360)
PHONE..............................805 543-1816
Bertha Foxford, *President*
Ann Tapper, *Officer*
Carla Swift, *Assoc VP*
Andy Bechinsky, *Senior VP*
Clarence Cabreros, *Senior VP*
EMP: 101
SQ FT: 19,700
SALES: 24.9MM **Privately Held**
WEB: www.sesloc.com
SIC: 6061 Federal credit unions

(P-9593)
SKYONE FEDERAL CREDIT UNION (PA)
14600 Aviation Blvd, Hawthorne (90250-6656)
P.O. Box 5003 (90251-5003)
PHONE..............................310 491-7500
Eileen C Rivera, *CEO*
Nataly Avila, *Officer*
Lisa Chavez, *Officer*
Anni Haroutunian, *Officer*
Ed Salazar, *Officer*
EMP: 58
SQ FT: 40,000
SALES: 16.5MM **Privately Held**
SIC: 6061 Federal credit unions

(P-9594)
SPECTRUM CREDIT UNION
500 12th St Ste 200, Oakland (94607-4084)
PHONE..............................510 251-6000
Jim Mooney, *CEO*
EMP: 200
SALES (est): 10.4MM **Privately Held**
SIC: 6061 Federal credit unions

(P-9595)
STANFORD FEDERAL CREDIT UNION (PA)
Also Called: SFCU
1860 Embarcadero Rd # 200, Palo Alto (94303-3320)
P.O. Box 10690 (94303-0843)
PHONE..............................650 725-1000
Jane S Duperrault, *Ch of Bd*
Tana Hutchison, *Treasurer*
Brian Thornton, *Vice Pres*
Jerry L Jobe, *Admin Sec*
Albert Finn, *HR Admin*
EMP: 61
SALES: 68.5MM **Privately Held**
SIC: 6061 Federal credit unions

(P-9596)
STAR ONE CREDIT UNION (PA)
1306 Bordeaux Dr, Sunnyvale (94089-1005)
P.O. Box 3643 (94088-3643)
PHONE..............................408 543-5202
Rick Heldebrant, *President*
Tammy Ward, *COO*
Scott Dunlap, *CFO*
Nya Munday, *Officer*
Elizabeth Rodriguez, *Officer*
EMP: 107
SQ FT: 25,000
SALES: 209.2MM **Privately Held**
SIC: 6061 Federal credit unions

(P-9597)
TELESIS COMMUNITY CREDIT UNION (PA)
9301 Winnetka Ave, Chatsworth (91311-6069)
PHONE..............................818 885-1226
Grace Mayo, *President*
Jean Faenza, *Exec VP*
EMP: 90
SQ FT: 17,000
SALES: 14.9MM **Privately Held**
SIC: 6061 6163 Federal credit unions; loan brokers

(P-9598)
TRAVIS CREDIT UNION
1300 E Covell Blvd, Davis (95616-1300)
PHONE..............................707 449-4000
EMP: 500
SALES (corp-wide): 106.6MM **Privately Held**
SIC: 6061 6062 Federal credit unions; state credit unions
PA: Travis Credit Union
1 Travis Way
Vacaville CA 95687
707 449-4000

(P-9599)
TRAVIS CREDIT UNION
1796 Tuolumne St, Vallejo (94589-2619)
PHONE..............................800 877-8328
EMP: 500
SALES (corp-wide): 106.6MM **Privately Held**
SIC: 6061 6022 6021 6029 Federal credit unions; state commercial banks; national commercial banks; commercial banks
PA: Travis Credit Union
1 Travis Way
Vacaville CA 95687
707 449-4000

(P-9600)
TRAVIS CREDIT UNION
2095 Diamond Blvd Ste 115, Concord (94520-5832)
PHONE..............................800 877-8328
Travis Credit, *Owner*
EMP: 500
SALES (corp-wide): 106.6MM **Privately Held**
SIC: 6061 6062 Federal credit unions; state credit unions
PA: Travis Credit Union
1 Travis Way
Vacaville CA 95687
707 449-4000

(P-9601)
TRAVIS CREDIT UNION
3263 Claremont Way, NAPA (94558-3313)
PHONE..............................800 877-8328
Marlene Myers, *Branch Mgr*
EMP: 500
SALES (corp-wide): 106.6MM **Privately Held**
SIC: 6061 6022 6029 Federal credit unions; state commercial banks; commercial banks
PA: Travis Credit Union
1 Travis Way
Vacaville CA 95687
707 449-4000

(P-9602)
TRAVIS CREDIT UNION (PA)
1 Travis Way, Vacaville (95687-3276)
P.O. Box 2069 (95696-2069)
PHONE..............................707 449-4000
Patsy Vanouwerkerk, *CEO*
Angela Deal, *Personnel Assit*
Michael Sabado, *Manager*
EMP: 300
SQ FT: 12,000
SALES: 106.6MM **Privately Held**
SIC: 6061 Federal credit unions

(P-9603)
TRAVIS CREDIT UNION
1515 K St, Sacramento (95814-4051)
PHONE..............................916 443-1446
EMP: 500

SALES (corp-wide): 106.6MM **Privately Held**
SIC: 6061 Federal credit unions
PA: Travis Credit Union
1 Travis Way
Vacaville CA 95687
707 449-4000

(P-9604)
TRAVIS CREDIT UNION
1194 W Olive Ave, Merced (95348-1952)
PHONE..............................209 723-0732
Patsy Vanouwerkerk, *CEO*
EMP: 500
SALES (corp-wide): 106.6MM **Privately Held**
SIC: 6061 Federal credit unions
PA: Travis Credit Union
1 Travis Way
Vacaville CA 95687
707 449-4000

(P-9605)
TRAVIS CREDIT UNION
5819 Lone Tree Way Ste A, Antioch (94531-8602)
PHONE..............................925 777-0573
Helen Raoufian, *Branch Mgr*
EMP: 500
SALES (corp-wide): 106.6MM **Privately Held**
SIC: 6061 6062 Federal credit unions; state credit unions
PA: Travis Credit Union
1 Travis Way
Vacaville CA 95687
707 449-4000

(P-9606)
TRAVIS CREDIT UNION
11 Cernon St, Vacaville (95688-2803)
PHONE..............................707 449-4000
Phil Christiansen, *Manager*
EMP: 500
SALES (corp-wide): 106.6MM **Privately Held**
SIC: 6061 Federal credit unions
PA: Travis Credit Union
1 Travis Way
Vacaville CA 95687
707 449-4000

(P-9607)
TRAVIS CREDIT UNION
2570 N Texas St, Fairfield (94533-1606)
PHONE..............................707 449-4000
Gloria Niccoli, *Manager*
EMP: 500
SALES (corp-wide): 106.6MM **Privately Held**
SIC: 6061 Federal credit unions
PA: Travis Credit Union
1 Travis Way
Vacaville CA 95687
707 449-4000

(P-9608)
TRAVIS CREDIT UNION
1372 E Main St, Woodland (95776-3551)
PHONE..............................800 877-8328
Jason Braga, *Manager*
EMP: 500
SALES (corp-wide): 106.6MM **Privately Held**
SIC: 6061 6022 6021 6029 Federal credit unions; state commercial banks; national commercial banks; commercial banks
PA: Travis Credit Union
1 Travis Way
Vacaville CA 95687
707 449-4000

(P-9609)
TRAVIS CREDIT UNION
2020 Harbison Dr, Vacaville (95687-3910)
PHONE..............................707 449-4000
Cathy Redman, *Branch Mgr*
EMP: 500
SALES (corp-wide): 106.6MM **Privately Held**
SIC: 6061 Federal credit unions
PA: Travis Credit Union
1 Travis Way
Vacaville CA 95687
707 449-4000

(P-9610)
TUCOEMAS FEDERAL CREDIT UNION (PA)
5222 W Cypress Ave, Visalia (93277-8305)
P.O. Box 5011 (93278-5011)
PHONE.................................559 737-5900
Linda Reese, *President*
Mike Ryan, *CFO*
Susan Warkentin, *Vice Pres*
Lidia Van Es, *Loan Officer*
EMP: 97
SALES: 7.3MM **Privately Held**
SIC: 6061 Federal credit unions

(P-9611)
TUCOEMAS FEDERAL CREDIT UNION
2300 W Whitendale Ave, Visalia (93277-6131)
P.O. Box 5011 (93278-5011)
PHONE.................................559 429-7094
John McHarry, *Manager*
EMP: 54
SQ FT: 19,413
SALES (corp-wide): 7.3MM **Privately Held**
SIC: 6061 Federal credit unions
PA: Tucoemas Federal Credit Union
5222 W Cypress Ave
Visalia CA 93277
559 737-5900

(P-9612)
UNCLE CREDIT UNION (PA)
2100 Las Positas Ct, Livermore (94551-7301)
PHONE.................................925 447-5001
Harold Roundtree, *CEO*
Jim Ott, *President*
Wendy Zanotelli, *COO*
Gina Bloomfield, *CFO*
Otis Nostrand, *Chairman*
EMP: 58
SQ FT: 17,000
SALES: 12.7MM **Privately Held**
WEB: www.unclecu.com
SIC: 6061 Federal credit unions

(P-9613)
UNIFY FINANCIAL FEDERAL CR UN (PA)
1899 Western Way Ste 100, Torrance (90501-1146)
P.O. Box 10018, Manhattan Beach (90267-7518)
PHONE.................................310 536-5000
Gordon M Howe, *Principal*
Gordon Howe, *COO*
Jenny Bell, *Officer*
Lisa Delgaizo, *Officer*
Susan Osa, *Assoc VP*
EMP: 80 **EST:** 1958
SALES: 111.2MM **Privately Held**
WEB: www.western.org
SIC: 6061 Federal credit unions

(P-9614)
UNITED SVCS AMER FEDERAL CR UN (PA)
Also Called: USA Federal Credit Union
9999 Willow Creek Rd, San Diego (92131-1117)
P.O. Box 26339 (92196-0339)
PHONE.................................858 831-8100
Martin Cassell, *President*
Jim Bedinger, *Vice Pres*
Ron Davis, *Vice Pres*
EMP: 90
SQ FT: 42,000
SALES (est): 18.8MM **Privately Held**
WEB: www.usafed.org
SIC: 6061 Federal credit unions

(P-9615)
UNIVERSITY CREDIT UNION
1500 S Sepulveda Blvd, Los Angeles (90025-3312)
PHONE.................................310 477-6628
Charles Bumbarger, *President*
Wendy Kollwitz, *Officer*
Patrick Aragon, *Vice Pres*
Steve Sercu, *Vice Pres*
Sandra Vanover, *Vice Pres*
EMP: 104

SALES: 15.5MM **Privately Held**
SIC: 6061 Federal credit unions

(P-9616)
USC CREDIT UNION
Also Called: U S C
3720 S Flower St, Los Angeles (90089-4303)
P.O. Box 2718 (90051-0718)
PHONE.................................213 821-7100
Gary J Perez, *President*
Gary Perez, *Executive*
Steve Smith, *Executive*
Valerie Ives, *Branch Mgr*
David Schauer-West, *Technology*
EMP: 56
SQ FT: 4,000
SALES: 19.9MM
SALES (corp-wide): 2.6B **Privately Held**
SIC: 6061 Federal credit unions
PA: University Of Southern California
3720 S Flower St Fl 3
Los Angeles CA 90089
213 740-7762

(P-9617)
VALLEY FIRST CREDIT UNION (PA)
1419 J St, Modesto (95354-1014)
P.O. Box 1411 (95353-1411)
PHONE.................................209 549-8511
Hank Barrett, *Exec Dir*
Fred Cruz, *CEO*
Dennis Barta, *CFO*
Gary Hall, *Treasurer*
Doug Button, *Vice Pres*
EMP: 90
SALES: 17.3MM **Privately Held**
SIC: 6061 Federal credit unions

(P-9618)
XCEED FINANCIAL CREDIT UNION (PA)
888 N Nash St, El Segundo (90245-2826)
PHONE.................................800 932-8222
Teresa Freeborn, *President*
Todd Helmerson, *Officer*
Bertha Gascon, *Vice Pres*
Courtnay Lynch, *Vice Pres*
Michael Stavrakis, *Vice Pres*
EMP: 96
SQ FT: 30,000
SALES: 33.1MM **Privately Held**
WEB: www.xfcu.org
SIC: 6061 Federal credit unions

6062 State Credit Unions

(P-9619)
ALLIANCE CREDIT UNION (PA)
3315 Almaden Expy Ste 55, San Jose (95118-1557)
P.O. Box 18460 (95158-8460)
PHONE.................................408 445-3386
Eileen M Lewis, *President*
Brian Dorcy, *CFO*
Ram Misra, *Bd of Directors*
Howard Watanabe, *Officer*
Jim Delyea, *Senior VP*
EMP: 73 **EST:** 1952
SQ FT: 40,000
SALES: 13.4MM **Privately Held**
SIC: 6062 State credit unions, not federally chartered

(P-9620)
ALTURA CREDIT UNION (PA)
2847 Campus Pkwy, Riverside (92507-0906)
PHONE.................................888 883-7228
Toll Free:.................................888 -
Mark Hawkins, *President*
Kevin Sherrell, *President*
Diana Wilcox, *CFO*
Luis Barrios, *Officer*
Ron Woodbury, *Exec VP*
EMP: 59
SQ FT: 60,000
SALES: 41.9MM **Privately Held**
SIC: 6062 State credit unions, not federally chartered

(P-9621)
AMERICAS CHRISTIAN CREDIT UN (PA)
Also Called: ACCU
2100 E Route 66 Ste 100, Glendora (91740-4623)
P.O. Box 5100 (91740-0808)
PHONE.................................626 208-5400
Mendell Thompson, *President*
Lucinda Garcia, *Officer*
Naomi Paris, *Officer*
Nicolette Harms, *Senior VP*
Terri Snyder, *Senior VP*
EMP: 83 **EST:** 1958
SQ FT: 22,000
SALES: 13.3MM **Privately Held**
SIC: 6062 State credit unions, not federally chartered

(P-9622)
BAY AREA CREDIT SERVICE LLC
10562 Caminito Flores, San Diego (92126-2804)
PHONE.................................858 653-3824
Roy Reese, *Principal*
EMP: 550
SALES (corp-wide): 22.3MM **Privately Held**
WEB: www.bayareacredit.com
SIC: 6062 State credit unions
PA: Bay Area Credit Service, Llc
4145 Shackleford Rd # 330
Norcross GA 30093
678 229-5010

(P-9623)
CALIFORNIA COAST CREDIT UNION (PA)
9201 Spectrum Center Blvd # 300, San Diego (92123-1407)
P.O. Box 502080 (92150-2080)
PHONE.................................858 495-1600
Marla Shepard, *CEO*
Ruth Peshkoff, *Ch of Bd*
Carol Walker, *Senior VP*
Charles Wallace, *Vice Pres*
Frederick Schwartz, *Admin Sec*
EMP: 150
SALES: 67.5MM **Privately Held**
WEB: www.calcoastcu.org
SIC: 6062 6163 State credit unions, not federally chartered; loan brokers

(P-9624)
CALIFORNIA COAST CREDIT UNION
8131 Allison Ave, La Mesa (91942-5523)
P.O. Box 502080, San Diego (92150-2080)
PHONE.................................858 495-1600
Gail Lillie, *Branch Mgr*
EMP: 55
SALES (est): 2.7MM
SALES (corp-wide): 67.5MM **Privately Held**
WEB: www.calcoastcu.org
SIC: 6062 State credit unions, not federally chartered
PA: California Coast Credit Union
9201 Spectrum Center Blvd # 300
San Diego CA 92123
858 495-1600

(P-9625)
CALIFORNIA CREDIT UNION (PA)
701 N Brand Blvd Ste 100, Glendale (91203-4231)
P.O. Box 29100 (91209-9100)
PHONE.................................818 291-6700
Steve O'Connell, *CEO*
Danny Pak, *President*
Jason Pugh, *President*
Hudson Lee, *CFO*
Mark Lovewell, *CFO*
EMP: 120
SALES: 93.6MM **Privately Held**
WEB: www.californiacu.org
SIC: 6062 6061 State credit unions, not federally chartered; federal credit unions

(P-9626)
CALIFORNIA CREDIT UNION
3550 W Century Blvd # 103, Inglewood (90303-1242)
PHONE.................................310 671-1080
Shawn T Thompson, *Branch Mgr*
EMP: 91
SALES (corp-wide): 93.6MM **Privately Held**
SIC: 6062 State credit unions, not federally chartered
PA: The California Credit Union
701 N Brand Blvd Ste 100
Glendale CA 91203
818 291-6700

(P-9627)
CHRISTIAN COMMUNITY CREDIT UN (PA)
255 N Lone Hill Ave, San Dimas (91773-2308)
P.O. Box 3012, Covina (91722-9012)
PHONE.................................626 915-7551
John T Walling, *President*
Jeremy Brown, *Officer*
Michael Garcia, *Officer*
David Estridge, *Exec VP*
Scott J Reitsma, *Senior VP*
EMP: 70 **EST:** 1957
SQ FT: 24,000
SALES: 30.1MM **Privately Held**
WEB: www.christiancommunitycu.com
SIC: 6062 State credit unions, not federally chartered

(P-9628)
COASTHILLS CREDIT UNION (PA)
Also Called: CSCU
3880 Constellation Rd, Lompoc (93436-1404)
P.O. Box 200 (93438-0200)
PHONE.................................805 733-7600
Jeff York, *President*
Marty Chatham, *CFO*
Amanda Hollingworth, *Officer*
Sandra Pickles, *Officer*
Jasmine Williams, *Officer*
EMP: 80
SQ FT: 30,000
SALES: 40.5MM **Privately Held**
WEB: www.coasthillsfederalcreditunion.com
SIC: 6062 State credit unions, not federally chartered

(P-9629)
EAGLE COMMUNITY CREDIT UNION (PA)
23021 Lake Center Dr, Lake Forest (92630-2836)
P.O. Box 5196 (92609-8696)
PHONE.................................949 588-9400
Sharon Updike, *CEO*
Rod Selbo, *Senior VP*
Mortiz Wohanke, *Senior VP*
Brooke Hazard, *Vice Pres*
Carol Rosas, *Vice Pres*
EMP: 75
SQ FT: 17,000
SALES: 7.9MM **Privately Held**
WEB: www.eaglecu.com
SIC: 6062 State credit unions, not federally chartered

(P-9630)
EDUCATIONAL EMPLOYEES CR UN
1460 W 7th St, Hanford (93230-4938)
PHONE.................................559 587-4460
Dianne Mitchell, *Owner*
EMP: 50
SALES (corp-wide): 80.3MM **Privately Held**
SIC: 6062 6061 State credit unions, not federally chartered; federal credit unions
PA: Educational Employees Credit Union
2222 W Shaw Ave
Fresno CA 93711
559 437-7700

PRODUCTS & SVCS

(P-9631)
EDUCATIONAL EMPLOYEES CR UN

3488 W Shaw Ave, Fresno (93711-3216)
P.O. Box 5242 (93755-5242)
PHONE...............................559 896-0222
Bruce L Barnett, *President*
Donna McGrady, *Administration*
Natalie Tomajan, *Director*
Carlos Romero, *Manager*
John J Otto, *Consultant*
EMP: 80
SQ FT: 17,939
SALES (corp-wide): 80.3MM **Privately Held**
SIC: 6062 State credit unions, not federally chartered
PA: Educational Employees Credit Union
2222 W Shaw Ave
Fresno CA 93711
559 437-7700

(P-9632)
EL MONTE COMMUNITY CREDIT UN

11718 Ramona Blvd, El Monte (91732-2310)
PHONE...............................626 444-0501
Evamarie Reta, *Officer*
EMP: 87
SQ FT: 3,405
SALES: 868.1K **Privately Held**
WEB: www.emcecu.org
SIC: 6062 State credit unions

(P-9633)
EVANGELICAL CHRISTIAN CR UN

955 W Imperial Hwy # 100, Brea (92821-3814)
PHONE...............................714 671-5700
EMP: 157
SALES (corp-wide): 37.2MM **Privately Held**
SIC: 6062 6061
PA: Evangelical Christian Credit Union
955 W Imperial Hwy # 100
Brea CA 92821
714 671-5700

(P-9634)
EVANGELICAL CHRISTIAN CR UN (PA)

Also Called: ECCU
955 W Imperial Hwy # 100, Brea (92821-3814)
P.O. Box 2400 (92822-2400)
PHONE...............................714 671-5700
Abel Pomar, *CEO*
Susan Rushing, *COO*
Gregory Talbott, *CFO*
Tom Honan, *Senior VP*
Patty Staples, *Senior VP*
EMP: 92
SQ FT: 125,000
SALES: 27.4MM **Privately Held**
WEB: www.ministrypartners.net
SIC: 6062 State credit unions, not federally chartered

(P-9635)
GOLDEN 1 CREDIT UNION

1282 Stabler Ln Ste 640, Yuba City (95993-2625)
PHONE...............................877 465-3361
Choni Weigman, *Manager*
EMP: 119
SALES (corp-wide): 344.3MM **Privately Held**
SIC: 6062 State credit unions
PA: Golden 1 Credit Union
8945 Cal Center Dr
Sacramento CA 95826
916 732-2900

(P-9636)
GOLDEN 1 CREDIT UNION (PA)

8945 Cal Center Dr, Sacramento (95826-3239)
P.O. Box 15966 (95852-0966)
PHONE...............................916 732-2900
Teresa Halleck, *President*
Richard Alfaro, *Officer*
Lisa Lemus, *Senior VP*
Greg Brown, *Vice Pres*

Tammy Davis, *Vice Pres*
EMP: 400 EST: 1933
SQ FT: 100,000
SALES: 344.3MM **Privately Held**
WEB: www.goldenone.com
SIC: 6062 State credit unions, not federally chartered

(P-9637)
GOLDEN 1 CREDIT UNION

Also Called: Unknown
2942 Main St, Susanville (96130-4730)
PHONE...............................530 251-0205
EMP: 80
SALES (corp-wide): 344.3MM **Privately Held**
SIC: 6062 State credit unions
PA: Golden 1 Credit Union
8945 Cal Center Dr
Sacramento CA 95826
916 732-2900

(P-9638)
KEYPOINT CREDIT UNION (PA)

2805 Bowers Ave Ste 105, Santa Clara (95051-0972)
PHONE...............................408 731-4100
T Bradford Canfield, *CEO*
Timothy M Kramer, *President*
John Herrick, *CFO*
Jeff Aana, *Manager*
Josh Herzog, *Manager*
EMP: 123
SQ FT: 60,715
SALES: 40.2MM **Privately Held**
WEB: www.keypointcu.com
SIC: 6062 State credit unions, not federally chartered

(P-9639)
KEYPOINT CREDIT UNION

2805 Bowers Ave Ste 105, Santa Clara (95051-0972)
PHONE...............................408 562-7011
Doug Schrock, *Branch Mgr*
EMP: 113
SALES (corp-wide): 40.2MM **Privately Held**
WEB: www.keypointcu.com
SIC: 6062 6061 State credit unions, not federally chartered; federal credit unions
PA: Keypoint Credit Union
2805 Bowers Ave Ste 105
Santa Clara CA 95051
408 731-4100

(P-9640)
LOS ANGELES POLICE CREDIT UN (PA)

Also Called: L A P F C U
16150 Sherman Way, Van Nuys (91406-3938)
P.O. Box 10188 (91410-0188)
PHONE...............................818 787-6520
Tyler E Izen, *Ch of Bd*
G Michael Padgett, *President*
Angelino Cayanan, *CFO*
Michael G Padgett, *CFO*
Warren D Spayth, *Treasurer*
EMP: 111
SQ FT: 30,000
SALES: 32.2MM **Privately Held**
WEB: www.lapfcu.org
SIC: 6062 6061 State credit unions, not federally chartered; federal credit unions

(P-9641)
MONTEREY CREDIT UNION (PA)

501 E Franklin St, Monterey (93940-3077)
P.O. Box 3288 (93942-3288)
PHONE...............................831 647-1000
David Laredo, *Chairman*
Ed Brown, *Vice Chairman*
J Stewart Fuller, *CEO*
Penprase Jim, *CFO*
Kathy Aliotti, *Branch Mgr*
EMP: 55
SQ FT: 10,000
SALES: 8.3MM **Privately Held**
SIC: 6062 State credit unions, not federally chartered

(P-9642)
NORTHROP GRUMMAN FEDERAL CR UN (PA)

879 W 190th St Ste 800, Gardena (90248-4205)
PHONE...............................310 808-4000
Stanley R Swenson Jr, *President*
Stephen Considine, *Vice Chairman*
Joe Demichele, *CFO*
Kathi Harper, *Chairman*
Georgetta A Wolff, *Vice Pres*
EMP: 60
SALES: 37.2MM **Privately Held**
SIC: 6062 State credit unions

(P-9643)
PATELCO CREDIT UNION

310 Hartz Ave, Danville (94526-3308)
PHONE...............................925 785-9487
EMP: 85
SALES (corp-wide): 178.4MM **Privately Held**
SIC: 6062 State credit unions
PA: Patelco Credit Union
5050 Hopyard Rd
Pleasanton CA 94588
800 358-8228

(P-9644)
PREMIER AMERICA CREDIT UNION (PA)

19867 Prairie St Lbby, Chatsworth (91311-6532)
P.O. Box 2178 (91313-2178)
PHONE...............................818 772-4000
John M Merlo, *President*
Nancy Wheeler-Chandler, *Vice Chairman*
Brad Cunningham, *CFO*
James Anderson, *Chairman*
Richard Ziebell, *Corp Secy*
EMP: 135
SQ FT: 80,000
SALES: 73.9MM **Privately Held**
WEB: www.premier.org
SIC: 6062 6163 State credit unions, not federally chartered; loan brokers

(P-9645)
PROVIDENT CREDIT UNION (PA)

303 Twin Dolphin Dr # 303, Redwood City (94065-1419)
P.O. Box 8007 (94063-0907)
PHONE...............................650 508-0300
Maurice Schmid, *Chairman*
Ludelle Morrow, *President*
Jim Ernest, *CEO*
Nicole Couch, *Officer*
Claudia Jimenez, *Officer*
EMP: 130
SQ FT: 150,000
SALES: 66.5MM **Privately Held**
SIC: 6062 State credit unions, not federally chartered

(P-9646)
SACRAMENTO CREDIT UNION (PA)

800 H St Ste 100, Sacramento (95814-2686)
P.O. Box 2351 (95812-2351)
PHONE...............................916 444-6070
Toll Free:......................................888 -
Bhavnesh Makin, *CEO*
James Batson, *CFO*
Jim Batson, *CFO*
Syuzana Manukyan, *Officer*
Blake Cairney, *Vice Pres*
EMP: 64
SQ FT: 39,138
SALES: 17.6MM **Privately Held**
WEB: www.sactocu.org
SIC: 6062 6163 State credit unions, not federally chartered; loan brokers

(P-9647)
SAFE CREDIT UNION (PA)

2295 Iron Point Rd # 100, Folsom (95630-8767)
PHONE...............................916 979-7233
Henry Wirz, *CEO*
James Allen, *President*
David Pope, *President*
Kathern Gaskins, *Treasurer*
Jason Cruce, *Sr Corp Ofcr*
EMP: 160

SQ FT: 57,000
SALES: 74.8MM **Privately Held**
SIC: 6062 State credit unions, not federally chartered

(P-9648)
SAFE CREDIT UNION

2295 Iron Point Rd # 100, Folsom (95630-8767)
PHONE...............................916 979-7233
Kristina Bruegenan, *Supervisor*
EMP: 160
SALES (corp-wide): 74.8MM **Privately Held**
SIC: 6062 6163 7389 6141 State credit unions, not federally chartered; loan agents; credit card service; automobile loans, including insurance
PA: Safe Credit Union
2295 Iron Point Rd # 100
Folsom CA 95630
916 979-7233

(P-9649)
SAN DIEGO COUNTY CREDIT UNION (PA)

6545 Sequence Dr, San Diego (92121-4363)
PHONE...............................877 732-2848
Irene Oberbauer, *President*
Theresa Halleck, *President*
Robert Marchand, *CFO*
Valerie Kwiatkowski, *Exec VP*
Heather Moshier, *Exec VP*
EMP: 239 EST: 1938
SQ FT: 50,000
SALES: 210.8MM **Privately Held**
WEB: www.sdccu.net
SIC: 6062 State credit unions, not federally chartered

(P-9650)
SAN DIEGO METROPOLITAN CR UN (PA)

9212 Balboa Ave, San Diego (92123-1514)
P.O. Box 719099 (92171-9099)
PHONE...............................619 297-4835
Stuart Camblin, *President*
Michelle Villa, *Vice Chairman*
Gloria Liberti, *Vice Pres*
Rebecca Ramos-Arzola, *Vice Pres*
Adele Sandberg, *Vice Pres*
EMP: 58
SQ FT: 20,000
SALES: 11.9MM **Privately Held**
WEB: www.sdmcu.com
SIC: 6062 State credit unions, not federally chartered

(P-9651)
SAN MATEO CREDIT UNION (PA)

350 Convention Way # 300, Redwood City (94063-1436)
P.O. Box 910 (94064-0910)
PHONE...............................650 363-1725
Berry Jolette, *President*
Magda Gonzalez, *Ch of Bd*
Motley Snuth, *Treasurer*
Jasmen Avedian, *Officer*
Valerie Alsip, *Vice Pres*
▲ EMP: 55
SQ FT: 18,300
SALES: 44.6MM **Privately Held**
SIC: 6062 State credit unions

(P-9652)
SAN MATEO CREDIT UNION

1515 S El Camino Real # 100, San Mateo (94402-3099)
PHONE...............................650 363-1725
Preston Monroe, *Principal*
EMP: 212
SALES (est): 6.2MM
SALES (corp-wide): 44.6MM **Privately Held**
SIC: 6062 State credit unions, not federally chartered
PA: San Mateo Credit Union
350 Convention Way # 300
Redwood City CA 94063
650 363-1725

(P-9653)

SCHOOLS FINANCIAL CREDIT UNION (PA)

1485 Response Rd Ste 126, Sacramento (95815-5261)
P.O. Box 526001 (95852-6001)
PHONE..............................916 569-5400
James P Jordan III, *President*
Todd Devoogd, *CFO*
Tim Marriott, *CFO*
David Menker, *Vice Pres*
Millard Baker, *Admin Mgr*
EMP: 150
SQ FT: 56,000
SALES: 52.3MM **Privately Held**
SIC: 6062 State credit unions, not federally chartered

(P-9654)

SIERRA CENTRAL CREDIT UNION (PA)

1351 Harter Pkwy, Yuba City (95993-2604)
PHONE..............................530 671-3009
John Cassidy, *CEO*
Ron Sweeney, *Exec VP*
EMP: 90
SQ FT: 8,000
SALES: 33MM **Privately Held**
WEB: www.sierracentral.com
SIC: 6062 State credit unions, not federally chartered

(P-9655)

SOUTHLAND CREDIT UNION (PA)

10701 Los Alamitos Blvd, Los Alamitos (90720-2353)
P.O. Box 7022, Downey (90241-7022)
PHONE..............................562 862-6831
Ferris R Foster, *CEO*
Tom Lent, *CFO*
Christopher Burns, *Vice Pres*
Bertrand Villavert, *Vice Pres*
Alexander Kort, *Branch Mgr*
EMP: 60
SALES: 23.5MM **Privately Held**
WEB: www.southlandcreditunion.com
SIC: 6062 State credit unions, not federally chartered

(P-9656)

SOUTHLAND CREDIT UNION

8545 Florence Ave, Downey (90240-4014)
PHONE..............................562 862-6831
Kathy Vitale, *Manager*
EMP: 55
SALES (corp-wide): 23.5MM **Privately Held**
WEB: www.southlandcreditunion.com
SIC: 6062 6141 State credit unions, not federally chartered; personal credit institutions
PA: Southland Credit Union
10701 Los Alamitos Blvd
Los Alamitos CA 90720
562 862-6831

(P-9657)

TECHNOLOGY CREDIT UNION

1562 S Bascom Ave, San Jose (95125-6108)
PHONE..............................408 467-2382
Steve Donahue, *Branch Mgr*
EMP: 74
SALES (corp-wide): 79.7MM **Privately Held**
SIC: 6062 6061 State credit unions, not federally chartered; federal credit unions
PA: Technology Credit Union
2010 N 1st St Ste 200
San Jose CA 95131
408 451-9111

(P-9658)

TECHNOLOGY CREDIT UNION

43848 Pcf Commons Blvd, Fremont (94538-3804)
PHONE..............................408 467-2385
Steven Fisher, *Owner*
Debra Bowman, *Senior VP*
Janikke Klem, *Vice Pres*
EMP: 74

SALES (corp-wide): 79.7MM **Privately Held**
SIC: 6062 State credit unions, not federally chartered
PA: Technology Credit Union
2010 N 1st St Ste 200
San Jose CA 95131
408 451-9111

(P-9659)

TECHNOLOGY CREDIT UNION (PA)

2010 N 1st St Ste 200, San Jose (95131-2024)
P.O. Box 1409 (95109-1409)
PHONE..............................408 451-9111
Kenneth Burns, *President*
Dean Davis, *President*
Barbara B Kamm, *CEO*
Richard Hanz, *Treasurer*
Mike Floyd, *Ch Credit Ofcr*
EMP: 133
SQ FT: 23,000
SALES: 79.7MM **Privately Held**
SIC: 6062 State credit unions, not federally chartered

(P-9660)

TECHNOLOGY CREDIT UNION

490 California Ave, Palo Alto (94306-1900)
PHONE..............................650 326-6445
Robert Hayes, *Branch Mgr*
EMP: 74
SALES (corp-wide): 79.7MM **Privately Held**
SIC: 6062 State credit unions, not federally chartered
PA: Technology Credit Union
2010 N 1st St Ste 200
San Jose CA 95131
408 451-9111

(P-9661)

VENTURA COUNTY CREDIT UNION (PA)

2575 Vista Del Mar Dr, Ventura (93001-3900)
PHONE..............................805 477-4000
Joseph Schroeder, *President*
Linda Sim, *CFO*
Annette Ortiz, *Officer*
Zerry Holefield, *Assoc VP*
Gavin Bradley, *Senior VP*
EMP: 84
SQ FT: 22,500
SALES: 44.1MM **Privately Held**
SIC: 6062 State credit unions, not federally chartered

(P-9662)

WESCOM CENTRAL CREDIT UNION (PA)

123 S Marengo Ave, Pasadena (91101-2428)
P.O. Box 7058 (91109-7058)
PHONE..............................888 493-7266
Toll Free:..............................888 -
Darren Williams, *Principal*
Whitney Bullock, *Officer*
Jean Grall, *Officer*
Cindy Law, *Officer*
Bryan Tinoco, *Officer*
EMP: 425
SQ FT: 90,000
SALES: 116.1MM **Privately Held**
WEB: www.wescom.org
SIC: 6062 State credit unions, not federally chartered

6081 Foreign Banks, Branches & Agencies

(P-9663)

HONG KONG & SHANGHAI BANKING

Also Called: Hong Kong Bank
770 Wilshire Blvd Ste 800, Los Angeles (90017-3719)
PHONE..............................213 626-2460
EMP: 60
SALES (corp-wide): 79.8B **Privately Held**
SIC: 6081

SALES (corp-wide): 79.7MM **Privately Held**
SIC: 6062 State credit unions, not federally chartered
PA: Technology Credit Union
2010 N 1st St Ste 200
San Jose CA 95131
408 451-9111

HQ: Hongkong And Shanghai Banking Corporation Limited, The
Hsbc Main Bldg
Central District HK
282 211-11

6082 Foreign Trade & Intl Banks

(P-9664)

PARIBAS ASSET MANAGEMENT INC

1 Front St Fl 23, San Francisco (94111-5325)
PHONE..............................415 772-1300
Francois Denis, *Principal*
William J La Herran, *Vice Pres*
EMP: 66 **Publicly Held**
WEB: www.bnpparibas.com
SIC: 6082 Foreign trade & international banking institutions
HQ: Paribas Asset Management, Inc.
787 7th Ave Fl 27
New York NY 10019

6091 Nondeposit Trust Facilities

(P-9665)

DEUTSCHE BANK NATIONAL TR CO

1761 E Saint Andrew Pl, Santa Ana (92705-4934)
PHONE..............................714 247-6054
F Jim Della Sala, *Principal*
David West, *Managing Dir*
EMP: 75
SALES (est): 9.2MM
SALES (corp-wide): 11.5B **Privately Held**
SIC: 6091 6021 Nondeposit trust facilities; national commercial banks
HQ: Deutsche Bank Trust Company Americas
60 Wall St Bsmt 1
New York NY 10005
212 250-2500

(P-9666)

SUNAMERICA INC (HQ)

1 Sun America Ctr Fl 38, Los Angeles (90067-6101)
PHONE..............................310 772-6000
Eli Broad, *Chairman*
Rodney Haviland, *President*
Kevin McGowan, *President*
Jay S Wintrob, *CEO*
Steve Kozman, *Officer*
EMP: 1000 **EST:** 1957
SQ FT: 95,845
SALES (est): 2.1B
SALES (corp-wide): 49.5B **Publicly Held**
SIC: 6091 6311 6211 6282 Nondeposit trust facilities; life insurance carriers; mutual funds, selling by independent salesperson; brokers, security; dealers, security; manager of mutual funds, contract or fee basis; pension & retirement plan consultants; pension, health & welfare funds
PA: American International Group, Inc.
80 Pine St Fl 4
New York NY 10005
212 770-7000

6099 Functions Related To Deposit Banking, NEC

(P-9667)

ACCURATE SERVICES INC

Also Called: Accurate Express
3429 Glendale Blvd, Los Angeles (90039-1814)
PHONE..............................323 906-1000
Ester Fishman, *CEO*
EMP: 107
SQ FT: 2,475
SALES (est): 14.4MM **Privately Held**
SIC: 6099 Check clearing services

(P-9668)

ACE CASH EXPRESS INC

6302 Van Buren Blvd, Riverside (92503-2051)
PHONE..............................951 509-3506
Michael Mc Knight, *Branch Mgr*
EMP: 105
SALES (corp-wide): 3B **Privately Held**
WEB: www.acecashexpress.com
SIC: 6099 Check cashing agencies
HQ: Ace Cash Express, Inc.
1231 Greenway Dr Ste 600
Irving TX 75038
972 550-5000

(P-9669)

ASCENDANTFX CAPITAL USA INC

3478 Buskirk Ave Ste 1000, Pleasant Hill (94523-4378)
PHONE..............................201 633-4667
Jason Mugford, *President*
Greg Allen, *Treasurer*
Bernard Beck, *Ch Credit Ofcr*
Dan Caputo, *Vice Pres*
Nabeel Siddiqui, *Principal*
EMP: 57
SALES (est): 8.8MM **Privately Held**
SIC: 6099 Foreign currency exchange
PA: Ascendantfx Capital Inc
200 Bay St N Suite 1625
Toronto ON M5J 2
416 943-0123

(P-9670)

ASSOCIATED FOREIGN EXCH INC (HQ)

Also Called: Afex
21045 Califa St, Woodland Hills (91367-5104)
PHONE..............................888 307-2339
Jan Vlietstra, *CEO*
Irving Barr, *Ch of Bd*
Fred Kunik, *President*
Richard Verasamy, *CFO*
Guido Schulz, *Exec VP*
EMP: 57
SALES (est): 25.3MM **Privately Held**
WEB: www.afex.com
SIC: 6099 Foreign currency exchange

(P-9671)

ASSOCTED FGN EXCH HOLDINGS INC (PA)

21045 Califa St, Woodland Hills (91367-5104)
PHONE..............................818 386-2702
Irving Barr, *Chairman*
Fred Kunik, *President*
Jan Vliestra, *CEO*
EMP: 89
SALES: 58MM **Privately Held**
SIC: 6099 Foreign currency exchange

(P-9672)

BLACKHAWK NETWORK INC (DH)

6220 Stoneridge Mall Rd, Pleasanton (94588-3260)
PHONE..............................925 226-9990
Talbott Roche, *President*
Mike Gionfriddo, *President*
Ben King, *President*
Tom Neale, *President*
Patrick Ramsey, *President*
EMP: 625 **EST:** 2005
SALES (est): 950.3MM
SALES (corp-wide): 83.2MM **Privately Held**
SIC: 6099 Electronic funds transfer network, including switching
HQ: Blackhawk Network Holdings, Inc.
6220 Stoneridge Mall Rd
Pleasanton CA 94588
925 226-9990

(P-9673)

BLACKHAWK NETWORK HOLDINGS INC (HQ)

6220 Stoneridge Mall Rd, Pleasanton (94588-3260)
PHONE..............................925 226-9990
Talbott Roche, *President*
Heather Blair, *Partner*
Nicole Watkins, *Partner*

Stephanie Wilson, *Partner*
Charles O Garner, *CFO*
EMP: 500
SQ FT: 149,000
SALES: 2.2B
SALES (corp-wide): 83.2MM **Privately Held**
WEB: www.safeway.com
SIC: 6099 Electronic funds transfer network, including switching
PA: Bhn Holdings, Inc.
6220 Stoneridge Mall Rd
Pleasanton CA 94588
925 226-9990

(P-9674)
COINBASE INC (PA)
Also Called: Blockr.io
548 Market St Ste 23008, San Francisco
(94104-5401)
PHONE....................415 275-2890
Brian David Armstrong, *CEO*
Brian Brooks,
Adam White, *Vice Pres*
Andy Ainess, *Principal*
Fred Ehrsam, *Principal*
EMP: 52
SALES (est): 44.9MM **Privately Held**
SIC: 6099 Foreign currency exchange

(P-9675)
CONTINENTAL CURRENCY SVCS INC (HQ)
Also Called: Continental Ex Money Order Co
1108 E 17th St, Santa Ana (92701-2600)
PHONE....................714 569-0300
Irving Barr, *Ch of Bd*
Fred Kunik, *President*
EMP: 50
SQ FT: 10,000
SALES (est): 11.7MM
SALES (corp-wide): 220.1MM **Privately Held**
SIC: 6099 Check cashing agencies
PA: Continental Currency Services, Inc.
1108 E 17th St
Santa Ana CA 92701
714 569-0300

(P-9676)
CONTINENTAL CURRENCY SVCS INC (PA)
Also Called: Cash It Here
1108 E 17th St, Santa Ana (92701-2600)
P.O. Box 10970 (92711-0970)
PHONE....................714 569-0300
Fred Kunik, *President*
Irving Barr, *Ch of Bd*
David Wilder, *COO*
Helen Cho, *Officer*
Rebecca Wischkaemper, *Officer*
EMP: 80
SQ FT: 12,500
SALES (est): 220.1MM **Privately Held**
SIC: 6099 Check cashing agencies; electronic funds transfer network, including switching; money order issuance

(P-9677)
CONTINENTAL EXCH SOLUTIONS INC (HQ)
Also Called: RIA FINANCIAL SERVICE
6565 Knott Ave, Buena Park (90620-1139)
PHONE....................714 522-7044
Juan C Bianchi, *CEO*
Timothy A Fanning, *COO*
Shawn D Fielder, *CFO*
Anthony Grandidge, *Senior VP*
Cindy Ashcraft, *Vice Pres*
EMP: 96
SALES: 539.7MM **Publicly Held**
SIC: 6099 Electronic funds transfer network, including switching

(P-9678)
CU COOPERATIVE SYSTEMS INC (PA)
Also Called: CO-OP NETWORK
9692 Haven Ave, Rancho Cucamonga
(91730-5891)
PHONE....................909 948-2500
Todd Clark, *President*
Tom Sargent, *Ch of Bd*
James Hanisch, *COO*
John Bommarito, *Treasurer*

Jill Deniro, *Officer*
EMP: 285
SALES: 399.9MM **Privately Held**
SIC: 6099 Automated teller machine (ATM) network; electronic funds transfer network, including switching

(P-9679)
DEBISYS INC (PA)
Also Called: Emida Technologies
27442 Portola Pkwy # 150, Foothill Ranch
(92610-2823)
PHONE....................949 699-1401
Dennis Andrews, *CEO*
Jim Wodach, *CFO*
Nidhi Gulati, *Technology*
Noemi Echeverria, *Accounts Mgr*
EMP: 80
SQ FT: 10,000
SALES (est): 59MM **Privately Held**
WEB: www.emida.net
SIC: 6099 Automated teller machine (ATM) network

(P-9680)
EDC SERVICE CORPORATION (DEL)
415 N Vineyard Ave # 205, Ontario
(91764-5493)
PHONE....................909 390-4747
Stephen Bezuidenhout, *President*
Wendy Bezuidenhout, *Vice Pres*
EMP: 60
SQ FT: 8,500
SALES (est): 5.6MM **Privately Held**
SIC: 6099 Automated clearinghouses

(P-9681)
FCTI INC (PA)
11766 Wilshire Blvd # 1100, Los Angeles
(90025-6561)
PHONE....................310 405-0022
Jeff Wernecke, *President*
Robel Gugsa, *CEO*
Sean Burke, *Senior VP*
Jesus Carrillo, *Vice Pres*
Joni Gaudes, *Vice Pres*
EMP: 72
SALES (est): 23MM **Privately Held**
WEB: www.fcti.net
SIC: 6099 Automated teller machine (ATM) network

(P-9682)
FINASTRA MERCHANT SERVICES INC (PA)
333 Bush St Fl 26, San Francisco
(94104-2806)
PHONE....................415 277-9900
Reuven Ben Menachem, *CEO*
Edward Ho, *President*
Bryan Schreiber, *Treasurer*
Mierzwa Dennis, *Vice Pres*
Santo Manna, *Admin Sec*
EMP: 60
SQ FT: 14,000
SALES (est): 53.3MM **Privately Held**
WEB: www.bankserv.com
SIC: 6099 Electronic funds transfer network, including switching

(P-9683)
FLAGSTAR BANCORP INC
949 S Coast Dr Ste 100, Costa Mesa
(92626-7828)
PHONE....................714 549-9100
Brett Baugh, *Loan Officer*
Mark Cook, *Loan Officer*
Alex Ford, *Loan Officer*
Ann Heinz, *Loan Officer*
Lisa Kwong, *Loan Officer*
EMP: 189 **Publicly Held**
SIC: 6099 Check clearing services
PA: Flagstar Bancorp, Inc.
5151 Corporate Dr
Troy MI 48098

(P-9684)
G P M M MONEY CENTERS INC
Also Called: Dollar Smart
1460 Doris Ave, Oxnard (93030-8771)
P.O. Box 6963 (93031-6963)
PHONE....................619 288-7607
Greg Palmer, *President*
Ryan Romero, *Business Mgr*

EMP: 50
SALES (est): 6.2MM **Privately Held**
SIC: 6099 Check cashing agencies

(P-9685)
GRANITE ESCROW SERVICES
439 N Canon Dr Ste 220, Beverly Hills
(90210-3933)
PHONE....................310 288-0110
Sue Nichols, *Branch Mgr*
Mark Fishman, *Banking Exec*
Lisa Rietz, *Banking Exec*
EMP: 58
SALES (corp-wide): 10MM **Privately Held**
SIC: 6099 Escrow institutions other than real estate
PA: Granite Escrow Services
450 Nwport Ctr Dr Ste 600
Newport Beach CA 92660
949 720-0110

(P-9686)
KINECTA ALTERNATIVE FIN (HQ)
Also Called: Nix Neighborhood Lending
1440 Rosecrans Ave, Manhattan Beach
(90266-3702)
PHONE....................310 538-2242
Thomas E Nix Jr, *President*
Darlene Gavin, *Vice Pres*
EMP: 60
SQ FT: 28,000
SALES: 27.8MM
SALES (corp-wide): 147MM **Privately Held**
WEB: www.nixcheckcashing.com
SIC: 6099 Check cashing agencies
PA: Kinecta Federal Credit Union
1440 Rosecrans Ave
Manhattan Beach CA 90266
310 643-5400

(P-9687)
LENLYN LIMITED WHICH WILL DO B (HQ)
6151 W Century Blvd, Los Angeles
(90045-5307)
P.O. Box 92192 (90009-2192)
PHONE....................310 417-3432
Bharat Shah, *CEO*
Aleta Lindsay, *Vice Pres*
Bharat Shas, *Vice Pres*
Mark Garrett, *Technology*
EMP: 75
SQ FT: 1,000
SALES (est): 17.8MM **Privately Held**
WEB: www.iceplc.com
SIC: 6099 Foreign currency exchange
PA: Lenlyn Holdings Limited
19-21 Shaftesbury Avenue
London
330 123-1430

(P-9688)
MANIFLO MONEY EXCHANGE INC
1442 Highland Ave, National City
(91950-4624)
PHONE....................619 434-7200
Florino Agpaoa, *President*
Ferdinand Agpaoa, *President*
Rodel Agpaoa, *Vice Pres*
EMP: 65
SQ FT: 1,500
SALES (est): 12.7MM **Privately Held**
WEB: www.maniflo.com
SIC: 6099 Electronic funds transfer network, including switching

(P-9689)
SERFIN FUNDS TRANSFER (PA)
1000 S Fremont Ave A-O, Alhambra
(91803-8800)
PHONE....................626 457-3070
Richard Stevenson, *President*
EMP: 100
SALES (est): 9.3MM **Privately Held**
SIC: 6099 Electronic funds transfer network, including switching

(P-9690)
TASQ TECHNOLOGY INC
8875 Washington Blvd A, Roseville
(95678-6214)
PHONE....................916 632-7600
Dan Mandel, *Branch Mgr*

Chumeng Thao, *Sales Staff*
Bill Burns, *Manager*
EMP: 325
SALES (corp-wide): 12B **Publicly Held**
SIC: 6099 Electronic funds transfer network, including switching
HQ: Tasq Technology, Inc.
1169 Canton Rd
Marietta GA 30066

(P-9691)
XOOM CORPORATION
425 Market St Ste 1200, San Francisco
(94105-5404)
PHONE....................415 777-4800
John Kunze, *President*
Ryno Blignaut, *CFO*
Christopher G Ferro, *Ch Credit Ofcr*
Julian King, *Senior VP*
Matt Hibbard, *Vice Pres*
EMP: 190
SQ FT: 35,552
SALES: 159MM
SALES (corp-wide): 13B **Publicly Held**
SIC: 6099 Electronic funds transfer network, including switching
HQ: Paypal, Inc.
2211 N 1st St
San Jose CA 95131
877 981-2163

6111 Federal Credit Agencies

(P-9692)
AGAMERICA FCB (PA)
3636 American River Dr # 100, Sacramento
(95864-5952)
PHONE....................651 282-8800
James D Kirk, *President*
David B Newlin, *CFO*
Roger J Cramer, *Ch Credit Ofcr*
Gregory J Buehne, *Senior VP*
Chris Doherty, *Vice Pres*
EMP: 85
SALES (est): 867K **Privately Held**
SIC: 6111 6163 Federal & federally sponsored credit agencies; loan brokers

(P-9693)
DEUTSCHE BANK NATIONAL TR CO (DH)
2000 Avenue Of The Stars, Los Angeles
(90067-4700)
PHONE....................213 620-8200
EMP: 52
SALES: 149.6MM
SALES (corp-wide): 11.5B **Privately Held**
SIC: 6111 National Consumer Cooperative Bank
HQ: Deutsche Bank Trust Company Americas
60 Wall St Bsmt 1
New York NY 10005
212 250-2500

(P-9694)
EDUCATIONAL CREDIT MGT CORP
Also Called: Ecmc-CA
P.O. Box 419045 (95741-9045)
PHONE....................800 367-1590
EMP: 293
SALES (corp-wide): 391.9MM **Privately Held**
SIC: 6111 Federal & federally sponsored credit agencies
PA: Educational Credit Management Corporation
111 Washington Ave S # 1400
Minneapolis MN 55401
651 221-0566

(P-9695)
FEDERAL HM LN BNK SAN FRNCISCO (PA)
600 California St, San Francisco
(94108-2704)
PHONE....................415 616-1000
John F Luikart, *Ch of Bd*
Deb Eldridge, *President*
Dean Schultz, *President*
Lisa B Macmillen, *COO*

Kenneth C Miller, *CFO*
▲ **EMP:** 262 **EST:** 1932
SQ FT: 108,147
SALES: 1.6B **Privately Held**
WEB: www.fhlbsf.com
SIC: 6111 Federal & federally sponsored credit agencies

(P-9696)
FRESNO-MADERA FEDERAL LAND

305 N I St, Madera (93637-3062)
P.O. Box 13069, Fresno (93794-3069)
PHONE..............................559 674-2437
Rob Kratz, *Manager*
EMP: 58
SALES (corp-wide): 10.2MM **Privately Held**
SIC: 6111 Federal Land Banks
PA: Fresno-Madera Federal Land Bank Association
4635 W Spruce Ave
Fresno CA 93722
559 277-7000

(P-9697)
LAW SCHOOL FINANCIAL INC

Also Called: Law School Loans
175 S Lake Ave Unit 200, Pasadena (91101-2629)
PHONE..............................626 243-1800
Harrison A Barnes, *President*
Dennis Geselowitz, *CFO*
EMP: 190
SQ FT: 25,000
SALES (est): 15.5MM **Privately Held**
WEB: www.lawschoolloans.com
SIC: 6111 Student Loan Marketing Association

(P-9698)
LBS FINANCIAL CREDIT UNION

1401 Quail St Ste 130, Newport Beach (92660-2772)
PHONE..............................714 893-5111
Laurie Skinner, *Manager*
Heather L Summers, *VP Mktg*
EMP: 82
SALES (corp-wide): 48MM **Privately Held**
SIC: 6111 6036 Federal & federally sponsored credit agencies; savings & loan associations, not federally chartered
PA: Lbs Financial Credit Union
5505 Garden Grove Blvd # 500
Westminster CA 92683
562 598-9007

(P-9699)
LBS FINANCIAL CREDIT UNION (PA)

5505 Garden Grove Blvd # 500, Westminster (92683-1894)
PHONE..............................562 598-9007
Jeffrey A Napper, *President*
Gene Allen, *Ch of Bd*
Dug Woog, *Treasurer*
Sean Hardeman, *Senior VP*
Kristin Sanchez, *Vice Pres*
EMP: 120
SQ FT: 63,000
SALES: 48MM **Privately Held**
SIC: 6111 6163 Federal & federally sponsored credit agencies; loan brokers

(P-9700)
YOSEMITE FARM CREDIT ACA (PA)

806 W Monte Vista Ave, Turlock (95382-7242)
P.O. Box 3278 (95381-3278)
PHONE..............................209 667-2366
Leonard Van Eldern, *President*
Tracy Sparks, *CFO*
Robert Fuller, *Vice Pres*
Brian Lemons, *Vice Pres*
Melba Miyamoto, *VP Mktg*
EMP: 60
SQ FT: 9,000
SALES: 108.4MM **Privately Held**
WEB: www.yosemitefarmcredit.com
SIC: 6111 Federal Land Banks

6141 Personal Credit Institutions

(P-9701)
AMERICAN HONDA FINANCE CORP (DH)

20800 Madrona Ave, Torrance (90503-4915)
P.O. Box 2200 (90509-2200)
PHONE..............................310 972-2239
Hideo Tamaka, *CEO*
John Weisickle, *CFO*
Stephan Smith, *Senior VP*
Scott Jepson, *Admin Sec*
Susan Kopplin, *Admin Asst*
EMP: 200 **EST:** 1980
SQ FT: 50,288
SALES: 2B
SALES (corp-wide): 144.1B **Privately Held**
WEB: www.americanhondafinancecorporation.com
SIC: 6141 Financing: automobiles, furniture, etc., not a deposit bank; automobile & consumer finance companies
HQ: American Honda Motor Co., Inc.
1919 Torrance Blvd
Torrance CA 90501
310 783-2000

(P-9702)
AMERICAN HONDA FINANCE CORP

10801 Walker St Ste 140, Cypress (90630-5042)
PHONE..............................714 816-8110
EMP: 72
SALES (corp-wide): 144.1B **Privately Held**
SIC: 6141 Financing: automobiles, furniture, etc., not a deposit bank; automobile & consumer finance companies
HQ: American Honda Finance Corporation
20800 Madrona Ave
Torrance CA 90503
310 972-2239

(P-9703)
AMERICAN UNION FINCL SVCS INC

210 S Orange Grove Blvd # 1, Pasadena (91105-1705)
PHONE..............................714 619-2520
David Villarreal, *Chairman*
EMP: 150
SALES (est): 11.4MM **Privately Held**
SIC: 6141 Consumer finance companies

(P-9704)
BALBOA CAPITAL CORPORATION (PA)

575 Anton Blvd Fl 12, Costa Mesa (92626-7169)
PHONE..............................949 756-0800
Patrick Byrne, *CEO*
Phil Silva, *President*
Robert Rasmussen, *COO*
Patrick Ontal, *Vice Pres*
David Shafer, *Vice Pres*
EMP: 200
SQ FT: 24,000
SALES (est): 113.2MM **Privately Held**
WEB: www.balboacapital.com
SIC: 6141 Automobile & consumer finance companies

(P-9705)
CASHCALL INC

1 City Blvd W Ste 102, Orange (92868-3621)
P.O. Box 66007, Anaheim (92816-6007)
PHONE..............................949 752-4600
John Paul Reddam, *CEO*
Ethan Taub, *Chief Mktg Ofcr*
Nicole Navarro, *Department Mgr*
Derrick Wheatley, *Branch Mgr*
Mike Turley, *Technology*
EMP: 1400
SALES (est): 399.2MM **Privately Held**
WEB: www.cashcall.com
SIC: 6141 Personal finance licensed loan companies, small

(P-9706)
COMMERCE WEST INSURANCE CO

6130 Stoneridge Mall Rd # 400, Pleasanton (94588-3279)
P.O. Box 8006 (94588-8606)
PHONE..............................925 730-6400
Jerald Fels, *President*
Michael Vrban, *CFO*
EMP: 60
SQ FT: 23,000
SALES: 106.7MM
SALES (corp-wide): 72.6K **Privately Held**
WEB: www.commercewest.net
SIC: 6141 Automobile & consumer finance companies
HQ: The Commerce Insurance Company
211 Main St
Webster MA 01570
508 943-9000

(P-9707)
CONSUMER PORTFOLIO SVCS INC

19500 Jamboree Rd, Irvine (92612-2411)
PHONE..............................949 788-5695
Charles E Bradley Jr, *Manager*
Gregory S Washer, *Bd of Directors*
EMP: 204 **Publicly Held**
WEB: www.consumerportfolio.com
SIC: 6141 Personal credit institutions
PA: Consumer Portfolio Services, Inc.
3800 Howard Hughes Pkwy
Las Vegas NV 89169

(P-9708)
CONSUMER PORTFOLIO SVCS INC

16355 Laguna Canyon Rd, Irvine (92618-3801)
PHONE..............................949 753-6800
Brian Rayhill, *Director*
EMP: 78 **Publicly Held**
SIC: 6141 Financing: automobiles, furniture, etc., not a deposit bank
PA: Consumer Portfolio Services, Inc.
3800 Howard Hughes Pkwy
Las Vegas NV 89169

(P-9709)
CREDIT SOLUTIONS CORP

13520 Evening Creek Dr N # 500, San Diego (92128-8110)
PHONE..............................858 650-0812
Michael A Joplin, *CEO*
Raecelle Joplin, *President*
Christophe Beyer, *General Counsel*
EMP: 110
SQ FT: 15,397
SALES (est): 20.4MM **Privately Held**
WEB: www.creditsolutionscorp.com
SIC: 6141 Financing: automobiles, furniture, etc., not a deposit bank

(P-9710)
ELEVATE CREDIT INC

11710 El Camino Real, San Diego (92130-2099)
PHONE..............................817 928-1500
EMP: 112
SALES (corp-wide): 673.1MM **Publicly Held**
SIC: 6141 Licensed loan companies, small
PA: Elevate Credit, Inc.
4150 Intl Plz Ste 300
Fort Worth TX 76109
817 928-1500

(P-9711)
FLURISH INC

Also Called: Lendup
225 Bush St Ste 1100, San Francisco (94104-4250)
PHONE..............................855 253-6387
Sasha Orloff, *CEO*
Bill Donnelly, *CFO*
Kathleen Fitzpatrick, *Vice Pres*
Robert Novick, *Vice Pres*
Jacob Rosenberg, *Admin Sec*
EMP: 80
SQ FT: 18,500
SALES: 12MM **Privately Held**
SIC: 6141 Consumer finance companies

(P-9712)
FORD MOTOR COMPANY

4900 Hopyard Rd Ste 220, Pleasanton (94588-3345)
PHONE..............................925 351-6205
Craig Krisan, *Branch Mgr*
EMP: 63
SQ FT: 10,000
SALES (corp-wide): 156.7B **Publicly Held**
WEB: www.ford.com
SIC: 6141 Installment sales finance, other than banks
PA: Ford Motor Company
1 American Rd
Dearborn MI 48126
313 322-3000

(P-9713)
FUNDING CIRCLE USA INC

Also Called: Endurance Lending Network
747 Front St Fl 4, San Francisco (94111-1922)
PHONE..............................855 385-5356
Sam Hodges, *Director*
Nick Colburn, *CFO*
Manpreet Dhot, *Officer*
Jerome Le Luel, *Officer*
David Spack, *Officer*
EMP: 55 **EST:** 2014
SALES (est): 53.9MM
SALES (corp-wide): 124.8MM **Privately Held**
SIC: 6141 Licensed loan companies, small
HQ: Funding Circle Ltd
71 Queen Victoria Street
London EC4V

(P-9714)
GREEN DOT CORPORATION (PA)

3465 E Foothill Blvd # 100, Pasadena (91107-6072)
P.O. Box 5100 (91117-0100)
PHONE..............................626 765-2000
Steven W Streit, *President*
William I Jacobs, *Ch of Bd*
Mary J Dent, *CEO*
Kuan Archer, *COO*
Mark L Shifke, *CFO*
EMP: 113 **EST:** 1999
SQ FT: 140,000
SALES: 890.1MM **Publicly Held**
WEB: www.greendotcorp.com
SIC: 6141 7389 Personal credit institutions; credit card service

(P-9715)
HSBC FINANCE CORPORATION

931 Corporate Center Dr, Pomona (91768-2642)
PHONE..............................909 623-3355
Mark Marks, *Principal*
EMP: 800
SALES (corp-wide): 79.6B **Privately Held**
WEB: www.household.com
SIC: 6141 7389 6351 6159 Consumer finance companies; credit card service; credit & other financial responsibility insurance; machinery & equipment finance leasing; mortgage bankers; life insurance carriers
HQ: Hsbc Finance Corporation
1421 W Shure Dr Ste 100
Arlington Heights IL 60004
224 880-7000

(P-9716)
HYUNDAI CAPITAL AMERICA (DH)

Also Called: Hyundai Finance
3161 Michelson Dr # 1900, Irvine (92612-4418)
PHONE..............................714 965-3000
Sam Sanghyuk Suh, *CEO*
Sukjoon Won, *President*
Jwa Jin Cho, *CEO*
Minsok Randy Park, *CFO*
Kwansun Ahn, *Vice Pres*
EMP: 76
SQ FT: 60,000
SALES (est): 106MM
SALES (corp-wide): 38B **Privately Held**
SIC: 6141 Automobile loans, including insurance

PRODUCTS & SVCS

HQ: Hyundai Motor America
10550 Talbert Ave
Fountain Valley CA 92708
714 965-3000

(P-9717)
HYUNDAI MOTOR AMERICA (HQ)
10550 Talbert Ave, Fountain Valley
(92708-6032)
P.O. Box 20850 (92728-0850)
PHONE..................714 965-3000
Kyung SOO Lee, *President*
Brian Smith, *COO*
Jerry Flannery, *Exec VP*
Ron Haughey, *Exec Dir*
Tom Vanderford, *Exec Dir*
◆ **EMP:** 345
SQ FT: 215,000
SALES (est): 351.5MM
SALES (corp-wide): 38B **Privately Held**
WEB: www.hmaservice.com
SIC: 6141 6153 5511 Automobile & consumer finance companies; short-term business credit; automobiles, new & used
PA: Hyundai Motor Company
12 Heolleung-Ro, Seocho-Gu
Seoul 06797
822 346-4111

(P-9718)
JMAC LENDING INC
2510 Redhill Ave, Santa Ana (92705-5542)
PHONE..................949 390-2688
MAI Christina Pham, *President*
Anne Nguyen, *Accounts Mgr*
Tom WEI, *Accounts Exec*
EMP: 60
SALES: 24MM **Privately Held**
WEB: www.jmaclending.com
SIC: 6141 Financing: automobiles, furniture, etc., not a deposit bank

(P-9719)
LOAN NOW
3100 S Harbor Blvd # 180, Santa Ana (92704-6823)
PHONE..................714 352-2250
Art Fedich, *Vice Pres*
Brenda Vasquez, *Executive*
Rebecca Vega, *QA Dir*
Lilian Tran, *Financial Analy*
Gabriela Mayorga, *Analyst*
EMP: 68
SALES (est): 5.1MM **Privately Held**
SIC: 6141 Personal credit institutions

(P-9720)
LOBEL FINANCIAL CORPORATION (PA)
1150 N Magnolia Ave, Anaheim (92801-2605)
P.O. Box 3000 (92803-3000)
PHONE..................714 995-3333
Harvey Lobel, *CEO*
Gary Lobel, *Corp Secy*
David Lobel, *Vice Pres*
Murray Lobel, *Vice Pres*
EMP: 66 **EST:** 1979
SQ FT: 11,000
SALES (est): 33.9MM **Privately Held**
SIC: 6141 Automobile loans, including insurance

(P-9721)
MECHANICS BANK
Crb Auto
18400 Von Karman Ave, Irvine (92612-1514)
PHONE..................855 272-2886
Bill Katafias, *CEO*
Michael Britton, *Assoc VP*
Matthew Mulkey, *Vice Pres*
Karen Ho, *Admin Asst*
Dawn McCrumn, *Regl Sales Mgr*
EMP: 270
SALES (corp-wide): 54.2MM **Privately Held**
SIC: 6141 Automobile loans, including insurance
HQ: The Mechanics Bank
1111 Civic Dr
Walnut Creek CA 94596
800 797-6324

(P-9722)
MITSUBISHI MOTORS CR AMER INC (DH)
6400 Katella Ave, Cypress (90630-5208)
P.O. Box 6014 (90630-0014)
PHONE..................714 799-4730
Dan Booth, *President*
Hideyuki Kitamura, *Treasurer*
Charles Tredway, *Exec VP*
Ellen Gleberman, *Admin Sec*
Denise Rice, *Manager*
EMP: 394
SQ FT: 32,256
SALES (est): 32.4MM
SALES (corp-wide): 20.5B **Privately Held**
WEB: www.acvl.com
SIC: 6141 6159 Automobile loans, including insurance; truck finance leasing; finance leasing, vehicles: except automobiles & trucks
HQ: Mitsubishi Motors North America, Inc.
6400 Katella Ave
Cypress CA 90630
714 799-4730

(P-9723)
MONTEREY FINANCIAL SVCS INC (PA)
4095 Avenida De La Plata, Oceanside (92056-5802)
P.O. Box 5199 (92052-5199)
PHONE..................760 639-3500
Robert Steinke, *President*
Mike Gray, *Exec VP*
Kathi Steinke, *Vice Pres*
Kathyleen Steinke, *Vice Pres*
Dustin Chung, *Engineer*
EMP: 110
SQ FT: 27,000
SALES: 12.9MM **Privately Held**
WEB: www.montereyfinancial.com
SIC: 6141 8721 7322 8742 Consumer finance companies; billing & bookkeeping service; collection agency, except real estate; financial consultant

(P-9724)
NATIONAL PLANNING CORPORATION
100 N Pacific Coast Hwy # 1800, El Segundo (90245-5612)
PHONE..................800 881-7174
John C Johnson, *President*
Patrick Carroll, *Treasurer*
Patricia McCallop, *Ch Credit Ofcr*
Caren Coleman, *Vice Pres*
Sarah Corce, *Vice Pres*
EMP: 150
SALES (est): 36.7MM **Privately Held**
SIC: 6141 Automobile & consumer finance companies

(P-9725)
NORTH AMERICAN ACCEPTANCE CORP
Also Called: An Open Check
3191 Red Hill Ave Ste 100, Costa Mesa (92626-3451)
PHONE..................714 868-3195
Marco J Rasic, *CEO*
Mary Clancey Rasic, *Vice Pres*
EMP: 123
SQ FT: 24,000
SALES (est): 16.6MM **Privately Held**
WEB: www.naacceptance.com
SIC: 6141 6719 Automobile & consumer finance companies; personal holding companies, except banks

(P-9726)
PAYOFF INC
Also Called: Happy Money
3200 Park Center Dr # 800, Costa Mesa (92626-1979)
PHONE..................949 430-0630
Scott Saunders, *CEO*
John Phamvan, *President*
Christopher Hilliard, *Ch Credit Ofcr*
Adam Zarlengo,
Ibrahim Dusi, *Officer*
EMP: 89
SQ FT: 19,500
SALES (est): 22.3MM **Privately Held**
SIC: 6141 Personal credit institutions

(P-9727)
TRADING FINANCIAL CREDIT LLC (PA)
Also Called: Trading Financial Capital
3055 Wilshire Blvd # 530, Los Angeles (90010-1145)
PHONE..................213 375-3113
Daniel Joelson, *President*
EMP: 50
SQ FT: 9,000
SALES: 7.5MM **Privately Held**
SIC: 6141 Personal credit institutions

(P-9728)
WELLS FARGO DEALER SVCS INC (DH)
23 Pasteur, Irvine (92618-3816)
P.O. Box 25341, Santa Ana (92799-5341)
PHONE..................949 727-1002
Thomas A Wolfe, *President*
J Keith Palmer, *Treasurer*
Dawn M Martin, *Exec VP*
Guy Du Bose, *Senior VP*
EMP: 350
SALES (est): 189.4MM
SALES (corp-wide): 97.7B **Publicly Held**
SIC: 6141 Consumer finance companies
HQ: Wells Fargo Bank, National Association
101 N Phillips Ave
Sioux Falls SD 57104
605 575-6900

(P-9729)
WILSHIRE CONSUMER CREDIT
Also Called: 1800-R-Ado
4751 Wilshire Blvd, Los Angeles (90010-3827)
P.O. Box 76809 (90076-0809)
PHONE..................323 692-8585
Ian Anderson, *President*
EMP: 50
SALES (est): 5.2MM **Privately Held**
SIC: 6141 Automobile & consumer finance companies

6153 Credit Institutions, Short-Term Business

(P-9730)
AFFIRM INC
Also Called: Affirm Identity
650 California St Fl 12, San Francisco (94108-2716)
PHONE..................415 984-0490
Max Levchin, *CEO*
Rob Pfeifer, *Owner*
Chip Overstreet, *President*
Huey Lin, *COO*
Carl Gish, *Chief Mktg Ofcr*
EMP: 200 **EST:** 2003
SALES (est): 35.8MM **Privately Held**
SIC: 6153 Working capital financing

(P-9731)
AMERICAN MERCHANT CENTER INC
6819 Sepulveda Blvd # 311, Van Nuys (91405-4463)
PHONE..................818 947-1700
Victor Olechno, *President*
Jeffrey Vaynberg, *Vice Pres*
Jenifer Nutzmann, *Sales Executive*
EMP: 70 **EST:** 1987
SQ FT: 5,000
SALES (est): 8.1MM **Privately Held**
WEB: www.americanmerchant.com
SIC: 6153 Credit card services, central agency collection

(P-9732)
BANK AMERICA NATIONAL ASSN
450 American St, Simi Valley (93065-6285)
PHONE..................805 520-5100
Danette Samilton, *Senior VP*
Karl Uselman, *Manager*
EMP: 100
SALES (corp-wide): 100.2B **Publicly Held**
SIC: 6153 Working capital financing

HQ: Bank Of America, National Association
100 S Tryon St
Charlotte NC 28202
704 386-5681

(P-9733)
BANKAMERICA FINANCIAL INC
Also Called: Bank of America
315 Montgomery St, San Francisco (94104-1856)
PHONE..................415 622-3521
James A Dern, *President*
Lewis W Teel, *Ch of Bd*
Michael K Riley, *Treasurer*
John Carson, *Senior VP*
Paul Ogorzelec, *Senior VP*
EMP: 1700
SALES (corp-wide): 100.2B **Publicly Held**
SIC: 6153 6141 6282 Factors of commercial paper; consumer finance companies; investment advisory service
PA: Bank Of America Corporation
100 N Tryon St Ste 170
Charlotte NC 28202
704 386-5681

(P-9734)
BLUEVINE CAPITAL INC
401 Warren St Ste 300, Redwood City (94063-1578)
PHONE..................888 216-9619
Eyal Lifshitz, *CEO*
Tina Chen, *Partner*
Ana Sirbu, *CFO*
Eric Mondloch, *Vice Pres*
Kairee Allomong, *Office Mgr*
EMP: 70
SALES (est): 703.6K **Privately Held**
SIC: 6153 Working capital financing

(P-9735)
COGENT FINANCIAL GROUP
5199 E Pacific Coast Hwy, Long Beach (90804-3309)
PHONE..................562 985-1388
Theodore Schlegel, *CEO*
EMP: 60
SQ FT: 6,500
SALES (est): 6.6MM **Privately Held**
WEB: www.cogentfinancialgroup.com
SIC: 6153 Purchasers of accounts receivable & commercial paper

(P-9736)
CONRAD ACCEPTANCE CORPORATION
Also Called: Conrad Credit
476 W Vermont Ave, Escondido (92025-6529)
PHONE..................760 735-5000
Keith Richenbacher, *President*
William Huss, *CFO*
John Page, *Vice Pres*
Bob Pranik, *Admin Sec*
Ernie Recesetar, *Director*
EMP: 50
SQ FT: 6,000
SALES (est): 5.4MM
SALES (corp-wide): 20.7MM **Privately Held**
SIC: 6153 Purchasers of accounts receivable & commercial paper
PA: Conrad Corporation
476 W Vermont Ave
Escondido CA 92025
800 826-6723

(P-9737)
EAST LOS ANGELES COMMUNITY UN (PA)
Also Called: Telacu
5400 E Olympic Blvd Fl 3, Commerce (90022-5147)
PHONE..................323 721-1655
David C Lizarraga, *Ch of Bd*
Paul Samuel, *CFO*
Michael D Lizarraga, *Exec VP*
Jay Bell, *Senior VP*
Ana Gonzalez, *Executive*
EMP: 50
SQ FT: 60,000

▲ = Import ▼=Export
◆ =Import/Export

SALES: 17.7MM **Privately Held**
WEB: www.telacu.com
SIC: **6153** 8322 6512 6514 Short-term business credit; multi-service center; non-residential building operators; dwelling operators, except apartments

(P-9738)
ENCORE CAPITAL GROUP INC (PA)
3111 Camino Del Rio N # 103, San Diego (92108-5721)
PHONE.....................877 445-4581
Ashish Masih, *President*
Michael P Monaco, *Ch of Bd*
Paul Grinberg, *President*
Jonathan C Clark, *CFO*
Gregory L Call, *Officer*
EMP: 83 **EST:** 1990
SQ FT: 118,000
SALES: 1.1B **Publicly Held**
WEB: www.encorecapitalgroup.com
SIC: **6153** Purchasers of accounts receivable & commercial paper

(P-9739)
GENERAL ELECTRIC COMPANY
3100 Zinfandel Dr Ste 255, Rancho Cordova (95670-6391)
P.O. Box 4596, New York NY (10163-4596)
PHONE.....................916 286-8020
EMP: 119
SALES (corp-wide): 122B **Publicly Held**
SIC: **6153** Short-term business credit
PA: General Electric Company
41 Farnsworth St
Boston MA 02210
617 443-3000

(P-9740)
HANA COMMERCIAL FINANCE INC
1000 Wilshire Blvd Fl 20, Los Angeles (90017-5645)
PHONE.....................213 240-1234
Suyong Kim, *CFO*
Sunnie Kim, *CEO*
Young Shim, *COO*
Suyoung Kim, *CFO*
EMP: 85 **EST:** 2016
SALES (est): 6.2MM **Privately Held**
SIC: **6153** Factoring services

(P-9741)
LENDINGCLUB CORPORATION (PA)
71 Stevenson St Ste 300, San Francisco (94105-2985)
PHONE.....................415 632-5600
Scott Sanborn, *President*
Kolya Klimenko, *President*
Sameer Gulati, *COO*
Carrie Dolan, *CFO*
Sandeep Bhandari, *Ch Credit Ofcr*
EMP: 88
SQ FT: 169,000
SALES: 574.5MM **Publicly Held**
SIC: **6153** Working capital financing

(P-9742)
MIDLAND CREDIT MANAGEMENT INC (HQ)
3111 Camino Del Rio N, San Diego (92108-5720)
P.O. Box 939069 (92193-9069)
PHONE.....................877 240-2377
Kenneth A Vecchione, *CEO*
Carl Gregory, *President*
Robin Pruitt, *Senior VP*
Andrew Asch, *Vice Pres*
Deepak Maheshwari, *Vice Pres*
EMP: 1800
SALES (est): 399.2MM
SALES (corp-wide): 1.1B **Publicly Held**
WEB: www.encorecapitalgroup.com
SIC: **6153** Short-term business credit
PA: Encore Capital Group, Inc.
3111 Camino Del Rio N # 103
San Diego CA 92108
877 445-4581

(P-9743)
NATIONS CAPITAL GROUP LLC
Also Called: Nations Surgery Center
5353 Balboa Blvd Ste 300, Encino (91316-2863)
PHONE.....................818 793-2050
Fax: 818 793-2059
EMP: 50
SALES (corp-wide): 5.1MM **Privately Held**
SIC: **6153**
PA: Nations Capital Group, Llc
5370 S Durango Dr
Las Vegas NV

(P-9744)
PACIFIC LIFE GLOBAL FUNDING
700 Newport Center Dr, Newport Beach (92660-6307)
PHONE.....................949 219-3011
William Gross, *Principal*
EMP: 56
SALES (est): 3.7MM
SALES (corp-wide): 12.8B **Privately Held**
SIC: **6153** Short-term business credit
HQ: Pacific Life Insurance Company
700 Newport Center Dr
Newport Beach CA 92660
949 219-3011

(P-9745)
PLAYSPAN LLC
2900 Gordon Ave Ste 201, Santa Clara (95051-0718)
P.O. Box 8999, San Francisco (94128-8999)
PHONE.....................408 617-9155
Alfred F Kelly Jr, *President*
Julie Whitehead, *CFO*
Lex Bayer, *General Mgr*
Andrew Magruder, *CTO*
Tony Weber, *Opers Staff*
EMP: 50
SQ FT: 3,500
SALES (est): 6.9MM **Publicly Held**
SIC: **6153** Credit card services, central agency collection
PA: Visa Inc.
900 Metro Center Blvd
Foster City CA 94404
-

(P-9746)
PROSPER FUNDING LLC
101 2nd St Fl 15, San Francisco (94105-3672)
PHONE.....................415 593-5400
Stephan Vermut, *Principal*
Eric Thaller, *Vice Pres*
Tauhid Rehman, *Director*
Ben Campbell, *Manager*
EMP: 140
SALES (est): 620.5K
SALES (corp-wide): 116.2MM **Privately Held**
SIC: **6153** Working capital financing
PA: Prosper Marketplace, Inc.
221 Main St Fl 3
San Francisco CA 94105
415 593-5400

(P-9747)
RIVIERA FINANCE OF TEXAS INC (PA)
220 Avenue I, Redondo Beach (90277-5617)
PHONE.....................310 540-3993
David B Clark, *President*
Kenneth J Wong, *CFO*
EMP: 200
SQ FT: 5,000
SALES (est): 16.2MM **Privately Held**
SIC: **6153** Factors of commercial paper

(P-9748)
SEQUOIA RESIDENTIAL FUNDING
1 Belvedere Pl Ste 330, Mill Valley (94941-2493)
PHONE.....................415 389-7373
George Bull, *CEO*
EMP: 90

SALES: 13.3MM **Publicly Held**
SIC: **6153** 7389 Working capital financing; financial services
PA: Redwood Trust, Inc.
1 Belvedere Pl Ste 300
Mill Valley CA 94941

(P-9749)
VEROS CREDIT LLC (PA)
2333 N Broadway Ste 400, Santa Ana (92706-1656)
P.O. Box 11914 (92711-1914)
PHONE.....................714 415-6185
Cyrus Bozorgi, *Mng Member*
Bijan Bozorgi,
EMP: 51
SALES (est): 15.1MM **Privately Held**
SIC: **6153** Working capital financing

(P-9750)
WELLS FARGO COML DIST FIN LLC
3100 Zinfandel Dr Ste 255, Rancho Cordova (95670-6391)
PHONE.....................916 636-2020
EMP: 94
SALES (corp-wide): 97.7B **Publicly Held**
SIC: **6153** Mercantile financing
HQ: Wells Fargo Commercial Distribution Finance, Llc
10 S Wacker Dr
Chicago IL 60606
847 747-6800

6159 Credit Institutions, Misc Business

(P-9751)
AMERICAN AGCREDIT FLCA (PA)
400 Aviation Blvd Ste 100, Santa Rosa (95403-1181)
P.O. Box 1120 (95402-1120)
PHONE.....................707 545-1200
Ron Carli, *CEO*
Byron Enix, *President*
Greg Somerhalder, *COO*
Christopher Call, *CFO*
John Horne, *Officer*
EMP: 91
SQ FT: 26,000
SALES (est): 118.5MM **Privately Held**
WEB: www.agloan.com
SIC: **6159** Agricultural credit institutions

(P-9752)
AMERICAN CAPITAL GROUP INC
Also Called: A C G
23382 Mill Creek Dr # 115, Laguna Hills (92653-7932)
PHONE.....................949 271-5800
Carl Heaton, *President*
Carl J Heaton, *President*
Wendy Page, *Admin Asst*
Sam Maffey, *Portfolio Mgr*
Burke Wiedel, *Controller*
EMP: 64
SALES (est): 11.9MM **Privately Held**
WEB: www.acgcapital.com
SIC: **6159** Equipment & vehicle finance leasing companies
PA: Nationwide Capital Holdings, Inc.
31726 Rncho Viejo Ste 111
San Juan Capistrano CA
949 271-5816

(P-9753)
ATEL CAPITAL GROUP (PA)
Also Called: Leasing Equipment
600 Montgomery St Fl 9, San Francisco (94111-2711)
PHONE.....................800 543-2835
Dean L Cash, *CEO*
Jeffrey Rosenthal, *President*
Paritosh K Choksi, *CFO*
Partichosh Choksi, *CFO*
Russell Wilder, *Officer*
EMP: 80
SALES (est): 26.8MM **Privately Held**
SIC: **6159** Machinery & equipment finance leasing

(P-9754)
BABCOCK & BROWN LATIN AMERICA
2 Harrison St Fl 6, San Francisco (94105-1671)
PHONE.....................415 512-1515
James Babcock, *President*
Camron Peters, *Vice Pres*
Peter Metzner, *Principal*
EMP: 85
SALES (est): 6.8MM
SALES (corp-wide): 708.8MM **Privately Held**
SIC: **6159** Loan institutions, general & industrial
HQ: Bbam Llc
50 California St Fl 14
San Francisco CA 94111
415 267-1600

(P-9755)
BANC AMERICA LSG & CAPITL LLC (DH)
555 California St Fl 4, San Francisco (94104-1506)
PHONE.....................415 765-7349
Eric Lundquist, *Managing Dir*
Daniel Monberg, *Vice Pres*
EMP: 150
SALES (est): 300.6MM
SALES (corp-wide): 100.2B **Publicly Held**
SIC: **6159** Machinery & equipment finance leasing
HQ: Bank Of America, National Association
100 S Tryon St
Charlotte NC 28202
704 386-5681

(P-9756)
ELECTRONIC COMMERCE LLC
1 City Blvd W Ste 1850, Orange (92868-3636)
PHONE.....................800 770-5520
Darnell Ponder, *Managing Prtnr*
Khaazra Maaranu, *Managing Prtnr*
EMP: 85
SQ FT: 7,000
SALES (est): 13.5MM **Privately Held**
SIC: **6159** Intermediate investment banks

(P-9757)
FUNDBOX INC
300 Montgomery St Ste 900, San Francisco (94104-1921)
PHONE.....................415 509-1343
Eyal Shinar, *CEO*
Prashant Fuloria, *COO*
Rose Zhong, *VP Finance*
Sharaya Magana, *Accounts Exec*
EMP: 150
SQ FT: 8,300
SALES: 300MM **Privately Held**
SIC: **6159** Small business investment companies
PA: Fundbox Ltd
23 Yehuda Halevy
Tel Aviv-Jaffa
362 468-06

(P-9758)
GENERAL ELECTRIC COMPANY
2995 Red Hill Ave Ste 100, Costa Mesa (92626-5984)
PHONE.....................714 434-4111
Teri Lo, *Manager*
EMP: 147
SALES (corp-wide): 122B **Publicly Held**
WEB: www.gecapital.com
SIC: **6159** Equipment & vehicle finance leasing companies; machinery & equipment finance leasing
PA: General Electric Company
41 Farnsworth St
Boston MA 02210
617 443-3000

(P-9759)
GENERAL ELECTRIC COMPANY
17901 Von Karman Ave # 600, Irvine (92614-6297)
P.O. Box 4596, New York NY (10163-4596)
PHONE.....................949 838-3043
Mark Dawejko, *Branch Mgr*
EMP: 159

SALES (corp-wide): 122B **Publicly Held**
WEB: www.gecapital.com
SIC: **6159** Equipment & vehicle finance
leasing companies
PA: General Electric Company
41 Farnsworth St
Boston MA 02210
617 443-3000

(P-9760)
INTERLINK
Also Called: Interlink Company The
10940 Wilshire Blvd, Los Angeles
(90024-3915)
PHONE....................310 734-1499
Shezad Rokerya, *Director*
Dr Charles Kohlhaas, *Vice Chairman*
Jason P Caramanis, *Exec VP*
EMP: 103
SQ FT: 4,000
SALES (est): 8.6MM **Privately Held**
SIC: **6159 8742** Intermediate investment
banks; banking & finance consultant

(P-9761)
NATIONWIDE FUNDING LLC
5520 Trabuco Rd Ste 100, Irvine
(92620-5705)
PHONE....................949 679-3600
Evan Lang, *Mng Member*
Josh Splinter,
EMP: 50
SQ FT: 12,000
SALES (est): 9.4MM **Privately Held**
SIC: **6159 7359** Machinery & equipment fi-
nance leasing; equipment rental & leasing

(P-9762)
PACIFIC CAPITAL COMPANIES
LLC
11620 Wilshire Blvd, Los Angeles
(90025-1706)
PHONE....................800 583-3015
Charles Anderson, *Managing Prtnr*
EMP: 150
SQ FT: 10,000
SALES (est): 17.8MM **Privately Held**
SIC: **6159** Automobile finance leasing

(P-9763)
PENTECH FINANCIAL SERVICES
INC (PA)
Also Called: Pentech Funding Services
75 E Santa Clara St # 1100, San Jose
(95113-1842)
PHONE....................408 879-2200
Benjamin Millerbis, *Ch of Bd*
Bruce Blanco, *CFO*
EMP: 51
SALES (est): 12MM **Privately Held**
WEB: www.pentechfinancial.com
SIC: **6159** Machinery & equipment finance
leasing

(P-9764)
TRINITY CAPITAL
CORPORATION (DH)
475 Sansome St Fl 19, San Francisco
(94111-3112)
PHONE....................415 956-5174
Don J McGrath, *CEO*
Jerry Newell, *President*
EMP: 74
SQ FT: 19,232
SALES (est): 35MM **Publicly Held**
WEB: www.trinitycapital.com
SIC: **6159 8741** Machinery & equipment fi-
nance leasing; management services
HQ: Bank Of The West
180 Montgomery St # 1400
San Francisco CA 94104
415 765-4800

(P-9765)
WELLS FARGO CAPITAL FIN
LLC (DH)
2450 Colo Ave Ste 3000w, Santa Monica
(90404)
PHONE....................310 453-7300
Peter E Schwab,
Jeff Carbery, *Exec VP*
Rocky Gor, *Senior VP*
Nichol Shuart, *Vice Pres*
Steven V Macko, *Managing Dir*
EMP: 73

SALES (est): 33.2MM
SALES (corp-wide): 97.7B **Publicly Held**
WEB: www.wellsfargo.com
SIC: **6159** Loan institutions, general & in-
dustrial
HQ: Wells Fargo Bank, National Associa-
tion
101 N Phillips Ave
Sioux Falls SD 57104
605 575-6900

(P-9766)
WESTLAKE SERVICES LLC (PA)
Also Called: Westlake Financial Services
4751 Wilshire Blvd # 100, Los Angeles
(90010-3847)
P.O. Box 76809 (90076-0809)
PHONE....................323 692-8800
Don Hankey, *Ch of Bd*
Ian Anderson, *President*
James Vagim, *President*
Paul Kerwin, *CFO*
Kent Hagan, *Vice Pres*
EMP: 169
SQ FT: 22,000
SALES (est): 40.4MM **Privately Held**
WEB: www.westlakefinancial.com
SIC: **6159 6141** Automobile finance leas-
ing; personal credit institutions

6162 Mortgage Bankers &
Loan Correspondents

(P-9767)
A D BILICH INC
Also Called: Preferred Financial
11 Crow Canyon Ct Ste 100, San Ramon
(94583-1981)
PHONE....................925 820-5557
Tim Barnes, *President*
Anthony D Bilich, *Owner*
Angela Bilich, *Admin Sec*
John Engstrom, *Controller*
Theresa Nolan, *Manager*
EMP: 50
SQ FT: 4,000
SALES (est): 7.8MM **Privately Held**
WEB: www.preferredfinancial.com
SIC: **6162** Mortgage bankers

(P-9768)
AGIRE MORTGAGE
CORPORATION
2125 E Katella Ave # 350, Anaheim
(92806-6072)
PHONE....................714 564-5821
Robin Auerbach, *President*
EMP: 50
SALES (est): 5.1MM **Privately Held**
SIC: **6162** Mortgage bankers

(P-9769)
ALL CALIFORNIA MORTGAGE
INC (PA)
17 E Sr Frncis Drke Bl200, Larkspur
(94939)
PHONE....................415 925-5225
Bruce Fonarow, *President*
Robert Knoll, *Partner*
Chuck Scoma, *Partner*
Jeffrey Drawdy, *Vice Pres*
Kevin Mulcahy, *Branch Mgr*
EMP: 66
SQ FT: 4,600
SALES (est): 7.9MM **Privately Held**
SIC: **6162** Mortgage bankers & correspon-
dents

(P-9770)
AMBER FINANCIAL GROUP LLC
(PA)
Also Called: Amber Mortgage
11415 W Bernardo Ct, San Diego
(92127-1639)
PHONE....................858 487-7209
Trena Papageorge,
Julian Kozar,
EMP: 110
SQ FT: 8,000
SALES (est): 7.6MM **Privately Held**
SIC: **6162** Mortgage bankers

(P-9771)
AMERICAN FINANCIAL
NETWORK INC (PA)
Also Called: Gateway Home Realty
10 Pointe Dr Ste 330, Brea (92821-7620)
PHONE....................909 606-3905
John B Sherman, *President*
John R Sherman, *Vice Pres*
EMP: 200
SQ FT: 8,000
SALES (est): 177.5MM **Privately Held**
SIC: **6162** Mortgage bankers

(P-9772)
AMERICAN INTERBANC MRTG
LLC
4 Park Plz Ste 650, Irvine (92614-2522)
PHONE....................714 957-9430
Jiangping JP He,
Nick Dang, *Technology*
Linda Chen, *Loan Officer*
Vanessa Nguyen, *Accountant*
Yana Guo, *Controller*
EMP: 50 EST: 1998
SALES (est): 7.5MM **Privately Held**
WEB: www.eloans4u.com
SIC: **6162 6163** Mortgage bankers; loan
brokers
PA: Seashine Financial Llc
4 Park Plz Ste 650
Irvine CA 92614

(P-9773)
AMERICAN INTERNET
MORTGAGE INC
Also Called: Aimloan.com, A Direct Lender
4121 Camino Del Rio S, San Diego
(92108-4103)
PHONE....................888 411-4246
Vincent J Kasperick, *President*
EMP: 106 EST: 1998
SQ FT: 4,500
SALES (est): 63.6MM **Privately Held**
SIC: **6162** Mortgage bankers

(P-9774)
AMERICAN PACIFIC MORTGAGE
CORP (PA)
Also Called: Big Valley Mortgage
3000 Lava Ridge Ct # 200, Roseville
(95661-2800)
PHONE....................916 960-1325
Kurt Reisig, *CEO*
Bill Lowman, *President*
David Mack, *COO*
Ralph Hints, *CFO*
Jim Black, *Officer*
EMP: 120
SQ FT: 35,000
SALES (est): 385.6MM **Privately Held**
WEB: www.apmmortgage.com
SIC: **6162** Mortgage bankers

(P-9775)
AMERICAN TRANSPORT INC
Also Called: Bankers Diversified Mortgage
3910 Prospect Ave Ste A, Yorba Linda
(92886-1776)
PHONE....................714 567-8000
David Hahnfeld, *President*
Diane G Hahnfeld, *Corp Secy*
David N Hartman, *Vice Pres*
EMP: 60
SQ FT: 32,000
SALES (est): 4MM **Privately Held**
WEB: www.bankersdiversified.com
SIC: **6162** Mortgage brokers, using own
money

(P-9776)
AMERICASH
3080 Bristol St Ste 300, Costa Mesa
(92626-3059)
PHONE....................714 994-7554
Paul Giangrande, *CEO*
Eric Harrington, *Vice Pres*
Michael Martin, *Vice Pres*
EMP: 50
SALES (est): 12.5MM **Privately Held**
WEB: www.americashloans.com
SIC: **6162** Mortgage bankers

(P-9777)
AMERIPATH MORTGAGE
CORPORATION
6410 Oak Cyn Ste 200, Irvine
(92618-5215)
PHONE....................949 753-9211
Paul B Akers, *President*
Kirk L Redding, *CEO*
Jo Beth Montoya, *Vice Pres*
EMP: 112
SQ FT: 22,286
SALES (est): 8.4MM **Privately Held**
WEB: www.amclend.com
SIC: **6162** Mortgage bankers

(P-9778)
ARCS COMMERCIAL
MORTGAGE CO LP (DH)
26901 Agoura Rd Ste 200, Calabasas
(91301-5109)
PHONE....................818 676-3274
Timothy White, *CEO*
EMP: 110
SQ FT: 15,000
SALES (est): 32.2MM
SALES (corp-wide): 18B **Publicly Held**
SIC: **6162** Mortgage bankers
HQ: Pnc Bank, National Association
222 Delaware Ave
Wilmington DE 19801
877 762-2000

(P-9779)
BANK AMERICA NATIONAL
ASSN
275 Valencia Ave, Brea (92823-6340)
PHONE....................949 474-8801
Pearl Bfar, *Administration*
Gary Bell, *Vice Pres*
EMP: 60
SALES (corp-wide): 100.2B **Publicly**
Held
SIC: **6162** Mortgage bankers
HQ: Bank Of America, National Association
100 S Tryon St
Charlotte NC 28202
704 386-5681

(P-9780)
BEAR STEARNS COMPANIES
LLC
Also Called: Bear Stern Residential Mrtg
1833 Alton Pkwy, Irvine (92606-4902)
PHONE....................949 856-8300
Troy Gotscahall, *Branch Mgr*
EMP: 780
SALES (corp-wide): 99.6B **Publicly Held**
WEB: www.bearstearns.com
SIC: **6162** Mortgage bankers
HQ: Bear Stearns Companies Llc
383 Madison Ave
New York NY 10179
212 272-2000

(P-9781)
BERKSHIRE MORTGAGE FIN
CORP
Also Called: Vauche Bank Berkshire Mort-
gage
7575 Irvine Center Dr # 200, Irvine
(92618-2987)
PHONE....................949 754-6300
Jeff Day, *Manager*
EMP: 80
SALES (corp-wide): 11.5B **Privately Held**
SIC: **6162** Mortgage bankers
HQ: Berkshire Mortgage Finance Corpora-
tion
1 North Beacon St Fl 14
Allston MA 02134
617 523-0066

(P-9782)
BROKER SOLUTIONS INC
233 Milford Dr, Corona Del Mar
(92625-3118)
PHONE....................800 450-2010
EMP: 89 **Privately Held**
SIC: **6162** Mortgage bankers & correspon-
dents
PA: Broker Solutions, Inc.
14511 Myford Rd Ste 100
Tustin CA 92780

(P-9783)
BSNAP LLC
4 Hutton Centre Dr Fl 10, Santa Ana
(92707-8713)
PHONE...................657 269-4410
EMP: 99
SALES (est): 2.4MM **Privately Held**
SIC: 6162

(P-9784)
CAL MUTUAL INC
2040 S Santa Cruz St # 115, Anaheim
(92805-6821)
PHONE...................888 700-4650
Dennis Shane Dailey, *President*
EMP: 87
SALES (est): 484K **Privately Held**
SIC: 6162 6531 Mortgage bankers & cor-
respondents; real estate agent, residential

(P-9785)
CALIBER HOME LOANS INC
6600 Koll Center Pkwy, Pleasanton
(94566-3256)
PHONE...................925 417-3491
Tim Soldati, *Principal*
EMP: 78
SALES (corp-wide): 2.4B **Privately Held**
SIC: 6162 Mortgage bankers & correspon-
dents
PA: Caliber Home Loans, Inc.
1525 S Belt Line Rd
Coppell TX 75019
800 401-6587

(P-9786)
CALIBER HOME LOANS INC
3700 Hilborn Rd Ste 700, Fairfield
(94534-7997)
PHONE...................707 432-1000
Sanjiv Das, *Principal*
Jessica Nix, *Manager*
EMP: 300
SALES (corp-wide): 2.4B **Privately Held**
SIC: 6162 Mortgage bankers & correspon-
dents
PA: Caliber Home Loans, Inc.
1525 S Belt Line Rd
Coppell TX 75019
800 401-6587

(P-9787)
CALIBER HOME LOANS INC
1111 Chapala St, Santa Barbara
(93101-3158)
PHONE...................805 883-6800
EMP: 79
SALES (corp-wide): 2.4B **Privately Held**
SIC: 6162 6141 Loan correspondents;
personal credit institutions
PA: Caliber Home Loans, Inc.
1525 S Belt Line Rd
Coppell TX 75019
800 401-6587

(P-9788)
CALIFORNIA EMPIRE BANCORP INC
10681 Fthill Blvd Ste 200, Rancho Cuca-
monga (91730)
PHONE...................909 484-7988
Lester Hills, *President*
Ken Emminger, *Vice Pres*
EMP: 50
SQ FT: 5,000
SALES (est): 3.5MM **Privately Held**
SIC: 6162 Mortgage bankers & correspon-
dents

(P-9789)
CAPITAL PLUS FINANCIAL CORP
909 W Laurel St Ste 250, San Diego
(92101-1224)
PHONE...................619 744-1900
Frank Sharpe, *President*
Doug Lipar, *Vice Pres*
Evelyn Cervantes, *Office Mgr*
EMP: 50
SQ FT: 5,000
SALES (est): 5.2MM **Privately Held**
SIC: 6162 Mortgage brokers, using own
money

(P-9790)
CENTURY FINANCE INCORPORATED
Also Called: Villagecraft Quality Furn
2461 Santa Monica Blvd, Santa Monica
(90404-2138)
PHONE...................310 281-3081
RC Zarate, *President*
Franceisca Zarate, *CFO*
Ezzio Delpino, *Corp Secy*
EMP: 56
SALES (est): 4.5MM **Privately Held**
SIC: 6162 2514 Mortgage bankers & cor-
respondents; metal household furniture

(P-9791)
CHAPEL FUNDING CORPORATION
26521 Rancho Pkwy S, Lake Forest
(92630-8329)
PHONE...................949 580-1800
Nina Mitchel, *President*
EMP: 165
SALES (est): 10.4MM **Privately Held**
WEB: www.chapelfunding.com
SIC: 6162 Mortgage bankers & correspon-
dents

(P-9792)
CITIGROUP INC
840 N Eckhoff St Ste 140, Orange
(92868-1054)
PHONE...................714 938-0748
Michael B Zeller, *Branch Mgr*
EMP: 100
SALES (corp-wide): 71.4B **Publicly Held**
WEB: www.citigroup.com
SIC: 6162 6163 Mortgage bankers & cor-
respondents; loan brokers
PA: Citigroup Inc.
388 Greenwich St
New York NY 10013
212 559-1000

(P-9793)
COUNTRYWIDE CAPITAL MKTS LLC (DH)
4500 Park Granada, Calabasas
(91302-1613)
PHONE...................818 225-3000
Angelo R Mozilo, *Ch of Bd*
Stanfard L Kurland, *CFO*
Ron Kripalani, *Director*
EMP: 182
SALES (est): 44.2MM
SALES (corp-wide): 100.2B **Publicly Held**
SIC: 6162 Mortgage brokers, using own
money
HQ: Countrywide Financial Corporation
4500 Park Granada
Calabasas CA 91302
818 225-3000

(P-9794)
COUNTRYWIDE FINANCIAL CORP (HQ)
4500 Park Granada, Calabasas
(91302-1613)
P.O. Box 7137, Pasadena (91109-7137)
PHONE...................818 225-3000
Angelo R Mozilo, *Ch of Bd*
David Sambol, *President*
Jack W Schakett, *COO*
Eric P Sieracki, *CFO*
David Kuhn, *Exec VP*
EMP: 1100
SQ FT: 225,000
SALES (est): 6.4B
SALES (corp-wide): 100.2B **Publicly Held**
WEB: www.countrywide.com
SIC: 6162 6211 6361 6411 Mortgage
bankers; brokers; security; dealers, secu-
rity; title insurance; life insurance agents;
loan brokers; real estate investors, except
property operators
PA: Bank Of America Corporation
100 N Tryon St Ste 170
Charlotte NC 28202
704 386-5681

(P-9795)
COUNTRYWIDE HOME LOANS INC (DH)
225 W Hillcrest Dr, Thousand Oaks
(91360-7883)
PHONE...................818 225-3000
Michael Schloessmann, *Ch of Bd*
Angelo R Mozilo, *Ch of Bd*
David Sambol, *President*
Carlos M Garcia, *COO*
Thomas K McLaughlin, *CFO*
EMP: 700 EST: 1969
SQ FT: 220,000
SALES (est): 579.7MM
SALES (corp-wide): 100.2B **Publicly Held**
WEB: www.mycountrywide.com
SIC: 6162 Mortgage bankers
HQ: Countrywide Financial Corporation
4500 Park Granada
Calabasas CA 91302
818 225-3000

(P-9796)
COUNTRYWIDE HOME LOANS INC
801 N Brand Blvd Ste 750, Glendale
(91203-3218)
PHONE...................818 550-8700
Lynda Martinlawley, *Manager*
EMP: 150
SALES (corp-wide): 100.2B **Publicly Held**
WEB: www.mycountrywide.com
SIC: 6162 Mortgage bankers
HQ: Countrywide Home Loans, Inc.
225 W Hillcrest Dr
Thousand Oaks CA 91360
818 225-3000

(P-9797)
CRESTLINE FUNDING CORPORATION
18851 Pardeen Ave, San Diego (92108)
PHONE...................949 863-8600
Scott M Brown, *President*
Brad Helman, *CFO*
Jeff Giger, *Executive*
Geoff Hickman, *Loan Officer*
Maddie Mullins, *Loan*
EMP: 50
SQ FT: 18,500
SALES (est): 12.3MM **Privately Held**
WEB: www.crestlinewholesale.com
SIC: 6162 Mortgage bankers

(P-9798)
DECISION READY SOLUTIONS INC
2855 Michelle Ste 350, Irvine (92606-1013)
PHONE...................949 400-1126
Ravi Ramanathan, *President*
Claudia Sanchez, *COO*
Tom Schmidt, *CFO*
Ranjeev Kumar, *Vice Pres*
Dan Mahler, *Security Dir*
EMP: 50 EST: 2011
SALES (est): 2MM **Privately Held**
SIC: 6162 7371 7372 Mortgage bankers;
computer software systems analysis &
design, custom; business oriented com-
puter software

(P-9799)
DIAMOND RIDGE CORPORATION
Also Called: Re/Max
121 S Mountain Ave, Upland (91786-6257)
PHONE...................909 949-0605
Jennifer Lynn Puglisi, *CEO*
Laura Aldridge, *Broker*
Debra Mares, *Broker*
Melvin Munguia, *Broker*
Bulenda Newson, *Broker*
EMP: 165
SALES (est): 231.4K **Privately Held**
SIC: 6162 Mortgage bankers & correspon-
dents

(P-9800)
DUXFORD FINANCIAL INC
Also Called: William Lyon Fin Services
4490 Von Karman Ave, Newport Beach
(92660-2008)
PHONE...................949 471-2010
William Lyon, *Ch of Bd*
EMP: 50
SALES (est): 5MM
SALES (corp-wide): 54.5MM **Privately Held**
WEB: www.duxford.com
SIC: 6162 Mortgage bankers & correspon-
dents
PA: Lyon Management Group, Inc.
4901 Birch St Frnt
Newport Beach CA 92660
949 252-9101

(P-9801)
ECI CORPORATION A CORP NEV (PA)
Also Called: Coast Capital
4300 Stevens Creek Blvd # 275, San Jose
(95129-1249)
PHONE...................408 941-9268
Robert Genisman, *CEO*
Pete Cline, *President*
Robin Cline, *Treasurer*
David Belleville, *Vice Pres*
Nina Genisman, *Admin Sec*
EMP: 70
SQ FT: 9,000
SALES (est): 5.4MM **Privately Held**
WEB: www.eci-corp.com
SIC: 6162 Mortgage brokers, using own
money

(P-9802)
EXECUTIVE FINANCIAL HM LN CORP
Also Called: Executive Home Loan
12501 Chandler Blvd, Valley Village
(91607-1941)
PHONE...................818 285-5626
Michael Nikravesh, *President*
Ron Fattal, *Vice Pres*
EMP: 50
SALES (est): 5MM **Privately Held**
SIC: 6162 Mortgage bankers & correspon-
dents

(P-9803)
FINANCE AMERICA LLC (HQ)
1901 Main St Ste 150, Irvine (92614-0516)
PHONE...................949 440-1000
Brian Libman,
Karen H Cornell,
Graham Fleming,
Arthur K Rice,
EMP: 207
SQ FT: 60,000
SALES (est): 154.2MM
SALES (corp-wide): 28.1MM **Privately Held**
WEB: www.closeasap.com
SIC: 6162 6163 Mortgage bankers; loan
brokers
PA: Lehman Brothers Holdings Inc.
277 Park Ave Fl 46
New York NY 10172
646 285-9000

(P-9804)
FINANCE AMERICA MORTGAGE LLC
13200 Crossroads Pkwy N, City of Industry
(91746-3459)
PHONE...................562 478-4664
Gabriel Garza, *Manager*
EMP: 293 **Privately Held**
SIC: 6162 Mortgage bankers
PA: Finance Of America Mortgage Llc
300 Welsh Rd Bldg 5
Horsham PA 19044

(P-9805)
FIRST CALIFORNIA MRTG CO II
1400 N Mcdowell Blvd # 300, Petaluma
(94954-6553)
P.O. Box 11868, San Rafael (94912-1868)
PHONE...................415 209-0910
Dennis M Hart, *Ch of Bd*
Christopher Hart, *President*
Elizabeth Armstrong, *Director*
EMP: 100
SALES (est): 12.8MM **Privately Held**
WEB: www.firstcal.net
SIC: 6162 Mortgage bankers & correspon-
dents

PRODUCTS & SVCS

(P-9806)
FIRST PRIORITY FINANCIAL INC
3700 Hilborn Rd Ste 700, Fairfield
(94534-7997)
PHONE..................707 432-1000
Timothy Kearns, *President*
David Soldati, *CFO*
Michael Soldati, *Vice Pres*
Aaron Lawrence, *CTO*
EMP: 300
SQ FT: 4,500
SALES (est): 1.6MM **Privately Held**
WEB: www.lendscape.com
SIC: 6162 Mortgage bankers & correspondents

(P-9807)
GENPACT MORTGAGE SERVICES INC (HQ)
Also Called: Moneyline Lending Services
15420 Laguna Canyon Rd, Irvine
(92618-2119)
PHONE..................949 417-5131
Gregory Gentek, *CEO*
Evan Gentry, *President*
Richard Belliston, *CFO*
Bradley J Barber, *Exec VP*
Taylor Woods, *Exec VP*
EMP: 85 EST: 1996
SQ FT: 17,000
SALES (est): 18MM **Privately Held**
SIC: 6162 6163 Mortgage brokers, using own money; loan brokers

(P-9808)
GOLDEN EMPIRE MORTGAGE INC
664 Shoppers Ln Ste A, Covina
(91723-3536)
PHONE..................626 967-3236
Joe Ewens, *Branch Mgr*
EMP: 72
SALES (corp-wide): 67.9MM **Privately Held**
SIC: 6162 Mortgage bankers & correspondents
PA: Golden Empire Mortgage, Inc.
1200 Discovery Dr Ste 300
Bakersfield CA 93309
661 328-1600

(P-9809)
GOLDEN EMPIRE MORTGAGE INC
Also Called: Gem Mortgage
420 Barstow Rd, Barstow (92311-2952)
PHONE..................760 256-3593
Tim Silva, *Branch Mgr*
EMP: 60
SALES (corp-wide): 67.9MM **Privately Held**
SIC: 6162 Mortgage bankers & correspondents
PA: Golden Empire Mortgage, Inc.
1200 Discovery Dr Ste 300
Bakersfield CA 93309
661 328-1600

(P-9810)
GOLDEN EMPIRE MORTGAGE INC (PA)
1200 Discovery Dr Ste 300, Bakersfield
(93309-7036)
PHONE..................661 328-1600
John Copeland, *Manager*
EMP: 80
SALES (est): 67.9MM **Privately Held**
SIC: 6162 Mortgage bankers

(P-9811)
GOLDEN EMPIRE MORTGAGE INC (PA)
2130 Chester Ave, Bakersfield
(93301-4471)
PHONE..................661 328-1600
Howard Kootstra, *CEO*
John Thomas, *Vice Pres*
Terry Bleecker, *Info Tech Dir*
Chris Bergam, *Controller*
EMP: 100
SQ FT: 25,000
SALES (est): 49.3MM **Privately Held**
WEB: www.gemcorp.com
SIC: 6162 Mortgage bankers

(P-9812)
GUARANTEED RATE INC
1455 Frazee Rd Ste 500, San Diego
(92108-4350)
PHONE..................760 310-6008
Trent Annicharico, *Branch Mgr*
Jon Solek, *Vice Pres*
Matt Veronesi, *Vice Pres*
EMP: 129 **Privately Held**
SIC: 6162 Mortgage bankers
PA: Guaranteed Rate, Inc.
3940 N Ravenswood Ave
Chicago IL 60613

(P-9813)
HCL FINANCE INC (PA)
Also Called: Home Community Lending
2560 Mission College Blvd, Santa Clara
(95054-1217)
PHONE..................408 845-9035
Hong Cheng, *President*
Nancy Cheng, *Vice Pres*
EMP: 107
SQ FT: 9,000
SALES (est): 7.6MM **Privately Held**
WEB: www.hclfinance.com
SIC: 6162 Mortgage bankers & correspondents

(P-9814)
HOME CAPITAL GROUP
948 N Grand Ave, Covina (91724-2045)
PHONE..................626 331-4213
Raymond Mark Gonzales, *Partner*
Rick Starr, *Partner*
EMP: 68
SALES (est): 3.4MM **Privately Held**
SIC: 6162 Mortgage bankers & correspondents

(P-9815)
HOMEQ SERVICING CORPORATION (DH)
4837 Watt Ave, North Highlands
(95660-5108)
PHONE..................916 339-6192
Arthur Lyon, *President*
Keith G Becher, *COO*
Mark K Metz, *Admin Sec*
EMP: 1000
SALES (est): 79.4MM
SALES (corp-wide): 1.1B **Publicly Held**
WEB: www.homeq.com
SIC: 6162 6163 6111 6159 Mortgage bankers; agents, farm or business loan; Student Loan Marketing Association; automobile finance leasing
HQ: Ocwen Loan Servicing, Llc
1661 Worthington Rd # 100
West Palm Beach FL 33409
561 682-8000

(P-9816)
HSBC FINANCE CORPORATION
21801 Ventura Bouelvard, Woodland Hills
(91364)
PHONE..................818 999-9175
EMP: 303
SALES (corp-wide): 79.6B **Privately Held**
WEB: www.household.com
SIC: 6162 Mortgage bankers
HQ: Hsbc Finance Corporation
1421 W Shure Dr Ste 100
Arlington Heights IL 60004
224 880-7000

(P-9817)
IMPAC MORTGAGE CORP
19500 Jamboree Rd, Irvine (92612-2411)
PHONE..................949 475-3600
Joseph R Tomkinson, *President*
Brendan Pawloski, *Executive*
Les Thomas, *Info Tech Mgr*
Deniece Negrete, *Manager*
Barbara Ramirez, *Manager*
EMP: 298
SALES (est): 62.6MM **Publicly Held**
SIC: 6162 Mortgage bankers
PA: Impac Mortgage Holdings, Inc.
19500 Jamboree Rd
Irvine CA 92612

(P-9818)
INTERNATIONAL HOME MORTGAGE
13601 Whittier Blvd # 311, Whittier
(90605-1968)
PHONE..................562 945-7753
Rick Arciniega, *Manager*
EMP: 75
SALES (est): 5.1MM **Privately Held**
SIC: 6162 Mortgage bankers & correspondents

(P-9819)
ISERVE RESIDENTIAL LENDING LLC
16745 W Bernardo Dr # 100, San Diego
(92127-1907)
PHONE..................858 486-4169
Doug Wilson, *Director*
Michael Wilson, *COO*
Dustin Jones, *Officer*
Angela Kidd, *Officer*
Robert Sanders, *Area Mgr*
EMP: 100
SALES (est): 18.9MM **Privately Held**
SIC: 6162 Bond & mortgage companies

(P-9820)
JMJ FINANCIAL GROUP (PA)
26800 Aliso Viejo Pkwy # 200, Aliso Viejo
(92656-2625)
PHONE..................949 340-6336
Virgil Kyle, *President*
Devin Langager, *Partner*
Thomas Kish, *COO*
Ryan Robertson, *CFO*
Erik Hoskins, *Officer*
EMP: 50
SQ FT: 10,000
SALES: 500MM **Privately Held**
SIC: 6162 Mortgage bankers

(P-9821)
JUST MORTGAGE INC
8577 Haven Ave Ste 306, Rancho Cucamonga (91730-4850)
PHONE..................562 908-5000
Eun H Choi, *CEO*
Sang H Jeung, *President*
Bryan Choi, *Vice Pres*
EMP: 118
SQ FT: 49,750
SALES (est): 15.9MM **Privately Held**
SIC: 6162 Mortgage bankers & correspondents

(P-9822)
KONDAUR CAPITAL CORPORATION (PA)
333 S Anita Dr Ste 400, Orange
(92868-3314)
PHONE..................714 352-2038
John Kontouis, *President*
EMP: 150
SALES (est): 2.2MM **Privately Held**
SIC: 6162 Mortgage bankers

(P-9823)
LAKE COUNTY HOME LOANS
Also Called: Selzer Home Loans
350 E Gobbi St, Ukiah (95482-5511)
PHONE..................707 462-4000
Richard Selzer, *Owner*
Elisa Moilanen, *Admin Sec*
EMP: 50
SALES (est): 4.4MM **Privately Held**
SIC: 6162 Mortgage bankers & correspondents

(P-9824)
LAND HOME FINANCIAL SVCS INC (PA)
1355 Willow Way Ste 250, Concord
(94520-8113)
PHONE..................925 676-7038
Bradley Harold Waite, *CEO*
Angela Warren, *President*
David Waite, *CFO*
Janelle Horne, *Officer*
Tiffany Jamieson, *Officer*
EMP: 50
SQ FT: 6,000
SALES (est): 19.2MM **Privately Held**
SIC: 6162 Loan correspondents

(P-9825)
LENOX FINANCIAL MORTGAGE CORP
Also Called: Weslend Financial
200 Sandpointe Ave # 800, Santa Ana
(92707-5783)
PHONE..................949 428-5100
Wesley C Hoaglund, *CEO*
Robert Oconnor, *Executive*
Derrick Sedberry, *Loan Officer*
Trinh Bui, *Business Mgr*
Julio Martinez, *Loan*
EMP: 105
SALES (est): 51.4MM **Privately Held**
SIC: 6162 Mortgage bankers

(P-9826)
LEON CHIEN CORP
Also Called: RE Max 2000 Realty
17843 Colima Rd, City of Industry
(91748-1729)
PHONE..................626 964-8302
Kuan Sung, *CEO*
EMP: 80
SALES (est): 8.5MM **Privately Held**
SIC: 6162 Mortgage bankers & correspondents

(P-9827)
LMB MORTGAGE SERVICES INC
Also Called: Lowermybills
4859 W Slauson Ave # 405, Los Angeles
(90056-3215)
PHONE..................310 348-6800
Steve Krenzer, *CEO*
Pat Gregory, *CFO*
EMP: 150
SALES (est): 20.3MM
SALES (corp-wide): 1.4B **Privately Held**
SIC: 6162 Mortgage bankers
PA: Rock Holdings Inc.
1074 Woodward Ave
Detroit MI 48226
313 373-7700

(P-9828)
LOANDEPOTCOM LLC
901 N Palm Canyon Dr, Palm Springs
(92262-4450)
PHONE..................760 797-6000
Anthony Hsieh, *Branch Mgr*
EMP: 1029 **Privately Held**
SIC: 6162 Mortgage bankers
PA: Loandepot.Com, Llc
26642 Towne Centre Dr
Foothill Ranch CA 92610

(P-9829)
LOANDEPOTCOM LLC (PA)
Also Called: Customer Loan Depot
26642 Towne Centre Dr, Foothill Ranch
(92610-2808)
PHONE..................949 474-1322
Anthony Hsieh, *CEO*
David Norris, *President*
Jon Frojen, *CFO*
Peter Macdonald, *Exec VP*
Bryan Sullivan, *Exec VP*
EMP: 963
SALES (est): 973.4MM **Privately Held**
WEB: www.loandepot.com
SIC: 6162 Mortgage bankers

(P-9830)
LONG BEACH INVESTMENT GROUP
Also Called: Dream Home & Investments Rlty
2041 Pacific Coast Hwy, Lomita
(90717-2685)
PHONE..................562 595-7277
Henry Salazar, *President*
EMP: 50
SQ FT: 6,000
SALES: 2.7MM **Privately Held**
SIC: 6162 Mortgage bankers & correspondents

(P-9831)
MASON MCDUFFIE MORTGAGE CORP (PA)
2010 Crow Canyon Pl # 400, San Ramon
(94583-1344)
PHONE..................925 242-4400

Marilyn Richardson, *CEO*
Jack Radin, *CFO*
Herb Tasker, *Chairman*
Bill Godfrey, *Exec VP*
Bill Simpson, *Exec VP*
EMP: 83
SALES (est): 6.2MM **Privately Held**
WEB: www.mmcdcorp.com
SIC: 6162 Mortgage bankers

(P-9832)
METRO HOME LOAN INC
Also Called: Metro City
15301 Ventura Blvd D300, Sherman Oaks
(91403-3102)
PHONE..............................818 461-9840
Paul Whiley, *Vice Pres*
EMP: 99
SALES (est): 5MM **Privately Held**
SIC: 6162 Mortgage bankers & correspondents

(P-9833)
MORTGAGE CAPITAL ASSOC INC
11150 W Olympic Blvd # 1160, Los Angeles
(90064-1826)
PHONE..............................310 477-6877
Jay Steren, *CEO*
EMP: 54
SALES (est): 6.9MM **Privately Held**
WEB: www.100percentloan.com
SIC: 6162 Mortgage bankers & correspondents

(P-9834)
MORTGAGE CAPITAL PARTNERS INC
12400 Wilshire Blvd # 900, Los Angeles
(90025-1030)
PHONE..............................310 295-2900
Carolyn W Chang, *President*
David Anthony, *Vice Pres*
Thomas Bayles, *Vice Pres*
Jordan Donolow, *Vice Pres*
Trevor Lane, *Vice Pres*
EMP: 80 **EST:** 2008
SALES (est): 11.2MM **Privately Held**
SIC: 6162 Mortgage bankers

(P-9835)
MOUNTAIN WEST FINANCIAL INC (PA)
Also Called: Mortgage Works Financial
1209 Nevada St Ste 200, Redlands
(92374-4581)
PHONE..............................909 793-1500
Gary H Martell Jr, *President*
Michael W Douglas, *Officer*
EMP: 391
SQ FT: 4,729
SALES (est): 76MM **Privately Held**
WEB: www.mwfinc.com
SIC: 6162 Mortgage bankers

(P-9836)
NETWORK CAPITAL FUNDING CORP (PA)
5 Park Plz Ste 800, Irvine (92614-8501)
PHONE..............................949 442-0060
Tri Nguyen, *President*
EMP: 345
SQ FT: 67,000
SALES (est): 49.6MM **Privately Held**
SIC: 6162 Mortgage bankers

(P-9837)
OCMBC INC
Also Called: Ocmban
19000 Macarthur Blvd # 200, Irvine
(92612-1420)
PHONE..............................714 479-0999
Rabi H Aziz, *CEO*
Madelina L Colon, *President*
Hector Chaidez, *Division Mgr*
Bernie Cavallucci, *Sales Mgr*
Sona Dominova, *Accounts Exec*
EMP: 70 **EST:** 2001
SQ FT: 12,500
SALES (est): 11.8MM **Privately Held**
WEB: www.helpufinance.com
SIC: 6162 Mortgage bankers

(P-9838)
ONEMAIN HOLDINGS INC
2401 Claribel Rd Ste C, Riverbank
(95367-9480)
PHONE..............................209 869-8030
Sean Craig, *Branch Mgr*
EMP: 146
SALES (corp-wide): 3.7B **Publicly Held**
SIC: 6162 Mortgage bankers & correspondents
PA: Onemain Holdings, Inc.
601 Nw 2nd St
Evansville IN 47708
812 424-8031

(P-9839)
ONEMAIN HOLDINGS INC
31712 Casino Dr Ste 6a, Lake Elsinore
(92530-4513)
PHONE..............................951 245-5029
EMP: 146
SALES (corp-wide): 3.7B **Publicly Held**
SIC: 6162 Mortgage bankers & correspondents
PA: Onemain Holdings, Inc.
601 Nw 2nd St
Evansville IN 47708
812 424-8031

(P-9840)
OPTIMA MORTGAGE CORPORATION
2081 Bus Ctr Dr Ste 230, Irvine (92612)
PHONE..............................714 389-4650
Mansour Sadeghi, *President*
Shiva Sadeghi, *Treasurer*
EMP: 55
SQ FT: 14,000
SALES: 5.1MM **Privately Held**
WEB: www.60minuteloan.com
SIC: 6162 Mortgage bankers

(P-9841)
OWNIT MORTGAGE SOLUTIONS INC
Also Called: Security Pacific Home Loans
4360 Park Terrace Dr # 100, Westlake Village (91361-5696)
PHONE..............................513 872-6922
Bill Dallas, *President*
Bruce Dickinson, *COO*
John Duhadway, *CFO*
John Du Hadway, *Vice Pres*
Brian Thompson, *VP Finance*
EMP: 500
SQ FT: 47,857
SALES (est): 35.7MM **Privately Held**
SIC: 6162 6163 Mortgage bankers & correspondents; loan brokers

(P-9842)
PARAMOUNT EQUITY MORTGAGE LLC
10888 White Rock Rd, Rancho Cordova
(95670-6044)
PHONE..............................916 290-9999
Hayes Barnard, *President*
EMP: 200
SALES (corp-wide): 113.1MM **Privately Held**
SIC: 6162 Mortgage bankers
PA: Paramount Equity Mortgage, Llc
8781 Sierra College Blvd
Roseville CA 95661
916 290-9999

(P-9843)
PARAMOUNT EQUITY MORTGAGE LLC
4200 Douglas Blvd, Granite Bay
(95746-5902)
PHONE..............................916 290-9999
Hayes Barnard, *President*
EMP: 100
SALES (corp-wide): 113.1MM **Privately Held**
SIC: 6162 Mortgage bankers
PA: Paramount Equity Mortgage, Llc
8781 Sierra College Blvd
Roseville CA 95661
916 290-9999

(P-9844)
PARAMOUNT EQUITY MORTGAGE LLC
22 Executive Park Ste 100, Irvine
(92614-2700)
PHONE..............................916 290-9999
Hayes Barnard, *President*
EMP: 150
SALES (corp-wide): 113.1MM **Privately Held**
SIC: 6162 Mortgage bankers
PA: Paramount Equity Mortgage, Llc
8781 Sierra College Blvd
Roseville CA 95661
916 290-9999

(P-9845)
PEOPLES CHOICE HOME (PA)
7515 Irvine Center Dr, Irvine (92618-2930)
PHONE..............................949 494-6167
Neil B Kornswiet, *CEO*
EMP: 55
SQ FT: 20,000
SALES (est): 16.9MM **Privately Held**
SIC: 6162 Mortgage companies, urban

(P-9846)
PLAZA HOME MORTGAGE INC (PA)
4820 Eastgate Mall # 100, San Diego
(92121-1993)
PHONE..............................858 346-1200
Kevin Parra, *President*
James Cutri, *Exec VP*
Michael Fontaine, *Exec VP*
Michael Modell, *Senior VP*
Karin Neidhart, *Senior VP*
EMP: 50
SQ FT: 1,000
SALES (est): 129.4MM **Privately Held**
WEB: www.plazahomemortgages.com
SIC: 6162 Mortgage bankers

(P-9847)
PRIVATE NAT MRTG ACCPTANCE LLC (HQ)
Also Called: Pennymac
6101 Condor Dr, Agoura Hills (91301)
PHONE..............................818 224-7401
Jeff Grogin,
Steve Bailey, *Security Dir*
EMP: 800
SALES (est): 138.7MM
SALES (corp-wide): 1.1B **Publicly Held**
SIC: 6162 Mortgage bankers
PA: Pennymac Financial Services, Inc.
3043 Townsgate Rd
Westlake Village CA 91361
818 224-7442

(P-9848)
PROVIDENT FINCL HOLDINGS INC
9245 Laguna Springs Dr # 13, Elk Grove
(95758-7987)
PHONE..............................916 709-3257
Chris Opfer, *Branch Mgr*
EMP: 84 **Publicly Held**
SIC: 6162 Mortgage bankers & correspondents
PA: Provident Financial Holdings, Inc.
3756 Central Ave
Riverside CA 92506

(P-9849)
PROVIDENT FUNDING ASSOC LP (PA)
851 Traeger Ave Ste 100, San Bruno
(94066-3091)
P.O. Box 5914, Santa Rosa (95402-5914)
PHONE..............................650 652-1300
Doug Pica, *General Ptnr*
Michelle Blake, *Partner*
Craig Pica, *Partner*
Ralph Pica, *Partner*
Jack Mullin, *Treasurer*
EMP: 50
SALES (est): 81.2MM **Privately Held**
SIC: 6162 Mortgage bankers

(P-9850)
PROVIDENT MRTG CPITL ASSOC INC
Also Called: P M C A
1633 Bayshore Hwy Ste 155, Burlingame
(94010-1515)
PHONE..............................650 652-1300
Craig Pica, *Ch of Bd*
Mark Lefanowicz, *CFO*
Michelle Blake, *Admin Sec*
John Kubiak, *CIO*
EMP: 600
SALES (est): 16.9MM **Privately Held**
SIC: 6162 Mortgage bankers

(P-9851)
PROVIDENT SAVINGS BANK
Also Called: Profed Mortgage
10370 Commerce Center Dr # 200, Rancho Cucamonga (91730-5806)
PHONE..............................909 484-6286
Debbie Baker, *General Mgr*
EMP: 50 **Publicly Held**
SIC: 6162 Mortgage bankers
HQ: Provident Savings Bank
6570 Magnolia Ave
Riverside CA 92506
951 782-6177

(P-9852)
QUALITY HOME LOANS
Also Called: Clear Credit Capital
27001 Agoura Rd Ste 200, Agoura Hills
(91301-5357)
PHONE..............................818 206-6600
Patrick Weaver, *President*
John T Gaiser, *President*
Randy Miller, *CFO*
Christopher Powell, *Vice Pres*
EMP: 220
SQ FT: 47,500
SALES: 18MM **Privately Held**
WEB: www.qualityhomeloans.com
SIC: 6162 Mortgage bankers & correspondents

(P-9853)
RATE IS LOW
Also Called: Ideal Home Sales
3744 Mt Diablo Blvd # 205, Lafayette
(94549-3694)
PHONE..............................925 299-9364
Ray Newby, *Manager*
EMP: 50
SALES (est): 3.1MM **Privately Held**
WEB: www.rateislow.com
SIC: 6162 Mortgage bankers & correspondents

(P-9854)
REAL ESTATE EQUITY EXCHANGE
Also Called: Unison
650 California St Fl 18, San Francisco
(94108-2722)
PHONE..............................415 992-4200
Thomas Stonholtz, *CEO*
EMP: 75
SALES (est): 279K **Privately Held**
SIC: 6162 Mortgage bankers & correspondents

(P-9855)
RESIDENTIAL BANCORP (PA)
22632 Goln Spgs Dr Ste 20, Diamond Bar
(91765)
PHONE..............................330 499-8333
Corey A Wood, *CEO*
William H James III, *President*
Michael J Luu, *CFO*
Tobias Hoy, *Exec VP*
Tom Wong, *Exec VP*
EMP: 57
SQ FT: 10,000
SALES (est): 10.8MM **Privately Held**
SIC: 6162 Mortgage bankers

(P-9856)
SEA BREEZE FINANCIAL SERVICES (PA)
Also Called: Sea Breeze Mortgage Services
18191 Von Karman Ave # 150, Irvine
(92612-7104)
P.O. Box 19079, Anaheim (92817-9079)
PHONE..............................949 223-9700

P
R
O
D
U
C
T
S

&

S
V
C
S

Leonard Hamilton, *President*
Curtis Green, *Executive*
EMP: 50
SQ FT: 50,000
SALES (est): 9.2MM **Privately Held**
SIC: 6162 Mortgage bankers & correspondents

(P-9857)
SECURITY NAT MSTR HOLDG CO LLC (PA)
323 5th St, Eureka (95501-0305)
P.O. Box 1028 (95502-1028)
PHONE...................707 442-2818
Robin P Arkley II, *CEO*
EMP: 140
SQ FT: 15,000
SALES (est): 48.3MM **Privately Held**
SIC: 6162 Mortgage bankers & correspondents

(P-9858)
SIERRA PACIFIC MORTGAGE CO INC
104 Traffic Way, Arroyo Grande (93420-3450)
PHONE...................805 489-6060
EMP: 88
SALES (corp-wide): 197.9MM **Privately Held**
SIC: 6162 Mortgage bankers
PA: Sierra Pacific Mortgage Company, Inc.
1180 Iron Point Rd # 200
Folsom CA 95630
916 932-1700

(P-9859)
SIERRA PACIFIC MORTGAGE CO INC (PA)
1180 Iron Point Rd # 200, Folsom (95630-8325)
PHONE...................916 932-1700
James Coffrini, *President*
Joe Waldherr, *Partner*
Gary Clark, *COO*
Amy Adamaitis, *Officer*
Joseph Bonhart, *Officer*
EMP: 580
SALES (est): 197.9MM **Privately Held**
WEB: www.premiumlending.com
SIC: 6162 Mortgage bankers

(P-9860)
STEARNS LENDING LLC (HQ)
4 Hutton Centre Dr Fl 10, Santa Ana (92707-8713)
PHONE...................714 513-7777
David C Schneider, *CEO*
Katherine Le, *President*
James Hecht, *COO*
Gary B Fabian, *CFO*
Kathleen L Vaughan, *Exec VP*
EMP: 350
SALES (est): 237.8MM **Privately Held**
WEB: www.stearns.com
SIC: 6162 Mortgage bankers & correspondents
PA: Stearns Holdings, Llc
4 Hutton Cntre Dr Fl 10 Flr 10
Santa Ana CA 92707
714 513-7273

(P-9861)
SUN WEST MORTGAGE COMPANY INC (PA)
18000 Studebaker Rd # 200, Cerritos (90703-2679)
PHONE...................800 453-7884
Pavan Agarwal, *CEO*
Hari S Agarwal, *President*
Sharda Agarwal, *Corp Secy*
Jim Trapinski, *Exec VP*
Anita Agarwal, *Vice Pres*
EMP: 61
SQ FT: 9,800
SALES (est): 33.5MM **Privately Held**
SIC: 6162 6163 Mortgage bankers; loan brokers

(P-9862)
TELACU INDUSTRIES INC (HQ)
5400 E Olympic Blvd # 300, Commerce (90022-5187)
PHONE...................323 721-1655
David Lizarraga, *CEO*

Michael D Lizarraga, *President*
EMP: 50
SQ FT: 17,000
SALES: 195.4K
SALES (corp-wide): 17.7MM **Privately Held**
SIC: 6162 6552 Subdividers & developers; loan correspondents
PA: East Los Angeles Community Union Inc
5400 E Olympic Blvd Fl 3
Commerce CA 90022
323 721-1655

(P-9863)
US CREDIT BANCORP INC
851 20th St, Santa Monica (90403-2002)
P.O. Box 1727 (90406-1727)
PHONE...................310 829-2112
Michel Rone, *President*
M Matsumote, *Corp Secy*
EMP: 85
SQ FT: 6,500
SALES: 45MM **Privately Held**
SIC: 6162 6799 Mortgage bankers; real estate investors, except property operators

(P-9864)
WALKER & DUNLOP INC
12100 Wilshire Blvd # 1500, Los Angeles (90025-7107)
PHONE...................301 215-5500
Willy Walker, *Manager*
EMP: 63 **Publicly Held**
SIC: 6162 6411 6531 Mortgage bankers; insurance agents, brokers & service; real estate agents & managers
PA: Walker & Dunlop, Inc.
7501 Wisconsin Ave 1200e
Bethesda MD 20814

(P-9865)
WELLS FARGO HOME MORTGAGE INC
5540 Fermi Ct Fl 2002, Carlsbad (92008-7325)
PHONE...................760 603-7000
Kathleen Vauthan, *Vice Pres*
Carolina McEnaney, *Marketing Mgr*
EMP: 400
SALES (corp-wide): 97.7B **Publicly Held**
WEB: www.wfhm.com
SIC: 6162 Mortgage bankers
HQ: Wells Fargo Home Mortgage Inc
1 Home Campus
Des Moines IA 50328
515 324-3707

(P-9866)
WOODSIDE GROUP INC
Also Called: Hillsborough
3509 Coffee Rd Ste D10, Modesto (95355-1358)
PHONE...................209 579-2030
Mike Golkin, *Manager*
EMP: 50
SALES (corp-wide): 143.4MM **Privately Held**
SIC: 6162 Mortgage bankers & correspondents
PA: Woodside Group, Llc
460 W 50 N Ste 200
Salt Lake City UT 84101
801 869-3950

6163 Loan Brokers

(P-9867)
ACA FINANCIAL GUARANTY CORP
7189 N Figueroa St, Los Angeles (90042-1279)
PHONE...................323 255-3583
Robert Snyder, *President*
Steven Joeseph Berkowitz, *CEO*
Allen Overton, *CFO*
Brian Foore, *Vice Pres*
Deboraa Kovacs, *Vice Pres*
EMP: 75
SQ FT: 6,500
SALES (est): 3.2MM **Privately Held**
SIC: 6163 Loan brokers

(P-9868)
ACCESS TO LOANS FOR LEARNING
1230 Rosecrans Ave # 560, Manhattan Beach (90266-2477)
PHONE...................310 979-4700
Chris Chapman, *President*
Charles Bull, *CEO*
EMP: 50
SALES: 61.8MM **Privately Held**
WEB: www.allstudentloan.org
SIC: 6163 Mortgage brokers arranging for loans, using money of others

(P-9869)
AFFILIATED FUNDING CORPORATION
Also Called: Inhouselender.com
5 Hutton Centre Dr # 1100, Santa Ana (92707-8714)
PHONE...................714 619-3100
Alfred Hanna, *President*
EMP: 70
SALES (est): 7.4MM **Privately Held**
WEB: www.inhouselender.com
SIC: 6163 Mortgage brokers arranging for loans, using money of others

(P-9870)
AMERICAN FUNDING
Also Called: American Realty
5369 Camden Ave Ste 240, San Jose (95124-5809)
PHONE...................408 269-4238
Ali Haider, *CEO*
EMP: 60
SALES (est): 4.8MM **Privately Held**
WEB: www.americanfunding.com
SIC: 6163 6531 Mortgage brokers arranging for loans, using money of others; real estate agents & managers

(P-9871)
AMERICAN LIBERTY CAPITAL CORP
Also Called: American Liberty Funding
19000 Macarthur Blvd # 400, Irvine (92612-1438)
P.O. Box 10059, Newport Beach (92658-0059)
PHONE...................949 623-0288
Christopher Chase, *President*
Mike R Chase, *Shareholder*
Chris Bull, *Corp Secy*
EMP: 105
SALES (est): 7.1MM **Privately Held**
SIC: 6163 Mortgage brokers arranging for loans, using money of others

(P-9872)
AMERICAN PACIFIC MORTGAGE CORP
300 Tamal Plz Ste 250, Corte Madera (94925-1170)
PHONE...................415 891-8706
Ryan Madden, *Branch Mgr*
Vince Breen, *Partner*
Ron Fiore, *Partner*
James Argo, *Officer*
Scarlet Kim, *Officer*
EMP: 50 **Privately Held**
SIC: 6163 Mortgage brokers arranging for loans, using money of others
PA: American Pacific Mortgage Corporation
3000 Lava Ridge Ct # 200
Roseville CA 95661

(P-9873)
AMERIQUEST CAPITAL CORPORATION (PA)
1100 W Twn Cntry Rd R, Orange (92868-4600)
PHONE...................714 564-0600
Aseem Mital, *President*
EMP: 400
SQ FT: 85,000
SALES (est): 520MM **Privately Held**
SIC: 6163 Mortgage brokers arranging for loans, using money of others

(P-9874)
CAL COAST FINANCIAL INC
39355 California St # 101, Fremont (94538-1447)
PHONE...................510 683-9850
Roger Bakshi, *CEO*
EMP: 70
SALES (est): 3.1MM **Privately Held**
SIC: 6163 Mortgage brokers arranging for loans, using money of others

(P-9875)
CINTIVA FINANCIAL CORPORATION
10145 Pacific Hts 800, San Diego (92121-4242)
PHONE...................877 246-8482
Richard A Myers, *President*
Niket Kulkarni, *Vice Pres*
Don Sarver, *Vice Pres*
EMP: 60
SQ FT: 12,500
SALES (est): 4MM **Privately Held**
WEB: www.cintiva.com
SIC: 6163 Mortgage brokers arranging for loans, using money of others

(P-9876)
CLEARPATH LENDING
15635 Alton Pkwy Ste 300, Irvine (92618-7332)
PHONE...................949 502-3577
Amir Ali Omid, *CEO*
Mark Hoagland, *Officer*
Janae Grupenhagen, *Admin Asst*
Lily Ali, *Loan Officer*
Jose Coutino, *Loan Officer*
EMP: 130 **EST:** 2012
SALES (est): 985.9K **Privately Held**
SIC: 6163 Mortgage brokers arranging for loans, using money of others

(P-9877)
CMG MORTGAGE INC (PA)
3160 Crow Canyon Rd # 400, San Ramon (94583-1382)
PHONE...................619 554-1327
Christopher M George, *CEO*
Tom Meyer, *Division VP*
Todd L Hempstead, *Senior VP*
Denise Tragale, *Vice Pres*
Marko Krosnjar, *Sales Staff*
EMP: 349
SQ FT: 5,500
SALES (est): 90.3MM **Privately Held**
WEB: www.pacificguarantee.com
SIC: 6163 Mortgage brokers arranging for loans, using money of others

(P-9878)
COMMERCE HOME MORTGAGE INC (HQ)
Also Called: Bank of Commerce Mortgage
3130 Crow Canyon Pl # 300, San Ramon (94583-1386)
PHONE...................925 830-1500
Scott Simonich, *President*
Lee Lieberman, *Partner*
Jeff Toomire, *President*
Mario De Tomasi, *CFO*
Allison Bates, *Officer*
EMP: 60
SQ FT: 1,400
SALES (est): 23.7MM
SALES (corp-wide): 50.7MM **Publicly Held**
SIC: 6163 Mortgage brokers arranging for loans, using money of others
PA: Bank Of Commerce Holdings
1901 Churn Creek Rd
Redding CA 96002
530 722-3952

(P-9879)
E&S FINANCIAL GROUP INC
Also Called: Capital Mortgage Services
4253 Transport St, Ventura (93003-5659)
PHONE...................805 644-1621
Jordan Eller, *President*
EMP: 70
SQ FT: 11,200
SALES (est): 2.6MM **Privately Held**
SIC: 6163 Mortgage brokers arranging for loans, using money of others

(P-9880)
E-LOAN INC (DH)
6230 Stoneridge Mall Rd, Pleasanton (94588-3260)
PHONE...................925 847-6200
Mark E Lefanowicz, *President*
EMP: 850
SQ FT: 118,000
SALES (est): 54.6MM
SALES (corp-wide): 2.1B **Publicly Held**
WEB: www.e-loan.com
SIC: 6163 6162 Mortgage brokers arranging for loans, using money of others; mortgage bankers & correspondents
HQ: Popular Finance Inc
326 Salud St El El Senorial Cond
Ponce PR 00716
787 844-2760

(P-9881)
EMERY FINANCIAL INC (PA)
Also Called: Wjbradley Mortgage Capital
620 Nwport Ctr Dr Ste 800, Newport Beach (92660)
PHONE...................949 219-0640
Bradford Sarvak, *President*
Jay Anderson, *Officer*
Matthew Sarvak, *Officer*
Peggy Suber, *Officer*
Dean Coney, *Loan Officer*
EMP: 60
SQ FT: 7,000
SALES (est): 15.2MM **Privately Held**
WEB: www.emeryfinancial.com
SIC: 6163 Mortgage brokers arranging for loans, using money of others

(P-9882)
ESNA CORPORATION
44300 Lowtree Ave Ste 100, Lancaster (93534-4166)
PHONE...................661 206-6010
Duane Faust, *President*
EMP: 50
SALES (est): 2.5MM **Privately Held**
SIC: 6163 Mortgage brokers arranging for loans, using money of others

(P-9883)
FIRST NATIONWIDE MORTGAGE CORP
18440 Bermuda St, Northridge (91326-3102)
PHONE...................818 209-3134
EMP: 133
SALES (corp-wide): 71.4B **Publicly Held**
SIC: 6163 6162 Mortgage brokers arranging for loans, using money of others; mortgage bankers & correspondents
HQ: First Nationwide Mortgage Corporation
5280 Corporate Dr
Frederick MD 21703

(P-9884)
GETRIGHT VENTURES INC
3675 Rocky Shore Ct, Vallejo (94591-6349)
PHONE...................510 402-4816
Joseph Pamplieda, *President*
Eddie E Bansag, *CFO*
EMP: 80
SALES (est): 3.4MM **Privately Held**
WEB: www.getrightrealty.com
SIC: 6163 Mortgage brokers arranging for loans, using money of others

(P-9885)
GUILD MORTGAGE COMPANY
3626 Fair Oaks Blvd, Sacramento (95864-7200)
PHONE...................916 486-6257
Mary Ann McGarry, *Branch Mgr*
EMP: 50
SALES (corp-wide): 1.2B **Privately Held**
SIC: 6163 Mortgage brokers arranging for loans, using money of others
PA: Guild Mortgage Company
5898 Copley Dr Fl 4
San Diego CA 92111
800 365-4441

(P-9886)
HARVEST SMALL BUSINESS FIN LLC
24422 Avenida De Carlota, Laguna Hills (92653)
PHONE...................949 446-8683
David Scherer, *President*
Evan Mitnick, *CFO*
Adam Seery, *Officer*
Todd Massas, *Exec VP*
EMP: 51
SALES: 3.4MM **Privately Held**
SIC: 6163 Mortgage brokers arranging for loans, using money of others

(P-9887)
HOMEBRIDGE FINANCIAL SERVICES
15301 Ventura Blvd, Sherman Oaks (91403-3102)
PHONE...................818 981-0606
Douglas Rotella, *President*
EMP: 1700 **Privately Held**
SIC: 6163 Mortgage brokers arranging for loans, using money of others
PA: Homebridge Financial Services, Inc.
194 Wood Ave S Fl 9
Iselin NJ 08830

(P-9888)
IZT MORTGAGE INC (PA)
Also Called: Ameritech Mortgage
3011 Citrus Cir Ste 202, Walnut Creek (94598-2631)
P.O. Box 492239, Los Angeles (90049-8239)
PHONE...................925 946-1858
Zoran Trajanovich, *CEO*
Irina Trajanovich, *President*
EMP: 50
SQ FT: 12,000
SALES (est): 10MM **Privately Held**
SIC: 6163 Mortgage brokers arranging for loans, using money of others

(P-9889)
J & P FINANCIAL INC (PA)
Also Called: Realty Executives
330 W Felicita Ave Ste E1, Escondido (92025-6534)
PHONE...................760 738-9000
Joe W Cobb Jr, *President*
Paula Cobb, *Vice Pres*
Tom Guthrie, *Real Est Agnt*
EMP: 50
SQ FT: 5,370
SALES (est): 10.7MM **Privately Held**
SIC: 6163 Mortgage brokers arranging for loans, using money of others

(P-9890)
KINGS PAWNSHOP
Also Called: Kings Jewelry and Loan
800 S Vermont Ave, Los Angeles (90005-1521)
PHONE...................213 383-5555
Sam Shocket, *President*
Marco Barraz, *General Mgr*
EMP: 52
SQ FT: 11,000
SALES (est): 7.8MM **Privately Held**
WEB: www.kingspawn.com
SIC: 6163 5944 Loan brokers; jewelry stores

(P-9891)
LENDINGCLUB ASSET MGT LLC
71 Stevenson St Ste 300, San Francisco (94105-2985)
PHONE...................415 632-5600
Carrie Dolan,
Russ Elmer, *Principal*
EMP: 258
SALES (est): 4.8MM **Publicly Held**
SIC: 6163 Loan brokers
PA: Lendingclub Corporation
71 Stevenson St Ste 300
San Francisco CA 94105

(P-9892)
LIBERTY AMERICAN MORTGAGE CORP (PA)
193 Blue Ravine Rd # 240, Folsom (95630-4756)
PHONE...................916 780-3000
Frank A Sousa, *President*
William Templeton, *Ch of Bd*
Dan Martinelli, *COO*
Jennifer Robinson, *CFO*
Patrick White, *Chairman*
EMP: 92
SQ FT: 18,000
SALES (est): 8MM **Privately Held**
WEB: www.libam.com
SIC: 6163 6162 Mortgage brokers arranging for loans, using money of others; mortgage bankers

(P-9893)
M & A MORTGAGE INC
1600 N Broadway Ste 1020, Santa Ana (92706-3930)
PHONE...................714 560-1970
EMP: 75
SALES (est): 25MM **Privately Held**
SIC: 6163

(P-9894)
MARK 1 MORTGAGE CORPORATION (PA)
1342 E Chapman Ave, Orange (92866-2219)
PHONE...................714 752-5700
Mark D Prather, *President*
EMP: 50
SQ FT: 8,000
SALES (est): 16.8MM **Privately Held**
SIC: 6163 Mortgage brokers arranging for loans, using money of others

(P-9895)
MERRILL LYNCH PIERCE FENNER
Also Called: Merrill Lynch Wealth MGT
800 E Colo Blvd Ste 400, Pasadena (91101)
PHONE...................626 304-1596
Lorenzo Detoma, *Vice Pres*
Ken Park, *Advisor*
EMP: 100
SALES (corp-wide): 100.2B **Publicly Held**
SIC: 6163 6211 Loan brokers; bond dealers & brokers
HQ: Merrill Lynch, Pierce, Fenner & Smith Incorporated
111 8th Ave
New York NY 10011
800 637-7455

(P-9896)
MISSION HILLS MORTGAGE CORP (HQ)
Also Called: Mission Hills Mortgage Bankers
18500 Von Karman Ave # 1100, Irvine (92612-0546)
PHONE...................714 972-3832
Jay Ledbetter, *President*
Brian Tilton, *Vice Pres*
Tim Cooper, *Site Mgr*
Robert Dewar, *Site Mgr*
Renee Jones, *Site Mgr*
EMP: 140
SQ FT: 27,000
SALES (est): 38.7MM
SALES (corp-wide): 132.1MM **Privately Held**
WEB: www.mhmc.com
SIC: 6163 Mortgage brokers arranging for loans, using money of others
PA: Tarbell Financial Corporation
1403 N Tustin Ave Ste 380
Santa Ana CA 92705
714 972-0988

(P-9897)
MORTGAGE CORP AMERICA INC
Also Called: Mortgage Corp of America
2315 Kuehner Dr Ste 115, Simi Valley (93063-3960)
PHONE...................805 582-2220
Bradley A Rice, *President*
Deena Monette, *Manager*

Christopher Bunce, *Real Est Agnt*
EMP: 60
SQ FT: 16,000
SALES (est): 5.1MM **Privately Held**
WEB: www.mcastar.com
SIC: 6163 Mortgage brokers arranging for loans, using money of others

(P-9898)
NATIONAL CREDIT INDUSTRIES INC
Also Called: Century 21
1100 Via Verde, San Dimas (91773-4401)
PHONE...................626 967-4355
Oscar Rodriguez, *President*
Ashley Alvarez, *Admin Sec*
Mireya Ruiz, *Admin Sec*
Lucy Hollingsworth, *Sales Mgr*
Dean Porter, *Sales Associate*
EMP: 90
SALES (est): 2MM **Privately Held**
SIC: 6163 Mortgage brokers arranging for loans, using money of others

(P-9899)
NEWWEST MORTGAGE COMPANY
Also Called: Newwest Funding
8255 Firestone Blvd # 101, Downey (90241-4800)
PHONE...................562 861-8393
David Samak, *President*
Kendra Samak, *Treasurer*
EMP: 60
SQ FT: 5,000
SALES (est): 5.1MM **Privately Held**
SIC: 6163 Mortgage brokers arranging for loans, using money of others

(P-9900)
PACIFIC BAY LENDING GROUP
Also Called: Bay Valley Mortgage
1 Centerpointe Dr Ste 330, La Palma (90623-2586)
PHONE...................714 367-5125
John Nelson, *CEO*
Christine Kim, *Officer*
Shane Park, *Vice Pres*
Andy Chung, *Accountant*
Victoria CHI, *Broker*
EMP: 100 EST: 2011
SALES (est): 3.8MM **Privately Held**
SIC: 6163 Loan brokers

(P-9901)
PACIFIC UNION INTL INC
135 W Napa St Ste 200, Sonoma (95476-6632)
PHONE...................707 934-2300
Jill Silvas, *Branch Mgr*
EMP: 539 **Privately Held**
SIC: 6163 Loan agents
PA: Pacific Union International, Inc.
1 Letterman Dr Bldg C
San Francisco CA 94129

(P-9902)
PENNYMAC CORP
27001 Agoura Rd, Agoura Hills (91301-5339)
PHONE...................818 878-8416
Stanford L Kurland, *President*
EMP: 597
SALES (est): 46.3MM **Privately Held**
SIC: 6163 Loan brokers
PA: Pennymac Mortgage Investment Trust
6101 Condor Dr
Moorpark CA 93021

(P-9903)
PINNACLE FUNDING GROUP INC
2092 Omega Rd Ste H, San Ramon (94583-1230)
PHONE...................925 552-5302
William Howard Paul III, *President*
EMP: 50
SQ FT: 5,000
SALES (est): 3.2MM **Privately Held**
SIC: 6163 Mortgage brokers arranging for loans, using money of others

P R O D U C T S & S V C S

(P-9904)
PROSPER MARKETPLACE INC (PA)
221 Main St Fl 3, San Francisco (94105-1911)
PHONE...................................415 593-5400
David Kimball, *CEO*
Ronald Suber, *President*
Aaron Vermut, *CEO*
Joshua M Tonderys, *COO*
Usama Ashraf, *CFO*
EMP: 55
SALES: 116.2MM **Privately Held**
SIC: 6163 Loan brokers

(P-9905)
REALTY ALLIANCE INC
Also Called: Loan Depot Group
20812 Ventura Blvd # 101, Woodland Hills (91364-2335)
PHONE...................................818 610-0080
Tulsi Bhatia, *President*
EMP: 70
SALES (est): 4.6MM **Privately Held**
SIC: 6163 6411 Mortgage brokers arranging for loans, using money of others; insurance agents, brokers & service

(P-9906)
SAND CANYON CORPORATION (HQ)
7595 Irvine Center Dr # 100, Irvine (92618-2958)
P.O. Box 57080 (92619-7080)
PHONE...................................949 727-9425
Robert Dubrish, *President*
Dale M Sugimoto, *CEO*
Steve Nadon, *COO*
William O'Neill, *CFO*
EMP: 100
SQ FT: 140,000
SALES (est): 180.7MM
SALES (corp-wide): 3.1B **Publicly Held**
WEB: www.oomc.com
SIC: 6163 6162 Loan brokers; mortgage bankers & correspondents
PA: H&R Block, Inc.
1 H&R Block Way
Kansas City MO 64105
816 854-3000

(P-9907)
SOCIAL FINANCE INC (PA)
Also Called: Sofi
1 Letterman Dr Ste 250, San Francisco (94129-2402)
PHONE...................................415 697-2049
Tom Hutton, *CEO*
Steve Freiberg, *CFO*
Joanne Bradford, *Chief Mktg Ofcr*
Lauren Crow, *Officer*
Shaunda Brown, *Business Dir*
EMP: 160
SQ FT: 20,000
SALES (est): 246.1MM **Privately Held**
SIC: 6163 Loan brokers

(P-9908)
SOCIAL FINANCE INC
375 Healdsburg Ave # 280, Healdsburg (95448-4151)
PHONE...................................707 473-9889
Michael Phillips, *Opers Mgr*
EMP: 419
SALES (corp-wide): 246.1MM **Privately Held**
SIC: 6163 Loan brokers
PA: Social Finance, Inc.
1 Letterman Dr Ste 250
San Francisco CA 94129
415 697-2049

(P-9909)
SRI (PA)
100 Bush St Ste 1650, San Francisco (94104-3942)
PHONE...................................415 989-5363
Oren Raphael, *President*
EMP: 50
SALES (est): 3.8MM **Privately Held**
SIC: 6163 Mortgage brokers arranging for loans, using money of others

(P-9910)
TARBELL FINANCIAL CORPORATION (PA)
1403 N Tustin Ave Ste 380, Santa Ana (92705-8691)
PHONE...................................714 972-0988
Donald Tarbell, *CEO*
Tina Jimov, *President*
Jin Lee, *COO*
Ronald Tarbell, *CFO*
Elizabeth Tarbell, *Admin Sec*
EMP: 100
SQ FT: 60,000
SALES (est): 132.1MM **Privately Held**
SIC: 6163 6531 6099 Mortgage brokers arranging for loans, using money of others; real estate brokers & agents; escrow institutions other than real estate

---

6211 Security Brokers & Dealers

(P-9911)
ABM JANITORIAL SERVICES INC
Also Called: ABM Securities
3580 Wilshire Blvd # 1130, Los Angeles (90010-2501)
PHONE...................................213 384-0600
EMP: 1500
SALES (corp-wide): 5.4B **Publicly Held**
SIC: 6211 Security brokers & dealers
HQ: Abm Janitorial Services, Inc.
1111 Fannin St Ste 1500
Houston TX 77002
713 654-8924

(P-9912)
ADVENT SECURITIES INVESTMENTS (PA)
Also Called: Olympic Security
9631 Alondra Blvd Ste 202, Bellflower (90706-3674)
PHONE...................................562 920-5467
Cynthia Jocson, *President*
Eric Sera, *Treasurer*
EMP: 50
SQ FT: 5,000
SALES (est): 32.4MM **Privately Held**
SIC: 6211 5699 Security brokers & dealers; uniforms

(P-9913)
ANALYTIC US MARKET NEUTRAL OFF
555 W 5th St Fl 50, Los Angeles (90013-1066)
PHONE...................................213 688-3015
Harindra Desilva, *President*
EMP: 70
SALES (est): 6.9MM **Privately Held**
SIC: 6211 Investment firm, general brokerage

(P-9914)
ATRIUM CAPITAL CORP
3000 Sand Hill Rd 2-130, Menlo Park (94025-7142)
PHONE...................................650 233-7878
Russell B Pyne, *Managing Dir*
Andy Baumbusch, *Principal*
Judy Hyrne, *Office Mgr*
EMP: 1505
SALES (est): 116.8MM **Privately Held**
WEB: www.atriumcapital.com
SIC: 6211 Investment firm, general brokerage

(P-9915)
B B & K FUND SERVICES INC
950 Tower Ln Ste 1900, Foster City (94404-2131)
PHONE...................................650 571-5800
Thomas Bailard, *CEO*
EMP: 50
SALES (est): 2.7MM
SALES (corp-wide): 4.5MM **Privately Held**
WEB: www.bailard.com
SIC: 6211 Security brokers & dealers

HQ: Bailard, Inc.
950 Tower Ln Ste 1900
Foster City CA 94404
650 571-5800

(P-9916)
BABCOCK & BROWN HOLDINGS INC (HQ)
1 Pier Ste 3, San Francisco (94111-2028)
PHONE...................................415 512-1515
James V Babcock, *Chairman*
EMP: 200
SALES (est): 203.6MM
SALES (corp-wide): 708.8MM **Privately Held**
SIC: 6211 Investment bankers

(P-9917)
BARCLAYS CAPITAL INC
Also Called: Lehman Brothers
10250 Santa Monica Blvd # 24, Los Angeles (90067-6482)
PHONE...................................310 481-4100
Barclay Perry, *Branch Mgr*
Michael Hartmeier, *Managing Dir*
Sonya Del Crognale, *Financial Exec*
EMP: 60
SALES (corp-wide): 35.4B **Privately Held**
WEB: www.lehmanbrothers.com
SIC: 6211 Investment firm, general brokerage
HQ: Barclays Capital Inc.
745 7th Ave
New York NY 10019
212 526-7000

(P-9918)
BBAM US LP
Also Called: Bbam Arcft Holdings 139 Labuan
50 California St Fl 14, San Francisco (94111-4683)
PHONE...................................415 267-1600
Steve Vissis, *CEO*
EMP: 349
SALES (est): 18.1MM
SALES (corp-wide): 708.8MM **Privately Held**
SIC: 6211 Investment bankers
HQ: Bbam Llc
50 California St Fl 14
San Francisco CA 94111
415 267-1600

(P-9919)
BROADREACH CAPITL PARTNERS LLC (PA)
855 El Camino Real, Palo Alto (94301-2305)
PHONE...................................650 331-2500
John A Foster, *Director*
Eli Khari,
Philip Flip F Maritz, *Director*
Craig G Vought, *Director*
EMP: 4010
SALES (est): 399.2MM **Privately Held**
WEB: www.broadreachcp.com
SIC: 6211 Investment firm, general brokerage

(P-9920)
BTIG LLC (PA)
Also Called: Baypoint Trading
600 Montgomery St Fl 6, San Francisco (94111-2708)
PHONE...................................415 248-2200
Scott Kovalik,
Brian Endres, *CFO*
Austin Hamilton, *Officer*
David Liu, *Vice Pres*
Matthew McLeod, *Vice Pres*
EMP: 77
SALES (est): 105MM **Privately Held**
SIC: 6211 Investment firm, general brokerage

(P-9921)
CANTOR FITZGERALD L P
1925 Century Park E # 700, Los Angeles (90067-2718)
PHONE...................................310 282-6500
Bill Wright, *Manager*
Joseph Wind, *Executive*
Benjamin Finkelstein, *Managing Dir*
Gary Wang, *Managing Dir*
Chris Larsen, *Sales Staff*
EMP: 100

SALES (corp-wide): 859.1MM **Privately Held**
SIC: 6211 Brokers, security
PA: Cantor Fitzgerald L P
499 Park Ave
New York NY 10022
212 938-5000

(P-9922)
CANYON PARTNERS INCORPORATED (HQ)
2000 Ave Of The Sts Fl 11, Los Angeles (90067)
PHONE...................................310 272-1000
Joshua S Friedman, *CEO*
Andrew Greene, *Partner*
Mitchell R Julis, *CEO*
John Simpson, *COO*
John Plaga, *CFO*
EMP: 57
SQ FT: 5,500
SALES (est): 24.6MM **Privately Held**
WEB: www.cjuf.com
SIC: 6211 Investment firm, general brokerage
PA: Canyon Partners, Llc
2000 Avenue Of The Stars # 11
Los Angeles CA 90067
310 272-1000

(P-9923)
CASEY SECURITIES INC (PA)
301 Pine St, San Francisco (94104-3301)
PHONE...................................415 544-5030
Richard Casey, *Ch of Bd*
George Gasparini, *President*
Kathleen Gallagher, *Vice Pres*
Scott Nelson, *Vice Pres*
EMP: 74 EST: 1976
SQ FT: 800
SALES (est): 7.6MM **Privately Held**
SIC: 6211 Brokers, security; stock brokers & dealers

(P-9924)
CASTLE & COOKE INC
Also Called: Castle & Cooke Mortgage
2099 S State College Blvd, Anaheim (92806-6142)
PHONE...................................714 385-9641
EMP: 3750
SALES (corp-wide): 911.7MM **Privately Held**
SIC: 6211 Mortgages, buying & selling
PA: Castle & Cooke, Inc.
1 Dole Dr
Westlake Village CA 91362
310 374-3952

(P-9925)
CHARLES SCHWAB CORPORATION (PA)
211 Main St Fl 17, San Francisco (94105-1901)
PHONE...................................415 667-7000
Walter W Bettinger II, *President*
Charles R Schwab, *Ch of Bd*
Joseph R Martinetto, *COO*
Peter B Crawford, *CFO*
David R Garfield, *Exec VP*
EMP: 150 EST: 1986
SQ FT: 569,000
SALES: 8.6B **Publicly Held**
WEB: www.schwab.com
SIC: 6211 6091 6282 7389 Brokers, security; investment bankers; investment firm, general brokerage; nondeposit trust facilities; investment advice; investment advisory service; financial services

(P-9926)
CHARLES SCHWAB CORPORATION
10770 Donner Pass Rd # 103, Truckee (96161-4881)
PHONE...................................530 448-8038
EMP: 52
SALES (corp-wide): 8.6B **Publicly Held**
SIC: 6211 Stock brokers & dealers
PA: The Charles Schwab Corporation
211 Main St Fl 17
San Francisco CA 94105
415 667-7000

(P-9927)
CHARLES SCHWAB CORPORATION
Also Called: Charles Schwab & Co Inc
3421 E Imperial Hwy, Brea (92823-6388)
PHONE..............................714 385-6000
Jane E Fry, *Branch Mgr*
EMP: 52
SALES (corp-wide): 8.6B **Publicly Held**
SIC: 6211 Security brokers & dealers
PA: The Charles Schwab Corporation
211 Main St Fl 17
San Francisco CA 94105
415 667-7000

(P-9928)
CHARLES SCHWAB CORPORATION
1400 Grant Ave Ste 101, Novato (94945-3155)
PHONE..............................415 294-3503
Michael Dolan, *President*
EMP: 53
SALES (corp-wide): 8.6B **Publicly Held**
SIC: 6211 Security brokers & dealers
PA: The Charles Schwab Corporation
211 Main St Fl 17
San Francisco CA 94105
415 667-7000

(P-9929)
CHARLES SCHWAB CORPORATION
12481 High Bluff Dr # 100, San Diego (92130-3583)
PHONE..............................858 523-2454
Greg Matthews, *Branch Mgr*
Dex Yudelson, *Associate*
EMP: 50
SALES (corp-wide): 8.6B **Publicly Held**
WEB: www.schwab.com
SIC: 6211 Brokers, security
PA: The Charles Schwab Corporation
211 Main St Fl 17
San Francisco CA 94105
415 667-7000

(P-9930)
CITIGROUP GLOBAL MARKETS INC
Also Called: Smith Barney
444 S Flower St Fl 35, Los Angeles (90071-2980)
P.O. Box 30367 (90030-0367)
PHONE..............................213 486-8811
Bruce Brereton, *Branch Mgr*
EMP: 180
SALES (corp-wide): 71.4B **Publicly Held**
WEB: www.salomonsmithbarney.com
SIC: 6211 Stock brokers & dealers
HQ: Citigroup Global Markets Inc.
388 Greenwich St Fl 18
New York NY 10013
212 816-6000

(P-9931)
CITIGROUP GLOBAL MARKETS INC
Also Called: Salomon Smith Barney
2381 Rosecrans Ave # 115, El Segundo (90245-4920)
PHONE..............................310 727-9533
Russ Bortonaro, *Branch Mgr*
EMP: 56
SALES (corp-wide): 71.4B **Publicly Held**
WEB: www.salomonsmithbarney.com
SIC: 6211 Security brokers & dealers
HQ: Citigroup Global Markets Inc.
388 Greenwich St Fl 18
New York NY 10013
212 816-6000

(P-9932)
CITIGROUP GLOBAL MARKETS INC
Also Called: Salomon Smith Barney
155 Cadillac Dr Fl 1, Sacramento (95825-5499)
PHONE..............................916 567-2056
Mike Dellisant, *Manager*
EMP: 50
SALES (corp-wide): 71.4B **Publicly Held**
WEB: www.salomonsmithbarney.com
SIC: 6211 Security brokers & dealers

HQ: Citigroup Global Markets Inc.
388 Greenwich St Fl 18
New York NY 10013
212 816-6000

(P-9933)
CITIGROUP GLOBAL MARKETS INC
4350 La Jolla Village Dr, San Diego (92122-1243)
PHONE..............................858 597-7777
Joe Capano, *Manager*
EMP: 71
SALES (corp-wide): 71.4B **Publicly Held**
WEB: www.salomonsmithbarney.com
SIC: 6211 Security brokers & dealers
HQ: Citigroup Global Markets Inc.
388 Greenwich St Fl 18
New York NY 10013
212 816-6000

(P-9934)
CITIGROUP GLOBAL MARKETS INC
Also Called: Smith Barney
21250 Hawthorne Blvd # 650, Torrance (90503-5506)
PHONE..............................310 540-9511
David Calomese, *Manager*
EMP: 50
SALES (corp-wide): 71.4B **Publicly Held**
WEB: www.salomonsmithbarney.com
SIC: 6211 Security brokers & dealers; stock brokers & dealers
HQ: Citigroup Global Markets Inc.
388 Greenwich St Fl 18
New York NY 10013
212 816-6000

(P-9935)
CITIGROUP GLOBAL MARKETS INC
Also Called: Smith Barney
1901 Main St Ste 800, Irvine (92614-0515)
PHONE..............................949 955-7500
John Konop, *General Mgr*
EMP: 85
SALES (corp-wide): 71.4B **Publicly Held**
WEB: www.salomonsmithbarney.com
SIC: 6211 6221 Investment firm, general brokerage; commodity contracts brokers, dealers
HQ: Citigroup Global Markets Inc.
388 Greenwich St Fl 18
New York NY 10013
212 816-6000

(P-9936)
CITIGROUP GLOBAL MARKETS INC
Also Called: Smith Barney
1225 Prospect St, La Jolla (92037-3687)
PHONE..............................858 456-4900
Erik Kivmkrugh, *Office Mgr*
EMP: 72
SALES (corp-wide): 71.4B **Publicly Held**
WEB: www.salomonsmithbarney.com
SIC: 6211 Security brokers & dealers; stock brokers & dealers
HQ: Citigroup Global Markets Inc.
388 Greenwich St Fl 18
New York NY 10013
212 816-6000

(P-9937)
CITIGROUP GLOBAL MARKETS INC
Also Called: Salomon Smith Barney
5250 N Palm Ave Ste 321, Fresno (93704-2213)
PHONE..............................559 438-2542
Jeff Branch, *Sales/Mktg Mgr*
EMP: 50
SALES (corp-wide): 71.4B **Publicly Held**
WEB: www.salomonsmithbarney.com
SIC: 6211 8742 Security brokers & dealers; stock brokers & dealers; financial consultant
HQ: Citigroup Global Markets Inc.
388 Greenwich St Fl 18
New York NY 10013
212 816-6000

(P-9938)
CITIGROUP GLOBAL MARKETS INC
Also Called: Smith Barney
609 Deep Valley Dr # 400, Rllng HLS Est (90274-3629)
P.O. Box 2809, Pls Vrds Pnsl (90274-8809)
PHONE..............................310 544-3600
Paul Tanzmen, *Manager*
EMP: 65
SALES (corp-wide): 71.4B **Publicly Held**
WEB: www.salomonsmithbarney.com
SIC: 6211 Stock brokers & dealers
HQ: Citigroup Global Markets Inc.
388 Greenwich St Fl 18
New York NY 10013
212 816-6000

(P-9939)
CITIGROUP GLOBAL MARKETS INC
456 W Foothill Blvd, Claremont (91711-2711)
PHONE..............................909 625-0781
Tony Battaglia, *Manager*
EMP: 60
SALES (corp-wide): 71.4B **Publicly Held**
WEB: www.salomonsmithbarney.com
SIC: 6211 Stock brokers & dealers
HQ: Citigroup Global Markets Inc.
388 Greenwich St Fl 18
New York NY 10013
212 816-6000

(P-9940)
CITIGROUP GLOBAL MARKETS INC
Also Called: Smith Barneys
2775 Sand Hill Rd Ste 120, Menlo Park (94025-7085)
PHONE..............................650 926-7600
Guy Dietrich, *Principal*
EMP: 103
SALES (corp-wide): 71.4B **Publicly Held**
WEB: www.salomonsmithbarney.com
SIC: 6211 Security brokers & dealers
HQ: Citigroup Global Markets Inc.
388 Greenwich St Fl 18
New York NY 10013
212 816-6000

(P-9941)
CITIGROUP INC
1 Sansome St Fl 27, San Francisco (94104-4426)
PHONE..............................415 617-8524
Chuck Prince, *President*
EMP: 60
SALES (corp-wide): 71.4B **Publicly Held**
WEB: www.citigroup.com
SIC: 6211 Investment bankers
PA: Citigroup Inc.
388 Greenwich St
New York NY 10013
212 559-1000

(P-9942)
CITIMORTGAGE INC
6160 Stoneridge Mall Rd # 150, Pleasanton (94588-3285)
PHONE..............................925 730-3800
Ernie Guzman, *Manager*
EMP: 50
SALES (corp-wide): 71.4B **Publicly Held**
SIC: 6211 Investment firm, general brokerage
HQ: Citimortgage, Inc.
1000 Technology Dr
O Fallon MO 63368
636 261-2484

(P-9943)
COLDWELL BANKER AND ASSOCIATES (PA)
Also Called: Coldwell Banker Inland Brokers
23823 Clinton Keith Rd # 102, Wildomar (92595-7734)
PHONE..............................951 304-2900
Raquel Wilks, *Manager*
Shannon Muller, *Office Admin*
Marla Obrien, *Office Admin*
Sarah Schlueter, *Office Admin*
Perri Leitao, *Executive Asst*
EMP: 60

SALES (est): 7.1MM **Privately Held**
SIC: 6211 Security brokers & dealers

(P-9944)
COUNTRYWIDE SECURITIES CORP
4500 Park Granada, Calabasas (91302-1613)
P.O. Box 7137, Pasadena (91109-7137)
PHONE..............................818 225-3000
Angelo Mozilo, *Ch of Bd*
Ranjit Kripalani, *President*
EMP: 275 **EST:** 1981
SALES (est): 41.7MM
SALES (corp-wide): 100.2B **Publicly Held**
SIC: 6211 Security brokers & dealers
HQ: Countrywide Capital Markets, Llc
4500 Park Granada
Calabasas CA 91302

(P-9945)
CREDIT SSSE SECURITIES USA LLC
10880 Wilshire Blvd, Los Angeles (90024-4101)
PHONE..............................213 253-2600
Reza Zafari, *Principal*
EMP: 75
SALES (corp-wide): 21.1B **Privately Held**
SIC: 6211 Investment bankers
HQ: Credit Suisse Securities (Usa) Llc
11 Madison Ave Bsmt 1b
New York NY 10010
212 325-2000

(P-9946)
CREDIT SUISSE (USA) INC
650 California St Fl 31, San Francisco (94108-2612)
PHONE..............................415 249-2100
Carey Timbrell, *Manager*
Jill Jensen, *Director*
EMP: 100
SALES (corp-wide): 21.1B **Privately Held**
SIC: 6211 Investment bankers
HQ: Credit Suisse (Usa), Inc.
11 Madison Ave Frnt 1
New York NY 10010
212 325-2000

(P-9947)
CREDIT SUISSE (USA) INC
650 California St Fl 28, San Francisco (94108-2609)
PHONE..............................415 678-3940
Susan Winegar, *Manager*
EMP: 50
SALES (corp-wide): 21.1B **Privately Held**
SIC: 6211 Investment bankers
HQ: Credit Suisse (Usa), Inc.
11 Madison Ave Frnt 1
New York NY 10010
212 325-2000

(P-9948)
DA DAVIDSON & CO
Also Called: Crowell, Weedon & Co.
624 S Grand Ave Ste 2600, Los Angeles (90017-3327)
PHONE..............................213 620-1850
Don Lardy, *Vice Pres*
James Cronk, *Opers Staff*
Marc Oliver, *Director*
Bill Fitzhugh, *Advisor*
EMP: 310
SALES (corp-wide): 381.6MM **Privately Held**
SIC: 6211 Stock brokers & dealers
HQ: D.A. Davidson & Co.
8 3rd St N
Great Falls MT 59401
406 727-4200

(P-9949)
DEUTSCHE BANK TR CO AMERICAS
101 California St # 4500, San Francisco (94111-5802)
PHONE..............................415 617-4200
Edmond Hon, *Vice Pres*
EMP: 130
SQ FT: 3,600

SALES (corp-wide): 11.5B **Privately Held**
WEB: www.db.com
SIC: **6211** Investment bankers
HQ: Deutsche Bank Trust Company Americas
60 Wall St Bsmt 1
New York NY 10005
212 250-2500

(P-9950)
EMBASSADOR PRIVATE SECURITIES
1341 Evans Ave, San Francisco (94124-1705)
PHONE..................................415 822-8811
Rj Hongisto, *Director*
Rj Hingisto, *Director*
David Culot, *Manager*
EMP: 55
SQ FT: 4,500
SALES (est): 4.7MM **Privately Held**
SIC: **6211** Security brokers & dealers

(P-9951)
FIRST ALLIED SECURITIES INC (PA)
655 W Broadway Fl 11, San Diego (92101-8487)
P.O. Box 85549 (92186-5549)
PHONE...................................619 702-9600
Adam Antoniades, *CEO*
Dustin Tenbroeck, *Managing Prtnr*
Kevin Keefe, *President*
Tiy O'Neal, *COO*
Gregg S Glaser, *CFO*
EMP: 75
SALES (est): 100.9MM **Privately Held**
SIC: **6211** Brokers, security; security brokers & dealers

(P-9952)
FOREX CAPITAL MARKETS LLC
201 Mission St Ste 290, San Francisco (94105-1859)
PHONE...................................415 343-4874
Chris Pelton, *Branch Mgr*
EMP: 95
SALES (corp-wide): 91.2MM **Privately Held**
SIC: **6211** Brokers, security
PA: Forex Capital Markets L.L.C.
55 Water St Fl 50
New York NY 10041
646 355-0839

(P-9953)
FRANKLIN TMPLETON INV SVCS LLC (DH)
Also Called: Franklin Templeton Investment
3344 Quality Dr, Rancho Cordova (95670-7361)
P.O. Box 2258 (95741-2258)
PHONE...................................916 463-1500
Charles B Johnson, *Ch of Bd*
Basil Fox, *President*
Greg Johnson, *President*
Robert Smith, *Senior VP*
May Tong, *Senior VP*
EMP: 1200
SQ FT: 40,000
SALES (est): 608.9MM
SALES (corp-wide): 6.3B **Publicly Held**
SIC: **6211** 6282 Traders, security; investment advisory service

(P-9954)
FREMONT MUTUAL FUNDS INC
333 Market St Ste 2600, San Francisco (94105-2127)
PHONE...................................800 548-4539
David L Redo, *CEO*
Michael Kosich, *President*
Vincent P Kuhn, *Exec VP*
Albert Kirschbaum, *Senior VP*
Peter Landini, *Senior VP*
EMP: 55
SQ FT: 19,000
SALES (est): 4.8MM **Privately Held**
SIC: **6211** Mutual funds, selling by independent salesperson

(P-9955)
GENSTAR CAPITAL LP
4 Embarcadero Ctr # 1500, San Francisco (94111-4106)
PHONE...................................415 834-2350
Jean-Pierre L Conte, *Partner*
Richard F Hoskins, *Partner*
Richard D Paterson, *Partner*
EMP: 560
SALES (est): 28.5MM **Privately Held**
SIC: **6211** Security brokers & dealers

(P-9956)
GI GP IV LLC (PA)
Also Called: GI Partners
188 The Embarcadero # 700, San Francisco (94105-1231)
PHONE...................................415 688-4800
Richard Magnuson, *Mng Member*
Rick Magnuson, *Managing Prtnr*
EMP: 50
SALES (est): 22.6MM **Privately Held**
SIC: **6211** 6512 Investment bankers; commercial & industrial building operation

(P-9957)
GOLD PARENT LP
11111 Santa Monica Blvd, Los Angeles (90025-3333)
PHONE...................................310 954-0444
Jonathan D Sokoloff, *Principal*
EMP: 3400 EST: 2016
SALES (est): 107.2MM **Privately Held**
SIC: **6211** Investment bankers

(P-9958)
GOLDMAN SACHS & CO
Also Called: Goldman Sachs
555 California St # 4500, San Francisco (94104-1675)
PHONE...................................415 393-7500
Eff Martin, *Partner*
Guy Muzio, *Partner*
Joyce Hsieh, *Vice Pres*
Ritu Kalra, *Vice Pres*
Gina Lytle, *Vice Pres*
EMP: 200
SALES (corp-wide): 42.2B **Publicly Held**
WEB: www.gs.com
SIC: **6211** 6282 Investment bankers; investment advice
HQ: Goldman Sachs & Co. Llc
200 West St Bldg 200 # 200
New York NY 10282
212 346-5440

(P-9959)
GOLDMAN SACHS & CO
Also Called: Goldman Sachs
2121 Avenue Stars 2600, Los Angeles (90067)
PHONE...................................310 407-5700
John Mallory, *Branch Mgr*
Jonathan Matz, *Vice Pres*
Rohin Bhasin, *Financial Exec*
EMP: 120
SALES (corp-wide): 42.2B **Publicly Held**
WEB: www.gs.com
SIC: **6211** Investment bankers
HQ: Goldman Sachs & Co. Llc
200 West St Bldg 200 # 200
New York NY 10282
212 346-5440

(P-9960)
GORES GROUP LLC (PA)
9800 Wilshire Blvd, Beverly Hills (90212-1804)
PHONE...................................310 209-3010
Alec Gores, *CEO*
Joseph Page, *COO*
Kurt Hans, *Senior VP*
Jeremy Rossen, *Senior VP*
Dewey Turner III, *Senior VP*
EMP: 60
SALES (est): 4.5B **Privately Held**
SIC: **6211** 7372 5734 Investment firm, general brokerage; prepackaged software; computer software & accessories

(P-9961)
GREEN EQUITY INVESTORS III L P
11111 Santa Monica Blvd # 2000, Los Angeles (90025-3333)
PHONE...................................310 954-0444

Jonathan D Sokoloff, *Partner*
Leonald G LP, *General Ptnr*
EMP: 1115
SQ FT: 15,000
SALES (est): 42.4MM **Privately Held**
SIC: **6211** Investment bankers

(P-9962)
HILLTOP SECURITIES INC
8350 Wilshire Blvd, Beverly Hills (90211-2327)
PHONE...................................800 765-2200
Peter Cappos, *Branch Mgr*
EMP: 50
SALES (corp-wide): 1.7B **Publicly Held**
SIC: **6211** Investment bankers
HQ: Hilltop Securities Inc.
1201 Elm St Ste 3500
Dallas TX 75270
214 859-1800

(P-9963)
IMPERIAL CAPITAL GROUP LLC (PA)
2000 Ave Of The, Los Angeles (90067)
PHONE...................................310 246-3700
Randall Wooster,
Lenny Bianco, *Senior VP*
Eric Groman, *Vice Pres*
Jason Reese,
EMP: 70
SQ FT: 14,909
SALES (est): 9.7MM **Privately Held**
SIC: **6211** Stock brokers & dealers

(P-9964)
IMPERIAL CAPITAL LLC (PA)
10100 Santa Monica Blvd # 2400, Los Angeles (90067-4136)
PHONE...................................310 246-3700
Randall Wooster, *CEO*
Tom Corcoran, *President*
Randall E Wooster, *CEO*
Mark Martis, *COO*
Harry Chung, *CFO*
EMP: 85
SALES (est): 32.7MM **Privately Held**
SIC: **6211** Investment bankers

(P-9965)
INVESTMENT TECH GROUP INC
400 Crprate Pinte Ste 855, Culver City (90230)
PHONE...................................310 216-6777
EMP: 150
SALES (corp-wide): 634.8MM **Publicly Held**
SIC: **6211** 7371
PA: Investment Technology Group, Inc.
1 Liberty Plz
New York NY 10006
212 588-4000

(P-9966)
JEFFERIES LLC
11100 Santa Monica Blvd # 12, Los Angeles (90025-3387)
PHONE...................................310 445-1199
Chris Kanoff, *Branch Mgr*
Irene Au, *President*
Sarah Choi, *Associate*
EMP: 60
SALES (corp-wide): 11.4B **Publicly Held**
SIC: **6211** Brokers, security; dealers, security
HQ: Jefferies Llc
520 Madison Ave Fl 10
New York NY 10022
212 284-2300

(P-9967)
JP MORGAN SECURITIES LLC
Also Called: Bear Stearns
14061 Mercado Dr, Del Mar (92014-2949)
PHONE...................................310 201-2693
EMP: 85
SALES (corp-wide): 106.2B **Publicly Held**
SIC: **6211**
HQ: J.P. Morgan Securities Llc
383 Madison Ave Fl 9
New York NY 10179
212 272-2000

(P-9968)
K A ASSOCIATES INC
1800 Avenue Of The Stars # 200, Los Angeles (90067-4204)
PHONE...................................310 556-2721
Richard Kayne, *CEO*
David Shladovsky, *Admin Sec*
EMP: 116
SALES: 1.3MM **Privately Held**
SIC: **6211** Security brokers & dealers

(P-9969)
LEAR CAPITAL INC
1990 S Bundy Dr Ste 600, Los Angeles (90025-5256)
PHONE...................................310 571-0190
John Ohanesian, *President*
Scott Robinson, *CFO*
Sandeep D'Souza, *Applctn Conslt*
Jason Liyanage, *Opers Mgr*
Cher Cusumano, *Mktg Dir*
EMP: 72
SQ FT: 4,500
SALES (est): 324MM **Privately Held**
WEB: www.goldcentral.com
SIC: **6211** Mineral, oil & gas leasing & royalty dealers

(P-9970)
LEERINK PARTNERS LLC
255 California St Fl 12, San Francisco (94111-4923)
PHONE...................................800 778-1164
Jeffrey Leerink, *CEO*
Dan McMullen, *Sales Staff*
EMP: 82 **Privately Held**
SIC: **6211** Brokers, security; investment bankers
PA: Leerink Partners Llc
1 Federal St Fl 37
Boston MA 02110

(P-9971)
LERETA LLC (PA)
1123 Park View Dr, Covina (91724-3748)
PHONE...................................626 543-1765
John Walsh, *CEO*
Glenn McCarthy, *President*
Daniel Telles, *President*
James V Micali, *COO*
Jim Micali, *COO*
EMP: 450
SQ FT: 40,000
SALES (est): 331MM **Privately Held**
SIC: **6211** 6541 6361 Tax certificate dealers; title search companies; real estate title insurance

(P-9972)
LPL HOLDINGS INC (HQ)
4707 Executive Dr, San Diego (92121-3091)
PHONE...................................858 450-9606
Mark Casady, *CEO*
Rebecca Power, *President*
Dan Schuck, *Exec VP*
Christopher Defrank, *Senior VP*
Doug M Oglesby, *Senior VP*
EMP: 84
SALES (est): 836.3MM **Publicly Held**
WEB: www.lpl.com
SIC: **6211** Brokers, security; dealers, security

(P-9973)
M L STERN & CO LLC (DH)
8350 Wilshire Blvd Fl 1, Beverly Hills (90211-2324)
PHONE...................................323 658-4400
Milford L Stern,
Richard Dimino, *Vice Pres*
Stephen F Kempa,
Michael Karp, *Asst Mgr*
Ron Calvin, *Accounts Exec*
EMP: 117
SQ FT: 8,100
SALES: 44.1MM
SALES (corp-wide): 1.7B **Publicly Held**
SIC: **6211** Brokers, security
HQ: Hilltop Securities Holdings Llc
200 Crescent Ct Ste 1330
Dallas TX 75201
214 855-2177

(P-9974)
MERLIN SECURITIES LLC
45 Fremont St Ste 3000, San Francisco
(94105-2256)
PHONE....................415 848-0269
Stephan P Vermut,
Robert Garrett, *Senior Partner*
Regina O'Neill,
EMP: 65
SALES (est): 9.3MM
SALES (corp-wide): 97.7B **Publicly Held**
SIC: 6211 Security brokers & dealers
HQ: Everen Capital Corporation
301 S College St
Charlotte NC 28202

(P-9975)
MERRILL LYNCH PIERCE FENNER
333 Middlefield Rd, Menlo Park
(94025-3552)
PHONE....................650 473-7888
Fax: 650 473-7800
EMP: 75
SALES (corp-wide): 95.1B **Publicly Held**
SIC: 6211
HQ: Merrill Lynch, Pierce, Fenner & Smith
Incorporated
111 8th Ave
New York NY 10011
800 637-7455

(P-9976)
MERRILL LYNCH PIERCE FENNER
16830 Ventura Blvd # 601, Encino
(91436-1707)
PHONE....................818 528-7809
Paul Pepperman, *Manager*
Craig Felten, *Advisor*
Kevin Muradyan, *Advisor*
William Peters, *Agent*
EMP: 57
SALES (corp-wide): 100.2B **Publicly Held**
WEB: www.merlyn.com
SIC: 6211 8742 Security brokers & dealers; financial consultant
HQ: Merrill Lynch, Pierce, Fenner & Smith
Incorporated
111 8th Ave
New York NY 10011
800 637-7455

(P-9977)
MERRILL LYNCH PIERCE FENNER
9560 Wilshire Blvd Fl 3, Beverly Hills
(90212-2430)
PHONE....................310 858-1500
Brad Dykes, *Branch Mgr*
Norman Saiger, *Vice Pres*
Susan Castruita, *Business Mgr*
Kevin Calderon, *Assistant VP*
Brenton Hamlet, *Advisor*
EMP: 50
SALES (corp-wide): 100.2B **Publicly Held**
WEB: www.merlyn.com
SIC: 6211 6282 Security brokers & dealers; investment advisory service
HQ: Merrill Lynch, Pierce, Fenner & Smith
Incorporated
111 8th Ave
New York NY 10011
800 637-7455

(P-9978)
MERRILL LYNCH PIERCE FENNER
16830 Ventura Blvd # 601, Encino
(91436-1707)
PHONE....................818 528-7800
Hugh Arian, *Manager*
Andrea Abeger, *Advisor*
EMP: 55
SALES (corp-wide): 100.2B **Publicly Held**
WEB: www.ml.com
SIC: 6211 Security brokers & dealers

(P-9979)
MERRILL LYNCH PIERCE FENNER
3075b Hansen Way, Palo Alto
(94304-1000)
PHONE....................650 842-2440
Huert Chang, *Branch Mgr*
EMP: 75
SALES (corp-wide): 100.2B **Publicly Held**
WEB: www.merlyn.com
SIC: 6211 Security brokers & dealers
HQ: Merrill Lynch, Pierce, Fenner & Smith
Incorporated
111 8th Ave
New York NY 10011
800 637-7455

(P-9980)
MERRILL LYNCH PIERCE FENNER
730 Patricia Dr, San Luis Obispo
(93405-1036)
PHONE....................661 802-0764
Martin B Epperson, *Principal*
EMP: 50
SALES (corp-wide): 100.2B **Publicly Held**
SIC: 6211 Brokers, security
HQ: Merrill Lynch, Pierce, Fenner & Smith
Incorporated
111 8th Ave
New York NY 10011
800 637-7455

(P-9981)
MERRILL LYNCH PIERCE FENNER
520 Newport Center Dr # 1900, Newport
Beach (92660-8808)
PHONE....................949 467-3760
David Gunta, *Branch Mgr*
John Acierno, *Finance*
Frank Buchholz, *Advisor*
Meredith Levin, *Advisor*
EMP: 240
SALES (corp-wide): 100.2B **Publicly Held**
SIC: 6211 Security brokers & dealers
HQ: Merrill Lynch, Pierce, Fenner & Smith
Incorporated
111 8th Ave
New York NY 10011
800 637-7455

(P-9982)
MERRILL LYNCH PIERCE FENNER
300 E Esplanade Dr, Oxnard (93036-1238)
PHONE....................800 964-5182
James Hardy, *Branch Mgr*
EMP: 240
SALES (corp-wide): 100.2B **Publicly Held**
SIC: 6211 Security brokers & dealers
HQ: Merrill Lynch, Pierce, Fenner & Smith
Incorporated
111 8th Ave
New York NY 10011
800 637-7455

(P-9983)
MERRILL LYNCH PIERCE FENNER
333 Middlefield Rd # 202, Menlo Park
(94025-3552)
PHONE....................650 473-7888
Deborah Germenis, *Branch Mgr*
Cory Goligoski, *Vice Pres*
Alice Chow, *Agent*
EMP: 240
SALES (corp-wide): 100.2B **Publicly Held**
SIC: 6211 Security brokers & dealers
HQ: Merrill Lynch, Pierce, Fenner & Smith
Incorporated
111 8th Ave
New York NY 10011
800 637-7455

(P-9984)
MERRILL LYNCH PIERCE FENNER
701 B St Ste 2350, San Diego
(92101-8125)
PHONE....................619 699-3700
Quinton Ellis, *Branch Mgr*
Mark Albers, *Exec Dir*
Marnie Maclaren, *Admin Mgr*
Nathan Labiak, *Finance*
Lawrence Brashears, *Manager*
EMP: 150
SALES (corp-wide): 100.2B **Publicly Held**
WEB: www.merlyn.com
SIC: 6211 8742 Security brokers & dealers; financial consultant
HQ: Merrill Lynch, Pierce, Fenner & Smith
Incorporated
111 8th Ave
New York NY 10011
800 637-7455

(P-9985)
MERRILL LYNCH PIERCE FENNER
50 W San Fernando St 16, San Jose
(95113-2429)
PHONE....................408 283-3000
Patricia Williams, *Manager*
Lois Eckmann, *Advisor*
Lyle Smith, *Advisor*
Peter Verbica, *Advisor*
Jim Yglesias, *Advisor*
EMP: 50
SALES (corp-wide): 100.2B **Publicly Held**
WEB: www.merlyn.com
SIC: 6211 6282 Security brokers & dealers; investment advice
HQ: Merrill Lynch, Pierce, Fenner & Smith
Incorporated
111 8th Ave
New York NY 10011
800 637-7455

(P-9986)
MERRILL LYNCH PIERCE FENNER
2049 Century Park E # 1100, Los Angeles
(90067-3101)
PHONE....................310 407-3900
Michael Rogers, *Branch Mgr*
Lance Polverini, *Vice Pres*
EMP: 120
SALES (corp-wide): 100.2B **Publicly Held**
WEB: www.merlyn.com
SIC: 6211 Security brokers & dealers
HQ: Merrill Lynch, Pierce, Fenner & Smith
Incorporated
111 8th Ave
New York NY 10011
800 637-7455

(P-9987)
MERRILL LYNCH PIERCE FENNER
1331 N Calif Blvd Ste 400, Walnut Creek
(94596-4561)
PHONE....................925 945-4800
Michael Dunn, *Branch Mgr*
Len Nathan, *Vice Pres*
Patricia Ancheta, *Financial Exec*
Tim Carlson, *Advisor*
EMP: 85
SALES (corp-wide): 100.2B **Publicly Held**
WEB: www.merlyn.com
SIC: 6211 8742 Security brokers & dealers; financial consultant
HQ: Merrill Lynch, Pierce, Fenner & Smith
Incorporated
111 8th Ave
New York NY 10011
800 637-7455

(P-9988)
MERRILL LYNCH PIERCE FENNER
101 California St Fl 24, San Francisco
(94111-5802)
PHONE....................415 274-7000
Jim Delancey, *Manager*
Christine Koh-Wong, *Vice Pres*

Charles Lewis, *Broker*
Randal T Avey, *Manager*
Andrew J Mayer, *Manager*
EMP: 50
SALES (corp-wide): 100.2B **Publicly Held**
WEB: www.merlyn.com
SIC: 6211 6282 Stock brokers & dealers; investment advice
HQ: Merrill Lynch, Pierce, Fenner & Smith
Incorporated
111 8th Ave
New York NY 10011
800 637-7455

(P-9989)
MERRILL LYNCH PIERCE FENNER
100 Spectrum Center Dr # 1100, Irvine
(92618-4962)
P.O. Box 2550, Laguna Hills (92654-2550)
PHONE....................949 859-2900
Pete Henvika, *Branch Mgr*
Andrew Binkerd, *Advisor*
Jeffrey Dewees, *Advisor*
Matthew M Egan, *Advisor*
Andrew Kopjak, *Advisor*
EMP: 90
SALES (corp-wide): 100.2B **Publicly Held**
WEB: www.merlyn.com
SIC: 6211 Security brokers & dealers
HQ: Merrill Lynch, Pierce, Fenner & Smith
Incorporated
111 8th Ave
New York NY 10011
800 637-7455

(P-9990)
MERRILL LYNCH PIERCE FENNER
7825 Fay Ave Ste 300, La Jolla
(92037-4255)
PHONE....................858 456-3600
Paul Sullivan, *Manager*
Neal Walton, *Manager*
Gary Wardein, *Manager*
Robert Wilcsek, *Manager*
Chrisanna Northrup, *Assistant*
EMP: 60
SALES (corp-wide): 100.2B **Publicly Held**
WEB: www.merlyn.com
SIC: 6211 Security brokers & dealers
HQ: Merrill Lynch, Pierce, Fenner & Smith
Incorporated
111 8th Ave
New York NY 10011
800 637-7455

(P-9991)
MIZUHO SECURITIES USA INC
3 Embarcadero Ctr # 1620, San Francisco
(94111-4049)
PHONE....................415 268-5500
EMP: 53
SALES (corp-wide): 33.4B **Privately Held**
SIC: 6211 Security brokers & dealers
HQ: Mizuho Securities Usa Llc
320 Park Ave Fl 12
New York NY 10022
212 282-3000

(P-9992)
MORGAN STANLEY
55 S Lake Ave Ste 800, Pasadena
(91101-2677)
PHONE....................626 405-9313
Alan Whitman, *Branch Mgr*
Kamran Hedjasi, *Agent*
Anny Shen, *Agent*
EMP: 60
SALES (corp-wide): 43.6B **Publicly Held**
SIC: 6211 Stock brokers & dealers
PA: Morgan Stanley
1585 Broadway
New York NY 10036
212 761-4000

(P-9993)
MORGAN STANLEY
4350 La Jolla Village Dr # 1000, San Diego
(92122-1247)
PHONE....................858 597-7777
Joe McDoval, *General Mgr*
EMP: 50

SALES (corp-wide): 43.6B **Publicly Held**
SIC: 6211 Security brokers & dealers
PA: Morgan Stanley
   1585 Broadway
   New York NY 10036
   212 761-4000

(P-9994)
MORGAN STANLEY
1901 Main St Ste 700, Irvine (92614-0514)
PHONE...................949 809-1200
Jeff Gilbert, *Manager*
EMP: 65
SALES (corp-wide): 43.6B **Publicly Held**
SIC: 6211 Security brokers & dealers
PA: Morgan Stanley & Co. Llc
   1585 Broadway
   New York NY 10036
   212 761-4000

(P-9995)
MORGAN STANLEY & CO LLC
407 Capitol Mall Ste 1900, Sacramento (95814)
PHONE...................916 444-8041
Henry Auwinger, *Branch Mgr*
EMP: 50
SALES (corp-wide): 43.6B **Publicly Held**
WEB: www.msvp.com
SIC: 6211 Stock brokers & dealers
HQ: Morgan Stanley & Co. Llc
   1585 Broadway
   New York NY 10036
   212 761-4000

(P-9996)
MORGAN STANLEY & CO LLC
5250 N Palm Ave Ste 321, Fresno (93704-2213)
PHONE...................559 431-5900
Gregory Conner, *Manager*
EMP: 50
SALES (corp-wide): 43.6B **Publicly Held**
WEB: www.msvp.com
SIC: 6211 Security brokers & dealers
HQ: Morgan Stanley & Co. Llc
   1585 Broadway
   New York NY 10036
   212 761-4000

(P-9997)
MORGAN STANLEY & CO LLC
2677 N Main St Fl 10, Santa Ana (92705-6633)
P.O. Box 11998 (92711-1998)
PHONE...................714 836-5181
Mark Albers, *Branch Mgr*
Jose Bohon, *Div Sub Head*
Ashby Jones, *Advisor*
EMP: 60
SALES (corp-wide): 43.6B **Publicly Held**
WEB: www.msvp.com
SIC: 6211 Stock brokers & dealers
HQ: Morgan Stanley & Co. Llc
   1585 Broadway
   New York NY 10036
   212 761-4000

(P-9998)
MORGAN STANLEY & CO LLC
101 W Broadway Ste 1800, San Diego (92101-8298)
PHONE...................619 236-1331
Eddie Dyer, *Branch Mgr*
EMP: 80
SQ FT: 13,000
SALES (corp-wide): 43.6B **Publicly Held**
WEB: www.msvp.com
SIC: 6211 Investment bankers
HQ: Morgan Stanley & Co. Llc
   1585 Broadway
   New York NY 10036
   212 761-4000

(P-9999)
MORGAN STANLEY & CO LLC
9100 Ming Ave Ste 205, Bakersfield (93311-1329)
PHONE...................661 663-8100
Tom Woodward, *Manager*
EMP: 53
SALES (corp-wide): 43.6B **Publicly Held**
WEB: www.msvp.com
SIC: 6211 Brokers, security

HQ: Morgan Stanley & Co. Llc
   1585 Broadway
   New York NY 10036
   212 761-4000

(P-10000)
MORGAN STANLEY & CO LLC
1999 Harrison St Ste 2200, Oakland (94612-3559)
PHONE...................510 839-8080
Renee Arst, *Manager*
EMP: 60
SALES (corp-wide): 43.6B **Publicly Held**
WEB: www.msvp.com
SIC: 6211 Security brokers & dealers
HQ: Morgan Stanley & Co. Llc
   1585 Broadway
   New York NY 10036
   212 761-4000

(P-10001)
MORGAN STANLEY & CO LLC
216 Lorton Ave, Burlingame (94010-4204)
PHONE...................650 340-6550
Jane Kelly, *Principal*
EMP: 75
SALES (corp-wide): 43.6B **Publicly Held**
WEB: www.msvp.com
SIC: 6211 Investment bankers
HQ: Morgan Stanley & Co. Llc
   1585 Broadway
   New York NY 10036
   212 761-4000

(P-10002)
MORGAN STANLEY & CO LLC
1453 3rd St Ste 200, Santa Monica (90401-3451)
P.O. Box 2310 (90407-2310)
PHONE...................310 319-5200
Thomas Padden, *Manager*
EMP: 65
SALES (corp-wide): 43.6B **Publicly Held**
WEB: www.msvp.com
SIC: 6211 Investment bankers
HQ: Morgan Stanley & Co. Llc
   1585 Broadway
   New York NY 10036
   212 761-4000

(P-10003)
MORGAN STANLEY & CO LLC
225 W Santa Clara St # 900, San Jose (95113-1746)
PHONE...................408 947-2200
William Svoboda, *Branch Mgr*
EMP: 60
SALES (corp-wide): 43.6B **Publicly Held**
WEB: www.msvp.com
SIC: 6211 Brokers, security
HQ: Morgan Stanley & Co. Llc
   1585 Broadway
   New York NY 10036
   212 761-4000

(P-10004)
MORGAN STANLEY & CO LLC
9665 Wilshire Blvd # 600, Beverly Hills (90212-2315)
PHONE...................310 285-4800
Margaret Black, *Manager*
EMP: 160
SALES (corp-wide): 43.6B **Publicly Held**
WEB: www.msvp.com
SIC: 6211 Security brokers & dealers
HQ: Morgan Stanley & Co. Llc
   1585 Broadway
   New York NY 10036
   212 761-4000

(P-10005)
MORGAN STANLEY & CO LLC
101 California St Fl 3, San Francisco (94111-5890)
PHONE...................415 693-6000
Renee Arst, *Manager*
EMP: 300
SALES (corp-wide): 43.6B **Publicly Held**
WEB: www.msvp.com
SIC: 6211 Brokers, security
HQ: Morgan Stanley & Co. Llc
   1585 Broadway
   New York NY 10036
   212 761-4000

(P-10006)
MYERS CAPITAL PARTNERS LLC
450 S Marengo Ave, Pasadena (91101-3113)
PHONE...................626 568-1398
William E Myers,
Kit McCullogh,
EMP: 50
SQ FT: 1,000
SALES (est): 8MM **Privately Held**
WEB: www.myerscapitalpartners.com
SIC: 6211 Investment firm, general brokerage

(P-10007)
NOMURA SECURITIES INTL INC
425 California St # 2600, San Francisco (94104-2211)
PHONE...................415 445-3831
John Denning, *Branch Mgr*
EMP: 340
SALES (corp-wide): 18.5B **Privately Held**
SIC: 6211 Dealers, security
HQ: Nomura Securities International, Inc.
   Worldwide Plaza 309 W 49t
   New York NY 10019
   212 667-9000

(P-10008)
PACIFIC GROWTH EQUITIES LLC
1 Bush St Fl 17, San Francisco (94104-4425)
PHONE...................415 274-6800
Thomas J Dietz, *CEO*
Kurtis Fechtmeyer, *Principal*
Richard Osgood,
EMP: 85
SQ FT: 34,000
SALES: 44MM **Privately Held**
WEB: www.pacgrow.com
SIC: 6211 Security brokers & dealers; investment bankers

(P-10009)
PARKSIDE LENDING LLC
180 Redwood St Ste 250, San Francisco (94102-3283)
PHONE...................415 771-3700
Alan Sagatelyan,
Clint Rosenthal, *President*
Hanford Chiu, *CFO*
Nathalie Lemaire, *Ch Credit Ofcr*
Laurie Blasko, *Officer*
EMP: 60
SQ FT: 5,097
SALES (est): 84.6MM **Privately Held**
WEB: www.parksidelending.com
SIC: 6211 Mortgages, buying & selling

(P-10010)
RBC CAPITAL MARKETS LLC
9665 Wilshire Blvd Fl 4, Beverly Hills (90212-2311)
PHONE...................310 273-7600
Elliot Katz, *Branch Mgr*
Brett Bartman, *Senior VP*
Phil Hammitt, *Senior VP*
Paul Lakon, *Senior VP*
Maria Lupu, *Vice Pres*
EMP: 50 **Privately Held**
WEB: www.hough.com
SIC: 6211 Investment bankers
HQ: Rbc Capital Markets, Llc
   60 S 6th St Ste 700
   Minneapolis MN 55402
   612 371-2711

(P-10011)
REYES HOLDINGS LLC
Also Called: Crest Beverage
8870 Liquid Ct, San Diego (92121-2234)
PHONE...................858 452-2300
Steve Souratas, *President*
EMP: 300 **Privately Held**
SIC: 6211 Distributors, security
PA: Reyes Holdings, L.L.C.
   6250 N River Rd Ste 9000
   Rosemont IL 60018

(P-10012)
ROTH CAPITAL PARTNERS LLC (PA)
888 San Clemente Dr # 400, Newport Beach (92660-6366)
PHONE...................800 678-9147
Byron Roth, *CEO*
John Chambers, *Vice Ch Bd*
Warren Dunnavant II, *Vice Pres*
Daniel Friedman, *Vice Pres*
Sherry He, *Vice Pres*
EMP: 100
SQ FT: 52,000
SALES (est): 55.7MM **Privately Held**
WEB: www.rothcp.com
SIC: 6211 Investment bankers; brokers, security

(P-10013)
SHAMROCK PLUS INC
Also Called: Shamrock Center
4444 W Lakeside Dr Lbby, Burbank (91505-4069)
PHONE...................818 845-4444
Stanley Gold, *President*
EMP: 50
SQ FT: 12,000
SALES (est): 3.4MM
SALES (corp-wide): 16.3MM **Privately Held**
SIC: 6211 Brokers, security; investment bankers; investment certificate sales
HQ: Shamrock Holdings Of California, Inc.
   4444 W Lakeside Dr Lbby
   Burbank CA 91505
   818 845-4444

(P-10014)
STANDARD PACIFIC CAPITAL LLC
101 California St Fl 36, San Francisco (94111-5831)
PHONE...................415 352-7100
Andrew Midler, *Mng Member*
Nicole Schwedhelm, *Research*
Lei Chen, *Analyst*
Alla Yakov Collins, *Controller*
Dan Martin,
EMP: 50
SQ FT: 9,000
SALES (est): 12.7MM **Privately Held**
SIC: 6211 Investment firm, general brokerage

(P-10015)
STOCKCROSS FINANCIAL SVCS INC (PA)
9464 Wilshire Blvd, Beverly Hills (90212-2707)
PHONE...................800 993-2015
Andrew Reich, *CEO*
EMP: 50
SQ FT: 8,000
SALES (est): 25.8MM **Privately Held**
WEB: www.stockcross.com
SIC: 6211 Brokers, security; dealers, security

(P-10016)
STONE & YOUNGBERG LLC (PA)
1 Ferry Plz, San Francisco (94111-4212)
PHONE...................415 445-2300
Terry Maas, *Principal*
Kenneth E Williams, *President*
Mitchell H Gage, *CFO*
B Craig Hutson, *Senior VP*
Kevin R Montoya, *Senior VP*
EMP: 130
SQ FT: 19,034
SALES (est): 35.7MM **Privately Held**
WEB: www.syllc.com
SIC: 6211 6282 Bond dealers & brokers; investment advice

(P-10017)
TAKENAKA PARTNERS LLC (PA)
801 S Figueroa St Ste 620, Los Angeles (90017-5556)
PHONE...................213 593-4011
Yukuo Takenaka, *President*
Yoshiko Nakaoki, *CFO*
Kathleen Agee, *Executive Asst*
Loy Valenzuela, *Human Res Mgr*
EMP: 50
SQ FT: 5,183

SALES (est): 7.5MM **Privately Held**
WEB: www.takenakapartners.com
SIC: 6211 Investment bankers

(P-10018)
TANIMURA BROTHERS
81 Hitchcock Rd, Salinas (93908-9449)
PHONE..........................831 424-0841
Tom Tanimura, *Partner*
George Tanimura, *Partner*
John Tanimura, *Partner*
EMP: 70 **EST:** 1948
SALES (est): 9.9MM **Privately Held**
SIC: 6211 Investment firm, general brokerage

(P-10019)
TCW FUNDS MANAGEMENT INC
865 S Figueroa St # 2100, Los Angeles
(90017-2588)
PHONE..........................213 244-0000
Thomas Larkin, *Ch of Bd*
Marc I Stern, *President*
William E Sonnebron, *CFO*
Ernest O Ellison, *Officer*
Alvin R Albe Jr, *Exec VP*
EMP: 550
SALES (est): 31.8MM
SALES (corp-wide): 205.6MM **Privately Held**
SIC: 6211 Security brokers & dealers
PA: The Tcw Group Inc
   865 S Figueroa St # 1800
   Los Angeles CA 90017
   213 244-0000

(P-10020)
THE CHARLES SCHWAB TRUST CO (HQ)
425 Market St Fl 7, San Francisco
(94105-5405)
PHONE..........................415 371-0518
James McCool, *CEO*
Steven Scheid, *CFO*
Nancy Larget, *Vice Pres*
Bill Jancouskas, *Managing Dir*
Denise Lockridge, *Associate*
EMP: 50
SALES (est): 54.3MM
SALES (corp-wide): 8.6B **Publicly Held**
SIC: 6211 Security brokers & dealers
PA: The Charles Schwab Corporation
   211 Main St Fl 17
   San Francisco CA 94105
   415 667-7000

(P-10021)
THOMAS WEISEL PARTNERS LLC (DH)
1 Montgomery St Ste 3700, San Francisco
(94104-5537)
PHONE..........................415 364-2500
Thomas Weisel,
Richard Spalding, *General Ptnr*
Bowman Wingard, *Partner*
Tracy Beaver, *Vice Pres*
Michael Carr, *Vice Pres*
EMP: 300
SALES (est): 74MM
SALES (corp-wide): 2.9B **Publicly Held**
WEB: www.tweisel.com
SIC: 6211 Investment bankers
HQ: Thomas Weisel Partners Group Inc.
   1 Montgomery St
   San Francisco CA 94104
   415 364-2500

(P-10022)
TRANSAMERICA SECURITIES SALES
1150 S Olive St Ste T25, Los Angeles
(90015-2214)
PHONE..........................213 741-7702
Sandy Brown, *President*
Dan S Trivers, *Principal*
EMP: 75
SALES (est): 6.1MM **Privately Held**
SIC: 6211 Security brokers & dealers

(P-10023)
TRANSMERICA FINCL ADVISORS INC
1150 S Olive St Ste T250, Los Angeles
(90015-2211)
PHONE..........................213 741-7702

Sandy Brown, *Branch Mgr*
EMP: 121
SALES (corp-wide): 593.2MM **Privately Held**
SIC: 6211 6282 Investment firm, general brokerage; manager of mutual funds, contract or fee basis
HQ: Transamerica Financial Advisors, Inc.
   570 Carillon Pkwy
   Saint Petersburg FL 33716
   727 557-2754

(P-10024)
UBS FINANCIAL SERVICES INC
777 S Figueroa St # 5100, Los Angeles
(90017-5800)
P.O. Box 90051 (90009-0051)
PHONE..........................213 972-1511
Wes Jennison, *Manager*
James Giordano, *Vice Pres*
EMP: 200
SALES (corp-wide): 29.4B **Privately Held**
SIC: 6211 Brokers, security
HQ: Ubs Financial Services Inc.
   1285 Ave Of The Americas
   New York NY 10019
   212 713-2000

(P-10025)
UBS FINANCIAL SERVICES INC
131 S Rodeo Dr Ste 200, Beverly Hills
(90212-2428)
PHONE..........................310 274-8441
Randall Grossblatt, *Manager*
John Buchanan, *Vice Pres*
Lane Goldstein, *Vice Pres*
Justin T Reese, *Vice Pres*
Mike Scandalios, *Vice Pres*
EMP: 100
SALES (corp-wide): 29.4B **Privately Held**
SIC: 6211 Bond dealers & brokers; brokers, security; stock brokers & dealers
HQ: Ubs Financial Services Inc.
   1285 Ave Of The Americas
   New York NY 10019
   212 713-2000

(P-10026)
UBS FINANCIAL SERVICES INC
600 W Broadway Ste 2100, San Diego
(92101-3356)
PHONE..........................619 236-0460
David Jones, *Manager*
Daniel Banks, *Manager*
Thomas Krumenacker, *Representative*
EMP: 130
SALES (corp-wide): 29.4B **Privately Held**
SIC: 6211 Dealers, security
HQ: Ubs Financial Services Inc.
   1285 Ave Of The Americas
   New York NY 10019
   212 713-2000

(P-10027)
UBS FINANCIAL SERVICES INC
555 California St # 3200, San Francisco
(94104-1608)
PHONE..........................415 954-6700
Loren Neumann, *Branch Mgr*
Richard Massey, *Vice Pres*
Alexander Taft, *Vice Pres*
Nick Tarrab, *Vice Pres*
Robert Vallercorse, *Vice Pres*
EMP: 175
SALES (corp-wide): 29.4B **Privately Held**
SIC: 6211 Stock brokers & dealers
HQ: Ubs Financial Services Inc.
   1285 Ave Of The Americas
   New York NY 10019
   212 713-2000

(P-10028)
UBS FINANCIAL SERVICES INC
888 San Clemente Dr # 300, Newport Beach (92660-6366)
PHONE..........................949 760-5308
Don Dalis, *Branch Mgr*
Scott G Purrelli, *Vice Pres*
Pamela Blazick, *Opers Mgr*
Ronald Meraz, *Director*
Michael Hammett, *Advisor*
EMP: 175
SALES (corp-wide): 29.4B **Privately Held**
SIC: 6211 Stock brokers & dealers

HQ: Ubs Financial Services Inc.
   1285 Ave Of The Americas
   New York NY 10019
   212 713-2000

(P-10029)
UBS FINANCIAL SERVICES INC
1610 Arden Way Ste 200, Sacramento
(95815-4041)
PHONE..........................916 648-7200
Tom Qvustgaard, *Branch Mgr*
John Lewis, *Vice Pres*
EMP: 50
SALES (corp-wide): 29.4B **Privately Held**
SIC: 6211 Security brokers & dealers
HQ: Ubs Financial Services Inc.
   1285 Ave Of The Americas
   New York NY 10019
   212 713-2000

(P-10030)
UBS FINANCIAL SERVICES INC
555 California St # 4650, San Francisco
(94104-1789)
PHONE..........................415 398-6400
Tony Tarrab, *Manager*
David Dicioccio, *Managing Dir*
EMP: 100
SALES (corp-wide): 29.4B **Privately Held**
SIC: 6211 Investment bankers; brokers, security
HQ: Ubs Financial Services Inc.
   1285 Ave Of The Americas
   New York NY 10019
   212 713-2000

(P-10031)
UBS FINANCIAL SERVICES INC
555 California St # 4650, San Francisco
(94104-1789)
PHONE..........................415 398-6400
Mark Zalinski, *Manager*
EMP: 60
SALES (corp-wide): 29.4B **Privately Held**
SIC: 6211 Security brokers & dealers
HQ: Ubs Financial Services Inc.
   1285 Ave Of The Americas
   New York NY 10019
   212 713-2000

(P-10032)
UBS SECURITIES LLC
555 California St # 4650, San Francisco
(94104-1789)
PHONE..........................415 352-5650
Kirt Engle, *Branch Mgr*
Karen Stinger, *Officer*
Jeffrey B Burke, *Vice Pres*
Angel K Chen, *Vice Pres*
Jeffrey P Nash, *Vice Pres*
EMP: 65
SALES (corp-wide): 29.4B **Privately Held**
SIC: 6211 Brokers, security; dealers, security
HQ: Ubs Securities Llc
   677 Washington Blvd
   Stamford CT 06901

(P-10033)
W R HAMBRECHT CO INC (PA)
Bay 3 Pier 1, San Francisco (94111)
PHONE..........................415 551-8600
William R Hambrecht, *Ch of Bd*
Jonathan Fayman, *CFO*
Clay Corbus, *Co-CEO*
EMP: 60 **EST:** 1998
SQ FT: 25,000
SALES (est): 21.4MM **Privately Held**
WEB: www.wrhambrecht.com
SIC: 6211 Investment bankers

(P-10034)
WADDELL & REED INC
695 Town Center Dr # 200, Costa Mesa
(92626-7128)
PHONE..........................714 437-7510
Daralee Barbera, *Director*
Dennis Logue, *Bd of Directors*
James Raines, *Bd of Directors*
Al Gumb, *District Mgr*
Valerie Tastad, *Producer*
EMP: 65 **Publicly Held**
SIC: 6211 8742 Security brokers & dealers; financial consultant

HQ: Waddell & Reed, Inc.
   6300 Lamar Ave
   Shawnee Mission KS 66202
   913 236-2000

(P-10035)
WEDBUSH SECURITIES INC (HQ)
1000 Wilshire Blvd # 800, Los Angeles
(90017-2466)
P.O. Box 30014 (90030-0014)
PHONE..........................213 688-8000
Edward W Wedbush, *President*
EMP: 300 **EST:** 1955
SQ FT: 100,000
SALES (est): 270.5MM
SALES (corp-wide): 280.1MM **Privately Held**
WEB: www.einvestmentbank.com
SIC: 6211 Brokers, security; stock brokers & dealers; bond dealers & brokers
PA: Wedbush, Inc.,
   1000 Wilshire Blvd # 900
   Los Angeles CA 90017
   213 688-8080

(P-10036)
WELLS FARGO CLEARING SVCS LLC
Also Called: Wells Fargo Advisors
777 S Figueroa St # 4700, Los Angeles
(90017-5800)
PHONE..........................213 486-5200
Tom Barker, *Manager*
EMP: 50
SALES (corp-wide): 97.7B **Publicly Held**
WEB: www.wachoviasec.com
SIC: 6211 8742 Stock brokers & dealers; financial consultant
HQ: Wells Fargo Clearing Services, Llc
   1 N Jefferson Ave
   Saint Louis MO 63103
   314 955-3000

(P-10037)
WELLS FARGO CLEARING SVCS LLC
Also Called: Wells Fargo Advisors
555 California St # 2300, San Francisco
(94104-1598)
PHONE..........................415 291-1200
Kevin Kitchin, *Manager*
Gary Garabedian, *Vice Pres*
Harry Gong, *Vice Pres*
Derek Holtzinger, *Vice Pres*
Beth Kirkland, *Manager*
EMP: 115
SALES (corp-wide): 97.7B **Publicly Held**
WEB: www.wachoviasec.com
SIC: 6211 6282 Stock brokers & dealers; investment advice
HQ: Wells Fargo Clearing Services, Llc
   1 N Jefferson Ave Fl 7
   Saint Louis MO 63103
   314 955-3000

(P-10038)
WELLS FARGO CLEARING SVCS LLC
Also Called: Wells Fargo Advisors
888 Prospect St Ste 220, La Jolla
(92037-4261)
PHONE..........................858 456-7706
Bill Ryan, *Manager*
Jerry Heavey, *Vice Pres*
Patrick Kearney, *Vice Pres*
Martin Levine, *Vice Pres*
Ellice J Papp, *Vice Pres*
EMP: 50
SALES (corp-wide): 97.7B **Publicly Held**
WEB: www.wachoviasec.com
SIC: 6211 Stock brokers & dealers
HQ: Wells Fargo Clearing Services, Llc
   1 N Jefferson Ave
   Saint Louis MO 63103
   314 955-3000

(P-10039)
WELLS FARGO CLEARING SVCS LLC
Also Called: Wells Fargo Advisors
3020 Old Ranch Pkwy # 190, Seal Beach
(90740-2765)
PHONE..........................562 594-1220
EMP: 50

SALES (corp-wide): 97.7B **Publicly Held**
SIC: 6211
HQ: Wells Fargo Clearing Services, Llc
1 N Jefferson Ave
Saint Louis MO 63103
314 955-3000

(P-10040)
WELLS FARGO CLEARING SVCS LLC
Also Called: Wells Fargo Advisors
5820 Canoga Ave Ste 100, Woodland Hills
(91367-6517)
PHONE....................818 226-2222
Jeff Bouchard, *Manager*
Thomas A Eisenstadt, *Vice Pres*
Mark Gale, *Vice Pres*
Barry Spadoni, *Vice Pres*
Marc Spiegel, *Vice Pres*
EMP: 60
SALES (corp-wide): 97.7B **Publicly Held**
WEB: www.wachoviasec.com
SIC: 6211 Stock brokers & dealers
HQ: Wells Fargo Clearing Services, Llc
1 N Jefferson Ave
Saint Louis MO 63103
314 955-3000

(P-10041)
WELLS FARGO SECURITIES LLC
600 California St Fl 17, San Francisco
(94108-2723)
PHONE....................415 645-0800
Eric Fornell, *Vice Chairman*
Abraham Mintz, *Vice Pres*
Dan Goggins, *Director*
EMP: 90
SALES (corp-wide): 97.7B **Publicly Held**
WEB: www.wellsfargosecurities.com
SIC: 6211 Investment bankers
HQ: Wells Fargo Securities, Llc
550 S Tryon St
Charlotte NC 28202
704 715-5320

(P-10042)
WINDJAMMER CAPITAL INVSTR III
Also Called: Westwind Equity Investors
610 Newport Center Dr # 1100, Newport
Beach (92660-6419)
PHONE....................949 706-9989
Robert Bartholomew, *Chairman*
Matt Anderson, *Vice Pres*
J Derek Watson, *Principal*
Derek J Watson, *Managing Dir*
Jeff Miehe, *Managing Dir*
EMP: 724
SALES (est): 46.2MM **Privately Held**
SIC: 6211 Investment firm, general brokerage

(P-10043)
ZELL ASSOCIATES INC (PA)
Also Called: Investment Real Estate
1777 Hamilton Ave # 1250, San Jose
(95125-5418)
PHONE....................408 978-1950
Sherman Zell, *President*
Sylvia Delpier, *Vice Pres*
Marie Jasinsky, *Director*
EMP: 72
SQ FT: 3,000
SALES (est): 15.3MM **Privately Held**
WEB: www.zell.com
SIC: 6211 6531 6552 Syndicate shares
(real estate, entertainment, equip.) sales;
real estate managers; real estate brokers
& agents; subdividers & developers

**6221 Commodity Contracts
Brokers & Dealers**

(P-10044)
APEX BULK COMMODITIES INC
14080 Slover Ave, Fontana (92337-7039)
PHONE....................909 854-9991
Steve Gale, *Branch Mgr*
EMP: 68
SALES (corp-wide): 74.9MM **Privately Held**
SIC: 6221 Commodity contracts brokers, dealers

PA: Apex Bulk Commodities, Inc.
12531 Violet Rd Ste A
Adelanto CA 92301
760 246-6077

(P-10045)
GLOBAL FUTURES EXCH & TRDG CO
303 17th St, Santa Monica (90402-2223)
PHONE....................818 996-0401
Kathy Hakimian, *President*
Francis Marcale, *Manager*
EMP: 80
SALES (est): 14.3MM **Privately Held**
WEB: www.gfetc.com
SIC: 6221 Commodity brokers, contracts

(P-10046)
MERRILL LYNCH PIERCE FENNER
145 S State College Blvd # 300, Brea
(92821-5844)
PHONE....................714 257-4400
Robert Max, *Manager*
Haseong Joo, *Vice Pres*
John Nam, *Vice Pres*
Colin Sinclair, *Vice Pres*
Cynthia C Wong, *Manager*
EMP: 69
SALES (corp-wide): 100.2B **Publicly Held**
WEB: www.merlyn.com
SIC: 6221 Commodity brokers, contracts;
commodity dealers, contracts
HQ: Merrill Lynch, Pierce, Fenner & Smith
Incorporated
111 8th Ave
New York NY 10011
800 637-7455

(P-10047)
MERRILL LYNCH PIERCE FENNER
800 E Colo Blvd Ste 400, Pasadena
(91101)
PHONE....................626 844-8500
Mark Mixon, *Manager*
Heidi Leu, *Manager*
Eric Callow, *Advisor*
Lawrence De Santis, *Advisor*
Anthony Gendal, *Advisor*
EMP: 80
SALES (corp-wide): 100.2B **Publicly Held**
WEB: www.merlyn.com
SIC: 6221 Commodity brokers, contracts;
commodity dealers, contracts
HQ: Merrill Lynch, Pierce, Fenner & Smith
Incorporated
111 8th Ave
New York NY 10011
800 637-7455

**6231 Security & Commodity
Exchanges**

(P-10048)
INTERCONTINENTAL EXCHANGE INC (HQ)
Also Called: Ice
1415 Moonstone, Brea (92821-2832)
PHONE....................770 857-4700
Jeffrey C Sprecher, *Ch of Bd*
Ben Jackson, *President*
Bruce Tupper, *President*
Brad Vannan, *President*
Charles A Vice, *President*
EMP: 383
SQ FT: 92,171
SALES (est): 2.3B
SALES (corp-wide): 4.6B **Publicly Held**
WEB: www.theice.com
SIC: 6231 Security & commodity exchanges
PA: Intercontinental Exchange, Inc.
5660 New Northside Dr # 300
Atlanta GA 30328
770 857-4700

(P-10049)
NYSE ARCA INC
115 Sansome St, San Francisco
(94104-3601)
PHONE....................415 393-4000
Philip D Defeo, *CEO*
David Diamond, *CFO*
Paul N Koutoulas, *Exec VP*
Peter Armstrong, *Senior VP*
Hark Yip, *Senior VP*
EMP: 265 EST: 1882
SALES (est): 512.9K
SALES (corp-wide): 4.6B **Publicly Held**
SIC: 6231 Stock exchanges
HQ: Nyse Group, Inc.
11 Wall St
New York NY 10005
212 656-3000

6282 Investment Advice

(P-10050)
ALLIANZ GLOBL INVSTORS AMER LP (HQ)
Also Called: Foreign Prnt Is Alanz AG Mnchn
680 Nwport Ctr Dr Ste 250, Newport Beach
(92660)
PHONE....................949 219-2200
Brian Gaffney, *President*
David Flattum, *Partner*
Alexandra Curtis, *Admin Sec*
Yvonne Cheng, *Human Res Dir*
Keith Andersen, *Director*
EMP: 100
SQ FT: 20,000
SALES (est): 707.9MM **Privately Held**
WEB: www.allianzinvestors.com
SIC: 6282 Investment advisory service;
manager of mutual funds, contract or fee
basis
PA: Allianz Se
Koniginstr. 28
Munchen 80802
893 800-0

(P-10051)
AMERICAN ADVISORS GROUP (PA)
3800 W Chapman Ave Fl 3, Orange
(92868-1638)
PHONE....................866 948-0003
Reza Jahangiri, *President*
Matt Engel, *CFO*
Martin Lenoir, *Chief Mktg Ofcr*
Becky Rhodes, *Officer*
Paul Fiore, *Exec VP*
EMP: 50
SQ FT: 4,500
SALES (est): 23.3MM **Privately Held**
SIC: 6282 Futures advisory service; investment advisory service

(P-10052)
AMERICAN CENTURY INV MGT INC
Also Called: American Century Investments
1665 Charleston Rd, Mountain View
(94043-1211)
PHONE....................650 965-8300
Randy Merk, *Branch Mgr*
Bob Gahagan, *Vice Pres*
Darrell Lee, *Vice Pres*
Kevin Sid, *Analyst*
Chris Evans, *Regl Sales Mgr*
EMP: 200
SALES (corp-wide): 777.3MM **Privately Held**
SIC: 6282 Investment advice
HQ: American Century Investment Management, Inc.
4500 Main St
Kansas City MO 64111
816 531-5575

(P-10053)
AMERICAN FINANCIAL NETWORK INC
8505 Florence Ave, Downey (90240-4014)
PHONE....................562 861-1414
Alejandro Ascencio, *Branch Mgr*
EMP: 92

SALES (corp-wide): 177.5MM **Privately Held**
SIC: 6282 Investment advice
PA: American Financial Network, Inc.
10 Pointe Dr Ste 330
Brea CA 92821
909 606-3905

(P-10054)
AMERICAN FINANCIAL NETWORK INC
14748 Pipeline Ave Ste A, Chino Hills
(91709-6024)
PHONE....................909 287-7585
EMP: 55
SALES (corp-wide): 177.5MM **Privately Held**
SIC: 6282 Investment advice
PA: American Financial Network, Inc.
10 Pointe Dr Ste 330
Brea CA 92821
909 606-3905

(P-10055)
AMERICAN FINANCIAL NETWORK INC
2125 Oak Grove Rd, Walnut Creek
(94598-2536)
PHONE....................925 705-7710
EMP: 81
SALES (corp-wide): 99.2MM **Privately Held**
SIC: 6282
PA: American Financial Network, Inc.
10 Pointe Dr Ste 330
Brea CA 92821
909 606-3905

(P-10056)
ANDERSON KAYNE CAPITAL
1800 Avenue Of The, Los Angeles (90067)
PHONE....................800 231-7414
Richard Kayne, *Chairman*
Edward Cerny, *Managing Prtnr*
Robert Sinnott, *CEO*
Frank Arentowicz Jr, *Managing Dir*
Justin Campeau, *Research Analys*
EMP: 300
SALES: 977.4K **Privately Held**
SIC: 6282 Investment advisory service

(P-10057)
ASSETMARK INC (HQ)
1655 Grant St Ste 1000, Concord
(94520-2789)
PHONE....................925 521-1040
Charles Goldman, *President*
Jason Thomas, *CEO*
Gary Zyla, *CFO*
Myra Rothfeld, *Chief Mktg Ofcr*
Jerry Chafkin, *Ch Invest Ofcr*
EMP: 50
SQ FT: 15,000
SALES (est): 39.2MM
SALES (corp-wide): 3.1B **Privately Held**
WEB: www.genworthwealth.com
SIC: 6282 Manager of mutual funds, contract or fee basis
PA: Huatai Securities Co., Ltd.
No.228,Jiangdong Middle Rd.
Nanjing 21000
258 338-7793

(P-10058)
AXA ADVISORS LLC
3435 Wilshire Blvd # 2500, Los Angeles
(90010-2011)
PHONE....................213 251-1600
Yong Parks, *Manager*
Kaising Lui, *Vice Pres*
Young Won, *Vice Pres*
Yujin OH, *Admin Asst*
Jenny Jung, *Info Tech Mgr*
EMP: 90 **Publicly Held**
WEB: www.axacs.com
SIC: 6282 Investment advisory service
HQ: Axa Advisors, Llc
1290 Ave Of Amrcs Fl Cnc1
New York NY 10104
212 554-1234

(P-10059)
AYCO COMPANY LP
17885 Von Karman Ave # 300, Irvine
(92614-5225)
PHONE....................949 955-1544

Emmett Clancy, *Manager*
America Moua, *Data Proc Staff*
Krystle St Claire, *Personnel Assit*
EMP: 150
SALES (corp-wide): 42.2B **Publicly Held**
WEB: www.ayco.com
SIC: 6282 8742 Investment counselors; financial consultant
HQ: The Ayco Company L P
　　321 Broadway
　　Saratoga Springs NY 12866
　　518 886-4000

(P-10060)
B B & K HOLDINGS (PA)
Also Called: Bailard
950 Tower Ln Ste 1900, Foster City
(94404-2131)
PHONE..................................650 571-5800
Thomas E Bailard, *Chairman*
Burney Sparks, *President*
Barbara Bailey, *Treasurer*
EMP: 50
SALES (est): 4.5MM **Privately Held**
SIC: 6282 Investment advisory service

(P-10061)
BAILARD INC (HQ)
950 Tower Ln Ste 1900, Foster City
(94404-2131)
PHONE..................................650 571-5800
Thomas E Bailard, *Ch of Bd*
Henry Newhall, *President*
Burnice E Sparks Jr, *President*
Louise Model, *Vice Pres*
Ronald Kaiser, *Principal*
EMP: 50
SQ FT: 150,000
SALES (est): 11.2MM
SALES (corp-wide): 4.5MM **Privately Held**
WEB: www.bailard.com
SIC: 6282 Investment advisory service
PA: B B & K Holdings
　　950 Tower Ln Ste 1900
　　Foster City CA 94404
　　650 571-5800

(P-10062)
BLACKROCK GLOBAL INVESTORS
400 Howard St, San Francisco
(94105-2618)
PHONE..................................415 670-2000
Patricia Dunn, *CEO*
Alex Litwinek, *Officer*
Blake Grossman, *Principal*
Carter Lyons, *Principal*
Kaustav Ghosh, *Assistant VP*
EMP: 1100
SQ FT: 65,000
SALES (est): 119.1MM **Publicly Held**
SIC: 6282 Investment advisory service
PA: Blackrock, Inc.
　　55 E 52nd St
　　New York NY 10055

(P-10063)
BLX GROUP LLC
777 S Figueroa St # 3200, Los Angeles
(90017-5800)
PHONE..................................213 612-2400
EMP: 60 EST: 2010
SQ FT: 13,000
SALES (est): 6.3MM **Privately Held**
SIC: 6282

(P-10064)
C2 FINANCIAL CORPORATION
3000 Citrus Cir Ste 118, Walnut Creek
(94598-2694)
PHONE..................................925 938-1300
Star Darden, *Branch Mgr*
EMP: 162
SALES (corp-wide): 8.2MM **Privately Held**
SIC: 6282 Investment advice
PA: C2 Financial Corporation
　　10509 Vista Sorrento Pkwy
　　San Diego CA 92121
　　858 312-4900

(P-10065)
C2 FINANCIAL CORPORATION
978 Burlingame Ave, Clovis (93612-0464)
PHONE..................................559 824-2300
EMP: 108
SALES (corp-wide): 8.2MM **Privately Held**
SIC: 6282 Investment advice
PA: C2 Financial Corporation
　　10509 Vista Sorrento Pkwy
　　San Diego CA 92121
　　858 312-4900

(P-10066)
C2 FINANCIAL CORPORATION
703 Sunset Ct, San Diego (92109-7024)
PHONE..................................858 220-2112
EMP: 216
SALES (corp-wide): 8.2MM **Privately Held**
SIC: 6282 Investment advice
PA: C2 Financial Corporation
　　10509 Vista Sorrento Pkwy
　　San Diego CA 92121
　　858 312-4900

(P-10067)
CALIBER CAPITAL GROUP LLC
5900 Katella Ave Ste A101, Cypress
(90630-5019)
PHONE..................................714 507-1998
David Kim,
EMP: 2214
SALES (est): 101.5MM **Privately Held**
SIC: 6282 8111 Investment advice; legal services

(P-10068)
CALLAN LLC (PA)
600 Montgomery St Ste 800, San Francisco
(94111-2710)
PHONE..................................415 974-5060
Ronald D Peyton, *CEO*
Gregory C Allen, *President*
Alina Vartanyan, *President*
Karen Witham, *President*
Ronald Peyton, *CEO*
EMP: 120 EST: 1973
SQ FT: 43,000
SALES (est): 43.8MM **Privately Held**
WEB: www.callan.com
SIC: 6282 8742 Investment advisory service; banking & finance consultant

(P-10069)
CAPITAL GROUP COMPANIES INC
11100 Santa Monica Blvd # 1500, Los Angeles (90025-3384)
PHONE..................................310 996-6238
David Fisher, *Ch of Bd*
Leonard Kim, *Managing Prtnr*
Jeff Brown, *Senior VP*
Will Thompson, *Vice Pres*
Hotak Chow, *Investment Ofcr*
EMP: 260
SALES (corp-wide): 2.2B **Privately Held**
WEB: www.capgroup.org
SIC: 6282 6722 Manager of mutual funds; contract or fee basis; management investment, open-end
PA: The Capital Group Companies Inc
　　333 S Hope St Fl 55
　　Los Angeles CA 90071
　　213 486-9200

(P-10070)
CAPITAL GROUP COMPANIES INC (PA)
Also Called: Capital Group, The
333 S Hope St Fl 55, Los Angeles
(90071-3061)
PHONE..................................213 486-9200
Philip De Toledo, *CEO*
Sandra Chuon, *President*
Mark Cuenca, *President*
Cindi Grossinger, *President*
Kevin Hogan, *President*
EMP: 800
SQ FT: 106,000

(P-10071)
CAPITAL GROUP COMPANIES INC
1 Market Plz Ste 1800, San Francisco
(94105-1018)
PHONE..................................213 486-1698
Chris Buchbinder, *Branch Mgr*
Stephanie Orr, *President*
Erin Covington, *Vice Pres*
Jeff Lager, *Vice Pres*
Kathleen G Kane, *General Mgr*
EMP: 413
SALES (corp-wide): 2.2B **Privately Held**
WEB: www.capgroup.org
SIC: 6282 6722 Manager of mutual funds; contract or fee basis; management investment, open-end
PA: The Capital Group Companies Inc
　　333 S Hope St Fl 55
　　Los Angeles CA 90071
　　213 486-9200

(P-10072)
CAPITAL GROUP COMPANIES INC
Also Called: Capital Group Private Markets
6455 Irvine Center Dr, Irvine (92618-4518)
PHONE..................................949 975-5000
EMP: 478
SALES (corp-wide): 2.2B **Privately Held**
WEB: www.capgroup.org
SIC: 6282 6091 6722 8741 Investment advice; nondeposit trust facilities; management investment, open-end; management services
PA: The Capital Group Companies Inc
　　333 S Hope St Fl 55
　　Los Angeles CA 90071
　　213 486-9200

(P-10073)
CAPITAL RESEARCH AND MGT CO (HQ)
333 S Hope St Fl 55, Los Angeles
(90071-3061)
PHONE..................................213 486-9200
R Michael Shanahan, *Ch of Bd*
James F Rothenberg, *Ch of Bd*
Timothy Armour, *CEO*
Susi Silverman, *Treasurer*
Gordon Crawford, *Senior VP*
EMP: 500
SALES (est): 1.1B
SALES (corp-wide): 2.2B **Privately Held**
SIC: 6282 Investment research; manager of mutual funds, contract or fee basis
PA: The Capital Group Companies Inc
　　333 S Hope St Fl 55
　　Los Angeles CA 90071
　　213 486-9200

(P-10074)
CAPITAL RESEARCH AND MGT CO
6455 Irvine Center Dr, Irvine (92618-4518)
P.O. Box 2205, Brea (92822-2205)
PHONE..................................949 975-5000
Damien Jordan, *Branch Mgr*
Christine Mueller, *Facilities Mgr*
EMP: 75
SALES (corp-wide): 2.2B **Privately Held**
SIC: 6282 6211 6726 6722 Investment research; manager of mutual funds, contract or fee basis; underwriters, security; investment offices; management investment, open-end
HQ: Capital Research And Management Company
　　333 S Hope St Fl 55
　　Los Angeles CA 90071
　　213 486-9200

(P-10075)
CHURCHILL MGT GROUP CORP
5900 Wilshire Blvd # 400, Los Angeles
(90036-5013)
PHONE..................................877 937-7110
Fred A Fern, *President*

Eileen Holmes, *CFO*
Anthony Pressimone, *Assoc VP*
David TSE, *Exec VP*
Ryan Murphy, *Senior VP*
EMP: 50
SALES (est): 12.5MM **Privately Held**
WEB: www.churchillmanagement.com
SIC: 6282 Investment counselors

(P-10076)
DEUTSCHE INV MGT AMERICAS INC
101 California St # 2400, San Francisco
(94111-5898)
PHONE..................................415 648-9408
Victor L Hymes, *Director*
Darrell Campos, *Vice Pres*
EMP: 50
SALES (corp-wide): 11.5B **Privately Held**
SIC: 6282 Investment advisory service
HQ: Deutsche Investment Management
　　Americas Inc.
　　345 Park Ave Uppr L-1
　　New York NY 10154
　　800 349-4281

(P-10077)
FIRST AMERICAN TRUST COMPANY (HQ)
5 First American Way, Santa Ana
(92707-5913)
P.O. Box 267 (92702-0267)
PHONE..................................714 560-7856
Toll Free:..................................877 -
Thomas M Kelley, *CEO*
Kelly Dudley, *COO*
Teri Pierce, *CFO*
Susan Heiner, *CFO*
Eric R McMullen, *Officer*
EMP: 54
SQ FT: 34,625
SALES: 82MM **Publicly Held**
SIC: 6282 Investment advisory service

(P-10078)
FMR LLC
1995 University Ave, Berkeley
(94704-1058)
PHONE..................................800 225-6447
EMP: 103
SALES (corp-wide): 15.9B **Privately Held**
SIC: 6282 Investment advisory service
PA: Fmr Llc
　　245 Summer St
　　Boston MA 02210
　　617 563-7000

(P-10079)
FMR LLC
1220 Rsville Pkwy Ste 100, Roseville
(95678)
PHONE..................................916 784-3649
Dave Taylor, *Principal*
Doug Juday, *Vice Pres*
EMP: 103
SALES (corp-wide): 15.9B **Privately Held**
SIC: 6282 Investment advisory service
PA: Fmr Llc
　　245 Summer St
　　Boston MA 02210
　　617 563-7000

(P-10080)
FORWARD MANAGEMENT LLC
Also Called: Webster Investment Management
101 California St # 1600, San Francisco
(94111-6100)
P.O. Box 1345, Denver CO (80201-1345)
PHONE..................................415 869-6300
John Blaisdell, *CEO*
Jeffrey P Cusack, *President*
John McGowan, *Sr Corp Ofcr*
James Halligan, *Bd of Directors*
Robert S Naka, *Senior VP*
EMP: 100
SQ FT: 22,000
SALES (est): 19.1MM
SALES (corp-wide): 91.4MM **Privately Held**
WEB: www.sierraclubfund.com
SIC: 6282 Investment advisory service
PA: Salient Partners, L.P.
　　4265 San Felipe St Fl 8
　　Houston TX 77027
　　713 993-4675

(P-10081)
FRANKLIN ADVISERS INC (HQ)
1 Franklin Pkwy, San Mateo (94403-1906)
PHONE..............................650 312-2000
Charles B Johnson, *Ch of Bd*
EMP: 1700
SQ FT: 120,000
SALES (est): 115.1MM
SALES (corp-wide): 6.3B **Publicly Held**
WEB: www.frk.com
SIC: 6282 Investment advice
PA: Franklin Resources, Inc.
   1 Franklin Pkwy
   San Mateo CA 94403
   650 312-2000

(P-10082)
FRANKLIN TEMPLETON SVCS LLC
1 Franklin Pkwy, San Mateo (94403-1906)
PHONE..............................650 312-3000
Martin L Flanagan, *President*
Charles B Johnson, *Ch of Bd*
EMP: 2500
SALES (est): 163MM
SALES (corp-wide): 6.3B **Publicly Held**
WEB: www.frk.com
SIC: 6282 Investment advice
PA: Franklin Resources, Inc.
   1 Franklin Pkwy
   San Mateo CA 94403
   650 312-2000

(P-10083)
FRANKLIN TMPLETON INV SVCS LLC
3366 Quality Dr, Rancho Cordova
(95670-7363)
PHONE..............................650 312-2000
Bavel Fox, *Branch Mgr*
EMP: 103
SALES (corp-wide): 6.3B **Publicly Held**
SIC: 6282 Investment advisory service
HQ: Franklin Templeton Investor Services, Llc
   3344 Quality Dr
   Rancho Cordova CA 95670
   916 463-1500

(P-10084)
FRANKLIN TMPLETON INV SVCS LLC
5130 Hacienda Dr Fl 4, Dublin
(94568-7598)
PHONE..............................925 875-2619
Priscilla Voyer, *Manager*
EMP: 200
SALES (corp-wide): 6.3B **Publicly Held**
SIC: 6282 Investment advisory service
HQ: Franklin Templeton Investor Services, Llc
   3344 Quality Dr
   Rancho Cordova CA 95670
   916 463-1500

(P-10085)
FUND SERVICES ADVISORS INC
777 S Figueroa St # 3200, Los Angeles
(90017-5800)
PHONE..............................213 612-2196
Mark Creger, *President*
EMP: 50
SQ FT: 2,000
SALES (est): 3.6MM **Privately Held**
WEB: www.bondlogistix.com
SIC: 6282 Investment advisory service

(P-10086)
HALL CAPITAL PARTNERS LLC (PA)
1 Maritime Plz Fl 5, San Francisco
(94111-3408)
PHONE..............................415 288-0544
Kathryn A Hall, *CEO*
John W Buoymaster, *President*
William Powers, *COO*
EMP: 90
SQ FT: 6,000
SALES (est): 45.7MM **Privately Held**
WEB: www.offithall.com
SIC: 6282 Investment advisory service

(P-10087)
HEARTHSTONE INC
24151 Ventura Blvd, Calabasas
(91302-1449)
PHONE..............................818 385-0005
James Pugash, *CEO*
Anthony Botte, *Senior VP*
Mark Porath, *Manager*
EMP: 70
SALES (est): 11.8MM **Privately Held**
WEB: www.hearthadvisors.com
SIC: 6282 Investment advice

(P-10088)
HIGHMARK CAPITAL MANAGEMENT
350 California St Fl 22, San Francisco
(94104-1435)
PHONE..............................800 582-4734
Earle Malm, *President*
Christian Anderson, *Vice Pres*
Robert Bigelow, *Vice Pres*
Cori Farwell, *Vice Pres*
Richard Grise, *Vice Pres*
EMP: 93
SALES (est): 13.9MM
SALES (corp-wide): 56.9B **Privately Held**
SIC: 6282 Investment advisory service
HQ: Mufg Union Bank, National Association
   400 California St Fl 14
   San Francisco CA 94104
   415 705-7000

(P-10089)
HOULIHAN LOKEY INC (PA)
10250 Constellation Blvd # 5, Los Angeles
(90067-6200)
PHONE..............................310 788-5200
Scott L Beiser, *CEO*
Irwin N Gold, *Ch of Bd*
Scott J Adelson, *President*
David A Preiser, *President*
J Lindsey Alley, *CFO*
EMP: 300
SALES: 963.3MM **Publicly Held**
WEB: www.hlhz.com
SIC: 6282 6211 Investment advice; security brokers & dealers; investment bankers

(P-10090)
INFINEX INVESTMENTS INC
550 Gateway Dr, NAPA (94558-7577)
PHONE..............................707 927-3578
EMP: 75 **Privately Held**
SIC: 6282 Investment advisory service
PA: Infinex Investments, Inc.
   538 Preston Ave
   Meriden CT 06450
   -

(P-10091)
JONES LANG LSALLE AMERICAS INC
2211 Michelson Dr, Irvine (92612-1384)
PHONE..............................949 296-3600
James Jasionowski, *Owner*
EMP: 161
SALES (corp-wide): 7.9B **Publicly Held**
SIC: 6282 Investment advice
HQ: Jones Lang Lasalle Americas, Inc.
   200 E Randolph St # 4300
   Chicago IL 60601
   312 782-5800

(P-10092)
KAGAN CAPITAL MANAGEMENT INC
Also Called: Paul Kagan Associates
126 Clock Tower Pl, Carmel (93923-8791)
PHONE..............................831 624-1536
Paul Kagan, *President*
Norman Glaser, *Vice Pres*
EMP: 85
SQ FT: 18,000
SALES (est): 7.1MM **Privately Held**
SIC: 6282 Investment advisory service

(P-10093)
KRAVITZ INVESTMENT SVCS INC
16030 Ventura Blvd # 200, Encino
(91436-2731)
PHONE..............................818 995-6100
Daniel Kravitz, *President*

(P-10094)
LWI FINANCIAL INC
Also Called: Loring Ward Advisor Services
10 Almaden Blvd Fl 15, San Jose
(95113-2226)
PHONE..............................408 260-3100
Alf Steele, *President*
Ronald Reynolds, *COO*
Meir Statman, *CFO*
Michael Clinton, *Officer*
Deborah Djeu, *Officer*
EMP: 60
SQ FT: 21,000
SALES (est): 13.2MM **Privately Held**
SIC: 6282 Investment advisory service

(P-10095)
MARLIN EQUITY PARTNERS LLC (PA)
338 Pier Ave, Hermosa Beach
(90254-3617)
PHONE..............................310 364-0100
David McGovern, *Mng Member*
Marcia Fish, *Officer*
Daniel Broadhurst, *Finance Dir*
Michael Williams, *Analyst*
Joshua Portillo, *Accountant*
EMP: 80
SQ FT: 16,000
SALES (est): 2.1B **Privately Held**
WEB: www.marlinequity.com
SIC: 6282 3661 Investment advisory service; telephones & telephone apparatus; multiplex equipment, telephone & telegraph

(P-10096)
MERCER GLOBAL SECURITIES LLC
1801 E Cabrillo Blvd A, Santa Barbara
(93108-2897)
PHONE..............................805 565-1681
Gene Dongieux Jr, *Mng Member*
Howard Rochestie,
Glen Wysel,
EMP: 77 EST: 1995
SALES (est): 6.6MM **Privately Held**
SIC: 6282 Investment advisory service

(P-10097)
MORGAN STANLEY
800 Nwport Ctr Dr Ste 500, Newport Beach
(92660)
P.O. Box 2000 (92658-8936)
PHONE..............................949 760-2440
Mark Zielinski, *Branch Mgr*
EMP: 60
SALES (corp-wide): 43.6B **Publicly Held**
SIC: 6282 6211 Investment advisory service; security brokers & dealers
PA: Morgan Stanley
   1585 Broadway
   New York NY 10036
   212 761-4000

(P-10098)
NEWLAND REAL ESTATE GROUP LLC (HQ)
4790 Eastgate Mall # 150, San Diego
(92121-2061)
PHONE..............................858 455-7503
Robert B McLeod, *President*
Daniel Epp, *Exec VP*
Tim Durie, *Senior VP*
Laurie Ford, *Vice Pres*
Douglas L Hageman, *Vice Pres*
EMP: 52
SQ FT: 12,000
SALES (est): 91.5MM **Privately Held**
SIC: 6282 6552 Investment advice; subdividers & developers

(P-10099)
OAKTREE CAPITAL MANAGEMENT LP (HQ)
333 S Grand Ave Ste 2800, Los Angeles
(90071-1530)
PHONE..............................213 830-6300
Bruce Karsh, *President*
Larry W Keele, *Partner*
D R Masson, *Partner*

Sheldon M Stone, *Partner*
David Kirchheimer, *CFO*
EMP: 120
SALES (est): 1.2B **Publicly Held**
WEB: www.oaktreecapital.com
SIC: 6282 6722 6211 Investment advisory service; management investment, open-end; security brokers & dealers

(P-10100)
ONEMAIN HOLDINGS INC
2278 Foothill Blvd, La Verne (91750-2944)
PHONE..............................909 392-5578
EMP: 146
SALES (corp-wide): 3.7B **Publicly Held**
SIC: 6282 Investment advice
PA: Onemain Holdings, Inc.
   601 Nw 2nd St
   Evansville IN 47708
   812 424-8031

(P-10101)
PACIFIC INVESTMENT MGT CO LLC (DH)
Also Called: Pimco
650 Newport Center Dr, Newport Beach
(92660-6392)
P.O. Box 6430 (92658-6430)
PHONE..............................949 720-6000
Emmanuel Roman, *CEO*
Jay Jacobs, *President*
Robin Shanahan, *COO*
Peter Strelow, *COO*
John Lane, *CFO*
EMP: 240
SQ FT: 25,000
SALES (est): 735MM **Privately Held**
SIC: 6282 Investment advice
HQ: Allianz Asset Management Of America Llc
   650 Newport Center Dr
   Newport Beach CA 92660
   949 219-2200

(P-10102)
PAYDEN AND RYGEL (PA)
333 S Grand Ave Ste 3200, Los Angeles
(90071-1552)
PHONE..............................213 625-1900
Joan Payden, *CEO*
Greg Morrison, *President*
Brian Matthews, *CFO*
Brad Hersh, *Treasurer*
Scott J Weiner, *Principal*
EMP: 140
SQ FT: 58,000
SALES (est): 86.8MM **Privately Held**
WEB: www.payden.com
SIC: 6282 6211 Investment counselors; security brokers & dealers

(P-10103)
PERFORMANT TECHNOLOGIES INC
333 N Canyons Pkwy # 100, Livermore
(94551-9478)
PHONE..............................925 960-4800
Lisa Im, *President*
Ian Johnston, *Officer*
Luis Aguilar, *Trust Officer*
Carmen Franklin, *Trust Officer*
Said Shawwa, *Vice Pres*
EMP: 350
SALES (est): 43.7MM **Publicly Held**
SIC: 6282 Investment advice
PA: Performant Financial Corporation
   333 N Canyons Pkwy # 100
   Livermore CA 94551

(P-10104)
PLAN MEMBER FINANCIAL CORP
Also Called: Planmember Services
6187 Carpinteria Ave, Carpinteria
(93013-2805)
PHONE..............................800 874-6910
Jon Ziehl, *CEO*
Mike Kulesza, *Partner*
Terrall Janeway, *COO*
Terry Janeway, *COO*
Bill Kemble, *CFO*
EMP: 100
SQ FT: 6,000

436   2019 Directory of California
Wholesalers and Services Companies   ▲ = Import ▼=Export
◆ =Import/Export

SALES (est): 34MM **Privately Held**
WEB: www.planmemberfinancialcorporation.com
SIC: 6282 Investment counselors

(P-10105)
PREMIERE FINANCIAL
Also Called: Premiere Properties
6498 Willow Pl, Carlsbad (92011-4212)
PHONE................760 518-5034
Richard Luichi, *Owner*
EMP: 100 **EST:** 2013
SALES: 400K **Privately Held**
SIC: 6282 8742 Investment advice; financial consultant

(P-10106)
PRESIDIO WEALTH MANAGEMENT LLC
101 California St # 2400, San Francisco (94111-5898)
PHONE................415 449-2500
Brodie Cobb, *Managing Prtnr*
Michael Russo, *Managing Prtnr*
Jeff Zlot, *Principal*
Thomas Emig, *Controller*
EMP: 50
SQ FT: 2,500
SALES (est): 4.2MM **Privately Held**
WEB: www.sncinvestment.com
SIC: 6282 Investment advisory service

(P-10107)
QUADION LLC
Also Called: Mar-Kell Seal
17651 Armstrong Ave, Irvine (92614-5727)
PHONE................714 546-0994
EMP: 1100 **EST:** 1945
SQ FT: 30,000
SALES: 110.7MM
SALES (corp-wide): 91.2B **Publicly Held**
SIC: 6282
HQ: Norwest Venture Capital Management, Inc.
80 S 8th St Ste 3600
Minneapolis MN 55402
612 215-1600

(P-10108)
RELATIONAL INVESTORS LLC
12400 High Bluff Dr # 600, San Diego (92130-3077)
PHONE................858 704-3333
David Batchelder, *Mng Member*
Ralph Whitworth,
EMP: 52 **EST:** 1996
SALES (est): 23.3MM **Privately Held**
SIC: 6282 Investment advisory service

(P-10109)
RESEARCH AFFILIATES CAPITAL LP
620 Nwport Ctr Ste 900, Newport Beach (92660)
PHONE................949 325-8700
Rob Arnott, *CEO*
Katrina F Sherrerd, *COO*
Trevor Schuesler, *Vice Pres*
Jason Hsu, *CIO*
EMP: 82
SALES (est): 10.4MM **Privately Held**
SIC: 6282 Investment advisory service; futures advisory service; investment research

(P-10110)
RESEARCH AFFILIATES LLC
620 Nwport Ctr Ste 900, Newport Beach (92660)
PHONE................949 325-8700
Rob Arnott, *CEO*
Katrina Sherrerd, *COO*
Joseph Hattesohl, *CFO*
Jeffrey Smith, *Officer*
Jeff Wilson, *Senior VP*
EMP: 80
SALES (est): 22.8MM **Privately Held**
WEB: www.researchaffiliates.com
SIC: 6282 Investment counselors

(P-10111)
RNC CAPITAL MANAGEMENT LLC
Also Called: Rnc Genter Capital Management
11601 Wilshire Blvd Ph, Los Angeles (90025-0509)
PHONE................310 477-6543
Dan Genter,
Manny Gutierrez, *Officer*
EMP: 65
SQ FT: 20,000
SALES (est): 19.3MM **Privately Held**
WEB: www.rncgenter.com
SIC: 6282 Investment counselors

(P-10112)
S&P GLOBAL INC
1566 Moffett St, Salinas (93905-3342)
PHONE................831 393-6044
David Taggard, *President*
EMP: 149
SALES (corp-wide): 6B **Publicly Held**
WEB: www.mcgraw-hill.com
SIC: 6282 Investment advisory service
PA: S&P Global Inc.
55 Water St
New York NY 10041
212 438-1000

(P-10113)
SB GROUP US INC
1 Circle Star Way Fl 1 # 1, San Carlos (94070-6235)
PHONE................650 562-8110
Ronald D Fisher, *CEO*
EMP: 59 **EST:** 2014
SALES (est): 111.9K
SALES (corp-wide): 85.9B **Publicly Held**
SIC: 6282 Investment advisory service
PA: Softbank Group Corp.
1-9-1, Higashishishibashi
Minato-Ku TKY 105-0
368 892-000

(P-10114)
STAMOS CAPITAL PARTNERS LP
2498 Sand Hill Rd, Menlo Park (94025-6940)
PHONE................650 233-5000
Peter Stamos, *CEO*
James Chenault, *Executive Asst*
Adam Afshar, *Technology*
Karina Leal, *Finance*
Jared Kanover, *General Counsel*
EMP: 55
SALES (est): 9.1MM **Privately Held**
SIC: 6282 Investment advisory service

(P-10115)
STANDARD POORS FINCL SVCS LLC
1 California St Fl 31, San Francisco (94111-5401)
PHONE................415 371-5000
Steve Zimmerman, *Manager*
EMP: 50
SALES (corp-wide): 6B **Publicly Held**
WEB: www.mcgraw-hill.com
SIC: 6282 Investment advisory service
HQ: Standard & Poor's Financial Services Llc
55 Water St Fl 49
New York NY 10041
212 438-2000

(P-10116)
TCW GROUP INC (PA)
Also Called: Trust Company of The West
865 S Figueroa St # 1800, Los Angeles (90017-2543)
PHONE................213 244-0000
David Lippman, *President*
David S Devito, *COO*
Richard M Villa, *CFO*
Meredith S Jackson, *Exec VP*
Heather Conforto Beatty, *Senior VP*
EMP: 450
SALES (est): 205.6MM **Privately Held**
SIC: 6282 6211 Investment advisory service; security brokers & dealers

(P-10117)
TPG SIXTH STREET PARTNERS LLC
345 California St Ste 330, San Francisco (94104-2606)
PHONE................415 743-1500
Alan Waxman,
EMP: 125
SALES (est): 3.3MM **Privately Held**
SIC: 6282 Investment advisory service

(P-10118)
TRANSAMERICA CBO I INC
600 Montgomery St Fl 16, San Francisco (94111-2718)
PHONE................415 983-4000
EMP: 64
SALES (est): 2.2MM **Privately Held**
SIC: 6282
HQ: Transamerica Corporation
4333 Edgewood Rd Ne
Cedar Rapids IA 52499
319 398-8511

(P-10119)
UNITED CPITL FNCL ADVISERS LLC
620 Nwport Ctr Dr Ste 500, Newport Beach (92660)
PHONE................949 999-8500
EMP: 77 **EST:** 2009
SALES (est): 17.2MM **Privately Held**
SIC: 6282 8742

(P-10120)
VIKING ASSET MANAGEMENT LLC
505 Sansome St Ste 1275, San Francisco (94111-3177)
PHONE................415 981-5300
Peter Bence, *Partner*
EMP: 1501
SALES (est): 55.6MM **Privately Held**
SIC: 6282 Investment advice

(P-10121)
WENTWORTH HAUSER & VIOLICH INC
301 Battery St Fl 4, San Francisco (94111-3237)
PHONE................415 981-6911
Steve Rhone, *CEO*
Judith Stevens, *President*
Earl Bell, *CFO*
Phillip Fox, *Exec VP*
George Springman, *CIO*
EMP: 78 **EST:** 1937
SQ FT: 14,000
SALES (est): 23MM **Privately Held**
WEB: www.lntyee.com
SIC: 6282 Investment advisory service
PA: Laird Norton Investment Management, Inc.
801 2nd Ave Ste 1300
Seattle WA 98104

(P-10122)
WETHERBY ASSET MANAGEMENT
580 California St Fl 8, San Francisco (94104-1029)
PHONE................415 399-9159
Debra L Wetherby, *President*
Chris Hauswirth, *COO*
Allan Jacobi, *CFO*
Steve Janowsky, *Principal*
Nichole Perry, *Office Mgr*
EMP: 55
SALES (est): 17.3MM **Privately Held**
WEB: www.wetherby.com
SIC: 6282 Investment advisory service

(P-10123)
WINDSTAR CAPITAL ADVISORS
10940 Wilshire Blvd, Los Angeles (90024-3915)
PHONE................310 505-3720
Jack Risko, *President*
EMP: 208
SALES (est): 12.5MM **Privately Held**
SIC: 6282 4213 Investment advice; heavy hauling

6289 Security & Commodity Svcs, NEC

(P-10124)
AMERICAN FUNDS SERVICE COMPANY
Also Called: Emerging Markets Growth Fund
6455 Irvine Center Dr, Irvine (92618-4518)
P.O. Box 6007, Indianapolis IN (46206-6007)
PHONE................949 975-5000
Josie Cortez, *Branch Mgr*
EMP: 50
SALES (corp-wide): 2.2B **Privately Held**
WEB: www.cganywhere.net
SIC: 6289 6282 Security transfer agents; investment advice
HQ: American Funds Service Company
6455 Irvine Center Dr
Irvine CA 92618
949 975-5000

(P-10125)
INTERACTIVE DATA CORPORATION
E Signal
919 E Hillsdale Blvd # 200, Foster City (94404-4249)
P.O. Box 5028, Hayward (94540)
PHONE................510 266-6000
Chuck Thompson, *President*
Radhika Subramanian, *Software Dev*
Marc Batten, *Director*
EMP: 150
SALES (corp-wide): 4.6B **Publicly Held**
WEB: www.interactivedata.com
SIC: 6289 Stock quotation service
HQ: Interactive Data Corporation
32 Crosby Dr
Bedford MA 01730

(P-10126)
STRATEGIC SECURITY SERVICES
Also Called: Strategic Secuirty Services
48521 Warm Springs Blvd # 302, Fremont (94539-7792)
PHONE................510 623-2355
Larry Reid, *Manager*
EMP: 190
SALES (corp-wide): 187.9MM **Publicly Held**
WEB: www.strategicsecurity.net
SIC: 6289 Protective committees
HQ: Strategic Security Services, Inc
3152 University Ave
San Diego CA
619 283-3976

6311 Life Insurance Carriers

(P-10127)
AMERICAN GEN LF INSUR CO DEL
Also Called: AIG
1 Montgomery St Fl 25, San Francisco (94104-4558)
PHONE................415 836-2700
Gordon Knight, *President*
Linda Sproule, *President*
Martin Elliott, *Vice Pres*
Linda Jiao, *Tech/Comp Coord*
Mark P Foletti, *Production*
EMP: 300
SALES (corp-wide): 49.5B **Publicly Held**
WEB: www.aiglifeinsurancecompany.com
SIC: 6311 Life insurance
HQ: American General Life Insurance Company Of Delaware
2727 Allen Pkwy Ste A
Houston TX 77019
713 522-1111

(P-10128)
ASSOCIATED INDEMNITY CORP
1465 N Mcdowell Blvd # 100, Petaluma (94954-6516)
P.O. Box 970, O Fallon MO (63366-0970)
PHONE................415 899-2000

D Andrew Torrance, *Chairman*
Jill E Paterson, *CFO*
Linda E Wright, *Treasurer*
Cynthia L Pevehouse, *Senior VP*
EMP: 2498
SQ FT: 240,000
SALES (est): 48.9MM **Privately Held**
WEB: www.firemansfund.com
SIC: 6311 6321 6331 6351 Life insur-
ance carriers; accident insurance carriers;
health insurance carriers; fire, marine &
casualty insurance & carriers; surety in-
surance
HQ: Fireman's Fund Insurance Company
    1465 N Mcdowell Blvd # 100
    Petaluma CA 94954
    415 899-2000

(P-10129)
ASSURANT INC
2677 N Main St Ste 600, Santa Ana
(92705-6629)
PHONE...................714 571-3900
Eric Juarez, *Branch Mgr*
EMP: 300
SALES (corp-wide): 6.4B **Publicly Held**
WEB: www.us.fortis.com
SIC: 6311 Life insurance
PA: Assurant, Inc.
    28 Liberty St Fl 41
    New York NY 10005
    212 859-7000

(P-10130)
AXA ADVISORS LLC
701 B St Ste 1500, San Diego
(92101-8170)
PHONE...................619 239-0018
Patrick Mead, *Exec VP*
David Moran, *Financial Exec*
George Chammas, *Advisor*
Stanley Ginsberg, *Advisor*
Sal Cocco, *Consultant*
EMP: 80 **Publicly Held**
WEB: www.axacs.com
SIC: 6311 6321 6411 6282
HQ: Axa Advisors, Llc
    1290 Ave Of Amrcs Fl Cnc1
    New York NY 10104
    212 554-1234

(P-10131)
**BEST LIFE AND HEALTH INSUR
CO**
17701 Mitchell N, Irvine (92614-6028)
P.O. Box 19721 (92623-9721)
PHONE...................949 253-4080
Donald R Lawrenz, *Ch of Bd*
Alfred Stoefell, *Shareholder*
Edith Christensen, *Executive Asst*
Ferdie Pascua, *Administration*
Nancy Mashhoud, *Accountant*
EMP: 60
SQ FT: 22,000
SALES (est): 31MM
SALES (corp-wide): 12.3MM **Privately
Held**
SIC: 6311 6324 Life insurance carriers;
hospital & medical service plans
PA: Pension Administrators Inc
    17701 Mitchell N
    Irvine CA 92614
    949 253-4080

(P-10132)
**BUILDERS & TRADESMENS
INSUR**
6610 Sierra College Blvd, Rocklin
(95677-4306)
PHONE...................916 772-9200
Norbert Hohlbein, *Principal*
Jeff Erickson, *Vice Pres*
Angela Jorgensen, *Sales Staff*
Erica Sanchez, *Sales Staff*
Kimberli Powers, *Assistant*
EMP: 61
SALES (est): 34.8MM **Privately Held**
WEB: www.btisonline.com
SIC: 6311 Life insurance

(P-10133)
**CENTURY-NATIONAL
INSURANCE CO (HQ)**
16650 Sherman Way Ste 200, Van Nuys
(91406-3782)
PHONE...................818 760-0880

Weldon Wilson, *CEO*
Michael Mahoney, *President*
Charlie Pidancet, *COO*
Judy Osborn, *CFO*
Marie Balicki, *Admin Sec*
EMP: 260
SQ FT: 41,000
SALES (est): 51.9MM **Publicly Held**
SIC: 6311 Life insurance carriers

(P-10134)
**EQUITABLE VARIABLE LF
INSUR CO**
701 B St Ste 1500, San Diego
(92101-8170)
PHONE...................619 239-0018
Jamie Smith, *Manager*
Brian Bickford, *Vice Pres*
EMP: 65
SALES (est): 7.5MM **Privately Held**
SIC: 6311 Life insurance

(P-10135)
FARMERS GROUP INC
Also Called: Farmers Insurance
700 S Flower St Ste 2800, Los Angeles
(90017-4215)
PHONE...................213 615-2500
Agie Lerner, *Legal Staff*
Ana Sanchez, *Office Mgr*
Vanessa Jackson, *Project Mgr*
Anuj Kanal, *Technology*
EMP: 60
SALES (corp-wide): 65.1B **Privately Held**
WEB: www.farmers.com
SIC: 6311 6799 Life insurance carriers;
real estate investors, except property op-
erators
HQ: Farmers Group, Inc.
    6301 Owensmouth Ave
    Woodland Hills CA 91367
    323 932-3200

(P-10136)
**GOLDEN STATE MUTL LF INSUR
CO (PA)**
1999 W Adams Blvd, Los Angeles
(90018-3500)
P.O. Box 26894, San Francisco (94126-
6894)
PHONE...................713 526-4361
Larkin Teasley, *President*
EMP: 100 **EST:** 1925
SQ FT: 57,000
SALES (est): 39.4MM **Privately Held**
SIC: 6311 Mutual association life insur-
ance; life insurance carriers; life reinsur-
ance

(P-10137)
**JACKSON NATIONAL LIFE
INSUR CO**
401 Wilshire Blvd # 1200, Santa Monica
(90401-1416)
PHONE...................310 899-7900
Clifford Jack, *President*
James Bull, *Info Tech Mgr*
Frank Ventura, *Info Tech Mgr*
EMP: 65
SALES (corp-wide): 55.4B **Privately Held**
WEB: www.jnl.com
SIC: 6311 Life insurance carriers; fraternal
protective associations; benevolent insur-
ance associations
HQ: Jackson National Life Insurance Co Inc
    1 Corporate Way
    Lansing MI 48951
    517 381-5500

(P-10138)
**JOHN ALDEN LIFE INSURANCE
CO**
20950 Warner Center Ln A, Woodland Hills
(91367-6560)
PHONE...................818 595-7600
Thomas Christenson, *Branch Mgr*
EMP: 65
SALES (corp-wide): 6.4B **Publicly Held**
WEB: www.jalden.com
SIC: 6311 Life insurance
HQ: Alden John Life Insurance Company
    501 W Michigan St
    Milwaukee WI 53203
    414 271-3011

(P-10139)
**MASSACHUSETTS MUTL LF
INSUR CO**
Also Called: Massmutual
8383 Wilshire Blvd # 600, Beverly Hills
(90211-2425)
PHONE...................323 965-6339
Grant D Fraser, *Branch Mgr*
David Streit, *Sales Staff*
Harvey Warren, *Author*
EMP: 60
SALES (corp-wide): 25.4B **Privately Held**
WEB: www.massmutual.com
SIC: 6311 Life insurance
PA: Massachusetts Mutual Life Insurance
    Company
    1295 State St
    Springfield MA 01111
    413 788-8411

(P-10140)
**NEW YORK LIFE INSURANCE
CO**
191 Sand Creek Rd Ste 200, Brentwood
(94513-2220)
PHONE...................925 809-7020
Dan Torres, *Branch Mgr*
EMP: 93
SALES (corp-wide): 25.1B **Privately Held**
SIC: 6311 Life insurance
PA: New York Life Insurance Company
    51 Madison Ave Bsmt 1b
    New York NY 10010
    212 576-7000

(P-10141)
**NEW YORK LIFE INSURANCE
CO**
4204 Riverwalk Pkwy # 200, Riverside
(92505-3391)
PHONE...................951 354-2094
Tim Crumbaker, *Branch Mgr*
Michael J O'Neill, *Sales Associate*
Timothy Crumbaker, *Manager*
Steven Cochran, *Agent*
Jose Lumbreras, *Agent*
EMP: 75
SALES (corp-wide): 25.1B **Privately Held**
WEB: www.newyorklife.com
SIC: 6311 Life insurance
PA: New York Life Insurance Company
    51 Madison Ave Bsmt 1b
    New York NY 10010
    212 576-7000

(P-10142)
**PACIFIC LIFE & ANNUITY
COMPANY**
700 Newport Center Dr, Newport Beach
(92660-6307)
P.O. Box 9000 (92658-9030)
PHONE...................949 219-3011
James Morris, *President*
Khanh T Tran, *CFO*
Audrey L Milfs, *Vice Pres*
Brian Klemens, *Controller*
Christina Q He, *Assistant VP*
EMP: 650
SQ FT: 125,000
SALES (est): 185.3MM
SALES (corp-wide): 12.8B **Privately Held**
SIC: 6311 6411 Life insurance carriers; in-
surance agents, brokers & service
HQ: Pacific Life Insurance Company
    700 Newport Center Dr
    Newport Beach CA 92660
    949 219-3011

(P-10143)
PATRA CORPORATION (PA)
1107 Inv Blvd Ste 100, El Dorado Hills
(95762)
PHONE...................415 595-9987
Dan Easterlin, *President*
Robin Newman, *COO*
Bob Murphy, *Officer*
Jessica Casteel, *Director*
EMP: 132 **EST:** 2007
SALES (est): 80.2MM **Privately Held**
SIC: 6311 Life insurance

(P-10144)
**PRINCIPAL FINANCIAL GROUP
INC**
500 N Brand Blvd Ste 1800, Glendale
(91203-3305)
PHONE...................818 243-7141
Jim Rhodes, *Branch Mgr*
Jennifer T Love, *Agent*
EMP: 80 **Publicly Held**
SIC: 6311 Life insurance
PA: Principal Financial Group, Inc.
    711 High St
    Des Moines IA 50392
    -

(P-10145)
**PRINCIPAL FINANCIAL GROUP
INC**
1350 E Spruce Ave Ste 100, Fresno
(93720-3373)
PHONE...................559 261-2000
William E Griffith, *Manager*
Melissa Bradley-Sperlin, *Sales Associate*
Geoffrey T Barry, *Agent*
Jennifer D Williams, *Agent*
EMP: 80 **Publicly Held**
SIC: 6311 Life insurance
PA: Principal Financial Group, Inc.
    711 High St
    Des Moines IA 50392
    -

(P-10146)
**SWISS RE AMERICA HOLDING
CORP**
Also Called: GE
27412 Carino Cir, Mission Viejo
(92692-5042)
PHONE...................858 485-5018
Deborah Boyce, *Branch Mgr*
EMP: 50
SALES (corp-wide): 33.1B **Privately Held**
SIC: 6311 Life reinsurance
HQ: Swiss Re America Holding Corporation
    5200 Metcalf Ave
    Overland Park KS 66202

(P-10147)
**TRANSAMERICA FINANCE
CORP**
1731 W Medical Center Dr, Anaheim
(92801-1837)
PHONE...................714 778-5100
Jim Karsch, *Manager*
EMP: 65
SALES (corp-wide): 593.2MM **Privately
Held**
SIC: 6311 6512 Life insurance; commer-
cial & industrial building operation
HQ: Transamerica Finance Corporation
    600 Montgomery St Fl 16
    San Francisco CA 94111
    415 983-4000

(P-10148)
**TRANSMRICA OCCIDENTAL LF
INSUR (DH)**
1150 S Olive St Fl 23, Los Angeles
(90015-2477)
P.O. Box 2101 (90078-2101)
PHONE...................213 742-2111
Ronald Wagley, *President*
Christopher Castro, *President*
Jeff Carnal, *Vice Pres*
John Holowasko, *Vice Pres*
Ali Fattahy, *Info Tech Mgr*
EMP: 2000 **EST:** 1906
SQ FT: 1,577,000
SALES (est): 2.8B
SALES (corp-wide): 593.2MM **Privately
Held**
WEB: www.transamerica.com
SIC: 6311 6371 6321 6324 Life insur-
ance carriers; life reinsurance; pension
funds; health insurance carriers; accident
insurance carriers; reinsurance carriers;
accident & health; group hospitalization
plans; investors

▲ = Import ▼=Export
◆ =Import/Export

(P-10149)
TRUCK UNDERWRITERS ASSOCIATION
Farmers Insurance
6303 Owensmouth Ave Fl 1, Woodland Hills (91367-2200)
PHONE................................323 932-3200
Jane Franklin, *Vice Pres*
Louis T Seletos, *COO*
Matt Lyon, *Vice Pres*
Todd Luzader, *Admin Mgr*
Doren Hohl, *Admin Sec*
EMP: 900
SQ FT: 275,000
SALES (corp-wide): 65.1B **Privately Held**
SIC: 6311 6331 6321 Life insurance; fire, marine & casualty insurance; accident & health insurance
HQ: Truck Underwriters Association
4680 Wilshire Blvd
Los Angeles CA 90010
323 932-3200

(P-10150)
ULTRALINK LLC
535 Anton Blvd Ste 200, Costa Mesa (92626-7680)
PHONE................................714 427-5500
Tony Ton, *Owner*
Vince Sheeran, *CEO*
Jack Baumann, *COO*
Dan Lieber, *Chairman*
Jeff Graves, *Vice Ch Bd*
EMP: 120
SALES (est): 31.4MM **Privately Held**
SIC: 6311 Life insurance carriers

(P-10151)
WELLPOINT INC
319 N San Dimas Ave Ste F, San Dimas (91773-2658)
PHONE................................805 375-1605
Clara Hua Wang, *Administration*
EMP: 200
SALES (est): 10.9MM **Privately Held**
SIC: 6311 6321 6324 6331 Life insurance; accident & health insurance; hospital & medical service plans; fire, marine & casualty insurance; surety insurance; insurance agents, brokers & service

(P-10152)
WILLIS INSURANCE SVCS CAL INC
4250 Executive Sq Ste 250, La Jolla (92037-9104)
PHONE................................858 678-2000
Jack Yelverton, *Branch Mgr*
EMP: 50 **Privately Held**
SIC: 6311 Life insurance
HQ: Willis Insurance Services Of California, Inc.
525 Market St Ste 3400
San Francisco CA 94105
415 955-0100

(P-10153)
ZENITH INSURANCE COMPANY
4460 Rosewood Dr Ste 300, Pleasanton (94588-3086)
PHONE................................925 460-0600
Jon Lindsay, *Manager*
Steve Bagby, *Sls & Mktg Exec*
Fred Martinez, *Marketing Staff*
Jim Ludman, *Manager*
EMP: 90
SALES (corp-wide): 16.2B **Privately Held**
SIC: 6311 6321 6324 6331 Life insurance; accident & health insurance; hospital & medical service plans; fire, marine & casualty insurance
HQ: Zenith Insurance Company
21255 Califa St
Woodland Hills CA 91367
818 713-1000

6321 Accident & Health Insurance

(P-10154)
21ST CENTURY LF & HLTH CO INC (PA)
Also Called: Lifecare Assurance Company
21600 Oxnard St Ste 1500, Woodland Hills (91367-4972)
P.O. Box 4243 (91365-4243)
PHONE................................818 887-4436
James M Glickman, *President*
Pamela Corbally, *President*
Paul Weber, *President*
Alan S Hughes, *CEO*
Daniel J Di Sipio, *CFO*
EMP: 246
SQ FT: 50,000
SALES (est): 167.8MM **Privately Held**
WEB: www.lifecareassurance.com
SIC: 6321 Health insurance carriers

(P-10155)
AGENT FRANCHISE LLC
9518 9th St Ste C2, Rancho Cucamonga (91730-4568)
PHONE................................949 930-5025
David Jackson,
EMP: 101
SQ FT: 14,980
SALES (est): 27.6MM **Privately Held**
SIC: 6321 Accident & health insurance

(P-10156)
ALTAMED HEALTH SERVICES CORP
535 S 2nd Ave, Covina (91723-3013)
PHONE................................626 214-1480
Robert Young, *Owner*
EMP: 69
SALES (corp-wide): 178.2MM **Privately Held**
SIC: 6321 Accident & health insurance carriers
PA: Altamed Health Services Corporation
2040 Camfield Ave
Commerce CA 90040
323 725-8751

(P-10157)
AON BENFIELD FAC INC
199 Fremont St Fl 15, San Francisco (94105-2299)
PHONE................................415 486-6900
Matt Davis, *Manager*
EMP: 200
SALES (corp-wide): 10B **Privately Held**
SIC: 6321 6311 Reinsurance carriers, accident & health; life insurance
HQ: Aon Benfield Fac Inc.
200 E Randolph St Fl 15
Chicago IL 60601
312 381-5300

(P-10158)
ARTA WESTERN MEDICAL GROUP
1665 Scenic Ave Ste 100, Costa Mesa (92626-1443)
PHONE................................949 260-6575
Baruch Fogel MD, *President*
EMP: 150
SALES: 15MM **Privately Held**
SIC: 6321 Health insurance carriers

(P-10159)
AUTO CLUB ENTERPRISES (PA)
3333 Fairview Rd Msa451, Costa Mesa (92626-1610)
P.O. Box 25001, Santa Ana (92799-5001)
PHONE................................714 850-5111
Robert T Bouttier, *CEO*
Thomas Mc Kernon, *President*
Robert Bouttier, *COO*
John F Boyle, *Treasurer*
Neiman Sharon, *Senior VP*
EMP: 1200
SQ FT: 700,000
SALES (est): 3.4B **Privately Held**
WEB: www.aaa-newmexico.com
SIC: 6321 Accident & health insurance

(P-10160)
AUTO CLUB ENTERPRISES
8761 Santa Monica Blvd, West Hollywood (90069-4538)
PHONE................................310 914-8500
Bob Szhwab, *Manager*
Michelle Gonsalves, *Branch Mgr*
EMP: 444
SALES (corp-wide): 3.4B **Privately Held**
WEB: www.aaa-newmexico.com
SIC: 6321 Accident & health insurance
PA: Auto Club Enterprises
3333 Fairview Rd Msa451
Costa Mesa CA 92626
714 850-5111

(P-10161)
B C LIFE & HEALTH INSURANCE CO
21555 Oxnard St, Woodland Hills (91367-4943)
PHONE................................818 703-2345
David Helwig, *President*
Kenneth C Zurek, *CFO*
Nicholas L Becker, *Principal*
Thomas Geiser, *Admin Sec*
EMP: 66
SALES (est): 18.7MM **Privately Held**
SIC: 6321 Indemnity plans health insurance, except medical service

(P-10162)
CAREMORE MEDICAL GROUP INC
12900 Park Plz Ste 150, Lakewood (90805)
PHONE................................562 622-2900
John Short, *Director*
EMP: 300 EST: 2011
SALES (est): 45.6MM
SALES (corp-wide): 90B **Publicly Held**
SIC: 6321 Health insurance carriers
PA: Anthem, Inc.
120 Monument Cir Ste 200
Indianapolis IN 46204
317 331-1476

(P-10163)
COUNTY OF KINGS
330 Campus Dr, Hanford (93230-4375)
PHONE................................559 584-1411
Kathy Mittlighder, *Director*
EMP: 110 **Privately Held**
SIC: 6321 9431 Accident & health insurance;
PA: County Of Kings
1400 W Lacey Blvd
Hanford CA 93230
559 582-0326

(P-10164)
E D D 2100
Also Called: Disability Insurance
3127 Transworld Dr # 150, Stockton (95206-4988)
PHONE................................209 941-6501
Judy Cruz, *Office Mgr*
Marcy Pruitt, *Managing Prtnr*
EMP: 92 EST: 1940
SALES (est): 18.7MM **Privately Held**
SIC: 6321 Disability health insurance

(P-10165)
HEALTHPOCKET INC
444 Castro St Ste 710, Mountain View (94041-2080)
PHONE................................800 984-8015
Bruce Telkamp, *CEO*
Sheldon Wang, *President*
EMP: 96
SALES (est): 28.1MM
SALES (corp-wide): 250.4MM **Publicly Held**
SIC: 6321 Health insurance carriers
PA: Health Insurance Innovations, Inc.
15438 N Florida Ave # 201
Tampa FL 33613
813 397-1187

(P-10166)
INLAND EMPIRE HEALTH PLAN (PA)
Also Called: Iehp
10801 6th St Ste 120, Rancho Cucamonga (91730-5987)
P.O. Box 1400 (91729-1400)
PHONE................................909 890-2000
Brad Gilbert, *CEO*
Chet Uma, *CFO*
Bob Buster, *Chairman*
Randee Roberts, *Finance Dir*
EMP: 855
SQ FT: 72,000
SALES (est): 329.7MM **Privately Held**
WEB: www.iehp.org
SIC: 6321 6324 Health insurance carriers; health maintenance organization (HMO), insurance only

(P-10167)
KINGS VIEW WORK EXPERIENCE CTR
703 I St, Los Banos (93635-4308)
PHONE................................209 826-8118
David Toliver, *Administration*
Irma Torrez, *Manager*
EMP: 50
SALES (est): 5MM **Privately Held**
SIC: 6321 7641 Disability health insurance; furniture repair & maintenance

(P-10168)
LIFECARE ASSURANCE COMPANY
21600 Oxnard St Fl 16, Woodland Hills (91367-4976)
PHONE................................818 887-4436
James Glickman, *President*
Alan S Hughes, *COO*
Daniel J Disipio, *CFO*
Peter Diffley, *Vice Pres*
Gwen D Franklin, *Vice Pres*
EMP: 246
SQ FT: 35,000
SALES: 386.3MM
SALES (corp-wide): 167.8MM **Privately Held**
WEB: www.lifecareassurance.com
SIC: 6321 6411 6311 Accident & health insurance; insurance agents, brokers & service; life insurance
PA: 21st Century Life And Health Company, Inc.
21600 Oxnard St Ste 1500
Woodland Hills CA 91367
818 887-4436

(P-10169)
MOLINA HEALTHCARE OF CALIFORNI
200 Oceangate Ste 100, Long Beach (90802-4317)
PHONE................................562 435-3666
Richard Chambers, *CEO*
Dr J Mario Molina, *President*
Terry Bayer, *COO*
Dr James Howatt, *Officer*
EMP: 2800
SALES (est): 329.7MM
SALES (corp-wide): 19.8B **Publicly Held**
SIC: 6321 8011 Health insurance carriers; clinic, operated by physicians
PA: Molina Healthcare, Inc.
200 Oceangate Ste 100
Long Beach CA 90802
562 435-3666

(P-10170)
SAN FRANCISCO REINSURANCE CO
1465 N Mcdowell Blvd, Petaluma (94954-6516)
PHONE................................415 899-2000
Joe Beneducci, *President*
EMP: 70
SQ FT: 240,000
SALES: 248.9MM **Privately Held**
WEB: www.firemansfund.com
SIC: 6321 Reinsurance carriers, accident & health
HQ: Fireman's Fund Insurance Company
1465 N Mcdowell Blvd # 100
Petaluma CA 94954
415 899-2000

PRODUCTS & SVCS

(P-10171)
SANTA BARBARA SAN LUIS OBISPO
Also Called: Cencal Health
4050 Calle Real, Santa Barbara
(93110-3413)
PHONE.........................800 421-2560
Robert Freeman, *CEO*
Kashina Bishop, *CFO*
Sherri Bennett, *Director*
EMP: 140
SALES (est): 64.8MM **Privately Held**
SIC: 6321 Accident & health insurance

(P-10172)
SANTE HEALTH SYSTEM INC (PA)
Also Called: Sante Community Physicians
7370 N Palm Ave Ste 101, Fresno
(93711-5782)
P.O. Box 1507 (93716-1507)
PHONE.........................559 228-5400
Mateo F Desoto, *CEO*
Scott Wells, *President*
Chris Cheney, *CFO*
Janine Stephenson, *Chief Mktg Ofcr*
Debbie Keena, *Vice Pres*
EMP: 76
SQ FT: 20,000
SALES (est): 154.9MM **Privately Held**
SIC: 6321 7371 Accident & health insurance; computer software development & applications

(P-10173)
STATE COMPENSATION INSUR FUND
2901 N Ventura Rd Ste 100, Oxnard
(93036-1126)
PHONE.........................888 782-8338
Martin Goldman, *Manager*
EMP: 400
SALES (corp-wide): 1.5B **Privately Held**
WEB: www.scif.com
SIC: 6321 9651 Disability health insurance; insurance commission, government;
PA: State Compensation Insurance Fund
333 Bush St Fl 8
San Francisco CA 94104
888 782-8338

(P-10174)
WESTERN HEALTH ADVANTAGE
2349 Gateway Oaks Dr # 100, Sacramento
(95833-4244)
PHONE.........................916 567-1950
Garry Maisel, *President*
Andrea Richardson, *CFO*
Rita Ruecker, *Treasurer*
Rick Heron, *Chief Mktg Ofcr*
Rebecca Downing, *Officer*
EMP: 100
SQ FT: 25,000
SALES: 726MM **Privately Held**
WEB: www.westernhealth.com
SIC: 6321 Health insurance carriers

6324 Hospital & Medical Svc Plans Carriers

(P-10175)
AETNA HEALTH CALIFORNIA INC
1 Embarcadero Ctr Ste 300, San Francisco
(94111-3628)
PHONE.........................415 645-8200
Sue Hallett, *Branch Mgr*
Becky Nguyen, *Technician*
Marisa Lin, *Manager*
Elaine Sibrel, *Assistant*
EMP: 80 **Publicly Held**
SIC: 6324 Health maintenance organization (HMO), insurance only
HQ: Aetna Health Of California, Inc.
2409 Camino Ramon
San Ramon CA 94583
925 543-9223

(P-10176)
AETNA HEALTH CALIFORNIA INC
727 Pueblo Pl, Chula Vista (91914-2426)
PHONE.........................619 656-3104
EMP: 51
SALES (corp-wide): 36.6B **Publicly Held**
SIC: 6324
HQ: Aetna Health Of California, Inc.
2409 Camino Ramon
San Ramon CA 94583
925 543-9000

(P-10177)
AETNA HEALTH CALIFORNIA INC (DH)
2409 Camino Ramon, San Ramon
(94583-4285)
PHONE.........................925 543-9223
John Brian Ternan, *CEO*
Pamela M Lemon, *Vice Pres*
Dan Swanson, *Executive*
Michael Thomas, *Executive*
Cindy Chandler, *Executive Asst*
EMP: 198
SALES (est): 304.6MM **Publicly Held**
SIC: 6324 Health maintenance organization (HMO), insurance only

(P-10178)
AGILON HEALTH INC
1 World Trade Ctr, Long Beach
(90831-0002)
PHONE.........................562 256-3800
Ron Kuerbide, *CEO*
Ted Halkias, *CFO*
EMP: 100
SQ FT: 12,000
SALES: 300MM **Privately Held**
SIC: 6324 Health maintenance organization (HMO), insurance only

(P-10179)
ALAMEDA ALLIANCE FOR HEALTH
1240 S Loop Rd, Alameda (94502-7084)
PHONE.........................510 747-4555
Ingrid Lamirault, *CEO*
Matthew Woodruff, *COO*
Gil Riojas, *CFO*
Michael Kaufman, *Managing Dir*
Brian Butcher, *Administration*
EMP: 135
SQ FT: 50,000
SALES (est): 116.9MM **Privately Held**
WEB: www.alamedaalliance.com
SIC: 6324 Health maintenance organization (HMO), insurance only

(P-10180)
ALIGNMENT HEALTH PLAN
Also Called: Citizens Choice Health Plan
1100 W Town & Country, Orange
(92868-4600)
PHONE.........................323 728-7232
Chuck Weber, *President*
Elizabeth Tejada, *COO*
Charlotte Leblanc,
EMP: 90
SALES (est): 50.2MM
SALES (corp-wide): 9.6MM **Privately Held**
WEB: www.mycchp.com
SIC: 6324 Health maintenance organization (HMO), insurance only
PA: Alignment Healthcare, Usa Llc
1100 W Town And Country R
Orange CA 92868
844 310-2247

(P-10181)
BLUE CROSS & BLUE SHIELD MICH
6300 Wilshire Blvd # 970, Los Angeles
(90048-5204)
PHONE.........................323 782-3046
Kenneth August, *Branch Mgr*
EMP: 203
SALES (corp-wide): 11.2B **Privately Held**
SIC: 6324 Hospital & medical service plans
PA: Blue Cross And Blue Shield Of Michigan Foundation
600 E Lafayette Blvd
Detroit MI 48226
313 225-9000

(P-10182)
BLUE CROSS OF CALIFORNIA (DH)
4553 La Tienda Rd, Westlake Village
(91362-3800)
PHONE.........................805 557-6050
Mark Morgan, *President*
Kenneth C Zurek, *CFO*
Thomas C Geiser, *Admin Sec*
EMP: 133
SQ FT: 427,104
SALES (est): 190.6MM
SALES (corp-wide): 90B **Publicly Held**
SIC: 6324 6411 Health maintenance organization (HMO), insurance only; insurance agents, brokers & service

(P-10183)
CALIFORNIA PHYSICIANS SERVICE
2020 17th St, Bakersfield (93301-4252)
PHONE.........................661 631-2277
Ricard Maiatico, *Owner*
EMP: 126
SALES (corp-wide): 17.6B **Privately Held**
WEB: www.blueshieldcafoundation.org
SIC: 6324 6321 Hospital & medical service plans; accident & health insurance
PA: California Physicians' Service
50 Beale St Bsmt 2
San Francisco CA 94105
415 229-5000

(P-10184)
CALIFORNIA PHYSICIANS SERVICE
Also Called: Blue Sheild of California
2066 Camel Ln Apt 24, Walnut Creek
(94596-5955)
PHONE.........................925 927-7419
John Durst, *Branch Mgr*
EMP: 232
SALES (corp-wide): 17.6B **Privately Held**
WEB: www.blueshieldcafoundation.org
SIC: 6324 Hospital & medical service plans
PA: California Physicians' Service
50 Beale St Bsmt 2
San Francisco CA 94105
415 229-5000

(P-10185)
CALIFORNIA PHYSICIANS SERVICE (PA)
Also Called: Blue Shield of California
50 Beale St Bsmt 2, San Francisco
(94105-1819)
P.O. Box 272540, Chico (95927-2540)
PHONE.........................415 229-5000
Paul Markovich, *President*
Bruce Bodoken, *Ch of Bd*
Karen Vigil, *CEO*
Heidi Kunz, *CFO*
Eric Book, *Chief Mktg Ofcr*
EMP: 900 EST: 1939
SQ FT: 120,000
SALES: 17.6B **Privately Held**
WEB: www.blueshieldcafoundation.org
SIC: 6324 Hospital & medical service plans

(P-10186)
CALIFORNIA PHYSICIANS SERVICE
4700 Bechelli Ln, Redding (96002-3506)
PHONE.........................530 351-6115
EMP: 158
SALES (corp-wide): 17.6B **Privately Held**
SIC: 6324 Hospital & medical service plans
PA: California Physicians' Service
50 Beale St Bsmt 2
San Francisco CA 94105
415 229-5000

(P-10187)
CALIFORNIA PHYSICIANS SERVICE
Also Called: Blue Shield of California
4203 Town Center Blvd, El Dorado Hills
(95762-7100)
P.O. Box 7168, San Francisco (94120-7168)
PHONE.........................916 350-7800
Eric Lam, *Director*
Sanjay Kumbagowdana, *Admin Asst*
Kimberly Mancini, *Analyst*

Elizabeth Fuentes, *Internal Med*
Andy Chasin, *General Counsel*
EMP: 260
SALES (corp-wide): 17.6B **Privately Held**
WEB: www.blueshieldcafoundation.org
SIC: 6324 6321 Hospital & medical service plans; accident & health insurance
PA: California Physicians' Service
50 Beale St Bsmt 2
San Francisco CA 94105
415 229-5000

(P-10188)
CALIFORNIA PHYSICIANS SERVICE
Also Called: Blue Shield of California
100 N Pacific Coast Hwy # 2000, El Segundo (90245-4359)
PHONE.........................310 744-2668
Aubrey Chernick, *Branch Mgr*
EMP: 126
SALES (corp-wide): 17.6B **Privately Held**
WEB: www.blueshieldcafoundation.org
SIC: 6324 Hospital & medical service plans
PA: California Physicians' Service
50 Beale St Bsmt 2
San Francisco CA 94105
415 229-5000

(P-10189)
CALIFORNIA PHYSICIANS SERVICE
Also Called: Blue Shield of California
6300 Canoga Ave Ste A, Woodland Hills
(91367-8000)
PHONE.........................818 598-8000
John Headberg, *Branch Mgr*
Lloyd Morgan, *Senior Mgr*
EMP: 400
SALES (corp-wide): 17.6B **Privately Held**
WEB: www.blueshieldcafoundation.org
SIC: 6324 Hospital & medical service plans
PA: California Physicians' Service
50 Beale St Bsmt 2
San Francisco CA 94105
415 229-5000

(P-10190)
CENTENE CORPORATION
550 Main St, Placerville (95667-5643)
PHONE.........................530 626-5773
EMP: 99 **Publicly Held**
SIC: 6324 Hospital & medical service plans
PA: Centene Corporation
7700 Forsyth Blvd Ste 800
Saint Louis MO 63105

(P-10191)
CENTENE CORPORATION
12033 Foundation Pl, Gold River
(95670-4502)
PHONE.........................314 505-6689
EMP: 70 **Publicly Held**
SIC: 6324 Hospital & medical service plans
PA: Centene Corporation
7700 Forsyth Blvd Ste 800
Saint Louis MO 63105

(P-10192)
CENTER FOR ELDERS INDEPENDENCE
Also Called: C E I
510 17th St Ste 400, Oakland
(94612-1570)
PHONE.........................510 433-1150
Peter Szutu, *President*
EMP: 225 EST: 1981
SALES: 65.4MM **Privately Held**
WEB: www.cei.elders.org
SIC: 6324 Hospital & medical service plans

(P-10193)
CHOC HEALTH ALLIANCE
1120 W La Veta Ave # 450, Orange
(92868-4224)
PHONE.........................714 565-5100
Roger Austin, *CEO*
EMP: 65
SALES (est): 20MM **Publicly Held**
WEB: www.chochealthalliance.com
SIC: 6324 Hospital & medical service plans

HQ: Anderson Schaller Inc
4500 E Cotton Center Blvd
Phoenix AZ 85040
602 659-1123

(P-10194)
CIGNA HEALTHCARE CAL INC
1 Front St Ste 1700, San Francisco
(94111-5392)
PHONE..............................415 374-2500
William Burke, *Branch Mgr*
Marlene Matsuoka, *Vice Pres*
Mike Nelsen, *Accounts Exec*
EMP: 226
SALES (corp-wide): 41.6B **Publicly Held**
SIC: 6324 Health maintenance organiza-
tion (HMO), insurance only
HQ: Cigna Healthcare Of California, Inc.
400 N Brand Blvd Ste 400 # 400
Glendale CA 91203
818 500-6262

(P-10195)
CIGNA HEALTHCARE CAL INC
(DH)
400 N Brand Blvd Ste 400 # 400, Glendale
(91203-2357)
P.O. Box 188045, Chattanooga TN (37422-
8045)
PHONE..............................818 500-6262
Leroy Volberding, *President*
Barry Ford, *Vice Pres*
Randy Mathews, *Vice Pres*
Nancy Ho, *Pharmacy Dir*
Randy Matthew, *MIS Mgr*
EMP: 400
SQ FT: 110,000
SALES (est): 276.9MM
SALES (corp-wide): 41.6B **Publicly Held**
SIC: 6324 Health maintenance organiza-
tion (HMO), insurance only
HQ: Healthsource, Inc.
2 College Park Dr
Hooksett NH 03106
603 268-7000

(P-10196)
CIGNA HEALTHCARE CAL INC
2801 Townsgate Rd Ste 121, Thousand
Oaks (91361-3029)
PHONE..............................805 230-8300
Peter Albert, *Director*
William Wilkins, *Manager*
EMP: 233
SALES (corp-wide): 41.6B **Publicly Held**
SIC: 6324 Group hospitalization plans
HQ: Cigna Healthcare Of California, Inc.
400 N Brand Blvd Ste 400 # 400
Glendale CA 91203
818 500-6262

(P-10197)
CIGNA HEALTHCARE CAL INC
5300 W Tulare Ave Ste 100, Visalia
(93277-3700)
PHONE..............................559 738-2000
Rich Keena, *Vice Pres*
Raemee Anderson, *Cust Mgr*
Vicki Clements, *Director*
EMP: 500
SALES (corp-wide): 41.6B **Publicly Held**
SIC: 6324 Health maintenance organiza-
tion (HMO), insurance only
HQ: Cigna Healthcare Of California, Inc.
400 N Brand Blvd Ste 400 # 400
Glendale CA 91203
818 500-6262

(P-10198)
COUNTY OF LOS ANGELES
Also Called: Community Health Plan
1000 S Fremont Ave Unit 4, Alhambra
(91803-8859)
PHONE..............................626 299-5300
Dave Beck, *Director*
EMP: 140 **Privately Held**
WEB: www.co.la.ca.us
SIC: 6324 9431 Hospital & medical serv-
ice plans; mental health agency adminis-
tration, government
PA: County Of Los Angeles
500 W Temple St Ste 437
Los Angeles CA 90012
213 974-1101

(P-10199)
DELTA DENTAL OF CALIFORNIA
1450 Frazee Rd Ste 200, San Diego
(92108-4341)
P.O. Box 261391 (92196-1391)
PHONE..............................619 683-2549
Delta California, *Branch Mgr*
EMP: 259
SALES (corp-wide): 5.8B **Privately Held**
SIC: 6324 Dental insurance
PA: Delta Dental Of California
560 Mission St Fl 13
San Francisco CA 94105
415 972-8300

(P-10200)
DELTA DENTAL OF CALIFORNIA
(PA)
560 Mission St Fl 13, San Francisco
(94105-2657)
PHONE..............................415 972-8300
Mike Castro, *Acting CEO*
Sandy Trent, *Volunteer Dir*
Gary D Radine, *President*
Nilesh Patel, *COO*
Alicia Weber, *Acting CFO*
EMP: 487 EST: 1955
SQ FT: 241,000
SALES: 5.8B **Privately Held**
WEB: www.deltadentalca.com
SIC: 6324 Dental insurance

(P-10201)
DELTA DENTAL OF CALIFORNIA
Also Called: Delta Dental Plan
11155 International Dr, Sacramento
(95826)
PHONE..............................916 853-7373
Tony Barth, *Branch Mgr*
Darlene E Gillespie, *Officer*
Perry Htay, *Administration*
Randy Alcantar, *Business Anlyst*
Jino An, *Technology*
EMP: 1000
SALES (corp-wide): 5.8B **Privately Held**
WEB: www.deltadentalca.com
SIC: 6324 Dental insurance
PA: Delta Dental Of California
560 Mission St Fl 13
San Francisco CA 94105
415 972-8300

(P-10202)
EBA & M CORPORATION (PA)
Also Called: Employees Benefit ADM & MGT
3505 Cadillac Ave O201, Costa Mesa
(92626-1447)
PHONE..............................714 668-8920
Bradl Gossen, *President*
Vernon Gossen, *President*
Mary Ann Wessel, *Senior VP*
Robin Pugh, *Administration*
John Stephens, *Applctn Conslt*
EMP: 75
SQ FT: 12,000
SALES (est): 30.7MM **Privately Held**
SIC: 6324 Hospital & medical service plans

(P-10203)
HEALDSBURG DIST HOSP
REHAB SVC
1540 Healdsburg Ave, Healdsburg
(95448-3253)
PHONE..............................707 433-9150
Stacy Smithson, *Manager*
EMP: 100
SALES (est): 20.1MM **Privately Held**
WEB: www.healdsburghospital.com
SIC: 6324 Hospital & medical service plans

(P-10204)
HEALTH NET INC (HQ)
21650 Oxnard St Fl 25, Woodland Hills
(91367-7829)
PHONE..............................818 676-6000
Jay M Gellert, *President*
James E Woys, *COO*
Rich Hall, *Officer*
Juanell Hefner, *Officer*
Angelee F Bouchard, *Senior VP*
EMP: 250
SQ FT: 115,488

(P-10205)
HEALTH NET INC
101 N Brand Blvd Ste 1500, Glendale
(91203-2659)
PHONE..............................818 543-9037
Kevin J Walker, *Manager*
EMP: 128 **Publicly Held**
SIC: 6324 Hospital & medical service plans
HQ: Health Net Of California, Inc.
21281 Burbank Blvd Fl 4
Woodland Hills CA 91367
818 676-6775

(P-10206)
HEALTH NET INC
Also Called: Fhpa
12033 Foundation Pl, Gold River
(95670-4502)
PHONE..............................916 935-3520
Jeffery Slynn, *Vice Pres*
Jeff Otwell, *Administration*
EMP: 300 **Publicly Held**
SIC: 6324 Hospital & medical service plans
HQ: Health Net Of California, Inc.
21281 Burbank Blvd Fl 4
Woodland Hills CA 91367
818 676-6775

(P-10207)
HEALTH NET CALIFORNIA INC
(DH)
21281 Burbank Blvd Fl 4, Woodland Hills
(91367-7073)
P.O. Box 9103, Van Nuys (91409-9103)
PHONE..............................818 676-6775
Jay Gellert, *Ch of Bd*
Patricia Clarey, *Ch Credit Ofcr*
Karen Blum, *Consultant*
EMP: 167
SQ FT: 150,000
SALES (est): 1.3B **Publicly Held**
SIC: 6324 8062 6311 6321 Hospital &
medical service plans; general medical &
surgical hospitals; life insurance carriers;
disability health insurance; accident &
health insurance carriers; workers' com-
pensation insurance; drug stores & propri-
etary stores

(P-10208)
HEALTH NET CALIFORNIA INC
155 Grand Ave Lbby, Oakland
(94612-3758)
PHONE..............................510 465-9600
Eric Johnson, *Manager*
Susan Sall, *Manager*
EMP: 450 **Publicly Held**
SIC: 6324 6321 Hospital & medical serv-
ice plans; accident & health insurance
HQ: Health Net Of California, Inc.
21281 Burbank Blvd Fl 4
Woodland Hills CA 91367
818 676-6775

(P-10209)
HEALTH NET COMMUNITY
SOLUTIONS
21650 Oxnard St Fl 25, Woodland Hills
(91367-7829)
PHONE..............................818 676-6000
EMP: 92
SALES (est): 3.4MM **Publicly Held**
SIC: 6324 Hospital & medical service plans
HQ: Health Net, Inc.
21650 Oxnard St Fl 25
Woodland Hills CA 91367

(P-10210)
HEALTH NET FEDERAL SVCS
LLC (DH)
2025 Aerojet Rd, Rancho Cordova
(95742-6418)
P.O. Box 2890 (95741-2890)
PHONE..............................916 935-5000
Thomas F Carrato, *President*
Nithya Rajaraman, *Analyst*
Mario Rodriguez, *Analyst*
Garrett Grinder, *Director*
Marilyn Perkola, *Manager*

EMP: 700
SQ FT: 100,000
SALES (est): 1B **Publicly Held**
SIC: 6324 Hospital & medical service plans
HQ: Health Net Of California, Inc.
21281 Burbank Blvd Fl 4
Woodland Hills CA 91367
818 676-6775

(P-10211)
HEALTH NET LIFE INSURANCE
CO
21281 Burbank Blvd, Woodland Hills
(91367-7073)
PHONE..............................800 865-6288
James Edwin Woys, *Principal*
EMP: 244
SALES (est): 44.3MM **Publicly Held**
WEB: www.healthnet.com
SIC: 6324 Hospital & medical service plans
HQ: Health Net, Inc.
21650 Oxnard St Fl 25
Woodland Hills CA 91367
-

(P-10212)
HEALTH PLAN OF SAN
JOAQUIN
7751 S Manthey Rd, French Camp
(95231-9802)
PHONE..............................209 942-6300
Amy Shinn, *CEO*
Alejandra Clyde, *Officer*
Nancy Raymond, *Officer*
Katherine Kutz, *Info Tech Dir*
Shelli Smith, *Information Mgr*
EMP: 120
SALES (est): 96.5MM **Privately Held**
SIC: 6324 Health maintenance organiza-
tion (HMO), insurance only

(P-10213)
HEALTHNET CALIFORNIA INC
Also Called: Healthnet Seniority Plus
1661 Golden Rain Rd, Seal Beach
(90740-4907)
PHONE..............................562 598-4043
Terry Anguiano Redd, *District Mgr*
EMP: 75
SALES (est): 6MM **Privately Held**
WEB: www.healthnetcalifornia.com
SIC: 6324 Health maintenance organiza-
tion (HMO), insurance only

(P-10214)
INLAND EMPIRE HEALTH PLAN
805 W 2nd St Ste C, San Bernardino
(92410-3255)
P.O. Box 1800, Rancho Cucamonga
(91729-1800)
PHONE..............................866 228-4347
EMP: 428 **Privately Held**
SIC: 6324 8742 Health maintenance or-
ganization (HMO), insurance only; hospi-
tal & health services consultant
PA: Inland Empire Health Plan
10801 6th St Ste 120
Rancho Cucamonga CA 91730

(P-10215)
INTER-VALLEY HEALTH PLAN
INC
300 S Park Ave Ste 300 # 300, Pomona
(91766-1546)
P.O. Box 6002 (91769-6002)
PHONE..............................909 623-6333
Ronald Bolding, *CEO*
Michael Nelson, *CFO*
Linda Carr, *Vice Pres*
Patricia Jacobson, *Vice Pres*
Don McCain, *Admin Sec*
EMP: 70
SQ FT: 54,700
SALES: 271.1MM **Privately Held**
WEB: www.ivhp.com
SIC: 6324 8011 Hospital & medical service
plans; offices & clinics of medical doctors

(P-10216)
KAISER FOUNDATION HOSPITALS
Also Called: Kaiser Foundation Health Plan
30116 Eigenbrodt Way, Union City
(94587-1225)
PHONE.....................510 675-5777
Colleen McKeown, *Manager*
EMP: 99
SALES (corp-wide): 94.1B **Privately Held**
SIC: 6324 Hospital & medical service plans
HQ: Kaiser Foundation Hospitals Inc
1 Kaiser Plz
Oakland CA 94612
510 271-6611

(P-10217)
KAISER FOUNDATION HOSPITALS
Also Called: Kaiser Foundation Health Plan
2350 Geary Blvd Fl 2, San Francisco
(94115-3305)
PHONE.....................415 833-2616
Sherri Moazi, *Pharmacist*
EMP: 85
SALES (corp-wide): 94.1B **Privately Held**
SIC: 6324 Hospital & medical service plans
HQ: Kaiser Foundation Hospitals Inc
1 Kaiser Plz
Oakland CA 94612
510 271-6611

(P-10218)
KAISER FOUNDATION HOSPITALS
Also Called: Kaiser Foundation Health Plan
393 E Walnut St, Pasadena (91188-0002)
PHONE.....................626 405-5000
David Lamm, *Branch Mgr*
Lena Townend, *Project Mgr*
Stephen Derose, *Research*
Cathy Romero, *Corp Comm Staff*
Javier Gomez, *Property Mgr*
EMP: 50
SALES (corp-wide): 94.1B **Privately Held**
WEB: www.kaiser.com
SIC: 6324 Hospital & medical service plans
HQ: Kaiser Foundation Hospitals Inc
1 Kaiser Plz
Oakland CA 94612
510 271-6611

(P-10219)
KAISER FOUNDATION HOSPITALS
Also Called: Kaiser Foundation Health Plan
1761 Broadway St Ste 210, Vallejo
(94589-2227)
PHONE.....................707 645-2720
Cynthia Chandler, *Director*
Schieree Harmon, *Admin Mgr*
EMP: 75
SALES (corp-wide): 94.1B **Privately Held**
WEB: www.kaiser.com
SIC: 6324 Hospital & medical service plans
HQ: Kaiser Foundation Hospitals Inc
1 Kaiser Plz
Oakland CA 94612
510 271-6611

(P-10220)
KAISER FOUNDATION HOSPITALS
Also Called: Kaiser Foundation Health Plan
820 Las Gallinas Ave, San Rafael
(94903-3410)
PHONE.....................415 444-3522
Bob Johnson, *Branch Mgr*
Carmen P Irizarry, *Psychiatry*
EMP: 100
SALES (corp-wide): 94.1B **Privately Held**
WEB: www.kaiser.com
SIC: 6324 Hospital & medical service plans
HQ: Kaiser Foundation Hospitals Inc
1 Kaiser Plz
Oakland CA 94612
510 271-6611

(P-10221)
KAISER FOUNDATION HOSPITALS
Also Called: Kaiser Foundation Health Plan
1550 W Manchester Ave, Los Angeles
(90047-5424)
PHONE.....................800 954-8000
EMP: 85
SALES (corp-wide): 94.1B **Privately Held**
SIC: 6324 Hospital & medical service plans
HQ: Kaiser Foundation Hospitals Inc
1 Kaiser Plz
Oakland CA 94612
510 271-6611

(P-10222)
KAISER FOUNDATION HOSPITALS
Also Called: Kaiser Foundation Health Plan
255 W Macarthur Blvd, Oakland
(94611-5641)
PHONE.....................510 752-7864
Albert Carver, *Branch Mgr*
EMP: 85
SALES (corp-wide): 94.1B **Privately Held**
SIC: 6324 Hospital & medical service plans
HQ: Kaiser Foundation Hospitals Inc
1 Kaiser Plz
Oakland CA 94612
510 271-6611

(P-10223)
KAISER FOUNDATION HOSPITALS
Also Called: Kaiser Foundation Health Plan
4785 N 1st St, Fresno (93726-0513)
PHONE.....................559 448-4555
EMP: 85
SALES (corp-wide): 94.1B **Privately Held**
SIC: 6324 Hospital & medical service plans
HQ: Kaiser Foundation Hospitals Inc
1 Kaiser Plz
Oakland CA 94612
510 271-6611

(P-10224)
KAISER FOUNDATION HOSPITALS
Also Called: Kaiser Foundation Health Plan
10305 Promenade Pkwy, Elk Grove
(95757-9400)
PHONE.....................916 544-6000
EMP: 85
SALES (corp-wide): 94.1B **Privately Held**
SIC: 6324 Hospital & medical service plans
HQ: Kaiser Foundation Hospitals Inc
1 Kaiser Plz
Oakland CA 94612
510 271-6611

(P-10225)
KAISER FOUNDATION HOSPITALS
Also Called: Kaiser Foundation Health Plan
14011 Park Ave, Victorville (92392-2413)
PHONE.....................888 750-0036
EMP: 85
SALES (corp-wide): 94.1B **Privately Held**
SIC: 6324 Hospital & medical service plans
HQ: Kaiser Foundation Hospitals Inc
1 Kaiser Plz
Oakland CA 94612
510 271-6611

(P-10226)
KAISER FOUNDATION HOSPITALS
Also Called: Kaiser Foundation Health Plan
17140 Bernardo Center Dr, San Diego
(92128-2093)
PHONE.....................619 528-5000
David Kvancz, *Branch Mgr*
EMP: 85
SALES (corp-wide): 94.1B **Privately Held**
SIC: 6324 Hospital & medical service plans
HQ: Kaiser Foundation Hospitals Inc
1 Kaiser Plz
Oakland CA 94612
510 271-6611

(P-10227)
KAISER FOUNDATION HOSPITALS
Also Called: Kaiser Foundation Health Plan
5893 Copley Dr, San Diego (92111-7906)
PHONE.....................619 528-5000
EMP: 85
SALES (corp-wide): 94.1B **Privately Held**
SIC: 6324 Hospital & medical service plans
HQ: Kaiser Foundation Hospitals Inc
1 Kaiser Plz
Oakland CA 94612
510 271-6611

(P-10228)
KAISER FOUNDATION HOSPITALS
Also Called: Kaiser Foundation Health Plan
27309 Madison Ave, Temecula
(92590-5685)
PHONE.....................866 984-7483
David Kvancz, *Vice Pres*
Vu Tinh, *Family Practiti*
EMP: 85
SALES (corp-wide): 94.1B **Privately Held**
SIC: 6324 Hospital & medical service plans
HQ: Kaiser Foundation Hospitals Inc
1 Kaiser Plz
Oakland CA 94612
510 271-6611

(P-10229)
KAISER FOUNDATION HOSPITALS
Also Called: Kaiser Foundation Health Plan
11001 Sepulveda Blvd, Mission Hills
(91345-1413)
PHONE.....................888 778-5000
EMP: 85
SALES (corp-wide): 94.1B **Privately Held**
SIC: 6324 Hospital & medical service plans
HQ: Kaiser Foundation Hospitals Inc
1 Kaiser Plz
Oakland CA 94612
510 271-6611

(P-10230)
KAISER FOUNDATION HOSPITALS
Also Called: Kaiser Foundation Health Plan
8001 Ventura Canyon Ave, Panorama City
(91402-6312)
PHONE.....................818 375-2028
Teresa Park, *Branch Mgr*
EMP: 85
SALES (corp-wide): 94.1B **Privately Held**
SIC: 6324 Hospital & medical service plans
HQ: Kaiser Foundation Hospitals Inc
1 Kaiser Plz
Oakland CA 94612
510 271-6611

(P-10231)
KAISER FOUNDATION HOSPITALS
Also Called: Kaiser Foundation Health Plan
27303 Sleepy Hollow Ave S, Hayward
(94545-4203)
PHONE.....................510 454-1000
EMP: 85
SALES (corp-wide): 15.7B **Privately Held**
SIC: 6324
HQ: Kaiser Foundation Hospitals Inc
1 Kaiser Plz
Oakland CA 94612
510 271-6611

(P-10232)
KAISER FOUNDATION HOSPITALS
Also Called: Kaiser Foundation Health Plan
5620 Mesmer Ave, Los Angeles
(90230-6315)
PHONE.....................800 954-8000
EMP: 85
SALES (corp-wide): 94.1B **Privately Held**
SIC: 6324 Hospital & medical service plans
HQ: Kaiser Foundation Hospitals Inc
1 Kaiser Plz
Oakland CA 94612
510 271-6611

(P-10233)
KAISER FOUNDATION HOSPITALS
Also Called: Rancho Cordova Medical Offices
10725 International Dr, Rancho Cordova
(95670-7967)
PHONE.....................916 631-3088
David Haddad, *Principal*
Wil Neria, *Engineer*
Vanessa Fontes, *Psychologist*
Marzieh Forghany, *Psychologist*
Sara L Koehler, *Obstetrician*
EMP: 50
SALES (corp-wide): 94.1B **Privately Held**
WEB: www.kaiserpermanente.org
SIC: 6324 Hospital & medical service plans
HQ: Kaiser Foundation Hospitals Inc
1 Kaiser Plz
Oakland CA 94612
510 271-6611

(P-10234)
KAISER FOUNDATION HOSPITALS
Also Called: Vaxaville Medical Offices
1 Quality Dr, Vacaville (95688-9494)
PHONE.....................707 624-4000
Murty Savitala, *Principal*
Guillermo Mendoza, *Med Doctor*
EMP: 50
SALES (corp-wide): 94.1B **Privately Held**
WEB: www.kaiserpermanente.org
SIC: 6324 Hospital & medical service plans
HQ: Kaiser Foundation Hospitals Inc
1 Kaiser Plz
Oakland CA 94612
510 271-6611

(P-10235)
KAISER FOUNDATION HOSPITALS
Also Called: Kaiser Foundation Health Plan
1011 S East St Fl 1, Anaheim
(92805-5749)
PHONE.....................714 284-6634
Ruth Ann Ferreria, *Manager*
Yolanda Cornejo, *Technology*
EMP: 100
SQ FT: 63,920
SALES (corp-wide): 94.1B **Privately Held**
WEB: www.kaiser.com
SIC: 6324 Hospital & medical service plans
HQ: Kaiser Foundation Hospitals Inc
1 Kaiser Plz
Oakland CA 94612
510 271-6611

(P-10236)
KAISER FOUNDATION HOSPITALS
Also Called: Kaiser Foundation Health Plan
25 N Via Monte, Walnut Creek
(94598-2510)
PHONE.....................925 926-3000
Phil Newbold, *Principal*
Virginia Martinez, *Executive Asst*
Oscar Miranda, *IT/INT Sup*
Richard Muir, *IT/INT Sup*
Nicole Thomas, *Engineer*
EMP: 70
SQ FT: 79,360
SALES (corp-wide): 94.1B **Privately Held**
WEB: www.kaiser.com
SIC: 6324 Hospital & medical service plans
HQ: Kaiser Foundation Hospitals Inc
1 Kaiser Plz
Oakland CA 94612
510 271-6611

(P-10237)
KAISER FOUNDATION HOSPITALS
Also Called: Kaiser Foundation Health Plan
2071 Herndon Ave, Clovis (93611-6101)
PHONE.....................559 324-5100
Angela H Kuo, *Med Doctor*
Toussaint Streat, *Family Practiti*
Hardeep S Chohan, *Internal Med*
Vinod Kumar, *Internal Med*
Melchor L Ong, *Internal Med*
EMP: 99
SQ FT: 67,465
SALES (corp-wide): 94.1B **Privately Held**
WEB: www.kaiser.com
SIC: 6324 Hospital & medical service plans

HQ: Kaiser Foundation Hospitals Inc
　　1 Kaiser Plz
　　Oakland CA 94612
　　510 271-6611

(P-10238)
KAISER FOUNDATION HOSPITALS
Also Called: Kaiser Foundation Health Plan
21263 Erwin St, Woodland Hills
(91367-3715)
PHONE...............................888 515-3500
EMP: 99
SALES (corp-wide): 94.1B **Privately Held**
WEB: www.kaiser.com
SIC: 6324 Hospital & medical service plans
HQ: Kaiser Foundation Hospitals Inc
　　1 Kaiser Plz
　　Oakland CA 94612
　　510 271-6611

(P-10239)
KAISER FOUNDATION HOSPITALS
Also Called: Kaiser Foundation Health Plan
1840 Sierra Gardens Dr, Roseville
(95661-2912)
PHONE...............................916 784-4050
Don Vu, *Principal*
EMP: 99
SQ FT: 102,150
SALES (corp-wide): 94.1B **Privately Held**
WEB: www.kaiser.com
SIC: 6324 Hospital & medical service plans
HQ: Kaiser Foundation Hospitals Inc
　　1 Kaiser Plz
　　Oakland CA 94612
　　510 271-6611

(P-10240)
KAISER FOUNDATION HOSPITALS
Also Called: Kaiser Foundation Health Plan
40595 Westlake Dr, Oakhurst
(93644-9024)
PHONE...............................559 658-8388
CHI Ly, *Principal*
EMP: 99
SALES (corp-wide): 94.1B **Privately Held**
WEB: www.kaiser.com
SIC: 6324 Hospital & medical service plans
HQ: Kaiser Foundation Hospitals Inc
　　1 Kaiser Plz
　　Oakland CA 94612
　　510 271-6611

(P-10241)
KAISER FOUNDATION HOSPITALS
Also Called: Kaiser Foundation Health Plan
2295 S Vineyard Ave, Ontario
(91761-7925)
PHONE...............................888 750-0036
Arlene Freeman, *Manager*
EMP: 99
SALES (corp-wide): 94.1B **Privately Held**
WEB: www.kaiser.com
SIC: 6324 Hospital & medical service plans
HQ: Kaiser Foundation Hospitals Inc
　　1 Kaiser Plz
　　Oakland CA 94612
　　510 271-6611

(P-10242)
KAISER FOUNDATION HOSPITALS
Also Called: Kaiser Foundation Health Plan
42575 Washington St, Palm Desert
(92211-8850)
PHONE...............................760 360-1475
EMP: 99
SALES (corp-wide): 94.1B **Privately Held**
WEB: www.kaiser.com
SIC: 6324 Hospital & medical service plans
HQ: Kaiser Foundation Hospitals Inc
　　1 Kaiser Plz
　　Oakland CA 94612
　　510 271-6611

(P-10243)
KAISER FOUNDATION HOSPITALS
Also Called: Kaiser Foundation Health Plan
888 S Hill Rd, Ventura (93003-8400)
PHONE...............................888 515-3500

Michael Steinbaum, *Manager*
EMP: 99
SALES (corp-wide): 94.1B **Privately Held**
WEB: www.kaiser.com
SIC: 6324 Hospital & medical service plans
HQ: Kaiser Foundation Hospitals Inc
　　1 Kaiser Plz
　　Oakland CA 94612
　　510 271-6611

(P-10244)
KAISER FOUNDATION HOSPITALS
Also Called: Kaiser Foundation Health Plan
3401 S Harbor Blvd, Santa Ana
(92704-7933)
PHONE...............................888 988-2800
Linh Kamikawa, *Principal*
Jenny Lee, *Pharmacist*
EMP: 99
SALES (corp-wide): 94.1B **Privately Held**
WEB: www.kaiser.com
SIC: 6324 Hospital & medical service plans
HQ: Kaiser Foundation Hospitals Inc
　　1 Kaiser Plz
　　Oakland CA 94612
　　510 271-6611

(P-10245)
KAISER FOUNDATION HOSPITALS
Also Called: Kaiser Foundation Health Plan
1717 Date Pike, San Bernardino (92404)
PHONE...............................888 750-0036
Jim Morrison, *Manager*
EMP: 99
SQ FT: 18,253
SALES (corp-wide): 94.1B **Privately Held**
WEB: www.kaiser.com
SIC: 6324 Hospital & medical service plans
HQ: Kaiser Foundation Hospitals Inc
　　1 Kaiser Plz
　　Oakland CA 94612
　　510 271-6611

(P-10246)
KAISER FOUNDATION HOSPITALS
Also Called: Kaiser Foundation Health Plan
11911 Central Ave, Chino (91710-1906)
PHONE...............................888 750-0036
Ken Lee, *Principal*
EMP: 99
SALES (corp-wide): 94.1B **Privately Held**
WEB: www.kaiser.com
SIC: 6324 Hospital & medical service plans
HQ: Kaiser Foundation Hospitals Inc
　　1 Kaiser Plz
　　Oakland CA 94612
　　510 271-6611

(P-10247)
KAISER FOUNDATION HOSPITALS
Also Called: Kaiser Foundation Health Plan
395 Hickey Blvd, Daly City (94015-2770)
PHONE...............................650 301-5860
Arthur Chin, *Principal*
Christine C Chen, *Obstetrician*
Veronica LI, *Pediatrics*
EMP: 99
SALES (corp-wide): 94.1B **Privately Held**
WEB: www.kaiser.com
SIC: 6324 Hospital & medical service plans
HQ: Kaiser Foundation Hospitals Inc
　　1 Kaiser Plz
　　Oakland CA 94612
　　510 271-6611

(P-10248)
KAISER FOUNDATION HOSPITALS
Also Called: Kaiser Foundation Health Plan
3553 Whipple Rd, Union City (94587-1507)
PHONE...............................510 675-2170
Mani Kammula, *Principal*
EMP: 99
SALES (corp-wide): 94.1B **Privately Held**
WEB: www.kaiser.com
SIC: 6324 Hospital & medical service plans
HQ: Kaiser Foundation Hospitals Inc
　　1 Kaiser Plz
　　Oakland CA 94612
　　510 271-6611

(P-10249)
KAISER FOUNDATION HOSPITALS
Also Called: Kaiser Foundation Health Plan
2417 Naglee Rd, Tracy (95304-7324)
PHONE...............................209 832-6339
EMP: 84
SALES (corp-wide): 94.1B **Privately Held**
WEB: www.kaiser.com
SIC: 6324 Hospital & medical service plans
HQ: Kaiser Foundation Hospitals Inc
　　1 Kaiser Plz
　　Oakland CA 94612
　　510 271-6611

(P-10250)
KAISER FOUNDATION HOSPITALS
Also Called: Kaiser Foundation Health Plan
901 El Camino Real, San Bruno
(94066-3009)
PHONE...............................650 742-2100
Allen Wu, *Principal*
EMP: 99
SALES (corp-wide): 94.1B **Privately Held**
WEB: www.kaiser.com
SIC: 6324 Hospital & medical service plans
HQ: Kaiser Foundation Hospitals Inc
　　1 Kaiser Plz
　　Oakland CA 94612
　　510 271-6611

(P-10251)
KAISER FOUNDATION HOSPITALS
Also Called: Kaiser Foundation Health Plan
3554 Round Barn Blvd, Santa Rosa
(95403-0929)
PHONE...............................707 571-3835
Jay Kelley, *Manager*
EMP: 99
SALES (corp-wide): 94.1B **Privately Held**
WEB: www.kaiser.com
SIC: 6324 Hospital & medical service plans
HQ: Kaiser Foundation Hospitals Inc
　　1 Kaiser Plz
　　Oakland CA 94612
　　510 271-6611

(P-10252)
KAISER FOUNDATION HOSPITALS
Also Called: Kaiser Foundation Health Plan
3925 Old Redwood Hwy, Santa Rosa
(95403-1719)
PHONE...............................707 393-4033
Clay Wheeler, *Principal*
EMP: 99
SALES (corp-wide): 94.1B **Privately Held**
WEB: www.kaiser.com
SIC: 6324 Hospital & medical service plans
HQ: Kaiser Foundation Hospitals Inc
　　1 Kaiser Plz
　　Oakland CA 94612
　　510 271-6611

(P-10253)
KAISER FOUNDATION HOSPITALS
Also Called: Kaiser Foundation Health Plan
1320 Standiford Ave, Modesto
(95350-0726)
PHONE...............................855 268-4096
Anita Vohra, *Principal*
EMP: 99
SALES (corp-wide): 94.1B **Privately Held**
WEB: www.kaiser.com
SIC: 6324 Hospital & medical service plans
HQ: Kaiser Foundation Hospitals Inc
　　1 Kaiser Plz
　　Oakland CA 94612
　　510 271-6611

(P-10254)
KAISER FOUNDATION HOSPITALS
Also Called: Kaiser Foundation Health Plan
5900 State Farm Dr # 100, Rohnert Park
(94928-2149)
PHONE...............................707 206-3000
Noel Smith, *Branch Mgr*
EMP: 85

SALES (corp-wide): 94.1B **Privately Held**
WEB: www.kaiser.com
SIC: 6324 Hospital & medical service plans
HQ: Kaiser Foundation Hospitals Inc
　　1 Kaiser Plz
　　Oakland CA 94612
　　510 271-6611

(P-10255)
KAISER FOUNDATION HOSPITALS
Also Called: Kaiser Foundation Health Plan
2417 Central Ave, Alameda (94501-4515)
PHONE...............................510 752-1190
Michael Gorin, *Branch Mgr*
EMP: 99
SALES (corp-wide): 94.1B **Privately Held**
WEB: www.kaiser.com
SIC: 6324 Hospital & medical service plans
HQ: Kaiser Foundation Hospitals Inc
　　1 Kaiser Plz
　　Oakland CA 94612
　　510 271-6611

(P-10256)
KAISER FOUNDATION HOSPITALS
Also Called: Kaiser Foundation Health Plan
969 Broadway, Oakland (94607-4017)
PHONE...............................510 251-0121
Mary Sage, *Branch Mgr*
Marilyn A Ancel, *Med Doctor*
EMP: 99
SALES (corp-wide): 94.1B **Privately Held**
WEB: www.kaiser.com
SIC: 6324 Hospital & medical service plans
HQ: Kaiser Foundation Hospitals Inc
　　1 Kaiser Plz
　　Oakland CA 94612
　　510 271-6611

(P-10257)
KAISER FOUNDATION HOSPITALS
Also Called: Kaiser Foundation Health Plan
9333 Rosecrans Ave, Bellflower
(90706-2141)
PHONE...............................562 461-3084
Arlene M Dolorico MD, *Manager*
EMP: 99
SALES (corp-wide): 94.1B **Privately Held**
WEB: www.kaiser.com
SIC: 6324 Hospital & medical service plans
HQ: Kaiser Foundation Hospitals Inc
　　1 Kaiser Plz
　　Oakland CA 94612
　　510 271-6611

(P-10258)
KAISER FOUNDATION HOSPITALS
Also Called: Kaiser Foundation Health Plan
2651 Highland Ave, Selma (93662-3392)
PHONE...............................559 898-6000
Hong-Hanh Ton-Nu, *Principal*
Michelle Humphreys, *Consultant*
EMP: 99
SQ FT: 37,081
SALES (corp-wide): 94.1B **Privately Held**
WEB: www.kaiser.com
SIC: 6324 Hospital & medical service plans
HQ: Kaiser Foundation Hospitals Inc
　　1 Kaiser Plz
　　Oakland CA 94612
　　510 271-6611

(P-10259)
KAISER FOUNDATION HOSPITALS
Also Called: Kaiser Foundation Health Plan
4201 W Chapman Ave, Orange
(92868-1505)
PHONE...............................714 748-7622
Doug Gustason, *Branch Mgr*
Robert M Bautista, *Med Doctor*
EMP: 99
SALES (corp-wide): 94.1B **Privately Held**
WEB: www.kaiser.com
SIC: 6324 Hospital & medical service plans
HQ: Kaiser Foundation Hospitals Inc
　　1 Kaiser Plz
　　Oakland CA 94612
　　510 271-6611

PRODUCTS & SVCS

(P-10260)
KAISER FOUNDATION HOSPITALS
Also Called: Kaiser Foundation Health Plan
1717 E Vista Chino Ste B2, Palm Springs (92262-3569)
PHONE..................866 370-1942
Ed McMahon, *Principal*
EMP: 99
SALES (corp-wide): 94.1B **Privately Held**
WEB: www.kaiser.com
SIC: 6324 Hospital & medical service plans
HQ: Kaiser Foundation Hospitals Inc
1 Kaiser Plz
Oakland CA 94612
510 271-6611

(P-10261)
KAISER FOUNDATION HOSPITALS
Also Called: Kaiser Foundation Health Plan
20790 Madrona Ave, Torrance (90503-3777)
PHONE..................800 780-1230
Shirley Oka, *Principal*
EMP: 99
SALES (corp-wide): 94.1B **Privately Held**
WEB: www.kaiser.com
SIC: 6324 Hospital & medical service plans
HQ: Kaiser Foundation Hospitals Inc
1 Kaiser Plz
Oakland CA 94612
510 271-6611

(P-10262)
KAISER FOUNDATION HOSPITALS
Also Called: Kaiser Foundation Health Plan
365 E Hillcrest Dr, Thousand Oaks (91360-5820)
PHONE..................888 515-3500
Beverly Torres, *Branch Mgr*
Jelyn Lu, *Family Practiti*
Joni L Jordan, *Internal Med*
EMP: 72
SALES (corp-wide): 94.1B **Privately Held**
WEB: www.kaiser.com
SIC: 6324 Hospital & medical service plans
HQ: Kaiser Foundation Hospitals Inc
1 Kaiser Plz
Oakland CA 94612
510 271-6611

(P-10263)
KAISER FOUNDATION HOSPITALS
Also Called: Kaiser Foundation Health Plan
3900 Alamo St, Simi Valley (93063-2111)
PHONE..................888 515-3500
Nami Kim, *Principal*
EMP: 99
SALES (corp-wide): 94.1B **Privately Held**
WEB: www.kaiser.com
SIC: 6324 Hospital & medical service plans
HQ: Kaiser Foundation Hospitals Inc
1 Kaiser Plz
Oakland CA 94612
510 271-6611

(P-10264)
KAISER FOUNDATION HOSPITALS
Also Called: Kaiser Foundation Health Plan
30400 Camino Capistrano, San Juan Capistrano (92675-1300)
PHONE..................888 988-2800
Patrick Roth, *Branch Mgr*
EMP: 99
SALES (corp-wide): 94.1B **Privately Held**
WEB: www.kaiser.com
SIC: 6324 Hospital & medical service plans
HQ: Kaiser Foundation Hospitals Inc
1 Kaiser Plz
Oakland CA 94612
510 271-6611

(P-10265)
KAISER FOUNDATION HOSPITALS
Also Called: Kaiser Foundation Health Plan
9961 Sierra Ave, Fontana (92335-6720)
P.O. Box None (92335)
PHONE..................909 427-3910
Gerald Mc Call, *Branch Mgr*

Jan Herrman, *Med Doctor*
Jack Yu, *Med Doctor*
Constance Koenig,
EMP: 99
SALES (corp-wide): 94.1B **Privately Held**
WEB: www.kaiser.com
SIC: 6324 Hospital & medical service plans
HQ: Kaiser Foundation Hospitals Inc
1 Kaiser Plz
Oakland CA 94612
510 271-6611

(P-10266)
KAISER FOUNDATION HOSPITALS
Also Called: Kaiser Foundation Health Plan
12200 Bellflower Blvd, Downey (90242-2804)
PHONE..................562 622-4190
Jim Harrington, *Branch Mgr*
Jacqueline Block, *Administration*
EMP: 99
SALES (corp-wide): 94.1B **Privately Held**
WEB: www.kaiser.com
SIC: 6324 Hospital & medical service plans
HQ: Kaiser Foundation Hospitals Inc
1 Kaiser Plz
Oakland CA 94612
510 271-6611

(P-10267)
KAISER FOUNDATION HOSPITALS
Also Called: CVS
5259 Mission Oaks Blvd, Camarillo (93012-5422)
PHONE..................805 482-0707
Brian Weiss, *Manager*
EMP: 99
SALES (corp-wide): 94.1B **Privately Held**
WEB: www.kaiser.com
SIC: 6324 Hospital & medical service plans
HQ: Kaiser Foundation Hospitals Inc
1 Kaiser Plz
Oakland CA 94612
510 271-6611

(P-10268)
KAISER FOUNDATION HOSPITALS
Also Called: Kaiser Foundation Health Plan
11666 Sherman Way, North Hollywood (91605-5831)
PHONE..................818 503-7082
Charles Ford, *Manager*
Brent Fratzke, *Vice Pres*
Karen Chang, *Director*
Kent Cox, *Director*
Cheryl Seifert, *Manager*
EMP: 53
SALES (corp-wide): 94.1B **Privately Held**
WEB: www.kaiser.com
SIC: 6324 Hospital & medical service plans
HQ: Kaiser Foundation Hospitals Inc
1 Kaiser Plz
Oakland CA 94612
510 271-6611

(P-10269)
KAISER FOUNDATION HOSPITALS
Also Called: Kaiser Foundation Health Plan
1625 I St, Modesto (95354-1121)
P.O. Box 577680 (95357-7680)
PHONE..................209 557-1000
Larry Stump, *Director*
Damon Ng, *Surgeon*
Amardeep S Deol, *Obstetrician*
Hongmei Meng, *Obstetrician*
Mayseng Lee, *Anesthesiology*
EMP: 60
SALES (corp-wide): 94.1B **Privately Held**
WEB: www.kaiser.com
SIC: 6324 Health maintenance organization (HMO), insurance only
HQ: Kaiser Foundation Hospitals Inc
1 Kaiser Plz
Oakland CA 94612
510 271-6611

(P-10270)
KAISER FOUNDATION HOSPITALS
Also Called: Kaiser Foundation Health Plan
200 N Lewis St Fl 1, Orange (92868-1538)
PHONE..................888 988-2800
Harriet Brown, *Director*
James De Fontes III, *Anesthesiology*
Siva Thuraiyur, *Manager*
EMP: 60
SALES (corp-wide): 94.1B **Privately Held**
WEB: www.kaiser.com
SIC: 6324 8011 Hospital & medical service plans; clinic, operated by physicians
HQ: Kaiser Foundation Hospitals Inc
1 Kaiser Plz
Oakland CA 94612
510 271-6611

(P-10271)
KAISER FOUNDATION HOSPITALS
Also Called: Kaiser Permanente
1900 E 4th St, Santa Ana (92705-3962)
PHONE..................714 967-4700
Martha Bieser, *Principal*
Dorothy L Siddall, *Family Practiti*
Jyotsna Thakkar, *Psychologist*
Tim Zung Tri Le, *Anesthesiology*
Paul C Rosandich, *Psychiatry*
EMP: 50
SALES (corp-wide): 94.1B **Privately Held**
WEB: www.kaiserpermanente.org
SIC: 6324 Hospital & medical service plans
HQ: Kaiser Foundation Hospitals Inc
1 Kaiser Plz
Oakland CA 94612
510 271-6611

(P-10272)
KAISER FUNDATION HLTH PLAN INC (PA)
1 Kaiser Plz, Oakland (94612-3610)
PHONE..................510 271-5800
Bernard J Tyson, *Ch of Bd*
John Rego, *Ch Radiology*
Gregory A Adams, *President*
Dave Underriner, *President*
Kathy Lancaster, *CFO*
EMP: 450 EST: 1955
SQ FT: 90,000
SALES (est): 94.1B **Privately Held**
WEB: www.kaiser.com
SIC: 6324 Health maintenance organization (HMO), insurance only

(P-10273)
KAISER FUNDATION HLTH PLAN INC
3801 Howe St, Oakland (94611-5312)
PHONE..................510 752-7644
EMP: 85
SALES (corp-wide): 94.1B **Privately Held**
SIC: 6324 Health maintenance organization (HMO), insurance only
PA: Kaiser Foundation Health Plan, Inc.
1 Kaiser Plz
Oakland CA 94612
510 271-5800

(P-10274)
KAISER FUNDATION HLTH PLAN INC
4460 Hacienda Dr, Pleasanton (94588-2761)
PHONE..................510 271-5800
Linsey Dicks, *Manager*
Manish Vipani, *Vice Pres*
Sudha Sharma, *Exec Dir*
Michael Won, *Program Mgr*
Fred Miller, *Administration*
EMP: 100
SALES (corp-wide): 94.1B **Privately Held**
WEB: www.kaiser.com
SIC: 6324 Health maintenance organization (HMO), insurance only
PA: Kaiser Foundation Health Plan, Inc.
1 Kaiser Plz
Oakland CA 94612
510 271-5800

(P-10275)
KAISER FUNDATION HLTH PLAN INC
1950 Franklin St Fl 3, Oakland (94612-5190)
PHONE..................510 987-2255
Jean Nudellman, *Manager*
EMP: 70
SALES (corp-wide): 94.1B **Privately Held**
WEB: www.kaiser.com
SIC: 6324 Health maintenance organization (HMO), insurance only
PA: Kaiser Foundation Health Plan, Inc.
1 Kaiser Plz
Oakland CA 94612
510 271-5800

(P-10276)
KAISER PERMANENTE ADMIN H
P.O. Box 12766 (94604-2766)
PHONE..................559 448-4405
EMP: 127
SALES (est): 11.7MM **Privately Held**
SIC: 6324 Hospital & medical service plans

(P-10277)
LIBERTY DENTAL PLAN CAL INC
340 Commerce Ste 100, Irvine (92602-1358)
PHONE..................949 223-0007
Amir Hossein Neshat, *Principal*
Stuart Gray, *COO*
Maja Kapic, *CFO*
John McCarthy, *General Mgr*
Eric Kim, *Info Tech Dir*
EMP: 300
SALES (est): 194.5MM **Privately Held**
SIC: 6324 Dental insurance

(P-10278)
LIBERTY DENTAL PLAN NEVADA INC
340 Commerce, Irvine (92602-1334)
PHONE..................888 703-6999
Amir Neshat, *President*
EMP: 54
SALES (est): 7.1MM **Privately Held**
SIC: 6324 Dental insurance

(P-10279)
LOCAL INITIATIVE HEALTH AUTHOR
Also Called: L.A. Care Health Plan
1055 W 7th St Fl 10, Los Angeles (90017-2750)
PHONE..................213 694-1250
John Baackes, *CEO*
Dino Kasdagly, *COO*
Marie Montgomery, *CFO*
Tim Reilly, *CFO*
Andrea Van Hook, *Bd of Directors*
EMP: 900
SALES (est): 329.7MM **Privately Held**
SIC: 6324 Health maintenance organization (HMO), insurance only

(P-10280)
MANAGED HEALTH NETWORK
7755 Center Ave Ste 700, Huntington Beach (92647-9126)
PHONE..................714 934-5519
Carol McLean, *Branch Mgr*
Dewitt Whitehurst, *Manager*
EMP: 580 **Publicly Held**
SIC: 6324 Hospital & medical service plans
HQ: Managed Health Network
2370 Kerner Blvd
San Rafael CA 94901
415 460-8168

(P-10281)
MANAGED HEALTH NETWORK (DH)
2370 Kerner Blvd, San Rafael (94901-5546)
P.O. Box 10207 (94912-0207)
PHONE..................415 460-8168
Jeffrey Bairstow, *CEO*
Jerry Coil, *President*
Steven Sell, *President*
Linda Brisbane, *COO*
Jonathan Wormhoudt, *COO*
EMP: 500
SQ FT: 97,314

SALES (est): 199.5MM **Publicly Held**
SIC: 6324 8099 8093 8011 Hospital &
medical service plans; health maintenance organization (HMO), insurance
only; medical services organization; specialty outpatient clinics; offices & clinics of
medical doctors

(P-10282)
MANAGED HEALTH NETWORK
2370 Kerner Blvd, San Rafael
(94901-5546)
P.O. Box 10207 (94912-0207)
PHONE....................................510 620-6143
John Crocker, *Branch Mgr*
EMP: 1100 **Publicly Held**
SIC: 6324 Hospital & medical service plans
HQ: Managed Health Network
2370 Kerner Blvd
San Rafael CA 94901
415 460-8168

(P-10283)
MHN SERVICES
2370 Kerner Blvd, San Rafael
(94901-5546)
PHONE....................................415 460-8300
Juanell Hefner, *President*
EMP: 1000
SALES: 87MM **Publicly Held**
SIC: 6324 8011 8742 8322 Hospital &
medical service plans; health mainte-
nance organization; management consult-
ing services; social service center
HQ: Health Net, Inc.
21650 Oxnard St Fl 25
Woodland Hills CA 91367

(P-10284)
MOLINA HEALTHCARE INC
1500 Hughes Way, Long Beach
(90810-1870)
PHONE....................................310 221-3031
Ravi Potlachervu, *Administration*
Sathiyaraj Thangavel, *Info Tech Mgr*
James Mandas, *Manager*
EMP: 269
SALES (corp-wide): 19.8B **Publicly Held**
SIC: 6324 6321 Hospital & medical serv-
ice plans; accident & health insurance
PA: Molina Healthcare, Inc.
200 Oceangate Ste 100
Long Beach CA 90802
562 435-3666

(P-10285)
ON LOK SENIOR HEALTH SERVICES (PA)
Also Called: On Lok Lifeways
1333 Bush St, San Francisco
(94109-5691)
PHONE....................................415 292-8888
Robert Edmondson, *CEO*
Grace LI, *COO*
Sue Wong, *CFO*
David Ng, *Executive*
Charlotte Carlson, *Associate Dir*
EMP: 570
SQ FT: 40,000
SALES: 120.9MM **Privately Held**
SIC: 6324 8082 Health maintenance or-
ganization (HMO), insurance only; home
health care services

(P-10286)
ON LOK SENIOR HEALTH SERVICES
Also Called: On Lok Life Ways
3683 Peralta Blvd, Fremont (94536-3708)
PHONE....................................510 249-2700
Janice Fujii, *Manager*
Sandra Aguayo, *Human Res Mgr*
EMP: 50
SALES (corp-wide): 120.9MM **Privately
Held**
SIC: 6324 8082 Health maintenance or-
ganization (HMO), insurance only; home
health care services
PA: On Lok Senior Health Services
1333 Bush St
San Francisco CA 94109
415 292-8888

(P-10287)
OPTUMRX INC
Also Called: Prescription Solutions
2858 Loker Ave E Ste 100, Carlsbad
(92010-6673)
P.O. Box 509075, San Diego (92150-9075)
PHONE....................................760 804-2399
Sean O'Rourke, *Manager*
Mac Cruz, *Mfg Staff*
Erin Paez, *Supervisor*
EMP: 400
SALES (corp-wide): 201.1B **Publicly
Held**
SIC: 6324 Hospital & medical service plans
HQ: Optumrx, Inc.
2300 Main St
Irvine CA 92614

(P-10288)
OPTUMRX INC (DH)
Also Called: Prescription Solutions
2300 Main St, Irvine (92614-6223)
P.O. Box 509075, San Diego (92150-9075)
PHONE....................................714 825-3600
Mark Thierer, *CEO*
Timothy Wicks, *President*
Jeff Park, *COO*
Jeffrey Grosklags, *CFO*
Todd Ebersole, *Vice Pres*
EMP: 300
SALES (est): 21.6B
SALES (corp-wide): 201.1B **Publicly
Held**
SIC: 6324 6321 Hospital & medical serv-
ice plans; accident & health insurance
HQ: United Healthcare Services Inc.
9900 Bren Rd E Ste 300w
Minnetonka MN 55343
952 936-1300

(P-10289)
PACIFICARE DENTAL
3110 W Lake Center Dr, Santa Ana
(92704-6917)
P.O. Box 25187 (92799-5187)
PHONE....................................661 631-8613
Jerry Vaccaro, *President*
EMP: 195 **EST:** 1972
SQ FT: 5,000
SALES (est): 55.9MM
SALES (corp-wide): 201.1B **Publicly
Held**
SIC: 6324 Dental insurance
HQ: Pacificare Health Plan Administrators,
Inc.
3120 W Lake Center Dr
Santa Ana CA 92704
714 825-5200

(P-10290)
PACIFICARE HEALTH PLAN ADMIN (DH)
3120 W Lake Center Dr, Santa Ana
(92704-6917)
P.O. Box 25186 (92799-5186)
PHONE....................................714 825-5200
David Reed, *Ch of Bd*
Coy F Baugh, *Treasurer*
Debra Lord, *Project Mgr*
Marilyn Drysch, *VP Finance*
Marcia Ford, *Accounts Mgr*
EMP: 400 **EST:** 1975
SQ FT: 220,000
SALES: 12.2B
SALES (corp-wide): 201.1B **Publicly
Held**
SIC: 6324 Group hospitalization plans

(P-10291)
PACIFICARE HEALTH SYSTEMS LLC (HQ)
5995 Plaza Dr, Cypress (90630-5028)
PHONE....................................714 952-1121
Howard Phanstiel, *CEO*
Felicia D Davis, *Partner*
Tim Rhatigan, *Vice Pres*
Christine Vargas, *Executive*
Nikkie Pool, *Executive Asst*
EMP: 550
SQ FT: 104,000

SALES (est): 12.7B
SALES (corp-wide): 201.1B **Publicly
Held**
WEB: www.pacificare.com
SIC: 6324 Health maintenance organiza-
tion (HMO), insurance only
PA: Unitedhealth Group Incorporated
9900 Bren Rd E Ste 300w
Minnetonka MN 55343
952 936-1300

(P-10292)
PACIFICDENTAL BENEFITS INC (PA)
2300 Clayton Rd Ste 1000, Concord
(94520-2168)
PHONE....................................925 363-6000
John Gaebel, *President*
Randy Breacher, *CFO*
Nilesh Patel, *Vice Pres*
EMP: 145
SQ FT: 18,530
SALES (est): 40.5MM **Privately Held**
SIC: 6324 6321 Dental insurance; acci-
dent & health insurance

(P-10293)
PARTNERSHIP HEALTH PLAN CAL
4665 Business Center Dr, Fairfield
(94534-1675)
PHONE....................................707 863-4100
Jack Horn, *CEO*
Liz Gibboney, *COO*
Gary Erickson, *CFO*
Noemi Perez, *Admin Asst*
Barbara Selig, *Project Mgr*
EMP: 290
SQ FT: 75,000
SALES (est): 231.9MM **Privately Held**
SIC: 6324 Health maintenance organiza-
tion (HMO), insurance only

(P-10294)
PERMANENTE MEDICAL GROUP INC
220 Oyster Point Blvd, South San Fran-
cisco (94080-1911)
PHONE....................................650 827-6500
Milan Patel, *Branch Mgr*
EMP: 70
SALES (corp-wide): 94.1B **Privately Held**
SIC: 6324 Hospital & medical service plans
HQ: The Permanente Medical Group Inc
1950 Franklin St Fl 18th
Oakland CA 94612
866 858-2226

(P-10295)
PERMANENTE MEDICAL GROUP INC
900 Veterans Blvd Ste 400, Redwood City
(94063-1742)
PHONE....................................650 598-2852
Diana Patino, *Principal*
EMP: 70
SALES (corp-wide): 94.1B **Privately Held**
SIC: 6324 Hospital & medical service plans
HQ: The Permanente Medical Group Inc
1950 Franklin St Fl 18th
Oakland CA 94612
866 858-2226

(P-10296)
PERMANENTE MEDICAL GROUP INC
1725 Eastshore Hwy, Berkeley
(94710-1703)
PHONE....................................510 559-5119
Susan Yee, *Administration*
Mario Villanueva, *Purch Agent*
EMP: 58
SALES (corp-wide): 94.1B **Privately Held**
WEB: www.permanente.net
SIC: 6324 Hospital & medical service plans
HQ: The Permanente Medical Group Inc
1950 Franklin St Fl 18th
Oakland CA 94612
866 858-2226

(P-10297)
PERMANENTE MEDICAL GROUP INC
2238 Geary Blvd, San Francisco
(94115-3416)
PHONE....................................415 833-2000
Philip R Madvig MD *Physn, Principal*
Gregory Chang,
Gregory V Mandrussow, *Emerg Med Spec*
Dee Marie Munoz, *Pharmacist*
EMP: 140
SALES (corp-wide): 94.1B **Privately Held**
WEB: www.permanente.net
SIC: 6324 Hospital & medical service plans
HQ: The Permanente Medical Group Inc
1950 Franklin St Fl 18th
Oakland CA 94612
866 858-2226

(P-10298)
PERMANENTE MEDICAL GROUP INC
1550 Gateway Blvd, Fairfield (94533-6901)
PHONE....................................707 427-4000
Laura Coffman, *Branch Mgr*
Georgina Jensen, *Med Doctor*
Pat Van Nordstrom, *Manager*
EMP: 50
SALES (corp-wide): 94.1B **Privately Held**
WEB: www.permanente.net
SIC: 6324 Hospital & medical service plans
HQ: The Permanente Medical Group Inc
1950 Franklin St Fl 18th
Oakland CA 94612
866 858-2226

(P-10299)
PERMANENTE MEDICAL GROUP INC
3555 Whipple Rd, Union City (94587-1507)
PHONE....................................510 675-4010
Deana Medinas, *Director*
Richard Barth, *Psychologist*
Laura Cayan, *Psychologist*
Teresa Matazzoni, *Psychologist*
Winnie Cheung, *Obstetrician*
EMP: 100
SALES (corp-wide): 94.1B **Privately Held**
WEB: www.permanente.net
SIC: 6324 Hospital & medical service plans
HQ: The Permanente Medical Group Inc
1950 Franklin St Fl 18th
Oakland CA 94612
866 858-2226

(P-10300)
PERMANENTE MEDICAL GROUP INC
Also Called: Kaiser Prmnnte Modesto Med
Ctr
4601 Dale Rd, Modesto (95356-9718)
PHONE....................................209 735-5000
Jennifer A Beard, *Principal*
Monie Abundiz, *Records Dir*
Anita Boronowsky, *Analyst*
Natalie Lee, *Anesthesiology*
Scott Knight, *Manager*
EMP: 63
SALES (corp-wide): 94.1B **Privately Held**
SIC: 6324 Hospital & medical service plans
HQ: The Permanente Medical Group Inc
1950 Franklin St Fl 18th
Oakland CA 94612
866 858-2226

(P-10301)
PHYSICIAN ASSOC SAN GABRIEL
199 S Los Robles Ave, Pasadena
(91101-2452)
PHONE....................................626 817-8300
Barton Wald MD, *President*
Theresa David, *COO*
EMP: 210
SALES (est): 65.1MM **Privately Held**
WEB: www.physicianassoc.com
SIC: 6324 Health maintenance organiza-
tion (HMO), insurance only

(P-10302)
PRIVATE MEDICAL-CARE INC
12898 Towne Center Dr, Cerritos
(90703-8546)
PHONE....................................562 924-8311
Robert Elliott, *President*

(PA)=Parent Co (HQ)=Headquarters (DH)=Div Headquarters
✪ = New Business established in last 2 years

EMP: 154 **EST:** 1970
SALES (est): 40.4MM
SALES (corp-wide): 5.8B **Privately Held**
WEB: www.deltadentalca.org
SIC: 6324 Dental insurance
PA: Delta Dental Of California
　　560 Mission St Fl 13
　　San Francisco CA 94105
　　415 972-8300

(P-10303)
PRUDENTIAL INSUR CO OF AMER
180 Montgomery St # 1900, San Francisco (94104-4278)
PHONE..................................415 486-3050
Tom Rhee, *Manager*
EMP: 97
SALES (corp-wide): 59.6B **Publicly Held**
SIC: 6324 6321 6311 6411 Health maintenance organization (HMO), insurance only; accident & health insurance; life insurance; insurance agents
HQ: The Prudential Insurance Company Of America
　　751 Broad St
　　Newark NJ 07102
　　973 802-6000

(P-10304)
REW INC
973 Higuera St Ste A, San Luis Obispo (93401-3614)
PHONE..................................805 541-1308
Robert Wacker, *CEO*
Sarah Robertson, *Admin Asst*
EMP: 63
SALES: 950K **Privately Held**
SIC: 6324 Hospital & medical service plans

(P-10305)
SAFEGUARD HEALTH ENTERPRISES (HQ)
95 Enterprise Ste 100, Aliso Viejo (92656-2605)
PHONE..................................949 425-4300
Steven J Baileys DDS, *Ch of Bd*
James E Buncher, *President*
Stephen J Baker, *COO*
Dennis L Gates, *CFO*
Ronald I Brendzel, *Senior VP*
EMP: 355
SQ FT: 68,000
SALES (est): 105.6MM
SALES (corp-wide): 62.3B **Publicly Held**
SIC: 6324 Dental insurance
PA: Metlife, Inc.
　　200 Park Ave
　　New York NY 10166
　　212 578-9500

(P-10306)
SCAN CALIFORNIA MANAGEMENT CO
3800 Kilroy Airport Way, Long Beach (90806-2494)
PHONE..................................562 989-5100
Chris Wing, *CEO*
EMP: 968
SALES (est): 1.1MM
SALES (corp-wide): 2.2B **Privately Held**
SIC: 6324 Hospital & medical service plans
PA: Scan Group
　　3800 Kilroy Arprt Way # 100
　　Long Beach CA 90806
　　562 308-2733

(P-10307)
SCAN GROUP (PA)
3800 Kilroy Arprt Way # 100, Long Beach (90806-2494)
PHONE..................................562 308-2733
Chris Wing, *CEO*
Vinod Mohan, *CFO*
Janet Kornblatt, *Admin Sec*
EMP: 306 **EST:** 1983
SALES (est): 2.2B **Privately Held**
SIC: 6324 Hospital & medical service plans

(P-10308)
SECOND OPINION MED GRP INC
2876 Sycamore Dr Ste 305, Simi Valley (93065-1550)
PHONE..................................805 496-4315
Rajeswari Ananda, *Principal*

Punita Khanna, *Vice Pres*
EMP: 99
SQ FT: 1,500
SALES (est): 13.1MM **Privately Held**
SIC: 6324 Hospital & medical service plans

(P-10309)
SENIOR CARE (PA)
Also Called: Scan Health Plan
3800 Kilroy Airport Way, Long Beach (90806-2494)
P.O. Box 22616 (90801-5616)
PHONE..................................562 989-5100
David Schmidt, *CEO*
Dennis Eder, *CFO*
Douglas Jaques, *Senior VP*
Rebecca Learner, *Senior VP*
Virginia Havai, *Vice Pres*
EMP: 857
SQ FT: 119,219
SALES (est): 329.7MM **Privately Held**
WEB: www.scanhealthplan.com
SIC: 6324 Health maintenance organization (HMO), insurance only

(P-10310)
SENIOR CARE
Also Called: Independence At Home lah
2501 Cherry Ave Ste 380, Long Beach (90755-2050)
PHONE..................................562 492-9878
Kit Donaldson, *Branch Mgr*
Denise Likar, *Exec Dir*
EMP: 55
SALES (est): 4.6MM
SALES (corp-wide): 329.7MM **Privately Held**
WEB: www.scanhealthplan.com
SIC: 6324 Health maintenance organization (HMO), insurance only
PA: Senior Care Action Network Foundation
　　3800 Kilroy Airport Way
　　Long Beach CA 90806
　　562 989-5100

(P-10311)
SHARP HEALTH PLAN
8520 Tech Way Ste 200, San Diego (92123-1450)
PHONE..................................858 499-8300
Melissa Hayden-Cook, *President*
Leslie Pels-Beck, *COO*
Rita Datko, *CFO*
Michael Byrd, *Vice Pres*
Dr Cary Shames, *Vice Pres*
EMP: 98
SALES: 322.6MM
SALES (corp-wide): 3.4B **Privately Held**
SIC: 6324 Health maintenance organization (HMO), insurance only
PA: Sharp Healthcare
　　8695 Spectrum Center Blvd
　　San Diego CA 92123
　　858 499-4000

(P-10312)
SOUTHERN CAL PRMNNTE MED GROUP
13652 Cantara St, Panorama City (91402-5423)
PHONE..................................800 272-3500
Arthur Phelps, *Branch Mgr*
Earle Johnson, *Officer*
Steve Spickler, *Vice Pres*
Francisco Meza, *Opers Staff*
Michele Turner, *Family Practiti*
EMP: 70
SALES (corp-wide): 3.5B **Privately Held**
SIC: 6324 Hospital & medical service plans
PA: Southern California Permanente Medical Group
　　393 Walnut Dr
　　Pasadena CA 91107
　　626 405-5704

(P-10313)
SOUTHERN CAL PRMNNTE MED GROUP
Also Called: Kaiser Foundation Health Plan
5855 Copley Dr Ste 250, San Diego (92111-7908)
PHONE..................................858 974-1000
Tom Cooper, *Manager*
Travis Van Ness, *Admin Asst*
James Badiner, *Director*
EMP: 75

SQ FT: 89,984
SALES (corp-wide): 3.5B **Privately Held**
WEB: www.kaiser.com
SIC: 6324 Health maintenance organization (HMO), insurance only
PA: Southern California Permanente Medical Group
　　393 Walnut Dr
　　Pasadena CA 91107
　　626 405-5704

(P-10314)
SOUTHERN CAL PRMNNTE MED GROUP
10800 Magnolia Ave, Riverside (92505-3043)
PHONE..................................866 984-7483
Jeffrey A Weisz, *Principal*
EMP: 262
SALES (corp-wide): 3.5B **Privately Held**
SIC: 6324 Hospital & medical service plans
PA: Southern California Permanente Medical Group
　　393 Walnut Dr
　　Pasadena CA 91107
　　626 405-5704

(P-10315)
SOUTHERN CAL PRMNNTE MED GROUP
1511 W Garvey Ave N, West Covina (91790-2138)
PHONE..................................626 960-4844
Jim Chomchai, *Psychiatry*
Novellyn Heard, *Psychiatry*
Jarvis Ngati, *Psychiatry*
Christine L Um, *Psychiatry*
EMP: 70
SALES (corp-wide): 3.5B **Privately Held**
SIC: 6324 Hospital & medical service plans
PA: Southern California Permanente Medical Group
　　393 Walnut Dr
　　Pasadena CA 91107
　　626 405-5704

(P-10316)
SOUTHERN CAL PRMNNTE MED GROUP
Also Called: Tustin Executive Center
17542 17th St Ste 300, Tustin (92780-1960)
PHONE..................................714 734-4500
Adamma Agufoh, *Director*
EMP: 70
SALES (corp-wide): 3.5B **Privately Held**
SIC: 6324 Hospital & medical service plans
PA: Southern California Permanente Medical Group
　　393 Walnut Dr
　　Pasadena CA 91107
　　626 405-5704

(P-10317)
SOUTHERN CAL PRMNNTE MED GROUP (PA)
Also Called: Kaiser Permanente
393 Walnut Dr, Pasadena (91107)
PHONE..................................626 405-5704
Bernard J Tyson, *Principal*
Diana Atkinson, *Project Mgr*
Marguerite Koster, *Technology*
Pam Asbill, *Analyst*
Javan Wygal, *Corp Comm Staff*
EMP: 60 **EST:** 1981
SQ FT: 600,000
SALES (est): 3.5B **Privately Held**
SIC: 6324 Health maintenance organization (HMO), insurance only

(P-10318)
SOUTHERN CAL PRMNNTE MED GROUP
Also Called: S C P M G
1255 W Arrow Hwy, San Dimas (91773-2340)
PHONE..................................909 394-2505
EMP: 50
SALES (corp-wide): 3.5B **Privately Held**
WEB: www.permanente.net
SIC: 6324 Health maintenance organization (HMO), insurance only

PA: Southern California Permanente Medical Group
　　393 Walnut Dr
　　Pasadena CA 91107
　　626 405-5704

(P-10319)
SOUTHERN CAL PRMNNTE MED GROUP
6860 Avenida Encinas, Carlsbad (92011-3201)
PHONE..................................619 528-5000
Walter Borschel, *Administration*
Luis Esquenazi, *Family Practiti*
EMP: 532
SALES (corp-wide): 3.5B **Privately Held**
SIC: 6324 Hospital & medical service plans
PA: Southern California Permanente Medical Group
　　393 Walnut Dr
　　Pasadena CA 91107
　　626 405-5704

(P-10320)
SOUTHERN CAL PRMNNTE MED GROUP
Also Called: Kaiser Permanente
9353 Imprl Hwy Grdn Med, Downey (90242)
PHONE..................................562 657-2200
Connie Pinkerton, *Project Mgr*
Richard Arnell, *Family Practiti*
Elizabeth Norheim, *Orthopedist*
Naren Gurbani, *Surgeon*
Jamie S Drinville, *Obstetrician*
EMP: 4341
SALES (corp-wide): 3.5B **Privately Held**
SIC: 6324 Hospital & medical service plans
PA: Southern California Permanente Medical Group
　　393 Walnut Dr
　　Pasadena CA 91107
　　626 405-5704

(P-10321)
SUPERIOR VISION SERVICES INC (PA)
11101 White Rock Rd # 150, Rancho Cordova (95670-6998)
PHONE..................................916 859-6218
Kirk Rothrock, *CEO*
Jonathan Bicknell, *CFO*
Brian Silverberg, *CFO*
Kimberley Hess, *Senior VP*
Stephanie Lucas, *Senior VP*
EMP: 53
SQ FT: 12,000
SALES (est): 50.6MM **Privately Held**
WEB: www.superiorvision.com
SIC: 6324 Hospital & medical service plans

(P-10322)
UHC OF CALIFORNIA (DH)
Also Called: Pacificare of California
5995 Plaza Dr, Cypress (90630-5028)
PHONE..................................714 952-1121
Brad A Bowlus, *Principal*
Michael Montevideo, *Treasurer*
Phyllis Graham, *Regional Mgr*
Lisa Espinosa, *Branch Mgr*
Joseph S Konowiecki, *Admin Sec*
EMP: 800
SALES (est): 257.3MM
SALES (corp-wide): 201.1B **Publicly Held**
WEB: www.rxsol.com
SIC: 6324 8732 Health maintenance organization (HMO), insurance only; commercial nonphysical research

(P-10323)
UNITED BEHAVIORAL HEALTH
Also Called: Pacificare
2300 Clayton Rd Ste 1000, Concord (94520-2168)
PHONE..................................925 246-1343
Fred Dodson, *Branch Mgr*
Kelly Ferber, *Accounts Mgr*
EMP: 150
SALES (corp-wide): 201.1B **Publicly Held**
WEB: www.unitedbehavioralhealth.com
SIC: 6324 Health maintenance organization (HMO), insurance only

HQ: United Behavioral Health
425 Market St Fl 18
San Francisco CA 94105
415 547-1403

(P-10324)
UNITEDHEALTH GROUP INC
Also Called: Pacificare Health Systems
7891 Moonmist Cir, Huntington Beach
(92648-5434)
PHONE.................................714 969-9050
Andrew Hall, *Branch Mgr*
EMP: 300
SALES (corp-wide): 201.1B **Publicly Held**
WEB: www.unitedhealthgroup.com
SIC: 6324 Health maintenance organization (HMO), insurance only
PA: Unitedhealth Group Incorporated
9900 Bren Rd E Ste 300w
Minnetonka MN 55343
952 936-1300

(P-10325)
UNITEDHEALTH GROUP INC
Also Called: Pacificare Health Systems
5701 Katella Ave, Cypress (90630-5006)
PHONE.................................952 936-1300
Mike Wallace, *Branch Mgr*
Tim Yee, *Vice Pres*
Frank Mesa, *Info Tech Mgr*
Ashok Neelameham, *Applctn Conslt*
Tracy Kamehaiku, *Business Mgr*
EMP: 100
SALES (corp-wide): 201.1B **Publicly Held**
WEB: www.unitedhealthgroup.com
SIC: 6324 Health maintenance organization (HMO), insurance only
PA: Unitedhealth Group Incorporated
9900 Bren Rd E Ste 300w
Minnetonka MN 55343
952 936-1300

(P-10326)
UNITEDHEALTH GROUP INC
2080 E 20th St, Chico (95928-7702)
PHONE.................................530 879-8251
Erica Lajoie, *Administration*
Shannon Cloud, *Opers Spvr*
Mark Franks, *Opers Staff*
EMP: 270
SALES (corp-wide): 201.1B **Publicly Held**
SIC: 6324 Health maintenance organization (HMO), insurance only
PA: Unitedhealth Group Incorporated
9900 Bren Rd E Ste 300w
Minnetonka MN 55343
952 936-1300

(P-10327)
VISION SERVICE PLAN (PA)
Also Called: C V S Optical Lab Div
3333 Quality Dr, Rancho Cordova
(95670-9757)
P.O. Box 997100, Sacramento (95899-7100)
PHONE.................................916 851-5000
James Robinson Lynch, *CEO*
Laura Costa, *COO*
Donald J Ball Jr, *CFO*
Gary Brooks, *Senior VP*
Gary Norman Brooks, *Vice Pres*
▲ **EMP:** 1600
SQ FT: 300,000
SALES (est): 3.2B **Privately Held**
WEB: www.vsp.com
SIC: 6324 5048 Hospital & medical service plans; ophthalmic goods

(P-10328)
VSP HOLDING COMPANY INC
3333 Quality Dr, Rancho Cordova
(95670-7985)
PHONE.................................916 851-5000
James Robinson Lynch, *CEO*
EMP: 52
SALES (est): 22.9MM **Privately Held**
SIC: 6324 Hospital & medical service plans

6331 Fire, Marine & Casualty Insurance

(P-10329)
AAA TRAVEL
1650 S Delaware St, San Mateo
(94402-2623)
PHONE.................................650 572-5600
Monica Iskander, *Manager*
EMP: 50
SALES (est): 3.8MM **Privately Held**
SIC: 6331 Automobile insurance

(P-10330)
ALLIANZ GLOBL RISKS US INSUR (DH)
2350 W Empire Ave, Burbank
(91504-3350)
P.O. Box 7780 (91510-7780)
PHONE.................................818 260-7500
Hugh Burgess, *CEO*
Paul Yun, *President*
Randy Renn, *CFO*
Edwin Van Zijll, *Vice Pres*
Victoria Gillette, *IT/INT Sup*
▲ **EMP:** 175
SQ FT: 20,000
SALES (est): 466.4MM **Privately Held**
SIC: 6331 Property damage insurance; fire, marine & casualty insurance & carriers; workers' compensation insurance
HQ: Fireman's Fund Insurance Company
1465 N Mcdowell Blvd # 100
Petaluma CA 94954
415 899-2000

(P-10331)
ALLIANZ GLOBL RISKS US INSUR
Also Called: Allianz Insurance Company
1465 N Mcdowell Blvd, Petaluma
(94954-6516)
PHONE.................................415 899-3758
Lori Oaks, *Manager*
EMP: 400 **Privately Held**
SIC: 6331 Fire, marine & casualty insurance
HQ: Allianz Global Risks Us Insurance Company
2350 W Empire Ave
Burbank CA 91504
818 260-7500

(P-10332)
ALLIANZ UNDERWRITERS INSUR CO
Also Called: Allianz Globl Corp & Specialty
2350 W Empire Ave, Burbank
(91504-3350)
PHONE.................................818 260-7500
Paul Yun, *Vice Pres*
Joel Kim, *Administration*
Lorrie Leonard, *Assistant VP*
EMP: 86
SALES (est): 39.4MM **Privately Held**
WEB: www.azoa.com
SIC: 6331 Fire, marine & casualty insurance
HQ: Allianz Of America, Inc.
55 Greens Farms Rd Ste 1
Westport CT 06880
203 221-8500

(P-10333)
ALLSTATE INSURANCE COMPANY
21950 Copley Dr Ste 130, Diamond Bar
(91765-4461)
PHONE.................................909 612-5504
EMP: 1005 **Publicly Held**
SIC: 6331 6351 Fire, marine & casualty insurance: stock; automobile insurance; property damage insurance; mortgage guarantee insurance
HQ: Allstate Insurance Company
2775 Sanders Rd
Northbrook IL 60062
847 402-5000

(P-10334)
AMERICAN AUTOMOBILE ASSCTN
Also Called: Csaa Insurance AAA
1501 Farmers Ln, Santa Rosa
(95405-7525)
P.O. Box 2906 (95405-0906)
PHONE.................................707 566-4000
Al Holcomb, *Branch Mgr*
EMP: 125
SALES (corp-wide): 907.9MM **Privately Held**
WEB: www.californiastateautomobileassociation.c
SIC: 6331 4724 6311 Automobile insurance; tourist agency arranging transport, lodging & car rental; life insurance
PA: American Automobile Association Of Northern California, Nevada & Utah
1900 Powell St Ste 1200
Emeryville CA 94608
800 922-8228

(P-10335)
AMERICAN AUTOMOBILE ASSOCIATIO
Also Called: Csaa Travel Agency
1277 Treat Blvd Ste 1000, Walnut Creek
(94597-8863)
PHONE.................................510 596-3669
EMP: 400
SALES (est): 13.4MM **Privately Held**
SIC: 6331 8699 Automobile insurance; automobile owners' association

(P-10336)
AMERICAN HOME ASSURANCE CO
777 S Figueroa St Ste 300, Los Angeles
(90017-5801)
PHONE.................................213 689-3500
Lynn Schwertner, *Branch Mgr*
EMP: 300
SALES (corp-wide): 49.5B **Publicly Held**
WEB:
www.americanhomeassuranceco.com
SIC: 6331 7371 Fire, marine & casualty insurance; custom computer programming services
HQ: American Home Assurance Co Inc
70 Pine St Fl 1
New York NY 10005
212 770-7000

(P-10337)
AMERICAN INSURANCE COMPANY INC
1465 N Mcdowell Blvd, Petaluma
(94954-6516)
PHONE.................................415 899-2000
Mike Larocco, *President*
Eileen Godwin, *Site Mgr*
Bob Lane, *Program Dir*
Shellie Filkins, *Consultant*
EMP: 4400
SALES (est): 329.7MM **Privately Held**
SIC: 6331 Fire, marine & casualty insurance
PA: Allianz Se
Koniginstr. 28
Munchen 80802
893 800-0

(P-10338)
AMICA MUTUAL INSURANCE COMPANY
3200 Park Center Dr # 650, Costa Mesa
(92626-7163)
PHONE.................................877 972-6422
Robert Mc Girr, *Principal*
EMP: 60
SALES (corp-wide): 2B **Privately Held**
WEB: www.amica.com
SIC: 6331 Fire, marine & casualty insurance: mutual
PA: Amica Mutual Insurance Company
100 Amica Way
Lincoln RI 02865
800 992-6422

(P-10339)
ARROWHEAD GEN INSUR AGCY INC (DH)
701 B St Ste 2100, San Diego
(92101-8197)
PHONE.................................619 881-8600
Chris L Walker, *CEO*
Peter C Arrowsmith, *General Ptnr*
Steve Boyd, *President*
Wendy Castelo, *President*
Robert T Kingsley, *President*
EMP: 240
SQ FT: 74,000
SALES (est): 222.3MM
SALES (corp-wide): 1.8B **Publicly Held**
SIC: 6331 6411 Automobile insurance; insurance agents, brokers & service
HQ: Arrowhead Management Company
701 B St Ste 2100
San Diego CA 92101
800 669-1889

(P-10340)
CA STE ATOM ASSOC INTR-INS BUR
Also Called: Via Magazine
150 Van Ness Ave, San Francisco
(94102-5200)
PHONE.................................415 565-2012
Kent Evans, *Branch Mgr*
EMP: 2000
SALES (corp-wide): 907.9MM **Privately Held**
WEB: www.viamagazine.com
SIC: 6331 2721 Automobile insurance; property damage insurance; magazines: publishing & printing
HQ: California State Automobile Association Inter-Insurance Bureau
1276 S California Blvd
Walnut Creek CA 94596
925 287-7600

(P-10341)
CA STE ATOM ASSOC INTR-INS BUR
Also Called: AAA
1650 S Delaware St, San Mateo
(94402-2623)
PHONE.................................650 572-5600
Rita Timewell, *Manager*
Lori Avila, *Sales Staff*
EMP: 100
SALES (corp-wide): 907.9MM **Privately Held**
WEB: www.viamagazine.com
SIC: 6331 6411 Automobile insurance; property & casualty insurance agent
HQ: California State Automobile Association Inter-Insurance Bureau
1276 S California Blvd
Walnut Creek CA 94596
925 287-7600

(P-10342)
CALIFORNIA AUTOMOBILE INSUR CO
Also Called: Cai Company
555 W Imperial Hwy, Brea (92821-4802)
P.O. Box 1150 (92822-1150)
PHONE.................................714 232-8669
George Joseph, *President*
Leo Lam, *CFO*
EMP: 800
SQ FT: 80,000
SALES (est): 617.8MM
SALES (corp-wide): 3.4B **Publicly Held**
WEB: www.californiaautomobileinsurance-company.com
SIC: 6331 Automobile insurance
PA: Mercury General Corporation
4484 Wilshire Blvd
Los Angeles CA 90010
323 937-1060

(P-10343)
CALIFORNIA CAPITAL INSUR CO (PA)
Also Called: Capital Insurance Group
2300 Garden Rd, Monterey (93940-5326)
P.O. Box 3110 (93942-3110)
PHONE.................................831 233-5500
L Arnold Chatterton, *President*
Andrew Doll, *COO*
Davis Tyndall, *CFO*

Walter Benett, *Vice Pres*
John Halberstadt, *Vice Pres*
EMP: 142
SQ FT: 50,000
SALES: 200.7MM **Privately Held**
SIC: 6331 Fire, marine & casualty insurance & carriers; automobile insurance

(P-10344)
CALIFORNIA CASUALTY MGT CO (HQ)
Also Called: California Casualty
1875 S Grant St Ste 800, San Mateo (94402-7030)
PHONE................................650 574-4000
Carl B Brown, *Ch of Bd*
Joseph L Volponi, *President*
Michael Ray, *CFO*
James R Englese, *Senior VP*
Michael Bower, *Vice Pres*
EMP: 135
SALES: 119.2MM
SALES (corp-wide): 239.8MM **Privately Held**
SIC: 6331 8741 Reciprocal interinsurance exchanges: fire, marine, casualty; management services
PA: California Casualty Indemnity Exchange
1900 Almeda De Las Pulgas
San Mateo CA 94403
650 574-4000

(P-10345)
CALIFORNIA STATE AUTOMOBILE (HQ)
Also Called: Triple A
1276 S California Blvd, Walnut Creek (94596-5123)
P.O. Box 22221, Oakland (94623-2221)
PHONE................................925 287-7600
James R Pouliot, *CEO*
Paula Downey, *President*
Tuan Chung, *Technology*
Carrie Tabor, *Human Resources*
Michele Salmon, *Marketing Staff*
EMP: 1600
SQ FT: 400,000
SALES (est): 880.6MM
SALES (corp-wide): 907.9MM **Privately Held**
WEB: www.viamagazine.com
SIC: 6331 Automobile insurance
PA: American Automobile Association Of Northern California, Nevada & Utah
1900 Powell St Ste 1200
Emeryville CA 94608
800 922-8228

(P-10346)
CALIFRNIA CSLTY INDEMNITY EXCH (PA)
1900 Almeda De Las Pulgas, San Mateo (94403-1222)
PHONE................................650 574-4000
Thomas R Brown, *Chairman*
Mike Ray, *CFO*
EMP: 130 **EST:** 1914
SQ FT: 90,000
SALES: 239.8MM **Privately Held**
SIC: 6331 Workers' compensation insurance; automobile insurance; property damage insurance; fire, marine & casualty insurance & carriers

(P-10347)
COMMERCIAL CARRIERS INSUR AGCY
4 Centerpointe Dr Ste 300, La Palma (90623-1074)
PHONE................................562 404-4900
Charles J Escalante, *President*
Henry H Escalante, *Ch of Bd*
Shannon S Walker, *Treasurer*
Helen M Escalante, *Admin Sec*
EMP: 208 **EST:** 1979
SQ FT: 16,000
SALES (est): 47.3MM
SALES (corp-wide): 13.2B **Privately Held**
WEB: www.cciainsurance.com
SIC: 6331 Fire, marine & casualty insurance

HQ: Meadowbrook, Inc.
26255 American Dr
Southfield MI 48034
248 358-1100

(P-10348)
COMPWEST INSURANCE COMPANY
3 Hutton Cntre Dr Ste 550, Santa Ana (92707)
PHONE................................714 641-9500
Ron Field, *Branch Mgr*
EMP: 67
SALES (corp-wide): 65.4MM **Privately Held**
SIC: 6331 Reciprocal interinsurance exchanges: fire, marine, casualty
PA: Compwest Insurance Company Inc
100 Pringle Ave Ste 515
Walnut Creek CA 94596
415 593-5100

(P-10349)
FACTORY MUTUAL INSURANCE CO
Also Called: FM Global
1333 N Calif Blvd Ste 200, Walnut Creek (94596-4559)
PHONE................................925 934-2200
Andrew Scanlon, *Branch Mgr*
Monique Modelo, *Admin Mgr*
Leslie Warren, *Admin Asst*
Damion McGee, *Technology*
Sara Whitecotton, *Accountant*
EMP: 109
SALES (corp-wide): 4.4B **Privately Held**
SIC: 6331 6411 Property damage insurance; insurance agents, brokers & service
PA: Factory Mutual Insurance Co
270 Central Ave
Johnston RI 02919
401 275-3000

(P-10350)
FACTORY MUTUAL INSURANCE CO
Also Called: FM Global
6320 Canoga Ave Ste 1100, Woodland Hills (91367-2578)
P.O. Box 9270, Van Nuys (91409-9270)
PHONE................................818 227-2200
John Labanieh, *Engineer*
Tim Malone, *Sales Staff*
Jeff Tenn, *Sales Staff*
Sham Ganguli, *Assistant VP*
EMP: 100
SALES (corp-wide): 4.4B **Privately Held**
SIC: 6331 Property damage insurance
PA: Factory Mutual Insurance Co
270 Central Ave
Johnston RI 02919
401 275-3000

(P-10351)
FARMERS GROUP INC (HQ)
Also Called: Farmers Insurance
6301 Owensmouth Ave, Woodland Hills (91367-2216)
P.O. Box 2450, Grand Rapids MI (49501-2450)
PHONE................................323 932-3200
Jeff Dailey, *CEO*
Steve Boshoven, *President*
Tony Desantis, *President*
Mhayse Samalya, *President*
Scott Lindquist, *CFO*
EMP: 2100 **EST:** 1927
SALES (est): 12B
SALES (corp-wide): 65.1B **Privately Held**
WEB: www.farmers.com
SIC: 6331 Automobile insurance; reciprocal interinsurance exchanges: fire, marine, casualty
PA: Zurich Insurance Group Ag
Zurich Versicherungs-Gesellschaft Ag
ZUrich ZH 8002
446 252-525

(P-10352)
FIREMANS FUND INSURANCE CO (HQ)
1465 N Mcdowell Blvd # 100, Petaluma (94954-6516)
PHONE................................415 899-2000
Gary Bhojwani, *Ch of Bd*

Antonio Derossi, *COO*
Kevin Walker, *CFO*
Robyn Hahn, *Chief Mktg Ofcr*
Christian Kortebein, *Senior VP*
EMP: 2242 **EST:** 1864
SQ FT: 240,000
SALES (est): 3.8B **Privately Held**
WEB: www.firemansfund.com
SIC: 6331 6351 6321 Fire, marine & casualty insurance & carriers; property damage insurance; fire, marine & casualty insurance: stock; workers' compensation insurance; surety insurance; credit & other financial responsibility insurance; liability insurance; reinsurance carriers, accident & health
PA: Allianz Se
Koniginstr. 28
Munchen 80802
893 800-0

(P-10353)
FIREMANS FUND INSURANCE CO
9275 Sky Park Ct, San Diego (92123-4386)
P.O. Box 85920 (92186-5920)
PHONE................................858 492-3019
Kelly Rauch, *Principal*
Mike Sprano, *Info Tech Mgr*
EMP: 131 **Privately Held**
WEB: www.firemansfund.com
SIC: 6331 Property damage insurance
HQ: Fireman's Fund Insurance Company
1465 N Mcdowell Blvd # 100
Petaluma CA 94954
415 899-2000

(P-10354)
FIREMANS FUND INSURANCE CO
2350 W Empire Ave Ste 200, Burbank (91504-3350)
PHONE................................818 953-6533
Karmyn Downs, *Manager*
EMP: 206 **Privately Held**
WEB: www.firemansfund.com
SIC: 6331 Property damage insurance
HQ: Fireman's Fund Insurance Company
1465 N Mcdowell Blvd # 100
Petaluma CA 94954
415 899-2000

(P-10355)
FRANK GATES SERVICE COMPANY
2400 E Katella Ave # 650, Anaheim (92806-5974)
PHONE................................800 994-4611
Gary Graham, *Manager*
Nancy Neely, *Accountant*
EMP: 60
SALES (corp-wide): 2.3B **Privately Held**
WEB: www.fgsc.com
SIC: 6331 Workers' compensation insurance
HQ: The Frank Gates Service Company
5000 Bradenton Ave # 100
Dublin OH 43017
614 793-8000

(P-10356)
GLENN E PORTER
3955 Coffee Rd, Bakersfield (93308-5024)
PHONE................................661 615-1500
Glenn E Porter, *Principal*
Glenn Porter, *Principal*
EMP: 50
SALES (est): 4.6MM **Privately Held**
SIC: 6331 Property damage insurance

(P-10357)
GOLDEN EAGLE INSURANCE CORP (DH)
525 B St Ste 1300, San Diego (92101-4421)
P.O. Box 85826 (92186-5826)
PHONE................................619 744-6000
J Paul Condrin III, *CEO*
Frank J Kotarba, *President*
Mitsu Diley, *Vice Pres*
EMP: 250 **EST:** 1997
SALES (est): 96.7MM
SALES (corp-wide): 38.3B **Privately Held**
SIC: 6331 Property damage insurance

HQ: Liberty Mutual Insurance Company
175 Berkeley St
Boston MA 02116
617 357-9500

(P-10358)
GREAT AMERICAN INSURANCE CO
5750 Wilshire Blvd 360, Los Angeles (90036-3697)
PHONE................................323 937-8600
Bob Nagaishi, *Branch Mgr*
EMP: 100 **Publicly Held**
SIC: 6331 Fire, marine & casualty insurance
HQ: Great American Insurance Company
301 E 4th St Fl 8
Cincinnati OH 45202
513 369-5000

(P-10359)
GREAT AMERICAN INSURANCE CO
725 S Figueroa St # 3400, Los Angeles (90017-5434)
PHONE................................213 430-4300
Thom Smith, *Division Pres*
Neil Bethel, *Senior VP*
Kirby Harness, *Vice Pres*
Rocio Garcia, *Division Mgr*
Alvin Esguerra, *Administration*
EMP: 142 **Publicly Held**
SIC: 6331 Fire, marine & casualty insurance
HQ: Great American Insurance Company
301 E 4th St Fl 8
Cincinnati OH 45202
513 369-5000

(P-10360)
HARTFORD CASUALTY INSURANCE CO
101 Montgomery St # 2700, San Francisco (94104-4179)
PHONE................................415 836-4800
William Reynolds, *Manager*
EMP: 600 **Publicly Held**
SIC: 6331 Fire, marine & casualty insurance: mutual; property damage insurance
HQ: Hartford Casualty Insurance Company
1 Hartford Plz
Hartford CT 06155
860 547-5000

(P-10361)
HERITAGE INDEMNITY COMPANY
23 Pasteur, Irvine (92618-3816)
PHONE................................303 987-5500
Adam Pope, *President*
EMP: 80
SALES (est): 5MM **Publicly Held**
SIC: 6331 Automobile insurance
PA: Amtrust Financial Services, Inc.
59 Maiden Ln Fl 43
New York NY 10038

(P-10362)
ICW GROUP HOLDINGS INC (PA)
15025 Innovation Dr, San Diego (92128-3455)
P.O. Box 85563 (92186-5563)
PHONE................................858 350-2400
Kevin M Prior, *CEO*
Ernest Rady, *Ch of Bd*
Sariborz Rostamian, *Treasurer*
EMP: 67 **EST:** 1974
SQ FT: 160,000
SALES (est): 344.9MM **Privately Held**
SIC: 6331 6411 Fire, marine & casualty insurance & carriers; insurance brokers

(P-10363)
INSURANCE COMPANY OF WEST (HQ)
Also Called: I C W
15025 Innovation Dr, San Diego (92128-3455)
P.O. Box 85563 (92186-5563)
PHONE................................858 350-2400
Kevin Prior, *President*
Ernest Rady, *Ch of Bd*
H Michael Freet, *Treasurer*

EMP: 146
SQ FT: 150,000
SALES (est): 371.5MM
SALES (corp-wide): 344.9MM **Privately Held**
SIC: 6331 Property damage insurance
PA: Icw Group Holdings, Inc.
15025 Innovation Dr
San Diego CA 92128
858 350-2400

(P-10364)
IVY INSURANCE GROUP INC (PA)
411 E Huntington Dr # 203, Arcadia (91006-3731)
PHONE.................................626 566-2116
James V O Donnell, *President*
William H T Bush, *Ch of Bd*
EMP: 69
SQ FT: 3,000
SALES (est): 10MM **Privately Held**
SIC: 6331 Fire, marine & casualty insurance: mutual; automobile insurance

(P-10365)
KRAMER-WILSON COMPANY INC (PA)
Also Called: Century National
6345 Balboa Blvd Ste 190, Encino (91316-1515)
P.O. Box 3999, North Hollywood (91609-0599)
PHONE.................................818 760-0880
Weldon Wilson, *CEO*
Kevin Wilson, *President*
Daniel Sherrin, *CFO*
Mary Ann Wagner, *Admin Sec*
EMP: 240
SQ FT: 41,000
SALES (est): 257.2MM **Privately Held**
WEB: www.cnico.com
SIC: 6331 Fire, marine & casualty insurance & carriers

(P-10366)
LIBERTY MUTUAL INSURANCE CO
101 Mission St Ste 740, San Francisco (94105-1737)
PHONE.................................415 957-1175
Gary Countryman, *Ch of Bd*
EMP: 150
SALES (corp-wide): 38.3B **Privately Held**
WEB: www.libertymutual.com
SIC: 6331 Fire, marine & casualty insurance
HQ: Liberty Mutual Insurance Company
175 Berkeley St
Boston MA 02116
617 357-9500

(P-10367)
LIBERTY MUTUAL INSURANCE CO
3633 Inland Empire Blvd # 280, Ontario (91764-4946)
P.O. Box 51486 (91761-0086)
PHONE.................................909 476-6688
Candi Peterson, *Sales/Mktg Mgr*
Don Leary, *Manager*
Caitlin Malone, *Agent*
EMP: 100
SALES (corp-wide): 38.3B **Privately Held**
WEB: www.libertymutual.com
SIC: 6331 6311 Fire, marine & casualty insurance; life insurance carriers
HQ: Liberty Mutual Insurance Company
175 Berkeley St
Boston MA 02116
617 357-9500

(P-10368)
LIBERTY MUTUAL INSURANCE CO
790 The City Dr S Ste 200, Orange (92868-4941)
P.O. Box 11020 (92856-8120)
PHONE.................................714 937-1400
Linda Vanauran, *Manager*
Eric Cady, *Project Mgr*
Virginia Bennett, *Human Resources*
EMP: 200

SALES (corp-wide): 38.3B **Privately Held**
WEB: www.libertymutual.com
SIC: 6331 6311 Fire, marine & casualty insurance; life insurance
HQ: Liberty Mutual Insurance Company
175 Berkeley St
Boston MA 02116
617 357-9500

(P-10369)
LIBERTY MUTUAL INSURANCE CO
20500 Belshaw Ave, Carson (90746-3506)
P.O. Box 212, Hingham MA (02043-0212)
PHONE.................................781 740-1920
Ronald Anderson, *Manager*
EMP: 155
SALES (corp-wide): 38.3B **Privately Held**
WEB: www.libertymutual.com
SIC: 6331 6311 Fire, marine & casualty insurance; life insurance carriers
HQ: Liberty Mutual Insurance Company
175 Berkeley St
Boston MA 02116
617 357-9500

(P-10370)
LIBERTY MUTUAL INSURANCE CO
1750 Howe Ave Ste 450, Sacramento (95825-3368)
PHONE.................................916 564-1792
Natalie Dougherty, *Manager*
Gunther Eger, *Opers Mgr*
John Rusk, *Sales Staff*
Anne Bower, *Manager*
Erin Burns, *Agent*
EMP: 340
SALES (corp-wide): 38.3B **Privately Held**
WEB: www.libertymutual.com
SIC: 6331 Fire, marine & casualty insurance
HQ: Liberty Mutual Insurance Company
175 Berkeley St
Boston MA 02116
617 357-9500

(P-10371)
MERCURY CASUALTY COMPANY (HQ)
Also Called: M C C
555 W Imperial Hwy, Brea (92821-4802)
P.O. Box 54600, Los Angeles (90054-0600)
PHONE.................................323 937-1060
Gabriel Tirador, *CEO*
George Joseph, *CEO*
EMP: 600 EST: 1962
SALES (est): 3.2B
SALES (corp-wide): 3.4B **Publicly Held**
SIC: 6331 6351 Automobile insurance; warranty insurance, home
PA: Mercury General Corporation
4484 Wilshire Blvd
Los Angeles CA 90010
323 937-1060

(P-10372)
MERCURY GENERAL CORPORATION (PA)
4484 Wilshire Blvd, Los Angeles (90010-3710)
P.O. Box 36662 (90036-0662)
PHONE.................................323 937-1060
Gabriel Tirador, *President*
George Joseph, *Ch of Bd*
Theodore R Stalick, *CFO*
Joshua Little, *Bd of Directors*
Allan Lubitz, *Senior VP*
EMP: 94 EST: 1961
SQ FT: 41,000
SALES: 3.4B **Publicly Held**
WEB: www.mercuryinsurance.com
SIC: 6331 6411 Automobile insurance; property damage insurance; fire, marine & casualty insurance & carriers; insurance agents, brokers & service

(P-10373)
MERCURY INSURANCE COMPANY
555 W Imperial Hwy, Brea (92821-4839)
P.O. Box 1150 (92822-1150)
PHONE.................................714 671-6700
Gave Tirador, *President*
EMP: 89

SALES (corp-wide): 3.4B **Publicly Held**
WEB: www.coveryourhome.com
SIC: 6331 6411 Fire, marine & casualty insurance; insurance agents, brokers & service
HQ: Mercury Insurance Company
4484 Wilshire Blvd
Los Angeles CA 90010
323 937-1060

(P-10374)
MERCURY INSURANCE COMPANY
Also Called: Mercury Insurance Group
104 Woodmere Rd, Folsom (95630-4705)
PHONE.................................916 353-4859
Beverly Ramm, *Vice Pres*
EMP: 89
SALES (corp-wide): 3.4B **Publicly Held**
WEB: www.coveryourhome.com
SIC: 6331 6411 Fire, marine & casualty insurance; insurance claim processing, except medical
HQ: Mercury Insurance Company
4484 Wilshire Blvd
Los Angeles CA 90010
323 937-1060

(P-10375)
MERCURY INSURANCE COMPANY
Also Called: Mercury Insurance Broker
1433 Santa Monica Blvd, Santa Monica (90404-1709)
PHONE.................................310 451-4943
Ken Donaldson, *Owner*
EMP: 89
SALES (corp-wide): 3.4B **Publicly Held**
WEB: www.coveryourhome.com
SIC: 6331 6411 Fire, marine & casualty insurance; insurance agents, brokers & service
HQ: Mercury Insurance Company
4484 Wilshire Blvd
Los Angeles CA 90010
323 937-1060

(P-10376)
MERCURY INSURANCE COMPANY
1700 Greenbriar Ln, Brea (92821-5971)
PHONE.................................714 255-5000
Ken Kitzmiller, *Branch Mgr*
EMP: 96
SALES (corp-wide): 3.4B **Publicly Held**
SIC: 6331 Fire, marine & casualty insurance
HQ: Mercury Insurance Company
4484 Wilshire Blvd
Los Angeles CA 90010
323 937-1060

(P-10377)
MERCURY INSURANCE COMPANY (HQ)
4484 Wilshire Blvd, Los Angeles (90010-3710)
P.O. Box 54600 (90054-0600)
PHONE.................................323 937-1060
Gabe Tirador, *CEO*
Ted Stalick, *CFO*
George Joseph, *Chairman*
Judith Walters, *Vice Pres*
EMP: 160
SQ FT: 40,809
SALES (est): 3.5B
SALES (corp-wide): 3.4B **Publicly Held**
WEB: www.coveryourhome.com
SIC: 6331 Fire, marine & casualty insurance
PA: Mercury General Corporation
4484 Wilshire Blvd
Los Angeles CA 90010
323 937-1060

(P-10378)
MERCURY INSURANCE COMPANY
9635 Gran Rdge Dr Ste 200, San Diego (92123)
P.O. Box 82167 (92138-2167)
PHONE.................................858 694-4100
Randy Petro, *Manager*
EMP: 100

SALES (corp-wide): 3.4B **Publicly Held**
WEB: www.coveryourhome.com
SIC: 6331 6411 Fire, marine & casualty insurance; insurance agents, brokers & service
HQ: Mercury Insurance Company
4484 Wilshire Blvd
Los Angeles CA 90010
323 937-1060

(P-10379)
MERCURY INSURANCE COMPANY
27200 Tourney Rd Ste 400, Valencia (91355-4997)
PHONE.................................661 291-6470
David Levy, *Manager*
EMP: 89
SALES (corp-wide): 3.4B **Publicly Held**
SIC: 6331 Fire, marine & casualty insurance
HQ: Mercury Insurance Company
4484 Wilshire Blvd
Los Angeles CA 90010
323 937-1060

(P-10380)
MERCURY INSURANCE SERVICES LLC
4484 Wilshire Blvd, Los Angeles (90010-3710)
PHONE.................................323 937-1060
Gabriel Tirador, *CEO*
EMP: 4000
SALES: 2.7B
SALES (corp-wide): 3.4B **Publicly Held**
SIC: 6331 Property damage insurance
HQ: Mercury Casualty Company
555 W Imperial Hwy
Brea CA 92821
323 937-1060

(P-10381)
METROMILE INC (PA)
690 Folsom St Ste 200, San Francisco (94107-1397)
PHONE.................................888 244-1702
Dan Preston, *CEO*
Carrie Dolan, *CFO*
Aman Bilon, *Executive Asst*
Jose Mercado, *CTO*
Stephanie Naulty, *Sales Associate*
EMP: 80
SALES (est): 123.5MM **Privately Held**
SIC: 6331 Automobile insurance

(P-10382)
MID CENTURY INSURANCE COMPANY
4680 Wilshire Blvd, Los Angeles (90010-3807)
P.O. Box 2478 (90051-0478)
PHONE.................................323 932-7116
Ron Coble, *Senior VP*
Bob Woudstra, *President*
EMP: 250
SQ FT: 210,000
SALES (est): 70.8MM
SALES (corp-wide): 65.1B **Privately Held**
SIC: 6331 6351 Automobile insurance; fidelity insurance
HQ: Farmers Insurance Exchange
6301 Owensmouth Ave # 300
Woodland Hills CA 91367
323 932-3200

(P-10383)
NATIONAL GENERAL INSURANCE CO
Also Called: GMAC Insurance
3633 Inland Empire Blvd # 700, Ontario (91764-4922)
PHONE.................................909 944-8085
Steven Wright, *Manager*
EMP: 86
SALES (corp-wide): 9.8B **Publicly Held**
SIC: 6331 Fire, marine & casualty insurance
HQ: National General Insurance Company
5757 Phantom Dr Ste 200
Hazelwood MO 63042
314 493-8000

P
R
O
D
U
C
T
S
&
S
V
C
S

(P-10384)
PACIFIC COMPENSATION INSUR CO
1 Baxter Way Ste 170, Westlake Village (91362-3819)
P.O. Box 5034, Thousand Oaks (91359-5034)
PHONE..................818 575-8500
Marc E Schmittlein, *President*
David Kuhn, *President*
Denise Richardson, *Officer*
Chris Closser, *Vice Pres*
Kris Mathis, *Vice Pres*
EMP: 150
SALES (est): 83.1MM **Privately Held**
WEB: www.edicwc.com
SIC: 6331 Workers' compensation insurance
HQ: Pacific Compensation Corporation
   1 Baxter Way Ste 170
   Westlake Village CA 91362

(P-10385)
PROGRESSIVE CORPORATION
Also Called: Progressive Insurance
2470 Via Mariposa, San Dimas (91773-4420)
PHONE..................626 232-1540
Aaron Cavazos, *Branch Mgr*
EMP: 86
SALES (corp-wide): 26.8B **Publicly Held**
SIC: 6331 Fire, marine & casualty insurance
PA: The Progressive Corporation
   6300 Wilson Mills Rd
   Mayfield Village OH 44143
   440 461-5000

(P-10386)
PROGRESSIVE CORPORATION
Also Called: Progressive Insurance
150 N Hill Dr Ste 9, Brisbane (94005-1023)
PHONE..................440 461-5000
EMP: 86
SALES (corp-wide): 26.8B **Publicly Held**
SIC: 6331 Fire, marine & casualty insurance
PA: The Progressive Corporation
   6300 Wilson Mills Rd
   Mayfield Village OH 44143
   440 461-5000

(P-10387)
REPUBLIC INDEMNITY CO AMER
100 Pine St Fl 14, San Francisco (94111-5116)
P.O. Box 7878 (94120-7878)
PHONE..................415 981-3200
Darryl Yim, *Vice Pres*
EMP: 100 **Publicly Held**
SIC: 6331 Workers' compensation insurance
HQ: Republic Indemnity Company Of America
   15821 Ventura Blvd # 370
   Encino CA 91436
   818 990-9860

(P-10388)
REPUBLIC INDEMNITY COMPANY CAL
Also Called: RICA
15821 Ventura Blvd # 370, Encino (91436-2936)
P.O. Box 20036 (91416-0036)
PHONE..................818 990-9860
Dwayne T Marioni, *President*
Shila Euper, *Admin Sec*
EMP: 127
SALES (est): 12.3MM **Publicly Held**
SIC: 6331 Fire, marine & casualty insurance
HQ: Republic Indemnity Company Of America
   15821 Ventura Blvd # 370
   Encino CA 91436
   818 990-9860

(P-10389)
REPUBLIC INDEMNITY COMPANY OF (DH)
15821 Ventura Blvd # 370, Encino (91436-2936)
P.O. Box 20036 (91416-0036)
PHONE..................818 990-9860
Dwayne Marioni, *CEO*
Emily Grund, *President*
Marion Chappel, *Senior VP*
Anu Ponto, *Analyst*
Kim Slagg, *Production*
EMP: 129
SQ FT: 70,000
SALES: 838.5MM **Publicly Held**
SIC: 6331 Workers' compensation insurance
HQ: Pennsylvania Company Inc
   1 E 4th St
   Cincinnati OH 45202
   513 579-2121

(P-10390)
RESIDENCE MUTUAL INSURANCE CO
2172 Dupont Dr Ste 220, Irvine (92612-1359)
P.O. Box 6019, Agoura Hills (91376-6019)
PHONE..................949 724-9402
Joe Crail, *President*
Michael Hardy, *CFO*
EMP: 65 EST: 1949
SQ FT: 35,000
SALES: 27.1MM **Privately Held**
SIC: 6331 Property damage insurance

(P-10391)
RICHARD J MENDOZA INC
501 2nd St Ste 330, San Francisco (94107-4131)
PHONE..................415 644-0180
Jeff Pallesen, *President*
Todd George, *Officer*
EMP: 95 EST: 2001
SALES (est): 15.2MM
SALES (corp-wide): 333MM **Publicly Held**
SIC: 6331 Fire, marine & casualty insurance
PA: Nv5 Global, Inc.
   200 S Park Rd Ste 350
   Hollywood FL 33021
   954 495-2112

(P-10392)
ROYAL SPECIALTY UNDWRT INC
Also Called: Rsui Group
15303 Ventura Blvd # 500, Sherman Oaks (91403-3110)
PHONE..................818 922-6700
Christine Chinen, *Administration*
Melanie Stevenson, *Vice Pres*
Myra Caagbay, *Administration*
Carisa Winters, *Administration*
Ron Cholaj, *Assistant VP*
EMP: 75
SALES (corp-wide): 6.4B **Publicly Held**
SIC: 6331 6411 Fire, marine & casualty insurance; insurance agents, brokers & service
HQ: Royal Specialty Underwriting, Inc.
   945 E Paces Ferry Rd Ne # 189
   Atlanta GA 30326
   404 231-2366

(P-10393)
SEQUOIA INSURANCE COMPANY (HQ)
31 Upper Ragsdale Dr, Monterey (93940-5771)
P.O. Box 1510 (93942-1510)
PHONE..................831 655-9612
Thomas G Moylan, *President*
EMP: 60
SALES (est): 35MM **Publicly Held**
WEB: www.sequoiains.com
SIC: 6331 Fire, marine & casualty insurance & carriers; property damage insurance

(P-10394)
STATE COMPENSATION INSUR FUND (PA)
Also Called: STATE FUND
333 Bush St Fl 8, San Francisco (94104-2806)
P.O. Box 8192, Pleasanton (94588-8792)
PHONE..................888 782-8338
Vernon Steiner, *President*
Hilda Padua, *President*
Rick Law, *COO*
Beatriz Sanchez, *COO*
Peter Guastamachio, *CFO*
EMP: 75
SQ FT: 80,000
SALES: 1.5B **Privately Held**
WEB: www.scif.com
SIC: 6331 Workers' compensation insurance

(P-10395)
STATE COMPENSATION INSUR FUND
Also Called: Santa Ana District Office
1750 E 4th St Fl 3, Santa Ana (92705-3929)
PHONE..................714 565-5000
Liz Glidden, *Manager*
Katarina Holstein, *Executive*
Mark Winsberg, *Sr Consultant*
Dina Camiolo, *Manager*
Tiruvur Mohanram, *Consultant*
EMP: 270
SALES (corp-wide): 1.5B **Privately Held**
WEB: www.scif.com
SIC: 6331 9651 Workers' compensation insurance; insurance commission, government;
PA: State Compensation Insurance Fund
   333 Bush St Fl 8
   San Francisco CA 94104
   888 782-8338

(P-10396)
STATE COMPENSATION INSUR FUND
Also Called: Bakersfield District Office
9801 Camino Media Ste 101, Bakersfield (93311-1312)
P.O. Box 21810 (93390-1810)
PHONE..................661 664-4000
Robert Kean, *Manager*
Mike La Deaux, *Executive*
Karel Davis, *Supervisor*
EMP: 190
SALES (corp-wide): 1.5B **Privately Held**
WEB: www.scif.com
SIC: 6331 9651 Workers' compensation insurance; insurance commission, government;
PA: State Compensation Insurance Fund
   333 Bush St Fl 8
   San Francisco CA 94104
   888 782-8338

(P-10397)
STATE COMPENSATION INSUR FUND
Also Called: Oakland District Office
2955 Peralta Oaks Ct, Oakland (94605-5319)
PHONE..................510 577-3000
Gary Dunlop, *Branch Mgr*
EMP: 200
SALES (corp-wide): 1.5B **Privately Held**
WEB: www.scif.com
SIC: 6331 9651 6321
PA: State Compensation Insurance Fund
   333 Bush St Fl 8
   San Francisco CA 94104
   888 782-8338

(P-10398)
STATE COMPENSATION INSUR FUND
Also Called: San Jose District Office
333 W San Carlos St # 950, San Jose (95110-2726)
PHONE..................888 782-8338
Jerry Madden, *Manager*
EMP: 210

SALES (corp-wide): 1.5B **Privately Held**
WEB: www.scif.com
SIC: 6331 9651 Workers' compensation insurance; insurance commission, government;
PA: State Compensation Insurance Fund
   333 Bush St Fl 8
   San Francisco CA 94104
   888 782-8338

(P-10399)
STATE COMPENSATION INSUR FUND
Also Called: Redding District Office
364 Knollcrest Dr, Redding (96002-0175)
P.O. Box 496049 (96049-6049)
PHONE..................888 782-8338
Michael Labeaux, *Manager*
David Olsen, *Analyst*
Dorothy Stewart, *Analyst*
EMP: 170
SALES (corp-wide): 1.5B **Privately Held**
WEB: www.scif.com
SIC: 6331 9651 Workers' compensation insurance; regulation, miscellaneous commercial sectors;
PA: State Compensation Insurance Fund
   333 Bush St Fl 8
   San Francisco CA 94104
   888 782-8338

(P-10400)
STATE COMPENSATION INSUR FUND
Also Called: San Diego District Office
10105 Pacific Hgts Blvd, San Diego (92121-4249)
PHONE..................888 782-8338
Lisa Middleton, *Manager*
EMP: 350
SALES (corp-wide): 1.5B **Privately Held**
WEB: www.scif.com
SIC: 6331 9651 Workers' compensation insurance; insurance commission, government;
PA: State Compensation Insurance Fund
   333 Bush St Fl 8
   San Francisco CA 94104
   888 782-8338

(P-10401)
STATE COMPENSATION INSUR FUND
Also Called: Fresno District Office
10 E Rver Pk Pl E Ste 110, Fresno (93720)
PHONE..................559 433-2700
John Putnam, *District Mgr*
Drake Gomez, *Technician*
Jose Mejia, *Analyst*
Patrick Taylor, *Consultant*
Monica Segura, *Underwriter*
EMP: 270
SALES (corp-wide): 1.5B **Privately Held**
WEB: www.scif.com
SIC: 6331 9651 Workers' compensation insurance; insurance commission, government;
PA: State Compensation Insurance Fund
   333 Bush St Fl 8
   San Francisco CA 94104
   888 782-8338

(P-10402)
STATE COMPENSATION INSUR FUND
Also Called: State Fund Office
655 N Central Ave Ste 200, Glendale (91203-1424)
P.O. Box 92503, Los Angeles (90009-2503)
PHONE..................213 576-7335
Linda Hoban, *Manager*
Mario Escalante, *Technology*
Marilyn Aguilera, *Auditor*
EMP: 185
SALES (corp-wide): 1.5B **Privately Held**
WEB: www.scif.com
SIC: 6331 9651 Workers' compensation insurance; insurance commission, government;
PA: State Compensation Insurance Fund
   333 Bush St Fl 8
   San Francisco CA 94104
   888 782-8338

(P-10403)
STATE COMPENSATION INSUR FUND
655 N Central Ave Ste 200, Glendale
(91203-1424)
P.O. Box 92503, Los Angeles (90009-2503)
PHONE....................323 266-5551
EMP: 185
SALES (corp-wide): 1.5B Privately Held
WEB: www.scif.com
SIC: 6331 9651 Workers' compensation
insurance; insurance commission, government;
PA: State Compensation Insurance Fund
333 Bush St Fl 8
San Francisco CA 94104
888 782-8338

(P-10404)
STATE COMPENSATION INSUR FUND
Also Called: Stockton District Office
3247 W March Ln Ste 110, Stockton
(95219-2363)
PHONE....................888 782-8338
Tom Clark, Manager
Belinda Walker, Manager
EMP: 200
SALES (corp-wide): 1.5B Privately Held
WEB: www.scif.com
SIC: 6331 9651 6411 Workers' compensation insurance; insurance commission, government; ; insurance agents, brokers & service
PA: State Compensation Insurance Fund
333 Bush St Fl 8
San Francisco CA 94104
888 782-8338

(P-10405)
STATE COMPENSATION INSUR FUND
Also Called: Los Angeles District Office
655 N Central Ave Ste 200, Glendale
(91203-1424)
P.O. Box 65005, Fresno (93650-5005)
PHONE....................888 782-8338
Linda Hoban, Manager
Beatriz Sanchez, Opers Mgr
Michael Banks, Manager
EMP: 185
SALES (corp-wide): 1.5B Privately Held
WEB: www.scif.com
SIC: 6331 9651 6321 Workers' compensation insurance; insurance commission, government; ; accident & health insurance
PA: State Compensation Insurance Fund
333 Bush St Fl 8
San Francisco CA 94104
888 782-8338

(P-10406)
STATE COMPENSATION INSUR FUND
Also Called: Sacramento District Office
2275 Gateway Oaks Dr, Sacramento
(95833-3224)
PHONE....................916 924-5100
Gary Dunlap, Manager
EMP: 325
SALES (corp-wide): 1.5B Privately Held
WEB: www.scif.com
SIC: 6331 9651 Workers' compensation
insurance; insurance commission, government;
PA: State Compensation Insurance Fund
333 Bush St Fl 8
San Francisco CA 94104
888 782-8338

(P-10407)
STATE COMPENSATION INSUR FUND
Also Called: Eureka District Office
800 W Harris St Ste 37, Eureka
(95503-3929)
PHONE....................707 443-9721
Steve Mackey, Branch Mgr
Arlene David, Technology
Sherry Brooks, Asst Mgr
EMP: 55

SALES (corp-wide): 1.5B Privately Held
WEB: www.scif.com
SIC: 6331 9651 Workers' compensation
insurance; insurance commission, government;
PA: State Compensation Insurance Fund
333 Bush St Fl 8
San Francisco CA 94104
888 782-8338

(P-10408)
STATE COMPENSATION INSUR FUND
Also Called: Riverside District Office
6301 Day St, Riverside (92507-0902)
PHONE....................888 782-8338
Barbara Katzka, Manager
William Zachry, Vice Pres
Jamie Towner-Joyce, Network Mgr
Gil D Santos, Chief Engr
Beverly Rosas, Counsel
EMP: 250
SALES (corp-wide): 1.5B Privately Held
WEB: www.scif.com
SIC: 6331 9651 Workers' compensation
insurance; insurance commission, government;
PA: State Compensation Insurance Fund
333 Bush St Fl 8
San Francisco CA 94104
888 782-8338

(P-10409)
STATE COMPENSATION INSUR FUND
5880 Owens Dr, Pleasanton (94588-3900)
PHONE....................925 523-5000
Patricia Smith, Manager
Joan Quintanilla, Regional Mgr
Bill Serrao, Info Tech Mgr
Bhargav Patel, Software Dev
Anusha Anand, Technology
EMP: 185
SALES (corp-wide): 1.5B Privately Held
WEB: www.scif.com
SIC: 6331 9441 Workers' compensation insurance; administration of social & manpower programs;
PA: State Compensation Insurance Fund
333 Bush St Fl 8
San Francisco CA 94104
888 782-8338

(P-10410)
STATE COMPENSATION INSUR FUND
5890 Owens Dr, Pleasanton (94588-3900)
PHONE....................888 782-8338
Alicia Reyes, Principal
Rachael Luong, Admin Asst
Orlando Cano, Info Tech Mgr
Harry Tang, Info Tech Mgr
Edison Wong, Prgrmr
EMP: 185
SALES (corp-wide): 1.5B Privately Held
SIC: 6331 Workers' compensation insurance
PA: State Compensation Insurance Fund
333 Bush St Fl 8
San Francisco CA 94104
888 782-8338

(P-10411)
STATE COMPENSATION INSUR FUND
Also Called: Los Angles Dst Off Policy Svcs
900 Corporate Center Dr, Monterey Park
(91754-7620)
P.O. Box 65005, Fresno (93650-5005)
PHONE....................323 266-5000
Joe Codron, Officer
Jerri Shaul, Broker
Jose Altamirano, Opers Mgr
Brenda Reid, Marketing Staff
Jennifer Arredondo, Manager
EMP: 150
SALES (corp-wide): 1.5B Privately Held
WEB: www.scif.com
SIC: 6331 9651 Workers' compensation
insurance; insurance commission, government;
PA: State Compensation Insurance Fund
333 Bush St Fl 8
San Francisco CA 94104
888 782-8338

(P-10412)
TRISTAR INSURANCE GROUP INC (PA)
Also Called: Tristart Risk Management
100 Oceangate Ste 700, Long Beach
(90802-4368)
PHONE....................562 495-6600
Thomas J Veale, President
Denise J Cotter, CFO
Joseph McLaughlin, Senior VP
Mary Ann Lubeskie, Vice Pres
Pamela Sheffield, Branch Mgr
EMP: 700
SQ FT: 9,000
SALES (est): 363.2MM Privately Held
SIC: 6331 8741 Workers' compensation
insurance; management services

(P-10413)
WAWANESA GENERAL INSURANCE CO
Also Called: Wawansea General Insurance
9050 Friars Rd Ste 200, San Diego
(92108-5800)
P.O. Box 82867 (92138-2867)
PHONE....................619 285-6020
Jeff Goy, CEO
Larry Smith, CFO
Angie Cantillon, Vice Pres
Richard Foote, Programmer Anys
Damion Cormier, Analyst
EMP: 500
SALES (est): 302.9MM
SALES (corp-wide): 2.3B Privately Held
SIC: 6331 Automobile insurance; property
damage insurance
PA: Wawanesa Mutual Insurance Company, The
191 Broadway Suite 900
Winnipeg MB R3C 3
204 985-3923

(P-10414)
WESTERN GENERAL HOLDING CO (PA)
5230 Las Virgenes Rd # 100, Calabasas
(91302-3448)
PHONE....................818 880-9070
Robert M Ehrlich, Ch of Bd
Daniel Mallut, President
Marlene Kushner, Admin Sec
EMP: 240 EST: 1999
SQ FT: 51,000
SALES (est): 98.7MM Privately Held
SIC: 6331 Fire, marine & casualty insurance

(P-10415)
WESTERN GENERAL INSURANCE CO
5230 Las Virgenes Rd, Calabasas
(91302-3448)
PHONE....................818 880-9070
Robert M Ehrlich, Ch of Bd
Denise M Tyson, COO
John Albanese, CFO
Daniel Mallut, Exec VP
Marleen Kushner, Admin Sec
EMP: 165
SQ FT: 51,000
SALES (est): 65.3MM
SALES (corp-wide): 98.7MM Privately Held
SIC: 6331 Automobile insurance
PA: Western General Holding Co
5230 Las Virgenes Rd # 100
Calabasas CA 91302
818 880-9070

(P-10416)
WORKERS COMPENSATION (PA)
Also Called: WCIRB
1221 Broadway Ste 900, Oakland
(94612-1995)
PHONE....................888 229-2472
William Mudge, President
Eric Riley, Officer
Dave Bellusci, Exec VP
David Bellusci, Senior VP
Brenda Keys, Senior VP
EMP: 207
SQ FT: 31,000
SALES: 38.5MM Privately Held
SIC: 6331 Workers' compensation insurance

(P-10417)
WORKMENS AUTO INSURANCE CO
714 W Olympic Blvd # 800, Los Angeles
(90015-1440)
PHONE....................213 742-8700
Jeanette Shammas, Ch of Bd
Nicholas J Lannotti, President
Denise M Tyson, President
EMP: 100
SALES (est): 67.3MM Privately Held
SIC: 6331 Fire, marine & casualty insurance

(P-10418)
ZENITH INSURANCE COMPANY (DH)
Also Called: Zenith A Fairfax Company, The
21255 Califa St, Woodland Hills
(91367-5021)
P.O. Box 9055, Van Nuys (91409-9055)
PHONE....................818 713-1000
Stanley R Zax, Ch of Bd
Darren Brown, President
Jack D Miller, President
Kari Van Gundy, CFO
Paul Ramont, Exec VP
EMP: 400 EST: 1950
SQ FT: 120,000
SALES (est): 1B
SALES (corp-wide): 16.2B Privately Held
SIC: 6331 Workers' compensation insurance; automobile insurance; agricultural insurance; property damage insurance
HQ: Zenith National Insurance Corp.
21255 Califa St
Woodland Hills CA 91367
818 713-1000

(P-10419)
ZENITH INSURANCE COMPANY
7676 Hazard Center Dr # 1200, San Diego
(92108-4517)
PHONE....................619 299-6252
Brian Anderson, Manager
Hector Lopez, HR Admin
Arlene Schroeder, Sales Executive
Dawne Pitts, Marketing Mgr
Amy Trexler, Nurse
EMP: 53
SALES (corp-wide): 16.2B Privately Held
SIC: 6331 6211 Workers' compensation insurance; underwriters, security
HQ: Zenith Insurance Company
21255 Califa St
Woodland Hills CA 91367
818 713-1000

6351 Surety Insurance Carriers

(P-10420)
AIA HOLDINGS INC (PA)
Also Called: Associated Bond
26560 Agoura Rd Ste 100, Calabasas
(91302-2015)
PHONE....................818 222-4999
Brian N Nairin, President
Eric Granof, President
Robert Kersnick, COO
Mark Francis, CFO
Jerry Watson, Officer
EMP: 51
SQ FT: 8,000
SALES (est): 23.1MM Privately Held
WEB: www.aiasurety.com
SIC: 6351 Fidelity or surety bonding

(P-10421)
AMERICAN CONTRS INDEMNITY CO (DH)
Also Called: HCC Surety Group
801 S Figueroa St Ste 700, Los Angeles
(90017-2523)
PHONE....................213 330-1309
Adam S Pessin, President
Michael Budnitsky, Vice Pres
CAM Fletcher, Vice Pres
Jeannie J Lee, Vice Pres
Paul A Yasilli, Vice Pres
EMP: 150

PRODUCTS & SVCS

SALES: 160MM
SALES (corp-wide): 2.1B **Privately Held**
WEB: www.hccsurety.com
SIC: 6351 Surety insurance bonding

(P-10422)
AXIOM HOME WARRANTY LLC
2015 Manhattan B, Redondo Beach (90278)
PHONE..............................844 562-9466
EMP: 112
SALES (est): 104.1K
SALES (corp-wide): 15.8MM **Privately Held**
SIC: 6351 Warranty insurance, home
PA: Wedgewood Inc.
2015 Manhattan Beach Blvd # 100
Redondo Beach CA 90278
310 640-3070

(P-10423)
BETA HEALTHCARE GROUP (PA)
1443 Danville Blvd, Alamo (94507-1911)
PHONE..............................925 838-6070
Tom Wander, *CEO*
Daniel J Sevilla Jr, *CFO*
Michael Willard, *CFO*
April Johnson, *Vice Pres*
Andrea Raub, *Vice Pres*
EMP: 60
SQ FT: 10,000
SALES (est): 34.4MM **Privately Held**
SIC: 6351 6411 Liability insurance; insurance agents, brokers & service

(P-10424)
CALIFORNIA PHYSICIANS SERVICE
6300 Canoga Ave Ste A, Woodland Hills (91367-8000)
PHONE..............................818 228-2010
David C Landress, *Manager*
EMP: 52
SALES (corp-wide): 17.6B **Privately Held**
WEB: www.blueshieldcafoundation.org
SIC: 6351 Surety insurance
PA: California Physicians' Service
50 Beale St Bsmt 2
San Francisco CA 94105
415 229-5000

(P-10425)
CAP-MPT (PA)
333 S Hope St Fl 8, Los Angeles (90071-3001)
PHONE..............................213 473-8600
Jim Weidner, *CEO*
Michael Wormley MD, *Ch of Bd*
John Donaldson, *CFO*
Nancy Brusegaard Johnson, *Senior VP*
Thomas Andre, *Vice Pres*
EMP: 140
SALES (est): 63.2MM **Privately Held**
SIC: 6351 Liability insurance

(P-10426)
DEVELOPERS SURETY INDEMNITY CO (DH)
Also Called: Insco Dico Group , The
17771 Cowan Ste 100, Irvine (92614-6044)
P.O. Box 19725 (92623-9725)
PHONE..............................949 263-3300
Walter Crowell, *President*
Harry C Crowell, *Ch of Bd*
David Rhodes, *Exec VP*
Jodi Traeger, *Info Tech Mgr*
EMP: 70
SQ FT: 25,000
SALES (est): 44.3MM **Publicly Held**
SIC: 6351 Fidelity or surety bonding
HQ: Insco Insurance Services, Inc.
17771 Cowan Ste 100
Irvine CA 92614
949 797-9243

(P-10427)
DOCTORS COMPANY INSURANCE SVCS
185 Greenwood Rd, NAPA (94558-7540)
P.O. Box 2900 (94558-0900)
PHONE..............................707 226-0100
Manuel F Puebla, *Ch of Bd*
Jack Meyer, *President*
Doug Boltz, *Vice Pres*

EMP: 300
SALES (est): 58.9MM
SALES (corp-wide): 393.7MM **Privately Held**
WEB: www.residentialsavingsmortgage.com
SIC: 6351 Liability insurance; fire, marine & casualty insurance
PA: The Doctors' Company An Interinsurance Exchange
185 Greenwood Rd
Napa CA 94558
707 226-0100

(P-10428)
FIDELITY NAT HM WARRANTY CO
1850 Gateway Blvd Ste 400, Concord (94520-8446)
PHONE..............................925 356-0194
Bill Jensen, *Manager*
Audra Woods, *Assistant VP*
EMP: 150
SALES (corp-wide): 7.6B **Publicly Held**
WEB: www.fnhw.com
SIC: 6351 Warranty insurance, home
HQ: Fidelity National Home Warranty Company
2950 Buskirk Ave Ste 201
Walnut Creek CA
-

(P-10429)
INDEMNITY COMPANY CALIFORNIA (DH)
17771 Cowan Ste 100, Irvine (92614-6044)
P.O. Box 19725 (92623-9725)
PHONE..............................949 263-3300
Harry C Crowell, *Chairman*
Fern Haberman, *CFO*
Sam Zaza, *CFO*
Walter A Crowell, *Admin Sec*
EMP: 71
SQ FT: 50,000
SALES (est): 9.5MM **Publicly Held**
SIC: 6351 Fidelity or surety bonding
HQ: Insco Insurance Services, Inc.
17771 Cowan Ste 100
Irvine CA 92614
949 797-9243

(P-10430)
KB HOME (PA)
10990 Wilshire Blvd Fl 5, Los Angeles (90024-3902)
PHONE..............................310 231-4000
Jeffrey T Mezger, *President*
Brett Dietz, *President*
Brian Kunec, *President*
Glen Longarini, *President*
Matt Mandino, *President*
EMP: 100
SALES: 4.3B **Publicly Held**
WEB: www.kbhome.com
SIC: 6351 6162 1531 Surety insurance; mortgage guarantee insurance; credit & other financial responsibility insurance; mortgage bankers & correspondents; speculative builder, single-family houses

(P-10431)
NATIONAL SURETY CORPORATION
1465 N Mcdowell Blvd # 100, Petaluma (94954-6516)
PHONE..............................415 899-2000
Lori D Fouche, *CEO*
EMP: 1000
SALES (est): 142.8MM **Privately Held**
SIC: 6351 Surety insurance
HQ: Fireman's Fund Insurance Company
1465 N Mcdowell Blvd # 100
Petaluma CA 94954
415 899-2000

(P-10432)
NMI HOLDINGS INC
2100 Powell St Fl 12th, Emeryville (94608-1894)
PHONE..............................855 530-6642
Bradley M Shuster, *Ch of Bd*
Claudia J Merkle, *President*
Adam Pollitzer, *CFO*
William J Leatherberry, *President*
Patrick Mathis, *Exec VP*
EMP: 276 **EST:** 2011

SQ FT: 47,000
SALES: 182.7MM **Privately Held**
SIC: 6351 Mortgage guarantee insurance

(P-10433)
XL SPECIALTY INSURANCE CORP
1340 Treat Blvd, Walnut Creek (94597-2101)
P.O. Box 8098 (94596)
PHONE..............................925 942-6142
Jim Bily, *Assistant VP*
EMP: 70 **Publicly Held**
SIC: 6351 Surety insurance
HQ: Xl Specialty Insurance Company
10 N Martingale Rd # 220
Schaumburg IL 60173
847 517-2990

6361 Title Insurance

(P-10434)
CALIFORNIA TITLE CO NTHRN CAL
1955 Hunts Ln Ste 102, San Bernardino (92408-3344)
PHONE..............................909 825-8800
Jim Sollami, *Manager*
Mark Medina, *Vice Pres*
EMP: 103 **Privately Held**
WEB: www.octitle.com
SIC: 6361 Title insurance
HQ: California Title Company Of Northern California
1551 N Tustin Ave Ste 300
Santa Ana CA 92705
714 558-2836

(P-10435)
CALIFORNIA TITLE COMPANY
2365 Northside Dr Ste 250, San Diego (92108-2719)
PHONE..............................619 516-5227
Jim Waterman, *President*
Chuck Bishop, *Assistant*
EMP: 65
SALES (est): 8.3MM
SALES (corp-wide): 27.9MM **Privately Held**
SIC: 6361 Title insurance
PA: California Title Company
28202 Cabot Rd Ste 625
Laguna Niguel CA 92677
949 582-8709

(P-10436)
CALIFORNIA TITLE COMPANY (PA)
28202 Cabot Rd Ste 625, Laguna Niguel (92677-1261)
PHONE..............................949 582-8709
Dave Erb, *President*
Jim Waterman, *President*
Christina Hattem, *CFO*
Dave Turner, *Officer*
David Skarman, *Vice Pres*
EMP: 65
SALES (est): 27.9MM **Privately Held**
SIC: 6361 Title insurance

(P-10437)
CHICAGO TITLE & ESCROW
316 W Mission Ave Ste 110, Escondido (92025-1731)
PHONE..............................760 746-3882
Joanne Lockard, *President*
Joann Lockard, *President*
Anne Radstinner, *Vice Pres*
EMP: 50
SALES (est): 6.8MM
SALES (corp-wide): 7.6B **Publicly Held**
WEB: www.fntg.com
SIC: 6361 Title insurance
PA: Fidelity National Financial, Inc.
601 Riverside Ave Fl 4
Jacksonville FL 32204
904 854-8100

(P-10438)
CHICAGO TITLE AND TRUST CO
535 N Brnd Blvrd Fl 3 Flr 3, Glendale (91203)
PHONE..............................818 548-0222
Mike Bossard, *Principal*

Kevin Lail, *Officer*
Edwin Ditlow, *Vice Pres*
Joyce Strazzulla, *Vice Pres*
Shane Pew, *Sales Staff*
EMP: 50
SALES (corp-wide): 7.6B **Publicly Held**
SIC: 6361 Real estate title insurance
HQ: Chicago Title And Trust Company
10 S La Salle St Ste 3100
Chicago IL 60603
312 223-2000

(P-10439)
CHICAGO TITLE COMPANY
701 B St Ste 1120, San Diego (92101-8103)
PHONE..............................619 230-6340
Madeline Lovejoy, *Principal*
Joe Goodman, *Principal*
Madeline G M Lovejoy, *Principal*
EMP: 107 **EST:** 1984
SQ FT: 2,650
SALES (est): 25.4MM **Privately Held**
SIC: 6361 Title insurance

(P-10440)
CHICAGO TITLE COMPANY
725 S Figueroa St Ste 200, Los Angeles (90017-5403)
PHONE..............................213 488-4375
Cheryl Yanez, *President*
Madeline Lovejoy, *Assistant VP*
Maria Leal, *Supervisor*
EMP: 70
SALES (est): 9.6MM
SALES (corp-wide): 7.6B **Publicly Held**
SIC: 6361 Title insurance
PA: Fidelity National Financial, Inc.
601 Riverside Ave Fl 4
Jacksonville FL 32204
904 854-8100

(P-10441)
CHICAGO TITLE COMPANY
7330 N Palm Ave Ste 101, Fresno (93711-5768)
PHONE..............................559 451-3700
Mark Barsotti, *Vice Pres*
Lisa Williams, *Agent*
EMP: 60 **EST:** 1989
SQ FT: 10,000
SALES (est): 4.5MM **Privately Held**
SIC: 6361 Real estate title insurance

(P-10442)
CHICAGO TITLE INSURANCE CO
105 Lake Forest Way, Folsom (95630-4708)
PHONE..............................916 985-0300
Steve Siqueiros, *Manager*
EMP: 50
SALES (corp-wide): 7.6B **Publicly Held**
SIC: 6361 Real estate title insurance
HQ: Chicago Title Insurance Company
4050 Calle Real
Santa Barbara CA 93110

(P-10443)
CHICAGO TITLE INSURANCE CO
500 E Esplanade Dr # 102, Oxnard (93036-2110)
PHONE..............................805 656-1300
Mike Hollins, *Manager*
EMP: 60
SALES (corp-wide): 7.6B **Publicly Held**
SIC: 6361 Real estate title insurance
HQ: Chicago Title Insurance Company
4050 Calle Real
Santa Barbara CA 93110
-

(P-10444)
CHICAGO TITLE INSURANCE CO
316 W Mission Ave Ste 110, Escondido (92025-1731)
PHONE..............................760 546-1000
Jo A Lockard, *Branch Mgr*
EMP: 60
SALES (corp-wide): 7.6B **Publicly Held**
SIC: 6361 Real estate title insurance
HQ: Chicago Title Insurance Company
4050 Calle Real
Santa Barbara CA 93110

(P-10445)
CHICAGO TITLE INSURANCE CO
925 Highland Pointe Dr # 340, Roseville
(95678-5423)
PHONE...................................916 783-7195
Patty Harris, *Vice Pres*
Laura Morales, *Officer*
Jean Williams, *Officer*
Brennon Mahon, *Sales Executive*
EMP: 293
SALES (corp-wide): 7.6B **Publicly Held**
SIC: 6361 Real estate title insurance
HQ: Chicago Title Insurance Company
  601 Riverside Ave
  Jacksonville FL 32204

(P-10446)
CHICAGO TITLE INSURANCE CO (HQ)
4050 Calle Real, Santa Barbara
(93110-3413)
PHONE...................................805 565-6900
Raymond R Quirk, *CEO*
William Halvorsen Jr, *President*
A Larry Sisk, *Treasurer*
Peter G Leemputte, *Vice Pres*
EMP: 150
SQ FT: 44,637
SALES (est): 329.7MM
SALES (corp-wide): 7.6B **Publicly Held**
SIC: 6361 Real estate title insurance
PA: Fidelity National Financial, Inc.
  601 Riverside Ave Fl 4
  Jacksonville FL 32204
  904 854-8100

(P-10447)
CHICAGO TITLE INSURANCE CO
120 N Floral St, Visalia (93291-6202)
P.O. Box 1191 (93279-1191)
PHONE...................................559 733-3814
Scott Collins, *President*
EMP: 64
SALES (corp-wide): 7.6B **Publicly Held**
SIC: 6361 Real estate title insurance
HQ: Chicago Title Insurance Company
  4050 Calle Real
  Santa Barbara CA 93110

(P-10448)
COMMONWEALTH LAND TITLE CO
6 Executive Cir Ste 100, Irvine
(92614-6732)
PHONE...................................949 460-4500
Carl Brown, *CEO*
EMP: 100
SALES (corp-wide): 7.6B **Publicly Held**
WEB: www.laurabarnetthomes.com
SIC: 6361 Title insurance
HQ: Commonwealth Land Title Insurance
  Company
  201 Cncourse Blvd Ste 200
  Glen Allen VA 23059
  904 854-8100

(P-10449)
CORINTHIAN TITLE COMPANY INC
5030 Camino De La Siesta, San Diego
(92108-3116)
PHONE...................................619 299-4800
Robert J Romano, *Co-CEO*
Natalie Castaneda, *President*
Michael Godwin, *COO*
Larry Vinti, *CFO*
Robert Romano, *Co-CEO*
EMP: 70
SQ FT: 6,000
SALES (est): 12.1MM **Privately Held**
SIC: 6361 Title insurance

(P-10450)
EQUITY TITLE COMPANY (DH)
801 N Brand Blvd Ste 400, Glendale
(91203-3261)
PHONE...................................818 291-4400
Jim Cossell, *President*
John Chadbourne, *Vice Pres*
Dindo De, *Vice Pres*
Corinne Holzman, *Vice Pres*
Larry Griffin, *Executive*
EMP: 80 EST: 1979

SALES (est): 35.5MM **Publicly Held**
SIC: 6361 Real estate title insurance

(P-10451)
FEDELITY NATIONAL TITLE CO ORG
5000 Van Nuys Blvd 500, Sherman Oaks
(91403-1793)
PHONE...................................818 758-6849
Richard Stine, *Principal*
EMP: 99 EST: 2010
SALES (est): 16.1MM **Privately Held**
SIC: 6361 Title insurance

(P-10452)
FIDELITY NATIONAL TITLE CO
42544 10th St W, Lancaster (93534-7079)
PHONE...................................818 881-7800
Cynthia L Fried, *President*
Madeline Barewald, *Assistant VP*
EMP: 50 EST: 1977
SALES (est): 11.8MM **Privately Held**
SIC: 6361 Real estate title insurance

(P-10453)
FIRST AMERICAN FINANCIAL CORP (PA)
1 First American Way, Santa Ana
(92707-5913)
PHONE...................................714 250-3000
Parker S Kennedy, *Ch of Bd*
George Livermore, *President*
Kathy Vian, *President*
Dennis J Gilmore, *CEO*
Mark E Seaton, *CFO*
EMP: 146
SQ FT: 490,000
SALES: 5.7B **Publicly Held**
SIC: 6361 6351 Title insurance; surety insurance

(P-10454)
FIRST AMERICAN MORTGAGE SVCS
3 First American Way, Santa Ana
(92707-5913)
PHONE...................................714 250-4210
Wes Mee, *President*
Jeanie Matten, *Senior VP*
Robert Lay, *Senior Mgr*
Tamra Carpenter, *Supervisor*
Margarita Mejia, *Supervisor*
EMP: 350
SALES (est): 134.2MM **Privately Held**
SIC: 6361 Title insurance

(P-10455)
FIRST AMERICAN TITLE INSUR CO (HQ)
1 First American Way, Santa Ana
(92707-5913)
P.O. Box 267 (92702-0267)
PHONE...................................800 854-3643
Dennis J Gilmore, *CEO*
Kurt Pfotenhauer, *Vice Chairman*
Kevin Wall, *President*
Curt Caspersen, *COO*
Curt G Johnson, *Vice Ch Bd*
EMP: 146
SALES (est): 2.6B **Publicly Held**
WEB: www.fatc.com
SIC: 6361 Real estate title insurance

(P-10456)
FIRST AMERICAN TITLE INSUR CO
411 Ivy St, San Diego (92101-2108)
PHONE...................................619 238-1776
Steve Mustin, *Manager*
Dan Baker, *Manager*
EMP: 160
SQ FT: 14,911 **Publicly Held**
WEB: www.fatc.com
SIC: 6361 6541 6531 Real estate insurance; title abstract offices; real estate agents & managers
HQ: First American Title Insurance Company
  1 First American Way
  Santa Ana CA 92707
  800 854-3643

(P-10457)
FIRST AMERICAN TITLE INSUR CO
1855 W Rdlands Blvd 100, Redlands
(92373)
PHONE...................................909 889-0311
Dan Williams, *Manager*
Paige Dejong, *VP Opers*
Jeff Bright, *Manager*
EMP: 140 **Publicly Held**
WEB: www.fatc.com
SIC: 6361 6541 Real estate title insurance; title abstract offices
HQ: First American Title Insurance Company
  1 First American Way
  Santa Ana CA 92707
  800 854-3643

(P-10458)
FIRST AMERICAN TITLE INSUR CO (HQ)
330 Soquel Ave, Santa Cruz (95062-2300)
PHONE...................................831 426-5000
Robert Schott, *President*
Ted Bigornia, *Officer*
Kimberly Delpolito, *Officer*
Shan Gould, *Officer*
Cassie Hanson, *Officer*
EMP: 230
SQ FT: 98,000
SALES (est): 232.6MM **Publicly Held**
WEB: www.fatcola.com
SIC: 6361 Real estate title insurance

(P-10459)
FIRST AMERICAN TITLE INSUR CO
899 Pacific St, San Luis Obispo
(93401-3635)
P.O. Box 1147 (93406-1147)
PHONE...................................805 543-8900
Kevin Irot, *Director*
Lisa Blasquez, *Officer*
EMP: 50 **Publicly Held**
WEB: www.fatc.com
SIC: 6361 Real estate title insurance
HQ: First American Title Insurance Company
  1 First American Way
  Santa Ana CA 92707
  800 854-3643

(P-10460)
FIRST AMERICAN TITLE INSUR CO
Also Called: First American Casualty Insur
9 First American Way, Santa Ana
(92707-5913)
PHONE...................................714 800-3000
Raymond Rai, *Branch Mgr*
Fahim Karim, *Technology*
EMP: 180 **Publicly Held**
WEB: www.fatc.com
SIC: 6361 Real estate title insurance
HQ: First American Title Insurance Company
  1 First American Way
  Santa Ana CA 92707
  800 854-3643

(P-10461)
FIRST AMERICAN TITLE INSUR CO
Also Called: First Amercn Lenders Advantage
1855 Gateway Blvd Ste 700, Concord
(94520-8455)
PHONE...................................925 798-2800
Tom Schlesinger, *Manager*
Jim Welch, *Vice Pres*
EMP: 70 **Publicly Held**
WEB: www.fatc.com
SIC: 6361 6541 Real estate title insurance; title & trust companies
HQ: First American Title Insurance Company
  1 First American Way
  Santa Ana CA 92707
  800 854-3643

(P-10462)
FIRST AMERICAN TITLE INSUR CO
First American Mortgage Svcs
3 First American Way, Santa Ana
(92707-5913)
PHONE...................................714 250-4000
Pat McLaughlin, *Branch Mgr*
Mike Williams, *President*
Marc Bonfigli, *Vice Pres*
Brian Lobuts, *Vice Pres*
Luis Ferreira, *IT/INT Sup*
EMP: 534 **Publicly Held**
SIC: 6361 6541 6531 Real estate title insurance; title abstract offices; real estate agents & managers
HQ: First American Title Insurance Company
  1 First American Way
  Santa Ana CA 92707
  800 854-3643

(P-10463)
FRONTIER TITLE CO (PA)
1499 Oliver Rd, Fairfield (94534-3492)
PHONE...................................707 427-5400
Leonard Gianno, *President*
Jeff Olson, *Exec VP*
EMP: 50
SQ FT: 10,000
SALES (est): 8.8MM **Privately Held**
WEB: www.frontiertitleco.com
SIC: 6361 Title insurance

(P-10464)
LAWYERS TITLE COMPANY
4542 Ruffner St Ste 200, San Diego
(92111-2239)
PHONE...................................858 650-3900
John Wall, *Branch Mgr*
EMP: 80
SQ FT: 1,800
SALES (corp-wide): 7.6B **Publicly Held**
SIC: 6361 Real estate title insurance
HQ: Lawyers Title Company
  7530 N Glenoaks Blvd
  Burbank CA 91504
  818 767-0425

(P-10465)
LAWYERS TITLE COMPANY (HQ)
7530 N Glenoaks Blvd, Burbank
(91504-1052)
PHONE...................................818 767-0425
Edward Zerwekh, *CEO*
Edward Beierle, *Senior VP*
Steve Bauer, *Vice Pres*
William Star, *Vice Pres*
Katie Smith, *Branch Mgr*
EMP: 50
SQ FT: 20,000
SALES (est): 107.9MM
SALES (corp-wide): 7.6B **Publicly Held**
SIC: 6361 6531 Real estate title insurance; escrow agent, real estate
PA: Fidelity National Financial, Inc.
  601 Riverside Ave Fl 4
  Jacksonville FL 32204
  904 854-8100

(P-10466)
LAWYERS TITLE INSURANCE CORP
18551 Von Karman Ave # 100, Irvine
(92612-1552)
PHONE...................................949 223-5575
Dan Williams, *Branch Mgr*
EMP: 70
SALES (corp-wide): 7.6B **Publicly Held**
WEB: www.diamondtitleco.com
SIC: 6361 6541 Real estate title insurance; title & trust companies
HQ: Lawyers Title Insurance Corporation
  601 Riverside Ave
  Jacksonville FL 32204
  888 866-3684

(P-10467)
NORTH AMERICAN TITLE CO INC
Also Called: N A T C
6612 Owens Dr 100, Pleasanton
(94588-3334)
PHONE...................................925 399-3000
Jim White, *Manager*

PRODUCTS & SVCS

EMP: 60
SQ FT: 32,000
SALES (corp-wide): 12.6B **Publicly Held**
WEB: www.natic.com
SIC: 6361 Real estate title insurance
HQ: North American Title Company, Inc.
1855 Gateway Blvd Ste 600
Concord CA 94520
925 935-5599

(P-10468)
OLD REPUBLIC TITLE COMPANY
101 N Brand Blvd Ste 1400, Glendale
(91203-2691)
PHONE..........................818 240-1936
Merv Morris, *President*
Preston Brede, *Officer*
Cathy Gaidano, *Officer*
Marci Goldsberry, *Officer*
Wendy McLaughlin, *Officer*
EMP: 645 **EST:** 1967
SQ FT: 25,000
SALES (est): 260.8MM
SALES (corp-wide): 6.2B **Publicly Held**
WEB: www.oldrepublictitle.com
SIC: 6361 Title insurance
HQ: Old Republic Title Holding Company, Inc.
275 Battery St Ste 1500
San Francisco CA 94111
415 421-3500

(P-10469)
OLD REPUBLIC TITLE COMPANY
584 S Main St, Salinas (93901-3347)
PHONE..........................831 757-8051
Ron Peterson, *President*
EMP: 50
SALES (corp-wide): 6.2B **Publicly Held**
WEB: www.ortc.com
SIC: 6361 Real estate title insurance
HQ: Old Republic Title Company
275 Battery St Ste 1500
San Francisco CA 94111
415 421-3500

(P-10470)
ORANGE CAST TITLE SOUTHERN CAL
2411 W La Palma Ave # 300, Anaheim
(92801-2639)
PHONE..........................714 822-3211
Barbara Kooey, *Manager*
Sharon Bewley, *Plant Mgr*
EMP: 100 **Privately Held**
SIC: 6361 Title insurance
PA: Orange Coast Title Company Of Southern California
1551 N Tustin Ave Ste 300
Santa Ana CA 92705
-

(P-10471)
STEWART TITLE CALIFORNIA INC (DH)
7676 Hazard Center Dr # 1400, San Diego
(92108-4516)
PHONE..........................619 692-1600
Steve Vivanco, *President*
Gregg Unrath, *Treasurer*
Deborah Britza, *Officer*
Brian Glaze, *Vice Pres*
Leslie Hopkins, *Vice Pres*
EMP: 140
SQ FT: 44,000
SALES (est): 217.2MM
SALES (corp-wide): 1.9B **Publicly Held**
WEB: www.stewarttitleco.com
SIC: 6361 Guarantee of titles
HQ: Stewart Title Company
1980 Post Oak Blvd Ste 80
Houston TX 77056
713 625-8100

(P-10472)
TICOR TITLE COMPANY CALIFORNIA
4210 Riverwalk Pkwy # 200, Riverside
(92505-3313)
PHONE..........................951 509-0211
Anthony Andre, *Branch Mgr*
EMP: 50

SALES (corp-wide): 7.6B **Publicly Held**
SIC: 6361 Real estate title insurance
HQ: Ticor Title Company Of California
1500 Quail St Ste 300
Newport Beach CA 92660
714 289-7100

(P-10473)
TICOR TITLE INSURANCE COMPANY (DH)
131 N El Molino Ave, Pasadena
(91101-1873)
PHONE..........................616 302-3121
John Rau, *Ch of Bd*
Gust Totlis, *CFO*
Peter Leemputte, *Treasurer*
Paul T Sands Jr, *Exec VP*
Bryan Willis, *Vice Pres*
EMP: 146
SQ FT: 44,637
SALES (est): 252.1MM
SALES (corp-wide): 7.6B **Publicly Held**
WEB: www.ticortitleindy.com
SIC: 6361 Real estate title insurance
HQ: Chicago Title And Trust Company
10 S La Salle St Ste 3100
Chicago IL 60603
312 223-2000

(P-10474)
WFG NATIONAL TITLE INSUR CO (PA)
Also Called: Alliance Title
700 N Brand Blvd Ste 1100, Glendale
(91203-1208)
PHONE..........................818 476-4000
Jeffrey Fox, *CEO*
Roberto Olivera, *President*
Chris White, *President*
James Lokay, *CFO*
Julie Alvarado, *Officer*
EMP: 75
SQ FT: 15,000
SALES (est): 103.8MM **Privately Held**
WEB: www.investorstitle.com
SIC: 6361 Title insurance

6371 Pension, Health & Welfare Funds

(P-10475)
ALAMEDA COUNTY EMPLOYEES RETIR
Also Called: Acera
475 14th St Ste 1000, Oakland
(94612-1916)
PHONE..........................510 628-3000
Charles Conrad, *General Mgr*
Catherine Walker, *CEO*
George Dewey, *Bd of Directors*
Darryl Walker, *Trustee*
Betty TSE, *Ch Invest Ofcr*
EMP: 70
SALES (est): 49.6MM **Privately Held**
WEB: www.acera.org
SIC: 6371 Pension funds

(P-10476)
ASSOCTED THIRD PTY ADMNSTRTORS
2831 Camino Del Rio S, San Diego
(92108-3802)
PHONE..........................619 358-8140
EMP: 200
SALES (corp-wide): 482.8MM **Privately Held**
SIC: 6371
PA: Associated Third Party Administrators Inc
222 N Sepulveda Blvd # 2000
El Segundo CA 90245
-

(P-10477)
CAL SOUTHERN UNITED FOOD
Also Called: U F C Pension Trust Fund
6425 Katella Ave, Cypress (90630-5246)
P.O. Box 6010 (90630-0010)
PHONE..........................714 220-2297
P Thompson, *Administration*
Dawn Fujihara, *Bookkeeper*
Carol Antonucci, *Human Res Mgr*
EMP: 240

SQ FT: 36,000
SALES (est): 108.2MM **Privately Held**
WEB: www.scufcwfunds.com
SIC: 6371 Pension funds

(P-10478)
CALIFOR STATE TEACH RETIRE SYS (DH)
Also Called: Cal Strs
100 Waterfront Pl, West Sacramento
(95605-2807)
P.O. Box 15275, Sacramento (95851-0275)
PHONE..........................800 228-5453
James D Mosman, *CEO*
Dana Dillon, *Ch of Bd*
Sharon Hendricks, *Ch of Bd*
Todd Golterman, *Technology*
Wing Wong, *Manager*
EMP: 130
SQ FT: 100,000
SALES (est): 549MM **Privately Held**
WEB: www.calstrs.com
SIC: 6371 Pension, health & welfare funds; administration of social & manpower programs;

(P-10479)
CALIFORNIA GOVRNMNT OPR AGNCY
Also Called: Califrnia Tchers Rtirement Sys
7667 Folsom Blvd Fl 3, Sacramento
(95826-2618)
PHONE..........................800 228-5453
James D Mosman, *Director*
EMP: 535 **Privately Held**
SIC: 6371 Pension, health & welfare funds
HQ: California Government Operations Agency
915 Capitol Mall Ste 200
Sacramento CA 95814
-

(P-10480)
CALIFORNIA PUBLIC EMPLYEES RET
Also Called: Calpers Investment Office
400 P St Ste 1204, Sacramento
(95814-5346)
PHONE..........................916 795-3000
Fred Buenrostro, *Manager*
Lisa Watson, *Officer*
Mark Marshall, *Administration*
Nelson Mina, *Administration*
Angela Lyons, *Investment Ofcr*
EMP: 150 **Privately Held**
WEB: www.calpers.net
SIC: 6371 9441 Pension funds; administration of social & manpower programs;
HQ: California Public Employees' Retirement System
400 Q St
Sacramento CA 95811
-

(P-10481)
CALIFORNIA PUBLIC EMPLYEES RET (DH)
400 Q St, Sacramento (95811-6201)
P.O. Box 942706 (94229-2706)
PHONE..........................916 795-3000
Anne Stausboll, *CEO*
Priya Mathur, *President*
Ronald E Gene Reich, *Officer*
Kathie Vaughn, *Officer*
Robert D Walton, *Officer*
EMP: 1600
SALES (est): 1.3B **Privately Held**
WEB: www.calpers.net
SIC: 6371 9441 Pension funds; administration of social & manpower programs;

(P-10482)
CHELBAY SCHULER & CHELBAY (PA)
Also Called: United Administrative Services
6800 Santa Teresa Blvd # 100, San Jose
(95119-1239)
P.O. Box 5057 (95150-5057)
PHONE..........................408 288-4400
Robert J Bradley, *President*
David Andresen, *Corp Secy*
Sharon Crist, *Vice Pres*
Debbie Hill, *Vice Pres*
Sandy Stephenson, *Vice Pres*
EMP: 100

SQ FT: 35,000
SALES (est): 46.6MM **Privately Held**
WEB: www.chelbayins.com
SIC: 6371 Pension funds

(P-10483)
COUNTY OF LOS ANGELES
Also Called: Public Social Services
27233 Camp Plenty Rd, Canyon Country
(91351-2634)
PHONE..........................661 298-3406
Hilda Ochoa, *Manager*
EMP: 60 **Privately Held**
WEB: www.co.la.ca.us
SIC: 6371 Union welfare, benefit & health funds
PA: County Of Los Angeles
500 W Temple St Ste 437
Los Angeles CA 90012
213 974-1101

(P-10484)
COUNTY OF SHASTA
Also Called: Shasta County Calworks
1400 California St, Redding (96001-1004)
PHONE..........................530 225-5000
Linda Parks, *Manager*
EMP: 90 **Privately Held**
WEB: www.rsdnmp.org
SIC: 6371 8748 Union welfare, benefit & health funds; employee programs administration
PA: County Of Shasta
1450 Court St Ste 308a
Redding CA 96001
530 225-5561

(P-10485)
EMPLOYEE BENEFITS SECURITY ADM
Also Called: Los Angeles Regional Office
1055 E Colo Blvd Ste 200, Pasadena
(91106)
PHONE..........................626 229-1000
EMP: 55 **Publicly Held**
SIC: 6371
HQ: Employee Benefits Security Administration
200 Constitution Ave Nw
Washington DC 20210
202 219-8233

(P-10486)
LIPMAN INSUR ADMNISTRATORS INC (PA)
39420 Liberty St Ste 260, Fremont
(94538-2297)
P.O. Box 5820 (94537-5820)
PHONE..........................510 796-4676
Frederic J Lipman, *President*
Janet Sylvester, *CFO*
Margaret Epstein, *Admin Sec*
Miriam Rivera, *Admin Asst*
EMP: 60
SQ FT: 14,000
SALES (est): 42.9MM **Privately Held**
SIC: 6371 Union welfare, benefit & health funds

(P-10487)
LOS ANGELES CNTY EMP RETIREMNT (PA)
Also Called: LACERA
300 N Lake Ave Ste 720, Pasadena
(91101-5674)
P.O. Box 7060 (91109-7060)
PHONE..........................626 564-6000
Gregg Rademather, *CEO*
David Kushner, *Ch Invest Ofcr*
Ana Chang, *Vice Pres*
Lisa Mazzocco, *Principal*
Sally Choi, *General Mgr*
EMP: 340
SQ FT: 85,000
SALES: 2B **Privately Held**
SIC: 6371 Pension funds

(P-10488)
MOTION PCTURE HLTH WLFARE FUND
11365 Ventura Blvd # 300, Studio City
(91604-3148)
P.O. Box 1999 (91614-0999)
PHONE..........................818 769-0007
Thomas Zimmerman, *Exec Dir*

Theodre Friesen, *CFO*
Long Voong, *IT/INT Sup*
Celso Perez, *Senior Mgr*
Gautam Tuli, *Assistant*
EMP: 215
SQ FT: 27,715
SALES (est): 20.9MM **Privately Held**
SIC: 6371 Union welfare, benefit & health funds

(P-10489)
MOTION PICTURE INDUSTRY PLANS
11365 Ventura Blvd # 300, Studio City (91604-3148)
PHONE...................................818 769-0007
David Wescoe, *CEO*
David Camp, *CFO*
Chuck Killian, *CFO*
Krysten Brennan, *Trustee*
Joel Manfredo, *CIO*
EMP: 150
SQ FT: 12,500
SALES (est): 92.5MM **Privately Held**
SIC: 6371 Pension, health & welfare funds

(P-10490)
NORCO FIRE DEPARTMENT
3902 Hillside Ave, Norco (92860-1515)
PHONE...................................951 737-8097
Ron Larson, *President*
EMP: 700
SALES (est): 245.4K **Privately Held**
SIC: 6371 Union funds

(P-10491)
PRODUCER -WRITERS GUILD
2900 W Alameda Ave # 1100, Burbank (91505-4267)
PHONE...................................818 846-1015
Jim Hedges, *Administration*
Alan Weidlich, *CIO*
Carol Davison, *Manager*
Andrea Gonzalez, *Manager*
Alan Hatanaka, *Manager*
EMP: 70
SQ FT: 30,000
SALES (est): 40.7MM **Privately Held**
WEB: www.wgaplans.org
SIC: 6371 Pension funds; pensions

(P-10492)
PUBLIC EMPLOYEES RETIREMENT
Also Called: Calpers
400 Q St, Sacramento (95811-6201)
PHONE...................................916 795-3400
Russell Fong, *Branch Mgr*
Robert Borrelli, *Officer*
Lakshmi Chennupati, *Officer*
Angela Glasgow, *Officer*
Cleon Pantell, *Officer*
EMP: 331 **Privately Held**
SIC: 6371 9441 Pension funds; administration of social & manpower programs;
HQ: California Public Employees' Retirement System
400 Q St
Sacramento CA 95811

(P-10493)
SCREEN ACTORS GUILD - AMERICAN
Also Called: Screen Actors Guild-Producers
3601 W Olive Ave Fl 2, Burbank (91505-4662)
P.O. Box 7830 (91510-7830)
PHONE...................................818 954-9400
Terence Young, *Admin Dir*
Daniel Leung, *Director*
Michael Maguire, *Manager*
EMP: 188
SALES (corp-wide): 59.7MM **Privately Held**
SIC: 6371 6411 Pensions; pension & retirement plan consultants
PA: Screen Actors Guild - American Federation Of Television And Radio Artists
5757 Wilshire Blvd Fl 7
Los Angeles CA 90036
415 391-7510

(P-10494)
UNITED ADMINISTRATIVE SERVICES
6800 Santa Teresa Blvd # 100, San Jose (95119-1239)
PHONE...................................408 288-4400
David Andresen, *President*
Sharon Crist, *Vice Pres*
EMP: 107
SQ FT: 35,000
SALES (est): 11.7MM
SALES (corp-wide): 46.6MM **Privately Held**
WEB: www.eebenefitplans.com
SIC: 6371 Pension funds; union welfare, benefit & health funds
PA: Chelbay, Schuler & Chelbay
6800 Santa Teresa Blvd # 100
San Jose CA 95119
408 288-4400

(P-10495)
WOODMONT REALTY ADVISORS INC
1050 Ralston Ave, Belmont (94002-2240)
PHONE...................................650 592-3960
Ronald V Granville, *CEO*
Howard Friedman, *President*
Caryn Kali, *CFO*
Sarah Davison, *Property Mgr*
Greg Perez, *Property Mgr*
EMP: 70
SQ FT: 10,000
SALES (est): 15.5MM **Privately Held**
WEB: www.wres.com
SIC: 6371 Pension funds
PA: Woodmont Real Estate Services, L.P.
1050 Ralston Ave
Belmont CA 94002

6399 Insurance Carriers, NEC

(P-10496)
AMERICAN INTL GROUP INC
Also Called: Sun America
777 S Figueroa St # 1800, Los Angeles (90017-5800)
PHONE...................................213 689-3500
Gregg Piltch, *President*
Melanie Taylor, *Underwriter*
EMP: 300
SALES (corp-wide): 49.5B **Publicly Held**
SIC: 6399 Deposit insurance
PA: American International Group, Inc.
80 Pine St Fl 4
New York NY 10005
212 770-7000

(P-10497)
CALIFRNIA INSUR GUARANTEE ASSN
Also Called: C I G A
101 N Brand Blvd Ste 600, Glendale (91203-2653)
P.O. Box 29066 (91209-9066)
PHONE...................................818 844-4300
Lawrence E Mulryan, *Director*
Wayne Wilson, *Exec Dir*
Devo Heller, *Info Tech Dir*
Feroz Merchhiya, *Info Tech Dir*
Armineh Oganesyan, *Business Anlyst*
EMP: 110 **EST:** 1969
SALES (est): 72.2MM **Privately Held**
WEB: www.caiga.org
SIC: 6399 Health insurance for pets

(P-10498)
FEDERAL DEPOSIT INSURANCE CORP
1333 S Mayflower Ave # 450, Monrovia (91016-4066)
PHONE...................................626 359-7152
Donald Powell, *Manager*
EMP: 123
SALES (corp-wide): 11.6B **Privately Held**
WEB: www.fdic.gov
SIC: 6399 9311 Federal Deposit Insurance Corporation (FDIC); finance, taxation & monetary policy;

PA: Federal Deposit Insurance Corporation
550 17th St Nw
Washington DC 20429
877 275-3342

(P-10499)
FEDERAL DEPOSIT INSURANCE CORP
Also Called: FDIC-San Frncisco Regional Off
25 Jessie St Ste 2300, San Francisco (94105-2780)
PHONE...................................415 546-0160
Stan Ivie, *Branch Mgr*
George Masa, *Principal*
Martin Briseno, *Admin Asst*
EMP: 150
SQ FT: 127,215
SALES (corp-wide): 11.6B **Privately Held**
WEB: www.fdic.gov
SIC: 6399 9311 Federal Deposit Insurance Corporation (FDIC); finance, taxation & monetary policy
PA: Federal Deposit Insurance Corporation
550 17th St Nw
Washington DC 20429
877 275-3342

(P-10500)
FEDERAL DEPOSIT INSURANCE CORP
Also Called: FDIC
5150 W Goldleaf Cir # 405, Los Angeles (90056-1662)
PHONE...................................323 545-9260
EMP: 123
SALES (corp-wide): 11.6B **Privately Held**
WEB: www.fdic.gov
SIC: 6399 9311 Federal Deposit Insurance Corporation (FDIC);
PA: Federal Deposit Insurance Corporation
550 17th St Nw
Washington DC 20429
877 275-3342

(P-10501)
FEDERAL DEPOSIT INSURANCE CORP
Also Called: F D I C
1532 Eureka Rd Ste 102, Roseville (95661-3054)
PHONE...................................916 789-8580
Andrea Davis, *Manager*
EMP: 123
SALES (corp-wide): 11.6B **Privately Held**
WEB: www.fdic.gov
SIC: 6399 9311 Federal Deposit Insurance Corporation (FDIC); finance, taxation & monetary policy;
PA: Federal Deposit Insurance Corporation
550 17th St Nw
Washington DC 20429
877 275-3342

(P-10502)
KANOPY INSURANCE CENTER LLC
545 N Mountain Ave # 205, Upland (91786-5055)
PHONE...................................877 513-2434
Ryan McClintock, *CEO*
EMP: 140 **EST:** 2013
SQ FT: 1,700
SALES: 650K **Privately Held**
SIC: 6399 6311 6351 Warranty insurance, automobile; life insurance; warranty insurance, home

(P-10503)
LISI INC
2677 N Main St Ste 350, Santa Ana (92705-6750)
PHONE...................................714 460-5153
Philip Lebherz, *Branch Mgr*
Jody Quinteros, *Executive Asst*
Mona Mehta, *Info Tech Dir*
Carroll Johnson, *Broker*
Rosalind Solano, *Broker*
EMP: 75
SALES (corp-wide): 48.4MM **Privately Held**
SIC: 6399 Deposit insurance
PA: Lisi, Inc.
1600 W Hillsdale Blvd # 100
San Mateo CA 94402
650 348-4131

(P-10504)
SQUARETRADE INC (DH)
360 3rd St Fl 6, San Francisco (94107-2154)
PHONE...................................415 541-1000
Ahmedulla Khaishgi, *President*
Mark Etnyre, *CFO*
Steve Abernethy, *Chairman*
Vince Tseng, *Officer*
Michael Costanza, *Vice Pres*
EMP: 146
SQ FT: 54,000
SALES: 1.3B **Publicly Held**
WEB: www.squaretrade.com
SIC: 6399 Warranty insurance, product; except automobile
HQ: Allstate Non Insurance Holdings Inc
2775 Sanders Rd Ste D
Northbrook IL 60062
847 402-5000

(P-10505)
TOPA INSURANCE COMPANY (HQ)
1800 Ave Of Stars # 1200, Los Angeles (90067-4200)
PHONE...................................310 201-0451
John E Anderson, *Ch of Bd*
Noshirwan Marfatia, *President*
Dan Sherrin, *CFO*
Harry W Degner, *Vice Ch Bd*
William S Anderson, *Admin Sec*
EMP: 79
SALES (est): 44.4MM
SALES (corp-wide): 391.4MM **Privately Held**
WEB: www.mcnabbins.com
SIC: 6399 Warranty insurance, product; except automobile
PA: Topa Equities, Ltd.
1800 Ave Of The
Los Angeles CA 90067
310 203-9199

6411 Insurance Agents, Brokers & Svc

(P-10506)
1-800-4-INSURE INSURANCE SVCS
Also Called: Low Cost Insurance
9310 Reseda Blvd, Northridge (91324-2926)
PHONE...................................818 701-3733
Amy Kong, *President*
EMP: 138
SQ FT: 8,000
SALES (est): 13.9MM **Privately Held**
SIC: 6411 Insurance agents, brokers & service

(P-10507)
21ST CENTURY INSURANCE COMPANY (DH)
6301 Owensmouth Ave, Woodland Hills (91367-2216)
PHONE...................................877 310-5687
Glenn A Pfeil, *CEO*
Richard R Andre, *Senior VP*
Michael J Cassanego, *Senior VP*
Dean E Stark, *Senior VP*
Barbary Baer, *Principal*
EMP: 1800
SQ FT: 412,000
SALES (est): 800.6MM
SALES (corp-wide): 65.1B **Privately Held**
SIC: 6411 Fire insurance underwriters' laboratories
HQ: 21st Century North America Insurance Company
3 Beaver Valley Rd
Wilmington DE 19803
877 310-5687

(P-10508)
ABD INSURANCE & FINCL SVCS INC (PA)
3 Waters Park Dr Ste 100, San Mateo (94403-1162)
PHONE...................................650 488-8565
Brian M Hetherington, *CEO*
Kurt De Grosz, *President*
Carolyn Locke, *President*

Kimily Phu, *President*
Helen Yu, *COO*
EMP: 72 **EST:** 2009
SQ FT: 14,000
SALES (est): 61.6MM **Privately Held**
SIC: 6411 Insurance brokers

(P-10509)
ACE FINANCIAL SERVICES INC
Also Called: Ace Property & Casualty
39300 Civic Center Dr # 290, Fremont
(94538-2338)
PHONE.....................510 790-4600
Angela Argiros, *Principal*
EMP: 70
SALES (corp-wide): 28.7B **Privately Held**
WEB: www.ace-ina.com
SIC: 6411 6331 Insurance agents, brokers
& service; fire, marine & casualty insurance
ance
HQ: Chubb Insurance Company
11133 Ave Of The Americas
New York NY 10019
212 642-7800

(P-10510)
ACE USA
39300 Civic Center Dr # 290, Fremont
(94538-2337)
PHONE.....................510 790-4695
EMP: 65
SALES (est): 3.8MM
SALES (corp-wide): 17.2B **Privately Held**
SIC: 6411
HQ: Ace Usa, Inc.
436 Walnut St
Philadelphia PA 19106
215 923-5352

(P-10511)
ADRIANAS INSURANCE SVCS INC (PA)
9445 Charles Smith Ave, Rancho Cucamonga (91730-5546)
PHONE.....................909 291-4040
Leon Fregoso, *President*
Kevin Antunez, *Broker*
EMP: 54
SALES (est): 71.5MM **Privately Held**
SIC: 6411 Insurance agents

(P-10512)
AIG DIRECT INSURANCE SVCS INC
9640 Gran Rdge Dr Ste 200, San Diego
(92123)
PHONE.....................858 309-3000
Ron Harris, *CEO*
Laura Huffman, *Exec VP*
Patty Karstein, *Vice Pres*
Kevin Wilshusen, *Vice Pres*
Mark Kobleur, *Manager*
EMP: 275
SQ FT: 24,000
SALES (est): 91.5MM
SALES (corp-wide): 49.5B **Publicly Held**
WEB: www.matrixdirect.com
SIC: 6411 Insurance agents
HQ: American General Life Insurance Company
2727 Allen Pkwy Ste A
Houston TX 77019
713 522-1111

(P-10513)
ALL MOTORISTS INSURANCE AGENCY
Also Called: W G Warranty and Insur Svcs
5230 Las Virgenes Rd # 100, Calabasas
(91302-3448)
PHONE.....................818 880-9070
Robert M Ehrlich, *President*
Patsy Brents, *Treasurer*
Daniel Mallut, *Exec VP*
Marleen F Kushner, *Admin Sec*
EMP: 250
SQ FT: 51,000
SALES (est): 33.4MM
SALES (corp-wide): 98.7MM **Privately Held**
WEB: www.westerngeneral.com
SIC: 6411 Insurance agents, brokers & service

PA: Western General Holding Co
5230 Las Virgenes Rd # 100
Calabasas CA 91302
818 880-9070

(P-10514)
ALLIANT INSURANCE SERVICES INC (PA)
1301 Dove St Ste 200, Newport Beach
(92660-2436)
P.O. Box 6450 (92658-6450)
PHONE.....................949 756-0271
Thomas Corbett, *Ch of Bd*
Faith Dolliver, *President*
Nathan Harrison, *President*
Greg Zimmer, *President*
Jerold Hall, *COO*
EMP: 170
SQ FT: 45,000
SALES (est): 1B **Privately Held**
WEB: www.alliantinsurance.com
SIC: 6411 8748 Insurance agents; business consulting

(P-10515)
ALLIANT INSURANCE SERVICES INC
701 B St Ste 600, San Diego (92101-8156)
PHONE.....................619 238-1828
Joyce Finizio, *Manager*
Debra V Horn, *Project Mgr*
Alexis Berlanga, *Technology*
Ashley Mitchell, *Accountant*
EMP: 100
SALES (corp-wide): 1B **Privately Held**
SIC: 6411 Insurance agents
PA: Alliant Insurance Services, Inc.
1301 Dove St Ste 200
Newport Beach CA 92660
949 756-0271

(P-10516)
ALLSTATE RESEARCH AND PLG CTR
4200 Bohannon Dr Ste 200, Menlo Park
(94025-1019)
PHONE.....................650 833-6200
Peggy Brinkmann, *Director*
Joel Winter, *Research Analys*
Polly Ziegler, *Associate*
EMP: 90
SALES (est): 9.1MM **Privately Held**
SIC: 6411 Insurance agents, brokers & service

(P-10517)
AMERICAN AUTOMOBILE
Also Called: Csaa Travel Agency
3055 Oak Rd, Walnut Creek (94597-2098)
PHONE.....................925 279-2300
John Wu, *Principal*
EMP: 67
SALES (corp-wide): 907.9MM **Privately Held**
WEB: www.californiastateautomobileassociation.c
SIC: 6411 7549 Insurance agents, brokers & service; inspection & diagnostic service, automotive
PA: American Automobile Association Of Northern California, Nevada & Utah
1900 Powell St Ste 1200
Emeryville CA 94608
800 922-8228

(P-10518)
AMERICAN FIDELITY ASSURANCE CO
Also Called: Educational Services Division
3200 Inland Empire Blvd # 260, Ontario
(91764-5513)
PHONE.....................909 941-1175
Suzanne Stokes, *Branch Mgr*
Chris Rodriguez, *Sales Mgr*
Brian Rossen, *Consultant*
Sara Beckley, *Accounts Exec*
EMP: 99 **Privately Held**
WEB: www.afadvantage.com
SIC: 6411 Insurance agents
HQ: American Fidelity Assurance Company
9000 Cameron Pkwy
Oklahoma City OK 73114
405 523-2000

(P-10519)
AMERICAN FIDELITY ASSURANCE CO
3649 W Beechwood Ave # 103, Fresno
(93711-0693)
PHONE.....................559 230-2107
Amanda Dillon, *Branch Mgr*
EMP: 99 **Privately Held**
SIC: 6411 Insurance agents
HQ: American Fidelity Assurance Company
9000 Cameron Pkwy
Oklahoma City OK 73114
405 523-2000

(P-10520)
AMERICAN GENERAL LIFE INSUR
455 Hickey Blvd Ste 500, Daly City
(94015-2631)
PHONE.....................650 994-6679
Yuriy Kushnir, *Sales Staff*
Roger Relph, *Administration*
EMP: 80
SALES (corp-wide): 49.5B **Publicly Held**
WEB: www.dejonghfinancial.com
SIC: 6411 6311 Insurance agents, brokers & service; life insurance
HQ: American General Life Insurance
1 Franklin Sq
Springfield IL 62703
217 528-2011

(P-10521)
AMERICAN INTL GROUP INC
Also Called: AIG Private Client Group
9350 Waxie Way Ste 300, San Diego
(92123-1052)
PHONE.....................619 682-4058
Jack Devlin, *Manager*
Bradley R McGowan, *Finance Mgr*
EMP: 150
SALES (corp-wide): 49.5B **Publicly Held**
WEB: www.aiglifeinsurancecompany.com
SIC: 6411 Insurance agents
PA: American International Group, Inc.
80 Pine St Fl 4
New York NY 10005
212 770-7000

(P-10522)
AMERICAN SPECIALTY HEALTH INC (PA)
10221 Wateridge Cir # 201, San Diego
(92121-2702)
PHONE.....................858 754-2000
George Devries III, *CEO*
Robert White, *President*
William Comer, *CFO*
William Komer Jr, *Treasurer*
Doug Metz, *Officer*
EMP: 146
SALES: 424MM **Privately Held**
SIC: 6411 8082 Insurance information & consulting services; home health care services

(P-10523)
AMERICAS FLOOD SERVICES INC
3350 Country Club Dr # 201, Cameron Park
(95682-8657)
P.O. Box 913112, Denver CO (80291-3112)
PHONE.....................916 636-9460
John F Gibson, *President*
EMP: 100
SQ FT: 5,000
SALES (est): 10.7MM
SALES (corp-wide): 161.5MM **Privately Held**
SIC: 6411 6331 Insurance agents; fire, marine & casualty insurance
PA: The Bruce Seibels Group Inc
1501 Lady St
Columbia SC 29201
803 748-2000

(P-10524)
AMWINS INSURANCE BRKG CAL LLC (HQ)
21550 Oxnard St Ste 1100, Woodland Hills
(91367-7106)
PHONE.....................818 772-1774
Michael Steven Decarlo,
George Maggay, *President*
Christine Mathias, *Executive Asst*

Carolyn Abbott, *Asst Broker*
John Boyle, *Asst Broker*
EMP: 60 **EST:** 1981
SQ FT: 16,000
SALES (est): 21.9MM
SALES (corp-wide): 697.8MM **Privately Held**
SIC: 6411 Insurance brokers
PA: Amwins Group, Inc.
4725 Piedmont Row Dr # 600
Charlotte NC 28210
704 749-2700

(P-10525)
ANCHOR GENERAL INSURANCE AGCY
10256 Meanley Dr, San Diego
(92131-3009)
P.O. Box 509020 (92150-9020)
PHONE.....................858 527-3600
Abdulla Badani, *President*
Shaukat Badani, *Vice Pres*
Michael Mitchell, *VP Sales*
Lorenzo Rosas, *Manager*
EMP: 203
SALES (est): 56.1MM **Privately Held**
SIC: 6411 Insurance agents

(P-10526)
ANDREINI & COMPANY (PA)
220 W 20th Ave, San Mateo (94403-1339)
PHONE.....................650 573-1111
Michael J Colzani, *CEO*
Craig Oden, *Managing Prtnr*
John Andreini, *President*
Don Kuhns, *Exec VP*
Ralph Neate, *Senior VP*
EMP: 95
SQ FT: 30,000
SALES (est): 73.5MM **Privately Held**
WEB: www.andreini.com
SIC: 6411 Insurance brokers; insurance agents

(P-10527)
ANKA BEHAVIORAL HEALTH INC
Also Called: Phoenix Home Lf Mutl Insur Co
2100 State St, Hemet (92543-7623)
PHONE.....................951 929-2744
Don Cox, *Administration*
EMP: 137
SALES (corp-wide): 40.4MM **Privately Held**
SIC: 6411 8051 Property & casualty insurance agent; mental retardation hospital
PA: Anka Behavioral Health, Incorporated
1850 Gateway Blvd Ste 900
Concord CA 94520
925 825-4700

(P-10528)
AON CONSULTING INC
707 Wilshire Blvd # 2500, Los Angeles
(90017-3534)
PHONE.....................818 506-4300
Richard Schumacher, *Manager*
EMP: 60
SQ FT: 18,000
SALES (corp-wide): 10B **Privately Held**
WEB: www.radford.com
SIC: 6411 7361 Insurance brokers; employment agencies
HQ: Aon Consulting, Inc.
200 E Randolph St LI3
Chicago IL 60601
312 381-1000

(P-10529)
AON CONSULTING INC
3461 Fair Oaks Blvd, Sacramento
(95864-5702)
PHONE.....................800 558-0655
Kelly McMillan, *Branch Mgr*
EMP: 61
SALES (corp-wide): 10B **Privately Held**
SIC: 6411 Insurance brokers
HQ: Aon Consulting, Inc.
200 E Randolph St LI3
Chicago IL 60601
312 381-1000

(P-10530)
AON CONSULTING INC
21900 Burbank Blvd # 101, Woodland Hills
(91367-6469)
PHONE..................................562 345-4700
EMP: 61
SALES (corp-wide): 10B **Privately Held**
SIC: 6411 Insurance brokers
HQ: Aon Consulting, Inc.
200 E Randolph St Ll3
Chicago IL 60601
312 381-1000

(P-10531)
AON CONSULTING INC
851 Van Ness Ave Fl 2, San Francisco
(94109-7876)
PHONE..................................800 283-1667
EMP: 61
SALES (corp-wide): 10B **Privately Held**
SIC: 6411 Insurance brokers
HQ: Aon Consulting, Inc.
200 E Randolph St Ll3
Chicago IL 60601
312 381-1000

(P-10532)
AON CONSULTING INC
160 Via Verde Ste 200, San Dimas
(91773-5121)
PHONE..................................800 815-1823
EMP: 61
SALES (corp-wide): 10B **Privately Held**
SIC: 6411 Insurance brokers
HQ: Aon Consulting, Inc.
200 E Randolph St Ll3
Chicago IL 60601
312 381-1000

(P-10533)
AON CONSULTING INC
199 Fremont St Fl 11, San Francisco
(94105-2291)
PHONE..................................415 486-6226
Matt Davis, *Manager*
EMP: 250
SALES (corp-wide): 10B **Privately Held**
SIC: 6411 Insurance brokers
HQ: Aon Consulting, Inc.
200 E Randolph St Ll3
Chicago IL 60601
312 381-1000

(P-10534)
AON CONSULTING INC
5000 E Spring St Ste 100, Long Beach
(90815-5217)
PHONE..................................562 496-2888
EMP: 68
SALES (corp-wide): 10B **Privately Held**
SIC: 6411 Insurance brokers
HQ: Aon Consulting, Inc.
200 E Randolph St Ll3
Chicago IL 60601
312 381-1000

(P-10535)
AON CONSULTING INC
255 S Lake Ave Ste 900, Pasadena
(91101-3001)
PHONE..................................626 683-5200
Joan Miles, *CEO*
EMP: 68
SALES (corp-wide): 10B **Privately Held**
SIC: 6411 Insurance brokers
HQ: Aon Consulting, Inc.
200 E Randolph St Ll3
Chicago IL 60601
312 381-1000

(P-10536)
AON CONSULTING & INSUR
SVCS
199 Fremont St Fl 14, San Francisco
(94105-2253)
PHONE..................................415 486-7500
Judy Vukovich, *Senior VP*
Gassia Gujral, *Project Mgr*
Clarissa Green, *Consultant*
Stephanie Le, *Consultant*
EMP: 85

SALES (est): 19.2MM
SALES (corp-wide): 10B **Privately Held**
WEB: www.radford.com
SIC: 6411 8742 Insurance brokers; medical insurance claim processing, contract
or fee basis; management consulting
services
HQ: Aon Consulting, Inc.
200 E Randolph St Ll3
Chicago IL 60601
312 381-1000

(P-10537)
AON RISK SVCS COMPANIES
INC
707 Wilshire Blvd # 2600, Los Angeles
(90017-3501)
PHONE..................................213 630-3200
Eric Stocker, *Branch Mgr*
Lizette Junor, *Director*
EMP: 71
SALES (corp-wide): 10B **Privately Held**
WEB: www.ecomponline.com
SIC: 6411 Insurance brokers
HQ: Aon Risk Services Companies, Inc.
200 E Randolph St Fl 14
Chicago IL 60601
312 381-1000

(P-10538)
APFELD & NEAL INSURANCE
SVCS
11022 Winners Cir Ste 100, Los Alamitos
(90720-2869)
PHONE..................................714 821-7041
Jay Apfeld, *Partner*
Gary Neal, *Partner*
EMP: 50
SQ FT: 7,000
SALES (est): 3.9MM **Privately Held**
SIC: 6411 Insurance agents

(P-10539)
APOLLO AGENCIES INC (PA)
Also Called: Ais, Associated Insurance Svc
700 W 1st St Ste 2, Tustin (92780-2948)
P.O. Box 3267, Mission Viejo (92690-1267)
PHONE..................................714 832-2100
Michael A Jacobs, *President*
Thomas Crandell, *Treasurer*
EMP: 72
SQ FT: 6,000
SALES (est): 9.1MM **Privately Held**
WEB: www.apolloinsurance.net
SIC: 6411 Insurance agents

(P-10540)
APPLIED UNDERWRITERS INC
950 Tower Ln Ste 1400, Foster City
(94404-2128)
P.O. Box 281900, San Francisco (94128-
1900)
PHONE..................................415 656-5000
Ellen Gardiner, *Vice Pres*
Katy Van Horn, *Executive Asst*
EMP: 50
SALES (corp-wide): 242.1B **Publicly**
Held
WEB: www.applieduw.com
SIC: 6411 Insurance agents, brokers &
service
HQ: Applied Underwriters, Inc.
10805 Old Mill Rd
Omaha NE 68154
402 342-4900

(P-10541)
ARROWHEAD MANAGEMENT
COMPANY (DH)
701 B St Ste 2100, San Diego
(92101-8197)
PHONE..................................800 669-1889
Patrick Kilkenny, *Ch of Bd*
Marianne Harmon, *Corp Secy*
EMP: 71
SALES (est): 270.3MM
SALES (corp-wide): 1.8B **Publicly Held**
WEB: www.arrowheadgrp.com
SIC: 6411 8741 Insurance agents, brokers
& service; administrative management
HQ: Arrowhead General Insurance Agency,
Inc.
701 B St Ste 2100
San Diego CA 92101
800 669-1889

(P-10542)
ARROYO INSURANCE
SERVICES INC (PA)
440 E Huntington Dr # 100, Arcadia
(91006-3750)
P.O. Box 661840 (91066-1840)
PHONE..................................626 799-9532
Robert J Knauf, *President*
Richard Beedle, *Corp Secy*
James Armitage, *Vice Pres*
Jim Simands, *Vice Pres*
Kathleen Grisanti, *Executive*
EMP: 52
SQ FT: 3,500
SALES (est): 43.1MM **Privately Held**
SIC: 6411 Insurance agents & brokers

(P-10543)
ARTHUR J GALLAGHER & CO
Also Called: Gallagher Bassett
18201 Von Karman Ave # 200, Irvine
(92612-1069)
PHONE..................................949 349-9800
Yvonne Norte, *Manager*
Christopher Lage, *President*
Brendon Pollis, *Producer*
Amber Seggie, *Assistant VP*
EMP: 50
SALES (corp-wide): 6.1B **Publicly Held**
SIC: 6411 Insurance brokers
PA: Arthur J. Gallagher & Co.
2850 Golf Rd Ste 1000
Rolling Meadows IL 60008
630 773-3800

(P-10544)
ARTHUR J GALLAGHER & CO
Also Called: Kemper Insurance
505 N Brand Blvd Ste 600, Glendale
(91203-3944)
PHONE..................................818 539-2300
Scott Firestone, *Branch Mgr*
Alexandra S Glickman, *Vice Chairman*
Carol Cattich, *President*
Shannon Kearney, *President*
Jose Llop, *President*
EMP: 200
SALES (corp-wide): 6.1B **Publicly Held**
WEB: www.ajg.com
SIC: 6411 Insurance brokers
PA: Arthur J. Gallagher & Co.
2850 Golf Rd Ste 1000
Rolling Meadows IL 60008
630 773-3800

(P-10545)
ARTHUR J GALLAGHER & CO
Also Called: Gallagher Construction Svcs
1 Market Spear Tower, San Francisco
(94105)
PHONE..................................415 546-9300
Douglas B Bowring, *President*
James F Buckley III, *Senior VP*
Joel Kornreich, *Vice Pres*
Laura Locke, *Vice Pres*
Scott Whiteside, *Executive*
EMP: 200
SQ FT: 20,000
SALES (corp-wide): 6.1B **Publicly Held**
WEB: www.ajg.com
SIC: 6411 Insurance brokers
PA: Arthur J. Gallagher & Co.
2850 Golf Rd Ste 1000
Rolling Meadows IL 60008
630 773-3800

(P-10546)
ARTHUR J GALLAGHER & CO
7910 N Ingram Ave Ste 201, Fresno
(93711-5828)
PHONE..................................559 436-0833
Mahlon Buck, *Manager*
Mike Gong, *President*
Katherine Cherry, *Accounts Mgr*
EMP: 55
SALES (corp-wide): 6.1B **Publicly Held**
WEB: www.ajg.com
SIC: 6411 Insurance brokers
PA: Arthur J. Gallagher & Co.
2850 Golf Rd Ste 1000
Rolling Meadows IL 60008
630 773-3800

(P-10547)
ARTHUR J GALLAGHER & CO
Also Called: Kemper Insurance
3697 Mt Diablo Blvd Ste 300, Lafayette
(94549-3747)
PHONE..................................925 299-1112
Douglas Bowring, *Branch Mgr*
Monica Kozak, *Client Mgr*
Susan Exline, *Agent*
Carla Colombana, *Supervisor*
EMP: 50
SALES (corp-wide): 6.1B **Publicly Held**
WEB: www.ajg.com
SIC: 6411 Insurance brokers
PA: Arthur J. Gallagher & Co.
2850 Golf Rd Ste 1000
Rolling Meadows IL 60008
630 773-3800

(P-10548)
ASSOCIATED PENSION CONS
INC (PA)
2035 Forest Ave, Chico (95928-7620)
P.O. Box 1282 (95927-1282)
PHONE..................................530 343-4233
Matt Blofsky, *President*
Marc Roberts, *Treasurer*
Linda Madsen, *Vice Pres*
Gloria Anderson, *Admin Asst*
John Olsen, *VP Opers*
EMP: 51
SQ FT: 20,000
SALES (est): 6.6MM **Privately Held**
SIC: 6411 Pension & retirement plan con-
sultants

(P-10549)
ASSUREDPARTNERS INC
1455 Response Rd Ste 260, Sacramento
(95815-5263)
PHONE..................................916 443-0200
EMP: 56 **Privately Held**
SIC: 6411 Insurance agents
PA: Assuredpartners, Inc.
200 Colonial Center Pkwy
Lake Mary FL 32746

(P-10550)
ATHENS INSURANCE SERVICE
INC
Also Called: Athens Administrators
2552 Stanwell Dr Ste 100, Concord
(94520-4851)
P.O. Box 4029 (94524-4029)
PHONE..................................925 826-1000
James C Jenkins, *Ch of Bd*
James R Jenkins, *President*
Jodi Ellington, *CFO*
EMP: 250
SALES (est): 56.8MM **Privately Held**
SIC: 6411 Insurance claim adjusters, not
employed by insurance company

(P-10551)
ATLAS GENERAL INSUR SVCS
LLC
4365 Executive Dr Ste 400, San Diego
(92121-2136)
PHONE..................................858 529-6700
William Trzos,
Greg Mosher, *President*
EMP: 153
SALES: 27MM **Privately Held**
SIC: 6411 Insurance agents

(P-10552)
AUTO INSUR SPCIALISTS-LONG
BCH
Also Called: A I S-Auto Insur Specialists
5000 E Spring St Ste 100, Long Beach
(90815-5217)
PHONE..................................562 496-2888
James F Caird, *President*
EMP: 60
SALES (est): 5MM
SALES (corp-wide): 10B **Privately Held**
SIC: 6411 6331 Insurance agents, brokers
& service; fire, marine & casualty insur-
ance
HQ: Aon Financial Services Group, Inc.
999 N Pacific Coast Hwy
El Segundo CA 90245
800 859-6511

PRODUCTS & SVCS

(P-10553)
AUTO INSURANCE
SPECIALISTS LLC (DH)
17785 Center Court Dr N # 110, Cerritos
(90703-8573)
PHONE..................562 345-6247
Mark Ribisi, *CEO*
Chris Bremer, *CFO*
Jerry Baker, *Vice Pres*
Mark Casas, *Vice Pres*
Lani Elkin, *Vice Pres*
EMP: 210
SQ FT: 45,000
SALES (est): 88.6MM
SALES (corp-wide): 3.4B **Publicly Held**
SIC: 6411 Insurance brokers

(P-10554)
AUTOMOBILE CLUB SOUTHERN
CAL (PA)
Also Called: A A A Automobile Club So Cal
2601 S Figueroa St, Los Angeles
(90007-3294)
P.O. Box 25001, Santa Ana (92799-5001)
PHONE..................213 741-3686
Robert T Bouttier, *Principal*
Zoo Babies, *President*
Peter R McDonald, *Senior VP*
Brian Deephouse, *Vice Pres*
Vicki Foshee, *Vice Pres*
EMP: 150
SQ FT: 425,000
SALES (est): 7.2B **Privately Held**
SIC: 6411 8699 Insurance agents; auto-
mobile owners' association

(P-10555)
AUTOMOBILE CLUB SOUTHERN
CAL
Also Called: AAA Auto Club
3333 Fairview Rd, Costa Mesa
(92626-1698)
PHONE..................714 885-1343
Becky Martinez, *Branch Mgr*
EMP: 200
SALES (corp-wide): 7.2B **Privately Held**
SIC: 6411 Insurance agents, brokers &
service
PA: Automobile Club Of Southern California
2601 S Figueroa St
Los Angeles CA 90007
213 741-3686

(P-10556)
AUTOMOBILE CLUB SOUTHERN
CAL
10540 Fthill Blvd Ste 100, Rancho Cuca-
monga (91730)
PHONE..................909 980-0233
Alice Holguin, *Branch Mgr*
Grace Curtis, *Office Mgr*
EMP: 108
SALES (corp-wide): 7.2B **Privately Held**
SIC: 6411 Insurance agents, brokers &
service
PA: Automobile Club Of Southern California
2601 S Figueroa St
Los Angeles CA 90007
213 741-3686

(P-10557)
AUTOMOBILE CLUB SOUTHERN
CAL
2666 Del Mar Heights Rd, Del Mar
(92014-3100)
PHONE..................858 481-7181
Tom McKernan, *Manager*
EMP: 108
SALES (corp-wide): 7.2B **Privately Held**
SIC: 6411 Insurance agents, brokers &
service
PA: Automobile Club Of Southern California
2601 S Figueroa St
Los Angeles CA 90007
213 741-3686

(P-10558)
AXA EQUITABLE LIFE INSUR CO
Also Called: Equitable Life Assurance
3777 La Jolla Village Dr, San Diego
(92122-1080)
PHONE..................858 552-1234
Alen Farwell, *Manager*
EMP: 70 **Publicly Held**
WEB: www.equitable.com

SIC: 6411 Insurance agents, brokers &
service
HQ: Axa Equitable Life Insurance Company
1290 Avenue Of The Americ
New York NY 10104
212 554-1234

(P-10559)
BARRY MCPHERSON INC
1932 E Deere Ave Ste 240, Santa Ana
(92705-5716)
PHONE..................425 343-5000
Kenneth B McPherson, *President*
EMP: 240
SALES (est): 26MM **Privately Held**
SIC: 6411 Insurance agents, brokers &
service

(P-10560)
BENEFICIAL ADMINISTRATION
CO
Also Called: Best Plans
17701 Mitchell N, Irvine (92614-6028)
PHONE..................949 756-1000
Jim Voegtlin, *President*
John Van Der Schraaf, *Treasurer*
Daniel Frey, *VP Admin*
Diana Abeta, *Admin Sec*
Dave Pitman, *Info Tech Dir*
EMP: 80 **EST:** 1970
SQ FT: 30,000
SALES (est): 9.6MM **Privately Held**
WEB: www.beneficialadmin.com
SIC: 6411 8741 Insurance agents, brokers
& service; management services

(P-10561)
BENEFIT & RISK MANAGEMENT
SVCS
80 Iron Point Cir Ste 200, Folsom
(95630-8593)
P.O. Box 2140 (95763-2140)
PHONE..................916 467-1200
Matthew Allen Schafer, *CEO*
Luke Schafer, *Vice Pres*
Paul Schafer, *Vice Pres*
Sean Groom, *Administration*
William Hardison, *Info Tech Dir*
EMP: 130
SQ FT: 15,000
SALES (est): 35.5MM **Privately Held**
WEB: www.brms-online.com
SIC: 6411 Insurance information & consult-
ing services

(P-10562)
BENETECH INC (PA)
3947 Lennane Dr Ste 250, Sacramento
(95834-1972)
P.O. Box 348570 (95834-8570)
PHONE..................916 484-6811
Robert L Brandon, *President*
James Casalegno, *Senior VP*
Christopher Blazek, *Vice Pres*
Robert Brandon, *Vice Pres*
Charles Bridges, *Vice Pres*
EMP: 60 **EST:** 1974
SQ FT: 20,000
SALES (est): 28.1MM **Privately Held**
SIC: 6411 Pension & retirement plan con-
sultants

(P-10563)
BENETECH INC
4420 Auburn Blvd Fl 2, Sacramento
(95841-4146)
P.O. Box 348570 (95834-8570)
PHONE..................916 484-6811
Kelly Roberts, *Manager*
Wes Jones, *CFO*
Janet Chapman, *Manager*
EMP: 50
SALES (corp-wide): 28.1MM **Privately
Held**
SIC: 6411 Pension & retirement plan con-
sultants
PA: Benetech, Inc
3947 Lennane Dr Ste 250
Sacramento CA 95834
916 484-6811

(P-10564)
BERKSHIRE HATHAWAY
HOMESTATES
2020 Camino Del Rio N, San Diego
(92108-1541)
PHONE..................619 686-8424
Michael Millwood, *Manager*
EMP: 70
SALES (corp-wide): 242.1B **Publicly
Held**
WEB: www.acpac.com
SIC: 6411 Insurance claim processing, ex-
cept medical
HQ: Berkshire Hathaway Homestates
50 California St Fl 14
San Francisco CA 94111

(P-10565)
BICKMORE AND ASSOCIATES
INC (DH)
Also Called: Bickmore Risk Svcs Consulting
1750 Creekside Oaks Dr # 200, Sacra-
mento (95833-3648)
PHONE..................916 244-1100
Greg L Trout, *CEO*
John Alltop, *President*
L Robert Kramer, *President*
Jeffrey C Grubbs, *COO*
Kailey Adams, *Admin Asst*
EMP: 70
SQ FT: 25,500
SALES (est): 43.4MM
SALES (corp-wide): 2.3B **Privately Held**
WEB: www.brsrisk.com
SIC: 6411 Insurance information & consult-
ing services
HQ: York Risk Services Group, Inc.
1 Upper Pond
Parsippany NJ 07054
973 404-1200

(P-10566)
BUILDERS & TRADESMENS
6610 Sierra College Blvd, Rocklin
(95677-4306)
PHONE..................916 772-9200
Norbert Hohlbein, *President*
Jeff Erickson, *Vice Pres*
Lisa Erickson, *Vice Pres*
Jeff Hohlbein, *Vice Pres*
Paul Hohlbein, *Vice Pres*
EMP: 75
SQ FT: 15,000
SALES (est): 62.6MM **Publicly Held**
WEB: www.btisinc.com
SIC: 6411 Insurance brokers; fire insur-
ance underwriters' laboratories
PA: Amtrust Financial Services, Inc.
59 Maiden Ln Fl 43
New York NY 10038

(P-10567)
C M A ALLIANCE
Also Called: Cornerstone Marketing Alliance
16542 Ventura Blvd # 210, Encino
(91436-2005)
PHONE..................818 981-0800
Steve Pato, *Owner*
EMP: 50 **EST:** 2001
SALES (est): 3.7MM **Privately Held**
WEB: www.cma-la.com
SIC: 6411 Insurance agents, brokers &
service

(P-10568)
CA STE ATOM ASSOC INTR-INS
BUR
Also Called: AAA
900 Miramonte Ave, Mountain View
(94040-2457)
P.O. Box 391840 (94039-1840)
PHONE..................650 623-3200
Jerry Hall, *Branch Mgr*
EMP: 60
SQ FT: 15,414
SALES (corp-wide): 907.9MM **Privately
Held**
WEB: www.viamagazine.com
SIC: 6411 Insurance claim processing, ex-
cept medical

HQ: California State Automobile Association Inter-Insurance Bureau
1276 S California Blvd
Walnut Creek CA 94596
925 287-7600

(P-10569)
CABRILLO GEN INSUR AGCY
INC
7071 Convoy Ct Ste 201, San Diego
(92111-1023)
P.O. Box 17425 (92177-7425)
PHONE..................858 244-0550
Robert Jester, *President*
Micheal McNitt, *Vice Pres*
EMP: 88 **EST:** 2005
SALES (est): 11.9MM **Privately Held**
SIC: 6411 Insurance agents, brokers &
service

(P-10570)
CAESAR AND SEIDER INSUR
SVCS (PA)
Also Called: Talbot Insurance & Fincl Svcs
40 E Alamar Ave Ste 4, Santa Barbara
(93105-3400)
P.O. Box 3310 (93130-3310)
PHONE..................805 682-2571
Thomas Caesar, *President*
Ray Seider, *Vice Pres*
EMP: 52 **EST:** 1954
SQ FT: 2,400
SALES (est): 7.3MM **Privately Held**
SIC: 6411 Insurance brokers

(P-10571)
CALIFORNIA CLINICAL TRIALS
3828 Delmas Ter 2, Culver City
(90232-2713)
PHONE..................310 945-1780
Murry Rosenthal, *CEO*
EMP: 200 **EST:** 1989
SALES (est): 16.3MM **Privately Held**
SIC: 6411 8731 Research services, insur-
ance; commercial physical research

(P-10572)
CALIFORNIA FAIR PLAN ASSN
3435 Wilshire Blvd # 1200, Los Angeles
(90010-1911)
PHONE..................213 487-0111
Stuart M Wilkinson, *President*
Elvira Evangelista, *Human Resources*
Raul Paez, *Supervisor*
EMP: 80
SALES (est): 17.7MM **Privately Held**
WEB: www.cfpnet.com
SIC: 6411 Insurance agents

(P-10573)
CALIFORNIA HEALTHCARE
Also Called: C.H.M.B.
700 La Terraza Blvd # 200, Escondido
(92025-3868)
PHONE..................760 520-1333
Bob Svendsen, *CEO*
Janet Boos, *President*
Vicki Brown, *Vice Pres*
Donna Forster, *Vice Pres*
James Trewin, *Vice Pres*
EMP: 135
SQ FT: 16,000
SALES (est): 52.2MM **Privately Held**
WEB: www.chmb.com
SIC: 6411 Medical insurance claim pro-
cessing, contract or fee basis

(P-10574)
CALIFRNIA PHYSCN
REIMBURSEMENT
1321 Butte St Apt 202, Redding
(96001-1065)
PHONE..................530 241-0473
Jane Rehberg, *President*
EMP: 73
SALES (est): 9.9MM **Privately Held**
WEB: www.cprbilling.com
SIC: 6411 Medical insurance claim pro-
cessing, contract or fee basis

(P-10575)
CAMICO MUTUAL INSURANCE CO (PA)
1800 Gateway Dr Ste 300, San Mateo (94404-4072)
PHONE..................................650 378-6874
Ricardo R Rosario, *President*
Robert P Evans, *Ch of Bd*
Jay H Stewart, *CFO*
Rachel Ehrlich, *Officer*
Judith Frederiksen, *Vice Pres*
EMP: 80
SQ FT: 22,000
SALES (est): 32.4MM **Privately Held**
SIC: 6411 Professional standards services, insurance

(P-10576)
CANNON COCHRAN MGT SVCS INC
Also Called: Ccmsi
18881 Von Karman Ave # 380, Irvine (92612-6580)
PHONE..................................949 474-6500
William Hougland, *Manager*
Andy Hougland, *Branch Mgr*
EMP: 59 **Privately Held**
SIC: 6411 Insurance agents
HQ: Cannon Cochran Management Services, Inc.
2 E Main St Towne Ctr
Danville IL 61832
217 446-1089

(P-10577)
CARLTON SENIOR LIVING INC
380 Branham Ln Ofc Ofc, San Jose (95136-4302)
PHONE..................................408 972-1400
Mandi Farrell, *Director*
EMP: 67
SALES (corp-wide): 29.6MM **Privately Held**
SIC: 6411 Pension & retirement plan consultants
PA: Senior Carlton Living Inc
4005 Port Chicago Hwy # 120
Concord CA 94520
925 338-2434

(P-10578)
CARNEGIE AGENCY INC
2101 Corp Cntr Dr Ste 150, Newbury Park (91320-1436)
PHONE..................................805 445-1470
John Smith, *President*
Chuck Smith, *Vice Pres*
EMP: 50
SQ FT: 40,000
SALES (est): 7.8MM **Privately Held**
WEB: www.cgia.com
SIC: 6411 Insurance agents, brokers & service

(P-10579)
CARTEL MARKETING INC
Also Called: Insure Express Insurance Svc
5230 Las Virgenes Rd # 250, Calabasas (91302-3448)
PHONE..................................818 483-1130
Robert M Humphreys, *Ch of Bd*
Jack Edelstein, *President*
Brian Murphy, *COO*
William Russell, *CFO*
Michael Neustadt, *Officer*
EMP: 102
SQ FT: 14,000
SALES (est): 23.3MM
SALES (corp-wide): 41.5MM **Privately Held**
WEB: www.cartel.net
SIC: 6411 Insurance agents & brokers
HQ: Expresslink, Inc.
16501 Ventura Blvd # 300
Encino CA 91436
818 788-5555

(P-10580)
CENTURY 21 A BETTER SVC RLTY
5831 Firestone Blvd Ste J, South Gate (90280-3718)
PHONE..................................562 806-1000
David Sarinana, *President*
Blanca Sarinana, *Vice Pres*

EMP: 97
SQ FT: 4,000
SALES (est): 16MM **Privately Held**
WEB: www.c21abetterservice.com
SIC: 6411 6531 Insurance agents, brokers & service; real estate agents & managers

(P-10581)
CHARLES M KAMIYA AND SONS INC
Also Called: Kamiya, Kenneth M Insurance
373 Van Ness Ave Ste 200, Torrance (90501-6239)
PHONE..................................310 781-2066
Kenneth Kamiya, *President*
Edward Kamiya, *Vice Pres*
EMP: 54
SALES (est): 7.5MM **Privately Held**
WEB: www.kamiyainsurance.com
SIC: 6411 Insurance agents

(P-10582)
CHOIC ADMINI INSUR SERVI
Also Called: California Choice
721 S Parker St Ste 200, Orange (92868-4772)
PHONE..................................714 542-4200
Ron Goldstein, *President*
Kevin J Counihan, *President*
Veronica Flores, *President*
Tamra Reise, *Senior VP*
Brenda Scott, *Senior VP*
EMP: 500
SALES (est): 105.1MM **Privately Held**
WEB: www.wordup.com
SIC: 6411 Insurance agents

(P-10583)
CHUBB US HOLDING INC
455 Market St Ste 500, San Francisco (94105-2539)
PHONE..................................415 547-4400
Steve Meyers, *Branch Mgr*
Norm Rafsol, *Branch Mgr*
Shannon Newman, *Human Res Dir*
Brian E Witzmann, *Manager*
EMP: 68
SALES (corp-wide): 28.7B **Privately Held**
WEB: www.ace.bm
SIC: 6411 Property & casualty insurance agent
HQ: Chubb Us Holding Inc.
1601 Chestnut St
Philadelphia PA 19192

(P-10584)
CHUBB US HOLDING INC
Also Called: Inamar
3131 Camino Del Rio N, San Diego (92108-5701)
PHONE..................................619 563-2400
Linda Andres, *Manager*
EMP: 212
SALES (corp-wide): 28.7B **Privately Held**
WEB: www.ace.bm
SIC: 6411 Insurance agents, brokers & service
HQ: Chubb Us Holding Inc.
1601 Chestnut St
Philadelphia PA 19192

(P-10585)
CHUBB US HOLDING INC
9200 Oakdale Ave, Chatsworth (91311-6500)
P.O. Box 3500, Woodland Hills (91365-3500)
PHONE..................................818 428-3600
James Perry, *Branch Mgr*
EMP: 150
SALES (corp-wide): 28.7B **Privately Held**
WEB: www.ace.bm
SIC: 6411 Property & casualty insurance agent; patrol services, insurance
HQ: Chubb Us Holding Inc.
1601 Chestnut St
Philadelphia PA 19192

(P-10586)
CLAIMS MANAGEMENT INC
1101 Crksde Rdge Dr 100, Roseville (95678)
P.O. Box 619079 (95661-9079)
PHONE..................................916 631-1250
Kathy Peterson, *President*
Patricia Spellins, *Train & Dev Mgr*
Kenny Seyer, *Training Spec*
Virginia Marsh, *Master*
John Scott, *Senior Mgr*
EMP: 130
SQ FT: 23,000
SALES (est): 21.2MM **Privately Held**
WEB: www.claimsmanagement.com
SIC: 6411 Insurance claim adjusters, not employed by insurance company

(P-10587)
CNA FINANCIAL CORPORATION
Also Called: CNA Insurance
1800 E Imperial Hwy # 200, Brea (92821-6062)
P.O. Box 6500 (92822-6500)
PHONE..................................714 255-2200
John C Magee III, *Branch Mgr*
EMP: 200
SALES (corp-wide): 13.7B **Publicly Held**
SIC: 6411 6531 Insurance brokers; fire, marine & casualty insurance
HQ: Cna Financial Corporation
151 N Franklin St Ste 700
Chicago IL 60606
312 822-5000

(P-10588)
CNA SURETY CORPORATION
1455 Frazee Rd Ste 801, San Diego (92108-4309)
PHONE..................................619 682-3550
Ron Fawcett, *Manager*
Jennifer Purdon, *Research Analys*
EMP: 71
SALES (corp-wide): 13.7B **Publicly Held**
SIC: 6411 Insurance agents
HQ: Cna Surety Corporation
333 S Wabash Ave Ste 41s
Chicago IL 60604
312 822-5000

(P-10589)
COASTAL SELECT INSURANCE CO
4820 Busineca Ctr Dr 20, Fairfield (94534)
PHONE..................................707 863-3700
Kevin Nish, *President*
Karen Padovese, *COO*
EMP: 50
SALES (est): 4.9MM **Privately Held**
WEB: www.pacificselectproperty.com
SIC: 6411 Insurance agents, brokers & service
PA: Geovera Holdings, Inc.
4820 Busineca Ctr Dr 20
Fairfield CA 94534

(P-10590)
COLDWELL BANKER
580 El Camino Real, San Carlos (94070-2412)
PHONE..................................650 596-5400
EMP: 80 EST: 2011
SALES (est): 5.7MM **Privately Held**
SIC: 6411

(P-10591)
COLLECTIVEHEALTH INC
Also Called: Collective Health
85 Bluxome St, San Francisco (94107-1664)
PHONE..................................650 376-3804
Ali Diab, *CEO*
Rajaie Batniji, *Officer*
Jude Komuves, *Officer*
Chris Willey, *Executive*
Kristin Spohn, *Business Dir*
EMP: 410 EST: 2013
SQ FT: 6,000
SALES (est): 2.9MM **Privately Held**
SIC: 6411 7379 7372 Medical insurance claim processing, contract or fee basis; ; business oriented computer software

(P-10592)
CONEXIS BNEFT ADMNISTRATORS LP (HQ)
721 S Parker St Ste 300, Orange (92868-4732)
PHONE..................................714 835-5006
Michael Close, *President*
EMP: 120
SQ FT: 57,000
SALES (est): 233.9MM
SALES (corp-wide): 383.5MM **Privately Held**
SIC: 6411 Insurance information & consulting services
PA: Word & Brown, Insurance Administrators, Inc.
721 S Parker St Ste 300
Orange CA 92868
714 835-5006

(P-10593)
CONFIE SEGUROS INC (HQ)
Also Called: Freeway Insurance
7711 Center Ave Ste 200, Huntington Beach (92647-9124)
PHONE..................................714 252-2500
Joseph Waked, *CEO*
Mordy Rothberg, *President*
Valeria Rico, *COO*
Robert Trebing, *CFO*
Chris Tedford, *Officer*
EMP: 146
SALES (est): 980.4MM
SALES (corp-wide): 981.3MM **Privately Held**
SIC: 6411 Insurance brokers
PA: Confie Seguros California, Inc.
7711 Center Ave Ste 200
Huntington Beach CA 92647
714 252-2649

(P-10594)
CORVEL CORPORATION
10750 4th St Ste 100, Rancho Cucamonga (91730-0980)
PHONE..................................909 257-3700
Lorie Gonzalez, *Branch Mgr*
Robert Cunningham, *Admin Asst*
Bryan Piattoni, *Regl Sales Mgr*
David Cuffia, *Supervisor*
EMP: 168
SALES (corp-wide): 558.3MM **Publicly Held**
WEB: www.corvel.com
SIC: 6411 Insurance agents, brokers & service
PA: Corvel Corporation
2010 Main St Ste 600
Irvine CA 92614
949 851-1473

(P-10595)
CORVEL ENTERPRISE COMP INC
2010 Main St Ste 600, Irvine (92614-7272)
PHONE..................................949 851-1473
Daniel J Starck, *CEO*
EMP: 99
SALES (est): 950K **Privately Held**
SIC: 6411 Insurance agents, brokers & service

(P-10596)
CREST FINANCIAL CORPORATION (DH)
12641 166th St, Cerritos (90703-2101)
P.O. Box 3190 (90703-3190)
PHONE..................................562 733-6500
Susan Scurti, *President*
Shannon S Walker, *CFO*
Michael Costello, *Senior VP*
Walter E Erker, *Vice Pres*
EMP: 62
SQ FT: 15,000
SALES (est): 32.4MM
SALES (corp-wide): 13.2B **Privately Held**
SIC: 6411 7311 Insurance agents; insurance information & consulting services; insurance adjusters; insurance agents & brokers; advertising agencies

(P-10597)
CSAA INSURANCE EXCHANGE (PA)
3055 Oak Rd, Walnut Creek (94597-2098)
P.O. Box 23392, Oakland (94623-0392)
PHONE...................800 922-8228
Paula Downey, *President*
Greg Meyer, *COO*
Marie Andel, *Officer*
Michael Zukerman, *Officer*
Stephen O'Connor, *CIO*
EMP: 106
SALES (est): 3.1B **Privately Held**
SIC: 6411 Insurance agents

(P-10598)
CSAC EXCESS INSURANCE AUTH
75 Iron Point Cir Ste 200, Folsom
(95630-8813)
PHONE...................916 850-7300
Michael Fleming, *CEO*
Rick Brush, *Officer*
Mike Pott, *Officer*
Jim Castle, *Sr Exec VP*
Ken Caldwell, *Exec VP*
EMP: 60
SQ FT: 13,613
SALES (est): 10.5MM **Privately Held**
WEB: www.csac-eia.org
SIC: 6411 Insurance agents

(P-10599)
CUSTOMZED SVCS ADMNSTRTORS INC
Also Called: Global Care Travel
4181 Ruffin Rd Ste 150, San Diego
(92123-1876)
P.O. Box 939057 (92193-9057)
PHONE...................858 810-2000
Guillaume Deybach, *CEO*
Huong Le, *Agent*
EMP: 140
SQ FT: 11,000
SALES (est): 55.9MM **Privately Held**
WEB: www.csatravelprotection.com
SIC: 6411 Insurance agents; travel agencies
PA: Enhancement Products Specialists Inc
5454 Ruffin Rd
San Diego CA

(P-10600)
CYBER POLICY
1 California St Ste 1100, San Francisco
(94111-5412)
PHONE...................877 626-9991
Keith Moore, *CEO*
EMP: 103
SALES (est): 10MM **Privately Held**
SIC: 6411 Insurance agents, brokers & service

(P-10601)
CYBER TECHNOLOGY LLC (PA)
Also Called: Smartfinancial
1901 Newport Blvd Ste 300, Costa Mesa
(92627-2290)
PHONE...................614 207-2955
Lev Barinskiy,
EMP: 50
SQ FT: 5,000
SALES (est): 5.6MM **Privately Held**
SIC: 6411 Insurance agents, brokers & service

(P-10602)
DEALEY RENTON AND ASSOCIATES
530 Water St Fl 7th, Oakland (94607-3547)
PHONE...................510 465-3090
Morgan West, *Principal*
Don Fitch, *Vice Pres*
Sherall Gradias, *Vice Pres*
Robin Rose, *Marketing Staff*
Angela Borg, *Accounts Mgr*
EMP: 55
SALES (est): 1.8MM **Privately Held**
SIC: 6411 Insurance brokers

(P-10603)
DEL AMO INSURANCE SERVICES
910 Lomita Blvd Ste E, Harbor City
(90710-2200)
PHONE...................310 534-3444
David Blunt, *President*
EMP: 60
SALES (est): 9.6MM **Privately Held**
SIC: 6411 Insurance agents, brokers & service

(P-10604)
DENTISTS INSURANCE COMPANY (HQ)
Also Called: Tdic
1201 K St Ste 1600, Sacramento
(95814-3925)
P.O. Box 1582 (95812-1582)
PHONE...................916 443-4567
Mark Soeth, *President*
EMP: 118
SQ FT: 12,000
SALES (est): 21.2MM
SALES (corp-wide): 21.4MM **Privately Held**
WEB: www.thedentists.com
SIC: 6411 Insurance agents, brokers & service
PA: California Dental Association Inc
1201 K St Fl 14
Sacramento CA 95814
916 443-0505

(P-10605)
DIBUDUO DFENDIS INSUR BRKS LLC (PA)
6873 N West Ave, Fresno (93711-4308)
P.O. Box 5479 (93755-5479)
PHONE...................559 432-0222
Matt Defendis, *Partner*
Mike De Fendis, *Partner*
Tony Canizales, *Vice Pres*
Debra Duckering, *Vice Pres*
Steve Ellsworth, *Vice Pres*
EMP: 93 EST: 1960
SQ FT: 22,000
SALES (est): 53MM **Privately Held**
WEB: www.dibu.com
SIC: 6411 Insurance agents

(P-10606)
DMA CLAIMS INC (PA)
Also Called: Dma Claims Services
330 N Brand Blvd Ste 230, Glendale
(91203-2380)
P.O. Box 26004 (91222-6004)
PHONE...................323 342-6800
Thomas J Reitze, *President*
EMP: 55
SQ FT: 20,000
SALES (est): 133MM **Privately Held**
WEB: www.davidmorse.com
SIC: 6411 Insurance claim adjusters, not employed by insurance company; insurance adjusters

(P-10607)
DMA CLAIMS INC
7188 Via Carmela, San Jose (95139-1125)
PHONE...................800 649-7602
Mark Rost, *Principal*
EMP: 64
SALES (corp-wide): 133MM **Privately Held**
SIC: 6411 Insurance adjusters
PA: Dma Claims, Inc.
330 N Brand Blvd Ste 230
Glendale CA 91203
323 342-6800

(P-10608)
DMA CLAIMS INC
Also Called: David Morse & Assoc.
330 N Brand Blvd Ste 230, Glendale
(91203-2380)
PHONE...................323 342-6800
Dan Mara, *Branch Mgr*
Dan Todd, *Agent*
EMP: 64
SALES (corp-wide): 133MM **Privately Held**
SIC: 6411 Insurance adjusters

PA: Dma Claims, Inc.
330 N Brand Blvd Ste 230
Glendale CA 91203
323 342-6800

(P-10609)
DOCTORS MANAGEMENT COMPANY (HQ)
185 Greenwood Rd, NAPA (94558-6270)
P.O. Box 2900 (94558-0900)
PHONE...................707 226-0100
Richard E Anderson, *CEO*
Eugene M Bullis, *CFO*
Kenneth R Chrisman, *Exec VP*
William J Gallagher, *Senior VP*
Michael Yacob, *Principal*
EMP: 200
SQ FT: 72,000
SALES (est): 232.2MM
SALES (corp-wide): 393.7MM **Privately Held**
SIC: 6411 Insurance information & consulting services; insurance claim processing, except medical
PA: The Doctors' Company An Interinsurance Exchange
185 Greenwood Rd
Napa CA 94558
707 226-0100

(P-10610)
EDGEWOOD PARTNERS INSUR CTR
1390 Willow Pass Rd # 800, Concord
(94520-7924)
PHONE...................415 356-3900
Joe Vineis, *Branch Mgr*
Ricky H Choi, *Senior VP*
Judi Bolanos, *Vice Pres*
Cindy Covington, *Vice Pres*
Mary Grandy, *Vice Pres*
EMP: 105 **Privately Held**
SIC: 6411 8742 Insurance brokers; property & casualty insurance agent; management consulting services
PA: Edgewood Partners Insurance Center, Inc.
1390 Willow Pass Rd # 800
Concord CA 94520

(P-10611)
EDGEWOOD PARTNERS INSUR CTR
1010 B St Ste 423, San Rafael
(94901-2921)
PHONE...................415 456-4323
Todd Sishman, *Branch Mgr*
EMP: 85 **Privately Held**
SIC: 6411 Insurance agents, brokers & service
PA: Edgewood Partners Insurance Center, Inc.
1390 Willow Pass Rd # 800
Concord CA 94520

(P-10612)
EDGEWOOD PRTNERS INSUR CTR INC (PA)
Also Called: Epic
1390 Willow Pass Rd # 800, Concord
(94520-7924)
P.O. Box 5900, San Mateo (94402-5900)
PHONE...................415 356-3900
John Hahn, *CEO*
Peter Garvey, *President*
Kathy Lopez, *President*
Kevin Harnetiaux, *COO*
Karman Chan, *CFO*
EMP: 65
SQ FT: 18,897
SALES (est): 434.8MM **Privately Held**
WEB: www.edgewoodins.com
SIC: 6411 Insurance brokers

(P-10613)
EHEALTH INC (PA)
440 E Middlefield Rd, Mountain View
(94043-4006)
PHONE...................650 584-2700
Ellen O Tauscher, *Ch of Bd*
Scott N Flanders, *CEO*
David Francis, *COO*
Derek N Yung, *CFO*

PA: Dma Claims, Inc.
330 N Brand Blvd Ste 230
Glendale CA 91203
323 342-6800

Tim Hannan, *Chief Mktg Ofcr*
EMP: 73
SQ FT: 36,012
SALES: 172.3MM **Publicly Held**
WEB: www.ehealthinsurance.com
SIC: 6411 Insurance agents; insurance agents & brokers; insurance information & consulting services

(P-10614)
EHEALTHINSURANCE SERVICES INC (HQ)
440 E Middlefield Rd, Mountain View
(94043-4006)
PHONE...................650 584-2700
Ellen O Tausche, *Principal*
Rob Lapstuen, *President*
Bill Shaughnessy, *President*
Jiang Wu, *President*
Samuel C Gibbs III, *Senior VP*
EMP: 100
SQ FT: 20,000
SALES (est): 59.5MM
SALES (corp-wide): 172.3MM **Publicly Held**
WEB: www.anysure.com
SIC: 6411 Insurance agents, brokers & service
PA: Ehealth, Inc.
440 E Middlefield Rd
Mountain View CA 94043
650 584-2700

(P-10615)
ESURANCE INSURANCE SVCS INC (HQ)
Also Called: PNC
650 Davis St, San Francisco (94111-1981)
PHONE...................415 875-4500
Gary C Tolman, *CEO*
Jonathan Adkisson, *CFO*
Alan Gellman, *Chief Mktg Ofcr*
Eric Brandt, *Officer*
Kerian Bunch, *Vice Pres*
EMP: 140 EST: 1999
SQ FT: 10,000
SALES (est): 357.6MM **Publicly Held**
SIC: 6411 Insurance agents

(P-10616)
EVIDERA ARCHIMEDES INC
450 Sansome St Ste 650, San Francisco
(94111-3380)
PHONE...................415 490-0400
Jon Williams, *President*
Lynn Okamoto, *Senior VP*
Josh Adler, *Vice Pres*
Denis Getsios, *Vice Pres*
Kevin Kelly, *Director*
EMP: 60
SALES (est): 12.4MM
SALES (corp-wide): 1B **Privately Held**
WEB: www.archimedesmodel.com
SIC: 6411 Insurance information & consulting services
HQ: Evidera, Inc.
7101 Wscnsin Ave Ste 1400
Bethesda MD 20814

(P-10617)
FARMERS GROUP INC
Also Called: Farmers Insurance
13950 Ramona Ave, Chino (91710-5427)
PHONE...................909 839-2020
Mike Dyer, *Branch Mgr*
Nicolas Corwin, *Manager*
EMP: 82
SALES (corp-wide): 65.1B **Privately Held**
WEB: www.farmers.com
SIC: 6411 4226 4225 Insurance agents, brokers & service; special warehousing & storage; general warehousing & storage
HQ: Farmers Group, Inc.
6301 Owensmouth Ave
Woodland Hills CA 91367
323 932-3200

(P-10618)
FARMERS GROUP INC
Also Called: Farmers Insurance
429 Llewellyn Ave, Campbell (95008-1948)
PHONE...................408 557-1100
William Garrity, *Manager*
Lynn Nice, *Executive*
EMP: 50

SALES (corp-wide): 65.1B **Privately Held**
WEB: www.farmers.com
SIC: **6411** Insurance agents, brokers & service
HQ: Farmers Group, Inc.
6301 Owensmouth Ave
Woodland Hills CA 91367
323 932-3200

(P-10619)
FARMERS GROUP INC
Also Called: Farmers Insurance
11555 Dublin Canyon Rd, Pleasanton
(94588-2815)
PHONE................................925 847-3100
Steve Dix, *Manager*
John McCarthy, *Manager*
EMP: 400
SALES (corp-wide): 65.1B **Privately Held**
WEB: www.farmers.com
SIC: **6411** Insurance agents, brokers & service
HQ: Farmers Group, Inc.
6301 Owensmouth Ave
Woodland Hills CA 91367
323 932-3200

(P-10620)
FARMERS GROUP INC
Also Called: Farmers Insurance
550 S Hill St Ste 1309, Los Angeles
(90013-2292)
PHONE................................818 249-3000
Leo Denlea Jr, *President*
EMP: 88
SALES (corp-wide): 65.1B **Privately Held**
WEB: www.farmers.com
SIC: **6411** Insurance agents, brokers & service
HQ: Farmers Group, Inc.
6301 Owensmouth Ave
Woodland Hills CA 91367
323 932-3200

(P-10621)
FARMERS GROUP INC
Also Called: Farmers Insurance
6518 Antelope Rd, Citrus Heights
(95621-1077)
PHONE................................916 727-4600
Bruce Bailey, *Manager*
EMP: 75
SALES (corp-wide): 65.1B **Privately Held**
WEB: www.farmers.com
SIC: **6411** Insurance agents, brokers & service
HQ: Farmers Group, Inc.
6301 Owensmouth Ave
Woodland Hills CA 91367
323 932-3200

(P-10622)
FARMERS GROUP INC
Also Called: Farmers Insurance
6303 Owensmouth Ave Fl 1, Woodland Hills
(91367-2200)
PHONE................................805 583-7400
EMP: 900
SALES (corp-wide): 74.2B **Privately Held**
SIC: **6411**
HQ: Farmers Group, Inc.
6301 Owensmouth Ave
Woodland Hills CA 91367
323 932-3200

(P-10623)
FARMERS INSURANCE EXCHANGE (DH)
6301 Owensmouth Ave # 300, Woodland Hills (91367-2268)
PHONE................................323 932-3200
Jeff Pailey, *CEO*
Ron Myhan, *CFO*
Melissa Joye, *Officer*
Anthony La Rosa, *Engineer*
Jeff Tateosian, *Broker*
EMP: 3000
SQ FT: 210,000
SALES (est): 1.8B
SALES (corp-wide): 65.1B **Privately Held**
SIC: **6411** Insurance agents, brokers & service
HQ: Farmers Group, Inc.
6301 Owensmouth Ave
Woodland Hills CA 91367
323 932-3200

(P-10624)
FARMERS INSURANCE EXCHANGE
411 E Pine St Ste A, Exeter (93221-1800)
PHONE................................559 594-4149
Sammy Harrell, *Branch Mgr*
EMP: 326
SALES (corp-wide): 65.1B **Privately Held**
SIC: **6411** Insurance agents, brokers & service
HQ: Farmers Insurance Exchange
6301 Owensmouth Ave # 300
Woodland Hills CA 91367
323 932-3200

(P-10625)
FCE BENEFIT ADMINISTRATORS INC (PA)
1528 S El Camino Real # 307, San Mateo (94402-3067)
PHONE................................650 341-0306
Gary Beckman, *President*
Tom Leon, *Exec VP*
Steve Porter, *Exec VP*
Rachel Campbell, *Executive*
Ricardo Maldonado, *Executive*
EMP: 150
SQ FT: 10,000
SALES (est): 36MM **Privately Held**
WEB: www.fcebenefit.com
SIC: **6411** Insurance agents

(P-10626)
FEDERAL INSURANCE COMPANY
21820 Burbank Blvd # 330, Woodland Hills (91367-6476)
P.O. Box 4208 (91365-4208)
PHONE................................818 596-6100
Walter Guzzo, *Branch Mgr*
EMP: 80
SQ FT: 1,000
SALES (corp-wide): 28.7B **Privately Held**
WEB: www.federalinsurancecompany.com
SIC: **6411** Property & casualty insurance agent
HQ: Federal Insurance Company
251 N Illinois St # 1100
Indianapolis IN 46204
908 903-2000

(P-10627)
FEDERAL INSURANCE COMPANY
Also Called: Chubb
275 Battery St Fl 12, San Francisco (94111-3305)
PHONE................................415 273-6300
Cliston Thomas, *Manager*
EMP: 100
SALES (corp-wide): 28.7B **Privately Held**
WEB: www.federalinsurancecompany.com
SIC: **6411** Insurance agents, brokers & service
HQ: Federal Insurance Company
251 N Illinois St # 1100
Indianapolis IN 46204
908 903-2000

(P-10628)
FIDELITY NATIONAL FINCL INC
1300 Dove St Ste 310, Newport Beach (92660-2417)
PHONE................................949 622-5000
Rob Vavrock, *Branch Mgr*
Jim John, *Exec VP*
Melissa Hall, *Vice Pres*
Meghann Sullivan, *Accounts Mgr*
Janette Delap, *Commercial*
EMP: 80
SALES (corp-wide): 7.6B **Publicly Held**
SIC: **6411** Insurance agents, brokers & service
PA: Fidelity National Financial, Inc.
601 Riverside Ave Fl 4
Jacksonville FL 32204
904 854-8100

(P-10629)
FINANCIAL PACIFIC INSURANCE CO
3850 Atherton Rd, Rocklin (95765-3700)
PHONE................................916 630-5000
Robert C Goodell, *Principal*
EMP: 81

SALES (est): 192.5K **Publicly Held**
SIC: **6411** Insurance agents, brokers & service
HQ: Financial Pacific Insurance Group, Inc
3880 Atherton Rd
Rocklin CA 95765
-

(P-10630)
FIRE INSURANCE EXCHANGE (PA)
4680 Wilshire Blvd, Los Angeles (90010-3807)
PHONE................................323 932-3200
Martin Feinstein, *CEO*
John Harrington, *President*
Ron Myhan, *Treasurer*
Doren Hohl, *Admin Sec*
Sreenivasarao Ravuri, *Analyst*
EMP: 2300
SALES: 1B **Privately Held**
SIC: **6411** Insurance agents, brokers & service

(P-10631)
FREEWAY INSURANCE (PA)
Also Called: South Coast Auto Insurance
7711 Center Ave Ste 200, Huntington Beach (92647-9124)
PHONE................................714 252-2500
Elias Assaf, *President*
Norm Hudson, *COO*
John Klaeb, *Vice Pres*
EMP: 120
SQ FT: 20,000
SALES (est): 115.5MM **Privately Held**
WEB: www.seguroahora.com
SIC: **6411** Insurance agents

(P-10632)
G J SULLIVAN CO INC
800 W 6th St Ste 1800, Los Angeles (90017-2701)
PHONE................................213 626-1000
Gerald J Sullivan, *President*
Steve Fetchet, *Vice Pres*
Lois Massa, *Vice Pres*
Ray Chen, *Analyst*
Dana Rogers, *HR Admin*
EMP: 60
SALES (est): 19.5MM
SALES (corp-wide): 75.2MM **Privately Held**
WEB: www.gjs.com
SIC: **6411** Insurance brokers
HQ: Gerald J. Sullivan & Associates, Inc. Insurance Brokers
800 W 6th St Ste 1800
Los Angeles CA
213 626-1000

(P-10633)
GEICO CORPORATION
2033 Arden Way Ste C, Sacramento (95825-2210)
PHONE................................707 448-7172
Vincent Harris, *Branch Mgr*
EMP: 147
SALES (corp-wide): 242.1B **Publicly Held**
SIC: **6411** Insurance agents, brokers & service
HQ: Geico Corporation
5260 Western Ave
Chevy Chase MD 20815
301 986-3000

(P-10634)
GEICO GENERAL INSURANCE CO
14111 Danielson St, Poway (92064-6886)
PHONE................................858 848-8200
Elizabeth Shew, *Principal*
Alex S Gomez, *Facilities Mgr*
EMP: 378
SALES (corp-wide): 242.1B **Publicly Held**
SIC: **6411** Insurance agents
HQ: Geico General Insurance Company
1 Geico Plz
Washington DC 20076

(P-10635)
GEOVERA SPECIALTY INSURANCE CO
1455 Oliver Rd, Fairfield (94534-3472)
PHONE................................707 863-3700
Karen Padovese, *President*
Frank Lazzeroni, *President*
Kevin Nish, *President*
Lori Gomez, *Vice Pres*
Mark Schroeder, *Director*
EMP: 60
SALES (est): 8.3MM **Privately Held**
WEB: www.homeinsurer.com
SIC: **6411** Insurance brokers
PA: Geovera Holdings, Inc.
4820 Busineca Ctr Dr 20
Fairfield CA 94534

(P-10636)
GGIS INSURANCE SERVICES INC
Also Called: Guardian General Insur Svcs
600 N Brand Blvd Ste 300, Glendale (91203-4207)
PHONE................................818 553-2110
EMP: 135
SALES (est): 12.7MM **Privately Held**
WEB: www.guardiangeneral.com
SIC: **6411**

(P-10637)
GOOD DEAL INSURANCE SERVICES
2140 S Hacienda Blvd A, Hacienda Heights (91745-7200)
PHONE................................626 275-6795
Chung Hwei Chang, *President*
EMP: 70
SQ FT: 4,000
SALES (est): 7.6MM **Privately Held**
SIC: **6411** Insurance agents

(P-10638)
GROSSLIGHT INSURANCE INC
Also Called: Kemper Insurance
1333 Westwood Blvd # 200, Los Angeles (90024-4949)
P.O. Box 24946 (90024-0946)
PHONE................................310 473-9611
Gilbert F Grosslight, *CEO*
Steven Schiewe, *President*
EMP: 60
SQ FT: 15,000
SALES (est): 16.4MM **Privately Held**
WEB: www.grosslight.com
SIC: **6411** Insurance agents

(P-10639)
GS LEVINE INSURANCE SVCS INC
10505 Sorrento Valley Rd # 200, San Diego (92121-1619)
PHONE................................858 481-8692
Gary S Levine, *CEO*
Ross Afsahi, *President*
Dick Avakian, *COO*
Judy King, *Manager*
Maiko Tanaka, *Accounts Mgr*
EMP: 62
SQ FT: 17,000
SALES (est): 11MM
SALES (corp-wide): 6.1B **Publicly Held**
WEB: www.gslevineins.com
SIC: **6411** Insurance brokers
PA: Arthur J. Gallagher & Co.
2850 Golf Rd Ste 1000
Rolling Meadows IL 60008
630 773-3800

(P-10640)
HAMILTON BRWART INSUR AGCY LLC
1282 W Arrow Hwy, Upland (91786-5040)
P.O. Box 1949 (91785-1949)
PHONE................................909 920-3250
Hamilton Brewart,
Derek Brewart,
EMP: 67
SQ FT: 12,000
SALES (est): 12.3MM **Privately Held**
WEB: www.hamiltonbrewart.com
SIC: **6411** Insurance agents; insurance brokers

PRODUCTS & SVCS

(P-10641)
HARTFORD FIRE INSURANCE CO
12009 Foundation Pl # 100, Gold River (95670-4534)
PHONE..............................916 294-1000
John Buckalew, *Manager*
EMP: 300 **Publicly Held**
WEB:
www.hartfordinvestmentscanada.com
SIC: 6411 Insurance agents
HQ: Hartford Fire Insurance Company
1 Hartford Plz
Hartford CT 06115
860 547-5000

(P-10642)
HARTFORD FIRE INSURANCE CO
777 S Figueroa St Ste 700, Los Angeles (90017-5861)
PHONE..............................213 452-5179
Rich Long, *Sales Staff*
EMP: 212 **Publicly Held**
WEB:
www.hartfordinvestmentscanada.com
SIC: 6411 Insurance agents
HQ: Hartford Fire Insurance Company
1 Hartford Plz
Hartford CT 06115
860 547-5000

(P-10643)
HEALTH COMP ADMINISTRATORS (PA)
621 Santa Fe Ave, Fresno (93721-2724)
P.O. Box 45018 (93718-5018)
PHONE..............................559 499-2450
Phillip Musson, *President*
Don Soper, *President*
Mike Bouskos, *Vice Pres*
Kelly Ferreira, *VP Admin*
Kelly Springsted, *VP Admin*
EMP: 185
SALES (est): 30.8MM **Privately Held**
SIC: 6411 Medical insurance claim processing, contract or fee basis

(P-10644)
HEALTHCOMP
Also Called: Healthcomp Administrators
621 Santa Fe Ave, Fresno (93721-2724)
P.O. Box 45018 (93718-5018)
PHONE..............................559 499-2450
Phillip Musson, *CEO*
Michael Bouskos, *CFO*
Marcia Fine, *Trust Officer*
Monique Bouskos, *Vice Pres*
Kelly Ferreira, *Vice Pres*
EMP: 260
SQ FT: 50,000
SALES (est): 58.9MM **Privately Held**
WEB: www.healthcomp.com
SIC: 6411 Medical insurance claim processing, contract or fee basis

(P-10645)
HEALTHSMART MANAGEMENT SERVICE
10855 Bus Ctr Dr Ste C, Cypress (90630)
P.O. Box 6300 (90630-0063)
PHONE..............................714 947-8600
Carol Houchins, *President*
Candice Chan,
Ginny Gamel,
Kerry Sargenti,
Marcus Yoon,
EMP: 90
SALES (est): 16.4MM **Privately Held**
WEB: www.healthsmartmso.com
SIC: 6411 8741 8721 Medical insurance claim processing, contract or fee basis; hospital management; business management; billing & bookkeeping service

(P-10646)
HEFFERNAN INSURANCE BROKERS
Also Called: Heffernan Group
180 Howard St Ste 200, San Francisco (94105-1663)
PHONE..............................800 829-9996
Jeffrey Hamlin, *Branch Mgr*
Paul Brown, *Vice Pres*
Tanner Fornesi, *Vice Pres*

Ed Lief, *Vice Pres*
Keith Newell, *Vice Pres*
EMP: 50
SALES (corp-wide): 172.9MM **Privately Held**
WEB: www.heffgroup.com
SIC: 6411 Insurance brokers
PA: Heffernan Insurance Brokers
1350 Carlback Ave
Walnut Creek CA 94596
925 934-8500

(P-10647)
HUB INTRNTIONAL INSUR SVCS INC
3636 American River Dr # 200, Sacramento (95864-5952)
PHONE..............................916 974-7800
Sergey Vorobets, *Producer*
Sharon Davis, *Accounts Mgr*
Sandi Pullen, *Accounts Mgr*
Brandy Brazil, *Underwriter*
EMP: 90 **Privately Held**
SIC: 6411 Insurance agents; insurance brokers
HQ: Hub International Insurance Services Inc.
3390 University Ave # 300
Riverside CA 92501
951 788-8500

(P-10648)
HUB INTRNTIONAL INSUR SVCS INC
Also Called: Der Manouel Insurance Group
548 W Cromwell Ave # 101, Fresno (93711-5714)
PHONE..............................559 447-4600
Victor Gunderson, *Vice Pres*
Jonathan Wiebe, *Admin Sec*
Britt Gosswiller, *Broker*
Karen Keyes, *Personnel*
Roger Allen, *Producer*
EMP: 71 **Privately Held**
SIC: 6411 Insurance agents
HQ: Hub International Insurance Services Inc.
3390 University Ave # 300
Riverside CA 92501
951 788-8500

(P-10649)
HUB INTRNTIONAL INSUR SVCS INC
40 E Alamar Ave, Santa Barbara (93105-3469)
PHONE..............................805 682-2571
Darren Tesars, *Manager*
Beth Mitchell, *Broker*
Betty Briggs, *Accounts Exec*
EMP: 52 **Privately Held**
SIC: 6411 Insurance agents
HQ: Hub International Insurance Services Inc.
3390 University Ave # 300
Riverside CA 92501
951 788-8500

(P-10650)
INSCO INSURANCE SERVICES INC (HQ)
Also Called: Developers Surety Indemnity Co
17771 Cowan Ste 100, Irvine (92614-6044)
P.O. Box 19725 (92623-9725)
PHONE..............................949 797-9243
Harry Crowell, *Ch of Bd*
Scott Rons, *Branch Mgr*
Gary Weintraub, *Finance Mgr*
Todd Nelson, *Manager*
EMP: 70
SQ FT: 50,000
SALES (est): 68.7MM **Publicly Held**
WEB: www.inscodico.com
SIC: 6411 6351 Property & casualty insurance agent; surety insurance bonding; liability insurance

(P-10651)
INSURANCE SERVICES AMERCN LLC
300 E Esplanade Dr # 2100, Oxnard (93036-1238)
PHONE..............................805 981-2220
Stanley Braun,
Nancy Braun,

Myrtle Solomon,
EMP: 70
SALES (est): 4.2MM **Privately Held**
SIC: 6411 Insurance agents & brokers

(P-10652)
INTEGRO USA INC
115 N El Molino Ave, Pasadena (91101-1804)
PHONE..............................626 795-9000
Steve Titus, *General Mgr*
EMP: 50
SALES (corp-wide): 307.6MM **Privately Held**
SIC: 6411 Insurance agents
HQ: Integro Usa Inc.
1 State St Fl 9
New York NY 10004
212 295-8000

(P-10653)
INTERCARE HOLDINGS INSUR SVCS
Also Called: Ihi
3010 Lava Ridge Ct # 110, Roseville (95661-3063)
P.O. Box 579 (95661-0579)
PHONE..............................916 677-2500
George McLeary, *CEO*
Anges Hoeberling, *Exec VP*
Richard R Rothman, *Exec VP*
Alan Avriett, *Vice Pres*
Sandra Jimenez, *Vice Pres*
EMP: 263
SALES (est): 29.4MM **Privately Held**
SIC: 6411 Insurance adjusters

(P-10654)
INTERNTNAL PRNSRANCE ASSOC LLC
504 Redwood Blvd Ste 240e, Novato (94947-6925)
PHONE..............................415 223-5548
David M Hofele, *Mng Member*
EMP: 50
SALES (est): 7.5MM **Privately Held**
SIC: 6411 Insurance brokers

(P-10655)
INTERWEST INSURANCE SVCS LLC (PA)
Also Called: Kemper Insurance
8950 Cal Center Dr Bldg 3, Sacramento (95826-3259)
PHONE..............................916 488-3100
Tom Williams, *Chairman*
Thomas Williams, *President*
Keith Schuler, *CEO*
Nancy Luttenbacher, *COO*
Donald Pollard, *CFO*
EMP: 173
SQ FT: 20,000
SALES (est): 218.1MM **Privately Held**
WEB: www.infosourcecafe.com
SIC: 6411 Insurance brokers

(P-10656)
INTERWEST INSURANCE SVCS LLC
Also Called: Lindo Hanna & Abbott
1357 E Lassen Ave Ste 100, Chico (95973-7824)
P.O. Box 8110 (95927-8110)
PHONE..............................530 895-1010
Keith Shuler, *CEO*
EMP: 70
SALES (corp-wide): 218.1MM **Privately Held**
WEB: www.infosourcecafe.com
SIC: 6411 Insurance brokers
PA: Interwest Insurance Services, Llc
8950 Cal Center Dr Bldg 3
Sacramento CA 95826
916 488-3100

(P-10657)
INVESMART INC
55 Almaden Blvd Ste 800, San Jose (95113-1612)
PHONE..............................408 961-2800
Kent Buckles, *CEO*
EMP: 55

SALES (est): 59MM
SALES (corp-wide): 38.6B **Privately Held**
WEB: www.stancorpfinancial.com
SIC: 6411 Pension & retirement plan consultants
HQ: Stancorp Financial Group, Inc.
1100 Sw 6th Ave
Portland OR 97204
971 321-7000

(P-10658)
JAMES C JENKINS INSUR SVC INC
Also Called: Athens Insurance
1390 Willow Pass Rd, Concord (94520-5200)
P.O. Box 696 (94522-0796)
PHONE..............................925 798-3334
John Hahn, *CEO*
Peter Garvey, *President*
Karman Chan, *CFO*
Jason Del Grande, *Vice Pres*
Michael Gonthier,
EMP: 125 **EST:** 1977
SQ FT: 30,000
SALES (est): 33.9MM **Privately Held**
SIC: 6411 Insurance brokers
PA: Edgewood Partners Insurance Center, Inc.
1390 Willow Pass Rd # 800
Concord CA 94520
-

(P-10659)
JAMES G PARKER INSURANCE ASSOC (PA)
Also Called: Bacome Insurance Agency
1753 E Fir Ave, Fresno (93720-3840)
P.O. Box 3947 (93650-3947)
PHONE..............................559 222-7722
James G Parker, *President*
Donna Eyman, *Partner*
Janice W Parker, *Treasurer*
Leroy Berrett, *Vice Pres*
John Cleveland, *Vice Pres*
EMP: 70
SQ FT: 13,000
SALES (est): 110.4MM **Privately Held**
SIC: 6411 Insurance agents

(P-10660)
JANET HILTON
Also Called: Allstate
990 W 190th St Ste 300, Torrance (90502-4461)
PHONE..............................310 851-7200
Janet Hilton, *Principal*
EMP: 100
SALES (est): 5MM **Privately Held**
SIC: 6411 Insurance agents, brokers & service

(P-10661)
KAERCHER CAMPBELL ASSOCIATE IN
600 Corporate Pointe # 1010, Culver City (90230-7600)
PHONE..............................310 556-1900
David Putman, *Ch of Bd*
Rod Austria, *President*
Allan Kaercher, *President*
Penni Campbell, *CEO*
Robert G Sattler, *Senior VP*
EMP: 119
SALES (est): 25.6MM **Privately Held**
SIC: 6411 Insurance agents, brokers & service

(P-10662)
KEENAN & ASSOCIATES
1791 Broadway St Ste 200, Redwood City (94063-2487)
P.O. Box 2707, Torrance (90509-2707)
PHONE..............................650 306-0616
Jessica Blakiston, *Manager*
EMP: 55 **Privately Held**
SIC: 6411 Insurance claim adjusters, not employed by insurance company
HQ: Keenan & Associates
2355 Crenshaw Blvd # 200
Torrance CA 90501
310 212-3344

(P-10663)
KEENAN & ASSOCIATES (HQ)
2355 Crenshaw Blvd # 200, Torrance
(90501-3395)
P.O. Box 4328 (90510-4328)
PHONE................................310 212-3344
John Keenan, *Ch of Bd*
Sean Smith, *CEO*
Davis Seres, *COO*
Henry Loubet, *Senior VP*
Keith Pippard, *Vice Pres*
EMP: 339
SQ FT: 80,000
SALES (est): 480.6MM **Privately Held**
WEB: www.keenanhealthcare.com
SIC: 6411 Insurance brokers

(P-10664)
KEENAN & ASSOCIATES
626 H St, Eureka (95501-1026)
PHONE................................707 268-1616
Kay Byrnes, *Manager*
EMP: 55 **Privately Held**
SIC: 6411 Insurance information & consult-
ing services
HQ: Keenan & Associates
2355 Crenshaw Blvd # 200
Torrance CA 90501
310 212-3344

(P-10665)
KEENAN & ASSOCIATES
3550 Vine St Ste 200, Riverside
(92507-4175)
P.O. Box 79991 (92513-1991)
PHONE................................951 788-0330
Karleen Smartiss, *Manager*
EMP: 65 **Privately Held**
WEB: www.keenanhealthcare.com
SIC: 6411 6371 Insurance brokers; pen-
sion, health & welfare funds
HQ: Keenan & Associates
2355 Crenshaw Blvd # 200
Torrance CA 90501
310 212-3344

(P-10666)
KEENAN & ASSOCIATES
2868 Prospect Park Dr # 600, Rancho Cor-
dova (95670-6020)
PHONE................................916 858-2981
Nancy Conner, *Manager*
EMP: 70 **Privately Held**
WEB: www.keenanhealthcare.com
SIC: 6411 Insurance agents, brokers &
service
HQ: Keenan & Associates
2355 Crenshaw Blvd # 200
Torrance CA 90501
310 212-3344

(P-10667)
KEENAN & ASSOCIATES
1740 Tech Dr Ste 300, San Jose (95110)
PHONE................................408 441-0754
Mickey Armstrong, *Manager*
EMP: 50 **Privately Held**
WEB: www.keenanhealthcare.com
SIC: 6411 Insurance brokers
HQ: Keenan & Associates
2355 Crenshaw Blvd # 200
Torrance CA 90501
310 212-3344

(P-10668)
KEENAN & ASSOCIATES
901 Calle Amanecer # 200, San Clemente
(92673-4211)
PHONE................................949 940-1760
Steve Gedestad, *Principal*
EMP: 55 **Privately Held**
WEB: www.keenanhealthcare.com
SIC: 6411 Insurance brokers
HQ: Keenan & Associates
2355 Crenshaw Blvd # 200
Torrance CA 90501
310 212-3344

(P-10669)
KORAM INSURANCE CENTER
INC
3807 Wilshire Blvd # 400, Los Angeles
(90010-3104)
PHONE................................323 660-1000
Edward Haan, *CEO*
James D Hahn, *Ch of Bd*

Edward M Hahn, *President*
Jaina Chang, *Vice Pres*
Mary Min, *Office Mgr*
EMP: 58 **EST:** 1974
SQ FT: 3,300
SALES (est): 5.8MM **Privately Held**
WEB: www.koraminsurance.com
SIC: 6411 Insurance agents

(P-10670)
LEAVITT GROUP ENTERPRISES
INC
785 E Washington Blvd # 4, Crescent City
(95531-8343)
PHONE................................707 465-6508
Debbie Koehlerschmidt, *Branch Mgr*
EMP: 130
SALES (corp-wide): 211MM **Privately
Held**
SIC: 6411 Insurance agents
PA: Leavitt Group Enterprises Inc
216 S 200 W
Cedar City UT 84720
435 586-1555

(P-10671)
LIBERTY MUTUAL INSURANCE
CO
19200 Von Karman Ave # 200, Irvine
(92612-8504)
PHONE................................310 316-9428
Lynnean Chisom, *Branch Mgr*
EMP: 110
SALES (corp-wide): 38.3B **Privately Held**
SIC: 6411 Insurance agents, brokers &
service
HQ: Liberty Mutual Insurance Company
175 Berkeley St
Boston MA 02116
617 357-9500

(P-10672)
LIBERTY MUTUAL INSURANCE
CO
13405 Folsom Blvd Ste 200, Folsom
(95630-4738)
PHONE................................916 294-9518
Charles Frazier, *Principal*
EMP: 107
SALES (corp-wide): 38.3B **Privately Held**
SIC: 6411 Insurance agents, brokers &
service
HQ: Liberty Mutual Insurance Company
175 Berkeley St
Boston MA 02116
617 357-9500

(P-10673)
LISI INC (PA)
1600 W Hillsdale Blvd # 100, San Mateo
(94402-3768)
PHONE................................650 348-4131
Philip Lebherz, *Ch of Bd*
Becky Patel, *CEO*
Ken Doyle, *Senior VP*
Kevin Timone, *Senior VP*
Tamara Henderson, *Vice Pres*
EMP: 140
SQ FT: 18,000
SALES (est): 48.4MM **Privately Held**
WEB: www.lisibroker.com
SIC: 6411 Insurance agents

(P-10674)
LOCKTON COMPANIES LLC-
PACIFI (HQ)
Also Called: Lockton Insurance Brokers
725 S Figueroa St Fl 35, Los Angeles
(90017-5435)
PHONE................................213 689-0500
Timothy J Noonan, *President*
Philip Hurrle, *Partner*
Dan Myers, *President*
Phillip Pierce, *President*
Leonard G Fodemski, *CFO*
EMP: 350
SQ FT: 72,300
SALES (est): 162.5MM
SALES (corp-wide): 1.9B **Privately Held**
SIC: 6411 Insurance brokers
PA: Lockton, Inc.
444 W 47th St Ste 900
Kansas City MO 64112
816 960-9000

(P-10675)
MANAGED CARE SYSTEMS
KERN CNTY
Also Called: MCS
5251 Office Park Dr # 405, Bakersfield
(93309-0404)
PHONE................................661 716-7100
Bob Severs, *CEO*
EMP: 80
SALES (est): 8.2MM **Privately Held**
SIC: 6411 7363 Medical insurance claim
processing, contract or fee basis; medical
help service

(P-10676)
MARKEL CORP
Also Called: Associated Intl Insur Co
21600 Oxnard St Ste 900, Woodland Hills
(91367-7834)
PHONE................................818 595-0600
Anthony Markel, *President*
Alan Kirshner, *Ch of Bd*
Steven Markel, *Vice Ch Bd*
Sue Bennett, *Admin Asst*
EMP: 276
SQ FT: 32,000
SALES (est): 28.9MM
SALES (corp-wide): 6B **Publicly Held**
SIC: 6411 Insurance brokers
HQ: Markel North America, Inc
4521 Highwoods Pkwy
Glen Allen VA 23060
804 747-0136

(P-10677)
MARKEL WEST INC
21600 Oxnard St Ste 400, Woodland Hills
(91367-4800)
PHONE................................818 595-0600
Anthony Markel, *President*
EMP: 50
SALES (est): 5.2MM
SALES (corp-wide): 6B **Publicly Held**
WEB: www.markelcorp.com
SIC: 6411 Insurance agents, brokers &
service
PA: Markel Corporation
4521 Highwoods Pkwy
Glen Allen VA 23060
804 747-0136

(P-10678)
MAROEVICH OSHEA &
COGHLAN
Also Called: M O C Insurance Services
44 Montgomery St Ste 1700, San Francisco
(94104-4704)
PHONE................................415 957-0600
Van Maroevich, *CEO*
Gerald Clifford, *CFO*
Jerry Clifford, *CFO*
Bill Grindell, *Exec VP*
Peter Brown, *Senior VP*
EMP: 60
SQ FT: 10,000
SALES (est): 17.6MM **Privately Held**
WEB: www.mocins.com
SIC: 6411 Insurance brokers

(P-10679)
MARSH & MCLENNAN AGENCY
LLC
1 Polaris Way Ste 300, Aliso Viejo
(92656-5358)
PHONE................................949 544-8460
Joe Tapias, *Branch Mgr*
Amy Fisher, *Opers Staff*
EMP: 86
SALES (corp-wide): 14B **Publicly Held**
WEB: www.barneyandbarney.com
SIC: 6411 Insurance brokers; life insurance
agents
HQ: Marsh & Mclennan Agency Llc
360 Hamilton Ave Ste 930
White Plains NY 10601

(P-10680)
MARSH & MCLENNAN AGENCY
LLC
201 California St Ste 900, San Francisco
(94111-5011)
PHONE................................415 243-4160
Paul Hering, *CEO*
Scott Reynolds, *Vice Pres*

EMP: 86
SALES (corp-wide): 14B **Publicly Held**
SIC: 6411 Insurance brokers; life insurance
agents
HQ: Marsh & Mclennan Agency Llc
360 Hamilton Ave Ste 930
White Plains NY 10601

(P-10681)
MARSH & MCLENNAN AGENCY
LLC
9171 Towne Centre Dr # 500, San Diego
(92122-1234)
PHONE................................858 457-3414
Paul Hering, *Branch Mgr*
Peter Epstine, *Vice Pres*
Laurie Carlson, *Executive*
Michael Grant, *Executive*
Sara Hayes, *Executive*
EMP: 200
SALES (corp-wide): 14B **Publicly Held**
SIC: 6411 Property & casualty insurance
agent; life insurance agents
HQ: Marsh & Mclennan Agency Llc
360 Hamilton Ave Ste 930
White Plains NY 10601

(P-10682)
MARSH & MCLENNAN
COMPANIES INC
777 S Figueroa St # 2200, Los Angeles
(90017-5820)
PHONE................................213 346-5555
Kris Davis, *Branch Mgr*
Dennis Donahue, *Vice Pres*
Kathleen Habermann, *Vice Pres*
John Heatherton, *Vice Pres*
Dennis McCaslin, *Vice Pres*
EMP: 80
SALES (corp-wide): 14B **Publicly Held**
WEB: www.seabury.com
SIC: 6411 Insurance brokers
PA: Marsh & Mclennan Companies, Inc.
1166 Avenue Of The Americ
New York NY 10036
212 345-5000

(P-10683)
MARSH USA INC
345 California St # 1300, San Francisco
(94104-2606)
PHONE................................415 743-8000
Mike Kelley, *Office Mgr*
Jennifer Spencer, *Senior VP*
Becky Anderson, *Vice Pres*
Yvonne Cho, *Vice Pres*
Christopher Davis, *Vice Pres*
EMP: 64
SALES (corp-wide): 14B **Publicly Held**
WEB: www.marsh.com
SIC: 6411 Insurance brokers
HQ: Marsh Usa Inc.
1166 Ave Of The Americas
New York NY 10036
212 345-6000

(P-10684)
MARSH USA INC
1735 Tech Dr Ste 790, San Jose (95110)
PHONE................................408 467-5600
Andrew Haaser, *Manager*
Ryan R Garvin, *Marketing Staff*
Manpreet S Gill, *Associate*
EMP: 62
SALES (corp-wide): 14B **Publicly Held**
SIC: 6411 Insurance brokers
HQ: Marsh Usa Inc.
1166 Ave Of The Americas
New York NY 10036
212 345-6000

(P-10685)
MAXSON YOUNG ASSOC INC
180 Montgomery St # 2100, San Francisco
(94104-4231)
PHONE................................415 228-6400
Vernon Chalfant, *CEO*
EMP: 120
SALES (est): 12.2MM **Privately Held**
SIC: 6411 Insurance adjusters

P R O D U C T S & S V C S

(P-10686)
MC GRAW COMMERCIAL INSUR SVC

Also Called: McGraw Insurance Services
8185 E Kaiser Blvd, Anaheim
(92808-2214)
PHONE..............................714 939-9875
Vivian Tafolla, *Principal*
EMP: 51
SALES (est): 3.2MM
SALES (corp-wide): 60.6MM **Privately Held**
SIC: 6411 Insurance agents, brokers & service
PA: Mc Graw Commercial Insurance Service, Inc
3601 Haven Ave
Menlo Park CA 94025
650 780-4800

(P-10687)
MC GRAW COMMERCIAL INSUR SVC (PA)

3601 Haven Ave, Menlo Park (94025-1064)
PHONE..............................650 780-4800
Michael J Mc Graw, *President*
Joan D Mc Graw, *Corp Secy*
John M Mc Graw, *Vice Pres*
Susan Valencia, *Vice Pres*
EMP: 90
SQ FT: 20,000
SALES (est): 60.6MM **Privately Held**
SIC: 6411 Insurance agents & brokers

(P-10688)
MC GRAW INSURANCE SERVICES CO

2200 Geng Rd Ste 200, Palo Alto
(94303-3358)
PHONE..............................650 780-4800
John V Mc Graw, *Ch of Bd*
Richard Fowler, *CFO*
Timothy Summers, *Exec VP*
Kyle Sackman, *Marketing Staff*
EMP: 100 **EST:** 1976
SQ FT: 20,000
SALES (est): 18.6MM **Privately Held**
SIC: 6411 Insurance agents

(P-10689)
MEDICAL EYE SERVICES INC

345 Baker St, Costa Mesa (92626-4518)
P.O. Box 25209, Santa Ana (92799-5209)
PHONE..............................714 619-4660
Aspasia Shappet, *President*
Chuck Kupfer, *CFO*
Karen Carnakis, *Regional Mgr*
David Grenell, *Regional Mgr*
Paul Vu, *Technology*
EMP: 100
SQ FT: 12,000
SALES (est): 24.6MM **Privately Held**
SIC: 6411 Insurance claim processing, except medical
PA: The Eye Care Network Of California Inc
345 Baker St
Costa Mesa CA

(P-10690)
MEDICAL INSURANCE EXCHANGE CAL

6250 Claremont Ave, Oakland
(94618-1324)
PHONE..............................510 596-4935
Dr Bradford Cohn, *President*
Dr William Donald, *Vice Chairman*
Dr Conrad Anderson, *Admin Sec*
EMP: 74
SQ FT: 13,000
SALES (est): 13MM **Privately Held**
WEB: www.miec.com
SIC: 6411 Loss prevention services, insurance

(P-10691)
METROPOLITAN LIFE INSUR CO

Also Called: MetLife
425 Market St Ste 960, San Francisco
(94105-2423)
PHONE..............................415 536-1065
Henry Loubouet, *Director*
Carol Palmer, *Manager*
EMP: 375

SALES (corp-wide): 62.3B **Publicly Held**
SIC: 6411 Insurance agents & brokers
HQ: Metropolitan Life Insurance Company (Inc)
501 Us Highway 22
Bridgewater NJ 08807
908 253-1000

(P-10692)
MICHAEL MAGUIRE & ASSOCIATES

611 Anton Blvd Ste 900, Costa Mesa
(92626-7684)
PHONE..............................714 435-7500
Michael Maguire, *Owner*
EMP: 50
SALES (est): 4.2MM **Privately Held**
SIC: 6411 8111 Insurance agents, brokers & service; general practice attorney, lawyer

(P-10693)
MITCHELL BUCKMAN INC (PA)

Also Called: Kemper Insurance
500 N Santa Fe St, Visalia (93292-5065)
P.O. Box 629 (93279-0629)
PHONE..............................559 733-1181
Clifford Dunbar, *Ch of Bd*
Stanley S Simpson, *Shareholder*
Lela Turbell, *Shareholder*
Jeffrey Boyle, *President*
Judy A Fussel, *President*
EMP: 80
SQ FT: 16,000
SALES (est): 50.1MM **Privately Held**
WEB: www.bminc.com
SIC: 6411

(P-10694)
MOMENTOUS INSURANCE BRKG INC

5990 Sepulvda Blvd # 550, Van Nuys
(91411-2536)
PHONE..............................818 933-2700
Diane Brinson Schiele, *President*
Erin Gaston, *Senior VP*
David Oliver, *Senior VP*
Michelle Boyer, *Principal*
Carla Cave, *Principal*
EMP: 78
SALES (est): 30.9MM **Privately Held**
SIC: 6411 Insurance agents; insurance brokers

(P-10695)
MORGAN KLEPPE & NASH

Also Called: Mkni
501 N Church St, Visalia (93291-5004)
P.O. Box 1390 (93279-1390)
PHONE..............................559 732-3436
Keith Kleppe, *Partner*
Gerry Folmer, *Partner*
EMP: 58
SQ FT: 2,500
SALES: 22MM **Privately Held**
WEB: www.morgankleppenash.com
SIC: 6411 Insurance agents

(P-10696)
MORRIS GRRITANO INSUR AGCY INC

1122 Laurel Ln, San Luis Obispo
(93401-5895)
P.O. Box 1189 (93406-1189)
PHONE..............................805 543-6887
Brendan Morris, *CEO*
David Morgan, *Shareholder*
Kelly Morgan, *Shareholder*
Kerry Pollock, *Shareholder*
John Pullock, *Shareholder*
EMP: 85
SQ FT: 14,000
SALES (est): 26.6MM **Privately Held**
WEB: www.morrisgarritano.com
SIC: 6411 Insurance agents; insurance brokers

(P-10697)
MULLIN TBG INSUR AGCY SVCS LLC (DH)

Also Called: Mullintbg
100 N Pacific Coast Hwy, El Segundo
(90245-4359)
PHONE..............................310 203-8770
Michael R Shute, *CEO*

Michael Glickman, *CFO*
EMP: 185
SALES (est): 97.1MM
SALES (corp-wide): 59.6B **Publicly Held**
WEB: www.mcg-chi.com
SIC: 6411 Insurance information & consulting services
HQ: The Prudential Insurance Company Of America
751 Broad St
Newark NJ 07102
973 802-6000

(P-10698)
NATIONAL RTREMENT PARTNERS INC (PA)

34700 Pacific Coast Hwy, Capistrano
Beach (92624-1351)
PHONE..............................949 488-8726
William R Chetney, *CEO*
Timothy O'Brien, *President*
Robert France, *COO*
Lawrence Craig Smith, *Officer*
Richard Darian, *Exec VP*
EMP: 53
SALES (est): 15.3MM **Privately Held**
WEB: www.n-r-p.com
SIC: 6411 Pension & retirement plan consultants

(P-10699)
NETWORKED INSURANCE AGENTS LLC

Also Called: Direct Access Insurance Svcs
443 Crown Point Cir Ste A, Grass Valley
(95945-9557)
PHONE..............................800 682-8476
George Biancardi, *President*
Tammy Magliola, *President*
Kelly McRae, *CFO*
Larry Oslie, *Exec VP*
EMP: 110
SQ FT: 15,000
SALES (est): 39.6MM
SALES (corp-wide): 697.8MM **Privately Held**
WEB: www.nia-ins.com
SIC: 6411 Insurance agents
PA: Amwins Group, Inc.
4725 Piedmont Row Dr # 600
Charlotte NC 28210
704 749-2700

(P-10700)
NEW ALLIANCE INSURANCE BROKERS

3700 Santa Fe Ave Ste 300, Long Beach
(90810-2171)
PHONE..............................424 205-6700
Marcello Povolo, *President*
Monica De La Cruz, *Office Mgr*
EMP: 50
SALES: 25MM **Privately Held**
SIC: 6411 Insurance agents

(P-10701)
NEW CENTURY INSURANCE SERVICES (PA)

16 N 2nd St, Alhambra (91801-3435)
PHONE..............................626 300-9000
Subert Wong, *President*
Simon Heng, *President*
Mark Narovlansky, *Exec VP*
Vibuel Saeheng, *Vice Pres*
Henry Ting, *Vice Pres*
EMP: 50
SQ FT: 15,000
SALES (est): 9.7MM **Privately Held**
WEB: www.newcenturyins.com
SIC: 6411 Insurance agents

(P-10702)
NEW YORK LIFE INSURANCE CO

1300 S El Cmno Real 400, San Mateo
(94402)
PHONE..............................650 571-1220
K B Sareen, *Manager*
Zachary E Whitman, *Sales Associate*
EMP: 400
SALES (corp-wide): 25.1B **Privately Held**
WEB: www.newyorklife.com
SIC: 6411 Insurance agents & brokers

PA: New York Life Insurance Company
51 Madison Ave Bsmt 1b
New York NY 10010
212 576-7000

(P-10703)
NEW YORK LIFE INSURANCE CO

675 Placentia Ave Ste 250, Brea
(92821-6171)
PHONE..............................714 255-5100
Michael V Ceci, *Branch Mgr*
Darren Durrill, *Vice Pres*
Kara Meyer, *Admin Asst*
Jennifer Hickson, *Director*
Hadi Hassan, *Advisor*
EMP: 58
SALES (corp-wide): 25.1B **Privately Held**
WEB: www.newyorklife.com
SIC: 6411 Insurance agents & brokers
PA: New York Life Insurance Company
51 Madison Ave Bsmt 1b
New York NY 10010
212 576-7000

(P-10704)
NEW YORK LIFE INSURANCE CO

3757 State St Ste 310, Santa Barbara
(93105-3133)
PHONE..............................805 898-7625
Mona Vargas, *Branch Mgr*
Dale Jones, *Manager*
EMP: 58
SALES (corp-wide): 25.1B **Privately Held**
WEB: www.newyorklife.com
SIC: 6411 Insurance agents & brokers
PA: New York Life Insurance Company
51 Madison Ave Bsmt 1b
New York NY 10010
212 576-7000

(P-10705)
NEW YORK LIFE INSURANCE CO

801 N Brand Blvd, Glendale (91203-1237)
PHONE..............................818 662-7500
Tigran Basmadkian, *Managing Prtnr*
Clode Moradi, *Advisor*
Richard Ragus, *Advisor*
Eszylfie Taylor, *Advisor*
Cynthia Ruffin, *Agent*
EMP: 58
SALES (corp-wide): 25.1B **Privately Held**
WEB: www.newyorklife.com
SIC: 6411 Insurance agents & brokers
PA: New York Life Insurance Company
51 Madison Ave Bsmt 1b
New York NY 10010
212 576-7000

(P-10706)
NEW YORK LIFE INSURANCE CO

1731 Tech Dr Ste 400, San Jose (95110)
PHONE..............................408 392-9782
Victor Vuong, *Partner*
Michal Grabowski, *Info Tech Dir*
Raymond Triplett, *Advisor*
EMP: 100
SALES (corp-wide): 25.1B **Privately Held**
WEB: www.newyorklife.com
SIC: 6411 Insurance agents & brokers
PA: New York Life Insurance Company
51 Madison Ave Bsmt 1b
New York NY 10010
212 576-7000

(P-10707)
NEW YORK LIFE INSURANCE CO

205 E Rver Pk Cir Ste 250, Fresno (93720)
PHONE..............................559 447-3900
Bert Moosios, *Agent*
EMP: 58
SALES (corp-wide): 25.1B **Privately Held**
WEB: www.newyorklife.com
SIC: 6411 Insurance agents & brokers
PA: New York Life Insurance Company
51 Madison Ave Bsmt 1b
New York NY 10010
212 576-7000

(P-10708)
NEW YORK LIFE INSURANCE CO
2020 Main St Ste 1200, Irvine
(92614-8235)
PHONE...........................949 797-2400
Christopher Prudhomme, *Owner*
Monzur A Mollah, *Sales Associate*
Scott Ziegelmeier, *Sales Associate*
Michael Furuta, *Advisor*
EMP: 70
SALES (corp-wide): 25.1B Privately Held
WEB: www.newyorklife.com
SIC: 6411 Insurance agents & brokers
PA: New York Life Insurance Company
     51 Madison Ave Bsmt 1b
     New York NY 10010
     212 576-7000

(P-10709)
NEW YORK LIFE INSURANCE CO
425 Market St Fl 16, San Francisco
(94105-2498)
PHONE...........................415 393-6060
Kevin Choi, *Manager*
EMP: 50
SALES (corp-wide): 25.1B Privately Held
WEB: www.newyorklife.com
SIC: 6411 Insurance agents & brokers
PA: New York Life Insurance Company
     51 Madison Ave Bsmt 1b
     New York NY 10010
     212 576-7000

(P-10710)
NEW YORK LIFE INSURANCE CO
2999 Douglas Blvd Ste 350, Roseville
(95661-3839)
PHONE...........................916 774-6200
Mark Ham, *Manager*
Rick Stivers, *Sales Executive*
Dean C Loftin, *Sales Associate*
John Wolff, *Director*
Sharon Stiles, *Advisor*
EMP: 100
SALES (corp-wide): 25.1B Privately Held
WEB: www.newyorklife.com
SIC: 6411 Insurance agents & brokers
PA: New York Life Insurance Company
     51 Madison Ave Bsmt 1b
     New York NY 10010
     212 576-7000

(P-10711)
NEW YORK LIFE INSURANCE CO
4365 Executive Dr Ste 800, San Diego
(92121-2130)
PHONE...........................858 623-8600
Antonio Montalvo, *Branch Mgr*
Cynthia R Bolker, *Advisor*
Trevor Isaacs, *Agent*
EMP: 140
SALES (corp-wide): 25.1B Privately Held
WEB: www.newyorklife.com
SIC: 6411 Insurance agents & brokers
PA: New York Life Insurance Company
     51 Madison Ave Bsmt 1b
     New York NY 10010
     212 576-7000

(P-10712)
NEW YORK LIFE INSURANCE CO
2633 Camino Ramon Ste 525, San Ramon
(94583-2174)
PHONE...........................415 999-9576
John Walker, *Manager*
EMP: 58
SALES (corp-wide): 25.1B Privately Held
WEB: www.newyorklife.com
SIC: 6411 Insurance agents & brokers
PA: New York Life Insurance Company
     51 Madison Ave Bsmt 1b
     New York NY 10010
     212 576-7000

(P-10713)
NEW YORK LIFE INSURANCE CO
300 E Esplanade Dr # 2050, Oxnard
(93036-0267)
PHONE...........................805 656-4598
Ashwani Kumarrana, *Principal*
Jane Choi, *Managing Dir*
John Higgins, *Advisor*
Judy Sun, *Advisor*
William Thomas, *Advisor*
EMP: 50
SALES (corp-wide): 25.1B Privately Held
WEB: www.newyorklife.com
SIC: 6411 Insurance agents & brokers
PA: New York Life Insurance Company
     51 Madison Ave Bsmt 1b
     New York NY 10010
     212 576-7000

(P-10714)
NEW YORK LIFE INSURANCE CO
6300 Wilshire Blvd # 1900, Los Angeles
(90048-5221)
PHONE...........................323 782-3000
Jerry M Fish, *Managing Prtnr*
Sheila Crimmins, *President*
Gregg Cicogna, *Info Tech Dir*
Mike Codina, *Manager*
Vivian Cosio, *Manager*
EMP: 50
SALES (corp-wide): 25.1B Privately Held
WEB: www.newyorklife.com
SIC: 6411 Insurance agents & brokers
PA: New York Life Insurance Company
     51 Madison Ave Bsmt 1b
     New York NY 10010
     212 576-7000

(P-10715)
NEW YORK LIFE INSURANCE CO
7112 N Fresno St Ste 100, Fresno
(93720-2949)
PHONE...........................559 447-3900
Janz Myderup, *Branch Mgr*
EMP: 100
SALES (corp-wide): 25.1B Privately Held
WEB: www.newyorklife.com
SIC: 6411 Insurance agents & brokers
PA: New York Life Insurance Company
     51 Madison Ave Bsmt 1b
     New York NY 10010
     212 576-7000

(P-10716)
NEW YORK LIFE INSURANCE CO
140 Via Verde Ste 200, San Dimas
(91773-5117)
PHONE...........................909 305-6500
Eddie Chao, *Manager*
EMP: 100
SALES (corp-wide): 25.1B Privately Held
WEB: www.newyorklife.com
SIC: 6411 Insurance agents & brokers
PA: New York Life Insurance Company
     51 Madison Ave Bsmt 1b
     New York NY 10010
     212 576-7000

(P-10717)
NNA INSURANCE SERVICES
9350 De Soto Ave, Chatsworth
(91311-4926)
P.O. Box 2402 (91313-2402)
PHONE...........................818 739-4071
Milton G Valera, *Ch of Bd*
Thomas A Heymann, *CEO*
Robert A Clarke, *CFO*
Deborah M Thaw, *Exec VP*
EMP: 204
SQ FT: 55,000
SALES (est): 44.9MM Privately Held
WEB: www.nationalnotary.com
SIC: 6411 Insurance agents, brokers & service

(P-10718)
NORCAL MUTUAL INSURANCE CO (PA)
575 Market St Fl 10, San Francisco
(94105-2885)
PHONE...........................415 397-9703
Theodore Scott Diener, *CEO*
Neil Simons, *President*
Jim Sunsari, *President*
Jaan Sidorov, *Bd of Directors*
Christoph Dugre, *Assoc VP*
EMP: 285
SALES (est): 311.7MM Privately Held
SIC: 6411 6331 Insurance agents; fire, marine & casualty insurance

(P-10719)
NORTHWEST INSURANCE AGENCY
Also Called: Bondi-Nderson Assoc Insur Brks
418 B St Ste 100, Santa Rosa
(95401-8500)
PHONE...........................707 573-1300
Mary Feli, *President*
EMP: 55
SALES (est): 5.2MM Privately Held
SIC: 6411 Insurance brokers

(P-10720)
NORTHWESTERN MUTL FINCL NETWRK (PA)
4225 Executive Sq, La Jolla (92037-9122)
PHONE...........................619 234-3111
Garrett J Bleakley, *Owner*
Devin Deverill, *Representative*
EMP: 120
SALES (est): 23MM Privately Held
SIC: 6411 Insurance agents

(P-10721)
OLD REPUBLIC CONTRACTORS INS
225 S Lake Ave Ste 900, Pasadena
(91101-3011)
PHONE...........................626 683-5200
Joan Miles, *CEO*
Oscar Burgos, *Senior VP*
Roberto Diaz-Albertini, *Senior VP*
Fil Gutierrez, *Vice Pres*
Chris Phillips, *Vice Pres*
EMP: 91
SALES (est): 19.4MM
SALES (corp-wide): 6.2B Publicly Held
SIC: 6411 Insurance agents, brokers & service
HQ: Old Republic General Insurance
     Group, Inc.
     307 N Michigan Ave # 1418
     Chicago IL 60601

(P-10722)
OLD REPUBLIC HM PROTECTION INC
2 Annabel Ln Ste 112, San Ramon
(94583-1377)
P.O. Box 5017 (94583-0917)
PHONE...........................925 866-1500
Gwen M Gallagher, *President*
Lorna Mello, *Senior VP*
Ed Adams, *Vice Pres*
Gail Stevens, *Vice Pres*
Terry Toole, *Vice Pres*
EMP: 305
SQ FT: 39,500
SALES (est): 101.2MM
SALES (corp-wide): 6.2B Publicly Held
WEB: www.orhp.com
SIC: 6411 Insurance agents
PA: Old Republic International Corporation
     307 N Michigan Ave
     Chicago IL 60601
     312 346-8100

(P-10723)
OMEGA INSURANCE SERVICES
Also Called: Word and Brown
721 S Parker St Ste 300, Orange
(92868-4732)
PHONE...........................714 973-0311
D P Thomas, *CEO*
Bill Mason, *President*
Angela Moran, *Senior VP*
Jeffrey Compangano, *Vice Pres*
Linh Huynh, *Vice Pres*
EMP: 50
SQ FT: 2,500
SALES (est): 17.3MM Privately Held
SIC: 6411 Insurance brokers

(P-10724)
OWEN & COMPANY
1455 Response Rd Ste 260, Sacramento
(95815-5263)
PHONE...........................916 993-2700
Jere Owen, *President*
John Owen, *Corp Secy*
EMP: 57
SQ FT: 4,741
SALES (est): 13.5MM Privately Held
SIC: 6411 8111 Insurance brokers; legal services

(P-10725)
PACIFIC INDEMNITY COMPANY
Also Called: Chubb
555 S Flower St Ste 300, Los Angeles
(90071-2427)
PHONE...........................213 622-2334
John Fennigan, *President*
Steven Goldman, *Exec VP*
Beth Mineau, *Vice Pres*
Chris Zupko, *Info Tech Mgr*
Lenea Sawyer, *Nurse*
EMP: 300
SALES (est): 57.2MM
SALES (corp-wide): 28.7B Privately Held
WEB: www.chubb.com
SIC: 6411 6331 6351 Property & casualty insurance agent; fire, marine & casualty insurance; mutual; surety insurance
HQ: Ina Chubb Holdings Inc
     436 Walnut St
     Philadelphia PA 19106
     215 640-1000

(P-10726)
PACIFIC PIONEER INSUR GROUP (PA)
Also Called: Pacific Pioneer Insur Group
6363 Katella Ave, Cypress (90630-5205)
PHONE...........................714 228-7888
Lin W Lan, *Founder*
Sherri Carlson, *Branch Mgr*
Laurie Eusebio, *Marketing Staff*
Daniel Fink, *Manager*
Colleen Eng, *Underwriter*
EMP: 104
SQ FT: 32,000
SALES (est): 17.5MM Privately Held
SIC: 6411 Insurance agents

(P-10727)
PACIFIC SPECIALTY INSURANCE CO
2200 Geng Rd Ste 200, Palo Alto
(94303-3358)
P.O. Box 40, Anaheim (92815-0040)
PHONE...........................650 780-4800
Timothy Joel Summers, *CEO*
John Mc Graw, *Shareholder*
Ann Mc Graw-Morrical, *Shareholder*
John Chu, *President*
Mike Mc Graw, *President*
EMP: 50
SQ FT: 20,000
SALES (est): 14.5MM Privately Held
WEB: www.pacificspecialty.com
SIC: 6411 Insurance agents
PA: Western Service Contract Corp.
     2200 Geng Rd Ste 200
     Palo Alto CA 94303

(P-10728)
PEGASUS RISK MANAGEMENT INC (PA)
Also Called: Status Medical Management
642 Galaxy Way, Modesto (95356-9606)
P.O. Box 5038 (95352-5038)
PHONE...........................209 574-2800
Ray Simon, *President*
Michelle Zaldua, *Human Res Dir*
Sharlene Russell, *Director*
EMP: 70
SQ FT: 10,000
SALES (est): 24.4MM Privately Held
WEB: www.statusmedical.com
SIC: 6411 Insurance claim processing, except medical

P
R
O
D
U
C
T
S

&

S
V
C
S

(P-10729)
PERR & KNIGHT INC (PA)
401 Wilshire Blvd Ste 300, Santa Monica
(90401-1454)
PHONE.................................310 230-9339
Timothy B Perr, *CEO*
Scott Knight, *Admin Mgr*
Chris Curry, *Manager*
Timothy Goggin, *Manager*
Jason Hudson, *Manager*
EMP: 93
SQ FT: 10,098
SALES (est): 36.4MM **Privately Held**
SIC: 6411 Loss prevention services, insurance; research services, insurance; reporting services, insurance

(P-10730)
PLANPRESCRIBER INC
440 E Middlefield Rd, Mountain View
(94043-4006)
PHONE.................................650 584-2700
Bruce A Telkamp, *CEO*
EMP: 298
SALES (est): 59.1MM
SALES (corp-wide): 172.3MM **Publicly Held**
SIC: 6411 Insurance agents, brokers & service
PA: Ehealth, Inc.
440 E Middlefield Rd
Mountain View CA 94043
650 584-2700

(P-10731)
PLEDGE INSURANCE BROKERAGE
2865 E Florence Ave, Huntington Park
(90255-5751)
PHONE.................................323 588-0223
Edward Fares, *Manager*
EMP: 70
SALES (est): 6.6MM **Privately Held**
SIC: 6411 Insurance brokers

(P-10732)
POLISEEK AIS INSUR SLTIONS INC
17785 Center Court Dr N # 250, Cerritos
(90703-8573)
PHONE.................................866 480-7335
Mark Ribisi, *President*
Chris Bremer, *CFO*
Lani Elkin, *VP Opers*
Romayne Levee, *VP Mktg*
Mark Casas, *VP Sales*
EMP: 70
SALES (est): 8.6MM
SALES (corp-wide): 3.4B **Publicly Held**
SIC: 6411 Insurance agents, brokers & service
HQ: Ais Management, Llc
17785 Center Court Dr N # 250
Cerritos CA 90703

(P-10733)
POLYCOMP ADMINISTRATIVE SVCS
3000 Lava Ridge Ct # 130, Roseville
(95661-2800)
PHONE.................................916 773-3480
Pamela Constantino, *Systems Mgr*
EMP: 50
SQ FT: 4,500
SALES (corp-wide): 33.5MM **Privately Held**
WEB: www.polycomp.net
SIC: 6411 Pension & retirement plan consultants
PA: Polycomp Administrative Services Inc
16030 Ventura Blvd # 200
Encino CA 91436
818 716-0111

(P-10734)
POMS & ASSOC INSUR BRKS INC (PA)
5700 Canoga Ave Ste 400, Woodland Hills
(91367-6594)
PHONE.................................818 449-9300
David A Poms, *CEO*
Jon Arima, *CFO*
Matthew Getty, *CFO*
Seth Ford Gilman, *Exec VP*

Seth Gilman, *Exec VP*
EMP: 90
SALES (est): 30.6MM **Privately Held**
SIC: 6411 Insurance brokers

(P-10735)
PRECEPT INC (DH)
Also Called: Precept Group The
130 Theory Ste 200, Irvine (92617-3065)
PHONE.................................949 955-1430
Wade R Olson, *President*
Roxane Langevin, *President*
Steve Williams, *President*
Steve Zarate, *COO*
Christopher H Coulter, *Chief Mktg Ofcr*
EMP: 90
SQ FT: 32,000
SALES (est): 46MM
SALES (corp-wide): 12.1B **Publicly Held**
WEB: www.preceptgroup.com
SIC: 6411 Insurance brokers
HQ: Mcgriff Insurance Services, Inc.
3605 Glenwood Ave Ste 190
Raleigh NC 27612
919 716-9907

(P-10736)
PREFERRED EMPLOYERS INSUR CO
9797 Aero Dr Ste 200, San Diego
(92123-1898)
P.O. Box 85478 (92186-5478)
PHONE.................................619 688-3900
Linda R Smith, *President*
Stephanie Graham, *President*
Eric Hansen, *Vice Pres*
Debbi Pacecca, *Administration*
Dale Piocos, *Engineer*
EMP: 70
SALES (est): 17.7MM
SALES (corp-wide): 7.6B **Publicly Held**
WEB: www.preferredworkcomp.com
SIC: 6411 Insurance information & consulting services
PA: W. R. Berkley Corporation
475 Steamboat Rd Fl 1
Greenwich CT 06830
203 629-3000

(P-10737)
PREMIER DEALER SERVICES INC
9449 Balboa Ave Ste 300, San Diego
(92123-4395)
PHONE.................................858 810-1700
John R Topits, *President*
Lisle Greenweller, *COO*
Kurt Wolery, *Senior VP*
A Kurt Wolery, *Admin Sec*
Mike Kissel, *Info Tech Mgr*
EMP: 100
SALES (est): 26.5MM **Privately Held**
WEB: www.pdsadm.com
SIC: 6411 Insurance agents, brokers & service

(P-10738)
PREMIERE AGENCY OF CALIFORNIA
Also Called: Placer Insurance
5 Sierra Gate Plz Fl 2nd, Roseville
(95678-6637)
P.O. Box 619052 (95661-9052)
PHONE.................................916 784-1008
Walter Klekowski, *President*
EMP: 65
SQ FT: 9,600
SALES (est): 12.4MM
SALES (corp-wide): 35.5B **Privately Held**
WEB: www.placerins.com
SIC: 6411 Insurance agents
HQ: Allied Group, Inc
1100 Locust St
Des Moines IA 50391
515 280-4211

(P-10739)
PRIMERICA FINANCIAL SVCS INC
27470 Jefferson Ave 5a, Temecula
(92590-2693)
PHONE.................................951 695-4325
Mary Simeta, *Manager*
EMP: 70 **Publicly Held**
SIC: 6411 Insurance agents & brokers

HQ: Primerica Financial Services, Inc.
3120 Breckinridge Blvd
Duluth GA 30099
800 544-5445

(P-10740)
PRIMERICA LIFE INSURANCE CO
260 Sheridan Ave Ste B42, Palo Alto
(94306-2046)
PHONE.................................650 323-2554
Omonike Wesipuryear, *Branch Mgr*
EMP: 121 **Publicly Held**
SIC: 6411 Insurance agents & brokers
HQ: Primerica Life Insurance Company
1 Primerica Pkwy
Duluth GA 30099
770 381-1000

(P-10741)
PRIMERICA LIFE INSURANCE CO
41307 12th St W Ste 200, Palmdale
(93551-1455)
PHONE.................................661 947-9070
Belia Rosales, *Branch Mgr*
EMP: 126 **Publicly Held**
SIC: 6411 Insurance agents & brokers
HQ: Primerica Life Insurance Company
1 Primerica Pkwy
Duluth GA 30099
770 381-1000

(P-10742)
PRIMERICA LIFE INSURANCE CO
175 N Cawston Ave, Hemet (92545-5277)
PHONE.................................951 652-6190
EMP: 126 **Publicly Held**
SIC: 6799 Insurance agents & brokers; investors
HQ: Primerica Life Insurance Company
1 Primerica Pkwy
Duluth GA 30099
770 381-1000

(P-10743)
PROFESSIONAL INSUR ASSOC INC (PA)
Also Called: Professsional Insurance
1100 Industrial Rd Ste 3, San Carlos
(94070-4131)
P.O. Box 1266 (94070-1266)
PHONE.................................650 592-7333
Paula Hammack, *President*
Devan Hammack, *Assoc VP*
Paul Hammack, *Vice Pres*
Anne Johnson, *Admin Asst*
Annalissa Trinidad, *Administration*
EMP: 50
SQ FT: 9,000
SALES (est): 67.8MM **Privately Held**
WEB: www.piainc.com
SIC: 6411 Insurance agents; insurance brokers

(P-10744)
PROPERTYPLUS INSUR AGCY INC
21820 Burbank Blvd # 130, Woodland Hills
(91367-6443)
PHONE.................................818 432-2640
EMP: 745
SALES (est): 81.7K
SALES (corp-wide): 26.8B **Publicly Held**
SIC: 6411 Real estate insurance agents
HQ: Arx Holding Corp.
1 Asi Way N
Saint Petersburg FL 33702
727 821-8765

(P-10745)
PROVIEW ADVANCED SOLUTIONS INC
130 Theory Ste 200, Irvine (92617-3065)
PHONE.................................949 752-2484
Alex Wasilewski III, *President*
EMP: 90
SALES (est): 10MM
SALES (corp-wide): 12.1B **Publicly Held**
WEB: www.preceptgroup.com
SIC: 6411 Insurance agents, brokers & service

HQ: Precept, Inc
130 Theory Ste 200
Irvine CA 92617
949 955-1430

(P-10746)
PRUDENTIAL INSUR CO OF AMER
3333 Michelson Dr Ste 820, Irvine
(92612-0655)
PHONE.................................949 440-5300
Jay Skolnick, *Manager*
EMP: 50
SALES (corp-wide): 59.6B **Publicly Held**
SIC: 6411 Insurance agents, brokers & service
HQ: The Prudential Insurance Company Of America
751 Broad St
Newark NJ 07102
973 802-6000

(P-10747)
PRUDENTIAL INSUR CO OF AMER
4 Embarcadero Ctr # 2700, San Francisco
(94111-4106)
PHONE.................................415 398-7310
Micheal Jamieson, *Manager*
Cornelia Cheng, *Vice Pres*
John Hall, *Managing Dir*
Tina Banninger, *Admin Asst*
Jocelyn Friel, *Director*
EMP: 80
SALES (corp-wide): 59.6B **Publicly Held**
SIC: 6411 Insurance agents, brokers & service
HQ: The Prudential Insurance Company Of America
751 Broad St
Newark NJ 07102
973 802-6000

(P-10748)
PRUDENTIAL INSUR CO OF AMER
15303 Ventura Blvd # 1550, Sherman Oaks
(91403-6624)
PHONE.................................818 990-2122
Craig Biggf, *Manager*
EMP: 50
SALES (corp-wide): 59.6B **Publicly Held**
SIC: 6411 Insurance agents, brokers & service
HQ: The Prudential Insurance Company Of America
751 Broad St
Newark NJ 07102
973 802-6000

(P-10749)
PRUDENTIAL INSUR CO OF AMER
5990 Sepulvda Blvd # 300, Van Nuys
(91411-2500)
PHONE.................................818 901-0028
EMP: 60
SALES (corp-wide): 41.4B **Publicly Held**
SIC: 6411
HQ: The Prudential Insurance Company Of America
751 Broad St
Newark NJ 07102
973 802-6000

(P-10750)
QBE FIRST INSURANCE AGENCY INC
9800 Muirlands Blvd, Irvine (92618-2515)
PHONE.................................949 206-6200
Becky Igo, *Principal*
EMP: 300 **Publicly Held**
WEB: www.zcsterling.com
SIC: 6411 Insurance agents
HQ: Qbe First Insurance Agency, Inc.
210 Interstate North Pkwy
Atlanta GA 30339
770 690-8400

(P-10751)
QUALIFIED BENEFITS INC
21021 Ventura Blvd # 100, Woodland Hills
(91364-2200)
PHONE.................................818 594-4900
Greg Taylor, *President*

▲ = Import ▼=Export
◆ =Import/Export

Angelo Mazzone, *Admin Sec*
EMP: 50
SQ FT: 11,500
SALES (est): 7.3MM **Privately Held**
WEB: www.qben.com
SIC: 6411 Pension & retirement plan consultants
PA: Qbi, Llc
    21031 Ventura Blvd # 1200
    Woodland Hills CA 91364

(P-10752)
QUALITY CLAIMS MANAGEMENT CORP
2763 Camino Del Rio S, San Diego
(92108-3708)
PHONE..................................619 450-8600
Ronald Reitz, *President*
Anne Schupack, *President*
Kevin McCarthy, *CFO*
Thomas Holthus, *Admin Sec*
Brian Reschke, *Business Anlyst*
EMP: 60
SQ FT: 8,000
SALES (est): 12.9MM **Privately Held**
WEB: www.qualityclaims.com
SIC: 6411 Insurance claim adjusters, not employed by insurance company

(P-10753)
R MC CLOSKEY INSURANCE AGENCY
Also Called: Tax and Financial Group
4001 Macarthur Blvd # 300, Newport Beach
(92660-2505)
PHONE..................................949 223-8100
Richard Mc Closkey, *President*
Art Veyna, *Partner*
Brian McNulty, *Managing Prtnr*
Paul Thomas, *Managing Prtnr*
Brian Freeman, *Senior VP*
EMP: 120
SQ FT: 15,000
SALES (est): 38.7MM **Privately Held**
WEB: www.tfgroup.com
SIC: 6411 Insurance agents; life insurance agents

(P-10754)
R S I INSURANCE BROKERS INC (PA)
2801 Bristol St Ste 200, Costa Mesa
(92626-5996)
PHONE..................................714 546-6616
Barry Rabune, *President*
Aaron Fawcett, *Vice Pres*
Ben Thomas, *Vice Pres*
Randee Grosso, *Technology*
Sandra Taber, *Human Res Mgr*
EMP: 52
SQ FT: 6,500
SALES (est): 55MM **Privately Held**
WEB: www.rsiinsurancebrokers.com
SIC: 6411 Insurance brokers

(P-10755)
RAMKADE INSURANCE SERVICES
Also Called: Time Financial Services
21550 Oxnard St Ste 500, Woodland Hills
(91367-7111)
PHONE..................................818 444-1340
Kate Kinkade, *President*
Patrick Ramsey, *Vice Pres*
EMP: 60
SALES (est): 7.5MM
SALES (corp-wide): 71.4B **Publicly Held**
WEB: www.timefin.com
SIC: 6411 Insurance agents
HQ: Citi Investor Services, Inc.
    105 Eisenhower Pkwy Ste 2
    Roseland NJ 07068

(P-10756)
RAMSELL PUBLIC HEALTH RX LLC
200 Webster St Ste 300, Oakland
(94607-4108)
PHONE..................................510 587-2600
Eric A Flowers,
Thomas Laker,
EMP: 51
SQ FT: 1,500

SALES (est): 3.8MM
SALES (corp-wide): 10.8MM **Privately Held**
SIC: 6411 Medical insurance claim processing, contract or fee basis
PA: Ramsell Corporation
    200 Webster St Ste 200 # 200
    Oakland CA 94607
    510 587-2659

(P-10757)
REHAB WEST INC
277 Rancheros Dr Ste 190, San Marcos
(92069-2982)
PHONE..................................619 518-3710
Sharon Douglas, *CEO*
Carol Holub, *CFO*
Kathy Galliher, *Office Mgr*
Carol Clark, *Admin Asst*
Tammy Rancourt, *Administration*
EMP: 50
SQ FT: 3,000
SALES: 5.5MM **Privately Held**
WEB: www.rehabwest.com
SIC: 6411 Medical insurance claim processing, contract or fee basis

(P-10758)
ROBERT MORENO INSURANCE SVCS
22860 Savi Ranch Pkwy, Yorba Linda
(92887-4610)
P.O. Box 87023 (92885-7023)
PHONE..................................714 525-5168
Robert B Moreno, *Owner*
Laura Moreno, *COO*
Ana Smith, *Business Mgr*
Stephen Grothues, *Controller*
Omar Gaitan, *Marketing Mgr*
EMP: 140 **EST:** 1978
SQ FT: 28,500
SALES (est): 28.1MM **Privately Held**
WEB: www.rmismga.com
SIC: 6411 Insurance agents

(P-10759)
RON FILICE ENTERPRISES INC
Also Called: Filice Insurance Agency
738 N 1st St Ste 202, San Jose
(95112-6371)
PHONE..................................408 294-0477
Ron Filice, *President*
Silvia G Lucero, *Officer*
Chris Lazio, *Exec VP*
Mike Chavez, *Vice Pres*
Michelle Filice, *Vice Pres*
EMP: 50
SQ FT: 3,000
SALES (est): 14.9MM **Privately Held**
SIC: 6411 Insurance agents

(P-10760)
RUTLEDGE CLAIMS MANAGEMENT INC
14286 Danielson St # 103, Poway
(92064-8819)
PHONE..................................858 883-2000
Thomas W Rutledge, *CEO*
EMP: 100
SALES (est): 16.5MM **Privately Held**
SIC: 6411 Insurance information & consulting services

(P-10761)
SACRAMNTO HSING RDVLPMENT AGCY
630 I St Fl 3, Sacramento (95814-2404)
PHONE..................................916 440-1376
La Shelle Dozier, *Branch Mgr*
Tanya Tran, *Program Mgr*
James Shields, *Administration*
Ranjit Rai, *CTO*
Kelly Tang, *Finance Mgr*
EMP: 125 **Privately Held**
SIC: 6411 Insurance agents, brokers & service
PA: Sacramento Housing And Redevelopment Agency
    801 12th St
    Sacramento CA 95814
    916 440-1390

(P-10762)
SAFE-GUARD PRODUCTS INTL LLC
18100 Von Karman Ave # 150, Irvine
(92612-0174)
PHONE..................................800 742-7896
Randy Barkowitz, *Branch Mgr*
EMP: 96 **Privately Held**
SIC: 6411 Property & casualty insurance agent
PA: Safe-Guard Products International Llc
    2 Concourse Pkwy Ste 500
    Atlanta GA 30328

(P-10763)
SAFECO INSURANCE COMPANY AMER
330 N Brand Blvd Ste 680, Glendale
(91203-2385)
PHONE..................................818 956-4250
Don Chambers, *Manager*
EMP: 160
SALES (corp-wide): 38.3B **Privately Held**
SIC: 6411 Insurance agents
HQ: Safeco Insurance Company Of America
    1001 4th Ave Ste 800
    Seattle WA 98185
    206 545-5000

(P-10764)
SCC ESA DEPT OF RISK MGMT
Also Called: ESA Risk Management
2310 N 1st St Ste 202, San Jose
(95131-1040)
PHONE..................................408 441-4207
EMP: 65
SALES (est): 2.8MM **Privately Held**
WEB: www.esariskmanagement.com
SIC: 6411

(P-10765)
SCHIRMER FIRE PROTECTION ENG
Also Called: AON
707 Wilshire Blvd # 2600, Los Angeles
(90017-3501)
PHONE..................................213 630-2020
Jacqueline Bychowski, *Office Mgr*
Mark Rochholz, *COO*
Helen Batsalkin, *Assistant VP*
EMP: 99
SALES (corp-wide): 339.5MM **Privately Held**
SIC: 6411 Insurance brokers
HQ: Schirmer Fire Protection Engineering Corporation
    200 E Randolph St
    Chicago IL 60601
    312 381-1000

(P-10766)
SCOTTISH AMERICAN INSURANCE (PA)
Also Called: Yates & Associates
2002 E Mcfadden Ave # 100, Santa Ana
(92705-4766)
PHONE..................................714 550-5050
Paul A Thomson, *CEO*
Carl Ledbetter, *President*
James M Yates, *President*
Gregory Martin, *CFO*
Catherine Huerta, *Admin Asst*
EMP: 69
SQ FT: 14,300
SALES (est): 17.2MM **Privately Held**
WEB: www.yates-assoc.com
SIC: 6411 Insurance brokers

(P-10767)
SEDGWICK CLAIMS MGT SVCS INC
3280 E Foothill Blvd # 350, Pasadena
(91107-3103)
P.O. Box 14435, Lexington KY (40512-4435)
PHONE..................................626 568-1415
Barbara Jones, *Principal*
Monica Soto, *Executive*
EMP: 70
SALES (corp-wide): 9.5B **Privately Held**
SIC: 6411 Insurance claim adjusters, not employed by insurance company

HQ: Sedgwick Claims Management Services, Inc.
    1100 Ridgeway Loop Rd # 200
    Memphis TN 38120
    901 415-7400

(P-10768)
SEDGWICK CLAIMS MGT SVCS INC
24025 Park Sorrento # 200, Calabasas
(91302-4018)
PHONE..................................818 591-9444
John Gernert, *Manager*
Kevin Hawkins, *Finance Dir*
Jeffery Bredehorn, *Controller*
John Koval, *Accounts Exec*
EMP: 200
SALES (corp-wide): 9.5B **Privately Held**
WEB: www.sedgwickcms.com
SIC: 6411 Insurance claim adjusters, not employed by insurance company
HQ: Sedgwick Claims Management Services, Inc.
    1100 Ridgeway Loop Rd # 200
    Memphis TN 38120
    901 415-7400

(P-10769)
SEDGWICK CLAIMS MGT SVCS INC
2101 Webster St, Oakland (94612-3011)
PHONE..................................510 302-3000
Athanasios Soha, *Branch Mgr*
William Etheridge, *President*
David Shaffer, *President*
Robert Shaffer, *Vice Pres*
Joyce Crain, *Admin Asst*
EMP: 70
SALES (corp-wide): 9.5B **Privately Held**
WEB: www.sedgwickcms.com
SIC: 6411 Insurance claim adjusters, not employed by insurance company
HQ: Sedgwick Claims Management Services, Inc.
    1100 Ridgeway Loop Rd # 200
    Memphis TN 38120
    901 415-7400

(P-10770)
SEDGWICK CLAIMS MGT SVCS INC
1851 Heritage Ln, Sacramento
(95815-4926)
PHONE..................................916 568-7394
EMP: 70
SALES (corp-wide): 9.5B **Privately Held**
SIC: 6411 Insurance claim adjusters, not employed by insurance company
HQ: Sedgwick Claims Management Services, Inc.
    1100 Ridgeway Loop Rd # 200
    Memphis TN 38120
    901 415-7400

(P-10771)
SELECTQUOTE INSURANCE SERVICES (PA)
595 Market St Fl 10, San Francisco
(94105-2899)
PHONE..................................415 543-7338
Charan J Singh, *President*
Robert Edwards, *COO*
Steven H Gerber, *Vice Pres*
Kellie Stewart, *Office Mgr*
Amy Spellman, *Executive Asst*
EMP: 200
SALES (est): 260.4MM **Privately Held**
WEB: www.selectquote.com
SIC: 6411 Life insurance agents

(P-10772)
SEQUOIA INSURANCE COMPANY
P.O. Box 1510, Monterey (93942-1510)
PHONE..................................916 933-9524
EMP: 72 **Publicly Held**
SIC: 6411
HQ: Sequoia Insurance Company
    31 Upper Ragsdale Dr
    Monterey CA 93940
    831 655-9612

PRODUCTS & SVCS

(P-10773)
SHAW & PETERSEN
INSURANCE INC
Also Called: Harbor's Insurance
1313 5th St, Eureka (95501-0660)
PHONE..........................707 443-0845
Maurice O Shaw Sr, *President*
Maurice O Shaw Jr, *Corp Secy*
Pat Krebs, *Receptionist*
EMP: 50
SQ FT: 3,000
SALES (est): 8.8MM **Privately Held**
WEB: www.shawandpetersen.com
SIC: 6411 Insurance agents

(P-10774)
SIGNATURE RESOURCES
INSURANCE
Also Called: John Hancock
19900 Macarthur Blvd # 920, Irvine
(92612-8417)
PHONE..........................949 930-2400
Gary Kaltenbach, *Owner*
Nina Manning, *Office Mgr*
William Barnett,
Susan Oleary,
Geoffrey Kaltenbach, *Mng Member*
EMP: 60
SQ FT: 1,800
SALES (est): 10.2MM **Privately Held**
WEB: www.signatureresources.net
SIC: 6411 Insurance agents & brokers

(P-10775)
SKYLES INSURANCE AGENCY
9840 Business Park Dr, Sacramento
(95827-1745)
PHONE..........................916 361-9585
Theron Skyles, *Partner*
John Dalton, *Administration*
Cindy Wingard, *Sales Associate*
EMP: 50
SALES (est): 6.6MM **Privately Held**
SIC: 6411 Insurance agents

(P-10776)
SPECIALTY RISK SERVICES INC
1 Pointe Dr Ste 220, Brea (92821-7626)
P.O. Box 7007, La Habra (90632-7007)
PHONE..........................714 674-1000
Sharon Bartholomew, *Principal*
EMP: 87
SALES (corp-wide): 9.5B **Privately Held**
SIC: 6411 Insurance agents, brokers &
service
HQ: Specialty Risk Services, Inc.
100 Corporate Dr Ste 211
Windsor CT 06095

(P-10777)
SPECIALTY RISK SERVICES INC
6140 Stoneridge Mall Rd # 245, Pleasanton
(94588-3233)
PHONE..........................877 809-9478
Eric Hansen, *Principal*
EMP: 117
SALES (corp-wide): 9.5B **Privately Held**
WEB: www.srsconnect.com
SIC: 6411 Insurance claim processing, ex-
cept medical; loss prevention services, in-
surance
HQ: Specialty Risk Services, Inc.
100 Corporate Dr Ste 211
Windsor CT 06095

(P-10778)
STATE FARM FIRE AND CSLTY
CO
Also Called: State Farm Insurance
5127 W Walnut Ave, Visalia (93277-3472)
PHONE..........................559 625-4330
Patrick Salazar, *Manager*
Elaine R Rider, *Agent*
EMP: 63
SALES (corp-wide): 39.5B **Privately Held**
WEB: www.statefarm.net
SIC: 6411 Insurance agents & brokers
HQ: State Farm Fire And Casualty Com-
pany
Three State Frm Plz S H-4
Bloomington IL 61710
309 766-2311

(P-10779)
STATE FARM FIRE AND CSLTY
CO
Also Called: State Farm Insurance
6400 State Farm Dr, Rohnert Park (94928)
PHONE..........................707 588-6011
Glen Dorsett, *Manager*
EMP: 500
SALES (corp-wide): 39.5B **Privately Held**
WEB: www.statefarm.net
SIC: 6411 Insurance agents & brokers
HQ: State Farm Fire And Casualty Com-
pany
Three State Frm Plz S H-4
Bloomington IL 61710
309 766-2311

(P-10780)
STATE FARM MUTL AUTO INSUR
CO
Also Called: State Farm Insurance
12122 S Halldale Ave # 200, Los Angeles
(90047-5320)
PHONE..........................309 766-2311
Rodrigo Salas, *Internal Med*
Stephan Buckley, *Manager*
Karl Lassiter, *Agent*
EMP: 326
SALES (corp-wide): 39.5B **Privately Held**
WEB: www.statefarm.com
SIC: 6411 Insurance agents & brokers
PA: State Farm Mutual Automobile Insur-
ance Company
1 State Farm Plz
Bloomington IL 61710
309 766-2311

(P-10781)
STATE FARM MUTL AUTO INSUR
CO
Also Called: State Farm Insurance
16656 Ventura Blvd # 203, Encino
(91436-1918)
PHONE..........................818 849-5126
EMP: 71
SALES (corp-wide): 39.5B **Privately Held**
SIC: 6411 Insurance agents & brokers
PA: State Farm Mutual Automobile Insur-
ance Company
1 State Farm Plz
Bloomington IL 61710
309 766-2311

(P-10782)
STATE FARM MUTL AUTO INSUR
CO
Also Called: State Farm Insurance
5050 El Camino Real # 108, Los Altos
(94022-1530)
PHONE..........................650 694-6767
Don M Parker, *Principal*
Jack Flesher, *Manager*
EMP: 72
SALES (corp-wide): 39.5B **Privately Held**
WEB: www.statefarm.com
SIC: 6411 Insurance agents & brokers
PA: State Farm Mutual Automobile Insur-
ance Company
1 State Farm Plz
Bloomington IL 61710
309 766-2311

(P-10783)
STATE FARM MUTL AUTO INSUR
CO
Also Called: State Farm Insurance
30125 Agoura Rd Ste 200, Agoura Hills
(91301-4322)
PHONE..........................818 597-4300
Dennis Pitta, *Branch Mgr*
EMP: 72
SALES (corp-wide): 39.5B **Privately Held**
WEB: www.statefarm.com
SIC: 6411 Insurance agents & brokers
PA: State Farm Mutual Automobile Insur-
ance Company
1 State Farm Plz
Bloomington IL 61710
309 766-2311

(P-10784)
STATE FARM MUTL AUTO INSUR
CO
Also Called: State Farm Insurance
1558 Fitzgerald Dr, Pinole (94564-2229)
PHONE..........................510 222-1102
Donald L Greco, *Owner*
EMP: 72
SALES (corp-wide): 39.5B **Privately Held**
WEB: www.statefarm.com
SIC: 6411 Insurance agents & brokers
PA: State Farm Mutual Automobile Insur-
ance Company
1 State Farm Plz
Bloomington IL 61710
309 766-2311

(P-10785)
STATE FARM MUTL AUTO INSUR
CO
Also Called: State Farm Insurance
1705 E 10th St Apt 201, Long Beach
(90813-6347)
PHONE..........................310 632-9810
Phil Davis, *Manager*
EMP: 72
SALES (corp-wide): 39.5B **Privately Held**
WEB: www.statefarm.com
SIC: 6411 Insurance agents & brokers
PA: State Farm Mutual Automobile Insur-
ance Company
1 State Farm Plz
Bloomington IL 61710
309 766-2311

(P-10786)
STATE FARM MUTL AUTO INSUR
CO
Also Called: State Farm Insurance
17122 Slover Ave Ste 106, Fontana
(92337-7588)
PHONE..........................909 349-2050
Lenita Graves, *Manager*
EMP: 72
SALES (corp-wide): 39.5B **Privately Held**
WEB: www.statefarm.com
SIC: 6411 Insurance agents & brokers
PA: State Farm Mutual Automobile Insur-
ance Company
1 State Farm Plz
Bloomington IL 61710
309 766-2311

(P-10787)
STATE FARM MUTL AUTO INSUR
CO
Also Called: State Farm Insurance
2019 24th St, Bakersfield (93301-3814)
PHONE..........................661 324-4077
Roger Hess, *Branch Mgr*
EMP: 72
SALES (corp-wide): 39.5B **Privately Held**
WEB: www.statefarm.com
SIC: 6411 Insurance agents & brokers
PA: State Farm Mutual Automobile Insur-
ance Company
1 State Farm Plz
Bloomington IL 61710
309 766-2311

(P-10788)
STATE FARM MUTL AUTO INSUR
CO
Also Called: State Farm Insurance
2555 Flores St Ste 175, San Mateo
(94403-2343)
PHONE..........................650 345-3571
Jake Bursalyan, *Manager*
Jake G Bursalyan, *Manager*
EMP: 72
SALES (corp-wide): 39.5B **Privately Held**
WEB: www.statefarm.com
SIC: 6411 Insurance agents & brokers
PA: State Farm Mutual Automobile Insur-
ance Company
1 State Farm Plz
Bloomington IL 61710
309 766-2311

(P-10789)
STATE FARM MUTL AUTO INSUR
CO
Also Called: State Farm Insurance
3351 Michelson Dr Ste 200, Irvine
(92612-4427)
PHONE..........................309 766-2311
Mike Memoly, *Owner*
Liz Schneider-Smith, *Recruiter*
Dick Horn, *Manager*
EMP: 72
SALES (corp-wide): 39.5B **Privately Held**
WEB: www.statefarm.com
SIC: 6411 Insurance agents & brokers
PA: State Farm Mutual Automobile Insur-
ance Company
1 State Farm Plz
Bloomington IL 61710
309 766-2311

(P-10790)
STATE FARM MUTL AUTO INSUR
CO
Also Called: State Farm Insurance
40315 Junction Dr Ste A, Oakhurst
(93644-9159)
PHONE..........................559 683-3467
Marilyn Rigg, *Branch Mgr*
EMP: 72
SALES (corp-wide): 39.5B **Privately Held**
WEB: www.statefarm.com
SIC: 6411 Insurance agents & brokers
PA: State Farm Mutual Automobile Insur-
ance Company
1 State Farm Plz
Bloomington IL 61710
309 766-2311

(P-10791)
STATE FARM MUTL AUTO INSUR
CO
Also Called: State Farm Insurance
5345 Fallbrook Ave, Woodland Hills
(91367-6112)
PHONE..........................818 887-1060
Gary Hoover, *Manager*
EMP: 72
SALES (corp-wide): 39.5B **Privately Held**
WEB: www.statefarm.com
SIC: 6411 Insurance agents & brokers
PA: State Farm Mutual Automobile Insur-
ance Company
1 State Farm Plz
Bloomington IL 61710
309 766-2311

(P-10792)
STATE FARM MUTL AUTO INSUR
CO
Also Called: State Farm Insurance
845 Via De La Paz Ste 12, Pacific Pal-
isades (90272-3627)
PHONE..........................310 454-0349
Vince Gurino, *Manager*
Trish Bowe, *Manager*
EMP: 72
SALES (corp-wide): 39.5B **Privately Held**
WEB: www.statefarm.com
SIC: 6411 Insurance agents & brokers
PA: State Farm Mutual Automobile Insur-
ance Company
1 State Farm Plz
Bloomington IL 61710
309 766-2311

(P-10793)
STATE FARM MUTL AUTO INSUR
CO
Also Called: State Farm Insurance
8040 W 3rd St, Los Angeles (90048-4307)
PHONE..........................323 852-6868
Daniel Williams, *Manager*
EMP: 72
SALES (corp-wide): 39.5B **Privately Held**
WEB: www.statefarm.com
SIC: 6411 Insurance agents & brokers
PA: State Farm Mutual Automobile Insur-
ance Company
1 State Farm Plz
Bloomington IL 61710
309 766-2311

(P-10794)

STATE FARM MUTL AUTO INSUR CO

Also Called: State Farm Insurance
4600 Ashe Rd Ste 308, Bakersfield
(93313-2040)
PHONE..................661 664-9663
Keith Stonebraker, *Branch Mgr*
Rosie Schweer, *Manager*
EMP: 72
SALES (corp-wide): 39.5B **Privately Held**
WEB: www.statefarm.com
SIC: 6411 Insurance agents
PA: State Farm Mutual Automobile Insurance Company
1 State Farm Plz
Bloomington IL 61710
309 766-2311

(P-10795)

STRATEGIC FINANCIAL GROUP

18191 Von Karman Ave # 100, Irvine
(92612-7103)
PHONE..................949 622-7200
Shawn Mackey, *Principal*
EMP: 50
SALES (est): 3.6MM **Privately Held**
SIC: 6411 Insurance agents

(P-10796)

SUN COAST GEN INSUR AGCY INC

23042 Mill Creek Dr, Laguna Hills
(92653-1214)
P.O. Box 30750 (92654-0750)
PHONE..................949 768-1132
Jeffrey Yeskin, *CEO*
David Yeskin, *President*
Larua Gibson, *CFO*
Scott Boren, *Chief Mktg Ofcr*
Rosie Garcia, *Technology*
EMP: 55
SQ FT: 13,000
SALES (est): 12.4MM **Privately Held**
WEB: www.suncoastinsurance.com
SIC: 6411 Insurance agents

(P-10797)

SUNLAND INSURANCE AGENCY

4961 E Kings Canyon Rd, Fresno
(93727-3812)
P.O. Box 779, Clovis (93613-0779)
PHONE..................559 251-7861
Michael Denman, *Owner*
EMP: 765
SALES (est): 166.4K
SALES (corp-wide): 3.4B **Publicly Held**
SIC: 6411 Insurance agents
HQ: Mercury Insurance Company
4484 Wilshire Blvd
Los Angeles CA 90010
323 937-1060

(P-10798)

SURVIVAL INSURANCE INC

Also Called: Survival Insurance Brkg A Cal
2550 N Hollywood Way # 120, Burbank
(91505-1055)
PHONE..................818 565-1584
Richard Acunto, *Ch of Bd*
Susan Mithoff, *Vice Pres*
EMP: 240
SQ FT: 10,000
SALES (est): 22.7MM **Privately Held**
SIC: 6411 Insurance brokers

(P-10799)

TBG INSURANCE SERVICES CORP

100 N Pacific Coast Hwy # 500, El Segundo (90245-4359)
PHONE..................310 203-8770
Michael R Shute, *CEO*
Michael Glickman, *CFO*
EMP: 260
SALES (est): 45.7MM **Privately Held**
SIC: 6411 8111 Insurance agents, brokers & service; legal services

(P-10800)

THOITS INSURANCE SERVICE INC

444 Castro St Ste 200, Mountain View
(94041-2051)
PHONE..................408 792-5400

Donald A Way, *CEO*
Eric Nielsen, *CFO*
Marianne K Chow, *Vice Pres*
Shanel Hudson, *Vice Pres*
Sean Lemmon, *Vice Pres*
EMP: 67
SQ FT: 16,250
SALES: 14.3MM **Privately Held**
WEB: www.thoits-insurance.com
SIC: 6411 Insurance agents

(P-10801)

TOKIO MARINE MANAGEMENT INC

800 E Colorado Blvd Ste 8, Pasadena
(91101-2103)
P.O. Box 7127 (91109-7127)
PHONE..................626 568-7600
Kaz Takashima, *Manager*
EMP: 250
SALES (corp-wide): 2.1B **Privately Held**
SIC: 6411 6331 6321 Insurance brokers; fire, marine & casualty insurance; accident & health insurance
HQ: Tokio Marine Management, Inc.
1221 Park Ave Ste 1500
New York NY 10128
212 297-6600

(P-10802)

TRAVELERS INDEMNITY COMPANY

Also Called: Travelers Insurance
21688 Gateway Center Dr # 300, Diamond Bar (91765-2451)
P.O. Box 660055, Dallas TX (75266-0055)
PHONE..................909 612-3000
Annet Ball, *Manager*
John Braddock, *Human Res Mgr*
Kety Lopez, *Opers Staff*
Peggy Smalley, *Manager*
Denise Pineda, *Consultant*
EMP: 200
SALES (corp-wide): 28.9B **Publicly Held**
WEB: www.travelers.com
SIC: 6411 6331 Insurance agents; fire, marine & casualty insurance
HQ: The Travelers Indemnity Company
1 Tower Sq
Hartford CT 06183
860 277-0111

(P-10803)

TRAVELERS PROPERTY CSLTY CORP

401 Lennon Ln, Walnut Creek
(94598-2508)
P.O. Box 13089, Sacramento (95813-3089)
PHONE..................925 945-4000
Julie Weisert, *Branch Mgr*
Jeison Aguilar, *Underwriter*
EMP: 300
SALES (corp-wide): 28.9B **Publicly Held**
WEB: www.travelerspc.com
SIC: 6411 Insurance agents
HQ: Travelers Property Casualty Corp.
1 Tower Sq 8ms
Hartford CT 06183

(P-10804)

TRAVELERS PROPERTY CSLTY CORP

145 S State College Blvd # 240, Brea
(92821-5818)
PHONE..................714 671-8000
Bob Plourde, *Branch Mgr*
EMP: 116
SALES (corp-wide): 28.9B **Publicly Held**
WEB: www.travelerspc.com
SIC: 6411 Insurance agents
HQ: Travelers Property Casualty Corp.
1 Tower Sq 8ms
Hartford CT 06183

(P-10805)

TRI-AD ACTUARIES INC

221 W Crest St Ste 300, Escondido
(92025-1737)
PHONE..................760 743-7555
Curtis Hamilton, *CEO*
Robert Krier, *CFO*

Thad Hamilton, *Vice Pres*
Judy Simons, *Vice Pres*
EMP: 117
SQ FT: 17,500
SALES (est): 40.5MM **Privately Held**
WEB: www.tri-ad.com
SIC: 6411 8742 Pension & retirement plan consultants; human resource consulting services

(P-10806)

TRISTAR RISK MANAGEMENT

203 N Golden Circle Dr # 200, Santa Ana
(92705-4011)
PHONE..................714 543-0700
Thomas Veale, *Branch Mgr*
EMP: 69
SALES (corp-wide): 363.2MM **Privately Held**
WEB: www.tristarrisk.com
SIC: 6411 8742 Inspection & investigation services, insurance; management consulting services
HQ: Tristar Risk Management
100 Oceangate Ste 700
Long Beach CA 90802
562 495-6600

(P-10807)

TRUE RATE INSURANCE AGENCY INC (PA)

2820 S Vermont Ave Ste 1, Los Angeles
(90007-2291)
PHONE..................323 735-1600
Samir Ramadan, *President*
EMP: 50
SQ FT: 1,900
SALES (est): 6.5MM **Privately Held**
WEB: www.truerateinsuranceagency.com
SIC: 6411 Insurance agents

(P-10808)

UNIFAX INSURANCE SYSTEMS INC

26050 Mureau Rd Fl 2, Calabasas
(91302-3174)
PHONE..................818 591-9800
Erwin Cheldin, *President*
Lester Aaron, *Treasurer*
Cary Cheldin, *Exec VP*
Michael Odmark, *Supervisor*
EMP: 80 EST: 1972
SQ FT: 50,000
SALES: 8.8MM
SALES (corp-wide): 36.7MM **Publicly Held**
WEB: www.crusaderinsurance.com
SIC: 6411 Insurance brokers
PA: Unico American Corporation
26050 Mureau Rd Fl 2
Calabasas CA 91302
818 591-9800

(P-10809)

UNITED CHINESE AMERICAN GENERA (PA)

Also Called: Uca General Insurance
6363 Katella Ave, Cypress (90630-5205)
PHONE..................714 228-7800
Robert Lan, *President*
Lin Lan, *Shareholder*
Ping Chen, *Corp Secy*
EMP: 50
SQ FT: 20,000
SALES (est): 10MM **Privately Held**
WEB: www.ucageneral.com
SIC: 6411 Insurance agents, brokers & service

(P-10810)

UNITED INSURANCE COMPANY

5601 E Slauson Ave # 105, Commerce
(90040-2997)
PHONE..................323 869-9381
Norman Petrousian, *District Mgr*
EMP: 50
SALES (est): 5.8MM **Privately Held**
SIC: 6411 Insurance agents

(P-10811)

UNITED STATES FIRE INSUR CO

Also Called: Crum & Forster
777 S Figueroa St # 1500, Los Angeles
(90017-5810)
PHONE..................213 797-3100

Mark Owens, *Manager*
Sean Ramones, *Analyst*
EMP: 53
SALES (corp-wide): 16.2B **Privately Held**
SIC: 6411 Insurance agents
HQ: United States Fire Insurance Company
305 Madison Ave
Morristown NJ 07960
973 490-6600

(P-10812)

UNUM LIFE INSURANCE CO AMER

Also Called: Unumprovident
655 N Central Ave, Glendale (91203-1422)
PHONE..................818 291-4739
Vicki Riggs, *Branch Mgr*
EMP: 195 **Publicly Held**
SIC: 6411 Insurance agents
HQ: Unum Life Insurance Company Of America
2211 Congress St
Portland ME 04122
207 575-2211

(P-10813)

USI INSURANCE SERVICES NAT

1350 Treat Blvd Ste 550, Walnut Creek
(94597-7999)
PHONE..................925 988-1700
Brian Heatherington, *Director*
EMP: 70 **Privately Held**
SIC: 6411 Insurance agents, brokers & service
HQ: Usi Insurance Services National, Inc.
150 N Michigan Ave # 3900
Chicago IL 60601
866 294-2571

(P-10814)

USI INSURANCE SERVICES NAT INC

1039a N Mcdowell Blvd, Petaluma
(94954-1173)
PHONE..................707 769-2900
Wayne Shira, *Manager*
EMP: 80 **Privately Held**
SIC: 6411 Insurance agents, brokers & service
HQ: Usi Insurance Services National, Inc.
150 N Michigan Ave # 3900
Chicago IL 60601
866 294-2571

(P-10815)

USI INSURANCE SERVICES NAT INC

5200 N Palm Ave Ste 114, Fresno
(93704-2225)
PHONE..................559 666-2001
Debra Powers, *Branch Mgr*
EMP: 70 **Privately Held**
SIC: 6411 Insurance agents, brokers & service
HQ: Usi Insurance Services National, Inc.
150 N Michigan Ave # 3900
Chicago IL 60601
866 294-2571

(P-10816)

USI INSURANCE SERVICES NAT INC

777 S Figueroa St # 2100, Los Angeles
(90017-5800)
PHONE..................213 253-6700
Alan Boring, *Director*
EMP: 123 **Privately Held**
SIC: 6411 Insurance agents, brokers & service
HQ: Usi Insurance Services National, Inc.
150 N Michigan Ave # 3900
Chicago IL 60601
866 294-2571

(P-10817)

USI INSURANCE SERVICES NAT INC

10940 White Rock Rd, Rancho Cordova
(95670-6182)
PHONE..................916 589-8000
Donna Flores, *Branch Mgr*
Roy Musgrove, *Vice Pres*
Kenneth Amerman, *Branch Mgr*
Maureen Schlimgen, *Accounts Mgr*
EMP: 210 **Privately Held**

SIC: 6411 Insurance agents, brokers & service
HQ: Usi Insurance Services National, Inc.
150 N Michigan Ave # 3900
Chicago IL 60601
866 294-2571

(P-10818)
USI INSURANCE SERVICES NAT INC
201 Mission St Ste 1100, San Francisco (94105-8100)
PHONE..............................628 201-9001
Samuel Jones, *Branch Mgr*
Erik Stenson, *Vice Pres*
EMP: 200 **Privately Held**
SIC: 6411 Insurance agents, brokers & service
HQ: Usi Insurance Services National, Inc.
150 N Michigan Ave # 3900
Chicago IL 60601
866 294-2571

(P-10819)
USI OF SOUTHERN CALIFORNIA INS
21700 Oxnard St Ste 1200, Woodland Hills (91367-7578)
PHONE..............................818 251-3000
Mike Rastigue, *President*
Mark Goldberg, *Vice Pres*
Bernadette Jackson, *Vice Pres*
Kelly Lee, *Executive Asst*
Jon Castellano, *Sales Staff*
EMP: 50
SQ FT: 15,000
SALES (est): 10.4MM **Privately Held**
WEB: www.usicondo.com
SIC: 6411 Insurance agents; life insurance agents
HQ: Usi Service Corporation
100 Summit Lake Dr # 400
Valhalla NY 10595
-

(P-10820)
USI SOUTH COAST
Also Called: Kemper Insurance
29a Technology Dr 200, Irvine (92618-2302)
PHONE..............................949 790-9200
Randy Joe Hartman, *Vice Pres*
Brian Cutick, *Architect*
EMP: 60
SQ FT: 5,000
SALES (est): 7.6MM **Privately Held**
SIC: 6411 7513 Insurance agents; property & casualty insurance agent; truck rental & leasing, no drivers

(P-10821)
VALUEOPTIONS OF CALIFORNIA
Also Called: Value Options-V B H
5665 Plaza Dr Ste 400, Cypress (90630-5037)
PHONE..............................800 228-1286
Juan Molina, *VP Opers*
Steve Rockowitz, *Ch of Bd*
Jolene Myrter, *CFO*
EMP: 200
SALES (est): 19.8MM
SALES (corp-wide): 501.8MM **Privately Held**
WEB: www.fhchealthsystems.com
SIC: 6411 6321 Insurance agents, brokers & service; accident & health insurance
PA: Fhc Health Systems, Inc
240 Corporate Blvd # 100
Norfolk VA 23502
757 459-5100

(P-10822)
VAN BEURDEN INSURANCE SVCS INC (PA)
Also Called: Kemper Insurance
1600 Draper St, Kingsburg (93631-1911)
P.O. Box 67 (93631-0067)
PHONE..............................559 634-7125
William J Van Beurden, *President*
Robin Hankins, *CFO*
Mike Beall, *Vice Pres*
Chris V Beurden, *Vice Pres*
Mark Karlie, *Vice Pres*
EMP: 67 **EST:** 1934

SQ FT: 20,000
SALES (est): 29.6MM **Privately Held**
WEB: www.vanbeurden.com
SIC: 6411 Insurance agents & brokers

(P-10823)
VEBA ADMINISTRATORS INC
Also Called: Benefit Planning
4640 Admiralty Way Fl 9, Marina Del Rey (90292-6630)
PHONE..............................310 577-1444
Guy Hocker, *President*
Richard Caplan, *Vice Pres*
Anthony Delfino, *Vice Pres*
EMP: 50
SALES (est): 7.3MM **Privately Held**
WEB: www.benplaninc.com
SIC: 6411 6141 Pension & retirement plan consultants; financing: automobiles, furniture, etc., not a deposit bank

(P-10824)
VELAPOINT LLC
16802 Aston, Irvine (92606-4835)
PHONE..............................877 434-1904
Kyal Moody, *Branch Mgr*
EMP: 77
SALES (corp-wide): 11.7MM **Privately Held**
SIC: 6411 Insurance agents, brokers & service
PA: Velapoint Llc
1100 Nw Compton Dr # 200
Beaverton OR 97006
503 608-3947

(P-10825)
W BROWN & ASSC PROPERTY & CSU
19000 Macarthur Blvd, Irvine (92612-1438)
PHONE..............................949 851-2060
Scott Brown, *President*
EMP: 60
SALES (est): 34.2MM **Privately Held**
SIC: 6411 Insurance agents

(P-10826)
WARNER PACIFIC INSUR SVCS INC (PA)
32110 Agoura Rd, Westlake Village (91361-4026)
PHONE..............................408 298-4049
John H Nelson, *CEO*
Kim Novak, *Bd of Directors*
David Nelson, *Vice Pres*
Dann Daggett, *Technology*
Jennifer Morrison, *Sales Executive*
EMP: 127
SQ FT: 10,000
SALES (est): 132.3MM **Privately Held**
SIC: 6411 Insurance brokers

(P-10827)
WESCOM HOLDINGS LLC (HQ)
123 S Marengo Ave, Pasadena (91101-2428)
PHONE..............................888 493-7266
Darren Williams, *CEO*
Kevin Vogt, *Officer*
Jorge Hernandez, *Loan*
Mark Semkin, *Manager*
EMP: 82
SALES (est): 3.2MM
SALES (corp-wide): 116.1MM **Privately Held**
SIC: 6411 6211 7371 Insurance agents, brokers & service; investment firm, general brokerage; computer software development & applications
PA: Wescom Central Credit Union
123 S Marengo Ave
Pasadena CA 91101
888 493-7266

(P-10828)
WESTERN GENERAL AGENCY INC
12200 Sylvan St Ste 140, North Hollywood (91606-3240)
P.O. Box 7001 (91615-0001)
PHONE..............................818 766-6500
Weldon Wilson, *President*
EMP: 55
SQ FT: 41,000

SALES (est): 5.2MM
SALES (corp-wide): 257.2MM **Privately Held**
WEB: www.cnico.com
SIC: 6411 Insurance agents
PA: Kramer-Wilson Company, Inc.
6345 Balboa Blvd Ste 190
Encino CA 91316
818 760-0880

(P-10829)
WESTERN UNITED INSURANCE CO
Also Called: Csaa Insur Group Walnut Creek
3349 Michelson Dr Ste 100, Irvine (92612-0688)
P.O. Box 24523, Oakland (94623-1523)
PHONE..............................800 959-9842
James B Schallert, *President*
EMP: 165
SQ FT: 50,000
SALES (est): 27.2MM
SALES (corp-wide): 907.9MM **Privately Held**
WEB: www.californiastateautomobileassociation.c
SIC: 6411 Insurance agents
PA: American Automobile Association Of Northern California, Nevada & Utah
1900 Powell St Ste 1200
Emeryville CA 94608
800 922-8228

(P-10830)
WESTWOOD INSURANCE AGENCY (DH)
8407 Fllbrook Ave Ste 200, Canoga Park (91304)
PHONE..............................818 990-9715
John Flynn, *President*
Mark Nettleton, *Vice Pres*
Karen Sherman, *Executive Asst*
Scott Davidson, *Analyst*
Vikki Siemons, *Cust Mgr*
EMP: 89
SQ FT: 17,765
SALES (est): 19.5MM **Publicly Held**
WEB: www.westwoodinsurance.com
SIC: 6411 Insurance agents
HQ: National General Lender Services, Inc.
210 Interstate N Pkwy
Atlanta GA 30339
770 690-8400

(P-10831)
WILSHIRE INSURANCE COMPANY
Also Called: Accidental Fire & Casualty
1206 W Avenue J Ste 100, Lancaster (93534-2953)
P.O. Box 7006 (93539-7006)
PHONE..............................661 940-7300
Stephen Stephano, *President*
Debbie Wrinkle, *Vice Pres*
Deborah Wrinkle, *Executive*
EMP: 50
SALES (est): 8MM **Privately Held**
SIC: 6411 Insurance agents

(P-10832)
WINTERTHUR U S HOLDINGS INC
888 S Figueroa St Ste 570, Los Angeles (90017-5449)
PHONE..............................213 228-0281
Ken McClelland, *Branch Mgr*
EMP: 240 **Privately Held**
SIC: 6411 6311 6331 Property & casualty insurance agent; life insurance; fire, marine & casualty insurance
HQ: Winterthur U. S. Holdings Inc
1 General Dr
Sun Prairie WI 53596
608 837-4440

(P-10833)
WINTON IRELAND STROM & GREEN (PA)
Also Called: Winton-Ireland, Strom and Gr
627 E Canal Dr, Turlock (95380-4022)
PHONE..............................209 667-0995
Michael Ireland, *President*
Ted Green, *Vice Pres*
Jeff Quinn, *Vice Pres*
Erin Harlan,

EMP: 88
SQ FT: 10,000
SALES (est): 18.7MM **Privately Held**
WEB: www.wintonireland.com
SIC: 6411 Insurance brokers

(P-10834)
WM MICHAEL STEMLER INC (PA)
Also Called: Delta Health Systems
3244 Brookside Rd Ste 200, Stockton (95219-2384)
P.O. Box 1227 (95201-1227)
PHONE..............................209 948-8483
William M Stemler, *CEO*
Richard Roge, *President*
Patti Silva, *Exec VP*
EMP: 110
SQ FT: 30,100
SALES: 24.8MM **Privately Held**
WEB: www.deltahealthsystems.com
SIC: 6411 Medical insurance claim processing, contract or fee basis

(P-10835)
WM MICHAEL STEMLER INC
7110 N Fresno St Ste 350, Fresno (93720-2933)
PHONE..............................559 228-4144
Robert Maes, *Branch Mgr*
EMP: 150
SALES (corp-wide): 24.8MM **Privately Held**
SIC: 6411 Medical insurance claim processing, contract or fee basis
PA: Wm. Michael Stemler, Incorporated
3244 Brookside Rd Ste 200
Stockton CA 95219
209 948-8483

(P-10836)
WOOD GUTMANN BOGART INSUR BRKG
Also Called: W G B
15901 Red Hill Ave # 100, Tustin (92780-7318)
PHONE..............................714 505-7000
Kevin S Bogart, *CEO*
Jason Cassidy, *Assoc VP*
Bill Holdren, *Exec VP*
Eric Schroeder, *Exec VP*
Angela Mullin, *Vice Pres*
EMP: 93
SALES (est): 30.5MM **Privately Held**
WEB: www.wgbib.com
SIC: 6411 Insurance agents

(P-10837)
WOODRUFF-SAWYER & CO (PA)
50 California St Fl 12, San Francisco (94111-4624)
PHONE..............................415 391-2141
Charles Rosson, *CEO*
Kristine Furrer, *Senior VP*
Stephen Gaitley, *Senior VP*
Charles Shoemaker, *Senior VP*
Melody Silberstein, *Senior VP*
EMP: 240
SQ FT: 54,000
SALES (est): 192.8MM **Privately Held**
SIC: 6411 Insurance brokers

(P-10838)
WORLDWIDE HOLDINGS INC (PA)
725 S Figueroa St # 1900, Los Angeles (90017-5496)
PHONE..............................213 236-4500
Donald R Davis, *Chairman*
Davis D Moore, *President*
Daniel Colacurcio, *Exec VP*
EMP: 85
SQ FT: 23,000
SALES (est): 75.2MM **Privately Held**
WEB: www.wwfi.com
SIC: 6411 Insurance agents, brokers & service

(P-10839)
WORXSITEHR INSUR SOLUTIONS INC
5000 Parkway Calabasas # 302, Calabasas (91302-1400)
PHONE..............................877 479-3591
EMP: 60

SQ FT: 2,500
SALES (est): 4.7MM Privately Held
SIC: 6411 7371

(P-10840)
YOURPEOPLE INC
Also Called: Zenefits Ftw Insurance Svcs
250 Brannan St 3, San Francisco
(94107-2007)
PHONE..................................415 798-9086
Parker Conrad, CEO
Avinash Anand, President
Rita Garg, President
David Sacks, CEO
Laks Srini, Officer
EMP: 700 EST: 2010
SALES: 158.4MM Privately Held
SIC: 6411 7372 Insurance brokers; business oriented computer software

(P-10841)
ZURICH AMERICAN INSURANCE CO
777 S Figueroa St Ste 400, Los Angeles
(90017-5802)
PHONE..................................213 270-0600
Yohei Miyamoto, Vice Pres
Victoria Ang, Legal Staff
EMP: 53
SALES (corp-wide): 65.1B Privately Held
SIC: 6411 Insurance agents, brokers & service
HQ: Zurich American Insurance Company
1299 Zurich Way
Schaumburg IL 60196
800 987-3373

(P-10842)
ZURICH AMERICAN INSURANCE CO
525 Market St Ste 2900, San Francisco
(94105-2737)
PHONE..................................415 538-7100
Bill Dougherty, Marketing Staff
Saul Partida, Facilities Mgr
Leah Kimball, Manager
EMP: 200
SALES (corp-wide): 65.1B Privately Held
WEB: www.zurichna.com
SIC: 6411 Insurance agents
HQ: Zurich American Insurance Company
1299 Zurich Way
Schaumburg IL 60196
800 987-3373

6512 Operators Of Nonresidential Bldgs

(P-10843)
14545 FRIAR LLC
14545 Friar St Ste 105, Van Nuys
(91411-2357)
PHONE..................................818 817-0082
Kambiz Merabi,
EMP: 52 EST: 2007
SQ FT: 3,000
SALES: 4.6MM Privately Held
SIC: 6512 6531 Nonresidential building operators; real estate agent, commercial

(P-10844)
5 DIAMOND PROTECTION INC
2901 W Macarthur Blvd, Santa Ana
(92704-6910)
PHONE..................................949 466-1367
Mohammad Sayed, President
Troy Sims, Director
EMP: 99
SALES: 200K Privately Held
SIC: 6512 Nonresidential building operators

(P-10845)
6500 HLLISTER AVE PARTNERS LLC
6500 Hollister Ave, Goleta (93117-3011)
PHONE..................................805 722-1362
Rob Ramirez, Manager
EMP: 100
SALES (est): 2MM Privately Held
SIC: 6512 Commercial & industrial building operation

(P-10846)
AAT TORREY RESERVE 6 LLC
11455 El Cmino Real Ste 2, San Diego
(92130)
PHONE..................................858 350-2600
John Chamberlain, Principal
EMP: 60
SALES (est): 1.3MM
SALES (corp-wide): 28.9MM Privately Held
SIC: 6512 Nonresidential building operators
PA: American Assets, Inc.
11455 El Cmno Rl Ste 140
San Diego CA 92130
858 350-2600

(P-10847)
ABBEY-PROPERTIES LLC (PA)
12447 Lewis St Ste 203, Garden Grove
(92840-6601)
PHONE..................................562 435-2100
Donald G Abbey,
EMP: 75
SQ FT: 276,000
SALES (est): 5.1MM Privately Held
WEB: www.theabbeyco.com
SIC: 6512 Commercial & industrial building operation

(P-10848)
ALEXANDER PROPERTIES COMPANY
2600 Camino Ramon Ste 201, San Ramon
(94583-5000)
P.O. Box 640 (94583-0640)
PHONE..................................925 866-0100
John T Waterhouse, CEO
Alexander Mehran, Principal
EMP: 50
SALES (est): 2.7MM Privately Held
SIC: 6512 Commercial & industrial building operation

(P-10849)
ALISAM OXNARD OPERATING
Also Called: Water Drops Express Carwash
212 26th St Ste 246, Santa Monica
(90402-2524)
PHONE..................................310 877-7179
Bob Bandabi, Mng Member
Sam Siam, Mng Member
EMP: 116
SALES: 32MM Privately Held
SIC: 6512 Nonresidential building operators

(P-10850)
ALLIED SWISS LIMITED
Also Called: Allied Swift
2636 Vista Pacific Dr, Oceanside
(92056-3514)
PHONE..................................760 941-1702
Wade Prescott, Partner
Bruce Damon, Ltd Ptnr
Robert Hively, Ltd Ptnr
Bonnie Prescott, Ltd Ptnr
Chip Prescott, Ltd Ptnr
EMP: 112
SQ FT: 21,000
SALES (est): 6.6MM Privately Held
WEB: www.alliedswiss.net
SIC: 6512 Commercial & industrial building operation

(P-10851)
ALPINE VILLAGE
Also Called: Alpine Inn Restaurant
833 Torrance Blvd Ste 1a, Torrance
(90502-1733)
PHONE..................................310 327-4384
Ursula Wilson, CEO
Brad Goodman, Controller
EMP: 250
SALES (est): 15.5MM Privately Held
WEB: www.alpinevillage.net
SIC: 6512 Commercial & industrial building operation

(P-10852)
AMERICARE HLTH RETIREMENT INC
Also Called: Silvergate San Marcos
1550 Security Pl Ofc, San Marcos
(92078-4063)
PHONE..................................760 744-4484
Melba Dunn, Administration
Dennis Prejusa, Director
EMP: 100
SQ FT: 51,071
SALES (corp-wide): 11.8MM Privately Held
WEB: www.americarehr.com
SIC: 6512 8051 Nonresidential building operators; skilled nursing care facilities
PA: Americare Health & Retirement, Inc.
140 Lomas Santa Fe Dr # 103
Solana Beach CA 92075
858 792-0696

(P-10853)
ANTELOPE VALLEY MALL
1233 W Rancho Vista Blvd # 405, Palmdale
(93551-3949)
PHONE..................................661 266-9150
Greg Lenners, General Mgr
George D Zamias Developer, Partner
EMP: 70
SALES (est): 3.6MM Privately Held
WEB: www.av-mall.com
SIC: 6512 Shopping center, property operation only

(P-10854)
APPLIED COMPANIES RE LLC
28020 Avenue Stanford, Valencia
(91355-1105)
P.O. Box 802078, Santa Clarita (91380-2078)
PHONE..................................661 257-0090
Mary Elizabeth Klinger, CEO
Joseph Klinger, Vice Pres
EMP: 50 EST: 1998
SALES (est): 158.4K Privately Held
SIC: 6512 Nonresidential building operators

(P-10855)
ARE- MARYLAND NO 31 LLC
385 E Colo Blvd Ste 299, Pasadena
(91101)
PHONE..................................626 578-0777
Lawrence Diamond, Exec VP
Scott Loftin, Exec Dir
Sam Barton, Info Tech Dir
Callie Supsinskas, Mktg Coord
EMP: 50
SALES (est): 574.7K Privately Held
SIC: 6512 Nonresidential building operators

(P-10856)
BAY WEST SHWPLACE INVSTORS LLC (PA)
Also Called: Sheplace Design Center
2 Henry Adams St Ste 450, San Francisco
(94103-5000)
PHONE..................................415 490-5800
Bill Poland, Manager
Tim Threadway, Chairman
EMP: 60 EST: 1983
SALES (est): 5MM Privately Held
SIC: 6512 5712 Commercial & industrial building operation; furniture stores

(P-10857)
BPR PROPERTIES BERKELEY LLC
953 Industrial Ave # 100, Palo Alto
(94303-4923)
PHONE..................................650 424-1400
Bhupendra B Patel,
Fred Destefano, Vice Pres
Sue Hefty, Vice Pres
Lacey Goldstein, General Mgr
Evelyn Curiel, Office Mgr
EMP: 130
SALES (est): 12.2MM Privately Held
SIC: 6512 Nonresidential building operators

(P-10858)
BRIDGE HOUSING ACQUISITION
1 Hawthorne St Ste 400, San Francisco
(94105-3909)
PHONE..................................415 989-1111
Carol Gilante, President
Lydia Tan, Vice Pres
EMP: 80
SALES: 78.1K Privately Held
SIC: 6512 Nonresidential building operators

(P-10859)
BUILDING SERVICES/SYSTEM INC
2575 Stanwell Dr, Concord (94520-4888)
PHONE..................................925 688-1234
Sam Martinovich, Principal
Sam Mardinovich, Principal
EMP: 99
SALES (est): 5.5MM Privately Held
SIC: 6512 Commercial & industrial building operation

(P-10860)
CASDEN BUILDERS LLC
9090 Wilshire Blvd Fl 3, Beverly Hills
(90211-1851)
PHONE..................................310 274-5553
Robert Hilderbrand,
Marilley Joe, Project Mgr
Mike Murray, Superintendent
EMP: 50
SALES (est): 1.6MM Privately Held
SIC: 6512 Nonresidential building operators

(P-10861)
CB RICHARD ELLIS STRTGC PRTNRS
515 S Flower St, Los Angeles
(90071-2201)
PHONE..................................213 683-4200
Richard Ellis,
EMP: 100
SALES (est): 3.6MM
SALES (corp-wide): 14.2B Publicly Held
WEB: www.cbrichardellis.com
SIC: 6512 Nonresidential building operators
PA: Cbre Group, Inc.
400 S Hope St Ste 25
Los Angeles CA 90071
213 613-3333

(P-10862)
CENTURY NATIONAL PROPERTIES (PA)
Also Called: Daytona Surfise
12200 Sylvan St Ste 250, North Hollywood
(91606-3229)
PHONE..................................818 760-0880
Weldon Wilson, President
Judith Osborne, Treasurer
Marie Balicki, Admin Sec
EMP: 61
SQ FT: 92,000
SALES (est): 2.9MM Privately Held
SIC: 6512 7011 Commercial & industrial building operation; motels

(P-10863)
CESAR CHAVEZ STUDENT CENTER
Also Called: Snackademic
1650 Holloway Ave Rm C134, San Francisco (94132-1722)
PHONE..................................415 338-7362
Guy Dalpe, Exec Dir
EMP: 130
SALES (est): 5MM Privately Held
SIC: 6512 Nonresidential building operators

(P-10864)
CITY OF ANAHEIM
Also Called: Anaheim Arena
2695 E Katella Ave, Anaheim (92806-5904)
PHONE..................................714 704-2400
Tim Ryan, Manager
EMP: 450 Privately Held
WEB: www.anaheim.net
SIC: 6512 7941 Nonresidential building operators; sports field or stadium operator, promoting sports events

---

PA: City Of Anaheim
200 S Anaheim Blvd
Anaheim CA 92805
714 765-5162

(P-10865)
CITY OF FAIRFIELD
Also Called: Fairfield Community Center
1000 Webster St, Fairfield (94533-4883)
PHONE..................707 428-7435
Karin McMillan, *Mayor*
EMP: 150 **Privately Held**
WEB: www.fairfieldpoa.com
SIC: 6512 Auditorium & hall operation
PA: City Of Fairfield
1000 Webster St
Fairfield CA 94533
707 428-7569

(P-10866)
DAVID D BOHANNON
ORGANIZATION (PA)
Also Called: San Lorenzo Village Shopg Ctr
60 31st Ave, San Mateo (94403-3404)
PHONE..................650 345-8222
David D Bohannon II, *President*
Scott Bohannon, *Senior VP*
Ernest Lotti Jr, *Vice Pres*
Frances E Nelson, *Director*
EMP: 61
SQ FT: 5,000
SALES (est): 7MM **Privately Held**
SIC: 6512 6552 Commercial & industrial
building operation; subdividers & developers

(P-10867)
DESERT HOT SPRINGS REAL
PROPER
Also Called: Desert Hot Springs Spa Hotel
10805 Palm Dr, Desert Hot Springs
(92240-2511)
PHONE..................760 329-6000
Lynn Byrnes, *CEO*
EMP: 85 **EST:** 1988
SQ FT: 44,070
SALES (est): 903.6K **Privately Held**
SIC: 6512 Nonresidential building operators

(P-10868)
DESERT SPRINGS HOTEL
10805 Palm Dr, Desert Hot Springs
(92240-2511)
PHONE..................760 251-3399
Lynn Byrnes, *President*
EMP: 50
SALES (est): 1.6MM **Privately Held**
SIC: 6512 Nonresidential building operators

(P-10869)
DONAHUE SCHRIBER RLTY
GROUP LP (PA)
200 Baker St Ste 100, Costa Mesa
(92626-4551)
PHONE..................714 545-1400
Patrick S Donahue, *CEO*
Lawrence P Casey, *President*
Lisa L Hirose, *Exec VP*
Mark L Whitfield, *Exec VP*
Warren Adair, *Vice Pres*
EMP: 100
SQ FT: 44,805
SALES (est): 26.2MM **Privately Held**
WEB: www.donahueschriber.com
SIC: 6512 Shopping center, property operation only

(P-10870)
DONAHUE SCHRIBER RLTY
GROUP LP
5082 N Palm Ave, Fresno (93704-2231)
PHONE..................714 545-1400
Elizabeth Schreiber, *Manager*
Kathy Stepp, *Admin Sec*
Taran Stokes, *Property Mgr*
Justin Labhart, *Manager*
EMP: 57
SALES (corp-wide): 26.2MM **Privately**
Held
SIC: 6512 Shopping center, property operation only

PA: Donahue Schriber Realty Group, L.P.
200 Baker St Ste 100
Costa Mesa CA 92626
714 545-1400

(P-10871)
DONAHUE SCHRIBER RLTY
GROUP LP
8020 E Santa Ana Cyn Rd, Anaheim
(92808-1110)
PHONE..................714 283-3535
Patrick S Donahue, *Branch Mgr*
EMP: 57
SALES (corp-wide): 26.2MM **Privately**
Held
SIC: 6512 Shopping center, property operation only
PA: Donahue Schriber Realty Group, L.P.
200 Baker St Ste 100
Costa Mesa CA 92626
714 545-1400

(P-10872)
DONAHUE SCHRIBER RLTY
GROUP LP
12925 El Camino Real J22, San Diego
(92130-1891)
PHONE..................858 793-5757
Pat Snow, *Branch Mgr*
EMP: 57
SALES (corp-wide): 26.2MM **Privately**
Held
WEB: www.donahueschriber.com
SIC: 6512 Shopping center, property operation only
PA: Donahue Schriber Realty Group, L.P.
200 Baker St Ste 100
Costa Mesa CA 92626
714 545-1400

(P-10873)
ENTREPRENEURIAL CAPITAL
CORP
4100 Nwport Pl Dr Ste 400, Newport Beach
(92660)
PHONE..................949 809-3900
John K Abel, *Principal*
EMP: 240
SALES (corp-wide): 33.2MM **Privately**
Held
SIC: 6512 Commercial & industrial building
operation
PA: Entrepreneurial Capital Corporation
4100 Newport Place Dr # 400
Newport Beach CA 92660
949 809-3900

(P-10874)
ESKATON (PA)
5105 Manzanita Ave Ste D, Carmichael
(95608-0523)
PHONE..................916 334-0296
Todd Murch, *CEO*
Trevor Hammond, *COO*
William Pace, *CFO*
Sheri Peifer, *Officer*
Karen Powell, *Social Dir*
EMP: 1400
SQ FT: 27,000
SALES (est): 4.3MM **Privately Held**
SIC: 6512 8051 Commercial & industrial
building operation; convalescent home
with continuous nursing care

(P-10875)
ETHAN CONRAD PROPERTIES
INC
1300 National Dr Ste 100, Sacramento
(95834-1981)
PHONE..................916 779-1000
Ethan Conrad, *President*
Ken Miller, *CFO*
Kenneth Miller, *CFO*
Chase Burke, *Vice Pres*
Grant Keeney, *Vice Pres*
EMP: 100
SQ FT: 45,063
SALES: 45MM **Privately Held**
WEB: www.ethanconradprop.com
SIC: 6512 Commercial & industrial building
operation

(P-10876)
FLORDO OAKLEY HALL
Also Called: Flor Do Oakley Club
520 2nd St, Oakley (94561-2158)
P.O. Box 466 (94561-0466)
PHONE..................925 625-4076
Joe Peisoto, *President*
Sam Billeci, *Treasurer*
Emidio Fonseca, *Treasurer*
David Alves, *Trustee*
Jose Peisoto, *Director*
EMP: 170
SQ FT: 5,000
SALES: 208.5K **Privately Held**
SIC: 6512 Auditorium & hall operation

(P-10877)
FOREST CITY RENTAL PRPTS
CORP
Oasis Fd Crt Antelope Vly Mall
1233 W Avenue P Ste 900, Palmdale
(93551-3950)
PHONE..................661 266-9150
Brian Gardner, *Manager*
EMP: 80
SALES (corp-wide): 911.9MM **Privately**
Held
SIC: 6512 Shopping center, property operation only; commercial & industrial building operation
HQ: Forest City Properties, Llc
127 Public Sq Ste 3100
Cleveland OH 44114
216 621-6060

(P-10878)
FRATERNAL ORDER EAGLES
1582
Also Called: EAGLES HALL
124 Vernon St, Roseville (95678-2631)
P.O. Box 766 (95678-0766)
PHONE..................916 782-2694
Charles Chase, *Admin Sec*
EMP: 120
SALES: 22.9K **Privately Held**
SIC: 6512 8641 Nonresidential building
operators; civic social & fraternal associations

(P-10879)
FRED H LUNDBLADE JR
Also Called: Lundblade Builders
939 Koster St Ste B, Eureka (95501-0106)
PHONE..................707 442-8049
Fred H Lundblade, *Owner*
EMP: 58
SALES (est): 2.5MM **Privately Held**
SIC: 6512 6513 1521 1541 Nonresidential building operators; apartment building
operators; single-family housing construction; industrial buildings & warehouses

(P-10880)
FREMONT PROPERTIES INC
199 Fremont St Ste 1900, San Francisco
(94105-2245)
PHONE..................415 284-8500
Allen Dachs, *CEO*
David Wall, *Exec VP*
Christopher Quiett, *Vice Pres*
Gry Faber, *Principal*
Suzanne Gagan, *Principal*
EMP: 50
SALES (est): 3.5MM
SALES (corp-wide): 18MM **Privately**
Held
SIC: 6512 Nonresidential building operators
PA: Fremont Investors, Inc.
199 Fremont St Fl 19
San Francisco CA 94105
415 284-8500

(P-10881)
G B & P CITRUS CO INC (PA)
1601 E Olympic Blvd # 111, Los Angeles
(90021-1936)
PHONE..................213 312-1380
Sam Perricone, *President*
Henry Beyer, *Vice Pres*
Paul Golub, *Admin Sec*
EMP: 98 **EST:** 1970

SALES (est): 5.3MM **Privately Held**
SIC: 6512 5148 2037 Commercial & industrial building operation; fruits; fruit
juices

(P-10882)
GEHR DEVELOPMENT
CORPORATION (HQ)
7400 E Slauson Ave, Commerce
(90040-3308)
PHONE..................323 728-5558
David Lifschitz, *CFO*
Alfred Somekh, *President*
EMP: 70
SALES (est): 5.1MM
SALES (corp-wide): 92.6MM **Privately**
Held
WEB: www.gehr.com
SIC: 6512 6513 Nonresidential building
operators; apartment building operators
PA: The Gehr Group Inc
7400 E Slauson Ave
Commerce CA 90040
323 728-5558

(P-10883)
GIRARDI AND KEEFE
1126 Wilshire Blvd, Los Angeles
(90017-1904)
PHONE..................213 489-5330
Thomas Girardi, *Partner*
Bob Keefe, *Partner*
John A Girardi,
EMP: 100
SQ FT: 21,000
SALES (est): 3.3MM **Privately Held**
SIC: 6512 Commercial & industrial building
operation

(P-10884)
GLENDALE ASSOCIATES LTD
Also Called: Apple Store Glendale Galleria
100 W Broadway Ste 100 # 100, Glendale
(91210-1230)
PHONE..................818 246-6737
Properties Knickerbocker, *Principal*
Knickerbocker Properties, *Partner*
EMP: 100
SALES (est): 6.1MM **Privately Held**
SIC: 6512 Shopping center, property operation only

(P-10885)
GONGS MARKET OF SANGER
INC (PA)
Also Called: Gong's Ventures
1825 Academy Ave, Sanger (93657-3798)
PHONE..................559 875-5576
William Gong, *President*
Bessie Gong Ohashi, *Corp Secy*
Thomas Gong, *Vice Pres*
EMP: 50
SQ FT: 35,000
SALES (est): 4.7MM **Privately Held**
SIC: 6512 Property operation, retail establishment

(P-10886)
GREENTREE PROPERTY MGT
INC
600 California St Fl 19, San Francisco
(94108-2710)
PHONE..................415 347-8600
Yat Pang Au, *President*
Leanne Leflet, *Admin Asst*
Jamie Millard, *Administration*
Eric Lakin, *Sr Project Mgr*
Marissa Rodriguez, *Case Mgr*
EMP: 50
SALES (est): 3.5MM **Privately Held**
SIC: 6512 Property operation, retail establishment

(P-10887)
GROSSMONT SHOPPING
CENTER CO
Also Called: Grossmont Center Management
5500 Grsmnt Ctr Dr # 213, La Mesa
(91942-3016)
PHONE..................619 465-2900
Thomas J Magee, *President*
EMP: 57 **EST:** 1960
SQ FT: 3,000

▲ = Import ▼=Export
◆ =Import/Export

SALES (est): 5.4MM **Privately Held**
SIC: **6512** Shopping center, property operation only

(P-10888)
GUMBINER SAVETT INC CPA
Also Called: Gumbiner, Savett, Finkel, Fing
1723 Cloverfield Blvd, Santa Monica
(90404-4017)
PHONE..................................310 828-9798
Louis Savett, *Ch of Bd*
Charles Gumbiner, *President*
Gary Finkel, *Exec VP*
Rodney Fingleson, *Vice Pres*
David Rose, *Vice Pres*
EMP: 90
SQ FT: 25,000
SALES (est): 11MM **Privately Held**
WEB: www.gscpa.com
SIC: **6512** Nonresidential building operators

(P-10889)
H D S I MANAGMENT
3460 S Broadway, Los Angeles
(90007-4409)
PHONE..................................323 231-1104
Noel Sweitzer, *Partner*
EMP: 50
SALES (est): 1.9MM **Privately Held**
SIC: **6512** Nonresidential building operators

(P-10890)
HAILWOOD INC
Also Called: Chase Bros Dairy
5755 Valentine Rd Ste 203, Ventura
(93003-7460)
PHONE..................................805 487-4981
Glywn S Chase Jr, *President*
Miriam Wille, *Corp Secy*
H M Chase, *Vice Pres*
EMP: 75
SQ FT: 1,600,000
SALES (est): 4.2MM **Privately Held**
SIC: **6512** 5143 5451 2024 Commercial & industrial building operation; dairy products, except dried or canned; dairy products stores; ice cream & frozen desserts

(P-10891)
HALSTEAD PARTNERSHIP
Also Called: Sundt Construction
2850 Gateway Oaks Dr # 450, Sacramento
(95833-4347)
PHONE..................................916 830-8000
John Wald, *Managing Prtnr*
Jerrie Waltz, *Administration*
EMP: 60
SALES (est): 7.3MM **Privately Held**
SIC: **6512** Nonresidential building operators

(P-10892)
HARDAGE INVESTMENTS INC
Also Called: Woodfin Suites
39150 Cedar Blvd, Newark (94560-5024)
PHONE..................................510 795-1200
Bill Marzonie, *Branch Mgr*
EMP: 50
SQ FT: 100,978 **Privately Held**
SIC: **6512** Nonresidential building operators
PA: Hardage Investments, Inc.
12671 High Bluff Dr # 300
San Diego CA

(P-10893)
HATHAWAY DINWIDDIE CNSTR GROUP
565 Laurelwood Rd, Santa Clara
(95054-2419)
PHONE..................................408 988-4200
Greg Cosko, *President*
EMP: 100 **Privately Held**
SIC: **6512** Commercial & industrial building operation
PA: Hathaway Dinwiddie Construction Group
275 Battery St Ste 300
San Francisco CA 94111

(P-10894)
HEALTH CARE WORKERS UNION (PA)
Also Called: Local 250 Health Care Wkrs Un
560 Thomas L Berkley Way, Oakland
(94612-1602)
PHONE..................................510 251-1250
Sal Rosselli, *President*
Sarah Steck, *Opers Mgr*
EMP: 200
SQ FT: 25,777
SALES (est): 8.3MM **Privately Held**
SIC: **6512** 8631 Commercial & industrial building operation; labor unions & similar labor organizations

(P-10895)
HFRM II INC (PA)
2051 Hilltop Dr Ste A18, Redding
(96002-0234)
PHONE..................................530 242-2010
Herbert F R Meyer Jr, *CEO*
Herbert F R Meyer III, *Shareholder*
Isaac Scott Meyer, *Shareholder*
Dara O'Farrell, *CFO*
Jan Pratt, *Admin Sec*
EMP: 260
SALES (est): 6.7MM **Privately Held**
WEB: www.meyercrest.com
SIC: **6512** Nonresidential building operators

(P-10896)
HUDSON TCHMART CMMERCE CTR LLC
5201 Great America Pkwy, Santa Clara
(95054-1122)
PHONE..................................408 451-4440
Mark Lammas, *COO*
Wendy Contreras, *Exec Sec*
EMP: 99 EST: 2015
SQ FT: 284,440
SALES (est): 1.2MM **Publicly Held**
SIC: **6512** Commercial & industrial building operation
PA: Hudson Pacific Properties, Inc.
11601 Wilshire Blvd Fl 6
Los Angeles CA 90025
-

(P-10897)
HYDROX PROPERTIES XII LLC
3170 Hilltop Mall Rd, Richmond
(94806-1921)
PHONE..................................510 262-7200
Mechanics Bank, *Principal*
EMP: 69
SALES (est): 3.3MM **Privately Held**
SIC: **6512** Nonresidential building operators

(P-10898)
ICW VALENCIA LLC
11455 El Camino Real, San Diego
(92130-2088)
PHONE..................................858 350-2600
John Chamberlain, *Principal*
EMP: 65
SALES (est): 1.4MM
SALES (corp-wide): 28.9MM **Privately Held**
SIC: **6512** Nonresidential building operators
PA: American Assets, Inc.
11455 El Cmno Rl Ste 140
San Diego CA 92130
858 350-2600

(P-10899)
INSIGNIA/ESG HT PARTNERS INC (DH)
11150 Santa Monica Blvd # 220, Los Angeles (90025-3380)
PHONE..................................310 765-2600
Mary Ann Tighe, *CEO*
John Powers, *President*
EMP: 325
SALES (est): 80.1MM
SALES (corp-wide): 14.2B **Publicly Held**
WEB: www.insigniaesg.com
SIC: **6512** Property operation, retail establishment

HQ: Cb Richard Ellis Real Estate Services, Llc
200 Park Ave Fl 19
New York NY 10166
212 984-8000

(P-10900)
INTEX RECREATION CORP
1665 Hughes Way, Long Beach
(90810-1835)
PHONE..................................310 549-5400
Kwai Kenny, *Exec Dir*
Phil Mimaki, *Creative Dir*
Carlos Bartra, *Engineer*
Norm Gold, *Controller*
Patrick Chik, *Opers Mgr*
EMP: 102
SALES (corp-wide): 171.8MM **Privately Held**
SIC: **6512** Nonresidential building operators
PA: Intex Recreation Corp
4001 Via Oro Ave Ste 210
Long Beach CA 90810
310 549-5400

(P-10901)
INVITATION HOMES
465 N Halstead St Ste 150, Pasadena
(91107-6017)
PHONE..................................805 372-2900
Luke Kochniuk, *President*
EMP: 80 EST: 2013
SALES (est): 4.3MM **Privately Held**
SIC: **6512** Nonresidential building operators

(P-10902)
JAMESON PROPERTIES CO INC
3530 Wilshire Blvd # 600, Los Angeles
(90010-2328)
PHONE..................................213 487-3770
Eric Kim, *General Mgr*
David Lee, *President*
Scott Burrin, *Managing Dir*
Victor Catalan, *Chief Engr*
EMP: 50
SQ FT: 4,000
SALES: 159.1K **Privately Held**
WEB: www.jamisonservices.com
SIC: **6512** Commercial & industrial building operation

(P-10903)
JOHNSON SERVICE GROUP INC
950 S Bascom Ave, San Jose
(95128-3536)
PHONE..................................408 728-9510
EMP: 850
SALES (corp-wide): 136.1MM **Privately Held**
SIC: **6512** Commercial & industrial building operation
PA: Johnson Service Group, Inc.
1 E Oakhill Dr Ste 200
Westmont IL 60559
630 655-3500

(P-10904)
LAGUNA COUNTRY MART LTD INC
Also Called: Lumberyard Plaza Mall
12410 Santa Monica Blvd, Los Angeles
(90025-2522)
PHONE..................................310 826-5635
Michael Koss, *President*
EMP: 50
SALES (est): 2.6MM **Privately Held**
SIC: **6512** Shopping center, property operation only

(P-10905)
LANSING MALL LTD PARTNERSHIP
Also Called: Southland Mall
1 Southland Mall, Hayward (94545-2125)
PHONE..................................510 782-3527
Veronica Curley, *General Mgr*
EMP: 50
SALES (corp-wide): 19.9MM **Privately Held**
WEB: www.mallofla.com
SIC: **6512** Shopping center, property operation only

HQ: Lansing Mall Limited Partnership
5330 W Saginaw Hwy
Lansing MI 48917
517 321-0145

(P-10906)
LANSING MALL LTD PARTNERSHIP
Also Called: Northridge Fashion Center
9301 Tampa Ave Ofc, Northridge
(91324-5627)
PHONE..................................818 885-9700
Daniele Gordon, *General Mgr*
EMP: 75
SALES (corp-wide): 19.9MM **Privately Held**
WEB: www.mallofla.com
SIC: **6512** Shopping center, property operation only
HQ: Lansing Mall Limited Partnership
5330 W Saginaw Hwy
Lansing MI 48917
517 321-0145

(P-10907)
LOS ANGELES CONVEN AND EXH
Also Called: Los Angeles Dept Convetion Tou
1201 S Figueroa St, Los Angeles
(90015-1308)
PHONE..................................213 741-1151
Brad Gessner, *General Mgr*
Annie Bebber, *Manager*
Abraham Reyes, *Manager*
EMP: 288
SQ FT: 867,000
SALES: 21.5MM **Privately Held**
WEB: www.laconventioninn.com
SIC: **6512** Commercial & industrial building operation; property operation, auditoriums & theaters

(P-10908)
MACERICH COMPANY
Also Called: Stonewood Ctr Mall Office
251 Stonewood St, Downey (90241-3935)
PHONE..................................562 861-9233
Charlie Hallums, *Manager*
EMP: 50
SALES (corp-wide): 993.6MM **Publicly Held**
WEB: www.macerich.com
SIC: **6512** Shopping center, property operation only
PA: Macerich Company
401 Wilshire Blvd Ste 700
Santa Monica CA 90401
310 394-6000

(P-10909)
MALIBU CONFERENCE CENTER INC
327 Latigo Canyon Rd, Malibu
(90265-2708)
PHONE..................................818 889-6440
Glen Gerson, *President*
EMP: 500
SALES: 35.6MM **Privately Held**
WEB: www.trainingsites.com
SIC: **6512** Commercial & industrial building operation

(P-10910)
MCCLELLAN FACILITIES SVCS LLC
3140 Peacekeeper Way, McClellan
(95652-2508)
PHONE..................................916 965-7100
Larry Kelley, *President*
Frank Meyers, *Vice Pres*
Megan Loewe, *General Mgr*
EMP: 52
SALES (est): 2.4MM **Privately Held**
SIC: **6512** Property operation, retail establishment

(P-10911)
MEGA MAIL MALL INC
128 Avenida Del Mar, San Clemente
(92672-4080)
PHONE..................................888 998-6245
Sara Chavez, *Manager*
EMP: 50

P
R
O
D
U
C
T
S

&

S
V
C
S

SALES (est): 1.5MM **Privately Held**
SIC: 6512 Shopping center, property operation only

(P-10912)
MFW PARTNERS
1120 Silverado St, La Jolla (92037-4524)
PHONE................................858 454-8857
Leah Hurwitz, *Managing Prtnr*
Esther Belinski, *Partner*
Anita Tobias, *Partner*
Evie Weinstock, *Partner*
EMP: 50
SALES (est): 2.2MM **Privately Held**
SIC: 6512 Nonresidential building operators

(P-10913)
MILLS CORPORATION
Also Called: Ontario Mills Shopping Center
1 Mills Cir Ste 1 # 1, Ontario (91764-5215)
PHONE................................909 484-8300
Laurence Siegel, *Branch Mgr*
EMP: 60 **Privately Held**
WEB: www.millscorp.com
SIC: 6512 Shopping center, property operation only
HQ: The Mills Corporation
5425 Wisconsin Ave # 300
Chevy Chase MD 20815
301 968-6000

(P-10914)
MILWOOD HEALTHCARE INC
Also Called: Maywood Acres Healthcare
2641 S C St, Oxnard (93033-4502)
PHONE................................626 274-4345
Alger Brion, *CEO*
Girlie Rozario, *Office Mgr*
EMP: 97
SQ FT: 10,000
SALES (est): 921K **Privately Held**
SIC: 6512 Nonresidential building operators

(P-10915)
MULLER-ING-GATEWAY LLC
23521 Paseo De Valencia # 200, Laguna Hills (92653-3107)
PHONE................................951 687-2900
Jon Muller, *President*
EMP: 80
SALES (est): 1.4MM **Privately Held**
SIC: 6512 Commercial & industrial building operation

(P-10916)
MUTH DEVELOPMENT CO INC
Also Called: Orco Block
11100 Beach Blvd, Stanton (90680-3219)
PHONE................................714 527-2239
Richard Muth, *President*
Dwayne Gleason, *Vice Pres*
Lynn Muth, *Vice Pres*
Tom Ruggeri, *Controller*
EMP: 80
SALES (est): 4.5MM **Privately Held**
SIC: 6512 Nonresidential building operators

(P-10917)
N G A ASSOCIATES
205 W Alvarado St, Fallbrook (92028-2025)
PHONE................................760 726-4015
George J Nicholas, *General Ptnr*
Michael Dancer, *Ltd Ptnr*
EMP: 50
SALES (est): 948.2K **Privately Held**
SIC: 6512

(P-10918)
NEDERLANDER OF CALIFORNIA INC
6233 Hollywood Blvd Fl 2, Los Angeles (90028-5310)
PHONE................................323 468-1700
James M Nederlander, *Chairman*
Robert Nederlander, *President*
EMP: 50 **EST:** 1975
SQ FT: 2,500
SALES (est): 3.5MM **Privately Held**
WEB: www.greektheatrela.com
SIC: 6512 7922 Theater building, ownership & operation; theatrical producers & services

(P-10919)
NEVINS-ADAMS PROPERTIES INC (PA)
Also Called: Nevins Adams Properties
920 Garden St Ste A, Santa Barbara (93101-7465)
PHONE................................805 963-2884
Henry Nevins, *President*
David Adams, *Chairman*
EMP: 250
SALES (est): 9.2MM **Privately Held**
WEB: www.nevinsadams.com
SIC: 6512 Commercial & industrial building operation

(P-10920)
NORTHRIDGE 07 A LLC
12411 Ventura Blvd, Studio City (91604-2407)
PHONE................................818 505-6777
Cathy Reynolds,
Alan Fox,
EMP: 80
SALES (est): 4.3MM **Privately Held**
SIC: 6512 Commercial & industrial building operation

(P-10921)
OATES BUZZ ENTERPRISES
Also Called: Folsom Manlove Venture
555 Capitol Mall Ste 900, Sacramento (95814-4606)
PHONE................................916 381-3600
Marvin L Oates, *Partner*
Carl Best, *Partner*
EMP: 100
SALES (est): 5.3MM **Privately Held**
SIC: 6512 6552 6531 Nonresidential building operators; subdividers & developers; real estate agents & managers

(P-10922)
OLEN COMMERCIAL REALTY CORP
Also Called: Olen Residential Realty
7 Corporate Plaza Dr, Newport Beach (92660-7904)
PHONE................................949 644-6536
Igor M Olenicoff, *President*
Andrei Olenicoff, *Corp Secy*
EMP: 400 **EST:** 1974
SQ FT: 44,000
SALES (est): 25.5MM **Privately Held**
SIC: 6512 Commercial & industrial building operation

(P-10923)
OLTMANS INVESTMENT COMPANY
Also Called: Oltmans Property Management
10005 Mission Mill Rd, Whittier (90601-1739)
P.O. Box 985 (90608-0985)
PHONE................................562 948-4242
J O Oltmans II, *President*
Basil C Johnson, *Managing Prtnr*
Robert Roy, *Managing Prtnr*
Gregory V Grupp, *Controller*
EMP: 50
SQ FT: 56,000
SALES (est): 3.2MM **Privately Held**
SIC: 6512 6552 Commercial & industrial building operation; subdividers & developers

(P-10924)
ONE TOWN CENTER ASSOCIATES LLC
3315 Fairview Rd, Costa Mesa (92626-1610)
PHONE................................714 435-2100
Stan Taeder, *Director*
Debbie Alcock, *Treasurer*
Karen Graham, *Associate Dir*
EMP: 50
SALES (est): 155K **Privately Held**
SIC: 6512 Commercial & industrial building operation

(P-10925)
PACIFIC EAGLE HOLDINGS CORP
353 Sacramento St Ste 360, San Francisco (94111-3688)
PHONE................................415 398-2473
Michael Simons, *Exec VP*
EMP: 87 **Privately Held**
SIC: 6512 6531 Commercial & industrial building operation; real estate managers
PA: Pacific Eagle Holdings Corporation
353 Sacramento St # 1788
San Francisco CA 94111

(P-10926)
PARAMOUNT THEATRE OF ARTS INC
2025 Broadway, Oakland (94612-2303)
PHONE................................510 893-2300
Leslee Stewart, *Director*
Robin Alexander, *Manager*
Sherre Giles, *Manager*
EMP: 60
SQ FT: 37,000
SALES: 2.4MM **Privately Held**
SIC: 6512 Theater building, ownership & operation

(P-10927)
PIER 39 LIMITED PARTNERSHIP (PA)
Beach Embarcadero Level 3, San Francisco (94133)
P.O. Box 193730 (94119-3730)
PHONE................................415 705-5500
Robert A Moor, *General Ptnr*
Molly M South, *Partner*
Frazer Thompson, *Vice Pres*
Charlotte Anderson-Jordan, *Admin Asst*
John Luu, *HR Admin*
EMP: 60 **EST:** 1968
SQ FT: 200,000
SALES: 40MM **Privately Held**
SIC: 6512 Commercial & industrial building operation

(P-10928)
PROPERTY INSIGHT
202 E Airport Dr Ste 210, San Bernardino (92408-3429)
PHONE................................909 876-6505
Frank Trujillo, *Principal*
Karen Schwartz, *Controller*
EMP: 200
SALES (est): 27.4MM
SALES (corp-wide): 7.6B **Publicly Held**
SIC: 6512 Nonresidential building operators
PA: Fidelity National Financial, Inc.
601 Riverside Ave Fl 4
Jacksonville FL 32204
904 854-8100

(P-10929)
PVCC INC (PA)
Also Called: Pacific View Companies
8100 La Mesa Blvd Ste 101, La Mesa (91942-6498)
PHONE................................619 463-4040
Charles I Feurzeig, *President*
Robert Teal, *CFO*
Charles R Swimmer, *Corp Secy*
James M Houck, *Vice Pres*
Robert Houck, *Vice Pres*
EMP: 62
SQ FT: 1,400
SALES (est): 5.8MM **Privately Held**
WEB: www.pacificviewcompanies.com
SIC: 6512 6513 Shopping center, property operation only; apartment building operators

(P-10930)
RP REALTY PARTNERS LLC
990 W 8th St Ste 600, Los Angeles (90017-2831)
PHONE................................310 207-6990
Stuart Ruben,
Howard Aminoff, *Exec VP*
Richard Costanzo, *Exec VP*
Yashaar Amin, *Vice Pres*
Rob Galanti, *Vice Pres*
EMP: 50

SALES (est): 4.4MM **Privately Held**
SIC: 6512 Commercial & industrial building operation

(P-10931)
SAN DEGO CNVNTION CTR CORP INC (PA)
111 W Harbor Dr, San Diego (92101-7822)
PHONE................................619 525-5000
Carol Wallace, *President*
Alfonso Sanchez, *Officer*
Dana Edward, *Vice Pres*
Karen Totaro, *General Mgr*
Melinda Moore, *Executive Asst*
EMP: 68
SALES (est): 91.1MM **Privately Held**
SIC: 6512 Nonresidential building operators

(P-10932)
SAN DIEGO THEATRES INC
Also Called: CIVIC THEATRE
1100 3rd Ave, San Diego (92101-4113)
P.O. Box 124920 (92112-4920)
PHONE................................619 615-4000
Donald M Telford, *CEO*
EMP: 200
SALES (est): 8MM **Privately Held**
WEB: www.sandiegotheatres.org
SIC: 6512 Theater building, ownership & operation

(P-10933)
SANTA MONICA CITY OF
Also Called: Civic Auditorium
1855 Main St, Santa Monica (90401-3209)
PHONE................................310 458-8551
Carole Curtin, *Manager*
EMP: 50 **Privately Held**
WEB: www.santamonicapd.org
SIC: 6512 9111 Auditorium & hall operation; mayors' offices
PA: City Of Santa Monica
1685 Main St
Santa Monica CA 90401
310 458-8411

(P-10934)
SDJ GENERAL PARTNERSHIP
2125 N Madera Rd Ste C, Simi Valley (93065-7711)
PHONE................................805 582-3200
Jawahar Tandon, *Partner*
Devinder Tandon, *Partner*
Sirjang Tandon, *Partner*
EMP: 70
SQ FT: 70,000
SALES (est): 2.9MM **Privately Held**
SIC: 6512 6513 Nonresidential building operators; apartment building operators

(P-10935)
SFI 2365 IRON POINT LLC
260 California St # 1100, San Francisco (94111-4396)
PHONE................................415 395-9701
Christopher Peatross, *President*
Deborah Abernathy, *Manager*
EMP: 50 **EST:** 2016
SALES (est): 695.4K **Privately Held**
SIC: 6512 Nonresidential building operators

(P-10936)
SFI CARLSBAD LLC
260 California St # 1100, San Francisco (94111-4396)
PHONE................................415 395-9701
Christopher Peatross,
EMP: 50 **EST:** 2015
SALES (est): 695.4K **Privately Held**
SIC: 6512 Nonresidential building operators

(P-10937)
SHENYANG ZHONG YI TIN-PLATING
Also Called: Professional Services Company
843 Clay St, San Francisco (94108-1614)
PHONE................................415 788-2280
Ku Hing Pong, *Principal*
EMP: 130
SQ FT: 250
SALES (est): 3.6MM **Privately Held**
SIC: 6512 5023 Nonresidential building operators; home furnishings

(P-10938)

SHOPPING CENTER MGT CORP
660 Stanford Shopping Ctr, Palo Alto
(94304-1400)
PHONE..........................650 617-8234
David B Longbine, *President*
EMP: 54
SALES (est): 2MM **Privately Held**
SIC: 6512 Shopping center, property operation only

(P-10939)

SHORENSTEIN COMPANY LLC
235 Montgomery St Fl 15, San Francisco
(94104-3102)
PHONE..........................415 772-7000
Douglas Shorenstein,
Tom Hart, *Exec VP*
John Boynton, *Vice Pres*
James Collins, *Vice Pres*
Paul Grafft, *Vice Pres*
EMP: 50
SALES (est): 4.3MM **Privately Held**
SIC: 6512 Commercial & industrial building operation

(P-10940)

SHORENSTEIN PROPERTIES LLC (PA)
235 Montgomery St Fl 16, San Francisco
(94104-3104)
PHONE..........................415 772-7000
Douglas W Shorenstein, *CEO*
Glenn A Shannon, *President*
Paula M Elliott, *Exec VP*
D Drew Dowsett, *Senior VP*
Katie McGettigan, *Senior VP*
EMP: 125
SQ FT: 20,000
SALES (est): 47.8MM **Privately Held**
SIC: 6512 Commercial & industrial building operation

(P-10941)

SIERRA VISTA 16 A LLC
12411 Ventura Blvd, Studio City
(91604-2407)
PHONE..........................818 505-6777
Cathy Reynolds, *Vice Pres*
Kristina Sheldon, *Supervisor*
EMP: 50
SALES (est): 632.2K **Privately Held**
SIC: 6512 Shopping center, community (100,000 - 300,000 sq ft)

(P-10942)

SIGNATURE SERVICES
4425 Jamboree Rd Ste 250, Newport
Beach (92660-3002)
PHONE..........................949 851-9391
Vanessa Sanchez, *Principal*
Chad Horning, *President*
Vanessa Viramontes, *Property Mgr*
EMP: 75
SALES (est): 7.8MM **Privately Held**
SIC: 6512 Commercial & industrial building operation

(P-10943)

SMG HOLDINGS INC
225 E Broadway 312, Glendale
(91205-1008)
P.O. Box 572559, Tarzana (91357-2559)
PHONE..........................310 432-2893
EMP: 69
SALES (corp-wide): 24.5B **Privately Held**
SIC: 6512 Nonresidential building operators
HQ: Smg Holdings, Llc
300 Cnshohckn State Rd # 450
Conshohocken PA 19428

(P-10944)

SMG HOLDINGS INC
Also Called: S M G
747 Howard St, San Francisco
(94103-3118)
PHONE..........................650 738-8737
Allan Crawford, *Finance*
EMP: 110

SALES (corp-wide): 24.5B **Privately Held**
WEB: www.smgworld.com
SIC: 6512 5812 8742 8741 Auditorium & hall operation; eating places; management consulting services; management services
HQ: Smg Holdings, Llc
300 Cnshohckn State Rd # 450
Conshohocken PA 19428

(P-10945)

SMG HOLDINGS INC
Also Called: Long Beach Convention Center
300 E Ocean Blvd, Long Beach
(90802-4825)
PHONE..........................562 499-7611
Charles Beirne, *General Mgr*
Catrin Lee, *Human Res Dir*
Louis Forgione, *Manager*
EMP: 69
SALES (corp-wide): 24.5B **Privately Held**
WEB: www.smgworld.com
SIC: 6512 Nonresidential building operators
HQ: Smg Holdings, Llc
300 Cnshohckn State Rd # 450
Conshohocken PA 19428

(P-10946)

SOLARI ENTERPRISES INC
1507 W Yale Ave, Orange (92867-3447)
PHONE..........................714 282-2520
Johrita Solari, *President*
Bruce Solari, *Vice Pres*
Stephanie Silvia, *Regional Mgr*
Maryann Oliver, *General Mgr*
Yanet Martinez, *Admin Asst*
EMP: 140
SQ FT: 8,400
SALES (est): 17.5MM **Privately Held**
SIC: 6512 Property operation, retail establishment

(P-10947)

SOTOYOME MEDICAL BUILDING LLC
Also Called: Redwood Regional Medical Group
990 Sonoma Ave Ste 15, Santa Rosa
(95404-4813)
PHONE..........................707 525-4000
Harold Phillips,
Sharon Debenedetti, *COO*
EMP: 80
SQ FT: 27,000
SALES (est): 9.8MM **Privately Held**
SIC: 6512 Commercial & industrial building operation

(P-10948)

SOUTH COAST PLAZA LLC (PA)
Also Called: South Coast Plaza Village
3333 Bristol St Ofc, Costa Mesa
(92626-1811)
PHONE..........................714 546-0110
N R Segerstrom, *Mng Member*
Debra Downing, *Exec Dir*
David Grant, *General Mgr*
Jennifer Toledo, *Admin Asst*
Debbie Corr, *Info Tech Dir*
EMP: 55
SQ FT: 8,000
SALES (est): 20.7MM **Privately Held**
WEB: www.blackstarrfrost.com
SIC: 6512 Shopping center, property operation only

(P-10949)

SOUTH COAST PLAZA LLC
Also Called: South Coast Plaza Mall
3333 Bristol St Ofc, Costa Mesa
(92626-1811)
PHONE..........................714 435-2000
David Grant, *Manager*
EMP: 60
SALES (corp-wide): 20.7MM **Privately Held**
WEB: www.blackstarrfrost.com
SIC: 6512 Shopping center, property operation only
PA: South Coast Plaza, Llc
3333 Bristol St Ofc
Costa Mesa CA 92626
714 546-0110

(P-10950)

SOUTHTOWN INDUSTRIAL PARK
Also Called: Neff Construction
1701 S Bon View Ave 104, Ontario
(91761-4412)
PHONE..........................909 947-3768
Kenneth L Neff, *President*
EMP: 50
SALES (est): 2.1MM **Privately Held**
SIC: 6512 Nonresidential building operators

(P-10951)

SPECTACOR MANAGEMENT GROUP
300 E Ocean Blvd, Long Beach
(90802-4825)
PHONE..........................562 436-3636
Charlie Beirne, *General Mgr*
EMP: 439
SQ FT: 4,000
SALES (est): 13.6MM **Privately Held**
SIC: 6512 Nonresidential building operators

(P-10952)

SUNAMERICA HSNG FND 1071
1 Sun America Ctr Fl 36, Los Angeles
(90067-6104)
PHONE..........................310 772-6000
Eric Geisler, *CFO*
EMP: 110
SALES (est): 3.2MM **Privately Held**
SIC: 6512 6513 Nonresidential building operators; apartment building operators

(P-10953)

SURTERRE PROPERTIES INC (PA)
1400 Newport Center Dr # 100, Newport
Beach (92660-0942)
PHONE..........................949 717-7100
Gary E Legrand, *CEO*
Gary Le Grand, *Sales Executive*
Jim Skelton, *Director*
EMP: 120
SALES (est): 13.4MM **Privately Held**
SIC: 6512 Nonresidential building operators

(P-10954)

TARIFF BUILDING ASSOCIATES LP (PA)
222 Kearny St Ste 200, San Francisco
(94108-4537)
PHONE..........................415 397-5572
Michael Depatie, *CEO*
Cheryl Lovelace, *Vice Pres*
Michael Thibodeau, *Info Tech Dir*
Cesar Herrera, *Project Mgr*
EMP: 60 EST: 1998
SALES (est): 1.3MM **Privately Held**
SIC: 6512 6513 Property operation, retail establishment; residential hotel operation

(P-10955)

TEGTMEIER ASSOCIATES INC
6701 Clark Rd, Paradise (95969-2833)
PHONE..........................530 872-7700
John Tegemeier, *President*
EMP: 58
SQ FT: 24,000
SALES (corp-wide): 3.3MM **Privately Held**
SIC: 6512 7841 5049 Theater building, ownership & operation; video disk/tape rental to the general public; theatrical equipment & supplies
PA: Tegtmeier Associates Inc.
14 Mansion Ct
Menlo Park CA 94025
650 847-1639

(P-10956)

TOM HOM INVESTMENT CORP
7660 Fay Ave Ste H, La Jolla (92037-4843)
PHONE..........................858 456-5000
Tom Hom, *Ch of Bd*
William Newbern, *President*
Les Harvey, *CFO*
EMP: 100
SQ FT: 2,000

(P-10957)

TOPA MANAGEMENT COMPANY (PA)
1800 Avenue Of The Stars # 1400, Los Angeles (90067-4220)
PHONE..........................310 203-9199
James Brooks, *CEO*
Jim Brooks, *President*
Jeanne Gettemy-Lazar, *CFO*
Darren Bell, *Vice Pres*
Paul Gienger, *Vice Pres*
EMP: 158
SALES (est): 14MM **Privately Held**
WEB: www.topamanagement.com
SIC: 6512 Commercial & industrial building operation

(P-10958)

US PROPERTY GROUP INC
Also Called: Manchester Center
1901 E Shields Ave # 203, Fresno
(93726-5313)
PHONE..........................559 227-1901
Kevin Mahieu, *Manager*
Moe Bagunu, *General Mgr*
Sandra Cortez, *Manager*
EMP: 50
SALES (est): 4.5MM **Privately Held**
WEB: www.manchester-center.com
SIC: 6512 Commercial & industrial building operation

(P-10959)

VALLEY PROPERTIES INC
10324 Balboa Blvd Lbby, Granada Hills
(91344-7363)
PHONE..........................818 360-3430
Peter J McKinnon, *President*
EMP: 90
SALES (est): 3.5MM **Privately Held**
SIC: 6512 Nonresidential building operators

(P-10960)

VIRGA INVESTMENT PROPERTY
430 S George Wash Blvd, Yuba City
(95993-9154)
PHONE..........................530 755-4409
Larry S Virga, *Owner*
EMP: 143
SALES: 300K **Privately Held**
SIC: 6512 Nonresidential building operators

(P-10961)

WEST SIDE REHAB CORPORATION
1755 Kings Way, Los Angeles (90069)
PHONE..........................323 231-4174
Dean Foley, *President*
EMP: 200
SQ FT: 1,500
SALES (est): 4.8MM **Privately Held**
SIC: 6512 Commercial & industrial building operation

(P-10962)

WEST VILLE PALM DESERT
Also Called: Palm Desert Town Center
72840 Highway 111 Ste 115, Palm Desert
(92260-3345)
PHONE..........................760 346-2121
Norie Bowlan, *Manager*
EMP: 50
SQ FT: 373,000
SALES (est): 3.1MM **Privately Held**
SIC: 6512 Shopping center, property operation only

(P-10963)

WESTFIELD LLC (DH)
2049 Century Park E # 4000, Los Angeles
(90067-3214)
PHONE..........................813 926-4600
Peter Lowy, *CEO*
Gregory Miles, *COO*
Philip Slavin, *CFO*
Mark Stefanel, *CFO*
Ron Goncalves, *Vice Pres*
EMP: 400
SQ FT: 120,000

SALES (est): 3.5MM **Privately Held**
SIC: 6512 Nonresidential building operators

P
R
O
D
U
C
T
S

&

S
V
C
S

SALES (est): 173.1MM **Privately Held**
WEB: www.westfieldamerica.com
SIC: 6512 Shopping center, property operation only
HQ: Westfield America, Inc.
　2049 Century Park E Fl 41
　Los Angeles CA 90067
　310 478-4456

(P-10964)
WESTFIELD AMERICA INC (HQ)
2049 Century Park E Fl 41, Los Angeles (90067-3101)
PHONE....................310 478-4456
Peter S Lowy, *CEO*
Mark A Stefanek, *CFO*
Elizabeth Westman, *Senior VP*
John Alderson, *Vice Pres*
Peter R Schwartz, *Director*
EMP: 200 **EST:** 1924
SALES (est): 181.4MM **Privately Held**
WEB: www.westfieldamerica.com
SIC: 6512 Shopping center, property operation only

(P-10965)
WESTFIELD AMERICA LTD PARTNR
2049 Century Park E # 4100, Los Angeles (90067-3101)
PHONE....................310 277-3898
John Widdup, *CEO*
Peter Lowy, *Partner*
Mark Stefanek, *CFO*
Hunter Lawrence, *Senior VP*
Craig Tanouye, *Senior VP*
EMP: 500
SALES (est): 8.9MM **Privately Held**
SIC: 6512 Shopping center, property operation only
HQ: Westfield, Llc
　2049 Century Park E # 4000
　Los Angeles CA 90067

(P-10966)
WESTLAKE DEVELOPMENT GROUP LLC (PA)
520 S El Camino Real # 900, San Mateo (94402-1722)
PHONE....................650 579-1010
T M Chang, *Mng Member*
William H C Chang,
EMP: 75
SQ FT: 80,000
SALES (est): 12.4MM **Privately Held**
WEB: www.westlake-global.com
SIC: 6512 6513 6531 Shopping center, property operation only; commercial & industrial building operation; apartment building operators; retirement hotel operation; real estate agents & managers

```
6513 Operators Of
Apartment Buildings
```

(P-10967)
10632 BOLSA AVENUE LP
Also Called: SYCAMORE COURT APT
500 Nwport Ctr Dr Ste 200, Newport Beach (92660)
P.O. Box 13326 (92658-5093)
PHONE....................949 673-1221
Shawn Boyd, *Principal*
EMP: 62 **EST:** 2017
SALES (est): 633.4K **Privately Held**
SIC: 6513 Apartment building operators

(P-10968)
1658 CAMDEN LLC
12147 Riverside Dr, North Hollywood (91607-3832)
PHONE....................818 769-1944
F Samuel Malik,
EMP: 50
SALES (est): 1.7MM **Privately Held**
SIC: 6513 Apartment building operators

(P-10969)
2ND FLOOR MAIN STREET CONCEPTS
126 Main St Ste 201, Huntington Beach (92648-8132)
PHONE....................714 969-9000
EMP: 50
SALES (est): 1.1MM **Privately Held**
SIC: 6513 Apartment building operators

(P-10970)
7410 WOODMAN AVENUE LLC
Also Called: Kaufman Properties
22837 Ventura Blvd # 201, Woodland Hills (91364-1224)
PHONE....................805 496-4336
Mark Kaufman,
Jill Pulido, *Info Tech Mgr*
Eddie Garravillo, *Manager*
David Villagomez, *Manager*
EMP: 100
SALES (est): 4.4MM **Privately Held**
SIC: 6513 Apartment building operators

(P-10971)
A COMMUNITY OF FRIENDS
3701 Wilshire Blvd # 700, Los Angeles (90010-2813)
PHONE....................213 480-0809
Dora Leong Gallo, *CEO*
Rachel Feldstein, *COO*
Dinde Patrick, *Office Mgr*
Kinette Cager, *Administration*
Brita Carlson, *Project Mgr*
EMP: 60
SQ FT: 5,800
SALES: 9MM **Privately Held**
WEB: www.acof.org
SIC: 6513 Apartment building operators

(P-10972)
AAH HUDSON LP
Also Called: Hudson Gardens
1255 N Hudson Ave, Pasadena (91104-2868)
PHONE....................626 794-9179
Victoria Miranda, *Comms Mgr*
Ellen Guccione, *Exec VP*
EMP: 3400
SALES: 200K **Publicly Held**
SIC: 6513 Apartment building operators
PA: Apartment Investment & Management Company
　4582 S Ulster St Ste 1100
　Denver CO 80237

(P-10973)
ALDERSLY RETIREMENT CENTER
Also Called: ALDERSLY RETIREMENT COMMUNITY
326 Mission Ave, San Rafael (94901-3425)
PHONE....................415 453-9271
Joanne Maxwell, *Administration*
Debra Shaw, *Marketing Staff*
David Eberhardt, *Food Svc Dir*
Tracey Brown, *Nursing Dir*
EMP: 75 **EST:** 1921
SQ FT: 3,000
SALES: 2.5MM **Privately Held**
WEB: www.aldersly.com
SIC: 6513 Retirement hotel operation

(P-10974)
ALL HALLOWS PRESERVATION LP
Also Called: All Hallows Garden Apartments
54 Navy Rd, San Francisco (94124-2825)
PHONE....................415 285-3909
Leeann Morein, *Senior VP*
George Buchanan, *Partner*
EMP: 3900
SALES: 950K **Publicly Held**
SIC: 6513 Apartment building operators
HQ: Aimco Properties, L.P.
　4582 S Ulster St Ste 1100
　Denver CO 80237

(P-10975)
ALTENHEIM INC
1720 Macarthur Blvd, Oakland (94602-1766)
PHONE....................510 530-4013

Cathy Hoopaugh, *Director*
EMP: 64 **EST:** 1890
SALES: 310.5K **Privately Held**
SIC: 6513 8051 Retirement hotel operation; skilled nursing care facilities; extended care facility

(P-10976)
AMERICAN BAPTIST HOMES OF WEST
Also Called: American Baptist Homes of West
460 E Fern Ave, Redlands (92373-6040)
PHONE....................909 335-3077
Mildred Makamure, *Manager*
EMP: 200
SALES (corp-wide): 178.8MM **Privately Held**
SIC: 6513 Retirement hotel operation
HQ: American Baptist Homes Of The West
　6120 Stoneridge Mall Rd # 300
　Pleasanton CA 94588
　925 924-7100

(P-10977)
AMERICAN BAPTIST HOMES OF WEST (HQ)
6120 Stoneridge Mall Rd # 300, Pleasanton (94588-3298)
PHONE....................925 924-7100
David B Ferguson, *CEO*
Christopher A Vito, *President*
Randy Stamper, *Chairman*
Sloan Bentley, *Senior VP*
Terese Farkas, *Senior VP*
EMP: 60 **EST:** 1955
SQ FT: 26,000
SALES: 175.8MM
SALES (corp-wide): 178.8MM **Privately Held**
WEB: www.abhow.com
SIC: 6513 Retirement hotel operation
PA: Humangood
　6120 Stoneridge Mall Rd
　Pleasanton CA 94588
　602 906-4024

(P-10978)
AMERICAN BAPTIST HOMES OF WEST
Also Called: Valle Verde Retirement Center
900 Calle De Los Amigos, Santa Barbara (93105-4435)
PHONE....................805 687-1571
Dawn Norrington, *Branch Mgr*
EMP: 200
SALES (corp-wide): 178.8MM **Privately Held**
WEB: www.abhow.com
SIC: 6513 8051 8052 Retirement hotel operation; convalescent home with continuous nursing care; intermediate care facilities
HQ: American Baptist Homes Of The West
　6120 Stoneridge Mall Rd # 300
　Pleasanton CA 94588
　925 924-7100

(P-10979)
AR PRESERVATION LP
201 Eddy St, San Francisco (94102-2715)
PHONE....................415 776-2151
Donald Falk, *Principal*
EMP: 99
SALES (est): 2.2MM **Privately Held**
SIC: 6513 Apartment building operators

(P-10980)
ASPEN APTS I
165 Eddy St, San Francisco (94102)
PHONE....................415 673-5879
EMP: 99
SALES (est): 3.4MM **Privately Held**
SIC: 6513

(P-10981)
ASPEN GROVE APARTMENTS LLC
450 E 8th St, Gilroy (95020-6650)
PHONE....................408 848-6400
Linda Mandolini, *Mng Member*
Kit Fong, *General Mgr*
EMP: 99
SALES (est): 1.6MM **Privately Held**
SIC: 6513 Apartment building operators

(P-10982)
BAYVIEW PRESERVATION LP
5 Commer Ct, San Francisco (94124-2713)
PHONE....................415 285-7344
Leeann Morein, *Senior VP*
Jennifer Hardee, *Partner*
David Robertson, *Partner*
EMP: 3900 **EST:** 2008
SALES (est): 31MM **Publicly Held**
SIC: 6513 Apartment building operators
HQ: Aimco Properties, L.P.
　4582 S Ulster St Ste 1100
　Denver CO 80237

(P-10983)
BEAR CREEK MANOR
2929 M St, Merced (95348-3215)
PHONE....................209 723-4674
H Davidson, *Principal*
EMP: 50
SALES (est): 1.1MM **Privately Held**
SIC: 6513 Apartment building operators

(P-10984)
BELMONT VILLAGE LP
Also Called: Belmont Village of Sunnyvale
1039 E El Camino Real, Sunnyvale (94087-7719)
PHONE....................408 720-8498
Dorothy Passarella, *Manager*
EMP: 60
SALES (corp-wide): 37.6MM **Privately Held**
SIC: 6513 Retirement hotel operation
PA: Belmont Village, L.P.
　7660 Woodway Dr Ste 400
　Houston TX 77063
　713 463-1700

(P-10985)
BELMONT VILLAGE LP
455 E Angeleno Ave, Burbank (91501-3077)
PHONE....................818 972-2405
Mary Jane Rodriguez, *Manager*
Leslie Brown, *Human Res Dir*
Jeffery Braine, *Chf Purch Ofc*
Jime Laylo, *QC Dir*
Michelle Scuillon, *Hlthcr Dir*
EMP: 60
SALES (corp-wide): 37.6MM **Privately Held**
SIC: 6513 Retirement hotel operation
PA: Belmont Village, L.P.
　7660 Woodway Dr Ste 400
　Houston TX 77063
　713 463-1700

(P-10986)
BELMONT VILLAGE LP
5701 Crestridge Rd, Rancho Palos Verdes (90275-4962)
PHONE....................310 377-9977
Judith Uy-Dillaruz, *Manager*
EMP: 60
SALES (corp-wide): 37.6MM **Privately Held**
SIC: 6513 Retirement hotel operation
PA: Belmont Village, L.P.
　7660 Woodway Dr Ste 400
　Houston TX 77063
　713 463-1700

(P-10987)
BELMONT VILLAGE LP
Also Called: Belmont Village of Hollywood
2051 N Highland Ave, Los Angeles (90068-1373)
PHONE....................323 874-7711
Kevin Ward, *Manager*
Eileen Ziedman, *Human Res Dir*
Anasheh Satoorian, *Nursing Dir*
Nadia Cantuna, *Hlthcr Dir*
EMP: 50
SQ FT: 96,800
SALES (corp-wide): 37.6MM **Privately Held**
SIC: 6513 Retirement hotel operation
PA: Belmont Village, L.P.
　7660 Woodway Dr Ste 400
　Houston TX 77063
　713 463-1700

(P-10988)
BIRTCHER/AETNA LAGUNA HILLS
Also Called: Wellington, The
24903 Moulton Pkwy Ofc, Laguna Hills (92653-6403)
PHONE..............................949 458-2311
Scott Mc Nutt, *Vice Pres*
EMP: 100
SQ FT: 292,000
SALES (est): 6.3MM **Privately Held**
SIC: 6513 Retirement hotel operation

(P-10989)
BRADDOCK & LOGAN INC
Also Called: Mission Pines Apts
3600 Pine St Apt 3600 # 3600, Martinez (94553-8505)
PHONE..............................925 229-1747
Russell Schaadt, *General Mgr*
Lorraine Guerra, *Manager*
EMP: 62
SALES (est): 1.6MM **Privately Held**
SIC: 6513 Apartment hotel operation

(P-10990)
BROADMOOR HOTEL (PA)
Also Called: The Broadmoore
1499 Sutter St, San Francisco (94109-5417)
PHONE..............................415 776-7034
Irene Lieberman, *President*
EMP: 220
SALES (est): 10.7MM **Privately Held**
WEB: www.granadasf.com
SIC: 6513 Residential hotel operation

(P-10991)
BROWNING APARTMENTS
1104 Browning Blvd, Los Angeles (90037-1662)
PHONE..............................213 252-8847
Tina Booth, *Manager*
EMP: 50
SALES: 55.4K **Privately Held**
SIC: 6513 Apartment building operators

(P-10992)
CAL SOUTHERN PRESBT HOMES
Also Called: Regents Point
19191 Harvard Ave Ofc, Irvine (92612-8624)
PHONE..............................949 854-9500
Melinda Forney, *Manager*
EMP: 175
SALES (corp-wide): 84.4MM **Privately Held**
WEB: www.scths.com
SIC: 6513 8052 8051 Retirement hotel operation; intermediate care facilities; skilled nursing care facilities
PA: Southern California Presbyterian Homes
516 Burchett St
Glendale CA 91203
818 247-0420

(P-10993)
CAL SOUTHERN PRESBT HOMES (PA)
516 Burchett St, Glendale (91203-1014)
PHONE..............................818 247-0420
John H Cochrane, *CEO*
Gerald W Dingivan, *CEO*
Ruben Grigorians, *Treasurer*
David Decker, *Bd of Directors*
Veronica Reyes, *Admin Asst*
EMP: 55
SQ FT: 11,000
SALES: 84.4MM **Privately Held**
WEB: www.scths.com
SIC: 6513 Retirement hotel operation

(P-10994)
CAL SOUTHERN PRESBT HOMES
Also Called: Windsor Manor
1230 E Windsor Rd Ofc, Glendale (91205-2674)
PHONE..............................818 244-7219
Marc Herrera, *Branch Mgr*
EMP: 110
SQ FT: 139,840

SALES (corp-wide): 84.4MM **Privately Held**
SIC: 6513 Retirement hotel operation
PA: Southern California Presbyterian Homes
516 Burchett St
Glendale CA 91203
818 247-0420

(P-10995)
CAL SOUTHERN PRESBT HOMES
Also Called: PARK PASEO
516 Burchett St, Glendale (91203-1014)
PHONE..............................818 247-0420
Gerald W Dingivan, *President*
Greg Bearce, *Vice Pres*
Dewayne McMullin, *Principal*
EMP: 55
SALES: 1.3MM **Privately Held**
WEB: www.parkpaseo.com
SIC: 6513 Retirement hotel operation

(P-10996)
CAL SOUTHERN PRESBT HOMES
Also Called: Royal Oaks
1763 Royal Oaks Dr Ofc, Duarte (91010-1989)
PHONE..............................626 357-1632
Tina Heaney, *Manager*
EMP: 161
SALES (corp-wide): 84.4MM **Privately Held**
WEB: www.scths.com
SIC: 6513 Retirement hotel operation
PA: Southern California Presbyterian Homes
516 Burchett St
Glendale CA 91203
818 247-0420

(P-10997)
CALIFORNIA ODD FELLOWS (PA)
Also Called: Meadows of NAPA Valley
1800 Atrium Pkwy, NAPA (94559-4837)
PHONE..............................707 257-7885
Wayne Panchesson, *Exec Dir*
Rina Famularcano, *Nursing Dir*
EMP: 100
SQ FT: 219,000
SALES (est): 1.5MM **Privately Held**
WEB: www.meadowsofnapavalley.org
SIC: 6513 8051 8322 Retirement hotel operation; convalescent home with continuous nursing care; old age assistance

(P-10998)
CALIFORNIA ODD FELLOWS
Also Called: Meadows Nappa Valley Care Ctr
1800 Atrium Pkwy, NAPA (94559-4837)
PHONE..............................707 257-7885
Wyane Panchesson, *Administration*
EMP: 65
SQ FT: 30,000
SALES (corp-wide): 1.5MM **Privately Held**
WEB: www.meadowsofnapavalley.org
SIC: 6513 8051 Apartment building operators; skilled nursing care facilities
PA: California Odd Fellows Housing Of Napa, Incorporated
1800 Atrium Pkwy
Napa CA 94559
707 257-7885

(P-10999)
CARMEL VLG RTIREMENT RESIDENCE
17077 San Mateo St # 3113, Fountain Valley (92708-7658)
PHONE..............................714 962-6667
S Butts, *President*
David Kuzmiak, *Nurse*
Cash Benton, *Director*
Rose Street, *Director*
EMP: 65
SQ FT: 117,670
SALES (est): 3.5MM **Privately Held**
SIC: 6513 Retirement hotel operation

(P-11000)
CASA SANDOVAL LLC
1200 Russell Way, Hayward (94541-7708)
PHONE..............................510 727-1700
Wai Tsin Chang,
EMP: 90
SQ FT: 215,000
SALES (est): 8.8MM **Privately Held**
WEB: www.casasandoval.com
SIC: 6513 Retirement hotel operation

(P-11001)
CHARLES & CYNTHIA EBERLY INC
Also Called: The Eberly Company
8383 Wilshire Blvd # 906, Beverly Hills (90211-2425)
PHONE..............................323 937-6468
Charles Eberly, *President*
Cynthia Eberly, *Vice Pres*
Jessica Avendano, *Assistant*
Sonia Godinez, *Supervisor*
EMP: 90
SALES (est): 7.4MM **Privately Held**
WEB: www.eberlyco.com
SIC: 6513 Apartment building operators

(P-11002)
CLASSIC PARK LANE PARTNERSHIP
Also Called: Park Lane A Classic Residenc
200 Glenwood Cir Ofc, Monterey (93940-6773)
PHONE..............................831 373-0101
Steve Brudnick, *Exec Dir*
Park Lane Investment, *Partner*
Jim Cox, *Director*
EMP: 83
SQ FT: 190,000
SALES (est): 3.1MM **Privately Held**
SIC: 6513 8361 Retirement hotel operation; home for the aged

(P-11003)
COMMERCIAL PROPERTY MANAGEMENT (PA)
3251 W 6th St Ste 109, Los Angeles (90020-5018)
PHONE..............................213 739-2000
David Soufer, *President*
EMP: 64
SQ FT: 4,500
SALES (est): 4MM **Privately Held**
WEB: www.cpmusa.com
SIC: 6513 Apartment building operators

(P-11004)
CONGRGTNAL CH RETIREMENT CMNTY
Also Called: Auburn Ravine Terrace
750 Auburn Ravine Rd, Auburn (95603-3820)
PHONE..............................530 823-6131
Deborah Stouff, *Admin Sec*
EMP: 85
SALES (est): 6.9MM **Privately Held**
SIC: 6513 Retirement hotel operation

(P-11005)
CREATIVE HOUSING & SERVICES
605 E Huntington Dr # 207, Monrovia (91016-6352)
PHONE..............................626 403-5454
George Mercer, *Director*
Scott Darrel, *Chairman*
Sylvia Karl, *Vice Pres*
EMP: 105
SQ FT: 6,000
SALES: 445.7K **Privately Held**
WEB: www.chmshousing.org
SIC: 6513 Apartment building operators

(P-11006)
CYPRESS GARDEN VILLAS
21600 Bloomfield Ave, Hawaiian Gardens (90716-2325)
PHONE..............................562 860-9260
Julia Forrester, *President*
EMP: 70
SALES (est): 1.2MM **Privately Held**
WEB: www.cypressgardensinn.com
SIC: 6513 Apartment building operators

(P-11007)
DOMINICAN OAKS CORPORATION
3400 Paul Sweet Rd Ofc, Santa Cruz (95065-1559)
PHONE..............................831 462-6257
Patience Beck, *Finance Mgr*
Sister Julie Hyer, *President*
Sally Boyd, *Administration*
Deborah Routley, *Administration*
Brenda Barber, *Human Res Dir*
EMP: 80
SALES: 11MM **Privately Held**
WEB: www.dominicanoaks.com
SIC: 6513 Retirement hotel operation

(P-11008)
E J WILLIAMS PROPERTY MGT
5637 N Pershing Ave Ste D, Stockton (95207-4943)
P.O. Box 7185 (95267-0185)
PHONE..............................209 473-4022
Ej Williams, *Principal*
EMP: 60
SALES (est): 360.6K **Privately Held**
SIC: 6513 Apartment building operators

(P-11009)
EAH ELENA GARDENS LP
Also Called: Elena Gardens Apartments
1902 Lakewood Dr, San Jose (95132-1409)
PHONE..............................415 295-8840
Cindy McAnally, *Principal*
EMP: 278
SALES: 4.2MM
SALES (corp-wide): 38.5MM **Privately Held**
WEB: www.centennialvillage.com
SIC: 6513 Apartment building operators
PA: Eah Inc.
22 Pelican Way
San Rafael CA 94901
415 258-1800

(P-11010)
EAST BAY ASIAN LOCAL DEV CORP
1825 San Pablo Ave # 200, Oakland (94612-1517)
PHONE..............................510 267-1917
Jeremy Liu, *Exec Dir*
Charise Fong, *COO*
Jean Bridges, *CFO*
Joshua Simon, *Exec Dir*
Anne Robertson, *Executive Asst*
EMP: 109
SQ FT: 78,000
SALES: 18MM **Privately Held**
WEB: www.ebaldc.org
SIC: 6513 Apartment building operators

(P-11011)
EDGEWOOD PROPERTIES (PA)
3096 Sandstone Rd, Alamo (94507-1617)
PHONE..............................925 838-2847
Jim Darst, *Partner*
Jim Rafton, *Partner*
EMP: 80
SQ FT: 600
SALES (est): 2.9MM **Privately Held**
SIC: 6513 Apartment building operators

(P-11012)
EMERITUS CORPORATION
Also Called: Villa Del Rey Retirement Inn
1351 E Washington Ave, Escondido (92027-1934)
PHONE..............................760 741-3055
Pam Judkins, *Branch Mgr*
EMP: 50
SQ FT: 60,000
SALES (corp-wide): 4.7B **Publicly Held**
WEB: www.emeraldestatesslc.com
SIC: 6513 Retirement hotel operation
HQ: Emeritus Corporation
3131 Elliott Ave Ste 500
Milwaukee WI 53214

(P-11013)
EMERITUS CORPORATION
Also Called: Creston Village
1919 Creston Rd Ofc, Paso Robles
(93446-4475)
PHONE..................805 239-1313
Tonya Hogue, *Director*
EMP: 50
SALES (corp-wide): 4.7B **Publicly Held**
WEB: www.emeraldestatesslc.com
SIC: 6513 Retirement hotel operation
HQ: Emeritus Corporation
3131 Elliott Ave Ste 500
Milwaukee WI 53214

(P-11014)
ENCORE SENIOR LIVING III LLC
Also Called: Encore Senior Vlg At Riverside
6280 Clay St, Riverside (92509-6005)
PHONE..................951 360-1616
Barbara Reece, *Director*
Brenda Jackson, *Social Dir*
EMP: 50 **Privately Held**
WEB: www.retirementinn.com
SIC: 6513 Retirement hotel operation
PA: Encore Senior Living Iii, Llc
400 Locust St Ste 820
Des Moines IA 50309

(P-11015)
ESSEX PROPERTY TRUST INC (PA)
1100 Park Pl Ste 200, San Mateo
(94403-7107)
PHONE..................650 655-7800
Michael J Schall, *President*
George M Marcus, *Ch of Bd*
Michael T Dance, *CFO*
Keith R Guericke, *Vice Ch Bd*
Gary Martin, *Bd of Directors*
EMP: 83
SQ FT: 39,600
SALES: 1.3B **Privately Held**
SIC: 6513 Apartment building operators

(P-11016)
FAIRWOOD ASSOCIATES APTS
Also Called: Fairwood Apartments
8893 Fair Oaks Blvd Ofc, Carmichael
(95608-2672)
PHONE..................916 944-0152
Leeann Morein, *Principal*
Arthur F Evans, *Partner*
The National Housing Partnersh, *Partner*
Jennifer Hardee, *Principal*
Joanette Stiron, *Manager*
EMP: 99
SALES: 500K **Publicly Held**
WEB: www.fairwoodapartments.com
SIC: 6513 Apartment building operators
PA: Apartment Investment & Management
Company
4582 S Ulster St Ste 1100
Denver CO 80237

(P-11017)
FATHERS OF ST CHARLES
Also Called: Villa Sclabrini Retirement Ctr
10631 Vinedale St, Sun Valley
(91352-2825)
PHONE..................818 768-6500
Ermete Nazzani, *Director*
Father E Nazzini, *Bd of Directors*
EMP: 188
SQ FT: 90,000
SALES: 5MM **Privately Held**
SIC: 6513 8051 Retirement hotel operation; skilled nursing care facilities

(P-11018)
FENTON SCRIPPS LANDING LLC
Also Called: H.G. Fenton Company
9970 Erma Rd, San Diego (92131-2425)
PHONE..................858 586-0206
Michael Neal, *Mng Member*
Andrea Norby, *Manager*
EMP: 99
SALES (est): 1.9MM **Privately Held**
SIC: 6513 Apartment building operators

(P-11019)
FIFTY PENINSULA PARTNERS
Also Called: Sterling Court
850 N El Camino Real Ofc, San Mateo
(94401-3787)
PHONE..................650 344-8200
S St Charles, *Exec Dir*
Sarah St Charles, *Exec Dir*
Joanne Coughlin, *Mktg Dir*
Ely Ramos, *Food Svc Dir*
EMP: 55
SALES (est): 4.8MM **Privately Held**
SIC: 6513 Retirement hotel operation

(P-11020)
FOREMOST HEALTHCARE CENTERS
Also Called: Health Care Developers
17581 Sultana St, Hesperia (92345-6552)
PHONE..................760 244-5579
Leonard Crites, *Owner*
Barbara Bandringa, *Owner*
Elizabeth Colon, *Administration*
Niru Vangala, *Administration*
Foremost Babette, *Bookkeeper*
EMP: 60
SALES (est): 1.7MM **Privately Held**
SIC: 6513 Apartment building operators

(P-11021)
FRED LEEDS PROPERTIES
3860 Crenshaw Blvd # 201, Los Angeles
(90008-1816)
PHONE..................310 826-2466
Fred Leeds, *President*
EMP: 50
SQ FT: 3,000
SALES (est): 3.4MM **Privately Held**
WEB: www.fredleedsproperties.com
SIC: 6513 Apartment building operators

(P-11022)
FRONT PORCH COMMUNITIES
849 Coast Blvd, La Jolla (92037-4223)
PHONE..................858 454-2151
Justin Weber, *Exec Dir*
David Weidert, *Exec Dir*
Margo McNeill, *Nursing Dir*
EMP: 100
SALES (corp-wide): 165.1MM **Privately Held**
SIC: 6513 8052 8361 Retirement hotel operation; intermediate care facilities; residential care
PA: Front Porch Communities And Services
- Casa De Manana, Llc
800 N Brand Blvd Fl 19
Glendale CA 91203
818 729-8100

(P-11023)
FRONT PORCH COMMUNITIES
Also Called: Wesley Palms
2567 2nd Ave Unit 312, San Diego
(92103-6579)
PHONE..................858 274-4110
Ben Gefke, *Manager*
Debbie Helmer, *Vice Pres*
Gregory Warren, *Analyst*
Karen Bixler, *Marketing Staff*
EMP: 330
SALES (corp-wide): 165.1MM **Privately Held**
SIC: 6513 Retirement hotel operation
PA: Front Porch Communities And Services
- Casa De Manana, Llc
800 N Brand Blvd Fl 19
Glendale CA 91203
818 729-8100

(P-11024)
FSQ RIO LAS PALMAS BUSINESS TR
877 E March Ln Apt 378, Stockton
(95207-5880)
PHONE..................209 957-4711
Sam Ogden, *Partner*
EMP: 54
SALES (est): 2.6MM **Publicly Held**
WEB: www.fivestarqualitycare.com
SIC: 6513 Retirement hotel operation
PA: Five Star Senior Living Inc.
400 Centre St
Newton MA 02458

(P-11025)
GABLES OF OJAI LLC
701 N Montgomery St, Ojai (93023-1844)
PHONE..................805 646-1446
Sue Collingsworth, *Director*
Barbara Nelson, *Office Mgr*
Donna Parsons, *Administration*
Carole Sullivan, *Supervisor*
EMP: 56
SALES (est): 2.7MM
SALES (corp-wide): 5.9MM **Privately Held**
WEB: www.gablesofojai.com
SIC: 6513 Retirement hotel operation
PA: The Parsons Group Inc
1 N Calle Chavez Ste 200
Santa Barbara CA 93101
805 564-3341

(P-11026)
GERSON BAKER & ASSOCIATES
Also Called: Westlake Village Apartments
333 Park Plaza Dr Ofc, Daly City
(94015-1538)
PHONE..................650 756-0959
Gerson Baker, *Owner*
Patsy Elbuhel, *Human Resources*
EMP: 100
SQ FT: 5,000
SALES (est): 6.5MM **Privately Held**
WEB: www.westlakevillageapts.com
SIC: 6513 Apartment hotel operation

(P-11027)
GK MANAGEMENT CO INC
Also Called: Studio Royale
3975 Overland Ave, Culver City
(90232-3722)
PHONE..................310 836-1812
Karen Longo, *Manager*
EMP: 60
SALES (corp-wide): 25.2MM **Privately Held**
WEB: www.gkind.com
SIC: 6513 Apartment building operators
PA: Gk Management Co., Inc.
5150 Overland Ave
Culver City CA 90230
310 204-2050

(P-11028)
HANK FISHER PROPERTIES INC (PA)
641 Fulton Ave Ste 200, Sacramento
(95825-4869)
PHONE..................916 485-1441
Nancy Fisher, *President*
EMP: 250 EST: 1976
SALES (est): 15.9MM **Privately Held**
SIC: 6513 Apartment building operators

(P-11029)
HARVEST FACILITY HOLDINGS LP
Also Called: Mission Cmmons Rtrment Rsdence
10 Terracina Blvd Ofc, Redlands
(92373-4800)
PHONE..................909 793-8691
John Degoucvia, *Manager*
EMP: 80 **Privately Held**
WEB: www.holidaytouch.com
SIC: 6513 Retirement hotel operation
HQ: Harvest Facility Holdings Lp
5885 Meadows Rd Ste 500
Lake Oswego OR 97035
503 370-7070

(P-11030)
HG FENTON COMPANY
7577 Mission Valley Rd # 200, San Diego
(92108-4432)
PHONE..................619 400-0120
Mike Neal, *CEO*
Robert Gottlieb, *CFO*
Henry Hunte, *Principal*
EMP: 84
SALES (est): 14.4MM **Privately Held**
SIC: 6513 6519 Apartment building operators; real property lessors

(P-11031)
HIGNELL INCORPORATED
Also Called: Sierra Manor Apts
1836 Laburnum Ave, Chico (95926-2375)
PHONE..................530 345-1965
Becky Nelson, *Branch Mgr*
EMP: 80
SALES (corp-wide): 41.1MM **Privately Held**
SIC: 6513 Apartment building operators
PA: Hignell, Incorporated
1750 Humboldt Rd
Chico CA 95928
530 894-0404

(P-11032)
INGLEWOOD MEADOWS KBS LP
1 S Locust St, Inglewood (90301-1808)
PHONE..................310 820-4888
Thomas Safran, *Partner*
EMP: 90
SALES: 1,000K **Privately Held**
SIC: 6513 Apartment building operators

(P-11033)
INTEGRAL SENIOR LIVING LLC (PA)
2333 State St Ste 300, Carlsbad
(92008-1691)
PHONE..................760 547-2863
Sue Farrow,
Terry Ervin, *President*
Tracee Degrande,
Suzanne Foley,
Vince Limburg,
EMP: 296
SALES (est): 33.3MM **Privately Held**
SIC: 6513 Retirement hotel operation

(P-11034)
INVESTORS MGT TR RE GROUP INC (PA)
Also Called: I M T
15303 Ventura Blvd # 200, Sherman Oaks
(91403-3110)
PHONE..................818 784-4700
John M Tesoriero, *President*
Glenn Killingsworth, *President*
Bryan Scher, *COO*
Frank Hutter, *CFO*
Scott Burns, *Vice Pres*
EMP: 50
SQ FT: 8,000
SALES (est): 18.3MM **Privately Held**
SIC: 6513 Apartment building operators

(P-11035)
IRVINE APT COMMUNITIES LP (HQ)
Also Called: I A C
110 Innovation Dr, Irvine (92617-3040)
PHONE..................949 720-5600
Raymond Watson, *Vice Chairman*
Mike Ellis, *Exec VP*
EMP: 200
SQ FT: 8,316
SALES: 68.3MM
SALES (corp-wide): 2.2B **Privately Held**
WEB: www.rental-living.com
SIC: 6513 6552 6798 Apartment building operators; subdividers & developers; real estate investment trusts
PA: The Irvine Company Llc
550 Newport Center Dr # 160
Newport Beach CA 92660
949 720-2000

(P-11036)
JEWISH SENIOR LIVING GROUP
302 Silver Ave, San Francisco
(94112-1510)
PHONE..................415 562-2600
Daniel Ruth, *President*
Kevin Krueger, *Executive*
Ken Diep, *Engineer*
Janet Garcia, *Accountant*
Terrence Scott, *Controller*
EMP: 60
SALES: 7.9MM **Privately Held**
SIC: 6513 Retirement hotel operation

(P-11037)
JOHN COLLINS CO INC
5155 Cedarwood Rd Mgr, Bonita
(91902-1942)
PHONE..............................818 227-2190
EMP: 97
SALES (corp-wide): 1.6MM Privately
Held
SIC: 6513 Apartment building operators
PA: The John Collins Co Inc
5135 N Harbor Dr
San Diego CA

(P-11038)
JOHN STEWART COMPANY
Also Called: Meadow Glen Apartments
2451 Meadowview Rd, Sacramento
(95832-1467)
PHONE..............................415 345-4400
David Lawler, Manager
EMP: 216
SALES (corp-wide): 118.2MM Privately
Held
SIC: 6513 Apartment building operators
PA: John Stewart Company
1388 Sutter St Ste 1100
San Francisco CA 94109
213 833-1860

(P-11039)
JONES & JONES MGT GROUP INC
8220 Topanga Canyon Blvd, Canoga Park
(91304-3844)
P.O. Box 6550, Woodland Hills (91365-
6550)
PHONE..............................818 594-0019
John D Jones, President
Helen Jones, CEO
Margaret Jones Dry, Vice Pres
Jennifer Nguyen, Regional Mgr
Krystal Dry, Associate
EMP: 142
SALES (est): 11.5MM Privately Held
SIC: 6513 Apartment building operators

(P-11040)
JP ALLEN INC
150 E Angeleno Ave, Burbank
(91502-1911)
PHONE..............................818 841-4770
Mark Crigler, President
Rich Reid, Finance Dir
EMP: 300
SQ FT: 100,000
SALES (est): 4MM Privately Held
SIC: 6513 7011 Apartment building opera-
tors; hotel, franchised

(P-11041)
KAMUNITY PROPERTIES (PA)
3760 State St, Santa Barbara
(93105-3168)
P.O. Box 30270 (93130-0270)
PHONE..............................805 682-5008
Joyce Trevillian, Owner
EMP: 50
SQ FT: 1,500
SALES (est): 2.1MM Privately Held
SIC: 6513 Apartment hotel operation

(P-11042)
KINGSLEY APARTMENTS
Also Called: Kingsley Court Apartments
1345 N Kingsley Dr, Los Angeles
(90027-5763)
PHONE..............................323 666-8862
Angelica Hovhannisyan, Manager
Gary Weiner, Director
Marietta Kartashyan, Manager
EMP: 80
SALES (est): 2.5MM Privately Held
SIC: 6513 Apartment building operators

(P-11043)
KISCO SENIOR LIVING LLC
Also Called: Drake Terrace
275 Los Ranchitos Rd, San Rafael
(94903-3673)
PHONE..............................415 491-1935
EMP: 95
SALES (corp-wide): 138.2MM Privately
Held
SIC: 6513 Retirement hotel operation

PA: Senior Kisco Living Llc
5790 Fleet St Ste 300
Carlsbad CA 92008
760 804-5900

(P-11044)
KISCO SENIOR LIVING LLC
1731 W Medical Center Dr, Anaheim
(92801-1837)
PHONE..............................714 872-9785
Carol Bush, Director
EMP: 72
SALES (corp-wide): 138.2MM Privately
Held
SIC: 6513 Retirement hotel operation
PA: Senior Kisco Living Llc
5790 Fleet St Ste 300
Carlsbad CA 92008
760 804-5900

(P-11045)
KISCO SENIOR LIVING LLC
Also Called: KRC Santa Margarita
21952 Buena Suerte, Rcho STA Marg
(92688-3903)
PHONE..............................949 888-2250
Rick Lansford, Branch Mgr
EMP: 100
SALES (corp-wide): 138.2MM Privately
Held
WEB: www.kiscosl.com
SIC: 6513 Retirement hotel operation
PA: Senior Kisco Living Llc
5790 Fleet St Ste 300
Carlsbad CA 92008
760 804-5900

(P-11046)
KISCO SENIOR LIVING LLC
1100 E Spruce Ave Ofc, Fresno
(93720-3314)
PHONE..............................559 449-8070
EMP: 55
SALES (corp-wide): 138.2MM Privately
Held
WEB: www.kiscosl.com
SIC: 6513 Retirement hotel operation
PA: Senior Kisco Living Llc
5790 Fleet St Ste 300
Carlsbad CA 92008
760 804-5900

(P-11047)
KISCO SENIOR LIVING LLC
Also Called: Oak View Snoma Hlls Apart-
ments
1350 Oak View Cir, Rohnert Park
(94928-6411)
PHONE..............................707 585-1800
Kim Healis, Branch Mgr
EMP: 66
SALES (corp-wide): 138.2MM Privately
Held
WEB: www.kiscosl.com
SIC: 6513 Retirement hotel operation
PA: Senior Kisco Living Llc
5790 Fleet St Ste 300
Carlsbad CA 92008
760 804-5900

(P-11048)
KISCO SENIOR LIVING LLC
Also Called: KRC Los Altos
1174 Los Altos Ave Ofc, Los Altos
(94022-1059)
PHONE..............................650 948-7337
Felora Lotfi, Branch Mgr
EMP: 50
SALES (corp-wide): 138.2MM Privately
Held
WEB: www.kiscosl.com
SIC: 6513 Retirement hotel operation
PA: Senior Kisco Living Llc
5790 Fleet St Ste 300
Carlsbad CA 92008
760 804-5900

(P-11049)
LA SALLE APARTMENTS
Also Called: La Salle Preservation
30 Whitfield Ct Ste 1, San Francisco
(94124-2840)
PHONE..............................415 647-0607
Leeann Morein, Principal
Jennifer Hardee, Principal
EMP: 99 EST: 2008

SALES (est): 2.5MM Privately Held
SIC: 6513 Apartment building operators

(P-11050)
LASSLEY ENTERPRISES INC
Also Called: Western Homes
1289 E Shaw Ave, Fresno (93710-7801)
P.O. Box 26988 (93729-6988)
PHONE..............................559 226-4300
Larry Lassley, President
Floyd Lassley, President
Terry Graham, Corp Secy
Lorraine Lassley, Vice Pres
EMP: 50 EST: 1963
SQ FT: 4,000
SALES (est): 1.7MM Privately Held
SIC: 6513 Apartment building operators

(P-11051)
LEGACY PARTNERS HOLLYWOOD
1600 Vine St, Los Angeles (90028-8818)
PHONE..............................949 930-7706
Tim O'Brien, Partner
Brandon Tran, Web Dvlpr
Andrew Koly, Mktg Dir
EMP: 91
SALES (est): 2.4MM Privately Held
SIC: 6513 Apartment building operators

(P-11052)
LEISURE CARE LLC
Also Called: Heritage Estates-Livermore
800 E Stanley Blvd, Livermore
(94550-2800)
PHONE..............................925 371-2300
EMP: 124
SALES (corp-wide): 128.3MM Privately
Held
SIC: 6513 Apartment building operators
PA: Leisure Care, Llc
999 3rd Ave Ste 4500
Seattle WA 98104
800 327-3490

(P-11053)
LEISURE CARE INC
Also Called: Norlyn Builders Newport Beach
1455 Superior Ave, Newport Beach
(92663-6127)
PHONE..............................949 645-6833
Connie Marvick, Administration
Newport Beach Plaza Retirement, General
Ptnr
M David Green, Ltd Ptnr
Jerome Pastor, Ltd Ptnr
Chuck Lytle, CEO
EMP: 60
SQ FT: 90,000
SALES (est): 4MM Privately Held
SIC: 6513 Retirement hotel operation

(P-11054)
LEXINGTON ASSOCIATES INC (PA)
1 Harbor Dr Ste 105, Sausalito
(94965-1433)
PHONE..............................415 332-8500
Richard Adams, President
EMP: 55
SQ FT: 4,400
SALES (est): 4.1MM Privately Held
SIC: 6513 Apartment building operators

(P-11055)
LINCOLN MARINERS ASSOC LTD
Also Called: Mariners Cove Apartments
4392 W Point Loma Blvd, San Diego
(92107-1128)
PHONE..............................619 225-1473
Leeann Morein, Principal
Jennifer Hardee, Principal
EMP: 99
SALES (est): 3.3MM Privately Held
WEB: www.marinerscoveapartments.com
SIC: 6513 Apartment building operators

(P-11056)
LIVING OPPORTUNITIES MGT CO
6900 Seville Ave, Huntington Park
(90255-4970)
PHONE..............................323 589-5956
EMP: 209

SALES (corp-wide): 11MM Privately Held
SIC: 6513 Apartment building operators
PA: Living Opportunities Management Co
3787 Worsham Ave
Long Beach CA 90808
562 595-7567

(P-11057)
LONGWOOD MANAGEMENT CORP
Also Called: California Villa
6728 Sepulveda Blvd, Van Nuys
(91411-1248)
PHONE..............................818 781-6348
Jackie Beltran, Administration
EMP: 50
SALES (corp-wide): 170MM Privately
Held
SIC: 6513 8361 Retirement hotel opera-
tion; residential care
PA: Longwood Management Corp.
4032 Wilshire Blvd Fl 6
Los Angeles CA 90010
213 389-6900

(P-11058)
LONGWOOD MANAGEMENT CORP
Also Called: Woodland Park Retirement Hotel
895 E Pasadena St, Pomona (91767-4930)
PHONE..............................818 884-7100
Susan Weisbarth, Manager
EMP: 68
SQ FT: 66,332
SALES (corp-wide): 170MM Privately
Held
SIC: 6513 Retirement hotel operation
PA: Longwood Management Corp.
4032 Wilshire Blvd Fl 6
Los Angeles CA 90010
213 389-6900

(P-11059)
LONGWOOD MANAGEMENT INC
Also Called: Huntington Rsdntial Rtrment Ht
20920 Earl St Ofc, Torrance (90503-4357)
PHONE..............................310 370-5828
Heather Argeta, Administration
Chiqui Olalia, Administration
EMP: 65
SALES (est): 2.1MM Privately Held
WEB: www.longwoodmanagement.com
SIC: 6513 Retirement hotel operation

(P-11060)
LOS ANGELES SENIOR CITIZEN
Also Called: PICO WOOSTER SENIOR
HOUSING
1425 S Wooster St, Los Angeles
(90035-3456)
PHONE..............................310 271-9670
Anne Friedrich, President
EMP: 55
SALES: 656.4K Privately Held
SIC: 6513 Retirement hotel operation

(P-11061)
M&M ASSEET MANAGEMENT GNL
2936 W El Segundo Blvd, Gardena
(90249-1558)
PHONE..............................310 769-6669
Ram K Mittal, Principal
Lillian Mittal, Principal
Evelyn Revellame, Controller
EMP: 99
SALES (est): 2.1MM Privately Held
SIC: 6513 Apartment building operators

(P-11062)
MARINA CITY CLUB LP A CALI
4333 Admiralty Way, Marina Del Rey
(90292-5469)
PHONE..............................310 822-0611
J H Snyder, Partner
Lewis Geyser, Partner
Lon Snyder, Partner
Milton Swimmer, Partner
Eileen Mc Carthy, Sales Dir
EMP: 125
SQ FT: 10,000

P R O D U C T S & S V C S

SALES (est): 7.6MM **Privately Held**
WEB: www.marinacityclub.net
SIC: 6513 7997 4493 Apartment building operators; membership sports & recreation clubs; marinas

(P-11063)
MAYER ASSOCIATES
9090 Wilshire Blvd Fl 3, Beverly Hills (90211-1851)
PHONE.....................310 274-5553
Alan I Casden, Partner
Alan Casden, Partner
EMP: 100
SALES (est): 2MM **Privately Held**
SIC: 6513 Apartment building operators

(P-11064)
MBK REAL ESTATE LTD A CALFOR
100 Lockewood Ln, Scotts Valley (95066-3900)
PHONE.....................831 438-7533
Kit Siemer, Exec Dir
EMP: 80
SALES (corp-wide): 45.9B **Privately Held**
SIC: 6513 Retirement hotel operation
HQ: Mbk Real Estate Ltd., A California Limited Partnership
4 Park Plz Ste 1000
Irvine CA 92614
949 789-8300

(P-11065)
MBK REAL ESTATE LTD A CALIFOR
Also Called: Ocean House Retirement Inn
2107 Ocean Ave Ofc, Santa Monica (90405-2282)
PHONE.....................310 399-3227
Lesley Henriksen, Exec Dir
EMP: 50
SALES (corp-wide): 45.9B **Privately Held**
SIC: 6513 Retirement hotel operation
HQ: Mbk Real Estate Ltd., A California Limited Partnership
4 Park Plz Ste 1000
Irvine CA 92614
949 789-8300

(P-11066)
MERCY HSING CALIFORNIA XXXIV
Also Called: Edith Witt Senior Community
66 9th St, San Francisco (94103-1427)
PHONE.....................415 503-0816
Abelle Cochico, Manager
Teresa Walorski, Administration
EMP: 99
SALES: 84.9K **Privately Held**
SIC: 6513 Apartment building operators

(P-11067)
MERRILL GARDENS LLC
350 Locust Dr Apt L215, Vallejo (94591-4226)
PHONE.....................707 553-2698
Frank Cook, Branch Mgr
EMP: 62 **Privately Held**
SIC: 6513 Retirement hotel operation
PA: Merrill Gardens L.L.C.
1938 Frview Ave E Ste 300
Seattle WA 98102

(P-11068)
MERRILL GARDENS LLC
4855 Snyder Ln Apt 152, Rohnert Park (94928-4863)
PHONE.....................707 585-7878
Jason Englehorn, Branch Mgr
EMP: 62 **Privately Held**
SIC: 6513 Retirement hotel operation
PA: Merrill Gardens L.L.C.
1938 Frview Ave E Ste 300
Seattle WA 98102

(P-11069)
MERRILL GARDENS LLC
Also Called: Merrill Gardens At Bankers Hl
2567 2nd Ave, San Diego (92103-6503)
PHONE.....................619 961-4990
Nancy Robinson, President
EMP: 63 **Privately Held**

SIC: 6513 Retirement hotel operation
PA: Merrill Gardens L.L.C.
1938 Frview Ave E Ste 300
Seattle WA 98102

(P-11070)
MERRILL GARDENS LLC
17200 Goldenwest St # 101, Huntington Beach (92647-9510)
PHONE.....................714 842-6569
EMP: 52 **Privately Held**
SIC: 6513 Retirement hotel operation
PA: Merrill Gardens L.L.C.
1938 Frview Ave E Ste 300
Seattle WA 98102

(P-11071)
MERRILL GARDENS LLC
2115 Winchester Blvd, Campbell (95008-3443)
PHONE.....................408 370-6431
EMP: 52 **Privately Held**
SIC: 6513 Retirement hotel operation
PA: Merrill Gardens L.L.C.
1938 Frview Ave E Ste 300
Seattle WA 98102

(P-11072)
MERRILL GARDENS LLC
3500 Lake Blvd, Oceanside (92056-4600)
PHONE.....................760 414-9880
EMP: 63 **Privately Held**
SIC: 6513 Retirement hotel operation
PA: Merrill Gardens L.L.C.
1938 Frview Ave E Ste 300
Seattle WA 98102

(P-11073)
MERRILL GARDENS LLC
1220 Suey Rd Bldg A, Santa Maria (93454-2687)
PHONE.....................805 310-4102
Ole Vonfrausing-Borch,
Stephen Start,
EMP: 70
SALES (est): 4.6MM **Privately Held**
SIC: 6513 Retirement hotel operation

(P-11074)
MERRILL GARDENS LLC
800 Oregon St, Sonoma (95476-6445)
PHONE.....................707 996-7101
Sunny Notimoh, Manager
EMP: 63 **Privately Held**
SIC: 6513 Retirement hotel operation
PA: Merrill Gardens L.L.C.
1938 Frview Ave E Ste 300
Seattle WA 98102

(P-11075)
MERRILL GARDENS LLC
430 N Union Rd, Manteca (95337-4367)
PHONE.....................209 823-0164
Travis Barnett, Manager
EMP: 63 **Privately Held**
SIC: 6513 Retirement hotel operation
PA: Merrill Gardens L.L.C.
1938 Frview Ave E Ste 300
Seattle WA 98102

(P-11076)
MERRILL GARDENS LLC
Also Called: Merrill Gardns At Chateau Whit
13250 Philadelphia St Ofc, Whittier (90601-4319)
PHONE.....................562 693-0505
Suzie Magpayo, Manager
EMP: 60 **Privately Held**
SIC: 6513 Retirement hotel operation
PA: Merrill Gardens L.L.C.
1938 Frview Ave E Ste 300
Seattle WA 98102

(P-11077)
MGD INC (PA)
Also Called: Garibaldi Company
3525 W Benjamin Holt Dr, Stockton (95219-3403)
PHONE.....................209 955-0535

Mark Garibaldi, President
Matt Errecart, Vice Pres
Diane McMurry, Controller
Mario Garibaldi, Property Mgr
Danielle Poladi, Manager
EMP: 100
SQ FT: 2,500
SALES (est): 11.6MM **Privately Held**
WEB: www.garibaldico.com
SIC: 6513 Apartment building operators

(P-11078)
MID-PENINSULA TYRELLA CORP (PA)
658 Bair Island Rd # 300, Redwood City (94063-2748)
PHONE.....................650 299-8000
Fran Wagstaff, Exec Dir
EMP: 65
SALES (est): 286.1K **Privately Held**
SIC: 6513 Apartment building operators

(P-11079)
MONARK LP
2804 W El Segundo Blvd, Gardena (90249-1551)
PHONE.....................310 769-6669
Evelyn Revellame, CFO
EMP: 99
SALES (est): 1.9MM **Privately Held**
SIC: 6513 Apartment building operators

(P-11080)
MONROE RESIDENCE CLUB
Also Called: Kenmore Residence Club
1499 Sutter St, San Francisco (94109-5417)
PHONE.....................415 771-9119
Irene Lieberman, Owner
EMP: 75
SQ FT: 1,000
SALES (est): 2MM **Privately Held**
WEB: www.monroeresidenceclub.com
SIC: 6513 Residential hotel operation

(P-11081)
MONTE VISTA RETIREMENT LODGE
Also Called: Monte Vista Village
2211 Massachusetts Ave, Lemon Grove (91945-3616)
PHONE.....................619 465-1331
Sidney Goodman, Partner
John Goodman, Partner
Donna Hanson, Partner
Amos Heilicher, Partner
Daniel Heilicher, Partner
EMP: 90
SALES (est): 5.6MM **Privately Held**
WEB: www.montevistalodge.com
SIC: 6513 Retirement hotel operation

(P-11082)
MP SHORELINE ASSOC LTD PARTNR
Also Called: Shorebreeze Apartments
460 N Shoreline Blvd, Mountain View (94043-4661)
PHONE.....................650 966-1327
Matt Franklin, President
EMP: 50
SALES: 2.7MM
SALES (corp-wide): 41.9K **Privately Held**
SIC: 6513 Apartment building operators
PA: Stanford Mid-Peninsula Urban Coalition
303 Vintage Park Dr # 250
Foster City CA 94404
650 356-2900

(P-11083)
MT VIEW APARTMENTS LLC
3170 Crow Canyon Pl # 165, San Ramon (94583-1347)
P.O. Box 308 (94583-0308)
PHONE.....................925 866-8429
Dennis Fuller,
EMP: 60
SALES (est): 2.9MM **Privately Held**
SIC: 6513 Apartment building operators

(P-11084)
NORMAND/WLSHIRE RTRMENT HT INC
Also Called: CALIFORNIA HEALTHCARE AND REHA
6700 Sepulveda Blvd, Van Nuys (91411-1248)
PHONE.....................818 373-5429
Jerry Catama, Administration
EMP: 99
SALES: 21.5MM **Privately Held**
SIC: 6513 8059 Retirement hotel operation; convalescent home

(P-11085)
NORTHGATE TERRACE APTS
1290 Northgate Dr Apt 48, Yuba City (95991-1565)
PHONE.....................530 671-2026
Dennis McLear, President
EMP: 100
SALES (est): 2MM **Privately Held**
SIC: 6513 Apartment hotel operation

(P-11086)
OAK CREEK APARTMENTS
Also Called: Gerson Bakar & Associates
1600 Sand Hill Rd, Palo Alto (94304-2047)
PHONE.....................650 327-1600
Gerson Bakar, Partner
A S Wilsey, General Ptnr
EMP: 50 **EST:** 1968
SQ FT: 300,000
SALES (est): 3.6MM
SALES (corp-wide): 42.1MM **Privately Held**
WEB: www.oakcreekapts.com
SIC: 6513 Apartment hotel operation
PA: Jalson Co., Inc.
201 Filbert St Ste 700
San Francisco CA 94133
415 391-1313

(P-11087)
OAKDALE HEIGHTS MGT CORP (PA)
250 Hemsted Dr Ste 100, Redding (96002-0940)
PHONE.....................530 222-6797
Michael Loudon, President
Jim Koenig, Shareholder
EMP: 347
SALES (est): 14MM **Privately Held**
SIC: 6513 Retirement hotel operation

(P-11088)
OCONNER WOODS A CALIFORNIA
3400 Wagner Heights Rd, Stockton (95209-4843)
PHONE.....................209 956-3400
Scot Sinclair, President
EMP: 100
SQ FT: 3,000
SALES (est): 3.6MM
SALES (corp-wide): 24.6MM **Privately Held**
SIC: 6513 Retirement hotel operation
PA: St. Joseph's Regional Housing Corporation
3400 Wagner Heights Rd
Stockton CA 95209
209 956-3400

(P-11089)
OCONNOR WOODS HOUSING CORP
3400 Wagner Heights Rd, Stockton (95209-4843)
PHONE.....................209 956-3400
Edward G Schoeder, President
Edward Schroeder, COO
Marcia Fitzgerald, Chief Mktg Ofcr
Scot Sinclair, Exec Dir
EMP: 100
SALES: 29.1MM
SALES (corp-wide): 24.6MM **Privately Held**
WEB: www.oconnorwoods.org
SIC: 6513 Retirement hotel operation
PA: St. Joseph's Regional Housing Corporation
3400 Wagner Heights Rd
Stockton CA 95209
209 956-3400

(P-11090)
OLIVE GROVE RETIREMENT RESORT
7858 California Ave, Riverside (92504-2599)
PHONE..................................951 687-2241
Kendall Jamison, *Director*
EMP: 65 EST: 1982
SQ FT: 170,000
SALES (est): 3.7MM **Privately Held**
WEB: www.olivegrove.com
SIC: 6513 Retirement hotel operation

(P-11091)
PAHC APARTMENTS INC
2595 E Byshore Rd Ste 200, Palo Alto (94303)
PHONE..................................650 321-9709
Marlene Prentergast, *President*
EMP: 50
SALES: 3.3MM **Privately Held**
SIC: 6513 Apartment building operators

(P-11092)
PANORAMA PARK APTS
401 W Columbus St Apt 64, Bakersfield (93301-5819)
PHONE..................................661 325-4047
Latanya Gordon, *Manager*
Leeann Morein, *Partner*
EMP: 99
SALES (est): 2.4MM **Privately Held**
SIC: 6513 Apartment building operators

(P-11093)
PARK NEWPORT LTD (PA)
Also Called: Park Newport Apartments
1 Park Newport, Newport Beach (92660-5004)
PHONE..................................949 644-1900
Gerson Bakar, *Owner*
Craig Capelouto, *Manager*
EMP: 75
SQ FT: 10,000
SALES (est): 4.2MM **Privately Held**
WEB: www.parknewport.com
SIC: 6513 Apartment hotel operation

(P-11094)
PARKWAY APARTMENTS LLC
3170 Crow Canyon Pl # 165, San Ramon (94583-1347)
PHONE..................................925 866-8429
Dennis Fuller, *Owner*
EMP: 50
SALES (est): 1.2MM **Privately Held**
SIC: 6513 Apartment building operators

(P-11095)
PASEO VLG HSING PARTNERS LP
1115 N Citron St, Anaheim (92801-2328)
PHONE..................................714 991-9172
Jim Brooks, *Controller*
Tesa Doleman,
EMP: 50
SALES (est): 1.8MM **Privately Held**
SIC: 6513 Apartment building operators

(P-11096)
PINOLE ASSISTED LIVING CMNTY
Also Called: PINOLE SENIOR VILLAGE
2850 Estates Ave, Pinole (94564-1416)
PHONE..................................510 758-1122
Tim McDonough, *President*
Melody Martini, *Vice Pres*
Debra Savoie, *Exec Dir*
EMP: 54
SALES: 4.1MM **Privately Held**
SIC: 6513 Retirement hotel operation

(P-11097)
PIONEER TOWERS RHF PARTNERS LP
515 P St Ofc, Sacramento (95814-6310)
PHONE..................................916 443-6548
Laverne R Joseph, *Managing Prtnr*
Deborah Stouff, *Principal*
EMP: 50
SALES: 2.3MM **Privately Held**
SIC: 6513 Apartment building operators

(P-11098)
PLB MANAGEMENT LLC
Also Called: Park Labrea Management
6200 W 3rd St, Los Angeles (90036-3157)
PHONE..................................323 549-5400
Dan James,
Greg Holihan,
EMP: 50
SALES (est): 3.4MM **Privately Held**
WEB: www.parklabrea.com
SIC: 6513 Apartment building operators

(P-11099)
PLUMMER VLG PRESERVATION LP
15450 Plummer St, North Hills (91343-2141)
PHONE..................................818 891-0646
Leeann Morein, *Partner*
Leeann Moreinm, *Partner*
EMP: 99
SALES: 950K **Publicly Held**
SIC: 6513 Apartment building operators
HQ: Aimco Properties, L.P.
4582 S Ulster St Ste 1100
Denver CO 80237
-

(P-11100)
PROVIDENT GROUP CROWN PNTE LLC
Also Called: Crown Pointe Retirement
737 Magnolia Ave Ofc, Corona (92879-7005)
PHONE..................................951 737-7482
Steve Hicks, *Mng Member*
Kathy Franco,
Debra Lockwood,
EMP: 56
SALES (est): 3.2MM **Privately Held**
SIC: 6513 Retirement hotel operation

(P-11101)
R & B REALTY GROUP
Also Called: Oakwood Garden Apts
3600 Barham Blvd, Los Angeles (90068-1106)
PHONE..................................323 851-3450
Tal Amquest, *Manager*
EMP: 100
SALES (corp-wide): 124.3MM **Privately Held**
SIC: 6513 Apartment building operators
PA: Oakwood Worldwide (Us) Lp
2222 Corinth Ave
Los Angeles CA 90064
800 888-0808

(P-11102)
R & B REALTY GROUP
Also Called: Oakwood Apartments
22122 Victory Blvd, Woodland Hills (91367-1937)
PHONE..................................818 710-5400
William Frill, *Manager*
EMP: 80
SALES (corp-wide): 124.3MM **Privately Held**
SIC: 6513 Apartment building operators
PA: Oakwood Worldwide (Us) Lp
2222 Corinth Ave
Los Angeles CA 90064
800 888-0808

(P-11103)
R & B REALTY GROUP
Also Called: Oakwood Apts
4111 Via Marina, Marina Del Rey (90292-5302)
PHONE..................................310 751-4545
Heather Hermann, *Manager*
EMP: 55
SALES (corp-wide): 124.3MM **Privately Held**
SIC: 6513 Apartment building operators
PA: Oakwood Worldwide (Us) Lp
2222 Corinth Ave
Los Angeles CA 90064
800 888-0808

(P-11104)
RAHF IV CASA PANORAMA LP
14555 Osborne St, Panorama City (91402-1820)
PHONE..................................216 621-6060

EMP: 50
SALES (est): 498.2K **Privately Held**
SIC: 6513 Apartment building operators

(P-11105)
RAHF IV GROVE LP
227 W H St, Ontario (91762-2717)
PHONE..................................216 621-6060
Angelo Pimpas, *Principal*
EMP: 50
SALES (est): 498.2K **Privately Held**
SIC: 6513 Apartment building operators

(P-11106)
RANCE KING PROPERTIES INC (PA)
Also Called: R K Properties
3737 E Broadway, Long Beach (90803-6104)
PHONE..................................562 240-1000
William Rance King Jr, *President*
Steve King, *Vice Pres*
Steven King, *Vice Pres*
John Freeborn, *Broker*
Heather Fitzgerald, *Property Mgr*
EMP: 104
SQ FT: 5,000
SALES (est): 14.8MM **Privately Held**
WEB: www.rkprop.com
SIC: 6513 Apartment building operators

(P-11107)
REGENCY HILL ASSOCIATES
Also Called: La Mirage
6560 Ambrosia Dr, San Diego (92124-3133)
PHONE..................................619 281-5200
David Nethercut, *President*
Marie Driscoll, *Director*
EMP: 58
SQ FT: 3,000
SALES (est): 3.2MM **Privately Held**
SIC: 6513 Apartment building operators

(P-11108)
RICK WEISS NEW HOPE APARTMENTS
1637 Appian Way, Santa Monica (90401-3249)
PHONE..................................310 395-1026
Reint Alberts, *Manager*
EMP: 50
SALES: 707K **Privately Held**
SIC: 6513 Apartment building operators

(P-11109)
SAN DIMAS RETIREMENT CENTER (PA)
Also Called: Longwood Management
834 W Arrow Hwy, San Dimas (91773-2418)
PHONE..................................909 599-8441
Frankie Ramirez, *Administration*
EMP: 70
SALES (est): 3.4MM **Privately Held**
SIC: 6513 8059 Retirement hotel operation; personal care home, with health care

(P-11110)
SANTA MONICA RHF HOUSING INC (PA)
911 N Studebaker Rd, Long Beach (90815-4900)
PHONE..................................562 257-5100
Laverne Joseph, *President*
John Von Rusten, *CFO*
EMP: 80
SALES: 970.5K **Privately Held**
WEB: www.mail2msright.com
SIC: 6513 Apartment building operators

(P-11111)
SATELLITE FIRST COMMUNITIES LP (PA)
1835 Alcatraz Ave, Berkeley (94703-2714)
PHONE..................................510 647-0700
Susan Friedland, *Exec Dir*
EMP: 54
SALES (est): 732.1K **Privately Held**
SIC: 6513 Apartment building operators

(P-11112)
SHOREVIEW PRESERVATION LP
35 Lillian Ct, San Francisco (94124-2822)
PHONE..................................415 647-6922
George Buchanan, *Partner*
EMP: 99
SALES: 950K **Publicly Held**
SIC: 6513 Apartment building operators
HQ: Aimco Properties, L.P.
4582 S Ulster St Ste 1100
Denver CO 80237

(P-11113)
SIGN OF DOVE
Also Called: Sunrise Retirement Villa
707 Sunrise Ave Ofc, Roseville (95661-4531)
PHONE..................................916 786-3277
Debbie Norman, *Manager*
EMP: 60 **Privately Held**
WEB: www.signdove.com
SIC: 6513 Retirement hotel operation
PA: Sign Of The Dove
22900 Ventura Blvd # 200
Woodland Hills CA 91364

(P-11114)
SILVERADO ORCHARDS (PA)
Also Called: Management Associates
601 Pope St Ofc, Saint Helena (94574-1275)
P.O. Box 102 (94574-0102)
PHONE..................................707 963-1461
Alan Baldwin, *General Ptnr*
L Meade Baldwin, *General Ptnr*
EMP: 100 EST: 1975
SQ FT: 80,000
SALES (est): 4.9MM **Privately Held**
WEB: www.silveradoorchards.com
SIC: 6513 Retirement hotel operation

(P-11115)
SNAPDRAGON PLACE 1 LP
702 County Square Dr, Ventura (93003-5450)
PHONE..................................805 659-3791
Nancy Conk, *Partner*
EMP: 86
SALES (est): 3.2MM **Privately Held**
SIC: 6513 Apartment building operators

(P-11116)
SOUTH BAY VLLA PRESERVATION LP
13111 S San Pedro St, Los Angeles (90061-2760)
PHONE..................................310 516-7325
Leeann Morein, *Vice Pres*
EMP: 99
SALES: 950K **Publicly Held**
SIC: 6513 Apartment building operators
HQ: Aimco Properties, L.P.
4582 S Ulster St Ste 1100
Denver CO 80237

(P-11117)
STEADFAST MANAGEMENT CO INC
Also Called: Flanders Pointe Apts
15520 Tustin Village Way, Tustin (92780-4211)
PHONE..................................714 542-2229
EMP: 105
SALES (corp-wide): 58.7MM **Privately Held**
SIC: 6513 6531 Apartment building operators; real estate managers
PA: Steadfast Management Company, Inc.
18100 Von Karman Ave
Irvine CA 92612
949 748-3000

(P-11118)
STERLING-ASE LTD PARTNERSHIP
Also Called: Sterling Inn
17738 Francesca Rd, Victorville (92395-5105)
PHONE..................................760 951-9507
Aaron Koelsch, *Managing Prtnr*
Bill Ziprick, *Ltd Ptnr*

PRODUCTS & SVCS

EMP: 125
SQ FT: 98,000
SALES (est): 5.3MM **Privately Held**
SIC: 6513 Retirement hotel operation

(P-11119)
STONESFAIR FINANCIAL CORP
577 Airport Blvd Ste 700, Burlingame
(94010-2024)
PHONE.....................................650 347-0442
Karl E Bakhtiari, *President*
Maryann Fair, *Director*
EMP: 60
SALES (est): 936.2K **Privately Held**
WEB: www.stonesfairfinancial.com
SIC: 6513 6514 Apartment building operators; residential building, four or fewer units: operation

(P-11120)
SUMMERVILLE SENIOR LIVING INC
10615 Jordan Rd, Whittier (90603-2932)
PHONE.....................................562 943-3724
Granger Cobb, *CEO*
EMP: 51
SALES (corp-wide): 4.7B **Publicly Held**
SIC: 6513 Apartment building operators
HQ: Summerville Senior Living, Inc.
3131 Elliott Ave Ste 500
Seattle WA 98121
206 298-2909

(P-11121)
SUMMERVILLE SENIOR LIVING INC
20801 Devonshire St, Chatsworth
(91311-3216)
PHONE.....................................818 341-2552
Ram Nemani, *Owner*
EMP: 51
SALES (corp-wide): 4.7B **Publicly Held**
SIC: 6513 Apartment building operators
HQ: Summerville Senior Living, Inc.
3131 Elliott Ave Ste 500
Seattle WA 98121
206 298-2909

(P-11122)
SUNRISE RETIREMENT VILLA
707 Sunrise Ave Ofc, Roseville
(95661-4531)
PHONE.....................................916 786-3277
Ed Latin, *General Ptnr*
Mike Klein, *General Ptnr*
EMP: 60
SQ FT: 180,000
SALES (est): 2.4MM **Privately Held**
SIC: 6513 Apartment building operators

(P-11123)
TANTRA LAKE PARTNERS LP
18802 Bardeen Ave, Irvine (92612-1521)
PHONE.....................................949 756-5959
Sares Regis Holdings, *General Ptnr*
EMP: 120 EST: 1998
SALES (est): 3.6MM **Privately Held**
SIC: 6513 Apartment building operators

(P-11124)
TERRACINA MEADOWS APTS
4500 Tynebourne St F105, Sacramento
(95834-2556)
PHONE.....................................916 419-0925
Gary Benn, *COO*
Tarna Sadler, *Manager*
EMP: 50
SALES (est): 1.3MM **Privately Held**
SIC: 6513 Apartment building operators

(P-11125)
THE PINES LTD
1423 E Washington Ave, El Cajon
(92019-2559)
PHONE.....................................619 447-1880
Helen Sue, *Partner*
Tim Sliger, *General Mgr*
EMP: 111
SALES (est): 4.1MM **Privately Held**
SIC: 6513 Apartment building operators

(P-11126)
TOPANGA VILLAS COMPANY
Also Called: Warner Villa
5807 Topanga Canyon Blvd, Woodland Hills
(91367-4626)
PHONE.....................................818 884-8017
Catherine Hayes, *Partner*
Universal Properties, *Partner*
EMP: 100
SALES (est): 4.4MM **Privately Held**
SIC: 6513 Apartment building operators

(P-11127)
TPG REFLECTIONS II LLC
Also Called: Tpg/Calstrs
515 S Flower St, Los Angeles
(90071-2201)
PHONE.....................................213 613-1900
James A Thomas,
Michael McGrath, *Manager*
EMP: 99
SALES: 950K **Privately Held**
SIC: 6513 Apartment building operators

(P-11128)
TREES APARTMENTS LLC
7030 Eigleberry St, Gilroy (95020-6465)
PHONE.....................................408 848-6400
Linda Mandolini, *President*
EMP: 99
SALES (est): 1.3MM **Privately Held**
SIC: 6513 Apartment building operators

(P-11129)
TUOLUMNE CITY INV GRP II LP
Also Called: Tuolumne Cy Senior Apartments
18402 Tuolumne Rd Apt 31, Tuolumne
(95379-9719)
PHONE.....................................209 928-1567
Rod Moore, *Principal*
EMP: 50
SALES (est): 872.6K **Privately Held**
SIC: 6513 Apartment building operators

(P-11130)
TURK & EDDY ASSOCIATES LP
201 Eddy St, San Francisco (94102-2715)
PHONE.....................................415 474-6524
Donald Falk, *Exec Dir*
EMP: 65
SALES (est): 883.8K **Privately Held**
SIC: 6513 Apartment building operators

(P-11131)
VENTAGE SENIOR HOUSING
Also Called: Avalon At Newport
4000 Hilaria Way, Newport Beach
(92663-3610)
PHONE.....................................949 631-3555
Mary Heilgeist, *Exec Dir*
Barbara Briscoe, *Exec Dir*
Caroline Tawfik, *Nursing Dir*
Helen Raptis, *Director*
EMP: 50
SQ FT: 41,704
SALES (est): 1.8MM **Privately Held**
SIC: 6513 Retirement hotel operation

(P-11132)
VILLA PASEO SENIOR RESIDENCES
Also Called: Villa Paseo Palms
2818 Ramada Dr, Paso Robles
(93446-3981)
PHONE.....................................805 227-4588
Jim Brooks, *Controller*
Tesa Doleman,
EMP: 99
SALES: 950K **Privately Held**
SIC: 6513 Apartment building operators

(P-11133)
VILLA SERRA CORPORATION
1320 Padre Dr Apt 103, Salinas
(93901-2162)
PHONE.....................................831 754-5532
Chuck Major, *Vice Pres*
EMP: 65
SQ FT: 160,000
SALES (est): 4.5MM **Privately Held**
SIC: 6513 8361 Retirement hotel operation; geriatric residential care

(P-11134)
VILLAGE GLEN APARTMENTS
633 S Pasadena Ave Apt 45, Glendora
(91740-6804)
PHONE.....................................626 963-4575
Julie Flores, *Manager*
EMP: 98
SALES (est): 1.5MM **Privately Held**
SIC: 6513 Apartment building operators

(P-11135)
VINTAGE SENIOR HOUSING LLC
Also Called: Vintage Simi Hills
5300 E Los Angeles Ave, Simi Valley
(93063-4136)
PHONE.....................................805 583-3500
John Peter,
EMP: 325
SALES (corp-wide): 25.9MM **Privately Held**
SIC: 6513 Retirement hotel operation
PA: Senior Vintage Housing Llc
23 Corporate Plaza Dr # 190
Newport Beach CA 92660
949 719-4080

(P-11136)
VINTAGE SENIOR LIVING CORP
27783 Center Dr, Mission Viejo
(92692-3603)
PHONE.....................................949 364-6210
EMP: 75
SALES (est): 503.9K **Privately Held**
SIC: 6513 Retirement hotel operation

(P-11137)
VINTAGE SENIOR MANAGEMENT INC
91 Napa Rd, Sonoma (95476-7691)
PHONE.....................................707 595-0009
EMP: 1161 **Privately Held**
SIC: 6513 Retirement hotel operation
PA: Senior Vintage Management Inc
23 Corporate Plaza Dr # 190
Newport Beach CA 92660

(P-11138)
VIVA GROUP INC
Also Called: Rent.com
11766 Wilshire Blvd # 300, Los Angeles
(90025-6570)
PHONE.....................................310 449-6400
Bill McKnight, *General Mgr*
Gretchen Humbert, *CFO*
Alain Avakian, *CTO*
Micah Neumark, *Software Dev*
Rosemary Ledesma, *Software Engr*
EMP: 100
SALES (est): 6.8MM **Privately Held**
SIC: 6513 7375 Apartment building operators; information retrieval services

(P-11139)
WAMC COMPANY INC (PA)
Also Called: Cal West Enterprises
7420 Clairemont Mesa Blvd, San Diego
(92111-1546)
PHONE.....................................858 454-2753
Peter Valenti, *President*
James Bashor, *Principal*
EMP: 85
SALES (est): 1.9MM **Privately Held**
SIC: 6513 Apartment building operators

(P-11140)
WILLMARK CMMNTIES UNIV VLG INC (PA)
9948 Hibert St Ste 210, San Diego
(92131-1034)
PHONE.....................................858 271-0582
Mark Schmidt, *President*
EMP: 78
SQ FT: 2,000
SALES (est): 5.3MM **Privately Held**
SIC: 6513 1522 Apartment building operators; multi-family dwellings, new construction; condominium construction

(P-11141)
WILLOW GLEN VILLA A
1660 Gaton Dr, San Jose (95125-4534)
PHONE.....................................408 266-1660
EMP: 70

SQ FT: 146,000
SALES: 3MM **Privately Held**
SIC: 6513

(P-11142)
WINDHAM AT SAINT AGNES
1100 E Spruce Ave Ofc, Fresno
(93720-3314)
PHONE.....................................559 449-8070
Sue Hefty, *Vice Pres*
Transamerica Realty Investment, *Owner*
EMP: 66
SQ FT: 200,000
SALES (est): 3.6MM **Privately Held**
SIC: 6513 Retirement hotel operation

(P-11143)
WINNRESIDENTIAL LTD PARTNR
Also Called: Hci
255 Washington Rd, Chowchilla
(93610-1909)
PHONE.....................................559 665-9600
EMP: 266
SALES (corp-wide): 6.9MM **Privately Held**
SIC: 6513 Apartment building operators
PA: Winnresidential Limited Partnership
6 Faneuil Hall Market Pl
Boston MA 02109
617 742-4500

(P-11144)
WOODLAND RESIDENTIAL SERVICES
Also Called: Wrs
1381 E Gum Ave, Woodland (95776-4275)
PHONE.....................................530 419-0059
Parm Kajley, *CEO*
Jack Kenealy, *Vice Pres*
Debbie Lancaster, *Manager*
EMP: 66
SALES (est): 3.2MM **Privately Held**
SIC: 6513 Apartment building operators

(P-11145)
WOODSPEAR PROPERTIES (PA)
810 Los Vallecitos Blvd # 201, San Marcos
(92069-1446)
PHONE.....................................760 761-4340
Steven Spierer, *Partner*
John A Woodward, *Partner*
Debbie Ware, *Admin Asst*
Libby Pecson, *Accounting Mgr*
Zakary Kessler, *General Counsel*
EMP: 50
SQ FT: 7,200
SALES (est): 4.7MM **Privately Held**
WEB: www.woodspearproperties.com
SIC: 6513 6512 Apartment building operators; nonresidential building operators

---

6514 Operators Of Dwellings, Except

(P-11146)
ACTION PROPERTY MANAGEMENT INC (PA)
2603 Main St Ste 500, Irvine (92614-4261)
PHONE.....................................949 450-0202
Matthew Holbrook, *CEO*
George Skrbin, *Exec VP*
Amanda Barry, *General Mgr*
Liza Dejesus, *General Mgr*
Robert Dishman, *General Mgr*
EMP: 90
SQ FT: 18,000
SALES (est): 71.8MM **Privately Held**
SIC: 6514 8641 Residential building, four or fewer units: operation; homeowners' association

(P-11147)
EAH INC (PA)
Also Called: Eah Housing
22 Pelican Way, San Rafael (94901-5545)
PHONE.....................................415 258-1800
Mary Murtagh, *CEO*
Laura Hall, *CEO*
Alvin Bonnett, *Senior VP*
Karen Belanger, *Vice Pres*
Al Bonnett, *Vice Pres*
EMP: 70 EST: 1968
SQ FT: 30,000

SALES: 38.5MM **Privately Held**
WEB: www.centennialvillage.com
SIC: 6514 Residential building, four or fewer units: operation

(P-11148)
HOME PORT INC
5030 Union Ave, San Jose (95124-5432)
PHONE................................408 377-4134
Peter Villareal, *Manager*
EMP: 99
SALES: 230.5K
SALES (corp-wide): 41.9K **Privately Held**
SIC: 6514 6513 Residential building, four or fewer units: operation; apartment building operators
PA: Stanford Mid-Peninsula Urban Coalition
303 Vintage Park Dr # 250
Foster City CA 94404
650 356-2900

(P-11149)
MENLO GATEWAY INC
Also Called: MIDPEN HOUSING
303 Vintage Park Dr # 250, Foster City (94404-1166)
PHONE................................650 356-2900
Mark Battey, *Chairman*
Peter Villareal, *Principal*
Luina Palchak, *Manager*
EMP: 99
SALES: 1.9MM
SALES (corp-wide): 41.9K **Privately Held**
SIC: 6514 6513 Residential building, four or fewer units: operation; apartment building operators
PA: Stanford Mid-Peninsula Urban Coalition
303 Vintage Park Dr # 250
Foster City CA 94404
650 356-2900

(P-11150)
MERRILL GARDENS
Also Called: Country Suites By Carlson
2860 Country Dr Ofc, Fremont (94536-5338)
PHONE................................510 790-1645
Dan Bodily, *Owner*
EMP: 65
SALES (est): 1.5MM **Privately Held**
SIC: 6514 Dwelling operators, except apartments

(P-11151)
MIDPEN RESIDENT SERVICES CORP
303 Vintage Park Dr # 250, Foster City (94404-1166)
PHONE................................650 356-2965
Fran Wagstaff, *President*
Lory Candelf, *Vice Pres*
EMP: 300
SALES: 6.3MM
SALES (corp-wide): 41.9K **Privately Held**
SIC: 6514 6513 Residential building, four or fewer units: operation; apartment building operators
PA: Stanford Mid-Peninsula Urban Coalition
303 Vintage Park Dr # 250
Foster City CA 94404
650 356-2900

(P-11152)
MP MORSE COURT ASSOCIATES
Also Called: Morse Court Apartments
825 Morse Ave, Sunnyvale (94085-3070)
PHONE................................408 734-9442
Matthew O Franklin, *Partner*
Luina Palchak, *Manager*
EMP: 99
SALES: 70K
SALES (corp-wide): 41.9K **Privately Held**
SIC: 6514 6513 Residential building, four or fewer units: operation; apartment building operators
PA: Stanford Mid-Peninsula Urban Coalition
303 Vintage Park Dr # 250
Foster City CA 94404
650 356-2900

(P-11153)
PROFESSIONAL COMMUNITY MGT CAL
Also Called: Pcm
27051 Towne Centre Dr # 200, Foothill Ranch (92610-2819)
PHONE................................949 768-7261
Jeffrey Olson, *CEO*
EMP: 80
SALES (corp-wide): 55MM **Privately Held**
WEB: www.pcm-ca.com
SIC: 6514 Dwelling operators, except apartments
PA: Professional Community Management Of California
27051 Towne Centre Dr # 200
Foothill Ranch CA 92610
800 369-7260

(P-11154)
SARATOGA COURT INC
Also Called: MID PENN HOUSING
18855 Cox Ave, Saratoga (95070-4159)
PHONE................................408 866-1392
Matthew Franklin, *President*
EMP: 99
SALES: 314.9K
SALES (corp-wide): 41.9K **Privately Held**
SIC: 6514 6513 Residential building, four or fewer units: operation; apartment building operators
PA: Stanford Mid-Peninsula Urban Coalition
303 Vintage Park Dr # 250
Foster City CA 94404
650 356-2900

(P-11155)
VIVENTE 1 INC
Also Called: MIDPEN HOUSING
2400 Enborg Ln, San Jose (95128-2641)
PHONE................................408 279-2706
Matthew O Franklin, *President*
EMP: 99
SALES: 446.8K
SALES (corp-wide): 41.9K **Privately Held**
SIC: 6514 6513 Residential building, four or fewer units: operation; apartment building operators
PA: Stanford Mid-Peninsula Urban Coalition
303 Vintage Park Dr # 250
Foster City CA 94404
650 356-2900

(P-11156)
VIVENTE 2 INC
5347 Dent Ave, San Jose (95118-2900)
PHONE................................408 279-2706
Matthew O Franklin, *President*
Peter Villareal, *Manager*
EMP: 99
SALES: 506.8K
SALES (corp-wide): 41.9K **Privately Held**
SIC: 6514 6513 Residential building, four or fewer units: operation; apartment building operators
PA: Stanford Mid-Peninsula Urban Coalition
303 Vintage Park Dr # 250
Foster City CA 94404
650 356-2900

6515 Operators of Residential Mobile Home

(P-11157)
BARBACCIA PROPERTIES
Also Called: Villa Theresa Mobile Home Park
165 Blossom Hill Rd, San Jose (95123-5938)
PHONE................................408 225-1010
Cy Barbaccia, *Partner*
Eva Antonio, *Partner*
Lena Barbaccia, *Partner*
Lou Barbaccia, *Partner*
EMP: 80
SQ FT: 5,000
SALES: 7MM **Privately Held**
SIC: 6515 7999 Mobile home site operators; golf driving range

(P-11158)
MOBILE HM COMMUNITIES OF AMER (PA)
1122 Willow St Ste 200, San Jose (95125-3103)
PHONE................................408 279-5200
G Jeffery Moore, *President*
Ron Zraick, *Corp Secy*
Rudy Steadler, *Vice Pres*
EMP: 150
SALES (est): 7.9MM **Privately Held**
SIC: 6515 Mobile home site operators

(P-11159)
R C ROBERTS & CO (PA)
Also Called: Sands Rv Resort
801 A St, San Rafael (94901-3010)
PHONE................................415 456-8600
Barbel Roberts,
Niels Roberts,
Scott Roberts,
EMP: 216 **EST:** 1977
SQ FT: 3,000
SALES (est): 11.4MM **Privately Held**
SIC: 6515 7011 6531 Mobile home site operators; resort hotel; real estate agents & managers

(P-11160)
WATERHOUSE MANAGEMENT CORP
500 Giuseppe Ct Ste 2, Roseville (95678-6305)
PHONE................................916 772-4918
Kenneth Watershouse, *President*
EMP: 150
SQ FT: 10,000
SALES (est): 10MM **Privately Held**
SIC: 6515 Mobile home site operators

(P-11161)
WESTWIND ENTERPRISES LTD (PA)
1515 The Alameda, San Jose (95126-2321)
PHONE................................408 998-8444
Ray K Farris II, *CEO*
EMP: 120 **EST:** 1982
SALES (est): 12MM **Privately Held**
WEB: www.westwindenterprises.com
SIC: 6515 Mobile home site operators

6519 Lessors Of Real Estate, NEC

(P-11162)
711 HOPE LP
3470 Wilshire Blvd # 700, Los Angeles (90010-2207)
PHONE................................213 365-5000
Pat Birgham, *Partner*
EMP: 250
SALES (est): 12.3MM **Privately Held**
SIC: 6519 6512 Real property lessors; commercial & industrial building operation

(P-11163)
A G PACEMAN INC
1100 Industrial Rd Ste 11, San Carlos (94070-4131)
PHONE................................650 592-7282
Darrell W Leong, *President*
Anna Leong, *Treasurer*
EMP: 55
SQ FT: 30,000
SALES (est): 2.6MM **Privately Held**
SIC: 6519 Real property lessors

(P-11164)
AB/SW 70 S LAKE OWNER LLC
70 S Lake Ave, Pasadena (91101-4703)
PHONE................................650 571-2200
Nancy Chau, *Vice Pres*
EMP: 50
SALES (est): 468.4K **Privately Held**
SIC: 6519 Real property lessors

(P-11165)
CALIFORNIA PARKING COMPANY (PA)
Also Called: Dnj Parking
768 Sansome St, San Francisco (94111-1704)
P.O. Box 2882 (94126-2882)
PHONE................................415 781-4896
Richard Puccinelli, *President*
Ron Britz, *Vice Pres*
Ronald Britz, *Vice Pres*
Robert Puccinelli, *Vice Pres*
EMP: 90
SQ FT: 1,300
SALES (est): 4.8MM **Privately Held**
WEB: www.californiaparking.com
SIC: 6519 6512 7521 Real property lessors; nonresidential building operators; parking lots

(P-11166)
CALIFRN/NVADA DEVELOPMENTS LLC
3010 Old Ranch Pkwy # 330, Seal Beach (90740-2764)
PHONE................................714 677-5721
James R Wheeler,
EMP: 147
SALES (est): 92.3K
SALES (corp-wide): 6.1B **Publicly Held**
SIC: 6519 Real property lessors
HQ: Ese Land Corporation
300 Liberty St
Peoria IL

(P-11167)
COLTON REAL ESTATE GROUP (PA)
Also Called: Mvp Partners
515 Cabrillo Park Dr # 305, Santa Ana (92701-5016)
PHONE................................949 475-4200
Dave Colton, *President*
John Clintock, *CFO*
John Mc Clintock, *CFO*
John McClintock, *Vice Pres*
Joe Campion, *Facilities Dir*
EMP: 55
SQ FT: 7,000
SALES (est): 7.1MM **Privately Held**
SIC: 6519 Real property lessors

(P-11168)
DREISBACH ENTERPRISES INC (PA)
Also Called: Dreisbach Freight Services
575 Maritime St, Oakland (94607-1011)
P.O. Box 7509 (94601-0509)
PHONE................................510 533-6600
Jason Dreisbach, *President*
Doretta Carrion, *CFO*
Val Nunes, *Vice Pres*
John Swinnerton, *Vice Pres*
Ronald Dreisbach, *Principal*
▲ **EMP:** 200
SQ FT: 100,000
SALES (est): 23.8MM **Privately Held**
WEB: www.dreisbach.com
SIC: 6519 1541 4222 4225 Real property lessors; industrial buildings & warehouses; warehousing, cold storage or refrigerated; general warehousing & storage

(P-11169)
EASTLAND TOWER PARTNERSHIP
Also Called: Eastland Executive Office
1932 E Garvey Ave S, West Covina (91791-1910)
PHONE................................626 858-2000
Ziad Alahassen, *Partner*
EMP: 50
SALES (est): 2MM **Privately Held**
SIC: 6519 Real property lessors

(P-11170)
ELEVATE PROPERTY SERVICES LP
19700 Fairchild Ste 150, Irvine (92612-2500)
PHONE................................562 219-2101
Andrew Layland, *Principal*
Kerrigan Capital LLC, *General Ptnr*

PRODUCTS & SVCS

EMP: 50
SALES (est): 2.5MM **Privately Held**
SIC: 6519 Real property lessors

(P-11171)
ESSEX QUEEN ANNE LLC
Also Called: Essex Property
1100 Park Pl Ste 200, San Mateo
(94403-7107)
PHONE..................................650 849-1600
Michael Schall, *President*
Mike Injayan, *Director*
Jason Kenworthy, *Director*
Simona Deleon, *Manager*
Rimi Dosanjh, *Manager*
EMP: 52
SALES (est): 18.1MM
SALES (corp-wide): 1.3B **Privately Held**
SIC: 6519 Real property lessors
HQ: Essex Portfolio, L.P.
925 E Meadow Dr
Palo Alto CA 94303

(P-11172)
EVERETT MALL 01 LLC
12411 Ventura Blvd, Studio City
(91604-2407)
PHONE..................................818 505-6777
Alan Fox,
EMP: 50
SALES (est): 1.1MM **Privately Held**
SIC: 6519 Real property lessors

(P-11173)
FREMONT REALTY CAPITAL LP
199 Fremont St Fl 19, San Francisco
(94105-2255)
PHONE..................................415 284-8665
Claude J Zinngrabe Jr, *Managing Prtnr*
Victor Kwok, *CFO*
Scott Downie, *Vice Pres*
Simon Naylor, *Vice Pres*
Doug Ricker, *Vice Pres*
EMP: 76
SQ FT: 100,000
SALES (est): 3.4MM
SALES (corp-wide): 37.6MM **Privately
Held**
WEB: www.fremontrealtycapital.com
SIC: 6519 8742 Real property lessors;
real estate consultant
PA: Fremont Group, L.L.C.
199 Fremont St Fl 19
San Francisco CA 94105
415 284-8880

(P-11174)
IC BP III HOLDINGS XV LLC
1 Sansome St Fl 15, San Francisco
(94104-4448)
PHONE..................................415 273-4250
Ray Kim, *Principal*
Mark Bailey,
EMP: 50 EST: 2015
SALES (est): 1MM **Privately Held**
SIC: 6519 7389 Sub-lessors of real estate;

(P-11175)
LAACO LTD (PA)
Also Called: Storage West
431 W 7th St, Los Angeles (90014-1601)
PHONE..................................213 622-1254
Karen L Hathaway, *President*
Bryan J Cusworth, *CFO*
Bryan Cusworth, *CFO*
John K Hathaway, *Vice Pres*
Steven K Hathaway, *Vice Pres*
EMP: 125
SQ FT: 100,000
SALES (est): 22.6MM **Privately Held**
SIC: 6519 7997 7011 5812 Real property
lessors; yacht club, membership; hotels;
resort hotel; eating places

(P-11176)
LYON REALTY
4340 Golden Center Dr A, Placerville
(95667-6280)
PHONE..................................530 295-4444
Teresa Burroughs, *Broker*
Mary Meyer, *Broker*
Shawn Allan, *Real Est Agnt*
EMP: 124 **Privately Held**
SIC: 6519 6531 Real property lessors;
real estate brokers & agents

PA: Lyon Realty
2280 Del Paso Rd Ste 100
Sacramento CA 95834

(P-11177)
**MAXIMUS REAL ESTATE
PARTNERS**
1 Maritime Plz Ste 1900, San Francisco
(94111-3509)
PHONE..................................415 584-4832
Robert Rosania, *CEO*
Seth Mallen, *Treasurer*
EMP: 100
SALES (est): 1.3MM **Privately Held**
SIC: 6519 Sub-lessors of real estate

(P-11178)
MT EDEN NURSERY CO INC (PA)
2124 Bering Dr, San Jose (95131-2013)
PHONE..................................408 213-5777
Yoshimi Shibata, *President*
EMP: 50
SALES (est): 2.8MM **Privately Held**
SIC: 6519 Farm land leasing

(P-11179)
OCEAN VIEW MANOR LP
Also Called: Ocean View Manor Apartments
3533 Empleo St, San Luis Obispo
(93401-7334)
PHONE..................................805 781-3088
John Fowler, *CEO*
Griffin Moore, *General Mgr*
EMP: 70 EST: 2016
SQ FT: 10,000
SALES (est): 587.4K **Privately Held**
SIC: 6519 Real property lessors

(P-11180)
PACIFIC EQUITIES CAPTL
Also Called: V G Pacific Equities
1640 S Sepulveda Blvd # 308, Los Angeles
(90025-7510)
P.O. Box 25991 (90025-0991)
PHONE..................................310 477-5300
David S Rosen, *President*
Ron Pelleg, *Exec Dir*
Harvey Rosen, *Admin Sec*
EMP: 75
SALES (est): 4.7MM **Privately Held**
WEB: www.pacificequities.net
SIC: 6519 Landholding office

(P-11181)
PLDA INC
2570 N 1st St 218, San Jose (95131-1035)
PHONE..................................408 273-4528
Jean-Yves Brena, *President*
EMP: 55
SALES (est): 1.8MM **Privately Held**
WEB: www.plda.com
SIC: 6519 Real property lessors

┌─────────────────────────┐
│ **6531 Real Estate Agents &** │
│ **Managers** │
└─────────────────────────┘

(P-11182)
1370 REALTY CORP
14545 Friar St Ste 101, Van Nuys
(91411-2357)
PHONE..................................818 817-0092
Kambiz Merabi, *President*
EMP: 180
SQ FT: 16,400
SALES (est): 4.9MM **Privately Held**
SIC: 6531 Real estate agents & managers

(P-11183)
1524 ABBOT KINNEY LLC
1746 Abbot Kinney Blvd, Venice
(90291-4839)
PHONE..................................310 907-6517
Tami Pardee, *Mng Member*
John Vaughan, *Buyer*
EMP: 60 EST: 2015
SALES (est): 1.5MM **Privately Held**
SIC: 6531 Real estate agent, commercial

(P-11184)
1755 EFM 1 LLC
1755 Kings Way, Los Angeles (90069)
PHONE..................................323 231-4174
Tim English,

Timothy English,
EMP: 70
SALES (est): 1.8MM **Privately Held**
SIC: 6531 6513 Rental agent, real estate;
apartment building operators

(P-11185)
2300 WEST EL SECUNDO LP
11916 Eucalyptus Ave, Hawthorne
(90250-2820)
PHONE..................................310 769-6669
Evelyn Revellame, *Controller*
EMP: 99
SALES (est): 2.1MM **Privately Held**
SIC: 6531 Real estate managers

(P-11186)
A F GILMORE COMPANY
6301 W 3rd St, Los Angeles (90036-3154)
P.O. Box 480314 (90048-1314)
PHONE..................................323 939-1191
Henry Hilty Jr, *President*
Ernest Mauritson, *Vice Pres*
EMP: 55 EST: 1915
SALES (est): 7MM **Privately Held**
SIC: 6531 Real estate managers

(P-11187)
**A G SPANOS MANAGEMENT
INC**
10100 Trinity Pkwy Fl 5, Stockton
(95219-7242)
P.O. Box 7126 (95267-0126)
PHONE..................................209 478-7954
Alexander G Spanos, *President*
Jeremiah T Murphy, *CFO*
George Spanos, *Corp Secy*
EMP: 50
SQ FT: 5,000
SALES (est): 1.7MM **Privately Held**
SIC: 6531 Real estate managers
PA: A.G. Spanos Companies
10100 Trinity Pkwy Fl 5
Stockton CA 95219

(P-11188)
ABBEY PARTNER VI
Also Called: Airpark Partners
7207 Arlington Ave Ste D, Riverside
(92503-1550)
PHONE..................................951 785-8800
Don Abbey, *Owner*
Brett Alerecht, *Vice Pres*
EMP: 50
SALES (est): 1MM
SALES (corp-wide): 5.1MM **Privately
Held**
WEB: www.theabbeyco.com
SIC: 6531 Real estate managers
PA: Abbey-Properties Llc
12447 Lewis St Ste 203
Garden Grove CA 92840
562 435-2100

(P-11189)
ABODE COMMUNITIES
1149 S Hill St Fl 7, Los Angeles
(90015-2219)
PHONE..................................213 629-2702
Robin Hughes, *President*
Rick Saperstein, *CFO*
Kenneth Krug, *Chairman*
Sandra Kulli, *Chairman*
Gio Aliano, *Vice Pres*
EMP: 150
SQ FT: 10,094
SALES (est): 6.3MM **Privately Held**
SIC: 6531 8712 8711 Housing authority
operator; architectural services; engineer-
ing services

(P-11190)
**ACTUAL REALITY PICTURES
INC**
Also Called: The Residence
16030 Ventura Blvd # 380, Encino
(91436-2778)
PHONE..................................818 325-8800
Rj Cutler, *President*
EMP: 50
SALES (est): 1.9MM **Privately Held**
SIC: 6531 Real estate brokers & agents

(P-11191)
ADAMS & BARNES INC
Also Called: Century 21
433 W Foothill Blvd, Monrovia
(91016-2025)
PHONE..................................626 358-1858
Lou Jean Barnes, *President*
Andrew Barnes, *Treasurer*
Thomas E Adams, *Vice Pres*
Stone Bradley, *Sales Staff*
Jacen Crehan, *Real Est Agnt*
EMP: 50
SALES (est): 3.9MM **Privately Held**
WEB: www.c21ab.com
SIC: 6531 Real estate agent, residential

(P-11192)
**AGUA CALIENTE
DEVELOPMENT AUTH**
5401 Dinah Shore Dr, Palm Springs
(92264-5970)
PHONE..................................760 699-6800
Richard M Milanovich, *Chairman*
EMP: 99
SALES (est): 5.8MM
SALES (corp-wide): 200.2MM **Privately
Held**
SIC: 6531 Real estate leasing & rentals
PA: Agua Caliente Band Of Cahuilla Indi-
ans
5401 Dinah Shore Dr
Palm Springs CA 92264
760 699-6800

(P-11193)
ALAIN PINEL REALTORS
Junipero Between 5 & 6 # 56, Carmel
(93921)
PHONE..................................831 622-1040
Ron Kirendole, *Manager*
EMP: 65
SALES (est): 2.9MM **Privately Held**
SIC: 6531 Real estate agent, residential;
real estate brokers & agents

(P-11194)
ALAIN PINEL REALTORS INC
2001 Union St Ste 200, San Francisco
(94123-4135)
PHONE..................................415 814-6690
Paul Hulme, *CEO*
Isabella Lanza, *Broker*
Todd Van Laanen, *Broker*
Peter Stein, *Real Est Agnt*
EMP: 62
SALES (corp-wide): 10.9MM **Privately
Held**
SIC: 6531 Real estate brokers & agents
PA: Alain Pinel Realtors, Inc.
12772 Sartga Snyvl Rd # 1000
Saratoga CA 95070
408 741-1111

(P-11195)
ALAIN PINEL REALTORS INC
101 Nellen Ave, Corte Madera
(94925-1180)
PHONE..................................415 755-1111
Steve Dickason, *Vice Pres*
EMP: 62
SALES (corp-wide): 10.9MM **Privately
Held**
SIC: 6531 Real estate agent, residential;
real estate brokers & agents
PA: Alain Pinel Realtors, Inc.
12772 Sartga Snyvl Rd # 1000
Saratoga CA 95070
408 741-1111

(P-11196)
ALAIN PINEL REALTORS INC
520 S El Camino Real # 100, San Mateo
(94402-1714)
PHONE..................................650 548-1111
Ron Gable, *Manager*
Robin Wrigley, *Broker*
Cindy Moscaret, *Real Est Agnt*
Colleen Parker, *Real Est Agnt*
EMP: 70
SALES (corp-wide): 10.9MM **Privately
Held**
SIC: 6531 Real estate brokers & agents
PA: Alain Pinel Realtors, Inc.
12772 Sartga Snyvl Rd # 1000
Saratoga CA 95070
408 741-1111

(P-11197)
ALAIN PINEL REALTORS INC
750 University Ave # 150, Los Gatos
(95032-7697)
PHONE..............................408 358-1111
Jeff Barnett, *Manager*
Laura Defilippo, *Real Est Agnt*
Dana C Pasquale, *Real Est Agnt*
Maria Stuart, *Real Est Agnt*
EMP: 55
SALES (corp-wide): 10.9MM **Privately Held**
SIC: 6531 Real estate agent, residential; real estate brokers & agents
PA: Alain Pinel Realtors, Inc.
12772 Sartga Snyvl Rd # 1000
Saratoga CA 95070
408 741-1111

(P-11198)
ALAIN PINEL REALTORS INC
2911 Cleveland Ave, Santa Rosa
(95403-2715)
PHONE..............................707 636-3800
Dennis Park, *Branch Mgr*
EMP: 51
SALES (est): 10.9MM **Privately Held**
SIC: 6531 Real estate agent, residential
PA: Alain Pinel Realtors, Inc.
12772 Sartga Snyvl Rd # 1000
Saratoga CA 95070
408 741-1111

(P-11199)
ALAIN PINEL REALTORS INC
900 Main St Ste 101, Pleasanton
(94566-6073)
PHONE..............................925 251-1111
Carol Rodoni, *Owner*
Timothy McGuire, *COO*
Kris Moxley, *Real Est Agnt*
EMP: 62
SALES (corp-wide): 10.9MM **Privately Held**
SIC: 6531 Real estate brokers & agents
PA: Alain Pinel Realtors, Inc.
12772 Sartga Snyvl Rd # 1000
Saratoga CA 95070
408 741-1111

(P-11200)
ALAIN PINEL REALTORS INC
1440 Chapin Ave Ste 200, Burlingame
(94010-4011)
PHONE..............................650 375-1111
Janice Woods, *Branch Mgr*
David Cauchi, *Sales Associate*
EMP: 62
SALES (corp-wide): 10.9MM **Privately Held**
SIC: 6531 Real estate brokers & agents
PA: Alain Pinel Realtors, Inc.
12772 Sartga Snyvl Rd # 1000
Saratoga CA 95070
408 741-1111

(P-11201)
ALAIN PINEL REALTORS INC
578 University Ave, Palo Alto (94301-1901)
PHONE..............................650 323-1111
Robert Gerlach, *Manager*
Scott Symon, *Property Mgr*
Estela Freeman, *Real Est Agnt*
Carol Lin, *Real Est Agnt*
Kathleen Wilson, *Real Est Agnt*
EMP: 120
SALES (corp-wide): 10.9MM **Privately Held**
SIC: 6531 Real estate brokers & agents
PA: Alain Pinel Realtors, Inc.
12772 Sartga Snyvl Rd # 1000
Saratoga CA 95070
408 741-1111

(P-11202)
ALAIN PINEL REALTORS INC
167 S San Antonio Rd # 1, Los Altos
(94022-3055)
PHONE..............................650 941-1111
Gary Wheeler, *Manager*
EMP: 100
SALES (corp-wide): 10.9MM **Privately Held**
SIC: 6531 Real estate brokers & agents

PA: Alain Pinel Realtors, Inc.
12772 Sartga Snyvl Rd # 1000
Saratoga CA 95070
408 741-1111

(P-11203)
ALAIN PINEL REALTORS INC
1550 El Camino Real # 100, Menlo Park
(94025-4117)
PHONE..............................650 462-1111
Mary Gebhardt, *Manager*
Chris Anderson, *Sales Staff*
EMP: 80
SALES (corp-wide): 10.9MM **Privately Held**
SIC: 6531 Real estate agent, residential; real estate brokers & agents
PA: Alain Pinel Realtors, Inc.
12772 Sartga Snyvl Rd # 1000
Saratoga CA 95070
408 741-1111

(P-11204)
ALAMEDA PRODUCE MARKET LLC
761 Terminal St Ste 2, Los Angeles
(90021-1111)
PHONE..............................213 221-3400
Richard Meruelo,
Miguel Echemendia, *Vice Pres*
EMP: 80 EST: 1997
SQ FT: 22,000
SALES (est): 4.6MM **Privately Held**
SIC: 6531 Real estate agent, commercial

(P-11205)
ALLIANCE BAY FUNDING INC
37600 Central Ct Ste 264, Newark
(94560-3440)
PHONE..............................510 742-6600
Dawar Lodin, *President*
EMP: 90
SALES (est): 4.7MM **Privately Held**
SIC: 6531 Real estate agents & managers

(P-11206)
ALLIANT ASSET MGT CO LLC (PA)
21600 Oxnard St Ste 1200, Woodland Hills
(91367-4949)
PHONE..............................818 668-2805
Shawn Horwitz, *Mng Member*
Scott Koticks,
Brian Goldberg, *Mng Member*
EMP: 81
SQ FT: 19,816
SALES (est): 18.7MM **Privately Held**
SIC: 6531 Broker of manufactured homes, on site

(P-11207)
ALLISON DOWDY
1045 College Ave, Santa Rosa
(95404-4112)
PHONE..............................707 303-3472
Allison Dowdy, *Principal*
EMP: 65
SALES: 300K **Privately Held**
SIC: 6531 Real estate brokers & agents

(P-11208)
ALLMARK INC (PA)
10070 Arrow Rte, Rancho Cucamonga
(91730-4194)
PHONE..............................909 989-7556
Wayne Slavitt, *CEO*
Michael Krcelic, *President*
Pat Price, *CFO*
Steve Strebel, *CFO*
Michael Payne, *Treasurer*
EMP: 65
SQ FT: 3,167
SALES (est): 9.1MM **Privately Held**
WEB: www.allmarkproperties.com
SIC: 6531 Real estate managers

(P-11209)
ALTERA REAL ESTATE
33522 Niguel Rd Ste 200, Dana Point
(92629-4009)
PHONE..............................949 547-7351
Matt Brabeck, *Principal*
EMP: 356
SALES (est): 6.9MM **Privately Held**
SIC: 6531 Real estate brokers & agents

(P-11210)
AMARIK PROPERTIES INC (PA)
Also Called: A P I Property Management
1400 Bristol St N Ste 220, Newport Beach
(92660-2965)
PHONE..............................714 505-5200
Richard Hauer, *President*
Margie Tabrizi, *VP Opers*
EMP: 75
SALES (est): 5.6MM **Privately Held**
SIC: 6531 Real estate managers

(P-11211)
AMERICAN MARKETING SYSTEMS INC
Also Called: Amsi Real Estate Services
2800 Van Ness Ave, San Francisco
(94109-1426)
PHONE..............................800 747-7784
Zoya Lee Smithton, *Director*
Robb Fleischer, *Director*
Ken Valencia, *Director*
Casey Belway, *Manager*
Gustavo L Chavez, *Real Est Agnt*
EMP: 75
SQ FT: 8,000
SALES (est): 20MM **Privately Held**
WEB: www.amsisf.com
SIC: 6531 Real estate brokers & agents

(P-11212)
AMERICAN REALTY CENTRE INC
120 S Glendale Ave, Glendale
(91205-1195)
PHONE..............................323 666-6111
Peter P Chorebanian, *President*
EMP: 55
SQ FT: 1,961
SALES (est): 3.2MM **Privately Held**
WEB: www.americanrealtycentre.com
SIC: 6531 Real estate agent, residential

(P-11213)
AMR APPRAISALS INC
Also Called: Got Appraisals
5000 Executive Pkwy # 270, San Ramon
(94583-4282)
P.O. Box 2426 (94583-7426)
PHONE..............................925 400-6066
Joe M Reid, *President*
EMP: 54
SALES (est): 5.6MM **Privately Held**
SIC: 6531 Appraiser, real estate

(P-11214)
APPRAISER LOFT LLC
3027 Townsgate Rd Ste 140, Westlake Village (91361-5871)
PHONE..............................858 832-8334
Aman Makka, *Mng Member*
EMP: 50 EST: 2007
SQ FT: 20,000
SALES (est): 2.6MM **Privately Held**
SIC: 6531 Appraiser, real estate

(P-11215)
ARCADIA MANAGEMENT SERVICE CO
5185 Cherry Ave Ste 10, San Jose
(95118-3783)
P.O. Box 5368 (95150-5368)
PHONE..............................408 286-4440
Michael Fletcher, *President*
EMP: 50
SALES (est): 3.1MM **Privately Held**
SIC: 6531 Cooperative apartment manager

(P-11216)
ARDENBROOK INC (PA)
Also Called: A.M. Services
4725 Thornton Ave, Fremont (94536-6408)
PHONE..............................510 797-7980
William Mathew Brooks, *President*
Jimmy Solidum, *Info Tech Mgr*
Fenny Lin, *Controller*
Ben Cisneros, *Manager*
EMP: 100
SALES (est): 13.5MM **Privately Held**
WEB: www.ardenbrook.com
SIC: 6531 Real estate managers

(P-11217)
AREA HOUSING AUTHORITY (PA)
1400 W Hillcrest Dr, Newbury Park
(91320-2721)
PHONE..............................805 480-9991
Douglas A Tapking, *Exec Dir*
George McGehee, *General Mgr*
Alexandria Banks, *Executive Asst*
Dennise Avila, *Info Tech Mgr*
Michael Nigh, *Controller*
EMP: 50
SQ FT: 24,000
SALES: 38.8MM **Privately Held**
WEB: www.ahacv.org
SIC: 6531 Housing authority operator

(P-11218)
ARGENT MANAGEMENT CO LLC
2392 Morse Ave, Irvine (92614-6234)
PHONE..............................949 777-4070
Rosemarie Dyvig, *Legal Staff*
David Cecchele, *Senior VP*
David Soyka, *Senior VP*
Eddie Byrne, *Vice Pres*
Travis Devan, *Vice Pres*
EMP: 72
SALES (est): 8.5MM **Privately Held**
SIC: 6531 Rental agent, real estate

(P-11219)
ARGENT MANAGEMENT LLC (PA)
Also Called: Suncal
2392 Morse Ave, Irvine (92614-6234)
PHONE..............................949 777-4000
Bruce Elieff, *Principal*
Robert Starkman, *Senior VP*
Michael Watson, *Vice Pres*
Steve Elieff, *Mng Member*
EMP: 333
SQ FT: 20,000
SALES (est): 14.6MM **Privately Held**
WEB: www.suncal.com
SIC: 6531 Real estate agents & managers

(P-11220)
ARGON ENTERPRISES INC
Also Called: Pacific Properties Realty
13658 Hawthorne Blvd, Hawthorne
(90250-5824)
PHONE..............................310 349-8777
Armando Gonzalez, *President*
EMP: 92
SQ FT: 5,000
SALES (est): 2.9MM **Privately Held**
SIC: 6531 Multiple listing service, real estate

(P-11221)
ARROYO & COATES INC
425 California St # 2000, San Francisco
(94104-2102)
PHONE..............................415 445-7800
Tom Coates, *Ch of Bd*
Brad Colton, *President*
Pedro Arroyo, *Corp Secy*
EMP: 60
SQ FT: 7,500
SALES (est): 3.3MM **Privately Held**
WEB: www.acventures.com
SIC: 6531 Real estate brokers & agents

(P-11222)
ASSOCIATED REALTORS
27411 Viana, Mission Viejo (92692-3211)
PHONE..............................949 813-1888
Heleen Chaban, *Partner*
Helene Chaban, *Partner*
Edward Coury, *Partner*
EMP: 80 EST: 1976
SQ FT: 5,000
SALES: 5MM **Privately Held**
WEB: www.ocrelocate.com
SIC: 6531 Real estate brokers & agents

(P-11223)
ASTRO REALTY INC
Also Called: Century 21
11305 183rd St, Cerritos (90703-5434)
PHONE..............................562 924-3381
Louis Rosencrance, *President*
EMP: 65
SALES (est): 2MM **Privately Held**
SIC: 6531 Real estate agent, residential

(P-11224)
ATLAS HOSPITALITY GROUP
1901 Main St Ste 175, Irvine (92614-0517)
PHONE...............................949 622-3400
Alan Reay, *President*
S Shah, *Vice Pres*
EMP: 90
SALES (est): 1.2MM **Privately Held**
WEB: www.atlashospitality.com
SIC: 6531 Real estate agent, commercial

(P-11225)
AUCHANTE INC
Also Called: Remax VIP
6730 Florence Ave, Bell Gardens
(90201-4946)
PHONE...............................562 231-1880
Eliazar Felix, *President*
Maria Felix, *Vice Pres*
EMP: 75
SQ FT: 15,000
SALES (est): 3.3MM **Privately Held**
SIC: 6531 Real estate agent, commercial

(P-11226)
AUCTIONCOM INC
1 Mauchly Ste 27, Irvine (92618-2305)
PHONE...............................800 499-6199
Jeffrey Frieden, *CEO*
Jake Seid, *President*
James Corum, *COO*
Tim Morse, *CFO*
Virginia Pierce, *CFO*
EMP: 200
SQ FT: 18,000
SALES (est): 14.2MM **Privately Held**
WEB: WWW.AUCTION.COM
SIC: 6531 Auction, real estate

(P-11227)
AUCTIONCOM LLC (PA)
1 Mauchly, Irvine (92618-2305)
PHONE...............................949 859-2777
Monte J M Koch, *CEO*
Sarah Andrews, *President*
Jeff Friesen, *President*
Philip Kates, *President*
Keith McLane, *President*
EMP: 83
SALES (est): 179MM **Privately Held**
SIC: 6531 Real estate agents & managers

(P-11228)
AVALONBAY COMMUNITIES INC
Also Called: Avalon At Penasquitos Hills
2050 Main St Ste 1200, Irvine
(92614-8280)
PHONE...............................949 955-6200
Chris Payne, *Vice Pres*
EMP: 50
SALES (corp-wide): 2.1B **Publicly Held**
WEB: www.avalonbay.com
SIC: 6531 Real estate managers
PA: Avalonbay Communities, Inc.
671 N Glebe Rd Ste 800
Arlington VA 22203
703 329-6300

(P-11229)
AVANTRA REAL ESTATE SERVICES
Also Called: Avantra Financial
148 E Fthill Blvd Ste 100, Arcadia (91006)
PHONE...............................626 357-7028
Robert B Doeppel, *CEO*
Vicky Hansen, *President*
Debbie Bello, *Treasurer*
Gina Olivares, *Admin Sec*
EMP: 50
SQ FT: 1,800
SALES (est): 35MM **Privately Held**
WEB: www.avantrahomes.com
SIC: 6531 Real estate agents & managers

(P-11230)
B F MANAGEMENT
117 N Fuller Ave, Los Angeles
(90036-2811)
PHONE...............................323 931-7776
Chaim Freeman, *Owner*
EMP: 70
SQ FT: 1,000
SALES (est): 990K **Privately Held**
SIC: 6531 Real estate agents & managers

(P-11231)
BARCELON ASSOCIATES MGT CORP
590 Lennon Ln Ste 110, Walnut Creek
(94598-5923)
PHONE...............................925 627-7000
Mark Barcelon, *CEO*
Sandy Barcelon, *Co-CEO*
Sean Barcelon, *Director*
Barry Cammer, *Director*
Rosewood Townhomes, *Supervisor*
EMP: 250
SQ FT: 3,000
SALES (est): 2.8MM **Privately Held**
WEB: www.barcelon.com
SIC: 6531 Real estate managers

(P-11232)
BAYCO FINANCIAL CORPORATION (PA)
24050 Madison St Ste 101, Torrance
(90505-6016)
PHONE...............................310 378-8181
Brenda McKenneth, *President*
Robert Cohen, *Ch of Bd*
Sheri Pfau, *Treasurer*
Mary Colin, *Vice Pres*
EMP: 53
SALES (est): 2MM **Privately Held**
SIC: 6531 Real estate managers

(P-11233)
BEACHSIDE REALTORS (PA)
Also Called: Century 21
19671 Beach Blvd Ste 101, Huntington
Beach (92648-5902)
PHONE...............................714 969-6100
Thomas Denny, *President*
EMP: 304
SQ FT: 13,000
SALES (est): 20.3MM **Privately Held**
WEB: www.mikelembeck.com
SIC: 6531 Real estate agent, residential

(P-11234)
BEACHSIDE REALTORS
Also Called: Century 21
15820 Whittier Blvd Ste B, Whittier
(90603-2572)
PHONE...............................562 947-7834
Shelley Reesman, *Manager*
EMP: 80
SALES (est): 1.8MM
SALES (corp-wide): 20.3MM **Privately Held**
WEB: www.mikelembeck.com
SIC: 6531 Real estate agent, residential
PA: Beachside Realtors
19671 Beach Blvd Ste 101
Huntington Beach CA 92648
714 969-6100

(P-11235)
BEETHOVEN HOLDINGS INC
Also Called: Keller William Realty
400 E Main St Ste 110, Visalia
(93291-6320)
PHONE...............................559 733-4100
Albert Meggers, *Principal*
Daisy Aldaco, *Real Est Agnt*
Jacob Castro, *Real Est Agnt*
Kimberly Hogue, *Real Est Agnt*
Rene Jaramillo, *Real Est Agnt*
EMP: 250
SALES (est): 12.2MM **Privately Held**
SIC: 6531 Real estate agent, residential

(P-11236)
BEITLER & ASSOCIATES INC (PA)
Also Called: Beitler Commercial Realty Svcs
825 S Barrington Ave, Los Angeles
(90049-6759)
PHONE...............................310 820-2955
Barry Beitler, *CEO*
Robert H Sargent, *CFO*
Robert Sargent, *CFO*
Ron Kassan, *Exec VP*
Joshua Gerson, *Vice Pres*
EMP: 120
SQ FT: 13,000
SALES (est): 10.3MM **Privately Held**
WEB: www.beitler.com
SIC: 6531 Real estate agent, commercial

(P-11237)
BERKADIA COMMERCIAL MRTG LLC
1 Better World Cir # 210, Temecula
(92590-3712)
PHONE...............................951 506-2787
EMP: 57 **Privately Held**
SIC: 6531 Real estate agent, commercial
PA: Berkadia Commercial Mortgage Llc
323 Norristown Rd Ste 300
Ambler PA 19002

(P-11238)
BERKELEY 75 HSING PARTNERS LP
1936 University Ave # 130, Berkeley
(94704-1003)
PHONE...............................510 705-1488
Jim Brooks, *Controller*
EMP: 50 EST: 2014
SALES (est): 1.7MM **Privately Held**
SIC: 6531 Real estate agents & managers

(P-11239)
BERKSHIRE HATTAWAY HOME SERVCS
Also Called: Mulhearn Group
16404 Colima Rd, Hacienda Heights
(91745-5502)
PHONE...............................626 913-2808
Bruce Mulhearn, *President*
James Liao, *Admin Sec*
Adrianna Deleon, *Real Est Agnt*
Linda Haslim, *Real Est Agnt*
James Mares, *Real Est Agnt*
EMP: 75
SALES (est): 3MM **Privately Held**
SIC: 6531 Real estate agent, residential

(P-11240)
BERRO MANAGEMENT
3950 Parmnt Blvd Ste 115, Lakewood
(90712)
PHONE...............................562 432-3444
Jack Berro, *President*
EMP: 52
SQ FT: 2,000
SALES (est): 2.9MM **Privately Held**
SIC: 6531 Real estate managers

(P-11241)
BETTER HOMES AND GARDENS MASON
5887 Lone Tree Way Ste A, Antioch
(94531-8625)
PHONE...............................925 776-2740
Melody Royal, *Manager*
Gina Alfaro, *Sales Associate*
Stephanie Schwartz, *Sales Associate*
Silvia Olson, *Real Est Agnt*
EMP: 60 EST: 2010
SALES (est): 1.4MM **Privately Held**
SIC: 6531 Real estate agents & managers

(P-11242)
BEVERLYWOOD REALTY INC
2800 S Robertson Blvd, Los Angeles
(90034-2406)
PHONE...............................310 836-8322
Stanley Shapiro, *President*
Cheryl Shapiro, *Director*
EMP: 50
SALES (est): 1.8MM **Privately Held**
WEB: www.beverlywoodha.com
SIC: 6531 Real estate brokers & agents

(P-11243)
BIRTCHER ANDRSON PROPERTY SVCS (PA)
27611 La Paz Rd Ste D, Laguna Niguel
(92677-3938)
PHONE...............................949 831-0707
Robert Anderson, *President*
Art B Birtcher, *CEO*
EMP: 60
SQ FT: 15,000
SALES (est): 9.5MM **Privately Held**
SIC: 6531 Real estate managers

(P-11244)
BLACK KNGHT RE DATA SLTONS LLC
Also Called: Black Knight Data & Analytics
3100 New York Dr, Pasadena
(91107-1524)
PHONE...............................626 808-9000
EMP: 203
SALES (est): 265.1K
SALES (corp-wide): 1B **Publicly Held**
SIC: 6531 Real estate brokers & agents
HQ: Black Knight Financial Services, Inc.
601 Riverside Ave
Jacksonville FL 32204
904 854-5100

(P-11245)
BLACKROCK HOLDCO 2 INC
Also Called: Metrick Property Management
50 California St Ste 200, San Francisco
(94111-4605)
PHONE...............................415 678-2000
Ron Zuzack, *Director*
EMP: 80 **Publicly Held**
WEB: www.blackrock.com
SIC: 6531 Real estate managers
HQ: Blackrock Holdco 2, Inc.
40 E 52nd St
New York NY 10022
212 754-5300

(P-11246)
BLAYNE PACELLI
12345 Ventura Blvd Ste A, Studio City
(91604-2511)
PHONE...............................310 383-6281
Blayne Joseph Pacelli, *Owner*
EMP: 85
SALES (est): 1.3MM **Privately Held**
SIC: 6531 Real estate brokers & agents

(P-11247)
BMR 21 ERIE ST LLC
17190 Bernardo Center Dr, San Diego
(92128-7030)
PHONE...............................858 485-9840
Alan D Gold, *CEO*
EMP: 71
SALES (est): 404.8K
SALES (corp-wide): 674.6MM **Privately Held**
SIC: 6531 Real estate brokers & agents
HQ: Biomed Realty, L.P.
17190 Bernardo Center Dr
San Diego CA 92128
858 485-9840

(P-11248)
BNC REAL ESTATE (PA)
Also Called: Nussbaum, Barry Company
990 Highland Dr Ste 203, Solana Beach
(92075-2427)
PHONE...............................858 481-3000
Barry Nussbaum, *President*
Richard Gelbart, *Senior VP*
EMP: 300
SQ FT: 900
SALES (est): 16.3MM **Privately Held**
WEB: www.bncrealestate.com
SIC: 6531 6799 Real estate managers;
real estate investors, except property operators

(P-11249)
BRADLEY MELISSA REAL ESTATE
851 Irwin St Ste 104, San Rafael
(94901-3343)
PHONE...............................415 459-1010
Melissa Bradley, *CEO*
Robert Bradley, *President*
Dan Bastien, *Broker*
Lee Hoskins, *Broker*
William Johnson, *Broker*
EMP: 100
SALES (est): 8.7MM **Privately Held**
SIC: 6531 Real estate brokers & agents

(P-11250)
BROSAMER & WALL LLC
1777 Oakland Blvd Ste 300, Walnut Creek
(94596-4063)
PHONE...............................925 932-7900
Charles Wall, *Mng Member*
Cynthia Lundquist, *Controller*

Robert Brosamer,
EMP: 50
SALES (est): 8.8MM **Privately Held**
SIC: 6531 8711 Rental agent, real estate; construction & civil engineering

(P-11251)
BRUNSWICK CORNER PARTNERSHIP
Also Called: Ray Stone
550 Howe Ave Ste 200, Sacramento
(95825-8339)
PHONE..................................916 649-7500
J Todd Stone, *Partner*
EMP: 50
SALES (est): 2.3MM **Privately Held**
SIC: 6531 Real estate agents & managers

(P-11252)
BUCHANAN STREET PARTNERS LP
3501 Jamboree Rd Ste 4200, Newport Beach (92660-2958)
PHONE..................................949 721-1414
Robert Brunswick, *CEO*
Timothy Ballard, *COO*
James Gill, *Vice Pres*
Kimberly Kanen, *Vice Pres*
Eric Snyder, *Principal*
EMP: 85
SALES (est): 4MM **Privately Held**
SIC: 6531 Real estate agents & managers

(P-11253)
BURKHIRE HAS A WAY HOME SERVC
Also Called: Prudential
16810 Ventura Blvd Fl 1, Encino
(91436-1778)
PHONE..................................818 501-4800
Kathy King, *Manager*
Bill Taylor, *Manager*
William T Taylor, *Asst Mgr*
EMP: 70 **EST:** 2000
SALES (est): 3MM **Privately Held**
WEB: www.homes2estates.net
SIC: 6531 Real estate agent, residential

(P-11254)
BURLEIGH POINT LTD (DH)
Also Called: Bbg
117 Waterworks Way, Irvine (92618-3110)
PHONE..................................949 428-3200
McNeil Seymour Fiske Jr, *CEO*
Ed Leasure, *President*
Paul Naude, *President*
Neil Fiske, *CEO*
Jeff Streader, *COO*
◆ **EMP:** 198
SQ FT: 80,000
SALES (est): 64.8MM **Publicly Held**
SIC: 6531 6513 Real estate agent, residential; residential hotel operation

(P-11255)
BUZZ OATES MANAGEMENT SERVICES
555 Capitol Mall Ste 900, Sacramento
(95814-4606)
PHONE..................................916 381-3843
Phil Oates, *Chairman*
Larry Allbaugh, *President*
Mike Stodden, *CFO*
Kimberly Chambers, *Vice Pres*
EMP: 50
SQ FT: 8,630
SALES (est): 5.2MM **Privately Held**
SIC: 6531 Real estate agent, commercial

(P-11256)
C B COAST NEWPORT PROPERTIES
Also Called: Coldwell Bnkr Rsdntial
840 Nwport Ctr Dr Ste 100, Newport Beach (92660)
PHONE..................................949 644-1600
Daniel F Bibb, *President*
Tom Queen, *Senior VP*
Gary Legrand, *VP Finance*
Edgar Reynoso, *Broker*
Cristi Ulrich, *Associate*
EMP: 100
SQ FT: 7,300

SALES (est): 3.8MM **Publicly Held**
WEB: www.cbestates.com
SIC: 6531 Real estate agent, residential; selling agent, real estate
HQ: Coldwell Banker Residential Real Estate
27271 Las Ramblas
Mission Viejo CA 92691
949 367-1800

(P-11257)
C C CONNECTION INC
Also Called: Re/Maxcc
2950 Buskirk Ave Ste 140, Walnut Creek
(94597-7773)
PHONE..................................925 937-0100
Robert Decker, *President*
Debbie Carter, *Treasurer*
Deborah Carter, *Manager*
EMP: 57
SQ FT: 4,200
SALES (est): 2.9MM **Privately Held**
WEB: www.re-pro.com
SIC: 6531 Real estate agent, residential

(P-11258)
C-21 SUPER STARS
Also Called: 21st Century Super Stars.
22342 Avenida Empresa, Rcho STA Marg
(92688-2140)
PHONE..................................949 389-1600
Phillip Romero, *Owner*
EMP: 90
SALES (est): 1.6MM **Privately Held**
SIC: 6531 Real estate agent, residential

(P-11259)
C21 PEAK
Also Called: Prellis Mortgage Company
11011 Balboa Blvd, Granada Hills
(91344-5008)
PHONE..................................818 363-1717
Ron Prechtl, *President*
Kathy Prechtl, *CFO*
Eric Oneil, *Maintence Staff*
Sarah McNeeley, *Maint Spvr*
Joey Trujillo, *Accounts Mgr*
EMP: 136
SQ FT: 7,400
SALES (est): 7.8MM **Privately Held**
WEB: www.c21allmoves.com
SIC: 6531 8741 Real estate agent, residential; management services

(P-11260)
CAL COAST FINANCIAL CORP (PA)
43801 Mssion Blvd Ste 201, Fremont
(94539)
PHONE..................................510 683-9850
Roger Bakshi, *CEO*
Naeem Wahab, *President*
Neeraj Datta, *Vice Pres*
Darron McCuller, *Office Mgr*
Jack Alexander, *Broker*
EMP: 75
SQ FT: 4,800
SALES (est): 4.8MM **Privately Held**
SIC: 6531 Real estate brokers & agents

(P-11261)
CALDWELL BANKER INC
Also Called: Coldwell Banker
40 Main St Ste E100, Vista (92083-5831)
PHONE..................................760 941-6888
Susan Anderson, *Office Mgr*
Jim Morrow, *President*
Polly A Savage, *Broker*
Travis Robbins, *Consultant*
Jim Delpy, *Real Est Agnt*
EMP: 80
SALES (est): 3.2MM **Privately Held**
SIC: 6531 Real estate agent, residential

(P-11262)
CALDWELL REALTY
14831 Whittier Blvd # 102, Whittier
(90605-1747)
PHONE..................................562 907-5655
Donald Caldwell, *Owner*
EMP: 60
SALES (est): 1.9MM **Privately Held**
SIC: 6531 Real estate agent, residential

(P-11263)
CALIFORNIA GOLDEN REALTY
26752 Calaroga Ave, Hayward
(94545-3505)
PHONE..................................408 822-6000
Renu Bhardwaj, *Principal*
Joel Gemmell, *General Mgr*
Igor Feoktistov, *Administration*
Yurek Gentry, *Technology*
George Koras, *Sales Staff*
EMP: 804
SALES (est): 34.7MM **Privately Held**
SIC: 6531 Real estate brokers & agents

(P-11264)
CANTAMAR PROPERTY MGT INC
Also Called: Meruelo Enterprises
9550 Firestone Blvd # 105, Downey
(90241-5560)
PHONE..................................562 862-4470
Alex Meruelo, *President*
EMP: 50
SALES (est): 3.4MM **Privately Held**
SIC: 6531 Real estate managers

(P-11265)
CARITAS MANAGEMENT CORPORATION
1358 Valencia St, San Francisco
(94110-3715)
PHONE..................................415 647-7191
Robert Zerrilla, *President*
EMP: 55
SQ FT: 3,000
SALES (est): 4.9MM
SALES (corp-wide): 29.4MM **Privately Held**
SIC: 6531 Real estate managers
PA: Mission Housing Development Corporation
474 Valencia St Ste 280
San Francisco CA 94103
415 864-6432

(P-11266)
CARLTON SENIOR LIVING
Also Called: Carlton Plaza of San Leandro
1000 E 14th St, San Leandro (94577-3787)
PHONE..................................510 636-0660
Harry Darrett, *Manager*
EMP: 65
SQ FT: 96,676
SALES (corp-wide): 29.6MM **Privately Held**
SIC: 6531 Real estate agents & managers
PA: Senior Carlton Living Inc
4005 Port Chicago Hwy # 120
Concord CA 94520
925 338-2434

(P-11267)
CARLTON SENIOR LIVING INC
6915 Elk Grove Blvd, Elk Grove
(95758-5526)
PHONE..................................916 714-2404
Kimberly Carlton, *Branch Mgr*
EMP: 50
SALES (corp-wide): 29.6MM **Privately Held**
SIC: 6531 Real estate managers
PA: Senior Carlton Living Inc
4005 Port Chicago Hwy # 120
Concord CA 94520
925 338-2434

(P-11268)
CARMEL PARTNERS INC (PA)
1000 Sansome St Fl 1, San Francisco
(94111-1342)
PHONE..................................415 273-2900
Ron Zeff, *CEO*
Quinn R Barton III, *Managing Prtnr*
Dan Garibaldi, *Managing Prtnr*
Mike Lahorgue, *President*
Dennis Markus, *CFO*
EMP: 120
SALES (est): 57.5MM **Privately Held**
WEB: www.carmelpartners.net
SIC: 6531 6519 Real estate agents & managers; real property lessors

(P-11269)
CARUSO MGT LTD A CAL LTD PRTNR
Also Called: Commons At Calabasas, The
101 The Grove Dr, Los Angeles
(90036-6221)
PHONE..................................323 900-8100
Rick Caruso, *Partner*
Peter Hayden, *President*
Carol Pacheco, *President*
David Williams, *Exec VP*
Brenda Heck, *Senior VP*
EMP: 100
SALES (est): 14.5MM **Privately Held**
SIC: 6531 Rental agent, real estate

(P-11270)
CASBN INVESTMENT INC
Also Called: RE Max Westlake Investments
345 Gellert Blvd Ste A, Daly City
(94015-2617)
PHONE..................................650 991-2800
Francis Ng, *President*
EMP: 60
SALES (est): 4.3MM **Privately Held**
SIC: 6531 6163 Real estate agent, residential; mortgage brokers arranging for loans, using money of others

(P-11271)
CASSIDY TRLY PROP MGT SN FRNCS
201 California St Ste 800, San Francisco
(94111-5002)
PHONE..................................415 781-8100
Mike Kamm, *CEO*
Todd Oliver, *Partner*
James Kovaleski, *Managing Prtnr*
Mark McNally, *Managing Prtnr*
Greg Moss, *Managing Prtnr*
EMP: 69 **EST:** 2010
SALES (est): 14MM
SALES (corp-wide): 5.7B **Privately Held**
SIC: 6531
HQ: Cushman & Wakefield, Inc.
225 W Wacker Dr Ste 3000
Chicago IL 60606
312 424-8000

(P-11272)
CB C&C PROPERTIES/COMM DI INC
2120 Churn Creek Rd, Redding
(96002-0738)
PHONE..................................530 221-7551
Steve Craft, *President*
EMP: 70
SALES (est): 1.6MM **Privately Held**
SIC: 6531 Real estate brokers & agents

(P-11273)
CB RICHARD ELLIS RE SVCS LLC
Also Called: Cbre Valuation and Advisory
355 S Grand Ave Ste 2700, Los Angeles
(90071-1596)
PHONE..................................213 613-3333
Cicily Dostalek, *Branch Mgr*
Val Achtemeier, *Exec VP*
Todd Millang, *Vice Pres*
Bob Morgan, *Vice Pres*
Bob Rosenthal, *Vice Pres*
EMP: 80
SALES (corp-wide): 14.2B **Publicly Held**
WEB: www.insigniafinancial.com
SIC: 6531 Real estate agent, commercial
HQ: Cb Richard Ellis Real Estate Services, Llc
200 Park Ave Fl 19
New York NY 10166
212 984-8000

(P-11274)
CBABR INC (PA)
Also Called: Coldwell Banker
31620 Rr Cyn Rd Ste A, Canyon Lake
(92587-9476)
PHONE..................................951 640-7056
Budge Huskey, *CEO*
Dennis M McCoy, *President*
Margaret McCoy, *Treasurer*
Jody Regus, *Vice Pres*
EMP: 73
SQ FT: 4,000

SALES (est): 3.7MM **Privately Held**
WEB: www.margaretmccoy.com
SIC: 6531 Real estate agent, residential

(P-11275)
CBRE INC
500 Capitol Mall Ste 2400, Sacramento
(95814-4752)
PHONE..................................916 446-6800
David Brennan, *Exec Dir*
Steven Smith, *Business Anlyst*
Anthony Burnett, *Asst Broker*
Angela Carlton, *Manager*
Kristy Gilger, *Manager*
EMP: 100
SALES (corp-wide): 14.2B **Publicly Held**
SIC: 6531 Real estate agent, commercial
HQ: Cbre, Inc.
　　400 S Hope St Ste 25
　　Los Angeles CA 90071
　　213 613-3333

(P-11276)
CBRE INC
2125 E Katella Ave # 100, Anaheim
(92806-6072)
P.O. Box 9410 (92812-7410)
PHONE..................................714 939-2100
Jeff Moore, *Branch Mgr*
EMP: 200
SALES (corp-wide): 14.2B **Publicly Held**
SIC: 6531 8742 Real estate agent, commercial; management consulting services
HQ: Cbre, Inc.
　　400 S Hope St Ste 25
　　Los Angeles CA 90071
　　213 613-3333

(P-11277)
CBRE INC
4900 Rivergrade Rd A110, Baldwin Park
(91706-1401)
PHONE..................................626 814-7900
Shashi Panat, *Manager*
EMP: 300
SALES (corp-wide): 14.2B **Publicly Held**
SIC: 6531 Real estate agent, commercial
HQ: Cbre, Inc.
　　400 S Hope St Ste 25
　　Los Angeles CA 90071
　　213 613-3333

(P-11278)
CBRE INC
15303 Ventura Blvd # 200, Van Nuys
(91403-3110)
PHONE..................................818 907-4600
Don Hudson, *Manager*
EMP: 60
SQ FT: 11,000
SALES (corp-wide): 14.2B **Publicly Held**
SIC: 6531 Real estate agent, commercial
HQ: Cbre, Inc.
　　400 S Hope St Ste 25
　　Los Angeles CA 90071
　　213 613-3333

(P-11279)
CBRE INC
225 W Santa Clara St # 1050, San Jose
(95113-1723)
PHONE..................................408 453-7400
Mark Schmidt, *Manager*
Brian Matteoni, *Vice Pres*
EMP: 100
SALES (corp-wide): 14.2B **Publicly Held**
SIC: 6531 Real estate agent, commercial
HQ: Cbre, Inc.
　　400 S Hope St Ste 25
　　Los Angeles CA 90071
　　213 613-3333

(P-11280)
CBRE INC
2221 Rosecrans Ave # 100, El Segundo
(90245-4931)
PHONE..................................310 363-4900
Myles Helm, *Director*
John Schumacher, *Exec VP*
Dean Haney, *Vice Pres*
Brian Held, *Vice Pres*
Ben Knight, *Vice Pres*
EMP: 175
SALES (corp-wide): 14.2B **Publicly Held**
SIC: 6531 Real estate agent, commercial

HQ: Cbre, Inc.
　　400 S Hope St Ste 25
　　Los Angeles CA 90071
　　213 613-3333

(P-11281)
CBRE INC
234 S Brand Blvd Ste 800, Glendale
(91204-1362)
PHONE..................................818 502-6700
David Josker, *Director*
EMP: 85
SALES (corp-wide): 14.2B **Publicly Held**
SIC: 6531 Real estate agent, commercial
HQ: Cbre, Inc.
　　400 S Hope St Ste 25
　　Los Angeles CA 90071
　　213 613-3333

(P-11282)
CBRE INC
Also Called: Cbre Capstone
1840 Century Park E # 900, Los Angeles
(90067-2110)
PHONE..................................310 550-2500
Jim Kruse, *Director*
Rocky Binswanger, *Vice Pres*
Adrienne Barr, *Sales Executive*
Nancy Jacobsen, *Receptionist*
Caitlin Hoffman, *Associate*
EMP: 90
SALES (corp-wide): 14.2B **Publicly Held**
SIC: 6531 Real estate agent, commercial
HQ: Cbre, Inc.
　　400 S Hope St Ste 25
　　Los Angeles CA 90071
　　213 613-3333

(P-11283)
CBRE INC
4365 Executive Dr # 1600, San Diego
(92121-2101)
PHONE..................................858 546-4600
John Frager, *Sales/Mktg Dir*
EMP: 160
SALES (corp-wide): 14.2B **Publicly Held**
SIC: 6531 Real estate agent, commercial
HQ: Cbre, Inc.
　　400 S Hope St Ste 25
　　Los Angeles CA 90071
　　213 613-3333

(P-11284)
CBRE INC
4141 Inland Empire Blvd # 100, Ontario
(91764-5025)
PHONE..................................909 418-2000
Joe Cesta, *Director*
David Consani, *Exec VP*
Cray Carlson, *Senior VP*
Kent Stalwick, *Senior VP*
Jason Chao, *Vice Pres*
EMP: 100
SALES (corp-wide): 14.2B **Publicly Held**
SIC: 6531 Real estate agent, commercial
HQ: Cbre, Inc.
　　400 S Hope St Ste 25
　　Los Angeles CA 90071
　　213 613-3333

(P-11285)
CBRE GROUP INC (PA)
400 S Hope St Ste 25, Los Angeles
(90071-2800)
PHONE..................................213 613-3333
Robert E Sulentic, *President*
Ray Wirta, *Ch of Bd*
Calvin W Frese Jr, *President*
Michael J Lafitte, *President*
Mike Lafitte, *CEO*
EMP: 250
SALES: 14.2B **Publicly Held**
WEB: www.cbrichardellis.com
SIC: 6531 6162 8742 Real estate agent,
commercial; real estate managers; appraiser, real estate; mortgage bankers;
real estate consultant

(P-11286)
CBSRR INC
Also Called: Coldwell Banker Sky Ridge Rlty
27206 Hwy 189, Blue Jay (92317)
P.O. Box 189, Lake Arrowhead (92352-0189)
PHONE..................................909 336-2131
Steve Keefe, *President*

Stephen Keefe, *President*
Jamie Keefe, *Vice Pres*
Joanne Johnson, *Sales Staff*
John Lorenz, *Associate*
EMP: 62
SALES (est): 4.8MM **Privately Held**
WEB: www.cbskyridge.com
SIC: 6531 Real estate agent, residential

(P-11287)
CEDAR MANAGEMENT LLC
Also Called: Cedar Signature
3233 Dnald Douglas Loop S, Santa Monica
(90405-3235)
P.O. Box 7484 (90406-7484)
PHONE..................................310 396-3100
Adam Pasori, *EMP: 80*
SQ FT: 10,000
SALES (est): 3.8MM **Privately Held**
SIC: 6531 Real estate managers

(P-11288)
CENTURY 21
301 Dickson Hill Rd Ste A, Fairfield
(94533-7203)
PHONE..................................707 429-2121
Linda Green, *President*
Laura Lee, *Vice Pres*
Susan Sheffer, *Manager*
Lauralee Ensign, *Real Est Agnt*
EMP: 50
SALES (est): 1.3MM **Privately Held**
SIC: 6531 Real estate agent, residential

(P-11289)
CENTURY 21 A BETTER SVC RLTY
8077 2nd St Fl Fl, Downey (90241)
PHONE..................................562 287-0230
David Sarinana, *President*
Nelson Sanchez, *Vice Pres*
EMP: 99
SALES (est): 2.1MM **Privately Held**
SIC: 6531 Real estate agent, residential

(P-11290)
CENTURY 21 ABLE INC
3202 Governor Dr Ste 100, San Diego
(92122-2939)
PHONE..................................858 450-2100
Tom Kumz, *President*
Geri Green, *Manager*
Melissa Pires, *Consultant*
Paulina Bretts, *Real Est Agnt*
EMP: 56
SALES (est): 1.7MM **Privately Held**
SIC: 6531 Real estate agent, residential

(P-11291)
CENTURY 21 ALPHA LLC
1630 W Campbell Ave Ste 1, Campbell
(95008-1500)
PHONE..................................408 369-2000
Ed Zimbrick, *Mng Member*
EMP: 89
SALES (est): 2.6MM **Privately Held**
WEB: www.century21alpha.com
SIC: 6531 Real estate agent, residential

(P-11292)
CENTURY 21 AMBER REALTY INC
21024 Wood Ave Apt A, Torrance
(90503-4143)
PHONE..................................310 625-4363
David Sheerin, *President*
EMP: 80
SALES (est): 3.5MM **Privately Held**
WEB: www.c21amber.com
SIC: 6531 Real estate agent, residential

(P-11293)
CENTURY 21 BEACHSIDE
6265 E 2nd St Ste 103, Long Beach
(90803-4613)
PHONE..................................562 430-2121
Ron Horn, *Principal*
Craig Smith, *Principal*
EMP: 71
SQ FT: 10,000
SALES (est): 1.8MM **Privately Held**
SIC: 6531 8611 Real estate agent, residential; business associations

(P-11294)
CENTURY 21 BEVERLYWOOD REALTY
2800 S Robertson Blvd, Los Angeles
(90034-2489)
PHONE..................................310 836-8321
Stanley Shaprio, *President*
Jerald Shapiro, *Vice Pres*
Sheryl Shaprio, *Vice Pres*
Nayeli Meza, *Opers Staff*
EMP: 55
SALES (est): 2.2MM **Privately Held**
SIC: 6531 7389 Real estate agent, residential; notary publics

(P-11295)
CENTURY 21 CREST
4005 Foothill Blvd, La Crescenta
(91214-1623)
PHONE..................................818 248-9100
Ray Mirzakhanian, *Owner*
EMP: 66
SALES (est): 1.1MM **Privately Held**
SIC: 6531 Real estate agent, residential
PA: E.A.M. Enterprises Inc.
　　4005 Foothill Blvd
　　La Crescenta CA 91214

(P-11296)
CENTURY 21 DSTNCTIVE PRPTS INC
Also Called: Century 21 Green Gable RE
1450 Ary Ln Ste A, Dixon (95620-4413)
PHONE..................................707 678-9211
Linda Green, *President*
EMP: 92
SQ FT: 2,200
SALES: 485K **Privately Held**
SIC: 6531 Real estate agent, residential

(P-11297)
CENTURY 21 EXCELLENCE
5207 Rosemead Blvd Ste 1, Pico Rivera
(90660-2734)
PHONE..................................562 948-4553
Manuel Davila, *Partner*
Mike Oycque, *Partner*
EMP: 50
SQ FT: 5,100
SALES (est): 2.6MM **Privately Held**
SIC: 6531 Real estate agent, residential

(P-11298)
CENTURY 21 EXCLUSIVE REALTORS
22831 Hawthorne Blvd, Torrance
(90505-3615)
PHONE..................................310 373-5252
EMP: 130 EST: 1998
SALES (est): 2.6MM **Privately Held**
SIC: 6531

(P-11299)
CENTURY 21 GOLDEN REALTY (PA)
482 N Rosemead Blvd, Pasadena
(91107-3000)
PHONE..................................626 797-6680
Carol Gharossian, *Administration*
Patrick Mc Ginley, *Executive*
Katheryn Henry, *Director*
EMP: 60
SALES (est): 3.2MM **Privately Held**
SIC: 6531 Real estate agent, residential

(P-11300)
CENTURY 21 HALEY & ASSOCIATES
699 Wshington Blvd Ste B5, Roseville
(95678)
PHONE..................................916 782-1500
James Haley, *President*
EMP: 72
SQ FT: 1,400
SALES: 1.9MM **Privately Held**
SIC: 6531 Real estate agent, residential

(P-11301)
CENTURY 21 HOME REALTORS (PA)
4110 Edison Ave Ste 210, Chino
(91710-8410)
PHONE..................................909 591-0158

Derek Wood, *President*
Amy Gaona, *Office Admin*
Candida Echeverria, *Broker*
EMP: 100
SQ FT: 11,000
SALES (est): 6MM **Privately Held**
SIC: 6531 Real estate agent, residential; escrow agent, real estate

(P-11302)
CENTURY 21 HOME REALTORS
Also Called: Century 21 King Realtors
8338 Day Creek Blvd # 101, Rancho Cucamonga (91739-9366)
P.O. Box 3424 (91729-3424)
PHONE...................................909 980-8000
Julio Cardenas, *Broker*
Alejandra Fernandez, *Admin Asst*
Andrew Espinoza, *Sales Mgr*
Carol Olivas, *Facilities Mgr*
EMP: 90 **Privately Held**
SIC: 6531 Real estate agent, residential
PA: Century 21 Home Realtors
4110 Edison Ave Ste 210
Chino CA 91710

(P-11303)
CENTURY 21 LANDMARK PROPERTIES
1650 Ximeno Ave Ste 120, Long Beach (90804-2179)
PHONE...................................562 422-0911
Fax: 562 428-1842
EMP: 50 **EST:** 1960
SALES (est): 2.3MM **Privately Held**
SIC: 6531

(P-11304)
CENTURY 21 LES RYAN REALTY (PA)
495 E Perkins St Ste A, Ukiah (95482-4573)
PHONE...................................707 468-0423
Les Ryan, *Owner*
EMP: 100
SALES (est): 4.7MM **Privately Held**
WEB: www.c21lesryan.com
SIC: 6531 6513 7011 Real estate agent, residential; apartment hotel operation; motels

(P-11305)
CENTURY 21 LES RYAN REALTY
1057 College Ave Ofc Ste, Santa Rosa (95404-4128)
PHONE...................................707 577-7777
Pat Provost, *Partner*
EMP: 75
SALES (corp-wide): 4.7MM **Privately Held**
WEB: www.c21lesryan.com
SIC: 6531 Real estate agent, residential
PA: Century 21 Les Ryan Realty
495 E Perkins St Ste A
Ukiah CA 95482
707 468-0423

(P-11306)
CENTURY 21 LUDECKE INC (PA)
34 E Foothill Blvd, Arcadia (91006-2305)
PHONE...................................626 445-0123
Michael W Ludecke, *President*
EMP: 100
SALES (est): 5.5MM **Privately Held**
WEB: www.c21ludecke.com
SIC: 6531 Real estate agent, residential

(P-11307)
CENTURY 21 MASTERS
480 W Rowland St Ste B, Covina (91723-2964)
PHONE...................................626 732-6184
Jody Fox, *Branch Mgr*
EMP: 52
SALES (corp-wide): 7.4MM **Privately Held**
SIC: 6531 Real estate agent, residential
PA: Century 21 Masters
1169 Fairway Dr Ste 100
Walnut CA 91789
909 595-6697

(P-11308)
CENTURY 21 SHOWCASE INC
7835 Church St, Highland (92346-4380)
PHONE...................................909 936-9334
Jeff Stoffel, *President*
EMP: 60
SALES (est): 2.9MM **Privately Held**
WEB: www.century21showcase.com
SIC: 6531 Real estate agent, residential

(P-11309)
CENTURY ADANALIAN & VASQUEZ
Also Called: Century 21
1415 W Shaw Ave, Fresno (93711-3608)
PHONE...................................559 244-6000
Bill Adanalian, *President*
Greg Vasquez, *Vice Pres*
Percy Saucedo, *Office Mgr*
Persival Saucedo, *Training Dir*
Connie T Colmenero, *Real Est Agnt*
EMP: 62
SQ FT: 4,250
SALES (est): 3.5MM **Privately Held**
SIC: 6531 Real estate agent, residential

(P-11310)
CENTURY PROPERTIES OWNERS ASSN
Also Called: Century, The
1 W Century Dr, Los Angeles (90067-3401)
PHONE...................................310 272-8580
Timothy Bowman, *Manager*
EMP: 50
SALES (est): 4.7MM **Privately Held**
SIC: 6531 Real estate agent, residential

(P-11311)
CH MARKET CENTER INC
Also Called: Keller Williams Realtors
4200 Chino Health Ste 325, Chino Hills (91709)
PHONE...................................909 628-9100
Nick Lanza, *President*
David Porchas, *President*
Suzi Moret, *Principal*
EMP: 75
SALES (est): 3.8MM **Privately Held**
SIC: 6531 Real estate agent, residential

(P-11312)
CHARLES DUNN CO INC
Also Called: Charles Dunn Raltor State Svcs
800 W 6th St Ste 800 # 800, Los Angeles (90017-2741)
PHONE...................................213 481-1800
Walter J Conn, *President*
Richard C Dunn, *President*
Eleanor B Dunn, *Vice Pres*
Joseph Dunn, *Admin Sec*
Matthew Dunn, *Assistant VP*
EMP: 200
SALES (est): 4.6MM **Privately Held**
SIC: 6531 Real estate brokers & agents

(P-11313)
CHARLES DUNN RE SVCS INC (PA)
800 W 6th St Ste 600, Los Angeles (90017-2709)
PHONE...................................213 270-6200
Walter Conn, *CEO*
Patrick Conn, *President*
EMP: 86
SQ FT: 30,000
SALES (est): 7.8MM **Privately Held**
WEB: www.charlesdunn.com
SIC: 6531 Real estate brokers & agents; real estate managers

(P-11314)
CHARTER REALTY GROUP INC (PA)
12400 Wilshire Blvd, Los Angeles (90025-1019)
PHONE...................................310 826-3174
Arnold L Porath, *President*
David Meltzer, *Vice Pres*
Paulette Gopaul, *District Mgr*
Carol Salomons, *Manager*
EMP: 80
SQ FT: 3,200
SALES (est): 8.5MM **Privately Held**
SIC: 6531 Rental agent, real estate

(P-11315)
CHILD DEVELOPMENT INCORPORATED
17341 Jacquelyn Ln, Huntington Beach (92647-5713)
PHONE...................................714 842-4064
EMP: 311
SALES (corp-wide): 28MM **Privately Held**
SIC: 6531 Real estate agents & managers
PA: Child Development Incorporated
350 Woodview Ave
Morgan Hill CA 95037
408 556-7300

(P-11316)
CHRISTIAN AND WAKEFIELD (PA)
Also Called: Burnham Real Estate
110 W A St Ste 900, San Diego (92101-3705)
P.O. Box 122910 (92112-2910)
PHONE...................................619 236-1555
Stath Karras, *President*
Mike Philbin, *Senior VP*
Jon Walz, *Senior VP*
EMP: 53
SQ FT: 22,000
SALES (est): 5.4MM **Privately Held**
SIC: 6531 Real estate brokers & agents

(P-11317)
CHRISTIAN CHURCH HOMES
Also Called: Westlake Christian Terrace - E
251 28th St, Oakland (94611-6063)
PHONE...................................510 893-2998
John Jordan, *Branch Mgr*
EMP: 219
SALES (corp-wide): 13.5MM **Privately Held**
SIC: 6531 Real estate agents & managers
PA: Christian Church Homes
303 Hegenberger Rd # 201
Oakland CA 94621
510 632-6712

(P-11318)
CIM GROUP LP (PA)
Also Called: Commercial Inv MGT Group
4700 Wilshire Blvd Ste 1, Los Angeles (90010-3854)
PHONE...................................323 860-4900
Avraham Shemesch, *Partner*
Eric P Rubenfeld, *Partner*
Chris Donohoe, *Vice Pres*
Jonathan Tao, *Investment Ofcr*
Macklin Turnrose, *Investment Ofcr*
EMP: 73
SALES (est): 238.1MM **Privately Held**
WEB: www.cimgroup.com
SIC: 6531 6798 6552 Real estate agent, commercial; real estate investment trusts; land subdividers & developers, commercial

(P-11319)
CITISCAPE PRPRTY MGT GROUP LLC
3450 3rd St Ste 1a, San Francisco (94124-1444)
PHONE...................................415 674-1440
Paul Mora, *Branch Mgr*
EMP: 64 **Privately Held**
SIC: 6531 Real estate managers
PA: Citiscape Property Management Group Llc
3450 3rd St Ste 1a
San Francisco CA 94124

(P-11320)
CITIVEST INC
4340 Von Karman Ave # 110, Newport Beach (92660-1201)
PHONE...................................949 474-0440
Dana Haynes, *President*
EMP: 90
SQ FT: 4,000
SALES (est): 10.4MM **Privately Held**
WEB: www.citivestinc.com
SIC: 6531 Real estate managers

(P-11321)
CLEARCAPITALCOM INC
10266 Truckee Airport Rd, Truckee (96161-3310)
PHONE...................................530 550-2500
Duane Andrews, *CEO*
Ronald Rowan, *CFO*
Becky Andrews, *Bd of Directors*
Kenon Chen, *Exec VP*
Beth Buell, *Vice Pres*
EMP: 140
SALES (corp-wide): 68.6MM **Privately Held**
SIC: 6531 Appraiser, real estate
PA: Clearcapital.Com, Inc.
300 E 2nd St Ste 1405
Reno NV 89501
775 470-5656

(P-11322)
CLEARCAPITALCOM INC
1410 Rocky Ridge Dr # 250, Roseville (95661-2811)
PHONE...................................530 582-5011
Duane Andrews, *CEO*
Joy He, *Technology*
Christopher Stobie, *Engineer*
EMP: 100
SALES (corp-wide): 76.2MM **Privately Held**
SIC: 6531 Real estate agents & managers
PA: Clearcapital.Com, Inc.
300 E 2nd St Ste 1405
Reno NV 89501
775 470-5656

(P-11323)
CLPF - SYCAMORE
6721 Sycamore Canyon Blvd, Riverside (92507-0751)
PHONE...................................212 883-2500
Stacey Magee, *Principal*
Kathy Handlon, *Principal*
EMP: 99
SALES (est): 950K **Privately Held**
SIC: 6531 Real estate agents & managers

(P-11324)
COAST TO COAST REALTY
Also Called: Century 21
18879 Brasilia Dr, Porter Ranch (91326-1919)
PHONE...................................818 360-2609
Debbie Abeyesinhe, *Owner*
EMP: 80
SALES (est): 2MM **Privately Held**
WEB: www.debbisellsthevalley.com
SIC: 6531 Real estate agent, residential

(P-11325)
COASTAL ALLIANCE HOLDINGS INC
Also Called: Coldwell Banker Coastl Aliance
1650 Ximeno Ave Ste 120, Long Beach (90804-2179)
PHONE...................................562 370-1000
Jack Irvin, *President*
EMP: 140
SALES (est): 6.6MM **Privately Held**
SIC: 6531 Real estate agent, residential

(P-11326)
COASTSIDE SENIOR HOUSING LIMIT
925 Main St, Half Moon Bay (94019-2379)
PHONE...................................415 355-7100
Jane Graf,
EMP: 50
SALES: 549K **Privately Held**
SIC: 6531 Real estate leasing & rentals

(P-11327)
COLDWELL BANKER
730 Alhambra Blvd Ste 150, Sacramento (95816-3885)
PHONE...................................916 447-5900
Michael Lippi, *Manager*
Malka Khan, *Office Admin*
Jeanine Roza, *Sales Associate*
Michael Onstead, *Director*
Wendi Reinl, *Manager*
EMP: 60
SALES (est): 2.6MM **Privately Held**
SIC: 6531 Real estate agent, residential

(P-11328)
COLDWELL BANKER
9332 Fuerte Dr, La Mesa (91941-4199)
PHONE..................................619 460-6600
Rick Hoffman, *President*
Martha A Price, *Broker*
Mike Habib, *Sales Executive*
Patricia Crisafulli, *Sales Staff*
Steve Wilson, *Manager*
EMP: 88
SQ FT: 4,000
SALES (est): 3.6MM **Privately Held**
SIC: 6531 Real estate agent, residential

(P-11329)
COLDWELL BANKER
740 Garden View Ct # 100, Encinitas
(92024-2474)
PHONE..................................760 753-5616
Jeff Hayes, *Manager*
Tatjana Jovanovic, *Asst Broker*
Lorie Brakas, *Sales Associate*
Grant Caldwell, *Sales Associate*
Karen Fields, *Sales Associate*
EMP: 75
SALES (est): 3.4MM **Privately Held**
SIC: 6531 Real estate agent, residential

(P-11330)
COLDWELL BANKER
1377 El Camino Real, Menlo Park
(94025-4210)
PHONE..................................650 324-4456
Chris Rafmussen, *Manager*
Regan Byers-Cinelli, *Asst Broker*
Beth Fishback, *Real Est Agnt*
Kelly Griggs, *Real Est Agnt*
Kim Hansen, *Real Est Agnt*
EMP: 80
SALES (est): 320.7K **Privately Held**
SIC: 6531 Real estate agent, residential

(P-11331)
COLDWELL BANKER
248 Main St Ste 200, Half Moon Bay
(94019-7120)
PHONE..................................650 726-1100
Greg Cowen, *Partner*
Stella Johnson, *Partner*
William Mahar, *Principal*
Rose Serdy, *Principal*
Marcia Kimball, *Real Est Agnt*
EMP: 50
SALES (est): 2.4MM **Privately Held**
SIC: 6531 Real estate agent, residential

(P-11332)
**COLDWELL BANKER
AFFILIATES**
161 S San Antonio Rd # 1, Los Altos
(94022-3031)
PHONE..................................650 941-7040
Fred Hibbard, *Manager*
Gary Van Zee, *Info Tech Mgr*
Carol Van Zee, *Manager*
Yuli Lyman, *Real Est Agnt*
EMP: 70
SQ FT: 9,000
SALES (est): 2.7MM **Privately Held**
SIC: 6531 Real estate agent, residential

(P-11333)
**COLDWELL BANKER AMARAL &
ASSOC**
3775 Main St Ste E, Oakley (94561-5793)
PHONE..................................925 439-7400
Arron Manwos, *Owner*
EMP: 65
SALES (est): 1.5MM **Privately Held**
SIC: 6531 Real estate agent, residential

(P-11334)
**COLDWELL BANKER HOME
SOURCE**
15500 W Sand St Ste 2, Victorville
(92392-2931)
PHONE..................................760 684-8100
Jason Lamoreaux, *Owner*
Chris Lamoreaux, *Owner*
EMP: 60
SALES (est): 1MM **Privately Held**
SIC: 6531 Real estate agent, residential

(P-11335)
**COLDWELL BANKER PREMIER
PRPTS**
1498 E Valley Rd, Santa Barbara
(93108-1241)
PHONE..................................805 565-2200
Chuck Farish, *President*
EMP: 70
SALES (est): 1.7MM **Privately Held**
WEB: www.betsyzwick.com
SIC: 6531 Real estate agent, residential

(P-11336)
**COLDWELL BANKER PROF
GROUP**
2860 Zanker Rd Ste 204, San Jose
(95134-2120)
PHONE..................................408 383-1044
Kathy Low, *Principal*
EMP: 90
SALES (est): 3MM **Privately Held**
WEB: www.kathylow.com
SIC: 6531 Real estate agent, residential

(P-11337)
**COLDWELL BANKER
PROPERTY SHOP**
727 W Ojai Ave, Ojai (93023-3726)
PHONE..................................805 646-7288
Dennis Guernsey, *President*
Larry Wilde Od, *Owner*
Erik Wilde, *Broker*
Sharon Maharry, *Real Est Agnt*
Christa Green, *Associate*
EMP: 60
SALES (est): 3.2MM **Privately Held**
WEB: www.ojaicoldwell.com
SIC: 6531 Real estate agent, residential

(P-11338)
COLDWELL BANKER RE CORP
15490 Ventura Blvd # 100, Sherman Oaks
(91403-3033)
PHONE..................................818 995-2424
Bill Dalton, *Branch Mgr*
Catherine Bess, *Broker*
Connie Harrison, *Broker*
Yolanda Thunderwolf, *Broker*
Lauren Tizabi, *Broker*
EMP: 60 **Publicly Held**
SIC: 6531 Real estate agent, residential
HQ: Coldwell Banker Real Estate Corporation
175 Park Ave
Madison NJ 07940
973 407-2000

(P-11339)
COLDWELL BANKER RE CORP
1000 Sunset Dr Ste 190, Roseville (95678)
PHONE..................................408 981-7200
Maxine Feil, *Manager*
EMP: 50 **Publicly Held**
WEB: www.coldwellbanker.com
SIC: 6531 Real estate agent, residential
HQ: Coldwell Banker Real Estate Corporation
175 Park Ave
Madison NJ 07940
973 407-2000

(P-11340)
COLDWELL BANKER RE CORP
501 W Redlands Blvd Ste A, Redlands
(92373-4642)
PHONE..................................909 792-4147
Sheila Cannon, *Owner*
Frank Faxon, *Manager*
Gloria Grochowski, *Manager*
Patricia Seymour, *Manager*
Peggy Wilcox, *Manager*
EMP: 50 **Publicly Held**
WEB: www.coldwellbanker.com
SIC: 6531 Real estate agent, residential
HQ: Coldwell Banker Real Estate Corporation
175 Park Ave
Madison NJ 07940
973 407-2000

(P-11341)
COLDWELL BANKER RE LLC
1045 Willow St, San Jose (95125-2346)
PHONE..................................408 491-1600
McKenzie Mckean, *Asst Broker*

Jess Flowers, *Broker*
Rachel Pham, *Broker*
Michael Uhri, *Broker*
Aleksey Astapenko, *Sales Associate*
EMP: 75
SALES (est): 39.9MM **Publicly Held**
SIC: 6531 Real estate agent, residential
PA: Realogy Holdings Corp.
175 Park Ave
Madison NJ 07940

(P-11342)
**COLDWELL BANKER
RESIDENTIAL RE (DH)**
27271 Las Ramblas, Mission Viejo
(92691-6392)
PHONE..................................949 367-1800
Robert Becker, *President*
Shawna Milanovic, *Graphic Designe*
Jan Palya, *Sales Staff*
EMP: 410
SQ FT: 6,000
SALES (est): 75.1MM **Publicly Held**
WEB: www.cbestates.com
SIC: 6531 Real estate agent, residential

(P-11343)
**COLDWELL BANKER
RESIDENTIAL RE**
15 E Foothill Blvd, Arcadia (91006-2399)
PHONE..................................626 445-5500
Jack Cooley, *Principal*
Cynthia Woo, *Office Mgr*
Brian Peralez, *Asst Broker*
Laura Mitchell-Davis, *Business Mgr*
Lisa Ta, *Broker*
EMP: 63
SALES (est): 3MM **Privately Held**
SIC: 6531 Real estate agent, residential

(P-11344)
**COLDWELL BANKER TOWN &
COUNTRY**
345 E Rowland St, Covina (91723-3153)
PHONE..................................626 966-3688
Norman Cox, *Manager*
Dewayne Sanders, *Broker*
Paul Lazo, *Sales Mgr*
EMP: 70
SQ FT: 7,000
SALES (est): 3.5MM **Privately Held**
WEB: www.cbtcsocal.com
SIC: 6531 Real estate agent, residential

(P-11345)
**COLDWELL BANKERS
RESIDENTIAL**
21060 Redwood Rd Ste 100, Castro Valley
(94546-5931)
PHONE..................................510 583-5400
Nelly Jagroop, *Manager*
Gregory Ricchini, *Broker*
Richard Dibona, *Consultant*
Leslie Drury, *Real Est Agnt*
Vanessa Klein, *Real Est Agnt*
EMP: 90
SALES (corp-wide): 4.5MM **Privately
Held**
WEB: www.laurarivera.com
SIC: 6531 Real estate agent, residential
PA: Coldwell Bankers Residential
604 Lindero Canyon Rd
Agoura Hills CA 91377
818 575-2660

(P-11346)
**COLDWELL BANKERS
RESIDENTIAL (PA)**
604 Lindero Canyon Rd, Agoura Hills
(91377-5455)
PHONE..................................818 575-2660
Irma Haldane, *Manager*
Randy Paller, *Admin Sec*
Beth Novak, *Real Est Agnt*
EMP: 104
SALES (est): 4.5MM **Privately Held**
WEB: www.sharonberman.com
SIC: 6531 Real estate agent, residential

(P-11347)
**COLDWELL BNKR FIRST CLASS
RLTY**
7825 Florence Ave A, Downey
(90240-3727)
PHONE..................................323 721-7430
Richard Estrada, *Manager*
Richard Estarda, *Manager*
EMP: 60
SALES (est): 2.3MM **Privately Held**
SIC: 6531 Real estate agent, residential

(P-11348)
**COLDWELL BNKR RESIDENTIAL
BRKG**
181 2nd Ave Ste 100, San Mateo
(94401-3830)
PHONE..................................650 558-6800
Eric Berggren, *Branch Mgr*
Bryant McFadyen, *Sales Associate*
Stacy Vollert, *Real Est Agnt*
Alexander Wilkas, *Associate*
EMP: 52 **Publicly Held**
SIC: 6531 Real estate agent, residential
HQ: Coldwell Banker Residential Brokerage
1855 Gateway Blvd Ste 750
Concord CA 94520
925 275-3000

(P-11349)
**COLDWELL BNKR RESIDENTIAL
BRKG**
500 Auburn Folsom Rd # 300, Auburn
(95603-5645)
PHONE..................................530 823-7653
Randi Greene, *Principal*
Charllis W Twilligear, *Real Est Agnt*
EMP: 52 **Publicly Held**
SIC: 6531 Real estate agent, residential
HQ: Coldwell Banker Residential Brokerage
1855 Gateway Blvd Ste 750
Concord CA 94520
925 275-3000

(P-11350)
**COLDWELL BNKR RESIDENTIAL
BRKG (DH)**
Also Called: Valley of California, Inc.
1855 Gateway Blvd Ste 750, Concord
(94520-3290)
PHONE..................................925 275-3000
Bruce G Zipf, *CEO*
Avram Goldman, *President*
Victoria Naidorf, *Vice Pres*
Melissa Huntsman, *Research*
Suzanne Chaix, *Mktg Coord*
EMP: 100
SALES (est): 19.3MM **Publicly Held**
WEB: www.cbnorcal.com
SIC: 6531 Real estate agent, residential

(P-11351)
**COLDWELL BNKR RESIDENTIAL
BRKG**
1427 Chapin Ave, Burlingame
(94010-4002)
PHONE..................................650 558-4200
Rachel Ni, *Branch Mgr*
Stephan Marshall, *Asst Broker*
Victor Zolezzi, *Asst Broker*
Maria Zamattia, *Broker*
Nick Corcoleotes, *Sales Associate*
EMP: 52 **Publicly Held**
SIC: 6531 Real estate agent, residential
HQ: Coldwell Banker Residential Brokerage
1855 Gateway Blvd Ste 750
Concord CA 94520
925 275-3000

(P-11352)
**COLDWELL BNKR RESIDENTIAL
BRKG**
2140 41st Ave Ste 100, Capitola
(95010-2067)
PHONE..................................831 462-9000
Spencer Hays, *Branch Mgr*
John Ribera, *Real Est Agnt*
EMP: 52 **Publicly Held**
SIC: 6531 Real estate agent, residential
HQ: Coldwell Banker Residential Brokerage
1855 Gateway Blvd Ste 750
Concord CA 94520
925 275-3000

(P-11353)
COLDWELL BNKR RESIDENTIAL BRKG
166 N Canon Dr Ste 200, Beverly Hills
(90210-5304)
PHONE....................310 273-3113
Betty Graham, *Manager*
Joyce Rey, *Asst Broker*
Katja Aronsson, *Broker*
Roni Heller, *Broker*
Joseph Reisman, *Broker*
EMP: 74 Publicly Held
WEB: www.bonnieo.com
SIC: 6531 Real estate agent, residential
HQ: Coldwell Banker Residential Brokerage
Company
27271 Las Ramblas
Mission Viejo CA 92691

(P-11354)
COLDWELL BNKR RESIDENTIAL BRKG
1801 Lombard St, San Francisco
(94123-2909)
PHONE....................415 447-8800
Mark Best, *Branch Mgr*
Jennifer Andary, *Broker*
Andrea Govoni, *Broker*
John Oloughlin, *Broker*
Marina Tsang, *Broker*
EMP: 52 Publicly Held
WEB: www.markbest.com
SIC: 6531 Real estate agent, residential
HQ: Coldwell Banker Residential Brokerage
1855 Gateway Blvd Ste 750
Concord CA 94520
925 275-3000

(P-11355)
COLDWELL BNKR RESIDENTIAL BRKG
1081 N Palm Canyon Dr, Palm Springs
(92262-4419)
PHONE....................760 325-4500
Thomas Ogle, *Branch Mgr*
Michael Paduano, *Broker*
EMP: 74 Publicly Held
WEB: www.bonnieo.com
SIC: 6531 Real estate agent, residential
HQ: Coldwell Banker Residential Brokerage
Company
27271 Las Ramblas
Mission Viejo CA 92691

(P-11356)
COLDWELL BNKR RESIDENTIAL BRKG
5034 Sunrise Blvd, Fair Oaks
(95628-4945)
PHONE....................916 966-8200
Donna Kopp, *Principal*
Mary Grebitus, *Asst Broker*
Terrence Murphy, *Broker*
Craig Diez, *Sales Associate*
Cathy Harman, *Property Mgr*
EMP: 52 Publicly Held
WEB: www.kathyfox.com
SIC: 6531 Real estate agent, residential
HQ: Coldwell Banker Residential Brokerage
1855 Gateway Blvd Ste 750
Concord CA 94520
925 275-3000

(P-11357)
COLDWELL BNKR RESIDENTIAL BRKG
21580 Yorba Linda Blvd, Yorba Linda
(92887-3748)
PHONE....................714 832-0020
Tom Iovenitti, *President*
John Israel, *Asst Broker*
Cheryl Ankeney, *Broker*
Kim Olson, *Broker*
Neicey Rustice, *Broker*
EMP: 50
SALES (est): 1.5MM Privately Held
SIC: 6531 Real estate agent, residential

(P-11358)
COLDWELL BNKR RESIDENTIAL BRKG
23647 Calabasas Rd, Calabasas
(91302-1502)
PHONE....................818 222-0023
Bill Dalton, *Manager*
Gregory McComb, *Asst Broker*
Denice Rice, *Broker*
Julie Bate, *Human Res Mgr*
Doug Arbetman, *Sales Associate*
EMP: 100 Publicly Held
WEB: www.bonnieo.com
SIC: 6531 Real estate agent, residential
HQ: Coldwell Banker Residential Brokerage
Company
27271 Las Ramblas
Mission Viejo CA 92691

(P-11359)
COLDWELL BNKR RESIDENTIAL BRKG
72605 Highway 111 Ste B2, Palm Desert
(92260-3392)
PHONE....................760 776-9898
Ron Gerlich, *Manager*
Carol Stephan, *Executive*
Cindy Guse, *Real Est Agnt*
Richard Ursem, *Real Est Agnt*
EMP: 100 Publicly Held
WEB: www.bonnieo.com
SIC: 6531 Real estate agent, residential
HQ: Coldwell Banker Residential Brokerage
Company
27271 Las Ramblas
Mission Viejo CA 92691

(P-11360)
COLDWELL BNKR RESIDENTIAL BRKG
45000 Club Dr, Indian Wells (92210-8856)
PHONE....................760 771-5454
Diane Busch, *Manager*
Jeffrey Fishbein, *Asst Broker*
Pamla Abramson, *Sales Associate*
Heather Smith, *Consultant*
Yvonne Roach, *Real Est Agnt*
EMP: 74 Publicly Held
WEB: www.bonnieo.com
SIC: 6531 Real estate agent, residential
HQ: Coldwell Banker Residential Brokerage
Company
27271 Las Ramblas
Mission Viejo CA 92691

(P-11361)
COLDWELL BNKR RESIDENTIAL BRKG
410 Sims Rd, Santa Cruz (95060-1326)
PHONE....................831 420-2628
EMP: 59 Privately Held
SIC: 6531 Real estate agent, residential
PA: Coldwell Banker Residential Brokerage
3 Parkway North Blvd # 400
Deerfield IL 60015

(P-11362)
COLDWELL BNKR RESIDENTIAL BRKG
3340 Walnut Ave Ste 110, Fremont
(94538-2215)
PHONE....................510 608-7600
Mitchell Grisso, *Technology*
Alex Cyriac, *Broker*
Paula Rasmussen, *Broker*
Josh Chen, *Sales Associate*
Michael Pinheiro, *Sales Associate*
EMP: 52 Publicly Held
SIC: 6531 Real estate agent, residential
HQ: Coldwell Banker Residential Brokerage
1855 Gateway Blvd Ste 750
Concord CA 94520
925 275-3000

(P-11363)
COLDWELL BNKR RSDENTIAL RE LLC
410 N Santa Cruz Ave, Los Gatos
(95030-5321)
PHONE....................408 355-1500
Karen Trolan, *Manager*
Felicia Whiteside, *Office Admin*
Rossana Marvin, *Broker*
Nathera Mawla, *Broker*
John Heringer, *Sales Associate*
EMP: 100 Publicly Held
SIC: 6531 Real estate agent, residential
HQ: Coldwell Banker Residential Real Estate Llc
6285 Barfield Rd Ste 100
Atlanta GA 30328
404 705-1500

(P-11364)
COLDWELL BNKR RSDNTIAL RE SVCS
4370 Town Center Blvd # 270, El Dorado Hills (95762-7140)
PHONE....................916 933-1155
Maxine Feil, *Branch Mgr*
Carrie Stinson, *Asst Broker*
Linda Bowers, *Broker*
Kathy Burk, *Sales Staff*
Larkin Bullard, *Real Est Agnt*
EMP: 65
SALES (corp-wide): 10.7MM Privately Held
SIC: 6531 Real estate agent, residential
PA: Coldwell Banker Residential Real Estate Services Inc
27271 Las Ramblas
Mission Viejo CA 92691
949 367-1800

(P-11365)
COLDWELL BNKR RSDNTIAL RE SVCS (PA)
27271 Las Ramblas, Mission Viejo
(92691-6392)
PHONE....................949 367-1800
Robert M Becker, *President*
Glynice Coleman, *President*
Gregory S Campbell, *Exec VP*
Robert J Arrigoni, *Senior VP*
Gregory Blackburn, *Vice Pres*
EMP: 75
SALES (est): 10.7MM Privately Held
WEB: www.mdeedy.com
SIC: 6531 Real estate agent, residential

(P-11366)
COLDWER BANKER PREVIEWS
Also Called: Coldwell Banker
9069 W Sunset Blvd # 100, West Hollywood (90069)
PHONE....................310 278-9470
Fran Hughes, *Manager*
Laurel Erickson, *Asst Broker*
Dana Williams, *Asst Broker*
Lauren Biedenharn, *Broker*
SOO Kim, *Broker*
EMP: 120
SALES (est): 2.8MM Privately Held
SIC: 6531 Real estate agent, residential

(P-11367)
COLLEGE PARK REALTY INC (PA)
Also Called: Re/Max
10791 Los Alamitos Blvd, Los Alamitos
(90720-2309)
PHONE....................562 594-6753
Barry Binder, *President*
Betty Binder, *Treasurer*
Carol Treadway, *Vice Pres*
Josh Jones, *Info Tech Dir*
Gay-Lynn Barnes, *Broker*
EMP: 146
SQ FT: 5,000
SALES (est): 9MM Privately Held
WEB: www.joannmurphy.com
SIC: 6531 Real estate agent, residential

(P-11368)
COLLEGE PARK REALTY INC
Also Called: Remax College Park Realty
2610 Los Coyotes Diagonal, Long Beach
(90815-1355)
PHONE....................562 982-0300
Marian Edwards, *Principal*
EMP: 50
SALES (corp-wide): 9MM Privately Held
WEB: www.joannmurphy.com
SIC: 6531 Real estate agents & managers

PA: College Park Realty Inc
10791 Los Alamitos Blvd
Los Alamitos CA 90720
562 594-6753

(P-11369)
COLLIERS INTERNATIONAL
101 2nd St Ste 1100, San Francisco
(94105-3652)
PHONE....................415 788-3100
Herbert Damner Jr, *Partner*
Alan Collenette, *Managing Dir*
Scott Harper, *Director*
EMP: 65
SALES (est): 7MM
SALES (corp-wide): 2.2B Privately Held
SIC: 6531 Real estate brokers & agents
HQ: Colliers International New England, Llc
160 Federal St Fl 11
Boston MA 02110
617 330-8000

(P-11370)
COLLIERS INTL PRPERTY CONS INC
4660 La Jolla Village Dr # 100, San Diego
(92122-4601)
PHONE....................858 455-1515
Tony Albin Senior, *Vice Pres*
EMP: 50
SALES (corp-wide): 2.2B Privately Held
SIC: 6531 Real estate agent, commercial
HQ: Colliers International Property Consultants Inc.
601 Union St Ste 3320
Seattle WA 98101
206 695-4200

(P-11371)
COLLIERS INTL PRPERTY CONS INC
301 University Ave # 100, Sacramento
(95825-5537)
PHONE....................916 929-5999
Randy Dixon, *Manager*
EMP: 100
SALES (corp-wide): 2.2B Privately Held
SIC: 6531 Real estate agent, commercial
HQ: Colliers International Property Consultants Inc.
601 Union St Ste 3320
Seattle WA 98101
206 695-4200

(P-11372)
COLLIERS PARRISH INTL INC
Also Called: Colliers Investment Services
450 W Santa Clara St, San Jose
(95113-1503)
PHONE....................408 282-3800
Mike Burke, *Manager*
Terry Healy, *Senior VP*
Marne Michaels, *Senior VP*
David Schmidt, *Senior VP*
David Buchholz, *Vice Pres*
EMP: 70
SALES (corp-wide): 20.6MM Privately Held
WEB: www.terraceaustin.com
SIC: 6531 Real estate agent, commercial
PA: Parrish Colliers International Inc
1 Almaden Blvd Ste 300
San Jose CA 95113
408 282-9799

(P-11373)
COLLIERS PARRISH INTL INC
1850 Mt Diablo Blvd # 200, Walnut Creek
(94596-4476)
PHONE....................925 279-1050
Edward Delbeccaro, *Manager*
Henry Englehardt, *Vice Pres*
Kevin Van Voorhis, *Plan/Corp Dev D*
Marie Turrin, *Admin Asst*
Terri Durkovic, *Opers Mgr*
EMP: 51
SALES (corp-wide): 20.6MM Privately Held
WEB: www.terraceaustin.com
SIC: 6531 Real estate brokers & agents
PA: Parrish Colliers International Inc
1 Almaden Blvd Ste 300
San Jose CA 95113
408 282-9799

PRODUCTS & SVCS

(P-11374)
COLONY MANAGEMENT INC
Also Called: Colony Advisors
1999 Ave Of The, Los Angeles (90067)
PHONE...................................310 282-8820
Thomas A Barrack, *CEO*
Mark Hedstrom, *CFO*
Michelle Nguyen, *Controller*
EMP: 75
SQ FT: 15,000
SALES (est): 4.7MM **Privately Held**
WEB: www.colonyinc.com
SIC: 6531 Real estate brokers & agents
PA: Colony Capital, Llc
2450 Broadway Ste 600
Santa Monica CA 90404

(P-11375)
COLONY NORTHSTAR INC
11601 Wilshire Blvd # 1600, Los Angeles (90025-0509)
PHONE...................................310 882-7230
Meiko Dixon, *Branch Mgr*
EMP: 77
SALES (corp-wide): 2.8B **Publicly Held**
SIC: 6531 Real estate managers
PA: Colony Capital, Inc.
515 S Flower St Fl 44
Los Angeles CA 90071
310 282-8820

(P-11376)
CONAM MANAGEMENT CORPORATION (PA)
3990 Ruffin Rd Ste 100, San Diego (92123-4805)
PHONE...................................858 614-7200
J Bradley Forrester, *CEO*
Robert Svatos, *CFO*
Daniel J Epstein, *Chairman*
Frazier Crawford, *Exec VP*
E Scott Dupree, *Senior VP*
EMP: 142
SQ FT: 45,634
SALES (est): 25.4MM **Privately Held**
SIC: 6531 Rental agent, real estate

(P-11377)
CONTINENTAL 155 5TH CORP
2041 Rosecrans Ave # 200, El Segundo (90245-4707)
PHONE...................................310 640-1520
Richard C Lundquist, *President*
Marcia Helfer, *Vice Pres*
EMP: 50
SALES (est): 1.4MM
SALES (corp-wide): 32.4MM **Privately Held**
WEB: www.continentaldevelopment.com
SIC: 6531 Real estate agent, commercial
PA: Continental Development Corporation
2041 Rosecrans Ave # 200
El Segundo CA 90245
310 640-1520

(P-11378)
COOK REALTY INC
Also Called: Cook Realty Sales
4305 Freeport Blvd, Sacramento (95822-2045)
PHONE...................................916 451-6702
Frank Cook, *President*
Barbara Cook, *Corp Secy*
Mark Warmack, *Office Mgr*
Atchan Vanpelt, *Sales Staff*
Ed Daniels, *Director*
EMP: 106
SALES (est): 5.7MM **Privately Held**
WEB: www.cookrealty.net
SIC: 6531 Real estate agent, residential; real estate brokers & agents

(P-11379)
CORE COMMUNICATIONS GROUP LLC
2749 Saturn St, Brea (92821-6705)
PHONE...................................714 729-8404
Arnold Valencia,
John Koos,
EMP: 58 EST: 2005
SALES (est): 5.3MM **Privately Held**
SIC: 6531 Real estate agents & managers

(P-11380)
CORE REALTY HOLDINGS MGT INC
Also Called: Crh Management
1600 Dove St Ste 450, Newport Beach (92660-2447)
PHONE...................................949 863-1031
Dougless Morehead, *CEO*
Marc Raskulinecz, *Senior VP*
David Kish, *Regional Mgr*
Alexandra Jernigan, *Admin Asst*
Erin Khamis, *Training Dir*
EMP: 99
SALES (est): 4.9MM **Privately Held**
SIC: 6531 Real estate managers

(P-11381)
CORELOGIC INC
201 Spear St Fl 4, San Francisco (94105-1669)
PHONE...................................714 250-6400
EMP: 50
SALES (corp-wide): 1.8B **Publicly Held**
SIC: 6531
PA: Corelogic, Inc.
40 Pacifica Ste 900
Irvine CA 92618
949 214-1000

(P-11382)
CORELOGIC INC
40 Pacifica Ste 900, Irvine (92618-7487)
PHONE...................................714 250-6400
EMP: 50
SALES (corp-wide): 1.8B **Publicly Held**
SIC: 6531
PA: Corelogic, Inc.
40 Pacifica Ste 900
Irvine CA 92618
949 214-1000

(P-11383)
CORINTHIAN REALTY LLC
3902 Smith St, Union City (94587-2616)
PHONE...................................510 487-8653
EMP: 60
SALES (est): 2.5MM **Privately Held**
SIC: 6531

(P-11384)
CORLAND COMPANIES (PA)
Also Called: Carlson
17542 17th St Ste 420, Tustin (92780-7928)
P.O. Box 807 (92781-0807)
PHONE...................................714 573-7780
Chis Hide, *President*
Patrick Galentine, *Vice Pres*
EMP: 60
SALES (est): 4.6MM **Privately Held**
SIC: 6531 Real estate managers

(P-11385)
CORONADO FINANCIAL CORP
Also Called: Prudential
940 Eastlake Pkwy, Chula Vista (91914-3558)
PHONE...................................619 946-1900
Corey Shepard, *President*
Jolene Shepard, *Treasurer*
EMP: 50
SQ FT: 10,000
SALES (est): 3.5MM **Privately Held**
SIC: 6531 Real estate agent, residential

(P-11386)
COSTAR GROUP INC
8910 University Center Ln # 300, San Diego (92122-1029)
PHONE...................................858 458-4900
Todd Thelen, *Manager*
Mike Burbach, *Vice Pres*
Laura Blumenauer, *Executive*
Martine Baechtel, *QA Dir*
Victor Marrero, *Web Dvlpr*
EMP: 230
SALES (corp-wide): 965.2MM **Publicly Held**
WEB: www.costar.com
SIC: 6531 Real estate agent, commercial
PA: Costar Group, Inc.
1331 L St Nw Ste 2
Washington DC 20005
202 346-6500

(P-11387)
COVELO INDIAN COMMUNITY CENTER
Also Called: C I C C
Hwy 162, Covelo (95428)
PHONE...................................707 983-8478
Otis Botherton, *Administration*
EMP: 100
SALES (est): 3MM **Privately Held**
SIC: 6531 Real estate agents & managers

(P-11388)
CROCKER GROUP LLC
1101 E Orangewood Ave, Anaheim (92805-6827)
PHONE...................................714 221-5621
Peter Barker, *Principal*
EMP: 75
SALES (est): 1.2MM **Privately Held**
SIC: 6531 Real estate agent, residential

(P-11389)
CUSHMAN & WAKEFIELD INC
Also Called: Terranomics
1350 Bayshore Hwy Ste 900, Burlingame (94010-1818)
PHONE...................................650 347-3700
Sheryl Simpson, *Branch Mgr*
John Brackett, *Partner*
Tom Christian, *Partner*
Staci E Cole, *Partner*
Jamie D'Alessandro, *Partner*
EMP: 50
SALES (corp-wide): 5.7B **Privately Held**
SIC: 6531 8742 Real estate leasing & rentals; real estate consultant
HQ: Cushman & Wakefield, Inc.
225 W Wacker Dr Ste 3000
Chicago IL 60606
312 424-8000

(P-11390)
CUSHMAN & WAKEFIELD CAL INC (DH)
1 Maritime Plz Ste 900, San Francisco (94111-3412)
PHONE...................................408 275-6730
Joseph Stettinius Jr, *CEO*
Randy Borron, *President*
Robert Alperin, *Vice Pres*
Jon Herman, *Managing Dir*
Don Morris, *Managing Dir*
EMP: 110 EST: 1887
SQ FT: 26,500
SALES (est): 309.2MM
SALES (corp-wide): 5.7B **Privately Held**
WEB: www.cushwake-nb.com
SIC: 6531 Real estate brokers & agents; real estate agent, commercial; real estate managers; appraiser, real estate
HQ: Cushman & Wakefield, Inc.
225 W Wacker Dr Ste 3000
Chicago IL 60606
312 424-8000

(P-11391)
CUSHMAN & WAKEFIELD CAL INC
18111 Von Karman Ave # 1000, Irvine (92612-7101)
PHONE...................................949 474-4004
Dee Shipley, *Sales/Mktg Mgr*
EMP: 50
SALES (corp-wide): 5.7B **Privately Held**
WEB: www.cushwake-nb.com
SIC: 6531 Real estate brokers & agents
HQ: Cushman & Wakefield Of California, Inc.
1 Maritime Plz Ste 900
San Francisco CA 94111
408 275-6730

(P-11392)
CWS APARTMENT HOMES LLC (PA)
Also Called: Cws Capital Partners
14 Corporate Plaza Dr # 210, Newport Beach (92660-7928)
PHONE...................................949 640-4200
Gary Carmell,
Steven J Sherwood,
EMP: 450 EST: 1998
SQ FT: 5,000
SALES (est): 30.3MM **Privately Held**
WEB: www.cwsapartments.com
SIC: 6531 Rental agent, real estate

(P-11393)
DAVID LYNG & ASSOCIATES INC
Also Called: America Dream Realty
1041 41st Ave Ste A, Santa Cruz (95062-4466)
PHONE...................................831 429-5700
Don Berig, *Owner*
Don Gerig, *Financial Exec*
EMP: 85
SALES (corp-wide): 6.2MM **Privately Held**
SIC: 6531 Real estate agent, residential
PA: David Lyng & Associates Inc
1041 41st Ave
Santa Cruz CA 95062
831 476-0100

(P-11394)
DAVID N SCHULTZ INC (PA)
715 N Central Ave Ste 300, Glendale (91203-4250)
PHONE...................................818 240-1070
David N Schultz, *President*
Jennifer Bertolet, *Senior VP*
Marvin Medows, *Vice Pres*
EMP: 155 EST: 1975
SQ FT: 15,744
SALES (est): 12.2MM **Privately Held**
SIC: 6531 Real estate agent, commercial; real estate managers

(P-11395)
DAYMARK REALTY ADVISORS INC
Also Called: Daymark Properties Realty
750 B St Ste 2620, San Diego (92101-8172)
P.O. Box 7369, Newport Beach (92658-7369)
PHONE...................................714 975-2999
Todd A Mikles, *CEO*
EMP: 400
SALES (est): 25.4MM **Privately Held**
SIC: 6531 Real estate brokers & agents

(P-11396)
DEAN GOODMAN INC
10833 Valley View St # 240, Cypress (90630-5046)
PHONE...................................714 229-8999
Candice H Miller, *President*
Amber Henson, *Admin Mgr*
Ray Pelaez, *Dean*
Adriana Soto, *Dean*
Mon Guadagno, *Manager*
EMP: 55
SALES (est): 4.8MM **Privately Held**
WEB: www.goodmandean.com
SIC: 6531 Appraiser, real estate

(P-11397)
DENOVA HOME SALES INC
Also Called: Denova Homes
1500 Willow Pass Ct, Concord (94520-1009)
PHONE...................................925 852-0545
David Sanson, *President*
Lori Sanson, *Vice Pres*
Joel Crawford, *Finance*
Mark Goode, *Sales Staff*
Linda Nelson-Gillis, *Sales Staff*
EMP: 84
SQ FT: 1,850
SALES (est): 9.3MM **Privately Held**
WEB: www.denovahomes.com
SIC: 6531 Real estate brokers & agents

(P-11398)
DESERT RESORT MANAGEMENT
42635 Melanie Pl Ste 103, Palm Desert (92211-9113)
PHONE...................................760 831-0172
Mark Dodge, *President*
EMP: 52
SQ FT: 11,000
SALES (est): 5.3MM **Privately Held**
SIC: 6531 Condominium manager; real estate managers

(P-11399)
DIABLO REALTY INC
Also Called: Pacific Mortgage Resources
975 Ygnacio Valley Rd, Walnut Creek
(94596-3825)
PHONE...............................925 933-9300
Linda Jean Anderson, *President*
Moses Guillory, *Corp Secy*
EMP: 50
SQ FT: 7,000
SALES (est): 3.5MM **Privately Held**
WEB: www.diablorealty.com
SIC: 6531 6163 Real estate brokers &
agents; mortgage brokers arranging for
loans, using money of others

(P-11400)
DIEZ & LEIS RE GROUP INC
Also Called: Prudential Norcal Realty
5120 Manzanita Ave # 120, Carmichael
(95608-0558)
PHONE...............................916 487-4287
Ron Leis, *President*
EMP: 60
SQ FT: 10,000
SALES (est): 3MM
SALES (corp-wide): 59.6B **Publicly Held**
SIC: 6531 Real estate agent, residential
HQ: Brer Affiliates Llc
18500 Von Karman Ave # 400
Irvine CA 92612
949 794-7900

(P-11401)
DILBECK INC (PA)
Also Called: Dilbeck Realtors
1030 Foothill Blvd, La Canada
(91011-3285)
PHONE...............................818 790-6774
Mark Dilbeck, *Ch of Bd*
Bruce Dilbeck, *Admin Sec*
Jennifer C Kim, *Broker*
Julie Mahoney, *Broker*
EMP: 70
SQ FT: 9,000
SALES (est): 6.6MM **Privately Held**
WEB: www.lacanadarealestate.com
SIC: 6531 Real estate agent, commercial;
real estate managers

(P-11402)
DILBECK INC
2943 Foothill Blvd, La Crescenta
(91214-3412)
PHONE...............................818 248-2248
Susan Lindsey, *Branch Mgr*
EMP: 80
SALES (corp-wide): 6.6MM **Privately
Held**
WEB: www.lacanadarealestate.com
SIC: 6531 Real estate agent, commercial
PA: Dilbeck Inc.
1030 Foothill Blvd
La Canada CA 91011
818 790-6774

(P-11403)
DILBECK INC
Also Called: Dilbeck Realtors
850 Hampshire Rd Ste A, Westlake Village
(91361-2800)
PHONE...............................805 379-1880
Chuck Lech, *Branch Mgr*
Kerri Dunton, *Real Est Agnt*
Charone Gilmore, *Real Est Agnt*
Judi Irwin, *Real Est Agnt*
Diane R Kane, *Real Est Agnt*
EMP: 50
SALES (corp-wide): 6.6MM **Privately
Held**
WEB: www.lacanadarealestate.com
SIC: 6531 Real estate agent, commercial;
real estate managers
PA: Dilbeck Inc.
1030 Foothill Blvd
La Canada CA 91011
818 790-6774

(P-11404)
DILBECK INC
Also Called: Dilbeck Realtors
225 E Colorado Blvd, Pasadena
(91101-1903)
PHONE...............................626 584-0101
Ray Hayes, *Manager*
EMP: 60

SALES (corp-wide): 6.6MM **Privately
Held**
WEB: www.lacanadarealestate.com
SIC: 6531 Real estate agent, commercial
PA: Dilbeck Inc.
1030 Foothill Blvd
La Canada CA 91011
818 790-6774

(P-11405)
**DONAHUE SCHRBER RLTY
GROUP INC (PA)**
200 Baker St Ste 100, Costa Mesa
(92626-4551)
PHONE...............................714 545-1400
Thomas Schriber, *Ch of Bd*
Patrick S Donahue, *President*
Larry Casey, *CFO*
EMP: 80
SQ FT: 20,000
SALES (est): 11.3MM **Privately Held**
WEB: www.montebellotowncenter.com
SIC: 6531 Real estate agent, commercial

(P-11406)
**DOUG ARNOLD REAL ESTATE
INC (PA)**
Also Called: Coldwell Banker
505 2nd St, Davis (95616-4618)
PHONE...............................530 758-3080
Doug Arnold, *President*
J David Taoramino, *Treasurer*
EMP: 50
SQ FT: 7,000
SALES (est): 4.4MM **Privately Held**
WEB: www.coldwellbankerdougarnold.com
SIC: 6531 Real estate agent, residential

(P-11407)
**DOUGLAS ELLIMAN REAL
ESTATE**
150 El Camino Dr, Beverly Hills
(90212-2733)
PHONE...............................310 595-3888
Collin Keanan, *General Mgr*
Stephen Kotler, *President*
EMP: 50
SALES (est): 498.6K **Privately Held**
SIC: 6531 Real estate agents & managers

(P-11408)
**DOUGLAS EMMETT REALTY
FUND 199**
808 Wilshire Blvd Ste 200, Santa Monica
(90401-1889)
PHONE...............................310 255-7700
Dan Emmett, *Principal*
EMP: 60
SALES (est): 1.4MM
SALES (corp-wide): 812MM **Privately
Held**
SIC: 6531 Real estate brokers & agents
PA: Douglas Emmett, Inc.
808 Wilshire Blvd Ste 200
Santa Monica CA 90401
310 255-7700

(P-11409)
DPPM INC
Also Called: Zephyr Real Estate
4040 24th St, San Francisco (94114-3716)
PHONE...............................415 695-7707
Fax: 415 695-1106
EMP: 80
SALES (corp-wide): 16.4MM **Privately
Held**
SIC: 6531
PA: Dppm, Inc.
850 7th St
San Francisco CA 94127
415 348-1212

(P-11410)
DREAM HOME ESTATES INC
2901 W Coast Hwy Ste 200, Newport
Beach (92663-4045)
PHONE...............................949 415-4646
David Prewitt, *CEO*
EMP: 50
SALES (est): 993K **Privately Held**
SIC: 6531 6799 8742 Selling agent, real
estate; real estate investors, except prop-
erty operators; real estate consultant

(P-11411)
**DUNLAP PROPERTY GROUP
INC**
801 E Chapman Ave Ste 233, Fullerton
(92831-3847)
P.O. Box 4308 (92834-4308)
PHONE...............................714 879-0111
Paul Dunlap, *President*
EMP: 55
SALES (est): 2.6MM **Privately Held**
SIC: 6531 Appraiser, real estate

(P-11412)
DYNAMIC REALTY CORP
800 S Barranca Ave # 260, Covina
(91723-3625)
PHONE...............................626 931-3200
Henry Melandez, *President*
EMP: 70
SALES (est): 2.2MM **Privately Held**
SIC: 6531 Real estate brokers & agents

(P-11413)
E-N REALTY II
Also Called: Century 21 E
1081 Grand Ave, Diamond Bar
(91765-2210)
PHONE...............................909 597-1736
John Newe, *President*
EMP: 50
SALES (est): 2.1MM **Privately Held**
SIC: 6531 Real estate agent, residential

(P-11414)
EAM ENTERPRISES INC (PA)
Also Called: Crest R E O & Relocation
4005 Foothill Blvd, La Crescenta
(91214-1623)
PHONE...............................818 248-9100
Razmik Mirzakhanian, *CEO*
EMP: 270
SQ FT: 5,000
SALES (est): 15.4MM **Privately Held**
SIC: 6531 Real estate agent, residential

(P-11415)
EAPPRAISEIT LLC (PA)
12395 First American Way, Poway
(92064-6897)
PHONE...............................800 281-6200
Anthony Merlo,
Rose Lusk, *Vice Pres*
Anna Rojas, *Executive*
Devid Feildman, *Principal*
Diane Swanson, *Director*
EMP: 65
SALES (est): 4.6MM **Privately Held**
WEB: www.eappraiseit.com
SIC: 6531 Appraiser, real estate

(P-11416)
**EAST CRSON II HSING
PRTNERS LP**
401 W Carson St, Carson (90745-2616)
PHONE...............................310 522-9606
Jim Brooks, *Controller*
EMP: 99
SALES (est): 1.8MM **Privately Held**
SIC: 6531 Real estate agents & managers

(P-11417)
**EDEN HOUSING MANAGEMENT
INC (PA)**
22645 Grand St, Hayward (94541-5031)
PHONE...............................510 582-1460
Linda Mandolini, *President*
Jan Peters, *COO*
Tony MA, *CFO*
Tracy Griffin, *Human Res Mgr*
Brian Gordon, *Property Mgr*
EMP: 50
SALES (est): 3.2MM **Privately Held**
SIC: 6531 Real estate managers

(P-11418)
ELIZABETH LARSON
3736 Jackson St, San Francisco
(94118-1609)
PHONE...............................415 409-7300
Elizabeth Larson, *Owner*
EMP: 60
SALES (est): 1.3MM **Privately Held**
WEB: www.elarsonphoto.com
SIC: 6531 Auction, real estate

(P-11419)
EMPIRE ESTATES INC
Also Called: Prudential
10750 Civic Center Dr # 100, Rancho Cu-
camonga (91730-3891)
PHONE...............................909 980-3100
Kim Senecal, *President*
EMP: 100
SQ FT: 4,500
SALES (est): 6.6MM **Privately Held**
WEB: www.kimsenecal.com
SIC: 6531 Real estate agent, residential

(P-11420)
**EMPIRE REALTY ASSOCIATES
INC**
380 Diablo Rd, Danville (94526-3468)
PHONE...............................925 217-5000
Judi Keenholtz, *CEO*
Brian Moggan, *General Mgr*
Dennis Burow, *Real Est Agnt*
Jennifer Hatter, *Real Est Agnt*
Jeanie Hess, *Real Est Agnt*
EMP: 60
SALES (est): 5.5MM **Privately Held**
WEB: www.empirera.com
SIC: 6531 Real estate agent, residential
PA: Pacific Union International, Inc.
1 Letterman Dr Bldg C
San Francisco CA 94129

(P-11421)
ERA REALTY CENTER
49 Placerville Dr, Placerville (95667-3901)
PHONE...............................530 295-2900
Dan Jacuzzi, *Owner*
Linda Capone, *Real Est Agnt*
EMP: 60
SALES (est): 2MM **Privately Held**
SIC: 6531 Real estate agent, residential

(P-11422)
ESSEX PROPERTIES LLC
18012 Sky Park Cir # 200, Irvine
(92614-6671)
PHONE...............................949 798-8100
Jim Niger, *President*
Burrel D Magnusson, *Chairman*
Linda Webber, *Vice Pres*
Trish Carlson, *Admin Asst*
Cindy Santos, *Admin Asst*
EMP: 75
SALES (est): 6.3MM **Privately Held**
SIC: 6531 Real estate agent, commercial

(P-11423)
EVANS/SIPES INC (PA)
Also Called: Re/Max
5720 Ralston St Ste 100, Ventura
(93003-7845)
PHONE...............................805 644-1242
Glenn Sipes, *President*
Jerry Beebe, *CFO*
Michael Sipes, *Vice Pres*
Krista Gaumer-Nowak, *Broker*
Gabriela Sandoval, *Consultant*
EMP: 250
SQ FT: 35,000
SALES (est): 19MM **Privately Held**
WEB: www.cynthialoughman.com
SIC: 6531 Real estate agent, residential

(P-11424)
EVOQ PROPERTIES INC
1318 E 7th St Ste 200, Los Angeles
(90021-1128)
PHONE...............................213 988-8890
Martin Caveroy, *CEO*
John Charles Maddux, *President*
Andrew Murray, *CFO*
Miguel Enrique Echemendia, *Officer*
Lynn Beckemeyer, *Exec VP*
EMP: 82
SALES (est): 6.4MM **Privately Held**
WEB: www.meruelomaddux.com
SIC: 6531 Real estate agent, commercial;
real estate agent, residential

P
R
O
D
U
C
T
S

&

S
V
C
S

(P-11425)
EXCELLNCE OF INLAND EMPIRE INC
Also Called: Century 21
9568 Archibald Ave 110, Rancho Cucamonga (91730-5710)
PHONE..................................909 758-4311
Ramiro Majia, President
Luis Oliver, CFO
EMP: 106
SQ FT: 8,874
SALES: 3.5MM Privately Held
SIC: 6531 7389 Real estate agent, residential; brokers' services

(P-11426)
EXPREAL INC
Also Called: Century 21 Experience
7168 Archibald Ave # 100, Alta Loma (91701-5061)
PHONE..................................909 373-4400
Peter Gottuso, Vice Pres
EMP: 99
SALES: 950K Privately Held
SIC: 6531 Real estate agent, residential

(P-11427)
F M TARBELL CO
18295 Collier Ave, Lake Elsinore (92530-2755)
PHONE..................................951 471-5333
Carol Rounsley, Manager
EMP: 70
SALES (corp-wide): 132.1MM Privately Held
SIC: 6531 Real estate agent, commercial
HQ: F. M. Tarbell Co
    1403 N Tustin Ave Ste 380
    Santa Ana CA 92705
    714 972-0988

(P-11428)
F M TARBELL CO
Also Called: Tarbel Realtors
39028 Winchester Rd # 101, Murrieta (92563-3505)
PHONE..................................951 677-3565
Joe McAllen, General Mgr
EMP: 80
SALES (corp-wide): 132.1MM Privately Held
SIC: 6531 Real estate agent, commercial
HQ: F. M. Tarbell Co
    1403 N Tustin Ave Ste 380
    Santa Ana CA 92705
    714 972-0988

(P-11429)
F M TARBELL CO
Also Called: Tarbell Realtors
321 S State College Blvd, Anaheim (92806-4118)
PHONE..................................714 772-8990
Fax: 714 772-3801
EMP: 55
SALES (corp-wide): 134.2MM Privately Held
SIC: 6531
HQ: F. M. Tarbell Co
    1403 N Tustin Ave Ste 380
    Santa Ana CA 92705
    714 972-0988

(P-11430)
F M TARBELL CO
Also Called: Tarbell Realtors
6396 E Santa Ana Cyn Rd, Anaheim (92807-2365)
PHONE..................................714 637-7240
Mercedes Sedano, Manager
EMP: 50
SALES (corp-wide): 132.1MM Privately Held
WEB: www.tarbell.com
SIC: 6531 Real estate brokers & agents
HQ: F. M. Tarbell Co
    1403 N Tustin Ave Ste 380
    Santa Ana CA 92705
    714 972-0988

(P-11431)
F M TARBELL CO (HQ)
Also Called: Tarbell Realtors
1403 N Tustin Ave Ste 380, Santa Ana (92705-8691)
PHONE..................................714 972-0988
Tina Jimov, President
Donald M Tarbell, CEO
Brenda Aguilar, Real Est Agnt
Adam Cervantes, Real Est Agnt
Eva De Fuente, Real Est Agnt
EMP: 110
SQ FT: 60,000
SALES (est): 24.1MM
SALES (corp-wide): 132.1MM Privately Held
WEB: www.tarbell.com
SIC: 6531 Real estate agent, residential
PA: Tarbell Financial Corporation
    1403 N Tustin Ave Ste 380
    Santa Ana CA 92705
    714 972-0988

(P-11432)
F M TARBELL CO
Also Called: Tarbell Realtors
315 Magnolia Ave, Corona (92879-3300)
PHONE..................................951 280-6040
Danny Vallejo, Manager
EMP: 190
SALES (corp-wide): 132.1MM Privately Held
WEB: www.tarbell.com
SIC: 6531 Real estate brokers & agents
HQ: F. M. Tarbell Co
    1403 N Tustin Ave Ste 380
    Santa Ana CA 92705
    714 972-0988

(P-11433)
F M TARBELL CO
Also Called: Tarbell Realtors
25201 La Paz Rd, Laguna Hills (92653-5118)
PHONE..................................949 830-6030
Dianne Montgomery, Manager
EMP: 62
SQ FT: 10,325
SALES (corp-wide): 132.1MM Privately Held
WEB: www.tarbell.com
SIC: 6531 Real estate agent, commercial
HQ: F. M. Tarbell Co
    1403 N Tustin Ave Ste 380
    Santa Ana CA 92705
    714 972-0988

(P-11434)
F M TARBELL CO
Also Called: Tarbell Realtors
27701 Scott Rd Ste 103, Menifee (92584-9434)
PHONE..................................951 301-5932
Kathy Ranier, Manager
EMP: 60
SALES (corp-wide): 132.1MM Privately Held
WEB: www.tarbell.com
SIC: 6531 Real estate brokers & agents
HQ: F. M. Tarbell Co
    1403 N Tustin Ave Ste 380
    Santa Ana CA 92705
    714 972-0988

(P-11435)
F M TARBELL CO
Also Called: Tarbell Realtors
31990 Temecula Pkwy # 101, Temecula (92592-5897)
PHONE..................................951 303-0307
West Ives, Manager
EMP: 135
SALES (corp-wide): 132.1MM Privately Held
WEB: www.tarbell.com
SIC: 6531 Real estate brokers & agents
HQ: F. M. Tarbell Co
    1403 N Tustin Ave Ste 380
    Santa Ana CA 92705
    714 972-0988

(P-11436)
F M TARBELL CO
Also Called: Tarbell Realtors
22632 Golden Springs Dr # 290, Diamond Bar (91765-4166)
PHONE..................................909 861-3100
Martha Figureoa, Manager
EMP: 90

SALES (corp-wide): 132.1MM Privately Held
WEB: www.tarbell.com
SIC: 6531 Real estate brokers & agents
HQ: F. M. Tarbell Co
    1403 N Tustin Ave Ste 380
    Santa Ana CA 92705
    714 972-0988

(P-11437)
F M TARBELL CO
Also Called: Tarbell Realtors
4040 Barranca Pkwy # 100, Irvine (92604-4766)
PHONE..................................714 639-0677
Clara Eisenman, Manager
EMP: 50
SALES (corp-wide): 132.1MM Privately Held
WEB: www.tarbell.com
SIC: 6531 Real estate brokers & agents
HQ: F. M. Tarbell Co
    1403 N Tustin Ave Ste 380
    Santa Ana CA 92705
    714 972-0988

(P-11438)
F M TARBELL CO
Also Called: Tarbell Realtors
4000 Barranca Pkwy # 160, Irvine (92604-4710)
PHONE..................................949 559-8451
Sheila Mayers, Manager
EMP: 72
SALES (corp-wide): 132.1MM Privately Held
WEB: www.tarbell.com
SIC: 6531 Real estate agent, residential
HQ: F. M. Tarbell Co
    1403 N Tustin Ave Ste 380
    Santa Ana CA 92705
    714 972-0988

(P-11439)
F M TARBELL CO
18295 Collier Ave, Lake Elsinore (92530-2755)
PHONE..................................951 471-5333
Carol Rounsley, Manager
EMP: 60
SALES (corp-wide): 132.1MM Privately Held
WEB: www.tarbell.com
SIC: 6531 Real estate brokers & agents
HQ: F. M. Tarbell Co
    1403 N Tustin Ave Ste 380
    Santa Ana CA 92705
    714 972-0988

(P-11440)
F M TARBELL CO
2409 S Vineyard Ave Ste A, Ontario (91761-6401)
PHONE..................................951 270-1022
Nancy Foster, Branch Mgr
George Ibarra, Real Est Agnt
EMP: 70
SALES (corp-wide): 132.1MM Privately Held
SIC: 6531 Real estate brokers & agents
HQ: F. M. Tarbell Co
    1403 N Tustin Ave Ste 380
    Santa Ana CA 92705
    714 972-0988

(P-11441)
F M TARBELL CO
Also Called: Tarbell Realtors
74245 Highway 111 Ste 100, Palm Desert (92260-4155)
PHONE..................................760 346-7405
Dan Trevino, Branch Mgr
EMP: 50
SALES (corp-wide): 132.1MM Privately Held
WEB: www.tarbell.com
SIC: 6531 Real estate brokers & agents
HQ: F. M. Tarbell Co
    1403 N Tustin Ave Ste 380
    Santa Ana CA 92705
    714 972-0988

(P-11442)
F M TARBELL CO
Also Called: Tarbell Realtors
1365 E 19th St Ste A, Upland (91784-4201)
PHONE..................................909 982-8881
Bill Velto, Manager
EMP: 102
SALES (corp-wide): 132.1MM Privately Held
WEB: www.tarbell.com
SIC: 6531 Real estate brokers & agents
HQ: F. M. Tarbell Co
    1403 N Tustin Ave Ste 380
    Santa Ana CA 92705
    714 972-0988

(P-11443)
FAR WEST MANAGEMENT CORP (PA)
17941 Mitchell S Ste A, Irvine (92614-6832)
P.O. Box 11976, Santa Ana (92711-1976)
PHONE..................................949 863-1757
Richard W Silver, CEO
Richard Franklin, Corp Secy
Bill Bird, Vice Pres
EMP: 53
SQ FT: 13,000
SALES (est): 6.6MM Privately Held
SIC: 6531 Condominium manager

(P-11444)
FELSON COMPANIES INC
1290 B St Ste 210, Hayward (94541-2996)
PHONE..................................510 538-1150
Joseph Felson, President
Joseph Lee Felson, President
Elliot Felson, Corp Secy
Victor Richard Felson, Vice Pres
EMP: 90
SQ FT: 4,000
SALES (est): 8.3MM Privately Held
SIC: 6531 Real estate managers

(P-11445)
FELSON MANAGEMENT CORP (PA)
1290 B St Ste 210, Hayward (94541-2996)
PHONE..................................510 538-1150
Joseph Lee Felson, President
Elliot Felson, CEO
Victor Richard Felson, CFO
EMP: 50
SQ FT: 3,750
SALES (est): 4.6MM Privately Held
SIC: 6531 6552 Real estate managers; subdividers & developers

(P-11446)
FESTIVAL MANAGEMENT CORP (PA)
Also Called: Festival Companies, The
5901 W Century Blvd # 700, Los Angeles (90045-5427)
PHONE..................................310 665-9610
Mark A Schurgin, CEO
Stuart L Mercer, Chairman
Rosalind Mark, Exec VP
Rosalind Schurgin, Exec VP
Karen Kennedy, Vice Pres
EMP: 85
SALES (est): 8.9MM Privately Held
SIC: 6531 Real estate leasing & rentals

(P-11447)
FILLMORE MARKETPLACE LP
Also Called: Fillmore Marketplace I
1223 Webster St, San Francisco (94115-5021)
PHONE..................................415 921-6514
Jim Brooks, Controller
EMP: 50
SALES (est): 1.1MM Privately Held
SIC: 6531 Real estate agents & managers

(P-11448)
FIRST & LA REALTY CORP (PA)
Also Called: Century 21 Hill Top Realtors
1301 E Los Angeles Ave, Simi Valley (93065-2882)
PHONE..................................805 581-0021
Robert Connlee, President
Pat Connlee, Treasurer
Susan Hill, Admin Sec

EMP: 67
SQ FT: 2,600
SALES (est): 3.7MM **Privately Held**
WEB: www.patconlee.com
SIC: 6531 Real estate agent, residential

(P-11449)
FIRST AMERCN PROF RE SVCS INC (PA)
200 Commerce, Irvine (92602-5000)
PHONE.................................714 250-1400
Larry Davidson, *President*
Mickey Allee, *Exec VP*
Eric Jones, *Vice Pres*
Brian Furst, *Technology*
Toni Carroll, *Business Mgr*
EMP: 240
SQ FT: 28,000
SALES (est): 10MM **Privately Held**
WEB: www.firstamsms.com
SIC: 6531 Real estate agents & managers

(P-11450)
FIRST AMERICAN TEAM REALTY INC (PA)
Also Called: Best Financial, The
2501 Cherry Ave Ste 100, Signal Hill (90755-2039)
PHONE.................................562 427-7765
Steve S Vong, *President*
Ron Jimenez, *Manager*
Jose Alamo, *Real Est Agnt*
Edgar Rodriguez, *Real Est Agnt*
EMP: 170
SQ FT: 3,300
SALES (est): 8.8MM **Privately Held**
WEB: www.firstamericanteam.com
SIC: 6531 Real estate agent, residential

(P-11451)
FIRST AMERICAN TITLE INSUR CO
1001 Galaxy Way Ste 101, Concord (94520-5736)
PHONE.................................925 356-7000
Connie Pickett, *Manager*
EMP: 80 **Publicly Held**
WEB: www.fatc.com
SIC: 6531 Real estate agents & managers
HQ: First American Title Insurance Company
1 First American Way
Santa Ana CA 92707
800 854-3643

(P-11452)
FIRST COMMUNITY INVESTMENTS
3636 E Florence Ave, Huntington Park (90255-5905)
PHONE.................................951 238-8322
Francisco Bernardino, *Owner*
Jimmy Hernandez,
EMP: 70
SQ FT: 250
SALES (est): 982.8K **Privately Held**
SIC: 6531 Real estate agent, commercial

(P-11453)
FIRST FAMILY HOMES
Also Called: Century 21
12027 Paramount Blvd, Downey (90242-2307)
PHONE.................................562 862-7373
William C Park, *President*
Soomi Park, *Corp Secy*
EMP: 50
SALES (est): 2.2MM **Privately Held**
WEB: www.century21prorealty.com
SIC: 6531 6798 Real estate agent, residential; real estate investment trusts

(P-11454)
FIRST MARIN REALTY INC
145 Lomita Dr, Mill Valley (94941-1403)
PHONE.................................415 383-9393
Douglas B Engel, *President*
Bruce Engel, *Ch of Bd*
Marcine Engel, *Vice Pres*
Brigetta Engle, *Vice Pres*
EMP: 60
SQ FT: 10,000
SALES (est): 3MM **Privately Held**
WEB: www.firstmarin.net
SIC: 6531 Real estate brokers & agents

(P-11455)
FIRST TEAM RE - ORANGE CNTY
74855 Country Club Dr, Palm Desert (92260-1961)
PHONE.................................760 340-9911
Todd Banks, *Branch Mgr*
EMP: 64
SALES (corp-wide): 63.6MM **Privately Held**
SIC: 6531 Real estate agent, residential; real estate brokers & agents
PA: First Team Real Estate - Orange County
108 Pacifica Ste 300
Irvine CA 92618
888 236-1943

(P-11456)
FIRST TEAM RE - ORANGE CNTY
Also Called: First Team S S Estate
1950 S Brea Canyon Rd # 1, Diamond Bar (91765-4015)
PHONE.................................909 861-1380
Jim Carrescia, *Manager*
Alicia Yong, *Corp Comm Staff*
Michael Chu, *Manager*
Barbara A Haywood, *Real Est Agnt*
Maria Koh, *Real Est Agnt*
EMP: 100
SALES (corp-wide): 70.7MM **Privately Held**
WEB: www.coastcitiesescrow.com
SIC: 6531 Real estate agent, residential; real estate brokers & agents
PA: First Team Real Estate - Orange County
108 Pacifica Ste 300
Irvine CA 92618
888 236-1943

(P-11457)
FIRST TEAM RE - ORANGE CNTY
18180 Yorba Linda Blvd # 501, Yorba Linda (92886-3901)
PHONE.................................714 223-2143
Bob Macculloch, *Manager*
Helen Chin, *Sales Staff*
Gayle Glew, *Director*
Pat McGinnis, *Manager*
Danelle Alstrup, *Real Est Agnt*
EMP: 100
SALES (corp-wide): 63.6MM **Privately Held**
WEB: www.coastcitiesescrow.com
SIC: 6531
PA: First Team Real Estate - Orange County
108 Pacifica Ste 300
Irvine CA 92618
888 236-1943

(P-11458)
FIRST TEAM RE - ORANGE CNTY
12501 Seal Beach Blvd # 100, Seal Beach (90740-2763)
PHONE.................................562 596-9911
Judy Sharp, *Manager*
Sara A Boehme, *Real Est Agnt*
Carole Campbell, *Real Est Agnt*
Aleta Esteibar, *Real Est Agnt*
June Freeman, *Real Est Agnt*
EMP: 150
SALES (corp-wide): 63.6MM **Privately Held**
WEB: www.coastcitiesescrow.com
SIC: 6531 Real estate agent, residential; real estate brokers & agents
PA: First Team Real Estate - Orange County
108 Pacifica Ste 300
Irvine CA 92618
888 236-1943

(P-11459)
FIRST TEAM RE - ORANGE CNTY
4 Corporate Plaza Dr # 100, Newport Beach (92660-7906)
PHONE.................................949 759-5747
Jennifer Berman, *Office Mgr*
Mary McCoy, *Real Est Agnt*

EMP: 55
SALES (corp-wide): 63.6MM **Privately Held**
WEB: www.coastcitiesescrow.com
SIC: 6531 Real estate brokers & agents
PA: First Team Real Estate - Orange County
108 Pacifica Ste 300
Irvine CA 92618
888 236-1943

(P-11460)
FIRST TEAM RE - ORANGE CNTY (PA)
Also Called: First Team Walk-In Realty
108 Pacifica Ste 300, Irvine (92618-7435)
PHONE.................................888 236-1943
Cameron Merage, *CEO*
Todd Bruechert, *Vice Pres*
Michelle Williams Harringto, *Vice Pres*
Anna Bennett, *Branch Mgr*
Mila Sealey, *Office Admin*
EMP: 160 **EST**: 1976
SQ FT: 8,000
SALES (est): 63.6MM **Privately Held**
WEB: www.coastcitiesescrow.com
SIC: 6531 Real estate agent, residential

(P-11461)
FIRST TEAM RE - ORANGE CNTY
Also Called: First State
20100 Brookhurst St, Huntington Beach (92646-4938)
PHONE.................................714 965-2244
Wally Malesh, *Manager*
Jerry Beusee, *Real Est Agnt*
Chris Delfs, *Real Est Agnt*
Michele Erwin, *Real Est Agnt*
Jose Herrera, *Real Est Agnt*
EMP: 100
SALES (corp-wide): 63.6MM **Privately Held**
WEB: www.coastcitiesescrow.com
SIC: 6531 Real estate brokers & agents
PA: First Team Real Estate - Orange County
108 Pacifica Ste 300
Irvine CA 92618
888 236-1943

(P-11462)
FIRST TEAM RE - ORANGE CNTY
42 64th Pl, Long Beach (90803-5676)
PHONE.................................562 346-5088
EMP: 78
SALES (corp-wide): 70.7MM **Privately Held**
SIC: 6531 Real estate agent, residential
PA: First Team Real Estate - Orange County
108 Pacifica Ste 300
Irvine CA 92618
888 236-1943

(P-11463)
FIRST TEAM RE - ORANGE CNTY
32451 Golden Lantern # 210, Laguna Niguel (92677-5344)
PHONE.................................949 240-7979
Mark Kojac, *General Mgr*
Brenda Thomas, *Agent*
Beau Beardslee, *Real Est Agnt*
Robert Blatman, *Real Est Agnt*
Jacqueline Chase, *Real Est Agnt*
EMP: 140
SALES (corp-wide): 70.7MM **Privately Held**
WEB: www.coastcitiesescrow.com
SIC: 6531 Real estate agent & agents
PA: First Team Real Estate - Orange County
108 Pacifica Ste 300
Irvine CA 92618
888 236-1943

(P-11464)
FIRST TEAM RE - ORANGE CNTY
Also Called: 1st Team Real Estate
17240 17th St, Tustin (92780-1940)
PHONE.................................714 544-5456
Michael Hampton, *Manager*

Asha Bans, *Agent*
Judith Casper, *Agent*
David Caballero, *Real Est Agnt*
Jay Gaylen, *Real Est Agnt*
EMP: 137
SALES (corp-wide): 63.6MM **Privately Held**
WEB: www.coastcitiesescrow.com
SIC: 6531 Real estate brokers & agents
PA: First Team Real Estate - Orange County
108 Pacifica Ste 300
Irvine CA 92618
888 236-1943

(P-11465)
FIRST TEAM RE - ORANGE CNTY
8028 E Santa Ana Cyn Rd, Anaheim (92808-1108)
PHONE.................................714 974-9191
Anna Bennet, *Manager*
Sandra Meucci, *Office Admin*
Alexander Thompson, *Broker*
Bruce Brown, *Real Est Agnt*
Tauna Crippen, *Real Est Agnt*
EMP: 63
SALES (corp-wide): 63.6MM **Privately Held**
WEB: www.coastcitiesescrow.com
SIC: 6531 Real estate brokers & agents
PA: First Team Real Estate - Orange County
108 Pacifica Ste 300
Irvine CA 92618
888 236-1943

(P-11466)
FIRST TEAM RE - ORANGE CNTY
26711 Aliso Creek Rd # 200, Aliso Viejo (92656-4820)
PHONE.................................949 389-0004
Michele Williams, *Branch Mgr*
EMP: 150
SALES (corp-wide): 63.6MM **Privately Held**
WEB: www.bhsi.com
SIC: 6531 Real estate agents & managers
PA: First Team Real Estate - Orange County
108 Pacifica Ste 300
Irvine CA 92618
888 236-1943

(P-11467)
FIRSTSERVICE RESIDENTIAL (HQ)
Also Called: Merit Property Management Inc
15241 Laguna Canyon Rd, Irvine (92618-3146)
PHONE.................................949 448-6000
Bob Cardoza, *President*
Katie Ward, *Principal*
EMP: 200
SQ FT: 21,000
SALES (est): 39MM
SALES (corp-wide): 1.7B **Privately Held**
SIC: 6531 Real estate managers
PA: Firstservice Corporation
1140 Bay St Suite 4000
Toronto ON M5S 2
416 960-9500

(P-11468)
FIRSTSRVICE RSIDENTIAL CAL INC (DH)
195 N Euclid Ave, Upland (91786-6055)
P.O. Box 1510 (91785-1510)
PHONE.................................909 981-4131
Glennon Gray, *President*
James Gray, *Vice Pres*
Kathy Johnston, *Division Mgr*
Louise Ceccarelli, *Corp Comm Staff*
Tad Creasey, *Property Mgr*
EMP: 69
SQ FT: 16,000
SALES (est): 7.5MM
SALES (corp-wide): 1.7B **Privately Held**
WEB: www.euclidmanagement.com
SIC: 6531 Real estate managers

(P-11469)
FKC PARTNERS A CAL LTD PARTNR
Also Called: Fkc Properties
180 N Rverview Dr Ste 100, Anaheim (92808)
PHONE...................714 528-9864
Paul Kramer,
Brett Albrecht, *Director*
EMP: 50
SALES (est): 2.4MM **Privately Held**
SIC: 6531 Real estate brokers & agents

(P-11470)
FLYNN PROPERTIES INC
225 Bush St Ste 1470, San Francisco (94104-4226)
PHONE...................415 835-0225
Greg Flynn, *President*
Penelope Welsh, *Executive*
Amjad Shehade, *Managing Dir*
Sylvia Hoang, *Accountant*
Diane Didriche, *Opers Staff*
EMP: 50
SALES (est): 4.8MM **Privately Held**
SIC: 6531 Real estate agent, commercial

(P-11471)
FOUNTAIN COURT ESSEX
22102 Clarendon St # 200, Woodland Hills (91367-6307)
PHONE...................818 227-2100
Michael Schall, *President*
EMP: 50
SALES (est): 1.2MM **Privately Held**
SIC: 6531 Rental agent, real estate

(P-11472)
FPI MANAGEMENT INC (PA)
800 Iron Point Rd, Folsom (95630-9004)
PHONE...................916 357-5300
Dennis Treadaway, *President*
Ken Hunt, *Shareholder*
Gary Quattrin, *Shareholder*
David Divine, *Vice Pres*
Tracie Freeman, *Vice Pres*
EMP: 50
SQ FT: 18,000
SALES (est): 89.5MM **Privately Held**
WEB: www.fpimgt.com
SIC: 6531 Real estate managers

(P-11473)
FRANK HOWARD ALLEN FINCL CORP
Also Called: Frank Howard Allen Real Estate
1016 Irwin St, San Rafael (94901-3320)
PHONE...................415 456-3000
Fred Angeli, *Manager*
EMP: 55 **Publicly Held**
WEB: www.fhallen.com
SIC: 6531 Real estate agent, residential
HQ: Frank Howard Allen Financial Corporation
1013 2nd St
Novato CA
415 897-4444

(P-11474)
FRANK HOWARD ALLEN FINCL CORP
460 Mission Blvd, Santa Rosa (95409-5351)
PHONE...................707 523-3000
Brian Connell, *Sales/Mktg Mgr*
Judy Freedman, *Real Est Agnt*
Joe Hernandez, *Real Est Agnt*
EMP: 71 **Publicly Held**
WEB: www.fhallen.com
SIC: 6531 Real estate agent, residential
HQ: Frank Howard Allen Financial Corporation
1013 2nd St
Novato CA
415 897-4444

(P-11475)
FUSION REAL ESTATE NETWORK INC
1300 National Dr Ste 170, Sacramento (95834-1991)
PHONE...................916 448-3174
Gwen Scott, *President*
James Becker, *Vice Pres*
Helen Whitelaw, *Vice Pres*

EMP: 90
SQ FT: 4,400
SALES (est): 5.2MM **Privately Held**
SIC: 6531 Real estate brokers & agents

(P-11476)
G M A C-ONE SOURCE REALTY
898 Jackman St, El Cajon (92020-3057)
PHONE...................619 405-6231
Greg Seaman, *Owner*
EMP: 56
SALES (est): 2.2MM **Privately Held**
SIC: 6531 Real estate agents & managers

(P-11477)
GEMMM CORP
587 W Los Angeles Ave, Moorpark (93021-1709)
PHONE...................805 267-2700
Dave Ward, *Branch Mgr*
EMP: 59
SALES (corp-wide): 8.5MM **Privately Held**
SIC: 6531 Real estate agents & managers
PA: Gemmm Corp
2860 E Thousand Oaks Blvd
Thousand Oaks CA 91362
805 496-0555

(P-11478)
GEMMM CORP
2211 Memory Ln, Westlake Village (91361-5524)
PHONE...................818 522-0740
Chris Doernes, *Branch Mgr*
EMP: 59
SALES (corp-wide): 8.5MM **Privately Held**
SIC: 6531 Real estate brokers & agents
PA: Gemmm Corp
2860 E Thousand Oaks Blvd
Thousand Oaks CA 91362
805 496-0555

(P-11479)
GEMMM CORP (PA)
Also Called: Prudential
2860 E Thousand Oaks Blvd, Thousand Oaks (91362-3201)
PHONE...................805 496-0555
Robert L Majorino, *President*
Anthony Principe, *CFO*
Robert Hamilton, *Vice Pres*
Lynn Gilbert, *Admin Sec*
Seth Backus, *Broker*
EMP: 100
SQ FT: 12,500
SALES (est): 8.5MM **Privately Held**
WEB: www.prucalhomes.com
SIC: 6531 Real estate agent, residential

(P-11480)
GIC REAL ESTATE INC (HQ)
1 Bush St Ste 1100, San Francisco (94104-4417)
PHONE...................415 229-1800
Adam Gallistel, *CEO*
EMP: 60
SQ FT: 10,000
SALES (est): 15.5MM **Privately Held**
SIC: 6531 6799 Real estate managers; real estate investors, except property operators

(P-11481)
GK MANAGEMENT CO INC (PA)
5150 Overland Ave, Culver City (90230-4914)
PHONE...................310 204-2050
Carole Glodney, *CEO*
Jona Goldrich, *Vice Pres*
EMP: 150
SALES (est): 25.2MM **Privately Held**
WEB: www.gkind.com
SIC: 6531 Real estate managers

(P-11482)
GK MANAGEMENT CO INC
5150 Overland Ave, Culver City (90230-4914)
PHONE...................310 204-2050
Carol Glodney, *President*
EMP: 150

SALES (corp-wide): 25.2MM **Privately Held**
WEB: www.gkind.com
SIC: 6531 6513 Real estate managers; apartment building operators
PA: Gk Management Co., Inc.
5150 Overland Ave
Culver City CA 90230
310 204-2050

(P-11483)
GK MANAGEMENT CO INC
Also Called: Coronado Royale
299 Prospect Pl, Coronado (92118-1967)
PHONE...................619 437-1777
Rudy Littlefield, *Manager*
EMP: 50
SALES (corp-wide): 25.2MM **Privately Held**
WEB: www.gkind.com
SIC: 6531 6513 Real estate managers; retirement hotel operation
PA: Gk Management Corp
5150 Overland Ave
Culver City CA 90230
310 204-2050

(P-11484)
GK MANAGEMENT CO INC
Also Called: Kittridge Gardens
6540 Wilbur Ave, Reseda (91335-5927)
PHONE...................818 705-8834
Jane Pouchino, *Manager*
EMP: 80
SALES (corp-wide): 25.2MM **Privately Held**
WEB: www.gkind.com
SIC: 6531 6513 Real estate managers; apartment building operators
PA: Gk Management Co., Inc.
5150 Overland Ave
Culver City CA 90230
310 204-2050

(P-11485)
GLENBOROUGH LLC (PA)
400 S El Camino Real # 1100, San Mateo (94402-1706)
PHONE...................650 343-9300
Andrew Batinovich, *CEO*
Terri Garnick, *Senior VP*
EMP: 60
SALES: 7MM **Privately Held**
SIC: 6531 Real estate managers

(P-11486)
GOLD COUNTRY MANAGEMENT INC
1825 Bell St Ste 100, Sacramento (95825-1020)
PHONE...................916 929-3003
James Gately, *President*
EMP: 70
SALES (est): 2.8MM **Privately Held**
SIC: 6531 Real estate managers

(P-11487)
GOLDEN RAIN FOUNDATION (PA)
Also Called: Rossmoor
1001 Golden Rain Rd, Walnut Creek (94595-2441)
P.O. Box 2070 (94595-0070)
PHONE...................925 988-7700
Stephen Adams, *CEO*
Steve Adams, *Executive*
Judith Perkins, *Executive*
Tess Haskett, *Finance*
Lucy Limon, *Opers Staff*
EMP: 59
SQ FT: 5,000
SALES (est): 26.4MM **Privately Held**
WEB: www.rossmoornews.com
SIC: 6531 8011 2711 7997 Real estate managers; offices & clinics of medical doctors; newspapers; golf club, membership

(P-11488)
GOODMAN NORTH AMERICA LLC
18201 Von Karman Ave, Irvine (92612-1000)
PHONE...................949 407-0100
Brandon Birtcher, *CEO*

Dan Grable, *COO*
Steve Williams, *Officer*
Anthony Alexander, *Associate Dir*
Charles Crossland, *Managing Dir*
EMP: 100
SALES (est): 10.2MM **Privately Held**
SIC: 6531 6552 1542 Real estate managers; land subdividers & developers, commercial; commercial & office building, new construction

(P-11489)
GRAND PACIFIC RESORTS INC (PA)
5900 Pasteur Ct Ste 200, Carlsbad (92008-7336)
P.O. Box 4068 (92018-4068)
PHONE...................760 431-8500
Timothy J Stripe, *Partner*
Diane Proulx, *President*
Crystal Gonzalez, *COO*
Nigel Lobo, *COO*
Randy Nakagawa, *Chief Mktg Ofcr*
EMP: 250
SQ FT: 22,000
SALES (est): 185.5MM **Privately Held**
WEB: www.grandpacificresorts.com
SIC: 6531 7011 Time-sharing real estate sales, leasing & rentals; hotels & motels

(P-11490)
GREENBRIAR MANAGEMENT COMPANY
Also Called: Greenbriar Homes Community
43160 Osgood Rd, Fremont (94539-5608)
PHONE...................510 497-8200
Gilbert M Meyer, *CEO*
Carol Meyer, *Vice Pres*
EMP: 100
SQ FT: 16,932
SALES (est): 6MM **Privately Held**
SIC: 6531 Cooperative apartment manager

(P-11491)
GREGA BROOKE SRA
18501 Riverside Dr, Sonoma (95476-4509)
P.O. Box 268 (95476-0268)
PHONE...................707 938-3362
Grega Brooke, *Principal*
EMP: 50
SALES (est): 1.3MM **Privately Held**
SIC: 6531 Appraiser, real estate

(P-11492)
GREYSTAR MANAGEMENT SVCS LP
6320 Canoga Ave Ste 1512, Woodland Hills (91367-2526)
PHONE...................818 596-2180
Grace White, *Owner*
EMP: 334 **Privately Held**
SIC: 6531 Real estate brokers & agents
PA: Greystar Management Services, L.P.
750 Bering Dr Ste 300
Houston TX 77057

(P-11493)
GRISWORLD REAL ESTATE MGT (PA)
5703 Oberlin Dr Ste 300, San Diego (92121-1743)
PHONE...................858 597-6100
Robert Griswold, *President*
Ted Smith, *Principal*
Sheri Griswold, *Regional Mgr*
Shelly Weld, *Regional Mgr*
Fay Dye, *Consultant*
EMP: 65
SQ FT: 3,000
SALES (est): 3.1MM **Privately Held**
WEB: www.griswoldremgmt.com
SIC: 6531 8111 Real estate managers; legal services

(P-11494)
GRUBB CO INC
1960 Mountain Blvd, Oakland (94611-2894)
PHONE...................510 339-0400
D J Grubb Jr, *President*
Robert A Belzer, *Vice Pres*
Laura Castillo, *Office Mgr*
Sherry Benninger, *Broker*
Julie Gardner, *Broker*

EMP: 53
SQ FT: 2,800
SALES (est): 5.3MM **Privately Held**
WEB: www.grubbco.com
SIC: 6531 Real estate agent, commercial

(P-11495)
GRUPE COMPANY (PA)
3255 W March Ln Ste 400, Stockton
(95219-2352)
P.O. Box 7576 (95267-0576)
PHONE...................................209 473-6000
Frank A Passadore, *President*
Greenlaw Grupe Jr, *Ch of Bd*
Mark Fischer, *CFO*
Angela Bridges, *Vice Pres*
Julie Dzubak, *Vice Pres*
EMP: 60 EST: 1960
SQ FT: 7,000
SALES (est): 87.6MM **Privately Held**
WEB: www.grupe.com
SIC: 6531 1542 Real estate agent, residential; real estate brokers & agents; commercial & office building, new construction

(P-11496)
GUARANTEE REAL ESTATE
756 W Shaw Ave Ste 105, Fresno
(93704-2223)
PHONE...................................559 650-6030
Sandy Darling, *Vice Pres*
J Scott Leonard, *CEO*
Laura Everson, *CFO*
Sandra Robertson, *Office Admin*
Jess Garcia, *Administration*
EMP: 50
SALES (est): 2.5MM **Privately Held**
SIC: 6531 Real estate brokers & agents

(P-11497)
GUARANTEE REAL ESTATE CORP
180 W Bullard Ave Ste 101, Clovis
(93612-0998)
PHONE...................................559 321-6040
Kyle Chaney, *Branch Mgr*
Amir Dehlan, *Real Est Agnt*
EMP: 51
SALES (corp-wide): 242.1B **Publicly Held**
SIC: 6531 Real estate brokers & agents
HQ: Guarantee Real Estate Corporation
3 E River Park Pl E
Fresno CA 93720
559 650-6000

(P-11498)
GUARANTEE REAL ESTATE CORP
6710 N West Ave Ste 108, Fresno
(93711-4300)
PHONE...................................559 431-8600
Allan Atchley, *Manager*
Awremce Reba, *Vice Pres*
EMP: 65
SALES (corp-wide): 242.1B **Publicly Held**
SIC: 6531 Real estate brokers & agents
HQ: Guarantee Real Estate Corporation
3 E River Park Pl E
Fresno CA 93720
559 650-6000

(P-11499)
HARMONY ESCROW INC
17100 Gillette Ave, Irvine (92614-5603)
PHONE...................................949 474-1134
Rande Johnsen, *President*
EMP: 60
SALES: 950K **Privately Held**
SIC: 6531 Real estate brokers & agents

(P-11500)
HARTWIG REALTY INC (PA)
Also Called: Coldwell Banker Hartwig Co
43912 20th St W, Lancaster (93534-5221)
PHONE...................................661 948-8424
Burl W Patterson, *President*
Conrad Engelhardt, *Vice Pres*
Angela Segura, *Broker*
Sharon Zumwalt, *Sales Associate*
Joe Hodge, *Sales Staff*
EMP: 89
SQ FT: 20,000

SALES (est): 5.3MM **Privately Held**
WEB: www.landinfonow.com
SIC: 6531 Real estate agent, residential

(P-11501)
HDSI MANAGEMENT INC (PA)
3460 S Broadway, Los Angeles
(90007-4409)
PHONE...................................323 231-1104
Noel L Sweitzer, *President*
Carlos Flores, *Accountant*
EMP: 65
SQ FT: 5,500
SALES (est): 5.7MM **Privately Held**
SIC: 6531 Real estate managers

(P-11502)
HELM MANAGEMENT CO (PA)
Also Called: Helm, The
4668 Nebo Dr Ste A, La Mesa
(91941-5200)
PHONE...................................619 589-6222
Tom Hensley, *President*
Jack Noy, *Sr Project Mgr*
EMP: 90
SQ FT: 1,176
SALES (est): 9.6MM **Privately Held**
WEB: www.helmmanagement.com
SIC: 6531 Real estate managers; time-sharing real estate sales, leasing & rentals; rental agent, real estate; condominium manager

(P-11503)
HINES INTERESTS LTD PARTNR
1 Hacker Way Bldg 10, Menlo Park
(94025-1456)
PHONE...................................650 518-6139
Melissa Perla, *Senior Mgr*
EMP: 170
SALES (corp-wide): 1.4B **Privately Held**
SIC: 6531 Real estate agent, commercial
PA: Hines Interests Limited Partnership
2800 Post Oak Blvd # 4800
Houston TX 77056
713 621-8000

(P-11504)
HMS AGRICULTURAL CORPORATION
46247 Arabia St, Indio (92201-5840)
P.O. Box 1787 (92202-1787)
PHONE...................................760 347-2335
Ole Fogh-Andersen, *President*
Earline Taylor, *Treasurer*
Linden Anderson, *Vice Pres*
Henry Bastidas, *Vice Pres*
EMP: 70 EST: 1975
SQ FT: 1,600
SALES (est): 4.5MM **Privately Held**
SIC: 6531 Real estate managers

(P-11505)
HOUSING ATHRTY OF THE CNTY OF
2160 41st Ave, Capitola (95010-2040)
PHONE...................................831 454-9455
Jennifer Panetta, *Exec Dir*
Beth Ahlgren, *Analyst*
Mark Failor, *Property Mgr*
EMP: 65
SALES: 58MM **Privately Held**
SIC: 6531 Real estate managers

(P-11506)
HUNT ENTERPRISES INC
Also Called: Shibui Apartments
2270 Sepulveda Blvd # 50, Torrance
(90501-5304)
PHONE...................................310 325-1496
EMP: 113
SQ FT: 53,813
SALES (corp-wide): 13.1MM **Privately Held**
SIC: 6531 Real estate leasing & rentals
PA: Hunt Enterprises, Inc.
4416 W 154th St
Lawndale CA 90260
310 675-3555

(P-11507)
HUNTER REALTY INC
Also Called: Prudential
2605 S Miller St Ste 101, Santa Maria
(93455-1774)
PHONE...................................805 346-8688

David Cabot, *President*
EMP: 155
SALES (est): 5.6MM **Privately Held**
SIC: 6531 Real estate agent, residential; real estate consultant

(P-11508)
HYATT VACATION OWNERSHIP INC
9615 Brighton Way M180, Beverly Hills
(90210-5140)
PHONE...................................310 285-0990
John Burlingame, *Exec VP*
EMP: 80
SALES (est): 1.3MM **Privately Held**
SIC: 6531 Real estate leasing & rentals

(P-11509)
I D PROPERTY CORPORATION
Also Called: Property I D
1001 Wilshire Blvd # 100, Los Angeles
(90017-2821)
PHONE...................................213 625-0100
Carlos Siderman, *President*
John Cote, *President*
Victor Marquez, *Executive*
Wendy Tejeda, *Executive*
Lori Wilson, *Sales Executive*
EMP: 120
SALES (est): 11.6MM **Privately Held**
SIC: 6531 8742 Real estate listing services; real estate consultant

(P-11510)
IC BP III HOLDINGS XII LLC
1 Sansome St Ste 1500, San Francisco
(94104-4449)
PHONE...................................415 549-5054
Aaron Snegg, *Manager*
EMP: 60
SALES (est): 2.5MM **Privately Held**
SIC: 6531 Real estate leasing & rentals

(P-11511)
IDS REAL ESTATE GROUP (PA)
Also Called: I S D
515 S Figueroa St Fl 16, Los Angeles
(90071-3301)
PHONE...................................213 627-9937
Murad M Siam, *CEO*
David G Mgrubllan, *President*
Mickey Siam, *COO*
Jeff Newman, *CFO*
Cathy Defazio, *Senior VP*
EMP: 75
SQ FT: 20,000
SALES (est): 10.1MM **Privately Held**
SIC: 6531 Real estate agent, commercial; real estate managers

(P-11512)
INLAND EMPIRE RE SOLUTIONS
Also Called: Remax Legends
8794 19th St, Alta Loma (91701-4608)
P.O. Box 129, Rancho Cucamonga (91739-0129)
PHONE...................................909 476-1000
Jodi Lee Nazi, *President*
Jodi Lee Nazir, *President*
EMP: 76
SQ FT: 5,600
SALES: 4MM **Privately Held**
SIC: 6531

(P-11513)
INLAND EMPIRE REAL ESTATE
8010 Haven Ave, Rancho Cucamonga
(91730-3047)
P.O. Box 1195 (91729-1195)
PHONE...................................909 944-2070
Ruben Mendez, *President*
EMP: 50
SALES (est): 1.8MM **Privately Held**
SIC: 6531 Real estate brokers & agents

(P-11514)
INMAN SPINOSA & BUCHAN INC
Also Called: Landmark Realty Center
28901 S Wstn Ave Ste 139, Rancho Palos
Verdes (90275)
PHONE...................................310 519-1080
Gordon Inman, *President*
Nancy Inman, *Treasurer*
Donna Buchan, *Vice Pres*
Keith Kelley, *Real Est Agnt*

EMP: 58
SALES (est): 3.4MM **Privately Held**
WEB: www.salsorrentino.com
SIC: 6531 6163 Real estate brokers & agents; mortgage brokers arranging for loans, using money of others

(P-11515)
INTERNET ESCROW SERVICES INC
180 Montgomery St Ste 650, San Francisco
(94104-4208)
PHONE...................................888 511-8600
Robert Barrie, *CEO*
Neil Katz, *CFO*
Jackson Elsegood, *General Mgr*
EMP: 69 EST: 1999
SALES: 7.5MM
SALES (corp-wide): 38MM **Privately Held**
WEB: www.internetescrowservices.com
SIC: 6531 Escrow agent, real estate
PA: Freelancer Limited
L 20 World Sq 680 George St
Sydney NSW 2000
285 992-700

(P-11516)
INTERO REAL ESTATE SERVICES
790 1st St, Gilroy (95020-4972)
PHONE...................................408 848-8400
Kathie Kingston, *President*
EMP: 62
SALES (est): 2.3MM **Privately Held**
SIC: 6531 Real estate agent, residential

(P-11517)
INTERO REAL ESTATE SVCS INC
12900 Saratoga Ave, Saratoga
(95070-4668)
PHONE...................................408 741-1600
Tom Tagnoli, *General Mgr*
EMP: 81
SALES (corp-wide): 242.1B **Publicly Held**
SIC: 6531 Real estate brokers & agents
HQ: Intero Real Estate Services, Inc.
10275 N De Anza Blvd
Cupertino CA 95014
408 342-3000

(P-11518)
INTERO REAL ESTATE SVCS INC
8255 Firestone Blvd # 200, Downey
(90241-4877)
PHONE...................................562 861-7242
Oscar Mendoza, *Principal*
EMP: 81
SALES (corp-wide): 242.1B **Publicly Held**
SIC: 6531 Real estate agent, commercial
HQ: Intero Real Estate Services, Inc.
10275 N De Anza Blvd
Cupertino CA 95014
408 342-3000

(P-11519)
INTERO REAL ESTATE SVCS INC
32145 Alvarado Niles Rd # 101, Union City
(94587-2930)
PHONE...................................510 489-8989
Joey Anudon, *Branch Mgr*
EMP: 81
SALES (corp-wide): 242.1B **Publicly Held**
SIC: 6531 Real estate agent, commercial; real estate brokers & agents
HQ: Intero Real Estate Services, Inc.
10275 N De Anza Blvd
Cupertino CA 95014
408 342-3000

(P-11520)
INTERO REAL ESTATE SVCS INC
5890 Silver Creek Vly Rd, San Jose
(95138-1027)
PHONE...................................408 574-5000
Robert Cruz, *Manager*
EMP: 150
SALES (corp-wide): 242.1B **Publicly Held**
SIC: 6531 6519 Real estate brokers & agents; real property lessors

HQ: Intero Real Estate Services, Inc.
10275 N De Anza Blvd
Cupertino CA 95014
408 342-3000

(P-11521)
INTERO REAL ESTATE SVCS INC
Also Called: Intero Silicon Valley
1900 Camden Ave, San Jose (95124-2942)
PHONE.....................408 558-3600
Terry Meyer, COO
EMP: 50
SALES (est): 1.9MM Privately Held
SIC: 6531 7389 Real estate agent, residential; office facilities & secretarial service rental

(P-11522)
INVESERVE CORPORATION
123 S Chapel Ave, Alhambra (91801-3951)
PHONE.....................626 458-3435
Norman Chang, President
Amy Chang, Vice Pres
Michael Fang, Advisor
EMP: 80
SQ FT: 1,000
SALES (est): 7.2MM Privately Held
WEB: www.inveserve.com
SIC: 6531 Real estate agent, commercial; real estate managers

(P-11523)
INZUNZA REAL ESTATE INC
Also Called: Entrepreneur Preferred
25310 Madison Ave Ste 101, Murrieta (92562-8908)
PHONE.....................951 544-8801
Jorge Inzunza, President
EMP: 60
SALES (est): 129.9K Privately Held
SIC: 6531 Real estate brokers & agents

(P-11524)
IVY REALTY
611 S Wilton Pl, Los Angeles (90005-3220)
PHONE.....................213 386-8888
J D Kym, CEO
Joana Chang, Real Est Agnt
Grace Kim, Real Est Agnt
Jessica Kim, Real Est Agnt
Jae Lee, Real Est Agnt
EMP: 50
SALES (est): 1.8MM Privately Held
WEB: www.ivyrealty.com
SIC: 6531 Real estate brokers & agents

(P-11525)
J BARON INC
Also Called: Re/Max
5299 Alton Pkwy, Irvine (92604-8604)
PHONE.....................949 451-1200
Tom Baron, President
Katy Obrejan, Broker
Andy Tseng, Broker
Alan Razani, Real Est Agnt
Jin Ah Lee, Associate
EMP: 96
SALES (est): 6MM Privately Held
SIC: 6531 Real estate agent, residential

(P-11526)
J H SYNDER CO LLC
5757 Wilshire Blvd Ph 30, Los Angeles (90036-3690)
PHONE.....................323 857-5546
Jerome Snyder, Managing Prtnr
Patrick Irvine, Vice Pres
Dan Schneider, Vice Pres
Mary Schwei, Executive
Jose Anaya, Info Tech Mgr
EMP: 60
SALES (est): 4.6MM Privately Held
SIC: 6531 Buying agent, real estate

(P-11527)
J M K INVESTMENTS INC (PA)
100 Saratoga Ave Ste 300, Santa Clara (95051-7337)
PHONE.....................408 249-2500
John Kehriotis, President
Megan Kehriotis, Controller
Isabella Rennie, Manager
EMP: 80
SQ FT: 1,200

SALES (est): 7.5MM Privately Held
SIC: 6531 6512 6162 Real estate agent, commercial; real estate managers; commercial & industrial building operation; mortgage brokers, using own money

(P-11528)
JALMAR PROPERTIES INC (PA)
12121 Wilshire Blvd # 1120, Los Angeles (90025-1164)
PHONE.....................310 207-8481
James H Donell, President
Stephen J Donell, President
David Donell, Exec VP
Sarah Bates, Vice Pres
Todd Donell, Vice Pres
EMP: 50
SALES (est): 4.5MM Privately Held
SIC: 6531 6799 6552 Real estate managers; real estate investors, except property operators; subdividers & developers

(P-11529)
JAMBOREE REALTY CORP (PA)
Also Called: Jamboree Management
22982 Mill Creek Dr, Laguna Hills (92653-1214)
PHONE.....................949 380-0300
Fred G Sparks, President
Richard M Tucker, CEO
Kathleen Tucker, Treasurer
Terri Boykin, Admin Asst
Lori Guay, Accounting Mgr
EMP: 120
SALES (est): 17.5MM Privately Held
SIC: 6531 Real estate agents & managers

(P-11530)
JB PARTNERS GROUP INC
18375 Ventura Blvd, Tarzana (91356-4218)
PHONE.....................818 668-8201
Robert E Hart, Principal
EMP: 127
SALES (est): 3.9MM
SALES (corp-wide): 19.7MM Privately Held
SIC: 6531 Real estate leasing & rentals
PA: The Laramar Group L L C
222 S Riverside Plz
Chicago IL 60606
312 669-1200

(P-11531)
JMS REALTORS LTD (PA)
Also Called: Realty Concepts
575 E Alluvial Ave # 101, Fresno (93720-2822)
PHONE.....................559 490-1500
John M Shamshoian, CEO
Eugene Savarino, Creative Dir
Katie Snyder, Admin Asst
Deanna Spellman, Broker
Ellen Armour, Opers Staff
EMP: 172 EST: 1991
SALES (est): 15.5MM Privately Held
SIC: 6531 7389 Real estate brokers & agents; brokers, contract services

(P-11532)
JOE CANPAGNA
Also Called: Prudential
2830 Shelter Island Dr, San Diego (92106-2733)
PHONE.....................619 222-0555
Joe Canpagna, Manager
EMP: 90 EST: 1998
SALES (est): 2MM Privately Held
WEB: www.bythewood.com
SIC: 6531 Real estate agent, residential

(P-11533)
JOHN G SHIPLEY
Also Called: Century 21
100 W Valencia Mesa Dr # 201, Fullerton (92835-3765)
PHONE.....................714 626-2000
John G Shipley, Owner
EMP: 90
SALES (est): 4MM Privately Held
WEB: www.c21discovery.com
SIC: 6531 Real estate agent, residential

(P-11534)
JOHN STEWART COMPANY
191 Heritage Ln, Dixon (95620-4873)
PHONE.....................707 676-5660

EMP: 78
SALES (corp-wide): 118.2MM Privately Held
SIC: 6531 Real estate managers
PA: John Stewart Company
1388 Sutter St Ste 1100
San Francisco CA 94109
213 833-1860

(P-11535)
JOHN STEWART COMPANY
888 S Figueroa St Ste 700, Los Angeles (90017-5320)
PHONE.....................213 787-2700
Monica Salirdano, Branch Mgr
Richard Himmelberger, Regional Mgr
Monica Solorzano, Sales Mgr
Melissa Bayles, Director
Peter Purtell, Director
EMP: 50
SALES (corp-wide): 118.2MM Privately Held
SIC: 6531 6513 Real estate managers; apartment building operators
PA: John Stewart Company
1388 Sutter St Ste 1100
San Francisco CA 94109
213 833-1860

(P-11536)
JOHN STEWART COMPANY (PA)
1388 Sutter St Ste 1100, San Francisco (94109-5454)
PHONE.....................213 833-1860
John K Stewart, Chairman
John Stewart, General Ptnr
Jack D Gardner, CEO
Noah Schwartz, COO
Michael Smith-Heimer, CFO
EMP: 80
SQ FT: 15,000
SALES (est): 118.2MM Privately Held
WEB: www.jsco.net
SIC: 6531 6552 6726 Real estate managers; subdividers & developers; investors syndicates

(P-11537)
JONES LANG LASALLE INC
4444 Mkt St Ste 1100, San Francisco (94111)
PHONE.....................415 395-4900
Chris Albrow, Manager
Wilfred Freeman, Chief Engr
Michelle Thomas, Property Mgr
EMP: 200
SALES (corp-wide): 7.9B Publicly Held
WEB: www.joneslanglasalle.com
SIC: 6531 Real estate agent, commercial
PA: Jones Lang Lasalle Incorporated
200 E Randolph St # 4300
Chicago IL 60601
312 782-5800

(P-11538)
JS TAMERS INC
468 N Camden Dr Ste 200, Beverly Hills (90210-4507)
PHONE.....................323 609-4101
Jordan T Seltzer, President
EMP: 50
SALES (est): 1.6MM Privately Held
SIC: 6531 Rental agent, real estate

(P-11539)
KELLER WILLIAMS REALTY
Also Called: Keller Williams Realtors
39 Calle De Los Ositos, Carmel Valley (93924-9711)
PHONE.....................831 622-6200
Bert Aronson, Principal
Ben Beesley, Real Est Agnt
Kristy Cosmero, Real Est Agnt
Jenifer A Jacobs, Real Est Agnt
EMP: 60
SALES (est): 1.6MM Privately Held
SIC: 6531 Real estate agent, residential

(P-11540)
KELLER WILLIAMS REALTY
Also Called: Keller Williams Realtors
100 N Citrus Ave, Covina (91723-2022)
PHONE.....................626 384-2803
John Hollander, Principal
EMP: 70 EST: 2015

SALES (est): 166.3K Privately Held
SIC: 6531 6519 Real estate agent, residential; real property lessors

(P-11541)
KELLER WILLIAMS REALTY
Also Called: Keller Williams Realtors
23670 Hawthorne Blvd # 100, Torrance (90505-5968)
PHONE.....................310 375-3511
Linda Hayden, Business Mgr
Vincenzo Oste, Manager
Rosa Chen, Real Est Agnt
Betty Fogg, Real Est Agnt
David Munoz, Real Est Agnt
EMP: 300
SALES (est): 8.8MM Privately Held
SIC: 6531 Real estate agent, residential

(P-11542)
KELLER WILLIAMS REALTY
Also Called: Keller Williams Realtors
12530 Hesperia Rd Ste 110, Victorville (92395-5848)
PHONE.....................760 951-5242
Brad Bodell, Owner
EMP: 99
SALES (est): 2.7MM Privately Held
SIC: 6531 Real estate agent, residential

(P-11543)
KELLER WILLIAMS REALTY
Also Called: Keller Williams Realtors
7898 Mission Grove Pkwy S # 102, Riverside (92508-5053)
PHONE.....................951 215-0787
Daniel Bell, Principal
Kimberly Campbell, Real Est Agnt
Debbie Galaviz, Real Est Agnt
Sue Miskelly, Real Est Agnt
EMP: 50
SALES (est): 950K Privately Held
SIC: 6531 Real estate agent, residential

(P-11544)
KELLER WILLIAMS REALTY INC
Also Called: Keller Williams Realtors
400 E Main St, Visalia (93291-6315)
PHONE.....................559 636-1235
EMP: 100
SALES (corp-wide): 113.3MM Privately Held
SIC: 6531
PA: Keller Williams Realty, Inc.
1221 S Mo Pac Expy # 400
Austin TX 78746
512 327-3070

(P-11545)
KELLER WLLAMS RLTY BVRLY HILLS
439 N Canon Dr Ste 300, Beverly Hills (90210-3909)
PHONE.....................310 432-6400
Paul Morris, Principal
Matthew Kessell, Financial Exec
John Harper, Real Est Agnt
EMP: 90
SALES (est): 4.8MM Privately Held
SIC: 6531 Real estate agent, residential

(P-11546)
KENNEDY-WILSON INC (PA)
151 El Camino Dr, Beverly Hills (90212-2704)
PHONE.....................310 887-6400
William McMorrow, Ch of Bd
Justin Enbody, CFO
John Pradhu, Vice Pres
Mary Ricks, Vice Pres
Matt Windisch, Vice Pres
EMP: 103
SALES (est): 36.6MM Privately Held
SIC: 6531 6799 Auction, real estate; real estate investors, except property operators

(P-11547)
KENNETH P SLAUGHT INC
200 E Carrillo St Ste 200 # 200, Santa Barbara (93101-2144)
PHONE.....................805 962-8989
Kenneth P Slaught, President
EMP: 50
SALES (est): 1.4MM Privately Held
SIC: 6531 Real estate brokers & agents

(P-11548)
KENNY PABST
248 Redondo Ave, Long Beach
(90803-5952)
PHONE.....................562 439-2147
George Pabst, *Owner*
EMP: 50
SALES (est): 1.3MM **Privately Held**
SIC: 6531 Real estate managers

(P-11549)
KEYSTONE PCF PROPERTY MGT INC (PA)
Also Called: Reflections and Enclave Hoa
16775 Von Karman Ave # 100, Irvine
(92606-4966)
PHONE.....................949 833-2600
Cary Treff, *President*
Denise Bergstrom, *COO*
Jared Jones, *CFO*
Gerry Kay, *CFO*
Jaime Chandler, *Vice Pres*
EMP: 56
SALES (est): 9.5MM **Privately Held**
WEB: www.canyonview.net
SIC: 6531 Real estate managers

(P-11550)
KILROY REALTY LP
2211 Michelson Dr Ste 330, Irvine
(92612-1388)
PHONE.....................949 788-1200
Doug Holte, *Senior VP*
EMP: 93
SALES (corp-wide): 719MM **Privately Held**
SIC: 6531 Real estate agent, residential
PA: Kilroy Realty, L.P.
12200 W Olympic Blvd # 200
Los Angeles CA 90064
310 481-8400

(P-11551)
KILROY REALTY LP
100 1st St Ste 250, San Francisco
(94105-4640)
PHONE.....................415 243-8803
Doug Holte, *Branch Mgr*
EMP: 116
SALES (corp-wide): 719MM **Privately Held**
SIC: 6531 6519 Real estate agents & managers; real property lessors
PA: Kilroy Realty, L.P.
12200 W Olympic Blvd # 200
Los Angeles CA 90064
310 481-8400

(P-11552)
KING MONSTER INC
Also Called: Realty One Group Solution
27451 Tourney Rd Ste 140, Valencia
(91355-6306)
PHONE.....................661 253-3000
Rich Szerman, *President*
Barabara Westover, *Treasurer*
Jean Szerman, *Vice Pres*
Patrick Raach, *Admin Sec*
EMP: 68
SQ FT: 5,000
SALES: 500K **Privately Held**
WEB: www.silvercreekrealty.com
SIC: 6531 Real estate agent, residential

(P-11553)
KOLL MANAGEMENT SERVICES INC
4343 Von Karman Ave, Newport Beach
(92660-2099)
PHONE.....................949 833-3030
Donald M Koll, *Ch of Bd*
EMP: 2400
SALES (est): 28.4MM **Privately Held**
SIC: 6531 8741 Real estate managers; management services

(P-11554)
KROPA REALTY
Also Called: Century 21
3093 Citrus Cir Ste 150, Walnut Creek
(94598-2693)
PHONE.....................925 937-4040
James Kropa, *Partner*
Maxine Chan, *Partner*
Tom Legault, *Manager*

EMP: 50
SQ FT: 2,500
SALES (est): 2.3MM **Privately Held**
WEB: www.kroparealty.com
SIC: 6531 Real estate agent, residential

(P-11555)
LA CIENEGA ASSOCIATES
Also Called: Beverly Center
8500 Beverly Blvd Ste 501, Los Angeles
(90048-6277)
PHONE.....................310 854-0071
Laurel Crary-Globus, *General Mgr*
Sheldon Gordon, *Partner*
A Alfred Taubman, *Partner*
Charlotte Warner, *Manager*
EMP: 75
SQ FT: 2,500
SALES (est): 5.7MM **Privately Held**
SIC: 6531 6512 Real estate brokers & agents; auditorium & hall operation

(P-11556)
LAGUNA WOODS VILLAGE
24351 El Toro Rd, Laguna Woods
(92637-4901)
P.O. Box 2220, Laguna Hills (92654-2220)
PHONE.....................949 597-4267
Milton John, *Director*
Russ Disbro, *Director*
EMP: 1000
SALES (est): 13.8K **Privately Held**
SIC: 6531 Real estate agents & managers

(P-11557)
LANE STUART COMPANY LLC
740 Lucille Ct, Moorpark (93021-1241)
P.O. Box 364 (93020-0364)
PHONE.....................805 553-9562
Stuart Lane, *Mng Member*
Gail Lane,
EMP: 55
SALES (est): 1.8MM **Privately Held**
SIC: 6531 Appraiser, real estate

(P-11558)
LAPHAM COMPANY INC
Also Called: Lapham Company Management
4844 Telegraph Ave, Oakland
(94609-2010)
PHONE.....................510 531-6000
Jon Shahoian, *President*
Jon M Shahoian, *President*
Menna Tesfatsion, *Vice Pres*
Jim Sweetman, *Controller*
Tony Collins, *Property Mgr*
EMP: 85 EST: 1947
SQ FT: 10,500
SALES (est): 7.9MM **Privately Held**
WEB: www.laphamcompany.com
SIC: 6531 Real estate agent, residential; real estate managers

(P-11559)
LARRY BLAIR REALTOR
2488 Junipero Serra Blvd, Daly City
(94015-1633)
PHONE.....................650 991-5267
Larry Blair, *Principal*
EMP: 50
SALES (est): 989.1K **Privately Held**
SIC: 6531 Real estate brokers & agents

(P-11560)
LBA REALTY LLC (PA)
3347 Michelson Dr Ste 200, Irvine
(92612-0687)
PHONE.....................949 833-0400
Philip A Belling, *Mng Member*
Attila Falvai, *COO*
Mike Memoly, *CFO*
Michael Coppola, *Vice Pres*
Tom Motherway, *Vice Pres*
EMP: 50
SALES (est): 28.8MM **Privately Held**
SIC: 6531 Real estate agent, commercial

(P-11561)
LEE & ASSOC COMM REAL EST SVCS
Also Called: Lee & Associates Coml RE Svcs
3535 Inland Empire Blvd, Ontario
(91764-4908)
PHONE.....................909 989-7771
Donald Kazanjian, *President*
Vincent Anthony, *Vice Pres*

Michael Chavez, *Vice Pres*
Douglas Earnhart, *Vice Pres*
Paul Earnhart, *Vice Pres*
EMP: 50
SALES (est): 4.7MM **Privately Held**
WEB: www.lee-assoc.com
SIC: 6531 8742 Real estate agent, commercial; real estate consultant

(P-11562)
LEE & ASSOCIATES COML RE SVCS (PA)
7700 Irvine Center Dr # 600, Irvine
(92618-2923)
PHONE.....................949 727-1200
John Matus, *Vice Pres*
Russ Johnson, *President*
Guy La Ferrara, *Corp Secy*
Mike Baker, *Vice Pres*
Jeff Bischofberger, *Agent*
EMP: 50
SQ FT: 8,500
SALES (est): 3.3MM **Privately Held**
SIC: 6531 Real estate agent, commercial

(P-11563)
LEE & ASSOCIATES REALTY GROUP
Also Called: LEE& Associates
100 Bayview Cir Ste 600, Newport Beach
(92660-2982)
PHONE.....................949 724-1000
Steve Jehorek, *President*
EMP: 50
SQ FT: 8,600
SALES (est): 3.9MM **Privately Held**
SIC: 6531 Real estate agent, commercial

(P-11564)
LEROY DURBIN
Also Called: Century 21
14620 Lakewood Blvd, Bellflower
(90706-2860)
PHONE.....................562 531-2001
Alex Lurchin, *Owner*
Leroy Durbin, *Owner*
EMP: 85
SALES (est): 2.1MM **Privately Held**
SIC: 6531 Real estate agent, residential

(P-11565)
LION CREEK SENIOR HOUSING PART
Also Called: Lion Creek Crossing V
6710 Lion Way, Oakland (94621-3370)
PHONE.....................510 878-9120
Jim Brooks, *Controller*
Tesa Doleman,
EMP: 99 EST: 2014
SALES (est): 2.6MM **Privately Held**
SIC: 6531 Real estate agents & managers

(P-11566)
LOIS LAUER REALTY
Also Called: Century 21
1998 Orange Tree Ln, Redlands
(92374-2841)
PHONE.....................909 748-7000
David Coy, *President*
Lawn Brian, *CEO*
Ann Bryan, *Treasurer*
Shirley Harrington, *Vice Pres*
Mike Hillard, *Technology*
EMP: 250
SQ FT: 17,000
SALES (est): 14MM **Privately Held**
WEB: www.loislauer.com
SIC: 6531 Real estate agent, residential

(P-11567)
LONG DRAGON REALTY CO INC
Also Called: Long Dragon Financial Service
2633 S Baldwin Ave, Arcadia (91007-8325)
PHONE.....................626 309-7999
Renee Ho, *CEO*
Robert Ho, *President*
George Ho, *Treasurer*
Wen LI, *General Mgr*
Vincent Chen, *Broker*
EMP: 120
SQ FT: 5,000

SALES (est): 6.7MM **Privately Held**
WEB: www.longdragonrealty.com
SIC: 6531 6163 6799 Real estate brokers & agents; mortgage brokers arranging for loans, using money of others; real estate investors, except property operators

(P-11568)
LOU BOZIGIAN
5900 Alleppo Ln, Palmdale (93551-2825)
PHONE.....................661 948-4737
Lou Bozigian, *President*
EMP: 60
SALES (est): 1.8MM **Privately Held**
WEB: www.coldwellbanker-bozigian.com
SIC: 6531 8742 Real estate brokers & agents; real estate consultant

(P-11569)
LOWE ENTERPRISES INC
11777 San Vicente Blvd # 900, Los Angeles
(90049-6615)
PHONE.....................310 820-6661
EMP: 221
SALES (corp-wide): 1B **Privately Held**
SIC: 6531 Real estate managers
PA: Lowe Enterprises, Inc.
11777 San Vicente Blvd # 900
Los Angeles CA 90049
310 820-6661

(P-11570)
LOWE ENTERPRISES INC (PA)
Also Called: Lei AG Seattle
11777 San Vicente Blvd # 900, Los Angeles
(90049-6615)
PHONE.....................310 820-6661
Robert J Lowe, *President*
Sara Bravo, *President*
Joseph Heredia, *President*
James Sabatier, *President*
Rick Swagerty, *President*
EMP: 125
SQ FT: 20,000
SALES (est): 1B **Privately Held**
WEB: www.ccpavilion.com
SIC: 6531 6552 Real estate managers; subdividers & developers

(P-11571)
LOYDA YU REAL ESTATE INC
860 Kuhn Dr Ste 200, Chula Vista
(91914-4517)
PHONE.....................619 475-7777
Loyda Calvano, *President*
EMP: 60
SALES (est): 212.6K **Privately Held**
SIC: 6531 Real estate agent, residential

(P-11572)
LRES CORPORATION (PA)
765 The City Dr S Ste 300, Orange
(92868-6916)
PHONE.....................714 520-5737
Roger Beane, *President*
Mark R Johnson, *President*
Paul Abbamonto, *COO*
Susheel Mantha, *CFO*
Richard Cimino, *Senior VP*
EMP: 91
SQ FT: 11,000
SALES: 27MM **Privately Held**
WEB: www.lrescorp.com
SIC: 6531 Real estate managers

(P-11573)
LYON REAL ESTATE
150 Natoma Station Dr # 300, Folsom
(95630-7965)
PHONE.....................916 355-7000
Michael Lyon, *CFO*
Dave Wilson, *CTO*
Peggie Ryan, *Database Admin*
Sara Veliz, *Asst Controller*
Ron Mott, *Broker*
EMP: 75
SALES (est): 2.3MM **Privately Held**
SIC: 6531 Real estate agent, residential; real estate brokers & agents

(P-11574)
LYON REALTY
8814 Madison Ave, Fair Oaks
(95628-3908)
PHONE.....................916 962-0111
Bryan Wurth, *Broker*

Steven C Barnes, *Real Est Agnt*
Suzanne Capestro, *Real Est Agnt*
Patty Crawford, *Real Est Agnt*
Peggy Kengle, *Real Est Agnt*
EMP: 218 Privately Held
SIC: 6531 Selling agent, real estate
PA: Lyon Realty
2280 Del Paso Rd Ste 100
Sacramento CA 95834
-

(P-11575)
LYON REALTY (PA)
2280 Del Paso Rd Ste 100, Sacramento
(95834-9701)
PHONE.....................916 574-8800
Patrick Shey, *President*
Rod Bouvia, *Broker*
Joann Kaleel, *Broker*
Tim Pierce, *Sales Associate*
Tong Veu, *Property Mgr*
EMP: 900
SALES (est): 19.6MM Privately Held
SIC: 6531 6519 Real estate agent, residential; real property lessors

(P-11576)
M & S ACQUISITION
CORPORATION (PA)
707 Wilshire Blvd # 5200, Los Angeles
(90017-3501)
PHONE.....................213 385-1515
Mark Santarsiero, *CFO*
Robert Kerslake, *Ch of Bd*
Paul Craig, *CFO*
Merle Atkins, *Exec VP*
John Spude, *Exec VP*
EMP: 115
SALES (est): 11.7MM Privately Held
SIC: 6531 8742 Appraiser, real estate; management consulting services

(P-11577)
M S E ENTERPRISES INC (PA)
Also Called: Marshall S Ezralow & Assoc
23622 Calabasas Rd # 200, Calabasas
(91302-1549)
PHONE.....................818 223-3500
Marshall S Ezralow, *President*
EMP: 90
SALES (est): 3.6MM Privately Held
WEB: www.ezralow.com
SIC: 6531 Real estate managers

(P-11578)
MACDONALD HOUSING
PARTNERS LP
Also Called: Trinity Plaza
350 Macdonald Ave Ste 100, Richmond
(94801-3097)
PHONE.....................510 620-0865
Jim Brooks, *Controller*
Tesa Doleman, *Manager*
EMP: 50 EST: 2009
SALES (est): 1.2MM Privately Held
SIC: 6531 Real estate agents & managers

(P-11579)
MACERICH COMPANY
10800 W Pico Blvd Ste 312, Los Angeles
(90064-2187)
PHONE.....................310 474-5940
Ken Raffensberger, *Manager*
EMP: 52
SALES (corp-wide): 993.6MM Publicly Held
SIC: 6531 Real estate agent, commercial
PA: Macerich Company
401 Wilshire Blvd Ste 700
Santa Monica CA 90401
310 394-6000

(P-11580)
MAJESTY ONE PROPERTIES
INC
6249 Quartz St, Rancho Cucamonga
(91701-3437)
PHONE.....................909 980-8000
Julio Cardenas, *President*
EMP: 130
SALES (est): 3.7MM Privately Held
SIC: 6531 Real estate agents & managers

(P-11581)
MALIBU REALTY INC
Also Called: Malibu Realty Property MGT
23838 Pacific Coast Hwy, Malibu
(90265-1513)
PHONE.....................310 457-5124
Eugene Calvin Barginear, *President*
Barbara Barginear, *CFO*
Jill Barginear-Getz, *Admin Sec*
EMP: 50
SALES (est): 767.4K Privately Held
WEB: www.caroldarrow.com
SIC: 6531 Real estate brokers & agents

(P-11582)
MANGOLD PROPERTY
MANAGEMENT
575 Calle Principal, Monterey
(93940-2811)
PHONE.....................831 372-1338
Thomas Mangold, *Owner*
EMP: 65
SQ FT: 13,000
SALES (est): 5.7MM Privately Held
WEB: www.mangoldproperties.com
SIC: 6531 Real estate managers

(P-11583)
MARCUS & MILLICHAP CAPITL
CORP
23975 Park Sorrento # 400, Calabasas
(91302-4014)
PHONE.....................818 212-2250
George Marcus, *President*
David Shillingtonas, *President*
Michael Shaffner, *Assoc VP*
Joe Linkogle, *Vice Pres*
Clifford Braly, *Research Analys*
EMP: 50
SALES (est): 2.9MM
SALES (corp-wide): 719.7MM Publicly Held
SIC: 6531 Real estate brokers & agents
HQ: Marcus & Millichap Real Estate Investment Services, Inc.
23975 Park Sorrento # 400
Calabasas CA 91302
-

(P-11584)
MARCUS & MILLICHAP REAL
ESTATE
Also Called: Ponderosa Mobile Estates
750 Battery St Fl 5, San Francisco
(94111-1531)
PHONE.....................415 391-9220
Jeffrey M Mishkin, *Sales Mgr*
Jeff Mishkin, *Manager*
EMP: 50
SALES (corp-wide): 90.7MM Privately Held
SIC: 6531 8742 Real estate brokers & agents; real estate consultant
HQ: Marcus & Millichap Real Estate Investment Services Of Indiana, Inc.
2626 Hanover St
Palo Alto CA 94304
650 494-1400

(P-11585)
MARCUS MILLICHAP REIS NEV
INC
23975 Park Sorrento # 400, Calabasas
(91302-4015)
PHONE.....................650 494-1400
George M Marcus, *Owner*
EMP: 70
SALES (est): 4.4MM
SALES (corp-wide): 719.7MM Publicly Held
SIC: 6531 Buying agent, real estate
PA: Marcus & Millichap, Inc.
23975 Park Sorrento # 400
Calabasas CA 91302
818 212-2250

(P-11586)
MARCUS MLLICHAP RE INV
SVCS INC (HQ)
Also Called: Instittional Property Advisors
23975 Park Sorrento # 400, Calabasas
(91302-4015)
PHONE.....................818 212-2250
William Millichap, *President*
Steve Gebing, *Director*

Joshua Jandris, *Director*
EMP: 50
SALES (est): 13.2MM
SALES (corp-wide): 719.7MM Publicly Held
SIC: 6531 Real estate agents & managers
PA: Marcus & Millichap, Inc.
23975 Park Sorrento # 400
Calabasas CA 91302
818 212-2250

(P-11587)
MARRAKESH MANAGEMENT
CORP
47000 Marrakesh Dr, Palm Desert
(92260-5805)
PHONE.....................760 568-2688
Barbara Valdivia, *Controller*
Dan Cooper, *Exec VP*
EMP: 50
SQ FT: 5,000
SALES: 704.3K Privately Held
WEB: www.marrakeshcountryclub.com
SIC: 6531 Real estate managers

(P-11588)
MASON-MCDUFFIE REAL
ESTATE INC
Also Called: Prudential
2095 Rose St Ste 100, Berkeley
(94709-1997)
PHONE.....................510 705-8611
Phina Chrisentery, *Manager*
EMP: 70
SALES (corp-wide): 33.1MM Privately Held
WEB: www.mohrparkneighbors.com
SIC: 6531 Real estate agent, residential
PA: Mason-Mcduffie Real Estate, Inc.
1555 Riviera Ave Ste E
Walnut Creek CA 94596
925 924-4600

(P-11589)
MASON-MCDUFFIE REAL
ESTATE INC
Also Called: Prudential
2051 Mt Diablo Blvd, Walnut Creek
(94596-4301)
PHONE.....................925 932-1000
Steve Curtis, *Manager*
EMP: 78
SALES (corp-wide): 33.1MM Privately Held
WEB: www.mohrparkneighbors.com
SIC: 6531 Real estate agent, residential
PA: Mason-Mcduffie Real Estate, Inc.
1555 Riviera Ave Ste E
Walnut Creek CA 94596
925 924-4600

(P-11590)
MASON-MCDUFFIE REAL
ESTATE INC
Also Called: Prudential
5887 Lone Tree Way Ste A, Antioch
(94531-8625)
PHONE.....................925 776-2740
Melody Royal, *Manager*
EMP: 52
SALES (corp-wide): 33.1MM Privately Held
WEB: www.mohrparkneighbors.com
SIC: 6531 Real estate agent, residential
PA: Mason-Mcduffie Real Estate, Inc.
1555 Riviera Ave Ste E
Walnut Creek CA 94596
925 924-4600

(P-11591)
MASON-MCDUFFIE REAL
ESTATE INC
21060 Redwood Rd Ste 100, Castro Valley
(94546-5931)
PHONE.....................510 886-7511
Gretchen Pearson, *Manager*
EMP: 50
SALES (corp-wide): 33.1MM Privately Held
WEB: www.mohrparkneighbors.com
SIC: 6531 Real estate agent, residential
PA: Mason-Mcduffie Real Estate, Inc.
1555 Riviera Ave Ste E
Walnut Creek CA 94596
925 924-4600

(P-11592)
MASON-MCDUFFIE REAL
ESTATE INC
Also Called: Predentials
3320 Grand Ave, Oakland (94610-2737)
PHONE.....................510 834-2010
Amberson McCulloch, *Manager*
Ernest Villafranca, *Real Est Agnt*
EMP: 80
SALES (corp-wide): 33.1MM Privately Held
WEB: www.mohrparkneighbors.com
SIC: 6531 Real estate agent, commercial
PA: Mason-Mcduffie Real Estate, Inc.
1555 Riviera Ave Ste E
Walnut Creek CA 94596
925 924-4600

(P-11593)
MASON-MCDUFFIE REAL
ESTATE INC
Also Called: Dutra Realty
5950 Stoneridge Dr, Pleasanton
(94588-2706)
PHONE.....................925 734-5000
Frank Cannella, *Manager*
Sue Condon, *Real Est Agnt*
EMP: 80
SALES (corp-wide): 33.1MM Privately Held
WEB: www.mohrparkneighbors.com
SIC: 6531 Real estate agent, residential
PA: Mason-Mcduffie Real Estate, Inc.
1555 Riviera Ave Ste E
Walnut Creek CA 94596
925 924-4600

(P-11594)
MATTHEWS RETAIL GROUP INC
Also Called: Matthews Real Estate Inv Svcs
841 Apollo St Ste 150, El Segundo
(90245-4724)
PHONE.....................866 889-0550
Kyle B Matthews, *President*
Radoslav Zlatkov, *CFO*
Redoslav Zlatkov, *CFO*
David Harrington, *Exec VP*
Chad Kurz, *Senior VP*
EMP: 59
SALES (est): 2.1MM Privately Held
SIC: 6531 7389 Real estate agent, commercial; financial services

(P-11595)
MAX SOMMERS REAL ESTATE
615 Esplanade Unit 312, Redondo Beach
(90277-4135)
PHONE.....................310 560-1499
Max Sommers, *Owner*
EMP: 75
SALES (est): 1.6MM Privately Held
SIC: 6531 Real estate agents & managers

(P-11596)
MBK REAL ESTATE COMPANIES
Also Called: MBK Laguna
4 Park Plz Ste 1000, Irvine (92614-2552)
PHONE.....................949 789-8300
Kain Matsumoto, *Chairman*
Kent Crandall, *CFO*
Edward Stokx, *CFO*
Karen Moore, *Exec Dir*
Amanda McCann, *Marketing Mgr*
EMP: 50
SALES (est): 6.5MM
SALES (corp-wide): 45.9B Privately Held
WEB: www.mitsui.co.jp
SIC: 6531 Real estate agents & managers
PA: Mitsui & Co., Ltd.
1-1-3, Marunouchi
Chiyoda-Ku TKY 100-0
332 851-111

(P-11597)
MBK REAL ESTATE LTD A
CALFOR (HQ)
4 Park Plz Ste 1000, Irvine (92614-2552)
PHONE.....................949 789-8300
Stefan Markowitz, *General Ptnr*
Kent Crandall, *CFO*
Jonathan Evans, *Analyst*
Corky Curtis, *Senior Mgr*
EMP: 58
SQ FT: 39,985

SALES (est): 10.7MM
SALES (corp-wide): 45.9B **Privately Held**
SIC: 6531 Real estate managers; auction, real estate
PA: Mitsui & Co., Ltd.
    1-1-3, Marunouchi
    Chiyoda-Ku TKY 100-0
    332 851-111

(P-11598)
MCM PARTNERS INC
Also Called: Prudential
6111 Johnson Ct Ste 110, Pleasanton
(94588-3373)
PHONE..................925 463-9500
Janet P Cristano, *President*
EMP: 65
SALES (est): 2.5MM **Privately Held**
SIC: 6531 Real estate agent, residential

(P-11599)
MCMILLIN RE & MRTG CO INC (PA)
Also Called: McMillin Escrow
4210 Bonita Rd Ste B, Bonita
(91902-1419)
PHONE..................619 475-0233
Scott Mc Millin, *President*
Robert Jones, *Treasurer*
Patricia Poole, *Exec VP*
David Johnston, *Senior VP*
Isabelle Hall, *Vice Pres*
EMP: 81
SALES (est): 5.3MM **Privately Held**
SIC: 6531 6163 Buying agent, real estate; escrow agent, real estate; mortgage brokers arranging for loans, using money of others

(P-11600)
MCMILLIN RE & MRTG CO INC
320 E H St, Chula Vista (91910-7483)
PHONE..................619 422-4500
Amrian Adan, *Manager*
EMP: 60
SALES (corp-wide): 5.3MM **Privately Held**
SIC: 6531 Buying agent, real estate
PA: Mcmillin Real Estate & Mortgage Company, Inc.
    4210 Bonita Rd Ste B
    Bonita CA 91902
    619 475-0233

(P-11601)
MELISSA BRADLEY RE INC
206 E Blithedale Ave, Mill Valley
(94941-2028)
PHONE..................415 388-5113
Mette Shirley, *Branch Mgr*
Noelle X Forfota, *Real Est Agnt*
EMP: 51
SALES (est): 7.3MM **Privately Held**
SIC: 6531 6519 Real estate brokers & agents; real property lessors
PA: Melissa Bradley Real Estate, Inc.
    55 Broadway Blvd
    Fairfax CA 94930
    415 455-1140

(P-11602)
MELISSA BRADLEY RE INC
3249 Browns Valley Rd, NAPA
(94558-5424)
PHONE..................707 258-3900
Carol Adler, *Branch Mgr*
EMP: 51
SALES (corp-wide): 7.3MM **Privately Held**
SIC: 6531 Real estate agent, residential
PA: Melissa Bradley Real Estate, Inc.
    55 Broadway Blvd
    Fairfax CA 94930
    415 455-1140

(P-11603)
MELISSA BRADLEY RE INC
1401 4th St, Santa Rosa (95404-4015)
PHONE..................707 536-0888
Robert Bradley, *Branch Mgr*
Alana Dwyer, *Broker*
Nancy Hoskins, *Sales Staff*
James Withington, *Consultant*
EMP: 51

SALES (corp-wide): 8.1MM **Privately Held**
SIC: 6531 Real estate brokers & agents
PA: Melissa Bradley Real Estate, Inc.
    55 Broadway Blvd
    Fairfax CA 94930
    415 455-1140

(P-11604)
MELISSA BRADLEY RE INC
1690 Tiburon Blvd, Belvedere Tiburon
(94920-2543)
PHONE..................415 435-2705
Arlene Manalo, *Branch Mgr*
Jo-Anne Fong, *Sales Staff*
Wayne Malen, *Sales Staff*
Dan Godfrey, *Agent*
EMP: 51
SALES (corp-wide): 8.1MM **Privately Held**
SIC: 6531 Real estate agent, residential
PA: Melissa Bradley Real Estate, Inc.
    55 Broadway Blvd
    Fairfax CA 94930
    415 455-1140

(P-11605)
MELISSA BRADLEY RE INC
1701 Novato Blvd Ste 100, Novato
(94947-3002)
PHONE..................415 209-1000
Julie Mello, *Branch Mgr*
Kirtis Donaldson, *Real Est Agnt*
Pamela S English, *Real Est Agnt*
Alan Kilpatrick, *Real Est Agnt*
EMP: 100
SALES (corp-wide): 8.1MM **Privately Held**
SIC: 6531 Real estate agent, residential
PA: Melissa Bradley Real Estate, Inc.
    55 Broadway Blvd
    Fairfax CA 94930
    415 455-1140

(P-11606)
MELISSA BRADLEY RE INC
44 Bolinas Rd, Fairfax (94930-1661)
PHONE..................415 485-4300
Vince Sheehan, *Branch Mgr*
EMP: 51
SALES (corp-wide): 7.3MM **Privately Held**
SIC: 6531 Real estate brokers & agents
PA: Melissa Bradley Real Estate, Inc.
    55 Broadway Blvd
    Fairfax CA 94930
    415 455-1140

(P-11607)
MERCY HOUSING CALIFORNIA XXVI
Also Called: Mercy Housing Calif Xxv
2512 River Plaza Dr, Sacramento
(95833-3677)
PHONE..................916 414-4400
Greg Sparks, *General Ptnr*
EMP: 60
SALES (est): 1.7MM
SALES (corp-wide): 322.3MM **Privately Held**
SIC: 6531 Real estate agents & managers
HQ: Mercy Housing California Xxv, A California Limited Partnership
    1256 Market St
    San Francisco CA 94102

(P-11608)
MERIDIAN MANAGEMENT GROUP
1145 Bush St, San Francisco (94109-5919)
PHONE..................415 434-9700
Randall Chapman, *President*
Gil Dowd, *Vice Pres*
Russell Flynn, *Vice Pres*
James R Wilson, *Admin Sec*
Sharon Lui, *Human Res Dir*
EMP: 160
SQ FT: 6,200
SALES (est): 15.3MM **Privately Held**
WEB: www.mmgroup.com
SIC: 6531 Real estate managers

(P-11609)
MERRILL GARDENS LLC
799 Yellowstone Dr, Vacaville
(95687-3449)
PHONE..................707 447-7496
Holly Sullins, *Branch Mgr*
EMP: 60 **Privately Held**
SIC: 6531 Real estate agents & managers
PA: Merrill Gardens L.L.C.
    1938 Frview Ave E Ste 300
    Seattle WA 98102

(P-11610)
MESA MANAGEMENT INC
1451 Quail St Ste 201, Newport Beach
(92660-2741)
P.O. Box 2990 (92658-9018)
PHONE..................949 851-0995
Steve Mensinger, *President*
Robert Lucas, *Vice Pres*
Aaron Schmiti, *Director*
EMP: 70
SQ FT: 5,000
SALES (est): 9.9MM **Privately Held**
WEB: www.mesamanagement.net
SIC: 6531 Real estate managers

(P-11611)
MGR SERVICES INC
1425 W Foothill Blvd # 300, Upland
(91786-8007)
PHONE..................909 981-4466
Michael Rademaker, *President*
Terry Padgitt, *Sales Mgr*
Tony Hermosillo, *Manager*
EMP: 73
SQ FT: 13,000
SALES (est): 5.7MM **Privately Held**
WEB: www.mgrservices.com
SIC: 6531 Selling agent, real estate; real estate managers

(P-11612)
MODULAR SYSTEMS INC
Also Called: MSI
800 Garden St Ste K, Santa Barbara
(93101-1596)
PHONE..................805 963-9350
Antonio R Romasanta, *President*
Angie Schultz, *Admin Sec*
EMP: 52
SQ FT: 6,000
SALES (est): 2.7MM **Privately Held**
SIC: 6531 8742 Real estate managers; management consulting services

(P-11613)
MOONSTONE MANAGEMENT CORP (PA)
Also Called: Moonstone Hotel Properties
2905 Burton Dr, Cambria (93428-4001)
PHONE..................805 927-4200
Dirk Winter, *President*
Christine Diacetis, *Regional Mgr*
Tina Terrell, *General Mgr*
Naomi Motta, *Admin Asst*
Matthhew Holder, *CIO*
EMP: 175
SQ FT: 5,000
SALES (est): 14.1MM **Privately Held**
SIC: 6531 Real estate managers

(P-11614)
MOSS & COMPANY INC (PA)
15300 Ventura Blvd # 418, Sherman Oaks
(91403-3140)
PHONE..................310 453-0911
Cindy Gray, *President*
Don Shields, *COO*
Chris Gray, *Exec VP*
Ronald Maurer, *Vice Pres*
Henriette Saffron, *Vice Pres*
EMP: 70
SQ FT: 10,000
SALES (est): 2.6MM **Privately Held**
SIC: 6531 Real estate managers

(P-11615)
MOUNTAIN HIGH RESORT ASSOC LLC
24512 Highway 2, Wrightwood (92397)
P.O. Box 3010 (92397-3010)
PHONE..................760 249-5808
Karl Kapuscinski,

Judy Pritts, *Human Res Dir*
John McColly, *VP Sales*
Joseph Stocking, *Marketing Mgr*
Michelle Roy,
EMP: 900
SALES (est): 45MM **Privately Held**
SIC: 6531 Real estate managers

(P-11616)
MOUNTAIN-PACIFIC FINANCIAL (PA)
Also Called: Re/Max
1010 Prospect St Ste 300, La Jolla
(92037-4109)
PHONE..................858 456-8420
Geoffrey Mountain, *President*
Wesley Christensen, *Broker*
Lisa Hall, *Broker*
Heather Caden, *Real Est Agnt*
Dave Dennis, *Real Est Agnt*
EMP: 70
SQ FT: 7,500
SALES (est): 3.8MM **Privately Held**
WEB:
www.distinctivepropertiesrealestate.com
SIC: 6531 Real estate agent, residential

(P-11617)
MOVE INC
8428 Calvin Ave, Northridge (91324-4212)
PHONE..................818 701-0012
Dan Laudo, *Branch Mgr*
EMP: 126
SALES (corp-wide): 9B **Publicly Held**
SIC: 6531 Real estate listing services
HQ: Move, Inc.
    3315 Scott Blvd Ste 250
    Santa Clara CA 95054
    408 558-7100

(P-11618)
MOVE INC (HQ)
Also Called: Realsuite SM
3315 Scott Blvd Ste 250, Santa Clara
(95054-3139)
PHONE..................408 558-7100
Steven H Berkowitz, *CEO*
Sunil Mehrotra, *President*
Eric Thorkilsen, *President*
Bryan Charap, *CFO*
Rachel C Glaser, *CFO*
EMP: 500
SQ FT: 32,405
SALES (est): 183.9MM
SALES (corp-wide): 9B **Publicly Held**
WEB: www.homestore.com
SIC: 6531 Real estate listing services; multiple listing service, real estate
PA: News Corporation
    1211 Ave Of The Americas
    New York NY 10036
    212 416-3400

(P-11619)
MOVE CO
30700 Russell Ranch Rd # 100, Westlake
Village (91362-9501)
PHONE..................805 557-2300
Lisa Farris, *Chief Mktg Ofcr*
Larry Peterson, *Vice Pres*
Julie Rice, *Info Tech Mgr*
Dave Overend, *Engineer*
Dan Wool, *Mktg Dir*
EMP: 110
SALES (est): 7.8MM **Privately Held**
SIC: 6531 Real estate agent, commercial

(P-11620)
MOVOTO LLC
1900 S Norfolk St Ste 310, San Mateo
(94403-1171)
PHONE..................888 766-8686
Shiro Takeuchi, *CEO*
Mark Brandemuehl, *COO*
EMP: 51
SALES (est): 1MM **Privately Held**
SIC: 6531 Real estate brokers & agents

(P-11621)
MP TICE OAKS ASSOCIATES A CA
Also Called: Tice Oaks Apartments
2150 Valley Blvd, Walnut Creek (94595)
PHONE..................650 356-2976
Matthew O Franklin, *Partner*
EMP: 99

SALES: 600K **Privately Held**
SIC: 6531 Real estate agents & managers

(P-11622)
MULHEARN
Also Called: Tifanny Mulhearn Realtors
11306 183rd St Ste 101, Cerritos
(90703-5408)
PHONE.................................562 860-2443
Bruce Mulhearn, *President*
Dick Allen, *Officer*
Maricela Flores, *Broker*
Johnny Salas, *Broker*
Kay Mascaro, *Real Est Agnt*
EMP: 70
SALES (est): 2.4MM **Privately Held**
WEB: www.prucarealty.com
SIC: 6531 Real estate brokers & agents

(P-11623)
MURCOR INC
Also Called: Pcv Murcor Real Estate Svcs
740 Corp Ctr Dr, Pomona (91768)
PHONE.................................909 623-4001
Keith D Murray, *President*
Cindy Nasser, *COO*
Tim Scherf, *COO*
Richard J Barkley, *Exec VP*
Jon D Van Deuren, *Exec VP*
EMP: 225
SALES (est): 17.8MM **Privately Held**
SIC: 6531 Appraiser, real estate

(P-11624)
NELSON SHELTON & ASSOCIATES
Also Called: Nelson, Shelton, & Associates
355 N Canon Dr, Beverly Hills
(90210-4704)
PHONE.................................310 271-2229
Mark Shelton, *Vice Pres*
Elsa Nelson, *Vice Pres*
EMP: 200
SALES (est): 7.2MM **Privately Held**
WEB: www.jeffmarkell.com
SIC: 6531 Real estate agent, residential

(P-11625)
NEVIN LEVY LLP A PARTNERSHIP
50 California St Ste 1500, San Francisco
(94111-4612)
PHONE.................................415 800-5770
Nathan Diehl, *Vice Chairman*
EMP: 63
SQ FT: 4,000
SALES (est): 1.6MM **Privately Held**
SIC: 6531 Buying agent, real estate

(P-11626)
NEW HOME PROFESSIONALS
Also Called: Estate Investment Group
6500 Dublin Blvd Ste 201, Dublin
(94568-3152)
P.O. Box 2398 (94568-0239)
PHONE.................................925 556-1555
Jay Lange, *President*
EMP: 150 EST: 1984
SALES (est): 6.1MM **Privately Held**
SIC: 6531 Real estate agents & managers

(P-11627)
NEWMARK & COMPANY RE INC
Also Called: Newmark Grubb Knight Frank
4675 Macarthur Ct # 1600, Newport Beach
(92660-1875)
PHONE.................................949 608-2000
Oliver Fleener, *Vice Pres*
Gary Allen, *Vice Pres*
Eva Horton, *Vice Pres*
Dana Hamric, *Associate Dir*
Nick Carey, *Broker*
EMP: 96
SALES (corp-wide): 3.3B **Publicly Held**
SIC: 6531 Real estate brokers & agents
HQ: Newmark & Company Real Estate, Inc.
125 Park Ave
New York NY 10017
212 372-2000

(P-11628)
NEWPORT PACIFIC CAPITAL CO INC (PA)
17300 Red Hill Ave # 280, Irvine
(92614-5656)
PHONE.................................949 852-5575
Michael Sullivan, *CEO*
Clarke Fairbrother, *President*
Katie Albright, *Regional Mgr*
Maria Horton, *Regional Mgr*
Steve Binder, *Office Mgr*
EMP: 150
SQ FT: 3,100
SALES (est): 18MM **Privately Held**
SIC: 6531 Rental agent, real estate; broker
of manufactured homes, on site

(P-11629)
NIJJAR REALTY INC (PA)
4900 Santa Anita Ave 2b, El Monte
(91731-1498)
P.O. Box 6085 (91734-2085)
PHONE.................................626 575-0062
Daljit Kler, *Principal*
Mike Nijjar, *President*
Swaranjit S Nijjar, *CEO*
Peter Nijjar, *Treasurer*
EMP: 70
SQ FT: 2,000
SALES (est): 6.7MM **Privately Held**
SIC: 6531 Real estate brokers & agents;
real estate agent, commercial; real estate
agent, residential

(P-11630)
NMMS TWIN PEAKS LLC
Also Called: PBR Twin Peaks
5850 Canoga Ave Ste 650, Woodland Hills
(91367-6573)
PHONE.................................818 710-6100
Sandra Kist,
Sanford Siegal,
EMP: 100
SALES (est): 4.9MM **Privately Held**
SIC: 6531 Real estate agent, commercial

(P-11631)
NMS PROPERTIES INC
1430 5th St Ste 101, Santa Monica
(90401-4423)
PHONE.................................310 475-7600
Naum Shekhter, *CEO*
Margot Shekhter, *President*
Dino Ciarmoli, *Exec VP*
Scott Walter, *Exec VP*
EMP: 95
SALES (est): 13.9MM **Privately Held**
SIC: 6531 Real estate managers

(P-11632)
NNJ SERVICES INC
9610 Waples St, San Diego (92121-2955)
PHONE.................................858 550-7900
Lelnor Hugus, *CEO*
Mike Packard, *President*
EMP: 250
SALES (est): 5.5MM **Privately Held**
WEB: www.nnj.com
SIC: 6531 Real estate agents & managers

(P-11633)
NOBLE TOWER PRESERVATION LP
1515 Lakeside Dr, Oakland (94612-4558)
PHONE.................................510 444-5228
Larry Lipton, *Principal*
Tesa Doleman, *Manager*
EMP: 99
SALES (est): 3.7MM **Privately Held**
SIC: 6531 Real estate agents & managers

(P-11634)
NORCAL GOLD INC
Also Called: Re/Max
2340 E Bidwell St, Folsom (95630-3455)
PHONE.................................916 984-8778
Michael Kooken, *Manager*
Sara Crouch, *Broker*
Todd Cackler, *Agent*
Debbie Woodruff, *Consultant*
Janice Dodson, *Real Est Agnt*
EMP: 50
SALES (corp-wide): 21.7MM **Privately Held**
SIC: 6531 Real estate agent, residential

PA: Norcal Gold, Inc.
5200 Sunrise Blvd Ste 5
Fair Oaks CA 95628
916 218-6700

(P-11635)
NORTHGATE TER CMNTY PARTNER LP
550 24th St, Oakland (94612-1757)
PHONE.................................510 465-9346
Fax: 510 465-0604
EMP: 50
SQ FT: 49,846
SALES (est): 1.8MM **Privately Held**
SIC: 6531

(P-11636)
NOURMAND & ASSOCIATES
421 N Beverly Dr Ste 200, Beverly Hills
(90210-4643)
PHONE.................................310 274-4000
Saeed Nourmand, *President*
Brendan Brown, *Real Est Agnt*
Geoffrey Peterson, *Real Est Agnt*
EMP: 50
SALES (est): 2.3MM **Privately Held**
WEB: www.andreabest.net
SIC: 6531 Real estate agent, residential

(P-11637)
NRT COMMERCIAL UTAH LLC
Also Called: Coldwell Banker
42 S Pasadena Ave, Pasadena
(91105-1943)
PHONE.................................626 449-5222
Dale Williamson, *Manager*
Shiun Lin, *Broker*
Armine Tagvoryan, *Marketing Mgr*
Eddie Kanouse, *Sales Associate*
Natalie Oginz, *Manager*
EMP: 100 **Publicly Held**
WEB: www.nrtinc.com
SIC: 6531 Real estate agent, residential
HQ: Nrt Commercial Utah Llc
175 Park Ave
Madison NJ 07940

(P-11638)
NSW REAL ESTATE HOLDINGS LLC
99 S Hill Dr Ste A, Brisbane (94005-1282)
PHONE.................................415 467-7600
Richard F Leao, *President*
EMP: 90
SALES (est): 8.4MM **Privately Held**
SIC: 6531 Real estate brokers & agents

(P-11639)
NUTEC ENTERPRISES INC
Also Called: Prudential
24200 Magic Mountain Pkwy # 105, Valencia (91355-4887)
PHONE.................................661 287-3200
Roxanna Ramey, *President*
Mark Jenkins, *Vice Pres*
EMP: 94
SQ FT: 5,000
SALES (est): 3.5MM **Privately Held**
WEB: www.scvfinehomes.com
SIC: 6531 Real estate agent, residential

(P-11640)
OAKTREE REAL ESTATE OPPORTUNIT
333 S Grand Ave Fl 28, Los Angeles
(90071-1504)
PHONE.................................213 830-6300
EMP: 1023 EST: 2014
SALES (est): 201.5K **Privately Held**
SIC: 6531 Real estate agents & managers
PA: Oaktree Capital Group Holdings, L.P.
333 S Grand Ave Fl 28
Los Angeles CA 90071

(P-11641)
OMNINET TWIN TOWERS GP LLC
9420 Wilshire Blvd # 400, Beverly Hills
(90212-3151)
PHONE.................................310 300-4100
Jacquie Felan,
EMP: 50 EST: 2012

SALES (est): 1.7MM **Privately Held**
SIC: 6531 Real estate agents & managers

(P-11642)
OMNINET TWIN TOWERS LP
9420 Wilshire Blvd # 400, Beverly Hills
(90212-3151)
PHONE.................................310 300-4110
Andrea Constantini, *Manager*
EMP: 50
SQ FT: 215,000
SALES (est): 2.7MM **Privately Held**
SIC: 6531 Fiduciary, real estate

(P-11643)
ON CENTRAL REALTY INC
1648 Colorado Blvd, Los Angeles (90041)
PHONE.................................323 543-8500
Vazrik Bonyadi, *Branch Mgr*
EMP: 355 **Privately Held**
SIC: 6531 6519 Real estate agents &
managers; real property lessors
PA: On Central Realty, Inc.
1625 W Glenoaks Blvd
Glendale CA 91201

(P-11644)
ORCHARD HOLDINGS GROUP INC
1 Venture Ste 300, Irvine (92618-7416)
PHONE.................................949 502-8300
James Saccacio, *President*
Larry Spencer, *Vice Pres*
Bud Reynolds, *Admin Sec*
EMP: 160
SQ FT: 1,300
SALES (est): 7.6MM **Privately Held**
SIC: 6531 Real estate agents & managers

(P-11645)
PACIFIC CITIES MANAGEMENT INC (PA)
Also Called: Westcal Management
6056 Rutland Dr Ste 1, Carmichael
(95608-0514)
P.O. Box 417127, Sacramento (95841-7127)
PHONE.................................916 348-1188
Michael Force, *President*
EMP: 55
SQ FT: 2,600
SALES (est): 4.2MM **Privately Held**
SIC: 6531 Real estate managers

(P-11646)
PACIFIC HOUSING MANAGEMENT (PA)
945 Katella St, Laguna Beach
(92651-3705)
PHONE.................................714 508-1777
Richard Hall, *President*
EMP: 60
SALES (est): 3.6MM **Privately Held**
WEB: www.sharonmichael.com
SIC: 6531 Real estate managers

(P-11647)
PACIFIC MEDICAL BUILDINGS LP
Also Called: P M B
3394 Carmel Mountain Rd # 200, San
Diego (92121-1066)
PHONE.................................858 794-1900
Jeffrey L Rush MD, *Mng Member*
Elizabeth A Powell,
Robert A Rosenthal,
Mark Toothacre,
EMP: 55
SQ FT: 5,000
SALES (est): 7MM **Privately Held**
SIC: 6531 Real estate managers

(P-11648)
PACIFIC MONARCH RESORTS INC
7 Grenada St, Laguna Niguel
(92677-4825)
PHONE.................................949 228-1396
EMP: 72
SALES (corp-wide): 16.6MM **Privately Held**
SIC: 6531 Real estate agents & managers

PA: Pacific Monarch Resorts, Inc.
4000 Macarthur Blvd # 600
Newport Beach CA 92660
949 609-2400

(P-11649)
PACIFIC MONARCH RESORTS INC (PA)
Also Called: Vacation Interval Realty
4000 Macarthur Blvd # 600, Newport Beach
(92660-2558)
PHONE................................949 609-2400
Mark D Post, *CEO*
Richard Muller, *President*
Nick Baldwin, *Vice Pres*
Carlton Post, *Director*
EMP: 100
SQ FT: 20,000
SALES (est): 16.6MM **Privately Held**
SIC: 6531 7011 Time-sharing real estate
sales, leasing & rentals; vacation lodges

(P-11650)
PACIFIC RIM REALTY GROUP
740 Lucille Ct, Moorpark (93021-1241)
P.O. Box 364 (93020-0364)
PHONE................................805 553-9562
Stuart Groten, *President*
EMP: 50
SALES: 950K **Privately Held**
SIC: 6531 Real estate brokers & agents

(P-11651)
PACIFIC UNION CO
1550 Tiburon Blvd Ste U, Belvedere
(94920-2516)
PHONE................................415 789-8686
EMP: 67
SALES (corp-wide): 59.1MM **Privately Held**
SIC: 6531 Real estate brokers & agents
PA: Pacific Union Co.
1699 Van Ness Ave 2
San Francisco CA 94109
415 929-7100

(P-11652)
PACIFIC UNION CO
1699 Van Ness Ave, San Francisco
(94109-3608)
PHONE................................415 474-6600
Linda Harrison, *Manager*
EMP: 65
SALES (corp-wide): 59.1MM **Privately Held**
WEB: www.sfcommercial.com
SIC: 6531 6552 Real estate agents &
managers; subdividers & developers
PA: Pacific Union Co.
1699 Van Ness Ave 2
San Francisco CA 94109
415 929-7100

(P-11653)
PACIFIC UNION INTL INC
23 Ross Cmn, Ross (94957-9900)
PHONE................................415 461-8686
Don Leisey, *Manager*
EMP: 270 **Privately Held**
SIC: 6531 Real estate brokers & agents
PA: Pacific Union International, Inc.
1 Letterman Dr Bldg C
San Francisco CA 94129

(P-11654)
PACIFIC UNION INTL INC
1900 Mountain Blvd # 102, Oakland
(94611-2800)
PHONE................................510 338-1379
EMP: 270 **Privately Held**
SIC: 6531 Real estate brokers & agents
PA: Pacific Union International, Inc.
1 Letterman Dr Bldg C
San Francisco CA 94129

(P-11655)
PACIFIC UNION RE GROUP (DH)
1699 Van Ness Ave 2, San Francisco
(94109-3608)
PHONE................................415 929-7100
Sandy Shaffer, *President*
Patrick Barber, *Manager*
EMP: 80
SQ FT: 700

SALES (est): 10.4MM
SALES (corp-wide): 2.1B **Privately Held**
WEB: www.bayarea-newhomes.com
SIC: 6531 6163 8741 Real estate agent,
commercial; mortgage brokers arranging
for loans, using money of others; financial
management for business
HQ: Gmac Home Services, Inc.
4 Walnut Grove Dr
Horsham PA 19044
215 682-4600

(P-11656)
PACIFIC UNION RESIDENTAL BRKG
1900 Mountain Blvd # 102, Oakland
(94611-2800)
PHONE................................510 339-6460
Pamela Hoffman, *President*
EMP: 72
SALES (est): 2.5MM
SALES (corp-wide): 2.1B **Privately Held**
WEB: www.bayarea-newhomes.com
SIC: 6531 Real estate agent, residential
HQ: Pacific Union Real Estate Group Ltd
1699 Van Ness Ave 2
San Francisco CA 94109
415 929-7100

(P-11657)
PACIFICA HOTEL COMPANY (HQ)
39 Argonaut, Aliso Viejo (92656-4152)
PHONE................................805 957-0095
Mike Barnard, *President*
Matt Marquis, *President*
Dale J Marquis, *CEO*
Todd Moreau, *Vice Pres*
Jorge Sanchez, *Technology*
EMP: 50 EST: 1993
SQ FT: 12,500
SALES: 44.2MM
SALES (corp-wide): 147.6MM **Privately Held**
WEB: www.cottage-inn.com
SIC: 6531 7011 Real estate brokers &
agents; real estate managers; hotels &
motels
PA: Invest West Financial Corp
1933 Cliff Dr Ste 1
Santa Barbara CA 93109
805 957-0095

(P-11658)
PALADIN REALTY PARTNERS LLC (PA)
10880 Wilshire Blvd, Los Angeles
(90024-4101)
PHONE................................310 914-2410
James R Worms,
John S Gerson,
Michael B Lenard,
EMP: 50
SALES (est): 3.4MM **Privately Held**
SIC: 6531 Real estate brokers & agents

(P-11659)
PANATTONI DEVELOPMENT CO INC (PA)
20411 Sw Birch St Ste 200, Newport Beach
(92660-1797)
PHONE................................916 381-1561
Carl Panattoni, *Chairman*
Rob Riner, *Partner*
Fredm Bohne, *Managing Prtnr*
Dudley Mitchell, *President*
Greg Thurman, *President*
EMP: 90
SQ FT: 7,000
SALES (est): 41.3MM **Privately Held**
SIC: 6531 Real estate agent, commercial

(P-11660)
PARAGON REAL ESTATE GROUP
350 Rhode Island St, San Francisco
(94103-5182)
PHONE................................415 323-4066
Jeff Salgado, *Principal*
EMP: 62
SALES (corp-wide): 2.9MM **Privately Held**
SIC: 6531 Real estate agent, residential

PA: Paragon Real Estate Group Of San
Francisco, Inc.
1400 Van Ness Ave
San Francisco CA 94109
415 292-2384

(P-11661)
PARAMUNT CONTRS DEVELOPERS INC
Also Called: Tops Auto Parks
6464 W Sunset Blvd # 700, Los Angeles
(90028-8001)
PHONE................................323 464-7050
Brad Folb, *President*
Brian Folb, *Exec VP*
EMP: 50
SQ FT: 102,000
SALES (est): 4.9MM **Privately Held**
WEB: www.folbart.com
SIC: 6531 1541 1521 Real estate man-
agers; industrial buildings & warehouses;
single-family housing construction

(P-11662)
PARK REGENCY INC
10146 Balboa Blvd, Granada Hills
(91344-7408)
PHONE................................818 363-6116
Joseph Alexander, *President*
Patrick Pace, *CFO*
Ken Engeron, *Vice Pres*
Kenneth Engeron, *Vice Pres*
Melody Cutler, *Info Tech Mgr*
EMP: 70
SQ FT: 4,500
SALES (est): 4.5MM **Privately Held**
WEB: www.parkregency.com
SIC: 6531 Real estate agent, residential;
real estate agent, commercial

(P-11663)
PARMA MANAGEMENT CO INC
6390 Greenwich Dr Ste 150, San Diego
(92122-5958)
P.O. Box 22209 (92192-2209)
PHONE................................858 457-4999
Leon Parma, *President*
David Kressin, *Vice Pres*
Michael Parma, *Vice Pres*
EMP: 50 EST: 2000
SALES (est): 4.7MM **Privately Held**
SIC: 6531 Real estate agents & managers

(P-11664)
PARWOOD PRESERVATION LP
Also Called: Northpointe Apartment Homes
5441 N Paramount Blvd, Long Beach
(90805-5128)
PHONE................................562 531-7880
Larry Lipton, *Partner*
EMP: 99
SALES (est): 4MM **Privately Held**
SIC: 6531 Real estate agents & managers

(P-11665)
PASSCO COMPANIES LLC (PA)
2050 Main St Ste 650, Irvine (92614-8265)
PHONE................................949 442-1000
William O Passo,
William H Winn, *President*
Thomas B Jahncke, *Senior VP*
Paul Mittmann, *Vice Pres*
Jeff Olshan, *VP Finance*
EMP: 68
SALES (est): 17.3MM **Privately Held**
WEB: www.passco.com
SIC: 6531 Real estate agents & managers

(P-11666)
PAUL CALVO AND COMPANY
1619 W Garvey Ave N # 201, West Covina
(91790-2144)
PHONE................................626 814-8000
Paul Calvo, *Owner*
Nelson Chavez,
EMP: 50
SALES (est): 3MM **Privately Held**
WEB: www.calvogroup.com
SIC: 6531 Real estate agent, commercial;
real estate managers

(P-11667)
PCS PROPERTY MANAGMENT LLC
11859 Wilshire Blvd # 600, Los Angeles
(90025-6616)
PHONE................................310 231-1000
Michael Ross, *Branch Mgr*
EMP: 136 **Privately Held**
SIC: 6531 Real estate managers
PA: Pcs Property Managment Llc
4500 Woodman Ave Ofc
Sherman Oaks CA 91423

(P-11668)
PEARSON REALTY (PA)
7480 N Palm Ave Ste 101, Fresno
(93711-5501)
PHONE................................559 432-6200
John Stewart, *CEO*
Richard Bonner, *Manager*
Frank Stepovich, *Agent*
Hersh Thompson, *Agent*
EMP: 65
SQ FT: 12,000
SALES (est): 5.4MM **Privately Held**
WEB: www.pearsonfarms.com
SIC: 6531 Real estate agent, residential;
appraiser, real estate

(P-11669)
PICKFORD REALTY INC
Also Called: Prudential
1015 Nipomo St Ste 100, San Luis Obispo
(93401-3890)
PHONE................................805 782-6000
Eric Pinpker, *Branch Mgr*
EMP: 51
SALES (corp-wide): 2.5MM **Privately Held**
SIC: 6531 Real estate agent, residential
HQ: Pickford Realty, Inc.
12544 High Bluff Dr # 420
San Diego CA 92130
888 995-7575

(P-11670)
PINNACLE ESTATE PROPERTIES (PA)
Also Called: Pinnacle Escrow Company
9137 Reseda Blvd, Northridge
(91324-3039)
PHONE................................818 993-4707
Dana Potter, *President*
Jeff Black, *CFO*
Diane Hahn, *Office Mgr*
Jennie Aldana, *Administration*
Leila Terwilliger, *Controller*
EMP: 120
SQ FT: 13,000
SALES (est): 10.4MM **Privately Held**
WEB: www.billparent.com
SIC: 6531 Real estate agent, commercial;
escrow agent, real estate

(P-11671)
PITTS & BACHMANN REALTORS INC
1436 State St, Santa Barbara
(93101-2512)
PHONE................................805 963-1391
Patty Tunnicliffe, *Manager*
Carol Mineau, *Manager*
EMP: 70
SALES (corp-wide): 4.4MM **Privately Held**
WEB: www.bridgetmurphyhomes.com
SIC: 6531 Real estate agents & managers
PA: Pitts & Bachmann Realtors Inc
1165 Coast Village Rd K
Santa Barbara CA 93108
805 682-6415

(P-11672)
PK NEVADA LLC
1317 5th St Fl 2, Santa Monica
(90401-1470)
PHONE................................310 255-0025
Kenneth Pressberg,
EMP: 50
SALES (est): 1.9MM **Privately Held**
WEB: www.pknevada.com
SIC: 6531 Real estate agents & managers

P R O D U C T S & S V C S

(P-11673)
PLAZA MANOR PRESERVATION LP
Also Called: Summer Crest Apartments
2615 E Plaza Blvd, National City
(91950-4017)
PHONE..................................619 475-2125
Larry Lipton, *Principal*
Las Palmas Foundation, *Partner*
Michael Herrington, *Partner*
EMP: 1828
SALES (est): 34.4MM **Privately Held**
SIC: 6531 Real estate agents & managers

(P-11674)
POMONA HOUSING PARTNERS LP
Also Called: Pomona Intergenerational
1731 W Holt Ave, Pomona (91768-3347)
PHONE..................................909 622-1010
Jim Brooks, *Controller*
Tesa Doleman,
EMP: 50 **EST:** 2014
SALES (est): 2MM **Privately Held**
SIC: 6531 Real estate agents & managers

(P-11675)
POWERHOUSE REALTY INC
Also Called: Century 21 Powerhouse Realty
3452 E Florence Ave, Huntington Park
(90255-5835)
PHONE..................................323 562-7777
Francisco Granadeno, *President*
Andrea Fernando, *Vice Pres*
EMP: 70
SALES (est): 4MM **Privately Held**
WEB: www.powerhouserealty.com
SIC: 6531 Real estate agent, residential

(P-11676)
PPM REAL ESTATE INC
3575 San Pablo Dam Rd, El Sobrante
(94803-7205)
P.O. Box 20621 (94820-0621)
PHONE..................................510 758-5636
Raymond D Smith, *President*
Ray Smith, *President*
EMP: 75
SALES (est): 3.1MM **Privately Held**
WEB: www.samuelchu.com
SIC: 6531 Real estate agent, residential

(P-11677)
PREFERRED BROKERS INC (PA)
Also Called: Coldwell Banker
9100 Ming Ave Ste 100, Bakersfield
(93311-1329)
PHONE..................................661 836-2345
John Mackessey, *President*
Gary Belter, *Vice Pres*
Susan Hallum, *Manager*
Katrina Costa, *Agent*
Jane Etcheverry, *Agent*
EMP: 70
SQ FT: 8,000
SALES (est): 4.9MM **Privately Held**
WEB: www.lesliewalters.com
SIC: 6531 Real estate agent, residential

(P-11678)
PREMIER VALLEY INC (PA)
Also Called: Century 21
1414 E F St Bldg A, Oakdale (95361-9251)
PHONE..................................209 847-6111
John Melo, *CEO*
Larry Matos, *Vice Pres*
Denny Dixon, *Manager*
Lana Dyer, *Real Est Agnt*
Kelley Mayfield, *Real Est Agnt*
EMP: 57
SQ FT: 5,522
SALES (est): 7MM **Privately Held**
SIC: 6531 8742 Real estate agent, residential; real estate consultant

(P-11679)
PRESCOTT COMPANIES (PA)
5950 La Place Ct Ste 200, Carlsbad
(92008-8852)
PHONE..................................760 634-4700
Gloria Todisco, *President*
Bonnie Grisandra, *Executive Asst*
EMP: 50
SQ FT: 11,000

SALES (est): 8.6MM **Privately Held**
SIC: 6531 Real estate agents & managers

(P-11680)
PRITCHETT RAPF AND ASSOCIATES
23732 Malibu Rd, Malibu (90265-4603)
PHONE..................................310 456-6771
Jim Rapf, *Partner*
Jack Pritchett, *Partner*
Vicki Salsberg, *Real Est Agnt*
EMP: 62
SALES (est): 4.2MM **Privately Held**
SIC: 6531 Rental agent, real estate

(P-11681)
PRO GROUP INC
Also Called: Keller Williams Realtors
4160 Temescal Canyon Rd # 500, Corona
(92883-4642)
PHONE..................................951 271-3000
James Brown, *President*
Jim Brown, *President*
Joseph Regan, *CFO*
David Clark, *Vice Pres*
Annie S Petrikin, *Real Est Agnt*
EMP: 195
SQ FT: 18,000
SALES (est): 6MM **Privately Held**
SIC: 6531 Real estate agent, residential

(P-11682)
PROFESSIONAL COMMUNITY MGT CAL (PA)
Also Called: P C M
27051 Towne Centre Dr # 200, Foothill
Ranch (92610-2819)
PHONE..................................800 369-7260
Donny Disbro, *CEO*
Russ Disbro, *Senior VP*
Elise Trent, *VP Human Res*
EMP: 50
SQ FT: 12,000
SALES (est): 55MM **Privately Held**
WEB: www.pcm-ca.com
SIC: 6531 Real estate managers

(P-11683)
PROFESSIONAL COMMUNITY MGT CAL
Also Called: Sun Lakes Country Club
850 Country Club Dr, Banning
(92220-5306)
PHONE..................................951 845-2191
Mike Bennett, *Manager*
EMP: 50
SALES (corp-wide): 55MM **Privately Held**
WEB: www.pcm-ca.com
SIC: 6531 Real estate managers
PA: Professional Community Management
Of California
27051 Towne Centre Dr # 200
Foothill Ranch CA 92610
800 369-7260

(P-11684)
PROFESSIONAL COMMUNITY MGT CAL
Also Called: Pcm
24351 El Toro Rd, Laguna Woods
(92637-4901)
PHONE..................................949 206-0580
Milt Johns, *Manager*
Jens Vreeland, *Technology*
Jackie Giacomazzi, *Human Res Mgr*
EMP: 134
SALES (corp-wide): 55MM **Privately Held**
WEB: www.pcm-ca.com
SIC: 6531 Real estate managers
PA: Professional Community Management
Of California
27051 Towne Centre Dr # 200
Foothill Ranch CA 92610
800 369-7260

(P-11685)
PROFESSIONAL COMMUNITY MGT CAL
Also Called: Leisure World Resales
23522 Paseo De Valencia, Laguna Hills
(92653)
P.O. Box 2220 (92654-2220)
PHONE..................................949 597-4200

Gabrielle Velten, *Manager*
EMP: 134
SALES (corp-wide): 55MM **Privately Held**
WEB: www.pcm-ca.com
SIC: 6531 Real estate managers
PA: Professional Community Management
Of California
27051 Towne Centre Dr # 200
Foothill Ranch CA 92610
800 369-7260

(P-11686)
PROLAND PROPERTY MANAGMENT LLC (PA)
Also Called: Hollingshead Management
2510 W 7th St Fl 2, Los Angeles
(90057-3802)
PHONE..................................213 738-8175
Ronald Gregg,
James Harris,
EMP: 80
SQ FT: 5,000
SALES (est): 5.8MM **Privately Held**
SIC: 6531 Real estate managers

(P-11687)
PROMETHEUS RE GROUP INC (PA)
1900 S Norfolk St Ste 150, San Mateo
(94403-1161)
PHONE..................................650 931-3400
Sanford N Diller, *CEO*
Bill Levia, *CFO*
Jackie Safier, *Exec VP*
John Ghio, *Vice Pres*
Paul Boatman, *Risk Mgmt Dir*
EMP: 140
SALES (est): 44.3MM **Privately Held**
WEB: www.prometheusreg.com
SIC: 6531 6552 Real estate managers;
land subdividers & developers, commercial; land subdividers & developers, residential

(P-11688)
PROPERTY MANAGEMENT ASSOC INC (PA)
Also Called: Capital Commercial Property
6011 Bristol Pkwy, Culver City
(90230-6601)
PHONE..................................323 295-2000
Thomas Spear, *President*
Patrick Lacey, *COO*
Joshua Fein, *CFO*
Jodie Mohr, *Portfolio Mgr*
Jennifer Ray, *Human Res Dir*
EMP: 130
SQ FT: 6,500
SALES (est): 13MM **Privately Held**
WEB: www.wemanageproperties.com
SIC: 6531 Real estate managers

(P-11689)
PROPERTY MANAGEMENT CONS (PA)
11717 Bernardo Plaza Ct # 220, San Diego
(92128-2412)
PHONE..................................858 485-9811
Richard L Grant, *Principal*
Bonnie Grant, *Corp Secy*
Gregory Grant, *Principal*
Vivian Worley, *Administration*
Jackie Couzens, *Property Mgr*
EMP: 50
SALES (est): 4.3MM **Privately Held**
SIC: 6531 Real estate managers

(P-11690)
PRUDENTIAL 24 HOUR REAL ESTATE
8635 Florence Ave Ste 101, Downey
(90240-4045)
PHONE..................................562 861-7257
Mel Berdelis, *Owner*
EMP: 80
SALES (est): 2.9MM **Privately Held**
WEB: www.prudential24hours.com
SIC: 6531 Real estate brokers & agents

(P-11691)
PRUDENTIAL CA REALTY
39275 Mssion Blvd Ste 103, Fremont
(94539)
PHONE..................................510 487-6088

William L Salgado, *President*
Grace Pinacate, *Admin Sec*
EMP: 58
SALES (est): 2.2MM **Privately Held**
WEB: www.kensmithrealty.com
SIC: 6531 Real estate agent, residential

(P-11692)
PRUDENTIAL CALIFORNIA REALTY
9003 Reseda Blvd Ste 105, Northridge
(91324-3942)
PHONE..................................818 993-8900
John Maquar, *President*
Sandy Weisberg, *Exec VP*
Jeff Kahn, *Sales Mgr*
EMP: 50
SALES (est): 2.2MM **Privately Held**
WEB: www.patrussell4re.com
SIC: 6531 Real estate agent, residential

(P-11693)
PRUDENTIAL CALIFORNIA REALTY
677 Portola Dr, San Francisco
(94127-1207)
PHONE..................................415 664-9400
Steven Spears, *President*
EMP: 90
SALES (est): 4.1MM **Privately Held**
WEB: www.propertyinsanfrancisco.com
SIC: 6531 Real estate agent, residential

(P-11694)
PRUDENTIAL CALIFORNIA REALTY
976 Main St Ste A, Ramona (92065-1970)
PHONE..................................858 487-3520
Jon Cook, *President*
Leeann Iacino, *COO*
EMP: 81
SQ FT: 1,200
SALES (est): 3.8MM **Privately Held**
WEB: www.wattshername.com
SIC: 6531 Real estate agent, residential

(P-11695)
PRUDENTIAL REALTY CORP
1430 Taraval St, San Francisco
(94116-2346)
PHONE..................................415 566-9800
Sam Cadelinia, *President*
Eli Keylin, *Broker*
Alice Lee, *Broker*
Frank Mack, *Broker*
Edison Ongpian, *Broker*
EMP: 66
SALES (est): 2.6MM **Privately Held**
SIC: 6531 Real estate agent, residential

(P-11696)
PS BUSINESS PARKS LP
701 Western Ave, Glendale (91201-2349)
PHONE..................................818 244-8080
Maria Hawthorne, *Partner*
Safu Rana, *Manager*
EMP: 99
SALES (est): 6.1MM
SALES (corp-wide): 402.1MM **Publicly Held**
SIC: 6531 Real estate agent, commercial
PA: Ps Business Parks, Inc.
701 Western Ave
Glendale CA 91201
818 244-8080

(P-11697)
QAL AFFILIATE INC
Also Called: Century 21 Golden Hills
2680 S White Rd Ste 150, San Jose
(95148-2079)
PHONE..................................408 238-5111
Bob Fernandez, *President*
Terry Castro, *Sales Staff*
Lillian Dang, *Agent*
Rahul Shah, *Real Est Agnt*
EMP: 50
SQ FT: 7,000
SALES (est): 2.6MM **Privately Held**
WEB: www.c21goldenhills.com
SIC: 6531 Real estate agent, residential

(P-11698)
R & B REALTY GROUP LP
Also Called: Oakwood Worldwide
2222 Corinth Ave, Los Angeles
(90064-1602)
PHONE................................310 478-1021
Howard F Ruby, *Partner*
Misty-Marie Jensen, *Executive*
Michael Duchateau, *Regional Mgr*
Darin Utterback, *Regional Mgr*
Angie Lener, *Branch Mgr*
EMP: 1500
SALES (est): 54.4MM **Privately Held**
SIC: 6531 Buying agent, real estate

(P-11699)
RAINBOW PROPERTIES INC
Also Called: Century 21
4812 Ostrom Ave, Lakewood (90713-2812)
PHONE................................323 562-0730
Zora Cervantes, *President*
Vince Cervantes, *Vice Pres*
EMP: 55
SALES (est): 2.9MM **Privately Held**
WEB: www.rainbowhomes.net
SIC: 6531 Real estate agent, residential

(P-11700)
RAINBOW REALTY CORPORATION
Also Called: Century 21
24221 Paseo De Valencia, Laguna Woods
(92637-3112)
PHONE................................949 770-9626
Frank J Hill, *President*
Michele Morris, *Credit Mgr*
Steve Bullock, *Agent*
Melanie Callahan, *Agent*
Gloria Einzig, *Agent*
EMP: 55
SALES (est): 3.4MM **Privately Held**
WEB: www.lizhead.net
SIC: 6531 Real estate agent, residential

(P-11701)
RAM COMMERCIAL ENTERPRISES INC
Also Called: Homepointe Property Management
5896 S Land Park Dr, Sacramento
(95822-3311)
P.O. Box 221660 (95822-8660)
PHONE................................916 429-1205
Robert Machado, *President*
Ann Ford, *General Mgr*
Kathy Carranco, *Office Mgr*
Kathy Garcia, *Office Mgr*
Derek Clark, *Property Mgr*
EMP: 50
SALES (est): 4.7MM **Privately Held**
WEB: www.homepointe.com
SIC: 6531 Real estate managers

(P-11702)
RAMSEY-SHILLING RESIDENTIAL RE
3360 Barham Blvd, Los Angeles
(90068-1473)
PHONE................................323 851-5512
Michael Alley, *Owner*
Paula Carpenter, *Real Est Agnt*
Susan Pfaltzgraf, *Real Est Agnt*
EMP: 75
SALES (est): 1.7MM **Privately Held**
SIC: 6531 Real estate agent, residential

(P-11703)
RANCHO MISSION VIEJO LLC (PA)
Also Called: Ladera Ranch
28811 Ortega Hwy, San Juan Capistrano
(92675-2023)
P.O. Box 9 (92693-0009)
PHONE................................949 240-3363
Anthony R Moiso, *Principal*
Gilbert G Aguirre, *Exec VP*
Michael Balsamo, *Senior VP*
Richard Broming, *Senior VP*
Gregory S Edwards, *Senior VP*
EMP: 60
SQ FT: 42,000
SALES (est): 11.4MM **Privately Held**
WEB: www.ranchomissionviejo.com
SIC: 6531 Real estate managers; escrow
agent, real estate

(P-11704)
RANCON REAL ESTATE CORPORATION (PA)
27740 Jefferson Ave # 100, Temecula
(92590-2698)
PHONE................................951 677-1800
Daniel L Stephenson, *Ch of Bd*
Andrew Bell, *Partner*
Michael Diaz, *President*
Sandy Tyler, *Vice Pres*
Misty Heredia, *Technology*
EMP: 60
SQ FT: 7,000
SALES (est): 11.3MM **Privately Held**
WEB: www.rancon.com
SIC: 6531 Real estate agent, residential;
real estate managers; escrow agent, real
estate

(P-11705)
RE MAX ADVANTAGE
Also Called: Re/Max
648 Yerington Ln, Lincoln (95648-8370)
PHONE................................800 247-4200
Britt Cooper, *President*
Michelle Cowles, *Sales Staff*
EMP: 80
SALES (est): 1.4MM **Privately Held**
SIC: 6531 Real estate agent, residential

(P-11706)
RE MAX ALL CITIES LK ARROWHEAD
28200 Highway 189, Lake Arrowhead
(92352-9700)
PHONE................................909 337-6111
Kelli Todd, *President*
EMP: 50
SALES (est): 1.1MM **Privately Held**
SIC: 6531 Real estate agent, residential

(P-11707)
RE MAX PARKSIDE REAL ESTATE
Also Called: RCA Properties
711 12th St, Paso Robles (93446-2206)
PHONE................................805 239-3310
Peter Dankin, *President*
Kaye D Rickerd, *Real Est Agnt*
EMP: 60
SALES (est): 4.2MM **Privately Held**
WEB: www.janstemperbrown.com
SIC: 6531 Real estate agent, residential

(P-11708)
RE/MAX
201 New Stine Rd Ste 300, Bakersfield
(93309-2659)
PHONE................................661 616-4040
Debra L Craig, *Owner*
EMP: 50
SALES (est): 1.5MM **Privately Held**
SIC: 6531 Real estate agent, residential

(P-11709)
RE/MAX LLC
Also Called: Remax Champions Real Estate
1071 E 16th St, Upland (91784-9148)
PHONE................................303 770-5531
None G Brmgr, *Branch Mgr*
EMP: 50
SALES (corp-wide): 195.9MM **Publicly Held**
SIC: 6531 Real estate agent, residential
HQ: Re/Max, Llc
5075 S Syracuse St
Denver CO 80237
303 770-5531

(P-11710)
RE/MAX BEACH CITIES REALTY MAR
400 S Sepulveda Blvd # 100, Manhattan
Beach (90266-6814)
PHONE................................310 376-2225
Robert Kenneth Todd, *Owner*
Patricia Hedstrom, *Executive*
Terry Ballentine, *Broker*
Sloane Sanders, *Broker*
Anthony Todora, *Sales Associate*
EMP: 150
SQ FT: 15,000
SALES (est): 5.7MM **Privately Held**
SIC: 6531 Real estate agent, residential

(P-11711)
RE/MAX MAGIC
11420 Ming Ave Ste 530, Bakersfield
(93311-1369)
PHONE................................661 616-4040
Debbie Banducci, *Owner*
EMP: 50
SALES (est): 546K **Privately Held**
SIC: 6531 Real estate agent, residential

(P-11712)
RE/MAX OF VALENCIA INC (PA)
25101 The Old Rd, Santa Clarita
(91381-2206)
PHONE................................661 255-2650
John O'Hare, *President*
John Ohare, *President*
Alice O'Hare, *Vice Pres*
Sean Daryani, *Broker*
Kristi Davalos, *Broker*
EMP: 125
SQ FT: 10,000
SALES (est): 7.5MM **Privately Held**
WEB: www.kathybost.com
SIC: 6531 8742 Real estate agent, residential; escrow agent, real estate; real estate consultant

(P-11713)
RE/MAX PLOS VRDES RLTY / EXCES
Also Called: Remax Estate Properties
450 Silver Spur Rd, Rancho Palos Verdes
(90275-3573)
PHONE................................310 541-5224
Kevin Mullen, *Manager*
Mary Thomas, *COO*
Charlene Phelps, *Office Mgr*
Jay Deai, *Property Mgr*
Yvonne Feng, *Property Mgr*
EMP: 50
SALES (corp-wide): 8.8MM **Privately Held**
WEB: www.realestatebymichele.com
SIC: 6531 Real estate agent, residential
PA: Re/Max Palos Verdes Realty/Exces
63 Malaga Cove Plz
Palos Verdes Estates CA 90274
310 378-9494

(P-11714)
REAL ESTATE AMERICA INC
2000 Powell St Ste 100, Emeryville
(94608-1774)
P.O. Box 494846, Port Charlotte FL
(33949-4846)
PHONE................................510 594-3100
Kareem K Macarthur, *President*
EMP: 55 **Privately Held**
SIC: 6531 Real estate brokers & agents
PA: Real Estate America, Inc.
10120 S Estrn Ave Ste 200
Henderson NV 89052

(P-11715)
REAL ESTATE CALIFORNIA DEPT
Also Called: Property Management
3737 Main St Ofc, Riverside (92501-3338)
PHONE................................951 715-0130
Bobie Sanchez, *Manager*
EMP: 100 **Privately Held**
SIC: 6531 9532 Real estate brokers &
agents; urban & community development;
HQ: California Department Of Real Estate
2201 Broadway Lowr
Sacramento CA

(P-11716)
REAL PROPERTY SYSTEMS INC
1443 E Washington Blvd, Pasadena
(91104-2650)
PHONE................................760 243-1143
Michael Palmer, *President*
EMP: 250
SALES (est): 6.2MM **Privately Held**
WEB: www.realpropertysystems.com
SIC: 6531 Real estate agents & managers

(P-11717)
REALOGY HOLDINGS CORP
Also Called: Artisan Sotheby's Intl. Realty
3554 Round Barn Blvd, Santa Rosa
(95403-0929)
PHONE................................707 284-1111
Eric Drew, *Branch Mgr*
Rosemarie Corrigan, *Sales Staff*
Johnny Drake, *Real Est Agnt*
Martin Schwartz, *Real Est Agnt*
EMP: 485 **Publicly Held**
SIC: 6531 Real estate agent, residential
PA: Realogy Holdings Corp.
175 Park Ave
Madison NJ 07940

(P-11718)
REALTOR SFR GREEN
4090 Mission Blvd, San Diego
(92109-5043)
PHONE................................858 488-4090
Brian Barber, *General Mgr*
EMP: 50
SALES (est): 1.1MM **Privately Held**
SIC: 6531 Real estate brokers & agents

(P-11719)
REALTY EXECUTIVES
26650 The Old Rd Ste 300, Valencia
(91381-0754)
PHONE................................661 286-8600
Jim Tanner, *President*
David Loyd, *Vice Pres*
Tiffany Bennett, *Broker*
Ken Putt, *Broker*
Vicki Repovich, *Broker*
EMP: 150
SALES (est): 4.9MM **Privately Held**
SIC: 6531 Real estate agent, residential

(P-11720)
REALTY ONE GROUP INC
19322 Jesse Ln, Riverside (92508-5072)
PHONE................................951 565-8105
EMP: 55
SALES (corp-wide): 22.1MM **Privately Held**
SIC: 6531 Real estate agent, residential
PA: Realty One Group, Inc.
7545 Irvine Center Dr # 250
Irvine CA 92618
949 596-4300

(P-11721)
REDFIN CORPORATION
655 Montgomery St # 1430, San Francisco
(94111-2631)
PHONE................................206 340-8794
Glenn Kelman, *Branch Mgr*
Saleem Buqeileh, *Real Est Agnt*
Mark Colwell, *Real Est Agnt*
Jennifer Tollenaar, *Real Est Agnt*
Miriam Westberg, *Real Est Agnt*
EMP: 337
SALES (corp-wide): 370MM **Publicly Held**
SIC: 6531 Real estate brokers & agents
PA: Redfin Corporation
1099 Stewart St Ste 600
Seattle WA 98101
206 576-8333

(P-11722)
REFERRAL REALTY INC
1601 S De Anza Blvd # 150, Cupertino
(95014-5358)
PHONE................................408 996-8100
Morise Nahouraii, *President*
Carl Zanger, *President*
Lisa Leung, *Broker*
Tom Cooper, *Agent*
Jill Hu, *Real Est Agnt*
EMP: 55
SQ FT: 5,800
SALES (est): 3.2MM **Privately Held**
WEB: www.referralrealty.com
SIC: 6531 Real estate brokers & agents

(P-11723)
REGENCY PARK SENIOR LIVING INC
Also Called: Regency Park El Molino
245 S El Molino Ave, Pasadena
(91101-2996)
PHONE................................626 578-0460

PRODUCTS & SVCS

Emil Fish, *President*
EMP: 81
SALES (corp-wide): 10.6MM **Privately Held**
SIC: 6531 Real estate agents & managers
PA: Regency Park Senior Living, Inc.
150 S Los Robles Ave # 480
Pasadena CA 91101
626 773-8800

(P-11724)
REGISTRY MONITORING INS SRVCS
Also Called: Rmis
5388 Sterling Center Dr, Westlake Village
(91361-4612)
PHONE..........................800 400-4924
Marvin Landon, *Chairman*
Hayden Landon, *President*
Matthew Mandery, *Software Dev*
John McKinney, *Software Dev*
Greg Sadikoff, *Controller*
EMP: 115
SALES (est): 17.2MM **Privately Held**
WEB: www.registrymonitoring.com
SIC: 6531 6411 Real estate agents & managers; insurance information & consulting services

(P-11725)
RELS LLC
Also Called: Rels Valuation
40 Pacifica Ste 900, Irvine (92618-7487)
PHONE..........................949 214-1000
Frank D Martell, *Officer*
EMP: 1300
SALES (est): 531K
SALES (corp-wide): 1.8B **Publicly Held**
WEB: www.rels.com
SIC: 6531 7323 Appraiser, real estate; commercial (mercantile) credit reporting bureau
PA: Corelogic, Inc.
40 Pacifica Ste 900
Irvine CA 92618
949 214-1000

(P-11726)
REMAX ACTIVE REALTY
Also Called: Remax Active Teal State
4056 Decoto Rd, Fremont (94555-3201)
PHONE..........................510 505-1660
Fay Louis, *Owner*
Bupinder Dev, *Broker*
EMP: 50 **EST:** 2001
SALES (est): 2MM **Privately Held**
SIC: 6531 Real estate agent, residential

(P-11727)
REMAX ALL STARS REALTY
765 N Main St, Corona (92880-1440)
PHONE..........................951 739-4000
Bret Meckes, *Owner*
Brian Bucsit, *Associate*
EMP: 64
SALES (est): 2.1MM **Privately Held**
SIC: 6531 Real estate agent, residential

(P-11728)
REMAX GOLD
Also Called: Re/Max
3620 Fair Oaks Blvd # 300, Sacramento
(95864-7263)
PHONE..........................916 609-2800
Pam Porter, *General Mgr*
Annvuletich Clark, *Broker*
Demetre Paraskevas, *Broker*
Nancy Beall, *Real Est Agnt*
Carol Calnero, *Real Est Agnt*
EMP: 85
SALES (est): 2.6MM **Privately Held**
WEB: www.goldcommercial.com
SIC: 6531 7389 Real estate agent, residential; brokers, business: buying & selling business enterprises

(P-11729)
REMAX METRO INC
Also Called: Re/Max
150 Paularino Ave Ste 125, Costa Mesa
(92626-3318)
PHONE..........................714 557-2544
Joseph Brodrick, *President*
EMP: 60
SALES (est): 2.3MM **Privately Held**
SIC: 6531 Real estate agent, residential

(P-11730)
REMAX OLSON
Also Called: Re/Max
30699 Russell Ranch Rd, Westlake Village
(91362-7315)
PHONE..........................805 267-4929
Todd Olson, *Owner*
Keith Myers, *President*
Henry Becker, *Broker*
David Cohan, *Broker*
Jordan Cohen, *Real Est Agnt*
EMP: 70
SALES (est): 3.4MM **Privately Held**
WEB: www.joedecarlo.com
SIC: 6531 Real estate agent, residential

(P-11731)
RETIREMENT HOUSING FOUNDATION (PA)
911 N Studebaker Rd # 100, Long Beach
(90815-4980)
PHONE..........................562 257-5100
Laverne R Joseph, *CEO*
Raymond East, *Ch of Bd*
Christina E Potter, *Vice Chairman*
Darryl M Sexton, *Vice Chairman*
Frank G Jahrling, *Treasurer*
EMP: 65
SALES: 37.3MM **Privately Held**
WEB: www.bixbyknolltowers.com
SIC: 6531 Real estate agents & managers

(P-11732)
RETIREMENT HOUSING FOUNDATION
Also Called: Plymouth Square
1319 N Madison St Ofc, Stockton
(95202-1001)
PHONE..........................209 466-4341
Gary Wiemers, *Administration*
EMP: 100
SALES (corp-wide): 37.3MM **Privately Held**
WEB: www.bixbyknolltowers.com
SIC: 6531 Real estate agents & managers
PA: Retirement Housing Foundation Inc
911 N Studebaker Rd # 100
Long Beach CA 90815
562 257-5100

(P-11733)
RICHARD REALTY GROUP INC
Also Called: Realty Group San Diego
2792 Gateway Rd Ste 103, Carlsbad
(92009-1749)
PHONE..........................760 603-8377
Bill Richard, *CEO*
Jan Richard, *CFO*
Janis Richard, *Vice Pres*
Steve Compos, *Real Est Agnt*
Daylene Grose, *Real Est Agnt*
EMP: 60 **EST:** 2009
SALES (est): 3.8MM **Privately Held**
SIC: 6531 Real estate agents & managers

(P-11734)
RIPHAGEN & BULLERDICK INC
Also Called: Re/Max
5925 Ball Rd, Cypress (90630-3245)
PHONE..........................714 763-2100
Gary Riphagen, *President*
Gerry Bullerdick, *Treasurer*
Kerry Louis, *Manager*
EMP: 50
SQ FT: 2,600
SALES (est): 4MM **Privately Held**
WEB: www.remaxtiffany.com
SIC: 6531 Real estate agent, residential

(P-11735)
RODEO REALTY INC
15300 Ventura Blvd # 101, Sherman Oaks
(91403-3103)
PHONE..........................818 986-7300
Jason Katzman, *Branch Mgr*
Ellen Grosser, *Real Est Agnt*
EMP: 76
SALES (corp-wide): 72.3MM **Privately Held**
SIC: 6531 Real estate brokers & agents
PA: Rodeo Realty, Inc.
9171 Wilshire Blvd # 321
Beverly Hills CA 90210
818 349-9997

(P-11736)
RODEO REALTY INC
11940 San Vicente Blvd, Los Angeles
(90049-5004)
PHONE..........................310 873-0100
Simon Pozi, *Manager*
EMP: 68
SALES (corp-wide): 72.3MM **Privately Held**
SIC: 6531 Real estate agent, residential
PA: Rodeo Realty, Inc.
9171 Wilshire Blvd # 321
Beverly Hills CA 90210
818 349-9997

(P-11737)
RODEO REALTY INC
Also Called: Paramount Properties Encino BR
17501 Ventura Blvd, Encino (91316-3836)
PHONE..........................818 285-3700
Syd Leibovitch, *President*
EMP: 76
SALES (est): 2.3MM
SALES (corp-wide): 72.3MM **Privately Held**
SIC: 6531 Real estate brokers & agents
PA: Rodeo Realty, Inc.
9171 Wilshire Blvd # 321
Beverly Hills CA 90210
818 349-9997

(P-11738)
RODEO REALTY INC
12345 Ventura Blvd Ste A, Studio City
(91604-2511)
PHONE..........................818 308-8273
Sib Leibovitch, *President*
EMP: 80
SALES (corp-wide): 72.3MM **Privately Held**
SIC: 6531 Real estate brokers & agents
PA: Rodeo Realty, Inc.
9171 Wilshire Blvd # 321
Beverly Hills CA 90210
818 349-9997

(P-11739)
RODEO REALTY INC (PA)
Also Called: Paramount Properties
9171 Wilshire Blvd # 321, Beverly Hills
(90210-5562)
PHONE..........................818 349-9997
Sydney Leibovitch, *CEO*
Linda Leibovitch, *Vice Pres*
Ilene Feldman, *Administration*
Ilene Klein, *Administration*
Sue Kogen, *Administration*
EMP: 76
SQ FT: 5,000
SALES (est): 72.3MM **Privately Held**
WEB: www.jennifer4homes.com
SIC: 6531 Real estate agent, residential

(P-11740)
RODEO REALTY INC
9338 Reseda Blvd Ste 102, Northridge
(91324-2986)
PHONE..........................818 349-9997
Teresa Todd, *Branch Mgr*
EMP: 100
SALES (corp-wide): 72.3MM **Privately Held**
WEB: www.jennifer4homes.com
SIC: 6531 Real estate brokers & agents
PA: Rodeo Realty, Inc.
9171 Wilshire Blvd # 321
Beverly Hills CA 90210
818 349-9997

(P-11741)
RODEO REALTY INC
23901 Calabasas Rd # 1050, Calabasas
(91302-3379)
PHONE..........................818 657-4609
Lu Duffy, *Branch Mgr*
EMP: 76
SALES (corp-wide): 72.3MM **Privately Held**
SIC: 6531 6519 6162 6141 Real estate brokers & agents; real property lessors; loan correspondents; personal credit institutions
PA: Rodeo Realty, Inc.
9171 Wilshire Blvd # 321
Beverly Hills CA 90210
818 349-9997

(P-11742)
RODEO REALTY INC
Also Called: Paramount Properties
21031 Ventura Blvd # 100, Woodland Hills
(91364-2208)
PHONE..........................818 999-2030
Demetra Kalizki, *Manager*
Alison De Caussin, *Real Est Agnt*
David Sunderland, *Real Est Agnt*
EMP: 100
SALES (corp-wide): 72.3MM **Privately Held**
WEB: www.jennifer4homes.com
SIC: 6531 Real estate brokers & agents
PA: Rodeo Realty, Inc.
9171 Wilshire Blvd # 321
Beverly Hills CA 90210
818 349-9997

(P-11743)
RONALD L WOLFE & ASSOC INC
Also Called: Wolfe & Associates
173 Chapel St, Santa Barbara
(93111-2333)
PHONE..........................805 964-6770
Ronald L Wolfe, *President*
Valerie McDonald, *Human Res Mgr*
Scott Marrison, *Director*
Mark Figueroa, *Manager*
Scott Wolfe, *Manager*
EMP: 50 **EST:** 1971
SQ FT: 5,000
SALES (est): 5MM **Privately Held**
WEB: www.rlwa.com
SIC: 6531 Real estate managers

(P-11744)
ROSANO PARTNERS
700 S Flower St Ste 2526, Los Angeles
(90017-4207)
PHONE..........................213 802-0300
Sagiv Rosano, *CEO*
Edgar Macias, *Manager*
EMP: 50
SALES (est): 3.9MM **Privately Held**
WEB: www.rosanopartners.com
SIC: 6531 Real estate agent, commercial

(P-11745)
ROW MANAGEMENT LTD INC
499 N Canon Dr, Beverly Hills
(90210-4887)
PHONE..........................310 887-3671
Kevin Shahin, *Branch Mgr*
EMP: 165
SALES (corp-wide): 50.8MM **Privately Held**
SIC: 6531 Real estate agents & managers
PA: Row Management Ltd. Inc.
1551 Sawgrass Corporate
Sunrise FL 33323
954 538-8400

(P-11746)
RSC ASSOCIATES INC (PA)
3120 Cohasset Rd Ste 5, Chico
(95973-0978)
PHONE..........................530 893-8228
Steven Baddely, *CEO*
Richard Gillaspie, *President*
Laura Carter, *CFO*
Cynthia Bryan, *Admin Sec*
EMP: 122
SQ FT: 3,000
SALES (est): 10.6MM **Privately Held**
SIC: 6531 Real estate managers

(P-11747)
RUBICON CORPORATION AMERICA
Also Called: Rubicon Realty
10425 Oklahoma Ave, Chatsworth
(91311-2450)
PHONE..........................818 765-2001
Nicholas M Cariglia, *President*
EMP: 50
SQ FT: 3,000
SALES (est): 1.7MM **Privately Held**
SIC: 6531 6163 Real estate brokers & agents; loan brokers

(P-11748)
RVTLZATION ANAHEIM II PARTNERS
1515 S Calle Del Mar, Anaheim (92802-2607)
PHONE..............................714 520-4041
Jim Brooks, *Partner*
EMP: 75 EST: 2014
SALES (est): 1.7MM **Privately Held**
SIC: 6531

(P-11749)
S D PROPERTY MANAGEMENT INC
Also Called: Four Seasons Landscaping
14937 Delano St, Van Nuys (91411-2123)
PHONE..............................323 658-7990
Steve Darrison, *President*
EMP: 60
SQ FT: 1,150
SALES (est): 3.1MM **Privately Held**
SIC: 6531 Real estate managers

(P-11750)
S P R E INC
Also Called: Security Pacific RE Brkg
3223 Blume Dr, Richmond (94806-5782)
PHONE..............................510 222-8340
Jack Burns Sr, *President*
Betty Couzens, *Corp Secy*
Ray De Gennaro, *Vice Pres*
EMP: 100
SQ FT: 16,000
SALES (est): 5.2MM **Privately Held**
WEB: www.spre.com
SIC: 6531 Real estate brokers & agents

(P-11751)
S&J STADTLER INC
Also Called: Remax Accord
5980 Stoneridge Dr # 122, Pleasanton (94588-4518)
PHONE..............................925 847-8900
Jerry Stadtler, *Owner*
EMP: 330
SALES (corp-wide): 21.8MM **Privately Held**
SIC: 6531 Real estate agent, residential
PA: S&J Stadtler Inc
   313 Sycamore Valley Rd W
   Danville CA 94526
   925 838-4100

(P-11752)
SAN DIEGO MORTGAGE & RE
9461 Grsmnt Smt Dr Ste D, La Mesa (91941-4165)
PHONE..............................619 334-7779
Mark Revetta, *President*
EMP: 50
SALES (est): 25MM **Privately Held**
SIC: 6531 Real estate brokers & agents

(P-11753)
SANTA ROSA & SONOMA CO REAL ES
1057 College Ave, Santa Rosa (95404-4128)
PHONE..............................707 524-1124
EMP: 50
SALES (est): 2MM **Privately Held**
SIC: 6531

(P-11754)
SATELLITE MANAGEMENT CO (PA)
Also Called: Ccts
1010 E Chestnut Ave, Santa Ana (92701-6497)
PHONE..............................714 558-2411
Ronald Jensen, *CEO*
Mary E Conzelman, *Vice Pres*
Helen M Jensen, *Vice Pres*
EMP: 121 EST: 1963
SQ FT: 800
SALES (est): 24.2MM **Privately Held**
WEB: www.satellitemanagement.com
SIC: 6531 Real estate managers

(P-11755)
SCHWEIZER RENA
Also Called: White House Properties
15720 Ventura Blvd # 100, Encino (91436-2914)
PHONE..............................818 501-7100

Marty William, *Owner*
Rena Schweizer, *Owner*
EMP: 60
SALES (est): 1.5MM **Privately Held**
WEB: www.realwinds.com
SIC: 6531 Real estate brokers & agents

(P-11756)
SCOTT PLACE ASSOCIATES
60 31st Ave, San Mateo (94403-3404)
PHONE..............................650 345-8222
David Bohannon, *General Ptnr*
EMP: 60
SALES (est): 2MM **Privately Held**
SIC: 6531 Real estate managers

(P-11757)
SEC PAC INC
Also Called: Security Pacific Real Estate
1555 Riviera Ave Ste E, Walnut Creek (94596-7321)
PHONE..............................925 938-9200
Allan Hibbard, *President*
Richard J Clancy, *Principal*
EMP: 60
SQ FT: 10,000
SALES (est): 2.8MM **Privately Held**
WEB: www.soldbymarian.com
SIC: 6531 Real estate agent, residential

(P-11758)
SECURITY PACIFIC RE BRKG
292 Violet Rd, Hercules (94547-1027)
PHONE..............................510 245-9901
Jack Burns Sr, *President*
Bill Prather, *Manager*
EMP: 90
SALES (est): 1.8MM **Privately Held**
WEB: www.billprather.com
SIC: 6531 Real estate brokers & agents

(P-11759)
SERVICE CORP INTERNATIONAL
Also Called: SCI
3500 Pacific View Dr, Corona Del Mar (92625-1112)
PHONE..............................949 644-2700
Ruby Louis, *Branch Mgr*
Rod Gomez, *Site Mgr*
EMP: 65
SALES (corp-wide): 3.1B **Publicly Held**
WEB: www.sci-corp.com
SIC: 6531 7261 Cemetery management service; crematory
PA: Service Corporation International
   1929 Allen Pkwy
   Houston TX 77019
   713 522-5141

(P-11760)
SFT REALTY GALWAY DOWNS LLC
Also Called: Kentina
38801 Los Porralitos, Temecula (92592)
P.O. Box 4404 Jeremie Dr
PHONE..............................951 232-1880
Kenneth C Smith, *Mng Member*
EMP: 70 EST: 2013
SQ FT: 2,000
SALES (est): 400K **Privately Held**
SIC: 6531 Real estate agents & managers

(P-11761)
SHE MANAGES PROPERTIES INC (PA)
9340 Hazard Way Ste B2, San Diego (92123-1228)
PHONE..............................619 291-6300
Karen Martinez, *President*
Jorge Martinez, *Corp Secy*
EMP: 65
SQ FT: 1,700
SALES (est): 10.2MM **Privately Held**
WEB: www.shemanages.com
SIC: 6531 Real estate managers

(P-11762)
SHEA HOMES ARIZONA LTD PARTNR
655 Brea Canyon Rd, Walnut (91789-3078)
PHONE..............................909 594-9500
EMP: 51

SALES (est): 92.7K
SALES (corp-wide): 2.2B **Privately Held**
SIC: 6531 Real estate agents & managers
HQ: Shea Homes Limited Partnership, A
   California Limited Partnership
   655 Brea Canyon Rd
   Walnut CA 91789

(P-11763)
SHEA PROPERTIES MGT CO INC
130 Vantis Dr Ste 200, Aliso Viejo (92656-2691)
P.O. Box 62814, Irvine (92602-6093)
PHONE..............................949 389-7000
Colm Macken, *CEO*
EMP: 347
SQ FT: 48,000
SALES (est): 26.9MM
SALES (corp-wide): 2.2B **Privately Held**
SIC: 6531 Rental agent, real estate
PA: J. F. Shea Co., Inc.
   655 Brea Canyon Rd
   Walnut CA 91789
   909 594-9500

(P-11764)
SHII LLC
Also Called: Frontier Communities
2151 E Cnvntn Ctr Way # 222, Ontario (91764-5429)
PHONE..............................909 354-8000
James Previti, *Mng Member*
Leigh Yetsko, *Administration*
Jan Hoffman, *Sales Staff*
Ed Hunter, *Sales Staff*
EMP: 50
SALES (est): 4.4MM **Privately Held**
SIC: 6531 Real estate brokers & agents

(P-11765)
SKYHILL FINANCIAL INC
5772 Bolsa Ave Ste 100, Huntington Beach (92649-1134)
PHONE..............................714 657-3938
Rosanne Covy, *President*
Angela Hess, *COO*
Michelle Meier, *Officer*
Sarah Tu, *Human Res Mgr*
Bryan Palomares, *Assistant VP*
EMP: 60
SALES (est): 3.6MM **Privately Held**
SIC: 6531 8741 Real estate managers; administrative management

(P-11766)
SMITH & SONS INVESTMENT CO
735 Ohms Way, Costa Mesa (92627-4305)
PHONE..............................949 646-9648
Walker Smith III, *President*
Kim S Lazarus, *Treasurer*
Clarke Smith, *Vice Pres*
EMP: 50
SQ FT: 4,700
SALES (est): 2.6MM **Privately Held**
SIC: 6531 Real estate agent, commercial; real estate managers

(P-11767)
SMITH COLEMAN INC
Also Called: Century 21
707 N La Brea Ave, Inglewood (90302-2203)
PHONE..............................310 671-8271
Ellis Smith, *President*
EMP: 50
SALES (est): 3.1MM **Privately Held**
WEB: www.joeltaylorrealestate.com
SIC: 6531 Real estate agent, residential

(P-11768)
SNOWCREEK PROPERTY MANAGEMENT
Also Called: Snow Creek Resort
1254 Old Mammoth Rd, Mammoth Lakes (93546)
P.O. Box 1647 (93546-1647)
PHONE..............................760 934-3333
Linda Dempsey, *Owner*
Julie Wright, *Vice Pres*
Jodi Melton, *Broker*
EMP: 50
SALES (est): 2.5MM **Privately Held**
WEB: www.snowcreekresort.com
SIC: 6531 Time-sharing real estate sales, leasing & rentals

(P-11769)
SOLANO GATEWAY REALTY INC (PA)
2420 Martin Rd Ste 100, Fairfield (94534-8610)
PHONE..............................707 422-1725
Stephen C Spencer, *President*
Bev Dorsett, *Vice Pres*
David Kellen, *Real Est Agnt*
EMP: 100
SALES (est): 5.2MM **Privately Held**
WEB: www.pamsigel.com
SIC: 6531 Real estate agent, residential

(P-11770)
SOLANO PACIFIC CORPORATION
Also Called: Coldwell Banker Solano Pacific
900 1st St, Benicia (94510-3218)
PHONE..............................707 745-6000
Richard A Bortolazzo, *CEO*
Joseph Banuat, *President*
EMP: 100
SQ FT: 5,000
SALES (est): 3.3MM **Privately Held**
SIC: 6531 Real estate agent, residential

(P-11771)
SOTHEBYS INTL RLTY INC
23405 Pacific Coast Hwy, Malibu (90265-4824)
PHONE..............................310 456-6431
Michael Novotny, *General Mgr*
Amy Alcini, *Real Est Agnt*
Jerel Taylor, *Real Est Agnt*
EMP: 50 **Publicly Held**
SIC: 6531 Real estate brokers & agents
HQ: Sotheby's International Realty, Inc.
   38 E 61st St
   New York NY 10065
   212 606-7660

(P-11772)
SOUTH COUNTY HOUSING CORP (PA)
16500 Monterey St Ste 120, Morgan Hill (95037-5193)
P.O. Box 4112, San Jose (95150-4112)
PHONE..............................510 582-1460
Dennis Lalor, *CEO*
John Cesare, *CFO*
Nestor Nu A EZ, *Finance*
EMP: 50
SQ FT: 13,000
SALES (est): 856.9K **Privately Held**
WEB: www.scounty.com
SIC: 6531 Real estate agent, residential

(P-11773)
SOVEREIGN CAPITL MGT GROUP INC
Also Called: Sovereign Capital MGT Group
750 B St Ste 2397, San Diego (92101-8124)
PHONE..............................619 294-8989
Todd A Mikles, *CEO*
William White, *President*
Peter Nguyen, *Info Tech Dir*
Chad Wardwell, *VP Finance*
Megan Moy, *Director*
EMP: 619
SALES (est): 4MM **Privately Held**
SIC: 6531 7389 Real estate agents & managers; financial services

(P-11774)
SPIEKER COMPANIES INC (PA)
1020 Corp Way Ste 100, Palo Alto (94303)
PHONE..............................650 968-2660
Richard T Spieker, *President*
Brian Feldstein, *Software Dev*
EMP: 157 EST: 1981
SQ FT: 3,000
SALES (est): 22.4MM **Privately Held**
SIC: 6531 Real estate managers

(P-11775)
STAR REAL ESTATE
19440 Goldenwest St, Huntington Beach (92648-2116)
PHONE..............................714 500-3300
Terry Reay, *Manager*
EMP: 90

SALES (corp-wide): 8.6MM Privately Held
SIC: 6531 Real estate agent, residential
PA: Star Real Estate
10540 Talbert Ave 100w
Fountain Valley CA 92708
714 754-6262

(P-11776)
STAR REAL ESTATE
12651 Newport Ave, Tustin (92780-2422)
PHONE...................................714 731-3777
Frank McDowell, *Branch Mgr*
EMP: 120
SALES (corp-wide): 8.6MM Privately Held
SIC: 6531 Real estate agent, residential
PA: Star Real Estate
10540 Talbert Ave 100w
Fountain Valley CA 92708
714 754-6262

(P-11777)
STAR REAL ESTATE SOUTH COUNTY
26711 Aliso Creek Rd 200a, Aliso Viejo (92656-4822)
PHONE...................................949 389-0004
Michelle Williams, *President*
EMP: 250 EST: 1976
SALES (est): 7.7MM Privately Held
SIC: 6531 6519 Real estate agent, residential; escrow agent, real estate; mine property leasing

(P-11778)
STARPOINT PROPERTY MGT LLC
Also Called: Vision Realty Managements
450 N Roxbury Dr Ste 1050, Beverly Hills (90210-4235)
PHONE...................................310 247-0550
Paul Daneshrad,
Jon Suematsu, *Regional Mgr*
Pat Haakstad, *Executive Asst*
Ethan Bui, *Info Tech Mgr*
Sheila Dameshrad,
EMP: 110
SALES (est): 8.8MM Privately Held
SIC: 6531 Real estate agents & managers

(P-11779)
STEVE ROBERSON
Also Called: Century 21
7825 Florence Ave, Downey (90240-3727)
PHONE...................................562 927-2626
Steve Roberson, *Owner*
EMP: 65 EST: 1977
SQ FT: 4,000
SALES (est): 2.9MM Privately Held
SIC: 6531 Real estate agent, residential

(P-11780)
STONESFAIR MANAGEMENT LLC (PA)
577 Airport Blvd Ste 700, Burlingame (94010-2024)
PHONE...................................650 401-3810
Karl E Bakhtiari,
Maryann Fair, *Vice Pres*
Andy Leong, *Controller*
Wilme Ng, *Human Resources*
Karl Bakhtiari,
EMP: 60
SALES (est): 7.1MM Privately Held
SIC: 6531 Real estate managers

(P-11781)
STRATEGIC PROPERTY MANAGEMENT
2055 3rd Ave Ste 200, San Diego (92101-2058)
PHONE...................................619 295-2211
Don Clausson, *Principal*
EMP: 75
SALES (est): 7.8MM Privately Held
WEB: www.stratprop.com
SIC: 6531 Real estate managers

(P-11782)
SVN INTERNATIONAL CORP
Also Called: Sperry Van Ness
11999 San Vicente Blvd # 215, Los Angeles (90049-5131)
PHONE...................................310 979-0800

David Rich, *Senior VP*
Kanna Sunkara, *Advisor*
EMP: 55 Privately Held
WEB: www.kittywallaceteam.com
SIC: 6531 Real estate agent, commercial
PA: Svn International Corp.
745 Atlantic Ave Fl 8
Boston MA 02111
-

(P-11783)
T ROYAL MANAGEMENT (PA)
7419 N Cedar Ave Ste 102, Fresno (93720-3640)
PHONE...................................559 447-9887
David Michael Thomas, *CEO*
James Ganson, *Shareholder*
EMP: 55
SQ FT: 5,000
SALES (est): 3.5MM Privately Held
WEB: www.royaltmanagement.com
SIC: 6531 Real estate managers

(P-11784)
TAHOE SEASONS RESORT TIME INTE
3901 Saddle Rd, South Lake Tahoe (96150-8707)
P.O. Box 16300 (96151-6300)
PHONE...................................530 541-6700
Michael Presley, *General Mgr*
EMP: 123
SALES (est): 10.5MM Privately Held
WEB: www.tahoeseasons.com
SIC: 6531 7011 5813 5812 Time-sharing real estate sales, leasing & rentals; hotels & motels; drinking places; eating places

(P-11785)
TARBELL FINANCIAL CORPORATION
1440 Industrial Park Ave, Redlands (92374-4517)
PHONE...................................909 335-0750
Maria Luevano, *Branch Mgr*
EMP: 60
SALES (corp-wide): 132.1MM Privately Held
SIC: 6531 Real estate agent, residential
PA: Tarbell Financial Corporation
1403 N Tustin Ave Ste 380
Santa Ana CA 92705
714 972-0988

(P-11786)
TEAM SPIRIT REALTY INC
6301 Beach Blvd Ste 225, Buena Park (90621-4031)
PHONE...................................714 562-0404
Edward Son, *President*
EMP: 50
SALES (est): 1.2MM Privately Held
SIC: 6531 Real estate agents & managers

(P-11787)
TEN-X LLC
1301 Shoreway Rd Ste 425, Belmont (94002-4154)
PHONE...................................800 793-6107
Monte J M Koch, *Branch Mgr*
EMP: 598 Privately Held
SIC: 6531 Real estate brokers & agents
PA: Auction.Com, Llc
1 Mauchly
Irvine CA 92618

(P-11788)
TEN-X LLC
Also Called: Auction.com
3050 S Del St Ste 201, San Mateo (94403)
PHONE...................................949 609-5376
EMP: 256 Privately Held
SIC: 6531 Real estate agents & managers
PA: Auction.Com, Llc
1 Mauchly
Irvine CA 92618

(P-11789)
TENDERLOIN HOUSING CLINIC INC (PA)
126 Hyde St, San Francisco (94102-3606)
PHONE...................................415 771-9850
Randall Shaw, *President*

Randy Shaw, *Exec Dir*
Rebecca Tang, *Admin Asst*
David Virgo, *Info Tech Dir*
Danny Smith, *Asst Director*
EMP: 250
SALES: 40.3MM Privately Held
WEB: www.thclinic.org
SIC: 6531 8111 Real estate agents & managers; legal services

(P-11790)
TERRA COASTAL PROPERTIES INC
Also Called: Prudential Malibu Realty
23405 Pacific Coast Hwy, Malibu (90265-4824)
PHONE...................................310 457-2534
Michael Novotny, *CEO*
EMP: 50
SALES (est): 2.4MM Privately Held
SIC: 6531 Real estate brokers & agents

(P-11791)
TERRA VISTA MANAGEMENT INC
Also Called: Terra Vista Management
2211 Pacific Beach Dr, San Diego (92109-5626)
PHONE...................................858 581-4200
Micheal Gelfand, *Branch Mgr*
EMP: 120
SALES (corp-wide): 13MM Privately Held
SIC: 6531 7033 4225 4226 Real estate managers; trailer parks & campsites; general warehousing & storage; special warehousing & storage; nonresidential building operators
PA: Vista Terra Management Inc
6310 San Vicente Blvd # 506
Los Angeles CA 90048
323 954-5900

(P-11792)
TERRY MEYER
Also Called: Coldwell Banker Residential RE
1712 Meridian Ave Ste C, San Jose (95125-5587)
PHONE...................................408 723-3300
Terry Meyer, *Principal*
Ned Laugharn, *Broker*
Brenda Hernandez, *Sales Executive*
Andrew Mirza, *Sales Associate*
James Nichols, *Sales Associate*
EMP: 61
SALES (est): 1.7MM Privately Held
SIC: 6531

(P-11793)
TEXACO INC
9525 Camino Media, Bakersfield (93311-1314)
PHONE...................................661 654-7000
Gary Wolff, *Manager*
EMP: 300
SALES (corp-wide): 141.7B Publicly Held
WEB: www.texaco.com
SIC: 6531 5511 1311 Real estate agents & managers; automobiles, new & used; crude petroleum production
HQ: Texaco Inc.
6001 Bollinger Canyon Rd
San Ramon CA 94583
925 842-1000

(P-11794)
THIRD & MISSION ASSOCIATES LLC
Also Called: Paramount
680 Mission St, San Francisco (94105-4000)
PHONE...................................415 341-8457
Jim Brooks, *Controller*
Tesa Doleman,
EMP: 50
SALES (est): 2.3MM Privately Held
SIC: 6531 Real estate managers

(P-11795)
THOMAS J HOBAN (PA)
Also Called: Hoban Management
215 W Lexington Ave, El Cajon (92020-4411)
PHONE...................................619 442-1665

Thomas J Hoban, *Owner*
Jacqueline Conger, *Executive Asst*
Arturo Gonzalez, *Maint Spvr*
Thomas J Castonguay,
Linda Dion, *Director*
EMP: 50
SQ FT: 1,700
SALES (est): 11.1MM Privately Held
WEB: www.hoban-management.com
SIC: 6531 Real estate brokers & agents; real estate managers

(P-11796)
THOMAS M OBINSON JR
7480 N Palm Ave Ste 101, Fresno (93711-5501)
PHONE...................................559 432-6200
Thomas Robinson, *Owner*
EMP: 55
SALES (est): 1.1MM Privately Held
SIC: 6531 Real estate agent, commercial

(P-11797)
TOPA BERKELEY LTD
1800 Avenue Of The Stars, Los Angeles (90067-4201)
PHONE...................................310 203-9199
John Anderson, *Owner*
EMP: 100
SALES (est): 2.8MM Privately Held
SIC: 6531 Real estate managers

(P-11798)
TRANSPACIFIC MANAGEMENT SVC
15661 Red Hill Ave # 205, Tustin (92780-7328)
PHONE...................................714 285-2626
William Sasser, *President*
Sherrie Fitchen, *Exec VP*
Michelle Pate, *Vice Pres*
EMP: 55
SALES (est): 5.4MM Privately Held
WEB: www.transpacinc.com
SIC: 6531 Real estate agents & managers

(P-11799)
TRANSWESTERN CORP POINTE LLC
600 Crprate Pinte Ste 250, Culver City (90230)
PHONE...................................310 642-1001
Dave Rock,
EMP: 99
SALES: 950K Privately Held
SIC: 6531 Real estate agent, commercial

(P-11800)
TRG INC
Also Called: Rosenthal Group, The
1350 Abbot Kinney Blvd # 101, Venice (90291-3893)
P.O. Box 837 (90294-0837)
PHONE...................................310 396-6750
R J Rosenthal, *President*
EMP: 100
SALES (est): 3.3MM Privately Held
WEB: www.trgnational.com
SIC: 6531 Real estate agents & managers

(P-11801)
TRILOGY REALTY GROUP INC
2025 N Mantle Ln, Santa Ana (92705-7614)
PHONE...................................937 206-0725
Garrett J Hilseth, *CEO*
Andrew Daggett, *Real Est Agnt*
EMP: 100 EST: 2014
SALES (est): 3MM Privately Held
SIC: 6531 Real estate agents & managers

(P-11802)
TRIMONT LAND COMPANY (DH)
Also Called: Northstar-At-Tahoe
5001 Northstar Dr, Truckee (96161-4236)
P.O. Box 129 (96160-0129)
PHONE...................................530 562-1010
Robert A Katz, *CEO*
Michael Barkin, *CFO*
EMP: 300
SALES (est): 20.7MM Publicly Held
SIC: 6531 7011 Real estate managers; ski lodge; resort hotel

(P-11803)
TROOP REAL ESTATE INC
4165 E Thousand Oaks Blvd # 100, Westlake Village (91362-3814)
PHONE..........................805 402-3028
Jeff Rosenblum, *Branch Mgr*
Patti Hepple, *Executive*
Samantha Kirkpatrick, *Broker*
Sharon Phelps, *Asst Mgr*
Maryann Baum, *Real Est Agnt*
EMP: 56
SALES (est): 1.5MM
SALES (corp-wide): 28.9MM **Privately Held**
SIC: 6531 Real estate agent, residential; real estate brokers & agents
PA: Troop Real Estate, Inc.
3200 E Los Angeles Ave
Simi Valley CA 93065
805 581-3200

(P-11804)
TROOP REAL ESTATE INC (PA)
3200 E Los Angeles Ave, Simi Valley (93065-3972)
PHONE..........................805 581-3200
Brian C Troop, *CEO*
Laura Lee Anthony, *President*
Deborah McCarthy, *COO*
Kristy Towry, *COO*
Janet Dorsey, *Branch Mgr*
EMP: 520
SQ FT: 10,000
SALES (est): 28.9MM **Privately Held**
WEB: www.scottpetto.com
SIC: 6531 Real estate agent, residential; real estate brokers & agents

(P-11805)
TRZ HOLDINGS II INC
Also Called: Brookfield Properties
725 S Figueroa St # 1850, Los Angeles (90017-5524)
PHONE..........................213 955-7170
Tim Callahan, *Manager*
EMP: 280
SALES (corp-wide): 31.9B **Publicly Held**
SIC: 6531 6552 Real estate managers; subdividers & developers
HQ: Trz Holdings Ii Llc
3 World Financial Ctr
New York NY 10281
212 693-8150

(P-11806)
UNITED CALIFORNIA REALTY INC
12829 Bear Valley Rd, Victorville (92392-9786)
PHONE..........................760 949-4040
Bob Gates, *President*
C V Tirone, *President*
Philip Tirone, *Corp Secy*
EMP: 65
SQ FT: 3,600
SALES (est): 3.2MM **Privately Held**
WEB: www.ucrproperties.com
SIC: 6531 Real estate agent, commercial

(P-11807)
UNIVERSE HOLDINGS DEV CO LLC
350 S Beverly Dr Ste 210, Beverly Hills (90212-4816)
PHONE..........................310 785-0077
Henry Manoucheri,
EMP: 50
SQ FT: 1,100
SALES (est): 1.9MM **Privately Held**
SIC: 6531 Real estate agents & managers

(P-11808)
US REAL ESTATE SERVICES INC
Also Called: Res.net
25520 Commercentre Dr # 1, Lake Forest (92630-8884)
PHONE..........................949 598-9920
Keith Guenther, *CEO*
Michael Bull, *CFO*
Gregory Metz, *Treasurer*
Garrett Mays, *Vice Pres*
Desirae Morales, *Manager*
EMP: 90
SQ FT: 37,000

SALES (est): 12.7MM **Privately Held**
WEB: www.usres.com
SIC: 6531 Real estate managers

(P-11809)
USA MULTIFAMILY MANAGEMENT
3200 Douglas Blvd Ste 200, Roseville (95661-4238)
PHONE..........................916 773-6060
Karen McCurdy, *President*
EMP: 130
SQ FT: 5,020
SALES (est): 758.8K
SALES (corp-wide): 1.1MM **Privately Held**
WEB: www.usapropfund.com
SIC: 6531 Real estate managers
PA: Usa Properties Fund, Inc.
3200 Douglas Blvd Ste 200
Roseville CA 95661
916 773-6060

(P-11810)
V TROTH INC
Also Called: Berkshire Hathaway
1801 W Avenue K Ste 101, Lancaster (93534-5999)
P.O. Box 2024 (93539-2024)
PHONE..........................661 948-4646
Debra K Anderson, *President*
Donald L Anderson, *Vice Pres*
Mark A Troth, *Admin Sec*
EMP: 75
SALES (est): 4.8MM **Privately Held**
SIC: 6531 8742 Real estate agent, residential; real estate consultant

(P-11811)
VALUATION CONCEPTS LLC
Also Called: Appraisal Trend
16350 Ventura Blvd D140, Encino (91436-5300)
PHONE..........................818 812-6233
Kendrick Jackson,
EMP: 90
SQ FT: 500
SALES (est): 1.9MM **Privately Held**
SIC: 6531 Appraiser, real estate

(P-11812)
VELOCITY COMMERCIAL CAPITL LLC
30699 Russell Ranch Rd, Westlake Village (91362-7315)
PHONE..........................818 532-3700
Christopher D Farrar,
Mark Szczepaniak, *CFO*
Lou Akel, *Ch Credit Ofcr*
Joseph Cowell, *Ch Credit Ofcr*
David Ryan, *Officer*
EMP: 50
SQ FT: 15,000
SALES (est): 10MM **Privately Held**
WEB: www.velocitycommercial.com
SIC: 6531 Real estate agent, commercial

(P-11813)
VILLAGEWAY MANAGEMENT INC
Also Called: Villageway Property Management
23041 Ave De La Carlta # 270, Laguna Hills (92653-1545)
PHONE..........................949 450-1515
Janet Walley, *President*
William Christiansen, *Treasurer*
Melanie Young, *Executive Asst*
Laura Gomez, *Human Res Dir*
Brittany Kitts, *Property Mgr*
EMP: 70 **EST:** 1969
SQ FT: 14,000
SALES (est): 5.9MM **Privately Held**
WEB: www.villageway.com
SIC: 6531 Real estate managers

(P-11814)
VISTA ANGLINA HSING PRTNERS LP
418 E Edgeware Rd, Los Angeles (90026-5693)
PHONE..........................213 482-4718
Tesa Doleman,
Jim Brooks, *Controller*
EMP: 50

SALES (est): 1.9MM **Privately Held**
SIC: 6531 Real estate agents & managers

(P-11815)
VISTA VALENCIA GROUP INC
Also Called: Coldwell Banker
25545 Via Paladar, Valencia (91355-3153)
PHONE..........................661 255-4600
Carol James, *CEO*
Roy Medows, *Bd of Directors*
Joan Byrd, *General Mgr*
Greg Handy, *General Mgr*
Diane Weber, *Info Tech Mgr*
EMP: 50
SALES (est): 3MM **Privately Held**
WEB: www.cbvista.com
SIC: 6531 Real estate agent, residential

(P-11816)
VOIT REAL ESTATE SERVICES LP
101 Shipyard Way Ste A, Newport Beach (92663-4447)
PHONE..........................949 644-8648
Bob Voit, *Managing Prtnr*
EMP: 130
SALES (est): 6.9MM **Privately Held**
WEB: www.voitco.com
SIC: 6531 Real estate agent, commercial

(P-11817)
WAGNER JACOBSON BROKERAGE INC
16400 Ventura Blvd # 333, Encino (91436-2137)
PHONE..........................323 872-1636
Michael Wagner, *President*
Charlotte Wagner, *Treasurer*
EMP: 50
SALES (est): 2.4MM **Privately Held**
SIC: 6531 Real estate brokers & agents

(P-11818)
WALSH VINEYARDS MANAGEMENT INC
1125 Golden Gate Dr, NAPA (94558-6188)
PHONE..........................707 255-1650
Tim Rodgers, *President*
Christopher Lynch, *CFO*
Vicki Thorpe, *Corp Secy*
Brian Shepard, *Vice Pres*
Towle Merritt, *General Mgr*
EMP: 250
SQ FT: 6,000
SALES (est): 27.4MM **Privately Held**
WEB: www.wvmgmt.com
SIC: 6531 Real estate managers

(P-11819)
WALTER E MCGUIRE RE INC
360 Primrose Rd, Burlingame (94010-4005)
PHONE..........................650 348-0222
Charles Moore, *President*
Reg Grady, *Real Est Agnt*
EMP: 180
SALES (est): 3.4MM
SALES (corp-wide): 20.4MM **Privately Held**
WEB: www.mcguire.com
SIC: 6531 Real estate brokers & agents
PA: Walter E. Mcguire Real Estate, Inc.
2001 Lombard St
San Francisco CA 94123
415 929-1500

(P-11820)
WALTER E MCGUIRE RE INC (PA)
2001 Lombard St, San Francisco (94123-2808)
PHONE..........................415 929-1500
Charles Moore, *CEO*
Andrew Weinberger, *Partner*
Alex Buehlmann, *COO*
Lauren Bensinger, *Business Dir*
Sean McKaig, *Info Tech Dir*
EMP: 262 **EST:** 1919
SQ FT: 10,000
SALES (est): 20.4MM **Privately Held**
WEB: www.mcguire.com
SIC: 6531 Real estate agent, residential

(P-11821)
WALTER E MCGUIRE RE INC
Also Called: Raymond Brown Company
17 Bluxome St, San Francisco (94107-1605)
PHONE..........................415 296-0123
Aldo Congi, *Manager*
Kristen Thompson, *Real Est Agnt*
EMP: 50
SALES (est): 1.5MM
SALES (corp-wide): 20.4MM **Privately Held**
WEB: www.mcguire.com
SIC: 6531 Real estate agent, residential
PA: Walter E. Mcguire Real Estate, Inc.
2001 Lombard St
San Francisco CA 94123
415 929-1500

(P-11822)
WALTER VOSS CYNTHIA RE MAX
6695 E Pacific Coast Hwy # 150, Long Beach (90803-4235)
PHONE..........................562 434-5980
Bob Stallings, *Owner*
EMP: 85
SALES (est): 1.4MM **Privately Held**
SIC: 6531 Real estate agent, residential

(P-11823)
WATERMARK RTRMENT CMMNTIES INC
3890 Nobel Dr, San Diego (92122-5786)
PHONE..........................858 597-8000
Barbara Wilkinson, *Manager*
EMP: 75 **Privately Held**
SIC: 6531 Real estate managers
HQ: Watermark Retirement Communities, Inc.
2020 W Rudasill Rd
Tucson AZ 85704
520 797-4000

(P-11824)
WAYPOINT REAL ESTATE GROUP LLC
1999 Harrison St Fl 22nd, Oakland (94612-4719)
PHONE..........................510 250-2200
Colin Wiel, *Mng Member*
Lane Auten,
Doug Brien,
EMP: 82
SALES (est): 7MM **Privately Held**
SIC: 6531 Real estate brokers & agents

(P-11825)
WELK RESORT GROUP INC (PA)
Also Called: Welk Resort Center
300 Rancheros Dr Ste 450, San Marcos (92069-2969)
PHONE..........................760 652-4913
Larry Welk, *CEO*
Jennifer Robinson, *Treasurer*
Heather Collins, *Admin Asst*
Susan Gardner, *Administration*
Oskar De Leon, *Sr Software Eng*
EMP: 50
SALES (est): 95.2MM **Privately Held**
WEB: www.welksandiego.com
SIC: 6531 6552 7992 7011 Time-sharing real estate sales, leasing & rentals; subdividers & developers; public golf courses; hotels & motels; eating places; tour operators

(P-11826)
WELLS & BENNETT REALTORS (PA)
1451 Leimert Blvd, Oakland (94602-1896)
PHONE..........................510 531-7000
Barton W Bennett, *Owner*
Jeannine Nelson, *Manager*
Tracy Lee L Butler, *Real Est Agnt*
Elisa Uribe, *Real Est Agnt*
EMP: 80
SQ FT: 5,000
SALES (est): 4.5MM **Privately Held**
WEB: www.wellsandbennett.com
SIC: 6531 6512 Real estate agent, commercial; real estate managers; nonresidential building operators; commercial & industrial building operation

(P-11827)
WESTCOE REALTORS INC
Also Called: Westcoe Escrow Division
7191 Magnolia Ave, Riverside
(92504-3805)
PHONE..............................951 784-2500
Rich Simonin, *Manager*
Susan Simonin, *President*
Richard Simonin, *Vice Pres*
Scott Hooks, *Broker*
Scott Beloian, *Real Est Agnt*
EMP: 65
SQ FT: 11,200
SALES (est): 4.3MM **Privately Held**
WEB: www.louanneludwig.com
SIC: 6531 Real estate agent, residential

(P-11828)
WESTERN AMERICA PROPERTIES LLC
111 N Sepulveda Blvd # 330, Manhattan Beach (90266-6813)
P.O. Box 1597 (90267-1597)
PHONE..............................310 374-4381
James Perley,
EMP: 89
SALES (est): 2.7MM **Privately Held**
SIC: 6531 Real estate agent, commercial

(P-11829)
WESTERN NATIONAL SECURITIES (PA)
8 Executive Cir, Irvine (92614-6746)
P.O. Box 19528 (92623-9528)
PHONE..............................949 862-6200
Michael K Hayde, *CEO*
James Gilly, *President*
Jerry Lapointe, *Principal*
Justin Woodworth, *Director*
EMP: 120 EST: 1981
SQ FT: 35,000
SALES (est): 17.1MM **Privately Held**
WEB: www.jpi.com
SIC: 6531 Real estate managers

(P-11830)
WESTLAKE REALTY GROUP INC (PA)
520 S El Camino Real # 900, San Mateo (94402-1722)
PHONE..............................650 579-1010
M Gary Wong, *President*
EMP: 66
SALES: 5MM **Privately Held**
SIC: 6531 Real estate agents & managers

(P-11831)
WESTMINSTER HOUSING PARTENERS
Also Called: Windsor Court/Stratford Place
8140 13th St, Westminster (92683-4794)
PHONE..............................714 891-3000
Jim Brooks, *Controller*
Tesa Doleman,
EMP: 50
SALES (est): 2.1MM **Privately Held**
SIC: 6531 Real estate agents & managers

(P-11832)
WHEATLAND SCHOOL DISTRICT
Also Called: Realty World
100 Wheatland Park Dr, Wheatland (95692-9286)
PHONE..............................530 633-3135
Justin Guzman, *President*
EMP: 85
SALES (corp-wide): 14MM **Privately Held**
SIC: 6531 Real estate agent, residential
PA: Wheatland School District
111 Main St
Wheatland CA 95692
530 633-3130

(P-11833)
WILLIAM L LYON & ASSOC INC
Also Called: Lyon & Associates Realtors
2801 J St, Sacramento (95816-4315)
PHONE..............................916 447-7878
Laure Woodgundlach, *Manager*
Janet Carlson, *Executive*
Paul Brecher, *Broker*
Dale Robertson, *Broker*
Eileen Nordman, *Sales Executive*
EMP: 55

SALES (est): 1.6MM
SALES (corp-wide): 65.8MM **Privately Held**
WEB: www.lyonre.com
SIC: 6531 Real estate agent, residential
PA: L Lyon William & Associates Inc
3640 American River Dr
Sacramento CA 95864
916 978-4200

(P-11834)
WILLIAM L LYON & ASSOC INC
Also Called: Lyon Realtors
8814 Madison Ave, Fair Oaks (95628-3908)
PHONE..............................916 535-0356
Clay Sigg, *Manager*
Kyle Thompson, *Office Mgr*
Anthony Metz, *Agent*
Sigrid Biddle, *Real Est Agnt*
EMP: 70
SALES (est): 2.1MM
SALES (corp-wide): 65.8MM **Privately Held**
WEB: www.lyonre.com
SIC: 6531 Real estate brokers & agents
PA: L Lyon William & Associates Inc
3640 American River Dr
Sacramento CA 95864
916 978-4200

(P-11835)
WILLIAMS KELLER REALTY
Also Called: Keller Williams Realtors
7005 Boardwalk Dr, Granite Bay (95746-9200)
PHONE..............................916 774-6700
William Hall, *President*
Paul Boudier, *Web Proj Mgr*
Boudier Paul, *Network Mgr*
EMP: 60
SALES (est): 2.2MM **Privately Held**
SIC: 6531 Real estate managers

(P-11836)
WILLIS ALLEN REAL ESTATE (PA)
1131 Wall St, La Jolla (92037-4579)
PHONE..............................858 459-4033
Andrew E Nelson, *President*
Jane Dreher, *Branch Mgr*
Josie Vara, *Office Mgr*
Clarissa Delgado, *Broker*
Bobby Graham, *Broker*
EMP: 50
SQ FT: 6,000
SALES (est): 4.6MM **Privately Held**
SIC: 6531 Real estate agent, residential

(P-11837)
WILLIS ALLEN REAL ESTATE
6024 Pasco Delicias, Rancho Santa Fe (92067)
P.O. Box 107 (92067-0107)
PHONE..............................858 756-2444
Gary Wheeler, *Manager*
EMP: 50
SALES (corp-wide): 4.6MM **Privately Held**
SIC: 6531 Real estate agent, residential
PA: Willis Allen Real Estate
1131 Wall St
La Jolla CA 92037
858 459-4033

(P-11838)
WILLOW GLEN HSING PARTNERS LP
465 Willow Glen Way # 100, San Jose (95125-6513)
PHONE..............................408 267-7252
Jim Brooks, *Controller*
Tesa Doleman,
EMP: 50 EST: 2014
SALES (est): 1.1MM **Privately Held**
SIC: 6531 Real estate brokers & agents

(P-11839)
WILMARK MANAGEMENT SERVICES (PA)
Also Called: Wilmark Development
9948 Hibert St Ste 210, San Diego (92131-1034)
PHONE..............................858 271-0583
Mark S Schmidt, *President*

EMP: 65
SALES (est): 3.2MM **Privately Held**
SIC: 6531 Real estate managers

(P-11840)
WINDERMERE REAL ESTATE EAST
71691 Highway 111, Rancho Mirage (92270-4441)
PHONE..............................760 568-2568
Bob Deville, *Principal*
EMP: 67
SALES (corp-wide): 13.5MM **Privately Held**
SIC: 6531 Real estate brokers & agents
PA: Windermere Real Estate East Inc
14405 Se 36th St Ste 100
Bellevue WA 98006
425 643-5500

(P-11841)
YORBA PROPERTIES CORP
Also Called: Re/Max
20459 Yorba Linda Blvd, Yorba Linda (92886-3043)
PHONE..............................714 777-5112
Gerry Bullerdick, *President*
Maryam Memon, *Broker*
Kelly Poole, *Real Est Agnt*
EMP: 75
SQ FT: 6,000
SALES (est): 3.4MM **Privately Held**
WEB: www.eastlakevillage.net
SIC: 6531 6163 Real estate agent, residential; mortgage brokers arranging for loans, using money of others

(P-11842)
YOUNG ESTATES
971 S Westlke Blvd 100, Westlake Village (91361)
PHONE..............................805 446-1800
Joan Young, *President*
Bill Carter, *Exec VP*
EMP: 80
SALES (est): 1.9MM **Privately Held**
SIC: 6531 Real estate agents & managers

(P-11843)
YOUNG REALTORS
Also Called: Joan Young Co Realtors
971 S Westlake Blvd # 100, Westlake Village (91361-3115)
PHONE..............................805 497-0947
Fax: 805 494-8986
EMP: 53
SALES (est): 1.5MM **Privately Held**
SIC: 6531

(P-11844)
Z & M ASSOCIATES INC
Also Called: Referral Realty Cupertino
1601 S Danza Blvd Ste 150, Cupertino (95014)
PHONE..............................408 996-8100
Moise Nahouraii, *President*
EMP: 85
SALES (est): 2.7MM **Privately Held**
SIC: 6531 Real estate agent, residential

(P-11845)
ZENITH HEALTH CARE
Also Called: Regency Park
245 S El Molino Ave, Pasadena (91101-2905)
PHONE..............................626 578-0460
Sandy Wooters, *Administration*
Nancy Oconnor, *Administration*
EMP: 70
SALES (est): 2MM **Privately Held**
WEB: www.zenithadm.com
SIC: 6531 Real estate agents & managers

(P-11846)
ZEPHYR PARTNERS RE-LLC
700 2nd St, Encinitas (92024-4459)
PHONE..............................858 558-3650
Brad Termini,
Chris Beucler, *COO*
Chuck Godlesky, *Officer*
Ryan Herrell, *Vice Pres*
Dean Loisel, *Vice Pres*
EMP: 50
SALES (est): 4MM **Privately Held**
SIC: 6531 Real estate agents & managers

6541 Title Abstract Offices

(P-11847)
CHICAGO TITLE INSURANCE CO
3127 Transworld Dr # 103, Stockton (95206-4988)
P.O. Box 7638 (95267-0638)
PHONE..............................209 952-5500
Lisa Westfall, *Branch Mgr*
EMP: 60
SALES (corp-wide): 7.6B **Publicly Held**
SIC: 6541 6361 6099 Title & trust companies; title insurance; escrow institutions other than real estate
HQ: Chicago Title Insurance Company
4050 Calle Real
Santa Barbara CA 93110

(P-11848)
FIRST AMERCN TITLE OF STOCKTON (PA)
2800 W March Ln Ste 210, Stockton (95219-8200)
PHONE..............................209 929-4800
Elmer Sanguinetti, *Director*
Cindy Freitas, *Officer*
EMP: 53
SALES (est): 2MM **Privately Held**
SIC: 6541 6099 Title & trust companies; escrow institutions other than real estate

(P-11849)
TIMESHARE RELIEF INC
Also Called: Transer America
15435 Park Point Ave # 106, Lake Elsinore (92532-0460)
PHONE..............................951 525-1539
Dave Halpern, *CEO*
Dave McMillian, *President*
Marcus Gillette, *Vice Pres*
Cindy Martin, *Vice Pres*
EMP: 170
SQ FT: 11,000
SALES (est): 7.5MM **Privately Held**
WEB: www.timesharerelief.com
SIC: 6541 Title abstract offices

(P-11850)
TITLE RECORDS INC
8926 Sunland Blvd, Sun Valley (91352-2843)
PHONE..............................818 767-9610
Brad Westover, *President*
Timothy Morgan, *Ch of Bd*
Kenneth Sean Pratt, *President*
EMP: 63
SQ FT: 88,000
SALES (est): 1.9MM **Privately Held**
SIC: 6541 Title search companies

6552 Land Subdividers & Developers

(P-11851)
A M S PARTNERSHIP (PA)
Also Called: La Mancha Development
1517 S Sepulveda Blvd, Los Angeles (90025-3311)
PHONE..............................310 312-6698
Marvin B Levine, *Partner*
Samuel Bachner, *Partner*
EMP: 60
SQ FT: 2,500
SALES (est): 7.7MM **Privately Held**
SIC: 6552 6512 Subdividers & developers; commercial & industrial building operation

(P-11852)
ALLEN DEVELOPMENT PARTNERS LLC (PA)
125 Sbridge 100, Visalia (93291)
PHONE..............................559 732-5425
Richard S Allen,
Kevin Noell,
EMP: 60 EST: 1993
SALES (est): 5MM **Privately Held**
SIC: 6552 Subdividers & developers

(P-11853)
AMCAL COMMUNITIES INC
30141 Agoura Rd Ste 100, Agoura Hills
(91301-2020)
PHONE..............................818 706-0694
Percival Vaz, *President*
EMP: 50
SALES (est): 4.4MM **Privately Held**
SIC: 6552 Land subdividers & developers,
residential

(P-11854)
**AMERICAN NWLAND
COMMUNITIES LP (PA)**
9820 Towne Centre Dr # 100, San Diego
(92121-1912)
PHONE..............................858 455-7503
Ladonna K Monsees, *CEO*
Dave Wood, *President*
Derek Thomas, *COO*
Daniel C Van Epp, *COO*
Vicki R Mullins, *CFO*
EMP: 50
SQ FT: 12,000
SALES (est): 119.3MM **Privately Held**
SIC: 6552 Land subdividers & developers,
commercial

(P-11855)
**ANNABEL INVESTMENT
COMPANY**
Also Called: Sunset Development Company
2600 Camino Ramon Ste 201, San Ramon
(94583-5000)
P.O. Box 640 (94583-0640)
PHONE..............................925 866-0100
Alexander Mehran, *Partner*
EMP: 100
SQ FT: 1,000,000
SALES (est): 5.9MM **Privately Held**
SIC: 6552 Subdividers & developers

(P-11856)
**BEVERLY HILLS COUNTRY
CLUB**
3084 Motor Ave, Los Angeles
(90064-4746)
PHONE..............................310 836-4400
Gene Axelrod, *Partner*
EMP: 130
SQ FT: 100,000
SALES (est): 15.6MM **Privately Held**
WEB: www.beverlyhillscc.com
SIC: 6552 6531 7997 Subdividers & de-
velopers; real estate agents & managers;
membership sports & recreation clubs

(P-11857)
**BRADDOCK & LOGAN GROUP II
LP**
4155 Blackhawk Plaza Cir # 201, Danville
(94506-4903)
PHONE..............................925 736-4000
Joseph Raphel, *General Ptnr*
EMP: 200
SALES (est): 8.5MM **Privately Held**
SIC: 6552 Subdividers & developers

(P-11858)
**BRIDGE HOUSING
CORPORATION (PA)**
600 California St Fl 9, San Francisco
(94108-2706)
PHONE..............................415 989-1111
Cinthia Parker, *President*
Susan Johnson, *Exec VP*
Kimberly McKay, *Exec VP*
Lydia Tan, *Exec VP*
Rebecca Hlebasko, *Vice Pres*
EMP: 90
SQ FT: 12,000
SALES (est): 23.8MM **Privately Held**
SIC: 6552 Land subdividers & developers,
residential

(P-11859)
**BROOKFELD BAY AREA
HLDINGS LLC**
Also Called: Brookfield Homes
500 La Gonda Way Ste 100, Danville
(94526-1747)
PHONE..............................925 743-8000
John J J Ryan,
Jay Lueckeman,

EMP: 60
SALES (est): 14.2MM **Privately Held**
SIC: 6552 Land subdividers & developers,
residential

(P-11860)
BURBANK HOUSING DEV CORP
790 Sonoma Ave, Santa Rosa
(95404-4713)
PHONE..............................707 526-9782
David W Spilman, *CEO*
Charles A Cornell, *President*
John Lowry, *President*
Stuart W Martin, *Treasurer*
Sandra Stribling, *Accountant*
EMP: 156
SQ FT: 9,850
SALES: 7.1MM **Privately Held**
SIC: 6552 Land subdividers & developers,
residential

(P-11861)
**CAREER DEV INST FOR
EXCPTNL**
1470 Marsh Way, Riverside (92501-1962)
PHONE..............................951 337-3678
Alan Schwerdt, *Principal*
EMP: 50 EST: 2015
SALES: 642.3K **Privately Held**
SIC: 6552 Subdividers & developers

(P-11862)
CARLTON SENIOR LIVING INC
Also Called: Chateau Pleasant Hill 2
2770 Pleasant Hill Rd Ofc, Concord
(94523-2086)
PHONE..............................925 935-1660
Linda Jackson, *Manager*
EMP: 65
SALES (corp-wide): 29.6MM **Privately
Held**
SIC: 6552 Subdividers & developers
PA: Senior Carlton Living Inc
4005 Port Chicago Hwy # 120
Concord CA 94520
925 338-2434

(P-11863)
CASDEN COMPANY LLC
9606 Santa Monica Blvd # 3, Beverly Hills
(90210-4420)
PHONE..............................310 274-5553
Alan I Casden,
Alan Casden,
Robert Decker, *Director*
EMP: 100
SQ FT: 40,000
SALES (est): 8.9MM **Privately Held**
SIC: 6552 Land subdividers & developers,
residential

(P-11864)
**CASTLE & COOKE
COMMERCIAL CA**
10000 Stockdale Hwy # 300, Bakersfield
(93311-3604)
PHONE..............................661 665-1540
Bruce Freeman, *President*
Bruce Davis, *Vice Pres*
Laura Whitaker, *Vice Pres*
Carol A Stringer, *Admin Sec*
Rosalinda Oasay, *Asst Treas*
EMP: 70
SQ FT: 19,602
SALES (est): 4.8MM
SALES (corp-wide): 911.7MM **Privately
Held**
WEB: www.castlecooke.net
SIC: 6552 Land subdividers & developers,
commercial
PA: Castle & Cooke, Inc.
1 Dole Dr
Westlake Village CA 91362
310 374-3952

(P-11865)
COLRICH COMMUNITIES INC
444 W Beech St Ste 300, San Diego
(92101-2942)
PHONE..............................858 350-7672
Richard Gabriel, *Ch of Bd*
Colin Seid, *President*
Maggie Lucas, *Admin Sec*
EMP: 60
SALES (est): 8.1MM **Privately Held**
SIC: 6552 Subdividers & developers

(P-11866)
**COMSTOCK CROSSER ASSOC
DEV INC**
Also Called: Comstock Homes
321 12th St Ste 200, Manhattan Beach
(90266-5354)
PHONE..............................310 546-5781
David Lauletta, *CEO*
Gary L Lyter, *CFO*
Dan Crosser, *Vice Pres*
Pete Perea, *Vice Pres*
Joseph Perri, *Finance*
EMP: 50
SQ FT: 7,000
SALES (est): 14.2MM **Privately Held**
WEB: www.comstock-homes.com
SIC: 6552 Land subdividers & developers,
residential

(P-11867)
COUNTY OF YUBA
Also Called: Yuba County Planning Dept
915 8th St Ste 123, Marysville
(95901-5273)
PHONE..............................530 749-5470
Kevin Mallen, *Branch Mgr*
EMP: 80 **Privately Held**
SIC: 6552 Subdividers & developers
PA: County Of Yuba
915 8th St Ste 109
Marysville CA 95901
530 749-7575

(P-11868)
CP DEVELOPMENT CO LLC
1 Sansome St Ste 3200, San Francisco
(94104-4436)
PHONE..............................415 995-1770
EMP: 58
SALES (est): 767.6K
SALES (corp-wide): 139.4MM **Publicly
Held**
SIC: 6552 Subdividers & developers
PA: Five Point Holdings, Llc
25 Enterprise Ste 300
Aliso Viejo CA 92656
949 349-1000

(P-11869)
DANCO COMMUNITIES
5251 Ericson Way Ste A, Arcata
(95521-9274)
PHONE..............................707 822-9000
Dan Johnson, *CEO*
Jill Kelley, *Risk Mgmt Dir*
Kathryn Hungerford, *Executive Asst*
EMP: 99
SALES (est): 1.3MM **Privately Held**
SIC: 6552 Subdividers & developers

(P-11870)
**DAVIDSON COMMUNITIES LLC
(PA)**
Also Called: Davidson Builders
1302 Camino Del Mar, Del Mar
(92014-2508)
PHONE..............................858 259-8500
William A Davidson,
Sarah Bancroft, *Office Mgr*
Jerry L Leaming,
William Davidson, *Manager*
EMP: 50
SQ FT: 14,000
SALES (est): 13.2MM **Privately Held**
WEB: www.davidsoncommunities.com
SIC: 6552 Subdividers & developers

(P-11871)
**DIABLO GRANDE LTD
PARTNERSHIP**
9521 Morton Davis Dr, Patterson
(95363-8610)
PHONE..............................209 892-7421
Donald Panoz, *Ltd Ptnr*
Jay Morton Davis, *Ltd Ptnr*
EMP: 100
SQ FT: 18,000
SALES (est): 6.7MM
SALES (corp-wide): 111.5MM **Privately
Held**
WEB: www.diablogrande.com
SIC: 6552 7011 7992 5812 Subdividers &
developers; resort hotel; public golf
courses; eating places

HQ: Elan Chateau Resorts Llc
100 Rue Charlemagne Dr
Braselton GA 30517

(P-11872)
DYA ASSOC
8335 W Sunset Blvd # 320, Los Angeles
(90069-1538)
PHONE..............................323 364-4270
David Yashar, *Principal*
EMP: 60 EST: 2015
SALES (est): 1.9MM **Privately Held**
SIC: 6552 Subdividers & developers

(P-11873)
EDAW INC (HQ)
300 California St Fl 5, San Francisco
(94104-1411)
PHONE..............................415 955-2800
Joseph E Brown, *CEO*
Jason Prior, *President*
Dana Waymire, *CFO*
Vaughan Davies, *Principal*
Jason Bowen, *Controller*
EMP: 120
SQ FT: 18,072
SALES (est): 121.8MM
SALES (corp-wide): 20.1B **Publicly Held**
WEB: www.edaw.com
SIC: 6552 0781 Subdividers & developers;
landscape architects
PA: Aecom
1999 Avenue Of The Stars # 2600
Los Angeles CA 90067
213 593-8000

(P-11874)
**EUREKA REALTY PARTNERS
INC (PA)**
Also Called: Craig Realty Group
4100 Macarthur Blvd # 200, Newport Beach
(92660-2064)
PHONE..............................949 224-4100
Steven L Craig, *CEO*
Donna Balderrama, *Vice Pres*
Rino Larosa, *Vice Pres*
Lori Smith, *Vice Pres*
Sally Terando, *Vice Pres*
EMP: 280
SQ FT: 15,000
SALES (est): 43.2MM **Privately Held**
WEB: www.craigrealtygroup.com
SIC: 6552 Land subdividers & developers,
commercial

(P-11875)
FC METROPOLITAN LOFTS INC
Also Called: Forrest City Development
949 S Hope St Ste 100, Los Angeles
(90015-1455)
PHONE..............................213 488-0010
Kevin Ratner, *President*
Ronald A Ratner, *President*
EMP: 80
SALES (est): 4.8MM **Privately Held**
SIC: 6552 Subdividers & developers

(P-11876)
FOOTHILL ESTATES INC
400 Griffin St, Salinas (93901-4344)
PHONE..............................831 422-7819
Frederick A Jensen, *President*
E A Jensen, *Agent*
EMP: 90
SALES (est): 4.7MM **Privately Held**
WEB: www.foothillestates.com
SIC: 6552 Land subdividers & developers,
residential

(P-11877)
**GOLDRICH & KEST INDUSTRIES
LLC (PA)**
5150 Overland Ave, Culver City
(90230-4914)
P.O. Box 3623 (90231-3623)
PHONE..............................310 204-2050
Warren Breslow,
EMP: 750
SQ FT: 5,000
SALES (est): 295.2MM **Privately Held**
SIC: 6552 Subdividers & developers

(P-11878)
GOLDRICHKEST (PA)
5150 Overland Ave, Culver City
(90230-4914)
P.O. Box 3623 (90231-3623)
PHONE.....................310 204-2050
Jona Goldrich, *President*
Sol Kest, *Vice Pres*
EMP: 276 EST: 1963
SQ FT: 5,000
SALES (est): 1.3MM **Privately Held**
SIC: 6552 Land subdividers & developers,
commercial

(P-11879)
**GROUPE DEVELOPMENT
ASSOCIATES**
Also Called: Brook Side Development
3255 W March Ln Fl 4, Stockton
(95219-2304)
P.O. Box 7576 (95267-0576)
PHONE.....................209 473-6000
Fritz Grupe, *Chairman*
EMP: 100
SQ FT: 500
SALES (est): 4MM **Privately Held**
SIC: 6552 Land subdividers & developers,
commercial; land subdividers & developers, residential

(P-11880)
HINES GS PROPERTIES INC
101 California St # 1000, San Francisco
(94111-5802)
PHONE.....................415 982-6200
James B Buie, *Exec VP*
John Carr, *Controller*
EMP: 50
SQ FT: 7,000
SALES (corp-wide): 1.4B **Privately Held**
SIC: 6552 Subdividers & developers
HQ: Hines Gs Properties, Inc.
2800 Post Oak Blvd
Houston TX 77056
713 621-8000

(P-11881)
**INVESTMENT CONCEPTS INC
(PA)**
Also Called: Vista Sun Apartments
1667 E Lincoln Ave, Orange (92865-1929)
PHONE.....................714 283-5800
George A Chami, *CEO*
George Mobayed, *COO*
Kaye Richey, *Senior VP*
Sam Benz, *Vice Pres*
Grace Imamura, *Vice Pres*
EMP: 192 EST: 1993
SALES (est): 39.8MM **Privately Held**
SIC: 6552 6531 Subdividers & developers;
real estate managers

(P-11882)
**KEITH DEVELOPMENT
CORPORATION**
2777 Cleveland Ave # 109, Santa Rosa
(95403-2763)
PHONE.....................707 528-8703
Joseph P Keith, *President*
Frank Denney, *Vice Pres*
Chris Coles, *Admin Sec*
EMP: 50
SQ FT: 2,000
SALES: 17MM **Privately Held**
SIC: 6552 1521 Land subdividers & developers, residential; new construction, single-family houses

(P-11883)
KING VENTURES
285 Bridge St, San Luis Obispo
(93401-5510)
PHONE.....................805 544-4444
John E King, *Owner*
Ben Neuman, *Business Mgr*
EMP: 126
SQ FT: 10,000
SALES (est): 9.4MM **Privately Held**
WEB: www.kingventures.net
SIC: 6552 6512 Land subdividers & developers, commercial; land subdividers & developers, residential; commercial & industrial building operation

(P-11884)
**LAND SERVICES LANDSCAPE
CONTRS**
901 Brown Rd, Fremont (94539-7089)
PHONE.....................510 656-8101
John Ahner, *President*
EMP: 80
SQ FT: 11,000
SALES (est): 9.5MM **Privately Held**
SIC: 6552 Subdividers & developers

(P-11885)
LODI DEVELOPMENT INC
Also Called: Anderson Homes
1420 S Mills Ave Ste E, Lodi (95242-4291)
P.O. Box 1237 (95241-1237)
PHONE.....................209 367-7600
Larry W Anderson, *President*
Bob Dolliver Sr, *COO*
Craig Barton, *CFO*
EMP: 50
SQ FT: 5,000
SALES (est): 3.3MM **Privately Held**
WEB: www.lodidevelopment.com
SIC: 6552 Land subdividers & developers,
commercial

(P-11886)
LOWE ENTERPRISES INC
11777 San Vincente Blvd S, Los Angeles
(90049)
PHONE.....................310 820-6661
Bob Lowe, *President*
Bill Wethe, *CFO*
Peter S Morgan, *Senior VP*
EMP: 100
SQ FT: 15,000
SALES (est): 4.5MM
SALES (corp-wide): 1B **Privately Held**
SIC: 6552 Land subdividers & developers,
commercial
HQ: Lowe Development Corporation-Reserve Manager
11777 San Vicente Blvd
Los Angeles CA 90049
310 820-6661

(P-11887)
**LOWE ENTERPRISES RE
GROUP**
Also Called: Lowe Enterprises Coml Group
11777 San Vicente Blvd # 900, Los Angeles
(90049-6615)
PHONE.....................310 820-6661
Bob Lowe, *President*
EMP: 90 EST: 1994
SQ FT: 10,000
SALES (est): 3.6MM
SALES (corp-wide): 1B **Privately Held**
WEB: www.loweenterprises.com
SIC: 6552 6531 Land subdividers & developers, commercial; real estate managers
PA: Lowe Enterprises, Inc.
11777 San Vicente Blvd # 900
Los Angeles CA 90049
310 820-6661

(P-11888)
M H PODELL COMPANY (PA)
Also Called: Nicholas A Stevens
22 Battery St Ste 404, Burlingame (94010)
PHONE.....................415 296-8800
Michael Podell, *President*
EMP: 51
SALES (est): 7.7MM **Privately Held**
WEB: www.mhpodell.com
SIC: 6552 6513 Subdividers & developers;
apartment building operators

(P-11889)
MAKAR PROPERTIES LLC (PA)
Also Called: Makallon La Jolla Properties
4100 Macarthur Blvd # 150, Newport Beach
(92660-2063)
P.O. Box 7080 (92658-7080)
PHONE.....................949 255-1100
Paul P Makarechian, *CEO*
Peter Ciaccia, *President*
Douglas Kiel, *COO*
Ben Mearig, *Vice Pres*
Tony Daly, *Business Dir*
EMP: 1200

SALES (est): 54.5MM **Privately Held**
SIC: 6552 1542 Land subdividers & developers, commercial; commercial & office building, new construction

(P-11890)
MEANY WILSON L P
4 Embarcadero Ctr # 3330, San Francisco
(94111-4184)
PHONE.....................415 905-5300
Thomas P Sullivan, *Partner*
EMP: 50
SQ FT: 22,000
SALES (est): 7MM **Privately Held**
WEB: www.wmspartners.com
SIC: 6552 6531 Land subdividers & developers, commercial; real estate agents & managers

(P-11891)
MEYER PROPERTIES CORP (PA)
4320 Von Karman Ave, Newport Beach
(92660-2004)
PHONE.....................949 862-0500
Robert E Meyer, *President*
EMP: 53
SQ FT: 5,200
SALES (est): 7.5MM **Privately Held**
WEB: www.meyerprop.com
SIC: 6552 6512 Land subdividers & developers, commercial; nonresidential building operators

(P-11892)
**MIDPEN HOUSING
CORPORATION**
303 Vintage Park Dr # 250, Foster City
(94404-1166)
PHONE.....................650 356-2900
Mark Battey, *CEO*
Matthew O Franklin, *President*
Pam Prasad, *Administration*
EMP: 300
SQ FT: 20,000
SALES: 22.3MM **Privately Held**
SIC: 6552 Land subdividers & developers,
residential

(P-11893)
**MORELAND PCF SNOQUALMIE
LLC**
5060 California Ave # 1150, Bakersfield
(93309-0728)
PHONE.....................661 322-1081
Terry L Moreland, *Ch of Bd*
Tammy Fleming, *President*
EMP: 150
SQ FT: 3,000
SALES (est): 11.1MM **Privately Held**
SIC: 6552 6512 Land subdividers & developers, commercial; commercial & industrial building operation

(P-11894)
**MOUNTAIN RETREAT
INCORPORATED**
111 Deerwood Rd Ste 100, San Ramon
(94583-4445)
P.O. Box 178 (94583-0178)
PHONE.....................925 838-7780
Thomas Porter, *President*
Peggy Porter, *Corp Secy*
Christopher Porter, *Vice Pres*
EMP: 100 EST: 1976
SQ FT: 8,000
SALES (est): 5.7MM **Privately Held**
SIC: 6552 6531

(P-11895)
**NATIONAL CMNTY
RENAISSANCE CAL (PA)**
9421 Haven Ave, Rancho Cucamonga
(91730-5886)
PHONE.....................909 483-2444
Steven J Pontell, *CEO*
Orlando Cabrera, *President*
Frank Taiese, *COO*
Tracy Thomas, *COO*
Richard Whittingham, *CFO*
EMP: 100
SALES: 53.3K **Privately Held**
SIC: 6552 Subdividers & developers

(P-11896)
**NEHEMIAH PROGRESSIVE
HOUSING D**
424 N 7th St Ste 250, Sacramento
(95811-0210)
PHONE.....................916 231-1999
Scott Syphax, *CEO*
Walt Mc Daniel, *CFO*
EMP: 60
SQ FT: 1,500
SALES (est): 316.5K **Privately Held**
WEB: www.nehemiahcorp.org
SIC: 6552 Land subdividers & developers,
residential
PA: Nehemiah Corporation Of America
640 Bercut Dr Ste A
Sacramento CA 95811

(P-11897)
NEWLAND GROUP INC (PA)
Also Called: Newland Northwest
4790 Eastgate Mall # 150, San Diego
(92121-2061)
PHONE.....................858 455-7503
Robert B Mc Leod, *President*
Ladonna Monsees, *President*
Fran Elgas, *Office Mgr*
Mark Sexton, *Administration*
Gary Gagne, *VP Accounting*
EMP: 50
SQ FT: 40,000
SALES (est): 18.5MM **Privately Held**
SIC: 6552 Subdividers & developers

(P-11898)
**NW MANOR COMMUNITY
PARTNERS LP**
17782 Sky Park Cir, Irvine (92614-6404)
PHONE.....................714 662-5565
Anand Kannan, *Partner*
Brian Brooks, *General Ptnr*
Perry Harenda, *General Ptnr*
Karen Buckland, *Project Mgr*
Caitlin Marroquin, *Project Mgr*
EMP: 85
SQ FT: 25,000
SALES (est): 3MM **Privately Held**
SIC: 6552 Subdividers & developers

(P-11899)
O & S HOLDINGS LLC
11611 San Vicente Blvd, Los Angeles
(90049-5106)
PHONE.....................310 207-8600
Gary Safady, *CEO*
Amy Lennox, *Administration*
Mark Safady, *Property Mgr*
Paul Orfalea, *
EMP: 50
SALES: 2MM **Privately Held**
WEB: www.osholdings.com
SIC: 6552 Land subdividers & developers,
commercial

(P-11900)
**OCEAN COLONY PARTNERS
LLC**
Also Called: Half Moon Bay Golf Links
2450 Cabrillo Hwy S # 200, Half Moon Bay
(94019-2266)
PHONE.....................650 726-5764
William E Barrett, *Partner*
EMP: 175
SQ FT: 6,000
SALES (est): 27.5MM **Privately Held**
SIC: 6552 7992 7389 Subdividers & developers; public golf courses; telephone services

(P-11901)
OLIVERMCMILLAN LLC (DH)
733 8th Ave, San Diego (92101-6407)
PHONE.....................619 321-1111
Morgan Dene Oliver, *CEO*
Paul Buss, *Vice Chairman*
Michael O'Hanlon, *COO*
Bill Persky, *CFO*
Erick Klafter, *General Mgr*
EMP: 51
SQ FT: 19,900

SALES (est): 74.5MM
SALES (corp-wide): 2.1B **Privately Held**
WEB: www.olivermcmillan.com
SIC: **6552** Land subdividers & developers, commercial; land subdividers & developers, residential
HQ: Brookfield Residential Properties Inc
4906 Richard Rd Sw
Calgary AB T3E 6
403 231-8900

(P-11902)
OLSON URBAN HOUSING LLC
Also Called: Olson Company, The
3010 Old Ranch Pkwy # 100, Seal Beach (90740-2750)
PHONE..................................562 596-4770
Steve Olson,
William E Holford, *President*
Todd J Olson, *President*
Stephen E Olson, *CEO*
Scott Laurie, *COO*
EMP: 60
SALES (est): 10.1MM **Privately Held**
SIC: **6552** Subdividers & developers

(P-11903)
PACIFIC UNION HOMES INC (PA)
675 Hartz Ave Ste 300, Danville (94526-3859)
PHONE..................................925 314-3800
Jeffrey W Abramson, *President*
Todd Deutscher, *CFO*
Matt Tunney, *Vice Pres*
Tammy Reyes, *Admin Sec*
Bruce Myers, *Director*
EMP: 75
SALES (est): 11.9MM **Privately Held**
WEB: www.pacificunionhomes.com
SIC: **6552** Subdividers & developers

(P-11904)
PARDEE HOMES
12220 El Camino Real # 300, San Diego (92130-2091)
PHONE..................................858 259-6390
Greg Sorich, *Branch Mgr*
Jim Forge, *Purch Mgr*
EMP: 50
SALES (corp-wide): 2.8B **Publicly Held**
WEB: www.pardeehomes.com
SIC: **6552** 6519 1542 1522 Subdividers & developers; real property lessors; nonresidential construction; residential construction; single-family housing construction
HQ: Pardee Homes
177 E Colo Blvd Ste 550
Pasadena CA 91105
310 955-3100

(P-11905)
PARDEE HOMES (DH)
177 E Colo Blvd Ste 550, Pasadena (91105)
PHONE..................................310 955-3100
Peter M Orser, *CEO*
Michael V McGee, *President*
Jon Lash, *COO*
William Bryan, *Treasurer*
Norbert Ackerman, *Marketing Staff*
EMP: 53
SQ FT: 35,000
SALES (est): 29MM
SALES (corp-wide): 2.8B **Publicly Held**
WEB: www.pardeehomes.com
SIC: **6552** 1531 Subdividers & developers; operative builders
HQ: Tri Pointe Holdings, Inc.
33663 Weyerhaeuser Way S
Federal Way WA 98001
949 438-1400

(P-11906)
PBP HOTEL LLC
Also Called: Double Tree Club Ht San Diego
1515 Hotel Cir S, San Diego (92108-3409)
PHONE..................................619 881-6900
Bu Patel,
Sunil Madhav,
John Murphy, *Mng Member*
EMP: 60
SQ FT: 6,000

SALES (est): 9MM
SALES (corp-wide): 67.4MM **Privately Held**
WEB: www.doubletreeclubsd.com
SIC: **6552** 7011 Land subdividers & developers, commercial; hotels & motels
PA: Tarsadia Hotels
620 Newport Center Dr # 1400
Newport Beach CA 92660
949 610-8000

(P-11907)
PDC CAPITAL GROUP LLC
250 Fischer Ave, Costa Mesa (92626-4515)
PHONE..................................866 500-8550
Emilio Francisco, *CEO*
Joseph N Franscisco, *Admin Sec*
Wilkin Acedera, *CTO*
EMP: 52
SQ FT: 25,000
SALES: 50MM **Privately Held**
SIC: **6552** Subdividers & developers

(P-11908)
PUBLIC INVESTMENT CORPORATION
4340 Eucalyptus Ave, Chino (91710-9705)
PHONE..................................310 451-5227
EMP: 199
SALES (corp-wide): 15.4MM **Privately Held**
SIC: **6552** Subdividers & developers
PA: Public Investment Corporation
1207 W Magnolia Blvd C
Burbank CA 91506
310 451-5227

(P-11909)
R F R CORPORATION
Also Called: Biltwell Roofing
3310 Verdugo Rd, Los Angeles (90065-2845)
PHONE..................................800 346-7663
Bruce Radenbaugh, *President*
Steven Radenbaugh, *Vice Pres*
EMP: 92
SQ FT: 1,000
SALES (est): 8.8MM **Privately Held**
WEB: www.biltwell.com
SIC: **6552** Subdividers & developers

(P-11910)
ROCKEFELLER GROUP DEV CORP
4 Park Plz Ste 840, Irvine (92614-3504)
PHONE..................................949 468-1800
Kevin Hackett, *President*
Tom McCormick, *Vice Pres*
EMP: 81
SALES (est): 6.6MM
SALES (corp-wide): 11.2B **Privately Held**
SIC: **6552** Land subdividers & developers, commercial
HQ: Rockefeller Group Development Corporation
1221 Ave Of Americas 17th Flr 17
New York NY 10020
212 282-2100

(P-11911)
RWR HOMES INC (PA)
1014 S Westlake Blvd # 14, Westlake Village (91361-3108)
PHONE..................................805 413-1792
R William Rheinschild, *President*
EMP: 65
SQ FT: 3,800
SALES (est): 8MM **Privately Held**
SIC: **6552** Subdividers & developers

(P-11912)
S P THOMAS CO OF NORTHERN CAL (PA)
1201 Plumber Way Ste 112, Roseville (95678-3565)
PHONE..................................916 786-2040
Stephen P Thomas, *President*
Grace Thomas, *Corp Secy*
Richard Smith, *Vice Pres*
EMP: 57
SQ FT: 2,000
SALES: 500K **Privately Held**
SIC: **6552** Land subdividers & developers, commercial

(P-11913)
SCC ACQUISITIONS INC
2392 Morse Ave, Irvine (92614-6234)
PHONE..................................949 777-4000
Bruce Elieff, *Principal*
Steve Elieff, *President*
Tom Rollins, *CFO*
EMP: 160
SQ FT: 20,392
SALES (est): 14.1MM **Privately Held**
SIC: **6552** Subdividers & developers
PA: Scd Holdings Corporation
2392 Morse Ave
Irvine CA 92614

(P-11914)
SEECON BUILT HOMES INC
4021 Port Chicago Hwy, Concord (94520-1134)
P.O. Box 4113 (94524-4113)
PHONE..................................925 671-7711
Albert Seeno Jr, *President*
EMP: 80
SQ FT: 16,000
SALES (est): 6MM **Privately Held**
SIC: **6552** 1542 1521 Land subdividers & developers, commercial; land subdividers & developers, residential; nonresidential construction; single-family housing construction

(P-11915)
SHAPELL INDUSTRIES LLC (HQ)
Also Called: S & S Construction Co
8383 Wilshire Blvd # 700, Beverly Hills (90211-2425)
PHONE..................................323 655-7330
Nathan Shapell, *CEO*
Margaret F Leong, *CFO*
David Shapell, *Exec VP*
Max Webb, *Senior VP*
Paul Mitsuuchi, *Controller*
EMP: 100
SQ FT: 25,000
SALES (est): 94MM
SALES (corp-wide): 5.8B **Publicly Held**
WEB: www.shapell.com
SIC: **6552** 6514 1522 Land subdividers & developers, residential; residential building, four or fewer units: operation; residential construction
PA: Toll Brothers, Inc.
250 Gibraltar Rd
Horsham PA 19044
215 938-8000

(P-11916)
SHERWOOD DEVELOPMENT COMPANY (PA)
2300 Norfield Ct, Thousand Oaks (91361-5354)
PHONE..................................805 496-1833
David H Murdock, *CEO*
Justin Murdock Jr, *Partner*
Tom Comber, *Vice Pres*
EMP: 50
SQ FT: 2,000
SALES (est): 10.9MM **Privately Held**
WEB: www.sherwoodcc.com
SIC: **6552** 7992 7991 5813 Subdividers & developers; public golf courses; physical fitness facilities; drinking places; eating places

(P-11917)
SIERRA PACIFIC DEVELOPMENT
1470 W Herndon Ave # 100, Fresno (93711-0552)
PHONE..................................559 256-1300
Paul Owhadi, *President*
EMP: 70
SQ FT: 14,000
SALES (est): 5.4MM **Privately Held**
SIC: **6552** Land subdividers & developers, commercial; land subdividers & developers, residential

(P-11918)
SIGNATURE PROPERTIES INC
4670 Willow Rd Ste 200, Pleasanton (94588-8588)
PHONE..................................925 463-1122
Mike Ghielmetti, *President*

EMP: 75
SQ FT: 24,000
SALES (est): 4.4MM **Privately Held**
SIC: **6552** Subdividers & developers

(P-11919)
SM 10000 PROPERTY LLC
Also Called: Michelle Pasternak
10000 Santa Monica Blvd, Los Angeles (90067-7000)
PHONE..................................305 374-5700
Roman Speron, *CEO*
EMP: 55
SALES (est): 1MM **Privately Held**
SIC: **6552** Subdividers & developers

(P-11920)
STEELWAVE INC (PA)
4000 E 3rd Ave Ste 500, Foster City (94404-4832)
PHONE..................................650 571-2200
Barry S Diraimondo, *CEO*
C Preston Butcher, *President*
Rick Wada, *Senior VP*
Robert Phipps, *Director*
EMP: 175
SALES (est): 352.8MM **Privately Held**
WEB: www.legacypartners.com
SIC: **6552** 8741 6531 6512 Land subdividers & developers, commercial; land subdividers & developers, residential; financial management for business; real estate agents & managers; nonresidential building operators

(P-11921)
STEELWAVE INC
2050 Main St Ste 230, Irvine (92614-8264)
PHONE..................................949 863-0390
Erik Hansen, *Senior VP*
EMP: 170
SALES (corp-wide): 352.8MM **Privately Held**
WEB: www.legacypartners.com
SIC: **6552** Land subdividers & developers, commercial; land subdividers & developers, residential
PA: Steelwave, Inc.
4000 E 3rd Ave Ste 500
Foster City CA 94404
650 571-2200

(P-11922)
STEELWAVE LLC
4000 E 3rd Ave Ste 500, Foster City (94404-4832)
PHONE..................................650 571-2200
Preston Butcher, *Mng Member*
Meghan Fauss, *President*
Paul Meyer, *CFO*
Melodie Borg, *Vice Pres*
Aaron Dwinell, *Vice Pres*
EMP: 1200
SALES (est): 49.4MM **Privately Held**
SIC: **6552** 8741 6531 Land subdividers & developers, commercial; financial management for business; real estate agents & managers

(P-11923)
STONE BROS MANAGEMENT (PA)
5250 Claremont Ave, Stockton (95207-5700)
PHONE..................................209 478-1791
Jay Allen, *Partner*
EMP: 70
SQ FT: 5,411
SALES (est): 10.3MM **Privately Held**
SIC: **6552** 6512 6513 6531 Subdividers & developers; commercial & industrial building operation; apartment building operators; real estate managers

(P-11924)
SUNDANCE FINANCIAL INC
2505 Congress St Ste 220, San Diego (92110-2847)
PHONE..................................619 298-9877
Russ R Richard, *President*
Jason Khoury, *Vice Pres*
Noel F Khoury, *Admin Sec*
EMP: 50 EST: 1971
SALES (est): 2.8MM **Privately Held**
WEB: www.legacybldg.com
SIC: **6552** Subdividers & developers

PRODUCTS & SVCS

(P-11925)
SUNRISE DESERT PARTNERS
Also Called: Toscana
300 Eagle Cir, Palm Desert (92211)
PHONE..................................760 404-1280
Mike Van, *Branch Mgr*
EMP: 100
SALES (corp-wide): 36.8MM **Privately Held**
WEB: www.indianridgecc.com
SIC: 6552 Land subdividers & developers, commercial; land subdividers & developers, residential
PA: Sunrise Desert Partners, A California Limited Partnership
300 Eagle Dance Cir
Palm Desert CA 92211
760 772-7227

(P-11926)
SUNRISE DESERT PARTNERS (PA)
Also Called: Sunrise Company
300 Eagle Dance Cir, Palm Desert (92211-7440)
PHONE..................................760 772-7227
William Bone, *Partner*
Gary Berger, *Exec VP*
Julie Bloom, *Vice Pres*
EMP: 200
SQ FT: 6,000
SALES (est): 36.8MM **Privately Held**
WEB: www.indianridgecc.com
SIC: 6552 Land subdividers & developers, commercial; land subdividers & developers, residential

(P-11927)
TAHOE LAKE PARTNERS LLC
855 Bordeaux Way Ste 200, NAPA (94558-7585)
P.O. Box 2490 (94558-0523)
PHONE..................................707 255-9890
Tim Wilkens, *CEO*
EMP: 68 EST: 2002
SALES (est): 5.5MM **Privately Held**
SIC: 6552 Land subdividers & developers, commercial

(P-11928)
TAYLOR MORRISON CALIFORNIA LLC
100 Spectrum Center Dr # 1450, Irvine (92618-4984)
PHONE..................................949 341-1200
Stephen J Wethor, *Mng Member*
Keith Croker, *Site Mgr*
Jyll Fuhler, *Consultant*
EMP: 250
SALES (est): 5.3MM
SALES (corp-wide): 3.8B **Publicly Held**
SIC: 6552 Land subdividers & developers, residential
PA: Taylor Morrison Home Corporation
4900 N Scottsdale Rd # 2000
Scottsdale AZ 85251
480 840-8100

(P-11929)
TD DESERT DEV LTD PARTNR (HQ)
Also Called: Rancho La Quinta Country Club
81570 Carboneras, La Quinta (92253-8219)
PHONE..................................760 777-1001
Nolan Sparks, *Vice Pres*
Marc McAlpine, *Senior VP*
EMP: 150
SALES (est): 55.1MM
SALES (corp-wide): 4.2B **Privately Held**
WEB: www.rancholaquinta.com
SIC: 6552 Land subdividers & developers, residential
PA: Drummond Company, Inc.
1000 Urban Center Dr # 300
Vestavia AL 35242
205 945-6500

(P-11930)
TOSCANA LAND LLC
300 Eagle Dance Cir, Palm Desert (92211-7440)
PHONE..................................760 772-7200
Toscana Land LP, *General Ptnr*
Phillip Smith, *President*

EMP: 100
SALES (est): 5.2MM **Privately Held**
SIC: 6552 Subdividers & developers

(P-11931)
TOWBES GROUP INC (PA)
21 E Victoria St Ste 200, Santa Barbara (93101-2605)
PHONE..................................805 962-2121
Michael Towbes, *CEO*
Craig Zimmerman, *President*
R D R Deaver, *CFO*
Michelle Konoske, *CFO*
Robert Skinner, *Exec VP*
EMP: 57
SQ FT: 7,250
SALES (est): 50.8MM **Privately Held**
SIC: 6552 6512 1542 Subdividers & developers; nonresidential building operators; nonresidential construction

(P-11932)
UNITED DEVELOPMENT GROUP INC
2805 Dickens St Ste 103, San Diego (92106-2764)
PHONE..................................858 244-0900
William Ayyad, *President*
Kit Sparks, *CFO*
Rebecca Ayyad, *Project Mgr*
EMP: 50
SQ FT: 3,000
SALES (est): 7.8MM **Privately Held**
SIC: 6552 Land subdividers & developers, commercial

(P-11933)
UNIWELL CORPORATION
2233 Ventura St, Fresno (93721-2915)
PHONE..................................559 268-1000
Steve Klein, *Manager*
EMP: 90
SALES (corp-wide): 28.3MM **Privately Held**
WEB: www.uniwell.com
SIC: 6552 Subdividers & developers
PA: Uniwell Corporation
21172 Figueroa St
Carson CA 90745
310 782-8888

(P-11934)
USA PROPERTIES FUND INC (PA)
3200 Douglas Blvd Ste 200, Roseville (95661-4238)
PHONE..................................916 773-6060
Geoffrey C Brown, *President*
Kristen Hawkins, *Treasurer*
Edward R Herzog, *Exec VP*
Michael McCleery, *Senior VP*
Karen McCurdy, *Senior VP*
EMP: 75
SQ FT: 10,500
SALES: 1.1MM **Privately Held**
WEB: www.usapropfund.com
SIC: 6552 6531 Subdividers & developers; real estate agents & managers

(P-11935)
VOIT DEVELOPMENT MANAGER INC
Also Called: Voit Commercial Brokerage
2020 Main St Ste 100, Irvine (92614-8218)
PHONE..................................949 851-5110
Fax: 949 261-9092
EMP: 57
SALES (corp-wide): 25.4MM **Privately Held**
SIC: 6552 6531
PA: Voit Development Manager, Inc.
101 Shipyard Way Ste M
Newport Beach CA 92663
949 644-8648

(P-11936)
WATT PROPERTIES INC (PA)
Also Called: Watt Commercial Properties
2716 Ocean Park Blvd # 2025, Santa Monica (90405-5207)
PHONE..................................310 314-2430
Janet Watt Van Huisen, *Ch of Bd*
Susan Rorison, *President*
James Maginn, *CEO*
Melanie Rush, *CFO*

Ryoko Takata, *Exec VP*
EMP: 78
SQ FT: 8,700
SALES (est): 17.7MM **Privately Held**
WEB: www.wattcommercial.com
SIC: 6552 6512 6531 Land subdividers & developers, commercial; shopping center, property operation only; real estate managers

(P-11937)
WESTFIELD AMERICA LTD PARTNR
2049 Century Park E Fl 41, Los Angeles (90067-3101)
PHONE..................................310 478-4456
Peter Lowy, *Partner*
EMP: 99
SQ FT: 81,909
SALES (est): 5.8MM **Privately Held**
SIC: 6552 Land subdividers & developers, commercial

6553 Cemetery Subdividers & Developers

(P-11938)
ALDERWOODS (DELAWARE) INC
Also Called: Lakewood Memorial Pk & Fnrl HM
900 Santa Fe Ave, Hughson (95326-9240)
PHONE..................................209 883-0411
Robin Warn, *Admin Mgr*
EMP: 50
SALES (corp-wide): 3.1B **Publicly Held**
WEB: www.memorialparkfuneral.com
SIC: 6553 7261 Cemeteries, real estate operation; funeral home
HQ: Alderwoods (Delaware), Inc.
1929 Allen Pkwy
Houston TX 77019

(P-11939)
CHAPEL OF CHIMES (DH)
Also Called: Alameda Chapel of The Chimes
32992 Mission Blvd, Hayward (94544-8277)
PHONE..................................510 471-3363
Andy Bryant, *President*
Gordon Swallow, *Treasurer*
Tinisha Redmond, *Executive Asst*
Raymond Lutnes, *Admin Asst*
Stephanie Brooks, *Sales Mgr*
EMP: 71
SQ FT: 10,000
SALES (est): 27.1MM
SALES (corp-wide): 35.1MM **Publicly Held**
WEB: www.bailingyuan.com
SIC: 6553 7261 Cemeteries, real estate operation; mausoleum operation; funeral home; crematory
HQ: Skylawn
32992 Mission Blvd
Hayward CA 94544
510 471-3363

(P-11940)
CHAPEL OF CHIMES
Also Called: Skylawn Memorial Park
100 Lifemark Rd, Redwood City (94062-4592)
P.O. Box 5070, San Mateo (94402-0070)
PHONE..................................650 349-4411
Rich McGown, *General Mgr*
EMP: 80
SALES (corp-wide): 35.1MM **Publicly Held**
WEB: www.bailingyuan.com
SIC: 6553 7261 Cemeteries, real estate operation; crematory
HQ: Chapel Of The Chimes
32992 Mission Blvd
Hayward CA 94544
510 471-3363

(P-11941)
FOREST LAWN MEMORIAL-PARK ASSN
Also Called: Forest Lawn Memorial & Mortuar
4471 Lincoln Ave, Cypress (90630-2507)
P.O. Box 1151, Glendale (91209-1151)
PHONE..................................714 828-3131
Don Gras, *Branch Mgr*
EMP: 80
SALES (corp-wide): 129.4MM **Privately Held**
SIC: 6553 7261 Cemeteries, real estate operation; funeral service & crematories
PA: Forest Lawn Memorial-Park Association
1712 S Glendale Ave
Glendale CA 91205
323 254-3131

(P-11942)
FOREST LAWN MEMORIAL-PARK ASSN
Also Called: Hollywood Hills
6300 Forest Lawn Dr, Los Angeles (90068-1096)
PHONE..................................323 254-7251
Wilma Joanis, *Branch Mgr*
Tina Deguzman, *Accountant*
Thelma Muniz, *Buyer*
EMP: 100
SALES (corp-wide): 129.4MM **Privately Held**
SIC: 6553 7261 Cemeteries, real estate operation; funeral service & crematories
PA: Forest Lawn Memorial-Park Association
1712 S Glendale Ave
Glendale CA 91205
323 254-3131

(P-11943)
FOREST LAWN MEMORIAL-PARK ASSN
1500 E San Antonio Dr, Long Beach (90807-1233)
PHONE..................................562 424-1631
Kim Evans, *Manager*
EMP: 60
SALES (corp-wide): 129.4MM **Privately Held**
SIC: 6553 7261 Cemeteries, real estate operation; crematory
PA: Forest Lawn Memorial-Park Association
1712 S Glendale Ave
Glendale CA 91205
323 254-3131

(P-11944)
HANIL DEVELOPMENT INC
Also Called: Aroma Wilshire Center
3680 Wilshire Blvd B01, Los Angeles (90010-2708)
PHONE..................................213 387-0111
Yeong Ik Kweon, *CEO*
Hyun Shin, *CFO*
Kee June Huh, *Vice Pres*
Jae Whang, *Executive*
Joung Ki Kim, *Exec Dir*
EMP: 50
SALES (est): 2.8MM **Privately Held**
WEB: www.aromaresort.com
SIC: 6553 Real property subdividers & developers, cemetery lots only

(P-11945)
LAKEWOOD MEM PK FNRL SVCS INC
Also Called: Lakewood Memorial Pk & Fnrl HM
900 Santa Fe Ave, Hughson (95326-9240)
PHONE..................................209 883-4465
Robin Warn, *President*
Jean Silva, *Executive*
EMP: 50 EST: 1988
SALES (est): 2.2MM **Privately Held**
SIC: 6553 7261 Cemeteries, real estate operation; funeral home

(P-11946)
OAKDALE MEMORIAL PARK (PA)
1401 S Grand Ave, Glendora (91740-5406)
PHONE..................................626 335-0281
Genny Delgado, *General Mgr*

EMP: 75 EST: 1890
SQ FT: 10,000
SALES (est): 8.9MM **Privately Held**
SIC: 6553 Cemeteries, real estate operation

(P-11947)
ROMAN CATHOLIC ARCHDIOCESE OF
Also Called: Holy Cross Cemetery
1500 Old Mission Rd, Daly City (94014)
PHONE..............................650 756-2060
Kathy Atkinson, *Director*
EMP: 55
SALES (corp-wide): 70.1MM **Privately Held**
WEB: www.strita.edu
SIC: 6553 Cemetery association
PA: The Roman Catholic Archdiocese Of San Francisco
1 Peter Yorke Way 1 # 1
San Francisco CA 94109
415 614-5500

(P-11948)
ROMAN CTHLIC BISHP OF SAN JOSE
Also Called: Gate of Heaven Cemetery
22555 Cristo Rey Dr, Los Altos (94024-7424)
PHONE..............................833 304-0763
April Ouellette, *Principal*
EMP: 1035
SALES (corp-wide): 57.7MM **Privately Held**
SIC: 6553 Cemeteries, real estate operation
PA: The Roman Catholic Bishop Of San Jose
1150 N 1st St Ste 100
San Jose CA 95112
408 983-0100

(P-11949)
ROSE HILLS COMPANY (HQ)
Also Called: Rose Hills Mem Pk & Mortuary
3888 Workman Mill Rd, Whittier (90601-1626)
PHONE..............................562 699-0921
Dennis Poulsen, *Ch of Bd*
Kenton Woods, *President*
Shawn Aylesworth, *Vice Pres*
Ophelia Camero, *Vice Pres*
Mary Guzman, *Vice Pres*
EMP: 595
SQ FT: 143,950
SALES (est): 185.4MM
SALES (corp-wide): 19.2MM **Privately Held**
WEB: www.rosehill.com
SIC: 6553 Real property subdividers & developers, cemetery lots only
PA: Rose Hills Holdings Corp.
3888 Workman Mill Rd
Whittier CA 90601
562 699-0921

(P-11950)
ROSE HILLS HOLDINGS CORP (PA)
Also Called: Rose Hills Mem Pk & Mortuary
3888 Workman Mill Rd, Whittier (90601-1626)
PHONE..............................562 699-0921
Pat Monroe, *CEO*
Jaciel Camacho, *Recruiter*
Ivette Gonzalez, *Advisor*
EMP: 680
SQ FT: 143,950
SALES (est): 19.2MM **Privately Held**
SIC: 6553 Cemetery subdividers & developers

(P-11951)
SERVICE CORP INTERNATIONAL
Also Called: SCI
1999 S El Camino Real, Oceanside (92054-5754)
PHONE..............................760 754-6600
Debra Allen, *General Mgr*
Debra Kurtz, *General Mgr*
EMP: 80

SALES (corp-wide): 3.1B **Publicly Held**
WEB: www.sci-corp.com
SIC: 6553 7261 Cemetery association; funeral service & crematories
PA: Service Corporation International
1929 Allen Pkwy
Houston TX 77019
713 522-5141

6712 Offices Of Bank Holding Co's

(P-11952)
BANAMEX USA BANCORP (DH)
2029 Century Park E Fl 42, Los Angeles (90067-2901)
PHONE..............................310 203-3440
Salvador Villar Jr, *President*
Francisco Moreno Sr, *Vice Pres*
EMP: 210
SALES (est): 62.6MM
SALES (corp-wide): 71.4B **Publicly Held**
SIC: 6712 6029 6022 Bank holding companies; commercial banks; state commercial banks

(P-11953)
GOLDEN PACIFIC BANCORP INC (PA)
1409 28th St, Sacramento (95816-6422)
PHONE..............................916 444-2450
Virginia A Varela, *CEO*
Edmund Gee, *Ch Credit Ofcr*
Lance Ethington, *Administration*
David Roche,
Cathy Lazzarone, *Manager*
EMP: 75
SALES (est): 18.7MM **Publicly Held**
SIC: 6712 Bank holding companies

(P-11954)
K-FED MUTUAL HOLDING COMPANY
1359 N Grand Ave, Covina (91724-1016)
PHONE..............................626 339-9663
James L Breeden, *Ch of Bd*
EMP: 110 **Privately Held**
SIC: 6712 Bank holding companies

(P-11955)
MECHANICS BANK
Also Called: Learner Financial
590 Ygnacio Valley Rd # 210, Walnut Creek (94596-3889)
PHONE..............................925 934-1601
EMP: 88
SALES (corp-wide): 54.2MM **Privately Held**
SIC: 6712 Bank holding companies
HQ: The Mechanics Bank
1111 Civic Dr
Walnut Creek CA 94596
800 797-6324

(P-11956)
MISSION VALLEY BANCORP
9116 Sunland Blvd, Sun Valley (91352-2052)
PHONE..............................818 394-2300
Tamara Gurney, *CEO*
EMP: 53
SALES: 1,000K **Privately Held**
WEB: www.missionvalleybank.com
SIC: 6712 Bank holding companies

(P-11957)
P & A HOLDINGS INC (PA)
Also Called: Blue Haven Pools
636 Broadway Ste 310, San Diego (92101-5410)
P.O. Box 126878 (92112-6878)
PHONE..............................619 233-3522
Terri Tuttle, *Vice Pres*
Ron Zaberer, *President*
EMP: 69 **Privately Held**
SIC: 6712 Bank holding companies

(P-11958)
SECURITY CALIFORNIA BANCORP
3403 10th St Ste 830, Riverside (92501-3666)
PHONE..............................951 368-2265

James A Robinson, *CEO*
Jim Robinson, *Ch of Bd*
Thomas Ferrer, *CFO*
Dolly L Nugent, *Ch Credit Ofcr*
EMP: 63 **Privately Held**
SIC: 6712 Bank holding companies

6719 Offices Of Holding Co's, NEC

(P-11959)
ABA HOLDINGS LLC
4777 Ruffner St, San Diego (92111-1519)
PHONE..............................858 565-4131
Steven B Andrade,
Richard Dine, *Purch Mgr*
Clyde C Blyleven,
Salomon Saenz, *Manager*
EMP: 200 **Privately Held**
SIC: 6719 Investment holding companies, except banks

(P-11960)
ABBEY MANAGEMENT COMPANY LLC
330 Golden Shore Ste 300, Long Beach (90802-4283)
PHONE..............................562 243-2100
Donald Abbey, *Mng Member*
Kevin Dillard, *Treasurer*
Dennis Loput Jr, *Admin Sec*
EMP: 60 **Privately Held**
SIC: 6719 Investment holding companies, except banks

(P-11961)
AF SOFTWARE HOLDINGS INC
1825 S Grant St Ste 900, San Mateo (94402-2675)
PHONE..............................888 317-3395
Bernadette Nixon, *CEO*
Carlton Baab, *CFO*
Kamil Chaudhary, *Admin Sec*
EMP: 349 **Privately Held**
SIC: 6719 Investment holding companies, except banks

(P-11962)
AF SOFTWARE PARENT INC
1825 S Grant St Ste 900, San Mateo (94402-2675)
PHONE..............................888 317-3395
Bernadette Nixon, *CEO*
Carlton Baab, *CFO*
Kamil Chaudhary, *Admin Sec*
EMP: 349 **Privately Held**
SIC: 6719 Investment holding companies, except banks

(P-11963)
ARCH BAY HOLDINGS LLC
327 W Maple Ave, Monrovia (91016-3331)
PHONE..............................949 679-2400
EMP: 60 EST: 2008 **Privately Held**
SIC: 6719

(P-11964)
BAVARIA HOLDINGS INC
1 Letterman Dr Bldg C, San Francisco (94129-2402)
PHONE..............................415 418-2900
Dipanjan Deb, *President*
Tom Ludwig, *COO*
Chris Adams, *Vice Pres*
My Le Nguyen, *Vice Pres*
Eugene Mesgar, *Vice Pres*
EMP: 615
SALES (corp-wide): 1.7B **Privately Held**
SIC: 6719 Investment holding companies, except banks
HQ: Francisco Partners, L.P.
1 Letterman Dr Bldg C
San Francisco CA 94129
415 418-2900

(P-11965)
BLUE EARTH INC (PA)
235 Pine St Ste 1100, San Francisco (94104-2744)
PHONE..............................702 608-5476
Johnny R Thomas, *CEO*
Laird Q Cagan, *Ch of Bd*
Ruben Fontes, *President*
Curtis McConnell, *President*

Robert C Potts, *President*
EMP: 108 EST: 2010 **Privately Held**
SIC: 6719 Personal holding companies, except banks

(P-11966)
BPAZ HOLDINGS 6 LLC
1 Sansome St Ste 1500, San Francisco (94104-4449)
PHONE..............................415 295-8080
Rob Saidi, *Vice Pres*
EMP: 80 **Privately Held**
SIC: 6719 Holding companies

(P-11967)
BRIDGE GROUP HH INC
5090 Shoreham Pl Ste 209, San Diego (92122-5935)
PHONE..............................858 455-5000
Jason Murray, *CEO*
EMP: 126 **Privately Held**
SIC: 6719 Investment holding companies, except banks

(P-11968)
CCC PROPERTY HOLDINGS LLC
Also Called: Contractors Cargo Company
500 S Alameda St, Compton (90221-3801)
P.O. Box 5290 (90224-5290)
PHONE..............................310 609-1957
Gerald Wheeler, *Ch of Bd*
Carla Ann Wheeler, *CFO*
Jerry Wheeler, *Chairman*
Kim Dorio, *Admin Sec*
EMP: 121 EST: 2009
SQ FT: 18,000 **Privately Held**
SIC: 6719 Investment holding companies, except banks

(P-11969)
CLEARBALANCE HOLDINGS LLC
3636 Nobel Dr Ste 250, San Diego (92122-1042)
PHONE..............................858 535-0870
Mitch Patridge, *CEO*
Susan Helscher, *Opers Staff*
EMP: 50 **Privately Held**
SIC: 6719 Investment holding companies, except banks

(P-11970)
COADNA HOLDINGS INC (HQ)
1020 Stewart Dr, Sunnyvale (94085-3914)
PHONE..............................408 736-1100
Jim Yuan, *President*
Irene Yum, *CFO*
Oliver Lu, *Officer*
Tom LI, *Senior VP*
EMP: 80 EST: 2000
SALES (corp-wide): 1.1B **Publicly Held**
SIC: 6719 3661 Investment holding companies, except banks; fiber optics communications equipment
PA: Ii-Vi Incorporated
375 Saxonburg Blvd
Saxonburg PA 16056
724 352-4455

(P-11971)
CONCRETE HOLDING CO CAL INC
15821 Ventura Blvd # 475, Encino (91436-2915)
PHONE..............................818 788-4228
Don Unmacht, *Principal*
Dominique Bidet, *Vice Pres*
EMP: 293
SQ FT: 4,000
SALES (corp-wide): 479.6MM **Privately Held**
SIC: 6719 Investment holding companies, except banks
HQ: National Cement Company, Inc.
15821 Ventura Blvd # 475
Encino CA 91436
818 728-5200

(P-11972)
CSU HOLDING COMPANY
531 Stone Rd, Benicia (94510-1113)
PHONE..............................707 746-0353
Jochen Michalski, *President*
EMP: 50 EST: 2002 **Privately Held**

SIC: **6719** Investment holding companies, except banks

(P-11973)
CYTOSPORT HOLDINGS INC
1340 Treat Blvd Ste 350, Walnut Creek (94597-7581)
PHONE...............707 751-3942
Robert King, *CEO*
EMP: 190
SALES (corp-wide): 9.1B **Publicly Held**
SIC: **6719** Investment holding companies, except banks
PA: Hormel Foods Corporation
1 Hormel Pl
Austin MN 55912
507 437-5611

(P-11974)
DELIMEX HOLDINGS INC
7878 Airway Rd, San Diego (92154-8305)
PHONE...............619 210-2700
Neil Harrison, *President*
Dori Reap, *CEO*
Christopher J Puma, *Vice Pres*
John B Puma, *Vice Pres*
Greggory R Surabian, *Vice Pres*
EMP: 550
SQ FT: 86,917
SALES (corp-wide): 26.2B **Publicly Held**
WEB: www.delimex.com
SIC: **6719** Personal holding companies, except banks
HQ: H J Heinz Finance Company
1 Ppg Pl Ste 3100
Pittsburgh PA 15222
412 456-5700

(P-11975)
DPR HOLDINGS LLC
Also Called: Massnexus
4804 Laurel Canyon Blvd, Studio City (91607-3717)
PHONE...............323 761-9829
Anthony Dickson, *Mng Member*
Mark Burton, *COO*
Chris Burns, *CFO*
EMP: 50 EST: 2011 **Privately Held**
SIC: **6719** Investment holding companies, except banks

(P-11976)
FINE CHEMICALS HOLDINGS CORP
Highway 50 And Hazel Ave, Rancho Cordova (95741)
PHONE...............916 357-6880
Fraser Preston, *President*
John Sobchak, *CFO*
Michael Gallagher, *Corp Secy*
EMP: 450 **Privately Held**
SIC: **6719** Investment holding companies, except banks

(P-11977)
FORTRESS HOLDING GROUP LLC
5500 E Santa Ana Canyon R, Anaheim (92807-3139)
PHONE...............714 202-8710
Loise Perez, *Chairman*
Adam Forbs, *President*
Erica Rodriguez, *Human Res Mgr*
EMP: 90 **Privately Held**
SIC: **6719** Investment holding companies, except banks

(P-11978)
GAF HOLDINGS INC
1300 E Mineral King Ave, Visalia (93292-6913)
P.O. Box 1431 (93279-1431)
PHONE...............559 734-3333
Don Groppetti, *President*
Peter Shellworth, *Sales Mgr*
EMP: 300 EST: 1999 **Privately Held**
SIC: **6719** Personal holding companies, except banks

(P-11979)
GBP INTERMEDIATE CORP (DH) ●
2321 Rosecrans Ave # 3255, El Segundo (90245-4985)
PHONE...............424 254-9774

EMP: 587 EST: 2018
SALES (corp-wide): 28.3MM **Privately Held**
SIC: **6719** Investment holding companies, except banks
HQ: Gbp Parent Corp.
2321 Rosecrans Ave # 3255
El Segundo CA 90245
424 254-9774

(P-11980)
GBP PARENT CORP (HQ)
2321 Rosecrans Ave # 3255, El Segundo (90245-4985)
PHONE...............424 254-9774
EMP: 587
SALES (corp-wide): 28.3MM **Privately Held**
SIC: **6719** Investment holding companies, except banks
PA: Pacific Avenue Capital Partners, Llc
2321 Rosecrans Ave # 3255
El Segundo CA 90245
424 254-9774

(P-11981)
GLOBAL HOLDINGS INC
1230 Rosecrans Ave # 660, Manhattan Beach (90266-2477)
PHONE...............818 905-6000
Sam Solakyan, *CEO*
EMP: 150 **Privately Held**
SIC: **6719** Investment holding companies, except banks

(P-11982)
GOLDEN WEST PACKG GROUP LLC (PA)
8333 24th Ave, Sacramento (95826-4809)
PHONE...............404 345-8365
Alan Ulman, *Principal*
EMP: 381
SALES (est): 20.5MM **Privately Held**
SIC: **6719** Investment holding companies, except banks

(P-11983)
GORES NORMENT HOLDINGS INC
10877 Wilshire Blvd # 1805, Los Angeles (90024-4341)
PHONE...............310 209-3010
Alex Gores, *Principal*
EMP: 246
SALES (corp-wide): 4.5B **Privately Held**
SIC: **6719** Investment holding companies, except banks
PA: The Gores Group Llc
9800 Wilshire Blvd
Beverly Hills CA 90212
310 209-3010

(P-11984)
GREENCYCLE US HOLDING INC (DH)
4686 Mercury St, San Diego (92111-2428)
PHONE...............858 677-0884
Hernan De La Vega, *CEO*
Marco Rudolph, *Exec VP*
Hendrick Dillinger, *Vice Pres*
Katya Leitner, *Vice Pres*
EMP: 80
SALES: 18MM
SALES (corp-wide): 200K **Privately Held**
SIC: **6719 4953** Investment holding companies, except banks; recycling, waste materials
HQ: Greencycle Gmbh
Stiftsbergstr. 1
Neckarsulm
713 294-2000

(P-11985)
HCO HOLDING I CORPORATION (HQ)
999 N Pacific Coast Hwy, El Segundo (90245-2714)
PHONE...............323 583-5000
Brian C Strauss, *CEO*
Jason Peel, *CFO*
Dori M Reap, *CFO*
Robert D Armstrong, *Senior VP*
James F Barry, *Senior VP*
◆ EMP: 100

SALES (est): 254.1MM **Privately Held**
WEB: www.henry.com
SIC: **6719** Investment holding companies, except banks
PA: Hnc Parent, Inc.
999 N Pacific Coast Hwy
El Segundo CA 90245
310 955-9200

(P-11986)
HEALTHFUSION HOLDINGS INC (HQ)
100 N Rios Ave, Solana Beach (92075-1238)
PHONE...............858 523-2120
Seth M Flam, *President*
Jonathan Flam, *CFO*
Gregory Chapman, *Sr Software Eng*
Karim Lakhani, *Sr Software Eng*
Corey Laulom, *Sales Dir*
EMP: 54 EST: 2000
SALES (est): 18.5MM
SALES (corp-wide): 531MM **Publicly Held**
WEB: www.healthfusion.com
SIC: **6719** Investment holding companies, except banks
PA: Nextgen Healthcare, Inc.
18111 Von Karman Ave
Irvine CA 92612
949 255-2600

(P-11987)
INDUSTRIAL GRWTH PARTNERS V LP
101 Mission St Ste 1500, San Francisco (94105-1731)
PHONE...............415 882-4550
Michael Beaumont, *Mng Member*
EMP: 200 **Privately Held**
SIC: **6719** Investment holding companies, except banks

(P-11988)
J BRAND HOLDINGS LLC
1318 E 7th St Ste 260, Los Angeles (90021-1131)
PHONE...............212 228-8181
Jeffrey Rudes,
EMP: 60
SALES (corp-wide): 19.1B **Privately Held**
SIC: **6719** Investment holding companies, except banks
PA: Fast Retailing Co., Ltd.
9-7-1, Akasaka
Minato-Ku TKY 107-0
368 650-050

(P-11989)
LEISURE SPORTS INC
4670 Willow Rd Ste 100, Pleasanton (94588-8587)
PHONE...............925 942-6301
Brian Amador, *Branch Mgr*
EMP: 350
SALES (corp-wide): 191.7MM **Privately Held**
WEB: www.leisuresportsinc.com
SIC: **6719** Investment holding companies, except banks; personal holding companies, except banks
PA: Leisure Sports, Inc.
4670 Willow Rd Ste 100
Pleasanton CA 94588
925 600-1966

(P-11990)
LIVERMORE SNIOR LVING ASSOC LP
Also Called: Leisure Care
900 E Stanley Blvd # 383, Livermore (94550-4089)
PHONE...............925 371-2300
Mike Palmer, *General Mgr*
EMP: 50 **Privately Held**
SIC: **6719** Investment holding companies, except banks

(P-11991)
MAFAB INC (PA)
1925 Century Park E # 650, Los Angeles (90067-2752)
PHONE...............714 893-0551
Ronald B Grey, *President*
Ronald Grey, *President*

EMP: 60
SQ FT: 3,600
SALES (est): 15.2MM **Privately Held**
SIC: **6719** Personal holding companies, except banks

(P-11992)
MILESTONE TOPCO INC (HQ)
901 Mariners Island Blvd, San Mateo (94404-1592)
PHONE...............650 376-2300
Steve Lucas, *CEO*
EMP: 949
SALES (corp-wide): 7.3B **Publicly Held**
SIC: **6719** Investment holding companies, except banks
PA: Adobe Inc.
345 Park Ave
San Jose CA 95110
408 536-6000

(P-11993)
MISSION ENERGY HOLDING COMPANY
2600 Michelson Dr # 1700, Irvine (92612-1550)
PHONE...............949 752-5588
Mark C Clarke, *CEO*
Thomas R McDaniel, *President*
W James Scilacci, *CFO*
EMP: 1890
SALES (corp-wide): 12.3B **Publicly Held**
WEB: www.edison.com
SIC: **6719** Personal holding companies, except banks
HQ: Edison Mission Group Inc.
2244 Walnut Grove Ave
Rosemead CA 91770
626 302-2222

(P-11994)
MLIM HOLDINGS LLC
350 Camino De La Reina, San Diego (92108-3003)
PHONE...............619 299-3131
Douglas Manchester, *Chairman*
John Lynch, *CEO*
EMP: 768 **Privately Held**
SIC: **6719** Investment holding companies, except banks

(P-11995)
NOVOZYMES US INC
1445 Drew Ave, Davis (95618-4880)
PHONE...............530 757-8100
Ejner Bech Jensen, *CEO*
Glen Medwin, *President*
EMP: 675 EST: 2000
SALES (corp-wide): 20.7B **Privately Held**
SIC: **6719** Investment holding companies, except banks
HQ: Novozymes A/S
Krogshojvej 36
BagsvArd 2880
444 600-00

(P-11996)
NRP HOLDING CO INC (PA)
1 Mauchly, Irvine (92618-2305)
PHONE...............949 583-1000
Jeffrey P Frieden, *President*
Ken Rivkin, *Exec VP*
Robert Friedman, *Vice Pres*
Robert D Friedman, *Vice Pres*
Jason Allnutt, *General Mgr*
EMP: 200
SQ FT: 40,000
SALES (est): 50.2MM **Privately Held**
SIC: **6719** Investment holding companies, except banks

(P-11997)
OMNI VENTURES GROUP LLC
300 Pasadena Ave, South Pasadena (91030-2905)
PHONE...............510 384-1033
Timothy Naple, *CEO*
EMP: 75 EST: 2007
SQ FT: 100,000 **Privately Held**
SIC: **6719** Investment holding companies, except banks

(P-11998)
PARIS BLUES INC (PA)
2397 Miguel Miranda Ave, Duarte
(91010-3319)
PHONE.....................................310 605-2000
Jose Quant, *President*
EMP: 95 **Privately Held**
SIC: 6719 Personal holding companies,
except banks

(P-11999)
PARPRO HOLDINGS CO LTD
9355 Airway Rd Ste 4, San Diego
(92154-7931)
PHONE.....................................619 498-9004
Matthew Dharm, *Officer*
Dan Torres, *Buyer*
EMP: 250
SALES (corp-wide): 185.1MM **Privately
Held**
SIC: 6719 Investment holding companies,
except banks
PA: Parpro Corporation
67-1, Tung Yuan Rd., Chung Li Ind.
Park,
Taoyuan City TAY 32063
345 255-35

(P-12000)
**PLATINUM GROUP COMPANIES
INC (PA)**
Also Called: Top Finance Company
22560 La Quilla Dr, Chatsworth
(91311-1221)
PHONE.....................................818 721-3800
David Mandel, *CEO*
Sandy To, *Treasurer*
Netzel Robert, *Info Tech Mgr*
Marilyn Vateri, *Finance*
Sandy Mandel, *Controller*
EMP: 125
SQ FT: 20,000
SALES (est): 46.6MM **Privately Held**
SIC: 6719 Personal holding companies,
except banks

(P-12001)
PROJECT BOAT HOLDINGS LLC
360 N Crescent Dr Bldg S, Beverly Hills
(90210-2529)
PHONE.....................................310 712-1850
Tom Gores,
Johnny O Lopez,
EMP: 3174 **Privately Held**
SIC: 6719 Investment holding companies,
except banks
PA: Platinum Equity, Llc
360 N Crescent Dr Bldg S
Beverly Hills CA 90210

(P-12002)
RIVER ROCK EQUIPMENT LLC
216 Kenroy Ln, Roseville (95678-4202)
PHONE.....................................916 791-1609
Warren Holt,
Bob Lettek,
EMP: 100
SQ FT: 2,500
SALES: 1MM **Privately Held**
SIC: 6719 Investment holding companies,
except banks

(P-12003)
**SAN FRANCISCO FORTY
NINERS**
4949 Mrie P Debartolo Way, Santa Clara
(95054-1156)
PHONE.....................................408 562-4949
John York, *Owner*
Les Schmidt, *COO*
EMP: 90 EST: 1977
SALES: 3.9MM **Privately Held**
SIC: 6719 Investment holding companies,
except banks

(P-12004)
**SANTA PAULA WATER WORKS
LTD**
9750 Washburn Rd, Downey (90241-5625)
PHONE.....................................562 923-0711
Henry H Wheeler Jr, *President*
Douglas K Martinet, *CFO*
Douglas Martinet, *Officer*
Danny Rodriguez, *Warehouse Mgr*

EMP: 70 **Privately Held**
WEB: www.parkwater.com
SIC: 6719 Investment holding companies,
except banks

(P-12005)
SHARESPOST INC
555 Montgomery St, San Francisco
(94111-2589)
PHONE.....................................800 279-7754
Carol Foster, *CFO*
EMP: 70 **Privately Held**
SIC: 6719 Holding companies

(P-12006)
**SKEFFINGTON ENTERPRISES
INC**
2200 S Yale St, Santa Ana (92704-4404)
PHONE.....................................714 540-1700
William J Skeffington, *President*
John Skeffington, *CFO*
EMP: 100
SQ FT: 180,000
SALES: 32.1MM **Privately Held**
SIC: 6719 Personal holding companies,
except banks

(P-12007)
**STANTEC HOLDINGS DEL III INC
(HQ)**
5500 Ming Ave Ste 300, Bakersfield
(93309-4627)
PHONE.....................................661 396-3770
Robert Gomes, *President*
EMP: 182
SALES (est): 30.3MM
SALES (corp-wide): 4B **Privately Held**
SIC: 6719 Investment holding companies,
except banks
PA: Stantec Inc
10220 103 Ave Nw Suite 400
Edmonton AB T5J 0
780 917-7000

(P-12008)
**STEELRIVER INFRASTURCTURE
PART (PA)**
1 Harbor Dr Ste 101, Sausalito
(94965-1433)
PHONE.....................................415 512-1515
Christopher P Kinney, *Partner*
John Anderson, *Partner*
Chris Kinney, *Partner*
Dennis Mahoney, *Partner*
Jay Elwell, *Chief Acct*
EMP: 200
SALES (est): 208.9MM **Privately Held**
SIC: 6719 Investment holding companies,
except banks

(P-12009)
**STURGEON SERVICES INTL INC
(PA)**
Also Called: Sturgeon & Son
3511 Gilmore Ave, Bakersfield
(93308-6205)
P.O. Box 2840 (93303-2840)
PHONE.....................................661 322-4408
Paul H Sturgeon, *President*
Oliver Sturgeon, *Ch of Bd*
Joe D'Angelo, *CFO*
Gina Blankenship, *Vice Pres*
John Powell, *General Mgr*
EMP: 50
SQ FT: 5,000
SALES (est): 182.8MM **Privately Held**
SIC: 6719 Personal holding companies,
except banks

(P-12010)
TOKAI INTL HOLDINGS INC (PA)
2055 S Haven Ave, Ontario (91761-0736)
PHONE.....................................909 930-5000
Felix M Hon, *CEO*
EMP: 50
SALES (est): 11.3MM **Privately Held**
SIC: 6719 Investment holding companies,
except banks

(P-12011)
**TRADESHIFT HOLDINGS INC
(HQ)**
612 Howard St Ste 100, San Francisco
(94105-3927)
PHONE.....................................800 381-3585

Christian Lanng, *CEO*
Jigish Avalani, *President*
Jeppe Rindom, *CFO*
Peter Van Pruissen, *CFO*
Daniel Spitzer, *Software Engr*
EMP: 80 EST: 2011
SALES: 31.9MM
SALES (corp-wide): 30.7MM **Privately
Held**
SIC: 6719 Investment holding companies,
except banks

(P-12012)
**TRANSAMERICA INTL
HOLDINGS**
600 Montgomery St Fl 16, San Francisco
(94111-2718)
PHONE.....................................415 983-4000
EMP: 220 **Privately Held**
SIC: 6719 Investment holding companies,
except banks
HQ: Transamerica Corporation
4333 Edgewood Rd Ne
Cedar Rapids IA 52499
319 398-8511

(P-12013)
TRESTLES HOLDINGS LLC
Also Called: Oaks Post Acute, The
450 Hayes Ln, Petaluma (94952-4010)
PHONE.....................................707 778-8686
Stephanie Walsh, *Principal*
Kevin Galbasini, *Principal*
Dan Gill, *Principal*
Cameron Rosenhan, *Principal*
EMP: 88 **Privately Held**
SIC: 6719 Holding companies

(P-12014)
TREX PARTNERS LLC
10455 Pacific Center Ct, San Diego
(92121-4339)
PHONE.....................................858 646-5300
Kenneth Tang,
Doug Bletcher, *Info Tech Dir*
Tod Barrett, *Webmaster*
EMP: 200 **Privately Held**
SIC: 6719 Investment holding companies,
except banks

(P-12015)
**USB SOLARCITY MASTER
TENANT**
393 Vintage Park Dr # 140, Foster City
(94404-1140)
PHONE.....................................650 963-5693
Lyndon Rive, *CEO*
Tara Hobbs,
EMP: 99
SALES (corp-wide): 11.7B **Publicly Held**
SIC: 6719 Holding companies
PA: Tesla, Inc.
3500 Deer Creek Rd
Palo Alto CA 94304
650 681-5000

(P-12016)
UTBLO INC
11061 Los Alamitos Blvd, Los Alamitos
(90720-3201)
PHONE.....................................562 493-3664
Wendi Rothman, *President*
EMP: 120
SQ FT: 12,000
SALES (corp-wide): 6.3B **Publicly Held**
WEB: www.lovinoven.com
SIC: 6719 Personal holding companies,
except banks
HQ: Treehouse Private Brands, Inc.
800 Market St Ste 2600
Saint Louis MO 63101

(P-12017)
VISIONARY INTEGRATION (PA)
Also Called: VIP
80 Iron Point Cir Ste 100, Folsom
(95630-8592)
PHONE.....................................916 985-9625
Jonna A Ward, *President*
EMP: 95
SQ FT: 9,000
SALES (est): 110.2MM **Privately Held**
SIC: 6719 Personal holding companies,
except banks

(P-12018)
YF ART HOLDINGS GP LLC
9130 W Sunset Blvd, Los Angeles
(90069-3110)
PHONE.....................................678 441-1400
Fred Boehler, *President*
EMP: 10600 **Privately Held**
SIC: 6719 Investment holding companies,
except banks

**6722 Management
Investment Offices**

(P-12019)
**ABSOLUTE RETURN
PORTFOLIO**
700 Newport Center Dr, Newport Beach
(92660-6307)
P.O. Box 9000 (92658-9030)
PHONE.....................................800 800-7646
EMP: 2079
SALES (est): 44.2MM
SALES (corp-wide): 12.8B **Privately Held**
SIC: 6722 Money market mutual funds
HQ: Pacific Life Fund Advisors Llc
700 Newport Center Dr
Newport Beach CA 92660

(P-12020)
**ADVANCED COMMERCIAL
CORPORATIO**
5900 Pasteur Ct Ste 200, Carlsbad
(92008-7336)
P.O. Box 4068 (92018-4068)
PHONE.....................................760 431-8500
Tim Stripe, *CEO*
David Brown, *President*
Cheryl Cunningham, *COO*
Angie Greenig, *Technology*
Steve Halterman, *Director*
EMP: 110
SALES (est): 12.2MM **Privately Held**
WEB: www.vacation-resales.com
SIC: 6722 Management investment, open-
end

(P-12021)
ALLIANCEBERNSTEIN LP
1999 Ave Of The Sts 215, Los Angeles
(90067)
PHONE.....................................310 286-6000
Alan D Croll, *Branch Mgr*
Maryann Best, *Managing Dir*
Daniel Eagan, *Managing Dir*
EMP: 60 **Publicly Held**
WEB: www.bernstein.com
SIC: 6722 Money market mutual funds
HQ: Alliancebernstein L.P.
1345 Avenue Of The Americ
New York NY 10105
212 969-1000

(P-12022)
AMCAP FUND INC
333 S Hope St Ste Levb, Los Angeles
(90071-3003)
PHONE.....................................213 486-9200
Marry Clemeson, *President*
Mary C Hall, *Treasurer*
Gordon Crawford, *Senior VP*
Paul G Haaga Jr, *Senior VP*
Walter Stern, *Principal*
EMP: 300
SQ FT: 2,000
SALES: 177.4MM **Privately Held**
SIC: 6722 Mutual fund sales, on own ac-
count

(P-12023)
**AMERICAN FUNDS DISTRS INC
(DH)**
333 S Hope St Ste Levb, Los Angeles
(90071-3003)
PHONE.....................................213 486-9200
Michael Johnston, *Ch of Bd*
Larry Clemmensen, *Ch of Bd*
Christopher Lanzafame, *President*
Ross McDonald, *President*
Peter Olsen, *President*
EMP: 116
SQ FT: 6,000

SALES: 1B
SALES (corp-wide): 2.2B **Privately Held**
SIC: 6722 Mutual fund sales, on own account; money market mutual funds
HQ: Capital Research And Management Company
　333 S Hope St Fl 55
　Los Angeles CA 90071
　213 486-9200

(P-12024)
AMERICAN MUTUAL FUND INC
333 S Hope St Fl 51, Los Angeles
(90071-1420)
PHONE..................213 486-9200
Jonathan B Lovelace Jr, *Ch of Bd*
James K Dunton, *Ch of Bd*
Robert G O'Donnell, *President*
Mary C Hall, *Treasurer*
Mary Hall, *Treasurer*
EMP: 200 **EST:** 1949
SQ FT: 5,000
SALES (est): 13.9MM **Privately Held**
SIC: 6722 Money market mutual funds

(P-12025)
ARES MANAGEMENT LP (PA)
2000 Avenue Of The Stars # 12, Los Angeles (90067-4733)
PHONE..................310 201-4100
Antony P Ressler, *Ch of Bd*
Ares M LLC, *General Ptnr*
Michael J Arougheti, *President*
Andrew Jurkowski, *Vice Pres*
Lucy Moffitt, *Vice Pres*
EMP: 86
SALES: 1.4B **Publicly Held**
SIC: 6722 Management investment, open-end

(P-12026)
ARES MANAGEMENT LLC
1999 Ave Of Stars Fl 37, Los Angeles
(90067-4650)
PHONE..................310 201-4100
Tony Ressler, *Branch Mgr*
EMP: 170
SALES (corp-wide): 1.4B **Publicly Held**
SIC: 6722 Management investment, open-end
HQ: Ares Management Llc
　2000 Avenue Of The Stars # 12
　Los Angeles CA 90067
　310 201-4100

(P-12027)
AURORA RESURGENCE FUND LP
10877 Wilshire Blvd # 2100, Los Angeles (90024-4341)
PHONE..................310 551-0101
Steven D Smith, *Managing Prtnr*
Anthony Disimone, *Partner*
Matt Homme, *Partner*
Peter Leibman, *Partner*
Ryan McCarthy, *Partner*
EMP: 700
SALES (est): 47.2MM **Privately Held**
SIC: 6722 Money market mutual funds

(P-12028)
BAY GROVE CAPITAL GROUP LLC (PA)
801 Montgomery St Fl 5, San Francisco
(94133-5151)
PHONE..................415 229-7953
Kevin Marchetti, *Managing Dir*
Adam Forste, *Managing Prtnr*
Michael Billings,
Geoff Colla,
David Ross,
EMP: 50
SALES (est): 53.6MM **Privately Held**
SIC: 6722 Management investment, open-end

(P-12029)
BLACKROCK FUNDS III
400 Howard St, San Francisco
(94105-2618)
PHONE..................415 597-2000
Mike Sobel, *Principal*
Sathish Balakrishnan, *Vice Pres*
Ken Yzurdiaga, *Vice Pres*
Deborah Ferris, *Principal*
Cesar Olano, *Network Enginr*

EMP: 56
SALES (est): 25.9MM **Privately Held**
SIC: 6722 Management investment, open-end

(P-12030)
BLACKROCK INSTNL TR NAT ASSN (HQ)
Also Called: Ishares
400 Howard St, San Francisco
(94105-2618)
PHONE..................415 597-2000
Laurence D Fink, *CEO*
Robert S Kapito, *President*
James Parsons, *President*
EMP: 600
SQ FT: 65,000
SALES: 1.5B **Publicly Held**
SIC: 6722 Money market mutual funds

(P-12031)
BRANDES INV PARTNERS INC (PA)
11988 Charmaine Way Ste 6, San Diego
(92131)
P.O. Box 919048 (92191-9048)
PHONE..................858 755-0239
Charles H Brandes, *Ch of Bd*
Christopher Garrett, *Partner*
Brent V Woods, *CEO*
Jeffrey A Busby, *Exec Dir*
Glenn R Carlson, *Exec Dir*
EMP: 121
SQ FT: 27,000
SALES (est): 119.9MM **Privately Held**
WEB: www.brandes.com
SIC: 6722 Money market mutual funds

(P-12032)
BROADRACH CPITL PRTNERS FUND I
248 Homer Ave, Palo Alto (94301-2722)
PHONE..................650 331-2500
EMP: 987
SALES (est): 20.2MM
SALES (corp-wide): 399.2MM **Privately Held**
SIC: 6722 Money market mutual funds
PA: Broadreach Capital Partners Llc
　855 El Camino Real
　Palo Alto CA 94301
　650 331-2500

(P-12033)
COLFIN ESH FUNDING LLC
2450 Broadway Fl 6, Santa Monica
(90404-3570)
PHONE..................310 282-8820
Richard B Saltzman, *President*
EMP: 268
SALES (est): 630.8K
SALES (corp-wide): 2.8B **Publicly Held**
SIC: 6722 Management investment, open-end
PA: Colony Capital, Inc.
　515 S Flower St Fl 44
　Los Angeles CA 90071
　310 282-8820

(P-12034)
DODGE & COX
555 California St # 4000, San Francisco
(94104-1538)
PHONE..................415 981-1710
Dana M Emery, *CEO*
Sheila Briones, *COO*
Barbara Duckett, *CFO*
John A Gunn, *Chairman*
Marian Z Baldauf, *Treasurer*
EMP: 195 **EST:** 1930
SQ FT: 45,000
SALES (est): 268.2MM **Privately Held**
WEB: www.dodgeandcox.com
SIC: 6722 Money market mutual funds

(P-12035)
ENCORE FUND LP
555 California St # 2975, San Francisco
(94104-1503)
PHONE..................415 676-4000
Jeff Skelton, *President*
John Dowd, *Vice Pres*
Collin Ross, *Vice Pres*
Samir Yajnik, *Vice Pres*
Steve Colamarino, *Managing Dir*

EMP: 70
SALES (est): 4.1MM **Privately Held**
SIC: 6722 Management investment, open-end

(P-12036)
FARALLON CAPITAL PARTNERS LP (PA)
1 Maritime Plz Ste 2100, San Francisco
(94111-3528)
PHONE..................415 421-2132
Chun R Ding, *Mng Member*
Paul Caldwell, *Exec Dir*
Colby Clark, *Managing Dir*
Rocky Fried, *Managing Dir*
Charles Gunawan, *Managing Dir*
EMP: 80
SQ FT: 8,000
SALES (est): 48.1MM **Privately Held**
SIC: 6722 Management investment, open-end

(P-12037)
FORTRESS INVESTMENT GROUP LLC
10250 Constellation Blvd # 2300, Los Angeles (90067-6200)
PHONE..................310 228-3030
Ian Schnider, *Director*
EMP: 74 **Privately Held**
SIC: 6722 Management investment, open-end
HQ: Fortress Investment Group Llc
　1345 Avenue Of The Americ
　New York NY 10105
　212 798-6100

(P-12038)
FORTRESS INVESTMENT GROUP LLC
42 Florida St Flr, San Francisco (94103)
PHONE..................415 284-7400
Douglas Doughty, *Managing Dir*
Dan Shea, *Managing Dir*
EMP: 74 **Privately Held**
SIC: 6722 Management investment, open-end
HQ: Fortress Investment Group Llc
　1345 Avenue Of The Americ
　New York NY 10105
　212 798-6100

(P-12039)
FRANKLIN RESOURCES INC (PA)
1 Franklin Pkwy, San Mateo (94403-1906)
PHONE..................650 312-2000
Gregory E Johnson, *Ch of Bd*
Jennifer M Johnson, *President*
Kenneth A Lewis, *CFO*
Rupert H Johnson Jr, *Vice Ch Bd*
Mariann Byerwalter, *Bd of Directors*
EMP: 76
SALES: 6.3B **Publicly Held**
WEB: www.frk.com
SIC: 6722 6726 Investment advice; management investment, open-end; management investment funds, closed-end

(P-12040)
KAYNE ANDERSON RUDNI
1800 Avenue Of The Stars # 200, Los Angeles (90067-4204)
PHONE..................310 229-9260
Stephen Rigali, *Exec VP*
Sheryl Sadis, *CFO*
Stephanie Gillman, *Bd of Directors*
Tom Connaghan, *Senior VP*
Lisa Holmes, *Vice Pres*
EMP: 60
SQ FT: 20,000
SALES (est): 13.7MM **Publicly Held**
WEB: www.kayne.com
SIC: 6722 Management investment, open-end
HQ: Virtus Partners, Inc.
　100 Pearl St Fl 9
　Hartford CT 06103

(P-12041)
MACFARLANE PARTNERS LLC (PA)
201 Spear St Ste 1000, San Francisco
(94105-1667)
PHONE..................415 356-2500
Victor B Macfarlane, *Ch of Bd*
Gregory M Vilkin, *President*
Susan A Kreusch, *CFO*
Katharine Ryan-Weiss, *Vice Pres*
David Dressler, *Principal*
EMP: 53
SQ FT: 14,000
SALES (est): 18.3MM **Privately Held**
SIC: 6722 Management investment, open-end

(P-12042)
MCMILLIN MANAGEMENT SVCS LP (HQ)
Also Called: McMillin Homes
2750 Womble Rd Ste 200, San Diego
(92106-6114)
PHONE..................619 477-4117
Scott McMillin, *General Ptnr*
Mark McMillin, *Partner*
EMP: 249
SQ FT: 24,000
SALES (est): 37.9MM
SALES (corp-wide): 50MM **Privately Held**
WEB: www.mcmillin.com
SIC: 6722 8611 Management investment, open-end; business associations
PA: Mcmillin Companies, Llc
　2750 Womble Rd Ste 200
　San Diego CA 92106
　619 477-4117

(P-12043)
ORANGE COUNTY EMPLOYEES RETIR
2223 S Wellington Ave, Santa Ana (92701)
PHONE..................714 558-6200
Raymond Fleming, *CEO*
Robert Kinsler, *Info Tech Mgr*
Michael Guerrero, *Accountant*
Toi Dang, *Manager*
EMP: 51
SALES (est): 7.6MM **Privately Held**
WEB: www.ocers.org
SIC: 6722 8111 Management investment, open-end; legal services

(P-12044)
PIMCO FUNDS DISTRIBUTION CO
840 Nwport Ctr Dr Ste 100, Newport Beach
(92660)
PHONE..................949 720-4761
Bill Gross, *CEO*
EMP: 300
SALES (est): 13.5MM **Privately Held**
SIC: 6722 Management investment, open-end

(P-12045)
R & S INVESTMENTS LLC
1 Bush St Fl 9, San Francisco
(94104-4468)
PHONE..................415 591-2700
G Randy Hecht, *Mng Member*
John Casconi, *President*
Matthew Fessler, *President*
Andrew Goodhand, *President*
Jason Muntner, *President*
EMP: 100
SALES (est): 21.8MM
SALES (corp-wide): 409.6MM **Publicly Held**
WEB: www.rsinvestments.com
SIC: 6722 Management investment, open-end
HQ: Victory Capital Management Inc.
　4900 Tiedeman Rd Fl 4
　Brooklyn OH 44144

(P-12046)
REO WORLD INC
170 Nwport Ctr Dr Ste 150, Newport Beach
(92660)
P.O. Box 1070, Corona Del Mar (92625-6070)
PHONE..................949 478-8000

Mark Cardelucci, *President*
Thomas F Crone, *COO*
EMP: 99
SALES: 950K **Privately Held**
WEB: www.reoworld.com
SIC: 6722 Management investment, open-end

(P-12047)
SUNAMERICA INVESTMENTS INC
1 Sun America Ctr Fl 38, Los Angeles (90067-6101)
PHONE....................310 772-6000
EMP: 200
SALES (est): 7.2MM
SALES (corp-wide): 52.3B **Publicly Held**
SIC: 6722
HQ: Sunamerica Inc.
    1 Sun America Ctr Fl 38
    Los Angeles CA 90067
    310 772-6000

(P-12048)
TEMPLETON FRANKLIN INTL TR
Also Called: Templton Fgn Smaller Companies
1 Franklin Pkwy, San Mateo (94403-1906)
PHONE....................650 312-2000
Gregory E Johnson, *CEO*
EMP: 50
SALES (est): 8.5MM **Privately Held**
SIC: 6722 Management investment, open-end

(P-12049)
US SMALL CPITL VALUE PORTFOLIO
1299 Ocean Ave Ste 150, Santa Monica (90401-1002)
PHONE....................310 395-8005
David Booth, *President*
Abbie J Smith, *Director*
EMP: 70
SALES (est): 5.5MM **Privately Held**
SIC: 6722 Money market mutual funds

(P-12050)
VANTAGEPOINT VENTURE PARTNERS
1001 Bayhill Dr Ste 300, San Bruno (94066-3061)
PHONE....................650 866-3100
Alan E Salzman, *Partner*
EMP: 56
SALES (est): 5.2MM
SALES (corp-wide): 15.5MM **Privately Held**
SIC: 6722 Mutual fund sales, on own account
PA: Vantagepoint Venture Partners
    1001 Bayhill Dr Ste 300
    San Bruno CA 94066
    650 866-3100

(P-12051)
VIHARAS GROUP INC
1919 W Artesia Blvd, Compton (90220-5397)
PHONE....................310 537-6700
Ashok Patel, *President*
EMP: 75 EST: 2007
SALES (est): 4.8MM **Privately Held**
SIC: 6722 Management investment, open-end

(P-12052)
WELLS FARGO ASSET MANAGEMENT
525 Market St Fl 10, San Francisco (94105-2718)
PHONE....................415 396-8000
EMP: 270
SALES (est): 6.4MM
SALES (corp-wide): 97.7B **Publicly Held**
SIC: 6722 Management investment, open-end
HQ: Everen Capital Corporation
    301 S College St
    Charlotte NC 28202

(P-12053)
WELLS FARGO INTL BOND CIT
525 Market St Fl 10, San Francisco (94105-2718)
PHONE....................415 396-4943
EMP: 231
SALES (est): 13.5MM
SALES (corp-wide): 97.7B **Publicly Held**
SIC: 6722 Money market mutual funds
HQ: Wells Capital Management Incorporated
    525 Market St Fl 10
    San Francisco CA 94105
    415 396-8000

(P-12054)
WESTERN ASSET CORE PLUS
385 E Colorado Blvd, Pasadena (91101-1923)
PHONE....................626 844-9400
Larry Clark, *Principal*
George Yeboah, *Controller*
EMP: 97
SALES (est): 251.6K
SALES (corp-wide): 3.1B **Publicly Held**
SIC: 6722 Money market mutual funds
HQ: Western Asset Management Company, Llc
    385 E Colorado Blvd # 250
    Pasadena CA 91101
    626 844-9265

(P-12055)
WESTERN ASSET MGT CO LLC (HQ)
385 E Colorado Blvd # 250, Pasadena (91101-1929)
PHONE....................626 844-9265
James W Hirschmann III, *CEO*
Jody Hiramoto, *Officer*
Andrew Kang, *Officer*
Vivian Lin, *Officer*
Colette Pontecorvo, *Officer*
▲ **EMP:** 50
SQ FT: 55,000
SALES (est): 221.1MM
SALES (corp-wide): 3.1B **Publicly Held**
SIC: 6722 Management investment, open-end
PA: Legg Mason Inc
    100 International Dr
    Baltimore MD 21202
    410 539-0000

(P-12056)
ZILLIONAIRE EMPRESS DANIELLE B
8549 Wilshire Blvd # 817, Beverly Hills (90211-3104)
PHONE....................310 461-9923
EMP: 1000
SQ FT: 300
SALES (est): 44.6MM **Privately Held**
SIC: 6722

6726 Unit Investment Trusts, Face-Amount Certificate Offices

(P-12057)
ASIA PACIFIC CAPITAL
345 Suth Fgroa St Ste 100, Los Angeles (90071)
PHONE....................213 628-8800
Eddy Chao, *CEO*
EMP: 85
SALES (est): 6.4MM **Privately Held**
WEB: www.apccusa.com
SIC: 6726 Investment offices

(P-12058)
CBRE INC (HQ)
400 S Hope St Ste 25, Los Angeles (90071-2800)
PHONE....................213 613-3333
Bob Sulentic, *President*
Jamie Dennison, *Senior Partner*
Thomas Monahan, *Vice Chairman*
Kenneth J Kay, *CFO*
Debbie Fan, *Treasurer*
EMP: 150

SALES (est): 9.9B
SALES (corp-wide): 14.2B **Publicly Held**
SIC: 6726 6531 Investment offices; real estate agent, commercial; real estate managers; appraiser, real estate
PA: Cbre Group, Inc.
    400 S Hope St Ste 25
    Los Angeles CA 90071
    213 613-3333

(P-12059)
CENTURY PK CAPITL PARTNERS LLC (PA)
2101 Rosecrans Ave # 4275, El Segundo (90245-4749)
PHONE....................310 867-2210
Martin A Sarafa,
Guy Zaczepinski, *Partner*
Charles W Roellig, *Managing Prtnr*
Martin Sarafa, *Managing Prtnr*
Paul J Wolf, *Managing Prtnr*
EMP: 160
SALES (est): 96.1MM **Privately Held**
WEB: www.cpclp.com
SIC: 6726 3569 3086 3448 Management investment funds, closed-end; firefighting apparatus & related equipment; carpet & rug cushions, foamed plastic; ramps: prefabricated metal

(P-12060)
CHRISTOPHER RANSOM CORPORATION (PA)
1300 Clay St Ste 600, Oakland (94612-1427)
P.O. Box 268 (94604-0268)
PHONE....................510 345-9144
Christopher N Ransom Jr, *CEO*
Christopher Ransom, *Ch of Bd*
EMP: 121 EST: 2013
SALES: 18MM **Privately Held**
SIC: 6726 Investment offices

(P-12061)
GLOBAL REACH 18 INC (PA)
10100 Santa Monica Blvd # 900, Los Angeles (90067-4003)
PHONE....................310 203-5850
Haim Saban, *CEO*
Adam Chesnoff, *President*
Fred Gluckman, *CFO*
Joel Andryc, *Ch Credit Ofcr*
Niveen Tadros, *Trustee*
EMP: 51
SALES (est): 50.4MM **Privately Held**
WEB: www.saban.com
SIC: 6726 6531 6799 Investment offices; real estate agents & managers; investors

(P-12062)
HAWAII PARENT CORP
600 Montgomery St Fl 32, San Francisco (94111-2807)
PHONE....................415 263-3660
Orlando Bravo, *Partner*
EMP: 495 EST: 2013
SALES (est): 18.1MM **Privately Held**
SIC: 6726 Investment offices

(P-12063)
INTERNATIONAL INDUSTRIAL PARK
5440 Morehouse Dr # 4000, San Diego (92121-1798)
PHONE....................858 623-9000
David Wick, *Vice Pres*
Lindsay Arobone, *Administration*
EMP: 99
SALES (est): 7.8MM **Privately Held**
SIC: 6726 Investment offices

(P-12064)
J ALEXANDER INVESTMENTS INC (PA)
Also Called: Investment Banking
922 S Barrington Ave A, Los Angeles (90049-5554)
PHONE....................213 687-8400
James Alexander, *President*
EMP: 70
SQ FT: 4,500
SALES (est): 10.1MM **Privately Held**
WEB: www.investmentbanking.com
SIC: 6726 Investment offices

(P-12065)
PARALLAX CAPITAL PARTNERS LLC (PA)
23332 Mill Creek Dr # 155, Laguna Hills (92653-1679)
PHONE....................949 296-4800
James Hale,
Lisa Hale,
Michael Hale,
William Koneval,
Scott Lencz,
EMP: 131
SALES (est): 18.3MM **Privately Held**
WEB: www.parallaxcap.com
SIC: 6726 Investment offices

(P-12066)
SILVER LAKE PARTNERS LP (PA)
2775 Sand Hill Rd Ste 100, Menlo Park (94025-7085)
PHONE....................650 233-8120
Jim Davidson, *Partner*
Yolande Jun, *Partner*
Harel Kodesh, *Partner*
Dan Hoevel, *Vice Pres*
Tezira Nabongo, *Vice Pres*
EMP: 70
SALES (est): 64.1MM **Privately Held**
SIC: 6726 Investment offices

(P-12067)
SILVER LAKE PARTNERS II LP
10080 N Wolfe Rd Sw3190, Cupertino (95014-2544)
PHONE....................408 454-4732
Andy Wagner, *Branch Mgr*
EMP: 97
SALES (corp-wide): 300MM **Privately Held**
SIC: 6726 Investment offices
PA: Silver Lake Partners Ii, L.P.
    2775 Sand Hill Rd Ste 100
    Menlo Park CA 94025
    650 233-8120

(P-12068)
SILVER LAKE PARTNERS II LP
Also Called: Silver Lake Financial
1 Market Plz, San Francisco (94105-1101)
PHONE....................415 293-4355
Roger Whittlin, *Manager*
EMP: 243
SALES (corp-wide): 300MM **Privately Held**
SIC: 6726 Investment offices
PA: Silver Lake Partners Ii, L.P.
    2775 Sand Hill Rd Ste 100
    Menlo Park CA 94025
    650 233-8120

(P-12069)
SPUS7 235 PINE LP
235 Pine St Ste 125, San Francisco (94104-2706)
PHONE....................231 683-4200
Pamela Craig, *General Ptnr*
Ming Lee, *General Ptnr*
Rick Klagstad, *General Mgr*
EMP: 99 EST: 2014
SQ FT: 25,000
SALES (est): 6.5MM **Privately Held**
SIC: 6726 Investment offices

(P-12070)
SPUS7 MIAMI ACC LP
515 S Flower St Ste 3100, Los Angeles (90071-2233)
PHONE....................213 683-4200
Mark Zikakis, *Principal*
Pamela Craig, *Partner*
EMP: 50 EST: 2014
SQ FT: 25,000
SALES (est): 5.8MM **Privately Held**
SIC: 6726 Investment offices

(P-12071)
T W M INDUSTRIES
Also Called: Carl's Jr.
3131 Crow Canyon Pl, San Ramon (94583-1325)
PHONE....................925 866-1156
John A Kubas, *President*
EMP: 858

SALES (corp-wide): 25.1MM **Privately Held**
SIC: 6726 Investment offices
PA: T W M Industries
899 Cherry Ave
San Bruno CA 94066
650 583-6491

(P-12072)
VECTOR TALENT II LLC
1 Market St Ste 2300, San Francisco
(94105-1414)
PHONE.................415 293-5000
Alex Slusky, *President*
EMP: 736
SALES (est): 49.9MM **Privately Held**
SIC: 6726 Investment offices

6732 Education, Religious & Charitable Trusts

(P-12073)
**BETHESDA UNIVERSITY
CALIFORNIA**
730 N Euclid St, Anaheim (92801-4115)
PHONE.................714 517-1945
Grace Sung Hae Kim, *Chancellor*
Uh Gin Kihm, *CFO*
William Min, *Officer*
Yoomin Kim, *Vice Pres*
David Kum, *Opers Mgr*
EMP: 70
SQ FT: 34,349
SALES: 4.2MM **Privately Held**
WEB: www.bethesdachristianuniversity.com
SIC: 6732 8221 Trusts: educational, religious, etc.; university

(P-12074)
**CALIFORNIA CMNTY
FOUNDATION (PA)**
221 S Figueroa St Ste 400, Los Angeles
(90012-3760)
PHONE.................213 413-4130
Antonia Hernandez, *President*
Tom Unterman, *Ch of Bd*
Steve Cobb, *CFO*
Peter Dunn, *Vice Pres*
Paul Schulz, *Vice Pres*
EMP: 53
SQ FT: 16,000
SALES (est): 243.2MM **Privately Held**
WEB: www.ccf-la.org
SIC: 6732 Charitable trust management

(P-12075)
**CALWORKS PARTNR
CONFERENCE**
5151 Murphy Canyon Rd # 220, San Diego
(92123-4440)
PHONE.................858 292-2900
Pat Rickard, *President*
EMP: 50
SALES (est): 6.2MM **Privately Held**
SIC: 6732 Educational trust management

(P-12076)
COMMUNITY PARTNERS INTL
2560 9th St Ste 315b, Berkeley
(94710-2567)
PHONE.................510 225-9676
Si Thura, *Exec Dir*
EMP: 117
SALES: 4.2MM **Privately Held**
SIC: 6732 Trusts: educational, religious, etc.

(P-12077)
**CREEKSIDE COMET
EDUCATION FUND**
6011 Massara St, Danville (94506-5004)
PHONE.................925 314-2000
Aaron Tarzian, *Principal*
EMP: 85
SALES (est): 3.9MM **Privately Held**
SIC: 6732 Educational trust management

(P-12078)
**HENRY J KAISER FMLY
FOUNDATION (PA)**
185 Berry St Ste 2000, San Francisco
(94107-1704)
PHONE.................650 854-9400

Drew Altman, *President*
Koonal Gandhi, *Senior VP*
Timothy Ortez, *Vice Pres*
EMP: 135
SQ FT: 185,000
SALES (est): 26.3MM **Privately Held**
SIC: 6732 Trusts: educational, religious, etc.

(P-12079)
**KRISHNMRTI FOUNDATION OF
AMER (PA)**
134 Besant Rd, Ojai (93023-2305)
P.O. Box 1560 (93024-1560)
PHONE.................805 646-2726
Jaap Sluijter, *Exec Dir*
Derek Dodds, *CFO*
Eric Fe, *Info Tech Mgr*
Gopal Krishnamurthy, *Program Dir*
Holly Johnson, *Associate*
EMP: 50 EST: 1969
SQ FT: 10,000
SALES: 4.9MM **Privately Held**
WEB: www.oakgroveschool.com
SIC: 6732 Educational trust management; charitable trust management

(P-12080)
MULLIGAN LIMITED
4281 Katella Ave Ste 228, Los Alamitos
(90720-6505)
PHONE.................714 484-6799
William Robert Thomas, *CEO*
EMP: 120
SALES (est): 6.5MM **Privately Held**
SIC: 6732 7929 Trusts: educational, religious, etc.; entertainment group

(P-12081)
**OAKLAND PUBLIC EDUCATION
FUND**
520 3rd St Ste 109, Oakland (94607-3503)
P.O. Box 71005 (94612-7105)
PHONE.................510 221-6968
Robert Spencer, *President*
Brian Stanley, *Exec Dir*
Jayo Macasaquit, *Human Resources*
Priya Jagannathan, *Manager*
EMP: 95 EST: 2003
SALES (est): 2.5MM **Privately Held**
SIC: 6732 Trusts: educational, religious, etc.

(P-12082)
**PENINSULA COMMUNITY
FOUNDATION**
Also Called: Center For Ventr Philanthropy
1700 S El Camino Real # 300, San Mateo
(94402-3047)
PHONE.................650 358-9369
Sterling K Speirn, *President*
George Chong, *Controller*
Roger Castle, *Assistant VP*
EMP: 55
SQ FT: 16,800
SALES: 200MM **Privately Held**
SIC: 6732 Charitable trust management

(P-12083)
**PERVERTED JSTICE
FUNDATION INC**
703 Pier Ave Ste B154, Hermosa Beach
(90254-3960)
PHONE.................310 910-9380
Xavier Von Erck, *President*
Dennis Kerr, *CFO*
EMP: 200
SALES (est): 105.6K **Privately Held**
SIC: 6732 Trusts: educational, religious, etc.

(P-12084)
UCLA FOUNDATION
10920 Wilshire Blvd # 200, Los Angeles
(90024-6502)
PHONE.................310 794-3193
Peter Hayashida, *Exec Dir*
Neal Axelrod, *Treasurer*
Jocelyn Smith, *Director*
EMP: 317
SALES: 305.4MM **Privately Held**
SIC: 6732 Educational trust management

(P-12085)
**UCR BOTANY AND PLANT
SCIENCES**
3401 Watkins Dr, Riverside (92507-4633)
PHONE.................951 827-5133
Michael Roose, *Principal*
EMP: 99
SALES (est): 6.2MM **Privately Held**
SIC: 6732 Trusts: educational, religious, etc.

(P-12086)
US GREEN BUILDING COUNCIL -
Also Called: US GREEN BUILDING COUN-
CIL INLA
2879 Breezy Meadow Ln, Corona
(92883-5915)
P.O. Box 2181, Redlands (92373-0721)
PHONE.................818 621-4880
Jennifer Ward, *CEO*
EMP: 99
SALES: 48.5K **Privately Held**
SIC: 6732 Trusts: educational, religious, etc.

6733 Trusts Except Educational, Religious & Charitable

(P-12087)
2100 TRUST LLC (PA)
625 N Grand Ave, Santa Ana (92701-4347)
PHONE.................877 469-7344
Erek J Delorenzi, *Principal*
EMP: 200
SALES (est): 2.5B **Privately Held**
SIC: 6733 Trusts

(P-12088)
**ANNENBERG FOUNDATION
TRUST (PA)**
37977 Bob Hope Dr, Rancho Mirage
(92270-2008)
PHONE.................760 202-2222
Geoffrey Cowan, *President*
Wallis Annenberg, *CEO*
Debbi Hinton, *CFO*
Charles Annenberg Weingarten, *Vice Pres*
Rosemary Anaya, *Executive*
EMP: 60
SALES: 26.8MM **Privately Held**
SIC: 6733 Trusts

(P-12089)
**CAPITAL GUARDIAN TRUST
COMPANY (HQ)**
333 S Hope St Fl 52, Los Angeles
(90071-3061)
PHONE.................213 486-9200
Richard C Barker, *Ch of Bd*
Robert Ronus, *President*
Teri Valenzuela, *President*
Barbara Brewer, *Vice Pres*
Bill Flumenbaum, *Vice Pres*
EMP: 100
SQ FT: 6,000
SALES (est): 52.2MM
SALES (corp-wide): 2.2B **Privately Held**
SIC: 6733 Trusts, except educational, religious, charity: management
PA: The Capital Group Companies Inc
333 S Hope St Fl 55
Los Angeles CA 90071
213 486-9200

(P-12090)
CARPENTER FUNDS
265 Hegenberger Rd # 100, Oakland
(94621-1443)
PHONE.................510 633-0333
David Lee, *CEO*
EMP: 79 EST: 1953
SQ FT: 60,956
SALES: 14.9MM **Privately Held**
WEB: www.carpenterfunds.com
SIC: 6733 Trusts, except educational, religious, charity: management

(P-12091)
**CHRISTMAS BONUS FUND OF
THE PL**
501 Shatto Pl Ste 5, Los Angeles
(90020-1730)
PHONE.................213 385-6161
Milton D Johnson, *Administration*
Mike Ayre, *Ch of Bd*
E A Norris, *Ch of Bd*
Allen Jones Jr, *Co-COB*
Raymond Forman, *Trustee*
EMP: 60
SQ FT: 70,000
SALES: 4.7MM **Privately Held**
SIC: 6733 Trusts, except educational, religious, charity: management

(P-12092)
**DEFINED CONTRIBUTION
TRUST FUN**
Also Called: SOUTHERN CALIFORNIA PIPE
TRADE
501 Shatto Pl Ste 500, Los Angeles
(90020-1730)
PHONE.................213 385-6161
Milton D Johnson, *CEO*
Mike Ayre, *Ch of Bd*
Raymond Forman, *Trustee*
Charles La Bouff, *Admin Sec*
EMP: 60
SQ FT: 70,000
SALES: 75.2MM **Privately Held**
SIC: 6733 Trusts, except educational, religious, charity: management

(P-12093)
**DEUTSCHE BANK NATIONAL TR
CO**
1761 E Saint Andrew Pl, Santa Ana
(92705-4934)
PHONE.................714 247-6000
Gary Vaughn, *Manager*
Paulina Rodriguez, *MIS Mgr*
Joseph Campbell, *Sales Staff*
EMP: 53
SALES (corp-wide): 11.5B **Privately Held**
SIC: 6733 6111 Trusts; banks for coopera-
tives
HQ: Deutsche Bank National Trust Co
2000 Avenue Of The Stars
Los Angeles CA 90067
213 620-8200

(P-12094)
DEVEREUX FOUNDATION
Also Called: Devereux Center In California
El Colegio Rd, Goleta (93117)
PHONE.................805 968-2525
Amy Evans, *Director*
Mr David Weisman, *Human Res Dir*
EMP: 350
SALES (corp-wide): 460.5MM **Privately
Held**
SIC: 6733 8361 8031 Trusts; group foster
home; offices & clinics of osteopathic
physicians
PA: Devereux Foundation
444 Devereux Dr
Villanova PA 19085
610 520-3000

(P-12095)
FIRST NATIONAL BANK (PA)
401 W A St Ste 200, San Diego
(92101-7917)
PHONE.................619 233-5588
Mike Perdue, *President*
EMP: 75
SALES (est): 62.5MM **Privately Held**
SIC: 6733 Trusts

(P-12096)
IMMIGRATION VOICE
3561 Homestead Rd 375, Santa Clara
(95051-5161)
PHONE.................408 204-2200
Aman Kapoor, *Owner*
Dilip Tekkedil, *Officer*
Rajatish Mukherjee, *Project Mgr*
Dheeraj Kohli, *VP Opers*
EMP: 99
SALES: 136.3K **Privately Held**
SIC: 6733 Trusts

(P-12097)
IMPAC SECURED ASSETS CORP
19500 Jamboree Rd, Irvine (92612-2411)
PHONE.................................949 475-3600
Ronald Martin Morrison, *Administration*
EMP: 92
SALES (est): 123.6K **Publicly Held**
SIC: 6733 Trusts
HQ: Impac Funding Corporation
   19500 Jamboree Rd
   Irvine CA 92612

(P-12098)
IRA SERVICES INC
1160 Industrial Rd Ste 1, San Carlos
(94070-4128)
PHONE.................................650 593-2221
Edwin Blue, *President*
Todd Yancey, *Officer*
Michael McNair, *Trust Officer*
Gary R Shumm, *Vice Pres*
Mary Marr, *Auditing Mgr*
EMP: 101
SQ FT: 16,000
SALES: 20MM **Privately Held**
WEB: www.ierinc.com
SIC: 6733 Trusts

(P-12099)
IRON WORKERS LOCAL 433
Also Called: California Field Ironwrkrs
252 Hillcrest Ave, San Bernardino
(92408-2120)
PHONE.................................909 884-5500
Fax: 909 885-0047
EMP: 50
SALES (est): 1.5MM **Privately Held**
SIC: 6733

(P-12100)
**IRONWRKER EMPLYEES
BENEFT CORP**
Also Called: Ironworkers Union
131 N El Molino Ave # 330, Pasadena
(91101-1873)
PHONE.................................626 792-7337
Dick Zampa, *President*
Lisanne Negrete, *Admin Asst*
Jennifer Janssen, *Exec Sec*
Mary J Merenda, *Representative*
EMP: 65
SQ FT: 19,000
SALES (est): 10.9MM **Privately Held**
SIC: 6733 Trusts, except educational, religious, charity: management; vacation funds for employees

(P-12101)
J D RUSH COMPANY INC (HQ)
5900 E Lerdo Hwy, Shafter (93263-4023)
PHONE.................................661 392-1900
James Varner, *CEO*
Paul Sahey, *Corp Secy*
Teri Seely, *Vice Pres*
EMP: 105
SQ FT: 3,000
SALES (est): 111MM **Privately Held**
SIC: 6733 Private estate, personal investment & vacation fund trusts
PA: Varner Family Limited Partnership
   5900 E Lerdo Hwy
   Shafter CA 93263
   661 399-1163

(P-12102)
**KAISER FOUNDATION
HOSPITALS**
Also Called: Otay Mesa Medical Offices
4650 Palm Ave, San Diego (92154-8404)
PHONE.................................619 662-5107
EMP: 454
SALES (corp-wide): 94.1B **Privately Held**
SIC: 6733 Trusts
HQ: Kaiser Foundation Hospitals Inc
   1 Kaiser Plz
   Oakland CA 94612
   510 271-6611

(P-12103)
**KAISER FOUNDATION
HOSPITALS**
Also Called: Kaiser Permanente
4647 Zion Ave, San Diego (92120-2507)
PHONE.................................619 528-5888

Kathy Roper, *Manager*
Charles Columbus, *Senior VP*
Jeff Johnson, *Exec Dir*
Brian Rees, *Technology*
Stephen Salvato, *Physician Asst*
EMP: 3000
SALES (corp-wide): 94.1B **Privately Held**
WEB: www.kaiserpermanente.org
SIC: 6733 8062 Trusts; general medical & surgical hospitals
HQ: Kaiser Foundation Hospitals Inc
   1 Kaiser Plz
   Oakland CA 94612
   510 271-6611

(P-12104)
**KAISER FOUNDATION
HOSPITALS**
Also Called: Martinez Medical Offices
200 Muir Rd, Martinez (94553-4672)
PHONE.................................925 372-1000
Bryan Fong, *Principal*
Pablo Baker, *Chief Engr*
Allen J Finley, *VP Mktg*
Ronald Heuberg, *Psychologist*
Ronald W Wyatt, *Surgeon*
EMP: 200
SALES (corp-wide): 94.1B **Privately Held**
WEB: www.kaiserpermanente.org
SIC: 6733 8011 Trusts; general & family practice, physician/surgeon
HQ: Kaiser Foundation Hospitals Inc
   1 Kaiser Plz
   Oakland CA 94612
   510 271-6611

(P-12105)
**KAISER FOUNDATION
HOSPITALS**
Also Called: Kaiser Permanente
5119 Pomona Blvd, Los Angeles
(90022-1711)
PHONE.................................323 881-5516
Judy Nantes, *Manager*
EMP: 50
SALES (corp-wide): 94.1B **Privately Held**
WEB: www.kaiserpermanente.org
SIC: 6733 Trusts
HQ: Kaiser Foundation Hospitals Inc
   1 Kaiser Plz
   Oakland CA 94612
   510 271-6611

(P-12106)
**KAISER FOUNDATION
HOSPITALS**
Also Called: Moreno Valley Heacock Med Offs
12815 Heacock St, Moreno Valley
(92553-2836)
PHONE.................................951 601-6174
Mark Ituah, *Principal*
EMP: 50
SALES (corp-wide): 94.1B **Privately Held**
WEB: www.kaiserpermanente.org
SIC: 6733 Trusts
HQ: Kaiser Foundation Hospitals Inc
   1 Kaiser Plz
   Oakland CA 94612
   510 271-6611

(P-12107)
**KAISER FOUNDATION
HOSPITALS**
Also Called: Kaiser Permanente
3285 Claremont Way, NAPA (94558-3313)
PHONE.................................707 258-2500
Debby Bacon, *Branch Mgr*
Andrea M Clarke, *Family Practiti*
Jonathan S Hernandez, *Family Practiti*
Bonnie L Richardson, *Family Practiti*
Julia Mueller, *Internal Med*
EMP: 200
SALES (corp-wide): 94.1B **Privately Held**
WEB: www.kaiserpermanente.org
SIC: 6733 8093 8062 Trusts, except educational, religious, charity: management; specialty outpatient clinics; general medical & surgical hospitals
HQ: Kaiser Foundation Hospitals Inc
   1 Kaiser Plz
   Oakland CA 94612
   510 271-6611

(P-12108)
**KAISER FOUNDATION
HOSPITALS**
Also Called: Kaiser Permanente
789 E Cooley Dr, Colton (92324-4007)
PHONE.................................909 427-5521
Barry A Wolfman, *Principal*
Richard L Henderson, *Psychiatry*
EMP: 793
SQ FT: 23,088
SALES (corp-wide): 94.1B **Privately Held**
WEB: www.kaiserpermanente.org
SIC: 6733 Trusts
HQ: Kaiser Foundation Hospitals Inc
   1 Kaiser Plz
   Oakland CA 94612
   510 271-6611

(P-12109)
**KAISER FOUNDATION
HOSPITALS**
Also Called: Corona Medical Offices
182 Granite St, Corona (92879-1288)
PHONE.................................866 984-7483
Randy Florence, *Branch Mgr*
EMP: 793
SALES (corp-wide): 94.1B **Privately Held**
SIC: 6733 8011 Trusts; internal medicine practitioners; general & family practice, physician/surgeon
HQ: Kaiser Foundation Hospitals Inc
   1 Kaiser Plz
   Oakland CA 94612
   510 271-6611

(P-12110)
**KAISER FOUNDATION
HOSPITALS**
Also Called: Orange County-Irvine Med Ctr
6640 Alton Pkwy, Irvine (92618-3734)
PHONE.................................949 932-5000
George Disalvo, *Branch Mgr*
David B Keschner, *Top Exec*
Marguerite Voorhees, *Risk Mgmt Dir*
Stephanie Prien, *Lab Dir*
Gwen Phillips, *Purch Dir*
EMP: 379
SALES (corp-wide): 94.1B **Privately Held**
SIC: 6733 Trusts
HQ: Kaiser Foundation Hospitals Inc
   1 Kaiser Plz
   Oakland CA 94612
   510 271-6611

(P-12111)
**MAKING WAVES EDUCATION
PROGRAM (PA)**
3220 Blume Dr Ste 250, San Pablo
(94806-5741)
PHONE.................................510 237-3434
Glenn Holsclaw, *Exec Dir*
Sherry Smith, *Managing Dir*
Damon Edwards, *Info Tech Dir*
Sheryl Weber, *Info Tech Dir*
Corina Garcia, *Opers Mgr*
EMP: 225
SQ FT: 12,000
SALES: 3.9MM **Privately Held**
SIC: 6733 Trusts, except educational, religious, charity: management

(P-12112)
**MANAGEMENT TRUST ASSN
INC**
100 E Thousand Oaks Blvd, Thousand
Oaks (91360-5713)
PHONE.................................805 496-5514
EMP: 109 **Privately Held**
SIC: 6733 Trusts
PA: The Management Trust Association Inc
   15661 Red Hill Ave # 201
   Tustin CA 92780

(P-12113)
**MANAGEMENT TRUST ASSN
INC**
9815 Carroll Canyon Rd, San Diego
(92131-1123)
PHONE.................................858 547-4373
Diane Houston, *Branch Mgr*
EMP: 109 **Privately Held**
SIC: 6733 Trusts

PA: The Management Trust Association Inc
   15661 Red Hill Ave # 201
   Tustin CA 92780

(P-12114)
**MANAGEMENT TRUST ASSN
INC**
4160 Temescal Canyon Rd # 202, Corona
(92883-4625)
PHONE.................................951 694-1758
EMP: 109 **Privately Held**
SIC: 6733 Trusts
PA: The Management Trust Association Inc
   15661 Red Hill Ave # 201
   Tustin CA 92780

(P-12115)
**MANAGEMENT TRUST ASSN
INC (PA)**
Also Called: Management Trust, The
15661 Red Hill Ave # 201, Tustin
(92780-7300)
PHONE.................................714 285-2626
William B Sasser, *CEO*
EMP: 58
SALES: 135MM **Privately Held**
SIC: 6733 Trusts

(P-12116)
MTC FINANCIAL INC
Also Called: Trustee Corps
17100 Gillette Ave, Irvine (92614-5603)
PHONE.................................949 252-8300
Fax: 949 634-1011
EMP: 50 EST: 1992
SALES (est): 4.7MM **Privately Held**
SIC: 6733

(P-12117)
**NORTHERN CAL RET CLKS-EMP
FUND**
190 N Wiget Ln Ste 110, Walnut Creek
(94598-2476)
PHONE.................................925 746-7530
Jeff Chapman, *Administration*
EMP: 120
SQ FT: 11,000
SALES (est): 4.2MM **Privately Held**
SIC: 6733 Vacation funds for employees

(P-12118)
**OPERATING ENGINEERS FUNDS
INC (PA)**
100 Corson St Ste 222, Pasadena
(91103-3892)
P.O. Box 7063 (91109-7063)
PHONE.................................866 400-5200
Mike Roddy, *CEO*
Matt Erieg, *COO*
Chuck Killian, *CFO*
Klairissa Sikorski, *Admin Asst*
Paul Egge, *CIO*
EMP: 135
SQ FT: 84,600
SALES (est): 47.2MM **Privately Held**
WEB: www.oefunds.com
SIC: 6733 Trusts, except educational, religious, charity: management

(P-12119)
**PMT CRDIT RISK TRNSF TR
2015-1**
3043 Townsgate Rd, Westlake Village
(91361-3027)
PHONE.................................818 224-7028
EMP: 239
SALES (est): 76.6K **Privately Held**
SIC: 6733 Trusts
PA: Pennymac Mortgage Investment Trust
   6101 Condor Dr
   Moorpark CA 93021

(P-12120)
**PMT CRDIT RISK TRNSF TR
2015-2**
3043 Townsgate Rd, Westlake Village
(91361-3027)
PHONE.................................818 224-7442
EMP: 239
SALES (est): 76.6K **Privately Held**
SIC: 6733 Trusts

PRODUCTS & SVCS

PA: Pennymac Mortgage Investment Trust
6101 Condor Dr
Moorpark CA 93021
-

(P-12121)
PNMAC GMSR ISSUER TRUST
3043 Townsgate Rd, Westlake Village
(91361-3027)
PHONE.............................818 746-2271
EMP: 1070
SALES (est): 84.3K
SALES (corp-wide): 1.1B **Publicly Held**
SIC: 6733 Trusts
PA: Pennymac Financial Services, Inc.
3043 Townsgate Rd
Westlake Village CA 91361
818 224-7442

(P-12122)
PROVIDENCE HEALTH SYSTEM
Also Called: Little Co Mary Hosp Pavilion
4320 Maricopa St, Torrance (90503-4314)
PHONE.............................310 543-5900
Mary Ann Young, *Manager*
EMP: 200
SALES (corp-wide): 17.6B **Privately Held**
WEB: www.lcmhs.org
SIC: 6733 8069 8051 Trusts; specialty
hospitals, except psychiatric; skilled nurs-
ing care facilities
HQ: Providence Health System-Southern
California
1801 Lind Ave Sw
Renton WA 98057
425 525-3355

(P-12123)
PROVIDENCE HEALTH SYSTEM
3551 Voyager St Ste 201, Torrance
(90503-1674)
PHONE.............................310 370-5895
EMP: 200
SALES (corp-wide): 17.6B **Privately Held**
SIC: 6733
HQ: Providence Health System-Southern
California
1801 Lind Ave Sw
Renton WA 98057
425 525-3355

(P-12124)
PROVIDENCE HEALTH SYSTEM
511 S Buena Vista St, Burbank
(91505-4809)
PHONE.............................818 846-8141
EMP: 200
SALES (corp-wide): 17.6B **Privately Held**
WEB: www.lcmhs.org
SIC: 6733 Trusts
HQ: Providence Health System-Southern
California
1801 Lind Ave Sw
Renton WA 98057
425 525-3355

(P-12125)
QUALITY LOAN SERVICE CORP
2763 Camino Del Rio S, San Diego
(92108-3708)
PHONE.............................619 645-7711
Kevin R McCarthy, *CEO*
Thomas J Holthus, *Ch of Bd*
Dave Owen, *COO*
Adriana Banuelos, *Trustee*
Victoria Logan, *Vice Pres*
EMP: 384
SALES (est): 30.7MM **Privately Held**
WEB: www.qualityloan.com
SIC: 6733 Trusts, except educational, reli-
gious, charity: management

(P-12126)
**SOHNEN BARRY AS CO
TRUSTEE**
8945 Eice Rd, Santa Fe Springs (90670)
PHONE.............................562 946-3531
Barry Sohnen, *President*
EMP: 50
SALES (est): 1.3MM **Privately Held**
SIC: 6733 Trusts

(P-12127)
**SOUTHERN CAL PIPE TRADES
ADM (PA)**
Also Called: Southern Cal Pipe Trades ADM
501 Shatto Pl Ste 500, Los Angeles
(90020-1730)
PHONE.............................213 385-6161
Milton D Johnson, *President*
Marcus Chin, *CFO*
EMP: 70
SQ FT: 70,000
SALES (est): 23.7MM **Privately Held**
WEB: www.marinavillage.net
SIC: 6733 6513 Trusts, except educa-
tional, religious, charity: management; re-
tirement hotel operation

(P-12128)
**TCW VALUE ADDED LTD
PARTNR**
865 S Figueroa St, Los Angeles
(90017-2543)
PHONE.............................213 244-0000
EMP: 53
SALES (est): 5MM
SALES (corp-wide): 205.6MM **Privately
Held**
SIC: 6733 Private estate, personal invest-
ment & vacation fund trusts
HQ: Tcw Asset Management Company Llc
865 S Figueroa St # 2100
Los Angeles CA 90017
213 244-0000

(P-12129)
**UFCW & EMPLOYERS TRUST
LLC (PA)**
1000 Burnett Ave Ste 200, Concord
(94520-2058)
PHONE.............................800 552-2400
Jody Osterweil, *Administration*
David Pipgras, *Business Anlyst*
May Gu, *Engineer*
Carol Munoz, *Accountant*
Mayra Rivas, *Hum Res Coord*
EMP: 110
SQ FT: 57,600
SALES (est): 26.8MM **Privately Held**
SIC: 6733 Trusts

(P-12130)
**VACATION AND HOLIDAY
BENEFIT F**
501 Shatto Pl Ste 5, Los Angeles
(90020-1730)
PHONE.............................213 385-6161
Milton D Johnson, *Administration*
Mike Ayre, *Ch of Bd*
E A Norris, *Ch of Bd*
Allen Jones Jr, *Co-COB*
Raymond Forman, *Trustee*
EMP: 60
SQ FT: 70,000
SALES (est): 3MM **Privately Held**
SIC: 6733 Trusts, except educational, reli-
gious, charity: management

(P-12131)
**VARNER FAMILY LTD
PARTNERSHIP (PA)**
5900 E Lerdo Hwy, Shafter (93263-4023)
PHONE.............................661 399-1163
James Varner, *General Ptnr*
EMP: 80
SALES (est): 111MM **Privately Held**
SIC: 6733 Private estate, personal invest-
ment & vacation fund trusts

(P-12132)
**WATTS HEALTH FOUNDATION
INC**
Also Called: Watts Health Center
10300 Compton Ave, Los Angeles
(90002-3628)
PHONE.............................323 357-6688
Clyde W Oden, *Manager*
EMP: 450
SALES (corp-wide): 31.9MM **Privately
Held**
WEB: www.sonnytran.com
SIC: 6733 8322 8011 Trusts; individual &
family services; offices & clinics of med-
ical doctors

HQ: Watts Health Foundation, Inc.
3405 W Imperial Hwy # 304
Inglewood CA 90303
310 424-2220

┌─────────────────────────┐
│ **6794 Patent Owners &**   │
│   **Lessors**   │
└─────────────────────────┘

(P-12133)
**ADVANCED FRESH CONCEPTS
CORP (PA)**
Also Called: A F C
19205 S Laurel Park Rd, Rancho
Dominguez (90220-6032)
PHONE.............................310 604-3630
Ryuji Ishii, *CEO*
Jeff Seiler, *Vice Pres*
Jeffery Seiler, *Vice Pres*
Michael Yoshino, *Technology*
Frederick Tam, *Asst Controller*
◆ **EMP:** 52
SQ FT: 60,000
SALES (est): 34MM **Privately Held**
WEB: www.afcsushi.com
SIC: 6794 2032 2092 5141 Patent own-
ers & lessors; Chinese foods: packaged
in cans, jars, etc.; fresh or frozen pack-
aged fish; food brokers

(P-12134)
BRER AFFILIATES LLC (DH)
Also Called: Prudential RE Affiliates Inc
18500 Von Karman Ave # 400, Irvine
(92612-0504)
PHONE.............................949 794-7900
John Vanderwall, *Ch of Bd*
Patti Ray, *Senior VP*
Ron Dashell, *Info Tech Dir*
EMP: 208
SQ FT: 55,500
SALES (est): 120.1MM
SALES (corp-wide): 59.6B **Publicly Held**
WEB: www.preacanada.com
SIC: 6794 6531 Franchises, selling or li-
censing; real estate agents & managers
HQ: The Prudential Insurance Company Of
America
751 Broad St
Newark NJ 07102
973 802-6000

(P-12135)
CEVA INC
1174 Castro St Ste 210, Mountain View
(94040-2569)
PHONE.............................650 417-7900
Gideon Wertheizer, *CEO*
Tanya Scott, *Managing Prtnr*
Peter McManamon, *Ch of Bd*
Yaniv Arieli, *CFO*
Eliyahu Ayalon, *Bd of Directors*
EMP: 278
SQ FT: 3,769
SALES (est): 87.5MM **Privately Held**
WEB: www.ceva-dsp.com
SIC: 6794 3674 Patent buying, licensing,
leasing; semiconductors & related de-
vices; integrated circuits, semiconductor
networks, etc.

(P-12136)
DOLBY LABS LICENSING CORP
100 Potrero Ave, San Francisco
(94103-4886)
PHONE.............................415 558-0200
Ray Dolby, *Chairman*
N William Jasper Jr, *President*
Andy Sherman, *Exec VP*
Steve Forshay, *Senior VP*
Priscilla Morgan, *Vice Pres*
EMP: 125
SQ FT: 50,000
SALES (est): 22.5MM
SALES (corp-wide): 1.1B **Publicly Held**
WEB: www.dolby.net
SIC: 6794 Patent buying, licensing, leasing
PA: Dolby Laboratories, Inc.
1275 Market St
San Francisco CA 94103
415 558-0200

(P-12137)
**EL POLLO LOCO HOLDINGS
INC (PA)**
3535 Harbor Blvd Ste 100, Costa Mesa
(92626-1494)
PHONE.............................714 599-5000
Stephen J Sather, *President*
Michael G Maselli, *Ch of Bd*
Kay L Bogeajis, *COO*
Douglas Ammerman, *Bd of Directors*
Mark Buller, *Bd of Directors*
EMP: 164
SQ FT: 29,880
SALES: 401.7MM **Publicly Held**
SIC: 6794 5812 Franchises, selling or li-
censing; Mexican restaurant

(P-12138)
LICENSALE INC
900 Bush St Apt 205, San Francisco
(94109-6379)
PHONE.............................604 681-6888
Benjamin Arazy, *President*
Mingsheng Qiu, *CFO*
EMP: 100
SALES: 25MM **Privately Held**
SIC: 6794 8748 Patent buying, licensing,
leasing; business consulting

(P-12139)
ORIGINAL PETES PIZZA INC
2001 J St, Sacramento (95811-3119)
PHONE.............................916 442-6770
Steve Presson, *President*
David Edmiston, *Vice Pres*
EMP: 50
SALES (est): 3.6MM **Privately Held**
SIC: 6794 5812 Franchises, selling or li-
censing; eating places

(P-12140)
**QUALCOMM INTERNATIONAL
INC (HQ)**
5775 Morehouse Dr, San Diego
(92121-1714)
PHONE.............................858 587-1121
Steve Altman, *President*
Derek Aberle, *Exec VP*
Ozcan Eren, *Admin Sec*
George Lee, *Software Engr*
Amod Bodas, *Manager*
EMP: 4000
SALES (est): 462.4MM
SALES (corp-wide): 22.2B **Publicly Held**
SIC: 6794 Patent buying, licensing, leasing
PA: Qualcomm Incorporated
5775 Morehouse Dr
San Diego CA 92121
858 587-1121

(P-12141)
**RELIGIOUS TECHNOLOGY
CENTER**
Also Called: RTC
1710 Ivar Ave Ste 1100, Los Angeles
(90028-5575)
PHONE.............................323 663-3258
Warren McShane, *President*
Barbara Griffin, *Treasurer*
Laurisse Stuckenbrock, *Admin Sec*
EMP: 67
SQ FT: 1,200
SALES (est): 10.9MM **Privately Held**
WEB: www.rtc.org
SIC: 6794 8661 Copyright buying & licens-
ing; religious organizations

(P-12142)
**RISK MANAGEMENT
SOLUTIONS INC (DH)**
7575 Gateway Blvd, Newark (94560-1193)
PHONE.............................510 505-2500
Karen White, *CEO*
Paul Dali, *Ch of Bd*
Stephen Robertson, *CFO*
Robert Muir-Wood, *Officer*
Paul Vandermarck, *Officer*
EMP: 140
SQ FT: 55,000
SALES (est): 176.8MM **Privately Held**
SIC: 6794 6411 Patent owners & lessors;
insurance information & consulting serv-
ices

HQ: Dmgi Land & Property Europe Ltd
5-7 Abbey Court
Exeter EX2 7
844 844-9966

(P-12143)
RPX CORPORATION (HQ)
1 Market Plz Lbby Bl-100, San Francisco
(94105-1002)
PHONE..................................866 779-7641
Dan McCurdy, *CEO*
Robert H Heath, *CFO*
Steven S Swank, *Officer*
Mallun Yen, *Exec VP*
Martin E Roberts, *Senior VP*
EMP: 62
SQ FT: 67,000
SALES: 330.4MM
SALES (corp-wide): 8.5MM **Privately Held**
SIC: 6794 8741 Patent owners & lessors; business management

(P-12144)
TENSILICA INC (HQ)
3393 Octavius Dr, Santa Clara
(95054-3004)
P.O. Box 202769, Dallas TX (75320-2769)
PHONE..................................408 986-8000
Jack Guedj, *President*
Chris Carney, *CFO*
Keith Van Sickle, *CFO*
Ashish Dixia, *Senior VP*
Beatrice Fu, *Senior VP*
EMP: 80
SQ FT: 20,000
SALES (est): 19.5MM
SALES (corp-wide): 1.9B **Publicly Held**
WEB: www.tensilica.com
SIC: 6794 9621 Patent owners & lessors; licensing agencies
PA: Cadence Design Systems, Inc.
2655 Seely Ave Bldg 5
San Jose CA 95134
408 943-1234

(P-12145)
UNIVERSAL STDIOS LICENSING INC
Also Called: Universal Studios Consmr Pdts
100 Universal City Plz, Universal City
(91608-1002)
PHONE..................................818 762-6284
Cynthia C Cleveland, *President*
EMP: 150
SALES (est): 16.4MM
SALES (corp-wide): 84.5B **Publicly Held**
WEB: www.universalstudios.com
SIC: 6794 Copyright buying & licensing
HQ: Universal Studios Company Llc
100 Universal City Plz
North Hollywood CA 91608
818 777-1000

(P-12146)
VIACOM CONSUMER PRODUCTS INC
5555 Melrose Ave, Los Angeles
(90038-3989)
PHONE..................................323 956-5634
Andrea Hein, *President*
Charles Phillips, *Vice Chairman*
William Schwartz, *Bd of Directors*
Mike Goldman, *Senior VP*
Terry Helton, *Senior VP*
EMP: 50 **EST:** 1991
SALES (est): 5.8MM
SALES (corp-wide): 13.2B **Publicly Held**
WEB: www.viacom.com
SIC: 6794 Patent buying, licensing, leasing
HQ: Paramount Pictures Corporation
5555 Melrose Ave
Los Angeles CA 90038
323 956-5000

(P-12147)
WONDERLAND MUSIC COMPANY INC
500 S Buena Vista St, Burbank
(91521-0001)
PHONE..................................818 840-1671
Chris Montan, *Principal*
EMP: 55
SALES (est): 3.6MM **Publicly Held**
SIC: 6794 Patent owners & lessors

HQ: Disney Enterprises, Inc.
500 S Buena Vista St
Burbank CA 91521
818 560-1000

(P-12148)
WSM INVESTMENTS LLC
Also Called: Topco Sales
3990b Heritage Oak Ct, Simi Valley
(93063-6716)
PHONE..................................818 332-4600
Scott Tucker, *CEO*
Martin Tucker, *Ch of Bd*
Michael Siegel, *COO*
Gabriel Scally, *Controller*
Louie Astorga, *Director*
▲ **EMP:** 145
SQ FT: 150,000
SALES (est): 20.1MM
SALES (corp-wide): 12.9MM **Privately Held**
WEB: www.topco-sales.com
SIC: 6794 5122 5099 4731 Performance rights, publishing & licensing; cosmetics; novelties, durable; freight forwarding
PA: Lover Health Science And Technology Incorporated Co., Ltd.
No.1208, Taihu Ave., Economic Development Zone
Changxing County 31310
572 612-1079

6798 Real Estate Investment Trusts

(P-12149)
AMERICAN HOMES TRUST
450 Camino Hermoso, San Marcos
(92078-8905)
PHONE..................................619 694-7821
Jesse Bookheim, *Owner*
EMP: 100
SQ FT: 23,000
SALES: 2MM **Privately Held**
SIC: 6798 Real estate investment trusts

(P-12150)
AMERICAN REALTY ADVISORS
515 S Flower St Ste 4900, Los Angeles
(90071-2220)
PHONE..................................818 545-1152
Stanley Iezman, *President*
Gregory A Blomstrand, *Principal*
Scott Darling, *Principal*
EMP: 58
SALES (est): 3.4MM **Privately Held**
SIC: 6798 Real estate investment trusts

(P-12151)
AMH PORTFOLIO ONE LLC
Also Called: Beazer Pre-Owned Rental Homes
30601 Agoura Rd Ste 200, Agoura Hills
(91301-2148)
PHONE..................................480 921-4600
David P Singelyn, *CEO*
EMP: 165 **EST:** 2014
SALES (est): 57MM
SALES (corp-wide): 960.4MM **Publicly Held**
SIC: 6798 Realty investment trusts
PA: American Homes 4 Rent
30601 Agoura Rd Ste 200
Agoura Hills CA 91301
805 413-5300

(P-12152)
ANCHOR LOANS LP
Also Called: Anchor Nationwide Loans
5230 Las Virgenes Rd # 105, Calabasas
(91302-3447)
PHONE..................................310 395-0010
Stephen Pollack, *CEO*
Lora Geis, *COO*
Bryan Thompson, *CFO*
Matt Ediger, *Vice Pres*
Lance Spencer, *Vice Pres*
EMP: 200
SALES (est): 213.3K **Privately Held**
SIC: 6798 Real estate investment trusts

(P-12153)
BIOMED REALTY LP (HQ)
17190 Bernardo Center Dr, San Diego
(92128-7030)
PHONE..................................858 485-9840
Alan D Gold, *Principal*
Kent Griffin, *Vice Pres*
EMP: 50
SQ FT: 61,286
SALES: 674.6MM **Privately Held**
WEB: www.biomedrealty.com
SIC: 6798 6531 Real estate investment trusts; real estate brokers & agents
PA: Biomed Realty Trust, Inc.
17190 Bernardo Center Dr
San Diego CA 92128
858 485-9840

(P-12154)
BROOKFIELD DTLA FUND OFFICE
355 S Grand Ave Ste 3300, Los Angeles
(90071-1592)
PHONE..................................213 626-3300
Dennis Friedrich, *Branch Mgr*
EMP: 70
SALES (corp-wide): 31.9B **Publicly Held**
SIC: 6798 Real estate investment trusts
HQ: Brookfield Dtla Fund Office Trust Inc.
4 Wrld Fncl Ctr Fl 15
New York NY 10281
212 417-7064

(P-12155)
CANYON VIEW CAPITAL INC
331 Soquel Ave Ste 100, Santa Cruz
(95062-2330)
PHONE..................................831 480-6335
Robert J Davidson, *CEO*
Alison Ruday, *Principal*
EMP: 80
SALES: 60MM **Privately Held**
SIC: 6798 Real estate investment trusts

(P-12156)
CORE REALTY HOLDINGS LLC (PA)
1600 Dove St Ste 450, Newport Beach
(92660-2447)
PHONE..................................949 863-1031
Doug Morehead, *Mng Member*
Jonathan Harmer, *CFO*
William Russ Colvin, *Chm Emeritus*
Tania Jernigan, *Vice Pres*
Gary Davi, *CIO*
EMP: 53
SALES (est): 31.4MM **Privately Held**
WEB: www.corerealtyholdings.com
SIC: 6798 Realty investment trusts

(P-12157)
DALLAS UNION HOTEL INC
Also Called: Sheraton
150 Corson St, Pasadena (91103-3839)
PHONE..................................626 356-1000
Leo Majich, *President*
Rona Bevando, *Treasurer*
Jeff Ford, *Vice Pres*
EMP: 170
SALES (est): 4MM
SALES (corp-wide): 47.2MM **Privately Held**
WEB: www.sheratongranddfw.com
SIC: 6798 Real estate investment trusts
PA: Operating Engineers Funds Inc
100 Corson St Ste 222
Pasadena CA 91103
866 400-5200

(P-12158)
DIGITAL REALTY TRUST LP
4 Embarcadero Ctr # 3200, San Francisco
(94111-4188)
PHONE..................................415 738-6500
A William Stein, *CEO*
Digital Realty Trust, *General Ptnr*
Jarrett B Appleby, *COO*
Andrew P Power, *CFO*
EMP: 1345
SALES: 2.1B
SALES (corp-wide): 2.4B **Privately Held**
SIC: 6798 Real estate investment trusts

PA: Digital Realty Trust, Inc.
4 Embarcadero Ctr # 3200
San Francisco CA 94111
415 738-6500

(P-12159)
EMT LLC (PA)
Also Called: Whitehall Asset Management
6600 Hunter Dr, Rohnert Park
(94928-2418)
PHONE..................................707 584-5123
Eugene J Burger,
Mark Epstein,
Thomas Haller,
EMP: 70
SQ FT: 18,000
SALES (est): 3.2MM **Privately Held**
SIC: 6798 6531 8742 Real estate investment trusts; real estate brokers & agents; management consulting services

(P-12160)
EQUINIX INC (PA)
1 Lagoon Dr Ste 400, Redwood City
(94065-1564)
PHONE..................................650 598-6000
Charles Meyers, *President*
Peter Van Camp, *Ch of Bd*
Keith D Taylor, *CFO*
Biju Baby, *Vice Pres*
Mike Campbell, *Security Dir*
EMP: 220
SALES: 4.3B **Publicly Held**
WEB: www.equinix.com
SIC: 6798 7374 Real estate investment trusts; computer processing services

(P-12161)
ESSEX MANAGEMENT CORPORATION (HQ)
925 E Meadow Dr, Palo Alto (94303-4299)
PHONE..................................650 494-3700
Keith Guericke, *President*
Michael J Schall, *CFO*
John Eudy, *Exec VP*
Craig Zimmerman, *Exec VP*
EMP: 60
SALES (est): 5.1MM
SALES (corp-wide): 1.3B **Privately Held**
SIC: 6798 Real estate investment trusts
PA: Essex Property Trust, Inc.
1100 Park Pl Ste 200
San Mateo CA 94403
650 655-7800

(P-12162)
ESSEX PROPERTY TRUST INC
8795 Folsom Blvd Ste 101, Sacramento
(95826-3720)
PHONE..................................916 381-0345
Laurie Bernhard, *Branch Mgr*
EMP: 70
SALES (corp-wide): 1.3B **Privately Held**
WEB: www.breproperties.com
SIC: 6798 Real estate investment trusts
PA: Essex Property Trust, Inc.
1100 Park Pl Ste 200
San Mateo CA 94403
650 655-7800

(P-12163)
GR HARDESTER LLC
21088 Calistoga Rd, Middletown
(95461-9300)
P.O. Box 308 (95461-0308)
PHONE..................................707 987-2325
Ross Hardester,
Walter Hardester,
EMP: 127 **EST:** 1999
SALES (est): 5.2MM **Privately Held**
SIC: 6798 Real estate investment trusts

(P-12164)
HCP INC (PA)
1920 Main St Ste 1200, Irvine
(92614-7230)
PHONE..................................949 407-0700
Thomas M Herzog, *CEO*
Brian Cartwright, *Ch of Bd*
Michael D McKee, *Ch of Bd*
Thomas M Klaritch, *COO*
Peter A Scott, *CFO*
EMP: 70
SALES: 1.8B **Publicly Held**
WEB: www.hcpi.com
SIC: 6798 Real estate investment trusts

(P-12165)
HUDSON PACIFIC PROPERTIES INC (PA)
11601 Wilshire Blvd Fl 6, Los Angeles (90025-0509)
PHONE..................310 445-5700
Victor J Coleman, *Ch of Bd*
Mark T Lammas, *COO*
Richard Fried, *Bd of Directors*
Jonathan Glaser, *Bd of Directors*
Robert Harris, *Bd of Directors*
EMP: 63
SALES: 728.1MM **Publicly Held**
SIC: 6798 Real estate investment trusts

(P-12166)
IMPAC MORTGAGE HOLDINGS INC (PA)
19500 Jamboree Rd, Irvine (92612-2411)
PHONE..................949 475-3600
Joseph R Tomkinson, *Ch of Bd*
William S Ashmore, *President*
Rian Furey, *President*
George A Mangiaracina, *President*
Brian Kuelbs, *CFO*
EMP: 564
SQ FT: 210,000
SALES: 138.7MM **Publicly Held**
SIC: 6798 Real estate investment trusts

(P-12167)
IRVINE EASTGATE OFFICE II LLC
Also Called: Irvine Company Office Property
550 Newport Center Dr, Newport Beach (92660-7011)
P.O. Box 2460 (92658-8960)
PHONE..................949 720-2000
Pam Van Nort, *Vice Pres*
Imelda Delherra, *Director*
Tony Terusa, *Director*
Crystal Saunders, *Manager*
EMP: 3000
SQ FT: 3,000
SALES (est): 329MM **Privately Held**
SIC: 6798 Real estate investment trusts

(P-12168)
JONES LANG LA SALLE
515 S Flower St Fl 13, Los Angeles (90071-2201)
PHONE..................213 239-6000
Peter Belisle, *General Mgr*
Maureen Hawley, *Sr Associate*
EMP: 80
SALES (est): 6.1MM **Privately Held**
SIC: 6798 Real estate investment trusts

(P-12169)
KILROY REALTY CORPORATION (PA)
12200 W Olympic Blvd # 200, Los Angeles (90064-1044)
PHONE..................310 481-8400
John Kilroy, *Ch of Bd*
Jeffrey Hawken, *COO*
Tyler Rose, *CFO*
Stephen Rosetta, *Exec VP*
Justin Smart, *Exec VP*
EMP: 86
SQ FT: 150,832
SALES: 719MM **Publicly Held**
WEB: www.kilroyrealty.com
SIC: 6798 Real estate investment trusts

(P-12170)
LBA REALTY FUND III - III LLC
3347 Michelson Dr Ste 200, Irvine (92612-0687)
PHONE..................949 833-0400
Perry Schonfeld, *Principal*
Aileen Chiang, *Accountant*
EMP: 99
SALES (est): 4.4MM **Privately Held**
SIC: 6798 Real estate investment trusts

(P-12171)
LBA RLTY FUND I-COMPANY IV LLC
3347 Michelson Dr Ste 950, Irvine (92612-1692)
PHONE..................949 955-9321
Michael Memoly,
EMP: 99

SALES (est): 7MM **Privately Held**
SIC: 6798 Real estate investment trusts

(P-12172)
MACERICH COMPANY (PA)
401 Wilshire Blvd Ste 700, Santa Monica (90401-1452)
PHONE..................310 394-6000
Arthur M Coppola, *CEO*
Steven R Hash, *Ch of Bd*
Edward C Coppola, *President*
Thomas E O'Hern, *CFO*
Ann C Menard,
EMP: 80 EST: 1965
SALES: 993.6MM **Publicly Held**
WEB: www.macerich.com
SIC: 6798 Real estate investment trusts

(P-12173)
MAGUIRE PROPERTIES TWR 17 LLC
1733 Ocean Ave Fl 4, Santa Monica (90401-3223)
PHONE..................310 857-1100
Martin Griffiths,
Alain Artin, *Technology*
EMP: 99
SALES (est): 5MM **Privately Held**
SIC: 6798 Real estate investment trusts

(P-12174)
MERABI & SONS LLC
14545 Friar St Ste 101, Van Nuys (91411-2357)
PHONE..................818 817-0006
Kambiz Merabi, *Managing Dir*
EMP: 135
SQ FT: 15,000
SALES: 1.5MM **Privately Held**
WEB: www.merabiandsons.com
SIC: 6798 Real estate investment trusts

(P-12175)
MERIDIAN INDUSTRIAL TRUST
455 Market St Ste 1700, San Francisco (94105-2456)
PHONE..................415 281-3900
Allen J Anderson, *CEO*
Milton K Reeder, *President*
Dennis D Higgs, *Senior VP*
EMP: 60
SALES: 66.1MM **Privately Held**
SIC: 6798 Real estate investment trusts

(P-12176)
MYRA INVESTMENT AND DEV CORP
47 W 6th St, Tracy (95376-4109)
PHONE..................209 834-2343
Abdul Siddiqi, *President*
EMP: 55
SQ FT: 2,500
SALES (est): 3.1MM **Privately Held**
SIC: 6798 Realty investment trusts

(P-12177)
ONE EMBARCADERO CENTER VENTURE
4 Embarcadero Ctr Ste 1, San Francisco (94111-4106)
PHONE..................415 772-0700
Bob Pester, *Regional Mgr*
EMP: 70
SALES (est): 4.1MM
SALES (corp-wide): 2.6B **Publicly Held**
SIC: 6798 Real estate investment trusts
HQ: Boston Properties Limited Partnership
800 Boylston St Ste 1900
Boston MA 02199
617 236-3300

(P-12178)
PACIFICA COMPANIES LLC (PA)
1775 Hancock St Ste 200, San Diego (92110-2036)
PHONE..................619 296-9000
Deepak Israni, *President*
Ashok Israni, *Chairman*
Cynthia Martinez, *Asst Sec*
EMP: 57
SALES (est): 442.6MM **Privately Held**
SIC: 6798 6512 Real estate investment trusts; nonresidential building operators

(P-12179)
PCCP LLC (PA)
555 California St # 3450, San Francisco (94104-1614)
PHONE..................415 732-7645
Donald H Kuemmeler,
Ryan Dodge, *Vice Pres*
William Lindsay, *Branch Mgr*
Whitney Allen, *Office Mgr*
Nicholas Colonna,
EMP: 58 EST: 1998
SQ FT: 5,400
SALES (est): 9.8MM **Privately Held**
WEB: www.pccpllc.com
SIC: 6798 Real estate investment trusts

(P-12180)
PMT ISSUER TRUST - FMSR ✪
3043 Townsgate Rd, Westlake Village (91361-3027)
PHONE..................818 224-7028
EMP: 239 EST: 2018
SALES (est): 91.4K **Privately Held**
SIC: 6798 Real estate investment trusts
PA: Pennymac Mortgage Investment Trust
6101 Condor Dr
Moorpark CA 93021

(P-12181)
PRIME ADMINISTRATION LLC
Also Called: Prime Group
357 S Curson Ave, Los Angeles (90036-5201)
P.O. Box 360859 (90036-1359)
PHONE..................323 549-7155
Daniel H James, *Chairman*
John C Atwater, *CEO*
Kris Bloom, *Exec VP*
Will Madison, *Vice Pres*
Chris Scroggin, *Vice Pres*
EMP: 522
SALES (est): 81.4MM **Privately Held**
SIC: 6798 Real estate investment trusts

(P-12182)
PROLOGIS INC (PA)
Bay 1 Pier 1, San Francisco (94111)
PHONE..................415 394-9000
Hamid R Moghadam, *Ch of Bd*
Nancy Ballester, *Partner*
Jesus Barrera, *Partner*
Katie Cassarino, *Partner*
Jacqui Colwell, *Partner*
EMP: 460
SALES: 2.6B **Publicly Held**
WEB: www.amb.com
SIC: 6798 Real estate investment trusts

(P-12183)
PROLOGIS LP (HQ)
Bay 1 Pier 1, San Francisco (94111)
PHONE..................415 394-9000
Hamid R Moghadam, *Ch of Bd*
Thomas S Olinger, *CFO*
Lori A Palazzolo,
Manel Vericat, *Opers Staff*
Caroline Melvin, *Corp Comm Staff*
EMP: 452
SALES: 2.6B **Publicly Held**
WEB: www.amb.com
SIC: 6798 6799 Real estate investment trusts; real estate investors, except property operators
PA: Prologis, Inc.
Bay 1 Pier 1
San Francisco CA 94111
415 394-9000

(P-12184)
PS BUSINESS PARKS INC (PA)
701 Western Ave, Glendale (91201-2349)
PHONE..................818 244-8080
Joseph D Russell Jr, *CEO*
Ronald L Havner Jr, *Ch of Bd*
Maria R Hawthorne, *President*
John W Petersen, *COO*
Jeffrey D Hedges, *CFO*
◆ EMP: 74
SALES: 402.1MM **Publicly Held**
WEB: www.psbusinessparks.com
SIC: 6798 Real estate investment trusts

(P-12185)
PUBLIC STORAGE (PA)
701 Western Ave, Glendale (91201-2349)
PHONE..................818 244-8080
Ronald L Havner Jr, *Ch of Bd*
Joseph D Russell, *President*
John Reyes, *CFO*
Lily Y Hughes,
EMP: 200
SALES: 2.6B **Publicly Held**
WEB: www.publicstorage.com
SIC: 6798 4225 Real estate investment trusts; miniwarehouse, warehousing; warehousing, self-storage

(P-12186)
QUAIL HILL INVESTMENTS INC
Also Called: Remax Value Properties
1124 Meridian Ave, San Jose (95125-4329)
PHONE..................408 978-9000
EMP: 110
SALES (est): 5.9MM **Privately Held**
WEB: www.colleenanddennisb.com
SIC: 6798

(P-12187)
SM BROADWAY CORP
Also Called: Hilton Newark Sremont
710 S Myrtle Ave Ste 285, Monrovia (91016-3423)
PHONE..................626 301-1198
Wen Shen Chang, *CEO*
EMP: 100 EST: 1994
SALES (est): 3.2MM **Privately Held**
SIC: 6798 Real estate investment trusts

(P-12188)
SUNSTONE HOTEL INVESTORS INC (PA)
200 Spectrum Center Dr, Irvine (92618-5003)
PHONE..................949 330-4000
John V Arabia, *President*
Douglas M Pasquale, *Ch of Bd*
Marc A Hoffman, *COO*
Bryan A Giglia, *CFO*
Andrew Batinovich, *Bd of Directors*
▲ EMP: 50
SALES: 1.1B **Publicly Held**
SIC: 6798 Real estate investment trusts

(P-12189)
T C W REALTY FUND VI
Also Called: C B Richard Ellis Investors
515 S Flower St Fl 31, Los Angeles (90071-2201)
PHONE..................213 683-4200
Bob Zerbst, *CEO*
Westmark Realty Advisors LLC, *General Ptnr*
Trust C West, *Trustee*
Parul Narain, *Officer*
Kenneth Rapp, *Exec VP*
EMP: 150
SQ FT: 24,000
SALES (est): 9.5MM **Privately Held**
SIC: 6798 Realty investment trusts

(P-12190)
TORREY AAT POINT LLC
11455 El Camino Real, San Diego (92130-2088)
PHONE..................858 350-2600
Ernest Rady, *CEO*
Robert Barton, *CFO*
EMP: 80
SALES (est): 4.4MM **Privately Held**
SIC: 6798 Real estate investment trusts

(P-12191)
US ADVISOR LLC
600 Trancas St, NAPA (94558-3083)
PHONE..................707 253-9953
Kevin Fitzgerald, *Mng Member*
Kathaleen Scanlon,
EMP: 73
SQ FT: 3,200
SALES (est): 3.6MM **Privately Held**
SIC: 6798 Real estate investment trusts

(P-12192)
WEST OAHU MALL ASSOCIATES
1880 Century Park E # 810, Los Angeles (90067-1600)
PHONE..................310 276-1290

Joseph Daneshgar, *Principal*
Bill Ketcham, *Principal*
EMP: 50
SALES (est): 2.9MM **Privately Held**
SIC: 6798 Real estate investment trusts

(P-12193)
WESTCOAST PERFORMANCE PDTS USA
Also Called: Zantos Living Trust
3100 E Coronado St, Anaheim
(92806-1914)
PHONE..................................714 630-4411
Robert Zantos, *President*
EMP: 70
SALES (corp-wide): 5.9MM **Privately Held**
WEB: www.westcoastinc.com
SIC: 6798 Real estate investment trusts
PA: Westcoast Performance Products
(Usa) Inc
3100 E Coronado St
Anaheim CA
714 630-4411

(P-12194)
WESTERN ASSET MRTG CAPITL CORP
385 E Colorado Blvd, Pasadena
(91101-1923)
PHONE..................................626 844-9400
Jennifer W Murphy, *President*
James W Hirschmann III, *Ch of Bd*
Jennifer Murphy, *COO*
Elliott Neumayer, *COO*
Lisa Meyer, *CFO*
EMP: 821
SALES: 154.7MM **Privately Held**
SIC: 6798 Real estate investment trusts

6799 Investors, NEC

(P-12195)
500 STARTUPS MANAGEMENT CO LLC
Also Called: Spacer.com
444 Castro St Ste 1200, Mountain View
(94041-2064)
PHONE..................................650 743-4738
Dave McClure, *Mng Member*
Matt Ellsworth, *Partner*
Khailee Ng, *Managing Prtnr*
Bedy Yang, *Managing Prtnr*
Meghan Christenson, *Office Mgr*
EMP: 120
SALES (est): 11.4MM **Privately Held**
SIC: 6799 Investors
HQ: Spacer.Com.Au Pty Ltd
Level 3
Pyrmont NSW 2009
130 050-0538

(P-12196)
ABS CAPITAL PARTNERS III LP
101 California St Fl 24, San Francisco
(94111-5802)
PHONE..................................415 617-2800
John Mallon, *Branch Mgr*
EMP: 100
SALES (est): 2.8MM **Privately Held**
SIC: 6799 Investors
PA: Abs Capital Partners Iii, L.P.
400 E Pratt St Ste 910
Baltimore MD 21202

(P-12197)
ADG CORPORATION
1871 Market St, San Francisco
(94103-1112)
PHONE..................................415 864-4090
David Levy, *President*
Gerald K Dowd, *Admin Sec*
EMP: 50
SALES (est): 2.4MM **Privately Held**
WEB: www.adg.vn
SIC: 6799 Venture capital companies

(P-12198)
ADMIRALTY PARTNERS INC
1170 Somera Rd, Los Angeles
(90077-2628)
PHONE..................................310 471-3772
Jon Kutler, *President*

EMP: 51
SALES (est): 1.8MM **Privately Held**
WEB: www.admiraltypartners.com
SIC: 6799 3675 Real estate investors, except property operators; electronic capacitors

(P-12199)
ARES MANAGEMENT LLC (HQ)
2000 Avenue Of The Stars # 12, Los Angeles (90067-4733)
PHONE..................................310 201-4100
Antony Ressler, *Mng Member*
Greg Margolies, *Senior Partner*
Seth Brufsky, *Vice Pres*
Tara Hicks, *Vice Pres*
Zhen Jiang, *Vice Pres*
EMP: 60
SALES (est): 926.5MM
SALES (corp-wide): 1.4B **Publicly Held**
SIC: 6799 Venture capital companies
PA: Ares Management, L.P.
2000 Avenue Of The Stars # 12
Los Angeles CA 90067
310 201-4100

(P-12200)
BARCLAYS CAPITAL INC
155 Linfield Dr, Menlo Park (94025-3741)
PHONE..................................650 289-6000
Stu Francis, *Branch Mgr*
Laurence Braham, *Technology*
Carl Chiou, *Director*
EMP: 70
SALES (corp-wide): 35.4B **Privately Held**
WEB: www.lehmanbrothers.com
SIC: 6799 Investors
HQ: Barclays Capital Inc.
745 7th Ave
New York NY 10019
212 526-7000

(P-12201)
BERTRAM CAPITAL MANAGEMENT LLC
800 Concar Dr Ste 100, San Mateo
(94402-7045)
PHONE..................................650 358-5000
Jeff Drazan, *Partner*
Ryan Craig, *Partner*
David Hellier, *Partner*
Jared Ruger, *Partner*
Ingrid Swenson, *Partner*
EMP: 261
SQ FT: 9,000
SALES (est): 44MM **Privately Held**
SIC: 6799 Venture capital companies

(P-12202)
BIRTCHER ANDRSON INVESTORS LLC
31910 Del Obispo St # 100, San Juan
Capistrano (92675-3182)
PHONE..................................949 545-0526
Robert M Anderson,
EMP: 50
SALES (est): 2.4MM **Privately Held**
SIC: 6799 Investors

(P-12203)
BRIDGE PARTNERS INC (PA)
1850 Mt Diablo Blvd # 410, Walnut Creek
(94596-4428)
PHONE..................................925 256-9448
Steve Klein, *President*
Ken Beall, *CFO*
Benjamin Jiang, *Analyst*
EMP: 62
SQ FT: 2,000
SALES (est): 9.9MM **Privately Held**
WEB: www.bridgepartners.com
SIC: 6799 6513 6514 8742 Real estate investors, except property operators; apartment building operators; dwelling operators, except apartments; real estate consultant

(P-12204)
BROADREACH CAPITL PARTNERS LLC
6430 W Sunset Blvd # 504, Los Angeles
(90028-7901)
PHONE..................................310 691-5760
Andre Ramillon, *Branch Mgr*
EMP: 1645

SALES (corp-wide): 399.2MM **Privately Held**
SIC: 6799 Investors
PA: Broadreach Capital Partners Llc
855 El Camino Real
Palo Alto CA 94301
650 331-2500

(P-12205)
BROADREACH CAPITL PARTNERS LLC
235 Montgomery St # 1018, San Francisco
(94104-2902)
PHONE..................................415 354-4640
John A Foster, *Branch Mgr*
EMP: 1316
SALES (corp-wide): 399.2MM **Privately Held**
SIC: 6799 Investors
PA: Broadreach Capital Partners Llc
855 El Camino Real
Palo Alto CA 94301
650 331-2500

(P-12206)
BUCHANAN FUND I LLC
620 Nwport Ctr Dr Ste 850, Newport Beach
(92660)
PHONE..................................949 721-1414
Timothy Ballard, *Mng Member*
EMP: 75 EST: 2000
SQ FT: 5,400
SALES (est): 3.5MM **Privately Held**
SIC: 6799 Real estate investors, except property operators

(P-12207)
BY-THE-BAY INVESTMENTS INC
37000 Fremont Blvd, Fremont
(94536-3604)
PHONE..................................510 793-2581
Javier Samaniego, *Branch Mgr*
EMP: 292 **Privately Held**
SIC: 6799 Investors
PA: By-The-Bay Investments, Inc.
360 Kiely Blvd Ste 270
San Jose CA 95129

(P-12208)
CALL TO ACTION LLC (PA)
11601 Wilshire Blvd Fl 23, Los Angeles
(90025-1759)
PHONE..................................310 996-7200
Colin Sapire, *Mng Member*
Richard Kam, *Marketing Mgr*
Lenny Sands,
▲ **EMP:** 100
SQ FT: 9,500
SALES (est): 38.3MM **Privately Held**
SIC: 6799 Investors

(P-12209)
CANESSA INVESTMENTS N V
9434 Cherokee Ln, Beverly Hills
(90210-1704)
PHONE..................................310 273-8543
Allen Martin, *Manager*
EMP: 50
SALES (est): 2.7MM **Privately Held**
SIC: 6799 Investors

(P-12210)
CARFINANCE CAPITAL LLC
7525 Irvine Center Dr # 250, Irvine
(92618-3066)
P.O. Box 57053 (92619-7053)
PHONE..................................800 900-5150
Dennis Morris,
Michael Ritter,
EMP: 522
SALES (est): 1.3MM **Privately Held**
SIC: 6799 6141 Investors; financing: automobiles, furniture, etc., not a deposit bank
PA: Flagship Credit Acceptance Llc
3 Christy Dr Ste 203
Chadds Ford PA 19317

(P-12211)
CASTER FAMILY ENTERPRISES INC
4607 Mission Gorge Pl, San Diego
(92120-4132)
PHONE..................................619 287-8893
Terrence R Caster, *President*

Barbara Caster, *Vice Pres*
Stella Cook, *Area Mgr*
Gregory Brown, *Info Tech Dir*
Sharon Brown, *Info Tech Mgr*
EMP: 125 EST: 1973
SQ FT: 250,000
SALES (est): 12.9MM **Privately Held**
WEB: www.castergrp.com
SIC: 6799 6512 6531 Real estate investors, except property operators; commercial & industrial building operation; real estate agents & managers

(P-12212)
CB RICHARD ELLIS STRATEGIC PAR
515 S Flower St Ste 3100, Los Angeles
(90071-2233)
PHONE..................................213 614-6862
Vance Maddocks, *Principal*
EMP: 62
SALES (est): 3.9MM **Privately Held**
SIC: 6799 Investors

(P-12213)
CCCC GROWTH FUND LLC
899 El Centro St, South Pasadena
(91030-3101)
PHONE..................................626 441-8770
Carl L Herrmann Jr, *Mng Member*
EMP: 61
SQ FT: 10,000
SALES (est): 5.2MM **Privately Held**
SIC: 6799 6411 Investors; insurance agents, brokers & service

(P-12214)
CHEVRON INVESTOR INC (HQ)
6001 Bollinger Canyon Rd, San Ramon
(94583-5737)
P.O. Box 5046 (94583-0946)
PHONE..................................925 842-1000
Howard Sheppard, *CEO*
John S Watson, *CEO*
Rex Mitchell, *Officer*
Miranda Palmisano, *Business Anlyst*
Pedro X Gama, *Project Mgr*
EMP: 300
SALES (est): 123.2MM
SALES (corp-wide): 141.7B **Publicly Held**
SIC: 6799 Investors
PA: Chevron Corporation
6001 Bollinger Canyon Rd
San Ramon CA 94583
925 842-1000

(P-12215)
CLEARVIEW CAPITAL LLC
12100 Wilshire Blvd # 800, Los Angeles
(90025-7140)
PHONE..................................310 806-9555
Larry Simon, *Branch Mgr*
EMP: 880
SALES (corp-wide): 281.9MM **Privately Held**
SIC: 6799 Venture capital companies
PA: Clearview Capital, Llc
1010 Washington Blvd # 1
Stamford CT 06901
203 698-2777

(P-12216)
COLONY CAPITL INV ADVISORS LLC
515 S Flower St Fl 44, Los Angeles
(90071-2201)
PHONE..................................310 282-8820
EMP: 57
SALES (est): 96.9K
SALES (corp-wide): 2.8B **Publicly Held**
SIC: 6799 Investors
PA: Colony Capital, Inc.
515 S Flower St Fl 44
Los Angeles CA 90071
310 282-8820

(P-12217)
CORRIDOR CAPITAL LLC (PA)
12400 Walsh Ave Ste 645, Los Angeles
(90066)
PHONE..................................310 442-7000
Craig L Enenstein, *CEO*
Jessamyn Davis, *CFO*
Edward A Monnier, *Managing Dir*
Cameron Reilly,

EMP: 126
SALES (est): 56.5MM **Privately Held**
SIC: 6799 Venture capital companies

(P-12218)
CRESTMONT CAPITAL LLC
2030 Main St, Irvine (92614-7219)
PHONE.................................800 949-0401
Gregory Keleshian,
EMP: 250
SALES (est): 6MM **Privately Held**
SIC: 6799 Investors

(P-12219)
CVF CAPITAL PARTNERS INC
Also Called: Central Valley Fund, The
1590 Drew Ave Ste 110, Davis
(95618-7849)
PHONE.................................530 757-7004
Jose C Blanco, *CEO*
Edward McNulty, *President*
Chris Carleson, *Vice Pres*
EMP: 150
SALES (est): 6.9MM **Privately Held**
SIC: 6799 Investors

(P-12220)
DAVIDON FIVE STAR CORP
Also Called: Davidon Homes
1600 S Main St Ste 150, Walnut Creek
(94596-5341)
PHONE.................................925 945-8000
Donald Chaiken, *Owner*
John Albini, *Vice Pres*
EMP: 80
SALES (est): 5MM **Privately Held**
SIC: 6799 Real estate investors, except
property operators

(P-12221)
EASIA GOLF INVESTMENT LLC
84000 Terra Lago Pkwy, Indio
(92203-9706)
PHONE.................................760 775-2000
Jon Lee, *General Mgr*
EMP: 60
SALES (est): 42MM **Privately Held**
SIC: 6799 Investors

(P-12222)
EAST HALL INVESTORS INC
Also Called: Keller Williams Realtors
11601 Blocker Dr Ste 200, Auburn
(95603-4650)
PHONE.................................530 328-1900
Daryl Rogers, *President*
EMP: 80
SALES (est): 5.3MM **Privately Held**
SIC: 6799 Investors

(P-12223)
EMP III INC
Also Called: Duarte Manor
1755 Mrtn Lthr Kng Jr Blv, Los Angeles
(90058-1522)
PHONE.................................323 231-4174
Ernie Piltil, *President*
Tim English, *CEO*
Scott Mason, *Vice Pres*
EMP: 80
SALES (est): 5.9MM **Privately Held**
SIC: 6799 Real estate investors, except
property operators

(P-12224)
**ENCORE CNSMR CAPITL FUND
II LP (PA)**
111 Pine St Ste 1825, San Francisco
(94111-5626)
PHONE.................................415 296-9850
Gary Smith, *CEO*
EMP: 88
SALES (est): 10MM **Privately Held**
SIC: 6799 Venture capital companies

(P-12225)
**END-TIME MESSAGE &
SUPPORT**
855 W 125th St, Los Angeles (90044-3811)
PHONE.................................323 756-6252
Alvin Labostrie, *Vice Pres*
EMP: 50
SALES (est): 2.1MM **Privately Held**
SIC: 6799 Real estate investors, except
property operators

(P-12226)
**ENGINEERED FOREST
PRODUCTS LLC**
Also Called: Future Homes International
1340 Bollinger Cyn, Moraga (94556-2742)
P.O. Box 6092 (94570-6092)
PHONE.................................925 376-0881
Gregory L Koepf,
Greg Koepf, *President*
Anne-Marie Koepf, *Admin Sec*
EMP: 100
SQ FT: 5,000
SALES: 100K **Privately Held**
SIC: 6799 Venture capital companies

(P-12227)
**FRANCISCO PARTNERS MGT LP
(PA)**
1 Letterman Dr Ste 410, San Francisco
(94129-1495)
PHONE.................................415 418-2900
Dipanjan Deb, *Managing Prtnr*
Benjamin Ball, *Partner*
Neil Garfinkel, *Partner*
David Golob, *Partner*
Eran Gorev, *Partner*
EMP: 50
SQ FT: 15,000
SALES (est): 1.7B **Privately Held**
WEB: www.franciscopartners.com
SIC: 6799 7372 Venture capital compa-
nies; application computer software

(P-12228)
**GAMUT CONSTRUCTION
COMPANY INC**
9340 Santa Anita Ave # 105, Rancho Cuca-
monga (91730-6149)
PHONE.................................909 948-0500
Mark Scarlatelli, *President*
Mark Scalatelli, *President*
Michelynn Scalatelli, *Corp Secy*
James White, *Vice Pres*
EMP: 75
SQ FT: 2,500
SALES (est): 4.8MM **Privately Held**
SIC: 6799 1521 Real estate investors, ex-
cept property operators; general remodel-
ing, single-family houses

(P-12229)
GOLDEN INTERNATIONAL
424 S Los Angeles St # 2, Los Angeles
(90013-1470)
PHONE.................................213 628-1388
Gl Hanbae, *Branch Mgr*
EMP: 2968
SALES (corp-wide): 153.5MM **Privately
Held**
SIC: 6799 Investors
PA: Golden International
36720 Palmdale Rd
Rancho Mirage CA 92270
760 568-1912

(P-12230)
**HARVARD GRAND INV INC A
CAL**
2 Civic Plaza Dr, Carson (90745-2231)
P.O. Box 761458, Los Angeles (90076-
1458)
PHONE.................................310 513-7560
Chang Hun Lee, *President*
Kathy Choy, *Controller*
EMP: 99 EST: 2007
SALES: 950K **Privately Held**
SIC: 6799 Investors

(P-12231)
**HELLMAN & FRIEDMAN
CAPITAL IV**
1 Maritime Plz Ste 1200, San Francisco
(94111-3531)
PHONE.................................415 788-5111
Warren Hellman, *Mng Member*
Allen Thorp,
EMP: 50
SALES (est): 14MM **Privately Held**
WEB: www.hf.com
SIC: 6799 Venture capital companies
PA: Hellman & Friedman Llc
1 Maritime Plz Ste 1200
San Francisco CA 94111

(P-12232)
HERCULES CAPITAL INC (PA)
400 Hamilton Ave Ste 310, Palo Alto
(94301-1805)
PHONE.................................650 289-3060
Manuel A Henriquez, *Ch of Bd*
Mark Harris, *CFO*
Mark R Harris, *CFO*
Melanie Grace, *Ch Credit Ofcr*
Thomas Fallon, *Bd of Directors*
EMP: 62
SQ FT: 14,500
SALES: 190.8MM **Publicly Held**
WEB: www.herculestech.com
SIC: 6799 Venture capital companies

(P-12233)
IDEALAB HOLDINGS LLC (PA)
130 W Union St, Pasadena (91103-3628)
PHONE.................................626 585-6900
Bill Gross, *CEO*
Marcia Goodstein, *President*
Craig Chrisney, *CFO*
Kristen Ding, *Vice Pres*
Wes Ferrari, *Vice Pres*
EMP: 626
SALES (est): 169.2MM **Privately Held**
WEB: www.idealab.com
SIC: 6799 5045 5734 Venture capital
companies; computer software; computer
software & accessories

(P-12234)
INCUBE LABS LLC (PA)
2051 Ringwood Ave, San Jose
(95131-1703)
PHONE.................................408 457-3700
Mir Imran, *CEO*
Mir Hashim, *Vice Pres*
Pratap Khanwilkar, *Vice Pres*
Phil Morgan, *Vice Pres*
Ben Tranchina, *Vice Pres*
EMP: 100
SQ FT: 24,000
SALES (est): 3.1MM **Privately Held**
SIC: 6799 Venture capital companies

(P-12235)
JH CAPITAL PARTNERS LP
451 Jackson St, San Francisco
(94111-1615)
PHONE.................................415 364-0300
John Hansen, *Partner*
EMP: 50
SALES (est): 1.7MM **Privately Held**
SIC: 6799 Venture capital companies

(P-12236)
**KLEINER PRKINS CFELD BYERS
LLC (PA)**
Also Called: Kpcb
2750 Sand Hill Rd, Menlo Park
(94025-7020)
PHONE.................................650 233-2750
Frank Caufield, *Partner*
John Doerr, *General Ptnr*
William Hearst III, *General Ptnr*
Tom Jermoluk, *General Ptnr*
Bill Joy, *General Ptnr*
EMP: 163 EST: 1984
SQ FT: 11,000
SALES (est): 37.6MM **Privately Held**
WEB: www.kpcb.com
SIC: 6799 3691 Venture capital compa-
nies; storage batteries

(P-12237)
**KLEINPARTNERS CAPITAL
CORP**
400 Continental Blvd # 600, El Segundo
(90245-5076)
PHONE.................................310 426-2055
Edward McMahon, *President*
Greg Klein, *Chairman*
EMP: 405
SALES (est): 13.6MM **Privately Held**
SIC: 6799 Investors

(P-12238)
KM FRESNO INVESTORS LLC
6222 Wilshire Blvd # 650, Los Angeles
(90048-5123)
PHONE.................................323 556-6600
David J Nagel, *President*
EMP: 50

SQ FT: 152,117
SALES (est): 2.8MM **Privately Held**
SIC: 6799 6531 Investors; real estate
managers

(P-12239)
**KOHLBERG KRAVIS ROBERTS
CO LP**
Also Called: K K R
2800 Sand Hill Rd Ste 200, Menlo Park
(94025-7080)
PHONE.................................650 233-6560
Michael Michelson, *Manager*
Mark Howard, *Officer*
Mitchell Rosenberg, *Human Resources*
Jim Momtazee, *Director*
Aaron Dickie, *Manager*
EMP: 55 **Publicly Held**
WEB: www.kkr.com
SIC: 6799 Investors
HQ: Kohlberg Kravis Roberts & Co. L.P.
9 W 57th St Ste 4200
New York NY 10019
212 750-8300

(P-12240)
**LIGHTHOUSE CAPITAL
FUNDING**
Also Called: Light House Group, The
15332 Antioch St Ste 540, Pacific Palisades
(90272-3628)
PHONE.................................310 230-8335
Gary Leshgold, *President*
Jennifer Napier, *VP Mktg*
Michelle Madden, *Marketing Staff*
Michael Wiggins, *Sr Associate*
Oliver Babcock, *Associate*
EMP: 50
SALES (est): 5.1MM **Privately Held**
WEB: www.lighthousecapitalfunding.net
SIC: 6799 Venture capital companies

(P-12241)
M & H REALTY PARTNERS LP
353 Sacramento St Fl 21, San Francisco
(94111-3620)
PHONE.................................415 693-9000
Peter Merlone, *Managing Prtnr*
EMP: 70
SALES (est): 4.2MM **Privately Held**
SIC: 6799 Real estate investors, except
property operators

(P-12242)
**MARLIN EQUITY PARTNERS III
LP (PA)**
338 Pier Ave, Hermosa Beach
(90254-3617)
PHONE.................................310 364-0100
David McGovern, *Mng Member*
George Kase,
Peter Spasov,
Nick Kaiser, *Mng Member*
EMP: 230
SALES (est): 15.7MM **Privately Held**
SIC: 6799 Venture capital companies

(P-12243)
**MATSUSHITA INTERNATIONAL
CORP (PA)**
1141 Via Callejon, San Clemente
(92673-6230)
PHONE.................................949 498-1000
Hiroyuki Matsushita, *President*
EMP: 80
SALES (est): 22.8MM **Privately Held**
SIC: 6799 3711 3714 Real estate in-
vestors, except property operators; auto-
mobile assembly, including specialty
automobiles; motor vehicle parts & acces-
sories

(P-12244)
**MCMILLIN COMMUNITIES INC
(PA)**
Also Called: McMillin Realty
2750 Womble Rd Ste 200, San Diego
(92106-6114)
PHONE.................................619 561-5275
Mark McMillin, *President*
Kenneth Baumgartner, *President*
Gary Beason, *CFO*
Bryce Jones, *Vice Pres*
Joe W Shielly, *General Mgr*
EMP: 1000

▲ = Import ▼=Export
◆ =Import/Export

SQ FT: 29,000
SALES (est): 97.8MM **Privately Held**
SIC: 6799 Investors

(P-12245)
MCMILLIN COMPANIES LLC (PA)
Also Called: McMillin Homes
2750 Womble Rd Ste 200, San Diego
(92106-6114)
PHONE..............................619 477-4117
Scott McMillin, *CEO*
Mark D McMillin, *President*
Robin Lewis, *Vice Pres*
Dennis Pulido, *Vice Pres*
Miesha Hunt, *Asst Controller*
EMP: 80 EST: 1998
SQ FT: 60,000
SALES: 50MM **Privately Held**
WEB: www.mcmillinrealty.com
SIC: 6799 Real estate investors, except
property operators

(P-12246)
MSD CAPITAL LP
100 Wilshire Blvd # 1450, Santa Monica
(90401-1110)
PHONE..............................310 458-3600
John Sauter, *Manager*
EMP: 52
SALES (corp-wide): 34.4MM **Privately
Held**
SIC: 6799 Venture capital companies; real
estate investors, except property opera-
tors; security speculators for own account
PA: Msd Capital L.P.
645 5th Ave Fl 21
New York NY 10022
212 303-1650

(P-12247)
N S B N INVESTMENTS LLC
9454 Wilshire Blvd Fl 4, Beverly Hills
(90212-2907)
PHONE..............................310 273-2501
Ken Miles,
William Esensten,
Jack Nienstein,
EMP: 75
SALES (est): 3.7MM **Privately Held**
WEB: www.nsbn.com
SIC: 6799 Investors

(P-12248)
NEW CIVIC COMPANY LTD
870 Market St Ste 1168, San Francisco
(94102-2916)
PHONE..............................415 986-1668
Zhonggen LI, *President*
Jun Chen, *Vice Pres*
EMP: 164
SALES (est): 10MM **Privately Held**
SIC: 6799 Investors

(P-12249)
NNN REALTY INVESTORS LLC
19700 Fairchild Ste 300, Irvine
(92612-2515)
P.O. Box 7369, Newport Beach (92658-
7369)
PHONE..............................714 667-8252
Jeffrey T Hanson, *President*
Michael Van Dusen, *Senior VP*
Fred D Cochran, *Vice Pres*
Todd A Mikles,
EMP: 458 EST: 1998
SQ FT: 18,800
SALES (est): 116.8K **Privately Held**
SIC: 6799 6531 Investors; real estate
managers

(P-12250)
NORWEST VENTURE PARTNERS VI LP
525 University Ave # 800, Palo Alto
(94301-1922)
PHONE..............................650 289-2243
EMP: 60
SALES (est): 2.1MM
SALES (corp-wide): 97.7B **Publicly Held**
SIC: 6799 Investors
HQ: Norwest Limited Lp, Lllp
420 Montgomery St
San Francisco CA

(P-12251)
NRLL LLC
Also Called: Land Disposition Company
1 Mauchly, Irvine (92618-2305)
PHONE..............................949 768-7777
Robert D Friedman,
Jeffrey Friedman,
EMP: 50
SQ FT: 18,000
SALES (est): 4MM
SALES (corp-wide): 47.1MM **Privately
Held**
WEB: www.landdisposition.com
SIC: 6799 Real estate investors, except
property operators
PA: Nrp Holding Co., Inc.
1 Mauchly
Irvine CA 92618
949 583-1000

(P-12252)
NUMERO UNO MARKET
4373 S Vermont Ave, Los Angeles
(90037-2411)
PHONE..............................323 231-9403
Philip Lopez, *President*
EMP: 80
SALES (corp-wide): 30MM **Privately
Held**
SIC: 6799 Investors
PA: Numero Uno Market
701 E Jefferson Blvd
Los Angeles CA 90011
323 846-5842

(P-12253)
NUMERO UNO MARKET
9127 S Figueroa St, Los Angeles
(90003-3905)
PHONE..............................213 381-1734
EMP: 80
SALES (corp-wide): 30MM **Privately
Held**
SIC: 6799 Investors
PA: Numero Uno Market
701 E Jefferson Blvd
Los Angeles CA 90011
323 846-5842

(P-12254)
OAKTREE HOLDINGS INC
333 S Grand Ave Ste 2800, Los Angeles
(90071-1530)
PHONE..............................213 830-6300
EMP: 1363 EST: 2014
SALES (est): 152.8K **Privately Held**
SIC: 6799 Investors
PA: Oaktree Capital Group Holdings, L.P.
333 S Grand Ave Fl 28
Los Angeles CA 90071
-

(P-12255)
OCM REAL ESTATE OPPORTUNITIES
333 S Grand Ave Fl 28, Los Angeles
(90071-1504)
PHONE..............................213 830-6300
EMP: 1023 EST: 2014
SALES (est): 246.9K **Privately Held**
SIC: 6799 Investors
PA: Oaktree Capital Group Holdings, L.P.
333 S Grand Ave Fl 28
Los Angeles CA 90071
-

(P-12256)
OTTS ASIA
Also Called: Newshire Investment
10015 Baring Cross St, Los Angeles
(90044-4511)
PHONE..............................562 259-3447
Asia Otts, *Owner*
Devon Moorer, *Owner*
EMP: 80
SALES (est): 1.5MM **Privately Held**
SIC: 6799 Investors

(P-12257)
P-WAVE HOLDINGS LLC
10877 Wilshire Blvd, Los Angeles
(90024-4341)
PHONE..............................310 209-3010
Alec Gores,
EMP: 2179 EST: 2012

SALES (est): 38.1MM **Privately Held**
SIC: 6799 Investors

(P-12258)
PEDESTAL CAPITAL II LLC
13111 Sycamore Dr, Norwalk (90650-8339)
PHONE..............................562 863-5555
Rui Zhao, *Principal*
Adam Stanchina, *Principal*
EMP: 80
SALES (est): 3.5MM **Privately Held**
SIC: 6799 Investors

(P-12259)
PLUG & PLAY LLC
Also Called: Plugandplaytechcenter.com
440 N Wolfe Rd, Sunnyvale (94085-3869)
PHONE..............................408 524-1400
Saeed Amidi, *CEO*
Alireza Masrour, *Managing Prtnr*
Candace Widdoes, *COO*
Charles Steinberg, *Bd of Directors*
Syed Azhar, *Vice Pres*
EMP: 150
SQ FT: 180,000
SALES: 20MM **Privately Held**
SIC: 6799 7389 Investors; office facilities
& secretarial service rental

(P-12260)
POULIN CORPORATION (PA)
Also Called: Liberty Ambulance
111 S Mahan St, Ridgecrest (93555-5430)
PHONE..............................760 375-6531
Cheryl Poulin, *President*
Brandalyn Sonnenberg, *Corp Secy*
EMP: 75
SALES (est): 7.6MM **Privately Held**
SIC: 6799 Real estate investors, except
property operators

(P-12261)
PYRAMID PEAK CORPORATION
450 Nwport Ctr Dr Ste 650, Newport Beach
(92660)
PHONE..............................949 769-8600
Cindy Ragsdale, *President*
Cindy Brown, *COO*
Lisa Jan, *Accountant*
EMP: 70
SALES (est): 7.9MM **Privately Held**
SIC: 6799 Investors

(P-12262)
R H O CAPITAL PARTNERS INC
525 University Ave # 1350, Palo Alto
(94301-1934)
PHONE..............................650 463-0300
Mark Leschley, *Principal*
Joshua Ruch, *Partner*
Peter Kalkanis, *CFO*
EMP: 50
SALES (est): 3.3MM **Privately Held**
SIC: 6799 Venture capital companies

(P-12263)
ROLL PROPERTIES INTL INC
Also Called: Paramout Farms
13646 Highway 33, Lost Hills (93249-9719)
PHONE..............................661 797-6500
Bill Bowers, *Manager*
Jay Menon, *Vice Pres*
Alycia Morris, *Executive Asst*
Russell Pair, *Engineer*
Silvana Hernandez, *Human Res Mgr*
EMP: 111
SALES (corp-wide): 55.2MM **Privately
Held**
WEB: www.roll.com
SIC: 6799 Real estate investors, except
property operators
PA: Roll Properties International, Inc.
11444 W Olympic Blvd # 10
Los Angeles CA 90064
310 966-5700

(P-12264)
RUSTIC CANYON GROUP LLC
Also Called: Rustic Canyon Partners
201 Santa Monica Blvd # 500, Santa Mon-
ica (90401-2213)
PHONE..............................310 998-8000
Nate Redmond, *Mng Member*
John Babcock,
Lee Bailey,
Michael Kim,

Renee Labran,
EMP: 75
SALES (est): 6.5MM **Privately Held**
WEB: www.rusticanyon.com
SIC: 6799 Venture capital companies

(P-12265)
SBE HOTEL GROUP LLC
8000 Beverly Blvd, Los Angeles
(90048-4504)
PHONE..............................323 655-8000
Sam Nazarian,
EMP: 65
SQ FT: 11,000
SALES (est): 4.5MM **Privately Held**
WEB: www.sbehotelgroup.com
SIC: 6799 Venture capital companies
HQ: Sbe Entertainment Group, Llc
2535 Las Vegas Blvd S
Los Angeles CA 90036
323 655-8000

(P-12266)
SEQUOIA CAPITAL OPERATIONS LLC
2800 Sand Hill Rd Ste 100, Menlo Park
(94025-7079)
PHONE..............................650 854-3927
Donald Valentine, *General Ptnr*
Doug Leone, *General Ptnr*
Douglas Leone, *General Ptnr*
Tom McMurray, *General Ptnr*
Bryan Schreier, *General Ptnr*
EMP: 89
SQ FT: 6,000
SALES (est): 46.7MM **Privately Held**
WEB: www.sequoiacap.com
SIC: 6799 Venture capital companies

(P-12267)
SITUS HOLDINGS LLC
101 Montgomery St # 2250, San Francisco
(94104-4161)
PHONE..............................415 374-2820
Steven J Powel, *CEO*
George Wisniewski, *Director*
EMP: 349
SALES (corp-wide): 72.2MM **Privately
Held**
SIC: 6799 6162 Investment clubs; bond &
mortgage companies
PA: Situs Holdings, Llc
5065 Westheimer Rd # 700
Houston TX 77056
713 328-4400

(P-12268)
STEELPOINT CAPITAL PARTNERS LP
2081 Faraday Ave, Carlsbad (92008-7230)
PHONE..............................858 764-8700
James A Caccavo, *General Ptnr*
Adam Dell, *General Ptnr*
Scott Tierney, *General Ptnr*
Jim Sullivan, *Partner*
Timothy Broadhead, *CFO*
EMP: 80
SALES (est): 8MM
SALES (corp-wide): 26.6MM **Privately
Held**
SIC: 6799 Investors
PA: Moore Capital Management, Lp
11 Times Sq Ste 36
New York NY 10036
212 782-7000

(P-12269)
SUNSTONE HOTEL INVESTORS LLC (PA)
120 Vantis Dr Ste 350, Aliso Viejo
(92656-2686)
PHONE..............................949 330-4000
Ken Cruse, *CEO*
Robert A Alter, *Ch of Bd*
Jon D Kline, *President*
David Sloan, *President*
Bryan Giglia, *CFO*
EMP: 51
SALES (est): 58.3MM **Privately Held**
WEB: www.sunstonehotels.com
SIC: 6799 7011 Real estate investors, ex-
cept property operators; hotels & motels

(P-12270)
TANO CAPITAL LLC
1 Franklin Pkwy, San Mateo (94403-1906)
PHONE..................................650 212-0330
Chuck Johnson, *Founder*
Candace Lyche, *Officer*
Peter Dabrowski, *Managing Dir*
Frank Liu, *Managing Dir*
Antoinette Vitug, *Technology*
EMP: 50
SALES (est): 4.8MM **Privately Held**
SIC: 6799 Investors

(P-12271)
TC PROPERTY MGT A CALIFORNI
1224 Cottonwood St Ofc, Woodland
(95695-4349)
PHONE..................................530 666-5799
Ted Caldwell, *President*
EMP: 80 EST: 1982
SALES (est): 4.1MM **Privately Held**
SIC: 6799 6531 Real estate investors, except property operators; real estate managers

(P-12272)
TCMI INC (PA)
Also Called: Technology Crossover Ventures
250 Middlefield Rd, Menlo Park
(94025-3560)
PHONE..................................650 614-8200
Nari Ansari, *Principal*
Christopher Marshall, *General Ptnr*
Jay Hoag, *President*
Richard Kimball, *CEO*
John Delfino, *Vice Pres*
EMP: 50 EST: 1995
SQ FT: 2,700
SALES (est): 24.4MM **Privately Held**
WEB: www.tcv.com
SIC: 6799 Venture capital companies

(P-12273)
TENNENBAUM CAPITL PARTNERS LLC (HQ)
Also Called: T C P
2951 28th St Ste 1000, Santa Monica
(90405-2993)
PHONE..................................310 566-1000
Lee Landrum, *Managing Prtnr*
Mark Holdsworth, *Managing Prtnr*
Michael Leitner, *Managing Prtnr*
Howard Levkowitz, *Managing Prtnr*
Philip Tseng, *Managing Prtnr*
EMP: 62
SQ FT: 15,850
SALES (est): 175.9MM **Publicly Held**
SIC: 6799 Venture capital companies

(P-12274)
TERA INVESTMENTS INC
Also Called: Chevron
4810 Chiles Rd, Davis (95618-4440)
PHONE..................................530 753-7129
Darshan Mundy, *CEO*
Charanjit Mundy, *Corp Secy*
James Mundy, *Vice Pres*
EMP: 50
SQ FT: 4,000
SALES: 21MM **Privately Held**
SIC: 6799 Investors

(P-12275)
THOMA BRAVO LLC
600 Montgomery St Fl 32, San Francisco
(94111-2807)
PHONE..................................415 263-3660
Seth Boro, *Branch Mgr*
Brian Jaffee, *Vice Pres*
EMP: 500 **Privately Held**
SIC: 6799 Venture capital companies
PA: Thoma Bravo, Llc
　　150 N Riverside Plz # 2800
　　Chicago IL 60606

(P-12276)
TRIDENT CAPITAL INC (PA)
400 S El Camino Real # 300, San Mateo
(94402-1728)
PHONE..................................650 289-4400
Donald Dixon, *President*
Linc Rembrandt, *Partner*
Lisa Lee, *CFO*

Taimur Shaikh, *Vice Pres*
Matthew Chagan, *Principal*
EMP: 124
SALES (est): 16.8MM **Privately Held**
WEB: www.tridentcap.com
SIC: 6799 Venture capital companies

(P-12277)
TRUE INVESTMENTS LLC
2260 University Dr, Newport Beach
(92660-3319)
PHONE..................................949 258-9720
Alan True, *CEO*
Eric Kim, *Senior VP*
Kent Ahlering, *Vice Pres*
Ted Farry, *Vice Pres*
Peter Nelson, *Executive*
EMP: 50
SALES (est): 4MM **Privately Held**
SIC: 6799 7372 Investors; application computer software

(P-12278)
ULTIMATE CREATIONS LLC
516 W Shaw Ave Ste 200, Fresno
(93704-2515)
PHONE..................................559 221-4936
Duwayne Turner,
EMP: 51
SALES (est): 1.2MM **Privately Held**
SIC: 6799 8742 Investors; real estate consultant

(P-12279)
VANTAGEPOINT MANAGEMENT INC (PA)
Also Called: Vantagepoint Capital Partners
1111 Bayhill Dr Ste 220, San Bruno
(94066-3198)
PHONE..................................650 866-3100
Alan E Salzman, *CEO*
Harold Friedman, *CFO*
Annette Bianchi, *Managing Dir*
Stephan Dolezalek, *Managing Dir*
Richard Harroch, *Managing Dir*
EMP: 65
SQ FT: 21,166
SALES (est): 14.4MM **Privately Held**
SIC: 6799 Venture capital companies

(P-12280)
WEDGEWOOD INC (PA)
2015 Manhattan Beach Blvd # 100, Redondo Beach (90278-1226)
PHONE..................................310 640-3070
Gregory L Geiser, *CEO*
Steve Meilicke, *CFO*
Magally Espinoza, *Officer*
Bob Morse, *Vice Pres*
David Wehrly, *Vice Pres*
EMP: 75
SQ FT: 3,200
SALES (est): 15.8MM **Privately Held**
SIC: 6799 Real estate investors, except property operators

(P-12281)
WESTAR CAPITAL ASSOC II LLC
949 S Coast Dr, Costa Mesa (92626-7737)
PHONE..................................714 481-5160
George Argyros, *Branch Mgr*
Sharon Bujacich, *Auditor*
John Clark, *VP Human Res*
EMP: 1184
SALES (corp-wide): 110.4MM **Privately Held**
SIC: 6799 Investors
PA: Westar Capital Associates Ii, Llc
　　949 S Coast Dr Ste 170
　　Costa Mesa CA 92626
　　714 481-5160

(P-12282)
WESTCORE DELTA LLC
Also Called: Westcore Croydon
4350 La Jolla Village Dr # 900, San Diego
(92122-1246)
P.O. Box 844405, Los Angeles (90084-4405)
PHONE..................................858 625-4100
Don Ankeny, *CEO*
Marc Brutten, *Ch of Bd*
EMP: 60
SQ FT: 14,000

SALES (est): 6MM **Privately Held**
SIC: 6799 Real estate investors, except property operators

(P-12283)
WESTPORT CAPITAL PARTNERS LLC
2121 Rosecrans Ave # 4325, El Segundo
(90245-4744)
PHONE..................................310 294-1234
Russel S Bernard, *Branch Mgr*
Erin Kerr, *Vice Pres*
Mathieu Durand, *Analyst*
Marian George, *Assistant VP*
EMP: 53 **Privately Held**
SIC: 6799 Investors
PA: Westport Capital Partners Llc
　　40 Danbury Rd
　　Wilton CT 06897

(P-12284)
WINDJMMER CAPITL INVESTORS LLC (PA)
610 Newport Center Dr, Newport Beach
(92660-6419)
PHONE..................................949 706-9989
Robert Bartholomew, *Mng Member*
Tony Sugalski, *Partner*
Jeff Dunnigan, *CFO*
Rob Quandt, *Managing Dir*
Helen Ruth, *Opers Staff*
EMP: 51
SALES (est): 4.9MM **Privately Held**
SIC: 6799 Investors

(P-12285)
WNC HOUSING LP
17782 Sky Park Cir, Irvine (92614-6404)
PHONE..................................714 662-5565
Willfred Cooper, *President*
Tom Riha, *CFO*
EMP: 50
SALES (est): 4.4MM **Privately Held**
SIC: 6799 Real estate investors, except property operators

7011 Hotels, Motels & Tourist Courts

(P-12286)
1000 AGUAJITO OP CO LLC
Also Called: Hilton Garden Inn Monterey
1000 Aguajito Rd, Monterey (93940-4801)
PHONE..................................831 373-6141
Jayson Zimmer, *General Mgr*
EMP: 77
SALES (est): 3.5MM **Privately Held**
SIC: 7011 Hotels

(P-12287)
120 SOUTH LOS ANGELES STREET H
Also Called: Kyoto Grand Hotel
120 S Los Angeles St, Los Angeles
(90012-3724)
PHONE..................................213 629-1200
Shannon King,
Joseph Kuhn,
EMP: 99
SALES (est): 4.2MM **Privately Held**
SIC: 7011 Hotels & motels

(P-12288)
1260 BB PROPERTY LLC
Also Called: Four Ssons Rsort Santa Barbara
1260 Channel Dr, Santa Barbara
(93108-2805)
PHONE..................................805 969-2261
Isadore Sharp, *Chairman*
J Allen Smith, *President*
Christine Judd, *Chief Mktg Ofcr*
Karen Earp, *General Mgr*
Graham Crossley, *Finance Dir*
EMP: 500
SALES (est): 36.9MM **Privately Held**
SIC: 7011 Hotels

(P-12289)
15TH & L INVESTORS LLC
1121 15th St, Sacramento (95814-4011)
PHONE..................................916 267-6805
Anthony R Giannoni, *Mng Member*

Shelly Moranville, *Mng Member*
EMP: 55
SALES (est): 2.8MM **Privately Held**
SIC: 7011 Hotel, franchised

(P-12290)
1835 COLUMBIA STREET LP
Also Called: Porto Vista Hotel
1835 Columbia St, San Diego
(92101-2505)
PHONE..................................619 564-3993
Moe Siry,
Mary Navarro, *Managing Dir*
Arnold Ming, *Finance*
Dave Threet, *Sales Staff*
Tom McMahan, *Director*
EMP: 60 EST: 2008
SALES (est): 4.2MM **Privately Held**
SIC: 7011 Hotels

(P-12291)
417 STOCKTON ST LLC
1180 S Beverly Dr Ste 508, Los Angeles
(90035-1157)
PHONE..................................323 327-9656
Jim Ciki, *Finance*
EMP: 60
SALES (est): 429.7K **Privately Held**
SIC: 7011 Hotels & motels

(P-12292)
425 NORTH POINT STREET LLC
Also Called: Tuscan Inn
101 California St Ste 950, San Francisco
(94111-5826)
PHONE..................................800 648-4626
Jan Misch,
EMP: 99
SALES (est): 5.6MM **Privately Held**
SIC: 7011 Hotels

(P-12293)
4290 EL CAMINO PROPERTIES LP
Also Called: Cabana Hotel
4290 El Camino Real, Palo Alto
(94306-4404)
PHONE..................................650 857-0787
Bhupendra B Patel, *Owner*
EMP: 146
SALES (est): 5.2MM **Privately Held**
SIC: 7011 Hotels

(P-12294)
48123 CA INVESTORS LLC
Also Called: Ventana Inn & Spa
48123 Highway 1, Big Sur (93920-9538)
PHONE..................................831 667-2331
Kent L Colwell, *Mng Member*
John D Benzie,
Shane Prince, *Director*
EMP: 152
SALES (est): 11.6MM **Privately Held**
WEB: www.ventanainn.com
SIC: 7011 5812 Bed & breakfast inn; eating places

(P-12295)
495 GEARY LLC
Also Called: Clift Hotels
495 Geary St, San Francisco (94102-1222)
PHONE..................................415 775-4700
Mary Coller, *Controller*
EMP: 220
SALES (est): 2MM **Privately Held**
SIC: 7011 Hotels & motels
HQ: Morgans Hotel Group Co. Llc
　　475 10th Ave Fl 11
　　New York NY 10018
　　212 277-4100

(P-12296)
51ST ST & 8TH AVE CORP
Also Called: Loews Coronado Bay Resort
4000 Coronado Bay Rd, Coronado
(92118-3290)
PHONE..................................619 424-4000
Johnathan M Tish, *Principal*
Barbara Vale, *Executive*
Kim Dopulos, *Associate Dir*
Roy Craft, *Marketing Staff*
Brandon Walton, *Sales Staff*
EMP: 550
SALES (est): 37.1MM **Privately Held**
SIC: 7011 Hotels

(P-12297)
550 FLOWER ST OPERATIONS LLC
Also Called: Standard Hotel, The
550 S Flower St, Los Angeles
(90071-2501)
PHONE.................................213 892-8080
Andre Balaz,
George Wu, *Asst Controller*
Ian Innocent, *Purch Mgr*
Michel Heredia, *Sales Mgr*
Jenni Boelkens, *Director*
EMP: 200
SQ FT: 172,197
SALES (est): 6MM **Privately Held**
WEB: www.standardhotel.com
SIC: 7011 5813 5812 Hotels; drinking places; eating places

(P-12298)
5TH AVENUE PARTNERS LLC
1047 5th Ave, San Diego (92101-5101)
PHONE.................................619 515-3000
Stephen Rebeil,
EMP: 300
SALES (est): 3.4MM **Privately Held**
SIC: 7011 Hotels

(P-12299)
6417 SELMA HOTEL LLC
Also Called: DREAM HOLLYWOOD
6417 Selma Ave, Los Angeles
(90028-7310)
PHONE.................................323 844-6417
Richard Heyman, *Mng Member*
EMP: 250
SALES: 6.8MM **Privately Held**
SIC: 7011 Hotels

(P-12300)
8110 AERO HOLDING LLC
Also Called: Sheraton
8110 Aero Dr, San Diego (92123-1715)
PHONE.................................858 277-8888
Lucy Burni, *Mng Member*
Nabih Geha, *Principal*
EMP: 210
SALES (est): 14.5MM **Privately Held**
WEB: www.sheratonfourpointshotel.com
SIC: 7011 5813 5812 Hotels & motels; drinking places; eating places

(P-12301)
901 WEST OLYMPIC BLVD LP
Also Called: Courtyard & Residence Inn La
901 W Olympic Blvd, Los Angeles
(90015-1327)
PHONE.................................347 992-5707
Greg Steinhauer, *Partner*
Homer Williams, *Partner*
EMP: 110
SQ FT: 286,000
SALES: 11.5MM **Privately Held**
SIC: 7011 Hotels

(P-12302)
A J ESPRIT
Also Called: Comfort Inn
5102 N Harbor Dr, San Diego
(92106-2356)
PHONE.................................619 223-8171
A J Esprit, *Manager*
A Esprit, *Human Res Dir*
EMP: 50
SALES (est): 1.2MM **Privately Held**
WEB: www.comfortinnattheharbor.com
SIC: 7011 Hotel, franchised

(P-12303)
ACCOR BUS & LEISURE N AMER LLC
Also Called: Hotel Sofitel
223 Twin Dolphin Dr, Redwood City
(94065-1414)
PHONE.................................650 598-9000
John Hutar, *Manager*
Gabriela Salazar, *Regional Mgr*
Rex Umbay, *Engineer*
Philippe Van Der Borght, *Finance Dir*
EMP: 200
SALES (corp-wide): 1B **Privately Held**
SIC: 7011 Hotels

HQ: Accor Business And Leisure North America, Llc
3470 Nw 82nd Ave Ste 600
Doral FL 33122

(P-12304)
ACCOR CORP
Also Called: Sofitel Los Angeles
8555 Beverly Blvd, Los Angeles
(90048-3303)
PHONE.................................310 278-5444
Gunter Zweimuller, *Manager*
Alwyn Quadras, *Info Tech Mgr*
Sandra Daddario, *Facilities Dir*
Bastien Chapel, *Director*
Thomas Kerschbaumer, *Director*
EMP: 200
SQ FT: 380,000
SALES (est): 7.9MM
SALES (corp-wide): 1B **Privately Held**
SIC: 7011 5812 Hotels; eating places
PA: Accor
82 Rue Henry Farman
Issy Les Moulineaux 92130
146 429-193

(P-12305)
ACCOR SERVICES US LLC
101 Wilshire Blvd, Santa Monica
(90401-1106)
PHONE.................................310 319-3122
Karl Buchta, *General Mgr*
Denise Martin, *Purchasing*
EMP: 275
SALES (corp-wide): 1B **Privately Held**
SIC: 7011 Hotels
HQ: Accor Services Us Llc
950 Mason St
San Francisco CA 94108
415 772-5000

(P-12306)
ACCOR SERVICES US LLC (DH)
Also Called: Fairmont Hotel
950 Mason St, San Francisco
(94108-6000)
PHONE.................................415 772-5000
April Schizley, *Manager*
Richard Davis, *Engineer*
Billy Lafferty, *Engineer*
Kevin Simmons, *Safety Dir*
Jeff Doane, *Sales Staff*
EMP: 1000
SQ FT: 2,100
SALES: 173.3MM
SALES (corp-wide): 1B **Privately Held**
SIC: 7011 Hotels
HQ: Fairmont Hotels & Resorts Inc
155 Wellington St W Suite 3300
Toronto ON M5V 0
416 874-2600

(P-12307)
AGUA CLNTE BAND CHILLA INDIANS
Also Called: Agua Caliente Casino & Resort
32250 Bob Hope Dr, Rancho Mirage
(92270-2704)
PHONE.................................760 321-2000
Ken Kettler, *Branch Mgr*
Frank Charolla, *CFO*
Laura Aviles, *Executive Asst*
David McCarthy, *Business Anlyst*
Beth Pasos, *Project Mgr*
EMP: 1000
SALES (corp-wide): 200.2MM **Privately Held**
WEB: www.hotwatercasino.com
SIC: 7011 Casino hotel
PA: Agua Caliente Band Of Cahuilla Indians
5401 Dinah Shore Dr
Palm Springs CA 92264
760 699-6800

(P-12308)
AGUA CLNTE BAND CHILLA INDIANS
Also Called: Spa Resort Casino
401 E Amado Rd, Palm Springs
(92262-6403)
PHONE.................................800 854-1279
Ramona Grinager, *Principal*
Savannah Cook, *Manager*
EMP: 1000

SALES (corp-wide): 200.2MM **Privately Held**
SIC: 7011 7991 Casino hotel; spas
PA: Agua Caliente Band Of Cahuilla Indians
5401 Dinah Shore Dr
Palm Springs CA 92264
760 699-6800

(P-12309)
AIRPORT CENTURY INN
Also Called: Travelodge
5547 W Century Blvd, Los Angeles
(90045-5913)
PHONE.................................310 649-4000
Lance Libscomb, *General Mgr*
Lance Lipscomb,
EMP: 59
SQ FT: 60,000
SALES (est): 4MM **Privately Held**
WEB: www.travelodgelax.com
SIC: 7011 6519 Inns; real property lessors

(P-12310)
AL ANWA USA INCORPORATED
Also Called: Marina International Hotel
4200 Admiralty Way, Marina Del Rey
(90292-5422)
PHONE.................................310 301-2000
Mohammed Khan, *Manager*
EMP: 120
SALES (corp-wide): 6MM **Privately Held**
WEB: www.marinaintlhotel.com
SIC: 7011 Hotels
PA: Al Anwa Usa Incorporated
2200 Nw 50th St Ste 240
Oklahoma City OK

(P-12311)
ALADDIN SONORA MOTOR INN
14260 Mono Way, Sonora (95370-8654)
PHONE.................................209 533-4971
David E Kalash, *Owner*
EMP: 50
SALES (est): 1.1MM **Privately Held**
WEB: www.aladdininn.com
SIC: 7011 5812 Motor inn; eating places

(P-12312)
ALBION RIVER INN INCORPORATED
3790 N Highway 1, Albion (95410-9781)
P.O. Box 100 (95410-0100)
PHONE.................................707 937-1919
Peter Wells, *President*
Flurry Healy, *Vice Pres*
EMP: 65
SQ FT: 15,000
SALES (est): 3.9MM **Privately Held**
WEB: www.albionriverinn.com
SIC: 7011 Resort hotel

(P-12313)
ALLIANCE RVRSIDE HSPTALITY LLC
Also Called: Courtyard By Mrriott Riverside
21520 Yorba Linda Blvd, Yorba Linda
(92887-3762)
PHONE.................................949 229-3168
Chiangsun Wang, *Mng Member*
EMP: 50
SALES (est): 3.8MM **Privately Held**
SIC: 7011 Resort hotel, franchised

(P-12314)
ALOFT ONTARIO-RANCHO CUCAMONGA
Also Called: Ihr Grnbuck Rncho Ccmnga Ventr
10480 4th St, Rancho Cucamonga
(91730-5893)
PHONE.................................909 484-2018
Cristina Riveroll, *Owner*
Yani Duran, *Director*
EMP: 55
SALES (est): 3MM **Privately Held**
SIC: 7011 Hotels

(P-12315)
ALPINE MEADOWS SKI AREA
Also Called: Alpine Meadows Ski Resort
2600 Alpine Meadows Rd, Alpine Meadows
(96146-9854)
PHONE.................................530 583-4232

John Cumming, *President*
Rick D Vaux, *CFO*
Nick Badami, *Admin Sec*
Sue Briggs, *Sales Staff*
EMP: 50 **EST:** 1959
SQ FT: 30,000
SALES (est): 4.5MM **Privately Held**
WEB: www.skialpine.com
SIC: 7011 Ski lodge; resort hotel
HQ: The Squaw Valley Development Company
1960 Squaw Valley Rd
Olympic Valley CA 96146
530 452-6985

(P-12316)
AMERICAN PROPERTY MANAGEMENT
Also Called: Pleasanton Hilton Hotel
7050 Johnson Dr, Pleasanton
(94588-3328)
PHONE.................................925 463-8000
Han-Ching Lin, *President*
Hui-Ying Chou, *Vice Pres*
Ron Raju, *Controller*
EMP: 190
SQ FT: 191,112
SALES (est): 10.2MM **Privately Held**
SIC: 7011 5813 5812 Hotels; drinking places; eating places

(P-12317)
AMERICAN PRPRTY-MNAGEMENT CORP
Also Called: U. S. Grant Hotel
326 Broadway, San Diego (92101-4812)
PHONE.................................619 232-3121
John Gallegon, *Manager*
EMP: 200
SALES (corp-wide): 172.2MM **Privately Held**
WEB: www.americanpropertymanagement-corp.com
SIC: 7011 Hotels & motels
PA: American Property-Management Corporation
8910 University Center Ln # 100
San Diego CA 92122
858 964-5500

(P-12318)
AMGREEN-KARENA HT PARTNR LTD (PA)
Also Called: Radisson Inn
5743 Corsa Ave Ste 200, Westlake Village
(91362-7312)
PHONE.................................818 707-9494
Jerald Greenstein, *Partner*
Joe Amorosa, *Partner*
EMP: 93
SALES (est): 3.6MM **Privately Held**
SIC: 7011 Hotels & motels

(P-12319)
AMSTAR/DAVIDSON ROBLES LLC
Also Called: Hilton Pasadena
168 S Los Robles Ave, Pasadena
(91101-2430)
PHONE.................................626 577-1000
Larry Mills,
Jenny Quintero, *Human Resources*
EMP: 99
SQ FT: 199,278
SALES (est): 6.8MM **Privately Held**
SIC: 7011 Hotels

(P-12320)
ANAHEIM CA LLC
Also Called: Doubltree Ht Anhim-Orange Cnty
100 The City Dr S, Orange (92868-3204)
PHONE.................................714 634-4500
Denise Pflum, *Manager*
EMP: 65
SALES (est): 5.6MM **Privately Held**
SIC: 7011 Hotels

(P-12321)
ANAHEIM HOTEL LLC
Also Called: Sheraton Pk Ht At Anheim Rsort
1855 S Harbor Blvd, Anaheim
(92802-3509)
PHONE.................................714 750-1811
Russ Cox, *Manager*
EMP: 200

(PA)=Parent Co (HQ)=Headquarters (DH)=Div Headquarters
✪ = New Business established in last 2 years

SALES (est): 2.7MM **Privately Held**
SIC: 7011 Hotels & motels
PA: Anaheim Hotel, Llc
575 E Parkcntr Blvd 500
Boise ID 83706

(P-12322)
ANAHEIM PARK HOTEL
Also Called: Wyndham Hotels & Resorts
222 W Houston Ave, Fullerton
(92832-3453)
PHONE..................714 992-1700
Fred Menoufi, *Partner*
Abdul El Mekligiange, *General Mgr*
EMP: 101
SQ FT: 174,123
SALES (est): 1.4MM **Privately Held**
SIC: 7011 YWCA/YWHA hotel; hotels

(P-12323)
ANAHEIM PARK INN AND CAMELOT
1520 S Harbor Blvd, Anaheim
(92802-2312)
PHONE..................714 635-7275
Suren Badalian, *Owner*
EMP: 75
SALES (est): 1.7MM **Privately Held**
WEB: www.bei-hotels.com
SIC: 7011 Motels

(P-12324)
ANAHEIM PLAZA HOTEL INC
Also Called: Anaheim Plaza Hotel & Suites
1700 S Harbor Blvd, Anaheim
(92802-2316)
PHONE..................714 772-5900
Saroj Patel, *President*
Rajni Patel, *Vice Pres*
Ligia Jaya, *Executive*
Cindy Treiber, *Director*
EMP: 150
SQ FT: 5,600
SALES (est): 4.5MM **Privately Held**
WEB: www.anaheimplazahotel.com
SIC: 7011 5812 5813 Motels; eating places; drinking places

(P-12325)
ANDERSEN HOTELS INC
Also Called: Hotel Laguna
92 Argonaut Ste 150, Aliso Viejo
(92656-4130)
PHONE..................949 494-1151
Claes Andersen, *President*
Georgia Andersen, *Vice Pres*
Stefan Andersen, *General Mgr*
EMP: 80
SQ FT: 40,000
SALES (est): 4.5MM **Privately Held**
WEB: www.hotellaguna.com
SIC: 7011 5812 5813 Resort hotel; American restaurant; bar (drinking places)

(P-12326)
APIC HOTELS GROUP LLC (HQ)
Also Called: Haiyi Hotels Worldwide
5 Thomas Mellon Cir # 305, San Francisco
(94134-2501)
PHONE..................415 692-1502
Jennifer Zhang,
Wilson Chen,
EMP: 200
SQ FT: 100,000
SALES (est): 1.2MM **Privately Held**
SIC: 7011 Resort hotel; resort hotel, franchised

(P-12327)
APPLE EIGHT HOSPITALITY MGT INC
Also Called: Courtyard Cypress
5865 Katella Ave, Cypress (90630-5008)
PHONE..................714 827-1010
Gary Liss, *Branch Mgr*
EMP: 65 **Privately Held**
WEB: www.dimdev.com
SIC: 7011 Hotels
HQ: Apple Eight Hospitality Management, Inc.
814 E Main St
Richmond VA 23219

(P-12328)
APPLE HOSPITALITY REIT INC
Also Called: Hilton Garden Inn Sacramento
2540 Venture Oaks Way, Sacramento
(95833-3200)
PHONE..................916 568-5400
Jeff Irving, *General Mgr*
EMP: 55 EST: 2007
SALES (est): 612.9K **Privately Held**
SIC: 7011 Hotels

(P-12329)
APPLE INNS INC
Also Called: Marina Inn
68 Monarch Bay Dr, San Leandro
(94577-6427)
PHONE..................510 895-1311
Audrey Velasquez, *Branch Mgr*
Peter Schultz, *President*
David Miller, *Vice Pres*
Janise Dawson, *Sales Staff*
EMP: 50
SALES (est): 2.9MM **Privately Held**
WEB: www.sanleandromarinainn.com
SIC: 7011 Motels

(P-12330)
APPLE NINE HOSPITALITY MGT
Also Called: Courtyard San Diego Central
8651 Spectrum Center Blvd, San Diego
(92123-1489)
PHONE..................858 573-0700
Matthew Spencer, *General Mgr*
David Buckley, *President*
Alex Wiley, *COO*
EMP: 87
SALES (est): 1.8MM **Privately Held**
SIC: 7011 Hotel, franchised

(P-12331)
ARAMARK SERVICES INC
800 Asilomar Blvd, Pacific Grove
(93950-3704)
P.O. Box 537 (93950-0537)
PHONE..................831 372-8016
Enos Esquivel, *Director*
Clement Ojugo, *Technology*
EMP: 210 **Publicly Held**
SIC: 7011 Hotels
HQ: Aramark Services, Inc.
1101 Market St Ste 45
Philadelphia PA 19107
215 238-3000

(P-12332)
ARETE HOTELS LLC
2229 Den Helder Dr, Modesto
(95356-0729)
PHONE..................209 602-7952
Kimberly Ali, *CEO*
Heather Houser, *Accountant*
EMP: 74
SALES (est): 280.3K **Privately Held**
SIC: 7011 Resort hotel

(P-12333)
ARGONAUT HOTEL
495 Jefferson St, San Francisco
(94109-1314)
PHONE..................415 563-0800
Micheal Ditatie, *CEO*
EMP: 175
SALES (est): 6.7MM **Privately Held**
SIC: 7011 Resort hotel; hotels

(P-12334)
ART PICCADILLY SHAW LLC (PA)
Also Called: Piccadilly Inn Shaw
2305 W Shaw Ave, Fresno (93711-3411)
PHONE..................559 348-5520
Ronald F Akin, *Manager*
EMP: 300
SALES (est): 6.8MM **Privately Held**
SIC: 7011 Hotels

(P-12335)
ART PICCADILLY SHAW LLC
Also Called: Piccadilly Inn Airport
5115 E Mckinley Ave, Fresno (93727-2033)
PHONE..................559 375-7760
Kathy Bell, *Branch Mgr*
EMP: 100

SALES (corp-wide): 6.8MM **Privately Held**
SIC: 7011 5813 5812 Hotels; drinking places; eating places
PA: Art Piccadilly Shaw Llc
2305 W Shaw Ave
Fresno CA 93711
559 348-5520

(P-12336)
ART PICCADILLY SHAW LLC
Piccadilly Inn-University
4961 N Cedar Ave, Fresno (93726-1062)
PHONE..................559 224-4200
Theresa Cross, *Branch Mgr*
EMP: 120
SALES (corp-wide): 6.8MM **Privately Held**
SIC: 7011 Motels
PA: Art Piccadilly Shaw Llc
2305 W Shaw Ave
Fresno CA 93711
559 348-5520

(P-12337)
ASCOT HOTEL LP
Also Called: Hotel Angeleno
170 N Church Ln, Los Angeles
(90049-2044)
PHONE..................310 476-6411
Mark Beccaria, *Partner*
EMP: 125 EST: 2008
SALES: 16.5MM **Privately Held**
SIC: 7011 Hotels

(P-12338)
ASHFORD TRS NICKEL LLC (PA)
Also Called: Walnut Creek Embassy Suites
1345 Treat Blvd, Walnut Creek
(94597-2173)
PHONE..................925 934-2500
Montgomery J Bennett,
EMP: 80
SALES (est): 4.4MM **Privately Held**
SIC: 7011 7389 Hotels; office facilities & secretarial service rental

(P-12339)
ATASCADERO HOTEL PARTNERS LLC
Also Called: Springhill Suites
900 El Camino Real, Atascadero
(93422-1424)
PHONE..................805 462-3500
Elizabeth Eberly, *Accounting Mgr*
EMP: 52
SALES (est): 251.7K **Privately Held**
SIC: 7011 Hotels & motels

(P-12340)
ATRIUM PLAZA LLC
Also Called: San Mateo Marriott
1770 S Amphlett Blvd, San Mateo
(94402-2708)
PHONE..................650 653-6000
Ron Anderhan,
Samantha Elgelda, *Office Mgr*
Kathy Nicholl, *Human Res Dir*
Sam Sattavorn, *Purch Dir*
Joy Garcia, *Director*
EMP: 208
SALES (est): 4.9MM **Privately Held**
SIC: 7011 Hotels

(P-12341)
AVIARA FSRC ASSOCIATES LIMITED
7100 Aviara Resort Dr, Carlsbad
(92011-4908)
PHONE..................760 603-6800
Robert Cima, *General Mgr*
Aviara Resort Club, *General Ptnr*
Hef IV LLC, *General Ptnr*
EMP: 1200 EST: 1995
SALES (est): 12.7MM
SALES (corp-wide): 51.3MM **Privately Held**
SIC: 7011 Resort hotel
PA: Aviara Resort Associates Limited Partnership, A California Limited Partnership
7100 Aviara Resort Dr
Carlsbad CA 92011
760 448-1234

(P-12342)
AVIARA RESORT ASSOCIATES (PA)
Also Called: Park Hyatt Aviara Resort
7100 Aviara Resort Dr, Carlsbad
(92011-4908)
PHONE..................760 448-1234
Maritz Wolff, *General Mgr*
Meredith Ferber, *Sales Staff*
EMP: 2100
SALES (est): 51.3MM **Privately Held**
SIC: 7011 Hotels

(P-12343)
AWH BURBANK HOTEL LLC
Also Called: Marriott Burbank
2500 N Hollywood Way, Burbank
(91505-1019)
PHONE..................813 843-6000
William Deforrest, *CEO*
Chad Cooley, *Vice Pres*
Russell Flicker, *Vice Pres*
Bernard Michael, *Vice Pres*
Jonathan Rosenfeld, *Vice Pres*
EMP: 176 EST: 2014
SALES (est): 7.6MM **Privately Held**
SIC: 7011 Hotels

(P-12344)
AYRES GROUP
Also Called: Ayres Hotel Manhattan Beach
14400 Hindry Ave, Hawthorne
(90250-6740)
PHONE..................310 220-6447
Ann Williams, *Manager*
EMP: 64
SQ FT: 85,082 **Privately Held**
SIC: 7011 Hotels
PA: Ayres Group
355 Bristol St
Costa Mesa CA 92626

(P-12345)
AYRES GROUP
Also Called: Ayres - Chino Hills
4785 Chino Hills Pkwy, Chino Hills
(91709-5849)
PHONE..................909 631-2922
Don Ayres III, *General Ptnr*
EMP: 61 **Privately Held**
SIC: 7011 Hotels
PA: Ayres Group
355 Bristol St
Costa Mesa CA 92626

(P-12346)
AYRES GROUP (PA)
355 Bristol St, Costa Mesa (92626-7922)
PHONE..................714 540-6060
Bruce F Ayres, *CEO*
EMP: 58
SALES (est): 61MM **Privately Held**
SIC: 7011 8741 1531 Hotels; management services; operative builders

(P-12347)
B H R OPERATIONS LLC
Also Called: Crown Plaza
777 Bellew Dr, Milpitas (95035-7900)
PHONE..................408 321-9500
Roy Escobar, *Mng Member*
Winnie Kwok, *General Mgr*
EMP: 100
SQ FT: 250,000
SALES (est): 1.8MM
SALES (corp-wide): 1.7B **Privately Held**
WEB: www.bristolhotels.com
SIC: 7011 Motel, franchised
HQ: Bristol Hotel & Resorts Inc.
3 Ravinia Dr Ste 100
Atlanta GA 30346

(P-12348)
B S A PARTNERS
Also Called: Residence Inn By Marriott
14419 Firestone Blvd, La Mirada
(90638-5912)
PHONE..................714 523-2800
Jim Gilbert, *General Mgr*
William Swank, *General Ptnr*
William E Swank Jr, *General Ptnr*
Kent Kittiwanich, *Human Res Mgr*
EMP: 80

SQ FT: 102,943
SALES (est): 3.4MM Privately Held
SIC: 7011 Hotels

(P-12349)
BADALIAN ENTERPRISES INC
Also Called: Park Inn
1540 S Harbor Blvd, Anaheim
(92802-2312)
PHONE..................714 635-4082
Ernest Badalian, President
Bonny Harutunian, Corp Secy
Greg Badalian, Vice Pres
Suren Badalian, Vice Pres
Patricia Coomb, Sales Staff
EMP: 90
SQ FT: 55,000
SALES (est): 6.1MM Privately Held
SIC: 7011 Hotels

(P-12350)
BALDWIN HOSPITALITY LLC
Also Called: Courtyard By Marriott
14635 Baldwin Ave, Baldwin Park (91706)
PHONE..................626 962-6000
Lina Mita, Branch Mgr
Kathy Vicario, Executive
Henry Zamora, General Mgr
EMP: 80
SQ FT: 148,187
SALES (corp-wide): 11MM Privately Held
SIC: 7011 Hotels & motels
PA: Baldwin Hospitality Llc
411 E Huntington Dr # 305
Arcadia CA 91006
626 446-2988

(P-12351)
BANEY CORPORATION
Also Called: Oxford Suites Chico
2035 Business Ln, Chico (95928-7628)
PHONE..................530 899-9090
Chris Coder, Manager
EMP: 52 Privately Held
WEB: www.oxfordsuites.com
SIC: 7011 Resort hotel; hotels
PA: Baney Corporation
475 Ne Bellevue Dr # 210
Bend OR 97701

(P-12352)
BARONA RESORT & CASINO
1932 Wildcat Canyon Rd, Lakeside
(92040-1553)
PHONE..................619 443-2300
Dean Allen, Senior VP
Nick Dillon, Exec VP
Troy Simpson, Exec VP
Linda Jordan, Senior VP
Michael Patterson, Vice Pres
EMP: 3500
SALES (est): 109.4MM Privately Held
WEB: www.barona.com
SIC: 7011 Resort hotel; casino hotel

(P-12353)
BARTELL HOTELS
Also Called: Humphreys Half Moon Inn
2303 Shelter Island Dr, San Diego
(92106-3109)
PHONE..................619 224-3411
Sergio Davies, Manager
EMP: 200
SALES (corp-wide): 61.5MM Privately
Held
WEB: www.holinnbayside.com
SIC: 7011 5812 5813 Motels; eating
places; cocktail lounge
PA: Bartell Hotels
4875 N Harbor Dr
San Diego CA 92106
619 224-1556

(P-12354)
BARTELL HOTELS
1710 W Mission Bay Dr, San Diego
(92109-7810)
PHONE..................619 222-6440
Kevin Konopasek, General Mgr
EMP: 200
SALES (corp-wide): 61.5MM Privately
Held
WEB: www.holinnbayside.com
SIC: 7011 4493 5812 Hotels; marinas;
eating places

PA: Bartell Hotels
4875 N Harbor Dr
San Diego CA 92106
619 224-1556

(P-12355)
BARTELL HOTELS
Also Called: Pacific Terrace
610 Diamond St, San Diego (92109-2444)
PHONE..................858 581-3500
Bob Kingery, Branch Mgr
EMP: 50
SALES (corp-wide): 61.5MM Privately
Held
SIC: 7011 Hotels
PA: Bartell Hotels
4875 N Harbor Dr
San Diego CA 92106
619 224-1556

(P-12356)
BARTELL HOTELS
Also Called: Best Western Island Palms
2051 Shelter Island Dr, San Diego
(92106-3105)
PHONE..................619 222-0561
Jim Finnegan, Manager
Andrea Davis, Sales Staff
EMP: 70
SQ FT: 56,500
SALES (corp-wide): 61.5MM Privately
Held
WEB: www.holinnbayside.com
SIC: 7011 Hotels
PA: Bartell Hotels
4875 N Harbor Dr
San Diego CA 92106
619 224-1556

(P-12357)
BARTELL HOTELS
Also Called: Sheraton
3299 Holiday Ct, La Jolla (92037-1830)
PHONE..................858 453-5500
Craig Reber, Owner
Desiree Ruiz, Manager
EMP: 81
SQ FT: 68,159
SALES (corp-wide): 61.5MM Privately
Held
WEB: www.holinnbayside.com
SIC: 7011 5812 Hotels; eating places
PA: Bartell Hotels
4875 N Harbor Dr
San Diego CA 92106
619 224-1556

(P-12358)
BASSLAKE LLC
39255 Marina Dr, Bass Lake (93604)
PHONE..................559 642-3121
Kyu Sun Choe, Principal
Sun Wha Choe, Principal
EMP: 99
SALES (est): 1MM Privately Held
SIC: 7011 Resort hotel

(P-12359)
**BAVARIAN LION COMPANY CAL
(PA)**
Also Called: Flamingo Resort Hotel
2777 4th St, Santa Rosa (95405-4795)
PHONE..................707 545-8530
Pierre Ehret, President
Janette Paule, Bookkeeper
Phil Krohn, Director
Lisa Parducci, Manager
David Sherman, Asst Mgr
EMP: 200 EST: 1976
SQ FT: 32,000
SALES (est): 16.9MM Privately Held
WEB: www.flamingohotel.com
SIC: 7011 7991 Resort hotel; health club

(P-12360)
**BAY CLUB HOTEL AND MARINA
A C**
Also Called: The Bay Club Hotel and Marina
2131 Shelter Island Dr, San Diego
(92106-3106)
PHONE..................619 224-8888
Frank Hope, Partner
Bob Collins, Partner
Chuck Hope, Partner
Ed Malone, Partner
Natalie Zaas, Sales Staff

EMP: 55
SQ FT: 200,000
SALES (est): 5.4MM Privately Held
WEB: www.bayclubhotel.com
SIC: 7011 6512 5812 5813 Resort hotel;
lessors of piers, docks, associated build-
ings & facilities; American restaurant; bars
& lounges

(P-12361)
BAYVIEW PROPERTIES INC
Also Called: Best Western
2600 Sand Dunes Dr, Monterey
(93940-3838)
PHONE..................831 655-7650
Allison Nord, Manager
EMP: 65
SALES (corp-wide): 5.9MM Privately
Held
WEB: www.montereybeachhotel.com
SIC: 7011 Hotels & motels
PA: Bayview Properties Inc
2600 Sand Dunes Dr
Monterey CA 93940
831 394-3321

(P-12362)
BAYVIEW PROPERTIES INC
Also Called: Carmel Mission Inn
3665 Rio Rd, Carmel (93923-8609)
PHONE..................831 624-1841
John Elford, Manager
EMP: 65
SQ FT: 40,000
SALES (corp-wide): 5.9MM Privately
Held
WEB: www.montereybeachhotel.com
SIC: 7011 Motel, franchised
PA: Bayview Properties Inc
2600 Sand Dunes Dr
Monterey CA 93940
831 394-3321

(P-12363)
BAYVIEW PROPERTIES INC (PA)
Also Called: Best Western, The Beach Resort
2600 Sand Dunes Dr, Monterey
(93940-3838)
PHONE..................831 394-3321
Theodore Richter, President
EMP: 99
SALES (est): 5.9MM Privately Held
WEB: www.montereybeachhotel.com
SIC: 7011 Hotels

(P-12364)
BEACH MOTEL PARTNERS LTD
Also Called: Harbor View Inn
28 W Cabrillo Blvd, Santa Barbara
(93101-3504)
PHONE..................800 755-0222
Antonio R Romasanta, Partner
Birgit Romasanta, Partner
Mark Romasanta, Manager
EMP: 60 EST: 1983
SQ FT: 40,000
SALES (est): 5.8MM Privately Held
SIC: 7011 Hotels

(P-12365)
BEAR RIVER CASINO
Also Called: Bear River Casino Hotel
11 Bear Paws Way, Loleta (95551-9684)
PHONE..................707 733-9644
John McGinnis, Executive Asst
Andrea Piazza, Security Dir
Jesse Reeves, Technical Staff
Nicole Dees, Accounting Mgr
Kyle Hudson, Cust Mgr
EMP: 286 Privately Held
SIC: 7011 Casino hotel
PA: Bear River Casino
27 Bear River Dr
Loleta CA 95551

(P-12366)
**BEHRINGER HARVARD
WILSHIRE BLV**
Also Called: Hotel Palomar
10740 Wilshire Blvd, Los Angeles
(90024-4493)
PHONE..................310 475-8711
Ravi Sikand, Partner
EMP: 99

SALES (est): 8.4MM Privately Held
SIC: 7011 6531 Hotels; real estate agents
& managers

(P-12367)
BELMONT CORPORATION
Also Called: Best Western
901 Park Ave, South Lake Tahoe
(96150-6938)
PHONE..................530 542-1101
Wilson Williford, President
EMP: 60
SALES (est): 3.9MM Privately Held
WEB: www.stationhouseinn.com
SIC: 7011 5012 Hotels; automobiles &
other motor vehicles

(P-12368)
**BELVEDERE HOTEL
PARTNERSHIP**
Also Called: Peninsula Beverly Hill's
9882 Santa Monica Blvd, Beverly Hills
(90212-1605)
PHONE..................310 551-2888
Ali Kasikci, Manager
EMP: 442
SALES (corp-wide): 14MM Privately
Held
WEB: www.patandmelody.com
SIC: 7011 6512 5813 5812 Hotels & mo-
tels; nonresidential building operators;
drinking places; eating places
PA: The Belvedere Hotel Partnership
421 N Beverly Dr Ste 350
Beverly Hills CA 90210
310 275-1001

(P-12369)
BELVEDERE PARTNERSHIP
Also Called: Peninsula Beverly Hills, The
9882 Santa Monica Blvd, Beverly Hills
(90212-1605)
PHONE..................310 551-2888
Robert Zarnegan, President
Nancy Kupka, Human Res Mgr
Mike Mandeville, Assistant
EMP: 400
SALES (est): 28.1MM Privately Held
SIC: 7011 Bed & breakfast inn; hotels

(P-12370)
BERESFORD CORPORATION
Also Called: Beresford Arms, The
635 Sutter St, San Francisco (94102-1017)
PHONE..................415 673-9900
Richard Osborn, Branch Mgr
EMP: 75
SALES (corp-wide): 6.4MM Privately
Held
WEB: www.beresford.com
SIC: 7011 Hotels
PA: Beresford Corporation
582 Market St Ste 912
San Francisco CA 94104
415 981-7386

(P-12371)
BEST WESTERN BAYSHORE INN
3500 Broadway, Eureka (95503-3810)
PHONE..................707 268-8005
Mark Watson, President
Emily Manfredonia, General Mgr
EMP: 50
SALES (est): 2.5MM Privately Held
WEB: www.bwbayshoreinn.com
SIC: 7011 Hotels & motels

(P-12372)
BEST WESTERN HILLTOP INN
2300 Hilltop Dr, Redding (96002-0508)
PHONE..................530 221-6100
Ed Rullman, General Ptnr
Steve Gaines, General Ptnr
Steven Wahrlich, General Ptnr
Tracy Wahrlich, General Ptnr
EMP: 50
SQ FT: 10,000
SALES (est): 2.8MM Privately Held
WEB: www.thehilltopinn.com
SIC: 7011 5812 5813 Hotels; eating
places; drinking places

(P-12373)
BEST WESTERN HOTEL TOMO
1800 Sutter St, San Francisco (94115-3220)
PHONE...................415 921-4000
Sean Salera, CFO
EMP: 50 EST: 2007
SALES (est): 1.1MM
SALES (corp-wide): 4.8MM Privately Held
SIC: 7011 Hotels
PA: Khp Iii Sf Sutter Llc
1800 Sutter St
San Francisco CA 94115
415 921-4000

(P-12374)
BEST WESTERN INTERNATIONAL INC
805 S Kaweah Ave, Exeter (93221-9361)
PHONE...................559 592-8118
Neil Patel, Manager
EMP: 80
SALES (corp-wide): 370.5MM Privately Held
SIC: 7011 Hotels & motels
PA: Best Western International, Inc.
6201 N 24th Pkwy
Phoenix AZ 85016
602 957-4200

(P-12375)
BEST WESTERN OXNARD INN
1156 S Oxnard Blvd, Oxnard (93030-7418)
PHONE...................805 483-9581
Jaysree Lad, Owner
Jace Lad, General Mgr
EMP: 50
SALES (est): 1.8MM Privately Held
WEB: www.bestwesternoxnardinn.com
SIC: 7011 Hotels & motels

(P-12376)
BEST WESTERN PLUS-HERITAGE INN
Also Called: Holiday Inn
111 E March Ln, Stockton (95207-5854)
PHONE...................209 474-3301
Ganatra Vasant, Mng Member
EMP: 50
SALES (est): 1.2MM Privately Held
SIC: 7011 Hotels & motels

(P-12377)
BEST WESTERN STOVALLS INN
Also Called: Best Western Park Place
1544 S Harbor Blvd, Anaheim (92802-2312)
PHONE...................714 776-4800
Lilian Wright, General Mgr
EMP: 50
SALES (est): 1.3MM
SALES (corp-wide): 22.2MM Privately Held
WEB: www.anaheiminn.com
SIC: 7011 Motels
PA: Best Western Stovalls Inn
1110 W Katella Ave
Anaheim CA 92802
714 956-4430

(P-12378)
BEST WESTERN STOVALLS INN (PA)
1110 W Katella Ave, Anaheim (92802-2805)
PHONE...................714 956-4430
James Stovall, Partner
Bill O'Connell, Partner
Minta Pettis-Stovall, Partner
Robert Stovall, Partner
EMP: 90
SQ FT: 4,800
SALES (est): 22.2MM Privately Held
WEB: www.anaheiminn.com
SIC: 7011 Inns

(P-12379)
BESTON DEVELOPMENT
Also Called: Bristol, The
1055 1st Ave, San Diego (92101-4808)
PHONE...................619 232-6315
EMP: 60

SALES: 2MM Privately Held
WEB: www.bristolhotelsandiego.com
SIC: 7011

(P-12380)
BEVERLY BLVD LEASECO LLC
Also Called: Sofitel
8555 Beverly Blvd, Los Angeles (90048-3303)
PHONE...................310 278-5444
Pierre-Louis Renou,
Sylvain Harribey, Executive
Priscilla Wright, Executive
Jeannine Kalthoff, Comms Mgr
David Hamerman, Security Dir
EMP: 100
SALES (est): 11.9MM
SALES (corp-wide): 1B Privately Held
SIC: 7011 Hotels & motels
HQ: Accor North America, Inc.
5055 Kelle Sprin Rd Ste 2
Addison TX 75001
972 360-9000

(P-12381)
BEVERLY HILLS LUXURY HOTEL LLC
1801 Century Park E # 1200, Los Angeles (90067-2334)
PHONE...................310 274-9999
Kenneth Bordewick, Mng Member
Ronnie Andrade, Technology
Mercedes Lucero, Director
EMP: 450
SALES (est): 22.3MM Privately Held
SIC: 7011 Resort hotel; hotels

(P-12382)
BEVERLY SUNSTONE HILLS LLC
Also Called: Residence Inn By Marriott
1177 S Beverly Dr, Los Angeles (90035-1119)
PHONE...................310 228-4100
Robert Alter, CEO
EMP: 60
SALES (est): 1.5MM Privately Held
SIC: 7011 Hotels & motels

(P-12383)
BH PARTN A CALIF LIMIT PARTNE (PA)
Also Called: Bahia Resort Hotels
998 W Mission Bay Dr, San Diego (92109-7803)
PHONE...................858 539-7635
Anne L Evans, General Ptnr
William L Evans, Partner
William Evans, Exec VP
Julia Debeers, Vice Pres
Janet Dooley, Risk Mgmt Dir
EMP: 300
SALES (est): 56MM Privately Held
WEB: www.missionbayresorts.com
SIC: 7011 6531 5812 Resort hotel; real estate managers; real estate leasing & rentals; eating places

(P-12384)
BH PARTN A CALIF LIMIT PARTNE
Also Called: The Lodge At Torrey Pines
11480 N Torrey Pines Rd A, La Jolla (92037-1045)
PHONE...................858 453-4420
Luis Badios, Manager
Stephanie Chavez, Executive Asst
Dan Ferbal, Human Res Dir
Michael Mena, Purch Mgr
Beth Webster, Natl Sales Mgr
EMP: 100
SALES (corp-wide): 56MM Privately Held
WEB: www.missionbayresorts.com
SIC: 7011 5813 5812 Hotels; drinking places; eating places
PA: Bh Partnership, A Califoria Limited Partnership
998 W Mission Bay Dr
San Diego CA 92109
858 539-7635

(P-12385)
BICYCLE CASINO LP
Also Called: Bicycle Hotel and Casino
888 Bicycle Casino Dr, Bell Gardens (90201-7617)
PHONE...................562 806-4646
Hashem Minaiy, CEO
EMP: 1500 EST: 1984
SALES (est): 10.8MM Privately Held
SIC: 7011 Casino hotel

(P-12386)
BIG RIVER LTD-DESIGN
Also Called: Big River Lodge
44850 Comptche Ukiah Rd, Mendocino (95460-9007)
P.O. Box 487 (95460-0487)
PHONE...................707 937-5615
Jeff Stanford, Co-Owner
Joan Stanford, Co-Owner
EMP: 70
SQ FT: 40,000
SALES (est): 3.6MM Privately Held
WEB: www.stanfordinn.com
SIC: 7011 5551 5941 5261 Resort hotel; canoes; kayaks; bicycle & bicycle parts; surfing equipment & supplies; nursery stock, seeds & bulbs; antiques; bathing suits; marine apparel

(P-12387)
BILTMORE HOTEL
2151 Laurelwood Rd, Santa Clara (95054-2796)
PHONE...................408 988-8411
Dafney Kang, Owner
Kay Gupta, Executive
Barbara Ratcliffe, General Mgr
Sharon Javier, Sales Staff
Christine Feeney, Manager
EMP: 110
SALES (est): 2.2MM Privately Held
SIC: 7011 Resort hotel

(P-12388)
BLACK MEADOW LANDING
156100 Black Meadow Rd, Parker Dam (92267)
P.O. Box 98 (92267-0098)
PHONE...................760 663-4901
George H Field Jr, Owner
EMP: 55
SQ FT: 100,000
SALES (est): 1.6MM Privately Held
WEB: www.blackmeadowlanding.com
SIC: 7011 7033 5411 5812 Motels; recreational vehicle parks; grocery stores, independent; restaurant, family; independent

(P-12389)
BLUE DEVILS LESSEE LLC
Also Called: Le Merdien Dlfina Santa Monica
530 Pico Blvd, Santa Monica (90405-1223)
PHONE...................310 399-9344
Jon Bortz, Ch of Bd
Cynthia Gonzales, Sales Mgr
Dan Sparacino, Sales Staff
Raymond Martz,
Bruno Santos, Director
EMP: 170
SALES (est): 24MM Privately Held
SIC: 7011 Resort hotel; hotels

(P-12390)
BLUE LAKE CASINO
777 Casino Way Blue Lk Blue Lake, Blue Lake (95525)
P.O. Box 1128 (95525-1128)
PHONE...................707 668-5101
Eric Ramos, President
EMP: 50
SALES (est): 5MM Privately Held
SIC: 7011 Casino hotel

(P-12391)
BODEGA BAY ASSOCIATES
Also Called: Bodega Bay Lodge
1100 Alma St Ste 106, Menlo Park (94025-3344)
PHONE...................650 330-8888
Ellis J Alden,
EMP: 95
SALES: 6.2MM Privately Held
SIC: 7011 Motels

(P-12392)
BOREAL RIDGE CORPORATION
Also Called: Boreal Ski Area
19749 Boreal Ridge Rd, Soda Springs (95728)
P.O. Box 39, Truckee (96160-0039)
PHONE...................530 426-1012
John Cumming, President
Jodi Churich, Vice Pres
EMP: 110
SQ FT: 10,000
SALES (est): 11.5MM
SALES (corp-wide): 108.4MM Privately Held
WEB: www.powdr.com
SIC: 7011 7999 Ski lodge; hotels; ski rental concession
PA: Powdr Corp.
1794 Olympic Pkwy Ste 210
Park City UT 84098
435 658-5500

(P-12393)
BOYKIN MGT CO LTD LBLTY CO
Also Called: Hampton Inn
3888 Greenwood St, San Diego (92110-4412)
PHONE...................619 299-6633
Tom Whelan, Principal
EMP: 50
SALES (corp-wide): 38.6MM Privately Held
WEB: www.wangyufei.com
SIC: 7011 Hotels & motels
PA: Boykin Management Company Limited Liability Company
8015 W Kenton Cir Ste 220
Huntersville NC 28078
704 896-2880

(P-12394)
BOYKIN MGT CO LTD LBLTY CO
Also Called: Radisson Inn
200 Marina Blvd, Berkeley (94710-1608)
PHONE...................510 548-7920
Neil Pasan, Manager
EMP: 300
SALES (corp-wide): 38.6MM Privately Held
WEB: www.wangyufei.com
SIC: 7011 5812 5813 Hotels & motels; eating places; drinking places
PA: Boykin Management Company Limited Liability Company
8015 W Kenton Cir Ste 220
Huntersville NC 28078
704 896-2880

(P-12395)
BRAEMAR PARTNERSHIP
Also Called: Catamaran Resort Hotel
3999 Mission Blvd, San Diego (92109-6959)
PHONE...................858 488-1081
Robert Gleason, CFO
The Trust of W D Evans, Partner
Anne L Evans, Managing Prtnr
Rocio Chavez, Human Res Mgr
Dayna Farris, Natl Sales Mgr
EMP: 350
SALES (est): 16.2MM Privately Held
WEB: www.catamaranresort.com
SIC: 7011 5812 5813 Resort hotel; American restaurant; cocktail lounge

(P-12396)
BRE DIAMOND HOTEL LLC
Also Called: Ritz-Carlton Halfmoon Bay
1 Miramontes Point Rd, Half Moon Bay (94019-2376)
PHONE...................650 712-7000
John Berndt, Manager
Cathy Oregon, Executive Asst
Stephanie Shaw, Info Tech Mgr
Alexis Turner, Accountant
Chrissy Johnson, Natl Sales Mgr
EMP: 116
SALES (corp-wide): 4.1MM Privately Held
WEB: www.shci.com
SIC: 7011 Hotels
HQ: Bre Diamond Hotel Llc
200 W Madison St Ste 1700
Chicago IL 60606
312 658-5000

▲ = Import ▼=Export
◆ =Import/Export

(P-12397)
BRE SELECT HOTELS OPER LLC
Also Called: Hilton
30 Ranch Dr, Milpitas (95035-5103)
PHONE..................................408 719-1313
Greg Juceam, *Exec VP*
Michelle O'Brien, *General Mgr*
Tabitha Christensen, *Manager*
EMP: 52 EST: 2013
SALES (est): 228.8K **Privately Held**
SIC: 7011 Hotels & motels

(P-12398)
BRE/JAPANTOWN OWNER LLC
Also Called: Hotel Kabuki
1625 Post St, San Francisco (94115-3603)
PHONE..................................415 922-3200
Craig Walterman, *General Mgr*
Katie Leung, *Accountant*
EMP: 100
SALES (est): 2.4MM **Privately Held**
SIC: 7011 Hotels

(P-12399)
BRIDGE BAY RESORT & MARINA
10300 Bridge Bay Rd, Redding (96003-9419)
PHONE..................................530 275-3021
Howard Weinberg,
EMP: 75
SALES (est): 5.3MM
SALES (corp-wide): 8.4MM **Privately Held**
WEB: www.sevencrown.com
SIC: 7011 Resort hotel
PA: Peloria Marinas Llc
2550 Via Tejon Ste 2b
Palos Verdes Estates CA 90274
310 363-7775

(P-12400)
BRIGHT BRISTOL STREET LLC
Also Called: Crowne Plaza Costa Mesa
3131 Bristol St, Costa Mesa (92626-3037)
PHONE..................................714 557-3000
Tom Van Winkle, *General Mgr*
Benjamin Shih, *Project Mgr*
Joseph Fan, *Manager*
EMP: 85
SALES (est): 303.6K **Privately Held**
SIC: 7011 Hotels

(P-12401)
BRILLIANCE INVESTMENT LLC
Also Called: Days Inn
8350 Edes Ave, Oakland (94621-1307)
PHONE..................................510 568-1880
Amit Motawala, *Mng Member*
EMP: 55
SQ FT: 70,000
SALES (est): 2MM **Privately Held**
SIC: 7011 5812 5813 Hotels; restaurant, family; independent; bars & lounges

(P-12402)
BRISAM LAX (DE) LLC
Also Called: Holiday Inn
9901 S La Cienega Blvd, Los Angeles (90045-5915)
PHONE..................................310 649-5151
Steve Hostetter, *General Mgr*
David Romero, *Sales Mgr*
Joann Endow, *Sales Staff*
Rodolfo Gutierrez, *Director*
EMP: 95
SALES (est): 4.1MM **Privately Held**
SIC: 7011 Hotels & motels

(P-12403)
BRISTOL HOTEL
1055 1st Ave, San Diego (92101-4808)
PHONE..................................619 232-6141
Eric Horodas, *Owner*
Lupe Veliz, *Admin Asst*
Kristina Alvarez, *Manager*
EMP: 90
SQ FT: 56,000
SALES (est): 4.6MM **Privately Held**
WEB: www.bristol.polhotels.com
SIC: 7011 5812 5813 Hotels; eating places; bars & lounges

(P-12404)
BROADMOOR HOTEL
Gaylord Suites
1465 65th St Apt 274, Emeryville (94608-1168)
PHONE..................................415 673-8445
Tony Daviduskis, *Branch Mgr*
Samuel Johnson, *Finance*
EMP: 75
SQ FT: 85,619
SALES (est): 928.6K
SALES (corp-wide): 10.7MM **Privately Held**
WEB: www.granadasf.com
SIC: 7011 6513 Hotels; apartment hotel operation
PA: Broadmoor Hotel
1499 Sutter St
San Francisco CA 94109
415 776-7034

(P-12405)
BROADMOOR HOTEL
Also Called: Granada Hotel
1000 Sutter St, San Francisco (94109-5818)
PHONE..................................415 673-2511
Tony Daviduskis, *Manager*
EMP: 70
SALES (est): 1.2MM
SALES (corp-wide): 10.7MM **Privately Held**
WEB: www.granadasf.com
SIC: 7011 Resort hotel
PA: Broadmoor Hotel
1499 Sutter St
San Francisco CA 94109
415 776-7034

(P-12406)
BROOKFIELD DTLA FUND OFFICE
Also Called: Westin Pasadena, The
191 N Los Robles Ave, Pasadena (91101-1707)
PHONE..................................626 792-2727
Jonathan Litvack, *General Mgr*
EMP: 70
SALES (corp-wide): 31.9B **Publicly Held**
WEB: www.maguireproperties.com
SIC: 7011 5812 5813 7299 Hotels; American restaurant; bars & lounges; banquet hall facilities
HQ: Brookfield Dtla Fund Office Trust Inc.
4 Wrld Fncl Ctr Fl 15
New York NY 10281
212 417-7064

(P-12407)
BROOKTRAILS LODGE LLC
24675 Birch St, Willits (95490-8476)
P.O. Box 297 (95490-0297)
PHONE..................................707 459-1596
Robert S Gitlin, *Manager*
EMP: 54
SQ FT: 87,120
SALES (est): 1MM **Privately Held**
SIC: 7011 Tourist camps, cabins, cottages & courts

(P-12408)
BSHH II LLC
Also Called: Bre El Segundo Property Owner
475 N Sepulveda Blvd, El Segundo (90245)
PHONE..................................310 356-4587
EMP: 50
SALES (est): 184.9K **Privately Held**
SIC: 7011

(P-12409)
BSHH II LLC
Also Called: Bre El Sgundo Property Owner B
525 N Pacific Coast Hwy, El Segundo (90245-4496)
PHONE..................................310 356-4577
Glenn Alba, *Director*
EMP: 70 EST: 2017
SALES (est): 246.8K **Privately Held**
SIC: 7011 Hotels & motels

(P-12410)
BURTON-WAY HOUSE LTD A CA
Also Called: Four Seasons Hotel
2 Dole Dr, Westlake Village (91362-7300)
PHONE..................................805 214-8075
Robert Cohen, *Branch Mgr*
Rob Hagelberg, *Manager*
EMP: 205
SALES (corp-wide): 31.1MM **Privately Held**
SIC: 7011 Hotels
PA: Burton Way Hotels, Ltd., A California Limited Partnership
2029 Century Park E # 2200
Los Angeles CA 90067
310 552-6623

(P-12411)
BURTON-WAY HOUSE LTD A CA
Also Called: Four Seasons Hotel
300 S Doheny Dr, Los Angeles (90048-3704)
PHONE..................................310 273-2222
Mehdi Efpekari, *General Mgr*
EMP: 225
SALES (corp-wide): 31.1MM **Privately Held**
SIC: 7011 5812 Hotels; eating places
PA: Burton Way Hotels, Ltd., A California Limited Partnership
2029 Century Park E # 2200
Los Angeles CA 90067
310 552-6623

(P-12412)
BURTON-WAY HOUSE LTD A CA (PA)
Also Called: Four Seasons Hotel
2029 Century Park E # 2200, Los Angeles (90067-2901)
PHONE..................................310 552-6623
Robert Cohen, *General Ptnr*
Joseph Cohen, *Partner*
EMP: 50
SALES (est): 31.1MM **Privately Held**
SIC: 7011 Hotels

(P-12413)
BY THE BLUE SEA LLC
Also Called: Shutters On The Beach
1 Pico Blvd, Santa Monica (90405-1063)
PHONE..................................310 458-0030
Tim Dubois, *President*
Klaus Mennekes, *Vice Pres*
EMP: 350
SALES (est): 22.4MM **Privately Held**
SIC: 7011 Hotels

(P-12414)
C N L HOTEL DEL PARTNERS LP
1500 Orange Ave, San Diego (92118-2918)
PHONE..................................619 522-8299
Todd Shallan, *Partner*
David Nadeau, *CFO*
EMP: 1100
SALES (est): 6.8MM **Privately Held**
SIC: 7011 Hotels

(P-12415)
C W HOTELS LTD
Also Called: JW Marriott Le Merigot
1740 Ocean Ave, Santa Monica (90401-3214)
PHONE..................................310 395-9700
Damien Hirsch, *General Mgr*
Paul Hortobagyi, *Manager*
EMP: 150
SALES (corp-wide): 6.3MM **Privately Held**
SIC: 7011 Hotels & motels
PA: C W Hotels Ltd
740 Centre View Blvd
Crestview Hills KY 41017
859 578-1100

(P-12416)
CABAZON BAND MISSION INDIANS
Fantasy Spring Resort Casino
84245 Indio Springs Dr, Indio (92203-3405)
PHONE..................................760 342-5000
Jim McCannon, *Manager*
EMP: 520 **Privately Held**

SIC: 7011 Casino hotel
PA: Cabazon Band Of Mission Indians
84245 Indio Springs Dr
Indio CA 92203
760 342-2593

(P-12417)
CACHE CREEK CASINO RESORT
14455 State Highway 16, Brooks (95606-9707)
P.O. Box 65 (95606-0065)
PHONE..................................530 796-3118
Bill Harland, *Vice Pres*
Mark Longshore, *Vice Pres*
Martha Cedano, *Admin Asst*
Daniel Ogden, *Sr Ntwrk Engine*
Tavis Feese, *Info Tech Mgr*
EMP: 2000
SALES (est): 111.6MM **Privately Held**
SIC: 7011 Casino hotel
PA: Yocha Dehe Wintun Nation
18960 County Rd 75 A
Brooks CA 95606
530 796-3400

(P-12418)
CALHOT ILLINIOS LLC
Also Called: Ramada Inn
5250 W El Segundo Blvd, Hawthorne (90250-4142)
PHONE..................................310 536-9800
Fred Groth, *General Mgr*
Kairey Choi, *Manager*
EMP: 160
SALES (est): 2.8MM **Privately Held**
SIC: 7011 5812 Hotels; eating places

(P-12419)
CALIFORNIA BISTRO AT FO
Also Called: Four Seasons Resort Aviara
7100 Aviara Resort Dr, Carlsbad (92011-4908)
PHONE..................................760 603-3700
Vince Parotta, *President*
EMP: 51
SALES (est): 2.2MM **Privately Held**
SIC: 7011 Resort hotel

(P-12420)
CALIFORNIA CLUB LUCKY LADY
Also Called: Lucky Lady Card Room
5526 El Cajon Blvd, San Diego (92115-3623)
PHONE..................................619 287-6690
Stanley Penn, *Owner*
EMP: 50
SQ FT: 7,000
SALES: 500K **Privately Held**
WEB: www.calicasinos.net
SIC: 7011 Casino hotel

(P-12421)
CALIFORNIA COMMERCE CLUB INC
Also Called: Commerce Casino
6131 Telegraph Rd, Commerce (90040-2501)
PHONE..................................323 721-2100
Haig Papaian, *CEO*
Dante Oliveto, *CFO*
Harvey Ross, *Vice Pres*
Andrew Schneiderman, *Vice Pres*
Ralph Wong, *Vice Pres*
EMP: 2600
SQ FT: 350,000
SALES (est): 105.9MM **Privately Held**
WEB: www.commercecasino.com
SIC: 7011 5812 Casino hotel; eating places

(P-12422)
CAMINO REAL GROUP LLC
Also Called: Hilton
840 E El Camino Real, Mountain View (94040-2808)
PHONE..................................650 964-1700
Garrett Ritter, *Manager*
EMP: 50
SALES (est): 3.6MM **Privately Held**
SIC: 7011 Hotels

P
R
O
D
U
C
T
S
&
S
V
C
S

(P-12423)
CAMPBELL HHG HOTEL DEV LP
Also Called: Courtyard By Marriott San Jose
655 Creekside Way, Campbell
(95008-0636)
PHONE.............................408 626-9590
Patricia Santini,
EMP: 50
SALES (est): 1.7MM **Privately Held**
SIC: 7011 7389 Hotels; office facilities &
secretarial service rental

(P-12424)
CANOGA HOTEL CORPORATION
Also Called: Hilton Wdlnd Hlls / Los Angeles
6360 Canoga Ave, Woodland Hills
(91367-2501)
PHONE.............................818 595-1000
James Evans, CFO
Deepak Mehra, General Mgr
EMP: 200
SALES (est): 3.9MM **Privately Held**
SIC: 7011 Resort hotel

(P-12425)
CANTERBURY HOTEL CORP
Also Called: Best Western Canterbury Hotel
750 Sutter St, San Francisco (94109-6417)
PHONE.............................415 345-3200
Dean Lehr, President
Jacqueline W Lehr, Ch of Bd
Frederick T Smith, Treasurer
Jon Lehr, Vice Pres
Matthew Jones, General Mgr
EMP: 110
SQ FT: 98,410
SALES (est): 3.3MM **Privately Held**
WEB: www.canterbury-hotel.com
SIC: 7011 5812 Hotels & motels; eating
places

(P-12426)
CAPITOL REGENCY LLC
Also Called: Hyatt Regency Sacramento
1209 L St, Sacramento (95814-3936)
PHONE.............................916 443-1234
Randy Verrue,
Brittany Hanson, Admin Asst
Brenda Kirian, Sales Dir
EMP: 360
SALES (est): 25.2MM **Privately Held**
SIC: 7011 Hotels

(P-12427)
**CARLTON HOTEL PROPERTIES
LP**
1075 Sutter St, San Francisco
(94109-5866)
PHONE.............................415 673-0242
Diane Feinstein, Partner
Richard Blum, Partner
Eileen Gartland, Partner
EMP: 55
SQ FT: 76,000
SALES (est): 3.8MM **Privately Held**
SIC: 7011 5812 Hotels; eating places

(P-12428)
CARMEL MISSION INN
3665 Rio Rd, Carmel (93923-8609)
PHONE.............................831 624-1841
Denise Morton, Sales Dir
Clayton Butterfield, Sales Mgr
Stacy Loving, Sales Staff
Kristen Phillips, Manager
EMP: 60
SALES (est): 1.3MM **Privately Held**
SIC: 7011 Inns

(P-12429)
CARMEL VALLEY RANCH
Also Called: Carmel Valley Ranch Hotel
1 Old Ranch Rd, Carmel (93923-8579)
PHONE.............................831 625-9500
Thomas Becker, General Mgr
Cv Ranch, General Ptnr
Scott Gill, Executive
Tim Wood, Executive
Gabrielle Wagemakers, Executive Asst
EMP: 250 EST: 1993
SALES (est): 23MM **Privately Held**
SIC: 7011 7997 6552 Resort hotel; tennis
club, membership; golf club, membership;
subdividers & developers

(P-12430)
**CARMEL VLY MRTG
BORROWER LLC**
Also Called: Carmel Valley Resort
1 Old Ranch Rd, Carmel (93923-8551)
PHONE.............................831 625-9500
Laura Bell, Principal
EMP: 99
SALES (est): 1.5MM **Privately Held**
SIC: 7011 Resort hotel

(P-12431)
CARNEROS INN LLC
Also Called: Poumtjack Hotels
4048 Sonoma Hwy, NAPA (94559-9745)
PHONE.............................707 299-4880
Keith Rogal, CEO
Nick Monroe, CFO
Philip Kendall, Vice Pres
Jonathan Vail, Info Tech Mgr
Jonathan Vale, Info Tech Mgr
EMP: 350
SQ FT: 50,000
SALES (est): 22.1MM **Privately Held**
SIC: 7011 Resort hotel; hotels

(P-12432)
**CARPENTERS SOUTHWEST
ADM CORP (PA)**
533 S Fremont Ave, Los Angeles
(90071-1712)
P.O. Box 17969 (90017-0969)
PHONE.............................213 386-8590
Douglas McCarron, CEO
Nina Gutierrez, Controller
Kristin Tingley, Manager
EMP: 70
SQ FT: 25,000
SALES (est): 45.1MM **Privately Held**
SIC: 7011 Hotels & motels

(P-12433)
CARPINTERIA MOTOR INN INC
Also Called: Best Western
4558 Carpinteria Ave, Carpinteria
(93013-1863)
PHONE.............................805 684-0473
Kevin Sweniak, General Mgr
EMP: 90
SALES (est): 1.9MM **Privately Held**
SIC: 7011 Hotels & motels

(P-12434)
**CARSON OPERATING COMPANY
LLC**
Also Called: Doubletree By Hilton Carson
2 Civic Plaza Dr, Carson (90745-2231)
PHONE.............................310 830-9200
Greg Guthrie, General Mgr
Leroy Russell, Controller
EMP: 90 EST: 2015
SALES (est): 1.9MM **Privately Held**
SIC: 7011 Hotels

(P-12435)
**CASA MADRONA HOTEL AND
SPA LLC**
801 Bridgeway, Sausalito (94965-2186)
PHONE.............................415 332-0502
John Warren Mays,
Brian Kelley, Controller
Jeremy Gaunt, Human Res Mgr
Steven Rauscher, Manager
EMP: 55
SQ FT: 18,000
SALES (est): 4.1MM **Privately Held**
WEB: www.casamadrona.com
SIC: 7011 5812 Hotels; eating places
PA: Olympus Real Estate Corp
5080 Spectrum Dr
Addison TX 75001

(P-12436)
CASA MUNRAS HOTEL LLC
700 Munras Ave, Monterey (93940-3110)
PHONE.............................831 375-2411
Karl K Hoagland III,
EMP: 82
SALES (est): 950K **Privately Held**
SIC: 7011 Hotels

(P-12437)
**CASA REAL ESTATE LTD
PARTNR**
Also Called: Estralla Inn & Spa
415 S Belardo Rd, Palm Springs
(92262-7307)
PHONE.............................760 320-4117
Elkor Trio, General Ptnr
EMP: 66
SALES (est): 4.2MM **Privately Held**
WEB: www.viceroypalmsprings.com
SIC: 7011 Resort hotel; hotels

(P-12438)
**CASTLBLACK PISMO BCH
OWNER LLC**
Also Called: Hilton Garden Inn Pismo
601 James Way, Pismo Beach
(93449-3502)
PHONE.............................805 773-6020
Gordon Jackson, Manager
Laura Benner, Vice Pres
EMP: 50
SALES (est): 1.3MM
SALES (corp-wide): 19.7MM **Privately
Held**
SIC: 7011 Motels
PA: Castleblack Owner Holdings, Llc
399 Park Ave Fl 18
New York NY 10022
212 547-2609

(P-12439)
**CASTLEHILL PROPERTIES INC
(PA)**
Also Called: Residnce Inn By Mrrott Stckton
3240 W March Ln, Stockton (95219-2341)
PHONE.............................209 472-9800
Jeff Carpenter, General Mgr
EMP: 58 EST: 1997
SALES (est): 5.3MM **Privately Held**
SIC: 7011 Hotels

(P-12440)
CAVALIER INN INC
Also Called: Cavalier Oceanfront Resort
9415 Hearst Dr, San Simeon (93452-9724)
PHONE.............................805 927-4688
Mona Rigdon, Principal
Michael Hanchett, Principal
EMP: 80
SALES (est): 599.6K **Privately Held**
SIC: 7011 Inns

(P-12441)
CAVALIER INN INCORPORATED
Also Called: Best Western
250 San Simeon Ave Ste 4c, San Simeon
(93452-9715)
PHONE.............................805 927-6444
Michael R Hanchett, President
Barbara J Hanchett, CFO
Michael Hanchett, Manager
EMP: 90
SALES (est): 4.8MM **Privately Held**
WEB: www.cavalierresort.com
SIC: 7011 Hotels & motels

(P-12442)
CAVALLO POINT LLC (PA)
601 Murray Cir, Sausalito (94965)
PHONE.............................415 339-4700
Peter Heinmann, Partner
Lonny Watne, Branch Mgr
Brendan Carlin, General Mgr
Jennifer Dykstra, Admin Sec
Mike Baroni, Engineer
EMP: 80 EST: 2007
SALES (est): 11.1MM **Privately Held**
SIC: 7011 Hotels

(P-12443)
CB-1 HOTEL
Also Called: Four Seasons Hotel
757 Market St, San Francisco
(94103-2001)
PHONE.............................415 633-3838
Douglas Housley, General Mgr
Frank Montalbano, Chief Engr
EMP: 99
SQ FT: 59,300
SALES (est): 6.8MM **Privately Held**
SIC: 7011 Hotels

(P-12444)
CDC SAN FRANCISCO LLC
Also Called: Intercontinental San Francisco
888 Howard St, San Francisco
(94103-3011)
PHONE.............................415 616-6512
Peter Koehler,
EMP: 99 EST: 2007
SALES (est): 950K **Privately Held**
SIC: 7011 Hotels

(P-12445)
CELEBRITY CASINOS INC
Also Called: Crystal Casino & Hotel
123 E Artesia Blvd, Compton (90220-4921)
PHONE.............................310 631-3838
Mark A Kelegian, President
Haig Kelegian Jr, CEO
EMP: 400
SQ FT: 190,000
SALES (est): 17.5MM **Privately Held**
SIC: 7011 Casino hotel

(P-12446)
CENTURY WILSHIRE INC
Also Called: Century Wilshire Hotel
9400 Culver Blvd, Culver City
(90232-2617)
PHONE.............................310 558-9400
Theodora Mallick, President
Monika Mallick, Corp Secy
Maya Mallick, Principal
EMP: 70
SQ FT: 38,000
SALES (est): 5.5MM **Privately Held**
WEB: www.centurywilshirehotel.com
SIC: 7011 Resort hotel; hotels

(P-12447)
CH CUPERTINO OWNER LLC
Also Called: Cypress Hotel
10050 S De Anza Blvd, Cupertino
(95014-2128)
PHONE.............................408 253-8900
David Hayes, Marketing Staff
EMP: 130
SALES (est): 8MM **Privately Held**
WEB: www.thecypresshotel.com
SIC: 7011 Hotels

(P-12448)
CHAMINADE LTD
Also Called: Chaminade At Santa Cruz
1 Chaminade Ln, Santa Cruz (95065-1524)
PHONE.............................831 475-5600
Tom O'Shea, General Mgr
James Birpo, General Ptnr
James Greggs, General Ptnr
Don Murchanson, General Ptnr
Paula Hamilton, Planning
EMP: 200 EST: 1979
SQ FT: 12,000
SALES: 10.3MM **Privately Held**
SIC: 7011 Resort hotel

(P-12449)
CHAMSON MANAGEMENT INC
Also Called: Doubletree Hotel
7 Hutton Centre Dr, Santa Ana
(92707-5753)
PHONE.............................714 751-2400
Jung-Hsiung Chiu, President
Magaly Marquez, Accounting Mgr
EMP: 90
SALES (est): 4.6MM **Privately Held**
SIC: 7011 Hotels

(P-12450)
CHATEAU LA JOLLA INN
233 Prospect St, La Jolla (92037-4600)
PHONE.............................858 459-4451
Toll Free:.............................888 -
Robert Collins, Partner
Jeff Fee, Partner
Wendy Matalon, Managing Dir
Jeffrey Sinnott, Controller
Kim Hollingsworth, Director
EMP: 50 EST: 1978
SQ FT: 40,000
SALES (est): 3.9MM **Privately Held**
WEB: www.chateaulajollainn.com
SIC: 7011 Inns

(P-12451)
CHESAPEAKE LODGING TRUST
Also Called: Le Meridian Hotel
333 Battery St Lbby, San Francisco
(94111-3234)
PHONE..............................415 296-2900
Joel Myers, *Director*
Jonathan Sembrana, *Purch Mgr*
Kelly Maclellan, *Sales Mgr*
Zachary Starke, *Director*
Randy Wilson, *Director*
EMP: 87
SALES (est): 9.8MM **Privately Held**
SIC: 7011 7021 Hotels; lodging house, ex-
cept organization

(P-12452)
CHIEF SAN DIEGO HOTEL LLC
601 Pacific Hwy, San Diego (92101-5914)
PHONE..............................619 239-2400
Andy Slater, *Vice Pres*
John D Smith, *General Mgr*
EMP: 100
SALES (est): 1.5MM
SALES (corp-wide): 25.4B **Privately Held**
SIC: 7011 Hotels & motels
HQ: Barings Real Estate Advisers Llc
1 Financial Plz
Hartford CT 06103

(P-12453)
**CHINA PEAK MOUNTAIN
RESORT LLC**
59265 Hwy 168, Lakeshore (93634)
P.O. Box 236 (93634-0236)
PHONE..............................559 233-2500
Tim Cohee, *CEO*
Michelle Vikupitz, *Marketing Staff*
Rich Bailey, *Manager*
Roger Myers, *Manager*
EMP: 74
SALES (est): 7.4MM **Privately Held**
SIC: 7011 Resort hotel

(P-12454)
CHIRAG HOSPITALITY INC
Also Called: Super 8 Motel
2440 Lombard St, San Francisco
(94123-2604)
PHONE..............................415 922-0244
Chirag Patel, *CEO*
Mishan Giri, *Manager*
EMP: 78
SALES (est): 159.9K **Privately Held**
SIC: 7011 Hotels & motels

(P-12455)
CHOA HOPE LLC
Also Called: Sioux City Ht & Conference Ctr
515 W Washington Ave, Escondido
(92025-1628)
PHONE..............................712 277-4101
Peter Parsons, *General Mgr*
EMP: 50
SALES (est): 1.9MM **Privately Held**
SIC: 7011 Hotels

(P-12456)
CHOICE HOTELS INTL INC
Also Called: Econo Lodge Inn & Suites
20688 Tracy Ave, Buttonwillow
(93206-9782)
PHONE..............................661 764-5207
EMP: 98
SALES (corp-wide): 1B **Publicly Held**
SIC: 7011 Hotel, franchised
PA: Choice Hotels International, Inc.
1 Choice Hotels Cir
Rockville MD 20850
301 592-5000

(P-12457)
**CHSP TRS FISHERMAN WHARF
LLC**
Also Called: Hyatt Fisherman's Wharf
555 N Point St, San Francisco
(94133-1311)
PHONE..............................415 563-1234
James Francis, *President*
EMP: 180
SALES (est): 1.8MM **Publicly Held**
SIC: 7011 5813 5812 Hotels & motels;
bars & lounges; eating places

PA: Chesapeake Lodging Trust
4300 Wilson Blvd Ste 625
Arlington VA 22203

(P-12458)
CHSP TRS LOS ANGELES LLC
Also Called: Hilton Checkers Los Angeles
535 S Grand Ave, Los Angeles
(90071-2601)
PHONE..............................213 624-0000
Eddie Andre, *Principal*
Paul Chambers, *Engineer*
EMP: 88
SALES (est): 1.9MM
SALES (corp-wide): 48.6MM **Privately
Held**
SIC: 7011 Hotels & motels
PA: Crestline Hotels & Resorts, Llc
3950 University Dr # 301
Fairfax VA 22030
571 529-6100

(P-12459)
**CHUKCHANSI GOLD RESORT
CASINO**
711 Lucky Ln, Coarsegold (93614-8206)
PHONE..............................866 794-6946
Richard Williams, *Owner*
Chanel Wright, *Officer*
BJ Martin, *General Mgr*
Cindy Meredith, *Admin Asst*
Amelia McLoughlin, *Administration*
EMP: 1400
SQ FT: 489,000
SALES (est): 43.7MM **Privately Held**
SIC: 7011 Casino hotel

(P-12460)
**CIM/OAKLAND CITY CENTER
LLC**
Also Called: Marriott
1001 Broadway, Oakland (94607-4019)
PHONE..............................510 451-4000
John Mazzoni, *Manager*
Avraham Shemesh, *Principal*
Emma Chao, *Finance*
Derrick Dawson, *Purch Mgr*
Thomas Foti, *Opers Staff*
EMP: 99
SALES (est): 9MM **Privately Held**
SIC: 7011 Hotels & motels

(P-12461)
CITRUS NORTH VENTURE
6591 Collins Dr Ste E11, Moorpark
(93021-1493)
PHONE..............................256 428-2000
Marc Pierguidi, *Admin Sec*
EMP: 99
SALES (est): 273.9K **Privately Held**
SIC: 7011 Hotel, franchised

(P-12462)
CITY OF SAN JOSE
Also Called: Dolce Hayes Mansion
200 Edenvale Ave, San Jose (95136-3309)
PHONE..............................408 226-6765
Cedric Fasbender, *General Mgr*
Jack Jackson, *Chief Engr*
Yves Hansel, *Asst Mgr*
EMP: 140 **Privately Held**
WEB: www.csjfinance.org
SIC: 7011 Hotels
PA: City Of San Jose
200 E Santa Clara St
San Jose CA 95113
408 535-3500

(P-12463)
**CLAREMONT HT PRPTS LTD
PARTNR**
Also Called: Claremont Hotel Club & Spa
41 Tunnel Rd, Berkeley (94705-2429)
PHONE..............................510 843-3000
Len Czarnecki, *Mng Member*
Michael Coughlin, *Finance Dir*
Guillermo Marquez, *Sales Staff*
Kevin Macdonald, *Director*
Kathy Marty, *Director*
EMP: 550
SALES (est): 16.3MM **Privately Held**
SIC: 7011 Resort hotel; hotels

(P-12464)
CLAREMONT STAR LP
Also Called: Doubletree Hotel
555 W Foothill Blvd, Claremont
(91711-3478)
PHONE..............................909 482-0124
Harry Wu, *Partner*
Shawn Chen, *Partner*
Andrew Behnke, *Executive*
EMP: 50
SALES (est): 3.5MM **Privately Held**
SIC: 7011 Hotels & motels

(P-12465)
**CLARION HOTEL SAN JOSE
AIRPORT**
1355 N 4th St, San Jose (95112-4783)
PHONE..............................408 453-5340
Ajay Shingal,
Ram Garg,
Mira Shingal,
EMP: 90
SALES (est): 3.1MM **Privately Held**
SIC: 7011 Hotels

(P-12466)
CLASSIC RIVERDALE INC
Also Called: Hyatt Hotel
200 Glenwood Cir, Monterey (93940-6741)
PHONE..............................831 373-0101
Matt Madison, *Partner*
EMP: 81
SALES (corp-wide): 79.7MM **Privately
Held**
WEB: www.hyattclassic.com
SIC: 7011 Hotels & motels
PA: Classic Riverdale, Inc.
200 W Madison St Ste 3700
Chicago IL 60606
312 803-8800

(P-12467)
**CLASSIC RSDENCE MGT LTD
PARTNR**
Also Called: Hyatt Hotel
200 Glenwood Cir Ofc, Monterey
(93940-6773)
PHONE..............................831 373-0101
Deann Daniel, *Exec Dir*
EMP: 100
SQ FT: 196,000
SALES (est): 3.8MM **Privately Held**
SIC: 7011 8322 Hotels & motels; senior
citizens' center or association

(P-12468)
CLOCKTOWER INN
Also Called: Ramada Clock Tower Inn
181 E Santa Clara St, Ventura
(93001-2715)
PHONE..............................805 652-0141
S Patel, *President*
Bahgat Tadros, *Asst Treas*
EMP: 65
SQ FT: 29,000
SALES (est): 3.3MM **Privately Held**
SIC: 7011 Hotels

(P-12469)
CLUB ONE CASINO INC
1033 Van Ness Ave, Fresno (93721-2006)
PHONE..............................559 497-3000
Kyle R Kirkland, *President*
George Sarantos, *President*
Chee Lee, *Info Tech Mgr*
Jeremy Newman, *Mktg Dir*
EMP: 325
SQ FT: 25,000
SALES (est): 13.2MM **Privately Held**
WEB: www.clubonecasino.com
SIC: 7011 Casino hotel

(P-12470)
**CLUB QUARTERS SAN
FRANCISCO**
424 Clay St, San Francisco (94111-3207)
PHONE..............................415 268-3606
Sanj Rai, *Manager*
Patrick Jackson, *General Mgr*
Joeann La Madrid, *Sales Executive*
EMP: 99
SALES (est): 3MM **Privately Held**
SIC: 7011 Hotels

(P-12471)
**CNCML A CALIFORNIA LTD
PARTNR**
Also Called: Plumpjack The
1920 Squaw Valley Rd, Olympic Valley
(96146)
P.O. Box 2407 (96146-2407)
PHONE..............................530 583-1578
Hilary Newsom, *President*
Jeremy Scherer, *Vice Pres*
Milham D Wakin, *Vice Pres*
Steve Lamb, *General Mgr*
Debi Martineau, *Controller*
EMP: 100
SQ FT: 20,000
SALES (est): 5.8MM **Privately Held**
SIC: 7011 5812 Resort hotel; eating
places

(P-12472)
CNI THL OPS LLC
Also Called: Sheraton Hotel San Jose
1801 Barber Ln, Milpitas (95035-7419)
PHONE..............................408 943-0600
Keon Marvasti, *Manager*
Luis Garcia, *Manager*
EMP: 98
SQ FT: 148,435
SALES (corp-wide): 11.1MM **Privately
Held**
WEB: www.hicrystallake.com
SIC: 7011 Hotels & motels
PA: Cni Thl Ops, Llc
515 S Flower St Fl 44
Los Angeles CA

(P-12473)
CNI THL PROPCO FE LLC
Also Called: Four Points Bakersfield
5101 California Ave, Bakersfield
(93309-1623)
PHONE..............................661 325-9700
Keon Marvasti,
EMP: 80
SALES (est): 599.6K **Privately Held**
SIC: 7011 Hotels & motels

(P-12474)
COLONY PALMS HOTEL LLC
572 N Indian Canyon Dr, Palm Springs
(92262-6030)
PHONE..............................760 969-1800
Al Wertheimer, *Owner*
Dan Burgess, *General Mgr*
Nicole Winslow, *General Mgr*
Arturo Ramirez, *Facilities Dir*
Luke Luger, *Manager*
EMP: 70 EST: 2011
SALES (est): 2.3MM **Privately Held**
SIC: 7011 Resort hotel; hotels

(P-12475)
COLUMBIA HOSPITALITY INC
Also Called: Inns of Monterey
652 Cannery Row, Monterey (93940-1021)
PHONE..............................831 646-8900
Randy Bernard, *Manager*
EMP: 120
SALES (corp-wide): 79.3MM **Privately
Held**
WEB: www.coastalhotel.com
SIC: 7011 5813 5812 Hotels; drinking
places; eating places
PA: Columbia Hospitality Inc
2200 Alaskan Way Ste 200
Seattle WA 98121
206 441-6666

(P-12476)
COLUMBIA HOSPITALITY INC
Also Called: Hotel Pacific
300 Pacific St, Monterey (93940-2418)
PHONE..............................831 373-5700
Randy Venard, *Manager*
EMP: 55
SALES (corp-wide): 79.3MM **Privately
Held**
WEB: www.coastalhotel.com
SIC: 7011 Hotels
PA: Columbia Hospitality Inc
2200 Alaskan Way Ste 200
Seattle WA 98121
206 441-6666

(P-12477)
COLUMBIA HOSPITALITY INC
Also Called: Victorian Inn
487 Foam St, Monterey (93940-1409)
PHONE..................................831 373-8000
Patrick Mallone, *Manager*
EMP: 50
SALES (corp-wide): 79.3MM **Privately Held**
WEB: www.coastalhotel.com
SIC: 7011 Hotels
PA: Columbia Hospitality Inc
2200 Alaskan Way Ste 200
Seattle WA 98121
206 441-6666

(P-12478)
COLUMBIA WOODLAKE LLC
500 Leisure Ln, Sacramento (95815-4207)
PHONE..................................206 728-9063
Alex Washburn, *President*
Leigh Noble, *CFO*
EMP: 90
SALES (est): 1.2MM **Privately Held**
SIC: 7011 Resort hotel

(P-12479)
COMFORT CALIFORNIA INC
Also Called: Comfort Inn
2775 Van Ness Ave, San Francisco
(94109-1423)
PHONE..................................415 928-5000
Todd Symynuk, *Branch Mgr*
EMP: 50
SALES (corp-wide): 198.1MM **Privately Held**
WEB: www.clarionanaheim.com
SIC: 7011 Hotels & motels
HQ: Comfort California, Inc.
10750 Columbia Pike # 300
Silver Spring MD 20901
301 592-3800

(P-12480)
COMFORT CALIFORNIA INC
Also Called: Clarion Hotel
616 W Convention Way, Anaheim
(92802-3401)
PHONE..................................714 750-3131
Mike Thomas, *Branch Mgr*
Naomi Bennett, *Manager*
EMP: 83
SALES (corp-wide): 198.1MM **Privately Held**
WEB: www.clarionanaheim.com
SIC: 7011 Hotels & motels
HQ: Comfort California, Inc.
10750 Columbia Pike # 300
Silver Spring MD 20901
301 592-3800

(P-12481)
COMFORT SUITES
Also Called: Comfort Inn
121 E Grand Ave, South San Francisco
(94080-4800)
PHONE..................................650 589-7100
David R Lane, *CFO*
Steven Nokes, *Partner*
EMP: 100
SQ FT: 5,000
SALES (est): 3.1MM **Privately Held**
SIC: 7011 Hotels & motels

(P-12482)
CONCORD HOTEL LLC
Also Called: Crowne Plaza Concord
45 John Glenn Dr, Concord (94520-5604)
PHONE..................................925 521-3751
Dave Warner,
Aaron Olson, *General Mgr*
Cathy Jackson, *Director*
EMP: 95
SALES: 8MM **Privately Held**
SIC: 7011 Hotels

(P-12483)
CONESTOGA HOTEL
Also Called: Holiday Inn
1240 S Walnut St, Anaheim (92802-2241)
PHONE..................................714 535-0300
Kevin Clayton, *General Mgr*
Mark Nunneley, *CFO*
Tom Van Winkle, *General Mgr*
EMP: 90
SQ FT: 150,000

SALES (est): 2.5MM **Privately Held**
WEB: www.conestogahotel.com
SIC: 7011 5812 5813 Hotels; American
restaurant; drinking places

(P-12484)
COPLEY PRESS INC
Borrego Sun, The
3845 Yaqui Pass, Borrego Springs
(92004-5000)
PHONE..................................760 767-0100
Greg Perlman, *President*
EMP: 187
SALES (corp-wide): 101.8MM **Privately Held**
WEB: www.copleynewspapers.com
SIC: 7011 Resort hotel
PA: The Copley Press Inc
7776 Ivanhoe Ave
La Jolla CA 92037
858 454-0411

(P-12485)
COUNTRY INN &SUITE BY CARLSON
231 N Vineyard Ave, Ontario (91764-4427)
PHONE..................................909 937-6000
Peter Bhakta, *Owner*
EMP: 50
SALES (est): 608.3K **Privately Held**
SIC: 7011 Hotels

(P-12486)
COUNTRYSIDE INN-CORONA LP
Also Called: Ayres Hotel Laguna Woods
24341 El Toro Rd, Laguna Woods
(92637-4901)
PHONE..................................949 588-0131
Vince Neale, *Manager*
EMP: 60
SALES (corp-wide): 34.4MM **Privately Held**
WEB: www.ayreshotelgroup.com
SIC: 7011 Resort hotel
PA: Countryside Inn-Corona, L.P.
1900 Bollero Pl
Corona CA 92882
714 540-6060

(P-12487)
COUNTRYSIDE INN-CORONA LP
Also Called: Countryside Suites By Ayres
325 Bristol St, Costa Mesa (92626-5998)
PHONE..................................714 549-0300
Steve Winning, *General Mgr*
EMP: 100
SALES (corp-wide): 34.4MM **Privately Held**
WEB: www.ayreshotelgroup.com
SIC: 7011 5813 5812 Hotels; drinking
places; eating places
PA: Countryside Inn-Corona, L.P.
1900 Bollero Pl
Corona CA 92882
714 540-6060

(P-12488)
COURTYARD BY MARRIOTT
595 Hotel Cir S, San Diego (92108-3403)
PHONE..................................619 291-5720
Veronica Butler, *Director*
Tracey Palmberg, *Sales Executive*
EMP: 60
SALES (est): 3MM **Privately Held**
SIC: 7011 Hotels & motels

(P-12489)
COURTYARD BY MARRIOTT
1605 Calle Joaquin, San Luis Obispo
(93405-7214)
PHONE..................................805 786-4200
James Flagg,
EMP: 55
SALES (est): 2.2MM **Privately Held**
SIC: 7011 Hotels & motels

(P-12490)
COURTYARD BY MARRIOTT
2500 Larkspur Landing Cir, Larkspur
(94939-1831)
PHONE..................................415 925-1800
Sam Pahlazan, *Principal*
EMP: 80
SALES (est): 1.9MM **Privately Held**
SIC: 7011 Hotels & motels

(P-12491)
COURTYARD BY MARRIOTT
1905 S Azusa Ave, Hacienda Heights
(91745-6850)
PHONE..................................626 965-1700
Michael Sweany, *Principal*
Maritza Mejia, *General Mgr*
EMP: 80
SALES (est): 2MM **Privately Held**
SIC: 7011 Hotels & motels

(P-12492)
COURTYARD MANAGEMENT CORP
21101 Ventura Blvd, Woodland Hills
(91364-2104)
PHONE..................................818 999-2200
J Willard Marriott, *Principal*
EMP: 55
SALES (corp-wide): 22.8B **Publicly Held**
SIC: 7011 Hotels
HQ: Courtyard Management Corporation
10400 Fernwood Rd
Bethesda MD 20817

(P-12493)
COURTYARD MANAGEMENT CORP
Also Called: Courtyard By Marriott
2250 Contra Costa Blvd, Pleasant Hill
(94523-3744)
PHONE..................................925 691-1444
Trace Moviel, *Branch Mgr*
EMP: 50
SALES (corp-wide): 22.8B **Publicly Held**
SIC: 7011 Hotels & motels
HQ: Courtyard Management Corporation
10400 Fernwood Rd
Bethesda MD 20817

(P-12494)
COURTYARD MANAGEMENT CORP
Also Called: Courtyard By Marriott
10683 White Rock Rd, Rancho Cordova
(95670-6002)
PHONE..................................916 638-3800
John Lister, *Branch Mgr*
EMP: 50
SALES (corp-wide): 22.8B **Publicly Held**
SIC: 7011 Hotels & motels
HQ: Courtyard Management Corporation
10400 Fernwood Rd
Bethesda MD 20817

(P-12495)
COURTYARD OXNARD
600 E Esplanade Dr, Oxnard (93036-2403)
PHONE..................................805 988-3600
Patricia Tewes, *General Mgr*
Maria Zavala, *Executive*
EMP: 80
SALES (est): 128.1K **Privately Held**
SIC: 7011 Hotels & motels

(P-12496)
COURTYARD-CENTRAL
Also Called: Courtyard By Marriott San Dieg
8651 Spectrum Center Blvd, San Diego
(92123-1489)
PHONE..................................858 573-0700
Brnet Andrus, *President*
Audun Poulsen, *CFO*
Sherly Chester, *Manager*
EMP: 70
SALES (est): 3.3MM **Privately Held**
WEB: www.cy-kearnymesa.com
SIC: 7011 7389 Hotels; office facilities &
secretarial service rental

(P-12497)
CPH MONARCH HOTEL LLC
Also Called: St Regis Resort Monarch Beach
1 Monarch Beach Resort, Dana Point
(92629-4085)
PHONE..................................949 234-3200
Paul Makarechian, *President*
EMP: 1100
SQ FT: 300,000

SALES (est): 56.1MM
SALES (corp-wide): 83.6MM **Privately Held**
SIC: 7011 Resort hotel
PA: Washington Real Estate Holdings Llc
600 University St # 2820
Seattle WA 98101
206 613-5300

(P-12498)
CREEDENCE LESSEE LLC
Also Called: Hotel Zoe
425 N Point St, San Francisco
(94133-1405)
PHONE..................................415 561-1100
Emily Chung, *Director*
EMP: 99 EST: 2015
SALES (est): 785.9K **Privately Held**
SIC: 7011 Hotels

(P-12499)
CRESTLINE HOTELS & RESORTS INC
Also Called: Kyoto Grand Hotel and Gardens
120 S Los Angeles St 11, Los Angeles
(90012-3724)
PHONE..................................213 629-1200
Richard Gaines, *General Mgr*
Joe Kuhn, *General Mgr*
John Jedic, *Human Res Dir*
Jeannette Garcia, *Human Resources*
EMP: 250
SALES (est): 4.8MM
SALES (corp-wide): 48.6MM **Privately Held**
SIC: 7011 5812 5813 Hotels; restaurant,
family: independent; drinking places
PA: Crestline Hotels & Resorts, Llc
3950 University Dr # 301
Fairfax VA 22030
571 529-6100

(P-12500)
CRESTLINE HOTELS & RESORTS LLC
Also Called: Renaissance Palm Springs Hotel
888 E Tahquitz Canyon Way, Palm Springs
(92262-6708)
PHONE..................................760 322-6000
Eric Hill, *Controller*
EMP: 200
SALES (corp-wide): 45.4MM **Privately Held**
WEB: www.crestlinehotels.com
SIC: 7011 Hotels & motels
PA: Crestline Hotels & Resorts, Llc
3950 University Dr # 301
Fairfax VA 22030
571 529-6100

(P-12501)
CROWN PLAZA SD
Also Called: Islands Restaurant & Lounge
2270 Hotel Cir N, San Diego (92108-2810)
PHONE..................................619 297-1101
Anna Cooper, *Manager*
EMP: 80
SALES (est): 2.2MM **Privately Held**
WEB: www.islandssushi.com
SIC: 7011 5812 Hotels; eating places

(P-12502)
CROWNE PLAZA LAX LLC
Also Called: Intercontntl Hotels Grp Resour
5985 W Century Blvd, Los Angeles
(90045-5477)
PHONE..................................310 258-1321
Paul Gibbs, *General Mgr*
EMP: 250
SALES (est): 6.5MM
SALES (corp-wide): 1.7B **Privately Held**
WEB: www.crowneplaza.com
SIC: 7011 Hotels & motels
HQ: Intercontinental Hotels Group Re-
sources, Inc.
3 Ravinia Dr Ste 100
Atlanta GA 30346
770 604-5000

(P-12503)
CRP CENTINELA LP
Also Called: Doubltree Los Angeles Westside
6161 W Centinela Ave, Culver City
(90230-6306)
PHONE..................................901 821-4117
Larry M Mills, *Partner*

EMP: 152
SALES: 950K
SALES (corp-wide): 3.6B **Publicly Held**
SIC: **7011** Hotels & motels
PA: The Carlyle Group L P
1001 Pennsylvania Ave Nw 220s
Washington DC 20004
202 729-5626

(P-12504)
CTC GROUP INC (DH)
Also Called: Doubletree Hotel
21333 Hawthorne Blvd, Torrance
(90503-5602)
PHONE....................................310 540-0500
John Huang, *CEO*
Tony Mayoral, *Executive*
Azman AWI, *Info Tech Dir*
Frances Hu, *Controller*
EMP: 145
SALES (est): 17MM
SALES (corp-wide): 2.7B **Publicly Held**
WEB: www.hiltontorrance.com
SIC: **7011** Hotels & motels

(P-12505)
CUPERTINO LESSEE LLC
Also Called: Juniper Hotel
10050 S De Anza Blvd, Cupertino
(95014-2128)
PHONE....................................908 253-8900
Peggy Chen, *General Mgr*
EMP: 120
SALES: 19.5MM **Privately Held**
SIC: **7011 5812** Hotels; American restaurant

(P-12506)
CUSTOM HOTEL LLC
8639 Lincoln Blvd, Los Angeles
(90045-3503)
PHONE....................................310 645-0400
Alisa Matthews, *General Mgr*
Jerry Peck, *Controller*
EMP: 100
SALES (est): 3.6MM
SALES (corp-wide): 231.8MM **Privately Held**
SIC: **7011** Hotels & motels
PA: Joie De Vivre Hospitality, Llc
1750 Geary Blvd
San Francisco CA 94115
415 835-0300

(P-12507)
CUSTOM HOUSE HOTEL LP
Also Called: Portola Hotel & Spa
2 Portola Plz, Monterey (93940-2419)
PHONE....................................831 649-4511
Dan Pollock,
EMP: 91
SALES (est): 10.7MM **Privately Held**
SIC: **7011** Bed & breakfast inn; hotels

(P-12508)
CWGP LIMITED PARTNERSHIP
Also Called: Marriott
1740 Ocean Ave, Santa Monica
(90401-3214)
PHONE....................................310 395-9700
Kai Beumer, *General Mgr*
Sig K Otloff, *General Mgr*
EMP: 100
SALES (est): 6.3MM **Privately Held**
WEB: www.lemerigotbeachhotel.com
SIC: **7011** Hotels & motels
PA: C W Hotels Ltd
740 Centre View Blvd
Crestview Hills KY 41017
859 578-1100

(P-12509)
CY GASLAMP LLC
Also Called: Courtyard San Diego Gaslamp
453 6th Ave, San Diego (92101-7007)
PHONE....................................619 544-1004
Tim Billing, *General Mgr*
Ana Dervi, *Accounts Mgr*
EMP: 65
SALES (est): 984.8K **Privately Held**
SIC: **7011** Hotels

(P-12510)
CY SAC OPERATOR LLC
Also Called: Courtyard Sacramento-Midtown
4422 Y St, Sacramento (95817-2220)
PHONE....................................916 455-6800
Colleen Jimenez,
Roshan Bhakta,
EMP: 67
SALES: 4.9MM **Privately Held**
SIC: **7011** Hotel, franchised

(P-12511)
D & W LLC
Also Called: Ramada Inn
3501 Rindge Ln, Redondo Beach
(90278-1420)
PHONE....................................310 345-0075
Paul Ding,
Jane Ding,
Jenny Wu,
EMP: 55
SQ FT: 80,000
SALES (est): 918.3K **Privately Held**
SIC: **7011** Hotels

(P-12512)
DARENSBURG ROGHAIR & RENIER
Also Called: Quailty Inn of Barstow
1520 E Main St, Barstow (92311-3230)
PHONE....................................760 256-6891
Charles Darensburg, *Partner*
EMP: 50
SALES (est): 1.2MM **Privately Held**
SIC: **7011 5812** Motel, franchised; American restaurant

(P-12513)
DAVIDSON HOTEL PARTNERS LP
Also Called: Agoura Hills Renaissance Hotel
30100 Agoura Rd, Agoura Hills
(91301-2004)
PHONE....................................818 707-1220
Larry Mills, *Partner*
Jason Fisk, *Engineer*
EMP: 120 **Privately Held**
SIC: **7011** Hotels
PA: Davidson Hotel Partners, L.P
1 Ravinia Dr Ste 1600
Atlanta GA 30346

(P-12514)
DAVIS HALLMARK PARTNERSHIP
Also Called: Hallmark Inn
110 F St, Davis (95616-4628)
PHONE....................................530 753-3320
Julian M Youmans, *Partner*
John Youmans, *Partner*
EMP: 50
SQ FT: 70,000
SALES (est): 2.8MM **Privately Held**
WEB: www.hallmarkinn.com
SIC: **7011** Hotel, franchised; hotels

(P-12515)
DAWN RANCH LODGE & RD HSE REST
16467 Hwy 116, Guerneville (95446-8328)
P.O. Box 45 (95446-0045)
PHONE....................................707 869-0656
Michael Clark, *President*
EMP: 65 EST: 1905
SQ FT: 23,226
SALES (est): 2.1MM **Privately Held**
SIC: **7011 5813 5812** Resort hotel; bar (drinking places); eating places

(P-12516)
DAYS INN BAKERSFIELD
Also Called: Regency Inn
818 Real Rd, Bakersfield (93309-1002)
PHONE....................................661 324-6666
Robert King, *President*
Michelle Diaz, *Telecom Exec*
EMP: 135
SQ FT: 40,000
SALES (est): 1.4MM **Privately Held**
SIC: **7011 5812 5813 7933** Motels; eating places; cocktail lounge; bowling centers

(P-12517)
DCP JL TRITON SF LLC
Also Called: Hotel Triton
342 Grant Ave, San Francisco
(94108-3607)
PHONE....................................844 808-0290
F Matthew Dinapoli,
Nicole Huebner, *Supervisor*
EMP: 50
SALES (est): 184.9K **Privately Held**
SIC: **7011** Hotels

(P-12518)
DESTINATION RESIDENCES LLC
Also Called: Shadow Mnt Rsort/Rcqut CL Tns
45750 San Luis Rey Ave, Palm Desert
(92260-4728)
PHONE....................................760 346-4647
Sindy Calhoun, *Manager*
EMP: 50
SALES (corp-wide): 1B **Privately Held**
WEB: www.destinationhotels.com
SIC: **7011 5699 6531** Resort hotel; sports apparel; condominium manager
HQ: Destination Residences Llc
10333 E Dry Creek Rd
Englewood CO 80112
303 799-3830

(P-12519)
DIAMOND INTL INVESTMENT LLC
3737 N Blackstone Ave, Fresno
(93726-5307)
PHONE....................................559 226-2200
Betty Qi,
Alvin Cachaper, *Manager*
EMP: 63 EST: 2015
SALES (est): 1.1MM **Privately Held**
SIC: **7011** Hotel, franchised

(P-12520)
DIAMOND MOUNTAIN CASINO
900 Skyline Dr, Susanville (96130-6071)
PHONE....................................530 252-1100
Campbell Jamieson, *Manager*
Matthew Wolcott, *COO*
Jill Ault, *Officer*
Bob Nay, *Security Dir*
Jake Fogal, *Info Tech Dir*
EMP: 135
SQ FT: 24,000
SALES (est): 9.7MM **Privately Held**
WEB: www.diamondmountaincasino.com
SIC: **7011** Casino hotel

(P-12521)
DIAMOND RESORTS LLC
Also Called: Palm Canyon Resort & Spa
2800 S Palm Canyon Dr, Palm Springs
(92264-9337)
PHONE....................................760 866-1800
Allison Wickerham, *Mng Member*
Stacy Bower, *CFO*
Carl Ellis, *Principal*
Kim Schaeffer, *Manager*
EMP: 100 EST: 2004
SALES: 300K **Privately Held**
WEB: www.palmcanyonresort.org
SIC: **7011 5812 7991** Resort hotel; American restaurant; spas

(P-12522)
DIAMONDROCK SAN DEGO TNANT LLC
Also Called: Westin San Diego
400 W Broadway, San Diego (92101-3504)
PHONE....................................619 239-4500
John Beaton,
Pamela Ford Green, *Accounting Mgr*
Karen Favory, *Human Res Dir*
Deidre Bengston, *Sales Staff*
Geralynn Penaflor, *Sales Staff*
EMP: 300
SQ FT: 337,717
SALES (est): 8.4MM
SALES (corp-wide): 870MM **Publicly Held**
SIC: **7011** Hotels
HQ: Diamondrock Hospitality Limited Partnership
3 Bethesda Metro Ctr
Bethesda MD 20814

(P-12523)
DIMENSION DEVELOPMENT TWO LLC
Also Called: Hampton Inn San Diego-Downtown
1531 Pacific Hwy, San Diego (92101-2413)
PHONE....................................619 233-8408
Mark Manis, *General Mgr*
EMP: 55
SALES (corp-wide): 64.2MM **Privately Held**
WEB: www.dimdev.com
SIC: **7011** Hotels
PA: Dimension Development Two, Llc
769 Highway 494
Natchitoches LA 71457
318 352-9519

(P-12524)
DIMENSION DEVELOPMENT TWO LLC
Also Called: Sheraton
11611 Bernardo Plaza Ct, San Diego
(92128-2408)
PHONE....................................858 485-9250
Douglas R Korn, *Branch Mgr*
EMP: 60
SALES (corp-wide): 64.2MM **Privately Held**
WEB: www.dimdev.com
SIC: **7011** Hotels
PA: Dimension Development Two, Llc
769 Highway 494
Natchitoches LA 71457
318 352-9519

(P-12525)
DISNEY ENTERPRISES INC
1150 W Magic Way, Anaheim (92802-2247)
PHONE....................................714 778-6600
Michael D Eisner, *President*
Cynthia J Garber, *Meeting Planner*
EMP: 3500 **Publicly Held**
SIC: **7011** Resort hotel
HQ: Disney Enterprises, Inc.
500 S Buena Vista St
Burbank CA 91521
818 560-1000

(P-12526)
DISNEY ENTERPRISES INC
1717 S Disneyland Dr, Anaheim
(92802-2308)
PHONE....................................714 999-0990
Samantha Muntz, *Principal*
EMP: 300 **Publicly Held**
SIC: **7011 5813 5812** Hotels; drinking places; eating places
HQ: Disney Enterprises, Inc.
500 S Buena Vista St
Burbank CA 91521
818 560-1000

(P-12527)
DISNEYLAND INTERNATIONAL
1580 S Disneyland Dr, Anaheim
(92802-2294)
PHONE....................................714 956-6746
EMP: 300 **Publicly Held**
SIC: **7011** Resort hotel
HQ: Disneyland International
770 The Cy Dr S Ste 6000
Orange CA 92868
714 490-3000

(P-12528)
DJONT/CMB SSF LEASING LLC
Also Called: Embassy Sites-So San Francisco
250 Gateway Blvd, South San Francisco
(94080-7018)
PHONE....................................650 589-3400
Rudy Ortiz, *General Mgr*
Dee Bradford, *Executive*
EMP: 60
SALES (est): 348.4K
SALES (corp-wide): 1.3B **Privately Held**
SIC: **7011** Hotels & motels
HQ: Rangers Sub I, Llc
3 Bethesda Metro Ctr # 1000
Bethesda MD 20814

(P-12529)
DKN HOTEL LLC (PA)
42 Corporate Park Ste 200, Irvine
(92606-3104)
PHONE.....................714 427-4320
Kiran Patel, *CEO*
Nilesh Patel, *Co-Owner*
John Jorgensen, *Vice Pres*
Bhalesh Gandhi, *Controller*
Dahya Lal,
EMP: 290 EST: 2002
SQ FT: 4,000
SALES (est): 38.7MM **Privately Held**
WEB: www.dknhotels.com
SIC: 7011 Hotels

(P-12530)
DKN HOTEL LLC
Also Called: Holiday Inn
1240 S Walnut St, Anaheim (92802-2241)
PHONE.....................714 535-0300
Niral Munshaw, *Branch Mgr*
EMP: 88
SALES (corp-wide): 38.7MM **Privately Held**
WEB: www.dknhotels.com
SIC: 7011 Hotels
PA: Dkn Hotel, Llc
42 Corporate Park Ste 200
Irvine CA 92606
714 427-4320

(P-12531)
DNC PRKS RESORTS AT TENAYA INC (DH)
Also Called: Tenaya Lodge
1122 Highway 41, Fish Camp (93623)
P.O. Box 159 (93623-0159)
PHONE.....................877 247-9241
Kevin T Kelly, *President*
Thomas Barney, *Vice Pres*
Stephanie Neal, *Human Resources*
EMP: 77
SALES (est): 6.9MM
SALES (corp-wide): 3B **Privately Held**
SIC: 7011 Resort hotel; hotels

(P-12532)
DNC PRKS RSRTS AT YOSEMITE INC
Also Called: Yosemite Concession Services
9001 Village Dr, Yosemite Ntpk (95389)
PHONE.....................209 372-1001
Dan Jensen, *President*
Paul Jensen, *Vice Pres*
Paul Jeppson, *Vice Pres*
Christy Contreras, *Area Mgr*
Audrey Lanting, *Asst Controller*
EMP: 1100
SALES (est): 55.6MM
SALES (corp-wide): 3B **Privately Held**
SIC: 7011 5399 5812 5947 Hotels; vacation lodges; country general stores; eating places; snack shop; gift shop; gasoline service stations; tours, conducted
HQ: Delaware North Companies Parks & Resorts, Inc.
250 Delaware Ave Ste 3
Buffalo NY 14202

(P-12533)
DODGE RIDGE CORPORATION
Also Called: Dodge Ridge Winter Sports Area
1 Dodge Ridge Rd, Pinecrest (95364)
PHONE.....................209 536-5300
Jason Reed, *CFO*
Bob Hohne, *CFO*
Dave Alley, *Senior Engr*
Erin Jensen, *Human Resources*
Jason Smith, *Opers Staff*
EMP: 350
SQ FT: 10,000
SALES (est): 13.1MM **Privately Held**
WEB: www.dodgeridge.com
SIC: 7011 7033 Ski lodge; campgrounds

(P-12534)
DOLCE INTERNATIONAL / NAPA LLC
1600 Atlas Peak Rd, NAPA (94558-1425)
PHONE.....................707 257-0200
Steven A Rudnitsky, *President*
EMP: 484

SALES (est): 2.2MM **Publicly Held**
SIC: 7011 Hotels & motels
HQ: Dolce International Holdings, Inc.
22 Sylvan Way
Parsippany NJ 07054
201 307-8700

(P-12535)
DOLPHIN BAY HT & RESIDENCE INC
Also Called: Dolphin Bay Hotel & Residences
2727 Shell Beach Rd, Shell Beach (93449-1602)
PHONE.....................805 773-4300
Richard J Loughead Jr, *CEO*
Christina Stieb, *Marketing Staff*
EMP: 90
SALES (est): 5MM **Privately Held**
SIC: 7011 Hostels; hotels

(P-12536)
DOLPHINS COVE RESORT LTD
465 W Orangewood Ave, Anaheim (92802-4759)
PHONE.....................714 980-0830
Winners Circle Resort Intnl In, *General Ptnr*
Jennifer Eaton, *General Mgr*
EMP: 90
SALES (est): 2.8MM **Privately Held**
SIC: 7011 Resort hotel

(P-12537)
DOMINION INTERNATIONAL INC
Also Called: Hampton Inn
2305 Longport Ct, Elk Grove (95758-7127)
PHONE.....................916 683-9545
Perry Ferrera, *General Mgr*
EMP: 100
SALES (est): 2.9MM **Privately Held**
SIC: 7011 Hotels & motels

(P-12538)
DONALD T STERLING CORPORATION
Also Called: Beverly Hills Plaza Hotel
10300 Wilshire Blvd, Los Angeles (90024-4772)
PHONE.....................310 275-5575
Zair Caceres, *Branch Mgr*
EMP: 80
SALES (corp-wide): 7.8MM **Privately Held**
SIC: 7011 Hotels
PA: Donald T. Sterling Corporation
9441 Wilshire Blvd Ph
Beverly Hills CA 90212
310 278-8000

(P-12539)
DOUBLETREE BY HILTON HOTEL
1985 E Grand Ave, El Segundo (90245-5015)
PHONE.....................310 322-0999
Jordan Austin, *General Mgr*
Mark Lewis, *Vice Pres*
EMP: 110 EST: 2011
SALES (est): 893.4K **Privately Held**
SIC: 7011 Hotels

(P-12540)
DOUBLETREE BY HILTON HOTEL
1515 Hotel Cir S, San Diego (92108-3409)
PHONE.....................619 881-6900
Victor Ravago, *Manager*
Evette Betancourt, *Accounting Mgr*
EMP: 70 EST: 2015
SALES (est): 642.7K **Privately Held**
SIC: 7011 Hotel, franchised

(P-12541)
DOUBLETREE HOTEL
888 Montebello Blvd, Rosemead (91770-4303)
PHONE.....................323 722-8800
Ying Ming Huang, *Partner*
EMP: 100
SQ FT: 110,000
SALES (est): 5.2MM **Privately Held**
SIC: 7011 Hotels & motels

(P-12542)
DOUBLTREE SUITES BY HILTON LLC
Also Called: Doubletree Hotel
2085 S Harbor Blvd, Anaheim (92802-3513)
PHONE.....................714 750-3000
Amrit K Patel,
Christopher Neilson, *Technology*
William R O'Connell,
Shirish H Patel,
Annice McCuller, *Director*
EMP: 175
SALES (est): 10.6MM **Privately Held**
WEB: www.orangewood.net
SIC: 7011 5812 Hotels; American restaurant

(P-12543)
DTRS SANTA MONICA LLC
Also Called: Loews Santa Monica Beach Hotel
1700 Ocean Ave, Santa Monica (90401-3214)
PHONE.....................310 458-6700
Paul Leclerc, *General Mgr*
John Thaeker, *Regional VP*
Gail Paul, *Software Dev*
Mercedes Smith, *Sales Staff*
Eric D Hassberger,
EMP: 300
SQ FT: 300,000
SALES (est): 20.7MM **Privately Held**
SIC: 7011 Resort hotel; hotels

(P-12544)
E H SUMMIT INC (PA)
Also Called: Luxe Sunset Boulevard Hotel
11461 W Sunset Blvd, Los Angeles (90049-2031)
PHONE.....................310 476-6571
Efrem Harkhan, *CEO*
EMP: 130
SALES (est): 13.9MM **Privately Held**
SIC: 7011 Hotels

(P-12545)
E H SUMMIT INC
360 N Rodeo Dr, Beverly Hills (90210-5177)
PHONE.....................310 273-0300
Efrem Harkhan, *President*
EMP: 65
SALES (est): 595.7K **Privately Held**
SIC: 7011 Hotels
PA: E. H. Summit, Inc.
11461 W Sunset Blvd
Los Angeles CA 90049
-

(P-12546)
EAST PALO ALTO HOTEL DEV INC
Also Called: Four Seasons Hotel Silicon Vly
2050 University Ave, East Palo Alto (94303-2248)
PHONE.....................650 566-1200
Tracy Mercer, *General Mgr*
EMP: 210
SALES (est): 9.1MM **Privately Held**
SIC: 7011 7389 Resort hotel; office facilities & secretarial service rental

(P-12547)
EASUN INC
2001 Point West Way, Sacramento (95815-4702)
PHONE.....................916 929-8855
Benjamin Shih, *Director*
EMP: 50
SALES: 20MM **Privately Held**
SIC: 7011 Hotels & motels

(P-12548)
ECONOMY INN
1243 E Main St, Barstow (92311-2408)
PHONE.....................760 256-5601
Mike Patel, *Owner*
EMP: 50
SALES (est): 960.4K **Privately Held**
WEB: www.elliott.com
SIC: 7011 Motels

(P-12549)
EDWARD THOMAS COMPANIES
Also Called: Jolly Roger Inn
640 W Katella Ave, Anaheim (92802-3411)
PHONE.....................714 782-7500
Fred Kokash, *Branch Mgr*
EMP: 100
SALES (corp-wide): 3.6MM **Privately Held**
WEB: www.jollyrogerhotel.com
SIC: 7011 5812 Motels; eating places
PA: The Edward Thomas Companies
9950 Santa Monica Blvd
Beverly Hills CA 90212
310 859-9366

(P-12550)
EDWARD THOMAS HOSPITALITY CORP
Also Called: Shutters On The Beach
1 Pico Blvd, Santa Monica (90405-1063)
PHONE.....................310 458-0030
Klaus Mennekes, *Branch Mgr*
Armella Stepan, *General Mgr*
EMP: 350
SALES (corp-wide): 17MM **Privately Held**
WEB: www.shuttersonthebeach.com
SIC: 7011 5812 7991 5813 Hotels & motels; eating places; physical fitness facilities; drinking places
PA: The Edward Thomas Hospitality Corp
9950 Santa Monica Blvd
Beverly Hills CA 90212
310 859-9366

(P-12551)
EL CORDOVA HOTEL
Also Called: Pacific Terrace Inn
1351 Orange Ave, Coronado (92118-2916)
PHONE.....................619 435-4131
Mark Francois, *General Mgr*
Robert Mc Ginnis, *Partner*
Jose Garcia, *General Mgr*
Robert Bottomley, *Manager*
Alex Hernandez, *Manager*
EMP: 100
SQ FT: 20,000
SALES (est): 3.5MM **Privately Held**
WEB: www.elcordovahotel.com
SIC: 7011 Resort hotel; motels

(P-12552)
EL DORADO ENTERPRISES INC
Also Called: Hustler Casino
1000 W Redondo Beach Blvd, Gardena (90247-4192)
PHONE.....................310 719-9800
Larry C Flynt, *CEO*
Alyona Kononova, *Info Tech Mgr*
EMP: 760
SALES (est): 31.1MM **Privately Held**
WEB: www.hustlergaming.com
SIC: 7011 Casino hotel

(P-12553)
EL RANCHO MOTEL INC
Also Called: Best Wstn El Rancho Inn Suites
1100 El Camino Real, Millbrae (94030-2098)
PHONE.....................650 588-8500
John C Wilms, *President*
Paul Wilms, *Vice Pres*
Art Schwass, *Technology*
EMP: 168
SQ FT: 23,958
SALES (est): 7.9MM **Privately Held**
WEB: www.elranchoinn.com
SIC: 7011 5812 5813 7991 Motels; eating places; drinking places; physical fitness facilities

(P-12554)
ELIZABETHAN INN ASSOCIATES LP
Also Called: The Sterling Hotel
1935 Wright St Apt 231, Sacramento (95825-1191)
PHONE.....................916 448-1300
Sandra Wasserman, *Partner*
EMP: 90
SQ FT: 15,000

SALES (est): 1.4MM **Privately Held**
WEB: www.sterlinghotel.com
SIC: 7011 5812 7299 Hotels; ethnic food
restaurants; banquet hall facilities

(P-12555)
ELK VALLEY CASINO INC
2500 Howland Hill Rd, Crescent City
(95531-9241)
PHONE...................................707 464-1020
Dale Miller, *Ch of Bd*
Larry Johnson, *General Mgr*
John Green, *Software Engr*
Michael White, *Mktg Dir*
Sean Norbury, *Director*
EMP: 125 EST: 1995
SQ FT: 35,000
SALES (est): 5.8MM **Privately Held**
WEB: www.elkvalleycasino.com
SIC: 7011 Casino hotel

(P-12556)
EMBARCADERO INN
ASSOCIATES
Also Called: Hotel Griffon
155 Steuart St, San Francisco
(94105-1206)
PHONE...................................415 495-2100
Edward Marinucci, *General Ptnr*
Pacific Union Investment Corpo, *General*
Ptnr
EMP: 125
SALES (est): 5MM **Privately Held**
WEB: www.hotelgriffon.com
SIC: 7011 5812 Hotels; family restaurants

(P-12557)
EMBASSY SUITES
MANAGEMENT LLC
4550 La Jolla Village Dr, San Diego
(92122-1248)
PHONE...................................858 453-0400
EMP: 102 EST: 2007
SALES (est): 868.3K **Privately Held**
SIC: 7011 Hotels

(P-12558)
EMERIK HOTEL CORP
Also Called: Luxe City Center
1020 S Figueroa St, Los Angeles
(90015-1305)
PHONE...................................213 748-1291
Emerson Glazer, *President*
Art Malmgren, *CFO*
John Kelly, *Vice Pres*
James Jones, *Admin Sec*
EMP: 90
SALES: 8MM **Privately Held**
WEB: www.hicitycenter.com
SIC: 7011 5813 5812 Hotels; bar (drink-
ing places); American restaurant

(P-12559)
ENCINA PEPPER TREE JOINT
VENTR (PA)
Also Called: Best Western
3850 State St, Santa Barbara
(93105-3112)
PHONE...................................805 687-5511
Jeanette Webber, *Managing Prtnr*
David Potter, *Partner*
Camille Shaar, *Partner*
Pamela Webber, *Partner*
Chivaun Clark, *General Mgr*
EMP: 70
SQ FT: 100,000
SALES: 12.9MM **Privately Held**
WEB: www.sbhotels.com
SIC: 7011 Hotels & motels

(P-12560)
EQUISTAR IRVINE COMPANY
LLC
Also Called: Hilton Irvine
18800 Macarthur Blvd, Irvine (92612-1410)
PHONE...................................949 833-3331
Meristar Mezzanine Borrower, *Manager*
EMP: 99
SALES (est): 5.2MM **Privately Held**
SIC: 7011 Hotels & motels

(P-12561)
ERGS AIM HOTEL REALTY LLC
Also Called: Embassy Suites Anaheim Or-
ange
400 N State College Blvd, Orange
(92868-1708)
PHONE...................................714 938-1111
Eric Pyland, *Business Mgr*
John Rogers, *CEO*
EMP: 75
SQ FT: 50,000
SALES (est): 1.9MM **Privately Held**
SIC: 7011 Hotels

(P-12562)
ERGS AIM HOTEL REALTY LLC
Also Called: Doubletree Suites Doheny
34402 Pacific Coast Hwy, Dana Point
(92624-1211)
PHONE...................................949 661-1100
Brian Nordahl,
Louisa Yeung, *Administration*
EMP: 54 EST: 2017
SALES (est): 212.6K **Privately Held**
SIC: 7011 Hotels & motels

(P-12563)
ESA P PRTFOLIO OPER LESSEE
LLC
Also Called: Extended Stay America
4881 Birch St, Newport Beach
(92660-2112)
PHONE...................................949 851-2711
William Arter, *Branch Mgr*
Russ Herbel, *Manager*
EMP: 50
SALES (corp-wide): 1.2B **Publicly Held**
WEB: www.weddingbells.net
SIC: 7011 Hotels
HQ: Esa P Portfolio Operating Lessee, Llc
11525 N Community House R
Charlotte NC 28277
980 345-1600

(P-12564)
ESA P PRTFOLIO OPER LESSEE
LLC
Also Called: Extended Stay America
1635 W Katella Ave, Orange (92867-3412)
PHONE...................................714 639-8608
Leilani Reynolds, *Branch Mgr*
EMP: 73
SALES (corp-wide): 1.2B **Publicly Held**
WEB: www.weddingbells.net
SIC: 7011 Hotels
HQ: Esa P Portfolio Operating Lessee, Llc
11525 N Community House R
Charlotte NC 28277
980 345-1600

(P-12565)
ET WHITEHALL SEASCAPE LLC
Also Called: Hotel Casa Del Mar
1910 Ocean Way, Santa Monica
(90405-1083)
PHONE...................................310 581-5533
Edward Slatkin,
Thomas Slatkin,
EMP: 202
SQ FT: 200,000
SALES (est): 12.2MM **Privately Held**
WEB: www.hotelcasadelmar.com
SIC: 7011 5812 Hotels; eating places

(P-12566)
EUROPEAN HOTL INVSTRS OF
CA
Also Called: Doubletree Hotel
1985 E Grandave, El Segundo (90245)
PHONE...................................310 322-0999
Tim River, *Manager*
EMP: 50
SALES (est): 1.7MM
SALES (corp-wide): 6.4MM **Privately**
Held
SIC: 7011 Hotels & motels
PA: European Hotel Investors I I, A Califor-
nia Limited Partnership
2532 Dupont Dr
Irvine CA 92612
949 474-7368

(P-12567)
EUROPEAN HOTL INVSTRS OF
CA (PA)
Also Called: O H I
2532 Dupont Dr, Irvine (92612-1524)
PHONE...................................949 474-7368
Timothy R Busch, *General Ptnr*
T R Busch Realty Corp, *Partner*
EMP: 80
SQ FT: 9,000
SALES (est): 6.4MM **Privately Held**
SIC: 7011 Hotels

(P-12568)
EVERGREEN DSTNTION
HLDINGS LLC
Also Called: Evergreen Lodge
33160 Evergreen Rd, Groveland
(95321-9772)
PHONE...................................209 379-2606
Brian Anderluh,
Nick Simon, *General Mgr*
Donna West, *Financial Exec*
Teri Marshall, *Sales Dir*
Dan Braun,
EMP: 75 EST: 1975
SQ FT: 6,000
SALES (est): 4.9MM **Privately Held**
SIC: 7011 5812 Resort hotel; eating
places

(P-12569)
EXECUTIVE INN INC
Also Called: Ramada Inn
1217 Wildwood Ave, Sunnyvale
(94089-2701)
PHONE...................................408 245-5330
Roger Chang, *President*
Jeffry S C Chang, *President*
Jeff Shannon, *General Mgr*
David C M Chang, *Admin Sec*
Karen Chau, *Manager*
EMP: 97
SQ FT: 15,400
SALES (est): 5.2MM **Privately Held**
SIC: 7011 Hotels & motels

(P-12570)
FARGO COLONIAL LLC
Also Called: Grande Colonial
910 Prospect St, La Jolla (92037-4144)
PHONE...................................858 454-2181
Roger Joseph,
Julieta Navas, *Sales Mgr*
Leslie Araiza-Lorenzo, *Marketing Staff*
Audra Gillespie, *Sales Staff*
Walfred Rodas, *Supervisor*
EMP: 63
SQ FT: 46,480
SALES: 9.6MM **Privately Held**
WEB: www.thegrandecolonial.com
SIC: 7011 5812 Hotels; eating places

(P-12571)
FC EL SEGUNDO LLC
Also Called: Cambria El Segundo Lax
199 Continental Blvd, El Segundo
(90245-4525)
PHONE...................................702 439-7945
Milton B Patipa, *Senior VP*
EMP: 75
SQ FT: 86,106
SALES (est): 341.8K **Privately Held**
SIC: 7011 Hotels

(P-12572)
FEDERTED INDANS GRTON
RNCHERIA
Graton Resort & Casino
630 Park Ct, Rohnert Park (94928-7906)
PHONE...................................707 588-7100
Greg Sarris, *Branch Mgr*
EMP: 313 **Privately Held**
SIC: 7011 Casino hotel
PA: Federated Indians Of Graton Rancheria
6400 Redwood Dr Ste 300
Rohnert Park CA 94928
619 917-9566

(P-12573)
FERRADO GARDEN COURT LLC
520 Cowper St Ste 100, Palo Alto
(94301-1826)
PHONE...................................650 543-2224
Ferrado Inmuebles SL, *Mng Member*

Barbara Gross,
EMP: 60
SQ FT: 63,620
SALES (est): 1MM **Privately Held**
WEB: www.gardencourt.com
SIC: 7011 Hotels

(P-12574)
FESS PRKER-RED LION GEN
PARTNR
Also Called: Doubletree Hotel
633 E Cabrillo Blvd, Santa Barbara
(93103-3611)
PHONE...................................805 564-4333
Fess Parker, *Partner*
Mary Friar, *Manager*
EMP: 325
SALES (est): 18.2MM **Privately Held**
SIC: 7011 Hotels & motels

(P-12575)
FIRST HOTELS INTERNATIONAL
INC
Also Called: Radisson Inn
295 N E St, San Bernardino (92401-1507)
P.O. Box 1805 (92402-1805)
PHONE...................................909 884-9364
James Deskus, *General Mgr*
Cindy Gardner, *Treasurer*
Choqchet Koski, *Controller*
Ivan Verheijen, *Manager*
EMP: 140
SALES (est): 2.8MM **Privately Held**
SIC: 7011 Hotels

(P-12576)
FITNESS RIDGE MALIBU LLC
Also Called: Biggest Lser Ftnes Rdge Malibu
277 Latigo Canyon Rd, Malibu
(90265-2707)
PHONE...................................818 874-1300
Michelle Kelsch,
Tami Clark,
Cameron Kelsch,
EMP: 56
SALES (est): 1.2MM **Privately Held**
SIC: 7011 7991

(P-12577)
FJS INC
Also Called: Anabella Hotel The
888 S Disneyland Dr # 400, Anaheim
(92802-1847)
PHONE...................................714 905-1050
Francis J Sparolini, *CEO*
C Y Chan, *President*
Nathan Fitzgerald, *General Mgr*
Brandon Jemison, *Office Mgr*
Rachel Moorhead, *Admin Sec*
EMP: 118
SALES (est): 9MM **Privately Held**
WEB: www.anabellahotel.com
SIC: 7011 Resort hotel

(P-12578)
FLORENCE VILLA HOTEL
Also Called: The Villa Florence Hotel
225 Powell St, San Francisco
(94102-2205)
PHONE...................................415 397-7700
Steve Miller, *General Mgr*
EMP: 200
SALES (est): 6.8MM
SALES (corp-wide): 1.1B **Privately Held**
WEB: www.villaflorence.com
SIC: 7011 5812 Hotels; eating places
PA: Lasalle Hotel Properties
7550 Wisconsin Ave # 100
Bethesda MD 20814
301 941-1500

(P-12579)
FLORENCE VILLA HOTEL LLC
225 Powell St, San Francisco
(94102-2205)
PHONE...................................415 397-7700
Sue Hefty,
Marit Davey,
EMP: 99
SALES (est): 1.2MM **Privately Held**
SIC: 7011 Hotels

P
R
O
D
U
C
T
S
&
S
V
C
S

(P-12580)
FORCE-OAKLEAF LP
Also Called: Courtyard By Marriott
6333 Bristol Pkwy, Culver City
(90230-6904)
PHONE.................................310 484-7000
Andy Eklov, *Partner*
EMP: 66
SQ FT: 167,792
SALES (est): 2MM **Privately Held**
SIC: 7011 Hotels

(P-12581)
FORGE-VIDOVICH MOTEL LIMITED
Also Called: Cupertino Inn
10889 N De Anza Blvd, Cupertino
(95014-0439)
PHONE.................................408 996-7700
John Vidovich, *General Ptnr*
Stephen J Vidovich, *General Ptnr*
Claudio Bono, *General Mgr*
Jerry Leap, *Marketing Staff*
EMP: 60
SQ FT: 8,323
SALES (est): 4.3MM **Privately Held**
WEB: www.cupertinoinn.com
SIC: 7011 Hotels

(P-12582)
FORTUNA ENTERPRISES LP
Also Called: Hilton
5711 W Century Blvd, Los Angeles
(90045-5672)
PHONE.................................310 410-4000
Henry H Hsu, *Partner*
Christine Hsu, *Partner*
David Hsu, *Partner*
Denise Clarke, *Sales Staff*
Doug Lennig, *Manager*
EMP: 450
SQ FT: 2,700
SALES (est): 29.7MM **Privately Held**
SIC: 7011 5812 5813 Hotels; eating
places; bar (drinking places)
HQ: Universal Fortuna Investment, Inc
5711 W Century Blvd # 1628
Los Angeles CA 90045

(P-12583)
FOUNDERS MANAGEMENT II CORP
Also Called: Crowne Plaza Hotel
1221 Chess Dr, Foster City (94404-1173)
PHONE.................................650 570-5700
Solomon Tsai, *Managing Dir*
Scott Castle, *General Mgr*
Debbie Millard, *Office Mgr*
Deena Castle, *Sales Dir*
EMP: 275
SQ FT: 280,000
SALES (est): 14.1MM **Privately Held**
SIC: 7011 5812 5813 Hotels; eating
places; bar (drinking places)

(P-12584)
FOUNTAINGROVE INN LLC
Also Called: Fountngrove Inn Conference Ctr
101 Fountaingrove Pkwy, Santa Rosa
(95403-1777)
P.O. Box 12277 (95406-2277)
PHONE.................................707 578-6101
Robert Miller,
Justin Hayman, *General Mgr*
Angelo Serro,
Andrew Watkins, *Manager*
EMP: 100
SQ FT: 79,200
SALES (est): 7.7MM **Privately Held**
WEB: www.fountaingroveinn.com
SIC: 7011 5812 Resort hotel; eating
places

(P-12585)
FOUR POINTS BY SHERATON
9750 Airport Blvd, Los Angeles
(90045-5404)
PHONE.................................310 645-4600
Jonh Vickers, *President*
EMP: 57
SALES (est): 2.9MM **Privately Held**
SIC: 7011 Hotels

(P-12586)
FOUR POINTS SAN JOSE DOWNTOWN
211 S 1st St, San Jose (95113-2702)
PHONE.................................408 282-8800
Randy Zimmerman, *General Mgr*
EMP: 50
SALES (est): 1.1MM **Privately Held**
SIC: 7011 Resort hotel; hotels

(P-12587)
FOUR SEASONS HOTEL INC
Also Called: Four Ssons Hotel-San Francisco
735 Market St Fl 6, San Francisco
(94103-2034)
PHONE.................................415 633-3441
Stan Bromley, *Branch Mgr*
EMP: 515
SALES (corp-wide): 5.5MM **Privately Held**
SIC: 7011 Hotels
HQ: Four Seasons Hotels Limited
1165 Leslie St
North York ON M3C 2
416 449-1750

(P-12588)
FOUR SEASONS HOTEL INC
2050 University Ave, East Palo Alto
(94303-2248)
PHONE.................................650 566-1200
Robert Whitfield, *Manager*
Marvin Wong, *Finance*
Cassie Conching, *Manager*
EMP: 515
SALES (corp-wide): 5.5MM **Privately Held**
SIC: 7011 Hotels
HQ: Four Seasons Hotels Limited
1165 Leslie St
North York ON M3C 2
416 449-1750

(P-12589)
FOUR SISTERS INNS
Also Called: 1906 Lodge
1060 Adella Ave, Coronado (92118-2908)
PHONE.................................619 437-1900
Susan Nelson, *General Mgr*
EMP: 154
SALES (corp-wide): 25MM **Privately Held**
SIC: 7011 Motels
PA: Four Sisters Inns
460 Alma St Ste 100
Monterey CA 93940
831 649-0908

(P-12590)
FPL LLC
Also Called: Wyndham Garden Pierpont Inn
550 San Jon Rd, Ventura (93001-3745)
PHONE.................................805 643-6144
EMP: 55
SALES (est): 968.1K **Privately Held**
SIC: 7011

(P-12591)
FREMONT MARRIOTT
46100 Landing Pkwy, Fremont
(94538-6437)
PHONE.................................510 413-3700
John Ault, *General Mgr*
EMP: 130
SALES (est): 567.6K **Privately Held**
SIC: 7011 Hotels

(P-12592)
FRENCH REDWOOD INC
Also Called: Hotel Sfitel San Francisco Bay
223 Twin Dolphin Dr, Redwood City
(94065-1414)
PHONE.................................650 598-9000
David O'Shaunessy, *President*
EMP: 228
SALES (est): 7.7MM
SALES (corp-wide): 1B **Privately Held**
WEB: www.hbsaward.com
SIC: 7011 5813 5812 Hotel, franchised;
drinking places; eating places
PA: Accor
82 Rue Henry Farman
Issy Les Moulineaux 92130
146 429-193

(P-12593)
FRESNO AIRPORT HOTELS LLC
Also Called: Wyndham Garden Fresno Airport
5090 E Clinton Way, Fresno (93727-1506)
PHONE.................................559 252-3611
Rohit Kumar, *President*
Leslie Beninga, *General Mgr*
EMP: 65
SALES (est): 2MM **Privately Held**
SIC: 7011 Inns

(P-12594)
FRESNO HOTEL PARTNERS LP
Also Called: Ramada Inn
324 E Shaw Ave, Fresno (93710-7610)
PHONE.................................559 224-4040
Arianna Navarro, *Sales Staff*
EMP: 60
SALES (est): 2.3MM **Privately Held**
SIC: 7011 7991 5812 7999 Hotels; physi-
cal fitness facilities; eating places; swim-
ming pool, non-membership

(P-12595)
G5 GLOBAL PARTNERS IX LLC
Also Called: Ramada Plz Ht San Dego/ Ht Cir
2151 Hotel Cir S, San Diego (92108-3314)
PHONE.................................619 291-6500
EMP: 75
SALES: 950K **Privately Held**
SIC: 7011

(P-12596)
GALLERIA PARK ASSOCIATES LLC
Also Called: Galleria Park Hotel
191 Sutter St, San Francisco (94104-4501)
PHONE.................................415 781-3060
James Lim, *General Mgr*
Fred De Stefano, *Exec VP*
Paul Frentsos, *Mng Member*
EMP: 68
SQ FT: 109,673
SALES: 8.5MM **Privately Held**
WEB: www.galleriapark.com
SIC: 7011 6512 5813 5812 Hotels; non-
residential building operators; drinking
places; eating places

(P-12597)
GARDEN COURT HOTEL
520 Cowper St Ste 100, Palo Alto
(94301-1826)
PHONE.................................650 322-9000
Norman Rosenblatt, *General Ptnr*
Irwin G Kasle, *General Ptnr*
Nan Rosenblatt, *General Ptnr*
Sanford H Webster, *General Ptnr*
EMP: 90
SQ FT: 67,000
SALES (est): 6.9MM **Privately Held**
SIC: 7011 5812 Hotels; eating places

(P-12598)
GASLAMP HOTEL MANAGEMENT INC
202 Island Ave, San Diego (92101-6826)
PHONE.................................619 234-0977
Dana Blasi, *President*
EMP: 168
SALES (est): 3.5MM **Privately Held**
SIC: 7011 8741 Resort hotel; hotel or
motel management

(P-12599)
GCCFC 2005-GG5 Y ST LTD PARTNR
Also Called: Courtyard By Marriott S
4422 Y St, Sacramento (95817-2220)
PHONE.................................916 455-6800
Ken Brewer, *General Mgr*
Beth Gamble, *Controller*
EMP: 70
SALES: 950K **Privately Held**
SIC: 7011 Hotels

(P-12600)
GEARY DARLING LESSEE INC
Also Called: Marker Hotel, The
501 Geary St, San Francisco (94102-1640)
PHONE.................................415 292-0100
Michael Depatie, *President*
EMP: 150
SQ FT: 20,000

SALES (est): 9.9MM
SALES (corp-wide): 1.1B **Privately Held**
WEB: www.monaco-sf.com
SIC: 7011 7991 5813 5812 Hotels; physi-
cal fitness facilities; drinking places; eat-
ing places; banquet hall facilities
PA: Lasalle Hotel Properties
7550 Wisconsin Ave # 100
Bethesda MD 20814
301 941-1500

(P-12601)
GENTRY ASSOCIATES LLC
Also Called: Park Manor Suites
525 Spruce St, San Diego (92103-5814)
PHONE.................................619 296-0057
Elizabeth Willis, *Mng Member*
EMP: 80
SALES (est): 3.7MM **Privately Held**
WEB: www.parkmanorsuites.com
SIC: 7011 5812 Resort hotel; eating
places

(P-12602)
GEORGIAN HOTEL
1415 Ocean Ave, Santa Monica
(90401-2101)
PHONE.................................310 395-9945
Richard Dodrill,
EMP: 55
SQ FT: 40,000
SALES (est): 4.8MM **Privately Held**
WEB: www.georgianhotel.com
SIC: 7011 5812 Hotels; American restau-
rant

(P-12603)
GFP OCEANSIDE BLOCK 21 LLC
Also Called: Springhill Suites Oceanside
110 N Myers St, Oceanside (92054-2603)
PHONE.................................760 722-1003
Kathleen Maola,
EMP: 99
SQ FT: 110,000
SALES (est): 2.1MM **Privately Held**
SIC: 7011 5812 Resort hotel, franchised;
seafood restaurants

(P-12604)
GGWH LLC
Also Called: Holiday Inn
9440 Santa Monica Blvd # 610, Beverly
Hills (90210-4653)
PHONE.................................310 786-1700
Emerson Glazer,
Ericka Glazer,
EMP: 50
SALES (est): 1MM **Privately Held**
SIC: 7011 5812 5813 Hotels & motels;
eating places; drinking places

(P-12605)
GHG PROPERTIES LLC
Also Called: Whittier Grand Hotel
7320 Greenleaf Ave, Whittier (90602-1620)
PHONE.................................562 945-8511
Grace Hu,
Joseph Fan, *Manager*
EMP: 80
SALES (est): 322.5K **Privately Held**
SIC: 7011 Hotels & motels

(P-12606)
GOLDEN DOOR PROPERTIES LLC
777 Deer Springs Rd, San Marcos
(92069-9757)
PHONE.................................760 744-5777
Joanne Conway, *Mng Member*
Kathy Van Ness, *COO*
Efren Augusto, *Info Tech Dir*
Carolina Cervantes, *Technology*
Melanie Flynn, *Technology*
EMP: 139
SQ FT: 50,000
SALES: 13.9MM **Privately Held**
SIC: 7011 Hotels & motels

(P-12607)
GOLDEN HOTEL LLC
Also Called: Radisson Suites Anaheim
7762 Beach Blvd, Buena Park
(90620-1935)
PHONE.................................714 739-5600
Hieu M Bui,

Rod Hertz, *General Mgr*
EMP: 65
SALES: 980K **Privately Held**
SIC: 7011 Hotels

(P-12608)
GOLDEN HOTELS LTD PARTNERSHIP
Also Called: Atrium Hotel
18700 Macarthur Blvd, Irvine (92612-1409)
PHONE.....................................949 833-2770
Mike Wang, *Partner*
Pacific Coast Realty Services, *General Ptnr*
John Wang, *Partner*
Scott Bruno, *Sales Dir*
Frederick Pina, *Manager*
EMP: 140
SQ FT: 120,000
SALES (est): 7.1MM **Privately Held**
WEB: www.atriumhotel.com
SIC: 7011 Resort hotel; hotels

(P-12609)
GOLDENPARK LLC
Also Called: Norwalk Marriott Hotel
16209 Paramount Blvd # 214, Paramount
(90723-5461)
PHONE.....................................562 863-5555
Dae In Kim,
Jane N Kim,
EMP: 100
SQ FT: 138,944
SALES (est): 4.7MM **Privately Held**
SIC: 7011 Hotel, franchised

(P-12610)
GOLETA HHG HOTEL DEV LP
Also Called: Hilton Garden Inn Santa
6878 Hollister Ave, Goleta (93117-3017)
PHONE.....................................805 562-5996
Yuly Rivera, *Admin Asst*
Patricia Santini, *Officer*
EMP: 60
SQ FT: 95,678
SALES (est): 205.3K **Privately Held**
SIC: 7011 Resort hotel, franchised

(P-12611)
GOODRICH LAX A CAL LTD PARTNR
Also Called: Quality Hotel Airport
310 W Longden Ave, Arcadia (91007-8235)
PHONE.....................................626 254-9988
Xi Min Yuan, *Partner*
EMP: 80
SALES: 4MM **Privately Held**
SIC: 7011 Hotels & motels

(P-12612)
GRAND DEL MAR RESORT LP
5300 Grand Del Mar Ct, San Diego
(92130-4901)
PHONE.....................................858 314-2000
Tom Voss, *Partner*
Jordan Snider, *Executive*
Lynn Donlou, *Admin Asst*
Michael Vinson, *CTO*
Edward Castillo, *Info Tech Mgr*
EMP: 570
SALES (est): 33MM **Privately Held**
SIC: 7011 Resort hotel; hotels

(P-12613)
GRAND PACIFIC CARLSBAD HT LP
Also Called: Sheraton Carlsbad Resort & Spa
5480 Grand Pacific Dr, Carlsbad
(92008-4723)
PHONE.....................................760 827-2400
Tim Shinkle, *CFO*
Erin Lindquist, *General Mgr*
John Wehner, *Engineer*
Janina Kershaw, *Controller*
Jeannie Curnutte, *Natl Sales Mgr*
EMP: 272
SALES (est): 19.2MM **Privately Held**
SIC: 7011 Resort hotel

(P-12614)
GRAND PACIFIC RESORTS SVCS LP
5900 Pasteur Ct Ste 200, Carlsbad
(92008-7336)
PHONE.....................................760 431-8500
Timothy Stripe, *Partner*

David Brown, *Partner*
Sherrie McIntosh, *Manager*
EMP: 120
SQ FT: 22,000
SALES (est): 5.6MM **Privately Held**
SIC: 7011 Resort hotel

(P-12615)
GRANLIBAKKEN MANAGEMENT CO LTD
Also Called: Granlibakken Ski Racquet Resort
725 Granlibakken Rd, Tahoe City (96145)
P.O. Box 6329 (96145-6329)
PHONE.....................................800 543-3221
Willem G C Parson, *President*
Norma Parson, *Treasurer*
EMP: 60
SALES: 7MM **Privately Held**
WEB: www.granlibakken.com
SIC: 7011 Resort hotel

(P-12616)
GRANVILLE HOTEL CORP
13111 Sycamore Dr, Norwalk (90650-8339)
PHONE.....................................562 863-5555
Lawrence Lui, *President*
James Evans, *CFO*
Anthony Carter, *Vice Pres*
EMP: 115
SALES (est): 1.2MM **Privately Held**
WEB: www.sheratonuptown.com
SIC: 7011 Hotel, franchised

(P-12617)
GREAT WESTERN HOTELS CORP
Also Called: Heritage Inn
1050 N Norma St, Ridgecrest
(93555-3151)
PHONE.....................................760 446-6543
Victoria Moore, *Manager*
EMP: 50
SALES (corp-wide): 10.7MM **Privately Held**
WEB: www.danapointmarinainn.com
SIC: 7011 Hotels
PA: Great Western Hotels Corp
    401 W Imperial Hwy
    La Habra CA 90631
    714 459-7500

(P-12618)
GREEN TREE CAPITAL LP
Also Called: Green Tree Inn
14173 Green Tree Blvd, Victorville
(92395-4343)
PHONE.....................................760 245-3461
Cathy Davis, *General Mgr*
Philip Elghanian,
EMP: 55
SQ FT: 52,647
SALES (est): 1.2MM **Privately Held**
SIC: 7011 Hotels & motels

(P-12619)
GREENS GROUP INC
9289 Research Dr, Irvine (92618-4286)
PHONE.....................................949 829-4902
Ashutosh Kadakia, *CFO*
EMP: 145
SQ FT: 2,526
SALES (est): 654.9K **Privately Held**
SIC: 7011 Resort hotel, franchised

(P-12620)
GREENWOOD HOLDINGS LLC
Also Called: Four Points San Diego-Seaworld
3888 Greenwood St, San Diego
(92110-4412)
PHONE.....................................619 299-6633
Imad T Mansour, *President*
EMP: 69
SALES: 5MM **Privately Held**
SIC: 7011 Hotels

(P-12621)
GRINGTEAM INC
Also Called: Doubletree Hotel
14455 Penasquitos Dr, San Diego
(92129-1603)
PHONE.....................................858 485-4145
Russ Tanakaya, *General Mgr*
EMP: 140
SALES (corp-wide): 2.7B **Publicly Held**
WEB: www.dtwarrenplace.com
SIC: 7011 Hotels & motels

HQ: Gringteam Inc
    21725 Gateway Center Dr
    Diamond Bar CA 91765
    -

(P-12622)
GRINGTEAM INC
Also Called: Doubletree Hotel
222 N Vineyard Ave, Ontario (91764-4428)
PHONE.....................................909 605-4222
Herman Haastrup, *Manager*
EMP: 343
SALES (corp-wide): 2.7B **Publicly Held**
WEB: www.dtwarrenplace.com
SIC: 7011 Hotels
HQ: Gringteam Inc
    21725 Gateway Center Dr
    Diamond Bar CA 91765

(P-12623)
GRINGTEAM INC
Also Called: Doubletree Hotel
2050 Gateway Pl, San Jose (95110-1011)
PHONE.....................................408 453-4000
David Costain, *General Mgr*
EMP: 350
SALES (corp-wide): 2.7B **Publicly Held**
WEB: www.dtwarrenplace.com
SIC: 7011 5812 Hotels; eating places
HQ: Gringteam Inc
    21725 Gateway Center Dr
    Diamond Bar CA 91765

(P-12624)
GRINGTEAM INC
Also Called: Doubltree By Hlton Ht Bkrsfeld
3100 Camino Del Rio Ct, Bakersfield
(93308-6245)
PHONE.....................................661 426-7919
Robert Balmer, *Manager*
Bill Murray, *General Mgr*
Carlos Navarro, *General Mgr*
EMP: 234
SALES (corp-wide): 2.7B **Publicly Held**
WEB: www.doralpmsprings.com
SIC: 7011 7299 Hotels; banquet hall facilities
HQ: Gringteam Inc
    21725 Gateway Center Dr
    Diamond Bar CA 91765

(P-12625)
GRINGTEAM INC
Also Called: Doubletree Hotel
201 E Macarthur Blvd, Santa Ana
(92707-5776)
PHONE.....................................714 825-3333
Marsha Hansen, *General Mgr*
EMP: 182
SALES (corp-wide): 2.7B **Publicly Held**
WEB: www.dtwarrenplace.com
SIC: 7011 Hotels & motels
HQ: Gringteam Inc
    21725 Gateway Center Dr
    Diamond Bar CA 91765

(P-12626)
GRINGTEAM INC
Also Called: Doubletree Hotel
2001 Point West Way, Sacramento
(95815-4702)
PHONE.....................................916 929-8855
Chris Mellini, *Manager*
EMP: 350
SALES (corp-wide): 2.7B **Publicly Held**
WEB: www.dtwarrenplace.com
SIC: 7011 5812 5813 7991 Hotels; eating places; bar (drinking places); physical fitness facilities
HQ: Gringteam Inc
    21725 Gateway Center Dr
    Diamond Bar CA 91765

(P-12627)
GRINGTEAM INC
Also Called: Doubletree Hotel
1150 9th St Frnt, Modesto (95354-0823)
PHONE.....................................209 526-6000
Cindy Power, *Manager*
EMP: 270

SALES (corp-wide): 2.7B **Publicly Held**
WEB: www.dtwarrenplace.com
SIC: 7011 5813 Hotels; drinking places
HQ: Gringteam Inc
    21725 Gateway Center Dr
    Diamond Bar CA 91765

(P-12628)
GRINGTEAM INC
Also Called: Doubletree By Hilton
7450 Hazard Center Dr, San Diego
(92108-4539)
PHONE.....................................619 297-5466
Karima Zaki, *Manager*
Leda Gonzalez, *Director*
EMP: 300
SALES (corp-wide): 2.7B **Publicly Held**
WEB: www.doralpalmsprings.com
SIC: 7011 5812 Hotels; eating places
HQ: Gringteam Inc
    21725 Gateway Center Dr
    Diamond Bar CA 91765

(P-12629)
GRINGTEAM INC
Also Called: Doubletree Hotel
835 Airport Blvd, Burlingame (94010-1922)
PHONE.....................................650 344-5500
Liza Normandy, *Branch Mgr*
David Chung, *Purch Mgr*
EMP: 175
SALES (corp-wide): 2.7B **Publicly Held**
WEB: www.doralpalmsprings.com
SIC: 7011 6512 5813 5812 Hotels; non-residential building operators; drinking places; eating places
HQ: Gringteam Inc
    21725 Gateway Center Dr
    Diamond Bar CA 91765

(P-12630)
GRINGTEAM INC
Also Called: Doubletree Hotel
34402 Pacific Coast Hwy, Dana Point
(92624-1211)
PHONE.....................................949 661-1100
Mike Peludo, *Manager*
EMP: 80
SALES (corp-wide): 2.7B **Publicly Held**
WEB: www.doralpalmsprings.com
SIC: 7011 Hotels & motels
HQ: Gringteam Inc
    21725 Gateway Center Dr
    Diamond Bar CA 91765

(P-12631)
GROSVENOR PROPERTIES LTD
Also Called: Best Western
380 S Airport Blvd, South San Francisco
(94080-6704)
PHONE.....................................650 873-3200
Jim McGuire, *Manager*
Fernando Alvarez, *Chief Engr*
David Huddleston, *Opers Mgr*
Roland Cinco, *Sales Mgr*
EMP: 160
SALES (est): 4.1MM
SALES (corp-wide): 11MM **Privately Held**
WEB: www.grosvenorsfo.com
SIC: 7011 5813 5812 7299 Hotels & motels; drinking places; eating places; banquet hall facilities
PA: Grosvenor Properties Ltd.
    222 Front St Fl 7
    San Francisco CA 94111
    415 421-5940

(P-12632)
GROSVENOR VISALIA ASSOCIATES
Also Called: Holiday Inn
9000 W Airport Dr, Visalia (93277-9511)
PHONE.....................................559 651-5000
Robert K Werbe, *General Ptnr*
EMP: 52
SQ FT: 163,415
SALES (est): 3.9MM **Privately Held**
SIC: 7011 Hotels & motels

(P-12633)
H C T INC
Also Called: Hyatt Regency Mission Bay Spa
1441 Quivira Rd, San Diego (92109-7805)
PHONE..........................619 224-1234
Mohsen Kaleghi, *President*
Mark S Hoplamazian, *President*
Kevin Hurley, *General Mgr*
Mohsen Khaleghi, *General Mgr*
Shaina Citrullo, *Sales Mgr*
EMP: 300
SALES (est): 16.3MM **Publicly Held**
SIC: 7011 4491 5813 5812 Hotels & motels; marine terminals; piers, incl. buildings & facilities; operation & maintenance; drinking places; eating places
PA: Chesapeake Lodging Trust
4300 Wilson Blvd Ste 625
Arlington VA 22203

(P-12634)
H D G ASSOCIATES
Also Called: Hotel Marmonte
1111 E Cabrillo Blvd, Santa Barbara
(93103-3701)
PHONE..........................805 963-0744
Ruth Grande, *President*
EMP: 125
SQ FT: 150,000
SALES (est): 3MM
SALES (corp-wide): 4.6B **Publicly Held**
WEB: www.hotelmarmonte.com
SIC: 7011 Hotels
HQ: Hyatt Corporation
150 N Riverside Plz
Chicago IL 60606
312 750-1234

(P-12635)
H2 HOTEL LLC
Also Called: Comfort Suites
219 Healdsburg Ave, Healdsburg
(95448-4103)
PHONE..........................707 431-2202
David Huish,
John Huish,
Scott Huish,
Shane Huish,
EMP: 80
SALES (est): 2.2MM **Privately Held**
SIC: 7011 Hotel, franchised; hotels

(P-12636)
HALF MOON BAY LODGE
Also Called: Best Wstn Half Moon Bay Lodge
2400 Cabrillo Hwy S, Half Moon Bay
(94019-2253)
PHONE..........................650 726-9000
Keith Wesstlmann, *Manager*
EMP: 50
SALES (est): 2.2MM **Privately Held**
SIC: 7011 Motels

(P-12637)
HAMPSTEAD LAFAYETTE HOTEL LLC
Also Called: Innsuites Hotels
2223 El Cajon Blvd, San Diego
(92104-1103)
PHONE..........................619 296-2101
James Green, *Manager*
EMP: 50
SALES (est): 1.2MM
SALES (corp-wide): 1.1MM **Privately Held**
WEB: www.lafayettehotelsd.com
SIC: 7011 Resort hotel; hotels
PA: Lafayette Hampstead Hotel Llc
2223 El Cajon Blvd
San Diego CA 92104
619 296-2101

(P-12638)
HAMPTON INN NORCO CORONA NORTH
1530 Hamner Ave, Norco (92860-2939)
PHONE..........................951 279-1111
Mahendra B Desai, *Executive Asst*
EMP: 80
SALES (est): 1.8MM **Privately Held**
SIC: 7011 Motels

(P-12639)
HANDLERY HOTELS INC
Also Called: Handlery Union Square Hotel
351 Geary St, San Francisco (94102-1801)
PHONE..........................415 781-7800
John Handlery, *Manager*
EMP: 150
SALES (corp-wide): 31.4MM **Privately Held**
WEB: www.handlery.com
SIC: 7011 Resort hotel
PA: Handlery Hotels, Inc.
180 Geary St Ste 700
San Francisco CA 94108
415 781-4550

(P-12640)
HANDLERY HOTELS INC
950 Hotel Cir N, San Diego (92108-2995)
PHONE..........................415 781-4550
John Martin, *Manager*
EMP: 150
SALES (corp-wide): 31.4MM **Privately Held**
WEB: www.handlery.com
SIC: 7011 5941 5812 5947 Hotels; golf goods & equipment; eating places; gift, novelty & souvenir shop; drinking places
PA: Handlery Hotels, Inc.
180 Geary St Ste 700
San Francisco CA 94108
415 781-4550

(P-12641)
HANFORD HOTELS LLC
17542 17th St Ste 450, Tustin
(92780-1964)
PHONE..........................714 210-0400
Donald E Sodaro, *Mng Member*
William A Caine Jr,
EMP: 189
SQ FT: 5,000
SALES (est): 2.8MM **Privately Held**
WEB: www.hanfordhotels.com
SIC: 7011 Hotels & motels

(P-12642)
HARBOR ISLAND HOTEL GROUP LP
Also Called: Four Points Sheraton Ventura
1050 Schooner Dr, Ventura (93001-4273)
PHONE..........................805 658-1212
Joseph Fan, *Managing Prtnr*
EMP: 80
SALES: 9MM **Privately Held**
SIC: 7011 Hotels

(P-12643)
HARBOR VIEW HOTEL VENTURES LLC
Also Called: Doubletree Ht San Diego Dwntwn
1646 Front St, San Diego (92101-2920)
PHONE..........................619 239-6800
Michael Gallegos, *Mng Member*
Rita Baca, *General Mgr*
Patricia Gallegos, *Sales Mgr*
Mario Garcia, *Sales Mgr*
Elizabeth Boman, *Marketing Staff*
EMP: 100
SALES (est): 6.5MM **Privately Held**
SIC: 7011 Hotels

(P-12644)
HARBOR VIEW HOTELS INC
Also Called: Hilton San Francisco
600 Airport Blvd, Burlingame (94010-1920)
PHONE..........................650 340-8500
James Evans, *CFO*
John Kellites, *Manager*
EMP: 99
SALES (est): 6MM **Privately Held**
WEB: www.sheratonsfo.com
SIC: 7011 Hotels

(P-12645)
HARDAGE GROUP OF COMPANIES
Also Called: Woodfin Suites Hotel Brea
3100 E Imperial Hwy, Brea (92821-6719)
PHONE..........................714 579-3200
Karla Barges, *Branch Mgr*
EMP: 55

SALES (corp-wide): 9MM **Privately Held**
WEB: www.woodfinsuitehotels.com
SIC: 7011 Hotels & motels
PA: The Hardage Group Of Companies
12730 High Bluff Dr # 250
San Diego CA

(P-12646)
HAVASU LANDING CASINO (PA)
1 Main St, Needles (92363)
PHONE..........................760 858-5380
Bethany Hopp, *CFO*
Dave Bartlett, *Info Tech Dir*
Denise Weddle, *Accounting Mgr*
Vickie Yount, *Marketing Staff*
John Csicsery, *Property Mgr*
EMP: 71
SALES (est): 3.9MM **Privately Held**
SIC: 7011 Casino hotel

(P-12647)
HAWAIIAN GARDENS CASINO
11871 Carson St, Hawaiian Gardens
(90716-1127)
PHONE..........................562 860-5887
David Moskowitz, *CEO*
Irving Moskowitz, *President*
Martha H Vital, *Administration*
Gerard Lara, *Project Mgr*
Louie Campos, *Purch Agent*
EMP: 1000
SALES (est): 41.4MM **Privately Held**
WEB: www.hgcasino.com
SIC: 7011 Casino hotel

(P-12648)
HAWAIIAN HOTELS & RESORTS INC
2830 Borchard Rd, Newbury Park
(91320-3810)
PHONE..........................805 480-0052
Edward J Hogan, *President*
Todd Castor, *Manager*
EMP: 100
SALES (est): 3.8MM
SALES (corp-wide): 7.2B **Privately Held**
WEB: www.hawaiihotels.com
SIC: 7011 Resort hotel; hotels
HQ: Pleasant Holidays, Llc
2404 Townsgate Rd
Westlake Village CA 91361

(P-12649)
HAYES MANSION CONFERENCE CTR
200 Edenvale Ave, San Jose (95136-3309)
PHONE..........................408 226-3200
Vickie Leong, *Principal*
Edward Robledo, *Manager*
EMP: 140
SALES (est): 4.6MM **Privately Held**
WEB: www.hayesmansion.com
SIC: 7011 Hotels

(P-12650)
HAZENS INVESTMENT LLC
Also Called: Sheraton
6101 W Century Blvd, Los Angeles
(90045-5310)
PHONE..........................310 642-1111
Orazio Parisi, *Admin Asst*
Fidelity Investment Insurance,
Blue Vista Investments,
Tonya Spencer, *Manager*
EMP: 395
SALES (est): 31.7MM **Privately Held**
WEB: www.edgemastery.com
SIC: 7011 Hotels

(P-12651)
HEI IRVINE LLC
2120 Main St, Irvine (92614-6219)
PHONE..........................949 553-8332
Gary Mendell, *Principal*
EMP: 78
SALES (est): 852.6K
SALES (corp-wide): 277.3MM **Privately Held**
SIC: 7011 Hotels
PA: Hei Hospitality, Llc
101 Merritt 7
Norwalk CT 06851
203 849-8844

(P-12652)
HEI LONG BEACH LLC
Also Called: Hilton Hotels
701 W Ocean Blvd, Long Beach
(90831-3100)
PHONE..........................562 983-3400
Clark Christopher, *Principal*
HEI Hospitality Fund Holdings,
EMP: 125
SALES (est): 5MM
SALES (corp-wide): 277.3MM **Privately Held**
SIC: 7011 Hotels
PA: Hei Hospitality, Llc
101 Merritt 7
Norwalk CT 06851
203 849-8844

(P-12653)
HEI MISSION VALLEY LP
Also Called: San Diego Mission Vly Hilton
901 Camino Del Rio S, San Diego
(92108-3515)
PHONE..........................619 299-2729
Dan Weber, *General Ptnr*
EMP: 220
SQ FT: 219,000
SALES (est): 3.7MM **Privately Held**
SIC: 7011 Hotels

(P-12654)
HHC TRS PORTSMOUTH LLC
Also Called: Renaissance Palm Springs
888 E Tahquitz Canyon Way, Palm Springs
(92262-6708)
PHONE..........................760 322-6000
David Kimichik,
EMP: 95 EST: 2003
SALES (est): 2.1MM **Privately Held**
SIC: 7011 Hotels & motels

(P-12655)
HHLP SAN DIEGO LESSEE LLC
Also Called: Marriott
530 Broadway, San Diego (92101-5206)
PHONE..........................619 446-3000
Ashish Parikh, *Manager*
EMP: 90
SQ FT: 1,000,000
SALES (est): 3.7MM **Privately Held**
SIC: 7011 Hotels & motels

(P-12656)
HI ANAHEIM LLC
100 W Katella Ave, Anaheim (92802)
PHONE..........................714 533-1500
Ajesh Patel,
EMP: 60
SALES (est): 205.3K **Privately Held**
SIC: 7011 Hotels

(P-12657)
HI FRESNO HOSPITALITY LLC
Also Called: Radisson Ht Frsno Cnfrence Ctr
1055 Van Ness Ave, Fresno (93721-2006)
PHONE..........................559 233-6650
Mukesh Shah, *Mng Member*
Leslie Beninga, *Sales Dir*
EMP: 70
SALES: 4MM **Privately Held**
SIC: 7011 Hotels

(P-12658)
HIGHLANDS INN INC
Also Called: Hyatt Carmel Highlands
120 Highland Dr, Carmel (93923-9607)
P.O. Box 1700 (93921-1700)
PHONE..........................831 620-1234
Mel Bettcher, *Principal*
Paul C Reed, *CEO*
EMP: 225
SALES (est): 3.5MM **Privately Held**
SIC: 7011 7389 Hotels & motels; timeshare condominium exchange

(P-12659)
HIGHLANDS INN INVESTORS II LP
Also Called: Hyatt Hotel
120 Highland Dr, Carmel (93923-9607)
PHONE..........................831 624-3801
Ulrich Samietz, *General Mgr*
Highlands Inn Investors, *Ltd Ptnr*
EMP: 260

▲ = Import ▼=Export
◆ =Import/Export

SALES (est): 7.7MM **Privately Held**
SIC: 7011 5812 5813 5947 Resort hotel; American restaurant; drinking places; gift, novelty & souvenir shop

(P-12660)
HILTON EL SEGUNDO LLC
Also Called: Hiltonm Grdn Inn Lax El Sgundo
2100 E Mariposa Ave, El Segundo
(90245-5002)
PHONE.................................310 726-0100
Brianna Akins,
EMP: 60 **EST:** 2013
SALES (est): 2MM **Privately Held**
SIC: 7011 Hotels

(P-12661)
HILTON GARDEN IN SAN MATEO
Also Called: Hilton Garden Hotel
2000 Bridgepointe Pkwy, Foster City
(94404-1586)
PHONE.................................650 522-9000
Derrick Hudson, *Manager*
Derek Hudson, *General Mgr*
EMP: 60
SALES (corp-wide): 3.7MM **Privately Held**
SIC: 7011 Hotels & motels
PA: Hilton Garden In San Mateo
2000 Bridgepointe Pkwy
Foster City CA 94404
650 522-9000

(P-12662)
HILTON GARDEN INN
510 Lewelling Blvd, San Leandro
(94579-1803)
PHONE.................................510 346-5533
Burt Knewson, *Manager*
EMP: 80
SALES (est): 2.5MM **Privately Held**
SIC: 7011 Hotels

(P-12663)
HILTON GARDEN INNS MGT LLC
6450 Carlsbad Blvd, Carlsbad
(92011-1058)
PHONE.................................760 476-0800
Robert Moore, *General Mgr*
Carlos Chang, *Controller*
EMP: 116
SALES (corp-wide): 2.7B **Publicly Held**
WEB: www.esirvine.com
SIC: 7011 Hotels & motels
HQ: Hilton Garden Inns Management Llc
7930 Jones Branch Dr
Mc Lean VA 22102
703 883-1000

(P-12664)
HILTON GARDEN INNS MGT LLC
2100 E Mariposa Ave, El Segundo
(90245-5002)
PHONE.................................310 726-0100
Barbara Bejan, *Manager*
EMP: 67
SQ FT: 87,198
SALES (corp-wide): 2.7B **Publicly Held**
SIC: 7011 Hotels & motels
HQ: Hilton Garden Inns Management Llc
7930 Jones Branch Dr
Mc Lean VA 22102
703 883-1000

(P-12665)
HILTON GARDEN INNS MGT LLC
2801 Constitution Dr Fl 2, Livermore
(94551-7613)
PHONE.................................925 292-2000
Joan Baldon, *Manager*
EMP: 50
SALES (corp-wide): 2.7B **Publicly Held**
SIC: 7011 Hotels & motels
HQ: Hilton Garden Inns Management Llc
7930 Jones Branch Dr
Mc Lean VA 22102
703 883-1000

(P-12666)
HILTON LOS ANGLES UNIVERSAL CY
555 Universal Hollywood Dr, Universal City
(91608-1001)
PHONE.................................818 506-2500
Juan Aquinde, *General Mgr*
EMP: 380

SALES (est): 16.2MM **Privately Held**
SIC: 7011 Hotels

(P-12667)
HILTON RESORT PALM SPRINGS
400 E Tahquitz Canyon Way, Palm Springs
(92262-6605)
PHONE.................................760 320-6868
Aftab Dada, *General Mgr*
Mike Leones, *Manager*
EMP: 200
SALES (est): 8.1MM **Privately Held**
WEB: www.hiltonpalmsprings.com
SIC: 7011 Hotels

(P-12668)
HILTON SAN FRANCISCO FINCL DST
750 Kearny St, San Francisco
(94108-1860)
PHONE.................................415 433-6600
Randall King, *Principal*
Michael Van, *Marketing Mgr*
J San Miguel, *Asst Director*
Lisa Russi, *Director*
EMP: 50
SALES (est): 3.6MM **Privately Held**
WEB: www.sanfranciscohiltonhotel.com
SIC: 7011 Hotels

(P-12669)
HILTON UNIVERSAL HOTEL
555 Universal Hollywood Dr, Universal City
(91608-1001)
PHONE.................................818 506-2500
Michelle Szeto, *Principal*
Juan Aquinde, *General Mgr*
LMI Unson, *Director*
Arnold Reyes, *Manager*
EMP: 99
SALES (est): 1.2MM
SALES (corp-wide): 13.5MM **Privately Held**
SIC: 7011 Hotels
HQ: Sun Hill Properties, Inc.
555 Universal Hollywood Dr
Universal City CA 91608
818 506-2500

(P-12670)
HILTON WOODLAND HILLS & TOWERS
6360 Canoga Ave, Woodland Hills
(91367-2501)
PHONE.................................818 595-1000
Ed Debries, *General Mgr*
Conoga Hotel Corporation, *Partner*
Lisa Barbaglto, *Executive*
EMP: 200
SALES (est): 7.1MM **Privately Held**
SIC: 7011 5813 5812 Resort hotel; drinking places; eating places

(P-12671)
HISTORIC MISSION INN CORP
Also Called: Mission Inn Hotel and Spa, The
3649 Mission Inn Ave, Riverside
(92501-3364)
P.O. Box 1433 (92502-1433)
PHONE.................................951 784-0300
Duane R Roberts, *President*
Cliff Day, *CFO*
Diana Rosure, *Vice Pres*
Stan Kantowski, *General Mgr*
Richard Shippee, *Admin Sec*
EMP: 460
SALES (est): 33.2MM **Privately Held**
WEB: www.missioninn.com
SIC: 7011 7991 Resort hotel; spas
PA: Entrepreneurial Capital Corporation
4100 Newport Place Dr # 400
Newport Beach CA 92660
949 809-3900

(P-12672)
HISTORICAL PROPERTIES INC (PA)
Also Called: Horton Grand Hotel
311 Island Ave, San Diego (92101-6923)
PHONE.................................619 230-8417
Doris J Rose, *President*
Santiago Ojeda, *CEO*
Maria Overton, *Controller*
Jennifer Nauta, *Sales Staff*

Jenny Schiller, *Sales Staff*
EMP: 96
SQ FT: 60,000
SALES (est): 8.6MM **Privately Held**
WEB: www.hortongrand.com
SIC: 7011 Hotels

(P-12673)
HIT PORTFOLIO I MISC TRS LLC
Also Called: Hyatt Hotel
8401 W Sunset Blvd, Los Angeles
(90069-1909)
PHONE.................................323 656-1234
Tim Flodin, *Manager*
Crystal Sandoval, *Human Res Dir*
Larisa Arbashevskaya, *Marketing Mgr*
Karina Nazarian, *Sales Staff*
Allison Wiltfong, *Assistant*
EMP: 165
SALES (corp-wide): 4.6B **Publicly Held**
WEB: www.hyatt.com
SIC: 7011 5812 5813 Hotels; restaurant; family; independent; bar (drinking places)
HQ: Hyatt Corporation
150 N Riverside Plz
Chicago IL 60606
312 750-1234

(P-12674)
HIT PORTFOLIO I MISC TRS LLC
3500 Market St, Riverside (92501-2841)
PHONE.................................909 240-9526
Donna Esparza, *General Mgr*
Jay Koury, *General Mgr*
EMP: 316
SALES (corp-wide): 4.6B **Publicly Held**
SIC: 7011 Hotels
HQ: Hyatt Corporation
150 N Riverside Plz
Chicago IL 60606
312 750-1234

(P-12675)
HIT PORTFOLIO I MISC TRS LLC
Also Called: Hyatt Hotel
50 Drumm St, San Francisco (94111-4804)
PHONE.................................415 788-1234
Matthew Adams, *Manager*
EMP: 900
SALES (corp-wide): 4.6B **Publicly Held**
WEB: www.hyatt.com
SIC: 7011 5812 5813 Hotels; eating places; bar (drinking places)
HQ: Hyatt Corporation
150 N Riverside Plz
Chicago IL 60606
312 750-1234

(P-12676)
HIT PORTFOLIO I MISC TRS LLC
Also Called: Hyatt House San Ramon
2323 San Ramon Vly Blvd, San Ramon
(94583-1607)
PHONE.................................925 743-1882
Pam Callahan, *Branch Mgr*
Kerry Knudson, *General Mgr*
Julie Thomas, *Manager*
EMP: 317
SALES (corp-wide): 4.6B **Publicly Held**
SIC: 7011 Hotels
HQ: Hyatt Corporation
150 N Riverside Plz
Chicago IL 60606
312 750-1234

(P-12677)
HIT PORTFOLIO I MISC TRS LLC
Also Called: Hyatt Hotel
200 S Pine Ave, Long Beach (90802-4537)
PHONE.................................562 432-0161
Steve Smith, *Manager*
Charles McInnish, *Engineer*
Mary Carley, *Director*
Kristin Abrams, *Manager*
Nancy Canzone, *Manager*
EMP: 500
SALES (corp-wide): 4.6B **Publicly Held**
WEB: www.hyatt.com
SIC: 7011 7299 Hotels; banquet hall facilities
HQ: Hyatt Corporation
150 N Riverside Plz
Chicago IL 60606
312 750-1234

(P-12678)
HIT PORTFOLIO I MISC TRS LLC
Also Called: Hyatt Regency Monterey
1 Old Golf Course Rd, Monterey
(93940-4908)
PHONE.................................831 372-1234
Michael Koffler, *Manager*
Neal Matsumoto, *Controller*
Paula Calvetti, *Human Res Dir*
Timothy Nelson, *Manager*
EMP: 420
SALES (corp-wide): 4.6B **Publicly Held**
WEB: www.hyatt.com
SIC: 7011 Hotels
HQ: Hyatt Corporation
150 N Riverside Plz
Chicago IL 60606
312 750-1234

(P-12679)
HIT PORTFOLIO I MISC TRS LLC
Also Called: Hyatt Hotel
17900 Jamboree Rd, Irvine (92614-6211)
PHONE.................................949 975-1234
Rod T Schinnerer, *General Mgr*
Madeline Douglass, *Director*
Andrea Miesen, *Manager*
Trish Santalla, *Manager*
EMP: 450
SALES (corp-wide): 4.6B **Publicly Held**
WEB: www.hyatt.com
SIC: 7011 7992 7991 5813 Hotels; public golf courses; physical fitness facilities; drinking places; eating places
HQ: Hyatt Corporation
150 N Riverside Plz
Chicago IL 60606
312 750-1234

(P-12680)
HIT PORTFOLIO I MISC TRS LLC
Also Called: Hyatt Grand Champion Resort
44600 Indian Wells Ln, Indian Wells
(92210-8707)
PHONE.................................760 341-1000
Allan Farwell, *Manager*
Melody Munger, *Admin Asst*
Vey Por, *MIS Mgr*
Denise Harnett, *Marketing Mgr*
Alexandra Magness, *Sales Mgr*
EMP: 500
SALES (corp-wide): 4.6B **Publicly Held**
WEB: www.hyatt.com
SIC: 7011 5813 5812 Hotels; drinking places; eating places
HQ: Hyatt Corporation
150 N Riverside Plz
Chicago IL 60606
312 750-1234

(P-12681)
HIT PORTFOLIO I MISC TRS LLC
Also Called: Hyatt Hotel
1107 Jamboree Rd, Newport Beach
(92660-6219)
PHONE.................................949 729-1234
Ruth Benjamin, *General Mgr*
Martha Collins, *Sales Associate*
Shelley Callahan, *Director*
Dylan Davidson, *Manager*
EMP: 300
SALES (corp-wide): 4.6B **Publicly Held**
WEB: www.hyatt.com
SIC: 7011 5813 5812 Hotels; drinking places; eating places
HQ: Hyatt Corporation
150 N Riverside Plz
Chicago IL 60606
312 750-1234

(P-12682)
HIT PORTFOLIO I MISC TRS LLC
55 E Brokaw Rd, San Jose (95112-4202)
PHONE.................................408 453-3006
Frank Palacios, *Principal*
EMP: 314
SALES (corp-wide): 4.6B **Publicly Held**
SIC: 7011 8741 Hotels; hotel or motel management
HQ: Hyatt Corporation
150 N Riverside Plz
Chicago IL 60606
312 750-1234

PRODUCTS & SVCS

(P-12683)
HIT PORTFOLIO I MISC TRS LLC
Also Called: Hyatt Regency San Francisco Ht
5 Embarcadero Ctr, San Francisco
(94111-4800)
PHONE.................................415 788-1234
Jerry Simmons, *General Mgr*
Vincent Savignano, *Executive*
Kelly Giannini, *Executive Asst*
Cecilia Santos, *Accountant*
Angela Au, *Hum Res Coord*
EMP: 600
SALES (corp-wide): 4.6B **Publicly Held**
WEB: www.hyatt.com
SIC: **7011** 5812 5813 Hotels; eating
places; drinking places
HQ: Hyatt Corporation
150 N Riverside Plz
Chicago IL 60606
312 750-1234

(P-12684)
HIT PORTFOLIO I MISC TRS LLC
Also Called: Andaz Sandiego
600 F St, San Diego (92101-6310)
PHONE.................................619 849-1234
Rusty Middleton, *Branch Mgr*
Rebecca Quezada, *Controller*
EMP: 200
SALES (corp-wide): 4.6B **Publicly Held**
SIC: **7011** Resort hotel
HQ: Hyatt Corporation
150 N Riverside Plz
Chicago IL 60606
312 750-1234

(P-12685)
HIT PORTFOLIO I NTC TRS LP
Also Called: Residence Inn La Lax El Segndo
2135 E El Segundo Blvd, El Segundo
(90245-4503)
PHONE.................................310 333-0888
EMP: 50
SALES (corp-wide): 621MM **Privately
Held**
SIC: **7011** Hotels
HQ: Hit Portfolio I Ntc Trs, Lp
3950 University Dr # 301
Fairfax VA 22030
571 529-6078

(P-12686)
HIT PORTFOLIO II NTC TRS LP
Also Called: Courtyard San Diego Carlsbad
5835 Owens Ave, Carlsbad (92008-6562)
PHONE.................................760 431-9399
Minda Zoloth, *Branch Mgr*
EMP: 50
SALES (corp-wide): 621MM **Privately
Held**
SIC: **7011** Hotels
HQ: Hit Portfolio Ii Ntc Trs, Lp
106 York Rd
Jenkintown PA

(P-12687)
HIT PORTFOLIO II TRS LLC
Also Called: Anaheim/Orange Hilton Suites
400 N State College Blvd, Orange
(92868-1708)
PHONE.................................714 938-1111
John Ault, *Manager*
EMP: 120
SALES (corp-wide): 2.7B **Publicly Held**
WEB: www.hiltondirect.com
SIC: **7011** 5812 Hotels; eating places
HQ: Hit Portfolio Ii Trs, Llc
7930 Jones Branch Dr
Mc Lean VA 22102
703 883-1000

(P-12688)
HMBL LLC
Also Called: Holiday Inn
8400 W Sunset Blvd Ste 3a, West Holly-
wood (90069-1934)
PHONE.................................323 656-8090
Robert Jackson,
Glen Grush,
Joel Leebove,
David Rose,
EMP: 125
SQ FT: 1,500
SALES (est): 2.4MM **Privately Held**
SIC: **7011** Hotels & motels

(P-12689)
HOLIDAY GARDEN SF CORP
Also Called: Residence In Anaheim
1700 S Clementine St, Anaheim
(92802-2902)
PHONE.................................714 533-3555
Hai-Ni Chen, *President*
EMP: 50 EST: 1997
SALES: 7MM **Privately Held**
SIC: **7011** Hotels & motels

(P-12690)
**HOLIDAY INN & SUITES
ANAHEIM**
1240 S Walnut St, Anaheim (92802-2241)
PHONE.................................714 535-0300
Eva Huang, *Principal*
Tom Van Winkle, *General Mgr*
EMP: 75
SALES (est): 1.2MM **Privately Held**
SIC: **7011** Hotels & motels

(P-12691)
**HOLIDAY INN EXPRESS
MERCED**
730 Motel Dr, Merced (95341-5151)
PHONE.................................209 383-0333
Kainth Brothers, *Principal*
EMP: 100
SALES (est): 2.1MM **Privately Held**
SIC: **7011** Hotels & motels

(P-12692)
**HOLIDAY INN HOTEL
TORRANCE**
19800 S Vermont Ave, Torrance
(90502-1138)
PHONE.................................310 781-9100
David Britton, *General Mgr*
EMP: 130
SQ FT: 95,000
SALES (est): 9.9MM **Privately Held**
SIC: **7011** Hotels & motels

(P-12693)
**HOLIDAY INN RNCHO
BERNARDO LLC**
17065 W Bernardo Dr, San Diego
(92127-1495)
PHONE.................................858 485-6530
Hsuan Jau Lin,
Yon Huang,
EMP: 55
SALES (est): 2.9MM **Privately Held**
SIC: **7011** Hotels & motels

(P-12694)
HOLLYWOOD STANDARD LLC
Also Called: Standard The
8300 W Sunset Blvd, Los Angeles
(90069-1516)
PHONE.................................323 822-3111
Andre Balazs,
Yvonne Lopez, *Human Res Mgr*
Jennifer Hall, *Sales Mgr*
Ian Innocent, *Manager*
EMP: 170
SALES (est): 6.7MM **Privately Held**
SIC: **7011** Hotels

(P-12695)
HOME AWAY INC
54432 Road 432, Bass Lake (93604)
PHONE.................................559 642-3121
Kyusun Choe, *President*
Sun Choe, *Admin Sec*
EMP: 65
SALES: 4MM **Privately Held**
SIC: **7011** Hotels & motels

(P-12696)
**HOMEWOOD SUITES
MANAGEMENT LLC**
1103 Embarcadero, Oakland (94606-5122)
PHONE.................................510 663-2700
Jason Oliveras, *Manager*
EMP: 50
SALES (corp-wide): 2.7B **Publicly Held**
WEB: www.esirvine.com
SIC: **7011** Hotels & motels
HQ: Homewood Suites Management Llc
7930 Jones Branch Dr
Mc Lean VA 22102
703 883-1000

(P-12697)
**HOMEWOOD VILLAGE
RESORTS LLC**
Also Called: Homewood Mountain Resort
5145 W Lake Blvd, Homewood (96141)
PHONE.................................530 525-2992
Todd Chapman, *CEO*
EMP: 50
SALES (est): 1.7MM **Privately Held**
SIC: **7011** Ski lodge

(P-12698)
HONEYMOON REAL ESTATE LP
Also Called: Avalon Hotel
9400 W Olympic Blvd, Beverly Hills
(90212-4552)
PHONE.................................310 277-5221
Brad Korzen, *Partner*
EMP: 90
SQ FT: 400,000
SALES (est): 5.5MM **Privately Held**
WEB: www.avalonhotel.com
SIC: **7011** Hotels

(P-12699)
**HONG KONG & SHANGHAI
HOTELS**
Also Called: The Peninsula Beverly Hills
9882 Santa Monica Blvd, Beverly Hills
(90212-1605)
PHONE.................................310 551-2888
Ali Kasikci, *Branch Mgr*
EMP: 75
SALES (est): 2.7MM
SALES (corp-wide): 740.3MM **Privately
Held**
WEB: www.hshgroup.com
SIC: **7011** Hotels & motels
PA: Hongkong And Shanghai Hotels, Lim-
ited, The
8/F St George's Bldg
Central District HK
284 077-88

(P-12700)
**HOSPITALITY VENTURES MGT
LLC**
Also Called: Embassy Suites
101 Mcinnis Pkwy, San Rafael
(94903-2773)
PHONE.................................415 499-9222
Rudy Otriz, *Manager*
David Tewelde, *Marketing Staff*
Vijay Kumar, *Director*
EMP: 65
SALES (corp-wide): 38.3MM **Privately
Held**
WEB: www.esirvine.com
SIC: **7011** 5812 5813 Hotels & motels;
eating places; drinking places
PA: Hospitality Ventures Management, Llc.
990 Hammond Dr Ste 325
Atlanta GA 30328
404 467-9299

(P-12701)
HOST HOTELS & RESORTS INC
Also Called: Marriott Fisherman's Wharf
1250 Columbus Ave, San Francisco
(94133-1327)
PHONE.................................415 775-7555
Michael Promos, *Branch Mgr*
EMP: 170
SALES (corp-wide): 5.3B **Publicly Held**
SIC: **7011** Hotels
PA: Host Hotels & Resorts, Inc.
6903 Rockledge Dr # 1500
Bethesda MD 20817
240 744-1000

(P-12702)
HOST HOTELS & RESORTS INC
1 Market Pl, San Diego (92101-7714)
PHONE.................................619 232-1234
Ted Kanatas, *Manager*
EMP: 170
SALES (corp-wide): 5.3B **Publicly Held**
WEB: www.hyatt.com
SIC: **7011** Hotels
PA: Host Hotels & Resorts, Inc.
6903 Rockledge Dr # 1500
Bethesda MD 20817
240 744-1000

(P-12703)
HOST HOTELS & RESORTS LP
Also Called: Newport Bch Marriott Ht & Spa
900 Newport Center Dr, Newport Beach
(92660-6206)
PHONE.................................949 640-4000
Paul Cahill, *General Mgr*
EMP: 100
SALES (corp-wide): 5.3B **Publicly Held**
WEB: www.scmarriott.com
SIC: **7011** 5813 5812 Hotels; drinking
places; eating places
HQ: Host Hotels & Resorts, L.P.
6903 Rockledge Dr # 1500
Bethesda MD 20817
240 744-1000

(P-12704)
HOST HOTELS & RESORTS LP
Also Called: Marriott
8757 Rio San Diego Dr, San Diego
(92108-1620)
PHONE.................................619 692-3800
Dan Stenz, *Branch Mgr*
Melanie Kahn, *General Mgr*
Dawn Medina-Amos, *Director*
EMP: 66
SALES (corp-wide): 5.3B **Publicly Held**
WEB: www.scmarriott.com
SIC: **7011** Hotels & motels
HQ: Host Hotels & Resorts, L.P.
6903 Rockledge Dr # 1500
Bethesda MD 20817
240 744-1000

(P-12705)
HOST HOTELS & RESORTS LP
Also Called: Hyatt Rgncy San Frncisco Arprt
1333 Bayshore Hwy, Burlingame
(94010-1804)
PHONE.................................650 347-1234
Keith Butz, *Manager*
EMP: 64
SALES (corp-wide): 5.3B **Publicly Held**
WEB: www.scmarriott.com
SIC: **7011** Hotels
HQ: Host Hotels & Resorts, L.P.
6903 Rockledge Dr # 1500
Bethesda MD 20817
240 744-1000

(P-12706)
HOST HOTELS & RESORTS LP
Also Called: JW Marriott Desert
74855 Country Club Dr, Palm Desert
(92260-1961)
PHONE.................................760 341-2211
Ken Forths, *Manager*
Peter Hurley, *Finance*
Joy Smith, *Purch Mgr*
Emily Bird, *Director*
Michelle Ianni, *Director*
EMP: 64
SALES (corp-wide): 5.3B **Publicly Held**
WEB: www.scmarriott.com
SIC: **7011** Hotels
HQ: Host Hotels & Resorts, L.P.
6903 Rockledge Dr # 1500
Bethesda MD 20817
240 744-1000

(P-12707)
HOST HOTELS & RESORTS LP
Also Called: Sheraton San Diego Ht & Marina
1380 Harbor Island Dr, San Diego
(92101-1007)
PHONE.................................619 291-2900
Joe Terzi, *Branch Mgr*
EMP: 66
SALES (corp-wide): 5.3B **Publicly Held**
WEB: www.scmarriott.com
SIC: **7011** Hotels
HQ: Host Hotels & Resorts, L.P.
6903 Rockledge Dr # 1500
Bethesda MD 20817
240 744-1000

(P-12708)
HOST HOTELS & RESORTS LP
Also Called: San Francisco Marriott Marquis
55 4th St, San Francisco (94103-3156)
PHONE.................................415 896-1600
Dan Kellher, *Manager*
Dan Kelleher, *President*
Greg Nickelson, *Manager*
EMP: 66

SALES (corp-wide): 5.3B **Publicly Held**
WEB: www.scmarriott.com
SIC: 7011 5813 5812 Hotels; drinking places; eating places
HQ: Host Hotels & Resorts, L.P.
6903 Rockledge Dr # 1500
Bethesda MD 20817
240 744-1000

(P-12709)
HOST HOTELS & RESORTS LP
1800 Old Bayshore Hwy, Burlingame
(94010-1203)
PHONE..................................650 692-9100
EMP: 66
SALES (corp-wide): 5.3B **Publicly Held**
WEB: www.scmarriott.com
SIC: 7011 Hotels
HQ: Host Hotels & Resorts, L.P.
6903 Rockledge Dr # 1500
Bethesda MD 20817
240 744-1000

(P-12710)
HOST HOTELS & RESORTS LP
Also Called: Ritz-Carlton Ht Marina Del Rey
4375 Admiralty Way, Venice (90292-5434)
PHONE..................................310 823-1700
Robert Thomas, *Branch Mgr*
EMP: 66
SALES (corp-wide): 5.3B **Publicly Held**
WEB: www.scmarriott.com
SIC: 7011 Hotels
HQ: Host Hotels & Resorts, L.P.
6903 Rockledge Dr # 1500
Bethesda MD 20817
240 744-1000

(P-12711)
HOST HOTELS & RESORTS LP
Also Called: Costa Mesa Marriott Suites
500 Anton Blvd, Costa Mesa (92626-1911)
PHONE..................................714 957-1100
Ronda Richardson, *General Mgr*
EMP: 66
SALES (corp-wide): 5.3B **Publicly Held**
WEB: www.scmarriott.com
SIC: 7011 5813 5812 Hotels; drinking places; eating places
HQ: Host Hotels & Resorts, L.P.
6903 Rockledge Dr # 1500
Bethesda MD 20817
240 744-1000

(P-12712)
HOST HOTELS & RESORTS LP
Also Called: Marriott
500 Bayview Cir, Newport Beach
(92660-2933)
PHONE..................................949 854-4500
Pam Ryan, *Manager*
Debbie Snavely, *Manager*
EMP: 66
SALES (corp-wide): 5.3B **Publicly Held**
WEB: www.scmarriott.com
SIC: 7011 7389 Hotels; office facilities & secretarial service rental
HQ: Host Hotels & Resorts, L.P.
6903 Rockledge Dr # 1500
Bethesda MD 20817
240 744-1000

(P-12713)
HOST HOTELS & RESORTS LP
Also Called: Westin Los Angeles Airport
5400 W Century Blvd, Los Angeles
(90045-5975)
PHONE..................................310 216-5858
Kimbell John, *CEO*
EMP: 66
SALES (corp-wide): 5.3B **Publicly Held**
WEB: www.scmarriott.com
SIC: 7011 Hotels
HQ: Host Hotels & Resorts, L.P.
6903 Rockledge Dr # 1500
Bethesda MD 20817
240 744-1000

(P-12714)
HOST HOTELS & RESORTS LP
Also Called: Marriott
1400 Park View Ave, Manhattan Beach
(90266-3714)
PHONE..................................310 546-7511
William Newton, *Director*
David Brown, *Engineer*

Ted Wells, *Manager*
EMP: 68
SALES (corp-wide): 5.3B **Publicly Held**
WEB: www.scmarriott.com
SIC: 7011 7997 Hotels; golf club, membership
HQ: Host Hotels & Resorts, L.P.
6903 Rockledge Dr # 1500
Bethesda MD 20817
240 744-1000

(P-12715)
HOST HOTELS & RESORTS LP
Also Called: Marriott
4100 Admiralty Way, Marina Del Rey
(90292-6207)
PHONE..................................310 301-3000
Susan Reardon, *Manager*
Janet Luna, *Director*
Mary Padgett, *Supervisor*
EMP: 66
SALES (corp-wide): 5.3B **Publicly Held**
WEB: www.scmarriott.com
SIC: 7011 5812 7389 Hotels; eating places; office facilities & secretarial service rental
HQ: Host Hotels & Resorts, L.P.
6903 Rockledge Dr # 1500
Bethesda MD 20817
240 744-1000

(P-12716)
HOST INTERNATIONAL INC
Also Called: Marriott
1661 Airport Blvd Ste 3e, San Jose
(95110-1216)
PHONE..................................408 294-1702
Fax: 408 294-4260
EMP: 180
SALES (corp-wide): 9.4MM **Privately Held**
SIC: 7011
HQ: Host International, Inc.
6905 Rockledge Dr Fl 1
Bethesda MD 20817
240 694-4100

(P-12717)
HOST INTERNATIONAL INC
3835 N Harbor Dr, San Diego
(92101-1073)
PHONE..................................619 231-5100
Cynthia Lias, *Branch Mgr*
Bob Mitchell, *Controller*
EMP: 193 **Privately Held**
SIC: 7011 Hotels
HQ: Host International, Inc.
6905 Rockledge Dr Fl 1
Bethesda MD 20817
240 694-4100

(P-12718)
HOTEL ADVENTURES LLC
17662 Irvine Blvd Ste 4, Tustin
(92780-3132)
PHONE..................................714 730-7717
Brad Perrin, *Mng Member*
EMP: 75
SALES (est): 2.8MM **Privately Held**
SIC: 7011 Hotels

(P-12719)
HOTEL CIRCLE INN & SUITES
2201 Hotel Cir S, San Diego (92108-3315)
PHONE..................................619 851-6800
Fred Sandoval, *Manager*
EMP: 50
SQ FT: 70,000
SALES (est): 3.2MM **Privately Held**
SIC: 7011 Motels

(P-12720)
HOTEL CIRCLE PROPERTY LLC
500 Hotel Cir N, San Diego (92108-3005)
PHONE..................................619 291-7131
EMP: 500
SALES (est): 6.1MM **Privately Held**
SIC: 7011 Resort hotel

(P-12721)
HOTEL CONTRACTING SERVICES INC
2140 Prof Dr Ste 150, Roseville (95661)
PHONE..................................916 865-4204
Ray Burns, *CEO*
Ann Edgerton, *Vice Pres*

James Murray, *Vice Pres*
EMP: 80
SALES (est): 3MM **Privately Held**
WEB: www.hotelcontractingservices.com
SIC: 7011 5812 7389 Hotels & motels; caterers;

(P-12722)
HOTEL DEL CORONADO LP
1500 Orange Ave, Coronado (92118-2986)
PHONE..................................619 522-8011
Brian Miller, *Partner*
Jessica Bridges, *Manager*
EMP: 51
SALES (est): 10MM **Privately Held**
SIC: 7011 Hotels

(P-12723)
HOTEL DIAMOND
220 W 4th St, Chico (95928-5315)
PHONE..................................530 893-3100
Wayne Cook, *Owner*
Amanda McGowan, *Sales Staff*
EMP: 50
SQ FT: 19,800
SALES (est): 1.6MM **Privately Held**
SIC: 7011 Hotels

(P-12724)
HOTEL DURANT A LTD PARTNERSHIP
Also Called: Henry's Pub
2600 Durant Ave, Berkeley (94704-1711)
PHONE..................................510 845-8981
Stephen Wahrlich, *General Ptnr*
Thunderbird Investors, *General Ptnr*
Tracy W Wahrlich Jr, *General Ptnr*
EMP: 84
SQ FT: 57,730
SALES (est): 4.5MM **Privately Held**
WEB: www.hoteldurant.com
SIC: 7011 5812 5813 6512 Hotels; American restaurant; bar (drinking places); nonresidential building operators

(P-12725)
HOTEL HEALDSBURG (PA)
25 Matheson St, Healdsburg (95448-4107)
PHONE..................................707 431-2800
Aziz Zhari, *Manager*
Most Rev Aziz Zhari, *Manager*
EMP: 56
SQ FT: 57,500
SALES (est): 7.1MM **Privately Held**
WEB: www.hotelhealdsburg.com
SIC: 7011 Hotels

(P-12726)
HOTEL HEALDSBURG
317 Healdsburg Ave, Healdsburg
(95448-4105)
PHONE..................................707 922-5399
Charlie Palmer, *Branch Mgr*
EMP: 60
SALES (corp-wide): 7.1MM **Privately Held**
SIC: 7011 Inns
PA: Hotel Healdsburg
25 Matheson St
Healdsburg CA 95448
707 431-2800

(P-12727)
HOTEL LA JOLLA
7955 La Jolla Shores Dr, La Jolla
(92037-3301)
PHONE..................................858 459-0261
Juliana Bancraft, *President*
Juan Cruz, *Chief Engr*
Lora Hepp, *Finance Dir*
EMP: 82
SALES (est): 4.5MM **Privately Held**
WEB: www.hotellajolla.com
SIC: 7011 Resort hotel; hotels

(P-12728)
HOTEL MAC RESTAURANT INC
50 Washington Ave, Richmond
(94801-3945)
PHONE..................................510 233-0576
William Burnett, *President*
EMP: 50 EST: 1978
SQ FT: 4,000

SALES (est): 3.4MM **Privately Held**
WEB: www.hotelmac.net
SIC: 7011 5812 5813 Hotels & motels; eating places; bar (drinking places)

(P-12729)
HOTEL NAPA II OPCO LP
Also Called: Homewood Suites
4755 Business Center Dr, Fairfield
(94534-1916)
PHONE..................................707 863-0300
Raymond Schulte, *Managing Prtnr*
EMP: 50
SALES (est): 203.4K **Privately Held**
SIC: 7011 Hotels & motels

(P-12730)
HOTEL NIKKO SAN FRANCISCO INC
222 Mason St, San Francisco
(94102-2115)
PHONE..................................415 394-1111
Vincent Rafanan, *CFO*
Solomon Walker, *Officer*
Anna Marie Presutti, *Vice Pres*
David Ng, *Info Tech Dir*
Russell Palacio, *Engineer*
EMP: 260
SQ FT: 540,000
SALES (est): 23.2MM
SALES (corp-wide): 717MM **Privately Held**
WEB: www.hotelnikkosf.com
SIC: 7011 5812 5813 7991 Resort hotel; eating places; bar (drinking places); health club; banquet hall facilities
HQ: Okura Nikko Hotel Management Co., Ltd.
2-4-11, Higashishinagawa
Shinagawa-Ku TKY 140-0
354 607-334

(P-12731)
HOTEL TONIGHT INC (PA)
901 Market St Ste 310, San Francisco
(94103-1752)
PHONE..................................800 208-2949
Sam Shank, *CEO*
Jared Simon, *COO*
Tony Grimminck, *CFO*
Ray Elias, *Chief Mktg Ofcr*
Amanda Richardson, *Vice Pres*
EMP: 69
SALES (est): 14.9MM **Privately Held**
SIC: 7011 Hotels

(P-12732)
HOTEL WHITCOMB
1231 Market St, San Francisco
(94103-1400)
PHONE..................................415 626-8000
Thomas Chan, *Controller*
Carla Santos, *Human Res Mgr*
Khaled AMR, *Sales Mgr*
Alisa Harvey, *Sales Staff*
Kevin Veasley, *Director*
EMP: 99 EST: 2007
SALES (est): 4.9MM **Privately Held**
SIC: 7011 Hotels

(P-12733)
HOWARD JOHNSON (PA)
1380 S Harbor Blvd, Anaheim
(92802-2310)
PHONE..................................714 776-6120
James P Edmondson, *President*
EMP: 125 EST: 1968
SQ FT: 200
SALES (est): 6.9MM **Privately Held**
SIC: 7011 Hotels & motels

(P-12734)
HPT TRS IHG-2 INC
Also Called: Candlewood Suites
481 El Camino Real, Santa Clara
(95050-4300)
PHONE..................................408 241-9305
Liz Olson, *Owner*
EMP: 74 **Publicly Held**
SIC: 7011 Hotels
HQ: Hpt Trs Ihg-2, Inc.
255 Washington St Ste 300
Newton MA 02458
617 964-8389

P R O D U C T S & S V C S

(P-12735)
HPT TRS IHG-2 INC
Also Called: Holiday Inn
1915 S Manchester Ave, Anaheim
(92802-3802)
PHONE................................714 748-7777
Sven Grunder, *General Mgr*
EMP: 100
SQ FT: 3,540 **Publicly Held**
WEB: www.sixcontinenthotels.com
SIC: 7011 Hotels & motels
HQ: Hpt Trs Ihg-2, Inc.
255 Washington St Ste 300
Newton MA 02458
617 964-8389

(P-12736)
HPT TRS IHG-2 INC
Also Called: Crowne Plaza
5985 W Century Blvd, Los Angeles
(90045-5477)
PHONE................................310 642-7500
Michael Payton, *Manager*
EMP: 100 **Publicly Held**
WEB: www.sixcontinenthotels.com
SIC: 7011 Hotels
HQ: Hpt Trs Ihg-2, Inc.
255 Washington St Ste 300
Newton MA 02458
617 964-8389

(P-12737)
HPT TRS IHG-2 INC
Also Called: Crowne Plaza
300 N Harbor Dr, Redondo Beach
(90277-2552)
PHONE................................310 318-8888
Paul Gibbs, *Branch Mgr*
EMP: 300 **Publicly Held**
WEB: www.sixcontinenthotels.com
SIC: 7011 Hotels
HQ: Hpt Trs Ihg-2, Inc.
255 Washington St Ste 300
Newton MA 02458
617 964-8389

(P-12738)
HPT TRS IHG-2 INC
Also Called: Staybridge Suites
900 Hamlin Ct, Sunnyvale (94089-1401)
PHONE................................408 745-1515
Tina Messenger, *Branch Mgr*
EMP: 50 **Publicly Held**
WEB: www.hptreit.com
SIC: 7011 Hotels
HQ: Hpt Trs Ihg-2, Inc.
255 Washington St Ste 300
Newton MA 02458
617 964-8389

(P-12739)
HST LESSEE BOSTON LLC
Also Called: Sheraton
1380 Harbor Island Dr, San Diego
(92101-1007)
PHONE................................619 692-2255
Joe Tursey, *General Mgr*
EMP: 60
SALES (corp-wide): 22.8B **Publicly Held**
SIC: 7011 Hotels
HQ: Hst Lessee Boston Llc
39 Dalton St
Boston MA 02199
617 236-2000

(P-12740)
HST LESSEE SAN DIEGO LP
Also Called: Sheraton San Diego Ht & Marina
1380 Harbor Island Dr, San Diego
(92101-1007)
PHONE................................619 291-2900
Joe Tursey, *Principal*
EMP: 473
SQ FT: 75,000
SALES (est): 30.3MM
SALES (corp-wide): 5.3B **Publicly Held**
WEB: www.sheratonsandiegohotelandma-
rina.com
SIC: 7011 5812 5947 5813 Hotels; eating
places; gift, novelty & souvenir shop;
drinking places; marinas
PA: Host Hotels & Resorts, Inc.
6903 Rockledge Dr # 1500
Bethesda MD 20817
240 744-1000

(P-12741)
HUMNIT HOTEL AT LAX LLC
Also Called: Concourse Hotel At
6225 W Century Blvd, Los Angeles
(90045-5311)
PHONE................................424 702-1234
Jina Luman, *Principal*
EMP: 99 EST: 2013
SQ FT: 49,500
SALES (est): 2.9MM **Privately Held**
SIC: 7011 Hotels

(P-12742)
HUNTINGTON HOTEL COMPANY
Also Called: Inn At Rancho Santa Fe, The
5951 Linea Del Cielo, Rancho Santa Fe
(92067)
PHONE................................858 756-1131
Scott Jenkins, *CEO*
Micah Severeid, *Executive*
Kathy Reese, *Sales Dir*
Rebecca Graves, *Sales Mgr*
Blake Polinski, *Manager*
EMP: 88
SQ FT: 5,000
SALES (est): 7.5MM **Privately Held**
SIC: 7011 5812 Resort hotel; eating
places

(P-12743)
HUOYEN INTERNATIONAL INC
Also Called: Crowne Plaza
1500 S Raymond Ave, Fullerton
(92831-5236)
PHONE................................714 635-9000
Hsi Jung Yang, *President*
EMP: 90
SQ FT: 144,698
SALES (est): 4.7MM **Privately Held**
SIC: 7011 Hotels

(P-12744)
HUSKIES LESSEE LLC
Also Called: Sir Francis Drake Hotel
450 Powell St, San Francisco
(94102-1504)
PHONE................................415 392-7755
John Price, *General Mgr*
EMP: 375
SALES (est): 32MM **Privately Held**
SIC: 7011 Hotels

(P-12745)
HYATT COPORATION AS AGENT OF B
7100 Aviara Resort Dr, Carlsbad
(92011-4908)
PHONE................................760 603-6851
Byron Peacock,
EMP: 58
SALES (est): 5.8MM **Privately Held**
SIC: 7011 Resort hotel

(P-12746)
HYATT CORPORATION
4001 Northstar Dr, Truckee (96161-4250)
PHONE................................530 562-3900
Beryl Guyon, *Branch Mgr*
EMP: 316
SALES (corp-wide): 4.6B **Publicly Held**
SIC: 7011 Vacation lodges
HQ: Hyatt Corporation
150 N Riverside Plz
Chicago IL 60606
312 750-1234

(P-12747)
HYATT CORPORATION
Also Called: Hyatt Los Angeles Airport
6225 W Century Blvd, Los Angeles
(90045-5311)
PHONE................................312 750-1234
Donald J Henderson, *Manager*
EMP: 500
SALES (corp-wide): 4.6B **Publicly Held**
SIC: 7011 5812 5813 Hotels; restaurant,
family; chain; bar (drinking places)
HQ: Hyatt Corporation
150 N Riverside Plz
Chicago IL 60606
312 750-1234

(P-12748)
HYATT CORPORATION
Also Called: Grand Hyatt San Francisco
345 Stockton St, San Francisco
(94108-4606)
PHONE................................415 848-6050
Steve Trent, *Manager*
Brittanie Martinez, *Social Dir*
Ed Randes, *Engineer*
Terry Henry, *Chief Engr*
Sara Frey, *Human Res Mgr*
EMP: 500
SALES (corp-wide): 4.6B **Publicly Held**
WEB: www.hyatt.com
SIC: 7011 5813 5812 6512 Hotels; drink-
ing places; eating places; nonresidential
building operators
HQ: Hyatt Corporation
150 N Riverside Plz
Chicago IL 60606
312 750-1234

(P-12749)
HYATT CORPORATION AS AGENT O
Also Called: Hyatt Regency Orange County
11999 Harbor Blvd, Garden Grove
(92840-2703)
PHONE................................714 750-1234
Kevin Kennedy, *Manager*
Brad Marman, *Project Dir*
Erin Deyager, *Sales Mgr*
Mari Mills, *Sales Mgr*
Anthony Flores, *Asst Director*
EMP: 300
SALES (corp-wide): 4.6B **Publicly Held**
WEB: www.hyatt.com
SIC: 7011 Hotels
HQ: Hyatt Corporation
150 N Riverside Plz
Chicago IL 60606
312 750-1234

(P-12750)
HYATT EQUITIES LLC
Also Called: Hyatt Hotel
1740 N 1st St, San Jose (95112-4508)
PHONE................................408 993-1234
Manou Mobesesahi, *Branch Mgr*
EMP: 253
SALES (corp-wide): 4.6B **Publicly Held**
SIC: 7011 Hotels & motels
HQ: Hyatt Equities, L.L.C.
71 S Wacker Dr Fl 14
Chicago IL 60606
312 750-1234

(P-12751)
HYATT HOTELS MANAGEMENT CORP
24500 Town Center Dr, Valencia
(91355-1322)
PHONE................................661 799-1234
Chris Aldiere, *Manager*
EMP: 140
SALES (corp-wide): 4.6B **Publicly Held**
WEB: www.hyattvacations.com
SIC: 7011 7299 5812 Hotels; banquet hall
facilities; caterers
HQ: Hyatt Hotels Management Corporation
71 S Wacker Dr Ste 1000
Chicago IL 60606
312 750-1234

(P-12752)
HYATT HOTELS MANAGEMENT CORP
Also Called: Regency Caterers By Hyatt
3777 Lajolla Village Dr, San Diego (92122)
PHONE................................858 552-1234
Chris Alteri, *Manager*
EMP: 485
SALES (corp-wide): 4.6B **Publicly Held**
WEB: www.hyattvacations.com
SIC: 7011 5812 5813 Hotels; caterers;
drinking places
HQ: Hyatt Hotels Management Corporation
71 S Wacker Dr Ste 1000
Chicago IL 60606
312 750-1234

(P-12753)
HYATT HOTELS MANAGEMENT CORP
285 N Palm Canyon Dr, Palm Springs
(92262-5525)
PHONE................................760 322-9000
Dania Duke, *Manager*
EMP: 200
SALES (corp-wide): 4.6B **Publicly Held**
WEB: www.hyattvacations.com
SIC: 7011 7299 5812 Hotels; banquet hall
facilities; caterers
HQ: Hyatt Hotels Management Corporation
71 S Wacker Dr Ste 1000
Chicago IL 60606
312 750-1234

(P-12754)
HYATT HOTELS MANAGEMENT CORP
4219 El Camino Real, Palo Alto
(94306-4405)
PHONE................................650 352-1234
Colleen Kareti, *General Mgr*
EMP: 365
SALES (corp-wide): 4.6B **Publicly Held**
WEB: www.hyattvacations.com
SIC: 7011 5813 5812 Hotels; drinking
places; eating places
HQ: Hyatt Hotels Management Corporation
71 S Wacker Dr Ste 1000
Chicago IL 60606
312 750-1234

(P-12755)
HYATT HOTELS MANAGEMENT CORP
1 Old Golf Course Rd, Monterey
(93940-4908)
PHONE................................831 372-1234
Mark Bastis, *General Mgr*
EMP: 500
SQ FT: 10,000
SALES (corp-wide): 4.6B **Publicly Held**
WEB: www.hyattvacations.com
SIC: 7011 Hotels
HQ: Hyatt Hotels Management Corporation
71 S Wacker Dr Ste 1000
Chicago IL 60606
312 750-1234

(P-12756)
HYATT REGENCY SANTA CLARA
5101 Great America Pkwy, Santa Clara
(95054-1118)
PHONE................................408 200-1234
Peter Reice, *General Mgr*
Paul Elwart, *Controller*
Pedro Gonzalez, *Human Res Dir*
Kimberly Boyer, *Sales Associate*
EMP: 76
SALES (est): 7MM **Privately Held**
SIC: 7011 Hotels

(P-12757)
I CYPRESS COMPANY
Also Called: Peeble Beach Resort
2700 17 Mile Dr Ste 3500, Pebble Beach
(93953-2668)
PHONE................................831 649-8500
EMP: 2368
SALES (corp-wide): 104.4MM **Privately Held**
SIC: 7011 Hotels & motels
PA: I Cypress Company
1700 17 Mile Dr
Pebble Beach CA 93953
831 647-7500

(P-12758)
I CYPRESS COMPANY (PA)
Also Called: Pebble Beach Company
1700 17 Mile Dr, Pebble Beach (93953)
P.O. Box 1418 (93953-1418)
PHONE................................831 647-7500
Bill Perocchi, *CEO*
Clint Eastwood, *Partner*
Cody Plott, *President*
David Heuck, *CFO*
Nasim Keynejad, *Human Res Mgr*
EMP: 2500
SALES (est): 104.4MM **Privately Held**
SIC: 7011 Resort hotel

(P-12759)
IA LODGING NAPA SOLANO TRS LLC
Also Called: NAPA Valley Marriott
3425 Solano Ave, NAPA (94558-2709)
PHONE......................707 253-8600
Amanda Hawkins-Vogel, *General Mgr*
EMP: 210
SQ FT: 200,000
SALES (est): 510.8K **Privately Held**
SIC: 7011 Resort hotel, franchised

(P-12760)
IHG MANAGEMENT (MARYLAND) LLC
Also Called: Crown Plaza Los Angeles
5985 W Century Blvd, Los Angeles (90045-5477)
PHONE......................310 642-7500
William Block, *Finance Dir*
Nicholas Knight, *General Mgr*
Olga Orellana, *Facilities Dir*
Ashley Schmitt, *Director*
EMP: 250
SQ FT: 14,000
SALES: 30MM **Privately Held**
SIC: 7011 Hotels

(P-12761)
IHMS (SF) LLC
Also Called: Campton Place, A Taj Hotel
340 Stockton St, San Francisco (94108-4609)
PHONE......................415 781-5555
Sanjay Jain,
Annahita Sarkari, *Executive*
Dinesh Bhatt, *General Mgr*
Rakesh Kant, *General Mgr*
Ajay Kulshreshta, *General Mgr*
EMP: 150
SALES (est): 8.8MM
SALES (corp-wide): 380.1MM **Privately Held**
SIC: 7011 Hotels
HQ: International Hotel Management Services Inc.
2 E 61st St
New York NY 10065

(P-12762)
INDIAN WELLS RESORT HOTEL
76661 Us Highway 111, Indian Wells (92210-8972)
PHONE......................760 345-6466
Brad Weimer, *President*
EMP: 50
SQ FT: 240,000
SALES (est): 3.6MM **Privately Held**
WEB: www.indianwellsresort.com
SIC: 7011 5812 Resort hotel; eating places

(P-12763)
INN AT SCOTTS VALLEY LLC
Also Called: Hilton Santa Cruz/Scotts Vly
6001 La Madrona Dr, Scotts Valley (95060-1057)
PHONE......................831 440-1000
Rich Higdon, *Mng Member*
EMP: 70
SQ FT: 130,000
SALES (est): 3.1MM **Privately Held**
SIC: 7011 Motels

(P-12764)
INTERCNTNNTAL HT GROUP RSURCES
Also Called: Holiday Inn
1300 Columbus Ave, San Francisco (94133-1328)
PHONE......................415 771-9000
Sheila Martin, *General Mgr*
EMP: 252
SALES (corp-wide): 1.7B **Privately Held**
WEB: www.sixcontinenthotels.com
SIC: 7011 8741 Hotels; hotel or motel management
HQ: Intercontinental Hotels Group Resources, Inc.
3 Ravinia Dr Ste 100
Atlanta GA 30346
770 604-5000

(P-12765)
INTERCONTINENTAL HOTELS
888 Howard St, San Francisco (94103-3011)
PHONE......................415 616-6500
Peter Koehler, *General Mgr*
EMP: 150
SALES (corp-wide): 1.7B **Privately Held**
WEB: www.southforkhotel.com
SIC: 7011 Hotels
HQ: Intercontinental Hotels Of San Francisco, Inc.
3 Ravinia Dr Ste 100
Atlanta GA 30346

(P-12766)
INTERCONTINENTAL HOTELS GROUP
Also Called: Crowne Plaza
17941 Von Karman Ave, Irvine (92614-6253)
PHONE......................949 863-1999
Jim Alexander, *Owner*
EMP: 180
SALES (corp-wide): 1.7B **Privately Held**
WEB: www.hptreit.com
SIC: 7011 Hotels
HQ: Intercontinental Hotels Group Resources, Inc.
3 Ravinia Dr Ste 100
Atlanta GA 30346
770 604-5000

(P-12767)
INTERCONTINENTAL HOTELS GROUP
Also Called: Hotel Indigo San Diego
509 9th Ave, San Diego (92101-7213)
PHONE......................619 727-4000
Raul Lopez, *General Mgr*
EMP: 60
SALES (corp-wide): 1.7B **Privately Held**
SIC: 7011 Hotels
HQ: Intercontinental Hotels Group Resources, Inc.
3 Ravinia Dr Ste 100
Atlanta GA 30346
770 604-5000

(P-12768)
INTERCONTINENTAL HOTELS GROUP
Also Called: Holiday Inn
50 8th St, San Francisco (94103-1409)
PHONE......................415 626-6103
Gino Lazzara, *General Mgr*
EMP: 160
SALES (corp-wide): 1.7B **Privately Held**
SIC: 7011 5813 5812 6512 Hotels; drinking places; eating places; nonresidential building operators
HQ: Intercontinental Hotels Group Resources, Inc.
3 Ravinia Dr Ste 100
Atlanta GA 30346
770 604-5000

(P-12769)
INTERCONTINENTAL HOTELS GROUP
Also Called: Holiday Inn
19800 S Vermont Ave, Torrance (90502-1126)
PHONE......................310 781-9100
David Britton, *General Mgr*
EMP: 74
SALES (corp-wide): 1.7B **Privately Held**
SIC: 7011 Hotels & motels
HQ: Intercontinental Hotels Group Resources, Inc.
3 Ravinia Dr Ste 100
Atlanta GA 30346
770 604-5000

(P-12770)
INTERCONTINENTAL HOTELS GROUP
Also Called: San Francisco Marriott Un Sq
480 Sutter St, San Francisco (94108-3901)
PHONE......................415 398-8900
John Simonich, *Branch Mgr*
EMP: 210

SALES (corp-wide): 1.7B **Privately Held**
WEB: www.southforkhotel.com
SIC: 7011 Hotels
HQ: Intercontinental Hotels Group Resources, Inc.
3 Ravinia Dr Ste 100
Atlanta GA 30346
770 604-5000

(P-12771)
INTERCONTINENTAL HOTELS GROUP
Also Called: Holiday Inn
5650 Calle Real, Goleta (93117-2319)
PHONE......................805 964-6241
Gary Opdahl, *General Mgr*
EMP: 65
SALES (corp-wide): 1.7B **Privately Held**
WEB: www.sixcontinenthotels.com
SIC: 7011 Hotels & motels
HQ: Intercontinental Hotels Group Resources, Inc.
3 Ravinia Dr Ste 100
Atlanta GA 30346
770 604-5000

(P-12772)
INTERCONTINENTAL HOTELS GROUP
Also Called: Holiday Inn
550 N Point St, San Francisco (94133-1312)
PHONE......................415 409-4600
Mike Cunningham, *Manager*
EMP: 50
SALES (corp-wide): 1.7B **Privately Held**
WEB: www.southforkhotel.com
SIC: 7011 Hotels & motels
HQ: Intercontinental Hotels Group Resources, Inc.
3 Ravinia Dr Ste 100
Atlanta GA 30346
770 604-5000

(P-12773)
INTERCONTINENTAL HOTELS GROUP
Also Called: Crowne Plaza Irvine-Orange Cou
17941 Von Karman Ave, Irvine (92614-6253)
PHONE......................949 863-1999
Martin Driskel, *Opers-Prdtn-Mfg*
EMP: 100
SALES (corp-wide): 1.7B **Privately Held**
WEB: www.southforkhotel.com
SIC: 7011 5813 5812 Hotels; drinking places; eating places
HQ: Intercontinental Hotels Group Resources, Inc.
3 Ravinia Dr Ste 100
Atlanta GA 30346
770 604-5000

(P-12774)
INTERCONTINENTAL HOTELS GROUP
2280 S Haven Ave, Ontario (91761-0739)
PHONE......................909 930-5555
Lori Whiting, *Manager*
EMP: 122
SALES (corp-wide): 1.7B **Privately Held**
WEB: www.southforkhotel.com
SIC: 7011 Hotels
HQ: Intercontinental Hotels Group Resources, Inc.
3 Ravinia Dr Ste 100
Atlanta GA 30346
770 604-5000

(P-12775)
INTERSTATE HOTELS RESORTS INC
Also Called: Sheraton
2500 Mason St, San Francisco (94133-1450)
PHONE......................415 362-5500
David Gievens, *Manager*
Michael Fontanilla, *Manager*
EMP: 250 **Privately Held**
WEB: www.sheratonokc.com
SIC: 7011 Hotels
HQ: Interstate Hotels & Resorts, Inc.
4501 Fairfax Dr Ste 500
Arlington VA 22203
703 387-3100

(P-12776)
INTERSTATE HOTELS RESORTS INC
Also Called: Marriott Los Angeles Downtown
333 S Figueroa St, Los Angeles (90071-1001)
PHONE......................213 617-1133
Guenet Kelelatchew, *Director*
EMP: 220
SQ FT: 143,000 **Privately Held**
WEB: www.sheratonokc.com
SIC: 7011 8741 Hotels; hotel or motel management
HQ: Interstate Hotels & Resorts, Inc.
4501 Fairfax Dr Ste 500
Arlington VA 22203
703 387-3100

(P-12777)
INTERSTATE HOTELS RESORTS INC
Also Called: Westin Bonaventure Ht & Suites
404 S Figueroa St 418a, Los Angeles (90071-1710)
PHONE......................213 624-1000
Peter Zen, *President*
EMP: 500 **Privately Held**
WEB: www.sheratonokc.com
SIC: 7011 Hotels
HQ: Interstate Hotels & Resorts, Inc.
4501 Fairfax Dr Ste 500
Arlington VA 22203
703 387-3100

(P-12778)
INTERSTATE HOTELS RESORTS INC
Also Called: Radisson Inn
32083 Alvarado Niles Rd, Union City (94587-2942)
PHONE......................510 489-2200
Peter San, *General Mgr*
EMP: 140 **Privately Held**
WEB: www.sheratonokc.com
SIC: 7011 5812 5813 Hotels; eating places; bar (drinking places)
HQ: Interstate Hotels & Resorts, Inc.
4501 Fairfax Dr Ste 500
Arlington VA 22203
703 387-3100

(P-12779)
INTERSTATE HOTELS RESORTS INC
Also Called: Hilton Sacramento Arden West
2200 Harvard St, Sacramento (95815-3306)
PHONE......................916 922-4700
Howard Harris, *General Mgr*
EMP: 200 **Privately Held**
WEB: www.sheratonokc.com
SIC: 7011 5812 5813 5947 Hotels; eating places; drinking places; gift, novelty & souvenir shop
HQ: Interstate Hotels & Resorts, Inc.
4501 Fairfax Dr Ste 500
Arlington VA 22203
703 387-3100

(P-12780)
IRP LAX HOTEL LLC
Also Called: Four Points by Sheraton LAX
9750 Airport Blvd, Los Angeles (90045-5404)
PHONE......................310 645-4600
Phil Baxter,
EMP: 240
SQ FT: 337,720
SALES (est): 6.8MM
SALES (corp-wide): 20.1B **Publicly Held**
SIC: 7011 Hotels
HQ: Tishman Hotel Corporation
666 5th Ave Fl 38
New York NY 10103

(P-12781)
ISLAND HOSPITALITY MGT LLC
Residence Inn By Marriott
750 Lakeway Dr, Sunnyvale (94085-4011)
PHONE......................408 720-1000
Hugo Hernandez, *Branch Mgr*
EMP: 50

P R O D U C T S & S V C S

SALES (corp-wide): 814.6MM **Privately Held**
WEB: www.napleshamptoninn.com
SIC: 7011 Hotels & motels
PA: Island Hospitality Management, Llc
222 Lakeview Ave Ste 200
West Palm Beach FL 33401
561 832-6132

(P-12782)
ISLAND HOSPITALITY MGT LLC
Also Called: Residence Inn By Marriott
2000 Winward Way, San Mateo
(94404-2472)
PHONE.............................650 574-4700
Omar Paredes, *Branch Mgr*
EMP: 60
SALES (corp-wide): 814.6MM **Privately Held**
WEB: www.napleshamptoninn.com
SIC: 7011 Hotels & motels
PA: Island Hospitality Management, Llc
222 Lakeview Ave Ste 200
West Palm Beach FL 33401
561 832-6132

(P-12783)
ISLAND HOSPITALITY MGT LLC
Residence Inn By Marriott
1080 Stewart Dr, Sunnyvale (94085-3917)
PHONE.............................408 720-8893
Kort Gursu, *Manager*
Stephen Peters, *Manager*
EMP: 59
SALES (corp-wide): 814.6MM **Privately Held**
WEB: www.napleshamptoninn.com
SIC: 7011 Hotels & motels
PA: Island Hospitality Management, Llc
222 Lakeview Ave Ste 200
West Palm Beach FL 33401
561 832-6132

(P-12784)
ISLAND HOSPITALITY MGT LLC
Also Called: Residence Inn By Marriott
2025 Convention Ctr Way, Ontario
(91764-4450)
PHONE.............................909 937-6788
Frank Palacios, *Branch Mgr*
EMP: 50
SALES (corp-wide): 814.6MM **Privately Held**
WEB: www.napleshamptoninn.com
SIC: 7011 Hotels & motels
PA: Island Hospitality Management, Llc
222 Lakeview Ave Ste 200
West Palm Beach FL 33401
561 832-6132

(P-12785)
ISLAND HOSPITALITY MGT LLC
Also Called: Summerfield Suites By Hyatt
400 Concourse Dr, Belmont (94002-4125)
PHONE.............................650 591-8600
Trinity Nguyen, *Branch Mgr*
Denise Eldrich, *General Mgr*
Alvin Magcale, *General Mgr*
EMP: 80
SALES (corp-wide): 814.6MM **Privately Held**
WEB: www.napleshamptoninn.com
SIC: 7011 Hotels
PA: Island Hospitality Management, Llc
222 Lakeview Ave Ste 200
West Palm Beach FL 33401
561 832-6132

(P-12786)
J5TH LLC
Also Called: Residence Inn By Mariott
356 6th Ave, San Diego (92101-7186)
PHONE.............................619 487-1200
Rajan Hansji, *Mng Member*
Sajan Hansji,
Dilip Kanji,
EMP: 55
SALES (est): 2.4MM **Privately Held**
SIC: 7011 7389 Hotels; office facilities & secretarial service rental

(P-12787)
JACK PARKER CORP
Also Called: Le Parker Meridien Palm Sprng
4200 E Palm Canyon Dr, Palm Springs
(92264-5230)
PHONE.............................760 770-5000
Adam Glick, *President*
Brandon McCurley, *General Mgr*
Alexandra Falcon, *Sales Mgr*
EMP: 177
SALES (est): 5.2MM **Privately Held**
SIC: 7011 Motels

(P-12788)
JC RESORTS INN
17550 Bernardo Oaks Dr, San Diego
(92128-2112)
PHONE.............................858 487-0700
Katherine Colachis, *Owner*
EMP: 80
SALES (est): 1.1MM **Privately Held**
SIC: 7011 Resort hotel

(P-12789)
JCK HOTELS LLC
Also Called: Holiday Inn
9888 Mira Mesa Blvd, San Diego
(92131-1025)
PHONE.............................858 635-5566
Brad Housewoorth,
Judy Fang,
George Liu,
Gloria Liu,
EMP: 55
SQ FT: 4,800
SALES (est): 3.1MM **Privately Held**
WEB: www.mmpcusa.com
SIC: 7011 Hotels & motels

(P-12790)
JHC INVESTMENT INC
Also Called: Dt Club Hotel Santa Ana
7 Hutton Centre Dr, Santa Ana
(92707-5753)
PHONE.............................714 751-2400
Jung-Hsiung Chiu, *President*
EMP: 70
SQ FT: 85,000
SALES (est): 2.7MM **Privately Held**
SIC: 7011 Hotels

(P-12791)
JJ GRAND HOTEL
620 S Harvard Blvd, Los Angeles
(90005-2510)
PHONE.............................213 383-3000
James Lee, *President*
Kuija Kim, *President*
EMP: 60
SALES (est): 1.4MM **Privately Held**
WEB: www.jjgrandhotel.com
SIC: 7011 Resort hotel; hotels

(P-12792)
JOIE DE VIVRE HOSPITALITY INC
Also Called: Wild Palms Hotel & Bar
910 E Fremont Ave, Sunnyvale
(94087-3702)
PHONE.............................408 738-0500
Steven C Y Chen, *President*
EMP: 51
SQ FT: 80,000
SALES (est): 4.8MM **Privately Held**
SIC: 7011 Motels

(P-12793)
JP ALLEN EXTENDED STAY
Also Called: Holiday Inn
150 E Angeleno Ave, Burbank
(91502-1911)
PHONE.............................818 841-4770
Chris Haven, *Manager*
EMP: 50
SALES (est): 2.3MM
SALES (corp-wide): 9.4MM **Privately Held**
SIC: 7011 Hotels & motels
PA: Jp Allen Extended Stay
450 Pioneer Dr
Glendale CA 91203
818 956-0202

(P-12794)
JP ALLEN EXTENDED STAY (PA)
Also Called: Days Inn
450 Pioneer Dr, Glendale (91203-1713)
PHONE.............................818 956-0202
Joe Perry, *Owner*
EMP: 76
SQ FT: 4,000
SALES (est): 9.4MM **Privately Held**
SIC: 7011 Hotels & motels

(P-12795)
JS HOSPITALITY GROUP LLC
Also Called: Courtyard Oxnard Ventura
600 E Esplanade Dr, Oxnard (93036-2403)
PHONE.............................805 988-3600
Joseph Fan,
EMP: 100
SALES: 5MM **Privately Held**
SIC: 7011 Hotels

(P-12796)
JWMCC LIMITED PARTNERSHIP
Also Called: Hyatt Hotel
2151 Avenue Of The Stars, Los Angeles
(90067-5004)
PHONE.............................310 277-1234
Ulrich Samietz, *General Mgr*
EMP: 353
SQ FT: 4,600
SALES (est): 4.7MM **Privately Held**
SIC: 7011 5812 Hotels; eating places

(P-12797)
KAIDAN HOSPITALITY LP
Also Called: Red Lion Hotel Redding
1830 Hilltop Dr, Redding (96002-0212)
PHONE.............................530 221-8700
EMP: 66
SALES (est): 2.9MM **Privately Held**
WEB: www.westcoasthotels.com
SIC: 7011 Hotels

(P-12798)
KALPANA LLC (PA)
620 Newport Center Dr # 1600, Newport
Beach (92660-8016)
PHONE.............................949 610-8200
Mayur Patel, *Principal*
Padmesh Patel, *Mng Member*
EMP: 300
SALES (est): 6.4MM **Privately Held**
SIC: 7011 Hotels

(P-12799)
KALPANA LLC
Also Called: San Dego Mission Vly Hilton Ht
901 Camino Del Rio S, San Diego
(92108-3515)
PHONE.............................619 543-9000
Jack Giacomini, *General Mgr*
Maria Armenion, *Marketing Staff*
EMP: 250
SALES (corp-wide): 6.4MM **Privately Held**
WEB: www.doralpalmsprings.com
SIC: 7011 5812 7299 Hotels; eating places; banquet hall facilities
PA: Kalpana, Llc
620 Newport Center Dr # 1600
Newport Beach CA 92660
949 610-8200

(P-12800)
KANG FAMILY PARTNERS LLC
Also Called: Santa Ynez Valley Marriott
555 Mcmurray Rd, Buellton (93427-9559)
PHONE.............................805 688-1000
Daphne Kang, *Mng Member*
Karla Azahar, *General Mgr*
Mike Hendrick, *General Mgr*
Jack Schlichting, *Manager*
EMP: 110
SALES: 6MM **Privately Held**
WEB: www.santaynezhotels.com
SIC: 7011 Hotel, franchised; hotels

(P-12801)
KAVA HOLDINGS INC (PA)
Also Called: Hotel Bel-Air
701 Stone Canyon Rd, Los Angeles
(90077-2909)
PHONE.............................310 472-1211
Hj Suharafadzil, *President*
Helen Smith, *President*
Christopher Cowdary, *CEO*

Franois Delahaye, *COO*
Eugenio Pirri, *Vice Pres*
EMP: 265
SQ FT: 30,000
SALES (est): 16.4MM **Privately Held**
WEB: www.hotelbelair.com
SIC: 7011 Resort hotel; hotels

(P-12802)
KEN REAL ESTATE LEASE LTD
Also Called: Anaheim Majestic Garden Hotel
900 S Disneyland Dr, Anaheim
(92802-1844)
PHONE.............................714 778-1700
Shigeru Sato, *President*
EMP: 99
SALES (est): 8.4MM **Privately Held**
SIC: 7011 Resort hotel

(P-12803)
KESARI HOSPITALITY LLC
445 Hotel Cir S, San Diego (92108-3402)
PHONE.............................619 298-1291
Kalpesh Kalthia, *Mng Member*
EMP: 72 EST: 2015
SQ FT: 18,774
SALES (est): 250.8K **Privately Held**
SIC: 7011 Resort hotel, franchised

(P-12804)
KEY INN LTD A CAL LTD PARTNR
Also Called: Key Inn & Suites
1611 El Camino Real, Tustin (92780-5203)
PHONE.............................714 832-3220
Ed Pankey, *Partner*
Peter Pankey, *Partner*
EMP: 50
SALES (est): 3.5MM **Privately Held**
WEB: www.keyinntustin.com
SIC: 7011 Motels

(P-12805)
KHANNA ENTPS - II LTD PARTNR
Also Called: Crowne Plz Scramento Northeast
5321 Date Ave, Sacramento (95841-2512)
PHONE.............................916 338-5800
Ravi Khanna, *Partner*
Anil Khanna, *Partner*
Ashwin Khanna, *Partner*
Rajesh Khanna, *Partner*
Brad Ross, *Sales Staff*
EMP: 114
SALES: 8MM **Privately Held**
WEB: www.sacnortheast.com
SIC: 7011 Hotels

(P-12806)
KHATRI INC
Also Called: Khatri Properties
1608 Sunrise Ave Ste 6, Modesto
(95350-4678)
PHONE.............................209 576-1481
Anil Khatri, *Manager*
EMP: 50
SQ FT: 10,662
SALES (corp-wide): 5.5MM **Privately Held**
SIC: 7011 Hotels & motels
PA: Khatri, Inc.
20700 Manter Rd
Castro Valley CA 94552
510 886-7909

(P-12807)
KHP II SAN DIEGO HOTEL LLC (PA)
Also Called: Palomar San Diego
1047 5th Ave, San Diego (92101-5101)
PHONE.............................619 515-3000
Nikki Leondakis, *Mng Member*
Drew Parker, *Sales Staff*
Mark Van Cooney,
Nicholas Gillio, *Asst Director*
EMP: 100
SALES: 8.6MM **Privately Held**
SIC: 7011 Hotels

(P-12808)
KHP III GOLETA LLC
Also Called: Goodland
5650 Calle Real, Goleta (93117-2319)
PHONE.............................805 964-6241

▲ = Import ▼=Export
◆ =Import/Export

Wesley Lau, *Principal*
Robert Cole, *General Mgr*
Alexis Schmidt, *Finance*
Martin Minev, *Accountant*
Courtney Guillory, *Sales Mgr*
EMP: 99 **EST:** 2016
SALES (est): 893.5K **Privately Held**
SIC: 7011 5812 Resort hotel; American restaurant

(P-12809)
KIMPTON HOTEL & REST GROUP LLC
Also Called: Serrano Hotel
405 Taylor St, San Francisco (94102-1701)
PHONE..................................415 885-2500
John Turner, *General Mgr*
Dalila Gutierrez, *Executive*
Benjamin Malmquist, *General Mgr*
Sarah Mendoza, *Asst Controller*
Maricar Miller, *Finance*
EMP: 100
SALES (corp-wide): 1.7B **Privately Held**
WEB: www.kuletos.com
SIC: 7011 7299 Hotels; banquet hall facilities
HQ: Kimpton Hotel & Restaurant Group Llc
222 Kearny St Ste 200
San Francisco CA 94108
415 397-5572

(P-12810)
KIMPTON HOTEL & REST GROUP LLC (HQ)
222 Kearny St Ste 200, San Francisco (94108-4537)
PHONE..................................415 397-5572
Mike Depatie, *CEO*
Donald Ogrady, *President*
Mike Defrino, *COO*
Niki Leondakis, *COO*
Ben Rowe, *CFO*
EMP: 100
SALES (est): 484.6MM
SALES (corp-wide): 1.7B **Privately Held**
WEB: www.kuletos.com
SIC: 7011 8741 6794 Hotels; hotel or motel management; franchises, selling or licensing
PA: Intercontinental Hotels Group Plc
Broadwater Park North Orbital Road
Uxbridge MIDDX UB9 5
189 551-2000

(P-12811)
KIMPTON HOTEL & REST GROUP LLC
Also Called: Kuleto's
221 Powell St, San Francisco (94102-2205)
PHONE..................................415 397-7720
Lan Shaw, *Manager*
EMP: 140
SALES (corp-wide): 1.7B **Privately Held**
WEB: www.kuletos.com
SIC: 7011 Hotels
HQ: Kimpton Hotel & Restaurant Group Llc
222 Kearny St Ste 200
San Francisco CA 94108
415 397-5572

(P-12812)
KIMPTON HOTEL & REST GROUP LLC
Also Called: Tuscan Inn
425 N Point St, San Francisco (94133-1405)
PHONE..................................415 561-1100
Jan Misch, *Manager*
EMP: 85
SALES (corp-wide): 1.7B **Privately Held**
WEB: www.kuletos.com
SIC: 7011 7299 5813 Hotels; banquet hall facilities; drinking places
HQ: Kimpton Hotel & Restaurant Group Llc
222 Kearny St Ste 200
San Francisco CA 94108
415 397-5572

(P-12813)
KIMPTON HOTEL & REST GROUP LLC
Also Called: Pescatore
2455 Mason St, San Francisco (94133-1401)
PHONE..................................415 561-1111
Leon Calahan, *Manager*
EMP: 74
SALES (corp-wide): 1.7B **Privately Held**
WEB: www.kuletos.com
SIC: 7011 Hotels
HQ: Kimpton Hotel & Restaurant Group Llc
222 Kearny St Ste 200
San Francisco CA 94108
415 397-5572

(P-12814)
KINGLEDON INC
Also Called: Ventura Beach Marriott Hotel
2055 Harbor Blvd, Ventura (93001-3707)
PHONE..................................805 643-6000
Chaohui Liu, *CEO*
Kathy Stanford, *Human Res Dir*
EMP: 150 **EST:** 2013
SALES (est): 3.1MM **Privately Held**
SIC: 7011 Hotels

(P-12815)
KINGS INN HOTEL SAN DIEGO
Also Called: Kings Inn Hotel & Grille
1333 Hotel Cir S, San Diego (92108-3491)
PHONE..................................619 297-2231
C Andro Petersen, *President*
Alfonso Gonzalez, *Human Res Dir*
Ana Cabrera, *Manager*
EMP: 70
SALES (est): 5.2MM **Privately Held**
SIC: 7011 Resort hotel; hotels

(P-12816)
KINTETSU ENTERPRISES CO AMER (HQ)
Also Called: Kintetsu Enterprises Co Amer
21241 S Wstn Ave Ste 100, Torrance (90501)
PHONE..................................310 782-9300
Hisao Hiro, *President*
EMP: 200 **EST:** 1961
SALES (est): 14MM
SALES (corp-wide): 11.4B **Privately Held**
WEB: www.miyakola.com
SIC: 7011 6512 Hotel, franchised; nonresidential building operators
PA: Kintetsu Group Holdings Co., Ltd.
6-1-55, Uehonmachi, Tennoji-Ku
Osaka OSK 543-0
667 753-355

(P-12817)
KINTETSU ENTERPRISES CO AMER
328 E 1st St, Los Angeles (90012-3902)
PHONE..................................213 617-2000
Akimasa Yoneda, *Branch Mgr*
EMP: 80
SALES (corp-wide): 11.4B **Privately Held**
WEB: www.miyakola.com
SIC: 7011 Hotels
HQ: Kintetsu Enterprises Company Of America
21241 S Wstn Ave Ste 100
Torrance CA 90501
310 782-9300

(P-12818)
KITTRIDGE HOTELS & RESORTS LLC
Also Called: Hard Rock Hotel Palm Springs
150 S Indian Canyon Dr, Palm Springs (92262-6604)
PHONE..................................760 325-9676
Stan Kantowski,
Andre Carpiac,
EMP: 64
SALES (est): 3MM **Privately Held**
WEB: www.hotelzoso.com
SIC: 7011 Hotels

(P-12819)
KMS FISHERMANS WHARF LP
Also Called: Tuscan Inn
425 N Point St, San Francisco (94133-1405)
PHONE..................................415 561-1100

Laura Meith, *Director*
Jan Misch, *Partner*
EMP: 110
SQ FT: 97,724
SALES (est): 3.2MM **Privately Held**
WEB: www.tuscaninn.com
SIC: 7011 Hotel, franchised

(P-12820)
KNOTTS BERRY FARM LLC
Also Called: Knott's Berry Farm Hotel
7675 Crescent Ave, Buena Park (90620-3947)
PHONE..................................714 995-1111
Stan Dlander, *Manager*
Katie Leong, *General Mgr*
Don Prescott, *General Mgr*
Jose Lopez, *Purchasing*
Kate Mendez, *Director*
EMP: 230
SALES (corp-wide): 1.3B **Publicly Held**
WEB: www.knotts.com
SIC: 7011 Resort hotel
HQ: Berry Knott's Farm Llc
8039 Beach Blvd
Buena Park CA 90620
714 827-1776

(P-12821)
KONOCTI VISTA CASINO (PA)
2755 Mission Rancheria Rd, Lakeport (95453-9612)
P.O. Box 57, Finley (95435-0057)
PHONE..................................707 262-1900
Sam Dornham, *General Mgr*
Larry Green, *CFO*
Marcus Mueck, *Technology*
Maria Bowers, *Accounting Mgr*
Grace Martinez, *Assistant*
EMP: 225
SALES (est): 11.6MM **Privately Held**
SIC: 7011 Casino hotel

(P-12822)
KSL RESORTS HOTEL DEL CORONADO
1500 Orange Ave, Coronado (92118-2918)
PHONE..................................619 435-6611
Bob Antes, *Principal*
EMP: 82
SALES (est): 2.1MM
SALES (corp-wide): 2.7B **Publicly Held**
SIC: 7011 Hotels
HQ: Hilton Supply Management Llc
7930 Jones Branch Dr # 400
Mc Lean VA 22102
703 883-1000

(P-12823)
KUMAR HOTELS INC
Also Called: Holiday Inn
545 N Humboldt Ave, Willows (95988-3502)
PHONE..................................530 934-8900
Pawan Kumar, *President*
EMP: 150
SALES (est): 4.6MM **Privately Held**
SIC: 7011 Hotels & motels

(P-12824)
L & S INVESTMENT CO INC
Also Called: Best Western
14173 Green Tree Blvd, Victorville (92395-4343)
PHONE..................................760 245-3461
Walter Schroeder, *Ch of Bd*
EMP: 100
SQ FT: 120,000
SALES (est): 1.7MM **Privately Held**
SIC: 7011 Hotels & motels

(P-12825)
L-O CORONADO HOTEL INC
1500 Orange Ave, Coronado (92118-2918)
PHONE..................................619 435-6611
Tod Shallon, *President*
EMP: 1350 **EST:** 1886
SALES (est): 8.1MM **Privately Held**
WEB: www.shopsatthedel.com
SIC: 7011 5812 5813 5941 Hotels; eating places; cocktail lounge; tennis goods & equipment

(P-12826)
L-O SOMA HOTEL INC
Also Called: Argent Hotel, The
50 3rd St, San Francisco (94103-3106)
PHONE..................................415 974-6400
Charles S Peck, *President*
Peter A Del Franco, *Exec VP*
Ronald A Silva, *Exec VP*
EMP: 420
SALES (est): 8.7MM
SALES (corp-wide): 1B **Privately Held**
WEB: www.destinationhotels.com
SIC: 7011 5812 Hotels; eating places
HQ: Destination Residences Llc
10333 E Dry Creek Rd
Englewood CO 80112
303 799-3830

(P-12827)
LA HOTEL VENTURE LLC
Also Called: Los Angeles Marriott Downtown
333 S Figueroa St, Los Angeles (90071-1001)
PHONE..................................213 617-1133
HEI Huang,
Reginald McDowell, *General Mgr*
Carl Sprayberry, *General Mgr*
Ronnie Lamm,
Ezri Manvar,
EMP: 400
SALES (est): 14.1MM **Privately Held**
SIC: 7011 Hotels & motels

(P-12828)
LA JOLLA BCH & TENNIS CLB INC
Also Called: Shores Restaurant
8110 Camino Del Oro, La Jolla (92037-3108)
PHONE..................................858 459-8271
John Cambel, *Manager*
EMP: 155
SALES (corp-wide): 28.2MM **Privately Held**
WEB: www.ljbtc.com
SIC: 7011 5812 5813 7299 Resort hotel; restaurant, family: independent; cocktail lounge; banquet hall facilities
PA: La Jolla Beach & Tennis Club, Inc.
2000 Spindrift Dr
La Jolla CA 92037
858 454-7126

(P-12829)
LA JOLLA COVE HOTEL & MOTEL
Also Called: La Jolla Cove Motel
1155 Coast Blvd, La Jolla (92037-3627)
P.O. Box 1067 (92038-1067)
PHONE..................................858 459-2621
Helen Jackman, *Vice Pres*
EMP: 78 **EST:** 1959
SQ FT: 78,000
SALES (est): 4.8MM **Privately Held**
WEB: www.lajollacove.com
SIC: 7011 Hotels

(P-12830)
LA POSTA CASINO
Also Called: La Posta Band Mission Indians
777 Crestwood Rd, Boulevard (91905)
PHONE..................................619 824-4100
Dwendolyn Prada, *President*
James Hill, *Corp Secy*
EMP: 140
SQ FT: 20,000
SALES (est): 3.3MM **Privately Held**
SIC: 7011 Casino hotel

(P-12831)
LAFAYETTE PARK HOTEL CORP (PA)
1100 Alma St Ste 106, Menlo Park (94025-3344)
PHONE..................................650 330-8888
Ellis J Alden, *President*
Katherine H Alden, *President*
EMP: 500
SQ FT: 2,500
SALES (est): 9.2MM **Privately Held**
WEB: www.lafayetteparkhotel.com
SIC: 7011 Hotels

(P-12832)
LAGUNA HILLS HOTEL DEV VENTR
Also Called: Holiday Inn
25205 La Paz Rd, Laguna Hills
(92653-5105)
PHONE.....................................949 586-5000
June Chen, *Partner*
Clement Chen, *President*
EMP: 100
SQ FT: 102,241
SALES (est): 2.4MM **Privately Held**
WEB:
www.holidayinngreaterlosangeles.com
SIC: 7011 5812 7299 Hotels; eating
places; banquet hall facilities

(P-12833)
LAKE ARRWHEAD RSORT OPRTOR INC (HQ)
Also Called: Marriott
27984 Hwy 189, Lake Arrowhead (92352)
PHONE.....................................909 336-1511
Carmen Rodriguez, *CEO*
Veronique Williams, *Administration*
EMP: 115
SALES (est): 11.8MM
SALES (corp-wide): 22.8B **Publicly Held**
WEB: www.laresort.com
SIC: 7011 5813 5812 Resort hotel; drink-
ing places; eating places
PA: Marriott International, Inc.
10400 Fernwood Rd
Bethesda MD 20817
301 380-3000

(P-12834)
LAKE NATOMA LODGING LP
Also Called: Lake Natoma Inn
702 Gold Lake Dr, Folsom (95630-2559)
PHONE.....................................916 351-1500
Robert Leach, *Partner*
Rick Fenstermaker, *General Ptnr*
Lynn Solberg, *General Mgr*
Elizabeth Kuwabara, *Manager*
EMP: 80
SQ FT: 82,000
SALES (est): 5.3MM **Privately Held**
WEB: www.lakenatomainn.com
SIC: 7011 Hotel, franchised; hotels

(P-12835)
LAMP LITER ASSOCIATES
Also Called: Lamp Liter Inn
3130 W Main St Ste A, Visalia
(93291-5765)
PHONE.....................................559 733-4328
Robert Lee, *General Mgr*
EMP: 75
SQ FT: 100,000
SALES (est): 3MM **Privately Held**
WEB: www.lampliter.net
SIC: 7011 5812 5813 Motels; eating
places; cocktail lounge

(P-12836)
LANDMARK HOTELS LLC
Also Called: Landmark Princess
312 Broadway St Ste 204, Laguna Beach
(92651-4335)
PHONE.....................................949 640-5040
Richard Packard, *President*
EMP: 150
SALES: 12.9MM **Privately Held**
SIC: 7011 Hotels

(P-12837)
LANGHAM HOTELS PACIFIC CORP
Also Called: Langham Hotels International
1401 S Oak Knoll Ave, Pasadena
(91106-4508)
PHONE.....................................617 451-1900
Ka Shui Lo, *President*
Brett Butcher, *Vice Pres*
Christie Joseph, *Social Dir*
Vicki Wang, *Social Dir*
Titania Shum, *Comms Mgr*
EMP: 61
SALES (est): 7.1MM **Privately Held**
SIC: 7011 Hotels; resort hotel

(P-12838)
LARKSPUR HSPTALITY DEV MGT LLC
Also Called: Hilton Garden Inn San
670 Gateway Blvd, South San Francisco
(94080-7014)
PHONE.....................................650 872-1515
Brian Fox, *General Mgr*
EMP: 100 **Privately Held**
SIC: 7011 Hotels
PA: Larkspur Hospitality Development And
Management Company, Llc
125 E Sir F Drake Blvd
Larkspur CA 94939

(P-12839)
LAV HOTEL CORP
Also Called: Whaling Bar & Grill
1132 Prospect St, La Jolla (92037-4533)
PHONE.....................................858 454-0771
Harry Collins, *President*
W M Allen Sr, *Bd of Directors*
W M Allen Jr, *Vice Pres*
Elvia Carrillo, *Facilities Dir*
Mike Allen, *Manager*
EMP: 250
SQ FT: 1,000
SALES (est): 13MM **Privately Held**
WEB: www.lavalencia.com
SIC: 7011 Hotels

(P-12840)
LAX HOSPITALITY LP
Also Called: Radisson Inn
6225 W Century Blvd, Los Angeles
(90045-5311)
PHONE.....................................310 670-9000
Sushli Israni, *Principal*
EMP: 200
SQ FT: 26,000
SALES (est): 11MM **Privately Held**
SIC: 7011 Hotels & motels

(P-12841)
LAX HOTEL VENTURES LLC
Also Called: Four Points Sheraton Lax
9750 Airport Blvd, Los Angeles
(90045-5404)
PHONE.....................................310 645-4600
EMP: 50
SALES: 950K **Privately Held**
SIC: 7011

(P-12842)
LAX PLAZA HOTEL
6333 Bristol Pkwy, Culver City
(90230-6904)
PHONE.....................................310 902-2202
Lindsay Butcher, *General Mgr*
EMP: 120
SALES (est): 1MM **Privately Held**
WEB: www.laxplazahotel.com
SIC: 7011 5812 5813 Hotels & motels;
eating places; bars & lounges

(P-12843)
LB FUNDING LLC
Also Called: Hilton Hotel Long Beach
701 W Ocean Blvd, Long Beach
(90831-3100)
PHONE.....................................562 983-3400
John Murphy,
EMP: 97 EST: 2013
SALES (est): 4.3MM **Privately Held**
SIC: 7011 Hotels

(P-12844)
LC TRS INC
Also Called: La Costa Resort & Spa
2100 Costa Del Mar Rd, Carlsbad
(92009-6823)
PHONE.....................................760 438-9111
Mike Shannon, *President*
Scott Dalecio, *Vice Pres*
Joseph Jimenez, *Engineer*
Stephanie Arcala, *Asst Controller*
Lauren Ewing, *Accountant*
EMP: 872
SQ FT: 5,000
SALES (est): 61.1MM **Privately Held**
SIC: 7011 5812 Resort hotel; eating
places

(P-12845)
LE MONTROSE HOTEL
Also Called: Le Montrose Suite Hotel
900 Hammond St Apt 434, West Hollywood
(90069-4443)
PHONE.....................................310 855-1115
John Douponce, *Managing Prtnr*
EMP: 69
SQ FT: 1,000
SALES (est): 3.9MM **Privately Held**
WEB: www.lemontrose.com
SIC: 7011 Hotels

(P-12846)
LEE-VICTORVILLE HOTEL CORP
Also Called: Green Tree Inn
14173 Green Tree Blvd, Victorville
(92395-4343)
PHONE.....................................760 245-3461
Walter M Schroeder, *President*
EMP: 105
SQ FT: 380,000
SALES (est): 5.4MM **Privately Held**
SIC: 7011 Bed & breakfast inn

(P-12847)
LEISURE SPORTS INC
Also Called: Renaissance Clubsport
2805 Jones Rd, Walnut Creek
(94597-7848)
PHONE.....................................925 938-3058
Brian Amador, *General Mgr*
Amy Tye, *Human Res Dir*
Susan Geyer, *Director*
EMP: 330
SALES (corp-wide): 191.7MM **Privately Held**
WEB: www.leisuresportsinc.com
SIC: 7011 Inns
PA: Leisure Sports, Inc.
4670 Willow Rd Ste 100
Pleasanton CA 94588
925 600-1966

(P-12848)
LH INDIAN WELLS OPERATING LLC
4500 Indian Wells Ln, Indian Wells (92210)
PHONE.....................................760 341-2200
Bob Low, *Principal*
EMP: 220
SALES (est): 4.2MM **Privately Held**
SIC: 7011 7991 Resort hotel; spas
PA: Lh Indian Wells Holding, Llc
11777 San Vicente Blvd
Los Angeles CA 90049

(P-12849)
LH UNIVERSAL OPERATING LLC
Also Called: Sheraton Universal Hotel
333 Unversal Hollywood Dr, Universal City
(91608-1001)
PHONE.....................................818 980-1212
Robert Lowe,
Virginia Clark, *General Mgr*
Alex Sorour, *General Mgr*
Renato Reyrata, *Asst Controller*
Gloria Poon, *Sales Mgr*
EMP: 280
SALES: 30MM **Privately Held**
SIC: 7011 Resort hotel; hotels

(P-12850)
LHO MSSION BAY RSIE LESSEE INC
Also Called: Hilton
1775 E Mission Bay Dr, San Diego
(92109-6801)
PHONE.....................................619 276-4010
Greg Fracassa, *Mng Member*
Don Dennis, *General Mgr*
EMP: 360
SALES (est): 20.1MM **Privately Held**
SIC: 7011 5812 5947 Hotels; eating
places; gift, novelty & souvenir shop

(P-12851)
LHO SANTA CRUZ ONE LESSE INC
Also Called: Chaminade of Santa Cruz
1 Chaminade Ln, Santa Cruz (95065-1524)
PHONE.....................................831 475-5600
Michael Barnello, *President*

Alfred Young, *COO*
Hans Weger, *CFO*
Robert Hagan, *Vice Pres*
EMP: 193
SQ FT: 50,000
SALES (est): 10.8MM
SALES (corp-wide): 1.1B **Privately Held**
SIC: 7011 Resort hotel
PA: Lasalle Hotel Properties
7550 Wisconsin Ave # 100
Bethesda MD 20814
301 941-1500

(P-12852)
LHOBERGE LESSEE INC
Also Called: L'Auberge Del Mar
1540 Camino Del Mar, Del Mar
(92014-2411)
PHONE.....................................858 259-1515
Jamie Sabatier, *CEO*
Charles Peck, *President*
Dennis Fischer, *Vice Pres*
Ronna Anderson, *Sales Staff*
Jennifer Joyner, *Manager*
EMP: 250
SQ FT: 84,312
SALES (est): 16.7MM **Privately Held**
WEB: www.laubergedelmar.com
SIC: 7011 Resort hotel

(P-12853)
LIBERTY STATION HHG HOTEL LP
Also Called: Courtyard By Marr San Diego Ai
2592 Laning Rd, San Diego (92106-6418)
PHONE.....................................619 221-1900
Kevin Keefer, *Partner*
EMP: 60
SALES (est): 2.8MM **Privately Held**
SIC: 7011 Hotels

(P-12854)
LIBERTY STATION HHG HOTEL LP
Also Called: Homewood Suites Libery Station
2576 Laning Rd, San Diego (92106-6418)
PHONE.....................................619 222-0500
Rick Brown, *General Mgr*
Kevin Keefer, *Partner*
EMP: 50
SALES (est): 2.6MM **Privately Held**
SIC: 7011 Hotels

(P-12855)
LINCOLN PLAZA HOTEL INC
123 S Lincoln Ave, Monterey Park
(91755-2914)
PHONE.....................................626 571-8818
Thira Ratanapreukskul, *President*
William H Roach, *Corp Secy*
EMP: 60
SQ FT: 95,600
SALES (est): 2.6MM **Privately Held**
WEB: www.lincolnplazahotel.net
SIC: 7011 Hotels

(P-12856)
LIONSGATE HT & CONFERENCE CTR
3410 Westover St, McClellan (95652-1005)
PHONE.....................................916 643-6222
Lary Kelly, *President*
Julie Vinson, *Director*
Marilou Will, *Director*
EMP: 90
SALES: 5MM **Privately Held**
SIC: 7011 Hotels

(P-12857)
LITTLE RIVER INN INC
Also Called: Little River Inn and Golf Crse
7901 N Highway 1, Little River
(95456-9527)
P.O. Box B (95456-0430)
PHONE.....................................707 937-5942
Charles D Hervilla, *CEO*
Susan Mc Kinney, *Vice Pres*
Edgar Rosas, *Maintence Staff*
Connie Reynolds, *Director*
Lynne Bearden, *Manager*
EMP: 100
SQ FT: 3,000

▲ = Import ▼=Export
◆ =Import/Export

SALES (est): 8.1MM **Privately Held**
WEB: www.littleriverinn.com
SIC: 7011 5812 Bed & breakfast inn; American restaurant

(P-12858)
LODGE AT TORREY PINES PARTNERS
998 W Mission Bay Dr, San Diego (92109-7803)
PHONE........................858 550-3908
Anne L Evans, *Partner*
David Cherashore, *Owner*
Philip Spada, *Principal*
Katie Campbell, *Natl Sales Mgr*
EMP: 275
SALES (est): 3.6MM **Privately Held**
WEB: www.lodgeattorreypines.com
SIC: 7011 5812 Resort hotel; coffee shop

(P-12859)
LODGEWORKS LP
1230 1st St, NAPA (94559-2930)
PHONE........................707 690-9800
Michael Collins, *Branch Mgr*
EMP: 60
SALES (est): 205.3K
SALES (corp-wide): 42.1MM **Privately Held**
SIC: 7011 Hotels & motels
PA: Lodgeworks, L.P.
　8100 E 22nd St N Bldg 500
　Wichita KS 67226
　316 681-5100

(P-12860)
LOEWS HOLLYWOOD HOTEL LLC
1755 N Highland Ave, Hollywood (90028-4403)
PHONE........................323 450-2235
Jonathan Tisch, *Ch of Bd*
Erika Ackerman, *Principal*
Brian Adams, *Security Dir*
Aaron Prince, *Technology*
Danny Smith, *Engineer*
EMP: 375 EST: 2012
SALES (est): 27.8MM
SALES (corp-wide): 13.7B **Publicly Held**
SIC: 7011 Hotels
PA: Loews Corporation
　667 Madison Ave Fl 7
　New York NY 10065
　212 521-2000

(P-12861)
LONE CYPRESS COMPANY LLC
US Open At Pebble Beach
17 Mile Dr, Pebble Beach (93953)
P.O. Box 567 (93953-0567)
PHONE........................831 624-3811
Robert Lapso, *Branch Mgr*
EMP: 1500
SALES (corp-wide): 119.8MM **Privately Held**
WEB: www.pebblebeach.com
SIC: 7011 7992 5813 5812 Resort hotel; public golf courses; drinking places; eating places
PA: Pebble Beach Resort Co Dba Lone Cypress Shop
　2700 17 Mile Dr
　Pebble Beach CA 93953
　831 647-7500

(P-12862)
LONG BEACH GOLDEN SAILS INC
Also Called: Best Western Golden Sails Ht
23545 Crenshaw Blvd # 100, Torrance (90505-5218)
PHONE........................562 596-1631
Luis Vasquez, *President*
Ruben Garza, *Vice Pres*
Vicki Arreguin, *Sales Staff*
EMP: 100
SQ FT: 150,000
SALES (est): 6.6MM **Privately Held**
WEB: www.goldensailshotel.com
SIC: 7011 5812 5813 Hotels; restaurant, family: independent; bar (drinking places)
PA: Abp Hotel, Llc
　2200 W Valley Blvd
　Alhambra CA 91803
　562 596-1631

(P-12863)
LONG POINT DEVELOPMENT LLC
Also Called: Terranea Resort
100 Terranea Way, Rancho Palos Verdes (90275-1013)
PHONE........................310 265-2800
Terri Haack, *General Mgr*
Jennifer Yang, *Executive Asst*
Jesse Freeman, *Engineer*
Francisco Salcedo, *Engineer*
Karen Schlesier, *VP Finance*
EMP: 1000 EST: 2004
SALES (est): 65.4MM **Privately Held**
SIC: 7011 Resort hotel

(P-12864)
LQ MANAGEMENT LLC
Also Called: La Quinta Inn
5249 W Century Blvd, Los Angeles (90045-5917)
PHONE........................310 645-2200
Ryan Thayer, *Branch Mgr*
EMP: 63 **Publicly Held**
WEB: www.neubayern.net
SIC: 7011 Hotels
HQ: Lq Management L.L.C.
　909 Hidden Rdg Ste 600
　Irving TX 75038
　214 492-6600

(P-12865)
LQR PROPERTY LLC
Also Called: La Quinta Resort & Club
49499 Eisenhower Dr, La Quinta (92253-2722)
PHONE........................760 564-4111
Stephen Strickland, *Executive*
Lynette Alarcon, *Accounting Mgr*
Linda Jones, *Controller*
Andrew Ferraro, *Asst Director*
Michelle Green, *Director*
EMP: 101
SALES (est): 9.2MM **Privately Held**
SIC: 7011 7999 Resort hotel; golf driving range

(P-12866)
M&C HOTEL INTERESTS INC
Also Called: Sheraton
530 Pico Blvd, Santa Monica (90405-1223)
PHONE........................310 399-9344
Lisa Nagahori, *Branch Mgr*
EMP: 55 **Privately Held**
WEB: www.richfield.com
SIC: 7011 Hotels & motels
HQ: M&C Hotel Interests, Inc.
　6560 Greenwood Plaza Blvd # 300
　Greenwood Village CO 80111

(P-12867)
M4DEV LLC
Also Called: Hilton Garden Inn
2137 Pacific Hwy Ste A, San Diego (92101-8472)
PHONE........................619 696-6300
Mayur Patel,
Daniel Velasquez, *Engineer*
Ryan Turnello, *Finance*
EMP: 100
SALES (est): 57.7K **Privately Held**
SIC: 7011 Hotels

(P-12868)
MADRONA MNR WINE CNTRY INN
1001 Westside Rd, Healdsburg (95448-9434)
PHONE........................707 433-4231
William R Konrad, *President*
Kevin West, *General Mgr*
Jason Heserly, *Facilities Dir*
Gertrude V Konrad,
Arielle Larson, *Director*
EMP: 55 EST: 1983
SQ FT: 1,800
SALES (est): 4.1MM **Privately Held**
WEB: www.madronamanor.com
SIC: 7011 5812 Bed & breakfast inn; Italian restaurant; Chinese restaurant; French restaurant; American restaurant

(P-12869)
MAJESTIC INDUSTRY HILLS LLC
Also Called: Pacific Plms Conference Resort
1 Industry Hills Pkwy, City of Industry (91744-5160)
PHONE........................626 810-4455
Scott Huntsman, *Branch Mgr*
John Semcken, *Principal*
EMP: 360
SALES (est): 4.6MM
SALES (corp-wide): 32MM **Privately Held**
SIC: 7011 7999 7389 7299 Resort hotel; tennis courts, outdoor/indoor: non-membership; convention & show services; banquet hall facilities
PA: Majestic Industry Hills, Llc
　1 Industry Hills Pkwy
　City Of Industry CA 91744
　562 692-9581

(P-12870)
MAJESTIC INDUSTRY HILLS LLC (PA)
Also Called: Pacific Plms Conference Resort
1 Industry Hills Pkwy, City of Industry (91744-5160)
PHONE........................562 692-9581
Edward P Roski Jr,
Pamela Golovkhin, *CFO*
Thomas H Cozzolino, *Vice Pres*
Matthew Vvhitfield, *Administration*
Sousan Madani, *Asst Controller*
EMP: 550
SALES (est): 32MM **Privately Held**
SIC: 7011 Hotels

(P-12871)
MAKAR ANAHEIM LLC
Also Called: Hilton
777 W Convention Way, Anaheim (92802-3425)
PHONE........................714 740-4431
Paul Makarechian,
Bruce Hayden, *CFO*
Carl Taylor, *Security Dir*
Shaun Robinson, *General Mgr*
Tom Abercrombie, *Info Tech Mgr*
EMP: 1200
SQ FT: 1,000,000
SALES (est): 38MM **Privately Held**
SIC: 7011 Hotels & motels

(P-12872)
MAMMOTH MOUNTAIN SKI AREA LLC (DH)
Also Called: Mammoth Mountain Inn
10001 Minaret Rd, Mammoth Lakes (93546)
P.O. Box 24 (93546-0024)
PHONE........................760 934-2571
Rusty Gregory, *President*
David Cummings, *Partner*
Mark Brownlie, *COO*
Erik Forsell, *Chief Mktg Ofcr*
Bruce Burton, *Vice Pres*
EMP: 347
SQ FT: 140,000
SALES (est): 137.9MM
SALES (corp-wide): 209.7MM **Privately Held**
WEB: www.mammothmotocross.com
SIC: 7011 5812 Ski lodge; resort hotel; eating places
HQ: Hawk Guarantor, Llc
　100 Saint Paul St Ste 800
　Denver CO 80206
　720 284-6400

(P-12873)
MANAS HOSPITALITY LLC
Also Called: Holiday Inn
445 Hotel Cir S, San Diego (92108-3402)
PHONE........................619 298-1291
Rajesh Chollera,
Hitesh Kalthia,
EMP: 50
SQ FT: 63,424
SALES (est): 816.3K **Privately Held**
SIC: 7011 Hotels & motels

(P-12874)
MANCHESTER GRAND RESORTS LP
Also Called: Hyatt Hotel
1 Market Pl Fl 33, San Diego (92101-7714)
PHONE........................619 232-1234
Mark S Hoplamazian, *CEO*
Richard V Gibbons, *Partner*
Douglas F Manchester, *Partner*
Gebhard F Rainer, *CFO*
Alexander Bremer, *Officer*
EMP: 900
SALES (est): 28.8MM
SALES (corp-wide): 4.6B **Publicly Held**
WEB: www.hyatt.com
SIC: 7011 Hotels & motels
HQ: Hyatt Corporation
　150 N Riverside Plz
　Chicago IL 60606
　312 750-1234

(P-12875)
MARIANIS INN & RESTAURANT
2500 El Camino Real, Santa Clara (95051-3098)
PHONE........................408 243-0312
Louis Mariani Sr, *President*
Dennis Mariani, *Principal*
EMP: 220 EST: 1953
SALES (est): 1.5MM **Privately Held**
SIC: 7011 5812 Motels; eating places

(P-12876)
MARINE CORPS UNITED STATES
Also Called: Camp Pendleton Billeting Fund
A St Bldg 1341, Camp Pendleton (92055)
PHONE........................760 430-4709
Monique Ramirez, *Director*
Jeanette Naputi, *Accounting Mgr*
EMP: 50 **Publicly Held**
WEB: www.usmc.mil
SIC: 7011 Hotels & motels
HQ: United States Marine Corps
　Pentagon Rm 4b544
　Washington DC 20380

(P-12877)
MARRIOT COURTYARD
Also Called: Courtyard By Marriott
580 Beach St, San Francisco (94133-1128)
PHONE........................415 775-1103
James Edmondson, *Owner*
EMP: 50 EST: 1995
SALES (est): 1.9MM **Privately Held**
SIC: 7011 Hotels & motels

(P-12878)
MARRIOTT GRAND RESIDENCE
1001 Heavenly Village Way, South Lake Tahoe (96150-6983)
PHONE........................530 542-8400
Steve Weitz, *President*
Marriot International, *Owner*
EMP: 320
SALES (est): 6.9MM **Privately Held**
SIC: 7011 Hotels & motels

(P-12879)
MARRIOTT HOTELS & RESORTS
1001 Broadway, Oakland (94607-4019)
PHONE........................510 451-4000
Steven Williams, *Director*
EMP: 80
SALES (est): 1.7MM **Privately Held**
SIC: 7011 Hotels

(P-12880)
MARRIOTT INTERNATIONAL INC
5835 Owens Ave, Carlsbad (92008-6562)
PHONE........................760 431-9399
Alicia Clements, *Branch Mgr*
EMP: 173
SALES (corp-wide): 22.8B **Publicly Held**
SIC: 7011 Hotels & motels
PA: Marriott International, Inc.
　10400 Fernwood Rd
　Bethesda MD 20817
　301 380-3000

PRODUCTS & SVCS

(P-12881)
MARRIOTT INTERNATIONAL INC
4381 Myra Ave, Cypress (90630-4131)
PHONE.....................................714 209-6586
EMP: 175
SALES (corp-wide): 22.8B **Publicly Held**
SIC: 7011 Hotels
PA: Marriott International, Inc.
10400 Fernwood Rd
Bethesda MD 20817
301 380-3000

(P-12882)
MARRIOTT INTERNATIONAL INC
9620 Airport Blvd, Los Angeles (90045-5402)
PHONE.....................................310 337-2800
Gregory Lehman, *Manager*
Jenny Ulch, *Finance*
EMP: 300
SALES (corp-wide): 22.8B **Publicly Held**
SIC: 7011 5813 5812 7389 Hotels; drinking places; eating places; office facilities & secretarial service rental
PA: Marriott International, Inc.
10400 Fernwood Rd
Bethesda MD 20817
301 380-3000

(P-12883)
MARRIOTT INTERNATIONAL INC
11966 El Camino Real, San Diego (92130-2592)
PHONE.....................................858 523-1700
Michael Woldowski, *Branch Mgr*
Lauren Walsh, *Financial Exec*
EMP: 167
SALES (corp-wide): 22.8B **Publicly Held**
SIC: 7011 5812 Hotels; American restaurant
PA: Marriott International, Inc.
10400 Fernwood Rd
Bethesda MD 20817
301 380-3000

(P-12884)
MARRIOTT INTERNATIONAL INC
5855 W Century Blvd, Los Angeles (90045-5614)
PHONE.....................................310 641-5700
Jim Burns, *General Mgr*
Karen A Englund, *General Mgr*
Cheryl Frazier, *Sales Mgr*
Carol Rosen, *Sales Staff*
Bill DEA, *Asst Director*
EMP: 900
SALES (corp-wide): 22.8B **Publicly Held**
SIC: 7011 7389 6513 Hotels; office facilities & secretarial service rental; residential hotel operation
PA: Marriott International, Inc.
10400 Fernwood Rd
Bethesda MD 20817
301 380-3000

(P-12885)
MARRIOTT INTERNATIONAL INC
299 2nd St, San Francisco (94105-3123)
PHONE.....................................415 947-0700
Lance Rohf, *Manager*
EMP: 100
SALES (corp-wide): 22.8B **Publicly Held**
SIC: 7011 6531 5812 5813 Hotels; real estate managers; eating places; drinking places
PA: Marriott International, Inc.
10400 Fernwood Rd
Bethesda MD 20817
301 380-3000

(P-12886)
MARRIOTT INTERNATIONAL INC
Also Called: Springhill Suites
900 Bayfront Ct, San Diego (92101-3007)
PHONE.....................................619 831-0225
Mike Murphy, *General Mgr*
EMP: 100

SALES (corp-wide): 22.8B **Publicly Held**
SIC: 7011 Hotels
PA: Marriott International, Inc.
10400 Fernwood Rd
Bethesda MD 20817
301 380-3000

(P-12887)
MARRIOTT INTERNATIONAL INC
46100 Landing Pkwy, Fremont (94538-6437)
PHONE.....................................510 413-3700
Orlando Carrasquillo, *Manager*
Yolanda Serranto, *Human Res Dir*
EMP: 200
SALES (corp-wide): 22.8B **Publicly Held**
SIC: 7011 7389 Hotels; office facilities & secretarial service rental
PA: Marriott International, Inc.
10400 Fernwood Rd
Bethesda MD 20817
301 380-3000

(P-12888)
MARRIOTT INTERNATIONAL INC
18000 Von Karman Ave, Irvine (92612-1004)
PHONE.....................................949 724-3606
Satinder Palpa, *Branch Mgr*
Rahul Vir, *General Mgr*
Bobby Shoemaker, *Planning*
Yugo Takahashi, *Opers Staff*
Mike Cooke, *Director*
EMP: 500
SALES (corp-wide): 22.8B **Publicly Held**
SIC: 7011 7389 Hotels; office facilities & secretarial service rental
PA: Marriott International, Inc.
10400 Fernwood Rd
Bethesda MD 20817
301 380-3000

(P-12889)
MARRIOTT INTERNATIONAL INC
4240 La Jolla Village Dr, La Jolla (92037-1407)
PHONE.....................................858 587-1414
Paul Corsinita, *Manager*
Dan Kaplan, *General Mgr*
Amy Konopasek, *Human Res Dir*
Esmeralda Florez, *Director*
David Merkel, *Director*
EMP: 337
SALES (corp-wide): 22.8B **Publicly Held**
SIC: 7011 Hotels
PA: Marriott International, Inc.
10400 Fernwood Rd
Bethesda MD 20817
301 380-3000

(P-12890)
MARRIOTT INTERNATIONAL INC
Also Called: Residence Inn By Marriott
5852 Stadium St, San Diego (92122-3305)
PHONE.....................................858 587-1770
Joe Kuhn, *Manager*
James Burkel, *Engineer*
Bill Billing, *Chief Engr*
George Flores, *Asst Mgr*
EMP: 89
SALES (corp-wide): 22.8B **Publicly Held**
SIC: 7011 Hotels & motels
PA: Marriott International, Inc.
10400 Fernwood Rd
Bethesda MD 20817
301 380-3000

(P-12891)
MARRIOTT INTERNATIONAL INC
38305 Cook St, Palm Desert (92211-1794)
PHONE.....................................760 776-0050
Michael Gerano, *Branch Mgr*
Eileen Collins, *Manager*
EMP: 167
SALES (corp-wide): 22.8B **Publicly Held**
SIC: 7011 Hotels & motels
PA: Marriott International, Inc.
10400 Fernwood Rd
Bethesda MD 20817
301 380-3000

(P-12892)
MARRIOTT INTERNATIONAL INC
Also Called: Residence Inn By Marriott
2135 E El Segundo Blvd, El Segundo (90245-4503)
PHONE.....................................310 333-0888
Ray Cruickshanks, *Manager*
EMP: 167
SALES (corp-wide): 22.8B **Publicly Held**
SIC: 7011 Hotels
PA: Marriott International, Inc.
10400 Fernwood Rd
Bethesda MD 20817
301 380-3000

(P-12893)
MARRIOTT INTERNATIONAL INC
Also Called: Residence Inn By Marriott
5400 Kearny Mesa Rd, San Diego (92111-1303)
PHONE.....................................858 278-2100
Doug Former, *Branch Mgr*
Shirley Walker, *President*
Jonathan Correll, *General Mgr*
Adam Lutz, *General Mgr*
EMP: 167
SALES (corp-wide): 22.8B **Publicly Held**
SIC: 7011 Hotels
PA: Marriott International, Inc.
10400 Fernwood Rd
Bethesda MD 20817
301 380-3000

(P-12894)
MARRIOTT INTERNATIONAL INC
4700 Airport Plaza Dr, Long Beach (90815-1252)
PHONE.....................................562 425-5210
Miran Ahmed, *Branch Mgr*
EMP: 210
SALES (corp-wide): 22.8B **Publicly Held**
SIC: 7011 Hotels
PA: Marriott International, Inc.
10400 Fernwood Rd
Bethesda MD 20817
301 380-3000

(P-12895)
MARRIOTT INTERNATIONAL INC
Also Called: Residence Inn By Marriott
2025 Convention Ctr Way, Ontario (91764-4450)
PHONE.....................................909 937-6788
Frank Palacios, *General Mgr*
Carlos Mendoza, *General Mgr*
EMP: 167
SALES (corp-wide): 22.8B **Publicly Held**
SIC: 7011 Hotels & motels
PA: Marriott International, Inc.
10400 Fernwood Rd
Bethesda MD 20817
301 380-3000

(P-12896)
MARRIOTT INTERNATIONAL INC
21850 Oxnard St, Woodland Hills (91367-3631)
PHONE.....................................818 887-4800
Clay Andrews, *Manager*
EMP: 167
SALES (corp-wide): 22.8B **Publicly Held**
SIC: 7011 Hotels
PA: Marriott International, Inc.
10400 Fernwood Rd
Bethesda MD 20817
301 380-3000

(P-12897)
MARRIOTT INTERNATIONAL INC
Also Called: Residence Inn By Marriott
1015 Montecito Dr, Corona (92879-1760)
PHONE.....................................951 371-0107
Fred Kokash, *Branch Mgr*
EMP: 167
SALES (corp-wide): 22.8B **Publicly Held**
SIC: 7011 Hotels & motels

PA: Marriott International, Inc.
10400 Fernwood Rd
Bethesda MD 20817
301 380-3000

(P-12898)
MARRIOTT INTERNATIONAL INC
Also Called: Courtyard By Marriott
2000 E Mariposa Ave, El Segundo (90245-5027)
PHONE.....................................310 322-0700
Steve Vandesteeg, *Manager*
EMP: 167
SALES (corp-wide): 22.8B **Publicly Held**
SIC: 7011 Hotels & motels
PA: Marriott International, Inc.
10400 Fernwood Rd
Bethesda MD 20817
301 380-3000

(P-12899)
MARRIOTT INTERNATIONAL INC
14400 Aviation Blvd, Hawthorne (90250-6654)
PHONE.....................................310 725-9696
David Laatz, *Branch Mgr*
EMP: 167
SALES (corp-wide): 22.8B **Publicly Held**
SIC: 7011 Hotels & motels
PA: Marriott International, Inc.
10400 Fernwood Rd
Bethesda MD 20817
301 380-3000

(P-12900)
MARRIOTT INTERNATIONAL INC
905 California St, San Francisco (94108-2289)
PHONE.....................................415 989-3500
Bill Love, *Branch Mgr*
EMP: 167
SALES (corp-wide): 22.8B **Publicly Held**
SIC: 7011 Hotels & motels
PA: Marriott International, Inc.
10400 Fernwood Rd
Bethesda MD 20817
301 380-3000

(P-12901)
MARRIOTT INTERNATIONAL INC
39802 Cedar Blvd, Newark (94560-5340)
PHONE.....................................510 657-4600
Scott Crunk, *Manager*
EMP: 167
SALES (corp-wide): 22.8B **Publicly Held**
SIC: 7011 Hotels & motels
PA: Marriott International, Inc.
10400 Fernwood Rd
Bethesda MD 20817
301 380-3000

(P-12902)
MARRIOTT INTERNATIONAL INC
4111 E Willow St, Long Beach (90815-1740)
PHONE.....................................562 595-0909
Lucas Fiamengo, *Manager*
Julie Buettner, *Office Mgr*
Juan Ochoa, *Chief Engr*
EMP: 167
SALES (corp-wide): 22.8B **Publicly Held**
SIC: 7011 Hotels & motels
PA: Marriott International, Inc.
10400 Fernwood Rd
Bethesda MD 20817
301 380-3000

(P-12903)
MARRIOTT INTERNATIONAL INC
1325 Broadway, Sonoma (95476-7505)
PHONE.....................................707 935-6600
Dave Dolquist, *General Mgr*
EMP: 200
SQ FT: 1,500
SALES (corp-wide): 22.8B **Publicly Held**
SIC: 7011 Hotels & motels

PA: Marriott International, Inc.
10400 Fernwood Rd
Bethesda MD 20817
301 380-3000

(P-12904)
MARRIOTT INTERNATIONAL INC
3130 S Harbor Blvd # 500, Santa Ana (92704-6829)
PHONE.................................714 545-5261
Wynne Prima, *Branch Mgr*
Latifa Khan, *President*
Ruth Rain, *Opers Mgr*
Melisa Rashid, *Manager*
MO Ross, *Manager*
EMP: 167
SALES (corp-wide): 22.8B **Publicly Held**
SIC: 7011 Hotels & motels
PA: Marriott International, Inc.
10400 Fernwood Rd
Bethesda MD 20817
301 380-3000

(P-12905)
MARRIOTT INTERNATIONAL INC
Also Called: Residence Inn By Marriott
700 Ellinwood Way, Pleasant Hill (94523-4700)
PHONE.................................925 689-1010
Trish Snowden, *Principal*
EMP: 167
SALES (corp-wide): 22.8B **Publicly Held**
SIC: 7011 Hotels & motels
PA: Marriott International, Inc.
10400 Fernwood Rd
Bethesda MD 20817
301 380-3000

(P-12906)
MARRIOTT INTERNATIONAL INC (PA)
500 Post St, San Francisco (94102-1229)
PHONE.................................415 929-2030
Lisa Definney, *General Mgr*
Akihito Ikeda, *Principal*
Donna Collings, *General Mgr*
Michael Lynch, *Sales Staff*
Lynn Pescherine, *Senior Mgr*
EMP: 99
SALES (est): 8.7MM **Privately Held**
SIC: 7011 Hotels & motels

(P-12907)
MARRIOTT INTERNATIONAL INC
900 W Olympic Blvd, Los Angeles (90015-1338)
PHONE.................................213 284-3862
Kimberly Bailey, *Manager*
EMP: 167
SALES (corp-wide): 22.8B **Publicly Held**
SIC: 7011 Hotels & motels
PA: Marriott International, Inc.
10400 Fernwood Rd
Bethesda MD 20817
301 380-3000

(P-12908)
MARRIOTT INTERNATIONAL INC
1800 Old Bayshore Hwy, Burlingame (94010-1203)
PHONE.................................650 692-9100
Stan Moore, *Manager*
Cliff Clark, *General Mgr*
Karen Navarro, *Human Resources*
Jeana Thayer, *Sales Mgr*
Maria Martinez, *Manager*
EMP: 167
SALES (corp-wide): 22.8B **Publicly Held**
SIC: 7011 7389 Hotels; office facilities & secretarial service rental
PA: Marriott International, Inc.
10400 Fernwood Rd
Bethesda MD 20817
301 380-3000

(P-12909)
MARRIOTT INTERNATIONAL INC
Also Called: Residence Inn By Marriott
900 Bayfront Ct, San Diego (92101-3007)
PHONE.................................619 831-0224
Evangelina Alaniz, *Accountant*
EMP: 99 EST: 2016
SALES (est): 485.2K **Privately Held**
SIC: 7011 Hotels

(P-12910)
MARRIOTT RSRTS HSPITALITY CORP
1091 Pinehurst Ln, Palm Desert (92260-1636)
PHONE.................................760 779-1200
EMP: 53 **Publicly Held**
SIC: 7011 Hotels & motels
HQ: Marriott Resorts Hospitality Corporation
6649 W Wood Blvd Ste 500
Orlando FL 32821
407 206-6000

(P-12911)
MARRIOTTS NEWPORT COAST VILLA
23000 Newport Coast Dr, Newport Beach (92657-2100)
PHONE.................................949 464-6000
Eric Penningroth, *Principal*
Charles Rokicki, *Sales Executive*
EMP: 56
SALES (est): 4.5MM **Privately Held**
SIC: 7011 Resort hotel

(P-12912)
MARRIOTTS SHADOW RIDGE
9003 Shadow Ridge Rd, Palm Desert (92211-2057)
PHONE.................................760 674-2600
John Faulk, *Owner*
EMP: 81
SALES (est): 7.5MM **Privately Held**
SIC: 7011 Resort hotel

(P-12913)
MARTIN RESORTS INC (PA)
1201 Palm St, San Luis Obispo (93408-3115)
P.O. Box 12060 (93406-2060)
PHONE.................................805 545-7900
Noreen Martin, *CEO*
Margaret Johnson, *COO*
Roger Philips, *CFO*
Laura Sherlock, *Vice Pres*
Cha E Fryburger, *General Mgr*
EMP: 252
SQ FT: 7,000
SALES (est): 13.9MM **Privately Held**
WEB: www.pismo.com
SIC: 7011 Resort hotel

(P-12914)
MASON STREET OPCO LLC
Also Called: Fairmont San Francisco
950 Mason St, San Francisco (94108-6000)
PHONE.................................415 772-5000
Seung Geon Kim, *President*
Kary Clark, *Human Res Mgr*
Daniel Kramer, *Asst Sec*
EMP: 850
SQ FT: 750,000
SALES: 112MM **Privately Held**
SIC: 7011 Hotels

(P-12915)
MAYFAIR HOTEL
1430 Amherst Ave Apt 5, Los Angeles (90025-0358)
PHONE.................................213 484-9789
Tung Shui Ng, *President*
EMP: 60 EST: 1979
SQ FT: 228,800
SALES (est): 3.8MM **Privately Held**
WEB: www.mayfairla.com
SIC: 7011 Hotels

(P-12916)
MBIPCH LLC
Also Called: Malibu Beach Inn
22211 Pacific Coast Hwy, Malibu (90265-5028)
PHONE.................................310 456-6444
Richard Sherman, *CEO*
Pauline Van Der Woude, *Manager*
EMP: 52
SALES (est): 3.3MM **Privately Held**
SIC: 7011 Resort hotel

(P-12917)
MBP LAND LLC
Also Called: Courtyard Marriott Mission Vly
595 Hotel Cir S, San Diego (92108-3403)
PHONE.................................619 291-5720
John Blem, *Mng Member*
EMP: 56
SALES: 750K
SALES (corp-wide): 194.5MM **Privately Held**
SIC: 7011 Hotels & motels
PA: Evolution Hospitality, Llc
1211 Puerta Del Sol # 170
San Clemente CA 92673
949 325-1350

(P-12918)
MCCLELLAN HOSPITALITY SVCS LLC
3140 Peacekeeper Way, Mcclellan (95652-2508)
PHONE.................................916 965-7100
Larry Kelley,
Douglas Hart,
EMP: 75
SALES (est): 1.2MM **Privately Held**
SIC: 7011 5812 Hotels & motels; caterers

(P-12919)
MENDOCINO HOTEL & RESORT CORP
Also Called: Mendocino Hotel & Grdn Suites
45080 Main St, Mendocino (95460)
PHONE.................................707 937-0511
Thomas Clark Kravis, *Owner*
Carlos Pena, *Executive*
Juan C Pena, *Executive*
Dan Clark, *Info Tech Mgr*
Cindy Rhinehart, *Data Proc Staff*
EMP: 80
SQ FT: 12,500
SALES (est): 3.2MM **Privately Held**
WEB: www.mendocinohotel.com
SIC: 7011 5812 5813 7299 Hotels; eating places; bars & lounges; banquet hall facilities

(P-12920)
MERISTAR SAN PEDRO HILTON LLC
Also Called: Hilton Port Los Angls-San Pdro
2800 Via Cabrillo Marina, San Pedro (90731-7223)
PHONE.................................310 514-3344
Paul Whetsell, *Mng Member*
Jeff Milnes, *CEO*
John Emery, *CFO*
EMP: 176
SALES (est): 1.6MM **Privately Held**
WEB: www.sheratonokc.com
SIC: 7011 Hotels
HQ: Interstate Hotels & Resorts, Inc.
4501 Fairfax Dr Ste 500
Arlington VA 22203
703 387-3100

(P-12921)
MERITAGE RESORT LLC
Also Called: Meritage Resort and Spa, The
875 Bordeaux Way, NAPA (94558-7524)
PHONE.................................707 251-1900
Timothy R Busch, *President*
Elisse Peck, *Executive*
Ashley Butler, *General Mgr*
Michael M Palmer, *General Mgr*
Ashley Thomas, *General Mgr*
EMP: 350
SALES (est): 17MM **Privately Held**
SIC: 7011 Hotels

(P-12922)
MERRITT HOSPITALITY LLC
Also Called: Hilton
701 W Ocean Blvd, Long Beach (90831-3100)
PHONE.................................562 983-3400
Grace Sun, *Sales Mgr*
Annette Dhein, *Vice Pres*
Helen McCaughan, *Sales Dir*
Richard Hoyt, *Director*
EMP: 250
SALES (corp-wide): 277.3MM **Privately Held**
SIC: 7011 7991 5813 5812 Hotels; physical fitness facilities; drinking places; eating places
HQ: Merritt Hospitality, Llc
101 Merritt 7 Ste 14
Norwalk CT 06851
203 849-8844

(P-12923)
MERRITT HOSPITALITY LLC
Also Called: Marriott
2701 Nutwood Ave, Fullerton (92831-5400)
PHONE.................................714 738-7800
Tom Beebon, *Manager*
EMP: 125
SALES (corp-wide): 277.3MM **Privately Held**
SIC: 7011 7991 5813 5812 Hotels; physical fitness facilities; drinking places; eating places
HQ: Merritt Hospitality, Llc
101 Merritt 7 Ste 14
Norwalk CT 06851
203 849-8844

(P-12924)
MESA PROPERTIES GP
25 Mauchly Ste 305, Irvine (92618-2331)
PHONE.................................949 857-1905
John Jourard, *Manager*
EMP: 60
SALES (est): 1.9MM **Privately Held**
SIC: 7011 Hotels

(P-12925)
METROPOLIS HOTEL MGT LLC
Also Called: Hotel Indigo Los Angles Dwntwn
899 Francisco St, Los Angeles (90017)
PHONE.................................213 683-4855
Raymond Vermolen, *General Mgr*
EMP: 120
SALES: 25MM
SALES (corp-wide): 1.7B **Privately Held**
SIC: 7011 Hotels & motels
HQ: Inter-Continental Hotels Corporation
3 Ravinia Dr Ste 100
Atlanta GA 30346
770 604-5000

(P-12926)
MHRP RESORT INC
Also Called: Mountain High Ski Resort
24510 Highway 2, Wrightwood (92397)
PHONE.................................760 249-5808
Russel S Bernard, *President*
W Gregory Geiger, *Vice Pres*
Kenneth Liang, *Vice Pres*
Marc Porosoff, *Vice Pres*
Ben Smith, *General Mgr*
EMP: 100
SALES (est): 5.7MM **Privately Held**
WEB: www.mountainhighskiresort.com
SIC: 7011 Ski lodge

(P-12927)
MIKADO HOTELS INC
Also Called: Mikado Best Western Hotel
12600 Riverside Dr, North Hollywood (91607-3411)
PHONE.................................818 763-9141
Jerome Frick, *CEO*
Edmond Petrossian, *President*
Diran Yahyayan, *Vice Pres*
EMP: 50
SQ FT: 71,500
SALES (est): 2.1MM **Privately Held**
SIC: 7011 5812 5813 Hotel, franchised; restaurant, lunch counter; cocktail lounge

(P-12928)
MILE POST PROPERTIES LLC
Also Called: La Quinta Inn
1050 Van Ness Ave, San Francisco (94109-6934)
PHONE.................................415 673-4711
Fred Reed, *General Mgr*
EMP: 100
SQ FT: 100,000
SALES (est): 1.6MM **Privately Held**
SIC: 7011 Hotels

(P-12929)
MILLBRAE WCP HOTEL II LLC
Also Called: Aloft Sfo
401 E Millbrae Ave, Millbrae (94030-3111)
PHONE.................................650 443-5500
Marc Swerdlow, *President*
Mark Zettl, *COO*
Chris Offutt, *General Mgr*
EMP: 50
SQ FT: 288,000
SALES (est): 3.7MM
SALES (corp-wide): 178.6MM **Privately Held**
SIC: 7011 Hotels
HQ: Ultima Hospitality, L.L.C.
30 S Wacker Dr Ste 3600
Chicago IL 60606
312 948-4500

(P-12930)
MISSION RANCH INC
26270 Dolores St, Carmel (93923-9215)
PHONE.................................831 624-6436
Roy Kaufman, *President*
Howard Bernstein, *Treasurer*
Clint Eastwood, *Director*
EMP: 50
SALES (est): 3.5MM **Privately Held**
SIC: 7011 7999 Resort hotel; tennis club, non-membership

(P-12931)
MISSION STUART HT PARTNERS LLC
Also Called: Hotel Vitale
8 Mission St, San Francisco (94105-1227)
PHONE.................................415 278-3700
Fax: 415 278-3750
EMP: 200
SALES (est): 10.8MM **Privately Held**
WEB: www.hotelvitale.com
SIC: 7011

(P-12932)
MISSION VALLEY HT OPERATOR INC
595 Hotel Cir S, San Diego (92108-3403)
PHONE.................................619 291-5720
Michael Medzigian, *President*
George Gudgeon, *Treasurer*
EMP: 75
SALES (est): 1.1MM **Privately Held**
SIC: 7011 Hotel, franchised

(P-12933)
MIYAKO HOTELS
328 E 1st St Ste 510, Los Angeles (90012-3902)
PHONE.................................213 617-2000
Akimasa Yoneda, *President*
EMP: 56
SALES (est): 2.3MM **Privately Held**
SIC: 7011 Hotel, franchised; hotels

(P-12934)
MODESTO HOSPITALITY LLC
Also Called: Doubltree By Hilton Ht Modesto
1150 9th St, Modesto (95354-0823)
PHONE.................................209 526-6000
EMP: 180
SALES (est): 424.9K **Privately Held**
SIC: 7011 Hotels & motels

(P-12935)
MODESTO HOSPITALITY LESSEE LLC
Also Called: Doubletree Hotel Modesto
1150 9th St Ste C, Modesto (95354-0857)
PHONE.................................209 526-6000
EMP: 99
SALES (est): 950K **Privately Held**
SIC: 7011

(P-12936)
MONO WIND CASINO
Also Called: Big Sandy Rancheria
37302 Rancheria Ln, Auberry (93602-9423)
P.O. Box 1060 (93602-1060)
PHONE.................................559 855-4350
Connie Lewis, *Principal*
Elizabeth D Kipp, *Principal*
Ronda Roman, *Payroll Mgr*
John Robertson, *Maintenance Dir*
EMP: 100

SALES (est): 6.6MM **Privately Held**
WEB: www.monowindcasino.com
SIC: 7011 5812 Casino hotel; restaurant, family; independent

(P-12937)
MONTAGE HOTELS & RESORTS LLC
Also Called: Montage Beverly Hills
225 N Canon Dr, Beverly Hills (90210-5301)
PHONE.................................310 499-4199
Alan Fuerstman, *Branch Mgr*
EMP: 450
SALES (est): 1MM
SALES (corp-wide): 117.9MM **Privately Held**
SIC: 7011 7991 Hotels; spas
PA: Montage Hotels & Resorts, Llc
3 Ada Ste 100
Irvine CA 92618
949 715-5002

(P-12938)
MONTAGE HOTELS & RESORTS LLC (PA)
Also Called: Montage Laguna Beach
3 Ada Ste 100, Irvine (92618-2322)
P.O. Box 52031, Phoenix AZ (85072-2031)
PHONE.................................949 715-5002
Alan Fuerstman, *Mng Member*
Jason Herthel, *President*
Dax Acosta, *Vice Pres*
Iqbal Bashir, *Vice Pres*
James D Bermingham, *Vice Pres*
EMP: 1770
SQ FT: 586,000
SALES (est): 117.9MM **Privately Held**
WEB: www.montagehotels.com
SIC: 7011 Hotels

(P-12939)
MONTCLAIR HOTELS MB LLC
Also Called: Holiday Inn
1050 Burnett Ave, Concord (94520-5713)
PHONE.................................925 687-5500
Stephanie Mullen, *General Mgr*
EMP: 75
SALES (est): 965.6K **Privately Held**
WEB: www.montclairhotels.com
SIC: 7011 Hotels & motels
PA: Montclair Hotels Mb, Llc
6600 Mannheim Rd
Rosemont IL 60018

(P-12940)
MONTECITO SEQUOIA INC
Also Called: Montecito Sequoia Lodge
8000 Generals Hwy, Kings Canyon Nationa (93633)
P.O. Box 858, Kcnp (93633-0858)
PHONE.................................559 565-3388
Virginia C Barnes, *President*
EMP: 61 EST: 1960
SALES (est): 2.2MM **Privately Held**
SIC: 7011 Resort hotel

(P-12941)
MONTEREY PLAZA HT LTD PARTNR
Also Called: Monterey Plaza Hotel & Spa
400 Cannery Row, Monterey (93940-7501)
PHONE.................................800 334-3999
John V Narigi, *General Ptnr*
EMP: 360
SALES (est): 24.5MM **Privately Held**
WEB: www.montereyplazahotel.com
SIC: 7011 Resort hotel; hotels

(P-12942)
MORGANS HOTEL GROUP LLC
Also Called: Miramar Hotel
1555 S Jameson Ln, Santa Barbara (93108)
PHONE.................................805 969-2203
Philip Dailey, *General Mgr*
EMP: 130 **Privately Held**
WEB: www.mondrianhotel.com
SIC: 7011 Hotels & motels
HQ: Morgans Hotel Group Management Llc
475 10th Ave Fl 11
New York NY 10018

(P-12943)
MORGANS HOTEL GROUP MGT LLC
Also Called: Mondrian Hotel
8440 W Sunset Blvd, Los Angeles (90069-1912)
PHONE.................................323 650-8999
David Weidlich, *General Mgr*
EMP: 200 **Privately Held**
WEB: www.mondrianhotel.com
SIC: 7011 5813 5812 Hotels; drinking places; eating places
HQ: Morgans Hotel Group Management Llc
475 10th Ave Fl 11
New York NY 10018

(P-12944)
MORGANS HOTEL GROUP MGT LLC
Also Called: Clift Hotel Four Season
495 Geary St, San Francisco (94102-1222)
PHONE.................................415 775-4700
Alexandra Walterstiel, *General Mgr*
EMP: 200
SQ FT: 271,387 **Privately Held**
WEB: www.mondrianhotel.com
SIC: 7011 5812 7991 5813 Hotels; eating places; physical fitness facilities; drinking places
HQ: Morgans Hotel Group Management Llc
475 10th Ave Fl 11
New York NY 10018

(P-12945)
MOTEL 6 OPERATING LP
5101 W Century Blvd, Inglewood (90304-1223)
PHONE.................................310 419-1234
Amad Serhat, *Manager*
Ray Sitzhugh, *General Mgr*
EMP: 53
SQ FT: 112,875
SALES (corp-wide): 570.8MM **Privately Held**
WEB: www.motel6.com
SIC: 7011 Hotels & motels
HQ: Motel 6 Operating L.P.
4001 Intl Pkwy Ste 500
Carrollton TX 75007
972 360-9000

(P-12946)
MOUNTAIN SPRINGS KIRKWOOD LLC
1501 Kirkwood Meadows Dr, Kirkwood (95646)
PHONE.................................209 258-6000
Charles E Cobb Jr, *Mng Member*
Tobin T Cobb,
Bud D Klein,
EMP: 200
SALES (est): 2MM **Privately Held**
SIC: 7011 Ski lodge; resort hotel

(P-12947)
MSR HOTELS & RESORTS INC
Also Called: Embassy Suites- Santa Clara
2885 Lakeside Dr, Santa Clara (95054-2805)
PHONE.................................408 496-6400
Teri Owens, *Branch Mgr*
EMP: 80
SALES (corp-wide): 43.6B **Publicly Held**
SIC: 7011 Hotels & motels
HQ: Msr Hotels & Resorts, Inc.
450 S Orange Ave
Orlando FL 32801
407 650-1000

(P-12948)
NAPA ES LEASING LLC
Also Called: Embassy Suites
1075 California Blvd, NAPA (94559-1061)
PHONE.................................707 253-9540
Reynaldo Zertuche, *General Mgr*
EMP: 117
SALES (est): 475.9K
SALES (corp-wide): 1.3B **Privately Held**
SIC: 7011 Hotels & motels
HQ: Rangers Sub I, Llc
3 Bethesda Metro Ctr # 1000
Bethesda MD 20814

(P-12949)
NAPA VALLEY LODGE LP
Also Called: Bodega Bay Lodge
103 Coast Highway 1, Bodega Bay (94923-9723)
PHONE.................................707 875-3525
Ellis Alden, *Owner*
EMP: 60
SALES (corp-wide): 4.7MM **Privately Held**
WEB: www.napavalleylodge.com
SIC: 7011 Vacation lodges
PA: Napa Valley Lodge L.P.
2230 Madison St
Yountville CA 94599
707 944-2468

(P-12950)
NARVEN ENTERPRISES INC
Also Called: Holiday Inn
1430 7th Ave Ste B, San Diego (92101-2815)
PHONE.................................619 239-2261
Behram Baxter, *President*
EMP: 75
SQ FT: 6,000
SALES (est): 5.6MM **Privately Held**
SIC: 7011 Hotels & motels

(P-12951)
NATIONAL HOSPITALITY LLC
Also Called: Royal Scandinavian Inn
400 Alisal Rd, Solvang (93463-3741)
P.O. Box 30 (93464-0030)
PHONE.................................805 688-8000
Cynthia Elwood, *Mng Member*
EMP: 80
SQ FT: 65,000
SALES (est): 1.7MM **Privately Held**
WEB: www.royalscandinavianinn.com
SIC: 7011 5812 7299 5813 Inns; eating places; banquet hall facilities; cocktail lounge

(P-12952)
NEW FIGUEROA HOTEL INC
1000 S Hope St Apt 201, Los Angeles (90015-1492)
PHONE.................................213 627-8971
Uno Thimansson, *President*
Elyse Omori, *Vice Pres*
Clay Andrews, *General Mgr*
Jacqui Cikra, *Sales Dir*
Tammy Nguyen, *Director*
EMP: 70
SQ FT: 200,000
SALES (est): 5.8MM **Privately Held**
SIC: 7011 5812 5813 Resort hotel; eating places; bars & lounges

(P-12953)
NEWARK COURTYARD BY MARRIOTT
34905 Newark Blvd, Newark (94560-1215)
PHONE.................................510 792-5200
Melody Lanthorn, *Manager*
EMP: 60
SALES (est): 1.9MM **Privately Held**
SIC: 7011 Hotels

(P-12954)
NEWPORT HOSPITALITY GROUP INC
Also Called: Holiday Inn
801 Truxtun Ave, Bakersfield (93301-4726)
PHONE.................................661 323-1900
Eric Iokal, *Manager*
EMP: 200
SALES (est): 2MM
SALES (corp-wide): 97.9MM **Privately Held**
WEB: www.newport-hospitality.com
SIC: 7011 Hotels
PA: Newport Hospitality Group Inc
1048 Irvine Ave Ste 365
Newport Beach CA
949 706-7002

(P-12955)
NEWPORT HOTEL CAPITAL LLC
Also Called: Hotel Menage
1221 S Harbor Blvd, Anaheim (92805-6004)
PHONE.................................714 758-0900
Rob Kaulfonic, *Vice Pres*

EMP: 123
SALES (est): 5.3MM **Privately Held**
SIC: 7011 5813 5812 Hotels; drinking places; eating places

(P-12956)
NHCA INC
Also Called: Crowne Plz Los Angeles Hbr Ht
2330 Grand Ave, Long Beach
(90815-1761)
PHONE.................................310 519-8200
SM Nasarudin, *CEO*
EMP: 151
SALES (est): 9.2MM **Privately Held**
WEB: www.sheratonlaharbor.com
SIC: 7011 Hotels

(P-12957)
NICKS COVE INC
23240 Ca 1, Marshall (94940)
PHONE.................................415 663-1033
Ruth Gibson, *Owner*
Nicks Cove, *President*
Wade Nakamine, *General Mgr*
Katrina Garrett, *Opers Mgr*
Alyssum Garcia, *Manager*
EMP: 70
SQ FT: 1,000
SALES (est): 1.5MM **Privately Held**
SIC: 7011 Hotels; bed & breakfast inn

(P-12958)
NOB HILL PROPERTIES INC
Also Called: Big Four Restaurant
1075 California St, San Francisco
(94108-2281)
PHONE.................................415 474-5400
John Cope, *President*
Newton Cope Sr, *Ch of Bd*
Newton Cope Jr, *Vice Pres*
EMP: 280
SALES (est): 17.6MM **Privately Held**
WEB: www.nobhillspa.com
SIC: 7011 5812 Hotels; eating places

(P-12959)
NOBLE AEW VINEYARD CREEK LLC
Also Called: Hyatt Vineyard Creek Ht & Spa
170 Railroad St, Santa Rosa (95401-6266)
PHONE.................................707 284-1234
Josephine Redrico, *Principal*
EMP: 99
SALES: 950K **Privately Held**
SIC: 7011 Hotels & motels

(P-12960)
NOBLE/UTAH LONG BEACH LLC
Also Called: Westin Long Beach Hotel, The
333 E Ocean Blvd, Long Beach
(90802-4827)
PHONE.................................562 436-3000
Mitesh B Shah, *Mng Member*
EMP: 250
SQ FT: 51,000
SALES (est): 8.1MM
SALES (corp-wide): 104.3MM **Privately Held**
SIC: 7011 Hotels & motels
PA: Noble Investment Group Llc
2000 Monarch Towe 3424
Atlanta GA 30326
404 262-9660

(P-12961)
NOIRO WEST LLC
Also Called: Sheraton Suites San Diego
701 A St, San Diego (92101-4611)
PHONE.................................619 819-6620
Richard M Kelleher,
Lydia Berlage, *Executive*
EMP: 200
SQ FT: 99,999
SALES (est): 9.1MM **Privately Held**
SIC: 7011 Hotels

(P-12962)
NORTHERN QUEEN INC
Also Called: Northern Queen Inn
400 Railroad Ave, Nevada City
(95959-2868)
PHONE.................................530 265-4492
Roy J Ramey, *President*
Jacqueline Ramey, *Treasurer*
Colleen Flores, *Vice Pres*
Diane Mansfield, *Systems Mgr*

EMP: 65
SQ FT: 32,000
SALES (est): 2MM **Privately Held**
SIC: 7011 6552 Motels; subdividers & developers

(P-12963)
NORTHWEST HOTEL CORPORATION (PA)
Also Called: Howard Johnson
1380 S Harbor Blvd, Anaheim
(92802-2310)
PHONE.................................714 776-6120
James P Edmondson, *President*
EMP: 62
SQ FT: 50,000
SALES (est): 7MM **Privately Held**
SIC: 7011 Hotels & motels

(P-12964)
NPL ANAHEIM INVESTMENTS LLC
Also Called: Homewood Suites Anaheim Resort
2010 S Harbor Blvd, Anaheim
(92802-3514)
PHONE.................................714 750-2010
Curtis Olson, *President*
Matthew Kaufman, *Corp Secy*
Ajesh Patel, *Vice Pres*
EMP: 68 EST: 2013
SQ FT: 165,000
SALES (est): 322.8K **Privately Held**
SIC: 7011 Hotels

(P-12965)
NREA-TRC 711 LLC
Also Called: Sheraton Downtown Los Angeles
711 S Hope St, Los Angeles (90017-3803)
PHONE.................................213 488-3500
EMP: 200
SQ FT: 470,000
SALES (est): 9.5MM **Privately Held**
SIC: 7011 Hotels

(P-12966)
OAK CREEK LP
Also Called: Holiday Inn
21725 Gateway Center Dr, Diamond Bar
(91765-2400)
PHONE.................................909 860-5440
Billy Mendez, *Partner*
Sammi Wang, *Principal*
Joe Subramaniam, *General Mgr*
Cesar Aparicio, *Chief Engr*
EMP: 60
SALES (est): 2.9MM **Privately Held**
SIC: 7011 Hotels & motels

(P-12967)
OAK VALLEY HOTEL LLC
2270 Hotel Cir N, San Diego (92108-2810)
PHONE.................................619 297-1101
Benjamin Shih,
EMP: 99
SALES (est): 675.5K **Privately Held**
SIC: 7011 Hotels

(P-12968)
OCEAN AVENUE LLC
Also Called: Fairmont Miramar Hotel
101 Wilshire Blvd, Santa Monica
(90401-1106)
PHONE.................................310 576-7777
Ellis O'Connor,
Matthew Lehman, *General Mgr*
Mathew Armstrong, *Info Tech Mgr*
Ashley Sun, *Sales Mgr*
An K Verbeeck, *Director*
EMP: 275
SQ FT: 209,000
SALES (est): 21.1MM **Privately Held**
SIC: 7011 7299 Hotels; banquet hall facilities

(P-12969)
OCEAN HOLIDAY LP
Also Called: Holiday Inn
1401 Carmelo Dr, Oceanside (92054-1012)
PHONE.................................760 231-7000
Joseph Fan, *Partner*
EMP: 55
SALES (est): 1.1MM **Privately Held**
SIC: 7011 Hotels & motels

(P-12970)
OCEAN PARK HOTELS INC (PA)
9777 Blue Larkspur Ln # 102, Monterey
(93940-6554)
PHONE.................................805 544-0812
James Flagg, *President*
Michael Chisholm, *Exec Dir*
EMP: 350
SALES (est): 9.1MM **Privately Held**
WEB: www.ophot.com
SIC: 7011 Hotels

(P-12971)
OCEAN PARK HOTELS INC
Also Called: Hilton
1000 Aguajito Rd, Monterey (93940-4801)
PHONE.................................831 373-6141
Cherie Davis, *General Mgr*
EMP: 115
SALES (est): 1.7MM
SALES (corp-wide): 9.1MM **Privately Held**
WEB: www.ophot.com
SIC: 7011 5813 8741 Hotels; drinking places; hotel or motel management
PA: Ocean Park Hotels, Inc.
9777 Blue Larkspur Ln # 102
Monterey CA 93940
805 544-0812

(P-12972)
OCEAN PARK HOTELS INC
Also Called: Hilton
27710 The Old Rd, Valencia (91355-1036)
PHONE.................................661 284-3200
Angela Peterson, *Branch Mgr*
EMP: 60
SALES (est): 1.4MM
SALES (corp-wide): 9.1MM **Privately Held**
WEB: www.ophot.com
SIC: 7011 Hotels
PA: Ocean Park Hotels, Inc.
9777 Blue Larkspur Ln # 102
Monterey CA 93940
805 544-0812

(P-12973)
OCEAN PARK HOTELS MMEX LLC
Also Called: Holiday Inn
27513 Wayne Mills Pl, Valencia
(91355-4980)
PHONE.................................661 284-2101
James Flagg,
EMP: 50
SQ FT: 5,322
SALES (est): 1.9MM **Privately Held**
SIC: 7011 Hotels & motels

(P-12974)
OCEANS ELEVEN CASINO
121 Brooks St, Oceanside (92054-3424)
PHONE.................................760 439-6988
Mark Kelegian, *Managing Prtnr*
Rachel Kinney, *Admin Asst*
Zaven Esmaili, *Manager*
EMP: 367 EST: 1996
SQ FT: 30,000
SALES (est): 15.9MM **Privately Held**
WEB: www.oceans11.com
SIC: 7011 Casino hotel

(P-12975)
OHI RESORT HOTELS LLC
Also Called: Wyndham Anaheim Garden Grove
12021 Harbor Blvd, Garden Grove
(92840-4001)
PHONE.................................714 867-5555
Jeremy Yujuico, *Principal*
Donna Coins, *Sales Staff*
Claudia Arbaiza, *Facilities Dir*
EMP: 98
SALES (est): 4.7MM **Privately Held**
SIC: 7011 Hotel, franchised

(P-12976)
OJAI VALLEY INN GOLF COURSE
Also Called: Ojai Valley Spa
905 Country Club Rd, Ojai (93023-3789)
PHONE.................................805 646-2420
Thad Hyland, *Director*
Doug Bowman, *Info Tech Mgr*

Vanessa Jimenez, *Human Res Mgr*
EMP: 600
SALES (est): 8.6MM **Privately Held**
WEB: www.ojaivalleyspa.com
SIC: 7011 7992 5941 Resort hotel; public golf courses; sporting goods & bicycle shops

(P-12977)
OLD TOWN FMLY HOSPITALITY CORP
Also Called: Fiesta De Reyes
4962 Concannon Ct, San Diego
(92130-2723)
PHONE.................................619 246-8010
Chuck Ross, *President*
EMP: 240 EST: 2009
SQ FT: 1,600
SALES: 16MM **Privately Held**
SIC: 7011 5812 Hotels; eating places

(P-12978)
OLS HOTELS & RESORTS LLC (PA)
16000 Ventura Blvd # 1010, Encino
(91436-2744)
PHONE.................................818 905-8280
John Fitts, *Principal*
Roger Vasey, *Exec VP*
Rick Ball, *Vice Pres*
Martti Mannoja, *Vice Pres*
Sarie Mannoja, *Vice Pres*
EMP: 2045
SQ FT: 9,500
SALES (est): 58.4MM **Privately Held**
WEB: www.outriggerlodging.com
SIC: 7011 Hotels

(P-12979)
OLS HOTELS & RESORTS LLC
Also Called: Marriott
14635 Bldwin Pk Towne Ctr, Baldwin Park
(91706-5548)
PHONE.................................626 962-6000
Peter Ehienberg, *Manager*
Jiyu Liang, *Human Res Dir*
EMP: 509
SALES (est): 3.9MM
SALES (corp-wide): 58.4MM **Privately Held**
WEB: www.outriggerlodging.com
SIC: 7011 Hotels & motels
PA: Ols Hotels & Resorts, Llc
16000 Ventura Blvd # 1010
Encino CA 91436
818 905-8280

(P-12980)
OLS HOTELS & RESORTS LP
Also Called: Le Parc Suite Hotel
733 W Knoll Dr, West Hollywood
(90069-5207)
PHONE.................................310 855-1115
Sam Ebeid, *CEO*
Ojan Ahmad, *Chief Engr*
Barry Podob, *Sales Dir*
EMP: 105
SALES (corp-wide): 58.4MM **Privately Held**
WEB: www.outriggerlodging.com
SIC: 7011 8741 Hotels; hotel or motel management
PA: Ols Hotels & Resorts, Llc
16000 Ventura Blvd # 1010
Encino CA 91436
818 905-8280

(P-12981)
OMNI HOTELS CORPORATION
41000 Bob Hope Dr, Rancho Mirage
(92270-4416)
PHONE.................................760 568-2727
EMP: 256
SALES (corp-wide): 1.2B **Privately Held**
SIC: 7011 Hotels
HQ: Omni Hotels Corporation
4001 Maple Ave Ste 500
Dallas TX 75219
972 871-5600

(P-12982)
OMNI HOTELS CORPORATION
675 L St, San Diego (92101-7022)
PHONE.................................619 231-6664
Ed Netzhammer, *Manager*
Michele Nash, *Finance*

P R O D U C T S & S V C S

Anthony Belef, *Human Res Dir*
Tawn McAllister, *Sales Mgr*
Chris Kramer, *Director*
EMP: 300
SALES (corp-wide): 1.2B **Privately Held**
WEB: www.omnihotels.com
SIC: 7011 Hotels & motels
HQ: Omni Hotels Corporation
4001 Maple Ave Ste 500
Dallas TX 75219
972 871-5600

(P-12983)
OMNI HOTELS CORPORATION
500 California St, San Francisco
(94104-1001)
PHONE............................415 677-9494
Michael Casey, *Branch Mgr*
Ruth Hirtzinger, *Sales Mgr*
Kelsey Angel, *Manager*
Adam Pickett, *Manager*
EMP: 264
SALES (corp-wide): 1.2B **Privately Held**
WEB: www.omnihotels.com
SIC: 7011 Hotels & motels
HQ: Omni Hotels Corporation
4001 Maple Ave Ste 500
Dallas TX 75219
972 871-5600

(P-12984)
OMNI HOTELS CORPORATION
251 S Olive St Fl 1, Los Angeles
(90012-3002)
PHONE............................213 617-3300
Bob Greeney, *General Mgr*
Mark Schwabenbauer, *General Mgr*
Carolyn Harber, *Info Tech Mgr*
Edwin Adolfo, *Purch Dir*
Mona Bantigue, *Asst Director*
EMP: 250
SALES (corp-wide): 1.2B **Privately Held**
WEB: www.omnihotels.com
SIC: 7011 Hotels & motels
HQ: Omni Hotels Corporation
4001 Maple Ave Ste 500
Dallas TX 75219
972 871-5600

(P-12985)
ONE NOB HILL ASSOCIATES LLC
Also Called: Intercontinental Mark Hopkins
999 California St, San Francisco
(94108-2250)
PHONE............................415 392-3434
Mary Ann Gonzales, *General Mgr*
EMP: 86
SALES (est): 2.1MM **Privately Held**
SIC: 7011 Hotels

(P-12986)
ONTARIO AIRPORT HOTEL CORP
Also Called: Hilton
4949 Great America Pkwy, Santa Clara
(95054-1216)
PHONE............................408 562-6709
James Evans, *CFO*
Gary Hauck, *Engineer*
Patricia Veron, *Human Res Mgr*
Karen Mathews, *Rector*
EMP: 127
SQ FT: 169,768
SALES (est): 9MM **Privately Held**
WEB: www.hiltonsantaclara.com
SIC: 7011 Hotels & motels

(P-12987)
ORCHARD INTERNATIONAL GROUP (PA)
Also Called: Orchard Hotel
665 Bush St, San Francisco (94108-3510)
PHONE............................415 362-8878
S C Huang, *President*
Robert Huang, *CEO*
Alejandra Almaraz, *Manager*
EMP: 100
SQ FT: 60,000
SALES: 12.4MM **Privately Held**
SIC: 7011 Hotels

(P-12988)
OTB ACQUISITION LLC
Also Called: Sierra Vista Extended Stay
770 S Brea Blvd Ste 227, Brea
(92821-5399)
PHONE............................520 458-0540
EMP: 119 **Privately Held**
SIC: 7011 Hotels & motels
PA: Otb Acquisition Llc
2201 W Royal Ln Ste 240
Irving TX 75063

(P-12989)
OUTRIGGER HOTELS HAWAII
Also Called: Marina International Hotel
4200 Admiralty Way, Venice (90292-5422)
PHONE............................310 301-2000
Mohammed Khan, *General Mgr*
EMP: 80
SALES (corp-wide): 144.5MM **Privately Held**
WEB: www.outriggerhawaii.com
SIC: 7011 6531 Hotels; real estate managers
PA: Outrigger Hotels Hawaii
2375 Kuhio Ave Fl 4
Honolulu HI 96815
808 921-6510

(P-12990)
OUTRIGGER HOTELS HAWAII
Grafton On Sunset, The
8462 W Sunset Blvd, West Hollywood
(90069-1912)
PHONE............................323 491-9015
Kevin Briggs, *Branch Mgr*
William Lopez, *Chief Engr*
Leota Rhaburn, *Sales Mgr*
Troy Berry, *Sales Staff*
Jason Jackson, *Manager*
EMP: 98
SALES (corp-wide): 144.5MM **Privately Held**
WEB: www.outriggerhawaii.com
SIC: 7011 Hotels
PA: Outrigger Hotels Hawaii
2375 Kuhio Ave Fl 4
Honolulu HI 96815
808 921-6510

(P-12991)
OVIS LLC
Also Called: Ojai Valley Inn & Spa
905 Country Club Rd, Ojai (93023-3734)
PHONE............................805 646-5511
Toll Free:............................888 -
Stephen Crown, *Mng Member*
Magdalena Morin, *CFO*
Luis Castro, *Executive*
Shaun O'Bryan, *General Mgr*
Blair Schwermer, *Admin Asst*
EMP: 600
SALES (est): 39.6MM **Privately Held**
WEB: www.ojairesort.com
SIC: 7011 5813 5812 Resort hotel; drinking places; eating places

(P-12992)
OXFORD PALACE HOTEL
745 S Oxford Ave, Los Angeles
(90005-2909)
PHONE............................213 382-7756
Bowhan Kim, *Principal*
Don W Chang, *Principal*
Bora Park, *Sales Dir*
Joann Lee, *Manager*
EMP: 96
SALES (est): 5.6MM **Privately Held**
WEB: www.oxfordhotel.com
SIC: 7011 5812 Resort hotel; Korean restaurant

(P-12993)
OXNARD BEACH HOTEL LP
350 E Port Hueneme Rd, Port Hueneme
(93041-3209)
PHONE............................805 488-6560
Joseph Fan, *Partner*
EMP: 50 **EST:** 2012
SALES (est): 1.1MM **Privately Held**
SIC: 7011 Hotels

(P-12994)
PACIFIC BEACH HOUSE LLC (PA)
Also Called: Beach House Ht - Half Moon Bay
4100 Cabrillo Hwy N, Half Moon Bay
(94019-5219)
P.O. Box 129 (94019-0129)
PHONE............................650 712-0220
Dana Daho, *General Mgr*
Margie Bennetts, *General Mgr*
Charlotte Papedis, *General Mgr*
Kevin Scanlon, *Controller*
Rachel Strom, *Director*
EMP: 95
SQ FT: 5,007
SALES (est): 4.4MM **Privately Held**
SIC: 7011 7999 Hotels; bathing beach, non-membership

(P-12995)
PACIFIC CAMBRIA INC
Also Called: Cambria Pines Lodge
2905 Burton Dr, Cambria (93428-4001)
PHONE............................805 927-6114
Dirk Winter, *President*
Tricia Anderson, *CTO*
Elizabeth Borges, *Controller*
Rebecca Ramos, *Sls & Mktg Exec*
Teri O'Rourke, *Sales Mgr*
EMP: 90
SQ FT: 70,000
SALES (est): 5.8MM **Privately Held**
WEB: www.cambriapineslodge.com
SIC: 7011 5812 5813 Hotels; resort hotel; restaurant, family: independent; bar (drinking places)

(P-12996)
PACIFIC CITY HOTEL LLC
Also Called: Pasea Hotel & Spa
21080 Pacific Coast Hwy, Huntington Beach (92648-5305)
PHONE............................714 698-6100
Lynette Dodd, *Asst Controller*
EMP: 300
SALES: 2.8MM **Privately Held**
SIC: 7011 Resort hotel; hotels

(P-12997)
PACIFIC GROVE ASLMAR OPER CORP
Also Called: Asilomar Conference Center
800 Asilomar Blvd, Pacific Grove
(93950-3704)
PHONE............................831 372-8016
Fax: 831 372-7227
EMP: 250
SQ FT: 20,000
SALES: 13.2MM **Privately Held**
SIC: 7011

(P-12998)
PACIFIC HOTEL DEV VENTR LP
Also Called: Sheraton Palo Alto
625 El Camino Real, Palo Alto
(94301-2301)
PHONE............................650 347-8260
Clement Chen, *Vice Pres*
Stephanie Johnson, *Director*
EMP: 200
SALES (est): 7MM **Privately Held**
SIC: 7011 Hotels

(P-12999)
PACIFIC HOTEL MANAGEMENT LLC
Also Called: Sheraton
1603 Powell St, Emeryville (94608-2436)
PHONE............................510 547-7888
Michelle Sims, *Owner*
EMP: 122
SALES (est): 4MM
SALES (corp-wide): 64.7MM **Privately Held**
SIC: 7011 Hotels
PA: Pacific Hotel Management, Llc
400 S El Camino Real # 200
San Mateo CA 94402
650 347-8260

(P-13000)
PACIFIC HOTEL MANAGEMENT LLC
Also Called: Courtyard By Marriott
3150 Garrity Way, Richmond (94806-1983)
PHONE............................510 262-0700
Curt Newport, *Branch Mgr*
Becky Ross, *General Mgr*
Chris Rokas, *Chief Engr*
EMP: 122
SALES (est): 3.6MM
SALES (corp-wide): 64.7MM **Privately Held**
WEB: www.pacifichotelmanagement.com
SIC: 7011 7389 Hotels; office facilities & secretarial service rental
PA: Pacific Hotel Management, Llc
400 S El Camino Real # 200
San Mateo CA 94402
650 347-8260

(P-13001)
PACIFIC HOTEL MANAGEMENT LLC
Also Called: Sheraton
625 El Camino Real, Palo Alto
(94301-2301)
PHONE............................650 328-2800
Jim Rebosio, *General Mgr*
Clement Chen, *Vice Pres*
Annie Tepe, *Social Dir*
John Groth, *Info Tech Dir*
Sagir Ahmed, *Controller*
EMP: 300
SALES (est): 5.5MM
SALES (corp-wide): 64.7MM **Privately Held**
SIC: 7011 Hotels
PA: Pacific Hotel Management, Llc
400 S El Camino Real # 200
San Mateo CA 94402
650 347-8260

(P-13002)
PACIFIC HOTEL MANAGEMENT INC
Also Called: Radison Hotel Newport Beach
4545 Macarthur Blvd, Newport Beach
(92660-2022)
PHONE............................949 608-1091
Ron Mavaddat, *President*
EMP: 140
SALES: 15MM **Privately Held**
SIC: 7011 Hotels

(P-13003)
PACIFIC HUNTINGTON HOTEL CORP
Also Called: Langham Huntington Hotel & Spa
1401 S Oak Knoll Ave, Pasadena
(91106-4508)
PHONE............................626 568-3900
Ying Shek Lo, *President*
Haruko Murphy, *Office Mgr*
Claudia Child, *Credit Mgr*
Louise O'Brien, *Director*
EMP: 600
SQ FT: 21,193
SALES (est): 1MM **Privately Held**
SIC: 7011 Resort hotel
PA: Langham Hotels International Limited
33/F Great Eagle Ctr
Wan Chai HK
218 623-88

(P-13004)
PACIFIC SNOW VALLEY RESORT LLC
Also Called: Holiday Inn Resort At Lodge
40650 Village Dr, Big Bear Lake (92315)
PHONE............................909 866-3121
Dennis Montes, *General Mgr*
EMP: 60 **Privately Held**
SIC: 7011 7299 5812 5813 Vacation lodges; banquet hall facilities; eating places; drinking places
PA: Pacific Snow Valley Resort Llc
1427 W Valley Blvd # 201
Alhambra CA 91803

(P-13005)

PACIFICA HIORANGE LP
Also Called: Hampton Inn
2720 Hotel Ter, Santa Ana (92705-5602)
PHONE..................................714 556-3838
Russell Fraser, *General Ptnr*
Arlene Kostock, *CFO*
EMP: 80 EST: 2012
SALES (est): 3.4MM **Privately Held**
SIC: 7011 Hotels & motels

(P-13006)

PACIFICA HOSTS INC
Also Called: Radisson Inn
6225 W Century Blvd, Los Angeles
(90045-5311)
PHONE..................................310 670-9000
Ashok Israni, *President*
EMP: 249
SALES (corp-wide): 136.1MM **Privately Held**
SIC: 7011 6552 5813 5812 Hotels & motels; subdividers & developers; drinking places; eating places
PA: Pacifica Hosts, Inc.
1775 Hancock St Ste 200
San Diego CA 92110
619 296-9000

(P-13007)

PACIFICA HOTEL & CONFERENCE CE
Also Called: Radisson Hotel La Westside
6161 W Centinela Ave, Culver City
(90230-6306)
PHONE..................................310 649-1776
Jim Collins, *General Ptnr*
Robert Leonard, *Partner*
EMP: 190
SALES (est): 4.9MM **Privately Held**
SIC: 7011 6512 5812 7389 Hotels; commercial & industrial building operation; eating places; convention & show services

(P-13008)

PACIFICA HOTEL COMPANY
Also Called: Shelter Point Hotel & Marina
1551 Shelter Island Dr, San Diego
(92106-3102)
PHONE..................................619 221-8000
Henric Larsen, *General Mgr*
EMP: 200
SALES (corp-wide): 147.6MM **Privately Held**
WEB: www.cottage-inn.com
SIC: 7011 4493 Hotels; marinas
HQ: Pacifica Hotel Company
39 Argonaut
Aliso Viejo CA 92656
805 957-0095

(P-13009)

PACIFICA HOTEL COMPANY
Also Called: Best Western Half Moon Bay
2400 Cabrillo Hwy S, Half Moon Bay
(94019-2253)
PHONE..................................650 726-9000
Curt Picillo, *Manager*
EMP: 50
SALES (corp-wide): 147.6MM **Privately Held**
WEB: www.cottage-inn.com
SIC: 7011 Hotels
HQ: Pacifica Hotel Company
39 Argonaut
Aliso Viejo CA 92656
805 957-0095

(P-13010)

PACIFICA SAN JOSE LP
Also Called: Wyndham San Jose
1775 Hancock St Ste 100, San Diego
(92110-2035)
PHONE..................................619 296-9000
Ashok Israni, *Partner*
Deepak Israni, *Partner*
Sushil Israni, *Partner*
EMP: 175
SALES: 12MM **Privately Held**
SIC: 7011 Hotels & motels

(P-13011)

PACKARD REALTY INC
Also Called: Holiday Inn
9901 S La Cienega Blvd, Los Angeles
(90045-5915)
PHONE..................................310 649-5151
Tommy Spencer, *General Mgr*
EMP: 85
SALES (est): 1.5MM **Privately Held**
WEB: www.hilax.com
SIC: 7011 Hotels & motels
PA: Packard Realty Inc.
9555 Chesapeake Dr # 202
San Diego CA 92123

(P-13012)

PALA CASINO SPA & RESORT
11154 Highway 76, Pala (92059-2904)
PHONE..................................760 510-5100
Toll Free:..................................877 -
Robert Smith, *Ch of Bd*
Garlon Banks, *President*
Bill Bembenek, *CEO*
Shauna Anton, *CFO*
Michael Crenshaw, *Vice Pres*
EMP: 1800 EST: 2000
SQ FT: 140,000
SALES (est): 80.1MM **Privately Held**
WEB: www.palacasino.com
SIC: 7011 Casino hotel

(P-13013)

PALA MESA LIMITED PARTNERSHIP
Also Called: Pala Mesa Resort
2001 Old Highway 395, Fallbrook
(92028-9771)
PHONE..................................760 728-5881
Tray Crayton, *President*
Kevin Poorbaugh, *General Mgr*
Amy Krausnick, *Asst Controller*
Deborah Ellis, *Human Res Mgr*
Ripley Vaughn, *Sales Staff*
EMP: 225
SALES (est): 8.8MM **Privately Held**
WEB: www.palamesa.com
SIC: 7011 Resort hotel

(P-13014)

PALMDALE RESORT INC
Also Called: Holiday Inn
38630 5th St W, Palmdale (93551-4208)
PHONE..................................661 947-8055
Toni Vilopas, *Owner*
EMP: 50
SQ FT: 71,394
SALES (est): 2.6MM **Privately Held**
WEB: www.hipalmdale.com
SIC: 7011 Hotels & motels

(P-13015)

PALMETTO HOSPITALITY
Also Called: Hilton Garden Inn Palo Alto
4216 El Camino Real, Palo Alto
(94306-4404)
PHONE..................................650 843-0795
Jason Boehm, *Vice Pres*
EMP: 50
SALES (est): 482.3K **Privately Held**
SIC: 7011 Hotels & motels

(P-13016)

PAN PCFIC HTELS RSRTS AMER INC
Also Called: Pan Pacific San Diego
400 W Broadway, San Diego (92101-3504)
PHONE..................................619 239-4500
Jim Hollister, *General Mgr*
Alice Cota, *Sales Staff*
EMP: 330
SALES (corp-wide): 16.2MM **Privately Held**
SIC: 7011 5812 Hotels; eating places
PA: Pan Pacific Hotels And Resorts America Inc.
500 Post St Ste 800
San Francisco CA 94102
415 732-7747

(P-13017)

PARADISE LESSEE INC
Also Called: Paradise Point Resort & Spa
1404 Vacation Rd, San Diego
(92109-7905)
PHONE..................................858 274-4630
David Hall, *General Mgr*
EMP: 350
SALES (est): 18.1MM
SALES (corp-wide): 1.1B **Privately Held**
WEB: www.paradisepoint.com
SIC: 7011 Resort hotel
PA: Lasalle Hotel Properties
7550 Wisconsin Ave # 100
Bethesda MD 20814
301 941-1500

(P-13018)

PARK HOTELS & RESORTS INC
Also Called: Hilton
633 E Cabrillo Blvd, Santa Barbara
(93103-3611)
PHONE..................................805 564-4333
Dean Feldmeier, *Manager*
EMP: 300
SALES (corp-wide): 2.7B **Publicly Held**
WEB: www.esirvine.com
SIC: 7011 Hotels & motels
PA: Park Hotels & Resorts Inc.
1775 Tysons Blvd Fl 7
Tysons VA 22102
571 302-5757

(P-13019)

PARK HOTELS & RESORTS INC
Also Called: Embassy Suites
901 E Calaveras Blvd, Milpitas
(95035-5419)
PHONE..................................408 942-0400
Bonnie Benson, *Manager*
Tara Weber, *CTO*
Brian Contildes, *Chief Engr*
Evangelina Sarracino, *Mktg Dir*
Anastasia Beals, *Marketing Staff*
EMP: 65
SALES (corp-wide): 2.7B **Publicly Held**
WEB: www.esirvine.com
SIC: 7011 5813 5812 Hotels & motels; drinking places; eating places
PA: Park Hotels & Resorts Inc.
1775 Tysons Blvd Fl 7
Tysons VA 22102
571 302-5757

(P-13020)

PARK HOTELS & RESORTS INC
Also Called: Embassy Suites Brea
900 E Birch St, Brea (92821-5812)
PHONE..................................714 990-6000
Jay Badillo, *Branch Mgr*
Lori Herrera, *Social Dir*
EMP: 60
SALES (corp-wide): 2.7B **Publicly Held**
SIC: 7011 Hotels
PA: Park Hotels & Resorts Inc.
1775 Tysons Blvd Fl 7
Tysons VA 22102
571 302-5757

(P-13021)

PARK HOTELS & RESORTS INC
Also Called: Hilton
1775 E Mission Bay Dr, San Diego
(92109-6801)
PHONE..................................619 276-4010
Patrick Duffy, *Director*
Carlos Nava, *Purch Dir*
Donna Daniel, *Marketing Mgr*
Shawn McAteer, *Director*
Jenny Miller, *Manager*
EMP: 360
SALES (corp-wide): 2.7B **Publicly Held**
SIC: 7011 5812 5947 Hotels; eating places; gift, novelty & souvenir shop
PA: Park Hotels & Resorts Inc.
1775 Tysons Blvd Fl 7
Tysons VA 22102
571 302-5757

(P-13022)

PARK HOTELS & RESORTS INC
Also Called: San Francisco Hilton & Towers
333 Ofarrell St, San Francisco
(94102-2116)
PHONE..................................415 771-1400
Holger B Gantz, *Manager*

William Boring, *Social Dir*
Michael Dunne, *General Mgr*
Jessica Parr, *Sales Mgr*
Chris Himpler, *Facilities Dir*
EMP: 330
SALES (corp-wide): 2.7B **Publicly Held**
WEB: www.esirvine.com
SIC: 7011 5812 7299 Hotels & motels; eating places; banquet hall facilities
PA: Park Hotels & Resorts Inc.
1775 Tysons Blvd Fl 7
Tysons VA 22102
571 302-5757

(P-13023)

PARK HOTELS & RESORTS INC
Also Called: Hilton
1 Hegenberger Rd, Oakland (94621-1405)
P.O. Box 2549 (94614-0549)
PHONE..................................510 635-5000
Mark Clement, *General Mgr*
Anna McKenzie, *Planning*
Lillian Virdure, *Telecom Exec*
Chuck Fisher, *Chief Engr*
Tara Capizano, *Marketing Staff*
EMP: 114
SALES (corp-wide): 2.7B **Publicly Held**
WEB: www.esirvine.com
SIC: 7011 5813 5812 Hotels & motels; drinking places; eating places
PA: Park Hotels & Resorts Inc.
1775 Tysons Blvd Fl 7
Tysons VA 22102
571 302-5757

(P-13024)

PARK HOTELS & RESORTS INC
Also Called: Hilton
10950 N Torrey Pines Rd, La Jolla
(92037-1006)
PHONE..................................858 450-4569
Patrick Duffy, *Manager*
Anthony Longa, *Manager*
Cheri Walter, *Manager*
EMP: 50
SALES (corp-wide): 2.7B **Publicly Held**
WEB: www.esirvine.com
SIC: 7011 5813 5812 Hotels & motels; drinking places; eating places
PA: Park Hotels & Resorts Inc.
1775 Tysons Blvd Fl 7
Tysons VA 22102
571 302-5757

(P-13025)

PARK HOTELS & RESORTS INC
Also Called: Embassy Suites
1075 California Blvd, NAPA (94559-1061)
PHONE..................................707 253-9540
Reynaldo Zertuche, *Manager*
EMP: 80
SQ FT: 83,251
SALES (corp-wide): 2.7B **Publicly Held**
WEB: www.esirvine.com
SIC: 7011 Hotels & motels
PA: Park Hotels & Resorts Inc.
1775 Tysons Blvd Fl 7
Tysons VA 22102
571 302-5757

(P-13026)

PARK HOTELS & RESORTS INC
Also Called: Hilton Hotels
700 N Haven Ave, Ontario (91764-4902)
PHONE..................................909 980-3420
Christopher J Nassetta, *Branch Mgr*
Chihiro Abe, *Manager*
EMP: 116
SALES (corp-wide): 2.7B **Publicly Held**
SIC: 7011 Hotels
PA: Park Hotels & Resorts Inc.
1775 Tysons Blvd Fl 7
Tysons VA 22102
571 302-5757

(P-13027)

PARK HOTELS & RESORTS INC
Also Called: Hilton
168 S Los Robles Ave, Pasadena
(91101-2430)
PHONE..................................626 577-1000
Todd Iacono, *Manager*
Elvira Nunez, *Executive Asst*
Alma Quintero, *Human Res Dir*
Javier Ricco, *Purch Agent*
EMP: 248

SALES (corp-wide): 2.7B **Publicly Held**
WEB: www.esirvine.com
SIC: 7011 5812 7389 7299 Hotels & motels; eating places; hotel & motel reservation service; banquet hall facilities; drinking places
PA: Park Hotels & Resorts Inc.
1775 Tysons Blvd Fl 7
Tysons VA 22102
571 302-5757

(P-13028)
PARK HOTELS & RESORTS INC
55 Cyril Magnin St, San Francisco (94102-2812)
PHONE....................415 392-8000
Steve Cowan, *General Mgr*
EMP: 500
SALES (corp-wide): 2.7B **Publicly Held**
SIC: 7011 5812 Hotels; American restaurant
PA: Park Hotels & Resorts Inc.
1775 Tysons Blvd Fl 7
Tysons VA 22102
571 302-5757

(P-13029)
PARK HOTELS & RESORTS INC
Also Called: Embassy Suites
1211 E Garvey St, Covina (91724-3666)
PHONE....................626 915-3441
Seig Heglund, *Manager*
EMP: 75
SALES (corp-wide): 2.7B **Publicly Held**
WEB: www.esirvine.com
SIC: 7011 7991 7359 7299 Hotels & motels; physical fitness facilities; equipment rental & leasing; banquet hall facilities
PA: Park Hotels & Resorts Inc.
1775 Tysons Blvd Fl 7
Tysons VA 22102
571 302-5757

(P-13030)
PARK HOTELS & RESORTS INC
Also Called: Hilton
9876 Wilshire Blvd, Beverly Hills (90210-3115)
PHONE....................310 415-3340
Beverly Hilton, *Principal*
Floyd Conklin, *Chief Engr*
Luis Rivas, *Production*
Paul Dreher, *Asst Director*
Mike Murdock, *Manager*
EMP: 113
SALES (corp-wide): 2.7B **Publicly Held**
WEB: www.esirvine.com
SIC: 7011 Hotels & motels
PA: Park Hotels & Resorts Inc.
1775 Tysons Blvd Fl 7
Tysons VA 22102
571 302-5757

(P-13031)
PARK HOTELS & RESORTS INC
Also Called: Hilton
4130 Lake Tahoe Blvd, South Lake Tahoe (96150-6965)
PHONE....................530 543-2126
John Steinbach, *Manager*
EMP: 250
SALES (corp-wide): 2.7B **Publicly Held**
WEB: www.esirvine.com
SIC: 7011 Hotels & motels
PA: Park Hotels & Resorts Inc.
1775 Tysons Blvd Fl 7
Tysons VA 22102
571 302-5757

(P-13032)
PARK HOTELS & RESORTS INC
Also Called: Embassy Suites
150 Anza Blvd, Burlingame (94010-1924)
PHONE....................650 342-4600
Christopher Beckman, *General Mgr*
EMP: 130
SALES (corp-wide): 2.7B **Publicly Held**
WEB: www.esirvine.com
SIC: 7011 5813 5812 Hotels; drinking places; eating places
PA: Park Hotels & Resorts Inc.
1775 Tysons Blvd Fl 7
Tysons VA 22102
571 302-5757

(P-13033)
PARK HOTELS & RESORTS INC
Also Called: Embassy Suites
211 E Huntington Dr, Arcadia (91006-3745)
PHONE....................626 445-8525
Stig Hedlund, *Manager*
EMP: 116
SALES (corp-wide): 2.7B **Publicly Held**
WEB: www.esirvine.com
SIC: 7011 Hotels & motels
PA: Park Hotels & Resorts Inc.
1775 Tysons Blvd Fl 7
Tysons VA 22102
571 302-5757

(P-13034)
PARK HOTELS & RESORTS INC
Also Called: Embassy Suites
8425 Firestone Blvd, Downey (90241-3843)
PHONE....................562 861-1900
Stig Hedlund, *Branch Mgr*
EMP: 100
SALES (corp-wide): 2.7B **Publicly Held**
WEB: www.esirvine.com
SIC: 7011 5813 5812 Hotels; drinking places; eating places
PA: Park Hotels & Resorts Inc.
1775 Tysons Blvd Fl 7
Tysons VA 22102
571 302-5757

(P-13035)
PARK HOTELS & RESORTS INC
Also Called: Embassy Suites
7762 Beach Blvd, Buena Park (90620-1935)
PHONE....................714 739-5600
Juergen Oswald, *General Mgr*
EMP: 65
SALES (corp-wide): 2.7B **Publicly Held**
WEB: www.esirvine.com
SIC: 7011 Hotels & motels
PA: Park Hotels & Resorts Inc.
1775 Tysons Blvd Fl 7
Tysons VA 22102
571 302-5757

(P-13036)
PARK HOTELS & RESORTS INC
Also Called: Hilton
700 N Haven Ave, Ontario (91764-4902)
PHONE....................909 980-0400
Robert Smith, *Branch Mgr*
EMP: 116
SALES (corp-wide): 2.7B **Publicly Held**
WEB: www.esirvine.com
SIC: 7011 5813 5812 Hotels & motels; drinking places; eating places
PA: Park Hotels & Resorts Inc.
1775 Tysons Blvd Fl 7
Tysons VA 22102
571 302-5757

(P-13037)
PARK HOTELS & RESORTS INC
Also Called: Hilton
225 W Valley Blvd, San Gabriel (91776-3743)
PHONE....................626 270-2700
Charles Noh, *Manager*
Amy Au, *Sls & Mktg Exec*
Julie Costanzo, *Sales Dir*
EMP: 116
SALES (corp-wide): 2.7B **Publicly Held**
WEB: www.esirvine.com
SIC: 7011 Hotels & motels
PA: Park Hotels & Resorts Inc.
1775 Tysons Blvd Fl 7
Tysons VA 22102
571 302-5757

(P-13038)
PARK HOTELS & RESORTS INC
Also Called: Embassy Suites
2120 Main St, Irvine (92614-6219)
PHONE....................949 553-8332
Mari Hnatt, *Manager*
Kenneth Beck, *Chief Mktg Ofcr*
EMP: 114
SALES (corp-wide): 2.7B **Publicly Held**
WEB: www.esirvine.com
SIC: 7011 Hotels & motels

PA: Park Hotels & Resorts Inc.
1775 Tysons Blvd Fl 7
Tysons VA 22102
571 302-5757

(P-13039)
PARK HOTELS & RESORTS INC
Also Called: Hilton
3050 Bristol St, Costa Mesa (92626-3036)
PHONE....................714 540-7000
Shaun Robinson, *General Mgr*
Lisa Amick, *Manager*
Scott Bruno, *Manager*
Brad Doell, *Manager*
EMP: 307
SALES (corp-wide): 2.7B **Publicly Held**
WEB: www.esirvine.com
SIC: 7011 5812 7299 Hotels; eating places; banquet hall facilities
PA: Park Hotels & Resorts Inc.
1775 Tysons Blvd Fl 7
Tysons VA 22102
571 302-5757

(P-13040)
PARK HOTELS & RESORTS INC
333 Ofarrell St, San Francisco (94102-2116)
PHONE....................415 771-1400
EMP: 89
SALES (corp-wide): 2.7B **Publicly Held**
WEB: www.hilton.com
SIC: 7011 Hotels
PA: Park Hotels & Resorts Inc.
1775 Tysons Blvd Fl 7
Tysons VA 22102
571 302-5757

(P-13041)
PARK HOTELS & RESORTS INC
Also Called: Embassy Suites
3100 E Frontera St, Anaheim (92806-2820)
PHONE....................714 632-1221
Margo Gilbert, *Manager*
EMP: 65
SALES (corp-wide): 2.7B **Publicly Held**
WEB: www.esirvine.com
SIC: 7011 8741 6794 Hotels; hotel or motel management; franchises, selling or licensing
PA: Park Hotels & Resorts Inc.
1775 Tysons Blvd Fl 7
Tysons VA 22102
571 302-5757

(P-13042)
PARK HOTELS & RESORTS INC
Also Called: Embassy Suites
250 Gateway Blvd, South San Francisco (94080-7018)
PHONE....................650 589-3400
Rudy Ortiz, *General Mgr*
EMP: 65
SALES (corp-wide): 2.7B **Publicly Held**
WEB: www.esirvine.com
SIC: 7011 Hotels & motels
PA: Park Hotels & Resorts Inc.
1775 Tysons Blvd Fl 7
Tysons VA 22102
571 302-5757

(P-13043)
PARK HOTELS & RESORTS INC
Also Called: Embassy Suites
901 Ski Run Blvd, South Lake Tahoe (96150-8569)
PHONE....................530 541-6122
Verla Younker, *Manager*
Phil Moulton, *Principal*
EMP: 50
SALES (corp-wide): 2.7B **Publicly Held**
WEB: www.esirvine.com
SIC: 7011 Hotels & motels
PA: Park Hotels & Resorts Inc.
1775 Tysons Blvd Fl 7
Tysons VA 22102
571 302-5757

(P-13044)
PARK INN BY RADISSON
3737 N Blackstone Ave, Fresno (93726-5307)
PHONE....................559 226-2200
Betty Qi, *Owner*
EMP: 75

SALES (est): 1.5MM **Privately Held**
SIC: 7011 Hotels

(P-13045)
PARK INN BY READISSON FRESNO
Also Called: Park Central Hotel Fresno
3737 N Blackstone Ave, Fresno (93726-5307)
PHONE....................559 226-2200
Lori Lascola, *General Mgr*
EMP: 62 EST: 2011
SALES (est): 2.8MM **Privately Held**
SIC: 7011 Hotels & motels

(P-13046)
PARK PLAZA HOTEL
150 Hegenberger Rd, Oakland (94621-1422)
PHONE....................510 635-5300
Tracy W Wahrlich Jr, *President*
Carl T Doughty, *General Ptnr*
Bert Taprizi, *General Ptnr*
Stephen Wahrlich, *General Ptnr*
EMP: 50
SALES (est): 1.5MM **Privately Held**
WEB: www.parkplazaoakland.com
SIC: 7011 Hotels

(P-13047)
PASADENA HOTEL DEV VENTR LP
Also Called: Sheraton Pasadena
303 Cordova St, Pasadena (91101-2426)
PHONE....................626 449-4000
Ray Serafin, *Principal*
David Iwane, *Principal*
Kathleen Blackman, *Sales Mgr*
Susan Dunn, *Sales Mgr*
Galia Zmud, *Manager*
EMP: 99
SALES (est): 6.6MM **Privately Held**
SIC: 7011 Hotels

(P-13048)
PASADENA RBLES ACQUISITION LLC
168 S Los Robles Ave, Pasadena (91101-2430)
PHONE....................626 577-1000
Vince Cuce, *Officer*
Cheree Goodall, *Office Mgr*
EMP: 99 EST: 2015
SQ FT: 85,000
SALES (est): 441.1K **Privately Held**
SIC: 7011 Hotels & motels

(P-13049)
PASKENTA BAND NOMLAKI INDIANS
Also Called: Rolling Hills Casino
2655 Everett Freeman Way, Corning (96021-9000)
P.O. Box 709 (96021-0709)
PHONE....................530 528-3500
Everett Freeman, *Chairman*
Ines Crosby, *Administration*
Jeremy Olson, *Purch Mgr*
EMP: 493
SALES (est): 14.9MM **Privately Held**
WEB: www.paskenta.org
SIC: 7011 Casino hotel

(P-13050)
PASO ROBLES INN LLC
Also Called: Paso Robles Hotel
1103 Spring St, Paso Robles (93446-2598)
PHONE....................805 238-2660
Paul Wallace, *General Mgr*
Tom Martin, *Owner*
Kim Eady, *Partner*
Andrew Litton, *Partner*
Ken Litton, *Partner*
EMP: 52
SALES (est): 2.5MM **Privately Held**
WEB: www.pasoroblesinn.com
SIC: 7011 5812 5813 Hotels; restaurant, family: independent; cocktail lounge

(P-13051)
PAUMA BAND OF MISSION INDIANS
Casino Pauma
777 Pauma Reservation Rd, Pauma Valley (92061)
P.O. Box 1067 (92061-1067)
PHONE..................................760 742-2177
Richard Darder, *CEO*
EMP: 500 **Privately Held**
WEB: www.casinopauma.com
SIC: 7011 Casino hotel
PA: Pauma Band Of Mission Indians
1010 Pauma Reservation Rd
Pauma Valley CA 92061
760 742-1289

(P-13052)
PEACOCK STES RESORT LTD PARTNR
1745 S Anaheim Blvd, Anaheim (92805-6518)
PHONE..................................714 535-8255
Sheldon Ginsburg, *General Ptnr*
Shell Development Corporation-, *General Ptnr*
Perry Snyderman, *General Ptnr*
Jeff Pink, *General Mgr*
Sandra Speers, *Sales Staff*
EMP: 60
SQ FT: 75,000
SALES (est): 2.2MM **Privately Held**
WEB: www.peacocksuitesresort.com
SIC: 7011 Resort hotel; hotels

(P-13053)
PEBBLE BCH RESRT CO DBA LONE C (PA)
Also Called: Pebble Beach Resorts
2700 17 Mile Dr, Pebble Beach (93953-2668)
P.O. Box 567 (93953-0567)
PHONE..................................831 647-7500
Bill Perocchi, *CEO*
Cody Plott, *President*
Dave Heuck, *CFO*
Paul Spengler, *Exec VP*
Mark Stilwell, *Exec VP*
EMP: 134
SQ FT: 2,197
SALES (est): 119.8MM **Privately Held**
WEB: www.pebblebeach.com
SIC: 7011 7992 5941 7991 Resort hotel; public golf courses; golf goods & equipment; tennis goods & equipment; physical fitness facilities

(P-13054)
PECHANGA DEVELOPMENT CORP
Also Called: Pechanga Resort & Casino
45000 Pechanga Pkwy, Temecula (92592-5810)
P.O. Box 9041 (92589-9041)
PHONE..................................951 695-4655
Patrick Murphy, *CEO*
Oda Becerra, *Partner*
Jerry Konchar, *CFO*
Christina McMenamin, *Treasurer*
Miusette Garcia, *Bd of Directors*
EMP: 4000
SALES (est): 206.1MM **Privately Held**
WEB: www.pechangarv.com
SIC: 7011 7929 7999 Casino hotel; entertainment service; gambling establishment

(P-13055)
PEEKAY INVESTMENTS PRPTS LLC
Also Called: Clarion Hotel
901 N China Lake Blvd, Ridgecrest (93555-3160)
PHONE..................................714 403-1923
Valerie Keval, *CEO*
EMP: 50
SALES (est): 223.7K **Privately Held**
SIC: 7011 Hotels & motels

(P-13056)
PEPPER TREE INN
Also Called: Rodeway Inn
645 N Lake Blvd, Tahoe City (96145)
P.O. Box 29 (96145-0029)
PHONE..................................530 583-3711
Thomas Brown, *Manager*

EMP: 65
SQ FT: 18,609
SALES (corp-wide): 4MM **Privately Held**
WEB: www.pismosands.com
SIC: 7011 Hotels & motels
PA: Pepper Tree Inn
998 Hilmar St
Santa Clara CA
-

(P-13057)
PEPPER TREE MOTEL
1241 E Holt Blvd, Ontario (91761-2028)
PHONE..................................909 988-2646
Yang Su, *Owner*
EMP: 60
SALES (est): 456.6K **Privately Held**
SIC: 7011 Motels

(P-13058)
PEPPERMILL CASINOS INC
4021 Port Chicago Hwy, Concord (94520-1122)
PHONE..................................925 671-7711
Ronald Rives, *Manager*
EMP: 200 **Privately Held**
WEB: www.thepeppermillcasinonv.com
SIC: 7011 7999 Casino hotel; gambling establishment
PA: Peppermill Casinos, Inc.
90 W Grove St Ste 600
Reno NV 89509

(P-13059)
PHF II BURBANK LLC
Also Called: Burbank Airport Mariott Hotel
2500 N Hollywood Way, Burbank (91505-1019)
PHONE..................................818 843-6000
Linda Davey, *Mng Member*
Sharon Estep, *Sales Mgr*
EMP: 220
SALES (est): 10MM **Privately Held**
SIC: 7011 Hotels & motels

(P-13060)
PHF RUBY LLC
Also Called: Pier 2620 Ht Fishermans Wharf
2620 Jones St, San Francisco (94133-1306)
PHONE..................................415 885-4700
Jose L Torres,
Jim Turner, *General Mgr*
Linda Hilton, *Sales Staff*
Anthony Kai Chiu Ceng,
EMP: 118
SALES (est): 7.6MM **Privately Held**
SIC: 7011 7991 5813 5812 Hotel, franchised; physical fitness facilities; drinking places; eating places

(P-13061)
PICCADILLY HOSPITALITY LLC
Also Called: Piccadilly Inn Shaw
2305 W Shaw Ave, Fresno (93711-3411)
PHONE..................................559 348-5520
Mu-Pien Chien, *President*
Gene Chien, *Vice Pres*
EMP: 50 EST: 2012
SALES (est): 1.4MM **Privately Held**
SIC: 7011 Resort hotel; hotels

(P-13062)
PIER PONT HOTEL LP
550 San Jon Rd, Ventura (93001-3745)
PHONE..................................805 643-6144
EMP: 50
SALES (est): 692.9K **Privately Held**
SIC: 7011

(P-13063)
PIERPONT INN INC
Also Called: Central Coast Management
550 San Jon Rd, Ventura (93001-3754)
P.O. Box 335, Grover Beach (93483-0335)
PHONE..................................805 643-0245
Subhash Patel, *President*
Mauline Patel, *Vice Pres*
EMP: 50 EST: 1956
SALES (est): 2.1MM **Privately Held**
WEB: www.pierpontinn.com
SIC: 7011 5812 Bed & breakfast inn; drive-in restaurant

(P-13064)
PINE & POWELL PARTNERS LLC
Also Called: Stanford Court Hotel
905 California St, San Francisco (94108-2201)
PHONE..................................415 989-3500
Naveen Kakarla,
Michael Baier,
Rosanna Harrison,
EMP: 99
SQ FT: 287,000
SALES (est): 301.3K **Privately Held**
SIC: 7011 Hotels & motels

(P-13065)
PINNACLE 1617 LLC
Also Called: Four Points By Sheraton
1617 1st Ave, San Diego (92101-3003)
PHONE..................................619 239-9600
Bharat Lall, *Mng Member*
Christine Gibbs, *Controller*
Lisa Kanemori, *Sales Mgr*
Kheam Taing, *Sales Staff*
Sue Depascale,
EMP: 50 EST: 2011
SALES (est): 4.5MM **Privately Held**
SIC: 7011 Hotels

(P-13066)
PINNACLE RVRSIDE HSPITALITY LP
Also Called: Riverside Marriott
3400 Market St, Riverside (92501-2826)
PHONE..................................951 784-8000
Dr Bharat Lall, *General Ptnr*
Melody Ortega, *Manager*
EMP: 190
SALES (est): 7.9MM **Privately Held**
SIC: 7011 Hotels

(P-13067)
PIONEER SQUARE HOTEL COMPANY
1940 Fillmore St, San Francisco (94115-2745)
PHONE..................................415 346-2323
Bart Seidler, *President*
EMP: 50
SALES (est): 1.5MM **Privately Held**
SIC: 7011 Hotels

(P-13068)
PISMO COAST VILLAGE INC
165 S Dolliver St, Pismo Beach (93449-2999)
PHONE..................................805 773-1811
Jay Jamison, *General Mgr*
Ronald Nunlist, *President*
Wayne Hardesty, *CFO*
Terris Hughes, *Exec VP*
Dwight Plumley, *Vice Pres*
EMP: 60
SALES (est): 8.2MM **Privately Held**
WEB: www.pismocoastvillage.com
SIC: 7011 Resort hotel

(P-13069)
PLAZA SUITES
3100 Lakeside Dr, Santa Clara (95054-2804)
PHONE..................................408 748-9800
Scott Seymore, *Principal*
Bond Patel, *Sales Dir*
Nancy Smith, *Manager*
EMP: 52
SALES (est): 3.5MM **Privately Held**
WEB: www.theplazasuites.com
SIC: 7011 Resort hotel; hotels

(P-13070)
PLEASANT CANYON HOTEL INC
Also Called: Residence Inn By Marriott
11920 Dublin Canyon Rd, Pleasanton (94588-2818)
PHONE..................................925 847-0535
James Evans, *CFO*
Melissa Emerick, *General Mgr*
EMP: 50 EST: 1996
SQ FT: 98,496
SALES (est): 3.4MM **Privately Held**
SIC: 7011 Hotels & motels

(P-13071)
PLEASANTON PROJECT OWNER LLC
Also Called: Marriott
11950 Dublin Canyon Rd, Pleasanton (94588-2818)
PHONE..................................925 847-7592
Dianna Teves, *General Mgr*
Takako Smith, *Finance Dir*
EMP: 60
SALES (est): 16MM **Privately Held**
SIC: 7011 Hotels & motels

(P-13072)
PONDEROSA ENTERPRISES (PA)
Also Called: Miners Inn, The
5181 Hwy 49 N, Mariposa (95338)
P.O. Box 2248 (95338-2248)
PHONE..................................209 742-7777
Ron Morehead, *President*
Ronald J Morehead, *President*
Chester J Morehead, *Corp Secy*
Ceslie Bradley, *Manager*
EMP: 50
SALES (est): 2.3MM **Privately Held**
WEB: www.bigfootsounds.com
SIC: 7011 5812 Motels; eating places

(P-13073)
PONTE VINEYARD INN
35001 Rancho Cal Rd, Temecula (92591-4008)
PHONE..................................951 587-6688
Sarah Martinez, *General Mgr*
Crystal Stadel, *Sales Dir*
EMP: 75 EST: 2012
SALES (est): 376K **Privately Held**
SIC: 7011 Hotels

(P-13074)
PORTFOLIO HOTELS & RESORTS LLC
Also Called: Casa Munras Garden Hotel
700 Munras Ave, Monterey (93940-3110)
PHONE..................................831 375-2411
Meredith Wood, *Principal*
EMP: 50
SALES (est): 751.9K **Privately Held**
SIC: 7011 Hotels
PA: Portfolio Hotels & Resorts, Llc
601 Oakmont Ln Ste 420
Westmont IL 60559
-

(P-13075)
PORTOFINO HOTEL PARTNERS LP
Also Called: Hotel Portofino
260 Portofino Way, Redondo Beach (90277-2033)
PHONE..................................310 379-8481
Glenn Bishop, *Principal*
Yvette Antoniou, *Sales Staff*
Michelle Baird, *Sales Staff*
Kim Coulehan, *Manager*
EMP: 151
SALES (est): 11.1MM **Privately Held**
WEB: www.hotelportofino.com
SIC: 7011 Hotels

(P-13076)
PORTOFINO INN & SUITES ANAHEIM
1831 S Harbor Blvd, Anaheim (92802-3509)
PHONE..................................714 782-7600
Jennifer Reihl, *Director*
Ricardo De La Torre, *Chief Engr*
Matthew Lacy, *Controller*
EMP: 727
SALES (est): 22.6MM
SALES (corp-wide): 67.4MM **Privately Held**
SIC: 7011 Inns
PA: Tarsadia Hotels
620 Newport Center Dr # 1400
Newport Beach CA 92660
949 610-8000

(P-13077)
POSADA ROYALE HOTEL & SUITES
1775 Madera Rd, Simi Valley (93065-3049)
PHONE..................................805 584-6300
Larry Rogers, *Partner*
Peter Zegers, *Partner*
EMP: 50
SQ FT: 55,000
SALES (est): 3.4MM Privately Held
WEB: www.posadaroyale.com
SIC: 7011 5812 7389 7299 Hotels; American restaurant; convention & show services; banquet hall facilities

(P-13078)
POST STREET RENAISSANCE
Also Called: Prescott Hotel, The
545 Post St, San Francisco (94102-1228)
PHONE..................................415 563-0303
John Dern, *President*
EMP: 300
SALES (est): 14.1MM
SALES (corp-wide): 1.7B Privately Held
WEB: www.prescotthotel.com
SIC: 7011 Resort hotel; hotels
HQ: Kimpton Hotel & Restaurant Group Llc
   222 Kearny St Ste 200
   San Francisco CA 94108
   415 397-5572

(P-13079)
PR RANCHO HOTEL LLC
11260 Point East Dr, Rancho Cordova
(95742-6232)
PHONE..................................916 638-4141
Viorica Sanchevici, *Principal*
Guneet Bajwa, *Principal*
Sheila Torres, *Sales Staff*
EMP: 53
SALES (est): 459K Privately Held
SIC: 7011 Hotels

(P-13080)
PRESIDIO HOTEL GROUP LLC
Also Called: Fairfield Inn
10713 White Rock Rd, Rancho Cordova
(95670-6031)
PHONE..................................916 631-7500
Sushil Patel, *Branch Mgr*
EMP: 74
SALES (corp-wide): 10.5MM Privately Held
SIC: 7011 Hotels & motels
PA: Presidio Hotel Group, Llc
   1011 10th St
   Sacramento CA 95814
   707 429-6000

(P-13081)
PROFICIENT LLC
Also Called: Crowne Plz Los Angeles Hbr Ht
601 S Palos Verdes St, San Pedro
(90731-3329)
PHONE..................................310 519-8200
Joyce Wang, *Principal*
EMP: 99
SALES (est): 2.9MM Privately Held
SIC: 7011 Inns

(P-13082)
PRUTEL JOINT VENTURE
Also Called: Ritz-Carlton Laguna Niguel
1 Ritz Carlton Dr, Dana Point (92629-4205)
PHONE..................................949 240-2000
W B Johnson, *Partner*
Prudential Realty, *Partner*
Paul Patterson, *CFO*
Brie Jones, *Social Dir*
Mike Williams, *Engineer*
EMP: 700
SALES (est): 29.2MM Privately Held
SIC: 7011 Hotels

(P-13083)
PT GAMING LLC
235 Oregon St, El Segundo (90245-4215)
PHONE..................................323 260-5060
Patrick Tierney, *Mng Member*
David Shindle, *COO*
Ed Evans, *Technology*
Jamie Breen, *Controller*
Rita Radics, *Human Res Mgr*
EMP: 700
SQ FT: 7,000

SALES (est): 17.5MM Privately Held
SIC: 7011 Casino hotel

(P-13084)
PYRAMID ADVISORS LLC
Also Called: Marriott
11950 Dublin Canyon Rd, Pleasanton
(94588-2818)
PHONE..................................925 847-6000
Norval Nelson, *General Mgr*
EMP: 70
SALES (corp-wide): 163.8MM Privately Held
SIC: 7011 Hotels
PA: Pyramid Advisors Limited Partnership
   1 Post Office Sq
   Boston MA 02109
   617 202-2033

(P-13085)
Q S H PROPERTIES INC
Also Called: Quality Inn
2701 Hotel Ter, Santa Ana (92705-5603)
PHONE..................................714 957-9200
Vahi M Melkonian, *President*
Cheng Wu, *Manager*
EMP: 52
SALES (est): 3.2MM Privately Held
SIC: 7011 Hotel, franchised

(P-13086)
Q S SAN LUIS OBISPO LP
Also Called: Quality Inn
1631 Monterey St, San Luis Obispo
(93401-2929)
PHONE..................................805 541-5001
George Newland, *Partner*
Harold Parker, *General Ptnr*
Robert Warmington, *General Ptnr*
Angela Kimball, *Sales Executive*
Winston Newland, *Manager*
EMP: 50
SALES (est): 2.5MM Privately Held
SIC: 7011 Hotels & motels

(P-13087)
QUAIL LODGE INC
Also Called: Covey, The
8205 Valley Greens Dr, Carmel
(93923-9513)
PHONE..................................831 624-1581
Clement Kwok, *CEO*
William Lawson Little, *Vice Pres*
EMP: 250
SQ FT: 20,000
SALES (est): 25.3MM Privately Held
WEB: www.quaillodge.com
SIC: 7011 7997 7389 5941 Resort hotel; golf club, membership; convention & show services; golf goods & equipment; eating places; subdividers & developers

(P-13088)
QUEENSBAY HOTEL LLC (PA)
444 W Ocean Blvd, Long Beach
(90802-4518)
PHONE..................................562 628-0625
Kambiz Babaoff, *Mng Member*
Michael Moskowitz,
EMP: 102
SALES (est): 2.5MM Privately Held
SIC: 7011 Hotels & motels

(P-13089)
QUEENSBAY HOTEL LLC
Also Called: Hotel Maya
700 Queensway Dr, Long Beach
(90802-6343)
PHONE..................................562 481-3910
Cherie Davis, *Manager*
EMP: 100
SALES (est): 6.3MM
SALES (corp-wide): 2.5MM Privately Held
SIC: 7011 Hotels
PA: Queensbay Hotel, Llc
   444 W Ocean Blvd
   Long Beach CA 90802
   562 628-0625

(P-13090)
R C HOTELS INC
Also Called: Hotel On Huntington Beach
7667 Center Ave, Huntington Beach
(92647-3073)
PHONE..................................714 891-0123

Toll Free:..................................877 -
Shu Chin Kou, *President*
Chris De Guzman, *Sales Mgr*
EMP: 60
SQ FT: 114,012
SALES (est): 3.3MM Privately Held
SIC: 7011 Resort hotel; hotels

(P-13091)
R P S RESORT CORP
1600 N Indian Canyon Dr, Palm Springs
(92262-4602)
PHONE..................................760 327-8311
Douglas McCarron, *President*
EMP: 250
SALES (est): 2.1MM
SALES (corp-wide): 45.1MM Privately Held
WEB: www.psriv.com
SIC: 7011 Resort hotel
HQ: The San Bernardino Hilton
   285 E Hospitality Ln
   San Bernardino CA 92408
   909 889-0133

(P-13092)
RADISSON HOTEL AT USC
Also Called: Radisson Inn
3540 S Figueroa St, Los Angeles
(90007-4313)
PHONE..................................213 748-4141
EMP: 120 EST: 1977
SALES (est): 587.4K Privately Held
SIC: 7011

(P-13093)
RADISSON HOTEL SANTA MARIA
3455 Skyway Dr, Santa Maria (93455)
PHONE..................................805 928-8000
Ryan Swack, *Principal*
EMP: 60
SQ FT: 60,000
SALES (est): 3MM Privately Held
SIC: 7011 5812 Hotels & motels; eating places

(P-13094)
RADISSON HT FISHERMANS WHARF
250 Beach St, San Francisco
(94133-1291)
PHONE..................................415 392-6700
John Sevilla, *General Mgr*
EMP: 100
SALES (est): 4.6MM Privately Held
SIC: 7011 Hotels

(P-13095)
RADLAX GATEWAY HOTEL LLC
Also Called: Radisson Inn
6225 W Century Blvd, Los Angeles
(90045-5311)
PHONE..................................310 670-9000
Peter Dumon, *Mng Member*
EMP: 300
SALES (est): 9.6MM Privately Held
SIC: 7011 Hotels & motels
PA: Portfolio Hotels & Resorts, Llc
   601 Oakmont Ln Ste 420
   Westmont IL 60559

(P-13096)
RAFFLES LRMITAGE BEVERLY HILLS
Also Called: L'Ermitage Hotel
9291 Burton Way, Beverly Hills
(90210-3709)
PHONE..................................310 278-3344
Jack Naderkhani, *General Mgr*
EMP: 249
SALES (est): 10MM
SALES (corp-wide): 31.7MM Privately Held
SIC: 7011 5813 5812 Hotels; drinking places; eating places
HQ: Raffles International Limited
   250 North Bridge Road
   Singapore 17910
   633 983-77

(P-13097)
RALEIGH ENTERPRISES INC (PA)
Also Called: Raleigh Holdings
5300 Melrose Ave Fl 4, Los Angeles
(90038-5114)
PHONE..................................310 899-8900
Kristen J Raleigh, *CEO*
George I Rosenthal, *Ch of Bd*
Mark Rosenthal, *President*
Dave Sehnem, *Vice Pres*
Dean Briones, *Info Tech Mgr*
EMP: 130
SQ FT: 20,000
SALES (est): 41.4MM Privately Held
WEB: www.raleighenterprises.com
SIC: 7011 Hotels

(P-13098)
RAMADA PLAZA HT ANAHEIM RESORT
515 W Katella Ave, Anaheim (92802-3609)
PHONE..................................714 991-6868
Stephen Hsu, *Owner*
EMP: 200
SALES (est): 3.3MM Privately Held
SIC: 7011 Hotels

(P-13099)
RANCHO BERNARDO PARTNERS LTD
Also Called: Radisson Inn
11520 W Bernardo Ct, San Diego
(92127-1602)
P.O. Box 1538, San Marcos (92079-1538)
PHONE..................................858 451-6600
Jonathan Jacobs, *Managing Prtnr*
EMP: 60
SQ FT: 87,214
SALES (est): 3.9MM Privately Held
SIC: 7011 Hotels & motels

(P-13100)
RANCHO LEONERO RESORT
5671 Palmer Way Ste E, Carlsbad
(92010-7256)
PHONE..................................760 438-2905
Genie Ireland, *Owner*
John Ireland, *Partner*
Eugenie Ireland, *Manager*
EMP: 50
SALES (est): 1.7MM Privately Held
SIC: 7011 Resort hotel

(P-13101)
RANCHO VALENCIA RESORT
5921 Valencia Cir, Rancho Santa Fe
(92067-9520)
P.O. Box 9126 (92067-4126)
PHONE..................................858 756-1123
Jeffrey Essakow, *Mng Member*
Mark Blevins, *Finance*
Kimberly Duran, *Accountant*
Claudia Pina, *Human Res Dir*
Oz Soykok, *Opers Staff*
EMP: 300
SALES (est): 24.8MM Privately Held
WEB: www.ranchovalencia.com
SIC: 7011 Resort hotel; hotels

(P-13102)
RECP CY OXNARD LLC
Also Called: Courtyard By Marriott Oxnard
600 E Esplanade Dr, Oxnard (93036-2403)
PHONE..................................805 604-7527
Mary Reece, *Principal*
Recp III Cal West Hotels LLC, *Mng Member*
EMP: 70
SQ FT: 103,000
SALES (est): 3.3MM Privately Held
SIC: 7011 Hotels & motels

(P-13103)
RECP RI OXNARD LLC
Also Called: Residnce Inn By Mrriott Oxnard
2101 W Vineyard Ave, Oxnard
(93036-2268)
PHONE..................................805 278-2200
Doug Pflaumer, *Manager*
Millicent Bennett, *Principal*
Recp III Cal West Hotels LLC, *Mng Member*
EMP: 150
SQ FT: 103,000
SALES (est): 4.3MM Privately Held
SIC: 7011 Hotels & motels

(P-13104)
RECP/WNDSOR SCRAMENTO VENTR LP
Also Called: Windsor Capital Hotel Group
4422 Y St, Sacramento (95817-2220)
PHONE................................916 455-6800
Mike Cryan, *CEO*
Recp Windsor Rim Sacramento GP, *General Ptnr*
EMP: 72
SALES (est): 1.9MM **Privately Held**
SIC: 7011 Hotels

(P-13105)
RED EARTH CASINO
3089 Norm Niver Rd, Thermal (92274-6550)
PHONE................................760 395-1200
Andrew Miranda, *General Mgr*
Nigel White, *Owner*
EMP: 150
SQ FT: 15,000
SALES (est): 9.3MM **Privately Held**
SIC: 7011 Casino hotel

(P-13106)
REDDING RANCHERIA (PA)
2000 Redding Rancheria Rd, Redding (96001-5528)
PHONE................................530 225-8979
Tracy Edward, *CEO*
Christi Hines, *CFO*
Tamra Olson, *CFO*
Monique Cassells, *Manager*
EMP: 60
SQ FT: 16,360
SALES (est): 36.5MM **Privately Held**
WEB: www.redding-rancheria.com
SIC: 7011 Hotels & motels

(P-13107)
REICHERT LENGFELD LTD PARTNR
Also Called: RI Properties
725 Folger Ave, Albany (94710-2809)
PHONE................................510 845-1077
Diana R Meyer, *Partner*
Herbert R Meyer, *General Ptnr*
EMP: 90
SQ FT: 1,500
SALES (est): 3.5MM **Privately Held**
SIC: 7011 Hotels & motels

(P-13108)
REMINGTON HOTEL CORPORATION
Also Called: Palm Springs Renaissance
888 E Tahquitz Canyon Way, Palm Springs (92262-6708)
PHONE................................760 322-6000
EMP: 85 **Privately Held**
SIC: 7011 Hotels
PA: Remington Hotel Corporation
14185 Dallas Pkwy # 1150
Dallas TX 75254

(P-13109)
REMINGTON HOTEL CORPORATION
Also Called: Holiday Inn
1150 S Beverly Dr, Los Angeles (90035-1120)
PHONE................................310 553-6561
Jack Jones, *Branch Mgr*
EMP: 2059 **Privately Held**
WEB: www.remingtonhotels.com
SIC: 7011 Hotels & motels
PA: Remington Hotel Corporation
14185 Dallas Pkwy # 1150
Dallas TX 75254

(P-13110)
REMINGTON LDGING HSPTALITY LLC
Bardessono Hotel
6526 Yount St, Yountville (94599-1270)
PHONE................................877 932-5333
Phillip G Sherburne, *Branch Mgr*
Jim Tredway, *General Mgr*
Tess Allen, *VP Mktg*
EMP: 830 **Privately Held**
SIC: 7011 Hotels

PA: Remington Lodging & Hospitality Llc
14185 Dallas Pkwy # 1150
Dallas TX 75254

(P-13111)
RENAISSANCE HOTEL CLUBSPORT
50 Enterprise, Aliso Viejo (92656-6026)
PHONE................................949 643-6700
Ed Tomlin, *General Mgr*
Michell Gullett, *Info Tech Mgr*
Damon Durante, *Sales Staff*
EMP: 61
SALES (est): 4.7MM **Privately Held**
SIC: 7011 Hotels & motels

(P-13112)
RENAISSANCE HOTEL HOLDINGS INC
1325 Broadway, Sonoma (95476-7505)
PHONE................................707 935-6600
Dave Dalquist, *General Mgr*
Gina Thayer, *Manager*
EMP: 99
SALES (est): 1.5MM **Privately Held**
SIC: 7011 Hotels

(P-13113)
RENAISSANCE HOTEL OPERATING CO
Also Called: Renaissance Indian Wells
44400 Indian Wells Ln, Indian Wells (92210-8708)
PHONE................................760 773-4444
Tom Tabler, *Principal*
EMP: 600
SALES (corp-wide): 22.8B **Publicly Held**
WEB: www.renaissancehotel.com
SIC: 7011 Hotel, franchised
HQ: Renaissance Hotel Operating Company, Inc
10400 Fernwood Rd
Bethesda MD 20817
301 380-3000

(P-13114)
RENAISSNCE ESMRALDA RESORT SPA
44400 Indian Wells Ln, Indian Wells (92210-8708)
PHONE................................760 773-4444
John Kalinski, *Principal*
Tom Tabler, *General Mgr*
Terry Venema, *Engineer*
Cara Marshall-Bryan, *Manager*
EMP: 67
SALES (est): 5MM **Privately Held**
SIC: 7011 Hotels

(P-13115)
RENESON HOTELS INC (PA)
Also Called: Carriage Inn
2700 Junipero Serra Blvd, Daly City (94015-1634)
PHONE................................650 449-5353
Alrene Flynn, *Chairman*
Garrett Grialou, *President*
Doug Sherer, *CFO*
Diane Grialou, *Admin Sec*
EMP: 100
SALES (est): 25.4MM **Privately Held**
WEB: www.renesonhotels.com
SIC: 7011 Motels

(P-13116)
RENESON HOTELS INC
Also Called: Hotel Britton
112 7th St, San Francisco (94103-2809)
PHONE................................415 621-7001
Norman Onaga, *General Mgr*
EMP: 150
SALES (corp-wide): 25.4MM **Privately Held**
WEB: www.renesonhotels.com
SIC: 7011 Hotels
PA: Reneson Hotels, Inc.
2700 Junipero Serra Blvd
Daly City CA 94015
650 449-5353

(P-13117)
RESERVATION RANCH (PA)
356 Sarina Rd N, Smith River (95567)
PHONE................................707 487-3516

Henry L Westbrook III, *Partner*
EMP: 160
SQ FT: 2,000
SALES (est): 5.4MM **Privately Held**
WEB: www.reservationranch.com
SIC: 7011 0241 Hotels & motels; dairy heifer replacement farm

(P-13118)
RESIDENCE INN BY MARRIOTT
5322 N Diana St, Fresno (93710-6700)
PHONE................................559 222-8900
Juliee May, *Manager*
Julee May, *General Mgr*
EMP: 80
SALES (est): 2.3MM **Privately Held**
SIC: 7011 Hotels & motels

(P-13119)
RESIDENCE INN BY MARRIOTT
1700 S Clementine St, Anaheim (92802-2909)
PHONE................................714 533-3555
Rosa Cook, *General Mgr*
EMP: 80
SALES (est): 1.3MM **Privately Held**
SIC: 7011 Hotels & motels

(P-13120)
RESIDENCE INN BY MARRIOTT
700 W Kimberly Ave, Placentia (92870-6329)
PHONE................................714 996-0555
Paulette Lombrodi, *Principal*
Audun Poulsen, *General Mgr*
Nancy Medrano, *Manager*
EMP: 80
SALES (est): 2MM **Privately Held**
SIC: 7011 Hotels

(P-13121)
RESIDENCE INN BY MARRIOTT
11002 Rancho Carmel Dr, San Diego (92128-4288)
PHONE................................858 673-1900
Casey Grieme, *Manager*
EMP: 80
SALES (est): 1.9MM **Privately Held**
SIC: 7011 Hotels & motels

(P-13122)
RESIDNCE INN BY MRRIOTT IRVINE
10 Morgan, Irvine (92618-2003)
PHONE................................949 380-3000
Camillo Bruce, *Manager*
Oscar Garcia, *Opers Mgr*
EMP: 80
SALES (est): 1.9MM **Privately Held**
SIC: 7011 Hotels

(P-13123)
RESORT AT PELICAN HILL LLC
22701 Pelican Hill Rd S, Newport Coast (92657-2008)
PHONE................................949 467-6800
Elia Gutierrez, *Director*
Tim La Duke, *Executive*
Omar Abreu, *General Mgr*
Jordan Griffin, *Admin Asst*
Amanda Taggart, *Admin Asst*
EMP: 187 EST: 2006
SALES (est): 23.4MM **Privately Held**
SIC: 7011 Resort hotel

(P-13124)
RIO VISTA DEVELOPMENT COMPANY (PA)
Also Called: Holiday Inn
4222 Vineland Ave, North Hollywood (91602-3318)
PHONE................................818 980-8000
Scott A Mills, *Principal*
Scott Mills, *General Ptnr*
Elizabeth Jacobs, *Human Res Dir*
Stella Pak, *Sales Executive*
Rhocelli Pascual, *Mktg Dir*
EMP: 135
SQ FT: 100,000
SALES (est): 11.5MM **Privately Held**
WEB: www.beverlygarland.com
SIC: 7011 Hotels & motels

(P-13125)
RITZ-CARLTON HOTEL COMPANY LLC
690 Market St, San Francisco (94104-5101)
PHONE................................415 781-9000
John Fitzgerald, *Branch Mgr*
EMP: 343
SALES (corp-wide): 22.8B **Publicly Held**
SIC: 7011 Hotels
HQ: The Ritz-Carlton Hotel Company Llc
10400 Fernwood Rd
Bethesda MD 20817
301 380-3000

(P-13126)
RITZ-CARLTON HOTEL COMPANY LLC
Also Called: Ritz Carlton
68900 Frank Sinatra Dr, Rancho Mirage (92270-5300)
PHONE................................760 321-8282
Carlton Ritz, *Branch Mgr*
Gary Ardrey, *General Mgr*
Amanda Kershaw, *Supervisor*
EMP: 349
SALES (corp-wide): 22.8B **Publicly Held**
SIC: 7011 Hotels
HQ: The Ritz-Carlton Hotel Company Llc
10400 Fernwood Rd
Bethesda MD 20817
301 380-3000

(P-13127)
RITZ-CARLTON HOTEL COMPANY LLC
1 Ritz Carlton Dr, Dana Point (92629-4206)
PHONE................................949 240-5020
Jannie Vanderoy, *Branch Mgr*
Paul Sanudo, *Administration*
EMP: 348
SALES (corp-wide): 22.8B **Publicly Held**
SIC: 7011 Hotels
HQ: The Ritz-Carlton Hotel Company Llc
10400 Fernwood Rd
Bethesda MD 20817
301 380-3000

(P-13128)
RITZ-CARLTON HOTEL COMPANY LLC
8301 Hollister Ave, Santa Barbara (93117-2474)
PHONE................................301 547-4700
EMP: 650
SALES (corp-wide): 22.8B **Publicly Held**
SIC: 7011 Hotels
HQ: The Ritz-Carlton Hotel Company Llc
10400 Fernwood Rd
Bethesda MD 20817
301 380-3000

(P-13129)
RITZ-CARLTON HOTEL COMPANY LLC
Also Called: Ritz-Carlton San Francisco
600 Stockton St, San Francisco (94108-2386)
PHONE................................415 773-6168
Edward Madey, *Manager*
Jo-Anne Hill, *President*
Nickolas Tice, *General Mgr*
Tyler Crist, *Info Tech Dir*
Paul Roa, *Director*
EMP: 500
SALES (corp-wide): 22.8B **Publicly Held**
WEB: www.ritz-carlton.com
SIC: 7011 Hotels
HQ: The Ritz-Carlton Hotel Company Llc
10400 Fernwood Rd
Bethesda MD 20817
301 380-3000

(P-13130)
RITZ-CARLTON HOTEL COMPANY LLC
Also Called: Ritz Carlton Rancho Mirage
68900 Frank Sinatra Dr, Rancho Mirage (92270-5300)
PHONE................................760 321-8282
James H Palllin Jr, *Manager*
EMP: 313

(PA)=Parent Co (HQ)=Headquarters (DH)=Div Headquarters
✿ = New Business established in last 2 years

2019 Directory of California
Wholesalers and Services Companies

561

PRODUCTS & SVCS

SALES (corp-wide): 22.8B **Publicly Held**
WEB: www.ritz-carlton.com
SIC: 7011 Hotels
HQ: The Ritz-Carlton Hotel Company Llc
10400 Fernwood Rd
Bethesda MD 20817
301 380-3000

(P-13131)
RITZ-CARLTON MARINA DEL REY
4375 Admiralty Way, Marina Del Rey
(90292-5434)
PHONE.....................310 823-1700
Robert Thomas, *Principal*
Lauren Lynch, *Corp Comm Staff*
Don Quimby, *Manager*
EMP: 74
SALES (est): 5.1MM **Privately Held**
SIC: 7011 Hotels

(P-13132)
RIVER ROCK ENTERTAINMENT AUTH
Also Called: River Rock Casino
3250 Highway 128, Geyserville
(95441-8908)
P.O. Box 607 (95441-0607)
PHONE.....................707 857-2777
David Fendrick, *CEO*
Joseph R Callahan, *CFO*
Jonathan Turner, *Administration*
Greg Bentall, *Finance Dir*
Yola Bawlec, *Exec Sec*
EMP: 616
SALES (est): 14.1MM **Privately Held**
SIC: 7011 Casino hotel

(P-13133)
RIVIERA REINCARNATE LLC
Also Called: Palm Sprng Riviera Resorts Spa
1600 N Indian Canyon Dr, Palm Springs
(92262-4602)
PHONE.....................760 327-8311
Jim Manion,
EMP: 78
SALES (est): 10.1MM **Privately Held**
SIC: 7011 Resort hotel

(P-13134)
RLJHGN EMERYVILLE LESSEE LP
Also Called: Hilton
1800 Powell St, Emeryville (94608-1808)
PHONE.....................510 658-9300
Mark Burden, *CEO*
Jeff Virgil, *CFO*
Dorota Wossner, *Social Dir*
EMP: 120
SQ FT: 476
SALES (est): 6.1MM **Privately Held**
SIC: 7011 Hotels

(P-13135)
RMS FOUNDATION INC
Also Called: Queen Mary Hotel
1126 Queens Hwy, Long Beach
(90802-6331)
PHONE.....................562 435-3511
Joseph F Prevratil, *President*
Leo Fuentes, *Executive*
Carol Cochrane, *Administration*
Chris Quintanilla, *Technology*
Daniel Quiroz, *Engineer*
EMP: 650
SQ FT: 750,000
SALES (est): 29.7MM **Privately Held**
WEB: www.queenmary.com
SIC: 7011 Hotels & motels
PA: City Of Long Beach
333 W Ocean Blvd Fl 10
Long Beach CA 90802
562 570-6450

(P-13136)
ROOSEVELT HOTEL LLC
Also Called: Hollywood Roosevelt Hotel
7000 Hollywood Blvd, Los Angeles
(90028-6003)
PHONE.....................323 466-7000
Goodwin Gaw, *Mng Member*
David Chan,
EMP: 200

SALES (est): 16.8MM **Privately Held**
WEB: www.hollywoodroosevelt.com
SIC: 7011 5813 5812 Hotels; drinking places; eating places

(P-13137)
ROPPONGI-TAHOE LP A CALIFORNI
Also Called: Lake Tahoe Resort Hotel
4130 Lake Tahoe Blvd, South Lake Tahoe
(96150-6965)
PHONE.....................530 544-5400
Kunihiro Nakayabu, *Managing Prtnr*
Masaru Saito, *Managing Prtnr*
Joseph McDaniel, *Controller*
EMP: 200
SALES (est): 12MM **Privately Held**
WEB: www.embassytahoe.com
SIC: 7011 Resort hotel; hotels

(P-13138)
ROSANNA INC
Also Called: Avenue of Arts Wyndham Hotel
3350 Avenue Of The Arts, Costa Mesa
(92626-1913)
PHONE.....................714 751-5100
Nick Price, *General Mgr*
Rachael Moorhead, *President*
Paul Sanford, *CEO*
Rosanna Chan, *Principal*
Robin Reid, *Director*
EMP: 151
SALES (est): 9.4MM **Privately Held**
SIC: 7011 5812 Hotels; food bars; caterers

(P-13139)
ROSCOE REAL ESTATE LTD PARTNR
Also Called: Elkor Properties
1819 Ocean Ave, Santa Monica
(90401-3215)
PHONE.....................310 260-7500
Vincent Piro, *General Mgr*
Elkor Trio LL LLC, *General Ptnr*
EMP: 80
SALES (est): 3.7MM **Privately Held**
WEB: www.viceroysantamonica.com
SIC: 7011 7389 Hotels; hotel & motel reservation service

(P-13140)
ROSEVILLE TOWNE PLACE SUITES
10569 Fairway Dr, Roseville (95678-3570)
PHONE.....................916 782-2232
Gary Tharaldson, *Principal*
Lynda Abrams, *Principal*
EMP: 99
SALES (est): 1.5MM **Privately Held**
SIC: 7011 Hotel, franchised

(P-13141)
ROSEWOOD HOTELS & RESORTS LLC
Also Called: Rosewood Sand Hill Hotel
2825 Sand Hill Rd, Menlo Park
(94025-7022)
PHONE.....................650 561-1500
Michael Casey, *Managing Dir*
Anthony Gutierrez, *Office Spvr*
John Terry, *Purchasing*
EMP: 300
SALES (est): 16.9MM **Privately Held**
SIC: 7011 Resort hotel; hotels

(P-13142)
ROYAL GORGE NORDIC SKI RESORT (PA)
Also Called: Royal Gorge Crss Cntry Ski Rst
9411 Hillside Rd, Soda Springs (95728)
PHONE.....................530 426-3871
John Slouber, *President*
Frances Wiesel, *Admin Sec*
EMP: 120 **EST:** 1971
SQ FT: 50,000
SALES (est): 4.5MM **Privately Held**
SIC: 7011 Ski lodge

(P-13143)
ROYAL HOSPITALITY INCORPORATED
Also Called: Ramada Inn
5550 Kearny Mesa Rd, San Diego
(92111-1304)
PHONE.....................858 278-0800
Maurice Coreia, *President*
Mary Holladay, *Sales Staff*
EMP: 60
SQ FT: 63,000
SALES (est): 4.9MM **Privately Held**
WEB: www.ramadasandiego.com
SIC: 7011 Inns

(P-13144)
RP SCS WSD HOTEL LLC
Also Called: W San Diego Hotel
421 W B St, San Diego (92101-3501)
PHONE.....................619 398-3020
Michael O'Donohue, *General Mgr*
Maria Veronica Rodriguez, *Finance Dir*
EMP: 60
SALES (est): 5MM **Privately Held**
SIC: 7011 Hotels

(P-13145)
RP/KINETIC PARC 55 OWNER LLC
Also Called: Parc 55 Hotel
55 Cyril Magnin St, San Francisco
(94102-2812)
PHONE.....................415 392-8000
Steve Barick,
Joeann Lamadrid, *President*
Peter Beheda, *Senior VP*
Gary Gutierrez, *Vice Pres*
Rob Gauthier, *General Mgr*
EMP: 450
SALES (est): 21.1MM
SALES (corp-wide): 7.1B **Publicly Held**
WEB: www.parc55hotel.com
SIC: 7011 Hotels
PA: The Blackstone Group L P
345 Park Ave Ste 1100
New York NY 10154
212 583-5000

(P-13146)
RPC OLD TOWN AVENUE OWNER LLC
Also Called: Fairfield Inn
3900 Old Town Ave, San Diego
(92110-2904)
PHONE.....................619 299-7400
Evan Hitter, *Director*
Amber Wilson, *Executive*
EMP: 55
SALES (est): 1.3MM **Privately Held**
SIC: 7011 Hotels & motels

(P-13147)
RPC OLD TOWN JEFFERSON
Also Called: San Diego Old Town
2435 Jefferson St, San Diego
(92110-3026)
PHONE.....................619 725-4221
Budd Barmeyer, *General Mgr*
Evan Hitter, *Director*
EMP: 60
SQ FT: 5,000
SALES (est): 4.2MM **Privately Held**
WEB: www.sunstonehotels.com
SIC: 7011 Hotels

(P-13148)
RPD HOTELS 18 LLC (PA)
Also Called: Vagabond Inns
2361 Rosecrans Ave # 150, El Segundo
(90245-7906)
PHONE.....................213 746-1531
Juan Sanchez Llaca, *President*
Les Biggins, *Vice Pres*
Chuck Valentino, *VP Opers*
Don Johnson,
Stewart Rubin,
EMP: 800
SALES (est): 26MM **Privately Held**
SIC: 7011 Motels

(P-13149)
RT PASAD HOTEL PARTNERS LP
Also Called: Courtyard By Marriott
180 N Fair Oaks Ave, Pasadena
(91103-3614)
PHONE.....................626 403-7000
Timothy Bristol, *General Mgr*
Jeff Hart, *General Mgr*
EMP: 140
SQ FT: 165,342
SALES (est): 7.2MM **Privately Held**
SIC: 7011 Hotels & motels

(P-13150)
RT SD-DENVER LP
Also Called: Residnce By Mria San Dego Cntl
5400 Kearny Mesa Rd, San Diego
(92111-1303)
PHONE.....................858 278-2100
J Correll, *General Mgr*
Jonathan Correll, *General Mgr*
EMP: 50
SALES (est): 131.9K **Privately Held**
SIC: 7011 Hotels & motels

(P-13151)
RUBICON B HACIENDA LLC
Also Called: Fairfield Inn
525 N Pacific Coast Hwy, El Segundo
(90245-4496)
PHONE.....................424 290-5000
Marc Gordon,
EMP: 56
SALES (est): 765.4K **Privately Held**
SIC: 7011 Inns

(P-13152)
RUBICON B HACIENDA LLC
Also Called: Aloft El Sgnd-Los Angles Arprt
475 N Pacific Coast Hwy, El Segundo
(90245-4446)
PHONE.....................424 290-5555
Louisa Yeung, *Administration*
EMP: 87
SALES (est): 409.5K **Privately Held**
SIC: 7011 Hotels & motels

(P-13153)
RUFFIN HOTEL CORP OF CAL
Also Called: Long Beach Marriott
4700 Airport Plaza Dr, Long Beach
(90815-1252)
PHONE.....................562 425-5210
Phillip G Ruffin, *President*
Jose Anezcua, *Opers Staff*
Jennifer Robinson, *Director*
Crystal Sierra, *Manager*
EMP: 260
SALES (est): 13.8MM **Privately Held**
WEB: www.lbmarriott.com
SIC: 7011 5812 5813 Hotels; eating places; coffee shop; drinking places

(P-13154)
RUNNING CREEK CASINO
635 E State Highway 20, Upper Lake
(95485-8793)
P.O. Box 788 (95485-0788)
PHONE.....................707 275-9209
Mike Caryl, *Finance Dir*
Raelene Cromwell, *Executive Asst*
Gerry Erickson, *Info Tech Dir*
Joe Denbo, *Mktg Dir*
EMP: 170 **EST:** 2011
SALES (est): 7.9MM **Privately Held**
SIC: 7011 5812 Casino hotel; eating places

(P-13155)
RYDE HOTEL LLC
Also Called: Ryde Motel
14340 State Highway 160, Walnut Grove
(95690-9742)
PHONE.....................916 776-1318
Toll Free:.....................888 -
Janice G Leroy,
EMP: 50 **EST:** 1997
SALES (est): 1.3MM **Privately Held**
WEB: www.rydehotel.com
SIC: 7011 5812 Hotels & motels; eating places

(P-13156)
S R H H INC
Also Called: Radisson Inn
1085 E El Camino Real, Sunnyvale
(94087-3755)
PHONE..........................408 247-0800
Donald Bramer, *President*
Gaylon Patterson, *Treasurer*
John Branagh, *Admin Sec*
EMP: 50
SQ FT: 150,000
SALES (est): 1.3MM **Privately Held**
SIC: 7011 5812 5813 Hotels & motels;
American restaurant; cocktail lounge

(P-13157)
S W K PROPERTIES LLC
Also Called: Holiday Inn
2726 S Grand Ave Lbby, Santa Ana
(92705-5404)
PHONE..........................714 481-6300
Rod Hurt, *Manager*
Barbara Smith, *Info Tech Mgr*
EMP: 66
SALES (corp-wide): 10MM **Privately Held**
SIC: 7011 Hotels
PA: S W K Properties Llc
3807 Wilshire Blvd # 1226
Los Angeles CA 90010
213 383-9204

(P-13158)
SACRAMENTO HOTEL PARTNERS LLC
100 Capitol Mall, Sacramento
(95814-3244)
PHONE..........................916 326-5000
Vishwa Nand, *Manager*
Robert Weight, *Manager*
EMP: 90
SALES (corp-wide): 4.9MM **Privately Held**
WEB: www.essacramento.com
SIC: 7011 Hotels & motels
PA: Sacramento Hotel Partners, Llc
100 Saratoga Ave Ste 300
Santa Clara CA 95051
408 249-2500

(P-13159)
SACRAMNTO FORTY NINER TRVL PLZ
Also Called: Sacramento 49er
2828 El Centro Rd, Sacramento
(95833-9602)
PHONE..........................916 927-4774
Tristen Griffith, *President*
Terrace Rust, *Vice Pres*
Matthew Hiibel, *Manager*
Paul Millette, *Manager*
EMP: 125 **EST:** 1976
SQ FT: 27,000
SALES (est): 7.8MM **Privately Held**
WEB: www.sacramento49er.com
SIC: 7011 5331 5812 5541 Motels; variety stores; restaurant, family: independent; truck stops

(P-13160)
SAGA SEAL CO LTD
Also Called: Pacific Inn, The
600 Marina Dr, Seal Beach (90740-6123)
PHONE..........................562 493-7501
Steve Bader, *President*
Gene Sugita, *General Mgr*
EMP: 80
SQ FT: 33,597
SALES (est): 4.3MM **Privately Held**
SIC: 7011 Hotels

(P-13161)
SAGE HOSPITALITY RESOURCES LLC
Also Called: Courtyard By Marriott
700 W Huntington Dr, Monrovia
(91016-3104)
PHONE..........................626 357-5211
Dennis Hollingdrake, *Manager*
EMP: 100
SALES (corp-wide): 394MM **Privately Held**
WEB: www.21chotel.com
SIC: 7011 Hotels

PA: Sage Hospitality Resources L.L.C.
1575 Welton St Ste 300
Denver CO 80202
303 595-7200

(P-13162)
SAGE HOSPITALITY RESOURCES LLC
Also Called: Homewood Suites Hilton Sfo
2000 Shoreline Ct, Brisbane (94005-1802)
PHONE..........................650 589-1600
Gina Merz, *Branch Mgr*
EMP: 67
SALES (corp-wide): 394MM **Privately Held**
WEB: www.21chotel.com
SIC: 7011 Hotels
PA: Sage Hospitality Resources L.L.C.
1575 Welton St Ste 300
Denver CO 80202
303 595-7200

(P-13163)
SAJAHTERA INC
Also Called: Beverly Hills Hotel
9641 Sunset Blvd, Beverly Hills
(90210-2938)
PHONE..........................310 276-2251
Junaidi Masri, *President*
Edward Mady, *General Mgr*
Adam Jones, *Info Tech Dir*
Ana Martinez, *Credit Mgr*
Bibi Bedoya, *Payroll Mgr*
EMP: 600
SQ FT: 10,758
SALES (est): 44.2MM
SALES (corp-wide): 507.9MM **Privately Held**
WEB: www.sajahtera.com
SIC: 7011 Resort hotel; hotels
HQ: Dorchester Group Limited
3 Tilney Street
London W1Y 5
207 319-7401

(P-13164)
SALT LAKE HOTEL ASSOCIATES LP (PA)
222 Kearny St Ste 200, San Francisco
(94108-4537)
PHONE..........................415 397-5572
Tom Lataur, *President*
EMP: 111
SALES (est): 3.6MM **Privately Held**
SIC: 7011 Hotels & motels

(P-13165)
SAN BERNARDINO HILTON (HQ)
285 E Hospitality Ln, San Bernardino
(92408-3411)
PHONE..........................909 889-0133
Douglas McCarron, *President*
Morgan McPherson, *Exec Dir*
Ronald Schoen, *Admin Sec*
Kenneth Morris, *Finance*
Najam Khan, *Contractor*
EMP: 152
SALES (est): 30.7MM
SALES (corp-wide): 45.1MM **Privately Held**
WEB: www.web66.com
SIC: 7011 6512 5812 Hotels; commercial & industrial building operation; eating places
PA: Carpenters Southwest Administrative Corporation
533 S Fremont Ave
Los Angeles CA 90071
213 386-8590

(P-13166)
SAN CARLOS ASSOCIATES LTD
Also Called: Monterey Marriott
350 Calle Principal, Monterey
(93940-2416)
PHONE..........................831 649-4234
Rene Boskoff, *General Mgr*
Andrew Leavitt, *Engineer*
EMP: 225
SALES (corp-wide): 5.7MM **Privately Held**
SIC: 7011 5813 5812 Hotels; bar (drinking places); grills (eating places)

PA: San Carlos Associates Ltd
1111 3rd Ave Ste 3030
Seattle WA
-

(P-13167)
SAN DEGO MRROTT MARQUIS MARINA
333 W Harbor Dr, San Diego (92101-7709)
PHONE..........................301 380-3000
Ray Warren, *Principal*
Tracey Palmberg, *Executive*
Dawn Myers, *Human Res Mgr*
Kate Bernstein, *Sales Staff*
Mark Erskine, *Director*
EMP: 50
SALES (est): 4.1MM **Privately Held**
SIC: 7011 Resort hotel

(P-13168)
SAN DIEGO FARAH PARTNERS
Also Called: Holiday Inn
1430 7th Ave Ste B, San Diego
(92101-2815)
PHONE..........................619 239-2261
Berham Baxter, *General Ptnr*
EMP: 50
SQ FT: 99,999
SALES (est): 2.1MM **Privately Held**
SIC: 7011 Hotels & motels

(P-13169)
SAN DIEGO HOTEL COMPANY LLC
Also Called: Marriott San Dego Gslamp Qrter
660 K St, San Diego (92101-7036)
PHONE..........................619 696-0234
James Evans, *CFO*
EMP: 135
SALES (est): 6.2MM **Privately Held**
WEB: www.sheratonuptown.com
SIC: 7011 Hotels

(P-13170)
SAN DIEGO HOTEL LEASE LLC
Also Called: Courtyard By Marriott
530 Broadway, San Diego (92101-5206)
PHONE..........................619 446-3000
J W Marriott, *Chairman*
Arne M Sorenson, *CEO*
Carl T Berquist, *Exec VP*
Lisa Morales, *Executive*
Joy Henricksen, *Sales Mgr*
EMP: 200
SQ FT: 126,742
SALES (est): 4.5MM **Privately Held**
SIC: 7011 Hotels & motels

(P-13171)
SAN DIEGO LESSEE LLC
Also Called: Doubletree By Hilton
7450 Hazard Center Dr, San Diego
(92108-4539)
PHONE..........................619 297-5466
Owen Wilcox,
Kevin J Jacobs, *CFO*
Sean Dell'orto, *Treasurer*
Kristin Campbell, *Exec VP*
Joseph Berger, *Senior VP*
EMP: 140
SALES: 20.3MM
SALES (corp-wide): 2.7B **Publicly Held**
SIC: 7011 Hotels
PA: Park Hotels & Resorts Inc.
1775 Tysons Blvd Fl 7
Tysons VA 22102
571 302-5757

(P-13172)
SAN DIEGO SHERATON CORPORATION
Also Called: Starwood Hotels & Resorts
1590 Harbor Island Dr, San Diego
(92101-1009)
PHONE..........................619 291-6400
Robert Cartwright, *General Mgr*
EMP: 850
SALES (est): 16.7MM
SALES (corp-wide): 22.8B **Publicly Held**
SIC: 7011 5813 5812 4493 Hotels; drinking places; eating places; marinas

HQ: Starwood Hotels & Resorts Worldwide, Llc
1 Star Pt
Stamford CT 06902
203 964-6000

(P-13173)
SAN FRANCISCO HOTEL ASSOCIATES
Also Called: Masa's
650 Bush St, San Francisco (94108-3509)
PHONE..........................415 392-4666
Michael Lennon, *Partner*
EMP: 80
SQ FT: 46,067
SALES (est): 1.8MM **Privately Held**
WEB: www.vintagecourt.com
SIC: 7011 5812 Hotels; French restaurant

(P-13174)
SAN FRANCISCO HOTEL GROUP LLC
Also Called: Loews Regency San Francisco
222 Sansome St, San Francisco
(94104-2703)
PHONE..........................415 276-9888
Yue-Tin Chang, *President*
Jonathan Tisch, *Chairman*
Tracy Lee, *Controller*
EMP: 183
SALES (est): 7.1MM
SALES (corp-wide): 13.7B **Publicly Held**
SIC: 7011 Resort hotel
HQ: Loews Hotels Holding Corporation
667 Madison Ave
New York NY 10065
212 521-2000

(P-13175)
SAN JOSE AIRPORT GARDEN HOTEL
1740 N 1st St, San Jose (95112-4508)
PHONE..........................408 793-3300
Ronald Werner, *Partner*
EMP: 99
SALES (est): 2.2MM **Privately Held**
SIC: 7011

(P-13176)
SAN JOSE AIRPORT HOTEL LLC
Also Called: Holiday Inn
1740 N 1st St, San Jose (95112-4508)
PHONE..........................408 793-3939
Manou Mobedshahi, *Mng Member*
Harry Engineer,
EMP: 230
SALES (est): 6.2MM **Privately Held**
SIC: 7011 Hotels & motels

(P-13177)
SAN JOSE FAIRMONT LESSEE LLC
170 S Market St Lbby, San Jose
(95113-2361)
PHONE..........................408 998-1900
Cirilo Custodio,
Jose Zarate, *Administration*
Alberto Mansilla, *Purch Mgr*
Marshall Jones, *Director*
EMP: 500
SALES: 69MM
SALES (corp-wide): 1B **Privately Held**
WEB: www.cp.ca
SIC: 7011 5812 5813 Resort hotel; ethnic food restaurants; cocktail lounge
HQ: Fairmont Hotels & Resorts Inc
155 Wellington St W Suite 3300
Toronto ON M5V 0
416 874-2600

(P-13178)
SAN JOSE LESSEE LLC
Also Called: Doubletree By Hilton San Jose
2050 Gateway Pl, San Jose (95110-1011)
PHONE..........................408 453-4000
Rowan Tejada, *Finance*
EMP: 99
SALES (est): 797.5K
SALES (corp-wide): 2.7B **Publicly Held**
SIC: 7011 Hotels & motels
HQ: Park Us Lessee Holdings Inc.
1600 Tysons Blvd Ste 1000
Mc Lean VA 22102
703 883-1052

(P-13179)
SAN MARCOS CATERERS INC
Also Called: Quails Inn Motel
1025 La Bonita Dr, San Marcos
(92078-5220)
PHONE..................760 744-0120
Gordon N Frazar, *President*
Ronald Frazar, *Corp Secy*
Dodi Holiday, *General Mgr*
EMP: 60
SALES (est): 4.3MM **Privately Held**
WEB: www.lakesanmarcosresort.com
SIC: 7011 5812 Motels; caterers

(P-13180)
SAN PSQUAL BAND MSSION INDIANS
Also Called: Valley View Casino
16300 Nyemii Pass Rd, Valley Center
(92082-6769)
P.O. Box 2379 (92082-2379)
PHONE..................760 291-5500
Toll Free:.....................866 -
Bruce Howards, *General Mgr*
Don Haig, *President*
Monique Gomez, *Manager*
EMP: 500 **Privately Held**
WEB: www.sanpasqualindians.org
SIC: 7011 Casino hotel
PA: San Pasqual Band Of Mission Indians
16400 Kumeyaay Way
Valley Center CA 92082

(P-13181)
SAN PSQUAL CSINO DEV GROUP INC
Also Called: Valley View Casino
16300 Nyemii Pass Rd, Valley Center
(92082-6769)
PHONE..................760 291-5500
Joe Navarro, *President*
Don Haig, *President*
Michael Gorczynski, *Treasurer*
Al Cope, *Vice Pres*
Silver Howard, *Vice Pres*
EMP: 50
SQ FT: 62,000
SALES (est): 4.5MM **Privately Held**
SIC: 7011 Casino hotel
PA: San Pasqual Band Of Mission Indians
16400 Kumeyaay Way
Valley Center CA 92082

(P-13182)
SAN RAFAEL HILLCREST LLC
Also Called: Four Points San Rafael
1010 Northgate Dr, San Rafael
(94903-2502)
PHONE..................415 479-8800
Beth Gamble,
EMP: 51
SQ FT: 50,000
SALES (est): 431K **Privately Held**
SIC: 7011 Hotels

(P-13183)
SAN YSIDRO BB PROPERTY LLC
Also Called: Stonehouse Restaurant
900 San Ysidro Ln, Santa Barbara
(93108-1325)
PHONE..................805 969-5046
Seamus McManus,
Franco De Bartolo, *Director*
EMP: 140
SQ FT: 4,415
SALES (est): 9MM **Privately Held**
WEB: www.sanysidroranch.com
SIC: 7011 5812 Hotels; eating places

(P-13184)
SANDM SAN DEGO MRRIOTT DEL MAR
11966 El Camino Real, San Diego
(92130-2592)
PHONE..................858 523-1700
Jenessa Schaniel, *Principal*
John Peart, *General Mgr*
EMP: 1000
SALES (est): 870.1K **Privately Held**
SIC: 7011 Hotels

(P-13185)
SANDWICH SPOT (PA)
1630 18th St, Sacramento (95811-6702)
PHONE..................916 492-2613
Tom Heally, *Principal*
EMP: 65
SALES (est): 7MM **Privately Held**
SIC: 7011 Bed & breakfast inn

(P-13186)
SANTA CLARA TENANT CORP
Also Called: Embassy Suites- Santa Clara
2885 Lakeside Dr, Santa Clara
(95054-2805)
PHONE..................408 496-6400
T Owens, *General Mgr*
Teri Owens, *General Mgr*
EMP: 90
SALES (est): 4.4MM
SALES (corp-wide): 1.4B **Privately Held**
SIC: 7011 Hotels & motels
PA: Ashford Hospitality Trust Inc
14185 Dallas Pkwy # 1100
Dallas TX 75254
972 490-9600

(P-13187)
SANTA CRUZ HOTEL ASSOCIATES
Also Called: West Coast Santa Cruz Hotel
175 W Cliff Dr, Santa Cruz (95060-5438)
PHONE..................831 426-4330
Brian Corbell, *President*
Robin Donozan, *General Mgr*
EMP: 150
SALES (est): 2.4MM **Privately Held**
SIC: 7011 Resort hotel

(P-13188)
SANTA MARIA HOTEL CORP
Also Called: Holiday Inn
2100 N Broadway, Santa Maria
(93454-1140)
PHONE..................805 928-6000
Lawrence Lui, *President*
EMP: 88
SALES (est): 4.1MM **Privately Held**
SIC: 7011 5812 7389 Hotels; eating places; convention & show services

(P-13189)
SANTA MONICA HOTEL OWNER LLC
Also Called: Doubletree Suites
1707 4th St, Santa Monica (90401-3301)
PHONE..................310 395-3332
EMP: 135
SALES (est): 4.3MM **Privately Held**
SIC: 7011 Hotels

(P-13190)
SANTA MONICA HSR LTD PARTNR
Also Called: Doubletree Hotel
1707 4th St, Santa Monica (90401-3301)
PHONE..................310 395-3332
Shashi Poudyal, *Manager*
EMP: 160
SALES (est): 4.7MM **Privately Held**
WEB: www.doubletreesantamonica.com
SIC: 7011 5812 Hotels; eating places

(P-13191)
SANTANA ROW HOTEL PARTNERS LP
355 Santana Row Ste 1010, San Jose
(95128-2050)
PHONE..................408 551-0010
Bonnie Best, *General Mgr*
EMP: 200 **Privately Held**
SIC: 7011 Hotels
PA: Santana Row Hotel Partners Lp
4400 Post Oak Pkwy
Houston TX 77027

(P-13192)
SARATOGA CAPITAL INC
Also Called: Hotel De Anza
233 W Santa Clara St, San Jose
(95113-1710)
PHONE..................408 286-1000
Alison McAennon, *Manager*
EMP: 65

SALES (corp-wide): 19.7MM **Privately Held**
WEB: www.saratogacapital.net
SIC: 7011 Hotels & motels
HQ: Saratoga Capital, Inc.
485 Alberto Way Ste 200
Los Gatos CA 95032
408 298-8600

(P-13193)
SAVE QUEEN LLC
429 Shoreline Village Dr I, Long Beach
(90802-8136)
PHONE..................562 435-3511
Sean Meddock, *Mng Member*
Edgar Stevens, *Technology*
Stewart Newell, *Human Res Mgr*
Sonja West, *Accounts Mgr*
EMP: 500 EST: 2007
SALES (est): 15.9MM **Privately Held**
SIC: 7011 Hotels

(P-13194)
SBEHG 465 S LA CIENEGA LLC
Also Called: S L S Hotel
465 S La Cienega Blvd, Los Angeles
(90048-4001)
PHONE..................310 247-0400
Manfred Moennich,
Chrystal Herndon, *Vice Pres*
Simon Sorpresi, *Managing Dir*
Scott Agnello, *Finance*
Claire Pignataro, *Sales Staff*
EMP: 500
SALES (est): 21.4MM **Privately Held**
WEB: www.granada-learning.com
SIC: 7011 Resort hotel; hotels

(P-13195)
SC HARP EL SEGUNDO LLC
1985 E Grand Ave, El Segundo
(90245-5015)
PHONE..................310 322-0999
Dave Harvey, *Mng Member*
EMP: 84
SALES: 950K **Privately Held**
SIC: 7011 Hotels & motels

(P-13196)
SD HOTEL CIRCLE LLC
Also Called: Homewood Suites San Diego Hote
2201 Hotel Cir S, San Diego (92108-3315)
PHONE..................619 881-6800
Mayur Patel, *Principal*
Louisa Yeung, *Administration*
EMP: 75
SALES (est): 256.8K **Privately Held**
SIC: 7011 Hotels & motels

(P-13197)
SD STADIUM HOTEL LLC
Also Called: Hilton Garded
3805 Murphy Canyon Rd, San Diego
(92123-4404)
PHONE..................858 278-9300
Mayur Patel,
Michael Mc Cullough, *Info Tech Dir*
Sandra Barnhart, *Sales Mgr*
Leeling Kirven, *Sales Staff*
EMP: 100
SALES (est): 2.8MM **Privately Held**
WEB: www.hioldtownhotel.com
SIC: 7011 Hotels & motels

(P-13198)
SE SAN DIEGO HOTEL LLC
1047 5th Ave, San Diego (92101-5101)
PHONE..................619 515-3000
Ador Bustamante, *Director*
Astrid Naujokaitis, *Accounting Mgr*
EMP: 51
SALES (est): 4.5MM **Privately Held**
SIC: 7011 Resort hotel

(P-13199)
SEACLIFF INN INC
Also Called: Best Western
7500 Old Dominion Ct, Aptos (95003-3807)
PHONE..................831 661-4671
Frank Giuliani, *President*
T J Scott, *Treasurer*
Norm BEI, *Vice Pres*
Coleen Giuliani, *Admin Sec*
Nikki Castro, *Human Res Dir*
EMP: 90

SQ FT: 60,000
SALES (est): 4.2MM **Privately Held**
WEB: www.seacliffinn.com
SIC: 7011 Hotels & motels

(P-13200)
SEASCAPE RESORT LTD A CALIF
Also Called: Sanderlings
19 Seascape Vlg, Aptos (95003-6102)
PHONE..................831 662-7120
Mark Holcomb, *General Ptnr*
EMP: 300
SQ FT: 45,000
SALES (est): 8MM **Privately Held**
WEB: www.seascaperesort.com
SIC: 7011 Resort hotel

(P-13201)
SEASIDE LAGUNA INN & SUITES
1661 S Coast Hwy, Laguna Beach
(92651-3228)
PHONE..................949 494-9717
Tino Farjad, *General Mgr*
EMP: 51
SQ FT: 27,500
SALES (est): 925.4K **Privately Held**
WEB: www.seacliffmotel.com
SIC: 7011 Hotels; motels

(P-13202)
SECOND STREET CORPORATION
Also Called: Huntley Hotel Santa Monica Bch
1111 2nd St, Santa Monica (90403-5003)
PHONE..................310 394-5454
Sohrab Sassounian, *President*
Dora Levy, *Shareholder*
Marschinda Felix, *COO*
Helal M El-Sherif, *CFO*
Shiva Aghaipour, *Vice Pres*
EMP: 250
SQ FT: 185,000
SALES (est): 17MM **Privately Held**
SIC: 7011 5812 Hotels; eating places

(P-13203)
SELECT HOTELS GROUP LLC
Also Called: Hyatt Pl Fremont/Silicon Vly
3101 W Warren Ave, Fremont
(94538-6428)
PHONE..................510 623-6000
John McEngee, *Manager*
EMP: 50
SALES (corp-wide): 4.6B **Publicly Held**
WEB: www.amerisuites.com
SIC: 7011 Hotels & motels
HQ: Select Hotels Group, L.L.C.
71 S Wacker Dr
Chicago IL 60606
312 750-1234

(P-13204)
SELECT HOTELS GROUP LLC
Also Called: Hyatt House Rancho Cordova
11260 Point East Dr, Rancho Cordova
(95742-6232)
PHONE..................916 638-4141
Brett Tmekei, *General Mgr*
EMP: 50
SALES (corp-wide): 4.6B **Publicly Held**
WEB: www.hallmarksuites.com
SIC: 7011 Hotel, franchised
HQ: Select Hotels Group, L.L.C.
71 S Wacker Dr
Chicago IL 60606
312 750-1234

(P-13205)
SELVI-VIDOVICH LP
Also Called: Grand Hotel The
865 W El Camino Real, Sunnyvale
(94087-1154)
PHONE..................408 720-8500
John Vidovich, *Managing Prtnr*
Al Selvi, *Partner*
Matt Heiser, *Controller*
EMP: 70
SQ FT: 90,805
SALES (est): 3.8MM **Privately Held**
WEB: www.thegrandhotel.com
SIC: 7011 Hotels

(P-13206)
SERVICE HOSPITALITY LLC
1050 Burnett Ave, Concord (94520-5713)
PHONE............................925 566-8820
Maryann Rhoe,
EMP: 70
SALES (est): 443.3K **Privately Held**
SIC: 7011 Seasonal hotel

(P-13207)
SETHI MANAGEMENT INC
183 Calle Magdalena # 101, Encinitas
(92024-3793)
PHONE............................760 652-4010
J P Sethi, *President*
Ganisha Sethi, *COO*
Gilbert Preciado, *Controller*
EMP: 99
SALES (est): 3.2MM **Privately Held**
SIC: 7011 Hotels & motels

(P-13208)
SEVEN RESORTS INC (PA)
9771 Irvine Center Dr, Irvine (92618-4343)
PHONE............................949 588-7100
David A Ohanesian, *President*
Jacqueline S Anderson, *Treasurer*
Lynda L Ohanesian-Druan, *Admin Sec*
EMP: 394
SALES (est): 10.7MM **Privately Held**
WEB: www.sevencrown.com
SIC: 7011 Resort hotel

(P-13209)
SEVEN SEAS ASSOCIATES LLC
Also Called: Seven Seas Best Western
411 Hotel Cir S, San Diego (92108-3402)
PHONE............................619 291-1300
Joe Toczylowski,
Desiree Govers, *Executive*
Eisler Family Trust,
Orwitz Family Trust,
Zolt Family Trust,
EMP: 108
SQ FT: 101,000
SALES (est): 8.7MM **Privately Held**
WEB: www.bw7seas.com
SIC: 7011 Motels

(P-13210)
SFD PARTNERS LLC
Also Called: Sir Francis Drake Hotel
450 Powell St, San Francisco
(94102-1504)
PHONE............................415 392-7755
John Price, *General Mgr*
EMP: 350
SALES (est): 2.8MM **Privately Held**
WEB: www.sirfrancisdrake.com
SIC: 7011 5812 5813 7389 Hotels; eating
places; drinking places; hotel & motel
reservation service

(P-13211)
SHAMROCK-HOSTMARK PALM DESRT
74700 Highway 111, Palm Desert
(92260-3806)
PHONE............................760 340-6600
Bob Cataldo,
Gerri Lynch,
EMP: 87
SALES (est): 3.1MM **Privately Held**
SIC: 7011 Hotels & motels

(P-13212)
SHAW HOSPITALITY GROUP INC
Also Called: Ramada Inn University
324 E Shaw Ave, Fresno (93710-7610)
PHONE............................559 224-4040
Raman Patel, *President*
Ashok Patel, *CFO*
EMP: 55
SQ FT: 91,168
SALES (est): 1.4MM **Privately Held**
SIC: 7011 Hotels & motels

(P-13213)
SHC BURBANK II LLC
Also Called: Marriott
2500 N Hollywood Way, Burbank
(91505-1019)
PHONE............................818 843-6000
EMP: 210

SALES (est): 10.7MM **Privately Held**
SIC: 7011

(P-13214)
SHEN ZHEN NEW WORLD II LLC
Also Called: Sheraton Universal Hotel
333 Unversal Hollywood Dr, Universal City
(91608-1001)
PHONE............................818 980-1212
Ming Yu,
EMP: 99
SALES (est): 2.9MM **Privately Held**
SIC: 7011 Hotels

(P-13215)
SHERATON CORPORATION
2500 Mason St, San Francisco
(94133-1450)
PHONE............................415 362-5500
Jim Sega, *Manager*
EMP: 300
SALES (corp-wide): 22.8B **Publicly Held**
SIC: 7011 Hotels
HQ: The Sheraton Corporation
1111 Westchester Ave
White Plains NY 10604
800 328-6242

(P-13216)
SHERATON CORPORATION
Also Called: Sheraton Gtwy Los Angeles Ht
6101 W Century Blvd, Los Angeles
(90045-5310)
PHONE............................310 642-1111
Michael Washington, *General Mgr*
EMP: 500
SALES (corp-wide): 22.8B **Publicly Held**
SIC: 7011 5813 5812 Hotels; drinking
places; eating places
HQ: The Sheraton Corporation
1111 Westchester Ave
White Plains NY 10604
800 328-6242

(P-13217)
SHERATON CORPORATION
Also Called: Sheraton Grand Sacramento Ht
1230 J St 13th, Sacramento (95814-2907)
PHONE............................916 447-1700
Gunter Stannius, *Manager*
EMP: 328
SALES (corp-wide): 22.8B **Publicly Held**
WEB: www.sheraton.com
SIC: 7011 Hotels
HQ: The Sheraton Corporation
1111 Westchester Ave
White Plains NY 10604
800 328-6242

(P-13218)
SHERATON CORPORATION
11960 Foothill Blvd, Rancho Cucamonga
(91739-9370)
PHONE............................909 204-6100
EMP: 328
SALES (corp-wide): 22.8B **Publicly Held**
SIC: 7011 Hotels
HQ: The Sheraton Corporation
1111 Westchester Ave
White Plains NY 10604
800 328-6242

(P-13219)
SHERATON CORPORATION
5990 Stoneridge Mall Rd, Pleasanton
(94588-3229)
PHONE............................925 463-3330
Marilyn Milligan, *Manager*
EMP: 328
SALES (corp-wide): 22.8B **Publicly Held**
SIC: 7011 Hotels
HQ: The Sheraton Corporation
1111 Westchester Ave
White Plains NY 10604
800 328-6242

(P-13220)
SHERATON HTL SAN DIEGO MSN VLY
Also Called: Sheraton San Diego Mission Vly
1433 Camino Del Rio S, San Diego
(92108-3521)
PHONE............................619 321-4602
Cynthia Adams Carlin, *Administration*
Sabra Baran, *General Mgr*
Kheam Taing, *General Mgr*

Brooke Vandenbrink, *Controller*
Alicia Ernenwein, *Human Res Dir*
EMP: 100
SALES (est): 2.5MM **Privately Held**
SIC: 7011 Hotels

(P-13221)
SHERTON GRDN GROVE ANHEIM S HT
12221 Harbor Blvd, Garden Grove
(92840-4005)
PHONE............................714 703-8400
Ronnie Lam, *Owner*
EMP: 80
SALES (est): 2.1MM **Privately Held**
SIC: 7011 Resort hotel

(P-13222)
SHERWOOD VALLEY RANCHERIA
Also Called: Sherwood Vllley Rnchria Casino
100 Kawi Pl, Willits (95490-4674)
PHONE............................707 459-7330
Kani Neves, *Manager*
EMP: 60 **Privately Held**
SIC: 7011 Casino hotel
PA: Sherwood Valley Rancheria
190 Sherwood Hill Dr
Willits CA 95490
707 459-9690

(P-13223)
SHORE HOTEL
1515 Ocean Ave, Santa Monica
(90401-2118)
PHONE............................310 458-1515
Julie Ward, *Principal*
Steve Farzam, *COO*
Gerry Peck, *General Mgr*
Roger Grajeda, *Engineer*
Laura Martinez, *Human Res Dir*
EMP: 56 EST: 2011
SALES (est): 3.8MM **Privately Held**
SIC: 7011 Resort hotel; hotels

(P-13224)
SHRI SIDHI VINAYAKA HOTEL INC
Also Called: Hilton
500 Leisure Ln, Sacramento (95815-4207)
PHONE............................855 922-5252
Vinod Kumar Sharma, *CEO*
EMP: 197
SALES (est): 5.7MM **Privately Held**
SIC: 7011 Hotels

(P-13225)
SIDJON CORPORATION
Also Called: Livermore Casino
3571 1st St, Livermore (94551-4901)
PHONE............................925 606-6135
Sidney Ahn, *CEO*
Kristen Salisbury, *Director*
EMP: 100 EST: 2007
SQ FT: 15,000
SALES (est): 3.2MM **Privately Held**
SIC: 7011 Casino hotel

(P-13226)
SIERRA AT TAHO SKI RESORTS
1111 Sierra At Tahoe Rd, Twin Bridges
(95735-9505)
PHONE............................530 659-7519
John Rice, *President*
George Gillette, *President*
EMP: 50 EST: 1996
SALES (est): 1.9MM **Privately Held**
SIC: 7011 Resort hotel, franchised

(P-13227)
SILICON VALLEY HWANG LLC
Also Called: Radisson Plaza Hotel Inn
1471 N 4th St, San Jose (95112-4716)
PHONE............................408 452-0200
John Simpson, *Principal*
EMP: 150
SQ FT: 112,218
SALES (est): 2.2MM **Privately Held**
SIC: 7011 Hotels & motels

(P-13228)
SILVERADO RSORT SVCS GROUP LLC
1600 Atlas Peak Rd, NAPA (94558-1425)
PHONE............................707 257-0200

Tim Wall, *Mng Member*
Roger Kent,
Johnny Miller,
EMP: 450
SALES (est): 26MM **Privately Held**
SIC: 7011 Resort hotel

(P-13229)
SIMI WEST INC
Also Called: Grand Vista Hotel
999 Enchanted Way, Simi Valley
(93065-1998)
PHONE............................805 583-2000
Tim Lasure, *Branch Mgr*
Tawny Byron, *General Mgr*
Marcia Foulks, *General Mgr*
Paul Gale, *Chief Engr*
Lea Foulks, *Sales Staff*
EMP: 115 **Privately Held**
SIC: 7011 5812 7299 Hotels & motels;
eating places; banquet hall facilities
PA: Simi West Inc
75110 Saint Charles Pl # 14
Palm Desert CA

(P-13230)
SINCLAIR COMPANIES
Also Called: Westgate Hotel
1055 2nd Ave, San Diego (92101-4811)
PHONE............................619 238-1818
Richard Cox, *Branch Mgr*
Fabrice Hardel, *Executive*
Beatriz Krause, *Manager*
EMP: 160
SALES (corp-wide): 3.9B **Privately Held**
SIC: 7011 Hotels
PA: The Sinclair Companies
550 E South Temple
Salt Lake City UT 84102
801 524-2700

(P-13231)
SISKIYOU DEVELOPMENT COMPANY
Also Called: HI Lo Motel
88 S Weed Blvd, Edgewood (96094-2607)
PHONE............................530 938-2731
Shawn Zanni, *Manager*
EMP: 65
SALES (corp-wide): 11.7MM **Privately Held**
WEB: www.sisdevco.com
SIC: 7011 Motels
PA: Siskiyou Development Company Inc
79 S Weed Blvd Ste 2
Weed CA 96094
530 938-2904

(P-13232)
SITA RAM LLC
Also Called: Best Western Amador Inn
200 S State Highway 49, Jackson
(95642-2548)
PHONE............................209 223-0211
Kumar Sharma,
Puwan Kumar,
EMP: 100
SQ FT: 8,000
SALES (est): 3.1MM **Privately Held**
WEB: www.sitaram.com
SIC: 7011 5812 5813 7991 Hotels & mo-
tels; eating places; bar (drinking places);
physical fitness facilities

(P-13233)
SIX CONTINENTS HOTELS INC
Also Called: Holiday Inn
19901 Prairie Ave, Torrance (90503-1687)
PHONE............................310 371-8525
John Bvell, *Manager*
EMP: 97
SALES (corp-wide): 1.7B **Privately Held**
SIC: 7011 Hotels & motels
HQ: Six Continents Hotels, Inc.
3 Ravinia Dr Ste 100
Atlanta GA 30346
770 604-2000

(P-13234)
SIX CONTINENTS HOTELS INC
Also Called: Holiday Inn
8244 Orion Ave, Van Nuys (91406-1344)
PHONE............................818 989-5010
Bob Yeager, *General Mgr*
EMP: 70

P R O D U C T S & S V C S

SALES (corp-wide): 1.7B **Privately Held**
SIC: 7011 5812 Hotels; restaurant, family:
　chain; box lunch stand
HQ: Six Continents Hotels, Inc.
　3 Ravinia Dr Ste 100
　Atlanta GA 30346
　770 604-2000

(P-13235)
SIX CONTINENTS HOTELS INC
Also Called: Holiday Inn
1020 S Figueroa St, Los Angeles
(90015-1305)
PHONE..................213 748-1291
Emerson Glazer, *President*
EMP: 100
SALES (corp-wide): 1.7B **Privately Held**
WEB: www.sixcontinenthotels.com
SIC: 7011 5812 5813 Hotels; eating
　places; bar (drinking places)
HQ: Six Continents Hotels, Inc.
　3 Ravinia Dr Ste 100
　Atlanta GA 30346
　770 604-2000

(P-13236)
SIX CONTINENTS HOTELS INC
Also Called: Holiday Inn
19800 S Vermont Ave, Torrance
(90502-1126)
PHONE..................310 781-9100
David Britton, *General Mgr*
EMP: 140
SALES (corp-wide): 1.7B **Privately Held**
WEB: www.sixcontinenthotels.com
SIC: 7011 Hotels
HQ: Six Continents Hotels, Inc.
　3 Ravinia Dr Ste 100
　Atlanta GA 30346
　770 604-2000

(P-13237)
SIX CONTINENTS HOTELS INC
Also Called: Holiday Inn
1355 N Harbor Dr, San Diego
(92101-3321)
PHONE..................619 232-3861
Tony Lovoy, *General Mgr*
EMP: 75
SALES (corp-wide): 1.7B **Privately Held**
WEB: www.sixcontinenthotels.com
SIC: 7011 Hotels & motels
HQ: Six Continents Hotels, Inc.
　3 Ravinia Dr Ste 100
　Atlanta GA 30346
　770 604-2000

(P-13238)
SIX CONTINENTS HOTELS INC
Also Called: Crown Plaza
11950 Dublin Canyon Rd # 609, Pleasanton
(94588-2818)
PHONE..................925 847-6000
Cathy Ryle, *Manager*
EMP: 75
SALES (corp-wide): 1.7B **Privately Held**
WEB: www.sixcontinenthotels.com
SIC: 7011 Hotels
HQ: Six Continents Hotels, Inc.
　3 Ravinia Dr Ste 100
　Atlanta GA 30346
　770 604-2000

(P-13239)
SIX CONTINENTS HOTELS INC
Also Called: Staybridge Suites
1110 A St, San Diego (92101-4732)
PHONE..................619 795-4000
Chris Jones, *Manager*
EMP: 97
SALES (corp-wide): 1.7B **Privately Held**
WEB: www.sixcontinenthotels.com
SIC: 7011 Hotels
HQ: Six Continents Hotels, Inc.
　3 Ravinia Dr Ste 100
　Atlanta GA 30346
　770 604-2000

(P-13240)
SIX CONTINENTS HOTELS INC
Also Called: Holiday Inn
700 National City Blvd, National City
(91950-1124)
PHONE..................619 474-2800
Larry Oneal, *General Mgr*
EMP: 80

SALES (corp-wide): 1.7B **Privately Held**
WEB: www.sixcontinenthotels.com
SIC: 7011 Hotels
HQ: Six Continents Hotels, Inc.
　3 Ravinia Dr Ste 100
　Atlanta GA 30346
　770 604-2000

(P-13241)
SJ HOTEL MANAGER LLC
Also Called: AC Hotel San Jose Downtown
350 W Santa Clara St, San Jose
(95113-1501)
PHONE..................401 946-4600
Elizabeth Procaccianti,
Michelle Joyal, *Administration*
EMP: 75
SALES (est): 1.9MM **Privately Held**
SIC: 7011 Hotels & motels

(P-13242)
SKY COURT USA INC
Also Called: Hyatt Westlake Plaza Hotel
880 S Westlake Blvd, Westlake Village
(91361-2905)
PHONE..................805 497-9991
Tetsuo Nishida, *President*
EMP: 180
SALES (est): 2.6MM **Privately Held**
SIC: 7011 Hotels

(P-13243)
SMITH RIVER LUCKY 7 CASINO
350 N Indian Rd, Smith River
(95567-9474)
PHONE..................707 487-7777
Terry Westrick, *Partner*
EMP: 70 **EST:** 1997
SALES (est): 5.2MM **Privately Held**
SIC: 7011 Casino hotel

(P-13244)
SMOKE TREE INC
Also Called: Smoke Tree Ranch
1850 Smoke Tree Ln, Palm Springs
(92264-1602)
PHONE..................760 327-1221
Lisa Bell, *Manager*
Brad Poncher, *Manager*
EMP: 85 **EST:** 1945
SALES (est): 5.7MM **Privately Held**
WEB: www.smoketreeinc.com
SIC: 7011 Resort hotel

(P-13245)
**SNOW SUMMIT SKI
CORPORATION (PA)**
880 Summit Blvd, Big Bear Lake (92315)
P.O. Box 77 (92315-0077)
PHONE..................909 866-5766
Richard C Kun, *President*
Wade Reeser, *COO*
Robert Tarras, *CFO*
Alan Macquoid, *Treasurer*
Robert Law, *Vice Pres*
EMP: 1000
SQ FT: 10,000
SALES (est): 62.6MM **Privately Held**
WEB: www.bearmtn.com
SIC: 7011 5812 Ski lodge; American
　restaurant

(P-13246)
**SONOMA HOTEL OPERATOR
INC**
Also Called: Fairmont Snoma Mission Inn
Spa
100 Boyes Blvd, Sonoma (95476-3678)
P.O. Box 1447 (95476-1447)
PHONE..................707 938-9000
Rick Corcoran, *General Mgr*
Karen Roenau, *Purch Agent*
Alice Fay, *Sales Mgr*
Michele Kelley, *Sales Mgr*
Chad Mendelman, *Sales Mgr*
EMP: 103 **Privately Held**
WEB: www.cp.ca
SIC: 7011 Hotels
HQ: Sonoma Hotel Operator, Inc.
　50 Rockefeller Plz
　New York NY 10020
　-

(P-13247)
SONOMA HOTEL PARTNERS LP
Also Called: Sheraton Sonoma Cnty
Petaluma
745 Baywood Dr, Petaluma (94954-5388)
PHONE..................707 283-2888
Scott Satterfield, *General Mgr*
EMP: 95
SQ FT: 134,732
SALES (est): 5.9MM **Privately Held**
SIC: 7011 Resort hotel; hotels

(P-13248)
SOULDRIVER LESSEE INC
Also Called: Hotel Solamar
435 6th Ave, San Diego (92101-7007)
PHONE..................619 819-9500
Maria Streedy, *President*
Marissa White, *Office Mgr*
Salvador Rojas, *Chief Engr*
Nina Leung, *Finance*
Alexis Schmidt, *Finance*
EMP: 80
SALES (est): 6.8MM **Privately Held**
SIC: 7011 Hotels

(P-13249)
**SOUTH COAST WESTIN HOTEL
CO**
Also Called: Starwood Hotels & Resorts
686 Anton Blvd, Costa Mesa (92626-1920)
PHONE..................714 540-2500
Steve Heyer, *CEO*
Bob Jenness, *Vice Pres*
Mike Hall, *Managing Dir*
EMP: 99
SALES (est): 7.9MM
SALES (corp-wide): 22.8B **Publicly Held**
SIC: 7011 5812 Hotels; eating places
HQ: Starwood Hotels & Resorts Worldwide,
　Llc
　1 Star Pt
　Stamford CT 06902
　203 964-6000

(P-13250)
SOUTHBOURNE INC
Also Called: Campton Place Hotel
340 Stockton St, San Francisco
(94108-4609)
PHONE..................415 781-5555
Reymond Dixon, *Director*
Maria Conlon, *Administration*
Nieves Trejo, *Chief Engr*
EMP: 131
SALES (est): 5.4MM **Privately Held**
WEB: www.camptonplace.com
SIC: 7011 Hotels
PA: Taj Hotels
　Nandafata Aral Korpana
　Wardha MH

(P-13251)
SPA RESORT CASINO (PA)
401 E Amado Rd, Palm Springs
(92262-6403)
PHONE..................888 999-1995
Kato Moy, *General Mgr*
Agvahgue Eahilla Indian, *Owner*
Steve Burt, *Senior Buyer*
Warren Chard, *Director*
EMP: 1000
SALES (est): 24.7MM **Privately Held**
SIC: 7011 Resort hotel; casino hotel

(P-13252)
SPECTRUM HOTEL GROUP LLC
Also Called: Double Three Htlirvinespectrum
90 Pacifica, Irvine (92618-3312)
PHONE..................949 471-8888
Timothy R Busch,
EMP: 100
SALES (est): 5.1MM **Privately Held**
SIC: 7011 7991 5812 Hotels; physical fit-
　ness facilities; eating places

(P-13253)
SPECTRUM HOTEL GROUP LLC
Also Called: Doubletree Hotel
90 Pacifica, Irvine (92618-3312)
PHONE..................949 471-8888
Tim Busch, *President*
EMP: 100

SALES (est): 2.7MM **Privately Held**
WEB: www.doubletreeirvinespectrum.com
SIC: 7011 7991 5812 Hotels; physical fit-
　ness facilities; eating places

(P-13254)
SPF CAPITAL REAL ESTATE LLC
Also Called: Crown Plaza La Harbor Hotel
601 S Palos Verdes St, San Pedro
(90731-3329)
PHONE..................310 519-8200
Tiegang Yin, *Principal*
Tim Yin, *Principal*
EMP: 99 **EST:** 2017
SALES (est): 651.4K **Privately Held**
SIC: 7011 Hotels

(P-13255)
SPIRE CONCESSIONS LLC
Also Called: Marriott Burbank
2500 N Hollywood Way, Burbank
(91505-1019)
PHONE..................818 843-6000
William Deforrest, *CEO*
William Keating, *President*
Chad Cooley, *Vice Pres*
Russell Flicker, *Vice Pres*
Bernard Michael, *Vice Pres*
EMP: 80
SALES (est): 2.1MM **Privately Held**
SIC: 7011 Hotels

(P-13256)
**SPORTSMENS LODGE HOTEL
LLC**
12825 Ventura Blvd, Studio City
(91604-2397)
PHONE..................818 769-4700
Mark Harlig,
Stephen Chavez, *General Mgr*
Ron Silva, *General Mgr*
Carmen Ruiz, *Technology*
Tiffany Flowers, *Controller*
EMP: 120
SQ FT: 100,000
SALES (est): 5.9MM **Privately Held**
WEB: www.slhotel.com
SIC: 7011 5812 5813 Hotels; American
　restaurant; cocktail lounge

(P-13257)
**SQUAW CREEK ASSOCIATES
LLC**
Also Called: Resort At Squaw Creek
400 Squaw Creek Rd, Alpine Meadows
(96146-9778)
P.O. Box 3333, Olympic Valley (96146-
3333)
PHONE..................530 581-6624
Andrea Baltzegar,
Andre Priemer, *General Mgr*
Eric Sather, *General Mgr*
Terry Ozanich, *Controller*
EMP: 600 **EST:** 1990
SALES (est): 34.9MM **Privately Held**
WEB: www.squawcreek.com
SIC: 7011 Resort hotel

(P-13258)
**SQUAW VALLEY DEVELOPMENT
CO (HQ)**
Also Called: Squaw Valley Ski
1960 Squaw Valley Rd, Olympic Valley
(96146)
P.O. Box 2007 (96146-2007)
PHONE..................530 452-6985
Andrew D Wirth, *CEO*
Lori Pommerenck, *Treasurer*
Megan Hallenberg, *Administration*
Heather Cooley, *Buyer*
Kendra Doyle, *Merchandising*
EMP: 88
SALES (est): 35.9MM **Privately Held**
SIC: 7011 5812 5813 7929 Hostels; ski
　lodge; eating places; bar (drinking
　places); entertainment service

(P-13259)
**SQUAW VALLEY SKI
CORPORATION (DH)**
1960 Squaw Valley Rd, Olympic Valley
(96146)
P.O. Box 2007 (96146-2007)
PHONE..................530 583-6985
Alexander C Cushing, *Ch of Bd*

▲ = Import ▼=Export
◆ =Import/Export

Steve La Grandeur, *President*
Mike Livak, *President*
Nancy R Wendt, *President*
Andy Wirth, *President*
EMP: 107
SQ FT: 200,000
SALES (est): 31.3MM **Privately Held**
SIC: 7011 Ski lodge
HQ: The Squaw Valley Development Company
1960 Squaw Valley Rd
Olympic Valley CA 96146
530 452-6985

(P-13260)
SS HERITAGE INN ONTARIO LLC ✪
3595 E Guasti Rd, Ontario (91761-3705)
PHONE.................................909 937-5000
Aimee Fyke, *Mng Member*
EMP: 99 **EST:** 2018
SALES (est): 597K **Privately Held**
SIC: 7011 Inns

(P-13261)
STANDARD HOLLYWOOD LESSEE LLC
Also Called: Standard Hollywood, The
8300 W Sunset Blvd, Los Angeles
(90069-1516)
PHONE.................................323 822-3102
B Reichelt, *Finance*
Kim Wattsman, *General Mgr*
Brian Reichelt, *Finance*
EMP: 200
SALES (est): 16MM **Privately Held**
SIC: 7011 Hotels & motels

(P-13262)
STANFORD HOTELS CORPORATION
Also Called: Hilton Santa Clara
4949 Great America Pkwy, Santa Clara
(95054-1216)
PHONE.................................408 330-0001
Peter Dolton, *Manager*
EMP: 195 **Privately Held**
SIC: 7011 Hotels
PA: Stanford Hotels Corporation
433 California St Ste 700
San Francisco CA 94104

(P-13263)
STANFORD HOTELS CORPORATION (PA)
433 California St Ste 700, San Francisco
(94104-2011)
PHONE.................................415 398-3333
Lawrence Lui, *President*
James Evans, *CFO*
◆ **EMP:** 50
SQ FT: 12,000
SALES (est): 32.1MM **Privately Held**
WEB: www.sheratonuptown.com
SIC: 7011 Hotels

(P-13264)
STANFORD PARK HOTEL
100 El Camino Real, Menlo Park
(94025-5292)
PHONE.................................650 322-1234
Ellis Alden, *Partner*
Western Lodging Flume Corpor, *Partner*
EMP: 212
SQ FT: 122,000
SALES (est): 11.7MM **Privately Held**
WEB: www.stanfordparkhotel.com
SIC: 7011 5813 5812 Resort hotel; drinking places; eating places

(P-13265)
STARLIGHT MANAGEMENT GROUP
Also Called: Wyndham Garden San Jose Arprt
1355 N 4th St, San Jose (95112-4714)
PHONE.................................408 334-7456
Ajay Shingal, *Vice Pres*
EMP: 99
SALES (est): 3.2MM **Privately Held**
SIC: 7011 Hotels & motels

(P-13266)
STARWOOD HOTEL
Also Called: Starwood Hotels & Resorts
5990 Green Valley Cir, Culver City
(90230-6907)
PHONE.................................310 641-7740
Ian Gee, *Mng Member*
EMP: 60
SALES (est): 3MM
SALES (corp-wide): 22.8B **Publicly Held**
SIC: 7011 Hotels & motels
HQ: Starwood Hotels & Resorts Worldwide, Llc
1 Star Pt
Stamford CT 06902
203 964-6000

(P-13267)
STARWOOD HOTELS & RESORTS
10480 4th St, Rancho Cucamonga
(91730-5893)
PHONE.................................909 484-2018
EMP: 195
SALES (corp-wide): 22.8B **Publicly Held**
SIC: 7011 Hotels & motels
HQ: Starwood Hotels & Resorts Worldwide, Llc
1 Star Pt
Stamford CT 06902
203 964-6000

(P-13268)
STARWOOD HOTELS & RESORTS
1230 J St, Sacramento (95814-2907)
PHONE.................................916 447-1700
EMP: 201
SALES (corp-wide): 22.8B **Publicly Held**
SIC: 7011 Hotels & motels
HQ: Starwood Hotels & Resorts Worldwide, Llc
1 Star Pt
Stamford CT 06902
203 964-6000

(P-13269)
STARWOOD HOTELS & RESORTS
181 3rd St, San Francisco (94103-3107)
PHONE.................................415 777-5300
Toni Knorr, *General Mgr*
EMP: 100
SALES (corp-wide): 22.8B **Publicly Held**
SIC: 7011 Hotel or motel management; casino hotel
HQ: Starwood Hotels & Resorts Worldwide, Llc
1 Star Pt
Stamford CT 06902
203 964-6000

(P-13270)
STARWOOD HOTELS & RESORTS
1010 Northgate Dr, San Rafael
(94903-2502)
PHONE.................................415 479-8800
Susan Bell, *General Mgr*
EMP: 140
SALES (corp-wide): 22.8B **Publicly Held**
SIC: 7011 5812 Hotels & motels; eating places
HQ: Starwood Hotels & Resorts Worldwide, Llc
1 Star Pt
Stamford CT 06902
203 964-6000

(P-13271)
STARWOOD HOTELS & RESORTS
401 E Millbrae Ave, Millbrae (94030-3111)
PHONE.................................650 692-6363
Tim Lucher, *Branch Mgr*
EMP: 99
SALES (corp-wide): 22.8B **Publicly Held**
SIC: 7011 Hotels & motels
HQ: Starwood Hotels & Resorts Worldwide, Llc
1 Star Pt
Stamford CT 06902
203 964-6000

(P-13272)
STARWOOD HOTELS & RESORTS
125 3rd St, San Francisco (94103-3107)
PHONE.................................415 284-4000
Elias Assaly, *Manager*
EMP: 195 **Privately Held**
SIC: 7011 Hotels & motels
HQ: Qatar Investment Authority
Ooredoo Building, P. O. Box 23224
West Bay Area, Diplomatic Stre
Doha
449 959-19

(P-13273)
STARWOOD HOTELS & RESORTS
910 Broadway Cir, San Diego
(92101-6114)
PHONE.................................619 239-2200
Doug Korn, *General Mgr*
EMP: 250
SALES (corp-wide): 22.8B **Publicly Held**
SIC: 7011 7991 6512 5812 Hotels & motels; physical fitness facilities; nonresidential building operators; eating places
HQ: Starwood Hotels & Resorts Worldwide, Llc
1 Star Pt
Stamford CT 06902
203 964-6000

(P-13274)
STARWOOD HTLS & RSRTS WRLDWDE
930 Hilgard Ave, Los Angeles
(90024-3033)
PHONE.................................310 208-8765
Parita Burmee, *Branch Mgr*
EMP: 185
SALES (corp-wide): 22.8B **Publicly Held**
SIC: 7011 Hotels & motels
HQ: Starwood Hotels & Resorts Worldwide, Llc
1 Star Pt
Stamford CT 06902
203 964-6000

(P-13275)
STARWOOD HTLS & RSRTS WRLDWDE
404 S Figueroa St, Los Angeles
(90071-1710)
PHONE.................................213 624-1000
Bryan Fitzgerald, *Manager*
EMP: 810
SALES (corp-wide): 22.8B **Publicly Held**
SIC: 7011 Hotels & motels
HQ: Starwood Hotels & Resorts Worldwide, Llc
1 Star Pt
Stamford CT 06902
203 964-6000

(P-13276)
STARWOOD HTLS & RSRTS WRLDWDE
71333 Dinah Shore Dr, Rancho Mirage
(92270-1501)
PHONE.................................760 328-5955
Ken Pilgrim, *Manager*
Dawn O'Flannery-Cleveland, *Sales Staff*
EMP: 486
SALES (corp-wide): 22.8B **Publicly Held**
SIC: 7011 Hotels & motels
HQ: Starwood Hotels & Resorts Worldwide, Llc
1 Star Pt
Stamford CT 06902
203 964-6000

(P-13277)
STARWOOD HTLS & RSRTS WRLDWDE
125 3rd St, San Francisco (94103-3107)
PHONE.................................415 284-4049
Barry Peterson, *Director*
EMP: 89
SALES (corp-wide): 22.8B **Publicly Held**
SIC: 7011 Hotels & motels

HQ: Starwood Hotels & Resorts Worldwide, Llc
1 Star Pt
Stamford CT 06902
203 964-6000

(P-13278)
STARWOOD HTLS & RSRTS WRLDWDE
2 New Montgomery St, San Francisco
(94105-3402)
PHONE.................................415 512-1111
T Staramelino, *Business Mgr*
EMP: 195
SALES (corp-wide): 22.8B **Publicly Held**
SIC: 7011 Hotels & motels
HQ: Starwood Hotels & Resorts Worldwide, Llc
1 Star Pt
Stamford CT 06902
203 964-6000

(P-13279)
STARWOOD HTLS & RSRTS WRLDWDE
6250 Hollywood Blvd, Los Angeles
(90028-5325)
PHONE.................................323 798-1300
Leon Young, *General Mgr*
EMP: 195
SALES (corp-wide): 22.8B **Publicly Held**
SIC: 7011 Hotels & motels
HQ: Starwood Hotels & Resorts Worldwide, Llc
1 Star Pt
Stamford CT 06902
203 964-6000

(P-13280)
STARWOOD HTLS & RSRTS WRLDWDE
601 W Mckinley Ave, Pomona
(91768-1635)
PHONE.................................909 622-2220
John Gilbert, *General Mgr*
EMP: 195
SALES (corp-wide): 22.8B **Publicly Held**
SIC: 7011 Hotels & motels
HQ: Starwood Hotels & Resorts Worldwide, Llc
1 Star Pt
Stamford CT 06902
203 964-6000

(P-13281)
STARWOOD HTLS & RSRTS WRLDWDE
1617 1st Ave, San Diego (92101-3003)
PHONE.................................619 239-9600
Gary Comeaux, *General Mgr*
EMP: 60
SALES (corp-wide): 22.8B **Publicly Held**
SIC: 7011 Hotels & motels
HQ: Starwood Hotels & Resorts Worldwide, Llc
1 Star Pt
Stamford CT 06902
203 964-6000

(P-13282)
STOCKBRIDGE/SBE HOLDINGS LLC
5900 Wilshire Blvd # 3100, Los Angeles
(90036-5013)
PHONE.................................323 655-8000
Sam Nazarian, *CEO*
EMP: 3000
SALES (est): 61MM **Privately Held**
SIC: 7011 Hotels; casino hotel

(P-13283)
STOCKTON HOTEL LTD
Also Called: Stockton Hilton Hotel
2323 Grand Canal Blvd, Stockton
(95207-6554)
PHONE.................................209 957-9090
Robert Hong, *General Ptnr*
Edward Hazard, *General Ptnr*
Claude Viergutz, *General Mgr*
Lilly McIntyre, *Controller*
EMP: 130
SALES (est): 206K **Privately Held**
SIC: 7011 Hotel, franchised

PRODUCTS & SVCS

(P-13284)
STONEBRIDGE MCWHINNEY LLC
Also Called: Hampton Inn
11747 Harbor Blvd, Garden Grove (92840-2701)
PHONE.....................714 703-8800
Thomas Long, *Manager*
EMP: 50
SALES (corp-wide): 9.7MM **Privately Held**
WEB: www.sleepinnpueblo.com
SIC: 7011 Hotels & motels
PA: Stonebridge Mcwhinney Llc
9100 E Panorama Dr # 300
Englewood CO 80112
303 785-3100

(P-13285)
STRESS RELIEF SERVICES
12603 Mariposa Rd, Victorville (92395-6004)
PHONE.....................760 241-7472
Nicole Williams, *Owner*
EMP: 60
SALES (est): 1.8MM **Privately Held**
SIC: 7011 Hotels

(P-13286)
SUN HILL PROPERTIES INC (HQ)
Also Called: Hilton Los Angls/Nversal Cy Ht
555 Universal Hollywood Dr, Universal City (91608-1001)
PHONE.....................818 506-2500
Denn Hu, *Ch of Bd*
EMP: 350
SALES (est): 19MM
SALES (corp-wide): 13.5MM **Privately Held**
WEB: www.sfbayleasing.com
SIC: 7011 Hotels, franchised
PA: Universal Paragon Corporation
150 Executive Park Blvd # 4000
San Francisco CA 94134
415 468-6676

(P-13287)
SUNNYSIDE RESORT
1850 W Lake Blvd, Tahoe City (96145)
P.O. Box 5969 (96145-5969)
PHONE.....................530 583-7200
Sandy Saxton, *President*
J Robert Thibaut, *Vice Pres*
Don Edelstein, *Human Res Mgr*
David Kim, *Manager*
EMP: 75
SALES (est): 3.6MM **Privately Held**
WEB: www.sunnysideresort.com
SIC: 7011 5812 5813 Resort hotel; American restaurant; bar (drinking places)

(P-13288)
SUNNYVALE SOF-X OWNER L P
Also Called: Sheraton Hotel Sunnyvale
1100 N Mathilda Ave, Sunnyvale (94089-1206)
PHONE.....................408 542-8264
Nick Antonopoulos, *Principal*
Anita Evans, *Principal*
EMP: 50
SQ FT: 120,000
SALES (est): 434K **Privately Held**
SIC: 7011 Seasonal hotel; hotels

(P-13289)
SUNSET TOWER HOTEL LLC
8358 W Sunset Blvd, Los Angeles (90069-1516)
PHONE.....................323 654-7100
E Peter Krulewitch, *Mng Member*
Jeffrey Klein, *Mng Member*
EMP: 52
SALES (est): 5.8MM **Privately Held**
SIC: 7011 Resort hotel; hotels

(P-13290)
SUNSHINE MIDTOWN LLC
Also Called: Radisson Hotel Phoenix Cy Ctr
631 W Katella Ave, Anaheim (92802-3410)
PHONE.....................602 604-4900
Nick Thompson, *General Mgr*
EMP: 50

SALES (est): 1.7MM **Privately Held**
SIC: 7011 7299 Hotels; banquet hall facilities

(P-13291)
SUNSTONE CENTER CRT LESSEE INC
200 Spectrum Center Dr # 21, Irvine (92618-5003)
PHONE.....................949 382-4000
John V Arabia, *CFO*
Lindsay Monge, *Vice Pres*
EMP: 160
SALES (est): 2.2MM
SALES (corp-wide): 1.1B **Publicly Held**
SIC: 7011 5812 5813 Hotels; eating places; drinking places
HQ: Sunstone Hotel Trs Lessee, Inc.
120 Vantis Dr Ste 350
Aliso Viejo CA

(P-13292)
SUNSTONE DURANTE LLC
Also Called: Hilton San Diego/Del Mar
15575 Jimmy Durante Blvd, Del Mar (92014-1901)
PHONE.....................858 792-5200
Scott Sloan, *Mng Member*
Damien Proctor, *Principal*
EMP: 250
SALES (est): 10.1MM **Privately Held**
SIC: 7011 Hotels

(P-13293)
SUNSTONE HOTEL INVESTORS INC
Also Called: Embassy Suites
9801 Airport Blvd, Los Angeles (90045-5407)
PHONE.....................310 215-1000
Phil Campaneli, *Manager*
EMP: 150
SALES (corp-wide): 58.3MM **Privately Held**
WEB: www.sunstonehotels.com
SIC: 7011 Hotels & motels
PA: Sunstone Hotel Investors, L.L.C.
120 Vantis Dr Ste 350
Aliso Viejo CA 92656
949 330-4000

(P-13294)
SUNSTONE HOTEL INVESTORS LLC
Also Called: Holiday Inn
14299 Firestone Blvd, La Mirada (90638-5523)
PHONE.....................714 739-8500
Dalla Rodriguez, *Manager*
EMP: 122 **Privately Held**
WEB: www.sunstonehotels.com
SIC: 7011 6512 5812 Hotels & motels; nonresidential building operators; eating places
HQ: Sunstone Hotel Investors, L.L.C.
120 Vantis Dr Ste 350
Aliso Viejo CA 92656
949 330-4000

(P-13295)
SUNSTONE HOTEL INVESTORS LLC
Also Called: Embassy Suites
39375 5th St W, Palmdale (93551-3886)
PHONE.....................661 267-6587
Randy Keller, *Manager*
EMP: 122
SALES (corp-wide): 58.3MM **Privately Held**
SIC: 7011 Hotels
PA: Sunstone Hotel Investors, L.L.C.
120 Vantis Dr Ste 350
Aliso Viejo CA 92656
949 330-4000

(P-13296)
SUNSTONE HOTEL INVESTORS LLC
2 Civic Plaza Dr, Carson (90745-2231)
PHONE.....................310 830-9200
John Schulv, *General Mgr*
EMP: 75 **Privately Held**
WEB: www.sunstonehotels.com

SIC: 7011 7991 5812 Hotels; physical fitness facilities; eating places
HQ: Sunstone Hotel Investors, L.L.C.
120 Vantis Dr Ste 350
Aliso Viejo CA 92656
949 330-4000

(P-13297)
SUNSTONE HOTEL INVESTORS LLC
Also Called: Holiday Inn
1617 1st Ave Ste 16, San Diego (92101-3003)
PHONE.....................619 239-6171
John Ault, *Manager*
EMP: 65
SALES (corp-wide): 58.3MM **Privately Held**
WEB: www.sunstonehotels.com
SIC: 7011 5812 Hotels; eating places
PA: Sunstone Hotel Investors, L.L.C.
120 Vantis Dr Ste 350
Aliso Viejo CA 92656
949 330-4000

(P-13298)
SUNSTONE HOTEL INVESTORS LLC
Also Called: Marriott
3425 Solano Ave, NAPA (94558-2709)
PHONE.....................707 253-8600
Micheal George, *Opers-Prdtn-Mfg*
EMP: 100 **Privately Held**
WEB: www.sunstonehotels.com
HQ: Sunstone Hotel Investors, L.L.C.
120 Vantis Dr Ste 350
Aliso Viejo CA 92656
949 330-4000

(P-13299)
SUNSTONE HOTEL INVESTORS LLC
Also Called: Hawthorn Suites
1752 S Clementine St, Anaheim (92802-2902)
PHONE.....................714 635-5000
Warren Nocon, *Branch Mgr*
EMP: 122 **Privately Held**
WEB: www.sunstonehotels.com
SIC: 7011 Hotels & motels
HQ: Sunstone Hotel Investors, L.L.C.
120 Vantis Dr Ste 350
Aliso Viejo CA 92656
949 330-4000

(P-13300)
SUNSTONE HOTEL INVESTORS LLC
6161 W Century Blvd, Los Angeles (90045-5310)
PHONE.....................310 649-1400
Connie White, *Mng Member*
Suthikiati Chirathivat, *President*
EMP: 122 **Privately Held**
WEB: www.sunstonehotels.com
SIC: 7011 Hotels & motels
HQ: Sunstone Hotel Investors, L.L.C.
120 Vantis Dr Ste 350
Aliso Viejo CA 92656
949 330-4000

(P-13301)
SUNSTONE HOTEL MANAGEMENT INC
Also Called: Marriott
3400 Market St, Riverside (92501-2826)
PHONE.....................951 784-8000
Tom Donahue, *Manager*
EMP: 200
SALES (corp-wide): 38.4MM **Privately Held**
WEB: www.sunstoneshopper.com
SIC: 7011 Hotels & motels
PA: Sunstone Hotel Management Inc
120 Vantis Dr Ste 350
Aliso Viejo CA 92656
949 297-4183

(P-13302)
SUNSTONE HOTEL MANAGEMENT INC (PA)
120 Vantis Dr Ste 350, Aliso Viejo (92656-2686)
PHONE.....................949 297-4183

Robert A Alter, *CEO*
Jon D Cline, *CFO*
Jill Johnson, *VP Human Res*
Dan Engle, *VP Sales*
EMP: 50
SQ FT: 1,200
SALES (est): 38.4MM **Privately Held**
WEB: www.sunstoneshopper.com
SIC: 7011 Hotels

(P-13303)
SUNSTONE HOTEL PROPERTIES INC
Also Called: Residence Inn By Marriott
1177 S Beverly Dr, Los Angeles (90035-1119)
PHONE.....................310 228-4100
Tom Beedon, *General Mgr*
EMP: 79 **Privately Held**
WEB: www.sunstonehotelproperties.com
SIC: 7011 Hotels & motels
HQ: Sunstone Hotel Properties Inc
120 Vantis Dr Ste 350
Aliso Viejo CA 92656

(P-13304)
SUNSTONE HOTEL PROPERTIES INC
Also Called: Residence Inn By Marriott
1700 N Sepulveda Blvd, Manhattan Beach (90266-5015)
PHONE.....................310 546-7627
Sandi Rae Kraft, *Branch Mgr*
EMP: 79 **Privately Held**
WEB: www.sunstonehotelproperties.com
SIC: 7011 Hotels & motels
HQ: Sunstone Hotel Properties Inc
120 Vantis Dr Ste 350
Aliso Viejo CA 92656

(P-13305)
SUNSTONE HOTEL PROPERTIES INC (DH)
Also Called: Hampton Inn
120 Vantis Dr Ste 350, Aliso Viejo (92656-2686)
PHONE.....................949 330-4000
Arthur Buser, *President*
EMP: 120
SALES (est): 111.8MM **Privately Held**
WEB: www.sunstonehotelproperties.com
SIC: 7011 Hotels & motels
HQ: Interstate Hotels & Resorts, Inc.
4501 Fairfax Dr Ste 500
Arlington VA 22203
703 387-3100

(P-13306)
SUNSTONE OCEAN LESSEE INC
200 Spectrum Center Dr # 21, Irvine (92618-5003)
PHONE.....................949 382-4000
John V Arabia, *CFO*
Lindsay Monge, *Treasurer*
Juan Lomeli, *Info Tech Mgr*
Judith Morgan, *Controller*
EMP: 275
SQ FT: 302,000
SALES (est): 5.2MM
SALES (corp-wide): 1.1B **Publicly Held**
SIC: 7011 Hotels & motels
HQ: Sunstone Hotel Trs Lessee, Inc.
120 Vantis Dr Ste 350
Aliso Viejo CA

(P-13307)
SUNSTONE TOP GUN LLC
Also Called: Embassy Stes San Dego-La Jolla
4550 La Jolla Village Dr, San Diego (92122-1248)
PHONE.....................858 453-0400
Sunstone Holdco,
EMP: 100
SALES (est): 2.4MM
SALES (corp-wide): 1.1B **Publicly Held**
SIC: 7011 Hotels
HQ: Sunstone Hotel Partnership, Llc
120 Vantis Dr Ste 350
Aliso Viejo CA 92656

▲ = Import ▼=Export
◆ =Import/Export

(P-13308)
SUNSTONE TOP GUN LESSEE INC
Also Called: Embassy Suites By Hilton San
4550 La Jolla Village Dr, San Diego
(92122-1248)
PHONE....................................949 330-4000
Kenneth E Cruse, *CEO*
John V Arabia, *CFO*
Lindsay Monge, *Treasurer*
EMP: 150 EST: 2006
SALES (est): 202.8K
SALES (corp-wide): 1.1B **Publicly Held**
SIC: 7011 Hotels & motels
HQ: Sunstone Hotel Trs Lessee, Inc.
120 Vantis Dr Ste 350
Aliso Viejo CA
-

(P-13309)
SVI LAX LLC
Also Called: Residence Inn By Marriot Lax/C
5933 W Century Blvd, Los Angeles
(90045-5471)
PHONE....................................310 281-0300
Robert A Alter,
EMP: 60
SQ FT: 213,000
SALES: 12MM **Privately Held**
SIC: 7011 Inns

(P-13310)
SWISS HOTEL GROUP INC
18 W Spain St, Sonoma (95476-5601)
PHONE....................................707 938-2884
Henry Marioni, *President*
EMP: 60 EST: 1929
SQ FT: 6,350
SALES: 2.3MM **Privately Held**
WEB: www.swisshotelsonoma.com
SIC: 7011 5813 5812 Hotels; bar (drinking places); steak restaurant

(P-13311)
SWVP DEL MAR HOTEL LLC
Also Called: DoubleTree by Hilton
11915 El Camino Real, San Diego
(92130-2539)
PHONE....................................858 481-5900
Tom Donahue, *Manager*
Kristina Grijalva, *Controller*
EMP: 120 EST: 2005
SALES (est): 5.4MM **Privately Held**
SIC: 7011 Hotels

(P-13312)
SWVP WESTLAKE LLC
Also Called: Hyatt Hotel
880 S Westlake Blvd, Westlake Village
(91361-2905)
PHONE....................................805 557-1234
David Coonan, *General Mgr*
EMP: 250
SALES (corp-wide): 2.9MM **Privately Held**
WEB: www.hyatt.com
SIC: 7011 5812 5813 Hotels; eating places; drinking places
PA: Swvp Westlake Llc
12790 El Camino Real
San Diego CA 92130
858 480-2900

(P-13313)
SYCAMORE MINERAL SPRING RESORT
1215 Avila Beach Dr, San Luis Obispo
(93405-8048)
PHONE....................................805 595-7302
Russell Kiessig, *President*
John King, *President*
Steve Gregory, *Vice Pres*
Charles Yates, *Vice Pres*
EMP: 65
SQ FT: 36,150
SALES (est): 2.9MM **Privately Held**
WEB: www.smsr.com
SIC: 7011 7991 Resort hotel; spas

(P-13314)
SYDELL HOTELS LLC
Also Called: Line Hotel, The
3515 Wilshire Blvd, Los Angeles
(90010-2301)
PHONE....................................213 381-7411

Doug Elpern,
Nahal Khatami,
Stephanie Saik, *Human Res Dir*
Holly Erker, *Sales Staff*
Courtney Kraushaar, *Sales Staff*
EMP: 130
SALES (est): 10.3MM
SALES (corp-wide): 22.5MM **Privately Held**
SIC: 7011 Resort hotel
PA: Sydell Group Llc
30 W 26th St Fl 12
New York NY 10010
646 810-0208

(P-13315)
T I C HOTELS INC
Also Called: Best Western Bayside Inn
555 W Ash St, San Diego (92101-3414)
PHONE....................................619 238-7577
Tracey Wicken, *General Mgr*
EMP: 55 **Privately Held**
WEB: www.tichotels.com
SIC: 7011 Hotels
HQ: T I C Hotels Inc
1811 State St Ste C
Santa Barbara CA 93101
805 898-0855

(P-13316)
T I C HOTELS INC
Also Called: Shorecliff Properties
2555 Price St, Pismo Beach (93449-2111)
PHONE....................................805 773-4671
Edward Brown, *Systems Mgr*
Barbara Parra, *General Mgr*
Karen Fyfe, *Human Res Dir*
Sandy Wirick, *Sales Executive*
EMP: 100 **Privately Held**
WEB: www.tichotels.com
SIC: 7011 5812 5813 Hotels; eating places; bar (drinking places)
HQ: T I C Hotels Inc
1811 State St Ste C
Santa Barbara CA 93101
805 898-0855

(P-13317)
T M MIAN & ASSOCIATES INC
Also Called: Hilton Garden Inn Calabasas
24150 Park Sorrento, Calabasas
(91302-4101)
PHONE....................................818 591-2300
Shawn Nicoles, *General Mgr*
EMP: 73
SALES (corp-wide): 4.6MM **Privately Held**
SIC: 7011 Hotel, franchised
PA: T. M. Mian & Associates, Inc.
1055 Regal Row
Dallas TX 75247
972 960-2024

(P-13318)
T M MIAN & ASSOCIATES INC
Also Called: Hilton
2000 Solar Dr, Oxnard (93036-2694)
PHONE....................................805 983-8600
T M Mian, *Partner*
Dolores Licon, *Info Tech Mgr*
EMP: 52
SALES (corp-wide): 4.6MM **Privately Held**
SIC: 7011 Hotel, franchised
PA: T. M. Mian & Associates, Inc.
1055 Regal Row
Dallas TX 75247
972 960-2024

(P-13319)
T-12 THREE LLC
Also Called: Hard Rock Hotel
207 5th Ave, San Diego (92101-6908)
PHONE....................................619 702-3000
Nilesh Madhav, *Mng Member*
Matt Greene, *General Mgr*
Brent Takeymia, *Info Tech Mgr*
Mark Andrews, *Engineer*
Burt Sharpe, *Chief Engr*
EMP: 356
SALES (est): 23.9MM **Privately Held**
SIC: 7011 Hotels

(P-13320)
TABLE MOUNTAIN CASINO
8184 Table Mountain Rd, Friant (93626)
P.O. Box 445 (93626-0445)
PHONE....................................559 822-7777
Frances Dandy, *Senior VP*
Ted Thay, *COO*
Troy Benne, *CFO*
Ricardo Nunez, *Executive*
Rick Peterson, *Engineer*
EMP: 1000
SQ FT: 30,000
SALES (est): 51.4MM **Privately Held**
WEB: www.tmcasino.com
SIC: 7011 Casino hotel

(P-13321)
TACHI PALACE HOTEL & CASINO
17225 Jersey Ave, Lemoore (93245-9760)
PHONE....................................559 924-7751
Tachi Yokut, *Owner*
Santa Yokut, *Owner*
Richard Laudale, *CFO*
Kelly Reinhart, *Officer*
Sharon Yarber, *Vice Pres*
EMP: 1500
SALES (est): 59.5MM **Privately Held**
SIC: 7011 Casino hotel

(P-13322)
TAHOE BEACH & SKI CLUB
3601 Lake Tahoe Blvd, South Lake Tahoe
(96150-8915)
PHONE....................................530 541-6220
Roy Fraser, *President*
Tamara Hollingsworth, *Manager*
EMP: 60
SALES (est): 2.9MM **Privately Held**
WEB: www.tahoebeachandski.com
SIC: 7011 6513 Resort hotel; apartment hotel operation

(P-13323)
TERRE DU SOLEIL LTD
Also Called: Auberge Du Soleil
180 Rutherford Hill Rd, Rutherford (94573)
P.O. Box B (94573-0902)
PHONE....................................707 963-1211
George Goeggel, *General Ptnr*
Robert Harmon, *General Ptnr*
Bradley Reynolds, *General Ptnr*
Claude Rouas, *General Ptnr*
Paul Lemieux, *Executive*
EMP: 280
SQ FT: 20,000
SALES (est): 18.4MM **Privately Held**
WEB: www.aubergedusoleil.com
SIC: 7011 5812 Resort hotel; French restaurant

(P-13324)
TESI INVESTMENT COMPANY LLC
Also Called: Best Western Pasada At Harbor
5005 N Harbor Dr, San Diego
(92106-2307)
PHONE....................................619 224-3254
Jorge Mendoza, *Mng Member*
Octavio Terrazas Jr, *President*
EMP: 60
SQ FT: 9,825
SALES (est): 1.8MM **Privately Held**
SIC: 7011 Hotels

(P-13325)
THOMAS EDWARD COMPANIES (PA)
9950 Santa Monica Blvd, Beverly Hills
(90212-1607)
PHONE....................................310 859-9366
Edward Slatkin, *Partner*
Thomas Slatkin, *Partner*
James Barela, *General Mgr*
Fran Fkuebler, *Office Mgr*
Jon Andera, *VP Finance*
EMP: 116
SQ FT: 1,000
SALES (est): 3.6MM **Privately Held**
WEB: www.jollyrogerhotel.com
SIC: 7011 Hotels & motels

(P-13326)
TIBURON HOTEL LLC
Also Called: Lodge At Tiburon, The
1651 Tiburon Blvd, Belvedere Tiburon
(94920-2511)
PHONE....................................415 435-5996
Mike Schuminsky, *Mng Member*
Eric Halliday, *General Mgr*
EMP: 77
SALES (est): 4.3MM **Privately Held**
SIC: 7011 7389 Hotels; office facilities & secretarial service rental

(P-13327)
TIC HOTELS INC
Also Called: Tic Worldwide
555 W Ash St, San Diego (92101-3414)
PHONE....................................619 238-7577
M Gardacio, *Vice Pres*
Suzy Briggs, *Corp Secy*
Tracy Wickens, *Sales Mgr*
T I C Hotels,
EMP: 50
SALES (est): 1MM **Privately Held**
SIC: 7011 Resort hotel

(P-13328)
TIC WORLD-WIDE CORP
Also Called: Best Western
555 W Ash St, San Diego (92101-3414)
PHONE....................................619 233-7500
Mamo Takeuchi, *President*
EMP: 55
SQ FT: 67,381
SALES (est): 3.7MM **Privately Held**
WEB: www.baysideinn.com
SIC: 7011 Hotels & motels

(P-13329)
TIDES CENTER
124 Turk St, San Francisco (94102-3926)
PHONE....................................415 359-9401
EMP: 178 **Privately Held**
SIC: 7011 Hotels & motels
PA: The Tides Center
The Prsdio 1014 Trney Ave
San Francisco CA 94129

(P-13330)
TODAYS HOTEL CORPORATION (PA)
Also Called: Holiday Inn
1500 Van Ness Ave, San Francisco
(94109-4606)
PHONE....................................415 441-4000
Ming Nin Zen, *President*
EMP: 109
SALES (est): 52.3MM **Privately Held**
WEB: www.goldengatewayhotel.com
SIC: 7011 Hotels

(P-13331)
TODAYS VI LLC
Also Called: Amerisuites
4760 Mills Cir, Ontario (91764-5223)
PHONE....................................909 980-2200
Peter Zen,
Paul Zen,
EMP: 60
SALES (est): 1.3MM **Privately Held**
SIC: 7011 Hotels & motels

(P-13332)
TORRES-MARTINEZ
Also Called: Red Earth Casino
3089 Norm Niver Rd, Thermal
(92274-6550)
PHONE....................................760 395-1200
David Seufert, *Branch Mgr*
EMP: 150 **Privately Held**
SIC: 7011 Casino hotel
PA: Torres-Martinez Desert Cahuilla Indians
66725 Martinez Rd
Thermal CA 92274
760 397-0300

(P-13333)
TORREYANA GRILLE
Also Called: Hilton
10950 N Torrey Pines Rd, La Jolla
(92037-1006)
PHONE....................................858 558-1500
Patrick Duffy, *President*
Naomi Higgins, *Director*

EMP: 60 EST: 2002
SALES (est): 3.6MM Privately Held
SIC: 7011 5812 Hotels & motels; grills (eating places)

(P-13334)
TOWNEPLACE SUITES
Also Called: TownePlace Suites By Marriott
700 E Campbell Ave, Campbell (95008-2104)
PHONE..................408 370-4510
Elece Otten, Owner
EMP: 80
SALES (est): 1.7MM Privately Held
SIC: 7011 Hotel, franchised

(P-13335)
TPG LA COMMERCE LLC
Also Called: Doubletree By Hilton La - Com
5757 Telegraph Rd, Commerce (90040-1513)
PHONE..................401 946-4600
Elizabeth Procaccianti,
Michelle Joyal, Administration
Guus Heijmans, Accountant
EMP: 100
SALES (est): 873.7K Privately Held
SIC: 7011 Resort hotel, franchised

(P-13336)
TR BIG SUR MANAGEMENT LLC
48123 Highway 1, Big Sur (93920-9538)
PHONE..................831 667-4212
Thomas Becker, Director
EMP: 50
SALES (est): 184.9K Privately Held
SIC: 7011 Resort hotel

(P-13337)
TR WARNER CENTER LP
Also Called: Warner Center Marriott Hotel
21850 Oxnard St, Woodland Hills (91367-3631)
PHONE..................818 887-4800
Clay Andrews, General Mgr
Jeff Nolte, Sales Staff
EMP: 300
SQ FT: 500,000
SALES (est): 10.2MM Privately Held
SIC: 7011 Hotels

(P-13338)
TRADEWINDS LODGE (PA)
Also Called: Cliff House Restaurant
400 S Main St, Fort Bragg (95437-4806)
PHONE..................707 964-4761
Dominic Affinito, Partner
EMP: 100
SQ FT: 19,000
SALES (est): 5MM Privately Held
SIC: 7011 5812 5813 6512 Motels; restaurant, family: independent; seafood restaurants; bars & lounges; commercial & industrial building operation; land subdividers & developers, commercial; land subdividers & developers, residential

(P-13339)
TRADEWINDS PARTNERSHIP
Also Called: Tradewinds Lodge Partnership
2920 Arden Way Ste F1, Sacramento (95825-1393)
PHONE..................916 333-5239
Michelle V Affinito, Partner
Michelle Affinito, CFO
EMP: 60
SALES (est): 950K Privately Held
SIC: 7011 1531 Hotels & motels; operative builders

(P-13340)
TRCF REDONDO LLC
Also Called: Homewood Suites Redondo
2430 Marine Ave, Redondo Beach (90278-1103)
PHONE..................310 536-1209
Brad Wagstaff, Manager
EMP: 50
SALES (est): 184.9K Privately Held
SIC: 7011 Hotels & motels

(P-13341)
TREVI PARTNERS A CALIF LP
Also Called: Tollhouse Hotel
140 S Santa Cruz Ave, Los Gatos (95030-6702)
PHONE..................408 395-7070
Marie Tallman, Manager
Amy Sands, Sales Mgr
EMP: 88 Privately Held
WEB: www.marinholidayinnexpress.com
SIC: 7011 5812 Hotels; eating places
HQ: Trevi Partners, A Calif. L.P.
6680 Regional St
Dublin CA 94568
925 828-7750

(P-13342)
TREVI PARTNERS A CALIF LP (HQ)
Also Called: Holiday Inn
6680 Regional St, Dublin (94568-2916)
PHONE..................925 828-7750
Micheal McDavid, General Mgr
EMP: 62
SALES (est): 15.8MM Privately Held
WEB: www.marinholidayinnexpress.com
SIC: 7011 Hotels & motels

(P-13343)
TREVI PARTNERS A CALIF LP
Also Called: Best Wstn Carmel Mission Inn
3665 Rio Rd, Carmel (93923-8609)
PHONE..................831 624-1841
Jose Cortega, Manager
EMP: 76 Privately Held
WEB: www.marinholidayinnexpress.com
SIC: 7011 Hotels
HQ: Trevi Partners, A Calif. L.P.
6680 Regional St
Dublin CA 94568
925 828-7750

(P-13344)
TREVI PARTNERS A CALIF LP (PA)
5955 Coronado Ln, Pleasanton (94588-8518)
PHONE..................925 225-4000
Michael Madden, Partner
EMP: 120
SALES (est): 15.8MM Privately Held
SIC: 7011 Hotels & motels

(P-13345)
TRI-STAR CCW MANAGEMENT L P
Also Called: Doubletree Hotel-Lax
1985 E Grand Ave, El Segundo (90245-5015)
PHONE..................310 322-0999
Harry Wu, Partner
Norman Chang, Partner
Shau An Chen, Partner
EMP: 99
SALES (est): 2.3MM Privately Held
SIC: 7011 Hotels

(P-13346)
TRIGILD INTERNATIONAL INC
Also Called: Ramada Inn
2151 Hotel Cir S, San Diego (92108-3314)
PHONE..................619 291-6500
EMP: 80
SALES (corp-wide): 36.7MM Privately Held
SIC: 7011
PA: Trigild International, Inc.
3323 Carmel Mountain Rd # 2
San Diego CA 92121
858 720-6700

(P-13347)
TUCSON HOTELS LP
Also Called: Holiday Inn
1800 Powell St, Oakland (94608-1808)
PHONE..................510 658-9300
Pat Goss, Manager
EMP: 300 Privately Held
WEB: www.embassysuitesoutdoorworld.com
SIC: 7011 5813 5812 7991 Hotels; motels; drinking places; eating places; physical fitness facilities

PA: Tucson Hotels Lp
2711 Centerville Rd # 400
Wilmington DE 19808

(P-13348)
TUCSON HOTELS LP
Also Called: Holiday Inn
300 J St, Sacramento (95814-2210)
PHONE..................916 446-0100
Liz Tavernese, Manager
EMP: 165 Privately Held
WEB: www.holidayinnportland.com
SIC: 7011 5812 5813 Hotels; restaurant, family: independent; bar (drinking places)
PA: Tucson Hotels Lp
2711 Centerville Rd # 400
Wilmington DE 19808

(P-13349)
TUCSON HOTELS LP
Also Called: Holiday Inn
300 J St, Sacramento (95814-2210)
PHONE..................916 446-0100
Liz Tavernese, Manager
EMP: 153 Privately Held
SIC: 7011 Hotels & motels
PA: Tucson Hotels Lp
2711 Centerville Rd # 400
Wilmington DE 19808

(P-13350)
TUCSON HOTELS LP
Also Called: Embassy Stes Monterey Bay Htl
1441 Canyon Del Rey Blvd, Seaside (93955-4729)
PHONE..................831 393-1115
Rick Weichert, Manager
Rob Lettman, Train & Dev Mgr
Andrea Jackson, Manager
EMP: 156 Privately Held
WEB: www.holidayinnportland.com
SIC: 7011 5813 5812 Hotels & motels; drinking places; eating places
PA: Tucson Hotels Lp
2711 Centerville Rd # 400
Wilmington DE 19808

(P-13351)
TYME MAIDU TRIBE-BERRY CREEK
Also Called: Gold Country Casino
4020 Olive Hwy, Oroville (95966-5527)
PHONE..................530 538-4560
Jim E Tribal, CEO
Leatha C Tribal, Treasurer
Jeff Fields, Officer
Grant Townsend, Vice Pres
Debra A Tribal, Vice Pres
EMP: 519
SALES (est): 32.9MM Privately Held
WEB: www.goldcountrycasino.com
SIC: 7011 Casino hotel

(P-13352)
UKA LLC
Also Called: Tarsadia Hotels
620 Newport Center Dr # 1400, Newport Beach (92660-8025)
PHONE..................949 610-8000
B U Patel, Mng Member
Pushpa Patel,
EMP: 50
SQ FT: 12,000
SALES (est): 466.2K Privately Held
SIC: 7011 Hotels

(P-13353)
UNITED AUBURN INDIAN COMMUNITY
Also Called: Thunder Valley Casino
1200 Athens Ave, Lincoln (95648-9328)
PHONE..................916 408-7777
Scott Garawitz, Branch Mgr
Michael Kuhn, President
Nancy Yang, President
Sean Dunne, Officer
Todd Deremer, Vice Pres
EMP: 1963 Privately Held
WEB: www.thundervalleyresort.com
SIC: 7011 Casino hotel

PA: United Auburn Indian Community
10720 Indian Hill Rd
Auburn CA 95603

(P-13354)
UNIVERSAL PARAGON CORPORATION (PA)
150 Executive Park Blvd # 4000, San Francisco (94134-3319)
PHONE..................415 468-6676
Denn Hu, Ch of Bd
EMP: 370
SQ FT: 200,000
SALES (est): 13.5MM Privately Held
WEB: www.sfbayleasing.com
SIC: 7011 6512 6552 Hotels; commercial & industrial building operation; land subdividers & developers, residential; land subdividers & developers, commercial

(P-13355)
UNIWELL CORPORATION
Also Called: Holiday Inn
7000 Beach Blvd, Buena Park (90620-1832)
PHONE..................714 522-7000
Tracy Myer, Branch Mgr
Sidney Chan, President
Elaine Chan, President
Teddy Katuari, Principal
EMP: 150
SALES (corp-wide): 28.3MM Privately Held
WEB: www.uniwell.com
SIC: 7011 5813 5812 Hotels; drinking places; eating places
PA: Uniwell Corporation
21172 Figueroa St
Carson CA 90745
310 782-8888

(P-13356)
UNIWELL FRESNO HOTEL LLC
Also Called: Doubletree By Hilton Fresno
2233 Ventura St, Fresno (93721-2915)
PHONE..................559 268-1000
Steve Klein,
Kristine Bacon, Manager
Kris Doyle, Manager
EMP: 100
SALES (est): 8.4MM Privately Held
SIC: 7011 Hotels

(P-13357)
UPHAM HOTEL
1404 De La Vina St # 93101, Santa Barbara (93101-3057)
PHONE..................805 962-0058
Carl Johnson, Owner
Jan Winn, General Mgr
EMP: 50
SALES (est): 1.3MM Privately Held
WEB: www.uphamhotel.com
SIC: 7011 Resort hotel

(P-13358)
URBAN COMMONS QUEENSWAY LLC
Also Called: Queen Mary, The
1126 Queens Hwy, Long Beach (90802-6331)
PHONE..................562 499-1611
Christopher Otamias,
EMP: 900 EST: 2016
SALES (est): 1.3MM Privately Held
SIC: 7011 Hotels

(P-13359)
US GRANT HOTEL VENTURES LLC
326 Broadway, San Diego (92101-4800)
PHONE..................619 744-2007
Daniel Tucker,
EMP: 80
SQ FT: 99,999
SALES (est): 7.2MM Privately Held
SIC: 7011 Resort hotel; hotels

(P-13360)
US HOTEL AND RESORT MGT INC
Also Called: Regency Inn
2544 Newport Blvd, Costa Mesa
(92627-1331)
PHONE......................949 650-2988
Peggy Chen, *Manager*
EMP: 83
SALES (corp-wide): 29MM **Privately Held**
WEB: www.regency-mgmt.com
SIC: 7011 Hotels
HQ: U.S. Hotel And Resort Management, Inc.
3211 W Sencore Dr
Sioux Falls SD 57107
605 334-2371

(P-13361)
V I P ASSOCIATES INC (PA)
Also Called: Comfort Inn
470 Camino El Estero, Monterey
(93940-3032)
PHONE......................831 646-1549
Chandrakant Patel, *President*
EMP: 50
SQ FT: 1,000
SALES (est): 856.1K **Privately Held**
WEB: www.stayatmonterey.com
SIC: 7011 5812 Hotel, franchised; fast-food restaurant, chain

(P-13362)
VAGABOND INN CORPORATION (HQ)
2361 Rosecrans Ave # 150, El Segundo
(90245-7906)
P.O. Box 3455 (90245-8591)
PHONE......................213 284-7533
Juan Llaca, *CEO*
Cindy Liao, *Marketing Staff*
EMP: 51
SALES (est): 9.6MM
SALES (corp-wide): 13.9MM **Privately Held**
SIC: 7011 Motels
PA: Vista Investments, Llc
2225 Campus Dr
El Segundo CA 90245
310 725-8200

(P-13363)
VALADON HOTEL LLC
Also Called: Petit Ermitage
8822 Cynthia St, West Hollywood
(90069-4502)
PHONE......................310 854-1114
Stefan Ashkenazy,
Leticia Guadian, *Hum Res Coord*
Adrian Ashkenazy,
Nancy Riese, *Director*
EMP: 80
SQ FT: 40,000
SALES (est): 7MM **Privately Held**
WEB: www.valadonhotel.com
SIC: 7011 Hotels

(P-13364)
VAN NESS HOTEL INC
1050 Van Ness Ave, San Francisco
(94109-6934)
PHONE......................415 673-4711
John M Scheurer, *President*
EMP: 90
SALES (est): 2.4MM **Privately Held**
SIC: 7011 Hotels

(P-13365)
VENTU PARK LLC
Also Called: Palm Garden Hotel
495 N Ventu Park Rd, Thousand Oaks
(91320-2707)
PHONE......................805 716-4200
Bob Zonitch, *Principal*
Michael Garik, *Principal*
Dave Warner, *Principal*
EMP: 70
SALES (est): 4MM **Privately Held**
SIC: 7011 Hotels

(P-13366)
VENTURA HSPTALITY PARTNERS LLC
Also Called: Crowne Plaza Ventura Beach
450 Harbor Blvd, Ventura (93001-2708)
PHONE......................805 648-2100
David Storm,
Akemi Shapiro, *Social Dir*
Molla Rosenberg, *Sales Mgr*
Julie Gonzalez, *Sales Staff*
Jodi Wagner, *Director*
EMP: 140
SQ FT: 143,000
SALES (est): 10MM **Privately Held**
SIC: 7011 Hotels

(P-13367)
VERASA MANAGEMENT LLC
1314 Mckinstry St, NAPA (94559-1900)
PHONE......................707 257-1800
Stewart Andersen, *Mng Member*
EMP: 94 EST: 2010
SALES (est): 3MM **Privately Held**
SIC: 7011 Hotels

(P-13368)
VICTORVLLE TRSURE HOLDINGS LLC
Also Called: Holiday Inn
15494 Palmdale Rd, Victorville
(92392-2408)
PHONE......................760 245-6565
Benjamin Gonzales, *General Mgr*
Jane Battle, *Supervisor*
EMP: 75
SALES (est): 796K **Privately Held**
SIC: 7011 5812 Hotels; American restaurant

(P-13369)
VINTNERS INN
4350 Barnes Rd, Santa Rosa
(95403-1514)
PHONE......................707 575-7350
Donald Carano,
Elena Reynoso, *Sales Staff*
EMP: 100
SQ FT: 30,670
SALES: 3.9MM **Privately Held**
WEB: www.vintnersinn.com
SIC: 7011 Motels; inns

(P-13370)
VISCAMAR LLC
Also Called: Presidian Hotel
300 S Court St, Visalia (93291-6214)
PHONE......................559 636-1111
H Drake Leddy,
EMP: 91
SQ FT: 134,055
SALES (est): 2.5MM **Privately Held**
SIC: 7011 Hotels

(P-13371)
VWI CONCORD LLC
Also Called: Hilton Concord
1970 Diamond Blvd, Concord
(94520-5718)
PHONE......................925 827-2000
Jack Hlavac, *General Mgr*
Jim Dunbar, *Officer*
EMP: 130
SALES (est): 9.7MM **Privately Held**
SIC: 7011 Hotels

(P-13372)
W LOS ANGELES
Also Called: Westwood Marquis Hotel & Grdns
930 Hilgard Ave, Los Angeles
(90024-3033)
P.O. Box 14029, Scottsdale AZ (85267-4029)
PHONE......................310 208-8765
George I Rosenthal, *President*
Mark Rosenthal, *COO*
Anil Sharma, *CFO*
Angela Baker, *Manager*
EMP: 330
SALES (est): 11MM
SALES (corp-wide): 41.4MM **Privately Held**
WEB: www.raleighenterprises.com
SIC: 7011 Resort hotel; hotels

PA: Raleigh Enterprises, Inc.
5300 Melrose Ave Fl 4
Los Angeles CA 90038
310 899-8900

(P-13373)
W-BEL AGE LLC
1020 N San Vicente Blvd, West Hollywood
(90069-3802)
PHONE......................310 854-1111
Laura Bell, *Principal*
EMP: 99
SALES (est): 875.8K **Privately Held**
SIC: 7011 Hotels & motels

(P-13374)
W-EMERALD LLC
Also Called: Westin San Diego
400 W Broadway, San Diego (92101-3504)
PHONE......................619 239-4500
John Beaton, *General Mgr*
EMP: 230
SQ FT: 99,999
SALES (est): 5.1MM **Privately Held**
SIC: 7011 Hotels

(P-13375)
W2005 NEW CNTURY HT PRTFLIO LP
Also Called: Sheraton Hotel Sunnyvale
1100 N Mathilda Ave, Sunnyvale
(94089-1206)
PHONE......................408 745-6000
Epenesa Pakola, *Manager*
EMP: 53 **Privately Held**
WEB: www.hicrystallake.com
SIC: 7011 Hotels & motels
PA: W2005 New Century Hotel Portfolio, L.P.
6011 Connection Dr
Irving TX 75039

(P-13376)
W2005 WYN HOTELS LP
Also Called: Doubletree Hotel
5757 Telegraph Rd, Commerce
(90040-1513)
PHONE......................323 887-8100
Steve Barick, *COO*
EMP: 81 EST: 1991
SALES (est): 4.2MM **Privately Held**
SIC: 7011 Hotels

(P-13377)
WALT DISNEY COMPANY
Also Called: Disneyland
1598 S Harbor Blvd, Anaheim
(92802-2312)
PHONE......................714 781-4278
Ed Greier, *Branch Mgr*
EMP: 170 **Publicly Held**
SIC: 7011 Resort hotel
PA: The Walt Disney Company
500 S Buena Vista St
Burbank CA 91521

(P-13378)
WALTERS FAMILY PARTNERSHIP
Also Called: Hilton Resort In Palm Spring
400 E Tahquitz Canyon Way, Palm Springs
(92262-6605)
PHONE......................760 320-6868
Lance Walters, *Partner*
EMP: 150
SQ FT: 200,000
SALES (est): 7.9MM **Privately Held**
SIC: 7011 5813 5812 Hotels; drinking places; eating places

(P-13379)
WARWICK CALIFORNIA CORPORATION
Also Called: Warwick Hotel San Francisco
490 Geary St, San Francisco (94102-1223)
PHONE......................415 992-3809
Richard Chiu, *President*
Joseph Tung, *Vice Pres*
EMP: 60
SQ FT: 23,386

SALES (est): 2.4MM **Privately Held**
WEB: www.warwicksf.com
SIC: 7011 7299 Hotels; banquet hall facilities
PA: Warwick Holdings Sa
Rue Eugene Ruppert 6
Luxembourg

(P-13380)
WASHINGTON INN LLC
Also Called: Holiday Inn
737 Washington Blvd, Marina Del Rey
(90292-5542)
PHONE......................310 821-4455
John Mathews,
Doug Pflumer, *General Mgr*
EMP: 80
SALES (est): 2.2MM **Privately Held**
SIC: 7011 Hotels & motels

(P-13381)
WATERFALL RESORT
5951 Encina Rd Ste 207, Goleta
(93117-6252)
PHONE......................805 879-3780
Chuck Beard, *Director*
EMP: 100
SALES (est): 4.6MM **Privately Held**
WEB: www.waterfallresort.com
SIC: 7011 Seasonal hotel

(P-13382)
WATERFRONT HOTEL LLC
Also Called: Hilton
21100 Pacific Coast Hwy, Huntington Beach
(92648-5307)
PHONE......................714 845-8000
John Gilbert, *Manager*
Douglas Thoene, *General Mgr*
Fernanda Lemos, *Sales Dir*
Linda Cunningham, *Marketing Staff*
Carolyn Lucas, *Sales Staff*
EMP: 298
SALES (est): 13MM **Privately Held**
WEB: www.waterfrontresort.com
SIC: 7011 5813 5812 7299 Hotels; drinking places; eating places; banquet hall facilities
PA: Waterfront Hotel Llc
660 Newport Center Dr
Newport Beach CA

(P-13383)
WATERFRONT PLAZA HOTEL LLC
10 Washington St, Oakland (94607-3751)
PHONE......................510 836-3800
Clyde R Gibb, *General Ptnr*
Thunderbird Investors, *General Ptnr*
EMP: 65 EST: 1964
SALES (est): 4.2MM **Privately Held**
SIC: 7011 Resort hotel; hotels

(P-13384)
WCO HOTELS INC (HQ)
Also Called: Disneyland Hotel
1150 W Magic Way, Anaheim (92802-2247)
PHONE......................323 636-3251
Tony Bruno, *President*
Cynthia Harriss, *Principal*
Hidel Amemiya, *VP Opers*
EMP: 62
SALES (est): 53.4MM **Publicly Held**
SIC: 7011 5812 Resort hotel; eating places

(P-13385)
WELCOME GROUP MANAGEMENT LLC
Also Called: Marriott
300 S Court St, Visalia (93291-6214)
PHONE......................310 378-6666
Amarjit Shokeen,
Carrie Groover, *Sales Dir*
EMP: 97
SQ FT: 3,224
SALES (est): 104.7K **Privately Held**
SIC: 7011 Hotels & motels

(P-13386)
WELK GROUP INC (PA)
Also Called: Welk Music Group
8860 Lawrence Welk Dr, Escondido
(92026-6403)
PHONE.................................760 749-3000
Jon Fredricks, *President*
Marc L Luzzatto, *COO*
Mario Trejo, *Plant Mgr*
Emily Parker, *Manager*
EMP: 345
SQ FT: 6,200
SALES (est): 100.2MM **Privately Held**
SIC: 7011 5099 Resort hotel; compact
   discs; tapes & cassettes, prerecorded

(P-13387)
WEST HOTEL PARTNERS LP (PA)
Also Called: Hilton San Jose and Towers
11828 La Grange Ave 200, Los Angeles
(90025-5212)
PHONE.................................310 477-3593
Lewis Wolff, *General Ptnr*
Philip Dinapoli, *Partner*
EMP: 246
SQ FT: 3,000
SALES (est): 7.7MM **Privately Held**
WEB: www.firstconf.com
SIC: 7011 5812 5813 7299 Hotels; eating
   places; drinking places; banquet hall facil-
   ities

(P-13388)
WEST HOTEL PARTNERS LP
Also Called: Hilton
300 Almaden Blvd, San Jose (95110-2703)
PHONE.................................408 947-4450
John Southwell, *Branch Mgr*
Silvia White, *Purchasing*
EMP: 200
SALES (est): 7.3MM
SALES (corp-wide): 7.7MM **Privately
Held**
WEB: www.firstconf.com
SIC: 7011 7371 6512 5813 Hotels; cus-
   tom computer programming services;
   nonresidential building operators; drinking
   places; eating places
PA: West Hotel Partners, L.P.
   11828 La Grange Ave 200
   Los Angeles CA 90025
   310 477-3593

(P-13389)
WEST INN & SUITES LLC
4970 Avenida Encinas, Carlsbad
(92008-4343)
PHONE.................................760 448-4500
Debbie Vought,
Veronica Garcia, *Administration*
Nick Seistrup, *Manager*
EMP: 80
SALES (est): 3.9MM **Privately Held**
WEB: www.westinnandsuites.com
SIC: 7011 Inns; hotels

(P-13390)
WEST SAN CRLOS HT PARTNERS LLC
Also Called: Hyatt Place San Jose Hotel
282 Almaden Blvd, San Jose (95113-2003)
PHONE.................................408 998-0400
F Matthew Dinapoli,
Michael Lerman, *General Mgr*
Tina Castaneda, *Administration*
EMP: 65
SALES (est): 1B **Privately Held**
SIC: 7011 Hotels

(P-13391)
WESTGROUP SAN DIEGO ASSOCIATES
Also Called: Paradise Point Resort
1404 Vacation Rd, San Diego
(92109-7905)
PHONE.................................858 274-4630
David Feeney, *Partner*
EMP: 500
SALES (est): 18.4MM **Privately Held**
SIC: 7011 Resort hotel

(P-13392)
WESTIN DESERT WILLOW
75 Willow Ridge, Palm Desert
(92260-0305)
PHONE.................................760 636-7003
Jim Moran, *General Mgr*
Warren Jerome, *Opers Staff*
EMP: 75
SALES (est): 3.5MM **Privately Held**
SIC: 7011 Hotels & motels

(P-13393)
WESTLAKE VILLAGE INN
Also Called: Westlake Inn Hotel
31943 Agoura Rd, Westlake Village
(91361-4427)
PHONE.................................818 889-0230
John Notter, *Owner*
Heidi Schatz, *Finance Mgr*
Mayra Andrade, *Human Res Dir*
Roxanne Stevenson, *Human Res Mgr*
David McCarthy, *VP Sales*
EMP: 150
SALES (est): 9.1MM **Privately Held**
WEB: www.westlakevillageinn.com
SIC: 7011 Resort hotel

(P-13394)
WESTLAND HOTEL CORPORATION
Also Called: Best Western Stockton Inn
4219 E Waterloo Rd, Stockton
(95215-2304)
PHONE.................................209 931-3131
Champ Patel, *Manager*
EMP: 50 **Privately Held**
SIC: 7011 Hotels
PA: Westland Hotel Corporation
   8885 Rio San Diego Dr
   San Diego CA
   -

(P-13395)
WESTPOST BERKELEY LLC
Also Called: Doubletree By Hilton Brky Mrna
200 Marina Blvd, Berkeley (94710-1608)
PHONE.................................510 548-7920
Moez Mangalgi, *Mng Member*
EMP: 99
SALES (est): 4.9MM **Privately Held**
SIC: 7011 Hotels

(P-13396)
WESTWARD HOSPITALITY MGT
200 Marina Blvd, Berkeley (94710-1608)
PHONE.................................510 548-7920
Patrick Birmingham, *Principal*
Rafael Fernandez, *Principal*
EMP: 99
SALES: 15MM **Privately Held**
SIC: 7011 Hotels & motels

(P-13397)
WHATEVER IT TAKES INC
Also Called: Desert Hot Springs Spa Hotel
10805 Palm Dr, Desert Hot Springs
(92240-2511)
PHONE.................................760 329-6000
Michael Bickford, *President*
EMP: 50
SQ FT: 50,000
SALES (est): 2.7MM **Privately Held**
SIC: 7011 5812 Hotels; eating places

(P-13398)
WHB CORPORATION
Also Called: Millennium Biltmore Hotel
506 S Grand Ave, Los Angeles
(90071-2602)
PHONE.................................213 624-1011
John Demola, *Branch Mgr*
Daniel Desbaillets, *COO*
Maselina Hansen, *Officer*
Colin Wang, *Vice Pres*
Sandra Avalos, *Executive*
EMP: 630 **Privately Held**
SIC: 7011 5812 5813 Hotels; eating
   places; drinking places
HQ: Whb Corporation
   7600 E Orchard Rd 230s
   Greenwood Village CO 80111
   303 779-2000

(P-13399)
WHGCA LLC
Also Called: Hilton Sacramento Arden West
2200 Harvard St, Sacramento
(95815-3306)
PHONE.................................916 922-4700
Alex Vargas, *Controller*
Howard Harris, *General Mgr*
EMP: 231
SALES (est): 6.2MM
SALES (corp-wide): 81.3MM **Privately
Held**
SIC: 7011 Hotels
HQ: Westminster Hospitality Inc
   5847 San Felipe St # 4650
   Houston TX 77057
   713 782-9100

(P-13400)
WIN RIVER HOTEL CORPORATION
Also Called: Hilton
5050 Bechelli Ln, Redding (96002-3539)
PHONE.................................530 226-5111
Glen Howard, *President*
EMP: 50
SALES (est): 2.7MM
SALES (corp-wide): 36.5MM **Privately
Held**
SIC: 7011 Hotels
PA: Redding Rancheria
   2000 Redding Rancheria Rd
   Redding CA 96001
   530 225-8979

(P-13401)
WIN TIME LTD (PA)
Also Called: Holiday Inn
9335 Kearny Mesa Rd, San Diego
(92126-4502)
PHONE.................................858 695-2300
Herman Lin, *General Ptnr*
Chue-Huang Chiu, *Partner*
Yi-Ho Huang, *Partner*
EMP: 250
SQ FT: 100,000
SALES (est): 17.6MM **Privately Held**
SIC: 7011 Hotels & motels

(P-13402)
WINDSOR CAPITAL GROUP INC
Also Called: Residence Inn By Marriott
2101 W Vineyard Ave, Oxnard
(93036-2268)
PHONE.................................805 988-0627
Doug Pflaumer, *Branch Mgr*
EMP: 100
SALES (corp-wide): 150MM **Privately
Held**
WEB: www.snowbirdpackage.com
SIC: 7011 Hotels
PA: Windsor Capital Group, Inc.
   3250 Ocean Park Blvd # 350
   Santa Monica CA 90405
   310 566-1100

(P-13403)
WINDSOR CAPITAL GROUP INC
Also Called: Pacific Suites Hotel
3250 Ocean Park Blvd # 350, Santa Monica
(90405-3257)
PHONE.................................310 566-1100
Michael D Cryan, *Manager*
EMP: 78
SALES (corp-wide): 150MM **Privately
Held**
WEB: www.snowbirdpackage.com
SIC: 7011 Hotels
PA: Windsor Capital Group, Inc.
   3250 Ocean Park Blvd # 350
   Santa Monica CA 90405
   310 566-1100

(P-13404)
WINDSOR CAPITAL GROUP INC
Also Called: Embassy Suites Arcadia
3250 Ocean Park Blvd # 350, Santa Monica
(90405-3257)
PHONE.................................310 566-1100
EMP: 78
SALES (corp-wide): 150MM **Privately
Held**
WEB: www.snowbirdpackage.com
SIC: 7011 Hotels

PA: Windsor Capital Group, Inc.
   3250 Ocean Park Blvd # 350
   Santa Monica CA 90405
   310 566-1100

(P-13405)
WINDSOR CAPITAL GROUP INC
Also Called: Embassy Suites Lompoc
3250 Ocean Park Blvd # 350, Santa Monica
(90405-3257)
PHONE.................................209 577-3825
EMP: 78
SALES (corp-wide): 150MM **Privately
Held**
WEB: www.snowbirdpackage.com
SIC: 7011 Hotels
PA: Windsor Capital Group, Inc.
   3250 Ocean Park Blvd # 350
   Santa Monica CA 90405
   310 566-1100

(P-13406)
WINDSOR CAPITAL GROUP INC
Also Called: Marriott
3250 Ocean Park Blvd # 350, Santa Monica
(90405-3257)
PHONE.................................209 577-3825
Shawn Williams, *Manager*
EMP: 78
SALES (corp-wide): 150MM **Privately
Held**
WEB: www.snowbirdpackage.com
SIC: 7011 Hotels & motels
PA: Windsor Capital Group, Inc.
   3250 Ocean Park Blvd # 350
   Santa Monica CA 90405
   310 566-1100

(P-13407)
WINDSOR CAPITAL GROUP INC
Also Called: Embassy Suites
900 E Birch St, Brea (92821-5812)
PHONE.................................714 990-6000
Regina Samy, *Manager*
EMP: 74
SQ FT: 48,164
SALES (corp-wide): 150MM **Privately
Held**
SIC: 7011 Hotels
PA: Windsor Capital Group, Inc.
   3250 Ocean Park Blvd # 350
   Santa Monica CA 90405
   310 566-1100

(P-13408)
WINDSOR CAPITAL GROUP INC
Also Called: Embassy Suites
29345 Rancho California, Temecula
(92591-5201)
PHONE.................................951 676-5656
Tom Demott, *General Mgr*
Greg Roberts, *General Mgr*
EMP: 75
SALES (corp-wide): 150MM **Privately
Held**
SIC: 7011 Hotels & motels
PA: Windsor Capital Group, Inc.
   3250 Ocean Park Blvd # 350
   Santa Monica CA 90405
   310 566-1100

(P-13409)
WINDSOR CAPITAL GROUP INC
3250 Ocean Park Blvd # 350, Santa Monica
(90405-3257)
PHONE.................................310 566-1100
EMP: 78
SALES (corp-wide): 150MM **Privately
Held**
WEB: www.snowbirdpackage.com
SIC: 7011 Hotels
PA: Windsor Capital Group, Inc.
   3250 Ocean Park Blvd # 350
   Santa Monica CA 90405
   310 566-1100

(P-13410)
WINDSOR CAPITAL GROUP INC
Also Called: Embassy Suites El Paso
3250 Ocean Park Blvd # 350, Santa Monica
(90405-3257)
PHONE.................................310 566-1100
EMP: 78

▲ = Import ▼=Export
◆ =Import/Export

SALES (corp-wide): 150MM **Privately Held**
WEB: www.snowbirdpackage.com
SIC: 7011 Hotels
PA: Windsor Capital Group, Inc.
3250 Ocean Park Blvd # 350
Santa Monica CA 90405
310 566-1100

(P-13411)
WINDSOR CAPITAL GROUP INC
Also Called: Embassy Suites
1325 E Dyer Rd, Santa Ana (92705-5615)
PHONE..................714 241-3800
Samuel Sansone, *Manager*
Tom Pugh, *General Mgr*
Laurie Mattson, *Sales Dir*
EMP: 87
SALES (corp-wide): 150MM **Privately Held**
SIC: 7011 5813 5812 Hotels; drinking places; eating places
PA: Windsor Capital Group, Inc.
3250 Ocean Park Blvd # 350
Santa Monica CA 90405
310 566-1100

(P-13412)
WINDSOR CAPITAL GROUP INC
Also Called: Marriott
1510 University Ave, Riverside (92507-4468)
PHONE..................951 276-1200
Jim Larson, *General Mgr*
EMP: 68
SALES (corp-wide): 150MM **Privately Held**
WEB: www.snowbirdpackage.com
SIC: 7011 Hotels
PA: Windsor Capital Group, Inc.
3250 Ocean Park Blvd # 350
Santa Monica CA 90405
310 566-1100

(P-13413)
WINDSOR CAPITAL GROUP INC
Also Called: Marriott
2355 N Main St, Walnut Creek (94596-3547)
PHONE..................925 934-2000
Patrick Nesbitt, *Branch Mgr*
EMP: 140
SALES (corp-wide): 150MM **Privately Held**
SIC: 7011 Hotels & motels
PA: Windsor Capital Group, Inc.
3250 Ocean Park Blvd # 350
Santa Monica CA 90405
310 566-1100

(P-13414)
WJ NEWPORT LLC
Also Called: Marriott
4500 Macarthur Blvd, Newport Beach (92660-2010)
PHONE..................949 476-2001
Wenjing Yang,
EMP: 190
SALES: 27.5MM **Privately Held**
SIC: 7011 5812 7389 Resort hotel; family restaurants;

(P-13415)
WMK SACRAMENTO LLC
Also Called: Doubltree By Hlton Scrmento Ht
2001 Point West Way, Sacramento (95815-4702)
PHONE..................916 929-8855
Ken Leone, *General Mgr*
Jonathan Wiser, *General Mgr*
EMP: 250
SALES: 17MM **Privately Held**
SIC: 7011 Hotel, franchised

(P-13416)
WOODFIN SUITE HOTELS LLC
Also Called: Chase Suite and Woodfin Hotels
12555 High Bluff Dr # 330, San Diego (92130-3005)
PHONE..................858 314-7910
Sam Hardage, *CEO*
Richard Meza, *CFO*
EMP: 780
SQ FT: 10,000
SALES (est): 29.2MM **Privately Held**
SIC: 7011 Hotels

(P-13417)
WORLD MARK OF OCEANSIDE
Also Called: World Mark By Trend West
1301 Carmelo Dr, Oceanside (92054-1089)
PHONE..................760 721-0890
Gene Hensley, *President*
EMP: 52
SALES (est): 2MM **Privately Held**
SIC: 7011 Resort hotel

(P-13418)
WORLD TRADE CTR HT ASSOC LTD
Also Called: Long Beach Hilton, The
701 W Ocean Blvd, Long Beach (90831-3100)
PHONE..................562 983-3400
Steve Holloway, *Controller*
Greater Los Angeles Trade Cent, *General Ptnr*
Matsushita International Corpo, *Ltd Ptnr*
EMP: 250
SALES (est): 7.3MM **Privately Held**
SIC: 7011 7991 5813 5812 Hotels; physical fitness facilities; drinking places; eating places

(P-13419)
WS HDM LLC
Also Called: Hilton San Diego/Del Mar
15575 Jimmy Durante Blvd, Del Mar (92014-1901)
PHONE..................858 792-5200
Al Hatfield, *Partner*
Scott Sloan, *General Mgr*
Kaylee Meyer, *Finance Dir*
EMP: 99 **EST:** 2012
SQ FT: 240,000
SALES (est): 2.9MM **Privately Held**
SIC: 7011 Resort hotel, franchised

(P-13420)
WS MMV HOTEL LLC
Also Called: San Diego Marriott Mission Vly
8757 Rio San Diego Dr, San Diego (92108-1620)
PHONE..................619 692-3800
EMP: 99 **EST:** 2016
SALES (est): 301.3K **Privately Held**
SIC: 7011 Hotels & motels

(P-13421)
WW LBV INC
Also Called: Radisson Inn
30100 Agoura Rd, Agoura Hills (91301-2004)
PHONE..................818 707-1220
Clay Andrews, *General Mgr*
EMP: 103
SALES (corp-wide): 81.3MM **Privately Held**
SIC: 7011 6022 5812 5813 Resort hotel; state commercial banks; caterers; drinking places
PA: Ww Lbv Inc.
2000 Hotel Plaza Blvd
Lake Buena Vista FL 32830
407 828-2424

(P-13422)
WW SAN DIEGO HARBOR ISLAND LLC
Also Called: Hilton
1960 Harbor Island Dr, San Diego (92101-1013)
PHONE..................619 291-6700
Shahid Kayani, *General Mgr*
Stephanie Sorn, *Info Tech Mgr*
Pamela Richardson, *Manager*
EMP: 120
SALES: 11.5MM
SALES (corp-wide): 81.3MM **Privately Held**
WEB: www.hiltonharborisland.com
SIC: 7011
PA: Ww Lbv Inc.
2000 Hotel Plaza Blvd
Lake Buena Vista FL 32830
407 828-2424

(P-13423)
WYNDHAM INTERNATIONAL INC
222 W Houston Ave, Fullerton (92832-3453)
PHONE..................714 992-1700
EMP: 102
SALES (corp-wide): 75MM **Privately Held**
WEB: www.wyndham.com
SIC: 7011 Hotel, franchised
HQ: Wyndham International, Inc
22 Sylvan Way
Parsippany NJ 07054
973 753-6000

(P-13424)
WYNDHAM INTERNATIONAL INC
888 E Tahquitz Canyon Way, Palm Springs (92262-6708)
PHONE..................760 322-6000
Jennie Hui, *Branch Mgr*
EMP: 102
SALES (corp-wide): 75MM **Privately Held**
WEB: www.wyndham.com
SIC: 7011 Hotel, franchised
HQ: Wyndham International, Inc
22 Sylvan Way
Parsippany NJ 07054
973 753-6000

(P-13425)
WYNDHAM INTERNATIONAL INC
Also Called: Wyndham San Dego At Emrald Plz
400 W Broadway, San Diego (92101-3504)
PHONE..................619 239-4500
John Beaton, *Branch Mgr*
Genna Polonia, *General Mgr*
EMP: 102
SALES (corp-wide): 75MM **Privately Held**
WEB: www.wyndham.com
SIC: 7011 Hotel, franchised
HQ: Wyndham International, Inc
22 Sylvan Way
Parsippany NJ 07054
973 753-6000

(P-13426)
WYNDHAM INTERNATIONAL INC
Also Called: Wyndham Hotels & Resorts
1 Old Ranch Rd, Carmel (93923-8551)
PHONE..................831 625-9500
Henry Dunwall, *Owner*
EMP: 102
SALES (corp-wide): 75MM **Privately Held**
WEB: www.wyndham.com
SIC: 7011 Hotels & motels
HQ: Wyndham International, Inc
22 Sylvan Way
Parsippany NJ 07054
973 753-6000

(P-13427)
WYNDHAM INTERNATIONAL INC
Also Called: Wyndham Garden Hotel
5757 Telegraph Rd, Commerce (90040-1513)
PHONE..................323 887-4331
Swiet Lana Cahill, *Manager*
EMP: 85
SALES (corp-wide): 75MM **Privately Held**
WEB: www.wyndham.com
SIC: 7011 5812 Hotels & motels; eating places
HQ: Wyndham International, Inc
22 Sylvan Way
Parsippany NJ 07054
973 753-6000

(P-13428)
WYNDHAM INTERNATIONAL INC
3350 Ave Of The Arts, Costa Mesa (92626-1913)
PHONE..................714 751-5100
Thomas Smalley, *General Mgr*
EMP: 100

SALES (corp-wide): 75MM **Privately Held**
WEB: www.wyndham.com
SIC: 7011 5812 5813 Hotels; eating places; drinking places
HQ: Wyndham International, Inc
22 Sylvan Way
Parsippany NJ 07054
973 753-6000

(P-13429)
WYNDHAM INTERNATIONAL INC
Also Called: Wyndham Hotels & Resorts
400 Concourse Dr, Belmont (94002-4125)
PHONE..................650 591-8600
Sylvia Chu, *Manager*
EMP: 50
SALES (corp-wide): 75MM **Privately Held**
WEB: www.wyndham.com
SIC: 7011 Hotels & motels
HQ: Wyndham International, Inc
22 Sylvan Way
Parsippany NJ 07054
973 753-6000

(P-13430)
WYNDHAM INTERNATIONAL INC
Also Called: Wyndham Hotels & Resorts
1350 N 1st St, San Jose (95112-4709)
PHONE..................408 451-3050
Gary Hageman, *Branch Mgr*
Joseph Harvey, *Finance*
EMP: 140
SALES (corp-wide): 75MM **Privately Held**
WEB: www.wyndham.com
SIC: 7011 5813 5812 Hotels; drinking places; eating places
HQ: Wyndham International, Inc
22 Sylvan Way
Parsippany NJ 07054
973 753-6000

(P-13431)
XANTERRA PARKS & RESORTS INC
Also Called: Furnace Creek Ranch & Inn
Hwy 190, Death Valley (92328)
P.O. Box 187 (92328-0187)
PHONE..................760 786-2345
Dominie Lenz, *Branch Mgr*
EMP: 215
SALES (corp-wide): 395.2MM **Privately Held**
WEB: www.amfac.com
SIC: 7011 Resort hotel
HQ: Parks Xanterra & Resorts Inc
6312 S Fiddlers Green Cir
Greenwood Village CO 80111
303 600-3400

(P-13432)
XLD GROUP LLC
Also Called: Torrance Marriott Hotel
3635 Fashion Way, Torrance (90503-4809)
PHONE..................310 316-3636
Pam Ryan, *General Mgr*
Jon Jackson, *Director*
Francis Martin, *Manager*
EMP: 66
SALES (est): 4.7MM
SALES (corp-wide): 3.5MM **Privately Held**
WEB: www.scmarriott.com
SIC: 7011 7389 Hotels; office facilities & secretarial service rental
PA: Xld Group, Llc
500 Sansome St Ste 502
San Francisco CA

(P-13433)
YHB LONG BEACH LLC
Also Called: Holiday Inn
2640 N Lakewood Blvd, Long Beach (90815-1715)
PHONE..................562 597-4401
Traycee Mayer, *Principal*
Eillen Labrador, *General Mgr*
Kim Mooyon, *General Mgr*
Robert Smit, *General Mgr*
Bess Cruz, *Sales Dir*
EMP: 90

P
R
O
D
U
C
T
S

&

S
V
C
S

SALES (est): 6.1MM **Privately Held**
WEB: www.hilongbeach.com
SIC: 7011 Hotels & motels

(P-13434)
YHB SAN FRANCISCO LLC
Also Called: Pickwick Hotel The
85 5th St, San Francisco (94103-1812)
PHONE..............................415 421-7500
Fred Kleisner, *CEO*
EMP: 65
SALES (est): 3.7MM **Privately Held**
WEB: www.thepickwickhotel.com
SIC: 7011 Hotels

(P-13435)
YOSEMITE MANAGEMENT GROUP LLC (PA)
Also Called: Bryce Canyon Resorts
11128 Hwy 140, El Portal (95318)
P.O. Box 650 (95318-0650)
PHONE..............................209 379-2817
Gerald Fischer,
Kevin Shelton, *Vice Pres*
Charles Fischer,
Christina Fischer,
Karane Fischer,
EMP: 75
SALES (est): 7.7MM **Privately Held**
WEB: www.yosemite-motels.com
SIC: 7011 Motels

(P-13436)
ZHG INC
Also Called: Monterey Beach Hotel
2600 Sand Dunes Dr, Monterey (93940-3838)
PHONE..............................831 394-3321
Theodore Richter, *President*
EMP: 85
SQ FT: 4,996
SALES (est): 2.6MM **Privately Held**
SIC: 7011 Hotels

7021 Rooming & Boarding Houses

(P-13437)
AISHA ACADEMY
706 S Pershing Ave, Stockton (95203-3243)
P.O. Box 4638, Inglewood (90309-4638)
PHONE..............................310 908-1962
Kelvin Williams, *Exec Dir*
Krystal Williams, *CFO*
EMP: 99
SQ FT: 139,800
SALES (est): 4.5K **Privately Held**
SIC: 7021 Rooming & boarding houses

(P-13438)
CAL POLY CORPORATION
Also Called: Housing Services
Cal Poly Bldg 31, San Luis Obispo (93407)
PHONE..............................805 756-1587
Alan Pepe, *Manager*
EMP: 70
SALES (corp-wide): 46.7MM **Privately Held**
WEB: www.calpolyarts.org
SIC: 7021 Dormitory, commercially operated
PA: Cal Poly Corporation
1 Grand Ave Bldg 15
San Luis Obispo CA 93407
805 756-1131

(P-13439)
CROCODILE BAY LODGE
Also Called: Lynch Creek Medical Management
731 Southpoint Blvd, Petaluma (94954-1495)
PHONE..............................707 559-7990
Robert T Williams, *Consultant*
John F Galloway, *Exec VP*
Robert T Wiliams, *Consultant*
EMP: 192
SQ FT: 2,500
SALES (est): 3MM **Privately Held**
WEB: www.crocodilebay.com
SIC: 7021 4724 Rooming & boarding houses; travel agencies

(P-13440)
INTERNATIONAL HOUSE
Also Called: INTERNATIONAL HOUSE AT U C BER
2299 Piedmont Ave Ste 535, Berkeley (94720-2392)
PHONE..............................510 642-9490
Robert M Berdahl, *Ch of Bd*
Joseph Lurie, *Exec Dir*
Adam Sterling, *Exec Dir*
Daniel Luecke, *Research*
Carroll Christman, *Director*
EMP: 162
SQ FT: 100,000
SALES: 15.5MM **Privately Held**
SIC: 7021 Rooming & boarding houses

(P-13441)
PACIFIC LABOR SERVICES INC
5690 Cypress Rd, Oxnard (93033-8509)
P.O. Box 824, Buellton (93427-0824)
PHONE..............................805 488-4625
Rafael Ramos, *President*
EMP: 50
SQ FT: 62,000
SALES: 1.1MM **Privately Held**
WEB: www.pacificlaborsourceinc.com
SIC: 7021 7363 7361

7032 Sporting & Recreational Camps

(P-13442)
ADVENTRES RLLING CROSS-COUNTRY
Also Called: Adventures Cross-Country
242 Redwd Hwy Frntge 1, Mill Valley (94941-6613)
PHONE..............................415 332-5075
Scott A Von Eschen, *President*
Jacob Swarsen, *Mktg Dir*
Kristin Eschen, *Hlthcr Dir*
Eben Coenen, *Director*
Whitney Hall, *Director*
EMP: 133
SQ FT: 2,500
SALES (est): 3.7MM **Privately Held**
WEB: www.adventurescrosscountry.com
SIC: 7032 Summer camp, except day & sports instructional

(P-13443)
ALISAL PROPERTIES (PA)
Also Called: Alisal Guest Ranch
1054 Alisal Rd, Solvang (93463-3033)
PHONE..............................805 688-6411
Palmer Jackson, *President*
Susanne Powell, *Corp Secy*
Joan Y Jackson, *Vice Pres*
EMP: 160
SQ FT: 10,000
SALES (est): 24.6MM **Privately Held**
WEB: www.alisal.com
SIC: 7032 7997 Sporting camps; golf club, membership

(P-13444)
ALLIANCE RDWODS CNFRNCE GRUNDS
6250 Bohemian Hwy, Occidental (95465-9105)
PHONE..............................707 874-3507
James Blake, *Exec Dir*
Sharon Akers, *Admin Sec*
Kevin Chandler, *Human Resources*
Abby Abrahams, *Manager*
Jason Sanders, *Manager*
EMP: 65
SQ FT: 1,392
SALES (est): 3.6MM **Privately Held**
WEB: www.allianceredwoods.com
SIC: 7032 Recreational camps; youth camps; Bible camp

(P-13445)
BEACHSPORTS INC
600 N Catalina Ave, Redondo Beach (90277-2134)
PHONE..............................310 372-2202
Jack Tingley, *President*
EMP: 50

SALES (est): 436.3K **Privately Held**
SIC: 7032 Summer camp, except day & sports instructional

(P-13446)
BIG LGUE DREAMS CONSULTING LLC
33700 Date Palm Dr, Cathedral City (92234-4731)
PHONE..............................760 324-5600
Steve Navarro, *Vice Pres*
EMP: 118
SALES (corp-wide): 45.7MM **Privately Held**
SIC: 7032 Recreational camps
PA: Big League Dreams Consulting, Llc
16333 Fairfield Ranch Rd
Chino Hills CA 91709
909 287-1700

(P-13447)
CALIFORNIA DEPT FISH WILDLIFE
Also Called: Sacramento Valley Region 2
1701 Nimbus Rd Ste A, Gold River (95670-4503)
PHONE..............................916 358-2900
Tina Bartlett, *Manager*
EMP: 200 **Privately Held**
WEB: www.caltaxidermy.com
SIC: 7032 7999 9512 Hunting camp; fishing lakes & piers, operation;
HQ: California Department Of Fish And Wildlife
1416 9th St Fl 12
Sacramento CA 95814

(P-13448)
CITY OF LOS ANGELES
Also Called: Parks & Recreation Dept
3200 Canyon Dr, Los Angeles (90068-2422)
PHONE..............................323 467-7193
Kathrynn Penny, *Director*
EMP: 50 **Privately Held**
WEB: www.lacity.org
SIC: 7032 9512 7999 Sporting & recreational camps; recreational program administration, government; ; recreation center
PA: City Of Los Angeles
200 N Spring St Ste 303
Los Angeles CA 90012
213 978-0600

(P-13449)
EASTER SEALS INC
Also Called: Camp Harmon Easter Seal Soc
16403 Highway 9, Boulder Creek (95006-9696)
PHONE..............................831 338-3383
Jennifer Whalen, *Manager*
EMP: 60
SALES (corp-wide): 73MM **Privately Held**
WEB: www.eastersealsinc.com
SIC: 7032 7033 Sporting & recreational camps; trailer parks & campsites
PA: Easter Seals, Inc.
141 W Jackson Blvd 1400a
Chicago IL 60604
312 726-6200

(P-13450)
GUIDED DISCOVERIES INC
Also Called: Desert Sun Science Center, The
26800 Saunders Meadows Rd, Idyllwild (92549)
P.O. Box 3399 (92549-3399)
PHONE..............................951 659-6062
Allen Tiso, *Director*
EMP: 50
SALES (est): 1MM
SALES (corp-wide): 17.1MM **Privately Held**
SIC: 7032 8299 Sporting & recreational camps; educational services
PA: Guided Discoveries, Inc.
27282 Calle Arroyo
San Juan Capistrano CA 92675
800 645-1423

(P-13451)
HUME LAKE CHRISTIAN CAMPS INC
64144 Hume Lake Rd Ofc, Miramonte (93628-9600)
PHONE..............................559 305-7770
Genie Coe, *Accountant*
Aubrie Wright, *Executive Asst*
Cameron Cadiz, *Admin Asst*
Amy Northrop, *Administration*
Michelle Wilcox, *Administration*
EMP: 78
SALES (corp-wide): 12.6MM **Privately Held**
SIC: 7032 Bible camp
PA: Hume Lake Christian Camps Inc
5545 E Hedges Ave
Fresno CA 93727
559 251-6055

(P-13452)
MAMMOTH MOUNTAIN LAKE CORP
10001 Minaret Rd, Mammoth Lakes (93546)
P.O. Box 24 (93546-0024)
PHONE..............................760 934-2571
Alan Gregory, *CEO*
Rusty Gregory, *Principal*
EMP: 450
SALES (est): 3.2MM
SALES (corp-wide): 209.7MM **Privately Held**
SIC: 7032 Sporting & recreational camps
HQ: Mammoth Mountain Ski Area, Llc
10001 Minaret Rd
Mammoth Lakes CA 93546
760 934-2571

(P-13453)
MOUNT HERMON ASSOCIATION INC (PA)
Also Called: Christian Conference Grounds
37 Conference Dr, Mount Hermon (95041)
PHONE..............................831 335-4466
Roger E Williams, *Exec Dir*
Jeremy Bentley, *Vice Pres*
Kerry Phibbs, *Associate Dir*
David Talbott, *Associate Dir*
Roger Williams, *Exec Dir*
EMP: 100
SQ FT: 10,000
SALES (est): 12.6MM **Privately Held**
WEB: www.mhcamps.org
SIC: 7032 5942 Bible camp; books, religious

(P-13454)
SILICON VALLEY MONTEREY BAY CO
29211 Highway 108, Long Barn (95335-9737)
PHONE..............................209 965-3432
Alan Buscaglia, *Branch Mgr*
EMP: 54
SALES (corp-wide): 4MM **Privately Held**
WEB: www.scouting.org
SIC: 7032 Boys' camp
PA: Silicon Valley Monterey Bay Council, Inc., Boy Scouts Of America
970 W Julian St
San Jose CA 95126
408 279-2086

(P-13455)
SILVER SPUR CHRISTIAN CAMP
17301 Silver Spur Dr, Tuolumne (95379-9638)
PHONE..............................209 928-4248
Stephen Johnson, *Director*
Marie Johnson, *Administration*
Kristen Hughes, *Relations*
EMP: 60
SALES (est): 2MM **Privately Held**
WEB: www.silverspur.com
SIC: 7032 7011 Recreational camps; hotels & motels

(P-13456)
UNITED CMPS CNFRENCES RETREATS (PA)
Also Called: UCCR
1304 Sthpint Blvd Ste 200, Petaluma (94954)
PHONE..............................707 762-3220

Mike Carr, *President*
Matthew Compton-Clark, *COO*
Richard Robinson, *Opers Staff*
EMP: 98
SQ FT: 1,700
SALES: 2.5MM **Privately Held**
WEB: www.uccr.org
SIC: 7032 Recreational camps; youth camps

(P-13457)
WESTMINSTER WOODS CAMP & CONFE
6510 Bohemian Hwy, Occidental (95465-9101)
PHONE............................707 874-2426
Sheila Denton, *Principal*
EMP: 50
SALES (est): 187.5K **Privately Held**
SIC: 7032 Sporting & recreational camps

(P-13458)
WINNARAINBOW INC (PA)
Also Called: CAMP WINNARAINBOW
1301 Henry St, Berkeley (94709-1928)
P.O. Box 1359, Laytonville (95454-1359)
PHONE............................510 525-4304
Jahanara Romney, *Director*
Dr Larry Brilliant, *Treasurer*
Hugh Romney, *Co-Director*
EMP: 50
SALES: 1.5MM **Privately Held**
WEB: www.wavygravy.net
SIC: 7032 Summer camp, except day & sports instructional

7033 Trailer Parks & Camp Sites

(P-13459)
BURLINGAME INDUSTRIES INC (PA)
Also Called: Eagle Roofing Products
3546 N Riverside Ave, Rialto (92377-3878)
PHONE............................909 355-7000
Robert C Burlingame, *Ch of Bd*
Kevin C Burlingame, *President*
Rich Jones, *CFO*
Seamus P Burlingame, *Exec VP*
Maria Altamirano, *Executive*
EMP: 100 **EST:** 1989
SQ FT: 100,000
SALES (est): 81.5MM **Privately Held**
SIC: 7033 0971 3559 3259 Campgrounds; hunting preserve; tile making machines; roofing tile, clay; asphalt felts & coatings

(P-13460)
BURLINGAME INDUSTRIES INC
Also Called: Resort Campground Intl
277 Lytle Creek Rd, Lytle Creek (92358-9751)
PHONE............................909 887-7038
Bob Boyter, *Manager*
EMP: 103
SALES (corp-wide): 81.5MM **Privately Held**
SIC: 7033 Campgrounds; campsite
PA: Burlingame Industries, Incorporated
3546 N Riverside Ave
Rialto CA 92377
909 355-7000

(P-13461)
CALIFORNIA LAND MGT SVCS CORP
Also Called: Calif Land Management
2165 Fallen Leaf Rd, South Lake Tahoe (96150)
PHONE............................530 544-5994
Gayle Ellis, *General Mgr*
EMP: 50
SALES (corp-wide): 12.7MM **Privately Held**
WEB: www.clm-services.com
SIC: 7033 Trailer parks & campsites
PA: California Land Management Services Corporation
675 Gilman St
Palo Alto CA 94301
650 322-1181

(P-13462)
COLORADO RIVER ADVENTURES INC (PA)
Also Called: Yuma Lakes Resort
2715 Parker Dam Rd, Earp (92242-9712)
P.O. Box 1088, Parker AZ (85344-1088)
PHONE............................760 663-3737
Phil Younis, *President*
Skip Russell, *General Mgr*
Debbie Crook, *Office Mgr*
Randy Wright, *Research*
Liz Walch, *Accounting Mgr*
EMP: 112
SQ FT: 6,500
SALES (est): 5.5MM **Privately Held**
WEB: www.coloradoriveradventures.com
SIC: 7033 8641 7032 Campgrounds; social club, membership; recreational camps

(P-13463)
COUNTY OF SAN MATEO
Also Called: Parks Department
455 County Ctr Fl 4, Redwood City (94063-9728)
PHONE............................650 363-4020
Eduardo Castillo, *Analyst*
Cecily Harris, *General Mgr*
EMP: 55 **Privately Held**
WEB: www.ci.sanmateo.ca.us
SIC: 7033 9199 Trailer park;
PA: County Of San Mateo
400 County Ctr
Redwood City CA 94063
650 363-4123

(P-13464)
DE ANZA CAMPLAND LLC (PA)
2211 Pacific Beach Dr, San Diego (92109-5626)
PHONE............................858 581-4200
Alvin Collins, *Principal*
EMP: 60
SALES (est): 1.7MM **Privately Held**
SIC: 7033 Trailer park

(P-13465)
EL CAPITAN CANYON LLC
11560 Calle Real, Santa Barbara (93117-9789)
PHONE............................805 685-3887
Roger Himovitz, *Mng Member*
Kendra Summers, *Sales Dir*
Robert Hansen, *Sales Mgr*
Kali McDonald, *Sales Mgr*
Jessica Adriano, *Sales Staff*
EMP: 62
SALES (est): 4.7MM **Privately Held**
WEB: www.elcapitanranch.com
SIC: 7033 Campgrounds

(P-13466)
EMERALD BROOK LLC
Also Called: Emerald Desert Rv Resort
76000 Frank Sinatra Dr, Palm Desert (92211-5031)
PHONE............................760 345-4770
Neil Brandom,
EMP: 50
SQ FT: 8,000
SALES (est): 1.7MM **Privately Held**
WEB: www.emeralddesert.com
SIC: 7033 7997 Recreational vehicle parks; golf club, membership

(P-13467)
SAN FRNCSCO NORTH/PETALUMA KOA
20 Rainsville Rd, Petaluma (94952-8121)
PHONE............................707 763-1492
William Wood, *President*
Judith Wood, *Corp Secy*
EMP: 50
SQ FT: 2,000
SALES (est): 2.3MM **Privately Held**
WEB: www.petalumakoakampground.com
SIC: 7033 4119 Campgrounds; sightseeing bus

(P-13468)
SILENT VALLEY CLUB INC
46305 Poppet Flats Rd, Banning (92220-9636)
PHONE............................951 849-4501
Patrick Buhrer, *Director*

Brenda Mejia, *CFO*
Jane Bryant, *Relations*
EMP: 70
SQ FT: 2,200
SALES: 2.7MM **Privately Held**
WEB: www.silentvalleyclub.com
SIC: 7033 Campgrounds

(P-13469)
THOUSAND TRAILS INC
Also Called: N A C O
31191 Hardin Flat Rd, Groveland (95321-9716)
PHONE............................209 962-0100
John Kimbrough, *Manager*
EMP: 50 **Publicly Held**
WEB: www.indianpt.com
SIC: 7033 Campgrounds
HQ: Thousand Trails, Inc.
2325 Highway 90
Gautier MS 39553
228 497-3594

(P-13470)
TRAILER PARK INC
4300 Soquel Dr Spc 90, Soquel (95073-2140)
PHONE............................831 462-3271
Mark Kalemos, *Principal*
EMP: 96 **Privately Held**
SIC: 7033 Trailer park
PA: Trailer Park, Inc.
6922 Hollywood Blvd Fl 12
Los Angeles CA 90028

7041 Membership-Basis Hotels

(P-13471)
AIRBNB INC (PA)
888 Brannan St Ste 300, San Francisco (94103-4931)
PHONE............................415 800-5959
Brian Chesky, *CEO*
Greg Greeley, *President*
Joe Gebbia,
Erin Clark, *Trust Officer*
Kim Roth, *Trust Officer*
EMP: 1032
SALES (est): 326.7MM **Privately Held**
SIC: 7041 Residence club, organization

(P-13472)
ASSOCIATED STUDENTS INC
333 S Twin Oaks Valley Rd, San Marcos (92096-0001)
PHONE............................760 750-4990
Susana Figueroa, *President*
Laura Poggi, *Exec Dir*
EMP: 50 **EST:** 1991
SALES: 1.3MM **Privately Held**
SIC: 7041 Boarding house, fraternity & sorority

(P-13473)
BERKELEY STUDENT COOP INC
2424 Ridge Rd, Berkeley (94709-1212)
PHONE............................510 848-1936
Janette E Stokley, *Exec Dir*
Palmer Buchholz, *President*
Marjorie Greene, *CFO*
Terra Steinkuehler, *Finance Mgr*
Marie Lucero, *Opers Mgr*
EMP: 100
SQ FT: 18,000
SALES: 11.2MM **Privately Held**
WEB: www.usca.org
SIC: 7041 Boarding house, organization

(P-13474)
CITY OF SUNNYVALE
Also Called: Housing Division
456 W Olive Ave, Sunnyvale (94086-7661)
P.O. Box 3707 (94088-3707)
PHONE............................408 730-7451
Gary Luebbers, *Principal*
EMP: 99 **Privately Held**
SIC: 7041 Rooming houses
PA: City Of Sunnyvale
456 W Olive Ave
Sunnyvale CA 94086
408 730-7415

(P-13475)
GAMMA PHI BETA SORORITY INC
Also Called: Delta PHI Chapter
890 Camino Pescadero, Goleta (93117-4768)
PHONE............................805 968-4221
Amber Setrakain, *President*
EMP: 90
SALES: 280.7K **Privately Held**
WEB: www.gammaphibetaucsb.com
SIC: 7041 8641 7011 Membership-basis organization hotels; university club; hotels & motels

(P-13476)
HEART CONSCIOUSNESS CHURCH (PA)
Also Called: Harbin Hot Springs
18424 Harbin Springs Rd, Middletown (95461-9687)
P.O. Box 782 (95461-0782)
PHONE............................707 987-2477
Robert F Hartley, *President*
Suzie Lecavalier, *Treasurer*
Julie Adams, *Vice Pres*
Sajjad Mahmud, *Vice Pres*
EMP: 110
SQ FT: 4,000
SALES: 4.8MM **Privately Held**
WEB: www.harbinhotsprings.com
SIC: 7041 Membership-basis organization hotels

(P-13477)
NATIONAL COMMUNITY RENAISSANCE (PA)
9421 Haven Ave Ste 100, Rancho Cucamonga (91730-5890)
PHONE............................909 483-2444
Steve Pontell, *President*
Tracy Thomas, *CFO*
Ciriaco Pinedo, *Exec VP*
Michael M Ruane, *Exec VP*
Doretta Bryan, *Vice Pres*
EMP: 51 **EST:** 1997
SALES: 5.6MM **Privately Held**
SIC: 7041 Lodging house, organization

(P-13478)
NAVY EXCHANGE SERVICE COMMAND
Also Called: Navy Bachelor Quarters
1395 Hussey Rd, Ridgecrest (93555)
PHONE............................760 939-8681
Mike Biddlingmeier, *Branch Mgr*
EMP: 95 **Publicly Held**
WEB: www.navy-nex.com
SIC: 7041 Lodging house, organization
HQ: Navy Exchange Service Command
3280 Virginia Beach Blvd
Virginia Beach VA 23452
757 631-3696

(P-13479)
PHI DELTA THETA INC
17740 Halsted St, Northridge (91325-2025)
P.O. Box 34082, Granada Hills (91394-4082)
PHONE............................818 885-9940
Jason McKnight, *President*
Bryan Guerrero, *Treasurer*
Evan Press, *Principal*
EMP: 50
SALES (est): 809.2K **Privately Held**
WEB: www.redarc.com
SIC: 7041 8641 Fraternities & sororities; fraternal associations

(P-13480)
RLJ HGN EMERYVILLE LESSEE LP
Also Called: Hilton Garden Inn Emeryville
1800 Powell St, Emeryville (94608-1808)
PHONE............................510 658-9300
EMP: 99
SQ FT: 89,000
SALES (est): 508.7K **Privately Held**
SIC: 7041 Membership-basis organization hotels

(P-13481)
SIGMA KAPPA SORORITY
2409 Warring St, Berkeley (94704-2593)
PHONE..................510 540-9142
Donna Jollymour, *President*
EMP: 80
SALES: 826.2K **Privately Held**
SIC: 7041 Sorority residential house

7211 Power Laundries, Family & Commercial

(P-13482)
AMERICAN ETC INC
Also Called: Royal Laundry
1140 San Mateo Ave, South San Francisco (94080-6602)
PHONE..................650 873-5353
Kenn T Edwards, *CEO*
Don Luckenbach, *President*
Martha A Guzman, *Controller*
Darlene Bell, *Opers Mgr*
Nick Hatzopoulos, *Opers Staff*
EMP: 325
SQ FT: 70,000
SALES (est): 21.1MM **Privately Held**
SIC: 7211 Power laundries, family & commercial

(P-13483)
ANITSA INC
Also Called: Valet Services
6032 Shull St, Bell Gardens (90201-6237)
PHONE..................213 237-0533
Margo Minisiam, *President*
Gary Von, *Executive*
Marilyn Enriquez, *Accounting Mgr*
Javier Martinez, *Human Resources*
Garo Minissian, *Opers Mgr*
EMP: 135
SQ FT: 65,000
SALES (est): 7.1MM **Privately Held**
WEB: www.anitsa.com
SIC: 7211 8742 Power laundries, family & commercial; industry specialist consultants

(P-13484)
BRAUN LINEN SERVICE INC
A-1 Pomona Linen
396 La Mesa St, Pomona (91766-2129)
P.O. Box 317 (91769-0317)
PHONE..................909 623-2678
Jim Moore, *Manager*
EMP: 100
SALES (corp-wide): 10.1MM **Privately Held**
SIC: 7211 7213 5947 Power laundries, family & commercial; linen supply; gifts & novelties
PA: Braun Linen Service, Inc.
16514 Garfield Ave
Paramount CA 90723
909 623-2678

(P-13485)
DEL MAR FRENCH LAUNDRY
508 Del Monte Ave, Monterey (93940-2405)
P.O. Box 1141 (93942-1141)
PHONE..................831 375-9597
Cedo Godspodnetich, *President*
Cynthia Godspodnetich, *Admin Sec*
EMP: 50
SQ FT: 12,150
SALES: 1MM **Privately Held**
SIC: 7211 Power laundries, family & commercial

(P-13486)
EMERALD TEXTILES LLC
1725 Dornoch Ct San Diego, San Diego (92154)
PHONE..................619 330-7077
Jaye Park, *President*
Glen McClanan, *CFO*
Jessica Vega, *Controller*
EMP: 400
SALES (est): 19.6MM **Privately Held**
SIC: 7211 Power laundries, family & commercial

PA: Encore Textiles, Inc.
1518 Paloma St Ste 101
Los Angeles CA 90021
213 493-4486

(P-13487)
LAMOURES INC (PA)
Also Called: Lamoure's Cleaners & Laundry
729 E Divisadero St, Fresno (93721-1044)
PHONE..................559 264-0241
Jean B Lamoure, *President*
Beverly Lamoure, *Corp Secy*
Joe Lamoure, *Vice Pres*
EMP: 98
SQ FT: 15,000
SALES (est): 1.3MM **Privately Held**
SIC: 7211 7216 Power laundries, family & commercial; curtain cleaning & repair

(P-13488)
MONTEREY BAY ACADAMY LAUNDRY
Also Called: Campus Laundry
675 Beach Dr, Watsonville (95076-1904)
PHONE..................831 728-1481
Tim Kuprock, *Principal*
Jay Ketelsen, *General Mgr*
Jay Ketelson, *Manager*
EMP: 70
SALES (est): 1.7MM **Privately Held**
SIC: 7211 7213 Power laundries, family & commercial; linen supply

(P-13489)
RADIANT SERVICES CORP (PA)
651 W Knox St, Gardena (90248-4409)
PHONE..................310 327-6300
Mina Keywanfar, *CEO*
Shahrokh Keywanfar, *President*
Jamshid Beroukhim, *Vice Pres*
Ester Manuel, *Controller*
Cyrus Shahbaz, *Opers Mgr*
EMP: 235
SALES (est): 15.5MM **Privately Held**
WEB: www.radiantservices.com
SIC: 7211 7216 Power laundries, family & commercial; drycleaning plants, except rugs

(P-13490)
ROYAL AIRLINE LINEN INC
125 N Ash Ave, Inglewood (90301-1648)
PHONE..................310 677-9885
Kathleen Cunningham, *CEO*
Kay Cunningham, *Vice Pres*
EMP: 100
SQ FT: 12,800
SALES (est): 5.8MM **Privately Held**
SIC: 7211 Laundry collecting & distributing outlet

(P-13491)
YUEN YEE LAUNDRY & CLEANERS
Also Called: Yee Yuen Linen Service
2575 S Normandie Ave, Los Angeles (90007-1598)
PHONE..................323 734-7205
Deborah Morikawa, *President*
Luis Lee, *Corp Secy*
Cynthia Louie, *Vice Pres*
EMP: 80
SQ FT: 20,000
SALES (est): 4.6MM **Privately Held**
WEB: www.yeeyuenlinen.com
SIC: 7211 Laundry collecting & distributing outlet

7212 Garment Pressing & Cleaners' Agents

(P-13492)
JOSEPH DIPUZO
Also Called: Superclean America
601 E Tahquitz Canyon Way # 120, Palm Springs (92262-6700)
P.O. Box 3006 (92263-3006)
PHONE..................760 325-1200
Joseph Dipuzo, *Owner*
EMP: 50
SALES (est): 701.6K **Privately Held**
SIC: 7212 Laundry & drycleaner agents

7213 Linen Sply

(P-13493)
ALSCO INC
1009 Factory St, Richmond (94801-2166)
PHONE..................510 237-9634
EMP: 84
SALES (corp-wide): 658.7MM **Privately Held**
SIC: 7213
PA: Alsco Inc.
505 E South Temple
Salt Lake City UT 84102
801 328-8831

(P-13494)
ALSCO INC
900 N Highland Ave, Los Angeles (90038-2413)
PHONE..................323 465-5111
Mike Keller, *Branch Mgr*
EMP: 180
SALES (corp-wide): 892.3MM **Privately Held**
WEB: www.amlinen.com
SIC: 7213 Uniform supply
PA: Alsco Inc.
505 E 200 S Ste 101
Salt Lake City UT 84102
801 328-8831

(P-13495)
ALSCO INC
2215 Palma Dr, Ventura (93003-6437)
PHONE..................805 650-6578
John Mc Carty, *Branch Mgr*
EMP: 85
SALES (corp-wide): 892.3MM **Privately Held**
SIC: 7213 5087 Uniform supply; laundry equipment & supplies
PA: Alsco Inc.
505 E 200 S Ste 101
Salt Lake City UT 84102
801 328-8831

(P-13496)
ALSCO INC
705 W Grape St, San Diego (92101-2212)
P.O. Box 122671 (92112-2671)
PHONE..................619 234-7291
Mike Scacco, *Branch Mgr*
Roberta Carleton, *Office Mgr*
Shane Harrison, *Manager*
EMP: 110
SALES (corp-wide): 892.3MM **Privately Held**
WEB: www.amlinen.com
SIC: 7213 Uniform supply
PA: Alsco Inc.
505 E 200 S Ste 101
Salt Lake City UT 84102
801 328-8831

(P-13497)
ALSCO INC
1575 Indiana St, San Francisco (94107-3529)
PHONE..................415 648-9266
Jonathan Silver, *Branch Mgr*
Nick Axsom, *General Mgr*
David Torres, *Chief Engr*
EMP: 100
SALES (corp-wide): 892.3MM **Privately Held**
WEB: www.amlinen.com
SIC: 7213 Uniform supply
PA: Alsco Inc.
505 E 200 S Ste 101
Salt Lake City UT 84102
801 328-8831

(P-13498)
ALSCO INC
1750 S Zeyn St, Anaheim (92802-2904)
P.O. Box 25068 (92825-5068)
PHONE..................714 774-4165
Scott Norris, *Manager*
Ray Schroeder, *District Mgr*
Kenneth Imaizumi, *Manager*
EMP: 100
SQ FT: 16,008

SALES (corp-wide): 892.3MM **Privately Held**
SIC: 7213 7218 Uniform supply; industrial launderers
PA: Alsco Inc.
505 E 200 S Ste 101
Salt Lake City UT 84102
801 328-8831

(P-13499)
ALSCO INC
3311 Industrial Dr, Santa Rosa (95403-2094)
PHONE..................707 523-3311
Denny Bunch, *General Mgr*
EMP: 100
SQ FT: 36,448
SALES (corp-wide): 892.3MM **Privately Held**
WEB: www.amlinen.com
SIC: 7213 Uniform supply
PA: Alsco Inc.
505 E 200 S Ste 101
Salt Lake City UT 84102
801 328-8831

(P-13500)
ALSCO INC
2275 Junction Ave, San Jose (95131-1211)
PHONE..................408 279-2345
Paul Johnson, *Manager*
Bob Warford, *Personnel Exec*
EMP: 110
SQ FT: 53,760
SALES (corp-wide): 892.3MM **Privately Held**
WEB: www.amlinen.com
SIC: 7213 7218 Uniform supply; industrial launderers
PA: Alsco Inc.
505 E 200 S Ste 101
Salt Lake City UT 84102
801 328-8831

(P-13501)
ALSCO INC
5159 Commercial Cir, Concord (94520-8597)
PHONE..................707 751-0652
Norman Underwood, *Branch Mgr*
EMP: 150
SALES (corp-wide): 892.3MM **Privately Held**
WEB: www.amlinen.com
SIC: 7213 Uniform supply
PA: Alsco Inc.
505 E 200 S Ste 101
Salt Lake City UT 84102
801 328-8831

(P-13502)
ALSCO INC
3391 Lanatt St, Sacramento (95819-1917)
PHONE..................916 454-5545
Michael Hollemdeck, *Branch Mgr*
Michael Hollenbeck, *Site Mgr*
EMP: 100
SALES (corp-wide): 892.3MM **Privately Held**
WEB: www.amlinen.com
SIC: 7213 Uniform supply
PA: Alsco Inc.
505 E 200 S Ste 101
Salt Lake City UT 84102
801 328-8831

(P-13503)
AMERICAN TEXTILE MAINT CO
Also Called: Medico Professional Linen Svc
1705 Hooper Ave, Los Angeles (90021-3111)
P.O. Box 4928, Long Beach (90804-0928)
PHONE..................213 749-4433
Kenny Immazumi, *Manager*
EMP: 50
SALES (corp-wide): 197.6MM **Privately Held**
WEB: www.amtextile.net
SIC: 7213 Uniform supply
PA: American Textile Maintenance Company
1667 W Washington Blvd
Los Angeles CA 90007
323 731-3132

(P-13504)
AMERICAN TEXTILE MAINT CO
Also Called: Republic Uniform
3001 E Anaheim St, Long Beach
(90804-3810)
PHONE..............................562 438-7656
Lawrence Pallan, *Manager*
EMP: 75
SALES (corp-wide): 197.6MM **Privately Held**
WEB: www.amtextile.net
SIC: 7213 Linen supply
PA: American Textile Maintenance Company
1667 W Washington Blvd
Los Angeles CA 90007
323 731-3132

(P-13505)
AMERICAN TEXTILE MAINT CO
Also Called: Republic Master Chefs Textile
3001 E Anaheim St, Long Beach
(90804-3810)
PHONE..............................562 438-1126
Lawrence Pallan, *Branch Mgr*
EMP: 92
SALES (corp-wide): 197.6MM **Privately Held**
SIC: 7213 Linen supply
PA: American Textile Maintenance Company
1667 W Washington Blvd
Los Angeles CA 90007
323 731-3132

(P-13506)
AMERICAN TEXTILE MAINT CO
Also Called: Master-Chef's Linen Rental
1664 W Washington Blvd, Los Angeles
(90007-1115)
PHONE..............................323 735-1661
Bob Brill, *Branch Mgr*
EMP: 130
SALES (corp-wide): 197.6MM **Privately Held**
WEB: www.amtextile.net
SIC: 7213 Towel supply; uniform supply
PA: American Textile Maintenance Company
1667 W Washington Blvd
Los Angeles CA 90007
323 731-3132

(P-13507)
AMERIPRIDE SERVICES INC
109 Calle Propano Ste C, Paso Robles
(93446-5950)
PHONE..............................805 239-9449
Matt Wenzel, *Branch Mgr*
Keith Jones, *Site Mgr*
EMP: 100 **Publicly Held**
WEB: www.ameripride.com
SIC: 7213 Uniform supply
HQ: Ameripride Services, Inc.
10801 Wayzata Blvd # 100
Minnetonka MN 55305
800 750-4628

(P-13508)
AMERIPRIDE SERVICES INC
3750 Eastside Rd, Redding (96001-3807)
PHONE..............................530 242-0564
J Oldham, *Branch Mgr*
Shane Battles, *Sales Executive*
EMP: 50 **Publicly Held**
SIC: 7213 Uniform supply
HQ: Ameripride Services, Inc.
10801 Wayzata Blvd # 100
Minnetonka MN 55305
800 750-4628

(P-13509)
AMERIPRIDE SERVICES INC
Also Called: Ameripride Unifom Svcs
335 Washington St, Bakersfield
(93307-2719)
PHONE..............................661 324-7941
Mike Beckwith, *General Mgr*
Jeremy Castillo, *Sales Staff*
Jerry Hill, *Sales Staff*
EMP: 110
SQ FT: 34,000 **Publicly Held**
WEB: www.ameripride.com
SIC: 7213 7218

HQ: Ameripride Services, Inc.
10801 Wayzata Blvd # 100
Minnetonka MN 55305
800 750-4628

(P-13510)
AMERIPRIDE SERVICES INC
4206 S B St, Stockton (95206-3990)
PHONE..............................209 982-0020
Walter Locke, *Branch Mgr*
EMP: 50 **Publicly Held**
WEB: www.ameripride.com
SIC: 7213 7218 Uniform supply; industrial launderers
HQ: Ameripride Services, Inc.
10801 Wayzata Blvd # 100
Minnetonka MN 55305
800 750-4628

(P-13511)
AMERIPRIDE SERVICES INC
2230 W Chapman Ave, Orange
(92868-2316)
PHONE..............................714 385-8991
Frank Saldana, *Branch Mgr*
EMP: 50 **Publicly Held**
WEB: www.ameripride.com
SIC: 7213 7218 Uniform supply; industrial launderers
HQ: Ameripride Services, Inc.
10801 Wayzata Blvd # 100
Minnetonka MN 55305
800 750-4628

(P-13512)
AMERIPRIDE SERVICES INC
3701 Collins Ave Ste 5b, Richmond
(94806-2079)
PHONE..............................800 748-6178
John Galletta, *Manager*
EMP: 50 **Publicly Held**
WEB: www.ameripride.com
SIC: 7213 7218 Uniform supply; industrial launderers
HQ: Ameripride Services, Inc.
10801 Wayzata Blvd # 100
Minnetonka MN 55305
800 750-4628

(P-13513)
AMERIPRIDE SERVICES INC
1356 Dayton St Ste R, Salinas
(93901-4427)
PHONE..............................800 882-5326
Jason Saathoff, *President*
EMP: 50 **Publicly Held**
WEB: www.ameripride.com
SIC: 7213 7218 Uniform supply; industrial launderers
HQ: Ameripride Services, Inc.
10801 Wayzata Blvd # 100
Minnetonka MN 55305
800 750-4628

(P-13514)
ARAMARK UNF & CAREER AP LLC
855 Mckendrie St, San Jose (95126-1295)
P.O. Box 28383 (95159-8383)
PHONE..............................408 243-9824
Brett Borba, *Manager*
EMP: 100 **Publicly Held**
WEB: www.aramark-uniform.com
SIC: 7213 7218 Uniform supply; industrial launderers
HQ: Aramark Uniform & Career Apparel, Llc
115 N First St Ste 203
Burbank CA 91502
818 973-3700

(P-13515)
ARAMARK UNF & CAREER AP LLC
15525 Garfield Ave, Paramount
(90723-4033)
P.O. Box 1799 (90723-1799)
PHONE..............................323 774-4216
Dave Canzani, *Owner*
EMP: 71 **Publicly Held**
WEB: www.aramark-uniform.com
SIC: 7213 Uniform supply
HQ: Aramark Uniform & Career Apparel, Llc
115 N First St Ste 203
Burbank CA 91502
818 973-3700

(P-13516)
ARAMARK UNF & CAREER AP LLC
5665 Eastgate Dr, San Diego
(92121-2817)
PHONE..............................858 550-1131
Stephen M Donly, *President*
Kady Aun, *Info Tech Mgr*
EMP: 50 **Publicly Held**
SIC: 7213 Uniform supply
HQ: Aramark Uniform & Career Apparel, Llc
115 N First St Ste 203
Burbank CA 91502
818 973-3700

(P-13517)
ARAMARK UNF & CAREER AP LLC
3333 N Sabre Dr, Fresno (93727-7816)
P.O. Box 1289, Clovis (93613-1289)
PHONE..............................559 291-6631
Anthony Mollica, *Sales/Mktg Mgr*
EMP: 200
SQ FT: 130,449 **Publicly Held**
WEB: www.aramark-uniform.com
SIC: 7213 Uniform supply
HQ: Aramark Uniform & Career Apparel, Llc
115 N First St Ste 203
Burbank CA 91502
818 973-3700

(P-13518)
ARAMARK UNF & CAREER AP LLC
440 Carolina St, San Francisco
(94107-2304)
PHONE..............................415 244-8332
Deborah Hupp, *Manager*
EMP: 250 **Publicly Held**
WEB: www.aramark-uniform.com
SIC: 7213 Uniform supply
HQ: Aramark Uniform & Career Apparel, Llc
115 N First St Ste 203
Burbank CA 91502
818 973-3700

(P-13519)
BRAUN LINEN SERVICE INC (PA)
Also Called: A-1 Pomona Linen
16514 Garfield Ave, Paramount
(90723-5304)
P.O. Box 348 (90723-0348)
PHONE..............................909 623-2678
Richard A Cornwell, *CEO*
William S Cornwell, *Vice Pres*
Peter Uy, *Admin Mgr*
EMP: 125
SQ FT: 28,000
SALES (est): 10.1MM **Privately Held**
SIC: 7213 Towel supply; table cover supply

(P-13520)
CAL SOUTHERN SERVICES
Also Called: Socal Uniform Rental
419 Mcgroarty St, San Gabriel
(91776-2302)
PHONE..............................626 281-5942
Theodore W Doll Jr, *President*
William Doll, *General Mgr*
James L Brittain, *Admin Sec*
EMP: 99
SALES (est): 3.1MM **Privately Held**
SIC: 7213

(P-13521)
CALIFORNIA LINEN SERVICES INC
40 E California Blvd, Pasadena
(91105-3203)
PHONE..............................626 564-4576
Brian O'Neil, *President*
Andy Oneil, *Opers Mgr*
Kelly Huizinga, *Manager*
Linda Harman, *Accounts Mgr*
EMP: 60
SALES (est): 2.3MM **Privately Held**
SIC: 7213 Uniform supply

(P-13522)
CINTAS CORPORATION
3201 Dnville Blvd Ste 285, Alamo (94507)
PHONE..............................925 743-1745

EMP: 54
SALES (corp-wide): 6.4B **Publicly Held**
SIC: 7213 5999 5912 5699 Uniform supply; alarm & safety equipment stores; drug stores & proprietary stores; uniforms & work clothing
PA: Cintas Corporation
6800 Cintas Blvd
Cincinnati OH 45262
513 459-1200

(P-13523)
CINTAS CORPORATION NO 3
2829 Workman Mill Rd, Whittier
(90601-1549)
PHONE..............................562 692-8741
Bryce Littlejohn, *General Mgr*
EMP: 100
SALES (corp-wide): 6.4B **Publicly Held**
WEB: www.cintas-corp.com
SIC: 7213 7218 Uniform supply; industrial launderers
HQ: Cintas Corporation No. 3
6800 Cintas Blvd
Mason OH 45040

(P-13524)
CINTAS CORPORATION NO 3
7735 Paramount Blvd, Pico Rivera
(90660-4308)
PHONE..............................562 368-3200
Robert Choonover, *Manager*
EMP: 150
SQ FT: 63,910
SALES (corp-wide): 6.4B **Publicly Held**
WEB: www.cintas-corp.com
SIC: 7213 Uniform supply
HQ: Cintas Corporation No. 3
6800 Cintas Blvd
Mason OH 45040

(P-13525)
CINTAS CORPORATION NO 3
2150 Proforma Ave, Ontario (91761-8518)
PHONE..............................909 930-9096
Jim Ewald, *President*
EMP: 150
SQ FT: 49,705
SALES (corp-wide): 6.4B **Publicly Held**
SIC: 7213 Uniform supply
HQ: Cintas Corporation No. 3
6800 Cintas Blvd
Mason OH 45040

(P-13526)
CINTAS CORPORATION NO 3
28334 Industry Dr, Valencia (91355-4103)
PHONE..............................661 310-7400
Eric Curtis, *Branch Mgr*
EMP: 94
SALES (corp-wide): 6.4B **Publicly Held**
WEB: www.cintas-corp.com
SIC: 7213 Uniform supply
HQ: Cintas Corporation No. 3
6800 Cintas Blvd
Mason OH 45040

(P-13527)
CITY TOWEL & DUST SERVICE INC
Also Called: Sunset Linen Service
3016 Dutton Ave, Santa Rosa
(95407-7886)
PHONE..............................707 542-0391
Michael Erwin, *President*
EMP: 50
SQ FT: 5,000
SALES (est): 3.3MM **Privately Held**
SIC: 7213 7211 Uniform supply; linen supply, non-clothing; laundry collecting & distributing outlet

(P-13528)
COMPLETE LINEN SVC
Also Called: Complete Linen Services
290 S Maple Ave, South San Francisco
(94080-6304)
PHONE..............................650 873-1221
Steve Bruni, *President*
Patrice Bruni, *Treasurer*
Colin Morf, *Vice Pres*
Kathy Lobos, *Admin Asst*

P
R
O
D
U
C
T
S

&

S
V
C
S

Tom Murphy, *Sales Staff*
EMP: 100
SQ FT: 14,000
SALES (est): 6.6MM **Privately Held**
WEB: www.completelinen.com
SIC: 7213 Linen supply

(P-13529)
DOMESTIC LINEN SUPPLY CO INC (HQ)
1600 Compton Ave, Los Angeles (90021-3142)
P.O. Box 21326 (90021-0326)
PHONE...................213 749-6300
Bruce L Colton, *President*
Leonard Colton, *Treasurer*
David J Colton, *Admin Sec*
EMP: 50
SQ FT: 49,454
SALES (est): 3MM
SALES (corp-wide): 38.3MM **Privately Held**
SIC: 7213 Uniform supply
PA: Domestic Linen Supply And Laundry Company
30555 Northwestern Hwy
Farmington Hills MI 48334
248 737-2000

(P-13530)
FOASBERG LAUNDRY & CLRS INC (PA)
Also Called: Crdn of Southern La County
640 E Wardlow Rd, Long Beach (90807-4624)
P.O. Box 17965 (90807-7965)
PHONE...................562 426-7345
James W Foasberg, *CEO*
Richard Foasberg, *Vice Pres*
EMP: 55
SQ FT: 40,000
SALES (est): 4.2MM **Privately Held**
SIC: 7213 7216 7211 7218 Uniform supply; drycleaning collecting & distributing agency; laundry collecting & distributing outlet; industrial launderers

(P-13531)
GBS LINENS INC (PA)
Also Called: GBS Party Linens
305 N Muller St, Anaheim (92801-5445)
PHONE...................714 778-6448
Pravin Mody, *President*
Ameer P Mody, *Vice Pres*
Sudha Mody, *Vice Pres*
Carol Trapschuh, *Social Dir*
Sujata Mody, *Admin Sec*
EMP: 100
SQ FT: 57,000
SALES (est): 12.3MM **Privately Held**
WEB: www.gbslinens.com
SIC: 7213 2392 7211 5023 Linen supply; household furnishings; power laundries; family & commercial; home furnishings; textile mill waste & remnant processing

(P-13532)
LA TAVOLA LLC (PA)
2655 Napa Valley Corp Dr, NAPA (94558)
PHONE...................707 257-3358
Betsy Stone, *President*
EMP: 91
SALES (est): 4.2MM **Privately Held**
SIC: 7213 Linen supply

(P-13533)
MISSION LINEN SUPPLY
Also Called: Mission Linen & Uniform Svc
2727 Industry St, Oceanside (92054-4810)
PHONE...................760 757-9099
Graig Rogers, *Principal*
Lupe Avalos, *Sales Staff*
EMP: 108
SALES (corp-wide): 192.2MM **Privately Held**
WEB: www.missions.com
SIC: 7213 7218 Uniform supply; industrial launderers
PA: Mission Linen Supply
717 E Yanonali St
Santa Barbara CA 93103
805 730-3620

(P-13534)
MISSION LINEN SUPPLY
Mission Linen & Uniform Svc
399 Errol St, Morro Bay (93442-1896)
PHONE...................805 772-4451
Josh Offil, *General Mgr*
EMP: 50
SALES (corp-wide): 192.2MM **Privately Held**
WEB: www.missions.com
SIC: 7213 Uniform supply
PA: Mission Linen Supply
717 E Yanonali St
Santa Barbara CA 93103

(P-13535)
MISSION LINEN SUPPLY
Also Called: Mission Linen & Uniform Svc
7520 Reese Rd, Sacramento (95828-3707)
PHONE...................916 423-3179
Peppy Secaile, *Manager*
Irving Dungca, *Area Mgr*
EMP: 125
SALES (corp-wide): 192.2MM **Privately Held**
WEB: www.missions.com
SIC: 7213 7218 Uniform supply; industrial launderers
PA: Mission Linen Supply
717 E Yanonali St
Santa Barbara CA 93103
805 730-3620

(P-13536)
MISSION LINEN SUPPLY
Also Called: Mission Linen & Uniform Svc
315 Kern St, Salinas (93905-2595)
PHONE...................831 424-1707
Mark Rogers, *Manager*
Linda Bartoli, *General Mgr*
EMP: 59
SALES (corp-wide): 192.2MM **Privately Held**
WEB: www.missions.com
SIC: 7213 Uniform supply
PA: Mission Linen Supply
717 E Yanonali St
Santa Barbara CA 93103
805 730-3620

(P-13537)
MISSION LINEN SUPPLY
Also Called: Mission Linen Supply & Svcs
1401 Summer St, Eureka (95501-2246)
PHONE...................707 443-8681
Jack Anderson, *General Mgr*
EMP: 58
SALES (corp-wide): 192.2MM **Privately Held**
WEB: www.missions.com
SIC: 7213 Uniform supply
PA: Mission Linen Supply
717 E Yanonali St
Santa Barbara CA 93103
805 730-3620

(P-13538)
MISSION LINEN SUPPLY
Also Called: Mission Linen & Uniform Svc
2555 S Orange Ave, Fresno (93725-1398)
PHONE...................559 268-0647
Allen Gregory, *Manager*
EMP: 75
SALES (corp-wide): 192.2MM **Privately Held**
WEB: www.missions.com
SIC: 7213 Uniform supply
PA: Mission Linen Supply
717 E Yanonali St
Santa Barbara CA 93103
805 730-3620

(P-13539)
MISSION LINEN SUPPLY
Also Called: Mission Linen & Uniform Svc
505 Maulhardt Ave, Oxnard (93030-7925)
PHONE...................805 485-6794
Matthew Aguelli, *Manager*
Jennifer Strong, *Office Mgr*
EMP: 55
SALES (corp-wide): 192.2MM **Privately Held**
WEB: www.missions.com
SIC: 7213 Towel supply

PA: Mission Linen Supply
717 E Yanonali St
Santa Barbara CA 93103
805 730-3620

(P-13540)
MISSION LINEN SUPPLY
Also Called: Mission Linen & Uniform Svc
30305 Union City Blvd, Union City (94587-1513)
PHONE...................510 429-7305
Ken Eggers, *Manager*
EMP: 120
SALES (corp-wide): 192.2MM **Privately Held**
WEB: www.missions.com
SIC: 7213 7218 Linen supply, non-clothing; linen supply, clothing; industrial launderers
PA: Mission Linen Supply
717 E Yanonali St
Santa Barbara CA 93103
805 730-3620

(P-13541)
MISSION LINEN SUPPLY
Also Called: Mission Linen & Uniform Svc
712 E Montecito St, Santa Barbara (93103-3295)
PHONE...................805 962-7687
Curtos Lopez, *Manager*
Sean Fallon, *Area Mgr*
Mario Witrado, *Area Mgr*
Karl Huff, *General Mgr*
Donald Oliveira, *General Mgr*
EMP: 50
SALES (corp-wide): 192.2MM **Privately Held**
WEB: www.missions.com
SIC: 7213 Uniform supply
PA: Mission Linen Supply
717 E Yanonali St
Santa Barbara CA 93103
805 730-3620

(P-13542)
MISSION LINEN SUPPLY
Also Called: Mission Linen & Uniform Svc
1340 W 7th St, Chico (95928-4907)
PHONE...................530 342-4110
Nick Katzenstein, *Manager*
David Simcox, *Area Mgr*
EMP: 50
SALES (corp-wide): 192.2MM **Privately Held**
WEB: www.missions.com
SIC: 7213 5699 Uniform supply; uniforms & work clothing
PA: Mission Linen Supply
717 E Yanonali St
Santa Barbara CA 93103
805 730-3620

(P-13543)
MISSION LINEN SUPPLY
Also Called: Mission Linen & Uniform Svc
435 W Market St, Salinas (93901-1498)
PHONE...................831 375-2491
Bill McCreary, *Manager*
EMP: 90
SALES (corp-wide): 192.2MM **Privately Held**
WEB: www.missions.com
SIC: 7213 Uniform supply
PA: Mission Linen Supply
717 E Yanonali St
Santa Barbara CA 93103
805 730-3620

(P-13544)
MISSION LINEN SUPPLY
Also Called: Mission Linen & Uniform Svc
619 W Avenue I, Lancaster (93534-2585)
PHONE...................661 948-5051
Bud McGuire, *General Mgr*
EMP: 100
SALES (corp-wide): 192.2MM **Privately Held**
SIC: 7213 2841 Uniform supply; soap & other detergents
PA: Mission Linen Supply
717 E Yanonali St
Santa Barbara CA 93103
805 730-3620

(P-13545)
MISSION LINEN SUPPLY
Also Called: Mission Linen & Uniform Svc
7524 Reese Rd, Sacramento (95828-3707)
PHONE...................916 423-3135
Ed Morrow, *Manager*
EMP: 150
SALES (corp-wide): 192.2MM **Privately Held**
WEB: www.missions.com
SIC: 7213 7218 Industrial launderers; uniform supply
PA: Mission Linen Supply
717 E Yanonali St
Santa Barbara CA 93103
805 730-3620

(P-13546)
MISSION LINEN SUPPLY
Also Called: Mission Linen & Uniform Svc
602 S Western Ave, Santa Maria (93458-5496)
PHONE...................805 922-3579
Bill Bently, *General Mgr*
EMP: 80
SALES (corp-wide): 192.2MM **Privately Held**
WEB: www.missions.com
SIC: 7213 Uniform supply
PA: Mission Linen Supply
717 E Yanonali St
Santa Barbara CA 93103
805 730-3620

(P-13547)
MISSION LINEN SUPPLY
Also Called: Mission Linen & Uniform Svc
5400 Alton Way, Chino (91710-7601)
PHONE...................909 393-5589
Mike Keller, *Manager*
Chet Gilliatt, *Branch Mgr*
EMP: 400
SALES (corp-wide): 192.2MM **Privately Held**
WEB: www.missions.com
SIC: 7213 7218 Linen supply, non-clothing; linen supply, clothing; industrial launderers
PA: Mission Linen Supply
717 E Yanonali St
Santa Barbara CA 93103
805 730-3620

(P-13548)
MORGAN SERVICES INC
Also Called: Morgan Linen Service
905 Yale St, Los Angeles (90012-1724)
PHONE...................213 485-9666
Mark Smith, *Branch Mgr*
Michelle Valenzuela, *Admin Asst*
David Morat, *Manager*
EMP: 100
SQ FT: 51,339
SALES (corp-wide): 38.6MM **Privately Held**
WEB: www.morganservices.com
SIC: 7213 7218 Linen supply; industrial launderers
PA: Morgan Services, Inc.
323 N Michigan Ave
Chicago IL 60601
312 346-3181

(P-13549)
PARK CLEANERS INC (PA)
Also Called: Park Uniform Rentals
419 Mcgroarty St, San Gabriel (91776-2302)
PHONE...................626 281-5942
James L Brittain, *President*
Ted Doll, *Vice Pres*
EMP: 75
SQ FT: 7,000
SALES (est): 2.4MM **Privately Held**
SIC: 7213 7216 Uniform supply; cleaning & dyeing, except rugs

(P-13550)
PRUDENTIAL OVERALL SUPPLY
Also Called: Store 17
5300 Gabbert Rd, Moorpark (93021-1772)
P.O. Box 11210, Santa Ana (92711-1210)
PHONE...................805 529-0833
Mark Stanton, *Manager*
Jon Locke, *Site Mgr*
Rebecca Kourey, *Plant Supt*

EMP: 56
SALES (corp-wide): 158.2MM **Privately Held**
WEB: www.pos-clean.com
SIC: 7213 5087 7218 Uniform supply; janitors' supplies; wiping towel supply
PA: Prudential Overall Supply
1661 Alton Pkwy
Irvine CA 92606
949 250-4855

(P-13551)
RFID CORPORATION
701 Willow Pass Rd Ste 10, Pittsburg (94565-1803)
PHONE...................................925 473-9978
John Burskens, *Plant Mgr*
EMP: 190 **Publicly Held**
SIC: 7213 Uniform supply
HQ: Rfid Corporation
1901 S Meyers Rd Ste 630
Oakbrook Terrace IL 60181
678 823-4100

(P-13552)
RFID TEXTILE SERVICES INC
300 E Commercial St, Pomona (91767-5506)
PHONE...................................909 623-5135
Albert Cunningham, *General Mgr*
EMP: 65 **Publicly Held**
SIC: 7213 Uniform supply
HQ: Rfid Textile Services, Inc.
1105 Lakewood Pkwy # 210
Alpharetta GA 30009
678 823-4100

(P-13553)
RICHARD K NEWMAN AND ASSOC INC (PA)
Also Called: Sparkle Uniform & Linen Svc
121 Monterey St, Bakersfield (93305-3406)
PHONE...................................661 634-1130
Jeffrey C Newman Sr, *Ch of Bd*
Jeffrey C Newman Jr, *President*
Mike Daniel, *COO*
Jeff Newman Jr, *Executive*
Alison Daniel, *Office Mgr*
EMP: 50
SQ FT: 26,000
SALES (est): 7.6MM **Privately Held**
WEB: www.sparklerental.com
SIC: 7213 7216 Linen supply, non-clothing; uniform supply; drycleaning collecting & distributing agency

(P-13554)
SYNERGY HEALTH NORTH AMER INC
2240 E Artesia Blvd, Long Beach (90805-1739)
PHONE...................................562 428-5858
Gary Metz, *Manager*
EMP: 72
SALES (corp-wide): 2.6B **Privately Held**
SIC: 7213 Linen supply
HQ: Synergy Health North America, Inc.
3903 Northdale Blvd 100e
Tampa FL 33624
813 891-9550

(P-13555)
UNIFIRST CORPORATION
4630 Beloit Dr Ste 40, Sacramento (95838-2449)
PHONE...................................916 929-3766
Jerald Satterlfield, *Branch Mgr*
EMP: 50
SALES (corp-wide): 1.7B **Publicly Held**
SIC: 7213 5949 5699 Uniform supply; needlework goods & supplies; uniforms
PA: Unifirst Corporation
68 Jonspin Rd
Wilmington MA 01887
978 658-8888

7215 Coin Operated Laundries & Cleaning

(P-13556)
ALL VALLEY WASHER SERVICE INC
15008 Delano St, Van Nuys (91411-2016)
PHONE...................................818 787-1100
Ron Feinstein, *President*
Billy Feinstein, *Treasurer*
Robert Feinstein, *Vice Pres*
Joan Heinmiller, *Sales Mgr*
Trini Valenzuela, *Marketing Staff*
EMP: 70
SQ FT: 11,000
SALES (est): 8.4MM **Privately Held**
WEB: www.allvalleywasher.com
SIC: 7215 6531 7359 5087 Laundry, coin-operated; real estate agents & managers; appliance rental; laundry equipment & supplies

(P-13557)
CLEAN KING LAUNDRY SYSTEMS INC
15431 Chatsworth St, Mission Hills (91345-1905)
P.O. Box 8689, Northridge (91327-8689)
PHONE...................................818 363-5500
Brian Merkel, *President*
EMP: 50
SALES (est): 1.5MM **Privately Held**
SIC: 7215 Coin-operated laundries & cleaning

(P-13558)
COINMACH CORPORATION (PA)
Also Called: Reliable Co
3628 San Fernando Rd, Glendale (91204-2944)
PHONE...................................818 637-4300
EMP: 80
SQ FT: 22,000
SALES (est): 4.6MM **Privately Held**
SIC: 7215 7211 5087

(P-13559)
CSC SERVICEWORKS HOLDINGS INC
Also Called: Kwik Wash Laundries
32910 Alvarado Niles Rd # 150, Union City (94587-3103)
PHONE...................................510 429-0900
Mike Hagen, *Manager*
Richard Lisowski, *Sales Staff*
EMP: 150
SALES (corp-wide): 356.6MM **Privately Held**
SIC: 7215 Laundry, coin-operated
PA: Csc Serviceworks Holdings, Inc.
303 Sunnyside Blvd # 70
Plainview NY 11803
516 349-8555

(P-13560)
OCEANSIDE LAUNDRY LLC
Also Called: Campus Laundry
675 Beach Dr, Watsonville (95076-1904)
PHONE...................................831 722-4358
Gregory Anderson, *President*
Malissa Edwards, *Human Res Dir*
Sherry Lee, *Sales Dir*
Raul Cuadra, *Manager*
EMP: 100
SALES (est): 8.1MM **Privately Held**
SIC: 7215 Coin-operated laundries & cleaning

(P-13561)
PRO-WASH INC
9117 S Main St, Los Angeles (90003-3722)
PHONE...................................323 756-6000
Steve Koo, *President*
EMP: 70
SQ FT: 20,000
SALES (est): 2.9MM **Privately Held**
WEB: www.prowashconsulting.com
SIC: 7215 Coin-operated laundries & cleaning

(P-13562)
WASH MLTFMILY LDRY SYSTEMS LLC (PA)
100 N Pacific Coast Hwy, El Segundo (90245-4359)
PHONE...................................310 643-8491
Mark C Good, *CEO*
Ross Van Horne, *Exec Dir*
EMP: 150
SQ FT: 130,000
SALES (est): 55.3MM **Privately Held**
WEB: www.weblaundry.com
SIC: 7215 Laundry, coin-operated

7216 Dry Cleaning Plants, Except Rug Cleaning

(P-13563)
CAMARO CLEANERS CORP (PA)
1515 Wedgewood Dr, Hillsborough (94010-7343)
PHONE...................................650 343-4296
Modesto Gomez, *CEO*
EMP: 85
SQ FT: 20,000
SALES (est): 543.4K **Privately Held**
SIC: 7216 Drycleaning plants, except rugs

(P-13564)
COIT SERVICES INC
1297 Logan Ave, Costa Mesa (92626-4004)
PHONE...................................949 760-0760
John Comer, *Branch Mgr*
Jan Carney, *President*
EMP: 50
SALES (corp-wide): 51.9MM **Privately Held**
SIC: 7216 7217 Drycleaning plants, except rugs; carpet & upholstery cleaning
PA: Coit Services, Inc.
897 Hinckley Rd
Burlingame CA 94010
650 243-8797

(P-13565)
CUSTOM COMMERCIAL DRY CLRS INC (PA)
Also Called: Frsteam By Custom Commercial
3201 Investment Blvd, Hayward (94545-3813)
PHONE...................................510 723-1000
Courtney Nicholas, *CEO*
Jim Nicholas, *President*
Ryan Meekma, *Vice Pres*
Holly Murry, *Vice Pres*
EMP: 50
SALES (est): 4.3MM **Privately Held**
SIC: 7216 Cleaning & dyeing, except rugs

(P-13566)
INTER-CITY CLEANERS
438 S Airport Blvd, South San Francisco (94080-6908)
PHONE...................................650 875-9200
Hans Gelfand, *Co-Owner*
Vera Gelfand, *Co-Owner*
EMP: 68
SQ FT: 9,000
SALES (est): 4.6MM **Privately Held**
WEB: www.intercitycleaners.com
SIC: 7216 7219 Cleaning & dyeing, except rugs; laundry, except power & coin-operated

(P-13567)
PICO CLEANER INC (PA)
9150 W Pico Blvd, Los Angeles (90035-1320)
PHONE...................................310 274-2431
Sharam Jahanbani, *CEO*
Simon Djahanbani, *President*
EMP: 80
SQ FT: 10,000
SALES (est): 5.6MM **Privately Held**
WEB: www.picocleaners.com
SIC: 7216 Cleaning & dyeing, except rugs; curtain cleaning & repair

---

(P-13568)
SANTA BARBARA FABRICARE INC
Also Called: Ablitt's Fine Cleaners
14 W Gutierrez St, Santa Barbara (93101-3423)
PHONE...................................805 963-6677
Neil Ablitt, *President*
R Neil Ablitt, *President*
Sue Ablitt, *Vice Pres*
Sean Nguyen, *General Mgr*
EMP: 50
SQ FT: 12,500
SALES (est): 3MM **Privately Held**
SIC: 7216 7211 7212 Cleaning & dyeing, except rugs; power laundries, family & commercial; valet apparel service

(P-13569)
SHADKOR INC
Also Called: Milt & Michael Master Dry Clrs
4021 W Alameda Ave, Burbank (91505-4335)
PHONE...................................818 953-4627
Thomas Agha, *President*
Milton Shortkoff, *Corp Secy*
EMP: 60
SQ FT: 4,345
SALES (est): 3.2MM **Privately Held**
SIC: 7216 Cleaning & dyeing, except rugs

(P-13570)
STERLING WESTWOOD INC
Also Called: Sterling Dry Cleaners
3405 Overland Ave, Los Angeles (90034-5405)
PHONE...................................310 287-2431
Harry Gershenson, *Manager*
EMP: 55
SALES (corp-wide): 2.1MM **Privately Held**
SIC: 7216 Drycleaning plants, except rugs
PA: Sterling Westwood Inc
1600 Westwood Blvd
Los Angeles CA 90024
310 474-8525

(P-13571)
VALETOR INC
Also Called: Hollyway Cleaners
8359 Santa Monica Blvd, Los Angeles (90069-4312)
PHONE...................................323 654-1271
Fatehali Amersi, *President*
EMP: 50
SQ FT: 4,000
SALES (est): 1.8MM **Privately Held**
SIC: 7216 7215 Cleaning & dyeing, except rugs; laundry, coin-operated

---

7217 Carpet & Upholstery Cleaning

(P-13572)
BONDED INC (PA)
Also Called: Bonded Carpet
7831 Ostrow St, San Diego (92111-3602)
P.O. Box 23910 (92193-3910)
PHONE...................................858 576-8400
Mitch Adler, *President*
Sherri Adler, *Vice Pres*
Mary Nelson, *Executive*
Amanda Deloach, *Administration*
Elva Espinoza, *Human Res Dir*
EMP: 80
SQ FT: 16,500
SALES (est): 6.6MM **Privately Held**
WEB: www.bondedcarpet.com
SIC: 7217 5713 Carpet & furniture cleaning on location; home furnishings; fireplace equipment & accessories

(P-13573)
C & S DRAPERIES INC
Also Called: Coit Restoration Services
4210 Kiernan Ave, Modesto (95356-9758)
PHONE...................................209 466-5371
Pete Bakker, *CEO*
Helen Bakker, *CEO*
EMP: 150
SQ FT: 50,000

(PA)=Parent Co (HQ)=Headquarters (DH)=Div Headquarters
✿ = New Business established in last 2 years
2019 Directory of California Wholesalers and Services Companies
579

SALES (est): 10.5MM Privately Held
SIC: 7217 Carpet & furniture cleaning on location; carpet & rug cleaning plant; carpet & rug cleaning & repairing plant

(P-13574)
CARPET SOLUTIONS
28126 Peacock Ridge Dr # 115, Rancho Palos Verdes (90275-7108)
PHONE..........................310 886-3800
Yenling Huan, *Owner*
EMP: 50 **EST:** 2011
SALES (est): 1.4MM **Privately Held**
SIC: 7217 1752 Carpet & upholstery cleaning; carpet laying

(P-13575)
CHROMA SYSTEMS
Also Called: Southcoast Dyeing & Finishing
3201 S Susan St, Santa Ana (92704-6838)
PHONE..........................714 557-8480
Peer Vinther, *Partner*
Monterey Carpets, *Partner*
Camelot Carpet Mills, *Partner*
EMP: 100
SQ FT: 200,000
SALES (est): 3.3MM **Privately Held**
SIC: 7217 2273 Carpet & rug dyeing plant; carpets & rugs

(P-13576)
COLT SERVICES INC
Also Called: Stanley Steemer Carpet Cleaner
9655 Via Excelencia, San Diego (92126-4555)
PHONE..........................858 271-9910
Toll Free:..........................888 -
Steven R Thompson, *President*
EMP: 100
SQ FT: 33,000
SALES (est): 9MM **Privately Held**
SIC: 7217 Carpet & furniture cleaning on location

(P-13577)
DESIGNERS LLC (PA)
Also Called: Nex Systems
235 Frank West Cir, Stockton (95206-4045)
PHONE..........................209 982-0600
Keith Bewley,
Doug Mc Kee, *CFO*
Adrian Henry, *General Mgr*
John Haberman, *Project Mgr*
James Rehn, *Marketing Staff*
EMP: 60
SQ FT: 8,000
SALES (est): 5.7MM **Privately Held**
WEB: www.nexsystems.com
SIC: 7217 Carpet & furniture cleaning on location

(P-13578)
EXPRESS CONTRACTORS INC
11625 Industry Ave, Fontana (92337-6931)
P.O. Box 310279 (92331-0279)
PHONE..........................951 360-6500
Amaer Alhamwi, *President*
Cesar Velarde, *Manager*
EMP: 100
SQ FT: 10,000
SALES (est): 9.1MM **Privately Held**
SIC: 7217 1752 1721 1743 Carpet & rug cleaning & repairing plant; carpet & rug cleaning plant; carpet & rug dyeing plant; carpet laying; painting & paper hanging; terrazzo, tile, marble, mosaic work

(P-13579)
J&M KEYSTONE INC
2709 Via Orange Way Ste A, Spring Valley (91978-1708)
PHONE..........................619 466-9876
Ronald D Martin, *CEO*
Dale Whittle, *Corp Secy*
James Bronson, *Vice Pres*
EMP: 80
SQ FT: 9,100
SALES (est): 14MM **Privately Held**
WEB: www.jmkeystone.com
SIC: 7217 1542 1799 8744 Carpet & furniture cleaning on location; commercial & office buildings, renovation & repair; steam cleaning of building exteriors; ; air duct cleaning; floor waxing; repairing fire damage, single-family houses

(P-13580)
STANLEY STEEMER OF LOS ANGLES (PA)
841 W Foothill Blvd, Azusa (91702-2815)
PHONE..........................626 791-9400
Kevin Pucci, *President*
Jeff Pucci, *Vice Pres*
Ryan Jourdain, *Opers Mgr*
EMP: 62
SQ FT: 100,000
SALES (est): 7MM **Privately Held**
SIC: 7217 1799 Carpet & furniture cleaning on location; post-disaster renovations

---

7218 Industrial Launderers

(P-13581)
AMERICAN TEXTILE MAINT CO
2201 E Carson St, Long Beach (90807-3043)
PHONE..........................562 424-1607
Steve Jones, *Manager*
EMP: 180
SALES (corp-wide): 197.6MM **Privately Held**
WEB: www.amtextile.net
SIC: 7218 7213 Industrial launderers; uniform supply
PA: American Textile Maintenance Company
1667 W Washington Blvd
Los Angeles CA 90007
323 731-3132

(P-13582)
AMERIPRIDE SERVICES INC
Also Called: Ameripride Uniform Services
1050 W Whites Bridge Ave, Fresno (93706-1328)
PHONE..........................559 266-0627
Matt Wencel, *Manager*
Deborah Money, *Officer*
Hector Moreno, *Engineer*
Carl Anderson, *Sales Executive*
Steve Plescia, *Sales Executive*
EMP: 100 **Publicly Held**
WEB: www.ameripride.com
SIC: 7218 7213 Radiation protective garment supply; linen supply
HQ: Ameripride Services, Inc.
10801 Wayzata Blvd # 100
Minnetonka MN 55305
800 750-4628

(P-13583)
ARAMARK UNF & CAREER AP LLC
1617 Jim Way, Modesto (95358-5703)
PHONE..........................209 368-9785
Manny Martinez, *General Mgr*
EMP: 60 **Publicly Held**
WEB: www.aramark-uniform.com
SIC: 7218 Industrial launderers
HQ: Aramark Uniform & Career Apparel, Llc
115 N First St Ste 203
Burbank CA 91502
818 973-3700

(P-13584)
ARAMARK UNF & CAREER AP LLC
115 N First St, Burbank (91502-1856)
P.O. Box 7891 (91510-7891)
PHONE..........................818 973-3700
EMP: 62 **Publicly Held**
SIC: 7218 Industrial launderers
HQ: Aramark Uniform & Career Apparel, Llc
115 N First St Ste 203
Burbank CA 91502
818 973-3700

(P-13585)
ARAMARK UNF & CAREER AP LLC
1419 National Dr, Sacramento (95834-1946)
P.O. Box 340910 (95834-0910)
PHONE..........................916 286-4100
Jeff Black, *Manager*
EMP: 300 **Publicly Held**
WEB: www.aramark-uniform.com
SIC: 7218 7213 Industrial launderers; uniform supply

HQ: Aramark Uniform & Career Apparel, Llc
115 N First St Ste 203
Burbank CA 91502
818 973-3700

(P-13586)
ARAMARK UNF & CAREER AP LLC (DH)
115 N First St Ste 203, Burbank (91502-1857)
P.O. Box 7891 (91510-7891)
PHONE..........................818 973-3700
Mike Fadden, *Mng Member*
Lorie Boodry, *Vice Pres*
Caralee Brown, *Vice Pres*
Terry Oberbroeckling, *Vice Pres*
Gene West, *Vice Pres*
EMP: 250
SQ FT: 63,000
SALES (est): 876.8MM **Publicly Held**
WEB: www.aramark-uniform.com
SIC: 7218 Industrial uniform supply; treated equipment supply: mats, rugs, mops, cloths, etc.; wiping towel supply
HQ: Aramark Uniform & Career Apparel Group, Inc.
1101 Market St Ste 45
Philadelphia PA 19107
215 238-3000

(P-13587)
ARAMARK UNF & CAREER AP LLC
755 Butte St, Redding (96001-0928)
PHONE..........................530 241-6433
Michael Brodeur, *Manager*
EMP: 70 **Publicly Held**
WEB: www.aramark-uniform.com
SIC: 7218 7213 Industrial launderers; uniform supply
HQ: Aramark Uniform & Career Apparel, Llc
115 N First St Ste 203
Burbank CA 91502
818 973-3700

(P-13588)
ARAMARK UNF & CAREER AP LLC
330 Chestnut St, Oakland (94607-2528)
PHONE..........................510 835-9285
Art Wake, *Branch Mgr*
Sue Harding, *Executive*
EMP: 200
SQ FT: 10,000 **Publicly Held**
WEB: www.aramark-uniform.com
SIC: 7218 Wiping towel supply
HQ: Aramark Uniform & Career Apparel, Llc
115 N First St Ste 203
Burbank CA 91502
818 973-3700

(P-13589)
ARAMARK UNF & CAREER AP LLC
4422 Dunham St, Los Angeles (90023-4113)
PHONE..........................323 266-0555
Alice Stewart, *General Mgr*
Boris Mezhebovsky, *Administration*
EMP: 230 **Publicly Held**
WEB: www.aramark-uniform.com
SIC: 7218 Industrial launderers
HQ: Aramark Uniform & Career Apparel, Llc
115 N First St Ste 203
Burbank CA 91502
818 973-3700

(P-13590)
ARAMARK UNF & CAREER AP LLC
3101 W Adams St, Santa Ana (92704-5807)
P.O. Box 20378, Fountain Valley (92728-0378)
PHONE..........................714 545-4877
Mark Papapendorf, *Manager*
Jose Deleon, *District Mgr*
Amy Nguyen, *Financial Exec*
John Bos, *Director*
EMP: 80
SQ FT: 15,317 **Publicly Held**
WEB: www.aramark-uniform.com
SIC: 7218 7213 Industrial launderers; uniform supply

HQ: Aramark Uniform & Career Apparel, Llc
115 N First St Ste 203
Burbank CA 91502
818 973-3700

(P-13591)
ARAMARK UNF & CAREER AP LLC
31148 San Antonio St, Hayward (94544-7906)
P.O. Box 5034 (94540)
PHONE..........................510 487-1855
Dave Tyquiengco, *Manager*
Kevin Thongsinthusak, *Executive*
EMP: 70 **Publicly Held**
WEB: www.aramark-uniform.com
SIC: 7218 Industrial uniform supply; treated equipment supply: mats, rugs, mops, cloths, etc.; wiping towel supply
HQ: Aramark Uniform & Career Apparel, Llc
115 N First St Ste 203
Burbank CA 91502
818 973-3700

(P-13592)
ARAMARK UNF & CAREER AP LLC
5000 Forni Dr, Concord (94520-1223)
P.O. Box 5826 (94524-0826)
PHONE..........................925 827-3782
Ray Rhode, *Manager*
EMP: 69 **Publicly Held**
WEB: www.aramark-uniform.com
SIC: 7218 7213 Industrial launderers; uniform supply
HQ: Aramark Uniform & Career Apparel, Llc
115 N First St Ste 203
Burbank CA 91502
818 973-3700

(P-13593)
ARAMARK UNF & CAREER AP LLC
5665 Eastgate Dr, San Diego (92121)
PHONE..........................858 550-5200
EMP: 196 **Publicly Held**
WEB: www.aramark-uniform.com
SIC: 7218 Industrial launderers
HQ: Aramark Uniform & Career Apparel, Llc
115 N First St Ste 203
Burbank CA 91502
818 973-3700

(P-13594)
ARAMARK UNF & CAREER AP LLC
15372 Cobalt St, Sylmar (91342-2729)
PHONE..........................818 364-8272
Brad Drummond, *Principal*
EMP: 63 **Publicly Held**
SIC: 7218 Industrial launderers
HQ: Aramark Uniform & Career Apparel, Llc
115 N First St Ste 203
Burbank CA 91502
818 973-3700

(P-13595)
ARAMARK UNF & CAREER AP LLC
440 N Canal St, South San Francisco (94080-4603)
PHONE..........................650 244-9332
David Techlingco, *Manager*
EMP: 70 **Publicly Held**
WEB: www.aramark-uniform.com
SIC: 7218 Industrial launderers
HQ: Aramark Uniform & Career Apparel, Llc
115 N First St Ste 203
Burbank CA 91502
818 973-3700

(P-13596)
ARAMARK UNIFORM SERVICES
1419 National Dr, Sacramento (95834-1946)
PHONE..........................916 286-4100
Gary Koolhof, *Principal*
Bill Ledbetter, *Purch Agent*
Gary Smith, *Sales Staff*
EMP: 99
SALES (est): 6.1MM **Publicly Held**
SIC: 7218 Industrial launderers

PA: Aramark
1101 Mkt St Aramark Twr Aramark Tower
Philadelphia PA 19107

(P-13597)
BOWSMITH INC (PA)
131 2nd St, Exeter (93221-1947)
P.O. Box 428 (93221-0428)
PHONE....................................559 592-9485
Allan L Smith, *CEO*
Kenneth Berg, *Vice Pres*
Tonnie Garnett, *Purch Mgr*
Richard Phillips, *Mfg Mgr*
Shannon Peacock, *Plant Mgr*
EMP: 75 EST: 1974
SQ FT: 14,400
SALES (est): 8.4MM **Privately Held**
WEB: www.bowsmith.com
SIC: 7218 4971 Industrial equipment launderers; irrigation systems

(P-13598)
CINTAS CORPORATION NO 2
2188 Del Franco St Ste 70, San Jose (95131-1583)
PHONE....................................408 292-6700
Scott Douglas Farmer, *Branch Mgr*
Jordan Pratt, *Sales Mgr*
Nick Pratt, *Sales Mgr*
Christina Harris, *Sales Staff*
Cynthia Manning, *Sales Staff*
EMP: 88
SALES (corp-wide): 6.4B **Publicly Held**
WEB: www.cintas-corp.com
SIC: 7218 Industrial uniform supply
HQ: Cintas Corporation No. 2
6800 Cintas Blvd
Mason OH 45040

(P-13599)
CINTAS CORPORATION NO 3
5500 Young St, Bakersfield (93311-9648)
PHONE....................................661 282-4300
EMP: 79
SALES (corp-wide): 6.4B **Publicly Held**
SIC: 7218 Industrial uniform supply
HQ: Cintas Corporation No. 3
6800 Cintas Blvd
Mason OH 45040

(P-13600)
CINTAS CORPORATION NO 3
675 32nd St, San Diego (92102-3301)
PHONE....................................619 239-1001
Kevin Nolan, *Branch Mgr*
EMP: 150
SQ FT: 7,000
SALES (corp-wide): 6.4B **Publicly Held**
WEB: www.cintas-corp.com
SIC: 7218 7213 Industrial uniform supply; uniform supply
HQ: Cintas Corporation No. 3
6800 Cintas Blvd
Mason OH 45040

(P-13601)
CINTAS CORPORATION NO 3
20929 Cabot Blvd, Hayward (94545-1155)
PHONE....................................510 352-6330
Stephen Dee, *Branch Mgr*
EMP: 79
SALES (corp-wide): 6.4B **Publicly Held**
WEB: www.cintas-corp.com
SIC: 7218 Industrial uniform supply
HQ: Cintas Corporation No. 3
6800 Cintas Blvd
Mason OH 45040

(P-13602)
CINTAS CORPORATION NO 3
20100 S Susana Rd, Compton (90221-5722)
PHONE....................................310 725-2850
Bryce Littlejohn, *Branch Mgr*
EMP: 79
SALES (corp-wide): 6.4B **Publicly Held**
SIC: 7218 Industrial uniform supply

(P-13603)
CINTAS CORPORATION NO 3
1231 National Dr, Sacramento (95834-1902)
PHONE....................................916 419-8519
Doyle Denny, *Manager*
EMP: 150
SALES (corp-wide): 6.4B **Publicly Held**
WEB: www.cintas-corp.com
SIC: 7218 Industrial uniform supply
HQ: Cintas Corporation No. 3
6800 Cintas Blvd
Mason OH 45040

(P-13604)
CINTAS CORPORATION NO 3
1851 S Wineville Ave, Ontario (91761-3667)
PHONE....................................909 390-4912
Adrian Sandoval, *Manager*
EMP: 79
SALES (corp-wide): 6.4B **Publicly Held**
WEB: www.cintas-corp.com
SIC: 7218 Industrial launderers
HQ: Cintas Corporation No. 3
6800 Cintas Blvd
Mason OH 45040

(P-13605)
CINTAS CORPORATION NO 3
220 Demeter St, East Palo Alto (94303-1303)
PHONE....................................650 589-4300
EMP: 79
SALES (corp-wide): 6.4B **Publicly Held**
SIC: 7218 Industrial uniform supply
HQ: Cintas Corporation No. 3
6800 Cintas Blvd
Mason OH 45040

(P-13606)
G&K SERVICES INC
5900 Alder Ave, Sacramento (95828-1110)
PHONE....................................916 381-5500
Rich Pland, *Branch Mgr*
Alberto Robles, *Plant Mgr*
Jerry Brigham, *Accounts Exec*
EMP: 80
SALES (corp-wide): 6.4B **Publicly Held**
WEB: www.gkservices.com
SIC: 7218 5699 7213 Industrial uniform supply; uniform supply
HQ: G&K Services, Llc
5995 Opus Pkwy Ste 500
Minnetonka MN 55343
952 912-5500

(P-13607)
G&K SERVICES LLC
1229 California Ave, Pittsburg (94565-4112)
PHONE....................................925 427-4401
Scott Hartesty, *Branch Mgr*
EMP: 50
SQ FT: 40,202
SALES (corp-wide): 6.4B **Publicly Held**
WEB: www.gkservices.com
SIC: 7218 7213 Industrial uniform supply; uniform supply
HQ: G&K Services, Llc
5995 Opus Pkwy Ste 500
Minnetonka MN 55343
952 912-5500

(P-13608)
GARMENT INDUSTRY LAUNDRY
710 W 58th St, Los Angeles (90037-4034)
PHONE....................................323 752-8335
Lyle Dean Foreman, *President*
Bjarne Schmidt, *Vice Pres*
EMP: 200
SQ FT: 30,000
SALES (est): 6.2MM **Privately Held**
SIC: 7218 7211 Industrial launderers; power laundries, family & commercial

(P-13609)
IMAGE FIRST HEALTHCRE LNDRY SP
Also Called: Image 1st
17818 S Figueroa St, Gardena (90248-4214)
PHONE....................................310 819-1463
Bryan Cunningham, *Manager*
Gino Giannettino, *Asst Mgr*
EMP: 144
SALES (corp-wide): 34.6MM **Privately Held**
SIC: 7218 Industrial clothing launderers
PA: Image First Healthcare Laundry Specialists, Inc.
900 E 8th Ave Ste 300
King Of Prussia PA 19406
484 253-7200

(P-13610)
INTERNATIONAL GARMENT FINISHER
Also Called: I G F
2144 W Gaylord St, Long Beach (90813-1034)
PHONE....................................562 983-7400
Richard Kim, *President*
EMP: 100
SALES (est): 3.4MM **Privately Held**
WEB: www.igf.com
SIC: 7218 Industrial launderers

(P-13611)
MISSION LINEN SUPPLY
Also Called: Mission Linen & Uniform Svc
435 W Market St, Salinas (93901-1498)
PHONE....................................831 424-1753
Bill McCreary, *Manager*
Joey Antonetti, *Area Mgr*
EMP: 150
SALES (corp-wide): 192.2MM **Privately Held**
WEB: www.missions.com
SIC: 7218 7213 Industrial uniform supply; linen supply
PA: Mission Linen Supply
717 E Yanonali St
Santa Barbara CA 93103
805 730-3620

(P-13612)
PRUDENTIAL OVERALL SUPPLY
6920 Bandini Blvd, Commerce (90040-3382)
PHONE....................................323 724-4888
Mark Albertson, *Manager*
Barry Easdale, *Executive*
Jennifer Shearer, *Sales Staff*
EMP: 100
SQ FT: 40,000
SALES (corp-wide): 158.2MM **Privately Held**
WEB: www.pos-clean.com
SIC: 7218 7213 5087 Industrial launderers; uniform supply; janitors' supplies
PA: Prudential Overall Supply
1661 Alton Pkwy
Irvine CA 92606
949 250-4855

(P-13613)
PRUDENTIAL OVERALL SUPPLY (PA)
1661 Alton Pkwy, Irvine (92606-4877)
P.O. Box 11210, Santa Ana (92711-1210)
PHONE....................................949 250-4855
Dan Clark, *CEO*
Donald Lahn, *Vice Chairman*
Thomas C Watts, *President*
Donald C Lahn, *Vice Ch Bd*
Stefan Schurter, *Executive*
▲ **EMP:** 95
SQ FT: 20,000
SALES: 158.2MM **Privately Held**
WEB: www.pos-clean.com
SIC: 7218 Wiping towel supply

(P-13614)
PRUDENTIAL OVERALL SUPPLY
Also Called: Prudential Dust Control
6997 Jurupa Ave, Riverside (92504-1009)
PHONE....................................951 687-0440
Jay Boyer, *General Mgr*
John Thompson, *CFO*
EMP: 127

SALES (corp-wide): 158.2MM **Privately Held**
WEB: www.pos-clean.com
SIC: 7218 Industrial launderers
PA: Prudential Overall Supply
1661 Alton Pkwy
Irvine CA 92606
949 250-4855

(P-13615)
PRUDENTIAL OVERALL SUPPLY
2485 Ash St, Vista (92081-8424)
PHONE....................................760 727-7163
Jason Thaffin, *Branch Mgr*
Scott Chafin, *General Mgr*
EMP: 95
SQ FT: 38,476
SALES (corp-wide): 158.2MM **Privately Held**
WEB: www.pos-clean.com
SIC: 7218 7213 5699 Industrial launderers; uniform supply; uniforms & work clothing
PA: Prudential Overall Supply
1661 Alton Pkwy
Irvine CA 92606
949 250-4855

(P-13616)
PRUDENTIAL OVERALL SUPPLY
Also Called: Prudential Cleanroom Services
1437 N Milpitas Blvd, Milpitas (95035-3154)
PHONE....................................408 719-0886
Tim Bleigh, *Manager*
EMP: 99
SQ FT: 30,201
SALES (corp-wide): 158.2MM **Privately Held**
WEB: www.pos-clean.com
SIC: 7218 Wiping towel supply
PA: Prudential Overall Supply
1661 Alton Pkwy
Irvine CA 92606
949 250-4855

(P-13617)
PRUDENTIAL OVERALL SUPPLY
Also Called: Prudential Cleanroom Services
6948 Bandini Blvd, Commerce (90040-3326)
PHONE....................................323 722-0636
Chris Wealch, *General Mgr*
Sandra Sepulveda, *Plant Supt*
Jerry Martin, *VP Sales*
EMP: 65
SQ FT: 21,925
SALES (corp-wide): 158.2MM **Privately Held**
WEB: www.pos-clean.com
SIC: 7218 7213 7349 Industrial launderers; uniform supply; cleaning service, industrial or commercial
PA: Prudential Overall Supply
1661 Alton Pkwy
Irvine CA 92606
949 250-4855

(P-13618)
PRUDENTIAL OVERALL SUPPLY
1260 E North Ave, Fresno (93725-1930)
PHONE....................................559 264-8231
Rick Ponce, *Branch Mgr*
Mark Willis, *General Mgr*
EMP: 80
SQ FT: 42,704
SALES (corp-wide): 158.2MM **Privately Held**
WEB: www.pos-clean.com
SIC: 7218 7213 Industrial launderers; linen supply
PA: Prudential Overall Supply
1661 Alton Pkwy
Irvine CA 92606
949 250-4855

(P-13619)
RFID TEXTILE SERVICES INC
1575 N Case St, Orange (92867-3635)
PHONE....................................714 998-6109
Alicia Silva, *Branch Mgr*
EMP: 194 **Publicly Held**
SIC: 7218 7213 Industrial launderers; uniform supply

P
R
O
D
U
C
T
S
&
S
V
C
S

HQ: Rfid Textile Services, Inc.
1105 Lakewood Pkwy # 210
Alpharetta GA 30009
678 823-4100

(P-13620)
RFID TEXTILE SERVICES INC
8190 Murray Ave, Gilroy (95020-4605)
PHONE..........................408 840-7504
John Beurskens, *Manager*
EMP: 89 **Publicly Held**
SIC: 7218 7213 Industrial launderers;
linen supply
HQ: Rfid Textile Services, Inc.
1105 Lakewood Pkwy # 210
Alpharetta GA 30009
678 823-4100

(P-13621)
SPECIALIZED LAUNDRY SVCS INC
Also Called: 1st Class Laundry Services
33485 Western Ave, Union City
(94587-3201)
PHONE..........................510 487-8297
Jefferey Lee Schlagel, *CEO*
EMP: 165
SQ FT: 24,000
SALES (est): 7.3MM **Privately Held**
SIC: 7218 Industrial launderers

(P-13622)
STONE BLUE INC
Also Called: Pink Diamonds
2501 E 28th St, Vernon (90058-1429)
PHONE..........................323 277-0008
Judy OH, *President*
EMP: 100
SQ FT: 70,000
SALES (est): 3.3MM **Privately Held**
SIC: 7218 Industrial clothing launderers

(P-13623)
UNIFIRST CORPORATION
819 N Hunter St, Stockton (95202-1706)
PHONE..........................209 941-8364
Peter Bernadicou, *Principal*
Joe Chiatello, *General Mgr*
EMP: 50
SALES (corp-wide): 1.7B **Publicly Held**
WEB: www.unifirst.com
SIC: 7218 7213 Industrial uniform supply;
uniform supply
PA: Unifirst Corporation
68 Jonspin Rd
Wilmington MA 01887
978 658-8888

(P-13624)
UNIFIRST CORPORATION
4041 Market St, San Diego (92102-4593)
PHONE..........................619 263-6116
Jesse Sandoval, *Manager*
Reginald Avalos, *Engineer*
EMP: 60
SQ FT: 22,685
SALES (corp-wide): 1.7B **Publicly Held**
WEB: www.unifirst.com
SIC: 7218 7213 Industrial uniform supply;
work clothing supply; radiation protective
garment supply; uniform supply
PA: Unifirst Corporation
68 Jonspin Rd
Wilmington MA 01887
978 658-8888

(P-13625)
UNIFIRST CORPORATION
700 Etiwanda Ave Ste C, Ontario
(91761-8608)
PHONE..........................909 390-8670
Jeff Martin, *Manager*
EMP: 130
SALES (corp-wide): 1.7B **Publicly Held**
WEB: www.unifirst.com
SIC: 7218 7213 Industrial uniform supply;
work clothing supply; radiation protective
garment supply; uniform supply
PA: Unifirst Corporation
68 Jonspin Rd
Wilmington MA 01887
978 658-8888

(P-13626)
UNIFIRST CORPORATION
4730 E Commerce Ave, Fresno
(93725-2222)
PHONE..........................559 233-0400
James Pirson, *Branch Mgr*
EMP: 60
SALES (corp-wide): 1.7B **Publicly Held**
SIC: 7218 Radiation protective garment
supply
PA: Unifirst Corporation
68 Jonspin Rd
Wilmington MA 01887
978 658-8888

(P-13627)
UNIFIRST CORPORATION
2016 Zanker Rd, San Jose (95131-2110)
PHONE..........................408 297-8101
EMP: 60
SALES (corp-wide): 1.7B **Publicly Held**
SIC: 7218 Radiation protective garment
supply
PA: Unifirst Corporation
68 Jonspin Rd
Wilmington MA 01887
978 658-8888

(P-13628)
WORKRITE UNIFORM COMPANY INC (DH)
1701 Lombard St Ste 200, Oxnard
(93030-8235)
PHONE..........................805 483-0175
Philip C Williamson, *CEO*
Keith Suddaby, *President*
Mark Adler, *Vice Pres*
John Marcelletti, *Info Tech Dir*
K'Ann Gregory, *Manager*
EMP: 385 **EST:** 1968
SALES (est): 26.4MM
SALES (corp-wide): 11.8B **Publicly Held**
SIC: 7218 Flame & heat resistant clothing
supply
HQ: Williamson-Dickie Manufacturing Company, Llc
509 W Vickery Blvd
Fort Worth TX 76104
817 336-7201

**7219 Laundry & Garment
Svcs, NEC**

(P-13629)
ARAMARK SERVICES INC
1405 E 58th Pl, Los Angeles (90001-1207)
PHONE..........................323 587-7661
Barry Eastill, *Manager*
EMP: 100
SQ FT: 22,000 **Publicly Held**
SIC: 7219 7218 Laundry, except power &
coin-operated; industrial launderers
HQ: Aramark Services, Inc.
1101 Market St Ste 45
Philadelphia PA 19107
215 238-3000

(P-13630)
CM LAUNDRY LLC
14919 S Figueroa St, Gardena
(90248-1720)
PHONE..........................310 436-6170
Luis Rodriguez,
Anthony Millar,
Ernesto Munoz, *Mng Member*
EMP: 100
SQ FT: 26,500
SALES (est): 4.9MM **Privately Held**
SIC: 7219 Laundry, except power & coin-operated

(P-13631)
DY-DEE SERVICE PASADENA INC
Also Called: California Linen Service
40 E California Blvd, Pasadena
(91105-3203)
PHONE..........................626 792-6183
Brian O'Neil, *President*
Andrew Oneil, *General Mgr*
Mary Hilliard, *Sales Mgr*
EMP: 60
SQ FT: 15,000

SALES (est): 4.6MM **Privately Held**
WEB: www.calinen.com
SIC: 7219 7213 Diaper service; linen supply

(P-13632)
DYDEE SERVICE OF PASEDENA
Also Called: California Linen
40 E California Blvd, Pasadena
(91105-3203)
PHONE..........................626 240-0115
Bryan O'Nell, *Owner*
Kelly Huizinga, *Manager*
EMP: 100 **EST:** 1938
SALES: 8MM **Privately Held**
SIC: 7219 Diaper service

(P-13633)
**FRENCH LAUNDRY
RESTAURANT CORP (PA)**
6540 Washington St, Yountville
(94599-1315)
PHONE..........................707 944-0167
Thomas Keller, *CEO*
EMP: 100
SALES (est): 3.7MM **Privately Held**
SIC: 7219 5812 French hand laundry;
French restaurant

(P-13634)
JOB OPTIONS INCORPORATED
1110 S Washington Ave, San Bernardino
(92408-2244)
PHONE..........................909 890-4612
EMP: 820
SQ FT: 35,800 **Privately Held**
WEB: www.joboptionsinc.org
SIC: 7219 Fur garment cleaning, repairing
& storage
PA: Job Options, Incorporated
3465 Camino DI Rio S 30
San Diego CA 92108

(P-13635)
KL CUTTING SERVICE INC
2250 Maple Ave, Los Angeles
(90011-1190)
PHONE..........................213 742-9001
Alex Palomino, *General Mgr*
Mark Feldman, *President*
EMP: 164 **EST:** 1997
SQ FT: 78,200
SALES (est): 7.8MM **Privately Held**
SIC: 7219 Garment making, alteration &
repair

(P-13636)
**PENINOU FRENCH LDRY &
CLRS INC (PA)**
101 S Maple Ave, South San Francisco
(94080-6303)
PHONE..........................800 392-2532
Todd Edwards, *CEO*
EMP: 90
SQ FT: 25,000
SALES (est): 6.2MM **Privately Held**
WEB: www.peninou.com
SIC: 7219 7216 French hand laundry;
drycleaning collecting & distributing
agency

(P-13637)
STAR LAUNDRY SERVICES INC
Also Called: Star Services
3410 Main St, San Diego (92113-3803)
PHONE..........................619 572-1009
Abraham Yang, *President*
Sonia Yang, *Opers Staff*
EMP: 80
SALES (est): 1.6MM **Privately Held**
SIC: 7219 Laundry, except power & coin-operated

(P-13638)
T POINTS INC
350 W Mrtn Lthr King Jr, Los Angeles
(90037-4529)
PHONE..........................323 846-9176
EMP: 50
SALES (est): 695.8K **Privately Held**
SIC: 7219

**7221 Photographic Studios,
Portrait**

(P-13639)
BAY PHOTO INC
2959 Park Ave Ste A, Soquel (95073-2863)
PHONE..........................831 475-6090
Larry Abitbol, *Principal*
EMP: 141
SALES (corp-wide): 33MM **Privately
Held**
SIC: 7221 Photographer, still or video
PA: Bay Photo, Inc.
920 Disc Dr
Scotts Valley CA
831 475-6686

(P-13640)
LIFETOUCH INC
7916 Alta Sunrise Ln, Citrus Heights
(95610-7904)
PHONE..........................916 535-7733
Chris Rousso, *Branch Mgr*
EMP: 80
SALES (corp-wide): 1.1B **Publicly Held**
WEB: www.lifetouch.com
SIC: 7221 Photographer, still or video
HQ: Lifetouch Inc.
11000 Viking Dr
Eden Prairie MN 55344
952 826-4000

(P-13641)
LIFETOUCH NAT SCHL STUDIOS INC
30351 Huntwood Ave, Hayward
(94544-7015)
PHONE..........................510 293-1818
John Capistran, *Manager*
Capistran John, *Manager*
EMP: 50
SALES (corp-wide): 1.1B **Publicly Held**
SIC: 7221 School photographer
HQ: Lifetouch National School Studios Inc.
11000 Viking Dr Ste 300
Eden Prairie MN 55344
952 826-4000

(P-13642)
LIFETOUCH PORTRAIT STUDIOS INC
9770 Carroll Centre Rd C, San Diego
(92126-6504)
PHONE..........................858 693-9197
Kim Clark, *Manager*
EMP: 50
SQ FT: 1,200
SALES (corp-wide): 1.1B **Publicly Held**
WEB: www.jcpportraits.com
SIC: 7221 Photographer, still or video;
school photographer
HQ: Lifetouch Portrait Studios Inc.
11000 Viking Dr
Eden Prairie MN 55344
952 826-4335

(P-13643)
SCHOOL PORTRAITS BY KRANZ
9992 Center Dr, Villa Park (92861-2715)
PHONE..........................714 545-1775
Gary Kranz, *President*
Judy Kranz, *Vice Pres*
EMP: 82
SQ FT: 14,455
SALES (est): 2.5MM **Privately Held**
SIC: 7221 School photographer

7231 Beauty Shops

(P-13644)
ALEXANDERS GRAND SALON
Also Called: Alexander's Grand Salon & Spa
5579 E Santa Ana Cyn Rd, Anaheim
(92807-3143)
PHONE..........................714 282-6438
Fax: 714 282-6446
EMP: 65
SALES (est): 1.3MM **Privately Held**
SIC: 7231

(P-13645)
ALLEN EDWARDS BEAUTY SALON (PA)
Also Called: Edwards, Allen Beauty Salon
16101 Ventura Blvd # 155, Encino
(91426-2500)
PHONE...................................818 981-7711
Paul Canter, *President*
Allen Edwards, *Admin Sec*
EMP: 100
SALES (est): 1.1MM **Privately Held**
SIC: 7231 Beauty shops

(P-13646)
AMADEUS SALON INC (PA)
2817 E Foothill Blvd, Pasadena
(91107-3463)
PHONE...................................626 795-0969
Joseph T Wong, *President*
GI Mui-Chow, *Vice Pres*
Tina Mui-Wong, *Admin Sec*
EMP: 80
SQ FT: 10,500
SALES (est): 2.3MM **Privately Held**
WEB: www.amadeusspa.com
SIC: 7231 7991 5999 Beauty shops;
spas; spas & hot tubs

(P-13647)
BEAUTY BAZAR INC
Also Called: La Belle Days Spas and Salons
36 Stanford Shopping Ctr, Palo Alto
(94304-1423)
PHONE...................................650 326-8522
Vella Schner, *Owner*
EMP: 80
SALES (est): 421.4K
SALES (corp-wide): 3.3MM **Privately Held**
WEB: www.labelledayspas.com
SIC: 7231 5999 Cosmetology & personal
hygiene salons; toiletries, cosmetics &
perfumes
PA: Beauty Bazar Inc
36 Stanford Shopping Ctr
Palo Alto CA 94304
415 433-7644

(P-13648)
BEAUTY RECOGNIZED LP
224 Via Rodeo Dr, Beverly Hills
(90210-5142)
PHONE...................................310 278-7646
Jose Eber,
EMP: 70
SALES (est): 909.8K **Privately Held**
SIC: 7231 Unisex hair salons

(P-13649)
CANTER/EDWARDS ENTERPRISES (PA)
Also Called: Allen Edwards Salons
23251 Collins St, Woodland Hills
(91367-4117)
PHONE...................................818 887-7330
Allen Edwards, *President*
Elissa Edwards, *Admin Director*
EMP: 50
SQ FT: 8,000
SALES (est): 919.2K **Privately Held**
SIC: 7231 Unisex hair salons

(P-13650)
CLASS ACT HAIR & NAIL SALON
2795 Bechelli Ln, Redding (96002-1924)
PHONE...................................530 223-3442
EMP: 69
SALES (est): 598.4K **Privately Held**
SIC: 7231

(P-13651)
CREATIVE NAIL DESIGN INC
Also Called: Revlon Professional
9560 Towne Centre Dr # 200, San Diego
(92121-1972)
PHONE...................................760 599-2900
James A Nordstrom, *CEO*
Jan Bragulla, *President*
Sennen Pamich, *President*
Chris Christopher, *CFO*
Mary Nordstrom, *Treasurer*
EMP: 105
SQ FT: 60,000
SALES (est): 8.9MM **Publicly Held**
SIC: 7231 Manicurist, pedicurist

PA: Revlon, Inc.
1 New York Plz
New York NY 10004

(P-13652)
DAGER CORPORATION (PA)
Also Called: Supercuts
8004 Flsom Hydre Aburn Rd, Folsom
(95630)
PHONE...................................916 989-4229
Glenn R James, *President*
EMP: 100
SALES (est): 1.9MM **Privately Held**
SIC: 7231 Unisex hair salons

(P-13653)
DUKE FINANCIAL CO INC
100 N Rancho Santa Fe Rd # 117, San
Marcos (92069-1280)
PHONE...................................858 694-1215
Ted Nelson, *President*
Craig Bingham, *VP Finance*
EMP: 184
SALES (est): 2.6MM **Privately Held**
SIC: 7231 6282 Hairdressers; investment
advisory service

(P-13654)
FABULOUS & COMPANY LLC
19553 Enadia Way, Reseda (91335-3620)
PHONE...................................818 261-7242
Maya Riley,
EMP: 50
SALES (est): 133.3K **Privately Held**
SIC: 7231 Beauty shops

(P-13655)
FEDERICO BEAUTY INSTITUTE
1515 Sports Dr Ste 100, Sacramento
(95834-1905)
PHONE...................................916 929-4242
Jeremy Frederico, *President*
EMP: 50
SALES (est): 1.2MM **Privately Held**
SIC: 7231 Beauty schools

(P-13656)
FERGUSON SALON MANAGEMENT
2946 State St Ste F, Carlsbad
(92008-2336)
P.O. Box 2804 (92018-2804)
PHONE...................................760 434-4141
Elizabeth Ferguson, *President*
EMP: 50
SQ FT: 1,000
SALES (est): 966K **Privately Held**
SIC: 7231 Hairdressers

(P-13657)
FERGUSON SALON MANAGEMENT INC
1104 Knowles Ave, Carlsbad (92008-1459)
P.O. Box 2804 (92018-2804)
PHONE...................................760 434-5008
Elizabeth Ferguson, *President*
Marvin Ferguson, *CFO*
EMP: 50
SALES (est): 2MM **Privately Held**
SIC: 7231 7241 Beauty shops; barber
shops

(P-13658)
FLORIDA BEAUTY FLORA INC
6205 Ventura Blvd, Ventura (93003-7226)
PHONE...................................805 642-1633
Ronen Koubi, *Branch Mgr*
EMP: 294
SALES (corp-wide): 55.9MM **Privately
Held**
SIC: 7231 Beauty shops
PA: Florida Beauty Flora, Inc.
3100 Nw 74th Ave
Miami FL 33122
305 503-1200

(P-13659)
GATES OF SPAIN WIBEL
2545 Mission St, Pasadena (91108-1691)
PHONE...................................626 441-3078
William J Bell, *President*
Susan Bell, *Co-Owner*
Vicki Lanzarotta, *Admin Sec*
EMP: 50 EST: 1959

SALES: 1MM **Privately Held**
SIC: 7231 Cosmetology & personal hygiene salons

(P-13660)
GF CARNEROS TENANT LLC
Also Called: Carneros Resort and Spa
4048 Sonoma Hwy, NAPA (94559-9745)
PHONE...................................707 299-4900
Monda Rigdon, *Principal*
Robert Heiser, *Principal*
EMP: 50
SALES (est): 581.5K **Privately Held**
SIC: 7231 Cosmetology & personal hy-
giene salons

(P-13661)
HAIR FASHION INC
Also Called: Cristophe Salon
348 N Beverly Dr, Beverly Hills
(90210-4701)
PHONE...................................310 274-0851
Cristopher Schatteman, *President*
Cristophe Schatteman, *President*
EMP: 80
SQ FT: 7,000
SALES (est): 2.4MM **Privately Held**
WEB: www.cristophesalon.com
SIC: 7231 Unisex hair salons

(P-13662)
HOSHALL CORPORATION
Also Called: Hoshall Designer Group
6608 Folsom Auburn Rd # 4, Folsom
(95630-2147)
PHONE...................................916 987-1995
William C Hoshall, *President*
EMP: 50 EST: 1964
SALES (est): 1.3MM **Privately Held**
WEB: www.hoshallssalonandspa.com
SIC: 7231 5621 5999 Manicurist, pedi-
curist; ready-to-wear apparel, women's;
cosmetics

(P-13663)
JOSEPH COZZA SALON INC (PA)
25 Egret Way, Mill Valley (94941-3248)
PHONE...................................415 433-3030
Joseph Bisazza, *President*
Joseph Cozza, *Corp Secy*
EMP: 60
SQ FT: 3,000
SALES (est): 2.7MM **Privately Held**
WEB: www.josephcozzasalon.com
SIC: 7231 Unisex hair salons

(P-13664)
JURLIQUE HLISTIC SKIN CARE INC (PA)
1411 5th St Ste 501, Santa Monica
(90401-2481)
PHONE...................................914 998-8800
Sam McKay, *CEO*
EMP: 50
SALES (est): 9.4MM **Privately Held**
SIC: 7231 Cosmetology & personal hy-
giene salons

(P-13665)
MINILUXE INC
11965 San Vicente Blvd, Los Angeles
(90049-5003)
PHONE...................................424 442-1630
EMP: 65
SALES (corp-wide): 15MM **Privately
Held**
SIC: 7231 Manicurist, pedicurist
PA: Miniluxe, Inc.
1 Faneuil Hall Sq Fl 7
Boston MA 02109
617 684-2731

(P-13666)
ORGANIC & SUSTAINABLE BUTY INC
5933 Bowcroft St, Los Angeles
(90016-4301)
PHONE...................................310 815-8201
Jessica Iclisoy, *President*
Arthur Iclisoy, *Managing Dir*
EMP: 50 EST: 2006

SALES (est): 1.9MM **Privately Held**
SIC: 7231 2844 Beauty shops; hair preparations, including shampoos; suntan lotions & oils; face creams or lotions

(P-13667)
PERSONLIZED BUTY DISCOVERY INC (PA)
Also Called: Ipsy
201 Baldwin Ave Fl 2, San Mateo
(94401-3914)
PHONE...................................888 769-4526
Marcelo Camberos, *CEO*
Jennifer Goldfarb, *President*
Fernando Madeira, *President*
Jorge Esteban Ochoa, *Vice Pres*
Mikhail Ulinich, *Vice Pres*
EMP: 57
SALES (est): 21.3MM **Privately Held**
SIC: 7231 Beauty shops

(P-13668)
PILGRIM PLACE IN CLAREMONT
Also Called: Pilgrim Place Beauty Salon
721 Harrison Ave, Claremont (91711-4539)
PHONE...................................909 621-9581
Will Cunitz, *Sales/Mktg Dir*
EMP: 180
SALES (corp-wide): 17.9MM **Privately
Held**
WEB: www.pilgrimplace.org
SIC: 7231 Beauty shops
PA: Pilgrim Place In Claremont
625 Mayflower Rd
Claremont CA 91711
909 399-5500

(P-13669)
PLATINUM STRANDS SALON
3443 E Chapman Ave, Orange
(92869-3812)
PHONE...................................714 532-2633
Donald Anderson, *Owner*
Sam Ardalan, *Owner*
Thomas Penna, *Manager*
EMP: 65
SALES (est): 818.2K **Privately Held**
SIC: 7231 Hairdressers

(P-13670)
REGIS CORPORATION
Also Called: Vidal Sassoon Salon
9403 Santa Monica Blvd, Beverly Hills
(90210-4604)
PHONE...................................310 274-8791
EMP: 50
SALES (corp-wide): 1.7B **Publicly Held**
SIC: 7231
PA: Regis Corporation
7201 Metro Blvd
Edina MN 55439
952 947-7777

(P-13671)
SALON LUJON INC
216 N Harbor Blvd, Fullerton (92832-3604)
PHONE...................................714 738-1882
Rale Whitesell, *Manager*
Lulu Poore, *Admin Sec*
EMP: 60
SQ FT: 3,000
SALES (est): 1.4MM **Privately Held**
SIC: 7231 7991 Unisex hair salons; spas

(P-13672)
SALON-SALON
1700 Mchenry Ave Ste 29, Modesto
(95350-4340)
PHONE...................................209 571-3500
Norma Foster Maddy, *Partner*
Chris Johnson, *Partner*
EMP: 55
SQ FT: 10,500
SALES (est): 1.7MM **Privately Held**
SIC: 7231 5621 5999 Hairdressers; bou-
tiques; hair care products

(P-13673)
SUPERCUTS ADMNISTRATIVE OFFICE (PA)
7750 El Cmino Real Ste 2g, Carlsbad
(92009)
PHONE...................................760 753-5543
Robert Jerome, *Owner*
EMP: 240
SQ FT: 750

PRODUCTS & SVCS

SALES: 6MM **Privately Held**
SIC: 7231 Unisex hair salons

(P-13674)
TONI & GUY HAIRDRESSING (PA)
1177 Newport Center Dr, Newport Beach (92660-6950)
PHONE.............................949 721-1666
Frank Chirico, *Partner*
Olivia Price, *Manager*
EMP: 80
SALES (est): 870.5K **Privately Held**
SIC: 7231 Hairdressers

(P-13675)
TRILOGY SQUAW SPA LLC
Also Called: Trilogy Day Spa
451 Manhattan Beach Blvd, Manhattan Beach (90266-5345)
PHONE.............................310 760-0044
Shandra Shaw,
EMP: 50
SALES (est): 1.3MM **Privately Held**
SIC: 7231 Facial salons

(P-13676)
ULTA BEAUTY INC
117 Ferrari Ranch Rd, Lincoln (95648-7421)
PHONE.............................916 581-4121
EMP: 110
SALES (corp-wide): 5.8B **Publicly Held**
SIC: 7231 Beauty shops
PA: Ulta Beauty, Inc.
1000 Remington Blvd # 120
Bolingbrook IL 60440
630 410-4800

(P-13677)
ULTA BEAUTY INC
755 E Betteravia Rd, Santa Maria (93454-7024)
PHONE.............................805 825-0093
EMP: 139
SALES (corp-wide): 5.8B **Publicly Held**
SIC: 7231 Beauty shops
PA: Ulta Beauty, Inc.
1000 Remington Blvd # 120
Bolingbrook IL 60440
630 410-4800

(P-13678)
ULTA BEAUTY INC
4941 Clairemont Dr Ste B, San Diego (92117-2730)
PHONE.............................858 581-9003
EMP: 110
SALES (corp-wide): 5.8B **Publicly Held**
SIC: 7231 Beauty shops
PA: Ulta Beauty, Inc.
1000 Remington Blvd # 120
Bolingbrook IL 60440
630 410-4800

(P-13679)
ULTA BEAUTY INC
2243 W Florida Ave, Hemet (92545-3610)
PHONE.............................951 652-2966
EMP: 110
SALES (corp-wide): 5.8B **Publicly Held**
SIC: 7231 Beauty shops
PA: Ulta Beauty, Inc.
1000 Remington Blvd # 120
Bolingbrook IL 60440
630 410-4800

(P-13680)
ULTA SALON COSMT FRAGRANCE INC
1229 S Lone Hill Ave, Glendora (91740-4507)
PHONE.............................909 592-5393
EMP: 147
SALES (corp-wide): 5.8B **Publicly Held**
SIC: 7231 Beauty shops
HQ: Ulta Salon, Cosmetics & Fragrance, Inc.
1000 Remington Blvd # 120
Bolingbrook IL 60440
630 410-4800

(P-13681)
ULTA SALON COSMT FRAGRANCE INC
9000 Ming Ave, Bakersfield (93311-1318)
PHONE.............................661 664-1402
EMP: 155
SALES (corp-wide): 5.8B **Publicly Held**
SIC: 7231 5999 Beauty shops; toiletries, cosmetics & perfumes
HQ: Ulta Salon, Cosmetics & Fragrance, Inc.
1000 Remington Blvd # 120
Bolingbrook IL 60440
630 410-4800

(P-13682)
ULTA SALON COSMT FRAGRANCE INC
Also Called: Ulta Beauty
2841 Countryside Dr, Turlock (95380-8403)
PHONE.............................209 664-1725
EMP: 155
SALES (corp-wide): 5.8B **Publicly Held**
SIC: 7231 Cosmetology & personal hygiene salons
HQ: Ulta Salon, Cosmetics & Fragrance, Inc.
1000 Remington Blvd # 120
Bolingbrook IL 60440
630 410-4800

(P-13683)
ULTA SALON COSMT FRAGRANCE INC
185 S Las Posas Rd, San Marcos (92078-2419)
PHONE.............................760 744-0853
EMP: 155
SALES (corp-wide): 5.8B **Publicly Held**
SIC: 7231 Beauty shops
HQ: Ulta Salon, Cosmetics & Fragrance, Inc.
1000 Remington Blvd # 120
Bolingbrook IL 60440
630 410-4800

7241 Barber Shops

(P-13684)
CUTTING EDGE PROTECTION I
381 Crosby St, Altadena (91001-5569)
PHONE.............................949 307-1596
Anthony Beaty, *President*
Greg Hammond, *Vice Pres*
EMP: 50
SALES (est): 335.8K **Privately Held**
WEB: www.tmbhollywood.com
SIC: 7241 Barber shops

(P-13685)
HAIRCUTTERS
1230 W Imperial Hwy Ste A, La Habra (90631-6961)
PHONE.............................562 690-2217
EMP: 92
SALES (corp-wide): 14.9MM **Privately Held**
SIC: 7241 7231
PA: The Haircutters
5160 Van Nuys Blvd
Sherman Oaks CA 91403
818 716-5319

7251 Shoe Repair & Shoeshine Parlors

(P-13686)
NAFTA SHOES INC
14632 Nelson Ave, City of Industry (91744-4346)
PHONE.............................626 369-9681
Ralph Chen, *President*
Angel Chen, *Vice Pres*
EMP: 100
SQ FT: 40,000
SALES (est): 2.3MM **Privately Held**
WEB: www.naftashoehospital.com
SIC: 7251 3144 3143 5139 Shoe repair shop; women's footwear, except athletic; men's footwear, except athletic; shoes

---

7261 Funeral Svcs & Crematories

(P-13687)
CHAPEL OF CHIMES
4499 Piedmont Ave, Oakland (94611-4293)
PHONE.............................510 654-1288
Marcie Russell, *Branch Mgr*
EMP: 50
SALES (corp-wide): 35.1MM **Publicly Held**
WEB: www.bailingyuan.com
SIC: 7261 Crematory
HQ: Chapel Of The Chimes
32992 Mission Blvd
Hayward CA 94544
510 471-3363

(P-13688)
CYPRESS FUNERAL SERVICES INC
Also Called: Cypress Lawn Funeral Home
1370 El Camino Real, Colma (94014-3239)
PHONE.............................650 550-8808
Kenneth E Varner, *President*
Armando Santana, *Managing Dir*
Ian Ho, *Planning*
Alvin Dougharty, *Director*
EMP: 150
SALES (est): 5.1MM **Privately Held**
SIC: 7261 Funeral home

(P-13689)
DESERT VIEW FUNERAL HOME
11478 Amargosa Rd, Victorville (92392-8125)
PHONE.............................760 244-0007
Jim Larkin, *CEO*
Terry Harmon, *Vice Pres*
EMP: 50
SALES (est): 1.1MM **Privately Held**
SIC: 7261 Funeral home

(P-13690)
F R A L P
1702 Fairhaven Ave, Santa Ana (92705-6821)
PHONE.............................714 633-1442
Fred Forgy Jr, *Partner*
Jack Stanley, *Partner*
EMP: 70 EST: 1911
SQ FT: 12,000
SALES (est): 2.2MM **Privately Held**
SIC: 7261 6512 6553 5999 Crematory; commercial & industrial building operation; mausoleum operation; gravestones, finished; flowers, fresh

(P-13691)
NEPTUNE MANAGEMENT CORPORATION
4065 Mowry Ave, Fremont (94538-1339)
PHONE.............................510 797-2269
EMP: 66 **Privately Held**
SIC: 7261 Funeral service & crematories
PA: Neptune Management Corporation
1250 S Pine Island Rd # 500
Plantation FL 33324

(P-13692)
NEPTUNE MANAGEMENT CORPORATION
9650 Fairway Dr 120, Roseville (95678-3537)
PHONE.............................916 771-5300
EMP: 66 **Privately Held**
SIC: 7261 Funeral home
PA: Neptune Management Corporation
1250 S Pine Island Rd # 500
Plantation FL 33324

(P-13693)
PIERCE BROTHERS (DH)
Also Called: SCI
10621 Victory Blvd, North Hollywood (91606-3918)
PHONE.............................818 763-9121
Oliver Yeo, *Manager*
R L Waltrip, *Ch of Bd*
David Anderson, *President*
Curtis Briggs, *Vice Pres*

Ray Gipson, *Vice Pres*
EMP: 80 EST: 1902
SQ FT: 10,000
SALES (est): 8.5MM
SALES: 3.1B **Publicly Held**
SIC: 7261 6553 Crematory; cemeteries, real estate operation
HQ: Sci Funeral Services Of New York, Inc.
1929 Allen Pkwy
Houston TX 77019
713 522-5141

(P-13694)
ROMAN CATH ARCH OF LOS ANGELS
Also Called: Holy Cross Cemetary & Masoleum
5835 W Slauson Ave, Culver City (90230-6505)
PHONE.............................310 836-5500
Maria Arascor, *Manager*
EMP: 50
SALES (corp-wide): 539.2MM **Privately Held**
WEB: www.smes.com
SIC: 7261 6553 Funeral service & crematories; cemetery subdividers & developers
PA: The Roman Catholic Archbishop Of Los Angeles
3424 Wilshire Blvd
Los Angeles CA 90010
213 637-7000

(P-13695)
ROMAN CATH ARCH OF LOS ANGELS
Also Called: Calvary Cemetery
199 N Hope Ave, Santa Barbara (93110-1609)
PHONE.............................805 687-8811
Gwen Hueston, *Branch Mgr*
EMP: 611
SALES (corp-wide): 539.2MM **Privately Held**
SIC: 7261 6553 Funeral service & crematories; cemetery subdividers & developers
PA: The Roman Catholic Archbishop Of Los Angeles
3424 Wilshire Blvd
Los Angeles CA 90010
213 637-7000

(P-13696)
ROSE HILLS MORTUARY INC
Also Called: Rose Hills Co
3888 Workman Mill Rd, Whittier (90601-1626)
P.O. Box 110 (90608-0110)
PHONE.............................562 699-0921
Dennis Poulsen, *Ch of Bd*
Mary C Guzman, *CFO*
Bruce Lazenby, *Exec Dir*
Ophelia Camero, *Administration*
Jin Chon, *Administration*
EMP: 850
SQ FT: 230,000
SALES (est): 15.1MM **Privately Held**
SIC: 7261 6553 Funeral home; cemetery subdividers & developers

(P-13697)
SAN DIEGO CEMETERY ASSN
Also Called: El Camino Mem Pk & Mortuary
5600 Carroll Canyon Rd, San Diego (92121-1702)
PHONE.............................858 453-2121
Adrienne Trousdale, *President*
Paul Hickman, *Treasurer*
Betty Flake, *Admin Sec*
EMP: 60
SQ FT: 10,000
SALES (est): 2.6MM **Privately Held**
SIC: 7261 6553 Funeral service & crematories; cemetery subdividers & developers

(P-13698)
SINAI TEMPLE
Also Called: Mt Sinai Mem Pk & Mortuary
5950 Forest Lawn Dr, Los Angeles (90068-1010)
PHONE.............................323 469-6000
Len Lawrence, *Manager*
Marc Graniger, *Finance Mgr*
Fay Foghi, *Accountant*
Victoria Zdor, *Controller*
Gail Levy, *Marketing Mgr*

EMP: 125
SQ FT: 22,633
SALES (corp-wide): 23.3MM **Privately Held**
WEB: www.mt-sinai.com
SIC: 7261 6553 Funeral home; cemeteries, real estate operation
PA: Temple Sinai
10400 Wilshire Blvd
Los Angeles CA 90024
310 475-6401

(P-13699)
STEWART ENTERPRISES INC
Also Called: El Camino Mem Pk & Mortuary
5600 Carroll Canyon Rd, San Diego
(92121-1702)
PHONE....................858 453-2121
Virginia McCuyston, *Manager*
EMP: 50
SALES (corp-wide): 3.1B **Publicly Held**
WEB: www.stewartenterprises.com
SIC: 7261 Funeral service & crematories
HQ: Stewart Enterprises, Inc.
1333 S Clearview Pkwy
New Orleans LA 70121
504 729-1400

(P-13700)
TEMPLE ISRAEL OF HOLLYWOOD (PA)
Also Called: Hillside Mem Pk & Mortuary
7300 Hollywood Blvd, Los Angeles
(90046-2999)
PHONE....................323 876-8330
Steve Sloan, *President*
David Cremin, *Treasurer*
Renee Mochkatel, *Vice Pres*
Jane Zuckerman, *Exec Dir*
Amanda Hedstrom, *Office Mgr*
EMP: 83
SQ FT: 15,000
SALES (est): 8.7MM **Privately Held**
SIC: 7261 8299 Funeral service & crematories; religious school

7291 Tax Return Preparation Svcs

(P-13701)
ANDERSEN TAX LLC
400 Suth Hope St Ste 2000, Los Angeles
(90071)
PHONE....................213 593-2300
Kurt Brune, *Managing Dir*
EMP: 154
SALES (corp-wide): 52.6MM **Privately Held**
SIC: 7291 Tax return preparation services
PA: Andersen Tax Llc
100 1st St Ste 1600
San Francisco CA 94105
415 764-2700

(P-13702)
CALIFORNIA DEPT TAX & FEE ADM
450 N St, Sacramento (95814-4311)
P.O. Box 942879 (94279-0001)
PHONE....................800 400-7115
Ester Cabrera, *Principal*
Nicolas Maduros, *Principal*
Jason Mallet, *Principal*
EMP: 99
SALES (est): 388.8K **Privately Held**
SIC: 7291 Tax return preparation services

(P-13703)
COMMONWEALTH EQUITY SVCS LLP
Also Called: Commonwealth Financial Network
20 Corporate Park Ste 150, Irvine
(92606-5183)
PHONE....................949 336-6440
Karen Caporaso, *Principal*
EMP: 56
SALES (corp-wide): 193.2MM **Privately Held**
SIC: 7291 Tax return preparation services
PA: Commonwealth Equity Services, Llc
29 Sawyer Rd Ste 2
Waltham MA 02453
781 736-7980

(P-13704)
EDGE FINANCIAL INC
10100 Santa Monica Blvd, Los Angeles
(90067-4003)
PHONE....................323 857-5809
Light Silver, *President*
EMP: 50
SQ FT: 3,500
SALES (est): 1MM **Privately Held**
WEB: www.stopirsdebt.com
SIC: 7291 7389 Tax return preparation services; legal & tax services

(P-13705)
EXACTAX INC (PA)
1100 E Orangethorpe Ave # 100, Anaheim
(92801-5168)
P.O. Box 61048 (92803-6148)
PHONE....................714 284-4802
Kevin Love, *President*
Franklin Pang, *Shareholder*
Richard Johnson, *Treasurer*
Michael Leonetti, *Vice Pres*
Bob Lynch, *Vice Pres*
EMP: 74
SQ FT: 18,000
SALES (est): 2.5MM **Privately Held**
WEB: www.exactax.com
SIC: 7291 7371 Tax return preparation services; computer software development

(P-13706)
H & R BLOCK INC
401 N Broadway Ste B, Santa Maria
(93454-4121)
PHONE....................805 349-9266
Bill Norris, *Branch Mgr*
EMP: 70
SALES (corp-wide): 3.1B **Publicly Held**
WEB: www.hrblock.com
SIC: 7291 Tax return preparation services
PA: H&R Block, Inc.
1 H&R Block Way
Kansas City MO 64105
816 854-3000

(P-13707)
H & R BLOCK INC
4300 Sonoma Blvd Ste 600, Vallejo
(94589-2211)
PHONE....................707 643-1856
Vince Largo, *Manager*
EMP: 200
SALES (corp-wide): 3.1B **Publicly Held**
WEB: www.hrblock.com
SIC: 7291 Tax return preparation services
PA: H&R Block, Inc.
1 H&R Block Way
Kansas City MO 64105
816 854-3000

(P-13708)
H&R BLOCK INC
Also Called: H & R Block
1745 Van Ness Ave, San Francisco
(94109-3620)
PHONE....................415 441-2666
Sharon Williams, *Manager*
EMP: 50
SALES (corp-wide): 3.1B **Publicly Held**
WEB: www.hrblock.com
SIC: 7291 Tax return preparation services
PA: H&R Block, Inc.
1 H&R Block Way
Kansas City MO 64105
816 854-3000

(P-13709)
HATFIELD INC
Also Called: Visor
5 3rd St Ste 525, San Francisco
(94103-3216)
PHONE....................415 802-8635
Gernot Zacke, *Director*
EMP: 50
SALES (est): 150.4K **Privately Held**
SIC: 7291 Tax return preparation services

(P-13710)
J B LAQUINDANUM & ASSOCIATES
2608 Springs Rd, Vallejo (94591-5713)
PHONE....................707 648-0501
J B Laquindanum, *Owner*
EMP: 50
SQ FT: 9,156

SALES (est): 527.6K **Privately Held**
SIC: 7291 Tax return preparation services

(P-13711)
OPTIMA TAX RELIEF LLC
3100 S Harbor Blvd # 250, Santa Ana
(92704-6823)
PHONE....................714 361-4636
Jesse Torres,
Jarrod Bassin, *Vice Pres*
Anthony T Doan, *Vice Pres*
Kevin Giordano, *Vice Pres*
Mick Cotten, *IT/INT Sup*
EMP: 180
SQ FT: 30,000
SALES (est): 13.1MM **Privately Held**
WEB: www.optimataxrelief.com
SIC: 7291 Tax return preparation services

7299 Miscellaneous Personal Svcs, NEC

(P-13712)
1NTEGER LLC
1437 7th St Ste 400, Santa Monica
(90401-2635)
PHONE....................424 320-2977
Joan Manning, *Principal*
EMP: 50
SALES (est): 310.5K **Privately Held**
SIC: 7299 Information services, consumer

(P-13713)
A-1 EVENT & PARTY RENTALS
Also Called: A1 Event & Party Rentals
251 E Front St, Covina (91723-1613)
PHONE....................626 967-0500
Chet Fortney, *President*
Rene Martinez, *Vice Pres*
EMP: 55
SQ FT: 40,000
SALES (est): 3.4MM **Privately Held**
SIC: 7299 7359 Party planning service; party supplies rental services

(P-13714)
AMERICAN CONSERVATORY THEATER
1117 Market St, San Francisco
(94103-1513)
PHONE....................415 439-2379
Heather Kitchen, *Principal*
Denys Baker, *Executive*
EMP: 109 **Privately Held**
SIC: 7299 Costume rental
PA: American Conservatory Theater
30 Grant Ave Fl 7
San Francisco CA 94108

(P-13715)
AMERICOR FUNDING INC
18200 Von Karman Ave # 600, Irvine
(92612-7146)
PHONE....................866 333-8686
Banir Ganatra, *CEO*
EMP: 170
SALES (est): 352.9K **Privately Held**
SIC: 7299 Debt counseling or adjustment service, individuals

(P-13716)
APPLE VLLEY/ VCTRVLLE CNSRTIUM
14955 Dale Evans Pkwy, Apple Valley
(92307-3061)
PHONE....................760 240-7000
Keneth J Henderson, *Exec Dir*
EMP: 65
SALES (est): 470.8K **Privately Held**
SIC: 7299 Information services, consumer

(P-13717)
AT YOUR HOME FAMILYCARE
6540 Lusk Blvd Ste C266, San Diego
(92121-2783)
PHONE....................858 625-0406
Laurie Edwards-Tate, *President*
EMP: 200
SQ FT: 2,000
SALES (est): 6.1MM **Privately Held**
WEB: www.atyourhomefamilycare.com
SIC: 7299 8082 Babysitting bureau; home health care services

(P-13718)
BABYCENTER LLC (DH)
163 Freelon St, San Francisco
(94107-1624)
PHONE....................415 537-0900
Mary Baker,
Tom Alessi, *Vice Pres*
Julie Demsey, *Vice Pres*
Linda Murray, *Vice Pres*
Zack Rogers, *Vice Pres*
EMP: 50
SALES (est): 3.5MM
SALES (corp-wide): 76.4B **Publicly Held**
WEB: www.babycenter.com
SIC: 7299 5999 Information services, consumer; infant furnishings & equipment
HQ: Johnson & Johnson Consumer Inc.
199 Grandview Rd
Skillman NJ 08558
908 874-1000

(P-13719)
BANQUET FACILITIES
Also Called: Indian Hills Golf Club
6000 Camino Real, Riverside
(92509-5310)
PHONE....................951 360-2081
John De Zoetez, *Manager*
EMP: 50
SALES (est): 391.3K **Privately Held**
SIC: 7299 Banquet hall facilities

(P-13720)
BELCAMPO GROUP INC
Also Called: Belcampo Meat
329 N Phillipe Ln, Yreka (96097-9413)
PHONE....................530 842-5200
Anya Sernald, *President*
EMP: 70
SALES (corp-wide): 17.4MM **Privately Held**
SIC: 7299 5421 Butcher service, processing only; meat markets, including freezer provisioners
PA: Belcampo Group, Inc.
65 Webster St
Oakland CA 94607
510 250-7810

(P-13721)
BEST VALET PARKING CORPORATION
12792 Valley View St # 201, Garden Grove
(92845-2510)
PHONE....................800 708-2538
Michael Raemer, *President*
EMP: 100
SQ FT: 650
SALES (est): 5MM **Privately Held**
SIC: 7299 Valet parking

(P-13722)
BUCKINGHAM PROPERTY MANAGEMENT
Also Called: Coventry Cove Apartments
12609 Moffatt Ln, Fresno (93730-9704)
PHONE....................559 322-1105
Cher Cha, *Principal*
EMP: 94
SALES (corp-wide): 10.7MM **Privately Held**
SIC: 7299 Apartment locating service
PA: Buckingham Property Management Inc
2170 N Winery Ave
Fresno CA 93703
559 452-8250

(P-13723)
CALIFORNIA SUN CENTERS INC
8265 Sierra College Blvd, Roseville
(95661-9403)
PHONE....................916 789-9767
Michael Blore, *CEO*
EMP: 80
SALES (est): 1MM **Privately Held**
SIC: 7299 5651 Tanning salon; family clothing stores

(P-13724)
CARFAX STUDIOS
3937 Carfax Ave, Long Beach
(90808-2210)
PHONE....................562 377-0223
Paul Levitt, *Principal*
EMP: 56 EST: 2009

P
R
O
D
U
C
T
S
&
S
V
C
S

SALES (est): 1.6MM **Privately Held**
SIC: 7299 Apartment locating service

(P-13725)
CATTLEMENS
Also Called: Cattlemens Restaurant
2882 Kitty Hawk Rd, Livermore
(94551-7666)
PHONE.....................925 447-1224
Jackie Gibson, *General Mgr*
EMP: 70
SALES (corp-wide): 19.5MM **Privately Held**
WEB: www.beststeakinthewest.com
SIC: 7299 5812 Banquet hall facilities; American restaurant
PA: Cattlemens
　　250 Dutton Ave
　　Santa Rosa CA 95407
　　707 528-1040

(P-13726)
CHOURA VENUE SERVICES
Also Called: Choura Vnue Svcs At Carson Ctr
4101 E Willow St, Long Beach
(90815-1740)
PHONE.....................562 426-0555
James Choura, *CEO*
Sandra Valdovinos, *Sales Executive*
EMP: 99
SALES (est): 6.7MM **Privately Held**
SIC: 7299 5812 Information services, consumer; caterers

(P-13727)
CINTAS CORPORATION NO 2
18050 Central Ave, Carson (90746-4006)
PHONE.....................310 635-8713
Cluadia Sanchez, *Manager*
EMP: 69
SALES (corp-wide): 6.4B **Publicly Held**
WEB: www.cintas-corp.com
SIC: 7299 Personal appearance services
HQ: Cintas Corporation No. 2
　　6800 Cintas Blvd
　　Mason OH 45040

(P-13728)
CINTAS CORPORATION NO 3
777 139th Ave, San Leandro (94578-3218)
PHONE.....................510 352-6330
Brian Delbecq, *General Mgr*
Luisa Orozco, *Site Mgr*
EMP: 50
SQ FT: 25,000
SALES (corp-wide): 6.4B **Publicly Held**
WEB: www.cintas-corp.com
SIC: 7299 2326 Clothing rental services; men's & boys' work clothing
HQ: Cintas Corporation No. 3
　　6800 Cintas Blvd
　　Mason OH 45040

(P-13729)
CLASSMATES MEDIA CORPORATION
21301 Burbank Blvd, Woodland Hills
(91367-6679)
PHONE.....................818 287-3600
Mark R Goldston, *Ch of Bd*
Paul J Pucino, *CFO*
Frederic A Randall Jr, *Exec VP*
Sarah Pynchon, *Vice Pres*
Jin Kim, *Sr Software Eng*
EMP: 346
SALES (est): 4.7MM **Publicly Held**
WEB: www.classmatesmedia.com
SIC: 7299 7389 Personal document & information services; advertising, promotional & trade show services
HQ: United Online, Inc.
　　21255 Burbank Blvd # 400
　　Woodland Hills CA 91367
　　818 287-3000

(P-13730)
CLUTTER INC (PA)
3526 Hayden Ave, Culver City
(90232-2413)
PHONE.....................800 805-4023
ARI Mir, *CEO*
EMP: 117

SALES (est): 29.3MM **Privately Held**
SIC: 7299 4212 Personal item care & storage services; moving services

(P-13731)
CONDUIT LNGAGE SPECIALISTS INC
22720 Ventura Blvd # 100, Woodland Hills
(91364-1305)
PHONE.....................859 299-3178
Art Mathews, *Branch Mgr*
EMP: 82
SALES (corp-wide): 9MM **Privately Held**
SIC: 7299 Personal appearance services
PA: Conduit Language Specialists, Inc.
　　5050 Bryan Station Rd
　　Lexington KY 40516
　　818 389-4333

(P-13732)
CONSUMER CREDIT COUNSELING SVC (PA)
Also Called: Credit Counselor of California
595 Market St Ste 1500, San Francisco
(94105-2824)
PHONE.....................415 788-0288
Kathryn Davis, *CEO*
EMP: 60 EST: 1969
SQ FT: 14,000
SALES (est): 6MM **Privately Held**
WEB: www.cccsf.org
SIC: 7299 Debt counseling or adjustment service, individuals

(P-13733)
CORINTHIAN INTL PRKG SVCS INC
Also Called: Corinthian Parking Services
19925 Stevens Creek Blvd B, Cupertino
(95014-2300)
PHONE.....................408 867-7275
Douglas E Knapp, *CEO*
Todd Fedde, *Vice Pres*
Kyle Baldasano, *Director*
Jonathan Covey, *Manager*
Laura Gomes, *Manager*
EMP: 500
SQ FT: 6,000
SALES (est): 18.5MM **Privately Held**
WEB: www.corinthianparking.com
SIC: 7299 7521 4119 Valet parking; parking garage; limousine rental, with driver

(P-13734)
CORPORATE SOUL LLC
433 Hudson St, Healdsburg (95448-4461)
PHONE.....................707 431-7781
Michele Boudreaux, *Mng Member*
EMP: 270
SQ FT: 2,000
SALES (est): 3.8MM **Privately Held**
WEB: www.corporatesoul.net
SIC: 7299 Massage parlor

(P-13735)
CP OPCO LLC (HQ)
Also Called: Classic Party Rentals
901 W Hillcrest Blvd A, Inglewood
(90301-2101)
PHONE.....................310 966-4900
EMP: 2300
SALES (est): 154.7MM
SALES (corp-wide): 1.9MM **Privately Held**
SIC: 7299

(P-13736)
CRYSTAL VALET PARKING INC
4477 Hollywood Blvd 209, Los Angeles
(90027-6006)
P.O. Box 27386 (90027-0386)
PHONE.....................323 663-7275
Greg Gee, *President*
EMP: 70
SALES (est): 1.1MM **Privately Held**
SIC: 7299 Valet parking

(P-13737)
DANERICA ENTERPRISES INC
Also Called: Tax Resolution Services, Co
23901 Calabasas Rd # 1068, Calabasas
(91302-3305)
PHONE.....................818 774-1813
Michael Rozbruch, *CEO*
R Brian Compton, *President*

Stephanie Riley, *Human Res Mgr*
Michael Castaneda, *Manager*
Alexis Castaneda, *Receptionist*
EMP: 100 EST: 1998
SQ FT: 15,000
SALES (est): 4.7MM **Privately Held**
WEB: www.taxresolution.com
SIC: 7299 Personal financial services

(P-13738)
DEBTMERICA LLC
Also Called: Debtmerica Relief
3100 S Harbor Blvd # 250, Santa Ana
(92704-6823)
PHONE.....................714 389-4200
Jesse Torres,
Sonia Duenas, *Human Res Mgr*
Harry Langenberg,
Tony Gaeta, *Consultant*
Marrietta Kelly, *Consultant*
EMP: 65
SQ FT: 15,000
SALES (est): 5MM **Privately Held**
WEB: www.debtmerica.com
SIC: 7299 Debt counseling or adjustment service, individuals

(P-13739)
DESTINATION RESIDENCES LLC
Also Called: Tesancia La Jlla Ht Spa Resort
9700 N Torrey Pines Rd, La Jolla
(92037-1102)
PHONE.....................858 550-1000
Charlie Peck, *President*
Kim Ponsoll, *Sales Mgr*
Christine Dingman, *Manager*
EMP: 256
SALES (corp-wide): 1B **Privately Held**
WEB: www.destinationhotels.com
SIC: 7299 7389 7991 7011 Banquet hall facilities; convention & show services; spas; hotels
HQ: Destination Residences Llc
　　10333 E Dry Creek Rd
　　Englewood CO 80112
　　303 799-3830

(P-13740)
DEVELOP POINT EDUCATION
9909 Topanga Canyon Blvd # 346,
Chatsworth (91311-3602)
PHONE.....................805 624-6171
Jim Negrete, *Principal*
EMP: 50
SALES (est): 585K **Privately Held**
SIC: 7299 Miscellaneous personal service

(P-13741)
EHARMONY INC (PA)
Also Called: Eharmony.com
10900 Wilshire Blvd, Los Angeles
(90024-6501)
P.O. Box 241810 (90024-9610)
PHONE.....................424 258-1199
Neil Clark Warren, *CEO*
Greg Steiner, *President*
Jeremy Verba, *CEO*
John Powers, *CFO*
Ken Walker,
EMP: 125
SQ FT: 6,000
SALES (est): 21.3MM **Privately Held**
WEB: www.eharmony.com
SIC: 7299 Dating service

(P-13742)
EMPYR INCORPORATED
11010 Roselle St Ste 150, San Diego
(92121-1226)
PHONE.....................888 664-5669
Jon Carder, *President*
Jarrod Cuzens, *Principal*
Peter Vogel, *General Mgr*
Jason Bausewein, *Sr Software Eng*
Ed Mitchell, *Sr Software Eng*
EMP: 65
SALES (est): 4.7MM **Privately Held**
SIC: 7299 Tax refund discounting

(P-13743)
EUROPRO INC (PA)
Also Called: Club Tan
9539 Langley Rd, Bakersfield
(93312-2140)
PHONE.....................661 615-6610
Rhonda Van Tassell, *President*

John Van Tassell, *President*
EMP: 98 EST: 1995
SQ FT: 1,400
SALES (est): 4.8MM **Privately Held**
WEB: www.EUROPROusa.com
SIC: 7299 Tanning salon

(P-13744)
EVEREST WTRPRFING RSTRTION INC
1270 Missouri St, San Francisco
(94107-3310)
PHONE.....................415 282-9800
Keith Goldstein, *President*
Mark Murray, *Vice Pres*
Andrina Howell, *Administration*
Arleen Campos, *Bookkeeper*
Aaron Busbee, *Opers Mgr*
EMP: 64
SQ FT: 5,000
SALES (est): 4.9MM **Privately Held**
WEB: www.everestsf.com
SIC: 7299 Home improvement & renovation contractor agency

(P-13745)
FREEDOM FINANCIAL NETWORK LLC (PA)
Also Called: Freedom Debt Relief
1875 S Grant St Ste 400, San Mateo
(94402-2676)
PHONE.....................650 393-6619
Bradford Stroh,
Cristina Huerta, *Admin Asst*
Robert Curtis, *Info Tech Dir*
Linda Luman, *VP Human Res*
Melissa Martinez, *Recruiter*
EMP: 77
SQ FT: 20,000
SALES (est): 20.8MM **Privately Held**
WEB: www.freedomfinancialnetwork.com
SIC: 7299 Debt counseling or adjustment service, individuals

(P-13746)
GALKOS CONSTRUCTION INC (PA)
15262 Pipeline Ln, Huntington Beach
(92649-1136)
PHONE.....................714 373-8545
Frank E Gialketsis, *President*
Lonnie Gailketsis, *Vice Pres*
Carin Orr, *Administration*
EMP: 60
SALES (est): 10.3MM **Privately Held**
WEB: www.galkos.com
SIC: 7299 Home improvement & renovation contractor agency

(P-13747)
HANDYMAN CONNECTION
1740 W Katella Ave Ste G, Orange
(92867-3434)
PHONE.....................714 288-0077
Rich Panitz, *President*
Linda Panitz, *Vice Pres*
EMP: 50
SQ FT: 1,000
SALES (est): 1.5MM **Privately Held**
WEB: www.omnigen.com
SIC: 7299 Handyman service

(P-13748)
HOMETOWN BUFFET INC
Also Called: Hometown Buffet 261
11471 South St, Cerritos (90703-6600)
PHONE.....................562 402-8307
Mary Woods, *General Mgr*
EMP: 51
SALES (corp-wide): 729.5MM **Privately Held**
WEB: www.hometownbuffet.com
SIC: 7299 Banquet hall facilities
HQ: Hometown Buffet Inc.
　　120 Chula Vis
　　San Antonio TX 78232
　　651 994-8608

(P-13749)
IDEAL PRODUCTS LLC
14724 Ventura Blvd Fl 200, Sherman Oaks
(91403-3514)
PHONE.....................818 217-2574
Mark Bess, *Mng Member*
Craig Shandler,

Michael Badar, *Mng Member*
EMP: 50
SALES (est): 2MM **Privately Held**
WEB: www.idealproduct.com
SIC: 7299 Information services, consumer

(P-13750)
IMPACT DESTINATIONS & EVENTS
Also Called: Impact Events
1005 Market St Unit 402, San Francisco
(94103-1627)
PHONE....................................415 766-4170
Dan Houdek, *President*
Salina Lohacharoen, *Sales Staff*
EMP: 50 EST: 2011
SALES (est): 254.9K **Privately Held**
SIC: 7299 Party planning service

(P-13751)
INFORMATION & REFERRAL FED LOS
Also Called: 211 La County
526 W Las Tunas Dr, San Gabriel
(91776-1111)
P.O. Box 726 (91778-0726)
PHONE....................................626 350-1841
Maribel Marin, *CEO*
Amy Latzer, *COO*
Laura Nelson, *CFO*
Laura Mejia, *Program Mgr*
Alana Hitchcock, *Executive Asst*
EMP: 100
SQ FT: 23,000
SALES (est): 8.8MM **Privately Held**
WEB: www.211-la.net
SIC: 7299 Information services, consumer

(P-13752)
INTERNATIONAL MISSING PERSONS
609 S Broder St, Anaheim (92804-3232)
P.O. Box 2542 (92814-0542)
PHONE....................................714 827-1947
Arthur Suchesk, *President*
Robert W Pershelli, *CFO*
J Cullins, *Admin Sec*
EMP: 55
SALES (est): 4.3MM **Privately Held**
SIC: 7299

(P-13753)
JENNY CRAIG INC (HQ)
5770 Fleet St, Carlsbad (92008-4700)
PHONE....................................760 696-4000
Monty Sharma, *CEO*
Patricia Larchet, *Ch of Bd*
Jim Kelly, *CFO*
Leesa Eichberger, *Chief Mktg Ofcr*
Alan V Dobies, *Vice Pres*
EMP: 220
SQ FT: 75,000
SALES (est): 134.2MM
SALES (corp-wide): 170.6MM **Privately Held**
WEB: www.jennycraig.com
SIC: 7299 6794 5149 5499 Diet center, without medical staff; franchises, selling or licensing; diet foods; dietetic foods
PA: North Castle Partners, L.L.C.
183 E Putnam Ave
Greenwich CT 06830
203 485-0216

(P-13754)
JENNY CRAIG WGHT LOSS CTRS INC (DH)
5770 Fleet St, Carlsbad (92008-4700)
PHONE....................................760 696-4000
Dana Fiser, *President*
Kent Kreh, *Ch of Bd*
Patti Larchet, *President*
Jenny Craig, *CEO*
James Kelly, *CFO*
EMP: 130
SQ FT: 50,000
SALES (est): 56.1MM
SALES (corp-wide): 170.6MM **Privately Held**
SIC: 7299 7991 Diet center, without medical staff; weight reducing clubs
HQ: Jenny Craig, Inc.
5770 Fleet St
Carlsbad CA 92008
760 696-4000

(P-13755)
JN PROJECTS INC
Also Called: Hellosign
301 Howard St Ste 200, San Francisco
(94105-6619)
PHONE....................................415 766-0273
Joseph Hartman Walla, *CEO*
Whitney Bouck, *COO*
Maranda Dziekonski, *Vice Pres*
MAI Ton, *Vice Pres*
Jack Dauer, *Executive*
EMP: 100
SQ FT: 13,600
SALES (est): 1.4MM **Privately Held**
SIC: 7299 Personal document & information services

(P-13756)
MASSAGE PLACE
2516 Overland Ave, Los Angeles
(90064-3333)
PHONE....................................310 204-3004
Michael Marylander, *Branch Mgr*
EMP: 200
SALES (corp-wide): 2.4MM **Privately Held**
SIC: 7299 Massage parlor
PA: The Massage Place
245 Main St
Venice CA 90291
310 399-5566

(P-13757)
MASTROIANNI FAMILY ENTPS LTD
Also Called: Jay's Catering
10581 Garden Grove Blvd, Garden Grove
(92843-1128)
PHONE....................................310 952-1700
Jay Mastroiannis, *President*
EMP: 78
SALES (corp-wide): 34.9MM **Privately Held**
WEB: www.jayscatering.com
SIC: 7299 Banquet hall facilities
PA: Mastroianni Family Enterprises Ltd.
10581 Garden Grove Blvd
Garden Grove CA 92843
714 636-6045

(P-13758)
MOUNTASIA OF SANTA CLARITA
Also Called: Mountasia Family Fun Center
21516 Golden Triangle Rd, Santa Clarita
(91350-2612)
PHONE....................................661 253-4386
Michael Fleming, *Partner*
David Fleming, *Partner*
EMP: 60
SALES (est): 1.7MM **Privately Held**
SIC: 7299 7999 Party planning service; skating rink operation services

(P-13759)
MOVE SALES INC (DH)
Also Called: Homestore Apartments & Rentals
3315 Scott Blvd Ste 250, Santa Clara
(95054-3139)
PHONE....................................805 557-2300
Steve Berkowitz, *CEO*
Maria Pietrosorte, *President*
Debbie Neuberger, *Senior VP*
Arul Daniel, *Vice Pres*
Mark Zone, *Executive*
EMP: 75
SALES (est): 12.3MM
SALES (corp-wide): 9B **Publicly Held**
SIC: 7299 Apartment locating service
HQ: Move, Inc.
3315 Scott Blvd Ste 250
Santa Clara CA 95054
408 558-7100

(P-13760)
ONE CALL PLUMBER GOLETA
140 Nectarine Ave Apt 4, Goleta
(93117-3359)
PHONE....................................805 284-0441
One Call Plumber Goleta, *Owner*
EMP: 99
SALES: 0 **Privately Held**
SIC: 7299 Handyman service

(P-13761)
PACIFIC EVENT PRODUCTIONS INC (PA)
Also Called: Pep Creations
6989 Corte Santa Fe, San Diego
(92121-3260)
PHONE....................................858 458-9908
Lawrence J Toll, *CEO*
George Duff, *President*
Lawrence Toll, *Vice Pres*
Amy Berner, *Social Dir*
Lisa Devine, *Social Dir*
EMP: 250
SQ FT: 30,000
SALES (est): 14.3MM **Privately Held**
WEB: www.pacificevents.com
SIC: 7299 Party planning service

(P-13762)
PACIFICA HEALTH AND MEDICAL
2650 Cmino Del Rio N 21, San Diego
(92108)
PHONE....................................619 688-1848
Jeff Sternberg, *President*
EMP: 104
SQ FT: 1,000
SALES (est): 2.2MM **Privately Held**
SIC: 7299 Diet center, without medical staff

(P-13763)
PALMDALE WOMANS CLUB
2141 E Avenue Q, Palmdale (93550-4040)
P.O. Box 901825 (93590-1825)
PHONE....................................661 266-3008
Shirley Haning, *President*
Helen Cleveland, *President*
Jackie Lawslo, *President*
EMP: 52
SQ FT: 3,215
SALES: 24.1K **Privately Held**
WEB: www.palmdalewomansclub.com
SIC: 7299 8699 Personal appearance services; charitable organization

(P-13764)
PALO ALTO HILLS GOLF AN
3000 Alexis Dr, Palo Alto (94304-1303)
PHONE....................................650 948-1800
Padmanabhan Srinagesh, *CEO*
Timothy Ralphs, *Executive*
David Root, *Executive*
Dirk Zander, *General Mgr*
Marian Paragas, *Controller*
EMP: 75
SQ FT: 25,000
SALES (est): 7.7MM **Privately Held**
WEB: www.pahgcc.com
SIC: 7299 7997 Banquet hall facilities; golf club, membership

(P-13765)
PARTY PANTRY GARDEN ROOM
12777 Knott St, Garden Grove
(92841-3903)
PHONE....................................714 899-0626
Lisa Waddell, *Owner*
EMP: 50 EST: 1971
SALES (est): 705.2K **Privately Held**
SIC: 7299 Banquet hall facilities

(P-13766)
PLAN-IT INTERACTIVE INC (PA)
150 W Industrial Way, Benicia
(94510-1016)
PHONE....................................707 752-6010
Skip Smith, *CEO*
Louis Smith, *President*
Greg Sloan, *Executive*
Kimberly Shirley, *Assistant*
EMP: 50
SQ FT: 24,000
SALES (est): 4.1MM **Privately Held**
WEB: www.interactivegame.com
SIC: 7299 Party planning service

(P-13767)
PPS PARKING INC
1800 E Garry Ave Ste 107, Santa Ana
(92705-5803)
P.O. Box 16635, Irvine (92623-6635)
PHONE....................................949 223-8707
Steve Paliska, *President*
Karen Such, *Senior VP*
EMP: 506

SQ FT: 5,000
SALES (est): 9.2MM **Privately Held**
SIC: 7299 8748 Valet parking; business consulting

(P-13768)
PRAETORIAN USA
Also Called: Praetorian Event Services
925 Lakeville St 129, Petaluma
(94952-3329)
PHONE....................................707 780-8020
Kathy J Kingman, *President*
Mark Solum, *Manager*
EMP: 99
SALES (est): 200K **Privately Held**
SIC: 7299 7389 Party planning service;

(P-13769)
PREMIER RESIDENTIAL SVCS LLC
43100 Cook St Ste 101, Palm Desert
(92211-3124)
P.O. Box 13250 (92255-3250)
PHONE....................................760 773-4081
Daniel Loera, *Mng Member*
Cindy Voyles, *Manager*
EMP: 60
SALES (est): 213.2K **Privately Held**
SIC: 7299 Miscellaneous personal service

(P-13770)
RAINCROSS HOSPITALITY CORP (PA)
Also Called: Riverside Aditorium Events Ctr
3637 5th St, Riverside (92501-2816)
PHONE....................................951 346-4700
Edward Weggeland, *President*
Debbie Guthrie, *Senior VP*
Mark Lewis, *Security Dir*
Marcy Hernandez, *Office Mgr*
Oscar Ornelas, *Engineer*
EMP: 56
SQ FT: 1,500
SALES (est): 5.6MM **Privately Held**
SIC: 7299 Banquet hall facilities; party planning service

(P-13771)
RETREAT & CONFERENCE CENTER
Also Called: De Lasalle Institute
4401 Redwood Rd, NAPA (94558-9708)
PHONE....................................707 252-3810
Linda Bausch, *Director*
EMP: 50 EST: 2001
SALES (est): 471.9K **Privately Held**
SIC: 7299 8661 Wedding chapel, privately operated; community church

(P-13772)
SALON TECHNIQUE
101 N Harbor Blvd, Fullerton (92832-3608)
PHONE....................................714 871-4247
Lynette Coryell, *Partner*
Pamela Coryell, *Partner*
EMP: 50 EST: 2010
SALES: 1.4MM **Privately Held**
SIC: 7299 7231 Massage parlor; facial salons; hairdressers

(P-13773)
SERVIZ INC
15303 Ventura Blvd # 1600, Sherman Oaks
(91403-3133)
PHONE....................................818 381-4826
Zorik Gordon, *CEO*
Michael Klien, *President*
Adam Wergeles, *Exec VP*
Jason Whitt, *Senior VP*
Max Dichter, *Vice Pres*
EMP: 70
SQ FT: 8,000
SALES (est): 12MM **Privately Held**
SIC: 7299 Home improvement & renovation contractor agency

(P-13774)
SKYPARK INC
Also Called: Airport Parking Services
1000 San Mateo Ave, San Bruno
(94066-1594)
PHONE....................................650 875-6655
Kim Kasser, *President*
Joe Galligan, *Ch of Bd*
Essayas Araya, *Office Mgr*

P R O D U C T S & S V C S

Shirley Krouse, *Admin Sec*
Susan D Porto, *Cust Mgr*
EMP: 75
SQ FT: 430,000
SALES (est): 5.5MM **Privately Held**
WEB: www.skypark.com
SIC: 7299 Valet parking

(P-13775)
SLC OPERATING LTD PARTNERSHIP
Also Called: Sheraton Universal Hotel
333 Unversal Hollywood Dr, North Hollywood (91608-1001)
PHONE....................818 980-1212
Silvio Campos, *Branch Mgr*
EMP: 350
SALES (corp-wide): 22.8B **Publicly Held**
SIC: 7299 7011 6512 5813 Banquet hall facilities; hotels; nonresidential building operators; drinking places; eating places
HQ: Slc Operating Limited Partnership
2231 E Camelback Rd # 400
Phoenix AZ 85016

(P-13776)
SOIREE VALET PARKING SERVICE
1470 Howard St, San Francisco (94103-2523)
PHONE....................415 284-9700
Jamie Dyos, *President*
Katie Dyos, *Business Dir*
Calvin Lun, *Opers Mgr*
Artem Shestopalov, *Prdtn Mgr*
EMP: 150
SQ FT: 3,000
SALES: 2.8MM **Privately Held**
WEB: www.soireevalet.com
SIC: 7299 7521 Valet parking; automobile parking

(P-13777)
TRUECAR INC (PA)
120 Broadway Ste 200, Santa Monica (90401-2385)
PHONE....................800 200-2000
Chip Perry, *President*
Alice Fluker, *Partner*
Daniel Lysaught, *Partner*
Jason Nierman, *Partner*
David Pributsky, *Partner*
EMP: 50
SQ FT: 38,000
SALES: 323.1MM **Publicly Held**
WEB: www.zag.com
SIC: 7299 5012 Information services, consumer; automotive brokers

(P-13778)
USA VALET PARKING LLC
980 9th St Ste 1620, Sacramento (95814-2719)
PHONE....................916 792-1055
Steven Baver, *Mng Member*
EMP: 50
SALES: 126.9K **Privately Held**
SIC: 7299 7521 Valet parking; outdoor parking services

(P-13779)
WATERCOURSE WAY
Also Called: Water Course Way
165 Channing Ave, Palo Alto (94301-2409)
PHONE....................650 462-2000
John Roberts, *Partner*
Watercourse Way, *Partner*
EMP: 120
SALES (est): 3.8MM **Privately Held**
WEB: www.watercourseway.com
SIC: 7299 Massage parlor

(P-13780)
WEDGEWOOD HSPITALITY GROUP INC
43385 Business Park Dr, Temecula (92590-3688)
PHONE....................951 491-8110
Daniel Bylund, *CFO*
EMP: 50
SQ FT: 5,000
SALES (est): 192K **Privately Held**
SIC: 7299 Banquet hall facilities

(P-13781)
WESTERN COSTUME LEASING
11041 Vanowen St, North Hollywood (91605-6314)
PHONE....................818 760-0900
Eddie Marks, *President*
Kristin Holbak, *Executive Asst*
EMP: 60
SQ FT: 150,000
SALES (est): 1.1MM
SALES (corp-wide): 6.5MM **Privately Held**
WEB: www.westerncostume.com
SIC: 7299 Costume rental
HQ: Western Costume Co.
11041 Vanowen St
North Hollywood CA 91605
818 760-0900

(P-13782)
Z VALET INC
Also Called: Z Valet & Shuttle Service
4221 Wilshire Blvd 170-11, Los Angeles (90010-3519)
PHONE....................323 954-3700
Daniel Ziv, *President*
EMP: 225
SQ FT: 1,500
SALES (est): 5.2MM **Privately Held**
WEB: www.zvalet.com
SIC: 7299 7363 8748 Valet parking; chauffeur service; business consulting

7311 Advertising Agencies

(P-13783)
180LA LLC
12555 W Jefferson Blvd # 200, Los Angeles (90066-7047)
PHONE....................310 382-1400
Michael Allen, *Mng Member*
William Gelner, *Creative Dir*
Eduardo Marques, *Creative Dir*
Pete Cline, *Managing Dir*
Savannah Carter, *Office Admin*
EMP: 110
SQ FT: 13,000
SALES: 24.4MM
SALES (corp-wide): 15.2B **Publicly Held**
WEB: www.180la.com
SIC: 7311 Advertising consultant
HQ: Tbwa Worldwide Inc.
488 Madison Ave
New York NY 10022

(P-13784)
72ANDSUNNY LLC
12101 Bluff Creek Dr, Playa Vista (90094-2627)
PHONE....................310 215-9009
John Boiler,
Sedef Onar, *Officer*
Chris Hutchinson, *Creative Dir*
Nai Gregory, *Admin Asst*
Glenn Cole,
EMP: 126
SALES (est): 41.7MM **Privately Held**
SIC: 7311 Advertising agencies

(P-13785)
A S I CORPORATION
Also Called: Bridgford Foods
1308 N Patt St, Anaheim (92801-2551)
PHONE....................714 526-5533
Allan L Bridgford, *Chairman*
Robert E Schulze, *President*
Raymond F Lancy, *Vice Pres*
William L Bridgford, *Admin Sec*
EMP: 200
SQ FT: 95,000
SALES (est): 13.8MM
SALES (corp-wide): 167.2MM **Publicly Held**
WEB: www.bridgford.com
SIC: 7311 2711 Advertising consultant; newspapers
HQ: Bridgford Foods Corporation
1308 N Patt St
Anaheim CA 92801
714 526-5533

(P-13786)
AAAZA INC
3250 Wilshire Blvd # 1901, Los Angeles (90010-1609)
PHONE....................213 380-8333
Zan Ng, *CEO*
Jeanine Kim, *Shareholder*
Peter Huang, *President*
EMP: 60
SQ FT: 3,000
SALES (est): 9.8MM **Privately Held**
WEB: www.aaaza.com
SIC: 7311 Advertising consultant

(P-13787)
ADLINK CABLE ADVERTISING LLC
11150 Santa Monica Blvd # 100, Los Angeles (90025-3380)
PHONE....................310 477-3994
Bob McCauley,
EMP: 120
SALES (est): 12MM **Privately Held**
WEB: www.adlink.com
SIC: 7311 Advertising consultant

(P-13788)
ADMARKETING INC
Also Called: Add Media
1801 Century Park E # 2100, Los Angeles (90067-2330)
PHONE....................310 203-8400
Jack Roth, *President*
Robert Roth, *Treasurer*
Marty Cagan, *Exec VP*
Bob Saltzburg, *Creative Dir*
Felicia Gaddis, *Executive Asst*
EMP: 55
SQ FT: 16,000
SALES (est): 12.4MM **Privately Held**
WEB: www.admarketingcreative.com
SIC: 7311 Advertising agencies

(P-13789)
ADROLL INC (PA)
2300 Harrison St Fl 2, San Francisco (94110-2013)
PHONE....................877 723-7655
Toby Gabriner, *CEO*
Scott Gifis, *Partner*
Peter Krivkovich, *COO*
Aaron Bell,
Suresh Khanna, *Vice Pres*
EMP: 83
SALES (est): 36.5MM **Privately Held**
SIC: 7311 Advertising consultant

(P-13790)
AIRPUSH INC
11400 W Olympic Blvd, Los Angeles (90064-1550)
PHONE....................877 944-2490
Asher Delug, *CEO*
David K Awamoto, *President*
Inman Breaux, *COO*
Matt Shaw, *Officer*
David Kawamoto, *Senior VP*
EMP: 140
SALES (est): 16.6MM **Privately Held**
SIC: 7311 Advertising agencies

(P-13791)
ALCONE MARKETING GROUP INC (HQ)
Also Called: Jeep Gear
4 Studebaker, Irvine (92618-2012)
PHONE....................949 595-5322
William Hahn, *CEO*
Sean Conciatore, *Ch Credit Ofcr*
Luis Camano, *Creative Dir*
Bill Hahn, *Principal*
EMP: 100
SQ FT: 90,000
SALES (est): 27.3MM
SALES (corp-wide): 15.2B **Publicly Held**
WEB: www.alconemarketing.com
SIC: 7311 Advertising agencies
PA: Omnicom Group Inc.
437 Madison Ave
New York NY 10022
212 415-3600

(P-13792)
AMOBEE INC (DH)
901 Marshall St 200, Redwood City (94063-2026)
PHONE....................650 353-4399
Kim Perell, *CEO*
Chad Bronstein, *Partner*
Domenic Venuto, *COO*
Craig Foster, *CFO*
Steve Hoffman, *CFO*
EMP: 130
SALES (est): 52.2MM
SALES (corp-wide): 13.3B **Privately Held**
WEB: www.amobee.com
SIC: 7311 Advertising agencies
HQ: Amobee Group Pte. Ltd.
8 Marina View
Singapore 01896
634 010-20

(P-13793)
AVIA TECH LLC
7220 Trade St Ste 300, San Diego (92121-2334)
PHONE....................858 777-5000
Dwight Gould, *CEO*
Cheryl Gould,
EMP: 56
SQ FT: 8,000
SALES (est): 9.2MM **Privately Held**
SIC: 7311 Advertising agencies

(P-13794)
AYZENBERG GROUP INC
49 E Walnut St, Pasadena (91103-3832)
PHONE....................626 584-4070
Eric Ayzenberg, *President*
EMP: 65
SQ FT: 10,000
SALES (est): 19.4MM **Privately Held**
WEB: www.ayzenberg.com
SIC: 7311 7336 Advertising consultant; commercial art & graphic design

(P-13795)
BASIS WORLDWIDE
1557 7th St, Santa Monica (90401-2605)
PHONE....................424 261-2354
Joe Dipietro, *CEO*
EMP: 50
SALES (est): 1.1MM **Privately Held**
SIC: 7311 Advertising consultant

(P-13796)
BATTERY MARKETING INC
Also Called: Battery Agency
6515 W Sunset Blvd # 200, Hollywood (90028-7261)
PHONE....................323 467-7267
Anson Sowby,
Philip Khosid, *Officer*
EMP: 52
SALES (est): 3.7MM **Privately Held**
SIC: 7311 Advertising consultant

(P-13797)
BBDO WORLDWIDE INC
600 California St Fl 8, San Francisco (94108-2726)
PHONE....................415 808-6200
Linda D Merrick, *Senior VP*
Linda Domercq, *Controller*
EMP: 60
SALES (corp-wide): 15.2B **Publicly Held**
WEB: www.bbdo.com
SIC: 7311 Advertising consultant
HQ: Bbdo Worldwide Inc.
1285 Ave Of The Amer
New York NY 10019
212 459-5000

(P-13798)
BDS MARKETING LLC (DH)
10 Holland, Irvine (92618-2504)
PHONE....................800 234-4237
Ken Kress, *CEO*
Scott McDaniel, *President*
David Tranberg, *Development*
Tracy Neff, *Services*
Randy Schrock, *Services*
EMP: 120

SALES (est): 94.4MM
SALES (corp-wide): 257.4MM **Privately Held**
WEB: www.bdsmarketing.com
SIC: **7311** 8743 8732 Advertising consultant; promotion service; commercial non-physical research
HQ: Bds Solutions Group, Llc
10 Holland
Irvine CA 92618
949 472-6700

(P-13799)
BDS SOLUTIONS GROUP LLC (DH)
10 Holland, Irvine (92618-2504)
PHONE....................949 472-6700
Mike Sunderland, *CEO*
Bob Salem, *CFO*
EMP: 1500
SALES (est): 94.4MM
SALES (corp-wide): 257.4MM **Privately Held**
SIC: **7311** Advertising consultant

(P-13800)
BUTLER SHINE STERN PRTNERS LLC
Also Called: Bssp
20 Liberty Ship Way, Sausalito (94965-3312)
PHONE....................415 331-6049
Greg Stern,
Dennis Moore, *CFO*
Matthew Curry, *Officer*
John Butler,
Mike Shine,
EMP: 139
SALES (est): 44.1MM **Privately Held**
SIC: **7311** Advertising consultant

(P-13801)
CADREON LLC
600 Battery St, San Francisco (94111-1817)
PHONE....................415 262-5900
Ian Johnson, *General Mgr*
Tushar Patel, *Senior VP*
Jason Chambers, *Vice Pres*
John George, *Vice Pres*
Chris Manolarakis, *Vice Pres*
EMP: 120
SALES (est): 11.6MM **Privately Held**
SIC: **7311** Advertising consultant
PA: Cadreon, Llc
100 W 33rd St Fl 8
New York NY 10001

(P-13802)
CADREON LLC
653 Front St, San Francisco (94111-1913)
PHONE....................415 262-5900
Quentin George, *Partner*
Erica Schmidt, *Exec VP*
Heather Prince, *Vice Pres*
Kimber Robbins, *Vice Pres*
Lee Stapleton, *Vice Pres*
EMP: 60
SALES (est): 9.8MM **Privately Held**
SIC: **7311** Advertising consultant
PA: Cadreon, Llc
100 W 33rd St Fl 8
New York NY 10001

(P-13803)
CASANOVA PNDRILL PBLICIDAD INC (PA)
275 Mccormick Ave Ste 1a, Costa Mesa (92626-3325)
PHONE....................949 474-5001
Daniel Nance, *President*
Laura Marella, *Vice Pres*
Jean Malley Vega, *Vice Pres*
Jose Molina, *Executive*
Andres Calvachi, *Accounting Mgr*
EMP: 55
SQ FT: 12,000
SALES (est): 10.4MM **Privately Held**
WEB: www.casanova.com
SIC: **7311** Advertising agencies

(P-13804)
COLOR AD INC
18601 S Santa Fe Ave, Compton (90221-5901)
PHONE....................310 632-5500
Lisa Scorziell, *Principal*
Rose Oldenkamp, *Vice Pres*
Keisha Palumbo, *Office Mgr*
Donna Terrano, *Administration*
Shafi Karim, *Project Mgr*
EMP: 50
SQ FT: 33,000
SALES (est): 15.9MM **Privately Held**
WEB: www.gocolorad.com
SIC: **7311** 2752 Advertising agencies; commercial printing, lithographic

(P-13805)
CREATIVE CHANNEL SERVICES LLC (HQ)
Also Called: C C S
12777 W Jefferson Blvd # 120, Los Angeles (90066-7038)
PHONE....................310 482-6500
Andy Restivo, *CEO*
Vida Roozen, *President*
Michael Butler, *CFO*
Hanoz Gandhi, *Exec VP*
George Plumb, *Exec VP*
EMP: 65
SALES (est): 33.9MM
SALES (corp-wide): 15.2B **Publicly Held**
WEB: www.creativechannel.com
SIC: **7311** Advertising agencies
PA: Omnicom Group Inc.
437 Madison Ave
New York NY 10022
212 415-3600

(P-13806)
CREW CREATIVE ADVERTISING LLC
7966 Beverly Blvd, Los Angeles (90048-4511)
PHONE....................310 451-3225
Damon Wolf, *Mng Member*
John Cain, *COO*
Jennifer Cain,
Charles Reimers,
Maria Reimers,
EMP: 165
SQ FT: 65,000
SALES (est): 11.1MM **Privately Held**
WEB: www.crewcreative.com
SIC: **7311** Advertising agencies

(P-13807)
D AUGUSTINE & ASSOCIATES
Also Called: Augustine Ideas
532 Gibson Dr Ste 250, Roseville (95678-5879)
PHONE....................916 774-9600
Debra Augustine, *CEO*
Robert Nelson, *COO*
Kimberly Ericksen, *Executive*
Michael Mezzanotte, *Creative Dir*
Brian Carey, *Business Dir*
EMP: 52
SQ FT: 7,500
SALES (est): 9.7MM **Privately Held**
SIC: **7311** Advertising consultant

(P-13808)
DAILEY & ASSOCIATES
Also Called: Interpublic Group of Companies
8687 Melrose Ave G300, Los Angeles (90069-5701)
PHONE....................310 360-3100
Thomas Lehr, *CEO*
Michael Perdigao, *Managing Prtnr*
Eugene Alejo Jr, *CFO*
Carlos Ariza, *Vice Pres*
Bret Covey, *Vice Pres*
EMP: 100 EST: 1964
SALES (est): 19.8MM
SALES (corp-wide): 7.8B **Publicly Held**
WEB: www.daileyads.com
SIC: **7311** Advertising consultant
PA: The Interpublic Group Of Companies Inc
909 3rd Ave Fl 7
New York NY 10022
212 704-1200

(P-13809)
DAVID & GOLIATH LLC
909 N Pacific Coast Hwy # 700, El Segundo (90245-2724)
PHONE....................310 445-5200
Yumi Prentice, *President*
Brian Dunbar, *Managing Prtnr*
Jerry Duran, *CFO*
Wells Davis, *Officer*
Bobby Pearce, *Officer*
EMP: 200
SQ FT: 1,000
SALES (est): 33.5MM
SALES (corp-wide): 385.8MM **Privately Held**
WEB: www.dngla.com
SIC: **7311** Advertising consultant
PA: Innocean Worldwide Inc.
308 Gangnam-Daero, Gangnam-Gu
Seoul 06253
822 201-6237

(P-13810)
DAVISELEN ADVERTISING INC (PA)
865 S Figueroa St # 1200, Los Angeles (90017-2543)
PHONE....................213 688-7000
Mark Davis, *CEO*
Teriann Hughes, *Partner*
Stan Kaplan, *Partner*
Jim Kelly, *Partner*
Malu Santamaria, *Partner*
EMP: 172
SQ FT: 32,000
SALES (est): 30.7MM **Privately Held**
WEB: www.daviselen.com
SIC: **7311** Advertising agencies

(P-13811)
DAVISELEN ADVERTISING INC
420 Stevens Ave Ste 240, Solana Beach (92075-2079)
PHONE....................858 847-0789
Jim Kelly, *Branch Mgr*
EMP: 61
SALES (corp-wide): 30.7MM **Privately Held**
SIC: **7311** Advertising consultant
PA: Daviselen Advertising, Inc.
865 S Figueroa St # 1200
Los Angeles CA 90017
213 688-7000

(P-13812)
DDB WORLDWIDE
340 Main St, Venice (90291-2524)
PHONE....................310 907-1500
Nick Bishop, *Manager*
Joanne Howes, *Partner*
Christopher Pultorak, *Vice Pres*
EMP: 175
SALES (corp-wide): 15.2B **Publicly Held**
SIC: **7311** Advertising agencies
HQ: Ddb Worldwide Communications Group, Inc.
437 Madison Ave Fl 11
New York NY 10022
212 415-2000

(P-13813)
DDB WORLDWIDE
600 California St Fl 7, San Francisco (94108-2731)
PHONE....................415 732-3600
Mary Moudry, *President*
Ryan De Leon, *Administration*
EMP: 160
SALES (corp-wide): 15.2B **Publicly Held**
SIC: **7311** Advertising consultant
HQ: Ddb Worldwide Communications Group, Inc.
437 Madison Ave Fl 11
New York NY 10022
212 415-2000

(P-13814)
DEDICATED MEDIA INC (PA)
909 N Pacific Coast Hwy # 320, El Segundo (90245-2734)
PHONE....................310 524-9400
Scott Yamano, *CEO*
Chris Berman, *COO*
Ryan Becker, *Vice Pres*
Brian Malone, *Vice Pres*
Monica Lee, *Accounts Mgr*

EMP: 53
SQ FT: 45,000
SALES (est): 15.3MM **Privately Held**
WEB: www.dedicatedla.com
SIC: **7311** Advertising consultant

(P-13815)
DEFY MEDIA LLC
8750 Wilshire Blvd # 200, Beverly Hills (90211-2707)
PHONE....................310 360-4141
Keith Richman,
Arsenio Jakovcich, *Info Tech Mgr*
EMP: 99
SALES (est): 2.5MM **Privately Held**
SIC: **7311** Advertising agencies

(P-13816)
DELPHI PRODUCTIONS INC (PA)
Also Called: Group Delphi
950 W Tower Ave, Alameda (94501-5049)
PHONE....................510 748-7494
Justin Hersh, *President*
Pete Bowes, *CFO*
Tony Erpelding, *Officer*
Kyle Wood, *Senior VP*
Sara Ost, *Vice Pres*
EMP: 142
SQ FT: 148,000
SALES (est): 54.3MM **Privately Held**
WEB: www.delphiproductions.com
SIC: **7311** Advertising agencies

(P-13817)
DEUTSCH LA INC
5454 Beethoven St, Los Angeles (90066-7017)
PHONE....................310 862-3000
Mike Sheldon, *CEO*
Demi Treisman, *Executive*
Neseem Ishaq, *Engineer*
Tyler West, *Business Mgr*
Nick Mariano, *Sales Staff*
EMP: 100 EST: 1995
SALES (est): 26.2MM
SALES (corp-wide): 7.8B **Publicly Held**
SIC: **7311** Advertising agencies
PA: The Interpublic Group Of Companies Inc
909 3rd Ave Fl 7
New York NY 10022
212 704-1200

(P-13818)
DGWB INC
Also Called: Dgwb Advg & Communications
217 N Main St Ste 200, Santa Ana (92701-4843)
PHONE....................714 881-2300
Mike Wiseman, *CEO*
Mike Weisman, *Partner*
Mike Shudak, *CFO*
Danika Petersen, *Executive*
John Gothold, *Principal*
EMP: 70
SALES (est): 19.5MM **Privately Held**
SIC: **7311** Advertising consultant

(P-13819)
DGWB VENTURES LLC
Also Called: Advertising
217 N Main St Ste 200, Santa Ana (92701-4843)
PHONE....................714 881-2308
Mike Weisman,
Madeline Dossin,
John Gothold,
Mike Shudak,
EMP: 95
SQ FT: 25,839
SALES (est): 832.9K **Privately Held**
SIC: **7311** Advertising consultant

(P-13820)
DIRECT PARTNERS INC (HQ)
12777 W Jefferson Blvd # 120, Los Angeles (90066-7038)
PHONE....................310 482-4200
Tom Harrison, *President*
Tom Parr, *CFO*
Barry Wagner, *Admin Sec*
EMP: 52
SQ FT: 31,000

PRODUCTS & SVCS

SALES (est): 11.1MM
SALES (corp-wide): 15.2B **Publicly Held**
WEB: www.directpartners.com
SIC: 7311 Advertising consultant
PA: Omnicom Group Inc.
  437 Madison Ave
  New York NY 10022
  212 415-3600

(P-13821)
DOREMUS & COMPANY
550 3rd St, San Francisco (94107-1805)
PHONE..................415 273-7800
Garrett Lawrence, *Manager*
Mike Goefft, *Exec Dir*
Thomas Lee, *Admin Asst*
Sal Allababidi, *Info Tech Mgr*
Shawn Fraser, *Manager*
EMP: 50
SALES (corp-wide): 15.2B **Publicly Held**
WEB: www.doremus.com
SIC: 7311 7319 Advertising consultant;
  sky writing
HQ: Doremus & Company
  200 Varick St Fl 11
  New York NY 10014
  212 366-3000

(P-13822)
E BUSINESS SOLUTIONS INC
1271 Dodson Way, Riverside (92507-2057)
PHONE..................800 660-2669
Travis Iverson, *CEO*
EMP: 50
SALES (est): 1.1MM **Privately Held**
SIC: 7311 Advertising agencies

(P-13823)
ELANCE INC (HQ)
441 Logue Ave Ste 150, Mountain View
(94043-4018)
PHONE..................650 316-7500
Stephane Kasriel, *President*
Brian Kinion, *CFO*
EMP: 147
SQ FT: 20,000
SALES (est): 47.5MM
SALES (corp-wide): 202.5MM **Publicly Held**
WEB: www.elance.com
SIC: 7311 Advertising consultant
PA: Upwork Inc.
  441 Logue Ave
  Mountain View CA 94043
  650 316-7500

(P-13824)
ELEVEN INC
Also Called: Eleven Communications
500 Sansome St Ste 100, San Francisco
(94111-3213)
PHONE 415 707-1111
Courtney Buechert, *CEO*
Michael Borosky, *Partner*
Alison Fowler, *Partner*
Jarett Hausske, *Partner*
Mike McKay, *Partner*
EMP: 120
SALES: 22MM **Privately Held**
WEB: www.eleveninc.com
SIC: 7311 Advertising agencies

(P-13825)
EPICENTRO ADVERTISING MKTG SVC
2370 Qume Dr Ste B, San Jose
(95131-1842)
PHONE..................408 453-0353
Maria Schabbing, *Owner*
EMP: 50
SALES (est): 5.1MM **Privately Held**
SIC: 7311 Advertising consultant

(P-13826)
EQAL INC
5250 Lankershim Blvd # 720, North Holly-
wood (91601-3188)
PHONE..................818 276-6300
Miles Beckett, *CEO*
Greg Goodfried, *President*
Robert Weiss, *COO*
Tyler Rubin, *CFO*
EMP: 154
SALES (est): 11.7MM
SALES (corp-wide): 1.1B **Publicly Held**
SIC: 7311 Advertising consultant

HQ: Everyday Health, Inc.
  345 Hudson St Rm 1600
  New York NY 10014
  646 728-9500

(P-13827)
EVANS HARDY & YOUNG INC
829 De La Vina St Ste 100, Santa Barbara
(93101-3285)
PHONE..................805 963-5841
Jim L Evans, *President*
Sue Andrews, *CFO*
Dennis Hardy, *Exec VP*
Lily Katz, *Senior VP*
John O'Brien, *Vice Pres*
EMP: 50
SQ FT: 5,000
SALES (est): 11.5MM **Privately Held**
WEB: www.ehy.com
SIC: 7311 Advertising consultant

(P-13828)
EXPONENTIAL INTERACTIVE INC (HQ)
5858 Horton St Ste 300, Emeryville
(94608-2183)
PHONE..................510 250-5500
Dilip Dasilva, *President*
Tim Brown, *Officer*
Philip Buxton, *Officer*
Amritpal Bedi, *Vice Pres*
Gill Brown, *Vice Pres*
EMP: 90 EST: 2000
SALES (est): 31.6MM
SALES (corp-wide): 1MM **Privately Held**
WEB: www.tribalfusion.com
SIC: 7311 Advertising consultant
PA: Exponential Interactive Uk Limited
  4th Floor 95 Southwark Street
  London
  203 411-7401

(P-13829)
FCB WORLDWIDE INC
Also Called: Draftfcb
1160 Battery St Ste 250, San Francisco
(94111-1216)
PHONE..................415 820-8545
Ian Beavis, *Branch Mgr*
EMP: 524
SALES (corp-wide): 7.8B **Publicly Held**
SIC: 7311 Advertising agencies
HQ: Fcb Worldwide, Inc.
  100 W 33rd St
  New York NY 10001
  212 885-3000

(P-13830)
FCB WORLDWIDE INC
1160 Battery St Ste 250, San Francisco
(94111-1216)
PHONE..................415 820-8000
Dominic Whittles, *President*
EMP: 180
SALES (corp-wide): 7.8B **Publicly Held**
WEB: www.pezzano.com
SIC: 7311 Advertising agencies
HQ: Fcb Worldwide, Inc.
  100 W 33rd St
  New York NY 10001
  212 885-3000

(P-13831)
FORTY FOUR GROUP LLC
Also Called: Origaudio
11397 Slater Ave, Fountain Valley
(92708-5416)
PHONE..................949 407-6360
Michael Szymczak,
Jason Lucash,
EMP: 58
SQ FT: 2,000
SALES (est): 442.8K **Privately Held**
SIC: 7311 Advertising agencies

(P-13832)
FULLSCREEN INC (HQ)
12180 Millennium Ste 100, Playa Vista
(90094-2951)
PHONE..................310 202-3333
George Strompolos, *CEO*
Bradley Hayes, *President*
Beau Bryant, *Senior VP*
Randy Ahn, *Vice Pres*
Polly Auritt, *Vice Pres*
EMP: 81 EST: 2011

SALES (est): 50.1MM
SALES (corp-wide): 1.9MM **Privately Held**
SIC: 7311 Advertising agencies
PA: Otter Media Holdings, Llc
  12180 Millennium
  Playa Vista CA 90094
  310 202-3333

(P-13833)
GIANT CREATIVE STRATEGY LLC
1700 Montgomery St # 485, San Francisco
(94111-1025)
PHONE..................415 655-5200
Steven Gold, *CEO*
Larry Caringi, *President*
Adam Gelling, *President*
Jeff Nemy, *CFO*
Eric Steckelman, *Officer*
EMP: 150
SQ FT: 24,000
SALES (est): 36MM
SALES (corp-wide): 260.2MM **Privately Held**
WEB: www.giantagency.com
SIC: 7311 Advertising agencies
PA: Huntsworth Plc
  8th Floor Holborn Gate
  London WC2A
  203 861-3999

(P-13834)
GL NEMIROW INC
Also Called: Terry Hines & Assoc
2550 N Hollywood Way, Burbank
(91505-1055)
PHONE..................818 562-9433
Grant W Nemirow, *President*
Ralph Terraciano, *CFO*
Norm Hayes, *IT/INT Sup*
EMP: 97
SALES (est): 14MM **Privately Held**
WEB: www.thatrailers.com
SIC: 7311 Advertising agencies

(P-13835)
GOODBY SLVERSTEIN PARTNERS INC
Also Called: Goodby Silverstein & Partners
720 California St, San Francisco
(94108-2440)
PHONE..................415 392-0669
Rich Silverstein, *CEO*
Brian McPherson, *Managing Prtnr*
Robert Riccardi, *Managing Prtnr*
Derek Robson, *Managing Prtnr*
Jeff Goodby, *President*
EMP: 200
SQ FT: 60,000
SALES (est): 58.1MM
SALES (corp-wide): 15.2B **Publicly Held**
WEB: www.omnicomgroup.com
SIC: 7311 Advertising consultant
PA: Omnicom Group Inc.
  437 Madison Ave
  New York NY 10022
  212 415-3600

(P-13836)
GREYSTRIPE INCORPORATED
30699 Russell Ranch Rd # 250, Westlake
Village (91362-7315)
PHONE..................415 644-1702
Michael Chang, *CEO*
Kurt Hawks, *COO*
Erica Chriss, *Senior VP*
Alvaro Bravo, *Vice Pres*
Andy Choi, *CTO*
EMP: 140
SALES (est): 3.1MM **Publicly Held**
SIC: 7311 Advertising agencies
HQ: Conversant, Llc
  30699 Russell Ranch Rd # 250
  Westlake Village CA 91362
  818 575-4500

(P-13837)
GRIZZARD CMMNCATIONS GROUP INC
2 N Lake Ave, Pasadena (91101-1858)
PHONE..................818 543-1315
Philip Stolberg, *Branch Mgr*
Mike Berry, *Creative Dir*
Anne Oparowski, *Buyer*
Larry Wilson, *Marketing Mgr*

EMP: 55
SALES (corp-wide): 15.2B **Publicly Held**
SIC: 7311 Advertising agencies
HQ: Grizzard Communications Group, Inc.
  3500 Lenox Rd Ne Ste 1900
  Atlanta GA 30326
  404 522-8330

(P-13838)
HOBBS HERDER ADVERTISING
Also Called: Hobbs/Herder Training
419 Main St, Huntington Beach
(92648-5199)
PHONE..................800 999-6090
Greg Herder, *Ch of Bd*
John Surge, *President*
Dennis Leblanc, *Vice Pres*
Scott Herder, *Technology*
Josh Hannum, *Consultant*
EMP: 85
SQ FT: 18,500
SALES (est): 12.7MM **Privately Held**
WEB: www.hobbsherder.com
SIC: 7311 Advertising consultant

(P-13839)
HORIZON MEDIA INC
1888 Century Park E # 700, Los Angeles
(90067-1702)
PHONE..................310 282-0909
Zach Rosenberg, *Branch Mgr*
Peter Bhusiririt, *Supervisor*
EMP: 250
SALES (corp-wide): 145.3MM **Privately Held**
SIC: 7311 Advertising agencies
PA: Horizon Media, Inc.
  75 Varick St Ste 1404
  New York NY 10013
  212 220-5000

(P-13840)
HORN GROUP INC
101 Montgomery St Fl 15, San Francisco
(94104-4147)
PHONE..................415 905-4000
Sabrina Horn, *President*
Todd Cadley, *Exec VP*
Kevin King, *Senior VP*
Katie Neuman, *Senior VP*
Smita Topolski, *Vice Pres*
EMP: 50
SQ FT: 13,000
SALES (est): 340K **Privately Held**
WEB: www.horngroup.com
SIC: 7311 Advertising agencies

(P-13841)
HVSF TRANSITION LLC
Also Called: Heat
1100 Sansome St, San Francisco
(94111-1205)
PHONE..................415 477-1999
John Elder, *President*
Elizabeth Warwick, *Office Mgr*
EMP: 60
SQ FT: 12,000
SALES (est): 11.5MM
SALES (corp-wide): 6.6B **Privately Held**
WEB: www.sfheat.com
SIC: 7311 Advertising consultant
HQ: Deloitte Consulting Llp
  30 Rockefeller Plz
  New York NY 10112
  212 492-4000

(P-13842)
I MEAN IT CREATIVE INC
1643 Buckingham Rd, Los Angeles
(90019-5904)
PHONE..................310 287-1000
Emrah Yucel, *President*
EMP: 50
SALES (est): 6.2MM **Privately Held**
SIC: 7311 Advertising agencies

(P-13843)
ICON MEDIA DIRECT INC (PA)
5910 Lemona Ave, Van Nuys (91411-3006)
PHONE..................818 995-6400
Nancy Lazkani, *CEO*
Seth Klein, *COO*
Minnie Dimesa, *Vice Pres*
Leslie Williams, *Office Mgr*
Lindsay Pritikin, *Executive Asst*
EMP: 90

SQ FT: 16,445
SALES (est): 18.6MM **Privately Held**
WEB: www.iconmediadirect.com
SIC: 7311 Advertising agencies

(P-13844)
IGNITE HEALTH LLC (PA)
7535 Irvine Center Dr # 200, Irvine
(92618-4951)
PHONE..................................949 861-3200
Matt Brown, *President*
Brian Lefkowitz, *Officer*
Richard E Fair,
Fabio Gratton,
Timothy J Riley,
EMP: 116
SQ FT: 15,000
SALES (est): 12.5MM **Privately Held**
WEB: www.ignitehealth.com
SIC: 7311 Advertising consultant

(P-13845)
IGNITED LLC (PA)
2150 Park Pl Ste 100, El Segundo
(90245-4714)
PHONE..................................310 773-3100
Eric Johnson, *CEO*
William Rosenthal, *COO*
Whitney Stephenson, *CFO*
Timothy Harsh, *Vice Pres*
Chalita Dasnanjali, *Director*
EMP: 126 EST: 1999
SQ FT: 55,000
SALES: 180MM **Privately Held**
WEB: www.ignitedminds.com
SIC: 7311 Advertising consultant

(P-13846)
**INNOCEAN WRLDWIDE
AMERICAS LLC (HQ)**
180 5th St Ste 200, Huntington Beach
(92648-7107)
PHONE..................................714 861-5200
Yun Jong Beak, *CFO*
Tim Blett, *COO*
Eddie Austin, *Vice Pres*
Fabrizia Cannalonga, *Vice Pres*
Jonathan Farjo, *Vice Pres*
EMP: 75
SALES (est): 36.5MM
SALES (corp-wide): 385.8MM **Privately
Held**
WEB: www.worldmarketinggroup.com
SIC: 7311 Advertising consultant
PA: Innocean Worldwide Inc.
    308 Gangnam-Daero, Gangnam-Gu
    Seoul 06253
    822 201-6237

(P-13847)
**INTER/MEDIA TIME BUYING
CORP (PA)**
Also Called: Inter/Media Advertising
22120 Clarendon St # 300, Woodland Hills
(91367-6315)
PHONE..................................818 995-1455
Robert B Yallen, *President*
Melanie Remneff, *Senior VP*
James Christensen, *Vice Pres*
Malena Cruz, *Vice Pres*
Joseph Poulose, *Vice Pres*
EMP: 50
SQ FT: 12,000
SALES (est): 21MM **Privately Held**
WEB: www.intermedia-advertising.com
SIC: 7311 Advertising agencies

(P-13848)
**INTERACTIVE MEDIA HOLDINGS
(DH)**
Also Called: Viant
4 Park Plz Ste 1500, Irvine (92614-3516)
PHONE..................................949 861-8888
Timothy C Vanderhook, *President*
Chris Vanderhook, *COO*
Roy E Luna, *CFO*
Larry Madden, *CFO*
Jon Ahuna, *Vice Pres*
EMP: 69
SALES (est): 22.8MM
SALES (corp-wide): 1.7B **Publicly Held**
SIC: 7311 7313 Advertising agencies;
    newspaper advertising representative

HQ: Time Inc.
    225 Liberty St Ste C2
    New York NY 10281
    212 522-1212

(P-13849)
**INTERTREND
COMMUNICATIONS INC**
228 E Broadway, Long Beach
(90802-4840)
PHONE..................................562 733-1888
Julia Huang, *CEO*
Susanna Jue, *General Mgr*
Stacy Liu, *Executive Asst*
Flo Kuraoka, *Administration*
Victoria Luong, *Planning*
EMP: 70
SQ FT: 10,000
SALES (est): 15.8MM **Privately Held**
WEB: www.intertrend.com
SIC: 7311 Advertising consultant

(P-13850)
ISEARCH MEDIA LLC
1710 S Amphlett Blvd # 320, San Mateo
(94402-2703)
PHONE..................................415 358-0882
Maury Domengeaux, *CEO*
Scott Rayden, *President*
Charles Hentrich, *CTO*
EMP: 65
SALES (est): 282.8K
SALES (corp-wide): 5.9MM **Privately
Held**
SIC: 7311 Advertising agencies
HQ: 3q Digital, Inc.
    155 Bovet Rd Ste 480
    San Mateo CA 94402
    650 539-4124

(P-13851)
IW GROUP (PA)
6300 Wilshire Blvd # 2150, Los Angeles
(90048-5232)
PHONE..................................310 289-5500
Bill Imada, *CEO*
Nita Song, *President*
Janice Huang, *Accounts Exec*
Hope Lee, *Accounts Exec*
EMP: 54
SQ FT: 7,500
SALES (est): 19.6MM **Privately Held**
WEB: www.iwgroupinc.com
SIC: 7311 8743 Advertising consultant;
    public relations services

(P-13852)
**J WALTER THOMPSON USA
LLC**
303 2nd St, San Francisco (94107-1366)
PHONE..................................415 268-5555
Greg Rowan, *Branch Mgr*
EMP: 66
SALES (corp-wide): 20.1B **Privately Held**
SIC: 7311 Advertising agencies
HQ: J. Walter Thompson U.S.A., Llc
    466 Lexington Ave Fl 2
    New York NY 10017
    212 210-7000

(P-13853)
**JACK MORTON WORLDWIDE
INC**
1840 Century Park E # 1800, Los Angeles
(90067-2119)
PHONE..................................310 967-2400
Gemma Roskam, *Principal*
Gemma Baker, *Office Mgr*
EMP: 53
SALES (corp-wide): 7.8B **Publicly Held**
SIC: 7311 7812 Advertising consultant;
    audio-visual program production
HQ: Jack Morton Worldwide Inc.
    500 Harrison Ave Ste 5r
    Boston MA 02118
    617 585-7000

(P-13854)
KANE & FINKEL LLC
Also Called: Kane Fnkle Hlthcare Cmmnc-
tions
534 4th St, San Francisco (94107-1621)
P.O. Box 128, Corte Madera (94976-0128)
PHONE..................................415 777-4990
EMP: 70

SQ FT: 15,000
SALES (est): 10MM **Privately Held**
WEB: www.kaneandfinkel.com
SIC: 7311 Advertising agencies

(P-13855)
KERN ORGANIZATION INC
Also Called: Kern Direct Marketing
20955 Warner Center Ln, Woodland Hills
(91367-6511)
PHONE..................................818 703-8775
Russell Kern, *President*
Zeke Ibarbia, *CFO*
Steven Orenstein, *CFO*
David Azulay, *Senior VP*
Tom Mackendrick, *Vice Pres*
EMP: 80
SQ FT: 11,350
SALES (est): 23.7MM
SALES (corp-wide): 15.2B **Publicly Held**
WEB: www.thekernorg.com
SIC: 7311 Advertising consultant
PA: Omnicom Group Inc.
    437 Madison Ave
    New York NY 10022
    212 415-3600

(P-13856)
KOVEL/FULLER LLC
9925 Jefferson Blvd, Culver City
(90232-3505)
PHONE..................................310 841-4444
John Fuller, *President*
J Reilly, *Vice Pres*
Leila Reynolds, *Vice Pres*
Guy Koppel, *Human Resources*
Graham McGuire, *Production*
EMP: 55
SQ FT: 40,000
SALES (est): 12.8MM **Privately Held**
WEB: www.kovelfuller.com
SIC: 7311 Advertising consultant

(P-13857)
LOCAL CORPORATION (PA)
Also Called: Local.com
7555 Irvine Center Dr, Irvine (92618-2930)
P.O. Box 50700 (92619-0700)
PHONE..................................949 784-0800
Frederick G Thiel, *Ch of Bd*
Kenneth S Cragun, *CFO*
Scott Reinke, *Officer*
Erick Herring, *Senior VP*
Randy Sesser, *Engineer*
EMP: 66
SQ FT: 34,612
SALES: 83.1MM **Publicly Held**
SIC: 7311 Advertising agencies

(P-13858)
LOS DEFENSORES INC
20101 Hamilton Ave # 300, Torrance
(90502-1351)
PHONE..................................310 519-4050
Mary Ann Walker, *President*
Amir Tamjidi, *Info Tech Mgr*
EMP: 50
SQ FT: 3,000
SALES (est): 3.7MM **Privately Held**
SIC: 7311 8111 Advertising agencies; gen-
    eral practice attorney, lawyer

(P-13859)
LOWCOM LLC
818 W 7th St Ste 700, Los Angeles
(90017-3430)
PHONE..................................213 408-0080
Lawrence Ng,
Fred Hsu,
EMP: 150
SALES (est): 9MM **Privately Held**
WEB: www.lowermybills.com
SIC: 7311 Advertising agencies

(P-13860)
MACHINTEL CORPORATION
4225 Executive Sq Ste 955, La Jolla
(92037-9152)
PHONE..................................617 517-3090
Mark Choudhari, *Ch of Bd*
EMP: 60 EST: 2010
SALES (est): 3.1MM **Privately Held**
SIC: 7311 Advertising agencies

(P-13861)
**MCCANN WORLD GROUP INC
(PA)**
Also Called: Universal McCann
653 Front St, San Francisco (94111-1913)
PHONE..................................415 262-5500
Daryl Lee, *CEO*
Sarah Personette, *President*
Jim Baller, *Vice Pres*
EMP: 68 EST: 2009
SALES (est): 15.3MM **Privately Held**
SIC: 7311 Advertising consultant

(P-13862)
**MCCANN-ERICKSON
CORPORATION (HQ)**
135 Main St Fl 21, San Francisco
(94105-1812)
PHONE..................................415 348-5600
Don Hov, *CFO*
Bernadette Chincuanco, *Managing Prtnr*
Nicole Gammino, *Vice Pres*
Hans Ullmark, *Div Sub Head*
Bettsy Sperry, *Managing Dir*
EMP: 100
SQ FT: 37,000
SALES (est): 14.9MM
SALES (corp-wide): 7.8B **Publicly Held**
SIC: 7311 Advertising agencies
PA: The Interpublic Group Of Companies
    Inc
    909 3rd Ave Fl 7
    New York NY 10022
    212 704-1200

(P-13863)
MEA DIGITAL WORX LLC
Also Called: Piston Agency
530 B St Ste 1900, San Diego
(92101-4472)
PHONE..................................619 238-8923
Michael Chaney, *CEO*
John Hartman, *President*
Andrew Resnick, *CFO*
Mark Burr, *Vice Pres*
Thomas Driver, *Marketing Staff*
EMP: 50
SALES (est): 9.6MM **Privately Held**
WEB: www.meadigital.com
SIC: 7311 8742 Advertising consultant;
    marketing consulting services

(P-13864)
MEDIAPLEX INC (DH)
30699 Russell Ranch Rd # 250, Westlake
Village (91362-7315)
PHONE..................................818 575-4500
Gregory R Raifman, *Ch of Bd*
Costa John, *COO*
Francis P Patchel, *CFO*
Ruiqing Jiang, *CTO*
Mark Joseph, *CTO*
EMP: 100
SALES (est): 5.8MM **Publicly Held**
WEB: www.mediaplex.com
SIC: 7311 Advertising agencies
HQ: Conversant, Llc
    30699 Russell Ranch Rd # 250
    Westlake Village CA 91362
    818 575-4500

(P-13865)
MEKANISM INC (PA)
640 2nd St Fl 3, San Francisco
(94107-4066)
PHONE..................................415 908-4000
Jason Harris, *CEO*
Tommy Means, *Partner*
Pete Caban, *CEO*
Michael Zlatoper, *COO*
Ana Dixon, *CFO*
EMP: 100
SALES (est): 21.8MM **Privately Held**
WEB: www.mekanism.com
SIC: 7311 Advertising agencies

(P-13866)
MENDELSOHN/ZIEN ADVG LLC
11901 Santa Monica Blvd # 618, Los Ange-
les (90025-2767)
PHONE..................................310 444-1990
Richard Zien,
Jordin Mendelsohn,
EMP: 75 EST: 1982
SQ FT: 7,000

PRODUCTS & SVCS

SALES (est): 8.7MM
SALES (corp-wide): 12.5B **Privately Held**
WEB: www.mzad.com
SIC: 7311 Advertising agencies
HQ: Hakuhodo Incorporated
5-3-1, Akasaka
Minato-Ku TKY 107-0
364 418-111

(P-13867)
MERINGCARSON HOLDINGS (PA)
1700 I St Ste 210, Sacramento
(95811-3018)
PHONE.................916 441-0571
David Mering, *CEO*
Colm Conn, *Senior Partner*
Lori Bartle, *President*
Lorie Brewster, *CFO*
Greg Carson, *Ch Credit Ofcr*
EMP: 85
SQ FT: 11,000
SALES (est): 25.1MM **Privately Held**
WEB: www.meringcarson.com
SIC: 7311 Advertising consultant

(P-13868)
METRO ONE TELECOM INC
4900 Rivergrade Rd B210, Irwindale
(91706-1401)
PHONE.................626 337-8100
Gary Brent, *Manager*
EMP: 150
SALES (corp-wide): 40.6MM **Publicly Held**
WEB: www.metro1.com
SIC: 7311 7389 Advertising agencies; telephone services
PA: Metro One Telecommunications, Inc.
1331 Nw Lovejoy St # 900
Portland OR 97209
503 643-9500

(P-13869)
MYPOINTSCOM LLC (HQ)
Also Called: My Points.com
44 Montgomery St Ste 1050, San Francisco
(94104-4621)
PHONE.................415 615-1100
Jeff Goldstein, *CFO*
Mark Harrington, *Exec VP*
Edward Zinser, *Exec VP*
Mv Krishnamurthy, *Senior VP*
Jordan Felsen, *Vice Pres*
EMP: 60
SALES (est): 10.8MM
SALES (corp-wide): 44.5MM **Privately Held**
WEB: www.mypoints.com
SIC: 7311 Advertising agencies
PA: Prodege, Llc
100 N Pacific Coast Hwy # 800
El Segundo CA 90245
310 294-9599

(P-13870)
NEXSTAR DIGITAL LLC
12777 W Jefferson Blvd, Los Angeles
(90066-7048)
PHONE.................310 971-9300
Morgan Harris, *Branch Mgr*
EMP: 100
SALES (corp-wide): 2.4B **Publicly Held**
SIC: 7311 Advertising agencies
HQ: Nexstar Digital, Llc
545 E John Carpenter Fwy
Irving TX 75062
972 373-8800

(P-13871)
OGILVY & MATHER WORLDWIDE INC
2425 Olympic Blvd 2200w, Santa Monica
(90404-4095)
PHONE.................310 280-2200
Hugh Branigan, *Sales & Mktg St*
Richard Salas, *Executive Asst*
EMP: 75
SALES (corp-wide): 20.1B **Privately Held**
SIC: 7311 Advertising consultant
HQ: Ogilvy & Mather Worldwide, Inc.
636 11th Ave
New York NY 10036
212 237-4000

(P-13872)
OMELET LLC (PA)
3540 Hayden Ave, Culver City
(90232-2413)
PHONE.................213 427-6400
Don Kurz, *CEO*
Naj Allana, *CFO*
Ryan Fey,
Shervin Samari,
EMP: 65
SQ FT: 7,500
SALES (est): 12.4MM **Privately Held**
SIC: 7311 Advertising consultant

(P-13873)
ONE PLANET OPS INC (PA)
Also Called: Buyerlink
1820 Bonanza St Ste 200, Walnut Creek
(94596-4376)
PHONE.................925 983-2800
Payam Zamani, *CEO*
Rudd Lippincott, *Vice Pres*
Armita Rostamian, *Vice Pres*
David Stein, *Vice Pres*
Michael Patterson, *Administration*
EMP: 121
SALES (est): 34.8MM **Privately Held**
WEB: www.reply.com
SIC: 7311 Advertising agencies

(P-13874)
OPENX TECHNOLOGIES INC (DH)
888 E Walnut St Fl 2, Pasadena
(91101-1897)
PHONE.................855 673-6948
Tim Cadogan, *CEO*
Marc Cristiano, *Partner*
Len Mendoza, *Partner*
John Gentry, *President*
Dan Sheehy, *President*
▲ **EMP:** 85
SALES (est): 55.9MM
SALES (corp-wide): 171.8MM **Privately Held**
SIC: 7311 Advertising agencies

(P-13875)
ORGANIC HOLDINGS INC
Also Called: Organic On
600 California St Fl 8, San Francisco
(94108-2726)
PHONE.................415 581-5300
Jonathan Nelson, *CEO*
Marita C Scarfi, *Exec VP*
Shane Ginsberg, *Director*
David Lewis, *Manager*
EMP: 350
SALES (est): 24MM **Privately Held**
SIC: 7311 7374 8742 7375 Advertising consultant; computer graphics service; management consulting services; information retrieval services

(P-13876)
OVERSEENET (PA)
550 S Hope St Ste 200, Los Angeles
(90071-2672)
PHONE.................213 408-0080
Debra Domeyer, *CEO*
Lawrence Ng, *President*
Dwayne Walker, *President*
Elizabeth Murray, *CFO*
Gene Chuang, *CTO*
EMP: 170
SQ FT: 54,000
SALES (est): 20.6MM **Privately Held**
WEB: www.oversee.net
SIC: 7311 Advertising agencies

(P-13877)
PEREIRA & ODELL LLC (PA)
215 2nd St Ste 100, San Francisco
(94105-3141)
PHONE.................415 284-9916
Nancy Daum, *CFO*
Andrew O'Dell, *CEO*
Dave Arnold, *Creative Dir*
Molly Parsley, *Comms Dir*
Jason Apaliski, *Exec Dir*
EMP: 73
SALES (est): 18MM **Privately Held**
WEB: www.pereiraodell.com
SIC: 7311 Advertising consultant

(P-13878)
PETROL ADVERTISING INC
443 N Varney St, Burbank (91502-1733)
PHONE.................323 644-3720
Alan J Hunter, *President*
Karl Stewart, *Partner*
Art Babayan, *Vice Pres*
Josh Alvarado, *Creative Dir*
John Conway, *Creative Dir*
EMP: 70
SALES (est): 17.1MM **Privately Held**
WEB: www.foodallergycure.com
SIC: 7311 Advertising consultant

(P-13879)
PHELPS GROUP
12121 W Bluff Dr Ste 200, Playa Vista
(90094)
PHONE.................310 752-4400
Jose Lozano, *CEO*
Ed Chambliss, *Managing Prtnr*
Glenn Schieke, *COO*
Robert Berry, *CFO*
Myles Watling, *CFO*
EMP: 50
SQ FT: 17,000
SALES (est): 21MM **Privately Held**
WEB: www.phelpsgroup.com
SIC: 7311 Advertising consultant

(P-13880)
POP-TENT INC
34221 Golden Lantern St # 202, Dana Point
(92629-2850)
PHONE.................949 313-7160
Rick Parkhill, *Chairman*
Andrew Jedynak, *CEO*
Sandy Dondici, *COO*
Tony Romeo, *Exec VP*
Dave Mann, *Vice Pres*
EMP: 55
SALES (est): 6MM **Privately Held**
SIC: 7311 Advertising agencies

(P-13881)
PORTER CRISPIN & LLC BOGUSKY
2110 Colorado Ave Ste 200, Santa Monica
(90404-3763)
PHONE.................305 859-2070
Ryan Skubic, *Manager*
EMP: 125
SALES (corp-wide): 1.5B **Publicly Held**
SIC: 7311 Advertising consultant
HQ: Crispin Porter & Bogusky Llc
6450 Gunpark Dr
Boulder CO 80301
305 859-2070

(P-13882)
POSTAER RUBIN AND ASSOCIATES (PA)
Also Called: R P Direct
2525 Colorado Ave Ste 100, Santa Monica
(90404-5576)
PHONE.................310 394-4000
Willam C Hagelstein, *CEO*
Gerrold R Rubin, *Ch of Bd*
Bill Hagelstein, *COO*
Vincent Mancuso, *CFO*
Jim Helberg, *Exec VP*
EMP: 148
SQ FT: 130,000
SALES (est): 62.6MM **Privately Held**
SIC: 7311 Advertising consultant

(P-13883)
PUBMATIC INC (PA)
305 Main St Fl 1, Redwood City
(94063-1729)
PHONE.................650 351-9162
Rajeev Goel, *CEO*
Amar Goel, *Ch of Bd*
Kirk McDonald, *President*
Steve Pantelick, *CFO*
Larry Harris, *Chief Mktg Ofcr*
EMP: 81
SQ FT: 4,000
SALES (est): 70.5MM **Privately Held**
SIC: 7311 Advertising agencies

(P-13884)
QUAD/GRAPHICS INC
Also Called: Sacramento Div
1201 Shore St, West Sacramento
(95691-3510)
PHONE.................916 371-9500
Dan Coffee, *Administration*
Bob Boone, *Opers Mgr*
Linda Myers, *Production*
EMP: 250
SALES (corp-wide): 4.1B **Publicly Held**
WEB: www.vertisinc.com
SIC: 7311 2759 2752 Advertising agencies; commercial printing; commercial printing, lithographic
PA: Quad/Graphics Inc.
N61w23044 Harrys Way
Sussex WI 53089
414 566-6000

(P-13885)
QUIGLY-SIMPSON HEPPELWHITE INC
Also Called: Quigley-Simpson La
11601 Wilshire Blvd Fl 7, Los Angeles
(90025-0509)
PHONE.................310 996-5800
Kathryn Browne, *CFO*
Gerald Bagg, *Ch of Bd*
Renee Hill Young, *Ch of Bd*
Duryea Ruffins, *President*
Alissa Stakgold, *President*
EMP: 150
SQ FT: 10,500
SALES (est): 39.4MM **Privately Held**
WEB: www.quigleysimpson.com
SIC: 7311 7319 Advertising agencies; media buying service

(P-13886)
RANKER INC
6420 Wilshire Blvd # 880, Los Angeles
(90048-5538)
PHONE.................323 782-1448
Clark Benson, *CEO*
Greg Morrow, *Officer*
EMP: 50
SALES (est): 2.3MM **Privately Held**
SIC: 7311 Advertising consultant

(P-13887)
RAPP WORLDWIDE INC
12777 W Jefferson Blvd, Los Angeles
(90066-7048)
PHONE.................310 563-7200
Collins Rapp, *Branch Mgr*
Milton Weaver, *Vice Pres*
Sebastian Werner, *Info Tech Dir*
Lauren Stokowski, *Project Mgr*
Megan Thompson, *Supervisor*
EMP: 100
SALES (corp-wide): 15.2B **Publicly Held**
SIC: 7311 Advertising consultant
HQ: Rapp Worldwide Inc.
437 Madison Ave
New York NY 10022

(P-13888)
REACHLOCAL INC (HQ)
21700 Oxnard St Ste 1600, Woodland Hills
(91367-7586)
PHONE.................818 274-0260
Sharon T Rowlands, *CEO*
Elisa Aguilar, *Partner*
Veronica Brokenberry, *Partner*
Jonathan Greer, *Partner*
Trent Hebert, *Partner*
EMP: 148
SQ FT: 38,592
SALES: 382.6MM
SALES (corp-wide): 3.1B **Publicly Held**
SIC: 7311 7375 Advertising consultant; on-line data base information retrieval
PA: Gannett Co., Inc.
7950 Jones Branch Dr
Mc Lean VA 22102
703 854-6000

(P-13889)
RED INTERACTIVE AGENCY LLC (PA)
3420 Ocean Park Blvd # 3080, Santa Monica (90405-3325)
PHONE.................310 399-4242

▲ = Import ▼=Export
◆ =Import/Export

Brian Lovell, *CEO*
Donny Makower, *President*
Derek Van Den Bosch, *COO*
Derek Bosch, *COO*
Andrew Feldman, *Vice Pres*
EMP: 100
SALES (est): 15.3MM **Privately Held**
SIC: 7311 Advertising consultant

(P-13890)
RED SKY INTERACTIVE
201 Mission St Fl 8, San Francisco
(94105-1834)
PHONE............................415 430-3200
Tim Smith, *CEO*
Howard Belk, *President*
Robert Murray, *CTO*
EMP: 110
SALES (est): 7MM **Privately Held**
SIC: 7311 Advertising agencies

(P-13891)
**RESCUE AGENCY PUB BENEFT
LLC (PA)**
2437 Morena Blvd, San Diego
(92110-4152)
PHONE............................619 231-7555
Kristin Carroll, *CEO*
Jeffrey Jordan, *President*
Dennis Triplett, *COO*
Michelle Bellon, *Vice Pres*
Tony Callico, *Vice Pres*
EMP: 70
SALES (est): 6MM **Privately Held**
SIC: 7311 8732 Advertising agencies; so-
ciological research

(P-13892)
RICHARDS GROUP INC
Also Called: Metro Pcs
888 S Figueroa St # 1400, Los Angeles
(90017-5449)
PHONE............................214 891-5700
Gene Howe, *Owner*
EMP: 175
SALES (corp-wide): 104.4MM **Privately
Held**
SIC: 7311 Advertising agencies
PA: The Richards Group Inc
2801 N Cntl Expy Ste 100
Dallas TX 75204
214 891-5700

(P-13893)
ROE HOLDINGS LLC
8437 Warner Dr, Culver City (90232-2428)
PHONE............................310 559-9222
Adam Roe, *Partner*
Lorraine Dahlinger, *Partner*
EMP: 62
SQ FT: 13,000
SALES (est): 5.2MM **Privately Held**
SIC: 7311 Advertising agencies

(P-13894)
ROSEMONT MEDIA LLC
1010 Turquoise St Ste 201, San Diego
(92109-1266)
PHONE............................858 200-0044
Mike Lubisich, *CFO*
Seth McKinney, *Creative Dir*
Corinne Michel, *Web Proj Mgr*
Scott Coburn, *Web Dvlpr*
Erin REA, *Graphic Designe*
EMP: 50
SALES (est): 1.2MM **Privately Held**
WEB: www.rosemontmedia.com
SIC: 7311 8742 Advertising consultant;
marketing consulting services

(P-13895)
ROUNDUP MEDIA LLC
Also Called: Network of One
5895 Blackwelder St, Culver City
(90232-7303)
PHONE............................310 841-2366
Aaron Debevoise, *Mng Member*
Sarah Arnett, *Vice Pres*
Matt Jessell, *Vice Pres*
Michael Windler, *Vice Pres*
Kristin Dunigan, *Manager*
EMP: 50
SQ FT: 7,200
SALES (est): 6.8MM **Privately Held**
SIC: 7311 Advertising consultant

(P-13896)
RUBICON PROJECT INC (PA)
12181 Bluff Creek Dr Fl 4, Los Angeles
(90094-3234)
PHONE............................310 207-0272
Michael Barrett, *CEO*
Frank Addant, *Ch of Bd*
Gregory R Raifman, *President*
David L Day, *CFO*
David Day, *Officer*
EMP: 138
SQ FT: 47,000
SALES: 155.5MM **Publicly Held**
SIC: 7311 Advertising agencies

(P-13897)
RUNYON SALTZMAN INC
Also Called: Rse
2020 L St Ste 100, Sacramento
(95811-4260)
PHONE............................916 446-9900
Christopher Holben, *President*
Estelle Saltzman, *Ch of Bd*
Paul McClure, *Vice Pres*
Scott Rose, *Vice Pres*
EMP: 65
SQ FT: 14,000
SALES: 39MM **Privately Held**
WEB: www.rs-e.com
SIC: 7311 8743 Advertising consultant;
public relations & publicity

(P-13898)
RW LYNCH CO INC (PA)
2333 San Ramon Valley Blv, San Ramon
(94583-4429)
P.O. Box 5159 (94583-5159)
PHONE............................925 837-3877
Randall W Lynch, *CEO*
Brian Lynch, *President*
Stephen Grazzini, *CFO*
Alyssa Granick, *Admin Asst*
Edward Francisco, *Info Tech Mgr*
EMP: 77
SQ FT: 19,000
SALES (est): 17.8MM **Privately Held**
WEB: www.lawonline.com
SIC: 7311 Advertising consultant

(P-13899)
**SAATCHI & SAATCHI N AMER
INC**
Team One Advertising
13031 W Jefferson Blvd, Los Angeles
(90094-7000)
PHONE............................310 437-2500
Amanda Taft, *President*
Patty Schiappa, *Officer*
Trevor Foley, *Associate Dir*
James Hendry, *Creative Dir*
Andrew Keegan, *Info Tech Dir*
EMP: 250
SALES (corp-wide): 13.6MM **Privately
Held**
WEB: www.saatchila.com
SIC: 7311 Advertising agencies
HQ: Saatchi & Saatchi North America, Inc.
1675 Broadway
New York NY 10019
212 463-2000

(P-13900)
SCORPION DESIGN LLC
27750 Entertainment Dr, Valencia
(91355-1091)
PHONE............................661 702-0100
Rustin Kretz, *CEO*
Paul Gordon, *Director*
EMP: 565
SQ FT: 100,000
SALES (est): 98.4MM **Privately Held**
WEB: www.scorpiondesign.com
SIC: 7311 Advertising agencies

(P-13901)
SEARCH AGENCY INC (PA)
11150 W Olym Blvd Ste 600, Los Angeles
(90064)
PHONE............................310 582-5700
David Hughes, *CEO*
Matt Kain, *CEO*
Peter Harington, *CFO*
David Otto Rahmel, *Vice Pres*
EMP: 90
SALES (est): 18.2MM **Privately Held**
SIC: 7311 Advertising agencies

(P-13902)
SHARETHIS INC (PA)
4005 Miranda Ave Ste 100, Palo Alto
(94304-1221)
PHONE............................650 641-0191
Dana Hayes Jr, *CEO*
Tim Schigel, *Ch of Bd*
Doug Dennis, *CFO*
Matt Gallatin, *CFO*
Paul Lentz, *Senior VP*
EMP: 50 **EST:** 2004
SALES (est): 12MM **Privately Held**
SIC: 7311 7313 7372 Advertising consult-
ant; electronic media advertising repre-
sentatives; prepackaged software

(P-13903)
**SIERRA WEATHERIZATION CO
INC**
43 E Main St Ste B, Los Gatos
(95030-6907)
PHONE............................408 354-1900
Peter Hofmann, *President*
Amy Diffenderfer, *Corp Secy*
EMP: 99
SALES (est): 12MM **Privately Held**
SIC: 7311 Advertising agencies

(P-13904)
SOLUTIONSET LLC
100 Montgomery St # 1500, San Francisco
(94104-4300)
PHONE............................415 367-6300
Tim Ross, *CEO*
Christopher R Averill, *CFO*
Libby Demeo, *Senior VP*
EMP: 200
SALES (est): 27.1MM **Publicly Held**
SIC: 7311 Advertising agencies
HQ: Epsilon Data Management, Llc
6021 Connection Dr
Irving TX 75039
469 262-0600

(P-13905)
STEEL HOUSE INC
3644 Eastham Dr, Culver City
(90232-2411)
PHONE............................310 773-3331
Mark Douglas, *CEO*
Rory Mitchell, *Ch Credit Ofcr*
Vin Bhardwaj, *Vice Pres*
Lindsey Breeden, *Vice Pres*
Chris Innes, *Vice Pres*
EMP: 160 **EST:** 2009
SALES (est): 10.9MM **Privately Held**
SIC: 7311 Advertising agencies

(P-13906)
**SUISSA MILLER ADVERTISING
LLC**
8687 Melrose Ave, West Hollywood
(90069-5701)
PHONE............................310 392-9666
David Suissa,
Bruce Miller,
EMP: 100
SQ FT: 40,000
SALES (est): 5.2MM **Privately Held**
SIC: 7311 Advertising agencies

(P-13907)
SWIRL INC
101 Montgomery St, San Francisco
(94129-1701)
PHONE............................415 276-8300
Martin Lauber, *Chairman*
Matt Hofherr, *Partner*
John Berg, *President*
Wayne Esplana, *CFO*
Greg Fischer, *Exec VP*
EMP: 60
SQ FT: 10,000
SALES (est): 574.6K **Privately Held**
WEB: www.swirl.net
SIC: 7311 Advertising agencies

(P-13908)
TAPJOY INC (PA)
111 Sutter St Fl 12, San Francisco
(94104-4541)
PHONE............................415 766-6900
Steve Wadsworth, *President*
Matthew Service, *COO*
Al Wood, *CFO*

George Garrick, *Chairman*
Peter Dille, *Chief Mktg Ofcr*
EMP: 54 **EST:** 2007
SALES (est): 14.9MM **Privately Held**
SIC: 7311 Advertising agencies

(P-13909)
TBWA WORLDWIDE INC
Also Called: Media Arts Lab
12539 Beatrice St, Los Angeles
(90066-7001)
PHONE............................310 305-4400
Larry Kelly, *Owner*
Dana Franklin, *Software Dev*
Kevin Lee, *Financial Analy*
Lisa Hill, *Analyst*
Karine Shahar, *Recruiter*
EMP: 133
SALES (corp-wide): 15.2B **Publicly Held**
SIC: 7311 Advertising consultant
HQ: Tbwa Worldwide Inc.
488 Madison Ave
New York NY 10022

(P-13910)
**TMP WORLDWIDE ADVERTISING
& CO**
330 N Brand Blvd Ste 1050, Glendale
(91203-2875)
PHONE............................818 539-2000
Gretchen Edwards, *Vice Pres*
Wendy De Haas, *Manager*
EMP: 74 **Privately Held**
SIC: 7311 Advertising agencies
PA: Tmp Worldwide Advertising & Commu-
nications, Llc
125 Broad St Fl 10
New York NY 10004

(P-13911)
TRAILER PARK INC
6922 Hollywood Blvd # 1200, Los Angeles
(90028-6132)
PHONE............................310 845-8400
Joel Johnston, *President*
EMP: 60 **Privately Held**
SIC: 7311 7812 Advertising agencies; mo-
tion picture & video production
PA: Trailer Park, Inc.
6922 Hollywood Blvd Fl 12
Los Angeles CA 90028

(P-13912)
TRAILER PARK INC (PA)
6922 Hollywood Blvd Fl 12, Los Angeles
(90028-6132)
P.O. Box 2950 (90078-2950)
PHONE............................310 845-3000
Tim Nett, *President*
James Hale, *Shareholder*
Matt Brubaker, *CEO*
Doug Troy, *COO*
Steven Bruno, *Vice Pres*
EMP: 100
SQ FT: 8,000
SALES (est): 36.4MM **Privately Held**
SIC: 7311 Advertising agencies

(P-13913)
**UNDERGROUND ELEPHANT
INC**
808 J St, San Diego (92101-7187)
PHONE............................800 466-4178
Jason Kulpa, *President*
William Huff, *CFO*
Jovel Lacson, *Vice Pres*
Michael Omalley, *Vice Pres*
James Riebel, *Vice Pres*
EMP: 100
SQ FT: 14,000
SALES (est): 23.8MM **Privately Held**
SIC: 7311 7371 Advertising consultant;
computer software development

(P-13914)
US INTERACTIVE DELAWARE
1270 Oakmead Pkwy Ste 318, Sunnyvale
(94085-4044)
PHONE............................408 863-7500
Sunil Mathur, *Branch Mgr*
Sunanda Kothapalli, *Office Mgr*
EMP: 130 **Privately Held**
SIC: 7311 Advertising consultant

PA: U.S. Interactive Corp Delaware
1270 Oakmead Pkwy Ste 318
Sunnyvale CA 94085

(P-13915)
VENABLES/BELL & PARTNERS LLC
Also Called: Vbp Orange
201 Post St Fl 2, San Francisco
(94108-5027)
PHONE..............................415 288-3300
Paul Venables, *Mng Member*
Paul Birks-Hay, *Partner*
Mary Johnstone, *Partner*
Venables Bell, *Creative Dir*
Justin Moore, *Creative Dir*
EMP: 190
SQ FT: 30,000
SALES (est): 54.8MM **Privately Held**
WEB: www.venablesbell.com
SIC: 7311 Advertising consultant

(P-13916)
VERTICAL SEARCH WORKS INC
1808 Aston Ave Ste 170, Carlsbad
(92008-7367)
PHONE..............................212 967-9502
EMP: 60
SALES (corp-wide): 12.3MM **Privately Held**
SIC: 7311
PA: Vertical Search Works, Inc.
336 W 37th St Rm 100
New York NY 10036
212 967-9502

(P-13917)
VISIONAIRE GROUP INC
Also Called: Tvgla
5340 Alla Rd Ste 100, Los Angeles
(90066-7036)
PHONE..............................310 823-1800
Dimitry Ioffe, *CEO*
Bryan Pettigrew, *President*
Jorge Cantero, *Creative Dir*
Jonathan Cook, *Creative Dir*
Julie Gargan, *Creative Dir*
EMP: 52
SALES (est): 9.9MM **Privately Held**
SIC: 7311 Advertising consultant

(P-13918)
VITRO LLC
2305 Historic Decatur Rd # 205, San Diego
(92106-6073)
PHONE..............................619 234-0408
Tom Sullivan, *President*
Mike Brower, *Director*
Eugene Kim, *Director*
Marc Wilson, *Director*
Nicole Samuel, *Accounts Exec*
EMP: 90
SALES (est): 16.4MM **Privately Held**
SIC: 7311 Advertising agencies

(P-13919)
VITROROBERTSON LLC
2305 Historic Decatur Rd, San Diego
(92106-6050)
PHONE..............................619 234-0408
John Vitro, *Principal*
Tom Sullivan, *President*
Alan Bonine, *Exec VP*
Marissa Walsh, *Executive*
John Hickman, *Comms Dir*
EMP: 89
SQ FT: 12,000
SALES (est): 17.3MM
SALES (corp-wide): 1.5B **Publicly Held**
WEB: www.vitrorobertson.com
SIC: 7311 Advertising consultant
PA: Mdc Partners Inc.
745 5th Ave Fl 19
New York NY 10151
646 429-1800

(P-13920)
WALKER ADVERTISING LLC
20101 Hamilton Ave # 300, Torrance
(90502-1351)
PHONE..............................310 519-4050
Mary Ann Walker, *CEO*
Fabiola Hinojosa, *Officer*
Josephine Nguyen, *Software Dev*

Myrna Yin, *Technology*
Inesa Conley, *Accountant*
EMP: 50
SALES (est): 14.1MM **Privately Held**
WEB: www.walkeradvertising.com
SIC: 7311 Advertising consultant

(P-13921)
YOUNG & RUBICAM INC
Also Called: Y & R
303 2nd St Ste N300, San Francisco
(94107-3638)
PHONE..............................415 882-0600
Michael Reese, *Branch Mgr*
Herman Brown, *Technology*
EMP: 120
SALES (corp-wide): 20.1B **Privately Held**
SIC: 7311 Advertising consultant
HQ: Young & Rubicam Llc
3 Columbus Cir
New York NY 10019
212 210-3000

(P-13922)
YUME INC (HQ)
601 Montgomery St # 1600, San Francisco
(94111-2603)
PHONE..............................650 591-9400
Ted Hastings, *President*
Dan Slivjanovski, *COO*
Ed Reginelli, *CFO*
Ed Haslam, *Treasurer*
Frank Barbieri, *Officer*
EMP: 80 **EST:** 2004
SQ FT: 20,400
SALES: 160.4MM **Privately Held**
SIC: 7311 Advertising consultant

(P-13923)
Z57 INC (DH)
10045 Mesa Rim Rd, San Diego
(92121-2913)
PHONE..............................858 623-5577
Steve Weber, *President*
Ryan Whitlock, *CEO*
Cynthia Sener, *Vice Pres*
Brian Angel, *Engineer*
Nick Oriti, *Finance*
EMP: 55
SALES (est): 8.4MM
SALES (corp-wide): 2.4B **Privately Held**
WEB: www.z57.com
SIC: 7311 Advertising agencies
HQ: Constellation Homebuilder Systems Inc.
888 S Dsnyland Dr Ste 430
Tustin CA 92780
714 768-6100

(P-13924)
ZEETOGROUP LLC
Also Called: Zeeto Media
925 B St Fl 5, San Diego (92101-4697)
PHONE..............................888 771-9194
Matthew Marcin, *Software Dev*
Stephan Goss, *CEO*
Shayne Cardwell, *Vice Pres*
Greg Kuchcik, *Human Res Dir*
Soojin Jun, *Hum Res Coord*
EMP: 55 **EST:** 2007
SALES (est): 17.2MM **Privately Held**
SIC: 7311 Advertising agencies

(P-13925)
ZVENTS INC
199 Fremont St Fl 4, San Francisco
(94105-6634)
PHONE..............................408 376-7346
Ethan Stock, *President*
EMP: 50
SALES (est): 6.1MM **Privately Held**
WEB: www.zvents.com
SIC: 7311 Advertising agencies

7312 Outdoor Advertising Svcs

(P-13926)
BAMKO INC
11620 Wilshire Blvd # 610, Los Angeles
(90025-1267)
PHONE..............................310 470-5859
▲ **EMP:** 150

SALES (est): 33.2MM **Privately Held**
WEB: www.bamko.net
SIC: 7312 7311

(P-13927)
MARKETSHARE INC (PA)
2001 Tarob Ct, Milpitas (95035-6825)
PHONE..............................408 262-0677
Frederick R Wilhelm, *CEO*
Alexis Bybel, *CFO*
John Lovell, *Vice Pres*
Dung Tran, *Art Dir*
Amelia Loy, *Assistant*
EMP: 99
SQ FT: 16,000
SALES (est): 13.5MM **Privately Held**
WEB: www.marketlineonline.com
SIC: 7312 3993 Billboard advertising;
electric signs

(P-13928)
MOBPARTNER INC
4151 Mddlfield Rd Ste 100, San Francisco
(94103)
PHONE..............................650 300-6388
Jamel Agaoua, *CEO*
EMP: 60
SALES (est): 3MM
SALES (corp-wide): 28.8MM **Privately Held**
SIC: 7312 Outdoor advertising services
PA: Mobpartner
89 91
Paris 75011
967 089-477

(P-13929)
OUTFRONT MEDIA INC
2635 N 1st St Ste 236, San Jose
(95134-2054)
PHONE..............................408 457-0111
EMP: 153
SALES (corp-wide): 1.5B **Publicly Held**
SIC: 7312 Outdoor advertising services
PA: Outfront Media Inc.
405 Lexington Ave Fl 17
New York NY 10174
212 297-6400

(P-13930)
OUTFRONT MEDIA LLC
1695 Eastshore Hwy, Berkeley
(94710-1733)
PHONE..............................510 527-3350
Rob Scheling, *Branch Mgr*
Greg Donner, *Vice Pres*
Gary Duckworth, *Div Sub Head*
Matt Molina, *Sales Mgr*
EMP: 100
SQ FT: 13,068
SALES (corp-wide): 1.5B **Publicly Held**
SIC: 7312 Outdoor advertising services
HQ: Outfront Media Llc
405 Lexington Ave Fl 14
New York NY 10174
212 297-6400

(P-13931)
VOLTA CHARGING LLC
155 De Haro St, San Francisco
(94103-5121)
PHONE..............................888 264-2208
Scott Mercer, *CEO*
Chris Wendel, *President*
Debra Crow, *CFO*
Dr Abdellah Cherkaoui, *Senior VP*
Jon Michaels, *Senior VP*
EMP: 60
SQ FT: 8,250
SALES (est): 645.6K **Privately Held**
SIC: 7312 Outdoor advertising services

7313 Radio, TV & Publishers Adv Reps

(P-13932)
101COMMUNICATIONS HOLDINGS LLC (HQ)
Also Called: 1105 Government Group
9201 Oakdale Ave Ste 101, Chatsworth
(91311-6546)
PHONE..............................818 734-1520
Neal Vitale, *President*
Jeffrey S Klein, *President*

Richard Vitale, *CFO*
Michael Valenti, *Exec VP*
EMP: 64
SQ FT: 21,000
SALES (est): 12.6MM
SALES (corp-wide): 136.4MM **Privately Held**
WEB: www.adtmag.com
SIC: 7313 7389 Printed media advertising
representatives; convention & show services
PA: 1105 Media, Inc.
6300 Canoga Ave Ste 1150
Woodland Hills CA 91367
818 814-5200

(P-13933)
AD RESULTS MEDIA LLC
111 C St, Encinitas (92024-3514)
PHONE..............................858 480-5223
Kurt Kaufer, *Manager*
EMP: 58
SALES (corp-wide): 2.8MM **Privately Held**
SIC: 7313 Electronic media advertising representatives
PA: Ad Results Media, Llc
320 Westcott St Ste 101
Houston TX 77007
713 783-1800

(P-13934)
APPSFLYER LTD
111 New Montgomery St, San Francisco
(94105-3605)
PHONE..............................415 636-9430
Armando Osuna, *Partner*
Sha Liang, *Partner*
Vrushali Khatav, *President*
Reshef Mann, *Officer*
Arnon Rotem-Gal-Oz, *Officer*
EMP: 80
SALES (est): 1.9MM **Privately Held**
SIC: 7313 Electronic media advertising representatives

(P-13935)
ATTN INC
729 Seward St, Los Angeles (90038-3503)
PHONE..............................323 413-2878
Jarrett Moreno, *CEO*
Matthew Segel, *President*
Philip Taylor, *Executive*
Mycah Seals, *Production*
Taryn Crouthers, *Sales Staff*
EMP: 200
SQ FT: 100,000
SALES (est): 1.6MM **Privately Held**
SIC: 7313 Radio, television, publisher representatives

(P-13936)
BEACHBODY LLC (PA)
Also Called: Product Partners
3301 Exposition Blvd Fl 3, Santa Monica
(90404-5082)
PHONE..............................310 883-9000
Carl Daikeler, *CEO*
Sue Collyns, *CFO*
Jon Congdon, *Chief Mktg Ofcr*
Brad Ramberg, *Exec VP*
Rose Pulver, *Comms Mgr*
EMP: 500
SALES (est): 166.5MM **Privately Held**
SIC: 7313 7999 Electronic media advertising representatives; physical fitness instruction

(P-13937)
BREITBART NEWS NETWORK LLC
Also Called: Bnn
149 S Barrington Ste 735, Los Angeles
(90049)
PHONE..............................424 371-0585
Laurence Solov, *CEO*
EMP: 60
SALES (est): 225.8K **Privately Held**
SIC: 7313 Electronic media advertising representatives

(P-13938)
BRITE MEDIA LLC
Also Called: Brite Promotions
16027 Ventura Blvd # 210, Encino
(91436-2876)
PHONE....................................818 826-5790
Greg Martin, *Branch Mgr*
EMP: 107
SALES (corp-wide): 22.4MM **Privately Held**
SIC: 7313 Electronic media advertising representatives
PA: Brite Media Llc
350 Frank Ogawa Plz
Oakland CA 94612
877 479-7777

(P-13939)
CANVAS WORLDWIDE LLC
12015 Bluff Creek Dr, Los Angeles
(90094-2930)
PHONE....................................424 303-4300
Kaya Lobaczewski, *President*
Scott Klatskin, *Vice Pres*
Matt Lawler, *Vice Pres*
EMP: 250
SALES (est): 40.9K
SALES (corp-wide): 385.8MM **Privately Held**
SIC: 7313 Electronic media advertising representatives
PA: Innocean Worldwide Inc.
308 Gangnam-Daero, Gangnam-Gu
Seoul 06253
822 201-6237

(P-13940)
CURTCO PUBLISHING LLC (PA)
Also Called: Worth Magazine
29160 Heathercliff Rd # 1, Malibu
(90265-6310)
PHONE....................................310 589-7700
Td Captital,
Weston Persido,
Marilyn Scott, *Manager*
EMP: 80
SQ FT: 7,680
SALES (est): 3.2MM **Privately Held**
WEB: www.worth.com
SIC: 7313 Printed media advertising representatives

(P-13941)
DAILY JOURNAL CORPORATION
915 E 1st St, Los Angeles (90012-4042)
PHONE....................................213 229-5500
Tu To, *Controller*
EMP: 50
SALES (corp-wide): 41.3MM **Publicly Held**
WEB: www.dailyjournal.com
SIC: 7313 Newspaper advertising representative
PA: Daily Journal Corporation
915 E 1st St
Los Angeles CA 90012
213 229-5300

(P-13942)
DANIEL J EDELMAN INC
Also Called: Edelman Public Relations
201 Baldwin Ave, San Mateo (94401-3914)
PHONE....................................650 762-2800
Bob Angus, *Branch Mgr*
Colleen Kuhn, *Executive*
Todd Irwin, *General Mgr*
Diane Zuniga, *Accounting Mgr*
Elena Fuhrmann, *Accounts Exec*
EMP: 100
SALES (corp-wide): 580.4MM **Privately Held**
SIC: 7313 8743 Electronic media advertising representatives; public relations & publicity
HQ: Daniel J. Edelman, Inc.
200 E Randolph St Fl 63
Chicago IL 60601
312 240-3000

(P-13943)
DANIEL J EDELMAN INC
Also Called: Edelman Public Relations
5900 Wilshire Blvd # 2400, Los Angeles
(90036-5022)
PHONE....................................323 857-9100
EMP: 53

SALES (corp-wide): 790.4MM **Privately Held**
SIC: 7313 8743
HQ: Daniel J. Edelman, Inc.
200 E Randolph St Fl 63
Chicago IL 60601
312 240-3000

(P-13944)
EDMUNDSCOM INC (HQ)
2401 Colorado Ave, Santa Monica
(90404-3585)
PHONE....................................310 309-6300
Peter Steinlauf, *Ch of Bd*
Seth Berkowitz, *President*
AVI Steinlauf, *CEO*
Allen Ollis, *CFO*
Ken Levin, *Exec VP*
EMP: 550
SALES: 212MM **Privately Held**
WEB: www.edmunds.com
SIC: 7313 Electronic media advertising representatives

(P-13945)
EL CLASIFICADO (PA)
11205 Imperial Hwy, Norwalk (90650-2229)
PHONE....................................323 837-4095
Martha C Dela Torre, *President*
Joseph Badame, *President*
Gil Garcia, *CFO*
EMP: 96
SALES (est): 12.4MM **Privately Held**
SIC: 7313 Newspaper advertising representative

(P-13946)
GHOST MANAGEMENT GROUP LLC
41 Discovery, Irvine (92618-3150)
PHONE....................................949 870-1400
Justin Hartfield, *CEO*
Doug Francis, *President*
Albert Lopez, *CFO*
Chris Beals, *General Counsel*
EMP: 175
SQ FT: 44,820
SALES: 40MM **Privately Held**
SIC: 7313 7371 Electronic media advertising representatives; computer software development & applications; custom computer programming services

(P-13947)
JAYLANEENTERTAINMENT CORP
585 Fernando Dr, Novato (94945-3333)
PHONE....................................707 820-2773
EMP: 65 EST: 2016
SALES (est): 941.1K **Privately Held**
SIC: 7313

(P-13948)
LEAF GROUP LTD (PA)
Also Called: Demand Media
1655 26th St, Santa Monica (90404-4016)
PHONE....................................310 656-6253
James R Quandt, *Ch of Bd*
Sean Moriarty, *CEO*
Brian Pike, *COO*
Rachel Glaser, *CFO*
Jantoon Reigersman, *CFO*
EMP: 143
SQ FT: 52,000
SALES: 128.9MM **Publicly Held**
WEB: www.demandmedia.com
SIC: 7313 7336 Electronic media advertising representatives; creative services to advertisers, except writers

(P-13949)
NAPASTYLE INC (PA)
360 Industrial Ct Ste A, NAPA (94558)
PHONE....................................707 251-5100
Renee Thomas Jacobs, *President*
EMP: 50
SALES (est): 6.6MM **Privately Held**
SIC: 7313 Radio, television, publisher representatives

(P-13950)
OBSCURA DIGITAL INCORPORATED
14 Louisiana St, San Francisco
(94107-4383)
PHONE....................................415 227-9979
Chris Lejeune, *CEO*
David Shulman, *CFO*
John Sierotko, *Officer*
Peter Sapienza, *Vice Pres*
Kimber Sterling, *Vice Pres*
EMP: 50
SQ FT: 40,000
SALES (est): 8.2MM
SALES (corp-wide): 1.5B **Publicly Held**
WEB: www.obscuradigital.com
SIC: 7313 Electronic media advertising representatives; printed media advertising representatives
PA: The Madison Square Garden Company
2 Penn Plz Fl 15
New York NY 10121
212 465-6000

(P-13951)
PAC-12 ENTEPRISES LLC
360 3rd St Ste 300, San Francisco
(94107-2163)
PHONE....................................415 580-4200
Lydia Murphy Stevens, *President*
David Aufhauser, *President*
Dave Hirsch, *President*
Kirk Reynolds, *President*
Terry Pierce, *COO*
EMP: 120
SQ FT: 11,000
SALES (est): 439MM **Privately Held**
WEB: www.pac-10.org
SIC: 7313 Electronic media advertising representatives

(P-13952)
PENSKE MEDIA CORPORATION (PA)
11175 Santa Monica Blvd, Los Angeles
(90025-3330)
PHONE....................................310 321-5000
Jay Penske, *CEO*
George Grobar, *COO*
Judith R Margolin, *Vice Pres*
EMP: 83
SALES (est): 33.3MM **Privately Held**
SIC: 7313 4899 Electronic media advertising representatives; data communication services

(P-13953)
PRODAY CO
2122 Union St, San Francisco
(94123-4004)
PHONE....................................517 980-1362
Sarah Kunst, *CEO*
EMP: 51
SALES: 3K **Privately Held**
SIC: 7313 Radio, television, publisher representatives

(P-13954)
QW MEDIA INTERNATIONAL LLC
620 Newport Center Dr # 11, Newport
Beach (92660-6420)
PHONE....................................949 200-4616
Marianne Moy, *Chairman*
Drian Hirabayashi, *Vice Pres*
Brian Hirabayashi, *Principal*
EMP: 50
SALES: 2MM **Privately Held**
SIC: 7313 Printed media advertising representatives

(P-13955)
SHED MEDIA US INC
3800 Barham Blvd Ste 410, Los Angeles
(90068-1042)
PHONE....................................323 904-4680
Nick Emmerson, *President*
Josh Mills, *Admin Sec*
Katie Greene, *Production*
Warren Small, *Editor*
EMP: 55
SALES (est): 9.8MM **Privately Held**
SIC: 7313 Electronic media advertising representatives

(P-13956)
STUDIO 71 LP
Also Called: Collective Digital Studio, LLC
8383 Wilshire Blvd Ste 10, Beverly Hills
(90211-2425)
PHONE....................................323 370-1500
Reza Isad,
Jordan Toplitzky, *CFO*
John Carle, *Vice Pres*
Federico Blanco, *General Counsel*
Nicole Andrewin,
EMP: 150 EST: 2011
SQ FT: 15,000
SALES: 60MM
SALES (corp-wide): 4.8B **Privately Held**
SIC: 7313 Electronic media advertising representatives
PA: Prosiebensat.1 Media Se
Medienallee 7
Unterfohring 85774
899 507-10

(P-13957)
THOUGHTFUL MEDIA GROUP INC
Also Called: Thoughtful Asia Limited
14724 Ventura Blvd # 1110, Sherman Oaks
(91403-3511)
PHONE....................................818 465-7500
Jak C Severson, *President*
Dan Thorman, *CFO*
Timothy Kwok, *Exec VP*
Ryan Yudell, *Senior VP*
Bani Tan, *Vice Pres*
EMP: 70
SALES (est): 4.4MM **Privately Held**
SIC: 7313 Electronic media advertising representatives

(P-13958)
TIME INC
2 Embarcadero Ctr # 1900, San Francisco
(94111-3914)
PHONE....................................415 982-5000
Tim Richards, *Manager*
EMP: 60
SALES (corp-wide): 2.2B **Publicly Held**
SIC: 7313 Magazine advertising representative
HQ: Time Inc.
225 Liberty St Ste C2
New York NY 10281
212 522-1212

(P-13959)
TIME INC
Time Magazine
11766 Wilshire Blvd # 1700, Los Angeles
(90025-6542)
PHONE....................................310 268-7200
Sally Masters, *Branch Mgr*
EMP: 200
SALES (corp-wide): 2.2B **Publicly Held**
SIC: 7313 Magazine advertising representative
HQ: Time Inc.
225 Liberty St Ste C2
New York NY 10281
212 522-1212

(P-13960)
TRAVELZOO USA INC
800 W El Camino Re, Mountain View
(94040)
PHONE....................................650 316-6956
Chris Loughlin, *CEO*
Ralph Bartel, *President*
Wayne Lee, *CFO*
Sandra Garcia, *Publisher*
EMP: 81
SALES (est): 17.8MM
SALES (corp-wide): 106.5MM **Publicly Held**
WEB: www.travelzoo.com
SIC: 7313 Electronic media advertising representatives
PA: Travelzoo
590 Madison Ave Rm 3700
New York NY 10022
212 484-4900

(P-13961)
ULTRADOT MEDIA
9908 Bell Ranch Dr, Santa Fe Springs
(90670-2972)
PHONE....................................562 906-0737

Bill Shears, *President*
EMP: 75
SALES (est): 3.7MM **Privately Held**
WEB: www.ultradotmedia.com
SIC: 7313 7336 Printed media advertising representatives; commercial art & graphic design

(P-13962)
WGA WEST INC
7000 W 3rd St, Los Angeles (90048-4321)
PHONE....................323 782-4512
Chris Keyser, *President*
Tery Lopez, *Director*
EMP: 100
SALES (est): 3.6MM **Privately Held**
SIC: 7313 Electronic media advertising representatives

7319 Advertising, NEC

(P-13963)
ADVERTISING CONSULTANTS INC (PA)
Also Called: American Crclation Innovations
330 Golden Shore Ste 410, Long Beach (90802-4271)
PHONE....................310 233-2750
Keith Somers, *President*
John G Walsh, *COO*
Kent Brown, *CFO*
Robert Somers, *Chairman*
EMP: 160 **EST:** 1966
SQ FT: 60,000
SALES (est): 19.1MM **Privately Held**
WEB: www.acicirculation.com
SIC: 7319 Distribution of advertising material or sample services

(P-13964)
AEGIS SOFTWARE INC
Also Called: Destination Webcam
5580 La Jolla Blvd # 436, La Jolla (92037-7651)
PHONE....................858 551-1652
Alan Edwards, *President*
EMP: 50
SALES (est): 3MM **Privately Held**
WEB: www.ecodb.com
SIC: 7319 Media buying service

(P-13965)
AMERICAN MDSG SPECIALISTS INC
958 Dainty Ave, Brentwood (94513-1206)
P.O. Box 2047 (94513-9047)
PHONE....................925 516-3220
Steve Nozet, *Branch Mgr*
EMP: 260
SALES (corp-wide): 24.9MM **Privately Held**
SIC: 7319 Display advertising service
PA: American Merchandising Specialists, Inc.
177 Barley Park Ln
Mooresville NC 28115
704 235-0144

(P-13966)
BAY AREA NEWS GROUP E BAY LLC (HQ)
6270 Houston Pl Ste A, Dublin (94568-3161)
PHONE....................925 302-1683
William Dean Singleton,
Joseph J Lodovic IV,
Michael Tully,
EMP: 74
SALES (est): 11.6MM
SALES (corp-wide): 9.3MM **Privately Held**
SIC: 7319 Media buying service
PA: California Newspapers Partnership
4 N 2nd St Fl 8
San Jose CA 95113
408 920-5333

(P-13967)
CARAT
85 2nd St Fl 6, San Francisco (94105-3464)
PHONE....................415 541-2700
A S Bracone, *Branch Mgr*
Laurent Oppenheim, *Senior VP*

Elissa Melendez, *Associate Dir*
Candace Davis, *Planning*
Danielle Mercer, *Finance*
EMP: 67
SALES (est): 6MM
SALES (corp-wide): 18.6MM **Privately Held**
SIC: 7319 Media buying service
PA: Carat
150 E 42nd St Fl 13
New York NY 10017
212 591-9100

(P-13968)
CARAT N AMER DNTSU AGEIS NTWRK
5800 Bristol Pkwy Fl 5, Culver City (90230-6696)
PHONE....................310 255-1000
John Barnes, *Branch Mgr*
Rob Hollander, *General Mgr*
Len Emig, *Director*
EMP: 135
SALES (corp-wide): 8.2B **Privately Held**
SIC: 7319 7313 Media buying service; printed media advertising representatives
HQ: Carat North America Dentsu Aegis Network
150 E 42nd St Fl 14
New York NY 10017
212 591-9100

(P-13969)
CBS INTERACTIVE INC
2900 W Alameda Ave, Burbank (91505-4220)
PHONE....................415 344-1813
EMP: 127
SALES (corp-wide): 13.7B **Publicly Held**
SIC: 7319 Distribution of advertising material or sample services
HQ: Cbs Interactive Inc.
235 2nd St
San Francisco CA 94105
-

(P-13970)
CBS INTERACTIVE INC (DH)
Also Called: Cbsi
235 2nd St, San Francisco (94105-3124)
PHONE....................415 344-2000
Jarl Mohn, *Ch of Bd*
Barry Briggs, *President*
Jim Lanzone, *President*
Joseph Gillespie, *Exec VP*
Andy Beal, *Vice Pres*
EMP: 600
SQ FT: 283,000
SALES (est): 254.6MM
SALES (corp-wide): 13.7B **Publicly Held**
WEB: www.mysimon.com
SIC: 7319 7375 4832 Distribution of advertising material or sample services; on-line data base information retrieval; radio broadcasting stations
HQ: Cbs Corporation
51 W 52nd St Bsmt 1
New York NY 10019
212 975-4321

(P-13971)
CIE DIGITAL LABS LLC (PA)
Also Called: Choice Internet
19900 Macarthur Blvd # 1000, Irvine (92612-8415)
PHONE....................949 381-6200
Anderee Berengian, *CEO*
Frances Lliles, *Office Mgr*
Brian Burlingame, *Accountant*
Evelyn Lee, *Human Res Dir*
Dennis L Suggs,
EMP: 55
SQ FT: 13,500
SALES (est): 9.4MM **Privately Held**
SIC: 7319 Display advertising service

(P-13972)
FASTCLICK INC
Also Called: Fastclick.com
530 E Montecito St, Santa Barbara (93103-3252)
PHONE....................805 689-9839
Kurt A Johnson, *President*
Fred Krupica, *CFO*
James Aviani, *CTO*
EMP: 87

SQ FT: 14,900
SALES (est): 4.8MM **Publicly Held**
WEB: www.fastclick.com
SIC: 7319 Circular & handbill distribution; coupon distribution
HQ: Conversant, Llc
30699 Russell Ranch Rd # 250
Westlake Village CA 91362
818 575-4500

(P-13973)
GILS DISTRIBUTING SERVICE (PA)
Also Called: Great Western Distributing Svc
718 E 8th St, Los Angeles (90021-1802)
PHONE....................213 627-0539
Feleciano Gil, *President*
Gloria Gil, *Treasurer*
Fidel Gil, *Vice Pres*
EMP: 112
SQ FT: 5,000
SALES (est): 5.3MM **Privately Held**
SIC: 7319 4215 Circular & handbill distribution; courier services, except by air

(P-13974)
IMAGE OPTIONS
80 Icon, Foothill Ranch (92610-3000)
PHONE....................949 586-7665
Tim Bennett, *CEO*
Brian Hite, *President*
Dave Bales, *COO*
Dave Brewer, *Vice Pres*
David Brewer, *Vice Pres*
EMP: 101
SQ FT: 22,000
SALES (est): 22.8MM **Privately Held**
SIC: 7319 7336 Display advertising service; commercial art & graphic design; art design services

(P-13975)
KSL MEDIA INC
15910 Ventura Blvd # 900, Encino (91436-2809)
PHONE....................212 468-3395
Kalman Liebowitz, *Ch of Bd*
Hank Cohen, *President*
Russell Meisels, *CFO*
EMP: 130
SQ FT: 13,000
SALES (est): 365.9MM **Privately Held**
WEB: www.kslmedia.com
SIC: 7319 Media buying service

(P-13976)
LEGGETT & PLATT INCORPORATED
Beeline Group
31023 Huntwood Ave, Hayward (94544-7007)
PHONE....................510 487-8063
Fax: 510 441-1782
EMP: 100
SALES (corp-wide): 3.7B **Publicly Held**
SIC: 7319
PA: Leggett & Platt, Incorporated
1 Leggett Rd
Carthage MO 64836
417 358-8131

(P-13977)
MEDIABRANDS WORLDWIDE INC
5700 Wilshire Blvd # 400, Los Angeles (90036-3659)
PHONE....................323 370-8000
Brett Whelan, *Senior VP*
Mandy Bubel, *Buyer*
Robert Ramon, *Manager*
Jennifer Iarossi, *Supervisor*
EMP: 300
SALES (corp-wide): 7.8B **Publicly Held**
WEB: www.wimc.com
SIC: 7319 Media buying service
HQ: Mediabrands Worldwide, Inc.
100 W 33rd St
New York NY 10001
212 605-7000

(P-13978)
NATIONAL CBLE CMMNICATIONS LLC
Also Called: Nca
11150 Santa Monica Blvd # 900, Los Angeles (90025-3380)
PHONE....................310 231-0745
Dori Wilde, *Manager*
EMP: 75
SALES (corp-wide): 84.5B **Publicly Held**
SIC: 7319 1799 7313 Transit advertising services; cable splicing service; radio, television, publisher representatives
HQ: National Cable Communications Llc
405 Lexington Ave Fl 6
New York NY 10174
212 548-3300

(P-13979)
ND SYSTEMS INC
5750 Hellyer Ave, San Jose (95138-1000)
PHONE....................408 776-0085
Jim Ciardella, *CFO*
EMP: 75
SALES (est): 4.5MM **Privately Held**
WEB: www.nationaldisplay.com
SIC: 7319 Display advertising service

(P-13980)
PALISADES MEDIA GROUP INC (PA)
Also Called: Palisades Interactive
1601 Cloverf Blvd 6000n, Santa Monica (90404-4178)
PHONE....................310 564-5400
Roger Schaffner, *Ch of Bd*
Laura Jean Bracken, *President*
Bruce Dennler, *President*
Russell Dean, *CFO*
Rhona Dass, *Senior VP*
EMP: 95
SQ FT: 13,000
SALES (est): 24.8MM **Privately Held**
WEB: www.palisadesmedia.com
SIC: 7319 Media buying service

(P-13981)
QUOTIENT TECHNOLOGY INC (PA)
400 Logue Ave, Mountain View (94043-4019)
PHONE....................650 605-4600
Steven R Boal, *Ch of Bd*
Kate Mueller, *Partner*
Mir M Aamir, *President*
Ronald J Fior, *CFO*
Connie Chen, *Officer*
EMP: 144
SQ FT: 91,000
SALES: 322.1MM **Publicly Held**
SIC: 7319 Coupon distribution

(P-13982)
REVENUE FRONTIER LLC
Also Called: Media Design Group
6922 Hollywood Blvd 2, Los Angeles (90028-6117)
PHONE....................310 584-9200
Greg Thomas, *CEO*
Ross McConnell, *President*
Patrick Romagnano, *CEO*
Michael Marrone, *Vice Pres*
Mike Scott, *Director*
EMP: 55
SALES (est): 7.5MM **Privately Held**
WEB: www.revenuefrontier.com
SIC: 7319 Media buying service

(P-13983)
SMALL BUSINESS ADVERTISING INC
24009 Ventura Blvd # 245, Calabasas (91302-1418)
PHONE....................818 262-8923
Stephen Tackett, *President*
EMP: 50
SALES (est): 765.5K **Privately Held**
SIC: 7319 8742 Advertising; marketing consulting services

(P-13984)
TURN INC (PA)
901 Marshall St 200, Redwood City (94063-2026)
PHONE....................650 353-4399

Bill Demas, *President*
Maureen Cullen, *Senior Partner*
Maureen Lee, *Senior Partner*
Mark Liao, *CFO*
Joe Nemeth, *CFO*
EMP: 111
SQ FT: 14,000
SALES (est): 51.1MM **Privately Held**
WEB: www.turn.com
SIC: 7319 Display advertising service

(P-13985)
US INTERNATIONAL MEDIA LLC (PA)
Also Called: US Outdoor
3415 S Sepulveda Blvd # 800, Los Angeles (90034-6060)
PHONE...................................310 482-6700
Dennis Holt, *CEO*
Doug Livingston, *COO*
Robyn Campbell, *Exec VP*
Sixto Castillo, *Exec VP*
Sherry Catchpole, *Exec VP*
EMP: 93
SQ FT: 5,000
SALES (est): 22MM **Privately Held**
WEB: www.usintlmedia.com
SIC: 7319 Media buying service

(P-13986)
VIANT TECHNOLOGY LLC (DH)
Also Called: Viant US
4 Park Plz Ste 1500, Irvine (92614-3516)
PHONE...................................949 861-8888
Timothy Vanderhook, *CEO*
Christopher Vanderhook, *COO*
Lawerence Madden, *CFO*
Cindy Yang, *Manager*
Marilyn Jacques, *Accounts Exec*
EMP: 200
SQ FT: 20,000
SALES (est): 35.4MM
SALES (corp-wide): 2.2B **Publicly Held**
SIC: 7319 Display advertising service
HQ: Time Inc.
225 Liberty St Ste C2
New York NY 10281
212 522-1212

(P-13987)
WEST COAST COUPON INC
9400 Oso Ave, Chatsworth (91311-6020)
PHONE...................................818 341-2400
Mark Fischer, *President*
Doug Rewers, *Vice Pres*
EMP: 50
SQ FT: 30,000
SALES (est): 8.3MM **Privately Held**
SIC: 7319 2731 5961 Coupon distribution; books: publishing & printing; computer software; mail order

---

7322 Adjustment & Collection Svcs

(P-13988)
ACCESS CAPITAL SERVICES INC (PA)
1625 E Shaw Ave Ste 137, Fresno (93710-8100)
P.O. Box 16187 (93755-6187)
PHONE...................................559 627-5221
Chris Lardiere, *President*
EMP: 54
SQ FT: 6,500
SALES (est): 3.2MM **Privately Held**
WEB: www.acscollectors.com
SIC: 7322 Collection agency, except real estate

(P-13989)
ACCOUNT CONTROL TECHNOLOGY INC
5531 Bus Park S Ste 100, Bakersfield (93309-1656)
PHONE...................................661 395-5702
Sam Shawwa, *Manager*
EMP: 50 **Privately Held**
WEB: www.accountcontrol.com
SIC: 7322 Collection agency, except real estate

HQ: Account Control Technology Inc.
21700 Oxnard St Ste 1400
Woodland Hills CA 91367
-

(P-13990)
ALLIED INTERSTATE INC (DH)
30699 Russell Ranch Rd # 250, Westlake Village (91362-7315)
PHONE...................................818 575-5400
Marwan Kashou, *General Mgr*
Jim Pond, *Opers Mgr*
Michelle Mc Laughling, *Manager*
EMP: 51
SQ FT: 10,000
SALES (est): 4.4MM **Privately Held**
SIC: 7322 8742 Adjustment & collection services; financial consultant
HQ: Intellirisk Management Corporation
335 Madison Ave Fl 27
New York NY 10017
646 274-3030

(P-13991)
ARS NATIONAL SERVICES INC (PA)
201 W Grand Ave, Escondido (92025-2603)
P.O. Box 463023 (92046-3023)
PHONE...................................800 456-5053
Jason Howerton, *President*
John Watson, *COO*
John Howerton, *Chairman*
Jim Beck, *Vice Pres*
Kathy Howerton, *Admin Sec*
EMP: 150
SQ FT: 33,000
SALES (est): 36.4MM **Privately Held**
WEB: www.arsnational.com
SIC: 7322 Collection agency, except real estate

(P-13992)
ATTORNEY RECOVERY SYSTEMS INC (PA)
18757 Burbank Blvd # 300, Tarzana (91356-3375)
PHONE...................................818 774-1420
Gene Bloom, *President*
Debbie Delgado, *Manager*
EMP: 70
SALES (est): 5.7MM **Privately Held**
WEB: www.legalcollection.com
SIC: 7322 8111 Collection agency, except real estate; legal services

(P-13993)
CAINE & WEINER COMPANY INC (PA)
5805 Sepulvda Blvd # 400, Van Nuys (91411-2532)
P.O. Box 55848, Sherman Oaks (91413-0848)
PHONE...................................818 226-6000
Greg A Cohen, *President*
Joneda Rizzo, *President*
Brad Robinson, *President*
Chris Mathews, *CFO*
Joe Batie, *Officer*
EMP: 90
SQ FT: 14,400
SALES (est): 24.9MM **Privately Held**
WEB: www.caine-weiner.com
SIC: 7322 Collection agency, except real estate

(P-13994)
CALIFORNIA BUSINESS BUREAU INC (PA)
Also Called: Medical Billing Services
1711 S Mountain Ave, Monrovia (91016-4256)
P.O. Box 5010 (91017-7110)
PHONE...................................626 303-1515
Michael J Sigal, *President*
Terry McSpadden, *Business Dir*
Brian Bonham, *Info Tech Mgr*
Yvette Sedberry, *Marketing Staff*
Angie Faulkner, *Manager*
EMP: 132 **EST:** 1973
SQ FT: 24,000
SALES (est): 11MM **Privately Held**
WEB: www.cbbinc.com
SIC: 7322 Collection agency, except real estate

(P-13995)
CB ASSOCIATES INC
11659 Haynes St, North Hollywood (91606-2530)
PHONE...................................424 777-8214
Candie Fernandez, *President*
Branden Fernandez, *COO*
Daniel Pettway Jr, *CFO*
EMP: 50
SALES (est): 1.7MM **Privately Held**
SIC: 7322 Collection agency, except real estate

(P-13996)
CBSJ FINANCIAL CORPORATION
1735 N 1st St Ste 250, San Jose (95112-4531)
PHONE...................................408 792-4600
Bertha Martin, *President*
EMP: 100 **EST:** 1983
SALES (est): 4.4MM **Privately Held**
WEB: www.cbsj.com
SIC: 7322 Collection agency, except real estate

(P-13997)
CMRE FINANCIAL SERVICES INC
3075 E Imperial Hwy # 200, Brea (92821-6753)
PHONE...................................714 528-3200
Jack C Nixon, *CEO*
Sandy Lawrence, *President*
Andrea Parr, *Corp Secy*
John Nixon, *Exec VP*
Patrick Nixon, *Vice Pres*
EMP: 450 **EST:** 2000
SQ FT: 35,000
SALES (est): 40.1MM **Privately Held**
WEB: www.cmrefsi.com
SIC: 7322 Collection agency, except real estate

(P-13998)
COLLECTECH SYSTEMS INC (DH)
2290 Agate Ct 1a, Simi Valley (93065-1935)
PHONE...................................818 597-7500
Steve Kent, *Exec VP*
EMP: 175
SQ FT: 19,376
SALES (est): 9.6MM **Privately Held**
SIC: 7322 Collection agency, except real estate
HQ: Intellirisk Management Corporation
335 Madison Ave Fl 27
New York NY 10017
646 274-3030

(P-13999)
COLLECTION TECHNOLOGY INC
Also Called: C T I
10801 6th St Ste 200, Rancho Cucamonga (91730-5904)
P.O. Box 2200 (91729-2200)
PHONE...................................800 743-4284
Chris Van Dellen, *CEO*
Paul Van Dellen, *President*
Divina Balli, *Accounting Mgr*
EMP: 100
SALES (est): 5.9MM **Privately Held**
WEB: www.collectiontechnology.com
SIC: 7322 Collection agency, except real estate

(P-14000)
CONRAD CREDIT CORPORATION
476 W Vermont Ave, Escondido (92025-6529)
P.O. Box 770 (92033-0770)
PHONE...................................760 735-5000
Keith Richenbacher, *President*
John Page, *Vice Pres*
Bob Pranik, *Admin Sec*
EMP: 50
SQ FT: 6,000
SALES (est): 5.9MM
SALES (corp-wide): 20.7MM **Privately Held**
SIC: 7322 Collection agency, except real estate

PA: Conrad Corporation
476 W Vermont Ave
Escondido CA 92025
800 826-6723

(P-14001)
CREDIT BUREAU NAPA COUNTY INC
Also Called: Chase Receivables
1247 Broadway, Sonoma (95476-7503)
PHONE...................................707 940-3000
Fred Merrill, *Chairman*
EMP: 145
SQ FT: 1,357
SALES (est): 13.5MM **Privately Held**
WEB: www.chaserec.com
SIC: 7322 Collection agency, except real estate

(P-14002)
FCI LENDER SERVICES INC
Also Called: F C I
8180 E Kaiser Blvd, Anaheim (92808-2277)
PHONE...................................714 974-1945
Michael W Griffith, *President*
EMP: 105
SQ FT: 19,000
SALES (est): 12.7MM **Privately Held**
WEB: www.trustfci.com
SIC: 7322 Adjustment & collection services

(P-14003)
FINANCIAL CREDIT NETWORK INC (PA)
1300 W Main St, Visalia (93291-5825)
P.O. Box 3084 (93278-3084)
PHONE...................................559 733-7550
Alicia Sundstrom, *President*
Kris Davisson, *Vice Pres*
EMP: 50
SQ FT: 11,000
SALES (est): 6.5MM **Privately Held**
WEB: www.fcnetwork.com
SIC: 7322 Collection agency, except real estate

(P-14004)
GC SERVICES LTD PARTNERSHIP
4900 Rivergrade Rd # 210, Irwindale (91706-1401)
PHONE...................................626 851-8227
David Jacques, *Manager*
EMP: 149
SALES (corp-wide): 246MM **Privately Held**
SIC: 7322 7373 7375 Collection agency, except real estate; computer integrated systems design; information retrieval services
PA: Gc Services Limited Partnership
6330 Gulfton St
Houston TX 77081
713 777-4441

(P-14005)
GRANT & WEBER (PA)
Also Called: Grant & Weber Travel
26610 Agoura Rd Ste 209, Calabasas (91302-2975)
P.O. Box 8669 (91372-8669)
PHONE...................................818 878-7700
Jimi Bingham, *CEO*
David Weinerman, *CFO*
Kim Mehr, *Vice Pres*
Spencer Weinerman, *Vice Pres*
Mary Kempski, *CIO*
EMP: 250
SQ FT: 30,000
SALES (est): 36.7MM **Privately Held**
WEB: www.grantweber.com
SIC: 7322 Collection agency, except real estate

(P-14006)
H P SEARS CO INC
Also Called: HP Sears Co.
2000 18th St, Bakersfield (93301-4292)
P.O. Box 2307 (93303-2307)
PHONE...................................661 325-5981
James P Sears, *President*
Chris Thompson, *General Mgr*
Susie Reddington, *Human Res Mgr*
Denise Garcia, *Accounts Exec*

P R O D U C T S & S V C S

Marshall Sanders, *Accounts Exec*
EMP: 60
SALES (est): 2.6MM Privately Held
SIC: 7322 Collection agency, except real estate

(P-14007)
H&H RESOLUTION LLC
151 Bernal Rd Ste 6, San Jose (95119-1306)
PHONE.....................408 362-2293
Daniel Oditt, *Mng Member*
EMP: 100
SALES (est): 1MM Privately Held
SIC: 7322 Collection agency, except real estate

(P-14008)
INTELLIRISK MANAGEMENT CORP
31229 Cedar Valley Dr, Westlake Village (91362-4036)
PHONE.....................818 575-5400
Jim Pond, *Branch Mgr*
EMP: 50 **Privately Held**
SIC: 7322 Adjustment & collection services
HQ: Intellirisk Management Corporation
335 Madison Ave Fl 27
New York NY 10017
646 274-3030

(P-14009)
J & L COLLECTIONS SERVICES INC
Also Called: J&L Teamworks
651 N Cherokee Ln Ste B2, Lodi (95240-4267)
PHONE.....................800 481-6006
Donald R Johnsen, *President*
Kenneth M Lamont, *CFO*
EMP: 85
SQ FT: 11,200
SALES: 6.5MM
SALES (corp-wide): 26.8MM Privately Held
SIC: 7322 Collection agency, except real estate
PA: Uscb, Inc.
355 S Grand Ave Ste 3200
Los Angeles CA 90071
213 985-2111

(P-14010)
JJ MAC INTYRE CO INC (PA)
4160 Temescal Canyon Rd, Corona (92883-4625)
P.O. Box 78150 (92877-0138)
PHONE.....................951 898-4300
Scott M Hall, *CEO*
Kenneth A Lee, *President*
EMP: 115
SQ FT: 28,254
SALES (est): 7.5MM Privately Held
WEB: www.jjmac.com
SIC: 7322 Collection agency, except real estate

(P-14011)
KINGS CREDIT SERVICES
96 Shaw Ave Ste 221, Clovis (93612-3842)
PHONE.....................559 322-2550
Randall Burchfield, *Owner*
Vicki Callahan, *Vice Pres*
Jeffrey Adams, *Director*
EMP: 55
SALES (est): 2.3MM Privately Held
SIC: 7322 Collection agency, except real estate

(P-14012)
L A COMMERCIAL GROUP INC (PA)
Also Called: Continental Commercial Group
317 S Brand Blvd, Glendale (91204-1701)
PHONE.....................818 551-6800
Robert Norman Merette, *President*
Herb Warme, *Vice Pres*
Rhett Tallas, *General Mgr*
John Unitas, *VP Mktg*
Richard Penn, *Mktg Dir*
EMP: 65
SQ FT: 5,650
SALES (est): 8.3MM Privately Held
SIC: 7322 Collection agency, except real estate

(P-14013)
NATIONAL COMMERCIAL SERVICES
6644 Valjean Ave Ste 100, Van Nuys (91406-5816)
PHONE.....................818 701-4400
Zoran Jovanoski, *President*
Zoran Jovanoski, *President*
Natalie Mansour, *Vice Pres*
Darlene Martinez, *Legal Staff*
EMP: 52
SQ FT: 4,500
SALES: 1.2MM Privately Held
WEB: www.ncslegalservices.com
SIC: 7322 Collection agency, except real estate

(P-14014)
OPTIO SOLUTIONS LLC
Also Called: Qualia Collection Services
1444 N Mcdowell Blvd, Petaluma (94954-6515)
PHONE.....................800 360-2827
Chris Schumacher, *CEO*
EMP: 200 **EST:** 2007
SALES: 11.7MM Privately Held
SIC: 7322 Collection agency, except real estate

(P-14015)
PCI COLLECTIONS INC
Also Called: P C I & Associates
402 W Broadway Fl 4, San Diego (92101-3554)
P.O. Box 3206, Gardena (90247-1406)
PHONE.....................619 595-3114
Emanuel Theodore Davis, *CEO*
EMP: 262
SALES (est): 10.8MM Privately Held
SIC: 7322 Collection agency, except real estate

(P-14016)
PERFORMANT RECOVERY INC
Also Called: DCS
17080 S Harlan Rd, Lathrop (95330-8739)
PHONE.....................209 858-3500
James Tracey, *Principal*
Carol Winston, *Supervisor*
EMP: 200 **Publicly Held**
SIC: 7322 Collection agency, except real estate
HQ: Performant Recovery, Inc.
333 N Canyons Pkwy # 100
Livermore CA 94551
209 858-3994

(P-14017)
PERFORMANT RECOVERY INC (HQ)
333 N Canyons Pkwy # 100, Livermore (94551-9478)
PHONE.....................209 858-3994
Lisa Im, *CEO*
Hakan Orvell, *CFO*
Lara Crapo, *General Mgr*
Bruce Calvin, *Admin Sec*
EMP: 118
SQ FT: 31,000
SALES (est): 53.6MM Publicly Held
SIC: 7322 8742 7371 Collection agency, except real estate; financial consultant; custom computer programming services

(P-14018)
PROFESSIONAL BUREAU OF COLLECT
9675 Elk Grove Florin Rd, Elk Grove (95624-2225)
PHONE.....................916 685-3399
Travis Justus, *Branch Mgr*
EMP: 115 **Privately Held**
SIC: 7322 Collection agency, except real estate
PA: Professional Bureau Of Collections Of Maryland, Inc.
5295 Dtc Pkwy
Greenwood Village CO 80111

(P-14019)
QUADRAMED CORPORATION
Also Called: Corona Rgional Med Ctr Bus Off
800 S Main St, Corona (92882-3420)
PHONE.....................951 736-6290

John Caldrone, *CEO*
EMP: 810
SALES (corp-wide): 2.1B Privately Held
WEB: www.quadramed.com
SIC: 7322 Collection agency, except real estate
HQ: Quadramed Corporation
2300 Corp Park Dr Ste 400
Herndon VA 20171
703 709-2300

(P-14020)
QUALIFIED BLLING CLLCTIONS LLC
Also Called: Q B C
4601 Wilshire Blvd Fl 3, Los Angeles (90010-3884)
PHONE.....................323 556-3470
Thomas Baker, *COO*
Peter Yeh, *COO*
Tom Baker, *Vice Pres*
Vlad Martynoff, *Info Tech Mgr*
Jack Chao, *Relations*
EMP: 200 **EST:** 1982
SALES (est): 3.4MM Privately Held
SIC: 7322 Collection agency, except real estate

(P-14021)
RM GALICIA INC
Also Called: Progressive Management Systems
1521 W Cameron Ave # 100, West Covina (91790-2738)
P.O. Box 2220 (91793-2220)
PHONE.....................626 813-6200
Timothy Chase Banta, *CEO*
Carole Ryan, *Vice Pres*
EMP: 125 **EST:** 1978
SQ FT: 20,000
SALES (est): 15.7MM Privately Held
WEB: www.pmscollects.com
SIC: 7322 Collection agency, except real estate

(P-14022)
SANTA CLARA COUNTY OF
Also Called: Revenue, Dept of
1555 Berger Dr Fl 1, San Jose (95112-2716)
P.O. Box 1897 (95109-1897)
PHONE.....................408 282-3200
Robert McGrath, *Branch Mgr*
Ed Bagsik
EMP: 75 **Privately Held**
WEB: www.countyairports.org
SIC: 7322 9311 Adjustment & collection services; taxation department, government;
PA: County Of Santa Clara
3180 Newberry Dr Ste 150
San Jose CA 95118
408 299-5105

(P-14023)
SEQUOIA CONCEPTS INC
Also Called: Sequoia Financial Services
28632 Roadside Dr Ste 110, Agoura Hills (91301-6074)
PHONE.....................818 409-6000
Roy Duplessis, *President*
Denise Duplessis, *Vice Pres*
Roy Deplessis II, *Admin Sec*
EMP: 75
SQ FT: 9,100
SALES (est): 8.5MM Privately Held
WEB: www.sequoiafinancial.com
SIC: 7322 Collection agency, except real estate

(P-14024)
UNIVERSAL ACCOUNTS INC
690 E Green St Ste 300, Pasadena (91101-2121)
PHONE.....................626 356-7900
Lon Yatman, *President*
Esther Yatman, *Exec VP*
Weng Tang, *Manager*
Weng L Tang, *Agent*
EMP: 60
SQ FT: 14,000
SALES (est): 5.1MM Privately Held
WEB: www.fhs-unifi.com
SIC: 7322 Collection agency, except real estate

(P-14025)
USCB INC
3535 Wilshire Blvd # 700, Los Angeles (90010)
PHONE.....................213 387-6181
Rose Erin, *Manager*
EMP: 75
SALES (corp-wide): 26.8MM Privately Held
WEB: www.uscbinc.com
SIC: 7322 Collection agency, except real estate
PA: Uscb, Inc.
355 S Grand Ave Ste 3200
Los Angeles CA 90071
213 985-2111

(P-14026)
USCB INC (PA)
Also Called: Uscb America
355 S Grand Ave Ste 3200, Los Angeles (90071-1591)
PHONE.....................213 985-2111
Albert Cadena, *Sales Executive*
Melvin F Shaw, *President*
Thomas Isgrigg, *Exec VP*
Sean Escobar, *Senior VP*
James Hughes, *Vice Pres*
EMP: 213
SQ FT: 34,000
SALES (est): 26.8MM Privately Held
WEB: www.uscbinc.com
SIC: 7322 8741 Collection agency, except real estate; management services

(P-14027)
VENGROFF WILLIAMS & ASSOC INC
2099 S State College Blvd # 300, Anaheim (92806-6149)
PHONE.....................714 889-6200
Robert Sherman, *Branch Mgr*
Joseph Torba, *President*
Michael Heinz, *Manager*
EMP: 213
SALES (corp-wide): 18.8MM Privately Held
SIC: 7322 Collection agency, except real estate
PA: Vengroff, Williams & Associates, Inc.
2211 Fruitville Rd
Sarasota FL 34237
941 363-5200

7323 Credit Reporting Svcs

(P-14028)
A-CHECK AMERICA INC (PA)
Also Called: A-Check America, Member Act 1
1501 Research Park Dr, Riverside (92507-2114)
P.O. Box 5615 (92517-5615)
PHONE.....................951 750-1501
Janice B Howroyd, *CEO*
Carlos Lacambra, *President*
Michael Hoyal, *CFO*
Gregg Hassler, *Vice Pres*
Christine Folmer, *Admin Asst*
EMP: 170
SQ FT: 30,000
SALES (est): 30.7MM Privately Held
WEB: www.acheckamerica.com
SIC: 7323 7375 Credit reporting services; information retrieval services

(P-14029)
A-CHECK AMERICA INC
1501 Research Park Dr, Riverside (92507-2114)
P.O. Box 29048, Glendale (91209-9048)
PHONE.....................800 872-2677
Carlos Lacambra, *Branch Mgr*
Dani Hughes, *Regl Sales Mgr*
EMP: 141
SALES (corp-wide): 30.7MM Privately Held
WEB: www.acheckamerica.com
SIC: 7323 7389 Credit reporting services; personal investigation service
PA: A-Check America, Inc.
1501 Research Park Dr
Riverside CA 92507
951 750-1501

▲ = Import ▼=Export
◆ =Import/Export

(P-14030)
ACEVA TECHNOLOGIES INC
1810 Gateway Dr Ste 360, San Mateo
(94404-4063)
PHONE..................................650 227-5500
Sundeep Jain, *Principal*
EMP: 200
SALES (est): 6.8MM
SALES (corp-wide): 9.1B **Publicly Held**
WEB: www.aceva.com
SIC: 7323 Credit clearinghouse
HQ: Fis Data Systems Inc.
    200 Campus Dr
    Collegeville PA 19426
    484 582-2000

(P-14031)
CLAIMREMEDI INC
2235 Mercury Way Ste 107, Santa Rosa
(95407-5472)
PHONE..................................707 827-1274
H Peter Bowhall, *CEO*
Bob Bleyhl, *Exec VP*
Keith Laliberty, *Info Tech Dir*
Ruby Ascencio, *Opers Staff*
EMP: 60
SALES: 7.5MM
SALES (corp-wide): 19MM **Privately Held**
SIC: 7323 Credit clearinghouse
PA: Esolutions, Inc.
    8215 W 108th Ter
    Overland Park KS 66210
    866 633-4726

(P-14032)
CORELOGIC INC
Also Called: Corelogic Info Solutions
11010 White Rock Rd, Rancho Cordova
(95670-6361)
PHONE..................................916 431-2146
Christine Christian, *Branch Mgr*
Cheri Schmieder, *Technology*
Patricia Bales, *Supervisor*
EMP: 95
SALES (corp-wide): 1.8B **Publicly Held**
SIC: 7323 Credit reporting services
PA: Corelogic, Inc.
    40 Pacifica Ste 900
    Irvine CA 92618
    949 214-1000

(P-14033)
CORELOGIC CREDCO LLC (HQ)
40 Pacifica Ste 900, Irvine (92618-7487)
PHONE..................................949 214-1000
Frank Martel, *President*
Jim Balas, *CFO*
Barry Sando, *Managing Dir*
Ranga Potluri, *Info Tech Mgr*
Steve Casey, *Technology*
EMP: 220 EST: 2005
SALES (est): 9.4MM
SALES (corp-wide): 1.8B **Publicly Held**
WEB: www.facredco.com
SIC: 7323 8748 Credit bureau & agency;
business consulting
PA: Corelogic, Inc.
    40 Pacifica Ste 900
    Irvine CA 92618
    949 214-1000

(P-14034)
DUN & BRADSTREET INC
Also Called: D&B
1 Embarcadero Ctr # 2060, San Francisco
(94111-3628)
PHONE..................................415 343-6540
EMP: 76 **Publicly Held**
SIC: 7323
HQ: Dun & Bradstreet, Inc
    103 Jfk Pkwy
    Short Hills NJ 07078
    973 921-5500

(P-14035)
EXPERIAN CORPORATION
475 Anton Blvd, Santa Ana (92704)
PHONE..................................714 830-7000
Rick Cortese, *CEO*
Craig Smith, *Ch of Bd*
Chris Callero, *President*
Margaret B Smith, *President*
Deborah Zuccarini, *President*
EMP: 5059
SQ FT: 323,000

SALES (est): 98.4MM
SALES (corp-wide): 4.6B **Privately Held**
SIC: 7323 Credit bureau & agency; commercial (mercantile) credit reporting bureau
HQ: Experian Na Unlimited
    Landmark House
    Nottingham NOTTS
    -

(P-14036)
EXPERIAN INFO SOLUTIONS INC (DH)
475 Anton Blvd, Costa Mesa (92626-7037)
P.O. Box 5001 (92628-5001)
PHONE..................................714 830-7000
Chris Callero, *CEO*
Craig Halley, *President*
Gary Kearns, *President*
Daniel Schotland, *President*
Jennifer Schulz, *President*
EMP: 3700
SQ FT: 323,000
SALES (est): 2B
SALES (corp-wide): 4.6B **Privately Held**
WEB: www.experian.com
SIC: 7323 Credit bureau & agency; commercial (mercantile) credit reporting bureau
HQ: Experian Holdings, Inc.
    475 Anton Blvd
    Costa Mesa CA 92626
    714 830-7000

(P-14037)
EXPERIAN INFO SOLUTIONS INC
18500 Von Karman Ave # 400, Irvine
(92612-0511)
PHONE..................................949 567-3731
Ed Ojdana, *President*
Scott Speice, *Engineer*
Blaine Lyerla, *Marketing Staff*
Dalonda Steinert, *Marketing Staff*
Gregory Bany, *Sales Staff*
EMP: 200
SALES (corp-wide): 4.6B **Privately Held**
WEB: www.experian.com
SIC: 7323 Commercial (mercantile) credit reporting bureau
HQ: Experian Information Solutions, Inc.
    475 Anton Blvd
    Costa Mesa CA 92626
    714 830-7000

(P-14038)
INFORMATIVE RESEARCH (PA)
13030 Euclid St Ste 209, Garden Grove
(92843-1334)
P.O. Box 2379 (92842-2379)
PHONE..................................714 638-2855
Randy Buckner, *CEO*
Sean Buckner, *President*
Perry Teague, *President*
Patrick Buckner, *Vice Pres*
Amy Montgomery, *Vice Pres*
EMP: 50 EST: 1946
SALES (est): 10.5MM **Privately Held**
WEB: www.informativeresearch.com
SIC: 7323 Credit reporting services

(P-14039)
MORTGAGE FAX INC
18685 Main St Ste 101, Huntington Beach
(92648-1719)
PHONE..................................714 899-2656
Joanne Ahmadi, *President*
EMP: 65
SQ FT: 8,500
SALES (est): 4.4MM **Privately Held**
WEB: www.mortgagefaxinc.com
SIC: 7323 Credit bureau & agency

7331 Direct Mail Advertising Svcs

(P-14040)
ADVANTAGE MAILING LLC (PA)
Also Called: Advantage Mailing Service
1600 N Kraemer Blvd, Anaheim
(92806-1410)
P.O. Box 66013 (92816-6013)
PHONE..................................714 538-3881
Tom Ling, *President*

Thomas C Ling, *President*
Brett Noss, *CFO*
EMP: 180
SQ FT: 60,000
SALES (est): 50.1MM **Privately Held**
WEB: www.advmailing.com
SIC: 7331 Mailing service

(P-14041)
ALL DIRECT MAIL SERVICES INC
Also Called: Mr Mailer
5091 4th St, Baldwin Park (91706-2173)
PHONE..................................818 833-7773
Dennis Zetting, *CEO*
Doug Zetting, *President*
Theresa Elkins, *Vice Pres*
Shirley Stephens, *Admin Sec*
EMP: 102
SQ FT: 50,000
SALES (est): 6.9MM **Privately Held**
WEB: www.admsi.com
SIC: 7331 Mailing service

(P-14042)
BUSINESS SERVICES NETWORK
1275 Fairfax Ave Ste 103, San Francisco
(94124-1759)
PHONE..................................415 282-8161
Harry Yue, *President*
Carlos Lamar, *Vice Pres*
Cindy Yue, *Vice Pres*
Norm Cosand, *VP Human Res*
EMP: 72
SQ FT: 31,120
SALES (est): 7.9MM **Privately Held**
WEB: www.bsnc.com
SIC: 7331 2752 7374 Mailing service; commercial printing, offset; data processing service

(P-14043)
DATABASE MARKETING GROUP INC
5 Peters Canyon Rd # 150, Irvine
(92606-1793)
PHONE..................................714 727-0800
John A Engstrom, *President*
Sharon M Engstrom, *Vice Pres*
Sharon Engstrom, *Vice Pres*
Yan Xia, *Vice Pres*
Scott Humphrey, *Business Dir*
EMP: 300
SQ FT: 12,000
SALES (est): 32MM **Privately Held**
WEB: www.dbmgroup.com
SIC: 7331 8742 Mailing service; marketing consulting services

(P-14044)
FINANCIAL STATEMENT SVCS INC (PA)
Also Called: Fssi
3300 S Fairview St, Santa Ana
(92704-7004)
PHONE..................................714 436-3326
Jennifer Dietz, *CEO*
Henry Perez, *COO*
Karen Elsbury, *CFO*
Jon Dietz, *Admin Sec*
Dan Palmquist, *VP Sales*
EMP: 144
SQ FT: 167,000
SALES: 19.2MM **Privately Held**
WEB: www.fssi-ca.com
SIC: 7331 7374 2759 Mailing service; data processing & preparation; laser printing

(P-14045)
HARTE-HANKS DIRECT MAIL/CALIFO
2337 W Commonwealth Ave, Fullerton
(92833-2997)
PHONE..................................714 738-5478
Larry Franklin, *Ch of Bd*
Richard Hockhouser, *President*
Donald R Crews, *Vice Pres*
EMP: 85
SQ FT: 65,000
SALES (est): 5.2MM
SALES (corp-wide): 383.9MM **Publicly Held**
SIC: 7331 Direct mail advertising services

PA: Harte Hanks, Inc.
    9601 Mcallister Fwy # 610
    San Antonio TX 78216
    210 829-9000

(P-14046)
INFOGROUP INC
951 Mariners Island Blvd # 130, San Mateo
(94404-1558)
PHONE..................................650 389-0700
Fax: 650 389-0707
EMP: 75
SALES (corp-wide): 151.6MM **Privately Held**
SIC: 7331 2741
PA: Infogroup Inc.
    1020 E 1st St
    Papillion NE 68046
    402 836-4500

(P-14047)
IRON MOUNTAIN FULFILLMENT (HQ)
Also Called: Iron Mountain Assurance Corp
565 Sinclair Frontage Rd, Milpitas
(95035-5413)
PHONE..................................408 945-1600
Mike Smith, *President*
EMP: 50
SALES (est): 16MM
SALES (corp-wide): 3.8B **Publicly Held**
WEB: www.comac.com
SIC: 7331 Direct mail advertising services
PA: Iron Mountain Incorporated
    1 Federal St Fl 7
    Boston MA 02110
    617 535-4766

(P-14048)
K/P LLC
13947 Washington Ave, San Leandro
(94578-3220)
PHONE..................................510 614-7800
Rich De Senglau, *Branch Mgr*
EMP: 50
SALES (corp-wide): 120MM **Privately Held**
WEB: www.kpcorporation.com
SIC: 7331 Direct mail advertising services
PA: Kp Llc
    13951 Washington Ave
    San Leandro CA 94578
    510 346-0729

(P-14049)
KP LLC
Also Called: Hunter Advertising Mail Co
13951 Washington Ave, San Leandro
(94578-3220)
PHONE..................................510 346-0729
Rich De Senglau, *President*
EMP: 140
SALES (corp-wide): 120MM **Privately Held**
WEB: www.kpcorporation.com
SIC: 7331 Direct mail advertising services
PA: Kp Llc
    13951 Washington Ave
    San Leandro CA 94578
    510 346-0729

(P-14050)
KP LLC
13951 Washington Ave, San Leandro
(94578-3220)
PHONE..................................510 614-7800
Scott Kane, *Manager*
EMP: 60
SQ FT: 6,000
SALES (corp-wide): 120MM **Privately Held**
WEB: www.kpcorporation.com
SIC: 7331 Mailing service
PA: Kp Llc
    13951 Washington Ave
    San Leandro CA 94578
    510 346-0729

(P-14051)
M M DIRECT MARKETING INC
14271 Corporate Dr, Garden Grove
(92843-5000)
PHONE..................................714 265-4100
Godfred P Otueye, *President*
EMP: 300

(PA)=Parent Co (HQ)=Headquarters (DH)=Div Headquarters
✪ = New Business established in last 2 years

2019 Directory of California
Wholesalers and Services Companies

599

P R O D U C T S & S V C S

SALES (est): 8.7MM
SALES (corp-wide): 46.8MM **Privately Held**
WEB: www.moneymailer.com
SIC: 7331 6794 Mailing service; franchises, selling or licensing
PA: Money Mailer, Llc
6261 Katella Ave Ste 200
Cypress CA 90630
714 889-3800

(P-14052)
MAILMARK ENTERPRISES LLC
8587 Canoga Ave, Canoga Park
(91304-2609)
PHONE..........................818 407-0660
Barry Silver,
EMP: 50
SQ FT: 15,500
SALES (est): 5.9MM **Privately Held**
WEB: www.mailmark.com
SIC: 7331 Mailing service

(P-14053)
MERCURY MAILING SYSTEMS INC
2727 Exposition Blvd, Los Angeles
(90018-4119)
PHONE..........................323 730-0307
Paul Hood, *President*
Cynthia Garcia, *VP Sales*
Gabie Perez, *Accounts Mgr*
EMP: 70
SQ FT: 20,000
SALES (est): 3.3MM **Privately Held**
SIC: 7331 Mailing service

(P-14054)
MONEY MAILER LLC (PA)
Also Called: Mm Advertising
6261 Katella Ave Ste 200, Cypress
(90630-5249)
PHONE..........................714 889-3800
Gary Mulloy,
Mike Lacombe, *Vice Pres*
Mike Tinz, *Vice Pres*
John Libby, *Regional Mgr*
Brian Frizek, *Sr Ntwrk Engine*
EMP: 250
SQ FT: 60,000
SALES (est): 46.8MM **Privately Held**
WEB: www.moneymailer.com
SIC: 7331 6794 Mailing service; franchises, selling or licensing

(P-14055)
MOPAR ENTERPRISES
Also Called: West Coast Mailing & Dist
1710 Dornoch Ct Ste A, San Diego
(92154-7235)
PHONE..........................858 492-1123
Parvin Salehi, *President*
EMP: 60
SQ FT: 49,278
SALES (est): 4.3MM **Privately Held**
SIC: 7331

(P-14056)
MRT INC
19781 Pauling, Foothill Ranch
(92610-2606)
PHONE..........................949 348-2292
Rick Theder, *President*
Tracy Vanevery, *Admin Sec*
EMP: 50
SQ FT: 18,000
SALES (est): 7.5MM **Privately Held**
WEB: www.impactorder.com
SIC: 7331 Direct mail advertising services

(P-14057)
PENSION ADMINISTRATORS INC (PA)
Also Called: Beneficial Administration
17701 Mitchell N, Irvine (92614-6028)
PHONE..........................949 253-4080
Donald R Lawrenz, *President*
John Der Schraaf, *Treasurer*
Daniel Frey, *Vice Pres*
Sam Deleese, *Data Proc Exec*
Annie Casey, *Info Tech Dir*
EMP: 105
SALES (est): 12.3MM **Privately Held**
SIC: 7331 6311 Mailing service; life insurance

(P-14058)
POMONA COLLEGE
333 N College Way, Claremont
(91711-4429)
PHONE..........................909 621-8000
David W Oxtoby, *President*
Stephanie Navarro, *President*
Jordan Snedcof, *Associate Dir*
Debra Dearinure, *Technician*
Faye Moore, *Technician*
EMP: 106
SALES (corp-wide): 193.4MM **Privately Held**
SIC: 7331 8221 Addressing service; college, except junior
PA: Pomona College
550 N College Ave
Claremont CA 91711
909 621-8135

(P-14059)
PREMIER MAILING INC
Also Called: Premier Mailing Services
14522 Garfield Ave, Paramount
(90723-3426)
PHONE..........................562 408-2134
Ramon Arribeno, *President*
Jose Aponte, *Sales Staff*
EMP: 50 **EST:** 1999
SQ FT: 5,200
SALES (est): 7.6MM **Privately Held**
SIC: 7331 Mailing service

(P-14060)
R R DONNELLEY & SONS COMPANY
Also Called: RR Donnelley
18915 S Laurel Park Rd, Rancho
Dominguez (90220-6005)
PHONE..........................310 784-8485
Kelly Martinez, *Vice Pres*
EMP: 50
SALES (corp-wide): 6.9B **Publicly Held**
SIC: 7331 Mailing service
PA: R. R. Donnelley & Sons Company
35 W Wacker Dr Ste 3650
Chicago IL 60601
312 326-8000

(P-14061)
REAL ESTATE IMAGE INC
Also Called: Advanced Image Direct
1415 S Acacia Ave, Fullerton (92831-5317)
PHONE..........................714 502-3900
Ty McMillin, *President*
Hugo Solorio, *Vice Pres*
Perry Wilson, *VP Sales*
Brett Furlong, *Cust Mgr*
Michelle Truong, *Account Dir*
EMP: 150
SQ FT: 136,000
SALES (est): 29.2MM **Privately Held**
WEB: www.advancedimagedirect.com
SIC: 7331 2752 Direct mail advertising services; commercial printing, lithographic

(P-14062)
SPECTRUM INFORMATION SVCS LLC (PA)
16 Technology Dr Ste 107, Irvine
(92618-2323)
PHONE..........................949 752-7070
Curtis Pilon, *President*
Jim Bradford, *CFO*
Glenn O Dell, *Vice Pres*
Glenn Odell, *Vice Pres*
EMP: 70
SQ FT: 142,000
SALES (est): 10MM **Privately Held**
SIC: 7331 7375 4731 Mailing service; information retrieval services; shipping documents preparation

(P-14063)
STAMPSCOM INC (PA)
1990 E Grand Ave, El Segundo
(90245-5013)
PHONE..........................310 482-5800
Kenneth T McBride, *Ch of Bd*
Kyle Huebner, *President*
Jeff Carberry, *CFO*
Sebastian Buerba, *Chief Mktg Ofcr*
Matt Lipson,
EMP: 825 **EST:** 1996
SQ FT: 99,600

SALES (est): 468.7MM **Publicly Held**
WEB: www.stamps.com
SIC: 7331 5961 4813 Mailing service; catalog & mail-order houses;

(P-14064)
T G T ENTERPRISES INC
Also Called: Anderson Direct Marketing
12650 Danielson Ct, Poway (92064-6822)
PHONE..........................858 413-0300
Ted Tietge, *CEO*
Randy Dale, *President*
Jennifer Jenkins, *President*
Vicky Ruegsegger, *Officer*
Scott Hopkins, *Exec VP*
EMP: 130
SQ FT: 77,000
SALES (est): 31.8MM **Privately Held**
WEB: www.andersondirectmail.com
SIC: 7331 2759 Mailing service; commercial printing

(P-14065)
TOWNE INC
Also Called: Towne Advertising
3441 W Macarthur Blvd, Santa Ana
(92704-6805)
PHONE..........................714 540-3095
Tarek Elkomi, *Branch Mgr*
EMP: 100
SALES (est): 6.8MM
SALES (corp-wide): 20.5MM **Privately Held**
SIC: 7331 7311 Mailing service; advertising agencies
PA: Towne, Inc.
3441 W Macarthur Blvd
Santa Ana CA 92704
714 540-3095

(P-14066)
TRANSMRCAN MLING FLFLLMENT INC
355 State Pl, Escondido (92029-1359)
PHONE..........................760 745-5343
Paul Barron, *CEO*
Eleanor Monica, *Vice Pres*
Jack Lazard, *Director*
Martin Benjamin, *Accounts Mgr*
EMP: 100
SALES (est): 16.8MM **Privately Held**
WEB: www.transamericanmailing.com
SIC: 7331 Mailing service

(P-14067)
VALASSIS COMMUNICATIONS INC
1575 Corporate Dr, Costa Mesa
(92626-1467)
PHONE..........................714 751-4006
Steve Scott, *Manager*
EMP: 52 **Privately Held**
WEB: www.valassis.com
SIC: 7331 Mailing service
HQ: Valassis Communications, Inc.
19975 Victor Pkwy
Livonia MI 48152
734 591-3000

(P-14068)
VALASSIS DIRECT MAIL INC
6955 Mowry Ave, Newark (94560-4924)
PHONE..........................510 505-6500
Debra Robinson, *Manager*
EMP: 100 **Privately Held**
WEB: www.advo.com
SIC: 7331 Mailing service
HQ: Valassis Direct Mail, Inc.
235 Great Pond Dr
Windsor CT 06095
800 437-0479

7334 Photocopying & Duplicating Svcs

(P-14069)
ABI ATTORNEYS SERVICE INC (PA)
Also Called: ABI VIP Attorney Service
2015 W Park Ave, Redlands (92373-6271)
P.O. Box 9240 (92375-2440)
PHONE..........................909 793-0613
Alice J Benge, *President*

Chuck Benge, *Corp Secy*
EMP: 80
SQ FT: 7,500
SALES (est): 6.1MM **Privately Held**
WEB: www.abivip.com
SIC: 7334 Photocopying & duplicating services

(P-14070)
AMERICAN LEGAL COPY-OR LLC
98 Battery St Ste 220, San Francisco
(94111-5509)
PHONE..........................415 777-4449
Kevin Brooks, *Manager*
EMP: 100 **Privately Held**
WEB: www.alcweb.com
SIC: 7334 Photocopying & duplicating services
PA: American Legal Copy-Or, Llc
1001 4th Ave Ste 300
Seattle WA 98154

(P-14071)
AMERICAN REPROGRAPHICS CO LLC
Also Called: Ford Graphics
934 Venice Blvd, Los Angeles
(90015-3230)
PHONE..........................213 745-3145
Juan Carlos, *Principal*
EMP: 100
SALES (corp-wide): 394.5MM **Publicly Held**
WEB: www.e-arc.com
SIC: 7334 7336 7374 Blueprinting service; commercial art & graphic design; computer graphics service
HQ: American Reprographics Company, L.L.C.
1981 N Broadway Ste 385
Walnut Creek CA 94596
925 949-5100

(P-14072)
AMERICAN REPROGRAPHICS CO LLC
Also Called: Brownie's Digital Imaging
1322 V St, Sacramento (95818-1418)
PHONE..........................916 443-1322
Jack Anderson, *Manager*
EMP: 80
SALES (corp-wide): 394.5MM **Publicly Held**
WEB: www.e-arc.com
SIC: 7334 Blueprinting service
HQ: American Reprographics Company, L.L.C.
1981 N Broadway Ste 385
Walnut Creek CA 94596
925 949-5100

(P-14073)
AMERICAN REPROGRAPHICS CO LLC
Also Called: ARC Imaging Resources
616 Monterey Pass Rd, Monterey Park
(91754-2419)
PHONE..........................626 289-5021
Doug Elffers, *Mng Member*
EMP: 52
SALES (corp-wide): 394.5MM **Publicly Held**
WEB: www.e-arc.com
SIC: 7334 Photocopying & duplicating services
HQ: American Reprographics Company, L.L.C.
1981 N Broadway Ste 385
Walnut Creek CA 94596
925 949-5100

(P-14074)
AMERICAN REPROGRAPHICS CO LLC
San Jose Blueprint
821 Martin Ave, Santa Clara (95050-2903)
PHONE..........................408 295-5770
Norma Mathews, *Human Res Mgr*
EMP: 90
SALES (corp-wide): 394.5MM **Publicly Held**
WEB: www.e-arc.com
SIC: 7334 Blueprinting service

HQ: American Reprographics Company,
L.L.C.
1981 N Broadway Ste 385
Walnut Creek CA 94596
925 949-5100

(P-14075)
**AMERICAN REPROGRAPHICS
CO LLC**
Also Called: Consolidated Reprographics
345 Clinton St, Costa Mesa (92626-6011)
PHONE..............................714 751-2680
Erick Hazell, *Vice Pres*
EMP: 150
SQ FT: 42,000
SALES (corp-wide): 394.5MM **Publicly
Held**
WEB: www.e-arc.com
SIC: 7334 Blueprinting service
HQ: American Reprographics Company,
L.L.C.
1981 N Broadway Ste 385
Walnut Creek CA 94596
925 949-5100

(P-14076)
**AMERICAN REPROGRAPHICS
CO LLC**
Also Called: Ocb Riverside
4295 Main St, Riverside (92501-3822)
PHONE..............................951 686-0530
Jesse De La Cruz, *General Mgr*
EMP: 75
SALES (corp-wide): 394.5MM **Publicly
Held**
WEB: www.ocbinc.com
SIC: 7334 Photocopying & duplicating
services
HQ: American Reprographics Company,
L.L.C.
1981 N Broadway Ste 385
Walnut Creek CA 94596
925 949-5100

(P-14077)
**ARC DOCUMENT SOLUTIONS
INC**
655 N Central Ave, Glendale (91203-1422)
PHONE..............................818 242-6555
Michael Cohanzard, *CEO*
EMP: 120
SALES (corp-wide): 394.5MM **Publicly
Held**
SIC: 7334 Blueprinting service
PA: Arc Document Solutions, Inc.
12657 Alcosta Blvd # 200
San Ramon CA 94583
925 949-5100

(P-14078)
**ARC DOCUMENT SOLUTIONS
INC**
1207 John Reed Ct Ste A, City of Industry
(91745-2421)
PHONE..............................626 333-7005
Steve Ostrander, *Manager*
EMP: 92
SALES (corp-wide): 394.5MM **Publicly
Held**
SIC: 7334 Photocopying & duplicating
services
PA: Arc Document Solutions, Inc.
12657 Alcosta Blvd # 200
San Ramon CA 94583
925 949-5100

(P-14079)
**ARC DOCUMENT SOLUTIONS
INC**
345 Clinton St, Costa Mesa (92626-6011)
PHONE..............................949 660-1150
Kevin Oermann, *Branch Mgr*
EMP: 100
SALES (corp-wide): 394.5MM **Publicly
Held**
SIC: 7334 Photocopying & duplicating
services
PA: Arc Document Solutions, Inc.
12657 Alcosta Blvd # 200
San Ramon CA 94583
925 949-5100

(P-14080)
**ARC DOCUMENT SOLUTIONS
INC**
American Reprographics Company
945 Bryant St Ste 1000, San Francisco
(94103-4523)
PHONE..............................415 495-8700
Soren Goodman, *General Mgr*
Suri Suriyakumar, *CEO*
Rick Ferry, *Principal*
EMP: 50
SALES (corp-wide): 394.5MM **Publicly
Held**
WEB: www.e-arc.com
SIC: 7334 Blueprinting service
PA: Arc Document Solutions, Inc.
12657 Alcosta Blvd # 200
San Ramon CA 94583
925 949-5100

(P-14081)
**ARC DOCUMENT SOLUTIONS
INC**
Also Called: Reliable Graphics
15019 Califa St, Van Nuys (91411-3003)
PHONE..............................818 908-0222
Danny Mesa, *Branch Mgr*
EMP: 120
SQ FT: 15,727
SALES (corp-wide): 394.5MM **Publicly
Held**
SIC: 7334 Blueprinting service
PA: Arc Document Solutions, Inc.
12657 Alcosta Blvd # 200
San Ramon CA 94583
925 949-5100

(P-14082)
**ASSOCTED REPRODUCTION
SVCS INC**
Also Called: ARS
13925 Whittier Blvd, Whittier (90605-2037)
PHONE..............................562 696-1181
John A Antonelli, *CEO*
John W Antonelli, *President*
Marsha Antonelli, *Vice Pres*
Ron Weingarten, *Info Tech Mgr*
Angelica Gonzalez, *Accountant*
EMP: 160
SQ FT: 25,000
SALES (est): 14.6MM **Privately Held**
WEB: www.arslegal.com
SIC: 7334 Photocopying & duplicating
services

(P-14083)
CRISP ENTERPRISES INC (PA)
Also Called: C2 Imaging
3180 Pullman St, Costa Mesa
(92626-3323)
PHONE..............................714 668-5955
Gary Crisp, *CEO*
William Govaars II, *Shareholder*
Arthur Gregory Lundeen III, *Shareholder*
Barry Malkin, *COO*
Julie Crisp, *Exec VP*
EMP: 60
SQ FT: 28,000
SALES (est): 28.6MM **Privately Held**
WEB: www.c2repro.com
SIC: 7334 Blueprinting service

(P-14084)
CTEK SOLUTIONS INC
Also Called: Auxilio Solutions, Inc.
27271 Las Ramblas Ste 200, Mission Viejo
(92691-8042)
PHONE..............................949 614-0700
Michael H McMillan, *CEO*
Bill Odell, *President*
EMP: 180 EST: 2004
SQ FT: 15,000
SALES: 60MM **Publicly Held**
SIC: 7334 8741 Photocopying & duplicat-
ing services; management services
PA: Cynergistek, Inc.
27271 Las Ramblas Ste 200
Mission Viejo CA 92691

(P-14085)
CYNERGISTEK INC (PA)
27271 Las Ramblas Ste 200, Mission Viejo
(92691-8042)
PHONE..............................949 614-0700

John D Abouchar, *Ch of Bd*
Michael McMillan, *CEO*
Paul T Anthony, *CFO*
Paul Anthony, *CFO*
Drexel Deford, *Bd of Directors*
EMP: 67
SQ FT: 17,000
SALES: 71.6MM **Publicly Held**
WEB: www.auxilio.net
SIC: 7334 8748 Photocopying & duplicat-
ing services; business consulting

(P-14086)
**FEDEX OFFICE & PRINT SVCS
INC**
2799 E Thousand Oaks Blvd, Thousand
Oaks (91362-3257)
PHONE..............................805 379-1552
Chris O'Neil, *Manager*
EMP: 50
SALES (corp-wide): 65.4B **Publicly Held**
WEB: www.kinkos.com
SIC: 7334 Photocopying & duplicating
services
HQ: Fedex Office And Print Services, Inc.
7900 Legacy Dr
Plano TX 75024
214 550-7000

(P-14087)
**FEDEX OFFICE & PRINT SVCS
INC**
13488 Maxella Ave, Marina Del Rey
(90292-4300)
PHONE..............................310 827-2297
Greg Johnson, *Manager*
EMP: 50
SALES (corp-wide): 65.4B **Publicly Held**
WEB: www.kinkos.com
SIC: 7334 Photocopying & duplicating
services
HQ: Fedex Office And Print Services, Inc.
7900 Legacy Dr
Plano TX 75024
214 550-7000

(P-14088)
**FEDEX OFFICE & PRINT SVCS
INC**
4360 E Main St Ste A, Ventura
(93003-8279)
PHONE..............................805 339-2000
Rick Schaub, *Manager*
EMP: 54
SALES (corp-wide): 65.4B **Publicly Held**
WEB: www.kinkos.com
SIC: 7334 Photocopying & duplicating
services
HQ: Fedex Office And Print Services, Inc.
7900 Legacy Dr
Plano TX 75024
214 550-7000

(P-14089)
**FEDEX OFFICE & PRINT SVCS
INC**
800 Wilshire Blvd, Los Angeles
(90017-2604)
P.O. Box Shire Blvd (90017)
PHONE..............................213 892-1700
Shawn Pendergast, *Branch Mgr*
EMP: 50
SALES (corp-wide): 65.4B **Publicly Held**
WEB: www.kinkos.com
SIC: 7334 Photocopying & duplicating
services
HQ: Fedex Office And Print Services, Inc.
7900 Legacy Dr
Plano TX 75024
214 550-7000

(P-14090)
KNOX SERVICES LLC (PA)
1522 Brookhollow Dr Ste 3, Santa Ana
(92705-5412)
PHONE..............................714 479-1650
Stephen L Knox,
Terry Ashman,
Steven L Bubel,
Robert C Porambo,
EMP: 70
SQ FT: 5,200
SALES (est): 4.5MM **Privately Held**
SIC: 7334 Photocopying & duplicating
services

(P-14091)
**OPTISOURCE TECHNOLOGIES
INC**
1855 W Katella Ave # 170, Orange
(92867-3441)
PHONE..............................714 288-0825
Trang Nguyen, *President*
David Nguyen, *President*
Lekhanh Tran, *Opers Mgr*
EMP: 50 EST: 1997
SQ FT: 5,500
SALES: 2.1MM **Privately Held**
WEB: www.optisource.com
SIC: 7334 Blueprinting service

(P-14092)
**SECOND IMAGE NATIONAL LLC
(PA)**
170 E Arrow Hwy, San Dimas
(91773-3336)
P.O. Box 52969, Houston TX (77052-2969)
PHONE..............................800 229-7477
Norman Fogwell, *CEO*
EMP: 145
SQ FT: 25,500
SALES (est): 23.7MM **Privately Held**
WEB: www.secondimage.net
SIC: 7334 Photocopying & duplicating
services

(P-14093)
UCLA COPY SERVICES
555 Westwood Plz Ste B, Los Angeles
(90095-8351)
PHONE..............................310 794-6371
James Muh, *Director*
David Aberbush, *Director*
EMP: 50
SALES (est): 3.4MM **Privately Held**
SIC: 7334 2759 Photocopying & duplicat-
ing services; commercial printing

(P-14094)
**V A ANDERSON ENTERPRISES
INC**
2680 Bishop Dr Ste 140, San Ramon
(94583-4453)
PHONE..............................925 866-6150
Fax: 925 866-6664
EMP: 73
SALES (corp-wide): 8.3MM **Privately
Held**
SIC: 7334
PA: V. A. Anderson Enterprises, Inc.
400 Atlas St
Brea CA 92821
714 990-6100

(P-14095)
XEROX CORPORATION
914 S Victory Blvd, Burbank (91502-2429)
PHONE..............................818 848-8676
Michael Simenian, *Branch Mgr*
EMP: 77
SALES (corp-wide): 10.2B **Publicly Held**
WEB: www.xerox.com
SIC: 7334 Photocopying & duplicating
services
PA: Xerox Corporation
201 Merritt 7
Norwalk CT 06851
203 968-3000

**7335 Commercial
Photography**

(P-14096)
**BRANDED ENTRMT NETWRK
INC (PA)**
15250 Ventura Blvd # 300, Sherman Oaks
(91403-3201)
PHONE..............................310 342-1500
Gary Shenk, *CEO*
Joe Schick, *CFO*
Kristin Glushon, *Exec VP*
Jim Mitchell, *Senior VP*
Brian Cohee, *CTO*
EMP: 233
SALES (est): 108.1MM **Privately Held**
WEB: www.corbis.com
SIC: 7335 Commercial photography

PRODUCTS & SVCS

(P-14097)
IMAGE OF CALIFORNIA INC (PA)
655 E 30th St, Los Angeles (90011-2021)
PHONE...........................213 896-0039
Susan Yoo, *CEO*
Tae Yoo, *President*
EMP: 60 EST: 1992
SALES (est): 4.9MM **Privately Held**
SIC: 7335 Photographic studio, commercial

(P-14098)
PRIMARY COLOR SYSTEMS CORP
401 Coral Cir, El Segundo (90245-4622)
PHONE...........................310 841-0250
Ed Phillips, *Branch Mgr*
EMP: 130
SALES (corp-wide): 61MM **Privately Held**
SIC: 7335 7384 Photographic studio, commercial; photofinishing laboratory
PA: Primary Color Systems Corporation
11130 Holder St
Cypress CA 90630
949 660-7080

(P-14099)
SECOND IMAGE NATIONAL LLC
700 E Bonita Ave, Pomona (91767-1906)
PHONE...........................909 445-8080
EMP: 72
SALES (corp-wide): 23.7MM **Privately Held**
SIC: 7335 Photographic studio, commercial
PA: Second Image National, Llc
170 E Arrow Hwy
San Dimas CA 91773
800 229-7477

┌─────────────────────────────┐
│ **7336 Commercial Art &**   │
│ **Graphic Design**   │
└─────────────────────────────┘

(P-14100)
ATELIER ACE LLC
3191 Casitas Ave Ste 116, Los Angeles (90039-2470)
PHONE...........................503 546-6836
Bradford Wilson, *President*
Kelly Sawdon, *Vice Pres*
Shannon Froh, *Manager*
EMP: 50
SALES: 10MM **Privately Held**
SIC: 7336 Creative services to advertisers, except writers

(P-14101)
BLT & ASSOCIATES INC
6430 W Sunset Blvd # 800, Los Angeles (90028-7911)
PHONE...........................323 860-4000
Clive Baillie, *President*
Dawn Baillie, *CFO*
Rick Lynch, *Vice Pres*
Kelly Hine, *Art Dir*
EMP: 170
SQ FT: 15,000
SALES (est): 20.2MM **Privately Held**
WEB: www.bltomato.com
SIC: 7336 Graphic arts & related design

(P-14102)
CHAMPION SIGNS INCORPORATED
7835 Wilkerson Ct, San Diego (92111-3606)
PHONE...........................858 751-2900
Ron Johnson, *President*
EMP: 50
SQ FT: 8,000
SALES (est): 3.2MM **Privately Held**
WEB: www.championsigns.net
SIC: 7336 Silk screen design

(P-14103)
CINNABAR
4571 Electronics Pl, Los Angeles (90039-1007)
PHONE...........................818 842-8190
Jonathan Katz, *President*
EMP: 200

SQ FT: 60,000
SALES (est): 19.6MM **Privately Held**
SIC: 7336 3999 7819 Graphic arts & related design; theatrical scenery; sound (effects & music production), motion picture; visual effects production

(P-14104)
CINNABAR CALIFORNIA INC
4571 Electronics Pl, Los Angeles (90039-1007)
PHONE...........................818 842-8190
Jonathan Katz, *Chairman*
Basil Katz, *CEO*
Leslie Crawford, *Vice Pres*
Kip Katz, *Vice Pres*
Jeff Crocker, *Project Mgr*
EMP: 60
SQ FT: 55,271
SALES: 16.7MM **Privately Held**
SIC: 7336 8712 1796 Art design services; architectural services; installing building equipment

(P-14105)
COLUMN FIVE MEDIA INC (PA)
5151 California Ave # 230, Irvine (92617-3205)
PHONE...........................949 614-0759
Jason Lankow, *CEO*
Asher Rumack, *Associate Dir*
Elizabeth Clawson, *Office Mgr*
Jenny Famularcano, *Software Dev*
Sean Parent, *Software Dev*
EMP: 50 EST: 2009
SALES: 5.5MM **Privately Held**
SIC: 7336 Graphic arts & related design

(P-14106)
CONSOLIDATED DESIGN WEST INC
Also Called: Cdw
1345 S Lewis St, Anaheim (92805-6431)
PHONE...........................714 999-1476
Victor John Perrillo, *CEO*
McKenzie Kiely, *Production*
Melissa Saldana, *Sales Executive*
Michael Brown, *Marketing Staff*
Steve Elliott, *Marketing Staff*
EMP: 80
SQ FT: 7,500
SALES (est): 17.1MM **Privately Held**
SIC: 7336 2754 Package design; commercial printing, gravure

(P-14107)
CONTINENTAL GRAPHICS CORP (HQ)
Also Called: Continental Data Graphics
4060 N Lakewood Blvd, Long Beach (90808-1700)
PHONE...........................714 503-4200
David Malmo, *CEO*
James Mills, *CFO*
Michael Parven, *Exec VP*
Calsee Hendrickson, *Vice Pres*
Zeyad Maasarani, *Comms Mgr*
EMP: 200
SQ FT: 45,000
SALES (est): 71MM
SALES (corp-wide): 93.3B **Publicly Held**
WEB: www.cdgnow.com
SIC: 7336 8741 8711 8999 Commercial art & graphic design; management services; engineering services; technical writing
PA: The Boeing Company
100 N Riverside Plz
Chicago IL 60606
312 544-2000

(P-14108)
COUNTY OF LOS ANGELES
Also Called: Gateway
1 Gateway Plz, Los Angeles (90012-3745)
P.O. Box 90012 (90009-0012)
PHONE...........................213 922-6210
Roger Snoball, *Owner*
EMP: 1000 **Privately Held**
WEB: www.co.la.ca.us
SIC: 7336 9621 Commercial art & graphic design; transportation department: government, non-operating;

PA: County Of Los Angeles
500 W Temple St Ste 437
Los Angeles CA 90012
213 974-1101

(P-14109)
CUSTOMLINE PROFESSIONAL
567 S Melrose St, Placentia (92870-6305)
PHONE...........................714 996-1333
Dan Mattox, *President*
EMP: 300
SQ FT: 60,000
SALES (est): 26.1MM **Privately Held**
WEB: www.customlinescreenprint.com
SIC: 7336 Silk screen design

(P-14110)
DANDREA GRAPHIC CORPORTION
Also Called: D'Andrea Graphics
6100 Gateway Dr, Cypress (90630-4840)
PHONE...........................310 642-0260
David D'Andrea, *CEO*
EMP: 80
SQ FT: 25,000
SALES (est): 17.8MM **Privately Held**
SIC: 7336 Graphic arts & related design

(P-14111)
DESTINATION MOON LP
Also Called: Turner Dockworth
615 Battery St Fl 6, San Francisco (94111-1808)
PHONE...........................415 675-7777
David Turner, *CEO*
Bruce Duckworth, *COO*
Greet Hods, *Creative Dir*
Joanne Chan, *General Mgr*
Gregory Holmes, *Executive Asst*
EMP: 70
SQ FT: 5,600
SALES (est): 8MM **Privately Held**
SIC: 7336 Graphic arts & related design

(P-14112)
DSH WEST INC
Also Called: Dsh Graphics
5455 Camino De Bryant, Yorba Linda (92887-4209)
PHONE...........................714 692-8777
Ron Herrera, *President*
Donna Herrera, *President*
EMP: 75
SALES: 7.8MM **Privately Held**
SIC: 7336 Creative services to advertisers, except writers; graphic arts & related design

(P-14113)
FINAL FILM
Also Called: Flash Point Graphix
3620 W Valhalla Dr, Burbank (91505-1127)
PHONE...........................323 467-0700
Thomas L Saliba, *Ch of Bd*
Guy S Claudy, *President*
Ron Dejesus, *President*
Gregory D Davidiian, *CEO*
Leslie Tolbert, *Vice Pres*
EMP: 62
SQ FT: 20,000
SALES (est): 10MM **Privately Held**
WEB: www.finalfilm.com
SIC: 7336 Graphic arts & related design

(P-14114)
FROG DESIGN INC (DH)
1130 Howard St, San Francisco (94103-3914)
PHONE...........................415 442-4804
Doreen Lorenzo, *CEO*
Toshi Mogi, *President*
Andy Zimmerman, *President*
Craig Ayers, *CFO*
Alec Cooper, *Vice Pres*
EMP: 122
SALES (est): 34.5MM
SALES (corp-wide): 1.1B **Privately Held**
WEB: www.frogdesign.com
SIC: 7336 Graphic arts & related design

(P-14115)
GEL PAK LLC
31398 Huntwood Ave, Hayward (94544-7818)
PHONE...........................510 576-2220
Jeanne Beacham, *Principal*

Priya Anand, *Admin Asst*
Joey Flores, *Technician*
Mike Tran, *Engineer*
EMP: 75
SALES (est): 217.5K
SALES (corp-wide): 25.8MM **Privately Held**
SIC: 7336 Package design
PA: Delphon Industries, Llc
31398 Huntwood Ave
Hayward CA 94544
510 576-2220

(P-14116)
HARDING MKTG CMMUNICATIONS INC (PA)
Also Called: Harding & Associates
377 S Daniel Way, San Jose (95128-5120)
PHONE...........................408 345-4545
James F Harding, *CEO*
Maria Richard, *CFO*
EMP: 70
SQ FT: 10,000
SALES (est): 11MM **Privately Held**
WEB: www.hardingmarketing.com
SIC: 7336 Graphic arts & related design

(P-14117)
IDEO LP (PA)
150 Forest Ave, Palo Alto (94301-1614)
PHONE...........................650 289-3400
Tim Brown, *President*
Charles Hayes, *Partner*
Davide Agnelli, *Managing Dir*
Melanie Bell, *Managing Dir*
Ethan Klein, *Web Dvlpr*
EMP: 135
SQ FT: 60,000
SALES (est): 47.2MM **Privately Held**
WEB: www.ideo.com
SIC: 7336 7389 8711 Commercial art & graphic design; design, commercial & industrial; engineering services

(P-14118)
LANDOR ASSOCIATES INTL LTD (DH)
1001 Front St, San Francisco (94111-1467)
PHONE...........................415 365-1700
Lois Jacobs, *CEO*
Cheryl Giovannoni, *President*
Ran Wadleigh, *CFO*
Craig Branigan, *Chairman*
Peter Law-Gisiko, *Principal*
EMP: 200
SQ FT: 44,000
SALES (est): 30.9MM
SALES (corp-wide): 20.1B **Privately Held**
SIC: 7336 Graphic arts & related design
HQ: Young & Rubicam Llc
3 Columbus Cir
New York NY 10019
212 210-3000

(P-14119)
LATERAL DESIGNS INC
Also Called: Logo Design Pros
639 Front St Fl 3, San Francisco (94111-1970)
PHONE...........................415 847-6618
Cliff Kaplan, *President*
EMP: 100
SALES: 5MM **Privately Held**
SIC: 7336 Graphic arts & related design

(P-14120)
MARKET TECH MEDIA CORPORATION
27220 Turnberry Ln # 190, Valencia (91355-1018)
PHONE...........................661 257-4745
Thomas Rice, *President*
Vance Kirby, *COO*
Richard Van Slyke, *Manager*
EMP: 100
SQ FT: 54,000
SALES (est): 7.9MM **Privately Held**
WEB: www.addcart.com
SIC: 7336 7311 Graphic arts & related design; advertising agencies

(P-14121)
MIRUM INC
Also Called: Digitaria
350 10th Ave Ste 1200, San Diego
(92101-8702)
PHONE....................619 237-5552
Daniel Khabie, *CEO*
Doug Hecht, *President*
Gary Correia, *CFO*
John Van Spyk, *Exec VP*
Jim McArthur, *Senior VP*
EMP: 200
SQ FT: 4,000
SALES (est): 27.2MM
SALES (corp-wide): 20.1B **Privately Held**
WEB: www.digitaria.com
SIC: 7336 Graphic arts & related design
HQ: J. Walter Thompson U.S.A., Llc
466 Lexington Ave Fl 2
New York NY 10017
212 210-7000

(P-14122)
MOTION THEORY INC
Also Called: Mirada
444 W Ocean Blvd Ste 1400, Long Beach
(90802-4522)
PHONE....................310 396-9433
Andrew Merkin, *Director*
Janell Perez, *CFO*
Vanessa Marzaroli, *Creative Dir*
Sascha Flick, *Mktg Dir*
Matthew Cullen,
EMP: 110 **EST:** 2000
SQ FT: 25,000
SALES (est): 27MM **Privately Held**
WEB: www.motiontheory.com
SIC: 7336 7371 7812 Graphic arts & related design; computer software development & applications; motion picture production

(P-14123)
MOTIVATIONAL SYSTEMS INC (PA)
2200 Cleveland Ave, National City
(91950-6412)
PHONE....................619 474-8246
Robert D Yound, *CEO*
Joe Jordan, *Treasurer*
Debra Bennett, *Vice Pres*
Andrew Cabrera, *Vice Pres*
Bob Charette, *Vice Pres*
EMP: 100 **EST:** 1975
SQ FT: 50,000
SALES (est): 25.6MM **Privately Held**
WEB: www.motivationalsystems.com
SIC: 7336 3993 Graphic arts & related design; signs & advertising specialties

(P-14124)
ONE K STUDIOS LLC
Also Called: 1k Studios
3400 W Olive Ave Ste 300, Burbank
(91505-5408)
PHONE....................818 531-3800
Matt Kennedy,
Steve Klinenberg,
Mitchell Rubinstein,
Jayson Won,
EMP: 50
SQ FT: 25,000
SALES (est): 5.7MM **Privately Held**
WEB: www.one-k.com
SIC: 7336 Commercial art & graphic design

(P-14125)
PLEASANTON UNIFIED SCHOOL DST
4665 Bernal Ave, Pleasanton (94566-7449)
PHONE....................925 462-5500
Lee Pomplin, *Branch Mgr*
EMP: 129
SALES (corp-wide): 179.3MM **Privately Held**
SIC: 7336 Commercial art & graphic design
PA: Pleasanton Unified School District
4665 Bernal Ave
Pleasanton CA 94566
925 462-5500

(P-14126)
PROLOGUE FILMS (PA)
Also Called: Title Boy
534 Victoria Ave, Venice (90291-4833)
PHONE....................310 589-9090
Kyle Cooper, *President*
Lisa Bolan, *Creative Dir*
EMP: 50
SALES (est): 4.8MM **Privately Held**
SIC: 7336 Graphic arts & related design

(P-14127)
PULP STUDIO INCORPORATED (PA)
Also Called: CGB
2100 W 139th St, Gardena (90249-2412)
P.O. Box 16231, Beverly Hills (90209-2231)
PHONE....................310 815-4999
Bernard Lax, *CEO*
Lynda N Lax, *President*
Kelly Lucatero, *Purchasing*
Karen Rains, *Natl Sales Mgr*
Katie Grimes, *Sales Associate*
EMP: 60
SQ FT: 36,000
SALES (est): 18.9MM **Privately Held**
WEB: www.pulpstudio.com
SIC: 7336 3229 Commercial art & graphic design; glass furnishings & accessories

(P-14128)
RYOT CORP
11995 Bluff Creek Dr, Playa Vista
(90094-2929)
PHONE....................323 356-1787
Bryn Mooser, *CEO*
Ricky Baba, *Creative Dir*
EMP: 100
SALES (est): 1MM **Privately Held**
SIC: 7336 7371 Still film producer; computer software development & applications

(P-14129)
TECH FLEX PACKAGE
12624 Daphne Ave, Hawthorne
(90250-3310)
PHONE....................323 241-1800
Neil Kinney, *President*
EMP: 50
SALES (est): 2MM **Privately Held**
SIC: 7336 Package design

(P-14130)
THE DESIGNORY INC (HQ)
211 E Ocean Blvd Ste 100, Long Beach
(90802-4850)
PHONE....................562 624-0200
Paul Hosea, *CEO*
Matt Radigan, *CFO*
Joel Fuller, *Exec VP*
Jay Brida, *Creative Dir*
Candy Ho, *Creative Dir*
EMP: 115
SALES (est): 13.8MM
SALES (corp-wide): 15.2B **Publicly Held**
WEB: www.designory.com
SIC: 7336 Graphic arts & related design
PA: Omnicom Group Inc.
437 Madison Ave
New York NY 10022
212 415-3600

(P-14131)
WILD SIDE WEST (PA)
Also Called: Wildside
311 Parkside Dr, San Fernando
(91340-3036)
PHONE....................818 837-5000
Faruk Gizatullin, *President*
Bernard Eveler, *Vice Pres*
Sean Gizatullin, *Vice Pres*
EMP: 80
SQ FT: 50,000
SALES (est): 5.9MM **Privately Held**
WEB: www.thewildside.com
SIC: 7336 Silk screen design

7338 Secretarial & Court Reporting Svcs

(P-14132)
ATKINSON-BAKER INC (PA)
500 N Brand Blvd Fl 3, Glendale
(91203-1945)
P.O. Box 29054 (91209-9054)
PHONE....................818 551-7300
Alan Atkinson Baker, *CEO*
Sheila Atkinson-Baker, *President*
Cristina Garcia, *Senior VP*
Deborah J Ackema, *Vice Pres*
April Hill, *Vice Pres*
EMP: 173
SQ FT: 23,000
SALES: 36.1MM **Privately Held**
WEB: www.atkinsonbaker.com
SIC: 7338 Court reporting service

(P-14133)
RETT INC
Also Called: Canedy Court Reporting
402 W Broadway Ste 400, San Diego
(92101-3554)
PHONE....................619 231-0403
Vicki Canedy, *President*
Blake Canedy, *CEO*
EMP: 100
SQ FT: 1,500
SALES: 2MM **Privately Held**
SIC: 7338 Court reporting service

(P-14134)
SOFTSCRIPT INC
2215 Campus Dr, El Segundo
(90245-0001)
PHONE....................310 451-2110
Howard Wisnicki, *CEO*
Ruien Shu, *Exec VP*
Claudia Mendoza, *Vice Pres*
Brandon Phillips, *Vice Pres*
Ofelia Aguirre, *Finance Mgr*
EMP: 1200
SALES (est): 49.5MM **Privately Held**
WEB: www.softscript.com
SIC: 7338 Secretarial & typing service

7342 Disinfecting & Pest Control Svcs

(P-14135)
A-ABLE INC (PA)
Also Called: Fume-A-Pest & Termite Control
17801 Ventura Blvd, Encino (91316-3616)
PHONE....................323 658-5779
Michael Herson, *President*
Jack Herson, *Vice Pres*
EMP: 65
SQ FT: 9,026
SALES (est): 4.2MM **Privately Held**
SIC: 7342 1799 Pest control in structures; termite control; steam cleaning of building exteriors

(P-14136)
ABLE EXTERMINATORS INC
68 N Sunset Ave, San Jose (95116-2036)
P.O. Box 5339 (95150-5339)
PHONE....................408 251-6500
Don Petree, *Vice Pres*
Shawna Petree, *Vice Pres*
EMP: 51
SQ FT: 4,000
SALES (est): 4.3MM **Privately Held**
WEB: www.ablexterm.com
SIC: 7342 Termite control; exterminating & fumigating

(P-14137)
ANTIMITE ASSOCIATES INC
5458 Complex St 401, San Diego
(92123-1118)
PHONE....................619 231-2900
Doug Lewis, *Branch Mgr*
EMP: 53
SALES (corp-wide): 10.3MM **Privately Held**
SIC: 7342 Pest control in structures; termite control

PA: Antimite Associates Inc.
6770 N Sunrise Blvd G200
Glendale AZ 85305
909 606-2300

(P-14138)
CARTWRIGHT TERMITE & PEST CTRL
51360 Calle Guatemala, La Quinta
(92253-2916)
P.O. Box 658 (92247-0658)
PHONE....................760 771-6091
Fax: 760 771-4881
EMP: 50
SALES (est): 2.6MM **Privately Held**
SIC: 7342

(P-14139)
CATS USA INC
Also Called: Cats U S A Pest Control
5683 Whitnall Hwy, North Hollywood
(91601-2213)
P.O. Box 151 (91603-0151)
PHONE....................818 506-1000
Hirotaka Otomo, *Ch of Bd*
Micheal Hunt, *Sales Executive*
EMP: 100
SQ FT: 3,900
SALES (est): 7MM
SALES (corp-wide): 813.6K **Privately Held**
SIC: 7342 Pest control in structures
HQ: Cats, Inc.
15-13, Nampeidaicho
Shibuya-Ku TKY 150-0
354 575-101

(P-14140)
CLARK PEST CTRL STOCKTON INC (PA)
555 N Guild Ave, Lodi (95240-0809)
P.O. Box 1480 (95241-1480)
PHONE....................209 368-7152
Joseph Clark, *CEO*
Jeffrey Clark, *Vice Pres*
Terry Clark, *Vice Pres*
EMP: 70
SQ FT: 2,500
SALES: 108.2MM **Privately Held**
SIC: 7342 Exterminating & fumigating; pest control in structures; termite control

(P-14141)
CLARK PEST CTRL STOCKTON INC
480 E Service Rd, Modesto (95358-9491)
PHONE....................209 524-6384
Ron Fair, *Manager*
EMP: 60
SALES (corp-wide): 108.2MM **Privately Held**
SIC: 7342 Pest control in structures
PA: Clark Pest Control Of Stockton, Inc.
555 N Guild Ave
Lodi CA 95240
209 368-7152

(P-14142)
CLARK PEST CTRL STOCKTON INC
5822 Roseville Rd, Sacramento
(95842-3071)
PHONE....................916 925-7000
Steven Adams, *Manager*
EMP: 100
SQ FT: 3,100
SALES (corp-wide): 108.2MM **Privately Held**
SIC: 7342 Exterminating & fumigating; pest control in structures
PA: Clark Pest Control Of Stockton, Inc.
555 N Guild Ave
Lodi CA 95240
209 368-7152

(P-14143)
CLARK PEST CTRL STOCKTON INC
811 U Banks, Vacaville (95688)
PHONE....................707 446-9748
Ron Gardner, *Manager*
EMP: 50
SQ FT: 1,300

PRODUCTS & SVCS

SALES (corp-wide): 108.2MM **Privately Held**
SIC: 7342 Pest control in structures
PA: Clark Pest Control Of Stockton, Inc.
555 N Guild Ave
Lodi CA 95240
209 368-7152

(P-14144)
CLARK PEST CTRL STOCKTON INC
4816 Clowes St, Stockton (95210-3506)
P.O. Box 1480, Lodi (95241-1480)
PHONE....................209 474-3204
Joe Dinubilo, *Manager*
EMP: 50
SALES (corp-wide): 108.2MM **Privately Held**
SIC: 7342 Pest control in structures
PA: Clark Pest Control Of Stockton, Inc.
555 N Guild Ave
Lodi CA 95240
209 368-7152

(P-14145)
CLARK PEST CTRL STOCKTON INC
199 Topaz St, Milpitas (95035-5430)
PHONE....................408 945-3600
Joe Gatto, *Branch Mgr*
EMP: 70
SALES (corp-wide): 108.2MM **Privately Held**
SIC: 7342 Pest control in structures
PA: Clark Pest Control Of Stockton, Inc.
555 N Guild Ave
Lodi CA 95240
209 368-7152

(P-14146)
CLARK PEST CTRL STOCKTON INC
2313 Research Dr, Livermore (94550-3824)
PHONE....................925 449-6203
Dave Erichsen, *Manager*
Kristeen Blevins, *Human Res Dir*
EMP: 60
SALES (corp-wide): 108.2MM **Privately Held**
SIC: 7342 Pest control in structures
PA: Clark Pest Control Of Stockton, Inc.
555 N Guild Ave
Lodi CA 95240
209 368-7152

(P-14147)
CLARK PEST CTRL STOCKTON INC
11285 White Rock Rd, Rancho Cordova (95742-6504)
PHONE....................916 635-7770
Robert Golubski, *Manager*
EMP: 50
SALES (corp-wide): 108.2MM **Privately Held**
SIC: 7342 Pest control in structures
PA: Clark Pest Control Of Stockton, Inc.
555 N Guild Ave
Lodi CA 95240
209 368-7152

(P-14148)
CORKYS PEST CONTROL INC
909 Rancheros Dr, San Marcos (92069-3028)
PHONE....................760 432-8801
Corky Mizer, *President*
EMP: 60
SQ FT: 5,000
SALES (est): 6.6MM **Privately Held**
SIC: 7342 0782 2879 5211 Pest control in structures; lawn & garden services; insecticides & pesticides; insulation material, building; landscape services; handyman service

(P-14149)
CRANE ACQUISITION INC
Also Called: Crane Pest Control
2700 Geary Blvd, San Francisco (94118-3406)
PHONE....................415 922-1666
Harold Stein, *President*
Harry J Cynkus, *Treasurer*

Eugene Iarocci, *Admin Sec*
EMP: 86
SQ FT: 6,000
SALES (est): 7.1MM
SALES (corp-wide): 1.6B **Publicly Held**
WEB: www.cranepestcontrol.com
SIC: 7342 Exterminating & fumigating; pest control services
PA: Rollins, Inc.
2170 Piedmont Rd Ne
Atlanta GA 30324
404 888-2000

(P-14150)
ECOLA SERVICES INC
15314 Devonshire St Ste F, Mission Hills (91345-2773)
PHONE....................818 920-7301
Susan Fries, *President*
Dennis McClure, *Regional Mgr*
Angie Gutierrez, *Cust Mgr*
EMP: 52
SQ FT: 10,000
SALES (est): 4.6MM **Privately Held**
WEB: www.ecolatermite.com
SIC: 7342 Termite control; pest control services

(P-14151)
HOMEGUARD INCORPORATED (PA)
Also Called: Redrocks Fumigation
510 Madera Ave, San Jose (95112-2918)
PHONE....................408 993-1900
James Steffenson Jr, *President*
Jim Hessling, *Treasurer*
Stacy Rife, *Admin Asst*
Corina Ruiz, *Controller*
Wendy Boston, *Manager*
EMP: 56
SQ FT: 6,000
SALES (est): 12.3MM **Privately Held**
SIC: 7342 Termite control

(P-14152)
LLOYD PEST CONTROL CO (PA)
935 Sherman St, San Diego (92110-4092)
PHONE....................619 298-9865
James A Ogle III, *President*
Ken Keith, *CFO*
Herb Field, *Vice Pres*
Thom Ball, *Info Tech Dir*
Mike Magnuson, *Opers Mgr*
EMP: 250
SALES (est): 17.1MM **Privately Held**
SIC: 7342 Exterminating & fumigating; pest control in structures

(P-14153)
LLOYD PEST CONTROL CO
566 E Dyer Rd, Santa Ana (92707-3737)
PHONE....................714 979-6021
Mike Magnuson, *Manager*
EMP: 50
SALES (corp-wide): 17.1MM **Privately Held**
SIC: 7342 Pest control in structures; termite control
PA: The Lloyd Pest Control Co
935 Sherman St
San Diego CA 92110
619 298-9865

(P-14154)
MCCLENAHAN PEST CONTROL INC
1 Arastradero Rd, Portola Valley (94028-8012)
PHONE....................650 326-8781
James M Mc Clenahan, *President*
Jeoffrey Dunster, *Manager*
EMP: 50
SALES (est): 1.6MM **Privately Held**
SIC: 7342 Pest control in structures

(P-14155)
OCONNOR PEST CONTROL VISALIA
1728 W Prospect Ave, Visalia (93291-2628)
PHONE....................559 366-4853
EMP: 100
SALES (est): 1MM **Privately Held**
SIC: 7342 Pest control in structures

(P-14156)
ROYCE CORPORATION (PA)
Also Called: Aai Termite Pest Control
4970 Salida Blvd, Salida (95368-9403)
P.O. Box 586 (95368-0586)
PHONE....................209 545-0789
Michael Rogers, *President*
Robert Capdeville, *Vice Pres*
EMP: 60
SQ FT: 6,500
SALES (est): 5.7MM **Privately Held**
SIC: 7342 Termite control; pest control in structures

(P-14157)
STATEWIDE PEST CONTROL CO INC (PA)
Also Called: Stanley Pest Control
2555 Loma Ave, South El Monte (91733-1417)
PHONE....................626 443-2847
Kevin Harness, *President*
Steve Wolfbrandt, *Branch Mgr*
Burdene Peterson, *Admin Sec*
Tony Ramirez, *Manager*
EMP: 106
SQ FT: 5,000
SALES: 14.2MM **Privately Held**
WEB: www.stanleypest.com
SIC: 7342 Pest control in structures

(P-14158)
TERMINIX INTL CO LTD PARTNR
3055 N California St, Burbank (91504-2005)
PHONE....................818 972-2037
Tarvis Braun, *Manager*
EMP: 50
SALES (corp-wide): 2.9B **Publicly Held**
SIC: 7342 Pest control services
HQ: The Terminix International Company Limited Partnership
150 Peabody Pl
Memphis TN 38103
901 766-1400

(P-14159)
TERMINIX INTL CO LTD PARTNR
6678 Owens Dr Ste 100, Pleasanton (94588-3324)
PHONE....................925 460-5063
Robert Castillo, *Sales/Mktg Mgr*
EMP: 70
SALES (corp-wide): 2.9B **Publicly Held**
SIC: 7342 Pest control services
HQ: The Terminix International Company Limited Partnership
150 Peabody Pl
Memphis TN 38103
901 766-1400

(P-14160)
TERMINIX INTL CO LTD PARTNR
649 S Waterman Ave Ste A, San Bernardino (92408-2365)
PHONE....................909 332-2479
Rodney Prince, *Principal*
EMP: 50
SALES (corp-wide): 2.9B **Publicly Held**
SIC: 7342 Pest control services
HQ: The Terminix International Company Limited Partnership
150 Peabody Pl
Memphis TN 38103
901 766-1400

(P-14161)
TERMINIX INTL CO LTD PARTNR
21113 Superior St, Chatsworth (91311-4309)
PHONE....................818 361-1191
Kyle Quinn, *Manager*
Keith Poindexter, *Branch Mgr*
Darren Moen, *Sales Executive*
EMP: 56
SALES (corp-wide): 2.9B **Publicly Held**
SIC: 7342 Pest control services
HQ: The Terminix International Company Limited Partnership
150 Peabody Pl
Memphis TN 38103
901 766-1400

(P-14162)
WESTERN EXTERMINATOR COMPANY
3333 W Temple St, Los Angeles (90026-4523)
PHONE....................310 274-9244
Paul Trammell, *Manager*
Angela Ortiz, *Human Res Dir*
EMP: 85
SQ FT: 10,264
SALES (corp-wide): 3.1B **Privately Held**
WEB: www.west-ext.com
SIC: 7342 Disinfecting & pest control services
HQ: Western Exterminator Company
305 N Crescent Way
Anaheim CA 92801
714 517-9000

(P-14163)
WESTERN EXTERMINATOR COMPANY
1985 W Wardlow Rd, Long Beach (90810-2037)
PHONE....................310 835-3513
Sandi Quintana, *Manager*
EMP: 50
SALES (corp-wide): 3.1B **Privately Held**
WEB: www.west-ext.com
SIC: 7342 Pest control services
HQ: Western Exterminator Company
305 N Crescent Way
Anaheim CA 92801
714 517-9000

(P-14164)
WESTERN EXTERMINATOR COMPANY
Also Called: Target Specialty Products
15415 Marquardt Ave, Santa Fe Springs (90670-5711)
P.O. Box 3408 (90670-1408)
PHONE....................562 802-2238
Rich Records, *Manager*
Gary Singh, *Administration*
Brayden Henrie, *Sales Staff*
EMP: 100
SALES (corp-wide): 3.1B **Privately Held**
WEB: www.west-ext.com
SIC: 7342 Disinfecting & pest control services
HQ: Western Exterminator Company
305 N Crescent Way
Anaheim CA 92801
714 517-9000

(P-14165)
YOUR WAY FUMIGATION INC
41880 Kalmia St Ste 170, Murrieta (92562-8838)
PHONE....................951 699-9116
Jose Manuel Aguilar, *President*
EMP: 90
SALES (est): 8.3MM **Privately Held**
SIC: 7342 Exterminating & fumigating

7349 Building Cleaning & Maintenance Svcs, NEC

(P-14166)
A1 BUILDING MANAGEMENT INC
2461 E Orangethorpe Ave # 200, Fullerton (92831-5302)
PHONE....................714 447-3800
Trent Pollack, *President*
EMP: 125
SALES (est): 1.8MM **Privately Held**
SIC: 7349 Building maintenance services

(P-14167)
ABM ELCTRCAL LTG SOLUTIONS INC
6940 Koll Center Pkwy # 100, Pleasanton (94566-3100)
PHONE....................408 399-3030
EMP: 65 **Privately Held**
SIC: 7349 Lighting maintenance service

(P-14168)
ABM ELCTRCAL LTG SOLUTIONS INC
14201 Franklin Ave, Tustin (92780-7008)
PHONE............................866 226-2838
Henrick C Slipsager, *CEO*
James S Lusk, *Exec VP*
Tracy K Price, *Exec VP*
Scott Tapia, *Sales Staff*
Sue Bremner, *Director*
EMP: 100
SQ FT: 4,803
SALES (est): 469K
SALES (corp-wide): 5.4B **Publicly Held**
WEB: www.sundownlighting.com
SIC: 7349 Lighting maintenance service
HQ: Abm Facility Solutions Group, Llc
    1201 Louisiana St
    Houston TX 77002
    832 214-5500

(P-14169)
ABM FACILITY SERVICES INC (DH)
Also Called: ABM Engineering
1266 14th St Ste 103, Oakland (94607-2205)
PHONE............................510 251-0381
Mike Latham, *CEO*
J E Benton III, *President*
Cornel Sneekes, *Exec VP*
George Sundby, *Senior VP*
Michael Hennessy, *Finance Dir*
EMP: 100
SALES (est): 60.5MM
SALES (corp-wide): 5.4B **Publicly Held**
SIC: 7349 Building maintenance services

(P-14170)
ABM INDUSTRIES INCORPORATED
5300 S Eastrn Ave Ste 110, Los Angeles (90040)
PHONE............................323 720-4020
Aide Jimenez, *Area Spvr*
Juleng Seng, *Accountant*
Jose Ferreras, *Manager*
Maria Franco, *Manager*
Mark Harrison, *Manager*
EMP: 50
SALES (corp-wide): 5.4B **Publicly Held**
SIC: 7349 Janitorial service, contract basis
PA: Abm Industries Incorporated
    1 Liberty Plz Fl 7
    New York NY 10006
    212 297-0200

(P-14171)
ABM JANITORIAL SERVICES INC
1335 N Plaza Dr Ste C, Visalia (93291-8838)
PHONE............................559 651-1612
Tony Bautista, *Branch Mgr*
EMP: 90
SALES (corp-wide): 5.4B **Publicly Held**
SIC: 7349 Janitorial service, contract basis
HQ: Abm Janitorial Services, Inc.
    1111 Fannin St Ste 1500
    Houston TX 77002
    713 654-8924

(P-14172)
ABM JANITORIAL SERVICES INC
4747 N Bendel Ave Ste 104, Fresno (93722-3962)
PHONE............................559 276-9096
Tony Bautista, *Manager*
EMP: 325
SALES (corp-wide): 5.4B **Publicly Held**
SIC: 7349 Janitorial service, contract basis
HQ: Abm Janitorial Services, Inc.
    1111 Fannin St Ste 1500
    Houston TX 77002
    713 654-8924

(P-14173)
ABM JANITORIAL SERVICES INC
6671 Owens Dr, Pleasanton (94588-3335)
PHONE............................925 924-0270
Greg Bu Puis, *Manager*
David Roe, *Vice Pres*

EMP: 267
SALES (corp-wide): 5.4B **Publicly Held**
SIC: 7349 Cleaning service, industrial or commercial
HQ: Abm Janitorial Services, Inc.
    1111 Fannin St Ste 1500
    Houston TX 77002
    713 654-8924

(P-14174)
ABM JANITORIAL SERVICES INC
830 Riverside Pkwy Ste 40, West Sacramento (95605-1505)
PHONE............................916 374-1739
Sean Petone, *Manager*
EMP: 320
SALES (corp-wide): 5.4B **Publicly Held**
SIC: 7349 Janitorial service, contract basis
HQ: Abm Janitorial Services, Inc.
    1111 Fannin St Ste 1500
    Houston TX 77002
    713 654-8924

(P-14175)
ABM JANITORIAL SERVICES INC
11955 Jack Benny Dr # 104, Rancho Cucamonga (91739-9230)
PHONE............................909 987-3700
Linda Mason, *District Mgr*
EMP: 105
SALES (corp-wide): 5.4B **Publicly Held**
SIC: 7349 Janitorial service, contract basis
HQ: Abm Janitorial Services, Inc.
    1111 Fannin St Ste 1500
    Houston TX 77002
    713 654-8924

(P-14176)
ABM JANITORIAL SERVICES INC
2385 Arch Airport Rd # 100, Stockton (95206-4404)
PHONE............................209 983-3923
Tony McGrat, *Manager*
Tony McGrath, *Branch Mgr*
EMP: 105
SALES (corp-wide): 5.4B **Publicly Held**
SIC: 7349 Janitorial service, contract basis
HQ: Abm Janitorial Services, Inc.
    1111 Fannin St Ste 1500
    Houston TX 77002
    713 654-8924

(P-14177)
ACCELERATED ENVMTL SVCS INC
23601 Taft Hwy, Bakersfield (93311)
P.O. Box 398, Taft (93268-0398)
PHONE............................661 765-4003
John E Neumann, *President*
EMP: 100
SQ FT: 25,440
SALES (est): 4.2MM **Privately Held**
SIC: 7349 Cleaning service, industrial or commercial

(P-14178)
ACCENT SERVICE COMPANY INC
2001 Lemnos Dr, Costa Mesa (92626-3535)
P.O. Box 9495, Newport Beach (92658-9495)
PHONE............................877 611-0131
Dan Yasui, *President*
EMP: 99
SQ FT: 200
SALES (est): 6MM **Privately Held**
WEB: www.accentsc.com
SIC: 7349 Building maintenance services

(P-14179)
ACME BUILDING MAINTENANCE CO (DH)
941 Catherine St, Alviso (95002)
PHONE............................408 263-5911
Richard Sanchez, *President*
Henry Sanchez, *Ch of Bd*
Solomon Wong, *Treasurer*
EMP: 80
SQ FT: 8,000

SALES (est): 25.7MM
SALES (corp-wide): 5.4B **Publicly Held**
SIC: 7349 Janitorial service, contract basis; building component cleaning service
HQ: Gca Services Group, Inc.
    1350 Euclid Ave Ste 1500
    Cleveland OH 44115
    800 422-8760

(P-14180)
ADHEI ENTERPRISES INC
Also Called: Knudtson Building Maint Svc
4627 Lemona Ave, Sherman Oaks (91403-2428)
PHONE............................818 788-7680
Jacqueline Campbell, *President*
Dayna Campbell, *Principal*
EMP: 50 **EST:** 1962
SALES (est): 1.2MM **Privately Held**
SIC: 7349 Janitorial service, contract basis

(P-14181)
ADVANCE BUILDING MAINTENANCE
9601 Wilshire Blvd Gl25, Beverly Hills (90210-5217)
PHONE............................310 247-0077
Forrest J Nolin, *President*
EMP: 500
SALES (est): 8.9MM **Privately Held**
WEB: www.advancemaintenance.com
SIC: 7349 Janitorial service, contract basis

(P-14182)
ADVANCED CLNROOM MCRCLEAN CORP
Also Called: A C M
3250 S Susan St Ste A, Santa Ana (92704-6807)
PHONE............................714 751-1152
Janet Ford, *CEO*
Jeff Stromberg, *CFO*
Brian Enright, *General Mgr*
Jennifer Nichols, *Supervisor*
EMP: 200
SQ FT: 3,500
SALES (est): 8.8MM **Privately Held**
WEB: www.advcleanroom.com
SIC: 7349 8734 Cleaning service, industrial or commercial; testing laboratories

(P-14183)
AESTHETIC MAINTENANCE CORP
Also Called: AMC
1625 Palo Alto St Ste 301, Los Angeles (90026)
PHONE............................213 353-1525
Curtiss Pierose, *President*
EMP: 50
SQ FT: 1,000
SALES (est): 1.9MM **Privately Held**
SIC: 7349 Janitorial service, contract basis

(P-14184)
ALL CARE INDUSTRIES INC
16747 1/2 Parkside Ave, Cerritos (90703-1840)
PHONE............................562 623-4009
Christopher Kim, *President*
Charles Lee, *Vice Pres*
EMP: 100
SALES: 1.7MM **Privately Held**
SIC: 7349 Janitorial service, contract basis

(P-14185)
ALL CONTROL CLEANING INC
124 N Aviador St Ste 1, Camarillo (93010-8321)
P.O. Box 341, Newbury Park (91319-0341)
PHONE............................805 987-4210
Lee Parrilla, *President*
Syeda Parrilla, *Admin Sec*
EMP: 52
SQ FT: 5,000
SALES (est): 1.5MM **Privately Held**
SIC: 7349 Building maintenance services

(P-14186)
ALL-RITE LEASING COMPANY INC
950 S Coast Dr Ste 110, Costa Mesa (92626-1778)
PHONE............................714 530-7074

Chris Schran, *President*
Pauline Rosenberg, *Corp Secy*
EMP: 269
SALES (est): 5.9MM **Privately Held**
SIC: 7349 Building maintenance services

(P-14187)
ALLSTATE BUILDING MAINTENANCE
4890 Saint Andrews Ave, Buena Park (90621-1072)
P.O. Box 3144, La Habra (90632-3144)
PHONE............................714 739-8080
Mike Ko, *Owner*
EMP: 100
SQ FT: 3,000
SALES (est): 1.4MM **Privately Held**
SIC: 7349 Building maintenance services

(P-14188)
AMERI-KLEEN
Also Called: Ameri-Kleen Building Services
313 W Beach St, Watsonville (95076-4508)
P.O. Box 2167 (95077-2167)
PHONE............................831 722-8888
Marisol Tavera, *Branch Mgr*
EMP: 450 **Privately Held**
SIC: 7349 Building maintenance services
PA: Ameri-Kleen
    119 W Beach St
    Watsonville CA 95076

(P-14189)
AMERI-KLEEN
Also Called: Ameri-Kleen Building Services
1023 E Grand Ave, Arroyo Grande (93420-2504)
PHONE............................805 546-0706
Dan Erpenbach, *Branch Mgr*
EMP: 250 **Privately Held**
SIC: 7349 Janitorial service, contract basis
PA: Ameri-Kleen
    119 W Beach St
    Watsonville CA 95076

(P-14190)
AMERICAN BLDG MAINT CO OF ILL
44870 Osgood Rd, Fremont (94539-6101)
PHONE............................510 573-1618
EMP: 50
SALES (corp-wide): 5.4B **Publicly Held**
SIC: 7349 Building maintenance services
HQ: American Building Maintenance Co Of Illinois, Inc
    420 Taylor St 200
    San Francisco CA 94102
    415 351-4386

(P-14191)
AMERICAN BLDG MAINT CO-WEST (HQ)
75 Broadway Ste 111, San Francisco (94111-1423)
PHONE............................415 733-4000
Henrik Slipsager, *President*
Douglas Bowlus, *Treasurer*
Harry H Kahn, *Admin Sec*
EMP: 150
SALES (est): 27.6MM
SALES (corp-wide): 5.4B **Publicly Held**
SIC: 7349 Janitorial service, contract basis
PA: Abm Industries Incorporated
    1 Liberty Plz Fl 7
    New York NY 10006
    212 297-0200

(P-14192)
AMERICAN BUILDING MAINT CO NY
101 California St, San Francisco (94111-5802)
PHONE............................415 733-4000
Henrik Slipsager, *President*
Dougles Bowlus, *Treasurer*
Scott Salmirs, *Exec VP*
EMP: 4530
SALES (est): 31.7MM
SALES (corp-wide): 5.4B **Publicly Held**
SIC: 7349 Janitorial service, contract basis

PA: Abm Industries Incorporated
1 Liberty Plz Fl 7
New York NY 10006
212 297-0200

(P-14193)
AMERICAN BUILDING SERVICE INC
4578 Crow Canyon Pl, Castro Valley
(94552-4804)
P.O. Box 32, San Leandro (94577-0003)
PHONE....................510 483-5120
Rui Donaldo Teixeira Canha, *President*
EMP: 100
SALES (est): 3.2MM **Privately Held**
SIC: 7349 Janitorial service, contract basis

(P-14194)
AMERICAN SERVICES AND PRODUCTS
Also Called: American Janitor Services
949 Camino Dos Rios, Thousand Oaks
(91360-2360)
PHONE....................805 375-2858
Dorothy Clemen, *President*
Mel Clemen, *Vice Pres*
Ron Clemen, *Admin Sec*
EMP: 60
SQ FT: 800
SALES: 1.2MM **Privately Held**
WEB: www.greenstoyotadirect.com
SIC: 7349 Janitorial service, contract basis

(P-14195)
ANDOVER MAINTENANCE INC
Also Called: Specialty Services
45 La Porte St, Arcadia (91006-2826)
PHONE....................626 254-1651
Daniel Tellez, *President*
Peter Richards, *Vice Pres*
Felix Morales, *Manager*
EMP: 73
SQ FT: 3,500
SALES (est): 3MM **Privately Held**
SIC: 7349 Janitorial service, contract basis

(P-14196)
AQUACLEAN JANITORIAL
9403 Compass Point Dr S, San Diego
(92126-5536)
P.O. Box 722557 (92172-2557)
PHONE....................858 537-9090
Amir B Chaudri, *President*
EMP: 65
SALES (est): 861.7K **Privately Held**
SIC: 7349 Building maintenance services

(P-14197)
ARAMARK FACILITY SERVICES LLC
941 W 35th St, Los Angeles (90007-4002)
PHONE....................213 740-8968
Ron Cote, *Manager*
EMP: 200 **Publicly Held**
SIC: 7349 Janitorial service, contract basis
HQ: Aramark Facility Services, Llc
1101 Market St
Philadelphia PA 19107
215 238-3000

(P-14198)
ARAMARK FACILITY SERVICES LLC
5301 Bolsa Ave Bldg 10, Huntington Beach
(92647-2048)
PHONE....................714 372-0683
Christopher Olsen-Bates, *Manager*
EMP: 50 **Publicly Held**
SIC: 7349 Janitorial service, contract
basis; building maintenance, except repairs
HQ: Aramark Facility Services, Llc
1101 Market St
Philadelphia PA 19107
215 238-3000

(P-14199)
AVALON BUILDING MAINTENANCE (PA)
3148 E La Palma Ave Ste A, Anaheim
(92806-2805)
PHONE....................714 693-2407
Steve J Healis, *CEO*
Tom Poston, *CFO*
Tom Devlin, *Admin Sec*

EMP: 220
SQ FT: 5,000
SALES (est): 8.5MM **Privately Held**
WEB: www.avaloncorona.com
SIC: 7349 Building maintenance services

(P-14200)
BERGENSONS PROPERTY SVCS INC
Also Called: Solve All Facility Services
3605 Ocean Ranch Blvd # 200, Oceanside
(92056-2695)
PHONE....................760 631-5111
Mark M Minasian, *CEO*
Kris McDevitt, *President*
Aram Minasian, *President*
Jay Garcia, *Exec VP*
James Henley, *Exec VP*
EMP: 2000
SQ FT: 2,000
SALES (est): 52.1MM **Privately Held**
WEB: www.bergensons.com
SIC: 7349 Building maintenance, except
repairs; janitorial service, contract basis

(P-14201)
BILLING SERVICES PLUS DBA APEX
70 Dorman Ave, San Francisco
(94124-1809)
PHONE....................415 604-3515
Gina Gregori, *Principal*
EMP: 99
SQ FT: 300
SALES (est): 470.9K **Privately Held**
SIC: 7349 Building & office cleaning serv-
ices; building cleaning service

(P-14202)
BISSELL BROTHERS JANITORIAL
Also Called: Bissell Bros Bldg Maint Servic
3207 Luyung Dr, Rancho Cordova
(95742-6862)
PHONE....................916 635-1852
David Bissell, *CEO*
EMP: 80
SQ FT: 2,400
SALES (est): 2.3MM **Privately Held**
WEB: www.cleaningcrew.com
SIC: 7349 Janitorial service, contract basis

(P-14203)
BRILLIANT GENERAL MAINTNC
Also Called: Bgm
954 Chestnut St, San Jose (95110-1504)
PHONE....................408 287-6708
Daniel Montes, *CEO*
Joel Sanchez, *CFO*
Eleuterio Pacheco, *Opers Mgr*
Daniel H Montes, *Marketing Staff*
Alberto Delgadillo, *Accounts Mgr*
EMP: 200
SQ FT: 6,000
SALES (est): 8.3MM **Privately Held**
SIC: 7349 Building maintenance, except
repairs; janitorial service, contract basis

(P-14204)
BRITEWORKS INC
620 N Commercial Ave, Covina
(91723-1309)
PHONE....................626 337-0099
Anita Ron, *President*
Gracie Corona, *Office Mgr*
EMP: 75
SQ FT: 4,800
SALES (est): 2.8MM **Privately Held**
WEB: www.briteworks.com
SIC: 7349 Janitorial service, contract basis

(P-14205)
C E B M INC
3100 E Cedar St Ste 17, Ontario
(91761-7695)
PHONE....................909 975-4440
William Dazalla, *President*
Robert Dazalla, *Vice Pres*
EMP: 50
SQ FT: 2,000
SALES (est): 1.2MM **Privately Held**
WEB: www.cebm.net
SIC: 7349 Janitorial service, contract basis

(P-14206)
CALDERON BUILDING MAINTENANCE
3822 Sherman St, San Diego (92110-4322)
P.O. Box 3550 (92163-1550)
PHONE....................619 269-5940
Andres J Calderon, *President*
Maria Calderon, *Admin Sec*
EMP: 90
SALES (est): 3.3MM **Privately Held**
WEB: www.calderoninc.com
SIC: 7349 Building maintenance services

(P-14207)
CALICO BUILDING SERVICES INC
15550 Rockfield Blvd C, Irvine
(92618-2791)
PHONE....................949 380-8707
Ron Strand, *President*
Orlando Fernandez, *Vice Pres*
Christopher Guidry, *Vice Pres*
Thomas Miquelon, *Vice Pres*
Rhyan Strand, *Admin Asst*
EMP: 185
SQ FT: 1,700
SALES (est): 9MM **Privately Held**
WEB: www.calicoweb.com
SIC: 7349 Janitorial service, contract basis

(P-14208)
CARRASCO HELEO
Also Called: Building Cleaning Systems
2510 N Grand Ave Ste 102, Santa Ana
(92705-8753)
PHONE....................714 639-1759
Heleo Carrasco, *President*
EMP: 130
SALES (est): 4.5MM **Privately Held**
WEB: www.buildingcleaningsystems.com
SIC: 7349 Janitorial service, contract basis

(P-14209)
CENTURY CONTRACT SERVICES INC
15815 Camino Codorniz, San Diego
(92127-5825)
P.O. Box 270589 (92198-2589)
PHONE....................858 672-4118
Edmund Rhee, *President*
EMP: 125
SQ FT: 3,000
SALES (est): 3.4MM **Privately Held**
SIC: 7349 Janitorial service, contract basis

(P-14210)
CITY OF LOS ANGELES
Also Called: General Services
3330 W 36th St, Los Angeles (90018-3610)
PHONE....................213 847-2799
Melody McCormick, *Branch Mgr*
EMP: 60 **Privately Held**
WEB: www.lacity.org
SIC: 7349 9611 Building maintenance
services; administration of general eco-
nomic programs
PA: City Of Los Angeles
200 N Spring St Ste 303
Los Angeles CA 90012
213 978-0600

(P-14211)
CITY OF PALMDALE
Also Called: Public Works Dept
39101 3rd St E, Palmdale (93550-3209)
PHONE....................661 267-5338
Gene Trevail, *Superintendent*
EMP: 135 **Privately Held**
SIC: 7349 9111 Building maintenance
services; mayors' offices
PA: City Of Palmdale
38300 Sierra Hwy
Palmdale CA 93550
661 267-5115

(P-14212)
CITY OF PASADENA
Also Called: Mayor Office
117 E Colorado Blvd, Pasadena
(91105-1938)
PHONE....................626 744-4311
Bill Bogaard, *Mayor*
EMP: 70 **Privately Held**
WEB: www.cityofpasadena.net

SIC: 7349 9111 Building maintenance
services; mayors' offices
PA: City Of Pasadena
100 N Garfield Ave
Pasadena CA 91101
626 744-4386

(P-14213)
CITY OF SALINAS
426 Work St, Salinas (93901-4308)
PHONE....................831 758-7233
Denise Estrada, *Director*
EMP: 89 **Privately Held**
WEB: www.co.monterey.ca.us
SIC: 7349 9224 Building maintenance
services; fire department, not including
volunteer
PA: City Of Salinas
200 Lincoln Ave
Salinas CA 93901
831 758-7489

(P-14214)
CITY OF SAN MATEO
Also Called: Corporate Yard
1949 Pacific Blvd, San Mateo
(94403-1430)
PHONE....................650 522-7300
Vernon Ficklind, *Manager*
EMP: 60 **Privately Held**
WEB: www.cityarts-sm.org
SIC: 7349 9111 Building maintenance
services; mayors' offices
PA: City Of San Mateo
330 W 20th Ave
San Mateo CA 94403
650 522-7000

(P-14215)
CJ MODEL HOME MAINTENANCE INC
240 Spring St, Pleasanton (94566-6626)
P.O. Box 5547 (94566-1547)
PHONE....................925 485-3280
Carrie Wevill, *President*
Richard Wevill, *Admin Sec*
EMP: 70
SQ FT: 2,200
SALES (est): 4.5MM **Privately Held**
WEB: www.cjsmodelhome.com
SIC: 7349 Building component cleaning
service

(P-14216)
CLARK BOOKER T (PA)
Also Called: First Building Maintenance
1569 Solano Ave, Berkeley (94707-2116)
P.O. Box 10947, Oakland (94610-0947)
PHONE....................510 482-8900
Booker T Clark, *Owner*
EMP: 50
SALES (est): 1.3MM **Privately Held**
WEB: www.1stmaint.com
SIC: 7349 4959 Janitorial service, contract
basis; sweeping service: road, airport,
parking lot, etc.

(P-14217)
CLEAN ENVIROMENT
4570 Alvarado Canyon Rd C, San Diego
(92120-4317)
PHONE....................619 521-0543
Steve G Ottman, *Owner*
Gloria Fernandes, *Admin Sec*
EMP: 60
SALES (est): 1.4MM **Privately Held**
SIC: 7349 Janitorial service, contract basis

(P-14218)
CLEAN-A-RAMA MAINT SVC LLC
526 Columbus Ave Fl 2, San Francisco
(94133-2802)
PHONE....................415 495-5298
Giuseppe Marchini,
Marcello Sebastiani,
EMP: 60
SQ FT: 800
SALES (est): 1.3MM **Privately Held**
SIC: 7349 Janitorial service, contract basis

▲ = Import ▼=Export
◆ =Import/Export

(P-14219)
COAST TO COAST WATER DAMAGE
Also Called: Coast To Coast Restoration
10881 La Tuna Canyon Rd, Sun Valley
(91352-2010)
PHONE...............................818 255-3323
Hayko Aldzhikyan, *President*
Marina Demirchyan, *Vice Pres*
EMP: 50
SQ FT: 9,000
SALES (est): 1.4MM **Privately Held**
WEB: www.c2crestoration.com
SIC: 7349 Building maintenance services

(P-14220)
COASTAL BUILDING SERVICES INC
718 N Hariton St, Orange (92868-1314)
PHONE...............................714 775-2855
Hipolito G Arias, *CEO*
Brett Dunstan, *CFO*
Lupe Godinez, *Admin Sec*
Alberto Melendez, *Opers Staff*
Rafael Perez, *Manager*
EMP: 300
SQ FT: 5,300
SALES (est): 8.9MM **Privately Held**
WEB: www.coastalbuildingservice.com
SIC: 7349 Janitorial service, contract basis

(P-14221)
COBB WATERBLASTING INC
Also Called: Cobb Property Services
1145 W Shelley Ct, Orange (92868-1200)
PHONE...............................714 769-2622
Mark Cobb, *President*
Dorothy Cobb, *Vice Pres*
William Roche, *Admin Sec*
EMP: 82 **EST:** 1989
SALES (est): 2.5MM **Privately Held**
SIC: 7349 Building cleaning service

(P-14222)
COME LAND MAINT SVC CO INC
1419 N San Fernando Blvd # 250, Burbank
(91504-4185)
PHONE...............................818 567-2455
Grace H Lee, *President*
William Lee, *Admin Sec*
EMP: 513
SQ FT: 12,750
SALES (est): 8.7MM
SALES (corp-wide): 4MM **Privately Held**
SIC: 7349 Janitorial service, contract basis
PA: Come Land, Inc.
1419 N San Fernando Blvd # 250
Burbank CA 91504
818 567-2455

(P-14223)
COMMON AREA MAINT SVCS INC (PA)
Also Called: CAM Services
5664 Selmaraine Dr, Culver City
(90230-6120)
PHONE...............................310 390-3552
Jim Swindle, *CEO*
David A Herrera, *President*
Sidney Young, *Principal*
Jonathan Arias, *Area Mgr*
Gardy Brill, *Manager*
EMP: 79
SQ FT: 4,000
SALES (est): 13MM **Privately Held**
WEB: www.camservices.com
SIC: 7349 Building maintenance, except repairs

(P-14224)
CONSOLIDATED CLEANING SERVICES
6353 Westover Dr, Oakland (94611-1603)
PHONE...............................510 663-2585
Joanne King, *President*
Michael Herling, *COO*
EMP: 100
SQ FT: 7,500
SALES (est): 3.4MM **Privately Held**
SIC: 7349 Building maintenance, except repairs; janitorial service, contract basis

(P-14225)
CONTRACT SERVICES GROUP INC
Also Called: Celex Solutions
480 Capricorn St, Brea (92821-3203)
P.O. Box 8815 (92822-5815)
PHONE...............................714 582-1800
John Pearce, *CEO*
Casey Pearce, *President*
EMP: 250
SALES (est): 9.6MM **Privately Held**
SIC: 7349 Janitorial service, contract basis

(P-14226)
CONTRLLED CNTMINATION SVCS LLC
Also Called: Controlled Contamination Svcs
6150 Lusk Blvd Ste B205, San Diego
(92121-2737)
PHONE...............................888 263-9886
Christopher Zines, *Mng Member*
Mark Cornish, *COO*
Eric Goldmann, *VP Sales*
Mike Zines,
Josh Bowman, *Manager*
EMP: 140
SQ FT: 2,000
SALES (est): 8.4MM **Privately Held**
SIC: 7349 Cleaning service, industrial or commercial

(P-14227)
CONTROLLED CONTAMINATION SVCS
Also Called: CCS
23595 Cabot Blvd Ste 115, Hayward
(94545-1681)
PHONE...............................510 728-1106
Brian Thaler, *Manager*
EMP: 66
SALES (est): 1.9MM **Privately Held**
SIC: 7349 Cleaning service, industrial or commercial

(P-14228)
CORPORATE BUILDING SVCS INC
3325 Wilshire Blvd # 1240, Los Angeles
(90010-1728)
PHONE...............................213 252-0999
Bruce Kim, *President*
Cindy Kim, *Admin Sec*
EMP: 200
SQ FT: 2,000
SALES: 3.5MM **Privately Held**
SIC: 7349 Janitorial service, contract basis

(P-14229)
CORPORATION SERVICE COMPANY
Also Called: Prentice Hall Legal Fincl Svcs
2710 Gateway Oaks Dr, Sacramento
(95833-3505)
PHONE...............................302 636-5400
Mark Sanchez, *Software Dev*
EMP: 100
SQ FT: 12,000
SALES (corp-wide): 439MM **Privately Held**
WEB: www.incspot.com
SIC: 7349 Building maintenance services
PA: Corporation Service Company Inc
251 Little Falls Dr
Wilmington DE 19808
302 636-5400

(P-14230)
COSTLESS MAINTENANCE SVCS CO
Also Called: Cmsc
3254 19th St, San Francisco (94110-1917)
PHONE...............................415 550-8819
Marlene Samson, *President*
Norma Edar, *Officer*
Guillermo Guzman, *Vice Pres*
EMP: 55
SALES: 1.8MM **Privately Held**
SIC: 7349 Janitorial service, contract basis

(P-14231)
COUNTY OF CONTRA COSTA
Also Called: General Services
2099 Arnold Industrial Wa, Concord
(94520-5321)
PHONE...............................925 646-5877
Jerry Redic, *Manager*
EMP: 100 **Privately Held**
SIC: 7349 9199 Building maintenance services; general government administration;
PA: County Of Contra Costa
625 Court St Ste 100
Martinez CA 94553
925 957-5280

(P-14232)
COUNTY OF CONTRA COSTA
Also Called: General Services
2467 Waterbird Way, Martinez
(94553-1457)
PHONE...............................925 313-7052
Roland Hindsman, *Manager*
EMP: 100 **Privately Held**
SIC: 7349 9199 Building maintenance services; general government administration;
PA: County Of Contra Costa
625 Court St Ste 100
Martinez CA 94553
925 957-5280

(P-14233)
COUNTY OF EL DORADO
El Dorado Cnty Bldg & Grounds
3000 Fairlane Ct Ste 2, Placerville
(95667-4100)
PHONE...............................530 621-5845
Bruce Pease, *Manager*
EMP: 76 **Privately Held**
WEB: www.filmtahoe.com
SIC: 7349 9111 Building maintenance services; executive offices
PA: County Of El Dorado
330 Fair Ln
Placerville CA 95667
530 621-5830

(P-14234)
COUNTY OF SACRAMENTO
Also Called: Airfield Maintenance
7207 Earhart Dr, Sacramento (95837-1104)
PHONE...............................916 874-0746
Terry Sutton, *Branch Mgr*
EMP: 80 **Privately Held**
WEB: www.sna.com
SIC: 7349 9311 Building maintenance services;
PA: County Of Sacramento
700 H St Ste 7650
Sacramento CA 95814
916 874-5544

(P-14235)
CREATIVE MAINTENANCE SYSTEMS
1340 Reynolds Ave Ste 111, Irvine
(92614-5503)
PHONE...............................949 852-2871
Bill Koop, *President*
Christina Alexander, *Vice Pres*
EMP: 100
SQ FT: 2,000
SALES (est): 2.3MM **Privately Held**
SIC: 7349 Building cleaning service

(P-14236)
CROSSROADS FACILITY SVCS INC
9300 Tech Center Dr # 100, Sacramento
(95826-2565)
PHONE...............................916 568-5230
David Deleonardis, *President*
Bill Walters, *Corp Secy*
EMP: 57
SQ FT: 5,700
SALES (est): 1MM **Privately Held**
SIC: 7349 1752 0781 Janitorial service, contract basis; wood floor installation & refinishing; landscape services

(P-14237)
CROWN BUILDING MAINTENANCE CO
1832 Tribute Rd Ste H, Sacramento
(95815-4309)
PHONE...............................916 920-9556
Jeff Marquis, *Principal*
EMP: 1111
SALES (corp-wide): 327.3MM **Privately Held**
SIC: 7349 1623 Building maintenance services; water, sewer & utility lines
PA: Crown Building Maintenance Co.
868 Folsom St
San Francisco CA 94107
415 981-8070

(P-14238)
CROWN BUILDING MAINTENANCE CO
Also Called: Able Building Maintenance
3300 W Macarthur Blvd, Santa Ana
(92704-6804)
PHONE...............................714 434-9494
Robert Hughes, *CEO*
EMP: 50
SALES (corp-wide): 327.3MM **Privately Held**
SIC: 7349 Janitorial service, contract basis
PA: Crown Building Maintenance Co.
868 Folsom St
San Francisco CA 94107
415 981-8070

(P-14239)
CROWN BUILDING MAINTENANCE CO
235 Pine St Ste 600, San Francisco
(94104-2745)
PHONE...............................303 680-3713
Dan Jaster, *Branch Mgr*
EMP: 494
SALES (corp-wide): 327.3MM **Privately Held**
SIC: 7349 8711 Janitorial service, contract basis; engineering services
PA: Crown Building Maintenance Co.
868 Folsom St
San Francisco CA 94107
415 981-8070

(P-14240)
CROWN BUILDING MAINTENANCE CO
5482 Complex St Ste 108, San Diego
(92123-1125)
PHONE...............................858 560-5785
Dan Jaster, *Branch Mgr*
EMP: 247
SALES (corp-wide): 327.3MM **Privately Held**
SIC: 7349 8711 Janitorial service, contract basis; engineering services
PA: Crown Building Maintenance Co.
868 Folsom St
San Francisco CA 94107
415 981-8070

(P-14241)
CROWN BUILDING MAINTENANCE CO
Also Called: Able Building Maintenance
2601 S Figueroa St # 299, Los Angeles
(90007-3254)
PHONE...............................213 765-7800
Brian Pagac, *Principal*
EMP: 50
SALES (corp-wide): 327.3MM **Privately Held**
WEB: www.ableserve.com
SIC: 7349 8711 Janitorial service, contract basis; engineering services
PA: Crown Building Maintenance Co.
868 Folsom St
San Francisco CA 94107
415 981-8070

(P-14242)
CROWN ENERGY SERVICES INC
Also Called: Able Engineering Services
2601 S Figueroa St Fl 1, Los Angeles
(90007-3254)
PHONE...............................213 765-7800

P
R
O
D
U
C
T
S

&

S
V
C
S

Ed Figueroa, *Manager*
EMP: 800 Privately Held
SIC: 7349 Building maintenance services
PA: Crown Energy Services, Inc.
868 Folsom St
San Francisco CA 94107
-

(P-14243)
CROWN FACILITY SOLUTIONS
3617 W Macarthur Blvd, Santa Ana
(92704-6847)
PHONE..................657 266-0821
Brent Shears, *President*
EMP: 50
SQ FT: 1,950
SALES: 1.2MM **Privately Held**
SIC: 7349 Building maintenance, except
repairs; janitorial service, contract basis

(P-14244)
CULVER-MELIN ENTERPRISES
Also Called: ServiceMaster
2150 Wardrobe Ave, Merced (95341-6400)
P.O. Box 2192 (95344-0192)
PHONE..................209 726-9182
David Melin, *President*
EMP: 70
SALES (est): 2.7MM **Privately Held**
SIC: 7349 Building maintenance services

(P-14245)
CUSHMAN & WAKEFIELD INC
800 W El Camino Real, Mountain View
(94040-2567)
PHONE..................408 664-5403
EMP: 131
SALES (corp-wide): 5.7B **Privately Held**
SIC: 7349 Janitorial service, contract basis
HQ: Cushman & Wakefield, Inc.
225 W Wacker Dr Ste 3000
Chicago IL 60606
312 424-8000

(P-14246)
CUSTOMIZED PERFORMANCE INC
780 Montague Expy Ste 201, San Jose
(95131-1316)
PHONE..................408 437-1720
Norberto Velez, *President*
EMP: 200
SQ FT: 5,000
SALES (est): 4.4MM **Privately Held**
WEB: www.customizedperformance.com
SIC: 7349 Janitorial service, contract basis

(P-14247)
D S P SERVICE INC
Also Called: D S P Janitorial Service
23762 Foley St Ste 3, Hayward
(94545-1662)
PHONE..................510 782-2200
Don Wallace, *President*
Dawn Wallace, *Corp Secy*
Gloria Wallace, *Vice Pres*
EMP: 50
SQ FT: 2,000
SALES: 1MM **Privately Held**
WEB: www.dspjanitorial.com
SIC: 7349 Janitorial service, contract basis

(P-14248)
DAN LOFGREN
Also Called: Central Cleaning Co
7707 Forsythia Ct, Pleasanton
(94588-4818)
PHONE..................925 846-6632
Dan Lofgren, *Owner*
EMP: 60
SALES: 1.5MM **Privately Held**
SIC: 7349 Building maintenance services

(P-14249)
DANISH ENVIRONMENT INC
9424 Eton Ave Ste G, Chatsworth
(91311-6936)
PHONE..................818 992-6722
Jens Grau, *President*
EMP: 70
SALES (est): 1.1MM **Privately Held**
WEB: www.danishenvironment.com
SIC: 7349 Janitorial service, contract basis

(P-14250)
DANLIL ENTERPRISE INC
Also Called: Sterling Building Services
1440 S State College Blvd, Anaheim
(92806-5724)
PHONE..................714 776-7705
Dan Rubio, *President*
EMP: 75
SQ FT: 2,000
SALES: 2.5MM **Privately Held**
WEB: www.jabezbs.com
SIC: 7349 Janitorial service, contract basis

(P-14251)
DAVE CALHOUN AND ASSOC LLC (PA)
2575 Stanwell Dr Ste 100, Concord
(94520-4838)
PHONE..................925 688-1234
Sam Martinovich, *CEO*
Dave Calhoun, *President*
Nick Van Lone, *Division Mgr*
Jesse Cunha, *Accounts Exec*
Robanne Olson, *Accounts Exec*
EMP: 195
SALES (est): 8.2MM **Privately Held**
WEB: www.bsminc.com
SIC: 7349 Building cleaning service

(P-14252)
DELTA TECH SERVICE INC (PA)
397 W Channel Rd, Benicia (94510-1117)
PHONE..................707 745-2080
Curtis S Johnson, *President*
G Leslie Johnson, *Shareholder*
Greg Niemuth, *CFO*
Karna Davis, *Vice Pres*
Matthew Webb, *General Mgr*
EMP: 75
SQ FT: 6,000
SALES: 24MM **Privately Held**
WEB: www.deltatechservice.com
SIC: 7349 Cleaning service, industrial or
commercial; chemical cleaning services

(P-14253)
DMS FACILITY SERVICES INC
Also Called: D M S
3137 Skyway Ct, Fremont (94539-5910)
PHONE..................510 656-9400
Loren Dotts, *Manager*
EMP: 800
SALES (corp-wide): 60.6MM **Privately Held**
WEB: www.dms-services.com
SIC: 7349 0782 Building maintenance, ex-
cept repairs; lawn & garden services
PA: Dms Facility Services, Inc.
1040 Arroyo Dr
South Pasadena CA 91030
626 305-8500

(P-14254)
DYNAMIC MAINTENANCE SVCS INC
837 Arnold Dr Ste 220, Martinez
(94553-6534)
PHONE..................925 228-7434
Arturo Ramos, *President*
Sue Moore, *CFO*
Susan K Moore, *CFO*
Violet Ramos, *Corp Secy*
Maria L Ramos, *Vice Pres*
EMP: 52 **EST:** 2006
SQ FT: 536
SALES: 1.8MM **Privately Held**
SIC: 7349 Janitorial service, contract basis

(P-14255)
EBM JANITORIAL SERVICES INC
Also Called: Excellent Building Maintenance
5260 Bonsai Ave Ste E, Moorpark
(93021-1768)
P.O. Box 204, Newbury Park (91319-0204)
PHONE..................805 523-3700
Matt Mullen, *President*
EMP: 70
SALES (est): 1.3MM **Privately Held**
SIC: 7349 Janitorial service, contract basis

(P-14256)
ELITE CRAFTSMAN (PA)
Also Called: Stockmar Industrial
2763 Saint Louis Ave, Long Beach
(90755-2025)
P.O. Box 90458 (90809-0458)
PHONE..................562 989-3511
William C Stockmar, *President*
George N Negrete, *Vice Pres*
Linda Pierson, *Admin Sec*
Linda S Pierson, *Admin Sec*
EMP: 130 **EST:** 1972
SQ FT: 10,000
SALES (est): 8.7MM **Privately Held**
SIC: 7349 Building maintenance services

(P-14257)
ELITE MAINTENANCE SERVICES INC
7770 Regents Rd Ste 113, San Diego
(92122-1967)
PHONE..................619 516-7000
Heidi Anderson, *President*
EMP: 55
SALES (est): 1.2MM **Privately Held**
SIC: 7349 Building cleaning service

(P-14258)
EMPIRE BUILDING SERVICES INC
1570 E Edinger Ave Ste D, Santa Ana
(92705-4909)
P.O. Box 26, Tustin (92781-0026)
PHONE..................714 836-7700
Suzanne De Rossett, *President*
Katie Doweling, *Admin Asst*
Karen Jimenez, *Admin Asst*
Mario Guevara, *Supervisor*
EMP: 80
SALES (est): 3.7MM **Privately Held**
SIC: 7349 Building cleaning service; janito-
rial service, contract basis

(P-14259)
ENVIRONMENT CONTROL
1849 N Helm Ave Ste 105, Fresno
(93727-1624)
PHONE..................559 456-9791
Dick Johns, *Partner*
Kit Seals, *Partner*
Patricia Cardenas, *Human Res Dir*
EMP: 50
SQ FT: 6,000
SALES (est): 1.2MM **Privately Held**
SIC: 7349 Janitorial service, contract basis

(P-14260)
EVERGREEN CLEANING SYSTEMS INC
3325 Wilshire Blvd # 622, Los Angeles
(90010-1747)
PHONE..................213 386-3260
John Lee, *President*
EMP: 50
SALES (est): 1.3MM **Privately Held**
SIC: 7349 Janitorial service, contract basis

(P-14261)
EXCEL BUILDING SERVICES LLC
1061 Serpentine Ln Ste H, Pleasanton
(94566-4793)
PHONE..................925 474-1080
Jennifer Fabrique, *CEO*
Jack Fabrique, *President*
Steve Sui, *CFO*
Scott Henley, *Exec VP*
Cindy Sui, *Accountant*
EMP: 1300 **EST:** 1998
SQ FT: 5,000
SALES (est): 50.7MM **Privately Held**
SIC: 7349 Janitorial service, contract basis

(P-14262)
FACILITY MASTERS INC (PA)
1604 Kerley Dr, San Jose (95112-4815)
PHONE..................408 436-9090
Ramsin Bitmansour, *CEO*
James Machado, *President*
Osvaldo Almeida, *Vice Pres*
EMP: 345
SQ FT: 7,000
SALES (est): 13.8MM **Privately Held**
SIC: 7349 Janitorial service, contract basis

(P-14263)
FAME SYSTEMS INC
301 Hearst Dr, Oxnard (93030-5158)
PHONE..................805 485-0808
Sal Mejia, *President*
Jesus Mejia, *Vice Pres*
Melina Mejia, *Manager*
EMP: 50
SALES: 2.5MM **Privately Held**
WEB: www.famesystems.com
SIC: 7349 Janitorial service, contract basis

(P-14264)
FIELDS CONSTRUCTION SERVICES
Also Called: Fields Win Clg Win Protection
5715 Southfront Rd Ste B1, Livermore
(94551-7807)
PHONE..................925 294-8183
Daniel Fields, *President*
EMP: 60
SALES (est): 1.5MM **Privately Held**
SIC: 7349 1799 Cleaning service, indus-
trial or commercial; coating, caulking &
weather, water & fireproofing

(P-14265)
FLAIR BUILDING SERVICES INC
Also Called: Flair Building Maintanance
3470 Edward Ave, Santa Clara
(95054-2130)
PHONE..................408 987-4040
Oscar Pena, *President*
Shirely McEvoy, *Treasurer*
EMP: 90
SQ FT: 2,400
SALES: 3.7MM **Privately Held**
SIC: 7349 Janitorial service, contract basis

(P-14266)
FLUOR FACILITY & PLANT SVCS
124 Blossom Hill Rd Ste H, San Jose
(95123-2397)
PHONE..................408 256-1333
Brett Heckel, *Finance*
EMP: 250
SALES (corp-wide): 19.5B **Publicly Held**
SIC: 7349 Building maintenance services
HQ: Fluor Facility & Plant Services, Inc
3 Polaris Way
Aliso Viejo CA
949 349-2000

(P-14267)
FLUOR INDUSTRIAL SERVICES INC
1 Enterprise, Aliso Viejo (92656-2606)
PHONE..................949 439-2000
David T Seaton, *CEO*
EMP: 1000 **EST:** 1986
SALES (est): 8.5MM
SALES (corp-wide): 19.5B **Publicly Held**
SIC: 7349 Building maintenance services
HQ: Fluor Enterprises, Inc.
6700 Las Colinas Blvd
Irving TX 75039
469 398-7000

(P-14268)
FOUNTAIN VALLEY SCHOOL DST
Also Called: South Valley School District
17330 Mount Herrmann St, Fountain Valley
(92708-4104)
PHONE..................714 668-5882
Joe Hastie, *Maint Spvr*
EMP: 75
SALES (corp-wide): 66.8MM **Privately Held**
SIC: 7349 Building maintenance services
PA: Fountain Valley School District
10055 Slater Ave
Fountain Valley CA 92708
714 668-5886

(P-14269)
FREMONT UNIFIED SCHOOL DST
43772 S Grimmer Blvd, Fremont
(94538-6308)
PHONE..................510 657-0761
Angel Castro, *Technology*
Susan Guerrero, *Education*
Anita Yepez, *Education*
Rebecca Kim, *Psychologist*

▲ = Import ▼=Export
◆ =Import/Export

Nina Lim, *Psychologist*
EMP: 73
SALES (corp-wide): 227.3MM **Privately Held**
SIC: 7349 Building maintenance services
PA: Fremont Unified School District
4210 Technology Dr
Fremont CA 94538
510 657-2350

(P-14270)
FRESNO UNIFIED SCHOOL DISTRICT
Also Called: Maintenance Department
4600 N Brawley Ave, Fresno (93722-3921)
PHONE...................................559 457-3074
Ron Tessada, *Director*
EMP: 170
SALES (corp-wide): 617.8MM **Privately Held**
WEB: www.fresno.k12.ca.us
SIC: 7349 Building maintenance services
PA: Fresno Unified School District
2309 Tulare St
Fresno CA 93721
559 457-3000

(P-14271)
GALAXY BUILDING SYSTEMS INC
23978 Craftsman Rd, Calabasas
(91302-1437)
PHONE...................................818 340-6557
Gerald C Baggett, *President*
EMP: 150 **EST:** 1968
SALES (est): 3.2MM **Privately Held**
WEB: www.galaxyservicesca.com
SIC: 7349 Janitorial service, contract basis

(P-14272)
GAMBOA SERVICE INC
Also Called: Corporate Image Maintenance
2116 S Wright St, Santa Ana (92705-5314)
PHONE...................................714 966-5325
Gilbert Gamboa, *President*
EMP: 55
SQ FT: 2,800
SALES (est): 2MM **Privately Held**
SIC: 7349 Janitorial service, contract basis

(P-14273)
GENERAL SERVICES CAL DEPT
9645 Butterfield Way # 1503, Sacramento
(95827-1501)
P.O. Box 277376 (95827-7376)
PHONE...................................916 845-4942
Jeff Henninger, *Director*
EMP: 120 **Privately Held**
WEB: www.4c.net
SIC: 7349 9199 Building maintenance services; general government administration;
HQ: California Department Of General Services
707 3rd St
West Sacramento CA 95605

(P-14274)
GENERAL SERVICES CAL DEPT
1304 O St Ste 301, Sacramento
(95814-5906)
PHONE...................................916 445-4566
Fred Lucy, *Principal*
EMP: 2000 **Privately Held**
WEB: www.4c.net
SIC: 7349 9199 Building maintenance services; general government administration;
HQ: California Department Of General Services
707 3rd St
West Sacramento CA 95605

(P-14275)
GENERAL SERVICES CAL DEPT
Also Called: Building and Property MGT BR
300 S Spring St Ste 1726, Los Angeles
(90013-1256)
PHONE...................................213 897-2241
Christopher Robles, *Regional Mgr*
EMP: 65 **Privately Held**
WEB: www.4c.net

SIC: 7349 9199 Building maintenance services; general government administration;
HQ: California Department Of General Services
707 3rd St
West Sacramento CA 95605

(P-14276)
GHOSSAIN & TRUELOCK ENTPS INC
Also Called: Custom Service Systems
783 Palmyrita Ave Ste A, Riverside
(92507-1817)
P.O. Box 5596 (92517-5596)
PHONE...................................951 781-9345
Kenneth Truelock, *President*
David L Truelock, *CEO*
Robert K Ghossain, *Bd of Directors*
Jayme Truelock, *Opers Mgr*
EMP: 80
SALES (est): 2.7MM **Privately Held**
WEB: www.cssclean.com
SIC: 7349 Janitorial service, contract basis

(P-14277)
GLEN ALPINE BUILDING SVCS INC
24685 Oneil Ave, Hayward (94544-1627)
P.O. Box 738 (94543-0738)
PHONE...................................510 582-7400
Janice Lynn Slade, *President*
EMP: 60
SALES: 1.8MM **Privately Held**
SIC: 7349 Janitorial service, contract basis

(P-14278)
GLENN BUILDING SERVICES INC
1148 N Lake Ave Apt 1, Pasadena
(91104-3729)
PHONE...................................626 398-8000
Christopher Garcia, *President*
Yvonne Pico, *Vice Pres*
EMP: 85
SALES: 600K **Privately Held**
SIC: 7349 Janitorial service, contract basis

(P-14279)
GLOBAL BUILDING SERVICES INC (PA)
25129 The Old Rd Ste 102, Stevenson Ranch (91381-2287)
PHONE...................................661 288-5733
Julio Belloso, *President*
Gabriel Torres, *Area Mgr*
Mike Lewis, *Supervisor*
EMP: 802
SALES (est): 37.3MM **Privately Held**
WEB: www.globalbuildingservices.com
SIC: 7349 Janitorial service, contract basis

(P-14280)
GMG JANITORIAL INC
70 Dorman Ave Ste 2, San Francisco
(94124-1809)
PHONE...................................415 642-2100
Gina Gregori, *President*
EMP: 220
SALES (est): 7.8MM **Privately Held**
SIC: 7349 Janitorial service, contract basis; building maintenance, except repairs

(P-14281)
GMI BUILDING SERVICES INC
8001 Vickers St, San Diego (92111-1917)
PHONE...................................858 279-6262
Larry Abrams, *President*
Alan Wagemester, *COO*
Nora Sinclair, *Financial Exec*
Michael Ibarra, *Accountant*
Dorothy Sorensen, *Human Res Mgr*
EMP: 225
SQ FT: 15,000
SALES (est): 9.2MM **Privately Held**
SIC: 7349 5087 Janitorial service, contract basis; janitors' supplies

---

(P-14282)
GMS JANITORIAL SERVICES INC
8690 Aero Dr Ste 115, San Diego
(92123-1757)
PHONE...................................858 569-6009
Rene Gonzalez, *President*
EMP: 66
SALES (est): 1.7MM **Privately Held**
SIC: 7349 Janitorial service, contract basis

(P-14283)
H U S D MAINTENANCE OPERATION
24400 Amador St, Hayward (94544-1302)
PHONE...................................510 784-2666
Joseph Zanini, *Director*
EMP: 80
SALES (est): 1.2MM **Privately Held**
SIC: 7349 Building maintenance services

(P-14284)
HARBOR BUILDING SERVICES
2701 Plaza Del Amo # 706, Torrance
(90503-7314)
PHONE...................................310 320-2966
Peter Lescord, *Owner*
EMP: 86
SQ FT: 3,000
SALES (est): 2.7MM **Privately Held**
SIC: 7349 Janitorial service, contract basis

(P-14285)
HARPERS MODEL HOME MAINTENANCE
Also Called: Harper's Model Homes Services
1949 5th St Ste 108, Davis (95616-4026)
P.O. Box 4590, El Dorado Hills (95762-0021)
PHONE...................................916 335-0282
Karen L Harper, *President*
Karen Harper, *President*
Garay Harper, *Admin Sec*
EMP: 70
SQ FT: 1,600
SALES (est): 1.8MM **Privately Held**
SIC: 7349 Building cleaning service

(P-14286)
HAYNES BUILDING SERVICE LLC
16027 Arrow Hwy Ste I, Baldwin Park
(91706-2064)
PHONE...................................626 359-6100
John P Scharler, *President*
Michael Franco, *Vice Pres*
EMP: 175
SQ FT: 20,000
SALES (est): 5.3MM **Privately Held**
WEB: www.haynesservices.com
SIC: 7349 Janitorial service, contract basis

(P-14287)
HUNTER EASTERDAY CORPORATION
1475 N Hundley St, Anaheim (92806-1323)
PHONE...................................714 238-3400
Sam Easterday, *CEO*
Manny Jones, *President*
Joanne Easterday, *CFO*
Gilbert Anzaldua, *Vice Pres*
EMP: 135
SQ FT: 4,400
SALES (est): 4.2MM **Privately Held**
WEB: www.ebmcorp.com
SIC: 7349 5087 Janitorial service, contract basis; building maintenance, except repairs; janitors' supplies

(P-14288)
HYDROCHEM LLC
Also Called: Hydro Chem Industrial Services
901 Loveridge Rd 592, Pittsburg
(94565-2811)
P.O. Box 1859 (94565-0859)
PHONE...................................925 432-1749
Jodi White, *Manager*
Elaido Velasquez, *Manager*
EMP: 65
SALES (corp-wide): 750MM **Privately Held**
WEB: www.hydrochem.com
SIC: 7349 Cleaning service, industrial or commercial

HQ: Hydrochem Llc
900 Georgia Ave
Deer Park TX 77536
713 393-5600

(P-14289)
INNOVATIONS BUILDING SVCS LLC
402 S Orange Ave Apt D, Monterey Park
(91755-7554)
PHONE...................................323 787-6068
Helbert Daniel Torres, *Principal*
EMP: 100
SALES (est): 1MM **Privately Held**
SIC: 7349 Building maintenance services

(P-14290)
INTEGRATED CLG SOLUTIONS INC
Also Called: I C S
3043 Mission St, San Francisco
(94110-4501)
PHONE...................................415 821-6757
Nicholas Mettler, *President*
Cori Holland, *Director*
EMP: 50
SQ FT: 2,500
SALES: 8MM **Privately Held**
WEB: www.nomoredirt.com
SIC: 7349 Janitorial service, contract basis

(P-14291)
INTEGRITY MANAGEMENT SVCS INC
141 W Dana St Ste 100, Nipomo
(93444-9152)
P.O. Box 976 (93444-0976)
PHONE...................................805 238-0905
Raul Torres, *President*
EMP: 200
SALES (est): 6.1MM **Privately Held**
SIC: 7349 Janitorial service, contract basis

(P-14292)
ISS FACILITY SERVICES INC
Also Called: Loma Cleaning Service
40563 Encyclopedia Cir, Fremont
(94538-2469)
PHONE...................................650 593-9774
Peter Beck, *Vice Pres*
EMP: 300
SALES (corp-wide): 12.6B **Privately Held**
SIC: 7349 Janitorial service, contract basis
HQ: Iss Facility Services, Inc.
1017 Central Pkwy N # 100
San Antonio TX 78232

(P-14293)
JABEZ BUILDING SERVICES INC
2094 Orange Ave, Costa Mesa
(92627-2101)
PHONE...................................714 776-7705
Daniel Rubio, *President*
Mary Rubio, *Vice Pres*
Fidel Reyes, *Opers Mgr*
EMP: 60
SALES (est): 1.4MM **Privately Held**
SIC: 7349 Janitorial service, contract basis

(P-14294)
JAN PRO CLG SYSTEMS STHERN CAL
2401 E Katella Ave # 525, Anaheim
(92806-5939)
PHONE...................................714 220-0500
Dave Rhodes, *Manager*
EMP: 50
SALES (est): 624.4K
SALES (corp-wide): 526K **Privately Held**
SIC: 7349 5087 Janitorial service, contract basis; service establishment equipment
PA: Jan Pro Cleaning Systems Of Southern California
3875 Hopyard Rd Ste 194
Pleasanton CA 94588
714 220-0500

P
R
O
D
U
C
T
S

&

S
V
C
S

(P-14295)
JANICO BUILDING MAINTENANCE
3001 Red Hill Ave 2-221, Costa Mesa (92626-4529)
PHONE...................714 444-4339
Shawn Dawson, *President*
EMP: 412
SQ FT: 5,000
SALES (est): 3.5MM **Privately Held**
SIC: 7349 Janitorial service, contract basis

(P-14296)
JANITORIAL EQUIPMENT SVCS INC
Also Called: King Janitorial Equipment Svcs
11752 Garden Grove Blvd # 100, Garden Grove (92843-1423)
PHONE...................951 205-8937
Javier Brito, *CFO*
EMP: 55
SALES: 950K **Privately Held**
SIC: 7349 Building maintenance services

(P-14297)
K & P JANITORIAL SERVICES
412 S Pacific Coast Hwy # 200, Redondo Beach (90277-3712)
PHONE...................310 540-8878
Kelly Lynch, *President*
EMP: 100
SALES (est): 3.2MM **Privately Held**
SIC: 7349 Janitorial service, contract basis

(P-14298)
KBM FCLITY SLTONS HOLDINGS LLC
Also Called: Kbm Building Services
7976 Engineer Rd Ste 200, San Diego (92111-1935)
PHONE...................858 467-0202
Brian Snow, *CEO*
Susan Cologna, *CFO*
Rene Tuthscher, *Vice Pres*
Shaun Gordon, *Director*
Robert Kennedy III, *Director*
EMP: 500
SQ FT: 10,000
SALES (est): 19.3MM
SALES (corp-wide): 25.9MM **Privately Held**
SIC: 7349 Janitorial service, contract basis
PA: Pristine Environments Inc
　7925 Jones Branch Dr Ll330
　Mc Lean VA 22102
　703 245-4751

(P-14299)
KM INDUSTRIAL INC
2375 W Esther St, Long Beach (90813-1029)
PHONE...................562 786-6200
Will Colon, *CEO*
Rich Bartel, *President*
EMP: 128
SALES (est): 6.1MM
SALES (corp-wide): 274.5MM **Privately Held**
SIC: 7349 Cleaning service, industrial or commercial
PA: K2 Industrial Services, Inc.
　3838 N Sam Houston Pkwy E
　Houston TX 77032
　850 477-6437

(P-14300)
LANDMARK SERVICES INC
410 N Fairview St, Santa Ana (92703-3412)
PHONE...................714 547-6308
Dan Rogers, *President*
EMP: 60
SQ FT: 130,000
SALES (est): 4MM **Privately Held**
SIC: 7349 Janitorial service, contract basis

(P-14301)
LEES MAINTENANCE SERVICE INC
14740 Keswick St, Van Nuys (91405-1205)
PHONE...................818 988-6644
Tyrone P Ingram, *President*
EMP: 275 EST: 1961
SQ FT: 3,000
SALES (est): 10.2MM **Privately Held**
WEB: www.leesmaint.com
SIC: 7349 5087 Janitorial service, contract basis; laundry & dry cleaning equipment & supplies

(P-14302)
LEWIS & TAYLOR LLC
Also Called: Lewis & Taylor Bldg Svc Contrs
440 Bryant St, San Francisco (94107-1303)
PHONE...................415 781-3496
Michael L Milstein, *President*
Mayela Ortiz, *Human Res Mgr*
Juan Vargas, *Opers Staff*
Dennis Sakurai, *Manager*
EMP: 150
SQ FT: 4,000
SALES: 6.4MM **Privately Held**
WEB: www.lewistaylor.com
SIC: 7349 Building maintenance, except repairs; janitorial service, contract basis; window cleaning; chemical cleaning services

(P-14303)
LIFE CYCLE ENGINEERING INC
2535 Camino Del Rio S # 250, San Diego (92108-3754)
PHONE...................619 785-5990
John Spencer, *Manager*
Thomas Hekman, *Program Mgr*
Adam B Duncan, *Engineer*
EMP: 80
SALES (corp-wide): 91.1MM **Privately Held**
WEB: www.lcesd.com
SIC: 7349 Building maintenance, except repairs
PA: Life Cycle Engineering, Inc.
　4360 Corporate Rd Ste 100
　North Charleston SC 29405
　843 744-7110

(P-14304)
LITTLE GIANT BLDG MAINT INC
15 Brooks Pl, Pacifica (94044-4403)
PHONE...................415 508-0282
David Dellanini, *President*
EMP: 230
SALES (corp-wide): 9.2MM **Privately Held**
SIC: 7349 7217 Window cleaning; carpet & upholstery cleaning
PA: Little Giant Building Maintenance, Inc.
　1485 Bay Shore Blvd # 117
　San Francisco CA 94124
　415 508-0282

(P-14305)
LODI UNIFIED SCHOOL DISTRICT
Also Called: Maintenance & Operations
1305 E Vine St, Lodi (95240-3179)
PHONE...................209 331-7181
Mike Matranga, *Manager*
EMP: 65
SALES (corp-wide): 360.5MM **Privately Held**
WEB: www.lodiusd.net
SIC: 7349 Building maintenance services
PA: Lodi Unified School District
　1305 E Vine St
　Lodi CA 95240
　209 331-7000

(P-14306)
LONG BEACH UNIFIED SCHOOL DST
Also Called: Maintenance
2425 Webster Ave, Long Beach (90810-3204)
PHONE...................562 997-7550
Joe Rasch, *Director*
Lisa Dutra, *Administration*
Phaloeuk Loeun, *Technician*
Susan Gavel, *Director*
EMP: 200
SALES (corp-wide): 867.6MM **Privately Held**
WEB: www.lbusd.k12.ca.us
SIC: 7349 School custodian, contract basis
PA: Long Beach Unified School District
　1515 Hughes Way
　Long Beach CA 90810
　562 997-8000

(P-14307)
LOS ANGELES UNIFIED SCHOOL DST
Also Called: Maintenance Dept
17729 S Figueroa St, Gardena (90248-4237)
PHONE...................310 808-1500
Roger Finstad, *Director*
EMP: 50
SALES (corp-wide): 3.8B **Privately Held**
WEB: www.lausd.k12.ca.us
SIC: 7349 School custodian, contract basis
PA: Los Angeles Unified School District
　333 S Beaudry Ave Ste 209
　Los Angeles CA 90017
　213 241-1000

(P-14308)
LUXERA INC
39300 Civic Center Dr # 140, Fremont (94538-2338)
PHONE...................510 456-7690
Leonard Simon Livschitz, *CEO*
EMP: 50 EST: 2010
SALES (est): 1MM **Privately Held**
SIC: 7349 Lighting maintenance service

(P-14309)
M-N-Z JANITORIAL SERVICES INC
2109 W Burbank Blvd, Burbank (91506-1231)
PHONE...................323 851-4115
Marc De Mauregne, *Exec VP*
Dennis Krebs, *Shareholder*
Zorina Russell Kroop, *President*
Gene Figueroa, *Project Mgr*
EMP: 110
SQ FT: 1,000
SALES (est): 2.9MM **Privately Held**
WEB: www.mnz.com
SIC: 7349 1799 Building maintenance, except repairs; construction site cleanup

(P-14310)
MAINTENANCE SERVICE FOR THE CY
Also Called: Public Works Superintendent
1616 Fortmann Way, Alameda (94501-1274)
PHONE...................510 865-3778
Lance Bryant, *Superintendent*
EMP: 51
SALES (est): 1MM **Privately Held**
SIC: 7349 Building maintenance services

(P-14311)
MAINTENANCE STAFF INC
122 W 8th St, Long Beach (90813-4371)
PHONE...................562 493-3982
Vivian M Frahm, *President*
EMP: 2600
SALES (est): 18MM **Privately Held**
WEB: www.maintenancestaff.com
SIC: 7349 Janitorial service, contract basis

(P-14312)
MARK GARCIA
Also Called: All In One Complete Bldg Svcs
5131 Ellsworth Rd Ste B, Vacaville (95688-9483)
P.O. Box 2383 (95696-2383)
PHONE...................707 446-4529
Mark Garcia, *Owner*
EMP: 60
SQ FT: 4,000
SALES: 250K **Privately Held**
SIC: 7349 1799 1521 Building maintenance services; cleaning new buildings after construction; cleaning building exteriors; repairing fire damage, single-family houses

(P-14313)
MAROTTO CORPORATION
Also Called: All American Maintenance
9524 Topanga Canyon Blvd, Chatsworth (91311-4011)
PHONE...................818 775-0320
Mario Marotto, *President*
EMP: 319
SQ FT: 1,000
SALES (est): 9.2MM **Privately Held**
SIC: 7349 1771 Building maintenance services; flooring contractor

(P-14314)
MASTER CLEAN USA INC
Also Called: Janitorial
5511 Ekwill St Ste D, Santa Barbara (93111-2361)
P.O. Box 8032, Goleta (93118-8032)
PHONE...................805 681-0950
Jessica Sanchez Hoseler, *CEO*
EMP: 50
SALES (est): 1.8MM **Privately Held**
SIC: 7349 7389 1799 Maid services, contract or fee basis; ; construction site cleanup

(P-14315)
MAXIM SERVICES LTD INC
2470 Estand Way, Pleasant Hill (94523-3912)
PHONE...................925 969-1907
Gregory Higgins, *President*
EMP: 60
SQ FT: 800
SALES (est): 1.7MM **Privately Held**
SIC: 7349 Janitorial service, contract basis

(P-14316)
MCKOWSKIS MAINT SYSTEMS INC
10979 San Dego Mission Rd, San Diego (92108-2431)
PHONE...................619 269-4600
James R McElwee, *President*
Paulina Zamora, *Security Dir*
EMP: 55 EST: 1979
SQ FT: 7,000
SALES (est): 5MM **Privately Held**
WEB: www.mckowskis.com
SIC: 7349 Janitorial service, contract basis

(P-14317)
MERCHANTS BUILDING MAINT CO
1639 E Edinger Ave Ste C, Santa Ana (92705-5013)
PHONE...................714 973-9272
George Rodriguez, *Branch Mgr*
EMP: 300
SALES (corp-wide): 128.1MM **Privately Held**
WEB: www.mbmonline.com
SIC: 7349 Building maintenance, except repairs
PA: Merchants Building Maintenance Company
　1190 Monterey Pass Rd
　Monterey Park CA 91754
　323 881-6701

(P-14318)
MERCHANTS BUILDING MAINT CO (PA)
1190 Monterey Pass Rd, Monterey Park (91754-3615)
PHONE...................323 881-6701
Theodore Haas, *CEO*
David Haas, *President*
Karen T Haas, *Treasurer*
Krista M Haas, *Vice Pres*
Lee Gorsuch, *Regional Mgr*
EMP: 96
SQ FT: 8,000
SALES (est): 128.1MM **Privately Held**
WEB: www.mbmonline.com
SIC: 7349 Janitorial service, contract basis

(P-14319)
MERCHANTS BUILDING MAINT CO
9555 Dist Ave 102, San Diego (92121)
PHONE...................858 455-0163
Eric Ruiz, *Manager*
Imelda Romero, *Cust Mgr*
EMP: 380
SALES (corp-wide): 128.1MM **Privately Held**
WEB: www.mbmonline.com
SIC: 7349 Janitorial service, contract basis
PA: Merchants Building Maintenance Company
　1190 Monterey Pass Rd
　Monterey Park CA 91754
　323 881-6701

(P-14320)
MERCHANTS BUILDING MAINT CO
1995 W Holt Ave, Pomona (91768-3352)
PHONE......................................909 622-8260
Angel Meza, *Branch Mgr*
Wallace Reid, *President*
Sharon Godinez, *Manager*
EMP: 220
SALES (corp-wide): 128.1MM **Privately Held**
WEB: www.mbmonline.com
SIC: 7349 7381 Janitorial service, contract basis; security guard service
PA: Merchants Building Maintenance Company
   1190 Monterey Pass Rd
   Monterey Park CA 91754
   323 881-6701

(P-14321)
MERCHANTS BUILDING MAINT CO
606 Monterey Paca Rd 20 Ste 202, Monterey Park (91754)
PHONE......................................323 881-8902
Michael A Palma,
Cesar Prado, *Branch Mgr*
Greg Whiting, *Branch Mgr*
Raquel Huamani, *Office Mgr*
Susan Penna, *Sales Executive*
EMP: 130
SALES (corp-wide): 128.1MM **Privately Held**
WEB: www.mbmonline.com
SIC: 7349 7381 Janitorial service, contract basis; detective & armored car services
PA: Merchants Building Maintenance Company
   1190 Monterey Pass Rd
   Monterey Park CA 91754
   323 881-6701

(P-14322)
METRO SERVICE SOUTH INC
3605 Cahuenga Blvd W, Los Angeles (90068-1205)
PHONE......................................310 995-8950
Michael Oddo, *President*
EMP: 100
SQ FT: 2,000
SALES (est): 1.2MM **Privately Held**
SIC: 7349 Building maintenance services

(P-14323)
MIDA INDUSTRIES INC
6101 Obispo Ave, Long Beach (90805-3799)
PHONE......................................562 616-1020
Michael T Drake, *President*
John Durfee, *President*
Dawit Kidane, *CFO*
John Valencia, *Vice Pres*
EMP: 250
SQ FT: 10,000
SALES (est): 14.9MM **Privately Held**
WEB: www.midaindustries.com
SIC: 7349 1799 Janitorial service, contract basis; asbestos removal & encapsulation

(P-14324)
MINTIE CORPORATION (PA)
Also Called: Mintie Technologies
1114 N San Fernando Rd, Los Angeles (90065-1126)
PHONE......................................323 225-4111
Kevin J Mintie, *CEO*
James M Mintie, *Exec VP*
Jim Bieritz, *Director*
Grace Domingo, *Manager*
EMP: 80
SQ FT: 8,000
SALES (est): 15.3MM **Privately Held**
WEB: www.mintie.com
SIC: 7349 Building cleaning service; air duct cleaning

(P-14325)
MOBLEY ENTERPRISES INC
Also Called: ServiceMaster
2260 Cooper Ave Ste F, Merced (95348-4362)
P.O. Box 3528 (95344-1528)
PHONE......................................209 726-9190
Jack Mobley, *President*

Amy Davis, *Manager*
EMP: 81
SQ FT: 3,000
SALES (est): 2.8MM **Privately Held**
SIC: 7349 Building maintenance services

(P-14326)
MOLLY MAID
24412 Muirlands Blvd A, Lake Forest (92630-3900)
PHONE......................................949 367-8000
Stephen Schatan, *Owner*
John Smith, *VP Finance*
EMP: 50
SQ FT: 2,000
SALES (est): 1MM **Privately Held**
SIC: 7349 7363 7299 Maid services, contract or fee basis; domestic help service; handyman service

(P-14327)
MONTEBELLO UNIFIED SCHOOL
Also Called: Maintenance & Operation Dept
500 Hendricks St Fl 2, Montebello (90640-1566)
PHONE......................................323 887-2140
Virgil Downs, *Principal*
EMP: 100
SALES (corp-wide): 296.9MM **Privately Held**
SIC: 7349 Building maintenance services
PA: Montebello Unified School District Protective League
   123 S Montebello Blvd
   Montebello CA 90640
   323 887-7900

(P-14328)
MORENO & ASSOCIATES INC
1260 Birchwood Dr, Sunnyvale (94089-2205)
PHONE......................................408 924-0353
Ernie Moreno, *President*
Paul Lima, *Vice Pres*
Sandra Cervantes, *Human Resources*
Felix Apreza, *Opers Spvr*
Alfredo Cortez, *Opers Spvr*
EMP: 60
SQ FT: 1,100
SALES (est): 2.6MM **Privately Held**
WEB: www.morenoclean.com
SIC: 7349 Janitorial service, contract basis

(P-14329)
NEALS JANITORIAL SERVICE
1588 Calco Creek Dr, San Jose (95127-4372)
PHONE......................................408 271-9944
Ralph B Neal, *Owner*
EMP: 50
SQ FT: 3,000
SALES (est): 1.2MM **Privately Held**
SIC: 7349 Janitorial service, contract basis; window cleaning

(P-14330)
NEXSENTIO INC
1346 Ridder Park Dr, San Jose (95131-2313)
PHONE......................................408 392-9249
Danielle Bunel, *Partner*
Rene Velazquez, *Vice Pres*
Aricela Castaneda, *Office Mgr*
EMP: 77 EST: 2006
SALES (est): 2.4MM **Privately Held**
SIC: 7349 7299 Janitorial service, contract basis; handyman service

(P-14331)
NMS MANAGEMENT INC
155 W 35th St Ste A, National City (91950-7922)
PHONE......................................619 425-0440
David Guaderrama, *President*
Sophia Guaderrama, *Exec VP*
EMP: 75
SQ FT: 8,300
SALES: 3MM **Privately Held**
SIC: 7349 0781 Building maintenance, except repairs; janitorial service, contract basis; landscape services

(P-14332)
NO MORE DIRT INC
1699 Valencia St, San Francisco (94110-5012)
PHONE......................................415 821-6757
Nicholas D Mettler, *President*
Jonathan Mack, *Accounts Mgr*
EMP: 150
SALES (est): 4.1MM **Privately Held**
SIC: 7349 Janitorial service, contract basis

(P-14333)
NORTH COAST CLEANING SERVICES
211 7th St, Eureka (95501-1701)
P.O. Box 177 (95502-0177)
PHONE......................................707 269-0838
Dave Toor, *President*
Charles Powell, *President*
EMP: 50
SALES (est): 1.4MM **Privately Held**
SIC: 7349 Janitorial service, contract basis

(P-14334)
NORTH STAR BUILDING MAINT INC
2828 Cochran St Ste 214, Simi Valley (93065-2780)
PHONE......................................805 518-0417
Glenn Rose, *President*
Jamie Rose, *Vice Pres*
Michael Paisley, *VP Sales*
EMP: 60
SQ FT: 800
SALES: 1MM **Privately Held**
SIC: 7349 Janitorial service, contract basis

(P-14335)
OAKLAND UNIFIED SCHOOL DST
Also Called: Facilities Management
955 High St, Oakland (94601-4404)
PHONE......................................510 535-2717
Timothy White, *Asst Supt*
Kylie Dalton, *Partner*
Maxine Jasper, *Office Mgr*
Veronica Del Rio, *Admin Sec*
Michael Ezeh, *Accountant*
EMP: 150
SALES (corp-wide): 658.8MM **Privately Held**
WEB: www.ousd.k12.ca.us
SIC: 7349 Building maintenance services
PA: Oakland Unified School District
   1000 Broadway Fl 4
   Oakland CA 94607
   510 434-7790

(P-14336)
OPTIMA BUILDING SERVICES MAINT
210 Mountain View Ave, Santa Rosa (95407-8203)
PHONE......................................707 586-6640
Adolfo Mendoza, *President*
EMP: 100
SALES (est): 2.3MM **Privately Held**
SIC: 7349 Building cleaning service

(P-14337)
PACIFIC BUILDING MAINT INC (PA)
Also Called: Servicmster Clean By Integrity
1601 Ives Ave Ste E, Oxnard (93033-1908)
PHONE......................................805 642-0214
Aaron Shia, *President*
Aaron Shiah, *President*
Jennifer Furst, *Manager*
EMP: 81
SQ FT: 1,600
SALES (est): 2.3MM **Privately Held**
WEB: www.pacificbuildingmaintenance.com
SIC: 7349 Cleaning service, industrial or commercial

(P-14338)
PACIFIC CLEANING SERVICE INC
3334 Pacific Coast Hwy # 205, Corona Del Mar (92625-2328)
PHONE......................................949 829-8790
Jeff Murray, *President*
EMP: 50

SQ FT: 1,500
SALES (est): 2.2MM **Privately Held**
WEB: www.pacificwindow.com
SIC: 7349 Window cleaning

(P-14339)
PACIFIC MAINTENANCE SVCS INC
1902 Verde Vista Dr, Redlands (92373-7322)
PHONE......................................909 793-7111
David Schulte, *President*
EMP: 200
SQ FT: 2,800
SALES (est): 3.1MM **Privately Held**
SIC: 7349 Building maintenance services

(P-14340)
PANAMA-BUENA VISTA UN SCHL DST
Also Called: District Office East
5901 Schirra Ct, Bakersfield (93313-2161)
PHONE......................................661 397-2205
Diane McConnell, *President*
EMP: 299
SALES (corp-wide): 203.4MM **Privately Held**
SIC: 7349 Building maintenance services
PA: Panama-Buena Vista Union School District
   4200 Ashe Rd
   Bakersfield CA 93313
   661 831-8331

(P-14341)
PARADISE BUILDING SERVICES
9664 Hermosa Ave, Rancho Cucamonga (91730-5812)
PHONE......................................909 399-0707
Chris Clifton, *President*
Susan Cutshaw, *Vice Pres*
EMP: 115
SQ FT: 5,500
SALES (est): 3MM **Privately Held**
SIC: 7349 Janitorial service, contract basis

(P-14342)
PARAGON COML BLDG MAINT INC
6731 32nd St Ste J, North Highlands (95660-3042)
PHONE......................................916 334-8801
Dwayne Willis, *President*
EMP: 80
SALES (est): 2.2MM **Privately Held**
SIC: 7349 Janitorial service, contract basis

(P-14343)
PARAMOUNT BLDG SOLUTIONS LLC
2045 California Ave # 101, Corona (92881-7231)
PHONE......................................951 272-4001
Glen Kucera, *Branch Mgr*
EMP: 237
SALES (corp-wide): 149.9MM **Privately Held**
SIC: 7349 Janitorial service, contract basis
PA: Paramount Building Solutions, Llc
   10235 S 51st St Ste 185
   Phoenix AZ 85044
   480 348-1177

(P-14344)
PBM MAINTENANCE CORP
Also Called: Professional Building Maint
8523 Lankershim Blvd, Sun Valley (91352-3127)
PHONE......................................818 771-1100
Fernando Real, *President*
David Lorin, *President*
EMP: 400
SQ FT: 40,000
SALES (est): 9.7MM **Privately Held**
WEB: www.pbmco.net
SIC: 7349 1799 Building maintenance services; steam cleaning of building exteriors

(P-14345)
PBMS INC
Also Called: Premier Building Maint Svcs
1909 Wilshire Blvd, Los Angeles (90057-3604)
PHONE......................................213 386-2552

P
R
O
D
U
C
T
S
&
S
V
C
S

Bryant S Kim, *President*
Kim Bryant, *Owner*
EMP: 100
SQ FT: 1,400
SALES (est): 3.3MM **Privately Held**
SIC: 7349 Janitorial service, contract basis

(P-14346)
PEERLESS BUILDING MAINT INC
4665 Mountain Lakes Blvd, Redding
(96003-1450)
PHONE....................530 222-6369
Jan Pauline Tuttle, *CEO*
Terry Tuttle, *President*
EMP: 100
SQ FT: 8,000
SALES: 3MM **Privately Held**
SIC: 7349 Janitorial service, contract basis

(P-14347)
PEERLESS MAINTENANCE SERVICE
1100 S Euclid St, La Habra (90631-6807)
P.O. Box 3900 (90632-3900)
PHONE....................714 871-3380
Linda Gabriel, *President*
David Gabriel, *Corp Secy*
EMP: 300
SQ FT: 2,000
SALES (est): 9.8MM **Privately Held**
WEB: www.peerlesssvc.com
SIC: 7349 Janitorial service, contract basis

(P-14348)
PEGASUS BUILDING SVCS CO INC (PA)
2343 Mira Mar Ave, Long Beach
(90815-1755)
PHONE....................562 961-1998
Judith Becker, *President*
Anna Corona, *Regional Mgr*
Laura Cortez, *Regional Mgr*
Betty Hernandez, *District Mgr*
Diana Lopez, *Human Res Mgr*
EMP: 350
SQ FT: 12,800
SALES (est): 11.4MM **Privately Held**
SIC: 7349 Janitorial service, contract basis

(P-14349)
PERFORMANCE BUILDING SERVICES
Also Called: Performance Cleanroom Services
22642 Lambert St Ste 409, Lake Forest
(92630-1645)
PHONE....................949 364-4364
James Chriss, *President*
Robert Lynch, *Vice Pres*
Ron Matthews, *Vice Pres*
Ramiro Teodoro, *Accounts Mgr*
EMP: 104
SALES: 5MM **Privately Held**
WEB: www.performance-now.com
SIC: 7349 7699 Janitorial service, contract basis; cleaning services

(P-14350)
PLATINUM CLG INDIANAPOLIS LLC
1522 2nd St, Santa Monica (90401-2303)
PHONE....................310 584-8000
William Hertz,
EMP: 460 **EST:** 2008
SALES (est): 12.2MM **Privately Held**
SIC: 7349 Building & office cleaning services

(P-14351)
PLATINUM FACILITIES SERVICES
1530 Oakland Rd Ste 120, San Jose
(95112-1241)
PHONE....................408 998-9004
Roger K Daniels, *President*
Sherry Jackson, *Finance Mgr*
Joseph Zanella, *Opers Mgr*
EMP: 150
SALES (est): 4.4MM **Privately Held**
SIC: 7349 Janitorial service, contract basis

(P-14352)
POLARIS BUILDING MAINTENANCE
2580 Wyandotte St Ste E, Mountain View
(94043-2366)
PHONE....................650 964-9400
Frank Schwarb, *President*
Roger Gomez, *Vice Pres*
EMP: 80
SQ FT: 2,700
SALES (est): 3.4MM **Privately Held**
SIC: 7349 Janitorial service, contract basis; building maintenance, except repairs

(P-14353)
PONDEROSA BUILDERS INC
Also Called: United Building Services
3300 W Macarthur Blvd, Santa Ana
(92704-6804)
PHONE....................714 434-9494
Robert Hughes, *President*
EMP: 800
SQ FT: 10,000
SALES (est): 11.4MM **Privately Held**
WEB: www.ubservices.com
SIC: 7349 Janitorial service, contract basis; window cleaning

(P-14354)
PREMIER FLOOR CARE INC (PA)
390 Carrol Ct Ste C, Brentwood
(94513-7376)
PHONE....................925 679-4901
Cedric Moore, *President*
EMP: 105
SALES (est): 2.5MM **Privately Held**
SIC: 7349 3589 Janitorial service, contract basis; commercial cleaning equipment

(P-14355)
PRIORITY BUILDING SERVICES LLC
Also Called: Priority Landscape Services
521 Mercury Ln, Brea (92821-4831)
PHONE....................714 255-2940
Simon Rocha, *President*
David Kraushaar, *Sales Mgr*
Scott Nankervis,
EMP: 375
SQ FT: 6,000
SALES (est): 15.2MM **Privately Held**
WEB: www.prioritybuildingservices.com
SIC: 7349 Cleaning service, industrial or commercial

(P-14356)
PRO BUILDING MAINTENANCE INC
149 N Maple St Ste H, Corona
(92880-1773)
PHONE....................951 279-3386
Carl Hoff, *CEO*
Christina L Hoff, *Principal*
EMP: 120
SQ FT: 1,600
SALES (est): 7.5MM **Privately Held**
SIC: 7349 Janitorial service, contract basis

(P-14357)
PROFESSIONAL JANITORIAL SVC
234 Eucalyptus Dr B, El Segundo
(90245-3820)
P.O. Box 646 (90245-0646)
PHONE....................310 410-1452
Michael Mc Grath, *President*
EMP: 50
SALES (est): 643.4K **Privately Held**
SIC: 7349 Building maintenance services

(P-14358)
PROFESSIONAL MAINT SYSTEMS INC
Also Called: Professional Maint Systems
4912 Naples St, San Diego (92110-3820)
P.O. Box 80038 (92138-0038)
PHONE....................619 276-1150
Karen Berry, *CEO*
Peter Alicea, *District Mgr*
EMP: 925
SQ FT: 9,000

SALES: 30MM **Privately Held**
WEB: www.pmsjanitorial.com
SIC: 7349 Janitorial service, contract basis

(P-14359)
PROPERTY MAINTENANCE COMPANY (PA)
Also Called: Dkd Property Management
255 W Julian St Ste 301, San Jose
(95110-2406)
PHONE....................408 297-7849
Sue Williams, *President*
EMP: 115 **EST:** 1979
SQ FT: 6,000
SALES (est): 2.3MM **Privately Held**
SIC: 7349 Building maintenance, except repairs

(P-14360)
PROTEC ASSOCIATION SERVICES (PA)
Also Called: Protec Building Services
10180 Willow Creek Rd, San Diego
(92131-1636)
PHONE....................858 569-1080
J David Rauch, *President*
Scot Clark, *Shareholder*
Russ Piccoli, *Shareholder*
Libbey Rauch, *Shareholder*
George Vanoofbree, *Shareholder*
EMP: 140
SQ FT: 12,500
SALES (est): 26.1MM **Privately Held**
SIC: 7349 Building maintenance services

(P-14361)
QUALITY COAST INCORPORATED
2462 Main St Ste H, Chula Vista
(91911-4671)
PHONE....................619 443-9192
Consuelo Rosengreen, *President*
Richard Rosengreen, *Treasurer*
EMP: 50
SALES (est): 1.7MM **Privately Held**
WEB: www.qualitycoast.com
SIC: 7349 Janitorial service, contract basis

(P-14362)
RAINBOW - BRITE INDUS SVCS LLC
463 E Salmon River Dr, Fresno
(93730-0860)
PHONE....................559 925-2580
Diana Tutson-Snowden, *CEO*
EMP: 100
SALES (est): 3.5MM **Privately Held**
SIC: 7349 Janitorial service, contract basis
PA: Santa Rosa Indian Community Of The
Santa Rosa Rancheria
16835 Alkali Dr
Lemoore CA 93245
559 924-1278

(P-14363)
RANSCAPES INC
30 Hughes Ste 209, Irvine (92618-1916)
P.O. Box 50580 (92619-0580)
PHONE....................866 883-9297
Ran Tomaino, *President*
Susan Tomaino, *Treasurer*
Joel Conchas, *Accounts Mgr*
EMP: 50
SQ FT: 2,000
SALES (est): 2.8MM **Privately Held**
WEB: www.ranscapes.com
SIC: 7349 Janitorial service, contract basis

(P-14364)
REDWOOD BUILDING MAINT CO
1364 N Mcdowell Blvd B, Petaluma
(94954-1116)
P.O. Box 750985 (94975-0985)
PHONE....................707 782-9100
Robert Stanley, *Owner*
EMP: 75
SQ FT: 2,000
SALES (est): 2.1MM **Privately Held**
WEB: www.rbmco.com
SIC: 7349 Janitorial service, contract basis

(P-14365)
RESOURCE COLLECTION INC
Also Called: Command Guard Services
3771 W 242nd St Ste 205, Torrance
(90505-6566)
PHONE....................310 219-3272
Martin Benom, *Ch of Bd*
Steven Jacobson, *Corp Secy*
Paula Benom, *Vice Pres*
Marilyn Jacobson, *Vice Pres*
EMP: 1400
SQ FT: 15,000
SALES (est): 16.4MM **Privately Held**
WEB: www.resourcecollection.com
SIC: 7349 7381 0782 3564 Air duct cleaning; guard services; lawn & garden services; air cleaning systems

(P-14366)
REYNOLDS CLEANING SERVICES INC
1472 Oddstad Dr, Redwood City
(94063-2607)
PHONE....................650 599-0202
James R Reynolds Jr, *President*
Charles Chantaca, *General Mgr*
Josh Juarbe, *Business Mgr*
Sonya Rodrigues, *Manager*
EMP: 110
SQ FT: 1,800
SALES (est): 3.2MM **Privately Held**
WEB: www.reynoldscleaning.com
SIC: 7349 Janitorial service, contract basis

(P-14367)
RHINO BUILDING SERVICES INC
6650 Flanders Dr Ste K, San Diego
(92121-3908)
PHONE....................858 455-1440
Cody Sears, *President*
EMP: 120
SQ FT: 110
SALES (est): 3.6MM **Privately Held**
WEB: www.rhinoliningsindustrial.com
SIC: 7349 Janitorial service, contract basis

(P-14368)
ROGAN BUILDING SERVICES INC
1531 7th St, Riverside (92507-4454)
P.O. Box 5787 (92517-5787)
PHONE....................951 248-1261
Byron Lee Rogan, *President*
Anne Rogan, *Admin Sec*
Cecelia Swiney, *Marketing Staff*
EMP: 50
SQ FT: 5,000
SALES (est): 1.6MM **Privately Held**
SIC: 7349 Building maintenance, except repairs; janitorial service, contract basis

(P-14369)
ROY JORGENSEN ASSOCIATES INC
19001 S Western Ave, Torrance
(90501-1106)
PHONE....................310 468-2478
Mark Thomas, *Principal*
EMP: 65
SALES (corp-wide): 120.2MM **Privately Held**
SIC: 7349 Building maintenance services
PA: Roy Jorgensen Associates, Inc.
3735 Buckeystown Pike
Buckeystown MD 21717
281 723-2099

(P-14370)
ROYAL CREST BUILDING MAINT
8601 Roland St Ste E, Buena Park
(90621-4809)
P.O. Box 391 (90621-0391)
PHONE....................714 562-5034
Robert Young, *President*
Carry Young, *Vice Pres*
Shaun Black, *Manager*
EMP: 50
SQ FT: 2,400
SALES (est): 1.6MM **Privately Held**
SIC: 7349 Janitorial service, contract basis

▲ = Import ▼=Export
◆ =Import/Export

(P-14371)
RUBICON ENTERPRISES INC
Also Called: RUBICON PROGRAMS
2500 Bissell Ave, Richmond (94804-1815)
PHONE..................................510 235-1516
Richard Aubry PHD, *Exec Dir*
EMP: 220
SALES: 4.3MM **Privately Held**
SIC: 7349 8322 8331 Building mainte-
nance services; social service center; job
training & vocational rehabilitation serv-
ices

(P-14372)
**RUBICON PROGRAMS
INCORPORATED (PA)**
2500 Bissell Ave, Richmond (94804-1815)
PHONE..................................510 235-1516
Jane Fischberg, *President*
Adrienne Kimball, *Admin Sec*
Hallie Friedman, *Administration*
Alexander Pfeifer-Rosenblum,
     Development
EMP: 75
SQ FT: 14,500
SALES: 15.9MM **Privately Held**
SIC: 7349 8322 8331 Building mainte-
nance services; social service center; job
training & vocational rehabilitation serv-
ices

(P-14373)
S J GENERAL BUILDING MAINT
919 Berryessa Rd Ste 10, San Jose
(95133-1087)
PHONE..................................408 392-0800
Armando Lamas, *President*
EMP: 60
SALES (est): 2.9MM **Privately Held**
SIC: 7349 Janitorial service, contract basis

(P-14374)
**SAN BERNARDINO CITY UNF
SCHOOL**
Also Called: Building Services
956 W 9th St, San Bernardino
(92411-2844)
PHONE..................................909 388-6100
Bob Leon, *Director*
EMP: 220
SALES (corp-wide): 469.2MM **Privately
Held**
WEB: www.sbcusd.k12.ca.us
SIC: 7349 8741 8211 Building mainte-
nance services; management services;
elementary & secondary schools
PA: San Bernardino City Unified School
     District
     777 N F St
     San Bernardino CA 92410
     909 381-1100

(P-14375)
**SAN DIEGO UNIFIED SCHOOL
DST**
Also Called: Maintenance Unit
4860 Ruffner St, San Diego (92111-1522)
PHONE..................................858 627-7130
William Fantos, *Director*
EMP: 1000
SALES (corp-wide): 966.4MM **Privately
Held**
WEB: www.sdcs.k12.ca.us
SIC: 7349 Building maintenance services
PA: San Diego Unified School District
     4100 Normal St
     San Diego CA 92103
     619 725-8000

(P-14376)
**SANTA CLARA VALLEY
CORPORATION**
Also Called: Swenson Developers and Contrs
715 N 1st St Ste 27, San Jose
(95112-6309)
PHONE..................................408 947-1100
Case Swenson, *President*
Lisa Swenson, *Admin Sec*
Heather Solis, *Project Mgr*
Kevin Young, *Project Mgr*
Aaron Gallaty, *Sales Staff*
EMP: 85
SQ FT: 1,200

SALES (est): 3.9MM **Privately Held**
SIC: 7349 0782 7623 7699 Building
maintenance, except repairs; janitorial
service, contract basis; lawn services; refrigeration service & repair; elevators: inspection, service & repair

(P-14377)
**SBM MANAGEMENT SERVICES
LP**
5241 Arnold Ave, McClellan (95652-1025)
PHONE..................................866 855-2211
Charles Somers, *CEO*
Ken Silva, *CFO*
Donald Tracy, *Exec VP*
Don Tracy, *Principal*
Ronald Alvarado, *Administration*
EMP: 300
SALES (est): 88.5MM **Privately Held**
SIC: 7349 Janitorial service, contract basis

(P-14378)
SBM SITE SERVICES LLC (PA)
Also Called: S B M
5241 Arnold Ave, McClellan (95652-1025)
PHONE..................................916 922-7600
Charles Somers, *Mng Member*
Craig Honig, *Officer*
Ken Silva, *Officer*
Don Tracy, *Exec VP*
Michael Abercrombie, *Vice Pres*
EMP: 5500
SQ FT: 25,000
SALES (est): 98.4MM **Privately Held**
SIC: 7349 Building maintenance services

(P-14379)
SBRM INC (PA)
Also Called: Servicmster Cmplete Rstoration
2342 Meyers Ave, Escondido (92029-1008)
PHONE..................................760 480-0208
Barbara Robert, *President*
Mike Gamez, *Admin Sec*
EMP: 70
SQ FT: 20,000
SALES (est): 11MM **Privately Held**
WEB: www.smsos.com
SIC: 7349 1521 Building maintenance
services; repairing fire damage, single-
family houses

(P-14380)
SCI CORP
303 Vintage Park Dr # 220, Foster City
(94404-1170)
P.O. Box 4007, Burlingame (94011-4007)
PHONE..................................650 578-1142
Carol Morrison, *CEO*
Maly Phang, *Accountant*
EMP: 100
SQ FT: 2,400
SALES: 3.1MM **Privately Held**
SIC: 7349 Janitorial service, contract basis

(P-14381)
SCV FACILITIES SERVICES
1907 W 75th St, Los Angeles (90047-2325)
PHONE..................................310 803-4588
Samuel Valdez, *Owner*
EMP: 72
SALES: 1.6MM **Privately Held**
SIC: 7349 7389 Janitorial service, contract
basis; cleaning service, industrial or com-
mercial;

(P-14382)
SEAFUS CORPORATION
Also Called: ServiceMaster
1365 Lowrie Ave, South San Francisco
(94080-6403)
PHONE..................................415 584-6100
David Decker, *President*
Beth Decker, *CFO*
EMP: 50
SQ FT: 4,500
SALES: 1,000K **Privately Held**
SIC: 7349 7217 Building maintenance
services; carpet & upholstery cleaning

(P-14383)
SERVI-TEK INC
Also Called: Servi-Tek Janitorial Services
3970 Sorrento Valley Blvd, San Diego
(92121-1416)
PHONE..................................858 638-7735
Bryan McMinn,

Maria Zarzosa, *QC Mgr*
Eric S Friz,
Kurt G Lester,
Bryan D McMinn,
EMP: 300
SQ FT: 2,000
SALES (est): 10.2MM **Privately Held**
WEB: www.servitek.org
SIC: 7349 Janitorial service, contract basis

(P-14384)
SERVICE BY MEDALLION
Also Called: Medallion Cnstr Clean-Up
411 Clyde Ave, Mountain View
(94043-2209)
PHONE..................................650 625-1010
Roland H Strick, *CEO*
David Godinez, *Shareholder*
Elias Nacif, *Vice Pres*
Roland F Strick, *Vice Pres*
Trino Cardenas, *District Mgr*
EMP: 490 EST: 1978
SQ FT: 7,000
SALES (est): 25.7MM **Privately Held**
WEB: www.servicebymedallion.com
SIC: 7349 Janitorial service, contract basis

(P-14385)
**SERVICEMASTER COMPANY
LLC**
1003 Hi Point St, Los Angeles
(90035-2607)
PHONE..................................760 298-7001
Samuel Druhora, *Branch Mgr*
EMP: 85
SALES (corp-wide): 2.9B **Publicly Held**
SIC: 7349 Building maintenance services
HQ: The Servicemaster Company Llc
     150 Peabody Pl Ste 103
     Memphis TN 38103
     901 597-1400

(P-14386)
**SERVICEMASTER COMPANY
LLC**
216 N Clara St, Santa Ana (92703-3518)
PHONE..................................714 245-1465
Gregg Gills, *Manager*
EMP: 200
SALES (corp-wide): 2.9B **Publicly Held**
WEB: www.servicemaster.com
SIC: 7349 Building maintenance services
HQ: The Servicemaster Company Llc
     150 Peabody Pl Ste 103
     Memphis TN 38103
     901 597-1400

(P-14387)
SERVICO BUILDING MAINT CO
13732b Carmel Ave, Glen Ellen (95442)
P.O. Box 25 (95442-0025)
PHONE..................................707 935-1224
Gary D'Acquisto, *President*
EMP: 100
SQ FT: 800
SALES (est): 2MM **Privately Held**
SIC: 7349 7217 Janitorial service, contract
basis; window cleaning; carpet & furniture
cleaning on location

(P-14388)
SERVPRO OF MENDOCINO
3001 S State St Ste 5, Ukiah (95482-6966)
PHONE..................................707 462-3848
Doug Bridges, *Principal*
EMP: 50
SALES (est): 430.6K **Privately Held**
SIC: 7349 Building maintenance services

(P-14389)
SFUSD BUILDING GROUND
834 Toland St, San Francisco
(94124-1314)
PHONE..................................415 695-5508
John Bitoff, *Director*
EMP: 100
SALES (est): 3.5MM **Privately Held**
SIC: 7349 Building maintenance services

(P-14390)
**SIGNATURE BUILDING MAINT
INC**
1330 White Oaks Rd, Campbell
(95008-6723)
P.O. Box 110340 (95011-0340)
PHONE..................................408 377-8066
Anna Murphy, *President*
Jeff Lolyd, *CFO*
Patrick Murphy, *General Mgr*
Tony Reyes, *Admin Sec*
Joe Megill, *Opers Mgr*
EMP: 80 EST: 1999
SQ FT: 1,800
SALES (est): 4.1MM **Privately Held**
WEB: www.signaturefacilities.com
SIC: 7349 Building cleaning service

(P-14391)
**SIGNIFICANT CLEANING SVCS
LLC**
1855 Hamilton Ave Ste 104, San Jose
(95125-5672)
P.O. Box 7702 (95150-7702)
PHONE..................................408 559-5959
Larry Lovaglia,
Anthony Lovaglia, *Project Mgr*
Nelson Celada, *Facilities Mgr*
John Ornales, *Manager*
Hugo Rosales, *Supervisor*
EMP: 105 EST: 1988
SQ FT: 250
SALES (est): 4.1MM **Privately Held**
WEB: www.significantcleaning.com
SIC: 7349 Cleaning service, industrial or
commercial

(P-14392)
SITE CREW INC
3185 Airway Ave Ste G, Costa Mesa
(92626-4601)
PHONE..................................714 668-0100
Tina Manavi, *CEO*
EMP: 300
SQ FT: 2,160
SALES (est): 8MM **Privately Held**
WEB: www.sitecrewinc.com
SIC: 7349 Janitorial service, contract basis

(P-14393)
SKYLSTAD-SCHOELEN CO INC
Also Called: ServiceMaster
3130 Skyway Dr Ste 701, Santa Maria
(93455-1800)
PHONE..................................805 349-0503
Linda Schoelen, *President*
Jeffrey Hopson, *Principal*
EMP: 80
SALES (est): 2.5MM **Privately Held**
SIC: 7349 Building maintenance services

(P-14394)
**SO CAL LAND MAINTENANCE
INC**
2965 E Coronado St, Anaheim
(92806-2502)
PHONE..................................714 231-1454
Stephen Guise, *Principal*
EMP: 72 EST: 2011
SALES (est): 958.1K **Privately Held**
SIC: 7349 Building maintenance services

(P-14395)
SODEXO OPERATIONS LLC
1325 Iris Ave Bldg 181, Imperial Beach
(91932-3751)
PHONE..................................619 429-5692
Rodrigo Domingo, *Branch Mgr*
EMP: 52
SALES (corp-wide): 139.1MM **Privately
Held**
SIC: 7349 Building maintenance services
HQ: Sodexo Operations, Llc
     9801 Washingtonian Blvd
     Gaithersburg MD 20878
     301 987-4000

(P-14396)
**SOUTHERN BUILDING MAINT
INC**
836 Crenshaw Blvd Ste 102, Los Angeles
(90005-3631)
PHONE..................................213 598-7071
Charles Chung, *CEO*
Kimberly Paek, *Principal*

EMP: 70
SALES: 950K Privately Held
SIC: 7349 Building maintenance services

(P-14397)
SOUTHERN CAL MAID SVC CRPT CLG
14909 Crenshaw Blvd # 209, Gardena
(90249-3665)
P.O. Box 1653 (90249-0653)
PHONE..............................310 675-0585
Rueben Trejo, President
EMP: 98
SALES (est): 1.8MM Privately Held
SIC: 7349 7217 Maid services, contract or
fee basis; carpet & furniture cleaning on
location

(P-14398)
SOUTHERN COUNTIES BLDG MAINT (PA)
1035 N Armando St Ste F, Anaheim
(92806-2607)
PHONE..............................805 928-9900
Ruben Garcia, President
EMP: 200 EST: 1978
SALES (est): 2.1MM Privately Held
SIC: 7349 Janitorial service, contract basis

(P-14399)
SPENCER BUILDING MAINTENANCE
10457 Old Placerville Rd, Sacramento
(95827-2508)
PHONE..............................916 922-1900
Aaron D Spencer, President
Jose Yanez, Opers Staff
Gordon Platt, Accounts Mgr
EMP: 307
SQ FT: 5,000
SALES (est): 10.9MM Privately Held
WEB: www.spencerservices.com
SIC: 7349 Janitorial service, contract basis

(P-14400)
STAR BRITE BUILDING MAINT
2688 Dawson Ave, Long Beach
(90755-2020)
PHONE..............................562 988-2829
Eric E Jenderko, President
EMP: 329 EST: 1989
SALES: 500K Privately Held
SIC: 7349 Janitorial service, contract basis

(P-14401)
STEVE AND BETH CHAPUT
Also Called: Molly Maid
1025 Sentinel Dr Ste 103, La Verne
(91750-3281)
PHONE..............................909 596-9994
Steve Chaput, Partner
Beth Chaput, Partner
EMP: 50
SALES (est): 1MM Privately Held
SIC: 7349 Maid services, contract or fee
basis

(P-14402)
SUMMIT BUILDING SERVICES INC
1128 Willow Pass Ct, Concord
(94520-1006)
PHONE..............................925 827-9500
Matt Colchico, Owner
Seth Pitzer, Office Mgr
EMP: 100
SALES (est): 2.5MM Privately Held
SIC: 7349 Janitorial service, contract basis

(P-14403)
SUNSET BUILDING MAINTANCE INC
Also Called: Sunset Building Maintenance
1920 Lafayette St Ste E, Santa Clara
(95050-3956)
PHONE..............................408 727-3408
Marisela Del Rio, President
EMP: 50
SQ FT: 1,000
SALES (est): 1.2MM Privately Held
SIC: 7349 Janitorial service, contract basis

(P-14404)
SUPERIOR ENVMTL SVCS INC
Also Called: SES
6383 Lake Arrowhead Dr, San Diego
(92119-3534)
P.O. Box 19784 (92159-0784)
PHONE..............................619 462-7079
Kevin Tullgren, President
Jared Dunn, Regional Mgr
Danny Sawyer, Regional Mgr
Jonathan Nieves, District Mgr
EMP: 50
SQ FT: 2,000
SALES: 1MM Privately Held
SIC: 7349 Cleaning service, industrial or
commercial

(P-14405)
SWAYZERS INCORPORATED
Also Called: Swayzer A-1 Sanitizing
1663 E Del Amo Blvd, Carson
(90746-2937)
P.O. Box 4365 (90749-4365)
PHONE..............................323 979-7223
Samuel Swayzer, President
Regina Swayzer, Vice Pres
EMP: 60
SALES (est): 1.7MM Privately Held
SIC: 7349 Building cleaning service

(P-14406)
THOREAU JANITORIAL SVCS INC
Also Called: Thoreau Services Nationwide
5120 W Goldleaf Cir # 10, Los Angeles
(90056-1292)
PHONE..............................310 822-8017
Nicki Frank, President
Dan Firestone, Shareholder
Robert Firestone, Shareholder
EMP: 150
SQ FT: 1,300
SALES (est): 5.3MM Privately Held
SIC: 7349 Building cleaning service

(P-14407)
TIM HOFER INC
Also Called: Environment Control
148 N Akers St, Visalia (93291-5121)
P.O. Box 6445 (93290-6445)
PHONE..............................559 732-6676
Timothy Hofer, President
Suzanne Hofer, Admin Sec
EMP: 103
SQ FT: 5,700
SALES: 2.6MM Privately Held
SIC: 7349 Janitorial service, contract basis

(P-14408)
TOTAL QUALITY MAINTENANCE INC
895 Commercial St, Palo Alto
(94303-4906)
PHONE..............................650 846-4700
Peter Vesanovic, President
Dee Vesanovic, Admin Sec
EMP: 180
SQ FT: 2,000
SALES (est): 5.8MM Privately Held
SIC: 7349 Janitorial service, contract basis

(P-14409)
TRINITY BUILDING SERVICES
430 N Canal St Ste 2, South San Francisco
(94080-4665)
PHONE..............................650 873-2121
Mike A Boschetto, President
EMP: 275
SALES (est): 9.5MM Privately Held
WEB: www.trinityservices.com
SIC: 7349 Janitorial service, contract basis

(P-14410)
TSCM CORPORATION
17791 Jamestown Ln, Huntington Beach
(92647-7134)
PHONE..............................714 841-1988
Margaret Pappano, President
Frank Pappano, Vice Pres
Frank J Pappano, Vice Pres
Jacki Wun, Office Mgr
Carlos Mendez, Info Tech Dir
EMP: 55

SALES: 4.7MM Privately Held
WEB: www.tscmcorp.com
SIC: 7349 1799 Building maintenance
services; steam cleaning of building exteriors

(P-14411)
TSI
789 W 20th St, Costa Mesa (92627-3487)
PHONE..............................949 515-7800
Thomas P Salazar, President
EMP: 100
SQ FT: 1,500
SALES (est): 1.7MM Privately Held
SIC: 7349 Building maintenance services

(P-14412)
TUTTLE FAMILY ENTERPRISES INC
Also Called: Peerless Building Maint Co
21020 Superior St, Chatsworth
(91311-4321)
PHONE..............................818 534-2566
Tim Tuttle, CEO
EMP: 350 EST: 1948
SALES (est): 10.7MM Privately Held
SIC: 7349 Building maintenance, except
repairs

(P-14413)
ULTIMATE MAINTENANCE SVCS INC
4237 Redondo Beach Blvd, Lawndale
(90260-3341)
PHONE..............................310 542-1474
Claudia Salomon, CFO
Paul Marmol, President
Sherly Garcia, Office Mgr
EMP: 50
SALES (est): 2MM Privately Held
WEB:
www.ultimatemaintenanceservices.com
SIC: 7349 Janitorial service, contract basis

(P-14414)
UNISERVE FACILITIES SVCS CORP (PA)
Also Called: Union Building Maintenance
2363 S Atlantic Blvd, Commerce
(90040-1256)
PHONE..............................213 533-1000
Sam M Hwang, Ch of Bd
Anthony Santana, COO
Eugene Hwang, Mktg Dir
James Jeon, Accounts Exec
EMP: 500
SQ FT: 5,000
SALES: 8.5MM Privately Held
SIC: 7349 Janitorial service, contract basis

(P-14415)
UNISERVE FACILITIES SVCS CORP
1200 Getty Center Dr, Los Angeles
(90049-1657)
PHONE..............................310 440-6747
F Jackson, Opers Staff
EMP: 620
SALES (corp-wide): 8.5MM Privately
Held
SIC: 7349 Janitorial service, contract basis
PA: Uniserve Facilities Services Corpora-
tion
2363 S Atlantic Blvd
Commerce CA 90040
213 533-1000

(P-14416)
UNITED BUILDING MAINT INC
8211 Sierra College Blvd, Roseville
(95661-9404)
PHONE..............................916 772-8101
Valerie Lynne Sherman, CEO
Paula Fischer, Vice Pres
EMP: 225
SQ FT: 2,500
SALES: 4.3MM Privately Held
SIC: 7349 Janitorial service, contract basis

(P-14417)
UNIVERSAL
Also Called: Clean Up
4632 Acacia Ave, San Bernardino
(92407-3539)
PHONE..............................909 882-5337

EMP: 100
SALES (est): 729.6K Privately Held
SIC: 7349 Building & office cleaning serv-
ices

(P-14418)
UNIVERSAL BLDG SVCS & SUP CO (PA)
3120 Pierce St, Richmond (94804-5996)
PHONE..............................510 527-1078
Grace Brusseau, CEO
Leonard Brusseau, President
EMP: 250 EST: 1963
SQ FT: 20,000
SALES (est): 34.4MM Privately Held
WEB: www.ubsco.com
SIC: 7349 5087 5169 Janitorial service,
contract basis; janitors' supplies; chemi-
cals & allied products

(P-14419)
UNIVERSAL BLDG SVCS & SUP CO
421 N Buchanan Cir, Pacheco
(94553-5142)
PHONE..............................925 934-5533
Frank Batra, Controller
EMP: 125
SALES (corp-wide): 34.4MM Privately
Held
WEB: www.ubsco.com
SIC: 7349 Janitorial service, contract basis
PA: Universal Building Services And Supply
Co.
3120 Pierce St
Richmond CA 94804
510 527-1078

(P-14420)
UNIVERSAL BLDG SVCS & SUP CO
430 Roberson Ln, San Jose (95112-1125)
PHONE..............................408 995-5111
Su Miles, Branch Mgr
EMP: 125
SALES (corp-wide): 34.4MM Privately
Held
WEB: www.ubsco.com
SIC: 7349 Janitorial service, contract basis
PA: Universal Building Services And Supply
Co.
3120 Pierce St
Richmond CA 94804
510 527-1078

(P-14421)
UNIVERSAL SITE SERVICES INC
3174 Luyung Dr Ste 3, Rancho Cordova
(95742-6576)
PHONE..............................916 635-1122
EMP: 56
SALES (corp-wide): 6.7MM Privately
Held
SIC: 7349 4959 0782 Building mainte-
nance, except repairs; road, airport &
parking lot maintenance services; lawn
services
PA: Universal Site Services, Inc.
760 E Capitol Ave
Milpitas CA 95035
800 647-9337

(P-14422)
UNIVERSAL SITE SERVICES INC (PA)
760 E Capitol Ave, Milpitas (95035-6812)
PHONE..............................800 647-9337
Gina Vella, President
Joseph Vella, Vice Pres
EMP: 54
SQ FT: 20,000
SALES: 6.7MM Privately Held
WEB: www.universalsweeping.com
SIC: 7349 4959 0782 Building mainte-
nance, except repairs; road, airport &
parking lot maintenance services; lawn
services

(P-14423)
US METRO GROUP INC
Also Called: Metro Building Maintenance
605 S Wilton Pl, Los Angeles (90005-3220)
PHONE..............................213 382-6435
Charles Kim, CEO

Jennifer Park, *CFO*
Philip Gregg, *General Mgr*
Jonathan Martinez, *Opers Staff*
Frank Smith, *Opers Staff*
EMP: 800
SQ FT: 40,000
SALES (est): 37.8MM **Privately Held**
SIC: 7349 Janitorial service, contract basis

(P-14424)
VARSITY CONTRACTORS INC
24155 Laguna Hills Mall, Laguna Hills
(92653-3667)
PHONE....................949 586-8283
EMP: 67
SALES (corp-wide): 547.1MM **Privately Held**
SIC: 7349 Janitorial service, contract basis
HQ: Varsity Contractors, Inc.
1055 S 3600 W Ste 101
Salt Lake City UT 84104
208 232-8598

(P-14425)
VISTA UNIVERSAL INC (PA)
2430 American Ave, Hayward
(94545-1810)
PHONE....................510 785-6166
David C Schneider, *President*
Carol Ekers, *Shareholder*
Mike Ekers, *Shareholder*
Libby A Schneider, *Shareholder*
Clarence E Schneider, *Treasurer*
EMP: 50
SQ FT: 23,000
SALES: 4.4MM **Privately Held**
WEB: www.vistau.com
SIC: 7349 1731 Lighting maintenance service; general electrical contractor

(P-14426)
WARD ENTERPRISES
2679 Buhach Rd, Atwater (95301-2504)
P.O. Box 413 (95301-0413)
PHONE....................209 358-0445
Waverly Pryor, *Partner*
Dennis Williams, *Partner*
EMP: 358
SQ FT: 5,284
SALES: 941K **Privately Held**
SIC: 7349 7217 5999 Janitorial service, contract basis; maid services, contract or fee basis; carpet & furniture cleaning on location; cleaning equipment & supplies

(P-14427)
WEST COAST MAINTENANCE INC
16312 S Main St, Gardena (90248-2822)
PHONE....................310 324-2511
Christopher Mehl, *President*
Mari Guzman, *Opers Staff*
EMP: 65
SALES: 840K **Privately Held**
WEB: www.westcoastmaintenance.com
SIC: 7349 Window cleaning

(P-14428)
WTMG INC (PA)
Also Called: ServiceMaster
2735 Teepee Dr Ste D, Stockton
(95205-2438)
PHONE....................209 954-1599
Blain Bibb, *President*
EMP: 60
SALES (est): 3.6MM **Privately Held**
SIC: 7349 Building maintenance services

(P-14429)
WURMS JANITORIAL SERVICE INC
544 Bateman Cir, Corona (92880-2011)
PHONE....................951 582-0003
Larry Stewart, *President*
Pam Costa, *Vice Pres*
EMP: 80
SALES: 1.4MM **Privately Held**
SIC: 7349 Janitorial service, contract basis

(P-14430)
ZWS/ABS JOINT VENTURE LLC
39899 Balentine Dr # 200, Newark
(94560-5355)
P.O. Box 1485 (94560-6485)
PHONE....................510 461-1433
Shavila Singh, *Mng Member*

EMP: 60
SALES: 2MM **Privately Held**
SIC: 7349 Building maintenance services

7352 Medical Eqpt Rental & Leasing

(P-14431)
APRIA HEALTHCARE LLC
2150 Trabajo Dr Ste B, Oxnard
(93030-8800)
PHONE....................805 278-6700
Tammy Martin, *Manager*
EMP: 115 **Privately Held**
WEB: www.apria.com
SIC: 7352 5999 7359 5047 Medical equipment rental; medical apparatus & supplies; equipment rental & leasing; medical & hospital equipment
HQ: Apria Healthcare Llc
26220 Enterprise Ct
Lake Forest CA 92630
949 639-2163

(P-14432)
APRIA HEALTHCARE LLC
10090 Willow Creek Rd, San Diego
(92131-1623)
PHONE....................858 653-6800
Bruce Bowman, *Branch Mgr*
EMP: 89 **Privately Held**
WEB: www.apria.com
SIC: 7352 Medical equipment rental
HQ: Apria Healthcare Llc
26220 Enterprise Ct
Lake Forest CA 92630
949 639-2163

(P-14433)
APRIA HEALTHCARE LLC
1931 Lundy Ave, San Jose (95131-1847)
PHONE....................949 639-2163
Josepf Ware, *Manager*
EMP: 55 **Privately Held**
WEB: www.apria.com
SIC: 7352 5999 Medical equipment rental; medical apparatus & supplies
HQ: Apria Healthcare Llc
26220 Enterprise Ct
Lake Forest CA 92630
949 639-2163

(P-14434)
APRIA HEALTHCARE LLC
3636 N Laughlin Rd # 190, Santa Rosa
(95403-1063)
PHONE....................707 543-0979
Jennifier Lasiter, *Principal*
Dwaine Burwell, *Manager*
EMP: 53 **Privately Held**
WEB: www.apria.com
SIC: 7352 Medical equipment rental
HQ: Apria Healthcare Llc
26220 Enterprise Ct
Lake Forest CA 92630
949 639-2163

(P-14435)
OPTION ONE HOME MED EQP INC
1220 Research Dr Ste A, Redlands
(92374-4563)
P.O. Box 40700, Mesa AZ (85274-0700)
PHONE....................909 478-5413
David Scheven, *CEO*
EMP: 117
SQ FT: 36,000
SALES (est): 11.9MM **Privately Held**
WEB: www.lifecaresoln.com
SIC: 7352 5999 Medical equipment rental; medical apparatus & supplies

(P-14436)
WOUNDCO HOLDINGS INC
10877 Wilshire Blvd, Los Angeles
(90024-4341)
PHONE....................310 551-0101
Timothy J Hart, *CEO*
EMP: 500
SALES (est): 20MM **Privately Held**
SIC: 7352 Medical equipment rental

7353 Heavy Construction Eqpt Rental & Leasing

(P-14437)
BIGRENTZ INC
Also Called: Bigrentz.com
1063 Mcgaw Ave Ste 200, Irvine
(92614-5553)
PHONE....................855 999-5438
Scott Cannon, *CEO*
Dallas Imbimbo, *Ch of Bd*
Neda Imbimbo, *CFO*
Stephen Jesson, *Exec VP*
Nicholas Kovacevich, *Vice Pres*
EMP: 75
SQ FT: 15,852
SALES (est): 27.3MM **Privately Held**
SIC: 7353 Earth moving equipment, rental or leasing

(P-14438)
D&D EQUIPMENT RENTAL LLC
2596 Mission St Ste 201, San Marino
(91108-1678)
PHONE....................562 595-4555
Gary Darnell,
John Allaire,
EMP: 50
SALES (est): 5.8MM **Privately Held**
WEB: www.ddrental.com
SIC: 7353 Earth moving equipment, rental or leasing

(P-14439)
EXTERRAN INC
3449 Santa Anita Ave, El Monte
(91731-2424)
PHONE....................626 455-0739
EMP: 51
SALES (corp-wide): 3.1B **Publicly Held**
SIC: 7353
HQ: Exterran, Inc.
16666 Northchase Dr
Houston TX 77060
281 836-7000

(P-14440)
GALENA EQUIPMENT RENTAL LLC
Also Called: Biggie Crane and Ritting
10700 Bigge St, San Leandro
(94577-1032)
PHONE....................510 638-8100
Brock Settlemier,
Reid Settlemeier,
Weston Settlemier,
EMP: 50
SALES (est): 8.6MM **Privately Held**
SIC: 7353 Cranes & aerial lift equipment, rental or leasing

(P-14441)
HARBOR INDUSTRIAL SERVICES
211 N Marine Ave, Wilmington
(90744-5724)
PHONE....................310 522-1193
W Michael Hawk, *President*
Steve Hessenauer, *VP Bus Dvlpt*
Billie Noble, *Admin Mgr*
EMP: 80 **EST:** 1993
SALES (est): 9.6MM **Privately Held**
WEB: www.harborindustrial.com
SIC: 7353 Cranes & aerial lift equipment, rental or leasing

(P-14442)
HAWTHORNE MACHINERY CO (PA)
Also Called: Hawthorne Cat
16945 Camino San Bernardo, San Diego
(92127-2499)
PHONE....................858 674-7000
Tee K Ness, *President*
David Ness, *COO*
Brian Verhoeven, *CFO*
Robert Price, *Exec VP*
Stephen E Wittman, *Vice Pres*
EMP: 200
SQ FT: 130,000

SALES (est): 195.6MM **Privately Held**
SIC: 7353 7699 5082 7359 Heavy construction equipment rental; construction equipment repair; construction & mining machinery; equipment rental & leasing

(P-14443)
HAWTHORNE MACHINERY CO (HQ)
Also Called: Caterpillar Authorized Dealer
16945 Camino San Bernardo, San Diego
(92127-2499)
PHONE....................858 674-7000
Tee K Ness, *CEO*
Bob Price, *Exec VP*
Paul Hawthorne, *Vice Pres*
Mike Johnson, *Vice Pres*
Steve Sager, *Vice Pres*
EMP: 100
SQ FT: 130,000
SALES (est): 13.6MM
SALES (corp-wide): 195.6MM **Privately Held**
WEB: www.hawthornelift.com
SIC: 7353 5084 Heavy construction equipment rental; industrial machinery & equipment
PA: Hawthorne Machinery Co.
16945 Camino San Bernardo
San Diego CA 92127
858 674-7000

(P-14444)
KING EQUIPMENT LLC
1690 Ashley Way, Colton (92324-4000)
PHONE....................909 986-5300
Ernie Quijada,
Sydney Reitz, *General Mgr*
Jennifer Beltran, *Admin Asst*
Jenna Madaris, *Admin Asst*
Casey Wheeler, *Admin Asst*
EMP: 73
SALES (est): 28.8MM **Privately Held**
SIC: 7353 Heavy construction equipment rental

(P-14445)
LLC BREWER CRANE
Also Called: Brewer Crane & Rigging
12570 Highway 67 Bldg 10, Lakeside
(92040-1159)
PHONE....................619 390-8252
Brent S Brewer, *President*
Brent K Garcia, *CFO*
Andre Silva, *Foreman/Supr*
Chris Campbell, *VP Sales*
Bob Abele, *Manager*
EMP: 72 **EST:** 1997
SQ FT: 2,500
SALES: 24MM **Privately Held**
WEB: www.brewercrane.com
SIC: 7353 Cranes & aerial lift equipment, rental or leasing

(P-14446)
M T M & M INC
Also Called: Pick-A-Part
3333 Peck Rd, Monrovia (91016-5001)
PHONE....................626 445-2922
Thomas Hutton, *President*
EMP: 100
SQ FT: 1,100
SALES (est): 7.5MM
SALES (corp-wide): 9.7B **Publicly Held**
WEB: www.pickapart.com
SIC: 7353 5093 Heavy construction equipment rental; scrap & waste materials
HQ: Pick-Your-Part Auto Wrecking
1235 S Beach Blvd
Anaheim CA 92804
800 962-2277

(P-14447)
MARCO CRANE & RIGGING CO
10168 Channel Rd, Lakeside (92040-1704)
PHONE....................619 938-8080
George Wheeler, *Sales/Mktg Mgr*
EMP: 70
SALES (corp-wide): 27MM **Privately Held**
WEB: www.marcocrane.com
SIC: 7353 Cranes & aerial lift equipment, rental or leasing

PA: Marco Crane & Rigging Co.
221 S 35th Ave
Phoenix AZ 85009
602 272-2671

(P-14448)
MAXIM CRANE WORKS LP
2373 S Mariposa Rd, Stockton
(95205-7811)
PHONE..........................209 464-7635
Darrel Sudduth, *Manager*
John Bambacigno, *Manager*
EMP: 150
SALES (corp-wide): 257.1MM **Privately Held**
WEB: www.maximcrane.com
SIC: 7353 Cranes & aerial lift equipment, rental or leasing
HQ: Maxim Crane Works, L.P.
1225 Wash Pike Ste 100
Bridgeville PA 15017
412 504-0200

(P-14449)
NATIONAL BUSINESS GROUP INC (PA)
Also Called: National Tube & Steel
15319 Chatsworth St, Mission Hills
(91345-2040)
PHONE..........................818 221-6000
James Mooneyham, *President*
EMP: 85
SQ FT: 24,000
SALES (est): 123.3MM **Privately Held**
WEB: www.fence-rental.com
SIC: 7353 5039 7359 3496 Earth moving equipment, rental or leasing; wire fence, gates & accessories; garage facility & tool rental; fencing, made from purchased wire; utility trailer rental

(P-14450)
NOBLE RENTS INC
8314 Slauson Ave, Pico Rivera
(90660-4323)
PHONE..........................855 767-4424
Nabil Kassam, *CEO*
Tom Caldaroni, *CFO*
Suzy Taherian, *Corp Secy*
EMP: 65 **EST:** 2011
SQ FT: 62,766
SALES: 13.4MM **Privately Held**
SIC: 7353 Heavy construction equipment rental

(P-14451)
NORTHWEST EXCAVATING INC
18201 Napa St, Northridge (91325-3374)
PHONE..........................818 349-5861
Susan Groff, *CEO*
Robbie Groff, *Vice Pres*
Cecille Bandalaria, *Executive Asst*
Jane Sotto, *Controller*
EMP: 72
SQ FT: 2,500
SALES (est): 15.2MM **Privately Held**
WEB: www.nwexc.com
SIC: 7353 1794 Heavy construction equipment rental; excavation & grading, building construction

(P-14452)
OFFSHORE CRANE & SERVICE CO (PA)
Also Called: T & T Truck & Crane Service
1375 N Olive St Ste A, Ventura
(93001-1375)
P.O. Box 1748 (93002-1748)
PHONE..........................805 648-3348
Earl G Holder, *CEO*
Tim Holder, *President*
Kimberly A Loft, *Treasurer*
Shawn Paul, *Vice Pres*
Jeff Helm, *General Mgr*
EMP: 52 **EST:** 1970
SQ FT: 11,000
SALES (est): 14.2MM **Privately Held**
SIC: 7353 4212 Cranes & aerial lift equipment, rental or leasing; truck rental with drivers

(P-14453)
PEED EQUIPMENT COMPANY
43466 Business Park Dr, Temecula
(92590-5526)
PHONE..........................951 657-0900

Carolyn Peed, *President*
Michael Peed, *Treasurer*
David Peed, *General Mgr*
EMP: 50
SQ FT: 17,000
SALES (est): 12.1MM **Privately Held**
SIC: 7353 7699 Heavy construction equipment rental; construction equipment repair

(P-14454)
RALPH D MITZEL INC
Also Called: Mitzel Company
1520 N Fairview St, Santa Ana
(92706-3111)
PHONE..........................714 554-4745
Ralph D Mitzel Jr, *President*
Bill Stehle, *CFO*
Arlene Mitzel, *Corp Secy*
John K Mitzel, *Vice Pres*
EMP: 100
SQ FT: 1,000
SALES (est): 13.2MM **Privately Held**
SIC: 7353 1794 Heavy construction equipment rental; excavation & grading, building construction

(P-14455)
RDO CONSTRUCTION EQUIPMENT CO
Also Called: John Deere Authorized Dealer
10108 Riverford Rd, Lakeside
(92040-2740)
PHONE..........................619 443-3758
Ron Offets, *President*
Christopher Scott, *General Mgr*
Bruce Johnson, *Manager*
Terrance Lacher, *Parts Mgr*
EMP: 60
SQ FT: 2,200
SALES (est): 13.2MM **Privately Held**
WEB: www.bbrental.com
SIC: 7353 5082 Heavy construction equipment rental; general construction machinery & equipment

(P-14456)
RJ ALLEN INC
10392 Stanford Ave, Garden Grove
(92840-6301)
PHONE..........................714 539-1022
Andrew Allen, *President*
Ron Markham, *Vice Pres*
EMP: 65
SQ FT: 20,000
SALES (est): 16.8MM **Privately Held**
WEB: www.rjalleninc.com
SIC: 7353 Heavy construction equipment rental

(P-14457)
SAVALA EQUIPMENT COMPANY INC (PA)
Also Called: Savala Equipment Rentals
16402 Construction Cir E, Irvine
(92606-4408)
PHONE..........................949 552-1859
Sean Savala, *President*
Scott Damon, *VP Sales*
EMP: 60
SQ FT: 3,200
SALES (est): 16.4MM **Privately Held**
WEB: www.savala.com
SIC: 7353 Cranes & aerial lift equipment, rental or leasing

(P-14458)
SHEEDY DRAYAGE CO (PA)
1215 Michigan St, San Francisco
(94107-3518)
P.O. Box 77004 (94107-0004)
PHONE..........................415 648-7171
Don Russell, *Chairman*
Richard Battaini, *President*
Michael A Battaini, *CEO*
Peter Hogan, *Corp Secy*
EMP: 80 **EST:** 1925
SQ FT: 25,000
SALES (est): 25MM **Privately Held**
WEB: www.sheedycrane.com
SIC: 7353 Cranes & aerial lift equipment, rental or leasing

(P-14459)
TONY R CRISALLI INC
3468 Campbell St, Riverside (92509-1029)
PHONE..........................951 727-0110
Tony R Crisalli, *President*
EMP: 50
SALES (est): 5.2MM **Privately Held**
SIC: 7353 Heavy construction equipment rental

(P-14460)
TRITON CONT INTL INC N AMER (DH)
456 Montgomery St Ste 800, San Francisco
(94104-1241)
PHONE..........................415 956-6311
Edward P Schneider, *CEO*
Glen Regier, *Vice Pres*
Jeff Wheatley, *Info Tech Mgr*
Geri Gualberto, *Accounting Mgr*
Katherine Wang, *Accounting Mgr*
EMP: 82
SALES (est): 21MM **Privately Held**
SIC: 7353 7359 Heavy construction equipment rental; shipping container leasing

(P-14461)
WASTE MGT COLLECTN RECYCL INC
1800 S Grand Ave, Santa Ana
(92705-4800)
PHONE..........................714 637-3010
Lee Hicks, *Principal*
Angelica Hernandez, *Hum Res Coord*
Eric Rasmussen, *Sales Dir*
Sissy Rivas, *Cust Mgr*
Hilario Perea, *Manager*
EMP: 350
SALES (est): 122.3MM
SALES (corp-wide): 14.4B **Publicly Held**
SIC: 7353 4953 Heavy construction equipment rental; refuse collection & disposal services
PA: Waste Management, Inc.
1001 Fannin St Ste 4000
Houston TX 77002
713 512-6200

(P-14462)
WESTERN PCF CRANE & EQP LLC (DH)
8600 Calabash Ave, Fontana (92335-3018)
PHONE..........................562 286-6618
Robert G Johnson, *President*
Robert G Jonhson, *President*
Matt Morrison, *Area Mgr*
Matt Noonan, *Sales Staff*
Steve Zaback, *Sales Staff*
EMP: 70
SQ FT: 45,000
SALES (est): 14.5MM
SALES (corp-wide): 193MM **Privately Held**
SIC: 7353 Cranes & aerial lift equipment, rental or leasing
HQ: Mi-Jack Products Inc.
3111 167th St
Hazel Crest IL 60429
708 596-5200

7359 Equipment Rental & Leasing, NEC

(P-14463)
(A) TOOL SHED INC (PA)
Also Called: A Tool Shed Equipment Rentals
3700 Soquel Ave, Santa Cruz
(95062-1774)
PHONE..........................831 477-7133
Robert Pedersen, *President*
Bruce Harmon, *General Mgr*
Star Luna, *Human Res Mgr*
Tim Heer, *Manager*
EMP: 72
SQ FT: 2,500
SALES (est): 20.3MM **Privately Held**
WEB: www.atoolshed.com
SIC: 7359 Tool rental

(P-14464)
A-THRONE CO INC
1850 E 33rd St, Long Beach (90807-5208)
PHONE..........................562 981-1197

Michael L Rice, *President*
Minerva Songco, *General Mgr*
Corey Vane, *Opers Mgr*
EMP: 55
SALES (est): 8.4MM **Privately Held**
WEB: www.athrone.com
SIC: 7359 1799 Portable toilet rental; fence construction

(P-14465)
ADVANCED TEST EQUIPMENT CORP
Also Called: Advanced Test Eqp Rentals
10401 Roselle St, San Diego (92121-1523)
PHONE..........................858 558-6500
James P Berg, *CEO*
Jill E Berg, *President*
John Reece, *Technology*
Gabriel Alcala, *Technical Staff*
Enrique Gonzalez, *Accounting Mgr*
EMP: 60
SQ FT: 25,000
SALES (est): 19.3MM **Privately Held**
WEB: www.atecorp.com
SIC: 7359 Equipment rental & leasing

(P-14466)
AFTER-PARTY2 INC (HQ)
Also Called: Classic Party Rentals
901 W Hillcrest Blvd, Inglewood
(90301-2100)
PHONE..........................310 202-0011
Jeff Black, *President*
Shawna Torres, *Human Resources*
Margot Kent, *Sales Staff*
Ana Sorto, *Sales Staff*
Gloeli Calderon, *Manager*
EMP: 200
SALES (est): 66.3MM **Publicly Held**
SIC: 7359 Party supplies rental services

(P-14467)
AFTER-PARTY2 INC
2310 E Imperial Hwy, El Segundo
(90245-2813)
PHONE..........................310 535-3660
Michael Stern, *Manager*
EMP: 59 **Publicly Held**
SIC: 7359 Tent & tarpaulin rental
HQ: After-Party2, Inc.
901 W Hillcrest Blvd
Inglewood CA 90301
310 202-0011

(P-14468)
AIR LEASE CORPORATION (PA)
2000 Avenue Of The Stars 1000n, Los Angeles (90067-4734)
PHONE..........................310 553-0555
John L Plueger, *President*
Steven F Udvar-Hazy, *Ch of Bd*
Pablo Chavez, *President*
Heidi Hyun, *President*
Sabrina Lemmens, *President*
EMP: 74
SALES: 1.5B **Publicly Held**
SIC: 7359 7389 Aircraft rental; aircraft & industrial truck rental services; financial services

(P-14469)
AJAX PORTABLE SERVICES
Also Called: Waste Management
11240 Commercial Pkwy, Castroville
(95012-3206)
PHONE..........................831 384-5000
David Steiner, *President*
Stephen Miceli, *District Mgr*
Kent Vuong, *Software Engr*
Adam Mallory, *Business Anlyst*
Maura Lavin, *Engineer*
EMP: 50
SALES (est): 5.3MM **Privately Held**
SIC: 7359 Portable toilet rental

(P-14470)
ALTA EQUIPMENT LEASING COMPANY
50 California St Fl 24, San Francisco
(94111-4624)
PHONE..........................415 875-1000
Michael J Sangiacomo, *President*
Archie L Humphrey, *COO*
Mark Lomele, *CFO*
EMP: 55

SALES (est): 3.5MM
SALES (corp-wide): 1.3B **Privately Held**
WEB: www.norcalwastesystemsofbutte-county.com
SIC: 7359 Equipment rental & leasing
PA: Recology Inc.
　50 California St Ste 2400
　San Francisco CA 94111
　415 875-1000

(P-14471)
AMADA CAPITAL CORPORATION
7025 Firestone Blvd, Buena Park (90621-1869)
PHONE..................................714 739-2111
Mike Guerin, *President*
David Kehrli, *Vice Pres*
EMP: 100
SQ FT: 103,000
SALES (est): 13.5MM
SALES (corp-wide): 2.8B **Privately Held**
SIC: 7359 Equipment rental & leasing
HQ: Amada North America, Inc
　7025 Firestone Blvd
　Buena Park CA 90621
　-

(P-14472)
ANDY GUMP INC
11551 Hart St, North Hollywood (91605-6204)
PHONE..................................818 255-0650
Gary Wood, *Manager*
Thomas Field, *Sales Mgr*
EMP: 70
SALES (est): 2.4MM
SALES (corp-wide): 21.6MM **Privately Held**
WEB: www.andygump.com
SIC: 7359 Portable toilet rental
PA: Andy Gump, Inc.
　26410 Summit Cir
　Santa Clarita CA 91350
　661 251-7721

(P-14473)
ARENA STUART RENTALS INC
454 S Abbott Ave, Milpitas (95035-5258)
PHONE..................................408 856-3232
Michael Berman, *President*
EMP: 150
SALES (est): 1.7MM **Privately Held**
SIC: 7359 5947 Party supplies rental services; party favors

(P-14474)
AUDIO VISUAL HEADQUARTERS (DH)
Also Called: Psav
16320 Arthur St, Cerritos (90703-2129)
PHONE..................................310 603-0652
Michael O'Brien, *President*
Pat Gephardt, *CFO*
James Hunter, *Technician*
Jacob Vanvolkenburgh, *Technician*
Jorge Contreras, *Technical Staff*
EMP: 50
SQ FT: 70,000
SALES (est): 33MM
SALES (corp-wide): 546.9MM **Privately Held**
WEB: www.avhq.com
SIC: 7359 7389 Audio-visual equipment & supply rental; convention & show services
HQ: Audio Visual Services Group, Inc.
　24105 Frampton Ave
　Harbor City CA 90710
　562 366-0620

(P-14475)
BA LEASING & CAPITAL CORP (DH)
555 California St Fl 4, San Francisco (94104-1506)
PHONE..................................415 765-1804
Richard Harris, *President*
K Thomas Rose, *COO*
Rod Hurd, *Treasurer*
Oliver James Warner, *Vice Pres*
EMP: 130 EST: 1955
SALES (est): 6.3MM
SALES (corp-wide): 100.2B **Publicly Held**
SIC: 7359 Equipment rental & leasing

HQ: Banc Of America Leasing & Capital, Llc
　555 California St Fl 4
　San Francisco CA 94104
　415 765-7349

(P-14476)
BAKERCORP (DH)
3020 Old Ranch Pkwy # 220, Seal Beach (90740-2765)
PHONE..................................562 430-6262
Bob Craycraft, *President*
Raymond Aronoff, *COO*
David Ignata, *CFO*
Neal Crost, *Division VP*
Jon Heslin, *Division VP*
EMP: 120
SQ FT: 7,500
SALES (est): 256.7MM
SALES (corp-wide): 6.6B **Publicly Held**
WEB: www.bakercorp.com
SIC: 7359 Equipment rental & leasing
HQ: Bakercorp International, Inc.
　7800 Dallas Pkwy Ste 500
　Plano TX 75024
　888 882-4895

(P-14477)
BAY CITIES CRANE & RIGGING INC (PA)
Also Called: Bragg Crane & Rigging
457 Parr Blvd, Richmond (94801-1133)
PHONE..................................510 232-7222
Marilynn Bragg, *President*
Mary Ann Pool, *Corp Secy*
Edward Gray, *Sales Staff*
Mike Lambert, *Sales Staff*
David McCabe, *Sales Staff*
EMP: 50 EST: 1970
SQ FT: 10,000
SALES (est): 6.4MM **Privately Held**
WEB: www.braggnorcal.com
SIC: 7359 7353 Equipment rental & leasing; cranes & aerial lift equipment, rental or leasing

(P-14478)
BBAM ARCFT HOLDINGS 137 LABUAN
50 California St Fl 14, San Francisco (94111-4683)
PHONE..................................415 267-1600
Steve Zissis, *CEO*
EMP: 100
SALES (est): 9.5MM **Privately Held**
SIC: 7359 Aircraft rental

(P-14479)
BRIGHT EVENT RENTALS LLC (PA)
Also Called: Wine Country Party & Events
1640 W 190th St, Torrance (90501-1113)
PHONE..................................310 202-0011
Michael Bjornstad, *Mng Member*
Casey Stone, *Principal*
Christine Pease, *Accounting Mgr*
Francisco Ledezma, *Opers Mgr*
Gama Sanchez, *Opers Staff*
EMP: 240
SALES (est): 76.2MM **Privately Held**
SIC: 7359 Party supplies rental services

(P-14480)
BRIGHT EVENT RENTALS LLC
Also Called: Event Rentals San Diego
7069 Consolidated Way, San Diego (92121-2688)
PHONE..................................858 496-9700
EMP: 510
SALES (corp-wide): 76.2MM **Privately Held**
SIC: 7359 Equipment rental & leasing
PA: Bright Event Rentals, Llc
　1640 W 190th St
　Torrance CA 90501
　310 202-0011

(P-14481)
BRIGHT EVENT RENTALS LLC
22674 Broadway Ste A, Sonoma (95476-8217)
PHONE..................................310 202-0011
Matt Wiltshire, *Manager*
EMP: 150

SALES (corp-wide): 76.2MM **Privately Held**
SIC: 7359 Equipment rental & leasing
PA: Bright Event Rentals, Llc
　1640 W 190th St
　Torrance CA 90501
　310 202-0011

(P-14482)
BROOK FURNITURE RENTAL INC
Also Called: Brook Furniture Clearance Ctr
30985 Santana St, Hayward (94544-7029)
PHONE..................................510 487-4440
Robert W Crawford, *Owner*
EMP: 50
SALES (corp-wide): 71.1MM **Privately Held**
WEB: www.bfr.com
SIC: 7359 Furniture rental
HQ: Brook Furniture Rental, Inc.
　100 N Field Dr Ste 220
　Lake Forest IL 60045
　847 810-4000

(P-14483)
CAI INTERNATIONAL INC (PA)
1 Market Plz Ste 900, San Francisco (94105-1101)
PHONE..................................415 788-0100
Hiromitsu Ogawa, *Ch of Bd*
David Remington, *Ch of Bd*
Victor M Garcia, *President*
Timothy B Page, *CFO*
Gary Sawka, *Bd of Directors*
▼ EMP: 94
SALES (est): 348.3MM **Publicly Held**
WEB: www.capps.com
SIC: 7359 Shipping container leasing

(P-14484)
CAL WEST GENERAL ENGRG INC
5480 Baltimore Dr Ste 215, La Mesa (91942-2066)
PHONE..................................619 469-5811
Ronald E Provience, *CEO*
Frank A Passiglia, *President*
EMP: 50
SQ FT: 2,000
SALES (est): 4.6MM **Privately Held**
SIC: 7359 Equipment rental & leasing

(P-14485)
CENTRAL VALLEY PARTY SUPPLY
Also Called: Grand Events
3250 Dale Rd Ste I, Modesto (95356-0578)
PHONE..................................209 569-0399
Ray Pogue, *Principal*
EMP: 50
SQ FT: 37,000
SALES (est): 3.7MM **Privately Held**
WEB: www.grand-events.com
SIC: 7359 Party supplies rental services

(P-14486)
CHOURA EVENTS
540 Hawaii Ave, Torrance (90503-5148)
PHONE..................................310 320-6200
James Ryan Choura, *CEO*
EMP: 80 EST: 2014
SALES: 8MM **Privately Held**
SIC: 7359 Party supplies rental services

(P-14487)
CITIZENS FINANCIAL SVCS INC
Also Called: Citizens Financial Svc.
3130 Harbor Blvd, Costa Mesa (92626-2507)
PHONE..................................714 751-6100
Jeff Holtshopple, *Branch Mgr*
EMP: 63
SALES (corp-wide): 56.7MM **Publicly Held**
SIC: 7359 Equipment rental & leasing
PA: Citizens Financial Services, Inc.
　15 S Main St
　Mansfield PA 16933
　570 662-2121

(P-14488)
COMPASS GROUP USA INC
Also Called: Canteen Vending
12640 Knott St, Garden Grove (92841-3902)
PHONE..................................714 899-2520
Ron Wanamaker, *Vice Pres*
EMP: 125
SALES (corp-wide): 28.9B **Privately Held**
WEB: www.compass-usa.com
SIC: 7359 7699 5962 Vending machine rental; vending machine repair; merchandising machine operators
HQ: Compass Group Usa, Inc.
　2400 Yorkmont Rd
　Charlotte NC 28217
　704 328-4000

(P-14489)
CONCORD JET SERVICE INC (PA)
1380 Galaxy Way Ste B, Concord (94520-4912)
P.O. Box 907 (94522-0907)
PHONE..................................925 682-4830
Kenneth Hoffman, *President*
Goy Fuller, *Principal*
EMP: 50
SALES (est): 4.4MM **Privately Held**
SIC: 7359 Aircraft rental

(P-14490)
CORT BUSINESS SERVICES CORP
14350 Grfield Ave Ste 500, Paramount (90723)
PHONE..................................562 582-1515
Pat Bockenstette, *Branch Mgr*
EMP: 70
SALES (corp-wide): 242.1B **Publicly Held**
SIC: 7359 Furniture rental
HQ: Cort Business Services Corporation
　15000 Conference
　Chantilly VA 20151
　703 968-8500

(P-14491)
CP OPCO LLC
Also Called: Classic Party Rentals
22674 Broadway A, Sonoma (95476-8217)
PHONE..................................707 253-2332
EMP: 59
SALES (corp-wide): 1.9MM **Privately Held**
SIC: 7359
HQ: Cp Opco, Llc
　901 W Hillcrest Blvd A
　Inglewood CA 90301
　310 966-4900

(P-14492)
CP OPCO LLC
Also Called: Classic Party Rentals
7069 Cnsld Way Ste 300, San Diego (92121)
PHONE..................................858 496-9700
EMP: 100
SALES (corp-wide): 1.9MM **Privately Held**
SIC: 7359
HQ: Cp Opco, Llc
　901 W Hillcrest Blvd A
　Inglewood CA 90301
　310 966-4900

(P-14493)
CP OPCO LLC
Also Called: Classic Party Rentals
333 S Grand Ave Ste 4070, Los Angeles (90071-1544)
PHONE..................................209 524-1966
EMP: 59
SALES (corp-wide): 1.9MM **Privately Held**
SIC: 7359
HQ: Cp Opco, Llc
　901 W Hillcrest Blvd A
　Inglewood CA 90301
　310 966-4900

P
R
O
D
U
C
T
S
&
S
V
C
S

(P-14494)
CP OPCO LLC
Also Called: Classic Party Rentals
11766 Wilshire Blvd # 380, Los Angeles
(90025-6538)
PHONE..........................310 966-4900
EMP: 59
SALES (corp-wide): 1.9MM **Privately Held**
SIC: 7359
HQ: Cp Opco, Llc
901 W Hillcrest Blvd A
Inglewood CA 90301
310 966-4900

(P-14495)
CP OPCO LLC
Also Called: Classic Party Rentals
22674 Broadway A, Sonoma (95476-8217)
PHONE..........................650 652-0300
Fax: 650 697-9090
EMP: 59
SALES (corp-wide): 1.9MM **Privately Held**
SIC: 7359
HQ: Cp Opco, Llc
901 W Hillcrest Blvd A
Inglewood CA 90301
310 966-4900

(P-14496)
CP OPCO LLC
Also Called: Classic Party Rentals
1120 Mark Ave, Carpinteria (93013-2918)
PHONE..........................805 566-3566
Fax: 805 566-3599
EMP: 59
SALES (corp-wide): 1.9MM **Privately Held**
SIC: 7359
HQ: Cp Opco, Llc
901 W Hillcrest Blvd A
Inglewood CA 90301
310 966-4900

(P-14497)
CP OPCO LLC
Also Called: Classic Party Rentals
3101 S Harbor Blvd, Santa Ana
(92704-6826)
PHONE..........................714 540-6111
EMP: 100
SALES (corp-wide): 1.9MM **Privately Held**
SIC: 7359
HQ: Cp Opco, Llc
901 W Hillcrest Blvd A
Inglewood CA 90301
310 966-4900

(P-14498)
CWF INC
Also Called: A-1 Party Rentals
251 E Front St, Covina (91723-1613)
PHONE..........................626 967-0500
Chet Fortney, *President*
EMP: 51
SALES: 950K **Privately Held**
SIC: 7359 Party supplies rental services

(P-14499)
DIAMOND ENVIRONMENTAL SVCS LP
807 E Mission Rd, San Marcos
(92069-3002)
PHONE..........................760 744-7191
Eric De Jong,
Eric Jong, *Project Mgr*
Don Sims, *Sales Staff*
EMP: 100 EST: 1997
SQ FT: 2,000
SALES (est): 21.7MM **Privately Held**
SIC: 7359 Portable toilet rental

(P-14500)
DISPATCH TRANSPORTATION LLC
Also Called: Dispatch Commodity Trucking
14032 Santa Ana Ave, Fontana
(92337-7035)
PHONE..........................909 355-5531
Bruce Degler,
Kim Pugmire,
EMP: 150
SQ FT: 3,500

SALES (est): 20.9MM **Privately Held**
WEB: www.proloaders.com
SIC: 7359 Equipment rental & leasing

(P-14501)
EAGLE HIGH REACH EQUIPMENT LLC
14241 Alondra Blvd, La Mirada
(90638-5501)
PHONE..........................619 265-2637
John Benjamin,
EMP: 70
SQ FT: 22,000
SALES (est): 4MM **Privately Held**
SIC: 7359 7353 5084 Equipment rental & leasing; cranes & aerial lift equipment, rental or leasing; materials handling machinery

(P-14502)
EL CAMINO RENTAL
1833 Oceanside Blvd Ste D, Oceanside
(92054-3456)
PHONE..........................760 722-7368
Bill Mahalic, *Owner*
Ted Donnelly, *General Mgr*
EMP: 50
SALES (est): 3.3MM **Privately Held**
WEB: www.elcaminorental.com
SIC: 7359 Party supplies rental services

(P-14503)
ELECTRO RENT CORPORATION (PA)
8511 Fllbrook Ave Ste 200, West Hills
(91304)
P.O. Box 605, Newbury Park (91319-0605)
PHONE..........................818 786-2525
Steven Markheim, *CEO*
Allen Sciarillo, *CFO*
Patrick Weisgarber, *Engineer*
Beverly Walin, *Manager*
Vinesh Mhalsekar, *Accounts Mgr*
EMP: 148 EST: 1965
SALES (est): 142MM **Privately Held**
SIC: 7359 7377 5065 5045 Electronic equipment rental, except computers; computer rental & leasing; electronic parts & equipment; computers & accessories, personal & home entertainment

(P-14504)
EZ ACCEPTANCE INC
7651 Ronson Rd, San Diego (92111-1511)
PHONE..........................858 278-8351
Ronald Zagami, *President*
Mike Toomey, *Vice Pres*
EMP: 140
SALES (est): 4.2MM **Privately Held**
SIC: 7359 Equipment rental & leasing

(P-14505)
FIFTH & SUNSET ENTERPRISES LLC
Also Called: 5th & Sunset Productions
12322 Exposition Blvd, Los Angeles
(90064-1014)
PHONE..........................310 979-0212
Bruce E Kramer, *President*
EMP: 85
SQ FT: 19,000
SALES: 12.5MM **Privately Held**
SIC: 7359 7335 Equipment rental & leasing; still & slide file production

(P-14506)
FREEMAN AUDIO VISUAL LLC
901 E South St, Anaheim (92805-5347)
PHONE..........................714 254-3400
Gabriele Buonacorsi, *Branch Mgr*
EMP: 200
SALES (corp-wide): 2.7B **Privately Held**
WEB: www.avwtelav.com
SIC: 7359 Audio-visual equipment & supply rental
HQ: Freeman Audio Visual, Llc
1600 Viceroy Dr Ste 100
Dallas TX 75235
214 445-1000

(P-14507)
H&E EQUIPMENT SERVICES INC
14241 Alondra Blvd, La Mirada
(90638-5501)
PHONE..........................714 522-6590
David Harkey, *Manager*
EMP: 110
SALES (corp-wide): 1B **Publicly Held**
WEB: www.engquist.com
SIC: 7359 7353 5084 Equipment rental & leasing; cranes & aerial lift equipment, rental or leasing; materials handling machinery
PA: H&E Equipment Services, Inc.
7500 Pecue Ln
Baton Rouge LA 70809
225 298-5200

(P-14508)
HANA FINANCIAL INC (PA)
1000 Wilshire Blvd Fl 20, Los Angeles
(90017-5645)
PHONE..........................213 240-1234
Sunnie S Kim, *CEO*
Kyle Kang, *Officer*
Michelle Maldonado, *Officer*
Michelle Yue, *Officer*
Charlotte Gardner, *Senior VP*
EMP: 85
SQ FT: 24,000
SALES (est): 16.8MM **Privately Held**
SIC: 7359 6153 6159 Equipment rental & leasing; factoring services; small business investment companies

(P-14509)
HERC RENTALS INC
Also Called: Herc Rentals 9741
5500 Commerce Blvd, Rohnert Park
(94928-1607)
PHONE..........................707 586-6491
Mark Hobson, *Regional Mgr*
Donovan Brian, *Controller*
Freeman Renee, *Recruiter*
Kathy Fagan, *Manager*
EMP: 58
SALES (corp-wide): 1.7B **Publicly Held**
SIC: 7359 Equipment rental & leasing
HQ: Herc Rentals Inc.
27500 Rverview Ctr Bldg 7
Bonita Springs FL 34134
800 654-6659

(P-14510)
HERC RENTALS INC
Also Called: Herc Rentals 9638
22422 S Alameda St, Carson (90810-1903)
PHONE..........................310 233-5000
Brian Dorte, *Manager*
EMP: 50
SQ FT: 19,494
SALES (corp-wide): 1.7B **Publicly Held**
WEB: www.hertzequip.com
SIC: 7359 Equipment rental & leasing
HQ: Herc Rentals Inc.
27500 Rverview Ctr Bldg 7
Bonita Springs FL 34134
800 654-6659

(P-14511)
HERC RENTALS INC
Also Called: Herc Rentals 9643
6315 Snow Rd, Bakersfield (93308-9531)
PHONE..........................661 392-3661
Matt Hudnall, *Branch Mgr*
Viola Pitcher, *Executive*
EMP: 225
SALES (corp-wide): 1.7B **Publicly Held**
SIC: 7359 Equipment rental & leasing
HQ: Herc Rentals Inc.
27500 Rverview Ctr Bldg 7
Bonita Springs FL 34134
800 654-6659

(P-14512)
HERC RENTALS INC
Also Called: Herc Rentals 9748
5251 Industrial Way, Benicia (94510-1034)
PHONE..........................707 747-4444
John Moyer, *Manager*
EMP: 50
SALES (corp-wide): 1.7B **Publicly Held**
SIC: 7359 Equipment rental & leasing

HQ: Herc Rentals Inc.
27500 Rverview Ctr Bldg 7
Bonita Springs FL 34134
800 654-6659

(P-14513)
HERC RENTALS INC
Also Called: Herc Rentals Prosolutions
7727 Oakport St, Oakland (94621-2026)
PHONE..........................510 633-2040
Ted Oshea, *Manager*
EMP: 225
SALES (corp-wide): 1.7B **Publicly Held**
SIC: 7359 Equipment rental & leasing
HQ: Herc Rentals Inc.
27500 Rverview Ctr Bldg 7
Bonita Springs FL 34134
800 654-6659

(P-14514)
HOLZMUELLER CORPORATION
Also Called: Holzmueller Productions
1000 25th St, San Francisco (94107-3509)
PHONE..........................415 826-8383
Richard P Gentschel, *President*
Carol Gentschel, *Vice Pres*
Will Hammersmith, *Prdtn Mgr*
Dave Tier, *Foreman/Supr*
Michael Hamlin, *Sales Mgr*
EMP: 50
SQ FT: 30,000
SALES (est): 6.2MM **Privately Held**
WEB: www.holzmueller.com
SIC: 7359 5719 1731 Sound & lighting equipment rental; lighting fixtures; electrical work

(P-14515)
HUB CONSTRUCTION SPC INC (PA)
Also Called: Hub Construction Sups & Eqp
379 S I St, San Bernardino (92410-2409)
P.O. Box 1269 (92402-1269)
PHONE..........................909 889-0161
Robert T Gogo, *President*
Bernice Gogo, *Corp Secy*
Casey Lester, *Technology*
James Hill, *Controller*
Dean Beatty, *Purch Agent*
EMP: 50
SQ FT: 25,000
SALES (est): 48.1MM **Privately Held**
SIC: 7359 5082 Equipment rental & leasing; construction & mining machinery

(P-14516)
IMPERIAL MRIDIAN COMPANIES INC
Also Called: Imca Capital
11901 Santa Monica Blvd # 338, Los Angeles (90025-2767)
PHONE..........................310 447-3460
Blake B Johnson, *President*
Emma Cabildo, *CFO*
EMP: 85
SQ FT: 10,200
SALES: 10MM **Privately Held**
SIC: 7359 Equipment rental & leasing

(P-14517)
J M EQUIPMENT COMPANY INC (PA)
Also Called: John Deere Authorized Dealer
321 Spreckels Ave, Manteca (95336-6007)
PHONE..........................209 522-3271
Ray Azevedo, *CEO*
Dave Baiocchi, *President*
Ed Henriquez, *President*
Vincent C Victorine, *CFO*
Audie Burgan, *Vice Pres*
EMP: 80
SQ FT: 7,000
SALES (est): 38.3MM **Privately Held**
WEB: www.jmequipment.com
SIC: 7359 5084 5999 Equipment rental & leasing; materials handling machinery; farm equipment & supplies; farm machinery; farm tractors

(P-14518)
JALUX AMERICAS INC (HQ)
390 N Pacific Coast Hwy # 2000, El Segundo (90245-4475)
PHONE..........................310 524-1000
Osamu Yamaguchi, *Principal*

Shinichi Matsuyama, *President*
Yu Katahira, *Treasurer*
Naohiko Habuki, *Corp Secy*
Hidebumi Mori, *Exec VP*
EMP: 50
SQ FT: 15,000
SALES: 21.8MM
SALES (corp-wide): 1.4B **Privately Held**
WEB: www.jaluxam.com
SIC: 7359 5088 5199 Aircraft rental; office machine rental, except computers; aircraft equipment & supplies; variety store merchandise
PA: Jalux Inc.
1-2-70, Konan
Minato-Ku TKY 108-0
363 678-800

(P-14519)
JC PARTY RENTALS INC
11562 Vanowen St, North Hollywood
(91605-6229)
PHONE..........................818 765-4819
Delmy Chavarria, *CEO*
Jose Urquilla, *President*
EMP: 52
SQ FT: 6,600
SALES: 653K **Privately Held**
SIC: 7359 Party supplies rental services

(P-14520)
JULES AND ASSOCIATES INC
515 S Figueroa St # 1900, Los Angeles
(90071-3336)
PHONE..........................213 362-5600
Jules Buenabenta, *President*
Michael Behar, *Senior VP*
Scott Monroe, *Senior VP*
Angel E Nevarez, *General Counsel*
EMP: 51
SQ FT: 15,000
SALES: 140MM **Privately Held**
WEB: www.julesandassociates.com
SIC: 7359 Equipment rental & leasing

(P-14521)
L A PARTY RENTS INC
13520 Saticoy St, Van Nuys (91402-6428)
PHONE..........................818 989-4300
Gerome Nehus, *President*
Kevin Dwyer, *Admin Asst*
Jerry Nehus, *CIO*
Rekha Sood, *Data Proc Staff*
Sukie Alvarado, *Consultant*
EMP: 100
SALES (est): 11.3MM **Privately Held**
WEB: www.lapartyrents.com
SIC: 7359 Party supplies rental services

(P-14522)
LOUNGE 22 LLC (PA)
211 N Brand Blvd, Glendale (91203-2609)
PHONE..........................818 502-0700
Armen S Gharabegian,
Armen Gharabegian,
EMP: 70
SALES (est): 3.7MM **Privately Held**
WEB: www.lounge22.com
SIC: 7359 5712 Furniture rental; furniture stores

(P-14523)
MACQURIE ARCFT LSG SVCS US INC
2 Embarcadero Ctr Ste 200, San Francisco
(94111-3801)
PHONE..........................415 829-6600
John R Willingham, *CEO*
Harry Forsythe, *Exec VP*
Nora Bergman, *Senior VP*
Lea Banducci, *Vice Pres*
Bruce Hogarth, *Vice Pres*
EMP: 60
SALES (est): 11.3MM **Privately Held**
SIC: 7359 Aircraft rental
HQ: Macquarie Airfinance (No 2) Limited
South Bank House
Dublin
-

(P-14524)
MCGRATH RENTCORP
Adler Tank Rentals
5700 Las Positas Rd, Livermore
(94551-7806)
PHONE..........................925 453-3312

Steve Adler, *Principal*
EMP: 94
SALES (corp-wide): 462MM **Publicly Held**
SIC: 7359 Equipment rental & leasing
PA: Mcgrath Rentcorp
5700 Las Positas Rd
Livermore CA 94551
925 606-9200

(P-14525)
MEETING SERVICES INC
Also Called: MSI PRODUCTION SERVICES
10895 Thornmint Rd Ste A, San Diego
(92127-2420)
PHONE..........................858 348-0100
John Brinkman, *CEO*
Tom Bollard, *Shareholder*
Ed Lafever, *Shareholder*
Ray Lucy, *Shareholder*
Suzanne Carlson, *Executive*
EMP: 90
SQ FT: 20,000
SALES: 12.7MM **Privately Held**
WEB: www.msiprod.com
SIC: 7359 7629 5049 Audio-visual equipment & supply rental; electrical equipment repair, high voltage; theatrical equipment & supplies

(P-14526)
MICROFINANCIAL INCORPORATED
2801 Townsgate Rd, Westlake Village
(91361-3003)
PHONE..........................805 367-8900
Richard Latour, *CEO*
EMP: 139
SALES (corp-wide): 62.5MM **Privately Held**
SIC: 7359 Business machine & electronic equipment rental services
HQ: Microfinancial Incorporated
1600 District Ave Ste 200
Burlington MA 01803
781 994-4800

(P-14527)
MICROLEASE INC (DH)
6060 Sepulveda Blvd, Van Nuys
(91411-2512)
PHONE..........................866 520-0200
Gordon Curwen, *Vice Pres*
Michael E Clark, *CEO*
Vince Petrecca, *Vice Pres*
Laurie Eubanks, *Executive Asst*
Patricia Alcala, *Human Res Mgr*
EMP: 85
SQ FT: 20,000
SALES (est): 57.7MM
SALES (corp-wide): 142MM **Privately Held**
WEB: www.microlease.com
SIC: 7359 Rental store, general
HQ: Microlease Limited
Unit 1 Waverley Industrial Estate
Harrow MIDDX HA1 4
208 420-0200

(P-14528)
MUFG AMERICAS LEASING CORP (DH)
445 S Figueroa St # 2700, Los Angeles
(90071-1602)
PHONE..........................213 488-3700
Hideya Takaishi, *CEO*
Rory Laughna, *President*
David A Meehan, *President*
Paul Nolan, *CFO*
Paul F Nolan, *Treasurer*
EMP: 100 **EST:** 1973
SALES (est): 13.7MM
SALES (corp-wide): 56.9B **Privately Held**
WEB: www.btmcapital.com
SIC: 7359 Equipment rental & leasing
HQ: Mufg Americas Holdings Corporation
1251 Ave Of The Americas
New York NY 10020
212 782-6800

(P-14529)
NATIONAL CNSTR RENTALS INC (HQ)
15319 Chatsworth St, Mission Hills
(91345-2040)
PHONE..........................818 221-6000

James R Mooneyham, *President*
W Robert Mooneyham, *President*
Stephanie Doan, *Accountant*
◆ **EMP:** 85
SQ FT: 23,000
SALES (est): 123.3MM **Privately Held**
WEB: www.rentnational.com
SIC: 7359 Equipment rental & leasing
PA: The National Business Group Inc
15319 Chatsworth St
Mission Hills CA 91345
818 221-6000

(P-14530)
OES EQUIPMENT LLC (PA)
37421 Centralmont Pl, Fremont
(94536-6536)
PHONE..........................510 284-1900
Peter Nosler,
Doug Woods,
EMP: 53
SQ FT: 20,000
SALES (est): 25MM **Privately Held**
SIC: 7359 Equipment rental & leasing

(P-14531)
OHANA PARTNERS INC (PA)
Also Called: Stuart Rental Company
454 S Abbott Ave, Milpitas (95035-5258)
PHONE..........................408 856-3232
Michael Berman, *CEO*
Andrew Sutton, *Vice Pres*
R Andrew Sutton, *Vice Pres*
Clara Ayala, *Controller*
Tina Padilla, *Buyer*
EMP: 60
SALES (est): 13.9MM **Privately Held**
WEB: www.stuartrental.com
SIC: 7359 5947 Party supplies rental services; tent & tarpaulin rental; gifts & novelties

(P-14532)
P J J ENTERPRISES INC
1250 Delevan Dr, San Diego (92102-2437)
PHONE..........................619 232-6136
John Lenore, *President*
Dorothy Lenore, *Treasurer*
Roger Carey, *Director*
EMP: 70 **EST:** 1966
SQ FT: 20,000
SALES (est): 2.7MM
SALES (corp-wide): 173.8MM **Privately Held**
WEB: www.johnlenore.com
SIC: 7359 Rental store, general
PA: Lenore John & Co
1250 Delevan Dr
San Diego CA 92102
619 232-6136

(P-14533)
PANAVISION INC (PA)
Also Called: Panavision Group
6101 Variel Ave, Woodland Hills
(91367-3722)
PHONE..........................818 316-1000
Ronald O Perlman, *Ch of Bd*
William C Bevins, *President*
Kimberly Snyder, *CEO*
Michael George, *COO*
Ross Landsbaum, *COO*
EMP: 440
SQ FT: 150,000
SALES (est): 151.5MM **Privately Held**
WEB: www.panastore.com
SIC: 7359 3861 3648 5063 Equipment rental & leasing; cameras & related equipment; stage lighting equipment; lighting fixtures

(P-14534)
PARKMERCED INVESTORS LLC
3711 19th Ave, San Francisco
(94132-2641)
PHONE..........................877 243-5544
Bruce Ward,
EMP: 50
SALES (est): 8.1MM **Privately Held**
SIC: 7359 Lawn & garden equipment rental

(P-14535)
PICO RENTS INC
Also Called: Pico Party Rents
13414 S Figueroa St, Los Angeles
(90061-1144)
PHONE..........................310 275-9431
William Edwards Jr, *President*
Darren G Edwards, *Admin Sec*
EMP: 60
SQ FT: 24,500
SALES (est): 8MM **Privately Held**
WEB: www.picopartyrents.com
SIC: 7359 Party supplies rental services

(P-14536)
PINAMAR LLC
Also Called: Special Events
6909 Las Positas Rd Ste D, Livermore
(94551-5113)
PHONE..........................925 243-8979
Weston Cook,
Jose Lazo, *Production*
Troy Porras, *Manager*
EMP: 60
SALES (est): 6.6MM **Privately Held**
WEB: www.pinamar.com
SIC: 7359 Party supplies rental services

(P-14537)
PSAV HOLDINGS LLC
111 W Ocean Blvd Ste 1110, Long Beach
(90802-4688)
PHONE..........................562 366-0138
J Michael McIlwain, *Exec Dir*
Teresa Wessling, *Vice Pres*
William Folger, *Area Mgr*
James Whitney Markowitz, *Admin Sec*
Gregory Bates, *Technician*
EMP: 8200
SALES (est): 98.4MM **Privately Held**
SIC: 7359 Equipment rental & leasing

(P-14538)
QUIXOTE STUDIOS LLC (PA)
Also Called: Quixote Production Vehicles
1011 N Fuller Ave, West Hollywood
(90046-6651)
PHONE..........................323 851-5030
Jordan T Kitaen,
Kaye Michaelson, *CFO*
Jeff Arnone, *Vice Pres*
Mario Campuzano, *Store Mgr*
Michael Matus, *Administration*
EMP: 50
SQ FT: 32,000
SALES (est): 22.4MM **Privately Held**
WEB: www.quixotestudios.com
SIC: 7359 Sound & lighting equipment rental

(P-14539)
R & D LEASING INC
Also Called: Blare's Air & Ground Services
19101 Kent Ave, Lemoore (93245-9137)
PHONE..........................559 924-1276
Roger Hewett, *President*
Diana Hewett, *Principal*
EMP: 67
SALES (est): 4MM **Privately Held**
SIC: 7359 Equipment rental & leasing

(P-14540)
RAPHAELS PARTY RENTALS INC (PA)
8606 Miramar Rd, San Diego
(92126-4326)
PHONE..........................858 444-1692
Raphael Silverman, *President*
Phillip Silverman, *Vice Pres*
Kitty Silverman, *Admin Sec*
Gary Armstead, *Project Mgr*
EMP: 175
SQ FT: 60,000
SALES (est): 14MM **Privately Held**
WEB: www.raphaels.com
SIC: 7359 Party supplies rental services

(P-14541)
S & S PORTABLE SERVICES INC
4511 Rowland Ave, El Monte (91731-1123)
PHONE..........................626 967-9300
Sergio D Diez, *President*
EMP: 99

P R O D U C T S & S V C S

SALES (est): 10.8MM **Privately Held**
SIC: 7359 Equipment rental & leasing

(P-14542)
S & S RENT-A-FENCE INC
Also Called: S & S Construction Services
4511 Rowland Ave, El Monte (91731-1123)
P.O. Box 367, Glendora (91740-0367)
PHONE.....................................818 896-7710
Sergio Diez, *CEO*
Steve Lakie, *Principal*
Steven R Parsell, *Principal*
EMP: 60 **EST:** 1978
SQ FT: 1,800
SALES (est): 5MM **Privately Held**
WEB: www.sandsrentafence.com
SIC: 7359 Portable toilet rental

(P-14543)
SEACASTLE INC
4000 Executive Pkwy # 240, San Ramon
(94583-4257)
PHONE.....................................925 480-3000
Kathleen Francis, *Vice Pres*
EMP: 65 **Privately Held**
SIC: 7359 Equipment rental & leasing
PA: Seacastle, Inc
    123 Tice Blvd Ste 210
    Woodcliff Lake NJ 07677

(P-14544)
SHOWROOM INTERIORS LLC
Also Called: Vesta Luxury Home Staging
1900 E 25th St, Vernon (90058-1130)
PHONE.....................................323 348-1551
Julianne Buckner, *Mng Member*
EMP: 105
SALES: 5MM **Privately Held**
SIC: 7359 Furniture rental
PA: Showroom, Inc
    1900 E 25th St
    Vernon CA 90058
    323 348-1551

(P-14545)
SIERRA EQUIPMENT LEASING INC
Also Called: Sierra Mountain Express
1140 Suncast Ln, El Dorado Hills
(95762-9313)
PHONE.....................................925 676-7300
Murray Zwicker, *President*
Carol Zwicker, *Treasurer*
EMP: 50
SALES (est): 10.1MM **Privately Held**
SIC: 7359 Industrial truck rental

(P-14546)
SR BRAY LLC
Also Called: Power Plus
2750 N Perris Blvd, Perris (92571-3234)
PHONE.....................................951 436-2920
Tony Maldonado, *Manager*
Nick Quinn, *Sales Mgr*
EMP: 50 **Privately Held**
SIC: 7359 Equipment rental & leasing
PA: S.R. Bray Llc
    1210 N Red Gum St
    Anaheim CA 92806

(P-14547)
TEXTAINER EQUIPMENT MGT US LTD (DH)
650 California St Fl 16, San Francisco
(94108-2720)
PHONE.....................................415 434-0551
Ernest Furtado, *CFO*
Brian Hogan, *Vice Pres*
Sameer Khurana, *Sr Ntwrk Engine*
Yani Najarro, *Opers Staff*
Michael Samsel, *Mktg Dir*
EMP: 55
SQ FT: 15,000
SALES (est): 10.1MM **Privately Held**
WEB: www.textainer.com
SIC: 7359 Shipping container leasing
HQ: Textainer Group Holdings Ltd
    650 California St Fl 16
    San Francisco CA 94108
    415 434-0551

(P-14548)
TEXTANER EQP INCOME FUND II LP
650 California St Fl 16, San Francisco
(94108-2720)
PHONE.....................................415 434-0551
Ernest J Furtado, *CFO*
EMP: 80
SQ FT: 15,000
SALES (est): 2.6MM **Privately Held**
SIC: 7359 Shipping container leasing

(P-14549)
TOWN & COUNTRY EVENT RENTALS (PA)
Also Called: Tacer
7725 Airport Bus Pkwy, Van Nuys (91406)
PHONE.....................................818 908-4211
Richard Loguercio, *CEO*
Chris Mackey, *Vice Pres*
Sherry Stimatz, *Branch Mgr*
Wayne Tay, *Branch Mgr*
David Searcy, *General Mgr*
EMP: 400
SQ FT: 1,100
SALES: 28MM **Privately Held**
WEB:
www.townandcountryeventrentals.com
SIC: 7359 Party supplies rental services

(P-14550)
UNITED RENTALS NORTH AMER INC
2911 E Fremont St, Stockton (95205-3913)
P.O. Box 8810 (95208-0810)
PHONE.....................................209 948-9500
Joe Doran, *Manager*
Mohammed Sayeed, *General Mgr*
Jeremy Davis, *Sales Staff*
EMP: 61
SALES (corp-wide): 6.6B **Publicly Held**
WEB: www.ur.com
SIC: 7359 Equipment rental & leasing
HQ: United Rentals (North America), Inc.
    100 Frederick St 700
    Stamford CT 06902
    203 622-3131

(P-14551)
UNITED RENTALS NORTH AMER INC
3455 San Gbriel Rver Pkwy, Pico Rivera
(90660-1450)
PHONE.....................................562 695-0748
Donnie Richardson, *Manager*
Erica Gomez, *Sales Staff*
EMP: 125
SALES (corp-wide): 6.6B **Publicly Held**
WEB: www.unitedrentals.com
SIC: 7359 Rental store, general
HQ: United Rentals (North America), Inc.
    100 Frederick St 700
    Stamford CT 06902
    203 622-3131

(P-14552)
UNITED SITE SERVICES CAL INC (PA)
242 Live Oak Ave, Irwindale (91706-1311)
PHONE.....................................626 462-9110
Debbi Thornton, *Manager*
EMP: 90
SQ FT: 2,400
SALES (est): 3.9MM **Privately Held**
WEB: www.americanclassicsanitation.com
SIC: 7359 Portable toilet rental

(P-14553)
UNITED SITE SERVICES CAL INC
3408 Hillcap Ave, San Jose (95136-1306)
PHONE.....................................408 295-2263
Ron Carapezzi, *CEO*
Frank Youngblood, *President*
Terence P Moriarty, *CFO*
Jim Youngblood, *Exec VP*
Dan Youngblood, *Vice Pres*
EMP: 200
SALES (est): 24.8MM
SALES (corp-wide): 212.9MM **Privately Held**
WEB: www.acmeandsons.com
SIC: 7359 Portable toilet rental

PA: United Site Services, Inc.
    118 Flanders Rd
    Westborough MA 01581
    508 594-2655

(P-14554)
VCI EVENT TECHNOLOGY INC
Also Called: Videocam
1261 S Simpson Cir, Anaheim
(92806-5530)
PHONE.....................................714 772-2002
Toll Free:...........................888 -
Evan H Goldschlag, *President*
Kirk Rhinehart, *Vice Pres*
Bryan Cook, *Technology*
EMP: 166
SALES (est): 22MM **Privately Held**
WEB: www.videocam.net
SIC: 7359 Audio-visual equipment & supply rental

(P-14555)
WESTERN OILFIELDS SUPPLY CO (PA)
Also Called: Rain For Rent
3404 State Rd, Bakersfield (93308-4538)
P.O. Box 2248 (93303-2248)
PHONE.....................................661 399-9124
Robert Lake, *CEO*
Maston Cunningham, *CFO*
Chris Lake, *Vice Pres*
Bruce Wyant, *Vice Pres*
Randy Hobbs, *Branch Mgr*
◆ **EMP:** 150 **EST:** 1934
SQ FT: 57,000
SALES (est): 40.7MM **Privately Held**
WEB: www.rainforrent.com
SIC: 7359 Equipment rental & leasing; farm machinery & equipment; irrigation equipment

(P-14556)
WESTERN PRECOOLING SYSTEMS
761 Commercial Ave, Oxnard
(93030-7233)
PHONE.....................................805 486-6371
Gary Elk, *Manager*
EMP: 60
SALES (corp-wide): 62.3MM **Privately Held**
WEB: www.wpsox.com
SIC: 7359 Equipment rental & leasing
PA: Western Precooling Systems
    43990 Fremont Blvd
    Fremont CA 94538
    510 656-2220

(P-14557)
WILLIS LEASE FINANCE CORP (PA)
773 San Marin Dr Ste 2215, Novato
(94945-1366)
PHONE.....................................415 408-4700
Charles F Willis IV, *Ch of Bd*
Brian R Hole, *President*
Felix Rodriguez, *COO*
Scott B Flaherty, *CFO*
Robert Keady, *Bd of Directors*
EMP: 80
SQ FT: 20,534
SALES: 274.8MM **Publicly Held**
WEB: www.wlfc.com
SIC: 7359 6159 5084 5088 Aircraft engines & engine parts; industrial machinery & equipment; aircraft rental

(P-14558)
WOW PARTY RENTAL INC
14575 Firestone Blvd, La Mirada
(90638-5914)
PHONE.....................................714 367-3380
Kevin Rahimi, *President*
Rodrigo Rodrigues, *Vice Pres*
EMP: 52
SQ FT: 22,000
SALES (est): 1.5MM **Privately Held**
SIC: 7359 Party supplies rental services

7361 Employment Agencies

(P-14559)
40 HRS INC
Also Called: 40 Hours Staffing
1669 Flanigan Dr, San Jose (95121-1682)
PHONE.....................................408 414-0158
Bryan Phan, *President*
Danny Tran, *Cust Mgr*
Van Ngo, *Accounts Mgr*
EMP: 1000
SQ FT: 3,000
SALES (est): 31.7MM **Privately Held**
SIC: 7361 Executive placement

(P-14560)
A S A P PROFESSIONAL SERVICES
Also Called: ASAP Professional Services
2440 Camino Ramon Ste 313, San Ramon
(94583-4391)
P.O. Box 1224 (94583-6224)
PHONE.....................................800 303-2727
Pam Sullivan, *President*
William Sullivan, *Vice Pres*
EMP: 80
SQ FT: 2,500
SALES (est): 4.7MM **Privately Held**
WEB: www.asapps.com
SIC: 7361 Employment agencies

(P-14561)
A-STAR STAFFING INC
3636 Camino Del Rio N # 102, San Diego
(92108-1722)
PHONE.....................................619 574-7600
Diana M Barnes, *President*
Dan Barnes, *Admin Sec*
Daniel R Barnes, *Admin Sec*
EMP: 165 **EST:** 1999
SQ FT: 2,400
SALES (est): 7.6MM **Privately Held**
WEB: www.astarstaffing.com
SIC: 7361 7363 Executive placement; placement agencies; help supply services; temporary help service

(P-14562)
AB CLOSING CORPORATION
Also Called: Kavaliro
1304 Southpoint Blvd, Petaluma
(94954-7464)
PHONE.....................................707 766-1777
Jane E Hynes, *Branch Mgr*
EMP: 71 **Privately Held**
SIC: 7361 Executive placement
PA: A.B. Closing Corporation
    12001 Res Pkwy Ste 344
    Orlando FL 32826

(P-14563)
ABSO
101 Creekside Ridge Ct # 2, Roseville
(95678-3595)
PHONE.....................................800 943-2589
William Greenblatt, *CEO*
Bradley Landin, *Vice Pres*
Natalie Voros, *Principal*
Nathan Wakefield, *Finance*
EMP: 135
SQ FT: 19,000
SALES: 5.8MM
SALES (corp-wide): 21.9MM **Privately Held**
WEB: www.absolutehire.com
SIC: 7361 Executive placement
PA: Sterling Infosystems, Inc.
    1 State St Fl 24
    New York NY 10004
    800 899-2272

(P-14564)
ACCELON INC
2410 Camino Ramon Ste 194, San Ramon
(94583-4328)
PHONE.....................................925 216-5735
Aizad Kamal, *CEO*
Unsa Kazmi Kamal, *CFO*
Manjiri Vilekar, *Exec Dir*
Vicky Chauhan, *Tech Recruiter*
Andy Paul, *Tech Recruiter*
EMP: 50
SQ FT: 1,500

SALES (est): 1.9MM **Privately Held**
SIC: **7361** 8742 Placement agencies;
labor contractors (employment agency);
construction project management consultant; business consultant

(P-14565)
ACCESS NURSES INC
5935 Cornerstone Ct W, San Diego
(92121-3737)
PHONE.................................858 458-4400
Alan Braynin, *CEO*
EMP: 100
SQ FT: 20,000
SALES (est): 4.8MM **Privately Held**
WEB: www.accessnurses.com
SIC: **7361** Nurses' registry

(P-14566)
**ACCOUNTABLE HEALTH STAFF
INC**
Also Called: Hrn Services
7777 Greenback Ln Ste 205, Citrus Heights
(95610-5800)
PHONE.................................916 286-7667
Tina Wilson, *Branch Mgr*
EMP: 371
SALES (corp-wide): 163.6MM **Privately
Held**
SIC: **7361** Employment agencies
PA: Accountable Healthcare Staffing, Inc.
999 W Yamato Rd Ste 210
Boca Raton FL 33431
561 235-7810

(P-14567)
ACT 1 GROUP INC (PA)
Also Called: Agile 1
1999 W 190th St, Torrance (90504-6202)
P.O. Box 2886 (90509-2886)
PHONE.................................310 532-1529
Janice B Howroyd, *CEO*
Bernard Howroyd, *President*
Carlton Bryant, *Exec VP*
Michael Hoyal, *Vice Pres*
Tina B Robinson, *Admin Sec*
EMP: 90
SQ FT: 18,026
SALES (est): 236.5MM **Privately Held**
WEB: www.act-1.com
SIC: **7361** 8741 Placement agencies; ad-
ministrative management

(P-14568)
**ALL HEALTH SERVICES CORP
(PA)**
206 W 8th St, Hanford (93230-4532)
PHONE.................................559 583-9101
Dave Matthews, *President*
Brenda Matthews, *CFO*
Michael Ross, *Vice Pres*
Jeremy Matthews, *Admin Sec*
Robert Garcia, *Director*
EMP: 65
SALES: 9MM **Privately Held**
WEB: www.allhs.net
SIC: **7361** Employment agencies

(P-14569)
ALOIS LLC
Also Called: Alois Staffing
548 Market St Ste 47970, San Francisco
(94104-5401)
PHONE.................................215 297-4492
Farhad Wadia, *CEO*
Kinjal Desai, *COO*
John Thomas,
EMP: 60
SALES: 3MM **Privately Held**
SIC: **7361** 7389 Employment agencies;

(P-14570)
ASGN INCORPORATED (PA)
26745 Malibu Hills Rd, Calabasas
(91301-5355)
PHONE.................................818 878-7900
Peter T Dameris, *CEO*
Jeremy M Jones, *Ch of Bd*
Theodore S Hanson, *President*
Edward L Pierce, *CFO*
William Brock, *Bd of Directors*
EMP: 148
SQ FT: 37,200

SALES (est): 2.6B **Publicly Held**
WEB: www.onassignment.com
SIC: **7361** 7363 Employment agencies;
temporary help service

(P-14571)
**ASSISTED HOME RECOVERY
INC (PA)**
Also Called: Assisted Home Care
8550 Balboa Blvd Lbby, Northridge
(91325-5808)
PHONE.................................818 894-8117
Elaine S Donley, *President*
Bill Donley, *Ch of Bd*
EMP: 110
SQ FT: 4,000
SALES (est): 11.5MM **Privately Held**
WEB: www.assistedca.com
SIC: **7361** Nurses' registry

(P-14572)
AVALON STAFFING LLC
550 Harvest Park Dr Ste B, Brentwood
(94513-4058)
PHONE.................................925 626-7138
Carisa Zink, *Mng Member*
John Zink, *Mng Member*
EMP: 70 EST: 2012
SQ FT: 1,500
SALES: 12MM **Privately Held**
SIC: **7361** Executive placement

(P-14573)
AYALA CORPORATION
Also Called: Ayala Farms
21510 S Chteau Fresno Ave, Riverdale
(93656-9673)
P.O. Box 187 (93656-0187)
PHONE.................................559 867-5700
Piedad Ayala, *President*
EMP: 150
SQ FT: 2,000
SALES (est): 9.2MM **Privately Held**
SIC: **7361** Labor contractors (employment
agency)

(P-14574)
**B & R FARM LABOR
CONTRACTOR**
422 Mockingbird Ln, Fillmore (93015-1673)
P.O. Box 366 (93016-0366)
PHONE.................................805 524-1346
Birtha Delara, *Owner*
EMP: 200
SALES (est): 7MM **Privately Held**
SIC: **7361** 0761 Labor contractors (em-
ployment agency); farm labor contractors

(P-14575)
BARONHR LLC
13085 Central Ave Ste 4, Chino
(91710-4184)
PHONE.................................909 517-3800
EMP: 119
SALES (corp-wide): 56.1MM **Privately
Held**
SIC: **7361** Employment agencies
PA: Baronhr, Llc
8101 E Kaiser Blvd # 110
Anaheim CA 92808
714 860-7800

(P-14576)
**BARRETT BUSINESS SERVICES
INC**
862 E Hospitality Ln, San Bernardino
(92408-3530)
PHONE.................................909 890-3633
EMP: 5002
SALES (corp-wide): 920.4MM **Publicly
Held**
SIC: **7361** Employment agencies
PA: Barrett Business Services Inc
8100 Ne Parkway Dr # 200
Vancouver WA 98662
360 828-0700

(P-14577)
BAY AREA TECHWORKERS (PA)
2000 Crow Canyon Pl # 150, San Ramon
(94583-4633)
PHONE.................................925 359-2200
Don Peed, *CEO*
Mark Thompson, *CFO*
HB Drake, *Vice Pres*

Rob Olsen, *Vice Pres*
Steve Powers, *Vice Pres*
EMP: 72
SQ FT: 11,422
SALES (est): 48.9MM **Privately Held**
WEB: www.techworkers.com
SIC: **7361** Placement agencies

(P-14578)
BOILING POINT REST SCA INC
13668 Valley Blvd Unit C2, City of Industry
(91746-2572)
PHONE.................................626 551-5181
CHI How Chou, *Chairman*
Michael Lin, *Vice Pres*
EMP: 300
SALES: 9.2MM **Privately Held**
SIC: **7361** 5812 Employment agencies;
Chinese restaurant

(P-14579)
**BULMARO CASTRO
CONTRACTORS**
Also Called: Bc Contractors
349 Belden St, Gonzales (93926)
P.O. Box 779 (93926-0779)
PHONE.................................831 675-2927
Bulmaro Castro, *President*
EMP: 200 EST: 1994
SQ FT: 1,500
SALES: 3.5MM **Privately Held**
SIC: **7361** 0761 Labor contractors (em-
ployment agency); farm labor contractors

(P-14580)
BUSINESS CONNECTIONS
Also Called: California Search Services
332 Pine St, Red Bluff (96080-3312)
PHONE.................................530 527-6229
Lynne Moule, *Owner*
EMP: 92
SALES (est): 3.8MM **Privately Held**
SIC: **7361** 7363 Employment agencies;
temporary help service

(P-14581)
**CALIFORNIA DEPT
REHABILITATION**
Also Called: San Francisco District Office
301 Howard St Ste 900, San Francisco
(94105-6606)
PHONE.................................415 904-7100
Theresa Woo, *Administration*
EMP: 60 **Privately Held**
WEB: www.carehab.org
SIC: **7361** 9431 Employment agencies;
HQ: California Department Of Rehabilita-
tion
721 Capitol Mall Fl 6
Sacramento CA 95814

(P-14582)
**CAMPOS DMETRIO FRM LABOR
CONTR**
Also Called: Campos Dmetrio Frm Labor
Contr
117 W Main St Ste 19, Woodland
(95695-2988)
P.O. Box 1288 (95776-1288)
PHONE.................................530 662-4143
Demetrio Campos, *President*
EMP: 100
SQ FT: 650
SALES (est): 4.4MM **Privately Held**
SIC: **7361** 0761 Labor contractors (em-
ployment agency); farm labor contractors

(P-14583)
**CANOGA PARK WORKSOURCE
CENTER**
Also Called: Arbor Employment & Training
21010 Vanowen St, Canoga Park
(91303-2804)
PHONE.................................818 596-4448
Gabe Ross, *President*
EMP: 50
SALES (est): 2MM **Privately Held**
SIC: **7361** Employment agencies

(P-14584)
**CARE PLUS NORTH OF SAN
DIEGO**
2337 Eastridge Loop, Chula Vista
(91915-1111)
PHONE.................................619 421-0807
George Khoury, *Owner*
EMP: 67
SALES (est): 4MM **Privately Held**
WEB: www.careplusinternational.com
SIC: **7361** Nurses' registry

(P-14585)
CAREER GROUP INC (PA)
Also Called: Fourthfloor Fashion Talent
10100 Santa Monica Blvd # 900, Los Ange-
les (90067-4138)
PHONE.................................310 277-8188
Michael B Levine, *CEO*
Susan Levine, *President*
Scott H Pick, *CFO*
EMP: 2100 EST: 1980
SQ FT: 11,986
SALES (est): 96.7MM **Privately Held**
SIC: **7361** Executive placement

(P-14586)
**CERTIFIED NURSING REGISTRY
INC**
2707 E Valley Blvd # 309, West Covina
(91792-3198)
PHONE.................................626 912-1877
Maria Cristina C Sy, *President*
Wilson Sy, *Vice Pres*
Cathy Chua, *Manager*
EMP: 125
SQ FT: 2,000
SALES: 2.5MM **Privately Held**
SIC: **7361** Registries

(P-14587)
CLC INCORPORATED (PA)
3001 Lava Ridge Ct # 250, Roseville
(95661-2838)
PHONE.................................916 789-7600
Brad Barron, *President*
Doug Abbott, *Senior VP*
Duncan Hay, *Vice Pres*
Katie Winkler, *Vice Pres*
Paul Heimburg, *Software Engr*
EMP: 50
SQ FT: 20,000
SALES (est): 10MM **Privately Held**
WEB: www.clclegalplans.com
SIC: **7361** Employment agencies

(P-14588)
**COAST PERSONNEL SERVICES
INC (PA)**
2295 De La Cruz Blvd, Santa Clara
(95050-3020)
P.O. Box 328 (95052-0328)
PHONE.................................408 653-2100
Larry K Bunker, *President*
Michael Avidano, *Vice Pres*
Larry Broun, *Vice Pres*
Corrina Moreno, *Payroll Mgr*
Carlos Castillo, *Accounts Mgr*
EMP: 1895
SQ FT: 7,500
SALES (est): 47.4MM **Privately Held**
WEB: www.coastjobs.com
SIC: **7361** Employment agencies

(P-14589)
CODE AMERICA INC
Also Called: Stat Registry Service
235 E Broadway Ste 960, Long Beach
(90802-7802)
PHONE.................................562 502-7365
Julius Irumundomon, *President*
EMP: 80
SQ FT: 700
SALES: 1MM **Privately Held**
SIC: **7361** Employment agencies

(P-14590)
**CONTEMPORARY SERVICES
CORP (PA)**
Also Called: C S C
17101 Superior St, Northridge
(91325-1961)
PHONE.................................818 885-5150
Damon Zumwalt, *CEO*
Jim Granger, *President*

P
R
O
D
U
C
T
S

&

S
V
C
S

Paul Erickson, *CFO*
Casey McNulty, *Social Dir*
Douglas Adams, *Security Mgr*
EMP: 148
SQ FT: 20,000
SALES (est): 328MM **Privately Held**
WEB: www.csc-usa.com
SIC: 7361 Employment agencies

(P-14591)
CONTINUING LF COMMUNITIES LLC (PA)
Also Called: La Costa Glen
1940 Levante St, Carlsbad (92009-5174)
PHONE..................................760 704-6400
Richard D Aschenbrenner, *Mng Member*
E Justin Wilson III, *CEO*
Darolyn Jorgensen, *Exec Dir*
Jo Baugh, *Executive Asst*
Donald Howard, *Administration*
EMP: 84
SALES (est): 19.9MM **Privately Held**
SIC: 7361 Employment agencies

(P-14592)
CONTRACT RECRUITING INC (PA)
Also Called: C R I
3625 Del Amo Blvd Ste 300, Torrance
(90503-1693)
PHONE..................................310 792-7100
Ladd Richland, *CEO*
Julie Lynn Richland, *President*
EMP: 60
SALES (est): 3.3MM **Privately Held**
WEB: www.contractrecruiting.com
SIC: 7361 Employment agencies

(P-14593)
COVENANT INDUSTRIES INC
Also Called: People Onesource
110 Pine Ave Ste 910, Long Beach
(90802-9447)
P.O. Box 7045, La Puente (91744-7045)
PHONE..................................951 808-3708
Statney Lattin, *CEO*
Joseph Randle El, *President*
Anna Roque, *Admin Sec*
EMP: 75
SQ FT: 2,500
SALES (est): 4.7MM **Privately Held**
WEB: www.covenantindustries.net
SIC: 7361 Employment agencies

(P-14594)
CREATIVE CIRCLE LLC (DH)
5900 Wilshire Blvd # 1100, Los Angeles
(90036-5036)
PHONE..................................323 930-2333
Lawrence Serf, *Mng Member*
Kristin Haverlock, *Vice Pres*
Sarah Adhami, *Executive*
Jenna Briggs, *Executive*
Jena Lepkowski, *Executive*
EMP: 65
SALES (est): 21.1MM
SALES (corp-wide): 2.6B **Publicly Held**
SIC: 7361 Executive placement
HQ: Mscp V Cc Parent, Llc
5900 Wilshire Blvd # 1100
Los Angeles CA 90036
323 634-0156

(P-14595)
CROSS COUNTRY HEALTHCARE INC
1700 Iowa Ave Ste 210, Riverside
(92507-2403)
PHONE..................................951 786-7683
EMP: 303
SALES (corp-wide): 865MM **Publicly Held**
SIC: 7361 Employment agencies
PA: Cross Country Healthcare, Inc.
5201 Congress Ave Ste 100
Boca Raton FL 33487
561 998-2232

(P-14596)
CROSSROADS DIVERSFD SVCS INC
7011 Sylvan Rd Ste A, Citrus Heights
(95610-3800)
PHONE..................................916 676-2540
Danny Marquez, *Principal*

EMP: 79
SALES (corp-wide): 10.4MM **Privately Held**
SIC: 7361 Executive placement
PA: Crossroads Diversified Services, Inc.
9300 Tech Center Dr # 100
Sacramento CA 95826
916 457-1900

(P-14597)
CUTTING EDGE STAFFING INC
27715 Jefferson Ave, Temecula
(92590-2660)
PHONE..................................951 587-0550
Lisa Fuess, *President*
EMP: 75
SALES (est): 3MM **Privately Held**
SIC: 7361 Placement agencies

(P-14598)
CVPARTNERS INC (HQ)
505 Sansome St Ste 1100, San Francisco
(94111-3174)
PHONE..................................415 543-8600
Kent Gray, *President*
Nancy Gray, *Vice Pres*
Ann King, *Vice Pres*
EMP: 161
SALES (est): 6.2MM
SALES (corp-wide): 117.9MM **Privately Held**
SIC: 7361 Employment agencies
PA: Addison Professional Financial Search Llc
125 S Wacker Dr Fl 27
Chicago IL 60606
312 424-0300

(P-14599)
CYBERCODERS INC
Also Called: Cyberscientific
6591 Irvine Center Dr # 200, Irvine
(92618-2129)
PHONE..................................949 885-5151
Heidi Golledge, *CEO*
Matt Miller, *COO*
Shane Lamb, *Vice Pres*
Chris Dececco, *Executive*
Anne Nguyen, *Office Admin*
EMP: 140
SALES (est): 17.2MM
SALES (corp-wide): 2.6B **Publicly Held**
WEB: www.cyberscientific.com
SIC: 7361 Executive placement
PA: Asgn Incorporated
26745 Malibu Hills Rd
Calabasas CA 91301
818 878-7900

(P-14600)
DECTON INC
19800 Macarthur Blvd # 600, Irvine
(92612-2435)
PHONE..................................949 851-0111
Steve Beal, *President*
EMP: 108
SALES (corp-wide): 31.4MM **Privately Held**
SIC: 7361 Labor contractors (employment agency)
PA: Decton, Inc.
19800 Macarthur Blvd # 600
Irvine CA 92612
562 229-3982

(P-14601)
DIAMONDPEO LLC
27442 Calle Arroyo Ste A, San Juan Capistrano (92675-6753)
PHONE..................................714 728-5186
Veronica Lake,
EMP: 180
SALES: 500K **Privately Held**
SIC: 7361 Employment agencies

(P-14602)
DIVERSITY BUS SOLUTIONS INC
2515 S Euclid Ave, Ontario (91762-6620)
PHONE..................................909 395-0243
Sandy Tribby, *CEO*
Sandra A Tribby, *Manager*
EMP: 200 **EST:** 2011
SALES (est): 1.3MM **Privately Held**
SIC: 7361 Employment agencies

(P-14603)
DURAN HUMAN CAPITAL PARTNERS
300 Orchard Cy Dr Ste 142, Campbell
(95008)
PHONE..................................408 540-0070
James Duran, *President*
EMP: 50
SALES (est): 2.9MM **Privately Held**
SIC: 7361 Executive placement

(P-14604)
DYNAMIC STAFFING INC (PA)
920 Reserve Dr Ste 150, Roseville
(95678-1382)
PHONE..................................916 773-3900
Michael J Reale, *President*
Keri J Case, *COO*
Steve Saucedo, *CFO*
Carl Cox, *Opers Staff*
Caesar Artolozaga, *Director*
EMP: 150
SQ FT: 2,768
SALES (est): 9.8MM **Privately Held**
SIC: 7361 Employment agencies

(P-14605)
E Z STAFFING INC (PA)
801 N Brand Blvd Ste 1120, Glendale
(91203-3239)
PHONE..................................818 845-2500
Abraham F Abirafeh, *President*
EMP: 298
SQ FT: 3,000
SALES (est): 13.1MM **Privately Held**
SIC: 7361 Nurses' registry

(P-14606)
EAGLE RESOURCES INC
516 W Boone St, Santa Maria
(93458-5614)
P.O. Box 6510 (93456-6510)
PHONE..................................805 922-0000
Guadalupe Castillo, *President*
Daniel Castillo Jr, *Vice Pres*
EMP: 100
SQ FT: 3,600
SALES: 4.2MM **Privately Held**
SIC: 7361 Labor contractors (employment agency)

(P-14607)
EASTRDGE PRSONNEL OF LAS VEGAS
530 Davis St, San Francisco (94111-1902)
PHONE..................................415 248-2567
EMP: 65
SALES (corp-wide): 9.1MM **Privately Held**
SIC: 7361 Employment agencies
PA: Eastridge Personnel Of Las Vegas Inc
2355 Northside Dr Ste 120
San Diego CA 92108
619 260-2000

(P-14608)
EASTRDGE PRSONNEL OF LAS VEGAS (PA)
Also Called: Eastridge Infotech
2355 Northside Dr Ste 120, San Diego
(92108-2714)
PHONE..................................619 260-2000
Robert Svet, *President*
EMP: 50
SALES (est): 9.1MM **Privately Held**
WEB: www.eastridge-infotech.com
SIC: 7361 Employment agencies

(P-14609)
ELITE NURSING SERVICES INC
1915 W Orangewood Ave # 110, Orange
(92868-2084)
PHONE..................................714 919-7898
Lee Hadfield, *President*
EMP: 50
SQ FT: 2,000
SALES: 2.3MM **Privately Held**
SIC: 7361 Nurses' registry

(P-14610)
ELITECARE MEDICAL STAFFING LLC
761 E Locust Ave Ste 103, Fresno
(93720-3023)
PHONE..................................559 438-7700

Steve Poggi,
Stacey Green, *Opers Mgr*
EMP: 60
SALES (est): 4MM **Privately Held**
SIC: 7361 Nurses' registry

(P-14611)
ELVIRA SANDOVAL
Also Called: Sandoval Labor Contractor
2154 Hill Rd, Williams (95987-5123)
P.O. Box 81 (95987-0081)
PHONE..................................530 473-5718
Elvira Sandoval, *Owner*
EMP: 170 **EST:** 1985
SALES (est): 7.6MM **Privately Held**
SIC: 7361 Employment agencies

(P-14612)
EMPLOYMENT DEV CAL DEPT
Also Called: Workforce Resource Center
1410 S Broadway Ste E, Santa Maria
(93454-6971)
PHONE..................................805 614-1550
Judy Kelley, *Branch Mgr*
EMP: 100 **Privately Held**
WEB: www.mpic.org
SIC: 7361 9441 8331 7338 Employment agencies; administration of social & manpower programs; ; job training & vocational rehabilitation services; secretarial & court reporting
HQ: California Department Of Employment Development
800 Capitol Mall 83
Sacramento CA 95814
916 654-8210

(P-14613)
EMPLOYMENT DEV CAL DEPT
Also Called: Edd Payroll Services
751 N St Fl 6, Sacramento (95814-4763)
P.O. Box 826880 (94280-0001)
PHONE..................................916 654-7867
Tina Campbell, *Chief*
EMP: 1000 **Privately Held**
WEB: www.mpic.org
SIC: 7361 9441 Employment agencies; administration of social & manpower programs;
HQ: California Department Of Employment Development
800 Capitol Mall 83
Sacramento CA 95814
916 654-8210

(P-14614)
EMPLOYNET INC
445 Tyler St, Monterey (93940-3039)
PHONE..................................831 316-1814
EMP: 2661
SALES (corp-wide): 30.6MM **Privately Held**
SIC: 7361 Employment agencies
PA: Employnet, Inc.
2555 Garden Rd Ste H
Monterey CA 93940
866 527-4473

(P-14615)
EMPLOYNET INC
838 S Main St Ste B, Salinas (93901-2408)
PHONE..................................831 233-9999
EMP: 1330
SALES (corp-wide): 30.6MM **Privately Held**
SIC: 7361 Employment agencies
PA: Employnet, Inc.
2555 Garden Rd Ste H
Monterey CA 93940
866 527-4473

(P-14616)
ESPARZA ENTERPRISES INC
3851 Fruitvale Ave A, Bakersfield
(93308-5111)
PHONE..................................661 831-0002
Irene Borland, *Manager*
EMP: 55
SALES (corp-wide): 98.4MM **Privately Held**
WEB: www.esparzaenterprises.com
SIC: 7361 Labor contractors (employment agency)

PA: Esparza Enterprises, Inc.
3851 Fruitvale Ave
Bakersfield CA 93308
661 831-0002

(P-14617)
ESPARZA ENTERPRISES INC
51335 Harrison St Ste 112, Coachella
(92236-1528)
PHONE..................................760 398-0349
Manuel Padilla, *Manager*
EMP: 680
SALES (corp-wide): 90.9MM **Privately Held**
SIC: 7361 Labor contractors (employment agency)
PA: Esparza Enterprises, Inc.
3851 Fruitvale Ave
Bakersfield CA 93308
661 831-0002

(P-14618)
EXECUTIVE PERSONNEL SERVICES
17842 Irvine Blvd Ste 236, Tustin
(92780-3244)
PHONE..................................714 310-9506
Mario Mendoza, *President*
Alinne Espinoza, *Vice Pres*
EMP: 300
SQ FT: 980
SALES (est): 179.3K **Privately Held**
SIC: 7361 Employment agencies

(P-14619)
EXPRESS PERSONNEL SERVICES
870 W Onstott Frontage Rd E, Yuba City
(95991-3500)
PHONE..................................530 671-9202
Tina Williams, *President*
Tom Williams, *Vice Pres*
EMP: 60
SALES (est): 1.8MM **Privately Held**
SIC: 7361 Employment agencies

(P-14620)
FINEZI INC
31080 Blvd Ste 212, Union City (94587)
PHONE..................................510 790-4768
Madhu Puttur, *President*
Adil Mohammad, *Administration*
Zeeshan Khan, *Technology*
Vijendra Shetty, *Technology*
Dhanraj Devadiga, *Recruiter*
EMP: 90
SALES (est): 4.9MM **Privately Held**
SIC: 7361 8742 Executive placement; management consulting services

(P-14621)
FIRST CALL NURSING SVCS INC
1313 N Milpitas Blvd # 210, Milpitas
(95035-3182)
PHONE..................................408 262-1533
Franklin Camillo, *CEO*
Celina Salazar-Camillo, *President*
EMP: 180
SALES (est): 11.4MM **Privately Held**
WEB: www.firstcallnursingservices.com
SIC: 7361 Nurses' registry

(P-14622)
FOWLER LABOR SERVICE INC
633 W Fresno St, Fowler (93625-9697)
PHONE..................................559 834-3723
Fax: 559 834-5949
EMP: 300
SQ FT: 3,250
SALES (est): 8.8MM **Privately Held**
SIC: 7361 0783

(P-14623)
FUENTES FARMS AG INC
2346 Glen Ave, Merced (95340-4059)
PHONE..................................209 722-7201
Edward Fuentes, *President*
EMP: 500
SALES (est): 12.4MM **Privately Held**
SIC: 7361 7363 0761 Labor contractors (employment agency); help supply services; farm labor contractors

(P-14624)
GARICH INC (PA)
Also Called: The Tristaff Group
6336 Greenwich Dr Ste A, San Diego
(92122-5922)
PHONE..................................858 453-1331
Gary O Van Eik, *President*
Rick Kail, *COO*
Amy Moser, *Vice Pres*
Alex Papike, *Vice Pres*
Richard N Papike, *Vice Pres*
EMP: 295
SQ FT: 9,000
SALES (est): 29.3MM **Privately Held**
SIC: 7361 8742 Employment agencies; management consulting services

(P-14625)
GARICH INC
Also Called: Tristaff Group
504 E Alvarado St Ste 201, Fallbrook
(92028-2364)
PHONE..................................951 302-4750
Trevor Nevis, *Manager*
EMP: 521
SALES (corp-wide): 29.3MM **Privately Held**
SIC: 7361 Employment agencies
PA: Garich Inc
6336 Greenwich Dr Ste A
San Diego CA 92122
858 453-1331

(P-14626)
GIGSURF INC
217 Dore St, San Francisco (94103-4307)
PHONE..................................415 894-2445
Nathan Goldfus, *CEO*
EMP: 450
SALES: 1.5MM **Privately Held**
SIC: 7361 Employment agencies

(P-14627)
GLOBAL HORIZONS INC
Also Called: Domestic Horizons
468 N Camden Dr Ste 200, Beverly Hills
(90210-4507)
PHONE..................................310 234-8475
Mordechai Orian, *President*
Robert Rutt, *CFO*
EMP: 400
SALES (est): 14.6MM **Privately Held**
WEB: www.gmpusa.com
SIC: 7361 Labor contractors (employment agency)

(P-14628)
GLOBAL NURSES ONLINE INC
5301 Beethoven St Ste 200, Los Angeles
(90066-7052)
PHONE..................................310 306-2760
Dorika Mamboleo, *President*
Dorika Beckett, *President*
EMP: 100
SALES (est): 5.1MM **Privately Held**
WEB: www.globalnursesonline.com
SIC: 7361 Nurses' registry

(P-14629)
GLOBAL STAFFING INC
Also Called: G T Global Staffing
5301 Beethoven St Ste 101, Los Angeles
(90066-7066)
P.O. Box 33025, Denver CO (80233-0025)
PHONE..................................303 451-5602
Ronald M Telanoff, *CEO*
Debbie Westmoreland, *Admin Sec*
EMP: 200
SALES (est): 6.1MM **Privately Held**
WEB: www.gtglobalstaffing.com
SIC: 7361 7363 Employment agencies; temporary help service

(P-14630)
GO-STAFF INC
9878 Complex Dr, Oceanside (92054)
PHONE..................................760 730-8520
EMP: 1472
SALES (corp-wide): 43.6MM **Privately Held**
SIC: 7361 Executive placement
PA: Go-Staff, Inc.
8798 Complex Dr
San Diego CA 92123
858 292-8562

(P-14631)
GO-STAFF INC
240 W Lincoln Ave, Anaheim (92805-2903)
PHONE..................................657 242-9350
EMP: 981
SALES (corp-wide): 43.6MM **Privately Held**
SIC: 7361 Executive placement
PA: Go-Staff, Inc.
8798 Complex Dr
San Diego CA 92123
858 292-8562

(P-14632)
GRANITE SOLUTIONS GROUPE INC
235 Montgomery St Ste 430, San Francisco
(94104-2907)
P.O. Box 3399, Diamond Springs (95619-3399)
PHONE..................................415 963-3999
Daniel Hector L'Abbe, *CEO*
Ann Bauer, *CFO*
John Henning, *Executive*
Michael Lacson, *Executive Asst*
Astrid Gravenor, *Recruiter*
EMP: 209
SQ FT: 3,582
SALES (est): 9.9MM **Privately Held**
WEB: www.granitesolutionsgroup.com
SIC: 7361 8742 Executive placement; management consulting services

(P-14633)
GROWERS COMPANY INC
21570 Potter Rd, Salinas (93908-9727)
P.O. Box 6217 (93912-6217)
PHONE..................................831 424-3850
Jesse Garcia, *Director*
EMP: 100
SALES (corp-wide): 20MM **Privately Held**
WEB: www.thegrowerscompany.com
SIC: 7361 Labor contractors (employment agency)
PA: The Growers Company Inc
15834 S Avenue G
Somerton AZ 85350
928 627-8080

(P-14634)
HARDESTY LLC (PA)
19800 Macar Boule Ste 820, Irvine (92612)
PHONE..................................949 407-6625
Karl Hardesty, *CEO*
Natl Arthur Cohen, *Partner*
Dan Corredor, *Partner*
Skip D'Orazio, *Partner*
David Tiffany, *Managing Dir*
EMP: 50
SQ FT: 5,000
SALES: 6MM **Privately Held**
SIC: 7361 Executive placement

(P-14635)
HARVEST TECHNICAL SERVICE INC
1839 Ygnacio Valley Rd # 390, Walnut
Creek (94598-3214)
PHONE..................................925 937-4874
Judy Fick, *President*
Chris Fick, *Admin Sec*
Carla Adcock, *HR Admin*
Samantha Gatewood, *Recruiter*
EMP: 150 **EST:** 1997
SQ FT: 1,000
SALES (est): 8.6MM **Privately Held**
WEB: www.harvtech.com
SIC: 7361 Executive placement

(P-14636)
HIRED HANDS INC
1754 2nd St Ste D, NAPA (94559-2452)
PHONE..................................707 265-6400
April Jacek, *Branch Mgr*
EMP: 125 **Privately Held**
SIC: 7361 Employment agencies
PA: Hired Hands Inc
1744 Novato Blvd Ste 200
Novato CA 94947

(P-14637)
HOLISTIC APPROACH INC
Also Called: Holistic Approach HM Hlth Care
4505 Precissi Ln Ste B, Stockton
(95207-6240)
PHONE..................................209 956-7050
Alice Sepulveda, *President*
Julian Sepulveda, *CFO*
Sylvia Sanchez, *Admin Sec*
EMP: 80
SQ FT: 6,000
SALES (est): 3.6MM **Privately Held**
SIC: 7361 8082 Nurses' registry; home health care services

(P-14638)
HOWARD FISCHER ASSOCIATES INC
10020 N De Anza Blvd # 101, Cupertino
(95014-2213)
PHONE..................................408 374-0580
Howard Fisher, *President*
Barry Ota, *Accountant*
Stanley Sitarski, *VP Opers*
Terry Garofalo, *Vice Pres*
EMP: 50
SALES (est): 1.5MM **Privately Held**
SIC: 7361 Executive placement

(P-14639)
HOWROYD-WRIGHT EMPLYMNT AGCY (HQ)
Also Called: Apple One Employment
327 W Broadway, Glendale (91204-1301)
PHONE..................................818 240-8688
Janice Bryant Howroyd, *CEO*
Bernard Howroyd, *President*
Michael Hoyal, *CFO*
Brett Howroyd, *Vice Pres*
Ruby Clark Bryant, *Finance*
EMP: 175
SQ FT: 27,000
SALES (est): 131.8MM
SALES (corp-wide): 236.5MM **Privately Held**
WEB: www.appleone.com
SIC: 7361 Labor contractors (employment agency); executive placement
PA: The Act 1 Group Inc
1999 W 190th St
Torrance CA 90504
310 532-1529

(P-14640)
HOWROYD-WRIGHT EMPLYMNT AGCY
Also Called: Appleone Employment Services
325 W Broadway, Glendale (91204-1301)
PHONE..................................818 240-8688
Marie Rounsavell, *Manager*
Rachel Borowski, *President*
EMP: 120
SALES (corp-wide): 236.5MM **Privately Held**
WEB: www.appleone.com
SIC: 7361 Labor contractors (employment agency)
HQ: Howroyd-Wright Employment Agency, Inc.
327 W Broadway
Glendale CA 91204
818 240-8688

(P-14641)
HYRIAN LLC
2355 Westwood Blvd, Los Angeles
(90064-2109)
PHONE..................................212 590-2567
Daniel Solmons,
Jason Berkowitz,
EMP: 110
SQ FT: 15,000
SALES (est): 3.9MM **Privately Held**
SIC: 7361 Executive placement

(P-14642)
IBFTECH INC
Also Called: Image Business Forms
343 Main St, El Segundo (90245-3814)
PHONE..................................424 217-8010
John Koch, *President*
Patricia Padilla, *Human Res Mgr*
Stephen Takahashi, *Recruiter*
EMP: 100
SQ FT: 4,000

PRODUCTS & SVCS

SALES (est): 92.8MM **Privately Held**
WEB: www.chiptonross.com
SIC: 7361 Executive placement

(P-14643)
IDC TECHNOLOGIES INC (PA)
920 Hillview Ct Ste 250, Milpitas
(95035-4560)
PHONE................................408 376-0212
Prateek Gattani, *CEO*
Yogen Malvia, *CFO*
Galvin Jha, *Vice Pres*
Priyanka Singh, *Executive*
Vikarant Sharma, *General Mgr*
EMP: 67
SQ FT: 4,000
SALES (est): 41.2MM **Privately Held**
SIC: 7361 Placement agencies

(P-14644)
IMPACT LOGISTICS
1155 S Milliken Ave Ste I, Ontario
(91761-8158)
PHONE................................909 937-9035
David Hamilton, *Principal*
EMP: 50
SALES (est): 1.7MM **Privately Held**
WEB: www.impactlogistics.com
SIC: 7361 Labor contractors (employment
agency)

(P-14645)
IMPACT SOLUTIONS LLC
3604 Ocean Ranch Blvd, Oceanside
(92056-2669)
PHONE................................760 231-0450
Toby Copeland,
EMP: 50
SQ FT: 3,000
SALES: 3.1MM **Privately Held**
SIC: 7361 Executive placement

(P-14646)
INCLINE INCORPORATED
Also Called: Hireforces
560 S Winchester Blvd # 500, San Jose
(95128-2560)
PHONE................................408 454-1140
Ray Ghamous, *President*
EMP: 120
SALES (est): 4.4MM **Privately Held**
WEB: www.inclineinc.com
SIC: 7361 Labor contractors (employment
agency)

(P-14647)
INDOSYS CORPORATION
3315 San Felipe Rd Ste 37, San Jose
(95135-2000)
PHONE................................408 705-1953
Sunil Kumar Bagai, *President*
Naina Bagai, *Vice Pres*
Sunil Bagai, *Human Res Mgr*
EMP: 140
SALES (est): 2.4MM **Privately Held**
WEB: www.indosys.com
SIC: 7361 Executive placement

(P-14648)
**INDUSTRIAL LABOR MGT
GROUP INC**
Also Called: Ilm Group, The
647 E E St Ste 105, Ontario (91764-4200)
PHONE................................323 582-4100
Gina Mendoza, *CEO*
Georgina Mendoza, *Owner*
EMP: 250
SQ FT: 2,000
SALES (est): 11.2MM **Privately Held**
SIC: 7361 Employment agencies

(P-14649)
**INNOVTIVE SCNTFIC SLUTIONS
INC**
Also Called: Innovative Staffing Resources
17581 Irvine Blvd Ste 202, Tustin
(92780-3124)
PHONE................................714 508-8620
Arlene Key Auster, *CEO*
Keith A Fiscus, *COO*
EMP: 120
SQ FT: 1,518
SALES (est): 7MM **Privately Held**
WEB: www.innstaff.com
SIC: 7361 Executive placement

(P-14650)
**INTERNET BOOKING
AGENCYCOM INC**
Also Called: Santa For Hirecom
232 Via Eboli, Newport Beach
(92663-4604)
PHONE................................949 673-7707
Robert Mindte, *CEO*
Felicia Mindte, *COO*
EMP: 500
SQ FT: 1,700
SALES (est): 16MM **Privately Held**
WEB: www.hireasanta.com
SIC: 7361 7922 Employment agencies;
theatrical producers & services

(P-14651)
**INTERNTIONAL LONGSHORE
WHSE UN**
Also Called: Ilwu Local 46
Bldng 608 Port Heneme Hbr, Port Huen-
eme (93041)
P.O. Box 100 (93044-0100)
PHONE................................805 488-2944
Larry Carlton, *Manager*
EMP: 100
SALES (corp-wide): 7.4MM **Privately
Held**
WEB: www.ilwu10.org
SIC: 7361 4491 Labor contractors (em-
ployment agency); marine cargo handling
PA: International Longshore & Warehouse
Union
1188 Franklin St Fl 4
San Francisco CA 94109
415 775-0533

(P-14652)
IQTALENT PARTNERS LLC
171 Main St Ste 284, Los Altos
(94022-2912)
PHONE................................888 501-4787
Tomislav Milic, *Mng Member*
Christopher Murdock,
EMP: 55
SALES (est): 256.3K **Privately Held**
SIC: 7361 Executive placement

(P-14653)
**IRVINE TECHNOLOGY
CORPORATION**
17900 Von Karman Ave # 100, Irvine
(92614-6249)
PHONE................................714 445-2624
Nicole McMackin, *President*
Kevin Orlando, *CFO*
Janet Thornby, *Vice Pres*
Michael Rose, *Admin Sec*
EMP: 160 EST: 2000
SQ FT: 8,000
SALES (est): 37.3MM **Privately Held**
WEB: www.irvinetechcorp.com
SIC: 7361 Executive placement

(P-14654)
JACKIE HOOFRING
Also Called: Avalon Staffing
3390 Auto Mall Dr, Westlake Village
(91362-3629)
PHONE................................818 961-7272
Jackie Hoofring, *Owner*
EMP: 50
SQ FT: 200
SALES: 1MM **Privately Held**
SIC: 7361 Employment agencies

(P-14655)
**JOSEPHINES PROF STAFFING
(PA)**
Also Called: Josephine's Personnel Services
2158 Ringwood Ave, San Jose
(95131-1720)
PHONE................................408 943-0111
Josephine Hughes, *President*
Victoria Picard, *Administration*
EMP: 250
SQ FT: 4,000
SALES (est): 13.1MM **Privately Held**
WEB: www.jps-inc.com
SIC: 7361 8742 8721 7363 Placement
agencies; management consulting serv-
ices; accounting, auditing & bookkeeping;
help supply services

(P-14656)
**KENT DANIELS & ASSOCIATES
INC**
Also Called: Daniels Kent Personnel Agency
680 Brea Canyon Rd # 258, Walnut
(91789-3007)
PHONE................................626 859-5018
Kimberly Ann Feith, *President*
Rick Feith, *Vice Pres*
Laura Vieyra, *HR Admin*
Madeline Zapanta, *Recruiter*
Susan Martin, *Manager*
EMP: 150
SALES: 1MM **Privately Held**
WEB: www.kentdaniels.com
SIC: 7361 Executive placement

(P-14657)
KFORCE INC
4510 Executive Dr Ste 325, San Diego
(92121-3069)
PHONE................................858 550-1645
Maryland Kaforey, *Manager*
Kathleen Mulvaney, *Tech Recruiter*
EMP: 66
SALES (corp-wide): 1.3B **Publicly Held**
WEB: www.kforce.com
SIC: 7361 Employment agencies
PA: Kforce Inc.
1001 E Palm Ave
Tampa FL 33605
813 552-5000

(P-14658)
KINETICOM INC (PA)
8885 Rio San Diego Dr # 210, San Diego
(92108-1626)
PHONE................................619 330-3100
Michael Wager, *CEO*
Casey Marquand, *CFO*
Blair Bode, *Vice Pres*
William Coyman, *Vice Pres*
Michael Steadman, *Vice Pres*
EMP: 79
SQ FT: 6,000
SALES (est): 30.9MM **Privately Held**
WEB: www.kineticom.com
SIC: 7361 Executive placement

(P-14659)
L&T STAFFING INC (PA)
Also Called: Staffing Solutions
950 W 17th St Ste E, Santa Ana
(92706-3573)
PHONE................................714 558-1821
Fortino Rivera, *CEO*
Lucia Montellano, *CFO*
EMP: 380
SQ FT: 1,500
SALES: 7MM **Privately Held**
SIC: 7361 Executive placement

(P-14660)
LA JOLLA NURSES HOME CARE
2223 Avenida De La Playa, La Jolla
(92037-3200)
PHONE................................858 454-9339
Brittany Solerno, *Director*
Martin Murphy, *Treasurer*
Sonia Cantor, *Personnel*
Billie Davis, *VP Opers*
Shannon Kehoe, *Nursing Dir*
EMP: 240
SALES (est): 2.2MM
SALES (corp-wide): 6.5MM **Privately
Held**
WEB: www.carehealthservices.com
SIC: 7361 8742 8082 Nurses' registry;
management consulting services; home
health care services
PA: Care Health Services, Inc
2290 10th Ave N Ste 304
Lake Worth FL 33461
561 433-8800

(P-14661)
LAUREL LABOR SERVICES INC
727 Richmind Ct, Santa Maria
(93455-7133)
P.O. Box 5792 (93456-5792)
PHONE................................805 928-0113
Lucy Laurel, *President*
EMP: 99
SQ FT: 950
SALES (est): 4.5MM **Privately Held**
SIC: 7361 Employment agencies

(P-14662)
LEADSTACK INC
1390 Market St Ste 200, San Francisco
(94102-5404)
PHONE................................628 200-3063
Kazi Ahmed, *CEO*
EMP: 64
SALES (est): 2.1MM **Privately Held**
SIC: 7361 Employment agencies

(P-14663)
**LOAN ADMINISTRATION
NETWRK INC**
Also Called: Lani
18952 Macarthur Blvd # 315, Irvine
(92612-1401)
PHONE................................949 752-5246
Charlene Nichols, *President*
Catherine Anderson, *Vice Pres*
Mila Fernandez, *Accounting Mgr*
Sunny Cahill, *Recruiter*
Bobbi Everett, *Recruiter*
EMP: 100
SQ FT: 4,000
SALES (est): 5.4MM **Privately Held**
WEB: www.lani.com
SIC: 7361 8742 Employment agencies; fi-
nancial consultant; training & develop-
ment consultant; banking & finance
consultant

(P-14664)
**LONG BEACH UNIFIED SCHOOL
DST**
Also Called: Long Bch Unfied Schl Dst Lbusd
999 Atlantic Ave Fl 3, Long Beach
(90813-4514)
PHONE................................562 491-1281
Ramon Curiel, *Branch Mgr*
EMP: 657
SALES (corp-wide): 867.6MM **Privately
Held**
SIC: 7361 Employment agencies
PA: Long Beach Unified School District
1515 Hughes Way
Long Beach CA 90810
562 997-8000

(P-14665)
LUIS ESPARZA SERVICES INC
183 Hwy 33, Maricopa (93252)
PHONE................................661 766-2344
Luis Esparza, *President*
EMP: 500
SALES (est): 7MM **Privately Held**
SIC: 7361 8631 Labor contractors (em-
ployment agency); labor unions & similar
labor organizations

(P-14666)
**MAGANA LABOR SERVICES
INC**
2896 W Telegraph Rd, Fillmore
(93015-9642)
PHONE................................805 524-0446
Juvenal Magana, *Owner*
Miguel Magana, *Human Res Dir*
EMP: 200
SALES (est): 9.9MM **Privately Held**
SIC: 7361 8631 Labor contractors (em-
ployment agency); labor unions & similar
labor organizations

(P-14667)
**MEGA FARM LABOR SERVICES
INC**
110 S Montclair St # 103, Bakersfield
(93309-3118)
P.O. Box 744, Delano (93216-0744)
PHONE................................661 229-8077
Belen Casimiro, *President*
EMP: 151
SALES (est): 4.4MM **Privately Held**
SIC: 7361 Labor contractors (employment
agency)

(P-14668)
MHS CUSTOMER SERVICE INC
7586 Trade St Ste C, San Diego
(92121-2427)
PHONE................................858 695-2151
Don T Fryer, *President*
Theresa Phebes, *Vice Pres*
EMP: 75
SQ FT: 8,600

SALES (est): 6.3MM **Privately Held**
SIC: 7361 1542 1531 7299 Labor contractors (employment agency); nonresidential construction; operative builders; handyman service

(P-14669)
MID VALLEY LABOR SERVICES INC
19358 Avenue 18 1/2, Madera (93637-9709)
P.O. Box 899 (93639-0899)
PHONE..................................559 661-6390
Samuel Mascarenas, *President*
Ben Mascarenas, *CFO*
EMP: 500
SQ FT: 2,132
SALES: 27MM **Privately Held**
WEB: www.midvalleybirthingservices.com
SIC: 7361 Labor contractors (employment agency)

(P-14670)
MYA SYSTEMS INC
27 Maiden Ln Ste 300, San Francisco (94108-5431)
PHONE..................................877 679-0952
Eyal Grayevsky, *CEO*
Braydan Young, *President*
James Maddox, *CTO*
EMP: 50
SQ FT: 1,500
SALES (est): 547.7K **Privately Held**
SIC: 7361 Placement agencies

(P-14671)
NETPOLARITY INC
900 E Campbell Ave, Campbell (95008-2366)
PHONE..................................408 971-1100
Haixia Zhang, *CEO*
David Chuang, *President*
Cathleen Lariviere, *General Mgr*
Alexander Chiang, *Tech Recruiter*
Bryan Corbin, *Tech Recruiter*
EMP: 500
SQ FT: 5,000
SALES (est): 44.2MM **Privately Held**
WEB: www.netpolarity.com
SIC: 7361 Placement agencies

(P-14672)
NETSOURCE INC
5955 Geary Blvd, San Francisco (94121-2006)
P.O. Box 590665 (94159-0665)
PHONE..................................415 831-3681
Lana Bondar, *President*
Riva Bondar, *Treasurer*
Eren Bondar, *Controller*
EMP: 55
SALES: 6MM **Privately Held**
WEB: www.netsourceweb.com
SIC: 7361 Executive placement

(P-14673)
NORTHWEST STAFFING RESOURCES
Also Called: Resource Staffing Group
701 University Ave # 120, Sacramento (95825-6700)
PHONE..................................916 960-2668
Windy Richard, *Manager*
EMP: 1880
SALES (corp-wide): 163.5MM **Privately Held**
WEB: www.nwstaffing.com
SIC: 7361 7363 Labor contractors (employment agency); temporary help service
PA: Northwest Staffing Resources, Inc.
851 Sw 6th Ave Ste 300
Portland OR 97204
503 323-9190

(P-14674)
NOVATIME TECHNOLOGY INC (HQ)
9680 Haven Ave Ste 200, Rancho Cucamonga (91730-5342)
PHONE..................................909 895-8100
Frank Su, *President*
Ian Sexton, *Senior VP*
Gil Sidhom, *Vice Pres*
Livia Gerardo, *Manager*
EMP: 60

SQ FT: 6,000
SALES (est): 18.8MM **Privately Held**
WEB: www.novatime.com
SIC: 7361 Executive placement
PA: Ascentis Corporation
11995 Singletree Ln # 400
Eden Prairie MN 55344
800 229-2713

(P-14675)
NPH MEDICAL SERVICES
Also Called: Nurses & Prof Hlth Care
555 Flying V St Ste 5, Chico (95928-7698)
PHONE..................................530 899-2255
SIS Gilmore, *President*
Jim Gilmore, *Vice Pres*
EMP: 76
SALES (est): 80K **Privately Held**
SIC: 7361 Nurses' registry

(P-14676)
NURSE PROVIDERS INC
Also Called: Nursing Registry
355 Gellert Blvd Ste 110, Daly City (94015-2668)
PHONE..................................650 992-8559
Sherri Burke, *President*
EMP: 800
SQ FT: 1,400
SALES (est): 19.3MM **Privately Held**
SIC: 7361 Nurses' registry

(P-14677)
NURSEFINDERS LLC (HQ)
12400 High Bluff Dr, San Diego (92130-3077)
P.O. Box 919024 (92191-9024)
PHONE..................................858 314-7427
Susan Salka, *CEO*
Ralph S Henderson, *President*
Denise L Jackson, *Senior VP*
EMP: 110
SQ FT: 22,000
SALES (est): 101.7MM
SALES (corp-wide): 1.9B **Publicly Held**
WEB: www.nursefinders.com
SIC: 7361 8082 7363 8049 Placement agencies; home health care services; help supply services; temporary help service; nurses, registered & practical
PA: Amn Healthcare Services, Inc.
12400 High Bluff Dr
San Diego CA 92130
866 871-8519

(P-14678)
NURSES INTERNET STAFFING SVCS (PA)
6055 E Wash Blvd Ste 409, Commerce (90040-2425)
PHONE..................................323 720-9900
Sonny Park, *President*
Sue Park, *CFO*
Andrew J Song, *Director*
EMP: 120
SALES (est): 5.7MM **Privately Held**
WEB: www.nursesinternet.com
SIC: 7361 Nurses' registry

(P-14679)
OFFICEWORKS INC
300 Frank H Ste 269, Oakland (94612)
PHONE..................................510 444-2161
EMP: 96
SALES (corp-wide): 18.8MM **Privately Held**
SIC: 7361 Employment agencies
PA: Officeworks, Inc.
3200 E Guasti Rd Ste 100
Ontario CA 91761
909 606-4100

(P-14680)
OFFICEWORKS INC
11801 Pierce St Fl 2, Riverside (92505-4400)
PHONE..................................951 784-2534
EMP: 96
SALES (corp-wide): 18.8MM **Privately Held**
SIC: 7361 Employment agencies
PA: Officeworks, Inc.
3200 E Guasti Rd Ste 100
Ontario CA 91761
909 606-4100

(P-14681)
ONLINE TECHNICAL SERVICES INC (PA)
1901 S Bascom Ave Ste 840, Campbell (95008-2210)
PHONE..................................408 378-1100
Hans Lemcke, *Ch of Bd*
Sean Anderson, *COO*
Brenton Hanlon, *Director*
Jim Piazza, *Director*
EMP: 50
SQ FT: 1,000
SALES (est): 2.4MM **Privately Held**
WEB: www.onlinetechnical.com
SIC: 7361 Placement agencies

(P-14682)
ORANGE COUNTY ONE STOP CENTER
Also Called: Coastal Community College
5405 Grdn Rd Blvd Ste 100, Westminster (92683)
PHONE..................................714 241-4900
Lois Wilkerson, *Director*
EMP: 55
SALES (est): 1.9MM **Privately Held**
WEB: www.coastalcommunitycollege.com
SIC: 7361 8742 Employment agencies; human resource consulting services

(P-14683)
OUTSOURCE CONSULTING SVCS INC (PA)
Also Called: Ocsi.co
505 14th St Ste 900, Oakland (94612-1468)
PHONE..................................510 986-0686
Sandra O Floyd, *President*
Kit Floyd, *Finance Other*
Carlie Stone, *Recruiter*
Lorraine Sepulveda, *Manager*
EMP: 75
SQ FT: 4,700
SALES (est): 5MM **Privately Held**
WEB: www.osource.com
SIC: 7361 Labor contractors (employment agency)

(P-14684)
P & P AGRILABOR
Highway 101 Floretta Rd, Chualar (93925)
PHONE..................................831 679-2307
P Concepcion Baclig, *Owner*
Purisima Concepcion Baclig, *Owner*
EMP: 80
SALES (est): 2.1MM **Privately Held**
SIC: 7361 Labor contractors (employment agency)

(P-14685)
PACIFIC GTWY WRKFRCE PRTNR INC
3447 Atlantic Ave, Long Beach (90807-4513)
PHONE..................................562 570-3700
Nick Schultz, *Exec Dir*
EMP: 50
SALES (est): 1.5MM **Privately Held**
SIC: 7361 Labor contractors (employment agency)

(P-14686)
PACIFIC RIM RESOURCES SRCH
14148 Brookhurst St, Garden Grove (92843-4656)
PHONE..................................714 638-0307
Trang Diem Tran, *CEO*
EMP: 200
SALES (est): 7.4MM **Privately Held**
WEB: www.prresources.net
SIC: 7361 Executive placement

(P-14687)
PARADIGM STAFFING SOLUTIONS
1970 Broadway Ste 615, Oakland (94612-2218)
PHONE..................................510 663-7860
Fax: 510 663-7866
EMP: 50
SALES (est): 2.3MM **Privately Held**
WEB: www.parastaffing.com
SIC: 7361

(P-14688)
PDS TECH INC
1798 Tech Dr Ste 130, San Jose (95110)
PHONE..................................408 916-4848
EMP: 1231
SALES (corp-wide): 262.4MM **Privately Held**
SIC: 7361 Employment agencies
PA: Pds Tech, Inc.
300 E John Carpenter Fwy # 700
Irving TX 75062
214 647-9600

(P-14689)
PDS TECH INC
3100 S Harbor Blvd # 135, Santa Ana (92704-6813)
PHONE..................................214 647-9600
Dj Englert, *Manager*
EMP: 82
SALES (corp-wide): 262.4MM **Privately Held**
WEB: www.pdstech.com
SIC: 7361 Employment agencies
PA: Pds Tech, Inc.
300 E John Carpenter Fwy # 700
Irving TX 75062
214 647-9600

(P-14690)
PEMER PACKING CO INC
20260 Spence Rd, Salinas (93908-9507)
P.O. Box 4783 (93912-4783)
PHONE..................................831 758-8586
Pedro Mercado, *President*
EMP: 800
SQ FT: 3,000
SALES (est): 36.1MM **Privately Held**
SIC: 7361 Labor contractors (employment agency)

(P-14691)
PEOPLE SCIENCE INC
951 Mariners Island Blvd, San Mateo (94404-1558)
PHONE..................................888 924-1004
Christine Nichlos, *CEO*
EMP: 50
SALES (corp-wide): 3.2MM **Privately Held**
SIC: 7361 Executive placement
PA: People Science Inc
595 Shrewsbury Ave # 102
Shrewsbury NJ 07702
888 924-1004

(P-14692)
PEOPLES CHOICE STAFFING INC
4218 Green River Rd # 101, Corona (92880-1634)
PHONE..................................951 735-0550
Denise Peoples, *President*
Wendell Peoples, *COO*
Marcell Peoples, *Business Mgr*
Candice Handley, *Manager*
EMP: 100
SALES: 14.5MM **Privately Held**
WEB: www.peopleschoicestaffing.com
SIC: 7361 Placement agencies

(P-14693)
PEOPLEWARE TECHNICAL RESOURCES
302 W Grand Ave Ste 4, El Segundo (90245-5108)
PHONE..................................310 640-2406
Sheryl Rooker, *President*
Jeff Thaler, *CFO*
EMP: 60
SQ FT: 3,000
SALES (est): 2.8MM **Privately Held**
WEB: www.peoplewareinc.com
SIC: 7361 7363 Placement agencies; help supply services

(P-14694)
PLUS GROUP INC
Also Called: Jobs Plus
2551 Sn Rmn Vlly Blvd 2, San Ramon (94583)
PHONE..................................925 831-8551
Patrick O'Donnell, *Branch Mgr*
Kelly Karmer, *Recruiter*
EMP: 100 **Privately Held**

P R O D U C T S & S V C S

WEB: www.tpgstaffing.com
SIC: 7361 7363 Temporary help service; executive placement
PA: The Plus Group Inc
　7425 Janes Ave Ste 201
　Woodridge IL 60517

(P-14695)
POSITIVE SOLUTION STAFFING LLC
15949 Oak Hill Dr, Chino Hills (91709-2467)
PHONE....................909 606-7512
Grace Rojas, *Mng Member*
Mary Rodriguez,
EMP: 106
SALES (est): 3MM **Privately Held**
SIC: 7361 Employment agencies

(P-14696)
PRECISE FIT LIMITED ONE LLC
Also Called: Pfitech
959 Suth Cast Dr Ste 200, Costa Mesa (92626)
PHONE....................310 824-1800
Richard Hernandez, *Marketing Staff*
Donald Zamba, *COO*
Roland Del Rio, *Officer*
Carl Cook, *Executive*
Tony Galindo, *CTO*
EMP: 380
SQ FT: 10,000
SALES: 20.5MM **Privately Held**
SIC: 7361 Employment agencies

(P-14697)
PREFERRED HLTHCARE RGISTRY INC
9089 Clairemont Mesa Blvd # 200, San Diego (92123-1225)
P.O. Box 17860 (92177-7860)
PHONE....................800 787-6787
Melanie Reiten, *President*
Rebecca Edwards Diata, *Vice Pres*
EMP: 170
SQ FT: 2,100
SALES (est): 7.9MM **Privately Held**
WEB: www.preferredregistry.com
SIC: 7361 7363 Employment agencies; temporary help service

(P-14698)
PREMIER HEALTHCARE SVCS LLC (HQ)
Also Called: Phs Staffing
815 Colorado Blvd Ste 400, Los Angeles (90041-1745)
PHONE....................626 204-7930
Anthony H Strange, *CEO*
EMP: 200
SALES (est): 26.7MM
SALES (corp-wide): 1B **Privately Held**
WEB: www.phs-staffing.com
SIC: 7361 Nurses' registry
PA: Aveanna Healthcare, Llc
　400 Interstate North Pkwy
　Atlanta GA 30339
　770 441-1580

(P-14699)
PREMIER INSITE GROUP INC
111 W Ocean Blvd Ste 400, Long Beach (90802-4633)
PHONE....................562 741-5018
Jose Castellanos, *President*
Juan Calderon, *Treasurer*
Sandra Picos, *Exec Dir*
EMP: 99
SQ FT: 1,628
SALES (est): 3.7MM **Privately Held**
SIC: 7361 Labor contractors (employment agency)

(P-14700)
PREMIER NURSING SERVICES INC (PA)
444 W Ocean Blvd Ste 1050, Long Beach (90802-8129)
PHONE....................562 437-4313
Issam Osman, *President*
Nancy Bauguess, *Admin Sec*
Othman Omar, *Project Mgr*
Heather Trzaska, *Opers Staff*
Waleed Omar, *Assistant*

EMP: 800
SQ FT: 2,000
SALES (est): 40.2MM **Privately Held**
WEB: www.premiernursing.com
SIC: 7361 Nurses' registry

(P-14701)
PRIVATE INDUSTRY CNCL SLNO CTY (PA)
Also Called: Workforce Inv Bd Solano Cnty
320 Campus Ln Ste A, Fairfield (94534-1566)
PHONE....................707 864-3370
Robert Bloom, *Exec Dir*
Taffy Della-Cioppa, *Principal*
EMP: 50
SALES: 4.2MM **Privately Held**
WEB: www.solanowib.org
SIC: 7361 Employment agencies

(P-14702)
PROFESSNAL CREER PLACEMENTSCOM
1990 N Calif Blvd Fl 8, Walnut Creek (94596-3742)
PHONE....................415 615-0688
Martin Shmagin, *CEO*
Cindy Sassler, *Vice Pres*
Maureen Stokes, *Opers Staff*
EMP: 50 EST: 2013
SQ FT: 1,459
SALES (est): 1.5MM **Privately Held**
SIC: 7361 Executive placement

(P-14703)
PROFESSNAL RGISTRY NETWRK CORP
20132 Canyon Dr, Yorba Linda (92886-6058)
PHONE....................714 394-4071
George Makridis, *President*
EMP: 105
SALES (est): 5.7MM **Privately Held**
WEB: www.prncorp.net
SIC: 7361 Registries

(P-14704)
PROFILE OF SANTA CRUZ
Also Called: Experience Unlimited
2045 40th Ave Ste B, Capitola (95010-2549)
PHONE....................831 479-0393
Lance Vera, *Exec Dir*
EMP: 70
SALES (est): 1.6MM **Privately Held**
WEB: www.santacruzprofile.org
SIC: 7361 Placement agencies

(P-14705)
PROLINX SERVICES INC
2033 Gateway Pl Ste 500, San Jose (95110-3712)
PHONE....................408 689-5777
Bryan Dunlap, *President*
Gerardo Ballester, *CFO*
EMP: 65 EST: 2008
SALES (est): 3.3MM
SALES (corp-wide): 5.7MM **Privately Held**
SIC: 7361 Employment agencies
PA: Tiffany Stuart Solutions, Inc.
　390 Diablo Rd Ste 220
　Danville CA 94526
　925 855-3600

(P-14706)
PROVEN SOLUTIONS INC
11150 Santa Monica Blvd # 1060, Los Angeles (90025-1575)
PHONE....................310 933-4544
EMP: 51 **Privately Held**
SIC: 7361 Employment agencies
PA: Proven Solutions, Inc.
　9444 Waples St Ste 440
　San Diego CA 92121

(P-14707)
PROVIDIAN STAFFING CORPORATION (PA)
Also Called: Providian Leasing
1249 S Diamond Bar Blvd, Diamond Bar (91765-4122)
PHONE....................909 598-9099
Rosa Gonzalez, *President*

EMP: 600
SQ FT: 3,940
SALES (est): 14.7MM **Privately Held**
SIC: 7361 Employment agencies

(P-14708)
PS NATIONAL INC
Also Called: Professional Staffing
17645 Chatsworth St, Granada Hills (91344-5602)
PHONE....................818 366-1300
Lee Leatherman, *President*
Ruth Leatherman, *Vice Pres*
EMP: 300 EST: 1977
SQ FT: 4,000
SALES (est): 12.7MM **Privately Held**
SIC: 7361 7363 Nurses' registry; help supply services

(P-14709)
PSINAPSE TECHNOLOGY LTD
1063 Serpentine Ln Ste A, Pleasanton (94566-4808)
PHONE....................925 225-0400
Sylvia Luneau, *President*
Kesha Boyd, *Admin Asst*
Kim Sopher, *Manager*
EMP: 90
SQ FT: 4,000
SALES (est): 3.7MM **Privately Held**
WEB: www.psinapse.com
SIC: 7361 Placement agencies

(P-14710)
PTS STAFFING SOLUTIONS
2860 Michelle Ste 150, Irvine (92606-1010)
PHONE....................949 268-4000
June Stein, *President*
David Stein, *Vice Pres*
Ronald Stein, *Vice Pres*
Russell Stein, *Vice Pres*
Tasha Huynh, *Tech Recruiter*
EMP: 220
SQ FT: 4,950
SALES: 30.6MM **Privately Held**
WEB: www.ptsstaffing.com
SIC: 7361 Employment agencies

(P-14711)
R N PRIORITY NURSING SERVICE
P.O. Box 234216 (92023-4216)
PHONE....................760 635-7776
Nancy Fournier, *Owner*
EMP: 60
SALES: 700K **Privately Held**
SIC: 7361 Nurses' registry

(P-14712)
RAMCO ENTERPRISES LP
325 Plaza Dr Ste 1, Santa Maria (93454-6929)
PHONE....................805 922-9888
EMP: 991
SALES (corp-wide): 85MM **Privately Held**
SIC: 7361 Executive placement
PA: Ramco Enterprises, L.P.
　710 La Guardia St
　Salinas CA 93905
　831 758-5272

(P-14713)
RAMCO ENTERPRISES LP
585 Auto Center Dr, Watsonville (95076-3764)
PHONE....................831 722-3370
EMP: 743
SALES (corp-wide): 85MM **Privately Held**
SIC: 7361 Employment agencies
PA: Ramco Enterprises, L.P.
　710 La Guardia St
　Salinas CA 93905
　831 758-5272

(P-14714)
RANDSTAD PROFESSIONALS US LLC
Also Called: Randstad Finance & Accounting
111 Anza Blvd Ste 202, Burlingame (94010-1932)
PHONE....................650 343-5111
Shannon Guzzetta, *Branch Mgr*
Anna Santiago, *HR Admin*
Angelo Hatzistratis, *Director*

EMP: 235
SALES (corp-wide): 27.4B **Privately Held**
SIC: 7361 Executive placement
HQ: Randstad Professionals Us, Llc
　150 Presidential Way Fl 4
　Woburn MA 01801

(P-14715)
RCSN INC
10221 Slater Ave Ste 214, Fountain Valley (92708-4751)
PHONE....................714 965-0244
Catherin Long, *CEO*
Ann Lee, *CFO*
Erick Nguyen, *Accounts Mgr*
EMP: 150
SQ FT: 400
SALES (est): 4.1MM **Privately Held**
SIC: 7361 Executive placement

(P-14716)
READYLINK INC
72030 Metroplex Dr, Thousand Palms (92276)
PHONE....................760 343-7000
Daniel Caliendo, *Principal*
EMP: 99
SALES (est): 4MM **Privately Held**
SIC: 7361 Employment agencies

(P-14717)
READYLINK HEALTHCARE
72030 Metroplex Dr, Thousand Palms (92276)
P.O. Box 1047 (92276-1047)
PHONE....................760 343-7000
Barry L Treash, *President*
Rebecca Ruiz, *Payroll Mgr*
Roberta Derrington, *Train & Dev Mgr*
Natashia Contreras, *Nurse*
Sheri Strebe, *Director*
EMP: 85
SALES (est): 8MM **Privately Held**
WEB: www.readylinkhealthcare.com
SIC: 7361 Labor contractors (employment agency)

(P-14718)
REAL TIME STAFFING SERVICES
Also Called: Select Staffing
301 Mentor Dr 210, Santa Barbara (93111-3339)
PHONE....................805 882-2200
Steve Sorensen, *Principal*
Virginia Pabloff, *Manager*
EMP: 99
SALES: 950K **Privately Held**
SIC: 7361 Employment agencies

(P-14719)
REDLANDS EMPLOYMENT SERVICES
Also Called: Redlands Staffing Services
4295 Jurupa St Ste 110, Ontario (91761-1429)
PHONE....................951 688-0083
Matt Tahlmeyer, *President*
Debbie Jahn, *Controller*
EMP: 363 **Privately Held**
SIC: 7361 Placement agencies
PA: Redlands Employment Services Inc
　499 W State St
　Redlands CA 92373

(P-14720)
RELIABLE NURSING SOLUTIONS
16057 Kamana Rd Ste B, Apple Valley (92307-0841)
PHONE....................760 946-9191
Carol Grigsby, *President*
EMP: 85
SQ FT: 1,200
SALES (est): 2.7MM **Privately Held**
WEB: www.reliablenursing.com
SIC: 7361 Placement agencies

(P-14721)
RENTERIA SANTIAGO J FARM LABO
137 W Kern Ave, Mc Farland (93250-1348)
PHONE....................661 792-0052

Santiago J Renteria, *Owner*
EMP: 150
SQ FT: 768
SALES (est): 6MM **Privately Held**
SIC: 7361 Labor contractors (employment agency)

(P-14722)
RESOURCES CONNECTION LLC (HQ)
Also Called: Resources Global Professionals
17101 Armstrong Ave # 100, Irvine (92614-5742)
PHONE..................................714 430-6400
Donald B Murray, *Ch of Bd*
Kate W Duchene, *President*
Tony Cherbak, *COO*
Herbert M Mueller, *CFO*
Tanja Cebula, *Exec VP*
EMP: 60 **EST:** 1999
SQ FT: 16,366
SALES: 583.4MM **Publicly Held**
WEB: www.resourcesconnection.com
SIC: 7361 8742 Executive placement; management consulting services

(P-14723)
RESPONSE 1 MEDICAL STAFFING
1101 Inv Blvd Ste 140, El Dorado Hills (95762)
PHONE..................................916 932-0430
Cheree Love, *CEO*
Gordon Helm, *Shareholder*
Gary Slavit, *Shareholder*
Lajuan Knorr, *CFO*
EMP: 150
SQ FT: 3,000
SALES: 12MM **Privately Held**
WEB: www.response1.com
SIC: 7361 Nurses' registry

(P-14724)
RIGHT CHOICE A HEALTH CARE
620 S Glendora Ave Ste A, Glendora (91740-6815)
P.O. Box 127 (91740-0127)
PHONE..................................626 335-1318
Mike Dababneh, *President*
EMP: 300
SQ FT: 3,000
SALES (est): 9MM **Privately Held**
WEB: www.right-choicestaffing.com
SIC: 7361 Employment agencies

(P-14725)
ROBERT HALF INTERNATIONAL INC
10 Almaden Blvd Ste 900, San Jose (95113-2268)
PHONE..................................408 961-2975
Catrina Simbe, *Branch Mgr*
EMP: 92
SALES (corp-wide): 5.2B **Publicly Held**
SIC: 7361 Placement agencies
PA: Robert Half International Inc.
2884 Sand Hill Rd Ste 200
Menlo Park CA 94025
650 234-6000

(P-14726)
ROBERT HALF INTERNATIONAL INC
865 S Figueroa St # 2600, Los Angeles (90017-5486)
PHONE..................................213 270-6731
Alicia Arzola, *Principal*
EMP: 92
SALES (corp-wide): 5.2B **Publicly Held**
WEB: www.rhii.com
SIC: 7361 Executive placement
PA: Robert Half International Inc.
2884 Sand Hill Rd Ste 200
Menlo Park CA 94025
650 234-6000

(P-14727)
ROBERT HALF INTERNATIONAL INC
50 California St Ste 1000, San Francisco (94111-4613)
PHONE..................................415 434-2429
EMP: 92
SALES (corp-wide): 5.2B **Publicly Held**
SIC: 7361 Placement agencies

PA: Robert Half International Inc.
2884 Sand Hill Rd Ste 200
Menlo Park CA 94025
650 234-6000

(P-14728)
ROBERT HALF INTERNATIONAL INC
39141 Civic Center Dr # 205, Fremont (94538-5823)
PHONE..................................510 744-6486
EMP: 92
SALES (corp-wide): 5.2B **Publicly Held**
SIC: 7361 Placement agencies
PA: Robert Half International Inc.
2884 Sand Hill Rd Ste 200
Menlo Park CA 94025
650 234-6000

(P-14729)
ROBERT HALF INTERNATIONAL INC
4 Lower Ragsdale Dr # 101, Monterey (93940-7835)
PHONE..................................831 241-9042
Gabby Ayala, *Manager*
EMP: 94
SALES (corp-wide): 5.2B **Publicly Held**
SIC: 7361 Placement agencies
PA: Robert Half International Inc.
2884 Sand Hill Rd Ste 200
Menlo Park CA 94025
650 234-6000

(P-14730)
ROBERT HALF INTERNATIONAL INC
1 City Blvd W Ste 1115, Orange (92868-3605)
PHONE..................................714 450-9838
Tina Fox, *Branch Mgr*
EMP: 92
SALES (corp-wide): 5.2B **Publicly Held**
SIC: 7361 Labor contractors (employment agency)
PA: Robert Half International Inc.
2884 Sand Hill Rd Ste 200
Menlo Park CA 94025
650 234-6000

(P-14731)
ROBERT HALF INTERNATIONAL INC
3000 Oak Rd, Walnut Creek (94597-2092)
PHONE..................................925 930-7766
Heath Harris, *Branch Mgr*
EMP: 92
SALES (corp-wide): 5.2B **Publicly Held**
SIC: 7361 Placement agencies
PA: Robert Half International Inc.
2884 Sand Hill Rd Ste 200
Menlo Park CA 94025
650 234-6000

(P-14732)
ROBERT HALF INTERNATIONAL INC
2280 Market St Ste 220, Riverside (92501-2120)
PHONE..................................951 779-9081
Jason Buchbinder, *Manager*
EMP: 92
SALES (corp-wide): 5.2B **Publicly Held**
SIC: 7361 Placement agencies
PA: Robert Half International Inc.
2884 Sand Hill Rd Ste 200
Menlo Park CA 94025
650 234-6000

(P-14733)
ROBERT HALF INTERNATIONAL INC
3100 Zinfandel Dr Ste 260, Rancho Cordova (95670-6391)
PHONE..................................916 852-1705
Chris Gardiner, *Branch Mgr*
EMP: 92
SALES (corp-wide): 5.2B **Publicly Held**
SIC: 7361 Placement agencies
PA: Robert Half International Inc.
2884 Sand Hill Rd Ste 200
Menlo Park CA 94025
650 234-6000

(P-14734)
ROBERT HALF INTERNATIONAL INC
Accountemps
10 Almaden Blvd Ste 900, San Jose (95113-2268)
PHONE..................................408 293-8611
Monique Cruz, *Principal*
EMP: 50
SALES (corp-wide): 5.2B **Publicly Held**
WEB: www.rhii.com
SIC: 7361 Employment agencies
PA: Robert Half International Inc.
2884 Sand Hill Rd Ste 200
Menlo Park CA 94025
650 234-6000

(P-14735)
ROBERT HALF INTERNATIONAL INC
4225 Executive Sq Ste 300, La Jolla (92037-9212)
PHONE..................................888 744-9202
Paige Thomas, *Manager*
EMP: 92
SALES (corp-wide): 5.2B **Publicly Held**
WEB: www.rhii.com
SIC: 7361 Employment agencies
PA: Robert Half International Inc.
2884 Sand Hill Rd Ste 200
Menlo Park CA 94025
650 234-6000

(P-14736)
ROBERT HALF INTERNATIONAL INC
Also Called: Accountemps
50 California St Ste 1000, San Francisco (94111-4613)
PHONE..................................415 434-1900
Katy Giggere, *Branch Mgr*
EMP: 140
SALES (corp-wide): 5.2B **Publicly Held**
WEB: www.rhii.com
SIC: 7361 7363 Executive placement; help supply services
PA: Robert Half International Inc.
2884 Sand Hill Rd Ste 200
Menlo Park CA 94025
650 234-6000

(P-14737)
ROBERT HALF INTERNATIONAL INC
Accountemps
1850 Gateway Dr Ste 200, San Mateo (94404-4061)
PHONE..................................650 574-8200
Stephanie Vinske, *Branch Mgr*
EMP: 50
SALES (corp-wide): 5.2B **Publicly Held**
SIC: 7361 Employment agencies
PA: Robert Half International Inc.
2884 Sand Hill Rd Ste 200
Menlo Park CA 94025
650 234-6000

(P-14738)
ROBERT HALF INTERNATIONAL INC
Also Called: Accountemps
2884 Sand Hill Rd Ste 200, Menlo Park (94025-7059)
PHONE..................................650 234-6000
Paul Gentzkow, *President*
Paulina Khokhlova, *Manager*
Joanie Umscheid, *Manager*
EMP: 99
SALES (corp-wide): 5.2B **Publicly Held**
WEB: www.rhii.com
SIC: 7361 Placement agencies
PA: Robert Half International Inc.
2884 Sand Hill Rd Ste 200
Menlo Park CA 94025
650 234-6000

(P-14739)
ROBERT HALF INTERNATIONAL INC
Also Called: Creative Group, The
2884 Sand Hill Rd Ste 200, Menlo Park (94025-7059)
PHONE..................................650 234-6000
Paul Gentzkow, *President*

Kyle Gray, *Branch Mgr*
Sana Khalid, *Recruiter*
Elaine Buhler, *Manager*
Jessica Gaylord, *Accounts Mgr*
EMP: 100
SALES (corp-wide): 5.2B **Publicly Held**
WEB: www.rhii.com
SIC: 7361 7363 Placement agencies; temporary help service
PA: Robert Half International Inc.
2884 Sand Hill Rd Ste 200
Menlo Park CA 94025
650 234-6000

(P-14740)
ROBERT HALF INTERNATIONAL INC
Also Called: Office Team
2884 Sand Hill Rd Ste 200, Menlo Park (94025-7059)
PHONE..................................650 234-6000
Chris Hoffmann, *President*
EMP: 92
SALES (corp-wide): 5.2B **Publicly Held**
SIC: 7361 Employment agencies
PA: Robert Half International Inc.
2884 Sand Hill Rd Ste 200
Menlo Park CA 94025
650 234-6000

(P-14741)
ROBERT HALF INTERNATIONAL INC
Also Called: Officeteam
18200 Von Karman Ave # 800, Irvine (92612-7158)
PHONE..................................949 476-3199
Heather Kwon, *Office Mgr*
EMP: 92
SALES (corp-wide): 5.2B **Publicly Held**
SIC: 7361 8721 Placement agencies; ship crew agency; auditing services
PA: Robert Half International Inc.
2884 Sand Hill Rd Ste 200
Menlo Park CA 94025
650 234-6000

(P-14742)
ROBERT HALF INTERNATIONAL INC
790 E Colo Blvd Ste 650, Pasadena (91101)
PHONE..................................626 463-2037
Tania Hablian, *Branch Mgr*
EMP: 92
SALES (corp-wide): 5.2B **Publicly Held**
WEB: www.rhii.com
SIC: 7361 7363 Placement agencies; temporary help service
PA: Robert Half International Inc.
2884 Sand Hill Rd Ste 200
Menlo Park CA 94025
650 234-6000

(P-14743)
ROBERT HALF INTERNATIONAL INC
990 W 190th St Ste 290, Torrance (90502-1046)
PHONE..................................310 719-1400
Steve Higginbotham, *Manager*
EMP: 92
SALES (corp-wide): 5.2B **Publicly Held**
WEB: www.rhii.com
SIC: 7361 Executive placement
PA: Robert Half International Inc.
2884 Sand Hill Rd Ste 200
Menlo Park CA 94025
650 234-6000

(P-14744)
ROBERT HALF INTERNATIONAL INC
3600 W Byshore Rd Ste 103, Palo Alto (94303)
PHONE..................................650 812-9790
Christina Marinovich, *Principal*
EMP: 92
SALES (corp-wide): 5.2B **Publicly Held**
SIC: 7361 Placement agencies
PA: Robert Half International Inc.
2884 Sand Hill Rd Ste 200
Menlo Park CA 94025
650 234-6000

PRODUCTS & SVCS

(P-14745)
ROBERT HALF INTERNATIONAL INC
Also Called: Office Team
2613 Camino Ramon, San Ramon (94583-4289)
PHONE............................925 913-1000
Max Messner, *Manager*
EMP: 50
SALES (corp-wide): 5.2B **Publicly Held**
WEB: www.rhii.com
SIC: 7361 7363 Placement agencies; temporary help service
PA: Robert Half International Inc.
2884 Sand Hill Rd Ste 200
Menlo Park CA 94025
650 234-6000

(P-14746)
ROBERT QUINTERO LABOR CONTG
1827 S Bardo St, Visalia (93277-4848)
PHONE............................559 732-6954
Robert Quintero, *Owner*
EMP: 50
SALES: 1MM **Privately Held**
SIC: 7361

(P-14747)
ROBERTAS LABOR CONTRACTING
137 Main St, Soledad (93960-3023)
P.O. Box I (93960-0860)
PHONE............................831 678-8176
Roberta Urquidez, *Owner*
EMP: 300
SALES (est): 9.2MM **Privately Held**
SIC: 7361 Labor contractors (employment agency)

(P-14748)
ROY CARRINGTON INC
Also Called: Human Resource Solutions
2460 Ceres Ave, Chico (95926-1057)
PHONE............................530 893-2100
Roy Carrington, *President*
EMP: 75
SALES: 1MM **Privately Held**
SIC: 7361 8721 Employment agencies; accounting, auditing & bookkeeping

(P-14749)
RYDEK ELETRONICS LLC
898 N Pacific Coast Hwy # 475, El Segundo (90245-2705)
PHONE............................310 641-9800
Doug Browning, *Principal*
Raymond Carlson, *Recruiter*
Heidi Rudolph, *Director*
EMP: 100
SALES (est): 3.2MM **Privately Held**
WEB: www.rydek.com
SIC: 7361 Employment agencies

(P-14750)
SA TECHNOLOGIES INC (PA)
5201 Great America Pkwy # 457, Santa Clara (95054-1146)
PHONE............................408 400-3900
Manoj Joshi, *CEO*
Priyanka Joshi, *President*
Charles Rich, *Business Dir*
Vivek Sharma, *Info Tech Dir*
Archana Panchal, *Technology*
EMP: 67
SQ FT: 3,500
SALES: 18MM **Privately Held**
WEB: www.satincorp.com
SIC: 7361 7379 Employment agencies; computer related consulting services

(P-14751)
SANDOVAL BROTHERS INC
36503 Mile End Rd, Soledad (93960-9689)
P.O. Box 1183 (93960-1183)
PHONE............................831 678-1465
Antonio Sandoval, *President*
EMP: 60 EST: 1997
SALES (est): 3.9MM **Privately Held**
SIC: 7361 Labor contractors (employment agency)

(P-14752)
SANTA ANA CITY OF
1000 E Santa Ana Blvd # 108, Santa Ana (92701-3900)
PHONE............................714 565-2600
Gus Chamoro, *Manager*
EMP: 50 **Privately Held**
SIC: 7361 9111 Employment agencies; mayors' offices
PA: City Of Santa Ana
20 Civic Center Plz Fl 8
Santa Ana CA 92701
714 647-5400

(P-14753)
SANTA CLARA VLY JOB CAREER CTR
725 E Main St Ste 101, Santa Paula (93060-2748)
PHONE............................805 933-8300
Art Hernandez, *Director*
EMP: 60
SALES (est): 1.3MM **Privately Held**
SIC: 7361 Employment agencies

(P-14754)
SCOTTS LABOR LEASING CO INC
Also Called: Scott's Glass Service
22560 Lucerne St, Carson (90745-4303)
P.O. Box 3683, Long Beach (90803-0683)
PHONE............................310 835-8388
Tom Scott, *President*
Cheri Scott, *Admin Sec*
Thomas Scott, *Safety Mgr*
EMP: 80
SQ FT: 1,000
SALES: 1.5MM **Privately Held**
SIC: 7361 Employment agencies

(P-14755)
SE SCHER CORPORATION
Also Called: Acrobat Staffing
2525 Camino Del Rio S, San Diego (92108-3717)
PHONE............................858 546-8300
Marc Caplan, *Branch Mgr*
Jessica Cox, *Assistant*
EMP: 918
SALES (corp-wide): 19.8MM **Privately Held**
SIC: 7361 Executive placement
PA: S.E. Scher Corporation
303 Hegenberger Rd # 300
Oakland CA 94621
415 431-8826

(P-14756)
SE SCHER CORPORATION
Also Called: Acrobat Staffing
6731 Five Star Blvd Ste C, Rocklin (95677-2680)
PHONE............................916 632-1363
Steve Scher, *CEO*
EMP: 459
SALES (corp-wide): 19.8MM **Privately Held**
SIC: 7361 Employment agencies
PA: S.E. Scher Corporation
303 Hegenberger Rd # 300
Oakland CA 94621
415 431-8826

(P-14757)
SECURE NURSING SERVICE INC
3333 Wilshire Blvd # 625, Los Angeles (90010-4106)
PHONE............................213 736-6771
Haesook Kim, *President*
Linda West, *Info Tech Dir*
EMP: 350 EST: 2001
SQ FT: 2,500
SALES (est): 6.5MM **Privately Held**
WEB: www.securenursing.com
SIC: 7361 Nurses' registry

(P-14758)
SELECT TEMPORARIES LLC (DH)
Also Called: Select Personnel Services
3820 State St, Santa Barbara (93105-3182)
PHONE............................805 882-2200
Thomas A Bickes, *President*
Stephen Biersmith, *President*

Gary Glaser, *President*
Shawn W Poole, *CFO*
Tom Bickes, *Bd of Directors*
EMP: 90
SQ FT: 30,000
SALES (est): 72.8MM
SALES (corp-wide): 584.5MM **Privately Held**
SIC: 7361 Executive placement
HQ: Employment Solutions Management, Inc.
1040 Crown Pointe Pkwy
Atlanta GA 30338
770 671-1900

(P-14759)
SHARF WOODWARD & ASSOCIATES
5900 Sepulvda Blvd # 104, Van Nuys (91411-2511)
PHONE............................818 989-2200
Bernard Sharf, *Co-President*
EMP: 90
SALES: 10MM **Privately Held**
WEB: www.swjobs.com
SIC: 7361 Employment agencies

(P-14760)
SIRACUSA ENTERPRISES INC
Also Called: Quality Temp Staffing
17737 Chtswrth St Ste 200, Granada Hills (91344-5628)
PHONE............................818 831-1130
Joe Alas, *President*
Marie Alas, *Vice Pres*
Angie Londono, *Recruiter*
EMP: 70
SALES: 3.7MM **Privately Held**
SIC: 7361 Employment agencies

(P-14761)
SMART CHOICE INVESTMENTS INC
Also Called: Brightstar Health
23332 Hawthorne Blvd # 203, Torrance (90505-3749)
PHONE............................310 944-6985
Maurice Geyen, *President*
EMP: 80 EST: 2008
SALES (est): 3.5MM **Privately Held**
SIC: 7361 8082 Nurses' registry; home health care services

(P-14762)
SNELLING EMPLOYMENT LLC
2203 Harvbor Bay Pkwy, Alameda (94502)
PHONE............................510 769-4400
Michelle Berkovich, *Manager*
EMP: 100
SALES (corp-wide): 4.1B **Privately Held**
SIC: 7361 7363 Labor contractors (employment agency); temporary help service
HQ: Snelling Employment, Llc
12801 N Cntl Expy Ste 600
Dallas TX 75243

(P-14763)
SOCAL SERVICES INC
Also Called: Tsg
6336 Greenwich Dr Ste 100, San Diego (92122-5922)
PHONE............................858 453-1331
Rich Papike, *President*
Gary Van Eik, *CEO*
Richard Papike, *CFO*
Richard J Kail, *Officer*
EMP: 250
SQ FT: 3,000
SALES (est): 15MM **Privately Held**
WEB: www.socalservices.com
SIC: 7361 7363 Employment agencies; temporary help service; office help supply service

(P-14764)
SOLEMNITY PERSONNEL
2008 Camfiled Ave, Commerce (90040)
PHONE............................323 718-3979
Peter Diaz, *Principal*
EMP: 50
SALES (est): 751.5K **Privately Held**
SIC: 7361 Employment agencies

(P-14765)
SPEC PERSONNEL LLC
Also Called: Spectra
1900 La Fytte St Unit 125, Santa Clara (95050)
PHONE............................408 727-8000
Andrew Bergen, *Branch Mgr*
EMP: 150
SALES (corp-wide): 46.6MM **Privately Held**
SIC: 7361 Employment agencies
PA: Spec Personnel, Llc
4625 Creekstone Dr # 130
Durham NC 27703
203 254-9935

(P-14766)
SPECIAL EVENTS STAFFING
1015 N Lake Ave Ste 205, Pasadena (91104-4575)
PHONE............................626 296-6771
Frank Barnes, *CEO*
EMP: 626
SQ FT: 900
SALES: 3.3MM **Privately Held**
SIC: 7361 Employment agencies

(P-14767)
STAFF ASSISTANCE INC (PA)
72 Moody Ct Ste 100, Thousand Oaks (91360-7426)
PHONE............................818 894-7879
Bill Donley, *Ch of Bd*
Elaine S Donley, *President*
EMP: 300
SQ FT: 800
SALES: 3.8MM **Privately Held**
SIC: 7361 Nurses' registry

(P-14768)
STAFF ASSISTANCE INC
Also Called: Assisted Home Care
72 Moody Ct Ste 100, Thousand Oaks (91360-7426)
PHONE............................805 371-9980
Elaine Thinney, *Branch Mgr*
John Solomon, *Info Tech Dir*
Aaron Bodie, *Marketing Staff*
Cinda Gennaro,
Elaine Phinney, *Director*
EMP: 300 **Privately Held**
SIC: 7361 8082 Nurses' registry; home health care services
PA: Staff Assistance Inc
72 Moody Ct Ste 100
Thousand Oaks CA 91360

(P-14769)
STAFFCHEX INC
20537 Devonshire St, Chatsworth (91311-3208)
PHONE............................818 709-6100
Steven Zingerman, *Principal*
EMP: 838
SALES (corp-wide): 65.2MM **Privately Held**
SIC: 7361 Employment agencies
PA: Staffchex, Inc.
790 The City Dr S Ste 180
Orange CA 92868
714 912-7500

(P-14770)
STAFFING SOLUTIONS INC
Also Called: Balance Staffing
2142 Bering Dr, San Jose (95131-2013)
PHONE............................408 980-9000
John Moss, *CEO*
Robert Feinstein, *President*
Anna Romay, *Business Mgr*
Nancy Mora, *Controller*
Lazara Casalla-Prieto, *Recruiter*
EMP: 80 EST: 1997
SQ FT: 4,000
SALES (est): 7.9MM **Privately Held**
SIC: 7361 7363 Placement agencies; help supply services

(P-14771)
STAR H-R
105 E 1st St, Cloverdale (95425-3701)
PHONE............................707 894-4404
EMP: 1012

SALES (corp-wide): 71.1MM **Privately Held**
SIC: **7361** Employment agencies
PA: Star H-R
   3820 Cypress Dr Ste 2
   Petaluma CA 94954
   707 762-4447

(P-14772)
SUNSHINE CLEARING CORPORATION
Also Called: Paragon Personel Services
1215 W Imperial Hwy # 210, Brea
(92821-3738)
PHONE..................714 829-0273
Brandy Rae Guzman, *President*
EMP: 50
SQ FT: 1,000
SALES (est): 1MM **Privately Held**
SIC: **7361** Placement agencies

(P-14773)
T W R FRAMING
1661 Railroad St, Corona (92880-2503)
PHONE..................951 279-2000
Tom Rhodes, *Owner*
Debbie Diter, *Controller*
Amy Strommer, *Director*
EMP: 100
SALES (est): 3.1MM **Privately Held**
WEB: www.twrframing.com
SIC: **7361** Labor contractors (employment agency)

(P-14774)
TALENT SPACE INC
2570 N 1st St Ste 400, San Jose
(95131-1045)
PHONE..................408 330-1900
Lisa Flores, *President*
Pearl Kearley, *Accounting Mgr*
Nick Kumar, *Recruiter*
Christina Boardman, *Art Dir*
Lynda Beauchesne, *Accounts Exec*
EMP: 80
SALES: 15MM **Privately Held**
SIC: **7361** Placement agencies

(P-14775)
TEAM-ONE EMPLYMENT SPCLSTS LLC
Also Called: Team One
2999 Overland Ave Ste 212, Los Angeles
(90064-4243)
PHONE..................310 481-4480
Frank Moran,
Joanne Geishecker, *Marketing Staff*
Faren Rose, *Manager*
EMP: 3281
SQ FT: 4,500
SALES: 35MM **Privately Held**
SIC: **7361** Placement agencies

(P-14776)
TECHLINK SYSTEMS INC (PA)
1 Post St Ste 300, San Francisco
(94104-5249)
PHONE..................415 732-7580
Jane Kim, *President*
Steve Kim, *COO*
Rupa RAO, *Associate Dir*
Reecha Pandey, *Administration*
James Steele, *Information Mgr*
EMP: 300
SQ FT: 3,000
SALES (est): 25.5MM **Privately Held**
WEB: www.techlinksystems.com
SIC: **7361** Placement agencies

(P-14777)
TECHNICAL TEMPS INC
Also Called: TTI
1096 Pecten Ct, Milpitas (95035-6805)
P.O. Box 610190, San Jose (95161-0190)
PHONE..................408 956-8256
Judith Kalune, *President*
EMP: 100
SQ FT: 1,000
SALES (est): 4.1MM **Privately Held**
WEB: www.technicaltemps.com
SIC: **7361** Executive placement

(P-14778)
TEG STAFFING INC
Also Called: Eastridge Workforce Solutions
2355 Northside Dr Ste 200, San Diego
(92108-2706)
PHONE..................619 260-2000
Adam Svet, *CEO*
Seth Stein, *President*
Jason Svet, *President*
Brandon Stanford, *CFO*
Erin Medina,
EMP: 1600
SALES (est): 17.9MM
SALES (corp-wide): 179.1MM **Privately Held**
SIC: **7361** Employment agencies
PA: Eplica, Inc.
   2355 Northside Dr Ste 120
   San Diego CA 92108
   619 260-2000

(P-14779)
TETRA TECH EXECUTIVE SVCS INC
3475 E Foothill Blvd, Pasadena
(91107-6024)
PHONE..................626 470-2400
Sam Box, *Principal*
EMP: 162
SALES (est): 5.9MM
SALES (corp-wide): 2.7B **Publicly Held**
WEB: www.tetratech.com
SIC: **7361** Employment agencies
PA: Tetra Tech, Inc.
   3475 E Foothill Blvd
   Pasadena CA 91107
   626 351-4664

(P-14780)
THOR INC (PA)
Also Called: Thor Agency
318 Avenue I, Redondo Beach
(90277-5601)
PHONE..................310 727-1777
Terry Thormodsgaard, *President*
Bob Fischer, *Vice Pres*
EMP: 52
SQ FT: 6,000
SALES (est): 3.6MM **Privately Held**
WEB: www.thorgroup.com
SIC: **7361** Labor contractors (employment agency)

(P-14781)
THOR GROUP INC (PA)
318 Avenue I, Redondo Beach
(90277-5601)
PHONE..................310 727-1777
Terry Thormodsgaard, *President*
Steve White, *Manager*
EMP: 50
SALES (est): 2.4MM **Privately Held**
SIC: **7361** Placement agencies

(P-14782)
TOTAL MANAGEMENT SVCS AMER INC
Also Called: Tms America
21151 S Wstn Ave Ste 139, Torrance
(90501)
PHONE..................310 328-0867
Pakaco Shimakage, *President*
EMP: 50
SALES: 1MM **Privately Held**
SIC: **7361** Executive placement

(P-14783)
TOTAL PROFESSIONAL NETWORK
Also Called: Core Medstaff
3946 Wilshire Blvd, Los Angeles
(90010-3303)
PHONE..................213 382-5550
Elizabeth Ann Poe, *President*
Therese Nery, *Vice Pres*
EMP: 100
SALES (est): 4.9MM **Privately Held**
WEB: www.coremedstaff.com
SIC: **7361** Nurses' registry

(P-14784)
TREELINE STAFFING
100 Broadway, San Francisco
(94111-1430)
PHONE..................415 819-7195

Boaz Mariles, *Principal*
EMP: 50
SALES (est): 636.4K **Privately Held**
SIC: **7361** Employment agencies

(P-14785)
TRI-STATE EMPLOYMENT SVC INC
450 Westmont Dr, San Pedro
(90731-1010)
PHONE..................310 521-9616
Neftali Torres, *Branch Mgr*
EMP: 465 **Privately Held**
SIC: **7361** Employment agencies
PA: Tri-State Employment Service Inc.
   160 Broadway Fl 15
   New York NY 10038
   -

(P-14786)
TRINET GROUP INC (PA)
1100 San Leandro Blvd # 300, San Leandro
(94577-1599)
PHONE..................510 352-5000
Burton M Goldfield, *President*
H Raymond Bingham, *Ch of Bd*
Olivier Kohler, *COO*
Richard Beckert, *CFO*
Brady Mickelsen,
EMP: 120
SALES: 3.2B **Publicly Held**
WEB: www.trinet.com
SIC: **7361 8721** Employment agencies; accounting, auditing & bookkeeping

(P-14787)
TRUE NORTH AR LLC
10971 Sun Center Dr # 200, Rancho Cordova (95670-9170)
PHONE..................916 369-9850
Manoj Sharma, *Branch Mgr*
EMP: 53
SALES (corp-wide): 5.4MM **Privately Held**
SIC: **7361** Employment agencies
PA: True North Ar, Llc
   100 Wood Hllow Dr Ste 200
   Novato CA 94945
   415 878-2200

(P-14788)
UAW-LBOR EMPLYMENT TRNING CORP
Also Called: One Stop Program
3965 S Vermont Ave, Los Angeles
(90037-1937)
PHONE..................323 730-7900
Audrey Holmes, *Branch Mgr*
EMP: 125
SALES (corp-wide): 9.2MM **Privately Held**
SIC: **7361** Employment agencies
PA: Uaw-Labor Employment And Training Corporation
   11010 Artesia Blvd # 100
   Cerritos CA 90703
   562 989-7700

(P-14789)
UAW-LBOR EMPLYMENT TRNING CORP (PA)
Also Called: LABOR EMPLOYMENT & TRAINING
11010 Artesia Blvd # 100, Cerritos
(90703-2551)
PHONE..................562 989-7700
Bruce Lee, *Chairman*
Robert Nelson, *President*
Phillip Tan, *CFO*
EMP: 155
SQ FT: 9,000
SALES: 9.2MM **Privately Held**
SIC: **7361 8331** Employment agencies; work experience center

(P-14790)
UNITED TEMP SERVICES INC
694 Albanese Cir, San Jose (95111-1001)
PHONE..................408 472-4309
EMP: 100
SALES: 1.5MM **Privately Held**
SIC: **7361 7363**

(P-14791)
VACO LAJOLLA LLC
Also Called: Vaco Technology
4250 Executive Sq Ste 750, La Jolla
(92037-9105)
PHONE..................858 642-0000
Brandy Sloatermen, *Mng Member*
Todd Sweat, *CFO*
Jerry Bostelman,
Jay Hollaman,
Brian Waller,
EMP: 58
SALES: 12.4MM **Privately Held**
SIC: **7361** Executive placement

(P-14792)
VALIDUS GROUP INC
Also Called: Ahr Professionals
1 Orchard Ste 210, Lake Forest
(92630-8314)
PHONE..................949 457-7606
Brian Demeo, *CEO*
EMP: 75
SALES (est): 3.2MM **Privately Held**
SIC: **7361** Placement agencies

(P-14793)
VALLEY HEALTH CARE SYSTEMS INC
Also Called: Valley Healthcare Staffing
1300 National Dr Ste 140, Sacramento
(95834-1981)
PHONE..................916 505-4112
Sejal Shah, *CEO*
Jason Beck, *President*
Steve Swan, *CTO*
Heather Swan, *Nurse*
Lisa Baker, *Manager*
EMP: 150
SQ FT: 5,000
SALES (est): 11.4MM
SALES (corp-wide): 27.6MM **Privately Held**
SIC: **7361** Nurses' registry
PA: Totalmed Staffing Inc.
   221 W College Ave
   Appleton WI 54911
   920 968-8708

(P-14794)
VALLEY LABOR SERVICE INC
39678 Road 84, Dinuba (93618-9588)
P.O. Box 775 (93618-0775)
PHONE..................559 591-5591
Jane Hobbs, *President*
Salvador Romero, *Vice Pres*
EMP: 100
SQ FT: 1,100
SALES (est): 5MM **Privately Held**
SIC: **7361** Labor contractors (employment agency)

(P-14795)
VERIZON COMMUNICATIONS INC
1800 Solar Dr, Oxnard (93030-2655)
PHONE..................805 988-5760
Tina Curts, *Principal*
EMP: 900
SALES (corp-wide): 126B **Publicly Held**
WEB: www.gte.com
SIC: **7361** Employment agencies
PA: Verizon Communications Inc.
   1095 Ave Of The Americas
   New York NY 10036
   212 395-1000

(P-14796)
VOTUM STAFFING INC
515 W Whittier Blvd, Montebello
(90640-5233)
PHONE..................310 499-4902
Giuseppe Veneziano, *CEO*
EMP: 450
SALES (est): 14.1MM **Privately Held**
SIC: **7361** Employment agencies

(P-14797)
WEDRIVEU HOLDINGS INC
700 Airport Blvd Ste 250, Burlingame
(94010-1937)
PHONE..................650 579-5800
Dennis Carlson, *CEO*
Brian F Sours, *Vice Pres*
Erick Vanwagenen, *Vice Pres*

Robert Miller, *General Mgr*
EMP: 99
SALES (est): 1MM **Privately Held**
SIC: 7361 Employment agencies

(P-14798)
WEST VALLEY ENGINEERING INC
3875 Hopyard Rd Ste 130, Pleasanton (94588-8505)
PHONE..............................925 416-9707
Mike Williams, *Branch Mgr*
EMP: 70
SALES (corp-wide): 49.5MM **Privately Held**
SIC: 7361 Employment agencies
PA: West Valley Engineering, Inc.
 390 Potrero Ave
 Sunnyvale CA 94085
 408 735-1420

(P-14799)
WMBE PAYROLLING INC
Also Called: TARGET CW
9475 Chesapeake Dr Ste A, San Diego (92123-1337)
PHONE..............................858 810-3000
Samer Khouli, *CEO*
Mitch Cook, *Officer*
Brian Smith, *Senior VP*
Stephanie Norling, *Associate Dir*
Courtney Hyma, *Executive Asst*
EMP: 75
SALES: 250.2MM **Privately Held**
SIC: 7361 Placement agencies

(P-14800)
XL STAFFING INC
Also Called: Excell Staffing & SEC Svcs
450 Fletcher Pkwy Ste 204, El Cajon (92020-2520)
PHONE..............................619 579-0442
William Mackey, *President*
EMP: 200
SQ FT: 1,100
SALES (est): 10.6MM **Privately Held**
SIC: 7361 7381 Placement agencies; security guard service

(P-14801)
YANG C PARK
Also Called: Cal Facilities Management Co
3703 Payne Ave, San Jose (95117-3413)
P.O. Box 9306 (95157-0306)
PHONE..............................408 260-8066
Toll Free:..............................888 -
Yang C Park, *Owner*
EMP: 100
SALES (est): 4.4MM **Privately Held**
SIC: 7361 7349 Labor contractors (employment agency); building maintenance services

(P-14802)
YOUR EXECUTIVE SOLUTIONS
9054 Slauson Ave, Pico Rivera (90660-4521)
PHONE..............................562 388-4150
Gani Gjonbalaj, *CEO*
EMP: 650
SQ FT: 2,000
SALES (est): 8.6MM **Privately Held**
SIC: 7361 Employment agencies

(P-14803)
ZENITH TALENT CORPORATION
3315 San Felipe Rd Ste 37, San Jose (95135-2000)
PHONE..............................844 467-2300
Sunil Bagai, *CEO*
Naina Bagai, *Vice Pres*
Sasi Kumar, *Technology*
EMP: 240
SALES: 9MM **Privately Held**
SIC: 7361 Executive placement

(P-14804)
ZOEL HOLDING COMPANY INC
2143 Hurley Way, Sacramento (95825-3253)
PHONE..............................916 646-3100
Ryan Johnson, *Branch Mgr*
Adam Reed, *Recruiter*
EMP: 131

SALES (corp-wide): 60.6MM **Privately Held**
SIC: 7361 Employment agencies
PA: Zoe Holding Company, Inc.
 3131 E Camelback Rd # 200
 Phoenix AZ 85016
 602 508-1883

7363 Help Supply Svcs

(P-14805)
24-HOUR MED STAFFING SVCS LLC
21700 Copley Dr Ste 270, Diamond Bar (91765-5489)
PHONE..............................909 895-8960
Erlinda R Stone,
Carlo Tan, *Accountant*
EMP: 110
SALES (est): 4MM **Privately Held**
SIC: 7363 Temporary help service

(P-14806)
A P R INC
Also Called: Alpha Professional Resources
100 E Thsnd Oaks Blvd, Thousand Oaks (91360)
PHONE..............................805 379-3400
Salvador Ramirez, *President*
Cliff Goodwin, *CFO*
Rick Ramirez, *Vice Pres*
Leslie Major, *Technology*
EMP: 125
SQ FT: 1,100
SALES: 6.3MM **Privately Held**
WEB: www.alphaprofessionals.com
SIC: 7363 7361 Temporary help service; employment agencies

(P-14807)
AARDVARK STAFFING INC
3017 Douglas Blvd Fl 3, Roseville (95661-3848)
PHONE..............................916 774-7115
Laura O'Boyle, *Principal*
EMP: 50
SALES: 2.5MM **Privately Held**
SIC: 7363 Temporary help service

(P-14808)
ADVANCE STAFFING INC
2060 Walsh Ave Ste 101, Santa Clara (95050-2568)
P.O. Box 391447, Mountain View (94039-1447)
PHONE..............................408 205-6154
Jose Badillo, *President*
EMP: 300
SQ FT: 1,043
SALES: 9MM **Privately Held**
SIC: 7363 Temporary help service

(P-14809)
ADVANCED MEDICAL REVIEWS INC
600 Crprate Pinte Ste 300, Culver City (90230)
PHONE..............................310 575-0900
Barak Mevorak, *CEO*
EMP: 61
SQ FT: 10,000
SALES (est): 4.5MM **Privately Held**
WEB: www.advancedmedicalreviews.com
SIC: 7363 Medical help service
PA: Examworks Group, Inc.
 3280 Peachtree Rd Ne
 Atlanta GA 30305

(P-14810)
AFFILIATED TEMPORARY HELP
4359 Florence Ave, Bell (90201-3525)
P.O. Box 124 (90201-0124)
PHONE..............................323 771-1383
John G Carbett, *President*
Ron Thomas, *Vice Pres*
EMP: 400
SQ FT: 1,100
SALES (est): 9.9MM **Privately Held**
SIC: 7363 8322 Temporary help service; individual & family services

(P-14811)
AGOSTINI AND ASSOCIATES INC
Also Called: Agostini Health Care Staffing
1470 Civic Ct Ste 1760, Concord (94520-7949)
P.O. Box 6337, Moraga (94570-6337)
PHONE..............................925 691-7300
Linda Hughes Agostini, *President*
Bobbie Duran, *COO*
Jules Agostini, *Corp Secy*
EMP: 50
SQ FT: 1,300
SALES (est): 2.1MM **Privately Held**
SIC: 7363 Medical help service

(P-14812)
ALLEGIS GROUP INC
1 Waters Park Dr, San Mateo (94403-1157)
PHONE..............................650 425-6950
EMP: 158
SALES (corp-wide): 12.3B **Privately Held**
SIC: 7363 Temporary help service
PA: Allegis Group, Inc.
 7301 Parkway Dr
 Hanover MD 21076
 410 579-3000

(P-14813)
ALTECH SERVICES INC
400 Continental Blvd Fl 6, El Segundo (90245-5074)
PHONE..............................888 725-8324
EMP: 320 **Privately Held**
SIC: 7363 7361 Help supply services; labor contractors (employment agency)
PA: Altech Services, Inc.
 695 Rte 46 W Ste 301b
 Fairfield NJ 07004

(P-14814)
AMERICAN EAGLE SERVICES INC
1320 Arrow Hwy, La Verne (91750-5218)
PHONE..............................574 859-2055
Jeni Bartolotti, *President*
John Bartolotti, *Vice Pres*
EMP: 70
SQ FT: 1,100
SALES: 3.7MM **Privately Held**
SIC: 7363 7513 Temporary help service; truck rental & leasing, no drivers

(P-14815)
AMN HEALTHCARE SERVICES INC (PA)
12400 High Bluff Dr, San Diego (92130-3077)
PHONE..............................866 871-8519
Douglas D Wheat, *Ch of Bd*
Diana Bowden, *President*
Jeff Decker, *President*
Ralph Henderson, *President*
Kelly Rakowski, *President*
EMP: 148
SQ FT: 199,418
SALES: 1.9B **Publicly Held**
WEB: www.amnhealthcare.com
SIC: 7363 Medical help service

(P-14816)
ANDERSON ASSOCIATES STAFFING (PA)
8200 Wilshire Blvd # 200, Beverly Hills (90211-2328)
PHONE..............................323 930-3170
Tom Anderson, *President*
EMP: 200 EST: 1997
SALES (est): 5.6MM **Privately Held**
WEB: www.andersonstaff.com
SIC: 7363 Temporary help service

(P-14817)
APEX STAFFING SERVICE
10134 6th St Ste A, Rancho Cucamonga (91730-5856)
PHONE..............................909 941-0267
Cynthia l Pacheco, *Partner*
Nick Saucedo, *Partner*
EMP: 50
SALES (est): 2.6MM **Privately Held**
SIC: 7363 Temporary help service

(P-14818)
ARCADIA SERVICES INC
4340 Redwood Hwy Ste 123, San Rafael (94903-2104)
PHONE..............................248 352-7530
John E Elliott II, *Branch Mgr*
EMP: 51
SALES (corp-wide): 147.7MM **Privately Held**
SIC: 7363 8082 Medical help service; home health care services
PA: Arcadia Services, Inc.
 20750 Civic Center Dr # 100
 Southfield MI 48076
 248 352-7530

(P-14819)
ASCENT SERVICES GROUP INC
1001 Galaxy Way Ste 408, Concord (94520-5758)
PHONE..............................925 627-4900
Joseph Nordlinger, *President*
Richard Lawrence, *CFO*
W Todd Peterson, *CFO*
Sudhir Sahu, *Chairman*
Max Levine, *Exec VP*
EMP: 450
SQ FT: 7,000
SALES (est): 48.1MM **Privately Held**
WEB: www.itascent.com
SIC: 7363 7379 Help supply services; computer related consulting services

(P-14820)
ASRC INDUSTRIAL SERVICES LLC (HQ)
2300 Clayton Rd Ste 1050, Concord (94520-2100)
PHONE..............................707 644-7455
Greg Johnson, *CEO*
Claudia Blaine, *Human Res Dir*
EMP: 143
SALES (est): 397.6MM
SALES (corp-wide): 2.8B **Privately Held**
SIC: 7363 Industrial help service
PA: Arctic Slope Regional Corporation
 3900 C St Ste 801
 Anchorage AK 99503
 907 339-6000

(P-14821)
AYA HEALTHCARE INC (PA)
5930 Cornerstone Ct W # 300, San Diego (92121-3741)
PHONE..............................858 458-4410
Alan Braynin, *President*
Crystal Erlendson, *Vice Pres*
Dan Walter, *Vice Pres*
Shelley Donovan, *VP Bus Dvlpt*
Kelly Correy, *General Mgr*
EMP: 74
SQ FT: 20,000
SALES (est): 77.2MM **Privately Held**
SIC: 7363 8049 Temporary help service; nurses, registered & practical

(P-14822)
B2B STAFFING SERVICES INC
Also Called: B2b Payroll Services
4501 Cerritos Ave Ste 201, Cypress (90630)
PHONE..............................714 243-4104
Brian Wigdor, *President*
Bruce Underwood, *CFO*
EMP: 300
SALES (est): 11.4MM **Privately Held**
SIC: 7363 Temporary help service

(P-14823)
BANYAN SOLUTIONS INC
Also Called: Banyon Transcription
2809 Blue Oak Ct, Brentwood (94513-4617)
PHONE..............................650 766-9338
Jyoti Challi, *President*
EMP: 63
SALES (est): 1.7MM **Privately Held**
SIC: 7363 7389 Medical help service;

(P-14824)
BEHAVIORAL INTERVENTION ASSN
Also Called: B I A
2354 Powell St A, Emeryville (94608-1738)
PHONE..............................510 652-7445

Hilary Stubblefield, *Exec Dir*
Fred Baldi, *COO*
Deanne Detmers, *Program Dir*
Hilary S Baldi, *Director*
EMP: 50
SALES: 4.3MM **Privately Held**
WEB: www.bia4autism.org
SIC: 7363 Domestic help service

(P-14825)
BUTLER INTERNATIONAL INC (PA)
3820 State St Ste A, Santa Barbara
(93105-3182)
PHONE.............................805 882-2200
Edward M Kopko, *Ch of Bd*
Mark Koscinski, *CFO*
James J Beckley, *Senior VP*
Ren E Ward, *Marketing Mgr*
EMP: 200
SALES (est): 97.2MM **Privately Held**
WEB: www.butler.com
SIC: 7363 8742 Help supply services; management consulting services

(P-14826)
BUTLER SERVICE GROUP INC (HQ)
3820 State St Ste A, Santa Barbara
(93105-3182)
PHONE.............................201 891-5312
Edward M Kopko, *President*
Michael C Hellriegel, *CFO*
R Scott Silver Hill, *Senior VP*
EMP: 100
SQ FT: 82,000
SALES (est): 32MM
SALES (corp-wide): 97.2MM **Privately Held**
SIC: 7363 8711 8748 3661 Engineering help service; engineering services; communications consulting; telephone & telegraph apparatus; general automotive repair shops
PA: Butler International, Inc.
3820 State St Ste A
Santa Barbara CA 93105
805 882-2200

(P-14827)
CALIFORNIA SCHL EMPLOYEES ASSN
4600 Santa Anita Ave, El Monte
(91731-1320)
PHONE.............................626 258-3300
Michael Leon, *Branch Mgr*
EMP: 295
SQ FT: 8,286
SALES (corp-wide): 65.6MM **Privately Held**
SIC: 7363 Help supply services
PA: California School Employees' Association
2045 Lundy Ave
San Jose CA 95131
408 473-1000

(P-14828)
CANON RECRUITING GROUP LLC
26531 Summit Cir, Santa Clarita
(91350-3049)
PHONE.............................661 252-7400
Laurie Grayem, *CEO*
Tim Grayem, *President*
EMP: 400
SQ FT: 7,500
SALES (est): 22MM **Privately Held**
SIC: 7363 7361 Office help supply service; executive placement

(P-14829)
CARDINAL POINT CAPTAINS INC
5005 Texas St Ste 104, San Diego
(92108-3722)
PHONE.............................760 438-7361
Jordan E Cousino, *CEO*
Heather Jenkins, *Accountant*
Pasquale Derosa, *Manager*
EMP: 56
SQ FT: 2,633
SALES (est): 1.1MM **Privately Held**
SIC: 7363 3812 Boat crew service; search & navigation equipment

(P-14830)
CARE MEDICAL TRNSP INC
Also Called: Care Ambulance
9770 Candida St, San Diego (92126-4536)
PHONE.............................858 653-4520
Kelvin Carlisle, *President*
EMP: 190
SQ FT: 14,000
SALES (est): 10.6MM **Privately Held**
SIC: 7363 Medical help service

(P-14831)
CHILDCARE CAREERS LLC
2000 Sierra Point Pkwy # 702, Brisbane
(94005-1874)
PHONE.............................650 372-0211
Jason Jones,
Sabah Raza, *Opers Staff*
Candice Wheeler, *Mktg Dir*
Cecilia De Ment, *Director*
Cecilia Dement, *Director*
EMP: 1000 **EST:** 2010
SQ FT: 6,300
SALES (est): 8.3MM **Privately Held**
SIC: 7363 7361 Temporary help service; teachers' agency

(P-14832)
CLEARPATH MANAGEMENT GROUP INC (PA)
1215 W Center St Ste 102, Manteca
(95337-4280)
PHONE.............................209 239-8700
Renee Fink, *CEO*
Judy Gnade, *CFO*
Jason Posel, *Senior VP*
David West, *Analyst*
EMP: 286
SQ FT: 3,171
SALES (est): 16.2MM **Privately Held**
SIC: 7363 Temporary help service

(P-14833)
CLEARPATH WORKFORCE MGT INC
1215 W Center St Ste 102, Manteca
(95337-4280)
PHONE.............................209 239-8700
Renee Fink, *CEO*
Judy Gnade, *CFO*
Jason Posel, *Senior VP*
Sue Ortiz, *Vice Pres*
EMP: 275
SQ FT: 3,171
SALES: 28.8MM
SALES (corp-wide): 16.2MM **Privately Held**
SIC: 7363 Temporary help service
PA: Clearpath Management Group, Inc.
1215 W Center St Ste 102
Manteca CA 95337
209 239-8700

(P-14834)
CLP RESOURCES INC
1485 Bay Shore Blvd # 138, San Francisco
(94124-3002)
PHONE.............................415 508-0910
Richard Webb, *Branch Mgr*
Toby Karlitz, *Executive*
EMP: 50
SALES (corp-wide): 2.5B **Publicly Held**
SIC: 7363 Temporary help service
HQ: Clp Resources, Inc.
1015 A St
Tacoma WA 98402
775 321-8000

(P-14835)
CLP RESOURCES INC
1260 N Dutton Ave, Santa Rosa
(95401-4659)
PHONE.............................707 569-0200
Dan Rosiak, *Branch Mgr*
EMP: 50
SALES (corp-wide): 2.5B **Publicly Held**
SIC: 7363 Temporary help service
HQ: Clp Resources, Inc.
1015 A St
Tacoma WA 98402
775 321-8000

(P-14836)
CLP RESOURCES INC
1000 Sunrise Ave Ste 8a, Roseville
(95661-5471)
PHONE.............................916 788-0300
EMP: 60
SALES (corp-wide): 2.1B **Publicly Held**
SIC: 7363
HQ: Clp Resources, Inc.
1015 A St
Tacoma WA 98402
775 321-8000

(P-14837)
CLP RESOURCES INC
570 El Cmino Real Ste 170, Redwood City
(94063)
PHONE.............................650 261-2100
Vince Vargas, *Director*
EMP: 200
SALES (corp-wide): 2.5B **Publicly Held**
SIC: 7363 Temporary help service
HQ: Clp Resources, Inc.
1015 A St
Tacoma WA 98402
775 321-8000

(P-14838)
CLP RESOURCES INC
4460 Redwood Hwy Ste 14, San Rafael
(94903-1953)
PHONE.............................415 446-7000
EMP: 50
SALES (corp-wide): 2.1B **Publicly Held**
SIC: 7363
HQ: Clp Resources, Inc.
1015 A St
Tacoma WA 98402
775 321-8000

(P-14839)
CLP RESOURCES INC
741 E Ball Rd Ste 100, Anaheim
(92805-5952)
PHONE.............................714 300-0510
Brian Rogers, *Manager*
EMP: 100
SALES (corp-wide): 2.5B **Publicly Held**
SIC: 7363 Temporary help service
HQ: Clp Resources, Inc.
1015 A St
Tacoma WA 98402
775 321-8000

(P-14840)
CLP RESOURCES INC
Also Called: Contractors Labor Pool of La
111 N First St Ste 100, Burbank
(91502-1851)
PHONE.............................818 260-9190
Guan Santos, *Manager*
EMP: 85
SALES (corp-wide): 2.5B **Publicly Held**
SIC: 7363 7361 Temporary help service; employment agencies
HQ: Clp Resources, Inc.
1015 A St
Tacoma WA 98402
775 321-8000

(P-14841)
CO TEAM STAFFING
1608 Sunrise Ave Ste D, Modesto
(95350-4678)
P.O. Box 2531, Ceres (95307-7931)
PHONE.............................209 578-4286
Hilario Vieyra, *Principal*
EMP: 90
SALES (est): 2MM **Privately Held**
SIC: 7363 Temporary help service

(P-14842)
COMPUTERIZED MANAGEMENT
40 W Cochran St, Simi Valley
(93065-6251)
P.O. Box 190 (93062-0190)
PHONE.............................805 522-5999
Daryl Favale, *Owner*
Dale Fazvale, *President*
Thomas Brajkovich, *Info Tech Mgr*
EMP: 60
SALES (est): 1.2MM **Privately Held**
WEB: www.cmsmanagement.net
SIC: 7363 8721 Medical help service; billing & bookkeeping service

(P-14843)
CPE PEO INC
9200 W Sunset Blvd, West Hollywood
(90069-3502)
PHONE.............................310 385-1000
Lee C Samson, *CEO*
Jay Cober, *President*
Grace Drulius, *CFO*
Harold Walt, *CFO*
Larry Feigen, *Vice Ch Bd*
EMP: 90
SQ FT: 11,000
SALES (est): 2.8MM **Privately Held**
SIC: 7363 Employee leasing service

(P-14844)
CPM LTD INC (PA)
Also Called: Manpower
1855 1st Ave Ste 300, San Diego
(92101-2668)
PHONE.............................619 237-9900
Philip Blair, *President*
Tony Evenson, *CFO*
Catherine Blair, *Treasurer*
Linda Katz, *Vice Pres*
Mel Katz, *Vice Pres*
EMP: 1400 **EST:** 1977
SALES (est): 73.7MM **Privately Held**
WEB: www.manpower-sd.com
SIC: 7363 Manpower pools

(P-14845)
CRAFT RESOURCES INC
220 S Pcifc Cst Hwy 112, Redondo Beach
(90277)
P.O. Box 7000 (90277-8710)
PHONE.............................310 937-3744
Stephen A Lawrence, *President*
EMP: 150
SQ FT: 2,000
SALES (est): 5.1MM **Privately Held**
WEB: www.craft-resources.com
SIC: 7363 7361 Industrial help service; employment agencies

(P-14846)
CULINARY SERVICES AMERICA INC
Also Called: Culinary Staffing Service
6363 Wilshire Blvd # 305, Los Angeles
(90048-5726)
PHONE.............................323 965-7582
Randy Hopp, *President*
Jessica Seastead, *Human Res Dir*
David Crego, *Recruiter*
EMP: 50
SQ FT: 1,200
SALES (est): 2.1MM **Privately Held**
SIC: 7363 7361 Temporary help service; employment agencies

(P-14847)
CW HEALTHCARE INC
2884 Wakefield Dr, Belmont (94002-2935)
PHONE.............................510 636-9000
Russell Jones, *President*
EMP: 50
SQ FT: 900
SALES (est): 1.3MM **Privately Held**
WEB: www.cwhealthcare.com
SIC: 7363 Medical help service

(P-14848)
DISCHARGE RESOURCE GROUP
Also Called: DRG Health Care Staffing
400 Oyster Point Blvd # 440, South San Francisco (94080-1979)
PHONE.............................650 877-8111
Lawrence Hix, *CEO*
Marsha Hix, *Treasurer*
Lucinda Ip, *Info Tech Mgr*
Georgia Abelardo, *Accounting Mgr*
Georgia Ip, *Accounting Mgr*
EMP: 250
SQ FT: 2,000
SALES (est): 12.3MM **Privately Held**
WEB: www.drgstaffing.com
SIC: 7363 7361 Temporary help service; medical help service; employment agencies

PRODUCTS & SVCS

(P-14849)
EMPLOYBRIDGE LLC (HQ)
Also Called: Select Staffing
301 Mentor Dr 210, Santa Barbara
(93111-3339)
PHONE..................805 882-2200
Thomas A Bickes, *President*
Fred R Herbert, *President*
Julie Mellin, *President*
Steve Mills, *President*
Paul J Sorensen, *President*
EMP: 148
SALES (est): 431.8MM
SALES (corp-wide): 584.5MM **Privately
Held**
WEB: www.selectpersonnel.com
SIC: 7363 Temporary help service
PA: Employbridge Holding Company
1040 Crown Pointe Pkwy # 1040
Atlanta GA 30338
770 671-1900

(P-14850)
EPLICA INC (PA)
Also Called: Eastridge ADM Staffing
2355 Northside Dr Ste 120, San Diego
(92108-2714)
PHONE..................619 260-2000
Robert Svet, *President*
Seth Stein, *Exec VP*
EMP: 175 EST: 1971
SQ FT: 15,000
SALES (est): 179.1MM **Privately Held**
WEB: www.hr-solutions.com
SIC: 7363 7361 Temporary help service;
employment agencies

(P-14851)
**ESPARZA ENTERPRISES INC
(PA)**
3851 Fruitvale Ave, Bakersfield
(93308-5111)
PHONE..................661 831-0002
Luis Esparza Jr, *President*
Maria Esparza, *Corp Secy*
Ruth Celedon, *Vice Pres*
EMP: 3500
SQ FT: 5,800
SALES (est): 98.4MM **Privately Held**
WEB: www.esparzaenterprises.com
SIC: 7363 7361 Help supply services;
labor contractors (employment agency)

(P-14852)
**FAMILY SVC AGCY SAN
FRANCISCO (PA)**
Also Called: Felton Institute
1500 Franklin St, San Francisco
(94109-4523)
PHONE..................415 474-7310
Albert Gilbert, *President*
Marvin L Davis, *CFO*
Derek Toliver, *Program Mgr*
Thom Brittany, *Admin Asst*
Zachary Cecil, *Admin Asst*
EMP: 70
SQ FT: 14,000
SALES: 19MM **Privately Held**
SIC: 7363 Help supply services

(P-14853)
**FERNANDES & SONS GEN
CONTRS**
2110 S Bascom Ave Ste 201, Campbell
(95008-3288)
PHONE..................408 626-9090
Larry Fernandes, *President*
EMP: 55
SALES (est): 4.8MM **Privately Held**
SIC: 7363 8299 Medical help service; edu-
cational services

(P-14854)
FLEXCARE LLC
Also Called: Flexcare Medical Staffing
990 Reserve Dr Ste 200, Roseville
(95678-1391)
PHONE..................866 564-3589
Nate Porter, *Mng Member*
EMP: 1000
SALES (est): 410.8K **Privately Held**
SIC: 7363 Temporary help service

(P-14855)
FREEDOM STAFF LEASING INC
3142 Pacific Coast Hwy, Torrance
(90505-6746)
P.O. Box 1689, Wilmington (90748-1689)
PHONE..................310 834-6621
Lofton Ryan Burris, *President*
EMP: 300
SQ FT: 1,000
SALES (est): 6.3MM **Privately Held**
WEB: www.freedompeo.com
SIC: 7363 Employee leasing service

(P-14856)
G R HELM INC
Also Called: Helm Technical Services
5050 Rbert J Mathews Pkwy, El Dorado
Hills (95762-5761)
PHONE..................916 933-9697
Gordon Helm, *President*
EMP: 85
SQ FT: 1,050
SALES (est): 3.3MM **Privately Held**
WEB: www.helmtech.com
SIC: 7363 7371 Labor resource services;
computer software development

(P-14857)
GENESIS HOME HEALTH INC
1687 Erringer Rd Ste 202, Simi Valley
(93065-6509)
PHONE..................805 520-7100
EMP: 50
SALES (est): 2.9MM **Privately Held**
SIC: 7363 7361

(P-14858)
GET HEAL INC
528 Palisades Dr Ste 176, Pacific Palisades
(90272-2844)
PHONE..................310 528-4957
EMP: 90
SALES (corp-wide): 10MM **Privately
Held**
SIC: 7363 Medical help service
PA: Get Heal, Inc.
1880 Century Park E # 711
Los Angeles CA 90067
310 528-4957

(P-14859)
**GOODWILL OF SILICON VALLEY
(PA)**
Also Called: INSTITUTE FOR CAREER DE-
VELOPME
1080 N 7th St, San Jose (95112-4425)
PHONE..................408 998-5774
Michael E Fox, *CEO*
Frank Kent, *CEO*
Christopher King, *COO*
Christopher Baker, *CFO*
Dale Achabal, *Treasurer*
EMP: 100
SQ FT: 180,000
SALES: 46.5MM **Privately Held**
SIC: 7363 5932 Help supply services;
used merchandise stores

(P-14860)
I N C BUILDERS INC
Also Called: Acme Staffing
1560 Ocotillo Dr Ste L, El Centro
(92243-4237)
PHONE..................760 352-4200
Rebecca Deal, *Manager*
EMP: 350
SALES (corp-wide): 8.3MM **Privately
Held**
SIC: 7363 Help supply services
PA: I N C Builders, Inc.
550 E 32nd St Ste 5a
Yuma AZ 85365
928 344-8367

(P-14861)
IASCO (PA)
1833 Castenada Dr, Burlingame
(94010-5716)
PHONE..................707 252-3522
Robert J Walters, *President*
K T Jack, *Ch of Bd*
Camille King, *Treasurer*
John R Lee, *Exec VP*
Richard Darrimon, *Manager*
EMP: 275 EST: 1959

SALES (est): 7.7MM **Privately Held**
WEB: www.iasco.com
SIC: 7363 Pilot service, aviation

(P-14862)
INFINITY NURSES CARE INC
39159 Paseo Padre Pkwy # 111, Fremont
(94538-1608)
PHONE..................510 713-8892
Angeles Santos, *President*
Richard Santos, *Vice Pres*
EMP: 100
SQ FT: 1,500
SALES: 15K **Privately Held**
SIC: 7363 8082 Medical help service;
home health care services

(P-14863)
INFINITY STAFFING SERVICE
710 Kirkpatric Ct, Hollister (95023-2817)
PHONE..................831 638-0360
Ramiro Rodriguez, *President*
John Blackmouth, *Manager*
EMP: 260
SALES (est): 1.1MM **Privately Held**
SIC: 7363 Temporary help service

(P-14864)
**INTERACTIVE MED
SPECIALISTS**
252 Waterside Cir, San Rafael
(94903-2795)
P.O. Box 287 (94903)
PHONE..................415 472-4204
Jaleh Ebrahimi, *President*
Oranous Ebrahimi, *Treasurer*
Ghazaleh Ebrahimi, *Vice Pres*
Oranus Ebrahimi, *Vice Pres*
EMP: 70
SALES (est): 2.8MM **Privately Held**
WEB: www.imsspecialists.com
SIC: 7363 Medical help service

(P-14865)
IQ PIPELINE LLC
1550 Hotel Cir N Ste 270, San Diego
(92108-2908)
PHONE..................858 483-7400
Chris Oberle, *EMP*
EMP: 100
SALES (est): 6.2MM **Privately Held**
SIC: 7363 Temporary help service

(P-14866)
JOHN PAUL USA (PA)
49 Stevenson St Ste 575, San Francisco
(94105-2943)
PHONE..................415 905-6088
David Amsellem, *CEO*
Amber Treshnell, *CEO*
Kim Augustine, *Vice Pres*
Paul McKnight, *Admin Sec*
Nora Healy, *Manager*
EMP: 94
SQ FT: 5,000
SALES (est): 31.6MM **Privately Held**
WEB: www.lesconcierges.com
SIC: 7363 Help supply services

(P-14867)
JUNE GROUP LLC
Also Called: Qualstaff Resources
9444 Waples St Ste 100, San Diego
(92121-2940)
PHONE..................858 450-4290
R Scott Silver-Hill, *Mng Member*
Charles Davis IV, *Recruiter*
Heather Gomez, *Recruiter*
Kristy Hernandez, *Recruiter*
Jesse Lafferty, *Recruiter*
EMP: 100
SQ FT: 4,200
SALES (est): 4.1MM **Privately Held**
SIC: 7363 Temporary help service

(P-14868)
KAMPS COMPANY
1262 Dupont Ct, Manteca (95336-6003)
PHONE..................209 823-8924
John Paul, *President*
John Kamps, *Shareholder*
EMP: 160
SQ FT: 3,000
SALES (est): 3MM **Privately Held**
SIC: 7363 Employee leasing service

PA: Kamps Propane, Inc.
1262 Dupont Ct
Manteca CA 95336

(P-14869)
KENSINGTON AGENCY INC
Also Called: Kensington Nursing Agency
8469 La Mesa Blvd, La Mesa
(91942-5335)
PHONE..................619 280-6993
David Keyte, *General Mgr*
Deaydre Pulliam, *COO*
EMP: 50
SQ FT: 1,000
SALES (est): 3.2MM **Privately Held**
SIC: 7363 Temporary help service

(P-14870)
**LABOR FNDERS OF THE PALM
BCHES**
Also Called: Labor Finders Staffing
4325 N Blackstone Ave, Fresno
(93726-1902)
PHONE..................559 221-2023
David Fritz, *Manager*
EMP: 60
SALES (corp-wide): 2.9MM **Privately
Held**
SIC: 7363 Temporary help service
PA: Labor Finders Of The Palm Beaches
Inc
1401 S Military Trl H-1
West Palm Beach FL 33415
561 439-0605

(P-14871)
LABOR READY INC
1405 Carmelo Dr 5112, Oceanside (92054)
PHONE..................760 433-4980
Frank Guttierez, *Manager*
EMP: 50
SALES (corp-wide): 2.5B **Publicly Held**
SIC: 7363 Temporary help service
HQ: Labor Ready Southwest, Inc.
1015 A St Unit A
Tacoma WA 98402
253 680-8487

(P-14872)
LANDMARK EVENT STAFFING
1965 Adams Ave, San Leandro
(94577-1005)
PHONE..................510 632-9000
Peter Kranske, *Branch Mgr*
EMP: 1603 **Privately Held**
SIC: 7363 Help supply services
PA: Landmark Event Staffing Services, Inc.
4131 Harbor Walk Dr
Fort Collins CO 80525

(P-14873)
**LOS ANGLES CNSRVTION
CORPS INC (PA)**
1400 N Spring St, Los Angeles
(90012-1924)
P.O. Box 861658 (90086-1658)
PHONE..................213 362-9000
Mercedes Morton, *President*
Wendy Butts, *CEO*
Albert Chavez, *Treasurer*
Teresa Cisneros Burton, *Admin Sec*
Nora Cabrera, *Admin Asst*
EMP: 92
SQ FT: 6,000
SALES: 19.6MM **Privately Held**
SIC: 7363 Temporary help service

(P-14874)
M K TECHNICAL SERVICES INC
4349 San Felipe Rd, San Jose
(95135-1507)
PHONE..................408 528-0401
Margie Menz King, *President*
Johnie Staggs, *Administration*
EMP: 50
SQ FT: 1,000
SALES: 5MM **Privately Held**
SIC: 7363 Temporary help service

(P-14875)
MAXIM HEALTHCARE SERVICES INC
631 River Oaks Pkwy, San Jose
(95134-1907)
PHONE................................408 914-7478
EMP: 283
SALES (corp-wide): 1.5B Privately Held
SIC: 7363 Medical help service
PA: Maxim Healthcare Services, Inc.
7227 Lee Deforest Dr
Columbia MD 21046
410 910-1500

(P-14876)
MAXIM HEALTHCARE SERVICES INC
500 E Esplanade Dr, Oxnard (93036-2110)
PHONE................................805 278-4593
EMP: 566
SALES (corp-wide): 1.5B Privately Held
SIC: 7363 Medical help service
PA: Maxim Healthcare Services, Inc.
7227 Lee Deforest Dr
Columbia MD 21046
410 910-1500

(P-14877)
MAXIM HEALTHCARE SERVICES INC
Also Called: Riverside Companion Services
1845 Bus Ctr Dr Ste 112, San Bernardino
(92408)
PHONE................................951 684-4148
Elijah Hall, Manager
Kevin Ramirez, Administration
EMP: 304
SALES (corp-wide): 1.5B Privately Held
WEB: www.maximstaffing.com
SIC: 7363 Medical help service
PA: Maxim Healthcare Services, Inc.
7227 Lee Deforest Dr
Columbia MD 21046
410 910-1500

(P-14878)
ME AND ME INC
Also Called: Employee Solutions
14536 Roscoe Blvd Ste 112, Van Nuys
(91402-4103)
P.O. Box 801795, Santa Clarita (91380-1795)
PHONE................................818 891-0197
Michael E Socha, President
EMP: 76
SALES: 2MM Privately Held
SIC: 7363 Medical help service

(P-14879)
MED STAFFING LLC
1860 Mowry Ave Ste 302, Fremont
(94538-1730)
PHONE................................510 795-0114
Ramesh C Karipineni MD,
Karen Parsons, Opers Mgr
EMP: 50
SALES (est): 750K Privately Held
SIC: 7363 Help supply services

(P-14880)
MEDICAL HOME SPECIALISTS INC
Also Called: Medical HM Care Professionals
2115 Churn Creek Rd, Redding
(96002-0732)
PHONE................................530 226-5577
Kathy A McKillop, CEO
Elaine Flores, COO
Kathy McKillop, Administration
EMP: 160
SQ FT: 1,600
SALES (est): 7.9MM Privately Held
WEB: www.medicalhomecarepros.com
SIC: 7363 Medical help service

(P-14881)
MEDICAL MANAGEMENT CONS INC (PA)
Also Called: MMC
8150 Beverly Blvd, Los Angeles
(90048-4513)
PHONE................................310 659-3835
Mashi Rahmani, President
Damian Castrellon, COO

Mark Peralejo, Administration
Nancy Barnes, Controller
Kimberly Andrade, Human Res Mgr
EMP: 50
SQ FT: 21,000
SALES (est): 71.4MM Privately Held
WEB: www.mmchr.com
SIC: 7363 8742 8748 8721 Help supply
services; hospital & health services consultant; employee programs administration; payroll accounting service

(P-14882)
MEDICAL SUPPORT SERVICES
6660 W Sunset Blvd Ste J, Los Angeles
(90028-7161)
PHONE................................323 860-7994
Raynoldo Fernandez, President
EMP: 100
SQ FT: 1,000
SALES (est): 2.5MM Privately Held
WEB: www.mssregistryinc.com
SIC: 7363 7361 Medical help service; employment agencies

(P-14883)
MERRITT HAWKINS & ASSOC LLC (HQ)
12400 High Bluff Dr, San Diego
(92130-3077)
PHONE................................858 792-0711
Susan Salka Fka Nowakowski, CEO
Brian Scott, CFO
John Dillon, Treasurer
Denise Jackson, Vice Pres
Maria Creps, Administration
EMP: 120
SQ FT: 96,000
SALES (est): 13.4MM
SALES (corp-wide): 1.9B Publicly Held
WEB: www.mhagroup.com
SIC: 7363 Medical help service
PA: Amn Healthcare Services, Inc.
12400 High Bluff Dr
San Diego CA 92130
866 871-8519

(P-14884)
MGA HEALTHCARE CALIFORNIA INC
879 W 190th St Ste 700, Gardena
(90248-4227)
PHONE................................310 324-5591
David T Zowine, President
Jimmy Mansoor, Recruiter
EMP: 50
SQ FT: 1,111
SALES (est): 2.5MM Privately Held
SIC: 7363 Temporary help service

(P-14885)
MSS NURSES REGISTRY INC
Also Called: Medical Support Services
6660 W Sunset Blvd Ste J, Los Angeles
(90028-7161)
PHONE................................323 467-5717
Raynoldo Fernandez, President
Teresita Fernandez, Principal
EMP: 99
SALES (est): 1.8MM Privately Held
SIC: 7363 Temporary help service

(P-14886)
NATIONAL BUILDER SERVICES INC
3835 E Thousand Oaks Blvd R, Westlake
Village (91362-3637)
PHONE................................714 634-7800
Joseph M Wiseman, President
EMP: 50
SQ FT: 1,700
SALES (est): 3.2MM Privately Held
WEB: www.tti-nbs.com
SIC: 7363 Employee leasing service

(P-14887)
NEW DAY STAFFING INC
5920 Friars Rd Ste 104, San Diego
(92108-1077)
PHONE................................619 481-5400
Julie Laurice, President
EMP: 150
SALES (est): 3.8MM Privately Held
SIC: 7363 Temporary help service

(P-14888)
NOW MEDICAL SERVICES INC
1641 1/2 Westwood Blvd, Los Angeles
(90024-5603)
PHONE................................310 479-4520
Larry Schapiro, President
EMP: 55
SQ FT: 1,700
SALES (est): 2.9MM Privately Held
SIC: 7363 4212 Help supply services; delivery service, vehicular

(P-14889)
PERSONNEL PREFERENCE INC
150 Boles St Ste A, Weed (96094-2586)
PHONE................................530 938-3909
Jill Tillinghast, President
EMP: 150
SALES (est): 5.7MM Privately Held
SIC: 7363 7361 Temporary help service; employment agencies

(P-14890)
PHARMACY TEMPS INC
Also Called: Nor-Cal Medical Temps
2125 Paradise Dr, Belvedere Tiburon
(94920-1939)
P.O. Box 736 (94920-0736)
PHONE................................415 459-5211
Kristina Glaves, President
EMP: 50
SALES: 700K Privately Held
SIC: 7363 Temporary help service

(P-14891)
PHOENIX ENGINEERING CO INC
Also Called: Phoenix Personnel
550 E Carson Plaza Dr # 112, Carson
(90746-7353)
P.O. Box 66395, Los Angeles (90066-0395)
PHONE................................310 532-1134
Silvia Lugo, President
EMP: 100
SQ FT: 1,700
SALES: 5.5MM Privately Held
WEB: www.phoenix-engineering.com
SIC: 7363 7361 Office help supply service; employment agencies

(P-14892)
PLANT MAINTENANCE INC
Also Called: Temporary Plant Cleaners
1330 Arnold Dr Ste 147, Martinez
(94553-6538)
P.O. Box 48 (94553-0115)
PHONE................................925 228-3285
Tim Hollz, President
Kenneth B Johnson, Vice Pres
EMP: 150 EST: 1996
SQ FT: 2,800
SALES: 2.3MM
SALES (corp-wide): 73.4MM Privately Held
WEB: www.montmech.com
SIC: 7363 Industrial help service
PA: Monterey Mechanical Co.
8275 San Leandro St
Oakland CA 94621
510 632-3173

(P-14893)
PLATINUM EMPIRE GROUP INC
Also Called: Platinum Healthcare Staffing
3521 Lomita Blvd Ste 202b, Torrance
(90505-5039)
PHONE................................310 821-5888
Arun Mahtani, President
Naveen Yadav, Technical Staff
Aaron Quiboloy, Human Res Mgr
Maluh Silvano, Manager
EMP: 120
SQ FT: 400
SALES (est): 1.3MM Privately Held
WEB: www.platinumhealthcarestaffing.com
SIC: 7363 Temporary help service

(P-14894)
PROCEL TEMPORARY SERVICES INC
222 W 6th St Ste 370, San Pedro
(90731-3348)
PHONE................................310 372-0560
Marilyn Stephens, President
EMP: 500
SQ FT: 4,600

SALES (est): 22.8MM Privately Held
SIC: 7363 Medical help service

(P-14895)
R L KLEIN & ASSOCIATES
3553 Atlantic Ave Ste A, Long Beach
(90807-5605)
PHONE................................562 427-5577
Bob Klein, Owner
EMP: 60
SQ FT: 2,100
SALES: 1,000K Privately Held
SIC: 7363 Temporary help service

(P-14896)
RANDSTAD NORTH AMERICA INC
7014 N Cedar Ave, Fresno (93720-3300)
PHONE................................559 297-0054
Tammy Wallace, Branch Mgr
EMP: 200
SALES (corp-wide): 27.4B Privately Held
SIC: 7363 Temporary help service
HQ: Randstad North America, Inc.
3625 Cumberland Blvd Se
Atlanta GA 30339
770 937-7000

(P-14897)
RANDSTAD NORTH AMERICA INC
106 E 7th St, Hanford (93230-4642)
PHONE................................559 582-2700
Fawn Perryman, Branch Mgr
EMP: 104
SALES (corp-wide): 27.4B Privately Held
WEB: www.placementpros.com
SIC: 7363 Temporary help service
HQ: Randstad North America, Inc.
3625 Cumberland Blvd Se
Atlanta GA 30339
770 937-7000

(P-14898)
RANDSTAD NORTH AMERICA INC
1110 W Visalia Rd Ste 116, Exeter
(93221-1481)
PHONE................................559 592-6700
Wendy Attaway, Manager
EMP: 254
SALES (corp-wide): 27.4B Privately Held
WEB: www.placementpros.com
SIC: 7363 Temporary help service
HQ: Randstad North America, Inc.
3625 Cumberland Blvd Se
Atlanta GA 30339
770 937-7000

(P-14899)
RANDSTAD NORTH AMERICA INC
27 Maiden Ln Ste 202, San Francisco
(94108-5440)
PHONE................................415 397-3384
Mark Rivard, Branch Mgr
Jessica Zucker, President
Dave Lindberg, Info Tech Mgr
EMP: 177
SALES (corp-wide): 27.4B Privately Held
WEB: www.placementpros.com
SIC: 7363 Temporary help service
HQ: Randstad North America, Inc.
3625 Cumberland Blvd Se
Atlanta GA 30339
770 937-7000

(P-14900)
REAL TIME INFORMATION SVCS INC
Also Called: Real-Time Staffing Services
191 W Shaw Ave Ste 106, Fresno
(93704-2826)
PHONE................................559 222-9400
EMP: 50
SALES (est): 2.3MM Privately Held
WEB: www.realtimeca.com
SIC: 7363

PRODUCTS & SVCS

(P-14901)
REDWOOD HEALTHCARE STAFFING
600 B St Ste 1570, San Diego
(92101-4560)
PHONE.....................619 238-4180
Genevieve Lavin, *President*
EMP: 60 **Privately Held**
SIC: 7363 Temporary help service
PA: Redwood Healthcare Staffing
1015 Gayley Ave
Los Angeles CA 90024
-

(P-14902)
REGISTRY NETWORK INC (PA)
1207 Carlsbad Village Dr X, Carlsbad
(92008-1958)
PHONE.....................760 966-3700
John Fusco, *President*
Eric Frehe, *COO*
Laura Moeller, *Vice Pres*
EMP: 190
SQ FT: 500
SALES (est): 5MM **Privately Held**
WEB: www.registrynetwork.net
SIC: 7363 7361 Medical help service;
nurses' registry

(P-14903)
RELIABLE HEALTH CARE SVCS INC
5705 Sepulveda Blvd, Culver City
(90230-6406)
PHONE.....................310 397-2229
William A Benbassat, *President*
EMP: 50
SALES (est): 2.7MM **Privately Held**
WEB: www.reliablehealthcare.com
SIC: 7363 Temporary help service

(P-14904)
REMEDYTEMP INC (DH)
Also Called: Remedy Intelligent Staffing
101 Enterprise Ste 100, Aliso Viejo
(92656-2604)
PHONE.....................949 425-7600
David Stephen Sorensen, *CEO*
Jeff R Mitchell, *CFO*
Richard Hulme, *Exec VP*
Lee Woods, *General Mgr*
John Neff, *Controller*
EMP: 143
SQ FT: 51,000
SALES (est): 56.4MM
SALES (corp-wide): 584.5MM **Privately Held**
WEB: www.remedystaff.com
SIC: 7363 7361 Temporary help service;
employment agencies

(P-14905)
RNCMBA INC
Also Called: Interim Services
4801 Truxtun Ave, Bakersfield
(93309-0605)
PHONE.....................661 395-1700
Darlyn Baker, *President*
Chuck Baker, *Vice Pres*
EMP: 125
SQ FT: 5,000
SALES (est): 5.4MM **Privately Held**
SIC: 7363 Temporary help service

(P-14906)
ROBERT A HALL
Also Called: Straight Edge
9769 Dawn Way, Windsor (95492-8879)
PHONE.....................707 837-8564
Robert Hall, *President*
Leslie Hall, *CFO*
Leslie A Hall, *Manager*
EMP: 60
SALES: 442.1K **Privately Held**
SIC: 7363 Manpower pools

(P-14907)
ROBERT HALF INTERNATIONAL INC (PA)
2884 Sand Hill Rd Ste 200, Menlo Park
(94025-7059)
PHONE.....................650 234-6000
Harold M Messmer Jr, *Ch of Bd*
Paul F Gentzkow, *President*
Ben Hirsh, *President*

Joshua Howarth, *President*
Pablo Markelis, *President*
▲ EMP: 100
SALES: 5.2B **Publicly Held**
WEB: www.rhii.com
SIC: 7363 7361 8748 8721 Temporary
help service; placement agencies; busi-
ness consulting; auditing services

(P-14908)
ROTH STAFFING COMPANIES LP (PA)
Also Called: Ultimate Staffing Services
450 N State College Blvd, Orange
(92868-1708)
PHONE.....................714 939-8600
Adam Roth, *Officer*
Ben Roth, *Ch of Bd*
Pam Sexauer, *Exec VP*
Staci Johnson, *Vice Pres*
Theresa Del Vecchio, *Executive*
◆ EMP: 80
SALES: 344.4MM **Privately Held**
WEB: www.ultimatestaffing.com
SIC: 7363 Help supply services

(P-14909)
RX PRO HEALTH LLC
12400 High Bluff Dr, San Diego
(92130-3077)
PHONE.....................858 369-4050
Susan R Salka, *CEO*
EMP: 1800
SQ FT: 175,000
SALES (est): 113.2K
SALES (corp-wide): 1.9B **Publicly Held**
WEB: www.amnhealthcare.com
SIC: 7363 Medical help service
PA: Amn Healthcare Services, Inc.
12400 High Bluff Dr
San Diego CA 92130
866 871-8519

(P-14910)
SAGE STAFFING CONSULTANTS INC (PA)
27441 Tourney Rd Ste 150, Valencia
(91355-5312)
PHONE.....................661 254-4026
Laura Kincaid, *CEO*
Greg Kincaid, *President*
Joanna Brison, *Manager*
EMP: 200
SQ FT: 5,000
SALES (est): 9.1MM **Privately Held**
WEB: www.sagestaffing.com
SIC: 7363 Temporary help service

(P-14911)
SE SCHER CORPORATION
1585 The Alameda, San Jose
(95126-2310)
PHONE.....................408 844-0772
Elizabeth Farley, *Opers Mgr*
Sonny Rendall, *Opers Mgr*
William Friedeberg,
Griffin Long, *Manager*
EMP: 612
SALES (corp-wide): 19.8MM **Privately Held**
SIC: 7363 Help supply services
PA: S.E. Scher Corporation
303 Hegenberger Rd # 300
Oakland CA 94621
415 431-8826

(P-14912)
SFN GROUP INC
114 Pacifica Ste 210, Irvine (92618-3320)
PHONE.....................949 727-8500
Tammy Hawkins, *Manager*
EMP: 75
SALES (corp-wide): 27.4B **Privately Held**
SIC: 7363 Temporary help service
HQ: Sfn Group, Inc.
2050 Spectrum Blvd
Fort Lauderdale FL 33309
954 308-7600

(P-14913)
SFN GROUP INC
Also Called: Spherion Staffing Group
3050 Bictor Ave Ste A, Redding (96002)
PHONE.....................530 222-3434
Sheryl Lakowski, *Branch Mgr*
EMP: 150

SALES (corp-wide): 27.4B **Privately Held**
SIC: 7363 Temporary help service
HQ: Sfn Group, Inc.
2050 Spectrum Blvd
Fort Lauderdale FL 33309
954 308-7600

(P-14914)
SPECTRUM PROF STAFFING INC
13520 Evening Creek Dr N # 300, San
Diego (92128-8105)
PHONE.....................800 644-1150
Raymond Lucia, *President*
EMP: 200
SALES (est): 4.5MM **Privately Held**
SIC: 7363 Employee leasing service

(P-14915)
STAFF TODAY INCORPORATED
212 E Rowland St 313, Covina
(91723-3146)
PHONE.....................800 928-5561
Paul Mwangi, *President*
EMP: 150
SALES (est): 770.2K **Privately Held**
SIC: 7363 7361 Temporary help service;
employment agencies

(P-14916)
STAR H-R (PA)
Also Called: Star Staffing
3820 Cypress Dr Ste 2, Petaluma
(94954-6964)
PHONE.....................707 762-4447
Carla Shevchuk, *President*
Lisa A Rogelstad, *Vice Pres*
Letty Smith, *Regional Mgr*
Juana Magana, *Administration*
Kara Crochett, *Opers Staff*
EMP: 2070
SALES (est): 71.1MM **Privately Held**
SIC: 7363 Temporary help service

(P-14917)
STENO EMPLOYMENT SERVICES INC
8560 Vineyard Ave Ste 208, Rancho Cuca-
monga (91730-4394)
PHONE.....................909 476-1404
Jaime Silguero, *CEO*
Ahmad Jackson, *President*
EMP: 2000
SALES (est): 40.1MM **Privately Held**
SIC: 7363 Employee leasing service

(P-14918)
SURGICAL STAFF INC
Surgical Staff, The
1523 G St, Sacramento (95814-1618)
PHONE.....................916 444-4424
Maryann Lesbirel, *Manager*
EMP: 200
SALES (corp-wide): 30.7MM **Privately Held**
WEB: www.mcnealtech.com
SIC: 7363 7361 Temporary help service;
employment agencies
PA: Surgical Staff, Inc.
120 Saint Matthews Ave
San Mateo CA 94401
650 558-3999

(P-14919)
TEGP INC
2375 Northside Dr Ste 360, San Diego
(92108-2713)
PHONE.....................619 584-3408
Michael Santos, *President*
EMP: 1500
SALES (est): 27.3MM
SALES (corp-wide): 179.1MM **Privately Held**
SIC: 7363 Temporary help service
PA: Eplica, Inc.
2355 Northside Dr Ste 120
San Diego CA 92108
619 260-2000

(P-14920)
TEMP UNLIMITED LLC
11306 183rd St Ste 301, Cerritos
(90703-5440)
P.O. Box 661358, Arcadia (91066-1358)
PHONE.....................562 860-3340
Carol Forrest, *President*

EMP: 80 EST: 2001
SALES (est): 2.7MM **Privately Held**
SIC: 7363 Temporary help service

(P-14921)
THERASTAFF INC
Also Called: Socal Staffing
2355 Northside Dr Ste 140, San Diego
(92108-4705)
PHONE.....................858 569-7555
William Stone, *President*
Carla A Marasigan, *Administration*
Kristy Gargano, *Manager*
EMP: 160
SQ FT: 3,600
SALES: 5.8MM **Privately Held**
WEB: www.therastaff.com
SIC: 7363 Medical help service

(P-14922)
TRANSFORCE INC
965 E Yosemite Ave Ste 7, Manteca
(95336-5943)
PHONE.....................209 952-2573
EMP: 50
SALES (est): 2.7MM **Privately Held**
SIC: 7363

(P-14923)
TRANSPORT DRIVERS INC
620 N Dmnd Bar Blvd Ste B, Diamond Bar
(91765-1074)
PHONE.....................800 497-6345
Ed Boyes, *Branch Mgr*
EMP: 500
SALES (corp-wide): 56.7MM **Privately Held**
WEB: www.transportdrivers.com
SIC: 7363 Medical help service
PA: Transport Drivers, Inc.
3540 Seven Bridges Dr # 300
Woodridge IL 60517
630 766-2721

(P-14924)
TRANSPORT DRIVERS INC
2131 S Grove Ave Ste D, Ontario
(91761-5697)
PHONE.....................909 937-3312
Ronald Formento Sr, *Branch Mgr*
EMP: 197
SALES (corp-wide): 56.7MM **Privately Held**
SIC: 7363 Truck driver services
PA: Transport Drivers, Inc.
3540 Seven Bridges Dr # 300
Woodridge IL 60517
630 766-2721

(P-14925)
TRUEBLUE INC
Also Called: Labor Ready
1362 Colusa Hwy, Yuba City (95993-9001)
PHONE.....................530 755-3291
Carol Pate, *Manager*
EMP: 125
SALES (corp-wide): 2.5B **Publicly Held**
WEB: www.laborready.com
SIC: 7363 Temporary help service
PA: Trueblue, Inc.
1015 A St
Tacoma WA 98402
253 383-9101

(P-14926)
TRUEBLUE INC
Also Called: Labor Ready
123 E Carrillo St, Santa Barbara
(93101-2110)
PHONE.....................805 963-5370
Adam Lockhart, *Manager*
EMP: 50
SALES (corp-wide): 2.5B **Publicly Held**
WEB: www.laborready.com
SIC: 7363 Temporary help service
PA: Trueblue, Inc.
1015 A St
Tacoma WA 98402
253 383-9101

(P-14927)
TWO ROADS PROF RESOURCES INC
5122 Bolsa Ave Ste 112, Huntington Beach
(92649-1050)
PHONE.....................714 901-3804

Tammy Gottschalk, *President*
Chris Hoff, *Vice Pres*
Michele Hoff, *Vice Pres*
Barry Vince, *Vice Pres*
Jackie Farber, *Tech Recruiter*
EMP: 110
SQ FT: 4,000
SALES (est): 5.6MM **Privately Held**
WEB: www.2roads.com
SIC: 7363 Temporary help service

(P-14928)
UNITED STATES DEPT OF NAVY
Also Called: Manpower
32444 Echo Ln Fl 3, San Diego
(92147-5100)
PHONE..............................619 524-1069
EMP: 175 **Publicly Held**
SIC: 7363 Manpower pools
HQ: United States Department Of The Navy
1200 Navy Pentagon
Washington DC 20350

(P-14929)
USA STAFFING INC
505 Higuera St, San Luis Obispo
(93401-6107)
PHONE..............................805 269-2677
Susan Elson, *Principal*
EMP: 75
SALES (est): 107.8K **Privately Held**
SIC: 7363 Temporary help service

(P-14930)
**VACAVILLE CONDOLESCENT
AND REH**
585 Nut Tree Ct, Vacaville (95687-3353)
PHONE..............................707 449-8000
Joseph M Niccoli Jr, *President*
EMP: 150
SALES (est): 666.8K **Privately Held**
SIC: 7363 Medical help service

(P-14931)
VANPIKE INC (PA)
6336 Greenwich Dr Ste 100, San Diego
(92122-5922)
PHONE..............................858 453-1331
Gary Van Eik, *President*
Richard Papike, *Vice Pres*
EMP: 60
SQ FT: 9,000
SALES: 26MM **Privately Held**
WEB: www.tristaff.com
SIC: 7363 7361 Temporary help service;
executive placement

(P-14932)
VOLT MANAGEMENT CORP
Also Called: Volt Workforce Solutions
19191 S Vt Ave Ste 950, Torrance
(90502-1098)
PHONE..............................310 316-8523
Rhona Driggs, *Branch Mgr*
EMP: 130
SALES (corp-wide): 1.1B **Publicly Held**
SIC: 7363 Help supply services
HQ: Volt Management Corp.
50 Charles Lindbergh Blvd
Uniondale NY 11553

(P-14933)
VOLT MANAGEMENT CORP
Also Called: Volt Temporary Services
2411 N Glassell St, Orange (92865-2717)
PHONE..............................714 921-7460
Rhona Driggs, *Branch Mgr*
EMP: 300
SALES (corp-wide): 1.1B **Publicly Held**
SIC: 7363 7373 Help supply services;
computer integrated systems design
HQ: Volt Management Corp.
50 Charles Lindbergh Blvd
Uniondale NY 11553

(P-14934)
VOLT MANAGEMENT CORP
Also Called: Volt Workforce Solutions
7676 Hazard Center Dr # 1000, San Diego
(92108-4503)
PHONE..............................858 576-3140
Rhona Driggs, *Branch Mgr*
EMP: 130

SALES (corp-wide): 1.1B **Publicly Held**
SIC: 7363 Help supply services
HQ: Volt Management Corp.
50 Charles Lindbergh Blvd
Uniondale NY 11553

(P-14935)
VOLT MANAGEMENT CORP
Also Called: Volt Workforce Solutions
7676 Hazard Center Dr # 1000, San Diego
(92108-4503)
PHONE..............................858 578-0920
Rhona Driggs, *Branch Mgr*
EMP: 130
SALES (corp-wide): 1.1B **Publicly Held**
SIC: 7363 Temporary help service
HQ: Volt Management Corp.
50 Charles Lindbergh Blvd
Uniondale NY 11553

(P-14936)
VOLT MANAGEMENT CORP
Also Called: Volt Workforce Solutions
7330 N Palm Ave Ste 105, Fresno
(93711-5768)
PHONE..............................559 435-1255
Scott Giroux, *Branch Mgr*
EMP: 130
SALES (corp-wide): 1.1B **Publicly Held**
SIC: 7363 7361 Temporary help service;
employment agencies
HQ: Volt Management Corp.
50 Charles Lindbergh Blvd
Uniondale NY 11553

(P-14937)
VOLT MANAGEMENT CORP
Also Called: Volt Workforce Solutions
2401 N Glassell St, Orange (92865-2705)
P.O. Box 3708 (92857-0708)
PHONE..............................714 921-8800
Scott Giroux, *Branch Mgr*
EMP: 130
SALES (corp-wide): 1.1B **Publicly Held**
SIC: 7363 Help supply services
HQ: Volt Management Corp.
50 Charles Lindbergh Blvd
Uniondale NY 11553

(P-14938)
VOLT MANAGEMENT CORP
Also Called: Volt Workforce Solutions
1544 Eureka Rd Ste 150, Roseville
(95661-3093)
PHONE..............................916 923-0454
Tim Chapman, *Branch Mgr*
EMP: 56
SALES (corp-wide): 1.1B **Publicly Held**
WEB: www.volt.com
SIC: 7363 Help supply services
HQ: Volt Management Corp.
50 Charles Lindbergh Blvd
Uniondale NY 11553

(P-14939)
VOLT MANAGEMENT CORP
Also Called: Volt Workforce Solutions
1650 Iowa Ave Ste 140, Riverside
(92507-2432)
PHONE..............................951 789-8133
Scott Giroux, *Branch Mgr*
EMP: 56
SALES (corp-wide): 1.1B **Publicly Held**
WEB: www.volt.com
SIC: 7363 Help supply services
HQ: Volt Management Corp.
50 Charles Lindbergh Blvd
Uniondale NY 11553

(P-14940)
VOLT MANAGEMENT CORP
Also Called: Volt Workforce Solutions
3558 Deer Park Dr 2, Stockton
(95219-2350)
PHONE..............................209 952-5627
Scott Giroux, *Branch Mgr*
EMP: 130
SALES (corp-wide): 1.1B **Publicly Held**
SIC: 7363 Help supply services

HQ: Volt Management Corp.
50 Charles Lindbergh Blvd
Uniondale NY 11553

(P-14941)
VOLT MANAGEMENT CORP
Also Called: Volt Workforce Solutions
1701 Solar Dr Ste 145, Oxnard
(93030-0137)
PHONE..............................805 485-0506
Scott Giroux, *Branch Mgr*
EMP: 130
SALES (corp-wide): 1.1B **Publicly Held**
SIC: 7363 Help supply services
HQ: Volt Management Corp.
50 Charles Lindbergh Blvd
Uniondale NY 11553

(P-14942)
WANNAJOB INC
Also Called: Construction Temps
2710 Saint Louis Ave, Signal Hill
(90755-2026)
PHONE..............................562 426-5272
William Davis, *President*
EMP: 75
SQ FT: 300
SALES (est): 2.4MM **Privately Held**
SIC: 7363 7361 Temporary help service;
employment agencies

(P-14943)
WEAVE INCORPORATED (PA)
Also Called: WEAVE
1900 K St Ste 200, Sacramento
(95811-4187)
PHONE..............................916 448-2321
Beth Hassett, *Exec Dir*
Garry Maisel, *Ch of Bd*
Priya Batra, *Principal*
Neil Forester, *Principal*
Bryan Merica, *Principal*
EMP: 100
SALES: 5.9MM **Privately Held**
WEB: www.weaveinc.org
SIC: 7363 8322 Domestic help service; in-
dividual & family services

(P-14944)
**WEST VALLEY ENGINEERING
INC (PA)**
Also Called: West Valley Staffing Group
390 Potrero Ave, Sunnyvale (94085-4116)
PHONE..............................408 735-1420
Michael F Williams, *President*
Teresa Kossayian, *CFO*
Jorge Martinez, *Administration*
Fay Wadia, *Finance Mgr*
Leonard Lucero, *Supervisor*
EMP: 72
SALES (est): 49.5MM **Privately Held**
SIC: 7363 Temporary help service

(P-14945)
WIGHTMAN ENTERPRISES INC
Also Called: Csl Solutions
8017 Sacramento St, Fair Oaks
(95628-7526)
PHONE..............................916 961-2959
Michelle Wightman, *President*
EMP: 60
SQ FT: 1,176
SALES (est): 2.3MM **Privately Held**
WEB: www.cslweb.com
SIC: 7363 Employee leasing service

(P-14946)
WORK FORCE SERVICES INC
Also Called: Work Force Staffing
300 Truxtun Ave, Bakersfield (93301-5314)
PHONE..............................661 327-5019
Brooks Whitehead, *President*
Brenda Bynum, *Accounting Dir*
EMP: 250
SQ FT: 1,600
SALES (est): 9.8MM **Privately Held**
WEB: www.workforcestaffing1.com
SIC: 7363 Temporary help service

(P-14947)
ZB REHAB STAFFING INC
Also Called: Thera Home Care
650 El Camino Real Ste M, Redwood City
(94063-1345)
PHONE..............................650 396-2207
Greg McCarthy, *CEO*
EMP: 75
SQ FT: 1,100
SALES: 2.5MM **Privately Held**
SIC: 7363 Help supply services

7371 Custom Computer Programming Svcs

(P-14948)
**22ND CENTURY
TECHNOLOGIES INC**
6203 San Ignacio Ave, San Jose
(95119-1371)
PHONE..............................866 537-9191
Satvinder Singh, *President*
EMP: 62
SALES (corp-wide): 81.7MM **Privately
Held**
SIC: 7371 Computer software systems
analysis & design, custom
PA: 22nd Century Technologies Inc.
220 Davidson Ave Ste 100b
Somerset NJ 08873
732 537-9191

(P-14949)
314E CORPORATION
47102 Mission Falls Ct # 219, Fremont
(94539-7835)
PHONE..............................510 371-6736
Abhishek Begerhotta, *President*
Matthew Rusch, *Assoc VP*
Alok Sharma, *Vice Pres*
Russell Tait, *Vice Pres*
Sabya Ray, *Technology*
EMP: 97
SQ FT: 10,078
SALES (est): 10.3MM **Privately Held**
WEB: www.314e.com
SIC: 7371 Custom computer programming
services

(P-14950)
3DNA CORP (PA)
Also Called: Nationbuilder
520 S Grand Ave Fl 2, Los Angeles
(90071-2600)
PHONE..............................213 394-4623
Jim H Gilliam, *President*
Chuck Collins, *Vice Pres*
Gina Davis, *Vice Pres*
Jesse Haff, *Vice Pres*
Cameron Orr, *Vice Pres*
EMP: 100
SALES (est): 11MM **Privately Held**
SIC: 7371 Computer software develop-
ment

(P-14951)
3K TECHNOLOGIES LLC
1114 Cadillac Ct, Milpitas (95035-3058)
PHONE..............................408 716-5900
Sireesha Chittabbathini,
Bala Krishna, *Tech Recruiter*
Kishore Gobireddy, *Business Mgr*
Krishna Chittabbathini,
Anita Kumar, *Manager*
EMP: 105
SQ FT: 2,000
SALES: 13.8MM **Privately Held**
SIC: 7371 Custom computer programming
services

(P-14952)
4D INC
95 S Market St Ste 240, San Jose
(95113-2311)
PHONE..............................408 557-4600
Laurent Ribardiere, *CEO*
Tracy Roberts, *President*
Phillipe Berthault, *CFO*
Vincent Migayrou, *CFO*
Thomas Maul, *Managing Dir*
EMP: 101

SALES (est): 11MM
SALES (corp-wide): 937.3K **Privately Held**
WEB: www.4d.com
SIC: 7371 7372 Computer software development & applications; prepackaged software
HQ: 4d
  Entree 4 Parc Des Erables
  Le Pecq 78230
  130 539-200

(P-14953)
5 NINE GROUP INC
Also Called: Franklin Data
1125 Lindero Canyon Rd, Westlake Village (91362-5474)
PHONE...............................805 880-2948
Matthew Blake, *Exec VP*
Henry Dicker, *Officer*
John Aben, *Exec VP*
EMP: 250
SQ FT: 14,000
SALES: 48MM **Privately Held**
SIC: 7371 Custom computer programming services

(P-14954)
6WIND USA INC
2975 Scott Blvd Ste 115, Santa Clara (95054-3314)
PHONE...............................408 816-1366
Eric Carmes, *President*
Charlie Ashton, *VP Mktg*
EMP: 88
SALES (est): 257.7K **Privately Held**
SIC: 7371 Computer software development

(P-14955)
ABACUS DATA SYSTEMS INC (HQ)
Also Called: Abacusnext
9171 Towne Centre Dr # 200, San Diego (92122-1267)
PHONE...............................858 452-4280
Alessandra Lezama, *CEO*
Mike Skelly, *CFO*
Chris Cardinal, *Exec VP*
Tomas Suros, *Admin Sec*
Jerome Fodor, *CTO*
EMP: 75
SQ FT: 10,000
SALES (est): 36.2MM
SALES (corp-wide): 20.4MM **Privately Held**
SIC: 7371 7374 Computer software systems analysis & design, custom; data processing & preparation; computer processing services; computer time-sharing
PA: Providence Strategic Growth Fund
  50 Kennedy Plz Fl 18
  Providence RI 02903
  401 751-1700

(P-14956)
ABACUS SERVICE CORPORATION
1725 23rd St, Sacramento (95816-7100)
PHONE...............................916 288-8948
Michelle Reuter, *Branch Mgr*
Ram Prasad, *Research Analys*
EMP: 300
SALES (corp-wide): 42.1MM **Privately Held**
SIC: 7371 Custom computer programming services
PA: Abacus Service Corporation
  25925 Telg Rd Ste 206
  Southfield MI
  248 324-9200

(P-14957)
ABBYY USA SOFTWARE HOUSE INC (DH)
890 Hillview Ct Ste 300, Milpitas (95035-4574)
PHONE...............................408 457-9777
Ding Yuan Tang, *CEO*
Arthur Whipple, *President*
Judy Hsu, *CFO*
Sheryl Lodolce, *CFO*
David Arthur, *Vice Pres*
EMP: 105 **EST:** 2000
SQ FT: 31,000

SALES: 37MM **Privately Held**
SIC: 7371 Computer software development
HQ: Abbyy Software Limited
  Egkomi, 2 Michail Karaoli
  Egkomi Nicosias
  226 806-35

(P-14958)
ABZOOBA INC
1551 Mccarthy Blvd # 204, Milpitas (95035-7437)
PHONE...............................650 453-8760
Vivek Vipul, *CEO*
Shikha Gupta, *Partner*
Pushpal Bhattacharya, *Vice Pres*
Pradeep Suryanarayan, *Vice Pres*
Arnab Bose, *Managing Dir*
EMP: 121 **EST:** 2010
SALES (est): 293.6K **Privately Held**
SIC: 7371 Computer software development

(P-14959)
ACCELERIZE INC (PA)
20411 Sw Birch St Ste 250, Newport Beach (92660-1771)
PHONE...............................949 515-2141
Brian Ross, *Ch of Bd*
Santi Pierini, *COO*
Michael Lin, *CFO*
Anthony Mazzarella, *CFO*
Damon Stein, *Admin Sec*
EMP: 97
SQ FT: 8,754
SALES: 24.1MM **Publicly Held**
SIC: 7371 8742 Computer software development & applications; marketing consulting services

(P-14960)
ACCESS SYSTEMS AMERICAS INC
3965 Freedom Cir Ste 200, Santa Clara (95054-1293)
PHONE...............................408 400-3000
Kiyo Oishi, *CEO*
Jeanne Seeley, *CFO*
Neale Foster, *Vice Pres*
Michael Kelley, *Vice Pres*
Michimasa Uematsu, *Vice Pres*
EMP: 518
SQ FT: 71,000
SALES (est): 35.1MM
SALES (corp-wide): 69.9MM **Privately Held**
WEB: www.palmsource.com
SIC: 7371 7372 Computer software development; software programming applications; prepackaged software
PA: Access Co.,Ltd.
  3, Kandaneribeicho
  Chiyoda-Ku TKY 101-0
  368 539-088

(P-14961)
ACHIEVO CORPORATION (PA)
1400 Terra Bella Ave E, Mountain View (94043-3062)
PHONE...............................925 498-8864
Sandy Wai-Yan Chau, *CEO*
Robert P Lee, *President*
Bernard Mathaisel, *COO*
Julio Leung, *CFO*
Darryl Quan, *CFO*
EMP: 66
SALES (est): 57.8MM **Privately Held**
WEB: www.achievo.com
SIC: 7371 Custom computer programming services

(P-14962)
ACTIVISION BLIZZARD INC
3420 Ocean Park Blvd # 2000, Santa Monica (90405-3304)
PHONE...............................310 581-4700
Rose Villasenor, *Opers Staff*
EMP: 140
SALES (corp-wide): 7B **Publicly Held**
WEB: www.blizzard.com
SIC: 7371 Computer software development
PA: Activision Blizzard, Inc.
  3100 Ocean Park Blvd
  Santa Monica CA 90405
  310 255-2000

(P-14963)
ADAPTAMED LLC
6699 Alvarado Rd Ste 2301, San Diego (92120-5241)
PHONE...............................877 478-7773
Aparna Reddy,
EMP: 120
SALES (est): 1.6MM **Privately Held**
SIC: 7371 Computer software development

(P-14964)
ADCOLONY INC
11400 W Olympic Blvd # 1200, Los Angeles (90064-1583)
PHONE...............................650 625-1262
William Kassoy, *CEO*
Stefan Adamczyk, *Vice Pres*
Ian Atkinson, *Vice Pres*
Tim O'Neil, *Vice Pres*
David Pokress, *Vice Pres*
EMP: 100
SALES (est): 17MM
SALES (corp-wide): 4.7MM **Privately Held**
SIC: 7371 Computer software development
PA: Adcolony Holdings Us, Inc.
  1875 S Grant St Ste 800
  San Mateo CA 94402
  650 625-1262

(P-14965)
ADDEPAR INC (PA)
303 Bryant St, Mountain View (94041-1552)
PHONE...............................855 464-6268
Eric Poirier, *CEO*
Derek Brown, *President*
Karen White, *President*
Nancy Hilker, *CFO*
Joe Lonsdale, *Chairman*
EMP: 85
SALES (est): 18.7MM **Privately Held**
SIC: 7371 Computer software development

(P-14966)
ADVANCED SOFTWARE DESIGN INC
Also Called: Advanced Software Dynamics
1371 Oakland Blvd Ste 100, Walnut Creek (94596-8407)
PHONE...............................925 975-0691
Manu Chatterjee, *CEO*
Sonali Singh, *President*
Shikha Chatterjee, *VP Opers*
EMP: 59
SQ FT: 1,200
SALES: 9MM **Privately Held**
WEB: www.asdglobal.com
SIC: 7371 7373 8711 8742 Computer software development; computer integrated systems design; engineering services; management consulting services

(P-14967)
ADVENT SOFTWARE INC (HQ)
Also Called: SS&c Advent
600 Townsend St Fl 5, San Francisco (94103-4945)
PHONE...............................415 543-7696
David Peter Hess Jr, *President*
Stephanie Dimarco, *Ch of Bd*
James Cox, *CFO*
Todd Gottula, *Exec VP*
Chris Momsen, *Exec VP*
EMP: 148
SQ FT: 158,264
SALES (est): 4MM
SALES (corp-wide): 1.6B **Publicly Held**
WEB: www.advent.com
SIC: 7371 7373 7372 6722 Custom computer programming services; computer integrated systems design; systems software development services; computer systems analysis & design; prepackaged software; management investment, open-end
PA: Ss&C Technologies Holdings, Inc.
  80 Lamberton Rd
  Windsor CT 06095
  860 298-4500

(P-14968)
AERA TECHNOLOGY INC
707 California St, Mountain View (94041-2005)
PHONE...............................408 524-2222
Ram Mohan, *President*
Valerie Preston, *Partner*
Travis Adlman, *CFO*
Tony Wessels, *Chief Mktg Ofcr*
Shariq Mansoor, *Officer*
EMP: 105
SALES (est): 1.3MM **Privately Held**
WEB: www.fusionops.com
SIC: 7371 Computer software development

(P-14969)
AESTIVA SOFTWARE INC
3551 Voyager St Ste 201, Torrance (90503-1674)
PHONE...............................310 697-0338
David M Silverberg, *President*
Eric Villicana, *Vice Pres*
EMP: 50
SALES (est): 3.9MM **Privately Held**
SIC: 7371 Computer software development

(P-14970)
AFTERSHOCK LA STUDIOS INC
3633 Lenawee Ave Ste 100, Los Angeles (90016-4310)
PHONE...............................650 450-9660
EMP: 60 **EST:** 2016
SALES (est): 891.1K **Privately Held**
SIC: 7371

(P-14971)
ALLDRAGON INTERNATIONAL INC
4285 Payne Ave 10028, San Jose (95117-3324)
PHONE...............................408 410-6248
Tom Gong, *CEO*
Connie Kang, *President*
EMP: 50
SALES: 150K **Privately Held**
SIC: 7371 Computer software development & applications

(P-14972)
ALLIANCE INFORMATION TECHNOLOG (PA)
Also Called: Allianceit
7041 Koll Center Pkwy # 140, Pleasanton (94566-3196)
PHONE...............................925 462-9787
Purushothama Polkampalli, *President*
Kalyani Mokkapati, *Managing Dir*
Kranthi Allianceit, *Business Mgr*
Nihanth K RAO, *Opers Mgr*
Shafia Mohammad, *Sales Staff*
EMP: 55
SQ FT: 2,000
SALES (est): 6.7MM **Privately Held**
SIC: 7371 8748 7379 7372 Computer software development; systems engineering consultant, ex. computer or professional; data processing consultant; prepackaged software

(P-14973)
ALOGENT HOLDINGS INC
5868 Owens Ave Ste 200, Carlsbad (92008-5517)
PHONE...............................760 410-9000
EMP: 80
SALES (est): 1.1MM
SALES (corp-wide): 202.5K **Privately Held**
SIC: 7371 Computer software development
PA: Alogent Holdings, Inc.
  350 Technology Pkwy # 200
  Norcross GA 30092
  770 752-6400

(P-14974)
ALPHA NET CONSULTING LLC
3080 Olcott St Ste C235, Santa Clara (95054-3281)
PHONE...............................408 330-0896
Gurderpinder Dhillon,
Surjit Bedi,
EMP: 85

SQ FT: 1,500
SALES: 18.6MM **Privately Held**
WEB: www.anetcorp.com
SIC: 7371 Custom computer programming services

(P-14975)
ALPHABET INC (PA)
1600 Amphitheatre Pkwy, Mountain View (94043-1351)
PHONE..................................650 253-0000
Larry Page, *CEO*
John L Hennessy, *Ch of Bd*
Sergey Brin, *President*
Ruth M Porat, *CFO*
Roger Ferguson, *Bd of Directors*
EMP: 55 EST: 1998
SALES: 110.8B **Publicly Held**
SIC: 7371 Computer software development & applications

(P-14976)
ALTIUM INC (HQ)
4225 Executive Sq Ste 700, La Jolla (92037-9181)
PHONE..................................858 864-1661
Aram Mirkazemi, *CEO*
Sergey Kostinsky, *President*
Kim Besharati, *Vice Pres*
Franz Maidl, *Managing Dir*
Mariann Sierra, *Executive Asst*
EMP: 92
SQ FT: 11,000
SALES: 38MM
SALES (corp-wide): 110.9MM **Privately Held**
SIC: 7371 Computer software development
PA: Altium Limited
L6 821 Pacific Hwy
Chatswood NSW 2067
294 101-005

(P-14977)
AMBER HOLDINGS INC
150 California St, San Francisco (94111-4500)
PHONE..................................415 765-6500
Robert F Smith, *President*
Brian N Sheth, *Vice Pres*
EMP: 1010
SALES (est): 22.5MM
SALES (corp-wide): 4.4B **Privately Held**
SIC: 7371 Computer software development
HQ: Vista Equity Partners Fund Iii, L.P.
4 Embarcadero Ctr # 2000
San Francisco CA 94111

(P-14978)
AMDOCS INC
Innovis
1104 Investment Blvd, El Dorado Hills (95762-5710)
PHONE..................................916 934-7000
Michael Saeger, *Manager*
Levina Till, *Executive Asst*
Manikandan Kumarappan, *Project Mgr*
Jeff Hill, *Technology*
Edwin Aviles, *Engineer*
EMP: 336 **Privately Held**
WEB: www.amdocs.com
SIC: 7371 7389 7374 Computer software systems analysis & design, custom; computer software development; software programming applications; financial services; data processing & preparation
HQ: Amdocs, Inc.
1390 Timberlake Manor Pkw
Chesterfield MO 63017
314 212-7000

(P-14979)
AMDOCS BCS INC
1104 Investment Blvd, El Dorado Hills (95762-5710)
PHONE..................................916 934-7000
EMP: 336
SALES (est): 557.9K
SALES (corp-wide): 3.5B **Privately Held**
SIC: 7371 7389 7374
HQ: Amdocs, Inc.
1390 Timberlake Manor Pkw
Chesterfield MO 63017
314 212-7000

(P-14980)
AMERICAN SUNRISE INC
7404 Santa Fe Canyon Pl, San Diego (92129)
PHONE..................................858 610-4766
John Zhang, *Officer*
EMP: 100
SQ FT: 4,000
SALES: 1MM **Privately Held**
SIC: 7371 7361 7379 Computer software development; employment agencies; computer related consulting services

(P-14981)
AMP TECHNOLOGIES LLC (PA)
445 Melrose Ct, San Ramon (94582-5103)
PHONE..................................877 442-2824
Neel Naicker, *CEO*
Arvind Sathyamoorthy, *CTO*
John Sherry, *Director*
EMP: 133
SALES (est): 10.1MM **Privately Held**
SIC: 7371 Computer software development & applications

(P-14982)
AMPLIFY EDUCATION INC
1032 Irving St Ste 445, San Francisco (94122-2216)
PHONE..................................562 209-7875
EMP: 82
SALES (corp-wide): 146.3MM **Privately Held**
SIC: 7371 Computer software development
PA: Amplify Education, Inc.
55 Washington St Ste 800
Brooklyn NY 11201
212 213-8177

(P-14983)
AMZN MOBILE LLC
525 Market St Fl 19, San Francisco (94105-2708)
PHONE..................................925 348-4580
EMP: 500
SALES (est): 7.8MM **Publicly Held**
SIC: 7371 Software programming applications
PA: Amazon.Com, Inc.
410 Terry Ave N
Seattle WA 98109

(P-14984)
ANAND SOFTWARE INC
4719 Quail Lakes Dr, Stockton (95207-5267)
PHONE..................................209 287-1708
Chaitanya Aluru, *CEO*
Michael Yin, *Shareholder*
EMP: 99
SALES: 3MM **Privately Held**
SIC: 7371 7373

(P-14985)
ANIMOTO LLC
333 Kearny St Fl 6, San Francisco (94108-3269)
PHONE..................................415 987-3139
Bradley C Jefferson, *CEO*
Russell G Keefe, *CFO*
EMP: 60
SQ FT: 15,000
SALES (est): 5.3MM **Privately Held**
SIC: 7371 Computer software development

(P-14986)
ANJANA SOFTWARE SOLUTIONS INC
1445 E Los Angeles Ave # 305, Simi Valley (93065-7818)
PHONE..................................805 583-0121
Saravana Kumarasamy, *President*
Kritik A Govindan, *Treasurer*
Venkatesh Ramachandran, *Vice Pres*
EMP: 75 EST: 2000
SQ FT: 3,000
SALES: 15.9MM
SALES (corp-wide): 10.6MM **Privately Held**
SIC: 7371 Computer software systems analysis & design, custom

PA: Anjana Software Solutions Private Limited
Module No. 306, Nsic Software Technology Park
Chennai TN 60003
444 684-6222

(P-14987)
ANNIE APP INC (DH)
23 Geary St Ste 400800, San Francisco (94108-5701)
PHONE..................................844 277-2664
Bertrand Schmitt, *CEO*
Marshall Nu, *COO*
Sujan Jain, *CFO*
Natasha Kehimkar, *Officer*
Ted Krantz, *Officer*
EMP: 66
SALES (est): 49.9MM **Privately Held**
SIC: 7371 Computer software development; computer software development & applications
HQ: Shanghai Qingtian Automatic Control Complete Set Equipment Co., Ltd.
Rm 3539,Building 24,No.2,Xincheng Road,Pudong New Dist.
Shanghai 20130
216 248-8355

(P-14988)
ANOMALI INCORPORATED
808 Winslow St, Redwood City (94063-1608)
PHONE..................................408 800-4050
Hugh Njemanze, *CEO*
Drew Hamer, *CFO*
Dan Barahona, *Chief Mktg Ofcr*
Colby Derodeff, *Officer*
Al Veach, *Officer*
EMP: 100
SALES (est): 4.9MM **Privately Held**
SIC: 7371 Computer software development

(P-14989)
APIGEE CORPORATION
1600 Amphitheatre Pkwy, Mountain View (94043-1351)
PHONE..................................408 343-7300
Chet Kapoor, *CEO*
Tim Wan, *CFO*
Ed Anuff, *Senior VP*
Brian Coulter, *Vice Pres*
Eric Cross, *Vice Pres*
EMP: 104
SQ FT: 41,000
SALES: 92MM
SALES (corp-wide): 110.8B **Publicly Held**
WEB: www.sonoasystems.com
SIC: 7371 Computer software development & applications
HQ: Google Llc
1600 Amphitheatre Pkwy
Mountain View CA 94043
650 253-0000

(P-14990)
APPLIED COMPUTER SOLUTIONS (HQ)
Also Called: ACS
15461 Springdale St, Huntington Beach (92649-1335)
PHONE..................................714 861-2200
Sandy Davis, *President*
Michael Davis, *COO*
Warren Barnes, *CFO*
Lancaster Cory, *Vice Pres*
Rogers Mathews, *Executive*
EMP: 70
SQ FT: 60,000
SALES (est): 75.7MM
SALES (corp-wide): 1.4B **Privately Held**
WEB: www.acs-g.com
SIC: 7371 Custom computer programming services; computer software development
PA: Pivot Technology Solutions, Inc
161 Bay St Suite 1020
Toronto ON M5J 2
647 788-2034

(P-14991)
APPLIED ENGINEERING MGT CORP
Also Called: Aem Corporation
760 Paseo Camarillo # 101, Camarillo (93010-6000)
P.O. Box 1263 (93011-1263)
PHONE..................................805 484-1909
Anne Morgan, *Branch Mgr*
Sharon Demonsabert, *President*
Kaylee Peterson, *Admin Asst*
Chris Kaczmarek, *Manager*
Kelly Lanier, *Assistant*
EMP: 250
SALES (est): 20.1MM
SALES (corp-wide): 47MM **Privately Held**
WEB: www.aemcorp.com
SIC: 7371 Computer software development
PA: Virginia Aem Corporation
13880 Dulles Corner Ln # 300
Herndon VA 20171
703 464-7030

(P-14992)
APPRENDRE TECHNOLOGIES INC
1781 S Campton Ave # 217, Anaheim (92805-6734)
PHONE..................................561 244-9917
Ron Broussard, *CEO*
Marsha Hall, *COO*
EMP: 99
SALES (est): 1.7MM
SALES (corp-wide): 2.6MM **Privately Held**
SIC: 7371 7372 8243 3699 Computer software development & applications; application computer software; software training, computer; electronic training devices; guard services; motion picture & video production
PA: Securecorp International Inc.
10299 Southern Blvd
Royal Palm Beach FL 33411
561 244-9917

(P-14993)
APPSTER INC
180 Sansome St Fl 4, San Francisco (94104-3713)
PHONE..................................415 926-2741
Esther Humphrey, *Administration*
EMP: 80
SALES (est): 3.7MM **Privately Held**
SIC: 7371 Computer software development & applications
PA: Appster Pty Ltd
L2 377 Lonsdale St
Melbourne VIC 3000

(P-14994)
APPTIVO INC
34364 Eucalyptus Ter, Fremont (94555-1983)
PHONE..................................650 906-1034
Bastin S Gerald, *CEO*
Randy Jacobs, *Manager*
EMP: 200 EST: 2009
SALES (est): 96.6K **Privately Held**
SIC: 7371 7389 Computer software development;

(P-14995)
ARCSOFT INC (PA)
46605 Fremont Blvd, Fremont (94538-6410)
PHONE..................................510 440-9901
Michael Deng, *President*
David Nagel, *Ch of Bd*
Todd Peters, *President*
Jennifer Pang, *CFO*
Sean Bi, *Senior VP*
EMP: 59
SQ FT: 26,000
SALES (est): 60.3MM **Privately Held**
WEB: www.arcsoft.com
SIC: 7371 5734 Computer software development; computer & software stores

PRODUCTS & SVCS

(P-14996)
ARCTOUCH LLC
303 2nd St Ste 800s, San Francisco
(94107-3631)
PHONE...................415 944-2000
Eric Shapiro, *CEO*
Jeremy Stephan, *Partner*
Adam Fingerman, *Officer*
Paulo Michels, *Engineer*
Ross Buffington, *Opers Staff*
EMP: 200
SQ FT: 1,500
SALES (est): 21MM
SALES (corp-wide): 20.1B **Privately Held**
SIC: 7371 Computer software development & applications
HQ: Grey Global Group Llc
200 5th Ave Bsmt B
New York NY 10010
212 546-2000

(P-14997)
ARCULES INC
17875 Von Karman Ave # 450, Irvine
(92614-6200)
PHONE...................949 439-0053
Andreas Pettersson, *CEO*
EMP: 70
SALES (est): 660K **Privately Held**
SIC: 7371 Software programming applications

(P-14998)
ARENA SOLUTIONS INC (PA)
989 E Hillsdale Blvd # 250, Foster City
(94404-4201)
PHONE...................650 513-3500
Craig Livingston, *CEO*
Jan Russo, *President*
Ken Bozzini, *CFO*
Andrea Pitts, *Vice Pres*
Eric Larkin, *CTO*
▲ EMP: 65
SALES (est): 19.9MM **Privately Held**
WEB: www.arenasolutions.com
SIC: 7371 Computer software development

(P-14999)
ARGO AI LLC (HQ)
100 W Evelyn Ave Ste 1, Mountain View
(94041-1471)
PHONE...................412 709-6992
Bryan Salesky, *CEO*
Peter Rander, *COO*
Daniel Beaven, *CFO*
Brett Browning, *Vice Pres*
EMP: 52 EST: 2016
SALES (est): 8.6MM
SALES (corp-wide): 156.7B **Publicly Held**
SIC: 7371 Software programming applications
PA: Ford Motor Company
1 American Rd
Dearborn MI 48126
313 322-3000

(P-15000)
ARICENT US INC (DH)
Also Called: Aricent Technologies
3979 Freedom Cir Ste 950, Santa Clara
(95054-1294)
PHONE...................408 329-7400
Frank Kern, *CEO*
Doreen Lorenzo, *President*
David Freedman, *CFO*
EMP: 50
SALES (est): 92.4MM
SALES (corp-wide): 1.1B **Privately Held**
WEB: www.emuzed.com
SIC: 7371 Computer software development
HQ: Altran Usa Holdings, Inc.
451 D St
Boston MA 02210
617 449-9790

(P-15001)
ARTIFICIAL SOLUTIONS INC
800 W El Camino Real, Mountain View
(94040-2567)
PHONE...................650 943-2325
EMP: 51

SALES (est): 40.9K **Privately Held**
SIC: 7371 Computer software development & applications

7371 Custom Computer Programming Svcs

(P-15001)
ARTIFICIAL SOLUTIONS INC
800 W El Camino Real, Mountain View
(94040-2567)
PHONE...................650 943-2325
EMP: 51
SALES (est): 40.9K **Privately Held**
SIC: 7371 Computer software development & applications

(P-15002)
ARTIZEN INCORPORATED
101 Golf Course Dr # 300, Rohnert Park
(94928-1718)
PHONE...................650 261-9400
Parker Painter, *President*
EMP: 150
SQ FT: 2,200
SALES (est): 11.9MM **Privately Held**
SIC: 7371 Computer software development & applications

(P-15003)
ASCENDIFY CORPORATION
580 California St Bsmt, San Francisco
(94104-1018)
PHONE...................415 528-5503
Matt Hendrickson, *CEO*
Kevin Grant, *Vice Pres*
Kelly King, *Vice Pres*
Derek Mercer, *Vice Pres*
Lauren Smith, *Vice Pres*
EMP: 50
SALES (est): 236.4K **Privately Held**
SIC: 7371 Computer software development

(P-15004)
ASHUNYA INC
642 N Eckhoff St, Orange (92868-1004)
PHONE...................714 385-1900
Melanie Merchant, *Principal*
EMP: 88
SALES (est): 7.8MM **Privately Held**
SIC: 7371 7372 7373 Computer software development & applications; application computer software; office computer automation systems integration; turnkey vendors, computer systems; value-added resellers, computer systems

(P-15005)
ATHOC INC (DH)
3001 Bishop Dr Ste 400, San Ramon
(94583-5005)
PHONE...................925 242-5660
Guy Miasnik, *President*
Douglas Doyle, *Officer*
Aviv Siegel, *Exec VP*
Ly Tran, *Exec VP*
Dubhe Beinhorn, *Vice Pres*
EMP: 61
SALES (est): 1.3MM
SALES (corp-wide): 932MM **Privately Held**
WEB: www.athoc.com
SIC: 7371 Computer software development
HQ: Blackberry Corp.
3001 Bishop Dr
San Ramon CA 94583
972 650-6126

(P-15006)
ATLAS DATABASE SOFTWARE CORP (PA)
Also Called: Atlas Development
26679 Agoura Rd Ste 200, Calabasas
(91302-3812)
PHONE...................818 340-7080
Robert D Atlas, *CEO*
Ana Villafane, *CFO*
Steven Atlas, *Vice Pres*
Lisa Conley, *Vice Pres*
Lori Markey, *Vice Pres*

EMP: 89
SQ FT: 15,000
SALES (est): 33.8MM **Privately Held**
WEB: www.atlasdev.com
SIC: 7371 Custom computer programming services

(P-15007)
ATLAZ INC
10721 Fair Oaks Blvd, Fair Oaks
(95628-7212)
PHONE...................415 671-6142
Mark Fedin, *CEO*
EMP: 70 EST: 2015
SALES (est): 1.2MM **Privately Held**
SIC: 7371

(P-15008)
ATRENTA INC (HQ)
690 E Middlefield Rd, Mountain View
(94043-4010)
PHONE...................408 453-3333
Ajoy K Bose, *President*
Bert Clement, *COO*
Solaiman Rahim, *Info Tech Dir*
Oleg Efimov, *Info Tech Mgr*
Oleg Esimov, *Info Tech Mgr*
EMP: 70
SQ FT: 8,000
SALES (est): 44.2MM
SALES (corp-wide): 2.7B **Publicly Held**
WEB: www.atrenta.com
SIC: 7371 Computer software systems analysis & design, custom
PA: Synopsys, Inc.
690 E Middlefield Rd
Mountain View CA 94043
650 584-5000

(P-15009)
AUDITBOARD INC (PA)
12800 Center Court Dr S # 100, Cerritos
(90703-9363)
PHONE...................877 769-5444
Daniel Kim, *Vice Pres*
Karen Gift, *CFO*
EMP: 50
SQ FT: 10,000
SALES (est): 5.1MM **Privately Held**
SIC: 7371 Computer software development

(P-15010)
AVANQUEST NORTH AMERICA LLC (HQ)
Also Called: Avanquest North America Inc.
23801 Calabasas Rd # 2005, Calabasas
(91302-1547)
PHONE...................818 591-9600
Roger Bloxberg, *CEO*
Todd Helfstein, *President*
Sharon Chiu, *CFO*
Cynthia Esters, *Officer*
Kelley Sanchez, *Vice Pres*
EMP: 80
SQ FT: 12,000
SALES (est): 59.8MM
SALES (corp-wide): 1.4MM **Privately Held**
WEB: www.novareg.com
SIC: 7371 Computer software development
PA: Claranova
Avanquest Blue Squad Bvrp Software Immeuble Vision Defense
La Garenne Colombes 92250
141 271-970

(P-15011)
AVENUESOCIAL INC
440 N Wolfe Rd, Sunnyvale (94085-3869)
PHONE...................510 275-4485
Salman Ghaznavi, *President*
EMP: 135
SQ FT: 1,000
SALES (est): 3MM **Privately Held**
SIC: 7371 Software programming applications

(P-15012)
AWAREPOINT CORPORATION (PA)
Also Called: Aware Point
600 W Broadway Ste 250, San Diego
(92101-3357)
PHONE...................858 345-5000

Tim Roche, *CEO*
EMP: 53
SALES (est): 17MM **Privately Held**
WEB: www.awarepoint.com
SIC: 7371 Software programming applications; computer software development

(P-15013)
AXCIENT INC (HQ)
1161 San Antonio Rd, Mountain View
(94043-1028)
PHONE...................650 314-7300
Matt Nachtrab, *CEO*
John Finegan, *CFO*
Justin Moore, *Security Dir*
Kevin Hoffman, *CTO*
EMP: 81
SALES (est): 43.4MM
SALES (corp-wide): 6MM **Privately Held**
WEB: www.axcient.com
SIC: 7371 Software programming applications
PA: Axcient Holdings, Llc
1161 San Antonio Rd
Mountain View CA 94043
650 314-7300

(P-15014)
AZUMIO INC (PA)
230 California Ave # 212, Palo Alto
(94306-1637)
PHONE...................719 310-3774
Bojan Bostjancic, *President*
Jennifer Grenz, *Vice Pres*
Eric Huynh, *Sr Project Mgr*
Jennifer Ta, *Editor*
EMP: 103
SALES (est): 5.9MM **Privately Held**
SIC: 7371 Computer software development

(P-15015)
B JACQUELINE AND ASSOC INC
Also Called: J B A
1192 N Lake Ave, Pasadena (91104-3739)
PHONE...................626 844-1400
Jacqueline Buickians, *President*
Gary Buickians, *Admin Sec*
Robert Bolliger, *Superintendent*
EMP: 300
SQ FT: 4,000
SALES (est): 16.8MM **Privately Held**
SIC: 7371 7379 Computer software development & applications; computer related consulting services

(P-15016)
BAAZ INC
Also Called: Baaz Global
1 Hallidie Plz Ste 200, San Francisco
(94102-2931)
PHONE...................408 621-6912
Ghanssan Salaneh, *CEO*
Michael Eisen, *Controller*
EMP: 75 EST: 2015
SALES (est): 144.5K
SALES (corp-wide): 4.7MM **Privately Held**
SIC: 7371 Computer software development & applications
PA: Rubix Global Holding, Inc.
1 Hallidie Plz Ste 200
San Francisco CA 94102
415 988-2606

(P-15017)
BABYFIRST AMERICAS LLC
10390 Santa Monica Blvd, Los Angeles
(90025-5058)
PHONE...................310 442-9853
Guy Oranim, *CEO*
Sharon Rechter, *President*
Karl Knipliy, *CFO*
EMP: 75
SALES: 13MM **Privately Held**
SIC: 7371 Computer software development & applications
PA: Bftv, Llc
10390 Santa Monica Blvd # 310
Los Angeles CA 90025
310 442-9853

(P-15018)
BAJA LIFE ONLINE PARTNERS
P.O. Box 4917 (92652-4917)
PHONE...................949 376-4619

Erik Cutter, *Partner*
EMP: 50
SALES (est): 1.8MM **Privately Held**
WEB: www.bajalife.com
SIC: 7371 4724 Custom computer programming services; travel agencies

(P-15019)
BAKBONE SOFTWARE INC (DH)
9540 Towne Centre Dr # 100, San Diego (92121-1989)
PHONE..................................858 450-9009
Michael S Dell, *CEO*
Stephen J Felice, *President*
Roy Hogsed, *Senior VP*
Kenneth Horner, *Senior VP*
Brian Tgladden, *Senior VP*
EMP: 72
SQ FT: 22,600
SALES (est): 23.4MM
SALES (corp-wide): 1.7B **Privately Held**
WEB: www.bakbone.com
SIC: 7371 7375 Computer software systems analysis & design, custom; information retrieval services
HQ: Quest Software, Inc.
4 Polaris Way
Aliso Viejo CA 92656
949 754-8000

(P-15020)
BASTILLE NETWORKS INC
499 Lake Ave, Santa Cruz (95062-3938)
PHONE..................................800 530-3341
Chris Risley, *CEO*
Ivan O'Sullivan, *Risk Mgmt Dir*
Sophie Koch, *Marketing Mgr*
Ben Campbell, *Director*
EMP: 50
SALES (est): 1MM **Privately Held**
SIC: 7371 Computer software development

(P-15021)
BEA SYSTEMS INC (HQ)
2315 N 1st St, San Jose (95131-1010)
PHONE..................................650 506-7000
Alfred S Chuang, *Ch of Bd*
Alan Button, *Partner*
Ted Kimes, *President*
Mark T Carges, *Exec VP*
Richard Geraffo, *Exec VP*
EMP: 1000
SQ FT: 236,000
SALES (est): 207.3MM
SALES (corp-wide): 39.8B **Publicly Held**
WEB: www.beasys.com
SIC: 7371 7372 Computer software development; prepackaged software
PA: Oracle Corporation
500 Oracle Pkwy
Redwood City CA 94065
650 506-7000

(P-15022)
BEAUTIES OF LIFE INC
Also Called: BI Daily
960 Jackson St, San Francisco (94133-4809)
PHONE..................................415 297-6765
Trung Vu, *CEO*
EMP: 150 **EST:** 2016
SALES: 7.2MM **Privately Held**
SIC: 7371 Computer software systems analysis & design, custom

(P-15023)
BENTLEY SYSTEMS INCORPORATED
1600 Riviera Ave Ste 300, Walnut Creek (94596-3570)
PHONE..................................925 933-2525
EMP: 80
SALES (corp-wide): 854.3MM **Privately Held**
SIC: 7371 8711
PA: Bentley Systems, Incorporated
685 Stockton Dr
Exton PA 19341
610 458-5000

(P-15024)
BIG BULB IDEAS INC
Also Called: Installmonetizer
5655 Silver Creek Vlley R, San Jose (95138-2473)
PHONE..................................408 888-2346
Vince Mundy, *CEO*
Lloyd Jacob, *Risk Mgmt Dir*
EMP: 50
SQ FT: 400
SALES: 20MM **Privately Held**
SIC: 7371 Computer software systems analysis & design, custom

(P-15025)
BIOCLINCA (PA)
Also Called: Synarc's
7707 Gateway Blvd Fl 3, Newark (94560-1160)
PHONE..................................415 817-8900
Claus Christiansen, *CEO*
Harry K Genant, *Chairman*
Aaron Timm, *Vice Pres*
John Leonard, *Administration*
Arkady Gliner, *Sr Software Eng*
EMP: 153
SQ FT: 40,000
SALES (est): 44MM **Privately Held**
WEB: www.synarc.com
SIC: 7371 Computer software development & applications

(P-15026)
BIRST INC
45 Fremont St Ste 1800, San Francisco (94105-2219)
PHONE..................................415 766-4800
Jay Larson, *CEO*
Samuel Wolff, *CFO*
Carl Tsukahara, *Chief Mktg Ofcr*
Brad Peters, *Officer*
Paul Staelin, *Officer*
EMP: 300
SQ FT: 36,171
SALES (est): 61.1MM
SALES (corp-wide): 3.1B **Privately Held**
SIC: 7371 Computer software development
HQ: Infor, Inc.
641 Ave Of The Americas # 4
New York NY 10011
646 336-1700

(P-15027)
BITFONE CORPORATION (PA)
32451 Golden Lantern # 301, Laguna Niguel (92677-5344)
PHONE..................................949 234-7000
Gene Wang, *President*
Hang Michael Xu, *CFO*
Harri Okkonen, *Senior VP*
Chris Cassapakis, *Vice Pres*
Carla Fitzgerald, *Vice Pres*
EMP: 50 **EST:** 2000
SQ FT: 11,000
SALES (est): 4.3MM **Privately Held**
WEB: www.bitfone.com
SIC: 7371 Computer software development

(P-15028)
BITTORRENT INC
612 Howard St Ste 400, San Francisco (94105-3944)
PHONE..................................408 641-4219
Aseem Mohanty, *President*
Chris Verzello, *Vice Pres*
Jaden Hsu, *Manager*
EMP: 50
SALES: 2MM **Privately Held**
SIC: 7371 Computer software development & applications

(P-15029)
BLACKARROW INC (HQ)
4 N 2nd St Ste 1100, San Jose (95113-1308)
PHONE..................................408 642-6400
Nick Troiano, *CEO*
Stephanie Mitchko-Beale, *COO*
Jonathan Batt, *CFO*
EMP: 55
SQ FT: 10,000
SALES (est): 10.8MM **Privately Held**
SIC: 7371 Computer software development & applications

(P-15030)
BLUEBEAM INC (PA)
55 S Lake Ave Ste 900, Pasadena (91101-2627)
PHONE..................................626 788-4100
Jon Elliott, *CEO*
Richard Lee, *President*
Jim Atkinson, *Officer*
EMP: 200
SALES (est): 33.4MM **Privately Held**
WEB: www.bluebeam.com
SIC: 7371 Computer software development

(P-15031)
BLUFOCUS INC
2233 N Ontario St 130, Burbank (91504-4503)
PHONE..................................818 294-7695
Paulette E Pantoja, *CEO*
Jake Ramirez, *Business Dir*
Paul Chang, *Office Mgr*
Juan Reyes, *CTO*
John Choi, *Production*
EMP: 60
SQ FT: 7,000
SALES (est): 5.9MM **Privately Held**
WEB: www.blufocus.com
SIC: 7371 8748 7379 Software programming applications; systems analysis & engineering consulting services; computer related consulting services

(P-15032)
BOWIE LIMITED
18351 Colima Rd Ste 255, Rowland Heights (91748-2791)
PHONE..................................716 610-2480
Guicai Zhang, *Principal*
EMP: 74 **EST:** 2017
SALES: 235K **Privately Held**
SIC: 7371 Computer software development & applications

(P-15033)
BPO MANAGEMENT SERVICES INC (PA)
8175 E Kaiser Blvd 100, Anaheim (92808-2214)
PHONE..................................714 972-2670
Patrick A Dolan, *Ch of Bd*
James Cortens, *President*
Donald W Rutherford, *CFO*
Koushik Dutta, *CTO*
Marc Maraccini, *Sales Staff*
EMP: 73
SQ FT: 5,871
SALES (est): 28.1MM **Privately Held**
SIC: 7371 Computer software development

(P-15034)
BRACKET GLOBAL LLC
303 2nd St Ste 700, San Francisco (94107-1366)
PHONE..................................415 293-1340
Kristen Dellaroca, *Branch Mgr*
Tony Puppo, *Associate Dir*
Simone Robinson, *Human Res Dir*
Eric Phanthavong, *Director*
EMP: 100
SALES (corp-wide): 64.2MM **Privately Held**
SIC: 7371 8748 Computer software development; telecommunications consultant
PA: Bracket Global Llc
575 E Swedesford Rd # 200
Wayne PA 19087
610 225-5900

(P-15035)
BRIENCE INC (DH)
Also Called: A Development Stage Company
128 Spear St Fl 3, San Francisco (94105-5147)
PHONE..................................415 974-5300
Roderick McGeary, *Ch of Bd*
James Drumright, *COO*
Stephen E Recht, *CFO*
Keyur Patel, *Officer*
Mark Losh, *Senior VP*
EMP: 90
SQ FT: 15,000
SALES (est): 10.1MM
SALES (corp-wide): 793.5MM **Privately Held**
WEB: www.brience.com
SIC: 7371 Computer software development & applications

(P-15036)
BRIGHTEDGE TECHNOLOGIES INC (PA)
989 E Hillsdale Blvd, Foster City (94404-2113)
PHONE..................................800 578-8023
Jim Yu, *President*
Krish Kumar, *COO*
Jim Emerich, *CFO*
William Cabrera, *Vice Pres*
Joshua Crossman, *Vice Pres*
EMP: 134
SALES (est): 90MM **Privately Held**
SIC: 7371 5045 Computer software development; computers, peripherals & software

(P-15037)
BRIGHTERION INC
150 Spear St Ste 1000, San Francisco (94105-5116)
PHONE..................................415 986-5600
Akli Adjaoute, *CEO*
EMP: 62
SQ FT: 15,000
SALES: 4MM **Privately Held**
WEB: www.brighterion.com
SIC: 7371 Computer software development

(P-15038)
BRISTLECONE INCORPORATED
10 Almaden Blvd Ste 600, San Jose (95113-2226)
PHONE..................................650 386-4000
Irfan A Khan, *President*
Naresh Hingorani, *Vice Pres*
Kulashekar Raghavan, *Vice Pres*
Bhaskar Ramanasundaram, *Vice Pres*
Tom Rauch, *Vice Pres*
EMP: 1300 **EST:** 1998
SQ FT: 10,000
SALES (est): 88.5MM
SALES (corp-wide): 7.4B **Privately Held**
WEB: www.bcone.com
SIC: 7371 8742 Software programming applications; management consulting services
PA: Mahindra And Mahindra Limited
Mahindra Towers, Dr. G M Bosale Marg
Mumbai MH 40001
222 490-1441

(P-15039)
BROADSOFT CONTACT CENTER INC
930 Hamlin Ct, Sunnyvale (94089-1401)
PHONE..................................408 338-0900
Prem Uppaluru, *CEO*
Arnab Mishra, *President*
Mike Shannahan, *CFO*
Gaya Vukkadala, *Senior VP*
Mukesh Sundaram, *CTO*
EMP: 50
SQ FT: 15,000
SALES (est): 6.9MM
SALES (corp-wide): 48B **Publicly Held**
SIC: 7371 8742 Computer software systems analysis & design, custom; management information systems consultant
HQ: Broadsoft, Inc.
9737 Washingtonian Blvd # 350
Gaithersburg MD 20878
301 977-9440

(P-15040)
BUILDINGMINDS INC
1200 Seaport Blvd, Redwood City (94063-5537)
PHONE..................................973 397-6510
Thomas Sparno, *Principal*
EMP: 50
SALES: 5MM **Privately Held**
SIC: 7371 Computer software development & applications

(P-15041)
BULLUP INC
4365 Via Scorpresa, San Diego (92124)
PHONE....................................566 997-2543
Xiangyu Sun, *CEO*
EMP: 50
SALES (est): 772K **Privately Held**
SIC: 7371 Computer software development & applications

(P-15042)
BY WIND INC
Also Called: Blue Harbor
15 Enterprise Ste 520, Aliso Viejo (92656-2656)
PHONE....................................949 385-6219
Jeffrey Danford, *CEO*
Jennifer Heil, *President*
Lisa Tran, *Finance Mgr*
Dan Charest, *Director*
EMP: 52
SQ FT: 4,500
SALES: 5MM **Privately Held**
SIC: 7371 6163 Computer software development; loan brokers

(P-15043)
BYND LLC
100 Montgomery St # 1102, San Francisco (94104-4331)
PHONE....................................415 944-2293
Nicholas Rappolt, *CEO*
Matthew Iliffe, *Partner*
Matt Basford, *General Mgr*
Denise Zocchi, *Project Mgr*
James Williams, *Finance*
EMP: 100 EST: 2004
SALES (est): 424.9K
SALES (corp-wide): 262.9MM **Privately Held**
SIC: 7371 Computer software development & applications
PA: Next Fifteen Communications Group Plc
75 Bermondsey Street
London SE1 3
207 908-6444

(P-15044)
C9 INC
177 Bovet Rd Ste 520, San Mateo (94402-3144)
PHONE....................................650 561-7855
Michael Howard, *CEO*
Stephen Lucas, *CFO*
Andy Twigg, *CTO*
EMP: 85
SALES (est): 44.1K
SALES (corp-wide): 85.8MM **Privately Held**
SIC: 7371 Software programming applications
PA: Insidesales.Com, Inc.
34 E 1700 S Ste A113
Provo UT 84606
801 754-9940

(P-15045)
CAKE CORPORATION
101 Redwood Ave, Redwood City (94061)
PHONE....................................650 215-7777
Mani Kulasooriya, *CEO*
Brian Beach, *Senior VP*
Shanil Fernando, *Vice Pres*
Paul Kelaita, *Vice Pres*
Jim O'Connor, *Vice Pres*
EMP: 100 EST: 2010
SALES (est): 1.4MM **Privately Held**
SIC: 7371 Computer software development & applications

(P-15046)
CALLFIRE INC
1410 2nd St Ste 200, Santa Monica (90401-3349)
PHONE....................................213 221-2289
Michel Veys, *Principal*
Komnieve Singh, *President*
Tj Thinakaran, *COO*
Tridivesh Kidambi, *CFO*
Vijesh Mehta, *Corp Secy*
EMP: 61
SALES (est): 13MM **Privately Held**
WEB: www.skyyconsulting.com
SIC: 7371 Computer software development

(P-15047)
CALLIDUS SOFTWARE INC (HQ)
Also Called: Calliduscloud
4140 Dublin Blvd Ste 400, Dublin (94568-7757)
PHONE....................................925 251-2200
Leslie Stretch, *President*
Roxanne Oulman, *CFO*
Mark Culhane, *Bd of Directors*
Kevin Klausmeyer, *Bd of Directors*
Murray Rode, *Bd of Directors*
EMP: 148
SQ FT: 109,000
SALES: 253MM
SALES (corp-wide): 27.6B **Privately Held**
WEB: www.callidussoftware.com
SIC: 7371 7372 Custom computer programming services; business oriented computer software
PA: Sap Se
Dietmar-Hopp-Allee 16
Walldorf 69190
622 774-7474

(P-15048)
CAMPAIGN MONITOR USA INC
123 Mission St Fl 26, San Francisco (94105-5140)
PHONE....................................888 533-8098
Alex Bard, *CEO*
EMP: 100 EST: 2014
SALES (est): 1.4MM
SALES (corp-wide): 89MM **Privately Held**
SIC: 7371 Computer software development
HQ: Campaign Monitor Pty Ltd
L38 201-5 Elizabeth St
Sydney NSW 2000
285 187-100

(P-15049)
CAPE CLEAR SOFTWARE INC
Also Called: Capeconnect
900 E Hamilton Ave # 100, Campbell (95008-0664)
PHONE....................................408 879-7365
Annrai O'Toole, *CEO*
David Clark, *Vice Pres*
James Pasley, *CTO*
EMP: 85 EST: 1999
SALES (est): 2.6MM **Privately Held**
WEB: www.capeclear.com
SIC: 7371 Computer software development

(P-15050)
CARBONFIVE INCORPORATED
Also Called: Carbon Five
585 Howard St Fl 2, San Francisco (94105-4677)
PHONE....................................415 546-0500
Don Thompson, *COO*
David Hendee, *Partner*
Mike Wynholds, *CEO*
James Brennan, *Software Dev*
Thomas Fisher, *Software Dev*
EMP: 62
SALES (est): 6.9MM **Privately Held**
WEB: www.carbonfive.com
SIC: 7371 Computer software development & applications

(P-15051)
CASK TECHNOLOGIES LLC (PA)
9350 Waxie Way Ste 210, San Diego (92123-1005)
P.O. Box 80337 (92138-0337)
PHONE....................................858 458-9951
Elizabeth Guezzale, *President*
Vanessa Dover, *Officer*
Gene Giraud, *Executive*
Michael Lemon, *General Mgr*
Zaid Omar, *General Mgr*
EMP: 180
SALES: 46.2MM **Privately Held**
SIC: 7371 7379 8742 8748 Computer software development & applications; computer related consulting services; management consulting services; business consulting; engineering services

(P-15052)
CATAPHORA INC (PA)
3425 Edison Way, Menlo Park (94025-1813)
P.O. Box 2007 (94026-2007)
PHONE....................................650 622-9840
Elizabeth B Charnock, *President*
EMP: 60
SQ FT: 25,000
SALES (est): 11.3MM **Privately Held**
WEB: www.cataphora.com
SIC: 7371 Computer software development

(P-15053)
CENTRIFY CORPORATION (PA)
3300 Tannery Way, Santa Clara (95054-2828)
PHONE....................................669 444-5200
Tom Kemp, *President*
Ally Zwahlen, *President*
Tim Steinkopf, *CFO*
Timothy Steinkopf, *CFO*
Bill Mann, *Senior VP*
EMP: 124
SQ FT: 8,300
SALES (est): 95.3MM **Privately Held**
WEB: www.centrify.com
SIC: 7371 Computer software development

(P-15054)
CERTENT INC (PA)
1548 Eureka Rd Ste 100, Roseville (95661-3083)
PHONE....................................925 730-4300
Michael Boese, *CEO*
Gordon Rausser, *Ch of Bd*
Ryan Stroub, *CFO*
Judy Ash, *Chief Mktg Ofcr*
Evan Condran, *Vice Pres*
EMP: 173
SALES (est): 34.4MM **Privately Held**
WEB: www.easiadmin.com
SIC: 7371 Computer software development

(P-15055)
CHASE CREDIT SYSTEMS INC
300 E Magnolia Blvd # 502, Burbank (91502-1145)
PHONE....................................818 762-6262
Perry Cohan, *President*
Ben Cohan, *Vice Pres*
EMP: 95
SALES (est): 3.9MM
SALES (corp-wide): 5.7B **Publicly Held**
SIC: 7371 Computer software systems analysis & design, custom
PA: Fiserv, Inc.
255 Fiserv Dr
Brookfield WI 53045
262 879-5000

(P-15056)
CHELSIO COMMUNICATIONS INC
209 N Fair Oaks Ave, Sunnyvale (94085-4423)
PHONE....................................408 962-3600
Kianoosh Naghshineh, *President*
William Delaney, *CFO*
Danny Gur, *Vice Pres*
Mehdi Mohtashemi, *Vice Pres*
Kun Taek Yim, *Vice Pres*
EMP: 130
SQ FT: 20,000
SALES (est): 19.5MM **Privately Held**
WEB: www.chelsio.com
SIC: 7371 Computer software systems analysis & design, custom
PA: Chelsio Communications Private Limited
2 Floor, Uniworth Plaza,
Bengaluru KA

(P-15057)
CHEQUE GUARD INC
512 S Verdugo Dr, Burbank (91502-2344)
PHONE....................................818 563-9335
Emil Ramzy, *President*
Alfred Ramzi, *CEO*
Louris Khalaf, *COO*
EMP: 54 EST: 2002
SQ FT: 6,000

(P-15058)
CHROME RIVER TECHNOLOGIES INC (PA)
5757 Wilshire Blvd # 270, Los Angeles (90036-5814)
PHONE....................................323 857-5800
Alan Richeimer, *President*
Elizabeth Meek, *Partner*
Dave Terry, *COO*
Daniel Machock, *CFO*
Julie Norquist Roy, *Chief Mktg Ofcr*
EMP: 53
SALES (est): 47.6MM **Privately Held**
SIC: 7371 Computer software development

SALES: 1.6MM **Privately Held**
SIC: 7371 2893 Computer software development; printing ink

(P-15059)
CIE GAMES LLC
500 Howard St Ste 300, San Francisco (94105-3027)
PHONE....................................415 800-6100
Dennis Suggs, *President*
Eric Ludwig, *CFO*
EMP: 50
SALES (est): 2.5MM
SALES (corp-wide): 286.8MM **Publicly Held**
SIC: 7371 Computer software development & applications
PA: Glu Mobile Inc.
875 Howard St Ste 100
San Francisco CA 94103
415 800-6100

(P-15060)
CIMATRON GIBBS LLC
Also Called: Gibbs & Associates
323 Science Dr, Moorpark (93021-2092)
PHONE....................................805 523-0004
Bill Gibbs, *Owner*
Jerry Foglesong, *Admin Asst*
Sabrina Hayes, *Administration*
Andy Heffner, *Engineer*
William F Gibbs,
EMP: 61
SQ FT: 22,500
SALES (est): 7.9MM **Publicly Held**
WEB: www.gibbsnc.com
SIC: 7371 Computer software development
PA: 3d Systems Corporation
333 Three D Systems Cir
Rock Hill SC 29730

(P-15061)
CITRIX SYSTEMS INC
4988 Great America Pkwy, Santa Clara (95054-1200)
PHONE....................................408 790-8000
Klaus Oerstermann, *Principal*
Janice Savage, *Partner*
Rajiv Sinha, *Vice Pres*
Chris Balzaretti, *Executive*
Gil Rosario, *Executive*
EMP: 95
SALES (corp-wide): 2.8B **Publicly Held**
WEB: www.citrix.com
SIC: 7371 Computer software development
PA: Citrix Systems, Inc.
851 W Cypress Creek Rd
Fort Lauderdale FL 33309
954 267-3000

(P-15062)
CITRUSBITS INC
5776 Stoneridge Mall Rd # 298, Pleasanton (94588-4513)
PHONE....................................925 452-6012
Harry Lee, *CEO*
EMP: 50 EST: 2007
SQ FT: 3,000
SALES (est): 1.5MM **Privately Held**
SIC: 7371 Computer software systems analysis & design, custom

(P-15063)
CLICK LABS INC
315 Montgomery St Fl 8, San Francisco (94104-1803)
PHONE....................................415 658-5227

▲ = Import ▼=Export
◆ =Import/Export

Samar Singla, *CEO*
Sarah Terrazas, *Vice Pres*
Rubal Singh, *Manager*
EMP: 501
SALES (est): 14.9MM **Privately Held**
SIC: 7371 Computer software development

(P-15064)
CLINAPPS INC
9530 Towne Centre Dr # 120, San Diego
(92121-1981)
PHONE.....................858 866-0228
Timothy W Elliott, *President*
Michelle Elliott, *Vice Pres*
Terri Fisher, *Vice Pres*
Tom Alvarez, *Manager*
EMP: 57
SQ FT: 7,000
SALES (est): 2.9MM
SALES (corp-wide): 64.2MM **Privately Held**
SIC: 7371 Computer software development
PA: Bracket Global Llc
575 E Swedesford Rd # 200
Wayne PA 19087
610 225-5900

(P-15065)
CLOUDERA INC (PA)
395 Page Mill Rd Ste 300, Palo Alto
(94306-2066)
PHONE.....................650 362-0488
Thomas J Reilly, *CEO*
Adam Weber, *Partner*
Michael A Olson, *Ch of Bd*
Jim Frankola, *CFO*
Scott Crawford, *Engineer*
EMP: 148
SQ FT: 225,000
SALES: 367.4MM **Publicly Held**
SIC: 7371 Custom computer programming services

(P-15066)
CLOUDPEOPLE GLOBAL
2485 Notre Dame Blvd, Chico
(95928-7161)
PHONE.....................530 591-7028
Sean Worthington, *President*
EMP: 50
SALES (est): 772K **Privately Held**
SIC: 7371 Computer software development & applications

(P-15067)
COGNITIVE MEDICAL SYSTEMS INC
9444 Waples St Ste 300, San Diego
(92121-2942)
PHONE.....................858 509-4949
Mary Lacroix, *CEO*
Doug Burke, *President*
Emory Fry, *CEO*
Ellen Change, *Vice Pres*
Jamie Gerkin, *Vice Pres*
EMP: 60
SQ FT: 12,000
SALES (est): 541.3K **Privately Held**
WEB: WWW.COGNITIVEmedicine.com
SIC: 7371 Computer software development & applications

(P-15068)
COGNITIVECLOUDS SOFTWARE INC
5433 Ontario Cmn, Fremont (94555-2930)
PHONE.....................415 234-3611
Prasanna Gopinath, *Principal*
EMP: 70
SALES (est): 1.1MM **Privately Held**
SIC: 7371 Computer software development & applications

(P-15069)
COMPULAW LLC
200 Crprate Pinte Ste 400, Culver City
(90230)
PHONE.....................310 553-3355
David Kalmick, *Mng Member*
Michael Armstrong,
Stephanie Hall,
Lois Kalmick,
Alex Manners,
EMP: 50

SQ FT: 15,000
SALES (est): 2.4MM
SALES (corp-wide): 4.6B **Publicly Held**
WEB: www.compulaw.com
SIC: 7371 Computer software development; computer software development & applications; software programming applications
HQ: Aderant Holdings, Inc.
500 Northridge Rd Ste 800
Atlanta GA 30350

(P-15070)
COMPUTER PROC UNLIMITED INC
Also Called: Cpu Medical Management Systems
9235 Activity Rd Ste 104, San Diego
(92126-4440)
PHONE.....................858 530-0875
Michael Stringer, *President*
Brian Castle, *CFO*
Doug Allem, *Treasurer*
Jean Campbell, *Senior VP*
Herald Bing, *Vice Pres*
EMP: 65
SQ FT: 11,250
SALES (est): 7.8MM
SALES (corp-wide): 208.3B **Publicly Held**
WEB: www.cpumms.com
SIC: 7371 5045 Computer software systems analysis & design, custom; computer peripheral equipment
PA: Mckesson Corporation
1 Post St Fl 18
San Francisco CA 94104
415 983-8300

(P-15071)
COMPUTER RESOURCES GROUP INC
275 Battery St Ste 800, San Francisco
(94111-3364)
PHONE.....................415 398-3535
Richard D Green, *Ch of Bd*
Allen Prestegard, *President*
EMP: 250
SQ FT: 12,000
SALES (est): 8.1MM **Privately Held**
SIC: 7371 7379 Custom computer programming services; computer related consulting services

(P-15072)
COMPUTER TASK GROUP INC
2033 Gateway Pl Fl 5, San Jose
(95110-3709)
PHONE.....................408 573-6070
Randolph A Marks, *Branch Mgr*
EMP: 230
SALES (corp-wide): 301.2MM **Publicly Held**
SIC: 7371 Custom computer programming services
PA: Computer Task Group, Incorporated
800 Delaware Ave
Buffalo NY 14209
716 882-8000

(P-15073)
COMPUTER TASK GROUP INC
Also Called: Ctg
101 Metro Dr Ste 530, San Jose
(95110-1341)
PHONE.....................800 992-5350
Larry Comstock, *Sales/Mktg Mgr*
EMP: 300
SALES (corp-wide): 301.2MM **Publicly Held**
WEB: www.ctg.com
SIC: 7371 7373 Custom computer programming services; computer systems analysis & design
PA: Computer Task Group, Incorporated
800 Delaware Ave
Buffalo NY 14209
716 882-8000

(P-15074)
COMPUTRITION INC (HQ)
8521 Fllbrook Ave Ste 100, Canoga Park
(91360)
P.O. Box 4689, Chatsworth (91313-4689)
PHONE.....................818 961-3999

Scott Saklad, *President*
Kim C Goldberg, *Vice Pres*
EMP: 60
SQ FT: 16,763
SALES (est): 12.9MM
SALES (corp-wide): 2.4B **Privately Held**
WEB: www.computrition.com
SIC: 7371 7372 Computer software development; prepackaged software
PA: Constellation Software Inc
20 Adelaide St E Suite 1200
Toronto ON M5C 2
416 861-2279

(P-15075)
COMPVUE INC
440 N Wolfe Rd, Sunnyvale (94085-3869)
PHONE.....................408 892-9909
Rakesh Gupta, *CEO*
Velu P Padmanabhan, *Technology*
EMP: 70
SALES: 981.7K **Privately Held**
SIC: 7371 Computer software development

(P-15076)
CONCERRO INC (DH)
9276 Scranton Rd Ste 400, San Diego
(92121-7714)
PHONE.....................858 882-8500
Graham Barnes, *CEO*
Cindy Watson, *COO*
Derrick Clackenbush, *CFO*
Michael E Meisel, *Vice Pres*
EMP: 60
SQ FT: 16,000
SALES (est): 5.9MM
SALES (corp-wide): 122B **Publicly Held**
SIC: 7371 Computer software development
HQ: Api Healthcare Corporation
1550 Innovation Way
Hartford WI 53027
262 673-6815

(P-15077)
CONNOTATE TECHNOLOGIES INC
2601 Main St Ste 830, Irvine (92614-5219)
PHONE.....................949 270-1916
Keith Cooper, *CEO*
Jake Roach, *Manager*
EMP: 50
SALES (corp-wide): 9.2MM **Privately Held**
SIC: 7371 Computer software writing services
PA: Connotate Technologies Inc.
317 George St Ste 320
New Brunswick NJ 08901
732 296-8844

(P-15078)
CONVERSEAI INC (HQ)
548 Market St, San Francisco
(94104-5401)
PHONE.....................415 919-7891
Anthony Lucas, *CEO*
EMP: 182
SALES (est): 32.2K
SALES (corp-wide): 111.2MM **Publicly Held**
SIC: 7371 Computer software development & applications
PA: Smartsheet Inc.
10500 Ne 8th St Ste 1300
Bellevue WA 98004
844 324-2360

(P-15079)
CORELYNX INC
11501 Dublin Blvd Ste 200, Dublin
(94568-2827)
PHONE.....................877 267-3599
Manash Chaudhuri, *CEO*
EMP: 103
SQ FT: 500
SALES (est): 3MM **Privately Held**
SIC: 7371 Computer software development

(P-15080)
CORETECHS STAFFING INC
50 Woodside Plz Ste 604, Redwood City
(94061-2500)
PHONE.....................650 363-7960

Andrew Adelman, *President*
Randall Stratton, *Principal*
EMP: 55
SALES (est): 5.7MM **Privately Held**
SIC: 7371 Computer software systems analysis & design, custom

(P-15081)
CORPTAX LLC
21550 Oxnard St Ste 700, Woodland Hills
(91367-7170)
PHONE.....................818 316-2400
Corey Caudill, *Technology*
EMP: 60 **Privately Held**
SIC: 7371 Computer software development
PA: Corptax, Llc
2100 E Lake Cook Rd # 800
Buffalo Grove IL 60089

(P-15082)
COURSERA INC (PA)
381 E Evelyn Ave, Mountain View
(94041-1530)
PHONE.....................650 963-9884
Jeff Maggioncalda, *CEO*
Lila Ibrahim, *COO*
John Madigan, *CFO*
Nikhil Sinha, *Officer*
Charlotte Crawford, *Admin Sec*
EMP: 52
SALES (est): 17.6MM **Privately Held**
SIC: 7371 Computer software development & applications

(P-15083)
COVERITY LLC (HQ)
185 Berry St Ste 6500, San Francisco
(94107-1728)
PHONE.....................415 321-5200
Anthony Bettencourt, *President*
Andy Chou, *President*
Jennifer Johnson, *Chief Mktg Ofcr*
Dave Peterson, *Chief Mktg Ofcr*
Matt Green, *Officer*
EMP: 80
SALES (est): 25.8MM
SALES (corp-wide): 2.7B **Publicly Held**
WEB: www.coverity.com
SIC: 7371 7372 Custom computer programming services; computer software development; software programming applications; prepackaged software
PA: Synopsys, Inc.
690 E Middlefield Rd
Mountain View CA 94043
650 584-5000

(P-15084)
CREATIVEBUG LLC
835 Market St Ste 700, San Francisco
(94103-1906)
PHONE.....................415 325-5926
Ursula Morgan, *CEO*
Julie Roehm, *Opers Staff*
EMP: 122
SALES (est): 13.5MM
SALES (corp-wide): 2.9B **Privately Held**
SIC: 7371 Computer software development & applications
HQ: Jo-Ann Stores, Llc
5555 Darrow Rd
Hudson OH 44236
330 656-2600

(P-15085)
CRESCENT STAFFING INC (PA)
Also Called: Crescent Solutions
17871 Mitchell N Ste 100, Irvine
(92614-6050)
PHONE.....................949 724-0304
Brian Fischbein, *CEO*
Pj Viloski, *President*
Nico Andino McGraw, *Business Mgr*
EMP: 195
SALES (est): 31.2MM **Privately Held**
WEB: www.crescent-enterprise.com
SIC: 7371 8748 7379 Computer software development; business consulting; computer related consulting services

PRODUCTS & SVCS

(P-15086)
CROSSCAP MEDIA SERVICES INC (PA)
311 California St Ste 320, San Francisco (94104-2605)
PHONE..................415 217-8860
Kenneth Craig Bushert, *President*
EMP: 72 EST: 2010
SALES (est): 5.9MM **Privately Held**
SIC: 7371 Computer software development; computer software development & applications

(P-15087)
CROSSLINK PROF TAX SLTIONS LLC (PA)
7575 W Linne Rd, Tracy (95304-9290)
P.O. Box 611 (95378-0611)
PHONE..................209 835-1360
Leroy E Petz, *President*
Charles W Petz, *Treasurer*
Reynold F Sbrilli, *Officer*
Reynold Sbrilli, *Officer*
Craig Petz, *Vice Pres*
EMP: 65
SALES (est): 22.1MM **Privately Held**
WEB: www.petzent.com
SIC: 7371 Software programming applications; computer software development & applications; computer software development

(P-15088)
CSC COVANSYS CORPORATION
34740 Tuxedo Cmn, Fremont (94555-2746)
PHONE..................510 304-3430
Chris Pensy, *Manager*
EMP: 150
SALES (corp-wide): 24.5B **Publicly Held**
SIC: 7371 Custom computer programming services
HQ: Csc Covansys Corporation
3170 Fairview Park Dr
Falls Church VA 22042
703 876-1000

(P-15089)
CSRA LLC
2727 Hamner Ave, Norco (92860-1927)
PHONE..................951 898-3015
Dennis Plambeck, *Manager*
EMP: 100
SALES (corp-wide): 30.9B **Publicly Held**
WEB: www.csc.com
SIC: 7371 Custom computer programming services
HQ: Csra Llc
3170 Fairview Park Dr
Falls Church VA 22042
703 641-2000

(P-15090)
CSS HOLDINGS INC
Also Called: Live Pos
7486 La Jolla Blvd, La Jolla (92037-5029)
PHONE..................888 884-9224
Liad Biton, *CEO*
Sammy Kahen, *President*
EMP: 70
SQ FT: 5,000
SALES (est): 5.8MM **Privately Held**
SIC: 7371 7379 Computer software development; computer related consulting services

(P-15091)
CU DIRECT CORPORATION (PA)
Also Called: Cudc
2855 E Guasti Rd Ste 500, Ontario (91761-1253)
P.O. Box 51482 (91761-0082)
PHONE..................909 481-2300
Antony Boutelle, *President*
Craig S Montesanti, *CFO*
Jerry Neemann, *Officer*
Kip Haas, *Exec VP*
Joe Greenwald, *Senior VP*
EMP: 175
SQ FT: 30,000
SALES (est): 60MM **Privately Held**
SIC: 7371 Computer software development

(P-15092)
CYBERDEFENDER CORPORATION
617 W 7th St Fl 10, Los Angeles (90017-3879)
PHONE..................323 449-0774
Kevin Harris, *CEO*
Igor Barash, *COO*
Sarah B Hicks, *Senior VP*
Steven R Okun, *Senior VP*
EMP: 379
SALES (est): 23.7MM **Privately Held**
WEB: www.networkdynamics.com
SIC: 7371 7372 Custom computer programming services; prepackaged software

(P-15093)
DAQRI LLC (PA)
1201 W 5th St Ste T800, Los Angeles (90017-1452)
PHONE..................213 375-8830
Roy Ashok, *CEO*
Robert Brass, *CFO*
Michael Lynch, *Officer*
Phil Greenhalgh, *Vice Pres*
Igor Komir, *Vice Pres*
EMP: 72 EST: 2007
SALES (est): 43.4MM **Privately Held**
SIC: 7371 Computer software development

(P-15094)
DASSAULT SYSTEMES AMERICAS
6320 Canoga Ave Fl 3, Woodland Hills (91367-2573)
PHONE..................818 999-2500
Kendall Pond, *President*
Paul Eberl, *Partner*
Holly Stratford, *President*
Thibault De Tersant, *CFO*
Victor Luster, *Info Tech Mgr*
EMP: 133
SALES (corp-wide): 1.7B **Privately Held**
SIC: 7371 Computer software development
HQ: Dassault Systemes Americas Corp.
175 Wyman St
Waltham MA 02451
781 810-3000

(P-15095)
DAYBREAK GAME COMPANY LLC
15051 Avenue Of Science, San Diego (92128-3430)
PHONE..................858 239-0500
John Smedley,
David Youssefi, *Vice Pres*
Jason Fermo, *Sr Ntwrk Engine*
Jeff Bolaris, *Technology*
Jennifer Perkins, *Counsel*
EMP: 450
SALES (est): 95.7MM **Privately Held**
SIC: 7371 Computer software development

(P-15096)
DAZ SYSTEMS LLC (DH)
880 Apollo St Ste 201, El Segundo (90245-4783)
PHONE..................310 640-1300
Walt Zipperman, *CEO*
Deborah Arnold, *President*
David Binkley, *COO*
Kevin Koontz, *Vice Pres*
Adam Stafford, *Vice Pres*
EMP: 60
SQ FT: 2,600
SALES (est): 46.5MM **Privately Held**
SIC: 7371 7372 Computer software development & applications; prepackaged software
HQ: Accenture Llp
161 N Clark St Ste 1100
Chicago IL 60601
312 693-0161

(P-15097)
DCM TECHNOLOGIES INC
Also Called: D C M Data Systems
39159 Paseo Padre Pkwy # 303, Fremont (94538-1698)
PHONE..................510 791-2182

Janakiram Kaki, *Vice Pres*
AC Biji, *Technology*
Mul Chand, *Technology*
Sanjeev Jain, *Senior Mgr*
Shilpa Kumari, *Manager*
EMP: 100
SALES (est): 11MM **Privately Held**
WEB: www.dcmds.com
SIC: 7371 Computer software systems analysis & design, custom
PA: Baap Technologies India Private Limited
No. 7
Coimbatore TN
422 259-0095

(P-15098)
DEALERSOCKET INC (PA)
100 Avenida La Pata, San Clemente (92673-6304)
P.O. Box 74866 (92673-0163)
PHONE..................949 900-0300
Sejal Pietrzak, *President*
Jose Arcilla, *COO*
Cameron Darby, *COO*
Gary Ito, *CFO*
Matthew Redden, *Vice Pres*
EMP: 60
SALES (est): 104.3MM **Privately Held**
WEB: www.firesocket.com
SIC: 7371 Computer software systems analysis & design, custom

(P-15099)
DECARTA INC
1455 Market St Fl 4, San Francisco (94103-1355)
PHONE..................408 294-8400
Kim J Fennell, *President*
Michael Seifert, *CFO*
Brent Hamby, *Vice Pres*
EMP: 96
SQ FT: 17,000
SALES (est): 10.1MM
SALES (corp-wide): 750.5MM **Privately Held**
WEB: www.decarta.com
SIC: 7371 Computer software development
PA: Uber Technologies, Inc.
1455 Market St Fl 4
San Francisco CA 94103

(P-15100)
DEMANDTEC LLC
1 Franklin Pkwy Bldg 910, San Mateo (94403-1906)
PHONE..................914 499-1900
Daniel R Fishback, *President*
William R Phelps, *COO*
Mark A Culhane, *CFO*
Michael A Bromme, *Senior VP*
EMP: 340
SQ FT: 82,000
SALES (est): 550.4K
SALES (corp-wide): 79.1B **Publicly Held**
WEB: www.demandtec.com
SIC: 7371 Computer software development
PA: International Business Machines Corporation
1 New Orchard Rd Ste 1 # 1
Armonk NY 10504
914 499-1900

(P-15101)
DENA CORP
185 Berry St Ste 3000, San Francisco (94107-1799)
PHONE..................415 375-3170
Shintaro Asako, *Principal*
Hiroaki Tokuda, *Asst Controller*
Kaiser Ng, *Finance*
EMP: 99 EST: 2014
SALES (est): 7.4MM **Privately Held**
SIC: 7371 Computer software development & applications

(P-15102)
DENKEN SOLUTIONS INC
220 Technology Dr Ste 220 # 220, Irvine (92618-2424)
PHONE..................949 630-5263
Rajendra Maddula, *Director*
Eddie Gallardo, *CEO*

Ephraim John, *IT/INT Sup*
Zufi Anna, *Technical Staff*
Raju Shanti, *Recruiter*
EMP: 120 EST: 2013
SQ FT: 4,000
SALES: 17.3MM **Privately Held**
SIC: 7371 8742 8748 Computer software systems analysis & design, custom; computer software development & applications; management consulting services; business consulting; systems analysis & engineering consulting services

(P-15103)
DEVICE ANYWHERE
777 Mariners Isl Blvd # 250, San Mateo (94404-5008)
PHONE..................650 655-6400
Faraz Syed, *Principal*
EMP: 68
SALES (est): 4.2MM **Privately Held**
SIC: 7371

(P-15104)
DEWMOBILE USA INC
2901 Tasman Dr Ste 107, Santa Clara (95054-1137)
PHONE..................408 550-2818
Shangpin Chang, *CTO*
EMP: 50
SALES (est): 1.5MM **Privately Held**
SIC: 7371 Computer software development & applications

(P-15105)
DFUSION SOFTWARE INC
Also Called: Total Immersion
5900 Wilshire Blvd # 2550, Los Angeles (90036-5013)
PHONE..................323 617-5577
Didier Lesteven, *CEO*
Sylvain Mittoux, *Vice Pres*
Pascal Mobuchon, *Vice Pres*
Bruno Uzzan, *Principal*
EMP: 50
SQ FT: 3,000
SALES (est): 3.8MM **Privately Held**
WEB: www.t-immersion.com
SIC: 7371 Computer software development

(P-15106)
DHAP DIGITAL INC
235 Montgomery St # 1320, San Francisco (94104-2902)
PHONE..................415 962-4900
Philip Dzilvelis, *President*
Arikko Howell, *Principal*
EMP: 50 EST: 1997
SQ FT: 12,000
SALES: 5MM **Privately Held**
WEB: www.dhap.com
SIC: 7371 Computer software systems analysis & design, custom

(P-15107)
DIGICENTURY CORPORATION
2303 Camino Ramon Ste 202, San Ramon (94583-1175)
PHONE..................408 213-0146
Emily Zhang, *CEO*
Weikai Xie, *President*
Jeana Nishihara, *Manager*
EMP: 67
SALES (est): 3.1MM **Privately Held**
WEB: www.digicentury.com
SIC: 7371 Computer software development

(P-15108)
DIGITAL CHOCOLATE INC
1855 S Grant St Ste 200, San Mateo (94402-7017)
PHONE..................650 372-1600
Trip Hawkins, *Ch of Bd*
Cheryl Dalrymple, *CFO*
EMP: 65
SALES (est): 6.5MM **Privately Held**
WEB: www.digitalchocolate.com
SIC: 7371 2741 Computer software development; miscellaneous publishing

(P-15109)
DIGITAL GUARDIAN INC
2101 Tasman Dr Ste 210, Santa Clara
(95054-1020)
PHONE...................................408 716-4200
EMP: 354
SALES (corp-wide): 85.2MM **Privately Held**
SIC: 7371 Computer software development & applications
PA: Digital Guardian, Inc.
860 Winter St Ste 3
Waltham MA 02451
781 788-8180

(P-15110)
DIGITE INC
21060 Homestead Rd # 220, Cupertino
(95014-0204)
PHONE...................................408 418-3834
Suhas S Patil, *Ch of Bd*
A V Sridhar, *CEO*
Raghunath Basavanahalli, *Senior VP*
Sudipta Lahiri, *Senior VP*
Mahesh Singh, *Senior VP*
EMP: 87
SQ FT: 3,000
SALES (est): 6.4MM **Privately Held**
WEB: www.digite.com
SIC: 7371 Computer software development

(P-15111)
DIMENSION DATA CLOUD SOLUTIONS (HQ)
5201 Great America Pkwy # 122, Santa Clara (95054-1125)
PHONE...................................408 567-2000
Robert J Ryan, *CEO*
Rick Dyer, *President*
Ray Solnik, *President*
Bryan Tolls, *CFO*
Richard Dym, *Chief Mktg Ofcr*
EMP: 75
SALES (est): 49.7MM **Privately Held**
WEB: www.opsource.net
SIC: 7371 Computer software development
PA: Dimension Data (Pty) Ltd
The Campus 57 Sloane St
Bryanston GP
115 750-000

(P-15112)
DISNEY INTERACTIVE STUDIOS INC
601 Circle Seven Dr, Glendale
(91201-2332)
PHONE...................................818 560-1000
Peter Casciani, *Manager*
EMP: 120 **Publicly Held**
SIC: 7371 Computer software development
HQ: Disney Interactive Studios, Inc.
500 S Buena Vista St
Burbank CA 91521
818 560-1000

(P-15113)
DISNEY INTERACTIVE STUDIOS INC
681 W Buena Vista St, Burbank
(91521-0001)
PHONE...................................818 553-5000
Gram Hoper, *Branch Mgr*
EMP: 120 **Publicly Held**
SIC: 7371 Computer software development
HQ: Disney Interactive Studios, Inc.
500 S Buena Vista St
Burbank CA 91521
818 560-1000

(P-15114)
DOCKER INC (PA)
144 Townsend St Ste 100, San Francisco
(94107-1915)
PHONE...................................800 764-4847
Steve Singh, *CEO*
James Grant, *Partner*
Dan Guzman, *Partner*
Rahim Ibrahim, *Partner*
Dylan Miller, *Partner*
EMP: 55

SALES (est): 17.8MM **Privately Held**
SIC: 7371 Computer software development & applications

(P-15115)
DOLPHIN IMAGING SYSTEMS LLC
9200 Oakdale Ave Ste 500, Chatsworth
(91311-6556)
PHONE...................................818 435-1368
Chester H Wang,
EMP: 50
SALES (est): 5.7MM
SALES (corp-wide): 5.4B **Publicly Held**
WEB: www.dolphinimaging.com
SIC: 7371 Computer software development
HQ: Patterson Dental Supply, Inc.
1031 Mendota Heights Rd
Saint Paul MN 55120
651 686-1600

(P-15116)
DORADO SOFTWARE INC
Also Called: Visiworks Software
4805 Golden Foothill Pkwy, El Dorado Hills
(95762-9651)
PHONE...................................916 673-1100
Timothy Sebring, *President*
Ed Kucala, *Vice Pres*
Edward Kurzenski, *Vice Pres*
Qiang Xiao, *QA Dir*
Brandon Norgaard, *Software Engr*
EMP: 80
SALES (est): 13MM **Privately Held**
WEB: www.doradosoftware.com
SIC: 7371 Computer software development

(P-15117)
DORANI LIMITED
777 S Alameda St, Los Angeles
(90021-1656)
PHONE...................................213 355-7230
Yan Liu,
EMP: 61
SALES (est): 902.8K **Privately Held**
SIC: 7371 Computer software development & applications

(P-15118)
DP TECHNOLOGY CORP (PA)
Also Called: Esprit
1150 Avenida Acaso, Camarillo
(93012-8719)
PHONE...................................805 388-6000
Daniel Frayssinet, *CEO*
Paul Ricard, *President*
Keith Jablonowski, *Regional Mgr*
Michael York, *Admin Asst*
Graham Starfelt, *Administration*
EMP: 60
SQ FT: 12,000
SALES (est): 18.4MM **Privately Held**
WEB: www.dptechnology.com
SIC: 7371 7373 7372 Computer software development; computer integrated systems design; prepackaged software

(P-15119)
DRAIOS INC
Also Called: Sysdig
1949 5th St Ste 104, Davis (95616-4026)
PHONE...................................916 521-3802
Suresh Vasudevan, *President*
Paul Murphy, *Vice Pres*
Martin Lewald, *Engineer*
Brooke Treseder, *Opers Staff*
Apurva Dave, *VP Mktg*
EMP: 64
SALES (corp-wide): 6.2MM **Privately Held**
SIC: 7371 Computer software development
PA: Draios, Inc.
85 2nd St Fl 8th
San Francisco CA 94105
530 758-2923

(P-15120)
DRCHRONO INC
328 Gibraltar Dr, Sunnyvale (94089-1326)
PHONE...................................650 600-2079
Michael Nusimow, *CEO*
Will Wagner, *President*
Daniel Kivatinos, *COO*

Bennett Thuener, *Vice Pres*
Barbara Gerke, *Office Mgr*
EMP: 50
SALES (est): 3.9MM **Privately Held**
SIC: 7371 Computer software development

(P-15121)
DSP GROUP INC (PA)
691 S Milpitas Blvd # 212, Milpitas
(95035-5478)
PHONE...................................408 986-4300
Ofer Elyakim, *CEO*
Dror Levy, *CFO*
Gabi Seligsohn, *Bd of Directors*
Norman Taffe, *Bd of Directors*
Patrick Tanguy, *Bd of Directors*
EMP: 71
SQ FT: 700
SALES: 124.7MM **Publicly Held**
WEB: www.dspg.com
SIC: 7371 3674 Computer software development; integrated circuits, semiconductor networks, etc.

(P-15122)
DTEX SYSTEMS INC
3055 Olin Ave Ste 2000, San Jose
(95128-2069)
PHONE...................................408 418-3786
Christy Wyatt, *CEO*
Bahman Mahbod, *COO*
Debbie Tuck, *CFO*
Steve Holton, *Officer*
Rajan Koo, *Senior VP*
EMP: 50
SALES (est): 4.9MM **Privately Held**
SIC: 7371 Computer software development

(P-15123)
E A COM INC
209 Redwood Shores Pkwy, Redwood City
(94065-1175)
PHONE...................................650 628-1500
E Stanton Mc Kee, *Exec VP*
Ruth A Kennedy, *Senior VP*
Bryan Neider, *Vice Pres*
EMP: 140
SALES (est): 21.6MM
SALES (corp-wide): 5.1B **Publicly Held**
WEB: www.ea.com
SIC: 7371 Computer software development
PA: Electronic Arts Inc.
209 Redwood Shores Pkwy
Redwood City CA 94065
650 628-1500

(P-15124)
E Z DATA INC (HQ)
251 S Lake Ave Ste 200, Pasadena
(91101-3075)
PHONE...................................626 585-3505
Dale Okuno, *President*
EMP: 51
SALES (est): 5.9MM
SALES (corp-wide): 363.9MM **Publicly Held**
WEB: www.ez-data.com
SIC: 7371 Computer software development
PA: Ebix, Inc.
1 Ebix Way Ste 100
Duluth GA 30097
678 281-2020

(P-15125)
ECONOSOFT INC
2375 Zanker Rd Ste 250, San Jose
(95131-1143)
PHONE...................................408 442-3663
Chander Shaiker, *President*
EMP: 72 **EST:** 2000
SALES (est): 3MM
SALES (corp-wide): 19.8MM **Privately Held**
SIC: 7371 Computer software systems analysis & design, custom
PA: Ace Technologies, Inc.
2375 Zanker Rd Ste 250
San Jose CA 95131
408 324-1203

(P-15126)
EFRONT FINANCIAL SOLUTIONS INC
135 Main St Ste 1330, San Francisco
(94105-1843)
PHONE...................................415 653-3239
Tarek Chouman, *CEO*
Matthew Bagley, *CFO*
Thibaut De Laval, *Chief Mktg Ofcr*
Tom Gardner, *Security Dir*
Michael Bischoff, *CTO*
EMP: 88
SALES (est): 1.3MM **Privately Held**
SIC: 7371 Computer software development & applications

(P-15127)
EGNYTE INC (PA)
1350 W Middlefield Rd, Mountain View
(94043-3061)
PHONE...................................650 968-4018
Vineet Jain, *President*
Jase Eskildsen, *Partner*
Kevin Patterson, *Partner*
Ben Rice, *President*
Benjamin Rice, *President*
EMP: 88 **EST:** 2008
SALES (est): 44.3MM **Privately Held**
SIC: 7371 Computer software development

(P-15128)
EHEALTHINSURANCE SERVICES INC
Also Called: Ehealth Insurance.com
11910 Foundation Pl # 100, Gold River
(95670-4537)
PHONE...................................916 608-6101
Robert Hurley, *Branch Mgr*
EMP: 120
SALES (corp-wide): 172.3MM **Publicly Held**
WEB: www.anysure.com
SIC: 7371 Computer software development
HQ: Ehealthinsurance Services, Inc.
440 E Middlefield Rd
Mountain View CA 94043
650 584-2700

(P-15129)
EINFOCHIPS INC (HQ)
2025 Gateway Pl Ste 270, San Jose
(95110-1007)
PHONE...................................408 496-1882
Pratul Shroff, *CEO*
Raj Sirohi, *COO*
Sribash Dey, *Exec VP*
Abhishek Binaykia, *Vice Pres*
Vijayaragavan Krishnaswamy, *Sr Software Eng*
EMP: 149
SQ FT: 6,178
SALES (est): 1.6B
SALES (corp-wide): 26.8B **Publicly Held**
SIC: 7371 7373 Computer software development; systems software development services; computer systems analysis & design; computer-aided system services; computer-aided design (CAD) systems service
PA: Arrow Electronics, Inc.
9201 E Dry Creek Rd
Centennial CO 80112
303 824-4000

(P-15130)
EINSTEIN INDUSTRIES INC
Also Called: Einstein Dental
6825 Flanders Dr, San Diego (92121-2905)
PHONE...................................858 459-1182
Robert C Silkey, *President*
Sergiy Zubatiy, *COO*
Ted Ricasa, *Vice Pres*
Robert Silkey, *Vice Pres*
John Bihn, *Regional Mgr*
EMP: 180
SALES (est): 26.7MM **Privately Held**
WEB: www.einsteindental.com
SIC: 7371 8742 8322 Computer software development; marketing consulting services; referral service for personal & social problems

(P-15131)
ELASTICSEARCH INC (PA)
800 W El Camino Real # 350, Mountain View (94040-2587)
PHONE..............................650 458-2620
Shay Banon, *CEO*
Lawrence Au, *Partner*
Doug Bleszinski, *President*
Craig Griffin, *President*
Kevin Kluge, *President*
EMP: 64
SQ FT: 30,000
SALES (est): 17.8MM **Privately Held**
SIC: 7371 Computer software development

(P-15132)
ELECTRONICS FOR IMAGING INC (PA)
Also Called: Efi
6750 Dumbarton Cir, Fremont (94555-3616)
PHONE..............................650 357-3500
Gill Cogan, *Ch of Bd*
Annmarie Berg, *Partner*
Bernie Lepore, *Partner*
Tom Offutt, *Partner*
Doug Richards, *Partner*
▼ EMP: 50
SQ FT: 119,000
SALES: 993.2MM **Publicly Held**
WEB: www.vutek.com
SIC: 7371 2899 Computer software development & applications; custom computer programming services; ink or writing fluids

(P-15133)
ELLATION INC (PA)
Also Called: Crunchyroll
835 Market St Ste 700, San Francisco (94103-1906)
PHONE..............................415 796-3560
Tom Pickett, *CEO*
Terry LI, *Vice Pres*
Jason Hubbard, *Info Tech Mgr*
Tristan Lemaster, *Technical Staff*
Robert Moineau, *Technical Staff*
EMP: 200
SALES (est): 4.9MM **Privately Held**
SIC: 7371 5932 Computer software development & applications; used merchandise stores

(P-15134)
ELLIE MAE INC
24025 Park Sorrento # 210, Calabasas (91302-4025)
PHONE..............................818 223-2000
EMP: 497
SALES (corp-wide): 417MM **Publicly Held**
SIC: 7371 Computer software systems analysis & design, custom
PA: Ellie Mae, Inc.
4420 Rosewood Dr Ste 500
Pleasanton CA 94588
925 227-7000

(P-15135)
EMBARCADERO SYSTEMS CORP
1601 Harbor Bay Pkwy # 120, Alameda (94502-3028)
PHONE..............................510 749-7400
Christopher R Redlich Jr, *Chairman*
Richard Beedenbender, *President*
John Sullivan, *Admin Sec*
EMP: 140
SQ FT: 27,000
SALES (est): 11.9MM **Privately Held**
WEB: www.esystem.com
SIC: 7371 Computer software development

(P-15136)
EMBRANE INC
2350 Mission College Blvd # 703, Santa Clara (95054-1556)
PHONE..............................408 550-2700
Bill Burns, *President*
Marco Di Benedetto, *CTO*
EMP: 50
SQ FT: 7,300

SALES (est): 5.3MM **Privately Held**
SIC: 7371 Computer software development

(P-15137)
EMETER CORPORATION
4000 E 3rd Ave Ste 400, Foster City (94404-4827)
PHONE..............................650 227-7770
Lisa Caswell, *President*
Guido Frantzen, *CFO*
Shannon Amerman, *Vice Pres*
Chris King, *Risk Mgmt Dir*
Larsh Johnson, *CTO*
EMP: 130
SQ FT: 30,000
SALES (est): 18.8MM
SALES (corp-wide): 97.7B **Privately Held**
WEB: www.emeter.com
SIC: 7371 Computer software development
HQ: Siemens Industry, Inc.
100 Technology Dr
Alpharetta GA 30005
770 740-3000

(P-15138)
ENGAGE TECHNOLOGIES INC
150 Spear St Ste 400, San Francisco (94105-1537)
PHONE..............................415 829-1400
John Doyle, *CEO*
Derek Newell, *President*
Siobhan Nolan Mangini, *CFO*
EMP: 428
SQ FT: 32,000
SALES (est): 3.8MM **Publicly Held**
SIC: 7371 Computer software systems analysis & design, custom
PA: Castlight Health, Inc.
150 Spear St Ste 400
San Francisco CA 94105
-

(P-15139)
ENVIANCE INC (HQ)
5780 Fleet St Ste 200, Carlsbad (92008-4714)
PHONE..............................760 496-0200
Amy Stelling, *CEO*
David McCurdy, *COO*
Jeffrey Pownell, *CFO*
Craig Ross, *CFO*
Joe McManus, *Vice Pres*
EMP: 69
SQ FT: 10,000
SALES (est): 33.4MM **Privately Held**
WEB: www.enviance.com
SIC: 7371 7374 Custom computer programming services; data processing & preparation

(P-15140)
ENVOY INC
410 Townsend St Ste 410 # 410, San Francisco (94107-1581)
PHONE..............................415 787-7871
Laurentiu Gadea, *CEO*
Kamal Mahyuddin, *Engineer*
Hollie Wegman, *VP Mktg*
Nate Starr, *Sales Staff*
Jon Long, *Manager*
EMP: 100 EST: 2013
SALES (est): 1.6K **Privately Held**
SIC: 7371 Computer software development & applications

(P-15141)
EPITEC INC
515 Olive Ave, Vista (92083-3439)
PHONE..............................760 650-2515
William Grivas, *President*
EMP: 900
SALES (corp-wide): 67MM **Privately Held**
SIC: 7371 Computer software systems analysis & design, custom
PA: Epitec, Inc.
24800 Denso Dr Ste 150
Southfield MI 48033
248 353-6800

(P-15142)
EPITOME ENTERPRISES LLC
821 Mary Pl, Claremont (91711-2273)
PHONE..............................909 625-4728

EMP: 60
SALES: 1.8MM **Privately Held**
WEB: www.epitomeenterprises.com
SIC: 7371

(P-15143)
EQUATOR LLC (HQ)
Also Called: Equator Business Solutions
6060 Center Dr Ste 500, Los Angeles (90045-8857)
PHONE..............................310 469-9500
Chris Saitta, *CEO*
Robert McKinley, *President*
John Vella, *Officer*
Dirk Meillinger, *Vice Pres*
Norm Cunthrampunt, *Admin Asst*
EMP: 200
SALES: 45.4MM **Privately Held**
SIC: 7371 Computer software development & applications

(P-15144)
ESCALATE INC (DH)
Also Called: Escalate Retail
10680 Treena St Ste 170, San Diego (92131-2443)
PHONE..............................858 457-3888
Stewart M Bloom, *CEO*
Mike Larkin, *COO*
Richard Harmatiuk, *Vice Pres*
EMP: 290
SQ FT: 59,000
SALES (est): 27.2MM
SALES (corp-wide): 764.5MM **Privately Held**
SIC: 7371 7373 5045 Custom computer programming services; computer integrated systems design; computers, peripherals & software

(P-15145)
ESSENTIAL PRODUCTS INC
380 Portage Ave, Palo Alto (94306-2244)
PHONE..............................650 300-0000
Andrew E Rubin, *CEO*
Niccolo De Masi, *President*
Meena Srinivasan, *CFO*
Matt Hershenson, *Co-Founder*
EMP: 82
SALES (est): 8MM **Privately Held**
SIC: 7371 Computer software systems analysis & design, custom

(P-15146)
ESTUATE INC
830 Hillview Ct Ste 280, Milpitas (95035-4564)
PHONE..............................408 946-0002
Prakash Balebail, *President*
Marc Hebert, *COO*
Nagaraja Kini, *CFO*
Prasanna Kulkarni, *Assoc VP*
Phil Hodsdon, *Vice Pres*
EMP: 67
SQ FT: 2,558
SALES: 12.3MM **Privately Held**
SIC: 7371 Computer software development

(P-15147)
ETRIGUE CORPORATION
6399 San Ignacio Ave # 200, San Jose (95119-1215)
PHONE..............................408 490-2900
Jeffrey A Holmes, *CEO*
EMP: 50
SQ FT: 43,000
SALES (est): 3.7MM **Privately Held**
SIC: 7371 Computer software development

(P-15148)
EVEG INC
16540 Aston, Irvine (92606-4805)
PHONE..............................844 221-3359
Peter Krish, *Mng Member*
EMP: 50
SALES (est): 215.9K **Privately Held**
SIC: 7371 Computer software development & applications

(P-15149)
EVEREST CONSULTING GROUP INC
39650 Mission Blvd, Fremont (94539-3000)
PHONE..............................510 494-8440
Raj Kamalanathan, *Manager*
EMP: 85
SALES (corp-wide): 21.7MM **Privately Held**
WEB: www.everestconsulting.net
SIC: 7371 Computer software development
PA: Everest Consulting Group Inc.
3840 Park Ave Ste 203
Edison NJ 08820
732 548-2700

(P-15150)
EVERGENT TECHNOLOGIES INC
1250 Borregas Ave, Sunnyvale (94089-1309)
PHONE..............................408 718-5453
Vijay Sajja, *CEO*
Charles Breed, *Senior VP*
Craig Barberich, *Vice Pres*
Bruce Lampert, *Vice Pres*
Sameer Kumar, *Sr Software Eng*
EMP: 57
SQ FT: 2,000
SALES: 5MM **Privately Held**
SIC: 7371 Computer software development

(P-15151)
EVERYONE COUNTS INC
4250 Executive Sq Ste 600, La Jolla (92037-9105)
PHONE..............................858 427-4673
Bill Kuncz, *CEO*
James Simmons, *Vice Pres*
Stefanie Histed, *Executive Asst*
Nissa Burger, *Admin Asst*
Vasiliy Bessonov, *Administration*
EMP: 70
SALES (est): 5.1MM
SALES (corp-wide): 800K **Privately Held**
SIC: 7371 Computer software development
PA: Votem Corp.
50 Public Sq Ste 200
Cleveland OH 44113
216 930-4300

(P-15152)
EVIDENTIO INC (HQ)
7901 Stoneridge Dr # 150, Pleasanton (94588-3677)
PHONE..............................855 933-1337
Mark McLaughlin, *CEO*
EMP: 117
SQ FT: 5,000
SALES: 8MM
SALES (corp-wide): 2.2B **Publicly Held**
SIC: 7371 Computer software systems analysis & design, custom; computer software development & applications
PA: Palo Alto Networks Inc.
3000 Tannery Way
Santa Clara CA 95054
408 753-4000

(P-15153)
EVISIONS INC (PA)
440 Exchange Ste 200, Irvine (92602-1390)
PHONE..............................949 833-1384
Joe Potenza, *President*
Penny Dobbs, *CFO*
Marianne D Jones, *Treasurer*
Adam P Shiell, *Sales Mgr*
EMP: 56
SQ FT: 15,000
SALES (est): 16.8MM **Privately Held**
SIC: 7371 Computer software development

(P-15154)
EVOX PRODUCTIONS LLC (PA)
2363 E Pacifica Pl 305, Compton (90220-6212)
PHONE..............................310 605-1400
David Falstrup,
Carol Falstrup, *CFO*

David Hirsch, *CFO*
Peter Avildsen, *Chief Mktg Ofcr*
Kelley Peters, *Vice Pres*
EMP: 58
SQ FT: 37,500
SALES (est): 11.4MM **Privately Held**
SIC: 7371 7335 Custom computer programming services; commercial photography

(P-15155)
EXIGEN (USA) INC (PA)
Also Called: Exigen Group
345 California St Fl 22, San Francisco (94104-2606)
PHONE.................................415 402-2600
Greg Shenkman, *CEO*
Alec Miloslavsky, *Ch of Bd*
Alex Kolt, *President*
Ivars Puksts, *COO*
Fazi Zand, *Vice Pres*
EMP: 550
SQ FT: 26,000
SALES (est): 49.2MM **Privately Held**
WEB: www.exigengroup.com
SIC: 7371 Computer software development

(P-15156)
FAMOUS SOFTWARE LLC (PA)
8080 N Palm Ave Ste 210, Fresno (93711-5797)
PHONE.................................559 438-3600
Kirk Parrish, *Human Res Mgr*
EMP: 60
SQ FT: 8,300
SALES: 10MM **Privately Held**
WEB: www.famoussoftware.com
SIC: 7371 7372 Computer software development; business oriented computer software

(P-15157)
FASTLY INC (PA)
475 Brannan St Ste 300, San Francisco (94107-5420)
P.O. Box 78266 (94107-8266)
PHONE.................................415 488-6329
Artur Bergman's, *CEO*
Hooman Beheshti, *President*
Joshua Bixby, *President*
Artur Bergman, *CEO*
William Kaufmann, *COO*
EMP: 68
SALES (est): 45.8MM **Privately Held**
SIC: 7371 Computer software development; computer software development & applications

(P-15158)
FCS SOFTWARE SOLUTIONS LIMITED
2375 Zanker Rd Ste 250, San Jose (95131-1143)
PHONE.................................408 324-1203
Dalip Kumar, *President*
Janak Sharma, *Director*
EMP: 99
SALES (est): 8.6MM **Privately Held**
SIC: 7371 Computer software development
PA: Fcs Software Solutions Limited
Plot No 83 Fcs House
Noida UP 20130

(P-15159)
FENDER DIGITAL LLC (HQ)
1575 N Gower St Ste 170, Los Angeles (90028-7179)
PHONE.................................323 462-2198
Ethan Katlan, *Principal*
EMP: 75
SQ FT: 25,000
SALES: 50MM
SALES (corp-wide): 816.3MM **Privately Held**
SIC: 7371 Computer software development & applications
PA: Fender Musical Instruments Corporation
17600 N Perimeter Dr # 100
Scottsdale AZ 85255
480 596-9690

(P-15160)
FINANCIAL INFORMATION NETWORK
Also Called: F I N
6656 Valjean Ave, Van Nuys (91406-5816)
P.O. Box 7954 (91409-7954)
PHONE.................................818 782-0331
Jerry Sears, *President*
Alan Shepoiser, *CFO*
Greg Bear, *Manager*
Steve Jelinski, *Manager*
EMP: 60
SQ FT: 6,000
SALES (est): 6.8MM **Privately Held**
WEB: www.fingps.com
SIC: 7371 7372 Custom computer programming services; prepackaged software

(P-15161)
FINANCIALFORCECOM INC (DH)
595 Market St Ste 2700, San Francisco (94105-2840)
PHONE.................................866 743-2220
Tod Nielsen, *President*
Joe Fuca, *President*
Gordy Brooks, *CFO*
Jeremy Roche, *Founder*
Fred Studer, *Chief Mktg Ofcr*
EMP: 80
SALES (est): 86.7MM **Privately Held**
SIC: 7371 Computer software development
HQ: Unit4 N.V.
Papendorpseweg 100
Utrecht 3528
184 444-444

(P-15162)
FLO HEALTH INC
541 Jefferson Ave Ste 100, Redwood City (94063-1700)
PHONE.................................510 303-9307
Maxim Scrobov, *CEO*
EMP: 78
SALES (corp-wide): 500K **Privately Held**
SIC: 7371 Computer software development & applications
PA: Flo Health, Inc.
1013 Centre Rd Ste 403b
Wilmington DE 19805
302 498-8369

(P-15163)
FLUID INC (DH)
1611 Telegraph Ave Fl 4, Oakland (94612-2143)
PHONE.................................877 343-3240
Vanessa Cartwright, *CEO*
Tamir Scheinok, *COO*
Michael Janiak, *Creative Dir*
Bermi Ferrer, *Engineer*
Kaye Sphr, *Human Res Dir*
EMP: 61
SQ FT: 7,000
SALES: 18.5MM
SALES (corp-wide): 68MM **Privately Held**
SIC: 7371 Computer software development
HQ: Astound Commerce Corporation
1111 Bayhill Dr Ste 425
San Bruno CA 94066
800 591-4710

(P-15164)
FNC INC
40 Pacifica Ste 900, Irvine (92618-7487)
PHONE.................................714 866-1099
Neil Olsen, *Officer*
David Johnson, *Executive*
Robert Chenen, *Analyst*
EMP: 52
SALES (est): 52.7MM **Privately Held**
SIC: 7371 Custom computer programming services
PA: Fnc, Inc.
1214 Office Park Dr
Oxford MS 38655
662 236-2020

(P-15165)
FOCUS 360 INC
27721 La Paz Rd Ste B, Laguna Niguel (92677-3949)
PHONE.................................949 234-0008
Steven G Ormonde, *President*
Brent C Chase, *Vice Pres*
EMP: 54
SQ FT: 18,300
SALES (est): 5.3MM **Privately Held**
WEB: www.focus360.com
SIC: 7371 Custom computer programming services

(P-15166)
FORESCOUT TECHNOLOGIES INC (PA)
190 W Tasman Dr, San Jose (95134-1700)
PHONE.................................408 213-3191
Michael Decesare, *President*
Yehezkel Yeshurun, *Ch of Bd*
Christopher Harms, *CFO*
David Dewalt, *Vice Ch Bd*
Rami Kalish, *Bd of Directors*
EMP: 147
SALES: 220.8MM **Publicly Held**
WEB: www.forescout.com
SIC: 7371 Computer software development

(P-15167)
FORMULA ONE SYSTEMS INC (HQ)
2850 E 29th St, Long Beach (90806-2313)
PHONE.................................562 424-7899
Patrick McMahon, *President*
EMP: 77
SQ FT: 23,000
SALES: 8MM
SALES (corp-wide): 40.6MM **Privately Held**
WEB: www.acom.com
SIC: 7371 Computer software development
PA: Acom Solutions, Inc.
2850 E 29th St
Long Beach CA 90806
562 424-7899

(P-15168)
FRECKLE EDUCATION INC
100 Bush St Ste 700, San Francisco (94104-3910)
PHONE.................................215 896-9896
Sidharph Kakkar, *President*
Brittany Med, *Executive*
Demond Walker, *Executive*
Alexandr Kurilin, *CTO*
Michelle Kim, *Analyst*
EMP: 50
SALES: 4MM **Privately Held**
SIC: 7371 Computer software development & applications

(P-15169)
FRONT PORCH INC (PA)
905 Mono Way, Sonora (95370-5206)
PHONE.................................209 288-5500
Zach Britton, *CEO*
Zachary Britton, *President*
Cheri Oteri, *CEO*
Bob Hohne, *CFO*
Robert Hohne Jr, *CFO*
EMP: 67
SQ FT: 1,022
SALES (est): 12.2MM **Privately Held**
WEB: www.adfirst.com
SIC: 7371 Computer software development

(P-15170)
FRONTECH N FUJITSU AMER INC
2933 Bunker Hill Ln # 101, Santa Clara (95054-1124)
PHONE.................................408 982-3697
John Mullerworth, *Manager*
EMP: 100
SALES (corp-wide): 38.4B **Privately Held**
WEB: www.fjicl.com
SIC: 7371 Computer software development

HQ: Fujitsu Frontech North America, Inc.
27121 Towne Centre Dr # 100
Foothill Ranch CA 92610

(P-15171)
FUJITSU GLOVIA INC (HQ)
200 Continental Blvd Fl 3, El Segundo (90245-4510)
PHONE.................................310 563-7000
Chikara Ono, *CEO*
Masahiro Cho, *CFO*
Jim Errington, *Exec VP*
Matt Snyder, *Info Tech Mgr*
EMP: 150
SQ FT: 53,000
SALES (est): 46.7MM
SALES (corp-wide): 38.4B **Privately Held**
SIC: 7371 7372 Computer software development; prepackaged software
PA: Fujitsu Limited
1-5-2, Higashishimbashi
Minato-Ku TKY 105-0
362 522-220

(P-15172)
FUSIONONE INC
55 Almaden Blvd Ste 500, San Jose (95113-1612)
PHONE.................................408 282-1200
Mike Mulica, *CEO*
Rick Onyon, *Ch of Bd*
Ed Battle, *CFO*
Jay Burrell, *Exec VP*
Alexander Tsarkov, *Vice Pres*
EMP: 90
SQ FT: 13,000
SALES (est): 3.6MM
SALES (corp-wide): 402.3MM **Publicly Held**
WEB: www.fusionone.com
SIC: 7371 Custom computer programming services
PA: Synchronoss Technologies, Inc.
200 Crossing Blvd Fl 8
Bridgewater NJ 08807
866 620-3940

(P-15173)
FUTURENET TECHNOLOGIES CORP
1320 Valley Vista Dr # 202, Diamond Bar (91765-3956)
PHONE.................................909 396-4000
Tom Liu, *President*
Wayne Wu, *COO*
Tony Towns, *Sales Dir*
EMP: 123
SQ FT: 9,650
SALES (est): 8.7MM **Privately Held**
WEB: www.futurenet-tech.com
SIC: 7371 Computer software development

(P-15174)
G2 DIRECT AND DIGITAL
Also Called: Grey Direct-E Marketing
612 Howard St Ste 400, San Francisco (94105-3944)
PHONE.................................415 421-1000
Felicia Montgomery, *Branch Mgr*
EMP: 50
SALES (corp-wide): 20.1B **Privately Held**
WEB: www.greydirect.com
SIC: 7371 Custom computer programming services
HQ: G2 Direct And Digital
777 3rd Ave Ste 37
New York NY 10017
212 537-3700

(P-15175)
GENEX (HQ)
800 Corporate Pointe # 100, Culver City (90230-7667)
PHONE.................................424 672-9500
Walter Schild, *CEO*
Gretchen Humbert, *CFO*
EMP: 130
SQ FT: 12,000
SALES (est): 10.6MM
SALES (corp-wide): 2.2B **Publicly Held**
WEB: www.genex.com
SIC: 7371 7379 4813 Computer software development & applications; computer related consulting services;

PA: Meredith Corporation
1716 Locust St
Des Moines IA 50309
515 284-3000

(P-15176)
GENIUM INC
585 Broadway St, Redwood City
(94063-3122)
PHONE...............................415 240-0442
Alexander Ledovskiy, *CEO*
Alex Iceman, *Exec Dir*
EMP: 150 **EST:** 2015
SALES: 4MM **Privately Held**
SIC: 7371 Computer software develop-

(P-15177)
GENUENT USA LLC
2240 Douglas Blvd Ste 100, Roseville
(95661-3874)
PHONE...............................916 772-3700
Greg Abel, *Manager*
EMP: 68
SALES (corp-wide): 12MM **Privately Held**
SIC: 7371 Custom computer programming services
HQ: Genuent Usa, Llc
1400 Post Oak Blvd # 200
Houston TX 77056
713 547-4444

(P-15178)
GIGYA INC (HQ)
2513 E Char Rd Ste 200, Mountain View
(94043)
PHONE...............................650 353-7230
Patrick Salyer, *CEO*
Rooly Elieverov, *President*
Jean-Francois Hervy, *CFO*
Derrick Arakaki, *Vice Pres*
Krayniy Sergey, *Vice Pres*
EMP: 76
SQ FT: 16,000
SALES (est): 40.4MM
SALES (corp-wide): 27.6B **Privately Held**
WEB: www.gigya-inc.com
SIC: 7371 Computer software develop-
ment & applications
PA: Sap Se
Dietmar-Hopp-Allee 16
Walldorf 69190
622 774-7474

(P-15179)
GIVA INC
1030 E El Camino Real, Sunnyvale
(94087-3759)
PHONE...............................408 260-9000
Ronald Avignone, *Founder*
Dan Switzer, *CTO*
EMP: 60 **EST:** 1999
SALES (est): 4.7MM **Privately Held**
SIC: 7371 Computer software develop-
ment

(P-15180)
GLOBAL TOUCHPOINTS INC
3005 Douglas Blvd Ste 108, Roseville
(95661-4267)
PHONE...............................916 878-5954
Naren Kini, *CEO*
Udayan Chanda, *President*
Sandhya Shenoy, *Treasurer*
Seema Chanda, *Admin Sec*
Bravim Chavan, *Business Anlyst*
EMP: 94
SQ FT: 2,174
SALES: 8.9MM **Privately Held**
SIC: 7371 7373 Computer software devel-
opment; computer software development
& applications; computer systems analy-
sis & design; systems integration services

(P-15181)
GLOBALLOGIC INC (PA)
1741 Tech Dr Ste 400, San Jose (95110)
PHONE...............................408 273-8900
Shashank Samant, *CEO*
Sameer Tikoo, *President*
Jim Dellamore, *COO*
Doug Ahrens, *CFO*
Charles Wayne Grubbs, *CFO*
EMP: 213

SALES (est): 406.5MM **Privately Held**
WEB: www.globallogic.com
SIC: 7371 7379 7373 Computer software
development; computer related consulting
services; systems engineering, computer
related

(P-15182)
GLOVIA INC
2250 E Imperial Hwy # 200, El Segundo
(90245-3508)
PHONE...............................310 563-7000
Howard Goldman, *Controller*
EMP: 200
SALES (est): 9.6MM **Privately Held**
SIC: 7371 Computer software develop-
ment & applications

(P-15183)
GLU MOBILE INC (PA)
875 Howard St Ste 100, San Francisco
(94103-3032)
PHONE...............................415 800-6100
Nick Earl, *President*
Niccolo M De Masi, *Ch of Bd*
Eric R Ludwig, *COO*
Eric Ball, *Bd of Directors*
Greg Brandeau, *Bd of Directors*
EMP: 131
SQ FT: 29,000
SALES: 286.8MM **Publicly Held**
WEB: www.glu.com
SIC: 7371 3944 Computer software devel-
opment & applications; computer software
writing services; computer code authors;
electronic games & toys

(P-15184)
GOOD SPORTS PLUS LTD
Also Called: ARC
370 Amapola Ave Ste 208, Torrance
(90501-7241)
PHONE...............................310 671-4400
Brad Lupien, *President*
Gary Lipsky, *President*
Kitty Cohen, *Vice Pres*
Daniel Castaneda, *Regional Mgr*
Stephanie Sajor, *Manager*
EMP: 300
SQ FT: 3,500
SALES (est): 9.9MM **Privately Held**
SIC: 7371 7997 Custom computer pro-
gramming services; outdoor field clubs

(P-15185)
GOOD TECHNOLOGY CORPORATION (HQ)
3001 Bishop Dr Ste 400, San Ramon
(94583-5005)
PHONE...............................408 352-9102
Christy Wyatt, *President*
Ronald J Fior, *CFO*
Cheryln Chin, *Senior VP*
Fr D Ric ARI S, *Senior VP*
Aira Cook, *Vice Pres*
EMP: 160 **EST:** 2014
SQ FT: 80,000
SALES (est): 160.3MM
SALES (corp-wide): 932MM **Privately Held**
WEB: www.good.com
SIC: 7371 7382 Computer software devel-
opment & applications; custom computer
programming services; protective de-
vices, security
PA: Blackberry Limited
2200 University Ave E
Waterloo ON N2K 0
519 888-7465

(P-15186)
GOOGLE LLC (HQ)
1600 Amphitheatre Pkwy, Mountain View
(94043-1351)
P.O. Box 2050 (94042-2050)
PHONE...............................650 253-0000
Sundar Pichai, *CEO*
Ruth M Porat, *CFO*
David C Drummond,
Nikesh Arora, *Senior VP*
Dan Dennison, *Administration*
▲ **EMP:** 250 **EST:** 2002
SQ FT: 4,800,000

SALES (est): 24.4B
SALES (corp-wide): 110.8B **Publicly Held**
WEB: www.google.com
SIC: 7371 7375 Computer software devel-
opment & applications; data base infor-
mation retrieval
PA: Alphabet Inc.
1600 Amphitheatre Pkwy
Mountain View CA 94043
650 253-0000

(P-15187)
GRACENOTE INC (DH)
2000 Powell St Ste 1500, Emeryville
(94608-1820)
PHONE...............................510 428-7200
Stephen White, *President*
Eric Allen, *Senior VP*
Tal Ball, *Senior VP*
Desmond Cussen, *Senior VP*
Brian Hamilton, *Senior VP*
EMP: 99
SALES (est): 78.9MM
SALES (corp-wide): 6.5B **Privately Held**
WEB: www.gracenote.com
SIC: 7371 Software programming applica-
tions

(P-15188)
GRAND INTELLIGENCE LLC
2880 Zanker Rd Ste 203, San Jose
(95134-2122)
PHONE...............................408 954-7368
Marylyn Lin, *Mng Member*
Dongyan Wang, *COO*
EMP: 100 **EST:** 2012
SALES: 10MM **Privately Held**
SIC: 7371 Computer software develop-
ment

(P-15189)
GREE INTERNATIONAL INC
275 Battery St Ste 1700, San Francisco
(94111-3369)
PHONE...............................415 409-5159
Naoki Aoyagi, *CEO*
Neil Haldar, *President*
Andrew Sheppard, *COO*
Shanti Bergel, *Senior VP*
Masaki Fujimoto, *CTO*
EMP: 250
SALES (est): 34.8MM
SALES (corp-wide): 701.8MM **Privately Held**
SIC: 7371 Computer software develop-
ment & applications; computer software
systems analysis & design, custom; soft-
ware programming applications
PA: Gree, Inc.
6-10-1, Roppongi
Minato-Ku TKY 106-0
357 709-500

(P-15190)
GREE INTERNATIONAL ENTRMT INC
185 Berry St Ste 590, San Francisco
(94107-9105)
PHONE...............................415 409-5200
Andrew Sheppard, *CEO*
Ryotaro Shima, *COO*
Shanti Bergel, *Senior VP*
Yoshikazu Tanaka, *Director*
EMP: 220 **EST:** 2016
SALES (est): 3.3MM
SALES (corp-wide): 701.8MM **Privately Held**
SIC: 7371 Computer software develop-
ment & applications
PA: Gree, Inc.
6-10-1, Roppongi
Minato-Ku TKY 106-0
357 709-500

(P-15191)
GRID NET INC (PA)
126 S Park St, San Francisco
(94107-1809)
PHONE...............................415 872-5097
Ray Bell, *CEO*
Andres Carvallo, *Officer*
William Bell, *Vice Pres*
Scott Maroney, *Vice Pres*
Jawed Sayed, *Vice Pres*
EMP: 52

SQ FT: 4,200
SALES (est): 3.8MM **Privately Held**
WEB: www.grid-net.com
SIC: 7371 Software programming applica-
tions; computer software development &
applications

(P-15192)
GROUP AVANTICA INC
Also Called: Avantica Technologies
2680 Bayshore Pkwy # 416, Mountain View
(94043-1022)
PHONE...............................650 248-9678
Mario Chaves, *CEO*
Luis C Chaves, *President*
EMP: 260
SALES (est): 17.3MM **Privately Held**
WEB: www.avantica.net
SIC: 7371 Computer software develop-
ment

(P-15193)
GTXCEL INC
2855 Telg Ave Ste 600, Berkeley (94705)
PHONE...............................800 609-8994
Becky Zehr, *Vice Pres*
Peter Stilson, *President*
EMP: 80
SQ FT: 10,000
SALES: 10MM **Privately Held**
SIC: 7371 Computer software develop-
ment

(P-15194)
GUIDEBOOK INC (PA)
340 Bryant St Ste 400, San Francisco
(94107-1442)
PHONE...............................650 319-7233
Jeff Lewis, *CEO*
Vadim Dolt, *President*
Chris Hart, *CFO*
Wayne Morris, *Vice Pres*
Mary Meinander, *Executive*
EMP: 90
SQ FT: 6,500
SALES (est): 12MM **Privately Held**
SIC: 7371 Computer software develop-
ment

(P-15195)
H & R ACCOUNTS INC
Also Called: Avadyne Health
3131 Camino Del Rio N, San Diego
(92108-5701)
PHONE...............................619 819-8844
Linda Hevern, *Branch Mgr*
EMP: 65
SALES (corp-wide): 39.1MM **Privately Held**
SIC: 7371 Computer software develop-
ment
PA: H & R Accounts, Inc.
5320 22nd Ave
Moline IL 61265
309 736-2255

(P-15196)
HACKEREARTH INC
38350 Fremont Blvd, Fremont
(94536-6060)
PHONE...............................650 461-4192
Sachin Gupta, *President*
EMP: 120
SALES (est): 1.5MM **Privately Held**
SIC: 7371 Custom computer programming
services

(P-15197)
HEAT WAVES LLC ✪
Also Called: Heat Software
1015 Campanile, Newport Beach
(92660-9031)
PHONE...............................323 753-8441
Andrews Mitchell,
EMP: 135 **EST:** 2018
SALES (est): 1.9MM **Privately Held**
SIC: 7371 Computer software develop-
ment & applications

(P-15198)
HEWLETT PACKARD
3000 Hanover St, Palo Alto (94304-1185)
PHONE...............................650 857-1501
EMP: 1835
SALES (est): 98.4MM **Privately Held**
SIC: 7371

646   2019 Directory of California
Wholesalers and Services Companies   ▲ = Import ▼=Export
◆ =Import/Export

(P-15199)
HGGC LLC (PA)
1950 University Ave # 350, East Palo Alto
(94303-2250)
PHONE..................................650 321-4910
Rich Lawson, *Mng Member*
Gary Crittenden, *Managing Prtnr*
Jon Huntsman, *Managing Prtnr*
James Learner, *Managing Prtnr*
Les Brown, *CFO*
EMP: 253
SALES (est): 151.1MM **Privately Held**
SIC: 7371 Computer software development & applications

(P-15200)
HONEYBOOK INC
539 Bryant St Ste 200, San Francisco
(94107-1269)
PHONE..................................770 403-9234
Oz Eliyahu, *CEO*
Jessica Burden, *Partner*
John Kramer, *COO*
Tina Hoang-To, *Officer*
Maya Wolkoon, *General Mgr*
EMP: 55
SALES: 1MM **Privately Held**
SIC: 7371 Computer software development

(P-15201)
HOUZZ INC (PA)
285 Hamilton Ave Fl 4, Palo Alto
(94301-2540)
PHONE..................................650 326-3000
ADI Tatarko, *CEO*
Deepa Mungara, *Partner*
Alon Cohen, *President*
Richard Wong, *CFO*
Liza Hausman, *Vice Pres*
EMP: 99
SALES (est): 57.9MM **Privately Held**
SIC: 7371 Computer software development

(P-15202)
HUMANITYCOM INC
50 Osgood Pl Ste 330, San Francisco
(94133-4644)
PHONE..................................415 230-0108
Chris Amani, *CEO*
David Charron, *President*
Kristina Dautovic, *QA Dir*
Milena Veletic, *Graphic Designe*
Aleksandra Vidic, *Accounting Mgr*
EMP: 50
SALES: 2.5MM **Privately Held**
SIC: 7371 Computer software development

(P-15203)
HVANTAGE TECHNOLOGIES INC
6700 Fllbrook Ave Ste 222, West Hills
(91307)
PHONE..................................818 661-6301
Krishna Baderia, *CEO*
EMP: 80
SALES (est): 1.2MM **Privately Held**
SIC: 7371 8748 7372 7373 Custom computer programming services; systems engineering consultant, ex. computer or professional; application computer software; business oriented computer software; systems engineering, computer related

(P-15204)
HYLAND SOFTWARE INC
2355 Main St Ste 100, Irvine (92614-4290)
PHONE..................................949 242-3100
Lloyd Warman, *Principal*
EMP: 60
SALES (corp-wide): 492.6MM **Privately Held**
WEB: www.onbase.com
SIC: 7371 Computer software development
HQ: Hyland Software, Inc.
　　28500 Clemens Rd
　　Westlake OH 44145

(P-15205)
HYPERGRID INC
110 Baytech Dr, San Jose (95134-2302)
PHONE..................................650 316-5524

Nariman Teymourian, *CEO*
Kevin Rains, *CFO*
Robert Taccini, *CFO*
Kelly Murphy, *Founder*
Mike O Neill, *Senior VP*
EMP: 64
SALES (est): 3.1MM **Privately Held**
SIC: 7371 5045 Computer software development; computers, peripherals & software

(P-15206)
HYUNDAI ATVER TLMTICS AMER INC
10550 Talbert Ave Fl 2, Fountain Valley
(92708-6032)
PHONE..................................949 381-6000
SOO Dong Park, *CEO*
Ui Chul Shi, *CFO*
Hyunho Lee, *Executive*
Changkick Sohn, *Executive*
Thomas Lee, *Finance Mgr*
EMP: 56
SALES (est): 7.7MM **Privately Held**
SIC: 7371 Computer software systems analysis & design, custom; computer software development & applications; software programming applications

(P-15207)
IBASET FEDERAL SERVICES LLC (PA)
27442 Portola Pkwy # 300, Foothill Ranch
(92610-2823)
PHONE..................................949 598-5200
Ladeira Poonian, *Chairman*
Vic Sial, *President*
Naveen Poonian, *COO*
Elizabeth Conley, *CFO*
Terri Carson, *Officer*
EMP: 75
SQ FT: 30,000
SALES (est): 43.8MM **Privately Held**
SIC: 7371 Computer software development

(P-15208)
IBS INTERPRIT INC (PA)
5860 El Camino Real, Carlsbad
(92008-8816)
PHONE..................................760 268-7299
Jan Steenkamp, *CEO*
Graham Ellis, *COO*
Ed Ott, *CFO*
EMP: 175
SALES (est): 8.7MM **Privately Held**
WEB: www.ibsinterprit.com
SIC: 7371 Computer software development

(P-15209)
IC COMPLIANCE LLC (PA)
Also Called: Talentwave
1065 E Hillsdale Blvd # 300, Foster City
(94404-1613)
PHONE..................................650 378-4150
Teresa Creech, *CEO*
Jim Hanrahan, *CFO*
Joe Russell, *CFO*
Catherine Chidyausiku, *Vice Pres*
Michael Soffel, *Vice Pres*
EMP: 2500
SQ FT: 5,100
SALES (est): 232.5MM **Privately Held**
WEB: www.gotoicon.com
SIC: 7371 8721 Computer software development & applications; payroll accounting service

(P-15210)
IDAPTIVE LLC
3300 Tannery Way, Santa Clara
(95054-2828)
PHONE..................................669 444-5400
Danny Kibel,
EMP: 130
SQ FT: 40,000
SALES: 30MM **Privately Held**
SIC: 7371 Computer software development

(P-15211)
ILLUMIO INC
160 San Gabriel Dr, Sunnyvale
(94086-5125)
PHONE..................................669 800-5000

Andrew Rubin, *CEO*
Remo Canessa, *CFO*
Alan Cohen, *Ch Credit Ofcr*
Matthew Glenn, *Vice Pres*
Christopher Khadan, *Vice Pres*
EMP: 140 EST: 2012
SALES (est): 5.5MM **Privately Held**
SIC: 7371 Computer software systems analysis & design, custom

(P-15212)
IMPERVA INC (PA)
3400 Bridge Pkwy Ste 200, Redwood City
(94065-1195)
PHONE..................................650 345-9000
Christopher S Hylen, *President*
Allan Tessler, *Ch of Bd*
Mike Burns, *CFO*
Geraldine Elliott, *Bd of Directors*
Charles Giancarlo, *Bd of Directors*
EMP: 144
SQ FT: 82,000
SALES (est): 321.7MM **Publicly Held**
WEB: www.imperva.com
SIC: 7371 Computer software development

(P-15213)
INDUS CORPORATION
1275 Columbus Ave, San Francisco
(94133-1301)
PHONE..................................415 202-1830
EMP: 60
SALES (corp-wide): 2.5B **Publicly Held**
SIC: 7371 7372 7373 7379
HQ: Indus Corporation
　　1515 Wilson Blvd Ste 1100
　　Arlington VA 22209
　　703 506-6700

(P-15214)
INNOPATH SOFTWARE INC (PA)
333 W El Camino Real # 290, Sunnyvale
(94087-8128)
P.O. Box 2454, Cupertino (95015-2454)
PHONE..................................408 962-9200
John Fazio, *President*
Naresh Bansal, *Vice Pres*
Adrian Chan, *Vice Pres*
Mark Fazio, *Vice Pres*
Eric King, *Vice Pres*
EMP: 100
SALES (est): 17MM **Privately Held**
WEB: www.innopath.com
SIC: 7371 Computer software development

(P-15215)
INNOVASYSTEMS INTL LLC
850 Beech St Unit 1006, San Diego
(92101-2895)
PHONE..................................619 955-5890
Chuck Davis, *Chief*
EMP: 79
SALES (corp-wide): 56.6MM **Privately Held**
SIC: 7371 Custom computer programming services
PA: Innovasystems International Llc
　　2385 Northside Dr Ste 300
　　San Diego CA 92108
　　619 756-6500

(P-15216)
INNOVASYSTEMS INTL LLC (PA)
2385 Northside Dr Ste 300, San Diego
(92108-2716)
PHONE..................................619 756-6500
Lynn Hutton, *Mng Member*
Mike McCoy, *COO*
Tom Flies, *Officer*
Kimberly Coleman, *Admin Asst*
Ian Chase, *Info Tech Mgr*
EMP: 99
SALES (est): 56.6MM **Privately Held**
WEB: www.innovasi.com
SIC: 7371 7373 7379 7376 Computer software systems analysis & design, custom; computer integrated systems design; computer related maintenance services; computer facilities management

(P-15217)
INSPIRA INC
4125 Blackford Ave # 255, San Jose
(95117-1711)
PHONE..................................408 247-9500
Ravindra Gudapati, *President*
EMP: 60
SQ FT: 2,908
SALES: 3MM **Privately Held**
SIC: 7371 Software programming applications

(P-15218)
INSTANT SYSTEMS INC
Also Called: Instantsys
40211 Dolerita Ave, Fremont (94539-3015)
PHONE..................................510 657-8100
Vipin K Chawla, *President*
Uzay Takaoglu, *Vice Pres*
Navnit Saurabh, *Marketing Mgr*
Mamta Chawla, *Director*
▲ EMP: 90
SALES (est): 3.4MM **Privately Held**
WEB: www.instantsys.com
SIC: 7371 7372 Custom computer programming services; computer software development & applications; business oriented computer software

(P-15219)
INSTART LOGIC INC
Also Called: Instart Labs
450 Lambert Ave, Palo Alto (94306-2219)
PHONE..................................888 418-5044
Sumit Dhawan, *CEO*
Mark Templeton, *Ch of Bd*
Manav Ratan Mital, *CEO*
Jony Hartono, *CFO*
Rafael Torres, *CFO*
EMP: 95
SALES (est): 18MM **Privately Held**
SIC: 7371 Computer software development; computer software development & applications

(P-15220)
INSTILL CORPORATION
777 Mariners Island Blvd # 400, San Mateo
(94404-5008)
PHONE..................................650 645-2600
Robert Bonavito, *CEO*
Michael Devries, *President*
Michael R Peckham, *CFO*
Nicholas Carnes, *Officer*
Shermann Min, *Officer*
EMP: 115
SQ FT: 28,427
SALES (est): 7.4MM **Privately Held**
WEB: www.instill.com
SIC: 7371 Computer software development

(P-15221)
INTEGRATED DYNMC SOLUTIONS INC
31194 La Baya Dr Ste 203, Westlake Village (91362-6433)
PHONE..................................818 707-8797
Nasrollah Gashtili, *CEO*
John Bryant, *Vice Pres*
Mercedes Guzman, *Tech Recruiter*
Nisha Hashim, *Tech Recruiter*
Joseph Varghese, *VP Human Res*
EMP: 50
SQ FT: 6,000
SALES: 2MM **Privately Held**
WEB: www.idspage.com
SIC: 7371 Computer software systems analysis & design, custom

(P-15222)
INTEL CORPORATION
2200 Mission College Blvd, Santa Clara
(95054-1549)
PHONE..................................503 696-8080
David Ryan, *Branch Mgr*
Nikhil Talpallikar, *Software Engr*
Nilanjan Das, *Engineer*
Dwikusuma Fransiska, *Engineer*
Michael Hugo, *Engineer*
EMP: 200
SALES (corp-wide): 62.7B **Publicly Held**
WEB: www.intel.com
SIC: 7371 Computer software development

PRODUCTS & SVCS

PA: Intel Corporation
2200 Mission College Blvd
Santa Clara CA 95054
408 765-8080

(P-15223)
INTELEX SYSTEMS INC
6320 Canoga Ave Ste 1546, Woodland Hills
(91367-2526)
PHONE..............................818 518-1100
Sreenath Bangar, *CEO*
EMP: 84 **EST:** 2006
SALES (est): 2.9MM **Privately Held**
SIC: 7371 7379 Computer software development; computer related services

(P-15224)
INTELLECTSOFT LLC
721 Colorado Ave Ste 101, Palo Alto
(94303-3973)
PHONE..............................650 300-4335
Paul Bach,
Artem Kozel, *Risk Mgmt Dir*
Dmitry Evdokimovich, *CIO*
Max Mironchik, *CTO*
Alexander Petrov, *Engineer*
EMP: 120
SQ FT: 1,000
SALES (est): 9MM **Privately Held**
SIC: 7371 Computer software development; computer software development & applications

(P-15225)
INTELLISWIFT SOFTWARE INC (PA)
Also Called: Magagnini
39600 Balentine Dr # 200, Newark
(94560-5304)
PHONE..............................510 490-9240
Parag Patel, *CEO*
Johnny Magagnini, *VP Bus Dvlpt*
Shannon Fox, *Executive*
Bob Patel, *Principal*
Anna Ashcraft, *Regional Mgr*
EMP: 225
SQ FT: 5,200
SALES (est): 75.2MM **Privately Held**
WEB: www.intelliswift.com
SIC: 7371 Custom computer programming services

(P-15226)
INTELLISYNC CORPORATION (HQ)
313 Fairchild Dr, Mountain View
(94043-2215)
PHONE..............................650 625-2185
Woodson Hobbs, *President*
Clyde Foster, *COO*
David Eichler, *CFO*
Robert Gerber, *Chief Mktg Ofcr*
Blair Hankins, *Technology*
EMP: 55
SQ FT: 33,821
SALES (est): 22MM
SALES (corp-wide): 27.3B **Privately Held**
SIC: 7371 7372 Computer software development; prepackaged software
PA: Nokia Oyj
Karaportti 3
Espoo 02610
104 488-000

(P-15227)
INTERACTIVE DATA CORPORATION
CMS Bondedge
2901 28th St Ste 300, Santa Monica
(90405-2972)
PHONE..............................310 664-2500
Andrew Hausman, *Manager*
EMP: 75
SALES (corp-wide): 4.6B **Publicly Held**
WEB: www.interactivedata.com
SIC: 7371 7372 Computer software development; prepackaged software
HQ: Interactive Data Corporation
32 Crosby Dr
Bedford MA 01730

(P-15228)
INTERANA INC
305 Walnut St Ste 300, Redwood City
(94063-1731)
PHONE..............................844 426-4678
Greg Smirin, *CEO*
Robin Davis, *Engineer*
Megan Maley, *Human Resources*
Dalley Michael, *Sales Staff*
Marge Anderson, *Manager*
EMP: 70
SQ FT: 18,000
SALES (est): 3.2MM **Privately Held**
SIC: 7371 Computer software development & applications

(P-15229)
INTERCOM INC
55 2nd St Ste 400, San Francisco
(94105-4560)
PHONE..............................831 920-7088
Eoghan McCabe, *CEO*
Des Traynor, *Officer*
Paul Adams, *Vice Pres*
Vikram Prakash, *Executive*
Ciaran Lee, *CTO*
EMP: 300
SALES (est): 32.4MM **Privately Held**
SIC: 7371 Computer software development

(P-15230)
INTERNATIONAL BUS MCHS CORP
Also Called: IBM
555 Bailey Ave, San Jose (95141-1003)
PHONE..............................408 463-2000
Lou Gerstner, *Manager*
Kevin Foster, *Partner*
Steve Mink, *Executive*
Gary Robinson, *Sr Software Eng*
Jeffrey Horton, *Information Mgr*
EMP: 1500
SALES (corp-wide): 79.1B **Publicly Held**
WEB: www.ibm.com
SIC: 7371 7372 5961 Computer software development; prepackaged software; catalog & mail-order houses
PA: International Business Machines Corporation
1 New Orchard Rd Ste 1 # 1
Armonk NY 10504
914 499-1900

(P-15231)
INTERNET BLUEPRINT INC
Also Called: Bidmail
1177 Warner Ave, Tustin (92780-6458)
PHONE..............................714 673-6000
Daniel Stapleton, *President*
Peter Amaraphornkul, *Info Tech Dir*
Jared Plumb, *Marketing Mgr*
EMP: 50
SALES (est): 4.9MM **Privately Held**
SIC: 7371 Computer software development & applications

(P-15232)
INTERNET SECURITY SYSTEMS INC
28350 Tamarack Ln, Santa Clarita
(91390-4038)
PHONE..............................661 296-5752
Lonny Esposito, *Manager*
EMP: 116
SALES (corp-wide): 79.1B **Publicly Held**
WEB: www.issx.com
SIC: 7371 Custom computer programming services
HQ: Internet Security Systems Inc
6303 Barfield Rd
Atlanta GA 30328

(P-15233)
INTERTRUST TECHNOLOGIES CORP (HQ)
920 Stewart Dr, Sunnyvale (94085-3921)
PHONE..............................408 616-1600
Talal G Shamoon, *CEO*
David P Maher, *Exec VP*
Gilles Boccon Gibod, *Senior VP*
Jeff McDow, *Senior VP*
Bill Rainey, *Senior VP*
EMP: 161

SQ FT: 58,000
SALES (est): 23.7MM
SALES (corp-wide): 10.9MM **Privately Held**
SIC: 7371 Computer software development; computer software development & applications
PA: Fidelio Acquisition Company, Llc
550 Madison Ave Fl 33
New York NY 10022
212 833-8000

(P-15234)
IPTOR SUPPLY CHAIN SYSTEMS USA (DH)
Also Called: I B S
915 Highland Pointe Dr # 250, Roseville
(95678-5421)
PHONE..............................916 542-2820
Doug Braun, *CEO*
Christian Paulsson, *COO*
Fredrik Sandelin, *CFO*
David Rode, *Vice Pres*
Bill Tomasi, *Vice Pres*
EMP: 153
SQ FT: 55,000
SALES (est): 24.7MM
SALES (corp-wide): 66.4MM **Privately Held**
WEB: www.ibsus.com
SIC: 7371 5045 Computer software development; computer software
HQ: Iptor Supply Chain Systems Ab
Hemvarnsgatan 8
Solna 171 5
862 723-00

(P-15235)
IQMS (PA)
2231 Wisteria Ln, Paso Robles
(93446-9820)
PHONE..............................805 227-1122
Randall C Flamm, *President*
Karen Sked, *President*
Matt Ouska, *CFO*
Nancy Flamm, *Vice Pres*
Gary Gross, *Vice Pres*
EMP: 130
SQ FT: 60,000
SALES (est): 37MM **Privately Held**
WEB: www.iqms.com
SIC: 7371 Computer software development

(P-15236)
IRDETO USA INC (DH)
3255 Scott Blvd Ste 3-101, Santa Clara
(95054-3019)
PHONE..............................760 268-7299
Barry Douglas Coleman, *CEO*
Loefie Engelbrecht, *President*
Gram Kill, *President*
Keddy Perry, *President*
Paul Ragland, *Vice Pres*
EMP: 70
SALES (est): 16.7MM
SALES (corp-wide): 57MM **Privately Held**
SIC: 7371 Computer software development
HQ: Mih Holdings Ltd
251 Oak Avenue
Johannesburg GP
112 893-024

(P-15237)
IRISE (PA)
2381 Rosecrans Ave # 100, El Segundo
(90245-7903)
PHONE..............................800 556-0399
Emmet B Keeffe III, *CEO*
Maurice Martin, *President*
Lionel Etrillard, *CFO*
Mitch Bishop, *Chief Mktg Ofcr*
Stephen Brickley, *Exec VP*
EMP: 94
SALES (est): 42.8MM **Privately Held**
SIC: 7371 Computer software development

(P-15238)
ISAAC FAIR CORPORATION
Also Called: Mindwave Software
3661 Valley Centre Dr, San Diego
(92130-3321)
PHONE..............................858 369-8000

Steve Gutschow, *Principal*
Michael Balon, *Admin Sec*
EMP: 88
SALES (corp-wide): 932.1MM **Publicly Held**
WEB: www.fairisaac.com
SIC: 7371 Computer software development
PA: Fair Isaac Corporation
181 Metro Dr Ste 700
San Jose CA 95110
408 535-1500

(P-15239)
ISCS INC
100 Great Oaks Blvd # 100, San Jose
(95119-1462)
PHONE..............................408 362-3000
Andy J Scurto, *President*
Myron Meier, *President*
Andy Scurto, *President*
Tim Shelton, *CFO*
Doug Moore, *CTO*
EMP: 201
SQ FT: 11,000
SALES (est): 24.9MM
SALES (corp-wide): 661MM **Publicly Held**
SIC: 7371 Software programming applications
PA: Guidewire Software, Inc.
1001 E Hillsdale Blvd # 8
Foster City CA 94404
650 357-9100

(P-15240)
ISHERIFF INC
555 Twin Dolphin Dr, Redwood City
(94065-2129)
PHONE..............................650 412-4300
Paul Lipman, *CEO*
Jon Botter, *President*
Eric Jenny, *CFO*
Marcus Smith, *CFO*
James Socas, *Chairman*
EMP: 235
SALES (est): 21.6MM
SALES (corp-wide): 42.8MM **Privately Held**
SIC: 7371 Software programming applications
PA: Mimecast Uk Limited
Citypoint, 1 Ropemaker Street
London EC2Y
207 843-2300

(P-15241)
JFROG INC (PA)
270 E Caribbean Dr, Sunnyvale
(94089-1007)
PHONE..............................408 329-1540
Shlomi Ben Haim, *CEO*
Goren Orit, *COO*
Jacob Shulman, *CFO*
Berznitsky Dror, *Vice Pres*
Notman Tali, *Vice Pres*
EMP: 61 **EST:** 2012
SALES (est): 18.5MM **Privately Held**
SIC: 7371 7372 Software programming applications; custom computer programming services; business oriented computer software

(P-15242)
JIANGSU JUWANG INFO TECH CO (PA)
195 Recino St, Fremont (94539-3835)
PHONE..............................510 967-3729
Song Han, *Owner*
EMP: 70
SALES (est): 2.2MM **Privately Held**
SIC: 7371 Computer software development & applications

(P-15243)
JM DRIVER LLC
Also Called: Lynx Technology
10620 Treena St Ste 224, San Diego
(92131-1140)
PHONE..............................855 596-9832
John Driver, *CEO*
Judie Endemann, *Vice Pres*
Jacob Berlin, *Sales Staff*
EMP: 51 **EST:** 2015

▲ = Import ▼=Export
◆ =Import/Export

SALES (est): 2.2MM **Privately Held**
SIC: **7371** Computer software development

(P-15244)
JUMPSHOT INC
333 Bryant St Ste 240, San Francisco
(94107-1443)
PHONE.....................415 212-9250
Deren Baker, *CEO*
Marcus Blatch, *Vice Pres*
Eli Goodman, *Vice Pres*
Alvin Jeng, *Vice Pres*
Hong Tsui, *Vice Pres*
EMP: 85
SALES (est): 188.1K **Privately Held**
SIC: **7371** Computer software development & applications

(P-15245)
JUMPSTART GAMES INC
500 W 190th St Ste 300, Gardena
(90248-4269)
PHONE.....................424 645-4311
David Lord, *CEO*
James Czulewicz, *Admin Sec*
EMP: 59
SALES (est): 12.5MM **Privately Held**
SIC: **7371 5734** Computer software systems analysis & design, custom; computer software development; software, computer games
HQ: Netdragon Websoft Holdings Limited
Rm 2201-5&11 20/F Harbour Ctr
Wan Chai HK

(P-15246)
KABAM INC (HQ)
575 Market St Ste 2450, San Francisco
(94105-2896)
PHONE.....................604 256-0054
Seungwon Lee, *President*
Nick Earl, *President*
Jangwon Seo, *CFO*
Paxton R Cooper, *Senior VP*
Doug Inamine, *Senior VP*
EMP: 92 EST: 2006
SALES (est): 112.7MM
SALES (corp-wide): 1.5B **Privately Held**
SIC: **7371** Computer software development & applications; computer software development
PA: Netmarble Corporation
20/F G-Valley Biz Plaza
Seoul 08379
821 588-5180

(P-15247)
KALLIDUS INC
Also Called: Skava
425 Market St Ste 2200, San Francisco
(94105-2434)
PHONE.....................877 554-2176
Arish Ali, *President*
Khurram Khan, *Officer*
Phil Spade, *Assoc VP*
Manu Gupta, *Vice Pres*
Gretchen Jones, *Executive Asst*
EMP: 100
SALES (est): 4.2MM
SALES (corp-wide): 9.6B **Privately Held**
WEB: www.skava.com
SIC: **7371** Computer software development
PA: Infosys Limited
Plot No. 44 & 97a, Electronics City
Bengaluru KA 56010
802 852-0362

(P-15248)
KAZEON SYSTEMS INC
2841 Mission College Blvd, Santa Clara
(95054-1838)
PHONE.....................650 641-8100
Fax: 650 641-8195
EMP: 80
SQ FT: 24,000
SALES (est): 3.9MM **Privately Held**
WEB: www.kazeon.com
SIC: **7371 7379**

(P-15249)
KEEP TRUCKIN INC (PA)
370 Townsend St, San Francisco
(94107-1607)
PHONE.....................855 434-3564
Obaid Khan, *President*
Shoaib Makani, *CEO*
Abigail Rogers, *Accounts Mgr*
Taurie Bjerken, *Accounts Exec*
Joel Rogers, *Accounts Exec*
EMP: 50
SALES (est): 80MM **Privately Held**
SIC: **7371** Computer software development & applications

(P-15250)
KOFAX INC (PA)
15211 Laguna Canyon Rd, Irvine
(92618-3146)
PHONE.....................949 783-1000
Reynolds C Bish, *CEO*
Cort Townsend, *CFO*
Kathleen Delaney, *Chief Mktg Ofcr*
Chris Huff, *Officer*
Howard Dratler, *Exec VP*
▼ EMP: 500
SQ FT: 100,000
SALES (est): 347.2MM **Privately Held**
SIC: **7371 3577** Computer software development; input/output equipment, computer

(P-15251)
KONG INC
251 Post St Ste 200, San Francisco
(94108-5021)
PHONE.....................415 754-9283
Augusto Marietti, *CEO*
EMP: 50 EST: 2009
SALES (est): 485.5K **Privately Held**
SIC: **7371** Computer software development & applications

(P-15252)
KRG TECHNOLOGIES INC
Also Called: K R G
25000 Ave Stnford Ste 243, Valencia
(91355)
PHONE.....................661 257-9967
Muthuramalingam Umapathi, *President*
Hemalatha Rajagopala, *Owner*
Balamurugan Subbiah, *Chairman*
Antony Biju, *Technology*
Balaji Bobby, *Technology*
EMP: 600
SQ FT: 780
SALES (est): 68.4MM **Privately Held**
WEB: www.krgtech.com
SIC: **7371** Computer software development & applications

(P-15253)
KUGGA INC
1841 Sunnyvale Ave, Walnut Creek
(94597-1811)
PHONE.....................925 639-0721
Yifan Ren, *CEO*
EMP: 60
SALES (est): 891.1K **Privately Held**
SIC: **7371** Computer software development & applications

(P-15254)
LANGUAGE WEAVER INC
Also Called: Sdl
6060 Center Dr Ste 150, Los Angeles
(90045-8808)
PHONE.....................310 437-7300
Mark Tapling, *CEO*
Daniel Marcu, *COO*
Kevin Knight, *Vice Pres*
Andrew Huang, *Engineer*
Don Kim, *Controller*
EMP: 55
SQ FT: 6,000
SALES (est): 7MM **Privately Held**
WEB: www.languageweaver.com
SIC: **7371** Computer software development
PA: Sdl Plc
Globe House
Maidenhead BERKS SL6 7

(P-15255)
LAXMI GROUP INC
Also Called: Importers Software
4699 Old Ironsides Dr # 100, Santa Clara
(95054-1824)
PHONE.....................408 329-7733
Gopal RAO, *President*
Shankar Ram, *Principal*
EMP: 60
SQ FT: 2,900
SALES (est): 6.4MM **Privately Held**
WEB: www.laxmigroup.com
SIC: **7371 7363** Computer software development; help supply services

(P-15256)
LEANTAAS INC
469 El Camino Real # 100, Santa Clara
(95050-4372)
PHONE.....................650 409-3501
Mohan Giridharadas, *CEO*
Lloyd Martin, *CFO*
Katie McDermott, *Marketing Staff*
Lauren Ullman, *Director*
Zakariya Ahmad, *Manager*
EMP: 90
SQ FT: 500
SALES (est): 883.6K **Privately Held**
SIC: **7371** Computer software development

(P-15257)
LEVER INC
989 Market St Ste 500, San Francisco
(94103-1708)
PHONE.....................415 458-2731
Sarah Nahm, *CEO*
Leela Srinivasan, *Chief Mktg Ofcr*
Rob Tomchick, *Vice Pres*
Nathaniel Smith, *CTO*
Amanda Bell, *Director*
EMP: 100 EST: 2014
SALES (est): 10MM **Privately Held**
SIC: **7371** Computer software development & applications

(P-15258)
LIGHTBEND INC
625 Market St Ste 1000, San Francisco
(94105-3312)
PHONE.....................877 989-7372
Mark Brewer, *Ch of Bd*
Steve Bean, *CFO*
Martin Odersky, *Chairman*
Kathleen Hayes, *Vice Pres*
Derek Henninger, *Vice Pres*
EMP: 72
SALES (est): 8.3MM **Privately Held**
SIC: **7371** Computer software development

(P-15259)
LIMINEX INC
Also Called: Goguardian
200 N Supulveda Blvd Ste, Hermosa Beach
(90254)
PHONE.....................310 963-3031
Aza Steel, *CEO*
Advait Shinde, *CTO*
EMP: 60 EST: 2014
SQ FT: 16,000
SALES (est): 1.1MM **Privately Held**
SIC: **7371** Computer software development

(P-15260)
LINDEN RESEARCH INC
Also Called: Linden Lab
945 Battery St, San Francisco
(94111-1305)
PHONE.....................415 243-9000
Ebbe Altberg, *CEO*
Bill Gurley, *Partner*
Bob Komin, *COO*
Malcolm Dunne, *CFO*
John Zdanowski, *CFO*
EMP: 330
SALES (est): 50.8MM **Privately Held**
WEB: www.lindenlab.com
SIC: **7371** Computer software development; computer software development & applications

(P-15261)
LOCATION LABS INC
2100 Powell St Fl 14, Emeryville
(94608-1826)
PHONE.....................510 601-7012
Egor Ioppe, *CEO*
Tasso Roumeliotis, *President*
Andrea Iannitti, *Sr Software Eng*
Patrick Hull, *Software Engr*
Stephen Kwong, *Software Engr*
EMP: 72
SALES (est): 3.5MM **Privately Held**
WEB: www.wavemarket.com
SIC: **7371** Computer software development

(P-15262)
LOCKHEED MARTIN ORINCON CORP (HQ)
10325 Meanley Dr, San Diego
(92131-3011)
PHONE.....................858 455-5530
Daniel Alspach, *Ch of Bd*
EMP: 200 EST: 1973
SQ FT: 41,000
SALES (est): 49.3MM **Publicly Held**
SIC: **7371 8731** Computer software development & applications; commercial physical research

(P-15263)
LOGILITY INC
4885 Greencraig Ln 200, San Diego
(92123-1664)
PHONE.....................858 565-4238
EMP: 55
SALES (corp-wide): 112.7MM **Publicly Held**
SIC: **7371 7372** Computer software development & applications; prepackaged software
HQ: Logility, Inc.
470 E Paces Ferry Rd Ne
Atlanta GA 30305
800 762-5207

(P-15264)
LOGIX DEVELOPMENT CORPORATION
473 Post St, Camarillo (93010-8553)
PHONE.....................888 505-6449
David K Howington, *CEO*
Pauline Malysko, *President*
Anne Howington, *Vice Pres*
Carla Wheeler, *Executive Asst*
Nikki Mitchell, *Controller*
EMP: 83
SALES (est): 5.2MM **Privately Held**
WEB: www.pop3.com
SIC: **7371** Computer software development

(P-15265)
LOGLOGIC INC
110 Rose Orchard Way, San Jose
(95134-1358)
PHONE.....................408 215-5900
Guy Churchward, *CEO*
Joseph Consul, *CFO*
EMP: 170
SALES (est): 12.1MM
SALES (corp-wide): 4.4B **Privately Held**
WEB: www.loglogic.com
SIC: **7371** Computer software development
HQ: Tibco Software Inc.
3307 Hillview Ave
Palo Alto CA 94304

(P-15266)
LUCID VR INC
4500 Great America Pkwy, Santa Clara
(95054-1283)
PHONE.....................408 391-0506
Han Jin, *CEO*
Adam Rowell, *CTO*
EMP: 79 EST: 2015
SALES (est): 323.3K **Privately Held**
SIC: **7371** Computer software development

(P-15267)
MACHINE ZONE INC (PA)
Also Called: Epic War
1050 Page Mill Rd, Palo Alto (94304-1019)
PHONE..................................650 320-1678
Kristen Dumont, *CEO*
Vincenzo Alagna, *President*
Tony Koinov, *President*
Eric Brown, *CFO*
Tory Valenzuela, *Officer*
EMP: 74
SALES (est): 101.8MM **Privately Held**
SIC: 7371 Computer software development

(P-15268)
MAGMA DESIGN AUTOMATION INC (HQ)
1650 Tech Dr Ste 100, San Jose (95110)
PHONE..................................408 565-7500
Rajeev Madhavan, *CEO*
Noriaki Kikuchi, *President*
Peter S Teshima, *CFO*
Gregory C Walker, *Senior VP*
Roy E Jewell, *Principal*
EMP: 410
SQ FT: 106,854
SALES (est): 34.9MM
SALES (corp-wide): 2.7B **Publicly Held**
WEB: www.magma-da.com
SIC: 7371 7373 Computer software development; computer integrated systems design
PA: Synopsys, Inc.
690 E Middlefield Rd
Mountain View CA 94043
650 584-5000

(P-15269)
MAINTECH INCORPORATED
2401 N Glassell St, Orange (92865-2705)
P.O. Box 13500 (92857-8500)
PHONE..................................714 921-8000
Tony Donato, *Vice Pres*
Noel Hughes, *Managing Dir*
Timothy Campagna, *Admin Asst*
Frank Sahanas Jr, *Info Tech Mgr*
Charles Peasley, *Software Engr*
EMP: 200
SQ FT: 1,200
SALES (corp-wide): 1.2MM **Privately Held**
SIC: 7371 3577 Computer software systems analysis & design, custom; computer peripheral equipment
HQ: Maintech, Incorporated
14 Commerce Dr Fl 2
Cranford NJ 07016
973 330-3200

(P-15270)
MAPR TECHNOLOGIES INC (PA)
Also Called: Mapr Data Technologies
4555 Great America Pkwy # 201, Santa Clara (95054-1244)
PHONE..................................408 914-2390
John Schroeder, *CEO*
Daniel K Atler, *CFO*
Steve Jenkins, *Vice Pres*
Geneva Lake, *Vice Pres*
Hayden Noriega, *Vice Pres*
EMP: 260
SQ FT: 55,000
SALES (est): 162.7MM **Privately Held**
SIC: 7371 Computer software development

(P-15271)
MARKET SCAN INFO SYSTEMS INC (PA)
815b Camarillo Springs Rd, Camarillo (93012-9472)
PHONE..................................805 823-4258
Stephen Smythe, *CEO*
Rusty West, *President*
Rustie G West, *CEO*
Nick Kulyk, *CTO*
Jessimyn Thomas, *Human Resources*
EMP: 150
SQ FT: 14,000
SALES (est): 20.2MM **Privately Held**
SIC: 7371 8732 Computer software development; market analysis, business & economic research

(P-15272)
MARKETO INC (DH)
901 Mariners Island Blvd, San Mateo (94404-1592)
PHONE..................................650 376-2300
Steve Lucas, *CEO*
Stephen Ceplenski, *Partner*
Jamie Anderson, *President*
Kate Fitzgerald, *President*
Yasutaka Fukuda, *President*
EMP: 148
SQ FT: 102,670
SALES: 209.8MM
SALES (corp-wide): 7.3B **Publicly Held**
SIC: 7371 7372 Computer software development; computer software writing services; prepackaged software
HQ: Milestone Holdco, Inc.
901 Mariners Island Blvd
San Mateo CA 94404
650 376-2300

(P-15273)
MARKLOGIC CORPORATION (PA)
999 Skyway Rd Ste 200, San Carlos (94070-2722)
PHONE..................................650 655-2300
Gary Bloom, *President*
Peter Norman, *CFO*
David Ponzini, *CFO*
Matt Biear, *Vice Pres*
Julie Globally, *Vice Pres*
EMP: 137 EST: 2004
SQ FT: 40,000
SALES (est): 109.8MM **Privately Held**
WEB: www.cerisent.com
SIC: 7371 Computer software development

(P-15274)
MARKMONITOR HOLDINGS INC
425 Market St Ste 500, San Francisco (94105-2464)
PHONE..................................415 278-8400
Irfan Salim, *President*
Tom Ryden, *Vice Pres*
EMP: 427
SALES (est): 19.8MM **Privately Held**
WEB: www.ftftech.com
SIC: 7371 Computer software development

(P-15275)
MAXPLORE TECHNOLOGIES INC
4450 Rosewood Dr Ste 200, Pleasanton (94588-3061)
PHONE..................................925 621-1400
Sam Mukherjee, *Principal*
EMP: 100
SALES (est): 1.6MM **Privately Held**
SIC: 7371 Computer software development & applications

(P-15276)
MEGA PROFESSIONAL INTL
Also Called: Mpic
995 Montague Expy Ste 121, Milpitas (95035-6827)
PHONE..................................408 946-1500
Monali Mehta, *CEO*
Bob Mehta, *President*
EMP: 52 EST: 1994
SALES (est): 3.1MM **Privately Held**
WEB: www.mpic.com
SIC: 7371 Computer software systems analysis & design, custom

(P-15277)
MEMSQL INC (PA)
534 4th St, San Francisco (94107-1621)
PHONE..................................855 463-6775
Eric Frenkiel, *CEO*
Ankur Goyal, *President*
Jerry Held, *Chairman*
Gary Orenstein, *Chief Mktg Ofcr*
Carl Wright, *Exec VP*
EMP: 50
SALES (est): 8.8MM **Privately Held**
SIC: 7371 Custom computer programming services

(P-15278)
MERA SOFTWARE SERVICES INC
2350 Mission College Blvd, Santa Clara (95054-1532)
PHONE..................................415 513-6401
Konstantin Nikashov, *CEO*
Juerg Lohri, *CFO*
James Hymel, *Senior VP*
Yury Menkov, *Vice Pres*
Andrey Ladygin, *Principal*
EMP: 1300
SALES (est): 27.2MM **Privately Held**
SIC: 7371 Computer software writing services

(P-15279)
METASWITCH NETWORKS
1751 Harbor Bay Pkwy # 125, Alameda (94502-3034)
PHONE..................................415 513-1500
John Lazar, *CEO*
Thomas L Cronan III, *CFO*
Graeme Macarthur, *Exec VP*
Chris Todd, *Exec VP*
EMP: 50
SALES (est): 9.5MM **Privately Held**
SIC: 7371 Computer software development
HQ: Metaswitch Limited
100 Church Street
Enfield MIDDX EN2 6
208 366-1177

(P-15280)
METRON-ATHENE INC (PA)
23046 Avnida De La Crlota Carlota, Laguna Hills (92653)
PHONE..................................949 588-5757
Paul Malton, *President*
David Kitley, *CFO*
John Howorth, *Senior VP*
Sarah Roper, *Software Engr*
Paul Shimell, *Director*
EMP: 75
SQ FT: 25,000
SALES (est): 4.2MM **Privately Held**
WEB: www.metron-athene.com
SIC: 7371 Computer software development

(P-15281)
MIDOKURA USA INC
315 Montgomery St Fl 8, San Francisco (94104-1803)
PHONE..................................888 512-0460
Dan Dumitriu, *CEO*
Adam Johnson, *Vice Pres*
Pino De Candia, *CTO*
Chris Calandro, *Regl Sales Mgr*
EMP: 50
SALES (est): 3.2MM **Privately Held**
SIC: 7371 Computer software development

(P-15282)
MINDSOURCE INC
555 Clyde Ave Ste 100, Mountain View (94043-2269)
PHONE..................................650 314-6400
David Clark, *President*
Gabriel Meza, *CFO*
Jurgen Verstraete, *Officer*
Puneet Sehgal, *Business Dir*
Victor Kumar, *Tech Recruiter*
EMP: 55
SQ FT: 3,200
SALES (est): 7MM **Privately Held**
WEB: www.mindsource.com
SIC: 7371 7372 Computer software development; application computer software

(P-15283)
MINERVA NETWORKS INC (PA)
2150 Gold St, Alviso (95002-3702)
PHONE..................................800 806-9594
Mauro Bonomi, *President*
Dr Jean-Georges Fritsch, *COO*
John Doerner, *CFO*
Jerome Barbedienne, *Vice Pres*
John Campos, *Vice Pres*
EMP: 100
SQ FT: 25,600
SALES (est): 14.1MM **Privately Held**
SIC: 7371 Software programming applications

(P-15284)
MIRNAVSEH INC
Also Called: World For US
8436 Florissant Ct, San Diego (92129-4408)
PHONE..................................858 335-2470
Vitaly Serov, *CEO*
Michael Morozov, *Chief Engr*
EMP: 90
SQ FT: 2,500
SALES (est): 5MM **Privately Held**
SIC: 7371 Computer software development

(P-15285)
MISSION CRITICAL TECH INC
2041 Rosecrans Ave # 220, El Segundo (90245-4789)
PHONE..................................310 246-4455
Yorgos Stylianos, *CEO*
EMP: 50
SQ FT: 3,000
SALES (est): 7.1MM **Privately Held**
WEB: www.mctinc.com
SIC: 7371 8331 7361 7379 Computer software development; job training & vocational rehabilitation services; executive placement; computer related consulting services

(P-15286)
MITCHELL INTERNATIONAL INC (HQ)
6220 Greenwich Dr, San Diego (92122-5913)
P.O. Box 229001 (92192-9001)
PHONE..................................858 368-7000
James Lindner, *Vice Ch Bd*
Jack Farnan, *President*
Alex Sun, *President*
Arthur J Long, *CFO*
Jesse Herrera, *Exec VP*
EMP: 148
SQ FT: 141,000
SALES (est): 3.2B **Publicly Held**
WEB: www.mitchell.com
SIC: 7371 Computer software development

(P-15287)
MOBILE PROGRAMMING LLC (PA)
30300 Agoura Rd Ste 140, Agoura Hills (91301-5406)
PHONE..................................310 584-6300
Ishwar Singh, *President*
Craig Ford, *Managing Dir*
EMP: 51
SALES (est): 4.4MM **Privately Held**
SIC: 7371 Computer software systems analysis & design, custom; computer software development & applications

(P-15288)
MOBILITYWARE INC
440 Exchange Ste 100, Irvine (92602-1390)
PHONE..................................949 788-9900
John Libby, *President*
Robert Jackson, *Vice Pres*
Natasha Dressler, *Executive Asst*
John Heard, *Sr Software Eng*
Ken Mason, *Sr Software Eng*
EMP: 58
SALES (est): 9.3MM **Privately Held**
SIC: 7371 Computer software development

(P-15289)
MODRINE LIMITED
750 N Diamond Bar Blvd, Diamond Bar (91765-1023)
PHONE..................................213 269-5466
Fang He, *Sales Mgr*
EMP: 69
SALES: 275K **Privately Held**
SIC: 7371 Computer software development & applications

(P-15290)
MOJO NETWORKS INC (PA)
5453 Great America Pkwy, Santa Clara (95054-3645)
PHONE..................................650 961-1111
Rick Wilmer, *CEO*

Tushar Saxena, *Partner*
Mike Anthofer, *CFO*
Freddy Mangum, *Chief Mktg Ofcr*
Anthony Paladino, *Managing Dir*
EMP: 86
SALES (est): 33.6MM **Privately Held**
WEB: www.airtightnetworks.net
SIC: 7371 Computer software development

(P-15291)
MONITISE AMERICAS INC
1 Embrcdero Cntre Fl 9 Flr 9, San Francisco (94111)
PHONE..............................415 526-7000
Elizabeth Buse, *CEO*
Anna Howard, *President*
Lisa Stanton, *President*
Lee Cameron, *CEO*
Brad Petzer, *CFO*
EMP: 61
SQ FT: 9,000
SALES (est): 13.7MM
SALES (corp-wide): 5.7B **Publicly Held**
WEB: www.clairmail.com
SIC: 7371 Computer software development
HQ: Monitise Limited
    Medius House, 3rd Floor
    London W1F 8
    203 005-3300

(P-15292)
MOOV CORPORATION
Also Called: Moovweb
123 Mission St Ste 1000, San Francisco (94105-5126)
PHONE..............................877 666-8932
Ajay Kapur, *CEO*
Chris Finlayson, *Executive*
Fady Awada, *Info Tech Mgr*
Doris Chen, *Accounting Mgr*
Maggie Lin, *Controller*
EMP: 105
SALES (est): 12.7MM **Privately Held**
SIC: 7371 Computer software development

(P-15293)
MOTIGA INC
100 Rdwood Shres Pkwy 4, Redwood City (94065)
PHONE..............................425 748-8509
Christopher Chung, *CEO*
Patrick Lambright, *CTO*
EMP: 77 **EST:** 2010
SQ FT: 1,400
SALES (est): 7MM **Privately Held**
SIC: 7371 Computer software development

(P-15294)
MOTION MATH INC
582 Market St Ste 511, San Francisco (94104-5306)
PHONE..............................415 590-2961
Jacob Klein, *CEO*
Gabriel Adauto, *CTO*
EMP: 120 **EST:** 2010
SALES (est): 3.5MM
SALES (corp-wide): 14MM **Privately Held**
SIC: 7371 Computer software development & applications
PA: Curriculum Associates, Llc
    153 Rangeway Rd
    North Billerica MA 01862
    978 667-8000

(P-15295)
MOTOROLA SOLUTIONS INC
805 E Middlefield Rd, Mountain View (94043-4025)
PHONE..............................650 318-3200
Maulik Desai, *Manager*
EMP: 60
SALES (corp-wide): 6.3B **Publicly Held**
WEB: www.motorola.com
SIC: 7371 Custom computer programming services
PA: Motorola Solutions, Inc.
    500 W Monroe St Ste 4400
    Chicago IL 60661
    847 576-5000

(P-15296)
MSHIFT INC
39899 Balentine Dr # 235, Newark (94560-5358)
PHONE..............................408 437-2740
Scott Moeller, *CEO*
Eric Buchbinder, *Officer*
Jeff Chen, *Vice Pres*
Alan Finke, *Vice Pres*
Jacqueline Snell, *Vice Pres*
EMP: 50
SALES (est): 6.8MM **Privately Held**
WEB: www.mobileshift.com
SIC: 7371 Computer software development & applications

(P-15297)
N A ARICENT INC
226 Airport Pkwy Ste 595, San Jose (95110-3704)
PHONE..............................408 324-1800
Pradeep Vajram, *President*
Sanjay Palasamudram, *COO*
Vijay Krishnamurthy, *CFO*
Vinod Kaushik, *Vice Pres*
EMP: 60
SALES (est): 4.7MM **Privately Held**
WEB: www.tforceinc.com
SIC: 7371 Custom computer programming services

(P-15298)
N MODEL INC (PA)
777 Mariners Island Blvd, San Mateo (94404-5008)
PHONE..............................650 610-4600
Jason Blessing, *CEO*
Charlie Abrams, *Partner*
David Barter, *CFO*
Charles Robel, *Chairman*
Mark Anderson, *Senior VP*
EMP: 137
SQ FT: 35,000
SALES (est): 131.1MM **Publicly Held**
WEB: www.modeln.com
SIC: 7371 Computer software development; computer software development & applications

(P-15299)
NANTMOBILE LLC
9920 Jefferson Blvd, Culver City (90232-3506)
PHONE..............................310 883-7888
Patrick Soon-Shiong,
EMP: 200
SALES (est): 3.7MM **Privately Held**
SIC: 7371 Computer software development

(P-15300)
NAVIS HOLDINGS LLC
55 Harrison St Ste 600, Oakland (94607-3776)
PHONE..............................510 267-5000
John Dillon, *CEO*
Jonathan Shields PHD, *CTO*
Erik Tiemroth PHD,
Peter Seiler, *Consultant*
EMP: 139
SALES (est): 7MM
SALES (corp-wide): 3.8B **Privately Held**
SIC: 7371 Computer software development
HQ: Hiab Usa Inc.
    12233 Williams Rd
    Perrysburg OH 43551
    419 482-6000

(P-15301)
NCIRCLE NETWORK SECURITY INC (DH)
101 2nd St Ste 400, San Francisco (94105-3645)
PHONE..............................415 625-5900
Abe Kleinfeld, *President*
Kelly E Lang, *CEO*
Mark Elchinoff, *CFO*
Beverly D'Elena, *Vice Pres*
Karl Hutter, *Vice Pres*
EMP: 63
SQ FT: 20,000

SALES (est): 11.2MM
SALES (corp-wide): 2.3B **Publicly Held**
WEB: www.ncircle.com
SIC: 7371 Computer software development & applications
HQ: Tripwire, Inc.
    101 Sw Main St Ste 1500
    Portland OR 97204
    503 276-7500

(P-15302)
NETEASE INFORMATION TECH CORP
2000 Sierra Point Pkwy # 800, Brisbane (94005-1845)
PHONE..............................415 612-7866
Zhuo Huang, *CEO*
Kathleen Asbury, *Manager*
Gordon Liu, *Manager*
EMP: 60 **EST:** 2014
SALES (est): 4.6MM **Privately Held**
SIC: 7371 Computer software development & applications

(P-15303)
NETSKOPE INC
270 3rd St, Los Altos (94022-3617)
PHONE..............................800 979-6988
Sanjay Beri, *CEO*
Abhay Kulkarni, *President*
Lebin Cheng, *Vice Pres*
Bob Gilbert, *Vice Pres*
Scott Hogrefe, *Vice Pres*
EMP: 100
SALES (est): 26.6MM **Privately Held**
SIC: 7371 Computer software development

(P-15304)
NETZERO INC (DH)
21301 Burbank Blvd Fl 3, Woodland Hills (91367-6697)
P.O. Box 5004 (91365-5004)
PHONE..............................805 418-2000
Mark R Goldston, *Ch of Bd*
Charles S Hilliard, *CFO*
Gerald Popek, *CTO*
Allison King, *Research*
EMP: 250
SQ FT: 48,000
SALES (est): 29.8MM **Publicly Held**
WEB: www.netzero.net
SIC: 7371 Computer software systems analysis & design, custom
HQ: United Online, Inc.
    21255 Burbank Blvd # 400
    Woodland Hills CA 91367
    818 287-3000

(P-15305)
NEUINTEL LLC (PA)
Also Called: Price Spider
20 Pacifica Ste 1000, Irvine (92618-7462)
PHONE..............................949 625-6117
Parsa Rohani,
Jon Pfortmiller, *President*
Anthony Ferry, *CEO*
Tim Marshall,
EMP: 80
SQ FT: 17,000
SALES (est): 16.5MM **Privately Held**
SIC: 7371 Computer software development

(P-15306)
NEVERSOFT ENTERTAINMENT INC
21255 Burbank Blvd # 600, Woodland Hills (91367-6744)
PHONE..............................818 610-4100
Joel Jewett, *President*
Sandy Jewett, *Data Proc Staff*
EMP: 170
SALES (est): 9.5MM
SALES (corp-wide): 7B **Publicly Held**
WEB: www.blizzard.com
SIC: 7371 7372 Computer code authors; prepackaged software
PA: Activision Blizzard, Inc.
    3100 Ocean Park Blvd
    Santa Monica CA 90405
    310 255-2000

(P-15307)
NEXA TECHNOLOGIES INC (HQ)
18552 Macarthur Blvd # 100, Irvine (92612-1235)
PHONE..............................972 590-8669
Eric Stoop, *President*
EMP: 65
SALES (est): 9.5MM **Privately Held**
WEB: www.nexatech.com
SIC: 7371 Computer software development

(P-15308)
NEXGENIX INC (PA)
2 Peters Canyon Rd # 200, Irvine (92606-1798)
PHONE..............................714 665-6240
Rick Dutta, *CEO*
Don Ganguly, *Ch of Bd*
Mark Iwanowski, *COO*
Dave R Andrade, *Vice Pres*
Ravi Renduchintala, *Vice Pres*
EMP: 258
SQ FT: 14,264
SALES (est): 25.1MM **Privately Held**
SIC: 7371 8748 4813 Computer software development; systems analysis or design;

(P-15309)
NEXTGEN HEALTHCARE INFO SYSTEM (HQ)
18111 Von Karman Ave, Irvine (92612-0199)
PHONE..............................949 255-2600
John Frantz, *President*
Roy Feague, *President*
Gene Gallogly, *President*
Daniel J Morefield, *COO*
Paul Holt, *CFO*
EMP: 65
SALES: 400MM
SALES (corp-wide): 531MM **Publicly Held**
SIC: 7371 5072 Computer software systems analysis & design, custom; hardware
PA: Quality Systems, Inc.
    18111 Von Karman Ave # 700
    Irvine CA 92612
    949 255-2600

(P-15310)
NIELSEN CLARITAS INC
9444 Waples St Ste 280, San Diego (92121-2985)
PHONE..............................858 622-0800
Karolina Roszel, *CTO*
Vanessa Hernandez, *Senior Mgr*
Robert Halford, *Director*
Elizabeth V Phillips, *Director*
Mimi Kim, *Manager*
EMP: 455
SALES (est): 12.6MM **Privately Held**
WEB: www.claritas.com
SIC: 7371 8742 Computer software development; marketing consulting services

(P-15311)
NITAI PARTNERS INC
1761 Reichert Way, Chula Vista (91913-4345)
PHONE..............................855 879-2847
Aditya Satsangi, *CEO*
Konisha Satsangi, *Principal*
EMP: 80 **EST:** 2011
SALES (est): 5MM **Privately Held**
SIC: 7371 7373 7372 7374 Computer software systems analysis & design, custom; systems integration services; business oriented computer software; data processing & preparation

(P-15312)
NITRO SOFTWARE INC
20 California St Ste 400, San Francisco (94111-4832)
PHONE..............................415 632-4894
Sam Chandler, *President*
Gina O Reilly, *COO*
Peter Bardwick, *CFO*
Richard Wenzel, *Treasurer*
Jeff Kreutz, *Vice Pres*
▼ **EMP:** 125
SQ FT: 6,000

SALES (est): 22.6MM
SALES (corp-wide): 20.8MM **Privately Held**
WEB: www.nitropdf.com
SIC: 7371 Computer software development
PA: Nitro Software Pty Ltd
    L4 246 Bourke St
    Melbourne VIC 3000
    399 290-400

(P-15313)
NOMINUM INC (HQ)
3355 Scott Blvd Fl 3, Santa Clara
(95054-3127)
PHONE..................................650 381-6000
Garry Messiana, *CEO*
Gopala Tumuluri, *COO*
Bob Verheecke, *CFO*
Pete Wisowaty, *Exec VP*
Srini Avirneni, *Senior VP*
EMP: 50
SQ FT: 15,000
SALES (est): 29.6MM
SALES (corp-wide): 2.5B **Publicly Held**
WEB: www.nominum.com
SIC: 7371 Computer software development
PA: Akamai Technologies, Inc.
    150 Broadway Ste 100
    Cambridge MA 02142
    617 444-3000

(P-15314)
NOODLE ANALYTICS INC
Also Called: Noodle.ai
604 Mission St Fl 9 Flr 9, Oakland (94605)
PHONE..................................415 412-2139
Stephen Pratt, *CEO*
Deepinder Dhingra,
Chelsea Hardaway, *Officer*
EMP: 100
SALES: 10MM **Privately Held**
SIC: 7371 Computer software development & applications

(P-15315)
NORTHROP GRUMMAN SYSTEMS CORP
9326 Spectrum Center Blvd, San Diego
(92123-1443)
PHONE..................................858 514-0400
James F Harvey, *General Mgr*
EMP: 260 **Publicly Held**
SIC: 7371 7379 Computer software development; computer related consulting services
HQ: Northrop Grumman Systems Corporation
    2980 Fairview Park Dr
    Falls Church VA 22042
    703 280-2900

(P-15316)
NORTHSTAR TECHNOLOGY CORP (PA)
32 Mauchly Ste C, Irvine (92618-2336)
PHONE..................................949 788-0738
Frances Chiang, *CEO*
Warren Matthews, *COO*
David Wills, *Project Mgr*
Phyllis Chang, *Human Resources*
EMP: 250
SQ FT: 1,500
SALES (est): 21.6MM **Privately Held**
SIC: 7371 Computer software development

(P-15317)
NOVALOGIC INC (PA)
27489 Agoura Rd Ste 300, Agoura Hills
(91301-2419)
PHONE..................................818 880-1997
John Garcia, *Ch of Bd*
John Butrovich, *Vice Pres*
Kyle Freeman, *Vice Pres*
David Seeholzer, *Vice Pres*
EMP: 100
SALES (est): 5.5MM **Privately Held**
WEB: www.novalogic.com
SIC: 7371 5734 7372 Computer software development & applications; software, business & non-game; prepackaged software

(P-15318)
NPARIO INC
350 Cambridge Ave Ste 330, Palo Alto
(94306-1578)
PHONE..................................650 461-9696
Bassel Ojjeh, *CEO*
EMP: 53
SALES (est): 2.5MM **Privately Held**
SIC: 7371 Computer software systems analysis & design, custom

(P-15319)
NTENT INC
1808 Aston Ave Ste 170, Carlsbad
(92008-7367)
PHONE..................................760 930-7600
Patti Stewart, *Manager*
EMP: 60
SALES (corp-wide): 8.9MM **Privately Held**
WEB: www.concera.com
SIC: 7371 Computer software development
PA: Ntent, Inc.
    135 W 41st St Frnt 2
    New York NY 10036
    212 967-9502

(P-15320)
NTS IT CARE INC
1605 S Main St Ste 125, Milpitas
(95035-6270)
PHONE..................................408 480-4083
Jagmeet Singh Virk, *President*
EMP: 180
SALES: 2MM **Privately Held**
SIC: 7371 Computer software development

(P-15321)
NUANCE COMMUNICATIONS INC
1005 Hamilton Ct, Menlo Park
(94025-1422)
PHONE..................................650 847-0000
Doug Neilsson, *Principal*
EMP: 150 **Publicly Held**
WEB: www.nuance.com
SIC: 7371 Computer software development
PA: Nuance Communications, Inc.
    1 Wayside Rd
    Burlington MA 01803

(P-15322)
NUNA INCORPORATED
Also Called: Nuna Health
650 Townsend St Ste 425, San Francisco
(94103-6221)
PHONE..................................415 942-5200
Jini Kim, *CEO*
Neil Austin, *Business Dir*
Katja Gussmann, *Executive Asst*
Joey Liaw, *Administration*
Clint Talbert, *VP Engrg*
EMP: 100
SQ FT: 25,000
SALES: 5MM **Privately Held**
SIC: 7371 Computer software development & applications

(P-15323)
NUTANIX INC (PA)
1740 Tech Dr Ste 150, San Jose (95110)
PHONE..................................408 216-8360
Dheeraj Pandey, *Ch of Bd*
Sudheesh Nair Vadakkedath, *President*
Duston M Williams, *CFO*
Howard Ting, *Chief Mktg Ofcr*
Sunil Potti,
EMP: 623
SQ FT: 176,000
SALES: 1.1B **Publicly Held**
SIC: 7371 Computer software development

(P-15324)
OBJECTIVE SYSTEMS INTEGRATORS (HQ)
Also Called: OSI
2365 Iron Point Rd # 170, Folsom
(95630-8711)
PHONE..................................916 467-1500
Mounir Ladki, *Principal*

Cheri Simko, *Vice Pres*
Beth Popham, *Executive Asst*
Curtis Crum, *Software Dev*
Danny Ho, *Software Engr*
EMP: 50
SQ FT: 14,000
SALES (est): 24.9MM
SALES (corp-wide): 3.9MM **Privately Held**
SIC: 7371 Computer software development
PA: Mycom France
    6 A 8
    Puteaux 92800
    147 730-651

(P-15325)
OBLONG INDUSTRIES INC (PA)
923 E 3rd St Ste 111, Los Angeles
(90013-1867)
PHONE..................................213 683-8863
John Underkoffler, *CEO*
Stewart Armstrong, *Officer*
David Kung, *Vice Pres*
Carlton Sparrell, *Vice Pres*
Tom Harvey, *Executive*
EMP: 140
SALES (est): 23.6MM **Privately Held**
SIC: 7371 Computer software development & applications

(P-15326)
OKTA INC (PA)
301 Brannan St Fl 1, San Francisco
(94107-3816)
PHONE..................................888 722-7871
Todd McKinnon, *Ch of Bd*
Charles Race, *President*
J Frederic Kerrest, *COO*
Jacques Frede Kerrest, *COO*
William E Losch, *CFO*
EMP: 148
SQ FT: 128,000
SALES: 259.9MM **Publicly Held**
SIC: 7371 Software programming applications

(P-15327)
OMNIUPDATE INC
1320 Flynn Rd Ste 100, Camarillo
(93012-8745)
PHONE..................................805 484-9400
Lance Merker, *President*
Tom Nalevanko, *Vice Pres*
Tom Smart, *Vice Pres*
Jeremy Rex, *Info Tech Mgr*
Priyank Bhatnagar, *Software Dev*
EMP: 60
SQ FT: 6,600
SALES: 10MM **Privately Held**
WEB: www.omniedit.com
SIC: 7371 7372 Computer software development; prepackaged software

(P-15328)
ONEBILL SOFTWARE INC
3080 Olcott St Ste D230, Santa Clara
(95054-3271)
PHONE..................................844 462-7638
Jk Chelladurai, *CEO*
Rajesh Jadhev, *Vice Pres*
Bob Maguire, *Vice Pres*
Kathy Mori, *Vice Pres*
Raj Padmanabhan, *Vice Pres*
EMP: 70
SALES (est): 2.1MM **Privately Held**
SIC: 7371 5734 Computer software development; computer software & accessories

(P-15329)
ONSOLVE LLC
3398 Carmel Mountain Rd # 100, San
Diego (92121-1044)
PHONE..................................858 724-1200
Wain Kellum, *Branch Mgr*
EMP: 90
SALES (corp-wide): 1B **Privately Held**
SIC: 7371 Computer software development & applications
HQ: Onsolve, Llc
    780 W Granada Blvd
    Ormond Beach FL 32174

(P-15330)
OOYALA INC (HQ)
2099 Gateway Pl Ste 600, San Jose
(95110-1048)
PHONE..................................650 961-3400
Jonathan Huberman, *CEO*
Jay Fulcher, *President*
David Wilson, *CFO*
Maria Flores, *Vice Pres*
Dave Hare, *Vice Pres*
EMP: 113
SALES (est): 110.2MM **Privately Held**
SIC: 7371 Software programming applications
PA: Ooyala Holdings, Inc.
    2099 Gateway Pl Ste 600
    San Jose CA 95110
    650 961-3400

(P-15331)
OPEN TEXT INC (HQ)
Also Called: Hightail
2950 S Delaware St, San Mateo
(94403-2199)
PHONE..................................650 645-3000
John Doolittle, *CEO*
Hormuz Adrianwala, *Vice Pres*
Steve Jewett, *Vice Pres*
Christopher Patterson, *Executive*
Jay Raulerson, *Executive*
EMP: 109
SALES (est): 221.5MM
SALES (corp-wide): 2.2B **Privately Held**
SIC: 7371 Computer software development
PA: Open Text Corporation
    275 Frank Tompa Dr
    Waterloo ON N2L 0
    519 888-7111

(P-15332)
OPERATION TECHNOLOGY INC (PA)
Also Called: Etap
17 Goodyear Ste 100, Irvine (92618-1822)
PHONE..................................949 462-0100
Farrokh Shokooh, *President*
Ben Boronow, *Vice Pres*
Nikta Nikzad Shokooh, *Admin Sec*
Cass Cunningham, *Sr Software Eng*
EMP: 90
SQ FT: 32,000
SALES (est): 18.2MM **Privately Held**
WEB: www.etap.com
SIC: 7371 8732 8249 Computer software development; research services, except laboratory; business training services

(P-15333)
OPSWAT INC (PA)
398 Kansas St, San Francisco
(94103-5130)
P.O. Box 77878 (94107-0878)
PHONE..................................415 590-7300
Benjamin Czarny, *President*
Patrick Tan, *CFO*
Frank Cohen, *Vice Pres*
Gary Mitchell, *Exec Dir*
Jeanelle Narine, *Office Mgr*
EMP: 58
SQ FT: 15,000
SALES (est): 11.4MM **Privately Held**
SIC: 7371 Computer software development

(P-15334)
OPTIMIZELY INC (PA)
631 Howard St Ste 100, San Francisco
(94105-3934)
PHONE..................................415 376-4598
Jay Larson, *CEO*
Julie Ritchie, *Partner*
Hiliary Robertson, *Partner*
Dan Siroker, *Chairman*
Carl Tsukahara, *Chief Mktg Ofcr*
EMP: 280
SQ FT: 76,000
SALES (est): 63.2MM **Privately Held**
SIC: 7371 Computer software development

(P-15335)
OPUS INSPECTION INC
1410 S Acacia Ave Ste A, Fullerton
(92831-5309)
PHONE..................................714 999-6727

Mike Golway, *Branch Mgr*
EMP: 55 **Privately Held**
WEB: www.esp-global.com
SIC: 7371 Computer software development
PA: Opus Inspection, Inc.
   7 Kripes Rd
   East Granby CT 06026
   -

(P-15336)
ORACLE AMERICA INC
4120 Network Cir, Santa Clara
(95054-1778)
PHONE..................................408 276-3331
Scott G McNealy, *Ch of Bd*
Ashok Krishnamurthi, *CEO*
Karen Willem, *CFO*
Rick Fabiano, *Principal*
Mark Leslie, *Principal*
EMP: 150
SALES (est): 14.8MM **Privately Held**
WEB: www.xsigo.com
SIC: 7371 Computer software development

(P-15337)
ORIGIN SYSTEMS INC
209 Redwood Shores Pkwy, Redwood City
(94065-1175)
PHONE..................................650 628-1500
EMP: 270
SQ FT: 175,000
SALES (est): 9.1MM
SALES (corp-wide): 4.5B **Publicly Held**
SIC: 7371
PA: Electronic Arts Inc.
   209 Redwood Shores Pkwy
   Redwood City CA 94065
   650 628-7272

(P-15338)
OSISOFT LLC (PA)
Also Called: OSI Software
1600 Alvarado St, San Leandro
(94577-2600)
P.O. Box 727 (94577-0427)
PHONE..................................510 297-5800
Dr J Patrick Kennedy, *Ch of Bd*
Eric Cardinal, *Partner*
Jenny Linton, *President*
Bob Guilbault, *COO*
Susanna Kass, *COO*
▲ **EMP:** 418
SQ FT: 55,000
SALES (est): 256.2MM **Privately Held**
WEB: www.osisoft.com
SIC: 7371 7372 7373 Custom computer programming services; application computer software; computer integrated systems design

(P-15339)
P MURPHY & ASSOCIATES INC
359 E Magnolia Blvd Ste G, Burbank
(91502-3211)
PHONE..................................818 841-2002
Phyliss Murphy, *President*
EMP: 121
SQ FT: 1,200
SALES (est): 8.8MM
SALES (corp-wide): 75.2MM **Privately Held**
WEB: www.pmurphy.com
SIC: 7371 Computer software development; employment agencies; executive placement
PA: Intelliswift Software, Inc.
   39600 Balentine Dr # 200
   Newark CA 94560
   510 490-9240

(P-15340)
PACKET DESIGN INC
1 Almaden Blvd Ste 1150, San Jose
(95113-2249)
PHONE..................................408 490-1000
Judy Estrin, *Chairman*
Jack Bradley, *CEO*
Steve Ackley, *Exec VP*
Jeff Raice, *Exec VP*
Daniel Ley, *Senior VP*
EMP: 56

SALES (est): 5.9MM **Privately Held**
WEB: www.packetdesign.com
SIC: 7371 Computer software development

(P-15341)
PACKETVIDEO CORPORATION (DH)
10350 Science Center Dr, San Diego
(92121-1129)
PHONE..................................858 731-5300
James C Brailean, *CEO*
John Driver, *Chief Mktg Ofcr*
Corbett Kull, *Vice Pres*
Kazunori Takagi, *Vice Pres*
Mike Mester, *Manager*
EMP: 100 **EST:** 1998
SQ FT: 22,000
SALES (est): 18.6MM
SALES (corp-wide): 110.7B **Privately Held**
WEB: www.packetvideo.com
SIC: 7371 7374 4812 Computer software development; data processing & preparation; radio telephone communication
HQ: Ntt Docomo, Inc.
   2-11-1, Nagatacho
   Chiyoda-Ku TKY 100-0
   351 561-111

(P-15342)
PALANTIR TECHNOLOGIES INC (PA)
100 Hamilton Ave Ste 300, Palo Alto
(94301-1651)
PHONE..................................650 815-0200
Alex Karp, *President*
Geoff Belknap, *Officer*
Erin Adam, *Executive Asst*
Nan Burton, *Executive Asst*
Nicole Harrison, *Executive Asst*
EMP: 148
SQ FT: 65,000
SALES (est): 386.5MM **Privately Held**
WEB: www.palantirtech.com
SIC: 7371 Computer software development

(P-15343)
PALANTIR USG INC (HQ)
635 Waverley St, Palo Alto (94301-2550)
PHONE..................................650 815-0200
Akash Jain, *President*
EMP: 190
SQ FT: 4,000
SALES: 3MM
SALES (corp-wide): 386.5MM **Privately Held**
SIC: 7371 Computer software development
PA: Palantir Technologies Inc.
   100 Hamilton Ave Ste 300
   Palo Alto CA 94301
   650 815-0200

(P-15344)
PANASAS INC (PA)
969 W Maude Ave, Sunnyvale
(94085-2802)
PHONE..................................408 215-6800
Faye Pairman, *President*
Tom Shea, *COO*
Stephanie Vinella, *CFO*
Jim Donovan, *Chief Mktg Ofcr*
Barbara Murphy, *Chief Mktg Ofcr*
EMP: 100
SQ FT: 20,000
SALES (est): 30.4MM **Privately Held**
WEB: www.panasas.com
SIC: 7371 Computer software development

(P-15345)
PATIENTSAFE SOLUTIONS INC (PA)
9330 Scranton Rd, San Diego
(92121-7704)
PHONE..................................858 746-3100
Si Luo, *President*
Bill Roof, *President*
Mark Young, *COO*
Balaji Sekar, *CFO*
Tim Needham, *Ch Credit Ofcr*
EMP: 83

SALES (est): 16MM **Privately Held**
WEB: www.patientsafesolutions.com
SIC: 7371 Software programming applications

(P-15346)
PATREON INC
600 Townsend St Ste 500, San Francisco
(94103-5696)
PHONE..................................415 967-2735
Jack Conte, *CEO*
Chelsea Wagenbrenner, *Opers Mgr*
EMP: 95
SALES (est): 10.3MM **Privately Held**
SIC: 7371 Computer software development & applications

(P-15347)
PATTERSON DENTAL SUPPLY INC
Also Called: Dolphin Imaging MGT Solutions
9200 Oakdale Ave Ste 500, Chatsworth
(91311-6556)
PHONE..................................818 435-1368
Sonya Lester, *Branch Mgr*
Joanna Tavanlar, *Manager*
EMP: 50
SALES (corp-wide): 5.4B **Publicly Held**
SIC: 7371 Computer software development & applications; computer software development
HQ: Patterson Dental Supply, Inc.
   1031 Mendota Heights Rd
   Saint Paul MN 55120
   651 686-1600

(P-15348)
PAYMENT PROCESSING INC
Also Called: Paypros
8200 Central Ave, Newark (94560-3448)
PHONE..................................510 795-2290
Charles R Smith, *CEO*
Eddie Myers, *President*
John Malnar, *CFO*
Chuck Riegel, *Exec VP*
Joe Monteil, *CIO*
EMP: 150
SQ FT: 59,000
SALES (est): 253.6K
SALES (corp-wide): 3.9B **Publicly Held**
WEB: www.paypros2.com
SIC: 7371 Computer software development & applications
PA: Global Payments Inc.
   3550 Lenox Rd Ne Ste 3000
   Atlanta GA 30326
   770 829-8000

(P-15349)
PDF SOLUTIONS INC (PA)
333 W San Carlos St, San Jose
(95110-2726)
PHONE..................................408 280-7900
John K Kibarian, *President*
Lucio L Lanza, *Ch of Bd*
Gregory Walker, *President*
Cees Hartgring, *Vice Pres*
Koji Maekawa, *Vice Pres*
EMP: 50
SQ FT: 28,600
SALES: 101.8MM **Publicly Held**
WEB: www.pdf.com
SIC: 7371 Computer software development

(P-15350)
PEPPERJAM LLC
Also Called: Adassured
408 Cassidy St Ste 101, Oceanside
(92054-5316)
PHONE..................................760 585-7150
EMP: 136
SALES (corp-wide): 18.2MM **Privately Held**
SIC: 7371 Computer software development & applications
PA: Pepperjam Llc
   7 S Main St
   Wilkes Barre PA 18701
   877 796-5700

(P-15351)
PERFECT WORLD ENTRMT INC
101 Redwood Shr Pkwy # 400, Redwood City (94065-1180)
PHONE..................................650 590-7700

Alan Chen, *CEO*
Yan Ji, *Vice Pres*
Bill Wang, *Vice Pres*
Robert H Xiao, *Vice Pres*
Kathy Chan, *Executive Asst*
EMP: 150 **EST:** 2007
SQ FT: 10,000
SALES (est): 26.7MM **Privately Held**
SIC: 7371 Computer software development & applications
HQ: Perfect World Co., Ltd.
   Rm 701-14,Building 5,No.1,Shangdi East Road,
   Beijing 10010
   105 780-5623

(P-15352)
PERNIXDATA INC
1740 Tech Dr Ste 150, San Jose (95110)
PHONE..................................408 724-8413
Poojan Kumar, *CEO*
Bala Narasimhan, *Vice Pres*
David Ducom, *Executive*
Mike Munoz, *Risk Mgmt Dir*
Satyam Vaghani, *CTO*
EMP: 75
SALES (est): 10.4MM **Publicly Held**
SIC: 7371 Computer software development & applications
PA: Nutanix, Inc.
   1740 Tech Dr Ste 150
   San Jose CA 95110
   -

(P-15353)
PERSISTENT SYSTEMS INC (HQ)
2055 Laurelwood Rd # 210, Santa Clara
(95054-2727)
PHONE..................................408 216-7010
Anand Deshpande, *CEO*
Jitendra Gokhale, *President*
Atul Khadilkar, *President*
Sudhir Kulkarni, *President*
Kiran Naik, *President*
EMP: 65
SQ FT: 25,500
SALES: 158MM
SALES (corp-wide): 268.8MM **Privately Held**
WEB: www.persistentsystems.com
SIC: 7371 Computer software development
PA: Persistent Systems Limited
   Bhageerath, 402 Senapati Bapat Road,
   Pune MH 41101
   206 703-0000

(P-15354)
PERSISTENT TLCOM SOLUTIONS INC
Also Called: Persistant Systems
2055 Laurelwood Rd # 210, Santa Clara
(95054-2729)
PHONE..................................408 216-7010
Dr Anand Suresh Deshpande, *CEO*
Jitendra Gokhale, *President*
Hari Haran, *President*
Atul Khadilkar, *President*
Sudhir Kulkarni, *President*
EMP: 50
SQ FT: 25,500
SALES (est): 4MM
SALES (corp-wide): 268.8MM **Privately Held**
SIC: 7371 Computer software development
HQ: Persistent Systems Inc.
   2055 Laurelwood Rd # 210
   Santa Clara CA 95054
   408 216-7010

(P-15355)
PERSONAGRAPH CORPORATION
920 Stewart Dr Ste 100, Sunnyvale
(94085-3923)
PHONE..................................408 616-1600
Mandar Shinde, *CEO*
Jason Davis, *Treasurer*
William Rainey, *Admin Sec*
EMP: 55 **EST:** 2012
SQ FT: 1,500
SALES (est): 183.9K **Privately Held**
SIC: 7371 Computer software systems analysis & design, custom

(P-15356)
PHACIL INC
601 California St # 1710, San Francisco
(94108-2822)
PHONE...................................415 901-1600
Sascha Mornell, *Principal*
EMP: 512
SALES (corp-wide): 108.5MM **Privately Held**
WEB: www.phacil.com
SIC: 7371 Computer software development
PA: Phacil, Inc.
8484 Westpark Dr Ste 600
Mc Lean VA 22102
703 526-1800

(P-15357)
PHILIPS HLTHCARE INFRMTICS INC (DH)
4430 Rosewood Dr Ste 200, Pleasanton
(94588-3050)
PHONE...................................650 293-2300
Deborah Disanzo, *CEO*
Davidi Gilo, *Ch of Bd*
Oran Muduroglu, *President*
Douglas Sinclair, *CFO*
Dana Cambra, *Vice Pres*
EMP: 148
SQ FT: 31,523
SALES (est): 92.5MM
SALES (corp-wide): 20.9B **Privately Held**
WEB: www.stentor.com
SIC: 7371 Computer software development & applications
HQ: Philips North America Llc
3000 Minuteman Rd Ms1203
Andover MA 01810
978 659-3000

(P-15358)
PHILOTIC INC
524 3rd St, San Francisco (94107-1805)
PHONE...................................510 730-1740
Jimmy Kittiyachavalit, *Mng Member*
EMP: 62
SALES (est): 3.6MM **Privately Held**
SIC: 7371 Custom computer programming services

(P-15359)
PICSART INC
351 California St Ste 650, San Francisco
(94104-2407)
PHONE...................................415 757-6800
Hovhannes Avoyan, *CEO*
Artavazd Mehrabyan, *COO*
Tammy H Nam, *COO*
Alan Chinn, *CFO*
Argam Derhartunian, *Vice Pres*
EMP: 100
SALES (est): 240K **Privately Held**
SIC: 7371 Computer software development

(P-15360)
PIVOT SYSTEMS INC
4320 Stevens Creek Blvd, San Jose
(95129-1202)
PHONE...................................408 435-1000
Rajesh Nair, *CEO*
Smita Nair, *Admin Sec*
EMP: 160
SQ FT: 40,000
SALES (est): 10.9MM **Privately Held**
WEB: www.pivotsys.com
SIC: 7371 Computer software development & applications

(P-15361)
PIVOTAL SOFTWARE INC (HQ)
Also Called: Pivotal Labs
875 Howard St Fl 5, San Francisco
(94103-3021)
PHONE...................................415 777-4868
Robert Mee, *CEO*
Paul Maritz, *Ch of Bd*
William Cook, *President*
Cynthia Gaylor, *CFO*
Andrew Cohen, *Senior VP*
EMP: 113
SQ FT: 66,510
SALES: 509.4MM
SALES (corp-wide): 78.6B **Publicly Held**
SIC: 7371 Computer software development & applications

PA: Dell Technologies Inc.
1 Dell Way
Round Rock TX 78682
800 289-3355

(P-15362)
PIVOTCLOUD INC
1230 Midas Way Ste 210, Sunnyvale
(94085-4068)
P.O. Box 620094, Redwood City (94062-0094)
PHONE...................................408 475-6090
Richard Gorman, *CEO*
Lorne Boden, *Vice Pres*
EMP: 50 EST: 2011
SALES (est): 1.8MM **Privately Held**
SIC: 7371 Computer software development & applications

(P-15363)
PIXELMAGS INC
1800 Century Park E # 600, Los Angeles
(90067-1508)
PHONE...................................310 598-7303
Mark Stubbs, *CEO*
Ryan Marquis, *COO*
Philip Lunn, *Chairman*
Benjamin Miller, *CTO*
EMP: 70
SQ FT: 5,425
SALES (est): 48MM **Privately Held**
WEB: www.pixelmags.com
SIC: 7371 Software programming applications

(P-15364)
PLAYHAVEN LLC
1447 2nd St Ste 200, Santa Monica
(90401-3404)
PHONE...................................310 308-9668
Mike Jones, *President*
Tom Dare, *Treasurer*
Greg Gilman, *Admin Sec*
EMP: 50 EST: 2014
SQ FT: 15,000
SALES (est): 851.9K
SALES (corp-wide): 53.6MM **Privately Held**
SIC: 7371 7311 Computer software development & applications; advertising agencies
PA: Rockyou, Inc.
1111 Broadway Ste 300
Oakland CA 94607
415 580-6400

(P-15365)
PLAYPHONE INC (PA)
100 Mathilda Pl Ste 160, Sunnyvale
(94086-6085)
PHONE...................................408 261-6200
Takahito Yasuki, *Chairman*
Ron Czerny, *CEO*
Bhaskar Roy,
Anders Evju, *Senior VP*
Thara Edson, *Vice Pres*
EMP: 61
SQ FT: 3,000
SALES (est): 11.3MM **Privately Held**
WEB: www.playphone.com
SIC: 7371 Computer software development

(P-15366)
POINT OF VIEW INC
947 N Del Sol Ln, Diamond Bar
(91765-1108)
PHONE...................................909 860-0705
Chris Warner, *President*
Mark Nausha, *Vice Pres*
Michael Terlecki, *Vice Pres*
EMP: 54
SQ FT: 10,000
SALES (est): 6.2MM **Privately Held**
WEB: www.pov-inc.com
SIC: 7371 Computer software development

(P-15367)
POLARIS NETWORKS INCORPORATED
14856 Holden Way, San Jose
(95124-4515)
PHONE...................................408 625-7273
Buddhadeb Biswas, *CEO*
Vikash Sharma, *Business Dir*

EMP: 70
SQ FT: 2,000
SALES (est): 2.4MM **Privately Held**
SIC: 7371 Computer software development

(P-15368)
POLARIS WIRELESS INC
301 N Whisman Rd, Mountain View
(94043-3969)
PHONE...................................408 492-8900
Manlio Allegra, *President*
Victor C Chun, *CFO*
Sridhar Kolar, *Vice Pres*
Victor Hwang, *Principal*
Robert Martin, *Sr Ntwrk Engine*
EMP: 50
SALES (est): 8.1MM **Privately Held**
WEB: www.polariswireless.com
SIC: 7371 8711 Computer software development; engineering services

(P-15369)
POLEXIS INC
10680 Treena St Fl 6, San Diego
(92131-2487)
PHONE...................................858 812-7300
Eric M Demarco, *President*
Deanna H Lund, *CFO*
Laura L Siegal, *Treasurer*
Michael W Fink, *Vice Pres*
Deborah Butera, *Admin Sec*
▲ EMP: 55
SQ FT: 20,000
SALES (est): 3MM **Publicly Held**
WEB: www.polexis.com
SIC: 7371 8742 Computer software development; management consulting services
HQ: Kratos Technology & Training Solutions, Inc.
10680 Treena St Fl 6
San Diego CA 92131
858 812-7300

(P-15370)
POLTEX COMPANY INC
Also Called: Interpoltex
14748 Wild Colt Pl, Jamul (91935-2121)
PHONE...................................619 669-1846
Andy Denysiak, *President*
Andy Novak, *Vice Pres*
EMP: 96
SALES (est): 6.8MM **Privately Held**
SIC: 7371 Computer software development

(P-15371)
POSTMAN INC
595 Market St Ste 1130, San Francisco
(94105-2818)
PHONE...................................415 796-6470
Abhinav Asthana, *President*
Kasey Byrne, *VP Mktg*
Claire Riley, *Manager*
EMP: 60
SALES (est): 268K **Privately Held**
SIC: 7371 Computer software development

(P-15372)
POWERREVIEWS OC LLC
180 Montgomery St # 1800, San Francisco
(94104-4205)
PHONE...................................415 315-9208
Ken Comee, *President*
Pete Lipovsek, *Vice Pres*
Matt Parsons, *Vice Pres*
David Hummel, *CTO*
Kira Meinzer, *VP Human Res*
EMP: 95
SALES (est): 5.7MM
SALES (corp-wide): 25MM **Privately Held**
WEB: www.powerreviews.com
SIC: 7371 Computer software development
PA: Powerreviews, Inc.
1 N Dearborn St Ste 800
Chicago IL 60602
312 447-6100

(P-15373)
PRACTICE FUSION INC (PA)
Also Called: Ringadoc
731 Market St Ste 400, San Francisco
(94103-2009)
PHONE...................................415 346-7700
Tom Langan, *CEO*
Joe Priest, *Partner*
Lisa Bari, *President*
Steve Filler, *COO*
Jonathan Malek, *Senior VP*
EMP: 93
SALES (est): 38.9MM **Privately Held**
WEB: www.practicefusion.com
SIC: 7371 Computer software development

(P-15374)
PRIME CLINICAL SYSTEMS (PA)
3675 Huntington Dr Ste A, Pasadena
(91107-5648)
PHONE...................................626 449-1705
Barry Ardelan, *President*
Hamid Amjadi, *Vice Pres*
Clifford Ermshar, *Vice Pres*
Mike Madri, *Vice Pres*
Mahsa Shakoori, *Software Engr*
EMP: 60
SQ FT: 5,000
SALES (est): 8MM **Privately Held**
SIC: 7371 Computer software development

(P-15375)
PRIYO INC
605 Tumbleweed Cmn, Fremont
(94539-6810)
PHONE...................................408 248-2507
Atm Zakaria, *CEO*
Abul Nuruzzaman, *CFO*
EMP: 50
SALES: 60K **Privately Held**
SIC: 7371 Computer software development & applications

(P-15376)
PRN LLC (HQ)
600 Montgomery St # 1800, San Francisco
(94111-2720)
PHONE...................................415 805-2525
Kevin Carbone, *CEO*
Jonathan Rosen, *Senior VP*
Ann Chico, *VP Sales*
Matt Aquino, *Editor*
EMP: 51
SQ FT: 46,000
SALES: 12MM **Privately Held**
SIC: 7371 Computer software development & applications

(P-15377)
PROCERA NETWORKS INC (HQ)
2055 Junction Ave Ste 105, San Jose
(95131-2115)
PHONE...................................510 230-2777
Lyndon Cantor, *CEO*
Andrew Kowal, *President*
Charles Constanti, *CFO*
Richard Deggs, *CFO*
Andy Lovit, *Senior VP*
▲ EMP: 61
SQ FT: 18,000
SALES (est): 41.3MM
SALES (corp-wide): 45.9MM **Privately Held**
WEB: www.proceranetworks.com
SIC: 7371 7372 Computer software development & applications; prepackaged software
PA: Kdr Holding, Inc.
47448 Fremont Blvd
Fremont CA 94538
510 230-2777

(P-15378)
PROCESSWEAVER INC
5201 Great America Pkwy # 300, Santa Clara (95054-1140)
PHONE...................................888 932-8373
Kumar Vidadala, *CEO*
EMP: 92
SALES: 9.1MM **Privately Held**
SIC: 7371 Computer software development

▲ = Import ▼ =Export
◆ =Import/Export

(P-15379)
PROCORE TECHNOLOGIES INC (PA)
6309 Carpinteria Ave, Carpinteria (93013-2924)
PHONE....................................866 477-6267
Craig F Courtemanche Jr, *CEO*
Steve Zahm, *President*
Robert Reed, *CFO*
Dennis Lyandres, *Risk Mgmt Dir*
Zachary Gross, *Sr Software Eng*
EMP: 119
SALES: 109.8MM **Privately Held**
SIC: 7371 Computer software development

(P-15380)
PRODEGE LLC (PA)
Also Called: Swagbucks
100 N Pacific Coast Hwy # 800, El Segundo (90245-4300)
PHONE....................................310 294-9599
Chuck Davis, *CEO*
Mendy Pinson, *President*
David Weinrot, *COO*
Brad Kates, *CFO*
Sarah Aibel, *Vice Pres*
EMP: 74 EST: 2005
SALES (est): 44.5MM **Privately Held**
SIC: 7371 8742 Computer software development & applications; marketing consulting services

(P-15381)
PROGRESSIVE COMPUTING LLC
3615 Krny Vlla Rd Ste 105, San Diego (92123)
PHONE....................................858 707-0707
Edward Miller, *Chairman*
EMP: 90
SALES (est): 7MM **Privately Held**
WEB: www.megamates.com
SIC: 7371 Computer software systems analysis & design, custom

(P-15382)
PROLIFICS TESTING INC
24025 Park Sorrento # 405, Calabasas (91302-4018)
PHONE....................................925 485-9535
Danis Yadegar, *President*
Claude Fenner, *Vice Pres*
Dale Lampson, *Vice Pres*
Rutesh Shah, *Vice Pres*
Armen Tekerian, *Vice Pres*
EMP: 60
SQ FT: 6,500
SALES (est): 7.9MM **Privately Held**
SIC: 7371 7372 Custom computer programming services; prepackaged software
HQ: Prolifics Application Services, Inc.
24025 Park Sorrento # 405
Calabasas CA 91302
646 201-4967

(P-15383)
PROOFPOINT INC (PA)
892 Ross Dr, Sunnyvale (94089-1443)
PHONE....................................408 517-4710
Gary Steele, *CEO*
Klaus Oestermann, *President*
Paul Auvil, *CFO*
Dana Evan, *Bd of Directors*
Jonathan Feiber, *Bd of Directors*
EMP: 148
SQ FT: 95,557
SALES: 515.2MM **Publicly Held**
WEB: www.proofpoint.com
SIC: 7371 Custom computer programming services; computer software systems analysis & design, custom; computer software development & applications

(P-15384)
PROSPANCE INC (PA)
4221 Bus Ctr Dr Ste 1, Fremont (94538)
PHONE....................................925 415-2394
Manish Bhardwaj, *President*
Kirk Muhlenbruck, *President*
Peter Anand, *CFO*
Manpreet Bajaj, *Vice Pres*
Rajesh Sinha, *Vice Pres*
EMP: 79

SQ FT: 2,400
SALES (est): 11.8MM **Privately Held**
SIC: 7371 Computer software development

(P-15385)
PSI FIRE
820 Eschenburg Dr, Gilroy (95020-5613)
PHONE....................................408 842-9308
Thomas Strickland, *Partner*
EMP: 50
SALES (est): 2.1MM **Privately Held**
WEB: www.psifire.com
SIC: 7371 Computer software development

(P-15386)
PUBLIC BELL INC
11277 Garden Grove Blvd # 200, Garden Grove (92843-1335)
PHONE....................................818 396-1675
Nelson Rasiah, *CTO*
EMP: 60
SALES (est): 1MM **Privately Held**
SIC: 7371 Computer software development & applications

(P-15387)
PULSE SECURE LLC (HQ)
2700 Zanker Rd Ste 200, San Jose (95134-2140)
PHONE....................................408 372-9600
Sudhakar Ramakrishna, *CEO*
Doug Erickson, *Partner*
Andreas Koch, *President*
Jeffrey C Key, *CFO*
Yoav Weiss, *Officer*
EMP: 85 EST: 2014
SALES (est): 28.4MM
SALES (corp-wide): 498.9MM **Privately Held**
SIC: 7371 4899 Computer software development & applications; communication signal enhancement network system
PA: Siris Capital Group, Llc
601 Lexington Ave Fl 59
New York NY 10022
212 231-0095

(P-15388)
QUADRIGA INC
Also Called: Taller Technologies
555 Clfornia Ave Ste 4925, San Francisco (94104)
PHONE....................................650 270-6326
Lucas E Fuller, *CEO*
EMP: 70
SALES (est): 1.5MM **Privately Held**
SIC: 7371 Custom computer programming services

(P-15389)
QUALYS INC (PA)
919 E Hillsdale Blvd Fl 4, Foster City (94404-2112)
PHONE....................................650 801-6100
Philippe F Courtot, *CEO*
Melissa B Fisher, *CFO*
Amer S Deeba, *Ch Credit Ofcr*
Howard Schmidt, *Bd of Directors*
Sumedh S Thakar,
EMP: 148
SQ FT: 50,000
SALES: 230.8MM **Publicly Held**
WEB: www.qualys.com
SIC: 7371 7372 Custom computer programming services; software programming applications; prepackaged software

(P-15390)
QUANTCAST CORPORATION (PA)
795 Folsom St Fl 5, San Francisco (94107-4226)
PHONE....................................800 293-5706
Konrad Feldman, *President*
Christina Cubeta, *Senior Partner*
Stephen Collins, *President*
Michael Kamprath, *President*
Rob Horler, *COO*
EMP: 57
SALES (est): 193.5MM **Privately Held**
SIC: 7371 Computer software development & applications

(P-15391)
QUANTROS INC (PA)
691 S Milpitas Blvd # 100, Milpitas (95035-5476)
PHONE....................................408 957-3300
Trey M Cook, *CEO*
Gerard Livaudais, *Chief Mktg Ofcr*
EMP: 100 EST: 1997
SQ FT: 13,000
SALES (est): 11.9MM **Privately Held**
WEB: www.quantros.com
SIC: 7371 Computer software development

(P-15392)
QUICKEN INC
Also Called: Quicken Sub, LLC
3760 Haven Ave, Menlo Park (94025-1012)
PHONE....................................650 564-3399
Eric Dunn, *CEO*
EMP: 120 EST: 2015
SQ FT: 10,000
SALES: 100MM **Privately Held**
SIC: 7371 Computer software development & applications
PA: Hig Capital Management, Inc.
1450 Brickell Ave Fl 31
Miami FL 33131

(P-15393)
RADIANT LOGIC INC
75 Rowland Way Ste 300, Novato (94945-5060)
PHONE....................................415 209-6800
Michel Prompt, *President*
Claude Samuelson, *Vice Pres*
Carol Mannella, *Office Mgr*
Divya Kandi, *QA Dir*
Sergiy Alymov, *Software Dev*
EMP: 79 EST: 1995
SQ FT: 10,718
SALES (est): 10.1MM **Privately Held**
WEB: www.radiantlogic.com
SIC: 7371 Computer software development

(P-15394)
RAINFOREST QA INC
600 Battery St Fl 2, San Francisco (94111-1820)
PHONE....................................650 866-1407
Fred Stevens Smith, *CEO*
Russell Smith, *President*
Derek Choy, *Vice Pres*
Heather Doshay, *Vice Pres*
Tran Kristina, *Office Mgr*
EMP: 120
SALES (est): 1.8MM **Privately Held**
SIC: 7371 Computer software development; software programming applications

(P-15395)
RAINTREE SYSTEMS INC
27307 Via Industria, Temecula (92590-3699)
PHONE....................................951 252-9400
Richard V Welty, *CEO*
Christopher Benson, *VP Bus Dvlpt*
Grace Rodriguez, *Executive Asst*
Tim McElroy, *Technology*
Darlyn Sullivan, *Opers Staff*
EMP: 58
SQ FT: 4,500
SALES (est): 8.2MM **Privately Held**
SIC: 7371 5045 5734 Computer software development; computer software; computer & software stores

(P-15396)
RAPID SOLUTIONS CONSULTING LLC
1900 S Norfolk St Ste 350, San Mateo (94403-1171)
PHONE....................................415 226-1131
Philip Martin, *CEO*
Mark Israelsen, *Vice Pres*
EMP: 50
SQ FT: 6,500
SALES (est): 1.5MM **Privately Held**
SIC: 7371 Computer software development & applications

(P-15397)
REAL ESTATE DIGITAL LLC
27081 Aliso Creek Rd # 200, Aliso Viejo (92656-5365)
PHONE....................................800 234-2139
Jay Gaskill, *CEO*
John Hensley, *Technology*
Shawn Brown, *Manager*
EMP: 108
SALES (est): 11MM
SALES (corp-wide): 2.4B **Privately Held**
SIC: 7371 Software programming applications
HQ: Constellation Homebuilder Systems Corp
75 Frontenac Dr
Markham ON L3R 6
888 723-2222

(P-15398)
REAL-TIME INNOVATIONS INC
Also Called: R T I
232 E Java Dr, Sunnyvale (94089-1318)
PHONE....................................408 990-7400
Stanley Schneider, *CEO*
Supreet Oberoi, *President*
Jody Schneider, *CFO*
Jody G Schneider, *CFO*
Gerardo Castellote, *Officer*
EMP: 90
SQ FT: 1,000
SALES (est): 14.5MM **Privately Held**
WEB: www.scopetools.com
SIC: 7371 7379 Computer software development; computer related consulting services

(P-15399)
RECIPROCITY INC
3043 Mission St, San Francisco (94110-4501)
PHONE....................................415 851-8667
Kenneth Lynch, *CEO*
Jeff Tchang, *CTO*
Rok Carl, *Software Engr*
Amy Peterson, *Opers Mgr*
Than Tran, *Director*
EMP: 50
SQ FT: 5,300
SALES (est): 1.7MM **Privately Held**
SIC: 7371 Computer software systems analysis & design, custom

(P-15400)
RED CONDOR INC
1300 Valley House Dr # 115, Rohnert Park (94928-4930)
PHONE....................................707 569-7419
Ron Longo, *President*
EMP: 60
SALES (est): 4.3MM **Privately Held**
WEB: www.redcondor.com
SIC: 7371 Custom computer programming services

(P-15401)
REDIS LABS INC
700 E El Camino Real # 250, Mountain View (94040-2813)
PHONE....................................415 930-9666
Ofer Bengal, *CEO*
Manish Gupta, *Chief Mktg Ofcr*
Jason Forget, *Officer*
Elad Ash, *Vice Pres*
Cihan Biyikoglu, *Vice Pres*
EMP: 51
SALES (est): 324K **Privately Held**
SIC: 7371 Computer software development
PA: Redis Labs Ltd
94 Alon Igal
Tel Aviv-Jaffa
732 805-177

(P-15402)
REFLEKTION INC (PA)
777 Mariners Island Blvd # 510, San Mateo (94404-5048)
PHONE....................................650 293-0800
Rajeev Madhavan, *CEO*
Ray Villeneuve, *President*
Kurt Heinemann, *Chief Mktg Ofcr*
Vivek Gupta, *Vice Pres*
Rajiv Katira, *Vice Pres*
EMP: 50

SALES (est): 6.5MM **Privately Held**
SIC: 7371 Computer software systems analysis & design, custom

(P-15403)
RELATED TECHNOLOGIES INC
81 Blue Ravine Rd Ste 230, Folsom (95630-4766)
P.O. Box 6975 (95763-6975)
PHONE..................916 357-5900
Cheryl Mal, *President*
Joel Solomon, *Vice Pres*
Cheryl Borgonah, *Marketing Staff*
EMP: 85 **EST:** 2001
SALES (est): 4.2MM **Privately Held**
WEB: www.relatedtechnologies.com
SIC: 7371 Computer software development

(P-15404)
RENOVATE AMERICA INC
Also Called: Hero
15073 Ave Of Science # 200, San Diego (92128-3453)
PHONE..................858 605-5333
Harold Lewis, *CEO*
Tony Jimenez, *President*
Patrick Moore, *COO*
Adam Garfinkle, *CFO*
Paige Wisdom, *CFO*
EMP: 119
SQ FT: 23,500
SALES (est): 28.1MM **Privately Held**
SIC: 7371 8742 Computer software development & applications; banking & finance consultant

(P-15405)
RESOLVE SYSTEMS LLC (PA)
2302 Martin Ste 225, Irvine (92612-1493)
PHONE..................949 325-0120
Martin B Savitt, *CEO*
Jim Livergood, *President*
Marin Sakhri, *Vice Pres*
Paul Gibson, *Admin Sec*
Thomas Tan, *Marketing Staff*
EMP: 65
SQ FT: 6,000
SALES (est): 15.9MM **Privately Held**
WEB: www.generationetech.com
SIC: 7371 Computer software development

(P-15406)
RESONATE INC (PA)
90 Great Oaks Blvd # 205, San Jose (95119-1314)
PHONE..................408 545-5500
Peter R Watkins, *Ch of Bd*
Evan Benoit, *Senior Partner*
Richard Hornstein, *CFO*
David Wheatley, *CFO*
Christopher Marino, *Founder*
EMP: 188
SQ FT: 38,000
SALES (est): 13.3MM **Privately Held**
SIC: 7371 7372 Computer software development & applications; business oriented computer software

(P-15407)
RESPONSYS INC (DH)
Also Called: Responsys.com
1100 Grundy Ln Ste 300, San Bruno (94066-3066)
PHONE..................650 745-1700
Daniel D Springer, *CEO*
Christian A Paul, *CFO*
Scott V Olrich, *Chief Mktg Ofcr*
Joan Burke, *Senior VP*
Julian Ong, *Senior VP*
EMP: 108
SQ FT: 72,000
SALES (est): 91.6MM
SALES (corp-wide): 39.8B **Publicly Held**
WEB: www.responsys.com
SIC: 7371 7372 Computer software development; business oriented computer software
HQ: Oc Acquisition Llc
500 Oracle Pkwy
Redwood City CA 94065
650 506-7000

(P-15408)
RESTAURANT IN A BOX LLC
3191 Red Hill Ave, Costa Mesa (92626-3451)
PHONE..................800 676-1281
Mitesh Gala, *CEO*
EMP: 50
SQ FT: 24,000
SALES (est): 1.3MM **Privately Held**
SIC: 7371 Computer software development & applications

(P-15409)
RETAIL PRO INTERNATIONAL LLC
Also Called: Retail Pro Software
400 Plaza Dr Ste 200, Folsom (95630-4746)
PHONE..................916 605-7200
Kerry Lemos, *CEO*
William Colley, *Senior VP*
Shaff Kassam, *Vice Pres*
Peter Latona, *Vice Pres*
Amit Lohia, *Vice Pres*
EMP: 70
SQ FT: 7,500
SALES (est): 13.6MM **Privately Held**
WEB: www.retailpro.com
SIC: 7371 7372 Computer software development; prepackaged software

(P-15410)
RETAILNEXT INC (PA)
60 S Market St Ste 1000, San Jose (95113-2336)
PHONE..................408 884-2162
Alexei Agratchev, *CEO*
Michael Manlapas, *President*
Kenton D Chow, *COO*
David Tognotti, *COO*
Andrew Skarupa, *CFO*
EMP: 77 **EST:** 2007
SQ FT: 12,000
SALES (est): 56.3MM **Privately Held**
SIC: 7371 Computer software development

(P-15411)
RHYTHMONE LLC
800 W El Camino Real, Mountain View (94040-2567)
PHONE..................650 961-9024
EMP: 70
SALES (corp-wide): 214.9MM **Privately Held**
SIC: 7371
HQ: Rhythmone, Llc
1 Market St Ste 1810
San Francisco CA 94111
415 655-1450

(P-15412)
RIGHTSCALE INC (PA)
402 E Gutierrez St, Santa Barbara (93101-1709)
PHONE..................805 500-4164
Michael Crandel, *President*
Bailey Caldwell, *President*
Josh Fraser, *President*
Ida Kane, *CFO*
Tim Miller, *Vice Pres*
EMP: 85 **EST:** 2007
SALES (est): 31.5MM **Privately Held**
SIC: 7371 Computer software development & applications

(P-15413)
RIOSOFT HOLDINGS INC
Also Called: Rio Seo
9255 Towne Centre Dr # 750, San Diego (92121-3017)
PHONE..................858 529-5005
Dema Zlotin, *CEO*
EMP: 50 **EST:** 2012
SALES (est): 152.7K **Privately Held**
SIC: 7371 Computer software development & applications

(P-15414)
RIOT GAMES INC (DH)
12333 W Olympic Blvd, Los Angeles (90064-1021)
PHONE..................310 828-7953
Brandon Beck, *CEO*
Mark Marrill, *President*
A Dyoan Jadeja, *CFO*

Dylan A Jadeja, *CFO*
Scott Gelb, *Officer*
EMP: 148 **EST:** 2006
SALES (est): 637.4MM **Privately Held**
SIC: 7371 7993 Custom computer programming services; video game arcade
HQ: Tencent Holdings Limited
29/F Three Pacific Place
Wan Chai HK
314 851-00

(P-15415)
ROBERT BOSCH START-UP PLTFM NA
Also Called: Mayfield Robotics
400 Convention Way, Redwood City (94063-1445)
PHONE..................248 876-6430
Michael Beebe, *CEO*
Sarah Osentoski, *COO*
Kaijen Hsiao, *CTO*
EMP: 50 **EST:** 2015
SALES (est): 1.3MM
SALES (corp-wide): 261.7MM **Privately Held**
SIC: 7371 Computer software development & applications
HQ: Robert Bosch Start-Up Platform North America Llc
2800 S 25th Ave
Broadview IL 60155
708 865-5200

(P-15416)
ROBOCA TECHNOLOGY
245 E Main St Ste 115, Alhambra (91801-7507)
PHONE..................561 501-3999
Yang Xiaoyan, *Owner*
EMP: 200
SALES: 20MM **Privately Held**
SIC: 7371 Computer software development & applications

(P-15417)
ROCKLEY PHOTONICS INC (HQ)
234 E Colo Blvd Ste 600, Pasadena (91101)
PHONE..................626 304-9960
Andrew George Rickman, *CEO*
Esthepany Aragon, *Manager*
EMP: 87
SALES (est): 16.6MM
SALES (corp-wide): 3.7MM **Privately Held**
SIC: 7371 Computer software development & applications

(P-15418)
ROSE INTERNATIONAL INC
450 N Brand Blvd Fl 6, Glendale (91203-2349)
PHONE..................636 812-4000
EMP: 151 **Privately Held**
SIC: 7371 8748 Computer software development; systems engineering consultant, ex. computer or professional
PA: Rose International, Inc.
16401 Swingley Ridge Rd
Chesterfield MO 63017

(P-15419)
RSA SECURITY LLC
Also Called: R S A Laboratories
2831 Mission College Blvd, Santa Clara (95054-1838)
PHONE..................650 529-9992
Carl Miller, *Branch Mgr*
C V Chang, *President*
James M Horn, *Principal*
EMP: 200
SALES (corp-wide): 78.6B **Publicly Held**
SIC: 7371 Computer software development
HQ: Rsa Security Llc
174 Middlesex Tpke
Bedford MA 01730
781 515-5000

(P-15420)
RUNA HR HOLDINGS INC
3067 E 1st St, Long Beach (90803-2536)
PHONE..................562 883-3546
Courtney McColgan, *CEO*
EMP: 55

SALES: 120K **Privately Held**
SIC: 7371 Computer software development & applications

(P-15421)
SAAMA TECHNOLOGIES INC (PA)
900 E Hamilton Ave, Campbell (95008-0664)
PHONE..................408 371-1900
Suresh Katta, *President*
Ken Coleman, *Ch of Bd*
Simon Ho, *CFO*
Scott Kleinberg, *CFO*
Rajeev Dadia, *Officer*
EMP: 237
SQ FT: 10,000
SALES (est): 83.6MM **Privately Held**
SIC: 7371 Computer software development

(P-15422)
SAFETRACES INC
6111 Johnson Ct Ste 200, Pleasanton (94588-3373)
PHONE..................925 398-8985
Anthony Zografos, *CEO*
EMP: 115 **EST:** 2016
SALES (est): 8.7MM **Privately Held**
SIC: 7371 Computer software development & applications

(P-15423)
SAGAN SYSTEMS INC
201 California St # 1300, San Francisco (94111-5015)
PHONE..................650 387-8485
Yolanda Ruiz, *VP Finance*
EMP: 60
SALES (est): 72.5K **Privately Held**
SIC: 7371 Computer software development & applications

(P-15424)
SAMBREEL SERVICES LLC
5857 Owens Ave Ste 300, Carlsbad (92008-5507)
PHONE..................760 266-5090
Kai Hankinson, *CEO*
Shawn E Bridgeman, *President*
EMP: 50
SALES (est): 6MM **Privately Held**
WEB: www.finialservices.com
SIC: 7371 Computer software development

(P-15425)
SAMSUNG SDS AMERICA INC
2665 N 1st St Ste 110, San Jose (95134-2033)
PHONE..................408 638-8800
Jh Kim, *Manager*
SOO Lee, *Vice Pres*
Juan Wee, *Business Mgr*
Kevin Gould, *Counsel*
EMP: 72
SALES (corp-wide): 4.1B **Privately Held**
SIC: 7371 Computer software development
HQ: Samsung Sds Global Scl America, Inc.
100 Challenger Rd Ste 601
Ridgefield Park NJ 07660
201 229-4456

(P-15426)
SANZARU GAMES INC
1065 E Hillsdale Blvd, Foster City (94404-1613)
PHONE..................650 312-1000
Glen Egan, *President*
Judah Baron, *Principal*
Martin Gerarro, *Principal*
Dave Grace, *Principal*
Paul Murray, *Principal*
EMP: 50 **EST:** 2006
SALES (est): 4.7MM **Privately Held**
SIC: 7371 Computer software development

(P-15427)
SAP LABS LLC
3475 Deer Creek Rd, Palo Alto (94304-1316)
PHONE..................650 849-4000
Ben Frommherz, *Manager*
Yolanda Ingram, *Info Tech Mgr*

Biju Balachandran, *Project Mgr*
Michael Sawi, *Project Mgr*
Nick Tingey, *Technology*
EMP: 53
SALES (corp-wide): 27.6B **Privately Held**
SIC: 7371 Computer software development & applications
HQ: Sap Labs, Llc
3410 Hillview Ave
Palo Alto CA 94304

(P-15428)
SAP LABS LLC (DH)
3410 Hillview Ave, Palo Alto (94304-1395)
PHONE................................650 849-4000
Heinz Roggemkemper, *Business Dir*
Elena Hartlieb, *Business Dir*
Karen Herrerias, *Marketing Staff*
Jenny Hill, *Marketing Staff*
Brian Tran, *Marketing Staff*
EMP: 300
SQ FT: 200,000
SALES (est): 63.9MM
SALES (corp-wide): 27.6B **Privately Held**
WEB: www.saplabs.com
SIC: 7371 Computer software development
HQ: Sap America, Inc.
3999 West Chester Pike
Newtown Square PA 19073
610 661-1000

(P-15429)
SAPHO INC
1150 Bayhill Dr Ste 325, San Bruno (94066-3004)
PHONE................................650 597-2746
Fouad Elnaggar, *President*
Peter Yared, *CTO*
Natalie Lambert, *VP Mktg*
Kristen Rumley, *Marketing Mgr*
EMP: 52
SALES (est): 3.9MM **Privately Held**
SIC: 7371 Computer software development & applications

(P-15430)
SATMETRIX SYSTEMS INC (PA)
1820 Gateway Dr Ste 300, San Mateo (94404-4024)
PHONE................................650 227-8300
Richard Owen, *President*
Brian Curry, *COO*
Raymond Yue, *CFO*
Marco Gutierrez, *Sales Staff*
EMP: 90
SQ FT: 20,000
SALES (est): 45.4MM **Privately Held**
SIC: 7371 Software programming applications

(P-15431)
SAVVIUS INC (HQ)
1340 Treat Blvd Ste 500, Walnut Creek (94597-7961)
PHONE................................925 937-3200
Larry Zulch, *President*
Eric Powell, *Admin Asst*
Brian Ferguson, *Controller*
Brad Hall, *Regl Sales Mgr*
Mandana Javaheri, *Manager*
EMP: 55
SQ FT: 30,000
SALES (est): 3.2MM **Privately Held**
WEB: www.wildpackets.com
SIC: 7371 Custom computer programming services

(P-15432)
SCENE7 INC
6 Hamilton Landing # 150, Novato (94949-8264)
PHONE................................415 506-6000
EMP: 75
SALES (est): 4.3MM **Privately Held**
WEB: www.scene7.com
SIC: 7371

(P-15433)
SD SQUARED NORTH AMERICA LTD
600 California St Fl 11, San Francisco (94108-2727)
PHONE................................650 721-1158
Sachin Dev Duggal, *CEO*

Varghese Cherian, *COO*
EMP: 125
SALES: 20MM **Privately Held**
SIC: 7371 Computer software development & applications

(P-15434)
SECUREAUTH CORPORATION (PA)
8845 Irvine Center Dr # 200, Irvine (92618-4248)
PHONE................................949 777-6959
Jeffrey Kukowski, *CEO*
Craig J Lund, *CEO*
Justin Dolly, *COO*
Tom Moyes, *CFO*
Nick Mansour, *Exec VP*
EMP: 79
SQ FT: 27,113
SALES: 12MM **Privately Held**
SIC: 7371 Computer software development

(P-15435)
SELECT DATA INC
4155 E La Palma Ave # 250, Anaheim (92807-1863)
PHONE................................714 577-1000
Edward A Buckley, *CEO*
Stephen Campbell, *COO*
Pete Poulis, *CFO*
Stacy Ashworth, *Officer*
Susan Carmichael, *Officer*
EMP: 121
SQ FT: 18,000
SALES (est): 18.6MM **Privately Held**
WEB: www.selectdata.com
SIC: 7371 7372 Computer code authors; prepackaged software

(P-15436)
SENTIENT TECHNOLOGIES USA LLC
1 California St Ste 2300, San Francisco (94111-5424)
PHONE................................415 422-9886
Antoine Blondeau, *CEO*
Julian Tandler, *President*
Fabrice Fischer, *CFO*
Tom Whittaker, *CTO*
Robert Lee, *Controller*
EMP: 50
SALES (est): 146.4K **Privately Held**
SIC: 7371 Computer software development; computer software development & applications
PA: Sentient Technologies (Hk) Limited
Dominion Ctr
Wan Chai HK

(P-15437)
SENTINEL ACQSTION HOLDINGS INC
2000 Avenue Of The Stars, Los Angeles (90067-4700)
PHONE................................310 201-4100
Matt Cwiertnia, *President*
EMP: 1463
SALES (est): 42.3MM **Privately Held**
SIC: 7371 7379 Computer software systems analysis & design, custom;

(P-15438)
SEQUOIA RETAIL SYSTEMS INC (DH)
660 W Dana St, Mountain View (94041-1302)
PHONE................................650 237-9000
Jim Zaorski, *CEO*
John Diaz, *COO*
Alan Vu, *Manager*
EMP: 52
SQ FT: 9,000
SALES (est): 8.6MM **Privately Held**
WEB: www.sequoiap.com
SIC: 7371 5942 5961 4813 Computer software development; college book stores; ;
HQ: Blackboard Inc.
1111 19th St Nw
Washington DC 20036
202 463-4860

(P-15439)
SERVICEMAX INC (DH)
4450 Rosewood Dr Ste 200, Pleasanton (94588-3061)
PHONE................................925 965-7859
Scott Berg, *COO*
David Milam, *Officer*
Michael Parry, *Sales Staff*
Lauri Armstrong, *Manager*
EMP: 69
SQ FT: 7,000
SALES (est): 41.9MM
SALES (corp-wide): 122B **Publicly Held**
WEB: www.maxplore.com
SIC: 7371 Computer software development
HQ: Ge Digital Llc
2623 Camino Ramon
San Ramon CA 94583
925 242-6200

(P-15440)
SES LLC
26561 Rancho Pkwy S, Lake Forest (92630-8301)
PHONE................................949 727-3200
Jim Griffith, *Principal*
Rashesh Mody, *Vice Pres*
Mike Pring, *Vice Pres*
Abhijeet Shegokar, *Program Mgr*
Patrick Bouzan, *Info Tech Dir*
EMP: 748
SALES (est): 17.9MM
SALES (corp-wide): 200.4K **Privately Held**
SIC: 7371 Computer software development & applications
HQ: Invensys Processs Systems, Inc.
10900 Equity Dr
Houston TX 77041
713 329-1600

(P-15441)
SFUSD JROTC BRIGADE
2162 24th Ave, San Francisco (94116-1723)
PHONE................................415 242-2546
Robert Powell, *Director*
EMP: 55
SALES (est): 2.1MM **Privately Held**
SIC: 7371 Computer software development

(P-15442)
SHIELDX NETWORKS INC
Also Called: Apeiro
4093 Oceanside Blvd Ste A, Oceanside (92056-5816)
PHONE................................760 724-2700
Ratinder Paul Singh Ahuja, *CEO*
Harjinder Singh, *President*
Manuel Nedbal, *Chief Engr*
Neny Hill, *Director*
EMP: 50
SALES (est): 4MM **Privately Held**
SIC: 7371 Computer software development & applications

(P-15443)
SHIFTPIXY INC
1 Venture Ste 150, Irvine (92618-7411)
PHONE................................949 207-7184
Scott W Absher, *President*
Patrice H Launay, *CFO*
John Holmes, *Manager*
EMP: 50
SALES (est): 20.2MM **Privately Held**
SIC: 7371 Computer software development & applications

(P-15444)
SHOPKICK INC
2317 Broadway St Fl 3, Redwood City (94063-1659)
PHONE................................650 763-8727
Cyriac Roeding, *CEO*
Alexis Rask, *CFO*
Kristy Stromberg, *Chief Mktg Ofcr*
Mariam Dombrovskaja, *VP Bus Dvlpt*
Sean Cooper, *Executive Asst*
EMP: 70
SQ FT: 8,000
SALES (est): 13.3MM **Privately Held**
SIC: 7371 Computer software development

(P-15445)
SIEMENS PRODUCT LIFE MGMT SFTW
Also Called: Siemens PLM Software
10824 Hope St, Cypress (90630-5214)
PHONE................................714 952-6500
Mike Sayen, *Manager*
Richard Bandurian, *Administration*
Rafael Nascimento, *QA Dir*
Sarang Baheti, *Software Dev*
Jianyong Wen, *Software Engr*
EMP: 75
SALES (corp-wide): 97.7B **Privately Held**
WEB: www.ugs.com
SIC: 7371 3695 Computer software development; magnetic & optical recording media
HQ: Siemens Product Lifecycle Management Software Inc.
5800 Granite Pkwy Ste 600
Plano TX 75024
972 987-3000

(P-15446)
SIFT SCIENCE INC
123 Mission St Fl 20, San Francisco (94105-1592)
PHONE................................415 882-7709
Jason Tan, *CEO*
Marc Olesen, *President*
Kevin Lee, *Trust Officer*
Freda Kreitzer, *Info Tech Mgr*
Paino Alex, *Software Engr*
EMP: 65
SALES (est): 6.4MM **Privately Held**
SIC: 7371 Computer software development

(P-15447)
SIGNALDEMAND INC
101 Montgomery St Ste 400, San Francisco (94104-4145)
PHONE................................415 356-0800
Mark Tice, *CEO*
Scott C Friend, *Partner*
Douglas Hickey, *Partner*
John G Simon, *Partner*
Bill Rupp, *President*
EMP: 50
SALES (est): 3MM **Publicly Held**
WEB: www.signaldemand.com
SIC: 7371 Computer software development
PA: Pros Holdings, Inc.
3100 Main St Ste 900
Houston TX 77002

(P-15448)
SILICON PRIME TECHNOLOGIES INC
4154 W 172nd St, Torrance (90504-1002)
PHONE................................310 279-0222
Quoc Dinh Tran Dinh, *CEO*
EMP: 50
SALES: 200K **Privately Held**
SIC: 7371 Computer software development & applications

(P-15449)
SKIRE INC
500 Oracle Pkwy, Redwood City (94065-1677)
PHONE................................650 289-2600
Massy Mendipour, *CEO*
Steve Apfelberg, *Chief Mktg Ofcr*
EMP: 70
SALES (est): 6.1MM
SALES (corp-wide): 39.8B **Publicly Held**
WEB: www.skire.com
SIC: 7371 Computer software development
PA: Oracle Corporation
500 Oracle Pkwy
Redwood City CA 94065
650 506-7000

(P-15450)
SKYLITE NETWORKS
43333 Osgood Rd, Fremont (94539-5659)
PHONE................................403 934-9349
Idress M Munir, *CEO*
EMP: 70

SALES (est): 81.7K **Privately Held**
SIC: 7371 Computer software development & applications

(P-15451)
SLEEPY GIANT ENTERTAINMENT INC
4 San Joaquin Plz Ste 200, Newport Beach (92660-5934)
PHONE.....................949 464-7986
EMP: 150 **EST:** 2007
SALES (est): 11.2MM **Privately Held**
SIC: 7371

(P-15452)
SMART ENERGY SYSTEMS LLC (PA)
19900 Macarthur Blvd, Irvine (92612-2445)
PHONE.....................909 703-9609
Ray Howlett,
EMP: 150
SALES: 70MM **Privately Held**
SIC: 7371 Computer software development & applications

(P-15453)
SMART ENERGY SYSTEMS LLC
Michelson Dr Ste 3370, Irvine (92612)
PHONE.....................909 703-9609
Ray Howlett,
EMP: 150
SALES (corp-wide): 70MM **Privately Held**
SIC: 7371 Computer software development & applications
PA: Smart Energy Systems Llc
　19900 Macarthur Blvd
　Irvine CA 92612
　909 703-9609

(P-15454)
SMARTDRIVE SYSTEMS INC (PA)
4790 Estgate Mall Ste 200, San Diego (92121)
PHONE.....................858 225-5550
Steve Mitgang, CEO
Jason Palmer, President
Michael J Baker, Vice Pres
Michael Baker, Vice Pres
Andy Deninger, Vice Pres
▲ **EMP:** 87
SQ FT: 18,000
SALES (est): 71.3MM **Privately Held**
WEB: www.smartdrive.net
SIC: 7371 Computer software development & applications

(P-15455)
SMILE FAMILY INC
Also Called: Sendbird
107 S Railroad Ave, San Mateo (94401)
PHONE.....................727 771-3641
John Kim, CEO
EMP: 60
SALES (est): 891.1K **Privately Held**
SIC: 7371 Computer software development & applications

(P-15456)
SNAP INC (PA)
Also Called: SNAPCHAT
2772 Dnald Douglas Loop N, Santa Monica (90405-2951)
PHONE.....................310 399-3339
Evan Spiegel, CEO
Michael Lynton, Ch of Bd
Tim Stone, CFO
Steven Horowitz, Vice Pres
Lara Sweet,
EMP: 148
SALES: 824.9MM **Publicly Held**
SIC: 7371 7372 Computer software development & applications; software programming applications; application computer software

(P-15457)
SNAPDOCS INC
100 Montgomery St # 2400, San Francisco (94104-4356)
PHONE.....................415 967-0136
Aaron King, President
EMP: 50 **EST:** 2013

SALES (est): 2.5MM **Privately Held**
SIC: 7371 Computer software development & applications

(P-15458)
SNOWFLAKE COMPUTING INC (PA)
100 S Ellsworth Ave, San Mateo (94401-3939)
PHONE.....................844 766-9355
Robert Muglia, CEO
Thomas Tuchscherer, CFO
Denise Persson, Chief Mktg Ofcr
Margo Smith,
Barbara Walkowski,
EMP: 65
SALES (est): 53.2MM **Privately Held**
SIC: 7371 Computer software development & applications; computer software development; software programming applications

(P-15459)
SOFTSOL RESOURCES INC (HQ)
46755 Fremont Blvd, Fremont (94538-6539)
PHONE.....................510 824-2000
Srini Madala, President
Rk Ghanta, Vice Pres
Kris Yalavarthy, Vice Pres
Krishna Magam, Tech Recruiter
Ashok Tata, Tech Recruiter
EMP: 200
SQ FT: 12,000
SALES (est): 16.1MM **Privately Held**
WEB: www.softsolusa.com
SIC: 7371 Computer software development

(P-15460)
SOFTWARE AG USA INC
1198 E Arques Ave, Sunnyvale (94085-4602)
P.O. Box 2000, Alviso (95002-2000)
PHONE.....................703 860-5050
Phillip Merrick, CEO
Bindu Nair, Sr Software Eng
Korin Yang, Software Engr
Saori Takahashi, Contractor
EMP: 160
SALES (corp-wide): 1B **Privately Held**
SIC: 7371 Computer software development
HQ: Software Ag Usa, Inc.
　11700 Plaza America Dr # 700
　Reston VA 20190
　703 860-5050

(P-15461)
SOLARTIS LLC
1601 N Sepulveda Blvd, Manhattan Beach (90266-5111)
PHONE.....................310 251-4861
Nicholas Richardson, President
Siby Nidhiry, CTO
EMP: 238
SALES (est): 12.3MM **Privately Held**
SIC: 7371 7374 7372 Computer software development; data processing & preparation; business oriented computer software

(P-15462)
SOLIDCORE SYSTEMS INC (DH)
3965 Freedom Cir, Santa Clara (95054-1206)
PHONE.....................408 387-8400
Anne Bonaparte, President
David Walker, Senior VP
Steve Albertolle, Vice Pres
Monico Mallari, Vice Pres
Jay Vaishnav, Vice Pres
EMP: 100
SQ FT: 2,000
SALES (est): 10MM **Privately Held**
WEB: www.solidcore.com
SIC: 7371 Computer software development
HQ: Mcafee, Llc
　2821 Mission College Blvd
　Santa Clara CA 95054
　888 847-8766

(P-15463)
SOLIX TECHNOLOGIES INC (PA)
4701 Patrick Henry Dr # 2001, Santa Clara (95054-1864)
PHONE.....................408 654-6446
SAI Gundavelli, CEO
Debra Reabock, Partner
Kishore Gadiraju, President
Pramod Gollahalli, Sr Software Eng
Ramanand Prasad, Info Tech Mgr
EMP: 60
SQ FT: 17,000
SALES: 10MM **Privately Held**
WEB: www.solix.com
SIC: 7371 Computer software development

(P-15464)
SONATA SOFTWARE NORTH AMER INC (HQ)
2201 Walnut Ave Ste 180, Fremont (94538-2334)
PHONE.....................510 791-7220
P Srikar Reddy, Principal
N E Devasahayam, Assoc VP
N Sridhara, Assoc VP
EMP: 66
SQ FT: 2,500
SALES: 47.2MM
SALES (corp-wide): 106.7MM **Privately Held**
WEB: www.odsi.com
SIC: 7371 Computer software development
PA: Sonata Software Limited
　1/4, A.P.S Trust Building
　Bengaluru KA 56001
　806 778-1999

(P-15465)
SONY CORPORATION OF AMERICA
Sony Interactive Studios Amer
2207 Bridgepointe Pkwy, Foster City (94404-5060)
PHONE.....................650 655-8000
Kelly Flock, Manager
EMP: 200
SALES (corp-wide): 80.1B **Privately Held**
SIC: 7371 Computer software development
HQ: Sony Corporation Of America
　25 Madison Ave Fl 27
　New York NY 10010
　212 833-8000

(P-15466)
SOUNDHOUND INC (PA)
Also Called: Mobile Application
5400 Betsy Ross Dr, Santa Clara (95054-1101)
PHONE.....................408 441-3200
Keyvan Mohajer, CEO
Amir Arbabi, President
Cheryl Lucanegro, President
Jay Eum, Bd of Directors
Larry Marcus, Officer
EMP: 61
SQ FT: 24,907
SALES (est): 25.4MM **Privately Held**
WEB: www.melodis.com
SIC: 7371 Software programming applications

(P-15467)
SOURCE INTERLINK MEDIA LLC
Also Called: Mind Over Eye
2221 Rosecrans Ave # 195, El Segundo (90245-4931)
PHONE.....................310 531-9394
Daniel Lin, Branch Mgr
Alex Gorodetzki, President
Levi Rugg, Creative Dir
Mike Ruiz, Creative Dir
Natalia Lax, Production
EMP: 55 **Privately Held**
SIC: 7371 7812 Computer software development & applications; motion picture & video production
PA: Ten Publishing Media, Llc
　831 S Douglas St Ste 100
　El Segundo CA 90245

(P-15468)
SPARK UNLIMITED INC
40 E Verdugo Ave 2, Burbank (91502-1931)
PHONE.....................818 788-1005
Craig Allen, CEO
EMP: 68
SALES (est): 6.8MM **Privately Held**
WEB: www.sparkunlimited.com
SIC: 7371 Computer software development

(P-15469)
SPERASOFT INC
2033 Gateway Pl Ste 500, San Jose (95110-3712)
PHONE.....................408 715-6615
Igor Efremov, CEO
Alexei Kudriashov, CFO
Anna Limarenko, Project Mgr
EMP: 375
SQ FT: 15,000
SALES: 16MM
SALES (corp-wide): 177.6MM **Privately Held**
SIC: 7371 Software programming applications
HQ: Keywords International Limited
　Whelan House
　Dublin

(P-15470)
SPRUCE TECHNOLOGY INC
3516 Browntail Way, San Ramon (94582-5245)
PHONE.....................925 415-8160
Muttu Nagubandi, Branch Mgr
EMP: 72
SALES (corp-wide): 13.7MM **Privately Held**
SIC: 7371 Computer software development & applications
PA: Spruce Technology Inc
　1149 Bloomfield Ave Ste G
　Clifton NJ 07012
　201 693-8843

(P-15471)
STARTEL CORPORATION (PA)
16 Goodyear B-125, Irvine (92618-3758)
PHONE.....................949 863-8700
William Lane, President
David Abrams, Purch Mgr
Steve Newell, Manager
Myrna Nunez, Manager
EMP: 60
SQ FT: 27,000
SALES (est): 10.5MM **Privately Held**
WEB: www.startelcorp.com
SIC: 7371 3661 Computer software development; communication headgear, telephone

(P-15472)
STARTUP FARMS INTL LLC
Also Called: Sufi
45690 Northport Loop E, Fremont (94538-6477)
PHONE.....................510 440-0110
Jasvir Gill, President
Kaval Kaur, CFO
Cassie Ku, Controller
EMP: 350
SALES (est): 287K **Privately Held**
WEB: www.startupfarms.com
SIC: 7371 Computer software development

(P-15473)
STONERIVER INC
770 The Cy Dr S Ste 5000, Orange (92868)
PHONE.....................714 705-8227
John Grundman, Principal
EMP: 333 **Privately Held**
SIC: 7371 Computer software development
HQ: Stoneriver, Inc.
　20 Horseneck Ln Ste 1
　Greenwich CT 06830
　303 729-7500

(P-15474)
STORYBOTS INC
4121 Redwood Ave, Los Angeles
(90066-5628)
PHONE..................................310 314-4394
Gregg Spiridellis, *CEO*
EMP: 90
SALES (est): 1.2MM **Privately Held**
SIC: 7371 Computer software development & applications

(P-15475)
STRANDS INC A DELAWARE CORP
999 Baker Way Ste 430, San Mateo
(94404-1581)
P.O. Box 331639, Miami FL (33233-1639)
PHONE..................................541 753-4426
Edward Chang, *CEO*
David Silverman, *President*
Jordi Teixido, *COO*
Marijke Van Daele, *Engineer*
Leandro Gimeno, *Business Mgr*
EMP: 50
SQ FT: 3,000
SALES (est): 3.8MM **Privately Held**
WEB: www.strands.com
SIC: 7371 Software programming applications

(P-15476)
STRANDS LABS INC
Also Called: Strands Finance
999 Baker Way Ste 430, San Mateo
(94404-1581)
PHONE..................................415 398-4333
EMP: 50
SALES (est): 3.1MM **Privately Held**
SIC: 7371

(P-15477)
STRATACARE LLC
17838 Gillette Ave Ste D, Irvine
(92614-6502)
P.O. Box 19600 (92623-9600)
PHONE..................................949 743-1200
Scott R Green, *CEO*
Steve Ditman, *CFO*
Robert McCaffrey, *Officer*
John Zavoli, *Officer*
Michael Josephs, *Vice Pres*
EMP: 250 **EST:** 1998
SALES (est): 899K
SALES (corp-wide): 10.2B **Publicly Held**
WEB: www.gensourcecorp.com
SIC: 7371 Computer software development & applications
HQ: Conduent Workers Compensation Holdings, Inc.
17838 Gillette Ave
Irvine CA 92614

(P-15478)
STREAMVECTOR INC
940 Stewart Dr 212, Sunnyvale
(94085-3912)
PHONE..................................760 203-3257
Lokesh Anand, *President*
Piyush Khemka, *Vice Pres*
EMP: 60
SALES (est): 880K **Privately Held**
SIC: 7371 Computer software development & applications

(P-15479)
STRIIM INC
575 Middlefield Rd, Palo Alto (94301-2150)
PHONE..................................425 894-1998
Ali Kutay, *President*
Don Knepper, *Officer*
Katherine Rincon, *Senior VP*
Kevin Colon, *Vice Pres*
Michelle Monica, *Executive Asst*
EMP: 50
SALES (est): 1MM **Privately Held**
SIC: 7371 Computer software development & applications

(P-15480)
STRIVR LABS INC
90 Middlefield Rd Ste 101, Menlo Park
(94025-3510)
PHONE..................................650 656-9987
Derek Belch, *President*
EMP: 75 **EST:** 2015

SALES (est): 5MM **Privately Held**
SIC: 7371 Computer software development & applications

(P-15481)
SUCCESSFACTORS INC (DH)
Also Called: Success Factors
1 Tower Pl Ste 1100, South San Francisco
(94080-1839)
PHONE..................................650 212-1296
Price Shawn, *President*
Suzanne Portugal, *Partner*
Mike Ettling, *President*
Matt Leone, *COO*
Klein Christian, *CFO*
EMP: 148
SQ FT: 58,700
SALES (est): 307.1MM
SALES (corp-wide): 27.6B **Privately Held**
SIC: 7371 Computer software development
HQ: Sap America, Inc.
3999 West Chester Pike
Newtown Square PA 19073
610 661-1000

(P-15482)
SUGARCRM INC (PA)
10050 N Wolfe Rd Sw2130, Cupertino
(95014-2528)
PHONE..................................408 454-6900
Larry Augustin, *Ch of Bd*
Andrew Chmyz, *CFO*
Steve Valenzuela, *CFO*
Karen Willem, *CFO*
Nick Halsey, *Chief Mktg Ofcr*
EMP: 210
SQ FT: 40,000
SALES (est): 39.6MM **Privately Held**
WEB: www.sugarcrm.com
SIC: 7371 Computer software development

(P-15483)
SUNGARD BI-TECH INC (DH)
890 Fortress St, Chico (95973-9023)
PHONE..................................530 891-5281
Aaron Johnson, *President*
Bruce Langston, *CFO*
EMP: 50
SALES (est): 12.6MM
SALES (corp-wide): 9.1B **Publicly Held**
WEB: www.bi-tech.com
SIC: 7371 Computer software development
HQ: Fis Data Systems Inc.
200 Campus Dr
Collegeville PA 19426
484 582-2000

(P-15484)
SYMITAR SYSTEMS INC
8985 Balboa Ave, San Diego (92123-1507)
PHONE..................................619 542-6700
Kathy Burress, *Principal*
Amy Goodrich, *Admin Sec*
Ramon Macias, *Administration*
John Clark, *Info Tech Dir*
Eben Maat, *Systs Prg Mgr*
EMP: 220
SALES (est): 22.9MM
SALES (corp-wide): 1.5B **Publicly Held**
SIC: 7371 Computer software development
PA: Jack Henry & Associates, Inc.
663 W Highway 60
Monett MO 65708
417 235-6652

(P-15485)
SYSINTELLI INC
9466 Black Mountain Rd # 200, San Diego
(92126-4550)
PHONE..................................858 271-1600
Ravindra Hanumara, *President*
Raja Yalamanchili, *Project Mgr*
Rushikesh Reddy, *Technical Staff*
Umesh Goud, *Recruiter*
Pradeep Medala, *Manager*
EMP: 123
SQ FT: 2,400
SALES (est): 4.5MM **Privately Held**
WEB: www.sysintelli.com
SIC: 7371 7379 Computer related consulting services; custom computer programming services

(P-15486)
SYSTECH SOLUTIONS INC (PA)
500 N Brand Blvd Ste 1900, Glendale
(91203-3308)
PHONE..................................818 550-9690
Arun Gollapudi, *President*
Ashish Parikh, *CFO*
Srinivasan Ramaswamy, *Vice Pres*
EMP: 81
SQ FT: 1,500
SALES (est): 25.1MM **Privately Held**
WEB: www.systechusa.com
SIC: 7371 Computer software systems analysis & design, custom

(P-15487)
SYSTEMS AND SOFTWARE ENTPS LLC (DH)
Also Called: Zodiac Inflight Innovations US
2929 E Imperial Hwy # 170, Brea
(92821-6716)
PHONE..................................714 854-8600
Matt Smith, *CEO*
Ed Barrera, *CFO*
Harry Gray, *Vice Pres*
Steve Hawkins, *CTO*
EMP: 73
SQ FT: 90,000
SALES (est): 65.4MM
SALES (corp-wide): 650.9MM **Privately Held**
WEB: www.imsinflight.com
SIC: 7371 Computer software systems analysis & design, custom
HQ: Zodiac Aerospace
Cs20001
Plaisir 78370
161 342-323

(P-15488)
T AND D COMMUNICATIONS INC (PA)
6761 Sierra Ct Ste F, Dublin (94568-2692)
PHONE..................................510 824-0010
Phillip Ernest Croan, *President*
Andrew Vargas, *CFO*
Patrick Croan, *Vice Pres*
James Vollmer, *Vice Pres*
Mark Weber, *Project Mgr*
EMP: 65
SQ FT: 3,000
SALES (est): 17.1MM **Privately Held**
WEB: www.t-and-d.com
SIC: 7371 Software programming applications

(P-15489)
TALENT & ACQUISITION LLC
100 W Broadway Ste 650, Long Beach
(90802-4466)
PHONE..................................213 742-1972
Quinn Fillmon, *Exec Dir*
Eric Gula, *Technical Staff*
Jennifer A Gordon, *Opers Staff*
EMP: 100
SALES (est): 2.1MM **Privately Held**
SIC: 7371 7379 7363 7361 Custom computer programming services; computer related consulting services; help supply services; employment agencies

(P-15490)
TAMTRON CORPORATION (DH)
6203 San Ignacio Ave # 110, San Jose
(95119-1371)
PHONE..................................408 323-3303
Fax: 408 246-5415
EMP: 60
SQ FT: 2,600
SALES (est): 3.8MM
SALES (corp-wide): 1.3B **Privately Held**
SIC: 7371
HQ: Impac Medical Systems, Inc
100 Mathilda Pl Fl 5
Sunnyvale CA 94086
408 830-8000

(P-15491)
TAPESTRY SOLUTIONS INC (HQ)
5643 Copley Dr, San Diego (92111-7903)
PHONE..................................858 503-1990
Geoff Evans, *President*
Jeremy Lowe, *President*
Mary Ann Wagner, *COO*

Mark Young, *CFO*
Vince Monteparpe, *Exec VP*
EMP: 125
SQ FT: 36,073
SALES (est): 80.6MM
SALES (corp-wide): 93.3B **Publicly Held**
SIC: 7371 5045 Custom computer programming services; computer software
PA: The Boeing Company
100 N Riverside Plz
Chicago IL 60606
312 544-2000

(P-15492)
TAULIA INC (PA)
250 Montgomery St Ste 400, San Francisco
(94104-3427)
PHONE..................................415 376-8280
Cedric Bru, *CEO*
Tina Ngo, *Partner*
Brady Cale, *President*
Jonathan Lowenhar, *President*
Courtney Ring, *President*
EMP: 85
SALES (est): 55.7MM **Privately Held**
SIC: 7371 Computer software development

(P-15493)
TAVANT TECHNOLOGIES INC (PA)
3965 Freedom Cir Ste 750, Santa Clara
(95054-1285)
PHONE..................................408 519-5400
Sarvesh Mahesh, *CEO*
Venkata Devana, *CFO*
Krishnan Pp, *Officer*
Hassan Rashid, *Senior VP*
Jerome Marr, *Principal*
EMP: 87
SALES (est): 108MM **Privately Held**
WEB: www.tavant.com
SIC: 7371 Computer software development; computer software systems analysis & design, custom

(P-15494)
TAX COMPLIANCE INC
10089 Willow Creek Rd # 300, San Diego
(92131-1699)
PHONE..................................858 547-4100
Carl Melcher, *Chairman*
Dave Shea, *CEO*
Jennifer Cortes, *Department Mgr*
Ivan Raykov, *Sr Software Eng*
Joy Trebbien, *QA Dir*
EMP: 52
SQ FT: 10,000
SALES (est): 8MM **Privately Held**
WEB: www.taxcomp.com
SIC: 7371 Computer software development
HQ: Mlm Information Services, Llc
780 3rd Ave
New York NY 10017
212 245-5310

(P-15495)
TCG SOFTWARE SERVICES INC
320 Commerce Ste 200, Irvine
(92602-1363)
PHONE..................................714 665-6200
Greg Blevins, *Branch Mgr*
EMP: 50 **Privately Held**
SIC: 7371 Custom computer programming services
PA: Tcg Software Services, Inc.
265 Davidson Ave Ste 220
Somerset NJ 08873

(P-15496)
TECH MAHINDRA (AMERICAS) INC
23461 S Pointe Dr Ste 370, Laguna Hills
(92653-1571)
PHONE..................................949 462-0640
EMP: 80
SALES (corp-wide): 3.6B **Privately Held**
SIC: 7371 Computer software development & applications
HQ: Tech Mahindra (Americas) Inc.
4965 Preston Park Blvd # 500
Plano TX 75093

(PA)=Parent Co (HQ)=Headquarters (DH)=Div Headquarters
✪ = New Business established in last 2 years

2019 Directory of California
Wholesalers and Services Companies

659

P R O D U C T S & S V C S

(P-15497)
TECHEXCEL INC (PA)
3675 Mt Diablo Blvd # 330, Lafayette
(94549-3792)
PHONE....................925 871-3900
Tieren Zhou, *President*
James Zhou, *CFO*
Rickard Jonsson, *Vice Pres*
Tingjin Xu, *Sr Software Eng*
Xiaojie Liu, *Software Engr*
EMP: 51
SQ FT: 11,187
SALES (est): 13MM **Privately Held**
WEB: www.techexcel.com
SIC: 7371 Computer software development

(P-15498)
TELESTREAM LLC (PA)
848 Gold Flat Rd, Nevada City
(95959-3208)
PHONE....................530 470-1300
Scott Puopolo, *CEO*
Jim Leighton, *Partner*
Gary Petruzzi, *Partner*
Chris Porter, *Partner*
Mark Cuny, *CFO*
EMP: 94
SALES (est): 56MM **Privately Held**
WEB: www.telestream.net
SIC: 7371 Computer software development & applications

(P-15499)
TELESYS SOFTWARE
1900 S Norfolk St Ste 221, San Mateo
(94403-1172)
PHONE....................650 522-9922
Bobby Bahl, *President*
Ed Lee, *Vice Pres*
EMP: 50
SQ FT: 4,000
SALES (est): 4.8MM **Privately Held**
WEB: www.telesys.com
SIC: 7371 Computer software development

(P-15500)
TEXXIS LIMITED
400 Spectrum Center Dr # 1, Irvine
(92618-4934)
PHONE....................213 631-3547
Wenwu Hu, *Director*
EMP: 72
SALES: 250K **Privately Held**
SIC: 7371 Computer software development & applications

(P-15501)
THINK PASSENGER INC (PA)
12100 Wilshire Blvd # 1950, Los Angeles
(90025-7120)
PHONE....................323 556-5400
Bahram Nour-Omid, *CEO*
Ramesh Pidikiti, *President*
Anthony Tam, *President*
Steve Howe, *COO*
Jessie Cooper, *Business Dir*
EMP: 60
SQ FT: 15,000
SALES (est): 9.2MM **Privately Held**
SIC: 7371 Computer software development

(P-15502)
THISMOMENT INC
690 Market St Unit 1101, San Francisco
(94104-5123)
PHONE....................415 200-4730
Vince Broady, *CEO*
Raffy Kaloustian, *President*
Trey Walker, *President*
John Walliser, *President*
Steve Bach, *CFO*
EMP: 135
SQ FT: 15,000
SALES (est): 17.9MM **Privately Held**
SIC: 7371 Computer software development

(P-15503)
THREATMETRIX INC
160 W Santa Clara St # 1400, San Jose
(95113-1701)
PHONE....................408 200-5700
Reed Taussig, *President*

Frank Teruel, *CFO*
Armen Najarian, *Chief Mktg Ofcr*
Alisdair Faulkner, *Officer*
Phil Steffora, *Officer*
EMP: 165
SQ FT: 10,000
SALES (est): 27.9MM
SALES (corp-wide): 9.7B **Privately Held**
SIC: 7371 7374 7382 Computer software development & applications; computer processing services; security systems services
HQ: Lexisnexis Risk Solutions Inc.
1000 Alderman Dr
Alpharetta GA 30005
678 694-6000

(P-15504)
TIBCO SOFTWARE INC (HQ)
3307 Hillview Ave, Palo Alto (94304-1204)
PHONE....................650 846-1000
Murray Rhode, *CEO*
Matt Quinn, *COO*
Bill Hughes, *Exec VP*
Jeffery McLellan, *Vice Pres*
Rafael C Toscano, *Vice Pres*
EMP: 148
SQ FT: 292,000
SALES (est): 783.4MM
SALES (corp-wide): 4.4B **Privately Held**
WEB: www.tibco.com
SIC: 7371 7373 Custom computer programming services; systems integration services
PA: Vista Equity Partners Management, Llc
4 Embarcadero Ctr # 2000
San Francisco CA 94111
415 765-6500

(P-15505)
TK CARSITES INC
2975 Red Hill Ave Ste 175, Costa Mesa
(92626-1209)
PHONE....................714 937-1239
Richard J Valenta, *CEO*
James Bradford, *President*
James Rucker, *Chief Mktg Ofcr*
Philip Sahyoun, *CTO*
EMP: 60
SQ FT: 8,000
SALES (est): 2.9MM
SALES (corp-wide): 26.3MM **Privately Held**
WEB: www.tkcarsites.com
SIC: 7371 Computer software development
PA: Search Optics, Llc
5770 Oberlin Dr
San Diego CA 92121
858 678-0707

(P-15506)
TOOLWIRE INC
7031 Koll Center Pkwy # 220, Pleasanton
(94566-3128)
PHONE....................925 227-8500
John Valencia, *President*
Brian Boyd, *Vice Pres*
John Catanzaro, *Vice Pres*
Cameron Crowe, *Vice Pres*
Jon Garcia, *Vice Pres*
EMP: 56
SQ FT: 12,500
SALES (est): 9.9MM **Privately Held**
WEB: www.toolwire.com
SIC: 7371 Computer software development

(P-15507)
TOWNS END STUDIOS LLC
699 8th St, San Francisco (94103-4901)
PHONE....................415 802-7936
Mark Pincus,
EMP: 1000
SALES (est): 8.9MM
SALES (corp-wide): 861.3MM **Publicly Held**
SIC: 7371 Computer software development & applications
PA: Zynga Inc.
699 8th St
San Francisco CA 94103
855 449-9642

(P-15508)
TRACKR INC
7410 Hollister Ave, Santa Barbara
(93117-2583)
PHONE....................855 981-1690
Christopher G Herbert, *CEO*
Christian J Smith, *President*
Tim Dir, *COO*
Nathan Kelly, *COO*
Matthew Pigeon, *CFO*
EMP: 100
SQ FT: 40,000
SALES: 44MM **Privately Held**
SIC: 7371 Computer software development & applications

(P-15509)
TRADE DESK INC (PA)
Also Called: THETRADEDESK
42 N Chestnut St, Ventura (93001-2662)
PHONE....................805 585-3434
Jeff T Green, *Ch of Bd*
Robert D Perdue, *COO*
Paul E Ross, *CFO*
Brian J Stempeck, *Ch Credit Ofcr*
Susan M Vobejda, *Chief Mktg Ofcr*
EMP: 95
SQ FT: 25,000
SALES: 308.2MM **Publicly Held**
SIC: 7371 7372 Software programming applications; prepackaged software; business oriented computer software; publishers' computer software

(P-15510)
TREASURE DATA INC
2565 Leghorn St, Mountain View
(94043-1613)
PHONE....................866 899-5386
Hiro Yoshikawa, *CEO*
Stephen Lee, *President*
Dan Weirich, *CFO*
Rob Glickman, *Chief Mktg Ofcr*
Noah Barr, *Vice Pres*
EMP: 100
SALES (est): 11.2MM **Privately Held**
SIC: 7371 7374 Custom computer programming services; optical scanning data service

(P-15511)
TRENDSHIFT LLC
13274 Fiji Way Ste 250, Marina Del Rey
(90292-7298)
P.O. Box 691233, West Hollywood (90069-9233)
PHONE....................866 644-8877
Ryan Weirich, *VP Finance*
EMP: 55
SALES (est): 2MM **Privately Held**
SIC: 7371 Computer software development & applications

(P-15512)
TRINUS CORPORATION
225 S Lake Ave Ste 1080, Pasadena
(91101-4892)
PHONE....................818 246-1143
Sanjay Kucheria, *CEO*
Harshada Kucheria, *President*
EMP: 50
SALES: 10MM **Privately Held**
SIC: 7371 Custom computer programming services

(P-15513)
TRYFACTA INC
Also Called: Systems America Public Sector
2950 Buskirk Ave Ste 160, Walnut Creek
(94597-7770)
PHONE....................408 419-9200
Ratika Tyagi, *CEO*
Nikhil Upadhyay, *Recruiter*
EMP: 351
SALES: 43.9MM **Privately Held**
SIC: 7371 7361 7373 8748 Computer software systems analysis & design, custom; labor contractors (employment agency); systems software development services; systems engineering consultant, ex. computer or professional

(P-15514)
TUNARI CORP INC
Also Called: Hara
2755 Campus Dr Ste 300, San Mateo
(94403-2538)
PHONE....................650 249-6740
Rodrigo J Prudencio, *CEO*
EMP: 59
SALES (est): 2.7MM
SALES (corp-wide): 6.6B **Publicly Held**
SIC: 7371 Computer software development
HQ: Verisae, Inc.
730 2nd Ave S Ste 600
Minneapolis MN 55402
612 455-2300

(P-15515)
UBICS INC
1050 Bridgeway, Sausalito (94965-2173)
PHONE....................415 289-1400
Vijay Mallya, *Branch Mgr*
EMP: 140 **Privately Held**
SIC: 7371 Custom computer programming services
PA: Ubics, Inc.
400 Sthpinte Blvd Ste 425
Canonsburg PA 15317

(P-15516)
UNX INC A DELAWARE CORP
Also Called: Universal Network Exchange
175 E Olive Ave Fl 2, Burbank
(91502-1821)
PHONE....................818 333-3300
J Scott Harrison, *CEO*
Andre Perold, *Ch of Bd*
David Collett, *CFO*
EMP: 95 EST: 1997
SQ FT: 16,000
SALES (est): 6.5MM **Privately Held**
WEB: www.unx.com
SIC: 7371 4813 6211 Computer software development & applications; ; security brokers & dealers

(P-15517)
USER ZOOM INC
10 Almaden Blvd Ste 250, San Jose
(95113-2226)
PHONE....................408 533-8619
Alfonso De La Nuez, *CEO*
Xavier Mestres, *Vice Pres*
Arthur Moan, *Vice Pres*
Matt Paulus, *Executive*
Ann Buckley, *Office Mgr*
EMP: 80 EST: 2007
SALES (est): 15.2MM **Privately Held**
SIC: 7371 Computer software development & applications

(P-15518)
UST GLOBAL INC (PA)
5 Polaris Way, Aliso Viejo (92656-5374)
PHONE....................949 716-8757
Paras Chandaria, *Chairman*
Rajesh Nair, *Partner*
Sajan Pillai, *CEO*
Arun Narayanan, *COO*
Krishna Sudheendra, *CFO*
EMP: 100 EST: 2007
SQ FT: 20,000
SALES (est): 885.9MM **Privately Held**
WEB: www.ust-global.com
SIC: 7371 Computer software development

(P-15519)
UTC FIRE SEC AMERICAS CORP INC
Also Called: Utc, Mas
2955 Red Hill Ave Ste 100, Costa Mesa
(92626-1207)
PHONE....................949 737-7800
Shin Voeks, *General Mgr*
Ron Darley, *District Mgr*
Frances Lee, *Sr Software Eng*
Vuong Vu, *Sr Software Eng*
Leslie Cushing, *Software Dev*
EMP: 60
SALES (corp-wide): 59.8B **Publicly Held**
SIC: 7371 5063 Computer software development & applications; computer software systems analysis & design, custom; alarm systems

HQ: Utc Fire & Security Americas Corporation, Inc.
8985 Town Center Pkwy
Lakewood Ranch FL 34202

(P-15520)
UTILITY SYSTEMS SCIENCE (PA)
Also Called: US 3
601 Parkcenter Dr Ste 209, Santa Ana
(92705-3542)
PHONE.....................714 542-1004
Gabriel A Chavez, *CEO*
Anthony Chavez, *CFO*
Mark Serres, *Vice Pres*
Bret Houston, *Software Engr*
EMP: 53
SALES (est): 7.9MM **Privately Held**
SIC: 7371 Computer software development

(P-15521)
VENDINI INC (PA)
660 Market St Ste 400, San Francisco
(94104-5004)
PHONE.....................415 693-9611
Mark Tacchi, *President*
Bill Schaefer, *President*
Michael Farrow, *CFO*
Susan Hollingshead,
Keith Goldberg, *Officer*
EMP: 67
SQ FT: 7,000
SALES (est): 22.7MM **Privately Held**
SIC: 7371 Computer software development

(P-15522)
VERINT AMERICAS INC
Blue Pumpkin
2250 Walsh Ave Ste 120, Santa Clara
(95050-2514)
PHONE.....................408 830-5400
Doron Aspitz, *Branch Mgr*
Ron Conway, *Bd of Directors*
Andi Fant, *Vice Pres*
Michael Maoz, *Vice Pres*
Elizabeth Ussher, *Vice Pres*
EMP: 100 **Publicly Held**
WEB: www.witness.com
SIC: 7371 8742 7372 Computer software writers, freelance; management consulting services; prepackaged software
HQ: Verint Americas Inc.
800 North Point Pkwy
Alpharetta GA 30005

(P-15523)
VERITAS TECHNOLOGIES LLC (HQ)
500 E Middlefield Rd, Mountain View
(94043-4000)
P.O. Box 7011 (94039-7011)
PHONE.....................650 933-1000
Greg Hughes, *CEO*
Mick Lopez, *CFO*
Ben Gibson, *Chief Mktg Ofcr*
Matt Cain,
John Gannon, *Exec VP*
EMP: 200
SALES (est): 156.4MM **Privately Held**
SIC: 7371 7375 Computer software development & applications; information retrieval services; data base information retrieval

(P-15524)
VERITAS US INC
500 E Middlefield Rd, Mountain View
(94043-4000)
PHONE.....................650 933-1000
William T Coleman, *CEO*
EMP: 200 **EST:** 2014
SALES: 1.2B **Privately Held**
SIC: 7371 Computer software development & applications

(P-15525)
VERIZON CONNECT NWF INC
9868 Scranton Rd Ste 1000, San Diego
(92121-1791)
PHONE.....................858 450-3245
Keith Schneider, *President*
Brad Lackey, *Administration*
Brian Madden, *Sales Mgr*

EMP: 95
SQ FT: 13,000
SALES (est): 21MM
SALES (corp-wide): 126B **Publicly Held**
WEB: www.networkcar.com
SIC: 7371 Computer software development & applications
HQ: Verizon Connect Inc.
2002 Summit Blvd Ste 1800
Brookhaven GA 30319
404 573-5800

(P-15526)
VERTAFORE FSC INC
28038 Dorothy Dr, Agoura Hills
(91301-2687)
PHONE.....................800 433-2550
Paul Areida, *President*
John Heitman, *Treasurer*
EMP: 130
SALES (est): 4.7MM
SALES (corp-wide): 352.6MM **Privately Held**
SIC: 7371 Custom computer programming services
PA: Vertafore, Inc.
999 18th St Ste 400
Denver CO 80202
800 444-4813

(P-15527)
VIDA HEALTH INC
100 Montgomery St Ste 750, San Francisco
(94104-4302)
PHONE.....................408 203-7959
Stephanie Tilenius, *CEO*
Ozan Onay, *Manager*
EMP: 100
SALES (est): 595.6K **Privately Held**
SIC: 7371 Computer software development & applications

(P-15528)
VIDHWAN INC
2 N Market St Ste 410, San Jose
(95113-1211)
PHONE.....................408 521-0167
EMP: 112
SALES (corp-wide): 24.7MM **Privately Held**
SIC: 7371 Custom computer programming services
PA: Vidhwan, Inc.
2 N Market St Ste 400
San Jose CA 95113
408 289-8200

(P-15529)
VISION SOLUTIONS INC (PA)
15300 Barranca Pkwy # 100, Irvine
(92618-2256)
PHONE.....................949 253-6500
Nicolaas Vlok, *President*
Maureen Eubeler, *Partner*
Don Scott, *CFO*
Wm Edward Vesely, *Chief Mktg Ofcr*
Alan Arnold, *Exec VP*
EMP: 90
SQ FT: 25,000
SALES: 145MM **Privately Held**
WEB: www.visionsolutions.com
SIC: 7371 7373 Computer software development; systems integration services

(P-15530)
VISION TECH SOLUTIONS LLC
222 N Pacific Coast Hwy # 1500, El Segundo (90245-5648)
PHONE.....................310 656-3100
David Nachman, *CEO*
Mike Truex, *Finance*
John Karambelas, *Sales Staff*
Martin Lind, *Services*
EMP: 60
SALES (est): 4.9MM
SALES (corp-wide): 61.8MM **Privately Held**
SIC: 7371 Computer software development & applications
PA: Granicus, Inc.
707 17th St Ste 4000
Denver CO 80202
415 357-3618

(P-15531)
VISUAL CONCEPTS ENTERTAINMENT
10 Hamilton Landing, Novato (94949-8207)
PHONE.....................415 479-3634
Gregory Thomas, *President*
Scott Patterson, *Vice Pres*
Tim Walter, *Info Tech Dir*
Brian Ramagli, *Software Engr*
Chad Riggleman, *Recruiter*
EMP: 200
SALES (est): 14.2MM **Publicly Held**
SIC: 7371 Computer software development
PA: Take-Two Interactive Software, Inc.
110 W 44th St
New York NY 10036

(P-15532)
VM SERVICES INC
1051 S East St, Anaheim (92805-5749)
PHONE.....................714 678-5200
Bernie Chong, *Branch Mgr*
EMP: 50
SALES (corp-wide): 2.9B **Privately Held**
WEB: www.venturemfg-usa.com
SIC: 7371 5734 3999 Computer software development; computer & software stores; barber & beauty shop equipment
HQ: Vm Services, Inc.
6701 Mowry Ave
Newark CA 94560
510 744-3720

(P-15533)
VM SERVICES INC (DH)
6701 Mowry Ave, Newark (94560-4927)
PHONE.....................510 744-3720
Chin Tong Wong, *CEO*
EMP: 120
SQ FT: 4,300
SALES (est): 106.6MM
SALES (corp-wide): 2.9B **Privately Held**
WEB: www.venturemfg-usa.com
SIC: 7371 Computer software development
HQ: Cebelian Holdings Pte Ltd
5006 Ang Mo Kio Avenue 5
Singapore
648 217-55

(P-15534)
VMWARE INC
Springsource
3400 Hillview Ave, Palo Alto (94304-1346)
PHONE.....................650 427-2100
Peter Cooper, *Principal*
EMP: 180
SALES (corp-wide): 78.6B **Publicly Held**
SIC: 7371 Computer software development & applications
HQ: Vmware, Inc.
3401 Hillview Ave
Palo Alto CA 94304
650 427-5000

(P-15535)
VMWARE INC (DH)
3401 Hillview Ave, Palo Alto (94304-1383)
PHONE.....................650 427-5000
Patrick Gelsinger, *CEO*
Hether Brice, *Partner*
Nancy Twomey, *Partner*
Michael Dell, *Ch of Bd*
Zane Rowe, *CFO*
EMP: 148
SQ FT: 1,592,802
SALES: 7.9B
SALES (corp-wide): 78.6B **Publicly Held**
SIC: 7371 7375 Computer software development; information retrieval services
HQ: Emc Corporation
176 South St
Hopkinton MA 01748
508 435-1000

(P-15536)
VMWARE INC
3305 Hillview Ave, Palo Alto (94304-1204)
P.O. Box 52100 (94303-0751)
PHONE.....................650 812-8200
George Symons, *Branch Mgr*
Sachin Prasad, *Administration*
Kurt Niska, *Senior Engr*
Alex Romanenko, *Manager*

EMP: 180
SALES (corp-wide): 78.6B **Publicly Held**
SIC: 7371 7375 Computer software development & applications; information retrieval services
HQ: Vmware, Inc.
3401 Hillview Ave
Palo Alto CA 94304
650 427-5000

(P-15537)
VOXIFY INC
1151 Marina Village Pkwy, Alameda
(94501-1017)
PHONE.....................510 545-3011
Madhu Ranganathan, *President*
John Gengarella, *President*
John Longinotti, *CFO*
EMP: 65
SALES (est): 6.4MM **Privately Held**
WEB: www.voxify.com
SIC: 7371 Computer software development

(P-15538)
VWISE INC
85 Enterprise Ste 320, Aliso Viejo
(92656-2504)
PHONE.....................949 716-1276
Tony F Mingo, *CEO*
Dave Ferrigno, *CFO*
EMP: 60
SALES (est): 3.2MM **Privately Held**
SIC: 7371 Computer software development

(P-15539)
VYSHNAVI INFORMATION TECHN
2603 Camino Ramon Ste 200, San Ramon
(94583-9137)
PHONE.....................408 454-6218
Ravi H Krishnamurthy, *CEO*
EMP: 150
SALES: 5.7MM **Privately Held**
SIC: 7371 7372 7373 Computer software development & applications; computer software systems analysis & design, custom; application computer software; business oriented computer software; systems software development services

(P-15540)
WALKME INC (HQ)
525 Market St Lbby, San Francisco
(94105-2709)
PHONE.....................855 492-5563
Dan Adika, *CEO*
Alea Stein, *Partner*
Rephael Sweary, *President*
Eyal Cohen, *Exec VP*
Richard Woolf, *Senior VP*
EMP: 60 **EST:** 2012
SALES: 5.1MM **Privately Held**
SIC: 7371 Computer software development
PA: Walkme Ltd
3 Kremnitzky
Tel Aviv-Jaffa
722 657-910

(P-15541)
WALZ GROUP LLC (HQ)
Also Called: Walz Postal Solutions
27398 Via Industria, Temecula
(92590-3699)
PHONE.....................951 491-6800
Rod Walz, *President*
Kevin Miller, *CFO*
Maria Moskver, *Ch Credit Ofcr*
Brad Knapp, *Exec VP*
Oya Babur, *Vice Pres*
EMP: 117
SQ FT: 40,000
SALES (est): 35.1MM
SALES (corp-wide): 78.2MM **Privately Held**
SIC: 7371 Computer software development & applications
PA: Lenderlive Network, Inc.
710 S Ash St Ste 200
Denver CO 80246
303 226-8000

PRODUCTS & SVCS

(P-15542)
WATERLINE DATA SCIENCE INC
615 National Ave Ste 100, Mountain View
(94043-2227)
PHONE..................650 868-4409
Kailash Ambwani, *CEO*
Kaycee Lai, *President*
Myoung Kang, *CFO*
Goldman Todd Chairperso, *Chief Mktg Ofcr*
Todd Goldman, *Chief Mktg Ofcr*
EMP: 75
SALES (est): 1.4MM **Privately Held**
SIC: 7371 Computer software development & applications

(P-15543)
WAY FORWARD TECHNOLOGY INC
28738 The Old Rd, Valencia (91355-1084)
PHONE..................661 286-2769
Voldi Way, *President*
Matt Bozon, *Creative Dir*
Walter Hecht, *Software Engr*
Andrew Aitchison, *Prgrmr*
Edward Fleischman, *Prgrmr*
EMP: 50
SQ FT: 10,000
SALES: 8.2MM **Privately Held**
WEB: www.wayforward.com
SIC: 7371 Computer software development

(P-15544)
WEBYOG INC
2900 Gordon Ave 100-7p, Santa Clara
(95051-0718)
PHONE..................408 512-1434
Rohit Nadhani, *CEO*
Sameer Kumar, *Sales Engr*
EMP: 250
SALES (est): 6.8MM **Privately Held**
SIC: 7371 Computer software development

(P-15545)
WIDEORBIT INC (PA)
1160 Battery St Ste 300, San Francisco
(94111-1212)
PHONE..................415 675-6700
Eric Mathewson, *CEO*
Vijay Kumar, *President*
Nathan Gans, *COO*
Margaret McCarthy, *CFO*
Mickey McClay Wilson, *Officer*
EMP: 124
SQ FT: 9,000
SALES (est): 35.3MM **Privately Held**
WEB: www.wideorbit.com
SIC: 7371 Computer software development

(P-15546)
WINMAX SYSTEMS CORPORATION
1900 Mccarthy Blvd # 301, Milpitas
(95035-7440)
PHONE..................408 894-9000
Suparna Bhattacharya, *President*
Vinnie Bandla, *Executive*
Dinesh Kumar, *Technical Staff*
Afton Usry-Papesh, *Opers Staff*
Nancy Gharib, *Manager*
EMP: 120
SQ FT: 1,900
SALES (est): 9.8MM **Privately Held**
WEB: www.winmaxcorp.com
SIC: 7371 8742 Computer software development; management consulting services

(P-15547)
WISE COMMERCE INC
1730 S El Camino Real # 500, San Mateo
(94402-3085)
PHONE..................855 469-4737
Arie Shpanya, *CEO*
Evan Walsh, *Engineer*
John Harrington, *Director*
EMP: 90
SALES (est): 230.4K **Privately Held**
SIC: 7371 Computer software development

(P-15548)
WORKDAY INC (PA)
6110 Stoneridge Mall Rd, Pleasanton
(94588-3211)
PHONE..................925 951-9000
Aneel Bhusri, *CEO*
David A Duffield, *Ch of Bd*
Chano Fernandez, *President*
Robynne D Sisco, *President*
James J Bozzini, *COO*
EMP: 148
SQ FT: 982,000
SALES: 2.1B **Publicly Held**
WEB: www.workday.com
SIC: 7371 Computer software development

(P-15549)
WORKFORCELOGIC
425 California St, San Francisco
(94104-2102)
PHONE..................707 939-4300
Catherine Candland, *CEO*
Steve Furtado, *CFO*
Gary D Nelson, *Chairman*
Stuart Thompto, *Senior VP*
Catherine Wingate, *Senior VP*
EMP: 100
SALES (est): 4.3MM
SALES (corp-wide): 2.8B **Privately Held**
SIC: 7371 7361 Computer software development; executive placement
PA: Zerochaos, Llc
420 S Orange Ave Ste 600
Orlando FL 32801
407 770-6161

(P-15550)
WORKSHARE TECHNOLOGY INC
650 California St Fl 7, San Francisco
(94108-2737)
PHONE..................415 590-7700
Brad Anthony Foy, *CEO*
Bruno Bossola, *President*
Thomas C Hoster, *CFO*
Nick Thomson, *Officer*
Barrie Hadfield, *Vice Pres*
EMP: 140
SQ FT: 15,000
SALES (est): 21.4MM
SALES (corp-wide): 23.4MM **Privately Held**
WEB: www.workshare.com
SIC: 7371 Computer software development
HQ: Workshare Limited
10-20 Fashion Street, Whitechapel
London E1 6P
207 426-0000

(P-15551)
WYNNE SYSTEMS INC (DH)
2603 Main St Ste 710, Irvine (92614-4263)
PHONE..................949 224-6300
John Bureau, *President*
Mike Stilwagner, *Vice Pres*
John Daniels, *Planning*
Danny Vu, *QA Dir*
Kevin Shaw, *Info Tech Mgr*
EMP: 69
SALES (est): 8.9MM
SALES (corp-wide): 2.4B **Privately Held**
WEB: www.unitedrentals.com
SIC: 7371 7372 Computer software development; prepackaged software
HQ: Volaris Group Inc
5800 Explorer Dr Suite 500
Mississauga ON L4W 5
905 267-5400

(P-15552)
XAMARIN INC (PA)
1355 Market St 3, San Francisco
(94103-1307)
PHONE..................855 926-2746
Nat Friedman, *CEO*
Andrew Yip, *Partner*
Derek Drennan, *President*
Stephanie Schatz, *Senior VP*
Keith Ballinger, *Vice Pres*
EMP: 250
SALES (est): 25.1MM **Privately Held**
SIC: 7371 Computer software development

(P-15553)
XYKA INC
5201 Great America Pkwy # 320, Santa
Clara (95054-1122)
PHONE..................408 340-1923
Rakesh Hegde, *CEO*
Nirav Chhaprapati, *President*
EMP: 50
SQ FT: 1,500
SALES (est): 2.4MM **Privately Held**
WEB: www.xyka.com
SIC: 7371 Computer software development & applications

(P-15554)
YARDI SYSTEMS INC (PA)
430 S Fairview Ave, Santa Barbara
(93117-3637)
PHONE..................805 699-2040
Anant Yardi, *President*
Jonathan Delong, *President*
Gordon Morrell, *COO*
John Pendergast, *Senior VP*
Fritz Schindelbeck, *Senior VP*
EMP: 380
SQ FT: 160,000
SALES (est): 493.5MM **Privately Held**
SIC: 7371 Computer software development

(P-15555)
YTEL INC
94 Icon, Foothill Ranch (92610-3000)
PHONE..................800 382-4913
Nick Newsom, *CEO*
Brian Keep, *COO*
Kevin O'Connor, *CFO*
Adam Johnson, *Sales Staff*
EMP: 100
SQ FT: 30,000
SALES: 20MM **Privately Held**
SIC: 7371 Computer software development & applications

(P-15556)
ZAPIER INC
548 Market St, San Francisco
(94104-5401)
PHONE..................770 988-0633
Charles Wade Foster, *CEO*
Matt Lukso, *Partner*
Jose Proenca, *Partner*
Tim Daniels, *CFO*
Bryan Helmig, *Founder*
EMP: 80 EST: 2013
SALES (est): 2.9MM **Privately Held**
SIC: 7371 Computer software development & applications

(P-15557)
ZEND TECHNOLOGIES USA INC
19200 Stevens Creek Blvd # 100, Cupertino (95014-2530)
PHONE..................408 253-8800
Andi Gutmans, *CEO*
Stu Schmidt, *President*
Curt Disibio, *CFO*
Daniel Moskowitz, *Treasurer*
Elaine Lennox, *Chief Mktg Ofcr*
EMP: 130
SALES (est): 15.6MM
SALES (corp-wide): 77.8MM **Privately Held**
SIC: 7371 Computer software development
PA: Rogue Wave Software, Inc.
1315 W Century Dr Ste 150
Louisville CO 80027
303 473-9118

(P-15558)
ZENTEK CORPORATION
3031 Stnfrd Rnch Rd 2, Rocklin (95765)
PHONE..................916 749-3610
Kristi Woehl, *Principal*
Michael Prendergast, *Business Mgr*
EMP: 100
SALES (est): 4.8MM **Privately Held**
SIC: 7371 8741 Computer software development & applications; management services

(P-15559)
ZESTFINANCE INC
1377 N Serrano Ave, Los Angeles
(90027-5623)
PHONE..................323 450-3000
Douglas Merrill, *CEO*
Michelle Sangster, *President*
Steven Fernald, *CFO*
Mike Armstrong, *Chief Mktg Ofcr*
Sonya Merrill, *Officer*
EMP: 61 EST: 2012
SALES (est): 11.4MM **Privately Held**
SIC: 7371 Computer software development

(P-15560)
ZIGNAL LABS INC
600 California St Fl 18, San Francisco
(94108-2711)
PHONE..................415 683-7871
Bob Deppisch, *Director*
Jonathan Dodson, *President*
Josh Ginsberg, *CEO*
Tracee Joice, *COO*
Chris Krook, *CFO*
EMP: 60 EST: 2011
SALES (est): 8.6MM **Privately Held**
SIC: 7371 Computer software development & applications

(P-15561)
ZL TECHNOLOGIES INC (PA)
860 N Mccarthy Blvd # 100, Milpitas
(95035-5110)
PHONE..................408 240-8989
Kon Leong, *President*
Nack Jung, *Software Engr*
Amit Chaudhary, *Network Enginr*
Ramesh Velampalayam, *Prgrmr*
Liwei Xu, *Research*
EMP: 50
SQ FT: 1,860
SALES (est): 14.7MM **Privately Held**
WEB: www.zlti.com
SIC: 7371 5045 Computer software systems analysis & design, custom; computer software

(P-15562)
ZONE24X7 INC (PA)
3150 Almaden Expy Ste 234, San Jose
(95118-1250)
PHONE..................408 268-8589
Llavaya Fernando, *President*
Tim Becera, *President*
Saw-Chin Fernando, *CFO*
Neschae Fernando, *Vice Pres*
Schayne Jallow, *Bus Dvlpt Dir*
EMP: 285
SQ FT: 1,000
SALES: 13MM **Privately Held**
WEB: www.zone24x7.com
SIC: 7371 Computer software development

7372 Prepackaged Software

(P-15563)
1ON1 LLC
12015 Waterfront Dr # 261, Playa Vista
(90094-2536)
PHONE..................310 448-5376
Susan Josephson, *Mng Member*
Todd Cherniawsky,
Nicole David,
Lorri Goddard,
Stephane Medam,
EMP: 50
SQ FT: 5,000
SALES: 20MM **Privately Held**
SIC: 7372 Application computer software

(P-15564)
ABB ENTERPRISE SOFTWARE INC
60 Spear St, San Francisco (94105-1506)
PHONE..................415 527-2850
Greg Dukat, *Branch Mgr*
EMP: 175
SALES (corp-wide): 34.3B **Privately Held**
WEB: www.indusinternational.com
SIC: 7372 Business oriented computer software

HQ: Abb Enterprise Software Inc.
400 Perimeter Ctr Ter 5
Atlanta GA 30346
678 830-1000

(P-15565)
ACCELA INC (PA)
2633 Camino Ramon Ste 500, San Ramon
(94583-9149)
PHONE....................925 659-3200
Ed Daihl, *CEO*
Lily Cheng, *Partner*
Robin Huey, *Partner*
Mark Jung, *Ch of Bd*
Jerald Lo, *President*
EMP: 150
SALES: 80MM **Privately Held**
WEB: www.accela.com
SIC: 7372 Business oriented computer
software

(P-15566)
ACTIVISION BLIZZARD INC
4 Hamilton Landing, Novato (94949-8256)
PHONE....................415 881-9100
EMP: 209
SALES (corp-wide): 7B **Publicly Held**
SIC: 7372 Home entertainment computer
software
PA: Activision Blizzard, Inc.
3100 Ocean Park Blvd
Santa Monica CA 90405
310 255-2000

(P-15567)
ACTIVISION BLIZZARD INC (PA)
3100 Ocean Park Blvd, Santa Monica
(90405-3032)
PHONE....................310 255-2000
Robert A Kotick, *CEO*
Brian G Kelly, *Ch of Bd*
Collister Johnson, *President*
Spencer Neumann, *CFO*
Kristin Binns, *Ch Credit Ofcr*
EMP: 333
SQ FT: 153,297
SALES: 7B **Publicly Held**
WEB: www.blizzard.com
SIC: 7372 Home entertainment computer
software

(P-15568)
ACTIVISION BLIZZARD INC
Blizzard Entertainment
3 Blizzard, Irvine (92618-3628)
P.O. Box 18979 (92623-8979)
PHONE....................949 955-1380
Frank Pearce, *Principal*
Mathew Smiley, *Administration*
Alex Serio, *Software Engr*
Alix Nguyen, *Graphic Designe*
Wan-Chun MA, *Engineer*
EMP: 85
SALES (corp-wide): 7B **Publicly Held**
WEB: www.blizzard.com
SIC: 7372 Prepackaged software
PA: Activision Blizzard, Inc.
3100 Ocean Park Blvd
Santa Monica CA 90405
310 255-2000

(P-15569)
ACTIVISION PUBLISHING INC (HQ)
3100 Ocean Park Blvd, Santa Monica
(90405-3032)
PHONE....................310 255-2000
Michael Griffith, *President*
Ron Doornink, *Ch of Bd*
Dave Cowling, *President*
Dan Rosensweig, *President*
Colin Schiller, *President*
EMP: 1306
SALES (est): 98.4MM
SALES (corp-wide): 7B **Publicly Held**
SIC: 7372 Home entertainment computer
software
PA: Activision Blizzard, Inc.
3100 Ocean Park Blvd
Santa Monica CA 90405
310 255-2000

(P-15570)
ADAPTIVE INSIGHTS INC (HQ)
3350 W Byshore Rd Ste 200, Palo Alto
(94303)
PHONE....................650 528-7500
Thomas F Bogan, *CEO*
James D Johnson, *CFO*
Connie Dewitt, *Chief Mktg Ofcr*
Frederick M Gewant, *Officer*
Bhaskar Himatsingka, *Officer*
EMP: 200
SQ FT: 30,000
SALES: 106.5MM
SALES (corp-wide): 2.1B **Publicly Held**
WEB: www.adaptiveplanning.com
SIC: 7372 Business oriented computer
software
PA: Workday, Inc.
6110 Stoneridge Mall Rd
Pleasanton CA 94588
925 951-9000

(P-15571)
ADEXA INC (PA)
5777 W Century Blvd # 1100, Los Angeles
(90045-5643)
PHONE....................310 642-2100
Khosrow Cyrus Hadavi, *CEO*
Kameron Hadavi, *Vice Pres*
John Hosford, *Vice Pres*
Nick Yanagibori, *Vice Pres*
William Green, *VP Business*
EMP: 50
SQ FT: 31,000
SALES (est): 20MM **Privately Held**
WEB: www.adexa.com
SIC: 7372 Business oriented computer
software

(P-15572)
ADOBE INC (PA)
345 Park Ave, San Jose (95110-2704)
PHONE....................408 536-6000
Shantanu Narayen, *Ch of Bd*
Rodman Likes, *President*
Mark Garrett, *CFO*
John Murphy, *CFO*
Amy Banse, *Bd of Directors*
EMP: 600
SQ FT: 391,000
SALES: 7.3B **Publicly Held**
WEB: www.adobe.com
SIC: 7372 Application computer software

(P-15573)
ADOBE SYSTEMS INCORPORATED
601 And 625 Townsend St, San Francisco
(94103)
PHONE....................415 832-2000
Les Schmidt, *Vice Pres*
Eric Robeson, *Engineer*
David Rich, *Director*
EMP: 1000
SALES (corp-wide): 7.3B **Publicly Held**
SIC: 7372 Application computer software
PA: Adobe Inc.
345 Park Ave
San Jose CA 95110
408 536-6000

(P-15574)
ADVENT RESOURCES INC
235 W 7th St, San Pedro (90731-3321)
PHONE....................310 241-1500
Ysidro Salinas, *Ch of Bd*
Timothy Gill, *CEO*
Vishal Ghelani, *Vice Pres*
Benjamin Gill, *Vice Pres*
Mitch Stahl, *Exec Dir*
EMP: 80
SQ FT: 22,000
SALES (est): 12.2MM **Privately Held**
WEB: www.adventresources.com
SIC: 7372 Prepackaged software

(P-15575)
AGENCYCOM LLC
5353 Grosvenor Blvd, Los Angeles
(90066-6913)
PHONE....................415 817-3800
Chan Suh, *CEO*
Jordan Warren, *President*
Rob Elliott, *CFO*
EMP: 400
SQ FT: 130,000

SALES (est): 22.4MM
SALES (corp-wide): 15.2B **Publicly Held**
WEB: www.agency.com
SIC: 7372 Application computer software
PA: Omnicom Group Inc.
437 Madison Ave
New York NY 10022
212 415-3600

(P-15576)
ALEKS CORPORATION
Also Called: Aleks Educational Systems
15640 Laguna Canyon Rd, Irvine (92618)
PHONE....................714 245-7191
R G Wilmot Lampros, *President*
Nicolas Thiery, *President*
Jean-Claude Falmagne, *Chairman*
Gildas Cadin, *Engineer*
Raymond Ramos, *Sales Staff*
EMP: 130
SQ FT: 50,000
SALES (est): 9.9MM **Privately Held**
WEB: www.aris.ss.uci.edu
SIC: 7372 Educational computer software

(P-15577)
ALFRESCO SOFTWARE INC (PA)
1825 S Grant St Ste 900, San Mateo
(94402-2675)
PHONE....................888 317-3395
Bernadette Nixon, *CEO*
Paul Holmes-Higgin, *President*
Doug Dennerline, *CEO*
Carlton Baab, *CFO*
Bob Pritchard, *Senior VP*
EMP: 80
SALES (est): 22.4MM **Privately Held**
SIC: 7372 Prepackaged software

(P-15578)
ALIENVAULT LLC (DH)
1100 Park Pl Ste 300, San Mateo
(94403-7108)
PHONE....................650 713-3333
Barmak Meftah, *President*
J Alberto Yepez, *Ch of Bd*
Chris Murphy, *President*
Brian Robins, *CFO*
Rita Selvaggi, *Chief Mktg Ofcr*
EMP: 61
SALES (est): 42MM
SALES (corp-wide): 160.5B **Publicly Held**
SIC: 7372 Business oriented computer
software
HQ: Alienvault, Inc.
1100 Park Pl Ste 300
San Mateo CA 94403
650 713-3333

(P-15579)
ALLDATA LLC
9650 W Taron Dr Ste 100, Elk Grove
(95757-8197)
PHONE....................916 684-5200
Stephen Odland,
Harry L Goldsmith,
Bob Olsen,
EMP: 76
SQ FT: 35,000
SALES (est): 43.3MM
SALES (corp-wide): 11.2B **Publicly Held**
WEB: www.alldata.com
SIC: 7372 Business oriented computer
software
PA: Autozone, Inc.
123 S Front St
Memphis TN 38103
901 495-6500

(P-15580)
ALTIUM LLC
4275 Executive Sq Ste 825, La Jolla
(92037-1478)
PHONE....................800 544-4186
Aram Mirkazemi,
Martin Ive, *Treasurer*
EMP: 75
SALES (est): 2.2MM **Privately Held**
SIC: 7372 Prepackaged software

(P-15581)
ALVENTIVE INC (PA)
2790 Walsh Ave, Santa Clara
(95051-0963)
P.O. Box 584, Cupertino (95015-0584)
PHONE....................408 969-8000
David Tiley, *Ch of Bd*
Dave Conner, *President*
EMP: 60
SQ FT: 44,895
SALES (est): 3.4MM **Privately Held**
WEB: www.alventive.com
SIC: 7372 7373 Prepackaged software;
computer-aided design (CAD) systems
service

(P-15582)
APPDIRECT INC (PA)
650 California St Fl 25, San Francisco
(94108-2606)
PHONE....................415 852-3924
Nicolas Desmarais, *Ch of Bd*
Angelica Patino, *Partner*
Daniel Saks, *President*
Michael Difilippo, *CFO*
Mark Beebe, *Vice Pres*
EMP: 59
SQ FT: 10,000
SALES (est): 24.2MM **Privately Held**
SIC: 7372 7371 Application computer soft-
ware; computer software development &
applications

(P-15583)
APPDYNAMICS LLC (HQ)
Also Called: Appdynamics, Inc.
303 2nd St Fl 8, San Francisco
(94107-1366)
PHONE....................415 442-8400
David Wadhwani, *President*
Dev Ittycheria, *Bd of Directors*
Daniel J Wright, *Senior VP*
Jim Cavanaugh, *Vice Pres*
Jeremy Duggan, *Vice Pres*
EMP: 135
SQ FT: 83,500
SALES: 150.5MM
SALES (corp-wide): 49.3B **Publicly Held**
SIC: 7372 Prepackaged software
PA: Cisco Systems, Inc.
170 W Tasman Dr
San Jose CA 95134
408 526-4000

(P-15584)
APPERY LLC
1340 Treat Blvd Ste 375, Walnut Creek
(94597-7590)
PHONE....................925 602-5504
Lynne Walter, *CFO*
Dimitry Binunsky, *Vice Pres*
EMP: 60
SQ FT: 7,200
SALES: 2MM **Privately Held**
SIC: 7372 Application computer software

(P-15585)
APPETIZE TECHNOLOGIES INC
6601 Center Dr W Ste 700, Los Angeles
(90045-1545)
PHONE....................877 559-4225
Max Roper, *CEO*
Jason Pratts, *COO*
Dan Machock, *CFO*
Mark Eastwood, *Officer*
Kevin Anderson, *Senior VP*
EMP: 110 **EST:** 2011
SALES (est): 257.6K **Privately Held**
SIC: 7372 Application computer software

(P-15586)
APPFOLIO INC (PA)
50 Castilian Dr Ste 101, Santa Barbara
(93117-5578)
PHONE....................805 364-6093
Jason Randall, *President*
Andreas Von Blottnitz, *Ch of Bd*
Ida Kane, *CFO*
Jonathan Walker, *CTO*
EMP: 130
SQ FT: 79,200
SALES: 143.8MM **Publicly Held**
SIC: 7372 Business oriented computer
software

PRODUCTS & SVCS

(P-15587)
APPFOLIO INC
Also Called: Mycase
9201 Spectrum, San Diego (92123)
PHONE..............................866 648-1536
Troy Alford, *Engineer*
EMP: 573
SALES (corp-wide): 143.8MM **Publicly Held**
SIC: 7372 Prepackaged software
PA: Appfolio, Inc.
50 Castilian Dr Ste 101
Santa Barbara CA 93117
805 364-6093

(P-15588)
APPLIED BIOSYSTEMS LLC (DH)
5791 Van Allen Way, Carlsbad (92008-7321)
PHONE..............................650 638-5000
David L Szekeres, *Mng Member*
Tony L White, *Ch of Bd*
Lars Holmkvist, *President*
Kathy P Ordonez, *President*
Dennis L Winger, *CFO*
▲ EMP: 120 EST: 1937
SQ FT: 51,000
SALES (est): 347.9MM
SALES (corp-wide): 20.9B **Publicly Held**
WEB: www.applera.com
SIC: 7372 3826 Prepackaged software; gas chromatographic instruments
HQ: Life Technologies Corporation
5781 Van Allen Way
Carlsbad CA 92008
760 603-7200

(P-15589)
APTELIGENT INC
1100 La Avenida St Ste A, Mountain View (94043-1453)
PHONE..............................415 371-1402
Pat Gelsinger, *CEO*
Scott Bajtos, *COO*
Sanjay Poonen, *COO*
Raghu Raghuram, *COO*
Rajiv Ramaswami, *COO*
EMP: 60
SALES (est): 3.8MM
SALES (corp-wide): 78.6B **Publicly Held**
SIC: 7372 Prepackaged software
HQ: Vmware, Inc.
3401 Hillview Ave
Palo Alto CA 94304
650 427-5000

(P-15590)
APTIV DIGITAL INC
2210 W Olive Ave Fl 2, Burbank (91506-2626)
PHONE..............................818 295-6789
Neil Jones, *President*
Christine Otto, *Director*
EMP: 85
SALES (est): 3.2MM
SALES (corp-wide): 826.4MM **Publicly Held**
WEB: www.tvguideinc.com
SIC: 7372 Home entertainment computer software
HQ: Rovi Guides, Inc.
2233 N Ontario St Ste 100
Burbank CA 91504

(P-15591)
ARIA SYSTEMS INC (PA)
100 Pine St Ste 2450, San Francisco (94111-5230)
PHONE..............................415 852-7250
Tom Dibble, *President*
Peter Worth, *Officer*
Michael Breslin, *Vice Pres*
Janice Kennealy, *Vice Pres*
Edward Popow, *Vice Pres*
▼ EMP: 62
SALES (est): 34MM **Privately Held**
WEB: www.ariasystems.com
SIC: 7372 Prepackaged software

(P-15592)
ARIBA INC (DH)
3420 Hillview Ave Bldg 3, Palo Alto (94304-1355)
PHONE..............................650 849-4000

Alex Atzberger, *CEO*
Marc Malone, *CFO*
Alicia Tillman, *Chief Mktg Ofcr*
Brad Brubaker, *Admin Sec*
Patrick Haines, *Human Resources*
EMP: 105
SQ FT: 86,000
SALES (est): 434.3MM
SALES (corp-wide): 27.6B **Privately Held**
WEB: www.ariba.com
SIC: 7372 Business oriented computer software
HQ: Sap America, Inc.
3999 West Chester Pike
Newtown Square PA 19073
610 661-1000

(P-15593)
ASPECT SOFTWARE INC
101 Academy Ste 130, Irvine (92617-3081)
PHONE..............................408 595-5002
James Foy, *Owner*
EMP: 50 **Privately Held**
SIC: 7372 Prepackaged software
HQ: Aspect Software, Inc.
2325 E Camelback Rd # 700
Phoenix AZ 85016
978 250-7900

(P-15594)
ASTORIA SOFTWARE
160 Spear St Ste 1100, San Francisco (94105-1546)
PHONE..............................415 956-3917
Michael Rosinski, *Branch Mgr*
Eric Kuhnen, *General Mgr*
EMP: 50 EST: 2010
SALES (est): 1.8MM **Privately Held**
SIC: 7372 Prepackaged software

(P-15595)
ATLASSIAN INC (DH)
1098 Harrison St, San Francisco (94103-4521)
PHONE..............................415 701-1110
Scott Farquhar, *CEO*
Doug Burgum, *Ch of Bd*
Denise Romero, *President*
Jay Simons, *President*
John Bruce, *CFO*
EMP: 101
SALES (est): 43.9MM **Privately Held**
WEB: www.atlassian.com
SIC: 7372 Business oriented computer software

(P-15596)
ATYPON SYSTEMS LLC (PA)
5201 Great America Pkwy # 510, Santa Clara (95054-1122)
PHONE..............................408 988-1240
Georgios Papadapoulos, *CEO*
Joshua Pyle, *President*
Gordon Tibbitts, *President*
Steve Castro, *CFO*
Jonathan Hevenstone, *Senior VP*
EMP: 60
SQ FT: 6,000
SALES (est): 13.2MM **Privately Held**
WEB: www.atypon.com
SIC: 7372 Application computer software

(P-15597)
AUDATEX NORTH AMERICA INC (DH)
Also Called: Audaexplore
15030 Ave Of, San Diego (92128)
PHONE..............................858 946-1900
Tony Aquila, *CEO*
Jack Pearlstein, *CFO*
Richard Palmer, *Vice Pres*
Don Tartre, *Vice Pres*
Ryan Hager, *VP Bus Dvlpt*
EMP: 200
SQ FT: 35,000
SALES (est): 144.6MM
SALES (corp-wide): 527.1MM **Privately Held**
SIC: 7372 Business oriented computer software

(P-15598)
AUTODESK INC
1 Market St, San Francisco (94105-1420)
PHONE..............................415 356-0700
Chris Bradshaw, *Vice Pres*

Yvonne Cekel, *Partner*
Wes Hamerstadt, *Partner*
Yannis Daubin, *Executive*
Tom Winter, *Executive*
EMP: 61
SALES (corp-wide): 2B **Publicly Held**
WEB: www.autodesk.com
SIC: 7372 Application computer software
PA: Autodesk, Inc.
111 Mcinnis Pkwy
San Rafael CA 94903
415 507-5000

(P-15599)
AUTODESK INC (PA)
111 Mcinnis Pkwy, San Rafael (94903-2700)
PHONE..............................415 507-5000
Andrew Anagnost, *President*
Kathe Rodd, *Partner*
Crawford W Beveridge, *Ch of Bd*
R Scott Herren, *CFO*
Kathleen Kewley, *Treasurer*
EMP: 400 EST: 1982
SQ FT: 220,000
SALES: 2B **Publicly Held**
WEB: www.autodesk.com
SIC: 7372 Application computer software

(P-15600)
AUTODESK INC
3950 Civic Center Dr, San Rafael (94903-5901)
PHONE..............................415 507-5000
Kathryn Najafi-Tagol, *Manager*
Thomas Georgens, *Bd of Directors*
Alexander Nikolayev, *Software Engr*
EMP: 250
SALES (corp-wide): 2B **Publicly Held**
WEB: www.autodesk.com
SIC: 7372 Application computer software
PA: Autodesk, Inc.
111 Mcinnis Pkwy
San Rafael CA 94903
415 507-5000

(P-15601)
AVOLENT INC
444 De Haro St Ste 100, San Francisco (94107-2350)
PHONE..............................415 553-6400
Doug Roberts, *CEO*
Mike Seashols, *Ch of Bd*
Bhupi Singh, *CFO*
Kevin Han, *Exec VP*
Tanya Johnson, *Vice Pres*
EMP: 80 EST: 1995
SQ FT: 60,000
SALES (est): 5.7MM **Privately Held**
SIC: 7372 Application computer software

(P-15602)
BADGEVILLE INC
805 Veterans Blvd Ste 307, Redwood City (94063-1737)
P.O. Box 2367 (94064-2367)
PHONE..............................650 323-6668
Jon Shalowitz, *President*
Stephanie Vinella, *CFO*
Karen Hsu, *Vice Pres*
Andy Pederson, *Vice Pres*
Roel Stalman, *Vice Pres*
EMP: 50 EST: 2010
SALES (est): 10.2MM **Privately Held**
SIC: 7372 Prepackaged software

(P-15603)
BARRA LLC (HQ)
Also Called: Barra, Inc.
2100 Milvia St, Berkeley (94704-1113)
PHONE..............................510 548-5442
Kamal Duggirala, *CEO*
Andrew Rudd, *Ch of Bd*
Aamir Sheikh, *President*
Greg Stockett, *CFO*
Susan Gledhill, *General Mgr*
EMP: 280
SQ FT: 35,000
SALES (est): 28.2MM **Publicly Held**
WEB: www.barra.com
SIC: 7372 8741 6282 Business oriented computer software; financial management for business; investment advisory service

(P-15604)
BARRACUDA NETWORKS INC (HQ)
3175 Winchester Blvd, Campbell (95008-6557)
PHONE..............................408 342-5400
William D Jenkins Jr, *President*
Dustin Driggs, *CFO*
Erin Hintz, *Chief Mktg Ofcr*
Zachary Levow, *Exec VP*
Fleming Shi, *Technology*
EMP: 225
SQ FT: 61,400
SALES: 352.6MM
SALES (corp-wide): 44.7MM **Privately Held**
WEB: www.barracudanetworks.com
SIC: 7372 7373 Prepackaged software; computer integrated systems design
PA: Barracuda Holdings, Llc
3175 Winchester Blvd
Campbell CA 95008
408 342-5400

(P-15605)
BDNA CORPORATION (PA)
339 Bernardo Ave Ste 206, Mountain View (94043-5232)
PHONE..............................650 625-9530
Constantin Delivanis, *CEO*
Ossama Hassanein, *Ch of Bd*
Walker White, *President*
Fred Hessabi, *CEO*
Dave Pomeroy, *CFO*
EMP: 64
SQ FT: 7,000
SALES (est): 17.5MM **Privately Held**
WEB: www.bdnacorp.com
SIC: 7372 Business oriented computer software

(P-15606)
BEATS MUSIC LLC
235 2nd St, San Francisco (94105-3124)
PHONE..............................415 590-5104
Timothy Cook, *CEO*
EMP: 95
SALES (est): 8.5MM
SALES (corp-wide): 265.6B **Publicly Held**
SIC: 7372 Prepackaged software
PA: Apple Inc.
1 Apple Park Way
Cupertino CA 95014
408 996-1010

(P-15607)
BETTERWORKS SYSTEMS INC
999 Main St, Redwood City (94063-1903)
PHONE..............................650 656-9013
Doug Dennerline, *CEO*
Mark Lambert, *CFO*
Mathew Geist, *Software Engr*
Justin Huang, *Software Engr*
Matthew Rasmus, *Software Engr*
EMP: 75
SALES: 8MM **Privately Held**
SIC: 7372 Publishers' computer software

(P-15608)
BIG SWITCH NETWORKS INC (PA)
3111 Coronado Dr Bldg A, Santa Clara (95054-3206)
PHONE..............................650 322-6510
Douglas Murray, *CEO*
Jeffrey Wang, *President*
Seamus Hennessy, *CFO*
Wendell Laidley, *CFO*
Gregg Holzrichter, *Chief Mktg Ofcr*
EMP: 53
SALES (est): 43.2MM **Privately Held**
SIC: 7372 Prepackaged software

(P-15609)
BILLCOM INC
1810 Embarcadero Rd, Palo Alto (94303-3308)
PHONE..............................650 353-3301
Rene Lacerte, *CEO*
Penny Lam, *Partner*
Yogesh Bhumralkar, *President*
Mark Orttung, *COO*
John Rettig, *CFO*
EMP: 140

SALES (est): 35.6MM **Privately Held**
SIC: 7372 Application computer software

(P-15610)
BIZMATICS INC (PA)
4010 Moorpark Ave Ste 222, San Jose
(95117-1843)
PHONE...............................408 873-3030
Vinay Deshpande, *CEO*
Chris Ferguson, *President*
Sneha Baing, *Executive*
Suvarna Gaikwad, *Software Engr*
Shashank Joshi, *Software Engr*
EMP: 250
SQ FT: 2,000
SALES: 5.9MM **Privately Held**
SIC: 7372 Business oriented computer
　software

(P-15611)
BLACKLINE SYSTEMS INC (HQ)
21300 Victory Blvd Fl 12, Woodland Hills
(91367-7734)
PHONE...............................818 746-4700
Therese Tucker, *CEO*
Jennifer T Pottle, *Partner*
Charles Best, *CFO*
Mark Partin, *CFO*
David Downing, *Chief Mktg Ofcr*
EMP: 108
SQ FT: 66,447
SALES (est): 123MM
SALES (corp-wide): 177MM **Publicly
Held**
WEB: www.blackline.com
SIC: 7372 Business oriented computer
　software
PA: Blackline, Inc.
　21300 Victory Blvd Fl 12
　Woodland Hills CA 91367
　818 223-9008

(P-15612)
BLIZZARD ENTERTAINMENT INC (HQ)
1 Blizzard, Irvine (92618-3628)
P.O. Box 18979 (92623-8979)
PHONE...............................949 955-1380
Mike Morhaime, *President*
J Allen Brack, *President*
Paul Sams, *President*
Frank Pearce, *Exec VP*
Chris Metzen, *Senior VP*
▲ **EMP:** 85
SALES (est): 62.1MM
SALES (corp-wide): 7B **Publicly Held**
SIC: 7372 5734 7819 Prepackaged soft-
　ware; software, computer games; repro-
　duction services, motion picture
　production
PA: Activision Blizzard, Inc.
　3100 Ocean Park Blvd
　Santa Monica CA 90405
　310 255-2000

(P-15613)
BLUE COAT LLC
350 Ellis St, Mountain View (94043-2202)
PHONE...............................408 220-2200
Greg Clark, *CEO*
Michael Fey, *President*
Thomas Seifert, *CFO*
Fran Rosch, *Exec VP*
Scott Taylor, *Exec VP*
EMP: 1583
SALES (est): 98.4MM
SALES (corp-wide): 4.8B **Publicly Held**
SIC: 7372 Prepackaged software
PA: Symantec Corporation
　350 Ellis St
　Mountain View CA 94043
　650 527-8000

(P-15614)
BORLAND SOFTWARE CORPORATION
951 Mariners Isl Blvd # 460, San Mateo
(94404-1558)
PHONE...............................650 286-1900
Gina Rosenberger, *Branch Mgr*
EMP: 100
SALES (corp-wide): 834.5MM **Privately
Held**
WEB: www.borland.com
SIC: 7372 Business oriented computer
　software

HQ: Borland Software Corporation
　8310 N Cpitl Of Texas Hwy
　Austin TX 78731
　512 340-2200

(P-15615)
BOX INC (PA)
900 Jefferson Ave, Redwood City
(94063-1837)
PHONE...............................877 729-4269
Aaron Levie, *Ch of Bd*
Stephanie Carullo, *COO*
Dylan Smith, *CFO*
Daniel Levin, *Bd of Directors*
David Leeb, *Senior VP*
EMP: 148 **EST:** 2005
SQ FT: 340,000
SALES: 506.1MM **Publicly Held**
SIC: 7372 Application computer software

(P-15616)
BQE SOFTWARE INC
3825 Del Amo Blvd Trrance Torrance, Tor-
rance (90503)
PHONE...............................310 602-4020
Shafat Qazi, *CEO*
Sharone Strauss, *Vice Pres*
Kari Weinberger, *Marketing Staff*
Jason Burkley, *Sales Staff*
Humza Khan, *Sales Staff*
EMP: 95
SQ FT: 20,000
SALES (est): 13.1MM **Privately Held**
WEB: www.billquick.com
SIC: 7372 5734 Application computer soft-
　ware; software, business & non-game

(P-15617)
BROADVISION INC (PA)
460 Seaport Ct Ste 102, Redwood City
(94063-5548)
PHONE...............................650 331-1000
Pehong Chen, *Ch of Bd*
James Dixon, *Bd of Directors*
Robert Lee, *Bd of Directors*
Francois Stieger, *Bd of Directors*
Richard Hughes, *Chief Mktg Ofcr*
EMP: 86
SQ FT: 16,399
SALES (est): 6.3MM **Publicly Held**
WEB: www.broadvision.com
SIC: 7372 Prepackaged software

(P-15618)
C3 IOT INC
1300 Seaport Blvd Ste 500, Redwood City
(94063-5592)
PHONE...............................650 503-2200
Thomas M Siebel, *CEO*
Ed Abbo, *President*
Rohit Sureka, *Sr Software Eng*
EMP: 125
SQ FT: 35,000
SALES (est): 24.6MM **Privately Held**
SIC: 7372 Business oriented computer
　software

(P-15619)
CA INC
3965 Freedom Cir Fl 6, Santa Clara
(95054-1286)
PHONE...............................800 225-5224
Vinod Peris, *Senior VP*
Sue Moynahan, *Director*
EMP: 166
SALES (corp-wide): 17.6B **Publicly Held**
SIC: 7372 Business oriented computer
　software
HQ: Ca, Inc.
　520 Madison Ave Fl 22
　New York NY 10022
　800 225-5224

(P-15620)
CA INC
10180 Telesis Ct Ste 500, San Diego
(92121-2787)
PHONE...............................631 342-6000
Greg Fox, *Manager*
Brian Dyson, *Sr Software Eng*
EMP: 100
SALES (corp-wide): 17.6B **Publicly Held**
WEB: www.cai.com
SIC: 7372 Prepackaged software

HQ: Ca, Inc.
　520 Madison Ave Fl 22
　New York NY 10022
　800 225-5224

(P-15621)
CADENCE DESIGN SYSTEMS INC (PA)
2655 Seely Ave Bldg 5, San Jose
(95134-1931)
PHONE...............................408 943-1234
Lip-Bu Tan, *President*
John B Shoven, *Ch of Bd*
Anirudh Devgan, *President*
Geoffrey G Ribar, *CFO*
Thomas P Beckley, *Senior VP*
EMP: 700
SALES: 1.9B **Publicly Held**
WEB: www.cadence.com
SIC: 7372 Prepackaged software; applica-
　tion computer software

(P-15622)
CARPARTS TECHNOLOGIES
32122 Camn Capistrano # 100, San Juan
Capistrano (92675-3734)
PHONE...............................949 488-8860
Charles Ruban, *CEO*
Cynthia Robbins, *President*
EMP: 163 **EST:** 2004
SQ FT: 1,400
SALES (est): 6.3MM **Privately Held**
WEB: www.crcs.com
SIC: 7372 Prepackaged software

(P-15623)
CATALYST DEVELOPMENT CORP
56925 Yucca Trl, Yucca Valley
(92284-7913)
PHONE...............................760 228-9653
Cary Harwin, *President*
Mike Stefanik, *Senior VP*
Kapil Desai, *Analyst*
EMP: 50
SALES (est): 3MM **Privately Held**
WEB: www.catalyst.com
SIC: 7372 Business oriented computer
　software

(P-15624)
CFS TAX SOFTWARE
Also Called: CFS Income Tax
1445 E Los Angeles Ave # 214, Simi Valley
(93065-2828)
P.O. Box 879 (93062-0879)
PHONE...............................805 522-1157
Ted Sullivan, *President*
Nolan Stacey, *Software Dev*
Juliana Caizzo, *Technology*
Roger Stock, *Technical Staff*
Juliana Caiazzo, *Sales Staff*
EMP: 60
SALES (est): 5.4MM **Privately Held**
WEB: www.taxtools.com
SIC: 7372 8721 Business oriented com-
　puter software; accounting, auditing &
　bookkeeping

(P-15625)
CHECK POINT SOFTWARE TECH INC (HQ)
959 Skyway Rd Ste 300, San Carlos
(94070-2723)
PHONE...............................650 628-2000
John Slavitt, *CEO*
Marius Nacht, *Ch of Bd*
Rafael Alegre, *President*
Jerry Ungerman, *President*
Eyal Desheh, *CFO*
EMP: 120
SALES (est): 222.6MM
SALES (corp-wide): 1.8B **Privately Held**
WEB: www.checkpoint.com
SIC: 7372 Operating systems computer
　software
PA: Check Point Software Technologies
　Ltd.
　5 Shlomo Kaplan
　Tel Aviv-Jaffa 67891
　375 345-55

(P-15626)
CHOWNOW INC
12181 Bluff Creek Dr # 200, Playa Vista
(90094-3232)
PHONE...............................888 707-2469
Eric Jaffe, *President*
Stuart Hathaway, *CFO*
Candice Taylor, *Recruiter*
Emily Neudorf, *Mktg Dir*
Jessica Springer, *Marketing Mgr*
EMP: 100
SQ FT: 25,000
SALES (est): 2.1MM **Privately Held**
SIC: 7372 Business oriented computer
　software

(P-15627)
CIPHERCLOUD INC (PA)
2581 Junction Ave Ste 200, San Jose
(95134-1923)
PHONE...............................408 519-6930
Pravin Kothari, *CEO*
Glenn Cobb, *Vice Pres*
Paul Culpepper, *Vice Pres*
Dev Ghoshal, *Vice Pres*
Harnish Kanani, *Vice Pres*
EMP: 90
SQ FT: 21,800
SALES (est): 40.3MM **Privately Held**
SIC: 7372 Prepackaged software

(P-15628)
CISCO IRONPORT SYSTEMS LLC (HQ)
170 W Tasman Dr, San Jose (95134-1706)
PHONE...............................650 989-6500
Scott Weiss, *CEO*
Tom Peterson, *President*
Craig Collins, *CFO*
Bob Kavner, *Chairman*
Kelly Bodnar Battles, *Vice Pres*
EMP: 260
SALES (est): 53.8MM
SALES (corp-wide): 49.3B **Publicly Held**
WEB: www.ironport.com
SIC: 7372 5045 Prepackaged software;
　computers, peripherals & software
PA: Cisco Systems, Inc.
　170 W Tasman Dr
　San Jose CA 95134
　408 526-4000

(P-15629)
CLEARSLIDE INC (DH)
45 Fremont St Fl 32, San Francisco
(94105-2258)
PHONE...............................877 360-3366
Dustin Grosse, *CEO*
Jim Benton, *Officer*
Sandra Wright, *Vice Pres*
Erin Stanwood, *Executive*
Mike Volk, *Executive*
EMP: 84
SALES (est): 27.5MM
SALES (corp-wide): 128.6MM **Privately
Held**
SIC: 7372 Business oriented computer
　software
HQ: Corel Corporation
　1600 Carling Ave Suite 100
　Ottawa ON K1Z 8
　613 728-8200

(P-15630)
CLEARWELL SYSTEMS INC
350 Ellis St, Mountain View (94043-2202)
PHONE...............................877 253-2793
Aaref Hilaly, *CEO*
Anup Singh, *CFO*
Venkat Rangan, *CTO*
EMP: 110
SQ FT: 17,000
SALES (est): 7.4MM
SALES (corp-wide): 4.8B **Publicly Held**
WEB: www.clearwellsystems.com
SIC: 7372 Business oriented computer
　software
PA: Symantec Corporation
　350 Ellis St
　Mountain View CA 94043
　650 527-8000

PRODUCTS & SVCS

(P-15631)
COLORTOKENS INC
2101 Tasman Dr Ste 201, Santa Clara
(95054-1020)
PHONE.................408 341-6030
Rajesh Parekh, *President*
EMP: 50
SALES (est): 1.3MM **Privately Held**
SIC: 7372 Business oriented computer
software

(P-15632)
COMMERCE VELOCITY LLC
1 Technology Dr Ste J725, Irvine
(92618-2353)
PHONE.................949 756-8950
Umesh Verma,
Ajay Chopra,
EMP: 50
SQ FT: 5,000
SALES (est): 6.8MM
SALES (corp-wide): 7.6B **Publicly Held**
WEB: www.cvelocity.com
SIC: 7372 Business oriented computer
software
PA: Fidelity National Financial, Inc.
601 Riverside Ave Fl 4
Jacksonville FL 32204
904 854-8100

(P-15633)
**COMPOSITE SOFTWARE LLC
(HQ)**
755 Sycamore Dr, Milpitas (95035-7411)
PHONE.................800 553-6387
Jim Green, *CEO*
Jon Bode, *CFO*
Marc Breissinger, *Exec VP*
Robert Eve, *Exec VP*
Che Wijesinghe, *Exec VP*
EMP: 74
SQ FT: 14,000
SALES (est): 16.7MM
SALES (corp-wide): 49.3B **Publicly Held**
WEB: www.compositesw.com
SIC: 7372 Prepackaged software
PA: Cisco Systems, Inc.
170 W Tasman Dr
San Jose CA 95134
408 526-4000

(P-15634)
**COMPULINK BUSINESS
SYSTEMS INC**
1100 Business Center Cir, Newbury Park
(91320-1129)
PHONE.................805 446-2050
Link Wilson, *President*
Mark Misteravich, *Executive*
Cole Galbraith, *CTO*
Cole Galbarith, *Info Tech Mgr*
Jose Melendez, *Technology*
EMP: 120
SQ FT: 15,000
SALES (est): 16.5MM **Privately Held**
WEB: www.compulink-software.com
SIC: 7372 Business oriented computer
software

(P-15635)
**COMPULINK MANAGEMENT
CTR INC**
Also Called: Laserfiche Document Imaging
3545 Long Beach Blvd, Long Beach
(90807-3941)
PHONE.................562 988-1688
Nien-Ling Wacker, *President*
Hedy Belttary, *Vice Pres*
Stephen Hall, *Vice Pres*
Jim Haney, *Vice Pres*
Thomas Phelps, *Vice Pres*
EMP: 170
SQ FT: 30,000
SALES (est): 37.3MM **Privately Held**
WEB: www.laserfiche.com
SIC: 7372 Business oriented computer
software

(P-15636)
CONTACTUAL INC
810 W Maude Ave, Sunnyvale
(94085-2910)
PHONE.................650 292-4408
Mansour Salame, *CEO*
David Sohm, *President*

David Chen, *Vice Pres*
Dani Shomron, *Vice Pres*
Richard W Southwick, *Vice Pres*
EMP: 50
SQ FT: 5,000
SALES (est): 3.3MM
SALES (corp-wide): 296.5MM **Publicly
Held**
WEB: www.contactual.com
SIC: 7372 Prepackaged software
PA: 8x8, Inc.
2125 Onel Dr
San Jose CA 95131
408 727-1885

(P-15637)
COPLEY PRESS INC
Also Called: Signon San Diego
2375 Northside Dr Ste 300, San Diego
(92108-2700)
PHONE.................619 718-5200
Ron James, *Manager*
EMP: 80
SALES (corp-wide): 101.8MM **Privately
Held**
WEB: www.copleynewspapers.com
SIC: 7372 2711 Prepackaged software;
newspapers
PA: The Copley Press Inc
7776 Ivanhoe Ave
La Jolla CA 92037
858 454-0411

(P-15638)
**CORNERSTONE ONDEMAND
INC (PA)**
1601 Cloverfield Blvd 620s, Santa Monica
(90404-4178)
PHONE.................310 752-0200
Adam L Miller, *Ch of Bd*
Stephen Pfeiffer, *President*
Kirsten Helvey, *COO*
Brian L Swartz, *CFO*
Vincent Belliveau, *Exec VP*
EMP: 148
SQ FT: 108,000
SALES (est): 481.9MM **Publicly Held**
WEB: www.cornerstoneondemand.com
SIC: 7372 Business oriented computer
software

(P-15639)
**COUPA SOFTWARE
INCORPORATED (PA)**
1855 S Grant St, San Mateo (94402-7016)
PHONE.................650 931-3200
Robert Bernshteyn, *Ch of Bd*
James Dinette, *Partner*
Chris Murdick, *Partner*
David Shanteler, *Partner*
Mark Riggs, *COO*
EMP: 111
SQ FT: 69,220
SALES: 186.7MM **Publicly Held**
WEB: www.coupa.com
SIC: 7372 Business oriented computer
software

(P-15640)
CRYSTAL DYNAMICS INC
1400a Saport Blvd Ste 300, Redwood City
(94063)
PHONE.................650 421-7600
Philip Rogers, *CEO*
Robert Dyer, *President*
John Horsley, *President*
John Miller, *President*
Kun Chen, *Info Tech Mgr*
EMP: 90
SQ FT: 26,000
SALES (est): 13MM
SALES (corp-wide): 2.3B **Privately Held**
WEB: www.crystald.com
SIC: 7372 Business oriented computer
software
HQ: Square Enix Limited
240 Blackfriars Road
London SE1 8
208 636-3000

(P-15641)
CUMULUS NETWORKS INC (PA)
185 E Dana St, Mountain View
(94041-1507)
PHONE.................650 383-6700
Jame Rivers, *CEO*

Nolan Leake, *Co-Owner*
Reza Malekzadeh, *Vice Pres*
Shrijeet Mukherjee, *Vice Pres*
Edward Leake, *Principal*
EMP: 124
SALES (est): 27MM **Privately Held**
SIC: 7372 7371 Publishers' computer soft-
ware; computer software development

(P-15642)
CYBREX CONSULTING INC
4470 W Sunset Blvd, Los Angeles
(90027-6302)
PHONE.................513 999-2109
Steve Kerver, *President*
EMP: 100
SQ FT: 1,000
SALES: 2MM **Privately Held**
SIC: 7372 8742 Prepackaged software;
real estate consultant

(P-15643)
CYLANCE INC (PA)
400 Spectrum Center Dr, Irvine
(92618-4934)
PHONE.................949 375-3380
Stuart McClure, *CEO*
David Stein, *Partner*
Daniel Doimo, *President*
Felix Marquardt, *President*
Brian Robins, *CFO*
EMP: 139 EST: 2012
SALES (est): 180.1MM **Privately Held**
SIC: 7372 Application computer software

(P-15644)
**D3PUBLISHER OF AMERICA
INC**
Also Called: D3 Go
15910 Ventura Blvd # 800, Encino
(91436-2810)
PHONE.................310 268-0820
Yoji Takenaka, *President*
Yuji ITOH, *Ch of Bd*
Hidetaka Tachibana, *CFO*
Russell Iriye, *Opers Staff*
Arthur Kawamoto, *Manager*
EMP: 63
SQ FT: 6,129
SALES (est): 8.4MM
SALES (corp-wide): 6.3B **Privately Held**
SIC: 7372 Home entertainment computer
software
HQ: D3 Publisher Inc.
1-9-5, Dogenzaka
Shibuya-Ku TKY 150-0
354 283-455

(P-15645)
DECISIONLOGIC LLC
9820 Willow Creek Rd # 310, San Diego
(92131-1112)
PHONE.................858 586-0202
David Evans, *President*
Ryley Johnson, *Opers Mgr*
Michelle Evans, *Opers Staff*
George Cashman, *Sales Staff*
EMP: 50
SALES (est): 3.3MM **Privately Held**
SIC: 7372 Business oriented computer
software

(P-15646)
DELPHIX CORP (PA)
1400 Saport Blvd Ste 200a, Redwood City
(94063)
PHONE.................650 494-1645
Chris Cook, *CEO*
Eric Schrock, *President*
Stewart Grierson, *CFO*
Jedidiah Yueh, *Officer*
Mike Stewart, *Senior VP*
EMP: 50
SQ FT: 18,000
SALES (est): 26.2MM **Privately Held**
SIC: 7372 Business oriented computer
software

(P-15647)
DEMANDBASE INC (PA)
680 Folsom St Ste 400, San Francisco
(94107-2159)
PHONE.................415 683-2660
Chris Golec, *CEO*
Peter Isaacson, *Chief Mktg Ofcr*
Alan Fletcher, *Officer*

Fatima Khan, *Officer*
Don Wight, *Officer*
EMP: 86
SALES (est): 57.2MM **Privately Held**
WEB: www.demandbase.com
SIC: 7372 Business oriented computer
software

(P-15648)
DINCLOUD INC
27520 Hawthorne Blvd # 185, Rllng HLS
Est (90274-3576)
PHONE.................310 929-1101
Mark Briggs, *CEO*
Mike L Chase, *Exec VP*
Ali M Dincmo, *Vice Pres*
EMP: 53
SQ FT: 1,500
SALES: 4MM
SALES (corp-wide): 43.1MM **Privately
Held**
SIC: 7372 Business oriented computer
software
PA: Premier Bpo, Inc.
128 N 2nd St Ste 210
Clarksville TN 37040
931 551-8888

(P-15649)
DISTILLERY INC
90 Heron Ct, San Quentin (94964)
PHONE.................415 505-5446
Adrian Szwarcburg, *President*
EMP: 55
SALES (est): 1.9MM **Privately Held**
SIC: 7372 Prepackaged software

(P-15650)
DOCTOR ON DEMAND INC
275 Battery St Ste 650, San Francisco
(94111-3332)
PHONE.................415 935-4447
Adam Jackson, *CEO*
Jennifer Nuckles, *Chief Mktg Ofcr*
Heather Johnson, *Vice Pres*
Yosselyn Dupuis, *Opers Staff*
Noah Slabotsky, *Sales Dir*
EMP: 100
SALES (est): 298.7K **Privately Held**
SIC: 7372 Application computer software

(P-15651)
DOCUSIGN INC (PA)
221 Main St Ste 1000, San Francisco
(94105-1925)
PHONE.................415 489-4940
Daniel D Springer, *President*
Keith J Krach, *Ch of Bd*
William Neil Hudspith, *President*
Kirsten O Wolberg, *COO*
Michael J Sheridan, *CFO*
EMP: 300
SQ FT: 117,231
SALES: 518.5MM **Publicly Held**
WEB: www.docusign.com
SIC: 7372 Prepackaged software

(P-15652)
**DORADO NETWORK SYSTEMS
CORP**
Also Called: Corelogic Dorado
555 12th St Ste 1100, Oakland
(94607-4049)
PHONE.................650 227-7300
Dain Ehring, *CEO*
Karen Camp, *CFO*
Adam Springer, *Senior VP*
Dave Parker, *VP Bus Dvlpt*
Rob Carpenter PHD, *CTO*
EMP: 140
SQ FT: 19,000
SALES (est): 11.7MM
SALES (corp-wide): 1.8B **Publicly Held**
WEB: www.dorado.com
SIC: 7372 Application computer software
PA: Corelogic, Inc.
40 Pacifica Ste 900
Irvine CA 92618
949 214-1000

(P-15653)
DOUBLEDUTCH INC (PA)
350 Rhode Island St # 375, San Francisco
(94103-5181)
PHONE.................800 748-9024
Bryan Parker, *CEO*

Brad Roberts, *CFO*
Emily He, *Chief Mktg Ofcr*
Lucian Beebe, *Vice Pres*
Lawrence Coburn, *Security Dir*
EMP: 65
SALES: 28MM **Privately Held**
SIC: 7372 Application computer software

(P-15654)
DRIVEAI INC
365 Ravendale Dr, Mountain View
(94043-5217)
PHONE.....................650 729-0499
Sameep Tandon, *CEO*
Swati Dube, *Co-Owner*
Brody Huval, *Co-Owner*
Jeff Kinske, *Co-Owner*
Joel Pazhayampallil, *Co-Owner*
EMP: 150 **EST:** 2015
SALES (est): 251.4K **Privately Held**
SIC: 7372 Prepackaged software

(P-15655)
DRIVER INC
438 Shotwell St, San Francisco
(94110-1914)
PHONE.....................415 999-4960
Will Polkinghorn, *CEO*
Amy Bronstien, *Executive Asst*
Tet Matsuguchi, *Engineer*
Pete Wild, *Opers Mgr*
EMP: 85
SALES (est): 2.7MM **Privately Held**
SIC: 7372 Educational computer software

(P-15656)
DROPBOX INC (PA)
333 Brannan St, San Francisco
(94107-1810)
PHONE.....................415 857-6800
Andrew W Houston, *Ch of Bd*
Dennis M Woodside, *COO*
Ajay V Vashee, *CFO*
Quentin J Clark, *Senior VP*
Rusty Pierce, *Office Mgr*
EMP: 148
SALES: 1.1B **Publicly Held**
SIC: 7372 Prepackaged software

(P-15657)
DRUVA INC (HQ)
150 Mathilda Pl Ste 450, Sunnyvale
(94086-6016)
PHONE.....................650 241-3501
Jaspreet Singh, *CEO*
Mahesh Patel, *CFO*
Sherry Lowe, *Chief Mktg Ofcr*
Wynn White, *Chief Mktg Ofcr*
Mike Palmer,
EMP: 58
SALES (est): 22.5MM **Privately Held**
SIC: 7372 Prepackaged software

(P-15658)
DWA NOVA LLC
1000 Flower St, Glendale (91201-3007)
PHONE.....................818 695-5000
Lincoln Wallen, *CEO*
Derek Chan, *COO*
EMP: 75
SQ FT: 10,000
SALES (est): 1.4MM **Privately Held**
SIC: 7372 Business oriented computer
software

(P-15659)
ECRIO INC
19925 Stevens Creek Blvd # 100, Cupertino (95014-2300)
PHONE.....................408 973-7290
Randy Granovetter, *CEO*
Tad Bogdan, *COO*
Nagesh Challa, *Officer*
Ted Goldstein, *Officer*
Lina Martin, *Vice Pres*
EMP: 90
SALES (est): 6.1MM **Privately Held**
WEB: www.ecrio.com
SIC: 7372 Prepackaged software

(P-15660)
EDGEWAVE INC
4225 Executive Sq # 1600, La Jolla
(92037-1487)
PHONE.....................800 782-3762
Louis E Ryan, *CEO*

Steve Kelley, *President*
Thalia R Gietzen, *CFO*
John Randall, *Vice Pres*
William R Baumel, *Principal*
EMP: 100
SQ FT: 37,000
SALES (est): 16.7MM **Privately Held**
WEB: www.edgewave.com
SIC: 7372 Operating systems computer
software

(P-15661)
EGAIN CORPORATION (PA)
1252 Borregas Ave, Sunnyvale
(94089-1309)
PHONE.....................408 636-4500
Ashutosh Roy, *Ch of Bd*
Eric Smit, *CFO*
Promod Narang, *Senior VP*
Todd Woodstra, *Senior VP*
Simon Broadbent, *Vice Pres*
EMP: 109
SQ FT: 42,541
SALES: 61.3MM **Publicly Held**
WEB: www.egain.com
SIC: 7372 7371 Prepackaged software;
application computer software; custom
computer programming services

(P-15662)
EGOMOTION INC
729 Minna St, San Francisco (94103-2707)
PHONE.....................415 849-4662
Kulveer Taggar, *CEO*
EMP: 50
SALES (est): 787.2K **Privately Held**
SIC: 7372 Business oriented computer
software

(P-15663)
EIS GROUP INC
731 Sansome St Fl 4, San Francisco
(94111-1723)
PHONE.....................415 402-2622
Alec Miloslavsky, *CEO*
Sergiy Synyanskyy, *CFO*
Nancy Kelly, *Senior VP*
Slava Kritov, *Senior VP*
Mark Binman, *Vice Pres*
EMP: 128
SQ FT: 16,803
SALES (est): 22.7MM **Privately Held**
SIC: 7372 Business oriented computer
software

(P-15664)
ELECTRONIC ARTS INC (PA)
Also Called: Ea
209 Redwood Shores Pkwy, Redwood City
(94065-1175)
PHONE.....................650 628-1500
Andrew Wilson, *CEO*
Lawrence F Probst III, *Ch of Bd*
Blake Jorgensen, *COO*
Vivek Paul, *Bd of Directors*
Christopher Bruzzo, *Chief Mktg Ofcr*
EMP: 475
SQ FT: 660,000
SALES: 5.1B **Publicly Held**
WEB: www.ea.com
SIC: 7372 Home entertainment computer
software

(P-15665)
ELECTRONIC CLEARING HOUSE INC (HQ)
730 Paseo Camarillo, Camarillo
(93010-6064)
PHONE.....................805 419-8700
Charles J Harris, *President*
Alice L Cheung, *CFO*
Karl Asplund, *Senior VP*
Rick Slater, *Vice Pres*
William Wied, *CIO*
EMP: 100
SQ FT: 32,669
SALES: 11.1MM
SALES (corp-wide): 5.9B **Publicly Held**
WEB: www.echo-inc.com
SIC: 7372 Business oriented computer
software
PA: Intuit Inc.
2700 Coast Ave
Mountain View CA 94043
650 944-6000

(P-15666)
ELLIE MAE INC (PA)
4420 Rosewood Dr Ste 500, Pleasanton
(94588-3059)
PHONE.....................925 227-7000
Jonathan Corr, *President*
Sigmund Anderman, *Ch of Bd*
Popi Heron, *CFO*
Brian Brown, *Exec VP*
Carina Cortez, *Exec VP*
EMP: 148 **EST:** 1997
SQ FT: 280,680
SALES: 417MM **Publicly Held**
WEB: www.elliemae.com
SIC: 7372 7371 Prepackaged software;
computer software systems analysis &
design, custom; computer software development & applications

(P-15667)
ENGAGIO INC
101 S San Mateo Dr Fl 4, San Mateo
(94401-3845)
PHONE.....................650 265-2264
Jon Miller, *CEO*
Heidi Bullock, *Chief Mktg Ofcr*
Cheryl Chavez, *Officer*
Scott Fehr, *Vice Pres*
Dan Gordon, *Vice Pres*
EMP: 50 **EST:** 2015
SALES: 531K **Privately Held**
SIC: 7372 Business oriented computer
software

(P-15668)
ENTCO LLC (DH)
Also Called: Autonomy Interwoven
1140 Enterprise Way, Sunnyvale
(94089-1412)
PHONE.....................312 580-9100
Jeremy K Cox,
John E Calonico Jr, *Senior VP*
Mercedes De Luca, *VP Info Sys*
Rishi Varma,
EMP: 400
SQ FT: 110,000
SALES (est): 54.8MM
SALES (corp-wide): 834.5MM **Privately
Held**
WEB: www.iwov.com
SIC: 7372 Business oriented computer
software
HQ: Micro Focus (Us), Inc.
700 King Farm Blvd # 125
Rockville MD 20850
301 838-5000

(P-15669)
ENTERPRISE SIGNAL INC
Also Called: Kloudgin
440 N Wolfe Rd, Sunnyvale (94085-3869)
PHONE.....................877 256-8303
Vikram Takru, *CEO*
Dharnesh Sethi, *CFO*
EMP: 65
SALES (est): 155.9K **Privately Held**
SIC: 7372 Business oriented computer
software

(P-15670)
EPICOR SOFTWARE CORPORATION
4120 Dublin Blvd Ste 300, Dublin
(94568-7759)
PHONE.....................925 361-9900
Pervez Qureshi, *Branch Mgr*
Noel Goggin, *Senior VP*
Janie West, *Vice Pres*
Dave Yusuf, *Vice Pres*
AIN Moin, *Executive*
EMP: 101 **Publicly Held**
SIC: 7372 Prepackaged software
HQ: Epicor Software Corporation
804 Las Cimas Pkwy # 200
Austin TX 78746

(P-15671)
ERI ECONOMIC RESEARCH INST INC
111 Academy Ste 270, Irvine (92617-3049)
PHONE.....................800 627-3697
Kerry Galvin, *CEO*
Steven Becker, *CFO*
Matt Skrinjar, *Manager*

EMP: 55
SALES (est): 2.2MM **Privately Held**
WEB: www.economicresearchinstitute.com
SIC: 7372 Application computer software;
business oriented computer software

(P-15672)
ESQ BUSINESS SERVICES INC (PA)
Also Called: E S Q
20660 Stevens, Cupertino (95014)
PHONE.....................925 734-9800
Iqbal S Sandhu, *Director*
Joe Haggarty, *President*
Neil Butani, *Officer*
Paul Sandhu, *CTO*
Raj Dhiman, *Technology*
EMP: 95
SQ FT: 300
SALES (est): 11.4MM **Privately Held**
WEB: www.esq.com
SIC: 7372 7379 Prepackaged software;
computer related consulting services

(P-15673)
EXADEL INC (PA)
1340 Treat Blvd, Walnut Creek
(94597-2101)
PHONE.....................925 363-9510
Fima Katz, *President*
Lev Shur, *President*
Lynne Walter, *CFO*
Dmitry Binunsky, *Vice Pres*
Janusz Fajkowski, *General Mgr*
EMP: 51
SALES (est): 18.6MM **Privately Held**
WEB: www.exadel.com
SIC: 7372 Application computer software

(P-15674)
FAIR ISAAC INTERNATIONAL CORP (HQ)
200 Smith Ranch Rd, San Rafael
(94903-5551)
PHONE.....................415 446-6000
Thomas G Grudnowski, *President*
Cheryl St John, *Cust Svc Dir*
EMP: 600
SALES (est): 51.2MM
SALES (corp-wide): 932.1MM **Publicly
Held**
SIC: 7372 Business oriented computer
software
PA: Fair Isaac Corporation
181 Metro Dr Ste 700
San Jose CA 95110
408 535-1500

(P-15675)
FILEMAKER INC (HQ)
5201 Patrick Henry Dr, Santa Clara
(95054-1164)
PHONE.....................408 987-7000
Dominique Philippe Goupil, *President*
Bill Epling, *CFO*
John F Pinheiro, *Vice Pres*
Albert Eisenstat, *Principal*
Steven Marcek, *CTO*
EMP: 230
SQ FT: 128,000
SALES (est): 79.1MM
SALES (corp-wide): 265.6B **Publicly
Held**
WEB: www.filemaker.com
SIC: 7372 Prepackaged software
PA: Apple Inc.
1 Apple Park Way
Cupertino CA 95014
408 996-1010

(P-15676)
FIORANO SOFTWARE INC
230 California Ave # 103, Palo Alto
(94306-1637)
PHONE.....................650 326-1136
Atul Saini, *CEO*
Madhav Vodnala, *President*
Anjali Saini, *CFO*
William La Forge, *Vice Pres*
EMP: 85
SALES (est): 6.7MM **Privately Held**
SIC: 7372 7371 Prepackaged software;
custom computer programming services;
computer software development

(P-15677)
FIREEYE INC (PA)
601 Mccarthy Blvd, Milpitas (95035-7932)
PHONE....................408 321-6300
Kevin R Mandia, *CEO*
Enrique Salem, *Ch of Bd*
Travis M Reese, *President*
Frank E Verdecanna, *CFO*
Alexa King, *Exec VP*
EMP: 148
SQ FT: 190,000
SALES: 751MM **Publicly Held**
WEB: www.fireeye.com
SIC: 7372 Prepackaged software

(P-15678)
FIVE9 INC (PA)
4000 Executive Pkwy # 400, San Ramon
(94583-4257)
PHONE....................925 201-2000
Rowan Trollope, *CEO*
Barry Zwarenstein, *CFO*
Michael Burkland, *Chairman*
Kevin Gavin, *Chief Mktg Ofcr*
Ryan Kam, *Chief Mktg Ofcr*
EMP: 144
SQ FT: 68,000
SALES: 200.2MM **Publicly Held**
WEB: www.five9.com
SIC: 7372 7374 Prepackaged software;
data processing & preparation

(P-15679)
FORGEROCK INC (PA)
201 Mission St Ste 2900, San Francisco
(94105-1858)
PHONE....................415 599-1100
Francis C Rosch, *CEO*
Priya Sharma, *Partner*
John Fernandez, *CFO*
John P Fernandez, *CFO*
Bob Humphrey, *Chief Mktg Ofcr*
EMP: 58
SQ FT: 15,000
SALES (est): 48.5MM **Privately Held**
SIC: 7372 5045 Prepackaged software;
computer software

(P-15680)
FORGEROCK US INC (HQ)
201 Mission St, San Francisco
(94105-1831)
PHONE....................415 599-1100
John Fernandez, *CFO*
Robert Humphrey, *Chief Mktg Ofcr*
Lasse Andresen, *CTO*
EMP: 73
SQ FT: 15,744
SALES (est): 14MM
SALES (corp-wide): 48.5MM **Privately
Held**
SIC: 7372 5045 Prepackaged software;
computer software
PA: Forgerock, Inc.
201 Mission St Ste 2900
San Francisco CA 94105
415 599-1100

(P-15681)
FORMATION INC
Also Called: Formation Systems
35 Stillman St, San Francisco
(94107-1361)
PHONE....................650 257-2277
Christian Hansen, *CEO*
Christian Selchau-Hansen, *CEO*
Ammon Haggerty, *Vice Pres*
EMP: 87
SQ FT: 10,000
SALES (est): 1.2MM **Privately Held**
SIC: 7372 Business oriented computer
software

(P-15682)
FORTINET INC (PA)
899 Kifer Rd, Sunnyvale (94086-5205)
PHONE....................408 235-7700
Ken Xie, *Ch of Bd*
Michael Xie, *President*
Keith Jensen, *CFO*
John Whittle, *Vice Pres*
EMP: 148
SQ FT: 162,000
SALES: 1.4B **Publicly Held**
WEB: www.fortinet.com
SIC: 7372 Prepackaged software

(P-15683)
**FOUNDATION 9
ENTERTAINMENT INC (PA)**
30211 A De Las Bandera200, Rancho
Santa Margari (92688)
PHONE....................949 698-1500
James N Hearn, *CEO*
John Goldman, *Ch of Bd*
David Mann, *President*
Steve Sardegna, *Exec VP*
Miguel Vazquez, *Finance Mgr*
EMP: 200
SALES (est): 38.1MM **Privately Held**
SIC: 7372 Home entertainment computer
software

(P-15684)
FOUNDSTONE INC
27201 Puerta Real Ste 400, Mission Viejo
(92691-8517)
PHONE....................949 297-5600
George Kurtz, *CEO*
Stuart McClure, *President*
Larry McIntosh, *Chief Mktg Ofcr*
William Chan, *Vice Pres*
Chris Prosise, *Vice Pres*
EMP: 80
SQ FT: 15,000
SALES (est): 4.9MM **Privately Held**
WEB: www.foundstone.com
SIC: 7372 Application computer software
HQ: Mcafee, Llc
2821 Mission College Blvd
Santa Clara CA 95054
888 847-8766

(P-15685)
FRONTAPP INC
525 Brannan St Ste 300, San Francisco
(94107-1632)
PHONE....................415 680-3048
Mathilde Collin, *CEO*
Laurent Perrin, *CTO*
EMP: 71
SQ FT: 11,000
SALES: 5MM **Privately Held**
SIC: 7372 Application computer software

(P-15686)
FRONTRANGE HOLDING INC
490 N Mccarthy Blvd, Milpitas
(95035-5118)
PHONE....................408 601-2800
Jon Temple, *CEO*
Ian Mc Ewan, *Vice Pres*
Duane Russell, *Info Tech Dir*
David Bellandi, *VP Mktg*
Gene Torre, *VP Mktg*
EMP: 383
SALES (est): 12.6MM **Privately Held**
SIC: 7372 7371 Prepackaged software;
computer software systems analysis &
design, custom

(P-15687)
FUSION MPHC HOLDING CORP
6800 Koll Center Pkwy, Pleasanton
(94566-7045)
PHONE....................925 201-2500
Paul Millie, *CFO*
EMP: 106 EST: 2007
SALES (est): 1.4MM
SALES (corp-wide): 150.5MM **Publicly
Held**
SIC: 7372 6719 Business oriented com-
puter software; investment holding com-
panies, except banks
PA: Fusion Connect, Inc.
420 Lexington Ave Rm 1718
New York NY 10170
212 201-2400

(P-15688)
G7 PRODUCTIVITY SYSTEMS
Also Called: Versacheck
16885 W Bernardo Dr # 290, San Diego
(92127-1618)
P.O. Box 270459 (92198-2459)
PHONE....................858 675-1095
Thomas Priebus, *President*
Teri Pfarr, *COO*
Jim Danforth, *CFO*
EMP: 60
SQ FT: 18,000

SALES (est): 3.9MM **Privately Held**
WEB: www.g7ps.com
SIC: 7372 Prepackaged software

(P-15689)
GE DIGITAL LLC (HQ)
2623 Camino Ramon, San Ramon
(94583-9130)
PHONE....................925 242-6200
EMP: 300
SALES (est): 121.1K
SALES (corp-wide): 122B **Publicly Held**
SIC: 7372 Business oriented computer
software
PA: General Electric Company
41 Farnsworth St
Boston MA 02210
617 443-3000

(P-15690)
GENERAL ELECTRIC COMPANY
2623 Camino Ramon, San Ramon
(94583-9130)
PHONE....................925 242-6200
Holly Gilthorpe, *Ch Credit Ofcr*
Rebecca Lawson, *Vice Pres*
Jennifer Schulze, *Vice Pres*
Ashima Puri, *Program Mgr*
Jim KAO, *Technical Mgr*
EMP: 67
SALES (corp-wide): 122B **Publicly Held**
SIC: 7372 Business oriented computer
software
PA: General Electric Company
41 Farnsworth St
Boston MA 02210
617 443-3000

(P-15691)
**GENESYS TELECOM LABS INC
(HQ)**
Also Called: Genesys Telecom Labs
2001 Junipero Serra Blvd, Daly City
(94014-3891)
PHONE....................650 466-1100
Paul Segre, *CEO*
Tom Eggemeier, *President*
David Sudbey, *Ch Credit Ofcr*
Reed Henry, *Chief Mktg Ofcr*
Peter Graf, *Officer*
EMP: 450
SQ FT: 156,000
SALES (est): 641.3MM
SALES (corp-wide): 69.9MM **Privately
Held**
WEB: www.genesyslabs.com
SIC: 7372 Business oriented computer
software
PA: Permira Advisers Llp
80 Pall Mall
London SW1Y
207 632-1000

(P-15692)
GIGAMON INC (HQ)
3300 Olcott St, Santa Clara (95054-3005)
PHONE....................408 831-4000
Paul A Hooper, *CEO*
Michelle Hodges, *Partner*
Shane Buckley, *President*
Dave Arkley, *CFO*
Kim Decarlis, *Chief Mktg Ofcr*
EMP: 126
SQ FT: 105,600
SALES: 310.8MM **Privately Held**
WEB: www.gigamon.com
SIC: 7372 3577 Prepackaged software;
computer peripheral equipment
PA: Ginsberg Holdco, Inc.
3300 Olcott St
Santa Clara CA 95054
408 831-4000

(P-15693)
GLOBALEX CORPORATION
Also Called: Revo Payments
2100 Abbot Kinney Blvd A, Venice
(90291-7003)
PHONE....................310 593-4833
Mike Corbera, *CEO*
Lolita Carrico, *Director*
EMP: 65 EST: 2003
SALES (est): 5.8MM **Privately Held**
SIC: 7372 Prepackaged software

(P-15694)
GOVERNMENTJOBSCOM INC
Also Called: Neogov
300 Continental Blvd # 565, El Segundo
(90245-5042)
PHONE....................310 426-6304
Damir Davidovic, *CEO*
Scott Letourneau, *President*
Robert Nishimuta, *Sr Software Eng*
Chris Rosenberger, *Info Tech Mgr*
Krishna Surendra, *Info Tech Mgr*
EMP: 130
SQ FT: 5,000
SALES (est): 18.9MM **Privately Held**
WEB: www.governmentjobs.com
SIC: 7372 Prepackaged software

(P-15695)
GRAYPAY LLC
6345 Balboa Blvd Ste 115, Encino
(91316-1517)
PHONE....................818 387-6735
Marc Geolina, *Mng Member*
Bryan Rainey,
EMP: 60 EST: 2015
SALES (est): 2.4MM **Privately Held**
SIC: 7372 Business oriented computer
software

(P-15696)
**GREEN HILLS SOFTWARE INC
(PA)**
30 W Sola St, Santa Barbara (93101-2599)
PHONE....................805 965-6044
Daniel O Dowd, *CEO*
Dave Kleidermacher, *President*
Michael W Liacko, *President*
Daniel O'Dowd, *CEO*
Brad Jackson, *COO*
EMP: 105
SALES (est): 76.5MM **Privately Held**
WEB: www.ghs.com
SIC: 7372 Prepackaged software

(P-15697)
GUAVUS INC (HQ)
2860 Junction Ave, San Jose (95134-1922)
PHONE....................650 243-3400
Anukool Lakhina, *CEO*
Michael Crane, *President*
Ty Nam, *COO*
Anupam Rastogi, *CTO*
EMP: 60
SALES (est): 39MM
SALES (corp-wide): 305.4MM **Privately
Held**
WEB: www.guavus.com
SIC: 7372 7371 Prepackaged software;
computer software development & appli-
cations
PA: Thales
Carpe Diem Esplanade Nord Tour Aig
Courbevoie 92400
157 778-000

(P-15698)
GUCK ARIBA
807 Eleventh Ave, Sunnyvale
(94089-4731)
PHONE....................650 390-1445
Jennifer Sinatra, *Managing Prtnr*
Dave Johnston, *Vice Pres*
Darlene French, *Executive*
Elke Koscher, *Executive*
Tim McKee, *Executive*
EMP: 147
SALES (est): 7MM **Privately Held**
SIC: 7372 Business oriented computer
software

(P-15699)
**GUIDANCE SOFTWARE INC
(HQ)**
1055 E Colo Blvd Ste 400, Pasadena
(91106)
PHONE....................626 229-9191
Patrick Dennis, *President*
Mandy Mueller, *Partner*
Barry Plaga, *COO*
Michael Harris, *Chief Mktg Ofcr*
Alfredo Gomez, *Senior VP*
EMP: 215 EST: 1997
SQ FT: 90,000

SALES: 110.5MM
SALES (corp-wide): 2.2B **Privately Held**
WEB: www.guidancesoftware.com
SIC: 7372 3572 Business oriented computer software; computer storage devices
PA: Open Text Corporation
275 Frank Tompa Dr
Waterloo ON N2L 0
519 888-7111

(P-15700)
GUIDEWIRE SOFTWARE INC (PA)
1001 E Hillsdale Blvd # 8, Foster City (94404-1642)
PHONE..................650 357-9100
Marcus S Ryu, *President*
Peter Gassner, *Ch of Bd*
Richard Hart, *CFO*
Ali Kheirolomoom,
Priscilla Hung, *Officer*
EMP: 148
SQ FT: 97,674
SALES: 661MM **Publicly Held**
WEB: www.guidewire.com
SIC: 7372 Business oriented computer software

(P-15701)
H2 WELLNESS INCORPORATED
11999 San Vicente Blvd, Los Angeles (90049-5131)
PHONE..................310 362-1888
Hooman Fakki, *CEO*
Houman Arasteh, *COO*
Russ Nash, *Bd of Directors*
Esfandiar Behrouz, *Director*
John Coleman, *Director*
EMP: 55
SALES (est): 3.5MM **Privately Held**
SIC: 7372 Application computer software

(P-15702)
HEALTHSTREAM INC
Also Called: Echo, A Heatlhstream Company
9605 Scranton Rd Ste 200, San Diego (92121-1768)
PHONE..................800 733-8737
Robert A Frist Jr, *Ch of Bd*
EMP: 306
SALES (corp-wide): 247.6MM **Publicly Held**
SIC: 7372 7371 Prepackaged software; custom computer programming services
PA: Healthstream, Inc.
209 10th Ave S Ste 450
Nashville TN 37203
615 301-3100

(P-15703)
HEARSAY SOCIAL INC (PA)
185 Berry St Ste 3800, San Francisco (94107-1725)
PHONE..................888 990-3777
Clara Shih, *CEO*
Michael H Lock, *President*
William Salisbury, *CFO*
Matt Green, *Officer*
Gaurav Agarwal, *Vice Pres*
EMP: 60
SALES (est): 13.5MM **Privately Held**
SIC: 7372 Publishers' computer software

(P-15704)
HEWLETT PACKARD ENTERPRISE CO
8000 Foothills Blvd, Roseville (95747-5200)
PHONE..................916 786-8000
Michael Ketcherside, *Branch Mgr*
Nick Gunn, *Vice Pres*
Cesar Sanchez, *Program Mgr*
Phong Lam, *Administration*
Kapil Gupta, *Info Tech Mgr*
EMP: 100
SQ FT: 64,000
SALES (corp-wide): 28.8B **Publicly Held**
SIC: 7372 Business oriented computer software
PA: Hewlett Packard Enterprise Company
3000 Hanover St
Palo Alto CA 94304
650 687-5817

(P-15705)
HEWLETT PACKARD ENTERPRISE CO (PA)
3000 Hanover St, Palo Alto (94304-1185)
PHONE..................650 687-5817
Antonio Neri, *President*
Patricia F Russo, *Ch of Bd*
Timothy C Stonesifer, *CFO*
Kirt P Karros, *Treasurer*
John F Schultz,
EMP: 148 **EST:** 2015
SALES: 28.8B **Publicly Held**
SIC: 7372 7379 3572 Business oriented computer software; computer related maintenance services; computer storage devices

(P-15706)
HORTONWORKS INC (PA)
5470 Great America Pkwy, Santa Clara (95054-3644)
PHONE..................408 916-4121
Robert Bearden, *Ch of Bd*
Scott Davidson, *COO*
Alan Fudge, *Risk Mgmt Dir*
Scott Reasoner,
Scott Gnau, *CTO*
EMP: 725
SQ FT: 92,000
SALES: 261.8MM **Publicly Held**
SIC: 7372 Application computer software

(P-15707)
IFWE INC (HQ)
848 Battery St, San Francisco (94111-1504)
PHONE..................415 946-1850
Dash Gopinath, *CEO*
Greg Tseng, *CEO*
Johann Schleier Smith, *CTO*
Erik Johannessen, *Engineer*
Louis Willacy, *Marketing Staff*
EMP: 87
SQ FT: 13,000
SALES (est): 30.7MM
SALES (corp-wide): 123.7MM **Publicly Held**
WEB: www.tagged.com
SIC: 7372 Application computer software
PA: The Meet Group Inc
100 Union Square Dr
New Hope PA 18938
215 862-1162

(P-15708)
IMAGEWARE SYSTEMS INC (PA)
10815 Rncho Brnrdo Rd 3 # 310, San Diego (92127)
PHONE..................858 673-8600
S James Miller Jr, *Ch of Bd*
Wayne Wetherell, *CFO*
David Harding, *Vice Pres*
David Lotze, *Vice Pres*
Mike Rerick, *Vice Pres*
EMP: 67
SQ FT: 9,927
SALES: 4.2MM **Publicly Held**
WEB: www.iwsinc.com
SIC: 7372 3699 Business oriented computer software; security control equipment & systems

(P-15709)
INDIUM SOFTWARE INC
1250 Oakmead Pkwy Ste 210, Sunnyvale (94085-4035)
PHONE..................408 501-8844
Harsha Nutalapati, *CEO*
Vijay Shankar Balaji, *President*
Shailesh Khanapur, *Assoc VP*
Bala S Selva, *Senior VP*
Tilak Dharmaraj, *Sales Staff*
EMP: 250
SALES (est): 12MM **Privately Held**
WEB: www.indiumsoft.com
SIC: 7372 Prepackaged software
HQ: Indium Software (India) Limited
2nd Floor Vds House,
Chennai TN 60008
-

(P-15710)
INFOR (US) INC
Also Called: MAI Systems
26250 Entp Way Ste 220, Lake Forest (92630)
PHONE..................678 319-8000
Barbara Nolan, *President*
Marvin Perkins, *Sales Staff*
EMP: 190
SALES (corp-wide): 3.1B **Privately Held**
SIC: 7372 Business oriented computer software
HQ: Infor (Us), Inc.
13560 Morris Rd Ste 4100
Alpharetta GA 30004
678 319-8000

(P-15711)
INFOR (US) INC
Also Called: Hansen Information Tech
11000 Olson Dr Ste 201, Rancho Cordova (95670-5642)
PHONE..................916 921-0883
Charles Hansen, *Manager*
EMP: 225
SALES (corp-wide): 3.1B **Privately Held**
SIC: 7372 Application computer software
HQ: Infor (Us), Inc.
13560 Morris Rd Ste 4100
Alpharetta GA 30004
678 319-8000

(P-15712)
INFORMATICA LLC (DH)
2100 Seaport Blvd, Redwood City (94063-5596)
PHONE..................650 385-5000
Anil Chakravarthy, *CEO*
Chris Cummins, *Partner*
Nick Voll, *Partner*
Sally Jenkins, *Officer*
Jo Stoner, *Officer*
EMP: 148
SQ FT: 290,000
SALES (est): 867.4MM
SALES (corp-wide): 1B **Privately Held**
WEB: www.metadataexchange.com
SIC: 7372 Prepackaged software

(P-15713)
INSIDESALESCOM INC
1269 Deep Creek Rd, Livermore (94550-8640)
PHONE..................385 207-7252
Chris Jhorgenson, *Branch Mgr*
EMP: 100
SALES (corp-wide): 85.8MM **Privately Held**
SIC: 7372 Publishers' computer software
PA: Insidesales.Com, Inc.
34 E 1700 S Ste A113
Provo UT 84606
801 754-9940

(P-15714)
INTAPP INC (PA)
200 Portage Ave, Palo Alto (94306-2242)
PHONE..................650 852-0400
John Hall, *CEO*
Stuart Douglass, *President*
Daniel Harsell, *President*
Kelvyn Stirk, *President*
Dan Tacone, *President*
EMP: 200
SALES: 100MM **Privately Held**
WEB: www.intapp.com
SIC: 7372 Business oriented computer software

(P-15715)
INTEGRAL DEVELOPMENT CORP (PA)
Also Called: Integral Engineering
850 Hansen Way, Palo Alto (94304-1017)
PHONE..................650 424-4500
Harpal Sandhu, *President*
Valerie Edwards, *COO*
Albert Yau, *CFO*
Patrick Barkhordarian, *Vice Pres*
Paul Calhoun, *Vice Pres*
EMP: 200
SQ FT: 35,000
SALES (est): 35MM **Privately Held**
WEB: www.integral.com
SIC: 7372 Business oriented computer software

(P-15716)
INTERACTIVE SOLUTIONS INC (HQ)
Also Called: Web Traffic School
283 4th St Ste 301, Oakland (94607-4320)
P.O. Box 209 (94604-0209)
PHONE..................510 214-9002
Isaak Tsifrin, *CEO*
Gary Golduber, *President*
Gary Tsifrin, *COO*
Mercy Gitau, *General Mgr*
EMP: 67
SQ FT: 14,000
SALES (est): 12.9MM
SALES (corp-wide): 18.2MM **Privately Held**
WEB: www.drivered.com
SIC: 7372 Prepackaged software
PA: Edriving Llc
283 4th St Ste 301
Oakland CA 94607
800 243-4008

(P-15717)
INTOUCH TECHNOLOGIES INC (PA)
Also Called: Intouch Health
7402 Hollister Ave, Goleta (93117-2583)
PHONE..................805 562-8686
Yulun Wang, *CEO*
Susan Wang, *Shareholder*
David Adornetto, *COO*
Stephen L Wilson, *CFO*
James Wright, *Assoc VP*
EMP: 301
SQ FT: 1,600
SALES (est): 23.6MM **Privately Held**
WEB: www.intouchhealth.com
SIC: 7372 Business oriented computer software

(P-15718)
INTUIT INC (PA)
2700 Coast Ave, Mountain View (94043-1140)
P.O. Box 7850 (94039-7850)
PHONE..................650 944-6000
Brad D Smith, *Ch of Bd*
Michelle M Clatterbuck, *CFO*
Scott D Cook, *Chairman*
Laura A Fennell, *Exec VP*
Sasan K Goodarzi, *Exec VP*
EMP: 70
SQ FT: 712,000
SALES: 5.9B **Publicly Held**
WEB: www.intuit.com
SIC: 7372 Business oriented computer software

(P-15719)
INTUIT INC
2700 Coast Ave Bldg 7, Mountain View (94043-1140)
PHONE..................650 944-6000
Brad Smith, *Branch Mgr*
EMP: 128
SALES (corp-wide): 5.9B **Publicly Held**
WEB: www.intuit.com
SIC: 7372 Business oriented computer software
PA: Intuit Inc.
2700 Coast Ave
Mountain View CA 94043
650 944-6000

(P-15720)
INTUIT INC
2535 Garcia Ave, Mountain View (94043-1111)
PHONE..................650 944-6000
Connie Berg, *Branch Mgr*
Ed Perez, *Partner*
Kelly Page, *Executive Asst*
Thomas Freese, *Sr Ntwrk Engine*
Alison G Reilly, *Systs Prg Mgr*
EMP: 128
SALES (corp-wide): 5.9B **Publicly Held**
WEB: www.intuit.com
SIC: 7372 Business oriented computer software
PA: Intuit Inc.
2700 Coast Ave
Mountain View CA 94043
650 944-6000

(P-15721)
INTUIT INC
141 Corona Way, Portola Valley
(94028-7437)
PHONE..................650 944-2840
EMP: 136
SALES (corp-wide): 5.9B **Publicly Held**
WEB: www.intuit.com
SIC: 7372 Business oriented computer
software
PA: Intuit Inc.
2700 Coast Ave
Mountain View CA 94043
650 944-6000

(P-15722)
INTUIT INC
180 Jefferson Dr, Menlo Park (94025-1115)
PHONE..................650 944-6000
Brad Smith, *Branch Mgr*
Jason Yip, *Business Anlyst*
Betsy Kha, *Marketing Staff*
Sally Shepherd, *Senior Mgr*
Pablo Espinosa, *Director*
EMP: 128
SALES (corp-wide): 5.9B **Publicly Held**
WEB: www.intuit.com
SIC: 7372 Business oriented computer
software
PA: Intuit Inc.
2700 Coast Ave
Mountain View CA 94043
650 944-6000

(P-15723)
INTUIT INC
Also Called: Turbotax
7545 Torrey Santa Fe Rd, San Diego
(92129-5704)
PHONE..................858 215-8000
Jason Jackson, *Branch Mgr*
William Moselle, *Business Dir*
Bradford Beidler, *Administration*
Muzaffar Malik, *Sr Software Eng*
Manny Ruiz, *Sr Software Eng*
EMP: 300
SALES (corp-wide): 5.9B **Publicly Held**
WEB: www.intuit.com
SIC: 7372 Business oriented computer
software
PA: Intuit Inc.
2700 Coast Ave
Mountain View CA 94043
650 944-6000

(P-15724)
IPOLIPO INC
Also Called: Jifflenow
440 N Wolfe Rd, Sunnyvale (94085-3869)
PHONE..................408 916-5290
Hari Shetty, *President*
Nancy Tannous, *Executive*
Traci Cummings, *Office Mgr*
Parth Mukherjee, *Mktg Dir*
Aaron Karpaty, *Sales Mgr*
EMP: 75 EST: 2006
SALES (est): 3.6MM **Privately Held**
SIC: 7372 Application computer software

(P-15725)
ISOLUTECOM INC (PA)
9 Northam Ave, Newbury Park
(91320-3323)
PHONE..................805 498-6259
Byron Nutley, *Ch of Bd*
Don Hyun, *President*
Thomas Mangle, *CFO*
Michael Brown, *CTO*
EMP: 50
SALES (est): 5.1MM **Privately Held**
WEB: www.isolute.com
SIC: 7372 Business oriented computer
software

(P-15726)
IXSYSTEMS INC (PA)
2490 Kruse Dr, San Jose (95131-1234)
PHONE..................408 943-4100
Mike Lauth, *CEO*
Andrew Madrid, *COO*
Brett Davis, *Exec VP*
Morgan Littlewood, *Senior VP*
Jeff Kaminsky, *General Mgr*
EMP: 60
SQ FT: 20,000

SALES (est): 17.8MM **Privately Held**
WEB: www.ixsystems.com
SIC: 7372 Operating systems computer
software

(P-15727)
KANA SOFTWARE INC (HQ)
Also Called: Verint
2550 Walsh Ave Ste 120, Santa Clara
(95051-1345)
PHONE..................650 614-8300
Mark Duffell, *CEO*
William A Bose, *President*
Brett White, *President*
Jeff Wylie, *CFO*
James Norwood, *Chief Mktg Ofcr*
EMP: 100
SQ FT: 40,000
SALES (est): 79.7MM **Publicly Held**
SIC: 7372 Application computer software

(P-15728)
KHAN ACADEMY INC
1200 Villa St Ste 200, Mountain View
(94041-2922)
P.O. Box 1630 (94042-1630)
PHONE..................650 336-5426
Salman Khan, *Exec Dir*
Jen Chong, *Partner*
Shantanu Sinha, *President*
Yin Lu, *Vice Pres*
Katherine Morris, *Vice Pres*
EMP: 85
SALES: 27.9MM **Privately Held**
SIC: 7372 Educational computer software

(P-15729)
KINGCOM(US) LLC (HQ)
3100 Ocean Park Blvd, Santa Monica
(90405-3032)
PHONE..................424 744-5697
EMP: 200
SALES (est): 16.9MM
SALES (corp-wide): 7B **Publicly Held**
SIC: 7372 Home entertainment computer
software
PA: Activision Blizzard, Inc.
3100 Ocean Park Blvd
Santa Monica CA 90405
310 255-2000

(P-15730)
KINTERA INC (HQ)
Also Called: Blackbaud Internet Solutions
9605 Scranton Rd Ste 200, San Diego
(92121-1768)
PHONE..................858 795-3000
Marc E Chardon, *CEO*
Alfred R Berkeley III, *Ch of Bd*
Richard Labarbera, *President*
Richard Davidson, *CFO*
Richard R Davidson, *Treasurer*
EMP: 76
SQ FT: 38,000
SALES (est): 38MM
SALES (corp-wide): 788.3MM **Publicly
Held**
WEB: www.kintera.org
SIC: 7372 Prepackaged software
PA: Blackbaud, Inc.
2000 Daniel Island Dr
Daniel Island SC 29492
843 216-6200

(P-15731)
KNO INC
2200 Mission College Blvd, Santa Clara
(95054-1537)
PHONE..................408 844-8120
Ronald D Dickel, *CEO*
Babur Habib, *CTO*
EMP: 70
SQ FT: 35,000
SALES (est): 9MM
SALES (corp-wide): 62.7B **Publicly Held**
SIC: 7372 Educational computer software
PA: Intel Corporation
2200 Mission College Blvd
Santa Clara CA 95054
408 765-8080

(P-15732)
KNOVA SOFTWARE INC (HQ)
10201 Torre Ave Ste 350, Cupertino
(95014-2131)
PHONE..................408 863-5800

Bruce Armstrong, *President*
Kent Heyman, *Ch of Bd*
Thomar Muise, *CFO*
Andy Feit, *Officer*
Sham Chotai, *Vice Pres*
EMP: 50
SQ FT: 16,800
SALES (est): 8.6MM
SALES (corp-wide): 559.6MM **Privately
Held**
WEB: www.knova.com
SIC: 7372 Business oriented computer
software
PA: Aptean, Inc.
4325 Alexander Dr Ste 100
Alpharetta GA 30022
770 351-9600

(P-15733)
**KONAMI DIGITAL ENTRMT INC
(DH)**
2381 Rosecrans Ave # 200, El Segundo
(90245-4922)
PHONE..................310 220-8100
Tomohiro Uesugi, *President*
Takahiro Azuma, *Vice Pres*
Chris Bartee, *Principal*
Kazumi Kitaue, *Principal*
EMP: 68
SQ FT: 53,596
SALES (est): 34.5MM
SALES (corp-wide): 2.2B **Privately Held**
SIC: 7372 Home entertainment computer
software
HQ: Konami Digital Entertainment Co., Ltd.
9-7-2, Akasaka
Minato-Ku TKY 107-0
357 710-573

(P-15734)
KPISOFT INC
50 California St Ste 1500, San Francisco
(94111-4612)
PHONE..................415 439-5228
Ravee Ramamoothie, *CEO*
EMP: 80
SQ FT: 4,000
SALES (est): 2.9MM **Privately Held**
SIC: 7372 Prepackaged software

(P-15735)
KRANEM CORPORATION
560 S Winchester Blvd, San Jose
(95128-2560)
PHONE..................650 319-6743
Ajay Batheja, *Ch of Bd*
Edward Miller, *CFO*
Luigi Caramico, *Vice Pres*
Christopher L Rasmussen, *Admin Sec*
EMP: 190
SALES: 8.3MM **Privately Held**
SIC: 7372 Business oriented computer
software

(P-15736)
**KRATOS TECH TRNING SLTIONS
INC (HQ)**
10680 Treena St Fl 6, San Diego
(92131-2487)
PHONE..................858 812-7300
Eric M Demarco, *President*
Kenneth Reagan, *President*
Deanna H Lund, *CFO*
Laura L Siegal, *Treasurer*
Phil Carrai, *Vice Pres*
EMP: 146
SQ FT: 25,000
SALES (est): 145.4MM **Publicly Held**
WEB: www.sys.com
SIC: 7372 Business oriented computer
software

(P-15737)
KRONOS INCORPORATED
240 Commerce, Irvine (92602-5004)
PHONE..................800 580-7374
Kaylee Uribe, *Branch Mgr*
David Alling, *Sr Software Eng*
Robert Murray, *Sr Software Eng*
Karen Katz, *Web Dvlpr*
Richard Bak, *Software Engr*
EMP: 56
SALES (corp-wide): 1B **Privately Held**
SIC: 7372 Business oriented computer
software

HQ: Kronos Incorporated
900 Chelmsford St # 312
Lowell MA 01851
978 250-9800

(P-15738)
KYRIBA CORP (HQ)
9620 Towne Cntre Dr 200, San Diego
(92121)
PHONE..................858 210-3560
Jean-Luc Robert, *CEO*
Timothy Ray, *President*
Didier Martineau, *COO*
Fabrice Levy, *CFO*
Fabrice Lvy, *CFO*
EMP: 50
SALES (est): 51.6MM
SALES (corp-wide): 25.3MM **Privately
Held**
WEB: www.kyriba.com
SIC: 7372 Prepackaged software
PA: Kyriba
247 Les Bureaux De La Colline
Saint Cloud 92210
177 920-040

(P-15739)
LASTLINE INC
6950 Hollister Ave # 101, Goleta
(93117-2896)
PHONE..................805 456-7075
EMP: 168 **Privately Held**
SIC: 7372 Prepackaged software
PA: Lastline, Inc.
203 Redwood Shores Pkwy
Redwood City CA 94065

(P-15740)
LAVANTE INC
5225 Hellyer Ave Ste 200, San Jose
(95138-1021)
P.O. Box 41058 (95160-1058)
PHONE..................408 754-1410
Frank Harbist, *President*
Tom Flynn, *Chief Mktg Ofcr*
Joe Flynn, *Officer*
Jason Welshonse, *Info Tech Mgr*
Vinay Ambekar, *Engineer*
EMP: 50
SALES (est): 8.4MM **Publicly Held**
WEB: www.auditsolutions.com
SIC: 7372 Business oriented computer
software
HQ: Prgx Usa, Inc.
600 Galleria Pkwy Se # 100
Atlanta GA 30339

(P-15741)
LAWINFOCOM INC
5901 Priestly Dr Ste 200, Carlsbad
(92008-8825)
PHONE..................760 510-3000
Gunter Enz, *President*
Cara Mae Harrison, *COO*
EMP: 68 EST: 1989
SQ FT: 10,000
SALES: 4.6MM **Privately Held**
WEB: www.lawinfo.com
SIC: 7372 8111 7375

(P-15742)
**LITHIUM TECHNOLOGIES LLC
(PA)**
1 Pier Ste 1 # 1, San Francisco
(94111-2028)
PHONE..................415 757-3100
Pete Hess, *CEO*
Robert Tarkoff, *President*
Jim Cox, *CFO*
Mark Culhane, *CFO*
Misha Logvinov, *Ch Credit Ofcr*
EMP: 92
SALES (est): 104.2MM **Privately Held**
WEB: www.lithium.com
SIC: 7372 Business oriented computer
software

(P-15743)
LIVEOFFICE LLC
Also Called: Advisorsquare
900 Corporate Pointe, Culver City
(90230-7609)
PHONE..................877 253-2793
Alexander Rusich,

Matt Hardy,
Jeffrey W Hausman,
Nikhil Menta,
Matt Smith,
EMP: 77
SQ FT: 15,000
SALES (est): 5.7MM
SALES (corp-wide): 4.8B **Publicly Held**
WEB: www.advisorsquare.com
SIC: 7372 Prepackaged software
PA: Symantec Corporation
        350 Ellis St
        Mountain View CA 94043
        650 527-8000

(P-15744)
LIVETIME SOFTWARE INC
276 Avocado St Apt C102, Costa Mesa
(92627-7302)
PHONE.................................415 905-4009
Darren Williams, *President*
EMP: 50
SALES (est): 2.7MM **Privately Held**
SIC: 7372 Prepackaged software

(P-15745)
LPA INSURANCE AGENCY INC
Also Called: Sat
4030 Truxel Rd Ste B, Sacramento
(95834-3767)
PHONE.................................916 286-7850
Michael Winkel, *President*
EMP: 56
SQ FT: 8,000
SALES (est): 3.3MM
SALES (corp-wide): 9.1B **Publicly Held**
WEB: www.sungard.com
SIC: 7372 Application computer software
HQ: Fis Data Systems Inc.
        200 Campus Dr
        Collegeville PA 19426
        484 582-2000

(P-15746)
**LYNX SOFTWARE
TECHNOLOGIES INC (PA)**
855 Embedded Way, San Jose
(95138-1030)
PHONE.................................408 979-3900
Inder Singh, *Chairman*
Gurjot Singh, *President*
Will Keegan, *CTO*
Ingrid Osborne, *Controller*
EMP: 52
SQ FT: 30,000
SALES (est): 15.6MM **Privately Held**
WEB: www.lynxworks.com
SIC: 7372 Business oriented computer
        software

(P-15747)
MALIKCO LLC
2121 N Calif Blvd Ste 290, Walnut Creek
(94596-7351)
PHONE.................................925 974-3555
Stephynie R Malik, *CEO*
Stephynie Malik, *General Mgr*
Alexandra O'Leary, *Business Mgr*
Devyn Wood, *Marketing Staff*
Dennis Dunnigan, *Director*
EMP: 50
SQ FT: 1,000
SALES (est): 4.8MM **Privately Held**
WEB: www.malikco.com
SIC: 7372 Operating systems computer
        software

(P-15748)
MAXIMUS HOLDINGS INC
2475 Hanover St, Palo Alto (94304-1114)
PHONE.................................650 935-9500
Dominic Gallello, *CEO*
Jim Johnson, *CFO*
Anshul Singh, *Executive*
EMP: 1006
SALES (est): 21.9MM
SALES (corp-wide): 569.5MM **Privately
Held**
SIC: 7372 Prepackaged software
PA: Symphony Technology Group, L.L.C.
        428 University Ave
        Palo Alto CA 94301
        650 935-9500

(P-15749)
MCAFEE INC
6707 Barnhurst Dr, San Diego
(92117-4208)
PHONE.................................858 967-2342
EMP: 82 **Privately Held**
SIC: 7372 Prepackaged software
HQ: Mcafee, Llc
        2821 Mission College Blvd
        Santa Clara CA 95054
        888 847-8766

(P-15750)
MCAFEE LLC (HQ)
2821 Mission College Blvd, Santa Clara
(95054-1838)
PHONE.................................888 847-8766
Christopher Young, *CEO*
Jean-Claude Broido, *President*
Tom Miglis, *President*
Michael Berry, *CFO*
Barry McPherson, *Exec VP*
▲ **EMP:** 148
SQ FT: 208,000
SALES (est): 1.5B **Privately Held**
WEB: www.mcafee.com
SIC: 7372 Application computer software

(P-15751)
MCAFEE FINANCE 2 LLC
2821 Mission College Blvd, Santa Clara
(95054-1838)
PHONE.................................888 847-8766
EMP: 1129
SALES (est): 10.3MM
SALES (corp-wide): 277.9MM **Privately
Held**
SIC: 7372 Prepackaged software
HQ: Mcafee Finance 1, Llc
        2821 Mission College Blvd
        Santa Clara CA 95054
        888 847-8766

(P-15752)
MCAFEE SECURITY LLC
2821 Mission College Blvd, Santa Clara
(95054-1838)
PHONE.................................866 622-3911
Michael Decesare, *President*
Bob Kelly, *CFO*
Edward Hayden, *Senior VP*
Louis Riley, *Senior VP*
EMP: 5030 **EST:** 2006
SQ FT: 208,000
SALES (est): 98.4MM **Privately Held**
SIC: 7372 Application computer software
HQ: Mcafee, Llc
        2821 Mission College Blvd
        Santa Clara CA 95054
        888 847-8766

(P-15753)
MEDALLIA INC (PA)
450 Concar Dr, San Mateo (94402-2681)
PHONE.................................650 321-3000
Leslie Stretch, *President*
Douglas Leone, *Partner*
Fred Mondragon, *President*
Aimey Presman, *President*
Frank Slootman, *President*
EMP: 145
SQ FT: 10,000
SALES (est): 507.7MM **Privately Held**
WEB: www.medallia.com
SIC: 7372 8732 Business oriented com-
        puter software; market analysis, business
        & economic research

(P-15754)
MEDATA INC (PA)
5 Peters Canyon Rd # 250, Irvine
(92606-1793)
PHONE.................................714 918-1310
Cy King, *CEO*
Tom Herndon, *President*
Thomas Herndon, *COO*
Bryan Lowe, *Officer*
T Don Theis, *Senior VP*
EMP: 51
SQ FT: 17,192
SALES (est): 114.3MM **Privately Held**
WEB: www.medata.com
SIC: 7372 6411 Business oriented com-
        puter software; medical insurance claim
        processing, contract or fee basis

(P-15755)
**MEDICAL TRANSCRIPTION
BILLING**
405 Kenyon St Ste 300, San Diego (92110)
PHONE.................................800 869-3700
EMP: 561
SALES (corp-wide): 31.8MM **Publicly
Held**
SIC: 7372 Prepackaged software
PA: Medical Transcription Billing, Corp.
        7 Clyde Rd
        Somerset NJ 08873
        732 873-5133

(P-15756)
MEDITAB SOFTWARE INC
333 Hegenberger Rd # 800, Oakland
(94621-1416)
PHONE.................................510 632-2021
Mike Patel, *President*
Marvin Chavez, *Partner*
Kal Patel, *COO*
Feros Khan, *Info Tech Mgr*
Amit Limba, *Prgrmr*
EMP: 250
SQ FT: 10,000
SALES (est): 27.9MM **Privately Held**
SIC: 7372 Business oriented computer
        software

(P-15757)
**MERCURY INTERACTIVE LLC
(HQ)**
3000 Hanover St, Palo Alto (94304-1112)
P.O. Box 60069, Sunnyvale (94088-0069)
PHONE.................................650 857-1501
Anthony Zingale, *President*
Nazley Davies, *Partner*
Moshe Egert, *President*
Jon E Flaxman, *Treasurer*
Jon White, *Admin Sec*
EMP: 350
SALES (est): 107MM
SALES (corp-wide): 28.8B **Publicly Held**
WEB: www.svca.mercuryinteractive.com
SIC: 7372 Prepackaged software
PA: Hewlett Packard Enterprise Company
        3000 Hanover St
        Palo Alto CA 94304
        650 687-5817

(P-15758)
METRICSTREAM INC (PA)
Also Called: Complianceonline
2479 E Byshore Rd Ste 260, Palo Alto
(94303)
PHONE.................................650 620-2900
Mikael Hagstroem, *CEO*
Gaurave Kapoor, *COO*
Steve Springsteel, *CFO*
Steven R Springsteel, *CFO*
Gunjan Sinha, *Chairman*
EMP: 150
SALES (est): 190.9MM **Privately Held**
SIC: 7372 Application computer software

(P-15759)
MICROSOFT CORPORATION
680 Vaqueros Ave, Sunnyvale
(94085-3523)
PHONE.................................650 964-7200
Susan Peletta, *Executive*
Lori Fazeli, *Partner*
Rukmini Iyer, *Partner*
Derek Loar, *Executive*
Jennifer Lyons, *Comms Dir*
EMP: 82
SALES (corp-wide): 110.3B **Publicly
Held**
SIC: 7372 Prepackaged software
PA: Microsoft Corporation
        1 Microsoft Way
        Redmond WA 98052
        425 882-8080

(P-15760)
MICROSOFT CORPORATION
7007 Friars Rd, San Diego (92108-1148)
PHONE.................................619 849-5872
Carolyn Allen, *Manager*
Sarah Forrest, *Manager*
Kleber Santos, *Manager*
EMP: 100

SALES (corp-wide): 110.3B **Publicly
Held**
SIC: 7372 Application computer software
PA: Microsoft Corporation
        1 Microsoft Way
        Redmond WA 98052
        425 882-8080

(P-15761)
MICROSOFT CORPORATION
1020 Entp Way Bldg B, Sunnyvale (94089)
PHONE.................................650 693-1009
William H Gates III, *Branch Mgr*
EMP: 103
SALES (corp-wide): 110.3B **Publicly
Held**
SIC: 7372 Prepackaged software
PA: Microsoft Corporation
        1 Microsoft Way
        Redmond WA 98052
        425 882-8080

(P-15762)
MICROSOFT CORPORATION
3 Park Plz Ste 1800, Irvine (92614-8541)
PHONE.................................949 263-3000
Sandy Thomas, *General Mgr*
Warren Kerby, *Info Tech Mgr*
Michael Ghekiere, *Technical Staff*
Juliet Helms, *Technical Staff*
Joseph Ruedlinger, *Sr Consultant*
EMP: 125
SALES (corp-wide): 110.3B **Publicly
Held**
WEB: www.microsoft.com
SIC: 7372 Application computer software
PA: Microsoft Corporation
        1 Microsoft Way
        Redmond WA 98052
        425 882-8080

(P-15763)
MICROSOFT CORPORATION
13031 W Jefferson Blvd # 200, Playa Vista
(90094-7001)
PHONE.................................213 806-7300
Evelyn Morgan, *Opers Mgr*
Austin Ogletree, *Partner*
Stephanie Friedman, *Executive*
Dean Suzuki, *Technology*
Matt Jackson, *Technical Staff*
EMP: 100
SALES (corp-wide): 110.3B **Publicly
Held**
WEB: www.microsoft.com
SIC: 7372 Application computer software
PA: Microsoft Corporation
        1 Microsoft Way
        Redmond WA 98052
        425 882-8080

(P-15764)
MICROSOFT CORPORATION
555 California St Ste 200, San Francisco
(94104-1504)
PHONE.................................415 972-6400
Teeka Miller, *Branch Mgr*
Laura Wallace, *Vice Pres*
Fernando Alvarado, *Executive*
Chris Fasano, *Executive*
Shelton Sunday, *Executive*
EMP: 160
SALES (corp-wide): 110.3B **Publicly
Held**
WEB: www.microsoft.com
SIC: 7372 Application computer software
PA: Microsoft Corporation
        1 Microsoft Way
        Redmond WA 98052
        425 882-8080

(P-15765)
MICROSOFT CORPORATION
2045 Lafayette St, Santa Clara
(95050-2901)
PHONE.................................408 987-9608
Jim Brown, *President*
EMP: 100
SALES (corp-wide): 110.3B **Publicly
Held**
WEB: www.microsoft.com
SIC: 7372 Application computer software
PA: Microsoft Corporation
        1 Microsoft Way
        Redmond WA 98052
        425 882-8080

P
R
O
D
U
C
T
S

&

S
V
C
S

(P-15766)
MJUS LLC (FKA MINDJET LLC)
275 Battery St Ste 1000, San Francisco
(94111-3333)
PHONE......................415 229-4344
Scott Raskin, *CEO*
Steve Glass, *President*
Steve Anderson, *CFO*
Francis Procaccia, *QA Dir*
Sasha Kipervarg, *Info Tech Dir*
EMP: 81
SQ FT: 15,140
SALES (est): 30.8MM
SALES (corp-wide): 31MM **Privately Held**
SIC: 7372 Business oriented computer software; educational computer software
PA: Spigit Holdings Corporation
275 Battery St Ste 1000
San Francisco CA 94111
415 229-4400

(P-15767)
MOBILEIRON INC (PA)
401 E Middlefield Rd, Mountain View
(94043-4005)
PHONE......................650 919-8100
Simon Biddiscombe, *President*
Tae Hea Nahm, *Ch of Bd*
Scott D Hill, *CFO*
Sohail Parekh, *Senior VP*
Gregory Randolph, *Senior VP*
EMP: 145
SQ FT: 78,000
SALES: 176.4MM **Publicly Held**
SIC: 7372 Prepackaged software

(P-15768)
MONTAVISTA SOFTWARE LLC (DH)
2315 N 1st St Fl 4, San Jose (95131-1010)
PHONE......................408 572-8000
Art Landro, *President*
Sanjay Uppal, *CFO*
Jason B Wacha, *Vice Pres*
James Ready, *CTO*
EMP: 150
SALES (est): 14.5MM **Privately Held**
WEB: www.mvista.com
SIC: 7372 Prepackaged software

(P-15769)
MSCSOFTWARE CORPORATION (HQ)
4675 Macarthur Ct Ste 900, Newport Beach
(92660-1845)
PHONE......................714 540-8900
Dominic Gallello, *President*
Eric Favre, *Vice Pres*
Michael Hoffmann, *Vice Pres*
Leo Kilfoy, *General Mgr*
Beate Funk-Klemke, *Administration*
EMP: 245 **EST:** 1963
SALES (est): 160.4MM
SALES (corp-wide): 18.8MM **Privately Held**
WEB: www.mscsoftware.com
SIC: 7372 Business oriented computer software
PA: Hexagon Ab
Lilla Bantorget 15
Stockholm 111 2
860 126-20

(P-15770)
MULESOFT INC
50 Fremont St Ste 300, San Francisco
(94105-2231)
PHONE......................415 229-2009
Greg Schott, *CEO*
Nick Trombetta, *President*
Matt Langdon, *CFO*
Vidya Peters, *Chief Mktg Ofcr*
Mark Dao, *Officer*
EMP: 841
SQ FT: 41,500
SALES: 296.4MM
SALES (corp-wide): 10.4B **Publicly Held**
WEB: www.mulesource.com
SIC: 7372 7371 Prepackaged software; computer software development
PA: Salesforce.Com, Inc.
1 Market Ste 300
San Francisco CA 94105
415 901-7000

(P-15771)
MUSICMATCH INC
16935 W Bernardo Dr # 270, San Diego
(92127-1634)
PHONE......................858 485-4300
Dennis Mudd, *CEO*
Peter Csathy, *President*
Gary Acord, *CFO*
Chris Allen, *Senior VP*
Don Leigh, *Senior VP*
EMP: 140
SQ FT: 20,000
SALES (est): 6.9MM **Publicly Held**
WEB: www.musicmatch.com
SIC: 7372 5734 Prepackaged software; software, business & non-game
PA: Altaba Inc.
140 E 45th St Ste 15a
New York NY 10017

(P-15772)
NC INTERACTIVE LLC
1900 S Norfolk St Ste 125, San Mateo
(94403-1175)
PHONE......................650 393-2200
Songyee Yoon, *CEO*
Eric Garay, *CFO*
Janet Lin, *General Counsel*
EMP: 99 **EST:** 2016
SQ FT: 16,692
SALES (est): 1.4MM **Privately Held**
SIC: 7372 Prepackaged software

(P-15773)
NEONROOTS LLC
8560 W Sunset Blvd # 500, West Holly-wood (90069-2311)
PHONE......................310 907-9210
Benjamin C Lee, *CEO*
EMP: 125 **EST:** 2012
SALES (est): 4.6MM **Privately Held**
SIC: 7372 Prepackaged software

(P-15774)
NET OPTICS INC
Also Called: Ixia
5301 Stevens Creek Blvd, Santa Clara
(95051-7201)
PHONE......................408 737-7777
Thomas B Miller, *CEO*
Robert Shaw, *President*
Dennis Omanoff, *COO*
Burt Podbere, *CFO*
Nadine Matityahu, *Corp Secy*
EMP: 85
SQ FT: 39,000
SALES (est): 9MM
SALES (corp-wide): 3.1B **Publicly Held**
WEB: www.netoptics.com
SIC: 7372 Operating systems computer software
HQ: Ixia
26601 Agoura Rd
Calabasas CA 91302
818 871-1800

(P-15775)
NETCUBE SYSTEMS INC
1275 Arbor Ave, Los Altos (94024-5330)
PHONE......................650 862-7858
Mallikarjuna Reddy, *President*
EMP: 75
SQ FT: 1,000
SALES: 35MM **Privately Held**
SIC: 7372 7379 7371 7361 Application computer software; computer related consulting services; custom computer programming services; employment agencies

(P-15776)
NETSUITE INC (DH)
Also Called: Oracle
2955 Campus Dr Ste 100, San Mateo
(94403-2539)
PHONE......................650 627-1000
Dorian Daley, *President*
Raghu Gnanasekaran, *Partner*
Erica Prado, *President*
James Dantow, *COO*
Evan Goldberg, *Exec VP*
EMP: 148
SQ FT: 165,000

SALES: 741.1MM
SALES (corp-wide): 39.8B **Publicly Held**
SIC: 7372 Business oriented computer software
HQ: Oc Acquisition Llc
500 Oracle Pkwy
Redwood City CA 94065
650 506-7000

(P-15777)
NETWORK AUTOMATION INC
3530 Wilshire Blvd # 1800, Los Angeles
(90010-2335)
PHONE......................213 738-1700
Dustin Snell, *CEO*
Graham Taylor, *CTO*
EMP: 50
SQ FT: 9,000
SALES (est): 3.9MM
SALES (corp-wide): 70.8MM **Privately Held**
WEB: www.networkautomation.com
SIC: 7372 Business oriented computer software
PA: Help/Systems, Llc
6455 City West Pkwy
Eden Prairie MN 55344
952 933-0609

(P-15778)
NEW BI US GAMING LLC
10920 Via Frontera # 420, San Diego
(92127-1729)
PHONE......................858 592-2472
Ian Bonner, *CEO*
Kimberly Armstrong, *Vice Pres*
Russell Schechter, *Vice Pres*
EMP: 92 **EST:** 2012
SALES (est): 5.8MM **Privately Held**
SIC: 7372 Prepackaged software

(P-15779)
NEW CAM COMMERCE SOLUTIONS LLC
5555 Garden Grove Blvd # 100, Westminster (92683-8227)
PHONE......................714 338-0200
Doug Roberson, *Mng Member*
EMP: 77
SQ FT: 26,000
SALES (est): 5.9MM
SALES (corp-wide): 23.1MM **Privately Held**
SIC: 7372 Business oriented computer software
PA: Celerant Technology Corp.
4830 Arthur Kill Rd Ste 3
Staten Island NY 10309
718 351-2000

(P-15780)
NEW RELIC INC (PA)
188 Spear St Ste 1200, San Francisco
(94105-1750)
PHONE......................650 777-7600
Lewis Cirne, *CEO*
Peter Fenton, *Ch of Bd*
Mark Sachleben, *CFO*
James Gochee, *President*
Matthew Flaming, *Vice Pres*
EMP: 148
SQ FT: 73,391
SALES: 355MM **Publicly Held**
SIC: 7372 Application computer software

(P-15781)
NEXENTA SYSTEMS INC
2025 Gateway Pl Ste 160, San Jose
(95110-1059)
PHONE......................408 791-3341
Tarkan Maner, *Ch of Bd*
Rick Martig, *CFO*
Tim Guleri, *Bd of Directors*
Evan Powell, *Officer*
Jon Ash, *Vice Pres*
EMP: 230
SALES (est): 35.1MM **Privately Held**
SIC: 7372 Operating systems computer software

(P-15782)
NEXTGEN HEALTHCARE INC (PA)
18111 Von Karman Ave, Irvine
(92612-0199)
PHONE......................949 255-2600

John R Frantz, *President*
Jeffrey H Margolis, *Ch of Bd*
Craig A Barbarosh, *Vice Chairman*
Scott E Bostick, *COO*
James R Arnold, *CFO*
EMP: 148
SQ FT: 83,100
SALES: 531MM **Publicly Held**
WEB: www.qsii.com
SIC: 7372 7373 Prepackaged software; computer integrated systems design

(P-15783)
NIGHTINGALE VANTAGEMED CORP (HQ)
10670 White Rock Rd, Rancho Cordova
(95670-6095)
PHONE......................916 638-4744
Steven Curd, *CEO*
Mark Cameron, *COO*
Liesel Loesch, *CFO*
Richard Altinger, *Vice Pres*
Jennifer Bentley, *VP Mktg*
EMP: 55
SALES (est): 10.9MM **Privately Held**
WEB: www.vantagemed.com
SIC: 7372 Business oriented computer software
PA: Nexia Health Technologies Inc
15 Allstate Prkwy 6th Fl
Markham ON L3R 5
905 415-3063

(P-15784)
NLYTE SOFTWARE AMERICAS LTD (DH)
2800 Campus Dr Ste 135, San Mateo
(94403-2554)
PHONE......................650 561-8200
Doug Sabella, *President*
Phil Kelly, *President*
Fred Dirla, *COO*
Owen Nisbett, *CFO*
Grant Bilbow, *Vice Pres*
EMP: 130
SALES (est): 19MM
SALES (corp-wide): 30.3MM **Privately Held**
SIC: 7372 Prepackaged software
HQ: Nlyte Software Americas Limited
26 Osiers Road
London SW18
208 877-7200

(P-15785)
NTRUST INFOTECH INC
230 Commerce Ste 180, Irvine
(92602-1336)
PHONE......................562 207-1600
Srikanth Ramachandran, *CEO*
Janakiraman Ramachandran, *COO*
Tom Scott, *Senior VP*
Ramki Krishnamoorthy, *Vice Pres*
Radha Krishnaraj, *Vice Pres*
EMP: 65 **EST:** 2003
SALES (est): 6.5MM **Privately Held**
SIC: 7372 7371 Business oriented computer software; computer software development & applications
PA: Ntrust Infotech Private Limited
3rd Floor Ganesh Towers
Chennai TN
-

(P-15786)
NUANCE COMMUNICATIONS INC
1198 E Arques Ave, Sunnyvale
(94085-4602)
PHONE......................781 565-5000
Charles Berger, *President*
Denise Danielson, *Program Mgr*
Katalin Vonberg, *Technology*
Bonnie Bartosik, *Purch Agent*
Regina Schmidt, *Marketing Staff*
EMP: 150
SQ FT: 60,000 **Publicly Held**
SIC: 7372 Application computer software
PA: Nuance Communications, Inc.
1 Wayside Rd
Burlington MA 01803
-

(P-15787)
NWP SERVICES CORPORATION (HQ)
535 Anton Blvd Ste 1100, Costa Mesa (92626-7699)
P.O. Box 19661, Irvine (92623-9661)
PHONE.....................................949 253-2500
Ron Reed, *President*
Lana Reeve,
Mike Haviken, *Exec VP*
Monique Black, *Human Resources*
Bob Smolarski, *Opers Staff*
EMP: 141
SQ FT: 21,171
SALES (est): 48.8MM
SALES (corp-wide): 670.9MM **Publicly Held**
WEB: www.nwpco.com
SIC: 7372 8721 Utility computer software; billing & bookkeeping service
PA: Realpage, Inc.
2201 Lakeside Blvd
Richardson TX 75082
972 820-3000

(P-15788)
ODDWORLD INHABITANTS INC
869 Monterey St, San Luis Obispo (93401-3224)
PHONE.....................................805 503-3000
Sherry McKenna, *CEO*
Lorne Lanning, *President*
Maurice Konkle, *COO*
EMP: 60
SQ FT: 15,000
SALES (est): 2.4MM **Privately Held**
WEB: www.oddworld.com
SIC: 7372 Application computer software

(P-15789)
ON24 INC (PA)
50 Beale St Ste 800, San Francisco (94105-1863)
PHONE.....................................877 202-9599
Sharat Sharan, *President*
Ian Halifax, *CFO*
Joe Hyland, *Chief Mktg Ofcr*
Mahesh Kheny, *Vice Pres*
Thomas Masotto, *Vice Pres*
EMP: 350
SQ FT: 28,353
SALES (est): 81.9MM **Privately Held**
WEB: www.on24.com
SIC: 7372 Business oriented computer software

(P-15790)
OPENTV INC (DH)
Also Called: Nagra
275 Sacramento St Ste SI1, San Francisco (94111-3831)
PHONE.....................................415 962-5000
Yves Pitton, *CEO*
Ben Bennett, *CEO*
Andr Kudelski, *CEO*
Wesley O Hoffman, *COO*
Shum Mukherjee, *CFO*
EMP: 150
SALES (est): 78.6MM
SALES (corp-wide): 1B **Privately Held**
SIC: 7372 Prepackaged software

(P-15791)
OPTIMUM SOLUTIONS GROUP LLC
419 Ponderosa Ct, Lafayette (94549-1812)
PHONE.....................................415 954-7100
G John Houtary,
Lisa Massman,
EMP: 109
SQ FT: 3,300
SALES (est): 4.5MM
SALES (corp-wide): 5.1B **Privately Held**
WEB: www.optimumsolutions.com
SIC: 7372 7371 8243 7374 Prepackaged software; computer software systems analysis & design, custom; data processing schools; computer graphics service
PA: Kpmg Llp
1676 Intl Dr Ste 1200
Mclean VA 22102
703 286-8000

(P-15792)
ORACLE AMERICA INC
Also Called: Sun Microsystems
4220 Network Cir, Santa Clara (95054-1780)
PHONE.....................................408 276-4300
Mark Toliver, *President*
Jesse Hsu, *Design Engr*
Jonathan Gibbons, *Technical Staff*
Peter Lam, *Technical Staff*
Ekaterina Pavlova, *Technical Staff*
EMP: 187
SALES (corp-wide): 39.8B **Publicly Held**
SIC: 7372 Prepackaged software
HQ: Oracle America, Inc.
500 Oracle Pkwy
Redwood City CA 94065
650 506-7000

(P-15793)
ORACLE AMERICA INC
475 Sansome St Fl 15, San Francisco (94111-3166)
PHONE.....................................415 908-3609
EMP: 58
SALES (corp-wide): 39.8B **Publicly Held**
SIC: 7372 Prepackaged software
HQ: Oracle America, Inc.
500 Oracle Pkwy
Redwood City CA 94065
650 506-7000

(P-15794)
ORACLE AMERICA INC
Also Called: Sun Microsystems
5815 Owens Dr, Pleasanton (94588-3939)
PHONE.....................................925 694-3314
Terri Beck, *Manager*
EMP: 75
SALES (corp-wide): 39.8B **Publicly Held**
SIC: 7372 Prepackaged software
HQ: Oracle America, Inc.
500 Oracle Pkwy
Redwood City CA 94065
650 506-7000

(P-15795)
ORACLE AMERICA INC
Also Called: Sun Microsystems
80 Railroad Ave, Milpitas (95035-4333)
PHONE.....................................408 635-3072
Bruce Webbe, *Manager*
EMP: 251
SALES (corp-wide): 39.8B **Publicly Held**
SIC: 7372 Prepackaged software
HQ: Oracle America, Inc.
500 Oracle Pkwy
Redwood City CA 94065
650 506-7000

(P-15796)
ORACLE AMERICA INC
Also Called: Sun Microsystems
9540 Towne Centre Dr, San Diego (92121-1988)
PHONE.....................................858 625-5044
Steven Nathan, *Manager*
EMP: 77
SALES (corp-wide): 39.8B **Publicly Held**
SIC: 7372 Prepackaged software
HQ: Oracle America, Inc.
500 Oracle Pkwy
Redwood City CA 94065
650 506-7000

(P-15797)
ORACLE AMERICA INC
Also Called: Sun Microsystems
4230 Leonard Stocking Dr, Santa Clara (95054-1777)
PHONE.....................................408 276-7534
Denise Shiffman, *VP Mktg*
Larry Williams, *COO*
Joe Fuentes, *Comms Mgr*
Michael Connaughton, *General Mgr*
William H Howard, *CIO*
EMP: 250
SALES (corp-wide): 39.8B **Publicly Held**
SIC: 7372 Prepackaged software
HQ: Oracle America, Inc.
500 Oracle Pkwy
Redwood City CA 94065
650 506-7000

(P-15798)
ORACLE CORPORATION
279 Barnes Rd, Tustin (92782-3748)
PHONE.....................................713 654-0919
John Czapko, *Branch Mgr*
EMP: 191
SALES (corp-wide): 39.8B **Publicly Held**
SIC: 7372 Business oriented computer software
PA: Oracle Corporation
500 Oracle Pkwy
Redwood City CA 94065
650 506-7000

(P-15799)
ORACLE CORPORATION
214 Clarence Ave, Sunnyvale (94086-5907)
PHONE.....................................650 607-5402
Jitendra Chinthakindi, *Principal*
EMP: 302
SALES (corp-wide): 39.8B **Publicly Held**
SIC: 7372 Business oriented computer software
PA: Oracle Corporation
500 Oracle Pkwy
Redwood City CA 94065
650 506-7000

(P-15800)
ORACLE CORPORATION
1408 Antigua Ln, Foster City (94404-3970)
PHONE.....................................650 678-3612
ARA Michaelian, *Principal*
EMP: 302
SALES (corp-wide): 39.8B **Publicly Held**
SIC: 7372 Business oriented computer software
PA: Oracle Corporation
500 Oracle Pkwy
Redwood City CA 94065
650 506-7000

(P-15801)
ORACLE CORPORATION
1490 Newhall St, Santa Clara (95050-6135)
PHONE.....................................408 421-2890
Stephanie Camarda, *Principal*
EMP: 302
SALES (corp-wide): 39.8B **Publicly Held**
SIC: 7372 Business oriented computer software
PA: Oracle Corporation
500 Oracle Pkwy
Redwood City CA 94065
650 506-7000

(P-15802)
ORACLE CORPORATION
231 Kerry Dr, Santa Clara (95050-6603)
PHONE.....................................408 276-5552
Annie Van Dalen, *Principal*
EMP: 302
SALES (corp-wide): 39.8B **Publicly Held**
SIC: 7372 Business oriented computer software
PA: Oracle Corporation
500 Oracle Pkwy
Redwood City CA 94065
650 506-7000

(P-15803)
ORACLE CORPORATION
3084 Thurman Dr, San Jose (95148-3143)
PHONE.....................................408 276-3822
Alasdair Rendall, *Principal*
EMP: 302
SALES (corp-wide): 39.8B **Publicly Held**
SIC: 7372 Business oriented computer software
PA: Oracle Corporation
500 Oracle Pkwy
Redwood City CA 94065
650 506-7000

(P-15804)
ORACLE CORPORATION
9515 Towne Centre Dr, San Diego (92121-1973)
PHONE.....................................858 202-0648
Michael Smith, *Technology*
Brandon Byers, *Technical Staff*
Shannon Kagey, *Manager*
EMP: 191

(P-15805)

(continued top of next column)
SALES (corp-wide): 39.8B **Publicly Held**
SIC: 7372 Business oriented computer software
PA: Oracle Corporation
500 Oracle Pkwy
Redwood City CA 94065
650 506-7000

(P-15805)
ORACLE CORPORATION
3532 Eastin Pl, Santa Clara (95051-2600)
PHONE.....................................650 506-9864
Maneesh Jain, *Principal*
Gia Nguyen, *Senior Engr*
EMP: 302
SALES (corp-wide): 39.8B **Publicly Held**
SIC: 7372 Business oriented computer software
PA: Oracle Corporation
500 Oracle Pkwy
Redwood City CA 94065
650 506-7000

(P-15806)
ORACLE CORPORATION
372 Calero Ave, San Jose (95123-4315)
PHONE.....................................408 390-8623
Aileen F Casanave, *Principal*
EMP: 302
SALES (corp-wide): 39.8B **Publicly Held**
SIC: 7372 Business oriented computer software
PA: Oracle Corporation
500 Oracle Pkwy
Redwood City CA 94065
650 506-7000

(P-15807)
ORACLE CORPORATION
475 Sansome St Fl 15, San Francisco (94111-3166)
PHONE.....................................415 402-7200
Victor Coskey, *Principal*
Trey Parsons, *Vice Pres*
Connor Thomas, *Vice Pres*
Minho Kim, *Sr Software Eng*
Rohit Koul, *Sr Software Eng*
EMP: 191
SALES (corp-wide): 39.8B **Publicly Held**
SIC: 7372 Business oriented computer software
PA: Oracle Corporation
500 Oracle Pkwy
Redwood City CA 94065
650 506-7000

(P-15808)
ORACLE CORPORATION
6224 Hummingbird Ln, Rocklin (95765-5929)
P.O. Box 3442 (95677-8469)
PHONE.....................................916 435-8342
Richard Gless, *Principal*
EMP: 302
SALES (corp-wide): 39.8B **Publicly Held**
SIC: 7372 Business oriented computer software
PA: Oracle Corporation
500 Oracle Pkwy
Redwood City CA 94065
650 506-7000

(P-15809)
ORACLE CORPORATION
5805 Owens Dr, Pleasanton (94588-3939)
PHONE.....................................877 767-2253
Bor R Fu, *Senior VP*
Clement Sciammas, *Vice Pres*
Sitaraman Swaminathan, *Executive*
Kevin Supan, *Info Tech Mgr*
Ricky Frost, *Software Engr*
EMP: 315
SALES (corp-wide): 39.8B **Publicly Held**
SIC: 7372 Business oriented computer software
PA: Oracle Corporation
500 Oracle Pkwy
Redwood City CA 94065
650 506-7000

(P-15810)
ORACLE CORPORATION
3925 Emerald Isle Ln, San Jose (95135-1708)
PHONE.....................................925 694-6258
Johnson Aremu, *Principal*

EMP: 306
SALES (corp-wide): 39.8B **Publicly Held**
SIC: 7372 Business oriented computer software
PA: Oracle Corporation
　500 Oracle Pkwy
　Redwood City CA 94065
　650 506-7000

(P-15811)
ORACLE CORPORATION
5863 Carmel Way, Union City
(94587-5170)
PHONE...................510 471-6971
Renzo Zagni, *Principal*
EMP: 302
SALES (corp-wide): 39.8B **Publicly Held**
SIC: 7372 Business oriented computer software
PA: Oracle Corporation
　500 Oracle Pkwy
　Redwood City CA 94065
　650 506-7000

(P-15812)
ORACLE CORPORATION
5750 Hannum Ave Ste 200, Culver City
(90230-6666)
PHONE...................310 258-7500
EMP: 302
SALES (corp-wide): 39.8B **Publicly Held**
SIC: 7372 Business oriented computer software
PA: Oracle Corporation
　500 Oracle Pkwy
　Redwood City CA 94065
　650 506-7000

(P-15813)
ORACLE CORPORATION
200 N Pacific Coast Hwy # 400, El Segundo (90245-5628)
PHONE...................310 343-7405
EMP: 306
SALES (corp-wide): 39.8B **Publicly Held**
SIC: 7372 Business oriented computer software
PA: Oracle Corporation
　500 Oracle Pkwy
　Redwood City CA 94065
　650 506-7000

(P-15814)
ORACLE CORPORATION
1001 Sunset Blvd, Rocklin (95765-3702)
PHONE...................916 315-3500
Chris Wilson, *Branch Mgr*
Nancy Peters, *VP Admin*
Nicole Stokes, *Admin Asst*
Liz Brock, *Administration*
Pavel Buenitsky, *Info Tech Dir*
EMP: 500
SALES (corp-wide): 39.8B **Publicly Held**
SIC: 7372 7371 Business oriented computer software; custom computer programming services
PA: Oracle Corporation
　500 Oracle Pkwy
　Redwood City CA 94065
　650 506-7000

(P-15815)
ORACLE SYSTEMS CORPORATION
200 N Pacific Coast Hwy # 400, El Segundo (90245-4340)
PHONE...................818 817-2900
Elizabeth Deitz, *General Mgr*
EMP: 70
SALES (corp-wide): 39.8B **Publicly Held**
WEB: www.forcecapital.com
SIC: 7372 Prepackaged software
HQ: Oracle Systems Corporation
　500 Oracle Pkwy
　Redwood City CA 94065
　650 506-7000

(P-15816)
ORACLE SYSTEMS CORPORATION
102 Santa Barbara Ave, Daly City
(94014-1045)
PHONE...................650 506-8648
EMP: 92

SALES (corp-wide): 39.8B **Publicly Held**
WEB: www.forcecapital.com
SIC: 7372 Prepackaged software
HQ: Oracle Systems Corporation
　500 Oracle Pkwy
　Redwood City CA 94065
　650 506-7000

(P-15817)
ORACLE SYSTEMS CORPORATION
301 Island Pkwy, Belmont (94002-4109)
PHONE...................650 654-7606
Sameer Patkar, *Vice Pres*
Thirupathi Annadi, *Technology*
Jennifer Tsai, *Technology*
Ramakrishna Gudia, *Manager*
EMP: 304
SALES (corp-wide): 39.8B **Publicly Held**
SIC: 7372 Prepackaged software
HQ: Oracle Systems Corporation
　500 Oracle Pkwy
　Redwood City CA 94065
　650 506-7000

(P-15818)
ORACLE SYSTEMS CORPORATION
500 Oracle Pwky, San Mateo (94403)
PHONE...................650 506-6780
Sayekumar Arumugam, *Principal*
EMP: 108
SALES (corp-wide): 39.8B **Publicly Held**
WEB: www.forcecapital.com
SIC: 7372 Prepackaged software
HQ: Oracle Systems Corporation
　500 Oracle Pkwy
　Redwood City CA 94065
　650 506-7000

(P-15819)
ORACLE SYSTEMS CORPORATION
10 Twin Dolphin Dr, Redwood City
(94065-1035)
PHONE...................650 506-0300
Richard Grogan, *Branch Mgr*
Ravi Sharma, *Technical Staff*
Yaldah Hakim, *Marketing Staff*
Richard Cardillo, *Sales Staff*
Robin Carlier, *Sales Staff*
EMP: 252
SALES (corp-wide): 39.8B **Publicly Held**
WEB: www.forcecapital.com
SIC: 7372 Prepackaged software
HQ: Oracle Systems Corporation
　500 Oracle Pkwy
　Redwood City CA 94065
　650 506-7000

(P-15820)
ORACLE SYSTEMS CORPORATION
5840 Owens Dr, Pleasanton (94588-3900)
PHONE...................925 694-3000
Apu Gupta, *Principal*
Randall Geyer, *Sr Software Eng*
Linda Tedjakusuma, *Sr Software Eng*
Matthew Taum, *Database Admin*
Dani Graham, *Director*
EMP: 252
SALES (corp-wide): 39.8B **Publicly Held**
WEB: www.forcecapital.com
SIC: 7372 5734 Prepackaged software; software, business & non-game
HQ: Oracle Systems Corporation
　500 Oracle Pkwy
　Redwood City CA 94065
　650 506-7000

(P-15821)
ORACLE SYSTEMS CORPORATION
2010 Main St Ste 450, Irvine (92614-7260)
PHONE...................949 224-1000
Dawn Lotez, *Manager*
EMP: 100
SALES (corp-wide): 39.8B **Publicly Held**
WEB: www.forcecapital.com
SIC: 7372 Prepackaged software
HQ: Oracle Systems Corporation
　500 Oracle Pkwy
　Redwood City CA 94065
　650 506-7000

(P-15822)
ORACLE SYSTEMS CORPORATION
17901 Von Karman Ave # 800, Irvine
(92614-6297)
PHONE...................949 623-9460
Fran Bracey, *Manager*
Don Kime, *Engineer*
Ralph Woodley, *Assistant*
EMP: 275
SALES (corp-wide): 39.8B **Publicly Held**
WEB: www.forcecapital.com
SIC: 7372 5045 Prepackaged software; computers, peripherals & software
HQ: Oracle Systems Corporation
　500 Oracle Pkwy
　Redwood City CA 94065
　650 506-7000

(P-15823)
ORACLE TALEO LLC
4140 Dublin Blvd Ste 400, Dublin
(94568-7757)
PHONE...................925 452-3000
Dorian Daley, *President*
Eric Ball, *CFO*
Guy Gauvin, *Exec VP*
Neil Hudspith, *Exec VP*
Jason Blessing, *Senior VP*
EMP: 1164
SQ FT: 47,500
SALES (est): 98.1MM
SALES (corp-wide): 39.8B **Publicly Held**
WEB: www.taleo.com
SIC: 7372 Business oriented computer software
PA: Oracle Corporation
　500 Oracle Pkwy
　Redwood City CA 94065
　650 506-7000

(P-15824)
PACIOLAN LLC (HQ)
Also Called: Ticketswest
5171 California Ave # 200, Irvine
(92617-3068)
PHONE...................949 476-2050
Dave Butler, *CEO*
Jane Kleinberger, *Ch of Bd*
Kimberly Boren, *CFO*
Steve Shaw, *CFO*
Teri Clark, *Admin Sec*
EMP: 70 **EST:** 1980
SALES (est): 29.2MM
SALES (corp-wide): 84.5B **Publicly Held**
WEB: www.paciolan.com
SIC: 7372 5045 Business oriented computer software; computers
PA: Comcast Corporation
　1701 Jfk Blvd
　Philadelphia PA 19103
　215 286-1700

(P-15825)
PATIENTPOP INC
214 Wilshire Blvd, Santa Monica
(90401-1202)
PHONE...................844 487-8399
Travis Schneider, *CEO*
Robert Palumbo, *Partner*
Jason Gardner, *CFO*
Luke Kervin, *Co-CEO*
Jeb Burrows, *Vice Pres*
EMP: 51
SALES (est): 1.1MM **Privately Held**
SIC: 7372 Business oriented computer software

(P-15826)
PATRON SOLUTIONS LLC
5171 California Ave # 200, Irvine
(92617-3066)
PHONE...................949 823-1700
Steve Shaw, *Owner*
EMP: 245
SALES (est): 17.4MM **Privately Held**
SIC: 7372 Application computer software

(P-15827)
PAXATA INC
1800 Seaport Blvd Fl 3, Redwood City
(94063-5543)
PHONE...................650 542-7897
Prakasa Nanduri, *CEO*
David Brewster, *Co-Owner*
Rik Tamm-Daniels, *President*

John Botros, *CFO*
Shankar Ganapathy, *Officer*
EMP: 90
SQ FT: 18,000
SALES (est): 8.7MM **Privately Held**
SIC: 7372 Business oriented computer software

(P-15828)
PAYLOCITY HOLDING CORPORATION
2107 Livingston St, Oakland (94606-5218)
PHONE...................847 956-4850
EMP: 398
SALES (corp-wide): 377.5MM **Publicly Held**
SIC: 7372 Prepackaged software
PA: Paylocity Holding Corporation
　1400 American Ln
　Schaumburg IL 60173
　847 463-3200

(P-15829)
PEOPLE CENTER INC
Also Called: Rippling
2443 Fillmore St, San Francisco
(94115-1814)
PHONE...................781 864-1232
Parker Conrad, *CEO*
Persona Sankaranarayana, *CTO*
EMP: 50
SQ FT: 4,000
SALES: 1MM **Privately Held**
SIC: 7372 Business oriented computer software

(P-15830)
PIERRY INC (PA)
557 Grand St, Redwood City (94062-2065)
PHONE...................800 860-7953
Josh Pierry, *CEO*
Ben Lee, *Chief Mktg Ofcr*
David Buchanan, *Officer*
Ozzie Thoreson, *Vice Pres*
Russell Zermani, *Vice Pres*
EMP: 50 **EST:** 2014
SALES (est): 7.8MM **Privately Held**
SIC: 7372 7311 Prepackaged software; advertising agencies

(P-15831)
PILLAR DATA SYSTEMS INC
2840 Junction Ave, San Jose (95134-1922)
PHONE...................408 503-4000
Michael L Workman, *CEO*
Nancy Holleran, *President*
Edward Hayes, *CFO*
Warren Webster, *Treasurer*
Adrian Jones, *Senior VP*
EMP: 409
SQ FT: 80,000
SALES (est): 29.3MM
SALES (corp-wide): 39.8B **Publicly Held**
WEB: www.pillardata.com
SIC: 7372 Prepackaged software
PA: Oracle Corporation
　500 Oracle Pkwy
　Redwood City CA 94065
　650 506-7000

(P-15832)
PLX TECHNOLOGY INC
1320 Ridder Park Dr, San Jose
(95131-2313)
PHONE...................408 435-7400
Hock Tan, *President*
Anthony Maslowski, *CFO*
Charlie Kawwas, *Senior VP*
Boon Chye Ooi, *Senior VP*
Andy Nallappan, *Vice Pres*
▲ **EMP:** 157
SQ FT: 55,000
SALES (est): 12.1MM
SALES (corp-wide): 17.6B **Publicly Held**
WEB: www.plxtech.com
SIC: 7372 3674 Business oriented computer software; integrated circuits, semiconductor networks, etc.
HQ: Avago Technologies Wireless (U.S.A.) Manufacturing Llc
　4380 Ziegler Rd
　Fort Collins CO 80525
　970 288-2575

▲ = Import ▼=Export
◆ =Import/Export

(P-15833)
POLARION SOFTWARE INC
1001 Marina Village Pkwy # 403, Alameda
(94501-6401)
PHONE..........................877 572-4005
Frank Schrder, *CEO*
George Briner, *CFO*
Stefano Rizzo, *Senior VP*
Nikolay Entin, *Vice Pres*
Jiri Walek, *Vice Pres*
EMP: 90
SALES (est): 7.2MM **Privately Held**
SIC: 7372 Prepackaged software

(P-15834)
PORTELLUS INC
2522 Chambers Rd Ste 100, Tustin
(92780-6962)
PHONE..........................949 250-9600
John Le, *President*
EMP: 80
SALES: 3.6MM **Privately Held**
WEB: www.portellus.com
SIC: 7372 Prepackaged software

(P-15835)
POWERSCHOOL GROUP LLC (HQ)
150 Parkshore Dr, Folsom (95630-4710)
PHONE..........................916 288-1636
Hardeep Gulati, *CEO*
Mark Oldemeyer, *CFO*
Chad Dirks, *Vice Pres*
Varughese George, *Vice Pres*
Alan Taylor, *Vice Pres*
EMP: 146
SALES (est): 69.6MM
SALES (corp-wide): 4.4B **Privately Held**
SIC: 7372 Prepackaged software
PA: Vista Equity Partners Management, Llc
    4 Embarcadero Ctr # 2000
    San Francisco CA 94111
    415 765-6500

(P-15836)
QAD INC (PA)
100 Innovation Pl, Santa Barbara
(93108-2268)
PHONE..........................805 566-6000
Pamela M Lopker, *Ch of Bd*
Tony Yip, *President*
Daniel Lender, *CFO*
Anton Chilton, *Exec VP*
Kara Bellamy, *Senior VP*
EMP: 148
SQ FT: 120,000
SALES: 305MM **Publicly Held**
WEB: www.qad.com
SIC: 7372 7371 Business oriented computer software; custom computer programming services

(P-15837)
QUEST SOFTWARE INC
Packettrap Networks
118 2nd St Fl 6, San Francisco
(94105-3620)
PHONE..........................415 373-2222
Steven M Goodman, *President*
EMP: 65
SALES (corp-wide): 1.7B **Privately Held**
SIC: 7372 Prepackaged software
HQ: Quest Software, Inc.
    4 Polaris Way
    Aliso Viejo CA 92656
    949 754-8000

(P-15838)
QUEST SOFTWARE INC
Also Called: Cloud Automation Division
4 Polaris Way, Aliso Viejo (92656-5356)
PHONE..........................949 754-8000
Alexa Ives, *Partner*
Brian Odonnell, *Partner*
Anne Simpson, *Partner*
Matt Vitale, *Vice Pres*
Pritesh Doshi, *Regional Mgr*
EMP: 80
SALES (corp-wide): 1.7B **Privately Held**
SIC: 7372 Prepackaged software
HQ: Quest Software, Inc.
    4 Polaris Way
    Aliso Viejo CA 92656
    949 754-8000

(P-15839)
QUMU INC
1100 Grundy Ln Ste 110, San Bruno
(94066-3072)
PHONE..........................650 396-8530
Jim Stewart, *CFO*
Chad Sears, *Vice Pres*
Dolores Rios, *Executive Asst*
Taimur Mirza, *Sr Software Eng*
Hamid Porasl, *Software Dev*
EMP: 56
SQ FT: 13,000
SALES (est): 9.5MM
SALES (corp-wide): 28.1MM **Publicly Held**
WEB: www.mediapublisher.com
SIC: 7372 Business oriented computer software
PA: Qumu Corporation
    510 1st Ave N Ste 305
    Minneapolis MN 55403
    612 638-9100

(P-15840)
REAL SOFTWARE SYSTEMS LLC (PA)
21255 Burbank Blvd # 220, Woodland Hills
(91367-6610)
PHONE..........................818 313-8000
Kent Sahin, *Mng Member*
Jenny Gonzales, *Consultant*
EMP: 60
SALES (est): 8MM **Privately Held**
WEB: www.realsoftwaresystems.com
SIC: 7372 Business oriented computer software

(P-15841)
REDSEAL INC
940 Stewart Dr Ste 101, Sunnyvale
(94085-3912)
PHONE..........................408 641-2200
Ray Rothrock, *Ch of Bd*
Pete Sinclair, *COO*
Bob Finley, *CFO*
Julie Parrish, *Chief Mktg Ofcr*
Gordon Adams, *Officer*
EMP: 100
SQ FT: 6,500
SALES (est): 21.3MM **Privately Held**
WEB: www.redseal.net
SIC: 7372 Prepackaged software

(P-15842)
REVJET
981 Industrial Rd Ste F, San Carlos
(94070-4150)
PHONE..........................650 508-2215
Patrick McNenny, *Vice Pres*
Bradley McKeon, *Vice Pres*
David Mackay, *Risk Mgmt Dir*
Serge Ioffe, *CTO*
Andriy Gusyev, *Engrg Dir*
EMP: 110 **EST:** 2017
SALES (est): 2.3MM **Privately Held**
SIC: 7372 Application computer software

(P-15843)
SABA SOFTWARE INC (PA)
4120 Dublin Blvd Ste 200, Dublin
(94568-7759)
PHONE..........................877 722-2101
Phil Saunders, *President*
Pete Low, *CFO*
Debbie Shotwell, *Executive*
Michelle Humphrey, *Executive*
Tina Garnaat, *Marketing Staff*
EMP: 100
SQ FT: 36,000
SALES (est): 196.6MM **Privately Held**
WEB: www.saba.com
SIC: 7372 7371 Application computer software; computer software development & applications

(P-15844)
SAGE SOFTWARE INC
1380 Tatan Trail Rd, Burlingame (94010)
PHONE..........................650 579-3628
Mau Chung Chang, *Branch Mgr*
EMP: 245
SALES (corp-wide): 2.2B **Privately Held**
SIC: 7372 Business oriented computer software

HQ: Sage Software International, Inc.
    271 17th St Nw Ste 1100
    Atlanta GA 30363
    866 996-7243

(P-15845)
SAGE SOFTWARE HOLDINGS INC (HQ)
6561 Irvine Center Dr, Irvine (92618-2118)
PHONE..........................866 530-7243
Stev Swenson, *CEO*
Mack Lout, *CFO*
Doug Meyer, *Vice Pres*
EMP: 400
SALES (est): 516.3MM
SALES (corp-wide): 2.2B **Privately Held**
SIC: 7372 7371 Business oriented computer software; custom computer programming services
PA: The Sage Group Plc.
    North Park Avenue
    Newcastle-Upon-Tyne NE13
    191 294-3000

(P-15846)
SALESFORCECOM INC (PA)
1 Market Ste 300, San Francisco
(94105-5188)
PHONE..........................415 901-7000
Marc Benioff, *Ch of Bd*
Keith Block, *President*
Mark Hawkins, *President*
Amy Weaver, *President*
Joe Allanson, *Senior VP*
EMP: 600 **EST:** 1999
SALES: 10.4B **Publicly Held**
WEB: www.salesforce.com
SIC: 7372 7375 Business oriented computer software; information retrieval services

(P-15847)
SAS INSTITUTE INC
Salesstock.com
1148 N Lemon St, Orange (92867-4701)
PHONE..........................949 250-9999
Shawn Anthony Stiltz, *Vice Pres*
EMP: 56
SALES (corp-wide): 3B **Privately Held**
SIC: 7372 Application computer software; business oriented computer software; educational computer software
PA: Sas Institute Inc.
    100 Sas Campus Dr
    Cary NC 27513
    919 677-8000

(P-15848)
SCHOOL INNOVATIONS ACHIEVEMENT (PA)
5200 Golden Foothill Pkwy, El Dorado Hills
(95762-9610)
PHONE..........................916 933-2290
Jeffrey C Williams, *CEO*
Jenn Abresch, *Partner*
Gemma Ball, *Partner*
Susan Cook, *COO*
Edgar Lopez, *Regional Mgr*
EMP: 95
SQ FT: 25,000
SALES: 14.8MM **Privately Held**
WEB: www.sia-us.com
SIC: 7372 8742 Prepackaged software; management consulting services

(P-15849)
SCOPELY INC (PA)
3530 Hayden Ave Ste A, Culver City
(90232-2413)
PHONE..........................323 400-6618
Walter Driver III, *President*
Eytan Elbaz, *Vice Pres*
Eric Futoran, *Vice Pres*
Mary Bloom, *Director*
Liz Liu, *Manager*
EMP: 200
SALES (est): 8.5MM **Privately Held**
SIC: 7372 Home entertainment computer software

(P-15850)
SHAREDATA INC
Also Called: Sharedta/E Trade Bus Solutions
2465 Augustine Dr, Santa Clara (95054)
PHONE..........................408 490-2500
Laura Fay, *President*

EMP: 53
SALES (est): 1.9MM **Privately Held**
SIC: 7372 Business oriented computer software

(P-15851)
SHOTSPOTTER INC
Also Called: SST
7979 Gateway Blvd Ste 210, Newark
(94560-1158)
PHONE..........................510 794-3100
Ralph A Clark, *President*
Alan R Stewart, *CFO*
Thomas Groos, *Bd of Directors*
Marc Morial, *Bd of Directors*
Paul S Ames, *Senior VP*
EMP: 76
SQ FT: 12,020
SALES: 23.7MM **Privately Held**
WEB: www.shotspotter.com
SIC: 7372 7382 Prepackaged software; security systems services

(P-15852)
SIGHT MACHINE INC
243 Vallejo St, San Francisco (94111-1511)
PHONE..........................888 461-5739
Jon Sobel, *CEO*
John Stone, *President*
Syed Hoda, *Chief Mktg Ofcr*
Jerry Wu, *Officer*
Kurt Demaagd, *Vice Pres*
EMP: 60
SQ FT: 6,500
SALES (est): 2MM **Privately Held**
SIC: 7372 Business oriented computer software

(P-15853)
SLACK TECHNOLOGIES INC (PA)
500 Howard St, San Francisco
(94105-3000)
PHONE..........................415 579-9153
Daniel Stewart Butterfield, *CEO*
April Underwood, *Officer*
Ved Kodipyaka, *Info Tech Dir*
Michelle Lusen, *Recruiter*
Adams Keith, *Chief*
EMP: 148
SALES (est): 272.4MM **Privately Held**
SIC: 7372 Business oriented computer software

(P-15854)
SMITH MICRO SOFTWARE INC (PA)
51 Columbia, Aliso Viejo (92656-1456)
PHONE..........................949 362-5800
William W Smith Jr, *Ch of Bd*
David Blakeney, *President*
Timothy C Huffmyer, *CFO*
Thomas Campbell, *Bd of Directors*
Samuel Gulko, *Bd of Directors*
EMP: 136
SQ FT: 24,688
SALES: 22.9MM **Publicly Held**
WEB: www.smithmicro.com
SIC: 7372 Business oriented computer software

(P-15855)
SNAPLOGIC INC (PA)
1825 S Grant St Ste 550, San Mateo
(94402-2719)
PHONE..........................888 494-1570
Gaurav Dhillon, *CEO*
Vaikom Krishnan, *President*
Bob Parker, *CFO*
Robert J Parker, *CFO*
David Downing, *Chief Mktg Ofcr*
EMP: 140
SALES (est): 28.8MM **Privately Held**
SIC: 7372 Business oriented computer software

(P-15856)
SOCIALIZE INC
450 Townsend St 102, San Francisco
(94107-1510)
PHONE..........................415 529-4019
Daniel R Odio, *CEO*
Sean Shadmand, *President*
Isaac Mosquera, *CTO*
EMP: 50

P R O D U C T S & S V C S

SALES (est): 2.8MM
SALES (corp-wide): 12MM **Privately Held**
SIC: 7372 Business oriented computer software
PA: Sharethis, Inc.
4005 Miranda Ave Ste 100
Palo Alto CA 94304
650 641-0191

(P-15857)
SOFTWARE AG INC
Also Called: Software AG of Virginia
2901 Tasman Dr Ste 219, Santa Clara
(95054-1138)
PHONE................................408 490-5300
Karl-Heinz Streibich, *Branch Mgr*
Artie Alvidrez, *Senior Mgr*
EMP: 119
SALES (corp-wide): 1B **Privately Held**
SIC: 7372 Application computer software
HQ: Software Ag, Inc.
11700 Plaza America Dr # 700
Reston VA 20190
703 860-5050

(P-15858)
SONIC SOLUTIONS HOLDINGS INC
2830 De La Cruz Blvd, Santa Clara
(95050-2619)
PHONE................................408 562-8400
Brian Botteri, *Manager*
EMP: 345
SALES (est): 120.6K
SALES (corp-wide): 826.4MM **Publicly Held**
SIC: 7372 Home entertainment computer software
PA: Tivo Corporation
2160 Gold St
San Jose CA 95002
408 519-9100

(P-15859)
SPIGIT INC
275 Battery St Ste 1000, San Francisco
(94111-3333)
PHONE................................855 774-4480
Scott Raskin, *President*
Stephen Anderson, *CFO*
Matt Chapman, *Vice Pres*
Doug Collins, *Vice Pres*
Steve Dilauro, *Vice Pres*
EMP: 99
SQ FT: 12,500
SALES (est): 13.9MM
SALES (corp-wide): 31MM **Privately Held**
SIC: 7372 Business oriented computer software
PA: Spigit Holdings Corporation
275 Battery St Ste 1000
San Francisco CA 94111
415 229-4400

(P-15860)
SPLUNK INC (PA)
270 Brannan St, San Francisco
(94107-2007)
PHONE................................415 848-8400
Douglas Merritt, *President*
Joe Massanova, *Partner*
Godfrey Sullivan, *Ch of Bd*
Susan St Ledger, *President*
David Conte, *CFO*
EMP: 160
SQ FT: 182,000
SALES: 1.2B **Publicly Held**
WEB: www.splunk.com
SIC: 7372 Business oriented computer software

(P-15861)
SQUARE INC (PA)
1455 Market St Ste 600, San Francisco
(94103-1332)
PHONE................................415 375-3176
Jack Dorsey, *Ch of Bd*
Sarah Friar, *CFO*
Jim McKelvey, *Bd of Directors*
Ajmere Dale, *Officer*
David Grodsky, *Officer*
EMP: 50
SQ FT: 338,910

SALES: 2.2B **Publicly Held**
SIC: 7372 Prepackaged software

(P-15862)
SRA OSS INC
5201 Great America Pkwy # 419, Santa
Clara (95054-1143)
PHONE................................408 855-8200
RAO Papolu, *President*
EMP: 160
SQ FT: 5,000
SALES (est): 15.6MM
SALES (corp-wide): 369.9MM **Privately Held**
WEB: www.sraoss.com
SIC: 7372 Publishers' computer software
HQ: Software Research Associates, Inc.
2-32-8, Minamiikebukuro
Toshima-Ku TKY 171-0
359 792-111

(P-15863)
STACKLA INC
33 New Montgomery St, San Francisco
(94105-4506)
PHONE................................415 528-4910
Damien Mahoney, *CEO*
Peter Cassaidy,
EMP: 63
SALES (est): 2.4MM **Privately Held**
SIC: 7372 Application computer software

(P-15864)
STALKER SOFTWARE INC
Also Called: Communigate Systems
125 Park Pl Ste 210, Richmond
(94801-3980)
PHONE................................415 569-2280
Vladimir Butenko, *President*
Philip Slater, *Executive*
Azdio Ballesteros, *Director*
EMP: 50
SALES (est): 5.6MM **Privately Held**
WEB: www.communigate.com
SIC: 7372 7371 Prepackaged software;
custom computer programming services

(P-15865)
STRATCITYCOM LLC
1317 Monterosso St, Danville
(94506-1960)
PHONE................................408 858-0006
Alfy Louis, *Mng Member*
EMP: 74
SQ FT: 3,400
SALES (est): 1.6MM **Privately Held**
SIC: 7372 Prepackaged software

(P-15866)
STRATEGIC INSIGHTS INC
Also Called: Brightscope
9191 Towne Centre Dr # 401, San Diego
(92122-1225)
PHONE................................858 452-7500
David Gaunt, *Vice Pres*
Paul Collins, *Sr Software Eng*
Chris Ferguson, *Sr Software Eng*
Marcus Planta, *Software Dev*
Justin Siu, *Software Engr*
EMP: 65 **Privately Held**
SIC: 7372 Business oriented computer software
PA: Strategic Insights, Inc.
805 3rd Ave
New York NY 10022

(P-15867)
STRATEGY COMPANION CORP
3240 El Camino Real # 120, Irvine
(92602-1384)
PHONE................................714 460-8398
Robert Sterling, *President*
Eric Halverson, *Partner*
Grace Lin, *Office Admin*
Al Siroon, *Sales Executive*
Bill Tang, *Manager*
EMP: 70
SALES (est): 5.5MM **Privately Held**
SIC: 7372 Prepackaged software
PA: Strategy Companion Corp.
Scotia Centre 4th Floor
George Town GR CAYMAN

(P-15868)
STREVUS INC
455 Market St Ste 1670, San Francisco
(94105-2472)
PHONE................................415 704-8182
Ken Hoang, *CEO*
Gregg Loos, *President*
Dmitri Korablev, *Vice Pres*
Ken Price, *Vice Pres*
Jennifer Turcotte, *Vice Pres*
EMP: 60
SALES (est): 5MM **Privately Held**
SIC: 7372 7371 Business oriented computer software; computer software development

(P-15869)
STRYDER CORP
Also Called: Handshake
225 Bush St Fl 12, San Francisco
(94104-4254)
P.O. Box 40770 (94140-0770)
PHONE................................415 981-8400
Garrett Lord, *Ch of Bd*
Ben Christensen, *Principal*
Scott Ringwelski, *Principal*
EMP: 100 **EST:** 2014
SALES (est): 404.2K **Privately Held**
SIC: 7372 7371 7379 Educational computer software; application computer software; business oriented computer software; computer software development & applications; computer related consulting services

(P-15870)
SYAPSE INC
303 2nd St Ste S650, San Francisco
(94107-2297)
PHONE................................650 924-1461
Gary J Kurtzman MD, *CEO*
Jonathan Hirsch, *President*
Dennis Shin, *Ch Credit Ofcr*
James Lim, *Senior VP*
Andreas Heid, *Vice Pres*
EMP: 87
SALES (est): 3.2MM **Privately Held**
SIC: 7372 Prepackaged software

(P-15871)
SYNERGEX INTERNATIONAL CORP
2330 Gold Meadow Way, Gold River
(95670-4471)
PHONE................................916 635-7300
Michele C Wong, *CEO*
Serena Channel, *Partner*
Vigfus A Asmundson, *Shareholder*
Georgia Petersen, *Shareholder*
Thomas J Powers, *Shareholder*
EMP: 55
SQ FT: 26,000
SALES (est): 8.8MM **Privately Held**
WEB: www.synergex.com
SIC: 7372 Business oriented computer software

(P-15872)
SYNOPSYS INC (PA)
690 E Middlefield Rd, Mountain View
(94043-4033)
PHONE................................650 584-5000
Aart J De Geus, *Ch of Bd*
CHI-Foon Chan, *President*
Trac Pham, *CFO*
Joseph W Logan, *Officer*
Ahsan Bootehsaz, *Vice Pres*
EMP: 500
SQ FT: 341,000
SALES: 2.7B **Publicly Held**
WEB: www.synopsys.com
SIC: 7372 Prepackaged software

(P-15873)
SYNOPSYS INC
199 S Los Robles Ave # 400, Pasadena
(91101-4634)
PHONE................................626 795-9101
George Bayz, *CEO*
Jake Jacobsen, *Technical Staff*
Geoff Suzuki, *Sales Staff*
EMP: 90
SALES (corp-wide): 2.7B **Publicly Held**
SIC: 7372 8711 Application computer software; engineering services

PA: Synopsys, Inc.
690 E Middlefield Rd
Mountain View CA 94043
650 584-5000

(P-15874)
SYNPLICITY INC (HQ)
690 E Middlefield Rd, Mountain View
(94043-4010)
PHONE................................650 584-5000
Gary Meyers, *President*
Alisa Yaffa, *Ch of Bd*
Andrew Dauman, *President*
John J Hanlon, *CFO*
Andrew Haines, *Senior VP*
EMP: 160
SQ FT: 66,212
SALES (est): 17.8MM
SALES (corp-wide): 2.7B **Publicly Held**
WEB: www.synplicity.com
SIC: 7372 Prepackaged software
PA: Synopsys, Inc.
690 E Middlefield Rd
Mountain View CA 94043
650 584-5000

(P-15875)
TALIX INC
660 3rd St Ste 302, San Francisco
(94107-1921)
PHONE................................628 220-3885
Derek Gordon, *President*
Paul Clip, *Vice Pres*
Shahyan Currimbhoy, *Vice Pres*
Ashmi Shah, *Vice Pres*
Niraj Katwala, *CTO*
EMP: 70
SALES (est): 2MM **Privately Held**
SIC: 7372 8099 Application computer software; blood related health services

(P-15876)
TANGOE INC
9920 Pcf Hts Blvd Ste 200, San Diego
(92121)
PHONE................................858 452-6800
Sandy Jimenez, *Branch Mgr*
EMP: 100
SALES (corp-wide): 383.5MM **Privately Held**
SIC: 7372 Application computer software
HQ: Tangoe Us, Inc.
169 Lackawanna Ave Ste 2b
Parsippany NJ 07054
973 257-0300

(P-15877)
TEKEVER CORPORATION
5201 Great America Pkwy, Santa Clara
(95054-1122)
PHONE................................408 730-2617
Michael L Margolis, *CEO*
Andre O Oliveira, *Vice Pres*
Robert Whitehouse, *Business Dir*
EMP: 70
SALES (est): 3.3MM **Privately Held**
WEB: www.tekever.com
SIC: 7372 Prepackaged software

(P-15878)
THOUSANDEYES INC (PA)
201 Mission St Ste 1700, San Francisco
(94105-8102)
PHONE................................415 513-4526
Mohit Lad, *CEO*
Mike Staiger, *CFO*
Sanjay Mehta, *Chief Mktg Ofcr*
Dave Fraleigh, *Vice Pres*
James Gibbon, *Executive*
EMP: 75
SALES (est): 17.4MM **Privately Held**
SIC: 7372 Business oriented computer software

(P-15879)
TI LIMITED LLC (PA)
20335 Ventura Blvd, Woodland Hills
(91364-2444)
PHONE................................323 877-5991
ARI Daniels,
Alberto Gamez,
EMP: 52 **EST:** 2016
SQ FT: 9,000
SALES: 9MM **Privately Held**
SIC: 7372 8748 Business oriented computer software; business consulting

▲ = Import ▼=Export
◆ =Import/Export

(P-15880)
TRAVIDIA INC (PA)
265 Airpark Blvd Ste 500, Chico
(95973-9519)
PHONE..............................530 343-6400
Rand Hutchison, *CEO*
Robert Clark, *Vice Pres*
James Green, *Vice Pres*
Bob Clark, *Director*
Chris Eckland, *Director*
EMP: 150
SQ FT: 10,000
SALES (est): 7.1MM **Privately Held**
WEB: www.travidia.com
SIC: 7372 Prepackaged software

(P-15881)
TRIBEWORX LLC
4 San Joaquin Plz Ste 150, Newport Beach
(92660-5934)
PHONE..............................800 949-3432
EMP: 75
SQ FT: 10,000
SALES (est): 4.9MM **Privately Held**
SIC: 7372

(P-15882)
TRION WORLDS, INC.
2400 Bridge Pkwy 100, Redwood City
(94065-1166)
PHONE..............................650 631-9800
EMP: 294
SALES (est): 55.1MM **Privately Held**
WEB: www.trionworld.com
SIC: 7372 Home entertainment computer
software

(P-15883)
TUBEMOGUL INC
1250 53rd St Ste 1, Emeryville
(94608-2965)
PHONE..............................510 653-0126
Brett Wilson, *President*
Derek Kruger, *Partner*
John Ratz, *Partner*
Robert Gatto, *COO*
Ron Will, *CFO*
EMP: 68
SQ FT: 49,000
SALES: 180.7MM
SALES (corp-wide): 7.3B **Publicly Held**
SIC: 7372 Application computer software
PA: Adobe Inc.
345 Park Ave
San Jose CA 95110
408 536-6000

(P-15884)
TZ HOLDINGS LP
567 San Nicolas Dr # 120, Newport Beach
(92660-6513)
PHONE..............................949 719-2200
Regina Paolillo, *Principal*
EMP: 2000
SALES (est): 46.9MM **Privately Held**
SIC: 7372 Prepackaged software

(P-15885)
ULTIMO SOFTWARE SOLUTIONS INC
33268 Central Ave 2, Union City
(94587-2010)
PHONE..............................408 943-1490
Venkatasubhash Pasumarthy, *President*
Smita Pasumarthi, *CFO*
Saurabh Srivastava, *Consultant*
EMP: 127
SQ FT: 4,000
SALES (est): 10.9MM **Privately Held**
WEB: www.ultimosoft.com
SIC: 7372 Prepackaged software

(P-15886)
UPSTANDING LLC
Also Called: Mobilityware
440 Exchange Ste 100, Irvine
(92602-1390)
PHONE..............................949 788-9900
Dave Yonamine,
Claudia Avitabile, *Office Mgr*
Carrie Collins, *Admin Asst*
Scott Hillier, *Technical Mgr*
John Libby,
EMP: 180
SQ FT: 48,000

SALES (est): 2.5MM **Privately Held**
WEB: www.upstanding.com
SIC: 7372 Business oriented computer
software

(P-15887)
URBAN TRADING SOFTWARE INC
21227 Foothill Blvd, Hayward
(94541-1517)
PHONE..............................877 633-6171
Soufyan Abouahmed, *Principal*
EMP: 50
SALES (est): 1.2MM **Privately Held**
SIC: 7372 Prepackaged software

(P-15888)
VEEVA SYSTEMS INC (PA)
4280 Hacienda Dr, Pleasanton
(94588-2719)
PHONE..............................925 452-6500
Peter P Gassner, *CEO*
Peter Harbin, *Partner*
Gordon Ritter, *Ch of Bd*
Matthew J Wallach, *President*
Timothy S Cabral, *CFO*
EMP: 114
SALES: 685.5MM **Publicly Held**
SIC: 7372 7371 7379 Prepackaged soft-
ware; software programming applications;
computer related consulting services

(P-15889)
VINDICIA INC
2988 Campus Dr Ste 300, San Mateo
(94403-2531)
PHONE..............................650 264-4700
Kris Nagel, *CEO*
Mark Elrod, *Exec VP*
Hurst Arthur, *Vice Pres*
Bryta Schulz, *Vice Pres*
Jason Knight, *Administration*
EMP: 135
SQ FT: 9,000
SALES (est): 15.3MM **Privately Held**
SIC: 7372 Business oriented computer
software
HQ: Amdocs, Inc.
1390 Timberlake Manor Pkw
Chesterfield MO 63017
314 212-7000

(P-15890)
VISUALON INC
2590 N 1st St Ste 100, San Jose
(95131-1021)
PHONE..............................408 645-6618
Andy Lin, *President*
Bill Lin, *Senior VP*
Sean Torsney, *Senior VP*
EMP: 120
SALES (est): 25MM **Privately Held**
WEB: www.visualon.com
SIC: 7372 Prepackaged software

(P-15891)
WEST COAST CONSULTING LLC (PA)
9233 Research Dr Ste 200, Irvine
(92618-4294)
PHONE..............................949 250-4102
Rajat Khurana,
Misty Chaudhry, *Executive*
Sagar Chand, *Tech Recruiter*
Yogesh Tomar, *Tech Recruiter*
Syed Shoaib, *Human Res Mgr*
EMP: 125
SALES (est): 14MM **Privately Held**
WEB: www.westcoastllc.com
SIC: 7372 Prepackaged software

(P-15892)
WIND RIVER SYSTEMS INC (HQ)
500 Wind River Way, Alameda
(94501-1162)
PHONE..............................510 748-4100
Jim Douglas, *CEO*
Shiva Kumar, *Partner*
Scot Morrision, *President*
Barry R Mainz, *COO*
Jane Bon, *CFO*
EMP: 148
SQ FT: 273,000

SALES (est): 349.9MM **Privately Held**
WEB: www.windriver.com
SIC: 7372 7373 Application computer software; systems software development
services

(P-15893)
WIND RIVER SYSTEMS INC
10505 Sorrento Valley Rd, San Diego
(92121-1618)
PHONE..............................858 824-3100
Brad Murdoch, *Vice Pres*
Arch Hughes, *Director*
EMP: 100 **Privately Held**
WEB: www.windriver.com
SIC: 7372 Prepackaged software
HQ: Wind River Systems, Inc.
500 Wind River Way
Alameda CA 94501
510 748-4100

(P-15894)
WME BI LLC
17075 Camino, San Diego (92127)
PHONE..............................877 592-2472
EMP: 60
SALES (est): 1.4MM **Privately Held**
SIC: 7372 Operating systems computer
software

(P-15895)
WORDSMART CORPORATION
10025 Mesa Rim Rd, San Diego
(92121-2913)
P.O. Box 366, La Jolla (92038-0366)
PHONE..............................858 565-8068
David Kay, *CEO*
EMP: 70
SQ FT: 12,375
SALES (est): 9.4MM **Privately Held**
WEB: www.wordsmart.com
SIC: 7372 Educational computer software

(P-15896)
XAVIENT INFO SYSTEMS INC
Also Called: Xavient Digital
2125 N Madera Rd Ste B, Simi Valley
(93065-7710)
PHONE..............................805 955-4111
Rajeev Tandon, *CEO*
Jessica Zhou, *Partner*
Saif Ahmad, *President*
Arshad Majeed, *Exec VP*
Kurt Eltz, *Senior VP*
EMP: 1800
SALES (corp-wide): 10.4B **Privately Held**
SIC: 7372 Business oriented computer
software
HQ: Telus International (U.S) Corp.
2251 S Decatur Blvd
Las Vegas NV 89102
702 238-7900

(P-15897)
XCELMOBILITY INC
2225 E Byshore Rd Ste 200, Palo Alto
(94303)
PHONE..............................650 320-1728
Zhixiong WEI, *Ch of Bd*
LI Ouyang, *CFO*
Ying Yang, *Admin Sec*
EMP: 98
SALES (est): 384.5K **Privately Held**
SIC: 7372 7999 Business oriented com-
puter software; gambling & lottery serv-
ices

(P-15898)
YUJA INC
2168 Ringwood Ave, San Jose
(95131-1720)
PHONE..............................888 257-2278
Ajit Singh, *President*
Nathan Arora, *Officer*
Nannette Don, *Sales Staff*
Boudreau Kline, *Manager*
Smith Isaac, *Accounts Mgr*
EMP: 125
SALES (est): 990K **Privately Held**
SIC: 7372 Prepackaged software

(P-15899)
ZENDESK INC (PA)
1019 Market St, San Francisco
(94103-1612)
PHONE..............................415 418-7506

Mikkel Svane, *Ch of Bd*
Adrian McDermott, *President*
Elena Gomez, *CFO*
Inamarie Johnson,
John Geschke, *Senior VP*
EMP: 148
SQ FT: 18,000
SALES: 430.4MM **Publicly Held**
SIC: 7372 Business oriented computer
software

(P-15900)
ZENPAYROLL INC (PA)
Also Called: Gusto
525 20th St, San Francisco (94107-4345)
PHONE..............................800 936-0383
Joshua D Reeves, *CEO*
Lauren Olson, *Partner*
Mike Dinsdale, *CFO*
Tomer London,
Lexi Reese, *Officer*
EMP: 500
SALES (est): 4.9MM **Privately Held**
SIC: 7372 Business oriented computer
software

(P-15901)
ZINIO SYSTEMS INC
114 Sansome St Fl 4, San Francisco
(94104-3803)
PHONE..............................415 494-2700
Rusty Lewis, *CEO*
Michelle Bottomley, *President*
Richard A Maggiotto, *President*
Virendra Vase, *COO*
Tom Nofziger, *CFO*
EMP: 75
SALES (est): 8.8MM **Privately Held**
WEB: www.zinio.com
SIC: 7372 Publishers' computer software

(P-15902)
ZSCALER INC (PA)
110 Rose Orchard Way, San Jose
(95134-1358)
PHONE..............................408 533-0288
Jay Chaudhry, *Ch of Bd*
Remo Canessa, *CFO*
Micheline Nijmeh, *Chief Mktg Ofcr*
Robert Schlossman,
Amit Sinha, *Exec VP*
EMP: 140
SQ FT: 56,000
SALES: 125.7MM **Publicly Held**
SIC: 7372 Prepackaged software

(P-15903)
ZUORA INC (PA)
3050 S Del St Ste 301, San Mateo (94403)
PHONE..............................800 425-1281
Tien Tzuo, *Ch of Bd*
Marc Diouane, *President*
Tyler Sloat, *CFO*
Brent R Cromley Jr, *Senior VP*
Jennifer W Pileggi, *Senior VP*
EMP: 300
SQ FT: 29,000
SALES: 167.9MM **Publicly Held**
SIC: 7372 Business oriented computer
software

(P-15904)
ZYRION INC
440 N Wolfe Rd, Sunnyvale (94085-3869)
PHONE..............................408 524-7424
EMP: 75
SQ FT: 6,000
SALES (est): 4.7MM **Privately Held**
SIC: 7372
PA: Kaseya Global Ireland Limited
Commerzbank House
Dublin

**7373 Computer Integrated
Systems Design**

(P-15905)
10UP INC
2765 Carradale Dr, Roseville (95661-4089)
PHONE..............................888 571-7130
Jacob Goldman, *Owner*
Ivan Lopez, *Engineer*
Veronica Bruce, *Finance Dir*

P
R
O
D
U
C
T
S

&

S
V
C
S

Taylor Lovett, *Director*
EMP: 95
SQ FT: 1,300
SALES (est): 6.1MM **Privately Held**
SIC: 7373 Systems software development services

(P-15906)
A10 NETWORKS INC (PA)
3 W Plumeria Dr, San Jose (95134-2111)
PHONE..............................408 325-8668
Lee Chen, *Ch of Bd*
Tom Constantino, *CFO*
Alan Henricks, *Bd of Directors*
Robert Cochran, *Exec VP*
Neil Wu Becker, *Vice Pres*
EMP: 837
SQ FT: 79,803
SALES (est): 235.4MM **Publicly Held**
WEB: www.a10networks.com
SIC: 7373 Systems integration services; systems software development services; computer system selling services

(P-15907)
ACOM SOLUTIONS INC (PA)
2850 E 29th St, Long Beach (90806-2313)
PHONE..............................562 424-7899
Patrick S McMahon, *President*
Steve Snider, *CFO*
Edward J Kennedy, *Chairman*
Mark Firmin, *Vice Pres*
James Scott, *Vice Pres*
▲ **EMP:** 50
SQ FT: 23,000
SALES (est): 40.6MM **Privately Held**
WEB: www.acom.com
SIC: 7373 Systems software development services

(P-15908)
ACTIAN CORPORATION (PA)
2300 Geng Rd Ste 150, Palo Alto (94303-3353)
PHONE..............................650 587-5500
Steve Shine, *CEO*
Lewis Black, *CFO*
Steven Springsteel, *CFO*
Tony Kavanagh, *Chief Mktg Ofcr*
Melissa Ribeiro,
EMP: 70
SQ FT: 20,000
SALES (est): 132.1MM **Privately Held**
WEB: www.ingres.com
SIC: 7373 7372 Systems software development services; business oriented computer software

(P-15909)
ACUMEN LLC
Also Called: Medric
500 Airport Blvd Ste 100, Burlingame (94010-1980)
PHONE..............................650 558-8882
Thomas Macurdy, *Mng Member*
Shally B Stanley, *Managing Dir*
Eddie Onaga, *General Mgr*
Catie Cappadona, *Admin Asst*
Thomas Joynt, *Administration*
EMP: 166
SALES (est): 29.9MM **Privately Held**
WEB: www.acumenllc.com
SIC: 7373 7379 8742 Systems software development services; computer related consulting services; data processing consultant; management consulting services; administrative services consultant

(P-15910)
AEROHIVE NETWORKS INC (PA)
1011 Mccarthy Blvd, Milpitas (95035-7920)
PHONE..............................408 510-6100
David K Flynn, *Ch of Bd*
Remo Canessa, *Bd of Directors*
Curtis Garner, *Bd of Directors*
David Greene, *Chief Mktg Ofcr*
John Ritchie, *Officer*
EMP: 624
SALES: 152.9MM **Publicly Held**
WEB: www.aerohive.com
SIC: 7373 Local area network (LAN) systems integrator

(P-15911)
ALEXANDRIA CLAYTON
Also Called: Net Eternity
2051 Hilltop Dr Ste A16c, Redding (96002-0264)
PHONE..............................530 262-5961
Alexandria Clayton, *Owner*
EMP: 50
SALES (est): 915K **Privately Held**
SIC: 7373 5961 Systems integration services;

(P-15912)
AMSNET INC (PA)
502 Commerce Way, Livermore (94551-7812)
PHONE..............................925 245-6100
Robert Tocci, *CEO*
Joe Moomau, *VP Opers*
EMP: 50
SQ FT: 15,000
SALES: 59.9MM **Privately Held**
SIC: 7373 1731 7378 Systems integration services; computer installation; computer maintenance & repair

(P-15913)
APRISO CORPORATION
301 E Ocean Blvd Ste 1200, Long Beach (90802-4839)
PHONE..............................562 951-8000
James Henderson, *CEO*
Carey Tokirio, *CFO*
Chris Brecher, *Exec VP*
Tom Comstock, *Exec VP*
Yves Vergnolle, *Senior VP*
EMP: 200
SALES (est): 6.7MM
SALES (corp-wide): 1.7B **Privately Held**
WEB: www.apriso.com
SIC: 7373 Computer integrated systems design
PA: Dassault Systemes
10 Rue Marcel Dassault
Velizy Villacoublay 78140
161 626-162

(P-15914)
APTTUS CORPORATION (PA)
1400 Fashion Island Blvd # 100, San Mateo (94404-2061)
PHONE..............................650 445-7700
Kirk Krappe, *CEO*
James E Ellis, *Partner*
Michael Jackson, *Partner*
Allison Wudel, *Partner*
George Kadifa, *Ch of Bd*
EMP: 134
SALES (est): 263.6MM **Privately Held**
SIC: 7373 Systems software development services

(P-15915)
ART & LOGIC INC
Also Called: Artlogic
87 N Raymond Ave, Pasadena (91103-3932)
PHONE..............................818 500-1933
Bob Bajoras, *President*
Paul Hershenson, *Co-Owner*
Tom Bajoras, *Owner*
Andrew Sherbrooke, *Vice Pres*
Jason Bagley, *Sr Software Eng*
EMP: 55
SQ FT: 1,500
SALES (est): 8MM **Privately Held**
WEB: www.artlogic.com
SIC: 7373 7371 7379 Systems software development services; custom computer programming services; computer related consulting services

(P-15916)
AT ROAD INC (HQ)
888 Tasman Dr, Milpitas (95035-7439)
PHONE..............................510 668-1638
Ken Colby, *President*
Michael Walker, *Exec VP*
Ian Gray, *Vice Pres*
Carol Rice-Murphy, *Vice Pres*
EMP: 350
SQ FT: 102,544

SALES (est): 17.5MM
SALES (corp-wide): 2.6B **Publicly Held**
SIC: 7373 7372 Systems integration services; prepackaged software; business oriented computer software
PA: Trimble Inc.
935 Stewart Dr
Sunnyvale CA 94085
408 481-8000

(P-15917)
ATAC (PA)
2770 De La Cruz Blvd, Santa Clara (95050-2624)
PHONE..............................408 736-2822
Mark Cochran, *Chairman*
Scott Simcox, *President*
Charles Winkleman, *CFO*
Jaclyn Mullick, *Admin Asst*
Tom Laird, *Sr Software Eng*
EMP: 81
SQ FT: 31,000
SALES: 21MM **Privately Held**
WEB: www.atac.com
SIC: 7373 7376 7379 8711 Computer integrated systems design; computer facilities management; computer related maintenance services; engineering services; physical research, noncommercial

(P-15918)
AUTOMATION ENGRG SYSTEMS INC
10815 Rancho Bernardo Rd, San Diego (92127-2186)
PHONE..............................858 967-8650
Leo Castaneda, *President*
Gary Mitchell, *Engineer*
Doug Strohl, *Engineer*
EMP: 80
SALES (est): 2.9MM **Privately Held**
SIC: 7373 Systems integration services

(P-15919)
AVEVA SOFTWARE LLC (DH)
Also Called: Wonderware
26561 Rancho Pkwy S, Lake Forest (92630-8301)
PHONE..............................949 727-3200
Ravi Gopinath, *President*
Lori Kane, *President*
James Danley, *Treasurer*
Paul Forney, *Vice Pres*
Jim Griffith, *Vice Pres*
EMP: 350
SALES: 264.3MM
SALES (corp-wide): 200.4K **Privately Held**
SIC: 7373 Computer integrated systems design
HQ: Schneider Electric Systems Usa, Inc.
38 Neponset Ave
Foxboro MA 02035
508 543-8750

(P-15920)
BELL INTEGRATOR INC (PA)
1735 N 1st St Ste 102, San Jose (95112-4530)
PHONE..............................650 943-2415
Andrey Korobitsyn, *CEO*
Eugene Pozdnikov, *COO*
Chris Pigott, *CTO*
Marina Shikhova, *Hum Res Coord*
EMP: 2500
SALES (est): 98.4MM **Privately Held**
SIC: 7373 8731 Systems integration services; computer (hardware) development

(P-15921)
BLUE COAT SYSTEMS LLC (HQ)
350 Ellis St, Mountain View (94043-2202)
PHONE..............................650 527-8000
Gregory S Clark, *CEO*
Donald W Alford, *President*
Michael Fey, *President*
David Yntemai, *President*
Nicholas R Noviello, *CFO*
EMP: 61
SQ FT: 234,000
SALES (est): 32.3MM
SALES (corp-wide): 4.8B **Publicly Held**
WEB: www.cacheflow.com
SIC: 7373 Computer integrated systems design

PA: Symantec Corporation
350 Ellis St
Mountain View CA 94043
650 527-8000

(P-15922)
BRILLIANT SFTWR SOLUTIONS INC
2400 Camino Ramon Ste 170, San Ramon (94583-4373)
PHONE..............................510 742-5120
Narendra Punati, *President*
Sreenivas Veerapaneni, *Vice Pres*
EMP: 75 **EST:** 2000
SALES (est): 5.2MM **Privately Held**
WEB: www.brilliantsoft.com
SIC: 7373 Systems integration services

(P-15923)
CACI INC - FEDERAL
1455 Frazee Rd Ste 700, San Diego (92108-4308)
PHONE..............................619 881-6000
J P London, *Ch of Bd*
EMP: 50
SALES (corp-wide): 4.3B **Publicly Held**
WEB: www.inventure.com
SIC: 7373 Computer integrated systems design
HQ: Caci, Inc. - Federal
1100 N Glebe Rd Ste 200
Arlington VA 22201
703 841-7800

(P-15924)
CADENT INC
Also Called: Orthocad
2560 Orchard Pkwy, San Jose (95131-1033)
PHONE..............................408 470-1000
Timothy Mack, *President*
Roger Blanchette, *CFO*
EMP: 130
SQ FT: 24,000
SALES (est): 12.4MM
SALES (corp-wide): 1.4B **Publicly Held**
WEB: www.orthocad.com
SIC: 7373 Computer systems analysis & design
HQ: Cadent Holdings, Inc.
2560 Orchard Pkwy
San Jose CA
-

(P-15925)
CALCULI CORPORATION
3945 Freedom Cir, Santa Clara (95054-1223)
PHONE..............................408 970-0007
Basheer Janjua, *CEO*
EMP: 50
SALES (est): 915K **Privately Held**
SIC: 7373 8711 Systems engineering, computer related; engineering services

(P-15926)
CAPTIVA SOFTWARE CORPORATION (DH)
10145 Pacific Hts Blvd, San Diego (92121-4234)
PHONE..............................858 320-1000
Reynolds C Bish, *President*
Patrick L Edsell, *Ch of Bd*
Rick E Russo, *CFO*
Howard Dratler, *Exec VP*
Jim Nicol, *Exec VP*
EMP: 80
SQ FT: 25,000
SALES (est): 19.7MM
SALES (corp-wide): 78.6B **Publicly Held**
SIC: 7373 7372 Office computer automation systems integration; prepackaged software
HQ: Emc Corporation
176 South St
Hopkinton MA 01748
508 435-1000

(P-15927)
CARLISLE RESEARCH CORPORATION
7100 Hayvenhurst Ave Ph F, Van Nuys (91406-3804)
PHONE..............................818 785-8677
Jimmy Carlisle, *President*

▲ = Import ▼=Export
◆ =Import/Export

EMP: 54
SQ FT: 52,250
SALES (est): 4.1MM **Privately Held**
WEB: www.cri-corp.com
SIC: 7373 7379 7372 7371 Computer integrated systems design; data processing consultant; prepackaged software; computer software systems analysis & design, custom; software, business & non-game

(P-15928)
CELESTIX NETWORKS INC
215 Fourier Ave Ste 140, Fremont (94539-7837)
PHONE...................510 668-0700
Yong Thye Lin, *CEO*
Bobby Chen, *Finance Dir*
Yong Ping Lin, *Director*
Mark Lloyd, *Director*
EMP: 70
SQ FT: 9,000
SALES (est): 12.3MM **Privately Held**
WEB: www.celestix.com
SIC: 7373 Systems software development services; systems engineering, computer related; systems integration services; local area network (LAN) systems integrator
PA: Celestix Networks Pte Ltd
62 Ubi Road 1
Singapore 40873

(P-15929)
CELLMATICS
2309 Masters Rd, Carlsbad (92008-3843)
PHONE...................760 692-2424
Rose Thomas, *CEO*
EMP: 50
SALES: 250K **Privately Held**
SIC: 7373 Computer integrated systems design

(P-15930)
CENTRO INC
115 Sansome St Ste 1200, San Francisco (94104-3630)
PHONE...................415 788-6190
EMP: 151
SALES (corp-wide): 23.6MM **Privately Held**
SIC: 7373 Systems software development services
PA: Centro, Inc.
11 E Madison St Ste 300
Chicago IL 60602
312 642-7348

(P-15931)
CGTECH (PA)
Also Called: Cgtech Vericut
9000 Research Dr, Irvine (92618-4214)
PHONE...................949 753-1050
Jon L Prun, *President*
Frankie Cates, *Admin Asst*
Heidi Edmonston, *Admin Asst*
Jia Yan, *Sr Software Eng*
Andrei Kvitsinski, *Software Dev*
EMP: 50
SQ FT: 27,000
SALES: 25.5MM **Privately Held**
WEB: www.cgtech.com
SIC: 7373 8243 Computer-aided design (CAD) systems service; computer-aided manufacturing (CAM) systems service; software training, computer

(P-15932)
CITADEL GROUP SOLUTIONS INC
1999 Avenue Of The Stars, Los Angeles (90067-6022)
PHONE...................310 649-7500
Gerald Marshall, *President*
EMP: 51 EST: 2016
SQ FT: 2,100
SALES (est): 929.3K **Privately Held**
SIC: 7373 Systems software development services

(P-15933)
CLINICOMP INTERNATIONAL INC (PA)
9655 Towne Centre Dr, San Diego (92121-1964)
PHONE...................858 546-8202

Chris Haudenschild, *Ch of Bd*
Eloisa Haudenschild, *CFO*
Sarah Crouch Chavez, *Vice Pres*
Sarah Crouch, *Vice Pres*
Jiao Fan, *Vice Pres*
EMP: 100
SQ FT: 42,000
SALES (est): 22.6MM **Privately Held**
WEB: www.clinicomp.com
SIC: 7373 7371 3571 Systems software development services; custom computer programming services; electronic computers

(P-15934)
CNET NETWORKS INC
235 2nd St, San Francisco (94105-3100)
PHONE...................415 344-2000
Mehdi Maghsoodnia, *Bd of Directors*
Matthew Barzun, *Officer*
Eric Schuldt, *Vice Pres*
Joanne Scott, *Vice Pres*
James Symington, *Vice Pres*
EMP: 905
SALES (est): 11.8MM
SALES (corp-wide): 13.7B **Publicly Held**
SIC: 7373 7371 Systems software development services; computer software development & applications
HQ: Cbs Interactive Inc.
235 2nd St
San Francisco CA 94105
-

(P-15935)
COGNIX AUTOMATION INC
3423 Torlano Pl, Pleasanton (94566-2114)
PHONE...................925 464-8822
Prasad Dasari, *President*
EMP: 50
SALES (est): 915K **Privately Held**
SIC: 7373 Office computer automation systems integration

(P-15936)
COMGLOBAL SYSTEMS INC (DH)
1315 Dell Ave, Campbell (95008-6609)
PHONE...................619 321-6000
Fax: 408 374-5209
EMP: 68
SQ FT: 600
SALES (est): 14.9MM
SALES (corp-wide): 335.6MM **Privately Held**
WEB: www.comglobal.com
SIC: 7373
HQ: Analex Corporation
11091 Sunset Hills Rd # 200
Reston VA 20171
703 956-8243

(P-15937)
CORDOBA CORPORATION
1401 N Broadway, Los Angeles (90012-1410)
PHONE...................213 895-0224
George Pla, *President*
Maria Mehranian, *COO*
EMP: 65
SALES (est): 5.4MM **Privately Held**
SIC: 7373 Computer integrated systems design

(P-15938)
CUBIC CORPORATION
Also Called: Cubic Defense Systems
9233 Balboa Ave, San Diego (92123-1513)
PHONE...................858 277-6780
Brigitte Jen, *Branch Mgr*
John Moran, *Officer*
Anthony Verna, *Vice Pres*
Donald Boyd, *Engineer*
Johannes Dharmawan, *Engineer*
EMP: 2000
SALES (corp-wide): 1.4B **Publicly Held**
SIC: 7373 Computer integrated systems design
PA: Cubic Corporation
9333 Balboa Ave
San Diego CA 92123
858 277-6780

(P-15939)
DATA CONTROL CORPORATION
P.O. Box 2069, Granite Bay (95746-2069)
PHONE...................916 774-4000
J Dale Debber, *President*
EMP: 67
SQ FT: 15,000
SALES (est): 3.9MM **Privately Held**
SIC: 7373 Systems software development services

(P-15940)
DATA DOMAIN LLC
2421 Mission College Blvd, Santa Clara (95054-1214)
PHONE...................408 980-4800
Frank Slootman, *President*
Michael P Scarpelli, *CFO*
Nick Bacica, *Senior VP*
Daniel R McGee, *Senior VP*
David L Schneider, *Senior VP*
EMP: 777
SQ FT: 200,000
SALES (est): 94.7MM
SALES (corp-wide): 78.6B **Publicly Held**
WEB: www.datadomain.com
SIC: 7373 Computer integrated systems design
HQ: Emc Corporation
176 South St
Hopkinton MA 01748
508 435-1000

(P-15941)
DATAPARK INC
1631 Neptune Dr, San Leandro (94577-3162)
PHONE...................510 483-7275
Steve Haralambiew, *President*
Lorenza Tomaz, *CFO*
EMP: 60
SQ FT: 9,900
SALES (est): 8.7MM **Privately Held**
WEB: www.dataparkgroup.com
SIC: 7373 Computer integrated systems design

(P-15942)
DELEGATA CORPORATION
2450 Venture Oaks Way # 400, Sacramento (95833-4226)
PHONE...................916 609-5400
Kais Menoufy, *President*
Charles Dunn, *Info Tech Dir*
Bob Martinez, *Pub Rel Dir*
Barbara Halsey, *Chief*
Kevin Malone, *Chief*
EMP: 100
SQ FT: 5,000
SALES (est): 13.8MM **Privately Held**
WEB: www.delegata.com
SIC: 7373 Computer integrated systems design

(P-15943)
DIGITAL KEYSTONE INC
21631 Stevns Crk Blvd A, Cupertino (95014-1169)
PHONE...................650 938-7301
Paolo Siccardo, *CEO*
Luc Vantalon, *CTO*
Freddie Bose, *QA Dir*
EMP: 50
SQ FT: 27,000
SALES (est): 4.4MM **Privately Held**
WEB: www.dkeystone.com
SIC: 7373 Computer integrated systems design

(P-15944)
DIGITAL NETWORKS GROUP INC
20382 Hermana Cir, Lake Forest (92630-8701)
PHONE...................949 428-6333
Jeff Davis, *CEO*
Michael Stammire, *President*
Bart Moran, *Vice Pres*
Chris Ursetta, *Admin Sec*
Gary Stanton, *Info Tech Mgr*
EMP: 100
SALES (est): 32.3MM
SALES (corp-wide): 51.7B **Privately Held**
WEB: www.digitalnetworksgroup.com
SIC: 7373 Computer integrated systems design

HQ: Avidex Industries, L.L.C.
13555 Ne Bel Red Rd # 226
Bellevue WA 98005
425 643-0330

(P-15945)
DIGITALIST USA LTD
128 Spear St Lbby, San Francisco (94105-5160)
PHONE...................949 278-1354
Jo Javier, *Vice Pres*
Mikael Laine, *Technology*
EMP: 1000
SALES (est): 43.3MM **Privately Held**
SIC: 7373 8731 Systems software development services; computer (hardware) development
HQ: Digitalist Group Oyj
Arkadiankatu 2
Helsinki 00100
505 814-075

(P-15946)
DIMENSION DATA NORTH AMER INC
5000 Hopyard Rd, Pleasanton (94588-3348)
PHONE...................925 226-8378
Scott Chudy, *Branch Mgr*
Anthony Beasley, *Executive*
George Bekmezian, *Engineer*
Deepti Jaiswal, *Manager*
EMP: 89
SALES (corp-wide): 110.7B **Privately Held**
SIC: 7373 Computer integrated systems design
HQ: Dimension Data North America, Inc.
110 Penn Plz Fl 16 Flr 16
New York NY 10119
212 613-1220

(P-15947)
DROISYS INC (PA)
4800 Patrick Henry Dr, Santa Clara (95054-1820)
PHONE...................408 874-8333
Sanjiv Goyal, *President*
Shum Mukherjee, *CFO*
Nita Goel, *Vice Pres*
Amit Kumar, *Admin Sec*
Dayal Gosain, *Administration*
EMP: 351
SQ FT: 3,374
SALES (est): 44.8MM **Privately Held**
WEB: www.droisys.com
SIC: 7373 7371 7379 Systems software development services; systems integration services; custom computer programming services; computer software writing services; computer related consulting services

(P-15948)
DYNCORP
Nas Nrth Is Bldg 1479, San Diego (92135)
P.O. Box 189002, Coronado (92178-9002)
PHONE...................619 522-2222
Mike Johnson, *Manager*
EMP: 115
SALES (corp-wide): 16.3B **Privately Held**
WEB: www.dyncorp.com
SIC: 7373 Systems software development services
PA: Dyncorp Llc
1700 Old Meadow Rd
Mc Lean VA 22102
571 722-0210

(P-15949)
E & J GALLO INC
3430 Tully Rd Ste 20, Modesto (95350-0840)
PHONE...................209 287-1716
Colleen Ellen Kenny, *CEO*
Michael Yin, *Principal*
EMP: 99
SALES (est): 2MM **Privately Held**
SIC: 7373 Computer integrated systems design

PRODUCTS & SVCS

(P-15950)
E2 CORP
Also Called: E2 Solutions
8121 Van Nuys Blvd # 308, Panorama City
(91402-5105)
PHONE..................................818 904-5660
Sonia Keshap, *President*
Lolita Munsayac, *Accountant*
Kevin Ragan, *Director*
EMP: 75
SQ FT: 1,550
SALES (est): 6.8MM **Privately Held**
WEB: www.e2solutions.com
SIC: 7373 7371 Computer integrated systems design; computer software systems analysis & design, custom

(P-15951)
ELECTRONIC DATA CARE INC
Also Called: E D C
23670 Hawthorne Blvd # 208, Torrance
(90505-8207)
PHONE..................................310 791-2600
Nabil Salem, *President*
Aref Rashad, *Vice Pres*
Jeff Woods, *Vice Pres*
Jeffrey Woods, *Vice Pres*
Amy Riddle, *VP Human Res*
EMP: 70
SQ FT: 2,500
SALES: 800K **Privately Held**
WEB: www.edatacare.com
SIC: 7373 8299 Systems integration services; educational services

(P-15952)
ELECTRONIC ONLINE SYSTEMS INTL
Also Called: E O S International
2292 Faraday Ave Frnt, Carlsbad
(92008-7237)
PHONE..................................760 431-8400
Scot Cheatham, *President*
Jeff Goodwin, *Vice Pres*
Greg Leiser, *Vice Pres*
Salvatore Provenza, *Vice Pres*
Jeff Smith, *Vice Pres*
EMP: 64
SQ FT: 22,000
SALES (est): 8.8MM **Privately Held**
WEB: www.eosintl.com
SIC: 7373 7371 7372 Turnkey vendors, computer systems; computer software development; prepackaged software

(P-15953)
ELITE INFORMATION GROUP INC (DH)
5100 W Goldleaf Cir # 100, Los Angeles
(90056-1284)
PHONE..................................323 642-5200
Christopher K Poole, *President*
Daniel Tacone, *COO*
Barry D Emerson, *CFO*
EMP: 400
SQ FT: 40,000
SALES (est): 28.6MM **Publicly Held**
WEB: www.eliteis.com
SIC: 7373 7372 Computer integrated systems design; systems software development services; systems integration services; business oriented computer software
HQ: Thomson Reuters Corporation
3 Times Sq
New York NY 10036
646 223-4000

(P-15954)
EMR CPR LLC
48511 Warm Springs Blvd # 206, Fremont
(94539-7746)
PHONE..................................408 471-6804
Edward Ohara, *CEO*
David Ohara, *COO*
EMP: 412
SALES (est): 1.2MM **Privately Held**
SIC: 7373 7374 Systems engineering, computer related; systems integration services; local area network (LAN) systems integrator; data entry service; data verification service

(P-15955)
ENQUERO INC
1551 Mccarthy Blvd # 207, Milpitas
(95035-7442)
PHONE..................................408 406-3203
Arvinder Pal Singh, *CEO*
Hemant Asher, *CFO*
Hemant S Asher, *Principal*
EMP: 80
SALES (est): 292.5K **Privately Held**
SIC: 7373 7379 Systems software development services;

(P-15956)
ERICSSON INC
100 Headquarters Dr, San Jose
(95134-1370)
PHONE..................................408 597-3600
Kevin A Denuccio, *Branch Mgr*
EMP: 1100
SALES (corp-wide): 23.8B **Privately Held**
SIC: 7373 Computer integrated systems design
HQ: Ericsson Inc.
6300 Legacy Dr
Plano TX 75024
972 583-0000

(P-15957)
FORCE10 NETWORKS INC
Also Called: Dell
350 Holger Way, San Jose (95134-1362)
PHONE..................................707 665-4400
Michael S Dell, *CEO*
James Hanley, *President*
Luu Nguyen, *President*
Sachi Sambandan, *President*
Mark Sanders, *President*
EMP: 582 EST: 1999
SQ FT: 97,000
SALES (est): 54.5MM **Privately Held**
WEB: www.force10networks.com
SIC: 7373 Computer integrated systems design

(P-15958)
FRANCISCO PARTNERS LP (HQ)
Also Called: FP
1 Letterman Dr Bldg C, San Francisco
(94129-2402)
PHONE..................................415 418-2900
Dipanjan Deb, *Managing Prtnr*
Chris Adams, *Partner*
Ben Ball, *Partner*
Peter Christodoulo, *Partner*
Neil Garfinkel, *Partner*
EMP: 60
SALES: 181.8MM
SALES (corp-wide): 1.7B **Privately Held**
SIC: 7373 7372 Systems integration services; prepackaged software
PA: Francisco Partners Management, L.P.
1 Letterman Dr Ste 410
San Francisco CA 94129
415 418-2900

(P-15959)
FRANCONNECT LLC
300 Carlsbad Village Dr 302a, Carlsbad
(92008-2990)
PHONE..................................760 720-5354
EMP: 101
SALES (corp-wide): 13.8MM **Privately Held**
SIC: 7373 Systems software development services
PA: Franconnect, Llc
11800 Sunrise Valley Dr # 900
Reston VA 20191
703 390-9300

(P-15960)
FRONTECH N FUJITSU AMER INC (DH)
Also Called: Ffna
27121 Towne Centre Dr # 100, Foothill
Ranch (92610-2826)
PHONE..................................949 855-5500
Yoshihiko Masuda, *President*
Tatsuo Horibe, *CFO*
Pat Cathey, *Senior VP*
Larry Fandel, *Senior VP*
Dick Zarski, *Senior VP*
EMP: 210

SQ FT: 90,000
SALES (est): 199.2MM
SALES (corp-wide): 38.4B **Privately Held**
WEB: www.fjicl.com
SIC: 7373 Computer systems analysis & design
HQ: Fujitsu Frontech Limited
1776, Yanokuchi
Inagi TKY 206-0
423 775-111

(P-15961)
FUJITSU AMERICA INC (DH)
1250 E Arques Ave, Sunnyvale
(94085-5401)
P.O. Box 3470 (94088-3470)
PHONE..................................408 746-6000
Mike Foster, *CEO*
Robert D Pryor, *President*
ARI Hovsepyan, *CFO*
Tom Duffy, *Officer*
Steve Della Rocchetta, *Exec VP*
EMP: 400
SALES (est): 1.4B
SALES (corp-wide): 38.4B **Privately Held**
SIC: 7373 Computer integrated systems design; systems software development services; systems integration services

(P-15962)
FUJITSU AMERICA INC
3113 Knights Bridge Rd, San Jose
(95132-1734)
PHONE..................................408 746-8419
Ratan Mohla, *Principal*
EMP: 100
SALES (corp-wide): 38.4B **Privately Held**
SIC: 7373 Computer integrated systems design
HQ: Fujitsu America Inc
1250 E Arques Ave
Sunnyvale CA 94085
408 746-6000

(P-15963)
FUJITSU AMERICA INC
317 Eureka St, San Francisco
(94114-2712)
PHONE..................................408 992-3561
EMP: 140
SALES (corp-wide): 38.4B **Privately Held**
SIC: 7373 Systems software development services
HQ: Fujitsu America Inc
1250 E Arques Ave
Sunnyvale CA 94085
408 746-6000

(P-15964)
FUJITSU AMERICA INC
2250 E Imperial Hwy # 200, El Segundo
(90245-3543)
PHONE..................................310 563-7000
Bob Pryor, *Branch Mgr*
EMP: 140
SALES (corp-wide): 38.4B **Privately Held**
SIC: 7373 Computer integrated systems design
HQ: Fujitsu America Inc
1250 E Arques Ave
Sunnyvale CA 94085
408 746-6000

(P-15965)
GEMALTO COGENT INC (DH)
639 N Rosemead Blvd, Pasadena
(91107-2147)
PHONE..................................626 325-9600
Olivier Piou, *CEO*
Michael Hollowich, *Exec VP*
Fong Liu, *Accountant*
EMP: 94
SQ FT: 151,000
SALES (est): 86MM
SALES (corp-wide): 3.5B **Privately Held**
WEB: www.cogentsystem.com
SIC: 7373 Computer-aided system services

(P-15966)
GENEA ENERGY PARTNERS INC
19100 Von Karman Ave # 550, Irvine
(92612-6571)
PHONE..................................714 694-0536
Jon Haahr, *Chairman*

David Balkin, *President*
Joseph Nugent, *President*
Keith Voysey, *CEO*
Cari Nicholson, *Executive Asst*
EMP: 85
SQ FT: 10,000
SALES (est): 14.5MM **Privately Held**
WEB: geneaenergy.com
SIC: 7373 Systems software development services

(P-15967)
GOBIG INC
338 Main St Unit 5c, San Francisco
(94105-2184)
PHONE..................................415 513-3029
Joachim Klein, *COO*
EMP: 50
SALES (est): 915K **Privately Held**
SIC: 7373 Systems software development services

(P-15968)
GROUPWARE TECHNOLOGY INC (PA)
541 Division St, Campbell (95008-6905)
PHONE..................................408 540-0090
Mike Thompson, *CEO*
Scott Sutter, *Exec VP*
Josh Avila, *Vice Pres*
John Barnes, *Vice Pres*
Anthony Miley, *Vice Pres*
EMP: 50
SQ FT: 14,000
SALES (est): 400MM **Privately Held**
WEB: www.groupwaretechnology.com
SIC: 7373 5045 Computer-aided system services; computers, peripherals & software; computer software

(P-15969)
HANDS-ON MOBILE AMERICAS INC (PA)
208 Utah St Ste 300, San Francisco
(94103-4890)
PHONE..................................415 580-6400
Jonathan Sacks, *CEO*
Dan Kranzler, *Ch of Bd*
Dave Arnold, *President*
Niccolo De Masi, *President*
Kevin Dent, *President*
EMP: 50 EST: 2001
SALES (est): 32.7MM **Privately Held**
WEB: www.mforma.com
SIC: 7373 Computer system selling services

(P-15970)
HEARTFLOW INC (PA)
1400 Seaport Blvd Bldg B, Redwood City
(94063-5594)
PHONE..................................650 241-1221
John Stevens, *CEO*
William C Weldon, *Ch of Bd*
Yoshiki Kawabata, *President*
Baird Radford, *CFO*
Michael Buck, *Ch Credit Ofcr*
EMP: 56
SQ FT: 3,400
SALES (est): 21.5MM **Privately Held**
SIC: 7373 Systems software development services

(P-15971)
HENRY BROS ELECTRONICS INC
Also Called: National Safe
1511 E Orangethorpe Ave A, Fullerton
(92831-5204)
PHONE..................................714 525-4350
Eric Demarco, *President*
Deanna Lund, *CEO*
Laura Siegal, *Treasurer*
Michael Fink, *Vice Pres*
Deborah Butera, *Admin Sec*
EMP: 200
SQ FT: 10,000
SALES (est): 17.2MM **Publicly Held**
WEB: www.hbe-ca.com
SIC: 7373 7382 5063 Computer integrated systems design; security systems services; burglar alarm systems
HQ: Henry Bros. Electronics, Inc.
17-01 Pollitt Dr Ste 5
Fair Lawn NJ 07410
201 794-6500

(P-15972)
HID GLOBAL SAFE INC
Also Called: Quantum Secure, Inc.
3590 N 1st St Ste 320, San Jose
(95134-1812)
PHONE..............................408 453-1008
Stefan Widing, *CEO*
Peter Giunchini, *Partner*
Rodney Glass, *COO*
Laura Crumbley, *CFO*
Ramesh Songukrishnasamy, *CIO*
EMP: 55
SALES (est): 9.6MM
SALES (corp-wide): 9B **Privately Held**
WEB: www.quantumsecure.com
SIC: 7373 7371 Systems software development services; computer software development & applications
HQ: Hid Global Corporation
611 Center Ridge Dr
Austin TX 78753
800 237-7769

(P-15973)
HUBB SYSTEMS LLC
Also Called: Data 911
12305 Crosthwaite Cir, Poway
(92064-6817)
PHONE..............................510 865-9100
Abigail Baker, *CEO*
Donald R Hubbard, *President*
Brian McCown, *CFO*
Doug Mosby, *General Mgr*
Fabrice Caporal, *Engineer*
EMP: 75
SALES (est): 15.2MM
SALES (corp-wide): 27.6MM **Privately Held**
SIC: 7373 7379 Turnkey vendors, computer systems; computer related consulting services
PA: Broadcast Microwave Services, Inc
12305 Crosthwaite Cir
Poway CA 92064
858 391-3050

(P-15974)
I LAN SYSTEMS INC
237 S Raymond Ave, Alhambra
(91801-3131)
PHONE..............................626 304-9021
Tom Reynolds, *President*
Virginia Reynolds, *Treasurer*
Mae LI Woo, *Admin Sec*
Trudy Woo, *Purch Agent*
EMP: 55
SQ FT: 1,000
SALES (est): 3.1MM **Privately Held**
SIC: 7373 Systems integration services

(P-15975)
ICYGEN LLC
940 Dwight Way Ste 13b, Berkeley
(94710-2528)
PHONE..............................510 540-7122
Milena Badjova,
Krasimir Koeff, *Project Mgr*
EMP: 80 EST: 1999
SALES (est): 4.4MM **Privately Held**
WEB: www.icygen.com
SIC: 7373 8742 Computer systems analysis & design; marketing consulting services

(P-15976)
IDONDEMAND INC
Also Called: ID On Demand
1900 Carnegie Ave Ste B, Santa Ana
(92705-5557)
PHONE..............................415 200-4546
Jennifer A Grigg, *Vice Pres*
Matthew Herscovitzh, *Principal*
EMP: 290
SALES (est): 41.2MM **Publicly Held**
SIC: 7373 Local area network (LAN) systems integrator
PA: Identiv, Inc.
2201 Walnut Ave Ste 100
Fremont CA 94538

(P-15977)
INDEPENDA INC
11455 El Camino Real # 365, San Diego
(92130-3036)
PHONE..............................800 815-7829

Kian Saneii, *CEO*
Melanie Sazegar, *Marketing Mgr*
EMP: 50
SALES (est): 5.5MM **Privately Held**
SIC: 7373 Systems software development services

(P-15978)
INSEEGO NORTH AMERICA LLC (DH)
Also Called: 1-Carasight Surveillance
9605 Scranton Rd Ste 300, San Diego
(92121-1789)
PHONE..............................541 685-9045
Michael Newman, *Admin Sec*
Birk Nelson, *Executive*
Roland Skinner, *Engineer*
Kelli Martin, *Hum Res Coord*
Patrick Downey, *Sales Staff*
EMP: 65
SQ FT: 36,000
SALES: 25MM
SALES (corp-wide): 219.3MM **Publicly Held**
WEB: www.feeneywireless.com
SIC: 7373 Computer integrated systems design
HQ: R.E.R. Enterprises, Inc.
1505 Westec Dr
Eugene OR 97402
541 685-9045

(P-15979)
INTEGRATED DECISION SYSTEMS
11150 W Olympic Blvd # 600, Los Angeles
(90064-1817)
PHONE..............................310 954-5530
Jerald Jackrel, *President*
Donald Potter, *CEO*
Philip Alford, *CFO*
Shahram Zaman, *Vice Pres*
Lawrence Kramer, *Principal*
EMP: 75
SALES (est): 4.4MM **Privately Held**
SIC: 7373 7372 Systems software development services; prepackaged software

(P-15980)
INTELLICUS TECH PVT LTD
720 University Ave # 130, Los Gatos
(95032-7609)
PHONE..............................408 213-3314
Praveen Kankiria, *CEO*
Jerry Malec, *President*
Anand Raman, *Vice Pres*
Pankaj Mittal, *CTO*
Rajesh Murthy, *VP Engrg*
EMP: 60
SQ FT: 1,000
SALES: 2MM **Privately Held**
SIC: 7373 Computer integrated systems design

(P-15981)
INTERNATIONAL BUS MCHS CORP
Also Called: IBM
30501 Agoura Rd Ste 100, Agoura Hills
(91301-4399)
PHONE..............................914 499-1900
Ricky Kurtz, *Manager*
EMP: 61
SALES (corp-wide): 79.1B **Publicly Held**
WEB: www.ibm.com
SIC: 7373 7379 Systems software development services; computer systems analysis & design; computer related consulting services
PA: International Business Machines Corporation
1 New Orchard Rd Ste 1 # 1
Armonk NY 10504
914 499-1900

(P-15982)
INTERNET CORP FOR ASSIGNED NAM (PA)
Also Called: I Cann
12025 Waterfront Dr # 300, Los Angeles
(90094-3220)
PHONE..............................310 823-9358
Cherine Chalaby, *Chairman*
Susanna Bennett, *COO*
Nigel Hickson, *Vice Pres*

Veni Markovski, *Vice Pres*
Christopher Mondini, *Vice Pres*
EMP: 160
SALES (est): 219.5MM **Privately Held**
WEB: www.icann.org
SIC: 7373 Systems software development services

(P-15983)
INTERSTATE ELECTRONICS CORP
3033 Science Park Rd, San Diego
(92121-1167)
PHONE..............................858 552-9500
Andrew Leuthe, *Principal*
EMP: 53
SALES (corp-wide): 9.5B **Publicly Held**
SIC: 7373 7379 5045 Systems engineering, computer related; computer related consulting services; computer software
HQ: Interstate Electronics Corporation
602 E Vermont Ave
Anaheim CA 92805
714 758-0500

(P-15984)
IP INFUSION INC (HQ)
3965 Freedom Cir Ste 200, Santa Clara
(95054-1293)
PHONE..............................408 400-1900
Koichi Narasaki, *Chairman*
Amit Chatterjee, *President*
Kiyo Oishi, *CEO*
Atsushi Ogata, *COO*
Shane Rigby, *COO*
EMP: 53
SQ FT: 11,900
SALES (est): 9.6MM
SALES (corp-wide): 69.9MM **Privately Held**
WEB: www.ipinfusion.com
SIC: 7373 Systems software development services
PA: Access Co.,Ltd.
3, Kandaneribeicho
Chiyoda-Ku TKY 101-0
368 539-088

(P-15985)
IPASS INC
15241 Laguna Canyon Rd # 100, Irvine
(92618-3146)
PHONE..............................650 232-4100
John Drosshan, *Manager*
EMP: 90 **Publicly Held**
SIC: 7373 Computer integrated systems design
PA: Ipass Inc.
3800 Bridge Pkwy
Redwood City CA 94065

(P-15986)
JACKSON TULL CHRTRED ENGINEERS
550 Continental Blvd # 195, El Segundo
(90245-5049)
PHONE..............................310 658-2132
Knox Tull, *President*
EMP: 50
SALES (corp-wide): 20MM **Privately Held**
WEB: www.jacksonandtull.com
SIC: 7373 8711 Systems engineering, computer related; civil engineering
PA: Jackson And Tull Chartered Engineers
2705 Bladensburg Rd Ne
Washington DC 20018
202 333-9100

(P-15987)
JUNIPER NETWORKS INC
Also Called: Proof of Concept Poc Lab
1137 Innovation Way B, Sunnyvale (94089)
PHONE..............................408 745-2000
Florin A Oprescu, *Principal*
Melissa Beauparlant, *Partner*
Phil Larson, *Partner*
Michael Tuttle, *Partner*
Domenico Di Mola, *Vice Pres*
EMP: 2000 **Publicly Held**
WEB: www.juniper.net
SIC: 7373 7372 Computer integrated systems design; prepackaged software

PA: Juniper Networks, Inc.
1133 Innovation Way
Sunnyvale CA 94089

(P-15988)
JUNIPER NETWORKS INC
Aurrion
6868 Cortona Dr Ste C, Goleta
(93117-1363)
PHONE..............................805 880-2000
EMP: 60 **Publicly Held**
SIC: 7373 Computer integrated systems design
PA: Juniper Networks, Inc.
1133 Innovation Way
Sunnyvale CA 94089

(P-15989)
JUNIPER NETWORKS INC
1215 K St Fl 17, Sacramento (95814-3954)
PHONE..............................916 503-1593
Gerald Chavez, *Branch Mgr*
EMP: 72 **Publicly Held**
WEB: www.juniper.net
SIC: 7373 7372 Computer integrated systems design; prepackaged software
PA: Juniper Networks, Inc.
1133 Innovation Way
Sunnyvale CA 94089

(P-15990)
JUNIPER NETWORKS INC
Also Called: Executive Briefing Center
1133 Innovation Way A, Sunnyvale
(94089-1228)
PHONE..............................888 586-4737
Kannan Kothandaraman, *Vice Pres*
Archana Baldwa, *Finance*
Rutesh Patel, *Finance*
Guhan Subbarayan, *Mfg Staff*
Gary Nichols, *Director*
EMP: 638 **Publicly Held**
WEB: www.juniper.net
SIC: 7373 7372 Computer integrated systems design; prepackaged software
PA: Juniper Networks, Inc.
1133 Innovation Way
Sunnyvale CA 94089

(P-15991)
KG OLDCO INC (HQ)
2270 Martin Ave, Santa Clara
(95050-2704)
PHONE..............................408 980-8550
Jeff Kaiser, *CEO*
Jason Gress, *President*
Jackie Nguyen, *Accounts Mgr*
EMP: 50
SQ FT: 13,130
SALES (est): 38.2MM
SALES (corp-wide): 38.8MM **Privately Held**
WEB: www.intervision.com
SIC: 7373 8712 Systems integration services; computer systems analysis & design; architectural services
PA: Netelligent Corporation
16401 Swingley Ridge Rd
Chesterfield MO 63017
314 392-6900

(P-15992)
KOAM ENGINEERING SYSTEMS INC
Also Called: K E S
7807 Convoy Ct Ste 200, San Diego
(92111-1213)
PHONE..............................858 292-0922
John S Yi, *President*
Richard Comber, *Vice Pres*
Erica Tofson, *Vice Pres*
Jim Meadows, *Director*
John Schiltz, *Director*
EMP: 105
SQ FT: 5,700
SALES (est): 26.1MM **Privately Held**
SIC: 7373 Computer integrated systems design

PRODUCTS & SVCS

(P-15993)
KRAFT & KENNEDY INC
1 Post St Ste 2600, San Francisco
(94104-5230)
PHONE..................................415 956-4000
Peter Kennedy, CEO
EMP: 60
SALES (corp-wide): 15.5MM **Privately Held**
WEB: www.kklsystems.com
SIC: 7373 7379 Computer integrated systems design; computer related consulting services
PA: Kraft & Kennedy, Inc.
630 3rd Ave Rm 1400
New York NY 10017
212 986-4700

(P-15994)
KUTIR CORPORATION
37600 Central Ct Ste 280, Newark
(94560-3438)
PHONE..................................510 402-4526
Gerry Ignatius, President
Ranjine Ramachandran, CFO
Prathiba Kalyan, Vice Pres
G L Kluttz, Vice Pres
Bhanu Morampudi, Vice Pres
EMP: 50
SALES (est): 7.4MM **Privately Held**
WEB: www.kutirtech.com
SIC: 7373 Systems software development services

(P-15995)
L3 TECHNOLOGIES INC
117 S Gold Canyon St, Ridgecrest
(93555-4121)
PHONE..................................760 375-0390
Jai Gupta, Manager
EMP: 100
SALES (corp-wide): 9.5B **Publicly Held**
SIC: 7373 8731 3761 1731 Systems engineering, computer related; computer systems analysis & design; systems integration services; commercial physical research; guided missiles & space vehicles; electrical work
PA: L3 Technologies, Inc.
600 3rd Ave Fl 34
New York NY 10016
212 697-1111

(P-15996)
LIFERAY INC (PA)
1400 Montefino Ave # 100, Diamond Bar
(91765-5501)
PHONE..................................877 543-3729
Bryan Cheung, CEO
Karen Newnam, Partner
Jorge Ferrer, President
Scott Tachiki, CFO
Paul Hinz, Chief Mktg Ofcr
EMP: 58
SALES (est): 3MM **Privately Held**
WEB: www.liferay.com
SIC: 7373 Systems software development services

(P-15997)
LIGHTCREST LLC
1112 Montana Ave Ste 705, Santa Monica
(90403-7219)
PHONE..................................888 320-8495
Zachary Fierstadt,
Evan Alexander, Business Dir
Thomas Swigert, Administration
Matthew Sibley, Sales Staff
Michael Hughes,
EMP: 50
SALES (est): 10MM **Privately Held**
SIC: 7373 Computer integrated systems design

(P-15998)
LILIEN LLC (HQ)
17 E Sir Francis Dr # 110, Larkspur
(94939-1708)
PHONE..................................415 389-7500
Geoffrey I Lilien, Mng Member
Eric Borsky, President
James Meydenbauer, Info Tech Mgr
Gary Belford, VP Sales
Dhruv Gulati,
EMP: 50
SQ FT: 6,200

SALES (est): 11.8MM
SALES (corp-wide): 62.9MM **Privately Held**
SIC: 7373 Computer integrated systems design
PA: Sysorex International, Inc
335 E Middlefield Rd
Mountain View CA 94043
650 967-2200

(P-15999)
LIQUIDATE DIRECT LLC
Also Called: Solid Commerce
2929 Washington Blvd Fl 2, Marina Del Rey
(90292-5546)
PHONE..................................800 750-7617
Eran Pick, CEO
Alon Berkovich, COO
Shawna Snukst, Bus Dvlpt Dir
EMP: 50 EST: 2003
SALES (est): 5.6MM **Privately Held**
SIC: 7373 7371 7379 Computer integrated systems design; custom computer programming services; computer related maintenance services

(P-16000)
LUCID DESIGN GROUP INC
304 12th St Ste 3c, Oakland (94607-4531)
PHONE..................................510 907-0400
Will Coleman, CEO
Vladisoav Shunturov, President
Scott Boutwell, Vice Pres
Kevin Burns, Vice Pres
Shelly Davenport, Vice Pres
EMP: 80
SALES (est): 11.6MM
SALES (corp-wide): 3.6B **Publicly Held**
WEB: www.luciddesigngroup.com
SIC: 7373 Systems software development services
PA: Acuity Brands, Inc.
1170 Peachtree St Ne
Atlanta GA 30309
404 853-1400

(P-16001)
MANTECH INTERNATIONAL CORP
8328 Clairemont Mesa Blvd, San Diego
(92111-1328)
PHONE..................................858 492-9938
Ronald Renfro, Exec Dir
EMP: 200
SALES (corp-wide): 1.7B **Publicly Held**
SIC: 7373 Systems software development services
PA: Mantech International Corporation
251 Corporate Park Dr
Herndon VA 20171
703 218-6000

(P-16002)
MANTECH INTERNATIONAL CORP
615 N Nash St Ste 200, El Segundo
(90245-2851)
PHONE..................................310 765-9324
EMP: 200
SALES (corp-wide): 1.7B **Publicly Held**
SIC: 7373 Systems software development services
PA: Mantech International Corporation
251 Corporate Park Dr
Herndon VA 20171
703 218-6000

(P-16003)
MILESTONE TECHNOLOGIES INC (PA)
3101 Skyway Ct, Fremont (94539-5910)
PHONE..................................510 651-2454
Nelson Eng, President
Edward Reginelli, CFO
Doug Tracy, Exec VP
Gary Bilovesky, Vice Pres
Natalie Heroux, Vice Pres
EMP: 116
SQ FT: 6,500
SALES (est): 133.1MM **Privately Held**
WEB: www.milestn.com
SIC: 7373 7374 Computer integrated systems design; data processing & preparation

(P-16004)
MIST SYSTEMS INC
1601 S De Anza Blvd # 248, Cupertino
(95014-5350)
PHONE..................................408 326-0346
Sujai Hajela, CEO
Brett Galloway, Ch of Bd
Laura Perrone, CFO
Bob Friday, CTO
Nirmala Venkataramani, Software Dev
EMP: 60
SALES (est): 7.6MM **Privately Held**
SIC: 7373 Local area network (LAN) systems integrator

(P-16005)
MOBICA US INC
2570 N 1st St Fl 2, San Jose (95131-1035)
PHONE..................................650 450-6654
Marcin Kloda, CEO
Rafael Janczyk, COO
Anna Orlova, Administration
Radoslaw Dumanski, Technical Staff
Pawel Olaszek, Accounts Mgr
EMP: 900 EST: 2012
SALES (est): 482.3K
SALES (corp-wide): 73.3MM **Privately Held**
SIC: 7373 Systems software development services
HQ: Mobica Limited
Crown House
Wilmslow SK9 1
162 544-6140

(P-16006)
MORPHOTRAK LLC (DH)
Also Called: Safran
5515 E La Palma Ave # 100, Anaheim
(92807-2116)
PHONE..................................714 238-2000
Celeste Thomasson, CEO
Florian Hebras, CFO
Clark Nelson, Vice Pres
Hieu Tran, Vice Pres
Diana Cullison, Executive Asst
EMP: 175
SQ FT: 32,000
SALES (est): 94.4MM
SALES (corp-wide): 4.5B **Privately Held**
WEB: www.morpho.com
SIC: 7373 Computer integrated systems design
HQ: Idemia Identity & Security France
11 Boulevard Gallieni
Issy Les Moulineaux 92130
158 112-500

(P-16007)
MOZILLA CORPORATION (HQ)
331 E Evelyn Ave Ste 100, Mountain View
(94041-1538)
PHONE..................................650 903-0800
Mitchell Baker, Ch of Bd
Chris Beard, CEO
James Cook, CFO
Jascha Kaykas-Wolff, Chief Mktg Ofcr
Larissa B Shapiro, Top Exec
EMP: 425
SQ FT: 15,000
SALES (est): 98.4MM
SALES (corp-wide): 421.2MM **Privately Held**
WEB: www.mozilla.com
SIC: 7373 Systems software development services
PA: Mozilla Foundation
331 E Evelyn Ave
Mountain View CA 94041
650 903-0800

(P-16008)
MSCSOFTWARE CORPORATION
Costa Mesa Office
4675 Macarthur Ct Ste 900, Newport Beach
(92660-1845)
PHONE..................................714 540-8900
Frank Perna, President
EMP: 350
SQ FT: 81,000

SALES (corp-wide): 18.8MM **Privately Held**
SIC: 7373 8711 7372 7371 Computer-aided engineering (CAE) systems service; engineering services; prepackaged software; custom computer programming services
HQ: Msc.Software Corporation
4675 Macarthur Ct Ste 900
Newport Beach CA 92660
714 540-8900

(P-16009)
NANTHEALTH INC (HQ)
9920 Jefferson Blvd, Culver City
(90232-3506)
PHONE..................................310 883-1300
Patrick Soon-Shiong, Ch of Bd
Ronald A Louks, COO
Bob Petrou, CFO
Michael Blaszyk, Bd of Directors
Sandeep Reddy, Chief Mktg Ofcr
EMP: 53
SQ FT: 8,000
SALES: 86.6MM
SALES (corp-wide): 127.9MM **Publicly Held**
SIC: 7373 Computer integrated systems design
PA: Nantworks, Llc
9920 Jefferson Blvd
Culver City CA 90232
310 883-1300

(P-16010)
NANTWORKS LLC (PA)
9920 Jefferson Blvd, Culver City
(90232-3506)
PHONE..................................310 883-1300
Charles N Kenworthy, Mng Member
EMP: 82
SALES (est): 127.9MM **Publicly Held**
SIC: 7373 Computer-aided system services

(P-16011)
NET EXPRESS
32 Snyder Way, Fremont (94536-1675)
PHONE..................................510 887-4395
Roland H Baker III, President
EMP: 65
SALES (est): 4.5MM **Privately Held**
SIC: 7373 Computer systems analysis & design

(P-16012)
NETAPP INC
300 Spectrum Center Dr # 900, Irvine
(92618-4925)
PHONE..................................949 754-6600
Chris White, Branch Mgr
Bob Moore, Executive
Igor Goldenberg, Database Admin
Robert Hunter, Technical Staff
Robert Boyce, Engineer
EMP: 209 **Publicly Held**
SIC: 7373 Computer integrated systems design
PA: Netapp, Inc.
1395 Crossman Ave
Sunnyvale CA 94089

(P-16013)
NETAPP INC
1299 Orleans Dr, Sunnyvale (94089-1138)
PHONE..................................408 822-3402
Joe McKinney, Accounts Mgr
EMP: 215 **Publicly Held**
SIC: 7373 Computer integrated systems design
PA: Netapp, Inc.
1395 Crossman Ave
Sunnyvale CA 94089

(P-16014)
NETAPP INC
6320 Canoga Ave Ste 1500, Woodland Hills
(91367-2563)
PHONE..................................818 227-5025
EMP: 209
SALES (corp-wide): 6.3B **Publicly Held**
SIC: 7373

▲ = Import ▼=Export
◆ =Import/Export

PA: Netapp, Inc.
495 E Java Dr
Sunnyvale CA 94089
408 822-6000

(P-16015)
NETAPP INC
1345 Crossman Ave, Sunnyvale
(94089-1114)
PHONE..................................408 419-5301
Pam Teshera, *Branch Mgr*
Pamela Hutcheson, *Opers Staff*
Justin Rojas, *Sales Staff*
Greg White, *Senior Mgr*
Tracy Windsor, *Director*
EMP: 209 Publicly Held
WEB: www.netapp.com
SIC: 7373 Computer integrated systems
design
PA: Netapp, Inc.
1395 Crossman Ave
Sunnyvale CA 94089
-

(P-16016)
NETAPP INC
3334 Meadowlands Ln, San Jose
(95135-1624)
PHONE..................................408 822-3803
EMP: 203
SALES (corp-wide): 6.3B Publicly Held
SIC: 7373
PA: Netapp, Inc.
495 E Java Dr
Sunnyvale CA 94089
408 822-6000

(P-16017)
**NETWORK INTGRTION
PARTNERS INC**
Also Called: Nic Partners
11981 Jack Benny Dr # 103, Rancho Cuca-
monga (91739-9232)
PHONE..................................909 919-2800
Franklin P Spaeth, *President*
EMP: 80
SQ FT: 6,000
SALES (est): 22.9MM Privately Held
SIC: 7373 Local area network (LAN) sys-
tems integrator

(P-16018)
**NEW DIRECTIONS TECH INC
(PA)**
Also Called: Ndti
137 W Drummond Ave Ste A, Ridgecrest
(93555-3583)
PHONE..................................760 384-2444
Cedric Knight, *President*
Bert Belisch, *CFO*
Adrian Miller, *Officer*
Michele E Hoopes, *Exec VP*
Ann Bucharelli, *Executive*
EMP: 65
SQ FT: 6,000
SALES (est): 26MM Privately Held
WEB: www.ndti.net
SIC: 7373 7374 8711 7371 Systems soft-
ware development services; data pro-
cessing & preparation; engineering
services; computer software development
& applications; computer facilities man-
agement

(P-16019)
**NORTHROP GRUMMAN
SYSTEMS CORP**
Also Called: Technical Services
P.O. Box 81, Moffett Field (94035-0081)
PHONE..................................650 604-6056
James R Blount, *Manager*
EMP: 120 Publicly Held
SIC: 7373 7374 Computer systems analy-
sis & design; computer processing serv-
ices
HQ: Northrop Grumman Systems Corpora-
tion
2980 Fairview Park Dr
Falls Church VA 22042
703 280-2900

(P-16020)
**NORTHROP GRUMMAN
SYSTEMS CORP**
5161 Verdugo Way, Camarillo
(93012-8603)
PHONE..................................805 987-9739
Jim Lueck, *Systems Staff*
Rian Hawkins, *Branch Mgr*
EMP: 60 Publicly Held
WEB: www.logicon.com
SIC: 7373 8731 8711 7371 Computer
systems analysis & design; commercial
physical research; engineering services;
custom computer programming services
HQ: Northrop Grumman Systems Corpora-
tion
2980 Fairview Park Dr
Falls Church VA 22042
703 280-2900

(P-16021)
NTT DATA INC
1000 Corporate Center Dr # 140, Monterey
Park (91754-7610)
PHONE..................................213 228-2500
Fax: 323 261-3030
EMP: 93
SALES (corp-wide): 93.3B Privately Held
SIC: 7373
HQ: Ntt Data, Inc.
5601 Gran Pkwy Ste 1000
Plano TX 75024
800 745-3263

(P-16022)
NURLOGIC DESIGN INC (DH)
5580 Morehouse Dr, San Diego
(92121-1709)
PHONE..................................858 455-7570
Rich Shine, *Manager*
David Matty, *President*
Hugh D Gerfin, *Treasurer*
Mike Brunolli, *CTO*
EMP: 60
SQ FT: 34,000
SALES (est): 2.9MM Privately Held
SIC: 7373 Computer integrated systems
design

(P-16023)
O2 MICRO INC
3118 Patrick Henry Dr, Santa Clara
(95054-1850)
PHONE..................................408 987-5920
Lynn Lin, *CEO*
Sterling Du, *President*
George Simion, *COO*
Perry Kuo, *CFO*
Johnny Chiang, *Vice Pres*
EMP: 100
SQ FT: 37,000
SALES (est): 15.9MM Privately Held
WEB: www.o2micro.com
SIC: 7373 Computer integrated systems
design
PA: O2micro International Limited
The Grand Pavillion
George Town GR CAYMAN KY1-1
-

(P-16024)
OASIS TECHNOLOGY INC
601 E Daily Dr Ste 226, Camarillo
(93010-5840)
PHONE..................................805 445-4833
George M Baldonado, *President*
Deborah Panish, *Officer*
Deborah Johnson, *Vice Pres*
Violeta Baldonado, *Admin Sec*
EMP: 65
SQ FT: 2,800
SALES: 3MM Privately Held
WEB: www.oasistechnology.com
SIC: 7373 5734 Computer system selling
services; personal computers

(P-16025)
**OBERMAN TIVOLI & PICKERT
INC**
Also Called: Media Services
500 S Sepulveda Blvd # 500, Los Angeles
(90049-3551)
PHONE..................................310 440-9600
Robert Oberman, *President*
Barry Oberman, *CEO*

Sanaa Wadsworth, *CFO*
EMP: 230
SALES (est): 24.8MM Privately Held
WEB: www.media-services.com
SIC: 7373 8721 8741 Systems software
development services; payroll accounting
service; business management

(P-16026)
**ONEMARKET NETWORK LLC
(HQ)**
835 Market St Ste 700, Los Angeles
(90067)
PHONE..................................415 638-9868
Don Kingsborough, *CEO*
Peter McInerney, *Vice Pres*
Kyle Spencer, *Vice Pres*
Larry Gordon, *Software Engr*
Jeremy Shapiro, *Engineer*
EMP: 175
SQ FT: 10,000
SALES (est): 6.9MM Privately Held
SIC: 7373 Computer integrated systems
design

(P-16027)
P-COVE ENTERPRISES INC
8745 Remmet Ave, Canoga Park
(91304-1519)
PHONE..................................818 341-1101
Jonathan Manhan, *CEO*
EMP: 59
SALES: 17MM Privately Held
SIC: 7373 Value-added resellers, computer
systems

(P-16028)
PACIFIC CROSSING LLC
95 Argonaut Ste 100, Aliso Viejo
(92656-4139)
PHONE..................................949 679-2588
Phyllis Johnson,
Walter Johnson,
EMP: 225
SQ FT: 1,500
SALES (est): 9.5MM Privately Held
WEB: www.pacificcrossing.com
SIC: 7373 Computer integrated systems
design

(P-16029)
PANZURA INC
695 Campbell Tech Pkwy # 225, Campbell
(95008-5076)
PHONE..................................408 457-8504
Randy Chou, *CEO*
Mark Santora, *Ch of Bd*
Pete Coticchia, *Vice Pres*
Rich Weber, *Vice Pres*
Darren Daugherty, *Principal*
EMP: 57 EST: 2008
SALES (est): 15MM Privately Held
SIC: 7373 5734 Computer integrated sys-
tems design; computer software & acces-
sories

(P-16030)
PARIVEDA SOLUTIONS INC
201 California St # 1250, San Francisco
(94111-5033)
PHONE..................................415 946-6100
Eric Wells, *Principal*
EMP: 197
**SALES (corp-wide): 39.7MM Privately
Held**
SIC: 7373 Computer systems analysis &
design
PA: Pariveda Solutions, Inc.
2811 Mckinney Ave Ste 220
Dallas TX 75204
214 777-4600

(P-16031)
PERSPECTA ENGINEERING INC
1315 Dell Ave, Campbell (95008-6609)
PHONE..................................408 961-3250
Joe Harris, *General Mgr*
EMP: 100
SALES (corp-wide): 13.5B Publicly Held
WEB: www.comglobal.com
SIC: 7373 1731 Systems software devel-
opment services; electrical work
HQ: Perspecta Engineering Inc.
15052 Conference Ctr Dr
Chantilly VA 20151
571 313-6000

(P-16032)
PINNACLE TELECOM INC (PA)
Also Called: Pti Solutions
8100 Sierra College Blvd, Roseville
(95661-9411)
PHONE..................................916 426-1000
Cecelia Lakatos Sullivan, *CEO*
Barbara Winters, *Chairman*
EMP: 50
SQ FT: 20,000
SALES: 12MM Privately Held
WEB: www.pinnacle-telecom.com
SIC: 7373 8741 1731 1623 Computer in-
tegrated systems design; management
services; electronic controls installation;
electric power line construction; computer
facilities management; computer related
maintenance services

(P-16033)
PIXIM INC
1730 N 1st St, San Jose (95112-4508)
PHONE..................................650 934-0550
Chris Adams, *CEO*
Randy Strahan, *President*
John Monti, *Vice Pres*
EMP: 51
SQ FT: 13,560
SALES (est): 7MM Privately Held
WEB: www.pixim.com
SIC: 7373 7361 Computer integrated sys-
tems design; employment agencies

(P-16034)
PLANET GROUP INC
5796 Armada Dr Ste 300, Carlsbad
(92008-4694)
PHONE..................................402 491-3560
Tom Nichting, *President*
David Gerheauser Jr, *Treasurer*
Sherry Magwire, *CTO*
EMP: 99
SALES: 950K Privately Held
SIC: 7373 Computer integrated systems
design

(P-16035)
PRIMITIVE LOGIC INC
704 Sansome St, San Francisco
(94111-1704)
PHONE..................................415 391-8080
Jill P Reber, *CEO*
Kevin Moos, *President*
Anisha Weber, *COO*
Mike McDermott, *Senior VP*
Kimberly Davis, *Vice Pres*
EMP: 63 EST: 1996
SQ FT: 10,000
SALES (est): 13.3MM Privately Held
WEB: www.primitivelogic.com
SIC: 7373 Computer integrated systems
design

(P-16036)
QCT LLC
1010 Rincon Cir, San Jose (95131-1325)
PHONE..................................510 270-6111
Alan Lam, *Mng Member*
Gary TSE, *Software Engr*
Olivia Chen, *Comp Spec*
George Deng, *Comp Spec*
Tonica Francis, *Comp Spec*
EMP: 1000
SALES (est): 6.5MM
SALES (corp-wide): 33.9B Privately Held
SIC: 7373 Systems integration services
PA: Quanta Computer Inc.
188, Wenhua 2nd Rd.,
Taoyuan City TAY 33383
332 723-45

(P-16037)
QSOLV INC
440 N Wolfe Rd Ste 26, Sunnyvale
(94085-3869)
PHONE..................................408 429-0918
Sujaya Viswanathan, *CEO*
Shell Scripting, *Partner*
Shyam Gopal, *President*
Sandy Shyam, *General Mgr*
EMP: 112

SALES (est): 3.9MM **Privately Held**
WEB: www.qsolv.net
SIC: 7373 7379 7371 Computer systems analysis & design; computer related consulting services; software programming applications

(P-16038)
QUEST MEDIA & SUPPLIES INC (PA)
9000 Fthills Blvd Ste 100, Roseville (95747)
P.O. Box 910 (95678-0910)
PHONE..............................916 338-7070
Timothy Burke, *CEO*
Vivian Aedo, *Partner*
Adam Burke, *Partner*
Cindy P Burke, *President*
Kathy Campbell, *COO*
EMP: 92
SQ FT: 9,500
SALES (est): 159.4MM **Privately Held**
WEB: www.questsys.com
SIC: 7373 Systems integration services

(P-16039)
QUEST SOFTWARE INC (HQ)
4 Polaris Way, Aliso Viejo (92656-5356)
PHONE..............................949 754-8000
Jeff Hawn, *CEO*
Marcelo Luis, *Partner*
Kevin E Brooks, *Vice Pres*
Thomas R Patterson Jr, *Vice Pres*
Philip Walsh, *Vice Pres*
EMP: 600
SQ FT: 170,000
SALES (est): 999.5MM
SALES (corp-wide): 1.7B **Privately Held**
WEB: www.quest.com
SIC: 7373 7379 7372 Computer integrated systems design; computer related consulting services; business oriented computer software
PA: Francisco Partners Management, L.P.
1 Letterman Dr Ste 410
San Francisco CA 94129
415 418-2900

(P-16040)
RAVENSWOOD SOLUTIONS INC
3065 Skyway Ct, Fremont (94539-5909)
PHONE..............................650 241-3661
Daniel Donoghue, *CEO*
Christopher Terndrup, *Exec Dir*
John Prausa,
EMP: 99 **EST:** 2015
SQ FT: 12,878
SALES (est): 6.3MM
SALES (corp-wide): 503.9MM **Privately Held**
SIC: 7373 7379 3679 8711 Systems engineering, computer related; computer related maintenance services; antennas, receiving; engineering services
PA: Sri International
333 Ravenswood Ave
Menlo Park CA 94025
650 859-2000

(P-16041)
RAYV INC
6380 Wilshire Blvd # 1006, Los Angeles (90048-5003)
PHONE..............................310 600-2959
Ron Zuckerman, *CEO*
Morris Azulay, *CFO*
Ori Birnbaum, *Vice Pres*
Omer Luzzatti, *CTO*
EMP: 50
SQ FT: 4,000
SALES (est): 3.2MM **Privately Held**
SIC: 7373 Computer integrated systems design

(P-16042)
REAL TIME LOGIC INC
4820 Estgate Mall Ste 200, San Diego (92121)
PHONE..............................858 812-7300
EMP: 88 **Publicly Held**
SIC: 7373 Computer integrated systems design
HQ: Real Time Logic, Inc.
12515 Academy Ridge Vw
Colorado Springs CO 80921
719 598-2801

(P-16043)
RESULT GROUP INC
2603 Main St Ste 710, Irvine (92614-4263)
PHONE..............................480 777-7130
William Derick Robson, *President*
David Griffiths, *Admin Sec*
EMP: 70
SALES (est): 5.4MM
SALES (corp-wide): 2.1B **Privately Held**
SIC: 7373 7372 Systems software development services; business oriented computer software
HQ: Wynne Systems, Inc.
2603 Main St Ste 710
Irvine CA 92614

(P-16044)
SAUCE LABS INC (PA)
116 New Montgomery St # 3, San Francisco (94105-3639)
PHONE..............................415 946-1117
Charles Ramsey, *CEO*
Paul Joachim, *CFO*
Tucker Callaway, *Officer*
Joe Alfaro, *Vice Pres*
Heather McLinden, *Vice Pres*
EMP: 55
SALES (est): 30.7MM **Privately Held**
SIC: 7373 Systems software development services

(P-16045)
SCIENCE APPLICATIONS INTL CORP
Also Called: Saic
4015 Hancock St, San Diego (92110-5121)
PHONE..............................858 826-3061
Gordon Saakamodo, *Manager*
Jeff Ferguson, *CEO*
Anthony Moraco, *CEO*
Barry Wallis, *Officer*
Richard Whiston, *Executive*
EMP: 600
SALES (corp-wide): 4.4B **Publicly Held**
WEB: www.saic.com
SIC: 7373 Systems engineering, computer related
PA: Science Applications International Corporation
12010 Sunset Hills Rd
Reston VA 20190
703 676-4300

(P-16046)
SCIENCE APPLICATIONS INTL CORP
Also Called: Saic
4242 Campus Point Ct, San Diego (92121-1513)
PHONE..............................858 826-6000
Raj Seksaria, *President*
Dave Clemons, *Vice Pres*
Gary Mills, *Software Engr*
Lilia Vaughn, *HR Admin*
Raymond S Bamford, *Director*
EMP: 350
SALES (corp-wide): 4.4B **Publicly Held**
WEB: www.saic.com
SIC: 7373 Systems engineering, computer related
PA: Science Applications International Corporation
12010 Sunset Hills Rd
Reston VA 20190
703 676-4300

(P-16047)
SECOM INTERNATIONAL (PA)
9610 Bellanca Ave, Los Angeles (90045-5508)
PHONE..............................310 641-1290
Ted Burton, *President*
Amir Behic, *CFO*
Terry Bixler, *Vice Pres*
John Martin, *Regional Mgr*
Linda Vose, *Admin Sec*
EMP: 52
SQ FT: 30,000
SALES (est): 8.4MM **Privately Held**
WEB: www.secomintl.com
SIC: 7373 3446 3559 7371 Turnkey vendors, computer systems; architectural metalwork; parking facility equipment & supplies; computer software systems analysis & design, custom

(P-16048)
SECURITY ON-DEMAND INC
12121 Scripps Summit Dr # 320, San Diego (92131-4609)
PHONE..............................858 563-5655
Peter Bybee, *CEO*
William Lyman, *CFO*
Glenn Dodds, *Vice Pres*
Paul Tobia, *Security Dir*
Joel Holland, *CTO*
EMP: 50 **EST:** 2001
SQ FT: 12,000
SALES: 3MM **Privately Held**
SIC: 7373 Computer integrated systems design

(P-16049)
SELLIGENT INC (HQ)
1300 Island Dr Ste 200, Redwood City (94065-5171)
PHONE..............................650 421-4200
John Hernandez, *CEO*
Frank Addante, *President*
Tricia Robinson-Pridemore, *President*
Chris Botting, *COO*
Steve Pantelick, *CFO*
EMP: 89
SALES (est): 34.6MM
SALES (corp-wide): 151.1MM **Privately Held**
WEB: www.strongmailsystems.com
SIC: 7373 Computer integrated systems design
PA: Hggc, Llc
1950 University Ave # 350
East Palo Alto CA 94303
650 321-4910

(P-16050)
SEMANTIC AI INC (PA)
Also Called: Semantic Research
4922 N Harbor Dr, San Diego (92106-2306)
PHONE..............................619 222-4050
Richard Harrison, *CEO*
Thomas Waltz, *CFO*
Dorie Kelly, *Manager*
EMP: 70
SQ FT: 2,600
SALES (est): 12MM **Privately Held**
WEB: www.semanticresearch.com
SIC: 7373 Systems software development services

(P-16051)
SEZZO LABS INC
313 Adeline Ave, San Jose (95136-4875)
PHONE..............................408 562-0081
Walter Simon, *President*
Edwin Chan, *CFO*
EMP: 50 **EST:** 2004
SQ FT: 5,000
SALES (est): 4.2MM **Privately Held**
WEB: www.ansi.com
SIC: 7373 Computer integrated systems design

(P-16052)
SIMULATIONS PLUS INC (PA)
42505 10th St W Ste 103, Lancaster (93534-7059)
PHONE..............................661 723-7723
Shawn M O'Connor, *CEO*
Walter S Woltosz, *Ch of Bd*
John A Dibella, *President*
John R Kneisel, *CFO*
EMP: 86
SQ FT: 13,500
SALES (est): 29.6MM **Publicly Held**
WEB: www.simulations-plus.com
SIC: 7373 Systems software development services

(P-16053)
SOFT MACHINES INC
Also Called: Smachines
3920 Freedom Cir, Santa Clara (95054-1240)
PHONE..............................408 969-0215
Mahesh Lingareddy, *CEO*
Mohammad Abdallah, *President*
Suresh Thirumandas, *Vice Pres*
Shawna Gonzales, *Admin Asst*
Eric Work, *Software Engr*
EMP: 65
SQ FT: 5,000

SALES (est): 9.3MM **Privately Held**
SIC: 7373 Systems software development services

(P-16054)
SOFTWARE DYNAMICS INCORPORATED
8501 Fllbrook Ave Ste 200, Canoga Park (91304)
PHONE..............................818 992-3299
Matthew Hale, *President*
Christopher J Stein, *Treasurer*
Richard Dobb, *Admin Sec*
EMP: 164
SQ FT: 40,000
SALES (est): 5.9MM **Publicly Held**
WEB: www.s1.com
SIC: 7373 7371 Computer systems analysis & design; computer software development
HQ: S1 Corporation
705 Westech Dr
Norcross GA 30092
678 966-9499

(P-16055)
SOLESTAGE INC
Also Called: Store & Online
17651 Railroad St, City of Industry (91748-1194)
PHONE..............................909 576-1309
Lane Wang, *CEO*
EMP: 50
SALES (est): 15MM **Privately Held**
SIC: 7373 7371 Value-added resellers, computer systems; computer software development & applications

(P-16056)
SONICWALL INC (PA)
1033 Mccarthy Blvd, Milpitas (95035-7920)
PHONE..............................800 509-1265
Bill Conner, *President*
Charles Canipe, *Partner*
Evan Kaplan, *President*
Ravi Chopra, *CFO*
Joe Nguyenle, *Officer*
EMP: 81
SQ FT: 86,000
SALES (est): 203.5MM **Privately Held**
WEB: www.sonicwall.com
SIC: 7373 Systems software development services

(P-16057)
SPARXENT INC (PA)
65 Enterprise, Aliso Viejo (92656-2705)
PHONE..............................949 222-2287
Steve Dewindt, *CEO*
Andrew Hyde, *CFO*
EMP: 50
SALES (est): 2.6MM **Privately Held**
SIC: 7373 Systems software development services

(P-16058)
SPIKE TECHNOLOGIES INC
2386 Lacey Dr, Milpitas (95035-6121)
PHONE..............................408 410-0624
Nikhil Modi, *President*
Pradeep Vajram, *COO*
EMP: 50
SALES (est): 3.2MM **Privately Held**
SIC: 7373 Systems engineering, computer related

(P-16059)
SSINFOTEK INC
15615 Alton Pkwy Ste 450, Irvine (92618-3308)
PHONE..............................949 732-3100
Prabhakara Pelluru, *President*
EMP: 50
SALES (est): 3.8MM **Privately Held**
SIC: 7373 Systems software development services

(P-16060)
STRATEGIC DATA SYSTEMS
Also Called: SDS
2020 Camino Del Rio N # 505, San Diego (92108-1544)
PHONE..............................619 546-7200
James Christopher, *President*
Eaton Jones, *Vice Pres*
Ryan Snyder, *Director*

EMP: 125
SQ FT: 3,000
SALES (est): 18.1MM **Privately Held**
WEB: www.sdatasystems.com
SIC: **7373** 7379 Systems software development services; computer related consulting services

(P-16061)
STRIPE INC
Also Called: Stripe Payments Company
185 Berry St Ste 550, San Francisco
(94107-9105)
PHONE..................................888 963-8955
Patrick Collison, *CEO*
Devesh Senapati, *Partner*
Billy Alvarado, *COO*
Shefali Roy, *Officer*
Maher Beg, *Software Engr*
EMP: 1100
SALES (est): 98.4MM **Privately Held**
SIC: **7373** Systems software development services

(P-16062)
SYSOREX USA (HQ)
101 Larkspur Landing Cir # 120, Larkspur
(94939-1749)
PHONE..................................415 389-7500
Nadir Ali, *CEO*
Mike Becker, *Manager*
EMP: 60
SQ FT: 2,800
SALES (est): 23.4MM
SALES (corp-wide): 45.1MM **Publicly Held**
WEB: www.lilien.com
SIC: **7373** Systems integration services
PA: Inpixon
2479 E Byshore Rd Ste 195
Palo Alto CA 94303
408 702-2167

(P-16063)
SYSTEM INTEGRATORS INC (HQ)
Also Called: Netlinx Publishing Solutions
1740 N Market Blvd, Sacramento
(95834-1997)
PHONE..................................916 830-2400
Paul Donlan, *President*
Allan Katzen, *Vice Pres*
Paul Nartey, *Opers Mgr*
EMP: 140
SQ FT: 70,000
SALES (est): 9.7MM **Privately Held**
SIC: **7373** 7372 7371 Computer integrated systems design; prepackaged software; custom computer programming services
PA: Net-Linx Ag
Kathe-Kollwitz-Ufer 76-79
Dresden
351 318-750

(P-16064)
TALEND INC (HQ)
800 Bridge Pkwy Ste 200, Redwood City
(94065-1156)
PHONE..................................650 539-3200
Mike Tuchen, *CEO*
Thomas Tuchscherer, *CFO*
Ashley Stirrup, *Chief Mktg Ofcr*
Nello Franco, *Senior VP*
Brad Stratton, *Senior VP*
EMP: 94
SQ FT: 1,200
SALES (est): 117.7MM
SALES (corp-wide): 60.1MM **Privately Held**
SIC: **7373** Computer systems analysis & design; systems integration services
PA: Talend
9 Rue Pages
Suresnes 92150
140 999-704

(P-16065)
TIBURON INC
9477 Waples St Ste 100, San Diego
(92121-2934)
PHONE..................................858 799-7000
Toney Eales, *CEO*
Blake Clark, *CFO*
Sean Raburn, *Principal*
EMP: 100

SQ FT: 18,647
SALES (est): 288.9K
SALES (corp-wide): 128.8MM **Privately Held**
WEB: www.tiburoninc.com
SIC: **7373** Computer integrated systems design
PA: Tritech Software Systems
9477 Waples St Ste 100
San Diego CA 92121
858 799-7000

(P-16066)
TRAMS INC (DH)
5777 W Century Blvd # 1200, Los Angeles
(90045-5674)
PHONE..................................310 641-8726
Lee B Rosen, *President*
EMP: 65
SQ FT: 14,500
SALES (est): 5.4MM **Publicly Held**
WEB: www.clientbase.com
SIC: **7373** Systems software development services
HQ: Sabre Glbl Inc.
3150 Sabre Dr
Southlake TX 76092
682 605-1000

(P-16067)
TRINITY TECHNOLOGY GROUP INC
2015 J St Ste 105, Sacramento
(95811-3124)
PHONE..................................916 779-0201
Randall E Duart, *CEO*
Timothy Purdy, *CFO*
Jane Duart, *Treasurer*
Stephen Williamson, *Vice Pres*
EMP: 67
SQ FT: 2,800
SALES (est): 14.8MM **Privately Held**
WEB: www.trinitytg.com
SIC: **7373** Systems software development services

(P-16068)
TWO PORE GUYS SYSTEM INC
101 Cooper St, Santa Cruz (95060-4526)
PHONE..................................821 420-0710
Jeremie Sutton Lumbroso, *Principal*
Jeremie Lumbroso, *CEO*
Michael Yin, *Principal*
EMP: 99
SALES: 18MM **Privately Held**
SIC: **7373** Computer integrated systems design

(P-16069)
UNISYS CORPORATION
9701 Jeronimo Rd Ste 100, Irvine
(92618-2076)
PHONE..................................949 380-5000
Carmen Lynch, *Manager*
EMP: 1000
SALES (corp-wide): 2.7B **Publicly Held**
WEB: www.unisys.com
SIC: **7373** Computer integrated systems design
PA: Unisys Corporation
801 Lakeview Dr Ste 100
Blue Bell PA 19422
215 986-4011

(P-16070)
UNITEK INC
Also Called: Interket Enterprise
41350 Christy St, Fremont (94538-3115)
PHONE..................................510 623-8544
Philip Kim, *CEO*
Russ Morrow, *Vice Pres*
EMP: 65
SQ FT: 20,000
SALES (est): 9.3MM **Privately Held**
WEB: www.unitekinc.com
SIC: **7373** 3679 3672 Turnkey vendors, computer systems; electronic circuits; printed circuit boards

(P-16071)
V-TEK SYSTEMS CORPORATION
21045 Ridge Park Dr, Yorba Linda
(92886-7808)
PHONE..................................909 396-5355
Bernard D Abrams, *President*
Mary Ellen Turino, *Human Resources*

EMP: 65
SQ FT: 19,000
SALES (est): 9.6MM **Privately Held**
WEB: www.v-tek.com
SIC: **7373** Computer integrated systems design

(P-16072)
VENCORE SVCS & SOLUTIONS INC
1315 Dell Ave, Campbell (95008-6609)
PHONE..................................408 961-3200
Carol Campbell, *President*
EMP: 50
SALES (corp-wide): 13.5B **Publicly Held**
SIC: **7373** Computer integrated systems design
HQ: Vencore Services And Solutions, Inc.
3076 Centreville Rd # 200
Herndon VA 20171
703 391-7017

(P-16073)
VERTISYSTEM INC
39300 Civic Center Dr # 230, Fremont
(94538-2338)
PHONE..................................510 794-8099
Shaloo Jeswani, *CEO*
Rakesh Sadhwani, *President*
Deebali Syed, *Vice Pres*
Smitha Prabhakaran, *Technical Mgr*
EMP: 110
SQ FT: 2,744
SALES (est): 9.8MM **Privately Held**
SIC: **7373** Systems software development services

(P-16074)
VICOR INC
855 Marina Bay Pkwy # 100, Richmond
(94804-6413)
PHONE..................................510 621-2000
Robert Kirk, *CEO*
Garry Mah, *CFO*
EMP: 72
SALES (est): 6.9MM
SALES (corp-wide): 9.1B **Publicly Held**
WEB: www.vicor.com
SIC: **7373** 7371 Systems engineering, computer related; computer software development
HQ: Metavante Corporation
4900 W Brown Deer Rd
Milwaukee WI 53223

(P-16075)
WAVESTRONG INC
5674 Stoneridge Dr # 225, Pleasanton
(94588-8500)
PHONE..................................925 549-2882
Harpreet Walia, *CEO*
Raj Khanna, *COO*
Mandeet Dhoat, *Vice Pres*
EMP: 94
SQ FT: 5,200
SALES (est): 12.4MM **Privately Held**
SIC: **7373** 7379 Computer integrated systems design; computer related consulting services

(P-16076)
WESCON TECHNOLOGY INC
4655 Old Ironsides Dr # 170, Santa Clara
(95054-1808)
PHONE..................................408 727-8818
Fred MA, *President*
Simon Minett, *COO*
Jason Huang, *Vice Pres*
Julie Wang, *Vice Pres*
Joanna Hsu, *Manager*
EMP: 140
SQ FT: 1,610
SALES (est): 15.3MM **Privately Held**
WEB: www.wescongroup.com
SIC: **7373** 7371 Computer integrated systems design; computer software writing services

(P-16077)
WEST PUBLISHING CORPORATION
Also Called: Elite
800 Crprate Pinte Ste 150, Culver City
(90230)
P.O. Box 51606, Los Angeles (90051-5906)
PHONE..................................424 243-2100
Salim Sunderji, *Vice Pres*
EMP: 174 **Publicly Held**
WEB: www.ruttergroup.com
SIC: **7373** 7371 Computer integrated systems design; custom computer programming services
HQ: West Publishing Corporation
610 Opperman Dr
Eagan MN 55123
651 687-7000

(P-16078)
XDIMENSIONAL TECHNOLOGIES INC
145 S State College Blvd # 160, Brea
(92821-5824)
PHONE..................................714 672-8960
Michael Walther, *Branch Mgr*
EMP: 60 **Privately Held**
WEB: www.xdimensional.com
SIC: **7373** Systems integration services
PA: Xdimensional Technologies Inc
450a Apollo St Ste A
Brea CA 92821

(P-16079)
XP SYSTEMS CORPORATION (HQ)
405 Science Dr, Moorpark (93021-2247)
PHONE..................................805 532-9100
John Edwards, *President*
Milton Denicholas, *Vice Pres*
Drew Foley, *Principal*
Tina Laramie, *Executive Asst*
Leela Dwaram, *QA Dir*
EMP: 200
SQ FT: 109,256
SALES (est): 21.9MM
SALES (corp-wide): 5.7B **Publicly Held**
WEB: www.xpsystems.com
SIC: **7373** Computer integrated systems design
PA: Fiserv, Inc.
255 Fiserv Dr
Brookfield WI 53045
262 879-5000

(P-16080)
ZENITH INFOTECH LIMITED
39675 Cedar Blvd Ste 240b, Newark
(94560-8541)
PHONE..................................510 687-1943
EMP: 145
SALES: 7.5MM **Privately Held**
WEB: www.zenithinfotech.com
SIC: **7373**
PA: Zenith Infotech Limited
29 & 30 Zenith House
Mumbai MH 40009

(P-16081)
ZMICRO INC (PA)
Also Called: Z Microsystems
9820 Summers Ridge Rd, San Diego
(92121-3083)
PHONE..................................858 831-7000
Jack Wade, *CEO*
Jason Wade, *President*
John Howell, *COO*
Rick Schmidt, *CFO*
Rick Elliot, *Vice Pres*
EMP: 57
SQ FT: 36,800
SALES (est): 20.1MM **Privately Held**
WEB: www.zmicro.com
SIC: **7373** 3577 3572 Computer integrated systems design; computer peripheral equipment; computer storage devices

P R O D U C T S & S V C S

7374 Data & Computer Processing & Preparation

(P-16082)
A S E C INTERNATIONAL INC
Also Called: Asec Group
11400 W Olympic Blvd, Los Angeles
(90064-1550)
PHONE....................803 939-4809
Evan Green, *President*
Del Snyder, *Exec VP*
Steve Seiler, *Admin Sec*
EMP: 700
SQ FT: 25,000
SALES (est): 21.8MM **Privately Held**
WEB: www.asecusa.com
SIC: 7374 Data processing service

(P-16083)
ACTIVIDENTITY CORPORATION
6623 Dumbarton Cir, Fremont
(94555-3603)
PHONE....................510 574-0100
Grant Evans, *Ch of Bd*
Jacques Kerrest, *COO*
John Boyer, *Senior VP*
Jerome Becquart, *Vice Pres*
Carolyn Newburn, *Vice Pres*
EMP: 218
SQ FT: 41,000
SALES (est): 16.4MM
SALES (corp-wide): 9B **Privately Held**
WEB: www.actividentity.com
SIC: 7374 Data verification service
HQ: Hid Global Corporation
611 Center Ridge Dr
Austin TX 78753
800 237-7769

(P-16084)
ALORICA INC (PA)
Also Called: Priority One Support
5 Park Plz Ste 1100, Irvine (92614-8502)
PHONE....................949 527-4600
Andy Lee, *President*
Kyle Baker, *President*
Jay King, *President*
Greg Haller, *COO*
Cindy Fiorillo, *CFO*
EMP: 100
SALES (est): 7.3B **Privately Held**
WEB: www.alorica.com
SIC: 7374 7389 7373 Data processing
service; telephone answering service;
telemarketing services; computer inte-
grated systems design

(P-16085)
AUTOMATIC DATA PROCESSING INC
Also Called: ADP
7000 Village Dr Ste 200, Buena Park
(90621-2287)
PHONE....................714 690-7000
Joseph Leung, *Principal*
Andrea Bereal, *Vice Pres*
Liz Coulter, *Vice Pres*
Devon Snedden, *Vice Pres*
Teddy Astorga, *Executive*
EMP: 117
SALES (corp-wide): 13.3B **Publicly Held**
SIC: 7374 8721 Data processing service;
payroll accounting service
PA: Automatic Data Processing, Inc.
1 Adp Blvd Ste 1 # 1
Roseland NJ 07068
973 974-5000

(P-16086)
AUTOMATIC DATA PROCESSING INC
Also Called: ADP
9445 Fairway View Pl # 200, Rancho Cuca-
monga (91730-0931)
PHONE....................800 225-5237
Bill Crawford, *Manager*
EMP: 200
SALES (corp-wide): 13.3B **Publicly Held**
SIC: 7374 Data processing service
PA: Automatic Data Processing, Inc.
1 Adp Blvd Ste 1 # 1
Roseland NJ 07068
973 974-5000

(P-16087)
AUTOMATIC DATA PROCESSING INC
Also Called: ADP
5153 Camino Ruiz Ste 100, Camarillo
(93012-8656)
PHONE....................805 383-8630
Erich Hillig, *Director*
Jeff Vlach, *Info Tech Mgr*
Jon Rust, *Technology*
Matt Grindstaff, *Manager*
EMP: 117
SALES (corp-wide): 13.3B **Publicly Held**
SIC: 7374 Data processing service
PA: Automatic Data Processing, Inc.
1 Adp Blvd Ste 1 # 1
Roseland NJ 07068
973 974-5000

(P-16088)
AUTOMATIC DATA PROCESSING INC
Also Called: ADP
600 California St Fl 11, San Francisco
(94108-2727)
PHONE....................800 225-5237
Steve Kapusta, *Manager*
Anamika Bhargava, *District Mgr*
Ashley McKenzie, *District Mgr*
Lisa Kavanaugh, *Technical Staff*
Christine Schindewolf, *Human Res Mgr*
EMP: 50
SALES (corp-wide): 13.3B **Publicly Held**
SIC: 7374 Data processing service
PA: Automatic Data Processing, Inc.
1 Adp Blvd Ste 1 # 1
Roseland NJ 07068
973 974-5000

(P-16089)
AUTOMATIC DATA PROCESSING INC
Also Called: ADP
620 W Covina Blvd, San Dimas
(91773-2956)
PHONE....................909 592-6411
Melanie Hardin, *Branch Mgr*
Victor Mak, *Vice Pres*
Rick Weber, *VP Mktg*
Heather Cooper, *Counsel*
Venkat Moganti, *Director*
EMP: 130
SALES (corp-wide): 13.3B **Publicly Held**
SIC: 7374 Data processing service
PA: Automatic Data Processing, Inc.
1 Adp Blvd Ste 1 # 1
Roseland NJ 07068
973 974-5000

(P-16090)
AUTOMATIC DATA PROCESSING INC
Also Called: ADP
720 Bay Rd, Redwood City (94063-2479)
PHONE....................800 225-5237
EMP: 130
SALES (corp-wide): 13.3B **Publicly Held**
SIC: 7374 Data processing service
PA: Automatic Data Processing, Inc.
1 Adp Blvd Ste 1 # 1
Roseland NJ 07068
973 974-5000

(P-16091)
AUTOMATIC DATA PROCESSING INC
Also Called: ADP
505 San Marin Dr Ste A110, Novato
(94945-1302)
PHONE....................415 899-7300
EMP: 130
SALES (corp-wide): 11.6B **Publicly Held**
SIC: 7374
PA: Automatic Data Processing, Inc.
1 Adp Blvd Ste 1
Roseland NJ 07068
973 974-5000

(P-16092)
AUTOMATIC DATA PROCESSING INC
Also Called: ADP
3972 Barranca Pkwy J610, Irvine
(92606-1204)
PHONE....................949 751-0360
EMP: 165
SALES (corp-wide): 13.3B **Publicly Held**
SIC: 7374 Data processing service
PA: Automatic Data Processing, Inc.
1 Adp Blvd Ste 1 # 1
Roseland NJ 07068
973 974-5000

(P-16093)
AUTOMATIC DATA PROCESSING INC
Also Called: ADP
820 N Mccarthy Blvd # 120, Milpitas
(95035-5115)
PHONE....................408 876-6600
Robert Thomas, *Branch Mgr*
Nga Tran, *Partner*
Chris Canales, *District Mgr*
Cara Cuison, *District Mgr*
Sergio Quilici, *District Mgr*
EMP: 450
SALES (corp-wide): 13.3B **Publicly Held**
SIC: 7374 8721 Data processing service;
accounting, auditing & bookkeeping
PA: Automatic Data Processing, Inc.
1 Adp Blvd Ste 1 # 1
Roseland NJ 07068
973 974-5000

(P-16094)
AUTOMATIC DATA PROCESSING INC
Also Called: ADP
5355 Orangethorpe Ave, La Palma
(90623-1095)
PHONE....................714 994-2000
Jim Wassik, *Branch Mgr*
Sean Mackay, *District Mgr*
John Oravitz, *District Mgr*
Wanda Mamaradlo, *Info Tech Dir*
Rick Bartlett, *Info Tech Mgr*
EMP: 78
SALES (corp-wide): 13.3B **Publicly Held**
SIC: 7374 Data processing service
PA: Automatic Data Processing, Inc.
1 Adp Blvd Ste 1 # 1
Roseland NJ 07068
973 974-5000

(P-16095)
AUTOMATIC DATA PROCESSING INC
ADP
4125 Hopyard Rd, Pleasanton
(94588-8534)
PHONE....................925 251-5300
Russ Deloach, *Officer*
Kenneth Wong, *Info Tech Mgr*
EMP: 78
SALES (corp-wide): 13.3B **Publicly Held**
SIC: 7374 8741 8742 Data processing
service; personnel management; man-
agement consulting services
PA: Automatic Data Processing, Inc.
1 Adp Blvd Ste 1 # 1
Roseland NJ 07068
973 974-5000

(P-16096)
AUTOMATIC DATA PROCESSING INC
Also Called: ADP
400 W Covina Blvd, San Dimas
(91773-2954)
PHONE....................800 225-5237
Rodney Hroblak, *Principal*
Robert Barnett, *Vice Pres*
Jorge Gonzalez, *District Mgr*
Anther Guilas, *Administration*
Mike Gill, *Programmer Anys*
EMP: 117
SALES (corp-wide): 13.3B **Publicly Held**
SIC: 7374 8721 Data processing service;
accounting, auditing & bookkeeping
PA: Automatic Data Processing, Inc.
1 Adp Blvd Ste 1 # 1
Roseland NJ 07068
973 974-5000

(P-16097)
AUTOMATIC DATA PROCESSING INC
Also Called: ADP
600 Crprate Pinte Ste 450, Los Angeles
(90230)
PHONE....................800 225-5237
Kevin Gramian, *Manager*
Ajit Kumar, *Chief*
Bryant Kwon, *Director*
Breeda Desmond, *Manager*
Jon Semizian, *Manager*
EMP: 70
SALES (corp-wide): 13.3B **Publicly Held**
SIC: 7374 8721 Data processing service;
payroll accounting service
PA: Automatic Data Processing, Inc.
1 Adp Blvd Ste 1 # 1
Roseland NJ 07068
973 974-5000

(P-16098)
AUTOMATIC DATA PROCESSING INC
Also Called: ADP
1450 Frazee Rd Ste 601, San Diego
(92108-4340)
PHONE....................619 293-4800
David Manriquez, *Branch Mgr*
Damon Iamele, *District Mgr*
Renee Luke, *Admin Sec*
Heather Zerrenner, *Consultant*
EMP: 100
SALES (corp-wide): 13.3B **Publicly Held**
SIC: 7374 Data processing service
PA: Automatic Data Processing, Inc.
1 Adp Blvd Ste 1 # 1
Roseland NJ 07068
973 974-5000

(P-16099)
BLEACHER REPORT INC
609 Mission St, San Francisco
(94105-3506)
PHONE....................415 777-5505
Mike Jacobsen, *CFO*
Ryan Oleary, *Producer*
Mark Smoyer, *Manager*
Tom Filip, *Editor*
Ian Kenyon, *Editor*
EMP: 65
SALES: 5.4MM **Privately Held**
SIC: 7374 Computer graphics service

(P-16100)
BMI IMAGING SYSTEMS INC (PA)
1115 E Arques Ave, Sunnyvale
(94085-3904)
PHONE....................916 924-6666
William D Whitney, *CEO*
Janice Harrison, *Corp Secy*
Penfold Brad, *Vice Pres*
Brad Gilbert, *Vice Pres*
Jim Modrall, *Vice Pres*
EMP: 60
SQ FT: 16,400
SALES: 9MM **Privately Held**
WEB: www.bmiimaging.com
SIC: 7374 5044 7334 Optical scanning
data service; microfilm equipment; photo-
copying & duplicating services

(P-16101)
CALIFORNIA SURVEY RES SVCS
15350 Sherman Way Ste 480, Van Nuys
(91406-4268)
PHONE....................818 780-2777
William Kaplan, *CEO*
Kenneth Gross, *President*
Terrie Kerr, *Research*
Hasmik Davtyan, *Manager*
EMP: 125
SQ FT: 10,000
SALES (est): 8.4MM **Privately Held**
WEB: www.calsurvey.com
SIC: 7374 8732 Data processing service;
market analysis or research

(P-16102)
CALIFRNIA HLTH HUMN SRVCS AGCY
Also Called: Hhsa Data Center
3301 S St, Sacramento (95816-7019)
PHONE....................916 739-7640

▲ = Import ▼=Export
◆ =Import/Export

John Moise, *Director*
EMP: 500 Privately Held
SIC: 7374 9431 Data processing & preparation; administration of public health programs;
HQ: California Health & Human Services Agency
1600 9th St Ste 460
Sacramento CA 95814

(P-16103)
CASTLIGHT HEALTH INC (PA)
150 Spear St Ste 400, San Francisco (94105-1537)
PHONE..................................415 829-1400
John C Doyle, *CEO*
Bryan Roberts, *Ch of Bd*
Derek Newell, *President*
Siobhan Nolan Mangini, *CFO*
Michael Eberhard, *Bd of Directors*
EMP: 94
SQ FT: 44,580
SALES: 131.4MM Publicly Held
SIC: 7374 7372 Data processing & preparation; prepackaged software

(P-16104)
CCH INCORPORATED
Also Called: Cch Computax
20101 Hamilton Ave # 200, Torrance (90502-1371)
PHONE..................................310 800-9800
Jessica Perez, *Human Res Mgr*
Rajkumar Govindaraj, *Info Tech Mgr*
Srinivas Lingineni, *Technology*
EMP: 350
SQ FT: 280,000
SALES (corp-wide): 5.2B Privately Held
WEB: www.cch.com
SIC: 7374 7372 7371 Data processing & preparation; prepackaged software; custom computer programming services
HQ: Cch Incorporated
2700 Lake Cook Rd
Riverwoods IL 60015
847 267-7000

(P-16105)
CHANGE HLTHCARE OPERATIONS LLC
241 Lombard St, Thousand Oaks (91360-5807)
PHONE..................................805 777-7773
Bob Ashworth, *Branch Mgr*
EMP: 75
SALES (corp-wide): 96.2MM Privately Held
SIC: 7374 8742 Data processing service; hospital & health services consultant
HQ: Change Healthcare Operations, Llc
3055 Lebanon Pike # 1000
Nashville TN 37214

(P-16106)
COMMUNITY HOSPITALS CENTL CAL
Also Called: Information Services Dept
1140 T St, Fresno (93721-1413)
P.O. Box 9732 (93794-9732)
PHONE..................................559 459-2916
Terri Lutz, *Branch Mgr*
Joshua Powell, *Programmer Anys*
EMP: 150
SALES (corp-wide): 1.6B Privately Held
SIC: 7374 8741 8062 Data processing & preparation; hospital management; hospital, AMA approved residency
PA: Community Hospitals Of Central California
2823 Fresno St
Fresno CA 93721
559 459-6000

(P-16107)
CORRECTONS RHBLTATION CAL DEPT
Also Called: Data Center
1920 Alabama Ave, Sacramento (95825)
P.O. Box 942883 (94283-0001)
PHONE..................................916 358-2319
Joe Penora, *Director*
EMP: 200 Privately Held
SIC: 7374 9223 Data processing service; correctional institutions;

HQ: California Department Of Corrections & Rehabilitation
1515 S St
Sacramento CA 95811

(P-16108)
COUNTY OF LOS ANGELES
Also Called: Voter Precinct Voter Reg Off
12400 Imperial Hwy, Norwalk (90650-3134)
PHONE..................................562 462-2094
Connie McCormack, *Branch Mgr*
EMP: 800 Privately Held
WEB: www.co.la.ca.us
SIC: 7374 9111 Data entry service; executive offices
PA: County Of Los Angeles
500 W Temple St Ste 437
Los Angeles CA 90012
213 974-1101

(P-16109)
COUNTY OF MARIN
Also Called: Computer Programming Dept
371 Bel Marin Keys Blvd # 100, Novato (94949-5662)
PHONE..................................415 499-7060
Daze Hill, *Director*
Yvonne Zupkow, *Admin Asst*
Barbara Layton, *Telecomm Mgr*
Deter Guglielmo, *Analyst*
Katherine Harrington, *Analyst*
EMP: 80 Privately Held
SIC: 7374 9111 Data processing service; county supervisors' & executives' offices
PA: County Of Marin
3501 Civic Center Dr # 258
San Rafael CA 94903
415 473-6358

(P-16110)
COUNTY OF SONOMA
Also Called: Sonoma County Data Processing
2615 Paulin Dr, Santa Rosa (95403-2804)
PHONE..................................707 527-2911
Daniel Fruchey, *Info Tech Dir*
Sabrina Doss, *Project Mgr*
EMP: 150
SQ FT: 13,000 Privately Held
WEB: www.sonomacompost.com
SIC: 7374 Data processing service
PA: County Of Sonoma
585 Fiscal Dr 100
Santa Rosa CA 95403
707 565-2431

(P-16111)
COUNTY OF SONOMA
Also Called: Information Systems Department
2300 Prof Dr Rear Door B, Santa Rosa (95403)
PHONE..................................707 527-2911
Mark Walsh, *Branch Mgr*
Hector Velasquez, *Network Analyst*
EMP: 75 Privately Held
WEB: www.sonomacompost.com
SIC: 7374 Data processing & preparation
PA: County Of Sonoma
585 Fiscal Dr 100
Santa Rosa CA 95403
707 565-2431

(P-16112)
COUNTY OF TUOLUMNE
Also Called: Information Systems & Services
2 S Green St, Sonora (95370-4618)
PHONE..................................209 533-5561
Gregg Jacob, *Manager*
Jacob Gregg, *Manager*
EMP: 500 Privately Held
WEB: www.tuolumne.courts.ca.gov
SIC: 7374 9111 7376 Data processing & preparation; county supervisors' & executives' offices; computer facilities management
PA: County Of Tuolumne
2 S Green St
Sonora CA 95370
209 533-5521

(P-16113)
CYBERSOURCE CORPORATION (HQ)
900 Metro Center Blvd, Foster City (94404-2172)
P.O. Box 8999, San Francisco (94128-8999)
PHONE..................................650 432-7350
Alfred F Kelly Jr, *President*
Scott R Cruickshank, *President*
Steven D Pellizzer, *CFO*
Robert J Ford, *Exec VP*
Perry Dembner, *Senior VP*
EMP: 115
SALES (est): 127.5MM Publicly Held
WEB: www.cybersource.com
SIC: 7374 Data processing service

(P-16114)
DATAPROSE INC
1451 N Rice Ave Ste A, Oxnard (93030-7991)
P.O. Box 451902, Omaha NE (68145-9002)
PHONE..................................805 278-7430
Glenn Carter, *President*
John Ray, *President*
Fred Fleet, *CFO*
Bill Murray, *Vice Pres*
Paul Orfalea, *Principal*
EMP: 65
SQ FT: 25,000
SALES (est): 2.4MM Publicly Held
SIC: 7374 7389 Service bureau, computer; fund raising organizations
PA: Csg Systems International, Inc.
6175 S Willow Dr Ste 100
Greenwood Village CO 80111

(P-16115)
DATASTAX INC (PA)
3975 Freedom Cir Ste 400, Santa Clara (95054-1258)
PHONE..................................650 389-6000
Billy Bosworth, *CEO*
Robert O'Donovan, *CFO*
Karl Van Den Bergh, *Chief Mktg Ofcr*
Matt Pfeil, *Officer*
Steve Rowland, *Exec VP*
EMP: 97 EST: 2011
SALES (est): 92.4MM Privately Held
SIC: 7374 Data processing & preparation

(P-16116)
DECISION MINDS
1525 Mccarthy Blvd # 224, Milpitas (95035-7453)
PHONE..................................408 309-8051
Murali Pabbisetty, *Owner*
Balati Ratagocalan, *Co-Owner*
Vidhya Sridaran, *Opers Mgr*
EMP: 135
SALES: 10MM Privately Held
SIC: 7374 Data entry service

(P-16117)
DELUXE MEDIA SERVICES
2130 N Hollywood Way, Burbank (91505-1522)
PHONE..................................818 526-3700
Joe Bigley, *General Mgr*
EMP: 500
SALES (est): 33.1MM Privately Held
SIC: 7374 Computer graphics service

(P-16118)
DOCLER MEDIA LLC (DH)
8000 Beverly Blvd, Los Angeles (90048-4504)
PHONE..................................424 777-3999
Balazs Sipocz, *CEO*
EMP: 62
SQ FT: 30,000
SALES: 22.3MM Privately Held
SIC: 7374 8741 Computer graphics service; computer processing services; administrative management
HQ: Docler Holding Sarl
Avenue John F. Kennedy 44
Luxembourg 1855
261 118-1

(P-16119)
DOCUMENT PROC SOLUTIONS INC (PA)
Also Called: Southern California Document
590 W Lambert Rd, Brea (92821-3914)
PHONE..................................714 482-2060
Felipe Heras, *President*
Ian Staley, *Regional Mgr*
Guadalupe Garcia, *Project Mgr*
Julie Mojica, *Accounting Mgr*
Lisa Ritter, *Accounting Mgr*
EMP: 85
SALES (est): 8.8MM Privately Held
WEB: www.dpsx.com
SIC: 7374 Data processing service

(P-16120)
E C WISE INC (PA)
1299 4th St Ste 505, San Rafael (94901-3031)
PHONE..................................415 355-9473
Jack Hakim, *CEO*
Tom Spitzer, *CFO*
Stan Shambaugh, *Info Tech Mgr*
Sean Smiley, *Info Tech Mgr*
Steven Libson, *Sales Associate*
EMP: 100 EST: 1998
SQ FT: 6,600
SALES (est): 8.5MM Privately Held
WEB: www.ecwise.com
SIC: 7374 Data processing service

(P-16121)
EDATA SOLUTIONS INC
39180 Liberty St Ste 125, Fremont (94538-2581)
PHONE..................................510 574-5380
Manan Kothari, *CEO*
EMP: 1000
SQ FT: 6,000
SALES: 1.1MM Privately Held
SIC: 7374 7371 Data processing service; computer software development & applications

(P-16122)
EMERALD CONNECT LLC (HQ)
15050 Avenue Of Sci 200, San Diego (92128)
PHONE..................................800 233-2834
Adam D Amsterdam, *Mng Member*
Sharon Greener, *Exec VP*
Heather Hinkle, *Exec VP*
Heidi Saucier, *Exec VP*
Dave Briggs, *Vice Pres*
EMP: 100
SQ FT: 35,000
SALES (est): 19.1MM
SALES (corp-wide): 4.3B Publicly Held
WEB: emeraldconnect.com
SIC: 7374 7331 Data processing service; mailing service
PA: Broadridge Financial Solutions, Inc.
5 Dakota Dr Ste 300
New Hyde Park NY 11042
516 472-5400

(P-16123)
EMOVE EXPRESS COMPANY
Also Called: Emovexpress.com
688 Matsonia Dr, Foster City (94404-1337)
PHONE..................................650 377-0913
Anthony Chiu, *Ch of Bd*
Steve Argyres, *President*
Teresa Hall, *CFO*
EMP: 56
SQ FT: 2,760
SALES (est): 2MM Privately Held
WEB: www.emoveexpress.com
SIC: 7374 Computer graphics service

(P-16124)
ENCLARITY INC
16815 Von Karman Ave # 125, Irvine (92606-2412)
PHONE..................................949 614-8110
Sean Downs, *CEO*
Paul Perleberg, *President*
Warren Gouk Andrea, *CFO*
Scott Marber, *Vice Pres*
Brian Smith, *Vice Pres*
EMP: 57
SQ FT: 3,500

SALES (est): 2.8MM
SALES (corp-wide): 9.7B **Privately Held**
WEB: www.enclarity.com
SIC: 7374 Data processing service
HQ: Lexisnexis Risk Solutions Inc.
1000 Alderman Dr
Alpharetta GA 30005
678 694-6000

(P-16125)

ENTERPRISE SERVICES LLC
3215 Prospect Park Dr, Rancho Cordova
(95670-6017)
PHONE..........................916 636-1000
Dennis Dormen, *Manager*
EMP: 800
SALES (corp-wide): 13.5B **Publicly Held**
WEB: www.eds.com
SIC: 7374 Data processing service
HQ: Enterprise Services Llc
5400 Legacy Dr
Plano TX 75024
703 245-9675

(P-16126)

ENTERPRISE SERVICES LLC
3990 Sherman St, San Diego (92110-4324)
PHONE..........................619 817-3851
Javier Berellez, *Manager*
EMP: 350
SALES (corp-wide): 13.5B **Publicly Held**
WEB: www.eds.com
SIC: 7374 Data processing & preparation
HQ: Enterprise Services Llc
5400 Legacy Dr
Plano TX 75024
703 245-9675

(P-16127)

ENTERPRISE SERVICES LLC
1 Hornet Way, El Segundo (90245-2804)
PHONE..........................310 331-1074
Nelson Lee, *Branch Mgr*
EMP: 138
SALES (corp-wide): 13.5B **Publicly Held**
WEB: www.eds.com
SIC: 7374 Data processing service
HQ: Enterprise Services Llc
5400 Legacy Dr
Plano TX 75024
703 245-9675

(P-16128)

EPOCHCOM LLC
2644 30th St Fl 2, Santa Monica
(90405-3061)
PHONE..........................310 664-5700
Joel Hall, *Mng Member*
Esther Martinez, *COO*
Harmik Gharapetian, *Vice Pres*
Christine Hull, *Vice Pres*
David Bonsukan, *Risk Mgmt Dir*
EMP: 150
SQ FT: 22,000
SALES (est): 15.7MM **Privately Held**
SIC: 7374 Data processing service

(P-16129)

FIERCE WOMBAT GAMES INC
910 E Hamilton Ave Fl 6, Campbell
(95008-0655)
PHONE..........................650 996-2910
Jonathan Buckheit, *CEO*
Michael Parrott, *Accountant*
EMP: 50 **EST:** 2010
SQ FT: 10,000
SALES: 50MM **Privately Held**
SIC: 7374 7371 Computer graphics serv-
ice; computer software development &
applications

(P-16130)

FIGURE EIGHT TECHNOLOGIES INC
940 Howard St, San Francisco
(94103-4114)
PHONE..........................415 471-1920
Lukas Biewald, *CEO*
Cameron Befus, *President*
Christopher Van Pelt, *COO*
Ryan Ferrier, *Vice Pres*
Vikram Kumar, *Vice Pres*
EMP: 60
SQ FT: 8,400
SALES (est): 7.5MM **Privately Held**
SIC: 7374 Computer graphics service

(P-16131)

FIRST DATABANK INC
701 Gateway Blvd Ste 600, San Francisco
(94188)
PHONE..........................650 588-5454
Joe Hirshmann, *Branch Mgr*
Joseph Palermo, *President*
Amanda Johnston, *Office Mgr*
Ayla-Mae Domingo, *Human Resources*
EMP: 100
SQ FT: 3,000
SALES (corp-wide): 6.6B **Privately Held**
WEB: www.firstdatabank.com
SIC: 7374 Data processing service
HQ: First Databank, Inc.
701 Gateway Blvd Ste 600
South San Francisco CA 94080
800 633-3453

(P-16132)

FISERV INC
19935 E Walnut Dr N, City of Industry
(91789-2818)
PHONE..........................909 595-9074
Mark Breithaupt, *Manager*
EMP: 79
SALES (corp-wide): 5.7B **Publicly Held**
WEB: www.fiserv.com
SIC: 7374 Data processing service
PA: Fiserv, Inc.
255 Fiserv Dr
Brookfield WI 53045
262 879-5000

(P-16133)

FISERV INC
19935 E Walnut Dr N, Walnut
(91789-2818)
PHONE..........................909 598-8700
Bill Costello, *Manager*
EMP: 72
SALES (corp-wide): 5.7B **Publicly Held**
SIC: 7374 Data processing service
PA: Fiserv, Inc.
255 Fiserv Dr
Brookfield WI 53045
262 879-5000

(P-16134)

FISERV INC
525 Almanor Ave, Sunnyvale (94085-3542)
PHONE..........................408 242-3011
EMP: 70
SALES (corp-wide): 5.7B **Publicly Held**
SIC: 7374 Data processing service
PA: Fiserv, Inc.
255 Fiserv Dr
Brookfield WI 53045
262 879-5000

(P-16135)

FISERV INC
405 Science Dr, Moorpark (93021-2247)
PHONE..........................805 532-9100
John Edwards, *Branch Mgr*
EMP: 71
SALES (corp-wide): 5.7B **Publicly Held**
SIC: 7374 7371 Data processing service;
computer software development & appli-
cations
PA: Fiserv, Inc.
255 Fiserv Dr
Brookfield WI 53045
262 879-5000

(P-16136)

FISERV INC
19935 E Walnut Dr N, Walnut
(91789-2818)
PHONE..........................909 595-9074
Jeff Conte, *Manager*
EMP: 62
SALES (corp-wide): 5.7B **Publicly Held**
WEB: www.fiserv.com
SIC: 7374 Data processing service
PA: Fiserv, Inc.
255 Fiserv Dr
Brookfield WI 53045
262 879-5000

(P-16137)

GENERAL SERVICES CAL DEPT
Office Physical Plg & Dev Csu
4665 Lampson Ave, Los Alamitos
(90720-5187)
PHONE..........................562 342-7212

James K Hightower, *Branch Mgr*
EMP: 100 **Privately Held**
WEB: www.4c.net
SIC: 7374 9199 Data processing service;
general government administration
HQ: California Department Of General
Services
707 3rd St
West Sacramento CA 95605

(P-16138)

GLINT INC
1100 Island Dr Ste 101, Redwood City
(94065-5187)
PHONE..........................650 817-7240
Jim Barnett, *CEO*
Dennis Jang, *CFO*
Mary Poppen, *Ch Credit Ofcr*
Jim Bell, *Chief Mktg Ofcr*
Chih-PO Wen, *Officer*
EMP: 100
SQ FT: 12,500
SALES: 5MM **Privately Held**
SIC: 7374 Data processing & preparation

(P-16139)

GREENSOFT TECHNOLOGY INC
155 S El Molino Ave # 100, Pasadena
(91101-2563)
PHONE..........................323 254-5961
Larry Yen, *President*
Jon Wu, *Vice Pres*
EMP: 121
SALES (est): 1.7MM **Privately Held**
SIC: 7374 Data processing service

(P-16140)

HACKERONE INC (PA)
300 Montgomery St # 1200, San Francisco
(94104-1914)
P.O. Box 166 (94104-0166)
PHONE..........................415 891-0777
Alex Rice, *CTO*
Soufiane Houri, *Vice Pres*
Scott Bostwick, *General Mgr*
Meredith Baker, *Executive Asst*
Tracy Nelson, *Executive Asst*
EMP: 55
SQ FT: 3,500
SALES (est): 5.3MM **Privately Held**
SIC: 7374 Data processing & preparation

(P-16141)

HARTE-HNKS MKT INTLLIGENCE INC (PA)
15015 Ave Of Science # 110, San Diego
(92128-3435)
PHONE..........................858 450-1667
Robert G Brown, *President*
Randall W Wussler, *Exec VP*
EMP: 150
SQ FT: 45,000
SALES (est): 25.6MM **Privately Held**
WEB: www.hartehanksmi.com
SIC: 7374 Data processing service

(P-16142)

HYVE SOLUTIONS CORPORATION (HQ)
44201 Nobel Dr, Fremont (94538-3178)
PHONE..........................855 869-6873
Kevin Murai, *CEO*
Peter Larocque, *President*
Stephanie Ballenger, *Credit Staff*
Cody Brooks, *Marketing Staff*
Lyn Caluma, *Sales Staff*
EMP: 3645
SALES (est): 4.4MM
SALES (corp-wide): 17B **Publicly Held**
SIC: 7374 Data processing & preparation
PA: Synnex Corporation
44201 Nobel Dr
Fremont CA 94538
510 656-3333

(P-16143)

I HOT LEADS
19671 Beach Blvd Ste 204, Huntington
Beach (92648-5905)
PHONE..........................714 960-8028
EMP: 56
SALES (est): 1.9MM **Privately Held**
WEB: www.ihotleads.com
SIC: 7374

(P-16144)

IKANO COMMUNICATIONS INC (PA)
Also Called: A & S Technologies
9221 Corbin Ave Ste 260, Northridge
(91324-1625)
PHONE..........................801 924-0900
Jim Murphy, *CEO*
Sam Ghahremanpour, *President*
George Mitsopoulos, *COO*
Dean Russ, *Vice Pres*
EMP: 91
SQ FT: 50,000
SALES (est): 32.7MM **Privately Held**
WEB: www.ikano.com
SIC: 7374 Data processing & preparation

(P-16145)

IMAGESCAN INC
390 S Fair Oaks Ave, Pasadena
(91105-2540)
PHONE..........................626 844-2050
Basker S Krishnan, *President*
Bryan Heesch, *Prgrmr*
Meher Kateli, *Manager*
EMP: 90
SQ FT: 4,000
SALES (est): 5MM **Privately Held**
WEB: www.imagescan-inc.com
SIC: 7374 Data entry service

(P-16146)

INFLECTION LLC
555 Twin Dolphin Dr # 200, Redwood City
(94065-2134)
PHONE..........................650 618-9910
Matthew Monahan,
Kristen McDonald, *Senior Partner*
Donald Landwirth, *COO*
Durbin Michele Don, *Vice Pres*
Terri Chavez, *Office Mgr*
EMP: 136
SQ FT: 22,914
SALES (est): 12.5MM **Privately Held**
SIC: 7374 Data processing & preparation

(P-16147)

INFLECTION RISK SOLUTIONS LLC
Also Called: Goodhire
555 Twin Dolphin Dr, Redwood City
(94065-2129)
PHONE..........................650 618-9910
Matthew Monahan, *Mng Member*
Jeremy Wood, *Executive*
EMP: 50
SQ FT: 7,000
SALES: 5MM **Privately Held**
SIC: 7374 Data processing & preparation

(P-16148)

INKO INDUSTRIAL CORPORATION
695 Vaqueros Ave, Sunnyvale
(94085-3524)
PHONE..........................408 830-1040
George Kuo, *President*
Charlie Chau, *Facilities Mgr*
Joe Mac,
EMP: 100
SQ FT: 80,000
SALES (est): 9.9MM **Privately Held**
WEB: www.pellicle-inko.com
SIC: 7374 Computer graphics service

(P-16149)

INTERNET BRANDS INC (PA)
909 N Pacific Coast Hwy # 11, El Segundo
(90245-2727)
PHONE..........................310 280-4000
Robert N Brisco, *CEO*
Paul Austin, *Partner*
Gregory T Perrier, *President*
Lisa Morita, *COO*
Scott Friedman, *CFO*
▲ **EMP:** 122
SQ FT: 54,000
SALES (est): 257.9MM **Privately Held**
WEB: www.carsdirect.com
SIC: 7374 Computer graphics service

(P-16150)
LEIDOS INC
Also Called: Sissc
1550 N Norma St, Ridgecrest
(93555-2556)
PHONE...............................858 826-7670
Doreen Ross, *Branch Mgr*
EMP: 253
SALES (corp-wide): 10.1B **Publicly Held**
WEB: www.saic.com
SIC: 7374 7373 Data processing & preparation; systems integration services
HQ: Leidos, Inc.
    11951 Freedom Dr Ste 500
    Reston VA 20190
    571 526-6000

(P-16151)
LENDER PROCESSING SERVICES INC
3100 New York Dr Ste 200, Pasadena
(91107-1524)
PHONE...............................626 808-9000
Brian Mushaney, *Vice Pres*
Aimee Hartmann, *Principal*
EMP: 99
SALES (est): 6MM **Privately Held**
SIC: 7374 Data processing & preparation

(P-16152)
LOS ANGELES UNIFIED SCHOOL DST
Also Called: Information Technology Agency
200 N Main St Ste 1400, Los Angeles
(90012-4127)
PHONE...............................213 847-6911
Jesse Juarros, *Manager*
EMP: 700
SALES (corp-wide): 3.8B **Privately Held**
WEB: www.lausd.k12.ca.us
SIC: 7374 Data processing service
PA: Los Angeles Unified School District
    333 S Beaudry Ave Ste 209
    Los Angeles CA 90017
    213 241-1000

(P-16153)
MARIN SOFTWARE INCORPORATED (PA)
123 Mission St Fl 27, San Francisco
(94105-1681)
PHONE...............................415 399-2580
Christopher Lien, *Ch of Bd*
Catriona M Fallon, *CFO*
Brad Kinnish, *CFO*
Nancy Koshiyama, *Officer*
Avik Dey, *Exec VP*
EMP: 116
SQ FT: 43,000
SALES: 74.9MM **Publicly Held**
SIC: 7374 Data processing & preparation

(P-16154)
MARKETLIVE INC
617 2nd St Ste D, Petaluma (94952-5160)
PHONE...............................707 780-1600
Ken Burke, *CEO*
Josh Baumrind, *Partner*
James Miller, *Exec VP*
EMP: 110
SQ FT: 35,000
SALES (est): 16.2MM
SALES (corp-wide): 59.8MM **Privately Held**
WEB: www.mmlive.com
SIC: 7374 Computer graphics service
PA: Kibo Software, Inc.
    717 N Harwood St Ste 1800
    Dallas TX 75201
    707 780-1600

(P-16155)
MERCHANT SERVICES INC (PA)
1 S Van Ness Ave Fl 5, San Francisco
(94103-5416)
PHONE...............................817 725-0900
Lorraine Stimmell, *CEO*
Le Tran-TI, *Senior VP*
Beth Dobyns, *Human Res Mgr*
EMP: 400
SQ FT: 58,336
SALES (est): 34MM **Privately Held**
WEB: www.msimerchantservices.com
SIC: 7374 Data processing service

(P-16156)
MERCURY DEFENSE SYSTEMS INC (HQ)
Also Called: Mercury Systems
10855 Bus Ctr Dr Bldg A, Cypress (90630)
PHONE...............................714 898-8200
Mark Aslett, *CEO*
Brian Perry, *President*
Kevin M Bisson, *CFO*
Gerald M Haines II, *Senior VP*
Peter Reese, *Vice Pres*
EMP: 84
SQ FT: 35,000
SALES (est): 17.6MM
SALES (corp-wide): 493.1MM **Publicly Held**
WEB: www.korelectronics.com
SIC: 7374 Data processing service
PA: Mercury Systems, Inc.
    50 Minuteman Rd
    Andover MA 01810
    978 256-1300

(P-16157)
MESSAGESOLUTION INC
1851 Mccarthy Blvd # 105, Milpitas
(95035-7448)
PHONE...............................408 383-0100
Jing Liang, *Branch Mgr*
EMP: 86
SALES (corp-wide): 13MM **Privately Held**
SIC: 7374 Data processing & preparation
PA: Messagesolution, Inc.
    1851 Mccarthy Blvd # 105
    Milpitas CA 95035
    408 383-0100

(P-16158)
MICRO HOLDING CORP
1 Maritime Plz Fl 12, San Francisco
(94111-3404)
PHONE...............................415 788-5111
Warren Hellman, *President*
EMP: 650
SALES (est): 182.3MM **Privately Held**
SIC: 7374 7389 Computer graphics service; advertising, promotional & trade show services
PA: Hellman & Friedman Llc
    1 Maritime Plz Ste 1200
    San Francisco CA 94111
    -

(P-16159)
MINDBODY INC (PA)
4051 Broad St Ste 220, San Luis Obispo
(93401-8723)
PHONE...............................877 755-4279
Richard Stollmeyer, *Ch of Bd*
Michael Mansbach, *President*
Brett White, *COO*
Kimberly Lytikainen,
Mark Baker, *Risk Mgmt Dir*
EMP: 109
SQ FT: 160,000
SALES: 182.6MM **Publicly Held**
SIC: 7374 7372 8741 Data processing & preparation; business oriented computer software; business management

(P-16160)
MOCANA CORPORATION
111 W Evelyn Ave Ste 210, Sunnyvale
(94086-6129)
PHONE...............................415 617-0055
James Isaacs, *CEO*
Najib Khouri-Haddad, *President*
Sandy Taylor, *CFO*
Steve Adelman, *Vice Pres*
Damien Eastwood, *General Counsel*
EMP: 69
SALES (est): 10.5MM **Privately Held**
WEB: www.mocana.com
SIC: 7374 7379 Computer graphics service;

(P-16161)
MOCEAN LLC
2440 S Sepulveda Blvd # 150, Los Angeles
(90064-1786)
PHONE...............................310 481-0808
Craig R Murray, *Mng Member*
Stuart Boone, *President*
Michael McIntyre, *President*
Doug Salkin, *Vice Pres*

Adam Rosenblatt, *Executive*
EMP: 200 EST: 2000
SALES (est): 27.1MM **Privately Held**
SIC: 7374 7822 Computer graphics service; motion picture distribution

(P-16162)
MOCHANIN LLC
Also Called: Mochahost.com
2880 Zanker Rd Ste 203, San Jose
(95134-2122)
PHONE...............................408 432-7259
Hristo Angelov, *Mng Member*
Jim Truong, *VP Sales*
Radostin Savov, *Mng Member*
EMP: 60
SALES (est): 211.3K **Privately Held**
SIC: 7374 Computer graphics service

(P-16163)
OSHYN INC
100 W Broadway Ste 330, Long Beach
(90802-9400)
PHONE...............................213 483-1770
Diego Rebosio, *CEO*
Pablo Bustamante, *Software Dev*
Jennifer Posthumus, *Consultant*
EMP: 75
SALES (est): 4.9MM **Privately Held**
WEB: www.oshyn.com
SIC: 7374 Computer graphics service

(P-16164)
PINE DATA PROCESSING INC
Also Called: Pine Company
10559 Jefferson Blvd, Culver City
(90232-3526)
P.O. Box 641836, Los Angeles (90064-6836)
PHONE...............................310 815-5700
Ben Pine, *Chairman*
Ken Holsenbeck, *President*
Carol Lewis, *Vice Pres*
EMP: 72
SQ FT: 11,500
SALES (est): 3.9MM **Privately Held**
WEB: www.pinedata.com
SIC: 7374 Data processing service

(P-16165)
PLANET LABS INC (PA)
346 9th St, San Francisco (94103-3809)
PHONE...............................415 829-3313
William Marshall, *CEO*
Leeza Frantz, *Partner*
Shireen Khan, *Partner*
Tom Barton, *COO*
David Oppenheimer, *CFO*
EMP: 76
SQ FT: 25,000
SALES (est): 92.5MM **Privately Held**
SIC: 7374 Data processing service

(P-16166)
PLEX SYSTEMS INC
4305 Hacienda Dr Ste 500, Pleasanton
(94588-8586)
PHONE...............................248 391-8001
EMP: 163 **Privately Held**
SIC: 7374 Data processing & preparation
PA: Plex Systems, Inc.
    900 Tower Dr Ste 1400
    Troy MI 48098

(P-16167)
PRICEMETRIX USA INC
3 Bridgeport Rd, Newport Coast
(92657-1014)
PHONE...............................714 357-6192
Brent Geddes, *CFO*
Doug Trott, *President*
EMP: 50
SALES (est): 1.5MM **Privately Held**
SIC: 7374 Data processing service

(P-16168)
PROSUM INC (PA)
Also Called: Prosum Technology Services
2201 Park Pl Ste 102, El Segundo
(90245-4909)
PHONE...............................310 404-1545
Ravi Chatwani, *CEO*
John Petri, *CFO*
Ken Aster, *Vice Pres*
Chad Heinrich, *Vice Pres*

Josh Tofteland, *Vice Pres*
EMP: 57 EST: 1996
SALES (est): 40.1MM **Privately Held**
WEB: www.prosum.com
SIC: 7374 8748 Data processing & preparation; systems engineering consultant, ex. computer or professional

(P-16169)
PROTOSOURCE CORPORATION
2511 W Shaw Ave Ste 102, Fresno
(93711-3325)
PHONE...............................559 490-8600
Andy Chu, *Principal*
EMP: 54
SALES (corp-wide): 9.3MM **Publicly Held**
SIC: 7374 Data processing service
PA: Protosource Corporation
    1236 Main St Ste 3
    Hellertown PA 18055
    610 814-0550

(P-16170)
QUALITY INV PRPTS SCRMENTO LLC
Also Called: Quality Tech Svcs Sacramento
1100 N Market Blvd, Sacramento
(95834-1931)
PHONE...............................916 679-2100
EMP: 78
SALES (est): 1.4MM
SALES (corp-wide): 446.5MM **Privately Held**
SIC: 7374
HQ: Qualitytech, Lp
    12851 Foster St
    Overland Park KS 66213
    -

(P-16171)
RESEARCH OF AMERICA
1232 Q St Ste 100, Sacramento
(95811-5801)
PHONE...............................916 443-4722
Rob Porber, *Owner*
Robert Proctor, *Vice Pres*
EMP: 135
SQ FT: 7,300
SALES (est): 8.2MM **Privately Held**
WEB: www.emhopinions.com
SIC: 7374 Data verification service

(P-16172)
RINGCENTRAL INC (PA)
20 Davis Dr, Belmont (94002-3002)
PHONE...............................650 472-4100
Vladimir Shmunis, *Ch of Bd*
David Sipes, *COO*
Mitesh Dhruv, *CFO*
Michael Machado, *Officer*
John Marlow, *Officer*
EMP: 80
SQ FT: 100,000
SALES: 501.5MM **Publicly Held**
WEB: www.ringcentral.com
SIC: 7374 4899 Data processing & preparation; data communication services

(P-16173)
ROCKSTAR SAN DIEGO
2200 Faraday Ave Ste 200, Carlsbad
(92008-7233)
PHONE...............................760 929-0700
Allan Wasserman, *President*
Kelly Gibson, *Human Res Dir*
Kevin Baca, *Director*
EMP: 125
SQ FT: 24,000
SALES (est): 7.7MM **Publicly Held**
WEB: www.rockstarsandiego.com
SIC: 7374 7372 Computer graphics service; prepackaged software
PA: Take-Two Interactive Software, Inc.
    110 W 44th St
    New York NY 10036

(P-16174)
RUITENG INTERNET TECHNOLOGY CO
18351 Colima Rd 255, Rowland Heights
(91748-2791)
PHONE...............................302 597-7438
Canzhi Zhen, *Owner*
EMP: 220
SQ FT: 500

SALES: 50MM **Privately Held**
SIC: 7374 Computer graphics service

(P-16175)
SANTA CRUZ COUNTY OF
Also Called: Information Services
701 Ocean St Rm 530, Santa Cruz
(95060-4015)
PHONE...................................831 454-2030
Kevin Bowling, *Director*
EMP: 70 **Privately Held**
WEB: www.scsheriff.com
SIC: 7374 Computer processing services
PA: County Of Santa Cruz
　　701 Ocean St Rm 520
　　Santa Cruz CA 95060
　　831 454-2100

(P-16176)
**SECURE ONE DATA SOLUTIONS
LLC**
11090 Artesia Blvd Ste D, Cerritos
(90703-2545)
PHONE...................................562 924-7056
David Sandobal, *President*
EMP: 50 **Privately Held**
SIC: 7374 Data punch service; data pro-
cessing service
PA: Secure One Data Solutions, Llc
　　2801 N 33rd Ave Ste 1
　　Phoenix AZ 85009

(P-16177)
SHOPPINGCOM INC
8000 Marina Blvd Ste 500, Brisbane
(94005-1886)
PHONE...................................650 616-6500
Gautam Thakar, *CEO*
Amir Ashkenazi, *President*
Hendrik Krampe, *CFO*
Robert J Krolik, *CFO*
Julie Barott, *Executive Asst*
EMP: 230
SALES (est): 15.2MM **Publicly Held**
SIC: 7374 Data processing & preparation
PA: Ebay Inc.
　　2025 Hamilton Ave
　　San Jose CA 95125

(P-16178)
SOCIABLE LABS INC
25 Division St, San Mateo (94402)
PHONE...................................415 225-8740
Naifan Gabbay, *President*
Peter O'Leary, *Vice Pres*
EMP: 50
SQ FT: 1,500
SALES (est): 3MM **Privately Held**
SIC: 7374 Computer graphics service

(P-16179)
SOCIETY6 LLC
1655 26th St, Santa Monica (90404-4016)
PHONE...................................310 394-6400
Sean Moriarty,
Dennis Yu, *Business Dir*
Rory Wood, *Mktg Dir*
EMP: 50
SQ FT: 25,000
SALES (est): 2MM **Publicly Held**
SIC: 7374 Data processing & preparation
PA: Leaf Group Ltd.
　　1655 26th St
　　Santa Monica CA 90404

(P-16180)
**SONY PICTURES IMAGEWORKS
INC**
9050 Washington Blvd, Culver City
(90232-2518)
PHONE...................................310 840-8000
Bob Osher, *President*
Ken Ralston, *Principal*
Stephanie Greco, *Department Mgr*
Ryan Cushman, *Info Tech Mgr*
Moti Cohen, *Software Engr*
EMP: 1000 **EST**: 1992
SALES (est): 98.4MM
SALES (corp-wide): 80.1B **Privately Held**
WEB: www.sonypictures.com
SIC: 7374 Computer graphics service

HQ: Sony Pictures Entertainment, Inc.
　　10202 Washington Blvd
　　Culver City CA 90232
　　310 244-4000

(P-16181)
**SOUTHBAY WEBSITE DESIGN
LLC**
Also Called: Phone App Company, The
1601 Pcf Cast Hwy Ste 290, Hermosa
Beach (90254)
PHONE...................................310 370-4043
Allen Rubin,
EMP: 60
SQ FT: 250
SALES: 500K **Privately Held**
SIC: 7374 7371 Computer graphics serv-
ice; computer software development &
applications

(P-16182)
STARK SERVICES
12444 Victory Blvd # 300, North Hollywood
(91606-3173)
PHONE...................................818 985-2003
Maricel Zabel, *President*
Elias Nunez, *Vice Pres*
Steve Pugh, *Vice Pres*
Michelle Alexander, *Accounts Mgr*
EMP: 75
SALES (est): 5.6MM **Privately Held**
WEB: www.starkservices.com
SIC: 7374 Data processing service

(P-16183)
STUBHUB INC (HQ)
Also Called: Stubhub.com
199 Fremont St Fl 4, San Francisco
(94105-6634)
PHONE...................................415 222-8400
Scott Cutler, *CEO*
Noah Goldberg, *COO*
Ajay Gopal, *CFO*
Jennifer Betka, *Chief Mktg Ofcr*
Raji Arasu, *Vice Pres*
EMP: 88
SQ FT: 20,000
SALES (est): 61.4MM **Publicly Held**
SIC: 7374 7922 Data processing & prepa-
ration; ticket agency, theatrical

(P-16184)
SUPPORTCOM INC (PA)
1200 Crossman Ave Ste 210, Sunnyvale
(94089-1123)
PHONE...................................650 556-9440
Richard A Bloom, *President*
Joshua E Schechter, *Ch of Bd*
EMP: 88
SQ FT: 6,283
SALES: 60.1MM **Publicly Held**
WEB: www.supportsoft.com
SIC: 7374 7372 Data processing & prepa-
ration; business oriented computer soft-
ware

(P-16185)
TASKUS INC (PA)
3221 Donald Douglas, Santa Monica
(90405-3213)
PHONE...................................888 400-8275
Bryce Maddock, *CEO*
Jaspar Weir, *President*
Joe Buggy, *COO*
Balaji Sekar, *CFO*
Jarrod Johnson, *Ch Credit Ofcr*
EMP: 50 **EST**: 2008
SQ FT: 17,000
SALES (est): 189.7MM **Privately Held**
SIC: 7374 Data processing service

(P-16186)
TEALIUM INC (PA)
11095 Torreyana Rd Fl 2, San Diego
(92121-1104)
PHONE...................................858 779-1344
Jeffrey W Lunsford, *CEO*
Adam Corey, *Partner*
Ali Behnam, *President*
Doug Lindroth, *CFO*
Mike Anderson, *Officer*
EMP: 79
SQ FT: 40,864
SALES (est): 43.5MM **Privately Held**
SIC: 7374 7371 Computer graphics serv-
ice; computer software development

(P-16187)
**TECHNOLOGY SERVICES CAL
DEPT**
Also Called: Teale Data Center
10860 Gold Center Dr # 100, Rancho Cor-
dova (95670-6024)
PHONE...................................916 464-3747
Carlos Ramos, *Exec Dir*
EMP: 50 **Privately Held**
WEB: www.osi.ca.gov
SIC: 7374 9199 Data processing & prepa-
ration; general government administra-
tion;
HQ: California Department Of Technology
　　Services
　　1325 J St Ste 1600
　　Sacramento CA 95814

(P-16188)
TECHNOSOCIALWORKCOM LLC
Also Called: Stria
4300 Resnik Ct Unit 103, Bakersfield
(93313-4836)
P.O. Box 21660 (93390-1660)
PHONE...................................661 617-6601
Jim Damian, *Mng Member*
Garrison Scott, *Vice Pres*
Robert Cleveland, *General Mgr*
Scott Garrison, *VP Sales*
Rory Banks,
EMP: 75
SQ FT: 10,000
SALES (est): 9.5MM **Privately Held**
WEB: www.goodsamaritanhospital.net
SIC: 7374 Computer graphics service

(P-16189)
TERIS LLC (PA)
Also Called: Teris Bay Area
2455 Faber Pl Ste 200, Palo Alto
(94303-3316)
P.O. Box 130114, Dallas TX (75313-0114)
PHONE...................................650 213-9922
Trevor Campion,
Christian Cogan, *Controller*
EMP: 85
SQ FT: 8,681
SALES (est): 5MM **Privately Held**
SIC: 7374 Data processing & preparation

(P-16190)
TERIS LLC
600 W Broadway Ste 300, San Diego
(92101-3352)
PHONE...................................619 231-3282
Adam Wells, *Branch Mgr*
EMP: 50
SALES (corp-wide): 5MM **Privately Held**
SIC: 7374 Data processing & preparation
PA: Teris, Llc
　　2455 Faber Pl Ste 200
　　Palo Alto CA 94303
　　650 213-9922

(P-16191)
TRULIA INC (HQ)
535 Mission St Fl 7, San Francisco
(94105-3223)
PHONE...................................415 648-4358
Peter Flint, *CEO*
Lloyd Frink, *President*
Jeff McConathy, *President*
Paul Levine, *COO*
Prashant Aggarwal, *CFO*
EMP: 357
SQ FT: 32,000
SALES: 251.9MM
SALES (corp-wide): 1B **Publicly Held**
SIC: 7374 Data processing & preparation
PA: Zillow Group, Inc.
　　1301 2nd Ave Fl 31
　　Seattle WA 98101
　　206 470-7000

(P-16192)
**TURBO DATA SYSTEMS INC
(PA)**
18302 Irvine Blvd Ste 200, Tustin
(92780-3464)
PHONE...................................714 573-5757
Roberta J Rosen, *President*
Carlos Mendez, *Treasurer*
EMP: 50
SQ FT: 10,000

SALES (est): 6.7MM **Privately Held**
WEB: www.turbodata.com
SIC: 7374 Data processing service

(P-16193)
UCC DIRECT SERVICES INC
330 N Brand Blvd Ste 700, Glendale
(91203-2336)
PHONE...................................818 662-4100
Walt Powell, *President*
EMP: 80
SALES (est): 2MM **Privately Held**
WEB: www.uccdirectservices.com
SIC: 7374 Data processing service

(P-16194)
UNITAS GLOBAL LLC (PA)
453 S Spring St Ste 201, Los Angeles
(90013-2566)
PHONE...................................213 785-6200
Patrick Shutt, *CEO*
Ian Gillott, *COO*
Bob Pollan, *CFO*
Grant A Kirkwood, *Founder*
Scott Walker, *Chief Mktg Ofcr*
EMP: 100
SQ FT: 9,000
SALES (est): 80MM **Privately Held**
SIC: 7374 Service bureau, computer

(P-16195)
UNIVERSITY CAL SAN DIEGO
Also Called: San Diego Supercomputer Cen-
ter
10100 Hopkins Dr, La Jolla (92093-0001)
P.O. Box 85608, San Diego (92186-5608)
PHONE...................................858 534-5000
Michael Norman, *Director*
Dilip Jeste, *Dean*
Yinliang Zhang, *Director*
Jan Zverina, *Director*
EMP: 300 **Privately Held**
WEB: www.generalatomics.com
SIC: 7374 8731 8221 9411 Data pro-
cessing & preparation; commercial physi-
cal research; university; administration of
educational programs;
HQ: University Of California, San Diego
　　9500 Gilman Dr
　　La Jolla CA 92093
　　858 534-2230

(P-16196)
**VELOCITY TECH SOLUTIONS
INC**
111 Pacifica Ste 320, Irvine (92618-7428)
PHONE...................................949 417-0260
EMP: 70
SALES (corp-wide): 168.2MM **Privately
Held**
SIC: 7374 Data processing & preparation
PA: Velocity Technology Solutions, Inc.
　　1901 Roxborough Rd # 406
　　Charlotte NC 28211
　　646 884-6600

(P-16197)
**VERIZON CONNECT TELO INC
(DH)**
Also Called: Telogis, Inc.
20 Enterprise Ste 100, Aliso Viejo
(92656-7104)
PHONE...................................949 389-5500
Ralph Mason, *CTO*
Jason Koch, *President*
David Mitchell, *President*
A Newth Morris IV, *President*
Susan Heystee, *Exec VP*
EMP: 150 **EST**: 2001
SQ FT: 55,700
SALES: 89MM
SALES (corp-wide): 126B **Publicly Held**
WEB: www.telogis.com
SIC: 7374 Data processing & preparation
HQ: Verizon Connect Inc.
　　2002 Summit Blvd Ste 1800
　　Brookhaven GA 30319
　　404 573-5800

(P-16198)
VITESSE LLC
1601 Willow Rd, Menlo Park (94025-1452)
PHONE...................................650 543-4800
Christopher R Gardner, *CEO*
EMP: 3000

SALES (est): 53.9MM
SALES (corp-wide): 40.6B **Publicly Held**
SIC: 7374 Data processing service
PA: Facebook, Inc.
1 Hacker Way Bldg 10
Menlo Park CA 94025
650 543-4800

(P-16199)
VOICE MAIL BROADCASTING CORP
Also Called: Vmbc
5 Columbia, Aliso Viejo (92656-1460)
PHONE..............................714 437-0600
Jesse Crowe, *CEO*
Melinda Chelliah, *CFO*
Joseph Cox, *Vice Pres*
Pablo Senzanonna, *Program Mgr*
Dan Tran, *Administration*
EMP: 76
SALES (est): 7.3MM **Privately Held**
SIC: 7374 Service bureau, computer

(P-16200)
VOICE PRINT INTERNATIONAL LLC (PA)
Also Called: V P I
160 Camino Ruiz, Camarillo (93012-6700)
PHONE..............................805 389-5200
Andrew D Marsh, *CEO*
Andrew Marsh, *CFO*
Scott Bindas, *Vice Pres*
Patrick Botz, *Vice Pres*
Darryl Corrigan, *Vice Pres*
EMP: 53
SALES (est): 22.2MM **Privately Held**
SIC: 7374 7389 Data processing & preparation; recording studio, noncommercial records

(P-16201)
YUB INC
520 Logue Ave, Mountain View (94043-4049)
PHONE..............................650 265-7316
Alastair Rampell, *President*
Edward Lim, *CTO*
EMP: 203
SQ FT: 5,000
SALES (est): 8.1MM **Publicly Held**
SIC: 7374 7311 Advertising agencies; computer time-sharing
PA: Quotient Technology Inc.
400 Logue Ave
Mountain View CA 94043

(P-16202)
ZILLOW GROUP INC
Also Called: New Home Feed
4100 Redwood Rd, Oakland (94619-2363)
PHONE..............................415 836-6760
EMP: 831
SALES (corp-wide): 1B **Publicly Held**
SIC: 7374 7371 Computer graphics service; software programming applications
PA: Zillow Group, Inc.
1301 2nd Ave Fl 31
Seattle WA 98101
206 470-7000

(P-16203)
ZYNGA INC (PA)
699 8th St, San Francisco (94103-4901)
PHONE..............................855 449-9642
Frank Gibeau, *CEO*
Mark Pincus, *Ch of Bd*
Bernard Kim, *President*
Matthew S Bromberg, *COO*
Gerard Griffin, *CFO*
EMP: 242
SQ FT: 669,000
SALES: 861.3MM **Publicly Held**
SIC: 7374 7372 Data processing & preparation; application computer software

┌─────────────────────────────┐
│ **7375 Information Retrieval** │
│ **Svcs** │
└─────────────────────────────┘

(P-16204)
23ANDME INC
349 Oyster Point Blvd # 100, South San Francisco (94080-1980)
PHONE..............................510 381-7237

EMP: 253 **Privately Held**
SIC: 7375 Information retrieval services
PA: 23andme, Inc.
899 W Evelyn Ave
Mountain View CA 94041

(P-16205)
23ANDME INC (PA)
899 W Evelyn Ave, Mountain View (94041-1225)
PHONE..............................650 961-7152
Anne Wojcicki, *CEO*
Karen Haynes, *Partner*
Andy Page, *President*
Steve Schwartz, *President*
Dean Schorno, *CFO*
EMP: 370
SALES (est): 65MM **Privately Held**
WEB: www.23andme.com
SIC: 7375 Information retrieval services

(P-16206)
ACCURATE BACKGROUND LLC (PA)
Also Called: Selectforce
7515 Irvine Center Dr, Irvine (92618-2930)
PHONE..............................800 784-3911
David C Dickerson, *CEO*
Tim Dowd, *President*
Piero Broccardo, *CFO*
Aaron Charbonnet, *Senior VP*
Naomi Mc Eachen, *VP Human Res*
EMP: 315
SQ FT: 98,024
SALES: 117.6MM **Privately Held**
WEB: www.accuratebackground.com
SIC: 7375 Information retrieval services

(P-16207)
ACXIOM CORPORATION
8801 Elmer Ln, Garden Grove (92841-1039)
PHONE..............................714 636-3093
Renee Heston, *Manager*
EMP: 50
SALES (corp-wide): 7.8B **Publicly Held**
WEB: www.acxiom.com
SIC: 7375 On-line data base information retrieval
HQ: Acxiom Llc
301 E Dave Ward Dr
Conway AR 72032
501 342-1000

(P-16208)
ACXIOM CORPORATION
100 Redwood Shores Pkwy, Redwood City (94065-1155)
PHONE..............................650 356-3400
Michael Gorman, *Senior VP*
Micki McLarty, *Vice Pres*
David Mariani, *VP Engrg*
EMP: 72
SALES (corp-wide): 7.8B **Publicly Held**
SIC: 7375 Information retrieval services
HQ: Acxiom Llc
301 E Dave Ward Dr
Conway AR 72032
501 342-1000

(P-16209)
AUTOWEB INC (PA)
18872 Macarthur Blvd, Irvine (92612-1408)
PHONE..............................949 225-4500
Jared Rowe, *President*
Michael J Fuchs, *Ch of Bd*
William A Ferriolo, *COO*
Kimberly S Boren, *CFO*
Michael Carpenter, *Bd of Directors*
EMP: 147
SQ FT: 26,000
SALES: 142.1MM **Publicly Held**
WEB: www.autobytel.com
SIC: 7375 On-line data base information retrieval

(P-16210)
CHANGEORG INC
383 Rhode Island St # 300, San Francisco (94103-5178)
PHONE..............................415 817-1840
Benj Rattay, *CEO*
Jennifer Dulski, *President*
Benj Rattray, *CEO*
Rahoul Seth, *CFO*

Durga Nandini, *Comms Dir*
EMP: 114
SQ FT: 10,000
SALES: 22MM **Privately Held**
SIC: 7375 On-line data base information retrieval

(P-16211)
COMPS INC
4535 Towne Centre Ct, San Diego (92121-8801)
PHONE..............................858 658-0576
Andrew Florance, *President*
Craig Farrington, *COO*
EMP: 175
SALES (est): 5.1MM
SALES (corp-wide): 965.2MM **Publicly Held**
SIC: 7375 Information retrieval services
PA: Costar Group, Inc.
1331 L St Nw Ste 2
Washington DC 20005
202 346-6500

(P-16212)
CONFI-CHEK INC (PA)
1915 21st St, Sacramento (95811-6813)
PHONE..............................800 718-8997
Rob Miller, *President*
EMP: 70
SQ FT: 6,000
SALES: 32MM **Privately Held**
WEB: www.confi-chek.com
SIC: 7375 Data base information retrieval

(P-16213)
CONVERSANT LLC (HQ)
30699 Russell Ranch Rd # 250, Westlake Village (91362-7319)
PHONE..............................818 575-4500
John Giuliani, *President*
Oded Benyo, *President*
John Pitstick, *CFO*
Scott Eagle, *Chief Mktg Ofcr*
Scott P Barlow, *Vice Pres*
EMP: 148
SQ FT: 41,500
SALES (est): 573.1MM **Publicly Held**
WEB: www.valueclick.com
SIC: 7375 4813 On-line data base information retrieval;

(P-16214)
CORVENTIS INC (PA)
2033 Gateway Pl Ste 100, San Jose (95110-3713)
PHONE..............................408 790-9300
John Russell, *President*
Abhi Chavan, *Vice Pres*
Kathy Lundberg, *Vice Pres*
Murali Srivathsa, *Vice Pres*
EMP: 61
SALES (est): 14.9MM **Privately Held**
SIC: 7375 Information retrieval services

(P-16215)
COUNTY OF LOS ANGELES
Also Called: Department of Mental Health
320 W Temple St Fl 9, Los Angeles (90012-3217)
PHONE..............................213 974-0515
Jacqueline Criddell, *Manager*
EMP: 150 **Privately Held**
WEB: www.co.la.ca.us
SIC: 7375 9131 Information retrieval services;
PA: County Of Los Angeles
500 W Temple St Ste 437
Los Angeles CA 90012
213 974-1101

(P-16216)
DIGITAL INSIGHT CORPORATION
5601 Lindero Canyon Rd # 100, Westlake Village (91362-6494)
PHONE..............................818 879-1010
Paul Nieman, *Principal*
EMP: 150
SALES (corp-wide): 6.5B **Publicly Held**
WEB: www.digitalinsight.com
SIC: 7375 Information retrieval services
HQ: Digital Insight Corporation
1300 Seaport Blvd Ste 300
Redwood City CA 94063

(P-16217)
DIGITAL INSIGHT CORPORATION (HQ)
Also Called: Intuit Financial Services
1300 Seaport Blvd Ste 300, Redwood City (94063-5591)
PHONE..............................818 879-1010
Jeffrey E Stiefler, *President*
Joseph M McDoniel, *Exec VP*
Tom Shen, *Exec VP*
Robert R Surridge, *Senior VP*
Nitin Agarwal, *Sr Software Eng*
EMP: 200
SQ FT: 46,000
SALES (est): 137.3MM
SALES (corp-wide): 6.5B **Publicly Held**
WEB: www.digitalsight.com
SIC: 7375 7372 7371 Information retrieval services; prepackaged software; custom computer programming services
PA: Ncr Corporation
864 Spring St Nw
Atlanta GA 30308
937 445-5000

(P-16218)
DRIVESAVERS INC
Also Called: Drivesavers Data Recovery
400 Bel Marin Keys Blvd, Novato (94949-5642)
PHONE..............................415 382-2000
Jay Hagan, *CEO*
Vicki O'Hara, *Partner*
Scott Moyer, *President*
Jacqueline Cunningham, *Executive*
Michael Hall, *CIO*
EMP: 90
SQ FT: 4,400
SALES: 20MM **Privately Held**
WEB: www.drivesavers.com
SIC: 7375 Information retrieval services

(P-16219)
E-TIMES CORPORATION LTD
601 S Figueroa St # 5000, Los Angeles (90017-3883)
PHONE..............................213 452-6720
Chiharu Nakahara, *President*
Ken Yasuda, *CFO*
EMP: 300
SALES (est): 12.5MM **Privately Held**
WEB: www.etimesltd.com
SIC: 7375 7374 8742 Information retrieval services; computer graphics service; administrative services consultant

(P-16220)
EDMUNDS HOLDING COMPANY (PA)
Also Called: Edmunds.com
2401 Colorado Ave, Santa Monica (90404-3585)
PHONE..............................310 309-6300
AVI Steinlauf, *CEO*
Seth Berkowitz, *President*
Charles Farrell, *CFO*
EMP: 650
SALES (est): 212MM **Privately Held**
SIC: 7375 Information retrieval services

(P-16221)
ELAVON INC
1281 9th Ave Unit 706, San Diego (92101-4645)
PHONE..............................954 776-7990
Kimberly Layton, *Manager*
David Dowling, *Production*
Jacqueline Flowers, *Director*
Melanie Miller, *Director*
Joseph Doherty, *Manager*
EMP: 514
SALES (corp-wide): 24B **Publicly Held**
SIC: 7375 Information retrieval services
HQ: Elavon, Inc.
2 Cncourse Pkwy Ste 800
Atlanta GA 30328
678 731-5000

(P-16222)
ELAVON INC
4234 Hacienda Dr Ste 250, Pleasanton (94588-2789)
PHONE..............................925 734-8939
EMP: 400

SALES (corp-wide): 24B **Publicly Held**
SIC: 7375 Information retrieval services
HQ: Elavon, Inc.
    2 Cncourse Pkwy Ste 800
    Atlanta GA 30328
    678 731-5000

(P-16223)
EXABLOX CORPORATION
1156 Sonora Ct, Sunnyvale (94086-5308)
PHONE................................408 773-8477
Douglas Brockett, *CEO*
Ramesh Iyer Balan, *Vice Pres*
Shridar Subramanian, *Risk Mgmt Dir*
Meagan Banning, *Office Mgr*
Tad Hunt, *CTO*
EMP: 51 EST: 2010
SALES (est): 6.9MM **Privately Held**
SIC: 7375 Data base information retrieval
PA: Storagecraft Technology Corporation
    380 W Data Dr Ste 300
    Draper UT 84020
    -

(P-16224)
FACEBOOK INC (PA)
1 Hacker Way Bldg 10, Menlo Park
(94025-1456)
PHONE................................650 543-4800
Mark Zuckerberg, *Ch of Bd*
David B Fischer, *Partner*
Sheryl K Sandberg, *COO*
David M Wehner, *CFO*
Antonio Lucio, *Chief Mktg Ofcr*
EMP: 800
SQ FT: 3,000,000
SALES: 40.6B **Publicly Held**
SIC: 7375 On-line data base information
   retrieval

(P-16225)
GLOBAL RISK MGT SOLUTIONS LLC
660 Nwport Ctr Dr Ste 600, Newport Beach
(92660)
PHONE................................949 759-8500
Gerard Smith, *President*
EMP: 200
SQ FT: 2,700
SALES (est): 14MM **Privately Held**
SIC: 7375 Information retrieval services

(P-16226)
GO2 SYSTEMS INC
Also Called: Go2systems
18400 Von Karman Ave Fl 9, Irvine
(92612-1514)
PHONE................................949 553-0800
S Lee Hancock, *President*
Scott Goldman, *COO*
Mark Buckner, *CFO*
Ward Kennedy, *CFO*
Edwin De Ferrante, *VP Mktg*
EMP: 75
SQ FT: 18,955
SALES (est): 3.2MM **Privately Held**
SIC: 7375 Information retrieval services

(P-16227)
GOOGLE LLC
1945 Charleston Rd, Mountain View
(94043-1201)
PHONE................................650 253-7323
Ryan Spurlock, *Branch Mgr*
Tony Fagan, *Director*
Mohit Kalra, *Associate*
EMP: 99
SALES (corp-wide): 110.8B **Publicly Held**
SIC: 7375 Data base information retrieval
HQ: Google Llc
    1600 Amphitheatre Pkwy
    Mountain View CA 94043
    650 253-0000

(P-16228)
GROUNDWORK OPEN SOURCE INC
333 Bryant St Ste 100, San Francisco
(94107-4103)
PHONE................................415 992-4500
Dave Lilly, *CEO*
Laura Horsky, *Engineer*
Roger Ruttimann, *Engineer*
Hans Kriel, *Opers Staff*
Wayne Dahler, *Regl Sales Mgr*

EMP: 100
SQ FT: 15,000
SALES (est): 9.3MM
SALES (corp-wide): 70.8MM **Privately Held**
WEB: www.groundworkopensource.com
SIC: 7375 7371 On-line data base information retrieval; custom computer programming services
HQ: Fox Technologies, Inc.
    6455 City West Pkwy
    Eden Prairie MN 55344
    800 328-1000

(P-16229)
GUIDANCE SOLUTIONS INC
4134 Del Rey Ave, Marina Del Rey
(90292-5604)
PHONE................................310 754-4000
Jason Meugniot, *CEO*
Jeff Herrera, *Partner*
John Provisor, *President*
Mike Hill, *Exec VP*
EMP: 50
SQ FT: 10,000
SALES (est): 8.8MM **Privately Held**
WEB: www.guidance.com
SIC: 7375 4813 On-line data base information retrieval;

(P-16230)
HIRERIGHT LLC (HQ)
3349 Michelson Dr Ste 150, Irvine
(92612-8881)
PHONE................................949 428-5800
Jurgen Leijdekker, *CEO*
Thomas Spaeth, *CFO*
Dawn Hirsch, *Officer*
Jim Weber, *Officer*
Gregg Freeman, *Vice Pres*
EMP: 148
SQ FT: 63,440
SALES (est): 161.8MM **Privately Held**
WEB: www.hireright.com
SIC: 7375 7374 Data base information retrieval; data verification service

(P-16231)
IAC SEARCH & MEDIA INC (HQ)
Also Called: Ask.com
555 12th St Ste 500, Oakland
(94607-3699)
PHONE................................510 985-7400
Doug Leeds, *CEO*
George S Lichter, *President*
Shane McGilloway, *COO*
Dominic Butera, *CFO*
Steven J Sordello, *CFO*
EMP: 200
SQ FT: 76,000
SALES (est): 119.4MM
SALES (corp-wide): 3.3B **Publicly Held**
WEB: www.ask.com
SIC: 7375 On-line data base information retrieval
PA: Iac/Interactivecorp
    555 W 18th St
    New York NY 10011
    212 314-7300

(P-16232)
INSURANCE SERVICES OFFICE INC
388 Market St Ste 750, San Francisco
(94111-5352)
PHONE................................415 874-4361
Jim Masek, *Branch Mgr*
Vincent McCarthy, *Vice Pres*
Robert Colvin, *Info Tech Dir*
Eric Good, *Engineer*
Mark Smith, *Manager*
EMP: 326 **Publicly Held**
SIC: 7375 Information retrieval services
HQ: Insurance Services Office, Inc.
    545 Washington Blvd Fl 12
    Jersey City NJ 07310
    201 469-2000

(P-16233)
INTERNET ARCHIVE
300 Funston Ave, San Francisco
(94118-2116)
PHONE................................415 561-6767
Brewster Kahle, *Director*
Kyrie Whitsett, *Partner*
Jefferson Bailey, *General Mgr*

Caitlin Olson, *Executive Asst*
Andy Bezella, *Administration*
EMP: 173
SALES: 13.9MM **Privately Held**
SIC: 7375 On-line data base information
   retrieval

(P-16234)
ISYNDICATE INC
455 9th St, San Francisco (94103-4410)
PHONE................................415 896-1900
Joel Mask, *CEO*
Ann-Marie McGowan, *COO*
Steven Dietsch, *CFO*
EMP: 54
SALES (est): 3.1MM **Privately Held**
SIC: 7375 On-line data base information
   retrieval

(P-16235)
JEPPESEN DATAPLAN INC
225 W Santa Clara St # 1600, San Jose
(95113-1752)
PHONE................................408 961-2825
Mark Van Tine, *President*
Jepson Fuller, *CFO*
Steve Altus, *Senior Mgr*
Jeff Harris, *Manager*
EMP: 118
SQ FT: 20,000
SALES (est): 10MM
SALES (corp-wide): 93.3B **Publicly Held**
WEB: www.jetplan.com
SIC: 7375 Information retrieval services
HQ: Jeppesen Sanderson, Inc.
    55 Inverness Dr E
    Englewood CO 80112
    303 799-9090

(P-16236)
LINKEDIN CORPORATION (HQ)
1000 W Maude Ave, Sunnyvale
(94085-2810)
PHONE................................650 687-3600
Jeff Weiner, *CEO*
Hywel Lo, *Partner*
Jian Lu, *President*
Maria Robinson, *President*
Steve Sordello, *CFO*
EMP: 148
SQ FT: 373,000
SALES: 2.9B
SALES (corp-wide): 110.3B **Publicly Held**
WEB: www.linkedin.com
SIC: 7375 On-line data base information
   retrieval
PA: Microsoft Corporation
    1 Microsoft Way
    Redmond WA 98052
    425 882-8080

(P-16237)
LOGICMONITOR INC (PA)
820 State St Fl 5, Santa Barbara
(93101-3271)
PHONE................................805 617-3884
Kevin McGibben, *CEO*
Richard Chen, *Partner*
Edward Shaughnessy, *CFO*
Steven Francis,
Dipan Mann, *Vice Pres*
EMP: 187
SALES (est): 30.5MM **Privately Held**
SIC: 7375 Information retrieval services

(P-16238)
LOWERMYBILLS, INC.
Also Called: Lowermybills.com
12181 Bluff Creek Dr, Playa Vista
(90094-2992)
PHONE................................310 348-6800
EMP: 68
SALES (est): 42.9MM **Privately Held**
SIC: 7375 Information retrieval services

(P-16239)
ONBOARDIQ INC
Also Called: Fountain
625 Market St Ste 500, San Francisco
(94105-3307)
PHONE................................480 433-1197
Kibaek Ryu, *President*
Nico Roberts, *COO*
EMP: 50

SALES: 5.5MM **Privately Held**
SIC: 7375 7371 Information retrieval services; computer software development & applications

(P-16240)
PERFORMANT FINANCIAL CORP (PA)
333 N Canyons Pkwy # 100, Livermore
(94551-9480)
PHONE................................925 960-4800
Lisa C Im, *Ch of Bd*
Michael Howell, *President*
Brian Golson, *Bd of Directors*
Harold T Leach Jr, *Officer*
Jeff Haughton, *Exec VP*
EMP: 96
SQ FT: 50,291
SALES: 132MM **Publicly Held**
WEB: www.performantcorp.com
SIC: 7375 Information retrieval services

(P-16241)
PINTEREST INC (PA)
808 Brannan St, San Francisco
(94103-4904)
PHONE................................650 561-5407
Tim Kendall, *President*
Pj Andersen, *Partner*
Brendon Augustine, *Partner*
Vivian Chow, *Partner*
Kylie Ratkovich, *Partner*
EMP: 400 EST: 2008
SALES (est): 90.1MM **Privately Held**
SIC: 7375 On-line data base information
   retrieval

(P-16242)
PLAID INC
85 2nd St Ste 400, San Francisco
(94105-3462)
PHONE................................415 799-1354
George Zachary Perret, *President*
Kelly Michael, *Sr Software Eng*
William Hockey, *CTO*
EMP: 110
SQ FT: 41,964
SALES: 2.5MM **Privately Held**
SIC: 7375 Information retrieval services

(P-16243)
QUORA INC
650 Castro St Ste 450, Mountain View
(94041-2026)
PHONE................................650 485-2464
Adam D Angelo, *CEO*
Aimee Catalano, *Partner*
Kelly Battles, *CFO*
Steven Trieu, *CFO*
Michael Alp, *Vice Pres*
EMP: 50 EST: 2009
SALES (est): 3.6MM **Privately Held**
SIC: 7375 Information retrieval services

(P-16244)
RELATIONEDGE LLC
10120 Pacific Heights Blv, San Diego
(92121-4210)
PHONE................................858 451-4665
Matthew Stoyka, *CEO*
EMP: 125
SALES: 17.4MM
SALES (corp-wide): 2B **Privately Held**
SIC: 7375 On-line data base information
   retrieval
HQ: Rackspace Us, Inc.
    1 Fanatical Pl
    Windcrest TX 78218
    210 312-4000

(P-16245)
RELX INC
Also Called: Lexisnexis
555 W 5th St Ste 4500, Los Angeles
(90013-3003)
PHONE................................213 627-1130
Tim Dawson, *Branch Mgr*
EMP: 70
SALES (corp-wide): 9.7B **Privately Held**
WEB: www.lexis-nexis.com
SIC: 7375 Information retrieval services
HQ: Relx Inc.
    230 Park Ave Ste 700
    New York NY 10169
    212 309-8100

692   2019 Directory of California
Wholesalers and Services Companies   ▲ = Import ▼=Export
◆ =Import/Export

(P-16246)
REPRINTS DESK INC
15821 Ventura Blvd # 165, Encino
(91436-5208)
PHONE..........................310 477-0354
Peter Derycz, *President*
Scott Ahlberg, *COO*
Alan Urban, *CFO*
Timothy Burleson, *Technology*
Marie Nyblom, *Technology*
EMP: 92
SQ FT: 2,500
SALES (est): 23MM **Publicly Held**
SIC: 7375 Information retrieval services
PA: Research Solutions, Inc.
15821 Ventura Blvd # 165
Encino CA 91436

(P-16247)
RESEARCH LIBRARIES GROUP INC
Also Called: R L G
777 Mariners Island Blvd # 550, San Mateo
(94404-5048)
PHONE..........................650 288-1288
James P Michalko, *President*
Robert J Scott, *Treasurer*
EMP: 100
SQ FT: 25,000
SALES (est): 4.4MM **Privately Held**
WEB: www.rlg.com
SIC: 7375 8731 7372 On-line data base
information retrieval; commercial physical
research; prepackaged software

(P-16248)
ROCKYOU INC (PA)
Also Called: Rockyou Media
1111 Broadway Ste 300, Oakland
(94607-4167)
PHONE..........................415 580-6400
Liza Marino, *CEO*
Josh Grant, *COO*
Sean Crawford, *Chief Mktg Ofcr*
Maia McCann, *Vice Pres*
Bill Schwidder, *Vice Pres*
EMP: 70
SALES (est): 53.6MM **Privately Held**
SIC: 7375 On-line data base information
retrieval

(P-16249)
SAGE SOFTWARE INC
7595 Irvine Center Dr # 200, Irvine
(92618-2957)
PHONE..........................949 753-1222
John Kang, *Branch Mgr*
Celina Oliver, *Partner*
Anne Seidel, *Partner*
Jennifer Warawa, *President*
Karen Mortham, *Exec VP*
EMP: 82
SALES (corp-wide): 2.2B **Privately Held**
SIC: 7375 7374 7372 3089 Information
retrieval services; data processing &
preparation; prepackaged software; plas-
tic processing
HQ: Sage Software International, Inc.
271 17th St Nw Ste 1100
Atlanta GA 30363
866 996-7243

(P-16250)
SALON MEDIA GROUP INC (PA)
870 Market St Ste 442, San Francisco
(94102-3018)
PHONE..........................415 870-7566
Jordan Hoffner, *CEO*
John Warnock, *Ch of Bd*
Elizabeth Hambrecht, *CFO*
David Daley, *Chief*
Justin Wohl, *Director*
EMP: 53
SQ FT: 2,405
SALES: 4.5MM **Publicly Held**
SIC: 7375 7383 On-line data base infor-
mation retrieval; news feature syndicate;
news pictures, gathering & distributing

(P-16251)
SCRIBD INC
333 Bush St Ste 2400, San Francisco
(94104-2806)
PHONE..........................415 896-9890
John Adler, *CEO*

Jared Fliesler, *COO*
Eric Shoup, *COO*
Simon Bond, *Chief Mktg Ofcr*
Julie Haddon, *Vice Pres*
EMP: 60
SALES (est): 11.1MM **Privately Held**
SIC: 7375 Information retrieval services

(P-16252)
TEUTONIC HOLDINGS LLC
9221 Corbin Ave Ste 260, Northridge
(91324-1625)
PHONE..........................818 264-4400
James Murphy, *CEO*
Sam Ghahremanpour, *President*
Doreen Paisano, *Human Resources*
EMP: 140
SALES: 41.7MM **Privately Held**
SIC: 7375 Data base information retrieval

(P-16253)
TINTRI INC
303 Ravendale Dr, Mountain View
(94043-5228)
PHONE..........................650 810-8200
Kieran Harty, *CTO*
Chris Gallamore, *Partner*
Yael Zheng, *Chief Mktg Ofcr*
Doug Kahn, *Exec VP*
Scott Buchanan, *Vice Pres*
EMP: 277
SQ FT: 127,000
SALES (est): 125.9MM
SALES (corp-wide): 231.8MM **Privately Held**
SIC: 7375 7374 Data base information re-
trieval; on-line data base information re-
trieval; data processing & preparation
PA: Datadirect Networks, Inc.
9351 Deering Ave
Chatsworth CA 91311
818 700-7600

(P-16254)
TRI-TECH INTERNET SERVICES INC
3465 Ocean View Blvd, Glendale
(91208-1508)
PHONE..........................818 548-5400
Jack Guiragosian, *President*
Gayle Butler, *CFO*
David Dginguerian, *Admin Sec*
EMP: 50 EST: 1998
SQ FT: 25,000
SALES: 20.5MM **Privately Held**
SIC: 7375 Information retrieval services

(P-16255)
TROJAN PROFESSIONAL SVCS INC
4410 Cerritos Ave, Los Alamitos
(90720-2549)
P.O. Box 1270 (90720-1270)
PHONE..........................714 816-7169
Mark Dunn, *CEO*
Ingrid M Kidd, *President*
Chris Iseri, *Admin Sec*
Nikki Myers, *Software Dev*
Gina Lopez, *Human Res Dir*
EMP: 99
SQ FT: 12,000
SALES (est): 11.8MM **Privately Held**
WEB: www.trojanonline.com
SIC: 7375 Data base information retrieval

(P-16256)
TWITTER INC (PA)
1355 Market St Ste 900, San Francisco
(94103-1337)
PHONE..........................415 222-9670
Jack Dorsey, *CEO*
Omid R Kordestani, *Ch of Bd*
Ned Segal, *CFO*
Vijaya Gadde,
EMP: 129 EST: 2006
SQ FT: 749,000
SALES: 2.4B **Publicly Held**
SIC: 7375 On-line data base information
retrieval

(P-16257)
UBER TECHNOLOGIES INC
900 Arastradero Rd Bldg B, Palo Alto
(94304-1332)
PHONE..........................832 610-0359
Chad Burton, *Manager*

EMP: 150
SQ FT: 140,000
SALES (corp-wide): 750.5MM **Privately Held**
SIC: 7375 On-line data base information
retrieval
PA: Uber Technologies, Inc.
1455 Market St Fl 4
San Francisco CA 94103

(P-16258)
VESTEK SYSTEMS INC (DH)
425 Market St Fl 6, San Francisco
(94105-2470)
PHONE..........................415 344-6000
Sam Campopiano, *President*
Virginia Chung, *Exec VP*
Brian Houston, *IT/INT Sup*
Lynn Roy PH, *Director*
EMP: 79
SQ FT: 18,000
SALES (est): 3.9MM
SALES (corp-wide): 124.6MM **Privately Held**
WEB: www.vestek.com
SIC: 7375 On-line data base information
retrieval

(P-16259)
VISCOMM INC (PA)
35 Leveroni Ct, Novato (94949-5721)
PHONE..........................415 454-7191
Howard J Fields, *President*
Robert Preger, *Ch of Bd*
Mehdi Khalvati, *Officer*
Dennis Neeley, *Vice Pres*
EMP: 56
SQ FT: 12,000
SALES: 2.7MM **Privately Held**
SIC: 7375 7372 4813 On-line data base
information retrieval; business oriented
computer software;

(P-16260)
WATER RESOURCES CAL DEPT
1416 9th St Rm 1225, Sacramento
(95814-5511)
PHONE..........................916 324-3812
Karen Bates, *President*
EMP: 50 **Privately Held**
WEB: www.water.ca.gov
SIC: 7375 9511 Data base information re-
trieval; water control & quality agency,
government;
HQ: California Department Of Water Re-
sources
1416 9th St
Sacramento CA 95814
916 653-9394

(P-16261)
WESTERN FELD INVSTIGATIONS INC (PA)
Also Called: Releasepoint
405 W Foothill Blvd 204, Claremont
(91711-2786)
PHONE..........................800 999-9589
Gerard F Halvey, *President*
Clair Halvey, *Vice Pres*
Derrick Halvey, *Vice Pres*
EMP: 100
SALES (est): 60MM **Privately Held**
WEB: www.wfi-inc.com
SIC: 7375 Information retrieval services

(P-16262)
YELP INC (PA)
140 New Montgomery St # 900, San Fran-
cisco (94105-3822)
PHONE..........................415 908-3801
Jeremy Stoppelman, *CEO*
Zach Anderson, *Partner*
Rebecca Campbell, *Partner*
Diane M Irvine, *Ch of Bd*
Joe Nachman, *COO*
EMP: 93
SALES: 846.8MM **Publicly Held**
SIC: 7375 On-line data base information
retrieval

(P-16263)
ZYME SOLUTIONS INC (PA)
240 Twin Dolphin Dr Ste D, Redwood City
(94065-1403)
PHONE..........................650 585-2258

Chandran Sankaran, *President*
Ashish Shete, *President*
Rajashree Majumdar, *CFO*
Adam Brenner, *Senior VP*
Edward Dimebro, *Senior VP*
EMP: 100
SALES (est): 32.6MM **Privately Held**
SIC: 7375 Information retrieval services

7376 Computer Facilities Management Svcs

(P-16264)
ALLIED DIGITAL SERVICES LLC (HQ)
680 Knox St Ste 200, Torrance
(90502-1358)
PHONE..........................310 431-2375
Paresh Shah, *CEO*
Gaurav Bahirvani, *Chief Mktg Ofcr*
Kapil Mehta, *Officer*
Sair Muhammad, *Exec VP*
Hubert Wong, *Vice Pres*
EMP: 110
SQ FT: 14,516
SALES (est): 28.9MM
SALES (corp-wide): 11.5MM **Privately Held**
WEB: www.allieddigital.net
SIC: 7376 Computer facilities management
PA: Allied Digital Services Limited
Premises No.13a ,13th Floor, Earnest
House
Mumbai MH 40002
226 681-6400

(P-16265)
CONTEMPORARY SERVICES CORP
4365 E Lowell St Ste A, Ontario
(91761-2226)
PHONE..........................909 740-3834
EMP: 65
SALES (corp-wide): 328MM **Privately Held**
SIC: 7376 Computer facilities management
PA: Contemporary Services Corporation
17101 Superior St
Northridge CA 91325
818 885-5150

(P-16266)
COUNTY OF SACRAMENTO
Also Called: Communication & Info Tech
799 G St, Sacramento (95814-1212)
PHONE..........................916 874-7752
Rami Zakaria, *Branch Mgr*
EMP: 395 **Privately Held**
WEB: www.sna.com
SIC: 7376 9631 Computer facilities man-
agement; communications commission,
government;
PA: County Of Sacramento
700 H St Ste 7650
Sacramento CA 95814
916 874-5544

(P-16267)
CSRA LLC
4045 Hancock St, San Diego (92110-5126)
PHONE..........................619 225-2600
Art Schrubb, *Manager*
Mike Wingo, *Technology*
EMP: 600
SALES (corp-wide): 30.9B **Publicly Held**
WEB: www.csc.com
SIC: 7376 Computer facilities management
HQ: Csra Llc
3170 Fairview Park Dr
Falls Church VA 22042
703 641-2000

(P-16268)
CSRA LLC
1520 Rr Ave Marie Is Marie Island, Vallejo
(94592)
PHONE..........................703 876-1026
Paul Branske, *CEO*
EMP: 147
SALES (corp-wide): 30.9B **Publicly Held**
SIC: 7376 Computer facilities management

HQ: Csra Llc
3170 Fairview Park Dr
Falls Church VA 22042
703 641-2000

(P-16269)
GLOBAL BLUE DVBE INC
5930 Price Ave, McClellan (95652-2402)
PHONE..................................916 632-2583
Dave Hornbeck, *President*
Michael Terpstra, *Vice Pres*
EMP: 75
SQ FT: 4,135
SALES (est): 11.1MM **Privately Held**
SIC: 7376 7379 7371 Computer facilities
management; computer related consult-
ing services; computer related mainte-
nance services; computer software
development & applications

(P-16270)
HCL AMERICA INC (DH)
330 Potrero Ave, Sunnyvale (94085-4194)
PHONE..................................408 733-0480
Shiv Nadar, *Chairman*
Manish Anand, *CEO*
Anil Chanana, *CFO*
Sanjay Singh, *Assoc VP*
Sanjay Tyagi, *Assoc VP*
EMP: 200
SQ FT: 31,000
SALES: 3.5B **Privately Held**
SIC: 7376 7371 8741 Computer facilities
management; computer software devel-
opment; management services

(P-16271)
NTT DATA SERVICES CORPORATION
6701 Center Dr W Ste 1000, Los Angeles
(90045-1566)
PHONE..................................310 342-3200
Sherry Cowan, *Manager*
EMP: 70
SALES (corp-wide): 110.7B **Privately
Held**
WEB: www.perotsystems.com
SIC: 7376 7379 Computer facilities man-
agement; computer related consulting
services
HQ: Ntt Data Services Corporation
7950 Legacy Dr
Plano TX 75024
972 577-0000

(P-16272)
RAGINGWIRE DATA CENTERS INC (DH)
Also Called: Raging Wire
1200 Striker Ave, Sacramento
(95834-1157)
P.O. Box 348060 (95834-8060)
PHONE..................................916 286-3000
Douglas S Adams, *President*
Joel Stone, *COO*
Kevin Dalton, *Senior VP*
Joe Goldsmith, *Senior VP*
Judi A Lee, *Senior VP*
▲ EMP: 275
SALES (est): 167.3MM
SALES (corp-wide): 110.7B **Privately
Held**
WEB: www.ragingwire.com
SIC: 7376 Computer facilities management
HQ: Ntt Communications Corporation
1-1-6, Uchisaiwaicho
Chiyoda-Ku TKY 100-0
335 008-111

(P-16273)
VERIZON BUS NETWRK SVCS INC
4340 Solar Way, Fremont (94538-6335)
PHONE..................................510 497-2500
Randy Cade, *Manager*
EMP: 75
SALES (corp-wide): 126B **Publicly Held**
WEB: www.gtl.net
SIC: 7376 Computer facilities management
HQ: Verizon Business Network Services
Inc.
1 Verizon Way
Basking Ridge NJ 07920
908 559-2000

7377 Computer Rental & Leasing

(P-16274)
2NDGEAR LLC (DH)
611 Anton Blvd Ste 700, Costa Mesa
(92626-7050)
PHONE..................................714 702-1023
John W Ford, *CEO*
EMP: 105
SALES (est): 2.3MM **Privately Held**
SIC: 7377 5045 Computer peripheral
equipment rental & leasing; computer pe-
ripheral equipment
HQ: Insight Investments Llc
611 Anton Blvd Ste 700
Costa Mesa CA 92626
714 939-2300

(P-16275)
INSIGHT INVESTMENTS LLC (HQ)
611 Anton Blvd Ste 700, Costa Mesa
(92626-7050)
PHONE..................................714 939-2300
John W Ford, *CEO*
Christopher Czaja, *CFO*
Mark Castellanos, *Vice Pres*
Michael Dundon, *Vice Pres*
EMP: 148
SQ FT: 30,000
SALES (est): 151.4MM **Privately Held**
WEB: www.insightinvestments.com
SIC: 7377 5045 Computer peripheral
equipment rental & leasing; computer pe-
ripheral equipment

7378 Computer Maintenance & Repair

(P-16276)
AMKOTRON INC
12620 Hiddencreek Way, Cerritos
(90703-2116)
PHONE..................................562 921-3330
Sunja Lee, *Branch Mgr*
EMP: 60
SALES (corp-wide): 8.5MM **Privately
Held**
SIC: 7378 5065 Computer peripheral
equipment repair & maintenance; elec-
tronic parts & equipment
PA: Amkotron, Inc.
16220 Bloomfield Ave
Cerritos CA 90703
562 921-3330

(P-16277)
APEX COMPUTER SYSTEMS INC
13875 Cerritos Corprt Dr A, Cerritos
(90703-2470)
PHONE..................................562 926-6820
Philip C Chen, *CEO*
Dennis Rice, *President*
Jessica C Chow, *CFO*
Jessica Chow, *CFO*
Michael Da Silva, *Vice Pres*
EMP: 60
SQ FT: 18,146
SALES (est): 23.6MM **Privately Held**
WEB: www.acsi2000.com
SIC: 7378 5734 Computer maintenance &
repair; computer & software stores

(P-16278)
BCP SYSTEMS INC
1560 S Sinclair St, Anaheim (92806-5933)
PHONE..................................714 202-3900
Carlos P Torres, *CEO*
William W Price, *President*
Amanda Apperson, *Administration*
Jennifer Marroquin, *Controller*
Trace Dibble, *Buyer*
EMP: 60

SALES (est): 10.1MM **Privately Held**
WEB: www.bcpsystems.com
SIC: 7378 3571 5063 Computer & data
processing equipment repair/mainte-
nance; computer peripheral equipment repair & maintenance; electronic
computers; electrical apparatus & equipment

(P-16279)
BIGBYTE CORPORATION
47430 Seabridge Dr, Fremont
(94538-6548)
PHONE..................................510 249-1100
Gary D Logan, *President*
EMP: 55
SQ FT: 7,500
SALES (est): 4MM **Privately Held**
WEB: www.bigbytecorp.com
SIC: 7378 Computer peripheral equipment
repair & maintenance

(P-16280)
COKEVA INC
Also Called: Applied Materials
9000 Foothills Blvd, Roseville
(95747-4411)
PHONE..................................916 462-6001
Ann D Nguyen, *CEO*
Ken Ueltzen, *President*
Dominick Derosa, *CFO*
Kevin Nguyen, *Vice Pres*
Lee Nguyen, *Vice Pres*
EMP: 181
SQ FT: 175,000
SALES (est): 30.5MM **Privately Held**
SIC: 7378 Computer maintenance & repair

(P-16281)
CONVOY INC
Also Called: Techmate
1020 Kearny St, San Francisco
(94133-4526)
PHONE..................................415 403-2770
Colin Barceloux, *CEO*
Scott Hasbrouck, *Executive*
EMP: 50
SQ FT: 5,000
SALES (est): 782.9K **Privately Held**
SIC: 7378 Computer maintenance & repair

(P-16282)
DST OUTPUT CALIFORNIA INC
5220 Rbert J Mathews Pkwy, El Dorado
Hills (95762-5705)
PHONE..................................916 939-4617
Kenneth Taylor, *Manager*
Marcus Lapilusa, *Admin Asst*
Adam Miller, *Admin Asst*
Rich Brown, *Administration*
Richard Rennecker, *Administration*
EMP: 95
SALES (est): 21MM
SALES (corp-wide): 4.3B **Publicly Held**
SIC: 7378 Computer maintenance & repair
HQ: Broadridge Customer Communica-
tions, Llc
2600 Southwest Blvd
Kansas City MO 64108

(P-16283)
ESL TECHNOLOGIES INC
8875 Washington Blvd B, Roseville
(95678-6214)
PHONE..................................916 677-4500
Donna Kwidzinski, *CEO*
Tjeu Blommaert, *President*
EMP: 350
SQ FT: 100,000
SALES (est): 23.3MM **Privately Held**
WEB: www.eslt.com
SIC: 7378 Computer peripheral equipment
repair & maintenance
HQ: Teleplan Holding Usa, Inc.
8875 Washington Blvd B
Roseville CA 95678
916 677-4500

(P-16284)
FAKOURI ELECTRICAL ENGRG INC
Also Called: F E E
30001 Comercio, Rcho STA Marg
(92688-2106)
PHONE..................................949 888-2400

Maryam Ewalt, *President*
Charles Ewalt, *COO*
John Oveisi, *CFO*
EMP: 79 EST: 1979
SQ FT: 15,000
SALES (est): 11.8MM **Privately Held**
WEB: www.fee-ups.com
SIC: 7378 8742 Computer maintenance &
repair; maintenance management con-
sultant

(P-16285)
FALCONWOOD INC
1011 Camino Del Rio S, San Diego
(92108-3531)
PHONE..................................619 297-9080
Bill Severi, *Principal*
EMP: 61
SALES (corp-wide): 21MM **Privately
Held**
SIC: 7378 8741 Computer & data pro-
cessing equipment repair/maintenance;
management services
PA: Falconwood, Inc.
2231 Crystal Dr Ste 801
Arlington VA 22202
703 888-4300

(P-16286)
GENERAL ELECTRIC COMPANY
1303 Bloomdale St, Duarte (91010-2501)
PHONE..................................626 359-7988
Edward Tabin, *Principal*
Richard Burke, *President*
Alta Yen, *Managing Dir*
EMP: 200
SALES (corp-wide): 122B **Publicly Held**
SIC: 7378 Computer maintenance & repair
PA: General Electric Company
41 Farnsworth St
Boston MA 02210
617 443-3000

(P-16287)
GUARDIAN COMPUTER SUPPORT
7075 Commerce Cir Ste D, Pleasanton
(94588-8015)
P.O. Box 5440, Walnut Creek (94596-
1440)
PHONE..................................925 251-8800
David Costa, *Principal*
Randy Swanson, *Principal*
EMP: 125
SQ FT: 24,000
SALES (est): 5.1MM **Privately Held**
WEB: www.guardiancomputer.com
SIC: 7378 Computer & data processing
equipment repair/maintenance

(P-16288)
INHOUSEIT INC
3193 Red Hill Ave, Costa Mesa
(92626-3432)
PHONE..................................949 660-5655
Glen Ackerman, *CEO*
Steve Bender, *President*
Mike Campbell, *Network Enginr*
Scott V Essen, *Director*
EMP: 70
SQ FT: 8,000
SALES (est): 12.2MM **Privately Held**
WEB: www.inhouseit.com
SIC: 7378 Computer & data processing
equipment repair/maintenance

(P-16289)
LOS ANGELES UNIFIED SCHOOL DST
Also Called: Information Technology
200 N Main St Ste 1400, Los Angeles
(90012-4127)
PHONE..................................213 485-3691
Marry K Kotzman, *Manager*
EMP: 150
SALES (corp-wide): 3.8B **Privately Held**
WEB: www.lausd.k12.ca.us
SIC: 7378 Computer & data processing
equipment repair/maintenance
PA: Los Angeles Unified School District
333 S Beaudry Ave Ste 209
Los Angeles CA 90017
213 241-1000

(P-16290)
ON-SITE LASERMEDIC CORPORATION (PA)
21540 Prairie St Ste D, Chatsworth (91311-5821)
PHONE.................818 775-9111
Gail Solomon, *CEO*
Ellen Zaldin, *President*
Jerry Richardson, *Admin Mgr*
Rodrigo Hernandez, *Technician*
Oscar Ruiz, *Technician*
EMP: 51
SQ FT: 6,000
SALES (est): 7.6MM **Privately Held**
WEB: www.onsitelasermedic.com
SIC: 7378 Computer & data processing equipment repair/maintenance

(P-16291)
QUEST INTL MONITOR SVC INC (PA)
60 Parker, Irvine (92618-1604)
PHONE.................949 581-9900
Shahnam Arshadi, *President*
Perry Aminzadeh, *CFO*
Kamyar Katouzian, *Vice Pres*
Claude Dir, *Executive*
Kelly Whitfield, *Admin Asst*
EMP: 60
SALES (est): 26MM **Privately Held**
WEB: www.questinc.com
SIC: 7378 7379 7371 7373 Computer maintenance & repair; computer related maintenance services; custom computer programming services; systems integration services; cathode ray tubes, including rebuilt; computer & software stores

(P-16292)
RAKWORX INC
17 Hammond Ste 404, Irvine (92618-1635)
PHONE.................949 215-1362
Yue Cong, *Vice Pres*
Zhiyong Ding, *President*
EMP: 150
SALES (est): 3.8MM **Privately Held**
SIC: 7378 3577 Computer & data processing equipment repair/maintenance; data conversion equipment, media-to-media: computer

(P-16293)
TELEPLAN SERVICE SOLUTIONS INC
8875 Washington Blvd B, Roseville (95678-6214)
PHONE.................916 677-4500
Russell Sproull, *CEO*
Pk Bala, *COO*
Jan Piet Valk, *CFO*
Jack Rockwood, *Vice Pres*
Michiel Van Der Ros, *Business Dir*
EMP: 75
SALES (est): 13.7MM **Privately Held**
SIC: 7378 Computer maintenance & repair
HQ: Teleplan Holding Usa, Inc.
8875 Washington Blvd B
Roseville CA 95678
916 677-4500

(P-16294)
THIRDWAVE TECHNOLOGY SERVICES
4054 Del Rey Ave Ste 207, Marina Del Rey (90292-5680)
PHONE.................310 563-2160
Sharmila Herr, *President*
EMP: 50
SALES (est): 1.4MM **Privately Held**
WEB: www.thirdwavets.com
SIC: 7378 Computer maintenance & repair

(P-16295)
TURNER TECHTRONICS INC
17845 Sky Park Cir, Irvine (92614-6112)
PHONE.................949 724-1339
Randy Hower, *Branch Mgr*
EMP: 118
SALES (corp-wide): 15.3MM **Privately Held**
WEB: www.turnertech.com
SIC: 7378 7372 Computer maintenance & repair; prepackaged software

PA: Turner Techtronics, Inc.
7675 N San Fernando Rd
Burbank CA 91505
818 973-1060

(P-16296)
TURNER TECHTRONICS INC (PA)
7675 N San Fernando Rd, Burbank (91505-1073)
PHONE.................818 973-1060
Brendan Turner, *President*
Charles Turner, *CFO*
Ellen Turner, *Vice Pres*
Megan Turner, *Marketing Mgr*
EMP: 140
SQ FT: 7,500
SALES (est): 15.3MM **Privately Held**
WEB: www.turnertech.com
SIC: 7378 7378 Computer & data processing equipment repair/maintenance; computer & software stores

(P-16297)
TUSA INC (PA)
Also Called: Terix Computer Service
986 Walsh Ave, Santa Clara (95050-2649)
PHONE.................888 848-3749
Bernd Appleby, *CEO*
EMP: 105
SALES (est): 30MM **Privately Held**
SIC: 7378 Computer maintenance & repair

(P-16298)
XEROX CORPORATION
2665 N 1st St Ste 200, San Jose (95134-2034)
PHONE.................408 953-2700
Tom Long, *Manager*
EMP: 200
SALES (corp-wide): 10.2B **Publicly Held**
WEB: www.xerox.com
SIC: 7378 7629 3861 5044 Computer peripheral equipment repair & maintenance; business machine repair, electric; photographic equipment & supplies; copying equipment; photocopy machines
PA: Xerox Corporation
201 Merritt 7
Norwalk CT 06851
203 968-3000

7379 Computer Related Svcs, NEC

(P-16299)
24 7AI INC (PA)
2001 All Programable, San Jose (95124-4356)
PHONE.................650 385-2247
Pallipuram V Kannan, *Ch of Bd*
Bruce Weiss, *Partner*
Matt Sato, *President*
Bill Robbins, *COO*
Brent Bowman, *CFO*
EMP: 109
SQ FT: 5,000
SALES (est): 921.1MM **Privately Held**
WEB: www.247customer.com
SIC: 7379

(P-16300)
741 STUDIOS LLC
2950 Buskirk Ave Ste 300, Walnut Creek (94597-6900)
PHONE.................925 407-2063
Lev Shur, *Legal Staff*
EMP: 200
SALES (est): 5MM **Privately Held**
SIC: 7379 Computer related consulting services

(P-16301)
A P R CONSULTING INC
17852 17th St Ste 206, Tustin (92780-2143)
PHONE.................714 544-3696
Darryl Stone, *Branch Mgr*
EMP: 590
SALES (corp-wide): 78.5MM **Privately Held**
SIC: 7379 7371 Computer related maintenance services; custom computer programming services

PA: A P R Consulting, Inc.
1370 Valley Vista Dr # 280
Diamond Bar CA 91765
909 396-5375

(P-16302)
ABTECH TECHNOLOGIES INC
Also Called: Abtech Support
2042 Corte Del Nogal D, Carlsbad (92011-1438)
PHONE.................760 827-5100
Robert Russell, *President*
Paul Storck, *Vice Pres*
Shawn Brown, *Office Mgr*
Caroline Wolfe, *Admin Asst*
Tony Vakilian, *Engineer*
EMP: 88
SALES (est): 18.4MM **Privately Held**
WEB: www.abtechsupport.com
SIC: 7379 Computer related consulting services

(P-16303)
ACER AMERICA CORPORATION (DH)
333 W San Carlos St, San Jose (95110-2726)
PHONE.................408 533-7700
Emmanuel Fromont, *CEO*
Marina Xu, *President*
Ming Wang, *CFO*
Nga Ly, *Treasurer*
John Nguyen, *Vice Pres*
EMP: 100
SALES (est): 93.3MM
SALES (corp-wide): 7.8B **Privately Held**
WEB: www.acersupport.com
SIC: 7379
HQ: Gateway, Inc.
7565 Irvine Center Dr # 150
Irvine CA 92618
949 471-7000

(P-16304)
ADCOM INTERACTIVE MEDIA INC
Also Called: Admedia
901 W Alameda Ave Ste 102, Burbank (91506-2849)
PHONE.................800 296-7104
Danny E Bibi, *Principal*
AVI Bibi, *COO*
AVI N Bibi, *Principal*
Daniel E Bibi, *Principal*
Lacey Stanford, *Principal*
EMP: 52
SALES (est): 6.9MM **Privately Held**
SIC: 7379

(P-16305)
ADD2NET INC (PA)
Also Called: Lunarpages
931 E La Habra Blvd, La Habra (90631-5505)
PHONE.................714 521-8150
George Natzic, *President*
Anoop Boonyarattapan, *Exec VP*
Sanit Khurasi, *Exec VP*
Harold Morrison, *Administration*
EMP: 50
SQ FT: 7,000
SALES (est): 9.9MM **Privately Held**
SIC: 7379

(P-16306)
ADVANCED RSRVATION SYSTEMS INC
2445 Truxtun Rd Ste 205, San Diego (92106-6154)
PHONE.................858 300-8600
Alec House, *President*
Dan Rhoads, *Shareholder*
Alan Suchdolski, *CEO*
Wayne Blum, *Vice Pres*
Keith Bockmier, *Vice Pres*
EMP: 65
SQ FT: 3,000
SALES (est): 8.7MM **Privately Held**
WEB: www.aresdirect.com
SIC: 7379

(P-16307)
ADVANTIS GLOBAL INC (PA)
301 Howard St Ste 1400, San Francisco (94105-6669)
PHONE.................415 850-1500
Bryan Barber, *CEO*
Jeff Taylor, *COO*
Randi Haaker, *Vice Pres*
Wora Iddhibhakdibong, *Tech Recruiter*
Sabrina Bennett, *Accounting Mgr*
EMP: 110 EST: 2007
SQ FT: 4,500
SALES: 40MM **Privately Held**
WEB: www.advantisglobal.com
SIC: 7379 Computer related consulting services;

(P-16308)
AGRIAN INC (PA)
352 W Spruce Ave, Clovis (93611)
PHONE.................559 437-5700
Nishan Majarian, *CEO*
Richard Machado, *President*
Andriana Majarian, *COO*
Joseph Middione, *COO*
Jeff Dearborn, *Officer*
EMP: 99
SQ FT: 3,500
SALES (est): 7.1MM **Privately Held**
SIC: 7379

(P-16309)
AICENT INC
900 E Hamilton Ave # 600, Campbell (95008-0671)
PHONE.................408 324-1316
Lynn Lui, *CEO*
Kallen Chan, *CFO*
EMP: 106 EST: 2000
SALES (est): 351.3K **Privately Held**
WEB: www.aicent.net
SIC: 7379 Data processing consultant

(P-16310)
ALLIANZ TECHNOLOGY AMERICA INC
1465 N Mcdowell Blvd, Petaluma (94954-6516)
PHONE.................415 899-2713
Axel Shell, *CEO*
Olav Spiegel, *COO*
Michael Schiebel, *CFO*
Ryan Gibson, *Admin Sec*
EMP: 120
SQ FT: 15,000
SALES (est): 36MM **Privately Held**
SIC: 7379
HQ: Allianz Technology International B.V.
Keizersgracht 484
Amsterdam
205 569-715

(P-16311)
ANAPLAN INC (PA)
50 Hawthorne St, San Francisco (94105-3902)
PHONE.................415 742-8199
Frank Calderoni, *President*
David H Morton Jr, *CFO*
Steven Birdsall, *Risk Mgmt Dir*
EMP: 108 EST: 2008
SQ FT: 55,000
SALES: 168.3MM **Publicly Held**
SIC: 7379

(P-16312)
APN SOFTWARE SERVICES INC (PA)
39899 Balentine Dr # 385, Newark (94560-5391)
PHONE.................510 623-5050
Aslam Chandiwalli, *President*
Srinivas Mallipog, *Executive*
Venkatesh Aithal, *Tech Recruiter*
Devesh K Upadhyay, *Tech Recruiter*
Wasif Rehman, *Technology*
EMP: 71
SQ FT: 3,500
SALES (est): 26.3MM **Privately Held**
WEB: www.apninc.com
SIC: 7379 Computer related consulting services

P R O D U C T S & S V C S

(P-16313)
ARXAN TECHNOLOGIES INC (PA)
650 California St Fl 2750, San Francisco (94108-2607)
PHONE..........................415 247-0900
Joe Sander, *CEO*
Charlie Velasquez, *CFO*
James Love, *Officer*
Mark Lorion, *Senior VP*
Rusty Carter, *Vice Pres*
EMP: 65
SALES (est): 20.5MM **Privately Held**
SIC: 7379 Computer related maintenance services

(P-16314)
ASCAR INC
110 E De La Guerra St, Santa Barbara (93101-2205)
P.O. Box 87 (93102-0087)
PHONE..........................805 966-3331
Roger Stettner, *CEO*
Thomas Laux, *Vice Pres*
EMP: 51
SALES (est): 92K
SALES (corp-wide): 51.9B **Privately Held**
SIC: 7379
HQ: Continental Advanced Lidar Solutions Us, Llc
6307 Crpinteria Ave Ste A
Santa Barbara CA 93103
805 318-2064

(P-16315)
ASSIGN CORPORATION
200 N Maryland Ave # 204, Glendale (91206-4274)
PHONE..........................818 247-7100
Umesh Lalwani, *CEO*
Tanuj Nigam, *Vice Pres*
Liandra Sapien, *Controller*
Deepa Achar, *Human Res Mgr*
EMP: 120
SQ FT: 1,300
SALES (est): 8MM **Privately Held**
WEB: www.assigncorp.com
SIC: 7379

(P-16316)
BENCHMARK INTERNET GROUP LLC
10621 Calle Lee Ste 141, Los Alamitos (90720-6798)
PHONE..........................562 286-6820
Denise Keller,
EMP: 100 EST: 2005
SALES (est): 6.8MM **Privately Held**
SIC: 7379 Computer related consulting services

(P-16317)
BESTITCOM INC (PA)
1464 Madera Rd, Simi Valley (93065-3077)
PHONE..........................602 667-5613
Harry Curtin, *CEO*
Susan Silberstein, *COO*
Rich Hybner, *CFO*
Fred Chen, *CTO*
John Yu, *Opers Staff*
EMP: 65
SQ FT: 20,000
SALES (est): 14.6MM **Privately Held**
WEB: www.bestit.com
SIC: 7379 Computer related consulting services; computer related maintenance services

(P-16318)
BIARCA INC (PA)
1060 Hyde Ave, San Jose (95129-3026)
PHONE..........................408 564-4465
Subhashini Rajana, *CEO*
Kris Rajana, *President*
EMP: 75 EST: 2016
SQ FT: 1,600
SALES (est): 4.6MM **Privately Held**
SIC: 7379 7371 Computer related consulting services; custom computer programming services

(P-16319)
BMR APPS INC
548 Market St, San Francisco (94104-5401)
PHONE..........................954 651-1412
William Schonbrun, *President*
EMP: 68
SALES (est): 4.9MM **Privately Held**
SIC: 7379

(P-16320)
BRADY COMPANY
795 Folsom St, San Francisco (94107-1243)
PHONE..........................415 644-0836
Robert L Brady, *Owner*
EMP: 53
SQ FT: 9,000
SALES: 5MM **Privately Held**
SIC: 7379 Computer related consulting services

(P-16321)
BRICSNET FM AMERICA INC
1820 Harvest Rd, Pleasanton (94566-5417)
PHONE..........................202 756-1840
Farid Jinian, *CEO*
Hector Rodriguez, *Ch of Bd*
Stuart Turner, *President*
EMP: 70
SALES (est): 6.2MM **Privately Held**
SIC: 7379 Computer related maintenance services

(P-16322)
CAPGEMINI AMERICA INC
1160 Battery St Ste 275, San Francisco (94111-1247)
PHONE..........................415 796-6777
EMP: 100
SALES (corp-wide): 353.3MM **Privately Held**
SIC: 7379 Computer related consulting services
HQ: Capgemini America, Inc.
79 5th Ave Fl 3
New York NY 10003

(P-16323)
CAPIOT SOFTWARE INC
3000 El Cam, Palo Alto (94306)
PHONE..........................650 766-2469
Anil Kshirsagar, *CEO*
Vasudeva Anumukonda, *COO*
Ashish Kapoor, *Vice Pres*
Hitesh Salla, *Vice Pres*
Sandil Srinivasan, *VP Sales*
EMP: 180 EST: 2014
SALES: 4.5MM **Privately Held**
SIC: 7379 7371 7389 Computer related consulting services; computer software development

(P-16324)
CELLARSTONE INC (PA)
Also Called: Qcommission
1650 Borel Pl Ste 100, San Mateo (94402-3529)
PHONE..........................650 242-0008
Gopi Mattel, *CEO*
Srini Rekapalli, *Vice Pres*
Beth Pineda, *Executive Asst*
EMP: 60
SQ FT: 800
SALES (est): 7.7MM **Privately Held**
WEB: www.cellarstone.com
SIC: 7379 8742 Computer related consulting services; management consulting services

(P-16325)
CENTRAL BUSINESS SOLUTIONS INC (PA)
37600 Central Ct Ste 214, Newark (94560-3456)
PHONE..........................510 573-5500
Anjul Katare, *President*
Kunal Joshi, *Tech Recruiter*
Akash Kumar, *Tech Recruiter*
Bitopi Ghosh, *Human Res Mgr*
Soumen Smith, *Recruiter*
EMP: 70
SALES (est): 5.7MM **Privately Held**
SIC: 7379

(P-16326)
CGI TECHNOLOGIES SOLUTIONS INC
505 14th St Fl 9, Oakland (94612-1406)
PHONE..........................510 238-5300
Shelley Bergum, *Branch Mgr*
Jose Guzman, *Info Tech Mgr*
EMP: 56
SALES (corp-wide): 8.6B **Privately Held**
SIC: 7379 Computer related consulting services
HQ: Cgi Technologies And Solutions Inc.
11325 Random Hills Rd
Fairfax VA 22030
703 267-8000

(P-16327)
CLOSINGCORP INC
3111 Camino Del Rio N # 200, San Diego (92108-5722)
PHONE..........................858 551-1500
Bob Jennings, *CEO*
Michael D Reynolds, *CFO*
Pat Carney, *Officer*
EMP: 63
SQ FT: 13,823
SALES (est): 14.2MM **Privately Held**
SIC: 7379 7375 4813 ; information retrieval services;

(P-16328)
COMERIT INC
2201 Francisco Dr # 140283, El Dorado Hills (95762-3713)
PHONE..........................888 556-5990
Greg Clark, *CEO*
Jesper Christensen, *Senior Partner*
David Perroni, *Senior Partner*
Jeff Johnston, *CFO*
Vishal Muchamarry, *Consultant*
EMP: 120
SQ FT: 3,500
SALES (est): 4.4MM **Privately Held**
SIC: 7379

(P-16329)
COMMERCIAL PRGRM SYSTEMS INC (PA)
Also Called: CPS
4400 Coldwater Canyon Ave # 200, Studio City (91604-1480)
PHONE..........................818 308-8560
Alan Strong, *CEO*
Phil Sawyer, *President*
Marjorie Kram, *Vice Pres*
Michele Stewart, *Vice Pres*
EMP: 146
SQ FT: 8,000
SALES (est): 15.2MM **Privately Held**
SIC: 7379 Data processing consultant

(P-16330)
COMPUTER SCIENCES CORPORATION
1111 Broadway Fl 13, Oakland (94607-4139)
PHONE..........................510 645-3000
William Cunningham, *Manager*
EMP: 100
SALES (corp-wide): 24.5B **Publicly Held**
WEB: www.csc.com
SIC: 7379 7373 Computer related consulting services; systems integration services
HQ: Computer Sciences Corporation
1775 Tysons Blvd Ste 1000
Tysons VA 22102
703 245-9675

(P-16331)
CONCENTRIX CORPORATION
44201 Nobel Dr, Fremont (94538-3178)
PHONE..........................510 668-3717
John Vitalie, *Branch Mgr*
EMP: 70
SALES (corp-wide): 17B **Publicly Held**
SIC: 7379 8742 7331 7311 Computer related maintenance services; management consulting services; direct mail advertising services; advertising agencies
HQ: Concentrix Corporation
3750 Monroe Ave
Pittsford NY 14534
585 218-5300

(P-16332)
CONNECTX INC
909 N Avi Blvd Unit 6, Manhattan Beach (90266)
PHONE..........................310 702-8686
Lance Arthur Parker, *President*
EMP: 50
SQ FT: 4,000
SALES (est): 842.8K **Privately Held**
SIC: 7379 Computer data escrow service

(P-16333)
COUNTY OF RIVERSIDE
4080 Lemon St Fl 3, Riverside (92501-3609)
PHONE..........................951 486-7700
Kevin Crawford, *Branch Mgr*
EMP: 50 **Privately Held**
SIC: 7379 Computer related consulting services
PA: County Of Riverside
4080 Lemon St Fl 11
Riverside CA 92501
951 955-1110

(P-16334)
COYOTE CREEK CONSULTING INC
1551 Mccarthy Blvd # 115, Milpitas (95035-7437)
PHONE..........................408 383-9200
Michael R Faster, *CEO*
Candi Faster, *Office Mgr*
Jeff Severance, *Engineer*
EMP: 65
SQ FT: 3,000
SALES (est): 11.2MM **Privately Held**
WEB: www.coyotecrk.com
SIC: 7379

(P-16335)
CROWDSTRIKE INC (HQ)
150 Mathilda Pl Ste 300, Sunnyvale (94086-6012)
PHONE..........................888 512-8906
George Kurtz, *CEO*
Michael Carpenter, *President*
Mike Carpenter, *President*
Colin Black, *COO*
Burt Podbere, *CFO*
EMP: 167
SQ FT: 16,000
SALES (est): 21.4MM
SALES (corp-wide): 74.2MM **Privately Held**
SIC: 7379 Computer related maintenance services
PA: Crowdstrike Holdings, Inc.
15440 Laguna Canyon Rd
Irvine CA 92618
888 512-8906

(P-16336)
CROWDSTRIKE HOLDINGS INC (PA)
15440 Laguna Canyon Rd, Irvine (92618-2138)
PHONE..........................888 512-8906
George Kurtz, *CEO*
Burt Podbere, *CFO*
Dmitri Alperovitch, *CTO*
EMP: 120
SQ FT: 5,000
SALES (est): 74.2MM **Privately Held**
SIC: 7379 Computer related maintenance services

(P-16337)
CSC CONSULTING INC
2100 E Grand Ave B360, El Segundo (90245-5055)
PHONE..........................310 563-2062
Alan Young, *Manager*
EMP: 75
SALES (corp-wide): 24.5B **Publicly Held**
SIC: 7379 Computer related consulting services
HQ: Csc Consulting, Inc.
1775 Tysons Blvd Fl 9
Tysons VA 22102
781 890-7446

(P-16338)
CSRA SYSTEMS & SOLUTIONS LLC
2727 Hamner Ave, Norco (92860-1927)
PHONE...............................951 735-3300
Kenneth Gunn, *Manager*
EMP: 50
SALES (corp-wide): 24.5B **Publicly Held**
SIC: 7379 Computer related consulting services
HQ: Csc Systems & Solutions Llc
   15000 Conference Ctr Dr
   Chantilly VA 20151

(P-16339)
CUSTOMER SRVC DLVRY PLTFRM CRP
Also Called: C S D P
15615 Alton Pkwy Ste 310, Irvine (92618-3308)
PHONE...............................717 896-8489
Jerry Edinger, *President*
David Englund, *CFO*
David Dorret, *Officer*
Dave Dorret, *CTO*
Ameet Rajadhyksha, *Senior Mgr*
EMP: 50
SQ FT: 5,000
SALES (est): 3.8MM **Privately Held**
WEB: www.csdpcorp.com
SIC: 7379 7373 Computer related consulting services; systems software development services

(P-16340)
DCM LIMITED
Also Called: Dcm Data Systems
39159 Paseo Padre Pkwy # 303, Fremont (94538-1698)
PHONE...............................510 494-2321
Ashok Choudhury, *President*
EMP: 60
SQ FT: 1,500 **Privately Held**
WEB: www.dcmusa.com
SIC: 7379 Computer related consulting services
PA: D C M Limited
   6th Floor, Vikrant Tower
   New Delhi DL 11000

(P-16341)
DEALERTRACK COLLTE MANAG SERVI
Also Called: Fdi Collateral Management
9750 Goethe Rd, Sacramento (95827-3500)
PHONE...............................916 368-5300
Mark O'Neil, *CEO*
Daniel L Wollenberg, *President*
Beverly Devine, *Exec VP*
Tony Panganiban, *Vice Pres*
Slava Filonenko, *Sr Software Eng*
EMP: 220
SQ FT: 84,900
SALES (est): 33.3MM
SALES (corp-wide): 32.8B **Privately Held**
WEB: www.fdielt.com
SIC: 7379 Computer related consulting services
HQ: Trivin, Inc.
   115 Poheganut Dr Ste 201
   Groton CT 06340
   860 448-3177

(P-16342)
DECLARA INC
977 Commercial St, Palo Alto (94303-4908)
PHONE...............................650 800-7695
Ramona Pierson, *CEO*
Pankaj Anand, *President*
Nelson Gonzalez, *Officer*
Bob Michitarian, *Officer*
Debra Chrapaty, *Executive*
EMP: 68
SQ FT: 3,000
SALES (est): 3.6MM **Privately Held**
SIC: 7379 Data processing consultant

(P-16343)
DEFENSEWEB TECHNOLOGIES INC
Also Called: Nliven
10188 Telesis Ct Ste 300, San Diego (92121-4779)
PHONE...............................858 272-8505
Robert Nascenzi, *CEO*
Marc Willard, *CEO*
Tonya Torgeson, *COO*
Kevin J Herdman, *CFO*
Jim Kesaris, *CFO*
EMP: 90
SQ FT: 21,352
SALES (est): 9.1MM
SALES (corp-wide): 53.7B **Publicly Held**
WEB: www.defenseweb.com
SIC: 7379 7371 Computer related consulting services; computer software development
PA: Humana Inc.
   500 W Main St Ste 300
   Louisville KY 40202
   502 580-1000

(P-16344)
DEL REY SYSTEMS AND TECH INC (PA)
7844 Convoy Ct, San Diego (92111-1210)
PHONE...............................858 874-8992
Nancy S Miller, *President*
EMP: 100
SQ FT: 5,000
SALES (est): 24.4MM **Privately Held**
WEB: www.drst.net
SIC: 7379 8732 ; merger, acquisition & reorganization research

(P-16345)
DELTA COMPUTER CONSULTING
25550 Hawthorne Blvd # 106, Torrance (90505-6831)
PHONE...............................310 541-9440
Marzieh Daneshvar, *President*
Masih Hakimpour, *Vice Pres*
EMP: 180
SQ FT: 2,000
SALES (est): 13.7MM **Privately Held**
WEB: www.deltacomputerconsulting.com
SIC: 7379 Computer related consulting services

(P-16346)
DELTA MAX
23 Curl Dr, Corona Del Mar (92625-1416)
P.O. Box 7188, Newport Beach (92658-7188)
PHONE...............................949 759-8529
Robert Swanson, *Owner*
EMP: 50
SALES (est): 2.2MM **Privately Held**
WEB: www.deltamax.com
SIC: 7379 Computer related consulting services

(P-16347)
DHARNE & COMPANY
19200 Von Karman Ave # 400, Irvine (92612-8553)
PHONE...............................949 293-5675
Nitin Dharne, *President*
Sahil Borate, *Officer*
Gina Wu, *Officer*
EMP: 80
SALES (est): 2.5MM **Privately Held**
SIC: 7379 Computer related services

(P-16348)
DIGITAL FOUNDRY INC
1707 Tiburon Blvd, Belvedere Tiburon (94920-2513)
PHONE...............................415 789-1600
Bradley W Stauffer, *President*
Robert Fraik, *Chairman*
Bonnie Albin Fraik, *Vice Pres*
Joe Carpenter, *Business Dir*
Andrew Lee, *Software Engr*
EMP: 50
SQ FT: 7,500
SALES (est): 5.3MM **Privately Held**
WEB: www.digitalfoundry.com
SIC: 7379 7371 Computer related consulting services; computer software development & applications

(P-16349)
DIGITAL REALTY TRUST INC (PA)
4 Embarcadero Ctr # 3200, San Francisco (94111-4188)
PHONE...............................415 738-6500
A William Stein, *CEO*
Laurence A Chapman, *Ch of Bd*
Jarrett B Appleby, *COO*
Andrew P Power, *CFO*
Andrew Power, *CFO*
EMP: 150
SALES: 2.4B **Privately Held**
WEB: www.digitalrealtytrust.com
SIC: 7379 7374 Data processing consultant; data processing service

(P-16350)
DIRECTAPPS INC (PA)
Also Called: Direct Technology
3009 Douglas Blvd Ste 300, Roseville (95661-3895)
PHONE...............................916 787-2200
Rick Nelson, *CEO*
Federico Michanie, *President*
Casey Stenzel, *CFO*
John Sercu, *Treasurer*
Wud Pocinwong, *Vice Pres*
EMP: 125
SQ FT: 19,000
SALES (est): 49MM **Privately Held**
WEB: www.directapps.com
SIC: 7379

(P-16351)
DTI SERVICES INC (PA)
601 S Figueroa St # 4300, Los Angeles (90017-5757)
PHONE...............................213 670-1100
Satoru Amano, *President*
Chad D Harmon, *CEO*
Ken Yasuda, *CFO*
Michael Frick, *Info Tech Dir*
EMP: 60 EST: 1996
SALES (est): 8.7MM **Privately Held**
WEB: www.dtiserv.com
SIC: 7379 4813 7374 7389 ; ; telephone communications broker; computer graphics service;

(P-16352)
DYNTEK INC (PA)
5241 California Ave # 150, Irvine (92617-3215)
PHONE...............................949 271-6700
Ron Ben-Yishay, *CEO*
Wade Stevenson, *President*
Karen S Rosenberger, *CFO*
Michael Gullard, *Chairman*
Jack Marks, *Vice Pres*
EMP: 105
SQ FT: 10,250
SALES (est): 66.6MM **Publicly Held**
WEB: www.dyntek.com
SIC: 7379 ; computer related consulting services

(P-16353)
EA CONSULTING INC
1024 Iron Point Rd, Folsom (95630-8013)
PHONE...............................916 357-6767
Chin K Wong, *CEO*
Robitah Mohd-Khatib, *President*
EMP: 50
SQ FT: 12,000
SALES (est): 3.2MM **Privately Held**
WEB: www.ea-inc.com
SIC: 7379 8748 Computer related consulting services; business consulting

(P-16354)
ECLIPSE SOLUTIONS INC
2150 River Plaza Dr # 380, Sacramento (95833-4138)
PHONE...............................916 565-8090
John Willis, *CEO*
Mike Watson, *President*
EMP: 84
SALES (est): 4.7MM
SALES (corp-wide): 379.7MM **Privately Held**
WEB: www.eclipsesolutions.com
SIC: 7379 8748 8742 8322 Computer related consulting services; business consulting; management consulting services; disaster service

(P-16355)
PA: Public Consulting Group, Inc.
   148 State St Fl 10
   Boston MA 02109
   617 426-2026

(P-16355)
EDMIN OPEN SYSTEMS INC (PA)
5471 Krny Vlla Rd Ste 310, San Diego (92123)
PHONE...............................858 712-9341
Peter Sibley, *CEO*
Rick Wells, *CFO*
Richard Datz, *Vice Pres*
D Clayton Hoyle, *Vice Pres*
Sage Ann Scheer, *Vice Pres*
EMP: 54
SQ FT: 15,000
SALES (est): 11.9MM **Privately Held**
WEB: www.edmin.com
SIC: 7379 7373 7371 Computer related consulting services; value-added resellers; computer systems; software programming applications

(P-16356)
ELITE TEK SERVICES INC
131 Mercer Way, Costa Mesa (92627-3797)
PHONE...............................714 881-5301
Stephanie Duplex, *President*
Scott Duplex, *Vice Pres*
EMP: 54
SALES (est): 4.8MM **Privately Held**
SIC: 7379 7361 Computer related consulting services; employment agencies

(P-16357)
EMERGE DIGITAL INC
Also Called: Emerge Digital Group
543 Howard St Lbby, San Francisco (94105-3015)
PHONE...............................415 839-5055
Chase Norlin, *CEO*
Alexander Rowland, *President*
Nelson Becerra, *Vice Pres*
Zachary Zarate, *Business Dir*
EMP: 88 EST: 2009
SALES (est): 6.6MM **Privately Held**
SIC: 7379 Computer related consulting services

(P-16358)
ENDSIGHT
1440 4th St Ste B, Berkeley (94710-1315)
PHONE...............................510 655-6500
Michael Chaput, *CEO*
Nici Courand, *Executive Asst*
EMP: 80
SALES (est): 7MM **Privately Held**
WEB: www.end-sight.com
SIC: 7379

(P-16359)
ETAIROS CONSULTING
6711 Studio Pl, Riverside (92509-5900)
PHONE...............................844 219-7027
EMP: 50
SQ FT: 4,000
SALES (est): 1.9MM **Privately Held**
SIC: 7379

(P-16360)
ETHERWAN SYSTEMS INC
2301 E Winston Rd, Anaheim (92806-5542)
PHONE...............................714 779-3800
Mitch Yang, *President*
John Marchiando, *President*
Mark Prowten, *Vice Pres*
Norman Law, *Technician*
Mars Pao, *Engineer*
EMP: 100 EST: 1996
SQ FT: 5,000
SALES (est): 9.6MM
SALES (corp-wide): 2B **Privately Held**
WEB: www.etherwan.com
SIC: 7379 3577 Computer related maintenance services; computer peripheral equipment
HQ: Etherwan Systems, Inc.
   8f, No. 2, Alley 6, Lane 235, Baoqiao Rd.
   New Taipei City 23145
   266 298-986

(PA)=Parent Co (HQ)=Headquarters (DH)=Div Headquarters
✿ = New Business established in last 2 years

2019 Directory of California
Wholesalers and Services Companies

697

P R O D U C T S & S V C S

(P-16361)
ETOUCH SYSTEMS CORP
6627 Dumbarton Cir, Fremont
(94555-3603)
PHONE.............................510 795-4800
Aniruddha Gadre, *CEO*
Amit Shah, *Surgery Dir*
Siddhartha Chakravarty, *Info Tech Mgr*
Samreen Akhter, *Tech Recruiter*
Viha Tyagi, *Tech Recruiter*
EMP: 600
SQ FT: 12,800
SALES: 75MM
SALES (corp-wide): 1B **Publicly Held**
WEB: www.etouch.net
SIC: 7379 ; computer related consulting
    services
PA: Virtusa Corporation
    132 Turnpike Rd Ste 300
    Southborough MA 01772
    508 389-7300

(P-16362)
EVENTBRITE INC (PA)
155 5th St Fl 7, San Francisco
(94103-2919)
PHONE.............................415 692-7779
Julia Hartz, *CEO*
Kevin Hartz, *Ch of Bd*
Randy Befumo, *CFO*
Omer Cohen,
Samantha Harnett, *Senior VP*
EMP: 148 EST: 2003
SALES: 201.6MM **Publicly Held**
SIC: 7379

(P-16363)
EVOTEK INC (PA)
Also Called: Evotek Solutions
6150 Lusk Blvd Ste 204, San Diego
(92121-2738)
PHONE.............................858 362-5083
Didi Gur, *CEO*
Jeff Klenner, *President*
Mari Rodish, *General Mgr*
David Clark, *Finance*
Torrie Bradley, *Mktg Coord*
EMP: 56
SALES: 100MM **Privately Held**
SIC: 7379 Computer related consulting
    services

(P-16364)
EXPERTS EXCHANGE LLC
Also Called: Experts Exch Exprts-Xchange-
    com
2701 Mcmillan Ave Ste 160, San Luis
    Obispo (93401-4744)
P.O. Box 1229 (93406-1229)
PHONE.............................805 787-0603
Randy Redberg, *Vice Pres*
Gene Richardson, *COO*
Adelaido Jimenez, *Admin Asst*
Phil Lips, *Administration*
Mark Olsen, *Sr Software Eng*
EMP: 55
SQ FT: 13,400
SALES (est): 5.5MM **Privately Held**
SIC: 7379

(P-16365)
FAIRWAY TECHNOLOGIES INC
7825 Fay Ave Ste 100, La Jolla
(92037-4247)
PHONE.............................858 454-4471
Michael Mannion, *COO*
Brett Humphrey, *CEO*
Casey Rubano, *Software Dev*
Gregory Charles, *Software Engr*
EMP: 90
SQ FT: 5,000
SALES (est): 3.9MM **Privately Held**
SIC: 7379 7371 Computer related consult-
    ing services; custom computer program-
    ming services; computer software
    systems analysis & design, custom; com-
    puter software development & applica-
    tions

(P-16366)
FMT CONSULTANTS LLC (PA)
Also Called: F M T
2310 Camino Vida Roble # 101, Carlsbad
(92011-1561)
PHONE.............................844 369-4593
Eric Casazza, *CEO*

Jim O'Grady, *Principal*
EMP: 51
SQ FT: 6,500
SALES: 9MM **Privately Held**
WEB: www.fmtconsultants.com
SIC: 7379

(P-16367)
**FNTI FIDELITY NAT TECH
IMAGIN**
2123 Ringwood Ave, San Jose
(95131-1725)
PHONE.............................408 942-1780
John Knight, *CEO*
Timothy L Plette, *CFO*
David L Walker, *Vice Pres*
EMP: 50
SQ FT: 8,000
SALES (est): 3MM **Privately Held**
SIC: 7379 Disk & diskette conversion serv-
    ice

(P-16368)
FORSYS INC
6036 Stevenson Blvd, Fremont
(94538-5250)
PHONE.............................408 409-2567
Jayaprasad Vejendla, *President*
Vijay Kiran, *Senior Mgr*
EMP: 75
SQ FT: 3,000
SALES (est): 20MM **Privately Held**
SIC: 7379 Computer related consulting
    services

(P-16369)
FORSYTHE TECHNOLOGY LLC
222 N Pacific Coast Hwy # 1426, El Se-
    gundo (90245-5648)
PHONE.............................424 217-6500
EMP: 64
SALES (corp-wide): 3.1B **Privately Held**
SIC: 7379 Computer related maintenance
    services
HQ: Forsythe Technology, Llc
    7770 Frontage Rd
    Skokie IL 60077
    847 213-7000

(P-16370)
FUNNY OR DIE INC
1041 N Formosa Ave, West Hollywood
(90046-6703)
PHONE.............................650 461-3929
Richard Glover, *CEO*
Mitch Galbraith, *COO*
Peter Morris, *Vice Pres*
Sebastian Rasino, *Information Mgr*
Taylor Treadwell, *Human Res Dir*
EMP: 50
SALES (est): 7.5MM **Privately Held**
SIC: 7379

(P-16371)
FUSIONZONE AUTOMOTIVE INC
1011 Swarthmore Ave, Pacific Palisades
(90272-2552)
PHONE.............................888 576-1136
Brett Sutherlin, *CEO*
Steve Greenfield, *President*
Karen Sutherlin, *COO*
Kevin Maloy, *CFO*
Mercedes Cruz, *General Mgr*
EMP: 50
SQ FT: 3,000
SALES (est): 3.6MM **Privately Held**
SIC: 7379 Computer related consulting
    services

(P-16372)
FUTURE DIAL INCORPORATED
392 Potrero Ave, Sunnyvale (94085-4116)
PHONE.............................408 245-8880
George C Huang, *CEO*
Sung L Choi, *President*
Steve Chan, *CEO*
Dwight Huang, *Vice Pres*
Jason LI, *Vice Pres*
EMP: 80 EST: 1999
SQ FT: 8,000
SALES (est): 11.6MM **Privately Held**
WEB: www.futuredial.com
SIC: 7379 Computer related maintenance
    services

(P-16373)
FUTURE STATE
2101 Webster St Ste 520, Oakland
(94612-3050)
PHONE.............................925 956-4200
Steven Laine, *President*
Lynette Phillips, *Vice Pres*
Shari McAneney, *Office Mgr*
Will French, *Recruiter*
Zoe Dunning, *Commissioner*
EMP: 90
SALES: 19.2MM **Privately Held**
SIC: 7379 8742 Data processing consult-
    ant; management consulting services

(P-16374)
GA SERVICES LLC
1681 Kettering, Irvine (92614-5613)
PHONE.............................949 752-6515
Fax: 949 606-1990
EMP: 50
SQ FT: 10,500
SALES (est): 3.6MM **Privately Held**
WEB: www.gasllc.com
SIC: 7379 7378

(P-16375)
GAMEFLY INC (PA)
6080 Center Dr Fl 8, Los Angeles
(90045-9205)
PHONE.............................310 568-8224
Dave Hodess, *President*
Stacey M Peterson, *CFO*
Terri Luke, *Vice Pres*
John Cmar, *Sr Software Eng*
Chris Gee, *Sr Software Eng*
EMP: 115
SALES (est): 34.3MM **Privately Held**
SIC: 7379

(P-16376)
GDR GROUP INC
3 Park Plz Ste 1700, Irvine (92614-8540)
PHONE.............................949 453-8818
Ellen Dorse, *Principal*
Lacie Oots, *COO*
Bruce Greenburg, *Principal*
Robert Redwitz, *Principal*
Aaron Housh, *Network Enginr*
EMP: 100
SALES (est): 17.3MM **Privately Held**
WEB: www.gdrgroup.com
SIC: 7379

(P-16377)
GEBBS SOFTWARE INTL INC
4640 Admiralty Way Fl 9, Marina Del Rey
(90292-6630)
PHONE.............................201 227-0088
Nitin Thakor, *CEO*
Kiran Salian, *Administration*
EMP: 85
SQ FT: 2,500
SALES: 15.4MM **Privately Held**
WEB: www.gebbs.com
SIC: 7379 Computer related consulting
    services
PA: Gebbs Software International Private
    Limited
    Gebbs House
    Mumbai MH

(P-16378)
GEEK SQUAD INC
2300 N Rose Ave, Oxnard (93036-2628)
PHONE.............................805 278-9555
Jonathan Roach, *Manager*
EMP: 88
SALES (corp-wide): 42.1B **Publicly Held**
SIC: 7379 Computer related consulting
    services
HQ: Geek Squad, Inc.
    1213 Washington Ave N
    Minneapolis MN 55401

(P-16379)
GEEK SQUAD INC
120 Imperial Hwy, Fullerton (92835-1019)
PHONE.............................800 433-5778
EMP: 88
SALES (corp-wide): 42.1B **Publicly Held**
SIC: 7379 Computer related consulting
    services

HQ: Geek Squad, Inc.
    1213 Washington Ave N
    Minneapolis MN 55401
    -

(P-16380)
GEEK SQUAD INC
1490 Fitzgerald Dr, Pinole (94564-2227)
PHONE.............................800 433-5778
Rex Santacera, *Branch Mgr*
Kyle Ciccarelli, *Agent*
EMP: 88
SALES (corp-wide): 42.1B **Publicly Held**
SIC: 7379 Computer related consulting
    services
HQ: Geek Squad, Inc.
    1213 Washington Ave N
    Minneapolis MN 55401

(P-16381)
GEEK SQUAD INC
901 S Coast Dr Ste F, Costa Mesa
(92626-1783)
PHONE.............................714 434-0132
EMP: 88
SALES (corp-wide): 42.1B **Publicly Held**
SIC: 7379 Computer related consulting
    services
HQ: Geek Squad, Inc.
    1213 Washington Ave N
    Minneapolis MN 55401

(P-16382)
GEEK SQUAD INC
3741 W Chapman Ave, Orange
(92868-1608)
PHONE.............................714 938-0380
EMP: 88
SALES (corp-wide): 42.1B **Publicly Held**
SIC: 7379 Computer related consulting
    services
HQ: Geek Squad, Inc.
    1213 Washington Ave N
    Minneapolis MN 55401
    -

(P-16383)
**GENERAL DYNAMICS INFO
TECH INC**
1615 Murray Canyon Rd # 600, San Diego
(92108-4314)
PHONE.............................619 881-8989
Dan Morrissey, *Branch Mgr*
EMP: 50
SALES (corp-wide): 30.9B **Publicly Held**
SIC: 7379 Computer related maintenance
    services
HQ: General Dynamics Information Tech-
    nology, Inc.
    3211 Jermantown Rd
    Fairfax VA 22030
    703 995-8700

(P-16384)
**GENERAL NETWORKS
CORPORATION**
3524 Ocean View Blvd, Glendale
(91208-1212)
PHONE.............................818 249-1962
Robert Todd Withers, *President*
Randall C Wise, *Ch of Bd*
Todd Withers, *President*
Cort Baker, *Vice Pres*
David Horwatt, *Vice Pres*
EMP: 60
SQ FT: 3,600
SALES: 12MM **Privately Held**
WEB: www.gennet.com
SIC: 7379 5045 7372 Computer related
    consulting services; terminals, computer;
    prepackaged software

(P-16385)
**GLOBAL BUSINESS SOLUTIONS
INC**
600 Anton Blvd Ste 1050, Costa Mesa
(92626-7055)
PHONE.............................714 257-1488
Johnnie R Carlin, *CEO*
John R Carlin, *CEO*
EMP: 258

SALES (est): 23.9MM **Privately Held**
WEB: www.gbscs.com
SIC: **7379** 8741 8742 Computer related consulting services; construction management; construction project management consultant

(P-16386)
GLOBAL SOFTWARE RESOURCES INC (PA)
Also Called: G S R
4447 Stoneridge Dr Ste 1, Pleasanton (94588-8325)
PHONE..................................925 249-2200
Prem J Hinduja, *President*
Venkat Krishnan, *Officer*
Satya Pappur, *Sr Software Eng*
Suzanne Griffith, *Human Res Dir*
Diane Walker, *Human Res Mgr*
EMP: 50
SALES (est): 6.7MM **Privately Held**
WEB: www.gsr-inc.com
SIC: **7379** 7371 Computer related consulting services; custom computer programming services

(P-16387)
GLOBALWAYS INC (PA)
42808 Christy St Ste 202, Fremont (94538-3119)
PHONE..................................510 580-1974
Uma Uppalapati, *President*
EMP: 68
SQ FT: 3,500
SALES (est): 5.8MM **Privately Held**
WEB: www.globalways.com
SIC: **7379** Computer related consulting services

(P-16388)
GRAYMETA INC
350 Via Las Brisas # 230, Newbury Park (91320-7045)
PHONE..................................855 202-2270
Tom Szabo, *CEO*
Tim Henderson, *President*
Rory Donnelly, *COO*
Josh Wiggins, *Risk Mgmt Dir*
John Motz, *CIO*
EMP: 50
SQ FT: 2,500
SALES (est): 811.3K **Privately Held**
SIC: **7379** 7374 7378 7371 Computer related maintenance services; data processing & preparation; computer & data processing equipment repair/maintenance; computer software development & applications

(P-16389)
HEADSTRONG CORPORATION
150 Mathilda Pl Ste 200, Sunnyvale (94086-6011)
PHONE..................................408 732-8700
Sandip Sahai, *Manager*
EMP: 60 **Privately Held**
WEB: www.headstrong.com
SIC: **7379** 8711 1731 Computer related consulting services; engineering services; electrical work
HQ: Headstrong Corporation
11921 Freedom Dr Ste 550
Reston VA 20190
703 272-6761

(P-16390)
HOMESTAR SYSTEMS INC
Also Called: Izmocars
230 California St Ste 510, San Francisco (94111-4331)
PHONE..................................415 694-6000
Tej Soni, *CEO*
Layton Judd, *Principal*
Gururaj Virupakshappa, *Administration*
Noman Saied, *Info Tech Mgr*
Craig Scudder, *Training Spec*
EMP: 85
SQ FT: 500
SALES (est): 7.7MM **Privately Held**
WEB: www.izmocars.com
SIC: **7379** Computer related consulting services

(P-16391)
HYPERMEDIA SYSTEMS INC
101 N Pacific Coast Hwy, El Segundo (90245-4318)
PHONE..................................213 452-6731
Michael Frick, *President*
Yumi Bustillos, *Admin Sec*
John Lee, *Administration*
Haridas Terhanian, *Administration*
Joshua Yarbrough, *Administration*
EMP: 85
SALES (est): 8.8MM **Privately Held**
WEB: www.hypermediasystems.com
SIC: **7379** Computer related consulting services

(P-16392)
IDRIVE INC
Also Called: Ibackup.com
26115 Mureau Rd Ste A, Calabasas (91302-3179)
PHONE..................................818 594-5972
Raghu Kulkarni, *Principal*
Vilabh Mishra, *President*
Emily Larson, *Admin Asst*
Kenny Nelson, *Admin Asst*
Pankti Shah, *Human Resources*
EMP: 70
SALES (est): 12.4MM **Privately Held**
WEB: www.pro-softnet.com
SIC: **7379** Computer related maintenance services; computer related consulting services

(P-16393)
INFOGAIN CORPORATION (PA)
485 Alberto Way Ste 100, Los Gatos (95032-5476)
PHONE..................................408 355-6000
Sunil Bhatia, *CEO*
Ayan Mukerji, *President*
Kapil K Nanda, *President*
Brian Rogan, *President*
Kulesh Bansal, *CFO*
EMP: 186
SQ FT: 14,487
SALES: 85.2MM **Privately Held**
WEB: www.infogain.com
SIC: **7379** 7373 8742 8748 Computer related consulting services; computer integrated systems design; management information systems consultant; systems engineering consultant, ex. computer or professional; data processing & preparation; electrical work

(P-16394)
INFOGEN LABS INC
18223 Charlton Ln, Porter Ranch (91326-3617)
PHONE..................................818 825-5024
Sanjeev Kuwadeker, *President*
Sid Patti, *VP Sales*
EMP: 70
SALES: 5MM **Privately Held**
SIC: **7379** Computer related consulting services

(P-16395)
INFORMATION TECH PARTNERS INC
Also Called: I T P
3003 N San Fernando Blvd, Burbank (91504-2525)
PHONE..................................800 789-7487
Michael Thompson, *President*
EMP: 60
SQ FT: 10,000
SALES (est): 13.5MM **Privately Held**
WEB: www.itpnet.com
SIC: **7379** Computer related consulting services

(P-16396)
INNOVA SOLUTIONS INC
3211 Scott Blvd Ste 202, Santa Clara (95054-3009)
PHONE..................................408 889-2020
Rajkumar Velagapudi, *CEO*
Malik Zegdi, *Exec VP*
Steven Craig, *Vice Pres*
Srinivas Jayanthi, *Vice Pres*
EMP: 160 EST: 2014
SQ FT: 4,656

SALES: 43MM **Privately Held**
SIC: **7379** Computer related consulting services

(P-16397)
INQBRANDS INC
Also Called: Ft USA
1801 E Holt Blvd Unit 101, Ontario (91761-2114)
PHONE..................................909 390-7788
Jinhua Shen, *CEO*
Rohn Monroe, *Vice Pres*
EMP: 55
SALES (est): 9.3MM
SALES (corp-wide): 182.7MM **Privately Held**
SIC: **7379**
PA: Focus Technology Co., Ltd.
12f, Unit A, Software Mansion, Xinghuo Rd., High Technology Dev
Nanjing 21000
256 667-7777

(P-16398)
INTEGRITS CORPORATION (PA)
5205 Kearny Villa Way # 200, San Diego (92123-1420)
PHONE..................................858 300-1600
Clarence M Carter Jr, *President*
Steve Fox, *COO*
Ivy Y Carter, *Vice Pres*
Michael Sosamon, *Vice Pres*
Mike Sosamon, *Vice Pres*
EMP: 50
SQ FT: 12,600
SALES: 6MM **Privately Held**
WEB: www.integrits.com
SIC: **7379** Computer related consulting services

(P-16399)
INTELLIPRO GROUP INC
3120 Scott Blvd 301, Santa Clara (95054-3326)
PHONE..................................408 200-9891
Grace MA, *CEO*
Tina Truong, *Vice Pres*
Xiaodong Wang, *Sr Software Eng*
Shivani Sharma, *Tech Recruiter*
Helen Gu, *Recruiter*
EMP: 380
SALES (est): 18.3MM **Privately Held**
SIC: **7379** Computer related consulting services

(P-16400)
INTERACTIVATE INC
707 Broadway Ste 1000, San Diego (92101-5324)
PHONE..................................619 814-1999
Jack Abbott Jr, *President*
EMP: 90
SALES (est): 4.9MM **Privately Held**
SIC: **7379**

(P-16401)
INTERMEDIA HOLDINGS INC (PA)
825 E Middlefield Rd, Mountain View (94043-4025)
PHONE..................................650 641-4000
Michael Gold, *CEO*
Christian Daugaard, *Partner*
Ron Dirienzo, *Partner*
Frankie White, *Partner*
Jonathan McCormick, *COO*
EMP: 60
SALES (est): 37.1MM **Privately Held**
SIC: **7379**

(P-16402)
INTERNATIONAL BUS MCHS CORP
Also Called: IBM
2350 Mission College Blvd, Santa Clara (95054-1532)
PHONE..................................408 850-8999
EMP: 529
SALES (corp-wide): 79.1B **Publicly Held**
SIC: **7379** Computer related consulting services
PA: International Business Machines Corporation
1 New Orchard Rd Ste 1 # 1
Armonk NY 10504
914 499-1900

(P-16403)
INTERNATIONAL BUS MCHS CORP
Also Called: IBM
1540 Scenic Ave, Costa Mesa (92626-1408)
PHONE..................................714 327-3501
William Kreidler, *Branch Mgr*
Alexander Kuang, *Lab Dir*
James Porter, *Sales Staff*
EMP: 381
SALES (corp-wide): 79.1B **Publicly Held**
SIC: **7379** Computer related consulting services
PA: International Business Machines Corporation
1 New Orchard Rd Ste 1 # 1
Armonk NY 10504
914 499-1900

(P-16404)
INTERNATIONAL BUS MCHS CORP
Also Called: IBM
1480 64th St Ste 200, Emeryville (94608-1292)
PHONE..................................510 652-6700
May Yang, *Manager*
EMP: 300
SALES (corp-wide): 79.1B **Publicly Held**
SIC: **7379** Computer related consulting services
PA: International Business Machines Corporation
1 New Orchard Rd Ste 1 # 1
Armonk NY 10504
914 499-1900

(P-16405)
INTERNATIONAL BUS MCHS CORP
Also Called: IBM
1001 E Hillsdale Blvd, Foster City (94404-1643)
PHONE..................................800 426-4968
Jessica Knuckles, *President*
Neli Momtaheni, *Technology*
Gaurav Deshpande, *Marketing Staff*
Kelly Overgaard, *Program Dir*
EMP: 396
SALES (corp-wide): 79.1B **Publicly Held**
SIC: **7379** 7371 3571 3572 Computer related consulting services; computer software development; software programming applications; minicomputers; mainframe computers; personal computers (microcomputers); computer storage devices; drum drives, computer; tape storage units, computer; semiconductors & related devices; microcircuits, integrated (semiconductor)
PA: International Business Machines Corporation
1 New Orchard Rd Ste 1 # 1
Armonk NY 10504
914 499-1900

(P-16406)
INTERNET-JOURNALS LLC
Also Called: Berkeley Electronic Press
2100 Milvia St Ste 300, Berkeley (94704-1113)
PHONE..................................510 665-1200
Jean-Gabriel Bankier, *CEO*
Ann Connolly, *Comms Dir*
Regan Smith, *Corp Comm Staff*
EMP: 52 EST: 1999
SALES (est): 5.8MM
SALES (corp-wide): 9.7B **Privately Held**
WEB: www.bepress.com
SIC: **7379**
HQ: Elsevier Inc.
230 Park Ave Fl 8
New York NY 10169
212 989-5800

(P-16407)
INTRATEK COMPUTER INC
9950 Irvine Center Dr, Irvine (92618-4357)
PHONE..................................949 334-4200
Allen Fahami, *Chairman*
Anthony Battey, *Shareholder*
Mohsen Fahami, *Shareholder*
Rodney Holdren, *Shareholder*
Jeffrey Shyshka, *CEO*

EMP: 310
SQ FT: 9,800
SALES: 11.6MM **Privately Held**
WEB: www.intrapc.com
SIC: 7379

(P-16408)
IP ACCESS INTERNATIONAL
31831 Cmno Capistrno 300a, San Juan
Capistrano (92675)
PHONE...................................949 655-1000
Bryan Hill, *President*
Bill Pitz, *Vice Pres*
Kim Graville, *Director*
Mike Gregg, *Director*
John Lewis, *Director*
EMP: 50
SQ FT: 10,000
SALES (est): 5.6MM **Privately Held**
WEB: www.ipinternational.net
SIC: 7379

(P-16409)
IP INTERNATIONAL INC
Also Called: Info Plus International
1510 Fashion Island Blvd # 104, San Mateo
(94404-1557)
PHONE...................................650 403-7800
Margaret Schaninger, *President*
Agustin Ramirez, *CFO*
EMP: 50
SQ FT: 2,500
SALES (est): 5.6MM **Privately Held**
WEB: www.infoplusintl.com
SIC: 7379 8748 Computer related consult-
ing services; business consulting

(P-16410)
ISPACE INC
2381 Rosecrans Ave # 110, El Segundo
(90245-4920)
PHONE...................................310 563-3800
Suresh Kothapalli, *CEO*
Ram Davaloor, *Vice Pres*
Ebrahim Mohammed, *Administration*
Rajiv Radhakrishnan, *Data Proc Staff*
Pankaj Khurana, *Tech Recruiter*
EMP: 120
SALES (est): 17.1MM **Privately Held**
WEB: www.ispace.com
SIC: 7379

(P-16411)
ISTS WORLDWIDE INC
2201 Walnut Ave Ste 210, Fremont
(94538-2355)
PHONE...................................510 794-1400
Viren Rana, *CEO*
Akash Jain, *President*
Linda S Perry, *Exec VP*
EMP: 106
SALES (est): 8.3MM **Privately Held**
WEB: www.istsinc.com
SIC: 7379 Computer related consulting
services

(P-16412)
ITALENT CORPORATION (PA)
Also Called: Italent Digital
27 Devine St Ste 20, San Jose
(95110-2279)
PHONE...................................408 496-6200
Renee Lalonde, *Partner*
Mark W Ciotek, *Ch of Bd*
Leslie Ottavi, *Exec VP*
Fred Walters, *Exec VP*
Josh Santomieri, *Vice Pres*
EMP: 150
SQ FT: 200,000
SALES (est): 20.4MM **Privately Held**
SIC: 7379 Computer related consulting
services

(P-16413)
ITCO SOLUTIONS INC
1003 Whitehall Ln, Redwood City
(94061-3687)
P.O. Box 610090 (94061-0090)
PHONE...................................650 367-0514
Ryan Edwards, *Director*
Chris Middleton, *Vice Pres*
Neetu Bassi, *Tech Recruiter*
Harpreet Sandhu, *Technology*
Tom Kramer, *Manager*
EMP: 295

SALES (est): 21.7MM **Privately Held**
WEB: www.itcosolutions.com
SIC: 7379

(P-16414)
ITEK SERVICES INC
25501 Arctic Ocean Dr, Lake Forest
(92630-8827)
PHONE...................................949 770-4835
Donald W Rowley, *CEO*
John Curl, *President*
Jon Thornton, *Project Mgr*
Rodrigo Romo, *Technical Staff*
Adrian Mauricio, *Engineer*
EMP: 100
SQ FT: 12,000
SALES: 24MM **Privately Held**
WEB: www.itekservice.com
SIC: 7379 Computer related maintenance
services

(P-16415)
ITRENEW INC (HQ)
8356 Central Ave, Newark (94560-3432)
PHONE...................................408 744-9600
Aidin Aghamiri, *CEO*
▲ EMP: 50
SQ FT: 72,000
SALES (est): 20.8MM
SALES (corp-wide): 3.6MM **Privately
Held**
SIC: 7379 7378 ; computer maintenance
& repair
PA: Intercept Parent, Inc.
110 E 59th St Fl 24
New York NY 10022
212 223-1383

(P-16416)
JOYENT INC
655 Montgomery St # 1600, San Francisco
(94111-2684)
PHONE...................................415 400-0600
Scott Hammond, *CEO*
Bill Fine, *Vice Pres*
Joshua Clulow, *Software Engr*
Cody Mello, *Software Engr*
Amrutha Kotikalapudi, *Network Enginr*
EMP: 120
SQ FT: 11,408
SALES (est): 23.1MM
SALES (corp-wide): 148.1B **Privately
Held**
WEB: www.joyent.com
SIC: 7379 Computer related consulting
services
HQ: Samsung Semiconductor, Inc.
3655 N 1st St
San Jose CA 95134
408 544-4000

(P-16417)
**KML ENTERPRISES CAREER
DEV LLC**
1900 S State College Blvd, Anaheim
(92806-0101)
PHONE...................................714 221-3100
Kevin M Landry,
EMP: 120
SQ FT: 20,000
SALES: 16.5MM **Privately Held**
SIC: 7379 8243 Computer related consult-
ing services; operator training, computer

(P-16418)
KORE1 INC
530 Technology Ste 150, Irvine
(92618-1350)
PHONE...................................949 706-6990
Brian Hunt, *CEO*
Steven Quarles, *Managing Dir*
EMP: 100
SALES: 8MM **Privately Held**
SIC: 7379

(P-16419)
LATTICE ENGINES INC (PA)
1820 Gateway Dr Ste 200, San Mateo
(94404-4059)
PHONE...................................877 460-0010
Shashi Upadhyay, *CEO*
Timothy Carruthers, *President*
Andrew Dong, *President*
Kent McCormick, *President*
Howie Shohet, *CFO*
EMP: 77

SALES (est): 41.6MM **Privately Held**
SIC: 7379 Computer related consulting
services

(P-16420)
**LOCKHEED MARTIN
GOVERNMENT SER**
500 N Via Val Verde, Montebello
(90640-2358)
PHONE...................................323 721-6979
Nate Sadorian, *Branch Mgr*
EMP: 50
SALES (corp-wide): 10.1B **Publicly Held**
SIC: 7379 7372 Computer related consult-
ing services; prepackaged software
HQ: Leidos Government Services, Inc.
700 N Frederick Ave
Gaithersburg MD 20879
856 486-5156

(P-16421)
LOGICTIER INC
7 41st Ave 76, San Mateo (94403-5105)
PHONE...................................650 235-6600
Mary Ann Byrnes, *CEO*
Omar Ahmad, *President*
Bill Zerella, *CFO*
Amanda Reed, *Exec VP*
Patrick Whalen, *Exec VP*
EMP: 200
SALES (est): 8.1MM **Privately Held**
SIC: 7379 1731 ; electrical work

(P-16422)
**LOGIN CONSULTING SERVICES
INC**
300 Continental Blvd # 530, El Segundo
(90245-5042)
PHONE...................................310 607-9091
Elece J Otten, *President*
Dan McKee, *Officer*
Lisa Borsa, *Executive*
Rose Villa, *Finance*
Aj Sarbuland, *Recruiter*
EMP: 75
SQ FT: 3,200
SALES (est): 7.9MM **Privately Held**
WEB: www.loginconsult.com
SIC: 7379

(P-16423)
MARKMONITOR INC (DH)
50 California St Ste 200, San Francisco
(94111-4605)
PHONE...................................415 278-8400
Hemant Gandhi, *Treasurer*
EMP: 86
SQ FT: 25,500
SALES (est): 43.9MM
SALES (corp-wide): 328.1K **Privately
Held**
WEB: www.markmonitor.com
SIC: 7379

(P-16424)
MAXONIC INC
2542 S Bascom Ave Ste 190, Campbell
(95008-5542)
PHONE...................................408 739-4900
Ajay Narain, *CEO*
Nitin Khanna, *President*
Ambrish Damani, *Regional Mgr*
Diane Osborne, *Admin Asst*
Kinjal Bhimani, *Tech Recruiter*
EMP: 65
SQ FT: 3,499
SALES (est): 14.5MM **Privately Held**
WEB: www.maxonic.com
SIC: 7379 7371 Computer related consult-
ing services; computer software develop-
ment & applications

(P-16425)
METABYTE INC
Also Called: Hotdoodle.com
39300 Civic Center Dr # 260, Fremont
(94538-2324)
PHONE...................................510 405-1117
Manu Mehta, *President*
Vijay Parjan, *Finance*
EMP: 100
SQ FT: 3,000
SALES: 12MM **Privately Held**
WEB: www.metabyte.com
SIC: 7379

(P-16426)
METIER LTD
1083 Vine St Ste 511, Healdsburg
(95448-4830)
PHONE...................................707 546-9300
Douglas Clark, *CEO*
Sandra Richardson, *COO*
Erin Baker, *Business Dir*
EMP: 55 EST: 1998
SALES (est): 6.9MM **Privately Held**
WEB: www.metier.com
SIC: 7379 Computer related consulting
services

(P-16427)
**MICROTEL COMPUTER
SYSTEMS INC**
5545 Daniels St, Chino (91710-9026)
PHONE...................................626 839-6038
Juliet Chui, *President*
EMP: 70
SQ FT: 17,000
SALES (est): 5.2MM **Privately Held**
WEB: www.microtelinc.com
SIC: 7379 Computer related consulting
services

(P-16428)
MULTIVEN INC
303 Twin Dolphin Dr # 600, Redwood City
(94065-1497)
P.O. Box 394, San Carlos (94070-0394)
PHONE...................................408 828-2715
EMP: 50
SQ FT: 2,000
SALES (est): 2.2MM **Privately Held**
WEB: www.multiven.com
SIC: 7379

(P-16429)
**MURPHY MCKAY & ASSOCIATES
INC**
3468 Mt Diablo Blvd B108, Lafayette
(94549-7103)
PHONE...................................925 283-9555
David D McKay, *Ch of Bd*
Timothy J Murphy, *President*
EMP: 50
SQ FT: 2,000
SALES (est): 7.5MM **Privately Held**
WEB: www.murphymckay.com
SIC: 7379 Computer related consulting
services

(P-16430)
NC INTERACTIVE LLC
Also Called: Ncsoft
1 Polaris Way Ste 110, Aliso Viejo
(92656-5358)
PHONE...................................512 623-8700
Songyee Yoon, *Principal*
EMP: 100
SALES (corp-wide): 1.4B **Privately Held**
SIC: 7379 Computer related consulting
services
HQ: Nc Interactive Llc
3180 139th Ave Se Ste 500
Bellevue WA 98005
206 588-7200

(P-16431)
NCC GROUP INC (HQ)
123 Mission St Ste 1020, San Francisco
(94105-5126)
PHONE...................................415 268-9300
Rob Cotton, *President*
Craig Motta, *President*
Craig Foster, *CFO*
Darren Maloney, *Treasurer*
Andy Grant, *Vice Pres*
EMP: 90
SQ FT: 12,000
SALES (est): 40.1MM
SALES (corp-wide): 325.1MM **Privately
Held**
SIC: 7379 Computer data escrow service
PA: Ncc Group Plc
Xyz Building, 2 Hardman Boulevard
Manchester M3 3A
161 209-5200

▲ = Import ▼=Export
◆ =Import/Export

(P-16432)
NETPACE INC
5000 Executive Pkwy # 530, San Ramon
(94583-4282)
PHONE.....................925 543-7760
Omar Khan, *President*
Vajih Khan, *Co-CEO*
Feroz Gul, *Software Engr*
Syed Ahmed, *Engineer*
Jaya Suresh, *Financial Exec*
EMP: 55
SQ FT: 4,000
SALES (est): 4.8MM **Privately Held**
WEB: www.netpace.com
SIC: 7379 Computer related consulting
services

(P-16433)
NEUDESIC LLC (PA)
Also Called: Neuron Esb
200 Spectrum Center Dr # 2000, Irvine
(92618-5013)
PHONE.....................949 754-4500
Parsa Rohani, *CEO*
Anthony Ferry,
Mike Hamilton, *Sr Consultant*
Andrie Tirta, *Sr Consultant*
Tim Marshall, *Mng Member*
EMP: 125
SQ FT: 15,150
SALES (est): 101.3MM **Privately Held**
SIC: 7379 Computer related consulting
services

(P-16434)
NORLAND GROUP
3350 Scott Blvd Ste 6501, Santa Clara
(95054-3125)
PHONE.....................408 855-8255
Mayling Liang, *President*
Sophie Kuo, *Accounting Mgr*
Reginald Malla, *Recruiter*
Karen Sandoval, *Recruiter*
EMP: 105
SQ FT: 2,200
SALES (est): 10.2MM **Privately Held**
WEB: www.norlandgroup.com
SIC: 7379 7361 Computer related consult-
ing services; employment agencies

(P-16435)
NOWCOM CORPORATION
Also Called: Hankey Group
4751 Wilshire Blvd # 205, Los Angeles
(90010-3860)
PHONE.....................323 938-6449
Don R Hankey, *President*
Vaibhav Deshpande, *Vice Pres*
Jay Kamdar, *Vice Pres*
Oliver Baes, *Administration*
Rosa Martinez, *Administration*
EMP: 54
SQ FT: 4,800
SALES (est): 14MM **Privately Held**
WEB: www.nowcom.com
SIC: 7379

(P-16436)
NTREPID LLC
10201 Wtridge Cir Ste 300, San Diego
(92121)
PHONE.....................858 866-1309
Mike Simpson, *Manager*
EMP: 80
SALES (est): 1.1MM **Privately Held**
SIC: 7379 Computer related maintenance
services
HQ: Ntrepid Llc
12801 Worldgate Dr # 800
Herndon VA 20170

(P-16437)
NUMBERS ONLY INC
4320 Stevens Creek Blvd, San Jose
(95129-1285)
PHONE.....................408 689-7258
EMP: 54
SALES (corp-wide): 16.1MM **Privately
Held**
SIC: 7379
PA: Numbers Only, Inc.
2615 E Southlake Blvd # 200
Southlake TX 76092
817 251-6200

(P-16438)
ODESUS INC (PA)
11766 Wilshire Blvd # 400, Los Angeles
(90025-6551)
PHONE.....................310 473-4600
Robert P Michaels, *President*
Krystal Long, *Vice Pres*
Teresa Boggs, *Admin Asst*
Jose Galvez, *Tech Recruiter*
Mark Lam, *Tech Recruiter*
EMP: 100
SQ FT: 3,000
SALES (est): 9MM **Privately Held**
WEB: www.odesus.com
SIC: 7379

(P-16439)
OLSON & ASSOC
3448 Lupine Cir Ste 102, Costa Mesa
(92626-1723)
PHONE.....................714 878-6649
Steven Olson, *CEO*
EMP: 60
SQ FT: 1,500
SALES (est): 4.7MM **Privately Held**
WEB: www.strategicgrowthsolutions.com
SIC: 7379 7389 Computer related consult-
ing services; personal service agents,
brokers & bureaus

(P-16440)
OMNIKRON SYSTEMS INC
20920 Warner Center Ln A, Woodland Hills
(91367-6526)
PHONE.....................818 591-7890
Sudipta K Ghosh, *President*
Jo Jandayan, *Executive Asst*
Mindy Peterson, *Admin Sec*
Heather King, *Systems Dir*
Jody Olivas, *Marketing Staff*
EMP: 100
SALES (est): 4.9MM **Privately Held**
WEB: www.omnikron.com
SIC: 7379 7375 5045 8243

(P-16441)
ONEHEALTH SOLUTIONS INC
420 Stevens Ave Ste 200, Solana Beach
(92075-2078)
PHONE.....................858 947-6333
Bruce Springer, *President*
John Shade, *COO*
Jeff Goe, *Senior VP*
Chuck Mitchell, *Vice Pres*
EMP: 100
SALES (est): 7.6MM
SALES (corp-wide): 53.1MM **Privately
Held**
SIC: 7379
PA: Viverae, Inc.
10670 N Cntl Expy Ste 700
Dallas TX 75231
214 827-4400

(P-16442)
OPAL SOFT INC
Also Called: Opalsoft
1288 Kifer Rd Ste 201, Sunnyvale
(94086-5326)
PHONE.....................408 267-2211
Omprakash Choudhary, *President*
Alkesh Choudhary, *CFO*
EMP: 80
SQ FT: 2,450
SALES (est): 13.3MM **Privately Held**
WEB: www.opalsoft.com
SIC: 7379 7371 8748 8713 ; computer
software systems analysis & design, cus-
tom; business consulting; photogrammet-
ric engineering; service bureau,
computer; computer facilities manage-
ment

(P-16443)
ORACLE CORPORATION (PA)
500 Oracle Pkwy, Redwood City
(94065-1677)
PHONE.....................650 506-7000
Safra A Catz, *CEO*
Lawrence J Ellison, *Ch of Bd*
Mark V Hurd, *CEO*
Jeffrey O Henley, *Vice Ch Bd*
Dorian E Daley, *Exec VP*
EMP: 2300
SQ FT: 2,100,000

SALES: 39.8B **Publicly Held**
WEB: www.oracle.com
SIC: 7379 8243 3571 3674 Computer related consulting services; software training, computer; minicomputers;
microprocessors; business oriented computer software

(P-16444)
**ORACLE SYSTEMS
CORPORATION (HQ)**
500 Oracle Pkwy, Redwood City
(94065-1677)
PHONE.....................650 506-7000
Safra A Catz, *CEO*
Lawrence J Ellison, *Ch of Bd*
Jeffrey O Henley, *Ch of Bd*
Mark V Hurd, *President*
Mark Hurd, *CEO*
EMP: 2300
SQ FT: 2,200,000
SALES (est): 4.4B
SALES (corp-wide): 39.8B **Publicly Held**
WEB: www.forcecapital.com
SIC: 7379 8243 7372 Data processing
consultant; software training, computer;
business oriented computer software
PA: Oracle Corporation
500 Oracle Pkwy
Redwood City CA 94065
650 506-7000

(P-16445)
ORGANIC INC
390 Amapola Ave Ste 8, Torrance
(90501-1400)
PHONE.....................310 543-4600
EMP: 71
SALES (corp-wide): 15.3B **Publicly Held**
SIC: 7379
HQ: Organic, Inc.
600 California St Fl 8
San Francisco CA 94108
415 581-5300

(P-16446)
ORGANIC INC (HQ)
600 California St Fl 8, San Francisco
(94108-2726)
PHONE.....................415 581-5300
Conor Brady, *Ch Credit Ofcr*
David Bryant, *Officer*
Mark Murata, *Officer*
Tina Leone Webber, *Controller*
Monik Sanghvi, *Marketing Staff*
EMP: 142
SQ FT: 23,000
SALES (est): 33.3MM
SALES (corp-wide): 15.2B **Publicly Held**
WEB: www.organic.com
SIC: 7379 8742 ; computer related con-
sulting services; marketing consulting
services
PA: Omnicom Group Inc.
437 Madison Ave
New York NY 10022
212 415-3600

(P-16447)
OSI DIGITAL INC
2525 Main St Ste 350, Irvine (92614-6685)
PHONE.....................949 724-8300
Kumar Yamani, *Owner*
Manoj Devireddy, *Vice Pres*
Adam Ruthruff, *Technology*
Candace Bracht, *Sr Consultant*
Sunil Meka, *Consultant*
EMP: 50 **Privately Held**
SIC: 7379 ; computer related consulting
services
PA: Osi Digital Inc.
5950 Canoga Ave Ste 300
Woodland Hills CA 91367

(P-16448)
OUTLOOK AMUSEMENTS INC
2900 W Alameda Ave # 400, Burbank
(91505-4220)
PHONE.....................818 433-3800
Jason Freeland, *CEO*
Cyrus Pejoumand, *President*
Tim Youd, *Co-President*
Tom Wszalek, *Senior VP*
Thomas Wszalek, *Vice Pres*
EMP: 150

SQ FT: 8,000
SALES (est): 25.9MM **Privately Held**
SIC: 7379

(P-16449)
**PACIFIC WEST CORPORATION
(PA)**
10369 Regis Ct, Rancho Cucamonga
(91730-3055)
PHONE.....................515 270-8181
Girish Reddy, *President*
EMP: 55
SQ FT: 2,500
SALES (est): 9.6MM **Privately Held**
SIC: 7379 Computer related consulting
services

(P-16450)
PACTRON
3000 Patrick Henry Dr, Santa Clara
(95054-1814)
PHONE.....................408 329-5500
Sriram Iyer, *CEO*
Prakash Kombupalayam, *COO*
K Prakash, *COO*
Ravi Iyer, *Executive*
Martin Barajas, *Engineer*
EMP: 99
SQ FT: 35,000
SALES (est): 20.3MM **Privately Held**
WEB: www.pactroninc.com
SIC: 7379 Computer related maintenance
services

(P-16451)
**PARTNERS INFORMATION TECH
INC (HQ)**
Also Called: Calance
7101 Village Dr, Buena Park (90621-2260)
PHONE.....................714 736-4487
Amit Govil, *Chairman*
Bill Darden, *CFO*
Asit Govil, *Treasurer*
Mark Goedde, *Vice Pres*
William Hylton, *Vice Pres*
EMP: 100
SQ FT: 46,000
SALES (est): 82MM **Privately Held**
SIC: 7379 ; computer related consulting
services

(P-16452)
PDS TECH INC
370 N Wstlake Blvd Stw120 Stw, Westlake
Village (91362)
PHONE.....................805 418-9862
Tony Mian, *Branch Mgr*
EMP: 1231
SALES (corp-wide): 262.4MM **Privately
Held**
SIC: 7379 7373 7371 Computer related
consulting services; computer integrated
systems design; computer software sys-
tems analysis & design, custom
PA: Pds Tech, Inc.
300 E John Carpenter Fwy # 700
Irving TX 75062
214 647-9600

(P-16453)
PEGASUS SQUIRE INC
12021 Wilshire Blvd Ste 7, Los Angeles
(90025-1206)
PHONE.....................866 208-6837
Scott Cooper, *CEO*
EMP: 100 **EST:** 2002
SALES (est): 4.6MM **Privately Held**
SIC: 7379 Computer related consulting
services

(P-16454)
**PERFORMANCE TECH
PARTNERS LLC**
11341 Gold Ex Dr Ste 160, Gold River
(95670)
PHONE.....................800 787-4143
John Podlipnik,
Jeff Forderer,
EMP: 106
SQ FT: 4,971
SALES: 30MM **Privately Held**
WEB: www.performtechnology.com
SIC: 7379

P R O D U C T S & S V C S

(P-16455)
PIVOT TECHNOLOGY SOLUTIONS LTD
11988 El Camino Real, San Diego (92130-3579)
PHONE..................647 788-2034
Kevin Shank, *CEO*
Shaun Maine, *COO*
John Flores, *Vice Pres*
Tony Villar, *Info Tech Mgr*
Derek Dunlap, *Finance*
EMP: 750
SALES (est): 102.3K
SALES (corp-wide): 1.4B **Privately Held**
SIC: 7379 7373 ; systems integration services
PA: Pivot Technology Solutions, Inc
161 Bay St Suite 1020
Toronto ON M5J 2
647 788-2034

(P-16456)
POINTSPEED INC
135 Wyndham Dr, Portola Valley (94028-7240)
PHONE..................650 638-3720
Norman Goldfarb, *President*
Ron Croce, *COO*
Michael Baltazar, *Vice Pres*
Sabet Chowdbury, *Vice Pres*
Jonathan Lewis, *Vice Pres*
EMP: 71
SALES (est): 2.7MM **Privately Held**
SIC: 7379 Computer related consulting services

(P-16457)
POUNCE CONSULTING INC
6080 Center Dr Ste 600, Los Angeles (90045-1540)
PHONE..................714 774-3500
Roger Viera, *CEO*
Josa A Velasco, *Treasurer*
Thania Herrera, *Office Admin*
Maria Jos Viera, *Legal Staff*
EMP: 250
SQ FT: 4,000
SALES (est): 11.9MM **Privately Held**
SIC: 7379 7361 Computer related consulting services; employment agencies
PA: Pounce Consulting, S.A. De C.V.
Av. 8 De Julio No. 1295
Guadalajara JAL. 44190

(P-16458)
PRAETORIAN GROUP (PA)
Also Called: Policeone Academy
200 Green St Ste 200 # 200, San Francisco (94111-1356)
PHONE..................415 962-8310
Mike Herning, *Ch of Bd*
Alex Ford, *CEO*
EMP: 50
SALES (est): 9.1MM **Privately Held**
WEB: www.policeone.com
SIC: 7379

(P-16459)
PRAMIRA INC
1422 Edinger Ave Ste 250, Tustin (92780-6299)
PHONE..................800 678-1169
Omar Houari, *CEO*
EMP: 125 EST: 2014
SQ FT: 6,000
SALES (est): 7.9MM **Privately Held**
SIC: 7379 8711 Computer related consulting services; engineering services

(P-16460)
PRECISEQ INC
11601 Wilshire Blvd Fl 5, Los Angeles (90025-1995)
PHONE..................310 709-6094
Mark Dorner, *Partner*
Guy Livneh, *Managing Prtnr*
EMP: 80
SQ FT: 1,200
SALES (est): 560K **Privately Held**
SIC: 7379 Computer related consulting services

(P-16461)
PRELUDE SYSTEMS INC (PA)
Also Called: Preludesys
5 Corporate Park Ste 140, Irvine (92606-3163)
PHONE..................949 208-7126
Kiran B Chandra, *CEO*
Rajamannar Abboy, *President*
Rangesh Rajaram, *Vice Pres*
Manoj K Chandra, *Sr Software Eng*
Senthilkumar Mani, *Programmer Anys*
EMP: 121
SQ FT: 4,900
SALES (est): 19MM **Privately Held**
SIC: 7379

(P-16462)
PRO-TEK CONSULTING (PA)
21300 Victory Blvd # 240, Woodland Hills (91367-2525)
PHONE..................805 807-5571
Raj Kessireddy, *CEO*
Divya Reddy Pyreddy, *Chairman*
Dev Raj, *Tech Recruiter*
EMP: 110 EST: 2010
SQ FT: 2,400
SALES (est): 14MM **Privately Held**
SIC: 7379

(P-16463)
PRODUCT QUALITY PARTNERS INC
450 Main St Ste 207, Pleasanton (94566-7071)
PHONE..................925 484-6491
Debra Levesque, *President*
Debra Hodtens, *President*
EMP: 54
SQ FT: 20,000
SALES: 600K **Privately Held**
WEB: www.qpqa.com
SIC: 7379 Computer related maintenance services

(P-16464)
PROLIFICS INC (DH)
24025 Park Sorrento # 405, Calabasas (91302-4037)
PHONE..................212 267-7722
Satya Bolli, *CEO*
Sam Ourfalian, *President*
David Mogel, *Admin Sec*
EMP: 255
SQ FT: 7,000
SALES (est): 53.1MM **Privately Held**
WEB: www.jyacc.com
SIC: 7379 7371 Computer related consulting services; computer software development
HQ: Prolifics Application Services, Inc.
24025 Park Sorrento # 405
Calabasas CA 91302
646 201-4967

(P-16465)
PROPEL SOFTWARE CORPORATION
1010 Rincon Cir, San Jose (95131-1325)
PHONE..................408 571-6300
Steven T Kirsch, *President*
Steven Manser, *COO*
EMP: 130
SQ FT: 30,000
SALES (est): 9.6MM **Privately Held**
WEB: www.propel.com
SIC: 7379 Computer related consulting services

(P-16466)
QUANTUM SOLUTIONS INC
5146 Douglas Fir Rd # 205, Calabasas (91302-1405)
PHONE..................818 577-4555
Hamid Akhavan, *CEO*
Eva Farooqi, *Administration*
EMP: 50
SQ FT: 14,641
SALES (est): 4.9MM **Privately Held**
SIC: 7379 8742 ; business consultant

(P-16467)
QUBERA SOLUTIONS INC
676 Gail Ave Apt 26, Sunnyvale (94086-8134)
PHONE..................650 294-4460

Prasad Jayaraman, *President*
Jacob Pszonowsky, *Vice Pres*
Nasr Shah, *Sr Software Eng*
Mihir Jariwala, *Manager*
Prasad Marrapu, *Consultant*
EMP: 50
SQ FT: 2,900
SALES: 8MM **Privately Held**
SIC: 7379 Computer related consulting services

(P-16468)
R S SOFTWARE INDIA LIMITED
1900 Mccarthy Blvd # 103, Milpitas (95035-7413)
PHONE..................408 382-1200
Rajnit Jain, *President*
Bibek Das, *Vice Pres*
Somnath Guha, *Sr Software Eng*
Subroto Mallick, *Info Tech Mgr*
Sumit Misra, *Business Mgr*
EMP: 96
SQ FT: 3,100
SALES (est): 11.1MM
SALES (corp-wide): 8.9MM **Privately Held**
WEB: www.rssoftware.com
SIC: 7379 7371 Computer related consulting services; computer software development
PA: R S Software (India) Limited
A - 2, Fmc Fortuna
Kolkata WB 70002
336 601-8899

(P-16469)
R SYSTEMS INC (HQ)
5000 Windplay Dr Ste 5, El Dorado Hills (95762-9319)
PHONE..................916 939-9696
Satinder S Rekhi, *CEO*
Lt Gen Baldev Singh, *President*
Ralph Kenney, *COO*
Raj Swaminathan, *COO*
Harpreet Rekhi, *Vice Pres*
EMP: 200
SQ FT: 7,000
SALES: 20.8MM
SALES (corp-wide): 38.6MM **Privately Held**
WEB: www.rsystems.com
SIC: 7379 7373 7374 Computer related consulting services; systems software development services; data processing & preparation
PA: R Systems International Limited
C 40, Sector 59
Noida UP 20130
120 258-7123

(P-16470)
RANDSTAD TECHNOLOGIES LP
8880 Rio San Diego Dr # 107, San Diego (92108-1634)
PHONE..................619 798-7300
Charity Cescolini, *Branch Mgr*
EMP: 64
SALES (corp-wide): 27.4B **Privately Held**
SIC: 7379 Computer hardware requirements analysis
HQ: Randstad Technologies, Llc
150 Presidential Way # 300
Woburn MA 01801
781 938-1910

(P-16471)
RIGHTPOINT CONSULTING LLC
1453 3rd Street Promenade, Santa Monica (90401-2397)
PHONE..................310 451-4619
EMP: 130 **Privately Held**
SIC: 7379
PA: Rightpoint Consulting, Llc
29 N Wacker Dr Fl 4
Chicago IL 60606

(P-16472)
RISKALYZE INC
373 Elm Ave, Auburn (95603-4524)
PHONE..................530 748-1660
Aaron Klein, *CEO*
Sarah Hutchinson, *Partner*
Matt Morris, *Partner*
Kyle Van Pelt, *Partner*
Andrew Palmer, *CFO*

EMP: 85
SALES (est): 5.2MM **Privately Held**
SIC: 7379

(P-16473)
RJT COMPUQUEST INC (PA)
Also Called: Apolis
222 N Pacific Coast Hwy, El Segundo (90245-5648)
PHONE..................310 378-6666
Amarjit Shokeen, *CEO*
Ashutosh Bansal, *Partner*
Rita Shokeen, *CFO*
Mayur Shah, *Exec VP*
Fred Degley, *Vice Pres*
EMP: 350
SQ FT: 8,000
SALES (est): 45.4MM **Privately Held**
SIC: 7379 7371 Computer related consulting services; custom computer programming services; software programming applications

(P-16474)
ROCKET FUEL INC (HQ)
2000 Seaport Blvd Ste 400, Redwood City (94063-5584)
PHONE..................650 595-1300
Mark Grether, *CEO*
Stephen Snyder, *CFO*
Eric Duerr, *Chief Mktg Ofcr*
Bill Keadle, *Officer*
Richard Song, *Officer*
EMP: 148
SALES: 456.2MM
SALES (corp-wide): 509MM **Privately Held**
SIC: 7379 7371 Computer related consulting services; computer software development & applications
PA: Sizmek Inc.
2500 Bee Caves Rd Ste 1
Austin TX 78746
512 469-5900

(P-16475)
SADA SYSTEMS INC
5250 Lankershim Blvd # 620, North Hollywood (91601-3188)
PHONE..................818 766-2400
Tony Safoian, *CEO*
Dana Berg, *COO*
Matt Lawrence, *COO*
Annie Safoian, *CFO*
Patrick Monaghan,
EMP: 106
SQ FT: 10,503
SALES: 28MM **Privately Held**
SIC: 7379 Computer related consulting services

(P-16476)
SAGE INTACCT INC (HQ)
300 Park Ave Ste 1400, San Jose (95110-2774)
PHONE..................408 878-0900
Maeve Naughton, *Partner*
Robert Kleinschmidt, *President*
Scott Lumish, *President*
Robert K Reid, *Exec VP*
Marc Linden, *Senior VP*
EMP: 50
SQ FT: 6,000
SALES (est): 26.3MM
SALES (corp-wide): 2.2B **Privately Held**
WEB: www.intacct.com
SIC: 7379 7371 Computer related consulting services; custom computer programming services
PA: The Sage Group Plc.
North Park Avenue
Newcastle-Upon-Tyne NE13
191 294-3000

(P-16477)
SCALEMATRIX HOLDINGS INC
5775 Kearny Villa Rd, San Diego (92123-1111)
PHONE..................888 349-9994
Paul G Marble, *Ch of Bd*
Mark Ortenzi, *CEO*
Emily Stebing, *CFO*
Jenny Friederichs, *Executive*
Linnette Hollman, *Admin Asst*
EMP: 75 EST: 2011
SQ FT: 85,461

SALES (est): 14.1MM **Privately Held**
SIC: 7379 Computer related consulting
services

(P-16478)
SCIENCE APPLICATIONS INTL CORP
Also Called: Saic Government Solutions
4015 Hancock St Ste 1000, San Diego
(92110-5121)
PHONE.....................................703 676-4300
Anthony Moraco, *Branch Mgr*
Jeff Ferguson, *CEO*
Anthony Morraco, *CEO*
EMP: 99
SALES (corp-wide): 4.4B **Publicly Held**
SIC: 7379 Computer related consulting
services
PA: Science Applications International Cor-
poration
12010 Sunset Hills Rd
Reston VA 20190
703 676-4300

(P-16479)
SEATECH CONSULTING GROUP INC
609 Deep Valley Dr # 200, Rllng HLS Est
(90274-3614)
PHONE.....................................310 356-6828
Chairul Irawan, *CEO*
EMP: 50
SALES: 3.5MM **Privately Held**
SIC: 7379

(P-16480)
SEAVER INTERNATIONAL
4169 Green Valley Schl Rd, Sebastopol
(95472-8944)
PHONE.....................................707 291-4929
Jesse Seaver, *Owner*
EMP: 89
SALES (est): 2.6MM **Privately Held**
SIC: 7379 Computer related consulting
services

(P-16481)
SENTEK CONSULTING INC
Also Called: Sentek Global
2811 Nimitz Blvd Ste G, San Diego
(92106-4311)
PHONE.....................................619 543-9550
Eric Basu, *CEO*
Dave Cully, *COO*
Jason Galetti, *COO*
Theresa Thomas, *Executive*
Brigitte Carino, *Office Mgr*
EMP: 132
SALES (est): 22.5MM **Privately Held**
WEB: www.sentekconsulting.com
SIC: 7379

(P-16482)
SERENE AST LLC (HQ)
3211 Scott Blvd Ste 201, Santa Clara
(95054-3009)
PHONE.....................................408 986-8544
Pravin Kumar, *CEO*
Shaji Zechariah, *President*
Amit Verma, *Manager*
EMP: 90
SQ FT: 4,816
SALES (est): 25MM
SALES (corp-wide): 69.3MM **Privately
Held**
WEB: www.serenecorp.com
SIC: 7379 Computer related consulting
services
PA: Applications Software Technology Llc
1755 Park St Ste 100
Naperville IL 60563
630 778-0707

(P-16483)
SHOWPAD INC (HQ)
301 Howard St Ste 1800, San Francisco
(94105-6614)
PHONE.....................................415 800-2033
Pieterjan Bouten, *CEO*
Lenz Briana, *President*
Jason Holmes, *President*
Hendrik Isebaert, *CEO*
Sofie Vermeulen, *Officer*
EMP: 350
SQ FT: 14,191

SALES (est): 4.4MM
SALES (corp-wide): 7MM **Privately Held**
SIC: 7379 Computer related maintenance
services
PA: Showpad Nv
Moutstraat 62
Gent 9000
230 939-17

(P-16484)
SITELITE HOLDINGS INC
111 Theory Fl 2, Irvine (92617-3039)
PHONE.....................................949 265-6200
Reddy Marri, *CEO*
Kumar Yamani, *Chairman*
EMP: 135 EST: 1999
SQ FT: 30,000
SALES (est): 6.2MM **Privately Held**
SIC: 7379 8742 Computer related consult-
ing services; management consulting
services

(P-16485)
SKYSLOPE INC
825 K St Fl 2, Sacramento (95814-3547)
PHONE.....................................916 833-2390
Tyler Smith, *CEO*
EMP: 100
SQ FT: 23,000
SALES: 5.8MM
SALES (corp-wide): 7.6B **Publicly Held**
SIC: 7379
PA: Fidelity National Financial, Inc.
601 Riverside Ave Fl 4
Jacksonville FL 32204
904 854-8100

(P-16486)
SMARTEK21 LLC
530 Lytton Ave Fl 2, Palo Alto
(94301-1541)
PHONE.....................................650 617-3221
EMP: 271 **Privately Held**
SIC: 7379 Computer related consulting
services
PA: Smartek21, Llc
12910 Totem Lake Blvd Ne # 105
Kirkland WA 98034
-

(P-16487)
SMASHON INC
1754 Tech Dr Ste 234, San Jose (95110)
PHONE.....................................855 762-7466
Tasawar Jalali, *CEO*
EMP: 50
SALES (est): 2.5MM **Privately Held**
SIC: 7379 Computer related maintenance
services; computer related consulting
services

(P-16488)
SOFTHQ
6494 Weathers Pl Ste 200, San Diego
(92121-2938)
PHONE.....................................858 658-9200
Sindhura Thummalasetty, *Principal*
Indrani Goswami, *Technology*
Bulagondla L Kumar, *Technology*
Surendra Recruiter, *Technology*
Srinivas Badiganti, *Recruiter*
EMP: 50
SALES (est): 9.9MM **Privately Held**
SIC: 7379

(P-16489)
SOFTWARE MANAGEMENT CONS INC (PA)
Also Called: Smci
500 Nth Brn Blvd Ste 1100, Glendale
(91203)
PHONE.....................................818 240-3177
Spencer L Karpf, *CEO*
Alden Metz, *President*
Bob Maltzman, *COO*
Susanna Dashknyan, *Vice Pres*
Jeff Elsasser, *VP Bus Dvlpt*
EMP: 320
SQ FT: 4,500
SALES (est): 53.2MM **Privately Held**
WEB: www.smci.com
SIC: 7379 7361 Computer related consult-
ing services; placement agencies

(P-16490)
SOLUGENIX CORPORATION
225 N Barranca St, West Covina
(91791-1688)
PHONE.....................................866 749-7658
Praveen Mallavarapu, *Manager*
EMP: 62
SALES (corp-wide): 42.8MM **Privately
Held**
SIC: 7379 Computer related maintenance
services
PA: Solugenix Corporation
601 Valencia Ave
Brea CA 92823
866 749-7658

(P-16491)
SONICOCOM INC
2202 S Figueroa St, Los Angeles
(90007-2049)
PHONE.....................................213 291-0475
Rodrigo Teijeiro, *President*
Gustavo Victorica, *CFO*
EMP: 90
SQ FT: 400
SALES (est): 3.6MM **Privately Held**
SIC: 7379

(P-16492)
SPARTA CONSULTING INC
111 Woodmere Rd Ste 200, Folsom
(95630-4750)
PHONE.....................................916 985-0300
Lokesh Sikaria, *CEO*
Paul Freudenberg, *Ch of Bd*
Vaibhav Nadgauda, *President*
Denise Ferre, *CFO*
Brent Kelton, *Exec VP*
EMP: 300 EST: 2007
SQ FT: 7,200
SALES (est): 38.4MM
SALES (corp-wide): 223.7MM **Privately
Held**
SIC: 7379 Computer related consulting
services
PA: Kpit Technologies Limited
Plot No-35 & 36, Rajiv Gandhi Infotech
Park,
Pune MH 41105
206 652-5000

(P-16493)
SRK GLOBAL CONSULTING
7225 Crescent Park W # 255, Los Angeles
(90094-2718)
PHONE.....................................310 295-2524
Steven Kahn, *Exec Dir*
EMP: 60
SALES (est): 500K **Privately Held**
SIC: 7379 Computer related consulting
services

(P-16494)
SRS CONSULTING INC
39465 Paseo Padre P, Fremont (94538)
PHONE.....................................510 252-0625
Sangeetha Chowhan, *CEO*
Shankar Chowhan, *President*
EMP: 58
SQ FT: 1,250
SALES (est): 7.9MM **Privately Held**
WEB: www.srsconsultinginc.com
SIC: 7379 7371 Computer related consult-
ing services; computer software develop-
ment

(P-16495)
STRATA INFORMATION GROUP INC
3935 Harney St Ste 203, San Diego
(92110-2849)
PHONE.....................................619 296-0170
Henry A Eimstad, *President*
Frank Vaskelis, *Corp Secy*
Kari Blinn, *Executive*
Emily Rudn, *Executive*
Linda Bettencourt, *Administration*
EMP: 93
SQ FT: 2,000
SALES: 17.4MM **Privately Held**
WEB: www.sigcorp.com
SIC: 7379

(P-16496)
SYMANTEC CORPORATION (PA)
350 Ellis St, Mountain View (94043-2202)
PHONE.....................................650 527-8000
Gregory S Clark, *CEO*
Daniel H Schulman, *Ch of Bd*
Michael D Fey, *President*
Nicholas R Noviello, *CFO*
Frank Dangeard, *Bd of Directors*
▲ EMP: 400
SQ FT: 794,000
SALES: 4.8B **Publicly Held**
WEB: www.symantec.com
SIC: 7379 7372 Computer related consult-
ing services; application computer soft-
ware

(P-16497)
SYNECTIC SOLUTIONS INC (PA)
Also Called: S S I
1701 Pacific Ave Ste 260, Oxnard
(93033-1887)
PHONE.....................................805 483-4800
Lynn Dines, *President*
Joel Dines, *CFO*
Toby Doane, *Vice Pres*
EMP: 80 EST: 1997
SQ FT: 5,000
SALES (est): 10.7MM **Privately Held**
WEB: www.synecsolu.com
SIC: 7379 8331 ; job training services

(P-16498)
SYNIVERSE TECHNOLOGIES LLC
181 Metro Dr Ste 450, San Jose
(95110-1344)
PHONE.....................................408 324-1830
EMP: 106
SALES (corp-wide): 793.5MM **Privately
Held**
SIC: 7379 Data processing consultant
HQ: Syniverse Technologies, Llc
8125 Highwoods Palm Way
Tampa FL 33647

(P-16499)
SYNOPTEK INC (PA)
19520 Jamboree Rd Ste 110, Irvine
(92612-2429)
PHONE.....................................949 241-8600
Tim Britt, *CEO*
Ricardo Ordonez, *CFO*
Philip Crippen, *Officer*
Brandon Maas, *Officer*
Jeff Pagano, *Officer*
EMP: 67
SALES (est): 107.4MM **Privately Held**
WEB: www.netsolutionsinc.com
SIC: 7379 Computer related consulting
services

(P-16500)
SYSTECH INTEGRATORS INC
2050 Gateway Pl, San Jose (95110-1011)
PHONE.....................................408 441-2700
Sam Tyagi, *CEO*
Rajeev Tyagi, *COO*
EMP: 240
SALES (est): 14.7MM **Privately Held**
WEB: www.systechi.com
SIC: 7379 Computer related consulting
services
HQ: Valores Corporativos Softtek, S.A. De
C.V.
Constitucion No. 3098 Ph. 1
Monterrey N.L. 64650

(P-16501)
T & T SOLUTIONS INC
7018 Owensmouth Ave # 201, Canoga Park
(91303-2073)
PHONE.....................................818 676-1786
Fax: 818 676-1272
EMP: 70
SQ FT: 2,100
SALES (est): 6.2MM **Privately Held**
WEB: www.ttsus.com
SIC: 7379

(P-16502)
TACIT KNOWLEDGE INC
27 Maiden Ln Fl 4, San Francisco
(94108-5444)
PHONE.................415 694-4322
Christopher Andrasick, *President*
Chase Hill, *COO*
Mike Hardy, *CFO*
Tjipto Sugijoto, *Managing Dir*
Scott Askew, *CTO*
EMP: 93
SALES (est): 8.2MM
SALES (corp-wide): 3.5B Publicly Held
WEB: www.tacitknowledge.com
SIC: 7379
HQ: Newgistics, Inc.
7171 Southwest Pkwy # 300
Austin TX 78735
-

(P-16503)
TACTICAL ENGRG & ANALIS INC
(PA)
6050 Santo Rd Ste 250, San Diego
(92124-6104)
P.O. Box 421425 (92142-1425)
PHONE.................858 573-9869
Robert Rosado, *President*
Lawrence Massaro, *CFO*
Julie Rapolla, *Executive*
David Andersen, *Business Dir*
Xavier Vargas, *Project Mgr*
EMP: 104
SQ FT: 14,000
SALES (est): 25MM Privately Held
WEB: www.tac-eng.com
SIC: 7379 8711 Computer related consult-
ing services; engineering services

(P-16504)
TALVIEW INC
3260 Hillview Ave, Palo Alto (94304-1220)
PHONE.................510 227-8227
Sanjoe Tom Jose, *CEO*
EMP: 200 EST: 2012
SALES (est): 2.7MM Privately Held
SIC: 7379

(P-16505)
TAOS MOUNTAIN LLC (PA)
121 Daggett Dr, San Jose (95134-2110)
PHONE.................408 324-2800
Ricardo Urrutia, *CEO*
Paul Smith, *Partner*
Hamilton Yu, *President*
Jeff Lucchesi, *COO*
Mary Hale, *CFO*
EMP: 335
SQ FT: 45,000
SALES (est): 87.4MM Privately Held
SIC: 7379 Computer related consulting
services

(P-16506)
TATA AMERICA INTL CORP
Also Called: Tata Consulting Services
5201 Great America Pkwy # 400, Santa
Clara (95054-1143)
PHONE.................408 569-5845
S K Bhattacharjee, *Manager*
Sunil Chauhan, *Partner*
Vinod Vishnumurthy, *Business Dir*
Dhanam Palanivel, *Technical Mgr*
Biswa R Pati, *Technical Mgr*
EMP: 100
SALES (corp-wide): 81.3MM Privately
Held
SIC: 7379 Computer related consulting
services
HQ: Tata America International Corporation
101 Park Ave Rm 2603
New York NY 10178
212 557-8038

(P-16507)
TECH-ED NETWORKS INC
10000 Allantown Dr # 175, Roseville
(95678-5996)
PHONE.................916 784-2005
Stephen Fassler, *President*
Ross Ramsey, *Vice Pres*
EMP: 111
SQ FT: 67,800

SALES (est): 6.6MM Privately Held
WEB: www.technetworks.com
SIC: 7379 Computer related consulting
services

(P-16508)
TECHNOLOGY RESOURCE
CENTER INC
2101 E 4th St Ste 130a, Santa Ana
(92705-3843)
PHONE.................714 542-1004
Gabriel Chavez, *President*
Anthony Chavez, *CFO*
Mark Serres, *Vice Pres*
EMP: 60
SQ FT: 2,000
SALES (est): 4.3MM Privately Held
WEB: www.trcinc.net
SIC: 7379 7361 Computer related consult-
ing services; employment agencies

(P-16509)
TECHNOLOGY SERVICES CAL
DEPT (DH)
Also Called: Dts
1325 J St Ste 1600, Sacramento
(95814-2941)
P.O. Box 1810, Rancho Cordova (95741-
1810)
PHONE.................916 319-9223
Marybel Batjer, *Admin Sec*
EMP: 94
SALES (est): 23.5MM Privately Held
WEB: www.osi.ca.gov
SIC: 7379

(P-16510)
TECTURA CORPORATION (PA)
951 Old County Rd 2-317, Belmont
(94002-2773)
PHONE.................650 273-4249
Duane W Bell, *CEO*
Dave Kempski, *CFO*
EMP: 50
SALES (est): 61.4MM Privately Held
SIC: 7379 Computer related consulting
services

(P-16511)
TERADATA CORPORATION
17095 Via Del Campo, San Diego
(92127-1711)
PHONE.................858 485-1220
Kathleen Edmons, *Branch Mgr*
Mary St Aubin, *General Mgr*
Brian Tinney, *Sr Ntwrk Engine*
Jeremy Browne, *Software Engr*
David Kunz, *Software Engr*
EMP: 800 Publicly Held
SIC: 7379 Computer related consulting
services
PA: Teradata Corporation
10000 Innovation Dr
Miamisburg OH 45342
-

(P-16512)
TIGERCONNECT
2110 Broadway, Santa Monica
(90404-2912)
PHONE.................310 401-1820
Jeffrey Evans, *CEO*
Sheila Saldana, *President*
Justin Nelson, *Officer*
Angie Inlow, *Vice Pres*
Tj Thomsen, *Vice Pres*
EMP: 50 EST: 2010
SALES (est): 946.7K Privately Held
SIC: 7379 Computer related maintenance
services

(P-16513)
TILLSTER INC (PA)
Also Called: Emn8
5959 Cornerstone Ct W # 100, San Diego
(92121-3764)
PHONE.................858 784-0800
Perse Faily, *CEO*
Ravi Singh, *President*
John Redding, *CFO*
Trevor Chong, *Senior VP*
Beth Sandell, *Vice Pres*
EMP: 70
SQ FT: 18,642

SALES (est): 34.3MM Privately Held
WEB: www.emn8.com
SIC: 7379 7373 Computer related maintenance services; systems integration services; computer system selling services

(P-16514)
TRADEBEAM INC
303 Twin Dolphin Dr # 600, Redwood City
(94065-1497)
PHONE.................650 653-4800
Fax: 650 653-4801
EMP: 100
SQ FT: 26,000
SALES (est): 4.8MM
SALES (corp-wide): 481.7MM Privately
Held
WEB: www.tradebeam.com
SIC: 7379
HQ: Cdc Software, Inc.
4325 Alexander Dr
Alpharetta GA 30022

(P-16515)
TRIAGE PARTNERS LLC
15717 Texaco Ave, Paramount
(90723-3923)
PHONE.................562 634-0058
EMP: 78
SALES (corp-wide): 25.6MM Privately
Held
SIC: 7379
PA: Triage Partners, L.L.C.
1715 N West Shore Blvd # 250
Tampa FL 33607
813 801-9869

(P-16516)
TRIANZ INC (HQ)
2350 Mission College Blvd, Santa Clara
(95054-1532)
PHONE.................408 387-5800
Srikanth Manchala, *President*
Anusuya Chaman, *CFO*
Ron Oehm, *Chairman*
Ganesh Arunachala, *Officer*
Ira Horowitz, *Vice Pres*
EMP: 120 EST: 2000
SQ FT: 18,000
SALES: 65.2MM Privately Held
WEB: www.trianz.com
SIC: 7379

(P-16517)
TRIFECTA MULTIMEDIA LLC
(PA)
Also Called: Trifecta Clinical
725 S Figueroa St # 4050, Los Angeles
(90017-5482)
PHONE.................626 355-1303
David Young,
Rick Ward, *Vice Pres*
Jessica Deroux, *Admin Asst*
Dan Brandt, *QA Dir*
Tarra Roshan, *QA Dir*
EMP: 50
SQ FT: 7,000
SALES (est): 7.6MM Privately Held
WEB: www.TRIFECTAMULTIMEDIA.com
SIC: 7379

(P-16518)
TRUSTARC INC
Also Called: Truste
835 Market St Ste 800, San Francisco
(94103-1906)
PHONE.................415 520-3400
Christopher Babel, *CEO*
Tim Sullivan, *CFO*
Michelle Hines, *Vice Pres*
Kevin Trilli, *Vice Pres*
Zeph Harben, *Info Tech Dir*
EMP: 100
SQ FT: 7,000
SALES (est): 12.8MM
SALES (corp-wide): 87.1K Privately Held
WEB: www.truste.com
SIC: 7379 8742 Computer related consult-
ing services; management consulting
services; marketing consulting services
PA: Truste Europe Ltd.
3rd Floor
London

(P-16519)
UNISH CORPORATION
4300 Stevens Creek Blvd # 126, San Jose
(95129-1263)
PHONE.................408 708-9300
Basavaraj Ullagaddi, *President*
EMP: 50
SALES (est): 2.4MM Privately Held
SIC: 7379

(P-16520)
UNITED STATES TECHNICAL
SVCS
Also Called: Usts
16541 Gothard St Ste 214, Huntington
Beach (92647-4436)
PHONE.................714 374-6300
Bob Polk, *President*
John Courtney, *CEO*
Cynthia Dugger, *Treasurer*
Dianne Cooper, *Admin Asst*
Dawyn Price, *Engineer*
EMP: 122
SQ FT: 2,500
SALES (est): 18.5MM Privately Held
WEB: www.usts.net
SIC: 7379

(P-16521)
UNITEK INFORMATION
SYSTEMS INC (PA)
Also Called: Unitek It Education
4670 Auto Mall Pkwy, Fremont
(94538-3197)
PHONE.................510 249-1060
Janis Paulson, *CEO*
Shiva Jahan, *CFO*
Navraj Bawa, *Vice Pres*
EMP: 55
SQ FT: 27,000
SALES (est): 23.6MM Privately Held
WEB: www.abriasoft.com
SIC: 7379 7371 Computer related consult-
ing services; custom computer program-
ming services

(P-16522)
US DATA MANAGEMENT LLC
(PA)
Also Called: Usdm Life Science
535 Chapala St, Santa Barbara
(93101-3411)
PHONE.................888 231-0816
Kevin Brown, *Mng Member*
Vega Finucan,
EMP: 148
SQ FT: 4,000
SALES (est): 20MM Privately Held
WEB: www.usdatamanagement.com
SIC: 7379 Computer related consulting
services

(P-16523)
VALLEY US INC
888 Saratoga Ave Ste 201, San Jose
(95129-2639)
PHONE.................408 260-7342
Sunita Kumari, *President*
EMP: 70
SALES (est): 2.8MM Privately Held
SIC: 7379 Computer related consulting
services

(P-16524)
VENTRUM LLC
2033 Gateway Pl Ste 500, San Jose
(95110-3712)
PHONE.................510 304-0852
Rahul Misra,
Rohita Misra,
EMP: 75
SALES: 8MM Privately Held
WEB: www.ventrum.com
SIC: 7379 Computer related consulting
services

(P-16525)
VERIZON DIGITAL MEDIA SVCS
INC (HQ)
13031 W Jefferson Blvd # 900, Los Angeles
(90094-7002)
PHONE.................310 396-7400
Ralf Jacob, *President*
Andre Amar, *Vice Pres*
Suzanne-Lee Haskell, *Vice Pres*

David Kahdian, *Vice Pres*
Jim Lambert, *Vice Pres*
EMP: 501
SQ FT: 50,000
SALES (est): 70.4MM
SALES (corp-wide): 126B **Publicly Held**
WEB: www.edgecast.com
SIC: 7379
PA: Verizon Communications Inc.
1095 Ave Of The Americas
New York NY 10036
212 395-1000

(P-16526)
VIRTIUM LLC
30052 Tomas, Rcho STA Marg
(92688-2127)
PHONE.....................949 888-2444
Robert P Healy,
Thomas Magee, *CFO*
Edward Peng, *Chairman*
Gary Drossel, *Vice Pres*
Scott Lawrence, *Pharmacy Dir*
EMP: 100
SALES (est): 51.8K **Privately Held**
SIC: 7379 Computer data escrow service

(P-16527)
VIRTUAL INSTRUMENTS CORP
2331 Zanker Rd, San Jose (95131-1109)
PHONE.....................408 579-4000
Philippe Vincent, *CEO*
Todd Osborne, *Partner*
Lorie Ross, *Partner*
Chris Carvacho, *President*
Tim Leow, *President*
EMP: 80
SALES (est): 23.1MM **Privately Held**
SIC: 7379 7371 Computer related consulting services; computer software development

(P-16528)
VISION SOLUTIONS INC
Also Called: Itera Software
15300 Barranca Pkwy # 100, Irvine
(92618-2200)
PHONE.....................949 253-6500
Daniel Neville, *Branch Mgr*
EMP: 52 **Privately Held**
WEB: www.visionsolutions.com
SIC: 7379 7371 Computer related consulting services; data processing consultant; computer software development & applications
PA: Vision Solutions, Inc.
15300 Barranca Pkwy # 100
Irvine CA 92618

(P-16529)
VORMETRIC INC (HQ)
Also Called: AES Networks
2860 Junction Ave, San Jose (95134-1922)
PHONE.....................408 433-6000
Alan Kessler, *President*
Ashvin Kamaraju, *President*
Wayne Lewandowski, *President*
Greg Paulsen, *CFO*
Roman Baudrit, *Vice Pres*
EMP: 79 **EST:** 2001
SQ FT: 56,000
SALES (est): 53.9MM
SALES (corp-wide): 305.4MM **Privately Held**
WEB: www.vormetric.com
SIC: 7379 Computer related maintenance services
PA: Thales
Carpe Diem Esplanade Nord Tour Aig
Courbevoie 92400
157 778-000

(P-16530)
WE SEE DRAGONS LLC
1100 Glendon Ave Ste 1700, Los Angeles
(90024-3588)
PHONE.....................310 361-5700
Zack Zalon, *Managing Prtnr*
EMP: 105
SALES: 45MM **Privately Held**
SIC: 7379 Computer related maintenance services

(P-16531)
WHITEGOLD SOLUTIONS INC
43 Fernwood Way Ste 210, San Rafael
(94901-2528)
PHONE.....................415 456-4493
Jack Zoken, *President*
EMP: 50
SALES (est): 3MM **Privately Held**
WEB: www.sift.com
SIC: 7379 Data processing consultant

(P-16532)
WHITEHAT SECURITY INC
1741 Tech Dr Ste 300, San Jose (95110)
PHONE.....................408 343-8300
Craig Hinkley, *CEO*
Terry Murphy, *CFO*
Joseph Feiman, *Security Dir*
Matthew Hutchinson, *VP Mktg*
EMP: 55
SALES (est): 14.4MM **Privately Held**
WEB: www.whitehatsec.com
SIC: 7379

(P-16533)
WINCERE INC
2350 Mission College Blvd # 290, Santa
Clara (95054-1575)
PHONE.....................408 841-4355
Himanshi Kansara, *President*
EMP: 210
SQ FT: 3,000
SALES (est): 13.6MM **Privately Held**
SIC: 7379 Computer related consulting services
PA: Wincere Solutions Private Limited
Regus Business Centre, Level 2
New Delhi DL 11002

(P-16534)
WORK TRUCK SOLUTIONS INC
2485 Notre Dame Blvd, Chico
(95928-7161)
PHONE.....................855 987-4544
Kathryn Schifferle, *CEO*
Kevin Kinell, *Technical Staff*
Ashley Hewitt, *Business Mgr*
Tony Solano, *VP Sales*
Gretchen Krugler, *Director*
EMP: 80
SALES (est): 5.6MM **Privately Held**
SIC: 7379 Computer related services

(P-16535)
WYNDGATE TECHNOLOGIES
4925 Robert J Mathews Pkw, El Dorado
Hills (95762-5700)
PHONE.....................916 404-8400
Michael Ruxnin, *Ch of Bd*
Tom Marcinek, *COO*
Morgan Polcheni, *Vice Pres*
EMP: 83
SALES (est): 5.3MM
SALES (corp-wide): 903.9MM **Publicly Held**
WEB: www.sttx.net
SIC: 7379 7371 7372 Computer related consulting services; custom computer programming services; prepackaged software
HQ: Global Med Technologies, Inc.
4925 Robert J Mathews Pkw
El Dorado Hills CA 95762
916 404-8400

(P-16536)
XANTRION INCORPORATED
651 Thomas L Berkley Way, Oakland
(94612-1344)
PHONE.....................510 272-4701
Tom Snyder, *COO*
Anne Bisagno, *President*
EMP: 50 **EST:** 2000
SQ FT: 10,000
SALES: 15.1MM **Privately Held**
SIC: 7379 ; computer related consulting services

(P-16537)
XAVOR CORPORATION
300 Spectrum Center Dr # 400, Irvine
(92618-4989)
PHONE.....................949 529-7372
Humayun Rashid, *President*
Dr Das Gupta, *Vice Pres*

Amara Masood, *Vice Pres*
EMP: 100
SQ FT: 14,000
SALES (est): 7.7MM **Privately Held**
SIC: 7379 1731 Computer related consulting services; electrical work

(P-16538)
XORIANT CORPORATION (PA)
1248 Reamwood Ave, Sunnyvale
(94089-2225)
PHONE.....................408 743-4400
Girish Gaitonde, *CEO*
Mehul Agarwal, *Partner*
Subu Subramanian, *President*
Arun Tendulkar, *COO*
Mahesh Nalavade, *CFO*
EMP: 134
SALES: 178MM **Privately Held**
WEB: www.xoriant.com
SIC: 7379 7371 Computer related consulting services; computer software development

(P-16539)
ZIONTECH SOLUTIONS INC
1900 Mccarthy Blvd # 415, Milpitas
(95035-7457)
PHONE.....................408 434-6001
Hymavathi Pentaparthi, *Principal*
Ashok Anumandla, *CEO*
Jyothi Veam, *Sales Staff*
EMP: 60 **EST:** 2008
SALES (est): 477.6K **Privately Held**
SIC: 7379

**7381 Detective & Armored
Car Svcs**

(P-16540)
A1 PROTECTIVE SERVICES INC
5 Thomas Mellon Cir, San Francisco
(94134-2501)
PHONE.....................415 467-7200
Paula Jones, *President*
EMP: 84
SQ FT: 900
SALES: 2MM **Privately Held**
SIC: 7381 Security guard service

(P-16541)
A1 PROTECTIVE SERVICES LLC
7000 Franklin Blvd, Sacramento
(95823-1881)
PHONE.....................916 421-3000
Paula Jones,
Brajah Norris,
EMP: 50
SALES (est): 227.8K **Privately Held**
SIC: 7381 Security guard service

(P-16542)
**ABC SECURITY SERVICE INC
(PA)**
1840 Embarcadero, Oakland (94606-5220)
P.O. Box 1709 (94604-1709)
PHONE.....................510 436-0666
Ana Chretien, *President*
Roger Chretien, *Vice Pres*
Mary Cordero, *Executive Asst*
Becky Hicklin, *Consultant*
EMP: 226
SQ FT: 17,000
SALES (est): 6.7MM **Privately Held**
WEB: www.abcsecurityinc.com
SIC: 7381 Security guard service

(P-16543)
ACTION FORCE SECURITY
1212 W Gardena Blvd Ste C, Gardena
(90247-4896)
PHONE.....................310 715-6053
Pedro Villatoro, *Owner*
EMP: 50
SALES (est): 880K **Privately Held**
SIC: 7381 Security guard service

(P-16544)
AI INC/CSC GROU
28001 Smyth Dr Ste 107, Valencia
(91355-4032)
PHONE.....................661 775-8400
Randy Andrews, *Partner*
EMP: 52 **EST:** 2016

SALES (est): 235K **Privately Held**
SIC: 7381 Guard services

(P-16545)
ALL ACTION SECURITY INC
20501 Ventura Blvd # 275, Woodland Hills
(91364-6413)
PHONE.....................800 482-7371
John Ayam, *President*
Daniel Charron, *Office Mgr*
Abbas Kosh, *Human Res Mgr*
EMP: 75
SALES (est): 2.1MM **Privately Held**
WEB: www.allactionsecurity.com
SIC: 7381 Security guard service

(P-16546)
**ALL NATION SECURITY SVCS
INC (PA)**
3701 Wilshire Blvd # 530, Los Angeles
(90010-2818)
PHONE.....................213 769-4510
Kathy Thabet, *President*
Sandra Torres, *General Mgr*
EMP: 250
SQ FT: 4,250
SALES (est): 4.9MM **Privately Held**
SIC: 7381 Security guard service

(P-16547)
**ALLIED PROTECTION SERVICES
INC**
19164 Van Ness Ave, Torrance
(90501-1101)
PHONE.....................310 330-8314
Leon Brooks, *President*
EMP: 78
SALES (est): 3.3MM **Privately Held**
WEB: www.alliedprotection.com
SIC: 7381 Security guard service

(P-16548)
ALLIED RISK MANAGEMENT INC
2010 W Avenue K 395, Lancaster
(93536-5229)
PHONE.....................661 305-0455
Howard Fuchs, *Director*
Eric Taylor, *General Mgr*
EMP: 99
SALES: 950K **Privately Held**
SIC: 7381 Security guard service

(P-16549)
**ALLIEDBARTON SECURITY
SVCS LLC**
765 The City Dr S Ste 150, Orange
(92868-6920)
PHONE.....................626 213-3100
Janet Melendez, *Manager*
EMP: 127
SALES (corp-wide): 3.2B **Privately Held**
SIC: 7381 Security guard service
HQ: Alliedbarton Security Services Llc
8 Tower Bridge 161 Wshgtn
Conshohocken PA 19428
610 239-1100

(P-16550)
**ALLIEDBARTON SECURITY
SVCS LLC**
3120 Chicago Ave Ste 190, Riverside
(92507-3431)
PHONE.....................951 801-7300
Paul Scrankowski, *Manager*
Aaron Lantz, *Supervisor*
EMP: 127
SALES (corp-wide): 3.2B **Privately Held**
SIC: 7381 Security guard service
HQ: Alliedbarton Security Services Llc
8 Tower Bridge 161 Wshgtn
Conshohocken PA 19428
610 239-1100

(P-16551)
**ALLIEDBARTON SECURITY
SVCS LLC**
637 E Albertoni St # 202, Carson
(90746-1539)
PHONE.....................310 324-1219
Chris Rike, *District Mgr*
EMP: 127
SALES (corp-wide): 3.2B **Privately Held**
SIC: 7381 Security guard service

PRODUCTS & SVCS

HQ: Alliedbarton Security Services Llc
8 Tower Bridge 161 Wshgtn
Conshohocken PA 19428
610 239-1100

(P-16552)
ALLIEDBARTON SECURITY SVCS LLC
8950 Cal Center Dr # 150, Sacramento
(95826-3236)
PHONE..................................916 489-8280
Rodney Carter, *Branch Mgr*
EMP: 150
SALES (corp-wide): 3.2B **Privately Held**
WEB: www.alliedsecurity.com
SIC: 7381 Security guard service
HQ: Alliedbarton Security Services Llc
8 Tower Bridge 161 Wshgtn
Conshohocken PA 19428
610 239-1100

(P-16553)
ALLIEDBARTON SECURITY SVCS LLC
300 E Esplanade Dr # 1510, Oxnard
(93036-1238)
PHONE..................................805 983-1204
Jenny Nelson, *Branch Mgr*
EMP: 93
SALES (corp-wide): 3.2B **Privately Held**
SIC: 7381 Security guard service
HQ: Alliedbarton Security Services Llc
8 Tower Bridge 161 Wshgtn
Conshohocken PA 19428
610 239-1100

(P-16554)
ALLIEDBARTON SECURITY SVCS LLC
Also Called: Initial Security
10330 Pioneer Blvd # 235, Santa Fe
Springs (90670-6012)
PHONE..................................562 906-4800
Larry Link, *Vice Pres*
EMP: 500
SALES (corp-wide): 3.2B **Privately Held**
SIC: 7381 Security guard service
HQ: Alliedbarton Security Services Llc
8 Tower Bridge 161 Wshgtn
Conshohocken PA 19428
610 239-1100

(P-16555)
ALLIEDBARTON SECURITY SVCS LLC
1600 Riviera Ave Ste 375, Walnut Creek
(94596-7377)
PHONE..................................510 839-4041
Kiet Phan, *District Mgr*
Matthew Goularte, *Opers Mgr*
EMP: 300
SALES (corp-wide): 3.2B **Privately Held**
WEB: www.alliedsecurity.com
SIC: 7381 Security guard service
HQ: Alliedbarton Security Services Llc
8 Tower Bridge 161 Wshgtn
Conshohocken PA 19428
610 239-1100

(P-16556)
ALLIEDBARTON SECURITY SVCS LLC
2540 N 1st St Ste 101, San Jose
(95131-1016)
PHONE..................................408 954-8274
Nanette Jacoby, *Principal*
Jason Brown, *Business Mgr*
Daniel Layfield, *Analyst*
Sharhonda Scott, *Opers Mgr*
Dennis Shaw, *Opers Mgr*
EMP: 500
SALES (corp-wide): 3.2B **Privately Held**
WEB: www.alliedsecurity.com
SIC: 7381 Security guard service; protec-
tive services, guard; private investigator;
detective agency
HQ: Alliedbarton Security Services Llc
8 Tower Bridge 161 Wshgtn
Conshohocken PA 19428
610 239-1100

(P-16557)
ALLIEDBARTON SECURITY SVCS LLC
7670 Opportunity Rd # 210, San Diego
(92111-2274)
PHONE..................................858 874-8200
Melone Widy, *Manager*
EMP: 400
SALES (corp-wide): 3.2B **Privately Held**
WEB: www.alliedsecurity.com
SIC: 7381 Security guard service
HQ: Alliedbarton Security Services Llc
8 Tower Bridge 161 Wshgtn
Conshohocken PA 19428
610 239-1100

(P-16558)
ALLIEDBARTON SECURITY SVCS LLC
3701 Wilshire Blvd # 600, Los Angeles
(90010-2804)
PHONE..................................800 418-6423
Veroin Higbee, *Manager*
Lisa Crane, *Admin Asst*
Greg Welch, *Business Mgr*
EMP: 300
SALES (corp-wide): 3.2B **Privately Held**
WEB: www.alliedsecurity.com
SIC: 7381 Security guard service; protec-
tive services, guard; private investigator
HQ: Alliedbarton Security Services Llc
8 Tower Bridge 161 Wshgtn
Conshohocken PA 19428
610 239-1100

(P-16559)
ALLIEDBARTON SECURITY SVCS LLC
765 The City Dr S Ste 105, Orange
(92868-6911)
PHONE..................................714 260-0805
Larry Crowl, *Principal*
William Evans, *Officer*
EMP: 160
SALES (corp-wide): 3.2B **Privately Held**
WEB: www.alliedsecurity.com
SIC: 7381 Security guard service
HQ: Alliedbarton Security Services Llc
8 Tower Bridge 161 Wshgtn
Conshohocken PA 19428
610 239-1100

(P-16560)
AMERICAN CORPORATE SEC INC (PA)
1 World Trade Ctr # 1240, Long Beach
(90831-1240)
PHONE..................................562 216-7440
Larry J Saye, *CEO*
Tim Lovette, *Human Res Mgr*
Andrew McPhee, *Human Resources*
EMP: 74
SALES (est): 35.9MM **Privately Held**
SIC: 7381 8721 Security guard service;
payroll accounting service

(P-16561)
AMERICAN CSTM PRIVATE SEC INC
446 E Vine St Ste A, Stockton
(95202-1116)
P.O. Box 8513 (95208-0513)
PHONE..................................209 369-1200
Rajesh Patti, *President*
EMP: 80
SQ FT: 1,100
SALES: 300K **Privately Held**
SIC: 7381 Security guard service

(P-16562)
AMERICAN EAGLE PRO
Also Called: American Eagle Protective Svcs
425 W Kelso St, Inglewood (90301-2539)
PHONE..................................310 412-0019
Veronica Bautista, *CEO*
Joelle Epoh, *Principal*
Alma Serrano, *Admin Sec*
EMP: 90 EST: 2011
SALES (est): 1.2MM **Privately Held**
SIC: 7381 Guard services

(P-16563)
AMERICAN FORCE PRIVATE SEC INC
1585 S D St Ste 208, San Bernardino
(92408-3236)
PHONE..................................909 384-9820
Shehab Abdelazim, *CEO*
EMP: 75
SALES (est): 1.7MM **Privately Held**
SIC: 7381 Security guard service; guard
services

(P-16564)
AMERICAN GUARD SERVICES INC (PA)
1125 W 190th St, Gardena (90248-4303)
PHONE..................................310 645-6200
Sherine Assal, *President*
Sherif Assal, *Vice Pres*
Adolfo Avendano, *Regional Mgr*
Usman Ahmad, *Area Spvr*
Nelson Cabrera, *Admin Sec*
EMP: 400
SQ FT: 28,000
SALES (est): 54.5MM **Privately Held**
SIC: 7381 Security guard service

(P-16565)
AMERICAN PATRIOT SECURITY
10293 Rockingham Dr # 104, Sacramento
(95827-2529)
P.O. Box 980071, West Sacramento
(95798-0071)
PHONE..................................916 706-2449
Scott Jacobs, *President*
Kelly Rochester, *Vice Pres*
EMP: 75
SQ FT: 1,200
SALES (est): 2.1MM **Privately Held**
WEB: www.americanpatriotsecurity.com
SIC: 7381 Security guard service

(P-16566)
AMERICAN PROTECTION GROUP INC (PA)
8551 Vesper Ave, Panorama City
(91402-2914)
PHONE..................................818 279-2433
John Chaverra, *CEO*
Anthony Brown, *Vice Pres*
EMP: 107
SQ FT: 3,000
SALES (est): 13.1MM **Privately Held**
SIC: 7381 5063 7382 Guard services;
burglary protection service; security guard
service; detective agency; alarm systems;
burglar alarm maintenance & monitoring

(P-16567)
AMERICAN SECURITY FORCE INC
5400 E Olympic Blvd # 225, Commerce
(90022-5154)
PHONE..................................323 722-8585
Albert Williams, *President*
EMP: 157
SQ FT: 3,700
SALES (est): 2.5MM **Privately Held**
SIC: 7381 7382 Protective services,
guard; private investigator; guard dog
rental; detective agency; burglar alarm
maintenance & monitoring

(P-16568)
AMERICAN-1 AIRTIGHT SEC CO
2510 N Grand Ave Ste 207, Santa Ana
(92705-8754)
P.O. Box 23130 (92711-3130)
PHONE..................................714 997-0605
Sid Asghari, *President*
EMP: 50
SALES: 1,000K **Privately Held**
WEB: www.spearsecurity.com
SIC: 7381 Security guard service

(P-16569)
ANDREWS INTERNATIONAL INC
455 N Moss St, Burbank (91502-1727)
PHONE..................................818 260-9586
John Adams, *Principal*
EMP: 177
SALES (corp-wide): 139.5MM **Privately Held**
SIC: 7381

PA: Andrews International, Inc.
455 N Moss St
Burbank CA 91502
818 487-4060

(P-16570)
ANDREWS INTERNATIONAL INC
455 N Moss St, Burbank (91502-1727)
PHONE..................................805 409-4160
Frank Alverez, *Branch Mgr*
EMP: 177
SALES (corp-wide): 139.5MM **Privately Held**
SIC: 7381 Security guard service
PA: Andrews International, Inc.
455 N Moss St
Burbank CA 91502
818 487-4060

(P-16571)
ANDREWS INTERNATIONAL INC (PA)
455 N Moss St, Burbank (91502-1727)
PHONE..................................818 487-4060
Randy Andrews, *President*
Ty Richmond, *COO*
James Wood, *COO*
Michael Topf, *CFO*
Obie R Moore III, *Exec VP*
EMP: 1700
SQ FT: 5,000
SALES (est): 139.5MM **Privately Held**
WEB: www.andrewinternational.com
SIC: 7381 Protective services, guard; se-
curity guard service

(P-16572)
ANDREWS INTERNATIONAL INC
455 N Moss St, Burbank (91502-1727)
PHONE..................................626 407-2290
Mike Wibben, *Vice Pres*
Steve Seyler, *Executive*
EMP: 200
SALES (corp-wide): 139.5MM **Privately Held**
SIC: 7381 Security guard service
PA: Andrews International, Inc.
455 N Moss St
Burbank CA 91502
818 487-4060

(P-16573)
ASSET PRIVATE SECURITY INC
36 Quail Run Cir Ste O, Salinas
(93907-2351)
PHONE..................................831 809-9779
Jay A Agamao, *CEO*
Allan Tucker, *COO*
Jorge Sareli, *CFO*
EMP: 77
SALES: 2.5MM **Privately Held**
SIC: 7381 Security guard service

(P-16574)
ATLAS SECURITY & PATROL INC
39465 Paseo Padre Pkwy # 2800, Fremont
(94538-1631)
PHONE..................................510 791-7380
Jason Solorzano, *Manager*
EMP: 50
SALES (corp-wide): 4MM **Privately Held**
SIC: 7381 Security guard service; private
investigator
PA: Atlas Security & Patrol, Inc.
3851 Charter Park Dr V
San Jose CA
408 972-2099

(P-16575)
BACO REALTY CORPORATION
6310 Stockton Blvd, Sacramento
(95824-4003)
PHONE..................................916 974-9898
EMP: 86
SALES (corp-wide): 37.1MM **Privately Held**
SIC: 7381 Guard services
PA: Baco Realty Corporation
51 Federal St Ste 202
San Francisco CA 94107
415 281-3700

(P-16576)
BAECHLER INVESTIGATIVE SVCS
1935 N Marshall Ave Ste C, El Cajon
(92020-1132)
PHONE.................................619 464-5600
Anthony Baechler, *President*
EMP: 53
SQ FT: 5,200
SALES (est): 1MM **Privately Held**
WEB: www.junes.com
SIC: 7381 Private investigator

(P-16577)
BALD EAGLE SECURITY SVCS INC
3626 Main St, San Diego (92113-3805)
P.O. Box 131350 (92170-1350)
PHONE.................................619 230-0022
Andrea Robinson, *President*
Dean Heilmann, *Manager*
EMP: 75
SALES (est): 234.2K **Privately Held**
SIC: 7381 Security guard service

(P-16578)
BARCOTT FRANK A SEC INVSTGTONS
Also Called: Barcott SEC & Investigations
6446 San Andres Ave, Cypress
(90630-5324)
P.O. Box 2278 (90630-1778)
PHONE.................................714 891-8556
Frank A Barcott, *President*
Carolyn Barcott, *Vice Pres*
EMP: 200
SALES (est): 5.2MM **Privately Held**
SIC: 7381 Security guard service; detective services

(P-16579)
BARRYS SECURITY SERVICES INC (PA)
16739 Van Buren Blvd, Riverside
(92504-5744)
PHONE.................................951 789-7575
Michelle Barry, *CEO*
Martin Morales, *Vice Pres*
Chase Blakney, *Human Res Dir*
EMP: 188
SQ FT: 5,000
SALES: 8.3MM **Privately Held**
WEB: www.weguard.biz
SIC: 7381 Security guard service

(P-16580)
BARRYS SECURITY SERVICES INC
5480 Katella Ave Ste 203, Los Alamitos
(90720-6823)
PHONE.................................562 493-7007
Carlos Nunez, *Branch Mgr*
EMP: 125
SALES (corp-wide): 8.3MM **Privately Held**
WEB: www.weguard.biz
SIC: 7381 Guard services
PA: Barry's Security Services, Inc.
16739 Van Buren Blvd
Riverside CA 92504
951 789-7575

(P-16581)
BEACH CITIES INVEST & PROTCTN
2500 Via Cabrillo Marina, San Pedro
(90731-7224)
PHONE.................................310 322-4724
Kevin R Hackie, *CEO*
Norma Chavarria, *Treasurer*
Nicholas Hackie, *Vice Pres*
Shana Alexander, *Admin Sec*
EMP: 300
SQ FT: 2,000
SALES (est): 4.1MM **Privately Held**
SIC: 7381 Detective services; private investigator

(P-16582)
BELL PRIVATE SECURITY INC
Also Called: R M B SEC Cnslting Invstgtions
18030 Brookhurst St, Fountain Valley
(92708-6756)
PHONE.................................714 964-9381
Robert M Bell, *President*
EMP: 90
SALES (est): 1.4MM **Privately Held**
WEB: www.bellprivatesecurity.com
SIC: 7381 Security guard service; private investigator

(P-16583)
BLACK BEAR SECURITY SERVICES
Also Called: Montana Investigation
2016 Oakdale Ave Ste B, San Francisco
(94124-2041)
PHONE.................................415 559-5159
Moura Borisova, *President*
EMP: 125
SQ FT: 3,000
SALES (est): 3.6MM **Privately Held**
WEB: www.blackbearsecurity.com
SIC: 7381 7382 Security guard service; security systems services

(P-16584)
BORGENS & BORGENS INC
Also Called: Delta Protective Services
141 E Acacia St Ste D, Stockton
(95202-1400)
P.O. Box 8633 (95208-0633)
PHONE.................................209 547-2980
L D Borgens, *President*
K R Borgens, *Vice Pres*
EMP: 85 EST: 1993
SQ FT: 2,475
SALES (est): 1.8MM **Privately Held**
WEB: www.deltaprotectiveservices.com
SIC: 7381 Security guard service

(P-16585)
BORUNDA PRIVATE SEC PATROL INC
1070 Brookhaven Dr, Clovis (93612-1913)
PHONE.................................559 299-2662
Ben Borunda, *CEO*
EMP: 50
SALES (est): 167.1K **Privately Held**
SIC: 7381 Security guard service

(P-16586)
BOYD & ASSOCIATES
445 E Esplanade Dr # 210, Oxnard
(93036-2126)
PHONE.................................805 988-8298
Kathy Correll, *Manager*
EMP: 100
SALES (corp-wide): 19.1MM **Privately Held**
WEB: www.boydsecurity.com
SIC: 7381 Security guard service
PA: Boyd & Associates
2191 E Thompson Blvd
Ventura CA 93001
818 752-1888

(P-16587)
BOYD & ASSOCIATES (PA)
2191 E Thompson Blvd, Ventura
(93001-3538)
PHONE.................................818 752-1888
Raymond G Boyd Sr, *Ch of Bd*
Daniel Boyd, *President*
Barbara K Boyd, *Vice Pres*
Eric Cardenas, *Opers Mgr*
EMP: 160
SQ FT: 8,000
SALES (est): 19.1MM **Privately Held**
WEB: www.boydsecurity.com
SIC: 7381 7382 Security guard service; detective services; security systems services

(P-16588)
BOYD & ASSOCIATES
3151 Airway Ave Ste K105, Costa Mesa
(92626-4613)
PHONE.................................714 835-5423
Fax: 714 835-5641
EMP: 150
SQ FT: 3,012
SALES (corp-wide): 19.4MM **Privately Held**
SIC: 7381
PA: Boyd & Associates
2191 E Thompson Blvd
Ventura CA 93001
818 752-1888

(P-16589)
BRINKS INCORPORATED
1120 Venice Blvd, Los Angeles
(90015-3289)
PHONE.................................818 503-8630
Dennis Dwyer, *Executive*
EMP: 136
SALES (corp-wide): 3.3B **Publicly Held**
WEB: www.brinksinc.com
SIC: 7381 Armored car services
HQ: Brink's, Incorporated
1801 Bayberry Ct Ste 400
Richmond VA 23226
804 289-9600

(P-16590)
BRINKS INCORPORATED
8178 Alpine Ave Unit A, Sacramento
(95826-4707)
PHONE.................................916 452-5279
Steve Morss, *Manager*
Dylene Campbell, *Human Resources*
EMP: 133
SALES (corp-wide): 3.3B **Publicly Held**
WEB: www.brinksinc.com
SIC: 7381 Armored car services
HQ: Brink's, Incorporated
1801 Bayberry Ct Ste 400
Richmond VA 23226
804 289-9600

(P-16591)
BRINKS INCORPORATED
4520 Federal Blvd Ste A, San Diego
(92102-2516)
PHONE.................................619 263-6615
Eric Holman, *Manager*
EMP: 120
SALES (corp-wide): 3.3B **Publicly Held**
WEB: www.brinksinc.com
SIC: 7381 Armored car services
HQ: Brink's, Incorporated
1801 Bayberry Ct Ste 400
Richmond VA 23226
804 289-9600

(P-16592)
BRINKS INCORPORATED
1630 Old Bayshore Hwy, San Jose
(95112-4304)
PHONE.................................408 436-7717
George Geovanni, *Manager*
EMP: 80
SALES (corp-wide): 3.3B **Publicly Held**
WEB: www.brinksinc.com
SIC: 7381 Armored car services
HQ: Brink's, Incorporated
1801 Bayberry Ct Ste 400
Richmond VA 23226
804 289-9600

(P-16593)
BRINKS INCORPORATED
1821 S Soto St, Los Angeles (90023-4210)
PHONE.................................323 262-2646
Eva Salas, *Manager*
Julian Moreira, *General Mgr*
EMP: 50
SALES (corp-wide): 3.3B **Publicly Held**
WEB: www.brinksinc.com
SIC: 7381 Armored car services
HQ: Brink's, Incorporated
1801 Bayberry Ct Ste 400
Richmond VA 23226
804 289-9600

(P-16594)
C & C SECURITY PATROL INC (PA)
4615 Enterprise Cmn, Fremont
(94538-6345)
PHONE.................................510 713-1260
Hermenegildo Couoh, *CEO*
Marcel Lopez, *Vice Pres*
Gareth Vicary, *Business Mgr*
Danny Bui, *QC Mgr*
EMP: 120
SALES (est): 5.9MM **Privately Held**
SIC: 7381 Security guard service

(P-16595)
C S I PATROL SERVICES
3605 Long Beach Blvd # 205, Long Beach
(90807-4013)
PHONE.................................562 981-8988
Dennis Cook, *President*
EMP: 55
SQ FT: 600
SALES (est): 1.6MM **Privately Held**
WEB: www.csipatrol.com
SIC: 7381 Protective services, guard; security guard service

(P-16596)
CALIFORNIA GUARD INC
Also Called: Ad Force Private Security
3108 N Cherryland Ave, Stockton
(95215-2222)
P.O. Box 55331 (95205-8831)
PHONE.................................209 465-8420
George Garcia, *CEO*
Surinder Singh Sandhu, *President*
EMP: 100
SALES (est): 3.5MM **Privately Held**
SIC: 7381 Security guard service

(P-16597)
CALIFORNIA SAFETY AGENCY
8932 Katella Ave Ste 108, Anaheim
(92804-6299)
PHONE.................................866 996-6990
EMP: 50
SALES (est): 1MM **Privately Held**
SIC: 7381

(P-16598)
CALIFORNIA SECURITY CONS
3108 N Cherryland Ave, Stockton
(95215-2222)
P.O. Box 55331 (95205-8831)
PHONE.................................209 465-8420
George Garcia, *President*
EMP: 200
SALES (est): 2.6MM **Privately Held**
SIC: 7381 Security guard service

(P-16599)
CENTRAL COAST PUB SAFETY INC
222 Carmen Ln Ste 202, Santa Maria
(93458-7777)
PHONE.................................805 556-4450
Carl Dougherty, *CEO*
EMP: 84
SALES (est): 968K **Privately Held**
SIC: 7381 8249 Protective services, guard; security guard service; medical training services

(P-16600)
CENTURION SECURITY INC
Also Called: Centurion Group, The
11454 San Vicente Blvd, Los Angeles
(90049-6208)
PHONE.................................818 755-0202
Steven Lemmer, *President*
David Rosenberg, *Corp Secy*
Daniel Cambell, *Vice Pres*
EMP: 200
SQ FT: 3,200
SALES (est): 6.4MM **Privately Held**
SIC: 7381 Security guard service

(P-16601)
CENTURION SECURITY SVCS INC (PA)
20102 Sw Cypress St, Newport Beach
(92660-0713)
PHONE.................................949 474-0444
Robyn Hamilton, *President*
Jeff Hamilton, *Vice Pres*
EMP: 54
SALES: 1.8MM **Privately Held**
SIC: 7381 Security guard service

(P-16602)
CHIEF PROTECTIVE SERVICES INC
Also Called: Assure Detective Agency
1344 W 6th St Ste 300, Corona
(92882-1641)
P.O. Box 1806 (92878-1806)
PHONE.................................951 738-0881
Steven Fernandez, *President*
EMP: 100
SQ FT: 3,000
SALES: 2.9MM **Privately Held**
SIC: 7381 Security guard service; private investigator

(P-16603)
CITADEL SECURITY INC
5199 E Pacific Cst Hwy # 200, Long Beach
(90804-3304)
PHONE......................562 248-2300
Brian Kelley, *CEO*
EMP: 150
SQ FT: 4,500
SALES (est): 2.4MM **Privately Held**
WEB: www.citadelsecurityinc.com
SIC: 7381 Security guard service

(P-16604)
CITY NATIONAL SEC SVCS INC
5901 W Century Blvd # 806, Los Angeles
(90045-5411)
PHONE......................310 641-6666
Chiraz Zouaoui, *Manager*
EMP: 80
SALES: 950K **Privately Held**
SIC: 7381 Security guard service

(P-16605)
CITY SECURITY CO INC
430 S Grfield Ave Ste 401, Alhambra
(91801)
PHONE......................626 458-2325
Bob Rysdon, *President*
EMP: 70
SALES (est): 1.3MM **Privately Held**
SIC: 7381 Security guard service

(P-16606)
CLASSIC PROTECTION INC
3208 Royal St, Los Angeles (90007-3657)
PHONE......................213 742-1238
Richard Ullman, *President*
EMP: 50
SQ FT: 1,000
SALES (est): 1.3MM **Privately Held**
SIC: 7381 Guard services; security guard
service

(P-16607)
COMMAND INTERNATIONAL SEC SVCS
6819 Sepulveda Blvd, Van Nuys
(91405-4463)
PHONE......................818 997-1666
Nafees Memon, *Owner*
EMP: 55
SQ FT: 700
SALES: 1.2MM **Privately Held**
SIC: 7381 Security guard service

(P-16608)
COMMAND SECURITY CORPORATION
8840 Warner Ave Ste 301, Fountain Valley
(92708-3234)
PHONE......................714 557-9355
John Dunlevy, *Regl Sales Mgr*
EMP: 168
SALES (corp-wide): 187.9MM **Publicly Held**
SIC: 7381 Security guard service
PA: Command Security Corporation
512 Herndon Pkwy Ste A
Herndon VA 20170
703 464-4735

(P-16609)
COMMAND SECURITY CORPORATION
890 Hillview Ct Ste 100, Milpitas
(95035-4573)
PHONE......................510 623-2355
Larry Reid, *President*
EMP: 168
SALES (corp-wide): 187.9MM **Publicly Held**
SIC: 7381 Security guard service
PA: Command Security Corporation
512 Herndon Pkwy Ste A
Herndon VA 20170
703 464-4735

(P-16610)
COMMAND SECURITY CORPORATION
Also Called: Aviation Safeguards
8929 S Sepulveda Blvd # 300, Los Angeles
(90045-3616)
PHONE......................310 981-4530
Sunny Williams, *Vice Pres*

Joe Conlon, *President*
EMP: 800
SALES (corp-wide): 187.9MM **Publicly Held**
WEB: www.cscny.com
SIC: 7381 7382 Security guard service;
security systems services
PA: Command Security Corporation
512 Herndon Pkwy Ste A
Herndon VA 20170
703 464-4735

(P-16611)
COMMAND SECURITY CORPORATION
Also Called: Aviation Safeguards
1701 Airport Blvd Ste 205, San Jose
(95110-1236)
PHONE......................650 574-0911
Earl Hartfield, *Manager*
EMP: 80
SALES (corp-wide): 187.9MM **Publicly Held**
WEB: www.cscny.com
SIC: 7381 Security guard service
PA: Command Security Corporation
512 Herndon Pkwy Ste A
Herndon VA 20170
703 464-4735

(P-16612)
COMMERCIAL PROTECTIVE SVCS INC
Also Called: CPS Security
3400 E Airport Way, Long Beach
(90806-2412)
PHONE......................310 515-5290
Christopher Coffey, *President*
William R Babcock, *CFO*
EMP: 1800
SQ FT: 10,000
SALES (est): 36MM **Privately Held**
SIC: 7381 Protective services, guard

(P-16613)
COMMONWEALTH INTERNATIONAL
968 Durfee Ave, South El Monte
(91733-4408)
PHONE......................626 279-9201
Jose Velasco, *President*
Emil Ayad, *Vice Pres*
EMP: 50
SALES (est): 1.3MM **Privately Held**
SIC: 7381 Armored car services

(P-16614)
COMPREHENSIVE SEC SVCS INC (PA)
10535 E Stockton Blvd G, Elk Grove
(95624-9758)
P.O. Box 246719, Sacramento (95824-6719)
PHONE......................916 683-3605
Bashir A Choudry, *President*
Jamal-Eddine Kabbaj, *Exec VP*
Omar Choudhry, *Director*
Nash Yakoub, *Manager*
EMP: 75
SQ FT: 3,300
SALES: 8.7MM **Privately Held**
WEB: www.comprehensivesecurity.net
SIC: 7381 7382 Security guard service;
security systems services

(P-16615)
CONTACT SECURITY INC
3000 E Birch St Ste 111, Brea
(92821-6261)
PHONE......................714 572-6760
Michelle Quesada, *President*
EMP: 250
SQ FT: 2,500
SALES (est): 4MM **Privately Held**
WEB: www.contactsecurity.com
SIC: 7381 Security guard service

(P-16616)
CONTEMPORARY SERVICES CORP
Also Called: Crowd Management
2650 E Shaw Ave, Fresno (93710-8284)
PHONE......................559 225-9325
Robert Humphrey, *Manager*
EMP: 200

SALES (corp-wide): 364.5MM **Privately Held**
WEB: www.csc-usa.com
SIC: 7381 Protective services, guard
PA: Contemporary Services Corporation
17101 Superior St
Northridge CA 91325
818 885-5150

(P-16617)
COURTESY SECURITY INC
Also Called: Securelion Security
37420 Cedar Blvd Ste D, Newark
(94560-4159)
PHONE......................888 572-5545
Ajmal Boomwal, *Principal*
EMP: 60
SALES (est): 263K **Privately Held**
SIC: 7381 Detective & armored car services

(P-16618)
COVENANT AVIATION SECURITY LLC
1000 Marina Blvd Ste 100, Brisbane
(94005-1839)
PHONE......................650 219-3473
Brian O Apos, *Manager*
EMP: 1100
SALES (corp-wide): 42.7MM **Privately Held**
SIC: 7381 Security guard service
HQ: Covenant Aviation Security, Llc
400 Quadrangle Dr Ste A
Bolingbrook IL 60440
630 771-0800

(P-16619)
CPS SECURITY SOLUTIONS INC (PA)
3400 E Airport Way, Long Beach
(90806-2412)
PHONE......................310 818-1030
Chris Coffey, *President*
William Babcock, *CFO*
Scott R Barnes, *Exec VP*
EMP: 67
SQ FT: 14,000
SALES (est): 47.9MM **Privately Held**
SIC: 7381 Security guard service

(P-16620)
CREATIVE SECURITY COMPANY INC
150 S Autumn St Ste B, San Jose
(95110-2515)
PHONE......................408 295-2600
Charles Wall, *President*
Brian Wall, *Vice Pres*
Mike Mattocks, *Security Dir*
Kendra Puckett, *Sales Staff*
EMP: 350
SQ FT: 12,000
SALES (est): 13MM **Privately Held**
WEB: www.creativesecurity.com
SIC: 7381 Security guard service; private
investigator

(P-16621)
CRIME IMPACT SECURITY PATROL
Also Called: Crime Impact Security & Patrol
3860 Crenshaw Blvd # 223, Los Angeles
(90008-1816)
PHONE......................323 296-6406
Darrin Jenkins, *President*
EMP: 55
SALES (est): 993.4K **Privately Held**
SIC: 7381 Security guard service

(P-16622)
CRIMETEK SECURITY
3448 N Golden State Blvd, Turlock
(95382-9709)
P.O. Box 845 (95381-0845)
PHONE......................209 668-6208
Edward Esmaili, *President*
Ed Esmaili, *Partner*
Rosy Esmaili, *Partner*
Joseph Givargis, *Manager*
EMP: 420 EST: 1999
SQ FT: 2,200
SALES (est): 12MM **Privately Held**
SIC: 7381 Security guard service; guard
services

(P-16623)
CYPRESS SECURITY LLC (PA)
478 Tehama St, San Francisco
(94103-4141)
PHONE......................866 345-1277
Kes Narbutas,
EMP: 83
SQ FT: 3,500
SALES (est): 30.5MM **Privately Held**
WEB: www.cypress-security.com
SIC: 7381 Security guard service

(P-16624)
CYPRESS SECURITY LLC
9926 Pioneer Blvd Ste 106, Santa Fe
Springs (90670-6243)
PHONE......................562 222-4197
Kes Narbutas, *CEO*
EMP: 80
SALES (corp-wide): 30.5MM **Privately Held**
SIC: 7381 Security guard service
PA: Cypress Security, Llc
478 Tehama St
San Francisco CA 94103
866 345-1277

(P-16625)
DAN CONNOLLY INC
Also Called: Armed Courier Service
855 Civic Center Dr Ste 5, Santa Clara
(95050-3962)
PHONE......................408 241-0910
Dan Connolly, *President*
EMP: 60
SQ FT: 6,000
SALES (est): 1.4MM **Privately Held**
WEB: www.armedcourierservice.com
SIC: 7381 Armored car services

(P-16626)
DANSK ENTERPRISES INC
Also Called: Nordic Security Services
3419 Via Lido 345, Newport Beach
(92663-3908)
PHONE......................714 751-0347
Peter Jensen, *President*
EMP: 100
SALES (est): 2.8MM **Privately Held**
WEB: www.nordicsec.com
SIC: 7381 Security guard service

(P-16627)
DELTA HAWKEYE SECURITY INC
7400 Shoreline Dr Ste 2, Stockton
(95219-5498)
PHONE......................209 957-3333
Dallas Faulkner, *Vice Pres*
Frank Passadore, *President*
Brian Millin, *Vice Pres*
EMP: 58
SQ FT: 2,000
SALES (est): 1.5MM
SALES (corp-wide): 87.6MM **Privately Held**
WEB: www.deltahawkeye.com
SIC: 7381 Security guard service
PA: The Grupe Company
3255 W March Ln Ste 400
Stockton CA 95219
209 473-6000

(P-16628)
DELTA ONE SECURITY INC
342 Acacia St, Fairfield (94533-3766)
PHONE......................707 425-9346
Robert Edwards, *President*
Betty Edwards, *CFO*
EMP: 60 EST: 2010
SALES (est): 1.4MM **Privately Held**
SIC: 7381 Security guard service

(P-16629)
DELTA PERSONNEL SERVICES INC
Also Called: Guardian Security Agency
1820 Galindo St Ste 3, Concord
(94520-2447)
PHONE......................925 356-3034
Judith Travers, *CEO*
Heather Travers, *Vice Pres*
EMP: 80
SQ FT: 4,300
SALES (est): 5.1MM **Privately Held**
SIC: 7381 Guard services

(P-16630)
DIEHARD SECURITY SOLUTIONS INC
1151 Harbor Bay Pkwy # 140, Alameda (94502-6591)
PHONE..................510 995-8450
Joseph Bando, *President*
Morgan Sorensen, *Office Mgr*
EMP: 107
SALES (est): 141.3K **Privately Held**
SIC: 7381 Guard services

(P-16631)
DLO ENTERPRISES INC
Also Called: Colt Security Services
41865 Boardwalk Ste 216, Palm Desert (92211-9033)
PHONE..................760 346-8033
Dennis L Oliver, *President*
EMP: 55
SALES (est): 1.1MM **Privately Held**
WEB: www.coltsecurity.com
SIC: 7381 Protective services, guard; security guard service

(P-16632)
DREW CHAIN SECURITY CORP
55 S Raymond Ave Ste 303, Alhambra (91801-7100)
PHONE..................626 457-8626
Kenneth Y Lee, *President*
Art Kasabyan, *COO*
EMP: 71
SQ FT: 800
SALES: 1MM **Privately Held**
WEB: www.alhambrahospital.com
SIC: 7381 Security guard service

(P-16633)
DRUM SECURITY SERVICE INC
4509 Callada Pl, Tarzana (91356-5101)
PHONE..................818 708-7914
Charles R Drum, *President*
EMP: 60
SALES (est): 947.1K **Privately Held**
SIC: 7381 Security guard service

(P-16634)
DUNBAR ARMORED INC
629 Whitney St, San Leandro (94577-1115)
PHONE..................510 569-7400
Ted Nguyen, *Manager*
EMP: 100
SALES (corp-wide): 3.3B **Publicly Held**
WEB: www.dunbararmored.com
SIC: 7381 Armored car services
HQ: Dunbar Armored, Inc.
50 Schilling Rd
Hunt Valley MD 21031
410 584-9800

(P-16635)
EAGLE SECURITY SERVICE INC
12903 S Normandie Ave, Gardena (90249-2123)
PHONE..................310 532-1626
Mohsen Kamel, *President*
EMP: 150
SQ FT: 5,000
SALES (est): 4.2MM **Privately Held**
SIC: 7381 Security guard service

(P-16636)
EASTSIDE GROUP CORPORATION
Also Called: Prudential Security Services
1830 W Olympic Blvd # 202, Los Angeles (90006-3734)
P.O. Box 531, Lynwood (90262-0531)
PHONE..................213 368-9777
Fernando Gonzales, *President*
Manny Martinez, *Vice Pres*
EMP: 125
SALES: 2.5MM **Privately Held**
SIC: 7381 Security guard service

(P-16637)
ELITE ENFRCMENT SEC SLTONS INC
29970 Technology Dr, Murrieta (92563-2645)
PHONE..................866 354-8308
Kevin Roncevich, *Branch Mgr*
EMP: 50

SALES (corp-wide): 5.6MM **Privately Held**
SIC: 7381 Security guard service
PA: Elite Enforcement Security Solutions Inc
1290 N Hancock St Ste 101
Anaheim CA 92807
866 354-8308

(P-16638)
ELITE SECURITY SERVICES INC
18006 Sky Park Cir # 205, Irvine (92614-6406)
P.O. Box 18073 (92623-8073)
PHONE..................949 222-2203
Betty Kaminski, *President*
Gene Kaminski, *Exec VP*
EMP: 450
SQ FT: 2,400
SALES (est): 5.2MM **Privately Held**
WEB: www.elitesecurityservices.net
SIC: 7381 7382 Guard services; security systems services

(P-16639)
ELITE SHOW SERVICES INC
2878 Camino Del Rio S # 260, San Diego (92108-3855)
PHONE..................619 574-1589
John Kontopuls, *President*
Gus Kontopuls, *Vice Pres*
Jim Polidan, *Branch Mgr*
Sally Hart, *Office Admin*
Karen Calderwood, *Human Res Mgr*
EMP: 3123
SALES (est): 75.2MM **Privately Held**
WEB: www.eliteshowservices.com
SIC: 7381 Security guard service

(P-16640)
EVENT GUARD SERVICES INC
1823 Business Center Dr, Duarte (91010-2902)
P.O. Box 26794, Los Angeles (90026-0794)
PHONE..................626 531-6772
Kelly Martin, *President*
Roman Vargas, *Social Dir*
EMP: 99
SALES (est): 2.1MM **Privately Held**
SIC: 7381 Security guard service

(P-16641)
EXECUSHELD PRTECTION GROUP LLC
301 Georgia St Ste 307, Vallejo (94590-5993)
PHONE..................707 439-6351
Michael Manibusan, *Principal*
Richard Berrios, *Principal*
Daniel Gonzalez, *Principal*
EMP: 75
SALES (est): 515K **Privately Held**
SIC: 7381 9221 Protective services, guard; security guard service; police protection

(P-16642)
EXECUSHIELD INC
4104 24th St Ste 501, San Francisco (94114-3615)
PHONE..................415 508-0825
Daniel Gonzalez, *President*
EMP: 55
SALES (est): 1.1MM **Privately Held**
WEB: www.execshield.com
SIC: 7381 Security guard service

(P-16643)
EXECUTIVE PROTECTION AGENCY K-
Also Called: Epak9
1175 N 2nd St Ste 102, El Cajon (92021-5033)
PHONE..................619 442-5771
Frank Whiteley, *President*
EMP: 50
SQ FT: 3,600
SALES (est): 993.4K **Privately Held**
SIC: 7381 Security guard service; guard services

(P-16644)
FIDELITY SECURITY SERVICES INC
25133 Avenue Tibbitts H, Valencia (91355-3494)
PHONE..................661 295-5007
Ahmadshah Ahmadi, *President*
Nazifa Ahmadi, *CFO*
EMP: 105
SQ FT: 1,000
SALES: 675K **Privately Held**
WEB: www.fidelitysecurityservices.com
SIC: 7381 Security guard service; guard services

(P-16645)
FIRST ALARM SEC & PATROL INC (PA)
Also Called: First Security Services
1731 Tech Dr Ste 800, San Jose (95110)
PHONE..................408 866-1111
Cal Horton, *President*
Jarl E Saal, *Chairman*
Teresa H Larkin, *Business Dir*
Vince Cardinale, *IT/INT Sup*
Omar Noory, *Opers Mgr*
EMP: 250
SALES (est): 43.5MM **Privately Held**
SIC: 7381 Security guard service

(P-16646)
FIRST INTERSTATE SECURITY INC
20548 Ventura Blvd # 118, Woodland Hills (91364-6225)
PHONE..................818 995-6664
Mike Ahmed, *President*
EMP: 210
SQ FT: 5,000
SALES (est): 3.4MM **Privately Held**
WEB: www.firstinterstateinc.com
SIC: 7381 Security guard service

(P-16647)
FIRSTCALL (PA)
Also Called: Steele Corp SEC Advisory Svcs
1 Sansome St Ste 3500, San Francisco (94104-4436)
PHONE..................415 781-4300
Kenneth Kurtz, *CEO*
EMP: 138
SQ FT: 5,000
SALES (est): 49.8MM **Privately Held**
SIC: 7381 8742 8748 Security guard service; management consulting services; agricultural consultant

(P-16648)
FPK SECURITY INC
Also Called: Fpk Investigaions
28348 Constellation Rd # 880, Valencia (91355-5097)
P.O. Box 55597 (91385-0597)
PHONE..................661 702-9091
Mark David, *CEO*
Robert Esquivel, *President*
Joe Madick, *Asst Director*
EMP: 365
SQ FT: 1,200
SALES (est): 8.9MM **Privately Held**
SIC: 7381 Private investigator

(P-16649)
FRASCO INC (PA)
Also Called: Frasco Investigative Services
215 W Alameda Ave, Burbank (91502-3060)
PHONE..................818 848-3888
John C Simmers, *President*
Jeff Davis, *President*
Laura Pfaffman, *CFO*
Todd Savar, *Officer*
Noelle Harling, *Vice Pres*
EMP: 65
SQ FT: 10,000
SALES (est): 20.6MM **Privately Held**
WEB: www.frasco.com
SIC: 7381 Private investigator

(P-16650)
FRESNO COUNTY PRIVATE SECURITY
2150 Tulare St, Fresno (93721-2103)
PHONE..................559 233-9800
Ronald Sawl, *President*

David McDonald, *Admin Mgr*
Robert Wilson, *Director*
EMP: 100
SALES (est): 2.2MM **Privately Held**
SIC: 7381 Security guard service

(P-16651)
G4S SECURE SOLUTIONS (USA)
4400 Ashe Rd Ste 206, Bakersfield (93313-2036)
PHONE..................661 834-3454
Thomas Robinson, *Branch Mgr*
EMP: 125
SALES (corp-wide): 10.3B **Privately Held**
SIC: 7381 Security guard service
HQ: G4s Secure Solutions (Usa) Inc.
1395 University Blvd
Jupiter FL 33458
561 622-5656

(P-16652)
G4S SECURE SOLUTIONS (USA)
4929 Wilshire Blvd # 601, Los Angeles (90010-3808)
PHONE..................323 938-9100
Yvonne Herod, *Manager*
Keith Boles, *General Mgr*
Yalda Assef, *Manager*
EMP: 300
SALES (corp-wide): 10.3B **Privately Held**
SIC: 7381 Security guard service
HQ: G4s Secure Solutions (Usa) Inc.
1395 University Blvd
Jupiter FL 33458
561 622-5656

(P-16653)
G4S SECURE SOLUTIONS (USA)
1450 Iowa Ave, Riverside (92507-0522)
PHONE..................951 341-3000
Richard McDale, *Manager*
Bob Schriener, *Business Mgr*
EMP: 300
SALES (corp-wide): 10.3B **Privately Held**
SIC: 7381 Security guard service
HQ: G4s Secure Solutions (Usa) Inc.
1395 University Blvd
Jupiter FL 33458
561 622-5656

(P-16654)
G4S SECURE SOLUTIONS (USA)
1 Annabel Ln Ste 208, San Ramon (94583-4360)
PHONE..................925 543-0008
EMP: 119
SALES (corp-wide): 11.8B **Privately Held**
SIC: 7381
HQ: G4s Secure Solutions (Usa) Inc
1395 University Blvd
Jupiter FL 33458
561 622-5656

(P-16655)
G4S SECURE SOLUTIONS USA INC
5030 Camino De La Siesta # 404, San Diego (92108-3120)
PHONE..................619 295-2394
Steven Fisher, *Systems Staff*
Camille Bangayan, *Administration*
Erin Fujioka, *Business Mgr*
EMP: 250
SQ FT: 1,500
SALES (corp-wide): 10.3B **Privately Held**
SIC: 7381 Security guard service
HQ: G4s Secure Solutions (Usa) Inc.
1395 University Blvd
Jupiter FL 33458
561 622-5656

(P-16656)
G4S SECURE SOLUTIONS USA INC
200 Pine St Fl 7, San Francisco (94104-2707)
PHONE..................415 591-0780
Stanley Lee, *Branch Mgr*
Kim Whitworth, *Business Mgr*
EMP: 119
SALES (corp-wide): 10.3B **Privately Held**
SIC: 7381 Security guard service
HQ: G4s Secure Solutions (Usa) Inc.
1395 University Blvd
Jupiter FL 33458
561 622-5656

(P-16657)
G4S SECURE SOLUTIONS USA INC
2300 E Katella Ave # 150, Anaheim (92806-6061)
PHONE.................714 939-4900
John Mc Elhaney, *Manager*
Brandon Joffe, *Manager*
EMP: 119
SALES (corp-wide): 10.3B **Privately Held**
SIC: 7381 Security guard service
HQ: G4s Secure Solutions (Usa) Inc.
1395 University Blvd
Jupiter FL 33458
561 622-5656

(P-16658)
G4S SECURE SOLUTIONS USA INC
5655 Lindero Canyon Rd # 504, Westlake Village (91362-4016)
PHONE.................818 889-1113
Yvonne Herrod, *Manager*
Quintin Ridley, *Manager*
EMP: 119
SALES (corp-wide): 10.3B **Privately Held**
SIC: 7381 Security guard service
HQ: G4s Secure Solutions (Usa) Inc.
1395 University Blvd
Jupiter FL 33458
561 622-5656

(P-16659)
GARDA CL TECHNICAL SVCS INC
15640 Roxford St, Sylmar (91342-1265)
PHONE.................818 362-7011
Ken Krogman, *Manager*
EMP: 55 **Privately Held**
WEB: www.gocashlink.com
SIC: 7381 Armored car services
HQ: Garda Cl Technical Services, Inc.
700 S Federal Hwy Ste 300
Boca Raton FL 33432

(P-16660)
GARDA CL WEST INC
372 S Arrowhead Ave, San Bernardino (92408-1307)
PHONE.................909 574-2676
Jim Chadwick, *Branch Mgr*
EMP: 50 **Privately Held**
SIC: 7381 Armored car services
HQ: Garda Cl West, Inc.
1612 W Pico Blvd
Los Angeles CA 90015
213 383-3611

(P-16661)
GARDA CL WEST INC (DH)
Also Called: Gcl W
1612 W Pico Blvd, Los Angeles (90015-2410)
PHONE.................213 383-3611
Stephan Cretier, *President*
Chris W Jamroz, *President*
Sean Salazar, *Assistant*
EMP: 375
SQ FT: 25,000
SALES (est): 53.8MM **Privately Held**
SIC: 7381 Armored car services

(P-16662)
GARDA CL WEST INC
301 N Lake Ave Ste 600, Pasadena (91101-5129)
PHONE.................800 883-8305
Duncan Longworth, *Branch Mgr*
Debbie Ray, *Vice Pres*
Hugues Trottier, *Vice Pres*
Gonzalo Aguirre, *District Mgr*
Ken Rose, *Human Res Mgr*
EMP: 70
SALES (corp-wide): 16.5MM **Privately Held**
SIC: 7381 Armored car services; security guard service
PA: Garda Cl West Inc
20325 E Walnut Dr N
Walnut CA 91789
323 668-2712

(P-16663)
GATEWAY SECURITY INC
5757 W Century Blvd, Los Angeles (90045-6401)
PHONE.................310 410-0790
Stephan Glassman, *Branch Mgr*
EMP: 818
SALES (corp-wide): 100.4MM **Privately Held**
SIC: 7381 Security guard service
PA: Gateway Security Inc.
604 Market St 608
Newark NJ 07105
973 465-8006

(P-16664)
GEIL ENTERPRISES INC (PA)
Also Called: CIS Security
1945 N Helm Ave Ste 102, Fresno (93727-1670)
PHONE.................559 495-3000
Sam Geil, *CEO*
Ryan Geil, *President*
Kim Evans, *Principal*
EMP: 107
SQ FT: 10,000
SALES (est): 36.4MM **Privately Held**
WEB: www.geilenterprises.com
SIC: 7381 7349 Protective services, guard; janitorial service, contract basis; building maintenance, except repairs

(P-16665)
GREEN VALLEY SECURITY INC
6049 Douglas Blvd Ste 28, Granite Bay (95746-6275)
PHONE.................916 797-4058
Anthony Urbancic, *President*
EMP: 60
SQ FT: 300
SALES (est): 1.2MM **Privately Held**
SIC: 7381 Security guard service

(P-16666)
GS1 GROUP INC
70 S Lake Ave Ste 945, Pasadena (91101-4991)
PHONE.................626 510-6384
Michael Vincent Severo, *CEO*
Ernesto Garcia, *President*
EMP: 68 EST: 2011
SALES: 1.2MM **Privately Held**
SIC: 7381 Security guard service; private investigator

(P-16667)
GUARD MANAGEMENT INC
Also Called: G M I
8001 Vickers St, San Diego (92111-1917)
PHONE.................858 279-8282
Larry Abrams, *President*
Bryan Allen, *Administration*
Melanie Bamba, *Business Mgr*
Heather Collins, *Business Mgr*
Katy Brant, *Human Res Dir*
EMP: 510
SALES (est): 11.1MM **Privately Held**
SIC: 7381 Security guard service

(P-16668)
GUARD-SYSTEMS INC (PA)
1190 Monterey Pass Rd, Monterey Park (91754-3615)
PHONE.................626 443-0031
Theodore Haas, *CEO*
Guillermo Amador, *Vice Pres*
Leo Austin, *Vice Pres*
Eric Macias, *Office Admin*
Rosie Rios, *Manager*
EMP: 1150
SQ FT: 8,000
SALES (est): 18.4MM **Privately Held**
WEB: www.guardsystemsinc.com
SIC: 7381 Security guard service; guard services

(P-16669)
GUARD-SYSTEMS INC
1910 S Archibald Ave M2, Ontario (91761-8502)
PHONE.................909 947-5400
Patrick Crawford, *Manager*
EMP: 300

SALES (corp-wide): 18.4MM **Privately Held**
WEB: www.guardsystemsinc.com
SIC: 7381 Protective services, guard; guard services; security guard service
PA: Guard-Systems, Inc.
1190 Monterey Pass Rd
Monterey Park CA 91754
626 443-0031

(P-16670)
GUARD-SYSTEMS INC
1190 Monterey Pass Rd, Monterey Park (91754-3615)
PHONE.................323 881-6711
Theodore Haas, *Branch Mgr*
EMP: 300
SALES (est): 2MM
SALES (corp-wide): 18.4MM **Privately Held**
WEB: www.guardsystemsinc.com
SIC: 7381 Security guard service
PA: Guard-Systems, Inc.
1190 Monterey Pass Rd
Monterey Park CA 91754
626 443-0031

(P-16671)
GUARD-SYSTEMS INC
Also Called: Guard Systems District 1
1190 Monterey Pass Rd, Monterey Park (91754-3615)
PHONE.................323 881-6715
Theodore Haas, *Owner*
EMP: 300
SALES (est): 2MM
SALES (corp-wide): 18.4MM **Privately Held**
WEB: www.guardsystemsinc.com
SIC: 7381 Security guard service
PA: Guard-Systems, Inc.
1190 Monterey Pass Rd
Monterey Park CA 91754
626 443-0031

(P-16672)
GUARDCO SECURITY SERVICES
1360 W 18th St, Merced (95340-4402)
PHONE.................209 723-4273
David Williams, *Owner*
John Lovett, *Human Res Dir*
EMP: 71
SQ FT: 1,000
SALES: 1.7MM **Privately Held**
WEB: www.guardcosecurity.com
SIC: 7381 Security guard service

(P-16673)
GUARDIAN EAGLE SECURITY INC
11400 W Olympic Blvd Fl 2, Los Angeles (90064-1579)
PHONE.................888 990-0002
Hassan M Galal, *CEO*
Fadwa Galal, *President*
Hassan Galal, *CEO*
Fathi M Galal, *Vice Pres*
Fathi Galal, *Vice Pres*
EMP: 500
SQ FT: 3,000
SALES (est): 8.1MM **Privately Held**
WEB: www.ges.net
SIC: 7381 Security guard service

(P-16674)
GUARDIAN NATIONAL INC
Also Called: Guardian National Security
20361 Prairie St Ste 1, Chatsworth (91311-8100)
PHONE.................800 700-1467
Mohammad Ramzan, *President*
Sarah Suleman, *Technology*
EMP: 50
SALES (est): 1.2MM **Privately Held**
SIC: 7381 Security guard service

(P-16675)
GUARDNOW INC (PA)
18663 Ventura Blvd # 217, Tarzana (91356-4100)
P.O. Box 67, Manhattan Beach (90267-0067)
PHONE.................877 482-7366
Mike Kator, *President*
EMP: 50 EST: 2011
SQ FT: 115

SALES: 5MM **Privately Held**
SIC: 7381 Security guard service

(P-16676)
GUARDSMARK LLC
4713 1st St Ste 215, Pleasanton (94566-7363)
PHONE.................925 484-4412
Charles Parker, *Manager*
EMP: 350
SALES (corp-wide): 741.7MM **Privately Held**
WEB: www.guardsmark.com
SIC: 7381 Security guard service
HQ: Guardsmark, Llc
1551 N Tustin Ave Ste 650
Santa Ana CA 92705
714 619-9700

(P-16677)
GUARDSMARK LLC
1225 W 190th St Ste 280, Gardena (90248-4305)
PHONE.................310 522-9603
Rebecca Wells, *Manager*
EMP: 60
SALES (corp-wide): 741.7MM **Privately Held**
WEB: www.guardsmark.com
SIC: 7381
HQ: Guardsmark, Llc
1551 N Tustin Ave Ste 650
Santa Ana CA 92705
714 619-9700

(P-16678)
GUARDSMARK LLC
3000 S Robertson Blvd # 150, Los Angeles (90034-3144)
PHONE.................310 287-3103
Rebekah Wells, *Principal*
EMP: 111
SALES (corp-wide): 741.7MM **Privately Held**
WEB: www.guardsmark.com
SIC: 7381 Security guard service
HQ: Guardsmark, Llc
1551 N Tustin Ave Ste 650
Santa Ana CA 92705
714 619-9700

(P-16679)
GUARDSMARK LLC (DH)
1551 N Tustin Ave Ste 650, Santa Ana (92705-8664)
PHONE.................714 619-9700
Steven S Jones, *CEO*
EMP: 131
SQ FT: 32,107
SALES (est): 276.3MM
SALES (corp-wide): 741.7MM **Privately Held**
WEB: www.guardsmark.com
SIC: 7381 8742 2721 Security guard service; private investigator; industry specialist consultants; periodicals: publishing only
HQ: Universal Protection Service, Lp
1551 N Tustin Ave Ste 650
Santa Ana CA 92705
714 619-9700

(P-16680)
GUARDSMARK LLC
350 Sansome St, San Francisco (94104-1304)
PHONE.................415 956-6070
Coley Buellesfeld, *Vice Pres*
EMP: 300
SALES (corp-wide): 741.7MM **Privately Held**
WEB: www.guardsmark.com
SIC: 7381 Security guard service
HQ: Guardsmark, Llc
1551 N Tustin Ave Ste 650
Santa Ana CA 92705
714 619-9700

(P-16681)
GUARDSMARK LLC
505 Alexis Ct, NAPA (94558-7526)
PHONE.................415 898-9022
Roy Sheets, *Branch Mgr*
William Kinane, *Vice Pres*
EMP: 112

SALES (corp-wide): 741.7MM **Privately Held**
SIC: **7381** Security guard service
HQ: Guardsmark, Llc
1551 N Tustin Ave Ste 650
Santa Ana CA 92705
714 619-9700

(P-16682)
GUARDSMARK LLC
101 S 1st St Ste 408, Burbank
(91502-1938)
PHONE.................................818 841-0288
Bob Carpenter, *Manager*
Jonathan Escalante, *Branch Mgr*
EMP: 118
SALES (corp-wide): 741.7MM **Privately Held**
WEB: www.guardsmark.com
SIC: **7381 7382** Security guard service;
security systems services
HQ: Guardsmark, Llc
1551 N Tustin Ave Ste 650
Santa Ana CA 92705
714 619-9700

(P-16683)
GUARDSMARK LLC
100 Hegenberger Rd # 130, Oakland
(94621-1447)
PHONE.................................510 562-7606
Ben Atkins, *Manager*
EMP: 250
SALES (corp-wide): 741.7MM **Privately Held**
WEB: www.guardsmark.com
SIC: **7381** Security guard service; private
investigator
HQ: Guardsmark, Llc
1551 N Tustin Ave Ste 650
Santa Ana CA 92705
714 619-9700

(P-16684)
GUARDSMARK LLC
4970 El Camino Real, Los Altos
(94022-1460)
PHONE.................................800 238-5878
Rania Terry, *Manager*
EMP: 118
SALES (corp-wide): 741.7MM **Privately Held**
SIC: **7381** Security guard service
HQ: Universal Protection Service, Lp
1551 N Tustin Ave Ste 650
Santa Ana CA 92705
714 619-9700

(P-16685)
GUARDSMARK LLC
5300 Lennox Ave Ste 102, Bakersfield
(93309-1662)
PHONE.................................661 325-5906
EMP: 111
SALES (corp-wide): 928.7MM **Privately Held**
SIC: **7381**
HQ: Guardsmark, Llc
6363 Poplar Ave Ste 300
Memphis TN 92705
901 761-2288

(P-16686)
GUARDSMARK LLC
5095 Murphy Canyon Rd # 301, San Diego
(92123-4346)
PHONE.................................858 499-0025
Ira Lipman, *Branch Mgr*
EMP: 111
SALES (corp-wide): 741.7MM **Privately Held**
WEB: www.guardsmark.com
SIC: **7381** Security guard service
HQ: Guardsmark, Llc
1551 N Tustin Ave Ste 650
Santa Ana CA 92705
714 619-9700

(P-16687)
GUARDSMARK LLC
600 W Shaw Ave Ste 200, Fresno
(93704-2420)
PHONE.................................559 243-1217
Ricardo Franco, *Branch Mgr*
EMP: 111

SALES (corp-wide): 741.7MM **Privately Held**
WEB: www.guardsmark.com
SIC: **7381** Security guard service
HQ: Guardsmark, Llc
1551 N Tustin Ave Ste 650
Santa Ana CA 92705
714 619-9700

(P-16688)
GUARDSMARK LLC
101 S 1st St Ste 408, Burbank
(91502-1938)
PHONE.................................818 841-0288
Scott Carpenter, *Manager*
EMP: 111
SALES (corp-wide): 741.7MM **Privately Held**
WEB: www.guardsmark.com
SIC: **7381** Security guard service
HQ: Guardsmark, Llc
1551 N Tustin Ave Ste 650
Santa Ana CA 92705
714 619-9700

(P-16689)
GUARDSMARK LLC
30 E San Joaquin St # 204, Salinas
(93901-2947)
PHONE.................................831 769-8981
Ira Litman,
EMP: 111
SALES (corp-wide): 741.7MM **Privately Held**
WEB: www.guardsmark.com
SIC: **7381** Security guard service
HQ: Guardsmark, Llc
1551 N Tustin Ave Ste 650
Santa Ana CA 92705
714 619-9700

(P-16690)
GUARDSMARK LLC
533 Airport Blvd Ste 303, Burlingame
(94010-2040)
PHONE.................................650 685-2400
David Connor, *Manager*
EMP: 111
SALES (corp-wide): 741.7MM **Privately Held**
WEB: www.guardsmark.com
SIC: **7381** Security guard service
HQ: Guardsmark, Llc
1551 N Tustin Ave Ste 650
Santa Ana CA 92705
714 619-9700

(P-16691)
GUARDSMARK LLC
1601 Bayshore Hwy Ste 350, Burlingame
(94010-1522)
PHONE.................................650 652-9130
EMP: 145
SALES (corp-wide): 928.7MM **Privately Held**
SIC: **7381**
HQ: Guardsmark, Llc
6363 Poplar Ave Ste 300
Memphis TN 92705
901 761-2288

(P-16692)
GUARDSMARK LLC
101 S 1st St Ste 408, Burbank
(91502-1938)
PHONE.................................818 841-0288
Seth Rapaport, *Manager*
EMP: 175
SALES (corp-wide): 741.7MM **Privately Held**
WEB: www.guardsmark.com
SIC: **7381** Security guard service
HQ: Guardsmark, Llc
1551 N Tustin Ave Ste 650
Santa Ana CA 92705
714 619-9700

(P-16693)
GUARDSMARK LLC
2900 Adams St Ste C10a, Riverside
(92504-8315)
PHONE.................................909 989-5345
Gary Parks, *Manager*
Larry Krininger, *Manager*
EMP: 295

SALES (corp-wide): 741.7MM **Privately Held**
WEB: www.guardsmark.com
SIC: **7381 7382** Security guard service;
security systems services
HQ: Guardsmark, Llc
1551 N Tustin Ave Ste 650
Santa Ana CA 92705
714 619-9700

(P-16694)
HAL-MAR-JAC ENTERPRISES
Also Called: McCoy's Patrol Service
1044 Potrero Cir, Suisun City (94585-4139)
PHONE.................................415 467-1470
Harold McCoy, *President*
Opal McCoy, *Admin Sec*
EMP: 110
SALES (est): 2.3MM **Privately Held**
SIC: **7381**

(P-16695)
HARVEST V CITIZENS PATROL
25098 Avenida Valencia, Homeland
(92548-9318)
P.O. Box 2255 (92548-2255)
PHONE.................................951 926-9763
Robert Gibbons, *Chairman*
Laura Daniels, *Treasurer*
Winn Barker, *Vice Pres*
John Lauda, *Principal*
Roy Yost, *Principal*
EMP: 127
SALES (est): 1.5MM **Privately Held**
SIC: **7381** Protective services, guard

(P-16696)
HIGHCOM SECURITY SERVICES
1900 Webster St Ste B, Oakland
(94612-2946)
PHONE.................................510 893-7600
Sammy Joselewitz, *President*
EMP: 60
SALES (est): 1.9MM **Privately Held**
WEB: www.highcomsecurityservices.com
SIC: **7381 8742** Security guard service;
management consulting services

(P-16697)
HMI ASSOCIATES INC
6800 Owensmouth Ave # 330, Canoga Park
(91303-3159)
PHONE.................................818 887-6800
Andrew Heider, *President*
Michael Moen, *Vice Pres*
EMP: 200
SALES (est): 1.8MM **Privately Held**
SIC: **7381**

(P-16698)
HORSEMEN INC
16911 Algonquin St, Huntington Beach
(92649-3812)
PHONE.................................714 847-4243
Patrick Carroll, *President*
Matt Carmichael, *Opers Mgr*
Andy Crimmins, *Opers Staff*
Cheryl Gall, *Consultant*
EMP: 100 EST: 1995
SALES (est): 3.9MM **Privately Held**
WEB: www.horsemeninc.com
SIC: **7381** Private investigator

(P-16699)
HYLTON SECURITY INC
1015 2nd St Fl 2, Sacramento
(95814-3255)
PHONE.................................916 442-1000
David J Hylton, *President*
Mindy A Hylton, *Senior VP*
EMP: 107
SQ FT: 1,500
SALES: 250K **Privately Held**
WEB: www.hyltonsecurity.com
SIC: **7381** Security guard service

(P-16700)
INTELLIGUARD SECURITY SERVICES
Also Called: Safety Dynamics
4663 Harbord Dr, Oakland (94618-2210)
PHONE.................................510 547-7656
John Weir, *President*
EMP: 130
SALES (est): 3.6MM **Privately Held**
SIC: **7381** Security guard service

(P-16701)
INTER-CON INVESTIGATORS INC
Also Called: Inter Con Systems
210 S De Lacey Ave, Pasadena
(91105-2048)
PHONE.................................626 535-2200
Enrique Hernandez Jr, *President*
Roland Hernandez, *Vice Pres*
EMP: 100
SQ FT: 17,000
SALES (est): 2.5MM **Privately Held**
SIC: **7381** Security guard service

(P-16702)
INTER-CON SECURITY SYSTEMS INC (PA)
210 S De Lacey Ave # 200, Pasadena
(91105-2048)
PHONE.................................626 535-2200
Enrique Hernandez Jr, *Ch of Bd*
Irene Gonzalez, *Partner*
Claudia Selene Mata, *COO*
Roland A Hernandez, *Vice Pres*
Adriana Vicente, *Admin Asst*
EMP: 120
SQ FT: 17,000
SALES (est): 421.9MM **Privately Held**
SIC: **7381** Security guard service

(P-16703)
INTERSTATE PROTECTIVE SERVICES
Also Called: Ips
20548 Ventura Blvd # 118, Woodland Hills
(91364-6225)
PHONE.................................818 995-6664
Nabila Helal, *CEO*
Michael Ahmed, *President*
Wil Hanna, *Principal*
Nancy Saenz, *Principal*
EMP: 99
SQ FT: 5,100
SALES: 4.8MM **Privately Held**
SIC: **7381** Security guard service

(P-16704)
IRONCLAD SECURITY SERVICES INC
3561 Homestead Rd Ste 600, Santa Clara
(95051-5161)
PHONE.................................408 773-2800
Bruce McAllister, *President*
Aner Medar, *Opers Staff*
EMP: 75
SQ FT: 4,000
SALES (est): 1MM **Privately Held**
SIC: **7381 7389** Protective services,
guard; security guard service; personal in-
vestigation service

(P-16705)
IUNLIMITED INCORPORATED
7801 Folsom Blvd Ste 203, Sacramento
(95826-2620)
PHONE.................................916 218-6198
Todd M Tano, *CEO*
Keith Jacobs, *President*
Jeff Walters, *Officer*
Jose Torres, *Regional Mgr*
Erin Frame, *Department Mgr*
EMP: 115
SALES: 8MM **Privately Held**
SIC: **7381** Private investigator

(P-16706)
J & E PRIVATE SECURITY CORP
3227 Producer Way Ste 110, Pomona
(91768-3919)
PHONE.................................909 594-1111
Megan Hsu, *Admin Sec*
Edwin Inocencio, *CFO*
EMP: 60
SALES: 1.7MM **Privately Held**
SIC: **7381** Guard services

(P-16707)
J WATERS INC
Also Called: Achates Security Agency
75 San Miguel Ave Ste 5, Salinas
(93901-3059)
P.O. Box 418 (93902-0418)
PHONE.................................831 424-1946
Mary Waters, *President*
Jeffrey S Waters, *Vice Pres*

EMP: 50
SALES (est): 989.5K Privately Held
WEB: www.achatessecurity.com
SIC: 7381 Security guard service

(P-16708)
JONES BOLD SECURITY INC
Also Called: Jbsprotection
7520 Sleepy Creek Ave, Fontana
(92336-2192)
PHONE.....................562 316-6552
Brandon Jones, Principal
EMP: 100
SALES (est): 393.1K Privately Held
SIC: 7381 Guard services

(P-16709)
K TECH SECURITY & PROTECT SVC
665 Alvin St, San Diego (92114-1817)
PHONE.....................619 858-5832
Kelly J Steppe, Owner
EMP: 127
SALES (est): 2.9MM Privately Held
WEB: www.k-techsecurity.com
SIC: 7381 Security guard service

(P-16710)
KAISER MED SECURITY SERVICES
2241 Geary Blvd, San Francisco
(94115-3415)
PHONE.....................415 833-3683
Dennis Hyams, Director
EMP: 100
SALES (est): 1.1MM Privately Held
SIC: 7381 Security guard service

(P-16711)
KING SECURITY SERVICES INC
1159 7th St, Novato (94945-2207)
PHONE.....................415 556-5464
Kimberly King, President
Jolanta King, CFO
Louis Siracusa, Vice Pres
EMP: 528
SQ FT: 2,000
SALES (est): 13.1MM Privately Held
WEB: www.kingsecurity.com
SIC: 7381 Security guard service; private investigator

(P-16712)
KYSMET SECURITY & PATROL INC
21 W Laurel Dr Ste 49, Salinas
(93906-3498)
PHONE.....................831 710-2425
Esteban Garcia, CEO
EMP: 50 EST: 2015
SALES (est): 1.1MM Privately Held
SIC: 7381 Detective & armored car services

(P-16713)
LAKE TAHOE SECRET WITNESS
1051 Al Tahoe Blvd, South Lake Tahoe
(96150-4502)
P.O. Box 14282 (96151-4282)
PHONE.....................530 541-6800
Pam Sullivan, Owner
EMP: 90 EST: 1997
SALES (est): 952.3K Privately Held
SIC: 7381 Detective services

(P-16714)
LANDMARK EVENT STAFFING
4790 Irvine Blvd Ste 105, Irvine
(92620-1998)
PHONE.....................714 293-4248
Peter Kranske, President
EMP: 916 Privately Held
SIC: 7381 Security guard service
PA: Landmark Event Staffing Services, Inc.
4131 Harbor Walk Dr
Fort Collins CO 80525

(P-16715)
LANTZ SECURITY SYSTEMS INC
101 N Westlake Blvd # 200, Westlake Village (91362-3753)
PHONE.....................805 496-5775
Terry Oestreich, Manager
EMP: 300 Privately Held

WEB: www.lantzsecurity.com
SIC: 7381 7382 Security guard service; security systems services
PA: Lantz Security Systems Inc
43440 Sahuayo St
Lancaster CA 93535

(P-16716)
LANTZ SECURITY SYSTEMS INC (PA)
43440 Sahuayo St, Lancaster
(93535-4659)
PHONE.....................661 949-3565
Jack E Lantz, President
Jose Reyes, Vice Pres
Damon Lantz, Marketing Staff
EMP: 60
SQ FT: 2,100
SALES (est): 12.9MM Privately Held
WEB: www.lantzsecurity.com
SIC: 7381 Security guard service

(P-16717)
LEGION CORPORATION
784 Geary St, San Francisco (94109-7302)
PHONE.....................800 750-0062
Joseph Shelley, CEO
Francois De La Roche, COO
EMP: 72
SALES (est): 1MM Privately Held
SIC: 7381 Security guard service

(P-16718)
LEGIONS PROTECTIVE SVCS LLC
17201 S Figueroa St, Gardena
(90248-3022)
PHONE.....................310 819-8881
Gregorio Campos, CEO
Armando Ojeda Jr, Vice Pres
EMP: 50
SQ FT: 1,000
SALES (est): 366.9K Privately Held
SIC: 7381 Security guard service

(P-16719)
LEVEL 9 SECURITY SERVICES
9020 Slauson Ave Ste 206, Pico Rivera
(90660-4578)
PHONE.....................562 949-7180
Jose Tellez, Owner
EMP: 50
SALES (est): 999.6K Privately Held
SIC: 7381 Security guard service

(P-16720)
LOCATOR SERVICES INC
Also Called: Able Patrol & Guard
4616 Mission Gorge Pl, San Diego
(92120-4133)
PHONE.....................619 229-6100
George Grauer,
Diane G Edwards, Vice Pres
George Grauer Jr, Vice Pres
Deborah L Kopki, Vice Pres
Christine Lowe, Admin Asst
EMP: 120
SQ FT: 4,500
SALES: 1.9MM Privately Held
WEB: www.ablepatrolandguard.com
SIC: 7381 Security guard service

(P-16721)
LOOMIS ARMORED US INC
897 Wrigley Way, Milpitas (95035-5407)
PHONE.....................408 273-1101
Ted Crane, General Mgr
EMP: 90
SALES (corp-wide): 2B Privately Held
WEB: www.loomisfargo.com
SIC: 7381 Armored car services
HQ: Loomis Armored Us, Llc
2500 Citywest Blvd # 2300
Houston TX 77042
713 435-6700

(P-16722)
LOOMIS ARMORED US LLC
3555 Aero Ct, San Diego (92123-1710)
PHONE.....................619 232-5106
Tim Bong, Manager
EMP: 70
SALES (corp-wide): 2B Privately Held
WEB: www.loomisfargo.com
SIC: 7381 Armored car services

HQ: Loomis Armored Us, Llc
2500 Citywest Blvd # 2300
Houston TX 77042
713 435-6700

(P-16723)
LOOMIS ARMORED US LLC
315 12th St, Sacramento (95814-0900)
PHONE.....................916 441-1091
Daryl Balko, General Mgr
EMP: 70
SALES (corp-wide): 2B Privately Held
WEB: www.loomisfargo.com
SIC: 7381 Armored car services
HQ: Loomis Armored Us, Llc
2500 Citywest Blvd # 2300
Houston TX 77042
713 435-6700

(P-16724)
LYONS SECURITY SERVICE INC
655 University Ave # 240, Sacramento
(95825-6707)
PHONE.....................916 925-9667
Robin Cheatam, Branch Mgr
EMP: 82 Privately Held
SIC: 7381 Protective services, guard
PA: Lyons Security Service, Inc.
2582 N Santiago Blvd
Orange CA 92867

(P-16725)
M & S SECURITY SERVICES INC
Also Called: Westside Security Patrol
2900 L St, Bakersfield (93301-2351)
PHONE.....................661 397-9616
Marvin Fuller Jr, President
Steve Fuller, President
Darlene Fuller, Corp Secy
Jimmy Watters, Executive
EMP: 100
SQ FT: 3,000
SALES (est): 3.4MM Privately Held
WEB: www.mssecurityservices.com
SIC: 7381 7382 1731 Protective services, guard; security systems services; burglar alarm maintenance & monitoring; fire detection & burglar alarm systems specialization

(P-16726)
MADERA PRIVATE SECURITY PATROL
910 W Yosemite Ave, Madera
(93637-4555)
PHONE.....................559 662-1546
Timothy Supple, Partner
Michael Gonzalez, Partner
Rebecca Supple, Partner
Rebecca Davis-Supple, Office Mgr
EMP: 78
SALES (est): 1.8MM Privately Held
WEB: www.maderaprivatesecurity.com
SIC: 7381 Protective services, guard; security guard service

(P-16727)
MAGNUS SECURITY
2667 Camino Del Rio S, San Diego
(92108-3707)
PHONE.....................619 546-7789
Marques Oliver, Principal
Marcus Oliver, Owner
EMP: 50 EST: 2013
SALES (est): 228.7K Privately Held
SIC: 7381 Security guard service

(P-16728)
MASTER LIGHTNING SEC SOLUTIONS
545 N Mountain Ave # 207, Upland
(91786-5055)
PHONE.....................310 419-2915
Peter Suaez, Principal
EMP: 70
SALES (est): 2MM Privately Held
SIC: 7381 Security guard service

(P-16729)
MAZAR CORP
Also Called: Gladiator Security Services
3200 E Guasti Rd Ste 100, Ontario
(91761-8661)
PHONE.....................909 292-8269
Mukhtar Ahmad Peerzay, President

Hares Kabir, CFO
Lamonte Sanders, Vice Pres
EMP: 62
SALES (est): 1.1MM Privately Held
SIC: 7381 Armored car services; security guard service

(P-16730)
MEMON AAMIR
Also Called: American Hrtg Protection Svcs
20832 Roscoe Blvd Ste 207, Winnetka
(91306-2058)
PHONE.....................818 339-8810
Aamir Memon, Owner
EMP: 50
SQ FT: 500
SALES (est): 887K Privately Held
SIC: 7381 Security guard service

(P-16731)
METROPOLITAN DST PRIVATE SEC
44262 Division St Ste A, Lancaster
(93535-3548)
PHONE.....................661 942-3999
Frederick Porras, President
EMP: 93
SQ FT: 1,200
SALES (est): 696.5K Privately Held
SIC: 7381 Security guard service

(P-16732)
MICHAEL MCCARTHY
Also Called: Loyal Svc Unt Spec Team
3233 E Broadway, Long Beach
(90803-5817)
PHONE.....................310 800-5367
Michael McCarthy, Owner
EMP: 50
SQ FT: 1,500
SALES (est): 292.8K Privately Held
SIC: 7381 4119 7361 Security guard service; local passenger transportation; employment agencies

(P-16733)
MISSION SECURITY AND PATROL
27 W Anapamu St Ste 141, Santa Barbara
(93101-3107)
PHONE.....................805 899-3039
Marcu Abandis, Owner
Marcus Abundis, President
Brian Fairrington, Director
EMP: 100
SALES (est): 2.1MM Privately Held
SIC: 7381 6411 Security guard service; patrol services, insurance

(P-16734)
MONUMENT SECURITY INC
24301 Suthland Dr Ste 312, Hayward
(94545)
PHONE.....................510 430-3540
Uatisone Nasaniai, Manager
EMP: 150 Privately Held
SIC: 7381
PA: Monument Security, Inc.
4926 43rd St Ste 10
Mcclellan CA 95652

(P-16735)
MONUMENT SECURITY INC (PA)
4926 43rd St Ste 10, McClellan
(95652-2618)
P.O. Box 399, North Highlands (95660-0399)
PHONE.....................916 564-4234
Scott McDonald, President
EMP: 150
SQ FT: 2,500
SALES (est): 36.3MM Privately Held
SIC: 7381 Security guard service

(P-16736)
MULHOLLAND SEC & PATROL INC
Also Called: Centurion Group, The
11454 San Vicente Blvd Fl, Los Angeles
(90049-6208)
PHONE.....................818 755-0202
David Rosenberg, President
Daniel Campbell, Vice Pres
Steven Lemmer, Vice Pres

Yael Sirota, *Executive*
EMP: 350
SQ FT: 2,500
SALES (est) 8.5MM **Privately Held**
WEB: www.mulhollandsecurity.com
SIC: 7381 Protective services, guard; security guard service

(P-16737)
NATIONAL PUBLIC SAFETY
490 N Magnolia Ave, El Cajon
(92020-3607)
P.O. Box 1136, Lemon Grove (91946-1136)
PHONE...................................619 401-9431
Natasha Frost, *CEO*
Douglas Frost, *President*
EMP: 56
SALES (est): 1.5MM **Privately Held**
SIC: 7381 Security guard service

(P-16738)
NATIONAL SECURITY INDUSTRIES
Also Called: National Security Santa Cruz
501 Mission St Ste 1a, Santa Cruz
(95060-3661)
PHONE...................................831 425-2052
James Clarke,
EMP: 300
SALES (est): 3.2MM **Privately Held**
SIC: 7381 Security guard service

(P-16739)
NATIONWIDE GUARD SERVICES INC
9327 Fairway View Pl # 200, Rancho Cucamonga (91730-0969)
PHONE...................................909 608-1112
John Woolen, *President*
Veronica Kemp, *Administration*
Johnathan Sullivan, *Planning*
Mari Bennett, *Director*
EMP: 56
SALES (est): 1.1MM **Privately Held**
WEB: www.nationwideguardservices.com
SIC: 7381 Security guard service

(P-16740)
NEW-JACK INDUSTRIES INC
2613 Manhattan Beach Blvd # 100, Redondo Beach (90278-1604)
PHONE...................................310 297-3605
W Tom Bragg, *President*
Ramon Rodriguez, *Vice Pres*
EMP: 400
SQ FT: 5,000
SALES (est): 4.1MM **Privately Held**
SIC: 7381 Security guard service

(P-16741)
NORTH AMERICAN SECURITY INC
550 E Carson Plaza Dr # 222, Carson
(90746-7371)
PHONE...................................310 630-4840
Arthur L Lopez, *President*
Kenneth Hillman, *Vice Pres*
Ken Hillman, *Technology*
Karen Savino, *Human Res Mgr*
Isidro Lopez, *Director*
EMP: 420
SQ FT: 1,000
SALES: 12.8MM **Privately Held**
SIC: 7381 Security guard service

(P-16742)
NORTH AMRCN SEC INVSTGTONS INC
550 E Carson Plaza Dr, Carson
(90746-3229)
PHONE...................................323 634-1911
Arthur Lopez, *CEO*
EMP: 500
SQ FT: 6,000
SALES (est): 5.2MM **Privately Held**
SIC: 7381 Private investigator

(P-16743)
NORTH STATE SECURITY INC
1970 Hartnell Ave, Redding (96002-2214)
P.O. Box 991348 (96099-1348)
PHONE...................................530 243-0295
Lance Boek, *President*
EMP: 100
SQ FT: 1,500

SALES: 1.4MM **Privately Held**
SIC: 7381 Security guard service

(P-16744)
NORTHEAST PROTECTIVE SVCS INC
Also Called: Neps Worldwide
16040 Peppertree Ln, La Mirada
(90638-3460)
PHONE...................................800 577-0899
Alan Burton, *President*
Frank Widder, *CFO*
Brenda Chavez, *Officer*
Josh Nordin, *Director*
EMP: 65
SALES: 1.5MM **Privately Held**
WEB:
www.northeastprotectiveservices.com
SIC: 7381 Protective services, guard

(P-16745)
OC SPECIAL EVENTS SEC INC
Also Called: Firearms Academy
1232 Village Way Ste K, Santa Ana
(92705-4746)
PHONE...................................714 541-4111
Richard Allum, *President*
David S Andersen, *Shareholder*
EMP: 102
SALES (est): 1.9MM **Privately Held**
SIC: 7381 Security guard service; guard services

(P-16746)
ODONA CENTRAL SECURITY INC
71 N San Gabriel Blvd, Pasadena
(91107-3749)
PHONE...................................323 728-8818
Fred Chen, *President*
EMP: 150
SQ FT: 2,000
SALES (est): 3.1MM **Privately Held**
WEB: www.odona.com
SIC: 7381 Security guard service

(P-16747)
OMEGA SECURITY SERVICES & CONS
10611 Garden Grove Ave # 2, Northridge
(91326-3211)
PHONE...................................818 831-1100
Motti Ben-Haim, *President*
Motti S Benhaim, *Office Mgr*
EMP: 70
SALES (est): 1.7MM **Privately Held**
WEB: www.omegasec.net
SIC: 7381 Guard services; security guard service

(P-16748)
ON-SCENE SECURITY SERVICES INC
P.O. Box 800147, Santa Clarita (91380-0147)
PHONE...................................661 263-2343
Larry Wilson, *President*
Deborah Wilson, *Vice Pres*
EMP: 50
SALES (est): 747.7K **Privately Held**
SIC: 7381 Security guard service

(P-16749)
ONTEL SECURITY SERVICES INC
708 L St, Modesto (95354-2240)
P.O. Box 579730 (95357-9730)
PHONE...................................209 521-0200
David Ackerman, *CEO*
David McCann, *COO*
Michael Ackerman, *CFO*
Roberta Gray, *Treasurer*
EMP: 71
SQ FT: 2,500
SALES (est): 2.4MM **Privately Held**
WEB: www.ontelsecurity.com
SIC: 7381 Security guard service

(P-16750)
OPSEC SPECIALIZED PROTECTION
44262 Division St Ste A, Lancaster
(93535-3548)
PHONE...................................661 942-3999

Anthony Cheval, *Exec Dir*
EMP: 99
SALES: 950K **Privately Held**
WEB:
www.opsecspecializedprotection.com
SIC: 7381 Security guard service

(P-16751)
OVERTON SECURITY SERVICES INC
39300 Civic Center Dr # 370, Fremont
(94538-2338)
PHONE...................................510 791-7380
Andrew Overton, *President*
Vicki Greiner, *CFO*
Sandra Overton, *Vice Pres*
Jonathan Casillas, *Security Dir*
Lupe Marin, *Opers Mgr*
EMP: 215
SALES (est): 20.2MM **Privately Held**
SIC: 7381 Security guard service

(P-16752)
PACIFIC PROTECTION SERVICES
22144 Clarendon St # 110, Woodland Hills
(91367-8201)
PHONE...................................818 313-9369
Melvin Staples, *Branch Mgr*
EMP: 97
SALES (corp-wide): 8.1MM **Privately Held**
SIC: 7381 Security guard service
PA: Pacific Protection Services Inc
22144 Clarendon St # 110
Woodland Hills CA 91367
818 313-9369

(P-16753)
PALADIN PRTCTION SPCALISTS INC
Also Called: Paladin Private Security
320 Commerce Cir, Sacramento
(95815-4213)
PHONE...................................916 331-3175
Louis G Aljens, *CEO*
Trinidad Batad, *Officer*
Joshua Morris, *Officer*
Matthew Carroll, *Vice Pres*
M Scott Johnson, *Vice Pres*
EMP: 135
SALES (est): 9.3MM **Privately Held**
WEB: www.paladinprivatesecurity.com
SIC: 7381 Security guard service

(P-16754)
PATROL MASTERS INC
1651 E 4th St Ste 150, Santa Ana
(92701-5173)
PHONE...................................714 426-2526
Samir Ahmad, *President*
EMP: 150 EST: 2006
SALES (est): 4.1MM **Privately Held**
SIC: 7381 Security guard service

(P-16755)
PEACE KEEPERS PRIVATE SECURITY
2734b Delta Fair Blvd, Antioch
(94509-4100)
PHONE...................................925 978-4140
Stuart M Welch, *President*
Stuart Welch, *President*
EMP: 60 EST: 1993
SALES: 800K **Privately Held**
SIC: 7381 Security guard service

(P-16756)
PERSONAL PROTECTIVE SVCS INC (PA)
398 Beach Rd Fl 2, Burlingame
(94010-2004)
P.O. Box 14007, Oakland (94614-2007)
PHONE...................................650 344-3302
Stan Teets, *President*
Corbby Johnson, *Opers Staff*
EMP: 100
SQ FT: 1,500
SALES (est): 2.4MM **Privately Held**
WEB: www.personalprotective.com
SIC: 7381 Protective services, guard; private investigator

(P-16757)
PLATINUM PROTECTION GROUP INC
8018 E Santa Ana Cyn Rd, Anaheim
(92808-1102)
PHONE...................................800 824-1097
Mark Van Holt,
EMP: 90
SALES: 500K **Privately Held**
WEB: www.platinumprotectiongroup.com
SIC: 7381 Security guard service; protective services, guard

(P-16758)
PLATT SECURITY SYSTEMS INC
Also Called: Platt Security Services
3275 E Grant St Ste D, Long Beach
(90755-1293)
PHONE...................................562 986-4484
Robert E Platt, *President*
Tamara Platt, *Treasurer*
Mark Platt, *Vice Pres*
Daenette Almond, *Human Res Mgr*
EMP: 150 EST: 1977
SQ FT: 2,200
SALES (est): 3.6MM **Privately Held**
WEB: www.plattsecurity.com
SIC: 7381 7382 Security guard service; security systems services

(P-16759)
PRE-EMPLOYCOM
3655 Meadow View Dr, Redding
(96002-9715)
PHONE...................................800 300-1821
Robert Mather, *CEO*
EMP: 100
SALES: 10MM **Privately Held**
SIC: 7381 8742 Private investigator; human resource consulting services

(P-16760)
PRE-EMPLOYCOM INC
3615 Meadow View Dr, Redding
(96002-9715)
P.O. Box 491570 (96049-1570)
PHONE...................................530 378-7680
Robert V Mather, *President*
EMP: 75
SQ FT: 10,500
SALES (est): 2.9MM **Privately Held**
WEB: www.pre-employ.com
SIC: 7381 Private investigator

(P-16761)
PRESTIGE SECURITY SERVICE INC
5855 Green Valley Cir # 207, Culver City
(90230-6968)
PHONE...................................310 670-5999
George Bernaba, *Owner*
Jay Bernaba, *Opers Staff*
EMP: 400
SALES (est): 7.5MM **Privately Held**
SIC: 7381 Security guard service

(P-16762)
PRIME INTERNATIONAL SECURITY
Also Called: Prime Security
1630 Centinela Ave # 209, Inglewood
(90302-6948)
P.O. Box 18348, Los Angeles (90018-0348)
PHONE...................................310 670-4565
Akubuo Okorie, *President*
Boniesace Nworgu, *Vice Pres*
EMP: 60
SALES (est): 1.5MM **Privately Held**
SIC: 7381 Security guard service

(P-16763)
PROBE INFORMATION SERVICES INC
6375 Auburn Blvd, Citrus Heights
(95621-5270)
P.O. Box 418429, Sacramento (95841-8429)
PHONE...................................916 676-1826
Ross O Stewart, *President*
Renea Abdin, *Vice Pres*
Dalene Bartholomew, *Vice Pres*
Rochelle Perham, *Admin Asst*
Van Haas, *VP Opers*
EMP: 101
SQ FT: 6,000

P R O D U C T S & S V C S

SALES: 7.3MM **Privately Held**
WEB: www.probeinfo.com
SIC: 7381 Private investigator

(P-16764)
PROFESSIONAL SECURITY CONS (PA)
11454 San Vicente Blvd # 2, Los Angeles
(90049-6208)
PHONE..............................310 207-7729
Moshe Alon, *President*
Ilene Alon, *Vice Pres*
Michael Lambos, *Vice Pres*
Grant Erickson, *Exec Dir*
Daniel Barajas, *Security Dir*
EMP: 103
SALES (est): 82MM **Privately Held**
SIC: 7381 7382 Security guard service;
security systems services

(P-16765)
PROFESSIONAL TECHNICAL SEC SVCS
1970 Broadway Ste 840, Oakland
(94612-2299)
PHONE..............................510 645-9200
EMP: 384
SALES (corp-wide): 11.5MM **Privately Held**
SIC: 7381 Guard services
PA: Professional Technical Security Services Inc
625 Market St Fl 9
San Francisco CA 94105
415 243-2100

(P-16766)
PROTECT-US
12397 Lewis St Ste 202, Garden Grove
(92840-4696)
PHONE..............................714 721-8127
Nadiya Aziz, *Principal*
EMP: 180
SALES (est): 624.3K **Privately Held**
SIC: 7381 Security guard service

(P-16767)
PROTECTED OUTCOMES CORPORATION
9663 Santa Monica Blvd, Beverly Hills
(90210-4303)
PHONE..............................203 545-9565
EMP: 87
SALES: 950K **Privately Held**
SIC: 7381

(P-16768)
PROTECTION SPECIALISTS
Also Called: Chad Garrett Investigations
6841 Whitsett Ave Apt 104, North Hollywood (91605-5456)
PHONE..............................818 503-1306
Chad Garrett, *Principal*
EMP: 500
SALES (est): 3.5MM **Privately Held**
SIC: 7381 Protective services, guard

(P-16769)
PUBLIC SECURITY INC
3860 Crenshaw Blvd # 223, Los Angeles
(90008-1816)
PHONE..............................323 293-9884
Darrin Jenkins, *Principal*
Willie Simmons, *Manager*
EMP: 50
SALES: 950K **Privately Held**
SIC: 7381 Security guard service

(P-16770)
R STANLEY SECURITY SERVICE
403 18th St, Bakersfield (93301-4930)
PHONE..............................661 634-9283
Rachelle Stanley, *President*
Charles Thompson, *Vice Pres*
Jenny James, *Manager*
EMP: 65
SQ FT: 3,000
SALES: 1MM **Privately Held**
SIC: 7381 7389 Security guard service;
convention & show services

(P-16771)
RANCHO SANTA FE PROTECTIVE SVC
Also Called: Rsf Protective Services
1991 Village Park Way # 100, Encinitas
(92024-1994)
PHONE..............................760 433-8887
Ron Boever, *President*
Denise Mueller, *Shareholder*
Richard Crooks, *Opers Staff*
Navio Bains, *Marketing Staff*
Gloria Ives, *Manager*
EMP: 50
SQ FT: 4,000
SALES: 1.2MM **Privately Held**
SIC: 7381 Security guard service

(P-16772)
REEL SECURITY CALIFORNIA INC
15303 Ventura Blvd # 1080, Sherman Oaks
(91403-5800)
PHONE..............................818 928-4737
Mario Inez Ramirez, *CEO*
Bradley Bush, *COO*
EMP: 99
SALES (est): 787.8K **Privately Held**
SIC: 7381 Guard services

(P-16773)
REV ENTERPRISES
Also Called: O & R
417 Arden Ave Ste 103, Glendale
(91203-4046)
PHONE..............................818 551-7111
J Antonio Revilla, *Principal*
EMP: 50
SALES: 1.1MM **Privately Held**
SIC: 7381 Detective & armored car services

(P-16774)
RJN INVESTIGATIONS INC
360 E 1st St Ste 696, Tustin (92780-3211)
P.O. Box 55451, Riverside (92517-0451)
PHONE..............................951 686-7638
Robert Nagle, *President*
Michael Gomez, *President*
Fred Martino, *Administration*
Miriam Lawrence, *QC Mgr*
EMP: 80
SALES (est): 4.8MM **Privately Held**
SIC: 7381 Detective agency; private investigator

(P-16775)
RMI INTERNATIONAL INC
Also Called: Rodbat Security Services
1919 Torrance Blvd, Torrance
(90501-2722)
PHONE..............................310 781-6768
Elena Rabinovich, *Branch Mgr*
EMP: 65
SALES (corp-wide): 25.5MM **Privately Held**
WEB: www.rmiintl.com
SIC: 7381 Security guard service; protective services, guard
PA: Rmi International Inc
8125 Somerset Blvd
Paramount CA 90723
562 806-9098

(P-16776)
RODGERS SECURITY SERVICE INC
Also Called: Rss
8726 S Sepulveda Blvd, Los Angeles
(90045-4014)
PHONE..............................310 684-3016
Tyrone Rodgers, *CEO*
EMP: 180 **EST:** 2011
SQ FT: 3,500
SALES: 2.5MM **Privately Held**
SIC: 7381 7382 Private investigator; security guard service; protective services, guard; detective services; burglar alarm maintenance & monitoring

(P-16777)
RORY V PARKER
Also Called: Bmt International SEC Svcs
818 27th St Ste 101, Oakland
(94607-3424)
PHONE..............................510 595-5543

Rory Parker, *Owner*
Patrick Charles, *Principal*
EMP: 222 **EST:** 2009
SQ FT: 2,200
SALES (est): 5.4MM **Privately Held**
SIC: 7381 Guard services

(P-16778)
ROYAL INVESTIGATION PATROL INC
2950 Merced St Ste 108, San Leandro
(94577-5636)
PHONE..............................510 352-6800
Edmund Young, *President*
EMP: 58 **EST:** 1974
SQ FT: 2,000
SALES (est): 1.2MM **Privately Held**
SIC: 7381 Protective services, guard; private investigator

(P-16779)
S C SECURITY INC
Also Called: Copper Eagle Patrol & Security
26752 Oak Ave Ste C, Santa Clarita
(91351-6620)
PHONE..............................661 251-6999
Isaiah Tally, *President*
William Corbett, *President*
George Streb, *Exec VP*
Deborah Corbett, *Admin Sec*
EMP: 50
SQ FT: 2,000
SALES (est): 1.3MM **Privately Held**
SIC: 7381 Security guard service; guard services

(P-16780)
SAFETY SECURITY PATROL LLC
560 N Arrowhead Ave 3b, San Bernardino
(92401-1219)
PHONE..............................909 888-7778
EMP: 63
SALES (est): 86.1K **Privately Held**
SIC: 7381

(P-16781)
SECTRAN SECURITY INCORPORATED (PA)
Also Called: Sectran Armored Truck Service
7633 Industry Ave, Pico Rivera
(90660-4301)
P.O. Box 7267, Los Angeles (90022-0967)
PHONE..............................562 948-1446
Fred Kunik, *President*
Efren Lizardi, *Branch Mgr*
Rony Ghaby, *General Mgr*
Erryna Pinon, *General Mgr*
Irving Barr, *Admin Sec*
EMP: 141
SQ FT: 19,736
SALES (est): 13.9MM **Privately Held**
SIC: 7381 Armored car services

(P-16782)
SECURE NET ALLIANCE
Also Called: Security Company
601 S Glenoaks Blvd # 409, Burbank
(91502-1474)
PHONE..............................818 848-4900
Levi Quintana, *CEO*
Jonathan Kraut, *Partner*
EMP: 50
SALES (est): 957.9K **Privately Held**
SIC: 7381 Security guard service; protective services, guard

(P-16783)
SECURITAS CRITICAL INFRASTRUCT
3914 Murphy Canyon Rd A120, San Diego
(92123-4491)
PHONE..............................858 560-0448
John Tucke, *Branch Mgr*
EMP: 868
SALES (corp-wide): 10.9B **Privately Held**
SIC: 7381 Security guard service
HQ: Securitas Critical Infrastructure Services, Inc.
13900 Lincoln Park Dr # 370
Herndon VA 20171

(P-16784)
SECURITAS CRITICAL INFRASTRUCT
1835 W Orangewood Ave # 250, Orange
(92868-2044)
PHONE..............................310 817-2177
Elijah Kimble, *Manager*
EMP: 1002
SALES (corp-wide): 10.9B **Privately Held**
SIC: 7381 Security guard service
HQ: Securitas Critical Infrastructure Services, Inc.
13900 Lincoln Park Dr # 370
Herndon VA 20171

(P-16785)
SECURITAS CRITICAL INFRASTRUCT
Rm 117 Bldg 7525, Vandenberg Afb
(93437)
PHONE..............................805 685-1100
Paul Jensen, *Branch Mgr*
EMP: 885
SALES (corp-wide): 10.9B **Privately Held**
SIC: 7381 Security guard service
HQ: Securitas Critical Infrastructure Services, Inc.
13900 Lincoln Park Dr # 370
Herndon VA 20171

(P-16786)
SECURITAS CRITICAL INFRASTRUCT
360 N Pacific Coast Hwy, El Segundo
(90245-4460)
PHONE..............................310 426-3300
Michael Kemppainen, *Branch Mgr*
EMP: 1750
SALES (corp-wide): 10.9B **Privately Held**
SIC: 7381 Security guard service
HQ: Securitas Critical Infrastructure Services, Inc.
13900 Lincoln Park Dr # 370
Herndon VA 20171

(P-16787)
SECURITAS SEC SVCS USA INC
5700 Ralston St, Ventura (93003-6050)
PHONE..............................805 650-6285
Silvia Portillo, *Manager*
Eddie Lucas, *Officer*
Michael Perenchio, *Branch Mgr*
EMP: 116
SALES (corp-wide): 10.9B **Privately Held**
SIC: 7381 Security guard service
HQ: Securitas Security Services Usa, Inc.
9 Campus Dr
Parsippany NJ 07054
973 267-5300

(P-16788)
SECURITAS SEC SVCS USA INC
2045 Hurley Way, Sacramento
(95825-3220)
PHONE..............................916 564-2009
Pete Niles, *President*
Joe Saputo, *President*
David Calhoun, *Officer*
Angela Scott, *Branch Mgr*
Andrea Barlow, *Analyst*
EMP: 181
SALES (corp-wide): 10.9B **Privately Held**
SIC: 7381 Security guard service
HQ: Securitas Security Services Usa, Inc.
9 Campus Dr
Parsippany NJ 07054
973 267-5300

(P-16789)
SECURITAS SEC SVCS USA INC
Also Called: Northern California Region
3115 W March Ln Ste A, Stockton
(95219-2393)
PHONE..............................209 943-1401
Kelly Davis, *Manager*
Freeman Johns, *Human Res Dir*
EMP: 120
SALES (corp-wide): 10.9B **Privately Held**
WEB: www.securitasinc.com
SIC: 7381 Protective services, guard

HQ: Securitas Security Services Usa, Inc.
9 Campus Dr
Parsippany NJ 07054
973 267-5300

(P-16790)
SECURITAS SEC SVCS USA INC
Also Called: Northern California Region
155 E Shaw Ave Ste 315, Fresno
(93710-7619)
PHONE..............................559 221-2302
Christopher Lewis, *Manager*
Kellee Cotten, *Human Res Mgr*
Kevin Geathers, *Human Res Mgr*
Roxana Quillen, *Human Res Mgr*
Daniel Reeves, *Human Res Mgr*
EMP: 116
SALES (corp-wide): 10.9B **Privately Held**
WEB: www.securitasinc.com
SIC: 7381 Security guard service
HQ: Securitas Security Services Usa, Inc.
9 Campus Dr
Parsippany NJ 07054
973 267-5300

(P-16791)
SECURITAS SEC SVCS USA INC
750 Terrado Plz Ste 107, Covina
(91723-3419)
PHONE..............................571 321-0913
Michael Persaud, *Branch Mgr*
EMP: 185
SALES (corp-wide): 10.9B **Privately Held**
SIC: 7381 Security guard service
HQ: Securitas Security Services Usa, Inc.
9 Campus Dr
Parsippany NJ 07054
973 267-5300

(P-16792)
SECURITAS SEC SVCS USA INC
425 Bush St Ste 400, San Francisco
(94108-3724)
PHONE..............................510 568-6818
Brad Lauer, *Assoc VP*
EMP: 188
SALES (corp-wide): 10.9B **Privately Held**
SIC: 7381 Security guard service
HQ: Securitas Security Services Usa, Inc.
9 Campus Dr
Parsippany NJ 07054
973 267-5300

(P-16793)
SECURITAS SEC SVCS USA INC
Also Called: Automotive Services Division
430 N Vineyard Ave # 335, Ontario
(91764-5494)
PHONE..............................909 974-3160
Dave Knutson, *Branch Mgr*
Mark De Ville, *Human Res Mgr*
Albert Jackson, *Supervisor*
EMP: 100
SALES (corp-wide): 10.9B **Privately Held**
WEB: www.securitasinc.com
SIC: 7381 Security guard service
HQ: Securitas Security Services Usa, Inc.
9 Campus Dr
Parsippany NJ 07054
973 267-5300

(P-16794)
SECURITAS SEC SVCS USA INC
Also Called: Southern California / Hawa Reg
2344 S 2nd St Ste C, El Centro
(92243-5606)
PHONE..............................760 353-8177
Manuel Andrade, *Branch Mgr*
EMP: 116
SALES (corp-wide): 10.9B **Privately Held**
WEB: www.securitasinc.com
SIC: 7381 Security guard service
HQ: Securitas Security Services Usa, Inc.
9 Campus Dr
Parsippany NJ 07054
973 267-5300

(P-16795)
SECURITAS SEC SVCS USA INC
Also Called: Northern California Region
2415 Larkspur Ln Ste B, Redding
(96002-0643)
PHONE..............................530 245-0256
Keith Adams, *Branch Mgr*
EMP: 75

SALES (corp-wide): 10.9B **Privately Held**
WEB: www.securitasinc.com
SIC: 7381 Security guard service; protec-
tive services, guard; detective services
HQ: Securitas Security Services Usa, Inc.
9 Campus Dr
Parsippany NJ 07054
973 267-5300

(P-16796)
SECURITAS SEC SVCS USA INC
Southern California / Hawa Reg
1550 Hotel Cir N Ste 440, San Diego
(92108-2933)
PHONE..............................619 641-0049
Kelly Senados, *Branch Mgr*
Lauren Winter, *Branch Mgr*
EMP: 178
SQ FT: 2,600
SALES (corp-wide): 10.9B **Privately Held**
WEB: www.securitasinc.com
SIC: 7381 Security guard service
HQ: Securitas Security Services Usa, Inc.
9 Campus Dr
Parsippany NJ 07054
973 267-5300

(P-16797)
SECURITAS SEC SVCS USA INC
Also Called: Western Operations Center
4330 Park Terrace Dr, Westlake Village
(91361-4630)
PHONE..............................818 706-4909
Edie Stafford, *Manager*
Paul R Amour, *President*
Pamela Williams, *Vice Pres*
Sean Keating, *Security Dir*
Norman Chavosky, *Branch Mgr*
EMP: 350
SALES (corp-wide): 10.9B **Privately Held**
WEB: www.securitasinc.com
SIC: 7381 Security guard service
HQ: Securitas Security Services Usa, Inc.
9 Campus Dr
Parsippany NJ 07054
973 267-5300

(P-16798)
SECURITAS SEC SVCS USA INC
Also Called: Northern California Region
1304 Sthpint Blvd Ste 110, Petaluma
(94954)
PHONE..............................707 586-1393
Michael Jack, *Branch Mgr*
EMP: 172
SALES (corp-wide): 10.9B **Privately Held**
WEB: www.securitasinc.com
SIC: 7381 Security guard service
HQ: Securitas Security Services Usa, Inc.
9 Campus Dr
Parsippany NJ 07054
973 267-5300

(P-16799)
SECURITAS SEC SVCS USA INC
Also Called: Southern California / Hawa Reg
5276 Hollister Ave # 204, Goleta
(93111-2073)
PHONE..............................805 967-8987
Linda Garcia, *Manager*
EMP: 116
SALES (corp-wide): 10.9B **Privately Held**
WEB: www.securitasinc.com
SIC: 7381 Security guard service
HQ: Securitas Security Services Usa, Inc.
9 Campus Dr
Parsippany NJ 07054
973 267-5300

(P-16800)
SECURITAS SEC SVCS USA INC
Also Called: Northern California Region
1606 Koster St Ste A, Eureka
(95501-0179)
PHONE..............................707 445-5463
Chris Peters, *Branch Mgr*
EMP: 82
SALES (corp-wide): 10.9B **Privately Held**
WEB: www.securitasinc.com
SIC: 7381 Security guard service
HQ: Securitas Security Services Usa, Inc.
9 Campus Dr
Parsippany NJ 07054
973 267-5300

(P-16801)
SECURITAS SEC SVCS USA INC
Northern California Region
2045 Hurley Way Ste 175, Sacramento
(95825-3220)
PHONE..............................916 569-4500
Wallace Lavery, *Principal*
Linda Brewer, *Human Res Mgr*
EMP: 200
SALES (corp-wide): 10.9B **Privately Held**
WEB: www.securitasinc.com
SIC: 7381 Security guard service
HQ: Securitas Security Services Usa, Inc.
9 Campus Dr
Parsippany NJ 07054
973 267-5300

(P-16802)
SECURITAS SEC SVCS USA INC
27450 Ynez Rd Ste 315, Temecula
(92591-4681)
PHONE..............................951 676-3954
Pat Mac Arthur, *Manager*
EMP: 116
SALES (corp-wide): 10.9B **Privately Held**
SIC: 7381 Security guard service
HQ: Securitas Security Services Usa, Inc.
9 Campus Dr
Parsippany NJ 07054
973 267-5300

(P-16803)
SECURITAS SEC SVCS USA INC
Also Called: Northern California Region
43-00 Cook St Ste 100, Palm Desert
(92211)
PHONE..............................559 221-2302
Kiet Phan, *Branch Mgr*
EMP: 200
SALES (corp-wide): 10.9B **Privately Held**
WEB: www.securitasinc.com
SIC: 7381 Security guard service
HQ: Securitas Security Services Usa, Inc.
9 Campus Dr
Parsippany NJ 07054
973 267-5300

(P-16804)
SECURITAS SEC SVCS USA INC
Also Called: Northern California Region
1611 Bunker Hill Way # 100, Salinas
(93906-6004)
PHONE..............................831 444-9607
Joseph Santos, *Manager*
EMP: 116
SALES (corp-wide): 10.9B **Privately Held**
WEB: www.securitasinc.com
SIC: 7381 Security guard service
HQ: Securitas Security Services Usa, Inc.
9 Campus Dr
Parsippany NJ 07054
973 267-5300

(P-16805)
SECURITAS SEC SVCS USA INC
Also Called: Northern California Region
7677 Oakport St Ste 725, Oakland
(94621-1962)
PHONE..............................925 746-0552
Nathan Wolfe, *Vice Pres*
Sean O'Brien, *Vice Pres*
Patricia Armstrong, *Human Res Mgr*
Raul Ramirez, *Manager*
EMP: 116
SALES (corp-wide): 10.9B **Privately Held**
WEB: www.securitasinc.com
SIC: 7381 Security guard service
HQ: Securitas Security Services Usa, Inc.
9 Campus Dr
Parsippany NJ 07054
973 267-5300

(P-16806)
SECURITAS SEC SVCS USA INC
Also Called: Southern California / Hawa Reg
1101 W Mckinley Ave, Pomona
(91768-1639)
PHONE..............................909 865-4356
Barry Gillies, *Branch Mgr*
EMP: 116
SALES (corp-wide): 10.9B **Privately Held**
WEB: www.securitasinc.com
SIC: 7381 Security guard service

HQ: Securitas Security Services Usa, Inc.
9 Campus Dr
Parsippany NJ 07054
973 267-5300

(P-16807)
SECURITAS SEC SVCS USA INC
Also Called: Southern California / Hawa Reg
6055 E Wash Blvd Ste 155, Commerce
(90040-2418)
PHONE..............................323 832-9074
Mike Kelly, *Branch Mgr*
EMP: 116
SALES (corp-wide): 10.9B **Privately Held**
WEB: www.securitasinc.com
SIC: 7381 Security guard service
HQ: Securitas Security Services Usa, Inc.
9 Campus Dr
Parsippany NJ 07054
973 267-5300

(P-16808)
SECURITAS SEC SVCS USA INC
Also Called: Southern California / Hawa Reg
1055 Wilshire Blvd, Los Angeles
(90017-2431)
PHONE..............................213 580-8825
Jeff Winter, *Principal*
Jessica Fitzsimmons, *Administration*
John Gill, *Database Admin*
Linnea Luker, *Analyst*
Michael Luke, *Director*
EMP: 116
SALES (corp-wide): 10.9B **Privately Held**
WEB: www.securitasinc.com
SIC: 7381 Security guard service
HQ: Securitas Security Services Usa, Inc.
9 Campus Dr
Parsippany NJ 07054
973 267-5300

(P-16809)
SECURITAS SEC SVCS USA INC
Also Called: Southern California / Hawa Reg
1500 W Carson St Ste 109, Long Beach
(90810-1401)
PHONE..............................562 427-2737
Ivory Phillips, *Assoc VP*
EMP: 116
SALES (corp-wide): 10.9B **Privately Held**
WEB: www.securitasinc.com
SIC: 7381 Security guard service
HQ: Securitas Security Services Usa, Inc.
9 Campus Dr
Parsippany NJ 07054
973 267-5300

(P-16810)
SECURITAS SEC SVCS USA INC
Also Called: Shared Services
400 Crenshaw Blvd Ste 200, Torrance
(90503-1736)
PHONE..............................310 787-0747
EMP: 181
SALES (corp-wide): 9.4B **Privately Held**
SIC: 7381
HQ: Securitas Security Services Usa, Inc.
2 Campus Dr
Parsippany NJ 07054
973 267-5300

(P-16811)
SECURITAS SEC SVCS USA INC
2870 Skypark Dr Ste 315, Torrance
(90505-5316)
PHONE..............................714 385-9745
Steven Lindsey, *Owner*
EMP: 116
SALES (corp-wide): 10.9B **Privately Held**
WEB: www.securitasinc.com
SIC: 7381 Security guard service
HQ: Securitas Security Services Usa, Inc.
9 Campus Dr
Parsippany NJ 07054
973 267-5300

(P-16812)
SECURITAS SEC SVCS USA INC
Also Called: Southern California / Hawa Reg
15428 Civic Dr Ste 305, Victorville
(92392-9772)
PHONE..............................760 245-1915
Bob Dorian, *Branch Mgr*
EMP: 150

SALES (corp-wide): 10.9B **Privately Held**
WEB: www.securitasinc.com
SIC: 7381 Security guard service
HQ: Securitas Security Services Usa, Inc.
  9 Campus Dr
  Parsippany NJ 07054
  973 267-5300

(P-16813)
SECURITAS SEC SVCS USA INC
Also Called: Automotive Services Division
16909 Parthenia St # 202, Northridge
(91343-4551)
PHONE...............................818 891-0458
Pat Salter, *Branch Mgr*
EMP: 150
SALES (corp-wide): 10.9B **Privately Held**
WEB: www.securitasinc.com
SIC: 7381 8742 8741 Security guard
  service; industry specialist consultants;
  management services
HQ: Securitas Security Services Usa, Inc.
  9 Campus Dr
  Parsippany NJ 07054
  973 267-5300

(P-16814)
SECURITAS SEC SVCS USA INC
4330 Park Terrace Dr, Westlake Village
(91361-4630)
PHONE...............................818 706-6800
Steve Lyndsay, *Branch Mgr*
Prasad Chandrupatla, *Info Tech Dir*
Joanne Mc Guff, *Human Resources*
Edie Stafford, *Director*
Jose Rodriguez, *Manager*
EMP: 116
SALES (corp-wide): 10.9B **Privately Held**
SIC: 7381 Security guard service
HQ: Securitas Security Services Usa, Inc.
  9 Campus Dr
  Parsippany NJ 07054
  973 267-5300

(P-16815)
SECURITECH SECURITY SERVICES
2733 N San Fernando Rd, Los Angeles
(90065-1318)
P.O. Box 65097 (90065-0097)
PHONE...............................213 387-5050
Serge Tachdjian, *President*
Adriana Alvarez, *Admin Sec*
EMP: 110
SALES (est): 9.2MM **Privately Held**
WEB: www.securitechguards.com
SIC: 7381 Security guard service

(P-16816)
SECURITY AMERICA INC
7120 Hayvenhurst Ave # 201, Van Nuys
(91406-3813)
PHONE...............................310 532-0121
Mary Garnica, *President*
Fred Garnica, *CEO*
Mark Carreno, *Vice Pres*
EMP: 84
SALES (est): 2.3MM **Privately Held**
WEB: www.securityamericainc.com
SIC: 7381 Security guard service

(P-16817)
SECURITY INDUST SPCIALISTS INC (PA)
6071 Bristol Pkwy, Culver City
(90230-6601)
PHONE...............................310 215-5100
John Spesak, *President*
Tom Seltz, *President*
Kit Knudsen, *COO*
Abel Sanchez,
Chuck Calderhead, *Officer*
EMP: 138
SQ FT: 9,000
SALES (est): 42.8MM **Privately Held**
WEB: www.securityindustryspecialists.com
SIC: 7381 5065 Security guard service;
  security control equipment & systems

(P-16818)
SECURITY ONE INC
1859 Streiff Ln, Santa Rosa (95403-2326)
PHONE...............................800 778-3017
Tom Kasnick, *President*
Valerie Kasnick, *Vice Pres*
EMP: 65 **EST:** 1998

SQ FT: 1,000
SALES (est): 1MM **Privately Held**
SIC: 7381 Guard services; security guard
  service; private investigator

(P-16819)
SEGURA ENTERPRISES INC
Also Called: Segura Security Services
1011 W Mccoy Ln, Santa Maria
(93455-1107)
PHONE...............................805 349-0550
Raul Segura, *CEO*
EMP: 100
SQ FT: 1,500
SALES (est): 7.3MM **Privately Held**
SIC: 7381 7382 Security guard service;
  security systems services

(P-16820)
SERVEXO
Also Called: Servexo Protective Service
879 W 190th St Ste 400, Gardena
(90248-4223)
P.O. Box 9017, San Pedro (90734-9017)
PHONE...............................323 527-9994
John Palmer, *CEO*
EMP: 50
SALES: 3MM **Privately Held**
SIC: 7381 Protective services, guard; se-
  curity guard service

(P-16821)
SHARP GUARD SERVICES INC
3450 Wilshire Blvd # 1000, Los Angeles
(90010-2208)
PHONE...............................213 739-1900
Ilham Chaouir, *President*
Mike Thabet, *Treasurer*
EMP: 521 **EST:** 1999
SALES (est): 4MM **Privately Held**
WEB: www.sharpgs.com
SIC: 7381 Security guard service

(P-16822)
SHERMAN SECURITY
7218 Hermosa Ave, Rancho Cucamonga
(91701-5929)
PHONE...............................909 941-4167
Daryl Enoch, *Partner*
Clarence Tanner, *Partner*
EMP: 102
SALES (est): 156.3K **Privately Held**
SIC: 7381 7389 Guard services;

(P-16823)
SHIELD SECURITY INC (DH)
1551 N Tustin Ave Ste 650, Santa Ana
(92705-8664)
PHONE...............................714 210-1501
Ed Klosterman Jr, *President*
Leo Green, *Vice Pres*
Kenneth Klosterman, *Vice Pres*
EMP: 300
SQ FT: 5,500
SALES (est): 24.5MM
SALES (corp-wide): 741.7MM **Privately Held**
SIC: 7381 Security guard service
HQ: Universal Protection Service, Lp
  1551 N Tustin Ave Ste 650
  Santa Ana CA 92705
  714 619-9700

(P-16824)
SHIELD SECURITY INC
21110 Vanowen St, Canoga Park
(91303-2821)
PHONE...............................818 239-5800
Kenneth Klosterman, *Branch Mgr*
EMP: 200
SALES (corp-wide): 741.7MM **Privately Held**
SIC: 7381 Security guard service
HQ: Shield Security, Inc.
  1551 N Tustin Ave Ste 650
  Santa Ana CA 92705
  714 210-1501

(P-16825)
SHIELD SECURITY INC
150 E Wardlow Rd, Long Beach (90807)
PHONE...............................562 283-1100
Leo Green, *Manager*
EMP: 450

SALES (corp-wide): 741.7MM **Privately Held**
SIC: 7381 Security guard service
HQ: Shield Security, Inc.
  1551 N Tustin Ave Ste 650
  Santa Ana CA 92705
  714 210-1501

(P-16826)
SHIELD SECURITY INC
265 N Euclid Ave, Upland (91786-6038)
PHONE...............................909 920-1173
Paul Srankowski, *Manager*
EMP: 300
SALES (corp-wide): 741.7MM **Privately Held**
SIC: 7381 Security guard service
HQ: Shield Security, Inc.
  1551 N Tustin Ave Ste 650
  Santa Ana CA 92705
  714 210-1501

(P-16827)
SIGNAL 88 LLC
821 S Rockefeller Ave, Ontario
(91761-8119)
PHONE...............................714 713-5306
Mark Anderson, *Branch Mgr*
EMP: 942
SALES (corp-wide): 35.4MM **Privately Held**
SIC: 7381 Guard services
PA: Signal 88, Llc
  3880 S 149th St Ste 102
  Omaha NE 68144
  877 498-8494

(P-16828)
SILICON VLY SEC & PATROL INC (PA)
1131 Luchessi Dr Ste 2, San Jose
(95118-3770)
PHONE...............................408 267-1539
Ray Higdon, *CEO*
Lisa Higdon, *President*
Gary Mills, *Vice Pres*
Stephanie Bownas, *Office Mgr*
Julianne Hinson, *Finance Mgr*
EMP: 225
SQ FT: 4,000
SALES (est): 6.7MM **Privately Held**
WEB: www.svsp.com
SIC: 7381 Security guard service

(P-16829)
SILVER SHIELD SECURITY
2107 N 1st St Ste 100, San Jose
(95131-2026)
PHONE...............................408 435-1111
Sabrina Wagner, *President*
Jay Wagner, *Vice Pres*
EMP: 105
SQ FT: 3,500
SALES (est): 1.3MM
SALES (corp-wide): 741.7MM **Privately Held**
WEB: www.silvershieldsecurity.com
SIC: 7381 Security guard service
HQ: Universal Protection Service, Lp
  1551 N Tustin Ave Ste 650
  Santa Ana CA 92705
  714 619-9700

(P-16830)
SOS SECURITY INCORPORATED
2601 Ocean Park Blvd # 208, Santa Monica
(90405-5229)
PHONE...............................310 392-9600
Doug Hamilton, *Manager*
Fred Silverman, *President*
EMP: 140
SALES (corp-wide): 106.2MM **Privately Held**
SIC: 7381 Security guard service; detec-
  tive agency
PA: Sos Security Incorporated
  1915 Us Highway 46 Ste 1
  Parsippany NJ 07054
  973 402-6600

(P-16831)
SOS SECURITY INCORPORATED
26250 Industrial Blvd # 48, Hayward
(94545-2922)
PHONE...............................510 782-4900
Michael Boone, *Vice Pres*

EMP: 140
SALES (corp-wide): 106.2MM **Privately Held**
SIC: 7381 Security guard service; detec-
  tive agency
PA: Sos Security Incorporated
  1915 Us Highway 46 Ste 1
  Parsippany NJ 07054
  973 402-6600

(P-16832)
SOS SECURITY LLC
331 N Beverly Dr Ste 3, Beverly Hills
(90210-4729)
PHONE...............................310 859-8248
EMP: 70
SALES (corp-wide): 107MM **Privately Held**
SIC: 7381 Security guard service
PA: Sos Security Llc
  1915 Us Highway 46 Ste 2
  Parsippany NJ 07054
  973 402-6600

(P-16833)
SPECTRUM SECURITY SERVICES INC
1633 E 4th St Ste 238, Santa Ana
(92701-5144)
PHONE...............................714 542-9600
Sam B Ersan, *President*
EMP: 97
SALES (corp-wide): 7.5MM **Privately Held**
SIC: 7381 Security guard service
PA: Spectrum Security Services, Inc.
  13967 Campo Rd Ste 101
  Jamul CA 91935
  619 669-6660

(P-16834)
SRS PROTECTION INC
2064 Eastman Ave Ste 110, Ventura
(93003-7787)
PHONE...............................805 744-7122
James Allen Rita, *CEO*
Robin Neubert, *Vice Pres*
EMP: 75 **EST:** 2013
SQ FT: 1,200
SALES: 500K **Privately Held**
SIC: 7381 Security guard service

(P-16835)
STAFF PRO INC
675 Convention Way, San Diego
(92101-7805)
PHONE...............................619 544-1774
Mike Hernandez, *Manager*
EMP: 198
SALES (corp-wide): 98.4MM **Privately Held**
WEB: www.staffpro.com
SIC: 7381 Security guard service
PA: Staff Pro Inc.
  15272 Jason Cir
  Huntington Beach CA 92649
  714 230-7200

(P-16836)
TRANS WEST INVESTIGATIONS INC
3255 Wilshire Blvd, Los Angeles
(90010-1404)
PHONE...............................213 381-1500
Edward W Beyer, *President*
James T Walsh, *CEO*
EMP: 57
SQ FT: 2,900
SALES (est): 1.2MM **Privately Held**
SIC: 7381 8111 Private investigator; legal
  services

(P-16837)
TRANS-WEST SECURITY SVCS INC
8503 Crippen St, Bakersfield (93311-8993)
PHONE...............................661 381-2900
Brooke L Antonioni, *President*
Duane Williams, *Exec VP*
Katy Williams, *Vice Pres*
Gilbert Cota, *Opers Mgr*
EMP: 300
SQ FT: 8,500

SALES (est): 11.2MM **Privately Held**
WEB: www.twsecurity.com
SIC: 7381 Security guard service

(P-16838)
TRANSCENDENT SECURITY SERVICES ✪
3553 Atl Ave Ste 1197, Long Beach (90807)
PHONE..................................562 850-3313
John Harris, *President*
EMP: 50 EST: 2018
SALES (est): 227.8K **Privately Held**
SIC: 7381 Security guard service

(P-16839)
TRIUMPH PROTECTION GROUP INC
853 Cotting Ct Ste D, Vacaville (95688-8701)
P.O. Box 852 (95696-0852)
PHONE..............................800 224-0286
Jeffrey David Field, *CEO*
Lisa Godden, *Accountant*
EMP: 150
SALES: 3MM **Privately Held**
SIC: 7381 Security guard service

(P-16840)
TURNER SECURITY SYSTEMS INC
Also Called: Don Turner and Associates
120 W Shields Ave, Fresno (93705-4101)
PHONE..............................559 486-3466
Donald A Turner, *President*
Michael Garaffa, *Office Mgr*
Gary Gannon, *Financial Exec*
Terry Campbell, *Sales Staff*
Mike Moua, *Accounts Mgr*
EMP: 190
SQ FT: 3,700
SALES (est): 7.2MM **Privately Held**
WEB: www.turnersec.com
SIC: 7381 Security guard service

(P-16841)
TYAN INC
Also Called: Security Specialists
1500 Glenoaks Blvd, San Fernando (91340-1780)
P.O. Box 3472, Van Nuys (91407-3472)
PHONE..............................818 785-5831
Nick Tsotsikyan, *President*
EMP: 55
SQ FT: 2,000
SALES (est): 2MM **Privately Held**
WEB: www.capatrol.com
SIC: 7381 Security guard service

(P-16842)
U S PRIVATE PROTECTION SEC INC
5555 Inglewood Blvd # 205, Culver City (90230-6250)
PHONE..............................310 301-0010
Dave Solomon, *President*
EMP: 180
SALES (est): 3.8MM **Privately Held**
SIC: 7381 Protective services, guard

(P-16843)
UNITED GUARD SECURITY INC
879 W 190th St Ste 510, Gardena (90248-4289)
PHONE..............................310 881-2984
Smail Zita, *CEO*
Chawki Nouizi, *Treasurer*
EMP: 120 EST: 2012
SALES (est): 143K **Privately Held**
SIC: 7381 Security guard service

(P-16844)
UNITY SEC & PROTECTIVE SVC
619 E Washington Blvd, Pasadena (91104-2260)
PHONE..............................323 695-7234
Jayson Lee, *President*
EMP: 78
SQ FT: 3,000
SALES (est): 1.4MM **Privately Held**
WEB: www.unitedprotection.com
SIC: 7381 Security guard service

(P-16845)
UNIVERSAL PROTECTION SVC LP
Also Called: Prestige Protection
2415 San Ramon Vly Blvd, San Ramon (94583-5381)
PHONE..............................805 496-4401
Tim Elsasser, *Branch Mgr*
EMP: 61
SALES (corp-wide): 741.7MM **Privately Held**
SIC: 7381
HQ: Universal Protection Service, Lp
1551 N Tustin Ave Ste 650
Santa Ana CA 92705
714 619-9700

(P-16846)
UNIVERSAL PROTECTION SVC LP
340 Golden Shore Ste 100, Long Beach (90802-4237)
PHONE..............................562 981-5700
Steve Salyer, *Owner*
Jessica Smith, *Division Mgr*
EMP: 58
SALES (corp-wide): 741.7MM **Privately Held**
SIC: 7381 Security guard service
HQ: Universal Protection Service, Lp
1551 N Tustin Ave Ste 650
Santa Ana CA 92705
714 619-9700

(P-16847)
UNIVERSAL PROTECTION SVC LP
21300 Victory Blvd # 230, Woodland Hills (91367-2525)
PHONE..............................818 227-1240
Jerry McConnell, *Branch Mgr*
EMP: 58
SALES (corp-wide): 741.7MM **Privately Held**
SIC: 7381 Security guard service
HQ: Universal Protection Service, Lp
1551 N Tustin Ave Ste 650
Santa Ana CA 92705
714 619-9700

(P-16848)
UNIVERSAL PROTECTION SVC LP (HQ)
Also Called: Allied Universal Security Svcs
1551 N Tustin Ave Ste 650, Santa Ana (92705-8664)
PHONE..............................714 619-9700
Brian Cescolini, *Partner*
Steve Jones, *Partner*
Louis Boulgarides, *President*
Philip Murray, *President*
Paul Sova, *President*
EMP: 148
SALES (est): 741.7MM **Privately Held**
SIC: 7381 Security guard service
PA: Universal Protection Gp, Llc
1551 N Tustin Ave Ste 650
Santa Ana CA 92705
714 619-9700

(P-16849)
UNIVERSAL PROTECTION SVC LP
1208 Vicente St, San Francisco (94116-3044)
PHONE..............................415 759-5056
David Nagle, *CEO*
EMP: 250
SALES (corp-wide): 741.7MM **Privately Held**
SIC: 7381 Security guard service
HQ: Universal Protection Service, Lp
1551 N Tustin Ave Ste 650
Santa Ana CA 92705
714 619-9700

(P-16850)
UNIVERSAL SERVICES AMERICA LP (DH)
Also Called: Allied Universal
1551 N Tustin Ave, Santa Ana (92705-8634)
P.O. Box 101034, Pasadena (91189-0003)
PHONE..............................714 619-9700

Steven Jones, *CEO*
Toni Ippolito, *CEO*
Chris Johnson, *Officer*
Julius McKinney, *Officer*
Scott Smith, *Officer*
EMP: 100
SALES: 2B
SALES (corp-wide): 3.2B **Privately Held**
SIC: 7381 7349 Security guard service; janitorial service, contract basis
HQ: Allied Universal Holdco Llc
1551 N Tustin Ave Ste 650
Santa Ana CA 92705
714 619-9700

(P-16851)
UNLIMITED SEC SPECIALISTS INC
13636 Ventura Blvd # 206, Sherman Oaks (91423-3700)
PHONE..............................877 310-4877
Jose Cardona, *Principal*
Alberto Alvarez, *Accounts Mgr*
EMP: 50
SALES: 2.5MM **Privately Held**
SIC: 7381 Security guard service

(P-16852)
US SECURITY ASSOCIATES INC
555 W Benjamin Holt Dr # 222, Stockton (95207-3860)
PHONE..............................209 476-7062
Perry Crawford, *Principal*
EMP: 108
SALES (corp-wide): 3.2B **Privately Held**
SIC: 7381 Security guard service
HQ: U.S. Security Associates, Inc.
200 Mansell Ct E Fl 5
Roswell GA 30076
-

(P-16853)
VENUE MANAGEMENT SYSTEMS INC
Also Called: V M S
2041 E Gladstone St Ste A, Glendora (91740-5385)
P.O. Box 25, San Dimas (91773-0025)
PHONE..............................626 445-6000
Charles E McIntyre, *President*
EMP: 3300
SQ FT: 35,000
SALES: 20MM **Privately Held**
WEB: www.vmscorporate.com
SIC: 7381 7363 8742 Detective & armored car services; employee leasing service; human resource consulting services

(P-16854)
W S B & ASSOCIATES INC
150 Executive Park Blvd # 4700, San Francisco (94134-3303)
PHONE..............................510 444-6266
Bobby Sisk, *President*
EMP: 100 **Privately Held**
SIC: 7381
PA: W S B & Associates Inc
1390 Market St Ste 314
San Francisco CA 94102
-

(P-16855)
W S B & ASSOCIATES INC (PA)
1390 Market St Ste 314, San Francisco (94102-5404)
PHONE..............................415 864-3510
Bobby Sisk, *CEO*
EMP: 77
SQ FT: 1,600
SALES (est): 6.6MM **Privately Held**
SIC: 7381 Security guard service

(P-16856)
WE TEAM SECURITY FIRM INC
12655 W Jefferson Blvd, Los Angeles (90066-7008)
PHONE..............................800 745-9051
Charli Beth Brown, *President*
EMP: 65
SALES (est): 139.2K **Privately Held**
SIC: 7381 Guard services

(P-16857)
WHELAN SECURITY CO
400 Continental Blvd, El Segundo (90245-5076)
PHONE..............................310 343-8628
Gregory Twardowski, *Branch Mgr*
EMP: 337
SALES (corp-wide): 204.1MM **Privately Held**
SIC: 7381 Guard services
PA: Whelan Security Co.
1699 S Hanley Rd Ste 350
Saint Louis MO 63144
314 644-3227

(P-16858)
WINDWALKER SECURITY PATROL INC
23987 Nw Frontage Rd, Acampo (95220)
P.O. Box 488 (95220-0488)
PHONE..............................209 333-3953
Richard V Edwards, *CEO*
Bb Edwards, *Shareholder*
EMP: 75
SALES (est): 1.4MM **Privately Held**
SIC: 7381 Security guard service

(P-16859)
WORLD PRIVATE SECURITY INC
16921 Parthenia St # 201, Northridge (91343-4568)
PHONE..............................818 894-1800
Fred Youssif, *President*
Jeannette Youssif, *Co-Owner*
EMP: 200
SALES: 4MM **Privately Held**
SIC: 7381 Security guard service

(P-16860)
WORLDWIDE SECURITY ASSOCIATES (HQ)
10311 S La Cienega Blvd, Los Angeles (90045-6109)
PHONE..............................310 743-3000
Andres Martinez, *President*
EMP: 300
SQ FT: 5,000
SALES (est): 23.1MM
SALES (corp-wide): 31.7MM **Privately Held**
WEB: www.wsainc.net
SIC: 7381 Security guard service
PA: Wsa Group Inc
19208 S Vermont Ave 200
Gardena CA 90248
310 743-3000

(P-16861)
WSA GROUP INC (PA)
19208 S Vermont Ave 200, Gardena (90248-4414)
PHONE..............................310 743-3000
Andres Martinez, *President*
James E Bush, *Vice Pres*
EMP: 50
SQ FT: 10,000
SALES (est): 31.7MM **Privately Held**
WEB: www.wsagroup.com
SIC: 7381 7349 Security guard service; janitorial service, contract basis

(P-16862)
XTREME SECURITY SERVICES INC
337 N Vineyard Ave # 210, Ontario (91764-5669)
PHONE..............................909 390-6818
Lawrence Polzin, *President*
EMP: 50
SALES: 1.2MM **Privately Held**
SIC: 7381 Security guard service

(P-16863)
YOSH ENTERPRISES INC
Also Called: Orion Security
675 E Gish Rd, San Jose (95112-2708)
PHONE..............................408 287-4411
Yosh Gahramani, *President*
Ashutosh Jha, *Managing Dir*
EMP: 400
SQ FT: 6,800

PRODUCTS & SVCS

SALES (est): 8.8MM **Privately Held**
WEB: www.orionsecurity.com
SIC: 7381 6531 8742 0782 Security guard service; private investigator; real estate managers; industrial & labor consulting services; lawn & garden services

7382 Security Systems Svcs

(P-16864)
3SCALE INC
995 Market St, San Francisco (94103-1702)
PHONE..................415 349-5187
Steven Willmott, *CEO*
Mark Cheshire, *COO*
David Lopez, *Software Engr*
Anna Grzywiska, *Hum Res Coord*
Laine Fuller, *VP Sales*
EMP: 50
SALES (est): 3MM **Privately Held**
SIC: 7382 Security systems services

(P-16865)
3VR SECURITY INC
814 Mission St Fl 4, San Francisco (94103-3034)
PHONE..................415 513-4577
Robert A Shipp, *CEO*
Charles F Ryan III, *CFO*
Masayuki Karahashi, *Vice Pres*
Uma Welingkar, *Vice Pres*
Clarissa Padilla, *Technology*
EMP: 90
SALES (est): 12.8MM **Publicly Held**
WEB: www.3vrsecurity.com
SIC: 7382 Protective devices, security
PA: Identiv, Inc.
2201 Walnut Ave Ste 100
Fremont CA 94538

(P-16866)
ACALVIO TECHNOLOGIES INC
2520 Mission College Blvd # 110, Santa Clara (95054-1238)
PHONE..................408 931-6160
Nat Natraj, *President*
Wade Lance, *Vice Pres*
Chad Scrupps, *Vice Pres*
EMP: 52
SQ FT: 4,166
SALES (est): 54.5K **Privately Held**
SIC: 7382 Security systems services

(P-16867)
ACS SECURITY INDUSTRIES INC
Also Called: A C S Security
1964 Westwood Blvd # 235, Los Angeles (90025-4683)
PHONE..................310 475-9016
Al Radi, *President*
EMP: 60
SALES (est): 5.2MM **Privately Held**
SIC: 7382 Security systems services

(P-16868)
ADMIRAL SECURITY SERVICES INC
2151 Salvio St Ste 260, Concord (94520-2406)
PHONE..................888 471-1128
Mohamed S Ahmed, *CEO*
Youssef Abdallah, *President*
Jeremy Drouin, *Human Resources*
EMP: 400
SQ FT: 1,500
SALES (est): 37.9MM **Privately Held**
SIC: 7382 7381 Security systems services; protective services, guard; security guard service; guard services

(P-16869)
ADT SECURITY CORPORATION
2150 John Glenn Dr # 100, Concord (94520-5671)
PHONE..................925 251-9088
Pete Sitch, *Branch Mgr*
Jeff Silva, *Manager*
EMP: 50
SALES (corp-wide): 2.9B **Publicly Held**
WEB: www.protectionone.com
SIC: 7382 5063 Burglar alarm maintenance & monitoring; alarm systems

HQ: The Adt Security Corporation
1501 W Yamato Rd
Boca Raton FL 33431
561 988-3600

(P-16870)
ADVANCED PROTECTION INDS INC
Also Called: National Monitoring Center
25341 Commercentre Dr # 100, Lake Forest (92630-8856)
PHONE..................800 662-1711
Michael Schubert, *President*
Scott Schubert, *Shareholder*
Woodie George Andrawos, *Exec VP*
Jessica Strojek, *Admin Mgr*
Demian Valle, *Info Tech Mgr*
EMP: 50
SALES (est): 9MM **Privately Held**
WEB: www.nmccentral.com
SIC: 7382 Burglar alarm maintenance & monitoring

(P-16871)
AERO PORT SERVICES INC (PA)
216 W Florence Ave, Inglewood (90301-1213)
PHONE..................310 623-8230
Chris Paik, *President*
Stephan Park, *CFO*
Jake Yoon, *CFO*
Julie Hong, *Treasurer*
Walter Vergara, *Chief Mktg Ofcr*
EMP: 53
SALES (est): 34.8MM **Privately Held**
WEB: www.aeroportservices.com
SIC: 7382 Security systems services

(P-16872)
AM-TEC TOTAL SECURITY INC (PA)
Also Called: Am-TEC Security
4075 Schaefer Ave, Chino (91710-5446)
PHONE..................909 573-4678
Jeff Torok, *President*
EMP: 55
SQ FT: 7,000
SALES (est): 280K **Privately Held**
SIC: 7382 Security systems services

(P-16873)
AMERICAN SERVICE INDUSTRIES
2930 W Imperial Hwy # 332, Inglewood (90303-3143)
PHONE..................323 779-4000
Tony Caminiti, *President*
Stephen E Kulp, *CEO*
John Congleton, *Senior VP*
EMP: 100
SQ FT: 1,200
SALES (est): 3.9MM **Privately Held**
SIC: 7382 7349 Protective devices, security; janitorial service, contract basis

(P-16874)
ARLO TECHNOLOGIES INC (HQ)
Also Called: NETGEAR
2200 Faraday Ave Ste 150, Carlsbad (92008-7224)
PHONE..................408 890-3900
Matthew McRae, *CEO*
Ralph E Faison, *Ch of Bd*
Christine M Gorjanc, *CFO*
Patrick J Collins III, *Senior VP*
Brian Busse, *Admin Sec*
EMP: 319
SALES (est): 11.7MM **Publicly Held**
SIC: 7382 7372 Security systems services; application computer software

(P-16875)
ASSERTIVE SECURITY SERVICES &
20501 Ventura Blvd # 150, Woodland Hills (91364-2330)
PHONE..................818 888-2405
Maryam Ayam, *President*
Daniel Charron, *Marketing Mgr*
EMP: 550
SALES (est): 28.1MM **Privately Held**
WEB: www.assertivesecurity.com
SIC: 7382 7381 Security systems services; security guard service

(P-16876)
ATLAS SECURITY INC
11862 Balboa Blvd Ste 395, Granada Hills (91344-2753)
PHONE..................323 876-1401
Jack Boyd, *President*
EMP: 50
SALES (est): 2.2MM **Privately Held**
SIC: 7382 Security systems services

(P-16877)
AUTHORIZED TAXI CAB
Also Called: A T S
6150 W 96th St, Los Angeles (90045-5218)
PHONE..................323 776-5324
Behzad Bitaraf, *President*
EMP: 60
SALES (est): 8.9MM **Privately Held**
SIC: 7382 Security systems services

(P-16878)
BAYER PROTECTIVE SERVICES INC
3436 Amrcn Rver Dr Ste 10, Sacramento (95864)
PHONE..................916 486-5800
Bryon A Bayer, *President*
Bryon Bayer, *President*
EMP: 165
SQ FT: 1,600
SALES (est): 10.8MM
SALES (corp-wide): 13.5MM **Privately Held**
WEB: www.bayerprotectiveservices.com
SIC: 7382 Security systems services
PA: First Security Services
850 San Jose Ave Ste 128
Clovis CA 93612
559 297-1444

(P-16879)
BLUEGILL TECHNOLOGIES LLC
Also Called: Bluegill Solar
11884 Welby Pl Ste 101, Moreno Valley (92557-6444)
PHONE..................877 765-2770
Aman Chowdhry, *President*
Jessica Sandoval, *Admin Asst*
EMP: 60
SQ FT: 1,100
SALES (est): 12MM **Privately Held**
SIC: 7382 7373 Security systems services; systems integration services

(P-16880)
BRIGHTCLOUD INC
4370 La Jolla Village Dr # 820, San Diego (92122-1277)
PHONE..................858 652-4803
Quinn Curtis, *President*
Hal Lonas, *President*
EMP: 125
SALES (est): 3.3MM
SALES (corp-wide): 153.3MM **Privately Held**
SIC: 7382 Security systems services
PA: Webroot Inc.
385 Interlocken Cres # 800
Broomfield CO 80021
303 442-3813

(P-16881)
CALLAN MANAGEMENT CORPORATION
Also Called: Western Area Security Services
2919 W Burbank Blvd Ste C, Burbank (91505-2351)
PHONE..................818 846-2215
Michael Butler, *President*
EMP: 300
SQ FT: 2,000
SALES (est): 14.5MM **Privately Held**
WEB: www.westernarea.com
SIC: 7382 7381 Security systems services; detective & armored car services

(P-16882)
CHRONICLE LLC
250 Mayfield Ave, Mountain View (94043)
PHONE..................650 214-5199
Ben Heben, *CFO*
Jan Kang,
EMP: 65

SALES (est): 965.6K
SALES (corp-wide): 110.8B **Publicly Held**
SIC: 7382 Security systems services
PA: Alphabet Inc.
1600 Amphitheatre Pkwy
Mountain View CA 94043
650 253-0000

(P-16883)
CLOUDFLARE INC (PA)
101 Townsend St, San Francisco (94107-1934)
PHONE..................650 319-8930
Matthew Prince, *President*
Kamilla Amirova, *Partner*
Rachele Gyorffy, *Partner*
Thomas Seifert, *CFO*
John Kaden, *General Mgr*
EMP: 72
SQ FT: 6,000
SALES (est): 31.4MM **Privately Held**
SIC: 7382 Security systems services

(P-16884)
CONTEMPORARY SERVICES CORP
369 Van Ness Way Ste 702, Torrance (90501-6245)
PHONE..................310 320-8418
Roy Sukimoto, *Branch Mgr*
EMP: 196
SALES (corp-wide): 328MM **Privately Held**
SIC: 7382 7381 7299 Security systems services; guard services; party planning service
PA: Contemporary Services Corporation
17101 Superior St
Northridge CA 91325
818 885-5150

(P-16885)
CONVERGINT TECHNOLOGIES LLC
5860 W Las Positas Blvd # 7, Pleasanton (94588-8557)
PHONE..................510 300-2800
Doug Lyle, *Branch Mgr*
Fred Michel, *Project Mgr*
Barry Woodward, *Project Mgr*
Lance Simpson, *Technology*
EMP: 50
SALES (corp-wide): 469.1MM **Privately Held**
SIC: 7382 Security systems services
PA: Convergint Technologies Llc
1 Commerce Dr
Schaumburg IL 60173
847 620-5000

(P-16886)
DELTA SCIENTIFIC CORPORATION (PA)
40355 Delta Ln, Palmdale (93551-3616)
PHONE..................661 575-1100
Harry D Dickinson, *CEO*
Bill Brunty, *President*
Richard I Winger, *CFO*
Keith Bobrosky, *Senior VP*
David Dickinson, *Vice Pres*
EMP: 200 **EST:** 1974
SQ FT: 200,000
SALES (est): 29.3MM **Privately Held**
WEB: www.deltascientific.com
SIC: 7382 Security systems services

(P-16887)
DIAL SECURITY (PA)
Also Called: Dial Communications
760 W Ventura Blvd, Camarillo (93010-8382)
P.O. Box 34781, Bethesda MD (20827-0781)
PHONE..................805 389-6700
William H Dundas, *President*
Erica Ayala, *Admin Asst*
Mark Snyder, *Manager*
EMP: 250
SQ FT: 12,000
SALES (est): 20.2MM **Privately Held**
WEB: www.dialcomm.com
SIC: 7382 7381 Protective devices, security; detective & armored car services

(P-16888)
DISTIL NETWORKS INC
115 Sansome St Ste 600, San Francisco
(94104-3618)
PHONE..............................415 423-0831
EMP: 55
SALES (corp-wide): 16.8MM **Privately Held**
SIC: 7382 Security systems services
PA: Distil Networks, Inc.
4501 Fairfax Dr Ste 120
Arlington VA 22203
866 598-6787

(P-16889)
DRIVE THRU TECHNOLOGY INC
Also Called: Dtt
1755 N Main St, Los Angeles (90031-2516)
PHONE..............................323 576-1400
Sam Naficy, President
Jeff Moran, CFO
Mark Simson, CFO
Thomas M Moran, Exec VP
Michael Sutton, Exec VP
EMP: 150
SQ FT: 17,000
SALES (est): 28.8MM **Privately Held**
WEB: www.dttusa.com
SIC: 7382 Confinement surveillance systems maintenance & monitoring

(P-16890)
ECAMSECURE
3400 E Airport Way, Long Beach
(90806-2412)
PHONE..............................888 246-0556
Christopher Coffey, President
William R Babcock, CFO
Eduardo Lira, Supervisor
EMP: 67
SQ FT: 3,500
SALES (est): 6.3MM **Privately Held**
SIC: 7382 5065 Security systems services; electronic parts & equipment

(P-16891)
EMAGINED SECURITY INC
2816 San Simeon Way, San Carlos
(94070-3611)
PHONE..............................415 944-2977
David Sockol, President
Eugene Schultz, Executive
Julianna Sockol, Info Tech Mgr
Chris Ingram, Director
Cory Dixon, Consultant
EMP: 50
SALES (est): 6.3MM **Privately Held**
WEB: www.emagined.com
SIC: 7382 Security systems services

(P-16892)
FED AIR SECURITY CORPORATION
210 S De Lacey Ave, Pasadena
(91105-2048)
PHONE..............................626 535-2200
Enrique Hernandez Jr, CEO
Chris R Sherman, CFO
EMP: 100
SQ FT: 16,000
SALES (est): 3.7MM **Privately Held**
SIC: 7382 Security systems services

(P-16893)
FIRST ALARM SEC & PATROL INC
5250 Claremont Ave, Stockton
(95207-5700)
PHONE..............................209 473-1110
EMP: 494
SALES (corp-wide): 43.5MM **Privately Held**
SIC: 7382 5063 Security systems services; transformers & transmission equipment
PA: First Alarm Security & Patrol, Inc.
1731 Tech Dr Ste 800
San Jose CA 95110
408 866-1111

(P-16894)
FIRST ALARM SEC & PATROL INC
1801 Oakland Blvd Ste 315, Walnut Creek
(94596-7017)
PHONE..............................925 295-1260
EMP: 329
SALES (corp-wide): 43.5MM **Privately Held**
SIC: 7382 Security systems services
PA: First Alarm Security & Patrol, Inc.
1731 Tech Dr Ste 800
San Jose CA 95110
408 866-1111

(P-16895)
FIRST ALARM SEC & PATROL INC
1240 Briggs Ave, Santa Rosa
(95401-4760)
PHONE..............................707 584-1110
EMP: 494
SALES (corp-wide): 43.5MM **Privately Held**
SIC: 7382 Security systems services
PA: First Alarm Security & Patrol, Inc.
1731 Tech Dr Ste 800
San Jose CA 95110
408 866-1111

(P-16896)
FIRST FIRE SYSTEMS INC (PA)
5947 Burchard Ave, Los Angeles
(90034-1701)
PHONE..............................310 559-0900
Juda Roshanzamir, President
Robbie Kashani, Executive
Ed Klapholz, Project Mgr
Abraham Velasco, Project Mgr
Cecil Christian, Technology
EMP: 100 EST: 1980
SQ FT: 9,400
SALES (est): 14.9MM **Privately Held**
WEB: www.firstfiresystems.com
SIC: 7382 Security systems services

(P-16897)
FIRSTLINE SECURITY SYSTEMS INC (PA)
2211 E Howell Ave, Anaheim (92806-6009)
PHONE..............................714 937-1440
Shelly Morefield, CEO
Steven Morefield, President
Tony Herrera, Technician
Gary Powell, Technician
John Cardos, Project Mgr
EMP: 55 EST: 1992
SQ FT: 7,776
SALES: 14MM **Privately Held**
SIC: 7382 Burglar alarm maintenance & monitoring

(P-16898)
G4S JUSTICE SERVICES LLC
Also Called: G4s Government Services
201 Technology Dr, Irvine (92618-2400)
PHONE..............................800 589-6003
Robert Contestabile, CEO
EMP: 220
SQ FT: 12,000
SALES (est): 11.9MM
SALES (corp-wide): 79.6MM **Privately Held**
SIC: 7382 3669 Fire alarm maintenance & monitoring; emergency alarms
PA: Sentinel Offender Services Llc
201 Technology Dr
Irvine CA 92618
949 453-1550

(P-16899)
GO GET EM INC
45248 Trevor Ave, Lancaster (93534-1614)
PHONE..............................702 985-5637
Michael Sprague, President
EMP: 60 **Privately Held**
SIC: 7382 Security systems services

(P-16900)
GUARD FORCE INTERNATIONAL INC
11566 Brookrun Ct, Riverside
(92505-5123)
P.O. Box 284, Austin TX (78767-0284)
PHONE..............................512 296-0316

Gordon Brooks, President
EMP: 50
SALES (est): 3MM **Privately Held**
SIC: 7382 Protective devices, security

(P-16901)
HIKVISION USA INC (HQ)
18639 Railroad St, City of Industry
(91748-1317)
PHONE..............................909 895-0400
Jeffrey He, CEO
Haifeng Xu, Treasurer
Sam Belbina, Vice Pres
Polo Cai, Vice Pres
Nick Tang, Vice Pres
EMP: 175 EST: 2007
SALES: 75MM
SALES (corp-wide): 6.3B **Privately Held**
SIC: 7382 Confinement surveillance systems maintenance & monitoring
PA: Hangzhou Hikvision Digital Technology
Co., Ltd.
No.555 Qianmo Road, Binjiang District
Hangzhou 31005
571 880-7599

(P-16902)
HOMELAND SECURITY SERVICES INC
31805 Temecula Pkwy, Temecula
(92592-8203)
P.O. Box 26052, Anaheim (92825-6052)
PHONE..............................714 956-2200
Leonard Bacani, President
Florencia Bacani, Vice Pres
EMP: 400
SQ FT: 250
SALES: 437.9K **Privately Held**
WEB: www.homelandsecurityservices.com
SIC: 7382 7381 Protective devices, security; detective & armored car services; detective services

(P-16903)
HONEYWELL INTERNATIONAL INC
1740 Creekside Oaks 150, Sacramento
(95833)
PHONE..............................916 923-7851
Mike Bishop, Manager
EMP: 100
SALES (corp-wide): 40.5B **Publicly Held**
WEB: www.honeywell.com
SIC: 7382 5075 Burglar alarm maintenance & monitoring; warm air heating & air conditioning
PA: Honeywell International Inc.
115 Tabor Rd
Morris Plains NJ 07950
973 455-2000

(P-16904)
ID ANALYTICS LLC
15253 Ave Of Science, San Diego
(92128-3437)
PHONE..............................858 312-6200
Scott Carter, CEO
Peter Boyes, COO
George Gelly, Officer
Daniel Rawlings, Officer
Steve Hanson, Vice Pres
EMP: 140 EST: 2002
SQ FT: 32,000
SALES (est): 19.9MM
SALES (corp-wide): 4.8B **Publicly Held**
WEB: www.idanalytics.com
SIC: 7382 Protective devices, security
HQ: Lifelock, Inc.
60 E Rio Salado Pkwy # 400
Tempe AZ 85281
480 682-5100

(P-16905)
IGOTCHU INC
4712 Admiralty Way # 997, Marina Del Rey
(90292-6905)
PHONE..............................818 987-1699
Seven Evans, President
EMP: 100
SALES (est): 1.1MM **Privately Held**
SIC: 7382 Security systems services

(P-16906)
INTREPID SECURITY SOLUTIONS
1999 S Bascom Ave Ste 700, Campbell
(95008-2205)
PHONE..............................855 379-2223
Rico Sciaky, CEO
EMP: 50
SQ FT: 150
SALES (est): 1.2MM **Privately Held**
SIC: 7382 Burglar alarm maintenance & monitoring

(P-16907)
IRON MOUNTAIN INCORPORATED
30481 Whipple Rd, Union City
(94587-1531)
P.O. Box 326 (94587-0326)
PHONE..............................510 798-6387
Keven Artis, Manager
EMP: 75
SALES (corp-wide): 3.8B **Publicly Held**
SIC: 7382 4226 3572 Security systems services; special warehousing & storage; computer storage devices
PA: Iron Mountain Incorporated
1 Federal St Fl 7
Boston MA 02110
617 535-4766

(P-16908)
JOHNSON CNTRLS SEC SLTIONS LLC
104 E Graham Pl, Burbank (91502-2027)
PHONE..............................818 428-6669
Carlo Alarc, Branch Mgr
April Sumague, Administration
EMP: 200 **Privately Held**
WEB: www.adt.com
SIC: 7382 Burglar alarm maintenance & monitoring
HQ: Johnson Controls Security Solutions
Llc
6600 Congress Ave
Boca Raton FL 33487
561 264-2071

(P-16909)
JOHNSON CNTRLS SEC SLTIONS LLC
1120 Palmyrita Ave # 280, Riverside
(92507-1744)
PHONE..............................951 787-0420
Tom Mannon, Manager
EMP: 100 **Privately Held**
WEB: www.adt.com
SIC: 7382 Burglar alarm maintenance & monitoring; fire alarm maintenance & monitoring
HQ: Johnson Controls Security Solutions
Llc
6600 Congress Ave
Boca Raton FL 33487
561 264-2071

(P-16910)
JOHNSON CNTRLS SEC SLTIONS LLC
3870 Murphy Canyon Rd # 140, San Diego
(92123-4446)
PHONE..............................561 988-3600
Greg Pavlicek, Manager
EMP: 122 **Privately Held**
WEB: www.adt.com
SIC: 7382 Burglar alarm maintenance & monitoring; fire alarm maintenance & monitoring
HQ: Johnson Controls Security Solutions
Llc
6600 Congress Ave
Boca Raton FL 33487
561 264-2071

(P-16911)
JOHNSON CNTRLS SEC SLTIONS LLC
150 N Hill Dr Ste 3, Brisbane (94005-1024)
PHONE..............................650 634-9000
Dan Zahhos, Manager
EMP: 60 **Privately Held**
WEB: www.adt.com
SIC: 7382 Burglar alarm maintenance & monitoring

HQ: Johnson Controls Security Solutions
Llc
6600 Congress Ave
Boca Raton FL 33487
561 264-2071

(P-16912)

JOHNSON CNTRLS SEC SLTIONS LLC

3825 Bay Center Pl B, Hayward
(94545-3619)
PHONE..................510 246-2862
Leo Brancheau, *General Mgr*
EMP: 70 **Privately Held**
WEB: www.adt.com
SIC: 7382 Burglar alarm maintenance &
monitoring; fire alarm maintenance &
monitoring
HQ: Johnson Controls Security Solutions
Llc
6600 Congress Ave
Boca Raton FL 33487
561 264-2071

(P-16913)

JOHNSON CNTRLS SEC SLTIONS LLC

7565 Irvine Center Dr # 100, Irvine
(92618-4918)
PHONE..................714 223-2300
Nels Jenson, *Manager*
EMP: 135 **Privately Held**
WEB: www.adt.com
SIC: 7382 Burglar alarm maintenance &
monitoring
HQ: Johnson Controls Security Solutions
Llc
6600 Congress Ave
Boca Raton FL 33487
561 264-2071

(P-16914)

JOHNSON CONTROLS

12728 Shoemaker Ave, Santa Fe Springs
(90670-6345)
PHONE..................562 405-3817
Andy Bernot, *Manager*
Donna Talley, *Executive*
EMP: 150 **Privately Held**
WEB: www.simplexgrinnell.com
SIC: 7382 1731 1711 Security systems
services; fire detection & burglar alarm
systems specialization; plumbing, heat-
ing, air-conditioning contractors
HQ: Johnson Controls Fire Protection Lp
4700 Exchange Ct Ste 300
Boca Raton FL 33431
561 988-7200

(P-16915)

KERN SECURITY CORPORATION

Also Called: Kern Security Systems
2701 Fruitvale Ave, Bakersfield
(93308-5905)
PHONE..................661 363-6874
John Affeld, *President*
Ronald C McVicar, *CFO*
EMP: 100
SQ FT: 4,000
SALES (est): 6.8MM
SALES (corp-wide): 55.1MM **Privately
Held**
WEB: www.kernsecurity.com
SIC: 7382 5999 1731 Burglar alarm main-
tenance & monitoring; fire alarm mainte-
nance & monitoring; alarm signal
systems; closed circuit television installa-
tion
PA: Security Signal Devices, Inc.
1740 N Lemon St
Anaheim CA 92801
800 888-0444

(P-16916)

KIMBERLITE CORPORATION

Sonitrol of Stockton
3728 Imperial Way, Stockton (95215-9686)
PHONE..................209 948-2551
Russ Borse, *Manager*
EMP: 55
SQ FT: 6,500

SALES (corp-wide): 11.7MM **Privately
Held**
SIC: 7382 1731 7359 5063 Burglar alarm
maintenance & monitoring; fire detection
& burglar alarm systems specialization;
electronic equipment rental, except computers; burglar alarm systems
PA: Kimberlite Corporation
3621 W Beechwood Ave
Fresno CA 93711
559 264-9730

(P-16917)

KIMBERLITE CORPORATION (PA)

Also Called: Sonitrol Security Systems
3621 W Beechwood Ave, Fresno
(93711-0648)
P.O. Box 9189 (93791-9189)
PHONE..................559 264-9730
Joey RAO Russell, *CEO*
Marselle Nikkel, *CFO*
Kenneth Berry, *Vice Pres*
Brian Petrille, *Vice Pres*
Marcos Reyes, *Vice Pres*
EMP: 58
SQ FT: 3,500
SALES (est): 11.7MM **Privately Held**
SIC: 7382 Burglar alarm maintenance &
monitoring; fire alarm maintenance &
monitoring; protective devices, security

(P-16918)

KOREA TCHNLGY CMMNICATIONS USA

Also Called: KT&c USA
10645 W Vanowen St, Burbank
(91505-1136)
PHONE..................213 381-0061
Jason JC Ra, *President*
H S Kwon, *CEO*
Joe Troiano, *Senior VP*
Danny Han, *Technical Staff*
Silvana Kim, *Sales Mgr*
EMP: 120
SALES (est): 6.7MM **Privately Held**
WEB: www.ktncusa.com
SIC: 7382 Security systems services

(P-16919)

LANTZ SECURITY SYSTEMS INC

4111 Las Virgenes Rd # 202, Calabasas
(91302-1886)
PHONE..................818 871-0193
EMP: 114
SALES (corp-wide): 9.7MM **Privately
Held**
SIC: 7382
PA: Lantz Security Systems Inc
43440 Sahuayo St
Lancaster CA 93535
661 949-3565

(P-16920)

LAW ENFORCEMENT OFFICERS INC

24000 Alicia Pkwy 17-229, Mission Viejo
(92691-3929)
PHONE..................855 477-3536
Erick Reyes, *CEO*
EMP: 130
SALES (est): 4.1MM **Privately Held**
SIC: 7382 Protective devices, security

(P-16921)

LIFE ALERT EMERGENCY RESPONSE (PA)

16027 Ventura Blvd # 400, Encino
(91436-2747)
PHONE..................800 247-0000
Isaac Shepher, *President*
Felix Leung, *CFO*
Miriam Shepher, *Senior VP*
Richard Chen, *Vice Pres*
Martin Yasin, *Software Engr*
EMP: 175
SQ FT: 29,489
SALES (est): 48.9MM **Privately Held**
WEB: www.lifealert.com
SIC: 7382 5731 Confinement surveillance
systems maintenance & monitoring; con-
sumer electronic equipment

(P-16922)

LYONS SECURITY SERVICE INC

P.O. Box 18955 (92817-8955)
PHONE..................714 401-4850
Kathleen Guidice, *President*
EMP: 75 EST: 2012
SALES (est): 2.7MM **Privately Held**
SIC: 7382 Security systems services

(P-16923)

MILLENNIUM ALARM SYSTEMS INC (PA)

5777 W Century Blvd # 1755, Los Angeles
(90045-5692)
PHONE..................310 337-1108
Niels Ole Staehr, *CEO*
Martin Askgaard, *CFO*
EMP: 50
SQ FT: 2,000
SALES (est): 11.3MM **Privately Held**
WEB: www.millenniumalarmsystems.com
SIC: 7382 Burglar alarm maintenance &
monitoring

(P-16924)

NATIONAL SECURITY INDUSTRIES

1217 Del Paso Blvd Ste A, Sacramento
(95815-3660)
PHONE..................916 779-0640
EMP: 279 **Privately Held**
SIC: 7382 Security systems services
PA: National Security Industries
940 Park Ave Frnt Frnt
San Jose CA 95126

(P-16925)

NETCONTINUUM INC

1454 Almaden Valley Dr, San Jose
(95120-3801)
PHONE..................408 961-5600
Varun Nagaraj, *CEO*
Gene Banman, *President*
EMP: 80
SQ FT: 31,000
SALES (est): 7.4MM **Privately Held**
SIC: 7382 Security systems services

(P-16926)

PACIFIC WEST SECURITY INC

Also Called: Sonitrol
1587 Schallenberger Rd, San Jose
(95131-2434)
PHONE..................801 748-1034
Paul Schumate, *President*
Kari Herzig, *COO*
Sandra Oswalt, *Corp Secy*
EMP: 60
SQ FT: 8,000
SALES (est): 6.7MM **Privately Held**
WEB: www.sonitrolsafetyzone.com
SIC: 7382 1731 Burglar alarm mainte-
nance & monitoring; fire alarm mainte-
nance & monitoring; fire detection &
burglar alarm systems specialization

(P-16927)

PLEXICOR INC (PA)

3598 Cadillac Ave, Costa Mesa
(92626-1416)
PHONE..................714 918-8700
Robert Klemme, *CEO*
EMP: 50
SALES (est): 4MM **Privately Held**
SIC: 7382 5063 1731 Security systems
services; electric alarms & signaling
equipment; safety & security specializa-
tion

(P-16928)

POST ALARM SYSTEMS (PA)

Also Called: Post Alarm Systems Patrol Svcs
47 E Saint Joseph St, Arcadia
(91006-2861)
PHONE..................626 446-7159
William Post, *President*
Bill Post, *Owner*
Lois Post, *Treasurer*
Robert Jennison, *Business Dir*
Gina Post-Franco, *General Mgr*
EMP: 98
SQ FT: 10,500

SALES (est): 12.6MM **Privately Held**
WEB: www.postalarm.com
SIC: 7382 1731 5063 Burglar alarm maintenance & monitoring; fire alarm maintenance & monitoring; protective devices,
security; fire detection & burglar alarm
systems specialization; electrical apparatus & equipment

(P-16929)

PROTECT-FOR-LESS SECURITY SVCS

Also Called: Pfl Security
72877 Dinah Shore Dr, Rancho Mirage
(92270-2763)
PHONE..................760 343-1192
Norman Southerby, *CEO*
Evelyn Frances Southerby, *President*
EMP: 50
SALES (est): 2.4MM **Privately Held**
SIC: 7382 Security systems services

(P-16930)

RAPISCAN SYSTEMS INC

2805 Columbia St, Torrance (90503-3804)
PHONE..................310 978-1457
Mal Maginnis, *President*
EMP: 160
SALES (est): 1.6MM **Privately Held**
SIC: 7382 Security systems services

(P-16931)

REALDEFENSE LLC

1541 Ocean Ave Ste 200, Santa Monica
(90401-2104)
PHONE..................310 693-5935
Gary Guseinov, *CEO*
EMP: 100
SALES (est): 1.2MM **Privately Held**
SIC: 7382 Security systems services

(P-16932)

REPUTATIONCOM INC (PA)

1400 A Sport Blvd Ste 401, Redwood City
(94063)
PHONE..................650 381-3056
Joe Fuca, *CEO*
Mark Phillips, *CFO*
Howard Bragman, *Vice Ch Bd*
Jason Grier, *Ch Credit Ofcr*
Colleen McCreary, *Officer*
EMP: 104
SALES (est): 29.4MM **Privately Held**
SIC: 7382 Security systems services

(P-16933)

SAFE SECURITY INC

2440 Camino Ramon Ste 200, San Ramon
(94583-4326)
P.O. Box 5164 (94583-5164)
PHONE..................925 830-4777
Paul F Sargenti, *President*
Jess Alvarado, *CFO*
Karen McQueen, *Marketing Mgr*
Wayne Jordan, *Director*
Sarah Ratcliffe, *Director*
EMP: 455
SALES (est): 49.9MM **Privately Held**
SIC: 7382 7539 Burglar alarm mainte-
nance & monitoring; automotive sound
system service & installation

(P-16934)

SECTEK INC

Bldg 15, Mountain View (94035)
PHONE..................650 604-1785
Wilfred D Blood, *Branch Mgr*
EMP: 55 **Privately Held**
WEB: www.sectek.com
SIC: 7382 Security systems services
PA: Sectek, Inc.
1930 Isaac Newton Sq W # 100
Reston VA 20190

(P-16935)

SECURITAS ELECTRONIC SEC INC

7002 Convoy Ct, San Diego (92111-1017)
PHONE..................858 812-7349
EMP: 99
SALES (corp-wide): 10.9B **Privately Held**
SIC: 7382 Security systems services

HQ: Securitas Electronic Security Inc.
3800 Tabs Dr
Uniontown OH 44685
855 331-0359

(P-16936)
SECURITAS SEC SVCS USA INC
Also Called: Northern California Region
1650 Borel Pl Ste 227, San Mateo
(94402-3508)
PHONE.....................650 358-1556
George King, *Branch Mgr*
Sanford White, *Branch Mgr*
EMP: 114
SALES (corp-wide): 10.9B **Privately Held**
WEB: www.securitasinc.com
SIC: 7382 Security systems services
HQ: Securitas Security Services Usa, Inc.
9 Campus Dr
Parsippany NJ 07054
973 267-5300

(P-16937)
SECURITY ALARM FING ENTPS INC
2440 Camino Ramon Ste 200, San Ramon
(94583-4326)
P.O. Box 5164 (94583-5164)
PHONE.....................925 830-4786
Paul Sargenti, *President*
Yolanda Zara, *Vice Pres*
Ann Atencio, *Office Mgr*
EMP: 70
SQ FT: 20,000
SALES (est): 10.7MM **Privately Held**
WEB: www.safefinancial.com
SIC: 7382 6141 Security systems services; financing: automobiles, furniture, etc., not a deposit bank

(P-16938)
SECURITY ON-SITE SERVICES INC
2210 Plaza Dr Ste 300, Rocklin
(95765-4406)
PHONE.....................916 988-6500
Martin A Steiner, *CEO*
Michael A McConnell, *COO*
EMP: 75 EST: 2013
SALES (est): 361K **Privately Held**
SIC: 7382 Security systems services

(P-16939)
SECURITY SIGNAL DEVICES INC (PA)
Also Called: Ssd Systems
1740 N Lemon St, Anaheim (92801-1047)
PHONE.....................800 888-0444
John F Affeld, *CEO*
Sheila Rossi, *Admin Sec*
EMP: 50 EST: 1969
SQ FT: 20,000
SALES (est): 55.1MM **Privately Held**
WEB: www.ssdsystems.com
SIC: 7382 1731 Security systems services; safety & security specialization; access control systems specialization; closed circuit television installation; fire detection & burglar alarm systems specialization

(P-16940)
SENTINEL MONITORING CORP (HQ)
220 Technology Dr Ste 200, Irvine
(92618-2424)
PHONE.....................949 453-1550
Robert Contestabile, *President*
EMP: 200
SALES (est): 5.1MM
SALES (corp-wide): 79.6MM **Privately Held**
WEB: www.sentrak.com
SIC: 7382 Confinement surveillance systems maintenance & monitoring
PA: Sentinel Offender Services Llc
201 Technology Dr
Irvine CA 92618
949 453-1550

(P-16941)
SENTINEL OFFENDER SERVICES LLC (PA)
201 Technology Dr, Irvine (92618-2400)
PHONE.....................949 453-1550

Robert Contestabile,
Salman Qureshi, *CTO*
Don Fulton, *Cust Mgr*
EMP: 85
SQ FT: 20,000
SALES (est): 79.6MM **Privately Held**
WEB: www.sentrak.com
SIC: 7382 Confinement surveillance systems maintenance & monitoring

(P-16942)
SKYBOX SECURITY INC (PA)
2077 Gateway Pl Ste 200, San Jose
(95110-1016)
PHONE.....................408 441-8060
Gideon Cohen, *CEO*
Lior Barak, *CFO*
Stewart Fox, *Exec VP*
Ravid Circus, *Vice Pres*
Michelle Cobb, *Vice Pres*
EMP: 64
SALES (est): 53MM **Privately Held**
WEB: www.skyboxsecurity.com
SIC: 7382 Security systems services

(P-16943)
SKYHIGH NETWORKS INC
900 E Hamilton Ave # 400, Campbell
(95008-0670)
PHONE.....................408 564-0278
Christopher D Young, *CEO*
Michael Berry, *CFO*
Allison Cerra, *Chief Mktg Ofcr*
Dawn Smith,
John Giamatteo, *Exec VP*
EMP: 99
SALES (est): 2.3MM **Privately Held**
SIC: 7382 Security systems services
HQ: Mcafee, Llc
2821 Mission College Blvd
Santa Clara CA 95054
888 847-8766

(P-16944)
SPECTRUM SECURITY SERVICES INC (PA)
13967 Campo Rd Ste 101, Jamul
(91935-3232)
P.O. Box 744 (91935-0744)
PHONE.....................619 669-6660
Sam Ersan, *President*
Porter Erent, *President*
Porter Trent, *COO*
Bill Treat, *Information Mgr*
EMP: 212
SQ FT: 1,200
SALES (est): 7.5MM **Privately Held**
WEB: www.spectrumsecurityservices.com
SIC: 7382 Security systems services

(P-16945)
STAFF PRO INC (PA)
15272 Jason Cir, Huntington Beach
(92649-1238)
PHONE.....................714 230-7200
Cory Meredith, *CEO*
Rose Davis, *Social Dir*
Jennifer Pacheco, *Director*
EMP: 2200
SQ FT: 10,000
SALES (est): 98.4MM **Privately Held**
WEB: www.staffpro.com
SIC: 7382 8741 Security systems services; management services

(P-16946)
TAD GROUP LLC
W Tower 5000 W Tow, Newport Beach
(92660)
PHONE.....................949 476-3601
Izan Todorov,
EMP: 150
SALES (est): 1.5MM **Privately Held**
SIC: 7382 7373 Security systems services; computer integrated systems design

(P-16947)
TALON EXECUTIVE SERVICES INC
151 Kalmus Dr Ste A103, Costa Mesa
(92626-5900)
PHONE.....................714 434-7476
Ronald William, *CEO*
Laurie Virtue, *Office Mgr*
Liz Russell, *Bookkeeper*
Martin Hanneman, *Manager*

EMP: 50
SQ FT: 2,000
SALES (est): 4.7MM **Privately Held**
WEB: www.talonexec.com
SIC: 7382 8742 Security systems services; management consulting services

(P-16948)
TTIK INC (PA)
Also Called: P C S C
3541 Challenger St, Torrance
(90503-1641)
PHONE.....................310 303-3600
Masami Kosaka, *President*
Hanan Rozner, *COO*
Robert K Takahashi, *CFO*
Henry Asao, *Vice Pres*
Alan Kosaka, *Vice Pres*
▲ **EMP:** 58
SQ FT: 28,000
SALES (est): 5.1MM **Privately Held**
SIC: 7382 Security systems services

(P-16949)
VERNON SECURITY INC
15317 Parmnt Blvd Ste 201, Paramount
(90723)
PHONE.....................562 790-8993
Jay Ellsworth, *President*
Dan Vincent, *Vice Pres*
Hector Parra, *Opers Mgr*
Elizabeth Getten, *Manager*
EMP: 100
SALES (est): 6.2MM **Privately Held**
SIC: 7382 Protective devices, security

(P-16950)
VOLUTONE LLC (PA)
Also Called: Volutone Distributing Co.
170 W Cochran St, Simi Valley
(93065-6215)
PHONE.....................805 520-8500
Neville Hansen, *President*
Trevor Hansen, *Vice Pres*
EMP: 88
SQ FT: 25,000
SALES (est): 17.7MM **Privately Held**
WEB: www.volutone.com
SIC: 7382 5065 Protective devices, security; sound equipment, electronic

(P-16951)
WARREN SECURITY SYSTEMS INC
1305 Francisco Blvd E, San Rafael
(94901-5501)
P.O. Box 3210 (94912-3210)
PHONE.....................415 456-7034
Warren V Glass III, *President*
EMP: 50
SALES (est): 2.9MM **Privately Held**
SIC: 7382 1731 Burglar alarm maintenance & monitoring; protective devices, security; electrical work

---

7383 News Syndicates

(P-16952)
ASSOCIATED PRESS
221 S Figueroa St Ste 300, Los Angeles
(90012-2553)
PHONE.....................213 626-1200
Anthony Marquez, *Manager*
EMP: 60
SALES (corp-wide): 510.1MM **Privately Held**
WEB: www.apme.com
SIC: 7383 News reporting services for newspapers & periodicals
PA: The Associated Press
200 Liberty St Fl 19
New York NY 10281
212 621-1500

(P-16953)
BLOOMBERG LP
345 California St Fl 35, San Francisco
(94104-2624)
PHONE.....................415 912-2960
Curtis McCool, *Planning*
Sarah Wilsak, *Research*
Ebru Boysan, *Sales Executive*
Robert Dellisanti, *Sales Staff*
Jeff Taylor, *Editor*

EMP: 100
SALES (corp-wide): 1.9B **Privately Held**
WEB: www.bloomberg.com
SIC: 7383 News reporting services for newspapers & periodicals
PA: Bloomberg L.P.
731 Lexington Ave Fl Ll2
New York NY 10022
212 318-2000

(P-16954)
BUENA VISTA TELEVISION (DH)
Also Called: Buena Vista TV Advg Sls
500 S Buena Vista St, Burbank
(91521-0001)
PHONE.....................818 560-1878
Janice Marinelli, *CEO*
Mort Marcus, *President*
Sal Sardo, *President*
Anne L Buettner, *CFO*
Jed Cohen, *Exec VP*
EMP: 129
SALES (est): 6.8MM **Publicly Held**
SIC: 7383 News feature syndicate
HQ: Disney Enterprises, Inc.
500 S Buena Vista St
Burbank CA 91521
818 560-1000

(P-16955)
GIGA OMNI MEDIA INC
1613a Lyon St, San Francisco
(94115-2414)
PHONE.....................415 974-6355
Paul Walborsky, *CEO*
Katie Chin, *Manager*
Natasha Leonova, *Manager*
EMP: 75
SALES (est): 7.8MM **Privately Held**
SIC: 7383 News pictures, gathering & distributing; press service

(P-16956)
MARKETWATCH INC (DH)
Also Called: C B S Marketwatch
201 California St Fl 13, San Francisco
(94111-5002)
PHONE.....................415 439-6400
Larry S Kramer, *Ch of Bd*
Kathleen B Yates, *President*
Paul Mattison, *CFO*
William Bishop, *Exec VP*
Doug Appleton, *Admin Sec*
EMP: 51
SQ FT: 24,000
SALES (est): 10.4MM
SALES (corp-wide): 9B **Publicly Held**
WEB: www.marketwatch.com
SIC: 7383 News ticker service
HQ: Dow Jones & Company, Inc.
1211 Avenue Of The Americ
New York NY 10036
609 627-2999

(P-16957)
MARKETWIRE INC (HQ)
100 N Pacific Coast Hwy, El Segundo
(90245-4359)
PHONE.....................310 765-3200
Michael Nowlan, *President*
James H Delaney, *COO*
Stephen Devito, *CFO*
Michael Shuler, *Senior VP*
Suresh Kumar, *Vice Pres*
EMP: 55 EST: 1998
SALES (est): 11.4MM
SALES (corp-wide): 3.9B **Publicly Held**
WEB: www.marketwire.com
SIC: 7383 Press service
PA: Nasdaq, Inc.
1 Liberty Plz Ste 4900
New York NY 10006
212 401-8700

(P-16958)
MELTWATER NEWS US INC (DH)
225 Bush St Ste 1000, San Francisco
(94104-4215)
P.O. Box 123408, Dallas TX (75312-3408)
PHONE.....................415 829-5900
Jorn Lyseggen, *CEO*
Filip Schoon, *Partner*
Adam Dealy, *COO*
Martin Hernandez, *CFO*
Marion Wallace, *Business Dir*
EMP: 54

(PA)=Parent Co (HQ)=Headquarters (DH)=Div Headquarters
✪ = New Business established in last 2 years

SALES (est): 218.7MM
SALES (corp-wide): 242.3MM **Privately Held**
SIC: 7383 News syndicates

(P-16959)
WRAP NEWS INC
Also Called: Wrap, The
2260 S Centinela Ave # 150, Los Angeles
(90064-1007)
PHONE..................................424 248-0612
Sharon Waxman, *President*
EMP: 50
SALES: 7.5MM **Privately Held**
SIC: 7383 News correspondents, independent; news pictures, gathering & distributing

7384 Photofinishing Labs

(P-16960)
ICON EXPOSURE INC
5450 Wilshire Blvd, Los Angeles
(90036-4218)
PHONE..................................323 933-1666
Ramesh Venugopal, *President*
Carlos Barrientos,
EMP: 57 EST: 1998
SQ FT: 11,600
SALES (est): 4.5MM **Privately Held**
SIC: 7384 Photofinishing laboratory

(P-16961)
J H MADDOCKS PHOTOGRAPHY
Also Called: Photocenter Imaging
40 E Verdugo Ave, Burbank (91502-1931)
PHONE..................................818 842-7150
Joe H Maddocks, *President*
Janet Maddocks, *Shareholder*
Vance Maddocks, *CEO*
Scott Maddocks, *Vice Pres*
Boris Winogradow, *Vice Pres*
EMP: 61
SQ FT: 15,000
SALES (est): 4.2MM **Privately Held**
WEB: www.photocenter.net
SIC: 7384 Film processing & finishing laboratory; film developing & printing

(P-16962)
JAKE HEY INCORPORATED
Also Called: A & I Color Laboratory
257 S Lake St, Burbank (91502-2111)
PHONE..................................323 856-5280
David Alexander, *President*
James Ishihara, *Vice Pres*
EMP: 144
SQ FT: 16,000
SALES (est): 7.2MM **Privately Held**
SIC: 7384 Photofinish laboratories

(P-16963)
PHOTO TLC INC
3925 Cypress Dr, Petaluma (94954-5900)
PHONE..................................415 462-0010
Ed Bernstein, *CEO*
EMP: 125
SQ FT: 30,000
SALES (est): 4.3MM **Privately Held**
SIC: 7384 Photographic services

(P-16964)
PICTURE IT ON CANVAS INC
1800 Seaport Blvd, Redwood City
(94063-5543)
PHONE..................................858 679-1200
Robert McKeon, *CEO*
Monica Denosta, *Senior VP*
Merete McCarthy, *Human Res Mgr*
Jason Richey, *Mktg Dir*
Brad Mangiameli, *Sales Mgr*
EMP: 65
SQ FT: 33,000
SALES (est): 10.7MM **Privately Held**
SIC: 7384 Photograph developing & retouching

(P-16965)
PRINTFUL INC
19749 Dearborn St, Chatsworth
(91311-6510)
PHONE..................................818 351-7181
Lauris Liberts, *Mng Member*
Davis Siksnans, *Founder*

EMP: 60 EST: 2010
SQ FT: 5,000
SALES (est): 1.7MM **Privately Held**
SIC: 7384 Film developing & printing

(P-16966)
SHUTTERFLY INC (PA)
2800 Bridge Pkwy Ste 100, Redwood City
(94065-1193)
PHONE..................................650 610-5200
Christopher North, *President*
Sarah Allbritten, *Partner*
Nicki Deuel, *Partner*
William J Lansing, *Ch of Bd*
Dwayne Black, *COO*
EMP: 148
SQ FT: 100,000
SALES: 1.1B **Publicly Held**
WEB: www.shutterfly.com
SIC: 7384 5946 Photofinishing laboratory; film developing & printing; camera & photographic supply stores; cameras; photographic supplies

(P-16967)
SUPER PHOTO LABORATORY INC
Also Called: Super Color Labs
979 N La Brea Ave, West Hollywood
(90038-2321)
PHONE..................................323 512-0247
Richard Kung, *President*
Josephine Kung, *Treasurer*
David Chang, *Vice Pres*
May Chang, *Admin Sec*
EMP: 55
SQ FT: 7,500
SALES (est): 4MM **Privately Held**
SIC: 7384 Photofinish laboratories

(P-16968)
TECHNICOLOR INC
Also Called: Technicolor Lab
2255 N Ontario St Ste 180, Burbank
(91504-4509)
PHONE..................................818 260-4577
Joe Berchtold, *President*
EMP: 400
SALES (est): 38.4MM **Privately Held**
SIC: 7384 Photofinish laboratories

7389 Business Svcs, NEC

(P-16969)
A F EVANS COMPANY INC
Also Called: Byron Park
1700 Tice Valley Blvd Ofc, Walnut Creek
(94595-1654)
PHONE..................................925 937-1700
Kirsten Korhsege, *Manager*
EMP: 70
SALES (corp-wide): 60.5MM **Privately Held**
WEB: www.afevans.com
SIC: 7389 Personal service agents, brokers & bureaus
PA: A. F. Evans Company, Inc.
    2033 N Main St Ste 340
    Walnut Creek CA 94596
    510 891-9400

(P-16970)
A J PARENT COMPANY INC (PA)
Also Called: Americas Printer.com
6910 Aragon Cir Ste 6, Buena Park
(90620-8103)
PHONE..................................714 521-1100
Arthur Parent, *CEO*
Mike Roccio, *Vice Pres*
Theresa Fatino, *Administration*
Bradley Schmidt, *Software Dev*
Melynda Bryan, *Human Res Dir*
EMP: 67
SALES (est): 18.1MM **Privately Held**
WEB: www.americaprinter.com
SIC: 7389 2752 Printers' services: folding, collating; commercial printing, lithographic

(P-16971)
AAA RESTAURANT FIRE CTRL INC
Also Called: AAA Fire Protection Service
30113 Union City Blvd, Union City
(94587-1511)
P.O. Box 3626, Hayward (94540-3626)
PHONE..................................510 786-9555
Brent Patterson, *President*
Jeanne Patterson, *Treasurer*
Karen Patterson, *Treasurer*
Brian Patterson, *Vice Pres*
Charisse Filteau, *Office Mgr*
EMP: 90
SQ FT: 10,000
SALES (est): 11.1MM **Privately Held**
WEB: www.aaafireprotection.com
SIC: 7389 Fire extinguisher servicing

(P-16972)
AARON THOMAS COMPANY INC (PA)
7421 Chapman Ave, Garden Grove
(92841-2115)
PHONE..................................714 894-4468
James T Chang, *Ch of Bd*
Thomas Bacon, *President*
Linda Bacon, *Treasurer*
Brian Robinson, *Principal*
Angie Mayfield, *Division Mgr*
EMP: 185
SQ FT: 207,000
SALES (est): 35.4MM **Privately Held**
WEB: www.packaging.com
SIC: 7389 Packaging & labeling services

(P-16973)
ABBA BAIL BONDS (PA)
900 Avila St Ste 2, Los Angeles
(90012-3871)
PHONE..................................213 680-1400
Scott Esparza, *Principal*
Joy Boiloue, *Manager*
Linda Olmeda, *Manager*
EMP: 50
SALES (est): 5.8MM **Privately Held**
SIC: 7389 Bail bonding

(P-16974)
ABI DOCUMENT SUPPORT SVCS LLC
11010 White Rock Rd # 160, Rancho Cordova (95670-6083)
PHONE..................................909 793-0613
Maggie Dragna, *Branch Mgr*
EMP: 50 **Privately Held**
SIC: 7389 5044 Microfilm recording & developing service; office equipment
HQ: Abi Document Support Services, Llc
    3534 E Sunshine St Ste L
    Springfield MO 65809

(P-16975)
ABI DOCUMENT SUPPORT SVCS LLC
10459 Mountain View Ave E, Loma Linda
(92354-2033)
PHONE..................................909 793-0613
David Benge, *Branch Mgr*
Debra Palazuelos, *Supervisor*
EMP: 100 **Privately Held**
SIC: 7389 5044 Microfilm recording & developing service; office equipment
HQ: Abi Document Support Services, Llc
    3534 E Sunshine St Ste L
    Springfield MO 65809

(P-16976)
ABSOLUTDATA TECHNOLOGIES INC
1320 Harbor Bay Pkwy # 170, Alameda
(94502-6506)
PHONE..................................510 748-9922
Anil Kaul, *President*
Jim Lord, *Senior VP*
Sudeshna Datta, *Vice Pres*
Suhale Kapoor, *Vice Pres*
Saurabh Mathur, *Executive*
EMP: 75
SQ FT: 1,600

SALES (est): 7.6MM **Privately Held**
WEB: www.absolutdata.com
SIC: 7389 7374 Personal service agents, brokers & bureaus; data processing service

(P-16977)
ABSOLUTE EXHIBITS INC (PA)
Also Called: Meroform Systems USA
1382 Valencia Ave Ste H, Tustin
(92780-6472)
PHONE..................................714 685-2800
Todd Koren, *President*
Jan Koren, *Co-President*
EMP: 65
SQ FT: 15,500
SALES (est): 23.8MM **Privately Held**
WEB: www.absoluteexhibits.com
SIC: 7389 Promoters of shows & exhibitions

(P-16978)
ACCESS BUSINESS GROUP INTL LLC
6500 Beach Blvd, Buena Park (90621)
PHONE..................................800 879-2732
Chris Thomas, *Research*
Anwar Abudagga, *Engineer*
Melisa Hernandez, *Buyer*
Rigo Monge, *Buyer*
Karl Waller, *Director*
EMP: 148
SALES (corp-wide): 8.7B **Privately Held**
WEB: www.accessbusinessgroupinternational.com
SIC: 7389 Personal service agents, brokers & bureaus
HQ: Access Business Group International Llc
    7575 Fulton St E
    Ada MI 49355
    616 787-6000

(P-16979)
ACCESS FINANCE INC
3415 S Sepulveda Blvd # 400, Los Angeles
(90034-6094)
PHONE..................................310 826-4000
Raquel Aguirre, *Manager*
EMP: 50
SALES (est): 184.3K **Privately Held**
SIC: 7389 Financial services

(P-16980)
ACCO ENGINEERED SYSTEMS INC
6446 E Washington Blvd, Commerce
(90040-1820)
PHONE..................................323 201-0931
Matt Deluca, *Principal*
Tim Karp, *Sales Engr*
EMP: 50
SALES (corp-wide): 768.2MM **Privately Held**
SIC: 7389 Automobile recovery service
PA: Acco Engineered Systems, Inc.
    6265 San Fernando Rd
    Glendale CA 91201
    818 244-6571

(P-16981)
ACCT HOLDINGS LLC
5949 Fair Oaks Blvd, Carmichael
(95608-5221)
PHONE..................................916 971-1981
EMP: 594
SALES (corp-wide): 373.6MM **Privately Held**
SIC: 7389 Telemarketing services
PA: Acct Holdings Llc
    1235 Westlakes Dr Ste 160
    Berwyn PA 19312
    610 695-0500

(P-16982)
ACCU-COUNT INVENTORY SVCS INC
Also Called: MSI Invntory Srvce-Los Angeles
1024 N Citrus Ave, Covina (91722-2739)
P.O. Box 814, Moorpark (93020-0814)
PHONE..................................805 231-6310
Mike M Naderi, *President*
EMP: 59
SQ FT: 800

SALES: 945.5K **Privately Held**
SIC: 7389 Inventory computing service

(P-16983)
ACTION SPORTS RETAILER
Also Called: Asr
31910 Del Obispo St # 200, San Juan
Capistrano (92675-3182)
PHONE...................................949 226-5744
Greg Farrar, *Principal*
EMP: 60
SALES (est): 1.4MM **Privately Held**
SIC: 7389 Trade show arrangement

(P-16984)
ACTIVE STORAGE INC
2295 Jefferson St, Torrance (90501-3302)
PHONE...................................818 709-1133
Alex Grossman, *CEO*
Steve Rizzone, *CEO*
Jane Wike, *CFO*
EMP: 50
SALES (est): 5.7MM **Privately Held**
SIC: 7389 Document storage service

(P-16985)
ADMINISTRATIVE SYSTEMS INC
1651 Response Rd Ste 350, Sacramento
(95815-5255)
P.O. Box 15437 (95851-0437)
PHONE...................................916 563-1121
Donald J Robinson, *President*
Paul Souza, *CFO*
Geraldine M Fong, *Corp Secy*
Keith Crane, *Vice Pres*
James R Powell, *Vice Pres*
EMP: 75
SALES (est): 11.8MM **Privately Held**
WEB: www.asipay.com
SIC: 7389 Personal service agents, bro-
kers & bureaus

(P-16986)
ADVANCED COMMUNICATION SERVICE
Also Called: Fphs2
2650 Flora Spiegel Way, Corona
(92881-3560)
PHONE...................................909 210-9328
Eddie Feghali, *President*
Jason Mokbel, *Exec VP*
William Scruggs, *Vice Pres*
Jon Harb, *Council Mbr*
EMP: 121
SQ FT: 2,400
SALES: 3.1MM **Privately Held**
SIC: 7389 Personal service agents, bro-
kers & bureaus

(P-16987)
AFFILIATED COMMUNICATIONS INC
Also Called: Alert Communications
3601 Calle Tecate Ste 200, Camarillo
(93012-5058)
P.O. Box 5720, Ventura (93005-0720)
PHONE...................................805 650-4949
Richard Starr, *President*
Monte L Widders, *Vice Pres*
Angel Elliott, *Human Res Mgr*
Sandra Rios, *Training Spec*
Frances Starr, *Sales Staff*
EMP: 50
SQ FT: 5,000
SALES (est): 7.5MM **Privately Held**
WEB: www.alertcommunications.com
SIC: 7389 5999 Telephone answering
service; telephone & communication
equipment

(P-16988)
AFFINITY AUTO PROGRAMS INC
Also Called: Costco Auto Program
10251 Vista Cerento Pkwy, San Diego
(92121)
PHONE...................................858 643-9324
Jeff Skeen, *President*
Bill Gregory, *President*
Gary Drean, *COO*
Joey Herschel, *Vice Pres*
Jason Petroske, *Mktg Dir*
EMP: 80
SQ FT: 34,000

SALES (est): 7.8MM **Privately Held**
WEB: www.costcoauto.com
SIC: 7389 Advertising, promotional & trade
show services

(P-16989)
AFM & SAG-AFTRA INTELLECTUAL
4705 Laurel Canyon Blvd # 400, Valley Vil-
lage (91607-5904)
PHONE...................................818 255-7980
Dennis Dreith, *Director*
Shari Hoffman, *COO*
Jennifer Leblanc, *CFO*
Eric Cowden, *Associate Dir*
John Felikian, *Associate Dir*
EMP: 70
SQ FT: 21,600
SALES: 54.3MM **Privately Held**
SIC: 7389 Fund raising organizations

(P-16990)
ALFREDS PICTURES FRAMES INC
Also Called: Heather Ann Creations
1580 Sunflower Ave, Costa Mesa
(92626-1511)
PHONE...................................714 434-4838
Pat Cochrane, *President*
Sandra Adams, *Manager*
EMP: 50
SQ FT: 40,000
SALES (est): 5.5MM **Privately Held**
WEB: www.heatherann.com
SIC: 7389 Interior decorating

(P-16991)
ALL-PRO BAIL BONDS INC (PA)
512 Via De La Valle # 303, Solana Beach
(92075-2715)
PHONE...................................858 481-1200
Steffan Gibbs, *CEO*
EMP: 63 EST: 2006
SALES (est): 16.5MM **Privately Held**
SIC: 7389 Bail bonding

(P-16992)
ALL-PRO BAIL BONDS INC
530 Hacienda Dr Ste 104d, Vista
(92081-6640)
PHONE...................................760 941-4100
Steffan Gibbs, *President*
EMP: 100
SALES (est): 6.9MM **Privately Held**
SIC: 7389 Bail bonding

(P-16993)
ALOM TECHNOLOGIES CORPORATION (PA)
48105 Warm Springs Blvd, Fremont
(94539-7498)
PHONE...................................510 360-3600
Hannah Kain, *President*
Jack Sexton, *CFO*
Tony Chiu, *Administration*
Brandon Marugg, *Info Tech Dir*
Lana Kaplenko, *Controller*
EMP: 95
SQ FT: 300,000
SALES (est): 42.2MM **Privately Held**
WEB: www.alom.com
SIC: 7389 4783 7374 7331 Packaging &
labeling services; packing goods for ship-
ping; data processing & preparation; di-
rect mail advertising services

(P-16994)
ALORICA CUSTOMER CARE INC
8885 Rio San Diego Dr, San Diego
(92108-1624)
PHONE...................................619 298-7103
EMP: 563
SALES (corp-wide): 7.3B **Privately Held**
SIC: 7389 Telemarketing services
HQ: Alorica Customer Care, Inc.
5085 W Park Blvd Ste 300
Plano TX
-

(P-16995)
ALPHA SWIMMING POOL & SPA
2600 Athena Pl, Fullerton (92833-2005)
PHONE...................................714 879-4667
Kim Moon, *Owner*

EMP: 51
SALES (est): 1.5MM **Privately Held**
SIC: 7389 Swimming pool & hot tub serv-
ice & maintenance

(P-16996)
ALTAF ZAHID ENGINEERING SVCS
42051 Orange Blossom Dr, Temecula
(92591-5543)
PHONE...................................760 481-9072
Shafiq Rassuli, *Director*
EMP: 50
SALES (est): 1.7MM **Privately Held**
SIC: 7389 Pipeline & power line inspection
service

(P-16997)
ALTEC PRODUCTS INC (PA)
23422 Mill Creek Dr # 225, Laguna Hills
(92653-7910)
PHONE...................................949 727-1248
Mark Ford, *CEO*
Brandt Morell, *President*
Frank Sansone, *CFO*
Mark Tague, *CFO*
Bill Brown, *Exec VP*
EMP: 80
SQ FT: 12,500
SALES (est): 17.1MM **Privately Held**
SIC: 7389 Telemarketing services; printing
broker

(P-16998)
AMERICA SHREDDING
6565 Smith Ave, Newark (94560-4217)
PHONE...................................702 262-3607
John Groenewold, *Vice Pres*
Kevin Duncomed, *President*
EMP: 90
SALES (est): 3.1MM **Privately Held**
WEB: www.americashredding.com
SIC: 7389 Document & office record de-
struction

(P-16999)
AMERICAN HEALTH CONNECTION
8484 Wilshire Blvd # 501, Beverly Hills
(90211-3243)
PHONE...................................424 226-0420
Yuriy Koltyar, *CEO*
Azabeh Williamson, *President*
EMP: 350
SQ FT: 3,000
SALES (est): 11.2MM **Privately Held**
SIC: 7389 Telemarketing services

(P-17000)
AMERICAS LEMONADE STAND INC
Also Called: Institutional Financing Svcs
5100 Park Rd, Benicia (94510-1136)
PHONE...................................707 745-1274
James M Cascino, *CEO*
Jose Ferreira Jr, *Ch of Bd*
Jack Hood, *CFO*
EMP: 250
SQ FT: 140,000
SALES (est): 10.7MM **Privately Held**
SIC: 7389 5094 5199 5145 Fund raising
organizations; jewelry & precious stones;
gifts & novelties; calendars; candy

(P-17001)
AMOEBA MUSIC INC
1855 Haight St, San Francisco
(94117-2790)
PHONE...................................415 831-1200
Joe Goldmark, *Manager*
EMP: 70
SALES (corp-wide): 8.9MM **Privately
Held**
WEB: www.ameebamusic.com
SIC: 7389 5999 5932 5735 Personal
service agents, brokers & bureaus;
posters; records, secondhand; video
discs & tapes, prerecorded
PA: Amoeba Music Inc.
2455 Telegraph Ave
Berkeley CA 94704
510 549-1125

(P-17002)
ANAHEIM/ORANGE CNTY VISITOR BU (PA)
Also Called: Visit Anaheim
2099 S State College Blvd, Anaheim
(92806-6142)
P.O. Box 4270 (92803-4270)
PHONE...................................714 765-8888
Jay Burress, *CEO*
Charles Ahlers, *President*
Mindy Abel, *Senior VP*
Christina Dawson, *Vice Pres*
Debbie Taylor, *Administration*
EMP: 56
SQ FT: 3,000
SALES: 16.5MM **Privately Held**
SIC: 7389 Convention & show services;
tourist information bureau

(P-17003)
ANDREW LAUREN COMPANY INC
15225 Alton Pkwy Unit 300, Irvine
(92618-2345)
PHONE...................................949 861-4222
Mark Noonan, *Principal*
EMP: 189 **Privately Held**
SIC: 7389 5713 Interior design services;
carpets
PA: The Andrew Lauren Company Inc
8909 Kenamar Dr Ste 101
San Diego CA 92121
-

(P-17004)
ANSIRA PARTNERS INC
Also Called: Co-Optimum
5000 Van Nuys Blvd, Sherman Oaks
(91403-1793)
PHONE...................................818 461-6100
Larry Feder, *Manager*
EMP: 60
SALES (corp-wide): 73.9MM **Privately
Held**
SIC: 7389 7331
PA: Ansira Partners, Inc.
2300 Locust St
Saint Louis MO 63103
314 783-2300

(P-17005)
ANSWER FINANCIAL INC (HQ)
15910 Ventura Blvd Fl 6, Encino
(91436-2803)
PHONE...................................818 644-4000
Robert J Slingerland, *CEO*
Darren Howard, *Chief Mktg Ofcr*
Daniel John Bryce, *Senior VP*
Peter Foley, *Senior VP*
John E Galaviz, *Senior VP*
EMP: 200
SQ FT: 45,000
SALES: 80MM **Publicly Held**
WEB: www.answerfinancial.com
SIC: 7389 6411 Brokers, business: buying
& selling business enterprises; property &
casualty insurance agent

(P-17006)
APERIO GROUP LLC
3 Harbor Dr Ste 204, Sausalito
(94965-1491)
PHONE...................................415 339-4300
Paul Solli,
Patrick Geddes,
Guy Lampard,
Robert L Newman,
EMP: 56
SALES (est): 3MM **Privately Held**
WEB: www.aperiogroup.com
SIC: 7389 Financial services

(P-17007)
APPLEBEE LEASING INC
4 Maidstone Dr, Newport Beach
(92660-4271)
P.O. Box 9878 (92658-1878)
PHONE...................................818 612-6218
William Applebee, *Administration*
EMP: 56
SALES (est): 2.7MM **Privately Held**
SIC: 7389 Personal service agents, bro-
kers & bureaus

(P-17008)
APPLIED LANGUAGE SOLUTIONS LLC
1250 W Sunflower, La Habra (90631-9286)
PHONE...................................800 579-5010
Gavin Wheeldon, *Mng Member*
EMP: 102
SALES (est): 4.3MM **Privately Held**
WEB: www.appliedlanguage.com
SIC: 7389 Translation services

(P-17009)
ARAMARK SERVICES INC
17044 Montanero Ave Ste 4, Carson
(90746-1338)
PHONE...................................310 635-5000
Chris Leonard, *Manager*
EMP: 67 **Publicly Held**
SIC: 7389 Coffee service
HQ: Aramark Services, Inc.
1101 Market St Ste 45
Philadelphia PA 19107
215 238-3000

(P-17010)
ARCANA CORPORATION
118 Nopalitos Way, Santa Barbara
(93103-3629)
P.O. Box 4400 (93140-4400)
PHONE...................................805 882-1305
Scot Smigel, *President*
EMP: 50
SALES (est): 3.6MM **Privately Held**
SIC: 7389 Hotel & motel reservation service

(P-17011)
ARRIVAL COMMUNICATIONS INC (DH)
1800 19th St, Bakersfield (93301-4315)
PHONE...................................661 322-7375
Richard Jalkut, *CEO*
Warren Heffelfinger, *President*
David Riordan, *COO*
Geoffrey Whynot, *CFO*
Tony Distefano, *Principal*
EMP: 75
SQ FT: 4,000
SALES (est): 6.6MM **Privately Held**
SIC: 7389 Design services
HQ: U.S. Telepacific Corp.
515 S Flower St Ste 4500
Los Angeles CA 90071
866 699-8242

(P-17012)
ASPIRIANT LLC
50 California St Ste 2600, San Francisco
(94111-4704)
PHONE...................................415 371-7800
Raymond Edwards, *Branch Mgr*
EMP: 50 **Privately Held**
SIC: 7389 Financial services
PA: Aspiriant, Llc
11100 Santa Monica Blvd
Los Angeles CA 90025

(P-17013)
ASSIST 65 PLUS
111 W 7th St Ste 211, Los Angeles
(90014-3933)
PHONE...................................323 557-4426
Kirbi Toure, *Partner*
EMP: 50 EST: 2011
SALES (est): 1.1MM **Privately Held**
SIC: 7389

(P-17014)
ASSOCIATED LANDSCAPE
Also Called: Associated Group
2420 S Eastern Ave, Commerce
(90040-1415)
PHONE...................................714 558-6100
Laurie Resnick, *President*
Patrick Skalka, *COO*
Lydia Monroe, *Vice Pres*
Greg Salmeri, *Vice Pres*
Stephanie Cervantes, *Project Mgr*
EMP: 90
SQ FT: 30,000

SALES (est): 13.1MM **Privately Held**
WEB: www.associatedgroup.biz
SIC: 7389 0781 Plant care service; decoration service for special events; landscape services

(P-17015)
AT&T CORP
5130 Hacienda Dr Fl 1, Dublin
(94568-7598)
PHONE...................................925 560-5011
Louis Casali, *Principal*
Antolin Canio, *Engineer*
Robert Ellis, *Sr Project Mgr*
Lloyd V Antwerp, *Senior Mgr*
EMP: 305
SALES (corp-wide): 160.5B **Publicly Held**
SIC: 7389 Personal service agents, brokers & bureaus
HQ: At&T Corp.
1 At&T Way
Bedminster NJ 07921
800 403-3302

(P-17016)
ATEL CORPORATION
600 Montgomery St Ste 900, San Francisco
(94111-2711)
PHONE...................................415 989-8800
Dean L Cash, *President*
Vasco Morais, *Exec VP*
Garner Millard, *Vice Pres*
Andrew Witherow, *Vice Pres*
Tim Kendall, *Database Admin*
EMP: 61
SQ FT: 2,000
SALES (est): 2.8MM **Privately Held**
SIC: 7389 Office facilities & secretarial service rental
PA: Atel Capital Group
600 Montgomery St Fl 9
San Francisco CA 94111

(P-17017)
ATLANTIC RECORDING CORP
3400 W Olive Ave, Burbank (91505-5538)
PHONE...................................818 238-6800
Aaron Bay-Schuck, *Manager*
EMP: 325 **Privately Held**
WEB: www.ledzep.com
SIC: 7389 Music recording producer
HQ: Atlantic Recording Corp
1633 Broadway Lowr 2c1
New York NY 10019
212 707-2000

(P-17018)
AUGMEDIX INC
1161 Mission St Ste 210, San Francisco
(94103-1571)
PHONE...................................855 720-2929
Ian Shakil, *CEO*
Pelu Tran, *President*
Reda Dehy, *CTO*
Jon Gallez, *Technology*
Ryan Gray, *Persnl Dir*
EMP: 92
SQ FT: 6,636
SALES (est): 3.9MM **Privately Held**
SIC: 7389 Handwriting analysis

(P-17019)
AUTHORITY TAX SERVICES LLC
Also Called: Tax Problem Center
777 S Figueroa St # 1900, Los Angeles
(90017-5817)
PHONE...................................213 486-5135
Wayne R Johnson, *President*
EMP: 60
SALES (est): 3.9MM **Privately Held**
SIC: 7389

(P-17020)
AUTOCRIB INC
2882 Dow Ave, Tustin (92780-7258)
PHONE...................................714 274-0400
Stephen Pixley, *CEO*
EMP: 150 EST: 1999
SQ FT: 25,000
SALES (est): 27.6MM **Privately Held**
SIC: 7389 3581 Inventory computing service; automatic vending machines

(P-17021)
AVANTI AGENCY CORPORATION
282 S Anita Dr, Orange (92868-3308)
P.O. Box 5406 (92863-5406)
PHONE...................................714 935-0900
Kenneth Thompson, *President*
Art Olson, *Marketing Staff*
EMP: 400
SALES (est): 14.6MM **Privately Held**
SIC: 7389 Personal service agents, brokers & bureaus

(P-17022)
AVAYA INC (HQ)
4655 Great America Pkwy, Santa Clara
(95054-1236)
PHONE...................................908 953-6000
Jim Chirico, *President*
Dino Di-Palma, *President*
Michael M Runda, *President*
Patrick O'Malley, *CFO*
Shefali Shah, *Officer*
EMP: 148
SALES (est): 3.7B **Publicly Held**
WEB: www.avaya.com
SIC: 7389 Telephone answering service; telephone directory distribution, contract or fee basis; telephone services

(P-17023)
AVITAS SYSTEMS INC
2882 Sand Hill Rd Ste 240, Menlo Park
(94025-7057)
PHONE...................................650 233-3900
Kenneth Alferez,
EMP: 51 EST: 2017
SQ FT: 6,000
SALES (est): 651.2K **Privately Held**
SIC: 7389 Industrial & commercial equipment inspection service; petroleum refinery inspection service; pipeline & power line inspection service

(P-17024)
B RILEY FINANCIAL INC (PA)
21255 Burbank Blvd # 400, Woodland Hills
(91367-6747)
PHONE...................................818 884-3737
Bryant R Riley, *Ch of Bd*
Thomas J Kelleher, *President*
Dan Shribman, *President*
Phillip J Ahn, *COO*
Kenneth Young, *Bd of Directors*
EMP: 127
SALES: 322.1MM **Publicly Held**
SIC: 7389 Financial services; merchandise liquidators

(P-17025)
BAD BOYS BAIL BONDS INC (PA)
595 Park Ave Ste 200, San Jose
(95110-2641)
PHONE...................................408 298-3333
Clifford J Stanley, *President*
Craig A Stanley, *Vice Pres*
George Wallace, *General Mgr*
EMP: 75
SQ FT: 3,000
SALES (est): 16MM **Privately Held**
SIC: 7389 Bail bonding

(P-17026)
BANKCARD SERVICES (PA)
21281 S Western Ave, Torrance
(90501-2958)
PHONE...................................213 365-1122
Monica Lee, *Associate*
EMP: 200
SALES (est): 17.1MM **Privately Held**
SIC: 7389 Credit card service

(P-17027)
BATES SAMPLE CASE COMPANY INC
Also Called: Bates Display & Packaging
5995 W Park Dr, Chino Hills (91709-6301)
PHONE...................................951 371-4922
Robert Sherman, *President*
Emmagene Sherman, *Corp Secy*
EMP: 60
SQ FT: 36,000
SALES (est): 8MM **Privately Held**
WEB: www.batesdisplay.com
SIC: 7389 Packaging & labeling services

(P-17028)
BENCHMARK-TECH CORPORATION
Also Called: Chaminade of Santa Cruz
1 Chaminade Ln, Santa Cruz (95065-1524)
PHONE...................................831 475-5600
Tom O'Shea, *Vice Pres*
Mike P Butler, *Controller*
Rebecca Stimler, *Sales Staff*
Aaron Ackerman, *Clerk*
EMP: 200
SQ FT: 61,000
SALES (est): 12.4MM **Privately Held**
SIC: 7389 Convention & show services

(P-17029)
BENEFICENT TECHNOLOGY INC
Also Called: Benetech
480 California Ave # 201, Palo Alto
(94306-1623)
PHONE...................................650 644-3400
James R Fruchterman, *CEO*
Betsy Beaumon, *President*
Brad Turner, *Vice Pres*
Theresa Chinte, *Executive*
Demetria Jones, *Admin Asst*
EMP: 50 EST: 2001
SALES: 12.9MM **Privately Held**
WEB: www.benetech.org
SIC: 7389 Personal service agents, brokers & bureaus

(P-17030)
BERSHTEL ENTERPRISES LLC (PA)
Also Called: We Pack It All
2745 Huntington Dr, Duarte (91010-2302)
PHONE...................................626 301-9214
Jack Bershtel, *President*
Sharon Bershtel, *CFO*
Gaby Gaiz, *Treasurer*
George Gellert, *Vice Pres*
Robert Gellert, *Vice Pres*
EMP: 145
SQ FT: 50,000
SALES (est): 31.5MM **Privately Held**
WEB: www.wepackitall.com
SIC: 7389 Packaging & labeling services

(P-17031)
BETTER LIVING BRANDS LLC
11555 Dublin Canyon Rd, Pleasanton
(94588-2815)
P.O. Box 99 (94566-0009)
PHONE...................................888 723-3929
Shannon Mahler, *Manager*
Sean Barrett, *Vice Pres*
EMP: 200
SQ FT: 20,000
SALES: 20MM **Privately Held**
SIC: 7389 Packaging & labeling services

(P-17032)
BEVERLY HILLS LINGUAL INST
8383 Wilshire Blvd # 250, Beverly Hills
(90211-2432)
PHONE...................................323 651-5000
Nevena Martinovic, *Consultant*
Aleksa Martinovic, *President*
EMP: 50
SALES (est): 1.9MM **Privately Held**
WEB: www.bhlingual.com
SIC: 7389 Translation services

(P-17033)
BEX PORTFOLIO LLC
925 E Meadow Dr, Palo Alto (94303-4233)
PHONE...................................650 494-3700
EMP: 92
SALES (est): 74.7K
SALES (corp-wide): 1.3B **Privately Held**
SIC: 7389 Financial services
HQ: Essex Portfolio, L.P.
925 E Meadow Dr
Palo Alto CA 94303

(P-17034)
BLAINE CONVENTION SERVICES INC
114 S Berry St, Brea (92821-4826)
PHONE...................................714 522-8270
Thomas W Blaine Sr, *President*
EMP: 960

▲ = Import ▼=Export
◆ =Import/Export

SQ FT: 107,000
SALES: 10.7MM **Privately Held**
WEB: www.blaineconventionservices.com
SIC: 7389 7359 2542 4731 Exhibit construction by industrial contractors; trade show arrangement; equipment rental & leasing; partitions & fixtures, except wood; domestic freight forwarding

(P-17035)
BLUE CHIP INVENTORY SERVICE
14852 Ventura Blvd # 112, Sherman Oaks (91403-3499)
PHONE..................818 461-1765
Gerard J Walsh, *President*
Carol F Edgington, *Vice Pres*
EMP: 70
SQ FT: 1,800
SALES (est): 3.7MM **Privately Held**
WEB: www.inventoryalliance.com
SIC: 7389 Inventory computing service

(P-17036)
BONHAMS BTTRFLDS ACTNEERS CORP (DH)
220 San Bruno Ave, San Francisco (94103-5018)
PHONE..................415 861-7500
Robert Brooks, *Principal*
Kristin Guiter, *President*
Sung-Hee Kim, *President*
Malcom Barber, *CEO*
Pactric Meade, *COO*
EMP: 150 **EST:** 1793
SQ FT: 45,000
SALES (est): 25.8MM
SALES (corp-wide): 228.4K **Privately Held**
SIC: 7389 Auctioneers, fee basis
HQ: Bonhams 1793 Limited
101 New Bond Street
London W1S 1
207 468-5868

(P-17037)
BONHAMS CORPORATION
220 San Bruno Ave, San Francisco (94103-5018)
PHONE..................415 861-7500
EMP: 140
SALES (est): 8.7MM **Privately Held**
SIC: 7389

(P-17038)
BOSHART AUTOMOTIVE TSTG SVCS
1840 S Carlos Ave 15, Ontario (91761-8005)
PHONE..................909 466-1602
Ken Boshart, *President*
Lynn Boshart, *Vice Pres*
EMP: 54
SQ FT: 13,567
SALES (est): 3.2MM **Privately Held**
SIC: 7389 7549 Inspection & testing services; emissions testing without repairs, automotive

(P-17039)
BOULEVARD ENTERTAINMENT INC
903 S Lake St Ste 202, Burbank (91502-2435)
P.O. Box 1188 (91507-1188)
PHONE..................818 840-6969
Scott Jacobson, *President*
David Jacobson, *Vice Pres*
EMP: 108
SALES (est): 4.5MM **Privately Held**
WEB: www.blvdent.com
SIC: 7389 Telephone services

(P-17040)
BOX BROS CORP
825 Wilshire Blvd, Santa Monica (90401-1809)
PHONE..................310 394-8660
Mark Frydman, *Branch Mgr*
EMP: 50
SQ FT: 6,930
SALES (corp-wide): 12.2MM **Privately Held**
SIC: 7389 Mailbox rental & related service; packaging & labeling services

PA: Box Bros. Corp.
22124 Ventura Blvd
Woodland Hills CA 91364
818 703-9393

(P-17041)
BRADFORD MESSENGER SERVICE
4955 E Andersen Ave # 118, Fresno (93727-1543)
PHONE..................559 252-0775
Liner Bluron, *Manager*
EMP: 60
SQ FT: 1,500
SALES (est): 1.6MM **Privately Held**
SIC: 7389 Courier or messenger service

(P-17042)
BRAGG INVESTMENT COMPANY INC (PA)
Also Called: Bragg Crane & Rigging
6251 N Paramount Blvd, Long Beach (90805-3713)
P.O. Box 727 (90801-0727)
PHONE..................562 984-2400
Marilynn Bragg, *CEO*
Dilip Patki, *CFO*
Mary A Pool, *Corp Secy*
Mike Roy, *Exec VP*
Scott Bragg, *Vice Pres*
EMP: 580
SQ FT: 50,000
SALES (est): 337.2MM **Privately Held**
SIC: 7389 7353 1791 Crane & aerial lift service; heavy construction equipment rental; structural steel erection

(P-17043)
BRIGHTCURRENT INC
426 17th St Ste 700, Oakland (94612-2850)
PHONE..................877 896-3306
John Bourne, *CEO*
EMP: 75
SQ FT: 20,000
SALES (est): 5.1MM
SALES (corp-wide): 16.5MM **Privately Held**
SIC: 7389 Telemarketing services
PA: Lpsh Holdings, Inc.
27368 Via Industria
Temecula CA 92590
855 647-5061

(P-17044)
BUTTER PADDLE
Also Called: Butter Paddle, The
33 N Santa Cruz Ave, Los Gatos (95030-5916)
PHONE..................408 395-1678
Doris Beccia, *President*
Mumuna Ali, *President*
Mary Ann Jeffri, *Store Mgr*
EMP: 70 **EST:** 1967
SQ FT: 2,000
SALES (est): 5.5MM **Privately Held**
SIC: 7389 Fund raising organizations

(P-17045)
CADFORCE INC
10811 Wash Blvd Ste 302, Culver City (90232-3660)
PHONE..................310 876-1800
James Katz, *Vice Pres*
Robert W Vanech, *Principal*
EMP: 800
SALES: 35MM **Privately Held**
WEB: www.cadforce.com
SIC: 7389 Drafting service, except temporary help

(P-17046)
CALIFORNIA CREDITS GROUP LLC
251 S Lake Ave Ste 400, Pasadena (91101-3051)
PHONE..................626 584-9800
John Simpson,
Jay Parker, *Vice Pres*
Marianne Serpa, *Associate Dir*
Esmeralda Rivera, *Tax Mgr*
Lan Hai, *Opers Staff*
EMP: 50

SALES (est): 5.9MM **Privately Held**
WEB: www.ccg.com
SIC: 7389 Personal service agents, brokers & bureaus

(P-17047)
CALIFORNIA HLTH COLLABORATIVE (PA)
1680 W Shaw Ave, Fresno (93711-3504)
PHONE..................559 221-6315
Gary Erickson, *Chairman*
Stephen Ramirez, *Exec Dir*
Stephanie Chandler, *Program Mgr*
Daisy Lopez, *Program Mgr*
Rueben Cuadrof, *Controller*
EMP: 68
SQ FT: 11,400
SALES: 7.2MM **Privately Held**
WEB: www.california.hometownlocator.com
SIC: 7389 Fund raising organizations

(P-17048)
CALIFORNIA SKATEPARKS
285 N Benson Ave, Upland (91786-5614)
PHONE..................909 949-1601
Joseph M Ciaglia Jr, *President*
Bill Minadeo, *Vice Pres*
Brian Pino, *Project Mgr*
Mario Rodriguez, *Project Mgr*
Ashley Ciaglia, *Marketing Mgr*
EMP: 150
SALES (est): 5.6MM **Privately Held**
SIC: 7389

(P-17049)
CALIFORNIA SUBSHINE INC
561 N Pacific Coast Hwy, Redondo Beach (90277-2104)
PHONE..................310 374-4900
EMP: 100
SALES (corp-wide): 4.5MM **Privately Held**
SIC: 7389
PA: California Subshine Inc.
251 N Linda Vista Ave
Ventura CA 93001
805 643-5400

(P-17050)
CALIFORNIA TRAFFIC CONTROL
Also Called: California Traffic Ctrl Svcs
3333 Cherry Ave, Long Beach (90807-4901)
PHONE..................562 595-7575
Delores Kepl, *CFO*
EMP: 70
SALES (est): 6.5MM **Privately Held**
SIC: 7389 Flagging service (traffic control)

(P-17051)
CALL CENTER SERVICES INTL LLC
809 Bowsprit Rd Ste 204, Chula Vista (91914-4527)
PHONE..................858 427-8500
Jose Erick Esparza, *President*
Mariana Alford, *Shareholder*
Jaime Edgar Esparza, *Shareholder*
Veronica Anguiano, *President*
Frank Esparza, *Vice Pres*
EMP: 60
SQ FT: 1,200
SALES (est): 6.2MM **Privately Held**
SIC: 7389 Telemarketing services

(P-17052)
CAMARILLO RANCH FOUNDATION
201 Camarillo Ranch Rd, Camarillo (93012-5081)
PHONE..................805 389-8182
Bruce Fuhrman, *Vice Pres*
EMP: 75
SALES: 796.2K **Privately Held**
SIC: 7389 Fund raising organizations

(P-17053)
CANON SOLUTIONS AMERICA INC
2382 Faraday Ave Ste 250, Carlsbad (92008-7262)
PHONE..................760 438-6990
EMP: 79

SALES (corp-wide): 43.8B **Privately Held**
SIC: 7389
HQ: Canon Solutions America, Inc.
1 Canon Park
Melville NY 11747
631 330-5000

(P-17054)
CAPITOL RECORDS LLC
Also Called: EMI Music Distribution
1750 Vine St, Los Angeles (90028-5274)
PHONE..................213 462-6252
Colin Finkelstein, *Mng Member*
Ben Moudry, *Info Tech Mgr*
EMP: 1500
SQ FT: 200,000
SALES (est): 98.4MM
SALES (corp-wide): 78.4MM **Privately Held**
WEB: www.capitolrecords.com
SIC: 7389 8999 Music & broadcasting services; music arranging & composing
HQ: Universal Music Group, Inc.
2220 Colorado Ave
Santa Monica CA 90404
310 865-4000

(P-17055)
CARDFLEX INC
2900 Bristol St Bldg F, Costa Mesa (92626-5981)
PHONE..................714 361-1900
Andrew M Phillips, *President*
EMP: 75
SALES (est): 8.4MM **Privately Held**
SIC: 7389 Credit card service

(P-17056)
CARDSERVICE INTERNATIONAL INC
Also Called: C S I
4565 Industrial St Ste 7k, Simi Valley (93063-3464)
PHONE..................800 217-4622
Chuck Burtzloft, *Branch Mgr*
EMP: 650
SALES (corp-wide): 12B **Publicly Held**
WEB: www.creditcardresults.com
SIC: 7389 7371 6153 Credit card service; custom computer programming services; short-term business credit
HQ: Cardservice International, Inc.
5898 Condor Dr 220
Moorpark CA 93021
805 648-1425

(P-17057)
CARDSERVICE INTERNATIONAL INC
Also Called: Csi
1538 W Commonwealth Ave, Fullerton (92833-2754)
PHONE..................714 773-1778
EMP: 56
SALES (corp-wide): 2B **Privately Held**
SIC: 7389
HQ: Cardservice International, Inc.
5898 Condor Dr 220
Moorpark CA 93021
805 648-1425

(P-17058)
CARDSERVICE INTERNATIONAL INC (HQ)
5898 Condor Dr 220, Moorpark (93021-2603)
PHONE..................805 648-1425
Don Headlund, *President*
Charles Burtzloff, *CEO*
EMP: 450
SQ FT: 34,000
SALES (est): 38.7MM
SALES (corp-wide): 12B **Publicly Held**
WEB: www.creditcardresults.com
SIC: 7389 6153 Credit card service; short-term business credit
PA: First Data Corporation
225 Liberty St Fl 29
New York NY 10281
800 735-3362

(P-17059)
CARECREDIT LLC
2995 Red Hill Ave Ste 100, Costa Mesa
(92626-5984)
PHONE.....................800 300-3046
Kurt Grossheim, *Principal*
Mario Cozzi, *President*
Mary Trammell, *President*
Gregory Pierce, *Vice Pres*
Denise Rogers, *Vice Pres*
EMP: 120
SQ FT: 12,000
SALES (est): 9.5MM
SALES (corp-wide): 16.7B **Publicly Held**
WEB: www.carecredit.com
SIC: 7389 8742 Financial services; bank-
ing & finance consultant
PA: Synchrony Financial
777 Long Ridge Rd
Stamford CT 06902
203 585-2400

(P-17060)
CASECENTRAL INC (DH)
Also Called: Casecentral.com
1055 E Colo Blvd Ste 400, Pasadena
(91106)
PHONE.....................415 989-2300
Christopher S Kruse, *President*
Randy Burrows, *Vice Pres*
Peter H Kruse, *Vice Pres*
Jay O'Connor, *Vice Pres*
Philip Sakakihara, *Vice Pres*
EMP: 60
SALES (est): 7.5MM
SALES (corp-wide): 2.2B **Privately Held**
WEB: www.casecentral.com
SIC: 7389 4813 4226 Legal & tax serv-
ices; ; document & office records storage
HQ: Guidance Software, Inc.
1055 E Colo Blvd Ste 400
Pasadena CA 91106
626 229-9191

(P-17061)
CASHEDGE INC
525 Almanor Ave Ste 150, Sunnyvale
(94085-3545)
PHONE.....................408 541-3900
McKenzie Lyons, *Principal*
Rommel Ringor, *Administration*
Metin Gokcen, *Director*
EMP: 100
SALES (corp-wide): 5.7B **Publicly Held**
WEB: www.cashedge.com
SIC: 7389 Financial services
HQ: Cashedge Inc.
215 Park Ave S Ste 1300
New York NY 10003
212 656-9000

(P-17062)
CATATI ROHNERT PARK INC
1400 Magnolia Ave, Rohnert Park
(94928-8129)
PHONE.....................707 792-4531
Jane Wheeler, *Principal*
EMP: 50
SALES (est): 2MM **Privately Held**
SIC: 7389 Personal service agents, bro-
kers & bureaus

(P-17063)
CENTRAL PAYMENT CO LLC
2350 Kerner Blvd Ste 300, San Rafael
(94901-5597)
PHONE.....................415 462-8335
Matthew Hyman, *Managing Prtnr*
Zachary Hyman, *Partner*
Ed Thomas, *Partner*
Eric Barth, *COO*
John Hinkle, *CFO*
EMP: 99
SALES (est): 13.1MM **Privately Held**
WEB: www.centralpaymentcorp.com
SIC: 7389 Credit card service

(P-17064)
CENTRAL SVC CTR & EXEC OFFS
1751 Plum Ln, Redlands (92374-4505)
PHONE.....................909 307-6555
Cynthia Harnish Breunig, *CEO*
EMP: 50

SALES (est): 851.3K **Privately Held**
SIC: 7389 Personal service agents, brokers & bureaus

(P-17065)
CENTRELINK INSUR & FINCL SVCS
Also Called: Centrelink Ins & Fincl Svcs
20750 Ventura Blvd # 300, Woodland Hills
(91364-2338)
PHONE.....................818 587-2001
Barry Wolfe, *President*
EMP: 90
SALES (est): 3.3MM **Privately Held**
SIC: 7389 8741 Financial services; finan-
cial management for business

(P-17066)
CENTURY BANKCARD SERVICES
25129 The Old Rd Ste 222, Stevenson
Ranch (91381-2281)
PHONE.....................818 700-3100
Scott Scherr, *President*
EMP: 55
SQ FT: 4,200
SALES (est): 3MM **Privately Held**
WEB: www.centurybankcard.com
SIC: 7389 Credit card service
PA: Pace Payment Systems, Inc.
30 Burton Hills Blvd
Nashville TN 37215

(P-17067)
CERAMIC DECORATING COMPANY INC
4651 Sheila St, Commerce (90040-1003)
PHONE.....................323 268-5135
Chad A Johnson, *CEO*
Allan Johnson, *President*
W Allan Johnson, *CEO*
Burnell D Johnson, *Admin Sec*
EMP: 50 EST: 1934
SQ FT: 30,290
SALES (est): 8.1MM **Privately Held**
WEB: www.ceramicdecoratingco.com
SIC: 7389 2396 Labeling bottles, cans,
cartons, etc.; lettering service; automotive
& apparel trimmings

(P-17068)
CESARS PRODUCTIONS
91 Miguel St, San Francisco (94131-2605)
PHONE.....................415 821-1156
Cesar Ascarrunz, *Owner*
EMP: 50
SALES (est): 2MM **Privately Held**
WEB: www.cesarsproductions.com
SIC: 7389 Music recording producer

(P-17069)
CETERA FINANCIAL GROUP INC (PA)
200 N Pacific Coast Hwy # 11, El Segundo
(90245-5628)
PHONE.....................866 489-3100
Robert Moore, *CEO*
Adam Antoniades, *President*
Thomas B Taylor, *President*
Catherine Bonneau, *COO*
Jeffrey Buchheister, *CFO*
EMP: 138
SQ FT: 70,000
SALES (est): 245.1MM **Privately Held**
SIC: 7389 6282 Financial services; invest-
ment advisory service

(P-17070)
CHANGE HEALTHCARE TECH LLC
5110 E Clinton Way # 101, Fresno
(93727-2040)
PHONE.....................559 455-4000
Glenda Josey, *Principal*
Denise Thompson, *Manager*
EMP: 120
SALES (corp-wide): 96.2MM **Privately
Held**
WEB: www.per-se.com
SIC: 7389 Personal service agents, bro-
kers & bureaus

HQ: Change Healthcare Technologies, Llc
5995 Windward Pkwy
Alpharetta GA 30005

(P-17071)
CHAPMAN UNIVERSITY
625 N Glassell St, Orange (92867)
PHONE.....................714 997-6821
Sukbae Tim, *Director*
Emily Fong, *Production*
Megan Belmonte, *Director*
Karina Ruiz, *Assistant*
Leanne Ewing, *Clerk*
EMP: 139
SALES (corp-wide): 437.7MM **Privately
Held**
SIC: 7389 Printers' services; folding, collat-
ing
PA: Chapman University
1 University Dr
Orange CA 92866
714 997-6815

(P-17072)
CHARLES SCHWAB CORPORATION
27580 Ynez Rd Ste A, Temecula
(92591-4667)
PHONE.....................951 587-2840
Mark Morgan, *Manager*
EMP: 77
SALES (corp-wide): 8.6B **Publicly Held**
SIC: 7389 6282 6211 Financial services;
investment advice; stock brokers & deal-
ers
PA: The Charles Schwab Corporation
211 Main St Fl 17
San Francisco CA 94105
415 667-7000

(P-17073)
CHERRY AVENUE AUCTION INC
4640 S Cherry Ave, Fresno (93706-5717)
PHONE.....................559 266-9856
William Mitchell, *President*
Margaret Mitchell, *Treasurer*
EMP: 50
SQ FT: 1,500
SALES (est): 3.2MM **Privately Held**
WEB: www.cherryavenueauction.com
SIC: 7389 Auctioneers, fee basis

(P-17074)
CIRTECH INC
250 E Emerson Ave, Orange (92865-3317)
PHONE.....................714 921-0860
Brad Reese, *President*
Frank E Reese, *CEO*
Juan Martinez, *Safety Mgr*
Dan Fernandez, *Sales Mgr*
Karen Bever, *Manager*
EMP: 50
SQ FT: 30,000
SALES (est): 1.7MM
SALES (corp-wide): 7MM **Privately Held**
WEB: www.cirtech.com
SIC: 7389 3672 Printed circuitry graphic
layout; printed circuit boards; wiring
boards
PA: Apct Holdings, Llc
3495 De La Cruz Blvd
Santa Clara CA 95054
408 727-6442

(P-17075)
CISCO SYSTEMS CAPITAL CORP (HQ)
170 W Tasman Dr, San Jose (95134-1706)
PHONE.....................610 386-5870
Kristine A Snow, *President*
David A Rogan, *President*
Prat Bhatt, *Treasurer*
David K Holland, *Treasurer*
John T Chambers, *Principal*
EMP: 143
SALES (est): 38.2MM
SALES (corp-wide): 49.3B **Publicly Held**
SIC: 7389 Financial services
PA: Cisco Systems, Inc.
170 W Tasman Dr
San Jose CA 95134
408 526-4000

(P-17076)
CISCO WEBEX LLC (HQ)
Also Called: Webex.com
170 W Tasman Dr, San Jose (95134-1706)
PHONE.....................408 435-7000
Subrah S Iyar,
Jeffrey Schmidt, *Vice Pres*
Praful Shah, *Vice Pres*
Andy Starr, *Vice Pres*
Philip A Long, *Info Tech Dir*
EMP: 1108
SQ FT: 160,000
SALES (est): 181MM
SALES (corp-wide): 49.3B **Publicly Held**
WEB: www.webex.com
SIC: 7389 4813 Teleconferencing serv-
ices; data telephone communications;
voice telephone communications
PA: Cisco Systems, Inc.
170 W Tasman Dr
San Jose CA 95134
408 526-4000

(P-17077)
CITY OF FRESNO
Also Called: Fresno Convention Center
700 M St, Fresno (93721-2715)
PHONE.....................559 445-8200
Michael Swinney, *Director*
Lyn Higginson, *Finance*
EMP: 60 **Privately Held**
WEB: www.fresnocitizencorps.org
SIC: 7389 9111 Convention & show serv-
ices; mayors' offices
PA: City Of Fresno
2600 Fresno St
Fresno CA 93721
559 621-7001

(P-17078)
CITY OF LONG BEACH
Also Called: Building Inspection
333 W Ocean Blvd Fl 4, Long Beach
(90802-4664)
PHONE.....................562 570-7298
Albert Sanchez, *Branch Mgr*
EMP: 300 **Privately Held**
SIC: 7389 Inspection & testing services
PA: City Of Long Beach
333 W Ocean Blvd Fl 10
Long Beach CA 90802
562 570-6450

(P-17079)
CITY OF LONG BEACH
Also Called: Long Bch Convention Entrmt Ctr
300 E Ocean Blvd, Long Beach
(90802-4825)
PHONE.....................562 436-3636
David Gordon, *Manager*
EMP: 300 **Privately Held**
WEB: www.polb.com
SIC: 7389 8611 6512 Convention & show
services; business associations; nonresi-
dential building operators
PA: City Of Long Beach
333 W Ocean Blvd Fl 10
Long Beach CA 90802
562 570-6450

(P-17080)
CITY OF PALO ALTO
Also Called: Water Quality Control Plant
2501 Embarcadero Way, Palo Alto
(94303-3326)
PHONE.....................650 329-2598
Richard Wetzel, *Branch Mgr*
EMP: 70 **Privately Held**
SIC: 7389 9111 8748 Sewer inspection
service; cloth cutting, bolting or winding;
city & town managers' offices; ; business
consulting
PA: City Of Palo Alto
250 Hamilton Ave
Palo Alto CA 94301
650 329-2571

(P-17081)
CITY OF RIVERSIDE
Also Called: Riverside Convention Center
3485 Mission Inn Ave, Riverside
(92501-3304)
PHONE.....................951 346-4700
Scott Megna, *General Mgr*
EMP: 100 **Privately Held**
SIC: 7389 Convention & show services

PA: City Of Riverside
3900 Main St Fl 7
Riverside CA 92522
951 826-5311

(P-17082)
CITY OF SAN JOSE
Also Called: Conventions Arts & Entrmt
408 Almaden Blvd, San Jose (95110-2709)
PHONE.................................408 277-5277
Nancy Johnson, *Branch Mgr*
Naresh Kapahi, *Finance*
Jennifer Rosenblatt, *Human Resources*
Kereli Sengstack, *Producer*
Beverley Locsin, *Sales Staff*
EMP: 300 Privately Held
WEB: www.csjfinance.org
SIC: 7389 9512 Convention & show services; land, mineral & wildlife conservation;
PA: City Of San Jose
200 E Santa Clara St
San Jose CA 95113
408 535-3500

(P-17083)
CITY OF SUNNYVALE
221 Commercial St, Sunnyvale (94085-4509)
P.O. Box 3707 (94088-3707)
PHONE.................................408 730-7510
James Craig, *Superintendent*
EMP: 200 Privately Held
SIC: 7389 Field warehousing
PA: City Of Sunnyvale
456 W Olive Ave
Sunnyvale CA 94086
408 730-7415

(P-17084)
CITY OF VISALIA
Also Called: Visalia Convention Center
303 E Acequia Ave, Visalia (93291-6341)
PHONE.................................559 713-4000
Wally Roeben, *General Mgr*
EMP: 60 Privately Held
SIC: 7389 Convention & show services
PA: Visalia, City Of (Inc)
707 W Acequia Ave
Visalia CA 93291
559 713-4565

(P-17085)
CITY RISE INC (PA)
Also Called: City Rise Services
1225 S Sacramento St, Lodi (95240-5703)
PHONE.................................209 333-0807
Nicole Beadles, *CEO*
EMP: 112 EST: 2014
SQ FT: 250,000
SALES (est): 1.5MM Privately Held
SIC: 7389 Flagging service (traffic control)

(P-17086)
CK ENTERPRISES INC
Also Called: World Tuned Radio
102 Copperwood Way Ste H, Oceanside (92058-3866)
PHONE.................................760 967-8863
Christopher Parks, *President*
EMP: 87
SALES (est): 2.5MM Privately Held
SIC: 7389

(P-17087)
CLUB SPORT OF FREMONT
46650 Landing Pkwy, Fremont (94538-6420)
PHONE.................................510 226-8500
Angela Grissar, *Business Mgr*
Guin Cloninger, *Partner*
EMP: 200
SALES (est): 13.8MM Privately Held
SIC: 7389 Artists' agents & brokers

(P-17088)
CLUM MORFORD DISTRIBUTING (PA)
Also Called: Can-West Directory Distrs
20 Ragsdale Dr Ste 100, Monterey (93940-7812)
PHONE.................................831 333-1100
Woodworth B Clum Jr, *President*
David Forey, *Senior VP*
Judy Carrillo, *Admin Sec*
EMP: 100

SALES (est): 4.4MM Privately Held
SIC: 7389 Telephone directory distribution, contract or fee basis

(P-17089)
CMG FINANCIAL SERVICES
3160 Crow Canyon Rd # 400, San Ramon (94583-1368)
PHONE.................................925 983-3073
Christopher M George, *CEO*
Julie Morris, *Partner*
Dana Booth, *Officer*
Ashley Mohammed, *Officer*
Jeffrey Putnam, *Officer*
EMP: 75
SALES (est): 13.5MM Privately Held
SIC: 7389 Financial services

(P-17090)
COAST ENVIRONMENTAL INC
2221 Las Palmas Dr Ste J, Carlsbad (92011-1528)
PHONE.................................760 929-9570
Dan Hughes, *President*
Andrew Laverty, *Project Engr*
Javier Alvarez, *Warehouse Mgr*
Lisa Smith, *Manager*
EMP: 60
SQ FT: 25,000
SALES (est): 6.7MM Privately Held
WEB: www.coastenvironmental.com
SIC: 7389 Safety inspection service

(P-17091)
COASTAL CLOSEOUTS INC
Also Called: West Coast Rags
100 Oceangate Ste 1200, Long Beach (90802-4324)
PHONE.................................323 589-7900
EMP: 52
SQ FT: 68,000
SALES (est): 4.1MM Privately Held
SIC: 7389

(P-17092)
COASTAL INTERNATIONAL INC (PA)
Also Called: Coastal Intl Cnstr Svcs
3 Harbor Dr Ste 211, Sausalito (94965-1491)
PHONE.................................415 339-1700
Bruce Green, *CEO*
Bob Hill, *Vice Pres*
Jesus Lopez, *Vice Pres*
Rich Rebecky, *Vice Pres*
Shelley Cowperthwait, *Admin Asst*
EMP: 600
SQ FT: 12,000
SALES (est): 47.5MM Privately Held
WEB: www.coastlintl.com
SIC: 7389 1542 1522 Trade show arrangement; nonresidential construction; residential construction

(P-17093)
COHESITY INC (PA)
300 Park Ave Ste 800, San Jose (95110-2773)
PHONE.................................408 645-0041
Mohit Aron, *CEO*
Lynn Lucas, *Chief Mktg Ofcr*
Riccardo Di Blasio, *Officer*
Diana Bustamante, *Executive*
Sarah Hirst, *Executive*
EMP: 65
SALES (est): 15.5MM Privately Held
SIC: 7389 Document storage service

(P-17094)
COMPLEX STUDIOS
Also Called: Complex The
2323 Corinth Ave, Los Angeles (90064-1701)
PHONE.................................310 477-1938
Walter Ulloa, *Owner*
EMP: 50
SQ FT: 19,000
SALES (est): 2.6MM Privately Held
SIC: 7389 Recording studio, noncommercial records

(P-17095)
COMPUMAIL INFORMATION SVCS INC
4057 Port Chicago Hwy # 300, Concord (94520-1160)
P.O. Box 6756 (94524-1756)
PHONE.................................925 689-7100
Monte G Bish, *President*
Frank Fribley, *CFO*
Michelle Lee Chung, *Controller*
EMP: 75
SQ FT: 22,000
SALES (est): 11.1MM Privately Held
WEB: www.compumailinc.com
SIC: 7389 Printers' services: folding, collating

(P-17096)
COMRADE INC
484 9th St, Oakland (94607-4048)
PHONE.................................510 277-3400
Thelton McMillian, *President*
Robin Borelli, *Partner*
Christy McMillian, *COO*
Stanley Rodrigues, *CFO*
Jeanette D Franks, *Project Mgr*
EMP: 50 EST: 2010
SQ FT: 4,596
SALES (est): 6.4MM Privately Held
SIC: 7389 8731 8742 7379 Product endorsement service; commercial physical research; marketing consulting services;
HQ: Ci&T, Inc.
630 Freedom Bus Ctr Dr # 300
King Of Prussia PA 19406
610 482-4810

(P-17097)
CONCEPT GREEN ENRGY SLTONS INC
13824 Yorba Ave, Chino (91710-5518)
PHONE.................................855 459-6535
Liang Gao, *President*
Henry F Hsieh, *Principal*
Jerry Krantiz, *VP Opers*
Michael Meng, *Opers Mgr*
EMP: 4000 EST: 2010
SALES (est): 98.4MM Privately Held
SIC: 7389 5211 Design services; energy conservation products

(P-17098)
CONFIRE J P A
1743 Miro Way, Rialto (92376-8630)
PHONE.................................909 356-2375
Richard Britt, *Director*
EMP: 60
SALES (est): 7.4MM Privately Held
SIC: 7389 Personal service agents, brokers & bureaus

(P-17099)
CONSOLDTED FIRE PROTECTION LLC (HQ)
153 Technology Dr Ste 200, Irvine (92618-2461)
PHONE.................................949 727-3277
Rob Salek, *CEO*
Keith Fielding, *President*
Kim Glasgow, *Executive*
Maddy Malin, *Executive*
Jonathan King, *Administration*
EMP: 800
SALES (est): 89.4MM Privately Held
SIC: 7389 Fire protection service other than forestry or public

(P-17100)
CONTI LIFE COMM PLEA LLC
Also Called: Stoneridge Creek Pleasanton
3300 Stoneridge Creek Way, Pleasanton (94588-2200)
PHONE.................................925 227-6800
Francis X Rodgers, *Exec Dir*
Troy Bourne, *Vice Pres*
Peter Cordingly, *Safety Mgr*
David Tsan, *Opers Staff*
Eric Myers, *Manager*
EMP: 51
SALES (est): 8.1MM Privately Held
SIC: 7389 Personal service agents, brokers & bureaus

(P-17101)
CORE GROUP INC (PA)
14544 Central Ave Ste 42, Chino (91710-9503)
PHONE.................................909 438-2626
John Goodman, *CEO*
Travis King, *President*
Michelle Alva, *Senior VP*
John Macdougall, *Vice Pres*
Diane Lanois, *Controller*
EMP: 136
SALES (est): 19.5MM Privately Held
SIC: 7389

(P-17102)
CORPORATE RISK HLDINGS III INC
Also Called: Hireright
3349 Michelson Dr Ste 150, Irvine (92612-8881)
PHONE.................................949 428-5839
John Fennelley, *CEO*
Thomas Spaeth, *CFO*
Dawn Hirsch, *Officer*
Jim Weber, *Officer*
Tony Magro, *Vice Pres*
EMP: 1700
SALES (est): 15MM Privately Held
SIC: 7389 Personal investigation service

(P-17103)
COUNTRY VILLA SERVICE CORP
39950 Vista Del Sol, Rancho Mirage (92270-3206)
PHONE.................................760 340-0053
Georgeanne Slapper, *Branch Mgr*
Penny Beltran, *Records Dir*
Tracy Hefner, *Marketing Staff*
EMP: 83
SALES (corp-wide): 125.3MM Privately Held
SIC: 7389 Personal service agents, brokers & bureaus
PA: Country Villa Service Corp.
2400 E Katella Ave # 800
Anaheim CA 92806
310 574-3733

(P-17104)
COUNTY OF LOS ANGELES
Also Called: Internal Services Dept
1100 N Eastern Ave, Los Angeles (90063-3200)
PHONE.................................323 267-2771
Linnette Bookman, *Superintendent*
EMP: 200 Privately Held
WEB: www.co.la.ca.us
SIC: 7389 9631 Telephone services; communications commission, government;
PA: County Of Los Angeles
500 W Temple St Ste 437
Los Angeles CA 90012
213 974-1101

(P-17105)
COUNTY OF MODOC
Also Called: Treasurer/Tax Collector
204 S Court St Ste 6, Alturas (96101-4138)
PHONE.................................530 233-6223
Cheryl Knoch, *Treasurer*
Linda Wilson, *General Mgr*
EMP: 250 Privately Held
WEB: www.modoccounty.us
SIC: 7389 Tax collection agency
PA: County Of Modoc
202 W 4th St Ste A
Alturas CA 96101
530 233-6400

(P-17106)
COUNTY OF MONTEREY
Also Called: Telecommunications Dept
855 E Laurel Dr Ste D, Salinas (93905-1300)
PHONE.................................831 755-4944
Chin Lavonne, *Branch Mgr*
EMP: 100 Privately Held
WEB: www.montereycountyfarmbureau.org
SIC: 7389 Personal service agents, brokers & bureaus
PA: County Of Monterey
168 W Alisal St Fl 2
Salinas CA 93901
831 755-5040

P R O D U C T S & S V C S

(P-17107)
COUNTY OF MONTEREY
Also Called: Dept of Building Inspection
240 Church St Ste 116, Salinas
(93901-2683)
P.O. Box 1208 (93902-1208)
PHONE..................................831 755-5027
Scott Hennessy, *Director*
EMP: 100 **Privately Held**
WEB: www.montereycountyfarmbureau.org
SIC: 7389 9111 8111 Building inspection
service; county supervisors' & executives'
offices; legal services
PA: County Of Monterey
168 W Alisal St Fl 2
Salinas CA 93901
831 755-5040

(P-17108)
CRAFTWORKS REST
BREWERIES INC
600 Polk St, San Francisco (94102-3328)
..................................415 292-5800
Alex Smith, *President*
EMP: 50 **Privately Held**
SIC: 7389 Personal service agents, bro-
kers & bureaus
PA: Craftworks Restaurants & Breweries,
Inc.
8001 Arista Pl Fl 5
Broomfield CO 80021
-

(P-17109)
CREATE MUSIC GROUP INC
1320 N Wilton Pl, Los Angeles
(90028-8527)
PHONE..................................310 623-0696
Jonathan Strauss, *CEO*
Alexandre Williams, *COO*
EMP: 85
SALES: 30MM **Privately Held**
SIC: 7389 7371 Music distribution sys-
tems; computer software development &
applications

(P-17110)
CREATIVE DESIGN CONS INC
(PA)
Also Called: C D C
2915 Red Hill Ave G201, Costa Mesa
(92626-7948)
PHONE..................................714 641-4868
Dana Eggerts, *Principal*
Brian Richardson, *Info Tech Mgr*
Rick Betts, *Project Mgr*
Shawna Bong, *Project Mgr*
Cassandra Hanhart, *Project Mgr*
EMP: 100
SQ FT: 9,988
SALES (est): 11.7MM **Privately Held**
WEB: www.cdcdesigns.com
SIC: 7389 Interior designer

(P-17111)
CREATIVE TECHNOLOGY
GROUP INC (DH)
14000 Arminta St, Panorama City
(91402-6080)
PHONE..................................818 779-2400
Graham Andrews, *President*
Stephen Gray, *COO*
Herb Brandt, *General Mgr*
Augie Dellapi, *General Mgr*
Sim Elwood, *General Mgr*
EMP: 80
SALES (est): 43.8MM
SALES (corp-wide): 17.7MM **Privately
Held**
WEB: www.avesco.com
SIC: 7389 Teleconferencing services
HQ: Creative Technology Group Limited
Unit E2
Crawley W SUSSEX
129 358-3400

(P-17112)
CREDIT CARD SERVICES INC
(PA)
Also Called: Bankcard Services
21281 S Western Ave, Torrance
(90501-2958)
PHONE..................................213 365-1122
Patrick S Hong, *CEO*
Dennis M Lee, *CFO*

Mimi Yi, *Purch Agent*
Yeseong Kim, *Marketing Staff*
Ju J Kim, *Manager*
EMP: 95
SQ FT: 17,000
SALES (est): 19.8MM **Privately Held**
WEB: www.e-bankcard.com
SIC: 7389 Credit card service

(P-17113)
CREDIT KARMA INC (PA)
760 Market St Ste 500, San Francisco
(94102-2410)
PHONE..................................415 510-5059
Kenneth Lin, *CEO*
Ryan Graciano, *President*
Joseph Kauffman, *CFO*
Ian Harshman, *Software Engr*
Charlie Ll, *Software Engr*
EMP: 148
SQ FT: 245,000
SALES (est): 134.2MM **Privately Held**
SIC: 7389 Credit card service

(P-17114)
CROSSCHECK INC (PA)
1440 N Mcdowell Blvd, Petaluma
(94954-6515)
P.O. Box 6008 (94955-6008)
PHONE..................................707 665-2100
J David Siembieda, *President*
Janet Cipriano, *President*
Christina Erasmy, *President*
Chris Pounds, *President*
Dave Kilat, *Exec VP*
EMP: 155
SALES (est): 22.5MM **Privately Held**
WEB: www.checksbynet.com
SIC: 7389 Credit card service

(P-17115)
CROSSROAD SERVICES INC
2360 Alvarado St, San Leandro
(94577-4314)
PHONE..................................510 895-5055
Steven Scheiner, *President*
Feroun Khan, *Vice Pres*
EMP: 419
SQ FT: 5,000
SALES: 21MM **Privately Held**
SIC: 7389 Inventory stocking service

(P-17116)
CRUZ HOFFSTETTER LLC
Also Called: Royal Crest Healthcare
519 W Badillo St, Covina (91722-3763)
PHONE..................................626 915-5621
Lydia Cruz, *President*
EMP: 60
SALES (est): 3.1MM **Privately Held**
SIC: 7389 Personal service agents, bro-
kers & bureaus

(P-17117)
CSDVRS LLC (PA)
Also Called: Zvrs
595 Menlo Dr, Rocklin (95765-3708)
PHONE..................................727 443-1218
Sherri Turpin,
Philip W Bravin, *President*
Dan Gatti, *President*
Lee Horner, *President*
Ryan Barry, *Vice Pres*
EMP: 250
SALES (est): 41.9MM **Privately Held**
SIC: 7389 5734 8731 Translation serv-
ices; computer software & accessories;
computer (hardware) development

(P-17118)
CSUB NURSING CLASS OF 2006
9001 Stockdale Hwy, Bakersfield
(93311-1022)
PHONE..................................408 219-5914
Michelle Concuora, *President*
EMP: 71
SALES: 2.3MM **Privately Held**
SIC: 7389 Fund raising organizations

(P-17119)
CURRENT TV LLC
118 King St, San Francisco (94107-1905)
PHONE..................................415 995-8328
David Bohrman,
Guy Barbaro,
Mark Golmon,

Paul Hollerbach,
Joel Hyatt,
EMP: 200
SQ FT: 27,000
SALES (est): 6.9MM **Privately Held**
WEB: www.currentmedia.com
SIC: 7389 Field audits, cable television
PA: Al Jazeera Media Network
Qatar Television Building Khalifa
Street
Doha
448 960-00

(P-17120)
CUSTOMFAB INC
Also Called: Fullclip USA
7345 Orangewood Ave, Garden Grove
(92841-1411)
PHONE..................................714 891-9119
Donald Martin Alhanati, *President*
Sharon Benson, *Office Mgr*
Brian Alhanati, *Technology*
Crisanto Sanchez, *Engineer*
Jill Alhanati, *Purch Mgr*
EMP: 250
SQ FT: 47,000
SALES (est): 28.9MM **Privately Held**
SIC: 7389 Sewing contractor

(P-17121)
CUTLER GROUP LP
101 Montgomery St Ste 700, San Francisco
(94104-4125)
PHONE..................................415 645-6745
Trent Cutler, *Managing Prtnr*
Anand Prakash, *Partner*
Doug Patterson, *Officer*
Steve Juno, *Managing Dir*
Carina Ho, *Office Mgr*
EMP: 50
SALES (est): 5.6MM **Privately Held**
SIC: 7389 Financial services

(P-17122)
CWPFL INC
1682 Langley Ave, Irvine (92614-5620)
PHONE..................................714 564-7900
Matthew K Stewart, *President*
Jeff Gunhus, *CEO*
Spencer Pepe, *CEO*
Jason Reed, *CEO*
EMP: 50
SALES (est): 1.6MM **Privately Held**
WEB: www.kleen-sales.com
SIC: 7389 Personal service agents, bro-
kers & bureaus

(P-17123)
D2J INC
6351 Regent St Ste 100, Huntington Park
(90255-3567)
PHONE..................................323 589-1374
Richard Kim, *President*
EMP: 90
SALES (est): 4MM **Privately Held**
SIC: 7389 Sewing contractor

(P-17124)
DAILYLOOK INC
2445 E 12th St Ste B, Los Angeles
(90021-2937)
PHONE..................................888 888-6645
Brian Ree, *CEO*
Richard Nam, *Finance Mgr*
Henry Barahona, *Director*
Michelle Gonzalez, *Supervisor*
EMP: 86
SALES (est): 919.9K **Privately Held**
SIC: 7389 Styling of fashions, apparel, fur-
niture, textiles, etc.

(P-17125)
DAVID SANTOS FARMING
720 Jefferson Ave, Los Banos
(93635-4713)
PHONE..................................209 826-1065
David Santos, *Owner*
EMP: 60
SALES (est): 5.6MM **Privately Held**
SIC: 7389 Personal service agents, bro-
kers & bureaus

(P-17126)
DECIMAL INC
Also Called: Ubiquity
1160 Battery St Ste 350, San Francisco
(94111-1238)
PHONE..................................855 980-6612
Chad Parks, *President*
Christopher Jasinski, *Partner*
Selby Mashakova, *Partner*
Mary Torgerson, *COO*
Kim Vo, *Administration*
EMP: 82
SQ FT: 5,000
SALES (est): 6.1MM **Privately Held**
WEB: www.decimal.com
SIC: 7389 Financial services

(P-17127)
DEDICATED MANAGEMENT
GROUP LLC
3876 E Childs Ave, Merced (95341-9520)
PHONE..................................209 385-0694
EMP: 141
SALES (corp-wide): 15.7MM **Privately
Held**
SIC: 7389
PA: Dedicated Management Group Llc
3651 Mars Hill Rd Ste 400
Watkinsville GA 30677
404 564-1201

(P-17128)
DEE SIGN CO
Also Called: American Sign
7950 Woodley Ave, Van Nuys
(91406-1260)
PHONE..................................818 904-3400
Braden Huenefeld, *Principal*
EMP: 55
SQ FT: 28,900
SALES (est): 3.2MM **Privately Held**
SIC: 7389 3993 Sign painting & lettering
shop; signs & advertising specialties

(P-17129)
DEKRA-LITE INDUSTRIES INC
Also Called: DI Imaging
3102 W Alton Ave, Santa Ana
(92704-6817)
PHONE..................................714 436-0705
Jeffrey Lopez, *CEO*
EMP: 80
SQ FT: 30,000
SALES (est): 13.3MM **Privately Held**
WEB: www.dekra-lite.com
SIC: 7389 5999 3999 Decoration service
for special events; art, picture frames &
decorations; Christmas lights & decora-
tions; advertising curtains

(P-17130)
DENIOS ROSEVILLE FARMERS
2013 Opportunity Dr, Roseville
(95678-3023)
PHONE..................................916 782-2704
Jeff Ronten, *CEO*
Ken Denio, *President*
Marilee Denio, *Corp Secy*
Jeff Ross, *Marketing Staff*
Lony Bauer, *Accounts Mgr*
EMP: 120
SQ FT: 18,212
SALES (est): 9.4MM **Privately Held**
WEB: www.denios.org
SIC: 7389 Flea market

(P-17131)
DFA OF CALIFORNIA
1050 Diamond St, Stockton (95205-7020)
P.O. Box 1727 (95201-1727)
PHONE..................................209 465-2289
Debra Pennell, *Principal*
EMP: 60
SALES (corp-wide): 9.7MM **Privately
Held**
WEB: www.dfaofca.com
SIC: 7389 Inspection & testing services
PA: Dfa Of California
710 Striker Ave
Sacramento CA 95834
916 561-5900

(P-17132)
DIABLO VLY COLLEGE
FOUNDATION (PA)
321 Golf Club Rd, Pleasant Hill
(94523-1544)
PHONE..........................925 685-1230
Mark G Edelstein, *President*
Katherine Guptill, *CEO*
EMP: 108
SQ FT: 1,000
SALES: 1MM **Privately Held**
WEB: www.dvc.edu
SIC: 7389 8221 Fund raising organizations; colleges universities & professional schools

(P-17133)
DMCG INC (PA)
Also Called: Bail Hotline Bail Bonds
3605 10th St, Riverside (92501-3619)
PHONE..........................951 683-9685
Daniel McGuire, *CEO*
Ben Srinivas, *CFO*
Cesar McGuire, *Exec VP*
Gilbert McGuire, *Exec VP*
Marco McGuire, *Exec VP*
EMP: 50
SQ FT: 15,000
SALES (est): 11.1MM **Privately Held**
SIC: 7389 Bail bonding

(P-17134)
DOCMAGIC INC
Also Called: Document Systems
1800 W 213th St, Torrance (90501-2832)
PHONE..........................800 649-1362
Dominic Iannitti, *President*
Gavin Ales, *Officer*
Shandi Smith, *Executive*
Alondra Sanders, *Office Mgr*
Jimmy Chen, *Administration*
EMP: 79
SQ FT: 20,000
SALES (est): 18MM **Privately Held**
WEB: www.docmagic.com
SIC: 7389 Legal & tax services

(P-17135)
DOCUMENT TECHNOLOGIES
LLC
275 Battery St Ste 250, San Francisco
(94111-3318)
PHONE..........................415 495-4100
Jonathan Kafka, *Branch Mgr*
EMP: 63
SALES (corp-wide): 589.6MM **Privately Held**
SIC: 7389 Document storage service
PA: Document Technologies, Llc
2 Ravinia Dr Ste 850
Atlanta GA 30346
770 390-2700

(P-17136)
DOCUMENT TECHNOLOGIES
LLC
350 S Figueroa St Ste 750, Los Angeles
(90071-1313)
PHONE..........................213 892-9000
John Davenport Jr, *Branch Mgr*
EMP: 71
SALES (corp-wide): 589.6MM **Privately Held**
SIC: 7389 Document storage service
PA: Document Technologies, Llc
2 Ravinia Dr Ste 850
Atlanta GA 30346
770 390-2700

(P-17137)
DOCUMENT TECHNOLOGIES
LLC
3600 W Bayshore Rd, Palo Alto
(94303-4239)
PHONE..........................650 485-2705
Victor Tan, *Branch Mgr*
EMP: 71
SALES (corp-wide): 589.6MM **Privately Held**
SIC: 7389 Document storage service
PA: Document Technologies, Llc
2 Ravinia Dr Ste 850
Atlanta GA 30346
770 390-2700

(P-17138)
DOUBLELINE CAPITAL LP
333 S Grand Ave Fl 18, Los Angeles
(90071-1504)
PHONE..........................213 633-8200
Jeffery E Gundlach, *Partner*
Philip A Barach, *Partner*
Henry V Chase, *Partner*
Louis Lucido, *COO*
Youse Guia, *Officer*
EMP: 111
SQ FT: 35,000
SALES (est): 18.5MM **Privately Held**
SIC: 7389 6719 Financial services; investment holding companies, except banks

(P-17139)
DRIVER SPG
1501 S Harris Ct, Anaheim (92806-5932)
PHONE..........................855 300-4774
Dana J Roberts, *CEO*
Karl Kreutziger, *President*
Matt Loorya, *Senior VP*
Aimee Siemianowsk, *Vice Pres*
Cecilia Ulloa, *Office Mgr*
EMP: 50
SQ FT: 7,000
SALES: 74MM **Privately Held**
SIC: 7389 Drive-a-way automobile service

(P-17140)
DUFF & PHELPS LLC
345 California St # 2100, San Francisco
(94104-2663)
PHONE..........................415 693-5300
Michael Lloyd, *Director*
David Larsen, *Managing Dir*
McGovern Mike, *Analyst*
EMP: 53
SALES (corp-wide): 558.1MM **Privately Held**
SIC: 7389 Financial services
HQ: Duff & Phelps, Llc
55 E 52nd St Fl 31
New York NY 10055
212 871-2000

(P-17141)
DUN & BRADSTREET
EMERGING (DH)
22761 Pacific Coast Hwy # 226, Malibu
(90265-5064)
PHONE..........................310 456-8271
Thomas J Manning, *CEO*
Wisdom Lu, *CFO*
Kathleen M Guinnessey, *Treasurer*
Susan D Beriont, *Vice Pres*
Chad Buechler, *Vice Pres*
EMP: 145
SALES (est): 66.7MM **Publicly Held**
SIC: 7389 Financial services
HQ: Dun & Bradstreet, Inc
103 Jfk Pkwy
Short Hills NJ 07078
973 921-5500

(P-17142)
DURINI LUIS CARLOS
ESTRADA
Also Called: Alltoss
100 W Broadway Ste 100 # 100, Glendale
(91210-1230)
PHONE..........................502 474-3112
Luis Estrada, *Owner*
EMP: 50
SALES (est): 978.2K **Privately Held**
SIC: 7389 Personal service agents, brokers & bureaus

(P-17143)
E & C FASHION INC
Also Called: Pacific Concept Laundry
3600 E Olympic Blvd, Los Angeles
(90023-3121)
PHONE..........................323 262-0099
William Moo Han Bae, *CEO*
Maria Bae, *President*
Elizabeth Bae, *Vice Pres*
Claudia Kye, *Vice Pres*
EMP: 300
SQ FT: 111,000
SALES (est): 33.1MM **Privately Held**
SIC: 7389 Sewing contractor

(P-17144)
E TRADESHOWGIRLSCOM
1 Ocean Rdg, Laguna Niguel (92677-9231)
PHONE..........................949 661-4177
Shelley Tippetts, *Owner*
EMP: 100 **EST:** 2000
SALES (est): 2.7MM **Privately Held**
SIC: 7389 Advertising, promotional & trade show services

(P-17145)
EAST BAY INNOVATIONS
2450 Washington Ave # 240, San Leandro
(94577-5996)
PHONE..........................510 618-1580
Tom Heinz, *Director*
Cathy Nielsen, *Treasurer*
Lindsay Moorehead, *Technology*
Tamy Ratto, *Director*
EMP: 60
SALES: 7.6MM **Privately Held**
WEB: www.eastbayinnovations.com
SIC: 7389 Personal service agents, brokers & bureaus

(P-17146)
ECONTACTLIVE INC
Also Called: Telecontact Resource Services
6436 Oakdale Rd, Riverbank (95367-9648)
PHONE..........................209 548-4300
Julie Hutchings, *CEO*
June Griffith, *Vice Pres*
Alice Martinez, *CTO*
David Schwerd, *Info Tech Mgr*
David Schwerdtfeger, *Technology*
EMP: 80
SQ FT: 42,000
SALES (est): 4MM **Privately Held**
WEB: www.eContactLive.com
SIC: 7389 Telemarketing services

(P-17147)
ELAINE NULL
1388 Sutter St Fl 11, San Francisco
(94109-5427)
PHONE..........................415 345-4428
EMP: 148
SALES (est): 10.1MM **Privately Held**
SIC: 7389 Personal service agents, brokers & bureaus

(P-17148)
ELECTRIC LIGHTWA
3700 Old Redwood Hwy, Santa Rosa
(95403-5738)
PHONE..........................707 284-4000
Shawn Shaw, *Branch Mgr*
Robert Guth, *President*
EMP: 72
SALES (corp-wide): 351.8MM **Privately Held**
SIC: 7389 4813 Telephone services; local & long distance telephone communications
PA: Electric Lightwave Communications, Inc.
18110 Se 34th St Bldg 1s
Vancouver WA 98683
360 558-6900

(P-17149)
ELLIE FASHION GROUP INC
1735 Stewart St Fl 2, Santa Monica
(90404-4021)
PHONE..........................818 355-3812
Marcus Greinke, *CEO*
EMP: 56
SQ FT: 7,000
SALES: 4MM **Privately Held**
SIC: 7389 Apparel designers, commercial

(P-17150)
EMAGIA CORPORATION
4701 P Henry Dr Bldg 20, Santa Clara
(95054)
PHONE..........................408 654-6575
Veena Gundavelli, *CEO*
Phyllis Saavedra, *Director*
John Symons, *Director*
EMP: 50
SALES (est): 3.4MM **Privately Held**
WEB: www.emagia.com
SIC: 7389 Financial services

(P-17151)
EMERALD EXPOSITIONS LLC
(HQ)
Also Called: Contract
31910 Del Obispo St # 200, San Juan
Capistrano (92675-3182)
PHONE..........................949 226-5700
Kosty Gilis, *CEO*
Joe Miranda, *Vice Pres*
Tina Nicholson, *Vice Pres*
Scott Pierce, *Vice Pres*
Suresh Ramalingam, *Managing Dir*
EMP: 384
SQ FT: 6,500
SALES (est): 154.1MM
SALES (corp-wide): 348.2MM **Publicly Held**
SIC: 7389 Trade show arrangement
PA: Emerald Expositions Events Inc.
31910 Del Obispo St
San Juan Capistrano CA 92675
949 226-5700

(P-17152)
ENTREPRENEURIAL
HOSPITALITY
Also Called: Riverside Convention Center
3485 Mission Inn Ave, Riverside
(92501-3304)
PHONE..........................951 346-4700
Duane Roberts, *Ch of Bd*
Richard Shippie, *President*
Ted Weggeland, *President*
Scott Megna, *Vice Pres*
EMP: 200
SQ FT: 75,000
SALES (est): 8.8MM **Privately Held**
SIC: 7389 Convention & show services

(P-17153)
EPHONAMATIONCOM INC
Also Called: Ansafone Contact Centers
145 E Columbine Ave, Santa Ana
(92707-4401)
P.O. Box 4678, Ocala FL (34478-4678)
PHONE..........................714 560-1000
Randy Harmat, *CEO*
Jennifer Oliveros, *Vice Pres*
EMP: 175
SQ FT: 18,900
SALES (est): 20.9MM **Privately Held**
SIC: 7389 Telephone answering service

(P-17154)
EQUILAR INC
1100 Marshall St, Redwood City
(94063-2595)
PHONE..........................877 441-6090
David Chun, *CEO*
Timothy Ranzetta, *President*
Courtney Yu, *Manager*
EMP: 110 **EST:** 2000
SALES (est): 21.3MM **Privately Held**
SIC: 7389 Financial services

(P-17155)
EREPUBLIC INC (PA)
Also Called: Government Technology
100 Blue Ravine Rd, Folsom (95630-4509)
PHONE..........................916 932-1300
Dennis McKenna, *CEO*
Margaret Mohr, *Chief Mktg Ofcr*
John Flynn, *Vice Pres*
Dee Pearson, *Vice Pres*
Randall Mott, *CIO*
EMP: 120
SQ FT: 36,000
SALES (est): 31.1MM **Privately Held**
WEB: www.erepublic.com
SIC: 7389 2759 2721 Convention & show services; publication printing; magazines: printing; periodicals

(P-17156)
ETC BUILDING & DESIGN INC
(PA)
Also Called: Essrig Taylor Constructions
6805 Nancy Ridge Dr, San Diego
(92121-2233)
PHONE..........................858 554-1150
Michael Essrig, *President*
Tom Ross, *Shareholder*
Chris Taylor, *Shareholder*
Benjamin Catalano, *CFO*
John Mentzer, *Vice Pres*

EMP: 143
SQ FT: 9,000
SALES (est): 21.5MM **Privately Held**
SIC: 7389 1711 1542 Safety inspection service; heating & air conditioning contractors; hospital construction

(P-17157)
EVERGREEN COMPANY INC
847 E Turner Rd, Lodi (95240-0734)
PHONE..................916 257-5994
Thomas W Bors, *CEO*
EMP: 60
SALES (est): 5.3MM **Privately Held**
SIC: 7389

(P-17158)
EXCELLENCE VENTURES INC
149 S Mednik Ave, Los Angeles (90022-1606)
PHONE..................323 262-6800
Recardo Davila, *CEO*
Manuel Davila, *President*
Ricardo Davila, *CEO*
EMP: 70
SQ FT: 4,000
SALES (est): 2.6MM **Privately Held**
SIC: 7389 Financial services

(P-17159)
FACT FOUNDATION
Also Called: FREDERICKA MANOR CARE CENTER
303 N Glenoaks Blvd, Burbank (91502-1116)
PHONE..................818 729-8105
Donna Shaw, *Principal*
Tim Detmen, *President*
EMP: 75
SALES: 816.1K
SALES (corp-wide): 165.1MM **Privately Held**
SIC: 7389 Fund raising organizations
PA: Front Porch Communities And Services - Casa De Manana, Llc
800 N Brand Blvd Fl 19
Glendale CA 91203
818 729-8100

(P-17160)
FACTER DIRECT LTD
4751 Wilshire Blvd # 140, Los Angeles (90010-3827)
PHONE..................323 634-1999
Larry Keefer, *Controller*
EMP: 170
SALES (est): 4.6MM
SALES (corp-wide): 8.8MM **Privately Held**
WEB: www.giftplanningdirect.com
SIC: 7389 8742 Telemarketing services; marketing consulting services
PA: Facter Direct Ltd
11500 W Olympic Blvd
Los Angeles CA
310 788-9000

(P-17161)
FAITH T & B PLATING INC
Also Called: Faith Bumper Service
8475 Forest St, Gilroy (95020-3646)
PHONE..................408 986-1226
Robert Foote, *President*
William Foote, *Vice Pres*
EMP: 66 EST: 1957
SQ FT: 22,000
SALES (est): 7.9MM **Privately Held**
SIC: 7389 Automobile recovery service

(P-17162)
FALLBROOK FIRE PROTECTION DST
315 E Ivy St, Fallbrook (92028-2138)
PHONE..................760 723-2010
Kermit Harrison, *President*
Herbert A Gaetjens, *Director*
Jsteve Johnson, *Director*
Pete Merritt, *Director*
Arlan H Peterson, *Director*
EMP: 69
SALES (est): 3.8MM **Privately Held**
SIC: 7389 Fire protection service other than forestry or public

(P-17163)
FAMILY PLG ASSOC MED GROUP
2777 Long Beach Blvd # 150, Long Beach (90806-1571)
PHONE..................562 595-5653
Edward C Allred, *Branch Mgr*
EMP: 73
SALES (corp-wide): 36.1MM **Privately Held**
SIC: 7389 Personal service agents, brokers & bureaus
PA: Family Planning Associates Medical Group
3050 E Airport Way
Long Beach CA 90806
213 738-7283

(P-17164)
FARMEX LAND MANAGEMENT INC
11156 E Annadale Ave, Sanger (93657-9727)
PHONE..................559 875-7181
James Yakligian, *President*
EMP: 125
SALES (est): 9.9MM **Privately Held**
SIC: 7389 Packaging & labeling services

(P-17165)
FEDERAL EXPRESS CORPORATION
Also Called: Fedex
2495 Faraday Ave, Carlsbad (92010-7225)
PHONE..................800 463-3339
Diane Coale, *Branch Mgr*
EMP: 167
SALES (corp-wide): 65.4B **Publicly Held**
WEB: www.federalexpress.com
SIC: 7389 Personal service agents, brokers & bureaus
HQ: Federal Express Corporation
3610 Hacks Cross Rd
Memphis TN 38125
901 369-3600

(P-17166)
FEDERAL EXPRESS CORPORATION
Also Called: Fedex
200 N Pacific Coast Hwy # 800, El Segundo (90245-4340)
PHONE..................800 463-3339
Fay Lester, *Manager*
William D Wacht, *Analyst*
Mary Gonzales, *Manager*
EMP: 500
SALES (corp-wide): 65.4B **Publicly Held**
WEB: www.federalexpress.com
SIC: 7389 Mailing & messenger services
HQ: Federal Express Corporation
3610 Hacks Cross Rd
Memphis TN 38125
901 369-3600

(P-17167)
FEDERAL EXPRESS CORPORATION
Also Called: Fedex
7275 Johnson Dr, Pleasanton (94588-3861)
PHONE..................800 463-3339
Tina Bier, *Manager*
EMP: 99
SALES (corp-wide): 65.4B **Publicly Held**
SIC: 7389 Courier or messenger service
HQ: Federal Express Corporation
3610 Hacks Cross Rd
Memphis TN 38125
901 369-3600

(P-17168)
FEDERAL EXPRESS CORPORATION
Also Called: Fedex
7000 Barranca Pkwy, Irvine (92618-3112)
PHONE..................800 463-3339
EMP: 350
SALES (corp-wide): 47.4B **Publicly Held**
SIC: 7389 4731 4581 4513
HQ: Federal Express Corporation
3610 Hacks Cross Rd
Memphis TN 38125
901 369-3600

(P-17169)
FEDERAL EXPRESS CORPORATION
Also Called: Fedex
3371 E Francis St, Ontario (91761-2914)
PHONE..................800 463-3339
Manny Vivamaco, *Manager*
EMP: 275
SALES (corp-wide): 65.4B **Publicly Held**
WEB: www.federalexpress.com
SIC: 7389 4513 4215 Courier or messenger service; air courier services; courier services, except by air
HQ: Federal Express Corporation
3610 Hacks Cross Rd
Memphis TN 38125
901 369-3600

(P-17170)
FEDEX CORPORATION
50 Cypress Ln, Brisbane (94005-1217)
PHONE..................415 657-0403
EMP: 50
SALES (corp-wide): 47.4B **Publicly Held**
SIC: 7389
PA: Fedex Corporation
942 Shady Grove Rd S
Memphis TN 38120
901 818-7500

(P-17171)
FENAGH ENGINEERING & TSTG LLC
9070 Center Ave, Rancho Cucamonga (91730-5327)
PHONE..................925 462-5151
John G Dooling,
Jonathan Felts,
EMP: 50
SQ FT: 7,500
SALES (est): 33.8K **Privately Held**
SIC: 7389 Inspection & testing services

(P-17172)
FIRST AMERICAN CARD SERVICE
25060 Hancock Ave Ste 103, Murrieta (92562-5959)
PHONE..................951 677-8720
Brian Rommele, *President*
EMP: 50
SALES (est): 1.4MM **Privately Held**
WEB: www.1stamericancardservice.com
SIC: 7389 Charge account service; credit card service

(P-17173)
FLAGSHIP CREDIT ACCEPTANCE LLC
7525 Irvine Center Dr, Irvine (92618-3066)
PHONE..................949 748-7172
EMP: 120 **Privately Held**
SIC: 7389 Financial services
PA: Flagship Credit Acceptance Llc
3 Christy Dr Ste 203
Chadds Ford PA 19317

(P-17174)
FREEMAN EXPOSITIONS LLC
901 E South St, Anaheim (92805-5347)
PHONE..................714 254-3400
Pattie Balding, *Manager*
Thanh Vu, *Info Tech Mgr*
EMP: 200
SALES (corp-wide): 2.7B **Privately Held**
SIC: 7389 Trade show arrangement
HQ: Freeman Expositions, Llc
1600 Viceroy Dr Ste 100
Dallas TX 75235
214 445-1000

(P-17175)
FREEMAN EXPOSITIONS LLC
245 S Spruce Ave, South San Francisco (94080-4581)
PHONE..................650 878-6023
Glenn Wyer, *Manager*
EMP: 95
SALES (corp-wide): 2.7B **Privately Held**
SIC: 7389 Trade show arrangement
HQ: Freeman Expositions, Llc
1600 Viceroy Dr Ste 100
Dallas TX 75235
214 445-1000

(P-17176)
FRESNO CNTY ECONOMIC OPPORTUNT
Also Called: Eoc Resource Development
1920 Mariposa Mall, Fresno (93721-2504)
PHONE..................559 263-1013
Roger Palomino, *Manager*
EMP: 500
SALES (corp-wide): 102.6MM **Privately Held**
SIC: 7389 Office facilities & secretarial service rental
PA: Fresno County Economic Opportunities Commission
1920 Mariposa Mall # 300
Fresno CA 93721
559 263-1010

(P-17177)
FRESNO METRO FLOOD CTRL DST
5469 E Olive Ave, Fresno (93727-2541)
PHONE..................559 456-3292
Bob Van Wyk, *General Mgr*
Jerry Lakeman, *Principal*
Jason Clarke, *Project Mgr*
Michael Maxwell, *Technical Staff*
Bob Notley, *Engineer*
EMP: 75 EST: 1955
SQ FT: 12,965
SALES (est): 7.4MM **Privately Held**
SIC: 7389 Personal service agents, brokers & bureaus

(P-17178)
FULL THROTTLE
125 E 56th St, Los Angeles (90011-5125)
PHONE..................323 474-8417
EMP: 172
SALES (est): 146.9K
SALES (corp-wide): 3.3B **Publicly Held**
SIC: 7389
HQ: Monster Beverage 1990 Corporation
1 Monster Way
Corona CA 92879
951 739-6200

(P-17179)
GALICE INC
30140 Tuttle Ct, Tehachapi (93561-7483)
PHONE..................323 731-8200
Cathrine A Lutz, *President*
EMP: 69 EST: 1991
SALES (est): 3.6MM **Privately Held**
WEB: www.galice.com
SIC: 7389 Interior decorating

(P-17180)
GARY R EDWARDS INC
3930 Utah St Ste C, San Diego (92104-2939)
PHONE..................619 299-8700
Gary R Edwards, *President*
EMP: 70
SALES (est): 4.3MM **Privately Held**
WEB: www.greinc.com
SIC: 7389 Subscription fulfillment services: magazine, newspaper, etc.

(P-17181)
GBS FINANCIAL CORP
Also Called: Wagner Financials
904 Manhattan Ave Ste 3, Manhattan Beach (90266-5538)
PHONE..................310 937-0073
EMP: 60
SALES (est): 1.9MM **Privately Held**
SIC: 7389

(P-17182)
GDF PARENT LLC
Also Called: Import Whl Univ Fund Raising
1510 1/2 W 228th St, Torrance (90501-5105)
PHONE..................714 743-7209
Yoelie Barag,
EMP: 75
SALES (est): 2.2MM **Privately Held**
SIC: 7389 Fund raising organizations

(P-17183)
GELFAND RENNERT & FELDMAN LLP (PA)
1880 Century Park E # 1600, Los Angeles (90067-1661)
PHONE.............................310 553-1707
Marshall M Gelfand, *Managing Prtnr*
Tyson Beem, *Partner*
Todd Gelfand, *Partner*
Norman Marcus, *Officer*
Cary Macmiller, *Managing Dir*
EMP: 200
SALES: 5K **Privately Held**
WEB: www.grfllp.com
SIC: 7389 8721 8741 Legal & tax services; accounting, auditing & bookkeeping; business management

(P-17184)
GENERAL ENVIRONMENTAL
Also Called: Stericycles Envmtl Solutions
11855 White Rock Rd, Rancho Cordova (95742-6603)
PHONE.............................916 351-0980
Matt Dickson, *Partner*
EMP: 55
SALES (est): 135.8K
SALES (corp-wide): 3.5B **Publicly Held**
SIC: 7389 Personal service agents, brokers & bureaus
HQ: Psc Environmental Services, Llc
5151 San Felipe St # 1100
Houston TX 77056
713 623-8777

(P-17185)
GENGO INC
307 2nd Ave, San Mateo (94401-3905)
PHONE.............................650 585-4390
Matthew Romaine, *CEO*
Andrea Belvedere, *President*
Matthew Skyrm, *COO*
EMP: 50
SALES (est): 778K **Privately Held**
SIC: 7389 Translation services

(P-17186)
GENTLE GIANT STUDIOS INC
7511 N San Fernando Rd, Burbank (91505-1044)
PHONE.............................818 504-3555
Karl Z Meyer, *President*
Jewell Morson, *Administration*
Dev Gilmore, *Director*
EMP: 56
SQ FT: 20,000
SALES (est): 7.4MM **Publicly Held**
WEB: www.gentlegiantstudios.com
SIC: 7389 Design services
HQ: 3d Systems, Inc.
333 Three D Systems Cir
Rock Hill SC 29730
803 326-3900

(P-17187)
GETTY IMAGES INC
Also Called: Gettyone Image Bank
6300 Wilshire Blvd # 1600, Los Angeles (90048-5227)
PHONE.............................323 202-4200
Anne Marion, *Branch Mgr*
EMP: 100
SALES (corp-wide): 312.9MM **Privately Held**
WEB: www.getty-images.com
SIC: 7389 Photography brokers
PA: Getty Images, Inc.
605 5th Ave S Ste 400
Seattle WA 98104
206 925-5000

(P-17188)
GLOBAL ASCENT INC
36 Waterworks Way, Irvine (92618-3107)
PHONE.............................714 930-6860
Gareth Ashworth, *CEO*
EMP: 50
SALES (est): 4.5MM
SALES (corp-wide): 1.2B **Publicly Held**
SIC: 7389 8711 Petroleum refinery inspection service; civil engineering
PA: Team, Inc.
13131 Dar Ashford Ste 600
Sugar Land TX 77478
281 331-6154

(P-17189)
GLOBAL CHECK SERVICE
1524 Graves Ave Ste C, El Cajon (92021-2991)
PHONE.............................619 449-5150
David James Homoki, *Partner*
Dalila Homoki, *Partner*
EMP: 200
SQ FT: 2,500
SALES (est): 8.5MM **Privately Held**
WEB: www.globalcheck.com
SIC: 7389 Check validation service; credit card service

(P-17190)
GLOBAL DEBT MANAGEMENT LLC (PA)
18881 Von Karman Ave # 1500, Irvine (92612-1582)
PHONE.............................949 825-7800
Banir Ganatra, *Mng Member*
Robert Guy,
EMP: 60
SQ FT: 3,400
SALES (est): 2.2MM **Privately Held**
SIC: 7389 Financial services

(P-17191)
GLOBAL EXPRNCE SPECIALISTS INC
5560 Katella Ave, Cypress (90630-5001)
PHONE.............................562 370-1500
EMP: 64 **Publicly Held**
SIC: 7389 Convention & show services
HQ: Global Experience Specialists, Inc.
7000 Lindell Rd
Las Vegas NV 89118
702 515-5500

(P-17192)
GLOBAL EXPRNCE SPECIALISTS INC
500 N Brand Blvd Ste 1860, Glendale (91203-3375)
PHONE.............................818 638-5959
Eddie Newquist, *Exec VP*
EMP: 65 **Publicly Held**
WEB: www.beckergroup.com
SIC: 7389 Design services
HQ: Global Experience Specialists, Inc.
7000 Lindell Rd
Las Vegas NV 89118
702 515-5500

(P-17193)
GLOBAL EXPRNCE SPECIALISTS INC
Also Called: Ges
491 C St, Chula Vista (91910-1604)
PHONE.............................619 498-6300
Tom Robins, *Manager*
EMP: 170 **Publicly Held**
WEB: www.gesexpo.com
SIC: 7389 Convention & show services
HQ: Global Experience Specialists, Inc.
7000 Lindell Rd
Las Vegas NV 89118
702 515-5500

(P-17194)
GLOBAL INNOVATION PARTNERS LLC
Also Called: GI Partners
188 The Embarcadero # 700, San Francisco (94105-1231)
PHONE.............................650 233-3600
Rick Magnuson, *Mng Member*
Roy Kelvin, *CFO*
Roman Braslavsky, *Vice Pres*
Mike Kirkman, *Vice Pres*
Mike Stuppler, *Vice Pres*
EMP: 100
SALES (est): 4.5MM **Privately Held**
SIC: 7389 Brokers, business: buying & selling business enterprises

(P-17195)
GLOBAL LANGUAGE SOLUTIONS LLC
19800 Macarthur Blvd, Irvine (92612-2421)
PHONE.............................949 798-1400
Olga Smirnova, *CEO*
Inna Kassatkina, *President*
Thanh V Dong, *Project Mgr*

Marilyn Nguyen, *Project Mgr*
Julia Tapia, *Project Mgr*
EMP: 100
SQ FT: 7,500
SALES (est): 7MM **Privately Held**
WEB: www.globallanguages.com
SIC: 7389 Translation services
PA: Welocalize, Inc.
241 E 4th St Ste 207
Frederick MD 21701

(P-17196)
GO WEST HOLDINGS LLC
795 Folsom St, San Francisco (94107-1243)
PHONE.............................888 670-0080
Victor Goree,
EMP: 145
SALES (est): 1.8MM **Privately Held**
SIC: 7389 Decoration service for special events

(P-17197)
GOODWILL SRVNG THE PPL OF STHR (PA)
Also Called: Links Sgn Lngg Intrprtng, Shrd
800 W Pacific Coast Hwy, Long Beach (90806-5243)
PHONE.............................562 435-3411
Janet McCarthy, *CEO*
EMP: 100
SQ FT: 80,000
SALES (est): 24.4MM **Privately Held**
WEB: www.goodwill-lbsb.org
SIC: 7389 8331 5932 Translation services; job training & vocational rehabilitation services; vocational training agency; used merchandise stores

(P-17198)
GOOGLE PAYMENT CORP
Also Called: Google Checkout
1600 Amphitheatre Pkwy, Mountain View (94043-1351)
PHONE.............................650 253-0000
EMP: 50
SALES (est): 6.6MM
SALES (corp-wide): 74.9B **Publicly Held**
SIC: 7389
HQ: Google Inc.
1600 Amphitheatre Pkwy
Mountain View CA 94043
650 253-0000

(P-17199)
GORDON & SCHWENKMEYER INC
1860 Howe Ave Ste 300, Sacramento (95825-1098)
PHONE.............................916 569-1740
Brett Carter, *Exec VP*
EMP: 70
SALES (corp-wide): 11.2MM **Privately Held**
WEB: www.gsitel.com
SIC: 7389 Personal service agents, brokers & bureaus
PA: Gordon & Schwenkmeyer Inc
20300 S Vt Ave Ste 210
Torrance CA 90502
310 615-2300

(P-17200)
GRAND PACIFIC RESORTS INC
Also Called: Resortime.com
5900 Pasteur Ct Ste 200, Carlsbad (92008-7336)
PHONE.............................760 431-8500
Sherri Weks, *Manager*
Cathy Fuchs, *Executive Asst*
Sherri Weeks, *VP Sales*
EMP: 200 **Privately Held**
WEB: www.grandpacificresorts.com
SIC: 7389 Personal service agents, brokers & bureaus
PA: Grand Pacific Resorts, Inc.
5900 Pasteur Ct Ste 200
Carlsbad CA 92008

(P-17201)
GRAND PERFORMANCES
350 S Grand Ave Ste A4, Los Angeles (90071-3461)
PHONE.............................213 687-2190

Craig Bloomgardner, *President*
Craig Bloomgarden, *President*
Katie Luna, *Administration*
Bria Chavez, *Marketing Mgr*
Nurit Smith, *Deputy Dir*
EMP: 55
SALES: 1.7MM **Privately Held**
SIC: 7389 Promoters of shows & exhibitions

(P-17202)
GRIDGAIN SYSTEMS INC
1065 E Hillsdale Blvd, Foster City (94404-1613)
PHONE.............................650 241-2281
Abe Kleinfeld, *President*
Eoin Connor, *CFO*
Andy Sacks, *Exec VP*
Terry Erisman, *Vice Pres*
Dianara Dube, *Info Tech Mgr*
EMP: 131
SALES (est): 470.3K **Privately Held**
SIC: 7389 Automobile recovery service

(P-17203)
GRILL ON THE ALLEY THE INC
6801 Hollywood Blvd, Los Angeles (90028-6136)
PHONE.............................323 856-5530
Katherine Sy, *Branch Mgr*
EMP: 1125
SALES (corp-wide): 25.2MM **Privately Held**
SIC: 7389 Design services
PA: Grill On The Alley, The, Inc
11661 San Vicente Blvd # 404
Los Angeles CA 90049
310 820-5559

(P-17204)
GRILL RECORDING STUDIO
4770 San Pablo Ave Ste C, Emeryville (94608-3028)
PHONE.............................510 531-4351
Levberlak Mhg, *Owner*
EMP: 51
SALES (est): 2MM **Privately Held**
SIC: 7389 Recording studio, noncommercial records

(P-17205)
GSA DESIGN INC
4551 San Fernando Rd # 102, Glendale (91204-3227)
PHONE.............................818 241-2558
Grigor Grigoryan, *President*
Narine Khachatryan, *CFO*
EMP: 150
SQ FT: 20,000
SALES: 7MM **Privately Held**
SIC: 7389 2386 Sewing contractor; garments, leather

(P-17206)
GUTHY-RENKER LLC
25892 Towne Centre Dr, Foothill Ranch (92610-3437)
PHONE.............................949 454-1400
Olly Efthyvoulos, *Branch Mgr*
EMP: 100
SALES (corp-wide): 370.7MM **Privately Held**
SIC: 7389 7374 Telemarketing services; data processing service
PA: Guthy-Renker Llc
100 N Pacific Coast Hwy # 1600
El Segundo CA 90245
760 773-9022

(P-17207)
HARINGA INC (PA)
Also Called: Premier Packaging/Assembly
14422 Best Ave, Santa Fe Springs (90670-5133)
P.O. Box 4707, Cerritos (90703-4707)
PHONE.............................800 499-9991
Victoria Haringa, *CEO*
Vicki Haringa, *President*
Randy Haringa, *General Mgr*
Candice Olson, *Opers Mgr*
Vincent Olson, *QC Mgr*
EMP: 77
SQ FT: 200,000
SALES (est): 13.2MM **Privately Held**
WEB: www.premierpkg.com
SIC: 7389 Packaging & labeling services

(P-17208)
HARRIS DIRECT
21250 Califa St Ste 114, Woodland Hills
(91367-5023)
PHONE.................818 357-2040
James Harris, *President*
EMP: 62
SQ FT: 3,800
SALES: 1.8MM **Privately Held**
SIC: 7389 7331 Telemarketing services;
direct mail advertising services

(P-17209)
HARTMANN STUDIOS INC (HQ)
1150 Brickyard Cove Rd, Point Richmond
(94801-4181)
PHONE.................510 232-5030
Thomas J Mahoney, *CEO*
EMP: 150
SALES (est): 1.5MM
SALES (corp-wide): 131.3MM **Privately Held**
SIC: 7389 Convention & show services
PA: Ita Group, Inc
4600 Westown Pkwy Ste 100
West Des Moines IA 50266
515 326-3400

(P-17210)
HARTMANN STUDIOS INCORPORATED
Also Called: Standard Party Rentals
70 W Ohio Ave Ste H, Richmond
(94804-2033)
PHONE.................510 232-5030
Matt Guelfi, *President*
Richard Olson, *CFO*
Matthew Guelfi, *Vice Pres*
Michael Guelfi, *Vice Pres*
Karim Kassab, *Vice Pres*
EMP: 150
SQ FT: 105,000
SALES (est): 22.5MM **Privately Held**
WEB: www.hartmann-studios.com
SIC: 7389 Investment holding companies,
except banks

(P-17211)
HCT PACKAGING INC (PA)
2800 28th St Ste 240, Santa Monica
(90405-6214)
PHONE.................310 260-7680
Tim Thorpe, *President*
Tara Corcoran, *Controller*
Christina Blanchard, *Director*
EMP: 125
SQ FT: 1,500
SALES (est): 24.3MM **Privately Held**
WEB: www.hctpackaging.com
SIC: 7389 Packaging & labeling services

(P-17212)
HEARTLAND PAYMENT SYSTEMS LLC
548 Shorebird Cir # 3101, Redwood City
(94065-1038)
PHONE.................650 678-2824
Gary Friedman, *Principal*
EMP: 99
SALES (corp-wide): 3.9B **Publicly Held**
SIC: 7389 Personal service agents, bro-
kers & bureaus
HQ: Heartland Payment Systems, Llc
10 Glenlake Pkwy Ste 324
Atlanta GA 30328
609 683-3831

(P-17213)
HEARTLAND PAYMENT SYSTEMS LLC
35804 Octopus Ln, Wildomar
(92595-8095)
PHONE.................909 609-1836
EMP: 97
SALES (corp-wide): 3.9B **Publicly Held**
SIC: 7389 Credit card service
HQ: Heartland Payment Systems, Llc
10 Glenlake Pkwy Ste 324
Atlanta GA 30328
609 683-3831

(P-17214)
HEARTLAND PAYMENT SYSTEMS LLC
1007 W College Ave Ste B, Santa Rosa
(95401-5046)
PHONE.................707 338-0510
Gregory Arena, *Principal*
EMP: 99
SALES (corp-wide): 3.9B **Publicly Held**
SIC: 7389 Personal service agents, bro-
kers & bureaus
HQ: Heartland Payment Systems, Llc
10 Glenlake Pkwy Ste 324
Atlanta GA 30328
609 683-3831

(P-17215)
HEARTLAND PAYMENT SYSTEMS LLC
207 S Broadway, Redondo Beach
(90277-3309)
PHONE.................424 247-8521
Gilbert Dowling, *Principal*
EMP: 99
SALES (corp-wide): 3.9B **Publicly Held**
SIC: 7389 Personal service agents, bro-
kers & bureaus
HQ: Heartland Payment Systems, Llc
10 Glenlake Pkwy Ste 324
Atlanta GA 30328
609 683-3831

(P-17216)
HEARTLAND PAYMENT SYSTEMS LLC
2225 Buena Vista Ave A, Walnut Creek
(94597-3513)
PHONE.................925 360-3258
Paul Bramblet, *Principal*
EMP: 99
SALES (corp-wide): 3.9B **Publicly Held**
SIC: 7389 Personal service agents, bro-
kers & bureaus
HQ: Heartland Payment Systems, Llc
10 Glenlake Pkwy Ste 324
Atlanta GA 30328
609 683-3831

(P-17217)
HEARTLAND PAYMENT SYSTEMS LLC
5325 Elkhorn Blvd, Sacramento
(95842-2526)
PHONE.................916 844-9548
James Bramblet, *Principal*
EMP: 99
SALES (corp-wide): 3.9B **Publicly Held**
SIC: 7389 Personal service agents, bro-
kers & bureaus
HQ: Heartland Payment Systems, Llc
10 Glenlake Pkwy Ste 324
Atlanta GA 30328
609 683-3831

(P-17218)
HEARTLAND PAYMENT SYSTEMS INC
510 Cerritos Way, Cathedral City
(92234-1617)
PHONE.................760 324-0133
EMP: 97
SALES (corp-wide): 2B **Publicly Held**
SIC: 7389
PA: Heartland Payment Systems, Inc.
90 Nassau St
Princeton NJ 30328
609 683-3831

(P-17219)
HEARTLAND PAYMENT SYSTEMS INC
Also Called: HEARTLAND PAYMENT SYS-
TEMS, INC.
1460 Golden Gate Ave # 5, San Francisco
(94115-4658)
PHONE.................415 518-4810
David Evan, *Principal*
EMP: 99
SALES (corp-wide): 3.9B **Publicly Held**
SIC: 7389 Personal service agents, bro-
kers & bureaus

HQ: Heartland Payment Systems, Llc
10 Glenlake Pkwy Ste 324
Atlanta GA 30328
609 683-3831

(P-17220)
HERBS POOL SERVICE INC
3769 Redwood Hwy, San Rafael
(94903-3998)
PHONE.................415 479-4040
Sandra L Scott, *CEO*
Herbert Dougan, *Agent*
EMP: 55 EST: 1958
SQ FT: 3,000
SALES (est): 6.6MM **Privately Held**
SIC: 7389 Swimming pool & hot tub serv-
ice & maintenance

(P-17221)
HIRSCH/BEDNER INTL INC (PA)
Also Called: Hba International
3216 Nebraska Ave, Santa Monica
(90404-4214)
PHONE.................310 829-9087
Rene G Kaerskov, *CEO*
Michael J Bedner, *Ch of Bd*
Howard Pharr, *President*
Bruce Jones, *Exec VP*
Jason Mitchell, *Pub Rel Dir*
EMP: 70
SQ FT: 14,000
SALES (est): 31.9MM **Privately Held**
WEB: www.hbadesign.com
SIC: 7389 Interior designer; interior design
services

(P-17222)
HOBBY LOBBY STORES INC
1301 W Pacheco Blvd Ste B, Los Banos
(93635-8627)
PHONE.................209 829-1807
EMP: 51
SALES (corp-wide): 4.5B **Privately Held**
SIC: 7389 5999 5945 5023 Interior design services; art, picture frames & decorations; hobbies; frames & framing,
picture & mirror
PA: Hobby Lobby Stores, Inc.
7707 Sw 44th St
Oklahoma City OK 73179
405 745-1100

(P-17223)
HOLLISTER PROCESS SERVICE
Also Called: Steven Snyder
341 Tres Pinos Rd Ste 201, Hollister
(95023-5582)
PHONE.................831 634-1479
Stephen Snyder, *Owner*
Gawnette Snyder, *Co-Owner*
EMP: 50
SALES: 65K **Privately Held**
SIC: 7389 Process serving service

(P-17224)
HOLLYWOOD SPORTS PARK LLC
Also Called: Giant Sportz Paintball Park
9030 Somerset Blvd, Bellflower
(90706-3402)
PHONE.................562 867-9600
Dennis Bukowski, *Mng Member*
Judy Bukowski,
Giovanni D'Egido,
EMP: 100
SQ FT: 20,000
SALES (est): 8.8MM **Privately Held**
WEB: www.hollywoodsportspark.com
SIC: 7389 Personal service agents, bro-
kers & bureaus

(P-17225)
HOOVER INSTITUTION
434 Galvez Mall, Stanford (94305-6003)
PHONE.................650 723-0603
John Raisian, *Director*
Jenny Mayfield, *President*
Irena Czernichowska, *Financial Exec*
Victor Hanson, *Teacher*
Laureen Schieron, *Director*
EMP: 200
SALES (est): 11.7MM **Privately Held**
SIC: 7389 Personal service agents, bro-
kers & bureaus

(P-17226)
HOSPITAL BUSINESS SERVICES INC
3300 E Guasti Rd, Ontario (91761-8655)
PHONE.................909 235-4400
Mike Sarian, *President*
Ken Wheeler, *Vice Pres*
EMP: 101
SALES (est): 3.6MM **Privately Held**
SIC: 7389 7349 Financial services; build-
ing maintenance services

(P-17227)
HUSTLE DIGITAL INC
12777 W Jefferson Blvd, Los Angeles
(90066-7048)
PHONE.................310 882-2680
Josh Mandel, *Vice Pres*
EMP: 50
SALES (est): 1.5MM **Privately Held**
SIC: 7389 Advertising, promotional & trade
show services

(P-17228)
HYDROPROCESSING ASSOCIATES LLC
Also Called: Hpa-USA
19122 S Santa Fe Ave, Compton
(90221-5910)
PHONE.................310 667-6456
Kees Ooms, *Branch Mgr*
EMP: 50 **Privately Held**
SIC: 7389 Petroleum refinery inspection
service
HQ: Hydroprocessing Associates, Llc
6016 Highway 63
Moss Point MS 39563

(P-17229)
ICON DESIGN AND DISPLAY INC
645 4th St Ste 212, Santa Rosa
(95404-4435)
PHONE.................707 284-3400
Mark Richard, *Ch of Bd*
Max Blum, *CEO*
EMP: 90
SQ FT: 44,000
SALES (est): 10.2MM **Privately Held**
WEB: www.icondisplay.com
SIC: 7389 Personal service agents, bro-
kers & bureaus

(P-17230)
IDEO LP
780 High St, Palo Alto (94301-2420)
PHONE.................650 289-3400
Tim Brown, *CEO*
EMP: 150
SALES (corp-wide): 47.2MM **Privately Held**
SIC: 7389 Design services
PA: Ideo Lp
150 Forest Ave
Palo Alto CA 94301
650 289-3400

(P-17231)
IDEO LP
28 The Embarcadero Annex, San Francisco
(94105-1252)
PHONE.................415 615-5000
Gretchen Addi, *Partner*
Daniel Fang, *Fellow*
EMP: 52
SALES (corp-wide): 47.2MM **Privately Held**
WEB: www.ideo.com
SIC: 7389 Design, commercial & industrial
PA: Ideo Lp
150 Forest Ave
Palo Alto CA 94301
650 289-3400

(P-17232)
IMG (PA)
Also Called: Demo Deluxe
4560 Dorinda Rd, Yorba Linda
(92887-1800)
PHONE.................714 974-1700
Jim Smith, *Partner*
Jerry Smith, *Partner*
EMP: 50
SQ FT: 3,600

SALES (est): 76.8MM **Privately Held**
WEB: www.demodeluxe.com
SIC: 7389 Demonstration service

(P-17233)
INDUSTRIAL STITCHTECH INC
520 Library St, San Fernando
(91340-2524)
PHONE..............................818 361-6319
Ed Perez, *President*
Amber Quinn, *Administration*
EMP: 150
SQ FT: 35,000
SALES (est): 10.9MM **Privately Held**
WEB: www.industrialstitchtech.com
SIC: 7389 Sewing contractor

(P-17234)
INFLUXDATA INC
799 Market St Ste 4, San Francisco
(94103-2001)
PHONE..............................415 295-1901
Alex Holmes, *Chief Mktg Ofcr*
EMP: 105
SALES (est): 90.3K **Privately Held**
SIC: 7389

(P-17235)
INGENIO LLC
182 Howard St 826, San Francisco
(94105-1611)
PHONE..............................415 992-8218
Devina Whitley, *Mng Member*
EMP: 57
SALES (est): 4.9MM **Privately Held**
SIC: 7389

(P-17236)
**INLAND INSPECTIONS
CONSULTING**
7338 Sycamore Canyon Blvd, Riverside
(92508-2334)
PHONE..............................951 697-1000
Carol Schumacher, *Manager*
EMP: 50
SALES (est): 1.7MM **Privately Held**
SIC: 7389 Safety inspection service

(P-17237)
INLAND-METRO SERVICES INC
1059 W 14th St, Upland (91786-2678)
PHONE..............................909 373-6810
Robert Ayala Sr, *President*
EMP: 55 EST: 2010
SQ FT: 750
SALES (est): 4.6MM **Privately Held**
SIC: 7389

(P-17238)
**INNOVATED PACKAGING
COMPANY**
38505 Cherry St Ste C, Newark
(94560-4700)
PHONE..............................510 713-3560
Ben F Polando, *President*
Adele Daszko, *Exec VP*
Donna Fernandez, *Senior VP*
Santina Polando, *Exec Sec*
EMP: 148
SQ FT: 110,000
SALES (est): 13.2MM **Privately Held**
WEB: www.innovpak.com
SIC: 7389 3086 Packaging & labeling
   services; packaging & shipping materials,
   foamed plastic

(P-17239)
**INNOVATIVE MERCH
SOLUTIONS LLC**
Also Called: IMS
21215 Burbank Blvd, Woodland Hills
(91367-7090)
PHONE..............................818 936-7800
Joe Kaplan,
Tim Jochner,
EMP: 250
SQ FT: 50,000
SALES (est): 12.8MM
SALES (corp-wide): 5.9B **Publicly Held**
WEB: www.innovativeclub.com
SIC: 7389 Credit card service
PA: Intuit Inc.
   2700 Coast Ave
   Mountain View CA 94043
   650 944-6000

(P-17240)
INNOVATIVE SILICON INC
4800 Great America Pkwy # 500, Santa
Clara (95054-1221)
P.O. Box 391657, Mountain View (94039-
1657)
PHONE..............................408 572-8700
Mark-Eric Jones, *CEO*
Michael Van Buskirk, *COO*
Jeff Lewis, *Senior VP*
EMP: 80
SQ FT: 11,000
SALES (est): 3.4MM **Privately Held**
WEB: www.innovativesilicon.com
SIC: 7389 Personal service agents, bro-
   kers & bureaus

(P-17241)
INSIKT INC
333 Bush St Ste 1700, San Francisco
(94104-2831)
PHONE..............................415 391-2431
James Michael Gutierrez, *CEO*
Chris Motes, *Vice Pres*
Ege Tanor, *Vice Pres*
Dan Sanford, *VP Finance*
Eric Burton, *Director*
EMP: 60
SALES (est): 3.3MM **Privately Held**
SIC: 7389 Financial services

(P-17242)
INSPECTORATE AMERICA CORP
3401 Jack Northrop Ave, Hawthorne
(90250-4428)
PHONE..............................800 424-0099
EMP: 148
SALES (corp-wide): 316.4MM **Privately
Held**
SIC: 7389 Petroleum refinery inspection
   service
HQ: Inspectorate America Corp
   12000 Aerospace Ave # 200
   Houston TX 77034
   713 944-2000

(P-17243)
INTEGRA TELECOM INC
101 Metro Dr, San Jose (95110-1314)
PHONE..............................408 758-7700
Robert Guth, *President*
EMP: 72
SALES (corp-wide): 351.8MM **Privately
Held**
SIC: 7389 4813 Telephone services; tele-
   phone communication, except radio
PA: Electric Lightwave Communications,
   Inc.
   18110 Se 34th St Bldg 1s
   Vancouver WA 98683
   360 558-6900

(P-17244)
**INTERIOR OFFICE SOLUTIONS
INC (PA)**
17800 Mitchell N, Irvine (92614-6004)
PHONE..............................949 724-9444
Jesse Bagley, *CEO*
Brian Airth, *Founder*
Ward Smith, *Admin Mgr*
Monique Ramirez, *Executive Asst*
Lisa Lamprich, *Business Mgr*
EMP: 50
SQ FT: 11,000
SALES (est): 87.8MM **Privately Held**
WEB: www.iosinc.com
SIC: 7389 5712 Design services; office
   furniture

(P-17245)
**INTERIOR OFFICE SOLUTIONS
INC**
444 S Flower St Ste 200, Los Angeles
(90071-2903)
PHONE..............................310 726-9067
Shireen Nadjlessi, *Branch Mgr*
EMP: 50
SALES (corp-wide): 87.8MM **Privately
Held**
SIC: 7389 5712 Design services; office
   furniture
PA: Interior Office Solutions, Inc.
   17800 Mitchell N
   Irvine CA 92614
   949 724-9444

(P-17246)
INTERIORS BY LINDA
49585 Brian Ct, La Quinta (92253-8127)
PHONE..............................760 341-9651
Linda Martin, *Owner*
EMP: 50 EST: 1999
SALES (est): 1.8MM **Privately Held**
SIC: 7389 Interior design services

(P-17247)
**INTERNATIONAL FDN FOR
KOREA UN**
3435 Wilshire Blvd # 480, Los Angeles
(90010-1901)
PHONE..............................213 550-2182
Willie Wang-Pyo Seung, *CEO*
EMP: 300 EST: 2017
SALES: 140K **Privately Held**
SIC: 7389 Business services

(P-17248)
INTERPAC TECHNOLOGIES INC
Also Called: Interpac Distribution Center
260 N Pioneer Ave, Woodland
(95776-5934)
PHONE..............................530 662-6363
Roderick W Miner, *President*
Corinne Christenson, *Vice Pres*
Stephen Cosenza, *Opers Mgr*
EMP: 75
SALES (est): 10.1MM **Privately Held**
WEB: www.interpactechnologies.com
SIC: 7389 Packaging & labeling services

(P-17249)
**INTERTEK TESTING SVCS NA
INC**
25791 Commercentre Dr, Lake Forest
(92630-8803)
PHONE..............................949 349-1684
Richard Adams, *Branch Mgr*
EMP: 60
SALES (corp-wide): 3.6B **Privately Held**
SIC: 7389 Inspection & testing services
HQ: Intertek Testing Services Na, Inc.
   3933 Us Route 11
   Cortland NY 13045
   607 753-6711

(P-17250)
INTERTEK USA INC
Also Called: Intertek Caleb Brett
1941 Freeman Ave Ste A, Signal Hill
(90755-1236)
PHONE..............................562 494-4999
Mark Phoreson, *Branch Mgr*
Crystal Scott, *Executive*
EMP: 50
SQ FT: 1,600
SALES (corp-wide): 3.6B **Privately Held**
WEB: www.itscb.com
SIC: 7389 Pipeline & power line inspection
   service
HQ: Intertek Usa Inc.
   200 Westlke Prk Blvd 40
   Houston TX 77079
   713 543-3600

(P-17251)
INVESTLINC GROUP LLC (PA)
Also Called: Investlinc Group, The
1230 Rosecrans Ave # 600, Manhattan
Beach (90266-2477)
PHONE..............................310 997-0580
Troy D Wiseman,
Paul Sanford, *Ch Invest Ofcr*
Jean-Marc Plantier, *Finance*
Luis Cifuentes, *Accountant*
Doris Stuart, *Controller*
EMP: 85
SALES (est): 2.9MM **Privately Held**
WEB: www.bfd-usa.com
SIC: 7389 Financial services

(P-17252)
IPAYMENT INC (DH)
30721 Russell Ranch Rd # 200, Westlake
Village (91362-7383)
PHONE..............................212 802-7200
Mark C Monaco, *CFO*
Philip J Ragona, *Exec VP*
Philip Ragona, *Exec VP*
Robert N Purcell,
EMP: 59
SQ FT: 3,800

SALES: 666.8MM
SALES (corp-wide): 1B **Privately Held**
WEB: www.ipaymentinc.com
SIC: 7389 Credit card service

(P-17253)
ISI INSPECTION SERVICES INC
1798 University Ave, Berkeley
(94703-1514)
PHONE..............................510 986-1157
Mike Zell, *Exec Dir*
EMP: 60 **Privately Held**
SIC: 7389 Inspection & testing services
PA: Isi Inspection Services, Inc.
   1798 University Ave
   Berkeley CA 94703

(P-17254)
**ISI INSPECTION SERVICES INC
(PA)**
1798 University Ave, Berkeley
(94703-1514)
PHONE..............................510 900-2101
Leslie A Sakai, *President*
Ed King, *Exec VP*
Terri Klepp, *Office Mgr*
Kasandra Horcasitas, *Admin Asst*
David Briggs, *Project Mgr*
EMP: 70
SQ FT: 9,700
SALES (est): 14MM **Privately Held**
WEB: www.inspectionservices.net
SIC: 7389 Inspection & testing services

(P-17255)
**J & J PRODUCTIONS
INCORPORATED**
1775 E Lincoln Ave # 205, Anaheim
(92805-4324)
PHONE..............................714 535-0951
Jack D George, *President*
Jessica George, *Vice Pres*
EMP: 50
SQ FT: 1,800
SALES (est): 2.8MM **Privately Held**
SIC: 7389 Fund raising organizations

(P-17256)
**JAPANESE ASSISTANCE
NETWRK INC**
Also Called: Jan
11135 Magnolia Blvd # 140, North Holly-
wood (91601-3183)
PHONE..............................818 505-6080
Genichi Kadono, *President*
Jj Nishikawa, *Controller*
EMP: 298
SQ FT: 1,700
SALES (est): 12.4MM
SALES (corp-wide): 1.8B **Privately Held**
WEB: www.jannetwork.com
SIC: 7389 Translation services
HQ: Relocation International,Inc.
   4-3-25, Shinjuku
   Shinjuku-Ku TKY 160-0
   353 128-702

(P-17257)
**JD WESSON & ASSOCIATES
INC**
3212 Jefferson St Ste 206, NAPA
(94558-3436)
PHONE..............................707 255-8667
Jim Wesson, *President*
EMP: 52
SALES (est): 3.2MM **Privately Held**
WEB: www.jdwesson.com
SIC: 7389 Personal investigation service

(P-17258)
JENCO PRODUCTIONS INC (PA)
401 S J St, San Bernardino (92410-2605)
PHONE..............................909 381-9453
Jennifer Imbriani, *President*
EMP: 160 EST: 1995
SQ FT: 50,000
SALES: 1.7MM **Privately Held**
WEB: www.jencoprod.com
SIC: 7389 Packaging & labeling services

**P
R
O
D
U
C
T
S

&

S
V
C
S**

(P-17259)
JILLIANS SAN FRANCISCO CA
101 4th St Ste 170, San Francisco
(94103-3003)
PHONE.................415 369-6100
Darren Daroches, *General Mgr*
Dan Smith, *President*
Marty Ryan, *General Mgr*
Bryan Galope, *Manager*
EMP: 60
SQ FT: 50,000
SALES (est): 2.9MM **Privately Held**
SIC: 7389 Personal service agents, bro-
kers & bureaus

(P-17260)
JIMMYS FASHIONS
3135 Chadney Dr, Glendale (91206-1004)
PHONE.................818 790-8932
Young Seok OH, *Owner*
EMP: 50
SALES (est): 2.3MM **Privately Held**
SIC: 7389 Sewing contractor

(P-17261)
JOHN HANCOCK LIFE INSUR CO
USA (DH)
865 S Figueroa St # 3320, Los Angeles
(90017-2543)
PHONE.................213 689-0813
Emeritus D'Alessandro, *CEO*
David F D'Alessandro, *President*
Ross Fryer, *President*
Gregory P Winn, *Treasurer*
Harold K Mosher, *Exec VP*
▲ EMP: 2000 EST: 1862
SQ FT: 3,600,000
SALES (est): 853.8MM
SALES (corp-wide): 45.6B **Privately Held**
WEB: www.jhcases.com
SIC: 7389 6351 6371 6321 Financial
services; mortgage guarantee insurance;
pensions; accident insurance carriers;
health insurance carriers
HQ: John Hancock Financial Services, Inc.
200 Clarendon St
Boston MA 02116
617 572-6000

(P-17262)
JOMAR INDUSTRIES INC
1500 W 139th St, Gardena (90249-2604)
PHONE.................323 770-0505
John H Stern, *President*
Margaret Stern, *CFO*
Margaret H Stern, *Corp Secy*
Jeff Stern, *Vice Pres*
EMP: 50
SQ FT: 25,000
SALES (est): 3.3MM **Privately Held**
SIC: 7389 3089 Packaging & labeling
services; coloring & finishing of plastic
products

(P-17263)
JONES DAY LIMITED
PARTNERSHIP
555 S Flower St Fl 50, Los Angeles
(90071-2452)
PHONE.................213 489-3939
Chris Lovrien, *Principal*
Erin L Burke, *Partner*
Lisa Y Takata, *Office Admin*
Lynette Telles, *Admin Sec*
Anna Raimer, *Info Tech Mgr*
EMP: 51
SALES (corp-wide): 833.4MM **Privately**
Held
SIC: 7389 8111 Personal service agents,
brokers & bureaus; legal services
PA: Jones Day Limited Partnership
901 Lakeside Ave E Ste 2
Cleveland OH 44114
216 586-3939

(P-17264)
JOPARI SOLUTIONS INC
1855 Gateway Blvd Ste 500, Concord
(94520-3277)
PHONE.................925 459-5200
John Stevens II, *CEO*
Scott A Hefner, *Senior VP*
EMP: 65

SALES (est): 8.7MM **Privately Held**
WEB: www.jopari.com
SIC: 7389 Financial services

(P-17265)
JPMORGAN CHASE BANK NAT
ASSN
1995 Santa Ana Ave, Costa Mesa
(92627-2252)
PHONE.................949 429-6071
EMP: 103
SALES (corp-wide): 99.6B **Publicly Held**
SIC: 7389 Personal service agents, bro-
kers & bureaus
HQ: Jpmorgan Chase Bank, National Asso-
ciation
1111 Polaris Pkwy
Columbus OH 43240
614 436-3055

(P-17266)
JPMORGAN CHASE BANK NAT
ASSN
502 Las Posas Rd, Camarillo
(93010-5705)
PHONE.................805 482-2902
Jane Morel, *Branch Mgr*
EMP: 223
SALES (corp-wide): 99.6B **Publicly Held**
SIC: 7389 6029 Financial services; com-
mercial banks
HQ: Jpmorgan Chase Bank, National Asso-
ciation
1111 Polaris Pkwy
Columbus OH 43240
614 436-3055

(P-17267)
JPMORGAN CHASE BANK NAT
ASSN
10790 Rancho Bernardo Rd, San Diego
(92127-5705)
PHONE.................858 605-3300
Cindy Dunks, *Principal*
Cheryl Hassoun, *Project Mgr*
EMP: 223
SALES (corp-wide): 99.6B **Publicly Held**
WEB: www.chase.com
SIC: 7389 Financial services
HQ: Jpmorgan Chase Bank, National Asso-
ciation
1111 Polaris Pkwy
Columbus OH 43240
614 436-3055

(P-17268)
K2 INDUSTRIAL SERVICES INC
2375 W Esther St, Long Beach
(90813-1029)
PHONE.................562 624-5800
Ron Biebel, *Controller*
Nicole Klaus, *Manager*
EMP: 50
SALES (corp-wide): 274.5MM **Privately**
Held
SIC: 7389 Personal service agents, bro-
kers & bureaus
PA: K2 Industrial Services, Inc.
3838 N Sam Houston Pkwy E
Houston TX 77032
850 477-6437

(P-17269)
KDS MARKETING
965 N Todd Ave, Azusa (91702-2226)
PHONE.................818 240-7000
Christopher Burks, *President*
Fred Burks, *Shareholder*
Angie Ingraham, *Sales Dir*
EMP: 110
SQ FT: 10,340
SALES (est): 9MM **Privately Held**
SIC: 7389 8742 Demonstration service;
management consulting services

(P-17270)
KDS PRINTING AND
PACKAGING INC
13397 Marlay Ave Ste A, Fontana
(92337-6946)
PHONE.................909 770-5400
Raymond Fecteau, *President*
Ray Fecteau, *Sales Staff*
EMP: 50
SQ FT: 35,000

SALES (est): 2.7MM **Privately Held**
WEB: www.kdspackaging.com
SIC: 7389 Printing broker

(P-17271)
KENEDCO INC
29363 Rancho Cal Rd, Temecula
(92591-5201)
PHONE.................951 699-9339
Kenneth G Miskam, *CEO*
EMP: 51
SALES (est): 2.1MM **Privately Held**
SIC: 7389

(P-17272)
KENNETH BRDWICK INTR
DSGNS INC
Also Called: Beverly Hills Luxury Interiors
1615 Westwood Blvd # 201, Los Angeles
(90024-5653)
PHONE.................310 274-9999
Kenneth Bordewick, *CEO*
Vivian Petreca, *Manager*
EMP: 73
SALES (est): 3.2MM **Privately Held**
WEB: www.kennethbordewickinteriorde-
signs.com
SIC: 7389 Interior designer

(P-17273)
KILCREW PRODUCTIONS
32811 Wesley St, Wildomar (92595-9759)
PHONE.................619 564-2080
Robert G Kilbride, *CEO*
Debora Kilbride, *CFO*
EMP: 57
SALES (est): 3.6MM **Privately Held**
SIC: 7389 Convention & show services

(P-17274)
KIM CHONG
Also Called: Union 76
2105 E 25th St, Los Angeles (90058-1125)
PHONE.................323 581-4700
Chong Kim, *Owner*
EMP: 59
SQ FT: 10,300
SALES (est): 4.7MM **Privately Held**
SIC: 7389 2395 Embroidering of advertis-
ing on shirts, etc.; embroidery products,
except schiffli machine

(P-17275)
KING-REYNOLDS VENTURES
LLC
Also Called: Costanoa
2001 Rossi Rd, Pescadero (94060-9732)
PHONE.................650 879-2136
John King,
Teri Giordani, *Sales Dir*
Thomas Reynolds,
Sharon Carpenter, *Manager*
Lance Miller, *Manager*
EMP: 75
SALES (est): 6.7MM **Privately Held**
WEB: www.costanoa.com
SIC: 7389 Financial services

(P-17276)
KIRSCHENMAN ENTERPRISES
SLS LP
12826 Edison Hwy, Edison (93220)
PHONE.................661 366-5736
Wayde Kirschenman, *General Ptnr*
EMP: 300
SQ FT: 5,000
SALES: 100MM **Privately Held**
SIC: 7389 Brokers, business: buying &
selling business enterprises

(P-17277)
KOBEY CORPORATION INC (PA)
Also Called: Kobey Swap Meet At Spt Arena
3740 Sports Arena Blvd # 2, San Diego
(92110-5128)
P.O. Box 81492 (92138-1492)
PHONE.................619 523-2700
Kimberly Kobey Pretto, *President*
Charles J Pretto, *Vice Pres*
Chuck Pretto, *Vice Pres*
Chris Haesloop, *General Mgr*
Joe Pretto, *Director*
EMP: 55
SQ FT: 1,800

SALES (est): 5.7MM **Privately Held**
SIC: 7389 Flea market

(P-17278)
KOOS MANUFACTURING INC
Also Called: Big Star
2741 Seminole Ave, South Gate
(90280-5550)
PHONE.................323 249-1000
U Yul Ku, *President*
Kee H Fong, *Vice Pres*
John Hur, *Vice Pres*
Nan J Ku, *Admin Sec*
EMP: 800
SQ FT: 180,000
SALES (est): 98.4MM **Privately Held**
WEB: www.koos.com
SIC: 7389 Sewing contractor

(P-17279)
KOUNTABLE INC
321 Pacific Ave Fl 3, San Francisco
(94111-1701)
PHONE.................310 613-5481
Chris Hale, *CEO*
Cherry Allen, *Exec VP*
Ian Goudy, *Exec VP*
Maika Hemphill, *Vice Pres*
EMP: 85 EST: 2014
SALES (est): 5.5MM **Privately Held**
SIC: 7389 Financial services

(P-17280)
KOURY ENGRG TSTG & INSPTN
14280 Euclid Ave, Chino (91710-8803)
PHONE.................310 851-8685
Richard Koury, *President*
EMP: 75
SQ FT: 5,000
SALES: 9MM **Privately Held**
WEB: www.kouryengineering.com
SIC: 7389 Building inspection service

(P-17281)
KPWR RADIO LLC
9550 Firestone Blvd # 105, Downey
(90241-5560)
PHONE.................562 745-2300
Alex Meruelo, *Mng Member*
EMP: 150
SALES: 27MM **Privately Held**
SIC: 7389 Music & broadcasting services
PA: Meruelo Group Llc
9550 Firestone Blvd # 105
Downey CA 90241
562 745-2300

(P-17282)
KSM MARKETING INC
Also Called: Keystone Marketing Specialists
10 Holland, Irvine (92618-2504)
PHONE.................949 597-2222
Karen Settle, *President*
EMP: 200
SQ FT: 12,000
SALES (est): 6.8MM **Privately Held**
WEB: www.keystone2000.com
SIC: 7389 Advertising, promotional & trade
show services

(P-17283)
L LYON DISTRIBUTING INC
254 W Stuart Ave, Redlands (92374-3136)
P.O. Box 8968 (92375-2168)
PHONE.................909 798-7129
Michael Lyon, *President*
Lori Lyon, *Vice Pres*
EMP: 50
SQ FT: 5,000
SALES (est): 4.1MM **Privately Held**
SIC: 7389 Merchandise liquidators

(P-17284)
LA IMPACT
5700 S Eastern Ave, Commerce
(90040-2924)
PHONE.................323 869-6874
Tony Ybarra, *Director*
EMP: 100
SALES (est): 6.7MM **Privately Held**
WEB: www.lacrcic.com
SIC: 7389 Personal service agents, bro-
kers & bureaus

(P-17285)
LA INC CONVENTION VISTORS BUR
333 S Hope St Ste 1800, Los Angeles
(90071-1430)
PHONE..............................213 236-2301
Mark Liberman, *Exec Dir*
Tia Sanford, *Sales Staff*
EMP: 75
SALES: 19.4MM **Privately Held**
WEB: www.lacvb.com
SIC: 7389 Advertising, promotional & trade
show services

(P-17286)
LA JOLLA GROUP INC
14350 Myford Rd, Irvine (92606-1002)
PHONE..............................949 428-2800
Toby Bost, *Owner*
EMP: 64
SALES (corp-wide): 33.8MM **Privately Held**
SIC: 7389 Apparel designers, commercial
PA: La Jolla Group, Inc.
14350 Myford Rd
Irvine CA 92606
949 428-2800

(P-17287)
LAKESIDE FIRE PROTECTION DST
12216 Lakeside Ave, Lakeside
(92040-1715)
PHONE..............................619 390-2350
Andy Parr, *Chief*
Tung Nguyen, *Business Anlyst*
Robert Schiwitz, *Comptroller*
Don Butz, *Fire Chief*
Scott Culkin,
EMP: 70
SALES: 14.6MM **Privately Held**
WEB: www.lakesidefire.com
SIC: 7389 Fire protection service other
than forestry or public

(P-17288)
LAKESIDE TAX & FINANCIAL SVCS
9748 Los Coches Rd Ste 3, Lakeside
(92040-4253)
PHONE..............................619 561-2681
Jodie Herzig, *President*
EMP: 68
SALES (est): 293.6K **Privately Held**
SIC: 7389 Financial services

(P-17289)
LAKEWOOD PARK HEALTH CENTER (PA)
12023 Lakewood Blvd, Downey
(90242-2699)
PHONE..............................562 869-0978
Daniel Zilafro, *President*
EMP: 285
SALES (est): 11MM **Privately Held**
SIC: 7389 Personal service agents, bro-
kers & bureaus

(P-17290)
LANGUAGE LINE SERVICES INC (DH)
Also Called: Teleinterpreters
1 Lower Ragsdale Dr # 2, Monterey
(93940-5747)
P.O. Box 202567, Dallas TX (75320-2567)
PHONE..............................800 752-6096
Scott W Klein, *CEO*
Jeffrey Grace, *CFO*
Solange Jerolimov, *CFO*
Michael Schmidt, *CFO*
Dennis G Dracup, *Chairman*
EMP: 53
SALES (est): 10.6MM
SALES (corp-wide): 126.1MM **Privately Held**
SIC: 7389 Translation services
HQ: Language Line Holdings, Inc.
1 Lower Ragsdale Dr # 2
Monterey CA 93940
831 648-5800

(P-17291)
LARK INDUSTRIES INC (HQ)
Also Called: Residential Design Service
4900 E Hunter Ave, Anaheim (92807-2057)
PHONE..............................714 701-4200
Tyron Johnson, *CEO*
Kendall Hoyd, *President*
Kip Cruze, *Exec VP*
Kelli A Finale, *Vice Pres*
Beverly Messemer, *Vice Pres*
EMP: 75
SALES (est): 46.1MM
SALES (corp-wide): 137.1MM **Publicly Held**
WEB: www.larkindustries.com
SIC: 7389 3281 Interior design services;
cut stone & stone products
PA: Select Interior Concepts, Inc.
4900 E Hunter Ave
Anaheim CA 92807
714 479-2517

(P-17292)
LAX INTERNATIONAL SERVICE CTR
Also Called: Worldway Airmail Center
5800 W Century Blvd, Los Angeles
(90009-5601)
PHONE..............................310 337-8764
Karen Padden, *General Mgr*
EMP: 65
SALES (est): 1.8MM **Privately Held**
SIC: 7389 Post office contract stations

(P-17293)
LEGEND MERCHANT GROUP INC
201 Mission St Ste 230, San Francisco
(94105-1883)
PHONE..............................415 957-9555
Chip Unsworth, *President*
EMP: 50
SALES (est): 3.2MM **Privately Held**
SIC: 7389 Financial services

(P-17294)
LENNAR PARTNERS OF LOS ANGELES (PA)
4350 Von Karman Ave # 200, Newport
Beach (92660-2041)
PHONE..............................949 885-8500
David Team, *Division Pres*
Rick Liebermann, *Managing Dir*
Diana Donaldson, *Human Resources*
Sheena Bellinger, *Manager*
EMP: 50
SALES (est): 9.5MM **Privately Held**
WEB: www.lennarpartners.com
SIC: 7389 Personal service agents, bro-
kers & bureaus

(P-17295)
LIFESIGNS NOW (PA)
2222 Laverna Ave Fl 1, Los Angeles
(90041-2654)
PHONE..............................323 550-4210
Emory Dively, *Director*
Denise Madland, *Manager*
EMP: 259 EST: 1986
SALES: 3.2MM **Privately Held**
WEB: www.lifesigns.com
SIC: 7389 Translation services

(P-17296)
LINDSAY FRUIT COMPANY LLC
Also Called: Yokohl Valley Packing
247 N Mount Vernon Ave, Lindsay
(93247-2440)
P.O. Box 907 (93247-0907)
PHONE..............................559 562-1327
Tim Bentley,
Rick Crocker, *Executive*
Henry Howison, *Manager*
EMP: 75
SALES (est): 5.9MM **Privately Held**
SIC: 7389 Packaging & labeling services

(P-17297)
LITIGTION RSRCES OF AMERICA-CA (PA)
Also Called: Legal Enterprise
4232-1 Las Virgenes Rd, Calabasas
(91302-3589)
PHONE..............................818 878-9227
Tony Maddocks, *President*

Rick Matsumoto, *Manager*
EMP: 75
SALES (est): 5.9MM **Privately Held**
SIC: 7389 8111 Document storage serv-
ice; general practice attorney, lawyer

(P-17298)
LIVE NATION ENTERTAINMENT INC
151 El Camino Dr Fl 3, Beverly Hills
(90212-2704)
PHONE..............................323 462-4785
Brooke Stanley, *Branch Mgr*
EMP: 70
SALES (corp-wide): 10.3B **Publicly Held**
SIC: 7389 Promoters of shows & exhibi-
tions
PA: Live Nation Entertainment, Inc.
9348 Civic Center Dr Lbby
Beverly Hills CA 90210
310 867-7000

(P-17299)
LIVE NATION ENTERTAINMENT INC (PA)
9348 Civic Center Dr Lbby, Beverly Hills
(90210-3642)
PHONE..............................310 867-7000
Greg Maffei, *Ch of Bd*
Ron Bension, *President*
Mark Campana, *President*
Arthur Fogel, *President*
Michael Rapino, *President*
EMP: 200
SALES: 10.3B **Publicly Held**
WEB: www.livenation.com
SIC: 7389 7922 7941 Promoters of shows
& exhibitions; entertainment promotion;
theatrical production services; theatrical
companies; legitimate live theater produc-
ers; sports clubs, managers & promoters

(P-17300)
LMS CORPORATION
300 Crprate Pinte Ste 301, Culver City
(90230)
PHONE..............................310 641-4222
Nola G Conway, *President*
EMP: 50
SQ FT: 2,712
SALES (est): 1.6MM **Privately Held**
WEB: www.thelmscorp.com
SIC: 7389 8742

(P-17301)
LONG BEACH UNIFIED SCHOOL DST
Also Called: Newcomb Academy
3351 Val Verde Ave, Long Beach
(90808-4456)
PHONE..............................562 493-3596
EMP: 803
SALES (corp-wide): 867.6MM **Privately Held**
SIC: 7389 Fund raising organizations
PA: Long Beach Unified School District
1515 Hughes Way
Long Beach CA 90810
562 997-8000

(P-17302)
LOON LLC
100 Mayfield Ave, Mountain View
(94043-4122)
PHONE..............................310 625-3449
Eleister Westgrath, *CEO*
EMP: 200 EST: 2000
SALES (est): 2.6MM **Privately Held**
SIC: 7389

(P-17303)
LOS ANGELES UNIFIED SCHOOL DST
Also Called: L A U S D
8525 Rex Rd, Pico Rivera (90660-6702)
PHONE..............................562 654-9007
Marc Monforte, *Branch Mgr*
Mar Tigno, *Principal*
EMP: 59
SALES (corp-wide): 3.8B **Privately Held**
WEB: www.lausd.k12.ca.us
SIC: 7389 Purchasing service

PA: Los Angeles Unified School District
333 S Beaudry Ave Ste 209
Los Angeles CA 90017
213 241-1000

(P-17304)
LOS ANGLES TRISM CONVENTION BD (PA)
333 S Hope St Ste 1800, Los Angeles
(90071-1430)
PHONE..............................213 624-7300
Ernest Wooden Jr, *CEO*
Alan I Rothenberg, *Ch of Bd*
Stefan J Dietrich, *CFO*
Adam Burke, *Officer*
John Boudouvas, *Vice Pres*
EMP: 50 EST: 1971
SALES: 43.7MM **Privately Held**
SIC: 7389 Convention & show services;
tourist information bureau

(P-17305)
LOYAL3 HOLDINGS INC
150 California St Ste 400, San Francisco
(94111-4566)
P.O. Box 26027 (94126-6027)
PHONE..............................415 981-0700
Barry L Schneider, *CEO*
James Iry, *President*
Peter Coleman, *CFO*
Dana Schmidt, *Ch Credit Ofcr*
Jeff Modisett, *Officer*
EMP: 80
SQ FT: 8,900
SALES (est): 10.8MM **Privately Held**
SIC: 7389 Financial services

(P-17306)
MABIE MARKETING GROUP INC
Also Called: California Marketing
8352 Clairemont Mesa Blvd, San Diego
(92111-1302)
PHONE..............................858 279-5585
John Mabie, *President*
Ramyar Ravansari, *CFO*
Samantha Galarneau, *Vice Pres*
Nate Ames, *Info Tech Dir*
Donald Kirchner, *Technology*
EMP: 200
SALES (est): 21MM **Privately Held**
WEB: www.calmarketing.com
SIC: 7389 Telemarketing services

(P-17307)
MACRO-PRO INC (PA)
Also Called: Micro-Pro Microfilming Svcs
2400 Grand Ave, Long Beach
(90815-1762)
P.O. Box 90459 (90809-0459)
PHONE..............................562 595-0900
Patty Waldeck, *President*
Eric Neitzel, *CFO*
Zuly Arguello, *Clerk*
EMP: 140
SQ FT: 24,000
SALES (est): 12.1MM **Privately Held**
WEB: www.macropro.com
SIC: 7389 7334 Legal & tax services; mi-
crofilm recording & developing service;
photocopying & duplicating services

(P-17308)
MADDEN CORPORATION
Also Called: Pam's Delivery Svc & Nat Msgnr
733 W Taft Ave, Orange (92865-4229)
PHONE..............................714 922-1670
Donald L Madden, *President*
EMP: 100
SQ FT: 7,000
SALES (est): 10.3MM **Privately Held**
SIC: 7389 Courier or messenger service

(P-17309)
MAGNOLIA VENTURES LTD
Also Called: C/O Longwood Management
4032 Wilshire Blvd Fl 6, Los Angeles
(90010-3425)
PHONE..............................213 389-6900
Jacob Freedman, *President*
EMP: 100
SALES (est): 3.7MM **Privately Held**
SIC: 7389 Personal service agents, bro-
kers & bureaus

PRODUCTS & SVCS

(P-17310)
MARINE TECHNICAL SERVICES INC
Also Called: Dockside Machine & Ship Repair
211 N Marine Ave, Wilmington (90744-5724)
P.O. Box 1301, San Pedro (90733-1301)
PHONE..................................310 549-8030
Dianne Marie Hawke, *President*
EMP: 75
SQ FT: 20,000
SALES (est): 11MM **Privately Held**
WEB: www.marinetechserv.com
SIC: 7389 7699 Crane & aerial lift service; nautical repair services

(P-17311)
MARINER SYSTEMS INC (PA)
114 C Ave, Coronado (92118-1435)
PHONE..................................305 266-7255
Carlos M Collazo, *President*
Neil Park, *CEO*
Sawyer Van Horn, *Accounts Mgr*
EMP: 66
SALES (est): 4.1MM **Privately Held**
WEB: www.marinersystems.net
SIC: 7389 7374 7372 7371 Telephone services; data processing service; prepackaged software; custom computer programming services

(P-17312)
MARMALADE LLC
Also Called: Marmalade Cafes
3894 Cross Creek Rd, Malibu (90265-4933)
PHONE..................................310 317-4242
Paul McGinley, *Branch Mgr*
EMP: 50
SALES (corp-wide): 20MM **Privately Held**
WEB: www.marmaladecafe.com
SIC: 7389 Personal service agents, brokers & bureaus
PA: Marmalade, Llc
  6800 Owensmouth Ave # 350
  Canoga Park CA 91303
  310 829-0093

(P-17313)
MARQUEZ BROTHERS ADVG AGCY
5801 Rue Ferrari, San Jose (95138-1857)
PHONE..................................408 960-2700
Gustavo Marquez, *President*
EMP: 100
SALES (est): 2.9MM **Privately Held**
SIC: 7389 Advertising, promotional & trade show services

(P-17314)
MARSH CONSULTING GROUP
2626 Summer Ranch Rd, Paso Robles (93446-8473)
PHONE..................................239 433-5500
Brad Heinrichs, *President*
Brad Gauen, *Consultant*
Geoffrey Marsh, *Consultant*
EMP: 70
SALES (est): 194.1K
SALES (corp-wide): 2.3MM **Privately Held**
WEB: www.mcgteam.com
SIC: 7389 Financial services
PA: Foster & Foster Consulting Actuaries, Inc.
  13420 Parker Commons Blvd
  Fort Myers FL 33912
  239 246-7168

(P-17315)
MARTYS CUTTING INC
Also Called: Marty's Cutting Service
2615 Fruitland Ave, Vernon (90058-2219)
PHONE..................................323 582-5758
Fax: 323 582-5272
EMP: 80
SQ FT: 57,000
SALES (est): 3.8MM **Privately Held**
WEB: www.marty-howard.com
SIC: 7389

(P-17316)
MB COATINGS INC
571 N Poplar St Ste G, Orange (92868-1023)
PHONE..................................714 625-2118
Michael Bartle, *President*
Amanda Bartle, *Vice Pres*
EMP: 80
SQ FT: 2,000
SALES: 5.9MM **Privately Held**
SIC: 7389 Hand painting, textile

(P-17317)
MEDIA ALL STARS INC
8525 Gibbs Dr Ste 206, San Diego (92123-1765)
PHONE..................................858 300-9600
Buddy Cummings, *President*
Joel Davies, *COO*
Mary Shvodian, *Officer*
Daniel Smith, *Opers Staff*
EMP: 53
SALES (est): 5.6MM **Privately Held**
WEB: www.mediaallstars.com
SIC: 7389 Fund raising organizations

(P-17318)
MEDUSIND SOLUTIONS INC (HQ)
31103 Rancho Viejo Rd, San Juan Capistrano (92675-1759)
PHONE..................................949 240-8895
Rajiv Sahney, *Chairman*
Robert Beck, *President*
Vipul Bansal, *CEO*
Dhiren Kapadia, *CFO*
Kranti Munje, *Senior VP*
EMP: 900
SALES (est): 50MM **Privately Held**
WEB: www.medusind.com
SIC: 7389 Personal service agents, brokers & bureaus

(P-17319)
MEGA APPRAISERS INC
14724 Ventura Blvd # 800, Sherman Oaks (91403-3508)
PHONE..................................818 246-7370
Levon Hairapetian, *President*
EMP: 600
SALES: 1.2MM **Privately Held**
SIC: 7389 Appraisers, except real estate

(P-17320)
MERCHANT OF TENNIS INC
1118 S La Cienega Blvd, Los Angeles (90035-2519)
PHONE..................................310 855-1946
Jay Banks, *Branch Mgr*
EMP: 189
SALES (corp-wide): 71.8MM **Privately Held**
SIC: 7389 Packaging & labeling services
PA: The Merchant Of Tennis Inc
  8737 Wilshire Blvd
  Beverly Hills CA 90211
  310 228-4000

(P-17321)
MERCHANT VALLEY CORPORATION
1808 Avondale Dr, Roseville (95747-8390)
PHONE..................................916 786-7227
Mahmood Merchant, *Principal*
EMP: 125
SALES (est): 1.5MM **Privately Held**
SIC: 7389

(P-17322)
MERCURY MESSENGER SERVICE INC
Also Called: Bestway Delivery
16735 Saticoy St Ste 104, Van Nuys (91406-2700)
PHONE..................................818 989-3115
Lionel Senker, *President*
EMP: 50
SQ FT: 1,500
SALES (est): 6.3MM **Privately Held**
SIC: 7389 4212 Courier or messenger service; delivery service, vehicular

(P-17323)
MERIBEAR PRODUCTIONS INC
Also Called: Meredith Baer & Associates
4100 Ardmore Ave, South Gate (90280-3246)
PHONE..................................310 204-5353
Meridith Baer, *President*
Caleb Morse, *CFO*
Anna Viola, *Office Mgr*
Ruben Ibarra, *Accounting Mgr*
Brett Baer, *Business Mgr*
▲ EMP: 90
SQ FT: 55,000
SALES (est): 13.9MM **Privately Held**
SIC: 7389 Interior design services; interior decorating

(P-17324)
MERICAL LLC (PA)
2995 E Miraloma Ave, Anaheim (92806-1805)
PHONE..................................714 238-7225
Jeffrey Stallings, *President*
Michael Schlinger, *CEO*
D Dean Baltzell, *CFO*
Elena Paraschiv, *Accounting Mgr*
George Sarkissian, *Controller*
EMP: 78
SQ FT: 92,000
SALES (est): 55.8MM **Privately Held**
SIC: 7389 Packaging & labeling services

(P-17325)
MERICAL LLC
Also Called: Merical/Vita-Pak
233 E Bristol Ln, Orange (92865-2715)
PHONE..................................714 283-9551
Claudia Ruffin, *Vice Pres*
Ian Morgan, *General Mgr*
Neil R Fournier, *Human Res Mgr*
Kim Butler, *Purchasing*
Jesus Martinez, *Buyer*
EMP: 322
SALES (corp-wide): 55.8MM **Privately Held**
SIC: 7389 Packaging & labeling services
PA: Merical, Llc
  2995 E Miraloma Ave
  Anaheim CA 92806
  714 238-7225

(P-17326)
MESSAGE BROADCASTCOM LLC
4685 Macarthur Ct Ste 250, Newport Beach (92660-1893)
PHONE..................................949 428-3111
William H Potter, *Mng Member*
Bill Joiner, *Officer*
Ato Manuud, *Executive*
Igor Kuznetsov, *Network Enginr*
Kyle Manchester, *Opers Mgr*
EMP: 50
SQ FT: 8,000
SALES (est): 6.4MM **Privately Held**
SIC: 7389 Telemarketing services

(P-17327)
MESSAGE CENTER COMMUNICATION
6779 Mesa Ridge Rd # 100, San Diego (92121-2996)
PHONE..................................858 974-7419
Gary Schaumann, *Owner*
EMP: 50
SALES (est): 1.8MM **Privately Held**
SIC: 7389 Telephone answering service

(P-17328)
METRICUS INC
P.O. Box 458 (94302-0458)
PHONE..................................650 328-2500
Jeanne J Fleming, *President*
Leonard C Schwarz, *CFO*
EMP: 119
SALES (est): 3.1MM **Privately Held**
WEB: www.metricus.com
SIC: 7389

(P-17329)
MICKWEE GROUP INC
Also Called: Mgi
5600 Mowry School Rd # 230, Newark (94560-5806)
PHONE..................................510 651-5527

Ronald Mickwee, *President*
EMP: 52
SALES (est): 3.1MM **Privately Held**
WEB: www.mickwee.com
SIC: 7389 8742 Telemarketing services; management consulting services

(P-17330)
MINIMALISMS INC
49 Missouri St Apt 10, San Francisco (94107-2484)
PHONE..................................415 309-3108
George Arriola, *President*
EMP: 52 EST: 2014
SALES: 250K **Privately Held**
SIC: 7389 Design services

(P-17331)
MIRIXA CORPORATION
5915 Hollis St Ste 201, Emeryville (94608-2067)
PHONE..................................510 596-3000
Rick Solano, *Branch Mgr*
EMP: 54
SALES (corp-wide): 47.4MM **Privately Held**
SIC: 7389 Personal service agents, brokers & bureaus
PA: Mirixa Corporation
  11600 Sunrse Vly Dr # 100
  Reston VA 20191
  703 683-1955

(P-17332)
MISSION COURIER INC
3204 Orange Grove Ave, North Highlands (95660-5806)
PHONE..................................916 484-1992
Marc Raty, *President*
Andy French, *Vice Pres*
EMP: 55
SQ FT: 11,000
SALES (est): 5.7MM **Privately Held**
SIC: 7389 Courier or messenger service

(P-17333)
MODERN DEV CO A LTD PARTNR
Also Called: Paramount Swap Meet
7900 All America City Way, Paramount (90723-3400)
PHONE..................................949 646-6400
Darren Kurkowski, *Branch Mgr*
EMP: 98
SALES (corp-wide): 17.7MM **Privately Held**
SIC: 7389 Flea market
PA: Modern Development Co, A Limited Partnership
  3146 Red Hill Ave Ste 220
  Costa Mesa CA 92626
  949 646-6400

(P-17334)
MOLD TESTING AND INSPECTION
Also Called: MT&i
4785 Sequoia Pl, Oceanside (92057-6126)
PHONE..................................760 643-1834
K W Huntington, *President*
Keith William Huntington, *President*
EMP: 75
SALES (est): 4.1MM **Privately Held**
SIC: 7389 Inspection & testing services

(P-17335)
MONTRENES FINANCIAL SVCS INC
Also Called: U S Merchant Services
27 Montpellier, Newport Beach (92660-6844)
PHONE..................................562 795-0450
Dan Montrenes, *President*
EMP: 100
SQ FT: 30,000
SALES (est): 5.2MM **Privately Held**
SIC: 7389 Credit card service

(P-17336)
MOTIVATIONAL MARKETING INC
Also Called: Motivational Fulfillment
15820 Euclid Ave, Chino (91708-9162)
PHONE..................................909 517-2200
Hal Altman, *CEO*

Andrea Stuhley, *Exec VP*
Anthony Altman, *Senior VP*
Tony Altman, *Vice Pres*
Cheryl Nataren, *Vice Pres*
EMP: 400
SQ FT: 300,000
SALES (est): 55.8MM **Privately Held**
WEB: www.mfpsinc.com
SIC: 7389 8748 8742 Telephone services; mailing & messenger services; business consulting; management consulting services

(P-17337)
MOULTON LOGISTICS MANAGEMENT (PA)
7850 Ruffner Ave, Van Nuys (91406-1619)
P.O. Box 8191 (91409-8191)
PHONE...................................818 997-1800
Aj Khubani, *CEO*
Lawrence Moulton, *President*
Tom Moulton, *Vice Pres*
Elaine Aspen, *Telecom Exec*
Ubaldo Lira, *Analyst*
EMP: 100
SQ FT: 108,000
SALES (est): 42.2MM **Privately Held**
WEB: www.moultonlogistics.com
SIC: 7389 4822 Subscription fulfillment services: magazine, newspaper, etc.; electronic mail

(P-17338)
MULTI-PAK CORPORATION
Also Called: Multipak
20131 Bahama St, Chatsworth (91311-6202)
PHONE...................................818 709-0508
Randall B Unthank, *President*
Victor Sandoval, *Manager*
EMP: 60
SQ FT: 20,000
SALES (est): 5.5MM **Privately Held**
WEB: www.multi-pak.com
SIC: 7389 Packaging & labeling services

(P-17339)
MULTIVISION INC (HQ)
Also Called: Bacon's Multivision
66 Franklin St Fl 3, Oakland (94607-3728)
PHONE...................................510 740-5600
Babak Farahi, *President*
EMP: 70
SALES (est): 9.4MM
SALES (corp-wide): 239MM **Privately Held**
WEB: www.multivision.com
SIC: 7389 Press clipping service
PA: Cision Us Inc.
130 E Randolph St Fl 7
Chicago IL 60601
312 922-2400

(P-17340)
MUSCOLINO INVENTORY SVC INC
1620 N Carptr Rd Ste D50, Modesto (95351)
PHONE...................................209 576-8469
Fax: 209 576-8469
EMP: 50
SALES (corp-wide): 67MM **Privately Held**
SIC: 7389
HQ: Muscolino Inventory Service, Inc.
320 W Chestnut Ave
Monrovia CA 91016
626 357-8600

(P-17341)
MX COURIER SYSTEMS INC
Also Called: Medical Ex Courier Systems
990 N Tustin St, Orange (92867-5903)
PHONE...................................714 288-8622
Mohammad A Zadsham, *President*
Akbar Heidarinia, *President*
EMP: 50
SQ FT: 1,200
SALES: 1.5MM **Privately Held**
SIC: 7389 4212 Courier or messenger service; delivery service, vehicular

(P-17342)
MZA EVENTS INC (PA)
3550 Wilshire Blvd # 1012, Los Angeles (90010-2412)
PHONE...................................213 201-1348
Craig R Miller, *CEO*
EMP: 50
SALES (est): 4.1MM **Privately Held**
WEB: www.mzainc.com
SIC: 7389 8742 Fund raising organizations; business planning & organizing services

(P-17343)
NATIONAL BUS INVSTIGATIONS INC
Also Called: MPS Security
25020 Las Brisas Rd Ste A, Murrieta (92562-4064)
PHONE...................................951 677-3500
Michael D Julian, *President*
Rafael Cisneros, *Security Mgr*
Ryan Hanhardt, *Manager*
Anthony Perez, *Manager*
Valerie Dovifaaz, *Accounts Mgr*
EMP: 60 **EST:** 1967
SQ FT: 2,000
SALES (est): 6MM **Privately Held**
SIC: 7389 7381 Personal investigation service; private investigator

(P-17344)
NATIONAL LGAL STUDIES INST INC
Also Called: Nlsi
23962 Alssndro Blvd Ste P, Moreno Valley (92553-8806)
P.O. Box 7562, Riverside (92513-7562)
PHONE...................................951 653-4240
Thersea Thompson, *CEO*
EMP: 50
SQ FT: 2,000
SALES (est): 2.4MM **Privately Held**
SIC: 7389 Paralegal service

(P-17345)
NATIONS DIRECT LENDER & IN
160 S Old Springs Rd # 260, Anaheim (92808-1229)
PHONE...................................800 969-7779
Jeff Store, *President*
Hal Lamm, *CFO*
EMP: 114
SQ FT: 18,000
SALES (est): 8.1MM **Privately Held**
WEB: www.signing-services.com
SIC: 7389 Drafting service, except temporary help

(P-17346)
NEFAB PACKAGING WEST LLC
8477 Central Ave, Newark (94560-3431)
PHONE...................................408 678-2516
Fredrik Solspher,
EMP: 60
SALES (est): 10MM
SALES (corp-wide): 454.3MM **Privately Held**
SIC: 7389 Packaging & labeling services
HQ: Nefab Companies, Inc.
204 Airline Dr Ste 100
Coppell TX 75019
866 332-4425

(P-17347)
NESTWISE LLC
9785 Towne Centre Dr, San Diego (92121-1968)
PHONE...................................855 444-6378
Esther Stearns, *CEO*
Beth Stelluto, *Chief Mktg Ofcr*
Burt White, *Ch Invest Ofcr*
Kandis Bates, *Officer*
Rudy Bethea, *Officer*
EMP: 383
SALES (est): 11.7MM **Publicly Held**
SIC: 7389 Financial services
PA: Lpl Financial Holdings Inc.
75 State St Ste 2401
Boston MA 02109

(P-17348)
NETBALL AMERICA INC
4686 Oceano Cir, Huntington Beach (92649-3224)
PHONE...................................949 307-4455
Sonya Ottaway, *President*
EMP: 50 **EST:** 2013
SALES (est): 108.4K **Privately Held**
SIC: 7389

(P-17349)
NEW CREW PRODUCTION CORP
200 W 138th St, Los Angeles (90061-1004)
PHONE...................................323 234-8880
Kris Park, *President*
Joseph Park, *Admin Sec*
EMP: 110
SQ FT: 20,000
SALES (est): 11.4MM **Privately Held**
WEB: www.newcrewproductioncorp.com
SIC: 7389 Sewing contractor

(P-17350)
NEW GLOBAL TELECOM INC
624 S Grand Ave Ste 2900, Los Angeles (90017-3881)
PHONE...................................213 489-3708
David Richardson, *Branch Mgr*
EMP: 56 **Privately Held**
WEB: www.ngt.com
SIC: 7389 Telephone services
PA: New Global Telecom, Inc.
143 Union Blvd Ste 400
Lakewood CO 80228
-

(P-17351)
NEWPORT DIVERSIFIED INC
Santa Fe Springs Swap Meet
13963 Alondra Blvd, Santa Fe Springs (90670-5814)
PHONE...................................562 921-4359
Rick Landis, *Sales & Mktg St*
Ron Westphal, *General Mgr*
Chris Woodson, *Opers Mgr*
EMP: 200
SQ FT: 10,846
SALES (corp-wide): 1.1MM **Privately Held**
WEB: www.nd-inc.com
SIC: 7389 5932 Flea market; used merchandise stores
PA: Newport Diversified, Inc.
4695 Macarthur Ct # 1420
Newport Beach CA 92660
949 851-1355

(P-17352)
NEWPORT DIVERSIFIED INC
Also Called: The Boardwalk
1286 Fletcher Pkwy, El Cajon (92020-1826)
PHONE...................................619 449-7800
Ron Westphal, *Manager*
EMP: 100
SALES (corp-wide): 1.1MM **Privately Held**
WEB: www.nd-inc.com
SIC: 7389 7996 Flea market; amusement parks
PA: Newport Diversified, Inc.
4695 Macarthur Ct # 1420
Newport Beach CA 92660
949 851-1355

(P-17353)
NEXT ISSUE MEDIA LLC (PA)
1 Apple Park Way, Cupertino (95014-0642)
PHONE...................................650 521-5151
John Loughlin, *CEO*
Keith Barraclough, *Exec VP*
Richard Quach, *Senior VP*
David Irvine, *Vice Pres*
Douglas Massey, *Vice Pres*
EMP: 75 **EST:** 2010
SALES (est): 12.4MM **Privately Held**
SIC: 7389 Subscription fulfillment services: magazine, newspaper, etc.

(P-17354)
NIELSEN MOBILE LLC (DH)
1010 Battery St, San Francisco (94111-1202)
PHONE...................................917 435-9301
Sid Gorham, *President*
Tom Stahl, *COO*

Jim Wandrey, *Treasurer*
Ryan O'Hearn, *Vice Pres*
Julie Oberhausen-Clar, *Engineer*
EMP: 180 **EST:** 2001
SQ FT: 38,000
SALES (est): 16.5MM
SALES (corp-wide): 6.5B **Privately Held**
WEB: www.telephia.com
SIC: 7389 Inspection & testing services

(P-17355)
NLC ENTERPRISES INCORPORATED
15710 Leffingwell Rd, Whittier (90604-3325)
PHONE...................................562 693-3590
Norman Carter, *Principal*
EMP: 50
SALES (est): 1.6MM **Privately Held**
SIC: 7389 Business services

(P-17356)
NNA SERVICES LLC
Also Called: Nna Insurance Services
9350 De Soto Ave, Chatsworth (91311-4926)
PHONE...................................818 739-4071
Milton G Valera, *Ch of Bd*
Thomas A Heymann, *CEO*
Robert A Clarke, *CFO*
Deborah M Thaw, *Exec VP*
EMP: 204
SQ FT: 55,000
SALES (est): 3.2MM **Privately Held**
SIC: 7389 6411 Notary publics; insurance agents, brokers & service

(P-17357)
NNNCC RANCH
7602 Monson Ave, Orange Cove (93646-9307)
PHONE...................................559 626-4890
Richard Nicholas, *Partner*
Richard M Nicholas, *Owner*
EMP: 100 **EST:** 2000
SQ FT: 2,238
SALES (est): 3.5MM **Privately Held**
SIC: 7389 Packaging & labeling services

(P-17358)
NOR-CAL BEVERAGE CO INC
Also Called: Norcal Beverage Co
1226 N Olive St, Anaheim (92801-2543)
PHONE...................................714 526-8600
William McFarland, *Manager*
EMP: 200
SALES (corp-wide): 248.5MM **Privately Held**
SIC: 7389 2033 Packaging & labeling services; canned fruits & specialties
PA: Nor-Cal Beverage Co., Inc.
2150 Stone Blvd
West Sacramento CA 95691
916 372-0600

(P-17359)
NORTHROP GRUMMAN SYSTEMS CORP
6411 W Imperial Hwy, Los Angeles (90045-6307)
PHONE...................................310 556-4911
Mark Shea, *Principal*
EMP: 303 **Publicly Held**
SIC: 7389 Personal service agents, brokers & bureaus
HQ: Northrop Grumman Systems Corporation
2980 Fairview Park Dr
Falls Church VA 22042
703 280-2900

(P-17360)
NOVATO FIRE PROTECTION DIST
95 Rowland Way, Novato (94945-5001)
PHONE...................................415 878-2690
Daniel Hom, *Finance*
Marc Revere, *Fire Chief*
EMP: 90
SALES (est): 6.1MM **Privately Held**
SIC: 7389 Fire protection service other than forestry or public

(P-17361)
NTH CONNECT TELECOM INC
2371 Bering Dr, San Jose (95131-1125)
PHONE..................408 922-0800
Steven Chen, *President*
EMP: 60
SALES (est): 7.1MM Privately Held
SIC: 7389 Telephone services

(P-17362)
NTH DEGREE INC
Also Called: N Th Degree
27092 Burbank, Foothill Ranch
(92610-2508)
PHONE..................714 734-4155
Scott Bennett, *Branch Mgr*
EMP: 50
SALES (corp-wide): 58.8MM Privately
Held
WEB: www.nthdegree.com
SIC: 7389 Convention & show services
PA: Nth Degree, Inc.
3237 Satellite Blvd # 600
Duluth GA 30096
404 296-5282

(P-17363)
**NUCOMPASS MOBILITY SVCS
INC (PA)**
6800 Koll Center Pkwy, Pleasanton
(94566-7045)
PHONE..................925 734-3434
Frank Patitucci, *CEO*
John Young, *President*
Ron Whitmill, *COO*
Lesley Dehoney, *Vice Pres*
Ken Klein, *Vice Pres*
EMP: 90
SALES (est): 17.5MM Privately Held
SIC: 7389 Relocation service

(P-17364)
**OAKTREE STRATEGIC INCOME
LLC**
333 S Grand Ave Fl 28, Los Angeles
(90071-1504)
PHONE..................213 830-6300
EMP: 682 EST: 2015
SALES (est): 52.4K Privately Held
SIC: 7389 Business services
PA: Oaktree Capital Group Holdings, L.P.
333 S Grand Ave Fl 28
Los Angeles CA 90071

(P-17365)
OC ACCESSORIES LLC
1968 S Coast Hwy Ste 195, Laguna Beach
(92651-3681)
PHONE..................949 229-2410
Don Seawell, *Principal*
Yesenia Cruz,
Tracy Zieve,
EMP: 58
SQ FT: 2,485
SALES (est): 792.6K Privately Held
SIC: 7389 Personal service agents, bro-
kers & bureaus

(P-17366)
**OCEAN BREEZE
MANUFACTURING**
1961 Hawkins Cir, Los Angeles
(90001-2255)
PHONE..................323 586-8760
Jamshid Daneshrad, *President*
Jackline Daneshrad, *Shareholder*
John Daneshrad, *Shareholder*
Shain Daneshrad, *Shareholder*
EMP: 80
SQ FT: 60,000
SALES (est): 1.5MM Privately Held
SIC: 7389 Sewing contractor

(P-17367)
OCEANX LLC (HQ)
100 N Pacific Coast Hwy, El Segundo
(90245-4359)
PHONE..................310 774-4088
Steve Adams, *Mng Member*
EMP: 99

SALES: 137MM
SALES (corp-wide): 370.7MM Privately
Held
SIC: 7389 4731 Subscription fulfillment
services: magazine, newspaper, etc.;
freight transportation arrangement
PA: Guthy-Renker Llc
100 N Pacific Coast Hwy # 1600
El Segundo CA 90245
760 773-9022

(P-17368)
ON-SITE MANAGER INC (HQ)
307 Orchard Cy Dr Ste 110, Campbell
(95008)
PHONE..................866 266-7483
Jake Harrington, *CEO*
Monte Jones, *President*
Gabriel Loera, *Program Mgr*
Lacey Smith, *Office Admin*
Scott Jones, *CTO*
EMP: 50
SALES (est): 11.2MM
SALES (corp-wide): 670.9MM Publicly
Held
WEB: www.on-sitemanager.com
SIC: 7389 Tenant screening service
PA: Realpage, Inc.
2201 Lakeside Blvd
Richardson TX 75082
972 820-3000

(P-17369)
ONE LEGAL INC
350 S Figueroa St Ste 385, Los Angeles
(90071-1208)
PHONE..................213 617-1212
Robert Battaglia, *President*
EMP: 60
SALES (est): 4.2MM Privately Held
SIC: 7389 Legal & tax services

(P-17370)
**ONTARIO CONVENTION
CENTER CORP**
Also Called: Smg Management Facility
2000 E Convention Ctr Way, Ontario
(91764-5633)
PHONE..................909 937-3000
Dick Walsh, *Mayor*
Michael K Krouse, *CEO*
EMP: 130
SQ FT: 225,000
SALES (est): 8.1MM Privately Held
WEB: www.ontariocc.com
SIC: 7389 9111 Convention & show serv-
ices; city & town managers' offices
PA: City Of Ontario
303 E B St
Ontario CA 91764
909 395-2012

(P-17371)
OPENTABLE INC (HQ)
1 Montgomery St Ste 700, San Francisco
(94104-4536)
PHONE..................415 344-4200
Christa Quarles, *CEO*
Matthew Roberts, *Ch of Bd*
Jeff McCombs, *CFO*
I Duncan Robertson, *CFO*
Joseph Essas, *CTO*
EMP: 123 EST: 1998
SQ FT: 50,965
SALES: 190MM
SALES (corp-wide): 12.6B Publicly Held
WEB: www.opentable.com
SIC: 7389 Restaurant reservation service
PA: Booking Holdings Inc.
800 Connecticut Ave
Norwalk CT 06854
203 299-8000

(P-17372)
OPTIMUM CX LLC
1288 W Mccoy Ln Ste C, Santa Maria
(93455-1054)
PHONE..................805 922-2999
Dan Ater, *Branch Mgr*
EMP: 230
SALES (corp-wide): 30.5MM Privately
Held
WEB: www.callfusion.com
SIC: 7389 Personal service agents, bro-
kers & bureaus

PA: Optimum Cx, Llc
11333 N Scottsdale Rd
Scottsdale AZ 85254
866 991-3888

(P-17373)
**ORA PACIFIC REGIONAL FIELD
OFF**
Also Called: Pacific Regional Laboratory SW
19701 Fairchild, Irvine (92612-2506)
PHONE..................949 608-2907
William Martin, *Director*
EMP: 85 Publicly Held
SIC: 7389 9431 Safety inspection service;
HQ: Ora Pacific Regional Field Office
1301 Clay St Ste 1180n
Oakland CA 94612

(P-17374)
**ORANGE CAST TITLE
SOUTHERN CAL (PA)**
1551 N Tustin Ave Ste 300, Santa Ana
(92705-8638)
P.O. Box 11825 (92711-1825)
PHONE..................714 558-2836
John L Marconi, *CEO*
Rich Mac Aluso, *President*
Fred Nilsen, *President*
Lori Romano, *COO*
Macaluso Rich, *Bd of Directors*
EMP: 100
SQ FT: 24,000
SALES (est): 166.3MM Privately Held
SIC: 7389 6361 6541 Personal service
agents, brokers & bureaus; title insur-
ance; title & trust companies

(P-17375)
**ORANGE CNTY ADULT
ACHVMENT CTR**
Also Called: My Day Counts
225 W Carl Karcher Way, Anaheim
(92801-2499)
PHONE..................714 744-5301
Michael Galliano, *CEO*
Aaron Flores, *CFO*
Patrick Faraday, *Vice Pres*
Richard Farmer, *Vice Pres*
Laurie Vinkavich, *Vice Pres*
▲ EMP: 105
SQ FT: 57,000
SALES: 10.5MM Privately Held
WEB: www.orangecountyarc.org
SIC: 7389 Packaging & labeling services

(P-17376)
ORANGE COURIER INC
3731 W Warner Ave, Santa Ana
(92704-5218)
P.O. Box 5308 (92704-0308)
PHONE..................714 384-3600
Evell T Stanley, *President*
EMP: 300
SQ FT: 150,000
SALES (est): 34.6MM Privately Held
WEB: www.orangecourier.com
SIC: 7389 4213 4225 Courier or messen-
ger service; trucking, except local; gen-
eral warehousing & storage

(P-17377)
OST TRUCKS AND CRANES INC
Also Called: Ost Crane Service
2951 N Ventura Ave, Ventura (93001-1210)
P.O. Box 237 (93002-0237)
PHONE..................805 643-9963
L Dennis Zermeno, *President*
Don D Zermeno, *Vice Pres*
Ron J Zermeno, *Vice Pres*
Kyley Andrews, *Manager*
EMP: 73
SQ FT: 3,000
SALES (est): 11.5MM Privately Held
WEB: www.ostcranes.com
SIC: 7389 4212 4225 Crane & aerial lift
service; local trucking, without storage;
general warehousing & storage

(P-17378)
OSTERHOUT GROUP INC
Also Called: Osterhout Design Group
153 Townsend St Ste 570, San Francisco
(94107-1976)
PHONE..................415 644-4000

Ralph F Osterhout, *President*
Chris White, *President*
Pete Jameson, *COO*
JP Moriarty, *CFO*
John Haddick, *Vice Pres*
EMP: 50
SQ FT: 2,200
SALES (est): 10.6MM Privately Held
SIC: 7389 Design, commercial & industrial

(P-17379)
OUR LADY OF GRACE P T G
2766 Navajo Rd, El Cajon (92020-2121)
PHONE..................619 466-0055
Susan Husc, *President*
Kathleen Malinosky, *President*
Gloria Green, *Treasurer*
Stephanie Hagenburger, *Treasurer*
Timothy Phariss, *Vice Pres*
EMP: 50
SALES (est): 3.5MM Privately Held
WEB: www.ourladyofkazanchurch.org
SIC: 7389 Fund raising organizations

(P-17380)
**OVERLAND PACIFIC & CUTLER
LLC (PA)**
Also Called: Pacific Relocation Consultants
3750 Schaufele Ave # 150, Long Beach
(90808-1779)
PHONE..................562 429-9391
Ray Armstrong, *CEO*
Barry McDaniel, *Vice Pres*
Steve Oliver, *Vice Pres*
Victoria Cook, *Program Mgr*
Min Saysay, *Program Mgr*
EMP: 55
SQ FT: 7,000
SALES (est): 18.7MM Privately Held
WEB: www.opcservices.com
SIC: 7389 Relocation service

(P-17381)
**OXNARD PERFRMN ARTS &
CONVTN**
Also Called: CITY OF OXNARD PERFORM-
ING ARTS
800 Hobson Way, Oxnard (93030-6723)
PHONE..................805 486-2424
Robert Holden, *CEO*
EMP: 50
SALES: 1.6MM Privately Held
SIC: 7389 Convention & show services;
tourist information bureau

(P-17382)
**PACIFIC COAST COMPANIES
INC**
10600 White Rock Rd # 100, Rancho Cor-
dova (95670-6294)
P.O. Box 419074 (95741-9074)
PHONE..................916 631-6500
David J Lucchetti, *President*
Dale Waldschmitt, *COO*
Joshua Kimerer, *CFO*
Daniel Yanagihara, *Vice Pres*
Ken Kerrick, *CIO*
EMP: 125
SALES (est): 18.9MM
SALES (corp-wide): 1.7B Privately Held
SIC: 7389 8742 Legal & tax services;
human resource consulting services
PA: Pacific Coast Building Products, Inc.
10600 White Rock Rd # 100
Rancho Cordova CA 95670
916 631-6500

(P-17383)
PACIFIC COAST PRODUCERS
650 S Guild Ave, Lodi (95240-3114)
PHONE..................209 365-9982
Jim Farmer, *Branch Mgr*
Molly Blask, *Purchasing*
Dan Newhall, *Manager*
EMP: 500
SALES (corp-wide): 668MM Privately
Held
SIC: 7389 5141 Packaging & labeling
services; groceries, general line
PA: Pacific Coast Producers
631 N Cluff Ave
Lodi CA 95240
209 367-8800

(P-17384)
PACIFIC MEDICAL INC (PA)
1700 N Chrisman Rd, Tracy (95304-9314)
P.O. Box 149 (95378-0149)
PHONE..............................800 726-9180
John M Petlansky, *CEO*
Jeffrey Leonard, *CFO*
Don Meng, *Officer*
Bob McCune, *Vice Pres*
Kevin Van Donselaar, *Business Dir*
EMP: 128
SQ FT: 18,000
SALES (est): 61.3MM **Privately Held**
WEB: www.pacmedical.com
SIC: 7389 7352 Brokers, contract services; medical equipment rental

(P-17385)
PARADIGM INDUSTRIES INC
13344 S Main St Ste C, Los Angeles
(90061-1638)
PHONE..............................310 965-1900
William Jun, *CEO*
Chu Kim, *President*
EMP: 80
SALES (est): 4.7MM **Privately Held**
WEB: www.paradigmindustries.com
SIC: 7389 Textile & apparel services

(P-17386)
PARCHMENT INC
3000 Lava Ridge Ct # 210, Roseville
(95661-2800)
PHONE..............................480 719-1646
Louis Delzompo, *Manager*
EMP: 58
SALES (corp-wide): 30.5MM **Privately Held**
SIC: 7389
PA: Parchment Inc.
6263 N Scotts Rd Ste 330
Scottsdale AZ 85250
480 719-1646

(P-17387)
PARKING CONCEPTS INC
12 Mauchly Ste I, Irvine (92618-6302)
PHONE..............................949 752-5558
Adrian Gonzales, *Branch Mgr*
Rocio Hernandez, *Admin Mgr*
Jim Mecham, *General Mgr*
Luis Portillo, *Manager*
EMP: 260
SALES (corp-wide): 58.5MM **Privately Held**
SIC: 7389 Personal service agents, brokers & bureaus
PA: Parking Concepts, Inc.
12 Mauchly Ste I
Irvine CA 92618
949 753-7525

(P-17388)
PARTNER HERO INC
1001 Avenida Pico C260, San Clemente
(92673-6957)
PHONE..............................888 968-2767
Shervin Talieh, *Administration*
EMP: 50 **EST:** 2014
SALES (est): 938.7K **Privately Held**
SIC: 7389 Telephone answering service

(P-17389)
PARTNERS CAPITAL GROUP INC (PA)
201 Sandpointe Ave # 500, Santa Ana
(92707-8716)
PHONE..............................949 916-3900
Mark Davin, *CEO*
Jason Bernal, *Vice Pres*
Mark Harmond, *Mktg Dir*
Trevor Teuscher, *Accounts Exec*
EMP: 80
SQ FT: 20,000
SALES (est): 57.8MM **Privately Held**
SIC: 7389 Financial services

(P-17390)
PARTOS AGENCY LLC
Also Called: Partos Company, The
227 Broadway Ste 204, Santa Monica
(90401-2370)
PHONE..............................310 458-7800
Walter Partos,
Laura Roman, *Office Mgr*
Ajay Ghosh, *Agent*
Martijn Hostetler, *Agent*
EMP: 70
SQ FT: 2,000
SALES (est): 3.8MM **Privately Held**
WEB: www.partos.com
SIC: 7389 7922 Authors' agents & brokers; talent agent, theatrical

(P-17391)
PASADENA CENTER OPERATING CO
Also Called: PASADENA CONVENTION CENTER
300 E Green St, Pasadena (91101-2399)
PHONE..............................626 795-9311
Michael Ross, *CEO*
Doug Finney, *General Mgr*
Mary Collins, *Executive Asst*
Tim Norman, *Technology*
Atish Shah, *VP Finance*
EMP: 116
SQ FT: 32,000
SALES (est): 23.6MM **Privately Held**
WEB: www.pasadenacal.com
SIC: 7389 Convention & show services

(P-17392)
PASSPRT ACCEPT FCLTY LOS ANGEL
Also Called: Sunset Station
1425 N Cherokee Ave, Los Angeles
(90093-2108)
PHONE..............................323 460-4811
Gerald Padilla, *General Mgr*
EMP: 60
SALES (est): 1.2MM **Privately Held**
SIC: 7389 Post office contract stations

(P-17393)
PATRICK K WILLIS COMPANY INC
Also Called: American Recovery Service
5118 Rbert J Mathews Pkwy, El Dorado Hills (95762-5703)
PHONE..............................800 398-6480
David Baker, *Senior VP*
John Foster, *Officer*
Christian Beyer, *Vice Pres*
Steven Schelk, *Risk Mgmt Dir*
Patrick K Willis, *Principal*
EMP: 300
SQ FT: 10,000
SALES (est): 3.2MM **Privately Held**
SIC: 7389 Repossession service

(P-17394)
PB CAR MOVERS
5510 W 120th St, Hawthorne (90250-3406)
PHONE..............................310 283-2741
Jose Desiderio, *Owner*
EMP: 60
SALES (est): 1.9MM **Privately Held**
SIC: 7389 Automobile recovery service

(P-17395)
PERFORMANCE TEAM FRT SYS INC
1651 California St Ste A, Redlands
(92374-2904)
PHONE..............................801 301-1732
EMP: 237
SALES (corp-wide): 372MM **Privately Held**
SIC: 7389 Personal service agents, brokers & bureaus
PA: Performance Team Llc
2240 E Maple Ave
El Segundo CA 90245
562 345-2200

(P-17396)
PERMITS TODAY LLC
140 S Lake Ave Ste 323, Pasadena
(91101-4787)
PHONE..............................626 585-2931
Scott Daves,
Margaret Sargent,
Carla Street,
Mario Zelaya, *Manager*
EMP: 75 **EST:** 1998
SALES: 2.5MM **Privately Held**
WEB: www.permitstoday.com
SIC: 7389 Personal service agents, brokers & bureaus

(P-17397)
PHOENIX INTL HOLDINGS INC
127 Press Ln, Chula Vista (91910-1011)
PHONE..............................619 207-0871
Kelvin Hall, *Branch Mgr*
EMP: 143 **Privately Held**
SIC: 7389 Marine reporting
PA: Phoenix International Holdings, Inc.
9301 Largo Dr W
Largo MD 20774

(P-17398)
PHOENIX TEXTILE INC
910 S Los Angeles St, Los Angeles
(90015-1726)
PHONE..............................213 239-9640
Fax: 213 228-1109
EMP: 70
SALES (corp-wide): 42.4MM **Privately Held**
SIC: 7389
PA: Phoenix Textile, Inc.
14600 S Broadway
Gardena CA 90248
310 715-7090

(P-17399)
PHONE WARE INC
8902 Activity Rd Ste A, San Diego
(92126-4471)
PHONE..............................858 530-8550
William J Nassir, *President*
Jim Rochford, *President*
Bolden Ellen, *CFO*
Hazel Nassir, *Exec VP*
Dianne Christiansen, *VP Bus Dvlpt*
EMP: 366
SQ FT: 20,000
SALES (est): 36.6MM **Privately Held**
WEB: www.phoneware.com
SIC: 7389 8742 Telemarketing services; marketing consulting services

(P-17400)
PIONEER THEATRES INC
Also Called: Roadium Open Air Market
2500 Redondo Beach Blvd, Torrance
(90504-1529)
PHONE..............................310 532-8183
William Fleischman, *President*
William Warnick, *Vice Pres*
EMP: 110
SQ FT: 3,000
SALES (est): 10.3MM **Privately Held**
WEB: www.pioneertheatre.org
SIC: 7389 5431 Flea market; fruit & vegetable markets

(P-17401)
PITNEY BOWES PRESORT SVCS INC
18550 S Broadwick St, Compton
(90220-6439)
PHONE..............................310 763-4615
Lori Butcher, *Branch Mgr*
EMP: 115
SALES (corp-wide): 3.5B **Publicly Held**
SIC: 7389 Presorted mail service
HQ: Pitney Bowes Presort Services, Inc.
10110 I St
Omaha NE 68127

(P-17402)
PITNEY BOWES PRESORT SVCS INC
125 Valley Dr, Brisbane (94005-1317)
PHONE..............................415 468-1660
Nick Saribalis, *Vice Pres*
Nicholas Saribalis, *President*
EMP: 70
SALES (corp-wide): 3.5B **Publicly Held**
WEB: www.psigroupinc.com
SIC: 7389 Presorted mail service
HQ: Pitney Bowes Presort Services, Inc.
10110 I St
Omaha NE 68127

(P-17403)
PIXIOR LLC (PA)
5901 S Eastern Ave, Commerce
(90040-4003)
PHONE..............................323 721-2221
Yassine Amallal, *Mng Member*
Simon Bouzaglou, *COO*
Elena Pickett, *Senior VP*
Gloria Harris, *Accountant*
Galina Turetskaya, *Accountant*
EMP: 89
SQ FT: 192,000
SALES (est): 15.9MM **Privately Held**
WEB: www.pixior.com
SIC: 7389 Advertising, promotional & trade show services

(P-17404)
PLASTIFLEX COMPANY INC (HQ)
601 E Palomar St Ste 424, Chula Vista
(91911-6976)
PHONE..............................619 662-8792
Gerald Green, *President*
Robert Sakiyama, *President*
David McIvor, *CEO*
Richard Loh, *Vice Pres*
Robert Deregge, *Principal*
EMP: 130
SQ FT: 48,000
SALES (est): 20.3MM **Privately Held**
WEB: www.plastiflex.com
SIC: 7389 Swimming pool & hot tub service & maintenance
PA: Plastiflex Suzhou Co., Ltd.
Block 10,Yangshan Science And Technology Industrial Park,No.8,Ji
Suzhou
512 667-2673

(P-17405)
PLUM HEALTHCARE GROUP LLC
Also Called: Redlands Health Care Group
1620 W Fern Ave, Redlands (92373-4918)
PHONE..............................909 793-2609
Mark Baliff,
Eddie Cook, *Technology*
Brittany Hernandez, *Graphic Designe*
Arnie Borromeo, *Director*
EMP: 80
SALES (est): 3.9MM **Privately Held**
WEB: www.plum.ca
SIC: 7389 Personal service agents, brokers & bureaus

(P-17406)
PRECISION IDEO INC
150 Forest Ave, Palo Alto (94301-1614)
PHONE..............................650 688-3400
Tim Brown, *President*
Duane Bray, *Partner*
Fred Dust, *Partner*
Tom Eich, *Partner*
Whitney Mortimer, *Partner*
EMP: 400
SALES (est): 20.5MM **Privately Held**
SIC: 7389 Design services

(P-17407)
PREMIER DISP & EXHIBITS INC (PA)
11261 Warland Dr, Cypress (90630-5033)
PHONE..............................562 431-2731
Christopher J Bullard, *CEO*
Stephen Amato, *Principal*
EMP: 84
SQ FT: 170,000
SALES (est): 25.7MM **Privately Held**
WEB: www.premierdisplays.com
SIC: 7389 Trade show arrangement

(P-17408)
PREMIER OFFICE CENTERS LLC (PA)
Also Called: Premier Business Centers
2102 Business Center Dr, Irvine
(92612-1001)
PHONE..............................949 253-4616
Jeffrey Reinstein, *CEO*
Sandra Mendoza, *Vice Pres*
Diana Alvarez, *General Mgr*
Vanessa Decker, *General Mgr*
Robin Riley, *General Mgr*
EMP: 50

PRODUCTS & SVCS

SALES (est): 63.8MM **Privately Held**
SIC: 7389 Office facilities & secretarial
　service rental

(P-17409)
PREVENT LIFE SAFETY SVCS INC
1410 Stealth St, Livermore (94551-9358)
PHONE...........................925 667-2088
Carol D Cohan, *President*
Jeff Norman, *Executive*
Kailey McLaughlin, *Mktg Dir*
EMP: 50
SALES (est): 2.4MM **Privately Held**
SIC: 7389 Fire protection service other
　than forestry or public

(P-17410)
PRO-TECH DESIGN & MFG INC
14561 Marquardt Ave, Santa Fe Springs
(90670-5137)
PHONE...........................562 207-1680
Pamela Mc Master, *CEO*
Aaron Swanson, *President*
David Mc Master, *CFO*
Jeff Swanson, *Vice Pres*
EMP: 60
SALES (est): 9MM **Privately Held**
WEB: www.protechdesign.net
SIC: 7389 8711 Packaging & labeling
　services; industrial engineers

(P-17411)
PROCALL SOLUTIONS INC
20 Ragsdale Dr Ste 100, Monterey
(93940-7812)
PHONE...........................800 733-9675
Dennis Hill, *Senior VP*
EMP: 120
SQ FT: 10,000
SALES: 5MM
SALES (corp-wide): 131.7MM **Privately
Held**
WEB: www.procallonline.com
SIC: 7389 Telemarketing services
PA: Product Development Corp
　30 Ragsdale Dr Ste 101
　Monterey CA 93940
　831 333-1100

(P-17412)
PRODUCT DEVELOPMENT CORP (PA)
30 Ragsdale Dr Ste 101, Monterey
(93940-5772)
PHONE...........................831 333-1100
Tim Dinovo, *President*
Bernie Clum, *Vice Chairman*
David Forey, *CFO*
Vince Gage, *Senior VP*
Edith Privratsky, *Senior VP*
EMP: 131
SQ FT: 10,700
SALES (est): 131.7MM **Privately Held**
WEB: www.pdceast.com
SIC: 7389 Telephone directory distribution,
　contract or fee basis

(P-17413)
PROFESSIONAL EXCHANGE SVC
4747 N 1st St Ste 140, Fresno
(93726-0517)
P.O. Box 1071 (93714-1071)
PHONE...........................559 229-6249
Cynthia Downing, *CEO*
Peggy Matsoura, *CFO*
Russell Nakaguchio, *Corp Secy*
Matt Haas, *Vice Pres*
Paul Bateman, *Principal*
EMP: 50 EST: 1980
SQ FT: 3,700
SALES (est): 5.5MM **Privately Held**
WEB: www.pesc.com
SIC: 7389 Telephone answering service

(P-17414)
PROFESSNAL CMMNCTONS NETWRK LP (PA)
6774 Magnolia Ave, Riverside
(92506-2908)
PHONE...........................951 275-9149
Diann K Johnston, *Partner*
Brian White, *Partner*
Jeff White, *Partner*

Diann Johnston, *General Mgr*
Donna Wuersch, *Finance Mgr*
EMP: 50
SQ FT: 4,000
SALES (est): 3.6MM **Privately Held**
SIC: 7389 Telephone answering service

(P-17415)
PROJECT SIX
13130 Burbank Blvd, Sherman Oaks
(91401-6037)
PHONE...........................818 781-0360
Barbera Firestone, *President*
EMP: 55
SALES: 3.4MM **Privately Held**
SIC: 7389 Tax title dealers

(P-17416)
PROLOGIC RDMPTION SLUTIONS INC (PA)
2121 Rosecrans Ave, El Segundo
(90245-4743)
PHONE...........................310 322-7774
William Atkinson, *CEO*
Paul Cooley, *President*
Robb Warwick, *CFO*
Kelly Fuller, *Ch Credit Ofcr*
Ross Ely, *Chief Mktg Ofcr*
EMP: 700
SALES (est): 39.5MM **Privately Held**
SIC: 7389 Coupon redemption service

(P-17417)
PS ENVIRONMENTAL SVCS INC
23775 Madison St, Torrance (90505-6006)
PHONE...........................310 373-6259
Joseph Gaglione, *President*
EMP: 62
SALES (est): 4.6MM **Privately Held**
WEB: www.psenvironmental.com
SIC: 7389 Air pollution measuring service

(P-17418)
PUNCTUS TEMPORIS TRANSLATIONS
5201 Great America Pkwy, Santa Clara
(95054-1122)
PHONE...........................510 309-0888
Jessica Cade, *Owner*
EMP: 50 EST: 2016
SALES (est): 641.1K **Privately Held**
SIC: 7389 Translation services

(P-17419)
QUALFAX INC
3605 Long Beach Blvd # 428, Long Beach
(90807-6020)
PHONE...........................562 988-1272
Daniel Wayne, *Treasurer*
Jim Wolf, *CEO*
EMP: 60
SALES (est): 2.5MM **Privately Held**
WEB: www.qualfax.com
SIC: 7389 8741 Tenant screening service;
　management services

(P-17420)
QUICKSILVER DELIVERY INC
Also Called: Quicksilver Delivery Service
129 Kissling St, San Francisco
(94103-3726)
PHONE...........................415 431-1600
Phil Mc Cafee, *President*
EMP: 65
SQ FT: 5,000
SALES (est): 3.3MM **Privately Held**
SIC: 7389 Courier or messenger service

(P-17421)
QUINSTREET INC (PA)
950 Tower Ln Ste 600, Foster City
(94404-4253)
PHONE...........................650 578-7700
Douglas Valenti, *Ch of Bd*
Gregory Wong, *CFO*
Martin J Collins, *Ch Credit Ofcr*
Tim Stevens, *Senior VP*
Suresh Kondamareddy, *Vice Pres*
EMP: 50
SQ FT: 63,998
SALES: 404.3MM **Publicly Held**
WEB: www.quinstreet.com
SIC: 7389 7372 Advertising, promotional &
　trade show services; prepackaged soft-
　ware; business oriented computer soft-
　ware

(P-17422)
R G CANNING ENTERPRISES INC
4515 E 59th Pl, Maywood (90270-3201)
PHONE...........................323 560-7469
Richard G Canning, *President*
Charles R Canning, *Vice Pres*
Tim Ellis, *General Mgr*
EMP: 215
SQ FT: 50,000
SALES (est): 12.1MM **Privately Held**
WEB: www.rgcshows.com
SIC: 7389 Promoters of shows & exhibi-
　tions

(P-17423)
RAILPROS FIELD SERVICES
1 Ada Ste 200, Irvine (92618-5341)
PHONE...........................877 315-0513
Johnny Johnson, *CEO*
Bill Pairman, *Manager*
EMP: 50
SQ FT: 900
SALES (est): 5.4MM
SALES (corp-wide): 9.7MM **Privately
Held**
SIC: 7389
PA: Railpros Field Services Inc
　1705 W Northwest Hwy # 150
　Grapevine TX 76051
　682 223-6897

(P-17424)
RALPH COLLAZO PACKING INC
72 E Main St Ste A, Heber (92249)
PHONE...........................760 353-0856
Ralph Collazo, *President*
EMP: 100
SALES (est): 8.8MM **Privately Held**
SIC: 7389 Packaging & labeling services

(P-17425)
RAYTHEON COMPANY
75 Coromar Dr, Goleta (93117-3088)
PHONE...........................805 562-2941
EMP: 66
SALES (corp-wide): 23.2B **Publicly Held**
SIC: 7389
PA: Raytheon Company
　870 Winter St
　Waltham MA 02451
　781 522-3000

(P-17426)
REGISTRATION CTRL SYSTEMS INC (PA)
Also Called: Rcs World Travel
1833 Portola Rd Unit B, Ventura
(93003-7797)
PHONE...........................805 654-0171
Edgar A Bolton, *President*
Duane Smeckert, *President*
Gary Bolton, *Vice Pres*
Gary Palmer, *Vice Pres*
Edgar Bolton, *Executive*
EMP: 65
SQ FT: 15,000
SALES (est): 3.3MM **Privately Held**
WEB: www.rcsreg.com
SIC: 7389 Convention & show services

(P-17427)
RESMEX PARTNERS LLC
438 Geary St, San Francisco (94102-1223)
PHONE...........................415 440-2737
Rallo Edwardo,
EMP: 50
SALES: 3MM **Privately Held**
SIC: 7389 Automobile recovery service

(P-17428)
RETAIL SERVICES WIS CORP
Also Called: W I S
13800 Heacock St D135c, Moreno Valley
(92553-3339)
PHONE...........................951 653-1472
Jeff Ferririak, *Manager*
EMP: 80
SALES (corp-wide): 39.4MM **Privately
Held**
WEB: www.wisusa.com
SIC: 7389 Inventory computing service

HQ: Retail Services Wis Corporation
　9265 Sky Park Ct Ste 100
　San Diego CA 92123
　858 565-8111

(P-17429)
RETAIL SERVICES WIS CORP
Also Called: W I S
9080 Telstar Ave Ste 313, El Monte
(91731-2840)
PHONE...........................626 288-1200
Tony Toledo, *Manager*
EMP: 60
SALES (corp-wide): 39.4MM **Privately
Held**
WEB: www.wisusa.com
SIC: 7389 Inventory computing service
HQ: Retail Services Wis Corporation
　9265 Sky Park Ct Ste 100
　San Diego CA 92123
　858 565-8111

(P-17430)
RETAIL SERVICES WIS CORP
3800 Watt Ave Ste 101, Sacramento
(95821-2622)
PHONE...........................916 485-3427
Craig Rust, *President*
EMP: 120
SALES (corp-wide): 39.4MM **Privately
Held**
WEB: www.wisusa.com
SIC: 7389 Inventory stocking service; in-
　ventory computing service
HQ: Retail Services Wis Corporation
　9265 Sky Park Ct Ste 100
　San Diego CA 92123
　858 565-8111

(P-17431)
RETAIL SERVICES WIS CORP
1838 N Tustin St Ste A, Orange
(92865-4650)
PHONE...........................714 637-3431
Rubin Vega, *Manager*
EMP: 65
SALES (corp-wide): 39.4MM **Privately
Held**
WEB: www.wisusa.com
SIC: 7389 Inventory computing service
HQ: Retail Services Wis Corporation
　9265 Sky Park Ct Ste 100
　San Diego CA 92123
　858 565-8111

(P-17432)
RETAIL SERVICES WIS CORP
21354 Nordhoff St Ste 108, Chatsworth
(91311-6910)
PHONE...........................818 772-4969
Mary Booher, *Branch Mgr*
EMP: 50
SALES (corp-wide): 39.4MM **Privately
Held**
WEB: www.wisusa.com
SIC: 7389 Inventory computing service
HQ: Retail Services Wis Corporation
　9265 Sky Park Ct Ste 100
　San Diego CA 92123
　858 565-8111

(P-17433)
RETAIL SERVICES WIS CORP
19420 Business Center Dr, Northridge
(91324-3541)
PHONE...........................818 407-2680
Scott Lopez, *Manager*
Kathleen McCormick, *Manager*
Tana Trinchero, *Manager*
Myra Zuniga, *Manager*
EMP: 80
SALES (corp-wide): 39.4MM **Privately
Held**
WEB: www.wisusa.com
SIC: 7389 Inventory computing service
HQ: Retail Services Wis Corporation
　9265 Sky Park Ct Ste 100
　San Diego CA 92123
　858 565-8111

(P-17434)
RETAIL SERVICES WIS CORP
1932 Eastman Ave, Ventura (93003-7706)
PHONE...........................805 644-5422
Paul Russ, *Branch Mgr*
EMP: 69

▲ = Import ▼=Export
◆ =Import/Export

SALES (corp-wide): 39.4MM Privately Held
WEB: www.wisusa.com
SIC: 7389 Inventory computing service
HQ: Retail Services Wis Corporation
9265 Sky Park Ct Ste 100
San Diego CA 92123
858 565-8111

(P-17435)
RGIS LLC
5500 Ming Ave Ste 185, Bakersfield
(93309-4623)
PHONE.............................661 827-9195
Laine Martin, *District Mgr*
EMP: 51
SALES (corp-wide): 7.1B Publicly Held
WEB: www.rgisinv.com
SIC: 7389 Inventory computing service
HQ: Rgis, Llc
2000 Taylor Rd
Auburn Hills MI 48326
248 651-2511

(P-17436)
RGIS LLC
1787 Mesa Verde Ave, Ventura
(93003-6531)
PHONE.............................805 644-0454
Darin Coupland, *Manager*
EMP: 75
SALES (corp-wide): 7.1B Publicly Held
WEB: www.rgisinv.com
SIC: 7389 Inventory computing service
HQ: Rgis, Llc
2000 Taylor Rd
Auburn Hills MI 48326
248 651-2511

(P-17437)
RGIS LLC
8801 Folsom Blvd Ste 173, Sacramento
(95826-3249)
PHONE.............................916 387-9692
Chris Massoni, *Vice Pres*
Marcus Duran, *Manager*
EMP: 100
SALES (corp-wide): 7.1B Publicly Held
WEB: www.rgisinv.com
SIC: 7389 Inventory computing service
HQ: Rgis, Llc
2000 Taylor Rd
Auburn Hills MI 48326
248 651-2511

(P-17438)
RGIS LLC
500 E Olive Ave Ste 240, Burbank
(91501-2171)
PHONE.............................248 651-2511
Bruce Hemingway, *Manager*
EMP: 140
SALES (corp-wide): 7.1B Publicly Held
WEB: www.rgisinv.com
SIC: 7389 Inventory computing service
HQ: Rgis, Llc
2000 Taylor Rd
Auburn Hills MI 48326
248 651-2511

(P-17439)
RGIS LLC
7567 Amador Valley Blvd, Dublin
(94568-2441)
PHONE.............................925 829-2875
Majid Jafarkhani, *Branch Mgr*
EMP: 85
SALES (corp-wide): 7.1B Publicly Held
WEB: www.rgisinv.com
SIC: 7389 Inventory computing service
HQ: Rgis, Llc
2000 Taylor Rd
Auburn Hills MI 48326
248 651-2511

(P-17440)
RGIS LLC
4320 Stevens Creek Blvd, San Jose
(95129-1202)
PHONE.............................408 243-9141
EMP: 65
SALES (corp-wide): 5.1B Publicly Held
SIC: 7389

HQ: Rgis, Llc
2000 Taylor Rd
Auburn Hills MI 48326
248 651-2511

(P-17441)
RGIS LLC
25115 Avenue Stanford, Valencia
(91355-1290)
PHONE.............................661 702-8987
Becky Conde, *Manager*
EMP: 79
SALES (corp-wide): 7.1B Publicly Held
WEB: www.rgisinv.com
SIC: 7389 Inventory stocking service
HQ: Rgis, Llc
2000 Taylor Rd
Auburn Hills MI 48326
248 651-2511

(P-17442)
RGIS LLC
20 Landing Cir Ste 100, Chico
(95973-7889)
PHONE.............................530 898-1015
Jacquelyn Pacconi, *Branch Mgr*
EMP: 65
SALES (corp-wide): 7.1B Publicly Held
WEB: www.rgisinv.com
SIC: 7389 Inventory computing service
HQ: Rgis, Llc
2000 Taylor Rd
Auburn Hills MI 48326
248 651-2511

(P-17443)
RGIS LLC
1041 W Badillo St, Covina (91722-4194)
PHONE.............................626 974-4841
James Roseman, *Manager*
EMP: 79
SALES (corp-wide): 7.1B Publicly Held
WEB: www.rgisinv.com
SIC: 7389 Inventory computing service
HQ: Rgis, Llc
2000 Taylor Rd
Auburn Hills MI 48326
248 651-2511

(P-17444)
RGIS LLC
1322 E Shaw Ave Ste 170, Fresno
(93710-7923)
PHONE.............................559 224-5898
Tim Butters, *Manager*
EMP: 60
SALES (corp-wide): 7.1B Publicly Held
WEB: www.rgisinv.com
SIC: 7389 Inventory computing service
HQ: Rgis, Llc
2000 Taylor Rd
Auburn Hills MI 48326
248 651-2511

(P-17445)
RGIS LLC
2000 E 4th St Ste 350, Santa Ana
(92705-3936)
PHONE.............................714 541-1431
Majel Becarra, *Branch Mgr*
EMP: 65
SALES (corp-wide): 7.1B Publicly Held
WEB: www.rgisinv.com
SIC: 7389 Inventory computing service
HQ: Rgis, Llc
2000 Taylor Rd
Auburn Hills MI 48326
248 651-2511

(P-17446)
RGIS LLC
2171 Junipero Serra Blvd # 400, Daly City
(94014-1984)
PHONE.............................650 757-6770
Alice Souza, *Manager*
EMP: 130
SALES (corp-wide): 7.1B Publicly Held
WEB: www.rgisinv.com
SIC: 7389 Inventory computing service
HQ: Rgis, Llc
2000 Taylor Rd
Auburn Hills MI 48326
248 651-2511

(P-17447)
RIVER CITY AUTO RECOVERY INC
3401 Fitzgerald Rd, Rancho Cordova
(95742-6815)
PHONE.............................916 851-1100
David Schmidt, *CFO*
EMP: 71
SQ FT: 15,000
SALES (est): 2.2MM
SALES (corp-wide): 316.5MM Privately Held
WEB: www.unitedroad.com
SIC: 7389 Repossession service
PA: United Road Services, Inc.
10701 Middlebelt Rd
Romulus MI 48174
734 946-3232

(P-17448)
ROAD SAFETY INC
4335 Pacific St Ste A, Rocklin
(95677-2104)
PHONE.............................916 543-4600
Melissa L Bamberg, *President*
Jason Bamberg, *CEO*
Andrea West, *Human Res Dir*
EMP: 120
SQ FT: 6,000
SALES (est): 14.3MM Privately Held
SIC: 7389 Flagging service (traffic control)

(P-17449)
RONSIN PHOTOCOPY INC (PA)
215 Lemon Creek Dr, Walnut (91789-2643)
PHONE.............................909 594-5995
Dennis Grant, *President*
Robert Alkema, *Ch of Bd*
Cheryl Alkema, *Corp Secy*
Dave Thomas, *Marketing Mgr*
Tom Alkema, *Marketing Staff*
EMP: 60
SQ FT: 12,000
SALES (est): 9.4MM Privately Held
WEB: www.ronsinphotocopy.com
SIC: 7389 Microfilm recording & developing service

(P-17450)
ROSE & SHORE INC
5151 Alcoa Ave, Vernon (90058-3715)
P.O. Box 58225 (90058-0225)
PHONE.............................323 826-2144
Irwin Miller, *President*
Carol Miller, *Admin Sec*
Carlos Enriquez, *Info Tech Dir*
James Craig, *VP Mfg*
EMP: 320
SQ FT: 60,000
SALES (est): 54MM Privately Held
WEB: www.rose-shore.com
SIC: 7389 5147 Packaging & labeling services; meats, cured or smoked

(P-17451)
SALT OF EARTH PRODUCTIONS INC
Also Called: Salt Catering
1437 S Robertson Blvd, Los Angeles
(90035-3414)
PHONE.............................818 399-1860
Tomas Rivera, *President*
EMP: 108
SALES (est): 1.6MM Privately Held
SIC: 7389 Decoration service for special events

(P-17452)
SAN DIEGO CAR ACCIDENT LAWYERS
Maple St, San Diego (92104)
PHONE.............................858 201-4178
Harry Keller, *Principal*
EMP: 50
SALES (est): 641.1K Privately Held
SIC: 7389 Business services

(P-17453)
SAN DIEGO TOURISM AUTHORITY (PA)
750 B St Ste 1500, San Diego
(92101-8131)
PHONE.............................619 232-3101
Joseph Terzi, *CEO*
Reint Reinders, *President*

Rick Meza, *CFO*
Christine Shimasaki, *Exec VP*
Sal Giametta, *Vice Pres*
EMP: 75
SQ FT: 2,100
SALES (est): 31.8MM Privately Held
SIC: 7389 Convention & show services; tourist information bureau

(P-17454)
SAN FRANCISCO FOUNDATION
1 Embarcadero Ctr # 1400, San Francisco
(94111-3703)
PHONE.............................415 733-8500
Sandra Hernandez MD, *Director*
EMP: 60
SQ FT: 22,000
SALES: 114.3MM Privately Held
SIC: 7389 Fund raising organizations

(P-17455)
SAN FRANCISCO TRAVEL ASSN
Also Called: SS TRAVEL
1 Front St Ste 2900, San Francisco
(94111-5333)
PHONE.............................415 974-6900
Joe D'Alessandro, *President*
Han Anh, *CFO*
Tina Wu, *CFO*
Bill Poland, *Treasurer*
Howard Pickett, *Chief Mktg Ofcr*
EMP: 70
SQ FT: 15,000
SALES: 32.9MM Privately Held
SIC: 7389 Convention & show services; tourist information bureau

(P-17456)
SANTA BARBARA CITY OF
Also Called: Pub Works/Community Dev
630 Garden St, Santa Barbara
(93101-1656)
PHONE.............................805 564-5485
Paul Casey, *Director*
Brenda Nielsen, *Admin Asst*
EMP: 200 Privately Held
WEB: www.citytv18.com
SIC: 7389 Safety inspection service
PA: City Of Santa Barbara
735 Anacapa St
Santa Barbara CA 93101
805 564-5334

(P-17457)
SANTA BARBARA PC USERS GROUP
462 S San Marcos Rd, Santa Barbara
(93111-2726)
PHONE.............................805 964-5411
Gerard L F Ching, *President*
Robert Winokur, *Info Tech Mgr*
EMP: 50 EST: 2001
SALES (est): 1.2MM Privately Held
SIC: 7389 Business services

(P-17458)
SARPA-FELDMAN ENTERPRISES INC
Also Called: Progressive Solutions
650 N King Rd, San Jose (95133-1715)
PHONE.............................408 982-1790
Mark E Sarpa, *CEO*
Scott R Feldman, *CFO*
Scott Feldman, *CFO*
Trang Nguyen, *Accountant*
Frances Gunther, *Production*
EMP: 56
SQ FT: 13,000
SALES (est): 9.3MM Privately Held
WEB: www.printhq.com
SIC: 7389 Printing broker

(P-17459)
SCA ENTERPRISES INC (PA)
Also Called: Southern Cal Appraisal Co
3817 W Magnolia Blvd, Burbank
(91505-2820)
P.O. Box 1455 (91507-1455)
PHONE.............................818 845-7621
Timothy S Davis, *CEO*
Paula Davis, *CFO*
Dan Karlson, *Info Tech Mgr*
Jaynie Castillo, *Recruiter*
Kelly Bicknell, *Opers Staff*
EMP: 107
SQ FT: 1,200

(PA)=Parent Co (HQ)=Headquarters (DH)=Div Headquarters
✪ = New Business established in last 2 years

2019 Directory of California
Wholesalers and Services Companies

741

P R O D U C T S & S V C S

SALES (est): 11.6MM Privately Held
SIC: 7389 Appraisers, except real estate

(P-17460)
SCHERZER INTERNATIONAL CORP (PA)
21650 Oxnard St Ste 300, Woodland Hills
(91367-4989)
PHONE.................................818 227-2770
Larry S Scherzer, President
Jessica Staheli, Vice Pres
David Lazar, Managing Dir
Carol Scherzer, Admin Sec
Andrew Duong, Admin Asst
EMP: 60
SQ FT: 11,400
SALES (est): 10.1MM Privately Held
SIC: 7389 Financial services

(P-17461)
SCREEN GEMS-EMI MUSIC INC
Also Called: EMI Publishing
2700 Colorado Ave Ste 100, Santa Monica
(90404-3581)
PHONE.................................310 586-2700
Martin N Bandier, CEO
EMP: 50
SALES (corp-wide): 3.2MM Privately Held
SIC: 7389 Music recording producer
HQ: Screen Gems-Emi Music Inc.
150 5th Ave Fl 7
New York NY 10011
212 786-8000

(P-17462)
SCRIP ADVANTAGE INC
4273 W Richert Ave # 110, Fresno
(93722-6333)
P.O. Box 13238 (93794-3238)
PHONE.................................559 320-0052
John Coyle, President
Robert Coyle, CFO
Bob Coyle, Vice Pres
EMP: 54 EST: 1999
SQ FT: 2,000
SALES: 136MM Privately Held
WEB: www.scripadvantage.com
SIC: 7389 Fund raising organizations

(P-17463)
SEARCH ENGINE OPTIMIZATION INC
5841 Edison Pl Ste 140, Carlsbad
(92008-6500)
PHONE.................................760 929-0039
Garry Grant, CEO
Krishnan Coughran, President
Yasser Aloosy, Engineer
Tyson Hymas, Director
Bryan Larkin, Director
EMP: 58
SQ FT: 15,000
SALES (est): 4.9MM Privately Held
WEB: www.seoinc.com
SIC: 7389 8742 Office facilities & secretarial service rental; marketing consulting services

(P-17464)
SEASIDE HOTEL LESSEE INC
Also Called: Viceroy Santa Monica
1819 Ocean Ave, Santa Monica
(90401-3215)
PHONE.................................310 260-7500
Janne Clare, General Mgr
Todd Yamakoa, General Mgr
Jay Thorson, Finance
EMP: 178
SALES: 26MM Privately Held
SIC: 7389 Hotel & motel reservation service; restaurant reservation service

(P-17465)
SEAVIEW INDUSTRIES
2501 Harbor Blvd, Costa Mesa
(92626-6143)
PHONE.................................714 957-5073
Tom Thomas, Manager
EMP: 50
SALES (est): 1.4MM Privately Held
WEB: www.seaviewgolf.com
SIC: 7389 Packaging & labeling services

(P-17466)
SERVICE CONTAINER COMPANY LLC
1754 Carr Rd Ste 204, Calexico
(92231-9509)
PHONE.................................858 391-7344
David Lenzen, Exec VP
Daniel Zdon, COO
Byron Wieberdink, CFO
Ronda Bayer, Vice Pres
Michael Snowball, Vice Pres
EMP: 75
SQ FT: 30,000
SALES (est): 4.1MM
SALES (corp-wide): 499.3MM Privately Held
WEB: www.servicecontainer.com
SIC: 7389 Packaging & labeling services
PA: Liberty Diversified International, Inc.
5600 Highway 169 N
New Hope MN 55428
763 536-6600

(P-17467)
SERVICE MASTER INDUSTRIES INC
2342 Meyers Ave, Escondido (92029-1008)
PHONE.................................760 480-0208
Mark Bower, General Mgr
Philip Fitzpatrick, President
Eylse Fitzpatrick, Vice Pres
Gerald Farley, Principal
EMP: 60
SALES (est): 4.1MM Privately Held
SIC: 7389 Personal service agents, brokers & bureaus

(P-17468)
SEVEN ONE INC (PA)
Also Called: Professional Tele Answering Svc
21540 Prairie St Ste E, Chatsworth
(91311-5814)
PHONE.................................818 904-3435
James Thompson, President
EMP: 83
SQ FT: 4,000
SALES (est): 5.1MM Privately Held
WEB: www.sevenone.com
SIC: 7389 Telephone answering service

(P-17469)
SHINWOO P&C USA INC
2177 Britannia Blvd # 203, San Diego
(92154-8307)
PHONE.................................619 407-7164
IL Kim, CEO
EMP: 600
SQ FT: 300
SALES (est): 43.5MM Privately Held
SIC: 7389 Packaging & labeling services

(P-17470)
SIGUE CORPORATION (PA)
13190 Telfair Ave, Sylmar (91342-3573)
PHONE.................................818 837-5939
Guillermo Dela Vina, CEO
Christina M Pappas, President
Alfredo Dela Vina, CFO
Enrique Carvajal, Vice Pres
Todd Sanders, General Mgr
EMP: 100
SQ FT: 3,000
SALES (est): 48.6MM Privately Held
SIC: 7389 4822 Financial services; telegraph & other communications

(P-17471)
SINECERA INC
Also Called: Crown Vly Precision Machining
5397 3rd St, Irwindale (91706-2085)
PHONE.................................626 962-1087
Mark M Miller, President
Lisa Miller, CFO
EMP: 80
SQ FT: 10,500
SALES (est): 8.8MM
SALES (corp-wide): 50.5MM Privately Held
SIC: 7389 Grinding, precision: commercial or industrial
PA: H-D Advanced Manufacturing Company
2200 Georgetown Dr # 300
Sewickley PA 15143
724 759-2850

(P-17472)
SKYBLUE SEWING MANUFACTURING
960 Mission St Fl 2, San Francisco
(94103-2911)
PHONE.................................415 777-9978
Huang Zhem, President
Freda Lau, Vice Pres
EMP: 50
SALES (est): 3MM Privately Held
SIC: 7389 Sewing contractor

(P-17473)
SMG FOOD AND BEVERAGE LLC (PA)
Also Called: Ontario Convention Center
2000 E Convention Ctr Way, Ontario
(91764-5633)
PHONE.................................909 937-3000
Victoria Van Damme, Mng Member
Dick Walsh, Mayor
John Burns,
Maureen Ginty,
EMP: 50
SALES (est): 12MM Privately Held
SIC: 7389 Convention & show services

(P-17474)
SMG HOLDINGS INC
848 M St Fl 2nd, Fresno (93721-2760)
PHONE.................................559 445-8100
William Overfelt, General Mgr
EMP: 336
SALES (corp-wide): 24.5B Privately Held
SIC: 7389 Convention & show services
HQ: Smg Holdings, Llc
300 Cnshohckn State Rd # 450
Conshohocken PA 19428
-

(P-17475)
SMITH-EMERY SAN FRANCISCO INC
1940 Oakdale Ave, San Francisco
(94124-2004)
P.O. Box 880550 (94188-0550)
PHONE.................................415 642-7326
James E Partridge, President
Helen Choe, CFO
EMP: 113
SQ FT: 10,160
SALES (est): 11.4MM Privately Held
SIC: 7389 8711 Inspection & testing services; engineering services

(P-17476)
SOBOBA BAND LUISENO INDIANS
Also Called: Soboba Casino
23333 Soboba Rd, San Jacinto (92583)
P.O. Box 817 (92581-0817)
PHONE.................................951 665-1000
Toll Free:.............................888 -
Richard Kline, Branch Mgr
Geneva Mojado, Vice Pres
Maggie Flynn, Purch Dir
Debbie Jordan, Purch Mgr
Shannon Hanna, Food Svc Dir
EMP: 900 Privately Held
WEB: www.soboba.com
SIC: 7389 7011 Personal service agents, brokers & bureaus; casino hotel
PA: Soboba Band Of Luiseno Indians
23906 Soboba Rd
San Jacinto CA 92583
951 654-2765

(P-17477)
SONY INTERACTIVE ENTRMT LLC (DH)
Also Called: Smss
2207 Bridgepointe Pkwy, Foster City
(94404-5060)
PHONE.................................310 981-1500
Sangita Patel, Vice Pres
Fumi Kanagawa, Exec VP
Ron Cushey, Vice Pres
EMP: 115
SALES (est): 74.6MM
SALES (corp-wide): 80.1B Privately Held
SIC: 7389 Music distribution systems
HQ: Sony Corporation Of America
25 Madison Ave Fl 27
New York NY 10010
212 833-8000

(P-17478)
SOROPTMIST INTL HUNTINGTON BCH
212 Utica Ave, Huntington Beach
(92648-2804)
PHONE.................................714 271-9305
Terry Rose, Partner
EMP: 50
SALES (est): 641.1K Privately Held
SIC: 7389

(P-17479)
SOUTHWEST DEALER SERVICES INC
1001 G St Ste 113, Sacramento
(95814-0834)
PHONE.................................925 753-0696
EMP: 150 Privately Held
SIC: 7389 Brokers, contract services
PA: Southwest Dealer Services, Inc.
8659 Research Dr Ste 100
Irvine CA 92618

(P-17480)
SOUTHWEST INSPECTION AND TSTG
Also Called: Southwest Inspection Testing
441 Commercial Way, La Habra
(90631-6168)
PHONE.................................562 941-2990
Steven L Godbey, President
Kathy Godbey, Treasurer
Charles L Godbey, Vice Pres
Jacob Godbey, Vice Pres
EMP: 75
SQ FT: 2,400
SALES (est): 8MM Privately Held
SIC: 7389 Building inspection service

(P-17481)
STACCATO COMMUNICATIONS INC
6195 Lusk Blvd Ste 200, San Diego
(92121-3723)
PHONE.................................858 812-0981
Rick Kornfeld, President
Marty Colombatto, Ch of Bd
Colin Macnab, COO
Mark Bowles, Vice Pres
Leopold B Mer, Vice Pres
EMP: 65
SALES (est): 2.9MM Privately Held
WEB: www.staccatocommunications.com
SIC: 7389 Personal service agents, brokers & bureaus

(P-17482)
STAGE II INC
Also Called: Stage II Design & Production
21 Channel Dr, Corte Madera
(94925-1845)
PHONE.................................415 285-8400
Chris McGregor, President
EMP: 50
SQ FT: 3,800
SALES (est): 3.5MM Privately Held
SIC: 7389 Decoration service for special events

(P-17483)
STANFORD LAW SCHL OFF FNCL AID
Crown Quadrangle 559, Stanford (94305)
PHONE.................................650 723-9247
Dewayne Barnes, Principal
EMP: 99
SALES: 950K Privately Held
SIC: 7389 Financial services

(P-17484)
STARCO GROUP INC
9160 Hyssop Dr, Rancho Cucamonga
(91730-6100)
PHONE.................................909 989-9898
Lin Lou, Administration
EMP: 60
SALES (est): 5MM Privately Held
SIC: 7389

(P-17485)

STERICYCLE COMM SOLUTIONS INC

2255 Watt Ave Ste 50, Sacramento
(95825-0504)
PHONE..................................888 370-6711
Gail Dawson, *Branch Mgr*
EMP: 54
SALES (corp-wide): 3.5B **Publicly Held**
SIC: 7389 Telephone answering service
HQ: Stericycle Communication Solutions,
Inc.
4010 Commercial Ave
Northbrook IL 60062
866 783-9820

(P-17486)

STERICYCLE COMM SOLUTIONS INC

612 S Harbor Blvd, Anaheim (92805-4526)
PHONE..................................714 991-9595
Jamie Lloyd, *Branch Mgr*
EMP: 50
SALES (corp-wide): 3.5B **Publicly Held**
SIC: 7389 Telephone answering service
HQ: Stericycle Communication Solutions,
Inc.
4010 Commercial Ave
Northbrook IL 60062
866 783-9820

(P-17487)

STERILE PROC SVCS AMER LLC

2240 E Artesia Blvd, Long Beach
(90805-1739)
PHONE..................................562 428-5858
Jacob Anderson,
Greg Anderson,
EMP: 50
SQ FT: 36,000
SALES (est): 1.1MM **Privately Held**
SIC: 7389 7349 Product sterilization serv-
ice; hospital housekeeping

(P-17488)

STERLING HSA INC

475 14th St Ste 120, Oakland
(94612-1900)
P.O. Box 71107 (94612-7207)
PHONE..................................800 617-4729
Cora M Tellez, *President*
Duarte Vatista, *COO*
Mark Maltun, *CFO*
Chris Bettner, *Exec VP*
Dawn West, *VP Finance*
EMP: 50
SALES (est): 7.2MM **Privately Held**
WEB: www.sterlinghsa.com
SIC: 7389 Financial services

(P-17489)

STRATEGIC OPERATIONS INC

4705 Ruffin Rd, San Diego (92123-1611)
PHONE..................................858 244-0559
Stuart Segall, *CEO*
EMP: 250
SQ FT: 12,000
SALES (est): 30.8MM **Privately Held**
WEB: www.strategic-operations.com
SIC: 7389 Personal service agents, bro-
kers & bureaus

(P-17490)

SUGAR FOODS CORPORATION

Also Called: Sygma Network, The
9500 El Dorado Ave, Sun Valley
(91352-1339)
PHONE..................................818 768-7900
Stephen Odell, *Partner*
EMP: 200
SALES (corp-wide): 286.3MM **Privately
Held**
WEB: www.sugarfoods.com
SIC: 7389 2099 2062 Packaging & label-
ing services; food preparations; cane
sugar refining
PA: Sugar Foods Corporation
950 3rd Ave Fl 21
New York NY 10022
212 753-6900

(P-17491)

SUGAR FOODS CORPORATION

Also Called: General Brands Packing
9500 El Dorado Ave, Sun Valley
(91352-1339)
PHONE..................................818 768-7900
Steven Odell, *Branch Mgr*
EMP: 100
SQ FT: 60,000
SALES (corp-wide): 294.2MM **Privately
Held**
WEB: www.sugarfoods.com
SIC: 7389 Packaging & labeling services
PA: Sugar Foods Corporation
950 3rd Ave Fl 21
New York NY 10022
212 753-6900

(P-17492)

SUN LIGHT & POWER

1035 Folger Ave, Berkeley (94710-2819)
PHONE..................................510 845-2997
Gary Gerber, *President*
Troy Tyler, *COO*
Zachary Gill, *Officer*
Margarette T Maceda, *Admin Asst*
Erinne Davis, *Project Mgr*
EMP: 63
SQ FT: 10,000
SALES (est): 11.3MM **Privately Held**
WEB: www.sunlightandpower.com
SIC: 7389 1796 3433 Design services;
power generating equipment installation;
solar heaters & collectors

(P-17493)

SUTTER HOME WINERY INC

Also Called: Trinchero Family Estates
18655 Jacob Brack Rd, Lodi (95242-9185)
PHONE..................................707 963-5928
EMP: 148
SALES (corp-wide): 196.8MM **Privately
Held**
SIC: 7389 Automobile recovery service
PA: Sutter Home Winery, Inc.
100 Saint Helena Hwy S
Saint Helena CA 94574
707 963-3104

(P-17494)

TACTICAL TELESOLUTIONS INC

2121 N California Blvd, Walnut Creek
(94596-3572)
PHONE..................................415 788-8808
Laura Hylton, *President*
Kurt Stenzel, *Vice Pres*
Kathy O'Toole, *Technology*
Kema Riley, *Technology*
Matt Weimer, *Technology*
EMP: 130
SQ FT: 15,000
SALES (est): 13.2MM **Privately Held**
WEB: www.tts-sf.com
SIC: 7389 Telemarketing services

(P-17495)

TALENTBURST INC

575 Market St Ste 3025, San Francisco
(94105-5840)
PHONE..................................415 813-4011
Kevin Callanan, *Vice Pres*
EMP: 115
SALES (corp-wide): 26.7MM **Privately
Held**
SIC: 7389 7375 Check validation service;
information retrieval services
PA: Talentburst, Inc.
679 Worcester St
Natick MA 01760
508 628-7516

(P-17496)

TATA COMMUNICATIONS AMER INC

Also Called: Bitgravity
700 Airport Blvd Ste 100, Burlingame
(94010-1931)
PHONE..................................650 262-0004
Srinivasan Cr, *Vice Pres*
Mehul Kapadia, *Managing Dir*
Alain Dessaire, *Network Enginr*
Aakratee Saini, *Technical Staff*
Ali Mohammad Fouladgar, *Engineer*
EMP: 62 **Privately Held**
SIC: 7389 Music & broadcasting services

HQ: Tata Communications (America) Inc.
2355 Dulles Corner Blvd # 700
Herndon VA 20171
703 657-8400

(P-17497)

TBWA CHIAT/DAY INC

5353 Grosvenor Blvd, Los Angeles
(90066-6913)
PHONE..................................310 305-5000
Lee Clow, *Branch Mgr*
Tanya Lesieur, *Officer*
Robin Rossi, *Executive*
Walter Velasquez, *QA Dir*
Khalid Best, *Graphic Designe*
EMP: 88
SALES (corp-wide): 15.2B **Publicly Held**
SIC: 7389 Interior design services
HQ: Tbwa Chiat/Day Inc.
488 Madison Ave Fl 7
New York NY 10022
212 804-1000

(P-17498)

TEAM SAN JOSE

408 Almaden Blvd, San Jose (95110-2709)
PHONE..................................408 295-9600
Karolyn Kirchgesler, *CEO*
Dave Costain, *COO*
Janette Divol, *CFO*
Janette Sutton, *CFO*
Kyle Schatzel, *Comms Mgr*
EMP: 900
SQ FT: 300,000
SALES: 8MM **Privately Held**
SIC: 7389 Convention & show services

(P-17499)

TECHNICON DESIGN CORPORATION

26522 La Alameda Ste 150, Mission Viejo
(92691-6545)
PHONE..................................949 218-1300
David Shall, *President*
Helen Thomas, *Exec VP*
Helen Carstens, *General Mgr*
Frank Goodchild, *Business Mgr*
Monica Chavez, *Recruiter*
EMP: 120
SQ FT: 1,000
SALES: 11.6MM
SALES (corp-wide): 21.3MM **Privately
Held**
WEB: www.techniconims.com
SIC: 7389 Design services
PA: Technicon Design Limited
Technicon House
Luton BEDS LU1 3
158 250-6600

(P-17500)

TEKWORKS INC (PA)

13000 Gregg St Ste B, Poway
(92064-7151)
PHONE..................................858 668-1705
William E Bourgeois, *CEO*
Dale Bourgeois, *Vice Pres*
Ryan Hardesty, *Vice Pres*
Dave Novak, *Vice Pres*
Brandon Watson, *Vice Pres*
EMP: 130
SALES (est): 44.7MM **Privately Held**
WEB: www.tekworkscomm.com
SIC: 7389 1731 Advertising, promotional &
trade show services; electrical work

(P-17501)

TELE-DIRECT COMMUNICATIONS

4741 Madison Ave Ste 200, Sacramento
(95841-2580)
PHONE..................................916 348-2170
A James Puff, *Chairman*
Thomas Coshow, *CEO*
Sandra Coggeshall, *Exec VP*
Jamei Puff, *Sales/Mktg Mgr*
EMP: 75
SQ FT: 6,000
SALES (est): 6.5MM **Privately Held**
WEB: www.tele-direct.com
SIC: 7389 5999 Telemarketing services;
telephone & communication equipment

(P-17502)

TELE-INTERPRETERS LLC

1 Lower Ragsdale Dr # 2, Monterey
(93940-5747)
P.O. Box 202572, Dallas TX (75320-2572)
PHONE..................................800 811-7881
Melanie Coto-Trevor,
EMP: 500
SQ FT: 10,000
SALES (est): 11.7MM
SALES (corp-wide): 126.1MM **Privately
Held**
WEB: www.teleinterpreters.com
SIC: 7389 Translation services
HQ: Language Line, Llc
1 Lower Ragsdale Dr # 2
Monterey CA 93940
831 648-5800

(P-17503)

TELECNTRIC COMMUNICATIONS INTL

12070 Telg Rd Ste 107, Santa Fe Springs
(90670)
PHONE..................................562 906-2555
CM Lee, *Owner*
EMP: 75
SALES (est): 920.2K **Privately Held**
SIC: 7389 Financial services

(P-17504)

TELECOM EVOLUTIONS LLC

9221 Corbin Ave Ste 260, Northridge
(91324-1625)
PHONE..................................818 264-4400
James Murphy, *Mng Member*
EMP: 50 EST: 2010
SALES: 22MM **Privately Held**
SIC: 7389 Telephone services

(P-17505)

TELECOM INC

2201 Broadway Ste 103, Oakland
(94612-3028)
PHONE..................................510 873-8283
Jon Martin, *President*
LI Tao, *CFO*
Greg Haggerty, *CTO*
Carlos Amaya, *Opers Mgr*
Lani Stackel, *Mktg Dir*
EMP: 100
SALES (est): 8.7MM **Privately Held**
WEB: www.telecominc.com
SIC: 7389 4813 8742 Telemarketing serv-
ices; data telephone communications;
marketing consulting services

(P-17506)

TEXAS INSTRUMENTS SUNNYVALE

165 Gibraltar Ct, Sunnyvale (94089-1301)
PHONE..................................408 541-9900
Andrew Hartland, *CFO*
EMP: 50
SQ FT: 12,070
SALES (est): 1.6MM
SALES (corp-wide): 14.9B **Publicly Held**
WEB: www.ti.com
SIC: 7389 Design services
PA: Texas Instruments Incorporated
12500 Ti Blvd
Dallas TX 75243
214 479-3773

(P-17507)

THOMPSON & RICH CRANE SERVICE

2373 E Mariposa Rd, Stockton
(95205-7811)
P.O. Box 30035 (95213-0035)
PHONE..................................209 465-3161
EMP: 50 EST: 1988
SALES (est): 2.5MM **Privately Held**
SIC: 7389

(P-17508)

THOMSON REUTERS (MARKETS) LLC

1 Sansome St, San Francisco
(94104-4448)
PHONE..................................415 677-2500
Ben Silverman, *Manager*
EMP: 60 **Publicly Held**
WEB: www.reuters.com

P R O D U C T S & S V C S

SIC: 7389 Personal service agents, brokers & bureaus
HQ: Reuters America Llc
3 Times Sq
New York NY 10036
646 223-4000

(P-17509)
THOUSAND OAKS PRTG & SPC INC
Also Called: T/O Printing
5334 Sterling Center Dr, Westlake Village (91361-4612)
PHONE............................818 706-8330
Steve Mahr, President
Lori Abrams, Admin Asst
Michael Berry, Administration
Beth Digirolamo, Human Res Dir
Ken Doolittle, Accounts Mgr
▲ EMP: 140
SQ FT: 60,000
SALES (est): 21.8MM
SALES (corp-wide): 6.9B Publicly Held
WEB: www.toprinting.com
SIC: 7389 2752 Printing broker; commercial printing, offset
HQ: Consolidated Graphics, Inc.
5858 Westheimer Rd # 400
Houston TX 77057
713 787-0977

(P-17510)
THYDE INC (PA)
300 El Sobrante Rd, Corona (92879-5757)
PHONE............................951 817-2300
Tim Hyde, President
EMP: 250
SQ FT: 70,000
SALES (est): 52.5MM Privately Held
WEB: www.hydeandhyde.com
SIC: 7389 Packaging & labeling services

(P-17511)
TIDAVATER INC
Also Called: Le Courier
2107 W Alameda Ave, Burbank (91506-2934)
PHONE............................818 848-4151
Fax: 818 848-5294
EMP: 150
SQ FT: 3,000
SALES (est): 5.2MM Privately Held
SIC: 7389 4513 4215

(P-17512)
TOMMY BAHAMA GROUP INC
610 Ventura Blvd Ste 1340, Camarillo (93010-5869)
PHONE............................805 482-8868
Janet Infante, Branch Mgr
EMP: 112
SALES (corp-wide): 1B Publicly Held
SIC: 7389 Apparel designers, commercial
HQ: Tommy Bahama Group, Inc.
400 Fairview Ave N # 488
Seattle WA 98109

(P-17513)
TOMMY BAHAMA GROUP INC
1720 Redwood Hwy Spc A019, Corte Madera (94925-1249)
PHONE............................415 737-0400
EMP: 112
SALES (corp-wide): 1B Publicly Held
SIC: 7389 Apparel designers, commercial
HQ: Tommy Bahama Group, Inc.
400 Fairview Ave N # 488
Seattle WA 98109

(P-17514)
TOWN & COUNTRY EVENT RENTALS
1 N Calle Cesar Chavez # 7, Santa Barbara (93103-5614)
PHONE............................805 770-5729
EMP: 400
SALES (corp-wide): 28MM Privately Held
SIC: 7389 Personal service agents, brokers & bureaus
PA: Town & Country Event Rentals, Inc
7725 Airport Bus Pkwy
Van Nuys CA 91406
818 908-4211

(P-17515)
TRAFFIC MANAGEMENT INC
Also Called: TMI
690 Quinn Ave, San Jose (95112-2635)
PHONE............................877 763-5999
Tina Becker, Branch Mgr
EMP: 50 Privately Held
SIC: 7389 8741 Flagging service (traffic control); management services
PA: Traffic Management, Inc.
2435 Lemon Ave
Signal Hill CA 90755
-

(P-17516)
TRAFFIC MANAGEMENT INC (PA)
2435 Lemon Ave, Signal Hill (90755-3462)
PHONE............................562 595-4278
Christopher H Spano, CEO
Jonathan Spano, COO
Micheel Spreuse, Senior VP
William Kearney, Vice Pres
Michael Flanagan, Regional Mgr
EMP: 144
SQ FT: 20,000
SALES (est): 206.5MM Privately Held
SIC: 7389 8741 Flagging service (traffic control); business management

(P-17517)
TRAILBLAZER TECHNOLOGIES
Also Called: Transcription Company, The
4100 W Burbank Blvd Fl 3, Burbank (91505-2121)
PHONE............................818 848-6500
Rich Brownstein, President
EMP: 60
SALES (est): 1.9MM Privately Held
SIC: 7389 Music & broadcasting services

(P-17518)
TRANS-PAK INCORPORATED
Also Called: Transpak Los Angeles
2601 S Garnsey St, Santa Ana (92707-3338)
PHONE............................310 618-6937
Charles Frasier, Principal
EMP: 108
SALES (corp-wide): 187.9MM Privately Held
SIC: 7389 Packaging & labeling services
PA: Transpak, Inc.
520 Marburg Way
San Jose CA 95133
408 254-0500

(P-17519)
TRANSPAK INC (PA)
520 Marburg Way, San Jose (95133-1619)
PHONE............................408 254-0500
Arlene Inch, Chairman
Bob Lally, President
Bert Inch, CEO
Ray Horner, COO
Chris Lee, CFO
EMP: 175
SALES: 187.9MM Privately Held
WEB: www.transpak.com
SIC: 7389 Packaging & labeling services

(P-17520)
TRAP
Also Called: Task Force For Reg Autostaff
1833 S Mountain Ave, Monrovia (91016-4270)
PHONE............................626 572-5610
EMP: 80
SALES (est): 2.4MM Privately Held
SIC: 7389

(P-17521)
TRILLIANT NETWORKS INC (PA)
1100 Island Dr Ste 201, Redwood City (94065-5187)
PHONE............................650 204-5050
Andy White, Principal
Mike Mortimer, Exec VP
Norma Formanek, Senior VP
Ryan Gerbrandt, Senior VP
Paul Karr, Senior VP
EMP: 65
SALES (est): 43.7MM Privately Held
SIC: 7389 Meter readers, remote

(P-17522)
TRILOGY FINANCIAL SERVICES INC (PA)
17011 Beach Blvd Ste 800, Huntington Beach (92647-5995)
PHONE............................714 843-9977
Jeff Motske, President
Ed Ghulamali, Managing Prtnr
Scott Naiman, Managing Prtnr
Joe Sirgy, Managing Prtnr
Gary Sussman, Managing Prtnr
EMP: 150
SQ FT: 6,500
SALES (est): 12.8MM Privately Held
WEB: www.asktrilogy.com
SIC: 7389 Financial services

(P-17523)
TRILOGY FINANCIAL SERVICES INC
12520 High Bluff Dr # 140, San Diego (92130-2061)
PHONE............................858 755-6696
Doug Stroot, Manager
Scott Babbitt, Vice Pres
Sean Covi, Vice Pres
Isaac Hansen, Vice Pres
Tom Bennett, Train & Dev Mgr
EMP: 50
SALES (est): 2MM
SALES (corp-wide): 12.8MM Privately Held
WEB: www.asktrilogy.com
SIC: 7389 Financial services
PA: Trilogy Financial Services, Inc.
17011 Beach Blvd Ste 800
Huntington Beach CA 92647
714 843-9977

(P-17524)
TRIMARK RAYGAL LLC
210 Commerce, Irvine (92602-1318)
PHONE............................949 474-1000
Victor Scott Moore, President
Eric Smith, Vice Pres
Dirk Hallett, Admin Sec
Gail Garvin-Golley, Administration
Dale Osburn, Director
EMP: 83
SQ FT: 21,000
SALES (est): 16.3MM
SALES (corp-wide): 6.3B Privately Held
WEB: www.raygal.com
SIC: 7389 Interior designer
HQ: Trimark Usa, Llc
505 Collins St
Attleboro MA 02703
508 399-2400

(P-17525)
TRINITY PACKING COMPANY INC
18700 E South Ave, Reedley (93654-9711)
PHONE............................559 743-3913
David E White, Branch Mgr
EMP: 294
SALES (corp-wide): 30MM Privately Held
SIC: 7389 Packaging & labeling services
PA: Trinity Packing Company, Inc.
7571 N Remington Ave # 104
Fresno CA 93711
559 433-3785

(P-17526)
TWO JINN INC (PA)
Also Called: Aladdin Bail Bonds
1000 Aviara Dr Ste 300, Carlsbad (92011-4218)
PHONE............................760 431-9911
Robert H Hayes, Ch of Bd
Leah Taniguchi, Controller
Sherry Tipps, Human Res Dir
EMP: 75
SALES (est): 53MM Privately Held
WEB: www.twojinn.com
SIC: 7389 Bail bonding

(P-17527)
UBS FINANCIAL SERVICES INC
50 W San Fernando St Fl 8, San Jose (95113-2414)
PHONE............................408 282-8402
Kirk Mandlin, Manager
John Moran, Vice Pres

Nancy Ubaldi, Vice Pres
Richard Gamboa, Agent
EMP: 50
SALES (corp-wide): 29.4B Privately Held
SIC: 7389 Financial services
HQ: Ubs Financial Services Inc.
1285 Ave Of The Americas
New York NY 10019
212 713-2000

(P-17528)
UBS FINANCIAL SERVICES INC
3801 University Ave # 300, Riverside (92501-3264)
PHONE............................951 684-6300
James Gallegos, Manager
EMP: 50
SALES (corp-wide): 29.4B Privately Held
SIC: 7389 Brokers, business: buying & selling business enterprises; authors' agents & brokers; speakers' bureau
HQ: Ubs Financial Services Inc.
1285 Ave Of The Americas
New York NY 10019
212 713-2000

(P-17529)
UBS FINANCIAL SERVICES INC
1200 Prospect St Ste 100, La Jolla (92037-3608)
P.O. Box 2268 (92038-2268)
PHONE............................858 454-9181
Lee Tripodi, Manager
Gary Goldmann, Vice Pres
Kurt Hoffman, Vice Pres
John Seiber, Vice Pres
Stephen Seiber, Vice Pres
EMP: 60
SALES (corp-wide): 29.4B Privately Held
SIC: 7389 Financial services; authors' agents & brokers; speakers' bureau
HQ: Ubs Financial Services Inc.
1285 Ave Of The Americas
New York NY 10019
212 713-2000

(P-17530)
UBS FINANCIAL SERVICES INC
200 S Los Robles Ave # 600, Pasadena (91101-4600)
PHONE............................626 449-1501
Donald Gorsch, Manager
Michael Naples, Advisor
EMP: 50
SALES (corp-wide): 29.4B Privately Held
SIC: 7389 Financial services
HQ: Ubs Financial Services Inc.
1285 Ave Of The Americas
New York NY 10019
212 713-2000

(P-17531)
UFS INTERNATIONAL LLC
16871 Millikan Ave, Irvine (92606-5011)
PHONE............................714 713-6311
Travis Phan, Owner
Robert Hrifko, COO
EMP: 150
SQ FT: 17,000
SALES (est): 10.8MM Privately Held
SIC: 7389 5044 7371 Financial services; office equipment; custom computer programming services

(P-17532)
UNITED EXCHANGE CORP (PA)
Also Called: Uec
5836 Corp Ave Ste 200, Cypress (90630)
PHONE............................562 977-4500
Eugene W Choi, CEO
Carol J Choi, President
Sean Akutagawa, Technology
Lynn Chang, Controller
Tom Blaylock, Opers Staff
EMP: 51
SQ FT: 100,000
SALES (est): 80MM Privately Held
WEB: www.ueccorp.com
SIC: 7389 5122 Packaging & labeling services; drugs, proprietaries & sundries

(P-17533)
UNITED EXPRESS MESSENGERS INC
1801 Century Park E # 520, Los Angeles (90067-2307)
PHONE..................310 261-2000
Shahin Abrishamchian, *President*
EMP: 60
SQ FT: 3,000
SALES (est): 4.8MM **Privately Held**
SIC: 7389 4212 Courier or messenger service; delivery service, vehicular

(P-17534)
UNITED PARCEL SERVICE INC
Also Called: UPS
14592 Palmdale Rd, Victorville (92392-2754)
PHONE..................760 241-5540
Hannah Chung, *Principal*
EMP: 1700
SALES (corp-wide): 65.8B **Publicly Held**
SIC: 7389 Mailbox rental & related service
PA: United Parcel Service, Inc.
55 Glenlake Pkwy
Atlanta GA 30328
404 828-6000

(P-17535)
UNITED PARCEL SERVICE INC OH
Also Called: UPS
3331 Industrial Dr Ste C, Santa Rosa (95403-2062)
PHONE..................678 339-3171
Karen Geerdes, *Manager*
EMP: 635
SALES (corp-wide): 65.8B **Publicly Held**
SIC: 7389 Mailbox rental & related service
HQ: United Parcel Service, Inc. (Oh)
55 Glenlake Pkwy
Atlanta GA 30328
404 828-6000

(P-17536)
UNITED PARCEL SERVICE INC OH
Also Called: UPS
2747 Vail Ave, Commerce (90040-2611)
PHONE..................323 837-1220
Steven Hill, *Principal*
Aracely Preciado, *Sales Staff*
EMP: 316
SALES (corp-wide): 65.8B **Publicly Held**
SIC: 7389 Mailing & messenger services
HQ: United Parcel Service, Inc. (Oh)
55 Glenlake Pkwy
Atlanta GA 30328
404 828-6000

(P-17537)
UNITED PARCEL SERVICE INC OH
Also Called: UPS
22 Brookline, Aliso Viejo (92656-1461)
PHONE..................949 643-6634
EMP: 316
SALES (corp-wide): 65.8B **Publicly Held**
SIC: 7389 Telephone services
HQ: United Parcel Service, Inc. (Oh)
55 Glenlake Pkwy
Atlanta GA 30328
404 828-6000

(P-17538)
UNITED PARCEL SERVICE INC OH
Also Called: UPS
3221 E Jurupa, Ontario (91764)
PHONE..................909 974-7250
Richard Ricardo, *General Mgr*
EMP: 635
SALES (corp-wide): 65.8B **Publicly Held**
WEB: www.upsscs.com
SIC: 7389 Mailbox rental & related service
HQ: United Parcel Service, Inc. (Oh)
55 Glenlake Pkwy
Atlanta GA 30328
404 828-6000

(P-17539)
UNITED PARCEL SERVICE INC OH
Also Called: UPS
1746 D St, South Lake Tahoe (96150-6227)
PHONE..................800 742-5877
EMP: 316
SALES (corp-wide): 65.8B **Publicly Held**
SIC: 7389 Personal service agents, brokers & bureaus
HQ: United Parcel Service, Inc. (Oh)
55 Glenlake Pkwy
Atlanta GA 30328
404 828-6000

(P-17540)
UNITED PARCEL SERVICE INC OH
Also Called: UPS
201 W Garvey Ave Ste 102, Monterey Park (91754-7425)
PHONE..................626 280-8012
Francis Fong, *Owner*
EMP: 635
SALES (corp-wide): 65.8B **Publicly Held**
WEB: www.upsscs.com
SIC: 7389 Mailing & messenger services
HQ: United Parcel Service, Inc. (Oh)
55 Glenlake Pkwy
Atlanta GA 30328
404 828-6000

(P-17541)
UNITED PARCEL SERVICE INC OH
Also Called: UPS
4607 Lakeview Canyon Rd, Westlake Village (91361-4028)
PHONE..................818 735-0945
Jim Penna, *Manager*
Jim Latenna, *Manager*
Howard Silber, *Manager*
EMP: 635
SALES (corp-wide): 65.8B **Publicly Held**
WEB: www.upsscs.com
SIC: 7389 Mailing & messenger services
HQ: United Parcel Service, Inc. (Oh)
55 Glenlake Pkwy
Atlanta GA 30328
404 828-6000

(P-17542)
UNITED PARCEL SERVICE INC OH
Also Called: UPS
11811 Landon Dr, Mira Loma (91752-4002)
PHONE..................951 749-3400
Paul Slater, *Principal*
Brandon Baxter, *Project Mgr*
Rita Avila, *Manager*
EMP: 316
SALES (corp-wide): 65.8B **Publicly Held**
SIC: 7389 Mailing & messenger services
HQ: United Parcel Service, Inc. (Oh)
55 Glenlake Pkwy
Atlanta GA 30328
404 828-6000

(P-17543)
UNITED PARCEL SERVICE INC OH
Also Called: UPS
48921 Warm Springs Blvd, Fremont (94539-7767)
PHONE..................800 742-5877
EMP: 316
SALES (corp-wide): 65.8B **Publicly Held**
SIC: 7389 Personal service agents, brokers & bureaus
HQ: United Parcel Service, Inc. (Oh)
55 Glenlake Pkwy
Atlanta GA 30328
404 828-6000

(P-17544)
UNITED PARCEL SERVICE INC OH
Also Called: UPS
91 W Easy St, Simi Valley (93065-1601)
PHONE..................866 553-1069
Louis Moody, *Principal*
EMP: 316

SALES (corp-wide): 65.8B **Publicly Held**
SIC: 7389 Mailing & messenger services
HQ: United Parcel Service, Inc. (Oh)
55 Glenlake Pkwy
Atlanta GA 30328
404 828-6000

(P-17545)
UNITED PAYMENT SERVICES INC
3537 Old Conejo Rd # 113, Newbury Park (91320-2157)
PHONE..................866 886-4833
Scott Rosen, *President*
Craig Rosen, *COO*
EMP: 480
SQ FT: 15,000
SALES: 4.1MM **Privately Held**
WEB: www.unitedpaymentservices.com
SIC: 7389 Credit card service

(P-17546)
UNITY COURIER SERVICE INC
1132 Beecher St, San Leandro (94577-1252)
PHONE..................510 568-8890
Michael Wynant, *Branch Mgr*
EMP: 60
SALES (corp-wide): 64.3MM **Privately Held**
WEB: www.unitycourier.com
SIC: 7389 Courier or messenger service
PA: Unity Courier Service, Inc.
3231 Fletcher Dr
Los Angeles CA 90065
323 255-9800

(P-17547)
UNIVERSAL CARD INC
Also Called: Merchant Services
9012 Research Dr Ste 200, Irvine (92618-4254)
PHONE..................949 861-4000
Jason W Moore, *President*
Robert Parisi, *Regional Mgr*
Beth Huebner, *Human Res Mgr*
Paul Burt, *Recruiter*
Nathan Jurczyk, *VP Opers*
EMP: 400
SQ FT: 40,000
SALES (est): 35.8MM **Privately Held**
WEB: www.merchantsvcs.com
SIC: 7389 Credit card service

(P-17548)
UNIVERSAL MUS INVESTMENTS INC (HQ)
2220 Colorado Ave, Santa Monica (90404-3506)
PHONE..................818 577-4700
Lucian C Grainge, *CEO*
Wendy Goldstein, *Senior VP*
Alasdair J McMullan, *Vice Pres*
Bernie Tan, *Associate Dir*
Marcella Gaither, *Principal*
EMP: 80
SALES (est): 24.9MM
SALES (corp-wide): 78.4MM **Privately Held**
SIC: 7389 7929 Music recording producer; musical entertainers; musicians
PA: Vivendi
42 Avenue De Friedland
Paris 75008
171 711-000

(P-17549)
UNIVERSAL MUSIC GROUP INC (HQ)
2220 Colorado Ave, Santa Monica (90404-3506)
PHONE..................310 865-4000
Lucian Grainge, *Co-CEO*
Mauro Deceglie, *Partner*
Jules Ferree, *Partner*
Darcus Beese, *President*
Joie Manda, *President*
▲ **EMP:** 100
SALES (est): 502MM
SALES (corp-wide): 78.4MM **Privately Held**
SIC: 7389 2741 Music recording producer; miscellaneous publishing

PA: Vivendi
42 Avenue De Friedland
Paris 75008
171 711-000

(P-17550)
UNIVERSAL MUSIC GROUP INC
10 Universal City Plz, Universal City (91608)
PHONE..................818 286-4000
Kent Earls, *Branch Mgr*
Ron Stuve, *Vice Pres*
Laura Jameson, *Exec Dir*
Tara Miller, *Controller*
Sarah Palmer, *Human Res Mgr*
EMP: 50
SALES (corp-wide): 78.4MM **Privately Held**
SIC: 7389 Music recording producer
HQ: Universal Music Group, Inc.
2220 Colorado Ave
Santa Monica CA 90404
310 865-4000

(P-17551)
UNIVERSITY STUDENT UNION INC
5151 State University Dr, Los Angeles (90032-4226)
PHONE..................323 343-2450
Joseph Aguirre, *Exec Dir*
Rowena Tran, *Asst Director*
EMP: 110
SALES (est): 3.6MM **Privately Held**
SIC: 7389 Personal service agents, brokers & bureaus

(P-17552)
UPS STORE INC (HQ)
Also Called: Mail Boxes Etc
6060 Cornerstone Ct W, San Diego (92121-3712)
PHONE..................858 455-8800
Walter T Davis, *CEO*
Tim Davis, *President*
Jeffrey Alianiello, *Vice Pres*
Kevin Foley, *Vice Pres*
Don Higginson, *Vice Pres*
EMP: 148
SQ FT: 66,000
SALES (est): 75.5MM
SALES (corp-wide): 65.8B **Publicly Held**
WEB: www.ups.com
SIC: 7389 8742 4783 Mailbox rental & related service; printers' services: folding, collating; packaging & labeling services; business consultant; packing goods for shipping
PA: United Parcel Service, Inc.
55 Glenlake Pkwy
Atlanta GA 30328
404 828-6000

(P-17553)
US BANKCARD SERVICES INC
17171 Gale Ave Ste 110, City of Industry (91745-1822)
PHONE..................888 888-8872
Christopher J Chang, *President*
EMP: 75
SQ FT: 3,000
SALES (est): 7.4MM **Privately Held**
WEB: www.topmsp.com
SIC: 7389 Credit card service

(P-17554)
US MERCHANTS FINCL GROUP INC
1625 Proforma Ave, Ontario (91761-7607)
PHONE..................909 923-3388
Larry Khemlani, *Manager*
Larry Khemlani, *Manager*
Cynthia Mayen, *Manager*
EMP: 150
SALES (corp-wide): 206.8MM **Privately Held**
SIC: 7389 7922 Personal service agents, brokers & bureaus; theatrical producers & services
PA: U.S. Merchants Financial Group, Inc.
1118 S La Cienega Blvd
Los Angeles CA 90035
310 855-1946

PRODUCTS & SVCS

(P-17555)
V A ANDERSON ENTERPRISES INC (PA)
Also Called: Kopy Kat Attorney Service
400 Atlas St, Brea (92821-3117)
P.O. Box 1029 (92822-1029)
PHONE..............................714 990-6100
Pat Flynn, *President*
Bob Flynn, *Vice Pres*
Perry Miller, *Manager*
EMP: 62
SQ FT: 10,000
SALES (est): 7.4MM **Privately Held**
WEB: www.kopykat.net
SIC: 7389 Microfilm recording & developing service

(P-17556)
V G CARELLI INTERNATIONAL CORP
1 Park Plz Ste 600, Irvine (92614-5987)
PHONE..............................310 247-8410
Vittorio G Carelli, *President*
Rebecca Mansdorf, *Director*
EMP: 50
SALES (est): 1.6MM **Privately Held**
SIC: 7389 Personal service agents, brokers & bureaus

(P-17557)
VALLEY INVENTORY SERVICE INC
1180 Horizon Dr Ste B, Fairfield (94533-1693)
P.O. Box 503 (94533-0050)
PHONE..............................707 422-6050
Jeffrey J Link, *President*
Veronica Link, *President*
Jack Link, *General Mgr*
Victoria Pellinen, *Manager*
EMP: 100 EST: 1970
SALES (est): 8.2MM **Privately Held**
WEB: www.valleycount.com
SIC: 7389 Inventory computing service

(P-17558)
VALLEY PRODUCTIONS INC
17247 La Canada Rd, Madera (93636-9249)
PHONE..............................559 661-6121
John Paye,
Steve Arsenault,
EMP: 50
SQ FT: 3,000
SALES (est): 1.5MM **Privately Held**
SIC: 7389 7922 Fund raising organizations; entertainment promotion

(P-17559)
VASTEK INC
1230 Columbia St Ste 1180, San Diego (92101-8520)
PHONE..............................925 948-5701
Vikash Mishra, *CEO*
Murry Vastek, *Tech Recruiter*
Suraj Sinha, *Recruiter*
EMP: 171
SQ FT: 1,600
SALES: 10.7MM **Privately Held**
SIC: 7389 7371 Air pollution measuring service; custom computer programming services

(P-17560)
VENTURE DESIGN SERVICES INC
451 Aviation Blvd Ste 215, Santa Rosa (95403-1055)
PHONE..............................707 524-8368
Robert Eves, *Branch Mgr*
EMP: 64
SALES (corp-wide): 13MM **Privately Held**
SIC: 7389 Design services
PA: Venture Design Services Inc.
1051 S East St
Anaheim CA 92805
714 765-3740

(P-17561)
VERIZON COMMUNICATIONS INC
2001 Broadway Fl 1, Santa Monica (90404-2909)
PHONE..............................310 315-7597
Steve Campanion, *Principal*
Suzanne L Haskell, *Sales Staff*
EMP: 60
SALES (corp-wide): 126B **Publicly Held**
WEB: www.gte.com
SIC: 7389 Telephone services
PA: Verizon Communications Inc.
1095 Ave Of The Americas
New York NY 10036
212 395-1000

(P-17562)
VERIZON COMMUNICATIONS INC
2801 Townsgate Rd Ste 300, Westlake Village (91361-3040)
PHONE..............................805 390-5417
Connie Murphree, *General Mgr*
EMP: 120
SALES (corp-wide): 126B **Publicly Held**
WEB: www.verizon.com
SIC: 7389 4812 Telemarketing services; radio telephone communication
PA: Verizon Communications Inc.
1095 Ave Of The Americas
New York NY 10036
212 395-1000

(P-17563)
VERIZON COMMUNICATIONS INC
18442 Arminta St, Reseda (91335-2012)
PHONE..............................818 438-1104
Randy Green, *Principal*
EMP: 744
SALES (corp-wide): 126B **Publicly Held**
SIC: 7389 Personal service agents, brokers & bureaus
PA: Verizon Communications Inc.
1095 Ave Of The Americas
New York NY 10036
212 395-1000

(P-17564)
VERIZON COMMUNICATIONS INC
18850 Orange St, Bloomington (92316-2425)
PHONE..............................909 421-5053
David Edmund, *Branch Mgr*
EMP: 776
SALES (corp-wide): 126B **Publicly Held**
WEB: www.verizon.com
SIC: 7389 Personal service agents, brokers & bureaus
PA: Verizon Communications Inc.
1095 Ave Of The Americas
New York NY 10036
212 395-1000

(P-17565)
VERIZON COMMUNICATIONS INC
700 S Flower St Ste 1700, Los Angeles (90017-4200)
PHONE..............................213 330-2556
Steve McNeely, *Branch Mgr*
Subbarao Akella, *Software Engr*
EMP: 776
SALES (corp-wide): 126B **Publicly Held**
WEB: www.verizon.com
SIC: 7389 Personal service agents, brokers & bureaus
PA: Verizon Communications Inc.
1095 Ave Of The Americas
New York NY 10036
212 395-1000

(P-17566)
VIAD CORP
5560 Katella Ave, Cypress (90630-5001)
PHONE..............................562 370-1500
Frank Carbone, *Branch Mgr*
Bill Kindig, *Opers Staff*
EMP: 85 **Publicly Held**
WEB: www.viad.com
SIC: 7389 Promoters of shows & exhibitions

PA: Viad Corp
1850 N Central Ave # 1900
Phoenix AZ 85004

(P-17567)
VIAN ENTERPRISES INC
1501 Industrial Dr, Auburn (95603-9018)
PHONE..............................530 885-1997
Christopher R Vian, *CEO*
Liz Popsicle, *President*
William Kirby, *CFO*
Carol Ann Vian, *Vice Pres*
Pam Vian, *Vice Pres*
EMP: 50
SALES (est): 8.7MM **Privately Held**
WEB: www.vianenterprises.com
SIC: 7389 Personal service agents, brokers & bureaus

(P-17568)
VISA USA INC (HQ)
900 Metro Center Blvd, Foster City (94404-2172)
P.O. Box 8999, San Francisco (94128-8999)
PHONE..............................650 432-3200
Alfred F Kelly Jr, *President*
Victor W Dahir, *CFO*
Kevin Burke, *Chief Mktg Ofcr*
Joshua R Floum, *Exec VP*
Douglas Michelman, *Exec VP*
EMP: 223
SALES (est): 485.3MM **Publicly Held**
WEB: www.moneychoices.com
SIC: 7389 Financial services

(P-17569)
VISIONFUND INTERNATIONAL
Also Called: VISION FUND INTERNATIONAL
800 W Chestnut Ave, Monrovia (91016-3106)
PHONE..............................626 303-8811
Scott Brown, *CEO*
Brad Stave, *Marketing Staff*
EMP: 85
SALES: 26.5MM
SALES (corp-wide): 1B **Privately Held**
SIC: 7389 Financial services
HQ: World Vision International
800 W Chestnut Ave
Monrovia CA 91016
626 303-8811

(P-17570)
VISUAL PAK SAN DIEGO LLC
2320 Paseo De Las Ave 2, San Diego (92154)
PHONE..............................847 689-1000
David Waldron, *Mng Member*
Clayton Bolke,
EMP: 250
SALES (est): 20.8MM **Privately Held**
SIC: 7389 Packaging & labeling services

(P-17571)
VITAL FARMLAND HOLDINGS LLC
3 Corte Las Casas, Belvedere Tiburon (94920-2012)
PHONE..............................415 465-2400
Craig Wichner, *Mng Member*
EMP: 54
SALES (est): 1.1MM **Privately Held**
SIC: 7389 Financial services

(P-17572)
VIVID SOLUTION
5959 W Century Blvd, Los Angeles (90045-6517)
PHONE..............................310 498-2559
Steve Huwang, *Principal*
EMP: 99
SALES (est): 1.9MM **Privately Held**
SIC: 7389 Business services

(P-17573)
VIVOPOOLS INC
825 S Primrose Ave Ste H, Monrovia (91016-3413)
PHONE..............................818 952-2121
William Johnson, *CEO*
Sal Hipolito, *Manager*
EMP: 55
SQ FT: 1,300

SALES: 5MM **Privately Held**
SIC: 7389 Swimming pool & hot tub service & maintenance

(P-17574)
VIVOPOOLS LLC
Also Called: North Bay Pool and Spa
245 W Foothill Blvd, Monrovia (91016-2152)
PHONE..............................888 702-8486
William Johnson, *Mng Member*
EMP: 63
SQ FT: 4,000
SALES (est): 7.6MM **Privately Held**
SIC: 7389 3589 5734 5091 Swimming pool & hot tub service & maintenance; swimming pool filter & water conditioning systems; computer software & accessories; swimming pools, equipment & supplies; swimming pool chemicals, equipment & supplies

(P-17575)
VOLCOM LLC (HQ)
Also Called: Stone Entertainment
1740 Monrovia Ave, Costa Mesa (92627-4407)
PHONE..............................949 646-2175
Jason Steris, *CEO*
Douglas P Collier, *CFO*
Tiffany Montgomery, *Bd of Directors*
Ryan Immegart, *Exec VP*
Tom D Ruiz, *Exec VP*
EMP: 200
SQ FT: 104,000
SALES (est): 88.7MM
SALES (corp-wide): 212.2MM **Privately Held**
WEB: www.volcoment.com
SIC: 7389 2253 7822 5136 Design services; music & broadcasting services; bathing suits & swimwear, knit; motion picture & tape distribution; men's & boys' clothing; women's & children's clothing
PA: Kering
40 Rue De Sevres
Paris 75007
145 646-100

(P-17576)
VXI GLOBAL SOLUTIONS LLC (PA)
220 W 1st St Fl 3, Los Angeles (90012-4105)
PHONE..............................213 739-4720
Eva Yi Hui Wang, *President*
Mark Hauge, *President*
Janet Kennedy, *President*
Jared Morrison, *COO*
David Zhou, *COO*
EMP: 1200
SALES (est): 1B **Privately Held**
WEB: www.vxi.com
SIC: 7389 Telemarketing services

(P-17577)
W SCOTT BLLARD DSIGN ARCH INC
Also Called: Ballard Clothing Design
1800 Century Park E # 600, Los Angeles (90067-1501)
PHONE..............................323 386-4740
W Scott Ballard, *CEO*
EMP: 50
SALES (est): 1.4MM **Privately Held**
SIC: 7389 Design services

(P-17578)
WALLIS FASHIONS INC
1100 8th Ave, Oakland (94606-3613)
PHONE..............................510 763-8018
Fax: 510 832-6882
EMP: 110
SALES (est): 5.2MM **Privately Held**
WEB: www.wallisfashions.com
SIC: 7389

(P-17579)
WARFIGHTER & FAMILY SERVICES
Also Called: Warfighter & Family Services C
2375 Recreation Way, San Diego (92136-5518)
PHONE..............................619 556-7168
A Quezada-Rmirez, *Accounting Mgr*

Anabel Quezada-Ramirez, *Accounting Mgr*
Olivia Austria, *Business Mgr*
EMP: 70
SALES (est): 1.6MM **Privately Held**
SIC: 7389 Personal service agents, bro-
kers & bureaus

(P-17580)
WARNER BROS RECORDS INC (DH)
3300 Warner Blvd, Burbank (91505-4694)
PHONE..........................818 846-9090
Todd Moscowitz, *President*
Rob Cavallo, *Ch of Bd*
Livia Tortella, *President*
Marty Greenfield, *CFO*
Murray Gitlin, *Exec VP*
EMP: 460
SQ FT: 85,000
SALES (est): 104MM **Privately Held**
WEB: www.warnerbrosrecords.com
SIC: 7389 Music recording producer;
recording studio, noncommercial records

(P-17581)
WASHINGTON INVENTORY SERVICE (DH)
Also Called: Wis
9265 Sky Park Ct Ste 100, San Diego
(92123-4375)
PHONE..........................858 565-8111
Jim Rose, *CEO*
Howard L Madden, *President*
Trey Graham, *CFO*
Chris Forsberg, *Exec VP*
Tom Compogiannis, *Vice Pres*
EMP: 135 EST: 1960
SQ FT: 30,000
SALES (est): 89.3MM **Publicly Held**
WEB: www.wisusa.com
SIC: 7389 Inventory computing service
HQ: Western Inventory Service Ltd
3770 Nashua Dr Suite 5
Mississauga ON L4V 1
905 677-1947

(P-17582)
WASHINGTON INVENTORY SERVICE
Also Called: Wis
7150 El Cajon Blvd, San Diego
(92115-1895)
PHONE..........................619 461-8198
Fax: 619 465-0362
EMP: 70
SALES (corp-wide): 671MM **Publicly Held**
SIC: 7389
HQ: Washington Inventory Service Inc
9265 Sky Park Ct Ste 100
San Diego CA 92123
858 565-8111

(P-17583)
WAWONA PACKING CO LLC
12133 Avenue 408, Cutler (93615-2056)
PHONE..........................559 528-4699
Brent Smittcamp,
Lisa Goeas,
Brandon Smittcamp,
Robert Smittcamp,
EMP: 400
SQ FT: 85,000
SALES (est): 19.3MM **Privately Held**
SIC: 7389 Packaging & labeling services

(P-17584)
WEBLY SYSTEMS INC
2603 Camino Ramon Ste 200, San Ramon
(94583-9137)
PHONE..........................888 444-6400
Taj Reneau, *CEO*
Bob McConnell, *CFO*
EMP: 50
SALES (est): 2MM **Privately Held**
SIC: 7389 Telephone services

(P-17585)
WELLS FARGO CAPITAL FIN INC (DH)
Also Called: Wfcf Technology E2040-030
2450 Colo Ave 3000w 3rd 3000 3rd, Santa
Monica (90404)
PHONE..........................310 453-7300
Henry K Jordan, *President*

Peter E Schwab, *Ch of Bd*
Steve Macko, *President*
Guy Fuchs, *COO*
Kevin M Coyle, *Exec VP*
EMP: 170 EST: 1971
SALES (est): 3.5MM
SALES (corp-wide): 97.7B **Publicly Held**
WEB: www.wffoothill.com
SIC: 7389 Financial services
HQ: The Foothill Group Inc
2450 Colo Ave Ste 3000w
Santa Monica CA 90404
310 453-7300

(P-17586)
WEST COAST LEGAL SERVICE INC
1245 S Winchester Blvd # 208, San Jose
(95128-3908)
PHONE..........................408 938-6520
Donald Russi, *President*
Susan Wertz, *Admin Sec*
EMP: 50 EST: 1972
SQ FT: 4,000
SALES (est): 3.6MM **Privately Held**
WEB: www.westcoastlegal.com
SIC: 7389 Legal & tax services; process
serving service

(P-17587)
WEST CORPORATION
170 N Church Ln, Los Angeles
(90049-2044)
PHONE..........................310 481-7878
Rick Patten, *Branch Mgr*
Jim Evans, *Director*
EMP: 198
SALES (corp-wide): 2.2B **Privately Held**
SIC: 7389 Telephone services; telemarket-
ing services
HQ: West Corporation
11808 Miracle Hills Dr
Omaha NE 68154
-

(P-17588)
WEST CORPORATION
3063 W Chapman Ave # 2353, Orange
(92868-1738)
PHONE..........................949 294-2801
Gavino D Bautista, *Principal*
EMP: 198
SALES (corp-wide): 2.2B **Privately Held**
SIC: 7389 Telephone services
HQ: West Corporation
11808 Miracle Hills Dr
Omaha NE 68154

(P-17589)
WEST SAFETY
Also Called: Positron Public Safety
3009 Douglas Blvd Ste 300, Roseville
(95661-3895)
PHONE..........................514 340-3314
Beth Meek, *President*
Chris Buxler, *Vice Pres*
EMP: 50
SALES (est): 32.7K
SALES (corp-wide): 2.2B **Privately Held**
SIC: 7389 Telephone services; telephone
answering service
HQ: West Corporation
11808 Miracle Hills Dr
Omaha NE 68154

(P-17590)
WEST UNFIED CMMNCTONS SVCS INC
1676 N California Blvd, Walnut Creek
(94596-4144)
PHONE..........................925 988-7112
Scott Etzler, *President*
EMP: 70
SALES (corp-wide): 2.2B **Privately Held**
SIC: 7389 Teleconferencing services
HQ: West Unified Communications Serv-
ices, Inc.
8420 W Bryn Mawr Ave # 1100
Chicago IL 60631

(P-17591)
WESTERN HOST INC (PA)
Also Called: Westin San Francisco Arprt Ht
1 Old Bayshore Hwy, Millbrae
(94030-3120)
P.O. Box 14019, Scottsdale AZ (85267-
4019)
PHONE..........................650 692-3500
Michael Dojlidko, *CEO*
EMP: 50 EST: 1974
SALES (est): 10.1MM **Privately Held**
SIC: 7389 7011 Office facilities & secretar-
ial service rental; hotels & motels

(P-17592)
WESTERN REPACKING LLLP
2771 French Camp Rd, Manteca
(95336-9689)
PHONE..........................916 668-8443
EMP: 53 **Privately Held**
SIC: 7389 Packaging & labeling services
PA: Western Repacking, Lllp
315 New Market Rd E
Immokalee FL 34142

(P-17593)
WESTPOINT MARKETING INTL INC
5901 Avalon Blvd, Los Angeles
(90003-1309)
P.O. Box 30144 (90030-0144)
PHONE..........................323 233-0233
Kee Sung Hong, *President*
John Hong, *Vice Pres*
EMP: 85
SALES (est): 2.9MM **Privately Held**
SIC: 7389

(P-17594)
WET (PA)
10847 Sherman Way, Sun Valley
(91352-4829)
PHONE..........................818 769-6200
Mark W Fuller, *CEO*
Shemi Hart, *CFO*
Kenneth Wynn, *Officer*
Tania Avedissian, *Senior VP*
Helen Park, *Senior VP*
▲ **EMP:** 148
SQ FT: 112,000
SALES (est): 74.7MM **Privately Held**
WEB: www.wetdesign.com
SIC: 7389 8711 3443 Design services;
engineering services; metal parts

(P-17595)
WILLITS PERPETUAL LLC
21600 Oxnard St, Woodland Hills
(91367-4976)
PHONE..........................818 668-6800
EMP: 75
SALES (est): 3.2MM **Privately Held**
SIC: 7389

(P-17596)
WILMAY INC
893 Oak Ave, Fillmore (93015-9621)
PHONE..........................805 524-2603
EMP: 80
SALES (est): 2.2MM **Privately Held**
SIC: 7389

(P-17597)
WINDSOR REDWOODS LP
790 Sonoma Ave, Santa Rosa
(95404-4713)
PHONE..........................707 526-1020
John Lowry, *Partner*
EMP: 52
SALES (est): 1.7MM **Privately Held**
SIC: 7389 Personal service agents, bro-
kers & bureaus

(P-17598)
WINNING PERFORMANCE PDTS INC
Also Called: Diplomat Packaging
13010 Bradley Ave, Sylmar (91342-3831)
PHONE..........................818 367-1041
Todd J Harding, *President*
Kim Harding, *Officer*
Barbara Rogers, *Officer*
EMP: 50
SQ FT: 60,000

SALES (est): 5.7MM **Privately Held**
WEB: www.diplomatpackaging.com
SIC: 7389 5013 Packaging & labeling
services; motorcycle parts

(P-17599)
WORLDLINK LLC (PA)
Also Called: Worldlink East
6100 Wilshire Blvd # 1400, Los Angeles
(90048-5111)
PHONE..........................323 866-5900
Toni E Knight, *Mng Member*
Gina Perez, *Executive*
Ryan Brommer, *Sales Staff*
Rex Janechuti, *Sales Staff*
Kayla Jung, *Sales Staff*
EMP: 72
SQ FT: 20,000
SALES (est): 8.5MM **Privately Held**
WEB: www.worldlinkmedia.com
SIC: 7389 Personal service agents, bro-
kers & bureaus

(P-17600)
Y M INTERNATIONAL INC (PA)
165 Valley Dr, Brisbane (94005-1340)
PHONE..........................415 467-3888
MEI Zhang, *President*
David Zhang, *Vice Pres*
EMP: 155
SQ FT: 60,000
SALES (est): 5MM **Privately Held**
WEB: www.ymintl.com
SIC: 7389 Sewing contractor

(P-17601)
YAPSTONE INC (PA)
Also Called: Rentpayment.com
2121 N Calif Blvd Ste 400, Walnut Creek
(94596-7305)
PHONE..........................866 289-5977
Tom Villante, *Ch of Bd*
Kelly Kay, *President*
Bryan Murphy, *President*
Mary Hentges, *CFO*
John Malnar, *CFO*
EMP: 120
SALES (est): 40MM **Privately Held**
WEB: www.rentpayment.com
SIC: 7389 Credit card service

(P-17602)
YC CABLE USA INC (HQ)
44061 Nobel Dr, Fremont (94538-3162)
PHONE..........................510 824-2788
Gary Hsu, *President*
KAO Y Fang, *Shareholder*
Wilson Tong, *Engineer*
Han Wang, *Purch Mgr*
Tam Ha, *Purchasing*
EMP: 70
SQ FT: 45,000
SALES (est): 21MM
SALES (corp-wide): 4.6MM **Privately Held**
SIC: 7389 3643 Field audits, cable televi-
sion; power line cable
PA: Y.C. Cable Co., Ltd.
5f, 12, Lane 270, Pei Shen Rd., Sec.
3,
New Taipei City 22205
226 629-656

(P-17603)
YELLOWPAGESCOM LLC (HQ)
Also Called: Dexyp
611 N Brand Blvd Ste 500, Glendale
(91203-1221)
PHONE..........................818 937-5500
David Krantz,
Williams Clenney, *CFO*
Sandra Barcena, *Treasurer*
Vivek Grover, *Principal*
Brad Mohs, *CTO*
EMP: 260
SALES (est): 56.7MM
SALES (corp-wide): 1.8B **Privately Held**
WEB: www.yellowpages.com
SIC: 7389 Telephone directory distribution,
contract or fee basis; telephone services
PA: Dex Media Holdings, Inc.
2200 W Airfield Dr
Dfw Airport TX 75261
972 453-7000

(P-17604)
ZS ASSOCIATES INC
400 S El Camino Real # 1500, San Mateo
(94402-1733)
PHONE..............................650 762-7800
Ty Curry, *Manager*
Craig Stinebaugh, *Admin Mgr*
Jennifer Gerstenberg, *Admin Asst*
Timur Shalizi, *Technical Mgr*
Brandon Bartell, *Business Anlyst*
EMP: 80
SALES (corp-wide): 291.2MM **Privately Held**
WEB: www.zsassociates.com
SIC: 7389 8742 Mapmaking services; marketing consulting services
PA: Zs Associates, Inc.
　　1560 Sherman Ave Ste 800
　　Evanston IL 60201
　　847 492-3600

7513 Truck Rental & Leasing, Without Drivers

(P-17605)
COUNTY OF INYO
224 N Edwards St, Independence (93526)
P.O. Box N (93526-0613)
PHONE..............................760 878-0292
Ron Juliff, *Manager*
EMP: 78
SQ FT: 4,173 **Privately Held**
SIC: 7513 Truck leasing, without drivers
PA: County Of Inyo
　　168 N Edwards
　　Independence CA 93526
　　760 878-0292

(P-17606)
PACCAR LEASING CORPORATION
Also Called: PacLease
2892 E Jensen Ave, Fresno (93706-5111)
PHONE..............................559 268-4344
Warren Auwae, *Manager*
EMP: 160
SALES (corp-wide): 19.4B **Publicly Held**
WEB: www.glsayre.com
SIC: 7513 Truck leasing, without drivers
HQ: Paccar Leasing Corporation
　　777 106th Ave Ne
　　Bellevue WA 98004
　　425 468-7400

(P-17607)
PARTS
2445 Evergreen Ave, West Sacramento
(95691-3011)
P.O. Box 716 (95691-0716)
PHONE..............................916 371-3115
Tim Hollman, *Principal*
EMP: 82
SALES (est): 1MM **Privately Held**
SIC: 7513 Truck rental & leasing, no drivers

(P-17608)
PENSKE AUTOMOTIVE GROUP INC
17 Woodland Ave, San Rafael
(94901-5301)
PHONE..............................415 492-1922
Jason Golpad, *Principal*
EMP: 50 **Publicly Held**
SIC: 7513 Truck rental & leasing, no drivers
PA: Penske Automotive Group, Inc.
　　2555 S Telegraph Rd
　　Bloomfield Hills MI 48302

(P-17609)
PENSKE AUTOMOTIVE GROUP INC
803 S 1st St, San Jose (95110-3123)
PHONE..............................408 293-7688
Ngoc Tran, *Branch Mgr*
EMP: 50 **Publicly Held**
SIC: 7513 Truck rental & leasing, no drivers

PA: Penske Automotive Group, Inc.
　　2555 S Telegraph Rd
　　Bloomfield Hills MI 48302

(P-17610)
PENSKE TRUCK LEASING CO LP
2300 E Olympic Blvd, Los Angeles
(90021-2537)
PHONE..............................213 628-1255
Alfred McCandless, *Vice Pres*
EMP: 50
SALES (corp-wide): 2.7B **Privately Held**
WEB: www.pensketruckleasing.com
SIC: 7513 Truck leasing, without drivers
PA: Penske Truck Leasing Co., L.P.
　　2675 Morgantown Rd
　　Reading PA 19607
　　610 775-6000

(P-17611)
PENSKE TRUCK LEASING CO LP
19646 Figueroa St, Long Beach
(90745-1001)
PHONE..............................310 327-3116
Chris Reynolds, *Manager*
Christina Darlak, *Branch Mgr*
EMP: 60
SQ FT: 9,680
SALES (corp-wide): 2.8B **Privately Held**
WEB: www.pensketruckleasing.com
SIC: 7513 Truck rental, without drivers
PA: Penske Truck Leasing Co., L.P.
　　2675 Morgantown Rd
　　Reading PA 19607
　　610 775-6000

(P-17612)
PENSKE TRUCK RENTAL INC
11200 Peoria St, Sun Valley (91352-1632)
PHONE..............................818 718-2536
Roger Penske, *President*
EMP: 50
SALES: 21MM **Privately Held**
SIC: 7513 Truck rental, without drivers

(P-17613)
RYDER INTEGRATED LOGISTICS INC
19133 Parthenia St, Northridge
(91324-3626)
PHONE..............................818 701-9332
Jerry Conrrad, *Branch Mgr*
Michael Senella, *Manager*
EMP: 50
SQ FT: 12,100
SALES (corp-wide): 7.3B **Publicly Held**
SIC: 7513 Truck rental, without drivers
HQ: Ryder Integrated Logistics, Inc.
　　11690 Nw 105th St
　　Medley FL 33178
　　305 500-3726

(P-17614)
RYDER TRUCK RENTAL INC
2700 3rd St, San Francisco (94107-3101)
PHONE..............................415 285-0756
Don Kelley, *Manager*
Gary Indes, *Controller*
Christopher Cornish, *Manager*
EMP: 110
SQ FT: 14,320
SALES (corp-wide): 7.3B **Publicly Held**
SIC: 7513 Truck rental, without drivers
HQ: Ryder Truck Rental, Inc.
　　11690 Nw 105th St
　　Medley FL 33178
　　305 500-3726

(P-17615)
RYDER TRUCK RENTAL INC
13630 Firestone Blvd, Santa Fe Springs
(90670-5600)
PHONE..............................562 921-0033
Adrianna Ducante, *Manager*
Dee Walker, *Site Mgr*
Lisa Anderson, *Manager*
EMP: 100
SQ FT: 15,680
SALES (corp-wide): 7.3B **Publicly Held**
SIC: 7513 Truck rental, without drivers

HQ: Ryder Truck Rental, Inc.
　　11690 Nw 105th St
　　Medley FL 33178
　　305 500-3726

(P-17616)
RYDER TRUCK RENTAL INC
9608 Santa Anita Ave, Rancho Cucamonga
(91730-6121)
PHONE..............................909 980-5084
Doreen Coddington, *Branch Mgr*
EMP: 75
SALES (corp-wide): 7.3B **Publicly Held**
SIC: 7513 4212 4213 4225 Truck leasing, without drivers; truck rental, without drivers; local trucking, without storage; trucking, except local; general warehousing; school buses; management services
HQ: Ryder Truck Rental, Inc.
　　11690 Nw 105th St
　　Medley FL 33178
　　305 500-3726

(P-17617)
U-HAUL CO OF CALIFORNIA (DH)
44511 S Grimmer Blvd, Fremont
(94538-6309)
PHONE..............................800 528-0463
Dave Adams, *President*
EMP: 150
SALES (est): 39.6MM
SALES (corp-wide): 3.6B **Publicly Held**
SIC: 7513 7519 4226 Truck rental & leasing, no drivers; trailer rental; special warehousing & storage
HQ: U-Haul International, Inc.
　　2727 N Central Ave
　　Phoenix AZ 85004
　　602 263-6011

(P-17618)
UNITED HAULING CORP
Also Called: National Cement
2620 Buena Vista St, Duarte (91010-3338)
PHONE..............................626 358-9417
Alfred Delmonte, *Branch Mgr*
EMP: 70
SALES (est): 1.8MM **Privately Held**
SIC: 7513 Truck rental & leasing, no drivers

(P-17619)
WILLIAM WARREN GROUP INC (PA)
201 Wilshire Blvd Ste 102, Santa Monica
(90401-1220)
P.O. Box 2034 (90406-2034)
PHONE..............................310 451-2130
William Warren Hobin, *President*
Kent Christensen, *COO*
Clark W Porter, *CFO*
Clark Porter, *CFO*
Gary Sugarman, *Officer*
EMP: 55
SQ FT: 1,500
SALES (est): 29.3MM **Privately Held**
SIC: 7513 Truck rental & leasing, no drivers

(P-17620)
WINNRESIDENTIAL LTD PARTNR
2350 W Shaw Ave Ste 148, Fresno
(93711-3400)
PHONE..............................559 435-3434
EMP: 443
SALES (corp-wide): 6.9MM **Privately Held**
SIC: 7513 Truck rental & leasing, no drivers
PA: Winnresidential Limited Partnership
　　6 Faneuil Hall Market Pl
　　Boston MA 02109
　　617 742-4500

7514 Passenger Car Rental

(P-17621)
ALAMO RENTAL (US) INC
Also Called: Alamo Rent A Car
9020 Aviation Blvd, Inglewood
(90301-2907)
PHONE..............................310 649-2242
Cesar Saurez, *Manager*

EMP: 100
SALES (corp-wide): 4.9B **Privately Held**
WEB: www.area-code-330.info
SIC: 7514 Rent-a-car service
HQ: Alamo Rental (Us) Inc.
　　600 Corporate Park Dr
　　Saint Louis MO 63105

(P-17622)
ALAMO RENTAL (US) INC
Also Called: Alamo Rent A Car
4500 Campus Dr Ste 300, Newport Beach
(92660-1815)
PHONE..............................949 852-0403
Gordon Schmierer, *Manager*
EMP: 50
SALES (corp-wide): 4.9B **Privately Held**
WEB: www.area-code-330.info
SIC: 7514 Rent-a-car service
HQ: Alamo Rental (Us) Inc.
　　600 Corporate Park Dr
　　Saint Louis MO 63105

(P-17623)
AVIS RENT A CAR SYSTEM INC
3450 E Airport Dr Ste 500, Ontario
(91761-7681)
PHONE..............................909 974-2192
Richard Kuehner, *Manager*
EMP: 80
SALES (corp-wide): 8.8B **Publicly Held**
WEB: www.avis.com
SIC: 7514 Rent-a-car service
HQ: Avis Rent A Car System, Inc.
　　6 Sylvan Way Ste 1
　　Parsippany NJ 07054
　　973 496-3500

(P-17624)
AVIS RENT A CAR SYSTEM INC
Also Called: Avis Budget Car Rentals
390 Doolittle Dr, San Leandro
(94577-1015)
PHONE..............................510 562-8828
Marie Peraida, *Manager*
EMP: 200
SALES (corp-wide): 8.8B **Publicly Held**
WEB: www.avis.com
SIC: 7514 Rent-a-car service
HQ: Avis Rent A Car System, Inc.
　　6 Sylvan Way Ste 1
　　Parsippany NJ 07054
　　973 496-3500

(P-17625)
AVIS RENT A CAR SYSTEM INC
1 Airport Dr, Oakland (94621-1430)
PHONE..............................510 577-6360
EMP: 80
SALES (corp-wide): 8.8B **Publicly Held**
WEB: www.cendant.com
SIC: 7514 Rent-a-car service
HQ: Avis Rent A Car System, Inc.
　　6 Sylvan Way Ste 1
　　Parsippany NJ 07054
　　973 496-3500

(P-17626)
AVIS RENT A CAR SYSTEM INC
Also Called: Avis Rent A Car Systems
6520 Mcnair Cir, Sacramento (95837-1120)
PHONE..............................916 922-5601
David McMillan, *Manager*
EMP: 200
SALES (corp-wide): 8.8B **Publicly Held**
SIC: 7514 Rent-a-car service
HQ: Avis Rent A Car System, Inc.
　　6 Sylvan Way Ste 1
　　Parsippany NJ 07054
　　973 496-3500

(P-17627)
AVIS RENT A CAR SYSTEM INC
513 Eccles Ave Ste A, South San Francisco
(94080-1906)
PHONE..............................650 616-0150
Bob Salermo, *Branch Mgr*
Craig Wallace, *Controller*
Alexandra Sweeney, *Manager*
Shirley Yeong, *Manager*
EMP: 100
SALES (corp-wide): 8.8B **Publicly Held**
WEB: www.cendant.com
SIC: 7514 Rent-a-car service

HQ: Avis Rent A Car System, Inc.
6 Sylvan Way Ste 1
Parsippany NJ 07054
973 496-3500

(P-17628)
AVIS RENT A CAR SYSTEM INC
4209 W Vanowen Pl, Burbank
(91505-1139)
PHONE...................................818 566-3001
Don Shelton, *Branch Mgr*
EMP: 80
SALES (corp-wide): 8.8B **Publicly Held**
WEB: www.avis.com
SIC: 7514 Rent-a-car service
HQ: Avis Rent A Car System, Inc.
6 Sylvan Way Ste 1
Parsippany NJ 07054
973 496-3500

(P-17629)
BHRAC LLC
Also Called: Beverly
9777 Wilshire Blvd # 517, Beverly Hills
(90212-1910)
PHONE...................................310 862-1933
David Sajasi,
Hugo Vargas, *Controller*
Ani Bsiabanian,
Allan Jerry Siemons,
Blair Stover,
EMP: 65
SALES: 13MM **Privately Held**
SIC: 7514 7515 Passenger car rental;
passenger car leasing

(P-17630)
DOLLAR THRIFTY AUTO GROUP INC
4420 Pacific Hwy, San Diego (92110-3107)
PHONE...................................619 298-7635
EMP: 722
SALES (corp-wide): 8.8B **Publicly Held**
SIC: 7514 Rent-a-car service
HQ: Dollar Thrifty Automotive Group, Inc.
8501 Williams Rd
Estero FL 33928
239 301-7000

(P-17631)
EAM INC (PA)
Also Called: Budget Rent-A-Car
5404 Whitsett Ave Ste 50, Valley Village
(91607-1615)
P.O. Box 2080, Grants Pass OR (97528-0258)
PHONE...................................213 342-1760
Korick Daniels, *President*
Donald Carr, *Vice Pres*
Eugene Mock, *Vice Pres*
EMP: 70
SQ FT: 1,500
SALES (est): 4.5MM **Privately Held**
SIC: 7514 Rent-a-car service

(P-17632)
ENTERPRISE HOLDINGS INC
780 W Pinedale Ave, Fresno (93711-5744)
PHONE...................................559 261-9221
Al Buroquez, *Branch Mgr*
EMP: 53
SALES (corp-wide): 4.9B **Privately Held**
SIC: 7514 Rent-a-car service
HQ: Enterprise Holdings, Inc.
600 Corporate Park Dr
Saint Louis MO 63105
314 512-5000

(P-17633)
ENTERPRISE RENT-A-CAR
78385 Varner Rd Ste D, Palm Desert
(92211-4118)
PHONE...................................760 772-0281
Jennifer Apruzzese, *Manager*
EMP: 51
SALES (corp-wide): 4.9B **Privately Held**
SIC: 7514 Passenger car rental
HQ: Enterprise Rent-A-Car Company Of
Los Angeles, Llc
333 City Blvd W Ste 1000
Orange CA 92868
657 221-4400

(P-17634)
ENTERPRISE RENT-A-CAR
2942 Kettner Blvd, San Diego
(92101-1111)
PHONE...................................619 297-0311
Doreen Bonner, *Manager*
EMP: 60
SALES (corp-wide): 4.9B **Privately Held**
WEB: www.area-code-330.info
SIC: 7514 Rent-a-car service
HQ: Enterprise Rent-A-Car Company Of
Los Angeles, Llc
333 City Blvd W Ste 1000
Orange CA 92868
657 221-4400

(P-17635)
ENTERPRISE RENT-A-CAR
28112 Camino Capistrano, Laguna Niguel
(92677-1136)
PHONE...................................949 373-9350
Sebrina Rokozit, *Manager*
EMP: 100
SALES (corp-wide): 4.9B **Privately Held**
SIC: 7514 Rent-a-car service
HQ: Enterprise Rent-A-Car Company Of
Los Angeles, Llc
333 City Blvd W Ste 1000
Orange CA 92868
657 221-4400

(P-17636)
ENTERPRISE RENT-A-CAR COMPAN
6320 Mcnair Cir, Sacramento (95837-1118)
PHONE...................................916 576-3164
Alfred Husary, *Manager*
EMP: 65
SALES (corp-wide): 4.9B **Privately Held**
WEB: www.area-code-330.info
SIC: 7514 Rent-a-car service
HQ: Enterprise Rent-A-Car Company Of
Sacramento, Llc
150 N Sunrise Ave
Roseville CA 95661

(P-17637)
FOX RENT A CAR INC (PA)
5500 W Century Blvd, Los Angeles
(90045-5914)
PHONE...................................310 342-5155
Allen Rezapour, *President*
Mike Jaberi, *Treasurer*
Joe Knight, *Exec VP*
Kevin Golchin, *Vice Pres*
Jerame Jackson, *Vice Pres*
EMP: 50
SQ FT: 73,500
SALES (est): 169.1MM **Privately Held**
SIC: 7514 Rent-a-car service

(P-17638)
GETAROUND INC (PA)
1177 Harrison St, San Francisco
(94103-4508)
PHONE...................................866 438-2768
Sam Zaid, *CEO*
Adam Kosmicki, *CFO*
Sylvano Carrasco, *Vice Pres*
Dhruv Raturi, *Software Engr*
Gagan Palrecha, *VP Opers*
EMP: 79
SALES (est): 21.7MM **Privately Held**
SIC: 7514 Rent-a-car service

(P-17639)
HERTZ CLAIM MANAGEMENT CORP
2923 Bradley St Ste 190, Pasadena
(91107-1502)
P.O. Box 7857, Burbank (91510)
PHONE...................................626 296-4760
Fax: 626 296-4799
EMP: 84
SALES (corp-wide): 8.8B **Publicly Held**
SIC: 7514
HQ: Hertz Claim Management Corporation
8501 Williams Rd
Estero FL 33928
239 301-7000

(P-17640)
HERTZ CORPORATION
2627 N Hollywood Way # 8, Burbank
(91505-1062)
PHONE...................................818 997-0414
James D Botsch, *Manager*
EMP: 50
SALES (corp-wide): 8.8B **Publicly Held**
WEB: www.hertz.com
SIC: 7514 Rent-a-car service
HQ: The Hertz Corporation
8501 Williams Rd
Estero FL 33928
239 301-7000

(P-17641)
HERTZ CORPORATION
1000 Walsh Ave, Santa Clara
(95050-2615)
PHONE...................................408 450-6025
Orland Savio, *Manager*
EMP: 100
SQ FT: 12,230
SALES (corp-wide): 8.8B **Publicly Held**
WEB: www.hertz.com
SIC: 7514 Rent-a-car service
HQ: The Hertz Corporation
8501 Williams Rd
Estero FL 33928
239 301-7000

(P-17642)
HERTZ CORPORATION
30 S Buchanan Cir, Pacheco (94553-5116)
PHONE...................................925 680-0316
Gerry Plescia, *President*
EMP: 99
SALES (corp-wide): 8.8B **Publicly Held**
SIC: 7514 Rent-a-car service
HQ: The Hertz Corporation
8501 Williams Rd
Estero FL 33928
239 301-7000

(P-17643)
HERTZ CORPORATION
177 S Airport Blvd, South San Francisco
(94080-6003)
PHONE...................................650 624-6391
Chuck Paterson, *Manager*
Brian Wong, *Administration*
EMP: 82
SALES (corp-wide): 8.8B **Publicly Held**
WEB: www.hertz.com
SIC: 7514 Rent-a-car service
HQ: The Hertz Corporation
8501 Williams Rd
Estero FL 33928
239 301-7000

(P-17644)
HERTZ CORPORATION
3111 N Kenwood St, Burbank
(91505-1041)
PHONE...................................818 569-6900
Rashida Barner, *Manager*
Lance Sorenson, *Sales Staff*
EMP: 99
SALES (corp-wide): 8.8B **Publicly Held**
SIC: 7514 Rent-a-car service
HQ: The Hertz Corporation
8501 Williams Rd
Estero FL 33928
239 301-7000

(P-17645)
MIDWAY RENT A CAR INC
Also Called: Midway Clinic Cars
1800 S Sepulveda Blvd, Los Angeles
(90025-4314)
PHONE...................................310 445-4355
Steve Rosen, *Manager*
EMP: 55 **Privately Held**
WEB: www.midway-group.com
SIC: 7514 Rent-a-car service
PA: Midway Rent A Car, Inc.
4751 Wilshire Blvd # 120
Los Angeles CA 90010

(P-17646)
NATIONAL RENTAL (US) INC
Also Called: National Rent A Car
7600 Earhart Rd Ste 4, Oakland
(94621-4558)
PHONE...................................510 877-4507

Babara Chappelle, *Principal*
EMP: 65
SALES (corp-wide): 4.9B **Privately Held**
WEB: www.specialtyrentals.com
SIC: 7514 Rent-a-car service
HQ: National Rental (Us) Inc.
6929 N Lakewood Ave # 100
Tulsa OK 74117

(P-17647)
NATIONAL RENTAL (US) INC
Also Called: National Rent A Car
2752 De La Cruz Blvd, Santa Clara
(95050-2624)
PHONE...................................408 492-0501
Thomas Currier, *Principal*
EMP: 100
SALES (corp-wide): 4.9B **Privately Held**
WEB: www.specialtyrentals.com
SIC: 7514 Rent-a-car service
HQ: National Rental (Us) Inc.
6929 N Lakewood Ave # 100
Tulsa OK 74117

(P-17648)
STAR LAX LLC
Also Called: Budget Rent-A-Car
150 S Doheny Dr, Beverly Hills
(90211-2545)
PHONE...................................310 642-4500
Jeffery Mirkin,
Linda King, *Principal*
EMP: 125
SALES (est): 9MM **Privately Held**
SIC: 7514 Rent-a-car service

(P-17649)
T C R LIMITED PARTNERSHIP
Also Called: Thrifty Car Rental
5440 W Century Blvd, Los Angeles
(90045-5912)
PHONE...................................310 645-1881
Brett Thomas, *Partner*
EMP: 120
SQ FT: 5,000
SALES (est): 3.2MM **Privately Held**
SIC: 7514 Rent-a-car service

(P-17650)
THRIFTY CAR RENTAL
780 Mcdonnell Rd Ste 1, San Francisco
(94128-3152)
PHONE...................................877 283-0898
James S Tennant, *President*
John Tennant, *Treasurer*
EMP: 140
SQ FT: 6,000
SALES (est): 4.9MM **Privately Held**
SIC: 7514 7513 7519 Rent-a-car service;
truck rental, without drivers; recreational
vehicle rental

(P-17651)
THRIFTY RENT-A-CAR SYSTEM INC
Also Called: Thrifty Car Rental
3500 Irvine Ave, Newport Beach
(92660-3106)
PHONE...................................949 757-0659
Marion Landazuri, *Manager*
EMP: 50
SALES (corp-wide): 8.8B **Publicly Held**
WEB: www.casinomagic.com
SIC: 7514 Rent-a-car service
HQ: Thrifty Rent-A-Car System, Inc.
8501 Williams Rd
Estero FL 33928
239 301-7000

7515 Passenger Car Leasing

(P-17652)
CITY LEASING & RENTALS
2111 Morena Blvd, San Diego
(92110-3440)
PHONE...................................619 276-6171
John Nieman, *President*
Dick Paullin, *Vice Pres*
Kenneth M Nieman, *Director*
EMP: 200

SALES (est): 3.9MM **Privately Held**
SIC: 7515 7514 5521 Passenger car leasing; passenger car rental; used car dealers

(P-17653)
EL CAJON MOTORS (PA)
Also Called: El Cajon Ford
1595 E Main St, El Cajon (92021-5902)
P.O. Box 1236 (92022-1236)
PHONE...................................619 579-8888
Paul F Leader, *President*
Andrew Breech, *Vice Pres*
John Blake, *Admin Sec*
▲ EMP: 100
SQ FT: 311,226
SALES (est): 11.9MM **Privately Held**
WEB: www.elcajonford.com
SIC: 7515 5511 Passenger car leasing; automobiles, new & used; pickups, new & used; vans, new & used

(P-17654)
ENTERPRISE RENT-A-CAR (DH)
333 City Blvd W Ste 1000, Orange (92868-5917)
PHONE...................................657 221-4400
Jack C Taylor, *Ch of Bd*
Pamela Nicholson, *COO*
William W Snyder, *CFO*
Andrew C Taylor, *Chairman*
Rose Langhorst, *Treasurer*
▲ EMP: 90
SQ FT: 30,000
SALES (est): 166.9MM
SALES (corp-wide): 4.9B **Privately Held**
SIC: 7515 7513 7514 Passenger car leasing; truck rental & leasing, no drivers; trucks, tractors & trailers: new & used; passenger car rental
HQ: Enterprise Holdings, Inc.
600 Corporate Park Dr
Saint Louis MO 63105
314 512-5000

(P-17655)
ENTERPRISE RENT-A-CAR COMPAN (DH)
150 N Sunrise Ave, Roseville (95661-2905)
PHONE...................................916 787-4500
Pamela Nicholson, *President*
Susan Irwin, *Vice Pres*
Theo Curtis, *Controller*
Lisa Holmes, *Manager*
Mark Reed, *Manager*
▲ EMP: 50
SALES (est): 62.1MM
SALES (corp-wide): 4.9B **Privately Held**
SIC: 7515 7514 5511 Passenger car leasing; rent-a-car service; automobiles, new & used
HQ: Enterprise Holdings, Inc.
600 Corporate Park Dr
Saint Louis MO 63105
314 512-5000

(P-17656)
MARTY FRANICH LEASING CO
Also Called: Chrysler Plymouth Dodge Jeep
555 Auto Center Dr, Watsonville (95076-3745)
PHONE...................................831 724-2463
Steven Franich, *President*
Robert H Culbertson, *Vice Pres*
EMP: 50 EST: 1960
SQ FT: 15,500
SALES (est): 2.5MM **Privately Held**
SIC: 7515 7513 Passenger car leasing; truck leasing, without drivers

(P-17657)
MIDWAY RENT A CAR INC
Also Called: Midway Car Rental
4201 Lankershim Blvd, North Hollywood (91602-2856)
PHONE...................................818 985-9770
Jeff Riesenberg, *Branch Mgr*
Dave Ross, *Area Mgr*
Damien Swan, *Branch Mgr*
Cynthia Tejeda, *Office Mgr*
Vincent Le, *City Mgr*
EMP: 151 **Privately Held**
SIC: 7515 7514 Passenger car leasing; passenger car rental

PA: Midway Rent A Car, Inc.
4751 Wilshire Blvd # 120
Los Angeles CA 90010

(P-17658)
MISSION TRUCK SALES
Also Called: Mission Valley Truck Center
780 E Brokaw Rd, San Jose (95112-1007)
PHONE...................................408 436-2920
Ernie Speno, *President*
Jeff Speno, *Vice Pres*
Saul Perez, *Manager*
EMP: 75
SALES (est): 2.2MM **Privately Held**
WEB: www.missionvalleyford.com
SIC: 7515 5511 5083 Passenger car leasing; automobiles, new & used; farm & garden machinery

---

7519 Utility Trailers & Recreational Vehicle Rental

(P-17659)
EL MONTE RENTS INC (HQ)
Also Called: El Monte Rv
12818 Firestone Blvd, Santa Fe Springs (90670-5404)
PHONE...................................562 404-9300
Kenneth Schork, *CEO*
Annemarie De Cort, *Marketing Mgr*
Lynn Van Geene, *Marketing Mgr*
Robert Huff, *Sales Associate*
EMP: 110
SALES (est): 43.2MM
SALES (corp-wide): 238.9MM **Privately Held**
WEB: www.elmonterv.com
SIC: 7519 5561 Motor home rental; motor homes
PA: Tourism Holdings Limited
Level 1
Auckland 1010
933 642-99

(P-17660)
QUIXOTE STUDIOS LLC
11473 Penrose St, Sun Valley (91352-3922)
PHONE...................................818 252-7722
Mikel Elliott, *Mng Member*
EMP: 50
SALES (corp-wide): 22.4MM **Privately Held**
SIC: 7519 5561 Trailer rental; travel trailers: automobile, new & used
PA: Quixote Studios Llc
1011 N Fuller Ave
West Hollywood CA 90046
323 851-5030

7521 Automobile Parking Lots & Garages

(P-17661)
ABM PARKING SERVICES
945 W 8th St, Los Angeles (90017-2505)
PHONE...................................213 955-7945
Mercedes Miranda, *Facilities Mgr*
EMP: 64 **Privately Held**
SIC: 7521 Parking lots
PA: Abm Parking Services
3585 Corporate Ct
San Diego CA 92123

(P-17662)
ABM PARKING SERVICES (PA)
3585 Corporate Ct, San Diego (92123-2415)
PHONE...................................619 235-4500
Paul Chacon, *General Mgr*
EMP: 120
SQ FT: 3,300
SALES (est): 4.4MM **Privately Held**
SIC: 7521 Parking lots; parking garage

(P-17663)
ACE PARKING MANAGEMENT INC
1901 Harrison St Ste 102, Oakland (94612-3589)
PHONE...................................510 589-2313
EMP: 108
SALES (corp-wide): 314.1MM **Privately Held**
SIC: 7521 Automobile parking
PA: Ace Parking Management, Inc.
645 Ash St
San Diego CA 92101
619 233-6624

(P-17664)
ACE PARKING MANAGEMENT INC
4352 La Jolla Village Dr, San Diego (92122-1233)
PHONE...................................858 552-0237
John Morgan, *Branch Mgr*
EMP: 167
SALES (corp-wide): 314.1MM **Privately Held**
SIC: 7521 Parking garage
PA: Ace Parking Management, Inc.
645 Ash St
San Diego CA 92101
619 233-6624

(P-17665)
ACE PARKING MANAGEMENT INC
711 Van Ness Ave, San Francisco (94102-3244)
PHONE...................................415 345-8354
Ed Tran, *General Mgr*
EMP: 51
SALES (corp-wide): 314.1MM **Privately Held**
SIC: 7521 Automobile parking
PA: Ace Parking Management, Inc.
645 Ash St
San Diego CA 92101
619 233-6624

(P-17666)
ACE PARKING MANAGEMENT INC
2101 Webster St, Oakland (94612-3011)
PHONE...................................510 272-9788
L Nick Dillard, *Principal*
EMP: 128
SALES (corp-wide): 314.1MM **Privately Held**
SIC: 7521 Parking lots
PA: Ace Parking Management, Inc.
645 Ash St
San Diego CA 92101
619 233-6624

(P-17667)
ACE PARKING MANAGEMENT INC
1330 Broadway Ste 915, Oakland (94612-2508)
PHONE...................................510 251-0509
EMP: 154
SALES (corp-wide): 314.1MM **Privately Held**
SIC: 7521 Parking lots
PA: Ace Parking Management, Inc.
645 Ash St
San Diego CA 92101
619 233-6624

(P-17668)
ACE PARKING MANAGEMENT INC
71 Fortune Dr Ste 916, Irvine (92618-2927)
PHONE...................................949 727-1470
John Duanno, *Manager*
EMP: 130
SALES (corp-wide): 314.1MM **Privately Held**
WEB: www.aceparking.com
SIC: 7521 Parking lots
PA: Ace Parking Management, Inc.
645 Ash St
San Diego CA 92101
619 233-6624

(P-17669)
ACE PARKING MANAGEMENT INC
110 W A St Ste 105, San Diego (92101-3702)
PHONE...................................619 238-4765
Henry Curiel, *Branch Mgr*
EMP: 103
SALES (corp-wide): 314.1MM **Privately Held**
SIC: 7521 Automobile parking
PA: Ace Parking Management, Inc.
645 Ash St
San Diego CA 92101
619 233-6624

(P-17670)
ACE PARKING MANAGEMENT INC
415 Taylor St, San Francisco (94102-1701)
PHONE...................................415 749-1949
Tom Abdul, *Owner*
EMP: 64
SALES (corp-wide): 314.1MM **Privately Held**
SIC: 7521 Parking lots
PA: Ace Parking Management, Inc.
645 Ash St
San Diego CA 92101
619 233-6624

(P-17671)
ACE PARKING MANAGEMENT INC (PA)
645 Ash St, San Diego (92101-3299)
PHONE...................................619 233-6624
Scott A Jones, *Chairman*
Steve Burton, *President*
John Baumgardner, *CEO*
Charles Blottin, *CFO*
Sasha Bradley, *Vice Pres*
EMP: 50
SQ FT: 10,000
SALES (est): 314.1MM **Privately Held**
WEB: www.aceparking.com
SIC: 7521 Parking lots; parking structure

(P-17672)
ACE PARKING MANAGEMENT INC
2050 Gateway Pl, San Jose (95110-1011)
PHONE...................................408 437-2185
Gregory V Wolcott, *Administration*
EMP: 77
SALES (corp-wide): 314.1MM **Privately Held**
SIC: 7521 Parking lots
PA: Ace Parking Management, Inc.
645 Ash St
San Diego CA 92101
619 233-6624

(P-17673)
ACE PARKING MANAGEMENT INC
21500 Pacific Coast Hwy, Huntington Beach (92648-5300)
PHONE...................................714 845-8000
Trevor Waiton, *Branch Mgr*
EMP: 123
SALES (corp-wide): 314.1MM **Privately Held**
SIC: 7521 Automobile parking
PA: Ace Parking Management, Inc.
645 Ash St
San Diego CA 92101
619 233-6624

(P-17674)
ACE PARKING MANAGEMENT INC
440 11th Ave, San Diego (92101-7203)
PHONE...................................619 230-0003
Doug Lakeman, *Branch Mgr*
EMP: 64
SALES (corp-wide): 314.1MM **Privately Held**
SIC: 7521 Parking garage
PA: Ace Parking Management, Inc.
645 Ash St
San Diego CA 92101
619 233-6624

(P-17675)
ACE PARKING MANAGEMENT INC
1 Market Pl, San Diego (92101-7714)
PHONE...................................619 232-1234
EMP: 108
SALES (corp-wide): 314.1MM **Privately Held**
SIC: 7521 Automobile parking
PA: Ace Parking Management, Inc.
    645 Ash St
    San Diego CA 92101
    619 233-6624

(P-17676)
AUTOMATE PARKING INC
8405 Pershing Dr Ste 301, Playa Del Rey (90293-7861)
PHONE...................................310 674-3396
EMP: 60
SQ FT: 1,000
SALES (est): 1MM **Privately Held**
SIC: 7521

(P-17677)
CAR PARK INC
6541 Hollywood Blvd, Hollywood (90028-6256)
PHONE...................................323 462-6060
Joseph Gharib, *President*
Rick Wilson, *Senior VP*
Isidro Mocon, *Finance*
Susan Charis, *Human Resources*
EMP: 110
SALES (est): 314.1K **Privately Held**
SIC: 7521 7299 Outdoor parking services; valet parking

(P-17678)
CENTRAL PARKING CORPORATION
1624 Franklin St Ste 722, Oakland (94612-2823)
PHONE...................................510 832-7227
EMP: 100
SALES (corp-wide): 1.5B **Publicly Held**
SIC: 7521
HQ: Central Parking Corporation
    507 Mainstream Dr
    Nashville TN 37228
    615 297-4255

(P-17679)
CENTRAL PARKING SYSTEM INC
3420 Bristol St Ste 225, Costa Mesa (92626-7136)
PHONE...................................714 751-2855
Peter Cho, *Manager*
EMP: 70
SALES (corp-wide): 1.5B **Publicly Held**
SIC: 7521 Automobile parking
HQ: Central Parking System, Inc.
    507 Mainstream Dr
    Nashville TN 37228
    615 297-4255

(P-17680)
CENTRAL PARKING SYSTEM INC
716 10th St Ste 101, Sacramento (95814-1807)
PHONE...................................916 441-1074
John Webster, *Branch Mgr*
EMP: 60
SALES (corp-wide): 1.5B **Publicly Held**
SIC: 7521
HQ: Central Parking System, Inc.
    1225 I St Nw Ste C100
    Washington DC 20005
    202 496-9650

(P-17681)
CENTURY PLAZA GARAGE
Also Called: American Building Maintenance
2049 Century Park E Ste D, Los Angeles (90067-3104)
PHONE...................................310 226-7495
Jose Ramos, *General Mgr*
JP Morgan Investment Mgmmt,
EMP: 135
SQ FT: 2,000
SALES (est): 3MM **Privately Held**
SIC: 7521 Outdoor parking services

(P-17682)
CITY OF BEVERLY HILLS
342 Foothill Rd, Beverly Hills (90210-3608)
PHONE...................................310 285-2552
Dan Pack, *Branch Mgr*
EMP: 500 **Privately Held**
WEB: www.bhcpr.org
SIC: 7521 9111 Automobile parking; mayors' offices
PA: City Of Beverly Hills
    455 N Rexford Dr
    Beverly Hills CA 90210
    310 285-1000

(P-17683)
CLASSIC PARKING INC
34 S Autumn St, San Jose (95110-2513)
PHONE...................................408 278-1444
Richard Flores, *CFO*
EMP: 345
SALES (corp-wide): 35.9MM **Privately Held**
SIC: 7521 Parking garage
PA: Classic Parking, Inc.
    3208 Royal St
    Los Angeles CA 90007
    213 742-1238

(P-17684)
IMPERIAL PARKING (US) LLC
Also Called: City Park
1740 Cesar Chavez Fl 2, San Francisco (94124-1134)
PHONE...................................415 495-3909
Tim Leonoudakis, *Branch Mgr*
Spencer Sechler, *Sales Staff*
EMP: 650
SALES (corp-wide): 443.7MM **Privately Held**
SIC: 7521 Parking lots; parking garage
PA: Imperial Parking (U.S.), Llc
    900 Haddon Ave Unit 333
    Collingswood NJ 08108
    856 854-7111

(P-17685)
IMPERIAL PARKING (US) LLC
195 N Access Rd, South San Francisco (94080-6905)
PHONE...................................650 871-5423
David Castagnola, *Branch Mgr*
EMP: 63
SALES (corp-wide): 443.7MM **Privately Held**
SIC: 7521 4724 4111 Automobile parking; travel agencies; airport transportation
PA: Imperial Parking (U.S.), Llc
    900 Haddon Ave Unit 333
    Collingswood NJ 08108
    856 854-7111

(P-17686)
IMPERIAL PARKING (US) LLC
Also Called: Sfo Shuttle Bus Company
360 Oak Rd Ste 1, Stanford (94305-4500)
PHONE...................................650 724-4309
Dave Gottlieb, *Branch Mgr*
EMP: 50
SALES (corp-wide): 443.7MM **Privately Held**
SIC: 7521 Parking lots; parking garage
PA: Imperial Parking (U.S.), Llc
    900 Haddon Ave Unit 333
    Collingswood NJ 08108
    856 854-7111

(P-17687)
IMPERIAL PARKING (US) LLC
Also Called: Sfo Shuttle Bus Company
7801 Earhart Rd, Oakland (94621-4529)
PHONE...................................510 382-2140
Dave Gottlieb, *Manager*
EMP: 50
SALES (corp-wide): 443.7MM **Privately Held**
SIC: 7521 Parking lots; parking garage
PA: Imperial Parking (U.S.), Llc
    900 Haddon Ave Unit 333
    Collingswood NJ 08108
    856 854-7111

(P-17688)
IMPERIAL PARKING INDUSTRIES (PA)
Also Called: I P I
6404 Wilshire Blvd B, Los Angeles (90048-5501)
PHONE...................................323 651-5588
Ali Yeganeh, *President*
Paul Gnasso, *Vice Pres*
Jose Mazariego, *Manager*
EMP: 100
SALES (est): 6.5MM **Privately Held**
SIC: 7521 Parking garage

(P-17689)
JIM & DOUG CARTERS AUTOMOTIVE
Also Called: Carters Details Plus
2612 N Hollywood Way, Burbank (91505-1020)
PHONE...................................818 842-5702
Douglas A Carter, *President*
Joan Carter, *Treasurer*
Derek Sweet, *Vice Pres*
EMP: 50
SQ FT: 10,000
SALES (est): 2.2MM **Privately Held**
SIC: 7521 Parking lots

(P-17690)
L AND R AUTO PARKS INC
Also Called: Joe's Auto Parks
707 Wilshire Blvd # 4300, Los Angeles (90017-3501)
PHONE...................................213 784-3018
Charles Bassett, *President*
Mark Funk, *CFO*
Gabriel Rubin, *Corp Secy*
Jeff Matsuno, *Vice Pres*
EMP: 250
SQ FT: 5,000
SALES (est): 13.3MM **Privately Held**
WEB: www.joesautoparks.com
SIC: 7521 7542 7371 Parking lots; carwashes; computer software development & applications

(P-17691)
L R INVESTMENT COMPANY
515 S Flower St Ste 3200, Los Angeles (90071-2215)
PHONE...................................213 627-8211
Scott Hutchison, *Partner*
Kenneth Oldam, *Partner*
EMP: 99
SALES (est): 6.2MM **Privately Held**
SIC: 7521 Automobile parking

(P-17692)
LINDBERGH PARKING INC
3705 N Harbor Dr, San Diego (92101-1021)
PHONE...................................619 291-1508
Maurice Gray, *President*
Scott Jones, *Corp Secy*
EMP: 150
SQ FT: 800
SALES (est): 3.1MM **Privately Held**
SIC: 7521 Parking garage

(P-17693)
LRW INVESTMENTS LLC
Also Called: Wally Park
9700 Bellanca Ave, Los Angeles (90045-5510)
PHONE...................................310 337-1944
Gilad Lumer, *Branch Mgr*
EMP: 60
SALES (corp-wide): 8MM **Privately Held**
WEB: www.wallypark.com
SIC: 7521 Automobile parking
PA: Lrw Investments Llc
    990 W 8th St Ste 600
    Los Angeles CA 90017
    213 629-3263

(P-17694)
MODERN PARKING INC
14110 Palawan Way, Marina Del Rey (90292-6231)
PHONE...................................310 821-1081
Arisur Rahnan, *Principal*
EMP: 80 **Privately Held**
SIC: 7521 Parking garage

PA: Modern Parking, Inc.
    1200 Wilshire Blvd # 300
    Los Angeles CA 90017

(P-17695)
PARK N FLY INC
Also Called: Park One Lax
6351 W Century Blvd, Los Angeles (90045-5355)
PHONE...................................310 417-3566
Yusef Dini, *Branch Mgr*
EMP: 51
SALES (corp-wide): 69.7MM **Privately Held**
WEB: www.parkholding.com
SIC: 7521 Parking lots
HQ: Park 'n Fly, Inc.
    2060 Mount Paran Rd Nw # 207
    Atlanta GA 30327
    404 264-1000

(P-17696)
PARKING COMPANY OF AMERICA
Also Called: Pcamp
523 W 6th St Ste 528, Los Angeles (90014-1225)
PHONE...................................562 862-2118
Alex Martin Chaves Jr, *President*
Eric Chaves, *President*
Pep Valdes, *Vice Pres*
Lupe Alvarado, *Human Resources*
Ricardo Delgado, *Opers Staff*
EMP: 100 EST: 1990
SQ FT: 4,000
SALES (est): 2.3MM **Privately Held**
SIC: 7521 Parking lots

(P-17697)
PARKING CONCEPTS INC
1036 Broxton Ave, Los Angeles (90024-2824)
PHONE...................................310 208-1611
Jorge Lopez, *Manager*
EMP: 50
SALES (corp-wide): 58.5MM **Privately Held**
WEB: www.parkingconcepts.net
SIC: 7521 Parking garage
PA: Parking Concepts, Inc.
    12 Mauchly Ste I
    Irvine CA 92618
    949 753-7525

(P-17698)
PARKING CONCEPTS INC
1801 Georgia St, Los Angeles (90015-3477)
PHONE...................................213 746-5764
Bob Hindle, *Manager*
Nicole Fletcher, *Mktg Dir*
EMP: 50
SALES (corp-wide): 58.5MM **Privately Held**
WEB: www.parkingconcepts.net
SIC: 7521 8748 Parking lots; traffic consultant
PA: Parking Concepts, Inc.
    12 Mauchly Ste I
    Irvine CA 92618
    949 753-7525

(P-17699)
PARKING CONCEPTS INC
14110 Palawan Way, Venice (90292-6231)
PHONE...................................310 821-1081
Frank Vargas, *General Mgr*
EMP: 180
SALES (corp-wide): 58.5MM **Privately Held**
WEB: www.parkingconcepts.net
SIC: 7521 8741 Parking lots; management services
PA: Parking Concepts, Inc.
    12 Mauchly Ste I
    Irvine CA 92618
    949 753-7525

(P-17700)
PARKING CONCEPTS INC
800 Wilshire Blvd, Los Angeles (90017-2604)
PHONE...................................213 623-2661
Juan Cortes, *Branch Mgr*
EMP: 50

(PA)=Parent Co (HQ)=Headquarters (DH)=Div Headquarters
✿ = New Business established in last 2 years

2019 Directory of California
Wholesalers and Services Companies

751

P R O D U C T S & S V C S

SALES (corp-wide): 58.5MM **Privately Held**
WEB: www.parkingconcepts.net
SIC: 7521 Parking garage
PA: Parking Concepts, Inc.
   12 Mauchly Ste I
   Irvine CA 92618
   949 753-7525

(P-17701)
PARKING CONCEPTS INC
12001 Vista Del Mar, Playa Del Rey
(90293-8518)
PHONE..................................310 322-5008
Zahid Hossian, *Branch Mgr*
EMP: 57
SALES (corp-wide): 58.5MM **Privately Held**
WEB: www.parkingconcepts.net
SIC: 7521 Parking garage
PA: Parking Concepts, Inc.
   12 Mauchly Ste I
   Irvine CA 92618
   949 753-7525

(P-17702)
PREFERRED VALET PARKING LLC
2568 Violet St, San Diego (92105-4567)
PHONE..................................619 233-7275
Nick Bernal,
EMP: 50
SALES (est) 976.7K **Privately Held**
SIC: 7521 7299 Parking lots; valet parking

(P-17703)
PRG PARKING CENTURY LLC
Also Called: Parking Spot, The
5701 W Century Blvd, Los Angeles
(90045-5629)
PHONE..................................310 642-0947
Geoffrey Okamoto, *General Mgr*
Prg Parking Holding LLC,
EMP: 100
SQ FT: 620,000
SALES (est): 3MM **Privately Held**
SIC: 7521 Parking garage

(P-17704)
PROFESSIONAL PARKING (PA)
2799 E 21st St, Signal Hill (90755-1007)
PHONE..................................714 722-0242
Caldin Ralph, *President*
Mario Montenegro, *COO*
EMP: 125
SALES (est): 6.2MM **Privately Held**
SIC: 7521 Parking garage

(P-17705)
RESORT PARKING SERVICES INC
39755 Berkey Dr B, Palm Desert
(92211-1106)
PHONE..................................760 328-4041
Mario Gardner, *President*
EMP: 120
SQ FT: 1,100
SALES (est): 4.3MM **Privately Held**
SIC: 7521 7299 Parking lots; indoor parking services; personal item care & storage services

(P-17706)
SERVICE PARKING CORPORATION
Also Called: Service Cleaning and Maint
3800 Barham Blvd Ste P1, Los Angeles
(90068-3097)
PHONE..................................323 851-2416
Aziz Azimi, *CEO*
Philip Chirino, *Vice Pres*
EMP: 65
SQ FT: 1,500
SALES (est): 1.8MM **Privately Held**
SIC: 7521 Parking garage

(P-17707)
SP PLUS CORPORATION
3470 Wilshire Blvd # 400, Los Angeles
(90010-3927)
PHONE..................................213 488-3100
Marjorie Jones, *Branch Mgr*
Paul Sian, *Vice Pres*
Ted Cotton, *Facilities Mgr*
Samir Elayyan, *Senior Mgr*

EMP: 60
SALES (corp-wide): 1.5B **Publicly Held**
SIC: 7521 Automobile parking
PA: Sp Plus Corporation
   200 E Randolph St # 7700
   Chicago IL 60601
   312 274-2000

(P-17708)
TPS PARKING MANAGEMENT LLC
Also Called: Parking Spot, The
9101 S Sepulveda Blvd, Los Angeles
(90045-4803)
PHONE..................................310 846-4747
Chris Fincutter, *Manager*
EMP: 70
SALES (corp-wide): 76.4MM **Privately Held**
SIC: 7521 Parking garage
PA: Tps Parking Management, Llc
   200 W Monroe St Ste 1500
   Chicago IL 60606
   312 781-9396

(P-17709)
UNIFIED VALET PARKING INC
99 S Chester Ave Fl 2, Pasadena
(91106-5805)
PHONE..................................818 822-5807
Mike Madjid Sabet, *President*
EMP: 57
SALES (est): 6.5MM **Privately Held**
SIC: 7521 Automobile parking

(P-17710)
VALET PARKING SVC A CAL PARTNR (PA)
6933 Hollywood Blvd, Los Angeles
(90028-6146)
PHONE..................................323 465-5873
Anthony Policella, *CEO*
EMP: 1268 **EST:** 1946
SQ FT: 10,000
SALES (est): 22.2MM **Privately Held**
WEB: www.valetparkingservice.com
SIC: 7521 7299 Parking lots; valet parking

7532 Top, Body & Upholstery Repair & Paint Shops

(P-17711)
ANAHEIM HILLS AUTO BODY INC
3500 E La Palma Ave, Anaheim
(92806-2116)
PHONE..................................714 632-8266
Robert Smith, *President*
EMP: 60
SQ FT: 33,000
SALES (est): 5.8MM **Privately Held**
WEB: www.anaheimhillsautobody.com
SIC: 7532 Body shop, automotive

(P-17712)
AUTO BODY MANAGEMENT INC
Also Called: Precision Auto Body
7654 Tampa Ave, Reseda (91335-1735)
PHONE..................................818 888-7654
Audrey Vasquev, *President*
EMP: 50
SALES: 4MM **Privately Held**
SIC: 7532 Body shop, automotive

(P-17713)
CALIBER BODYWORKS TEXAS INC
1100 Colorado Ave, Santa Monica
(90401-3010)
PHONE..................................310 392-7662
EMP: 100 **Privately Held**
SIC: 7532 Body shop, automotive
HQ: Caliber Bodyworks Of Texas, Inc.
   401 E Corp Dr Ste 150
   Lewisville TX 75057
   469 948-9500

(P-17714)
CALIBER BODYWORKS TEXAS INC
1399 Logan Ave, Costa Mesa
(92626-4006)
PHONE..................................714 436-5010
EMP: 150 **Privately Held**
SIC: 7532 Body shop, automotive
HQ: Caliber Bodyworks Of Texas, Inc.
   401 E Corp Dr Ste 150
   Lewisville TX 75057
   469 948-9500

(P-17715)
CALIBER BODYWORKS TEXAS INC
Also Called: Caliber Collision Centers
5 Auto Center Dr, Tustin (92782-8402)
PHONE..................................714 665-3905
David Adams, *Branch Mgr*
EMP: 100 **Privately Held**
SIC: 7532 Body shop, automotive
HQ: Caliber Bodyworks Of Texas, Inc.
   401 E Corp Dr Ste 150
   Lewisville TX 75057
   469 948-9500

(P-17716)
CALIBER BODYWORKS TEXAS INC
Also Called: Caliber Collision Centers
3517 Hillcap Ave, San Jose (95136-1391)
PHONE..................................408 972-0300
Abel Silva, *Branch Mgr*
EMP: 100 **Privately Held**
SIC: 7532 Body shop, automotive
HQ: Caliber Bodyworks Of Texas, Inc.
   401 E Corp Dr Ste 150
   Lewisville TX 75057
   469 948-9500

(P-17717)
CALIBER BODYWORKS TEXAS INC
20601 Valley Blvd, Walnut (91789-2731)
PHONE..................................909 598-1113
Brad Wilson, *General Mgr*
Cindy Sanders, *Human Res Dir*
EMP: 50 **Privately Held**
SIC: 7532 Body shop, automotive
HQ: Caliber Bodyworks Of Texas, Inc.
   401 E Corp Dr Ste 150
   Lewisville TX 75057
   469 948-9500

(P-17718)
CALIBER HOLDINGS CORPORATION
Also Called: Classic Collision Center 2
3020 Riverside Dr, Los Angeles
(90039-2014)
P.O. Box 39437 (90039-0437)
PHONE..................................323 913-4000
Madjid Berenji, *Branch Mgr*
EMP: 60 **Privately Held**
WEB: www.classicpasadena.com
SIC: 7532 Body shop, automotive
PA: Caliber Holdings Corporation
   401 E Corp Dr Ste 150
   Lewisville TX 75057

(P-17719)
EUGENE N TOWNSEND
Also Called: Gene Townsend's Auto Body
609 S Marshall Ave, El Cajon (92020-4214)
PHONE..................................619 442-8807
Eugene N Townsend, *Owner*
EMP: 55
SQ FT: 60,000
SALES (est): 3.4MM **Privately Held**
SIC: 7532 Body shop, automotive; paint shop, automotive

(P-17720)
FAITH QUALITY AUTO BODY INC
41130 Nick Ln, Murrieta (92562-7012)
PHONE..................................951 698-8215
Lee Amaradio, *President*
EMP: 60
SALES (est): 6MM **Privately Held**
WEB: www.faithqualityautobody.com
SIC: 7532 Body shop, automotive

(P-17721)
FORNACA INC (PA)
Also Called: Frank Toyata & Scion
2400 National City Blvd, National City
(91950-6628)
P.O. Box 540 (91951-0540)
PHONE..................................866 308-9461
James Fornaca, *CEO*
Gary Fenelli, *Vice Pres*
Ronald Fornaca, *Vice Pres*
Janice Ulrich, *Administration*
Jerry Drewett, *Info Tech Mgr*
EMP: 140
SQ FT: 150,000
SALES (est): 28.6MM **Privately Held**
WEB: www.frankmotors.com
SIC: 7532 5531 5511 Top & body repair & paint shops; automotive & home supply stores; automotive parts; automobiles, new & used

(P-17722)
FOUNTAIN VALLEY BODY WORKS M2
Also Called: Fvbw
17481 Newhope St, Fountain Valley
(92708-4277)
PHONE..................................714 751-8812
David March, *President*
Laurie March, *Vice Pres*
EMP: 50 **EST:** 1975
SQ FT: 50,000
SALES: 6MM **Privately Held**
WEB: www.fountainvalleybodyworks.com
SIC: 7532 Body shop, automotive; paint shop, automotive

(P-17723)
GOLDEN STATE COLLISION CENTERS
841 Galleria Blvd, Roseville (95678-1331)
PHONE..................................916 772-1666
Dave Finkelstein, *President*
Michelle Finkelstein, *Vice Pres*
EMP: 75
SQ FT: 14,000
SALES: 11MM **Privately Held**
WEB: www.goldenstatecollision.com
SIC: 7532 Paint shop, automotive; body shop, automotive

(P-17724)
GREENWALDS AUTOBODY FRAMEWORKS (PA)
1814 Roosevelt Ave, National City
(91950-5537)
PHONE..................................619 477-2600
Karen Greenwald, *Owner*
Daniel Greenwald, *Owner*
EMP: 70
SQ FT: 13,325
SALES (est): 6MM **Privately Held**
SIC: 7532 Body shop, automotive

(P-17725)
HARRYS AUTO BODY INC
Also Called: Harry's Auto Collision
1013 S La Brea Ave, Los Angeles
(90019-6902)
PHONE..................................323 933-4600
Harry Barseghian, *President*
Sally Courtois, *Marketing Staff*
Dean Wolf, *Accounts Mgr*
▲ **EMP:** 65
SQ FT: 5,000
SALES (est): 9.4MM **Privately Held**
SIC: 7532 Body shop, automotive

(P-17726)
HOLMES BODY SHOP INC (PA)
466 Foothill Blvd, La Canada Flintridge
(91011-3518)
PHONE..................................626 795-6447
Thomas V Holmes, *President*
EMP: 64
SQ FT: 300,000
SALES (est): 8.1MM **Privately Held**
WEB: www.holmesbodyshop.com
SIC: 7532 Body shop, automotive; collision shops, automotive

(P-17727)
LABAYA BEACHCOMBER LP
3101 Sturgis Rd, Oxnard (93030-7971)
PHONE..................................805 278-6688

Daniel Mohr, *Managing Prtnr*
Edward Mohr, *Partner*
EMP: 50
SQ FT: 25,000
SALES (est): 1.9MM **Privately Held**
SIC: 7532 Collision shops, automotive

(P-17728)
MARCOS AUTO BODY INC (PA)
1390 E Palm St, Altadena (91001-2042)
PHONE..............................626 286-5691
Marco G Maimone, *President*
Mike Gregorian, *President*
Lillian Maimone, *Treasurer*
Carl Canzano, *Vice Pres*
EMP: 100
SQ FT: 14,000
SALES (est): 4.7MM **Privately Held**
WEB: www.marcosautobody.com
SIC: 7532 7539 Body shop, automotive; frame & front end repair services

(P-17729)
MARINA AUTO BODY SHOP INC
721 Washington Blvd, Marina Del Rey (90292-5542)
PHONE..............................310 822-6615
Tom Williamson, *President*
Bill Hubbard, *Manager*
EMP: 50
SQ FT: 24,000
SALES (est): 2.2MM **Privately Held**
WEB: www.marinaautobody.com
SIC: 7532 Body shop, automotive; paint shop, automotive

(P-17730)
MIKE ROSES AUTO BODY INC
Also Called: Meks's Auto Body
2001 Fremont St, Concord (94520-2616)
PHONE..............................925 686-1739
Michelle Banducci, *Manager*
EMP: 50
SALES (corp-wide): 9.5MM **Privately Held**
SIC: 7532 Upholstery & trim shop, automotive; body shop, trucks
PA: Mike Rose's Auto Body, Inc.
2260 Via De Mercados
Concord CA 94520
925 689-1739

(P-17731)
MULLAHEY CHEVROLET INC
Also Called: Cone Collision Center
11899 Woodruff Ave, Downey (90241-5631)
PHONE..............................714 871-2545
Timothy Mullahey, *President*
EMP: 50 **EST:** 1998
SQ FT: 11,000
SALES (est): 3.8MM **Privately Held**
WEB: www.mullaheychevrolet.com
SIC: 7532 5511 Collision shops, automotive; new & used car dealers

(P-17732)
PK AUTOBODY INC
Also Called: Z J'S Auto Body
361 N Minnewawa Ave, Clovis (93612-0208)
PHONE..............................559 298-9691
Pam Hartley, *CEO*
Jay Bruno, *President*
Ed Bruno, *CFO*
David Rodriguez, *CFO*
Horace Bruno, *Vice Pres*
EMP: 50
SQ FT: 23,000
SALES (est): 4MM **Privately Held**
SIC: 7532 Body shop, automotive

(P-17733)
PLATINUM EQUITY PARTNERS INC
3131 S Standard Ave, Santa Ana (92705-5642)
PHONE..............................714 444-3100
Hamid Hojati, *President*
Ingrid Cramer, *Vice Pres*
Elham Hojati, *Vice Pres*
EMP: 145
SQ FT: 45,000
SALES (est): 5.1MM **Privately Held**
SIC: 7532 Body shop, automotive

(P-17734)
PRESTIGE AUTO COLLISION INC
23726 Via Fabricante, Mission Viejo (92691-3145)
PHONE..............................949 470-6031
Bernie Gates, *President*
Laurie Gates, *Treasurer*
Amy Beckner, *Info Tech Mgr*
EMP: 65
SQ FT: 10,000
SALES (est): 4.7MM **Privately Held**
WEB: www.prestigeautocollision.com
SIC: 7532 Collision shops, automotive

(P-17735)
PRESTIGE TOO AUTO BODY INC
11899 Woodruff Ave, Downey (90241-5631)
PHONE..............................310 787-8852
Ben L Guerra, *President*
EMP: 50
SALES (est): 4.7MM **Privately Held**
WEB: www.prestigetooautobody.com
SIC: 7532 Body shop, automotive; collision shops, automotive

(P-17736)
PRIDE COLLISION CENTERS INC (PA)
Also Called: Pride Auto Body
7950 Haskell Ave, Van Nuys (91406-1923)
PHONE..............................818 909-0660
Randy Stabler, *President*
Jay Russell, *Vice Pres*
Robert Turchan, *Vice Pres*
Steve Morris, *Opers Staff*
Shawn Sgambellone, *Parts Mgr*
EMP: 65
SQ FT: 44,000
SALES (est): 9.8MM **Privately Held**
SIC: 7532 Body shop, automotive

(P-17737)
REDLANDS FORD INC
1121 W Colton Ave, Redlands (92374-2935)
PHONE..............................909 793-3211
Steve Rojas, *CEO*
Tracey Hooper, *Treasurer*
Luis Perez, *Sales Mgr*
Monica Alvarado, *Sales Staff*
Trever Desherlia, *Manager*
EMP: 85
SALES (est): 9.5MM **Privately Held**
WEB: www.redlandsford.com
SIC: 7532 5511 Body shop, automotive; automobiles, new & used

(P-17738)
SERVICE KING HOLDINGS LLC
Also Called: Service King Cllision Repr Ctr
7801 Oakport St, Oakland (94621-2024)
PHONE..............................510 562-9650
Sherman Pung, *Site Mgr*
EMP: 88
SALES (corp-wide): 347.9MM **Privately Held**
SIC: 7532 Body shop, automotive
PA: Service King Holdings, Llc
2375 N Glenville Dr
Richardson TX 75082
972 960-7595

(P-17739)
SERVICE KING HOLDINGS LLC
Also Called: Service King Cllision Repr Ctr
4660 Alvarado Canyon Rd, San Diego (92120-4304)
PHONE..............................619 219-3927
EMP: 59
SALES (corp-wide): 347.9MM **Privately Held**
SIC: 7532 Body shop, automotive
PA: Service King Holdings, Llc
2375 N Glenville Dr
Richardson TX 75082
972 960-7595

(P-17740)
SERVICE KING HOLDINGS LLC
Also Called: Service King Cllision Repr Ctr
18065 Euclid St, Fountain Valley (92708-6107)
PHONE..............................714 962-2600
EMP: 75

SALES (corp-wide): 347.9MM **Privately Held**
SIC: 7532 Body shop, automotive
PA: Service King Holdings, Llc
2375 N Glenville Dr
Richardson TX 75082
972 960-7595

(P-17741)
SERVICE KING PAINT & BODY LLC
6080 Dublin Blvd, Dublin (94568-7581)
PHONE..............................925 301-8481
EMP: 150
SALES (corp-wide): 7.1B **Publicly Held**
SIC: 7532 Body shop, automotive
HQ: Service King Paint & Body, Llc
2375 N Glenville Dr
Richardson TX 75082
972 960-7595

(P-17742)
SONSHINE COLLISION SERVICES
Also Called: Sonshine Auto Body
17200 Jasmine St, Victorville (92395-5836)
PHONE..............................760 243-3185
Gary L Cooper, *CEO*
Darlene T Cooper, *Treasurer*
Terry Thomas, *Vice Pres*
Aaron P Cooper, *Admin Sec*
Jeannine Blanchard, *Accountant*
EMP: 60
SALES (est): 4.7MM **Privately Held**
SIC: 7532 Collision shops, automotive

(P-17743)
SONSHINE NORTH AUTOBODY
17200 Jasmine St, Victorville (92395-5836)
PHONE..............................760 245-3183
Gary Cooper, *Owner*
EMP: 60
SALES (est): 1.4MM **Privately Held**
SIC: 7532 Body shop, automotive

(P-17744)
STERLING COLLISION CENTER LLC (PA)
Also Called: Sea Breeze Collision
1111 Bell Ave Ste A, Tustin (92780-6463)
PHONE..............................714 259-1111
Ray Shaai, *General Ptnr*
EMP: 65
SALES (est): 6.6MM **Privately Held**
SIC: 7532 Body shop, automotive

(P-17745)
WILLIAMSON ENTERPRISES INC
Also Called: Marina Autobody
721 Washington Blvd, Marina Del Rey (90292-5542)
PHONE..............................310 822-6615
Thomas C Williamson, *President*
Abbie Woods, *Executive*
Kathlene R Williamson, *Admin Sec*
EMP: 51
SQ FT: 24,000
SALES (est): 5.3MM **Privately Held**
WEB: www.williamsonenterprises.com
SIC: 7532 Body shop, automotive

(P-17746)
Y & S ENTERPRISES INC (PA)
Also Called: Y & S Auto Body Shop
1441 N Gaffey St, San Pedro (90731-1325)
PHONE..............................310 548-1120
Younan Safar, *CEO*
Maher Kyrillos, *Controller*
Rose Safar, *Director*
EMP: 50
SQ FT: 71,000
SALES (est): 5.1MM **Privately Held**
WEB: www.yandsautobody.com
SIC: 7532 Body shop, automotive

(P-17747)
ZIKAKIS AUTO HOLDINGS LLC (PA)
Also Called: Lompoc Honda Body Shop
1224 N H St, Lompoc (93436-3302)
PHONE..............................805 736-4595
Christopher A Zikakis, *Mng Member*
Steve Munoz, *Rector*
Ken Belch, *Manager*

Frank Villalobos, *Manager*
EMP: 50
SQ FT: 10,000
SALES (est): 4MM **Privately Held**
WEB: www.lompochonda.com
SIC: 7532 Body shop, automotive

7534 Tire Retreading & Repair Shops

(P-17748)
AAA SIGNS INC
Also Called: Total Tire Recycling
2020 Railroad Dr, Sacramento (95815-3515)
PHONE..............................916 568-3456
Gary Matranga, *President*
Danny L Matranga, *Officer*
Nancy Gray, *Office Mgr*
EMP: 54
SQ FT: 14,000
SALES (est): 5.6MM **Privately Held**
SIC: 7534 7353 Tire retreading & repair shops; cranes & aerial lift equipment, rental or leasing

(P-17749)
NEW PRIDE CORPORATION
2757 E Del Amo Blvd, Compton (90221-6005)
PHONE..............................310 631-7000
Edward Eunjong Kim, *President*
EMP: 50 **Privately Held**
SIC: 7534 1799 Rebuilding & retreading tires; antenna installation
HQ: New Pride Tire, Inc.
333 Hegenberger Rd # 705
Oakland CA 94621
510 567-8800

(P-17750)
RUBBER DUST INC (PA)
Also Called: J & O'S Commercial Tire Center
533 S 13th St, Richmond (94804-3702)
PHONE..............................510 237-6344
Charlie T Talbot, *CEO*
John A Talbot, *President*
Bonnie Talbot, *Corp Secy*
Edward Talbot, *Vice Pres*
▼ **EMP:** 57
SQ FT: 40,000
SALES: 7.3MM **Privately Held**
WEB: www.jandotire.com
SIC: 7534 7538 Tire repair shop; general automotive repair shops

7536 Automotive Glass Replacement Shops

(P-17751)
ALL STAR GLASS INC (PA)
1845 Morena Blvd, San Diego (92110-3699)
PHONE..............................619 275-3343
Bob Scharaga, *CEO*
Mark V Doren, *COO*
Hermeen Scharaga, *Treasurer*
Janet Scharaga, *Vice Pres*
▲ **EMP:** 50
SQ FT: 15,512
SALES: 24.9MM **Privately Held**
SIC: 7536 Automotive glass replacement shops

(P-17752)
SAFELITE FULFILLMENT INC
Also Called: Safelite Autoglass
261 Richards Blvd, Sacramento (95811-0216)
PHONE..............................916 442-4715
Frank Primer, *Manager*
EMP: 80 **Privately Held**
WEB: www.belronus.com
SIC: 7536 4225 Automotive glass replacement shops; general warehousing & storage
HQ: Safelite Fulfillment, Inc.
7400 Safelite Way
Columbus OH 43235
614 210-9000

PRODUCTS & SVCS

7537 Automotive Transmission Repair Shops

(P-17753)
PDQ AUTOMATIC TRANSM PARTS INC
8380 Tiogawoods Dr, Sacramento
(95828-5048)
PHONE......................916 681-7701
John G Hicks Jr, *President*
John Hicks Sr, *Treasurer*
Tracy Hicks, *Vice Pres*
Amy Hicks, *Admin Sec*
▲ EMP: 62
SQ FT: 33,600
SALES (est): 11.8MM **Privately Held**
WEB: www.pdqparts.com
SIC: 7537 Automotive transmission repair shops

7538 General Automotive Repair Shop

(P-17754)
AUTO TOWN INC
2150 E Hammer Ln, Stockton
(95210-4122)
P.O. Box 690368 (95269-0368)
PHONE.......(209) 473-2513
Paul C Wondries, *President*
EMP: 70 EST: 1947
SQ FT: 40,000
SALES (est): 2.1MM **Privately Held**
SIC: 7538 5511 General automotive repair shops; automobiles, new & used

(P-17755)
BAE SYS SIERRA DETROIT ALLISON (DH)
1755 Adams Ave, San Leandro
(94577-1001)
PHONE......................510 635-8991
Cindy Bergstrom, *President*
Wade Sperry, *Vice Pres*
EMP: 95
SQ FT: 45,000
SALES (est): 6.8MM
SALES (corp-wide): 2.2B **Publicly Held**
SIC: 7538 5084 5085 Diesel engine repair: automotive; engines & parts, diesel; industrial supplies
HQ: Bae Systems Resolution Inc.
1000 La St Ste 4950
Houston TX 77002
713 868-7700

(P-17756)
BREWSTERS AUTOMOTIVE INC
17357 Los Angeles St, Yorba Linda
(92886-1723)
PHONE......................714 528-4683
John M Brewster, *President*
Karen Brewster, *Treasurer*
EMP: 70 EST: 1973
SALES (est): 4.6MM **Privately Held**
SIC: 7538 7542 General automotive repair shops; carwashes

(P-17757)
CITY OF LONG BEACH
Also Called: Long Beach City Fleet Services
2600 Temple Ave, Long Beach
(90806-2209)
PHONE......................562 570-2828
Dan Burlenbach, *General Mgr*
John Seevers, *Superintendent*
EMP: 250 **Privately Held**
WEB: www.polb.com
SIC: 7538 9111 General automotive repair shops; mayors' offices
PA: City Of Long Beach
333 W Ocean Blvd Fl 10
Long Beach CA 90802
562 570-6450

(P-17758)
CRYSTAL CHRYSLER PLYMUTH DODGE
36444 Auto Park Dr, Cathedral City
(92234-6500)
PHONE......................760 324-9375

Robert Sherr, *President*
Savannah Trevino, *Advisor*
EMP: 78
SALES (est): 8.3MM **Privately Held**
WEB: www.crystalchrysler.com
SIC: 7538 5511 General automotive repair shops; automobiles, new & used

(P-17759)
FLT INC
Also Called: Folsom Lake Toyota
12747 Folsom Blvd, Folsom (95630-8097)
PHONE......................916 355-1500
Charles G Peterson, *President*
Pam Peterson, *Admin Sec*
Jeff Bear, *Manager*
EMP: 125
SALES (est): 9.2MM **Publicly Held**
WEB: www.folsomlaketoyota.com
SIC: 7538 5511 7532 5531 General automotive repair shops; automobiles, new & used; pickups, new & used; body shop, automotive; automotive parts; automobiles, used cars only
PA: Group 1 Automotive, Inc.
800 Gessner Rd Ste 500
Houston TX 77024

(P-17760)
FORTRESS RESOURCES LLC (PA)
Also Called: Royal Truck Body
24200 Main St, Carson (90745-6325)
PHONE......................562 633-9951
Dudley De Zonia Jr, *President*
Ann De Zonia, *Admin Sec*
EMP: 122
SQ FT: 53,000
SALES: 25MM **Privately Held**
SIC: 7538 General truck repair

(P-17761)
GARRICK MOTORS INC
559 S Pine St, Escondido (92025-4021)
PHONE......................760 489-2656
Gary Myers, *Branch Mgr*
Paul Sinclair, *Advisor*
EMP: 138
SALES (corp-wide): 107MM **Privately Held**
SIC: 7538 7532 General automotive repair shops; body shop, automotive
PA: Garrick Motors, Inc.
231 E Lincoln Ave
Escondido CA 92026
760 746-0601

(P-17762)
GIBBS INTERNATIONAL INC (PA)
Also Called: Gibbs International Truck Ctrs
2201 Ventura Blvd, Oxnard (93036-7902)
P.O. Box 5206 (93031-5206)
PHONE......................805 485-0551
Edward A Gibbs, *President*
Mark Rapin, *Sales Mgr*
George Wishart, *Sales Staff*
EMP: 135
SQ FT: 25,000
SALES: 59MM **Privately Held**
WEB: www.gibbstrucks.com
SIC: 7538 5511 4212 Truck engine repair, except industrial; trucks, tractors & trailers: new & used; local trucking, without storage

(P-17763)
GLENN E THOMAS COMPANY INC
Also Called: GLENN E THOMAS DODGE CHRIYSLAR
2100 E Spring St, Long Beach
(90755-2115)
PHONE......................562 426-5111
Robert W Davis, *President*
Allen King, *CFO*
J Allen King, *CFO*
Brad Davis, *Vice Pres*
John Davis, *General Mgr*
EMP: 90
SQ FT: 38,000

SALES (est): 13.2MM **Privately Held**
WEB: www.getdodge.com
SIC: 7538 5511 General automotive repair shops; pickups, new & used; automobiles, new & used

(P-17764)
GRAND AUTO CARE
Also Called: Grand Auto Repair
744 N Grand Ave, Covina (91724-2402)
PHONE......................626 331-8390
Ellie Fingerfield, *Owner*
EMP: 50
SALES (est): 1MM **Privately Held**
SIC: 7538 7539 7542 General automotive repair shops; brake repair, automotive; washing & polishing, automotive

(P-17765)
GRIMMWAY ENTERPRISES INC
2171 W Bannister Rd, Brawley
(92227-9653)
PHONE......................760 344-0204
Cheryl Chaney, *Principal*
EMP: 182
SALES (corp-wide): 2.1B **Privately Held**
SIC: 7538 General automotive repair shops
PA: Grimmway Enterprises, Inc.
14141 Di Giorgio Rd
Arvin CA 93203
800 301-3101

(P-17766)
HAMBLINS BDY PNT FRAME SP INC
Also Called: Hamblin's Auto & Body Shop
7590 Cypress Ave, Riverside (92503-1904)
PHONE......................951 689-8440
Rod Perry, *President*
EMP: 70
SALES (est): 5.9MM **Privately Held**
WEB: www.hamblinsbodyandpaint.com
SIC: 7538 7532 General automotive repair shops; body shop, automotive

(P-17767)
HAWTHORNE MACHINERY CO
Also Called: Caterpillar
16945 Camino San Bernardo, San Diego
(92127-2499)
PHONE......................858 674-7000
Bob Price, *Manager*
EMP: 100
SALES (corp-wide): 195.6MM **Privately Held**
SIC: 7538 5084 7359 5085 Diesel engine repair: automotive; engines & parts, air-cooled; equipment rental & leasing; industrial supplies; marine crafts & supplies
PA: Hawthorne Machinery Co.
16945 Camino San Bernardo
San Diego CA 92127
858 674-7000

(P-17768)
J&R FLEET SERVICES LLC
210 Saint Katherine Dr, La Canada
Flintridge (91011-4109)
PHONE......................909 820-7000
Javier G Rodriguez,
Ricardo Rodriguez,
Roberto Rodriguez,
EMP: 70
SQ FT: 30,000
SALES (est): 7.9MM **Privately Held**
SIC: 7538 General truck repair

(P-17769)
LANCASTER COMM SVCS FNDTN
46008 7th St W, Lancaster (93534-7602)
PHONE......................661 723-6230
Randy Williams, *Manager*
EMP: 70 **Privately Held**
WEB: www.poppyfestival.com
SIC: 7538 9111 General automotive repair shops; mayors' offices
PA: The Lancaster Community Services Foundation Inc
44993 Fern Ave
Lancaster CA 93534
661 723-6000

(P-17770)
LINCOLN WITT MERCURY
Also Called: Auto Collection
728 N Escondido Blvd, Escondido
(92025-1704)
PHONE......................760 233-3333
Edward Witt,
EMP: 100
SALES (corp-wide): 39.5MM **Privately Held**
WEB: www.sdautoconnect.com
SIC: 7538 5521 5511 7532 General automotive repair shops; used car dealers; new & used car dealers; top & body repair & paint shops; passenger car leasing; truck rental & leasing, no drivers
PA: Witt Lincoln Mercury
588 Camino Del Rio N
San Diego CA 92108
619 358-5000

(P-17771)
LITHIA MOTORS INC
3077 E Hammer Ln, Stockton
(95212-2801)
PHONE......................209 956-1930
David Maldonado, *Branch Mgr*
EMP: 50
SALES (corp-wide): 10B **Publicly Held**
SIC: 7538 General automotive repair shops
PA: Lithia Motors, Inc.
150 N Bartlett St
Medford OR 97501
541 776-6401

(P-17772)
MAGNUSSENS DODGE CRYSLER JEEP
1901 Grass Valley Hwy, Auburn
(95603-2852)
PHONE......................530 885-2900
Bernie Magnussen, *President*
Larry Carmen, *Owner*
Damon Wied, *Manager*
EMP: 60
SALES (est): 2.7MM **Privately Held**
SIC: 7538 5511 General automotive repair shops; pickups, new & used

(P-17773)
NORMANDINS
Also Called: Normandin Chrysler Jeep
900 Cptl Expy Aut Mall, San Jose
(95136-1102)
PHONE......................877 330-0391
Lon Normandin, *Owner*
Mark Normandin, *President*
Paul Normandin, *Exec VP*
Doug Kasch, *Store Mgr*
Ben Zahra, *Finance Mgr*
EMP: 119
SQ FT: 12,000
SALES (est): 18.2MM **Privately Held**
WEB: www.normandinchrysler.com
SIC: 7538 5511 General automotive repair shops; new & used car dealers

(P-17774)
OC IV A CALIFORNIA LP
Also Called: Oil Changers
4511 Willow Rd Ste 1, Pleasanton
(94588-2735)
PHONE......................925 734-5800
Lawrence Read, *CEO*
LMC Properties IV, *General Ptnr*
Charles Pass, *CFO*
EMP: 50
SALES (est): 663.3K **Privately Held**
SIC: 7538 General automotive repair shops

(P-17775)
PAPE TRUCKS INC
Also Called: Pape' Kenworth
2892 E Jensen Ave, Fresno (93706-5111)
P.O. Box 407, Eugene OR (97440-0407)
PHONE......................559 268-4344
Charles Davis, *General Mgr*
Tena Dimond, *General Mgr*
Jeff Harris, *Finance Mgr*
Veronica Lopez, *Opers Mgr*
Steve Brown, *Sales Staff*
EMP: 77

▲ = Import ▼=Export
◆ =Import/Export

SALES (corp-wide): 587.9MM **Privately Held**
SIC: 7538 5511 5531 General truck repair; trucks, tractors & trailers: new & used; truck equipment & parts
HQ: Pape' Trucks, Inc.
355 Goodpasture Island Rd
Eugene OR 97401

(P-17776)
PARK PLACE FORD LLC
555 W Foothill Blvd, Upland (91786-3853)
PHONE..............................909 946-5555
Timothy Park,
EMP: 83 EST: 2012
SQ FT: 15,000
SALES (est): 6.3MM **Privately Held**
SIC: 7538 7532 7549 5561 General automotive repair shops; collision shops, automotive; emissions testing without repairs, automotive; inspection & diagnostic service, automotive; travel trailers: automobile, new & used

(P-17777)
PEP BOYS MANNY MOE JACK OF CAL
11456 Washington Blvd, Whittier (90606)
PHONE..............................562 908-4400
Luis Suarez, *Manager*
EMP: 50
SQ FT: 35,341
SALES (corp-wide): 21.7B **Publicly Held**
WEB: www.apdnow.com
SIC: 7538 5531 7549 General automotive repair shops; automotive parts; inspection & diagnostic service, automotive
HQ: The Pep Boys Manny Moe & Jack Of California
3111 W Allegheny Ave
Philadelphia PA 19132
215 430-9095

(P-17778)
PREMIER AUTO W COVINA LLC
777 W Orangethorpe Ave, Placentia (92870-6824)
PHONE..............................626 858-7202
Troy Duhon, *Mng Member*
EMP: 60
SQ FT: 10,000
SALES: 5.7MM **Privately Held**
SIC: 7538 General automotive repair shops

(P-17779)
QUALITY AUTO CRAFT INC
3295 Bernal Ave Ste B, Pleasanton (94566-6298)
PHONE..............................925 426-0120
Ivo Soares, *President*
EMP: 1614
SQ FT: 10,000
SALES (est): 30MM **Privately Held**
SIC: 7538 7532 General automotive repair shops; body shop, automotive

(P-17780)
RAYMAK AUTOMOTIVE INC
Also Called: Falcon Auto Repair
15600 S Main St, Gardena (90248-2219)
PHONE..............................310 329-8910
Kamyar Najmi, *President*
EMP: 50
SQ FT: 38,000
SALES: 7.2MM **Privately Held**
SIC: 7538 General automotive repair shops

(P-17781)
ROCKET SMOG INC
11413 W Washington Blvd, Los Angeles (90066-6012)
PHONE..............................310 390-7664
Ann Sadeck, *President*
EMP: 59
SQ FT: 9,000
SALES (est): 287.3K **Privately Held**
SIC: 7538 General automotive repair shops

(P-17782)
RP AUTOMOTIVE INC (PA)
2010 E Garvey Ave S, West Covina (91791-1911)
PHONE..............................626 430-9011
Roger S Penske Jr, *President*
Roy Durham, *General Mgr*
EMP: 130
SALES (est): 2MM **Privately Held**
SIC: 7538 General automotive repair shops

(P-17783)
SEIDNER-MILLER AUTOMOTIVE INC
1253 S Lone Hill Ave, Glendora (91740-4507)
PHONE..............................909 394-3500
Peter Miller, *Vice Pres*
Pierce Caine, *Sales Mgr*
EMP: 50
SALES (est): 1.8MM **Privately Held**
SIC: 7538 General automotive repair shops

(P-17784)
SIEMENS MOBILITY INC
5301 Price Ave, McClellan (95652-2401)
PHONE..............................916 621-2700
Christopher Maynard, *Vice Pres*
EMP: 100
SALES (corp-wide): 97.7B **Privately Held**
SIC: 7538 3743 General truck repair; train cars & equipment, freight or passenger
HQ: Siemens Mobility, Inc.
1 Penn Plz Frnt 11
New York NY 10119
916 717-8174

(P-17785)
SOUTHERN CALIFORNIA FLEET SVC
6726 Nicolett St, Riverside (92504-1843)
PHONE..............................951 272-8655
Tom Franchina, *CEO*
EMP: 50
SALES (est): 2.1MM **Privately Held**
WEB: www.socalfleet.com
SIC: 7538 General truck repair

(P-17786)
SOUTHERN CALIFORNIA MAR ASSN
3333 Fairview Rd, Costa Mesa (92626-1610)
PHONE..............................714 850-4004
Betty Chew, *Director*
Greg Backley, *Vice Pres*
Jim Doran, *Empl Rel Mgr*
EMP: 58
SALES (est): 9.6MM **Privately Held**
SIC: 7538 General automotive repair shops

(P-17787)
TEAMROSS INC
Also Called: Team Superstores
301 Auto Mall Pkwy, Vallejo (94591-3870)
PHONE..............................707 643-9000
Kenneth B Ross, *President*
Trish Gress, *Treasurer*
Michael Drinker, *Vice Pres*
EMP: 95
SQ FT: 57,000
SALES (est): 7.9MM **Privately Held**
SIC: 7538 5511 General automotive repair shops; automobiles, new & used

(P-17788)
TED FORD JONES INC (PA)
Also Called: Ken Grody Ford
6211 Beach Blvd, Buena Park (90621-2307)
P.O. Box 2154 (90621-0654)
PHONE..............................714 521-3110
Kenneth B Grody, *President*
Ken Grody, *President*
Billy Raymond, *CFO*
Curt Maletych, *Vice Pres*
Kurt Maletych, *Vice Pres*
▼ EMP: 110
SQ FT: 4,500

SALES (est): 32MM **Privately Held**
WEB: www.kengrody.com
SIC: 7538 5511 General automotive repair shops; automobiles, new & used

(P-17789)
TOYOTA-SUNNYVALE INC (PA)
898 W El Camino Real, Sunnyvale (94087-1153)
PHONE..............................408 245-6640
Adam Simms, *President*
Tom Price, *Vice Pres*
Mike Shum, *General Mgr*
Negal Ryan, *Finance Mgr*
Mike New, *Finance*
EMP: 120
SQ FT: 35,000
SALES (est): 19.5MM **Privately Held**
WEB: www.toyotasunnyvale.com
SIC: 7538 5511 5521 5531 General automotive repair shops; automobiles, new & used; used car dealers; automotive & home supply stores

(P-17790)
VOLKSWAGEN SOUTH COAST
1450 Auto Mall Dr, Santa Ana (92705-4732)
PHONE..............................657 231-5600
Peter Maldonado, *General Mgr*
Armond Hayrapetian, *Finance Mgr*
EMP: 65
SALES (est): 45.5K **Privately Held**
SIC: 7538 5521 General automotive repair shops; used car dealers

> # 7539 Automotive Repair Shops, NEC

(P-17791)
ALASKA DIESEL ELECTRIC
425 S Hacienda Blvd, City of Industry (91745-1123)
PHONE..............................626 934-6211
Peter B Hill Jr, *President*
EMP: 119
SALES (est): 3.1MM
SALES (corp-wide): 181.2MM **Privately Held**
SIC: 7539 Automotive repair shops
PA: Valley Power Systems, Inc.
425 S Hacienda Blvd
City Of Industry CA 91745
626 333-1243

(P-17792)
CALTECK USA INC
33 Goldenrod, Irvine (92614-7923)
PHONE..............................949 786-4854
David Carmi, *General Mgr*
▲ EMP: 50
SALES (est): 1MM **Privately Held**
SIC: 7539 Electrical services

(P-17793)
DISCOUNT TIRE CTR
Also Called: Discount Tire Center
19545 Parthenia St Ste 3, Northridge (91324-3462)
PHONE..............................818 993-4758
Sebouh Donoyan, *CEO*
Steve Donoyan, *Manager*
EMP: 66 EST: 2002
SQ FT: 500
SALES (est): 3.5MM **Privately Held**
SIC: 7539 5531 Automotive repair shops; automotive tires

(P-17794)
EDF RENEWABLES SERVICES INC (HQ)
Also Called: Enxco
15445 Innovation Dr, San Diego (92128-3432)
PHONE..............................858 521-3575
Tristan Grimbert, *President*
John Marchand, *President*
Greg Oliver, *Admin Asst*
EMP: 65
SQ FT: 70,000

SALES (est): 104MM
SALES (corp-wide): 569.6MM **Privately Held**
SIC: 7539 Alternators & generators, rebuilding & repair
PA: Edf Renewables, Inc.
15445 Innovation Dr
San Diego CA 92128
858 521-3300

(P-17795)
HIGH SUMMIT LLC
Also Called: Special Events
6909 Las Positas Rd Ste D, Livermore (94551-5113)
PHONE..............................925 605-2900
Weston Cook,
Elizabeth Clark, *Manager*
Christine Cook, *Manager*
Danielle Landman, *Manager*
EMP: 50
SALES (est): 3.3MM **Privately Held**
SIC: 7539 Automotive repair shops

(P-17796)
NBCCAT CORP
Also Called: X M G M
1044 Madruga Rd, Lathrop (95330-9779)
PHONE..............................209 858-0283
Richard Gray, *Manager*
EMP: 51
SALES (corp-wide): 6.2MM **Privately Held**
SIC: 7539 Automotive repair shops
PA: Nbccat Corp
7431 W 90th St
Bridgeview IL 60455
708 793-5191

(P-17797)
SACRAMENTO MUNICPL UTILITY DST
6201 S St, Sacramento (95817-1818)
P.O. Box 15830 (95852-0830)
PHONE..............................916 452-3211
Jan Shoory, *General Mgr*
EMP: 2000
SALES (corp-wide): 1.5B **Privately Held**
SIC: 7539 Electrical services
PA: Sacramento Municipal Utility District
6201 S St
Sacramento CA 95817
916 452-3211

(P-17798)
SAN FRANCISCO CITY & COUNTY
200 Paul Ave B, San Francisco (94124-3100)
PHONE..............................415 550-4600
Peter Aviles, *Office Mgr*
Michael Braun, *Supervisor*
EMP: 110 **Privately Held**
SIC: 7539 9311 7538
PA: City & County Of San Francisco
1 Dr Carlton B Goodlett P
San Francisco CA 94102
415 554-7500

(P-17799)
VERNON AUTOPARTS INC
1559 W 134th St, Gardena (90249-2215)
PHONE..............................323 249-7545
Mike Klapper, *President*
Mary Ann Klapper, *Corp Secy*
David Klapper, *Vice Pres*
EMP: 54
SQ FT: 100,000
SALES (est): 468.6K
SALES (corp-wide): 7.2MM **Privately Held**
SIC: 7539 3714 3694 3592 Machine shop, automotive; motor vehicle parts & accessories; engine electrical equipment; carburetors, pistons, rings, valves; power transmission equipment; pumps & pumping equipment
PA: Electrical Rebuilders Sales, Inc.
1559 W 134th St
Gardena CA 90249
323 249-7545

7542 Car Washes

(P-17800)
ALL HNDS CRWASH DTAIL CTR LUBE
22952 Pacific Park Dr, Aliso Viejo (92656-3389)
PHONE..................949 716-3600
Raul Valerio, *President*
Carlos Valerio, *CFO*
EMP: 60
SQ FT: 92,000
SALES (est): 1.3MM **Privately Held**
WEB: www.allhandscarwash.com
SIC: 7542 Washing & polishing, automotive

(P-17801)
AUTO WORLD CAR WASH LLC
15951 Los Gatos Blvd, Los Gatos (95032-3428)
PHONE..................408 345-6532
Jeff Locastro, *CEO*
EMP: 1597
SALES (est): 2.7MM
SALES (corp-wide): 66.5MM **Privately Held**
SIC: 7542
PA: California Secured Investments, Llc
14225 Lora Dr Apt 96
Los Gatos CA

(P-17802)
BEACH AND LA MIRADA CAR WASH
5231 Beach Blvd, Buena Park (90621-1229)
PHONE..................714 994-1099
Efrain Garcia, *Manager*
Harry Acebedo, *Systs Prg Mgr*
EMP: 50
SALES (est): 1.4MM **Privately Held**
SIC: 7542 Carwashes

(P-17803)
BOWIE ENTERPRISES
Also Called: Red Carpet Car Wash
1920 S Mooney Blvd, Visalia (93277-4450)
PHONE..................559 732-2988
Scott Rotse, *Manager*
EMP: 53
SALES (corp-wide): 13.7MM **Privately Held**
WEB: www.redcarpetcarwash.com
SIC: 7542 Washing & polishing, automotive
PA: Bowie Enterprises
4411 N Blackstone Ave
Fresno CA 93726
559 227-6221

(P-17804)
BOWIE ENTERPRISES (PA)
Also Called: Red Carpet Car Wash
4411 N Blackstone Ave, Fresno (93726-1904)
PHONE..................559 227-6221
David Bowie, *President*
James M Bowie, *Ch of Bd*
Karen Bowie, *Treasurer*
Kathryn Bowie, *Admin Sec*
EMP: 60
SQ FT: 7,700
SALES (est): 13.7MM **Privately Held**
WEB: www.redcarpetcarwash.com
SIC: 7542 5541 Carwash, automatic; filling stations, gasoline

(P-17805)
BOWIE ENTERPRISES
Also Called: Red Carpet Car Wash
801 W Shaw Ave, Clovis (93612-3218)
PHONE..................559 292-6565
EMP: 65
SALES (corp-wide): 13.7MM **Privately Held**
WEB: www.redcarpetcarwash.com
SIC: 7542 Washing & polishing, automotive
PA: Bowie Enterprises
4411 N Blackstone Ave
Fresno CA 93726
559 227-6221

(P-17806)
CANEPAS CAR WASH (PA)
642 N Hunter St, Stockton (95202-2022)
PHONE..................209 948-1636
Remo J Canepa, *President*
Marion Canepa, *Corp Secy*
Steven Canepa, *Vice Pres*
EMP: 60
SQ FT: 30,000
SALES (est): 2.4MM **Privately Held**
SIC: 7542 5541 5947 Washing & polishing, automotive; filling stations, gasoline; gift shop

(P-17807)
CAR WASH PARTNERS INC
3201 Panama Ln, Bakersfield (93313-3732)
PHONE..................661 837-9485
John Lai, *President*
EMP: 150
SALES (corp-wide): 2.7MM **Privately Held**
SIC: 7542 Carwashes
PA: Car Wash Partners, Inc.
222 E 5th St
Tucson AZ 85705
520 615-4000

(P-17808)
CHARLES FENLEY ENTERPRISES
Also Called: Chevron
1109 Oakdale Rd, Modesto (95355-4065)
P.O. Box 577200 (95357-7200)
PHONE..................209 523-2832
Gene Rooney, *Manager*
EMP: 50
SALES (corp-wide): 9.1MM **Privately Held**
SIC: 7542 5541 5948 7549 Carwash, automatic; filling stations, gasoline; luggage, except footlockers & trunks; leather goods, except luggage & shoes; lubrication service, automotive
PA: Charles Fenley Enterprises
1121 Oakdale Rd Ste 7
Modesto CA 95355
209 576-0381

(P-17809)
CIRCLE MARINA CAR WASH INC
Also Called: Circle Marina Hand Car Wash
4800 E Pacific Coast Hwy, Long Beach (90804-3243)
PHONE..................562 494-4698
John C Wang, *President*
EMP: 50
SALES (est): 1.9MM **Privately Held**
SIC: 7542 Washing & polishing, automotive

(P-17810)
CLASSIC CAR WASH INC (PA)
871 E Hamilton Ave Ste C, Campbell (95008-0602)
P.O. Box 5993, San Jose (95150-5993)
PHONE..................408 371-2414
Frank Dorsa, *President*
Robert Miller, *CFO*
EMP: 150
SQ FT: 1,500
SALES (est): 4.7MM **Privately Held**
WEB: www.classiccarwash.net
SIC: 7542 Carwash, automatic; washing & polishing, automotive

(P-17811)
COAST CARWASH LP
Also Called: Coast Hand Car Wash
5677 E 7th St, Long Beach (90804-4430)
PHONE..................562 961-5555
James Yang, *Partner*
Gregory Yang, *Partner*
Jerry Yang, *Partner*
Peter Yang, *Partner*
EMP: 50 EST: 1998
SALES (est): 3MM **Privately Held**
WEB: www.coastcarwash.com
SIC: 7542 7538 Carwashes; general automotive repair shops

(P-17812)
DUCKYS OF SAN CARLOS INC
Also Called: Ducky's Car Wash
1301 Old County Rd, San Carlos (94070-5201)
PHONE..................650 637-1301
Steve Munkdale, *President*
EMP: 50
SALES (est): 907.9K **Privately Held**
SIC: 7542 Washing & polishing, automotive

(P-17813)
DYNAMIC AUTO IMAGES INC
Also Called: Dynamic Detail
1407 N Batavia St Ste 102, Orange (92867-3525)
PHONE..................714 981-4367
Tom Miller, *President*
EMP: 300
SQ FT: 2,500
SALES (est): 13.2MM **Privately Held**
WEB: www.dynamicautoimages.com
SIC: 7542 7532 Washing & polishing, automotive; collision shops, automotive

(P-17814)
ENCINO CENTER CAR WASH INC
16300 Ventura Blvd, Encino (91436-2116)
PHONE..................818 788-6300
EMP: 50
SALES (est): 1MM **Privately Held**
SIC: 7542 5541 5947

(P-17815)
GEORGE FASCHING
Also Called: Faschings Car Wash
425 N Santa Anita Ave, Arcadia (91006-2876)
PHONE..................626 446-0654
George Fasching, *Owner*
Geri Fasching, *Co-Owner*
EMP: 50 EST: 1977
SQ FT: 60,000
SALES (est): 1.8MM **Privately Held**
SIC: 7542 5541 Carwash, automatic; washing & polishing, automotive; filling stations, gasoline

(P-17816)
GIEG CHEVRON LLC
Also Called: Splash Fast Lube
905 Abbott St 945, Salinas (93901-4361)
PHONE..................831 755-8000
Ron Gieg, *Mng Member*
Dale Gieg, *Co-Owner*
EMP: 60 EST: 1998
SALES (est): 1.3MM **Privately Held**
SIC: 7542 5541 Carwashes; filling stations, gasoline

(P-17817)
HLW CORP
Also Called: Shine and Bright Hand Car Wash
11166 Venice Blvd, Culver City (90232-3921)
PHONE..................310 838-7100
John Watkins, *President*
Monica Dixon, *Manager*
EMP: 50
SQ FT: 600
SALES (est): 1.6MM **Privately Held**
WEB: www.hlwcorp.com
SIC: 7542 Washing & polishing, automotive

(P-17818)
IN & OUT CAR WASH INC
Also Called: Spot Free Car Wash
3615 Monte Real, Escondido (92029-7911)
PHONE..................619 316-8492
Donald Macek, *President*
Denis McKnight, *Vice Pres*
EMP: 50
SQ FT: 20,000
SALES (est): 2MM **Privately Held**
WEB: www.inoutcarwash.com
SIC: 7542 Washing & polishing, automotive

(P-17819)
JACKS CAR WASH 3
6745 N West Ave, Fresno (93711-4304)
PHONE..................559 438-8201

EMP: 60
SALES (est): 117.5K **Privately Held**
SIC: 7542 5947 5812 Carwash, self-service; gift shop; coffee shop

(P-17820)
JEMTOWN INC
Also Called: Five Star Auto Repr & Car Wash
6818 Five Star Blvd, Rocklin (95677-2660)
PHONE..................916 315-0555
James A Sperlazza, *President*
Mary Sperlazza, *Vice Pres*
Kieran Griffin, *Manager*
EMP: 50
SALES (est): 2.1MM **Privately Held**
SIC: 7542 Washing & polishing, automotive

(P-17821)
JKF AUTO SERVICE INC
Also Called: Five Star Auto Repair and Wash
6818 Five Star Blvd, Rocklin (95677-2660)
PHONE..................916 315-0555
Jeff Finerman, *President*
Karen W Finerman, *Vice Pres*
EMP: 60
SALES (est): 1.3MM **Privately Held**
SIC: 7542 7549 7539 Washing & polishing, automotive; lubrication service, automotive; automotive repair shops

(P-17822)
LAKEWOOD SOUTH CAR WASH LLC
Also Called: Rossmoor Carwash
11031 Alamitos Ave, Los Alamitos (90720)
PHONE..................562 430-4975
Foster A Hooper, *Principal*
Alex Quiroz, *General Mgr*
EMP: 50 EST: 1965
SALES (est): 1.2MM **Privately Held**
SIC: 7542 Washing & polishing, automotive

(P-17823)
LARK AVENUE CAR WASH
Also Called: Classic Car Washes
5005 Almaden Expy, San Jose (95118-2049)
P.O. Box 5993 (95150-5993)
PHONE..................408 371-2565
Chuck Mina, *Site Mgr*
EMP: 72
SQ FT: 7,859
SALES (corp-wide): 11.6MM **Privately Held**
SIC: 7542 Carwashes
PA: Lark Avenue Car Wash
871 E Hamilton Ave
Campbell CA 95008
408 371-2414

(P-17824)
LARK AVENUE CAR WASH
Also Called: Chevron
981 E Hamilton Ave, Campbell (95008-0648)
PHONE..................408 377-2525
Mike Davis, *Principal*
EMP: 60
SALES (corp-wide): 11.6MM **Privately Held**
SIC: 7542 Carwashes
PA: Lark Avenue Car Wash
871 E Hamilton Ave
Campbell CA 95008
408 371-2414

(P-17825)
LITTLE SISTERS TRUCK WASH INC
72189 Varner Rd, Thousand Palms (92276-3364)
PHONE..................760 343-3448
Bob Crogan, *Manager*
EMP: 60 **Privately Held**
SIC: 7542 Washing & polishing, automotive; truck wash
PA: Little Sisters Truck Wash Inc
25 Rolling View Ln
Fallbrook CA 92028

(P-17826)
LITTLE SISTERS TRUCK WASH INC
8899 Three Flags Ave, Oak Hills (92344-0497)
PHONE....................................760 947-4448
Joe McSann, *Manager*
EMP: 65 **Privately Held**
SIC: 7542 Washing & polishing, automotive; truck wash
PA: Little Sisters Truck Wash Inc
25 Rolling View Ln
Fallbrook CA 92028
-

(P-17827)
LITTLE SISTERS TRUCK WASH INC
14264 Valley Blvd, Fontana (92335-5293)
PHONE....................................909 549-1862
Tod Kerns, *Manager*
EMP: 65 **Privately Held**
SIC: 7542 Washing & polishing, automotive; truck wash
PA: Little Sisters Truck Wash Inc
25 Rolling View Ln
Fallbrook CA 92028
-

(P-17828)
LITTLE SISTERS TRUCK WASH INC
2960 Lenwood Rd, Barstow (92311-9571)
PHONE....................................760 253-2277
B J Elmanza, *Manager*
EMP: 70
SQ FT: 2,482 **Privately Held**
SIC: 7542 Washing & polishing, automotive; truck wash
PA: Little Sisters Truck Wash Inc
25 Rolling View Ln
Fallbrook CA 92028
-

(P-17829)
LITTLE SISTERS TRUCK WASH INC (PA)
Also Called: Little Sister's Truck Wash
25 Rolling View Ln, Fallbrook (92028-9234)
P.O. Box 1530, Bonsall (92003-1530)
PHONE....................................760 731-3170
Renald J Anelle, *President*
Cathy Anelle, *Corp Secy*
William F Wire, *Vice Pres*
EMP: 69
SALES (est): 8.1MM **Privately Held**
SIC: 7542 Washing & polishing, automotive; truck wash

(P-17830)
LOZANO INC
Also Called: Lozano Car Wash
2690 W El Camino Real, Mountain View (94040-1117)
PHONE....................................650 941-0590
Manuel J Lozano, *President*
Claudia Rozriduez, *Manager*
EMP: 107
SQ FT: 500
SALES (est): 3.5MM **Privately Held**
WEB: www.lozano.net
SIC: 7542 Carwash, automatic

(P-17831)
M K H INC
Also Called: Cruisers Carwash & Diner
8870 Tampa Ave, Northridge (91324-3519)
PHONE....................................818 882-9274
Mike Harn, *President*
EMP: 60
SALES (est): 1.2MM **Privately Held**
SIC: 7542 5812 Washing & polishing, automotive; diner

(P-17832)
MISSION CAR WASH
Also Called: Mission Car Wash & Quik Lube
59 Mission Cir, Santa Rosa (95409-5304)
PHONE....................................707 537-2040
Tim Mitchell, *Owner*
Rebecca Boling, *Buyer*
EMP: 50
SQ FT: 6,157

SALES (est): 1.4MM **Privately Held**
SIC: 7542 Washing & polishing, automotive

(P-17833)
NORCO HILLS CAR WASH
Also Called: Norco Auto Wash
18020 Magnolia St, Fountain Valley (92708-5603)
PHONE....................................951 279-4398
Steve Hart, *Partner*
Robert Keane, *Partner*
EMP: 50
SALES (est): 2.4MM **Privately Held**
SIC: 7542 Washing & polishing, automotive

(P-17834)
PLAZA HAND CARWASH INC
Also Called: Prime Stop
23100 Alssndro Blvd Ste B, Moreno Valley (92553-9670)
PHONE....................................951 697-4420
Bob Sherrick, *President*
EMP: 50
SQ FT: 15,000
SALES (est): 1.1MM **Privately Held**
SIC: 7542 5087 Carwash, automatic; carwash equipment & supplies

(P-17835)
PRECISION AUTO DETAILING LLC
700 Serramonte Blvd, Colma (94014-3220)
PHONE....................................650 992-9775
Anthony Caprini,
EMP: 80
SALES (est): 2MM **Privately Held**
SIC: 7542 5087 Washing & polishing, automotive; carwash equipment & supplies

(P-17836)
PRESTIGE CAR WASH LAFAYETTE LP
Also Called: Lafayette Car Wash
3319 Mt Diablo Blvd, Lafayette (94549-4011)
PHONE....................................925 283-1190
Jesse Wellen, *Partner*
EMP: 50
SQ FT: 2,000
SALES (est): 1.6MM **Privately Held**
WEB: www.lafayettecarwash.com
SIC: 7542 7532 Washing & polishing, automotive; body shop, automotive

(P-17837)
RUSSELL FISHER PARTNERSHIP
Also Called: Bella Terra Carwash
16061 Beach Blvd, Huntington Beach (92647-3802)
PHONE....................................714 842-4453
Ruben Hernandez, *Site Mgr*
Alphonso Perez, *Manager*
Juan Rojas, *Manager*
EMP: 50
SALES (est): 2.5MM
SALES (corp-wide): 3.6MM **Privately Held**
SIC: 7542 Washing & polishing, automotive
PA: Russell Fisher Partnership
18971 Beach Blvd
Huntington Beach CA 92648
909 930-5420

(P-17838)
RUSSELL FISHER PARTNERSHIP (PA)
Also Called: Huntington Beach Car Wash
18971 Beach Blvd, Huntington Beach (92648-2009)
PHONE....................................909 930-5420
Eddie R Fischer, *Partner*
Mario Gomez, *Manager*
EMP: 80
SQ FT: 3,000
SALES (est): 3.6MM **Privately Held**
SIC: 7542 Washing & polishing, automotive

(P-17839)
SUDS CAR WASH INC
4620 Post St, El Dorado Hills (95762-7102)
PHONE....................................916 673-6300
Jeffery A Lowe, *President*
Ashley Lowe, *Vice Pres*
EMP: 50
SALES (est): 1.7MM **Privately Held**
SIC: 7542 Washing & polishing, automotive

(P-17840)
TEAM DYKSPRA (PA)
2315 California Ave, Corona (92881-6655)
PHONE....................................951 898-6482
Lenny Dykstra, *President*
EMP: 60
SALES (est): 3.1MM **Privately Held**
SIC: 7542 7549 Carwashes; automotive maintenance services

(P-17841)
VERNON TRUCK WASH INC
3308 Bandini Blvd, Vernon (90058-4113)
PHONE....................................323 267-0706
Armen Keshishyan, *President*
EMP: 105
SQ FT: 800
SALES (est): 2.6MM **Privately Held**
SIC: 7542 Truck wash

(P-17842)
VLADIGOR INVESTMENT INC
Also Called: Tower Car Wash
1601 Mission St, San Francisco (94103-2413)
PHONE....................................415 558-9274
Igor Paskhover,
Lisa Syelsky, *Vice Pres*
EMP: 90
SQ FT: 25,000
SALES (est): 3.4MM **Privately Held**
SIC: 7542 Washing & polishing, automotive

(P-17843)
WEST LAKE TOUCHLESS CAR WASH
223 87th St, Daly City (94015-1644)
PHONE....................................650 992-5344
Fred Tautenhan, *Owner*
Dean Tautenhahn, *Persnl Dir*
EMP: 50
SALES (est): 1.1MM **Privately Held**
WEB: www.westlaketouchlesscarwash.com
SIC: 7542 5541 Carwash, automatic; gasoline service stations

7549 Automotive Svcs, Except Repair & Car Washes

(P-17844)
AA AUTMTIVE PERSONNEL SVCS INC
2251 Federal Ave, Los Angeles (90064-1403)
PHONE....................................310 914-3012
Alvaro Marcin, *President*
EMP: 200
SALES (est): 4.1MM **Privately Held**
SIC: 7549 Automotive maintenance services

(P-17845)
ABSOLUTE TOWING-HOLLENBECK DIV
4760 Valley Blvd, Los Angeles (90032-3834)
PHONE....................................323 225-9294
Todd Q Smart, *President*
EMP: 50 **EST:** 1998
SQ FT: 111,000
SALES (est): 3.9MM **Privately Held**
SIC: 7549 Towing service, automotive

(P-17846)
ALAMITOS ENTERPRISES LLC (PA)
Also Called: Jiffy Lube
3311 Katella Ave, Los Alamitos (90720-2337)
PHONE....................................562 596-1827
Michael Biddle, *Mng Member*
Mike Biddle, *Vice Pres*
Patrick Novak, *Administration*
Robert Curry,
EMP: 70
SQ FT: 2,500
SALES (est): 10.3MM **Privately Held**
SIC: 7549 Lubrication service, automotive

(P-17847)
ALLIED GARDENS TOWING INC (HQ)
9150 Chesapeake Dr # 240, San Diego (92123-1061)
PHONE....................................619 563-4060
Edward S Bischop, *President*
EMP: 60 **EST:** 1970
SQ FT: 1,500
SALES (est): 2.3MM
SALES (corp-wide): 615.1MM **Publicly Held**
SIC: 7549 Towing service, automotive
PA: Miller Industries, Inc.
8503 Hilltop Dr
Ooltewah TN 37363
423 238-4171

(P-17848)
ALLIED LUBE TEXAS LP (PA)
4440 Von Karman Ave # 100, Newport Beach (92660-2011)
PHONE....................................949 486-4008
Anthony Fancicola, *Owner*
Bob Seidmeyer, *Vice Pres*
Robert Angus, *Finance Mgr*
Tiffany Preijers-Pompa, *HR Admin*
Maggie Chapdelaine, *VP Mktg*
EMP: 57 **EST:** 2005
SALES (est): 11.9MM **Privately Held**
SIC: 7549 Lubrication service, automotive

(P-17849)
AMERIT FLEET SOLUTIONS INC (HQ)
1331 N Calif Blvd Ste 150, Walnut Creek (94596-4535)
PHONE....................................877 512-6374
Gary Herbold, *Chairman*
Dan Williams, *CEO*
Amein Punjani, *COO*
David Allinson, *CFO*
Kent Bates, *CFO*
EMP: 100
SALES: 160MM **Privately Held**
SIC: 7549 Inspection & diagnostic service, automotive

(P-17850)
ARS WEST LLC
780 W El Norte Pkwy, Escondido (92026-3984)
PHONE....................................760 480-6631
Jennie Anderson, *President*
EMP: 86
SALES (corp-wide): 39.2MM **Privately Held**
SIC: 7549 5499 Automotive maintenance services; dried fruit
PA: Ars West Llc
2204 S El Camino Real # 314
Oceanside CA 92054
760 730-5137

(P-17851)
AUTOMOTIVE TSTG & DEV SVCS INC (PA)
400 Etiwanda Ave, Ontario (91761-8637)
PHONE....................................909 390-1100
Devon Larry Smith, *CEO*
Kay Smith, *Corp Secy*
Linwood Farmer, *Vice Pres*
Jason Link, *Manager*
George Keeble, *Supervisor*
▲ **EMP:** 200
SQ FT: 24,000

SALES (est): 18.4MM **Privately Held**
WEB: www.automotivetesting.com
SIC: 7549 8734 8711 Emissions testing without repairs, automotive; testing laboratories; engineering services

(P-17852)
BEAUDRY R V SAN MARCOS INC
Also Called: Beaudry Rv
251 Travelers Way, San Marcos (92069-2797)
P.O. Box 26925, Tucson AZ (85726-6925)
PHONE.................................760 736-8800
Robert Beaudry, *President*
Marty Holman, *COO*
EMP: 104
SQ FT: 14,000
SALES (est): 1.6MM **Privately Held**
SIC: 7549 5561 Automotive maintenance services; recreational vehicle parts & accessories

(P-17853)
BOWIE ENTERPRISES
Also Called: Red Carpet Car Wash
4411 N Blackstone Ave, Fresno (93726-1904)
PHONE.................................559 227-3400
EMP: 72
SALES (corp-wide): 13.7MM **Privately Held**
SIC: 7549 7538 Lubrication service, automotive; general automotive repair shops
PA: Bowie Enterprises
4411 N Blackstone Ave
Fresno CA 93726
559 227-6221

(P-17854)
C & D TOWING SPECIALISTS INC (PA)
Also Called: Auto Repair Specialist
8332 Case St, La Mesa (91942-2919)
PHONE.................................619 463-8697
Charles Sturrock, *CEO*
Shirlee Sturrock, *Admin Sec*
EMP: 70
SQ FT: 2,000
SALES (est): 3.9MM **Privately Held**
WEB: www.cdtowing.com
SIC: 7549 7521 Towing service, automotive; automobile storage garage

(P-17855)
CA STE ATOM ASSOC INTR-INS BUR
Also Called: AAA
4400 Capitola Rd Ste 100, Capitola (95010-3571)
P.O. Box 250 (95010-0250)
PHONE.................................831 824-9128
Donald Foley, *Branch Mgr*
EMP: 100
SALES (corp-wide): 907.9MM **Privately Held**
WEB: www.viamagazine.com
SIC: 7549 Towing services
HQ: California State Automobile Association Inter-Insurance Bureau
1276 S California Blvd
Walnut Creek CA 94596
925 287-7600

(P-17856)
CAR SPA INC
996 Mountain Ave, Norco (92860-3160)
PHONE.................................951 279-1422
Jesus Medina, *Manager*
EMP: 50
SALES (corp-wide): 39.8MM **Privately Held**
WEB: www.car-spa.com
SIC: 7549 7542 Lubrication service, automotive; washing & polishing, automotive
PA: Car Spa, Inc.
4835 Lyndo B Johns Fwy St
Dallas TX 75244
469 374-0280

(P-17857)
COMPLETE COACH WORKS (HQ)
Also Called: John Deere Authorized Dealer
1863 Service Ct, Riverside (92507-2341)
PHONE.................................951 682-2557
Dale E Carson, *President*
Michael Dominici, *CFO*
Aaron Timlick, *General Mgr*
Terri Carson, *Admin Sec*
Camelia Cocan, *Admin Asst*
▲ EMP: 280
SALES (est): 26.7MM
SALES (corp-wide): 57.1MM **Privately Held**
SIC: 7549 5082 Trailer maintenance; construction & mining machinery
PA: D/T Carson Enterprises, Inc.
42882 Ivy St
Murrieta CA 92562
951 684-9585

(P-17858)
COUNTY OF MADERA
Also Called: Madera County Road Department
200 W 4th St, Madera (93637-3548)
PHONE.................................559 675-7811
Johannes Hoeversz, *Manager*
Richard Cortez, *Manager*
EMP: 84 **Privately Held**
WEB: www.madera-county.com
SIC: 7549 Road service, automotive
PA: County Of Madera
209 W Yosemite Ave
Madera CA 93637
559 675-7726

(P-17859)
COVEY AUTO EXPRESS INC (PA)
Also Called: Pacific Towing
1444 El Pinal Dr, Stockton (95205-2642)
PHONE.................................253 826-0461
Michael D Covey, *President*
Kathy Covey, *Vice Pres*
Mark Kahler, *General Mgr*
Chelsey Moris, *Administration*
Gary Kudla, *Controller*
EMP: 150
SQ FT: 19,000
SALES (est): 21.5MM **Privately Held**
SIC: 7549 Towing service, automotive; towing services

(P-17860)
EVGO SERVICES LLC
11390 W Olympic Blvd Fl 2, Los Angeles (90064-1607)
PHONE.................................310 954-2900
Cathy Zoi, *CEO*
Christoper O'Donnell, *CFO*
Jay Goldman, *Vice Pres*
Jonathan Levy, *Vice Pres*
Olga Shevorenkova, *Vice Pres*
EMP: 75
SQ FT: 10,000
SALES (est): 2.8MM **Privately Held**
SIC: 7549 Automotive maintenance services

(P-17861)
EZ LUBE LLC (PA)
3540 Howard Way Ste 200, Costa Mesa (92626-1496)
PHONE.................................714 556-1312
Guy Marsala, *President*
Roger Dunlap, *VP Opers*
Mark D Goodman, *Mng Member*
EMP: 60
SQ FT: 2,000
SALES (est): 22.5MM **Privately Held**
WEB: www.ezlube.com
SIC: 7549 Lubrication service, automotive; inspection & diagnostic service, automotive

(P-17862)
HIGH STREET HAND CAR WASH INC
Also Called: High St Car Wash Lube & Oil
569 High St, Oakland (94601-3905)
PHONE.................................510 536-4333
Chong B Kim, *President*
EMP: 51

SQ FT: 3,123
SALES (est): 2MM **Privately Held**
SIC: 7549 7542 Lubrication service, automotive; carwashes

(P-17863)
HONDA PERFORMANCE DEV INC
25145 Anza Dr, Santa Clarita (91355-3416)
PHONE.................................661 294-7300
Eddie Navarrette, *General Mgr*
Eric Berkman, *President*
Lee Niffenegger, *Engineer*
Russell Machida, *Purchasing*
Marc Sours, *Prdtn Mgr*
◆ EMP: 88
SQ FT: 100,000
SALES (est): 15.2MM
SALES (corp-wide): 144.1B **Privately Held**
SIC: 7549 High performance auto repair & service
HQ: American Honda Motor Co., Inc.
1919 Torrance Blvd
Torrance CA 90501
310 783-2000

(P-17864)
J C TOWING INC
2501 Faivre St, Chula Vista (91911-4603)
PHONE.................................619 429-1492
Gardner J Clark IV, *President*
EMP: 52
SQ FT: 2,000
SALES (est): 3.2MM **Privately Held**
SIC: 7549 Towing services

(P-17865)
LITHIA AUTOMOTIVE GROUP INC
Also Called: Nissan of Stockton
1020 S Beckman Rd, Lodi (95240-3152)
PHONE.................................209 956-6500
Brian Castonguay, *Branch Mgr*
EMP: 50
SQ FT: 20,000
SALES (corp-wide): 26.3MM **Privately Held**
SIC: 7549 5599 7538 Automotive maintenance services; aircraft dealers; general automotive repair shops
PA: Lithia Automotive Group Inc
163 S 9th St
Springfield OR 97477
541 747-3374

(P-17866)
METROPRO ROAD SERVICES INC (PA)
Also Called: A & P Towing-Metropro Rd Svcs
2550 S Garnsey St, Santa Ana (92707-3337)
PHONE.................................714 556-7600
Bradley T Humphreys, *CEO*
Jody Campbell, *President*
Jean Noutary, *General Mgr*
Michael Kirkland, *Manager*
EMP: 100
SQ FT: 85,000
SALES (est): 7.3MM **Privately Held**
SIC: 7549 Towing services

(P-17867)
MOC PRODUCTS COMPANY INC
9840 Kitty Ln, Oakland (94603-1070)
PHONE.................................510 635-1230
George Logan, *Branch Mgr*
EMP: 68
SALES (corp-wide): 64.6MM **Privately Held**
WEB: www.mocproducts.com
SIC: 7549 Automotive maintenance services
PA: Moc Products Company, Inc.
12306 Montague St
Pacoima CA 91331
818 794-3500

(P-17868)
POISON SPYDER CUSTOMS INC
Also Called: Transamerican Auto Parts
1177 W Lincoln St Ste 100, Banning (92220-4524)
PHONE.................................951 849-5911
Larry McRae, *President*

Cheri McRae, *Officer*
◆ EMP: 884 EST: 2009
SALES (est): 29.9MM **Privately Held**
SIC: 7549 Automotive customizing services, non-factory basis
PA: Tap Worldwide, Llc
400 W Artesia Blvd
Compton CA 90220

(P-17869)
REDHILL TOWING & AUTOBODY
428 Irwin St, San Rafael (94901-5113)
PHONE.................................415 456-8943
Joe Paz Jr, *President*
Linda Paz, *Vice Pres*
EMP: 54
SQ FT: 7,000
SALES (est): 4.4MM **Privately Held**
WEB: www.redhilltowing.com
SIC: 7549 Towing service, automotive; towing services

(P-17870)
S AND R TOWING INC (PA)
1060 Airport Rd, Oceanside (92058-1209)
P.O. Box 4366, Carlsbad (92018-4366)
PHONE.................................760 722-6686
Steve Dugan, *President*
Charles Russell, *CFO*
Ric Johnsen, *Info Tech Mgr*
Rusty Russell, *Webmaster*
EMP: 50
SQ FT: 2,400
SALES (est): 8.3MM **Privately Held**
WEB: www.srtow.com
SIC: 7549 Towing service, automotive; towing services

(P-17871)
SEARS ROEBUCK AND CO
40680 Winchester Rd, Temecula (92591-5504)
PHONE.................................951 719-3528
Dan Larue, *Manager*
EMP: 93
SALES (corp-wide): 16.7B **Publicly Held**
SIC: 7549 Automotive maintenance services
HQ: Sears, Roebuck And Co.
3333 Beverly Rd
Hoffman Estates IL 60179
847 286-2500

(P-17872)
SEARS ROEBUCK AND CO
Also Called: Sears Auto Center
1235 Colusa Ave, Yuba City (95991-3693)
PHONE.................................530 751-4628
Cathy Nicholls, *Branch Mgr*
EMP: 100
SALES (corp-wide): 16.7B **Publicly Held**
SIC: 7549 Automotive maintenance services
HQ: Sears, Roebuck And Co.
3333 Beverly Rd
Hoffman Estates IL 60179
847 286-2500

(P-17873)
STRLNG PATH MEDCL CORP
3030 Old Ranch Pkwy # 430, Seal Beach (90740-2760)
PHONE.................................562 799-8900
Changgao Yang, *President*
EMP: 50
SALES (est): 532.6K **Privately Held**
SIC: 7549 Inspection & diagnostic service, automotive

(P-17874)
SUNBELT TOWING INC (PA)
Also Called: Western Towing
4370 Pacific Hwy, San Diego (92110-3106)
PHONE.................................619 297-8697
Steven Hendrickson, *President*
Cindy Florian, *Cust Mgr*
Larry White, *Manager*
EMP: 70
SALES: 8.5MM **Privately Held**
WEB: www.perfectionautobody.net
SIC: 7549 7532 Towing service, automotive; top & body repair & paint shops

▲ = Import ▼=Export
◆ =Import/Export

(P-17875)
TEGSCO LLC
Also Called: Autoreturn
450 7th St, San Francisco (94103-4532)
PHONE...............................415 575-2340
Ray Krouse,
Raymond Krouse,
John Wicker,
EMP: 60
SQ FT: 15,000
SALES (est): 6.3MM **Privately Held**
SIC: 7549 Towing service, automotive

(P-17876)
TOYOTA LOGISTICS SERVICES
1340 Cesar E Chavez Pkwy, San Diego
(92113-2133)
PHONE...............................619 531-0157
Antonio Venejas, *Principal*
EMP: 210
SALES (corp-wide): 275.7B **Privately
Held**
SIC: 7549 8999 Automotive maintenance
services; artists & artists' studios
HQ: Toyota Logistics Services, Inc
19001 S Western Ave
Torrance CA 90501
310 618-5009

(P-17877)
TOYOTA LOGISTICS SERVICES
(DH)
19001 S Western Ave, Torrance
(90501-1106)
PHONE...............................310 618-5009
Randy Pflughaupt, *CEO*
Allen Decarr, *President*
Donald Esmond, *Principal*
▼ EMP: 176
SQ FT: 600
SALES (est): 62.8MM
SALES (corp-wide): 275.7B **Privately
Held**
SIC: 7549 3711 Automotive maintenance
services; motor vehicles & car bodies
HQ: Toyota Motor Sales Usa Inc
6565 Hdqtr Dr Apt W1 3c
Plano TX 75024
310 468-4000

(P-17878)
TOYOTA LOGISTICS SERVICES
785 Edison Ave, Long Beach (90813-2657)
PHONE...............................562 437-6767
Audie Freeman, *Manager*
EMP: 289
SALES (corp-wide): 275.7B **Privately
Held**
SIC: 7549 Automotive maintenance serv-
ices
HQ: Toyota Logistics Services, Inc
19001 S Western Ave
Torrance CA 90501
310 618-5009

(P-17879)
UNITED ROAD TOWING INC
1516 S Bon View Ave, Ontario
(91761-4407)
PHONE...............................909 923-6100
Gabriel Ramirez, *Manager*
EMP: 56
SALES (est): 881.6K
SALES (corp-wide): 152.1MM **Privately
Held**
WEB: www.unitedroad.com
SIC: 7549 Towing service, automotive; tow-
ing services
HQ: United Road Towing, Inc.
9550 Bormet Dr Ste 304
Mokena IL 60448
708 390-2200

(P-17880)
UNITED ROAD TOWING INC
945 W Brockton Ave, Redlands
(92374-2903)
PHONE...............................909 798-4863
Gabriel Ramirez, *Manager*
EMP: 56
SALES (est): 429.2K
SALES (corp-wide): 152.1MM **Privately
Held**
WEB: www.unitedroad.com
SIC: 7549 Towing services

HQ: United Road Towing, Inc.
9550 Bormet Dr Ste 304
Mokena IL 60448
708 390-2200

(P-17881)
VALVOLINE INTERNATIONAL
INC
Also Called: Valvoline Instant Oil Change
9520 John St, Santa Fe Springs
(90670-2904)
PHONE...............................562 906-6200
Brian Nichols, *Branch Mgr*
EMP: 50
SALES (corp-wide): 2B **Publicly Held**
SIC: 7549 Automotive maintenance serv-
ices
HQ: Valvoline International, Inc.
100 Valvoline Way
Lexington KY 40509
-

7622 Radio & TV Repair Shops

(P-17882)
BLACK & WHITE TV INC
8756 Dorrington Ave, West Hollywood
(90048-1724)
PHONE...............................310 855-1040
Jeffrey Fischgrund, *President*
EMP: 50
SALES (est): 771.8K **Privately Held**
SIC: 7622 Television repair shop

(P-17883)
JVC AMERICAS CORP
Also Called: Jvc Company of America
5665 Corporate Ave, Cypress
(90630-4727)
PHONE...............................714 527-7500
Ron Serasio, *Manager*
EMP: 60
SQ FT: 82,000 **Privately Held**
SIC: 7622 Radio & television repair

(P-17884)
JVC AMERICAS CORP
Also Called: Jvc Service & Engineering
11925 Pike St, Santa Fe Springs
(90670-2955)
PHONE...............................562 463-8110
EMP: 80 **Privately Held**
SIC: 7622

(P-17885)
MINILEC SERVICE INC
Also Called: Minilec Service-Los Angeles BR
9207 Deering Ave Ste A, Chatsworth
(91311-6959)
PHONE...............................818 341-1125
EMP: 50
SQ FT: 7,000
SALES (corp-wide): 6.6MM **Privately
Held**
SIC: 7622 4812
PA: Minilec Service Inc.
9207 Deering Ave Ste A
Chatsworth CA 91311
818 773-6300

(P-17886)
PRECISION TELEVISION INC
Also Called: Precision TV
2350 Stanwell Dr, Concord (94520-4822)
PHONE...............................925 825-5296
Derrick W Behrens, *CEO*
Robert Behrens, *Vice Pres*
EMP: 54
SQ FT: 5,500
SALES (est): 7.5MM **Privately Held**
SIC: 7622 Television repair shop

(P-17887)
SOHNEN ENTERPRISES INC
(PA)
13225 Marquardt Ave, Santa Fe Springs
(90670-4831)
P.O. Box 2884 (90670-0884)
PHONE...............................562 903-4957
Barry Sohnen, *President*
Nathan Balsam, *Vice Pres*
Bryan Chase, *Admin Sec*
Jean Pouchoulen, *Sales Associate*

Larry Sohnen, *Asst Sec*
◆ EMP: 50
SQ FT: 132,000
SALES (est): 12.4MM **Privately Held**
WEB: www.sohnen.com
SIC: 7622 5065 7629 Radio repair shop;
video repair; communication equipment
repair; sound equipment, electronic; video
equipment, electronic; telephone equipment; communication equipment; electrical repair shops

(P-17888)
SYNTELESYS INC
Also Called: Ytech
2550 Corp Pl Ste C108, Monterey Park
(91754)
PHONE...............................323 859-2160
Carey Chrisman, *President*
▼ EMP: 50
SALES (est): 3.2MM **Privately Held**
SIC: 7622 7313 Antenna repair & installa-
tion; electronic media advertising repre-
sentatives

7623 Refrigeration & Air Conditioning Svc & Repair Shop

(P-17889)
ACCO ENGINEERED SYSTEMS
INC
3421 S Malt Ave, Commerce (90040-3127)
PHONE...............................323 727-7765
Eric Porras, *Branch Mgr*
Minh Phan, *Design Engr*
Jose Carreon, *Foreman/Supr*
Michael Gamet, *Manager*
Brian Icban, *Supervisor*
EMP: 70
SQ FT: 77,399
SALES (corp-wide): 768.2MM **Privately
Held**
WEB: www.accoair.com
SIC: 7623 1711 Air conditioning repair;
plumbing, heating, air-conditioning con-
tractors
PA: Acco Engineered Systems, Inc.
6265 San Fernando Rd
Glendale CA 91201
818 244-6571

(P-17890)
BROWER MECHANICAL INC
Also Called: Honeywell Authorized Dealer
4060 Alvis Ct, Rocklin (95677-4012)
PHONE...............................530 749-0808
Jeff Brower, *President*
Duane Knickerbocker, *Vice Pres*
Troy Bagwell, *Cust Mgr*
Gina Vierra, *Commercial*
EMP: 75
SQ FT: 5,000
SALES (est): 17.2MM **Privately Held**
WEB: www.browermechanical.com
SIC: 7623 7629 Air conditioning repair;
electrical household appliance repair

(P-17891)
CARRIER CORPORATION
Also Called: Carrier Commercial Service
1168 National Dr Ste 60, Sacramento
(95834-1979)
PHONE...............................916 928-9500
Craig Sweeney, *Branch Mgr*
EMP: 50
SALES (corp-wide): 59.8B **Publicly Held**
WEB: www.carrier.com
SIC: 7623 Air conditioning repair
HQ: Carrier Corporation
13995 Pasteur Blvd
Palm Beach Gardens FL 33418
800 379-6484

(P-17892)
CLIMA-TECH INC
187 W Orangethorpe Ave G, Placentia
(92870-6932)
PHONE...............................909 613-5513
William C Valenzuela, *CEO*
Ada Roberts, *CFO*
Husein Aziz, *Exec VP*
EMP: 89

SQ FT: 11,500
SALES (est): 13.6MM **Privately Held**
SIC: 7623 1711 Refrigeration service & repair; refrigeration contractor; heating & air
conditioning contractors

(P-17893)
COMMERCIAL MECHANICAL
SVC INC (PA)
Also Called: C M Service
981 Bing St, San Carlos (94070-5321)
PHONE...............................650 610-8440
Thomas Fewell, *President*
EMP: 50
SALES (est): 5MM **Privately Held**
WEB: www.fm-svcs.com
SIC: 7623 Refrigeration repair service; air
conditioning repair

(P-17894)
CONTROL AIR CONDITIONING
CORP
1390 Armorlite Dr, San Marcos
(92069-1342)
PHONE...............................760 744-2727
Mike Eepn, *Branch Mgr*
EMP: 190
SALES (corp-wide): 110.3MM **Privately
Held**
SIC: 7623 1711 Refrigeration service & re-
pair; heating systems repair & mainte-
nance
PA: Control Air Conditioning Corporation
5200 E La Palma Ave
Anaheim CA 92807
714 777-8600

(P-17895)
GMH INC
Also Called: West Coast Air Conditioning
561 Kinetic Dr Ste A, Oxnard (93030-7947)
PHONE...............................805 485-1410
Michael C Haase, *President*
Jim Clower, *Vice Pres*
Gina Haase, *Vice Pres*
Brent Brubaker, *Project Mgr*
Chris Pyne, *Project Mgr*
EMP: 50 EST: 1976
SQ FT: 5,600
SALES (est): 13.4MM **Privately Held**
WEB: www.westcoast-air.com
SIC: 7623 1711 Refrigeration repair serv-
ice; air conditioning repair; refrigeration
contractor; warm air heating & air condi-
tioning contractor

(P-17896)
RECURVE INC
220 Montgomery St Ste 820, San Francisco
(94104-3439)
PHONE...............................510 540-4860
Andy Leventhal, *CEO*
Matthew Golden, *President*
EMP: 52
SQ FT: 8,000
SALES (est): 3.6MM **Privately Held**
SIC: 7623 Air conditioning repair

(P-17897)
SUNBELT CONTROLS INC
Also Called: Honeywell Authorized Dealer
4511 Willow Rd Ste 4, Pleasanton
(94588-2735)
PHONE...............................925 660-3900
Josh Reding, *Branch Mgr*
EMP: 50
SALES (corp-wide): 814.8MM **Privately
Held**
SIC: 7623 1711 Refrigeration service & re-
pair; septic system construction
HQ: Sunbelt Controls, Inc.
6265 San Fernando Rd
Glendale CA 91201
-

(P-17898)
WESTERN ALLIED SERVICE
COMPANY
12046 Florence Ave, Santa Fe Springs
(90670-4406)
P.O. Box 3628 (90670-1628)
PHONE...............................562 941-3243
Steve Kieve, *CEO*
EMP: 300
SQ FT: 15,000

SALES (est): 10.4MM **Privately Held**
SIC: 7623 Air conditioning repair

7629 Electrical & Elex Repair Shop, NEC

(P-17899)
AAR MANUFACTURING INC
AAR Composites
5307 Luce Ave Bldg 243e, McClellan
(95652-2440)
PHONE....................916 830-7011
Eloy Herrera, *Branch Mgr*
EMP: 73
SALES (corp-wide): 1.7B **Publicly Held**
SIC: 7629 Electronic equipment repair
HQ: Aar Manufacturing, Inc.
　1100 N Wood Dale Rd
　Wood Dale IL 60191
　630 227-2000

(P-17900)
AAR MANUFACTURING INC
AAR Mobility Systems
5239 Luce Ave Bldg 243d, McClellan
(95652-2427)
PHONE....................800 422-2213
Lee Krantz, *Branch Mgr*
Eloy Herrera, *Business Dir*
EMP: 73
SALES (corp-wide): 1.7B **Publicly Held**
SIC: 7629 Electronic equipment repair
HQ: Aar Manufacturing, Inc.
　1100 N Wood Dale Rd
　Wood Dale IL 60191
　630 227-2000

(P-17901)
ABLE CABLE INC (PA)
Also Called: A C I Communications
5115 Douglas Fir Rd Ste A, Calabasas
(91302-2588)
PHONE....................818 223-3600
Russell Ramas, *President*
David Gardner, *CFO*
Michael Collette, *Vice Pres*
Anthony Buschelman, *Accountant*
Jim Hailfinger, *Sales Staff*
EMP: 175
SQ FT: 3,500
SALES (est): 14.8MM **Privately Held**
WEB: www.acicommunications.com
SIC: 7629 1731 4813 Telephone set repair; telephone & telephone equipment installation; fiber optic cable installation; telephone communication, except radio

(P-17902)
CPI ECONCO DIVISION (DH)
Also Called: Econco Broadcast Service
1318 Commerce Ave, Woodland
(95776-5908)
PHONE....................530 662-7553
David P Elliot, *President*
Joel Littman, *Corp Secy*
Heidi Lindberg, *Info Tech Mgr*
Todd Baker, *Engineer*
Paul Cochran, *Engineer*
◆ **EMP:** 73
SQ FT: 50,000
SALES (est): 9.4MM **Privately Held**
SIC: 7629 3671 Electrical repair shops; vacuum tubes

(P-17903)
DUTHIE ELECTRIC SERVICE CORP
Also Called: Duthie Power Services
2335 E Cherry Indus Cir, Long Beach
(90805-4416)
PHONE....................562 790-1772
Christina Duthie, *President*
Richard Duthie, *Corp Secy*
Rick Duthie, *Vice Pres*
Kevin Gates, *Sales Mgr*
Peter Thornton, *Sales Engr*
EMP: 50
SQ FT: 17,000
SALES: 13.5MM **Privately Held**
WEB:
SIC: 7629 7359 Generator repair; equipment rental & leasing

(P-17904)
GDSA-LINCOLN INC (PA)
Also Called: Weco Aerospace Systems
1501 Aviation Blvd, Lincoln (95648-9388)
PHONE....................916 645-8961
William Weygandt, *President*
Robert Weygandt, *CFO*
Kathleen Weygandt, *Admin Sec*
Elisabeta Bejenariu, *Purchasing*
▲ **EMP:** 55 **EST:** 1971
SQ FT: 7,800
SALES (est): 4.2MM **Privately Held**
SIC: 7629 5088 Aircraft electrical equipment repair; aircraft equipment & supplies

(P-17905)
JJR ENTERPRISES INC (PA)
Also Called: Caltronics Business Systems
10491 Old Placerville Rd # 150, Sacramento (95827-2531)
PHONE....................916 363-2666
Daniel F Reilly, *CEO*
Anne Long, *CFO*
John J Reilly, *Chairman*
Ryan Tellez, *Executive*
Mark Demee, *Branch Mgr*
EMP: 95
SQ FT: 30,000
SALES: 53.7MM **Privately Held**
WEB: www.caltronics.net
SIC: 7629 5044 7359 Business machine repair, electric; office equipment; equipment rental & leasing

(P-17906)
NSG TECHNOLOGY INC
Also Called: Hon Hai Precision Industry
1705 Junction Ct Ste 200, San Jose
(95112-1023)
PHONE....................408 547-8700
Ted Dubbs, *CEO*
Albert LI, *Business Dir*
MEI Huang, *Program Mgr*
Amy Lau, *Program Mgr*
Cindy LI, *Program Mgr*
▲ **EMP:** 280 **EST:** 1995
SALES (est): 43MM
SALES (corp-wide): 60.3B **Privately Held**
SIC: 7629 Electronic equipment repair
HQ: Maxwell Holdings Limited
　C/O Vistra (Cayman) Limited
　George Town GR CAYMAN

(P-17907)
PETERSON MACHINERY CO (PA)
Also Called: Peterson Cat
955 Marina Blvd, San Leandro
(94577-3440)
P.O. Box 5258 (94577-0610)
PHONE....................541 302-9199
Duane S Doyle, *CEO*
Mark Ehni, *President*
Mark Macguidwin, *CFO*
Bill Bean, *General Mgr*
Annette Crespo, *Admin Asst*
EMP: 79
SALES (est): 67.4MM **Privately Held**
WEB: www.petersonholding.com
SIC: 7629 Electrical repair shops

(P-17908)
RAYTHEON COMPANY
988 Inner Loop Rd, Fort Irwin (92310)
P.O. Box 10079 (92310-0079)
PHONE....................760 386-2572
Denise Lapage, *Branch Mgr*
Richard Stikkers, *Manager*
EMP: 500
SALES (corp-wide): 25.3B **Publicly Held**
SIC: 7629 1731 Electrical equipment repair services; electrical work
PA: Raytheon Company
　870 Winter St
　Waltham MA 02451
　781 522-3000

(P-17909)
SCHROFF INC
Also Called: Pentair Equipment Protection
7328 Trade St, San Diego (92121-3435)
PHONE....................858 740-2400
Robert Bradley, *Branch Mgr*
EMP: 120

SALES (corp-wide): 352.2K **Privately Held**
SIC: 7629 3469 Electronic enclosures, stamped or pressed metal; telecommunication equipment repair (except telephones)
HQ: Schroff, Inc.
　1665 Utica Ave S Ste 700
　Saint Louis Park MN 55416
　763 204-7700

(P-17910)
SCOTTEL VOICE & DATA INC
Also Called: Black Box Network Services
6100 Center Dr Ste 720, Los Angeles
(90045-9228)
PHONE....................310 737-7300
George Robertson, *General Mgr*
Rachelle Phillips, *Admin Asst*
Linda Hunt, *Technical Staff*
Stephen Murnane, *Sales Dir*
EMP: 130
SQ FT: 5,200
SALES (est): 30.8MM
SALES (corp-wide): 774.6MM **Publicly Held**
WEB: www.scottel.com
SIC: 7629 1731 Telecommunication equipment repair (except telephones); telephone & telephone equipment installation
PA: Black Box Corporation
　1000 Park Dr
　Lawrence PA 15055
　724 746-5500

(P-17911)
SEARS ROEBUCK AND CO
Also Called: Sears Service Center
1406 N Johnson Ave, El Cajon
(92020-1681)
PHONE....................619 590-3812
John Copelan, *Branch Mgr*
EMP: 142
SALES (corp-wide): 16.7B **Publicly Held**
SIC: 7629
HQ: Sears, Roebuck And Co.
　3333 Beverly Rd
　Hoffman Estates IL 60179
　847 286-2500

(P-17912)
SERVICE SOLUTIONS GROUP LLC
Also Called: Barkers Food Machinery
5367 2nd St, Irwindale (91706-6608)
PHONE....................626 960-9390
Robert Zachary Barasch, *Branch Mgr*
Scott Risley, *Manager*
EMP: 60
SALES (corp-wide): 2.9B **Privately Held**
SIC: 7629 7623 5046 5078 Electrical equipment repair services; refrigeration repair service; restaurant equipment & supplies; commercial refrigeration equipment; plumbing fittings & supplies; electronic parts & equipment
HQ: Service Solutions Group, Llc
　800 Aviation Pkwy
　Smyrna TN 37167
　615 462-4000

(P-17913)
SIEMENS INDUSTRY INC
1585 Parkway Blvd, West Sacramento
(95691-5017)
PHONE....................916 371-2600
EMP: 51 **Privately Held**
SIC: 7629 1731 Electrical repair shops; electrical work
PA: Republic Intelligent Transportation Services, Inc.
　371 Bel Marin Blvd
　Novato CA 94949

(P-17914)
SIMCO ELECTRONICS (PA)
3131 Jay St Ste 100, Santa Clara
(95054-3336)
PHONE....................408 734-9750
Brian Kenna, *CEO*
Bradford G Phillips, *CFO*
Sophia Tran, *HR Admin*
Todd Lee, *Opers Spvr*
Sam Klooster, *Director*
EMP: 75 **EST:** 1962

SQ FT: 24,222
SALES (est): 59.2MM **Privately Held**
WEB: www.simco.com
SIC: 7629 8734 5045 7379 Electrical repair shops; calibration & certification; computer software; computer related consulting services; computer related maintenance services

(P-17915)
TELENET VOIP INC
850 N Park View Dr, El Segundo
(90245-4914)
PHONE....................310 253-9000
Asghar Ghassemy, *President*
Nicol Payab, *Vice Pres*
Doug Amos, *Executive*
Michael Merkel, *General Mgr*
Jose Pino, *Technician*
EMP: 65
SQ FT: 11,000
SALES (est): 12.2MM **Privately Held**
WEB: www.telenetusa.net
SIC: 7629 7379 7382 3612 Telephone set repair; computer related consulting services; security systems services; transmission & distribution voltage regulators

(P-17916)
TESTEQUITY LLC (PA)
6100 Condor Dr, Moorpark (93021-2608)
PHONE....................805 498-9933
Neil McKinnon, *CFO*
Don Sinclair, *Vice Pres*
Dan Copsey,
Carol Newton, *Director*
Thomas Martinez, *Associate*
▲ **EMP:** 168
SQ FT: 75,000
SALES (est): 129.2MM **Privately Held**
SIC: 7629 3825 Electrical equipment repair services; test equipment for electronic & electrical circuits

(P-17917)
TOSHIBA BUS SOLUTIONS USA INC (DH)
9740 Irvine Blvd, Irvine (92618-1608)
PHONE....................949 462-6000
Mark Mathews, *CEO*
EMP: 118
SALES (est): 128.9MM
SALES (corp-wide): 37B **Privately Held**
SIC: 7629 5044 5999 Business machine repair, electric; office equipment; business machines & equipment
HQ: Toshiba America Business Solutions, Inc.
　25530 Commercentre Dr
　Lake Forest CA 92630
　949 462-6000

(P-17918)
USACO SERVICE CORP
Also Called: Kenwood Service Center West
16205 Distribution Way, Cerritos
(90703-2329)
PHONE....................562 483-8747
Stewart Park, *President*
▲ **EMP:** 150
SALES (est): 6.4MM **Privately Held**
WEB: www.usacoservice.com
SIC: 7629 Electrical repair shops

7631 Watch, Clock & Jewelry Repair

(P-17919)
ADVANCE SERVICES INC
8021 Kern Ave, Gilroy (95020-4051)
PHONE....................408 767-2797
Vanessa Valencia, *Manager*
EMP: 2167 **Privately Held**
SIC: 7631 Watch, clock & jewelry repair
PA: Advance Services, Inc.
　12702 Wsport Pkwy Ste 201
　La Vista NE 68138

(P-17920)
M & G JEWELERS INC
10823 Edison Ct, Rancho Cucamonga
(91730-3868)
PHONE.............................909 989-2929
Juan Guevara, *President*
Michael Insalago, *Vice Pres*
Adolfo Burbano, *Info Tech Mgr*
Brian Groce, *Accounting Mgr*
Ryan Tigner, *VP Opers*
EMP: 68
SQ FT: 8,432
SALES (est): 10.7MM **Privately Held**
WEB: www.mandgjewelers.com
SIC: 7631 Watch, clock & jewelry repair

7641 Reupholstery & Furniture Repair

(P-17921)
CORP OF CHURCH OF CHRIST LD ST
Also Called: Los Angeles Deseret Industries
2720 E 11th St, Los Angeles (90023-3404)
PHONE.............................323 268-7281
Dessin Meyer, *Director*
EMP: 130
SALES (corp-wide): 3.9B **Privately Held**
WEB: www.lds.org
SIC: 7641 5932 7629 8331 Furniture repair & maintenance; furniture, secondhand; household appliances, used; electrical household appliance repair; job training & vocational rehabilitation services
PA: Corporation Of The President Of The Church Of Jesus Christ Of Latter-Day Saints
50 E North Temple
Salt Lake City UT 84150
801 240-1000

(P-17922)
MOYES CUSTOM FURNITURE INC
3431 E La Palma Ave Ste 3, Anaheim
(92806-2022)
PHONE.............................714 729-0234
Brian Moyes, *President*
Jane Moyes, *Corp Secy*
David Moyes, *Administration*
EMP: 50
SQ FT: 59,000
SALES (est): 3.7MM **Privately Held**
WEB: www.moyesfurniture.com
SIC: 7641 2512 Reupholstery; upholstered household furniture

7692 Welding Repair

(P-17923)
HAYES WELDING INC (PA)
Also Called: Valew Welding & Fabrication
12522 Violet Rd, Adelanto (92301-2704)
P.O. Box 310 (92301-0310)
PHONE.............................760 246-4878
Roger L Hayes, *CEO*
Velma D Hayes, *President*
Vernon L Hayes, *Vice Pres*
Patrick Cavanagh, *Plant Mgr*
▲ **EMP:** 86
SQ FT: 45,000
SALES (est): 14.5MM **Privately Held**
WEB: www.valew.com
SIC: 7692 3465 3714 3713 Welding repair; automotive stampings; body parts, automobile: stamped metal; fenders, automobile: stamped or pressed metal; fuel systems & parts, motor vehicle; truck & bus bodies; fabricated plate work (boiler shop)

(P-17924)
JABIL SILVER CREEK INC (HQ)
Also Called: Wolfe Engineering, Inc.
5981 Optical Ct, San Jose (95138-1400)
PHONE.............................669 255-2900
John P Wolfe, *CEO*
Rita Wolfe, *Vice Pres*
Pete Leon, *Manager*
▲ **EMP:** 115
SQ FT: 76,000
SALES (est): 25.5MM
SALES (corp-wide): 22.1B **Publicly Held**
WEB: www.wolfe-engr.com
SIC: 7692 8711 3674 3317 Welding repair; engineering services; semiconductors & related devices; steel pipe & tubes; fabricated pipe & fittings
PA: Jabil Inc.
10560 Dr Martin Luther
Saint Petersburg FL 33716
727 577-9749

(P-17925)
SOUTHCOAST WELDING & MFG LLC
2591 Faivre St Ste 1, Chula Vista
(91911-7146)
PHONE.............................619 429-1337
Patrick Shoup, *President*
Leo Mathieu, *CFO*
Jay Parast, *Vice Pres*
Elizabeth Molina, *Human Res Dir*
Frank McGhee, *Prdtn Mgr*
EMP: 270
SQ FT: 82,000
SALES (est): 30.3MM **Privately Held**
SIC: 7692 Welding repair

(P-17926)
WELDLOGIC INC
2651 Lavery Ct, Newbury Park
(91320-1502)
PHONE.............................805 375-1670
Robert Elizarraz, *President*
Jack Froschauer, *Vice Pres*
Rick Heminuk, *Vice Pres*
Amil Zagheb, *Electrical Engi*
▲ **EMP:** 65
SQ FT: 25,000
SALES (est): 11.6MM **Privately Held**
WEB: www.weldlogic.com
SIC: 7692 Welding repair

7699 Repair Shop & Related Svcs, NEC

(P-17927)
AER TECHNOLOGIES INC
650 Columbia St, Brea (92821-2912)
PHONE.............................714 871-7357
Kim Quick, *CEO*
Michael McGroarty, *President*
Ingrid Osborne, *Admin Sec*
Cameron Quick, *Business Mgr*
EMP: 320
SQ FT: 50,000
SALES (est): 32.9MM **Privately Held**
SIC: 7699 Precision instrument repair

(P-17928)
AERO-ENGINES INC
2641 Roseview Ave, Los Angeles
(90065-1123)
PHONE.............................323 663-3961
Otis Perera, *President*
Antonio Ortega, *Vice Pres*
▲ **EMP:** 60
SQ FT: 41,000
SALES (est): 4.6MM **Privately Held**
SIC: 7699 3724 Aircraft & heavy equipment repair services; aircraft engines & engine parts

(P-17929)
AL-TAR SERVICES INC
823 Kifer Rd, Sunnyvale (94086-5204)
P.O. Box 1929, Evergreen CO (80437-1929)
PHONE.............................866 522-3499
Melissa Mia Castro, *President*
Dustin Castro, *COO*
EMP: 54
SQ FT: 15,000
SALES (est): 4.9MM **Privately Held**
WEB: www.al-tar.com
SIC: 7699 Laboratory instrument repair

(P-17930)
ALL AMERICAN SERVICE & SUPS
1776 All American Way, Corona
(92879-2070)
P.O. Box 2229 (92878-2229)
PHONE.............................951 736-3880

Daniel D Sisemore, *President*
Mark A Luer, *Principal*
Thomas Toscas, *Admin Sec*
EMP: 90
SALES (est): 7.8MM **Privately Held**
SIC: 7699 Construction equipment repair

(P-17931)
ALLSTAR COMMERCIAL CLEANING
4805 Mercury St Ste H, San Diego
(92111-2110)
PHONE.............................858 715-0500
Michael Paul McCarthy, *CEO*
Adam Bolio, *Co-Owner*
EMP: 50
SALES (est): 1.6MM **Privately Held**
SIC: 7699 Cleaning services

(P-17932)
AMERICAN RESIDENTIAL SVCS LLC
Also Called: Rescue Rooter Bay Area South
2305 Paragon Dr, San Jose (95131-1309)
P.O. Box 640845 (95164-0845)
PHONE.............................408 435-3810
Earnest Bell, *Manager*
EMP: 60
SALES (corp-wide): 2.4B **Privately Held**
WEB: www.ars.com
SIC: 7699 1711 Sewer cleaning & rodding; plumbing contractors
PA: American Residential Services Llc
965 Ridge Lake Blvd # 201
Memphis TN 38120
901 271-9700

(P-17933)
AMERICAN VISION WINDOWS INC
2125 N Madera Rd Ste A, Simi Valley
(93065-7709)
PHONE.............................805 582-1833
William Herren, *CEO*
Al Alfieri, *Vice Pres*
Monica Estrada, *Vice Pres*
Oscar Colmenares, *General Mgr*
John Herren, *General Mgr*
EMP: 215
SALES (est): 31.9MM **Privately Held**
SIC: 7699 1799 5031 Door & window repair; home/office interiors finishing, furnishing & remodeling; metal doors, sash & trim

(P-17934)
ANCON MARINE
2209 Zeus Ct, Bakersfield (93308-6867)
PHONE.............................310 952-8160
Bill Boyd, *Principal*
EMP: 73
SALES (corp-wide): 186.6MM **Privately Held**
SIC: 7699 7349 Tank repair & cleaning services; cleaning service, industrial or commercial
PA: Ancon Marine
22707 Wilmington Ave
Carson CA 90745
310 522-5110

(P-17935)
ARNIES SUPPLIES SERVICE LTD
1501 N Ditman Ave, Los Angeles
(90063-2501)
P.O. Box 26, Philadelphia PA (19105-0026)
PHONE.............................323 263-1696
Arnold Espino, *President*
EMP: 60
SQ FT: 806
SALES (corp-wide): 6.6MM **Privately Held**
SIC: 7699 Pallet repair
PA: Arnie's Supply Service Ltd.
1541 N Ditman Ave
Los Angeles CA 90063
323 263-1696

(P-17936)
AUTOMATED SYSTEMS AMERICA INC
Also Called: Asai
101 N Brand Blvd Ste 1230, Glendale
(91203-2677)
PHONE.............................877 500-0002

John Thomas Steely, *President*
Jackie Steely, *CFO*
EMP: 52
SQ FT: 1,200
SALES (est): 47MM **Privately Held**
WEB: www.asaiatm.com
SIC: 7699 3578 6099 Automated teller machine (ATM) repair; automatic teller machines (ATM); automated teller machine (ATM) network

(P-17937)
CHROMALLOY SAN DIEGO CORP
7007 Consolidated Way, San Diego
(92121-2604)
PHONE.............................858 877-2800
Armand F Lauzon Jr, *CEO*
Carlo Luzzatto, *President*
Bob Shambaugh, *COO*
David G Albert, *Vice Pres*
Michael Beffel, *Vice Pres*
EMP: 120
SQ FT: 120,000
SALES (est): 17.5MM
SALES (corp-wide): 3.6B **Publicly Held**
WEB: www.chromalloysatx.com
SIC: 7699 3724 Aircraft & heavy equipment repair services; aircraft engines & engine parts
HQ: Chromalloy American Llc
330 Blaisdell Rd
Orangeburg NY 10962
845 230-7355

(P-17938)
CLEAN HRBORS ES INDUS SVCS INC
Also Called: Brand Precision
4501 California Ct, Benicia (94510-1021)
PHONE.............................707 745-1581
Mark Davis, *Manager*
EMP: 60
SALES (corp-wide): 2.9B **Publicly Held**
WEB: www.onyxindustrial.com
SIC: 7699 8748 Waste cleaning services; sewer cleaning & rodding; environmental consultant
HQ: Clean Harbors Es Industrial Services, Inc.
4760 World Houston Pkwy # 100
Houston TX 77032
713 672-8004

(P-17939)
CLEAN POWER FINANCE INC
50 Osgood Pl Ste 400, San Francisco
(94133-4644)
PHONE.............................899 525-2123
Gary Kremen, *President*
Rajiv Ghatalia, *Ch of Bd*
Michael Pope, *CFO*
Shawn Tabak, *CFO*
Kristian Hanelt, *Senior VP*
EMP: 140 **EST:** 2006
SALES (est): 13.7MM
SALES (corp-wide): 21.6MM **Privately Held**
SIC: 7699 7389 Cleaning services; financial services
PA: Spruce Financial, Inc.
50 Osgood Pl Ste 400
San Francisco CA 94133
866 525-2123

(P-17940)
CLEANING SERVICES
7828 Monterey St, Gilroy (95020-4537)
PHONE.............................408 778-9251
Michael Jones, *President*
EMP: 50
SALES (est): 1.7MM **Privately Held**
WEB: www.makeitclean.com
SIC: 7699 Cleaning services

(P-17941)
COLLECTORS UNIVERSE INC (PA)
1610 E Saint Andrew Pl, Santa Ana
(92705-4931)
P.O. Box 6280, Newport Beach (92658-6280)
PHONE.............................949 567-1234
Joseph J Orlando, *CEO*
A Clinton Allen, *Ch of Bd*
Joseph J Wallace, *CFO*

(PA)=Parent Co (HQ)=Headquarters (DH)=Div Headquarters
✪ = New Business established in last 2 years

2019 Directory of California
Wholesalers and Services Companies

761

PRODUCTS & SVCS

Gary Smith, *Officer*
Dawn Sanchez, *Risk Mgmt Dir*
EMP: 82
SQ FT: 48,500
SALES: 68.4MM **Publicly Held**
WEB: www.collectors.com
SIC: 7699 Hobby & collectors services

(P-17942)
D S R INC
Also Called: Mr Rooter
3503 Arundell Cir Ste A, Ventura
(93003-4916)
PHONE..............................805 275-0039
Richard Svestak, *President*
EMP: 70
SQ FT: 6,200
SALES (est): 2MM **Privately Held**
SIC: 7699 Sewer cleaning & rodding

(P-17943)
DESIGN MACHINE AND MFG
2491 Simpson St, Kingsburg (93631-9501)
PHONE..............................559 897-7374
Abe Wiabe, *Owner*
John Zweigle, *General Mgr*
EMP: 50
SALES (est): 282.9K **Privately Held**
SIC: 7699 Industrial machinery & equip-
ment repair

(P-17944)
DICALITE MINERALS CORP
36994 Summit Lake Rd, Burney
(96013-9636)
PHONE..............................530 335-5451
Raymond Perlman, *President*
Derek J Cusack, *VP Opers*
M B Greenley, *VP Sales*
◆ **EMP:** 70
SQ FT: 3,000
SALES (est): 9.7MM **Privately Held**
WEB: www.dicalite-dicaperl.com
SIC: 7699 Filter cleaning

(P-17945)
FOSTER DAIRY FARMS
1472 Hall Rd, Hickman (95323-9615)
PHONE..............................209 874-9605
Ronald Hill, *Manager*
EMP: 200
SALES (corp-wide): 320.5MM **Privately
Held**
SIC: 7699 Farm machinery repair
PA: Foster Dairy Farms
529 Kansas Ave
Modesto CA 95351
209 576-3400

(P-17946)
GENERAL ELECTRIC COMPANY
2264 E Avion Ave, Ontario (91761-7794)
PHONE..............................909 605-7603
Bob Ritch, *Manager*
EMP: 500
SALES (corp-wide): 122B **Publicly Held**
SIC: 7699 4581 5088 Aircraft & heavy
equipment repair services; airports, flying
fields & services; aircraft & parts
PA: General Electric Company
41 Farnsworth St
Boston MA 02210
617 443-3000

(P-17947)
GENESIS TECH PARTNERS LLC
21540 Plummer St Ste A, Chatsworth
(91311-4143)
PHONE..............................800 950-2647
Sandy D Morford,
Haresh Satiani,
EMP: 175
SQ FT: 3,000
SALES (est): 3.3MM **Publicly Held**
SIC: 7699 Medical equipment repair, non-
electric
HQ: Cohr, Inc.
10510 Twin Lakes Pkwy
Charlotte NC 28269
704 948-5700

(P-17948)
GLOBAL DEV STRATEGIES INC
9985 Businesspark Ave A, San Diego
(92131-1132)
P.O. Box 26997 (92196-0997)
PHONE..............................858 408-1173
Marlene Stephens, *President*
Brandon Campbell, *CFO*
EMP: 60
SALES (est): 14.7MM **Privately Held**
WEB: www.globalstrategy.biz
SIC: 7699 Garage door repair

(P-17949)
HAWKER PACIFIC AEROSPACE
11240 Sherman Way, Sun Valley
(91352-4942)
PHONE..............................818 765-6201
Bernd Riggers, *CEO*
Katie Higgins, *CFO*
Troy Trower, *CFO*
Blas Maidagan, *Exec VP*
Brian Carr, *Vice Pres*
▲ **EMP:** 355
SQ FT: 193,000
SALES (est): 45.8MM
SALES (corp-wide): 41.9B **Privately Held**
WEB: www.hawker.com
SIC: 7699 5088 3728 Hydraulic equip-
ment repair; aircraft & parts; aircraft parts
& equipment
HQ: Lufthansa Technik Ag
Weg Beim Jager 193
Hamburg 22335
405 070-3667

(P-17950)
HOFFMAN SOUTHWEST CORP
Also Called: Roto-Rooter
1183 N Kraemer Pl, Anaheim (92806-1923)
PHONE..............................714 630-0404
Don Hatcher, *Manager*
EMP: 50
SALES (corp-wide): 16.9MM **Privately
Held**
SIC: 7699 1711 Sewer cleaning & rodding;
plumbing contractors
PA: Hoffman Southwest Corp.
23311 Madero
Mission Viejo CA 92691
800 784-7473

(P-17951)
HOFFMAN SOUTHWEST CORP
Also Called: Roto-Rooter
8930 Center Ave, Rancho Cucamonga
(91730-5328)
PHONE..............................909 397-0567
Dan Chavez, *Manager*
Linda Davies, *Admin Asst*
Jerry Martinez, *Manager*
EMP: 52
SALES (corp-wide): 16.9MM **Privately
Held**
SIC: 7699 Sewer cleaning & rodding
PA: Hoffman Southwest Corp.
23311 Madero
Mission Viejo CA 92691
800 784-7473

(P-17952)
HOFFMAN TEXAS INC
24971 Avenue Stanford, Valencia
(91355-1278)
PHONE..............................661 257-9200
Gary Thomas, *Manager*
EMP: 50
SQ FT: 6,936
SALES (corp-wide): 16.9MM **Privately
Held**
WEB: www.rw-rotorooter.com
SIC: 7699 Sewer cleaning & rodding
HQ: Hoffman Texas, Inc.
23311 Madero
Mission Viejo CA 92691
949 380-4161

(P-17953)
HRD AERO SYSTEMS INC
Also Called: Hrd Oxygens
25555 Avenue Stanford, Valencia
(91355-1101)
PHONE..............................661 295-0670
Tom Salamone, *President*
EMP: 65
SQ FT: 8,000

SALES (est): 1.2MM **Privately Held**
WEB: www.hrd-aerosystems.com
SIC: 7699 Aircraft & heavy equipment repair services; aircraft flight instrument repair; aviation propeller & blade repair

(P-17954)
HRD AERO SYSTEMS INC (PA)
25555 Avenue Stanford, Valencia
(91355-1101)
PHONE..............................661 295-0670
Tom Salamone, *President*
Tim McBride, *CFO*
Rich OHM, *Officer*
Paul Zapata, *Regional Mgr*
Albert Leon, *MIS Dir*
◆ **EMP:** 110
SQ FT: 70,000
SALES (est): 19.1MM **Privately Held**
SIC: 7699 8711 Aircraft & heavy equip-
ment repair services; aircraft flight instru-
ment repair; aviation propeller & blade
repair; aviation &/or aeronautical engi-
neering

(P-17955)
HYDRATECH LLC (HQ)
1331 S West Ave, Fresno (93706-2530)
PHONE..............................559 233-0876
John J McMahon Jr,
Dave Ogden, *CFO*
Ginny Zhou, *Executive*
Leon N Nolgn III,
Lin Dellanina, *Director*
▲ **EMP:** 53
SQ FT: 40,000
SALES (est): 8.6MM
SALES (corp-wide): 501.5MM **Privately
Held**
WEB: www.mvphydratech.com
SIC: 7699 Hydraulic equipment repair
PA: Ligon Industries, Llc
1927 1st Ave N Ste 500
Birmingham AL 35203
205 322-3302

(P-17956)
IMAGE 2000 (PA)
26037 Huntington Ln, Valencia
(91355-1145)
PHONE..............................818 781-2200
Joe Blatchford, *CEO*
Richard Campbell, *President*
EMP: 50
SQ FT: 22,557
SALES (est): 28MM **Privately Held**
SIC: 7699 5999 Photographic equipment
repair; photocopy machines

(P-17957)
**INDUS LIGHT & MAGIC (VANCO)
LL**
1110 Gorgas Ave, San Francisco
(94129-1406)
PHONE..............................415 292-4671
Steve Condiotti, *CEO*
Kevin Wooley, *Vice Pres*
Janet Lewin, *Executive*
Gretchen Libby, *Executive*
Thomas Chan, *Administration*
▲ **EMP:** 98
SALES (est): 21.6MM **Publicly Held**
SIC: 7699 Industrial equipment services
HQ: Lucasfilm Ltd. Llc
1110 Gorgas Ave Bldg C-Hr
San Francisco CA 94129
415 623-1000

(P-17958)
**INLAND BUSINESS MACHINES
INC (DH)**
1326 N Market Blvd, Sacramento
(95834-1912)
PHONE..............................916 928-0770
Liz Stafford, *President*
David Whitten, *Accounts Mgr*
EMP: 79
SALES (est): 16MM
SALES (corp-wide): 10.2B **Publicly Held**
WEB: www.ibs-team.com
SIC: 7699 5044 5999 Printing trades ma-
chinery & equipment repair; office equip-
ment; photocopy machines

(P-17959)
**INNOVATIVE MEDICAL
SOLUTIONS**
3002 Dow Ave Ste 110, Tustin
(92780-7247)
PHONE..............................714 505-7070
James Stevens, *President*
Stephen Ohare, *Officer*
Elizabeth Stevens, *Vice Pres*
EMP: 58
SALES: 3MM **Privately Held**
SIC: 7699 5047 Hospital equipment repair
services; medical & hospital equipment

(P-17960)
KONE INC
9850 Businesspark Ave, San Diego
(92131-1121)
PHONE..............................858 578-5100
Jeff Blum, *Manager*
Kevin Wigley, *Program Dir*
EMP: 80
SALES (corp-wide): 732.3MM **Publicly
Held**
WEB: www.us.kone.com
SIC: 7699 3534 Elevators: inspection,
service & repair; elevators & moving stair-
ways
HQ: Kone Inc.
4225 Naperville Rd # 400
Lisle IL 60532
630 577-1650

(P-17961)
**LA HYDRO-JET ROOTER SVC
INC**
Also Called: La Hydrojet
10639 Wixom St, Sun Valley (91352-4603)
PHONE..............................818 768-4225
Daniel Baldwin, *President*
Lori Baldwin, *CFO*
Janet Parker, *Assistant*
EMP: 68 **EST:** 1991
SALES (est): 9MM **Privately Held**
SIC: 7699 Sewer cleaning & rodding

(P-17962)
**MATTHEWS INTERNATIONAL
CORP**
580 S State St Ste 8, San Jacinto
(92583-4035)
PHONE..............................951 654-9123
Robert Ochoa, *Manager*
EMP: 50 **EST:** 1850
SQ FT: 1,200
SALES (est): 392.2K **Privately Held**
SIC: 7699 Industrial equipment services

(P-17963)
N & S TRACTOR CO (PA)
600 S St 59, Merced (95341-6543)
P.O. Box 910 (95341-0910)
PHONE..............................209 383-5888
Arthur R Nutcher, *CEO*
Mary Wallace, *Corp Secy*
Stephanie Nutcher, *Vice Pres*
Matt Freitas, *Marketing Staff*
David Bybee, *Sales Staff*
▲ **EMP:** 60
SQ FT: 8,700
SALES (est): 12.5MM **Privately Held**
WEB: www.nstractor.com
SIC: 7699 5083 Farm machinery repair;
agricultural machinery & equipment

(P-17964)
**NIACC-AVITECH
TECHNOLOGIES INC (PA)**
245 W Dakota Ave, Clovis (93612-5608)
PHONE..............................559 291-2500
Jeff Andrews, *CEO*
Thomas S Irwin, *Treasurer*
Todd Rose, *General Mgr*
Elizabeth R Letendre, *Admin Sec*
Rayan Kabeer, *Engineer*
EMP: 80
SALES (est): 13.7MM **Privately Held**
WEB: www.niacctech.com
SIC: 7699 3471 Aircraft flight instrument
repair; plating of metals or formed prod-
ucts

(P-17965)
OTIS ELEVATOR COMPANY
Also Called: United Technologies
711 E Ball Rd Ste 200, Anaheim
(92805-5960)
PHONE..................................714 758-9593
Bob McLeese, *Branch Mgr*
Joe Marquez, *Purchasing*
EMP: 50
SALES (corp-wide): 59.8B **Publicly Held**
WEB: www.otis.com
SIC: 7699 1796 Elevators: inspection,
service & repair; elevator installation &
conversion
HQ: Otis Elevator Company
1 Carrier Pl
Farmington CT 06032
860 674-3000

(P-17966)
OTIS ELEVATOR COMPANY
444 Spear St Ste 100, San Francisco
(94105-1642)
PHONE..................................415 546-0880
Rob Neill, *Branch Mgr*
George V Klan, *Analyst*
EMP: 150
SALES (corp-wide): 59.8B **Publicly Held**
WEB: www.otis.com
SIC: 7699 1796 Miscellaneous building
item repair services; elevators: inspection,
service & repair; elevator installation &
conversion
HQ: Otis Elevator Company
1 Carrier Pl
Farmington CT 06032
860 674-3000

(P-17967)
OVERMILLER INC
Also Called: Roto-Rooter
195 Mason Cir, Concord (94520-1213)
PHONE..................................925 798-2122
Billy Joe Bristol, *President*
Mardell A Bristol, *Vice Pres*
EMP: 53
SQ FT: 12,000
SALES (est): 7MM **Privately Held**
SIC: 7699 1711 Sewer cleaning & rodding;
plumbing contractors

(P-17968)
PACIFIC GAS TURBINE CENTER LLC
7007 Consolidated Way, San Diego
(92121-2604)
PHONE..................................858 877-2910
Graham Bell,
◆ **EMP:** 101
SQ FT: 110,000
SALES (est): 4MM **Privately Held**
SIC: 7699 Industrial equipment services;
engine repair & replacement, non-auto-
motive

(P-17969)
PACWEST INSTRUMENT LABS INC
Also Called: Pacific Southwest Instruments
1721 Railroad St, Corona (92880-2511)
PHONE..................................951 737-0790
Jim Joubert, *President*
Boon Lee, *CFO*
Ray McDonald, *Vice Pres*
EMP: 51
SQ FT: 37,000
SALES (est): 10.1MM **Privately Held**
WEB: www.psilabs.com
SIC: 7699 7629 Aircraft flight instrument
repair; aircraft electrical equipment repair

(P-17970)
PEGGS COMPANY INC (PA)
4851 Felspar St, Riverside (92509-3024)
PHONE..................................253 584-9548
Chresten Revelle Nelson, *CEO*
John L Peggs, *President*
Frank Loera, *Purchasing*
◆ **EMP:** 100
SQ FT: 80,000

SALES (est): 28.4MM **Privately Held**
WEB: www.thepeggscompany.com
SIC: 7699 3496 5046 7359 Shopping
cart repair; miscellaneous fabricated wire
products; commercial equipment; equipment rental & leasing

(P-17971)
PKL SERVICES INC
14265 Danielson St C1, Poway
(92064-8818)
PHONE..................................858 679-1755
Samuel Flores Jr, *President*
Paul Callan, *Exec VP*
David K Howell, *Vice Pres*
Mike Naylor, *Vice Pres*
Michael Nisley, *Vice Pres*
EMP: 160
SQ FT: 6,000
SALES (est): 16.8MM **Privately Held**
WEB: www.pklservices.com
SIC: 7699 Aircraft & heavy equipment re-
pair services

(P-17972)
POMONA VALLEY MOTORCYCLES INC
Also Called: Pomona Valley Harley-Davidson
8710 Central Ave, Montclair (91763-5100)
PHONE..................................909 981-9500
Barbara Pennell, *President*
Barbara E Pennell, *President*
David A Pennell, *CFO*
William Sherred, *Sales Staff*
Brittany Overlin, *Parts Mgr*
EMP: 53
SQ FT: 26,000
SALES (est): 4.8MM **Privately Held**
WEB: www.pvhd.com
SIC: 7699 5571 Motorcycle repair service;
motorcycle parts & accessories

(P-17973)
PROPAK LOGISTICS INC
1300 S F St, Porterville (93257-5969)
PHONE..................................559 782-8696
EMP: 66 **Privately Held**
SIC: 7699 Pallet repair
PA: Propak Logistics, Inc.
1100 Garrison Ave
Fort Smith AR 72901

(P-17974)
PROPULSION CONTROLS ENGRG (PA)
1620 Rigel St, San Diego (92113-3832)
P.O. Box 13606 (92170-3606)
PHONE..................................619 235-0961
David P Clapp, *CEO*
John P Reilly III, *Corp Secy*
Ehrich Steinmetz, *General Mgr*
Kenny Vega, *Admin Asst*
Alex Chambosse, *Technical Staff*
EMP: 70
SQ FT: 22,000
SALES (est): 23.4MM **Privately Held**
WEB: www.pcehawaii.com
SIC: 7699 Boiler repair shop

(P-17975)
PSC INDUSTRIAL OUTSOURCING LP
Also Called: Hydrochempsc
19340 Van Ness Ave, Torrance
(90501-1103)
PHONE..................................310 325-1600
Peter Raynor, *Branch Mgr*
EMP: 137
SALES (corp-wide): 750MM **Privately Held**
SIC: 7699
PA: Psc Industrial Outsourcing, Lp
900 Georgia Ave
Deer Park TX 77536
713 393-5600

(P-17976)
RAYMOND HANDLING CONCEPTS CORP (DH)
Also Called: Rhcc
41400 Boyce Rd, Fremont (94538-3113)
PHONE..................................510 745-7500
James Wilcox, *President*
Donald Jones, *Vice Pres*

Al Seiler, *Vice Pres*
Samantha Barrows, *Admin Asst*
Ron Curtis, *VP Finance*
EMP: 60
SQ FT: 32,000
SALES (est): 44.7MM
SALES (corp-wide): 18.8B **Privately Held**
WEB: www.raymondhandling.com
SIC: 7699 5084 7359 7629 Industrial ma-
chinery & equipment repair; materials
handling machinery; equipment rental &
leasing; electrical repair shops
HQ: The Raymond Corporation
22 S Canal St
Greene NY 13778
607 656-2311

(P-17977)
RETRONIX INTERNATIONAL INC
Also Called: Retronix Semiconductors
65 Enterprise, Aliso Viejo (92656-2705)
PHONE..................................949 388-6930
Anthony Boswell, *President*
Mark Diamond, *COO*
Stuart Proctor, *Vice Pres*
EMP: 90
SQ FT: 5,000
SALES (est): 7.8MM **Privately Held**
SIC: 7699 Industrial machinery & equip-
ment repair

(P-17978)
ROTO ROOTER PLUMBING & DRAIN S
2141 Industrial Ct Ste B, Vista
(92081-7905)
PHONE..................................951 658-8541
Craig Nunez, *General Mgr*
EMP: 50
SALES (est): 1.4MM **Privately Held**
SIC: 7699 Sewer cleaning & rodding

(P-17979)
ROTO-ROOTER SERVICES COMPANY
220 Demeter St, East Palo Alto
(94303-1303)
PHONE..................................650 322-2366
Cory Feverson, *Branch Mgr*
EMP: 75
SALES (corp-wide): 1.6B **Publicly Held**
SIC: 7699 Sewer cleaning & rodding
HQ: Roto-Rooter Services Company
255 E 5th St Ste 2500
Cincinnati OH 45202
513 762-6690

(P-17980)
RS CALIBRATION SERVICES INC
1047 Serpentine Ln # 500, Pleasanton
(94566-4786)
PHONE..................................925 462-4217
Ralph Sabiel, *President*
Debbie Sabiel, *Treasurer*
Mike Vollman, *Vice Pres*
Michele Rediger, *Executive*
Nick Bean, *Administration*
EMP: 50
SQ FT: 5,000
SALES (est): 11.2MM **Privately Held**
WEB: www.rscalibration.com
SIC: 7699 8734 Professional instrument
repair services; calibration & certification

(P-17981)
S A CAMP PUMP COMPANY
Also Called: SA Camp Pump and Drilling Co
17876 Zerker Rd, Bakersfield
(93308-9221)
P.O. Box 82575 (93380-2575)
PHONE..................................661 399-2976
James S Camp, *President*
John Ferguson, *Office Mgr*
Josh Alvidrez, *Sales Staff*
Gerrit Otten, *Sales Staff*
Valerie Bailey, *Clerk*
EMP: 60 **EST:** 1952
SQ FT: 10,000
SALES (est): 11.5MM
SALES (corp-wide): 18.1MM **Privately Held**
WEB: www.sacamp.net
SIC: 7699 Agricultural equipment repair
services; pumps & pumping equipment

PA: S A Camp Companies
17876 Zerker Rd
Bakersfield CA 93308
661 399-4451

(P-17982)
SANACT INC (PA)
Also Called: Roto-Rooter
5717 Brisa St, Livermore (94550-2511)
PHONE..................................510 483-2324
Rodney Allen Wray, *CEO*
▼ **EMP:** 175
SQ FT: 18,000
SALES (est): 24.4MM **Privately Held**
SIC: 7699 Sewer cleaning & rodding

(P-17983)
SCHINDLER ELEVATOR CORPORATION
2000 Avenue Of The Stars, Los Angeles
(90067-4700)
PHONE..................................310 785-9775
EMP: 88
SALES (corp-wide): 10.3B **Privately Held**
SIC: 7699 Elevators: inspection, service &
repair
HQ: Schindler Elevator Corporation
20 Whippany Rd
Morristown NJ 07960
973 397-6500

(P-17984)
SCHINDLER ELEVATOR CORPORATION
16450 Fthill Blvd Ste 200, Sylmar (91342)
PHONE..................................818 336-3000
Lance Howard, *Manager*
Ronan Lebaut, *General Mgr*
John Meadows, *Sales Staff*
EMP: 240
SALES (corp-wide): 10.3B **Privately Held**
WEB: www.us.schindler.com
SIC: 7699 Elevators: inspection, service &
repair
HQ: Schindler Elevator Corporation
20 Whippany Rd
Morristown NJ 07960
973 397-6500

(P-17985)
SCIENTIFIC CONCEPTS INC
303 Vintage Park Dr # 220, Foster City
(94404-1166)
PHONE..................................650 578-1142
Charles Morrison Sr, *President*
Klahn Gboloh Jorbah, *Vice Pres*
Carol Morrison, *Admin Sec*
EMP: 350
SQ FT: 23,000
SALES (est): 20.4MM **Privately Held**
WEB: www.scientificconceptsinc.com
SIC: 7699 Cleaning services

(P-17986)
SEARS ROEBUCK AND CO
100 Brea Mall, Brea (92821-5996)
PHONE..................................714 256-7328
Penny Bishop, *Manager*
EMP: 200
SALES (corp-wide): 16.7B **Publicly Held**
SIC: 7699
HQ: Sears, Roebuck And Co.
3333 Beverly Rd
Hoffman Estates IL 60179
847 286-2500

(P-17987)
SEARS ROEBUCK AND CO
Also Called: Direct Delivery Center
5691 E Philadelphia St, Ontario
(91761-2805)
PHONE..................................909 390-4210
Rick Ings, *Manager*
EMP: 125
SALES (corp-wide): 16.7B **Publicly Held**
SIC: 7699 7629
HQ: Sears, Roebuck And Co.
3333 Beverly Rd
Hoffman Estates IL 60179
847 286-2500

(P-17988)
SECURITY CENTRAL INC
Also Called: Reed Brothers Security
4432 Telegraph Ave, Oakland
(94609-2018)
PHONE..................................510 652-2477
Ronald Reed, *President*
Randall Reed, *Treasurer*
Michael Salk, *Vice Pres*
EMP: 51
SQ FT: 19,000
SALES (est): 10.3MM **Privately Held**
SIC: 7699 5099 3446 5999 Locksmith
shop; locks & lock sets; fences or posts,
ornamental iron or steel; electronic parts
& equipment

(P-17989)
**SOUTH BAY SAND BLASTING
AND TA**
Also Called: Sbsbtc
326 W 30th St, National City (91950-7206)
P.O. Box 13009, San Diego (92170-3009)
PHONE..................................619 238-8338
Canuto Lopez, *CEO*
Johnny Sanchez, *Manager*
Barbara Schilf, *Manager*
EMP: 100
SQ FT: 60,000
SALES (est): 13.5MM **Privately Held**
SIC: 7699 4212 Ship boiler & tank clean-
ing & repair, contractors; ship scaling,
contractors; hazardous waste transport

(P-17990)
**SOUTHBAY SNDBLST & TANK
CLG**
3589 Dalbergia St, San Diego
(92113-3810)
P.O. Box 13009 (92170-3009)
PHONE..................................619 238-8338
Adam Juarez, *President*
EMP: 100 EST: 2015
SALES (est): 703.1K **Privately Held**
SIC: 7699 4212 Ship boiler & tank clean-
ing & repair, contractors; ship scaling,
contractors; hazardous waste transport

(P-17991)
SPEEDY LOCKSMITH
429 Avnida De La Estrella, San Clemente
(92672)
P.O. Box 5075, Oceanside (92052-5075)
PHONE..................................760 439-5000
Micky Abdallah, *Owner*
EMP: 70
SALES: 320K **Privately Held**
WEB: www.speedylocksmith.com
SIC: 7699 Locksmith shop

(P-17992)
**SUNVAIR AEROSPACE GROUP
INC (PA)**
29145 The Old Rd, Valencia (91355-1015)
PHONE..................................661 294-3777
Udo Reider, *CEO*
Glenn Miller, *CFO*
EMP: 80 EST: 2014
SQ FT: 77,000
SALES: 30MM **Privately Held**
SIC: 7699 Aircraft & heavy equipment re-
pair services

(P-17993)
**SURVIVAL SYSTEMS INTL INC
(PA)**
Also Called: Ssi
34140 Valley Center Rd, Valley Center
(92082-6017)
P.O. Box 1855 (92082-1855)
PHONE..................................760 749-6800
Mark Beatty, *Vice Pres*
George Beatty, *Shareholder*
Helen Beatty, *Shareholder*
Colin Hooper, *Vice Pres*
Tony Mora, *CTO*
▲ EMP: 95
SQ FT: 100,000
SALES (est): 18MM **Privately Held**
WEB: www.survivalsystemsint.net
SIC: 7699 3531 3086 Industrial equip-
ment services; boat building & repair; life saving &
survival equipment, non-medical: repair;
winches; plastics foam products

(P-17994)
**TECH KNOWLEDGE
ASSOCIATES LLC**
Also Called: Tka
1 Centerpointe Dr Ste 200, La Palma
(90623-2529)
PHONE..................................714 735-3810
Joe Randolph, *CEO*
Ed Wong, *CFO*
Steve Gilbert, *Exec VP*
EMP: 80
SALES: 45.2MM
SALES (corp-wide): 17.6B **Privately Held**
SIC: 7699 Medical equipment repair, non-
electric
HQ: St. Joseph Health System
3345 Michelson Dr Ste 100
Irvine CA 92612
949 381-4000

(P-17995)
TED LEVINE DRUM CO (PA)
1817 Chico Ave, South El Monte
(91733-2943)
P.O. Box 3246 (91733-0246)
PHONE..................................626 579-1084
Ozzie Levine, *President*
Harvey Kale, *COO*
Mario Hernandez, *Department Mgr*
Guillermo Sandoval, *Business Mgr*
Tom Campbell, *Plant Mgr*
EMP: 80
SQ FT: 200,000
SALES (est): 14.5MM **Privately Held**
WEB: www.tldrumco.com
SIC: 7699 4959 3412 Industrial equip-
ment services; sanitary services; metal
barrels, drums & pails

(P-17996)
**THARP TRUCK RENTAL INC
(PA)**
Also Called: Depot
15243 Road 192, Porterville (93257-8967)
PHONE..................................559 782-5800
Morris A Tharp, *CEO*
Carol R Tharp, *Corp Secy*
Casey O Tharp, *Vice Pres*
◆ EMP: 125
SQ FT: 5,000
SALES (est): 11.2MM **Privately Held**
WEB: www.emtharp.com
SIC: 7699 5013 5511 5012 Agricultural
equipment repair services; motor vehicle
supplies & new parts; trucks, tractors &
trailers: new & used; automobiles & other
motor vehicles

(P-17997)
**THYSSENKRUPP ELEVATOR
CORP**
1965 Gillespie Way # 101, El Cajon
(92020-0500)
PHONE..................................619 596-7220
Jeff Hansen, *Manager*
EMP: 100
SALES (corp-wide): 48.7B **Privately Held**
WEB: www.tyssenkrupp.com
SIC: 7699 Elevators: inspection, service &
repair
HQ: Thyssenkrupp Elevator Corporation
11605 Haynes Bridge Rd # 650
Alpharetta GA 30009
678 319-3240

(P-17998)
**THYSSENKRUPP ELEVATOR
CORP**
16290 Shoemaker Ave, Cerritos
(90703-2241)
PHONE..................................323 278-9888
Toll Free:..................................877 -
Joe Gonzalles, *Manager*
Marie Beth Der, *Vice Pres*
Maricela Estrada, *Project Mgr*
EMP: 50
SALES (corp-wide): 48.7B **Privately Held**
WEB: www.thyssenkruppelevator.com
SIC: 7699 1796 Miscellaneous building
item repair services; elevator installation
& conversion
HQ: Thyssenkrupp Elevator Corporation
11605 Haynes Bridge Rd # 650
Alpharetta GA 30009
678 319-3240

(P-17999)
**TURBINE REPAIR SERVICES
LLC (PA)**
1838 E Cedar St, Ontario (91761-7763)
PHONE..................................909 947-2256
Victor M Sanchez, *Mng Member*
Dave Meyer,
Danny Sanchez,
Cesar Siordia,
Michael Dorrel, *Mng Member*
EMP: 56
SQ FT: 12,000
SALES (est): 10.8MM **Privately Held**
WEB: www.steamandgas.com
SIC: 7699 Mechanical instrument repair

(P-18000)
**UNICO INDUSTRIAL SERVICE
CO (PA)**
945 Tyler St, Benicia (94510-2915)
P.O. Box 887 (94510-0887)
PHONE..................................707 736-8787
Dean Gordon Potter, *CEO*
D Gordon Potter, *President*
EMP: 50
SQ FT: 10,000
SALES (est): 3.5MM **Privately Held**
WEB: www.unicoservices.com
SIC: 7699 3599 Industrial machinery &
equipment repair; machine shop, jobbing
& repair

(P-18001)
**UNITED CALIFORNIA GLASS &
DOOR**
745 Cesar Chavez, San Francisco
(94124-1211)
PHONE..................................415 824-8500
Judith Ticktin, *President*
▲ EMP: 70
SQ FT: 31,000
SALES (est): 10.2MM **Privately Held**
WEB: www.ucgd.com
SIC: 7699 1793 Door & window repair;
glass & glazing work

(P-18002)
UNITED SERVICE TECH INC
21801 Cactus Ave Ste A, Riverside
(92518-3020)
PHONE..................................714 224-1406
Robert J Heidkamp, *CEO*
Sandra Smelcer, *Treasurer*
Rodger Smelcer, *Vice Pres*
Greg Haan, *General Mgr*
Terrie Heidkamp, *Admin Sec*
EMP: 56
SQ FT: 2,400
SALES (est): 8.8MM **Privately Held**
SIC: 7699 5963 Industrial equipment serv-
ices; food services, direct sales

(P-18003)
**UPWIND BLADE SOLUTIONS
INC**
2869 Historic Decatur Rd # 100, San Diego
(92106-6176)
PHONE..................................866 927-3142
Marty Crotty, *CEO*
Bo Thisted, *President*
Bryan Coggins, *CFO*
EMP: 119
SALES (est): 2.9MM
SALES (corp-wide): 11.7B **Privately Held**
SIC: 7699 Pumps & pumping equipment
repair
HQ: Upwind Solutions, Inc.
2869 Historic Decatur Rd # 100
San Diego CA 92106

(P-18004)
VSS SALES INC (PA)
Also Called: Vss Compressor Service
16220 Garfield Ave, Paramount
(90723-4804)
P.O. Box 1898 (90723-1898)
PHONE..................................562 630-0606
Thomas F Vaughan, *President*
David Newton, *Treasurer*
Keven Vaughan, *Vice Pres*
Patricia Vaughan, *Vice Pres*
Greg Boyd, *Accounting Mgr*
EMP: 60
SQ FT: 10,000

SALES (est): 4.4MM **Privately Held**
WEB: www.vsssales.com
SIC: 7699 1796 1711 Industrial equipment services; installing building equipment; mechanical contractor

(P-18005)
WARDLOW 2 LP (PA)
333 S Grand Ave Ste 4070, Los Angeles
(90071-1544)
PHONE..................................562 432-8066
Steven B McLeod, *Partner*
Joe Gregorio, *Partner*
Gail Parris, *CFO*
Scott Baker, *General Mgr*
Joe Kantoris, *Info Tech Mgr*
EMP: 99
SALES (est): 53.3MM **Privately Held**
WEB: www.brockwaymoran.com
SIC: 7699 Construction equipment repair

(P-18006)
WESTERN PUMP INC (PA)
3235 F St, San Diego (92102-3315)
PHONE..................................619 239-9988
Dennis Rethmeier, *CEO*
Ryan Rethmeier, *President*
Janice C Rethmeier, *Corp Secy*
▲ EMP: 55
SQ FT: 10,000
SALES (est): 13.9MM **Privately Held**
WEB: www.westernpump.com
SIC: 7699 5084 1799 3728 Tank repair &
cleaning services; petroleum industry ma-
chinery; petroleum storage tanks, pump-
ing & draining; aircraft parts & equipment

(P-18007)
WEYGANDT & ASSOCIATES
Also Called: Weco Aerospace Systems
1501 Avi Blvd Ste 100, Lincoln (95648)
PHONE..................................916 543-0431
William Weygandt, *President*
Harold Weygandt, *President*
EMP: 50
SQ FT: 7,800
SALES (est): 3.3MM **Privately Held**
SIC: 7699 Aircraft & heavy equipment re-
pair services

**7812 Motion Picture & Video
Tape Production**

(P-18008)
**A ITS LAUGH PRODUCTIONS
INC**
Also Called: Would You Rather - Season 1
914 N Victory Blvd, Burbank (91502-1632)
PHONE..................................818 848-8787
Amanda C Ramey, *CEO*
EMP: 100
SALES (est): 410.7K **Privately Held**
SIC: 7812 Video production

(P-18009)
**ABC FAMILY WORLDWIDE INC
(HQ)**
500 S Buena Vista St, Burbank
(91521-0001)
PHONE..................................818 560-1000
Robert A Iger, *President*
EMP: 500
SALES (est): 42.3MM **Publicly Held**
SIC: 7812 4841 Cartoon production, tele-
vision; cable & other pay television serv-
ices

(P-18010)
ABM DISTRIBUTORS INC
811 W 7th St Ste 1040, Los Angeles
(90017-3408)
PHONE..................................310 401-0434
Alander Pulliam, *CEO*
EMP: 87
SALES (est): 555K **Privately Held**
SIC: 7812 Television film production

(P-18011)
ADVANCED DIGITAL SERVICES INC (PA)
Also Called: A D S
948 N Cahuenga Blvd, Los Angeles
(90038-2615)
PHONE...............................323 962-8585
Thomas Engdahl, *President*
Andrew McIntyre, *Ch of Bd*
Valerie Kroll, *President*
Brad Weyl, *COO*
David Lee, *Info Tech Dir*
▲ EMP: 87
SQ FT: 33,000
SALES (est): 8.8MM **Privately Held**
WEB: www.adshollywood.com
SIC: 7812 7819 Video tape production;
film processing, editing & titling: motion
picture

(P-18012)
ALLDAYEVERYDAY PRODUCTIONS LLC
2028 E 7th St, Los Angeles (90021-1302)
PHONE...............................323 556-6200
Arrow Kruse,
Ross Vinstein, *CFO*
Michael Karbelnikoff, *Finance*
EMP: 50 EST: 2014
SQ FT: 5,000
SALES (est): 1MM **Privately Held**
SIC: 7812 Video production

(P-18013)
ALLIED ENTERTAINMENT GROUP INC (PA)
Also Called: Allied Artists International
273 W Allen Ave, City of Industry (91746)
PHONE...............................626 330-0600
Greg Hammond, *President*
Robert Fitzpatrick, *Treasurer*
John Mason, *Vice Pres*
Ashley D Posner, *Vice Pres*
Kim Richards, *Admin Sec*
◆ EMP: 325
SQ FT: 60,000
SALES: 30MM **Privately Held**
SIC: 7812 Motion picture & video production

(P-18014)
AMBLIN/RELIANCE HOLDING CO LLC
Also Called: Story Teller
100 Universal City Plz, Universal City
(91608-1002)
PHONE...............................818 733-6272
Lindson Harding, *Mng Member*
EMP: 99
SALES (est): 2.5MM **Privately Held**
SIC: 7812 7929 Motion picture production;
entertainment group

(P-18015)
AND SYNDICATED PRODUCTIONS INC
3500 W Olive Ave Ste 1000, Burbank
(91505-5515)
PHONE...............................818 308-5200
▲ EMP: 100
SALES (est): 6.2MM **Privately Held**
SIC: 7812

(P-18016)
ANE PRODUCTIONS INC
3500 W Olive Ave Ste 1000, Burbank
(91505-5515)
PHONE...............................818 972-0777
EMP: 60
SALES (est): 883.9K **Privately Held**
SIC: 7812 Motion picture production & distribution, television

(P-18017)
ANONYMOUS CONTENT LLC (PA)
3532 Hayden Ave, Culver City
(90232-2413)
PHONE...............................310 558-6000
Steve Golin,
Steve Golin,
▲ EMP: 60 EST: 1999

SALES (est): 9.6MM **Privately Held**
WEB: www.anonymouscontent.com
SIC: 7812 Video production

(P-18018)
ARTISAN ENTERTAINMENT INC
2700 Colorado Ave Ste 200, Santa Monica
(90404-5502)
PHONE...............................310 449-9200
Wayne Levin, *President*
James W Barge, *CFO*
James Keegan, *CFO*
Erin Austin, *Exec VP*
David Ginsburg, *Exec VP*
EMP: 1000
SALES (est): 341MM
SALES (corp-wide): 3.2B **Privately Held**
SIC: 7812 Motion picture production; motion picture production & distribution;
music video production; video tape production
HQ: Lions Gate Entertainment Inc.
2700 Colorado Ave Ste 200
Santa Monica CA 90404
310 449-9200

(P-18019)
ASSOCIATED ENTRMT RELEASING (PA)
Also Called: Associated Television Intl
4401 Wilshire Blvd, Los Angeles
(90010-3703)
P.O. Box 4180 (90078-4180)
PHONE...............................323 934-7044
David McKenzie, *President*
Murray Drechsler, *CFO*
Murray Dreschler, *CFO*
Richard Casares, *Exec VP*
Barry Thurston, *Administration*
EMP: 50 EST: 1976
SQ FT: 35,000
SALES (est): 10.5MM **Privately Held**
WEB: www.associatedtelevision.com
SIC: 7812 Motion picture production & distribution

(P-18020)
ATLAS DIGITAL LLC (PA)
170 S Flower St, Burbank (91502-2122)
P.O. Box 4110 (91503-4110)
PHONE...............................323 762-2626
Shawn Sanbar, *Owner*
Carrie Iino, *Admin Mgr*
Steve Sauber, *Software Dev*
Greg Evanski, *Technician*
Ryan Hammer, *Technician*
EMP: 75
SQ FT: 13,000
SALES (est): 12.8MM **Privately Held**
SIC: 7812 Video production

(P-18021)
ATLAS ENTERTAINMENT INC
9200 W Sunset Blvd Ste 10, West Hollywood (90069-3608)
PHONE...............................310 786-4900
Charles V Roven, *President*
Alex Gartner, *Partner*
Brent Maduro, *Finance*
Marilyn Mordecai, *Assistant*
Melinda Whitaker, *Assistant*
EMP: 50
SALES (est): 3.2MM **Privately Held**
SIC: 7812 Motion picture production & distribution

(P-18022)
AVOCA PRODUCTIONS INC
Also Called: The Newly Wed
10202 Washington Blvd, Culver City
(90232-3119)
PHONE...............................310 244-4000
Steve Mosko, *President*
EMP: 60
SALES (est): 1.1MM
SALES (corp-wide): 80.1B **Privately Held**
WEB: www.sonypictures.com
SIC: 7812 Television film production
HQ: Sony Pictures Entertainment, Inc.
10202 Washington Blvd
Culver City CA 90232
310 244-4000

(P-18023)
BACHELOR PRODUCTIONS INC
2121 Avenue Of The Stars, Los Angeles
(90067-5010)
PHONE...............................310 567-9249
Desiree Varni, *Accountant*
EMP: 99
SALES (est): 850.1K **Privately Held**
SIC: 7812 Motion picture & video production

(P-18024)
BLAIR TELEVISION INC
Also Called: Blair TV
11111 Santa Monica Blvd # 1900, Los Angeles (90025-3333)
PHONE...............................714 537-5923
Nancy Dodson, *Manager*
EMP: 55 **Privately Held**
SIC: 7812 Motion picture & video production
HQ: Blair Television Inc
200 Park Ave Fl 17
New York NY 10166
212 230-5900

(P-18025)
BRENTWOOD CMMNCATIONS INTL INC
Also Called: BCII
16135 Roscoe Blvd, North Hills
(91343-6226)
PHONE...............................818 333-3680
Bud W Brutsman, *President*
EMP: 50
SALES: 5.8MM **Privately Held**
SIC: 7812 Television film production

(P-18026)
BRILLSTEIN ENTRMT PARTNERS LLC (PA)
Also Called: Brillstein Grey Entertainment
9150 Wilshire Blvd # 350, Beverly Hills
(90212-3427)
PHONE...............................310 205-5100
Brad Grey, *President*
Joanne Colonna, *Manager*
EMP: 290
SALES (est): 18.5MM **Privately Held**
SIC: 7812 Television film production

(P-18027)
BUNIM-MURRAY PRODUCTIONS
Also Called: Bmp
1015 Grandview Ave, Glendale
(91201-2205)
PHONE...............................818 756-5100
Jonathan Murray, *CEO*
Gil Goldschein, *CEO*
Mark Lebowitz, *CFO*
Jon Murray, *Chairman*
▲ EMP: 150
SQ FT: 20,000
SALES (est): 18.9MM
SALES (corp-wide): 99.7K **Privately Held**
SIC: 7812 Television film production
HQ: Banijay Entertainment
5 Rue Francois 1er
Paris
143 189-191

(P-18028)
BVS ENTERTAINMENT INC (DH)
500 S Buena Vista St, Burbank
(91521-0001)
PHONE...............................818 460-6917
Griffith Foxley, *President*
David K Thompson, *Admin Sec*
EMP: 50
SQ FT: 111,000
SALES (est): 5.9MM **Publicly Held**
SIC: 7812 7822 Cartoon production, television; motion picture distribution; television & video tape distribution
HQ: Abc Family Worldwide, Inc.
500 S Buena Vista St
Burbank CA 91521
818 560-1000

(P-18029)
CAFFEINE PRODUCTIONS
1040 N Las Palmas Ave, Los Angeles
(90038-2409)
PHONE...............................323 860-8111
Jen Gore, *Director*

Greg Choa, *Owner*
EMP: 80
SQ FT: 10,000
SALES (est): 890.6K
SALES (corp-wide): 13.2B **Publicly Held**
WEB: www.caffeineproductions.com
SIC: 7812 Television film production
HQ: Comedy Partners
345 Hudson St Fl 9
New York NY 10014

(P-18030)
CARA COMMUNICATIONS CORP
Also Called: Vin Dibona Productions
12233 W Olympic Blvd # 170, Los Angeles
(90064-1034)
PHONE...............................310 442-5600
Vincent Dibona, *President*
Sharon Arnett, *Vice Pres*
Janet Ghio, *Office Mgr*
Stephanie Rondeau, *Production*
EMP: 50
SALES (est): 4.4MM **Privately Held**
SIC: 7812 7819 7922 Television film production; directors, independent: motion picture; television program, including commercial producers

(P-18031)
CINOVATION INC
6527 San Fernando Rd, Glendale
(91201-2108)
P.O. Box 909, Pacific Palisades (90272-0909)
PHONE...............................818 246-3160
Rick Baker, *President*
EMP: 100
SQ FT: 24,000
SALES (est): 1.9MM **Privately Held**
SIC: 7812 Motion picture production

(P-18032)
CNX MEDIA INC
1 Beach St Ste 300, San Francisco
(94133-1228)
PHONE...............................415 229-8300
James Hornthal, *Ch of Bd*
Allan Horlick, *President*
Angela Pumo Cohen, *Exec VP*
Tim Wentworth, *Data Proc Staff*
Nancy Strong, *VP Mktg*
EMP: 90
SQ FT: 15,000
SALES (est): 5.1MM **Privately Held**
SIC: 7812 Video tape production

(P-18033)
COLUMBIA PICTURES INDS INC (DH)
10202 Washington Blvd, Culver City
(90232-3119)
PHONE...............................310 244-4000
Michael Lynton, *CEO*
Doug Belgrad, *President*
Andrew Gumpert, *President*
Hannah Minghella, *President*
Matt Tolmach, *President*
EMP: 200
SALES (est): 70.1MM
SALES (corp-wide): 80.1B **Privately Held**
WEB: www.columbiapictures.com
SIC: 7812 Motion picture production & distribution
HQ: Sony Pictures Entertainment, Inc.
10202 Washington Blvd
Culver City CA 90232
310 244-4000

(P-18034)
COOKIE JAR ENTRMT USA INC
4100 W Alameda Ave # 101, Burbank
(91505-4195)
PHONE...............................818 955-5400
Andy Heyward, *President*
Brad Brooks, *President*
Steve Voleti, *CFO*
EMP: 110
SQ FT: 27,000
SALES (est): 4.6MM
SALES (corp-wide): 6.6MM **Privately Held**
SIC: 7812 Television film production

PA: Dic Entertainment Holdings, Inc.
4100 W Alameda Ave Fl 4
Burbank CA 91505
818 955-5400

(P-18035)
CORPORATE PRODUCTION DESIGNS
1427 Goodman Ave, Redondo Beach
(90278-4004)
PHONE..........................310 937-9663
Bill Ganz, *President*
EMP: 50 **EST:** 1997
SALES (est): 1.7MM **Privately Held**
SIC: 7812 Video production

(P-18036)
CYBERNET ENTERTAINMENT LLC (PA)
1800 Mission St, San Francisco
(94103-3502)
PHONE..........................415 865-0230
Peter Ackworth, *Mng Member*
Matthew Devney, *Admin Asst*
Adam Boyd, *HR Admin*
EMP: 93
SALES (est): 11.6MM **Privately Held**
SIC: 7812 Video production

(P-18037)
DALAKLIS MCKEOWN ENTERTAINMENT
2517 Crest Dr, Manhattan Beach
(90266-2135)
PHONE..........................310 545-0120
Charles Dalaklis, *President*
Theresa McKeown, *COO*
EMP: 75
SQ FT: 12,000
SALES (est): 13.5MM **Privately Held**
WEB: www.dmetv.net
SIC: 7812 Television film production

(P-18038)
DCP RIGHTS LLC
2900 Olympic Blvd, Santa Monica
(90404-4127)
PHONE..........................310 255-4600
Allen Shapiro, *President*
Kyla Druckman, *Sales Mgr*
EMP: 50
SQ FT: 45,637
SALES (est): 366.9K **Privately Held**
SIC: 7812 Motion picture & video produc-

(P-18039)
DELUXE MEDIA SERVICES LLC
1377 N Serrano Ave, Los Angeles
(90027-5623)
PHONE..........................323 462-6171
John Suh, *Principal*
Karen Clifton, *Vice Pres*
Marty Siegall, *Manager*
EMP: 900 **EST:** 2012
SALES (est): 44.2MM **Privately Held**
SIC: 7812 Video production

(P-18040)
DIGITAL DOMAIN 30 INC (PA)
12641 Beatrice St, Los Angeles
(90066-7003)
PHONE..........................310 314-2800
Daniel Seah, *CEO*
Frank Ming WEI, *Vice Chairman*
Od Welch, *President*
Amit Chopra, *COO*
Daniel Rosen, *Vice Pres*
EMP: 300
SALES: 75MM **Privately Held**
SIC: 7812 Video production

(P-18041)
DIGITAL KITCHEN LLC
3585 Hayden Ave, Culver City
(90232-2412)
PHONE..........................310 499-9255
Cythia Bimon, *Manager*
EMP: 50
SALES (corp-wide): 12.5B **Privately Held**
SIC: 7812 7819 Video production; serv-
ices allied to motion pictures

HQ: Digital Kitchen, Llc
600 W Fulton St Ste 400
Chicago IL 60661
-

(P-18042)
DISNEY ENTERPRISES INC (HQ)
500 S Buena Vista St, Burbank
(91521-0001)
P.O. Box 3232, Anaheim (92803-3232)
PHONE..........................818 560-1000
Robert Iger, *President*
◆ **EMP:** 2325 **EST:** 1986
SALES (est): 4.5B **Publicly Held**
SIC: 7812 6794 5331 7996 Motion picture production & distribution; motion picture production & distribution; television;
video tape production; television film production; copyright buying & licensing;
music royalties, sheet & record; performance rights, publishing & licensing; variety
stores; theme park, amusement; ice
hockey club

(P-18043)
DISNEY ENTERPRISES INC
3235 S Buena Vista St, Burbank
(91521-0001)
PHONE..........................818 560-3692
EMP: 300 **Publicly Held**
SIC: 7812 Television film production
HQ: Disney Enterprises, Inc.
500 S Buena Vista St
Burbank CA 91521
818 560-1000

(P-18044)
DISNEY INCORPORATED (DH)
500 S Buena Vista St, Burbank
(91521-0001)
PHONE..........................818 560-1000
Matthew L McGinnis, *CEO*
Sanford M Litvack, *President*
Kevin Brockman, *Exec VP*
Bernardo Silva, *Vice Pres*
Donovan Foster, *Exec Dir*
▲ **EMP:** 150
SALES (est): 30.4MM **Publicly Held**
WEB: www.wdwnews.com
SIC: 7812 Motion picture production & dis-
tribution
HQ: Disney Enterprises, Inc.
500 S Buena Vista St
Burbank CA 91521
818 560-1000

(P-18045)
DREAMWORKS ANIMATION LLC
Also Called: Dreamworks Animation TV
1000 Flwr St Cmpnile Bldg, Glendale
(91201)
PHONE..........................818 695-5000
Lewis Coleman,
Olivia Canter, *Vice Pres*
Catherine Giddings, *Executive*
Annie Morita, *Executive*
Vicki Lan, *Admin Sec*
EMP: 69
SALES (est): 87.2MM
SALES (corp-wide): 84.5B **Publicly Held**
SIC: 7812 Motion picture & video produc-
tion
HQ: Dwa Holdings, Llc
1000 Flower St
Glendale CA 91201
818 695-5000

(P-18046)
DREAMWORKS ANIMATION PUBG LLC
1000 Flower St, Glendale (91201-3007)
PHONE..........................818 695-5000
EMP: 297 **EST:** 2014
SALES (est): 3.7MM
SALES (corp-wide): 84.5B **Publicly Held**
SIC: 7812 Motion picture & video produc-
tion
HQ: Dwa Holdings, Llc
1000 Flower St
Glendale CA 91201
818 695-5000

(P-18047)
DUCKPUNK PRODUCTIONS INC
10728 Westminster Ave, Los Angeles
(90034-5516)
PHONE..........................310 836-3818
Mellissa Tong, *President*
EMP: 100
SALES: 202.3K **Privately Held**
SIC: 7812 7311 7335 7819 Commercials,
television: tape or film; advertising agencies; commercial photography; services
allied to motion pictures; directors, independent: motion picture

(P-18048)
DWA HOLDINGS LLC (HQ)
1000 Flower St, Glendale (91201-3007)
PHONE..........................818 695-5000
Mellody Hobson, *Ch of Bd*
Ann Daly, *President*
Jeffrey Katzenberg, *CEO*
Fazal Merchant, *CFO*
Rob Sherwood, *Vice Pres*
EMP: 83
SQ FT: 500,000
SALES (est): 915.8MM
SALES (corp-wide): 84.5B **Publicly Held**
WEB: www.dreamworksanimation.com
SIC: 7812 Cartoon motion picture produc-
tion
PA: Comcast Corporation
1701 Jfk Blvd
Philadelphia PA 19103
215 286-1700

(P-18049)
EARTHBOUND PRODUCTIONS LLC
849 N Occidental Blvd, Los Angeles
(90026-2925)
PHONE..........................504 734-3337
Mandy M Gagliardi,
EMP: 100
SALES (est): 984.1K **Privately Held**
SIC: 7812 Television film production

(P-18050)
EFILM LLC
Also Called: E Film Digital Labratories
1144 N Las Palmas Ave, Los Angeles
(90038-1209)
PHONE..........................323 463-7041
Aria Mehrabi,
Joachim Zell, *Vice Pres*
Grant Janssen, *Administration*
Mae Capalla, *Software Engr*
Kevin Braun, *Research*
EMP: 150
SALES (est): 15.6MM **Privately Held**
WEB: www.efilm.com
SIC: 7812 Video production
HQ: Deluxe Laboratories, Inc.
2400 W Empire Ave Ste 200
Burbank CA 91504
323 462-6171

(P-18051)
FILM ROMAN LLC
6320 Canoga Ave Ste 450, Woodland Hills
(91367-2561)
PHONE..........................818 748-4000
Dana Booton, *Manager*
EMP: 200
SQ FT: 87,000
SALES (corp-wide): 3.2B **Privately Held**
SIC: 7812 Cartoon motion picture produc-
tion; cartoon production, television
HQ: Film Roman, Llc.
8900 Liberty Cir
Englewood CO 80112
720 852-6327

(P-18052)
FILM ROMAN LLC
6320 Canoga Ave Ste 450, Woodland Hills
(91367-2561)
PHONE..........................818 748-4000
Glenn Curtis, *Mng Member*
Carin Davis, *President*
John W Hyde, *President*
Bill Schultz, *Exec VP*
Brett Coker, *Vice Pres*
EMP: 200
SQ FT: 81,000
SALES (est): 8.3MM **Privately Held**
SIC: 7812 Television film production

(P-18053)
FILMQUEST PICTURES CORPORATION
15331 Stonewood Ter, Sherman Oaks
(91403-4917)
PHONE..........................818 905-1006
Eric Steven Stahl, *President*
EMP: 175
SALES (est): 3.6MM **Privately Held**
SIC: 7812 Motion picture production & dis-
tribution

(P-18054)
FOX ANIMATION STUDIOS INC
5700 Wilshire Blvd # 325, Los Angeles
(90036-3659)
PHONE..........................323 857-8800
John McKenna, *President*
▲ **EMP:** 310
SALES (est): 9.1MM
SALES (corp-wide): 30.4B **Publicly Held**
WEB: www.foxmovies.com
SIC: 7812 Motion picture production & dis-
tribution; video tape production; motion
picture production & distribution, televi-
sion; cartoon motion picture production
HQ: Twentieth Century Fox Film Corpora-
tion
10201 W Pico Blvd
Los Angeles CA 90064
310 369-1000

(P-18055)
FRIENDS OF MAX ROSE LLC
1639 11th St Ste 260, Santa Monica
(90404-3759)
PHONE..........................424 901-1260
Paul Currie,
EMP: 58 **EST:** 2011
SALES (est): 1MM **Privately Held**
SIC: 7812 Motion picture production

(P-18056)
GLOBAL ASYLUM INCORPORATED
Also Called: Asylum, The
440 W Los Feliz Rd, Glendale
(91204-2776)
PHONE..........................323 850-1214
Paul Bales, *CFO*
EMP: 50 **EST:** 1997
SALES (est): 3.9MM **Privately Held**
SIC: 7812 Motion picture production & dis-
tribution

(P-18057)
GLOBAL EAGLE ENTERTAINMENT INC
2941 Alton Pkwy, Irvine (92606-5142)
PHONE..........................949 608-8700
Rick Warren,
Ian Mattair, *Director*
EMP: 140 **Publicly Held**
SIC: 7812 Video production
PA: Global Eagle Entertainment Inc.
6100 Center Dr Ste 1020
Los Angeles CA 90045
-

(P-18058)
HARPO PRODUCTIONS INC
Also Called: Harpo Entertainment Group
1041 N Formosa Ave, West Hollywood
(90046-6703)
PHONE..........................312 633-1000
Oprah Winfrey, *Ch of Bd*
Tim Bennett, *President*
Doug Pattison, *CFO*
Bill Becker, *Vice Pres*
EMP: 200
SQ FT: 100,000
SALES (est): 17.2MM **Privately Held**
SIC: 7812 Television film production; video
tape production

(P-18059)
HELINET AVIATION SERVICES LLC (PA)
16303 Waterman Dr, Van Nuys
(91406-1222)
PHONE..........................818 902-0229
Jim McGowan, *President*
Kathryn Purwin, *Ch of Bd*
EMP: 53
SQ FT: 10,000

SALES (est): 9MM Privately Held
SIC: 7812 7359 4522 Motion picture & video production; aircraft & industrial truck rental services; helicopter carriers, non-scheduled

(P-18060)
HIGHPOINT PRODUCTIONS INC
13400 Rverside Dr Ste 300, Sherman Oaks (91423)
PHONE..............................818 728-7600
Gary Benz, *President*
Michael Branton, *Vice Pres*
EMP: 100
SALES (est): 9.4MM Privately Held
WEB: www.grbtv.com
SIC: 7812 Television film production

(P-18061)
HISTORIC TW INC
Also Called: Time Warner
106 Disney Productions, Burbank (91521-0001)
PHONE..............................818 954-3096
Alan Horn, *CEO*
EMP: 50
SALES (corp-wide): 160.5B Publicly Held
SIC: 7812 3652 Motion picture & video production; master records or tapes, preparation of
HQ: Historic Tw Inc.
75 Rockefeller Plz
New York NY 10019

(P-18062)
IF LIVE LLC (PA)
2254 S Sepulveda Blvd, Los Angeles (90064-1812)
PHONE..............................323 957-6868
Alan Walter Fields,
Peter Frankfurt,
Francis Houghton,
EMP: 70 EST: 2001
SALES (est): 832.2K Privately Held
SIC: 7812 Motion picture & video production

(P-18063)
IGNITION CREATIVE LLC
12959 Coral Tree Pl, Los Angeles (90066-7020)
PHONE..............................310 315-6300
Ron Moler,
Doug Dezzani, *Creative Dir*
Martin Kistler, *Creative Dir*
Eric Leung, *Engineer*
Kelly Gans,
EMP: 65
SALES (est): 12MM Privately Held
WEB: www.ignitionla.com
SIC: 7812 Video production

(P-18064)
IMAGINARY FORCES LLC (PA)
2254 S Sepulveda Blvd, Los Angeles (90064-1812)
PHONE..............................323 957-6868
Peter Frankfurt,
Linda Nakagawa, *CFO*
Charles Khoury, *Creative Dir*
Chip Houghton, *Managing Dir*
Margaret Blakemore, *Executive Asst*
EMP: 85
SALES (est): 10.2MM Privately Held
WEB: www.imaginaryforces.com
SIC: 7812 Motion picture & video production

(P-18065)
JEOPARDY PRODUCTIONS INC
10202 Washington Blvd, Culver City (90232-3119)
PHONE..............................310 244-8855
Rocky Schmitt, *CEO*
EMP: 125 EST: 1984
SALES (est): 2MM
SALES (corp-wide): 80.1B Privately Held
WEB: www.jeopardy.com
SIC: 7812 Television film production
HQ: Sony Pictures Entertainment, Inc.
10202 Washington Blvd
Culver City CA 90232
310 244-4000

(P-18066)
JIM HENSON COMPANY INC (PA)
Also Called: Henson Recording Studio
1416 N La Brea Ave, Los Angeles (90028-7506)
PHONE..............................323 856-6680
Lisa Henson, *CEO*
Cheryl Henson, *President*
Peter Schube, *President*
Halle Stanford, *President*
Brian Henson, *CEO*
EMP: 65
SQ FT: 7,000
SALES (est): 12MM Privately Held
WEB: www.farscape.com
SIC: 7812 Motion picture production & distribution; television film production

(P-18067)
LEGEND3D INC
1500 N El Centro Ave # 100, Los Angeles (90028-9229)
PHONE..............................858 793-4420
Ian Jessel, *President*
Tom Sinnott, *COO*
Mark Steffler, *CFO*
Steven Wolkenstein, *CFO*
Barry Sandrew, *Ch Credit Ofcr*
EMP: 86
SQ FT: 50,000
SALES (est): 15MM Privately Held
SIC: 7812 Motion picture & video production

(P-18068)
LGH DIGITAL MEDIA INC
Also Called: Larsons Studios
6520 W Sunset Blvd, Los Angeles (90028-7202)
PHONE..............................323 469-3986
Richard Larson, *President*
A Richard Larson, *President*
Dave Cottrell, *CFO*
Jim Henderson, *Exec VP*
Nisha Sharma, *Accounting Mgr*
EMP: 50
SALES (est): 5.6MM Privately Held
SIC: 7812 Motion picture & video production

(P-18069)
LINNE ENTERTAINMENT LLC
1250 N June St Apt 305, Los Angeles (90038-1387)
PHONE..............................213 425-1146
Eric Hall,
EMP: 50
SALES (est): 15.2K Privately Held
SIC: 7812 7389 Motion picture & video production;

(P-18070)
LIONS GATE ENTERTAINMENT INC (HQ)
2700 Colorado Ave Ste 200, Santa Monica (90404-5502)
PHONE..............................310 449-9200
Jon Feltheimer, *Ch of Bd*
Steven Beeks, *President*
Joseph Drake, *President*
Erik Feig, *President*
Jared Goetz, *President*
EMP: 55
SALES (est): 2.1B
SALES (corp-wide): 3.2B Privately Held
SIC: 7812 Motion picture production & distribution
PA: Lions Gate Entertainment Corp
250 Howe St Fl 20
Vancouver BC V6C 3
877 848-3866

(P-18071)
LIONS GATE FILMS INC
2700 Colorado Ave Ste 200, Santa Monica (90404-5502)
PHONE..............................310 449-9200
Jon Feltheimer, *President*
Steve Beeks, *COO*
James Keegan, *CFO*
Kate Nexon, *Sales Mgr*
Lorna Mann, *Director*
EMP: 147
SQ FT: 30,000

SALES (est): 9MM
SALES (corp-wide): 3.2B Privately Held
WEB: www.lionsgatefilms.com
SIC: 7812 Motion picture & video production
HQ: Lions Gate Entertainment Inc.
2700 Colorado Ave Ste 200
Santa Monica CA 90404
310 449-9200

(P-18072)
LMNO PRODUCTIONS INC
Also Called: Lmno Cable Group
15821 Ventura Blvd # 320, Encino (91436-2928)
PHONE..............................818 995-5555
Eric Schotz, *President*
Ned Davis, *Vice Pres*
David Reed, *Info Tech Mgr*
Lilly Silbert, *Finance*
Jason Coughlan, *Opers Mgr*
EMP: 200
SALES (est): 14.6MM Privately Held
SIC: 7812 Television film production

(P-18073)
LOOKOUT PRODUCTIONS LLC
3748 W 9th St Apt 403, Los Angeles (90019-2117)
PHONE..............................310 408-5687
Gustavo Morales, *Mng Member*
Douglas Wirth,
EMP: 50
SQ FT: 1,500
SALES (est): 559.9K Privately Held
SIC: 7812 Motion picture & video production

(P-18074)
LUCASFILM LTD LLC (HQ)
Also Called: Lucasfilm Coml Productions
1110 Gorgas Ave Bldg C-Hr, San Francisco (94129-1406)
P.O. Box 29901 (94129-0901)
PHONE..............................415 623-1000
Kathleen Kennedy, *President*
Colum Slevin, *Vice Pres*
Lisa Ullmann, *Vice Pres*
Richard Dunn, *Executive*
Rayne Roberts, *Executive*
▲ EMP: 250
SALES (est): 69.2MM Publicly Held
WEB: www.lucasfilm.com
SIC: 7812 6794 Motion picture production & distribution; television film production; patent owners & lessors

(P-18075)
MARK HERZOG & COMPANY INC
4640 Lankershim Blvd, North Hollywood (91602-1841)
PHONE..............................818 762-4640
Mark Herzog, *President*
Raleigh Stewart, *Creative Dir*
EMP: 64
SQ FT: 12,500
SALES (est): 6.3MM Privately Held
WEB: www.herzogproductions.com
SIC: 7812 Television film production

(P-18076)
MEDIA VNTURES ENTRMT GROUP LLC
1547 14th St, Santa Monica (90404-3302)
PHONE..............................310 260-3171
Hans Zimmer, *President*
EMP: 50
SALES (est): 1.3MM Privately Held
SIC: 7812 Video tape production

(P-18077)
MEDIAPLATFORM INC
Also Called: Vcall
8383 Wilshire Blvd # 460, Beverly Hills (90211-2446)
PHONE..............................310 909-8410
Jim McGovern, *CEO*
Mike Newman, *President*
Dena Kendros, *Vice Pres*
Amzi Jackson, *General Mgr*
Eric Vargo, *Sr Software Eng*
EMP: 60

SALES (est): 3.2MM Publicly Held
WEB: www.vodium.com
SIC: 7812 7819 7822 8743 Motion picture & video production; services allied to motion pictures; motion picture & tape distribution; public relations services
HQ: Precisionir Group Inc.
601 Moorefield Park Dr
North Chesterfield VA

(P-18078)
MERLOT FILM PRODUCTIONS INC
Also Called: CBS Network News
7800 Beverly Blvd, Los Angeles (90036-2112)
PHONE..............................323 575-2906
Bruce C Taub, *CEO*
Lesile Moondes, *President*
David Strauss, *CFO*
Claudia E Morf, *Treasurer*
Leo Gorius, *Vice Pres*
EMP: 200
SALES (est): 6MM
SALES (corp-wide): 13.7B Publicly Held
SIC: 7812 4833 Motion picture & video production; television broadcasting stations
HQ: Cbs Broadcasting Inc.
51 W 52nd St
New York NY 10019
212 975-4321

(P-18079)
METHOD STUDIOS LLC
3401 Exposition Blvd, Santa Monica (90404-5050)
PHONE..............................310 434-6500
Dan Glass, *Creative Dir*
Todd Davidovich, *Opers Staff*
Gabby Gourrier, *Producer*
Alyssa Giuliano, *Sales Staff*
Jason Lin, *Director*
EMP: 104
SALES (est): 7.1MM Privately Held
SIC: 7812 Video production
HQ: Deluxe Entertainment Services Group Inc.
2400 W Empire Ave
Los Angeles CA 90027

(P-18080)
METRO-GOLDWYN-MAYER INC (DH)
Also Called: MGM
245 N Beverly Dr, Beverly Hills (90210-5319)
PHONE..............................310 449-3000
Gary Barber, *CEO*
Tricia Samuels, *COO*
Ken Schapiro, *COO*
Lesley Freeman, *Officer*
John Bryan, *Exec VP*
EMP: 300
SQ FT: 131,400
SALES (est): 66MM
SALES (corp-wide): 1.1B Privately Held
WEB: www.mgm.com
SIC: 7812 Motion picture production & distribution; motion picture production & distribution, television; television film production; video production
HQ: Mgm Holdings Ii, Inc.
245 N Beverly Dr
Beverly Hills CA 90210
310 449-3000

(P-18081)
MIRAMAX FILM NY LLC
1901 Avenue Of The Stars # 2000, Los Angeles (90067-6021)
PHONE..............................310 409-4321
Steven Schoch, *CEO*
EMP: 80
SALES (est): 9.9MM Privately Held
SIC: 7812 Video production
PA: Bein Media Group Wll
Tv And Radio Complex Tv Roundabout
Doha
445 777-77

PRODUCTS & SVCS

(P-18082)
NEP GROUP INC
Screenworks Nep
1580 Magnolia Ave, Corona (92879-2073)
PHONE......................951 279-8877
Tom McCracken, *Branch Mgr*
Cheri Navarro, *Administration*
EMP: 50
SALES (corp-wide): 100.3MM **Privately
Held**
SIC: 7812 Television film production
PA: Nep Group, Inc.
2 Beta Dr
Pittsburgh PA 15238
412 826-1414

(P-18083)
NEP GROUP INC
7635 Airport Bus Pkwy, Van Nuys (91406)
PHONE......................412 423-1354
EMP: 100
SALES (corp-wide): 100.3MM **Privately
Held**
SIC: 7812 Television film production
PA: Nep Group, Inc.
2 Beta Dr
Pittsburgh PA 15238
412 826-1414

(P-18084)
**NEW PARADIGM PRODUCTIONS
INC (PA)**
Also Called: Edelman Productions
39 Mesa St Ste 212, San Francisco
(94129-1019)
PHONE......................415 924-8000
Steve Edelman, *President*
EMP: 100
SQ FT: 8,500
SALES (est): 19.7MM **Privately Held**
WEB: www.edelmanproductions.com
SIC: 7812 Video production

(P-18085)
**NEW REGENCY PRODUCTIONS
INC (PA)**
Also Called: Regency Enterprises
10201 W Pico Blvd Bldg 12, Los Angeles
(90064-2606)
PHONE......................310 369-8300
Arnon Milchan, *Principal*
Yariv Milchan, *President*
Brad Weston, *CEO*
Jonathan Fischer, *COO*
Mimi Mtseng, *CFO*
▼ **EMP:** 75
SQ FT: 13,000
SALES (est): 11.7MM **Privately Held**
WEB: www.newregency.com
SIC: 7812 Video production

(P-18086)
NOVASTAR POST INC
23466 Hatteras St, Woodland Hills
(91367-3020)
P.O. Box 25724, Miami FL (33102-5724)
PHONE......................323 467-5020
Greg Geddes, *President*
Bob Sky, *Vice Pres*
EMP: 52
SQ FT: 7,900
SALES (est): 1.5MM **Privately Held**
WEB: www.novastarpost.com
SIC: 7812 Audio-visual program production

(P-18087)
NW ENTERTAINMENT INC (PA)
Also Called: New Wave Entertainment
2660 W Olive Ave, Burbank (91505-4525)
PHONE......................818 295-5000
Paul Apel, *CEO*
Brian Volk-Weiss, *President*
Rick Nowak, *COO*
Greg Woertz, *CFO*
Gary Lister, *Senior VP*
▲ **EMP:** 92
SQ FT: 40,000
SALES (est): 17.7MM **Privately Held**
WEB: www.newwaveent.com
SIC: 7812 Motion picture production

(P-18088)
**ORION PICTURES
CORPORATION**
245 N Beverly Dr, Beverly Hills
(90210-5319)
PHONE......................310 449-3000
Alex Yemenidjian, *Ch of Bd*
Daniel J Taylor, *Treasurer*
EMP: 1000
SALES (est): 89.2K
SALES (corp-wide): 1.1B **Privately Held**
SIC: 7812 Motion picture production & dis-
tribution
HQ: Metro-Goldwyn-Mayer, Inc.
245 N Beverly Dr
Beverly Hills CA 90210

(P-18089)
P J VIDEO SERVICES INC
Also Called: Post Factory
630 The City Dr S Ste 100, Orange
(92868-4926)
PHONE......................714 705-6088
Todd C Yates, *President*
Johnathan Hicks, *Vice Pres*
John Merrell, *Opers Mgr*
EMP: 55 **EST:** 1987
SQ FT: 17,000
SALES (est): 5.4MM **Privately Held**
WEB: www.gearmonkeyrentals.com
SIC: 7812 Video tape production; video
production

(P-18090)
**PARAMOUNT PICTURES
CORPORATION (HQ)**
Also Called: Paramount Studios
5555 Melrose Ave, Los Angeles
(90038-3197)
PHONE......................323 956-5000
Jim Gianopulos, *Ch of Bd*
Fred T Gallo, *President*
Adam Goodman, *President*
Dennis Maguire, *President*
David Stainton, *President*
▲ **EMP:** 1700 **EST:** 1912
SALES (est): 314.9MM
SALES (corp-wide): 13.2B **Publicly Held**
WEB: www.paramount.com
SIC: 7812 5099 4833 7829 Motion pic-
ture production & distribution, television;
motion picture production & distribution;
video cassettes, accessories & supplies;
television broadcasting stations; motion
picture distribution services
PA: Viacom Inc.
1515 Broadway
New York NY 10036
212 258-6000

(P-18091)
**PARAMOUNT TELEVISION
SERVICE**
Also Called: Paramount Pictures
5555 Melrose Ave Rm 204, Los Angeles
(90038-3996)
PHONE......................323 956-5000
EMP: 1800
SALES (est): 9.2MM
SALES (corp-wide): 13.2B **Publicly Held**
WEB: www.paramount.com
SIC: 7812 Motion picture production & dis-
tribution, television; motion picture pro-
duction & distribution
HQ: Paramount Pictures Corporation
5555 Melrose Ave
Los Angeles CA 90038
323 956-5000

(P-18092)
PARTICIPANT MEDIA LLC (PA)
331 Foothill Rd Fl 3, Beverly Hills
(90210-3669)
PHONE......................310 550-5100
Jeff Skoll, *CEO*
Joshua Couch, *President*
Jeffrey Ivers, *COO*
Andy Kim, *CFO*
Mae Smith, *Receptionist*
EMP: 65
SALES (est): 10.4MM **Privately Held**
WEB: www.participantproductions.com
SIC: 7812 Video production

(P-18093)
PIE TOWN PRODUCTIONS INC
5433 Laurel Canyon Blvd, North Hollywood
(91607-2114)
PHONE......................818 255-9300
Tara Sandler, *President*
Dana Besnoy, *Vice Pres*
Drew Hallmann, *Executive*
Laura Stover, *Executive*
Jeff Bloom, *Opers Staff*
EMP: 160
SALES (est): 8.3MM **Privately Held**
WEB: www.pietownproductions.com
SIC: 7812 Television film production

(P-18094)
PIXAR
Also Called: Pixar Animation Studios
1200 Park Ave, Emeryville (94608-3677)
PHONE......................510 922-3000
James W Morris, *CEO*
Bob Morgan, *COO*
Liz Gazzano, *Bd of Directors*
John Lasseter, *Exec VP*
Robin Chandler, *Vice Pres*
▲ **EMP:** 850
SQ FT: 247,000
SALES (est): 149.1MM **Publicly Held**
WEB: www.martinreddy.net
SIC: 7812 7372 7371 Cartoon motion pic-
ture production; commercials, television:
tape or film; prepackaged software; com-
puter software development
PA: The Walt Disney Company
500 S Buena Vista St
Burbank CA 91521

(P-18095)
**PLAYBOY ENTERPRISES INC
(PA)**
Also Called: Playboy Magazine
9346 Civic Center Dr # 200, Beverly Hills
(90210-3604)
PHONE......................310 424-1800
Ben Kohn, *CEO*
David Israel, *President*
Bob Meyers, *President*
Randy A Nicolau, *President*
Alex L Vaickus, *President*
▲ **EMP:** 95 **EST:** 1953
SALES (est): 45.3MM **Privately Held**
WEB: www.playboy.com
SIC: 7812 4841 2721 Motion picture pro-
duction; video production; cable & other
pay television services; periodicals

(P-18096)
**PLAYBOY ENTRMT GROUP INC
(HQ)**
2300 W Empire Ave, Burbank
(91504-3341)
PHONE......................323 276-4000
Brinda Viloa, *Director*
James Griffiths, *President*
Rebecca Pizzello, *Executive Asst*
Valerie Golson, *Mktg Dir*
Jessica Lewis, *Mktg Dir*
EMP: 139
SALES (est): 7.9MM
SALES (corp-wide): 45.3MM **Privately
Held**
SIC: 7812 Video tape production
PA: Playboy Enterprises, Inc.
9346 Civic Center Dr # 200
Beverly Hills CA 90210
310 424-1800

(P-18097)
POST MODERN EDIT LLC
4551 Glencoe Ave Ste 210, Marina Del Rey
(90292-7930)
PHONE......................310 396-7375
EMP: 70
SALES (est): 853.1K **Privately Held**
SIC: 7812 Video production
PA: Post Modern Edit, Llc
2941 Alton Pkwy
Irvine CA 92606

(P-18098)
POST MODERN EDIT LLC (PA)
2941 Alton Pkwy, Irvine (92606-5142)
PHONE......................949 608-8700

Rick Warren,
Hamid Samnani,
Frank Alvarez, *Manager*
Chris Lovett, *Editor*
◆ **EMP:** 51
SQ FT: 22,000
SALES (est): 7.2MM **Privately Held**
WEB: www.postmoderngroup.com
SIC: 7812 Video production

(P-18099)
PRG (CALIFORNIA) INC
Also Called: Fourth Phase Los Angeles
1245 Aviation Pl, San Fernando
(91340-1459)
PHONE......................818 252-2600
Jeremiah Harris, *President*
James Riendeau, *Vice Pres*
▲ **EMP:** 50
SALES (est): 6.7MM **Privately Held**
SIC: 7812 Video production

(P-18100)
**PURPLE LANGUAGE SERVICES
CO**
595 Menlo Dr, Rocklin (95765-3708)
PHONE......................916 435-8216
Dan Luis, *CEO*
John Ferron, *CFO*
Ed Reginelli, *Vice Pres*
EMP: 140
SALES (est): 6.3MM
SALES (corp-wide): 216.8MM **Privately
Held**
WEB: www.purple.us
SIC: 7812 Video production
PA: Purple Communications, Inc.
595 Menlo Dr
Rocklin CA 95765
888 600-4780

(P-18101)
**PUTTIN ON PRODUCTIONS
CORP**
Also Called: POPS
2010 N Sepulveda Blvd A, Manhattan
Beach (90266-2906)
P.O. Box 397 (90267-0397)
PHONE......................310 546-5544
Julia Mirkovich, *Principal*
Susan Liebson, *Business Mgr*
EMP: 50
SALES (est): 376.3K **Privately Held**
SIC: 7812 7911 Motion picture & video
production; dance studio & school

(P-18102)
QUADRA PRODUCTIONS INC
Also Called: Wheel of Fortune
10202 Washington Blvd, Culver City
(90232-3119)
PHONE......................310 244-1234
Harry Friedman, *President*
EMP: 130
SALES (est): 4.9MM
SALES (corp-wide): 80.1B **Privately Held**
WEB: www.sonypictures.com
SIC: 7812 Television film production
HQ: Sony Pictures Entertainment, Inc.
10202 Washington Blvd
Culver City CA 90232
310 244-4000

(P-18103)
RADLEYS
3780 Wilshire Blvd, Los Angeles
(90010-2805)
PHONE......................310 765-2223
Christian Thompson, *Mng Member*
Drake Chandler, *Graphic Designe*
Elizabeth Lisk, *Controller*
Brandon Pleus, *Production*
Chad Itskowitz, *Producer*
EMP: 50
SALES (est): 1.9MM **Privately Held**
SIC: 7812 Television film production

(P-18104)
**RANCH HAND ENTERTAINMENT
INC**
11333 Moorpark St Pmb 441, Studio City
(91602-2618)
PHONE......................612 396-2632
Peter Williams, *President*
Jonathan Ward, *Vice Pres*

EMP: 68
SALES (est): 784K **Privately Held**
SIC: 7812 7389 Television film production;

(P-18105)
REGENT WORLDWIDE SALES LLC
10990 Wilshire Blvd, Los Angeles (90024-3913)
PHONE.................................310 806-4288
Stephen P Jarchow,
Paul Colichman,
EMP: 50
SALES (est): 12MM **Privately Held**
SIC: 7812 Motion picture production & distribution

(P-18106)
REILLY WORLDWIDE INC
3000 Olympic Blvd, Santa Monica (90404-5073)
PHONE.................................310 449-4065
James M Burnett, *President*
EMP: 50
SALES (est): 1.1MM **Privately Held**
SIC: 7812 Television film production

(P-18107)
REMOTE CONTROL PRODUCTIONS (PA)
1547 14th St, Santa Monica (90404-3302)
PHONE.................................310 260-0171
Hans Zimmer, *President*
EMP: 50
SALES (est): 6MM **Privately Held**
SIC: 7812 Video tape production

(P-18108)
RESPOND 2 LLC
Also Called: R2c Group
727 Ansome St, San Francisco (94111)
PHONE.................................415 398-4200
Mark Yesayian, *Branch Mgr*
EMP: 65
SALES (corp-wide): 25MM **Privately Held**
SIC: 7812 Video production
PA: Respond 2 Llc
207 Nw Park Ave
Portland OR 97209
503 222-0025

(P-18109)
RHYTHM AND HUES INC (PA)
Also Called: Rhythm & Hues Studios
2100 E Grand Ave Ste A, El Segundo (90245-5055)
PHONE.................................310 448-7500
John Hughes, *President*
Keith Goldfarb, *Shareholder*
Pauline TSO, *Corp Secy*
Gary Nolin, *Manager*
Derek Spears, *Supervisor*
EMP: 53
SALES (est): 15MM **Privately Held**
WEB: www.floatingmuseum.com
SIC: 7812 Cartoon production, television; commercials, television: tape or film

(P-18110)
ROCK PAPER SCISSORS LLC
2308 Broadway, Santa Monica (90404-2916)
PHONE.................................310 586-0600
Angus Wall,
Arleen Rosenberg, *CFO*
Eve Kornblum, *Executive*
Tommy Asbee, *Engineer*
Rob Larose, *Engineer*
EMP: 50
SQ FT: 9,000
SALES (est): 6.9MM **Privately Held**
WEB: www.a52.com
SIC: 7812 8999 Commercials, television: tape or film; editorial service

(P-18111)
ROUNDABOUT ENTERTAINMENT INC
Also Called: Secuto Music
217 S Lake St, Burbank (91502-2111)
PHONE.................................818 842-9300
Craig S Clark, *CEO*
Tiffany Price, *Treasurer*
Mike Esfahanian, *Vice Pres*

Isabel Olmos, *Admin Asst*
Ross Millard, *Info Tech Mgr*
EMP: 84
SQ FT: 6,000
SALES (est): 9.2MM **Privately Held**
WEB: www.roundabout.com
SIC: 7812 Video production

(P-18112)
RSA FILMS INC (PA)
634 N La Peer Dr, West Hollywood (90069-5602)
PHONE.................................310 659-1577
Jules Daly, *President*
Susan Tamas, *Office Mgr*
Raymond Chu, *CIO*
Marlene Muller, *Project Mgr*
Autumn Hymes, *Production*
EMP: 57
SALES (est): 8.3MM **Privately Held**
WEB: www.rsafilms.com
SIC: 7812 Commercials, television: tape or film; music video production

(P-18113)
SCALELAB LLC
10351 Santa Monica Blvd # 404, Los Angeles (90025-6935)
PHONE.................................310 526-7524
David Brenner, *Mng Member*
Maximilien Desmarais, *President*
Tyler Wells, *Senior VP*
Richard Scotten, *CTO*
Gus Schultz, *Manager*
EMP: 50
SALES (est): 56.7K **Privately Held**
SIC: 7812 Video production

(P-18114)
SCRIPT TO SCREEN INC
200 N Tustin Ave Ste 200 # 200, Santa Ana (92705-3817)
PHONE.................................714 558-3287
Barbara L Kerry, *Ch of Bd*
W E Mitchell, *President*
Alex Dinsmoor, *Exec VP*
Kenneth P Kerry, *Vice Pres*
Catherine Gudvangen, *Producer*
EMP: 75
SQ FT: 6,000
SALES (est): 7MM **Privately Held**
WEB: www.scripttoscreen.com
SIC: 7812 Video production; motion picture production

(P-18115)
SDI MEDIA USA INC (DH)
Also Called: Sdi Media USA
6060 Center Dr Ste 100, Los Angeles (90045-8835)
PHONE.................................323 602-5455
Walter Schonfeld, *CEO*
Rick Sanchez, *CFO*
Mary Ann Fialkowski, *Exec VP*
Scott Rose, *Exec VP*
Ron Cook, *Vice Pres*
EMP: 87
SQ FT: 13,000
SALES (est): 30.6MM
SALES (corp-wide): 176.1K **Privately Held**
WEB: www.sdimediagroup.com
SIC: 7812 Motion picture & video production
HQ: Sdi Media Group Limited
1000 Great West Road
Brentford MIDDX
208 232-4930

(P-18116)
SHADOW ANIMATION LLC
940 N Mansfield Ave, Los Angeles (90038-2312)
PHONE.................................323 466-7771
Alex Bulkley, *Owner*
Corey Campodonico,
EMP: 50
SALES (est): 3.2MM **Privately Held**
WEB: www.shadowmachine.com
SIC: 7812 Audio-visual program production

(P-18117)
SMUK INC
3800 Barham Blvd Ste 410, Los Angeles (90068-1042)
PHONE.................................323 904-4680

Nick Emmerson, *President*
EMP: 200
SALES (est): 2MM **Privately Held**
SIC: 7812 Television film production

(P-18118)
SONY ELECTRONICS INC
Also Called: Urban Sony Service Center
14450 Myford Rd, Irvine (92606-1001)
PHONE.................................714 508-7634
Jim Whitehouse, *Principal*
EMP: 101
SALES (corp-wide): 80.1B **Privately Held**
SIC: 7812 7622 5731 Motion picture & video production; video repair; high fidelity stereo equipment
HQ: Sony Electronics Inc.
16535 Via Esprillo Bldg 1
San Diego CA 92127
858 942-2400

(P-18119)
SONY ELECTRONICS INC
835 Howard St, San Francisco (94103-3009)
PHONE.................................415 833-4796
Yvonne Miranda, *Principal*
EMP: 300
SALES (corp-wide): 80.1B **Privately Held**
SIC: 7812 7832 Motion picture production & distribution; motion picture production & distribution; television; motion picture theaters, except drive-in
HQ: Sony Electronics Inc.
16535 Via Esprillo Bldg 1
San Diego CA 92127
858 942-2400

(P-18120)
SONY PICTURES ENTRMT INC
9050 Washington Blvd, Culver City (90232-2518)
PHONE.................................310 840-8000
Kym Wulfe, *President*
EMP: 500
SALES (corp-wide): 80.1B **Privately Held**
WEB: www.sonypictures.com
SIC: 7812 Motion picture & video production
HQ: Sony Pictures Entertainment, Inc.
10202 Washington Blvd
Culver City CA 90232
310 244-4000

(P-18121)
SONY PICTURES ENTRMT INC (DH)
Also Called: Sony Pictures Studios
10202 Washington Blvd, Culver City (90232-3119)
PHONE.................................310 244-4000
Tony Vinciquerra, *CEO*
Kristine Belson, *President*
David Bishop, *President*
Rory Bruer, *President*
Dwight Caines, *President*
▲ **EMP:** 3000
SALES (est): 429.2MM
SALES (corp-wide): 80.1B **Privately Held**
WEB: www.sonypictures.com
SIC: 7812 7822 7832 Motion picture production & distribution; motion picture production & distribution; television; distribution, exclusive of production: motion picture; distribution for television: motion picture; motion picture theaters, except drive-in
HQ: Sony Corporation Of America
25 Madison Ave Fl 27
New York NY 10010
212 833-8000

(P-18122)
SONY PICTURES STUDIOS INC
1250 S Beverly Glen Blvd # 112, Los Angeles (90024-5204)
PHONE.................................310 244-4000
Jack Kindberg, *President*
Jared Jussim, *Admin Sec*
EMP: 380
SALES (est): 8.1MM
SALES (corp-wide): 80.1B **Privately Held**
WEB: www.sonypictures.com
SIC: 7812 Motion picture production

HQ: Sony Pictures Entertainment, Inc.
10202 Washington Blvd
Culver City CA 90232
310 244-4000

(P-18123)
SONY PICTURES TELEVISION INC (DH)
10202 Washington Blvd, Culver City (90232-3119)
PHONE.................................310 244-7625
Steve Mosko, *CEO*
Drew Shearer, *CFO*
Linda Bershad, *Vice Pres*
Kerstin G Ehne, *VP Sales*
Kerstin G Hne, *VP Sales*
▲ **EMP:** 300
SALES: 6MM
SALES (corp-wide): 80.1B **Privately Held**
WEB: www.sonypicturestelevision.com
SIC: 7812 Motion picture production & distribution, television
HQ: Sony Pictures Entertainment, Inc.
10202 Washington Blvd
Culver City CA 90232
310 244-4000

(P-18124)
SPORTVISION INC
6657 Kaiser Dr, Fremont (94555-3608)
PHONE.................................510 736-2925
Rhonda Brewer, *Manager*
Mark Osborne, *QA Dir*
Jonathan Hirschberg, *Engineer*
Andrew Lorenz, *Manager*
EMP: 50
SALES (corp-wide): 38.6MM **Privately Held**
SIC: 7812 7371 Commercials, television: tape or film; custom computer programming services
HQ: Sportvision, Inc.
4619 N Ravenswood Ave # 304
Chicago IL 60640
773 293-4300

(P-18125)
STARGATE FILMS INC
Also Called: Stargate Digital
1001 El Centro St, South Pasadena (91030-5206)
PHONE.................................626 403-8403
Sam Nicholson, *President*
Jason Lucas, *CFO*
Jim Railey, *Exec VP*
Darren Frankel, *Vice Pres*
Pete Ware, *Principal*
EMP: 65
SQ FT: 50,000
SALES (est): 7.4MM **Privately Held**
SIC: 7812 Motion picture production; television film production

(P-18126)
STU SEGALL PRODUCTIONS INC
4705 Ruffin Rd, San Diego (92123-1611)
PHONE.................................858 974-8988
Stu Segall, *President*
Kevin Waskow, *Vice Pres*
Christopher Burke, *Financial Exec*
Scott Brazil, *Director*
EMP: 200
SQ FT: 1,000
SALES (est): 14MM **Privately Held**
WEB: www.stusegall.com
SIC: 7812 Video production

(P-18127)
STUDY TAPES
Also Called: PINE KNOLL PUBLICATIONS
1341 Pine Knoll Cres, Redlands (92373-6545)
PHONE.................................909 792-0111
Dr Gerald A Kirk, *Partner*
Cheryl J Kirk, *Partner*
▲ **EMP:** 52 **EST:** 1972
SALES: 265.2K **Privately Held**
WEB: www.pineknoll.org
SIC: 7812 5735 Video tape production; audio tapes, prerecorded

(P-18128)
T25CL ENTERTAINMENT LLC
1074 55th St, Oakland (94608-2746)
PHONE.................................951 308-2040

Andre Ward, *CEO*
Ricardo Burgess, *CTO*
Rosalyn Jordan Mills, *Director*
EMP: 229
SQ FT: 8,000
SALES (est): 63MM **Privately Held**
SIC: 7812 7929 Motion picture & video production; entertainment service

(P-18129)
TAFT BROADCASTING COMPANY LLC
23755 Z St, March ARB (92518-2077)
PHONE..........................951 413-2337
Robert Dawson, *Branch Mgr*
EMP: 80
SALES (corp-wide): 5.7MM **Privately Held**
WEB: www.taftbroadcasting.com
SIC: 7812 7389 Television film production; video tape production; music & broadcasting services
PA: Taft Broadcasting Company, Llc
1118 Heights Blvd
Houston TX 77008
713 692-2900

(P-18130)
TALL PONY PRODUCTIONS INC
300 Loma Metisse Rd, Malibu (90265-3059)
P.O. Box 1026 (90265-1026)
PHONE..........................310 456-7495
Anthony Eaton, *President*
EMP: 150
SQ FT: 2,000
SALES (est): 3.4MM **Privately Held**
WEB: www.tallponyproductions.com
SIC: 7812 Television film production

(P-18131)
TECHNICOLOR NEW MEDIA INC
250 E Olive Ave Ste 300, Burbank (91502-1211)
PHONE..........................818 480-5100
Dave Weaphers, *President*
EMP: 50
SALES (est): 3.4MM **Privately Held**
SIC: 7812 Audio-visual program production

(P-18132)
TIME WARNER CABLE ENTPS LLC
3500 W Olive Ave Ste 1000, Burbank (91505-5515)
PHONE..........................818 972-0808
EMP: 75
SALES (corp-wide): 41.5B **Publicly Held**
SIC: 7812 Television film production
HQ: Time Warner Cable Enterprises Llc
400 Atlantic St Ste 6
Stamford CT 06901

(P-18133)
TOPANGA PRODUCTIONS INC
10202 Wash Blvd Ste 1132, Culver City (90232-3119)
PHONE..........................310 244-4000
Steve Mosko, *CEO*
EMP: 50
SALES (est): 66.5K
SALES (corp-wide): 80.1B **Privately Held**
WEB: www.sonypictures.com
SIC: 7812 Motion picture & video production
HQ: Sony Pictures Entertainment, Inc.
10202 Washington Blvd
Culver City CA 90232
310 244-4000

(P-18134)
TOUCHSTONE TELEVISION PROD LLC (PA)
500 S Buena Vista St, Burbank (91521-0001)
PHONE..........................323 671-5116
Mark Pedowitz, *President*
EMP: 50
SALES (est): 11.9MM **Privately Held**
SIC: 7812 Non-theatrical motion picture production, television

(P-18135)
TRIAGE ENTERTAINMENT INC
6701 Center Dr W Ste 300, Los Angeles (90045-2482)
PHONE..........................310 417-4800
Stuart M Schreiberg, *President*
Stephen Kroopnick, *Exec VP*
John Bravakis, *Vice Pres*
EMP: 60
SQ FT: 15,000
SALES (est): 6.9MM **Privately Held**
WEB: www.triageinc.com
SIC: 7812 Motion picture & video production

(P-18136)
TRICOR ENTERTAINMENT INC
Also Called: Chinaamerica Film Distributors
1613 Chelsea Rd, San Marino (91108-2419)
PHONE..........................626 282-5184
Craig Darian, *Chairman*
Howard Kazanjian, *Co-COB*
Sally Austin, *Exec VP*
William E Wegner, *General Counsel*
EMP: 240
SQ FT: 350,000
SALES (est): 3.6MM **Privately Held**
SIC: 7812 Motion picture production; television film production

(P-18137)
TTT WEST COAST INC
3000 W Alameda Ave # 125, Burbank (91505-4437)
PHONE..........................818 972-0500
Mike Darnell, *President*
EMP: 200
SALES (est): 5MM
SALES (corp-wide): 2.2B **Publicly Held**
SIC: 7812 Motion picture production; television film production
HQ: Time Inc.
225 Liberty St Ste C2
New York NY 10281
212 522-1212

(P-18138)
TURNER BROADCASTING SYSTEM INC
Also Called: TNT Originals
3500 W Olive Ave Ste 1500, Burbank (91505-4630)
PHONE..........................818 977-5452
Sandra Dewey, *Vice Pres*
Julianne Gorman, *Director*
Cuong Pham, *Manager*
EMP: 50
SALES (corp-wide): 160.5B **Publicly Held**
WEB: www.turner.com
SIC: 7812 Television film production
HQ: Turner Broadcasting System, Inc.
1 Cnn Ctr Nw 14sw
Atlanta GA 30303
404 575-7250

(P-18139)
TWENTIETH CENTURY FOX HOME E (DH)
10201 W Pico Blvd, Los Angeles (90064-2651)
PHONE..........................310 369-1000
K Rupert Murdoch,
Rod Conti, *Opers Staff*
Mary Navia, *Opers Staff*
EMP: 1000
SQ FT: 25,000
SALES (est): 85.4MM
SALES (corp-wide): 30.4B **Publicly Held**
SIC: 7812 Motion picture & video production
HQ: Twentieth Century Fox Film Corporation
10201 W Pico Blvd
Los Angeles CA 90064
310 369-1000

(P-18140)
TWENTIETH CNTURY FOX FILM CORP (DH)
Also Called: Fox Films Entertainment
10201 W Pico Blvd, Los Angeles (90064-2606)
P.O. Box 900, Beverly Hills (90213-0900)
PHONE..........................310 369-1000
K Rupert Murdoch, *Ch of Bd*
Florence Grace, *Vice Pres*
Paul Krinsky, *Exec Dir*
Jeff Shell, *Branch Mgr*
Derek Grier, *Network Mgr*
◆ **EMP:** 75 **EST:** 1915
SQ FT: 25,000
SALES (est): 345.3MM
SALES (corp-wide): 30.4B **Publicly Held**
WEB: www.foxmovies.com
SIC: 7812 Motion picture production & distribution; video tape production; motion picture production & distribution, television; television film production
HQ: Fox Entertainment Group, Llc
1211 Ave Of The Americas
New York NY 10036
212 852-7000

(P-18141)
UNIVERSAL CITY STUDIOS LLC (DH)
Also Called: Universal Creative
100 Universal City Plz, Universal City (91608-1085)
PHONE..........................800 864-8377
Kimberley D Harris,
Eliot Sekuler, *President*
Scott Abraham, *Vice Pres*
Glen Connally, *Vice Pres*
Claudia Soriano, *Comp Spec*
EMP: 58
SALES (est): 15.2MM
SALES (corp-wide): 84.5B **Publicly Held**
SIC: 7812 Motion picture production & distribution
HQ: Nbcuniversal Media, Llc
30 Rockefeller Plz Fl 2
New York NY 10112
212 664-4444

(P-18142)
UNIVERSAL STUDIOS INC
1295 Los Angeles St Ste 1, Glendale (91204-2403)
PHONE..........................818 262-4301
Kate Sullivan, *Branch Mgr*
EMP: 155
SALES (corp-wide): 84.5B **Publicly Held**
WEB: www.universalstudios.com
SIC: 7812 Motion picture & video production
HQ: Universal Studios Company Llc
100 Universal City Plz
North Hollywood CA 91608
818 777-1000

(P-18143)
UNIVERSAL STUDIOS INC
MCA Music
4123 Lankershim Blvd, North Hollywood (91602-2828)
PHONE..........................818 753-0000
George Smith, *Manager*
EMP: 100
SALES (corp-wide): 84.5B **Publicly Held**
WEB: www.universalstudios.com
SIC: 7812 Motion picture & video production
HQ: Universal Studios Company Llc
100 Universal City Plz
North Hollywood CA 91608
818 777-1000

(P-18144)
UNIVERSAL STUDIOS INC
3900 Lankershim Blvd, Studio City (91604)
PHONE..........................818 777-2351
Edgar Bromfrom Jr, *Manager*
EMP: 155
SALES (corp-wide): 84.5B **Publicly Held**
WEB: www.universalstudios.com
SIC: 7812 Motion picture & video production
HQ: Universal Studios Company Llc
100 Universal City Plz
North Hollywood CA 91608
818 777-1000

(P-18145)
UNIVERSAL STUDIOS COMPANY LLC
Also Called: MCA Music
1000 Univ Studio Blvd 2, Universal City (91608-1008)
PHONE..........................818 622-4455
James Warren, *Manager*
Kathy Mandato, *Senior VP*
EMP: 400
SALES (corp-wide): 84.5B **Publicly Held**
WEB: www.universalstudios.com
SIC: 7812 Motion picture & video production
HQ: Universal Studios Company Llc
100 Universal City Plz
North Hollywood CA 91608
818 777-1000

(P-18146)
UNIVERSAL STUDIOS COMPANY LLC (DH)
100 Universal City Plz, North Hollywood (91608-1002)
PHONE..........................818 777-1000
Adam Fogelson, *Chairman*
Ron Meyer, *Vice Chairman*
Sean Gamble, *CFO*
Donna Langley, *Chairman*
Michael Daruty, *Vice Pres*
▲ **EMP:** 168 **EST:** 1924
SQ FT: 100,000
SALES (est): 1.1B
SALES (corp-wide): 84.5B **Publicly Held**
WEB: www.universalstudios.com
SIC: 7812 3652 2741 5947 Motion picture production & distribution; television film production; phonograph records, prerecorded; magnetic tape (audio): prerecorded; compact laser discs, prerecorded; music, sheet: publishing & printing; gift shop; novelties; jewelry stores; gift items, mail order; novelty merchandise, mail order; jewelry, mail order
HQ: Nbcuniversal Media, Llc
30 Rockefeller Plz Fl 2
New York NY 10112
212 664-4444

(P-18147)
UNIVERSAL STUDIOS COMPANY LLC
MCA Music
100 Universal City Plz # 3, Universal City (91608-1002)
PHONE..........................818 777-1000
Larry Miller, *Manager*
Craig Arkenau, *Director*
EMP: 155
SALES (corp-wide): 84.5B **Publicly Held**
WEB: www.universalstudios.com
SIC: 7812 Motion picture & video production
HQ: Universal Studios Company Llc
100 Universal City Plz
North Hollywood CA 91608
818 777-1000

(P-18148)
UNIVERSAL STUDIOS COMPANY LLC
2440 S Sepulveda Blvd # 100, Los Angeles (90064-1784)
PHONE..........................310 235-4749
David Renzer, *Principal*
James Harrington, *Senior VP*
Chris Monaco, *Senior VP*
Liz Alvarado, *Vice Pres*
Dan Bess, *Vice Pres*
EMP: 125
SALES (corp-wide): 84.5B **Publicly Held**
WEB: www.universalstudios.com
SIC: 7812 Motion picture & video production
HQ: Universal Studios Company Llc
100 Universal City Plz
North Hollywood CA 91608
818 777-1000

(P-18149)
UNIVERSAL STUDIOS COMPANY LLC
Also Called: Universal City
2220 Colorado Ave, Santa Monica
(90404-3506)
PHONE.................................310 865-5000
Darcey Graver, *Principal*
Jesus Naranjo, *Director*
Carla Espinoza, *Receptionist*
EMP: 100
SALES (corp-wide): 84.5B **Publicly Held**
SIC: 7812 Motion picture production & distribution
HQ: Universal Studios Company Llc
100 Universal City Plz
North Hollywood CA 91608
818 777-1000

(P-18150)
UP STAGE INC
Also Called: Stage Right Production Svcs
30757 Canwood St, Agoura (91301-2022)
PHONE.................................818 879-8781
Thomas Peachee, *President*
Lisa Peachee, *Admin Sec*
EMP: 50
SALES (est): 895.5K **Privately Held**
SIC: 7812 Commercials, television: tape or film

(P-18151)
VIACOM NETWORKS
Also Called: Mtv Networks
1575 N Gower St Ste 100, Los Angeles
(90028-6488)
PHONE.................................310 752-8000
Anthony Disanto, *President*
Jeremy Gonzalez, *President*
Kimberly Rach, *Senior VP*
Bill Hutten, *Vice Pres*
Elaine Nefsky, *Info Tech Dir*
EMP: 3645
SALES (est): 106.8MM **Privately Held**
SIC: 7812 7822 Television film production; motion picture & tape distribution

(P-18152)
WAD PRODUCTIONS INC
Also Called: Ellen Degeneres Show, The
3500 W Olive Ave Ste 1000, Burbank
(91505-5515)
PHONE.................................818 260-5673
Greg Gorden, *President*
Neha Modha, *Internal Med*
Liz Patrick, *Director*
Stephanie Guerrieri, *Manager*
EMP: 99
SALES (est): 5.4MM **Privately Held**
SIC: 7812 Motion picture & video production

(P-18153)
WALT DISNEY COMPANY
601 Circle Seven Dr, Glendale
(91201-2332)
PHONE.................................818 553-4222
Jan Smith, *Branch Mgr*
EMP: 120 **Publicly Held**
SIC: 7812 Motion picture production & distribution; motion picture production & distribution, television; video tape production; television film production
PA: The Walt Disney Company
500 S Buena Vista St
Burbank CA 91521

(P-18154)
WALT DISNEY RECORDS DIRECT (DH)
500 S Buena Vista St, Burbank
(91521-0007)
PHONE.................................818 560-1000
Alan H Bergman, *Senior VP*
Rob Moore, *CFO*
Nick Franklin, *Senior VP*
Marsha Reed, *Admin Sec*
Kevin Constantine, *Engineer*
◆ EMP: 2990
SQ FT: 600,000

SALES (est): 102.1MM **Publicly Held**
WEB: www.radiodisney.com
SIC: 7812 Motion picture production & distribution; motion picture production & distribution, television; non-theatrical motion picture production; non-theatrical motion picture production, television
HQ: Disney Enterprises, Inc.
500 S Buena Vista St
Burbank CA 91521
818 560-1000

(P-18155)
WARNER BROS ENTERTAINMENT INC
Also Called: Warner Bros. Paint Department
4000 Warner Blvd, Burbank (91522-0002)
PHONE.................................818 954-1817
Ron Stansberry, *Manager*
EMP: 120
SALES (corp-wide): 160.5B **Publicly Held**
SIC: 7812 7384 Television film production; home movies, developing & processing
HQ: Warner Bros. Entertainment Inc.
4000 Warner Blvd
Burbank CA 91522
818 954-6000

(P-18156)
WARNER BROS ENTERTAINMENT INC
Also Called: Warner Bros. Legal Department
4000 Warner Blvd, Burbank (91522-0002)
PHONE.................................818 954-7232
Peter Roch, *President*
Bonnie Hill, *Vice Pres*
Gabriel J Pasette, *Vice Pres*
Carmen Velez, *General Mgr*
Pranav Sharma, *Project Mgr*
EMP: 447
SALES (corp-wide): 160.5B **Publicly Held**
SIC: 7812 8111 Television film production; specialized legal services
HQ: Warner Bros. Entertainment Inc.
4000 Warner Blvd
Burbank CA 91522
818 954-6000

(P-18157)
WARNER BROS ENTERTAINMENT INC
Also Called: Warner Bros Studio Facilities
4000 Warner Blvd, Burbank (91522-0002)
PHONE.................................818 954-3000
David Camp, *Manager*
EMP: 168
SALES (corp-wide): 160.5B **Publicly Held**
SIC: 7812 Motion picture production; television film production
HQ: Warner Bros. Entertainment Inc.
4000 Warner Blvd
Burbank CA 91522
818 954-6000

(P-18158)
WARNER BROS ENTERTAINMENT INC
Also Called: Warner Bros Domestic TV Dist
4000 Warner Blvd Bldg 118, Burbank
(91522-0002)
PHONE.................................818 954-5301
Mike Troxler, *Branch Mgr*
EMP: 168
SALES (corp-wide): 160.5B **Publicly Held**
SIC: 7812 Motion picture production & distribution, television
HQ: Warner Bros. Entertainment Inc.
4000 Warner Blvd
Burbank CA 91522
818 954-6000

(P-18159)
WARNER BROS ENTERTAINMENT INC
DC Entertainment
4000 Warner Blvd, Burbank (91522-0002)
PHONE.................................818 954-6000
Diane Nelson, *President*
EMP: 125

SALES (corp-wide): 160.5B **Publicly Held**
SIC: 7812 Motion picture & video production
HQ: Warner Bros. Entertainment Inc.
4000 Warner Blvd
Burbank CA 91522
818 954-6000

(P-18160)
WARNER BROS ENTERTAINMENT INC (DH)
Also Called: Victory Studio
4000 Warner Blvd, Burbank (91522-0002)
PHONE.................................818 954-6000
Kevin Tsujihara, *CEO*
Alan Horn, *President*
Jeff Brown, *Exec VP*
Susan Kantor, *Exec VP*
Dee Dee Myers, *Exec VP*
◆ EMP: 1938
SALES (est): 722MM
SALES (corp-wide): 160.5B **Publicly Held**
SIC: 7812 Television film production

(P-18161)
WARNER BROS ENTERTAINMENT INC
Warner Bros. Animation
4000 Warner Blvd, Burbank (91522-0002)
PHONE.................................818 954-3000
Nina Naranja, *Branch Mgr*
George Aluzzi, *President*
James Davidson, *Manager*
EMP: 168
SALES (corp-wide): 160.5B **Publicly Held**
SIC: 7812 Cartoon motion picture production
HQ: Warner Bros. Entertainment Inc.
4000 Warner Blvd
Burbank CA 91522
818 954-6000

(P-18162)
WARNER BROS ENTERTAINMENT INC
4000 Warner Blvd Bldg 30, Burbank
(91522-0002)
PHONE.................................818 954-2181
Randy Hoffman, *Branch Mgr*
EMP: 168
SALES (corp-wide): 160.5B **Publicly Held**
SIC: 7812 Motion picture production & distribution, television
HQ: Warner Bros. Entertainment Inc.
4000 Warner Blvd
Burbank CA 91522
818 954-6000

(P-18163)
WARNER BROS HOME ENTRMT INC (DH)
4000 Warner Blvd Bldg 160, Burbank
(91522-0002)
P.O. Box 9153, Canton MA (02021-9153)
PHONE.................................818 954-6000
James Cardwell, *President*
Mark Kaufman, *Exec VP*
Christian Davin, *Senior VP*
David Haddad, *Senior VP*
Jeff Baker, *Vice Pres*
▲ EMP: 80
SQ FT: 12,000
SALES (est): 58.4MM
SALES (corp-wide): 160.5B **Publicly Held**
SIC: 7812 Motion picture & video production
HQ: Warner Bros. Entertainment Inc.
4000 Warner Blvd
Burbank CA 91522
818 954-6000

(P-18164)
WARNER BROS INTL TV DIST INC
4000 Warner Blvd, Burbank (91522-0002)
PHONE.................................818 954-6000
Jeffrey R Schlesinger, *President*
Monique Esclavissat, *Exec VP*
Sarah Godfrey, *Senior Mgr*
Margee Schubert, *Director*

EMP: 99
SALES (est): 2MM
SALES (corp-wide): 160.5B **Publicly Held**
SIC: 7812 Motion picture & video production
HQ: Warner Bros. Entertainment Inc.
4000 Warner Blvd
Burbank CA 91522
818 954-6000

(P-18165)
WARNER BROTHERS STUDIOS
4000 Warner Blvd, Burbank (91522-0001)
PHONE.................................818 954-5000
Gary Credle, *Principal*
Alan Horn, *COO*
Jack Nguyen, *Senior VP*
Nevin Shalit, *Vice Pres*
Niki Sherrod, *Vice Pres*
▲ EMP: 74
SALES (est): 12.8MM **Privately Held**
WEB: www.warnerbros.com
SIC: 7812 Motion picture & video production

(P-18166)
WATCHIT MEDIA INC
655 Montgomery St # 1000, San Francisco
(94111-2635)
PHONE.................................702 740-1700
James R Lavelle, *Ch of Bd*
John Dong, *CFO*
No L McDaniel, *Marketing Mgr*
EMP: 140
SALES (est): 2.5MM **Privately Held**
WEB: www.cotl.com
SIC: 7812 7822 Motion picture production & distribution, television; film exchange for television: motion picture

(P-18167)
WEINSTEIN COMPANY LLC
9100 Wilshire Blvd 700w, Beverly Hills
(90212-3466)
PHONE.................................424 204-4800
Harvey Weinstein, *Manager*
Isaac Mizrahi, *Vice Pres*
Marissa Moffitt, *Executive Asst*
Adam Bernardi, *Editor*
EMP: 60
SALES (corp-wide): 39.5MM **Privately Held**
SIC: 7812 Audio-visual program production
PA: The Weinstein Company Llc
99 Hudson St Fl 4
New York NY 10013
212 845-8600

(P-18168)
WESTWIND MEDIA INC
100 W Alameda Ave, Burbank
(91502-2208)
PHONE.................................818 972-9000
John A Bidasio, *President*
EMP: 55
SQ FT: 20,000
SALES (est): 3.4MM **Privately Held**
SIC: 7812 Non-theatrical motion picture production, television

(P-18169)
WESTWIND STUDIOS LLC
Also Called: Westwind Media
100 W Alameda Ave, Burbank
(91502-2208)
PHONE.................................818 972-9000
John A Bidasio, *Mng Member*
Stephen Cannell,
Leland Postil,
EMP: 50
SQ FT: 20,000
SALES: 9MM **Privately Held**
SIC: 7812 Motion picture production; television film production

(P-18170)
WRITTEN ON MY SKIN LLC
7119 W Sunset Blvd # 316, Los Angeles
(90046-4411)
PHONE.................................312 504-5100
Rod Roberts, *Mng Member*
EMP: 50
SALES (est): 275.6K **Privately Held**
SIC: 7812 Motion picture production

(P-18171)
YES VIDEOCOM INC (PA)
2805 Bowers Ave Ste 230, Santa Clara
(95051-0971)
PHONE.................................408 907-7600
Michael Chang, *CEO*
▲ **EMP:** 350
SQ FT: 36,000
SALES (est): 33.1MM **Privately Held**
WEB: www.yesvideo.com
SIC: 7812 Motion picture production

(P-18172)
ZEFR INC
Also Called: Movieclips.com
4101 Redwood Ave, Los Angeles
(90066-5603)
PHONE.................................310 392-3555
Rich Raddon, *President*
Alan Joos, *Partner*
Toby Byrne, *President*
Jeremy Greenspan, *President*
Gabi Loeb, *CFO*
EMP: 200
SALES (est): 15.1MM **Privately Held**
SIC: 7812 Motion picture production

(P-18173)
ZOIC INC
Also Called: Zoic Studios
3582 Eastham Dr, Culver City
(90232-2409)
PHONE.................................310 838-0770
Loni Peristere, *CEO*
Chris Jones, *President*
Tim McBride, *Treasurer*
Patrick Mooney, *General Mgr*
Alex Hopkins, *Executive Asst*
EMP: 125
SQ FT: 15,000
SALES (est): 14MM **Privately Held**
WEB: www.zoicstudios.com
SIC: 7812 Video production

**7819 Services Allied To
Motion Picture Prdtn**

(P-18174)
525 STUDIOS INC
1632 5th St, Santa Monica (90401-3318)
PHONE.................................310 525-1234
Od Welch, *President*
EMP: 70
SQ FT: 19,000
SALES (est): 1.2MM **Privately Held**
SIC: 7819 TV tape services: editing, transfers, etc.

(P-18175)
A FILML INC
Also Called: FILML.A
6255 W Sunset Blvd Fl 12, Los Angeles
(90028-7428)
PHONE.................................213 977-8600
Paul Audley, *President*
Denise Gutches, *CFO*
Art Yoon, *Exec VP*
Daniel Poissant, *Office Admin*
Corina Sandru, *Admin Sec*
EMP: 70
SALES: 12.7MM **Privately Held**
WEB: www.filmla.com
SIC: 7819 Services allied to motion pictures

(P-18176)
ACADEMY FOUNDATION (HQ)
8949 Wilshire Blvd, Beverly Hills
(90211-1907)
PHONE.................................310 247-3000
Bruce Davis, *Exec Dir*
Brian Hatcher, *Technology*
Dawn Mori, *Director*
EMP: 60
SQ FT: 35,000
SALES: 72.3MM
SALES (corp-wide): 123.6MM **Privately Held**
WEB: www.academyfoundation.com
SIC: 7819 Services allied to motion pictures

PA: Academy Of Motion Picture Arts & Sciences
8949 Wilshire Blvd
Beverly Hills CA 90211
310 247-3000

(P-18177)
ALLIANCE FUNDING GROUP
Also Called: Alliance Capital Markets
3745 W Chapman Ave # 200, Orange
(92868-1656)
PHONE.................................800 978-8817
Brijesh Ashok Patel, *President*
Shawn M Donohue, *Vice Pres*
Vishal V Masani, *Vice Pres*
EMP: 80 **EST:** 1998
SQ FT: 25,000
SALES (est): 18.7MM **Privately Held**
WEB: www.alliancefunds.com
SIC: 7819 7377 6159 7353 Equipment & prop rental, motion picture production; computer rental & leasing; equipment & vehicle finance leasing companies; machinery & equipment finance leasing; earth moving equipment, rental or leasing; equipment rental & leasing

(P-18178)
ANT FARM LLC
1027 W Edgeware Rd, Los Angeles
(90026-5131)
PHONE.................................323 850-0700
Doug Brandt, *CEO*
Bryan Schmoldt, *Administration*
Norm Haddeman, *CTO*
Sam Frankiel, *Technology*
Barbara Glazier,
EMP: 120
SALES (est): 15.4MM **Privately Held**
SIC: 7819 Film processing, editing & titling: motion picture

(P-18179)
AVONGARD PRODUCTS USA LTD
Also Called: Hydraulx
12777 W Jefferson Blvd # 100, Los Angeles
(90066-7048)
PHONE.................................310 319-2300
David Strause, *President*
Gregor D Strause, *CEO*
Colin Strause, *Vice Pres*
Linda Strause, *Admin Sec*
Chad Vanhorn, *Production*
EMP: 50
SQ FT: 8,000
SALES (est): 7.8MM **Privately Held**
WEB: www.avongard.com
SIC: 7819 Visual effects production

(P-18180)
BAY AREA VIDEO COALITION INC
Also Called: Bavc
2727 Mariposa St Fl 2, San Francisco
(94110-1401)
PHONE.................................415 861-3282
Ken Ikeda, *Director*
Kelly Haydon, *Info Tech Mgr*
Innesa Goldman, *Accountant*
Vicki Nunez, *Controller*
Christine Sugrue, *Opers Staff*
EMP: 55 **EST:** 1977
SQ FT: 25,000
SALES (est): 4.7MM **Privately Held**
WEB: www.bavc.org
SIC: 7819 8249 Video tape or disk reproduction; vocational schools

(P-18181)
CHAPMAN/LEONARD STUDIO EQP INC (PA)
12950 Raymer St, North Hollywood
(91605-4211)
PHONE.................................323 877-5309
Leonard Chapman, *President*
Michael Chapman, *Corp Secy*
David Bullard, *Graphic Designe*
Elsa Echeverria, *Personnel Assit*
Dennis J Fraser, *Director*
▲ **EMP:** 145
SQ FT: 300,000
SALES (est): 24.3MM **Privately Held**
WEB: www.chapman-leonard.com
SIC: 7819 Studio property rental, motion picture; equipment rental, motion picture

(P-18182)
CINELEASE INC (HQ)
5375 W San Fernando Rd, Los Angeles
(90039-1013)
PHONE.................................855 441-5500
Steven Ortiz, *President*
Brian Macdonald, *President*
Scott Massengill, *Treasurer*
Joseph Ball, *Vice Pres*
J Jeffrey Zimmerman, *Admin Sec*
▲ **EMP:** 50
SALES (est): 11.5MM
SALES (corp-wide): 1.7B **Publicly Held**
SIC: 7819 Equipment rental, motion picture
PA: Herc Holdings Inc.
27500 Riverview Center Bl
Bonita Springs FL 34134
239 301-1000

(P-18183)
CMS LLNL
7000 East Ave Msl090, Livermore
(94550-9698)
PHONE.................................925 422-5584
Stan Stone,
EMP: 56
SALES (est): 8.7MM **Privately Held**
SIC: 7819 Laboratory service, motion picture

(P-18184)
COMPANY 3 INC
1661 Lincoln Blvd Ste 400, Santa Monica
(90404-3741)
PHONE.................................310 255-6600
Stefan Sonnenfeld, *President*
Emily Schaeberle, *Executive Asst*
Daniel Schamper, *Business Mgr*
Katherine Andrews, *Producer*
Kayla Kossi, *Client Mgr*
EMP: 59
SALES (est): 6.5MM
SALES (corp-wide): 1.9B **Publicly Held**
SIC: 7819 Services allied to motion pictures
PA: Deluxe Corporation
3680 Victoria St N
Shoreview MN 55126
651 483-7111

(P-18185)
CONDOR PRODUCTIONS LLC
245 N Beverly Dr, Beverly Hills
(90210-5319)
PHONE.................................310 449-3000
Kathryn Rose-Remlinger, *Accountant*
EMP: 99
SQ FT: 5,000
SALES (est): 401.6K **Privately Held**
SIC: 7819 TV tape services: editing, transfers, etc.

(P-18186)
DELUXE DIGITAL DIST INC
2400 W Empire Ave Ste 200, Los Angeles
(90027)
PHONE.................................818 260-6202
Cyril Drabinsky, *CEO*
Warren Stein, *Exec VP*
Jeff Cuneo, *Engineer*
Alejandro Barcena, *Director*
Kelly Delany, *Director*
EMP: 50
SALES (est): 5MM **Privately Held**
SIC: 7819 Services allied to motion pictures

(P-18187)
DELUXE LABORATORIES INC (DH)
Also Called: Color By Deluxe
2400 W Empire Ave Ste 200, Burbank
(91504-3355)
PHONE.................................323 462-6171
Cyril Drabinsky, *CEO*
Mike Gunter, *CFO*
Scott Ehrlich, *Exec VP*
Dashiell Morrison, *Exec VP*
Warren Stein, *Exec VP*
▲ **EMP:** 626 **EST:** 1990
SQ FT: 150,000
SALES (est): 70.5MM **Privately Held**
SIC: 7819 Film processing, editing & titling: motion picture

(P-18188)
DIRECTORS GUILD AMERICA INC (PA)
Also Called: D G A
7920 W Sunset Blvd # 600, Los Angeles
(90046-3334)
PHONE.................................310 289-2000
Jay D Roth, *Exec Dir*
Michael Apted, *President*
Brian O'Rourke, *CFO*
Joan Sumpter, *CFO*
Scott Berger, *Treasurer*
EMP: 110
SQ FT: 100,000
SALES: 26.2MM **Privately Held**
WEB: www.directors-guild.com
SIC: 7819 8631 Directors, independent: motion picture; labor unions & similar labor organizations

(P-18189)
DTS INC (HQ)
5220 Las Virgenes Rd, Calabasas
(91302-1064)
PHONE.................................818 436-1000
Jon E Kirchner, *CEO*
Brian D Towne, *President*
Melvin L Flanigan, *CFO*
Kevin Doohan, *Chief Mktg Ofcr*
Kris M Graves, *Exec VP*
▲ **EMP:** 150
SQ FT: 89,000
SALES: 138.2MM
SALES (corp-wide): 373.7MM **Publicly Held**
WEB: www.dtsonline.com
SIC: 7819 3651 Services allied to motion pictures; household audio & video equipment
PA: Xperi Corporation
3025 Orchard Pkwy
San Jose CA 95134
408 321-6000

(P-18190)
ENCORE MEDIA SERVICES INC
24853 Avenue Rockefeller, Valencia
(91355-3468)
PHONE.................................661 705-1323
Steve Kalson, *CFO*
EMP: 86
SALES: 21.5MM **Privately Held**
SIC: 7819 3652 Services allied to motion pictures; compact laser discs, prerecorded

(P-18191)
ESC ENTERTAINMENT INC
4000 Warner Blvd, Burbank (91522-0001)
PHONE.................................818 954-1018
Tom Davila, *President*
Ed Jones, *CEO*
Tom Settle, *CFO*
EMP: 250
SQ FT: 61,000
SALES (est): 16.1MM **Privately Held**
SIC: 7819 Visual effects production

(P-18192)
FOTO-KEM INDUSTRIES INC (PA)
Also Called: Foto Kem Film & Video
2801 W Alameda Ave, Burbank
(91505-4405)
P.O. Box 7755 (91510-7755)
PHONE.................................818 846-3102
William F Brodersen, *CEO*
Robert Semmer, *COO*
Melaine Diego, *Bd of Directors*
Mike Brodersen, *Officer*
Rosanna Marino, *Senior VP*
▲ **EMP:** 500
SQ FT: 43,000
SALES (est): 82.3MM **Privately Held**
WEB: www.fotokem.com
SIC: 7819 Laboratory service, motion picture; developing & printing of commercial motion picture film

(P-18193)
FOTO-KEM INDUSTRIES INC
Also Called: Fotokem
2801 W Olive Ave, Burbank (91505-4578)
PHONE.................................818 846-3102
William Brodersen, *President*

▲ = Import ▼=Export
◆ =Import/Export

Ronnie Bordey, *Technical Mgr*
Shawn Leonard, *Engineer*
Thomas Ennis, *VP Sales*
EMP: 500
SALES (corp-wide): 82.3MM **Privately Held**
WEB: www.fotokem.com
SIC: 7819 Laboratory service, motion picture; developing & printing of commercial motion picture film
PA: Foto-Kem Industries, Inc.
2801 W Alameda Ave
Burbank CA 91505
818 846-3102

(P-18194)
FUSEFX LLC
14823 Califa St, Van Nuys (91411-3108)
PHONE..................................818 237-5052
David Altenau, *CEO*
Tim Jacobsen, *Officer*
Jason Fotter, *CTO*
EMP: 300
SQ FT: 12,500
SALES (est): 1.9MM **Privately Held**
SIC: 7819 Visual effects production

(P-18195)
HIGH TECHNOLOGY VIDEO INC
Also Called: H T V
10900 Ventura Blvd, Studio City
(91604-3340)
PHONE..................................323 969-8822
Jim Hardy, *CEO*
Steve Weiner, *Chairman*
Steve Tannen, *Chief Mktg Ofcr*
Steve Galloway, *Senior VP*
Sandy Crawford, *General Mgr*
EMP: 73
SQ FT: 30,000
SALES (est): 11.5MM **Privately Held**
WEB: www.htvinc.net
SIC: 7819 Video tape or disk reproduction

(P-18196)
HOLLYWOOD RNTALS PROD SVCS LLC (PA)
5300 Melrose Ave, Los Angeles
(90038-5111)
PHONE..................................818 407-7800
Mark A Rosenthal, *Mng Member*
▲ **EMP:** 100
SQ FT: 100,000
SALES (est): 13.7MM **Privately Held**
WEB: www.hollywoodrentals.com
SIC: 7819 Equipment rental, motion picture

(P-18197)
IMAX CORPORATION (HQ)
12582 Millennium, Los Angeles
(90094-2823)
PHONE..................................310 255-5500
Richard Gelfond, *CEO*
Greg Foster, *President*
Heather Anthony, *Vice Pres*
◆ **EMP:** 80
SALES (est): 13.4MM
SALES (corp-wide): 380.7MM **Privately Held**
WEB: www.imaxcorporation.com
SIC: 7819 Visual effects production
PA: Imax Corporation
2525 Speakman Dr
Mississauga ON L5K 1
905 403-6500

(P-18198)
JACKSON SHRUB SUPPLY INC
11505 Vanowen St, North Hollywood
(91605-6232)
PHONE..................................818 982-0100
Gary Jackson, *President*
EMP: 60
SQ FT: 16,000
SALES (est): 4.1MM **Privately Held**
WEB: www.jacksonshrub.com
SIC: 7819 Services allied to motion pictures

(P-18199)
LUMA PICTURES INC
1424 2nd St, Santa Monica (90401-2345)
PHONE..................................310 888-8738
Payam Shohadai, *President*
Matt Lydecker, *Creative Dir*
John Betdul, *Principal*

Kevin McCartney, *Info Tech Mgr*
Chadd Dombrova, *Director*
EMP: 171
SQ FT: 5,500
SALES (est): 2.7MM **Privately Held**
WEB: www.lumapictures.com
SIC: 7819 Visual effects production

(P-18200)
MBS EQUIPMENT COMPANY (PA)
Also Called: Tm Motion Picture Eqp Rentals
1600 Rosecrans Ave 4b, Manhattan Beach
(90266-3708)
PHONE..................................310 558-3100
Tom May, *President*
EMP: 77
SALES (est): 23.2MM **Privately Held**
SIC: 7819 Equipment rental, motion picture

(P-18201)
MODERN VIDEOFILM INC
Also Called: Mod Vid Film
1733 Flower St, Glendale (91201-2022)
PHONE..................................818 637-6800
Mark Smirnoff, *Manager*
EMP: 125
SALES (corp-wide): 30.7MM **Privately Held**
WEB: www.mvfinc.com
SIC: 7819 Video tape or disk reproduction; film processing, editing & titling: motion picture; TV tape services: editing, transfers, etc.
PA: Modern Videofilm, Inc.
2300 W Empire Ave
Burbank CA 91504
818 840-1700

(P-18202)
MODERN VIDEOFILM INC (PA)
Also Called: Mvf World Wide Services
2300 W Empire Ave, Burbank
(91504-3341)
PHONE..................................818 840-1700
Scott Avila, *CEO*
Cooper Crouse, *President*
Roxanna Sassanian, *CFO*
Walt Bigelow, *Engineer*
Timothy Suzuki, *Supervisor*
EMP: 230
SQ FT: 100,000
SALES (est): 30.7MM **Privately Held**
WEB: www.mvfinc.com
SIC: 7819 Video tape or disk reproduction; film processing, editing & titling: motion picture; TV tape services: editing, transfers, etc.

(P-18203)
MUSIC COLLECTIVE LLC
12711 Ventura Blvd # 110, Studio City
(91604-2432)
PHONE..................................818 508-3303
Alan Ett, *Owner*
EMP: 50
SALES (est): 1.9MM **Privately Held**
WEB: www.aemg.com
SIC: 7819 Sound (effects & music production), motion picture

(P-18204)
NATIONAL FILM LABORATORIES
Also Called: Crest Digital
900 Glenneyre St, Laguna Beach
(92651-2707)
PHONE..................................323 466-0281
Stephen R Stein, *CEO*
Ronald Stein, *President*
Lorraine Ross, *Corp Secy*
EMP: 157
SQ FT: 50,000
SALES (est): 7.4MM **Privately Held**
WEB: www.concorddisc.com
SIC: 7819 7812 Film processing, editing & titling: motion picture; reproduction services, motion picture production; motion picture & video production

(P-18205)
NEG OPERATIONS LLC
401 Wilshire Blvd # 1070, Santa Monica
(90401-1428)
PHONE..................................310 777-1940
Peter Hurwitz, *CEO*

Scott Frosch, *CFO*
EMP: 250
SQ FT: 1,500
SALES: 150MM **Privately Held**
SIC: 7819 Reproduction services, motion picture production

(P-18206)
NEW DEAL STUDIOS INC
1812 W Burbank Blvd, Burbank
(91506-1315)
PHONE..................................310 578-9929
Shannon Gans, *CEO*
Matthew Gratzner, *Vice Pres*
Ian Hunter, *Admin Sec*
EMP: 52
SQ FT: 20,000
SALES (est): 4.2MM **Privately Held**
SIC: 7819 Visual effects production

(P-18207)
OMEGA/CINEMA PROPS INC
5857 Santa Monica Blvd, Los Angeles
(90038-2001)
PHONE..................................323 466-8201
E Jay Krause, *President*
Cheryl Jordan, *Corp Secy*
▲ **EMP:** 90
SQ FT: 300,000
SALES (est): 11.6MM **Privately Held**
WEB: www.omegacinemaprops.com
SIC: 7819 Equipment rental, motion picture

(P-18208)
PIXELOGIC MEDIA PARTNERS LLC
4000 W Alameda Ave # 110, Burbank
(91505-4305)
PHONE..................................818 861-2001
John Suh,
Robert Seidel,
Jeffrey Demoss, *Manager*
EMP: 250
SQ FT: 20,000
SALES (est): 4.4MM **Privately Held**
SIC: 7819 Reproduction services, motion picture production

(P-18209)
POINT360
1133 N Hollywood Way, Burbank
(91505-2528)
PHONE..................................818 556-5700
Brian Ehrlich, *Manager*
EMP: 100
SALES (corp-wide): 37.5MM **Publicly Held**
WEB: www.vdimultimedia.com
SIC: 7819 Editing services, motion picture production; equipment & prop rental, motion picture production
PA: Point.360
2701 Media Center Dr
Los Angeles CA 90065
818 565-1400

(P-18210)
POINT360 (PA)
Also Called: Digital Film Labs
2701 Media Center Dr, Los Angeles
(90065-1700)
PHONE..................................818 565-1400
Haig S Bagerdjian, *Ch of Bd*
Alan R Steel, *CFO*
David Weathers, *Exec VP*
Hawk Hamilton, *Vice Pres*
John Schweizer, *Vice Pres*
EMP: 123
SQ FT: 64,600
SALES: 37.5MM **Publicly Held**
WEB: www.vdimultimedia.com
SIC: 7819 7822 7829 Video tape or disk reproduction; motion picture & tape distribution; television & video tape distribution; motion picture distribution services

(P-18211)
POST GROUP INC (PA)
1415 N Cahuenga Blvd, Los Angeles
(90028-8198)
PHONE..................................323 462-2300
Frederic Rheinstein, *Chairman*
Lloyd Guillen, *President*
Vincent Lyons, *President*
Duke Gallagher, *Admin Sec*
Geoff Horn, *Admin Asst*

EMP: 110
SQ FT: 40,000
SALES (est): 12.7MM **Privately Held**
WEB: www.postgroup.com
SIC: 7819 7812 Editing services, motion picture production; film processing, editing & titling: motion picture; TV tape services: editing, transfers, etc.; motion picture & video production

(P-18212)
PRIME FOCUS NORTH AMERICA INC (HQ)
Also Called: Prime Focus World
5750 Hannum Ave Ste 100, Culver City
(90230-6666)
PHONE..................................323 461-7887
Namit Malhotra, *CEO*
Robert Hummel, *CEO*
Oliver Welch, *COO*
Massoud Entekhabi, *CFO*
Sue Murphree, *CFO*
EMP: 85
SQ FT: 50,000
SALES (est): 10.2MM
SALES (corp-wide): 3.6MM **Privately Held**
WEB: www.postlogic.com
SIC: 7819 Sound (effects & music production), motion picture
PA: Arlique Media Investments Plc
160 Great Portland Street
London W1W 5
207 268-5086

(P-18213)
QUIXOTE MM LLC
Also Called: Movie Movers
1011 N Fuller Ave Ste B, West Hollywood
(90046-6658)
PHONE..................................323 851-5030
Mikel Elliott, *Mng Member*
EMP: 50
SALES (est): 4MM **Privately Held**
SIC: 7819 Equipment rental, motion picture

(P-18214)
RALEIGH ENTERPRISES INC
Also Called: Raleigh Studios
5300 Melrose Ave Fl 3, Los Angeles
(90038-5113)
PHONE..................................323 466-3111
Michael Moore, *Branch Mgr*
EMP: 130
SQ FT: 68,388
SALES (corp-wide): 41.4MM **Privately Held**
WEB: www.raleighenterprises.com
SIC: 7819 7359 6512 Services allied to motion pictures; equipment rental & leasing; nonresidential building operators
PA: Raleigh Enterprises, Inc.
5300 Melrose Ave Fl 4
Los Angeles CA 90038
310 899-8900

(P-18215)
RELIANCE MEDIA WORKS VFX INC
1800 Vine St, Los Angeles (90028-5250)
PHONE..................................818 557-7333
Benkatash Roddam, *President*
George Murphy, *Officer*
Ashish R Agarwal, *Admin Sec*
EMP: 50
SQ FT: 25,000
SALES (est): 5.1MM **Privately Held**
SIC: 7819 Visual effects production
PA: Reliance Adae
Fl 7 B Wing, Trade World Senapati
Bapat Marg
Mumbai MH

(P-18216)
SEIBO LLC (PA)
425 Via Corta Ste 304, Palos Verdes Estates (90274-1360)
P.O. Box 773 (90274-0773)
PHONE..................................310 465-1700
Dave Oberman, *CEO*
Jeff Boldenweck, *Exec VP*
Chris Toone, *Vice Pres*
Alison Clougherty, *Client Mgr*
EMP: 55

PRODUCTS & SVCS

SALES: 40MM **Privately Held**
SIC: 7819 Visual effects production

(P-18217)
SIX POINT HARNESS
1759 Glendale Blvd, Los Angeles
(90026-1761)
PHONE...................323 462-3344
Brendan Burch, *Principal*
Dave Vamos, *Opers Staff*
Andy Fiedler, *Production*
Cash McBride, *Production*
EMP: 50
SALES (est): 2.5MM **Privately Held**
SIC: 7819 Services allied to motion pictures

(P-18218)
SKYLAR FILM STUDIOS LLC
13589 Mindanao Way # 11, Marina Del Rey
(90292-6950)
PHONE...................424 653-8902
Jamie Skylar, *CEO*
Dylan Johnson, *Managing Dir*
EMP: 200 **EST:** 2010
SQ FT: 200,000
SALES (est): 2.7MM **Privately Held**
SIC: 7819 Services allied to motion pictures

(P-18219)
STAN WINSTON INC
Also Called: Stan Winston Studio
340 Parkside Dr, San Fernando
(91340-3035)
PHONE...................818 782-0870
Stan Winston, *President*
Brian Gilbert, *Vice Pres*
EMP: 80
SQ FT: 10,538
SALES (est): 2.1MM **Privately Held**
WEB: www.stanwinston.com
SIC: 7819 Visual effects production

(P-18220)
STEREO D LLC
Also Called: Stereod
3355 W Empire Ave Fl 1, Burbank
(91504-3160)
P.O. Box 892164, Temecula (92589-2164)
PHONE...................818 861-3100
William Sherak, *President*
Aaron Parry, *Exec VP*
Milton Adamou, *Vice Pres*
Prafull Gade, *Vice Pres*
Andrew Eick, *Production*
EMP: 275
SQ FT: 55,000
SALES (est): 24.9MM **Privately Held**
SIC: 7819 Editing services, motion picture production
HQ: Deluxe Entertainment Services Group
Inc.
2400 W Empire Ave
Los Angeles CA 90027

(P-18221)
TECHNCLOR CRATIVE SVCS USA INC (DH)
6040 W Sunset Blvd, Los Angeles
(90028-6402)
PHONE...................818 260-3800
Timothy Sarnoff, *CEO*
Richard Andrews, *President*
Claude Gagnon, *CEO*
John Hancock, *Admin Sec*
EMP: 300
SQ FT: 25,000
SALES (est): 27.8MM
SALES (corp-wide): 63.6MM **Privately Held**
WEB: www.vidfilm.com
SIC: 7819 Video tape or disk reproduction
HQ: Technicolor Thomson Group, Inc
2233 N Ontario St Ste 300
Burbank CA 91504
818 260-3600

(P-18222)
TECHNCLOR CRATIVE SVCS USA INC
Technicolor Complete Post
6040 W Sunset Blvd, Los Angeles
(90028-6402)
PHONE...................323 467-1244

Mike Doggett, *Manager*
Heather Sanchez, *Personnel Exec*
EMP: 150
SALES (corp-wide): 63.6MM **Privately Held**
WEB: www.vidfilm.com
SIC: 7819 TV tape services: editing, transfers, etc.; sound (effects & music production), motion picture
HQ: Technicolor Creative Services Usa, Inc.
6040 W Sunset Blvd
Los Angeles CA 90028
818 260-3800

(P-18223)
TECHNCLOR VDOCASSETTE MICH INC (DH)
Also Called: Technicolor Video Service
3233 Mission Oaks Blvd, Camarillo
(93012-5138)
PHONE...................805 445-1122
Lanni Ormonvo, *President*
John H Oliphant, *Admin Sec*
▲ **EMP:** 500
SQ FT: 300,000
SALES (est): 42.6MM
SALES (corp-wide): 63.6MM **Privately Held**
SIC: 7819 Video tape or disk reproduction
HQ: Technicolor Thomson Group, Inc
2233 N Ontario St Ste 300
Burbank CA 91504
818 260-3600

(P-18224)
TECHNICOLOR INC (DH)
3233 Mission Oaks Blvd, Camarillo
(93012-5097)
PHONE...................805 445-1122
Quinton Lily, *President*
▲ **EMP:** 55
SALES (est): 11.8MM
SALES (corp-wide): 63.6MM **Privately Held**
WEB: www.technicolor.com
SIC: 7819 Video tape or disk reproduction
HQ: Technicolor Thomson Group, Inc
2233 N Ontario St Ste 300
Burbank CA 91504
818 260-3600

(P-18225)
TECHNICOLOR HM ENTRMT SVCS INC
Also Called: Technicolor - Funimation Ent
1778 Zinetta Rd Ste F, Calexico
(92231-9510)
PHONE...................760 357-3372
EMP: 268
SALES (corp-wide): 63.6MM **Privately Held**
SIC: 7819 Video tape or disk reproduction
HQ: Technicolor Home Entertainment Services, Inc.
3233 Mission Oaks Blvd
Camarillo CA 93012

(P-18226)
TECHNICOLOR HM ENTRMT SVCS INC
Also Called: Accounts Payable Department
5491 E Philadelphia St, Ontario
(91761-2807)
P.O. Box 2459, Rancho Cucamonga
(91729-2459)
PHONE...................909 974-2016
EMP: 301
SALES (corp-wide): 63.6MM **Privately Held**
SIC: 7819 Video tape or disk reproduction
HQ: Technicolor Home Entertainment Services, Inc.
3233 Mission Oaks Blvd
Camarillo CA 93012

(P-18227)
TECHNICOLOR HM ENTRMT SVCS INC (DH)
Also Called: Technicolor Video Services
3233 Mission Oaks Blvd, Camarillo
(93012-5097)
PHONE...................805 445-1122

Lanny Raimondo, *CEO*
Orlando F Raimondo, *President*
Patricia Dave, *CFO*
◆ **EMP:** 500
SQ FT: 5,000
SALES (est): 434.3MM
SALES (corp-wide): 63.6MM **Privately Held**
SIC: 7819 Video tape or disk reproduction
HQ: Technicolor Usa, Inc.
101 W 103rd St
Indianapolis IN 46290
818 260-3651

(P-18228)
TECHNICOLOR THOMSON GROUP
Also Called: Technicolor Hollywood
6040 W Sunset Blvd, Los Angeles
(90028-6402)
PHONE...................323 817-6600
Michael Doggett, *Manager*
Tom Cotton, *President*
EMP: 573
SALES (corp-wide): 63.6MM **Privately Held**
SIC: 7819 Video tape or disk reproduction; developing & printing of commercial motion picture film
HQ: Technicolor Thomson Group, Inc
2233 N Ontario St Ste 300
Burbank CA 91504
818 260-3600

(P-18229)
TECHNICOLOR THOMSON GROUP
2255 N Ontario St Ste 100, Burbank
(91504-3194)
PHONE...................818 260-3600
Juliana Bacchus, *Branch Mgr*
EMP: 301
SQ FT: 200,000
SALES (corp-wide): 63.6MM **Privately Held**
WEB: www.technicolor.com
SIC: 7819 2759 Film processing, editing & titling: motion picture; TV tape services: editing, transfers, etc.; commercial printing
HQ: Technicolor Thomson Group, Inc
2233 N Ontario St Ste 300
Burbank CA 91504
818 260-3600

(P-18230)
TECHNICOLOR THOMSON GROUP
Technicolor Entertainment Svcs
5491 E Philadelphia St, Ontario
(91761-2807)
PHONE...................909 974-2222
Mary Nakagawa, *Manager*
EMP: 300
SALES (corp-wide): 63.6MM **Privately Held**
WEB: www.technicolor.com
SIC: 7819 Video tape or disk reproduction; developing & printing of commercial motion picture film
HQ: Technicolor Thomson Group, Inc
2233 N Ontario St Ste 300
Burbank CA 91504
818 260-3600

(P-18231)
TECHNICOLOR THOMSON GROUP
3301 Mission Oaks Blvd, Camarillo
(93012-5048)
PHONE...................805 445-1122
Orlando Raimondo, *CEO*
EMP: 2000
SALES (corp-wide): 63.6MM **Privately Held**
WEB: www.technicolor.com
SIC: 7819 Video tape or disk reproduction
HQ: Technicolor Thomson Group, Inc
2233 N Ontario St Ste 300
Burbank CA 91504
818 260-3600

(P-18232)
TEN PUBLISHING MEDIA LLC (PA)
831 S Douglas St Ste 100, El Segundo
(90245-4956)
PHONE...................310 531-9900
Scott P Dickey, *CEO*
Peter H Englehart, *Ch of Bd*
Chris Argentieri, *President*
Bill Sutman, *CFO*
Jonathan Anastas, *Chief Mktg Ofcr*
EMP: 230
SALES (est): 74.3MM **Privately Held**
WEB: www.sourceinterlink.com
SIC: 7819 Visual effects production

(P-18233)
WALT DISNEY IMAGINEERING (DH)
1401 Flower St, Glendale (91201-2421)
P.O. Box 25020 (91221-5020)
PHONE...................818 544-6500
Thomas O Staggs, *CEO*
Martin A Sklar, *Vice Ch Bd*
Craig Russell, *Exec VP*
Markus Gross, *Vice Pres*
Jessica Hodgins, *Vice Pres*
▲ **EMP:** 1011
SQ FT: 100,000
SALES (est): 92.8MM **Publicly Held**
SIC: 7819 8712 1542 8741 Visual effects production; architectural services; custom builders, non-residential; management services; engineering services
HQ: Disney Enterprises, Inc.
500 S Buena Vista St
Burbank CA 91521
818 560-1000

7822 Motion Picture & Video Tape Distribution

(P-18234)
ABC CABLE NETWORKS GROUP
Also Called: Buena Vista Pictures Dist
698 S Buena Vista St, Burbank
(91521-0001)
PHONE...................818 560-4365
Cindy Cohen-Hiller, *Vice Ch Bd*
Chuch Viane, *President*
EMP: 190 **Publicly Held**
WEB: www.breakbar.com
SIC: 7822 Distribution, exclusive of production: motion picture
HQ: Abc Cable Networks Group
500 S Buena Vista St
Burbank CA 91521
818 460-7477

(P-18235)
BLEACHER REPORT INC
153 Kearny St Fl 2, San Francisco
(94108-4808)
PHONE...................415 777-5505
Dave Finocchio, *CEO*
Josh Abrams, *Vice Pres*
Bill McCandless, *Vice Pres*
Joe Yanarella, *Vice Pres*
Adam Lefkoe, *Social Dir*
EMP: 128
SALES (est): 12.3MM
SALES (corp-wide): 160.5B **Publicly Held**
SIC: 7822 4833 4841 7812 Motion picture distribution; television broadcasting stations; cable television services; motion picture production
HQ: Turner Broadcasting System, Inc.
1 Cnn Ctr Nw 14sw
Atlanta GA 30303
404 575-7250

(P-18236)
BUENA VISTA INTERNATIONAL INC (HQ)
500 S Buena Vista St, Burbank
(91521-0001)
PHONE...................818 560-1000
David M Hollis, *CEO*
Mark D Zoradi, *President*
David Hughes, *Treasurer*
▲ **EMP:** 50

SALES (est): 7.9MM **Publicly Held**
WEB: www.filmes.net
SIC: 7822 Distribution, exclusive of production: motion picture; distribution for television: motion picture

(P-18237)
DISNEY INTERFINANCE CORP
500 S Buena Vista St, Burbank
(91521-0001)
PHONE.................................818 560-1000
David K Thompson, *President*
EMP: 360
SALES (est): 1.7MM **Publicly Held**
SIC: 7822 Distribution, exclusive of production: motion picture
HQ: Disney Enterprises, Inc.
    500 S Buena Vista St
    Burbank CA 91521
    818 560-1000

(P-18238)
ERO-TECH CORP
2301 S El Camino Real, San Mateo
(94403-2213)
PHONE.................................415 468-5600
David Sturman, *President*
▲ **EMP:** 100
SALES (est): 2.6MM **Privately Held**
SIC: 7822 5192 Video tapes, recorded: wholesale; magazines

(P-18239)
IMAGE ENTERTAINMENT INC (DH)
6320 Canoga Ave Ste 790, Woodland Hills
(91367-2561)
PHONE.................................818 407-9100
Miguel Penella, *COO*
Drew Wilson, *CFO*
Diana Flaherty, *Vice Pres*
▲ **EMP:** 63
SQ FT: 30,000
SALES (est): 10.9MM
SALES (corp-wide): 2.8B **Publicly Held**
WEB: www.image-entertainment.com
SIC: 7822 Motion picture & tape distribution
HQ: Rlj Entertainment, Inc.
    8515 Georgia Ave Ste 650
    Silver Spring MD 20910
    301 608-2115

(P-18240)
METROLUX THEATRES
Also Called: Metrolux 14 Theatres
8727 W 3rd St, Los Angeles (90048-3843)
PHONE.................................310 858-2800
EMP: 70
SALES (est): 2.5MM **Privately Held**
SIC: 7822 Motion picture & tape distribution

(P-18241)
MORGAN CREEK PRODUCTIONS (PA)
10351 Santa Monica Blvd # 200, Los Angeles (90025-6937)
PHONE.................................310 432-4848
James Robinson, *Ch of Bd*
EMP: 60
SQ FT: 3,497
SALES (est): 2.7MM **Privately Held**
SIC: 7822 Motion picture & tape distribution

(P-18242)
REVOLUTION STUDIOS DIST CO LP (PA)
225 Santa Monica Blvd # 900, Santa Monica (90401-2209)
PHONE.................................310 255-7000
Joe Roth, *Mng Member*
Jeffrey Small, *CFO*
▲ **EMP:** 60
SALES (est): 2.4MM **Privately Held**
SIC: 7822 Motion picture & tape distribution

(P-18243)
SONY DADC NEW MDIA SLTIONS INC
4499 Glencoe Ave, Marina Del Rey
(90292-6357)
PHONE.................................310 760-8500

Scott Hamilton, *President*
EMP: 200 **EST:** 2015
SQ FT: 20,000
SALES (est): 401.6K **Privately Held**
SIC: 7822 7374 Motion picture & tape distribution; data processing & preparation

(P-18244)
TWENTIETH CNTURY FOX INTL CORP (DH)
10201 W Pico Blvd Bldg 1, Los Angeles
(90064-2606)
P.O. Box 900, Beverly Hills (90213-0900)
PHONE.................................310 969-5300
Pat Wyatt, *Ch of Bd*
Bob Delellis, *President*
Craig Sloan, *President*
Dean Hallett, *CFO*
David Miller, *Treasurer*
▲ **EMP:** 400
SQ FT: 115,000
SALES (est): 66.8MM
SALES (corp-wide): 30.4B **Publicly Held**
SIC: 7822 7922 Motion picture distribution; television program, including commercial producers
HQ: Twentieth Century Fox Film Corporation
    10201 W Pico Blvd
    Los Angeles CA 90064
    310 369-1000

(P-18245)
UNITED ARTISTS PRODUCTIONS INC
10250 Constellation Blvd # 19, Los Angeles
(90067-6200)
PHONE.................................310 449-3000
Christopher McGurk, *President*
EMP: 200
SALES (est): 1MM
SALES (corp-wide): 1.1B **Privately Held**
WEB: www.unitedartists.com
SIC: 7822 Distribution, exclusive of production: motion picture; distribution for television: motion picture
HQ: United Artists Pictures Inc.
    10250 Constellation Blvd
    Los Angeles CA 90067
    -

(P-18246)
UNITED ARTISTS TELEVISION CORP
10250 Constellation Blvd # 27, Los Angeles
(90067-6200)
PHONE.................................310 449-3000
EMP: 150
SALES (est): 448.9K
SALES (corp-wide): 1.1B **Privately Held**
SIC: 7822 Distribution, exclusive of production: motion picture
HQ: United Artists Pictures Inc.
    10250 Constellation Blvd
    Los Angeles CA 90067
    -

(P-18247)
VPD IV INC (PA)
Also Called: Video Products Distributors
150 Parkshore Dr, Folsom (95630-4710)
PHONE.................................916 605-1500
Tim Shannahan, *President*
Russ Frazier, *Senior VP*
Marty Jorgensen, *Senior VP*
▲ **EMP:** 175
SQ FT: 70,000
SALES (est): 24MM **Privately Held**
WEB: www.vpdinc.com
SIC: 7822 5092 Video tapes, recorded: wholesale; video games

(P-18248)
VUBIQUITY INC
15301 Ventura Blvd Bldg E, Sherman Oaks
(91403-5885)
PHONE.................................818 526-5000
Darcy Antonellis, *Branch Mgr*
EMP: 200 **Privately Held**
SIC: 7822 Motion picture & tape distribution
HQ: Vubiquity, Inc.
    3900 W Alameda Ave Ste 17
    Burbank CA 91505
    -

(P-18249)
WARNER BROS TRANSATLANTIC INC (DH)
4000 Warner Blvd, Burbank (91522-0002)
PHONE.................................818 977-0018
Barry M Meyer, *CEO*
Jeremy Williams, *President*
Ralph Peterson, *Treasurer*
Dean Hale, *Officer*
Scott Phelan, *Officer*
▲ **EMP:** 900
SALES (est): 424.8MM
SALES (corp-wide): 160.5B **Publicly Held**
WEB: www.juwannamann.com
SIC: 7822 Distribution, exclusive of production: motion picture

(P-18250)
WARNER BROS TRANSATLANTIC INC
3300 W Olive Ave Ste 200, Burbank
(91505-4658)
PHONE.................................818 977-6384
Scott Levy, *Branch Mgr*
Dave Hedrick, *Vice Pres*
Lawrence Smith, *Info Tech Dir*
EMP: 515
SALES (corp-wide): 160.5B **Publicly Held**
SIC: 7822 Distribution, exclusive of production: motion picture
HQ: Warner Bros. (Transatlantic), Inc.
    4000 Warner Blvd
    Burbank CA 91522
    818 977-0018

(P-18251)
WARNER BROS TRANSATLANTIC INC
Also Called: Telepictures
3500 W Olive Ave Ste 1000, Burbank
(91505-5515)
PHONE.................................818 972-0777
Khuyem Phan, *Branch Mgr*
Joshua Barber, *Counsel*
EMP: 515
SALES (corp-wide): 160.5B **Publicly Held**
SIC: 7822 Distribution, exclusive of production: motion picture
HQ: Warner Bros. (Transatlantic), Inc.
    4000 Warner Blvd
    Burbank CA 91522
    818 977-0018

7829 Services Allied To Motion Picture Distribution

(P-18252)
MOVIES ANYWHERE LLC
500 S Buena Vista St, Burbank
(91521-0001)
PHONE.................................818 560-0038
Karin Gilford, *General Mgr*
Elissa Brown, *Vice Pres*
Jessica Kahn, *Vice Pres*
Tina Rubin, *VP Mktg*
Beth Baier, *Asst Chief*
EMP: 52
SALES (est): 254.4K **Publicly Held**
SIC: 7829 Film delivery, motion picture
HQ: Disney Enterprises, Inc.
    500 S Buena Vista St
    Burbank CA 91521
    818 560-1000

(P-18253)
OUR ALCHEMY LLC (PA)
5900 Wilshire Blvd Fl 18, Los Angeles
(90036-5013)
PHONE.................................310 893-6289
Bill Lee,
Scott Guthrie, *Co-President*
Kelly Summers, *Co-President*
EMP: 80
SQ FT: 30,000
SALES (est): 5.1MM **Privately Held**
SIC: 7829 Motion picture distribution services

(P-18254)
PACIFIC THEATERS
Also Called: Northridge Fashion Center 10
9400 Shirley Ave, Northridge (91324-2413)
PHONE.................................818 501-5121
Joshua Watts, *Manager*
EMP: 60
SALES (est): 1.1MM **Privately Held**
SIC: 7829 Motion picture distribution services

(P-18255)
WALT DISNEY PICTURES AND TV
500 S Buena Vista St, Burbank
(91521-0007)
PHONE.................................818 560-1000
Bob Iger, *CEO*
Robert Matschullat, *Vice Chairman*
Alan Bergman, *President*
Richard W Cook, *Chairman*
Fred Langhammer, *Bd of Directors*
▲ **EMP:** 56
SALES (est): 6.6MM **Publicly Held**
SIC: 7829 Motion picture distribution services
HQ: Disney Enterprises, Inc.
    500 S Buena Vista St
    Burbank CA 91521
    818 560-1000

7832 Motion Picture Theaters, Except Drive-In

(P-18256)
AMC ENTERTAINMENT INC
4549 Mills Cir, Ontario (91764-5220)
PHONE.................................909 476-1288
Adam Aron, *Owner*
EMP: 50 **Publicly Held**
SIC: 7832 Exhibitors, itinerant: motion picture
HQ: Amc Entertainment Inc.
    11500 Ash St
    Leawood KS 66211
    913 213-2000

(P-18257)
AMERICAN MULTI-CINEMA INC
Also Called: AMC
125 E Palm Ave, Burbank (91502-1834)
PHONE.................................818 953-4020
Breanna Corrigan, *Manager*
EMP: 70 **Publicly Held**
WEB: www.arrowheadtownecenter.com
SIC: 7832 Motion picture theaters, except drive-in
HQ: American Multi-Cinema, Inc.
    1 Amc Way
    Leawood KS 66211
    913 213-2000

(P-18258)
AMERICAN MULTI-CINEMA INC
Also Called: AMC
7037 Friars Rd, San Diego (92108-1129)
PHONE.................................619 296-0370
Brian Fuller, *Manager*
EMP: 50 **Publicly Held**
WEB: www.arrowheadtownecenter.com
SIC: 7832 Exhibitors, itinerant: motion picture
HQ: American Multi-Cinema, Inc.
    1 Amc Way
    Leawood KS 66211
    913 213-2000

(P-18259)
AMERICAN MULTI-CINEMA INC
Also Called: AMC
450 N Atlantic Blvd, Monterey Park
(91754-1057)
PHONE.................................626 407-0240
EMP: 61 **Publicly Held**
SIC: 7832 Exhibitors, itinerant: motion picture
HQ: American Multi-Cinema, Inc.
    1 Amc Way
    Leawood KS 66211
    913 213-2000

(P-18260)
AMERICAN MULTI-CINEMA INC
Also Called: AMC
1414 N Azusa Ave, Covina (91722-1251)
PHONE..........................626 974-8624
John Eisner, *Manager*
EMP: 60 **Publicly Held**
WEB: www.arrowheadtownecenter.com
SIC: 7832 Exhibitors, itinerant: motion picture
HQ: American Multi-Cinema, Inc.
1 Amc Way
Leawood KS 66211
913 213-2000

(P-18261)
AMERICAN MULTI-CINEMA INC
Also Called: AMC
1000 Van Neca Ave Ste A, San Francisco
(94109)
PHONE..........................415 674-4630
Shawn Eisern, *Manager*
EMP: 50 **Publicly Held**
SIC: 7832 Motion picture theaters, except
drive-in
HQ: American Multi-Cinema, Inc.
1 Amc Way
Leawood KS 66211
913 213-2000

(P-18262)
AMERICAN MULTI-CINEMA INC
Also Called: AMC
2591 Airport Dr, Torrance (90505-6137)
PHONE..........................310 326-5011
Craig Adams, *Sales/Mktg Mgr*
Peter Lieu, *Managing Dir*
EMP: 120 **Publicly Held**
WEB: www.arrowheadtownecenter.com
SIC: 7832 Exhibitors, itinerant: motion picture
HQ: American Multi-Cinema, Inc.
1 Amc Way
Leawood KS 66211
913 213-2000

(P-18263)
AMERICAN MULTI-CINEMA INC
Also Called: AMC
20 City Blvd W Ste E1, Orange
(92868-3130)
PHONE..........................714 769-4288
Scott Shellenbergar, *Manager*
EMP: 90 **Publicly Held**
WEB: www.arrowheadtownecenter.com
SIC: 7832 Motion picture theaters, except
drive-in
HQ: American Multi-Cinema, Inc.
1 Amc Way
Leawood KS 66211
913 213-2000

(P-18264)
AMERICAN MULTI-CINEMA INC
Also Called: AMC
1001 S Lemon St Ste A, Fullerton
(92832-3007)
PHONE..........................714 992-6961
Brian Lind, *Manager*
EMP: 50 **Publicly Held**
WEB: www.arrowheadtownecenter.com
SIC: 7832 Exhibitors, itinerant: motion picture
HQ: American Multi-Cinema, Inc.
1 Amc Way
Leawood KS 66211
913 213-2000

(P-18265)
AMERICAN MULTI-CINEMA INC
Also Called: AMC
42 Miller Aly, Pasadena (91103-3643)
PHONE..........................626 585-8900
EMP: 50 **Publicly Held**
SIC: 7832
HQ: American Multi-Cinema, Inc.
1 Amc Way
Leawood KS 66211
913 213-2000

(P-18266)
AMERICAN MULTI-CINEMA INC
Also Called: AMC
12300 Civic Center Dr, Norwalk
(90650-3171)
PHONE..........................562 864-6206

Gary Orland, *Executive*
EMP: 50 **Publicly Held**
WEB: www.arrowheadtownecenter.com
SIC: 7832 Exhibitors, itinerant: motion picture
HQ: American Multi-Cinema, Inc.
1 Amc Way
Leawood KS 66211
913 213-2000

(P-18267)
AMERICAN MULTI-CINEMA INC
Also Called: AMC
10250 Snta Mnca Bld Ste 196, Los Angeles
(90067)
PHONE..........................310 228-5500
Rick Walsh, *Branch Mgr*
EMP: 50 **Publicly Held**
SIC: 7832 Motion picture theaters, except
drive-in
HQ: American Multi-Cinema, Inc.
1 Amc Way
Leawood KS 66211
913 213-2000

(P-18268)
AMERICAN MULTI-CINEMA INC
Also Called: AMC
1640 Cmino Del Rio N 20, San Diego
(92108)
PHONE..........................619 296-2737
Kathy Dominguez, *Manager*
EMP: 75 **Publicly Held**
WEB: www.arrowheadtownecenter.com
SIC: 7832 Exhibitors, itinerant: motion picture
HQ: American Multi-Cinema, Inc.
1 Amc Way
Leawood KS 66211
913 213-2000

(P-18269)
AMERICAN MULTI-CINEMA INC
Also Called: AMC
1560 S Azusa Ave, City of Industry
(91748-1603)
PHONE..........................626 810-7949
Favio Adane, *General Mgr*
EMP: 59 **Publicly Held**
SIC: 7832 Exhibitors, itinerant: motion picture
HQ: American Multi-Cinema, Inc.
1 Amc Way
Leawood KS 66211
913 213-2000

(P-18270)
AMERICAN MULTI-CINEMA INC
Also Called: AMC
1475 N Montebello Blvd, Montebello
(90640-2584)
PHONE..........................323 722-4583
Rachell Hatton, *General Mgr*
EMP: 50 **Publicly Held**
WEB: www.arrowheadtownecenter.com
SIC: 7832 Exhibitors, itinerant: motion picture
HQ: American Multi-Cinema, Inc.
1 Amc Way
Leawood KS 66211
913 213-2000

(P-18271)
ARCLIGHT CINEMA COMPANY
15301 Ventura Blvd Bldg A, Sherman Oaks
(91403-3102)
PHONE..........................818 501-0753
Christopher S Forman, *Branch Mgr*
EMP: 92
SALES (corp-wide): 13.9MM **Privately
Held**
SIC: 7832 Motion picture theaters, except
drive-in
PA: Arclight Cinema Company
6360 W Sunset Blvd
Los Angeles CA 90028
323 464-4226

(P-18272)
ARCLIGHT CINEMA COMPANY
120 N Robertson Blvd Fl 3, Los Angeles
(90048-3115)
PHONE..........................323 464-1465
Christopher S Forman, *Branch Mgr*
EMP: 171

SALES (corp-wide): 13.9MM **Privately
Held**
SIC: 7832 Motion picture theaters, except
drive-in
PA: Arclight Cinema Company
6360 W Sunset Blvd
Los Angeles CA 90028
323 464-4226

(P-18273)
**BRENDEN THEATRE
CORPORATION**
531 Davis St, Vacaville (95688-4632)
PHONE..........................707 469-0180
Tim Kruse, *Branch Mgr*
EMP: 70
SALES (corp-wide): 18.7MM **Privately
Held**
WEB: www.brendantheaters.com
SIC: 7832 Exhibitors, itinerant: motion picture
PA: Brenden Theatre Corporation
1985 Willow Pass Rd Ste C
Concord CA 94520
925 677-0462

(P-18274)
**BRENDEN THEATRE
CORPORATION**
1021 10th St Frnt, Modesto (95354-0888)
PHONE..........................209 491-7770
Saul Trujllo, *General Mgr*
EMP: 100
SALES (corp-wide): 18.7MM **Privately
Held**
WEB: www.brendantheaters.com
SIC: 7832 Exhibitors, itinerant: motion picture
PA: Brenden Theatre Corporation
1985 Willow Pass Rd Ste C
Concord CA 94520
925 677-0462

(P-18275)
**BRENDEN THEATRE
CORPORATION (PA)**
1985 Willow Pass Rd Ste C, Concord
(94520-2533)
PHONE..........................925 677-0462
John Brenden, *President*
EMP: 189
SQ FT: 70,000
SALES (est): 18.7MM **Privately Held**
WEB: www.brendantheaters.com
SIC: 7832 Motion picture theaters, except
drive-in

(P-18276)
CAL GRAN THEATRES LLC
Also Called: Valley Drive-In Theatre
3170 Santa Maria Way, Santa Maria
(93455-2102)
PHONE..........................805 934-1582
Bob Gran, *President*
Diane Gran, *General Mgr*
EMP: 50
SQ FT: 1,200
SALES (est): 1MM **Privately Held**
SIC: 7832 7833 Motion picture theaters,
except drive-in; drive-in motion picture
theaters

(P-18277)
CENTURY STADIUM
Also Called: Century Stadium 21
1590 Ethan Way, Sacramento
(95825-2298)
PHONE..........................916 922-4241
Donna Sheila, *Owner*
EMP: 73
SALES (est): 1.2MM **Privately Held**
SIC: 7832 Motion picture theaters, except
drive-in

(P-18278)
CINEMA CITY THEATERS
5635 E La Palma Ave, Anaheim
(92807-2109)
PHONE..........................714 970-0865
Meghan Walsh, *Manager*
EMP: 50
SALES (est): 1.1MM **Privately Held**
WEB: www.cinemacitytheatres.com
SIC: 7832 Motion picture theaters, except
drive-in

(P-18279)
CINEMARK 16 BAYFAIR
15555 E 14th St Ste 600, San Leandro
(94578-1970)
PHONE..........................510 276-9684
Anthony Tan, *Branch Mgr*
EMP: 60
SALES (est): 606.3K **Privately Held**
SIC: 7832 Motion picture theaters, except
drive-in

(P-18280)
CINEMARK USA INC
Also Called: Century Huntington Beach & Xd
7777 Edinger Ave Ste 170, Huntington
Beach (92647-8690)
PHONE..........................714 373-4573
Kevin Cron, *Branch Mgr*
EMP: 90 **Publicly Held**
SIC: 7832 Motion picture theaters, except
drive-in
HQ: Cinemark Usa, Inc.
3900 Dallas Pkwy Ste 500
Plano TX 75093
972 665-1000

(P-18281)
**CINEMASTAR LUXURY
THEATERS**
1949 Avenida Del Oro # 100, Oceanside
(92056-5829)
PHONE..........................760 945-2500
Jack R Crosby, *President*
EMP: 350
SALES (est): 4.1MM **Privately Held**
WEB: www.cinemastar.com
SIC: 7832 Motion picture theaters, except
drive-in

(P-18282)
CINEPOLIS LUXURY CINEMAS
6420 Wilshire Blvd # 900, Los Angeles
(90048-5502)
PHONE..........................323 556-6340
Rafael Ossio, *Officer*
Neil Baron, *Vice Pres*
April Mendoza, *Vice Pres*
Estrella Ayala, *Executive*
Giselle Cruz, *Executive*
EMP: 87
SALES (est): 396.1K **Privately Held**
SIC: 7832 Motion picture theaters, except
drive-in

(P-18283)
**COMMERCE CENTER
THEATRES**
Also Called: Pacific Thtres Cmmerce Theatre
950 Goodrich Blvd, Commerce
(90022-4110)
PHONE..........................323 722-5577
Roberta Sanchez, *Manager*
EMP: 60
SALES (est): 562.8K **Privately Held**
SIC: 7832 Motion picture theaters, except
drive-in

(P-18284)
**DE ANZA LAND & LEISURE
CORP**
Also Called: South Bay Drive In Theatre
2170 Coronado Ave, San Diego
(92154-2022)
PHONE..........................619 423-2727
Veronica Sarabia, *Branch Mgr*
EMP: 50
SALES (corp-wide): 12.6MM **Privately
Held**
SIC: 7832 Motion picture theaters, except
drive-in
PA: De Anza Land & Leisure Corp.
4407 State St
Montclair CA 91763
909 628-0019

(P-18285)
DECURION CORPORATION (PA)
120 N Robertson Blvd Fl 3, Los Angeles
(90048-3115)
PHONE..........................310 659-9432
Michael R Forman, *President*
Jeffrey Koblentz, *COO*
James Cotter, *Vice Pres*
Jerome Forman, *Vice Pres*
Stephen Green, *Vice Pres*

EMP: 100
SQ FT: 31,000
SALES (est): 204.8MM **Privately Held**
SIC: 7832 7833 Motion picture theaters, except drive-in; drive-in motion picture theaters

(P-18286)
EDWARDS BREA 10 WEST
255 W Birch St, Brea (92821-4965)
PHONE..............................714 672-4136
Mike Campbell, *President*
EMP: 50
SALES (est): 780.9K **Privately Held**
SIC: 7832 Motion picture theaters, except drive-in

(P-18287)
EDWARDS THEATRES CIRCUIT INC
Also Called: Jurupa Stadium Cinema 14
8032 Limonite Ave, Riverside (92509-6107)
PHONE..............................951 361-1917
EMP: 62
SALES (corp-wide): 1.1B **Privately Held**
SIC: 7832 Motion picture theaters, except drive-in
HQ: Edwards Theatres Circuit, Inc.
   300 Newport Center Dr
   Newport Beach CA 92660
   949 640-4600

(P-18288)
EDWARDS THEATRES CIRCUIT INC
Also Called: Mesa Pointe Stadium 12
901 S Coast Dr, Costa Mesa (92626-1747)
PHONE..............................714 428-0962
Minh Duong, *Branch Mgr*
EMP: 62
SALES (corp-wide): 1.1B **Privately Held**
SIC: 7832 Motion picture theaters, except drive-in
HQ: Edwards Theatres Circuit, Inc.
   300 Newport Center Dr
   Newport Beach CA 92660
   949 640-4600

(P-18289)
EDWARDS THEATRES CIRCUIT INC
Also Called: Rancho San Diego Cinema 16
2951 Jamacha Rd, El Cajon (92019-4342)
PHONE..............................619 660-3460
EMP: 62
SALES (corp-wide): 1.1B **Privately Held**
SIC: 7832 Motion picture theaters, except drive-in
HQ: Edwards Theatres Circuit, Inc.
   300 Newport Center Dr
   Newport Beach CA 92660
   949 640-4600

(P-18290)
EDWARDS THEATRES CIRCUIT INC
Also Called: Kaleidoscope Stadium Cinema
27741 Crown Valley Pkwy # 323, Mission Viejo (92691-6532)
PHONE..............................949 582-4078
EMP: 62
SALES (corp-wide): 1.1B **Privately Held**
SIC: 7832 Motion picture theaters, except drive-in
HQ: Edwards Theatres Circuit, Inc.
   300 Newport Center Dr
   Newport Beach CA 92660
   949 640-4600

(P-18291)
EDWARDS THEATRES CIRCUIT INC
Also Called: Mira Mesa Stadium 18
10733 Westview Pkwy, San Diego (92126-2963)
PHONE..............................858 635-7716
Peter Brandon, *Branch Mgr*
EMP: 62
SALES (corp-wide): 1.1B **Privately Held**
SIC: 7832 Motion picture theaters, except drive-in
HQ: Edwards Theatres Circuit, Inc.
   300 Newport Center Dr
   Newport Beach CA 92660
   949 640-4600

(P-18292)
EDWARDS THEATRES CIRCUIT INC
Also Called: South Coast Village
1561 W Sunflower Ave, Santa Ana (92704-7436)
PHONE..............................714 557-5701
EMP: 62
SALES (corp-wide): 1.1B **Privately Held**
SIC: 7832 Motion picture theaters, except drive-in
HQ: Edwards Theatres Circuit, Inc.
   300 Newport Center Dr
   Newport Beach CA 92660
   949 640-4600

(P-18293)
EDWARDS THEATRES CIRCUIT INC (DH)
300 Newport Center Dr, Newport Beach (92660-7529)
PHONE..............................949 640-4600
W James Edwards III, *Ch of Bd*
Steve Coffey, *President*
Joan Randolph, *Vice Pres*
Marcella Sheldon, *Admin Sec*
EMP: 118
SQ FT: 30,000
SALES (est): 78.3MM
SALES (corp-wide): 1.1B **Privately Held**
SIC: 7832 Motion picture theaters, except drive-in
HQ: Regal Cinemas, Inc.
   101 E Blount Ave Ste 100
   Knoxville TN 37920
   865 922-1123

(P-18294)
EDWARDS THEATRES CIRCUIT INC
Also Called: Long Beach Stadium Cinemas 26
7501 Carson Blvd, Long Beach (90808-2365)
PHONE..............................562 429-3321
EMP: 62
SALES (corp-wide): 1.1B **Privately Held**
SIC: 7832 6512 Motion picture theaters, except drive-in; theater building, ownership & operation
HQ: Edwards Theatres Circuit, Inc.
   300 Newport Center Dr
   Newport Beach CA 92660
   949 640-4600

(P-18295)
EDWARDS THEATRES CIRCUIT INC
Also Called: San Marcos Stadium Cinema 18
1180 W San Marcos Blvd, San Marcos (92078-4009)
PHONE..............................760 471-3734
Jerry Jorgensen, *Manager*
EMP: 100
SALES (corp-wide): 1.1B **Privately Held**
SIC: 7832 Motion picture theaters, except drive-in
HQ: Edwards Theatres Circuit, Inc.
   300 Newport Center Dr
   Newport Beach CA 92660
   949 640-4600

(P-18296)
EDWARDS THEATRES CIRCUIT INC
Also Called: Cerritos Cinemas 10
12761 Towne Center Dr, Artesia (90703-8545)
PHONE..............................562 403-1133
James Edwards III, *Branch Mgr*
EMP: 60
SALES (corp-wide): 1.1B **Privately Held**
SIC: 7832 Motion picture theaters, except drive-in
HQ: Edwards Theatres Circuit, Inc.
   300 Newport Center Dr
   Newport Beach CA 92660
   949 640-4600

(P-18297)
EDWARDS THEATRES CIRCUIT INC
Also Called: Temecula Stadium Cinemas 15
40750 Winchester Rd, Temecula (92591-5524)
PHONE..............................951 296-0144
EMP: 62
SALES (corp-wide): 1.1B **Privately Held**
SIC: 7832 Motion picture theaters, except drive-in
HQ: Edwards Theatres Circuit, Inc.
   300 Newport Center Dr
   Newport Beach CA 92660
   949 640-4600

(P-18298)
EDWARDS THEATRES CIRCUIT INC
Also Called: Edwards Theaters
680 Ventura Blvd, Camarillo (93010-5877)
PHONE..............................805 383-8866
J D Powers, *Manager*
EMP: 62
SALES (corp-wide): 1.1B **Privately Held**
SIC: 7832 Motion picture theaters, except drive-in
HQ: Edwards Theatres Circuit, Inc.
   300 Newport Center Dr
   Newport Beach CA 92660
   949 640-4600

(P-18299)
EDWARDS THEATRES CIRCUIT INC
Also Called: Edwards Cinemas University
4245 Campus Dr, Irvine (92612-2752)
PHONE..............................949 854-8811
Mike Peterson, *Branch Mgr*
EMP: 62
SALES (corp-wide): 1.1B **Privately Held**
SIC: 7832 Motion picture theaters, except drive-in
HQ: Edwards Theatres Circuit, Inc.
   300 Newport Center Dr
   Newport Beach CA 92660
   949 640-4600

(P-18300)
EDWARDS THEATRES CIRCUIT INC
Also Called: Simi Valley Plaza 10
1457 E Los Angeles Ave, Simi Valley (93065-2807)
PHONE..............................805 526-4329
Dominiqua Lint, *Branch Mgr*
EMP: 62
SALES (corp-wide): 1.1B **Privately Held**
SIC: 7832 Motion picture theaters, except drive-in
HQ: Edwards Theatres Circuit, Inc.
   300 Newport Center Dr
   Newport Beach CA 92660
   949 640-4600

(P-18301)
EDWARDS THEATRES CIRCUIT INC
Also Called: Santa Maria Cinema 10
1521 S Bradley Rd, Santa Maria (93454-8014)
PHONE..............................805 347-1164
Santa Edwards, *Manager*
EMP: 62
SALES (corp-wide): 1.1B **Privately Held**
SIC: 7832 Motion picture theaters, except drive-in
HQ: Edwards Theatres Circuit, Inc.
   300 Newport Center Dr
   Newport Beach CA 92660
   949 640-4600

(P-18302)
HARKINS THEATRES INC
3100 Chino Ave, Chino Hills (91709)
PHONE..............................909 627-8010
Sarah Yeats, *Principal*
EMP: 70 **Privately Held**
SIC: 7832 Motion picture theaters, except drive-in
PA: Harkins Theatres, Inc.
   7511 E Mcdonald Dr
   Scottsdale AZ 85250

(P-18303)
KRIKORIAN PREMIERE THEATRE LLC
410 S Myrtle Ave, Monrovia (91016-2812)
PHONE..............................626 305-7469
Ted Goldbeck, *Branch Mgr*
Elizabeth Holliday, *Sales Associate*
Michelle Newcombe, *Manager*
Sandra Simental, *Manager*
Gene Gausselin, *Cashier*
EMP: 110
SALES (corp-wide): 68.5MM **Privately Held**
WEB: www.krikorianmetroplex.com
SIC: 7832 Motion picture theaters, except drive-in
PA: Krikorian Premiere Theatre Llc
   2275 W 190th St
   Torrance CA 90504
   310 856-1270

(P-18304)
KRIKORIAN PREMIERE THEATRE LLC
25 Main St, Vista (92083-5800)
PHONE..............................760 945-7469
EMP: 110
SALES (corp-wide): 68.5MM **Privately Held**
SIC: 7832 Motion picture theaters, except drive-in
PA: Krikorian Premiere Theatre Llc
   2275 W 190th St
   Torrance CA 90504
   310 856-1270

(P-18305)
KRIKORIAN PREMIERE THEATRE LLC
8540 Whittier Blvd, Pico Rivera (90660-2520)
PHONE..............................562 205-3456
Todd Cummings, *Branch Mgr*
EMP: 66
SALES (corp-wide): 68.5MM **Privately Held**
SIC: 7832 Motion picture theaters, except drive-in
PA: Krikorian Premiere Theatre Llc
   2275 W 190th St
   Torrance CA 90504
   310 856-1270

(P-18306)
METROPLEX THEATRES LLC
2275 W 190th St Ste 201, Torrance (90504-6007)
PHONE..............................310 856-1270
George Krikorian,
EMP: 600
SALES (est): 8.9MM **Privately Held**
SIC: 7832 Motion picture theaters, except drive-in

(P-18307)
NORTH AMERICAN CINEMAS INC
Also Called: Airport Cinemas 12
409 Aviation Blvd, Santa Rosa (95403-1069)
PHONE..............................707 571-1412
Nicholas Mann, *General Mgr*
EMP: 365 **Privately Held**
WEB: www.northamericacinemas.com
SIC: 7832 Motion picture theaters, except drive-in
PA: North American Cinemas, Inc.
   917 College Ave
   Santa Rosa CA 95404

(P-18308)
PACIFIC THEATERS INC (PA)
120 N Robertson Blvd Fl 3, Los Angeles (90048-3113)
PHONE..............................310 657-8420
Michael Forman, *Ch of Bd*
Christopher Forman, *CEO*
Gary Marcotte, *CFO*
Kevin Elms, *Treasurer*
EMP: 120 **EST:** 1950
SQ FT: 25,000

SALES (est): 8MM **Privately Held**
SIC: 7832 7812 Exhibitors, itinerant: motion picture; motion picture production & distribution, television

(P-18309)
PACIFIC THEATERS INC
Also Called: Beach Cities 16 Cinemas
831 S Nash St, El Segundo (90245-4708)
PHONE..............................310 607-0007
Gaye Clemson, *Manager*
EMP: 55
SALES (corp-wide): 7.2MM **Privately Held**
SIC: 7832 Motion picture theaters, except drive-in
PA: Pacific Theaters, Inc
120 N Robertson Blvd Fl 3
Los Angeles CA 90048
310 657-8420

(P-18310)
PACIFIC THEATERS INC
4821 Del Amo Blvd, Lakewood (90712-2504)
PHONE..............................562 634-1183
Bill Bayam, *Manager*
Penny McNamee, *Manager*
EMP: 80
SALES (corp-wide): 7.2MM **Privately Held**
SIC: 7832 Exhibitors, itinerant: motion picture
PA: Pacific Theaters, Inc
120 N Robertson Blvd Fl 3
Los Angeles CA 90048
310 657-8420

(P-18311)
PACIFIC THEATRES ENTRMT CORP (HQ)
120 N Robertson Blvd Fl 3, Los Angeles (90048-3113)
PHONE..............................310 659-9432
Christopher Forman, *Ch of Bd*
Joe Robinson, *Administration*
EMP: 100 EST: 1962
SQ FT: 3,000
SALES (est): 7.8MM
SALES (corp-wide): 204.8MM **Privately Held**
WEB: www.pacifictheatres.com
SIC: 7832 Motion picture theaters, except drive-in
PA: The Decurion Corporation
120 N Robertson Blvd Fl 3
Los Angeles CA 90048
310 659-9432

(P-18312)
READING ENTERTAINMENT INC (HQ)
500 Citadel Dr Ste 300, Commerce (90040-1575)
PHONE..............................213 235-2226
Robert F Smerling, *President*
Andrzej Matyczynski, *CFO*
Terri Alvarez, *Vice Pres*
Ellen Cotter, *Vice Pres*
Wayne Smith, *Exec Dir*
▲ EMP: 78
SQ FT: 3,300
SALES (est): 3.2MM
SALES (corp-wide): 279.7MM **Publicly Held**
SIC: 7832 Motion picture theaters, except drive-in
PA: Reading International, Inc.
5995 Sepulveda Blvd Fl 3
Culver City CA 90230
213 235-2240

(P-18313)
READING INTERNATIONAL INC
41090 California Oaks Rd, Murrieta (92562-5749)
PHONE..............................951 696-7045
Dolly Woodland, *General Mgr*
EMP: 50
SALES (corp-wide): 279.7MM **Publicly Held**
SIC: 7832 Motion picture theaters, except drive-in

PA: Reading International, Inc.
5995 Sepulveda Blvd Fl 3
Culver City CA 90230
213 235-2240

(P-18314)
READING INTERNATIONAL INC
Also Called: Angelika Film Center and Cafe
11620 Carmel Mountain Rd, San Diego (92128-4621)
PHONE..............................858 207-2606
Chris Herbert, *General Mgr*
EMP: 60
SALES (corp-wide): 279.7MM **Publicly Held**
SIC: 7832 5812 5182 Motion picture theaters, except drive-in; cafe; wine & distilled beverages
PA: Reading International, Inc.
5995 Sepulveda Blvd Fl 3
Culver City CA 90230
213 235-2240

(P-18315)
READING INTERNATIONAL INC
2508 Land Park Dr, Sacramento (95818-2224)
PHONE..............................916 442-0985
EMP: 734
SALES (corp-wide): 279.7MM **Publicly Held**
SIC: 7832 Motion picture theaters, except drive-in
PA: Reading International, Inc.
5995 Sepulveda Blvd Fl 3
Culver City CA 90230
213 235-2240

(P-18316)
READING INTERNATIONAL INC (PA)
5995 Sepulveda Blvd Fl 3, Culver City (90230-6400)
PHONE..............................213 235-2240
Ellen M Cotter, *Ch of Bd*
Margaret Cotter, *Vice Chairman*
Devasis Ghose, *CFO*
Guy Adams, *Bd of Directors*
Judy Codding, *Bd of Directors*
EMP: 138
SQ FT: 11,700
SALES: 279.7MM **Publicly Held**
SIC: 7832 7922 6512 6531 Motion picture theaters, except drive-in; theatrical producers & services; nonresidential building operators; real estate agents & managers

(P-18317)
REGAL CINEMAS INC
Also Called: Natomas Marketplace 16
3561 Truxel Rd, Sacramento (95834-3641)
PHONE..............................916 419-0205
Ricks Hescock, *Manager*
EMP: 60
SALES (corp-wide): 1.1B **Privately Held**
WEB: www.regalcinemas.com
SIC: 7832 Motion picture theaters, except drive-in
HQ: Regal Cinemas, Inc.
101 E Blount Ave Ste 100
Knoxville TN 37920
865 922-1123

(P-18318)
REGAL CINEMAS INC
550 Deep Valley Dr # 339, Rllng HLS Est (90274-7603)
PHONE..............................310 544-3042
Christy Alexander, *Manager*
EMP: 80
SALES (corp-wide): 1.1B **Privately Held**
WEB: www.regalcinemas.com
SIC: 7832 Motion picture theaters, except drive-in
HQ: Regal Cinemas, Inc.
101 E Blount Ave Ste 100
Knoxville TN 37920
865 922-1123

(P-18319)
REGENCY THEATERS INC
26901 Agoura Rd Ste 150, Agoura Hills (91301-5114)
PHONE..............................818 224-3825
Lyndon H Golin, *President*

Monica Golin, *CFO*
Andrew Gualtieri, *District Mgr*
Dwight Morgan, *District Mgr*
Crystal Whittaker, *Marketing Staff*
EMP: 50
SQ FT: 1,000
SALES: 4MM **Privately Held**
WEB: www.regencymovies.com
SIC: 7832 Motion picture theaters, except drive-in

(P-18320)
SANBORN THEATRES INC
41090 Calif Oaks Rd, Murrieta (92562-5749)
PHONE..............................909 296-9728
Arthur Sanborn, *Branch Mgr*
EMP: 70
SALES (corp-wide): 10.9MM **Privately Held**
SIC: 7832 Motion picture theaters, except drive-in
PA: Sanborn Theatres Inc
13 Corporate Plaza Dr # 110
Newport Beach CA 92660
949 640-2370

(P-18321)
SILVER CINEMAS ACQUISITION CO (PA)
Also Called: Landmark Theatres
2222 S Barrington Ave, Los Angeles (90064-1206)
PHONE..............................310 473-6701
Mark Cuban, *President*
George T Mundorff, *CEO*
Todd Wagner, *CEO*
Paul Duchouquette, *Vice Pres*
Maren Beckman, *General Mgr*
EMP: 52
SALES (est): 83.4MM **Privately Held**
SIC: 7832 Motion picture theaters, except drive-in

(P-18322)
UA GALAXY LOS CERRITOS
Also Called: Ua Galaxy Los Cerritos 33
4900 E 4th St, Ontario (91764-5229)
PHONE..............................562 865-6499
Mike Friextad, *Manager*
EMP: 70
SALES (est): 939.4K **Privately Held**
SIC: 7832 Motion picture theaters, except drive-in

(P-18323)
WESTSTAR CINEMAS INC
Also Called: Mann's Theatres
6801 Hollywood Blvd # 335, Los Angeles (90028-6136)
PHONE..............................323 461-3331
Laval How, *Manager*
EMP: 95
SALES (corp-wide): 26.5MM **Privately Held**
WEB: www.manntheatres.com
SIC: 7832 Motion picture theaters, except drive-in
PA: Weststar Cinemas, Inc
16530 Ventura Blvd # 500
Encino CA 91436
818 784-6266

(P-18324)
WF CINEMA HOLDINGS LP
Also Called: Village 8
180 Promenade Way Ste R, Westlake Village (91362-3826)
PHONE..............................805 379-8966
Joseph Leptore, *Manager*
EMP: 50
SALES (corp-wide): 26.5MM **Privately Held**
WEB: www.manntheatres.com
SIC: 7832 Motion picture theaters, except drive-in
PA: Weststar Cinemas, Inc
16530 Ventura Blvd # 500
Encino CA 91436
818 784-6266

7833 Drive-In Motion Picture Theaters

(P-18325)
CENTURY THEATRES INC
Also Called: Century 14
1555 Eureka Rd, Roseville (95661-3040)
PHONE..............................916 797-3466
Ray Syufy, *President*
EMP: 70 **Publicly Held**
WEB: www.centurytheaters.com
SIC: 7833 7832 Drive-in motion picture theaters; motion picture theaters, except drive-in
HQ: Century Theatres, Inc
3900 Dallas Pkwy Ste 500
Plano TX 75093
972 665-1000

(P-18326)
CENTURY THEATRES INC
3200 Klose Way, Richmond (94806-5792)
PHONE..............................510 758-9626
Makisha Jones, *Manager*
EMP: 90 **Publicly Held**
WEB: www.centurytheaters.com
SIC: 7833 7832 Drive-in motion picture theaters; motion picture theaters, except drive-in
HQ: Century Theatres, Inc
3900 Dallas Pkwy Ste 500
Plano TX 75093
972 665-1000

(P-18327)
CENTURY THEATRES INC
Also Called: Century 8
12827 Victory Blvd, North Hollywood (91606-3012)
PHONE..............................818 508-1943
Terrell Hammack, *Branch Mgr*
EMP: 60 **Publicly Held**
WEB: www.centurytheaters.com
SIC: 7833 7832 Drive-in motion picture theaters; motion picture theaters, except drive-in
HQ: Century Theatres, Inc
3900 Dallas Pkwy Ste 500
Plano TX 75093
972 665-1000

(P-18328)
MISSION DRIVE-IN THEATRE CO
Also Called: Los Angeles Dr-In Theatre Co
4407 State St, Montclair (91763-6034)
PHONE..............................909 465-9219
William Oldknow, *Managing Prtnr*
Charles P Skouras III, *Partner*
Charles P Skouras Jr, *Partner*
Diane M Skouras, *Partner*
Christianna Skouras-Marin, *Partner*
EMP: 60
SQ FT: 500
SALES (est): 3.2MM **Privately Held**
WEB: www.missiontiki.com
SIC: 7833 6515 5932 Drive-in motion picture theaters; mobile home site operators; used merchandise stores

(P-18329)
NATIONWIDE THEATRES CORP (HQ)
120 N Robertson Blvd Fl 3, Los Angeles (90048-3115)
PHONE..............................310 657-8420
Christopher Forman, *President*
Nora Dashwood, *COO*
EMP: 75
SQ FT: 25,000
SALES (est): 40.5MM
SALES (corp-wide): 204.8MM **Privately Held**
SIC: 7833 7832 Drive-in motion picture theaters; motion picture theaters, except drive-in
PA: The Decurion Corporation
120 N Robertson Blvd Fl 3
Los Angeles CA 90048
310 659-9432

7841 Video Tape Rental

(P-18330)
NETFLIX INC
121 Albright Way, Los Gatos (95032-1801)
PHONE......................................408 540-3700
EMP: 2000 **Publicly Held**
SIC: 7841 Video tape rental
PA: Netflix, Inc.
100 Winchester Cir
Los Gatos CA 95032
-

(P-18331)
NETFLIX INC (PA)
100 Winchester Cir, Los Gatos
(95032-1815)
PHONE......................................408 540-3700
Reed Hastings, *Ch of Bd*
David Wells, *CFO*
Rachel Whetstone, *Ch Credit Ofcr*
Kelly Bennett, *Chief Mktg Ofcr*
Greg Peters,
EMP: 166
SQ FT: 600,000
SALES: 11.6B **Publicly Held**
SIC: 7841 Video disk/tape rental to the
general public

7911 Dance Studios, Schools & Halls

(P-18332)
CLOVIS UNIFIED SCHOOL DISTRICT
885 Gettysburg Ave, Clovis (93612-3906)
PHONE......................................559 327-3900
EMP: 284
SALES (corp-wide): 315MM **Privately Held**
SIC: 7911 Dance instructor & school services
PA: Clovis Unified School District
1450 Herndon Ave
Clovis CA 93611
559 327-9000

(P-18333)
FOUNDATION FOR DANCE EDUCATION
Also Called: Inland Pacific Ballet
9061 Central Ave, Montclair (91763-1622)
PHONE......................................909 482-1590
Victoria Koenig, *Exec Dir*
▲ **EMP:** 51
SALES: 480K **Privately Held**
SIC: 7911 Dance studios, schools & halls

(P-18334)
GABRIELLA FOUNDATION
639 S Commwl Ave Ste B, Los Angeles
(90005)
PHONE......................................213 365-2491
Liza Bercovici, *Exec Dir*
Staci Armao, *Opers Staff*
EMP: 82
SALES: 1.7MM **Privately Held**
WEB: www.gabriellaaxelradfoundation.org
SIC: 7911 8211 Children's dancing school;
elementary & secondary schools

7922 Theatrical Producers & Misc Theatrical Svcs

(P-18335)
42ND STREET MOON
601 Van Ness Ave, San Francisco
(94102-3200)
PHONE......................................415 255-8207
J Patterson McBaine, *President*
Joe Mader, *Managing Dir*
Ken Levin, *Director*
Greg Mackellan, *Director*
Dyan McBride, *Director*
EMP: 50
SALES: 700.4K **Privately Held**
SIC: 7922 Theatrical producers & services

(P-18336)
4WALL ENTERTAINMENT INC
400 N Berry St, Brea (92821-3104)
PHONE......................................702 263-3858
EMP: 130
SALES (corp-wide): 150MM **Privately Held**
SIC: 7922 Theatrical producers & services
PA: 4wall Entertainment, Inc.
3165 W Sunset Rd Ste 100
Las Vegas NV 89118
702 263-3858

(P-18337)
4WALL ENTERTAINMENT INC
5435 W San Fernando Rd, Los Angeles
(90039-1014)
PHONE......................................818 252-7481
Kathy Torjman, *CEO*
EMP: 86
SALES (corp-wide): 150MM **Privately Held**
SIC: 7922 Theatrical producers & services
PA: 4wall Entertainment, Inc.
3165 W Sunset Rd Ste 100
Las Vegas NV 89118
702 263-3858

(P-18338)
ADAIR ENTERPRISES
Also Called: American Way Cultural Center
2390 N American Way, Orange
(92865-2502)
PHONE......................................714 998-5551
Richard Adair, *Partner*
Marty Adair, *Partner*
EMP: 53 **EST:** 1982
SQ FT: 35,000
SALES (est): 1MM **Privately Held**
WEB: www.awccevents.com
SIC: 7922 Performing arts center production

(P-18339)
ADVENTIST MEDIA CENTER INC (PA)
Also Called: It Is Written
11291 Pierce St, Riverside (92505-2705)
P.O. Box 101, Simi Valley (93062-0101)
PHONE......................................805 955-7777
Daniel R Jackson, *CEO*
Daniel Jackson, *Ch of Bd*
Marshall Chase, *President*
Charles Reel, *Treasurer*
Warren Judd, *Vice Pres*
▲ **EMP:** 76 **EST:** 1972
SQ FT: 76,000
SALES (est): 14.3MM **Privately Held**
WEB: www.sdamedia.org
SIC: 7922 Television program, including
commercial producers

(P-18340)
AEG PRESENTS LLC (DH)
425 W 11th St, Los Angeles (90015-3459)
PHONE......................................323 930-5700
Randy Phillips,
Montana Hauser, *Partner*
Andrew Bersch, *Vice Pres*
Reeves Price, *Vice Pres*
Jessica Vonhoven, *Executive*
▲ **EMP:** 140
SQ FT: 16,400
SALES (est): 36.7MM **Privately Held**
SIC: 7922 Entertainment promotion
HQ: Anschutz Entertainment Group, Inc
1100 S Flower St
Los Angeles CA 90015
213 337-5052

(P-18341)
AGENCY FOR PERFORMING ARTS INC (PA)
405 S Beverly Dr Ste 500, Beverly Hills
(90212-4425)
PHONE......................................310 557-9049
James Gosnell, *President*
Betsy Berg, *Senior VP*
Manfred Westphal, *Senior VP*
Jeff Witjas, *Senior VP*
Jay Gilbert, *Vice Pres*
EMP: 145 **EST:** 1962
SALES (est): 12.9MM **Privately Held**
WEB: www.apa-agency.com
SIC: 7922 Theatrical producers & services

(P-18342)
AMERICAN CONSERVATORY
415 Geary St, San Francisco (94102-1222)
PHONE......................................415 749-2228
Roger Wahther, *Manager*
EMP: 70
SALES (corp-wide): 27.4MM **Privately Held**
WEB: www.acts-at.com
SIC: 7922 Repertory, road or stock companies: theatrical
PA: American Conservatory Theatre Foundation
30 Grant Ave Fl 7
San Francisco CA 94108
415 834-3200

(P-18343)
AMERICAN CONSERVATORY
Also Called: A C T Box Office
405 Geary St, San Francisco (94102-1222)
PHONE......................................415 749-2228
Cheryl Sorokin, *Branch Mgr*
EMP: 70
SALES (corp-wide): 27.4MM **Privately Held**
WEB: www.acts-at.com
SIC: 7922 Repertory, road or stock companies: theatrical
PA: American Conservatory Theatre Foundation
30 Grant Ave Fl 7
San Francisco CA 94108
415 834-3200

(P-18344)
BEN BOLLINGER PRODUCTIONS INC
Also Called: Bollingers Candelight Pavilion
455 W Foothill Blvd, Claremont
(91711-2701)
PHONE......................................909 626-3296
Ben Bollinger, *President*
EMP: 70
SALES (est): 3.3MM **Privately Held**
SIC: 7922 8999 Legitimate live theater
producers; music arranging & composing

(P-18345)
BERKELEY REPERTORY THEATRE (PA)
2025 Addison St, Berkeley (94704-1103)
PHONE......................................510 204-8901
Susan Medak, *Managing Dir*
David Lorenc, *General Mgr*
Karen Racanelli, *General Mgr*
Theresa Von Klug, *General Mgr*
Andrew Susskind, *Executive Asst*
▲ **EMP:** 66
SQ FT: 20,000
SALES: 20.7MM **Privately Held**
WEB: www.berkeleyrep.org
SIC: 7922 Performing arts center production

(P-18346)
BREAK FLOOR PRODUCTIONS LLC (PA)
Also Called: Jump Dance Convention
5446 Satsuma Ave, North Hollywood
(91601-2837)
PHONE......................................818 432-1234
Jacquelyn Stroming, *Mng Member*
George Gregory, *Prdtn Dir*
EMP: 50
SALES: 5MM **Privately Held**
WEB: www.breakthefloor.com
SIC: 7922 Theatrical producers

(P-18347)
BROADWAY BY BAY
853 Industrial Rd Ste H, San Carlos
(94070-3324)
P.O. Box 728 (94070-0728)
PHONE......................................650 579-5565
Waren Doan, *President*
Sarah Dunn-Rankin, *Volunteer Dir*
Samantha Cardenas, *Marketing Staff*
Alicia Jeffrey, *Director*
EMP: 140
SQ FT: 1,600
SALES: 1.2MM **Privately Held**
WEB: www.bbbay.org
SIC: 7922 Ticket agency, theatrical

(P-18348)
BROADWAY SACRAMENTO (PA)
Also Called: Music Circus
1510 J St Ste 200, Sacramento
(95814-2099)
PHONE......................................916 446-5880
Richard Lewis, *President*
Laura Hunter, *Store Mgr*
Dori Gough, *Executive Asst*
Stephanie Tabor, *Accountant*
Corinne Wihl, *Human Res Mgr*
▲ **EMP:** 150
SQ FT: 7,000
SALES: 18.4MM **Privately Held**
WEB: www.calmt.com
SIC: 7922 Theatrical companies

(P-18349)
BULLY PICTURES INC (PA)
1220 Cabrillo Ave, Venice (90291-3704)
PHONE......................................310 395-6500
Jason Forest, *Principal*
EMP: 103
SALES (est): 2MM **Privately Held**
SIC: 7922 Television program, including
commercial producers

(P-18350)
CALIFORNIA REPERTORY COMPANY
Also Called: California University Long Bch
1250 N Bellflower Blvd # 124, Long Beach
(90840-0124)
PHONE......................................562 985-7891
Joanne Gordon, *Director*
Howard Burman, *Director*
Christina Ramos, *Director*
EMP: 50
SALES: 2.2MM **Privately Held**
SIC: 7922 6512 Theatrical producers &
services; theater building, ownership &
operation

(P-18351)
CALIFORNIA SHAKESPEARE THEATER
Also Called: Cal Shakes
701 Heinz Ave, Berkeley (94710-2732)
PHONE......................................510 548-3422
Jonathan Moscone, *Director*
EMP: 225 **EST:** 1974
SALES: 5.7MM **Privately Held**
WEB: www.calshakes.org
SIC: 7922 Plays, road & stock companies

(P-18352)
CALIFORNIA TICKETSCOM INC
1855 Gateway Blvd Ste 630, Concord
(94520-3200)
PHONE......................................925 671-4000
Terry Wojtulewicz, *Branch Mgr*
John Burns, *Info Tech Mgr*
EMP: 200
SALES (corp-wide): 194.3MM **Privately Held**
WEB: www.tickets.com
SIC: 7922 7999 Ticket agency, theatrical;
ticket sales office for sporting events, contract
HQ: California Tickets.Com Inc.
555 Anton Blvd Fl 11
Costa Mesa CA 92626
714 327-5400

(P-18353)
CALIFORNIA TICKETSCOM INC (DH)
555 Anton Blvd Fl 11, Costa Mesa
(92626-7675)
PHONE......................................714 327-5400
Joe Choti, *President*
Derek Goodnature, *President*
Cristine Hurley, *CFO*
Derek Palmer, *Exec VP*
Steven Reed, *Vice Pres*
▲ **EMP:** 89
SALES (est): 18.5MM
SALES (corp-wide): 194.3MM **Privately Held**
WEB: www.tickets.com
SIC: 7922 7999 5961 5045 Ticket
agency, theatrical; ticket sales office for
sporting events, contract; catalog & mail-
order houses; computers, peripherals &
software

HQ: Mlb Advanced Media, L.P.
75 9th Ave Fl 5
New York NY 10011
212 485-3444

(P-18354)
CENTER THTRE GROUP LOS ANGELES (PA)
601 W Temple St, Los Angeles (90012-2621)
PHONE..................213 972-7344
Michael Ritchie, *CEO*
William Ahmanson, *Ch of Bd*
Kiki Ramos Gindler, *President*
Cheryl Shepherd, *CFO*
Bruce L Ross, *Treasurer*
▲ **EMP:** 130
SQ FT: 20,000
SALES: 48.8MM **Privately Held**
WEB: www.ctgla.org
SIC: 7922 Theatrical companies

(P-18355)
CITY & COUNTY OF SAN FRANCISCO
Also Called: Zellerbach Rehearsal Hall
401 Van Ness Ave Ste 110, San Francisco (94102-4521)
PHONE..................415 621-6600
Elizabeth Maury, *Manager*
Rob Levin, *Manager*
EMP: 100 **Privately Held**
SIC: 7922 9199 Performing arts center production; general government administration; ;
PA: City & County Of San Francisco
1 Dr Carlton B Goodlett P
San Francisco CA 94102
415 554-7500

(P-18356)
CITY & COUNTY OF SAN FRANCISCO
Also Called: War Memorial Prfrmg Art Ctr
401 Van Ness Ave Ste 110, San Francisco (94102-4521)
PHONE..................415 621-6600
Elizabeth Murray, *Finance*
Jim Whipple, *Officer*
Colleen Burke-Hill, *Administration*
Stephanie Smith, *Administration*
Lisa Chau, *Business Mgr*
EMP: 100 **Privately Held**
SIC: 7922 9199 6512 Performing arts center production; general government administration; ; nonresidential building operators
PA: City & County Of San Francisco
1 Dr Carlton B Goodlett P
San Francisco CA 94102
415 554-7500

(P-18357)
CITY OF CONCORD
Also Called: Concord Pavillion
2000 Kirker Pass Rd, Concord (94521-1642)
PHONE..................925 692-2400
Doug Warrick, *General Mgr*
EMP: 400 **Privately Held**
WEB: www.cpd.ci.concord.ca.us
SIC: 7922 6512 Theatrical companies; theater building, ownership & operation
PA: City Of Concord
1950 Parkside Dr
Concord CA 94519
925 671-3000

(P-18358)
CITY OF DOWNEY
Also Called: Downey Civic Theatre
8435 Firestone Blvd, Downey (90241-3843)
P.O. Box 607 (90241-0607)
PHONE..................562 861-8211
Gerald Caton, *Manager*
EMP: 97 **Privately Held**
WEB: www.dpoa.org
SIC: 7922 Legitimate live theater producers
PA: City Of Downey
11111 Brookshire Ave
Downey CA 90241
562 869-7331

(P-18359)
COVENANT PLAYERS (PA)
1741 Fiske Pl, Oxnard (93033-1864)
P.O. Box 2900 (93034-2900)
PHONE..................805 486-7155
Robin Johnson-Tanner, *Owner*
Peter Iverson, *Vice Pres*
Gail Crabtree, *Director*
Bobbi Johnson-Tanner, *Director*
Bobbi Johnsontanner, *Director*
EMP: 220
SQ FT: 19,424
SALES: 405.2K **Privately Held**
WEB: www.covenantplayers.org
SIC: 7922 8661 Performing arts center production; religious organizations

(P-18360)
CREATING ARTS COMPANY
Also Called: Cac Studios
4380 Hillview Dr, Malibu (90265-2832)
PHONE..................310 804-0223
Shannon Sukovaty, *CEO*
Todd Skinner, *President*
EMP: 50
SALES: 250K **Privately Held**
SIC: 7922 Theatrical companies

(P-18361)
CREATIVE ARTISTS AGENCY LLC (PA)
Also Called: C A A
2000 Avenue Of The Stars # 100, Los Angeles (90067-4705)
PHONE..................424 288-2000
Steve Hasker, *CEO*
Kevin Gelbard, *Partner*
Steve Lafferty, *Managing Prtnr*
Rick Nicita, *Chairman*
Mark Cheatham, *Vice Pres*
EMP: 800
SALES (est): 112.7MM **Privately Held**
WEB: www.caa.com
SIC: 7922 Agent or manager for entertainers

(P-18362)
DAVIE BROWN ENTERTAINMENT INC
12777 W Jefferson Blvd # 120, Los Angeles (90066-7038)
PHONE..................310 979-1980
James Davie, *CEO*
Stephanie Cohen, *President*
Tom Meyer, *President*
Russell Meisels, *CFO*
Adam Smith, *Exec VP*
EMP: 60
SQ FT: 16,100
SALES: 18.5MM
SALES (corp-wide): 15.2B **Publicly Held**
WEB: www.davie-brown.com
SIC: 7922 Entertainment promotion
HQ: The Marketing Arm Inc
1999 Bryan St Fl 18
Dallas TX 75201

(P-18363)
DELICATE PRODUCTIONS INC (PA)
874 Verdulera St, Camarillo (93010-8371)
PHONE..................415 484-1174
James Steve Dabbs, *CEO*
Christopher Smyth, *CFO*
Angus Thomson, *Vice Pres*
Steven I Gilbard, *Principal*
EMP: 79
SQ FT: 19,937
SALES (est): 7.1MM **Privately Held**
WEB: www.delicate.com
SIC: 7922 7359 Equipment rental, theatrical; sound & lighting equipment rental

(P-18364)
ELVIS SCHOENBERG PRODUCTION
549 Marie Ave, Los Angeles (90042-1305)
PHONE..................323 344-1745
Ross Wright, *President*
EMP: 50
SALES (est): 662.1K **Privately Held**
SIC: 7922 Theatrical producers & services

(P-18365)
ENDEMOL
9255 W Sunset Blvd # 1100, West Hollywood (90069-3309)
PHONE..................310 860-9914
David Goldberg, *Chairman*
EMP: 70 EST: 2012
SALES: 170MM **Privately Held**
SIC: 7922 Television program, including commercial producers

(P-18366)
EPICENTER LIVE INC
4040 Mahaila Ave Unit A, San Diego (92122-5807)
PHONE..................424 235-4835
Devon Joseph, *President*
Keith A Joseph, *Exec Dir*
EMP: 150
SALES (est): 2.6MM **Privately Held**
SIC: 7922 Concert management service

(P-18367)
FRIENDS OF CULTURAL CENTER INC
Also Called: McCallum Theatre
73000 Fred Waring Dr, Palm Desert (92260-2800)
PHONE..................760 346-6505
Ted Giatas, *President*
William Towers, *Chairman*
Ron Gregroire, *Treasurer*
Betty Wolf, *Vice Pres*
Alan Zon, *Opers Staff*
EMP: 100
SQ FT: 66,000
SALES: 15.3MM **Privately Held**
WEB: www.mccallum-theatre.org
SIC: 7922 Theatrical producers & services

(P-18368)
GERSH AGENCY INC (PA)
9465 Wilshire Blvd Fl 6, Beverly Hills (90212-2605)
PHONE..................310 274-6611
Robert Gersh, *President*
Beatrice Gersh, *Vice Pres*
David Gersh, *Vice Pres*
EMP: 100 EST: 1949
SQ FT: 15,000
SALES (est): 11.1MM **Privately Held**
WEB: www.gershagency.com
SIC: 7922 Talent agent, theatrical

(P-18369)
GREAT AMERICAN MUSIC HALL
859 Ofarrell St, San Francisco (94109-7005)
PHONE..................415 885-0750
Dawn Holiday, *CEO*
Kit Carter, *Manager*
EMP: 50
SQ FT: 6,000
SALES (est): 1.3MM **Privately Held**
WEB: www.musichallsf.com
SIC: 7922 5813 Entertainment promotion; cocktail lounge

(P-18370)
GREENWAY ARTS ALLIANCE INC
544 N Fairfax Ave, Los Angeles (90036-1771)
PHONE..................323 655-7679
Molly Miles, *Chairman*
Phloe Pontaoe, *Opers Staff*
Nijeul Porter, *Director*
D Pierson Blaetz, *Manager*
Whitney Weston, *Manager*
EMP: 79
SALES: 1.7MM **Privately Held**
SIC: 7922 8299 Theatrical companies; art school, except commercial

(P-18371)
HARPO INC
Also Called: Harpo Studios
1041 N Formosa Ave, West Hollywood (90046-6703)
PHONE..................312 633-1000
Oprah Winfrey, *President*
Erik Logan, *President*
Sheri Salata, *President*
Douglas J Pattison, *CFO*
Jon Sinclair, *Vice Pres*

EMP: 70
SQ FT: 88,000
SALES (est): 8.2MM **Privately Held**
SIC: 7922 Television program, including commercial producers

(P-18372)
INNOVATIVE ARTISTS TALENT AGNY (PA)
1505 10th St, Santa Monica (90401-2805)
PHONE..................310 656-0400
Scott Harris, *President*
Jonathan Howard, *Vice Pres*
Jim Stein, *Project Mgr*
Robert Haas, *Agent*
EMP: 75
SALES (est): 6MM **Privately Held**
WEB: www.iany.com
SIC: 7922 7819 Talent agent, theatrical; casting bureau, motion picture

(P-18373)
INTERNATIONAL CREATIVE MGT INC (HQ)
Also Called: I C M
10250 Constellation Blvd, Los Angeles (90067-6200)
PHONE..................310 550-4000
Jeff Berg, *Ch of Bd*
Rick Levy, *Managing Prtnr*
Robert Murphy, *CFO*
Nancy Josephson, *Co-President*
Ed Limato, *Co-President*
▲ **EMP:** 220
SQ FT: 72,000
SALES (est): 36.5MM **Privately Held**
WEB: www.icmtalent.com
SIC: 7922 8699 Talent agent, theatrical; literary, film or cultural club
PA: Icm Holdings Inc
40 W 57th St Fl 16
New York NY 10019
212 556-5600

(P-18374)
INTERNATIONAL CREATIVE MGT INC
Also Called: I C M
10250 Constellation Blvd # 1, Los Angeles (90067-6200)
PHONE..................310 550-4000
Jeff Derg, *Manager*
EMP: 200
SALES (corp-wide): 36.5MM **Privately Held**
SIC: 7922 Booking agency, theatrical
HQ: International Creative Management, Inc.
10250 Constellation Blvd
Los Angeles CA 90067
310 550-4000

(P-18375)
J C ENTERTAINMENT LTG SVCS INC
Also Called: E L S
5435 W San Fernando Rd, Los Angeles (90039-1014)
PHONE..................818 252-7481
John Allen Chuck, *CEO*
Todd Richards, *CFO*
Kevin Dowling, *Vice Pres*
Derek Smith, *Vice Pres*
EMP: 80
SQ FT: 69,000
SALES (est): 9.6MM **Privately Held**
WEB: www.elslights.com
SIC: 7922 5719 Equipment rental, theatrical; lighting, lamps & accessories

(P-18376)
JOHN GORE ORGANIZATION INC
255 S B St, San Mateo (94401-4017)
PHONE..................650 340-0469
EMP: 78
SALES (corp-wide): 555.1MM **Privately Held**
SIC: 7922 Entertainment promotion
PA: The John Gore Organization Inc
1619 Broadway Fl 9
New York NY 10019
917 421-5400

▲ = Import ▼=Export
◆ =Import/Export

(P-18377)
KID STOCK INC
1539 Funston Ave, San Francisco
(94122-3530)
PHONE..............................415 753-3737
Jane Sullivan, *Deputy Dir*
Noel Donahue, *Deputy Dir*
EMP: 80
SALES: 432.5K **Privately Held**
WEB: www.kidstockinc.org
SIC: 7922 Community theater production

(P-18378)
LA LIVE PROPERTIES LLC
800 W Olympic Blvd # 305, Los Angeles
(90015-1360)
PHONE..............................213 763-7700
Donna Johnson, *VP Finance*
EMP: 50
SALES (est): 5.8MM **Privately Held**
WEB: www.lalive.com
SIC: 7922 6512 Theatrical producers &
services; property operation, auditoriums
& theaters
HQ: Anschutz Entertainment Group, Inc.
1100 S Flower St
Los Angeles CA 90015
213 337-5052

(P-18379)
LAGUNA PLAYHOUSE (PA)
606 Laguna Canyon Rd, Laguna Beach
(92651-1837)
P.O. Box 1747 (92652-1747)
PHONE..............................949 497-2787
Karen Wood, *CEO*
Bob Crowson, *CFO*
Veltria Roman, *Treasurer*
Ellen Richard, *Exec Dir*
Richard Stein, *Exec Dir*
EMP: 250
SQ FT: 19,000
SALES: 4.4MM **Privately Held**
WEB: www.lagunaplayhouse.com
SIC: 7922 Community theater production

(P-18380)
**LIVE NATION ENTERTAINMENT
INC**
7060 Hollywood Blvd Ste 2, Los Angeles
(90028-6030)
PHONE..............................213 639-6178
Michael Rapino, *Branch Mgr*
EMP: 86
SALES (corp-wide): 10.3B **Publicly Held**
SIC: 7922 Entertainment promotion
PA: Live Nation Entertainment, Inc.
9348 Civic Center Dr Lbby
Beverly Hills CA 90210
310 867-7000

(P-18381)
LIVE NATION WORLDWIDE INC
6500 Wilshire Blvd # 200, Los Angeles
(90048-4920)
PHONE..............................323 966-5066
Terry Dreher, *Principal*
EMP: 130
SALES (corp-wide): 10.3B **Publicly Held**
WEB: www.sfx.com
SIC: 7922 Theatrical producers & services
HQ: Live Nation Worldwide, Inc.
430 W 15th St
New York NY 10011
917 421-5100

(P-18382)
LIVE NATION WORLDWIDE INC
9348 Civic Center Dr Lbby, Beverly Hills
(90210-3642)
PHONE..............................310 867-7000
Kathy Willard, *CEO*
Jonathan Dolgen, *Bd of Directors*
Jimmy Iovine, *Bd of Directors*
Mark Shapiro, *Bd of Directors*
EMP: 8800
SALES (est): 291K
SALES (corp-wide): 10.3B **Publicly Held**
SIC: 7922 Theatrical producers & services
PA: Live Nation Entertainment, Inc.
9348 Civic Center Dr Lbby
Beverly Hills CA 90210
310 867-7000

(P-18383)
LUCAS DIGITAL LTD (DH)
3155 Kerner Blvd, San Rafael
(94901-5410)
PHONE..............................415 258-2000
James Morris, *President*
EMP: 500
SALES (est): 6.4MM **Publicly Held**
WEB: www.ldlhr.com
SIC: 7922 7819 Theatrical producers &
services; sound (effects & music produc-
tion), motion picture
HQ: Lucasfilm Ltd. Llc
1110 Gorgas Ave Bldg C-Hr
San Francisco CA 94129
415 623-1000

(P-18384)
**LUTHER BURBANK MEM
FOUNDATION**
50 Mark West Springs Rd, Santa Rosa
(95403-1457)
PHONE..............................707 546-3600
Richard Nowlin, *Exec Dir*
Robin Seltzer, *Director*
J David Siembieda, *Director*
Anita Wiglesworth, *Director*
EMP: 74
SQ FT: 120,000
SALES: 11.2MM **Privately Held**
WEB: www.lbc.net
SIC: 7922 8299 6519 Performing arts
center production; music & drama
schools; real property lessors

(P-18385)
MAGIC MOUNTAIN LLC
Also Called: Six Flags Magic Mountain
26101 Magic Mountain Pkwy, Valencia
(91355-1052)
P.O. Box 5500 (91380-5500)
PHONE..............................661 255-4100
Bonnie Rabjohn,
Tim Tim Burkhart, *Vice Pres*
Casey Bustle, *Administration*
Scott McClellan, *Finance*
Mike Wolf, *Manager*
▲ EMP: 300
SALES (est): 11.1MM
SALES (corp-wide): 1.3B **Publicly Held**
SIC: 7922 7996 Entertainment promotion;
theme park, amusement
PA: Six Flags Entertainment Corp
924 E Avenue J
Grand Prairie TX 75050
972 595-5000

(P-18386)
MCGUIRE TALENT INC
8608 Utica Ave Ste 220, Rancho Cuca-
monga (91730-4879)
PHONE..............................909 527-7006
EMP: 80
SQ FT: 2,200
SALES: 2MM **Privately Held**
SIC: 7922

(P-18387)
MOUNTAIN PLAY ASSOCIATION
1556 4th St B, San Rafael (94901-2713)
PHONE..............................415 383-1100
Sara Pearson, *Director*
EMP: 50
SQ FT: 650
SALES: 985.3K **Privately Held**
SIC: 7922 Theatrical producers & services

(P-18388)
NEWPORT TELEVISION LLC
4880 N 1st St, Fresno (93726-0514)
PHONE..............................559 761-0243
EMP: 123
SALES (corp-wide): 51.2MM **Privately
Held**
SIC: 7922 Television program, including
commercial producers
PA: Newport Television Llc
460 Nichols Rd Ste 250
Kansas City MO 64112
816 751-0200

(P-18389)
NFL PROPERTIES LLC
Also Called: Nfl Network
10950 Wash Blvd Ste 100, Culver City
(90232-4032)
PHONE..............................310 840-4635
Steve Bernstein, *Principal*
Lorey Zlotnick, *Senior VP*
Hovanes Gambaryan, *Sr Software Eng*
Paul Tabor, *Info Tech Dir*
Antoine Boyer, *Software Engr*
EMP: 300
SALES (corp-wide): 58.5MM **Privately
Held**
SIC: 7922 Television program, including
commercial producers
PA: Nfl Properties Llc
345 Park Ave Bsmt Lc1
New York NY 10154
212 450-2000

(P-18390)
OLD GLOBE THEATRE
1363 Old Globe Way, San Diego
(92101-1696)
P.O. Box 122171 (92112-2171)
PHONE..............................619 234-5623
Michael G Murphy, *CEO*
Louis Spisto, *CEO*
Mark Somers, *CFO*
Keely Tidrow, *Officer*
Amy Allison, *General Mgr*
▲ EMP: 500
SALES: 21.6MM **Privately Held**
WEB: www.theoldglobe.org
SIC: 7922 Performing arts center produc-
tion

(P-18391)
OPERA SAN JOSE INC
2149 Paragon Dr, San Jose (95131-1312)
PHONE..............................408 437-4450
Irene Dalis, *Exec Dir*
George Crow, *President*
Laurie Warner, *Vice Pres*
Bryan Ferraro, *Comms Mgr*
Larry Hancock, *General Mgr*
EMP: 100
SQ FT: 25,000
SALES: 4.3MM **Privately Held**
SIC: 7922 7929 Opera company; enter-
tainers & entertainment groups

(P-18392)
PARADIGM MUSIC LLC (PA)
360 N Crescent Dr, Beverly Hills
(90210-4874)
PHONE..............................310 288-8000
Sam Gores, *Ch of Bd*
Lucy Stille, *Partner*
Colby Casoria, *Chairman*
Sam Alpert, *Vice Pres*
April Perroni, *Vice Pres*
EMP: 70
SALES (est): 8.2MM **Privately Held**
WEB: www.michaelokeefe.com
SIC: 7922 Talent agent, theatrical

(P-18393)
**PERFORMING ARTS CENTER OF
LA C**
Also Called: Music Center
135 N Grand Ave, Los Angeles
(90012-3013)
PHONE..............................213 972-7211
John Emerson, *Ch of Bd*
Lisa Specht, *Ch of Bd*
Stephen Rountree, *President*
William Meyerchak, *CFO*
Jennifer Samsel, *Assistant VP*
▲ EMP: 250
SQ FT: 24,000
SALES: 70.4MM **Privately Held**
WEB: musiccenter.org
SIC: 7922 Theatrical producers & services;
equipment rental, theatrical; concert man-
agement service; ticket agency, theatrical
PA: The Music Center Of Los Angeles
County Inc
135 N Grand Ave Ste 201
Los Angeles CA 90012
213 972-8007

(P-18394)
**PLAYWRIGHTS FOUNDATION
INC**
1616 16th St Ste 350, San Francisco
(94103-5164)
PHONE..............................415 626-2176
Amy Mueller, *Director*
Linda Brewer, *President*
Jill Maclean, *Producer*
Marcy Straw, *Marketing Staff*
Karen Piemme, *Manager*
EMP: 73
SQ FT: 1,200
SALES: 249.3K **Privately Held**
SIC: 7922 Legitimate live theater produc-
ers

(P-18395)
**PRDCTIONS N FREMANTLE
AMER INC (DH)**
Also Called: Fremantle Media
2900 W Alameda Ave # 800, Burbank
(91505-4220)
PHONE..............................818 748-1100
Thom Beers, *CEO*
Donna Redier Linsk, *COO*
Dan Goldberg, *Exec VP*
Debra Bergman, *Senior VP*
Ellen Goldstein, *Vice Pres*
EMP: 100
SALES (est): 18.2MM
SALES (corp-wide): 82.3MM **Privately
Held**
SIC: 7922 Television program, including
commercial producers
HQ: Fremantlemedia Group Limited
1 Stephen Street
London W1T 1
207 691-6000

(P-18396)
**PREMIERE RADIO NETWORK
INC (DH)**
Also Called: Prn Radio Networks
15260 Ventura Blvd # 400, Sherman Oaks
(91403-5307)
PHONE..............................818 377-5300
Stephen C Lehman, *CEO*
Kraig T Kitchin, *President*
Timothy M Kelly, *Exec VP*
Steve Akopyan, *Vice Pres*
Dennis Brownlee, *Vice Pres*
EMP: 200
SQ FT: 15,000
SALES (est): 17MM **Publicly Held**
WEB: www.premrad.com
SIC: 7922 7389 4832 Radio producers;
advertising, promotional & trade show
services; radio broadcasting stations
HQ: Jacor Communications Company
200 E Basse Rd
San Antonio TX 78209
210 822-2828

(P-18397)
**PRODUCTION SPECIAL EVENTS
SVCS**
17326 Devonshire St, Northridge
(91325-1543)
PHONE..............................818 831-5326
Wendy Moodie, *President*
Terry Merkle, *Vice Pres*
EMP: 50 **EST: 1997**
SALES (est): 2.1MM **Privately Held**
SIC: 7922 Entertainment promotion

(P-18398)
RADFORD STUDIO CENTER INC
Also Called: CBS Studio Center
4024 Radford Ave, Studio City
(91604-2101)
PHONE..............................818 655-5000
Michael Klausman, *President*
Nina Tassler, *Ch of Bd*
Bill Rimpau, *Top Exec*
Jamie Barnett, *Vice Pres*
Esther Walker, *Exec Dir*
EMP: 300
SALES (est): 31.3MM
SALES (corp-wide): 13.7B **Publicly Held**
WEB: www.cbssc.com
SIC: 7922 6512 7999 Television program,
including commercial producers; nonresi-
dential building operators; martial arts
school

HQ: Cbs Broadcasting Inc.
51 W 52nd St
New York NY 10019
212 975-4321

(P-18399)
ROSE BRAND WIPERS INC
11440 Sheldon St, Sun Valley
(91352-1121)
PHONE..................................818 505-6290
Tina Carlin, *Principal*
Victoria Williamson, *Opers Staff*
EMP: 82
SALES (corp-wide): 135.2MM **Privately Held**
SIC: 7922 Costume & scenery design services
PA: Rose Brand Wipers, Inc.
4 Emerson Ln
Secaucus NJ 07094
201 809-1730

(P-18400)
SACRAMENTO THEATRICAL LTG LTD
Also Called: S T L
950 Richards Blvd, Sacramento
(95811-0333)
PHONE..................................916 447-3258
John W Cox, *CEO*
Kaye Newton, *Vice Pres*
Bobbie Odehnal, *Manager*
EMP: 65
SQ FT: 60,000
SALES (est): 6.6MM **Privately Held**
WEB: www.stl-ltd.com
SIC: 7922 5063 Equipment rental, theatrical; lighting fixtures

(P-18401)
SAN DIEGO OPERA ASSOCIATION (PA)
233 A St Ste 500, San Diego (92101-4095)
PHONE..................................619 232-7636
Michael Lowry, *Finance*
Michael Lowery, *Officer*
EMP: 50 EST: 1945
SQ FT: 11,000
SALES: 9.3MM **Privately Held**
SIC: 7922 Opera company

(P-18402)
SAN FRANCISCO BALLET ASSN
455 Franklin St, San Francisco
(94102-4471)
PHONE..................................415 865-2000
Glenn McCoy, *CEO*
Donald B Paterson, *CFO*
J Stuart Francis, *Treasurer*
Jennifer Peterian, *Treasurer*
Nicole Lugtu, *Officer*
▲ EMP: 250
SQ FT: 70,000
SALES: 25.3MM **Privately Held**
SIC: 7922 7911 Ballet production; dance studio & school

(P-18403)
SAN FRANCISCO OPERA ASSN
301 Van Ness Ave, San Francisco
(94102-4509)
PHONE..................................415 861-4008
John A Gunn, *Chairman*
Karl O Mills, *Vice Chairman*
Keith B Geeslin, *President*
David Gockley, *CEO*
Michael Simpson, *CFO*
◆ EMP: 1050 EST: 1932
SALES: 39.5MM **Privately Held**
SIC: 7922 Opera company

(P-18404)
SHOW CALL PRODUCTIONS INC
5212 Lenore Dr, San Diego (92115-1638)
P.O. Box 13333, La Jolla (92039-3333)
PHONE..................................619 602-0656
Gary Zugel, *CEO*
EMP: 400 EST: 2006
SALES (est): 2.6MM **Privately Held**
SIC: 7922 Concert management service

(P-18405)
SOUTH COAST REPERTORY INC
Also Called: SCR
655 Town Center Dr, Costa Mesa
(92626-1918)
P.O. Box 2197 (92628-2197)
PHONE..................................714 708-5500
Martin Benson, *Art Dir*
Terry Schomburg, *COO*
David Krajanowski, *Vice Pres*
Kimberly Uhlman, *Executive*
Lauren Hovey, *Social Dir*
EMP: 60
SQ FT: 40,000
SALES: 9.9MM **Privately Held**
SIC: 7922 Repertory, road or stock companies: theatrical

(P-18406)
STEVE SILVER PRODUCTIONS INC
678 Green St Ste 2, San Francisco
(94133-3846)
PHONE..................................415 421-4284
EMP: 94
SALES (corp-wide): 3.7MM **Privately Held**
SIC: 7922
PA: Silver Steve Productions Inc
470 Columbus Ave Ste 204
San Francisco CA 94133
415 421-4284

(P-18407)
TENNIS CHANNEL INC (HQ)
2850 Ocean Park Blvd # 150, Santa Monica
(90405-6217)
PHONE..................................310 392-1920
Ken Solomon, *CEO*
William Simon, *COO*
EMP: 70
SALES (est): 8.8MM
SALES (corp-wide): 2.7B **Publicly Held**
WEB: www.thetennischannel.com
SIC: 7922 Television program, including commercial producers
PA: Sinclair Broadcast Group, Inc.
10706 Beaver Dam Rd
Hunt Valley MD 21030
410 568-1500

(P-18408)
THINKWELL GROUP INC
2710 Media Center Dr, Los Angeles
(90065-1746)
PHONE..................................818 333-3444
Joseph Zenas, *CEO*
Francois Bergeron, *COO*
Craig Hanna, *Officer*
Francois Girard, *Senior VP*
Kelly Ryner, *Senior VP*
▲ EMP: 75
SQ FT: 23,000
SALES (est): 11MM **Privately Held**
SIC: 7922 7389 Theatrical producers & services; interior design services

(P-18409)
TICKETMASTER ENTERTAINMENT LLC
8800 W Sunset Blvd, West Hollywood
(90069-2105)
PHONE..................................800 653-8000
Ron Bension, *Mng Member*
EMP: 4390
SALES (est): 53.3MM
SALES (corp-wide): 10.3B **Publicly Held**
SIC: 7922 Ticket agency, theatrical; agent or manager for entertainers
PA: Live Nation Entertainment, Inc.
9348 Civic Center Dr Lbby
Beverly Hills CA 90210
310 867-7000

(P-18410)
TICKETSCOM LLC (DH)
Also Called: Tickets.com, Inc.
535 Anton Blvd Ste 250, Costa Mesa
(92626-7694)
PHONE..................................714 327-5400
Joe Choti, *President*
Larry D Witherspoon, *President*
Cristine Hurley, *CFO*
John Walker, *Principal*
Curt Clausen, *Admin Sec*

EMP: 50
SALES: 75MM
SALES (corp-wide): 194.3MM **Privately Held**
SIC: 7922 7372 Ticket agency, theatrical; application computer software
HQ: Mlb Advanced Media, L.P.
75 9th Ave Fl 5
New York NY 10011
212 485-3444

(P-18411)
TRISTAR TELEVISION MUSIC INC
10202 Washington Blvd, Culver City
(90232-3119)
PHONE..................................310 244-4000
Eric Tannenbaum, *President*
EMP: 50
SALES (est): 696.3K
SALES (corp-wide): 80.1B **Privately Held**
WEB: www.paulleydenonline.com
SIC: 7922 Television program, including commercial producers
HQ: Sony Pictures Releasing International Corporation
10202 Washington Blvd
Culver City CA 90232
310 244-4000

(P-18412)
TURNING POINT FOR GOD
Also Called: Turning Point Ministries
10007 Riverford Rd, Lakeside
(92040-2772)
PHONE..................................619 258-3600
David P Jeremiah, *CEO*
Donna Jeremiah, *Admin Sec*
EMP: 55
SALES: 52.6MM **Privately Held**
SIC: 7922 Radio producers

(P-18413)
WILLIAM MORRIS ENDEAVOR
Also Called: William Morris Agency
2624 Military Ave, Los Angeles
(90064-3132)
PHONE..................................310 285-9000
Mark Edkins, *Manager*
EMP: 500
SALES (corp-wide): 53.3MM **Privately Held**
WEB: www.rupaul.com
SIC: 7922 Talent agent, theatrical
PA: William Morris Endeavor Entertainment, Llc
11 Madison Ave Fl 18
New York NY 10010
212 586-5100

(P-18414)
WILLIAM MORRIS ENDEAVOR
Also Called: William Morris Consulting
9601 Wilshire Blvd Fl 3, Beverly Hills
(90210-5219)
PHONE..................................310 285-9000
Chris Newman, *Vice Pres*
Matt Edelman, *Marketing Staff*
EMP: 393
SALES (corp-wide): 53.3MM **Privately Held**
WEB: www.rupaul.com
SIC: 7922 Talent agent, theatrical
PA: William Morris Endeavor Entertainment, Llc
11 Madison Ave Fl 18
New York NY 10010
212 586-5100

(P-18415)
WILLIAM MORRIS ENDEAVOR EN (HQ)
9601 Wilshire Blvd Fl 3, Beverly Hills
(90210-5219)
PHONE..................................310 285-9000
Tom Strickler, *Mng Member*
Peter Klein, *CFO*
Corey Fitelson, *Vice Pres*
Kelly Weiss, *Vice Pres*
Charity Johnson, *Finance*
EMP: 180

SALES (est): 16.4MM
SALES (corp-wide): 53.3MM **Privately Held**
WEB: www.endeavorla.com
SIC: 7922 Theatrical talent & booking agencies
PA: William Morris Endeavor Entertainment, Llc
11 Madison Ave Fl 18
New York NY 10010
212 586-5100

7929 Bands, Orchestras, Actors & Entertainers

(P-18416)
19 ENTERTAINMENT WORLDWIDE LLC
Also Called: 19 Management
401 Wilshire Blvd Lbby, Santa Monica
(90401-1453)
PHONE..................................310 777-1940
Iain Pirie, *President*
Scott Frosch, *CFO*
Maria Diaz, *Finance Dir*
EMP: 60
SALES (est): 2.7MM **Privately Held**
WEB: www.19.co.uk
SIC: 7929 Entertainment service

(P-18417)
51 MINDS ENTERTAINMENT LLC
Also Called: Mindless Entertainment
5200 Lankershim Blvd # 200, North Hollywood (91601-3180)
PHONE..................................323 466-9200
Mark Cronin,
Angela Aguilera, *Vice Pres*
Courtland Cox, *Vice Pres*
Chris Kinsella, *Vice Pres*
Maria Vaznaugh, *Office Mgr*
▼ EMP: 60
SALES (est): 2.8MM
SALES (corp-wide): 2.1B **Privately Held**
WEB: www.51minds.com
SIC: 7929 7812 Entertainers; television film production
HQ: Endemol Usa Holding, Inc.
5161 Lankershim Blvd # 400
North Hollywood CA 91601
310 860-9914

(P-18418)
ANSCHUTZ ENTRMT GROUP INC (HQ)
Also Called: AEG Worldwide
1100 S Flower St, Los Angeles
(90015-2180)
PHONE..................................213 337-5052
Tim Leiweke, *President*
Scott Bosarge, *President*
Sean Ryan, *President*
Chris Wright, *President*
Dan Beckerman, *CFO*
EMP: 168
SALES (est): 53.7MM **Privately Held**
SIC: 7929 Entertainment service

(P-18419)
ARAMARK SPT & ENTRMT GROUP LLC
525 W Santa Clara St, San Jose
(95113-1520)
PHONE..................................408 999-5735
John Heberden, *Principal*
EMP: 106 **Publicly Held**
WEB: www.aramarksports.com
SIC: 7929 Entertainers & entertainment groups
HQ: Aramark Sports And Entertainment Group, Llc
1101 Market St
Philadelphia PA 19107
215 238-3000

(P-18420)
ARAMARK SPT & ENTRMT GROUP LLC
3400 S Figueroa St, Los Angeles
(90007-4348)
PHONE..................................213 740-1224
EMP: 120 **Publicly Held**

SIC: 7929 Entertainment service
HQ: Aramark Sports And Entertainment
Group, Llc
1101 Market St
Philadelphia PA 19107
215 238-3000

(P-18421)
ARAMARK SPT & ENTRMT GROUP LLC
886 Cannery Row, Monterey (93940-1023)
PHONE..............................831 648-9809
EMP: 106 **Publicly Held**
SIC: 7929 Entertainers & entertainment groups
HQ: Aramark Sports And Entertainment
Group, Llc
1101 Market St
Philadelphia PA 19107
215 238-3000

(P-18422)
ARAMARK SPT & ENTRMT GROUP LLC
5001 Great America Pkwy, Santa Clara (95054-1119)
PHONE..............................408 748-7030
Jerry McCarthy, *Manager*
EMP: 100 **Publicly Held**
WEB: www.aramarksports.com
SIC: 7929 Entertainment service
HQ: Aramark Sports And Entertainment
Group, Llc
1101 Market St
Philadelphia PA 19107
215 238-3000

(P-18423)
ARTISTIC ENTRMT SVCS LLC
120 N Aspan Ave, Azusa (91702-4224)
PHONE..............................626 334-9388
Craig Bugajski, *Mng Member*
Kurt Boyer, *Project Mgr*
Julio Gonzalez, *Purch Mgr*
EMP: 60
SALES (est): 10MM **Privately Held**
SIC: 7929 Entertainers & entertainment groups

(P-18424)
BAKERSFIELD SYMPHONY ORCH
1328 34th St Ste A, Bakersfield (93301-2154)
PHONE..............................661 323-7928
Kari Heilman, *Exec Dir*
Audrey Boyle, *Vice Pres*
Nicole Barnett, *Corp Comm Staff*
Oneida Rodenburg, *Manager*
EMP: 75
SALES: 938.1K **Privately Held**
WEB: www.bakersfieldsymphony.org
SIC: 7929 Symphony orchestras

(P-18425)
BENTO BOX ENTERTAINMENT LLC
5161 Lankershim Blvd # 1, North Hollywood (91601-4964)
PHONE..............................818 333-7700
Scott Greenberg,
Anneliese Waddington, *Admin Sec*
Cherri Accetta, *Human Res Dir*
Sydney Bright, *Manager*
EMP: 300
SALES (est): 6.6MM **Privately Held**
SIC: 7929 Entertainment service

(P-18426)
BERKELEY SYMPHONY ORCHESTRA
1942 University Ave # 207, Berkeley (94704-1246)
PHONE..............................510 841-2800
Gary Ginstling, *Exec Dir*
Ian Harwood, *Associate Dir*
Theresa Gabel, *Exec Dir*
James Kleinmann, *Exec Dir*
Rene Mandel, *Exec Dir*
EMP: 50
SALES: 1.3MM **Privately Held**
SIC: 7929 Symphony orchestras

(P-18427)
BONANZA PRODUCTIONS INC
4000 Warner Blvd, Burbank (91522-0001)
P.O. Box 1667 (91507-1667)
PHONE..............................818 954-4212
John A Rogovin, *CEO*
Jonathan Rosenfeld, *Director*
EMP: 1000 EST: 1991
SALES (est): 13.6MM **Privately Held**
SIC: 7929 Entertainment group

(P-18428)
CZND INC
8444 Wilshire Blvd Fl 5, Beverly Hills (90211-3200)
PHONE..............................323 378-6505
Luigi Picarazzi, *President*
EMP: 68
SALES (est): 140.1K **Privately Held**
SIC: 7929 Entertainment service

(P-18429)
DANNY MAHAGNA SHAPPRIE
73280 Highway 111, Palm Desert (92260-3915)
PHONE..............................760 341-5070
Danny Mahagna Shapprie, *Principal*
EMP: 50
SALES (est): 265.2K **Privately Held**
SIC: 7929 Entertainment service

(P-18430)
DELUXE ENTRMT SVCS GROUP INC (PA)
2400 W Empire Ave Ste 200, Burbank (91504-3355)
PHONE..............................818 565-3600
EMP: 98 EST: 1932
SALES (est): 38.3MM **Privately Held**
SIC: 7929

(P-18431)
DOUBLE G PRODUCTIONS LTD
11301 W Olympic Blvd # 115, Los Angeles (90064-1653)
PHONE..............................310 479-0978
Louie Irizarry, *Branch Mgr*
EMP: 74
SALES (corp-wide): 2.3MM **Privately Held**
WEB: www.doubleg.com
SIC: 7929 Disc jockey service
PA: Double G Productions Ltd
1055 Stewart Ave Fl 2
Bethpage NY 11714
516 932-8342

(P-18432)
ENTERTINMENT STUDIOS MEDIA INC (PA)
1925 Century Park E # 1025, Los Angeles (90067-2701)
PHONE..............................310 277-3500
Byron A Folks, *President*
Eric Gould Evp, *CIO*
EMP: 65
SQ FT: 5,000
SALES: 10MM **Privately Held**
SIC: 7929 Entertainers & entertainment groups

(P-18433)
ENTITLEMENT LLC
1236 Euclid St, Santa Monica (90404-1041)
PHONE..............................224 336-2669
Ted Lauck,
EMP: 50
SALES (est): 117.4K **Privately Held**
SIC: 7929 Entertainment service

(P-18434)
FORUM ENTERPRISES INC
333 W Florence Ave, Inglewood (90301-1103)
PHONE..............................310 330-7300
Gerard McCallum, *Exec VP*
EMP: 50
SALES (est): 545.7K **Privately Held**
WEB: www.thelaforum.com
SIC: 7929 4832 Entertainment service; sports

(P-18435)
GENTRY GROUP LLC
555 N Rockingham Ave, Los Angeles (90049-2639)
PHONE..............................310 968-5399
Brandon Kahen,
EMP: 50
SALES (est): 117.4K **Privately Held**
SIC: 7929 Entertainment service

(P-18436)
HOB ENTERTAINMENT LLC
1350 Disneyland Dr, Anaheim (92802)
PHONE..............................714 778-2583
Kristen Kowlminsky, *Branch Mgr*
EMP: 240
SALES (corp-wide): 10.3B **Publicly Held**
WEB: www.hob.ca
SIC: 7929 Entertainment service
HQ: Hob Entertainment, Llc
7060 Hollywood Blvd
Los Angeles CA 90028

(P-18437)
HOB ENTERTAINMENT LLC
8430 W Sunset Blvd, West Hollywood (90069-1910)
PHONE..............................323 848-5100
Arich Berghammer, *Principal*
EMP: 230
SALES (corp-wide): 10.3B **Publicly Held**
WEB: www.hob.ca
SIC: 7929 Entertainment service
HQ: Hob Entertainment, Llc
7060 Hollywood Blvd
Los Angeles CA 90028

(P-18438)
HOB ENTERTAINMENT LLC
1055 5th Ave, San Diego (92101-5101)
PHONE..............................619 299-2583
Jim Biasore, *Manager*
EMP: 220
SALES (corp-wide): 10.3B **Publicly Held**
WEB: www.hob.ca
SIC: 7929 Entertainment service
HQ: Hob Entertainment, Llc
7060 Hollywood Blvd
Los Angeles CA 90028

(P-18439)
HOB ENTERTAINMENT LLC (DH)
Also Called: House of Blues
7060 Hollywood Blvd, Los Angeles (90028-6014)
PHONE..............................323 769-4600
Michael Rapino, *CEO*
Joseph C Kaczorowski, *President*
Peter Cyffka, *Senior VP*
EMP: 172
SQ FT: 53,000
SALES (est): 102MM
SALES (corp-wide): 10.3B **Publicly Held**
WEB: www.hob.ca
SIC: 7929 Entertainment service
HQ: Live Nation Worldwide, Inc.
430 W 15th St
New York NY 10011
917 421-5100

(P-18440)
HOUSE OF BLUES CONCERTS INC (DH)
6255 W Sunset Blvd Fl 16, Los Angeles (90028-7403)
PHONE..............................323 769-4977
Joe Kazoworski, *President*
EMP: 150
SALES (est): 15.5MM
SALES (corp-wide): 10.3B **Publicly Held**
WEB: www.hob.com
SIC: 7929 Entertainers & entertainment groups

(P-18441)
IMPERIAL PROJECT INC
Also Called: Bare Elegance
1947 S Myrtle Ave, Monrovia (91016-4854)
PHONE..............................310 671-3263
Michael Woods, *Treasurer*
David Amos, *President*

EMP: 60
SQ FT: 1,500
SALES (est): 809.1K **Privately Held**
WEB: www.bareelegance.com
SIC: 7929 5813 Entertainment service; night clubs

(P-18442)
INSOMNIAC INC
9441 W Olympic Blvd, Beverly Hills (90212-4541)
PHONE..............................323 874-7020
Pasquale Rotella, *CEO*
Simon Rust Lamb, *CFO*
John Boyle, *Officer*
Meelo Solis, *Executive*
Bunny Eachon, *Creative Dir*
▲ EMP: 86
SALES (est): 6MM **Privately Held**
SIC: 7929 Entertainment service

(P-18443)
INSOMNIAC HOLDINGS LLC
9441 W Olympic Blvd, Beverly Hills (90212-4541)
PHONE..............................323 874-7020
Michael Rapino,
George Chan, *Accounting Mgr*
Pasquale Rotella,
EMP: 125
SQ FT: 5,000
SALES: 120MM
SALES (corp-wide): 10.3B **Publicly Held**
SIC: 7929 Entertainers & entertainment groups
PA: Live Nation Entertainment, Inc.
9348 Civic Center Dr Lbby
Beverly Hills CA 90210
310 867-7000

(P-18444)
ISRAEL POPS ORCHESTRA
4841 Alonzo Ave, Encino (91316-3607)
PHONE..............................818 343-6450
Michael Isaacson, *President*
EMP: 50
SALES (est): 439.4K **Privately Held**
SIC: 7929 Orchestras or bands

(P-18445)
KADEN CASH LLC
15845 Jackson Dr, Fontana (92336-1763)
PHONE..............................818 714-4665
Kevin Buckley,
EMP: 50 EST: 2017
SALES (est): 127.4K **Privately Held**
SIC: 7929 Entertainment service

(P-18446)
LIVE MEDIA LLC
1580 Magnolia Ave, Corona (92879-2073)
PHONE..............................951 279-8877
Tom McCracken,
EMP: 50
SALES (est): 14.5MM
SALES (corp-wide): 100.3MM **Privately Held**
SIC: 7929 Entertainment service
PA: Nep Group, Inc.
2 Beta Dr
Pittsburgh PA 15238
412 826-1414

(P-18447)
LIVE NATION ENTERTAINMENT INC
6255 W Sunset Blvd Fl 16, Los Angeles (90028-7403)
PHONE..............................323 468-1160
Greg Trojan, *Principal*
Nikhil Deshpande, *Info Tech Mgr*
Adolfo Guzman, *QC Mgr*
EMP: 70
SALES (corp-wide): 10.3B **Publicly Held**
SIC: 7929 Entertainers & entertainment groups
PA: Live Nation Entertainment, Inc.
9348 Civic Center Dr Lbby
Beverly Hills CA 90210
310 867-7000

PRODUCTS & SVCS

(P-18448)
LOS ANGELES CHMBER ORCHSTRA
350 S Figueroa St Ste 183, Los Angeles (90071-1117)
PHONE...................213 622-7001
Andrea Laguni, *Exec Dir*
Thomas Mallen, *CFO*
Eva Moravcik, *Executive*
Scott Harrison, *Exec Dir*
Nicole Santos, *Marketing Staff*
EMP: 60
SALES: 5.3MM **Privately Held**
WEB: www.laco.org
SIC: 7929 Orchestras or bands

(P-18449)
LOS ANGELES PHILHARMONIC ASSN (PA)
Also Called: L A Philharmonic
151 S Grand Ave, Los Angeles (90012-3034)
P.O. Box 1951 (90078-1951)
PHONE...................213 972-7300
Deborah Borda, *CEO*
Mike Demartini, *CFO*
David C Bohnett, *Chairman*
Shana Mathur, *Vice Pres*
Alan Wayte, *Admin Sec*
EMP: 2000
SQ FT: 13,467
SALES (est): 169.5MM **Privately Held**
WEB: www.laphil.com
SIC: 7929 Symphony orchestras

(P-18450)
MAKER STUDIOS INC (HQ)
3515 Eastham Dr, Culver City (90232-2440)
PHONE...................310 606-2182
Courtney Holt, *CEO*
Lisa Donovan, *CFO*
Cherie Hurwitz, *Director*
Breanna Carter, *Manager*
Margaret Chang, *Manager*
EMP: 250
SQ FT: 20,000
SALES (est): 23.3MM **Publicly Held**
SIC: 7929 Entertainment service

(P-18451)
MARINE BAND SAN DIEGO
1400 Russell Ave, San Diego (92140-5594)
PHONE...................619 524-1754
Edward Hayes, *Chief*
EMP: 50
SALES (est): 339.7K **Privately Held**
WEB: www.marines.mil
SIC: 7929 Entertainers

(P-18452)
MPC PRODUCTIONS LLC
12035 Killion St, Sherman Oaks (91401)
PHONE...................310 418-8115
Rick Nicolet,
EMP: 75
SALES (est): 176.9K **Privately Held**
SIC: 7929 Entertainment service

(P-18453)
ORCHARD HORROR FILM LLC
15715 Woodvale Rd, Encino (91436-3416)
PHONE...................212 203-6147
Brandon Menchen, *Mng Member*
EMP: 50 EST: 2017
SALES (est): 117.4K **Privately Held**
SIC: 7929 Entertainment service

(P-18454)
PACIFIC SYMPHONY
17620 Fitch Ste 100, Irvine (92614-6081)
PHONE...................714 755-5788
Jjohn Forsyte, *President*
John E Forsyte, *CEO*
Rhonda Halverson, *Vice Pres*
Kelli Frager, *Manager*
EMP: 60
SQ FT: 5,750
SALES: 19MM **Privately Held**
WEB: www.psyo.org
SIC: 7929 Symphony orchestras

(P-18455)
PALA BAND OF MISSION INDIANS
3478 Sunset Dr, Fallbrook (92028-9579)
PHONE...................760 207-2603
Ryan McQueen Rusnell, *Branch Mgr*
EMP: 173 **Privately Held**
SIC: 7929 Entertainers & entertainment groups
PA: Pala Band Of Mission Indians
12196 Pala Mission Rd
Pala CA 92059
760 891-3500

(P-18456)
POP MEDIA NETWORKS LLC (DH)
Also Called: Tvguide.com
5510 Lincoln Blvd Ste 400, Playa Vista (90094-1900)
PHONE...................323 856-4000
Allen Shapiro, *Chairman*
Ryan O'Hara, *President*
Brad Schwartz, *President*
Debra Wichser, *CFO*
David Mandell, *Exec VP*
EMP: 60
SALES (est): 10MM
SALES (corp-wide): 3.2B **Privately Held**
SIC: 7929 7313 7379 Entertainment service; electronic media advertising representatives;
HQ: Lions Gate Entertainment Inc.
2700 Colorado Ave Ste 200
Santa Monica CA 90404
310 449-9200

(P-18457)
SAN BERNARDINO SYMPHONY
198 N Arrowhead Ave 2b, San Bernardino (92408-1011)
PHONE...................909 381-5388
Mary Schnepp, *President*
Charles Bradley, *Exec Dir*
Anne Viricel, *Med Doctor*
EMP: 80
SALES: 514.6K **Privately Held**
WEB: www.sanbernardinosymphony.org
SIC: 7929 Symphony orchestras

(P-18458)
SAN DIEGO SYMPHONY ORCHESTRA
1245 7th Ave, San Diego (92101-4398)
PHONE...................619 235-0800
Edward B Gill, *Exec Dir*
EMP: 110
SALES: 27MM **Privately Held**
SIC: 7929 Symphony orchestras; orchestras or bands

(P-18459)
SAN FRANCISCO SYMPHONY INC (PA)
201 Van Ness Ave, San Francisco (94102-4585)
PHONE...................415 552-8000
Brent Assink, *CEO*
James Kirk, *CFO*
Mark Koenig, *CFO*
Randy Baysinger, *Bd of Directors*
Margo Kieser, *Bd of Directors*
▲ EMP: 400 EST: 1911
SALES: 91.1MM **Privately Held**
SIC: 7929 Symphony orchestras

(P-18460)
SANTA CRUZ COUNTY SYMPHONY
307 Church St, Santa Cruz (95060-3811)
PHONE...................831 462-0553
Mary James, *President*
Jan Derecho, *Exec Dir*
Virginia Wright, *Exec Dir*
EMP: 50
SALES: 1.2MM **Privately Held**
WEB: www.santacruzsymphony.com
SIC: 7929 Symphony orchestras

(P-18461)
SANTA ROSA RNCHRIA GAMING COMM
17225 Jersey Ave, Lemoore (93245-9760)
P.O. Box 668 (93245-0668)
PHONE...................559 924-6948
Abby Ramirez, *Principal*
EMP: 55
SALES (est): 1MM **Privately Held**
SIC: 7929 Entertainment service

(P-18462)
SAS ENTERTAINMENT PARTNERS INC
6224 Greenleaf Ave, Whittier (90601-3528)
PHONE...................213 400-1901
Miles Williams, *President*
EMP: 50
SALES (est): 117.4K **Privately Held**
SIC: 7929 Entertainment service

(P-18463)
SKY ZONE LLC (HQ)
1201 W 5th St Ste T340, Los Angeles (90017-1489)
PHONE...................310 734-0300
Jeffrey Platt, *CEO*
▲ EMP: 59
SALES (est): 11.7MM
SALES (corp-wide): 1.6MM **Privately Held**
SIC: 7929 Entertainment service

(P-18464)
SLEEPY GIANT ENTERTAINMENT INC
3501 Jamboree Rd Ste 5000, Newport Beach (92660-2959)
PHONE...................714 460-4113
Matthew Hannus, *CEO*
David S Lee, *Admin Sec*
◆ EMP: 58
SALES: 1.5MM **Privately Held**
SIC: 7929 Entertainment service

(P-18465)
SOCAL SPORTSNET LLC
100 Park Blvd, San Diego (92101-7405)
PHONE...................619 795-5000
Ron Fowler,
EMP: 600 EST: 2012
SALES (est): 1.2MM **Privately Held**
SIC: 7929 Entertainment service

(P-18466)
SONY PICTURES ENTRMT INC
9336 Washington Blvd, Culver City (90232-2628)
PHONE...................310 202-1234
Margi Bertram, *Manager*
EMP: 500
SALES (corp-wide): 80.1B **Privately Held**
WEB: www.sonypictures.com
SIC: 7929 Entertainers
HQ: Sony Pictures Entertainment, Inc.
10202 Washington Blvd
Culver City CA 90232
310 244-4000

(P-18467)
SONY PICTURES ENTRMT INC
6527 W 82nd St, Los Angeles (90045-2841)
PHONE...................310 244-3558
Kriege Janz, *Branch Mgr*
EMP: 500
SALES (corp-wide): 80.1B **Privately Held**
SIC: 7929 Entertainers
HQ: Sony Pictures Entertainment, Inc.
10202 Washington Blvd
Culver City CA 90232
310 244-4000

(P-18468)
STREAMRAY INC
Also Called: Hotbox
910 E Hamilton Ave Fl 6, Campbell (95008-0655)
PHONE...................408 745-5449
Mallorie Burak, *CEO*
EMP: 315
SALES (est): 697.3K **Privately Held**
SIC: 7929 Entertainment group

(P-18469)
TURTLE ENTERTAINMENT AMERICA
Also Called: Esl
1212 Chestnut St, Burbank (91506-1627)
PHONE...................818 861-7315
Han Park, *President*
Yvette Marinez-Ray, *COO*
Craig Levine, *Exec VP*
Paul Brewer, *Vice Pres*
Kevin Rosenblatt, *Vice Pres*
EMP: 50
SALES (est): 1.8MM
SALES (corp-wide): 2B **Privately Held**
SIC: 7929 Entertainment service
HQ: Turtle Entertainment Gmbh
Schanzenstr. 23
Koln 51063
221 880-4490

(P-18470)
TWENTY MILE PRODUCTIONS LLC
11833 Miss Ave Ste 101, Los Angeles (90025-6135)
PHONE...................412 251-0767
Karen Wacker,
Margaret Ellison,
EMP: 150
SALES (est): 716K **Privately Held**
SIC: 7929 Entertainment group

(P-18471)
UBI SOFT ENTERTAINMENT
625 3rd St Fl 3, San Francisco (94107-1918)
PHONE...................415 547-4000
Yves Guillemot, *President*
Christian Guillemot, *Exec VP*
Chris Early, *Vice Pres*
Victor Fajardo, *Admin Mgr*
Josie MAI, *Planning*
EMP: 51 EST: 2011
SALES (est): 4.5MM
SALES (corp-wide): 1.2B **Privately Held**
SIC: 7929 Entertainers & entertainment groups
PA: Ubisoft Entertainment
107 Avenue Henri Freville
Rennes 35200
299 932-068

(P-18472)
UNIVERSAL MUSIC GROUP INC
Also Called: Verve Music Group
2220 Colorado Ave, Santa Monica (90404-3506)
PHONE...................310 865-4000
Charles Ciongoli, *Exec VP*
Rob Cromar, *President*
James Krents, *Vice Pres*
EMP: 100
SALES (corp-wide): 78.4MM **Privately Held**
SIC: 7929 Entertainment service
HQ: Universal Music Group, Inc.
2220 Colorado Ave
Santa Monica CA 90404
310 865-4000

(P-18473)
US AIRFORCE BAND OF GOLDEN W
551 Waldron St Bldg 240, Travis Afb (94535)
PHONE...................707 424-2263
Michael Manch, *Principal*
EMP: 50
SALES (est): 488.9K **Privately Held**
SIC: 7929 Orchestras or bands

(P-18474)
WALT DISNEY COMPANY
3900 W Alameda Ave Rm 845, Burbank (91505-4316)
PHONE...................818 567-5590
Ramona Barnes, *Principal*
EMP: 2002 **Publicly Held**
SIC: 7929 Entertainment service
PA: The Walt Disney Company
500 S Buena Vista St
Burbank CA 91521

(P-18475)
WERM INVESTMENTS LLC
Also Called: Exchange La
14242 Ventura Blvd # 212, Sherman Oaks
(91423-2771)
PHONE......................................213 627-8070
ADI McBain, *Mng Member*
Camil Sayadeh,
EMP: 50
SALES (est): 297.4K **Privately Held**
SIC: 7929 Entertainment service

7933 Bowling Centers

(P-18476)
3900 WEST LANE BOWL INC
3900 West Ln, Stockton (95204-2436)
PHONE......................................209 466-6100
Richard Ghio, *President*
Rudy Antonini, *Corp Secy*
Correen Edgerly, *Programmer Anys*
EMP: 50
SQ FT: 20,000
SALES (est): 2.1MM **Privately Held**
WEB: www.westlanebowl.net
SIC: 7933 5812 5813 Ten pin center;
American restaurant; beer garden (drink-
ing places)

(P-18477)
AMF BOWLING CENTERS INC
1201 W Beverly Blvd, Montebello
(90640-4142)
PHONE......................................323 728-9161
Norris Runnels, *Manager*
EMP: 50
SALES (corp-wide): 81.2MM **Privately
Held**
WEB: www.kidsports.org
SIC: 7933 7999 Ten pin center; tourist at-
tractions, amusement park concessions &
rides
HQ: Amf Bowling Centers, Inc.
7313 Bell Creek Rd
Mechanicsville VA 23111

(P-18478)
AMF BOWLING CENTERS INC
1819 30th St, Bakersfield (93301-1928)
PHONE......................................661 324-4966
Rick Mossman, *Branch Mgr*
EMP: 50
SALES (corp-wide): 81.2MM **Privately
Held**
WEB: www.kidsports.org
SIC: 7933 7999 Ten pin center; tourist at-
tractions, amusement park concessions &
rides
HQ: Amf Bowling Centers, Inc.
7313 Bell Creek Rd
Mechanicsville VA 23111

(P-18479)
AMF BOWLING CENTERS INC
22771 Centre Dr, Lake Forest
(92630-1747)
PHONE......................................949 770-0055
Darryl Messiah, *Branch Mgr*
EMP: 50
SALES (corp-wide): 81.2MM **Privately
Held**
WEB: www.kidsports.org
SIC: 7933 5813 Ten pin center; bar (drink-
ing places)
HQ: Amf Bowling Centers, Inc.
7313 Bell Creek Rd
Mechanicsville VA 23111

(P-18480)
BDP BOWL INC
Also Called: Classic Bowling Center
900 King Plz, Daly City (94015-4450)
PHONE......................................650 878-0300
Robert Devincenzi, *President*
Richard J Bocci, *Treasurer*
Richard Bocci, *Treasurer*
Matthew Devincenzi, *Business Dir*
Rob Petroni, *General Mgr*
EMP: 50
SQ FT: 50,000

SALES (est): 1.9MM **Privately Held**
WEB: www.classicbowling.com
SIC: 7933 Ten pin center

(P-18481)
BOWLERO CORP
Also Called: Brunswick Covino Lanes
1060 W San Bernardino Rd, Covina
(91722-4160)
PHONE......................................626 339-1286
Javier Guzman, *Manager*
EMP: 53
SALES (corp-wide): 358.9MM **Privately
Held**
SIC: 7933 Bowling centers
PA: Bowlero Corp.
222 W 44th St
New York NY 10036
212 777-2214

(P-18482)
BOWLERO CORP
Also Called: West Covina Lanes
675 S Glendora Ave, West Covina
(91790-3705)
PHONE......................................626 960-3636
Joe Carridoza, *Manager*
EMP: 55
SQ FT: 57,259
SALES (corp-wide): 358.9MM **Privately
Held**
SIC: 7933 Ten pin center
PA: Bowlero Corp.
222 W 44th St
New York NY 10036
212 777-2214

(P-18483)
BOWLERO CORP
Also Called: Brunswick Deer Creks Lnes 213
7930 Haven Ave Ste 101, Rancho Cuca-
monga (91730-3056)
PHONE......................................909 945-9392
Venesa Boudreau, *Assistant VP*
EMP: 50
SALES (corp-wide): 358.9MM **Privately
Held**
SIC: 7933 Ten pin center
PA: Bowlero Corp.
222 W 44th St
New York NY 10036
212 777-2214

(P-18484)
BOWLERO CORP
Also Called: Brunswick Cal Oaks Bowl
40440 California Oaks Rd, Murrieta
(92562-5828)
PHONE......................................951 698-2202
John Tang, *Branch Mgr*
EMP: 50
SALES (corp-wide): 358.9MM **Privately
Held**
SIC: 7933 Ten pin center
PA: Bowlero Corp.
222 W 44th St
New York NY 10036
212 777-2214

(P-18485)
CAL BOWL ENTERPRISES LLC
2500 Carson St, Lakewood (90712-4198)
PHONE......................................562 421-8448
Charles Knistler,
EMP: 50
SALES (est): 836.6K **Privately Held**
SIC: 7933 Bowling centers

(P-18486)
COVINA BOWL INC
675 S Glendora Ave, West Covina
(91790-3705)
PHONE......................................626 339-1286
Leonard A Brutocao, *President*
Angelo Brutocao, *Treasurer*
EMP: 80
SQ FT: 60,000
SALES (est): 1.4MM **Privately Held**
SIC: 7933 5812 5813 7999 Ten pin cen-
ter; American restaurant; drinking places;
billiard parlor

(P-18487)
CRENSHAW BOWLING
Also Called: Palos Verdes Bowl
24600 Crenshaw Blvd, Torrance
(90505-5307)
PHONE......................................310 326-5120
George Brant, *Vice Pres*
Charlotte Melsh, *Marketing Staff*
EMP: 50
SQ FT: 40,000
SALES (est): 1.6MM **Privately Held**
SIC: 7933 5812 5813 Ten pin center;
snack bar; bar (drinking places)

(P-18488)
FOLSOM RECREATION CORP
Also Called: Lake Bowl
511 E Bidwell St, Folsom (95630-3118)
PHONE......................................916 983-4411
Wally Dreher, *President*
Sue Dreher, *Vice Pres*
Dan Dreher, *General Mgr*
Jeremy Dreher, *General Mgr*
Carly Dreher, *Bookkeeper*
EMP: 70
SQ FT: 18,000
SALES (est): 4.1MM **Privately Held**
SIC: 7933 Ten pin center

(P-18489)
FOURTH STREET BOWL
1441 N 4th St, San Jose (95112-4716)
PHONE......................................408 453-5555
Ken Nakatsu, *President*
MAI Shimizu, *Admin Asst*
EMP: 50
SQ FT: 31,450
SALES (est): 3.1MM **Privately Held**
WEB: www.4thstreetbowl.com
SIC: 7933 5813 5812 Bowling centers;
bar (drinking places); coffee shop

(P-18490)
FREMONT SPORTS INC
Also Called: Cloverleaf Bowl
40645 Fremont Blvd Ste 3, Fremont
(94538-4368)
PHONE......................................510 656-4411
James Chambers, *CEO*
Donald F Hillman, *President*
Mike Hillman, *Manager*
EMP: 50
SQ FT: 40,000
SALES (est): 2.4MM **Privately Held**
WEB: www.cloverleafbowl.com
SIC: 7933 5812 5813 Ten pin center; food
bars; bar (drinking places)

(P-18491)
GABLE HOUSE INC
Also Called: Gable House Bowl
22501 Hawthorne Blvd, Torrance
(90505-2509)
PHONE......................................310 378-2265
Michael Cogan, *President*
EMP: 100
SQ FT: 80,000
SALES (est): 4.7MM **Privately Held**
WEB: www.gablehousebowl.com
SIC: 7933 5813 5812 Ten pin center; bar
(drinking places); snack bar

(P-18492)
**LUCKY STRIKE
ENTERTAINMENT LLC**
6801 Hollywood Blvd # 143, Los Angeles
(90028-6138)
PHONE......................................818 933-3752
David Bradley, *General Mgr*
Gail Stoltze, *Vice Pres*
EMP: 87 **Privately Held**
SIC: 7933 Bowling centers
HQ: Lucky Strike Entertainment, Llc
15260 Ventura Blvd # 1110
Sherman Oaks CA 91403
323 467-7776

(P-18493)
**LUCKY STRIKE
ENTERTAINMENT LLC**
15260 Ventura Blvd # 1110, Sherman Oaks
(91403-5346)
PHONE......................................818 933-0872
Mark P'Pool, *Branch Mgr*
EMP: 131 **Privately Held**

(P-18494)
**LUCKY STRIKE
ENTERTAINMENT LLC**
20 City Blvd W Ste G2, Orange
(92868-3131)
PHONE......................................248 374-3420
Ismail Saleem, *Branch Mgr*
EMP: 88 **Privately Held**
SIC: 7933 Ten pin center
HQ: Lucky Strike Entertainment, Llc
15260 Ventura Blvd # 1110
Sherman Oaks CA 91403
323 467-7776

(P-18495)
MCHENRY BOWL INC
3700 Mchenry Ave, Modesto (95356-1597)
PHONE......................................209 571-2695
Garrard Marsh, *President*
Dallas Kadry, *Treasurer*
W Jerry Marsh, *Vice Pres*
Maxine Marsh, *Admin Sec*
EMP: 50
SQ FT: 52,000
SALES (est): 1.6MM **Privately Held**
WEB: www.mchenrybowl.com
SIC: 7933 5813 5941 Ten pin center; bar
(drinking places); bowling equipment &
supplies

(P-18496)
NATIONWIDE THEATRES CORP
Also Called: Cal Coffee Shop
2500 Carson St, Lakewood (90712-4107)
PHONE......................................562 421-8448
Tom Moeller, *Manager*
EMP: 60
SALES (corp-wide): 204.8MM **Privately
Held**
SIC: 7933 5813 5812 Ten pin center;
cocktail lounge; coffee shop
HQ: Nationwide Theatres Corp.
120 N Robertson Blvd Fl 3
Los Angeles CA 90048
310 657-8420

(P-18497)
PINSETTERS INC
Also Called: Country Club Lanes
2600 Watt Ave, Sacramento (95821-6296)
PHONE......................................916 488-7545
Greg Kassis, *Ch of Bd*
Dave Haness, *President*
Jim Kassis, *Corp Secy*
Dave Kassis, *Vice Pres*
Kerry Kassis, *Vice Pres*
EMP: 70
SQ FT: 70,000
SALES (est): 2.7MM **Privately Held**
SIC: 7933 5812 5813 Ten pin center;
snack bar; bar (drinking places)

(P-18498)
SPARE-TIME INC
429 W Lockeford St, Lodi (95240-2058)
PHONE......................................209 371-0241
Dennis Kaufman, *Principal*
EMP: 226
SALES (corp-wide): 37.1MM **Privately
Held**
SIC: 7933 Ten pin center
PA: Spare-Time, Inc.
11344 Coloma Rd Ste 350
Gold River CA 95670
916 859-5910

(P-18499)
**STARS RECREATION CENTER
LP**
155 Browns Valley Pkwy, Vacaville
(95688-3011)
PHONE......................................707 455-7827
Ernest E Sousa, *Partner*
Kenneth Sousa, *Partner*
EMP: 50
SQ FT: 65,000
SALES (est): 2.2MM **Privately Held**
SIC: 7933 Ten pin center

(P-18500)
STRIKES UNLIMITED INC
5681 Lonetree Blvd, Rocklin (95765-3735)
PHONE..................................916 626-3600
Kari Pegram, *CEO*
Kathi Miller, *General Mgr*
Armando Pacheco, *General Mgr*
Prakash Chandra, *Controller*
Nancy Hill, *Bookkeeper*
EMP: 90 EST: 2011
SQ FT: 54,000
SALES (est): 3.5MM Privately Held
SIC: 7933 5812 Ten pin center; eating
places

(P-18501)
**UNITED STTES BOWL
CONGRESS INC**
12895 Arbor Ln, Red Bluff (96080-9387)
PHONE..................................530 527-9049
Fred Zastrow, *Branch Mgr*
EMP: 51
SALES (corp-wide): 32.9MM Privately
Held
SIC: 7933 Ten pin center
PA: United States Bowling Congress, Inc.
621 Six Flags Dr
Arlington TX 76011
817 385-8200

**7941 Professional Sports
Clubs & Promoters**

(P-18502)
**ACE HIGH ENTERTAINNMENT
LLC**
125 Sconce Way, Sacramento
(95838-4744)
PHONE..................................916 243-5515
Rodney Shead, *CEO*
EMP: 50
SALES (est): 403.3K Privately Held
SIC: 7941 5812 7922 Sports field or sta-
dium operator, promoting sports events;
Sushi bar; ethnic food restaurants; Chi-
nese restaurant; theatrical talent & book-
ing agencies

(P-18503)
**ANAHEIM ARENA
MANAGEMENT LLC**
Also Called: AAM
2695 E Katella Ave, Anaheim (92806-5904)
PHONE..................................714 704-2400
Tim Ryan, *President*
Michael Schulman, *Ch of Bd*
Chris Johnston, *President*
Angela Wergechik, *Vice Pres*
Mike Wing, *CIO*
EMP: 600
SQ FT: 106,000
SALES (est): 37.9MM Privately Held
WEB: www.hondacenter.com
SIC: 7941 Sports field or stadium operator,
promoting sports events

(P-18504)
**ANAHEIM DUCKS HOCKEY
CLUB LLC (PA)**
2695 E Katella Ave, Anaheim (92806-5904)
PHONE..................................714 940-2900
Michel Schulman, *Mng Member*
Bob Murray, *Exec VP*
Tim Ryan, *Exec VP*
David McNab, *Senior VP*
Jay Scott, *Vice Pres*
EMP: 82
SALES (est): 12.7MM Privately Held
SIC: 7941 Sports clubs, managers & pro-
moters

(P-18505)
ANGELS BASEBALL LP (PA)
Also Called: Los Angeles Angels of Anaheim
2000 E Gene Autry Way, Anaheim
(92806-6143)
PHONE..................................714 940-2000
Dennis Kuhl, *General Ptnr*
Bill Beverage, *Partner*
Molly Jolly, *Partner*
Richard McClemmy, *Partner*
Tim Mead, *Partner*
EMP: 1000 EST: 1996

SALES (est): 61.7MM Privately Held
SIC: 7941 Baseball club, professional &
semi-professional

(P-18506)
**ANSCHUTZ SO CALIF SPORTS
COMPL**
Also Called: Stop Hop Center
18400 Avalon Blvd Ste 100, Carson
(90746-2180)
PHONE..................................310 630-2000
Kedie Pendolfo,
Anschutz Grp,
EMP: 160
SALES (est): 4.6MM Privately Held
SIC: 7941 Soccer club
HQ: Anschutz Entertainment Group, Inc.
1100 S Flower St
Los Angeles CA 90015
213 337-5052

(P-18507)
**ATHLETICS INVESTMENT
GROUP LLC (PA)**
Also Called: Oakland Athletics
7000 Coliseum Way Ste 3, Oakland
(94621-1917)
P.O. Box 2220 (94621-0120)
PHONE..................................510 638-4900
Lewis N Wolff, *Mng Member*
David Rinetti, *Vice Pres*
Mike Selleck, *Vice Pres*
Billy Beane, *General Mgr*
Carolyn Jones, *Executive Asst*
EMP: 162 EST: 1901
SALES (est): 23.8MM Privately Held
SIC: 7941 Baseball club, professional &
semi-professional

(P-18508)
**BIG LEAGUE DREAMS JURUPA
LLC**
10550 Cntu Gllano Rnch Rd, Mira Loma
(91752-3261)
PHONE..................................951 685-6900
Scott Parks Letellier, *CEO*
Jeffrey Odekirk,
Richard Odekirk,
EMP: 57
SALES (est): 2.9MM Privately Held
SIC: 7941 7999 Sports field or stadium
operator, promoting sports events; recre-
ation center

(P-18509)
**BIG LGUE DRAMS CHINO HILLS
LLC**
16333 Fairfield Ranch Rd, Chino Hills
(91709-8816)
PHONE..................................909 287-6900
Rick Odekirk,
Jeff Odekirk,
EMP: 93
SALES (est): 2.2MM Privately Held
WEB: www.baseballfirst.com
SIC: 7941 Sports field or stadium operator,
promoting sports events

(P-18510)
**BIG LGUE DREAMS
CONSULTING LLC**
2155 Trumble Rd, Perris (92571-9211)
PHONE..................................619 846-8855
EMP: 118
SALES (corp-wide): 45.7MM Privately
Held
SIC: 7941 Sports field or stadium operator,
promoting sports events
PA: Big League Dreams Consulting, Llc
16333 Fairfield Ranch Rd
Chino Hills CA 91709
909 287-1700

(P-18511)
**BIG LGUE DREAMS
CONSULTING LLC**
2100 S Azusa Ave, West Covina
(91792-1507)
PHONE..................................626 839-1100
Jeffrey Odekirk, *Principal*
EMP: 118
SALES (corp-wide): 45.7MM Privately
Held
SIC: 7941 Sports field or stadium operator,
promoting sports events

PA: Big League Dreams Consulting, Llc
16333 Fairfield Ranch Rd
Chino Hills CA 91709
909 287-1700

(P-18512)
BIG3 BASKETBALL LLC
644 S Figueroa St, Los Angeles
(90017-3411)
PHONE..................................213 417-2013
Jeff Kwatinetz, *CEO*
O'Shea Jackson Sr, *Principal*
EMP: 67
SALES (est): 2.7MM Privately Held
SIC: 7941 Basketball club

(P-18513)
CAA SPORTS LLC (HQ)
2000 Avenue Of The Stars # 100, Los An-
geles (90067-4705)
PHONE..................................424 288-2000
Michael A Rubel,
EMP: 67
SALES (est): 12.5MM
SALES (corp-wide): 112.7MM Privately
Held
SIC: 7941 Sports promotion
PA: Creative Artists Agency, Llc
2000 Avenue Of The Stars # 100
Los Angeles CA 90067
424 288-2000

(P-18514)
**CHARGERS FOOTBALL
COMPANY LLC (PA)**
Also Called: Los Angeles Chargers
3333 Susan St, Costa Mesa (92626-1632)
P.O. Box 609609, San Diego (92160-9609)
PHONE..................................619 280-2121
Dean A Spanos, *President*
Jeanne Bonk, *CFO*
Alex Spanos, *Chairman*
Alexander G Spanos, *Bd of Directors*
Jeanne M Bonk, *Exec VP*
EMP: 70
SALES (est): 15.4MM Privately Held
SIC: 7941 Football club

(P-18515)
CITY OF GLENDALE
541 W Chevy Chase Dr, Glendale
(91204-1813)
PHONE..................................818 548-3950
Daniel Hardgrove, *Manager*
EMP: 80 Privately Held
WEB: www.glendaleca.com
SIC: 7941 9111 Sports clubs, managers &
promoters; mayors' offices
PA: City Of Glendale
141 N Glendale Ave Fl 2
Glendale CA 91206
818 548-2085

(P-18516)
COTO DE CAZA GOLF CLUB INC
25291 Vista Del Verde, Trabuco Canyon
(92679-4900)
PHONE..................................949 766-7886
Jack Deal, *Director*
Marc Chasman, *Director*
EMP: 135
SALES (est): 2.6MM
SALES (corp-wide): 11.2MM Privately
Held
WEB: www.coto-de-caza.com
SIC: 7941 5813 7992 7991 Professional
& semi-professional sports clubs; drinking
places; public golf courses; physical fit-
ness facilities; eating places
PA: Coto De Caza Limited
24800 Chrisanta Dr
Mission Viejo CA
-

(P-18517)
**FORTY NINERS FOOTBALL CO
LLC**
Also Called: San Francisco 49ers
4949 Mrie P Debartolo Way, Santa Clara
(95054-1156)
PHONE..................................408 562-4949
Denise Debartolo York, *Principal*
Brano Perkovich, *Ch Invest Ofcr*
Keena Turner, *Vice Pres*
Tom Gamble, *Executive*
Keith Yanagi, *Executive*

PA: Big League Dreams Consulting, Llc
16333 Fairfield Ranch Rd
Chino Hills CA 91709
909 287-1700

EMP: 99
SALES (est): 13.6MM Privately Held
SIC: 7941 Football club

(P-18518)
FOX BSB HOLDCO INC
Also Called: Dodger Stadium
1000 Vin Scully Ave, Los Angeles
(90090-1112)
PHONE..................................323 224-1500
Steve Soboroff, *Vice Chairman*
Jamie McCourt, *Vice Chairman*
Ron Wheeler, *CEO*
Dannis Mannion, *COO*
Peter Wilhelm, *CFO*
EMP: 5182
SQ FT: 20,000
SALES (est): 155.1MM
SALES (corp-wide): 706.7MM Privately
Held
WEB: www.ladodgers.com
SIC: 7941 Baseball club, professional &
semi-professional
PA: Guggenheim Partners, Llc
330 Madison Ave Rm 201
New York NY 10017
212 739-0700

(P-18519)
**GOLDEN STATE WARRIORS
LLC**
1011 Broadway, Oakland (94607-4027)
PHONE..................................510 986-2200
Christopher Cohan, *Mng Member*
Mike Kitts, *Partner*
Jennifer Cabalquinto, *CFO*
Chip Bowers, *Chief Mktg Ofcr*
John Beaven, *Vice Pres*
EMP: 100 EST: 1962
SALES (est): 16.4MM Privately Held
WEB: www.gs-warriors.com
SIC: 7941 Basketball club

(P-18520)
**HOTROLLERGIRL
PRODUCTIONS**
11890 Silver Spur St, Ojai (93023-4181)
PHONE..................................530 521-2745
Kristin Longstreet, *Owner*
EMP: 100 EST: 2015
SALES (est): 377.6K Privately Held
SIC: 7941 7231 7221 Stadium event op-
erator services; beauty shops; photogra-
pher, still or video

(P-18521)
**INLAND EMPRE 66ERS BSEBLL
CLB**
280 S E St, San Bernardino (92401-2009)
PHONE..................................909 888-9922
David Elmore, *CEO*
Donna Tuttle, *President*
Jhon Fonsaker, *CFO*
John Fonseca, *Controller*
Matt Kowallis, *Mktg Dir*
EMP: 110
SQ FT: 600
SALES (est): 5.4MM
SALES (corp-wide): 44.4MM Privately
Held
WEB: www.ie66ers.com
SIC: 7941 Baseball club, professional &
semi-professional
PA: The Elmore Group Ltd
19 N Grant St Ste 2
Hinsdale IL
630 325-6228

(P-18522)
**KINGS ARENA LTD
PARTNERSHIP**
Also Called: Maloof Sport Entertainment
1 Sports Pkwy, Sacramento (95834-2300)
PHONE..................................916 928-0000
Gavin Maloof, *Managing Prtnr*
John Rinehart, *Partner*
John Thomas, *Partner*
EMP: 60 EST: 1992
SALES (est): 7.1MM Privately Held
SIC: 7941 Boxing & wrestling arena

(P-18523)
LA SPORTS PROPERTIES INC
Also Called: Los Angeles Clippers
1212 S Flower St Fl 5, Los Angeles
(90015-2123)
PHONE...................213 742-7500
Dick Parsons, *CEO*
Andrew Roeser, *Exec VP*
EMP: 195
SQ FT: 5,000
SALES (est): 15.1MM **Privately Held**
WEB: www.clippers.com
SIC: 7941 Basketball club

(P-18524)
LOS ANGELES DODGERS LLC
1000 Vin Scully Ave, Los Angeles
(90090-1112)
PHONE...................323 224-1507
Stan Kasten, *President*
EMP: 1360
SALES (est): 4.2MM **Privately Held**
SIC: 7941 Stadium event operator services

(P-18525)
LOS ANGELES LAKERS INC
Also Called: La Lakers
2275 E Mariposa Ave, El Segundo
(90245-5029)
PHONE...................310 426-6000
Jeanie Buss, *President*
Joseph McCormack, *Senior VP*
Kiesha Nix, *Exec Dir*
Ron Rockoff, *Exec Dir*
Alison Bogli, *Senior Mgr*
EMP: 150
SQ FT: 12,000
SALES (est): 1.3MM **Privately Held**
WEB: www.lakers.com
SIC: 7941 Basketball club

(P-18526)
LOS ANGELES RAMS LLC (PA)
Also Called: St Louis Rams
29899 Agoura Rd, Agoura Hills
(91301-2493)
PHONE...................314 982-7267
E Stanley Kroenke, *General Ptnr*
Lucia Rodriguez, *Owner*
Chip Rosenbloom, *Owner*
Kevin Demoff, *COO*
Les Snead, *General Mgr*
EMP: 100
SALES (est): 26.6MM **Privately Held**
WEB: www.stlouisrams.com
SIC: 7941 Football club

(P-18527)
LOS ANGLES KINGS HOCKEY CLB LP
555 N Nash St, El Segundo (90245-2818)
P.O. Box 912 (90245-0912)
PHONE...................310 535-4502
Dean Lombardi, *General Mgr*
Kelly Cheeseman, *COO*
Tiffany Frost, *Executive Asst*
Robyn Dutton, *Marketing Staff*
Ashley Grossman, *Sales Staff*
EMP: 119 **Privately Held**
WEB: www.lakings.com
SIC: 7941 Ice hockey club
PA: The Los Angeles Kings Hockey Club LP
800 W Olympic Blvd
Los Angeles CA 90015

(P-18528)
LOS ANGLES KINGS HOCKEY CLB LP (PA)
Also Called: L A Kings
800 W Olympic Blvd, Los Angeles
(90015-1360)
PHONE...................888 546-4752
Toll Free:...................888
Timothy Leiweke, *Partner*
Dan Beckerman, *CFO*
Joe Leibfried, *Vice Pres*
Johnathan Lowe, *Vice Pres*
Scott Servetnick, *Executive*
EMP: 120
SALES (est): 3.3MM **Privately Held**
WEB: www.lakings.com
SIC: 7941 Ice hockey club

(P-18529)
MANDALAY SPORTS ENTRMT LLC (PA)
Also Called: Mandalay Baseball Properties
4751 Wilshire Blvd Fl 3, Los Angeles
(90010-3844)
PHONE...................323 549-4300
Hank Stickney, *CEO*
Anthony Lott, *Ch of Bd*
Peter Guber, *CEO*
Jimmy Bailey, *CFO*
Jason Berman, *Vice Pres*
EMP: 72
SALES (est): 7.2MM **Privately Held**
SIC: 7941 Sports clubs, managers & promoters

(P-18530)
PADRES LP
Also Called: San Diego Padres
100 Park Blvd Petco Park, San Diego
(92101)
P.O. Box 122000 (92112-2000)
PHONE...................619 795-5000
Mike Dee,
Ronda Sedillo,
Katie Jackson, *Director*
Ellen Lopresti, *Manager*
Nicole Miller, *Manager*
EMP: 1100
SQ FT: 3,000
SALES (est): 398.6K **Privately Held**
SIC: 7941 Baseball club, professional & semi-professional

(P-18531)
RIVER CY BASBAL INV GROUP LLC (PA)
400 Ball Park Dr, West Sacramento
(95691-2824)
PHONE...................916 376-4700
Art Savage,
Alan Ledford,
Dan Vistica,
EMP: 60
SALES (est): 2.8MM **Privately Held**
SIC: 7941 7999 6512 Baseball club, professional & semi-professional; concession operator; nonresidential building operators

(P-18532)
SACRAMENTO RIVER CATS BASEBALL
400 Ball Park Dr, West Sacramento
(95691-2824)
PHONE...................916 376-4700
Art Savage,
Chip Maxson, *General Mgr*
Angela Kroeker, *Executive Asst*
Javier Navarro, *Engineer*
Madeline Strika, *Controller*
EMP: 50
SALES (est): 6.2MM
SALES (corp-wide): 2.8MM **Privately Held**
WEB: www.rivercats.net
SIC: 7941 Baseball club, professional & semi-professional
PA: River City Baseball Investment Group Llc
400 Ball Park Dr
West Sacramento CA 95691
916 376-4700

(P-18533)
SAN FRANCISCO FORTY NINERS (PA)
4949 Mrie P Debartolo Way, Santa Clara
(95054-1156)
PHONE...................408 562-4949
Denise Debartolo York, *Ch of Bd*
Peter Harris, *President*
Larry Macneil, *CFO*
Denise York, *Bd of Directors*
Robert Alberino, *Vice Pres*
EMP: 120
SQ FT: 50,000
SALES (est): 164.5MM **Privately Held**
WEB: www.sf49ers.com
SIC: 7941 Football club

(P-18534)
SAN JOSE SHARKS LLC
Also Called: HP Pavilion At San Jose
525 W Santa Clara St, San Jose
(95113-1500)
PHONE...................408 999-6810
Greg Jamison, *President*
Neda Tabatabaie, *Vice Pres*
Jeenette Miller, *Administration*
Jay Shulist, *Opers Mgr*
Patrick Doherty, *Opers Staff*
EMP: 170
SALES (est): 15.1MM **Privately Held**
WEB: www.hppsj.com
SIC: 7941 Ice hockey club

(P-18535)
SHARKS SPORTS & ENTRMT LLC
Also Called: SSE Merchandise
525 W Santa Clara St, San Jose
(95113-1520)
PHONE...................408 287-7070
Hasso Plattner, *Mng Member*
Charles Faas, *Exec VP*
Flavil Hampsten, *Exec VP*
Rich Sotelo, *Vice Pres*
Rebeca Davichick, *Executive Asst*
EMP: 800
SALES (est): 31.9MM **Privately Held**
SIC: 7941 Sports field or stadium operator, promoting sports events

(P-18536)
UNITED STTES OLYMPIC COMMITTEE
Also Called: Arco Olympic Training Center
2800 Olympic Pkwy, Chula Vista
(91915-6002)
PHONE...................619 656-1500
Tracie Lamb, *Director*
EMP: 50
SALES (corp-wide): 336MM **Privately Held**
WEB: www.usoc.org
SIC: 7941 Manager of individual professional athletes
PA: United States Olympic Committee Inc
1 Olympic Plz
Colorado Springs CO 80903
719 632-5551

7948 Racing & Track Operations

(P-18537)
CALIFORNIA SPEEDWAY CORP
Also Called: Auto Club Speedway
9300 Cherry Ave, Fontana (92335-2562)
PHONE...................909 429-5000
William Miller, *President*
Ray Wilkings, *Vice Pres*
Erin Macdonald, *Executive*
Erin Fernandez, *Accountant*
Chastain Navarro, *Opers Staff*
EMP: 50 **EST:** 1994
SALES (est): 4.8MM
SALES (corp-wide): 671.4MM **Publicly Held**
SIC: 7948 Automotive race track operation
HQ: 88 Corporation
1801 W Intl Speedway Blvd
Daytona Beach FL 32114
386 254-2700

(P-18538)
CHURCHILL DOWNS INCORPORATED
800 W El Camino Real # 400, Mountain View (94040-2589)
PHONE...................502 638-3879
Ted Gay, *President*
EMP: 900
SALES (corp-wide): 882.6MM **Publicly Held**
SIC: 7948 7993 Race track operation; thoroughbred horse racing; gambling machines, coin-operated
PA: Churchill Downs Incorporated
600 N Hurstbourne Pkwy # 400
Louisville KY 40222
502 636-4400

(P-18539)
DEL MAR THOROUGHBRED CLUB
Also Called: Surfside Race Place At Del Mar
2260 Jimmy Durante Blvd, Del Mar
(92014-2216)
P.O. Box 700 (92014-0700)
PHONE...................858 755-1141
Joe Harper, *President*
Mike Ernst, *CFO*
Lori Hall, *Officer*
Craig Dado, *Vice Pres*
Craig Fravel, *Vice Pres*
▲ **EMP:** 400 **EST:** 1970
SALES (est): 37.7MM **Privately Held**
WEB: www.dmtc.com
SIC: 7948 Thoroughbred horse racing

(P-18540)
LOS ANGELES TURF CLUB INC (DH)
Also Called: Santa Anita Park
285 W Huntington Dr, Arcadia
(91007-3439)
P.O. Box 60014 (91066-6014)
PHONE...................626 574-6330
Gregory C Avioli, *CEO*
Frank Stronach, *Ch of Bd*
George Haines II, *President*
Sherwood Chillingworth, *Exec VP*
Frank Demarco Jr, *Vice Pres*
▲ **EMP:** 168 **EST:** 1964
SALES (est): 33.4MM
SALES (corp-wide): 38.9B **Privately Held**
WEB: www.santaanita.com
SIC: 7948 Horse race track operation
HQ: Magna Car Top Systems Of America, Inc.
2725 Commerce Pkwy
Auburn Hills MI 48326
248 836-4500

(P-18541)
NATIONAL HOT ROD ASSOCIATION (PA)
Also Called: Nhra
2035 E Financial Way, Glendora
(91741-4602)
P.O. Box 5555 (91740-0950)
PHONE...................626 914-4761
Wally Parks, *Director*
Tom Compton, *President*
Richard Wells, *Admin Sec*
EMP: 200 **EST:** 1951
SQ FT: 30,000
SALES: 99.2MM **Privately Held**
WEB: www.nhra.com
SIC: 7948 2711 2741 Automotive race track operation; newspapers: publishing only, not printed on site; miscellaneous publishing

(P-18542)
PACIFIC RACING ASSOCIATION
Also Called: Golden Gate Fields
1100 Eastshore Hwy, Albany (94710-1002)
P.O. Box 6027 (94706-0027)
PHONE...................510 559-7300
Frank Stronach, *President*
TW Johnson, *Security Dir*
Mary Hile, *Admin Asst*
Juan Leon, *Info Tech Mgr*
Bob Hemmer, *Analyst*
EMP: 140
SALES: 63MM **Privately Held**
WEB: www.goldengatefields.com
SIC: 7948 Horses, racing

(P-18543)
PHILIP DAMATO RACING LLC
28202 Palmada, Mission Viejo
(92692-1422)
PHONE...................949 830-7027
Philip D'Amato,
EMP: 55 **EST:** 2014
SALES (est): 227.3K **Privately Held**
SIC: 7948 Horses, racing

(P-18544)
SMISC HOLDINGS
Hwy 121, Sonoma (95476)
PHONE...................707 938-8448
Steve Page, *Manager*
EMP: 50

SALES (corp-wide): 453.5MM **Publicly Held**
SIC: 7948 Motor vehicle racing & drivers
HQ: Smisc Holdings, Llc
  5239 Zmax Blvd
  Harrisburg NC 28075
  704 455-9453

(P-18545)
SPEEDWAY SONOMA LLC
Also Called: Infineon Raceway
Hwy 37 N, Sonoma (95476)
PHONE..............................707 938-8448
Bruton Smith,
Sarah Grasal,
▲ EMP: 60
SALES (est): 4.3MM
SALES (corp-wide): 453.5MM **Publicly Held**
WEB: www.infineonraceway.com
SIC: 7948 Automotive race track operation
HQ: Speedway Motorsports, Inc.
  5555 Concord Pkwy S
  Concord NC 28027

7991 Physical Fitness Facilities

(P-18546)
2 G FITNESS LLC
Also Called: Studio By Clubsport, The
730 Camino Ramon Ste 200, Danville
(94526-4263)
PHONE..............................925 838-9200
Patrick J O'Brien, *Mng Member*
Steve Gilmour, *Owner*
Pj Bunce, *Manager*
EMP: 62
SALES (est): 1.1MM
SALES (corp-wide): 191.7MM **Privately Held**
SIC: 7991 Physical fitness facilities
PA: Leisure Sports, Inc.
  4670 Willow Rd Ste 100
  Pleasanton CA 94588
  925 600-1966

(P-18547)
24 HOUR FITNESS USA INC
Also Called: Folsom Sport Club
1006 Riley St, Folsom (95630-3266)
PHONE..............................916 984-1924
Doug Coelho, *Manager*
Travis Owens, *Manager*
EMP: 50
SALES (corp-wide): 535.4MM **Privately Held**
SIC: 7991 Health club
HQ: 24 Hour Fitness Usa, Inc.
  12647 Alcosta Blvd # 500
  San Ramon CA 94583
  925 543-3100

(P-18548)
24 HOUR FITNESS USA INC
39300 Paseo Padre Pkwy, Fremont
(94538-1629)
PHONE..............................510 795-6666
Tammy Egan, *Manager*
EMP: 50
SALES (corp-wide): 535.4MM **Privately Held**
SIC: 7991 Health club
HQ: 24 Hour Fitness Usa, Inc.
  12647 Alcosta Blvd # 500
  San Ramon CA 94583
  925 543-3100

(P-18549)
24 HOUR FITNESS USA INC
5964 La Place Ct, Carlsbad (92008-8829)
P.O. Box 2409 (92018-2409)
PHONE..............................760 918-4790
Geoff Singer, *Branch Mgr*
Jerry Mc Cauley, *Manager*
EMP: 59
SALES (corp-wide): 535.4MM **Privately Held**
WEB: www.extremephysiques.net
SIC: 7991 Health club

HQ: 24 Hour Fitness Usa, Inc.
  12647 Alcosta Blvd # 500
  San Ramon CA 94583
  925 543-3100

(P-18550)
24 HOUR FITNESS USA INC
Also Called: Boulder Active Club
1265 Laurel Tree Ln # 100, Carlsbad
(92011-4221)
PHONE..............................760 602-5001
S Woodard, *Principal*
EMP: 80
SALES (corp-wide): 535.4MM **Privately Held**
SIC: 7991 Health club
HQ: 24 Hour Fitness Usa, Inc.
  12647 Alcosta Blvd # 500
  San Ramon CA 94583
  925 543-3100

(P-18551)
24 HOUR FITNESS USA INC
Also Called: Beverly Hills Active Club
9911 W Pico Blvd Ste A, Los Angeles
(90035-2708)
PHONE..............................310 553-7600
Julian Jekines, *Manager*
EMP: 60
SALES (corp-wide): 535.4MM **Privately Held**
SIC: 7991 Health club
HQ: 24 Hour Fitness Usa, Inc.
  12647 Alcosta Blvd # 500
  San Ramon CA 94583
  925 543-3100

(P-18552)
24 HOUR FITNESS USA INC
Also Called: Pasadena Sport Club
525 E Colorado Blvd Bsmt, Pasadena
(91101-5229)
PHONE..............................626 795-7121
Mike Priebe, *General Mgr*
EMP: 55
SALES (corp-wide): 535.4MM **Privately Held**
SIC: 7991 Health club
HQ: 24 Hour Fitness Usa, Inc.
  12647 Alcosta Blvd # 500
  San Ramon CA 94583
  925 543-3100

(P-18553)
24 HOUR FITNESS USA INC
Also Called: Rancho Cucamonga Sport Club
11787 Foothill Blvd, Rancho Cucamonga
(91730-3907)
PHONE..............................909 944-1000
Bobby Serrano, *Branch Mgr*
EMP: 100
SALES (corp-wide): 535.4MM **Privately Held**
SIC: 7991 Health club
HQ: 24 Hour Fitness Usa, Inc.
  12647 Alcosta Blvd # 500
  San Ramon CA 94583
  925 543-3100

(P-18554)
24 HOUR FITNESS USA INC
Also Called: West Hollywood Sport Club
8612 Santa Monica Blvd, West Hollywood
(90069-4110)
PHONE..............................310 652-7440
Robin Morris, *Manager*
EMP: 50
SALES (corp-wide): 535.4MM **Privately Held**
SIC: 7991 Health club
HQ: 24 Hour Fitness Usa, Inc.
  12647 Alcosta Blvd # 500
  San Ramon CA 94583
  925 543-3100

(P-18555)
24 HOUR FITNESS USA INC
Also Called: Costa Mesa Sport Club
555 W 19th St, Costa Mesa (92627-2753)
PHONE..............................949 650-3600
Andy Breton, *Manager*
EMP: 85
SALES (corp-wide): 535.4MM **Privately Held**
SIC: 7991 Health club

HQ: 24 Hour Fitness Usa, Inc.
  12647 Alcosta Blvd # 500
  San Ramon CA 94583
  925 543-3100

(P-18556)
24 HOUR FITNESS USA INC
(HQ)
12647 Alcosta Blvd # 500, San Ramon
(94583-4436)
P.O. Box 2689, Carlsbad (92018-2689)
PHONE..............................925 543-3100
Chris Roussos, *CEO*
Frank Napolitano, *President*
Patrick Flanagan, *CFO*
▲ EMP: 183
SALES (est): 535.4MM **Privately Held**
WEB: www.extremephysiques.net
SIC: 7991 Health club
PA: 24 Hour Fitness Worldwide, Inc.
  12647 Alcosta Blvd # 500
  San Ramon CA 94583
  925 543-3100

(P-18557)
24 HOUR FITNESS USA INC
Also Called: Anaheim Gateway Sport Club
1430 N Lemon St, Anaheim (92801-1200)
PHONE..............................714 525-9924
Dalia Shoham, *Manager*
EMP: 50
SALES (corp-wide): 535.4MM **Privately Held**
SIC: 7991 Health club
HQ: 24 Hour Fitness Usa, Inc.
  12647 Alcosta Blvd # 500
  San Ramon CA 94583
  925 543-3100

(P-18558)
24 HOUR FITNESS USA INC
Also Called: Chula Vista Active Club
1660 Broadway Ste 19, Chula Vista
(91911-4857)
PHONE..............................619 425-6600
Louis Carranza, *Manager*
EMP: 65
SALES (corp-wide): 535.4MM **Privately Held**
SIC: 7991 Health club
HQ: 24 Hour Fitness Usa, Inc.
  12647 Alcosta Blvd # 500
  San Ramon CA 94583
  925 543-3100

(P-18559)
24 HOUR FITNESS USA INC
Also Called: Glendale Super-Sport Club
450 N Brand Blvd Ste 100, Glendale
(91203-2345)
PHONE..............................818 247-4334
David Crisalli, *Branch Mgr*
EMP: 100
SALES (corp-wide): 535.4MM **Privately Held**
SIC: 7991 Health club
HQ: 24 Hour Fitness Usa, Inc.
  12647 Alcosta Blvd # 500
  San Ramon CA 94583
  925 543-3100

(P-18560)
24 HOUR FITNESS USA INC
Also Called: Citrus Heights Sport Club
12647 Alcosta Blvd # 500, San Ramon
(94583-4436)
PHONE..............................916 722-7588
Tom Hatfield, *Director*
EMP: 70
SALES (corp-wide): 535.4MM **Privately Held**
SIC: 7991 Health club
HQ: 24 Hour Fitness Usa, Inc.
  12647 Alcosta Blvd # 500
  San Ramon CA 94583
  925 543-3100

(P-18561)
24 HOUR FITNESS USA INC
Also Called: Santa Monica Sport Club
2929 31st St, Santa Monica (90405-3036)
PHONE..............................310 450-4464
Tina Rodriguez, *Manager*
EMP: 98

SALES (corp-wide): 535.4MM **Privately Held**
SIC: 7991 Health club
HQ: 24 Hour Fitness Usa, Inc.
  12647 Alcosta Blvd # 500
  San Ramon CA 94583
  925 543-3100

(P-18562)
24 HOUR FITNESS USA INC
Also Called: Foothill Ranch Sport Club
26781 Rancho Pkwy, Lake Forest
(92630-8706)
PHONE..............................949 830-4213
Rick Roe, *Manager*
EMP: 60
SALES (corp-wide): 535.4MM **Privately Held**
SIC: 7991 Health club
HQ: 24 Hour Fitness Usa, Inc.
  12647 Alcosta Blvd # 500
  San Ramon CA 94583
  925 543-3100

(P-18563)
24 HOUR FITNESS USA INC
Also Called: San Mateo Sport Club
500 El Camino Real, Burlingame
(94010-5159)
PHONE..............................650 343-7922
Paul Draubot, *Branch Mgr*
EMP: 50
SALES (corp-wide): 535.4MM **Privately Held**
SIC: 7991 Health club
HQ: 24 Hour Fitness Usa, Inc.
  12647 Alcosta Blvd # 500
  San Ramon CA 94583
  925 543-3100

(P-18564)
24 HOUR FITNESS USA INC
1640 Camino Del Rio N # 315, San Diego
(92108-1525)
PHONE..............................619 294-2424
Denver Warth, *Manager*
EMP: 50
SALES (corp-wide): 535.4MM **Privately Held**
SIC: 7991 Health club
HQ: 24 Hour Fitness Usa, Inc.
  12647 Alcosta Blvd # 500
  San Ramon CA 94583
  925 543-3100

(P-18565)
24 HOUR FITNESS USA INC
Also Called: Canoga Park/West Hills Club
6653 Fallbrook Ave, Canoga Park
(91307-3520)
PHONE..............................818 887-2582
Nichole Lorenz, *Branch Mgr*
EMP: 68
SALES (corp-wide): 535.4MM **Privately Held**
SIC: 7991 Health club
HQ: 24 Hour Fitness Usa, Inc.
  12647 Alcosta Blvd # 500
  San Ramon CA 94583
  925 543-3100

(P-18566)
24 HOUR FITNESS USA INC
Also Called: Whittier Active Club
10125 Whittwood Dr, Whittier
(90603-2314)
PHONE..............................562 943-3771
Bryan Mirchof, *Manager*
EMP: 60
SALES (corp-wide): 535.4MM **Privately Held**
SIC: 7991 Health club
HQ: 24 Hour Fitness Usa, Inc.
  12647 Alcosta Blvd # 500
  San Ramon CA 94583
  925 543-3100

(P-18567)
24 HOUR FITNESS USA INC
Also Called: Walnut Creek Active Club
2033 N Main St Ste 110, Walnut Creek
(94596-3737)
PHONE..............................925 930-7900
Scott Pendel, *General Mgr*
EMP: 60

▲ = Import ▼=Export
◆ =Import/Export

SALES (corp-wide): 535.4MM **Privately Held**
WEB: www.extremephysiques.net
SIC: 7991 Health club
HQ: 24 Hour Fitness Usa, Inc.
    12647 Alcosta Blvd # 500
    San Ramon CA 94583
    925 543-3100

(P-18568)
24 HOUR FITNESS USA INC
Also Called: Mountain View Sport Club
550 Showers Dr Ste 1, Mountain View
(94040-1438)
PHONE..................................650 941-2268
Oshkar Gobani, *General Mgr*
EMP: 50
SALES (corp-wide): 535.4MM **Privately Held**
SIC: 7991 Health club
HQ: 24 Hour Fitness Usa, Inc.
    12647 Alcosta Blvd # 500
    San Ramon CA 94583
    925 543-3100

(P-18569)
24 HOUR FITNESS USA INC
Also Called: Rancho Penasquitos Sport Club
10025 Carmel Mountain Rd, San Diego
(92129-3229)
PHONE..................................858 538-4400
Connie Lauda, *Manager*
EMP: 50
SALES (corp-wide): 535.4MM **Privately Held**
SIC: 7991 Health club
HQ: 24 Hour Fitness Usa, Inc.
    12647 Alcosta Blvd # 500
    San Ramon CA 94583
    925 543-3100

(P-18570)
24 HOUR FITNESS USA INC
Also Called: Hayward Active Club
24727 Amador St, Hayward (94544-1801)
PHONE..................................510 264-3275
Stephanie Johnson, *Manager*
EMP: 75
SALES (corp-wide): 535.4MM **Privately Held**
SIC: 7991 Health club
HQ: 24 Hour Fitness Usa, Inc.
    12647 Alcosta Blvd # 500
    San Ramon CA 94583
    925 543-3100

(P-18571)
24 HOUR FITNESS WORLDWIDE INC (PA)
12647 Alcosta Blvd # 500, San Ramon
(94583-4436)
PHONE..................................925 543-3100
Brenden Egen, *Principal*
David Galvan, *Vice Pres*
EMP: 100 EST: 2001
SALES (est): 535.4MM **Privately Held**
WEB: www.24hourfitness.com
SIC: 7991 Health club

(P-18572)
24 HOUR FITNESS WORLDWIDE INC
1601 Pcf Cast Hwy Ste 100, Hermosa Beach (90254)
PHONE..................................310 374-4524
Tommy Cassidy, *Manager*
EMP: 50
SALES (corp-wide): 535.4MM **Privately Held**
WEB: www.24hourfitness.com
SIC: 7991 Health club
PA: 24 Hour Fitness Worldwide, Inc.
    12647 Alcosta Blvd # 500
    San Ramon CA 94583
    925 543-3100

(P-18573)
ADDISON-PENZAK JEWISH COMMUNIT
14855 Oka Rd Ste 201, Los Gatos
(95032-1956)
PHONE..................................408 358-3636
Nate Stein, *CEO*
Rebecca Geshuri, *Vice Chairman*
Stuart Phillips, *CFO*

Nettie Azoulay, *General Mgr*
Stephanie McShurley, *Executive Asst*
EMP: 236
SALES: 8.3MM **Privately Held**
WEB: www.svjcc.org
SIC: 7991 8299 Physical fitness facilities;
educational services

(P-18574)
ADVENTUREPLEX
1701 Marine Ave, Manhattan Beach
(90266-4100)
PHONE..................................310 546-7708
Kate Hurley, *Manager*
EMP: 50
SALES (est): 1.7MM **Privately Held**
WEB: www.adventureplex.com
SIC: 7991 Physical fitness facilities

(P-18575)
B A M I INC
Also Called: 24 Hour In Motion Fitness
1293 E 1st Ave, Chico (95926-1548)
PHONE..................................530 343-5678
Carleton J Sommer, *President*
Lance Baxman, *Accountant*
Adeliz King, *Director*
Marie Phillips, *Director*
Lori Pine, *Director*
EMP: 50
SQ FT: 19,400
SALES (est): 2.3MM **Privately Held**
WEB: www.inmotionfitness.net
SIC: 7991 Health club

(P-18576)
BACK STREET FITNESS INC
Also Called: Health Quest
3175 California Blvd, NAPA (94558-3307)
PHONE..................................707 254-7200
Anthony Giovannoni, *President*
Mary A Schaffer, *Director*
EMP: 50
SALES (est): 1.4MM **Privately Held**
WEB: www.napahealthquest.com
SIC: 7991 Exercise facilities

(P-18577)
BAY CLUBS INC
Also Called: Decathlon Club
3250 Central Expy, Santa Clara
(95051-0828)
PHONE..................................408 738-2582
Erin Rucker, *Manager*
EMP: 90
SALES (corp-wide): 83.4MM **Privately Held**
WEB: www.pacclub.com
SIC: 7991 7997 5813 5812 Athletic club
& gymnasiums, membership; member-
ship sports & recreation clubs; drinking
places; eating places
HQ: Bay Clubs, Inc.
    1 Lombard St
    San Francisco CA 94111
    415 781-1874

(P-18578)
BAY CLUBS INC
Also Called: Sanctuary, The
200 Redwood Shr Pkwy, Redwood City
(94065-1100)
PHONE..................................650 593-1112
Erin Cker, *Manager*
EMP: 79
SALES (corp-wide): 86.2MM **Privately Held**
WEB: www.pacclub.com
SIC: 7991 7997 5812 5699 Health club;
swimming club, membership; tennis club,
membership; racquetball club, member-
ship; eating places; sports apparel; sport-
ing goods & bicycle shops
HQ: Bay Clubs, Inc.
    1 Lombard St
    San Francisco CA 94111
    415 781-1874

(P-18579)
BEING FIT INC (PA)
Also Called: Being Fit Fitness Centers
8292 Mira Mesa Blvd, San Diego
(92126-2604)
PHONE..................................858 549-3456
Lenny Hecht, *President*
EMP: 60

SALES (est): 700K **Privately Held**
WEB: www.beingfit.net
SIC: 7991 Exercise facilities

(P-18580)
BEING FIT INC
4971 Clairemont Dr Ste A, San Diego
(92117-2785)
PHONE..................................858 483-9294
Lennie Heck, *President*
EMP: 56
SALES (corp-wide): 700K **Privately Held**
WEB: www.beingfit.net
SIC: 7991 Aerobic dance & exercise
classes; health club
PA: Being Fit, Inc
    8292 Mira Mesa Blvd
    San Diego CA 92126
    858 549-3456

(P-18581)
BLADIUM INC (PA)
Also Called: Bladium Sports Clubs
800 W Tower Ave Bldg 40, Alameda
(94501-5048)
PHONE..................................510 814-4999
Brad C Shook, *President*
David Walsh, *CFO*
Derek Schulte, *Program Mgr*
EMP: 120
SQ FT: 115,000
SALES (est): 3.5MM **Privately Held**
WEB: www.bladium.com
SIC: 7991 Athletic club & gymnasiums,
membership

(P-18582)
BURN 60 LLC
159 S Barrington Pl, Los Angeles
(90049-3305)
PHONE..................................310 476-5656
Drew Gerstein, *Owner*
Kristy Catchpole, *Vice Pres*
EMP: 50
SALES (est): 351.2K **Privately Held**
SIC: 7991 5993 Aerobic dance & exercise
classes; tobacco stores & stands

(P-18583)
CALIFORNIA FAMILY HEALTH LLC
Also Called: California Family Fitness
8569 Bond Rd Ste 130, Elk Grove
(95624-9522)
PHONE..................................916 685-3355
Eric Sorenson, *Manager*
Dave Stauffer, *President*
EMP: 50 **Privately Held**
SIC: 7991 Health club
PA: California Family Health Llc
    8680 Greenback Ln Ste 108
    Orangevale CA 95662

(P-18584)
CALISTOGA SPA INC
Also Called: Calistoga Spa Hot Springs
1006 Washington St, Calistoga
(94515-1499)
PHONE..................................707 942-6269
Bradley L Barrett, *President*
Michael Lennon, *General Mgr*
Diane Barrett, *Admin Sec*
EMP: 65
SQ FT: 50,000
SALES (est): 2.5MM **Privately Held**
WEB: www.calistogaspa.com
SIC: 7991 Spas

(P-18585)
CAPITAL ATHLETIC CLUB INC
1515 8th St, Sacramento (95814-5503)
PHONE..................................916 442-3927
Ken Hoffman, *President*
Jane Coolidge, *Admin Mgr*
Veronica Gomez, *Admin Asst*
Rosie Riem, *Administration*
Jonna Edwinson, *Director*
EMP: 64
SQ FT: 52,000
SALES (est): 2MM **Privately Held**
WEB: www.capitalac.com
SIC: 7991 Health club

(P-18586)
CLUB AT LOS GATOS INC
14428 Big Basin Way Ste A, Saratoga
(95070-6010)
PHONE..................................408 867-5110
David S Wilson, *CEO*
EMP: 60
SALES (est): 160.6K **Privately Held**
SIC: 7991 Physical fitness clubs with train-
ing equipment; health club

(P-18587)
CLUBSPORT SAN RAMON LLC
Also Called: Oakwood Athletic Club
4000 Mt Diablo Blvd, Lafayette
(94549-3498)
PHONE..................................925 283-4000
Michael Reardon, *Manager*
EMP: 170
SQ FT: 63,749
SALES (corp-wide): 9.7MM **Privately Held**
WEB: www.clubsportsr.com
SIC: 7991 7997 Athletic club & gymnasi-
ums, membership; membership sports &
recreation clubs
PA: Clubsport San Ramon, Llc
    350 Bollinger Canyon Ln
    San Ramon CA 94582
    925 735-1182

(P-18588)
CLUBSPORT SAN RAMON LLC (PA)
Also Called: Spa At Club Sport
350 Bollinger Canyon Ln, San Ramon
(94582-4592)
PHONE..................................925 735-1182
Dennis Garrison,
John Moore, *Partner*
Al Schaffer, *Partner*
Mike Reardon, *General Mgr*
Andrea Ramirez, *Manager*
EMP: 350
SQ FT: 70,000
SALES (est): 9.7MM **Privately Held**
WEB: www.clubsportsr.com
SIC: 7991 Health club

(P-18589)
CRUNCH LLC
Also Called: Crunch Fitness
8000 W Sunset Blvd # 220, West Holly-
wood (90046-2439)
PHONE..................................323 654-4550
Amita Balla, *Branch Mgr*
Sean Renzetti, *Opers Mgr*
Anita Balla, *Manager*
EMP: 75 **Privately Held**
SIC: 7991 Physical fitness clubs with train-
ing equipment
PA: Crunch, Llc
    220 W 19th St
    New York NY 10011

(P-18590)
CRUNCH LLC
Also Called: Embarcadero, The
345 Spear St Ste 104, San Francisco
(94105-1659)
PHONE..................................415 495-1939
Mahogany Lenard, *Branch Mgr*
EMP: 224 **Privately Held**
SIC: 7991 Health club
PA: Crunch, Llc
    220 W 19th St
    New York NY 10011

(P-18591)
CRUNCH FITNESS
19867 Prairie St Ste 200, Chatsworth
(91311-6533)
PHONE..................................805 522-5454
Teresa Frost, *General Mgr*
Tobin Lindstrom, *Training Spec*
EMP: 65
SQ FT: 22,000
SALES (est): 1.4MM **Privately Held**
WEB: www.oakridgefitness.com
SIC: 7991 Athletic club & gymnasiums,
membership

(P-18592)
DECATHLON CLUB INC
3250 Central Expy, Santa Clara
(95051-0873)
PHONE....................408 738-2582
Kayte Bandcraft, *Manager*
EMP: 200
SQ FT: 100,000
SALES (est): 5MM **Privately Held**
SIC: 7991 5812 Physical fitness clubs with
training equipment; eating places

(P-18593)
DEEPAK CHOPRA LLC
2013 Costa Del Mar Rd, Carlsbad
(92009-6801)
PHONE....................760 494-1600
Deepak Chopra,
EMP: 50
SALES (est): 1.5MM **Privately Held**
WEB: www.chopra.com
SIC: 7991 Health club

(P-18594)
EQUINOX HOLDINGS INC
Also Called: Equinox Fitness Club
747 Market St, San Francisco
(94103-2001)
PHONE....................415 243-0492
Amie Skidmore, *General Mgr*
EMP: 500
SALES (corp-wide): 10.6B **Privately Held**
SIC: 7991 Health club
HQ: Equinox Holdings, Inc.
895 Broadway Fl 3
New York NY 10003
212 677-0180

(P-18595)
EQUINOX-76TH STREET INC
301 Pine St, San Francisco (94104-3301)
PHONE....................415 398-0747
Patrick Ahern, *Manager*
EMP: 75
SALES (corp-wide): 10.6B **Privately Held**
SIC: 7991 Health club
HQ: Equinox-76th Street, Inc.
895 Broadway Fl 3
New York NY 10003

(P-18596)
EQUINOX-76TH STREET INC
Also Called: Equinox Fitness Club
19540 Jamboree Rd, Irvine (92612-8448)
PHONE....................949 296-1700
Herb Umphreyville, *General Mgr*
EMP: 90
SALES (corp-wide): 10.6B **Privately Held**
SIC: 7991 Health club
HQ: Equinox-76th Street, Inc.
895 Broadway Fl 3
New York NY 10003

(P-18597)
**EXECUTIVE FITNESS
MANAGEMENT**
Also Called: World Gym Fitness Centers
226 E Palm Ave, Burbank (91502-1227)
P.O. Box 10997 (91510-0997)
PHONE....................818 259-6753
Manny Kazanjian, *President*
EMP: 50
SALES (est): 512K **Privately Held**
SIC: 7991 Health club

(P-18598)
EXECUTIVES OUTLET INC
Also Called: Decathalon Club
1 Lombard St Lbby, San Francisco
(94111-1127)
PHONE....................415 433-6044
James Gerber, *President*
Sandra Hoeffer, *Vice Pres*
Mindy Steiner, *Vice Pres*
David Smith, *Admin Sec*
EMP: 150
SQ FT: 100,000
SALES: 7.8MM
SALES (corp-wide): 46.3MM **Privately
Held**
SIC: 7991 7997 Athletic club & gymnasi-
ums, membership; racquetball club, mem-
bership

PA: Bay Club Holdings Iii, Llc
1 Lombard St Lbby
San Francisco CA 94111
415 781-1874

(P-18599)
FITNESS 2000 INC
35145 Newark Blvd, Newark (94560-1219)
PHONE....................510 791-2481
Mike Patel, *President*
Sonia Patel, *Principal*
Jay Patel, *Manager*
EMP: 50
SALES (est): 658.3K **Privately Held**
SIC: 7991 Health club

(P-18600)
FITNESS EVOLUTION
Also Called: Gold's Gym
4120 Dale Rd Ste G, Modesto
(95356-9239)
PHONE....................209 545-9055
David Knapp,
EMP: 70 EST: 2001
SQ FT: 35,000
SALES (est): 1.2MM **Privately Held**
SIC: 7991 Athletic club & gymnasiums,
membership

(P-18601)
FITNESS INTERNATIONAL LLC
Also Called: La Fitness
24491 Alicia Pkwy, Mission Viejo
(92691-4506)
PHONE....................949 421-6082
Lisa Guidno, *Branch Mgr*
EMP: 50
SALES (corp-wide): 173MM **Privately
Held**
SIC: 7991 Physical fitness clubs with train-
ing equipment
PA: Fitness International, Llc
3161 Michelson Dr Ste 600
Irvine CA 92612
949 255-7200

(P-18602)
FITNESS INTERNATIONAL LLC
Also Called: L A Fitness Sports Clubs
10535 Heater Ct, San Diego (92121-4111)
PHONE....................858 550-5912
Joe Torrice, *Manager*
EMP: 50
SALES (corp-wide): 173MM **Privately
Held**
WEB: www.proresultsfit.com
SIC: 7991 Physical fitness clubs with train-
ing equipment
PA: Fitness International, Llc
3161 Michelson Dr Ste 600
Irvine CA 92612
949 255-7200

(P-18603)
**GEORGE BROWNS SPORTS
CLUB (PA)**
Also Called: Gb3
1155 N Fowler Ave Ste 500, Clovis
(93611-8192)
PHONE....................559 297-8656
George Brown, *President*
EMP: 70
SALES (est): 1.2MM **Privately Held**
SIC: 7991 Health club

(P-18604)
GILROY FITNESS INC (PA)
Also Called: Gilroy Health and Fitness
8540 Church St, Gilroy (95020-4231)
PHONE....................408 848-1234
Joe Gigantino, *President*
Rosa Munoz, *Bookkeeper*
Raymond Butler, *Opers Mgr*
Carlos Bishop, *Maintence Staff*
EMP: 50
SQ FT: 27,000
SALES (est): 1MM **Privately Held**
WEB: www.gilroyfitness.com
SIC: 7991 Health club

(P-18605)
**GOLDS GYM INTERNATIONAL
INC**
39 S Altadena Dr, Pasadena (91107-4256)
PHONE....................626 304-1133
Frank Jordan, *Manager*

EMP: 55
SALES (corp-wide): 1.2B **Privately Held**
SIC: 7991 Athletic club & gymnasiums,
membership
HQ: Gold's Gym International, Inc.
125 E J Carpentr Fwy 13
Irving TX 75062
972 444-8527

(P-18606)
HARBOR BAY CLUB INC
200 Packet Landing Rd, Alameda
(94502-6599)
P.O. Box 1450 (94501-0158)
PHONE....................510 521-5414
C Timothy Hoppen, *President*
Timothy Hoppen, *President*
Debbi Douglas, *Bd of Directors*
Louise Howard, *Mktg Dir*
Vince Piro, *Facilities Mgr*
EMP: 83
SQ FT: 30,000
SALES (est): 2.9MM **Privately Held**
WEB: www.harborbayclub.com
SIC: 7991 5813 5941 5812 Athletic club
& gymnasiums, membership; aerobic
dance & exercise classes; bar (drinking
places); golf goods & equipment; eating
places
PA: Harbor Bay Club Associates, A Califor-
nia Limited Partnership
1141 Harbor Bay Pkwy Fl 2
Alameda CA 94502

(P-18607)
**HEALTHSPORT LTD A LTD
PARTNR (PA)**
Also Called: Healthsport-Arcata
300 Dr Martin Luther, Arcata (95521)
PHONE....................707 822-3488
Susan Johnson, *Partner*
Bill Spaeth, *Personnel*
EMP: 115
SQ FT: 24,560
SALES (est): 3.4MM **Privately Held**
WEB: www.healthsport.com
SIC: 7991 Health club

(P-18608)
HERCULES FITNESS
600 Alfred Nobel Dr, Hercules
(94547-1834)
PHONE....................510 724-2900
Steve Buchanan, *Owner*
Kathrina Delrosario, *Asst Mgr*
EMP: 50 EST: 2008
SALES (est): 766.1K **Privately Held**
SIC: 7991 Athletic club & gymnasiums,
membership

(P-18609)
HOLLYWOOD SPA INC
Also Called: Hollywood Spa, The
5636 Vineland Ave, North Hollywood
(91601-2028)
PHONE....................323 464-0445
Rosa Klein, *CEO*
Peter D Sykes, *President*
EMP: 50
SQ FT: 20,000
SALES (est): 1.8MM **Privately Held**
WEB: www.hollywoodspa.com
SIC: 7991 Health club

(P-18610)
**IN SHAPE MANAGEMENT
COMPANY**
Also Called: In Shape Health Clubs
6 S El Dorado St, Stockton (95202-2804)
PHONE....................209 472-2231
Morton Rothbard, *President*
Paul Rothbard, *CEO*
Rob Farrens, *CFO*
EMP: 300
SQ FT: 60,000
SALES (est): 9MM **Privately Held**
SIC: 7991 Health club

(P-18611)
**IN-SHAPE HEALTH CLUBS LLC
(PA)**
Also Called: In-Shape City
6 S El Dorado St Ste 700, Stockton
(95202-2804)
PHONE....................209 472-2231
Francesca Schuler, *CEO*
Morton Rothbard, *President*
Paul Rothbard, *Treasurer*
Rob Farrens, *Vice Pres*
Damian Weber, *District Mgr*
EMP: 50
SQ FT: 60,000
SALES (est): 22.7MM **Privately Held**
WEB: www.inshapeclubs.com
SIC: 7991 Health club

(P-18612)
IN-SHAPE HEALTH CLUBS LLC
101 S Tracy Blvd, Tracy (95376-4620)
PHONE....................209 836-2504
Robin Phillip, *Manager*
EMP: 113
SALES (corp-wide): 22.7MM **Privately
Held**
WEB: www.inshapeclubs.com
SIC: 7991 Health club
PA: In-Shape Health Clubs, Llc
6 S El Dorado St Ste 700
Stockton CA 95202
209 472-2231

(P-18613)
**INSTITUTE FOR ONE WORLD
HEALTH**
600 California St Fl 11, San Francisco
(94108-2727)
PHONE....................650 392-2510
Victoria G Hale, *Ch of Bd*
EMP: 50 EST: 2000
SALES (est): 30.6MM **Privately Held**
SIC: 7991 Health club

(P-18614)
**JACKOVICS ENTERPRISES INC
(PA)**
Also Called: Fitness SF
150 Nellen Ave Ste 250, Corte Madera
(94925-1199)
PHONE....................415 348-6377
Sebastyen Jackovics, *President*
Zsolt Jackovicks, *Vice Pres*
Judy Jackovics, *Admin Sec*
Brian Heminger, *Personnel*
Don Dickerson, *Opers Staff*
EMP: 200
SALES (est): 4.7MM **Privately Held**
SIC: 7991 Athletic club & gymnasiums,
membership

(P-18615)
JAZZERCISE INC (PA)
2460 Impala Dr, Carlsbad (92010-7226)
PHONE....................760 476-1750
Judi Sheppard Missett, *CEO*
Andrew Blocksidge, *President*
Sally Baldridge, *CFO*
Shanna Missett Nelson, *Exec VP*
EMP: 100
SQ FT: 24,228
SALES (est): 12.2MM **Privately Held**
WEB: www.jazzercise.com
SIC: 7991 6794 5961 Aerobic dance &
exercise classes; franchises, selling or li-
censing; fitness & sporting goods, mail
order

(P-18616)
JEFF STOVER INC
Also Called: Chico Sports Club
260 Cohasset Rd Ste 190, Chico
(95926-2282)
PHONE....................530 345-9427
Jeff Stover, *President*
Jimmie Purkey, *General Mgr*
Jennifer Jellison, *Director*
EMP: 85
SQ FT: 11,000
SALES (est): 3.2MM **Privately Held**
WEB: www.chicosportsclub.com
SIC: 7991 7997 Health club; membership
sports & recreation clubs

(P-18617)
KEISERS HOLDINGS LLC
411 S West Ave, Fresno (93706-1320)
PHONE......................................559 265-4700
Dennis Keiser,
EMP: 80
SALES (est): 646.9K **Privately Held**
SIC: 7991 Physical fitness facilities

(P-18618)
KENNEDY ATHLETIC CLUB (PA)
3534 El Camino Real, Atascadero
(93422-2532)
PHONE......................................805 466-6775
Kevin P Kennedy, *General Ptnr*
Barbara Kennedy, *General Ptnr*
EMP: 85
SQ FT: 30,000
SALES (est): 2.7MM **Privately Held**
WEB: www.kennedyclubs.com
SIC: 7991 Health club

(P-18619)
KENNEDY CLUB FITNESS
188 Tank Farm Rd, San Luis Obispo
(93401-7528)
PHONE......................................805 781-3488
Brett Weaver,
Barbara Kennedy,
Kevin Kennedy,
EMP: 70
SQ FT: 50,000
SALES (est): 552.7K **Privately Held**
SIC: 7991 Athletic club & gymnasiums,
membership

(P-18620)
L & O ALISO VIEJO LLC
Also Called: Renaissnce Clbsport Aliso Vejo
50 Enterprise, Aliso Viejo (92656-6026)
PHONE......................................949 643-6700
Ed Tomlin, *Mng Member*
EMP: 80
SALES (est): 2.2MM **Privately Held**
SIC: 7991 7011 Spas; hotels

(P-18621)
L A FITNESS INTL LLC
Also Called: L A Fitness Sports Clubs
1760 S Victoria Ave, Ventura (93003-6592)
PHONE......................................805 289-9907
Eric Bjerkens, *Manager*
EMP: 60
SALES (corp-wide): 173MM **Privately Held**
WEB: www.proresultsfit.com
SIC: 7991 Physical fitness facilities
PA: Fitness International, Llc
3161 Michelson Dr Ste 600
Irvine CA 92612
949 255-7200

(P-18622)
LA BONNE VIE INC
2723 Shell Beach Rd, Shell Beach
(93449-1629)
PHONE......................................805 773-5003
Maureen Raynaud-Loughead, *Principal*
EMP: 100
SALES (est): 128.7K **Privately Held**
SIC: 7991 Spas

(P-18623)
LA BOXING FRANCHISE CORP
1241 E Dyer Rd Ste 100, Santa Ana
(92705-5611)
PHONE......................................714 668-0911
Anthony Geisler, *President*
▲ **EMP:** 173
SALES (est): 5.1MM
SALES (corp-wide): 35.4MM **Privately Held**
SIC: 7991 Physical fitness facilities
PA: U Gym, Llc
1501 Quail St Ste 100
Newport Beach CA 92660
714 668-0911

(P-18624)
LA PETITE BALEEN INC
Also Called: La Petite Baleen Swim School
434 San Mateo Ave, San Bruno
(94066-4417)
PHONE......................................650 588-7665
John Kolbisen, *Owner*
Joan Monaghan, *Sales Executive*

EMP: 80
SALES (corp-wide): 8.1MM **Privately Held**
WEB: www.swimlpb.com
SIC: 7991 7999 Physical fitness facilities;
swimming instruction
PA: La Petite Baleen, Inc
775 Main St
Half Moon Bay CA
-

(P-18625)
LEISURE SPORTS INC
Also Called: Clubsport of Fremont
46650 Landing Pkwy, Fremont
(94538-6420)
PHONE......................................510 226-8500
Dan Detrick, *General Mgr*
EMP: 200
SALES (corp-wide): 191.7MM **Privately Held**
WEB: www.leisuresportsinc.com
SIC: 7991 Athletic club & gymnasiums,
membership
PA: Leisure Sports, Inc.
4670 Willow Rd Ste 100
Pleasanton CA 94588
925 600-1966

(P-18626)
LIVERMORE VALLEY TENNIS CLUB
2000 Arroyo Rd, Livermore (94550-6027)
PHONE......................................925 443-7700
Kim Fuller, *General Ptnr*
Roy Rasmussen, *General Ptnr*
Desiree Bailey, *Director*
EMP: 100 EST: 1972
SQ FT: 51,758
SALES (est): 3.1MM **Privately Held**
WEB: www.lvtc.com
SIC: 7991 5941 Athletic club & gymnasi-
ums, membership; sporting goods & bicy-
cle shops; tennis goods & equipment

(P-18627)
LOS ANGELES ATHLETIC CLUB INC
431 W 7th St, Los Angeles (90014-1691)
PHONE......................................213 625-2211
Karen Hathaway, *President*
Bryan Cusworth, *CFO*
EMP: 175
SALES (est): 1.5MM
SALES (corp-wide): 22.6MM **Privately Held**
SIC: 7991 Athletic club & gymnasiums,
membership
PA: Laaco, Ltd.
431 W 7th St
Los Angeles CA 90014
213 622-1254

(P-18628)
LOVE LIFTED US YOUTH SERVICES
6356 Van Nuys Blvd # 229, Van Nuys
(91401-2627)
P.O. Box 2131, North Hills (91393-2131)
PHONE......................................818 471-0594
Ashley D Oshilaja, *CEO*
EMP: 50 EST: 2015
SALES (est): 52.3K **Privately Held**
SIC: 7991 Physical fitness facilities

(P-18629)
MARINER SQUARE ATHLETIC INC
2227 Mariner Square Loop, Alameda
(94501-1021)
PHONE......................................510 523-8011
Kathy Wagner, *President*
Diana Thomas, *General Mgr*
Kevin Truglio, *General Mgr*
Mike Daniels, *Maintence Staff*
Camille Hammond, *Manager*
EMP: 100 EST: 1975
SQ FT: 60,000
SALES (est): 3.6MM **Privately Held**
WEB: www.marinersq.com
SIC: 7991 7997 Athletic club & gymnasi-
ums, membership; membership sports &
recreation clubs

(P-18630)
MAXIMUM FITNESS LLC
Also Called: Gold's Gym
135 Dobbins St, Vacaville (95688-3929)
PHONE......................................707 447-0606
Richard A Martindale,
David Conner,
EMP: 50 EST: 1997
SQ FT: 27,000
SALES (est): 1.9MM **Privately Held**
SIC: 7991 Athletic club & gymnasiums,
membership

(P-18631)
MCCALL GYM GROUP INC (PA)
Also Called: Golds Gym San Jose
1893 Monterey Hwy Ste 250, San Jose
(95112-6138)
PHONE......................................408 271-2416
Jerry Mc Call, *President*
EMP: 52
SALES (est): 3.8MM **Privately Held**
WEB: www.mccallgymgroup.com
SIC: 7991 Athletic club & gymnasiums,
membership

(P-18632)
MILLENIUM ATHLETIC CLUB LLC
Also Called: Goleta Valley Athletic Club
170 Los Carneros Way, Goleta
(93117-3012)
PHONE......................................805 562-3845
Jarrod Schwartz,
Sean Yeager-Diamond, *Personnel*
Gordon Schwartz,
David Arico, *Manager*
▲ **EMP:** 65
SQ FT: 30,000
SALES (est): 2.4MM **Privately Held**
WEB: www.gvac.com
SIC: 7991 Health club

(P-18633)
MONIQUE SURACI
Also Called: Murrieta Day Spa
41885 Ivy St, Murrieta (92562-8607)
PHONE......................................951 677-8111
Monique Suraci, *Owner*
Adrienne Crane, *Director*
EMP: 60
SALES (est): 1.7MM **Privately Held**
SIC: 7991 Spas

(P-18634)
MUSCLE IMPROVEMENT INC
Also Called: Gold's Gym
200 N Harbor Dr, Redondo Beach
(90277-2507)
PHONE......................................310 374-5522
Fax: 310 372-4741
EMP: 70
SQ FT: 21,000
SALES (est): 3.2MM **Privately Held**
SIC: 7991

(P-18635)
MUSCLEBOUND INC (PA)
Also Called: Golds Gym
19835 Nordhoff St, Northridge
(91324-3331)
PHONE......................................818 349-0123
Angel J Banos, *President*
William Banos, *Vice Pres*
Michelle McLemore, *Vice Pres*
Ricardo Gomez, *Facilities Mgr*
Luis Enriquez, *Maintence Staff*
EMP: 350
SQ FT: 8,625
SALES (est): 11.5MM **Privately Held**
SIC: 7991 Athletic club & gymnasiums,
membership

(P-18636)
MV HOSPITALITY INC
Also Called: Mount View Hotel
1457 Lincoln Ave, Calistoga (94515-1417)
PHONE......................................707 942-6877
Steve Carver, *Manager*
Mike Woods, *President*
Rick Howard, *Vice Pres*
Skip Williams, *Info Tech Mgr*
EMP: 50
SALES (est): 2.5MM **Privately Held**
WEB: www.mountviewhotel.com
SIC: 7991 7011 Spas; hotels

(P-18637)
NC FIT INC
647 N Santa Cruz Ave C, Los Gatos
(95030-4351)
PHONE......................................408 910-6748
Jason Khalipa, *Branch Mgr*
EMP: 88
SALES (corp-wide): 3.6MM **Privately Held**
SIC: 7991 Physical fitness clubs with train-
ing equipment
PA: Nc Fit, Inc.
2280 S Bascom Ave Ste A
Campbell CA 95008
408 822-9597

(P-18638)
OLYMPIX FITNESS LLC
4101 E Olympic Plz, Long Beach (90803)
PHONE......................................562 366-4600
Eden Paul,
EMP: 91 EST: 2016
SALES (est): 89K **Privately Held**
SIC: 7991 Physical fitness facilities

(P-18639)
PERFECT WORKOUT INC (PA)
150 N El Camino Real, Encinitas
(92024-2849)
PHONE......................................949 943-7281
Matt Hedman, *CEO*
Josh Hedman, *Opers Staff*
EMP: 60
SALES (est): 5.1MM **Privately Held**
SIC: 7991 Athletic club & gymnasiums,
membership

(P-18640)
PF WEST LLC
Also Called: Planet Fitness
101 Lucas Valley Rd # 150, San Rafael
(94903-1700)
PHONE......................................415 479-9600
Roger Bates, *Mng Member*
EMP: 105
SQ FT: 1,500
SALES (est): 3.1MM **Privately Held**
SIC: 7991 Physical fitness clubs with train-
ing equipment

(P-18641)
PISMO BEACH ATHLETIC CLUB
1751 Price St, Pismo Beach (93449-2230)
PHONE......................................805 773-3011
Henry F Myers, *President*
Ryan Tomich, *Executive*
EMP: 50
SALES (est): 1.7MM **Privately Held**
WEB: www.pbac.com
SIC: 7991 Health club

(P-18642)
PRESTON WYNNE SPA INC
14567 Big Basin Way A2, Saratoga
(95070-6039)
PHONE......................................408 741-1750
Peggy Wynne-Borgman, *President*
EMP: 56
SQ FT: 4,700
SALES (est): 1.5MM **Privately Held**
WEB: www.prestonwynne.com
SIC: 7991 Spas

(P-18643)
PRIME TIME ATHLETIC CLUB INC
1730 Rollins Rd, Burlingame (94010-2297)
PHONE......................................650 204-3662
John Michael, *President*
Jerry Bruton, *Sales Staff*
Ray Jungwirth,
EMP: 80 EST: 1979
SQ FT: 35,000
SALES (est): 3.3MM **Privately Held**
WEB: www.primetimeathleticclub.com
SIC: 7991 Athletic club & gymnasiums,
membership

(P-18644)
REACH FITNESS CLUB
1235 Radio Rd Ste 120, Redwood City
(94065-1315)
PHONE......................................650 327-3224
Darryl Brandon, *Branch Mgr*
Lynn Hill, *Accountant*

Missy Caudill, *Site Mgr*
Garrett Anderson, *Opers Mgr*
EMP: 55
SALES (corp-wide): 5.5MM **Privately Held**
WEB: www.reachfitness.com
SIC: 7991 5699 Health club; sports apparel
PA: Reach Fitness Club
1235 Radio Rd Ste 120
Redwood City CA 94065
650 817-9050

(P-18645)
REDWOOD HEALTH CLUB (PA)
3101 S State St, Ukiah (95482-6938)
PHONE..................................707 468-0441
Rob Marthe Deomont, *Partner*
Kathy Tobin, *Manager*
Melissa Tobin, *Manager*
EMP: 85
SQ FT: 20,000
SALES (est): 1.2MM **Privately Held**
WEB: www.redwoodhealthclub.com
SIC: 7991 7997 5812 5813 Health club; racquetball club, membership; tennis club, membership; snack bar; drinking places

(P-18646)
SALUTARY SPORTS CLUBS INC
Also Called: Sports Club of El Dorado
4242 Sports Club Dr, Shingle Springs (95682-9546)
P.O. Box 659 (95682-0659)
PHONE..................................530 677-5705
Don Lynd, *Manager*
EMP: 50
SALES (corp-wide): 7.8MM **Privately Held**
SIC: 7991 Physical fitness facilities
PA: Salutary Sports Clubs, Inc.
3442 Browns Valley Rd # 100
Vacaville CA 95688
707 446-2350

(P-18647)
SALVATION ARMY
6845 University Ave, San Diego (92115-5829)
PHONE..................................619 269-1404
Cindy Foley, *Principal*
James Knaggs, *President*
David Hudson, *Vice Pres*
EMP: 300
SALES (est): 8.6MM **Privately Held**
SIC: 7991 8661 7032 7922 Physical fitness clubs with training equipment; miscellaneous denomination church; sporting & recreational camps; community theater production

(P-18648)
SAN FRANCISCO TENNIS CLUB
645 5th St, San Francisco (94107-1516)
PHONE..................................415 777-9000
Jim Hinckley, *President*
Thomas Kanar, *Corp Secy*
Jeff Janke, *Vice Pres*
EMP: 100
SQ FT: 300,000
SALES: 209.4K
SALES (corp-wide): 477MM **Privately Held**
WEB: www.sftennis.com
SIC: 7991 7997 5813 Physical fitness facilities; membership sports & recreation clubs; drinking places
HQ: Clubcorp Usa, Inc.
3030 Lyndon B Johnson Fwy
Dallas TX 75234
972 243-6191

(P-18649)
SANTA CLARITA ATHLETIC CLUB
23942 Lyons Ave Ste 106, Newhall (91321-2475)
PHONE..................................661 255-3365
Charles Hamilton, *President*
Michelle Marbach, *Vice Pres*
Ann Hamilton, *Admin Sec*
EMP: 78
SQ FT: 64,000

SALES: 5MM **Privately Held**
WEB: www.santaclaritaathleticclub.com
SIC: 7991 5812 8699 Health club; athletic club & gymnasiums, membership; cafe; athletic organizations

(P-18650)
SANTEE SYSTEMS SERVICES II LL
229 E Gage Ave, Los Angeles (90003-1533)
PHONE..................................323 445-0044
EMP: 50 **EST:** 2012
SQ FT: 10,000
SALES (est): 1.4MM **Privately Held**
SIC: 7991

(P-18651)
SIM INVESTMENT CORPORATION (PA)
Also Called: Right Stuff Health Club, The
1600 W Campbell Ave, Campbell (95008-1526)
PHONE..................................408 874-0610
Paul Infald, *President*
Dave Morrison, *Vice Pres*
EMP: 300
SQ FT: 1,200
SALES (est): 5.7MM **Privately Held**
SIC: 7991 Health club

(P-18652)
SIM INVESTMENT CORPORATION
Also Called: Right Stuff Health Club, The
1329 Blossom Hill Rd, San Jose (95118-3801)
PHONE..................................408 445-3310
Enrico Dileonardo, *General Mgr*
EMP: 60
SALES (corp-wide): 5.7MM **Privately Held**
SIC: 7991 Health club
PA: S.I.M. Investment Corporation
1600 W Campbell Ave
Campbell CA 95008
408 874-0610

(P-18653)
SK SANCTUARY DAY SPA SALON LLC
6919 La Jolla Blvd, La Jolla (92037-5427)
PHONE..................................858 459-2400
Steven Krant, *Mng Member*
Lyn Krant,
EMP: 50
SALES (est): 2.4MM **Privately Held**
WEB: www.sk-sanctuary.com
SIC: 7991 Spa

(P-18654)
SOUND MIND AND BODY INC
117 Via Yella, Newport Beach (92663-5536)
PHONE..................................206 547-2706
Richard Harrington, *President*
Victoria Aldrich, *Vice Pres*
Dennis Rose, *Vice Pres*
EMP: 60
SALES (est): 1.3MM **Privately Held**
WEB: www.smbgym.com
SIC: 7991 Health club

(P-18655)
SPA CAS PALMAS
Also Called: Spa Las Palmas of Marriot Intl
41000 Bob Hope Dr, Rancho Mirage (92270-4416)
PHONE..................................760 836-3106
Dawn Ferraro, *Exec Dir*
EMP: 50
SALES (est): 763.8K **Privately Held**
SIC: 7991 Spas

(P-18656)
SPA DREAMS
6419 Hesperia Ave, Reseda (91335-6225)
PHONE..................................818 298-1120
Yvette Vink, *Owner*
EMP: 100
SALES: 350K **Privately Held**
SIC: 7991 Spas

(P-18657)
SPA HAVENS LP
Also Called: Cal-A-Vie
29402 Spa Haven Way, Vista (92084-2234)
PHONE..................................760 945-2055
John Havens, *Owner*
Gary McGivoney, *Vice Pres*
Cayley Macgregor, *Executive Asst*
Bret Rotheram, *Info Tech Mgr*
Dell Meeks, *Financial Exec*
▲ **EMP:** 105
SALES (est): 8.6MM **Privately Held**
WEB: www.calavie.com
SIC: 7991 Spas

(P-18658)
SPA PARTNERS INC
Also Called: Mount View Spa
1457 Lincoln Ave, Calistoga (94515-1417)
PHONE..................................707 942-5789
Thomas M Gottlieb, *President*
EMP: 50
SALES: 4.2MM **Privately Held**
SIC: 7991 Spa

(P-18659)
SPAD HOLDINGS LLC
Also Called: Total Woman - Westlake Village
966 S Westlake Blvd Ste 4, Westlake Village (91361-3153)
PHONE..................................805 496-9978
Natalie Roberts, *Branch Mgr*
Larissa Solomos, *Personnel*
Nicole Cole, *Supervisor*
EMP: 70
SALES (corp-wide): 26.6MM **Privately Held**
WEB: www.totalwomanspa.com
SIC: 7991 Physical fitness clubs with training equipment; spas
HQ: Spad Holdings, Llc
10805 Rnch Bernardo Rd120
San Diego CA 92127
-

(P-18660)
SPAD HOLDINGS LLC
24245 Magic Mountain Pkwy, Valencia (91355-3401)
PHONE..................................661 286-0229
Carol Steen, *Branch Mgr*
EMP: 60
SALES (corp-wide): 26.6MM **Privately Held**
SIC: 7991 Physical fitness facilities
HQ: Spad Holdings, Llc
10805 Rnch Bernardo Rd120
San Diego CA 92127
-

(P-18661)
SPAD HOLDINGS LLC
Also Called: Total Woman - Placentia
860 N Rose Dr, Placentia (92870-7522)
PHONE..................................714 993-6003
Lori Colagrossi, *Branch Mgr*
EMP: 50
SALES (corp-wide): 26.6MM **Privately Held**
WEB: www.totalwomanspa.com
SIC: 7991 Physical fitness clubs with training equipment; spas
HQ: Spad Holdings, Llc
10805 Rnch Bernardo Rd120
San Diego CA 92127

(P-18662)
SPAD HOLDINGS LLC
Also Called: Total Woman - Irvine
14280 Culver Dr Ste B, Irvine (92604-0347)
PHONE..................................949 733-0473
Mary Gladwill, *Branch Mgr*
EMP: 70
SALES (corp-wide): 26.6MM **Privately Held**
WEB: www.totalwomanspa.com
SIC: 7991 Physical fitness clubs with training equipment; spas
HQ: Spad Holdings, Llc
10805 Rnch Bernardo Rd120
San Diego CA 92127

(P-18663)
SPAD HOLDINGS LLC
Also Called: Total Woman - Warner Center
6100 Topanga Canyon Blvd # 1310, Woodland Hills (91367-3627)
PHONE..................................818 710-7606
Gina Licali, *Branch Mgr*
Julie Thornberg, *General Mgr*
EMP: 70
SALES (corp-wide): 26.6MM **Privately Held**
WEB: www.totalwomanspa.com
SIC: 7991 Physical fitness clubs with training equipment; spas
HQ: Spad Holdings, Llc
10805 Rnch Bernardo Rd120
San Diego CA 92127

(P-18664)
SPAD HOLDINGS LLC
Also Called: Total Woman - Northridge
19456 Nordhoff St, Northridge (91324-2417)
PHONE..................................818 772-8900
Mina Keshavarzi, *Manager*
Paige Rider, *Supervisor*
EMP: 70
SALES (corp-wide): 26.6MM **Privately Held**
WEB: www.totalwomanspa.com
SIC: 7991 Physical fitness clubs with training equipment; spas
HQ: Spad Holdings, Llc
10805 Rnch Bernardo Rd120
San Diego CA 92127

(P-18665)
SPAD HOLDINGS LLC
Also Called: Total Woman - Glendale
601 N Brand Blvd, Glendale (91203-1211)
PHONE..................................818 552-2027
Teryn Radvany, *Branch Mgr*
EMP: 70
SALES (corp-wide): 26.6MM **Privately Held**
WEB: www.totalwomanspa.com
SIC: 7991 Physical fitness clubs with training equipment; spas
HQ: Spad Holdings, Llc
10805 Rnch Bernardo Rd120
San Diego CA 92127

(P-18666)
SPARE-TIME INC
Also Called: Natomas Racquet Club
2450 Natomas Park Dr, Sacramento (95833-2938)
PHONE..................................916 649-0909
Joe Rose, *Manager*
EMP: 70
SALES (corp-wide): 37.1MM **Privately Held**
WEB: www.sparetimeinc.com
SIC: 7991 Health club
PA: Spare-Time, Inc.
11344 Coloma Rd Ste 350
Gold River CA 95670
916 859-5910

(P-18667)
SPORT CENTER FITNESS INC
Also Called: King Harbor Sports Center
819 N Harbor Dr, Redondo Beach (90277-2006)
PHONE..................................310 376-9443
Michael Marinelli, *President*
EMP: 73
SQ FT: 25,000
SALES (est): 514.9K **Privately Held**
WEB: www.sportcenterfitness.com
SIC: 7991 7999 Health club; tennis courts, outdoor/indoor: non-membership

(P-18668)
SPORTSMEN OF STANISLAUS INC
Also Called: S O S CLUB
819 Sunset Ave, Modesto (95351-3756)
P.O. Box 3031 (95353-3031)
PHONE..................................209 578-5801
Aaron Andrews, *General Mgr*
Bryan Manley, *Ch of Bd*
Emily Kennerly, *Personnel Exec*

EMP: 100
SQ FT: 70,000
SALES: 986.6K **Privately Held**
SIC: 7991 5812 8641 7997 Athletic club & gymnasiums, membership; eating places; civic social & fraternal associations; membership sports & recreation clubs; drinking places

(P-18669)
SWEETWATER GARDENS INC
955 Ukiah, Mendocino (95460)
P.O. Box 337 (95460-0337)
PHONE..............................707 937-4140
John Carl Fliessbach, *President*
EMP: 50
SQ FT: 1,250
SALES (est): 1.2MM **Privately Held**
SIC: 7991 5499 7011 7299 Spas; juices, fruit or vegetable; motels; massage parlor

(P-18670)
THINK TOGETHER
12016 Telegraph Rd, Santa Fe Springs (90670-3784)
PHONE..............................562 236-3835
EMP: 704
SALES (corp-wide): 47.1MM **Privately Held**
SIC: 7991 Physical fitness facilities
PA: Think Together
2101 E 4th St Ste 200b
Santa Ana CA 92705
714 543-3807

(P-18671)
TOTAL WOMAN
860 N Rose Dr, Placentia (92870-7522)
PHONE..............................714 993-6003
Lori Colagrossi, *Manager*
Cheryle Bujarski, *Sales Staff*
EMP: 65
SALES (est): 989.7K **Privately Held**
SIC: 7991 Physical fitness facilities

(P-18672)
U GYM LLC
470 N Mckinley St, Corona (92879-1291)
PHONE..............................951 808-3850
Shawna Winters, *General Mgr*
Andrew Hennebelle, *Director*
EMP: 97
SALES (corp-wide): 35.4MM **Privately Held**
SIC: 7991 Health club
PA: U Gym, Llc
1501 Quail St Ste 100
Newport Beach CA 92660
714 668-0911

(P-18673)
U GYM LLC (PA)
Also Called: Ufc Gym
1501 Quail St Ste 100, Newport Beach (92660-2797)
PHONE..............................714 668-0911
Brent Leffel,
Adam Fedlack, *Senior VP*
Jason Figorski, *General Mgr*
Jordan Robinson, *Administration*
Alexis Nwaekeke, *Graphic Designe*
EMP: 70 EST: 2008
SALES (est): 35.4MM **Privately Held**
SIC: 7991 5699 Physical fitness clubs with training equipment; shirts, custom made

(P-18674)
WESTLAKE NAIL SPA
233 Lake Merced Blvd, Daly City (94015-3113)
PHONE..............................650 994-7777
Loi Duong, *Owner*
EMP: 68
SALES (est): 762.9K **Privately Held**
SIC: 7991 Spas

(P-18675)
WI SPA LLC
2700 Wilshire Blvd, Los Angeles (90057-3202)
PHONE..............................213 487-2700
Stuart Whang,
Jonathan Suh, *Manager*
EMP: 50
SALES (est): 1.7MM **Privately Held**
SIC: 7991 Spas

(P-18676)
XI ENTERPRISE INC
2140 E Palmdale Blvd, Palmdale (93550-1202)
PHONE..............................661 266-3200
Shah Roshan, *CEO*
EMP: 75
SALES (est): 1.2MM **Privately Held**
SIC: 7991 Physical fitness facilities

(P-18677)
YOGA WORKS INC (HQ)
Also Called: Yogaworks
5780 Uplander Way, Culver City (90230-6606)
PHONE..............................310 664-6470
Phillip Swain, *CEO*
Jay Decoons, *President*
Jessica Johnson, *Regional Mgr*
Kiernan Aileen, *General Mgr*
Allison Korycki, *Teacher*
EMP: 50
SQ FT: 6,000
SALES (est): 8.4MM
SALES (corp-wide): 54.5MM **Publicly Held**
SIC: 7991 5961 5651 Exercise salon; mail order house; unisex clothing stores
PA: Yogaworks, Inc.
5780 Uplander Way
Culver City CA 90230
310 664-6470

(P-18678)
YOGAWORKS INC (PA)
Also Called: MYYOGAWORKS
5780 Uplander Way, Culver City (90230-6606)
PHONE..............................310 664-6470
Rosanna C McCollough, *President*
Peter L Garran, *Ch of Bd*
Vance Y Chang, *CFO*
Vance Chang, *CFO*
Kurt C Donnell, *Exec VP*
EMP: 60 EST: 1987
SALES: 54.5MM **Publicly Held**
SIC: 7991 7999 5961 5651 Yoga instruction; mail order house; unisex clothing stores; exercise salon

---
7992 Public Golf Courses

(P-18679)
ALISO VIEJO GOLF CLUB INC
Also Called: Aliso Viejo Country Club
33 Santa Barbara Dr, Aliso Viejo (92656-1622)
PHONE..............................949 598-9200
Lorraine Grassman, *General Mgr*
Lorraine Gerassman, *General Mgr*
EMP: 110
SQ FT: 8,000
SALES (est): 6.5MM
SALES (corp-wide): 477MM **Privately Held**
WEB: www.alisogolf.com
SIC: 7992 Public golf courses
HQ: Clubcorp Usa, Inc.
3030 Lyndon B Johnson Fwy
Dallas TX 75234
972 243-6191

(P-18680)
ALONDRA GOLF COURSE INC
Also Called: Three Rivers Golf Course
16400 Prairie Ave, Lawndale (90260-3037)
PHONE..............................310 217-9915
Steve OH, *President*
EMP: 52
SQ FT: 12,000
SALES (est): 2.9MM **Privately Held**
SIC: 7992 5941 5812 Public golf courses; golf goods & equipment; restaurant, family: independent

(P-18681)
AMERICAN GOLF CORPORATION
Also Called: Lakewood Country Club
3101 Carson St, Lakewood (90712-4005)
PHONE..............................562 421-0550
Gary Kossick, *General Mgr*
EMP: 50

SALES (corp-wide): 588MM **Privately Held**
WEB: www.americangolf.com
SIC: 7992 Public golf courses; golf club, membership
PA: American Golf Corporation
909 N Pacific Coast Hwy
El Segundo CA 90245
310 664-4000

(P-18682)
AMERICAN GOLF CORPORATION
Also Called: Recreation Park Golf Course 18
5001 Deukmejian Dr, Long Beach (90804-4311)
PHONE..............................562 494-4424
Tim Dunlop, *Branch Mgr*
Jack Duty, *Sales Staff*
EMP: 50
SQ FT: 2,000
SALES (corp-wide): 588MM **Privately Held**
WEB: www.americangolf.com
SIC: 7992 Public golf courses
PA: American Golf Corporation
909 N Pacific Coast Hwy
El Segundo CA 90245
310 664-4000

(P-18683)
AMERICAN GOLF CORPORATION
Also Called: La Mirada Country Club
15501 Alicante Rd, La Mirada (90638-3112)
PHONE..............................562 943-7123
Dill Crawford, *Manager*
EMP: 65
SALES (corp-wide): 588MM **Privately Held**
WEB: www.americangolf.com
SIC: 7992 Public golf courses
PA: American Golf Corporation
909 N Pacific Coast Hwy
El Segundo CA 90245
310 664-4000

(P-18684)
AMERICAN GOLF CORPORATION
Also Called: Wood Ranch Golf Club
301 Wood Ranch Pkwy, Simi Valley (93065-6600)
PHONE..............................805 527-9663
Mark Kelly, *Manager*
EMP: 70
SALES (corp-wide): 588MM **Privately Held**
WEB: www.americangolf.com
SIC: 7992 7997 7299 Public golf courses; golf club, membership; banquet hall facilities
PA: American Golf Corporation
909 N Pacific Coast Hwy
El Segundo CA 90245
310 664-4000

(P-18685)
AMERICAN GOLF CORPORATION
Also Called: Coyote Hills Golf Course
1440 E Bastanchury Rd, Fullerton (92835-2822)
PHONE..............................714 672-6800
Brent Boznanski, *Manager*
Mike Hallowell, *Director*
Mark Kuramoto, *Manager*
EMP: 100
SALES (corp-wide): 588MM **Privately Held**
WEB: www.americangolf.com
SIC: 7992 7997 7299 5812 Public golf courses; membership sports & recreation clubs; banquet hall facilities; eating places
PA: American Golf Corporation
909 N Pacific Coast Hwy
El Segundo CA 90245
310 664-4000

(P-18686)
ANTIOCH PUBLIC GOLF CORP
Also Called: LONE TREE GOLF COURSE
4800 Golf Course Rd, Antioch (94531-8012)
P.O. Box 2115 (94531-2115)
PHONE..............................925 706-4220
Ollie Anderson, *President*
Jonathan Hork, *Executive*
Crystal Biggs, *Relations*
EMP: 58
SALES: 2.8MM **Privately Held**
SIC: 7992 5941 7999 5812 Public golf courses; golf goods & equipment; golf driving range; restaurant, family: independent

(P-18687)
BARONA CREEK GOLF CLUB
1932 Wildcat Canyon Rd, Lakeside (92040-1553)
PHONE..............................619 387-7018
Clifford Lachappa, *Chairman*
Dean Allen, *CFO*
Mike Murphy, *Info Tech Mgr*
Dawn Michel, *Project Mgr*
Sheila Lavery, *Human Res Mgr*
EMP: 60
SALES (est): 3.1MM **Privately Held**
SIC: 7992 Public golf courses

(P-18688)
BIG SKY COUNTRY CLUB LLC
Also Called: Lost Canyons Golf Course
3301 Lost Canyons Dr, Simi Valley (93063-7168)
PHONE..............................805 522-4653
Jay Collaite,
Liz Leaver, *Controller*
New Delos Ptnr,
EMP: 100 EST: 1997
SQ FT: 30,000
SALES (est): 2.7MM **Privately Held**
WEB: www.lostcanyons.com
SIC: 7992 5941 5812 Public golf courses; golf, tennis & ski shops; eating places

(P-18689)
BLACK GOLD GOLF CLUB
1 Black Gold Dr, Yorba Linda (92886-2383)
PHONE..............................714 961-0060
Eric Lohman, *General Mgr*
Jim Goss, *General Mgr*
Dave Bosak, *Technology*
Todd Elder, *Sales Staff*
Jon Lyng, *Director*
EMP: 90
SALES (est): 3.1MM **Privately Held**
SIC: 7992 Public golf courses

(P-18690)
BSL GOLF CORP
Also Called: Bayonet/Blackhorse Golf Course
1 Mcclure Way, Seaside (93955-7100)
PHONE..............................831 899-7271
Joe Priddy, *Manager*
EMP: 150
SALES (corp-wide): 9.1MM **Privately Held**
WEB: www.bayonetblackhorse.com
SIC: 7992 Public golf courses
PA: Bsl Golf Corp.
402 Heights Blvd
Houston TX 77007
713 522-4547

(P-18691)
CALIFORNIA FUJI INTERNATIONAL
Also Called: Malibu Country Club
901 Encinal Canyon Rd, Malibu (90265-2405)
P.O. Box 3126, Westlake Village (91359-0126)
PHONE..............................818 889-6680
Norihisa Koda, *General Mgr*
Takashi Nozu, *President*
Motohiro Nozu, *Vice Pres*
EMP: 50
SQ FT: 11,000
SALES: 4MM
SALES (corp-wide): 13.7MM **Privately Held**
WEB: www.malibucountryclub.net
SIC: 7992 5812 Public golf courses; eating places

PRODUCTS & SVCS

PA: Tokyo Leisure Development Co.,Ltd.
3-12, Kioicho
Chiyoda-Ku TKY 102-0
352 750-922

(P-18692)
CALIFORNIA OAK VALLEY GOLF
Also Called: Oak Valley Golf Club
1888 Golf Club Dr, Beaumont
(92223-9700)
PHONE.....................951 769-9771
Mike Pearson, *Manager*
Evlyon Then, *Manager*
EMP: 50
SQ FT: 1,000
SALES (est): 2.4MM **Privately Held**
SIC: 7992 Public golf courses

(P-18693)
CHAMPIONSHIP GOLF SERVICES INC
2340 Silver Oak Cir, Corona (92882-6025)
P.O. Box 79156 (92877-0171)
PHONE.....................951 272-4340
Steven Plummer, *President*
Cheri Plummer, *CFO*
EMP: 145
SALES: 5.9MM **Privately Held**
SIC: 7992 Public golf courses

(P-18694)
CITY OF CONCORD
4050 Port Chicago Hwy, Concord
(94520-1121)
PHONE.....................925 686-6262
Joe Fernandez, *Manager*
EMP: 60
SQ FT: 3,200 **Privately Held**
WEB: www.cpd.ci.concord.ca.us
SIC: 7992 9111 Public golf courses; mayors' offices
PA: City Of Concord
1950 Parkside Dr
Concord CA 94519
925 671-3000

(P-18695)
CITY OF DELANO
Also Called: City Corporation Yard
725 S Lexington St, Delano (93215-3617)
PHONE.....................661 721-3350
Phil Newhouse, *Branch Mgr*
Craig Wilson, *Vice Pres*
EMP: 50 **Privately Held**
SIC: 7992 Public golf courses
PA: City Of Delano
1015 11th Ave
Delano CA 93215
661 721-3300

(P-18696)
CITY OF OXNARD
Also Called: River Ridge Gulf Course
2401 W Vineyard Ave, Oxnard
(93036-2218)
PHONE.....................805 983-4653
Otto Kenny, *General Mgr*
EMP: 100 **Privately Held**
WEB: www.oxnardtourism.com
SIC: 7992 Public golf courses
PA: City Of Oxnard
300 W 3rd St Uppr Fl4
Oxnard CA 93030
805 385-7803

(P-18697)
CITY OF PASADENA
Also Called: Brookside Golf Course
1133 Rosemont Ave, Pasadena
(91103-2401)
PHONE.....................626 543-4708
EMP: 60 **Privately Held**
SIC: 7992 9111
PA: City Of Pasadena
100 N Garfield Ave
Pasadena CA 91101
626 744-4386

(P-18698)
CLUBCORP USA INC
Also Called: Turkey Creek Golf Club
1525 Highway 193, Lincoln (95648-9639)
PHONE.....................916 434-9100
Brent Cohen, *Manager*
EMP: 50

SALES (corp-wide): 477MM **Privately Held**
WEB: www.remington-gc.com
SIC: 7992 5941 5813 5812 Public golf courses; sporting goods & bicycle shops; drinking places; eating places
HQ: Clubcorp Usa, Inc.
3030 Lyndon B Johnson Fwy
Dallas TX 75234
972 243-6191

(P-18699)
COUNTY OF LOS ANGELES
Also Called: Parks and Recreation Dept
1875 Fairplex Dr, Pomona (91768-1240)
PHONE.....................909 629-1166
Chad Hackman, *General Mgr*
EMP: 55 **Privately Held**
WEB: www.co.la.ca.us
SIC: 7992 9512 7299 Public golf courses; recreational program administration, government; ; wedding chapel, privately operated
PA: County Of Los Angeles
500 W Temple St Ste 437
Los Angeles CA 90012
213 974-1101

(P-18700)
COURSECO INC (PA)
1039 N Mcdowell Blvd B, Petaluma
(94954-1173)
PHONE.....................707 763-0335
Michael Sharp, *CEO*
John C Telischak, *Shareholder*
Tom Bugbee, *President*
Thomas B Isaak, *President*
Craig Hazel, *CFO*
EMP: 1025
SALES (est): 31.7MM **Privately Held**
WEB: www.courseco.com
SIC: 7992 Public golf courses

(P-18701)
COYOTE CREEK GOLF CLUB
1 Coyote Creek Golf Dr, Morgan Hill
(95037-9052)
P.O. Box 2527 (95038-2527)
PHONE.....................408 463-1400
Stephan Vigiano, *General Mgr*
EMP: 75
SQ FT: 12,000
SALES (est): 5.2MM **Privately Held**
WEB: www.coyotecreekgolf.com
SIC: 7992 5812 5941 Public golf courses; eating places; sporting goods & bicycle shops

(P-18702)
CROCKETT & COINC
Also Called: Bonita Golf Club
5540 Sweetwater Rd, Bonita (91902-2137)
PHONE.....................619 267-1103
Clayton Crockett, *Principal*
EMP: 58
SALES (corp-wide): 4.9MM **Privately Held**
WEB: www.bonitagolfclub.com
SIC: 7992 5812 Public golf courses; eating places
PA: Crockett & Co.Inc.
5120 Robinwood Rd Ste A22
Bonita CA 91902
619 267-6410

(P-18703)
CRSTB PARTNERS LLC
Also Called: Twelve Bridges Golf Club
3075 Twelve Bridges Dr, Lincoln (95648)
PHONE.....................916 645-7200
Chris S Member, *Principal*
EMP: 110
SALES (est): 1.4MM **Privately Held**
SIC: 7992 Public golf courses

(P-18704)
CYPRESS RIDGE GOLF COURSE
780 Cypress Ridge Pkwy, Arroyo Grande
(93420-6524)
PHONE.....................805 474-7979
Dennis Sullivan, *Owner*
Jodi Sailors, *Relations*
EMP: 50
SALES (est): 1.8MM **Privately Held**
SIC: 7992 6531 Public golf courses; real estate agents & managers

(P-18705)
D C GOLF A CA PARTNERSHIP
Also Called: Eaton Canyon Golf Course
1456 E Mendocino St, Altadena
(91001-2600)
PHONE.....................626 797-3821
Doug Colliflower, *Managing Prtnr*
EMP: 50
SQ FT: 6,000
SALES (est): 1.7MM **Privately Held**
WEB: www.dcgolf.info
SIC: 7992 5812 Public golf courses; American restaurant

(P-18706)
DESERT WILLOW GOLF RESORT INC
Also Called: Desert Willow Golf Course
38995 Desert Willow Dr, Palm Desert
(92260-1674)
PHONE.....................760 346-0015
Richard Mogensen, *General Mgr*
EMP: 150
SQ FT: 33,000
SALES (est): 8.3MM **Privately Held**
WEB: www.desertwillow.com
SIC: 7992 Public golf courses

(P-18707)
DONOVAN BROS GOLF LLC
Also Called: Tierra Rejada Golf Course
15187 Tierra Rejada Rd, Moorpark
(93021-9756)
PHONE.....................805 531-9300
Michael Donovan,
Jerry Crumpler,
Ted Kruger,
Brian Durtschi, *Manager*
EMP: 60
SALES (est): 3MM **Privately Held**
WEB: www.donovanbrosgolf.com
SIC: 7992 Public golf courses

(P-18708)
DONOVAN GOLF COURSES MGT (PA)
Also Called: Willowick Golf Course
3017 W 5th St, Santa Ana (92703-1827)
PHONE.....................714 554-0672
William J Donovan Sr, *President*
Elana C Donovan, *Vice Pres*
Dan Donovan, *Manager*
William Donovan, *Manager*
EMP: 120 **EST:** 1975
SQ FT: 1,500
SALES (est): 6.3MM **Privately Held**
WEB: www.willowickgolf.com
SIC: 7992 Public golf courses

(P-18709)
DONOVAN GOLF COURSES MGT
Also Called: Western Hills Golf & Cntry CLB
1800 Carbon Canyon Rd, Chino (91708)
PHONE.....................714 528-6400
Michael Donovan, *General Mgr*
EMP: 50
SALES (corp-wide): 6.3MM **Privately Held**
WEB: www.willowickgolf.com
SIC: 7992 Public golf courses
PA: Donovan Golf Courses Management, Inc
3017 W 5th St
Santa Ana CA 92703
714 554-0672

(P-18710)
EAGLE GLEN COUNTRY CLUB LLC
Also Called: Eagle Glen Golf Club
1800 Eagle Glen Pkwy, Corona
(92883-0620)
PHONE.....................951 272-4653
Jim Previty, *Chairman*
Tiffany Elsner, *Sales Mgr*
EMP: 60
SQ FT: 26,000
SALES (est): 4MM **Privately Held**
WEB: www.eagleglengc.com
SIC: 7992 Public golf courses

(P-18711)
EL PRADO GOLF COURSE LP
6555 Pine Ave, Chino (91708-9192)
PHONE.....................909 597-1751

Bruce Jenke, *General Ptnr*
Anthony Foo, *Partner*
G Barton Heuler, *Partner*
Walter Heuler, *Partner*
Greg Entrup, *Director*
EMP: 80
SQ FT: 5,000
SALES (est): 4.5MM **Privately Held**
SIC: 7992 Public golf courses

(P-18712)
EMPIRE GOLF INC (PA)
Also Called: Fairgrounds Golf Center
14670 Cantova Way Ste 228, Rancho Murieta (95683-9005)
P.O. Box 689, Sloughhouse (95683-0689)
PHONE.....................916 314-3150
Rod Metzler, *President*
EMP: 75
SQ FT: 1,500
SALES (est): 5.2MM **Privately Held**
SIC: 7992 8742 Public golf courses; business consultant

(P-18713)
FOUNTAIN GROVE GOLF & ATHC CLB
1525 Fountaingrove Pkwy, Santa Rosa
(95403-1778)
PHONE.....................707 521-3207
Greg Sabens, *Manager*
EMP: 75
SQ FT: 33,000
SALES: 5MM **Privately Held**
WEB: www.fountaingrovegolf.com
SIC: 7992 7299 5941 7997 Public golf courses; banquet hall facilities; golf goods & equipment; golf club, membership

(P-18714)
FOUR SEASONS RESORT AVIARA
Also Called: Aviar Golf Club
7447 Batiquitos Dr, Carlsbad (92011-4732)
PHONE.....................760 603-6900
James Bellington, *Manager*
EMP: 74
SALES (corp-wide): 5.5MM **Privately Held**
SIC: 7992 7011 Public golf courses; hotels
HQ: Four Seasons Hotels Limited
1165 Leslie St
North York ON M3C 2
416 449-1750

(P-18715)
GLEN ANNIE GOLF CLUB
405 Glen Annie Rd, Goleta (93117-1427)
PHONE.....................805 968-6400
Richard Nahas, *General Mgr*
EMP: 80
SALES (est): 2.7MM **Privately Held**
SIC: 7992 Public golf courses

(P-18716)
GREEN RIVER GOLF CORPORATION
Also Called: Green River Golf Course
5215 Green River Rd, Corona
(92880-9404)
PHONE.....................714 970-8411
Judy Saguchi, *President*
EMP: 100
SQ FT: 30,000
SALES (est): 6.8MM **Privately Held**
WEB: www.playgreenriver.com
SIC: 7992 5941 5813 5812 Public golf courses; sporting goods & bicycle shops; drinking places; eating places
PA: Courseco, Inc.
1039 N Mcdowell Blvd B
Petaluma CA 94954

(P-18717)
HAYWARD AREA RECREATION PKDIST
Also Called: Sky West Golf Course
1401 W Golf Course Rd, Hayward
(94541-4619)
PHONE.....................510 317-2300
Dan Eiamana, *Branch Mgr*
Lee Hernandez, *Manager*
EMP: 50
SQ FT: 2,400

SALES (corp-wide): 34.9MM **Privately Held**
SIC: 7992 Public golf courses
PA: Hayward Area Recreation & Pk.Dist
1099 E St
Hayward CA 94541
510 670-1665

(P-18718)
HERITAGE GOLF GROUP INC
Also Called: Valencia Country Club
27330 Tourney Rd, Valencia (91355-1806)
PHONE.................................661 254-4401
Jim Fitzsimmons, *Manager*
EMP: 100
SALES (corp-wide): 583.7MM **Privately Held**
WEB: www.talegagolfclub.com
SIC: 7992 Public golf courses
HQ: Heritage Golf Group, Llc
12750 High Bluff Dr # 400
San Diego CA 92130
858 720-0694

(P-18719)
HERITAGE GOLF GROUP LLC
Also Called: Talega Golf Club
990 Avenida Talega, San Clemente (92673-6849)
PHONE.................................949 369-6226
David Foster, *Branch Mgr*
EMP: 70
SALES (corp-wide): 583.7MM **Privately Held**
WEB: www.talegagolfclub.com
SIC: 7992 Public golf courses
HQ: Heritage Golf Group, Llc
12750 High Bluff Dr # 400
San Diego CA 92130
858 720-0694

(P-18720)
HIGH TIDE AND GREEN GRASS INC
Also Called: River Ridge Golf Club
2401 W Vineyard Ave, Oxnard (93036-2218)
PHONE.................................805 981-8722
Carl Kanny, *President*
John Kanny, *Vice Pres*
Otto Kanny, *Vice Pres*
EMP: 84
SQ FT: 27,000
SALES (est): 3.5MM **Privately Held**
SIC: 7992 5812 Public golf courses; snack bar

(P-18721)
INDIAN VALLEY GOLF CLUB INC
3035 Novato Blvd, Novato (94947-1002)
P.O. Box 351 (94948-0351)
PHONE.................................415 897-1118
Jeff Mc Andrew, *President*
Fermin Vergara, *Vice Pres*
EMP: 50
SQ FT: 4,000
SALES: 2.6MM **Privately Held**
WEB: www.ivgc.com
SIC: 7992 5941 Public golf courses; golf goods & equipment

(P-18722)
INSTITUTE LLC
14830 Foothill Ave, Morgan Hill (95037-9595)
PHONE.................................408 782-7101
Steven Sorenson, *Owner*
EMP: 50
SQ FT: 200
SALES (est): 2.2MM **Privately Held**
SIC: 7992 Public golf courses

(P-18723)
J G GOLFING ENTERPRISES INC
Also Called: San Bernardino Golf Club
1494 S Waterman Ave, San Bernardino (92408-2805)
P.O. Box 3632, Running Springs (92382-3632)
PHONE.................................909 885-2414
Tom Shelf, *President*
EMP: 50
SQ FT: 4,000

SALES (est): 2.1MM **Privately Held**
WEB: www.sanbernardinogolfclub.com
SIC: 7992 Public golf courses

(P-18724)
KOLLWOOD GOLF OPERATING LP
Also Called: Kollstar Golf Company
4343 Von Karman Ave, Newport Beach (92660-2099)
PHONE.................................949 833-3025
Joseph Woodard, *Partner*
Donald M Koll, *Partner*
EMP: 400
SALES (est): 3.8MM **Privately Held**
SIC: 7992 Public golf courses

(P-18725)
LAGUNA BCH GOLF BNGLOW VLG LLC
Also Called: Aliso Creek Inn and Golf Crse
31106 Coast Hwy, Laguna Beach (92651-8130)
PHONE.................................949 499-2271
Mark Christy, *Mng Member*
Kurt Bjorkman, *General Mgr*
Mark Slymen, *Info Tech Mgr*
Johnny Sanabria, *Accounting Mgr*
Lisa Rosecrans, *Human Resources*
EMP: 65
SQ FT: 10,000
SALES (est): 5.7MM **Privately Held**
WEB: www.alisocreekinn.com
SIC: 7992 7011 Public golf courses; hotels

(P-18726)
LAKESIDE GOLF CLUB
4500 W Lakeside Dr, Burbank (91505-4088)
P.O. Box 2386, Toluca Lake (91610-0386)
PHONE.................................818 984-0601
Jerry Fard, *Manager*
Michael E Henry, *CEO*
Isabel Cruz, *Controller*
EMP: 98
SQ FT: 25,000
SALES: 12.4MM **Privately Held**
WEB: www.lakesidegolfclub.com
SIC: 7992 Public golf courses

(P-18727)
LB HILLS GOLF CLUB LLC
Also Called: Golf Club At Terra Lago, The
84000 Terra Lago Pkwy, Indio (92203-9706)
PHONE.................................760 775-2000
Jeff Walser, *Partner*
John Lee, *General Mgr*
Neil Sauer, *Manager*
EMP: 100
SALES (est): 4.1MM **Privately Held**
WEB: www.golfclub-terralago.com
SIC: 7992 7991 7299 Public golf courses; physical fitness facilities; banquet hall facilities

(P-18728)
LINCOLN HILLS GOLF CLUB
1005 Sun City Ln, Lincoln (95648-8443)
PHONE.................................916 543-9200
Marker Brian, *President*
John Reuer, *Manager*
EMP: 50
SALES (est): 2.2MM **Privately Held**
WEB: www.lincolnhillsclub.com
SIC: 7992 7997 Public golf courses; golf club, membership

(P-18729)
LOS SERRANOS GOLF CLUB
Also Called: Los Serranos Golf & Cntry CLB
15656 Yorba Ave, Chino Hills (91709-3129)
PHONE.................................909 597-1769
John A Kramer Jr, *CEO*
Gloria Kramer, *Shareholder*
John A Kramer Sr, *President*
David Kramer, *Treasurer*
Ronald Kramer, *Vice Pres*
EMP: 135
SQ FT: 41,896
SALES (est): 9.1MM **Privately Held**
WEB: www.losserranoscountryclub.com
SIC: 7992 5812 5813 Public golf courses; American restaurant; snack shop; cocktail lounge

(P-18730)
LOS VERDES MNS GOLF CNTRY CLB
Also Called: Los Verdes Golf Curse
7000 Los Verdes Dr Ste 1, Rancho Palos Verdes (90275-5600)
PHONE.................................310 377-7370
Bob Lockhart, *General Mgr*
Fred Weibell, *Principal*
EMP: 50
SALES: 87.1K **Privately Held**
SIC: 7992 Public golf courses

(P-18731)
MADERAS GOLF CLUB
17750 Old Coach Rd, Poway (92064-6621)
PHONE.................................858 451-8100
Bill O'Brien, *General Mgr*
EMP: 80
SALES (est): 3MM **Privately Held**
SIC: 7992 Public golf courses

(P-18732)
MADISON CLUB OWNERS ASSN
Also Called: Madison Club, The
53035 Meriwether Way, La Quinta (92253-5535)
P.O. Box 1558 (92247-1558)
PHONE.................................760 777-9320
Douglas Siebold, *CEO*
Brian Ellis, *Principal*
EMP: 125
SQ FT: 70,000
SALES (est): 10.1MM **Privately Held**
SIC: 7992 Public golf courses

(P-18733)
MESA VERDE PARTNERS
Also Called: Costa Mesa Country Club
1701 Golf Course Dr, Costa Mesa (92626-5049)
PHONE.................................714 540-7500
Scott Henderson, *Partner*
Jim Fetterly, *Superintendent*
EMP: 100
SQ FT: 12,000
SALES (est): 3.6MM
SALES (corp-wide): 5.3MM **Privately Held**
SIC: 7992 7997 5813 5812 Public golf courses; membership sports & recreation clubs; drinking places; eating places
PA: Santa Anita Associates
405 S Santa Anita Ave
Arcadia CA 91006
626 447-2764

(P-18734)
MF DAILY OXNARD RANCH PARTNR
Also Called: Soule Park Golf Course
1033 E Ojai Ave, Ojai (93023-3018)
P.O. Box 758 (93024-0758)
PHONE.................................805 646-5633
Don Miller, *General Mgr*
Tim Wolfe, *Officer*
EMP: 50
SQ FT: 13,000
SALES (est): 1.3MM **Privately Held**
SIC: 7992 5941 5812 Public golf courses; golf goods & equipment; eating places

(P-18735)
MILE SQUARE GOLF COURSE
10401 Warner Ave, Fountain Valley (92708-1604)
PHONE.................................714 962-5541
David A Rainville, *Partner*
EMP: 109
SQ FT: 12,000
SALES (est): 5.9MM **Privately Held**
WEB: www.milesquaregolfcourse.com
SIC: 7992 7999 5812 Public golf courses; golf driving range; American restaurant

(P-18736)
MONARCH BAY GOLF RESORT
13800 Monarch Bay Dr, San Leandro (94577-6401)
PHONE.................................510 895-2162
Roland Smith, *CEO*
David Price, *President*
EMP: 100
SALES (est): 1.7MM **Privately Held**
SIC: 7992 Public golf courses

(P-18737)
MONARCH BEACH GOLF LINKS (HQ)
50 Monarch Beach Resort N, Dana Point (92629-4084)
PHONE.................................949 240-8247
Hale Kelly, *Director*
John Gray, *Assistant*
EMP: 80
SALES (est): 4.6MM **Privately Held**
WEB: www.monarchbeachgolf.com
SIC: 7992 Public golf courses

(P-18738)
MORTON GOLF LLC
Also Called: Haggin Oaks Golf Shop
3645 Fulton Ave, Sacramento (95821-1808)
PHONE.................................916 481-4653
Terry Daubert, *Principal*
Jack Gillette, *Controller*
Marlene Kawaguchi, *Buyer*
Warene Weathers, *Inv Control Mgr*
Kathleen Morton,
EMP: 100
SQ FT: 13,800
SALES (est): 12.3MM **Privately Held**
WEB: www.mortongolfsales.com
SIC: 7992 5941 5813 5812 Public golf courses; golf goods & equipment; drinking places; eating places

(P-18739)
MOTHERLODE INVESTORS LLC
Also Called: Greenlaw Grupe Jr Operating Co
711 Mccauley Ranch Rd, Angels Camp (95222-9562)
PHONE.................................209 736-8112
Greenlaw Grupe,
EMP: 85
SALES (est): 2.4MM **Privately Held**
SIC: 7992

(P-18740)
NEW DISCOVERY INC
Also Called: Discovery Bay Golf & Cntry CLB
2600 Cherry Hills Dr, Byron (94505-1430)
P.O. Box 907, Concord (94522-0907)
PHONE.................................925 634-0505
Keneth H Hofmann, *President*
EMP: 75
SALES (est): 18MM **Privately Held**
SIC: 7992 Public golf courses

(P-18741)
OAKMONT GOLF CLUB INC (PA)
7025 Oakmont Dr, Santa Rosa (95409-6301)
PHONE.................................707 538-2454
John Yacobellis, *Director*
John Theilade, *Director*
EMP: 60
SQ FT: 4,000
SALES: 3.8MM **Privately Held**
WEB: www.oakmontgc.com
SIC: 7992 7997 5941 Public golf courses; golf club, membership; golf goods & equipment

(P-18742)
OCEAN LINKS CORPORATION
Also Called: Half Moon Bay Golf Links
2 Miramontes Point Rd, Half Moon Bay (94019-2377)
PHONE.................................650 726-1800
Mark Kendall, *President*
Michael Herold, *Sales Staff*
Yunus Yilmaz, *Food Svc Dir*
Brett Bergschneider, *Director*
Mischa Szymanski, *Director*
▼ EMP: 100
SQ FT: 6,000
SALES (est): 3.7MM **Privately Held**
SIC: 7992 Public golf courses

(P-18743)
POPPY HILLS INC
3200 Lopez Rd, Pebble Beach (93953-2900)
PHONE.................................831 625-1513
Lyn Nelson, *President*
Manny Sousa, *Superintendent*
EMP: 60
SQ FT: 8,000

SALES (est): 1.6MM **Privately Held**
SIC: **7992** 5941 5812 Public golf courses;
golf goods & equipment; eating places
PA: Poppy Holding Inc
3200 Lopez Rd
Pebble Beach CA 93953

(P-18744)
POPPY RIDGE INC
Also Called: Poppy Ridge Golf Course
4280 Greenville Rd, Livermore
(94550-9720)
PHONE.....................925 456-8229
Paul Porter, *President*
Raymond Evernham, *Executive*
Jennifer Barbara, *Marketing Mgr*
Chris Bitticks, *Director*
Todd Cook, *Superintendent*
EMP: 75
SALES (est): 4.3MM **Privately Held**
SIC: **7992** Public golf courses
PA: Poppy Holding Inc
3200 Lopez Rd
Pebble Beach CA 93953

(P-18745)
PREMIER GOLF PROPERTIES LP
Also Called: Cottonwood Golf Club
3121 Willow Glen Dr, El Cajon
(92019-4604)
PHONE.....................619 442-9891
Daryl Idler, *Partner*
EMP: 90
SALES (est): 4.8MM **Privately Held**
WEB: www.cottonwoodgolf.com
SIC: **7992** Public golf courses

(P-18746)
PRESERVE GOLF CLUB INC
1 Rancho San Carlos Rd, Carmel
(93923-7999)
PHONE.....................831 620-6871
Thomas Gray, *President*
EMP: 50
SQ FT: 20,000
SALES: 4MM **Privately Held**
SIC: **7992** Public golf courses

(P-18747)
PRIMM VALLEY GOLF CLUB
1 Yates Wells Rd, Nipton (92364)
PHONE.....................702 679-5509
Keith Flatt, *Director*
Dustin Flatt, *General Mgr*
▲ EMP: 70
SALES (est): 2.5MM **Privately Held**
SIC: **7992** Public golf courses

(P-18748)
PYJ V A CALIFORNIA LTD PARTNR
Also Called: Westlake Village Golf Course
4812 Lakeview Canyon Rd, Westlake Village (91361-4030)
PHONE.....................805 495-8437
Clinton Airey, *General Mgr*
EMP: 60
SQ FT: 7,131
SALES: 3MM **Privately Held**
SIC: **7992** 7999 6531 5091 Public golf
courses; golf services & professionals;
real estate managers; golf equipment

(P-18749)
QUARRY AT LA QUINTA INC (PA)
41865 Boardwalk Ste 214, Palm Desert
(92211-9033)
PHONE.....................760 777-1100
William Morrow, *President*
EMP: 60
SALES (est): 5.5MM **Privately Held**
SIC: **7992** Public golf courses

(P-18750)
RANCH GOLF CLUB
4601 Hill Top View Ln, San Jose
(95138-2707)
PHONE.....................408 270-0557
Mike Higuera Jr, *Superintendent*
Kristy Park, *General Mgr*
Thomas Mejia,
Julie Pascua, *Manager*
EMP: 75

SQ FT: 2,880
SALES (est): 5.3MM **Privately Held**
SIC: **7992** Public golf courses

(P-18751)
RAWITSER GOLF SHOP MIKE
Also Called: San Jose Municipal Golf Course
1560 Oakland Rd, San Jose (95131-2430)
PHONE.....................408 441-4653
Mike Rawitser, *President*
Berne Finch, *Director*
EMP: 50
SQ FT: 2,500
SALES (est): 1.9MM **Privately Held**
WEB: www.sjmuni.com
SIC: **7992** Public golf courses

(P-18752)
ROBINSON RANCH GOLF LLC
27734 Sand Canyon Rd, Santa Clarita
(91387-3639)
PHONE.....................818 885-0599
Bill McNair,
EMP: 120 EST: 1999
SALES (est): 8.4MM **Privately Held**
WEB: www.robinsonranchgolf.com
SIC: **7992** 7997 Public golf courses; membership sports & recreation clubs

(P-18753)
ROOSTER RUN GOLF CLUB INC
2301 E Washington St, Petaluma
(94954-3897)
PHONE.....................707 778-1211
Rob Watson, *President*
John Nice, *Vice Pres*
EMP: 50
SALES (est): 2.8MM **Privately Held**
WEB: www.roosterrun.com
SIC: **7992** 5812 Public golf courses; eating places

(P-18754)
RUBY HILL GOLF CLUB LLC
3400 W Ruby Hill Dr, Pleasanton
(94566-3604)
PHONE.....................925 417-5840
Jim Ghielmetti,
Chef Harold, *Executive*
Michael Rood, *General Mgr*
Anne Fay, *Director*
Melisa Johnson, *Director*
EMP: 100 EST: 1994
SALES (est): 8.1MM **Privately Held**
WEB: www.rubyhill.com
SIC: **7992** Public golf courses

(P-18755)
SAN JUAN GOLF INC
Also Called: San Juan Hill Country Club
32120 San Juan Creek Rd, San Juan
Capistrano (92675-3840)
PHONE.....................949 493-1167
Tony Kato, *President*
Mike Abee, *General Mgr*
Ashley Demien, *Food Svc Dir*
Stacey Strausbaugh, *Director*
EMP: 50
SALES (est): 3.3MM **Privately Held**
SIC: **7992** 5812 5941 Public golf courses;
eating places; golf goods & equipment

(P-18756)
SAN JUAN OAKS LLC
Also Called: San Juan Oaks Golf Club
3825 Union Rd, Hollister (95023-9135)
PHONE.....................831 636-6113
Kenneth Gimelli,
Rachele Giusiana, *Human Resources*
Brandie Brewster, *Sales Staff*
Gail Grammatico, *Director*
EMP: 80
SQ FT: 1,800
SALES (est): 6.9MM **Privately Held**
WEB: www.sanjuanoaks.com
SIC: **7992** 5941 5812 5813 Public golf
courses; golf goods & equipment; eating
places; bar (drinking places); banquet
hall facilities

(P-18757)
SAND CANYON LLC
Also Called: Strawberry Farms Golf Club
11 Strawberry Farm Rd, Irvine
(92612-2300)
PHONE.....................949 551-2560

Doug Decinces, *Partner*
EMP: 80
SALES (est): 4.2MM **Privately Held**
WEB: www.sandcanyon.com
SIC: **7992** Public golf courses

(P-18758)
SANTA ANITA ASSOCIATES (PA)
Also Called: Santa Anita Golf Course
405 S Santa Anita Ave, Arcadia
(91006-3509)
PHONE.....................626 447-2764
Scott L Henderson, *Managing Prtnr*
Mike Donavan, *Partner*
EMP: 60
SQ FT: 16,000
SALES (est): 5.3MM **Privately Held**
SIC: **7992** 5812 7999 7299 Public golf
courses; American restaurant; golf cart,
power, rental; golf driving range; banquet
hall facilities

(P-18759)
SANTA TERESA GOLF CLUB
Also Called: Santa Teresa Golf Center
260 Bernal Rd, San Jose (95119-1809)
PHONE.....................408 225-2650
Mike Rawitser, *Partner*
Lawrence Lobue, *General Ptnr*
Victor Lobue, *General Ptnr*
John Mc Enery III, *General Ptnr*
Rudy Steadler, *General Ptnr*
EMP: 70
SQ FT: 5,300
SALES (est): 4.3MM **Privately Held**
WEB: www.all-seasons-golf.com
SIC: **7992** Public golf courses

(P-18760)
SCGA GOLF COURSE MGT INC
39500 Robrt Trnt Jnes Pkw, Murrieta
(92563-5849)
PHONE.....................951 677-7446
Jon Bilger, *President*
EMP: 72
SQ FT: 4,000
SALES: 2.5MM
SALES (corp-wide): 7MM **Privately Held**
WEB: www.scgamembersclub.com
SIC: **7992** 5812 5941 7999 Public golf
courses; eating places; golf goods &
equipment; golf driving range
PA: Southern California Golf Association
3740 Cahuenga Blvd
North Hollywood CA 91604
818 980-3630

(P-18761)
SHAPELL INC
9000 S Gale Ridge Rd, San Ramon
(94582-9174)
PHONE.....................925 735-4253
Joey Pickavance, *Manager*
EMP: 75
SALES (est): 934.5K **Privately Held**
SIC: **7992** Public golf courses

(P-18762)
SIERRA LAKES GOLF CLUB
16600 Clubhouse Dr, Fontana
(92336-5138)
PHONE.....................909 350-2500
Dave Lewis, *President*
Rick Danruther, *Manager*
EMP: 60
SALES (est): 3.4MM **Privately Held**
WEB: www.sierralakes.com
SIC: **7992** Public golf courses

(P-18763)
SILVER ROCK RESORT GOLF CLUB
79179 Ahmanson Ln, La Quinta
(92253-5715)
PHONE.....................760 777-8884
Randy Duncan, *Manager*
Doug Vonbank, *Controller*
Willie Lopez, *Superintendent*
EMP: 100
SALES (est): 4.5MM **Privately Held**
SIC: **7992** Public golf courses

(P-18764)
SISKIYOU LAKE GOLF RESORT INC
Also Called: Mount Shasta Resort
1000 Siskiyou Lake Blvd, Mount Shasta
(96067-9482)
PHONE.....................530 926-3030
John Cullison, *President*
John Fryer, *Director*
EMP: 80
SALES (est): 5.5MM **Privately Held**
WEB: www.mtshastaresort.com
SIC: **7992** 5941 7011 5812 Public golf
courses; golf goods & equipment; tourist
camps, cabins, cottages & courts; American restaurant

(P-18765)
STEELE CANYON GOLF CLUB CORP (PA)
3199 Stonefield Dr, Jamul (91935-1527)
PHONE.....................619 441-6900
Lawrence M Taylor, *CEO*
Barry Rice, *Food Svc Dir*
Colin Radchenko, *Manager*
Antonio Osuna, *Superintendent*
Paul Spangler, *Supervisor*
EMP: 53 EST: 1991
SALES (est): 6.2MM **Privately Held**
SIC: **7992** Public golf courses

(P-18766)
STEVINSON RANCH-SAVANNAH GP
Also Called: Stevinson Ranch Golf Club
2700 Van Clief Rd, Stevinson
(95374-9619)
PHONE.....................209 668-8200
Dee Roadman,
EMP: 80
SALES (est): 5.4MM **Privately Held**
WEB: www.stevinsonranch.com
SIC: **7992** 7999 5941 7299 Public golf
courses; golf driving range; golf goods &
equipment; banquet hall facilities; hotels
& motels; eating places

(P-18767)
STONETREE GOLF LLC
Also Called: Stonetree Management
9 Stonetree Ln, Novato (94945-3541)
PHONE.....................415 209-6744
Warren Spieker, *Partner*
Bill Bunce, *Partner*
Dennis Singleton, *Partner*
EMP: 50
SALES (est): 5.1MM **Privately Held**
WEB: www.blackpt.com
SIC: **7992** 5941 5812 Public golf courses;
golf, tennis & ski shops; family restaurants

(P-18768)
STRAWBERRY FARMS GOLF CLUB LLC
11 Strawberry Farm Rd, Irvine
(92612-2300)
PHONE.....................949 551-2560
Doug Decinese,
EMP: 75
SALES (est): 3.6MM **Privately Held**
WEB: www.strawberryfarmsgolf.com
SIC: **7992** Public golf courses

(P-18769)
SUN CITY RSVLLE CMNTY ASSN INC (PA)
Also Called: TIMBER CREEK GOLF COURSE
7050 Del Webb Blvd, Roseville
(95747-8040)
PHONE.....................916 774-3880
Dewolfe Emory, *CEO*
Earl Wiklund, *Exec Dir*
Jason Smith, *Director*
Chris Hall, *Manager*
EMP: 200 EST: 1994
SALES: 11.2MM **Privately Held**
WEB: www.scr-cc.com
SIC: **7992** 5812 Public golf courses; eating places; caterers

(P-18770)
SUNOL VLY GOLF &
RECREATION CO
Also Called: Sunol Valley Golf Course
5117 Mount Tam Cir, Pleasanton
(94588-3676)
PHONE...................................925 862-2404
Ron Ivaldi, *General Ptnr*
Lisa Grannzella, *Partner*
Brian Richardson, *General Mgr*
Carol Richardson, *Office Mgr*
Perry Lee, *Technology*
EMP: 100
SALES (est): 4MM **Privately Held**
WEB: www.sunolvalley.com
SIC: 7992 5812 5813 7997 Public golf
courses; coffee shop; snack shop; cock-
tail lounge; membership sports & recre-
ation clubs; sporting goods & bicycle
shops

(P-18771)
TAHOE DONNER GOLF COURSE
INC
11509 Northwoods Blvd, Truckee
(96161-6000)
PHONE.....................................530 587-9455
Mike Peters, *Executive Asst*
EMP: 75
SALES: 5MM **Privately Held**
SIC: 7992 5813 5812 Public golf courses;
bar (drinking places); American restaurant

(P-18772)
TRADITION GOLF CLUB
ASSOCIATES
78505 Avenue 52, La Quinta (92253-2802)
PHONE.....................................760 564-3355
David Champman, *General Mgr*
Beth Bland, *Director*
EMP: 60
SALES (est): 2MM **Privately Held**
SIC: 7992 Public golf courses

(P-18773)
TRADITIONS GOLF LLC
Also Called: Cinnabar Hills Golf Club
23600 Mckean Rd, San Jose (95141-1001)
PHONE.....................................408 323-5200
Bill Baron,
D Scott Hoyt, *General Mgr*
Lee Brandenburg,
Paul Pugh,
EMP: 100
SQ FT: 25,000
SALES (est): 7.5MM **Privately Held**
WEB: www.cinnabarhills.com
SIC: 7992 Public golf courses

(P-18774)
TRILOGY GOLF AT LA QUINTA
60151 Trilogy Pkwy, La Quinta
(92253-7640)
PHONE.....................................760 771-0707
Tom Williams, *Manager*
Ralph Bernhisel, *General Mgr*
Marge Deschaak, *Office Admin*
EMP: 64
SALES (est): 2.4MM
SALES (corp-wide): 2.2B **Privately Held**
WEB: www.jfshea.com
SIC: 7992 Public golf courses
HQ: J.F. Shea Construction, Inc.
655 Brea Canyon Rd
Walnut CA 91789
909 595-4397

(P-18775)
VB GOLF LLC
Also Called: Mariner's Point Golf Course
2401 E 3rd Ave, Foster City (94404-1067)
PHONE.....................................650 573-7888
Chris Aliaga, *Manager*
Sergio Garcia, *Partner*
William Verbrugge, *Partner*
EMP: 55
SALES (est): 2.7MM **Privately Held**
SIC: 7992 Public golf courses

(P-18776)
VH PROPERTY CORP
1 Ocean Trl, Rancho Palos Verdes (90275)
PHONE.....................................310 303-3210
Donald Trump Jr, *Director*
Tom Sperandeo, *Controller*

EMP: 300
SQ FT: 39,883
SALES (est): 6.6MM **Privately Held**
SIC: 7992 Public golf courses

(P-18777)
VINTNERS GOLF CLUB
Also Called: Lakeside Grill, The
7901 Solano Ave, Yountville (94599-1453)
PHONE.....................................707 944-1992
Mike Stead, *Owner*
Jason Boldt, *General Mgr*
EMP: 50 EST: 1999
SALES (est): 2.2MM **Privately Held**
WEB: www.vintnersgolfclub.com
SIC: 7992 Public golf courses

(P-18778)
WESTRIDGE GOLF INC
1400 S La Habra Hills Dr, La Habra
(90631-6998)
PHONE.....................................562 690-4200
J C Song, *General Mgr*
EMP: 75
SQ FT: 15,000
SALES (est): 4.4MM **Privately Held**
WEB: www.westridgegolf.com
SIC: 7992 Public golf courses

(P-18779)
WINDSOR GOLF CLUB INC
1340 19th Hole Dr, Windsor (95492-6829)
PHONE.....................................707 838-7888
Charlie Gibson, *General Mgr*
Larry Wasm, *Treasurer*
Brove O'Brien, *Vice Pres*
Alex Wright, *Principal*
Tami Sullberg, *General Mgr*
EMP: 60
SALES (est): 2.8MM **Privately Held**
WEB: www.windsorgolf.com
SIC: 7992 5941 Public golf courses; golf
goods & equipment

(P-18780)
WOODLEY LAKES GOLF
COURSE
6331 Woodley Ave, Van Nuys
(91406-6473)
PHONE.....................................818 780-6886
Phil Rigs, *Manager*
EMP: 70
SALES (est): 2.6MM **Privately Held**
SIC: 7992 Public golf courses

| **7993 Coin-Operated** |
| **Amusement Devices &** |

(P-18781)
CAMPO BAND MISSIONS
INDIANS
Also Called: Golden Acorn Casino & Trvl Ctr
1800 Golden Acorn Way, Campo
(91906-2301)
P.O. Box 310 (91906-0310)
PHONE.....................................619 938-6000
Don Trimble, *Manager*
Bill West, *CFO*
Larry Drouse, *General Mgr*
Annah Ceballos, *Admin Sec*
Leroy Berg, *Info Tech Mgr*
EMP: 330
SALES (est): 11.7MM **Privately Held**
SIC: 7993 5812 Gambling establishments
operating coin-operated machines; Ameri-
can restaurant
PA: Campo Band Of Missions Indians
36190 Church Rd
Campo CA 91906
619 478-9046

(P-18782)
EMOTIV SYSTEMS INC
1770 Post St Ste 350, San Francisco
(94115-3606)
PHONE.....................................415 503-3601
Tan Le, *President*
EMP: 50
SALES (est): 1.8MM **Privately Held**
SIC: 7993 Game machines

(P-18783)
INDUSTRY EVENTS
25501 Narbonne Ave, Lomita (90717-2511)
PHONE.....................................310 834-3422
John Bayouth, *Principal*
EMP: 50
SALES (est): 1.4MM **Privately Held**
SIC: 7993 Amusement arcade

(P-18784)
LOOFS LITE A LINE
2500 Long Beach Blvd, Long Beach
(90806-3112)
PHONE.....................................562 436-2978
Michael Sincola, *Owner*
Ettamay Errock, *Partner*
EMP: 50
SQ FT: 10,005
SALES (est): 1.1MM **Privately Held**
SIC: 7993 Arcades

(P-18785)
MOORETOWN RANCHERIA
Also Called: Feather Falls Casino
3 Alverda Dr, Oroville (95966-9379)
PHONE.....................................530 533-3885
Tom Yarbrough, *General Mgr*
Jerry Morgan, *CTO*
Dori Moura, *Human Res Dir*
EMP: 340 **Privately Held**
WEB: www.drumvision.com
SIC: 7993 7999 Gambling establishments
operating coin-operated machines; gam-
bling establishment
PA: Mooretown Rancheria
1 Alverda Dr
Oroville CA 95966

(P-18786)
PACHINKO WORLD INC
5912 Bolsa Ave 108, Huntington Beach
(92649-1105)
PHONE.....................................714 895-7772
Shinichi Hirabayashi, *CEO*
Yoneji Hirabayashi, *Ch of Bd*
Akinori Hirabayashi, *COO*
Haruo Miyano, *Admin Sec*
EMP: 195
SQ FT: 500
SALES (est): 9MM **Privately Held**
SIC: 7993 7999 5812 5194 Game ma-
chines; pinball machines; amusement ar-
cade; game parlor; Japanese restaurant;
cigarettes

(P-18787)
PLAYTIKA SANTA MONICA LLC
2701 Ocean Park Blvd # 220, Santa Monica
(90405-5237)
PHONE.....................................310 622-7380
Michael Demartino, *General Mgr*
EMP: 130
SALES (est): 3.2MM **Privately Held**
SIC: 7993 Video game arcade

(P-18788)
SCANDIA RECREATION
CENTERS
Also Called: Scandia Amusement Park
1155 S Wanamaker Ave, Ontario
(91761-7839)
PHONE.....................................909 390-3092
Scott Larson, *President*
Sharilyn Christensen, *Shareholder*
Mark Larson, *Shareholder*
Sara Larson, *Shareholder*
Todd Larson MD, *Shareholder*
EMP: 75
SQ FT: 92,480
SALES (est): 1.7MM **Privately Held**
SIC: 7993 7999 7996 Coin-operated
amusement devices; miniature golf
course operation; amusement parks

(P-18789)
SEGA ENTERTAINMENT USA
INC
Also Called: Gameworks
12777 W Jefferson Blvd # 100, Los Angeles
(90066-7034)
PHONE.....................................909 987-4263
Jerome Seeney, *Branch Mgr*
EMP: 60

SALES (corp-wide): 3B **Privately Held**
SIC: 7993 Mechanical games, coin-operated
HQ: Sega Entertainment Usa Inc
600 N Brand Blvd Fl 5
Glendale CA 91203
310 217-9500

| **7996 Amusement Parks** |

(P-18790)
APEX PARKS GROUP LLC (PA)
27061 Aliso Creek Rd # 100, Aliso Viejo
(92656-5322)
PHONE.....................................949 349-8461
John Fitzgerald, *CEO*
Greg Borman, *Senior VP*
Ken Kobane, *Vice Pres*
Rebecca Tortorelli, *Vice Pres*
Craig Stieglitz, *General Mgr*
EMP: 127 EST: 2014
SALES (est): 39.9MM **Privately Held**
SIC: 7996 Amusement parks

(P-18791)
CASINO MORONGO
49500 Seminole Dr, Cabazon
(92230-2202)
P.O. Box 366 (92230-0366)
PHONE.....................................951 849-3080
Gene Stachowksi, *Principal*
Joseph Osterloh, *Director*
EMP: 57
SALES (est): 5MM **Privately Held**
SIC: 7996 Amusement parks

(P-18792)
CEDAR FAIR LP
Great America Theme Park
4701 Great America Pkwy, Santa Clara
(95054-1287)
P.O. Box 1776 (95052-1776)
PHONE.....................................408 988-1776
David Mannix, *Systems Mgr*
Roger Ross, *Comms Mgr*
Brian Christensen, *Sales Staff*
Ernesto Lopez, *Director*
Armando Amezcua, *Supervisor*
EMP: 120
SALES (corp-wide): 1.3B **Publicly Held**
WEB: www.cedarfair.com
SIC: 7996 Theme park, amusement
PA: Cedar Fair, L.P.
1 Cedar Point Dr
Sandusky OH 44870
419 626-0830

(P-18793)
CITY OF OXNARD
Also Called: Streets Street Tree Inquiries
1060 Pacific Ave, Oxnard (93030-7337)
PHONE.....................................805 385-7950
Michael Henderson, *Director*
Sergio Cervantes, *Supervisor*
EMP: 100 **Privately Held**
WEB: www.oxnardtourism.com
SIC: 7996 Amusement parks
PA: City Of Oxnard
300 W 3rd St Uppr Fl4
Oxnard CA 93030
805 385-7803

(P-18794)
CITY OF VALLEJO
Also Called: Marine World/Africa USA
1001 Fairgrounds Dr, Vallejo (94589-4001)
PHONE.....................................707 644-4000
Joe Meck, *Vice Pres*
EMP: 350 **Privately Held**
WEB: www.ci.vallejo.ca.us
SIC: 7996 Theme park, amusement
PA: City Of Vallejo
555 Santa Clara St
Vallejo CA 94590
707 648-4575

(P-18795)
COUNTY OF SACRAMENTO
Also Called: Department of Regional Parks
10361 Rockingham Dr # 100, Sacramento
(95827-2519)
PHONE.....................................916 363-8383
Ron Suter, *Manager*
Janet Baker, *Principal*
Jill Ritzman, *Manager*

P
R
O
D
U
C
T
S

&

S
V
C
S

EMP: 82 **Privately Held**
WEB: www.sna.com
SIC: 7996 Amusement parks
PA: County Of Sacramento
700 H St Ste 7650
Sacramento CA 95814
916 874-5544

(P-18796)
DISCOVERY SCNCE CTR
ORNGE CNTY
2500 N Main St, Santa Ana (92705-6600)
PHONE..................................866 552-2823
Daniel Bolar, *Ch of Bd*
Joseph Adams, *President*
Lisa Charrier, *President*
Brie Griset Smith, *Vice Pres*
Luis Almonte, *Technology*
▲ EMP: 135
SALES: 12MM **Privately Held**
WEB: www.discoverycube.org
SIC: 7996 Amusement parks

(P-18797)
DISNEYLAND INTERNATIONAL
105 S Harbor Blvd, Anaheim (92805)
PHONE..................................714 781-4000
James Rasulo, *Manager*
EMP: 203 **Publicly Held**
SIC: 7996 Amusement parks
HQ: Disneyland International
770 The Cy Dr S Ste 6000
Orange CA 92868
714 490-3000

(P-18798)
DISNEYLAND INTERNATIONAL
(DH)
500 S Buena Vista St, Burbank
(91521-0001)
PHONE..................................818 560-1000
James Thomas, *President*
James Cora, *Ch of Bd*
Robert S Risteen, *Treasurer*
Doris Smith, *Admin Sec*
David A Hughes, *Asst Treas*
EMP: 200
SALES (est): 147MM **Publicly Held**
SIC: 7996 Theme park, amusement
HQ: Disney Enterprises, Inc.
500 S Buena Vista St
Burbank CA 91521
818 560-1000

(P-18799)
FESTIVAL FUN PARKS LLC
3500 Polk St, Riverside (92505-1824)
PHONE..................................951 785-3000
EMP: 68 **Privately Held**
SIC: 7996 Amusement parks
HQ: Festival Fun Parks, Llc
4590 Macarthur Blvd # 400
Newport Beach CA 92660
949 261-0404

(P-18800)
FESTIVAL FUN PARKS LLC
Also Called: Malibu Grand Prix 51
4590 Macarthur Blvd # 400, Newport Beach
(92660-2027)
PHONE..................................949 261-0404
Margi Marshall, *Information Mgr*
Amanda Blazey, *Mktg Coord*
EMP: 50 **Privately Held**
SIC: 7996 Kiddie park
HQ: Festival Fun Parks, Llc
4590 Macarthur Blvd # 400
Newport Beach CA 92660
949 261-0404

(P-18801)
GILROY GARDENS FAMILY
THEME PK
3050 Hecker Pass Rd, Gilroy (95020-9411)
PHONE..................................408 840-7100
Michael Bonfante, *Director*
Barb Granter, *President*
Eva Trenberth, *Human Resources*
Walter Dunckel, *Opers Staff*
Josh Korbel, *Foreman/Supr*
EMP: 204
SALES: 15.8MM **Privately Held**
SIC: 7996 Amusement parks

(P-18802)
HARDCORE SKATEPARKS INC
285 N Benson Ave, Upland (91786-5614)
PHONE..................................909 949-1601
Joseph M Ciaglia Jr, *CEO*
EMP: 150
SALES (est): 560.8K **Privately Held**
SIC: 7996 Amusement parks

(P-18803)
LEGOLAND CALIFORNIA LLC
1 Legoland Dr, Carlsbad (92008-4610)
PHONE..................................760 918-5346
John Jakobson,
Mercedes Casey, *Social Dir*
Shawn Greiner, *Social Dir*
Frank Idris, *General Mgr*
John Ussher, *General Mgr*
▲ EMP: 400
SALES (est): 36.4MM
SALES (corp-wide): 2.1B **Privately Held**
WEB: www.legoland.com
SIC: 7996 Theme park, amusement
HQ: Merlin Entertainments Group Limited
3 Market Close
Poole BH15
120 266-6900

(P-18804)
MALIBU CASTLE
27061 Aliso Creek Rd # 100, Aliso Viejo
(92656-5322)
PHONE..................................210 341-6663
EMP: 50
SQ FT: 6,980
SALES: 3.1MM **Privately Held**
SIC: 7996
HQ: Festival Fun Parks, Llc
4590 Macarthur Blvd # 400
Newport Beach CA 92660
949 261-0404

(P-18805)
MOUNTASIA FAMILY FUN
CENTER
21516 Golden Triangle Rd, Santa Clarita
(91350-2612)
PHONE..................................661 253-4386
David Fleming, *Owner*
Mike Fleming, *Partner*
Mike Henn, *General Mgr*
EMP: 60
SQ FT: 22,000
SALES: 2.4MM **Privately Held**
WEB: www.mountasiafuncenter.com
SIC: 7996 Theme park, amusement

(P-18806)
MULLIGAN LIMITED (PA)
Also Called: Mulligan Family Fun Center
4281 Katella Ave Ste 228, Los Alamitos
(90720-6505)
PHONE..................................714 484-6799
Rob Thomas, *Principal*
Georgia Claessens, *Partner*
EMP: 58
SALES (est): 4MM **Privately Held**
WEB: www.mulliganfun.com
SIC: 7996 Amusement parks

(P-18807)
MULLIGAN LTD A CAL LTD
PARTNR
Also Called: Mulligan Family Fun Center
24950 Madison Ave, Murrieta
(92562-9714)
PHONE..................................951 696-9696
Micheal Brooks, *Manager*
EMP: 95 **Privately Held**
WEB: www.mulliganfun.com
SIC: 7996 7999 Theme park, amusement;
tourist attractions, amusement park con-
cessions & rides
PA: Mulligan Limited
4281 Katella Ave Ste 228
Los Alamitos CA 90720

(P-18808)
SANTA CRUZ SEASIDE
COMPANY (PA)
400 Beach St, Santa Cruz (95060-5416)
PHONE..................................831 423-5590
Charles L Canfield, *President*
Jo Anne Dlott, *Vice Pres*

Robert Bosken, *Risk Mgmt Dir*
Patricia Isaak, *Admin Asst*
Stacy Phelps, *Admin Asst*
▲ EMP: 299
SQ FT: 8,000
SALES: 55.2MM **Privately Held**
WEB: www.scseaside.com
SIC: 7996 7011 7933 6531 Pier, amuse-
ment; motels; bowling centers; real estate
agents & managers

(P-18809)
SANTA MONICA AMUSEMENTS
LLC
Also Called: Pacific Park
380 Santa Monica Pier, Santa Monica
(90401-3128)
PHONE..................................310 451-9641
Mary Ann Powell, *CEO*
Sharon Augenstein, *CFO*
David Gillam, *CFO*
Jeff Klocke, *Vice Pres*
Flor Perez, *Executive Asst*
EMP: 325
SQ FT: 70,000
SALES (est): 22.9MM **Privately Held**
WEB: www.pacpark.com
SIC: 7996 Theme park, amusement

(P-18810)
SIX FLAGS ENTERTAINMENT
CORP
Also Called: Waterworld USA
1600 Exposition Blvd, Sacramento
(95815-5104)
PHONE..................................916 924-3747
Keith Regardons, *Director*
EMP: 300
SALES (corp-wide): 1.3B **Publicly Held**
WEB: www.sixflags.com
SIC: 7996 Theme park, amusement
PA: Six Flags Entertainment Corp
924 E Avenue J
Grand Prairie TX 75050
972 595-5000

(P-18811)
SLIDECO RECREATION INC
Also Called: Waterworks Park
151 N Boulder Dr, Redding (96003-4607)
PHONE..................................530 246-9550
David Enns, *President*
EMP: 75
SQ FT: 1,000
SALES (est): 2.2MM **Privately Held**
WEB: www.waterworkspark.com
SIC: 7996 5812 Theme park, amusement;
snack bar

(P-18812)
WALT DISNEY COMPANY
1133 Flower St, Glendale (91201)
PHONE..................................818 544-6500
Grant Crabtree, *Vice Pres*
EMP: 714 **Publicly Held**
SIC: 7996 Kiddie park
PA: The Walt Disney Company
500 S Buena Vista St
Burbank CA 91521

(P-18813)
WALT DISNEY COMPANY
650 S Buenavista St, Burbank (91501)
PHONE..................................818 553-7333
Sylvian Goessens, *Branch Mgr*
EMP: 250 **Publicly Held**
SIC: 7996 Kiddie park
PA: The Walt Disney Company
500 S Buena Vista St
Burbank CA 91521

┌─────────────────────────────┐
│ **7997 Membership Sports &** │
│ **Recreation Clubs** │
└─────────────────────────────┘

(P-18814)
1334 PARTNERS LP
Also Called: MANHATTAN COUNTRY CLUB
1330 Park View Ave, Manhattan Beach
(90266-3704)
PHONE..................................310 546-5656
Keith Brackpool, *Partner*
EMP: 100

SQ FT: 80,000
SALES: 54.7K **Privately Held**
WEB: www.manhattancc.com
SIC: 7997 6512 7991 5813 Country club,
membership; commercial & industrial
building operation; physical fitness facilities; drinking places; eating places

(P-18815)
16700 ROSCOE ASSOCIATES
LLC
Also Called: Maguire Aviation
16700 Roscoe Blvd, Van Nuys
(91406-1100)
PHONE..................................818 989-2300
Robert F Maguire III, *Mng Member*
Alec Maguire, *President*
Cary Stalding, *CFO*
EMP: 70
SALES: 15MM **Privately Held**
SIC: 7997 Aviation club, membership

(P-18816)
A A A FIVE STAR ADVENTURES
611 S Palm Canyon Dr, Palm Springs
(92264-7213)
PHONE..................................760 320-1500
A D Kesson, *Principal*
EMP: 50
SALES (est): 619.2K **Privately Held**
SIC: 7997 Membership sports & recreation
clubs

(P-18817)
ACADEMY SWIM CLUB
Also Called: Santa Clarita Swim Club
28079 Smyth Dr, Valencia (91355-4023)
PHONE..................................661 702-8585
Nikki Miller, *President*
Jim Miller, *Vice Pres*
Dakota Miller, *Program Dir*
EMP: 55
SALES (est): 187.7K **Privately Held**
SIC: 7997 7999 Swimming club, member-
ship; swimming instruction

(P-18818)
ADVENTURES IN HOSPITALITY
INC
Also Called: Barbara Worth Resort
633 W Canal St, Calexico (92231-3503)
PHONE..................................760 356-2806
Suzanna Esparza, *President*
EMP: 65
SQ FT: 15,000
SALES (est): 3.5MM **Privately Held**
WEB: www.bwresort.com
SIC: 7997 Country club, membership; golf
club, membership

(P-18819)
AGI HOLDING CORP (PA)
Also Called: Affinity Group
2575 Vista Del Mar Dr, Ventura
(93001-3900)
P.O. Box 6888, Englewood CO (80155-
6888)
PHONE..................................805 667-4100
Mr Stephen Adams, *CEO*
Joe McAdams, *President*
Michael Schneider, *COO*
Mark Boggess, *CFO*
Brenda Hutchinson, *Prdtn Mgr*
▲ EMP: 59
SQ FT: 74,000
SALES (est): 488.7MM **Privately Held**
SIC: 7997 2741 Membership sports &
recreation clubs; directories: publishing &
printing; newsletter publishing

(P-18820)
AIRPORT CLUB
Also Called: Airport Health Club
432 Aviation Blvd, Santa Rosa
(95403-1069)
PHONE..................................707 528-2582
Bob Page, *President*
Vickie Morse, *Corp Secy*
Russell Tow, *Vice Pres*
EMP: 120
SQ FT: 44,000
SALES (est): 6MM **Privately Held**
SIC: 7997 7991 Membership sports &
recreation clubs; physical fitness facilities

(P-18821)
ALMADEN GOLF & COUNTRY CLUB
6663 Hampton Dr, San Jose (95120-5536)
PHONE..................................408 323-4812
Robert Osshalem, *General Mgr*
Michael Gardner, *Manager*
EMP: 60
SQ FT: 26,000
SALES: 6MM **Privately Held**
WEB: www.almadengcc.com
SIC: 7997 Country club, membership; golf club, membership

(P-18822)
ALMADEN VALLEY ATHLETIC CLUB
Also Called: Avac
5400 Camden Ave, San Jose (95124-5897)
PHONE..................................408 445-4900
Joseph Shank, *General Ptnr*
Court Aquatic Sports, *General Ptnr*
Kristin Cordova, *Site Mgr*
EMP: 70
SQ FT: 20,000
SALES (est): 4MM **Privately Held**
SIC: 7997 Tennis club, membership

(P-18823)
ALTA SIERRA COUNTRY CLUB INC
11897 Tammy Way, Grass Valley (95949-6626)
PHONE..................................530 273-2041
Del Clement, *President*
Jim Hansen, *Treasurer*
Doug Bulman, *Vice Pres*
Carl Guastaferro, *Admin Sec*
EMP: 50
SQ FT: 21,500
SALES (est): 3.6MM **Privately Held**
WEB: www.altasierracc.com
SIC: 7997 Golf club, membership

(P-18824)
ALTA VISTA COUNTRY CLUB LLC
777 Alta Vista St, Placentia (92870-5101)
PHONE..................................714 524-1591
Karl Reul, *Mng Member*
EMP: 60
SQ FT: 6,751,800
SALES (est): 217.1K **Privately Held**
SIC: 7997 Golf club, membership

(P-18825)
ALTADENA TOWN AND COUNTRY CLUB
2290 Country Club Dr, Altadena (91001-3202)
PHONE..................................626 345-9088
David Edens, *President*
Peggy Stahlheber, *Vice Pres*
Matthew Zboray, *Executive*
Kelly Bash, *Office Mgr*
Margot Flynn, *Office Mgr*
EMP: 80
SQ FT: 50,000
SALES: 4MM **Privately Held**
SIC: 7997 Country club, membership

(P-18826)
AMERICAN GOLF CORPORATION
Also Called: Lomas Santa Fe Country Club
1505 Lomas Santa Fe Dr, Solana Beach (92075-2103)
PHONE..................................858 755-6768
Lynn Ferrer, *Sales/Mktg Mgr*
EMP: 150
SALES (corp-wide): 588MM **Privately Held**
WEB: www.americangolf.com
SIC: 7997 Country club, membership; golf club, membership
PA: American Golf Corporation
909 N Pacific Coast Hwy
El Segundo CA 90245
310 664-4000

(P-18827)
AMERICAN GOLF CORPORATION
Also Called: Sunset Hills Country Club
4155 Erbes Rd, Thousand Oaks (91360-6842)
PHONE..................................805 495-5407
Scott Richmond, *Manager*
EMP: 75
SALES (corp-wide): 588MM **Privately Held**
WEB: www.americangolf.com
SIC: 7997 Country club, membership; golf club, membership
PA: American Golf Corporation
909 N Pacific Coast Hwy
El Segundo CA 90245
310 664-4000

(P-18828)
AMERICAN GOLF CORPORATION
Also Called: Rancho San Joaquin Golf Course
1 Ethel Coplen Way, Irvine (92612-1716)
PHONE..................................949 786-1224
Steve Jeffrey, *Manager*
EMP: 125
SALES (corp-wide): 588MM **Privately Held**
WEB: www.americangolf.com
SIC: 7997 7992 Golf club, membership; public golf courses
PA: American Golf Corporation
909 N Pacific Coast Hwy
El Segundo CA 90245
310 664-4000

(P-18829)
AMERICAN GOLF CORPORATION (PA)
909 N Pacific Coast Hwy, El Segundo (90245-2724)
PHONE..................................310 664-4000
Jim Hinckley, *CEO*
Paul Major, *President*
Keith Brown, *COO*
Mike Moecker, *CFO*
Rick Rosen, *CFO*
EMP: 150
SALES (est): 588MM **Privately Held**
WEB: www.americangolf.com
SIC: 7997 7999 5812 5941 Golf club, membership; tennis club, membership; golf services & professionals; eating places; golf goods & equipment; public golf courses

(P-18830)
AMERICAN GOLF CORPORATION
Also Called: Mountain Gate Country Club
12445 Mountain Gate Dr, Los Angeles (90049-1115)
PHONE..................................310 476-2411
Terry Anglan, *Manager*
Michael Dejordy, *General Mgr*
Meredith Anderson, *Director*
Nicole Chapman, *Director*
Adrian Killigrew, *Director*
EMP: 140
SQ FT: 20,000
SALES (corp-wide): 588MM **Privately Held**
WEB: www.americangolf.com
SIC: 7997 Tennis club, membership; country club, membership; golf club, membership
PA: American Golf Corporation
909 N Pacific Coast Hwy
El Segundo CA 90245
310 664-4000

(P-18831)
AMERICAN GOLF CORPORATION
Also Called: Reserve At Spanos Park, The
6301 W Eight Mile Rd, Stockton (95219-8702)
P.O. Box 7126 (95267-0126)
PHONE..................................209 477-4653
Barry Ruhl, *Manager*
EMP: 50

SALES (corp-wide): 588MM **Privately Held**
WEB: www.americangolf.com
SIC: 7997 7992 Golf club, membership; public golf courses
PA: American Golf Corporation
909 N Pacific Coast Hwy
El Segundo CA 90245
310 664-4000

(P-18832)
AMERICAN GOLF CORPORATION
Also Called: Yorba Linda Country Club
19400 Mountain View Ave, Yorba Linda (92886-5530)
PHONE..................................714 779-2461
Scott Lester, *District Mgr*
Shuji Inada, *Buyer*
EMP: 55
SQ FT: 19,800
SALES (corp-wide): 588MM **Privately Held**
WEB: www.americangolf.com
SIC: 7997 Golf club, membership
PA: American Golf Corporation
909 N Pacific Coast Hwy
El Segundo CA 90245
310 664-4000

(P-18833)
AMERICAN GOLF CORPORATION
Also Called: Desert Rose Golf Course
68311 Paseo Real, Cathedral City (92234-6767)
PHONE..................................702 431-2191
EMP: 78
SALES (corp-wide): 560.6MM **Privately Held**
SIC: 7997 7999 7992
PA: American Golf Corporation
6080 Center Dr Ste 500
Los Angeles CA 90245
310 664-4000

(P-18834)
AMERICAN GOLF CORPORATION
Also Called: Black Lake Golf Course
1490 Golf Course Ln, Nipomo (93444-9307)
PHONE..................................805 343-1214
Bill Burney, *Manager*
Robert Ogden, *General Mgr*
EMP: 70
SQ FT: 3,000
SALES (corp-wide): 588MM **Privately Held**
WEB: www.americangolf.com
SIC: 7997 Country club, membership; golf club, membership
PA: American Golf Corporation
909 N Pacific Coast Hwy
El Segundo CA 90245
310 664-4000

(P-18835)
AMERICAN GOLF CORPORATION
Also Called: Seacliff Country Club
6501 Palm Ave, Huntington Beach (92648-2611)
PHONE..................................714 536-8866
Mike Cress, *General Mgr*
EMP: 100
SQ FT: 20,000
SALES (corp-wide): 588MM **Privately Held**
WEB: www.americangolf.com
SIC: 7997 Golf club, membership
PA: American Golf Corporation
909 N Pacific Coast Hwy
El Segundo CA 90245
310 664-4000

(P-18836)
AMERICAN GOLF CORPORATION
Also Called: Diamond Bar Golf Course
22751 Golden Springs Dr, Diamond Bar (91765-2218)
PHONE..................................909 861-5757
Andy Melnyk, *Manager*
EMP: 70

SALES (corp-wide): 588MM **Privately Held**
WEB: www.americangolf.com
SIC: 7997 7992 Golf club, membership; public golf courses
PA: American Golf Corporation
909 N Pacific Coast Hwy
El Segundo CA 90245
310 664-4000

(P-18837)
AMERICAN GOLF CORPORATION
Also Called: Oakhurst Country Club
1001 Peacock Creek Dr, Clayton (94517-2201)
PHONE..................................925 672-9737
Craig Wong, *General Mgr*
EMP: 100
SALES (corp-wide): 588MM **Privately Held**
WEB: www.americangolf.com
SIC: 7997 Golf club, membership
PA: American Golf Corporation
909 N Pacific Coast Hwy
El Segundo CA 90245
310 664-4000

(P-18838)
AMERICAN GOLF CORPORATION
Also Called: Summitpointe Golf Club
1500 Country Club Dr, Milpitas (95035-3456)
PHONE..................................408 262-8813
Lance Fong, *General Mgr*
EMP: 50
SALES (corp-wide): 588MM **Privately Held**
WEB: www.americangolf.com
SIC: 7997 Golf club, membership
PA: American Golf Corporation
909 N Pacific Coast Hwy
El Segundo CA 90245
310 664-4000

(P-18839)
AMERICAN GOLF CORPORATION
Also Called: El Camino Country Club
3202 Vista Way, Oceanside (92056-3607)
PHONE..................................760 757-2100
Ted Axe, *Manager*
Anne Handley, *Sales Staff*
Cindy Melfi, *Director*
Natalie Anderson, *Relations*
EMP: 75
SALES (corp-wide): 588MM **Privately Held**
WEB: www.americangolf.com
SIC: 7997 Golf club, membership
PA: American Golf Corporation
909 N Pacific Coast Hwy
El Segundo CA 90245
310 664-4000

(P-18840)
AMERICAN GOLF CORPORATION
Also Called: Los Verdes Golf Course
7000 Los Verdes Dr Ste 1, Rancho Palos Verdes (90275-5600)
PHONE..................................310 377-7370
Mike Shank, *Branch Mgr*
Tyson Johnson, *Sales Staff*
EMP: 55
SALES (corp-wide): 588MM **Privately Held**
WEB: www.americangolf.com
SIC: 7997 Golf club, membership
PA: American Golf Corporation
909 N Pacific Coast Hwy
El Segundo CA 90245
310 664-4000

(P-18841)
AMERICAN GOLF CORPORATION
16782 Graham St, Huntington Beach (92649-3754)
PHONE..................................714 846-1364
Brent Boznanski, *Manager*
EMP: 55

PRODUCTS & SVCS

SALES (corp-wide): 588MM **Privately Held**
WEB: www.americangolf.com
SIC: 7997 Golf club, membership
PA: American Golf Corporation
909 N Pacific Coast Hwy
El Segundo CA 90245
310 664-4000

(P-18842)
AMERICAN GOLF CORPORATION
Also Called: Seascape Golf Club
610 Clubhouse Dr Rear, Aptos
(95003-4868)
PHONE.................................831 688-3213
Steve Argo, *Manager*
EMP: 60
SALES (corp-wide): 588MM **Privately Held**
WEB: www.americangolf.com
SIC: 7997 5941 5812 Golf club, membership; golf goods & equipment; eating places
PA: American Golf Corporation
909 N Pacific Coast Hwy
El Segundo CA 90245
310 664-4000

(P-18843)
AMERICAN GOLF CORPORATION
Also Called: Monterey Country Club
41500 Monterey Ave, Palm Desert
(92260-2173)
PHONE.................................760 568-9311
Rod Winger, *Manager*
John Kulow, *General Mgr*
EMP: 50
SALES (corp-wide): 588MM **Privately Held**
WEB: www.americangolf.com
SIC: 7997 Golf club, membership
PA: American Golf Corporation
909 N Pacific Coast Hwy
El Segundo CA 90245
310 664-4000

(P-18844)
AMERICAN GOLF CORPORATION
Also Called: Simi Hills Golf Course
5031 Alamo St, Simi Valley (93063-1949)
PHONE.................................805 522-0803
Brian Reed, *Branch Mgr*
Jackie Cochran, *Director*
EMP: 50
SALES (corp-wide): 588MM **Privately Held**
WEB: www.americangolf.com
SIC: 7997 5941 7992 Golf club, membership; golf goods & equipment; public golf courses
PA: American Golf Corporation
909 N Pacific Coast Hwy
El Segundo CA 90245
310 664-4000

(P-18845)
ANNANDALE GOLF CLUB
1 N San Rafael Ave, Pasadena
(91105-1299)
PHONE.................................626 796-6125
Christoff Granger, *General Mgr*
Rebecca Bedrick, *Vice Pres*
Michael Beam, *General Mgr*
Tom Lease, *Controller*
Susy Gorlach, *Human Res Dir*
EMP: 125
SQ FT: 10,000
SALES: 11.2MM **Privately Held**
WEB: www.annandalegolf.com
SIC: 7997 Golf club, membership

(P-18846)
ANTELOPE VALLEY COUNTRY CLUB
39800 Country Club Dr, Palmdale
(93551-2970)
PHONE.................................661 947-3142
Mark Range, *General Mgr*
EMP: 150 EST: 1952
SQ FT: 22,000

SALES (est): 2.8MM **Privately Held**
WEB: www.palmdalegolf.com
SIC: 7997 Country club, membership

(P-18847)
ANTIOCH ROTARY CLUB
324 G St, Antioch (94509-1255)
P.O. Box 692 (94509-0069)
PHONE.................................925 757-1800
EMP: 50 EST: 2010
SALES (est): 1.7MM **Privately Held**
SIC: 7997

(P-18848)
APPLE VALLEY GOLF CLUB
Also Called: Apple Valley Golf Course
15200 Rancherias Rd, Apple Valley
(92307-5201)
PHONE.................................760 242-3653
Ned R Curtis, *CEO*
Todd Edwards, *Principal*
EMP: 170
SQ FT: 21,471
SALES (est): 5.2MM **Privately Held**
WEB: www.applevalleycountryclub.net
SIC: 7997 Country club, membership

(P-18849)
ARDEN HILLS COUNTRY CLUB INC
1220 Arden Hills Ln, Sacramento
(95864-5378)
PHONE.................................916 482-6111
Jeralyn Favero, *President*
Brett Favero, *Admin Sec*
Minnetta McAdams, *Controller*
Meredith Cassady, *Personnel Exec*
Lauren Morgan, *Human Res Dir*
EMP: 70
SALES (est): 5.9MM **Privately Held**
WEB: www.ardenhills.net
SIC: 7997 Country club, membership

(P-18850)
ASSOCIATED KOI CLUBS AMERICA
P.O. Box 10879, Costa Mesa (92627-0272)
PHONE.................................949 650-5225
Robert Finnegan, *Chairman*
EMP: 75
SALES: 34.1K **Privately Held**
SIC: 7997 Membership sports & recreation clubs

(P-18851)
ATSUGI KOKUSAI KANKO USA INC
28095 John F Kennedy Dr, Moreno Valley
(92555-6301)
PHONE.................................951 924-4444
Hideo Komuro, *President*
EMP: 55
SQ FT: 21,000
SALES (est): 978.8K
SALES (corp-wide): 14.9MM **Privately Held**
WEB: www.hawaiikaigolf.com
SIC: 7997 5812 Membership sports & recreation clubs; eating places
PA: Atsugi Kokusai Kanko Co., Ltd.
1-13-23, Shintomi
Chuo-Ku TKY 104-0
335 533-280

(P-18852)
BAKERSFIELD COUNTRY CLUB
4200 Country Club Dr, Bakersfield
(93306-3700)
P.O. Box 6007 (93386-6007)
PHONE.................................661 871-4000
Jon Van Boening, *President*
EMP: 75
SQ FT: 30,000
SALES: 5.6MM **Privately Held**
WEB: www.bakersfieldcountryclub.com
SIC: 7997 5812 5813 Country club, membership; eating places; bar (drinking places)

(P-18853)
BALBOA BAY CLUB INC (HQ)
1221 W Coast Hwy Ste 145, Newport
Beach (92663-5092)
PHONE.................................949 645-5000
David Wooten, *President*

W D Ray, *CEO*
EMP: 275
SALES (est): 17MM
SALES (corp-wide): 30.2MM **Privately Held**
SIC: 7997 7011 Country club, membership; resort hotel
PA: International Bay Clubs, Llc
1221 W Coast Hwy Ste 145
Newport Beach CA 92663
949 645-5000

(P-18854)
BALBOA YACHT CLUB
1801 Bayside Dr, Corona Del Mar
(92625-1898)
PHONE.................................949 673-3515
Howard Ness, *President*
EMP: 50 EST: 1924
SQ FT: 23,000
SALES: 6.5MM **Privately Held**
WEB: www.balboayachtclub.com
SIC: 7997 Yacht club, membership

(P-18855)
BAY CLUB GOLDEN GATEWAY LLC
Also Called: Bay Club Golden Gateway Inc
370 Drumm St, San Francisco
(94111-2010)
PHONE.................................415 616-8800
Broc Stevens, *General Mgr*
Rachel Ruperto, *President*
David Smith, *Admin Sec*
EMP: 50
SQ FT: 8,000
SALES (est): 1.8MM
SALES (corp-wide): 46.3MM **Privately Held**
WEB: www.ggtsc.com
SIC: 7997 7999 7991 Tennis club, membership; swimming club, membership; swimming instruction; health club
PA: Bay Club Holdings Iii, Llc
1 Lombard St Lbby
San Francisco CA 94111
415 781-1874

(P-18856)
BAY CLUBS INC
Also Called: Bay Club Marin
220 Corte Madera Town Ctr, Corte Madera
(94925-1208)
PHONE.................................415 945-3000
Maegan Devlin, *Manager*
EMP: 68
SALES (corp-wide): 86.2MM **Privately Held**
WEB: www.pacclub.com
SIC: 7997 Membership sports & recreation clubs
HQ: Bay Clubs, Inc.
1 Lombard St
San Francisco CA 94111
415 781-1874

(P-18857)
BAY CLUBS INC
Also Called: Racquetball World
22235 Sherman Way, Canoga Park
(91303-1058)
PHONE.................................818 884-5034
Harold Wright, *Branch Mgr*
EMP: 80
SQ FT: 85,294
SALES (corp-wide): 86.2MM **Privately Held**
SIC: 7997 7299 7991 Racquetball club, membership; personal appearance services; physical fitness facilities
HQ: Bay Clubs, Inc.
1 Lombard St
San Francisco CA 94111
415 781-1874

(P-18858)
BEACH CLUB
201 Palisades Beach Rd, Santa Monica
(90402-1401)
PHONE.................................310 395-3254
Gregg Patterson, *Exec Dir*
EMP: 60 EST: 1923
SQ FT: 35,000

SALES: 7.6MM **Privately Held**
WEB: www.beachclub.com
SIC: 7997 5812 5813 Beach club, membership; eating places; bar (drinking places)

(P-18859)
BEAR CREEK GOLF CLUB INC
Also Called: Bear Creek Golf & Country Club
22640 Bear Creek Dr N, Murrieta
(92562-3015)
PHONE.................................951 677-8621
Peter Hanson, *General Mgr*
Rich Gillete, *President*
EMP: 85
SQ FT: 28,000
SALES: 2.9MM **Privately Held**
WEB: www.bearcreekgc.com
SIC: 7997 7992 Golf club, membership; public golf courses

(P-18860)
BEAR CREEK PARTNERS LLC
22640 Bear Creek Dr N, Murrieta
(92562-3015)
PHONE.................................951 677-8621
Richard H Gillette, *Mng Member*
Gary Mineo, *Controller*
Tim Gardner, *Director*
EMP: 65
SALES (est): 2.5MM **Privately Held**
SIC: 7997 Golf club, membership

(P-18861)
BEL-AIR COUNTRY CLUB
10768 Bellagio Rd, Los Angeles
(90077-3799)
PHONE.................................310 472-9563
Joseph Wagner, *General Mgr*
Peter Best, *CEO*
Martha Gamez, *Executive*
Karen Decker, *Human Res Mgr*
Courtney Quider, *Purch Mgr*
EMP: 140
SQ FT: 10,000
SALES: 13.9MM **Privately Held**
WEB: www.bel-aircc.com
SIC: 7997 5941 Country club, membership; golf goods & equipment

(P-18862)
BELMONT ATHLETIC CLUB
4918 E 2nd St, Long Beach (90803-5318)
PHONE.................................562 438-3816
John Doyle, *Partner*
Bill Fraser, *Ltd Ptnr*
Patrick Gormley, *Ltd Ptnr*
Barry Miller, *Ltd Ptnr*
Joyce Pokstaff, *Ltd Ptnr*
EMP: 65 EST: 1980
SQ FT: 25,000
SALES (est): 2.9MM **Privately Held**
WEB: www.belmontathleticclub.com
SIC: 7997 7991 Racquetball club, membership; athletic club & gymnasiums, membership

(P-18863)
BERKELEY COUNTRY CLUB
7901 Cutting Blvd, El Cerrito (94530-1877)
PHONE.................................510 233-7550
Richard Pettler, *President*
Ken Kipp, *Treasurer*
Charles Ibbotson, *Vice Pres*
Ron Svien, *General Mgr*
Bob Langbein, *Admin Sec*
EMP: 60
SQ FT: 12,000
SALES (est): 3.7MM **Privately Held**
SIC: 7997 Country club, membership

(P-18864)
BERMUDA DUNES COUNTRY CLUB
42765 Adams St, Bermuda Dunes
(92203-7937)
PHONE.................................760 360-2481
Ed Cooney, *CEO*
Steve Hubbard, *President*
Perry Dickey, *COO*
George Neidhardt, *Treasurer*
Leon Webrand, *Vice Pres*
EMP: 50
SQ FT: 40,000

SALES: 4.3MM **Privately Held**
WEB: www.bermudadunescc.com
SIC: 7997 Country club, membership

(P-18865)
BIG CANYON COUNTRY CLUB
1 Big Canyon Dr, Newport Beach
(92660-5299)
PHONE..............................949 644-5404
Donald Tippett, *CEO*
William Stamply, *President*
Lisa Curlee, *Comms Mgr*
Lisa Daley, *Comms Mgr*
Gloria Bridges, *Human Res Dir*
EMP: 180
SQ FT: 50,000
SALES: 20.4MM **Privately Held**
WEB: www.bigcanyoncc.org
SIC: 7997 Country club, membership

(P-18866)
BIG LGUE DREAMS CONSULTING LLC
20155 Viking Way, Redding (96003-8293)
PHONE..............................530 223-1177
Brandi Merkel, *Principal*
EMP: 109
SALES (corp-wide): 45.7MM **Privately Held**
SIC: 7997 Outdoor field clubs
PA: Big League Dreams Consulting, Llc
16333 Fairfield Ranch Rd
Chino Hills CA 91709
909 287-1700

(P-18867)
BIGHORN GOLF CLUB
255 Palowet Dr, Palm Desert (92260-7311)
PHONE..............................760 773-2468
Carl T Cardinalli, *President*
Joe Curtis, *Treasurer*
Theresa Maggio, *Vice Pres*
Greg Proper, *Executive*
Marilyn Gillespie, *Administration*
EMP: 190
SALES (est): 16.9MM **Privately Held**
SIC: 7997 7992 Country club, membership; public golf courses

(P-18868)
BIRNAM WOOD GOLF CLUB
1941 E Valley Rd, Santa Barbara
(93108-1427)
PHONE..............................805 969-2223
Robert Thornburgh, *President*
Michael-Mc Gardner, *COO*
Robert Trent Jones, *Principal*
Mitch Vargas, *Security Dir*
Marty Moore, *Superintendent*
EMP: 145
SQ FT: 45,000
SALES (est): 10.6MM **Privately Held**
WEB: www.birnamwoodgolfclub.com
SIC: 7997 7992 5812 Golf club, membership; public golf courses; eating places

(P-18869)
BLACKHAWK COUNTRY CLUB
599 Blackhawk Club Dr, Danville
(94506-4522)
PHONE..............................925 736-6500
Michael G Burton, *CEO*
Larry Marx, *President*
Kevin Dunne, *COO*
EMP: 230
SQ FT: 35,743
SALES: 17.2MM **Privately Held**
WEB: www.blackhawkcc.org
SIC: 7997 7992 5812 Golf club, membership; tennis club, membership; public golf courses; eating places

(P-18870)
BOYS & GIRLS CLB OF PENINSULA
401 Pierce Rd, Menlo Park (94025-1240)
PHONE..............................650 322-6255
Peter Fortenbaugh, *Exec Dir*
Shannon Petrello, *General Mgr*
Daniel Keough, *Admin Asst*
Gladys Maloata, *Administration*
Cindy McIntyre, *Finance Dir*
EMP: 60 EST: 1975
SQ FT: 2,000

SALES: 9MM **Privately Held**
SIC: 7997 Membership sports & recreation clubs

(P-18871)
BOYS AND GIRLS CLUB
22450 Mulholland Hwy, Calabasas
(91302-5180)
PHONE..............................818 225-8406
Natalie Gonzales, *Director*
EMP: 50
SALES (est): 86K **Privately Held**
SIC: 7997 Membership sports & recreation clubs

(P-18872)
BRAEMAR COUNTRY CLUB INC
4001 Reseda Blvd, Tarzana (91356-5330)
P.O. Box 570217 (91357-0217)
PHONE..............................323 873-6880
Steven Held, *Manager*
EMP: 199
SQ FT: 20,000
SALES (est): 7.9MM
SALES (corp-wide): 477MM **Privately Held**
WEB: www.braemarclub.com
SIC: 7997 Country club, membership
HQ: Clubcorp Usa, Inc.
3030 Lyndon B Johnson Fwy
Dallas TX 75234
972 243-6191

(P-18873)
BRENTWOOD COUNTRY CLUB
590 S Burlingame Ave, Los Angeles
(90049-4896)
PHONE..............................310 451-8011
Linda Briskman, *President*
Rosemary Bryan, *Director*
Dave Smith, *Director*
EMP: 120
SALES (est): 520.9K **Privately Held**
SIC: 7997 7999 Country club, membership; golf services & professionals

(P-18874)
BRIDGES AT GALE RANCH LLC
Also Called: Bridges Golf Club, The
9000 S Gale Ridge Rd, San Ramon
(94582-9174)
PHONE..............................925 735-4253
Joey Pickavance, *Manager*
EMP: 90
SALES (est): 4.9MM **Privately Held**
WEB: www.thebridgesgolf.com
SIC: 7997 Golf club, membership

(P-18875)
BROOKSIDE COUNTRY CLUB
3603 Saint Andrews Dr, Stockton
(95219-1868)
PHONE..............................209 956-6200
Barney Kramer, *CEO*
New England Life, *Partner*
EMP: 70
SQ FT: 5,000
SALES: 3.2MM **Privately Held**
WEB: www.brooksidegolf.net
SIC: 7997 7999 5941 5812 Country club, membership; swimming club, membership; tennis club, membership; golf driving range; golf goods & equipment; eating places

(P-18876)
BURLINGAME COUNTRY CLUB
80 New Place Rd, Hillsborough
(94010-6499)
PHONE..............................650 696-8100
Ralston P Roberts, *CEO*
EMP: 70 EST: 1893
SALES (est): 8.2MM **Privately Held**
WEB: www.burlingamecc.org
SIC: 7997 Country club, membership

(P-18877)
BUSINESS AND SUPPORT SERVICES
P.O. Box 6001 (92278-6001)
PHONE..............................760 830-6873
EMP: 70 **Publicly Held**
SIC: 7997 Membership sports & recreation clubs

HQ: Business And Support Services
3044 Catlin Ave
Quantico VA 22134
703 432-0109

(P-18878)
CALABASAS COUNTRY CLUB
4515 Park Entrada, Calabasas
(91302-1469)
PHONE..............................818 222-8111
Robert W Linn, *Principal*
EMP: 74
SALES (est): 427.1K
SALES (corp-wide): 5.3MM **Privately Held**
SIC: 7997 Golf club, membership
PA: Knight-Calabasas Llc
4515 Park Entrada
Calabasas CA 91302
818 222-3200

(P-18879)
CALIFORNIA COUNTRY CLUB
Also Called: S R Mutual Funds
1509 Workman Mill Rd, City of Industry
(90601-1499)
PHONE..............................626 333-4571
Will Bayer, *General Mgr*
ARA Cho, *Executive*
Helen Bates, *Administration*
Ted Parker, *Director*
EMP: 60 EST: 1956
SALES (est): 4.9MM **Privately Held**
WEB: www.golfccc.com
SIC: 7997 Country club, membership

(P-18880)
CALIFORNIA MOTORCYCLE CLUB
742 45th Ave, Oakland (94601-4429)
PHONE..............................510 534-6222
Mark Norris, *Exec Dir*
Larry Steward, *Principal*
Chuck Younglund, *
EMP: 75
SQ FT: 2,232
SALES: 88.2K **Privately Held**
WEB: www.oaklandmc.org
SIC: 7997 Membership sports & recreation clubs

(P-18881)
CALIFRNIA GOLF CLB SAN FRNCSCO
844 W Orange Ave, South San Francisco
(94080-3125)
PHONE..............................650 588-9021
Jon McGovern, *CEO*
Junaid Sheikh, *Treasurer*
Henry Bullock, *Vice Pres*
Gregory Spencer, *Exec Dir*
Steven Ruwe, *Admin Sec*
EMP: 74
SQ FT: 30,000
SALES: 7.9MM **Privately Held**
SIC: 7997 Golf club, membership

(P-18882)
CAMERON PARK COUNTRY CLUB INC
3201 Royal Dr, Cameron Park
(95682-8559)
PHONE..............................530 672-9840
J Poindexter, *Manager*
Jack Mehl, *President*
Mark Carson, *CEO*
Don Seese, *CFO*
Joe William, *Vice Pres*
EMP: 60
SQ FT: 50,000
SALES: 3.8MM **Privately Held**
WEB: www.cameronparkcc.com
SIC: 7997 Country club, membership

(P-18883)
CANYON CREST COUNTRY CLUB INC
Also Called: Golf Pro Shop
975 Country Club Dr, Riverside
(92506-3699)
PHONE..............................951 274-7900
Robert H Dedman, *Ch of Bd*
James Maser, *Officer*
Frank Gore, *Exec VP*
Richard S Poole, *Exec VP*

Sidney Simmons, *Exec VP*
EMP: 85
SQ FT: 4,000
SALES (est): 4.2MM
SALES (corp-wide): 433.7MM **Privately Held**
WEB: www.canyoncrestcc.com
SIC: 7997 5812 5813 Golf club, membership; American restaurant; bar (drinking places)
HQ: Clubcorp Usa, Inc.
3030 Lyndon B Johnson Fwy
Dallas TX 75234
972 243-6191

(P-18884)
CASTLEWOOD COUNTRY CLUB
707 Country Club Cir, Pleasanton
(94566-9743)
PHONE..............................925 846-2871
Jerry Olson, *CEO*
Rick Hankins, *President*
Jerry Olsen, *CEO*
Tom Rutherford, *General Mgr*
John Vest, *General Mgr*
EMP: 167 EST: 1954
SQ FT: 55,000
SALES: 12.4MM **Privately Held**
WEB: www.castlewoodcc.org
SIC: 7997 Golf club, membership

(P-18885)
CATHEDRAL OAKS TENNIS SWIM ATH
Also Called: Cathedral Oaks Athletic Club
5800 Cathedral Oaks Rd, Goleta
(93117-1898)
PHONE..............................805 964-7762
Julie Main, *Exec Dir*
Richard Ortale, *Shareholder*
Charlott Valentine, *Vice Pres*
EMP: 75
SQ FT: 8,000
SALES (est): 2.7MM **Privately Held**
SIC: 7997 7991 Swimming club, membership; athletic club & gymnasiums, membership

(P-18886)
CATTA VERDERA COUNTRY CLUB
1111 Catta Verdera, Lincoln (95648-9649)
PHONE..............................916 645-7200
Deke Kastner, *Manager*
EMP: 90
SQ FT: 196,020
SALES (est): 3.5MM **Privately Held**
SIC: 7997 Golf club, membership; country club, membership

(P-18887)
CHAPMAN GOLF DEVELOPMENT LLC
Also Called: Tradition Golf Club
78505 Avenue 52, La Quinta (92253-2802)
PHONE..............................760 564-8723
David Chapman, *Mng Member*
Victoria Khaligov, *CFO*
Heidi Risk, *General Mgr*
Wendy Parks, *Accountant*
Beth Bland, *Hlthcr Dir*
EMP: 100
SALES: 12.3MM **Privately Held**
SIC: 7997 Golf club, membership

(P-18888)
CHARDONNAY/ CLUB SHAKESPEARE
Also Called: Chardonnay Golf Club
2555 Jamieson Canyon Rd, NAPA (94558)
PHONE..............................707 257-1900
Jack Barry, *President*
EMP: 100
SQ FT: 24,000
SALES (est): 3.3MM **Privately Held**
WEB: www.chardonnaygolfclub.com
SIC: 7997 Golf club, membership

(P-18889)
CITIZENS DEVELOPMENT CORP (PA)
Also Called: Lake San Marcos Resort
1105 La Bonita Dr, San Marcos
(92078-5296)
PHONE..............................760 744-0120

Ronald N Frazar, *President*
EMP: 59
SALES (est): 3.4MM **Privately Held**
SIC: 7997 Country club, membership

(P-18890)
CITY CLUB LLC
Also Called: City Club of San Francisco
155 Sansome St Fl 9, San Francisco
(94104-3687)
PHONE...............................415 362-2480
Martin Brown, *Owner*
Brian Reed, *President*
EMP: 65
SQ FT: 25,000
SALES (est): 3.6MM **Privately Held**
WEB: www.cityclubsf.com
SIC: 7997 8641 5812 Membership sports
& recreation clubs; civic social & fraternal
associations; caterers

(P-18891)
CLAREMONT COUNTRY CLUB
5295 Broadway Ter, Oakland (94618-1498)
PHONE...............................510 653-6789
Harold Peter Smith, *CEO*
Warren Chip Brown, *President*
Richard W Kraber, *Treasurer*
Thomas C Crosby, *Vice Pres*
Alec Churchward, *General Mgr*
EMP: 85 **EST:** 1903
SQ FT: 479,160
SALES: 11.4MM **Privately Held**
WEB: www.claremontcountryclub.org
SIC: 7997 Country club, membership

(P-18892)
CLAREMONT TENNIS CLUB
Also Called: Claremont Club, The
1777 Monte Vista Ave, Claremont
(91711-2916)
PHONE...............................909 625-9515
Michael G Alpert, *President*
Geoffrey Clark, *Vice Pres*
Cathy Garner, *Director*
Antionette Mara, *Director*
Bart Hitt, *Assistant*
EMP: 200
SQ FT: 40,000
SALES (est): 11.2MM **Privately Held**
SIC: 7997 7991 5812 Membership sports
& recreation clubs; health club; eating
places

(P-18893)
**CLUB AT SHNNDOAH SPRNG
VLG INC**
32700 Desert Moon Dr, Thousand Palms
(92276-3713)
PHONE...............................760 343-3497
Ronald Safren, *President*
Gary Safren, *Treasurer*
Ronald Edwards, *Vice Pres*
Gary Copp, *Controller*
EMP: 50 **EST:** 2006
SALES: 3MM **Privately Held**
SIC: 7997 Country club, membership

(P-18894)
CLUB NAUTIQUE (PA)
1150 Ballena Blvd Ste 161, Alameda
(94501-7314)
PHONE...............................510 521-5544
Don Durant, *President*
Judith Ann Durant, *Admin Sec*
Colin Williams, *Opers Staff*
David Baizer, *Sales Staff*
Mary Suddaby, *Manager*
EMP: 80
SQ FT: 4,800
SALES (est): 3.5MM **Privately Held**
WEB: www.clubnautique.net
SIC: 7997 Boating club, membership

(P-18895)
CLUB OF SUNRISE COUNTRY
71601 Country Club Dr, Rancho Mirage
(92270-3546)
PHONE...............................760 328-6549
Bill Athan, *General Mgr*
Eric Charos, *General Mgr*
EMP: 64
SQ FT: 15,000

SALES: 3.3MM **Privately Held**
SIC: 7997 5812 5941 Country club, membership; American restaurant; golf, tennis
& ski shops

(P-18896)
CLUB ONE AT PETALUMA
1201 Redwood Way, Petaluma
(94954-6533)
PHONE...............................707 766-8080
Yalda Teranchi, *General Mgr*
EMP: 90
SALES (est): 775.7K **Privately Held**
SIC: 7997 Membership sports & recreation
clubs

(P-18897)
CLUBCORP USA INC
5690 Cancha De Golf, Rancho Santa Fe
(92091-4408)
PHONE...............................858 756-2471
Jim Macdonough, *General Mgr*
EMP: 180
SALES (corp-wide): 433.7MM **Privately
Held**
WEB: www.remington-gc.com
SIC: 7997 Country club, membership
HQ: Clubcorp Usa, Inc.
3030 Lyndon B Johnson Fwy
Dallas TX 75234
972 243-6191

(P-18898)
**CONTRA COSTA COUNTRY
CLUB**
801 Golf Club Rd, Pleasant Hill
(94523-1101)
PHONE...............................925 798-7135
Bill Wampler, *Manager*
EMP: 69
SQ FT: 20,000
SALES: 5.3MM **Privately Held**
SIC: 7997 5812 5813 Golf club, member-
ship; American restaurant; drinking places

(P-18899)
**COPPER RIVER COUNTRY CLUB
LP (PA)**
2140 E Clubhouse Dr, Fresno
(93730-7020)
P.O. Box 25850 (93729-5850)
PHONE...............................559 434-5200
William R Tatham Sr, *Partner*
Renne Antognoli, *Partner*
Michael F Tatham, *Partner*
William T Tatham Jr, *Partner*
Chris Huerta, *Administration*
EMP: 62
SALES (est): 4.2MM **Privately Held**
SIC: 7997 Golf club, membership

(P-18900)
CORDEVALLE GOLF CLUB LLC
1 Cordevalle Club Dr, San Martin
(95046-9472)
PHONE...............................408 695-4500
Earl Wilson,
EMP: 250 **EST:** 1999
SALES (est): 9.3MM **Privately Held**
WEB: www.cordevalle.com
SIC: 7997 Golf club, membership

(P-18901)
**CORRAL DE TIERRA COUNTRY
CLUB**
81 Corral De Tierra Rd, Salinas
(93908-9477)
PHONE...............................831 484-1325
Mike Oprish, *President*
William Bennett, *Executive*
Dominic Guzzo, *General Mgr*
David Webb, *General Mgr*
Patrick Carter, *Admin Sec*
EMP: 100 **EST:** 1959
SQ FT: 15,000
SALES (est): 7.7MM **Privately Held**
WEB: www.corraldetierracc.com
SIC: 7997 Country club, membership

(P-18902)
CORRAL DEL TIERRA
81 Corral De Tierra Rd, Salinas
(93908-9474)
PHONE...............................831 372-6244
Dominic Guzzo, *Manager*

EMP: 70
SALES: 40.3K **Privately Held**
SIC: 7997 Golf club, membership

(P-18903)
**COTO DE CAZA GOLF RACQUET
CLB**
Also Called: Coto De Caza Golf Racquet CLB
25291 Vista Del Verde, Trabuco Canyon
(92679-4900)
PHONE...............................949 858-4100
John Rosenbluth, *General Mgr*
EMP: 160
SQ FT: 44,000
SALES (est): 7.8MM
SALES (corp-wide): 477MM **Privately
Held**
WEB: www.remington-gc.com
SIC: 7997 7992 7991 5813 Racquetball
club, membership; public golf courses;
physical fitness facilities; drinking places;
eating places
HQ: Clubcorp Usa, Inc.
3030 Lyndon B Johnson Fwy
Dallas TX 75234
972 243-6191

(P-18904)
COURTSIDE TENNIS CLUB
Also Called: Courtside Club
14675 Winchester Blvd, Los Gatos
(95032-1890)
PHONE...............................408 395-7111
James Hinckley, *President*
Jim Gerber, *President*
EMP: 90
SQ FT: 100,000
SALES (est): 3.7MM
SALES (corp-wide): 477MM **Privately
Held**
WEB: www.courtsideclub.com
SIC: 7997 7991 5812 Membership sports
& recreation clubs; physical fitness facili-
ties; eating places
HQ: Clubcorp Usa, Inc.
3030 Lyndon B Johnson Fwy
Dallas TX 75234
972 243-6191

(P-18905)
**CROSBY NATIONAL GOLF CLUB
LLC**
17102 Bing Crosby Blvd, Rancho Santa Fe
(92067)
PHONE...............................858 756-6310
Rhonda Hill, *Director*
Ron Cropley, *Principal*
EMP: 70
SALES (est): 4.8MM **Privately Held**
SIC: 7997 Golf club, membership

(P-18906)
**CRYSTAL AIRE COUNTRY CLUB
GOLF**
Also Called: Crystalaire Country Club
15701 Boca Raton Ave, Llano
(93544-1211)
PHONE...............................661 944-2112
Mike Carpenter, *President*
Jane Reason, *Treasurer*
Dick McDonald, *Vice Pres*
Laura Litten, *Director*
EMP: 50
SALES (est): 1.9MM **Privately Held**
WEB: www.crystalairecc.com
SIC: 7997 5812 Golf club, membership;
American restaurant

(P-18907)
**CRYSTAL SPRINGS GOLF
PARTNERS**
Also Called: Crystal Springs Golf Course
6650 Golf Course Dr, Burlingame
(94010-6543)
PHONE...............................650 342-4188
Tom Issak, *President*
John Teleshek, *CFO*
Natalia Aldana, *Director*
EMP: 50
SALES (est): 3.9MM **Privately Held**
WEB: www.playcrystalsprings.com
SIC: 7997 Country club, membership

(P-18908)
DEL MAR COUNTRY CLUB INC
6001 Clubhouse Dr, Rancho Santa Fe
(92067)
P.O. Box 9866 (92067-4866)
PHONE...............................858 759-5500
Madeleine Pickens, *President*
EMP: 90
SQ FT: 18,000
SALES (est): 7.5MM **Privately Held**
WEB: www.delmarcountryclub.com
SIC: 7997 Golf club, membership; country
club, membership

(P-18909)
DEL PASO COUNTRY CLUB
3333 Marconi Ave, Sacramento
(95821-6293)
PHONE...............................916 489-3681
Chris Shanks, *Controller*
Eric Hatzenbiler, *CEO*
EMP: 105
SALES (est): 7.6MM **Privately Held**
WEB: www.delpasocountryclub.com
SIC: 7997 5941 5812 Country club, mem-
bership; sporting goods & bicycle shops;
eating places

(P-18910)
**DEL RIO GOLF & COUNTRY
CLUB**
801 Stewart Rd, Modesto (95356-9639)
PHONE...............................209 341-2414
John Bellizzi, *Principal*
Duncan Reno, *Officer*
Jay Ward, *Admin Sec*
Emmy Paulos, *Controller*
Christina Alger, *Human Res Dir*
EMP: 112
SQ FT: 48,000
SALES (est): 7.2MM **Privately Held**
WEB: www.delriocountryclub.com
SIC: 7997 5941 Country club, member-
ship; golf club, membership; tennis club,
membership; sporting goods & bicycle
shops

(P-18911)
**DESERT FALLS COUNTRY CLUB
INC**
1111 Desert Falls Pkwy, Palm Desert
(92211-1709)
PHONE...............................760 340-5646
Tim Scogan, *President*
EMP: 90
SALES (est): 5MM
SALES (corp-wide): 477MM **Privately
Held**
WEB: www.desert-falls.com
SIC: 7997 5812 7992 7299 Golf club,
membership; eating places; public golf
courses; banquet hall facilities
HQ: Clubcorp Usa, Inc.
3030 Lyndon B Johnson Fwy
Dallas TX 75234
972 243-6191

(P-18912)
DESERT PRINCESS HOME
28555 Landau Blvd, Cathedral City
(92234-3508)
PHONE...............................760 322-1655
Lynn Gilliam, *President*
EMP: 50
SALES (est): 2.8MM **Privately Held**
WEB: www.desertprincess.com
SIC: 7997 Country club, membership

(P-18913)
DHCCNP
Also Called: DESERT HORIZONS COUN-
TRY CLUB
44900 Desert Horizons Dr, Indian Wells
(92210-7401)
PHONE...............................760 340-4646
Jurgen Gross, *Manager*
Armida Trujillo, *Merchandise Mgr*
EMP: 86 **EST:** 1979
SQ FT: 30,000
SALES: 5MM **Privately Held**
WEB: www.deserthorizonscc.com
SIC: 7997 7992 5812 Country club, mem-
bership; public golf courses; eating places

(P-18914)
DIABLO COUNTRY CLUB
1700 Club House Rd, Diablo (94528)
PHONE.....................925 837-4221
Tom Gibbons, *CEO*
Steven Buck, *General Mgr*
Piper Harris, *Director*
EMP: 80
SQ FT: 52,000
SALES: 11MM **Privately Held**
WEB: www.diablocc.com
SIC: 7997 5812 5813 5941 Country club, membership; eating places; drinking places; sporting goods & bicycle shops

(P-18915)
DIABLO COUNTRY CLUB
Also Called: Golf Pro. Shop
1700 Clubhouse Rd, Diablo (94528)
PHONE.....................925 837-4221
Larry Marx, *General Mgr*
EMP: 50
SQ FT: 38,199
SALES (est): 1.3MM **Privately Held**
SIC: 7997 Golf club, membership

(P-18916)
EAGLE RIDGE GOLF CNTRY CLB LLC
Also Called: Eagle Ridge Golf Club
2951 Club Dr, Gilroy (95020-3043)
PHONE.....................408 846-4531
Mark Gurnow, *Mng Member*
EMP: 125
SALES (est): 3.9MM **Privately Held**
WEB: www.eagleridgegc.com
SIC: 7997 7992 5812 Country club, membership; public golf courses; eating places

(P-18917)
EAGLE VNES VNYRDS GOLF CLB LLC
580 S Kelly Rd, American Canyon (94503-5600)
P.O. Box 2398, NAPA (94558-0239)
PHONE.....................707 257-4470
Tokutaro Umezawa,
Nobu Mizuhara, *Vice Pres*
Michael Stirling, *Director*
Alisa Hartman, *Manager*
EMP: 70
SALES (est): 3.7MM **Privately Held**
SIC: 7997 Golf club, membership

(P-18918)
EL CABALLERO COUNTRY CLUB
18300 Tarzana Dr, Tarzana (91356-4216)
PHONE.....................818 654-3000
Bary West, *President*
Peter Jimenez, *CFO*
Gary Diamond, *Treasurer*
EMP: 125
SQ FT: 20,000
SALES: 11MM **Privately Held**
SIC: 7997 7992 5812 Country club, membership; public golf courses; eating places

(P-18919)
EL DORADO COUNTRY CLUB
46000 Fairway Dr, Indian Wells (92210-8631)
PHONE.....................760 346-8081
Geoff Hasley, *President*
Wade Miller, *General Mgr*
EMP: 200
SQ FT: 50,000
SALES (est): 13MM **Privately Held**
WEB: www.eldoradocountryclub.com
SIC: 7997 5812 Golf club, membership; eating places

(P-18920)
EL MACERO COUNTRY CLUB INC
44571 Clubhouse Dr, El Macero (95618-1073)
PHONE.....................530 753-3363
Steven Backman, *General Mgr*
Chad Bennett, *Opers Staff*
Kevin Estrella, *Director*
Channan Anchondo, *Manager*
Kyle Kircher, *Assistant*
EMP: 60
SQ FT: 21,000

SALES: 3.6MM **Privately Held**
SIC: 7997 5941 5812 5813 Golf club, membership; golf goods & equipment; American restaurant; bar (drinking places)

(P-18921)
FAIRBANKS RANCH CNTRY CLB INC
15150 San Dieguito Rd, Rancho Santa Fe (92067)
P.O. Box 8586 (92067-8586)
PHONE.....................858 259-8811
Mike Kendall, *CEO*
Brad Forrester, *President*
Robert Macier, *CEO*
Stan Kinsey, *Vice Pres*
EMP: 180
SQ FT: 35,000
SALES: 12.7MM **Privately Held**
WEB: www.fairbanksranch.com
SIC: 7997 Country club, membership

(P-18922)
FAMILY MRALE WLFARE RECREATION
Also Called: Fmwr
1317 Normandy Dr, Fort Irwin (92310)
PHONE.....................760 380-3493
Brian Contreras, *Principal*
Marion Taylor, *CFO*
Tricia Berg, *Officer*
Sonia Bonet-Betancourt, *Director*
EMP: 99
SALES (est): 350.4K **Privately Held**
SIC: 7997 5812 8361 8351 Membership sports & recreation clubs; family restaurants; residential care for children; child day care services

(P-18923)
FARMS GOLF CLUB INC
Also Called: Red Tail Golf Assoc
8500 San Andrews Rd, Rancho Santa Fe (92067)
P.O. Box 2769 (92067-2769)
PHONE.....................858 756-5585
Scott Heyn, *Manager*
Bruce Bennetts, *Manager*
EMP: 63
SALES (est): 1.9MM **Privately Held**
SIC: 7997 Golf club, membership

(P-18924)
FIG GARDEN GOLF COURSE INC
7700 N Van Ness Blvd, Fresno (93711-0499)
PHONE.....................559 439-2928
David Knott, *President*
David T Knott, *President*
Marie D Knott, *Admin Sec*
Bill Reitz, *Sales Executive*
EMP: 55
SQ FT: 8,000
SALES (est): 3.5MM **Privately Held**
WEB: www.figgardengolf.com
SIC: 7997 5941 5812 Golf club, membership; golf goods & equipment; coffee shop

(P-18925)
FOREST PARK CABANA CLUB
2911 Pruneridge Ave, Santa Clara (95051-5652)
P.O. Box 2151 (95055-2151)
PHONE.....................408 244-1884
Jo Ann Frink, *President*
EMP: 50
SALES: 277.7K **Privately Held**
WEB: www.forestparkcabanaclub.com
SIC: 7997 Swimming club, membership

(P-18926)
FORT WASH GOLF & CNTRY CLB
Also Called: FORT, THE
10272 N Millbrook Ave, Fresno (93730-3400)
PHONE.....................559 434-1702
Dean Pryor, *President*
Bruce Waltz, *President*
EMP: 95
SALES: 4.3MM **Privately Held**
SIC: 7997 5813 5812 Golf club, membership; cocktail lounge; American restaurant

(P-18927)
FRIENDLY HILLS COUNTRY CLUB
8500 Villaverde Dr, Whittier (90605-1398)
PHONE.....................562 698-0331
Dave Goodrich, *COO*
Peter Phan, *Executive*
Taylor Stewart, *Marketing Staff*
Chris Banner, *Director*
Brandon Morgan, *Director*
EMP: 110 **EST:** 1969
SQ FT: 42,000
SALES (est): 3.9MM **Privately Held**
WEB: www.friendlyhillscc.com
SIC: 7997 Country club, membership

(P-18928)
GLENDORA COUNTRY CLUB
2400 Country Club Dr, Glendora (91741)
PHONE.....................626 335-4051
Jack Stoughton, *CEO*
Mike Kerstetter, *President*
Jim Leahy, *CEO*
Bill McKinley, *Treasurer*
EMP: 90
SQ FT: 10,000
SALES: 5MM **Privately Held**
SIC: 7997 5812 5813 Country club, membership; eating places; drinking places

(P-18929)
GLENROCK GROUP
Also Called: Golf Club At Boulder Ridge
1000 Old Quarry Rd, San Jose (95123-2454)
PHONE.....................408 323-9900
Glenda Garcia, *Vice Pres*
Rocke Garcia, *President*
EMP: 75
SALES (est): 988.3K **Privately Held**
SIC: 7997 Membership sports & recreation clubs

(P-18930)
GOLF INVESTMENT LLC (PA)
200 Avenida La Pata, San Clemente (92673-6301)
PHONE.....................949 498-6604
Shahin Vosough,
EMP: 100
SQ FT: 42,250
SALES (est): 2.7MM **Privately Held**
WEB: www.golfinvestment.com
SIC: 7997 7992 Golf club, membership; public golf courses

(P-18931)
GRANITE BAY GOLF CLUB
9600 Golf Club Dr, Granite Bay (95746-6721)
PHONE.....................916 791-5379
Bob Kunz, *General Mgr*
EMP: 120
SQ FT: 1,440
SALES (est): 4.7MM
SALES (corp-wide): 477MM **Privately Held**
WEB: www.granitebayclub.com
SIC: 7997 5812 7299 Golf club, membership; eating places; wedding chapel, privately operated
HQ: Clubcorp Usa, Inc.
3030 Lyndon B Johnson Fwy
Dallas TX 75234
972 243-6191

(P-18932)
GREEN VALLEY COUNTRY CLUB
35 Country Club Dr, Fairfield (94534-1305)
PHONE.....................707 864-1101
Tom Snell, *President*
EMP: 75
SALES: 5.2MM **Privately Held**
WEB: www.greenvalleycc.com
SIC: 7997 Country club, membership

(P-18933)
HACIENDA GOLF CLUB
718 East Rd, La Habra Heights (90631-8155)
PHONE.....................562 694-1081
Frank Cordeiro, *Officer*
Lane Greenlee, *CFO*
Russell Sylte, *General Mgr*

Veronica Barajas, *Admin Asst*
Cheryl Martenson, *Controller*
EMP: 95
SQ FT: 30,000
SALES: 5.9MM **Privately Held**
WEB: www.haciendagolfclub.com
SIC: 7997 5812 5813 Golf club, membership; American restaurant; bar (drinking places)

(P-18934)
HCC INVESTORS LLC
Also Called: Lennar
18550 Seven Bridges Rd, Rancho Santa Fe (92091-0216)
P.O. Box 1322 (92067-1322)
PHONE.....................858 759-7200
Jon Jaffe,
Patty Aguirre, *Controller*
EMP: 120
SQ FT: 35,000
SALES (est): 3.5MM **Privately Held**
SIC: 7997 Golf club, membership

(P-18935)
HILLCREST COUNTRY CLUB
10000 W Pico Blvd, Los Angeles (90064-3400)
PHONE.....................310 553-8911
John Jameson, *President*
John Goldsmith, *CEO*
Tom Driefus, *CFO*
Chester Firestien, *Principal*
Leonard Fisher, *Principal*
EMP: 180
SQ FT: 69,081
SALES: 22.1MM **Privately Held**
WEB: www.hcc-la.com
SIC: 7997 Country club, membership

(P-18936)
HUMBOLDT YACHT CLUB
2479 Wrigley Rd, Eureka (95503-9618)
P.O. Box 445 (95502-0445)
PHONE.....................707 443-1469
Tom Elfers, *Principal*
Wayne Sutherland, *Treasurer*
EMP: 75
SALES (est): 1MM **Privately Held**
SIC: 7997 Yacht club, membership

(P-18937)
INDIAN WELLS COUNTRY CLUB INC
Also Called: Iw Golf Club, Inc
46000 Club Dr, Indian Wells (92210-8870)
PHONE.....................760 345-2561
Gabe Codding, *General Mgr*
James Hinckley, *President*
Jack Lupton, *Treasurer*
Douglas Howe, *Exec VP*
Erin Dougherty, *General Mgr*
EMP: 60
SQ FT: 65,000
SALES (est): 5MM
SALES (corp-wide): 477MM **Privately Held**
WEB: www.remington-gc.com
SIC: 7997 Country club, membership
HQ: Clubcorp Usa, Inc.
3030 Lyndon B Johnson Fwy
Dallas TX 75234
972 243-6191

(P-18938)
INTERNATIONAL BAY CLUBS LLC (PA)
Also Called: Balboa Bay Club and Resort
1221 W Coast Hwy Ste 145, Newport Beach (92663-5037)
PHONE.....................949 645-5000
Todd M Pickup, *CEO*
David Wooten, *President*
EMP: 500
SQ FT: 330,000
SALES (est): 30.2MM **Privately Held**
WEB: www.balboabayclub.com
SIC: 7997 4493 6552 7011 Country club, membership; beach club, membership; marinas; land subdividers & developers, residential; hotels & motels

(P-18939)
INTERVEC PHOENIX TRAVEL CLUB
1456 Seacoast Dr Unit 4a, Imperial Beach (91932-3198)
PHONE..................828 728-5287
Donna Weston, *President*
EMP: 130
SALES (est): 5.5MM **Privately Held**
SIC: 7997 Membership sports & recreation clubs

(P-18940)
JACK KRAMER CLUB
11 Montecillo Dr, Rllng HLS Est (90274-4297)
PHONE..................310 326-4404
Craig Purcell, *General Mgr*
Connie Spencer, *President*
Bruce Ostermann, *General Mgr*
EMP: 50
SQ FT: 4,000
SALES (est): 1.2MM **Privately Held**
WEB: www.jackkramerclub.com
SIC: 7997 5941 5812 7999 Tennis club, membership; swimming club, membership; tennis goods & equipment; snack bar; swimming instruction; aerobic dance & exercise classes

(P-18941)
JONATHAN CLUB
Also Called: Jonathan Beach Club
850 Palisades Beach Rd, Santa Monica (90403-1008)
PHONE..................310 393-9245
Ernie Dunn, *Manager*
Jeremy Samson, *Finance Mgr*
EMP: 150
SQ FT: 12,784
SALES (corp-wide): 39.4MM **Privately Held**
WEB: www.jc.org
SIC: 7997 5812 8641 Beach club, membership; grills (eating places); civic social & fraternal associations
PA: Jonathan Club
545 S Figueroa St
Los Angeles CA 90071
213 624-0881

(P-18942)
KNIGHT-CALABASAS LLC (PA)
Also Called: Calabasas Country Club
4515 Park Entrada, Calabasas (91302-1453)
PHONE..................818 222-3200
Mike Calabassas,
Greg Elowe, *CFO*
Robert W Linn, *General Mgr*
Karen Seidman, *Controller*
EMP: 75
SQ FT: 2,000
SALES (est): 5.3MM **Privately Held**
SIC: 7997 Golf club, membership; country club, membership

(P-18943)
KNIGHT-CALABASAS LLC
Also Called: Peacock Gap Golf & Country Clb
333 Biscayne Dr, San Rafael (94901-1577)
PHONE..................415 453-4940
Bobby Yokito, *Partner*
Tricia Harris, *Director*
EMP: 60
SALES (est): 1.8MM
SALES (corp-wide): 5.3MM **Privately Held**
SIC: 7997 Golf club, membership
PA: Knight-Calabasas Llc
4515 Park Entrada
Calabasas CA 91302
818 222-3200

(P-18944)
LA CANADA FLINTRIDGE CNTRY CLB
5500 Godbey Dr, La Canada (91011-1836)
PHONE..................818 790-0611
Gilbert Dreyfus, *President*
Shi Wang, *CFO*
Evelyn Dreyfus, *Admin Sec*
EMP: 80 EST: 1977
SQ FT: 24,000

SALES (est): 7MM **Privately Held**
SIC: 7997 Country club, membership

(P-18945)
LA CUMBRE COUNTRY CLUB
4015 Via Laguna, Santa Barbara (93110-2298)
PHONE..................805 687-2421
Brian Bahman, *General Mgr*
Lanita Pattenaude, *Human Resources*
Chuck Pressley, *Facilities Mgr*
Karen Webb, *Director*
Michael Amador, *Manager*
EMP: 100
SQ FT: 8,000
SALES: 7.4MM **Privately Held**
SIC: 7997 Golf club, membership; country club, membership

(P-18946)
LA JOLLA BCH & TENNIS CLB INC (PA)
Also Called: Marine Room Restaurant
2000 Spindrift Dr, La Jolla (92037-3237)
PHONE..................858 454-7126
William J Kellogg, *CEO*
Jeannie Porter, *CFO*
Rob Walsh, *Vice Pres*
Caitlin Boehrig, *Executive Asst*
Pierrette Featherby, *Admin Asst*
▲ EMP: 165
SQ FT: 3,500
SALES (est): 28.2MM **Privately Held**
WEB: www.ljbtc.com
SIC: 7997 8742 Membership sports & recreation clubs; food & beverage consultant

(P-18947)
LA JOLLA COUNTRY CLUB INC
7301 High Ave, La Jolla (92037-5210)
PHONE..................858 454-9601
Andrew Gorton, *General Mgr*
Michael Mooney, *General Mgr*
Deborah Nixon, *Administration*
Jorge Dominguez, *Facilities Dir*
Rachel Carter, *Director*
EMP: 122 EST: 1928
SQ FT: 39,000
SALES: 10.6MM **Privately Held**
WEB: www.lajollacc.com
SIC: 7997 5812 5941 5813 Golf club, membership; eating places; golf goods & equipment; bar (drinking places); public golf courses

(P-18948)
LA QUINTA COUNTRY CLUB
77750 Avenue 50, La Quinta (92253-2204)
PHONE..................760 564-4151
Ernest Moore, *CFO*
Bradd Bennick, *Executive*
Tamarah Bennick, *Human Resources*
Ricardo Prado, *Opers Staff*
Tana Bustamante,
EMP: 55
SQ FT: 36,000
SALES: 6.7MM **Privately Held**
SIC: 7997 Country club, membership

(P-18949)
LA RINCONADA COUNTRY CLUB INC (PA)
Also Called: LA RINCONADA GOLF AND COUNTRY
14595 Clearview Dr, Los Gatos (95032-1799)
PHONE..................408 395-4181
Steve Vindasius, *CEO*
Mac Niven, *General Mgr*
Tom Schunn, *General Mgr*
Janett Antle, *Admin Asst*
Meriam Issaq,
EMP: 78
SQ FT: 100,000
SALES: 10.9MM **Privately Held**
WEB: www.larinconadacc.com
SIC: 7997 5813 5812 Country club, membership; bar (drinking places); eating places

(P-18950)
LAACO LTD
Also Called: California Yacht Club
4469 Admiralty Way, Marina Del Rey (90292-5415)
PHONE..................310 823-4567
Steve Hathaway, *President*
EMP: 100
SALES (corp-wide): 22.6MM **Privately Held**
SIC: 7997 4493 Yacht club, membership; marinas
PA: Laaco, Ltd.
431 W 7th St
Los Angeles CA 90014
213 622-1254

(P-18951)
LAGUNA WOODS GOLF CLUB
Also Called: Laguna Woods Village Golf Club
24122 Moulton Pkwy, Laguna Hills (92637-2781)
PHONE..................949 597-4336
Joel Walker, *Director*
Roger Teel, *Director*
▲ EMP: 50
SALES (est): 736.9K **Privately Held**
SIC: 7997 Golf club, membership

(P-18952)
LAHONTAN GOLF CLUB
12700 Lodgetrail Dr, Truckee (96161-5125)
PHONE..................530 550-2400
Jon Madonna, *President*
Kelly Gold, *Branch Mgr*
Steve Harris, *Admin Sec*
Tracy Murdock, *Controller*
EMP: 150 EST: 1996
SQ FT: 500,000
SALES (est): 10.3MM **Privately Held**
SIC: 7997 Golf club, membership

(P-18953)
LAKE MERCED GOLF & COUNTRY CLB
2300 Junipero Serra Blvd, Daly City (94015-1630)
PHONE..................650 755-2233
Dale Holub, *CEO*
Donna Lowe, *General Mgr*
EMP: 75
SQ FT: 38,000
SALES: 7MM **Privately Held**
WEB: www.lmgc.org
SIC: 7997 5813 Country club, membership; golf club, membership; tennis club, membership; bars & lounges

(P-18954)
LAKES COUNTRY CLUB ASSN INC (PA)
Also Called: Lakes Country Club, The
161 Old Ranch Rd, Palm Desert (92211-3211)
PHONE..................760 568-4321
Gerald Lee Hagood, *President*
Sandy Seddon, *COO*
Ron Phipps, *CFO*
Frank Melon, *Principal*
Jim Gammon, *Manager*
EMP: 300
SQ FT: 3,600
SALES (est): 14MM **Privately Held**
WEB: www.thelakescc.com
SIC: 7997 5941 5812 Country club, membership; sporting goods & bicycle shops; eating places

(P-18955)
LANCASTER JETHAWKS
45116 Valley Central Way, Lancaster (93536-1508)
PHONE..................661 726-5400
Peter A Carfagna, *CEO*
Pete Carfagna, *President*
Brad Seymour, *President*
Derek Sharp, *General Mgr*
William Thornhill, *General Mgr*
EMP: 80
SALES (est): 2.7MM **Privately Held**
SIC: 7997 Baseball club, except professional & semi-professional

(P-18956)
LAS POSAS CLUB INC
230 Ramona Pl, Camarillo (93010-8406)
P.O. Box 3089 (93011-3089)
PHONE..................805 482-1811
Barbara Stevens, *President*
EMP: 75
SALES: 45.1K **Privately Held**
SIC: 7997 Country club, membership

(P-18957)
LAS POSAS COUNTRY CLUB
Also Called: Lpcc
955 Fairway Dr, Camarillo (93010-8499)
PHONE..................805 482-4518
Sandy McNolty, *Controller*
Charles Burns, *CEO*
Thomas Walling, *CEO*
Alfonso Arechiga, *Executive*
Dena Levy, *Principal*
EMP: 100
SALES: 5.1MM **Privately Held**
SIC: 7997 7992 5812 0781 Country club, membership; tennis club, membership; public golf courses; eating places; landscape counseling & planning

(P-18958)
LONE CYPRESS COMPANY LLC
Also Called: Beach & Tennis Club
1567 Cypress Dr, Pebble Beach (93953)
P.O. Box 1128 (93953-1128)
PHONE..................831 625-8507
Steve Hurst, *Branch Mgr*
EMP: 100
SALES (corp-wide): 119.8MM **Privately Held**
WEB: www.pebblebeach.com
SIC: 7997 7999 5812 7991 Beach club, membership; swimming club, membership; tennis services & professionals; caterers; physical fitness facilities
PA: Pebble Beach Resort Co Dba Lone Cypress Company
2700 17 Mile Dr
Pebble Beach CA 93953
831 647-7500

(P-18959)
LONG BEACH YACHT CLUB
6201 E Appian Way, Long Beach (90803-4199)
PHONE..................562 598-9401
Louis Izurieta, *General Mgr*
Robert Frazer, *Ch of Bd*
Matthew Williston, *Executive*
Louis Izureita, *General Mgr*
Amy York, *VP Finance*
EMP: 63
SQ FT: 25,000
SALES: 5.8MM **Privately Held**
WEB: www.lbyc.org
SIC: 7997 Yacht club, membership

(P-18960)
LOS ALTOS GOLF AND COUNTRY CLB
1560 Country Club Dr, Los Altos (94024-5907)
PHONE..................650 947-3100
Bill Schneider, *President*
Grace Ikan, *Accountant*
Claudia Westrum, *Buyer*
Tracy Goodwin, *Director*
Mike Stevenson, *Director*
EMP: 70
SALES: 13.3MM **Privately Held**
WEB: www.lagcc.com
SIC: 7997 Country club, membership

(P-18961)
LOS AMIGOS COUNTRY CLUB INC
Also Called: Los Amigos Golf Course
7295 Quill Dr, Downey (90242-2001)
PHONE..................562 923-9696
Donald Duffin Sr, *President*
Tina Nunez, *Vice Pres*
Anne Hunter, *Admin Sec*
EMP: 65
SALES (est): 3.9MM **Privately Held**
WEB: www.losamigoscountryclub.com
SIC: 7997 Golf club, membership

2019 Directory of California
Wholesalers and Services Companies

▲ = Import ▼=Export
◆ =Import/Export

(P-18962)
LOS ANGELES 2024 EXPLORATORY
10960 Wilshire Blvd, Los Angeles
(90024-3702)
PHONE..............................310 407-0539
Casey Wasserman, *Chairman*
EMP: 50 **EST:** 2014
SALES: 17.7MM **Privately Held**
SIC: 7997 Membership sports & recreation clubs

(P-18963)
LOS ANGELES COUNTRY CLUB
10101 Wilshire Blvd, Los Angeles
(90024-4703)
PHONE..............................310 276-6104
Kirk O Reese, *Principal*
Alan Green, *Security Dir*
Shannon Dunne, *Executive Asst*
Terri Buchanan, *Asst Controller*
Ben Saberi, *Accountant*
EMP: 250 **EST:** 1898
SQ FT: 75,000
SALES: 17.6MM **Privately Held**
WEB: www.thelacc.org
SIC: 7997 Country club, membership; golf club, membership; tennis club, membership

(P-18964)
LOS ANGELES ROYAL VISTA GOLF C
Also Called: Los Angles Ryal Vsta Golf Crse
20055 Colima Rd, Walnut (91789-3502)
PHONE..............................909 595-7471
Don Crooker, *Manager*
EMP: 80
SQ FT: 37,948
SALES (corp-wide): 42.2MM **Privately Held**
SIC: 7997 7299 7992 Golf club, membership; banquet hall facilities; public golf courses
HQ: Los Angeles Royal Vista Golf Courses, Inc.
770 Kapiolani Blvd # 506
Honolulu HI 96813
808 592-4800

(P-18965)
MARBELLA COUNTRY CLUB
Also Called: NATIONAL GOLF PROPERTIES
30800 Golf Club Dr, San Juan Capistrano
(92675-5415)
PHONE..............................949 248-3700
Dan Riker, *Manager*
Ted Clark, *Treasurer*
Jeffrey Krifle, *General Mgr*
Phil Kempler, *Admin Sec*
EMP: 140
SQ FT: 43,000
SALES: 6.8K **Privately Held**
WEB: www.marbellacc.net
SIC: 7997 Country club, membership
PA: National Golf Properties Llc
2951 28th St Ste 3000
Santa Monica CA 90405

(P-18966)
MARBELLA GOLF & COUNTRY CLUB
30800 Golf Club Dr, San Juan Capistrano
(92675-5415)
PHONE..............................949 248-3700
Rod Hayden, *President*
Gary Lisenbee, *Treasurer*
David Neish, *Vice Pres*
Larry De Pope, *General Mgr*
Robert Hatch, *Admin Sec*
EMP: 114
SQ FT: 43,000
SALES (est): 4MM **Privately Held**
SIC: 7997 Country club, membership

(P-18967)
MARIN COUNTRY CLUB INC
500 Country Club Dr, Novato (94949-5896)
PHONE..............................415 382-6700
Ryan Wilson, *CEO*
Jackie Woodard, *Merchandise Mgr*
Susan Conroy, *Marketing Staff*
Marco Zuniga, *Maintence Staff*
Ken Doherty, *Director*

EMP: 75
SQ FT: 5,000
SALES: 7.8MM **Privately Held**
WEB: www.marincountryclub.com
SIC: 7997 5812 Country club, membership; golf club, membership; tennis club, membership; swimming club, membership; eating places

(P-18968)
MAYACAMA GOLF CLUB LLC
1240 Mayacama Club Dr, Santa Rosa
(95403-8251)
PHONE..............................707 569-2900
Johnathan Wilhelm, *Managing Prtnr*
Jonathan Wilhelm, *Managing Prtnr*
Greg Brown, *General Mgr*
Tracy Bell, *Executive Asst*
Jan Bowers, *Human Res Dir*
EMP: 120
SQ FT: 5,000
SALES (est): 11.4MM **Privately Held**
SIC: 7997 Golf club, membership

(P-18969)
MEADOW CLUB
1001 Bolinas Rd, Fairfax (94930-2200)
P.O. Box 129 (94978-0129)
PHONE..............................415 453-3274
John Grehan, *General Mgr*
EMP: 81
SQ FT: 3,000
SALES: 9.4MM **Privately Held**
WEB: www.meadowclub.com
SIC: 7997 Golf club, membership

(P-18970)
MENIFEE MANAGEMENT CORP
Also Called: Menifee Lakes Country Club
3200 E Guasti Rd Ste 100, Ontario
(91761-8661)
PHONE..............................951 672-4824
Chiao-Tung Geroge Chang, *CEO*
EMP: 100
SALES (est): 4.7MM **Privately Held**
SIC: 7997 Country club, membership

(P-18971)
MENLO CIRCUS CLUB
190 Park Ln, Atherton (94027-4194)
PHONE..............................650 322-4616
Steve De Laet, *CEO*
Nora B Stent, *President*
Matt Quinlan, *CFO*
Jason Asbra, *General Mgr*
Susie Frimel, *Admin Sec*
EMP: 70 **EST:** 1923
SQ FT: 14,000
SALES: 9.2MM **Privately Held**
SIC: 7997 Country club, membership

(P-18972)
MESA VERDE COUNTRY CLUB
3000 Club House Rd, Costa Mesa
(92626-3599)
PHONE..............................714 549-0377
John Hayhoe, *CEO*
Robert Heflin, *President*
Christopher Chun, *Executive*
Patricia Smith, *Controller*
Nicole Capp, *Sales Staff*
EMP: 125
SQ FT: 34,000
SALES: 8.9MM **Privately Held**
WEB: www.mesaverdecc.com
SIC: 7997 Country club, membership

(P-18973)
METROPOLITAN CLUB
640 Sutter St, San Francisco (94102-1097)
PHONE..............................415 673-0600
Clint Prescott, *General Mgr*
Kayne Maynard, *President*
Margaret Handelman, *Treasurer*
Gibbs Freeman, *General Mgr*
EMP: 65
SQ FT: 101,662
SALES: 5.6MM **Privately Held**
WEB: www.metropolitanclubsf.org
SIC: 7997 Membership sports & recreation clubs

(P-18974)
MID VLLEY RACQUETBALL ATHC CLB
Also Called: Mid-Valley Athletic Club
18420 Hart St, Reseda (91335-4317)
PHONE..............................818 705-6500
Ray Haizlip, *President*
Harold Wright, *President*
Jeannie Henning, *Vice Pres*
Christina Hughes, *Admin Sec*
EMP: 120 **EST:** 1979
SQ FT: 75,000
SALES (est): 2.2MM **Privately Held**
SIC: 7997 7991 Racquetball club, membership; physical fitness facilities

(P-18975)
MILLBRAE RACQUET CLUB
301 Santa Paula Ave, Millbrae
(94030-2026)
P.O. Box 344 (94030-0344)
PHONE..............................650 583-4345
Hector Johns, *President*
EMP: 82
SALES: 44.3K **Privately Held**
SIC: 7997 Tennis club, membership

(P-18976)
MISSION HILLS COUNTRY CLUB INC
34600 Mission Hills Dr, Rancho Mirage
(92270-1300)
PHONE..............................760 324-9400
Josh Tanner, *General Mgr*
Doug Howe, *Exec VP*
EMP: 130
SQ FT: 75,000
SALES (est): 9.7MM
SALES (corp-wide): 477MM **Privately Held**
WEB: www.remington-gc.com
SIC: 7997 7992 5812 Country club, membership; public golf courses; eating places
HQ: Clubcorp Usa, Inc.
3030 Lyndon B Johnson Fwy
Dallas TX 75234
972 243-6191

(P-18977)
MISSION VIEJO COUNTRY CLUB
26200 Country Club Dr, Mission Viejo
(92691-5905)
PHONE..............................949 582-1550
Michael Lance Kennedy, *Mng Member*
Enrique Martinez, *Principal*
Chad Pettit, *Principal*
Veronica Alva Roman, *Accountant*
Scot Dey, *Superintendent*
EMP: 103
SALES: 6.2MM **Privately Held**
WEB: www.missionviejocc.com
SIC: 7997 7991 5812 7299 Country club, membership; physical fitness facilities; eating places; banquet hall facilities

(P-18978)
MODESTO COURT ROOM INC
2012 Mchenry Ave, Modesto (95350-3212)
PHONE..............................209 577-1060
Lloyd Overholtzer, *President*
Sheri Walker, *Vice Pres*
EMP: 90
SQ FT: 43,000
SALES (est): 1.6MM **Privately Held**
WEB: www.modestocourtroom.net
SIC: 7997 5941 Swimming club, membership; racquetball club, membership; handball club, membership; sporting goods & bicycle shops

(P-18979)
MONTECITO COUNTRY CLUB INC
920 Summit Rd, Santa Barbara
(93108-2326)
P.O. Box 1170 (93102-1170)
PHONE..............................805 969-0800
Tai Warner, *President*
Michael Blackwell, *Executive*
Hiro Suzuki, *General Mgr*
Kelly Woodard,
EMP: 100
SQ FT: 10,000

SALES (est): 6.2MM
SALES (corp-wide): 188.7MM **Privately Held**
WEB: www.montecitocc.com
SIC: 7997 5812 5813 Country club, membership; eating places; bar (drinking places)
PA: Tsukamoto Corporation Co., Ltd.
1-6-5, Nihombashihoncho
Chuo-Ku TKY 103-0
332 791-330

(P-18980)
MONTEREY PENINSULA COUNTRY CLB
Also Called: Mpcc
3000 Club Rd, Pebble Beach (93953-2542)
PHONE..............................831 373-1556
Robert Perry Smith, *CEO*
Michael Bowhay, *Exec Dir*
Joan Lucido, *Accounting Mgr*
Rick Busman, *Finance*
Anne Musson,
EMP: 130
SQ FT: 70,000
SALES: 23.6MM **Privately Held**
WEB: www.mpccpb.org
SIC: 7997 Country club, membership

(P-18981)
MORAGA CNTRY CLB HMOWNERS ASSN
1600 Saint Andrews Dr, Moraga
(94556-1194)
PHONE..............................925 376-2200
Frank Meln, *General Mgr*
EMP: 100 **EST:** 1973
SQ FT: 10,000
SALES (est): 5.5MM **Privately Held**
WEB: www.moragacc.com
SIC: 7997 Country club, membership

(P-18982)
NAMASTA INC
Also Called: North American Studio Alliance
2313 Hastings Dr, Belmont (94002-3317)
PHONE..............................650 591-3639
Bernard Slede, *President*
Margaret LI, *General Mgr*
EMP: 50
SALES (est): 852K **Privately Held**
WEB: www.namasta.com
SIC: 7997 Membership sports & recreation clubs

(P-18983)
NAPA GOLF ASSOCIATES LLC
Also Called: Chardonnay
2555 Jameson Canyon Rd, NAPA (94558)
PHONE..............................707 257-1900
Kenneth E Laird,
Gus Gianulias,
Jim Gianulias,
EMP: 84
SQ FT: 24,000
SALES (est): 2MM
SALES (corp-wide): 433.7MM **Privately Held**
WEB: www.remington-gc.com
SIC: 7997 Golf club, membership
HQ: Clubcorp Usa, Inc.
3030 Lyndon B Johnson Fwy
Dallas TX 75234
972 243-6191

(P-18984)
NAPA VALLEY COUNTRY CLUB
3385 Hagen Rd, NAPA (94558-3849)
PHONE..............................707 252-1111
Todd Jeffrey Meginness, *CEO*
Todd Meginness, *COO*
George Hise, *Treasurer*
Mike Wilson, *Vice Pres*
Patrick Smorra, *Admin Sec*
▲ **EMP:** 80
SQ FT: 8,000
SALES: 6.4MM **Privately Held**
WEB: www.napavalleycc.com
SIC: 7997 5813 5812 Country club, membership; bar (drinking places); eating places

(P-18985)
NATIONAL GOLF PROPERTIES INC
Also Called: San Geronimo Golf Course
5800 Sir Francis Drake, San Geronimo (94963)
P.O. Box 130 (94963-0130)
PHONE..............................415 488-4030
Heather Loivos, *Manager*
EMP: 98 **Privately Held**
WEB: www.nationalgolfproperties.com
SIC: 7997 Golf club, membership
PA: National Golf Properties Llc
2951 28th St Ste 3000
Santa Monica CA 90405
-

(P-18986)
NEW DISCOVERY INC
Also Called: Discovery Bay Ctry Club
1475 Clubhouse Dr, Byron (94505-9241)
PHONE..............................925 783-6613
Mark Tissot, *Manager*
Jenelle Tissot, *Manager*
EMP: 60
SALES (corp-wide): 9.3MM **Privately Held**
SIC: 7997 Golf club, membership
PA: New Discovery Inc
1380 Galaxy Way
Concord CA
-

(P-18987)
NEWPORT BEACH COUNTRY CLUB INC
1 Clubhouse Dr, Newport Beach (92660-7107)
PHONE..............................949 644-9550
David Wooten, *President*
Gerald Johnson, *CFO*
Jerry Anderson, *Vice Pres*
EMP: 90
SALES (est): 5.5MM
SALES (corp-wide): 30.2MM **Privately Held**
WEB: www.newportbeachcc.com
SIC: 7997 7991 5941 5813 Country club, membership; physical fitness facilities; sporting goods & bicycle shops; drinking places; eating places
PA: International Bay Clubs, Llc
1221 W Coast Hwy Ste 145
Newport Beach CA 92663
949 645-5000

(P-18988)
NOR-WALL INC (PA)
Also Called: Cal Courts
518 W Clark St, Eureka (95501-0103)
PHONE..............................707 445-5445
Agetha Nord, *President*
Glen Wallace, *President*
EMP: 50
SQ FT: 9,000
SALES (est): 1.8MM **Privately Held**
WEB: www.calcourtsfitness.com
SIC: 7997 Tennis club, membership; racquetball club, membership

(P-18989)
NORTH RANCH COUNTRY CLUB
4761 Valley Spring Dr, Westlake Village (91362-4399)
PHONE..............................818 889-3531
Mark Bagaaso, *CEO*
Scott London, *Treasurer*
Jeff Miller, *Director*
EMP: 160
SQ FT: 53,000
SALES: 12MM **Privately Held**
SIC: 7997 5812 5941 Country club, membership; eating places; sporting goods & bicycle shops

(P-18990)
NORTH RIDGE COUNTRY CLUB
7600 Madison Ave, Fair Oaks (95628-3400)
PHONE..............................916 967-5717
Dennis Tootelian, *CEO*
Rink Sanford, *General Mgr*
EMP: 75
SQ FT: 5,000

SALES: 5.7MM **Privately Held**
WEB: www.northridgegolf.com
SIC: 7997 Country club, membership; golf club, membership

(P-18991)
OAKDALE GOLF AND COUNTRY CLUB
243 N Stearns Rd, Oakdale (95361-9247)
PHONE..............................209 847-2984
Tom Brennan, *President*
Rick Schultz, *General Mgr*
Rachel Walsh, *Finance Mgr*
Scott Pinkelman, *Teacher*
Chris Carroll, *Manager*
EMP: 55
SQ FT: 12,000
SALES: 3.9MM **Privately Held**
WEB: www.oakdalegcc.org
SIC: 7997 Country club, membership

(P-18992)
OAKMONT COUNTRY CLUB
3100 Country Club Dr, Glendale (91208-1799)
PHONE..............................818 542-4260
Pat Dahlson, *CEO*
John Schiller, *President*
Michael Hyler, *COO*
Pierangelo Ramponi, *Executive*
Jonathan Goglia, *Assistant*
EMP: 125
SQ FT: 37,000
SALES: 10.3MM **Privately Held**
SIC: 7997 Country club, membership; golf club, membership; swimming club, membership

(P-18993)
OASIS PALM DSERT HMOWNERS ASSN
Also Called: Oasis Country Club
42330 Casbah Way, Palm Desert (92211-7660)
PHONE..............................760 345-5661
Robert Masata, *President*
Roy McGowen, *President*
EMP: 52
SALES (est): 2.4MM **Privately Held**
SIC: 7997 Country club, membership

(P-18994)
OLYMPIC INVESTORS LTD
Also Called: Walnut Creek Spt & Fitnes CLB
1908 Olympic Blvd, Walnut Creek (94596-5023)
PHONE..............................925 322-8996
Linda Hansen, *Partner*
Sam Beler, *General Ptnr*
George Valerio, *General Ptnr*
Robert F Wattles, *General Ptnr*
EMP: 90
SQ FT: 25,000
SALES (est): 4.9MM **Privately Held**
WEB: www.wcsf.net
SIC: 7997 7991 5812 7999 Membership sports & recreation clubs; physical fitness facilities; eating places; physical fitness instruction

(P-18995)
ORINDA COUNTRY CLUB
315 Camino Sobrante, Orinda (94563-1899)
PHONE..............................925 254-4313
Jeff Bause, *President*
John Townsend, *Executive*
Tracy Alcaide, *Comms Dir*
George Parker, *General Mgr*
Jennifer Ontiveros, *Admin Asst*
EMP: 90
SALES: 12MM **Privately Held**
WEB: www.orindacc.org
SIC: 7997 Country club, membership

(P-18996)
PACIFIC CLUB (PA)
4110 Macarthur Blvd, Newport Beach (92660-2012)
PHONE..............................949 955-1123
Douglas M Ammerman, *President*
Richard M Ortwein, *Treasurer*
Heather Fisher, *Executive*
Joe Gatto, *General Mgr*
Thomas R Acklum, *Admin Sec*
EMP: 77

SQ FT: 28,000
SALES (est): 6.8MM **Privately Held**
WEB: www.pacificclub.org
SIC: 7997 Country club, membership; eating places; bar (drinking places)

(P-18997)
PACIFIC GOLF & COUNTRY CLUB
200 Avenida La Pata, San Clemente (92673-6301)
PHONE..............................949 498-6604
Tom Frost, *Manager*
EMP: 90
SQ FT: 27,000
SALES (est): 1.8MM
SALES (corp-wide): 2.7MM **Privately Held**
WEB: www.pacificgc.com
SIC: 7997 7992 Golf club, membership; public golf courses
PA: Golf Investment Llc
200 Avenida La Pata
San Clemente CA 92673
949 498-6604

(P-18998)
PALM DSERT RCRTL FCLITIES CORP
Also Called: Pdrfc
38995 Desert Willow Dr, Palm Desert (92260-1674)
P.O. Box 14290 (92255-4290)
PHONE..............................760 346-0015
Richard Mogensen, *General Mgr*
Francois Gaertner, *Executive*
Derek White, *General Mgr*
Jason Wilkinson, *Administration*
Lisa Lozano, *Accountant*
EMP: 100
SQ FT: 10,000
SALES: 2.5MM **Privately Held**
WEB: www.cityofpalmdesert.com
SIC: 7997 Membership sports & recreation clubs
PA: City Of Palm Desert
73510 Fred Waring Dr
Palm Desert CA 92260
760 346-0611

(P-18999)
PALOMAR GEM & MINERAL CLUB
2120 Mission Rd Ste 260, Escondido (92029-1014)
P.O. Box 1583 (92033-1583)
PHONE..............................760 743-0809
Mike Nelson, *Principal*
Don Parsley, *Manager*
EMP: 70
SALES (est): 692.5K **Privately Held**
SIC: 7997 Membership sports & recreation clubs

(P-19000)
PALOS VERDES BEACH & ATHC CLB
389 Paseo Del Mar, Palos Verdes Estates (90274-1267)
P.O. Box 158 (90274-0158)
PHONE..............................310 375-8777
Jane Williamson, *Manager*
EMP: 88
SQ FT: 5,000
SALES: 1.7MM **Privately Held**
SIC: 7997 Swimming club, membership

(P-19001)
PASADENA MODEL RAILROAD CLUB
5458 Alhambra Ave, Los Angeles (90032-3102)
PHONE..............................323 222-1718
Steve Phillips, *President*
William James, *Principal*
EMP: 55
SQ FT: 6,596
SALES: 16.6K **Privately Held**
SIC: 7997 Membership sports & recreation clubs

(P-19002)
PAUMA VALLEY COUNTRY CLUB
15835 Pauma Valley Dr, Pauma Valley (92061-1612)
P.O. Box 206 (92061-0206)
PHONE..............................760 742-1230
Butt Suze, *President*
Paul Devine, *General Mgr*
EMP: 76 EST: 1961
SQ FT: 3,000
SALES (est): 6.4MM **Privately Held**
SIC: 7997 Country club, membership

(P-19003)
PLANTATION GOLF CLUB INC
50994 Monroe St, Indio (92201-9709)
P.O. Box 1657, La Quinta (92247-1657)
PHONE..............................760 775-3688
Art Schillings, *General Mgr*
EMP: 54
SQ FT: 16,000
SALES: 6.3MM **Privately Held**
SIC: 7997 Golf club, membership

(P-19004)
PORTER VALLEY COUNTRY CLUB
Also Called: Porter Valley Catering
19216 Singing Hills Dr, Northridge (91326-1799)
PHONE..............................818 360-1071
Robert H Dedman, *Ch of Bd*
John Beckett, *President*
Doug Howe, *Exec VP*
EMP: 110
SQ FT: 18,000
SALES (est): 5.1MM
SALES (corp-wide): 477MM **Privately Held**
WEB: www.remington-gc.com
SIC: 7997 5812 5941 Golf club, membership; steak restaurant; sporting goods & bicycle shops
HQ: Clubcorp Usa, Inc.
3030 Lyndon B Johnson Fwy
Dallas TX 75234
972 243-6191

(P-19005)
RACQUET CLUB OF IRVINE
Also Called: Rci
5 Ethel Coplen Way Ste 5 # 5, Irvine (92612-1797)
PHONE..............................949 786-3000
Spearman Industry, *President*
EMP: 54
SQ FT: 15,000
SALES (est): 1.4MM **Privately Held**
SIC: 7997 Tennis club, membership

(P-19006)
RAMS HILL COUNTRY CLUB
1881 Rams Hill Rd, Borrego Springs (92004-5400)
PHONE..............................760 767-4259
Wesley Porter, *President*
Don Davis, *Exec VP*
EMP: 60
SQ FT: 40,000
SALES (est): 2.8MM **Privately Held**
SIC: 7997 Country club, membership

(P-19007)
RANCHO BERNARDO GOLF CLUB
Also Called: COUNTY CLUB OF RANCHO BERNARDO
17550 Bernardo Oaks Dr, San Diego (92128-2112)
PHONE..............................858 487-1134
Robert Schwanhausser, *CEO*
Scott Bentley, *General Mgr*
John Kersey, *Admin Sec*
EMP: 67
SQ FT: 23,000
SALES: 2.8MM **Privately Held**
WEB: www.ccofrb.com
SIC: 7997 Golf club, membership

(P-19008)
RANCHO MURIETA COUNTRY CLUB
7000 Alameda Dr, Rancho Murieta (95683-9148)
PHONE..................................916 354-2400
Robert Wright, *CEO*
Vince Lepera, *President*
Buzz Breedlove, *Treasurer*
Dick Stenstrom, *Vice Pres*
Johnny Frink, *Executive*
EMP: 90
SQ FT: 40,000
SALES (est): 6.8MM **Privately Held**
WEB: www.ranchomurietacc.com
SIC: 7997 Country club, membership; golf club, membership

(P-19009)
RANCHO SANTA FE ASSOCIATION A
Also Called: Rancho Sante Fe Golf Club
5827 Viadelacumere, Rancho Santa Fe (92067)
P.O. Box A (92067-0359)
PHONE..................................858 756-1182
Stephen Nordstrom, *Manager*
EMP: 100
SALES (corp-wide): 16.3MM **Privately Held**
SIC: 7997 Golf club, membership
PA: Rancho Santa Fe Association
17022 Avenida De Acacias
Rancho Santa Fe CA 92067
858 756-1174

(P-19010)
RB ANGLERS CLUB
12578 Cresta Pl, San Diego (92128-2312)
PHONE..................................858 487-6484
Richard Studinka, *President*
EMP: 75
SALES (est): 735.7K **Privately Held**
SIC: 7997 Membership sports & recreation clubs

(P-19011)
RED HILL COUNTRY CLUB
8358 Red Hl Cntry Clb Dr, Rancho Cucamonga (91730-1899)
PHONE..................................909 982-1358
Rob Mocskley, *President*
EMP: 92
SQ FT: 20,000
SALES (est): 4.8MM **Privately Held**
WEB: www.redhillcc.com
SIC: 7997 5812 Country club, membership; eating places

(P-19012)
REDLANDS COUNTRY CLUB
1749 Garden St, Redlands (92373-7248)
PHONE..................................909 793-2661
Scott Reding, *President*
Kurt Burmeister, *General Mgr*
Jason Murphy, *General Mgr*
Kathy Knudsen, *Director*
Ruben Mendoza, *Asst Mgr*
EMP: 80
SQ FT: 22,000
SALES (est): 5.6MM **Privately Held**
SIC: 7997 5812 5813 Country club, membership; tennis club, membership; golf club, membership; snack shop; diner; bar (drinking places)

(P-19013)
RESERVE CLUB
49400 Desert Butte Trl, Indian Wells (92210-7075)
PHONE..................................760 674-2222
Kenneth Novack, *President*
C Ted McCarter, *Treasurer*
Ben Wiley, *Human Res Dir*
EMP: 80
SQ FT: 10,000
SALES (est): 8.5MM **Privately Held**
SIC: 7997 Country club, membership

(P-19014)
RICHMOND COUNTRY CLUB
1 Markovich Ln, Richmond (94806-1825)
PHONE..................................510 231-2241
Mac Niven, *General Mgr*
EMP: 57

SQ FT: 30,000
SALES (est): 4MM **Privately Held**
SIC: 7997 Country club, membership

(P-19015)
RIVER ISLAND COUNTRY CLUB INC
31989 River Island Dr, Porterville (93257-9611)
PHONE..................................559 781-2917
Terry Treece, *Director*
Dale Waller, *Executive*
Jimmy Pettis, *Director*
Corey Carlson, *Manager*
EMP: 52
SQ FT: 13,500
SALES (est): 2.8MM **Privately Held**
SIC: 7997 Golf club, membership; country club, membership

(P-19016)
RIVER RIDGE GOLF CLUB
2401 W Vineyard Ave, Oxnard (93036-2218)
PHONE..................................805 981-8724
Otto Kanny, *General Mgr*
EMP: 92
SALES (est): 1.7MM **Privately Held**
SIC: 7997 Golf club, membership

(P-19017)
RIVERVIEW GOLF AND COUNTRY CLB
4200 Bechelli Ln, Redding (96002-3533)
PHONE..................................530 224-2254
Ralph Stroch, *President*
Ralph Storch, *President*
Kim Pickering, *Comptroller*
Chad Ohmer, *Manager*
Lynette Trotter, *Manager*
EMP: 72
SQ FT: 30,000
SALES (est): 3.2MM **Privately Held**
WEB: www.riverviewgolf.net
SIC: 7997 5812 5813 Country club, membership; eating places; bar (drinking places)

(P-19018)
RODDY RANCH PBC LLC
Also Called: Golf Club At Roddy Ranch
1 Tour Way, Antioch (94531-9053)
PHONE..................................925 978-4653
Jack Roddy,
EMP: 55
SQ FT: 1,400
SALES (est): 5.3MM **Privately Held**
WEB: www.roddyranch.com
SIC: 7997 Golf club, membership

(P-19019)
ROSE BOWL AQUATICS CENTER
360 N Arroyo Blvd, Pasadena (91103-3201)
PHONE..................................626 564-0330
Judy Biggs, *Exec Dir*
Kurt Knop, *Principal*
Sandra Hilts, *Finance*
Timothy Unger, *Human Res Mgr*
Jeff Julian, *Mktg Dir*
EMP: 80
SALES (est): 7.6MM **Privately Held**
WEB: www.rosebowlpolo.com
SIC: 7997 Boating & swimming clubs

(P-19020)
ROTARY CLB PCF GROVE CHAR FUND
706 Forest Ave, Pacific Grove (93950-4283)
PHONE..................................831 372-3877
Kenneth Petersen, *Principal*
EMP: 77
SALES (est): 98.5K **Privately Held**
SIC: 7997 Membership sports & recreation clubs

(P-19021)
ROUND HILL COUNTRY CLUB
Also Called: Rh
3169 Roundhill Rd, Alamo (94507-1735)
PHONE..................................925 934-8211
Debby Grauman, *CEO*
Greg Tachiera, *CEO*

John Hattab, *Director*
EMP: 50 EST: 1965
SALES (est): 5.6MM **Privately Held**
SIC: 7997 Country club, membership

(P-19022)
ROUND HILL ENTERPRISES
Also Called: Round Hill Golf & Country Club
3169 Roundhill Rd, Alamo (94507-1735)
PHONE..................................925 934-8211
Arthur Davis, *President*
Jack Mahoney, *COO*
Leonard D'Orazio, *CFO*
Theodore Budach, *Vice Pres*
Lori Primasing, *Admin Sec*
EMP: 180 EST: 1959
SQ FT: 20,000
SALES (est): 5.8MM **Privately Held**
WEB: www.rhcountryclub.com
SIC: 7997 5812 5813 Country club, membership; American restaurant; bar (drinking places)

(P-19023)
SADDLEBACK VLY
25631 Peter A Hartman Way, Mission Viejo (92691-3142)
PHONE..................................949 586-1234
Don Cuzick, *Principal*
EMP: 56
SALES (est): 4MM **Privately Held**
SIC: 7997 Membership sports & recreation clubs

(P-19024)
SALESIAN BOYS AND GIRLS CLUB
680 Filbert St, San Francisco (94133-2805)
PHONE..................................415 397-3068
Russell Gumina, *Exec Dir*
Randal Demartini, *Asst Director*
EMP: 79
SALES (est): 2.4MM **Privately Held**
SIC: 7997 Membership sports & recreation clubs

(P-19025)
SAN DIEGO COUNTRY CLUB INC
88 L St, Chula Vista (91911-1499)
PHONE..................................619 422-8895
David Morris, *General Mgr*
EMP: 80
SQ FT: 36,140
SALES (est): 5.1MM **Privately Held**
WEB: www.sdcc.cc
SIC: 7997 Country club, membership; golf club, membership

(P-19026)
SAN DIMAS GOLF INC
Also Called: Via Verde Country Club
1400 Avenida Entrada, San Dimas (91773-4004)
PHONE..................................909 599-8486
Kwan O Lee, *President*
Dal Eun Lee, *Shareholder*
Dal H Lee, *Vice Pres*
Dal K Lee, *Admin Sec*
EMP: 70 EST: 1975
SQ FT: 21,887
SALES (est): 4.5MM **Privately Held**
WEB: www.viaverdecountryclub.com
SIC: 7997 Country club, membership

(P-19027)
SAN GABRIEL COUNTRY CLUB
350 E Hermosa Dr, San Gabriel (91775-2346)
PHONE..................................626 287-9671
Tom Dukes, *President*
Bill Johnson, *General Mgr*
EMP: 80 EST: 1904
SQ FT: 48,000
SALES (est): 8.4MM **Privately Held**
WEB: www.sangabrielcc.com
SIC: 7997 Country club, membership

(P-19028)
SAN JOAQUIN COUNTRY CLUB
3484 W Bluff Ave, Fresno (93711-0199)
PHONE..................................559 439-3483
Jeffrey Newman, *President*
Melissa Allen, *Manager*
EMP: 63
SQ FT: 39,615

SALES: 3.1MM **Privately Held**
SIC: 7997 5812 5813 Country club, membership; American restaurant; bar (drinking places)

(P-19029)
SAN JOSE COUNTRY CLUB
15571 Alum Rock Ave, San Jose (95127-2799)
PHONE..................................408 258-4901
Chris Simpson, *General Mgr*
Jason Green, *General Mgr*
Lauren Embry, *Admin Asst*
UT Lu, *Asst Controller*
Jacquelyn Chac, *Director*
EMP: 70
SQ FT: 24,000
SALES: 5.6MM **Privately Held**
SIC: 7997 7299 Ice sports; color consultant

(P-19030)
SAN LUIS OBISPO GOLF
Also Called: Slogcc
255 Country Club Dr, San Luis Obispo (93401-8921)
PHONE..................................805 543-3400
David Cole, *President*
Carol Kerwin, *Admin Sec*
Hugh Payne, *Director*
Christopher Simpson, *Manager*
EMP: 110
SQ FT: 10,000
SALES (est): 6MM **Privately Held**
SIC: 7997 Country club, membership

(P-19031)
SANTA ANA COUNTRY CLUB
20382 Newport Blvd, Santa Ana (92707-5396)
PHONE..................................714 556-3000
Joseph J Wagner, *CEO*
Pamela Paulson, *Director*
EMP: 100
SALES (est): 8.8MM **Privately Held**
SIC: 7997 Country club, membership

(P-19032)
SANTA BARBARA ATHLETIC CLB INC
520 Castillo St, Santa Barbara (93101-3400)
PHONE..................................805 966-6147
Gordon Mc Cay, *President*
Eric Geeb, *General Mgr*
Laura Lewis, *Admin Sec*
Debbie Chatfield, *Director*
Melissa Valdez, *Director*
EMP: 80
SQ FT: 21,600
SALES (est): 2.3MM **Privately Held**
SIC: 7997 Membership sports & recreation clubs

(P-19033)
SANTA CLARA WOMENS CLUB
Also Called: Santa Clara Woman's Club Adobe
3260 The Alameda, Santa Clara (95050-4329)
P.O. Box 367 (95052-0367)
PHONE..................................408 246-8000
Marlene O'Donnell, *President*
EMP: 92
SALES (est): 1.1MM **Privately Held**
SIC: 7997 Membership sports & recreation clubs

(P-19034)
SANTA LUCIA PRESERVE COMPANY
1 Rancho San Carlos Rd, Carmel (93923-7999)
PHONE..................................831 620-6760
Tom Gray, *Principal*
Richard Tanner, *Purch Mgr*
Candace Allen, *Manager*
Leif Utegaard, *Manager*
EMP: 96
SALES (est): 8.6MM **Privately Held**
SIC: 7997 Country club, membership

P
R
O
D
U
C
T
S

&

S
V
C
S

(P-19035)
SANTA ROSA GOLF & COUNTRY CLUB
333 Country Club Dr, Santa Rosa (95401-5599)
PHONE...................707 546-3485
Eric L Affeldt, *CEO*
EMP: 100
SQ FT: 40,000
SALES (est): 7.7MM
SALES (corp-wide): 477MM **Privately Held**
WEB: www.santarosagolf.com
SIC: 7997 Country club, membership
HQ: Clubcorp Holdings, Inc.
   3030 Lbj Fwy Ste 600
   Dallas TX 75234
   972 243-6191

(P-19036)
SANTALUZ CLUB INC
8170 Caminito Santaluz E, San Diego (92127-2577)
PHONE...................858 759-3120
Steve Cowell, *CEO*
Timothy A Kaehr, *CFO*
Michael Forsum, *Vice Pres*
James Hoselton, *Vice Pres*
Jim Macdonough, *General Mgr*
EMP: 120
SQ FT: 19,000
SALES (est): 11.7MM **Privately Held**
WEB: www.santaluz.com
SIC: 7997 Country club, membership

(P-19037)
SANYO FOODS CORP AMERICA
Also Called: Tustin Ranch Golf Club
12442 Tustin Ranch Rd, Tustin (92782-1000)
PHONE...................714 730-1611
Steve Plummer, *Branch Mgr*
EMP: 117
SALES (corp-wide): 71B **Privately Held**
SIC: 7997 Golf club, membership
HQ: Sanyo Foods Corporation Of America
   11955 Monarch St
   Garden Grove CA 92841
   714 891-3671

(P-19038)
SATICOY COUNTRY CLUB
4450 Clubhouse Dr, Somis (93066-9798)
PHONE...................805 647-1153
Douglas Taxton, *President*
James R Van Wyck, *CEO*
Kathy Sube, *Financial Exec*
Amy Hogue, *Accountant*
Nadia Chapman, *Mktg Dir*
EMP: 80
SALES: 4.2MM **Privately Held**
WEB: www.saticoycountryclub.com
SIC: 7997 Country club, membership; golf club, membership

(P-19039)
SEBASTOPOL RIFLE & PISTOL CLUB
343 Flynn St, Sebastopol (95472)
P.O. Box 575 (95473-0575)
PHONE...................707 824-0184
Greg Bolker, *President*
Greg Bolken, *President*
Garry Goss, *Treasurer*
Barry McLaren, *Vice Pres*
EMP: 72
SALES: 38.6K **Privately Held**
SIC: 7997 Membership sports & recreation clubs

(P-19040)
SEQUOIA WOOD COUNTRY CLUB
1000 Cypress Point Dr, Arnold (95223)
P.O. Box 930 (95223-0930)
PHONE...................209 795-1000
Norm Kestner, *President*
EMP: 64
SQ FT: 13,000
SALES (est): 2.3MM **Privately Held**
WEB: www.sequoiawoods.com
SIC: 7997 5812 5813 Golf club, membership; eating places; bar (drinking places)

(P-19041)
SERRANO ASSOCIATES LLC
Also Called: Serrano Country Club
5005 Serrano Pkwy, El Dorado Hills (95762-7511)
PHONE...................916 939-3333
Kevitt Sale, *Manager*
EMP: 100
SALES (corp-wide): 10.1MM **Privately Held**
WEB: www.serranoassociates.com
SIC: 7997 5941 5813 5812 Golf club, membership; sporting goods & bicycle shops; drinking places; eating places
PA: Serrano Associates, Llc
   4525 Serrano Pkwy
   El Dorado Hills CA 95762
   916 939-3333

(P-19042)
SERRANO COUNTRY CLUB INC
5005 Serrano Pkwy P, El Dorado Hills (95762-7511)
PHONE...................916 933-5005
Dean Cummings, *President*
Bob Stangroom, *General Mgr*
Laura Lewis, *Accounting Mgr*
Tazim Venkataya, *Controller*
Ken Zinky, *Facilities Mgr*
EMP: 105
SALES: 7.8MM **Privately Held**
WEB: www.serranocountryclub.com
SIC: 7997 Golf club, membership

(P-19043)
SEVEN LAKES HM ASSN CNTRY CLB
1 Desert Lakes Dr, Palm Springs (92264-5520)
PHONE...................760 328-2695
Silas Dreher, *General Mgr*
Diane Hale, *Administration*
EMP: 50
SQ FT: 6,000
SALES (est): 884.7K **Privately Held**
SIC: 7997 8641 Country club, membership; homeowners' association

(P-19044)
SEVEN OAKS COUNTRY CLUB
2000 Grand Lakes Ave, Bakersfield (93311-2931)
P.O. Box 11165 (93389-1165)
PHONE...................661 664-6404
David H Murdock, *CEO*
Bruce Freeman, *President*
Don Ciota, *General Mgr*
Eryn Urban, *Director*
EMP: 125
SQ FT: 39,000
SALES (est): 7.9MM **Privately Held**
WEB: www.sevenoakscountryclub.com
SIC: 7997 Country club, membership

(P-19045)
SHADY CANYON GOLF CLUB INC
100 Shady Canyon Dr, Irvine (92603-0301)
PHONE...................949 856-7000
James T Wood, *CEO*
Thomas Heggi, *President*
Robert Leenhouts, *Principal*
Bernard Lee, *Accountant*
Melissa Loos, *Director*
EMP: 113
SALES: 186.4K **Privately Held**
WEB: www.shadycanyongolfclub.com
SIC: 7997 Country club, membership

(P-19046)
SHERWOOD COUNTRY CLUB
320 W Stafford Rd, Thousand Oaks (91361-5087)
PHONE...................805 496-3036
Lance Fisher, *General Mgr*
Garrett Yokoyama, *Executive*
Melanie Kohagen, *Executive Asst*
Jean Gojkovich, *Human Res Dir*
Heze Katalbas, *Maintence Staff*
EMP: 113 **EST:** 1989
SALES: 14.5MM **Privately Held**
WEB: www.sherwoodcc.com
SIC: 7997 Country club, membership

(P-19047)
SIERRA VIEW COUNTRY CLUB
105 Alta Vista Ave, Roseville (95678-1647)
P.O. Box 676 (95678-0676)
PHONE...................916 782-3741
Barry Macdonald, *CEO*
Steve Rainwater, *President*
Traci Burres, *Executive*
John Welch, *General Mgr*
Thomas Broxham, *Director*
EMP: 75
SQ FT: 5,000
SALES: 1.8MM **Privately Held**
WEB: www.sierraviewcc.com
SIC: 7997 5812 5813 Golf club, membership; American restaurant; bar (drinking places)

(P-19048)
SILVER CREEK VLY CNTRY CLB INC
5460 Country Club Pkwy, San Jose (95138-2215)
PHONE...................408 239-5775
Rene Devos, *General Mgr*
Steven Backman, *General Mgr*
Alan Deck, *General Mgr*
Robert E Lee, *General Mgr*
Stacey Leando, *Finance*
EMP: 180
SALES (est): 9MM **Privately Held**
WEB: www.scvcc.com
SIC: 7997 5941 Country club, membership; sporting goods & bicycle shops

(P-19049)
SILVERADO RESORT AND SPA
1600 Atlas Peak Rd, NAPA (94558-1425)
PHONE...................707 257-0200
Setsuo Okawa, *CEO*
Isao Okawa, *Ch of Bd*
EMP: 600
SQ FT: 2,000
SALES (est): 75.8K **Privately Held**
WEB: www.silveradoresort.com
SIC: 7997 Country club, membership
HQ: Silverado Napa Corp
   1600 Atlas Peak Rd
   Napa CA 94558
   707 226-1325

(P-19050)
SNOWBOUNDERS SKI CLUB
5402 Tattershall Ave, Westminster (92683-3447)
PHONE...................714 892-4897
Lowe Jacobson, *President*
EMP: 80
SALES: 47.9K **Privately Held**
SIC: 7997

(P-19051)
SOUTH HILLS COUNTRY CLUB
2655 S Citrus St, West Covina (91791-3405)
PHONE...................626 339-1231
James Wendoll, *CEO*
Chris Banner, *General Mgr*
Linn Aparicio, *Controller*
Candice Allen, *Opers Mgr*
Alex Godinez, *Manager*
EMP: 78
SQ FT: 34,000
SALES: 5.7MM **Privately Held**
WEB: www.southhillscountryclub.org
SIC: 7997 5813 5812 Country club, membership; golf club, membership; bar (drinking places); American restaurant

(P-19052)
SOUTHWESTERN YACHT CLUB INC
2702 Qualtrough St, San Diego (92106-3415)
PHONE...................619 222-0438
Jeff Wheeler, *General Mgr*
Craig Wong, *General Mgr*
EMP: 50
SQ FT: 10,000
SALES: 4.1MM **Privately Held**
WEB: www.southwesternyc.org
SIC: 7997 4493 5812 5813 Yacht club, membership; yacht basins; eating places; bar (drinking places)

(P-19053)
SPANISH HILLS COUNTRY CLUB (PA)
999 Crestview Ave, Camarillo (93010-8493)
PHONE...................805 389-1644
Joe Topper, *President*
Steve Thomas, *CEO*
Grant Webster, *Controller*
Rachel Gluckman, *Director*
EMP: 150
SQ FT: 42,000
SALES (est): 10.1MM **Privately Held**
WEB: www.spanishhillscc.com
SIC: 7997 Country club, membership

(P-19054)
SPARE-TIME INC
Also Called: Broadstone Raquet Club
820 Halidon Way, Folsom (95630-8406)
PHONE...................916 983-9180
Gavin Russo, *General Mgr*
EMP: 80
SALES (corp-wide): 37.1MM **Privately Held**
WEB: www.sparetimeinc.com
SIC: 7997 7991 Racquetball club, membership; health club
PA: Spare-Time, Inc.
   11344 Coloma Rd Ste 350
   Gold River CA 95670
   916 859-5910

(P-19055)
SPARE-TIME INC
11344 Coloma Rd Ste 350, Gold River (95670-6302)
PHONE...................916 859-5910
David Anderson, *Branch Mgr*
EMP: 59
SALES (corp-wide): 37.1MM **Privately Held**
SIC: 7997 Racquetball club, membership
PA: Spare-Time, Inc.
   11344 Coloma Rd Ste 350
   Gold River CA 95670
   916 859-5910

(P-19056)
SPARE-TIME INC
Also Called: Johnson Ranch Racquet Club
2501 Eureka Rd, Roseville (95661-6400)
PHONE...................916 782-2600
Tim Munson, *General Mgr*
EMP: 60
SQ FT: 21,584
SALES (corp-wide): 37.1MM **Privately Held**
WEB: www.sparetimeinc.com
SIC: 7997 Racquetball club, membership
PA: Spare-Time, Inc.
   11344 Coloma Rd Ste 350
   Gold River CA 95670
   916 859-5910

(P-19057)
SPARE-TIME INC
Also Called: Gold River Racquet Club
2201 Gold Rush Dr, Gold River (95670-4466)
PHONE...................916 638-7001
Mike Burchett, *General Mgr*
EMP: 50
SALES (corp-wide): 37.1MM **Privately Held**
WEB: www.sparetimeinc.com
SIC: 7997 Racquetball club, membership
PA: Spare-Time, Inc.
   11344 Coloma Rd Ste 350
   Gold River CA 95670
   916 859-5910

(P-19058)
SPARE-TIME INC
Also Called: Laguna Creek Racquet Club
9570 Racquet Ct, Elk Grove (95758-4349)
PHONE...................916 859-5910
Kimberley Miller, *Manager*
EMP: 59
SALES (corp-wide): 37.1MM **Privately Held**
WEB: www.sparetimeinc.com
SIC: 7997 7999 7991 Racquetball club, membership; racquetball club, non-membership; health club

PA: Spare-Time, Inc.
11344 Coloma Rd Ste 350
Gold River CA 95670
916 859-5910

(P-19059)
SPE GO HOLDINGS INC
Also Called: Mount Woodson Country Club
16422 N Woodson Dr, Ramona
(92065-6800)
PHONE.....................................858 638-0672
Steve Dawe, *Exec VP*
Amanda Rangel, *General Mgr*
Scott Hardy, *Superintendent*
EMP: 50
SALES (corp-wide): 14.2B **Publicly Held**
SIC: 7997 Country club, membership
HQ: Spe Go Holdings, Inc.
11575 Great Oaks Way # 210
Alpharetta GA 30022
401 621-4200

(P-19060)
SPRING VALLEY LAKE
COUNTRY CLB
13229 Spring Valley Pkwy, Victorville
(92395)
PHONE.....................................760 245-5356
Erick Affeldt, *CEO*
Osmar Castro, *General Mgr*
Jon Sabo, *General Mgr*
Maria Punsal, *Corp Comm Staff*
EMP: 90
SALES (est): 4MM
SALES (corp-wide): 477MM **Privately Held**
WEB: www.remington-gc.com
SIC: 7997 Country club, membership
HQ: Clubcorp Usa, Inc.
3030 Lyndon B Johnson Fwy
Dallas TX 75234
972 243-6191

(P-19061)
SPRINGS CLUB INC
Also Called: Springs Country Club, The
1 Duke Dr, Rancho Mirage (92270-3647)
PHONE.....................................760 328-0254
Robert Middlemas, *CEO*
Daniel Cooper, *COO*
Ronda Allen, *Principal*
Douglas R Hart, *Principal*
Doug Lober, *Principal*
EMP: 65
SQ FT: 36,000
SALES (est): 5.5MM **Privately Held**
SIC: 7997 5812 5813 Golf club, membership; tennis club, membership; American restaurant; cocktail lounge

(P-19062)
ST FRANCIS YACHT CLUB
700 Marina Blvd, San Francisco
(94123-1044)
PHONE.....................................415 563-6363
Jim Diepenbrock, *CEO*
Blake Kennedy, *Asst Controller*
Nora Cotter, *Food Svc Dir*
Penelope Smith,
Ryan Stiles, *Asst Director*
◆ **EMP:** 110
SQ FT: 20,000
SALES: 16.4MM **Privately Held**
WEB: www.stfyc.com
SIC: 7997 4493 Yacht club, membership; marinas

(P-19063)
STOCKDALE COUNTRY CLUB
7001 Stockdale Hwy, Bakersfield
(93309-1313)
P.O. Box 9727 (93389-9727)
PHONE.....................................661 832-0310
Sam Monroe, *President*
Michael Davis, *CEO*
Linda Voiland, *Vice Pres*
Susan Greer, *General Mgr*
Linda Turner, *Controller*
EMP: 100 **EST:** 1925
SQ FT: 12,000
SALES: 5.7MM **Privately Held**
WEB: www.stockdalecountryclub.com
SIC: 7997 Country club, membership

(P-19064)
STONEBRAE LP
Also Called: TPC Stonebrea
222 Country Club Dr, Hayward
(94542-7927)
PHONE.....................................510 728-7878
Lisa Hinman, *General Mgr*
Erin Crawford, *Project Mgr*
EMP: 67
SALES (est): 5MM **Privately Held**
SIC: 7997 Country club, membership

(P-19065)
SYCAMORE CC INC
Also Called: The Golf Club of California
3742 Flowerwood Ln, Fallbrook
(92028-8013)
PHONE.....................................760 451-3700
William Lyon, *President*
EMP: 60
SQ FT: 4,320
SALES (est): 2.5MM **Publicly Held**
WEB: www.lyonhomes.com
SIC: 7997 Golf club, membership
PA: William Lyon Homes
4695 Macarthur Ct Ste 800
Newport Beach CA 92660

(P-19066)
TEHAMA GOLF CLUB LLC
4 Tehama, Carmel (93923-9622)
PHONE.....................................831 622-2200
Roy D Kaufman,
Howard M Bernstein,
EMP: 95
SALES (est): 5.8MM **Privately Held**
WEB: www.tehamagolfclub.com
SIC: 7997 Golf club, membership

(P-19067)
TENNIS EVERYONE
INCORPORATED
Also Called: Rolling Hills Club
351 San Andreas Dr, Novato (94945-1206)
PHONE.....................................415 897-2185
Chuk Trieve, *President*
Andrea Pozzi, *Officer*
Anna Levinson, *Exec Dir*
Marybeth Bradley, *General Mgr*
Robin Freitas, *General Mgr*
EMP: 85 **EST:** 1973
SQ FT: 19,000
SALES (est): 3MM **Privately Held**
WEB: www.rollinghillsclub.com
SIC: 7997 Swimming club, membership

(P-19068)
THE VALLEY CLUB OF
MONTECITO
1901 E Valley Rd, Santa Barbara
(93108-1427)
PHONE.....................................805 969-2215
John S Degroot, *CEO*
Palmer Jackson, *President*
EMP: 50 **EST:** 1931
SQ FT: 3,000
SALES: 6.5MM **Privately Held**
SIC: 7997 Golf club, membership

(P-19069)
THE WOODBRIDGE GOLF
CNTRY CLB
800 E Woodbridge Rd, Woodbridge
(95258-9628)
P.O. Box 806 (95258-0806)
PHONE.....................................209 369-2371
Jerry Leonard, *CEO*
Ernie Micelli, *General Mgr*
Mindy Adolf, *Admin Asst*
Kristine Roberson,
Catherine Kading, *Director*
EMP: 79
SQ FT: 20,000
SALES: 3.8MM **Privately Held**
SIC: 7997 Country club, membership

(P-19070)
THUNDERBIRD COUNTRY CLUB
70737 Country Club Dr, Rancho Mirage
(92270-3500)
P.O. Box 5005 (92270-1065)
PHONE.....................................760 328-2161
Brian Rice, *CEO*
David Shepler, *COO*

Donna Potts, *Vice Pres*
Michaell Crandall, *General Mgr*
Julie Gomez, *Office Mgr*
EMP: 60
SQ FT: 30,000
SALES: 8.7MM **Privately Held**
WEB: www.thunderbirdcc.org
SIC: 7997 5812 7011 Country club, membership; eating places; hotels & motels

(P-19071)
TIBURON PENINSULA CLUB INC
1600 Mar West St, Belvedere Tiburon
(94920-1830)
P.O. Box 436 (94920-0436)
PHONE.....................................415 789-7900
Gerry Pang, *Principal*
Jerry Pang, *General Mgr*
Laura Jones, *Bookkeeper*
Malcolm Lacey, *Opers Staff*
Brendan Curry, *Director*
EMP: 50
SQ FT: 6,674
SALES: 5.8MM **Privately Held**
WEB: www.tiburonpc.org
SIC: 7997 Swimming club, membership; tennis club, membership

(P-19072)
TIERRA OAKS GOLF CLUB INC
19700 La Crescenta Dr, Redding
(96003-7474)
PHONE.....................................530 275-0795
Shawn Sich, *General Mgr*
EMP: 90
SALES (est): 3.5MM **Privately Held**
WEB: www.lockefordsprings.com
SIC: 7997 6531 Golf club, membership; real estate agents & managers
PA: Spring Lockeford Golf Course Inc
16360 N Highway 88
Lodi CA 95240

(P-19073)
TOSCANA COUNTRY CLUB INC
76009 Via Club Villa, Indian Wells
(92210-7851)
PHONE.....................................760 404-1444
Paul K Levy, *CEO*
James Butzbach, *Security Dir*
Beth Hunter, *General Mgr*
Tony Carrillo, *Asst Controller*
Patricia Daniels, *Buyer*
EMP: 150
SALES (est): 8MM **Privately Held**
SIC: 7997 Country club, membership

(P-19074)
TY INVESTMENT INC
1015 21st St Unit A, Santa Monica
(90403-4567)
PHONE.....................................619 448-4242
Toru Mise, *President*
EMP: 75
SALES (est): 3.9MM **Privately Held**
WEB: www.carltonoaksgolf.com
SIC: 7997 Country club, membership; golf club, membership

(P-19075)
UNITED STATES PONY CLUBS
7010 Hidden Valley Pl, Granite Bay
(95746-9456)
PHONE.....................................916 791-1223
Linda Gurnee, *Director*
EMP: 82
SALES: 58.2K **Privately Held**
SIC: 7997 Membership sports & recreation clubs

(P-19076)
VALLEY-HI COUNTRY CLUB
9595 Franklin Blvd, Elk Grove
(95758-9532)
PHONE.....................................916 684-2120
Edgar Gill, *CEO*
Nick West, *Principal*
Jim Davis, *General Mgr*
Judi Santiago, *Office Mgr*
Sean McPhedran, *Technology*
EMP: 50
SQ FT: 20,000
SALES: 3.2MM **Privately Held**
WEB: www.valleyhicc.com
SIC: 7997 Country club, membership

(P-19077)
VILLAGE WEST YACHT CLUB
6633 Embarcadero Dr, Stockton
(95219-3329)
PHONE.....................................209 478-8992
Fred Von Helf, *President*
Margaret Armstrong, *CFO*
EMP: 100
SALES (est): 1.8MM **Privately Held**
SIC: 7997 7941 Yacht club, membership; sports clubs, managers & promoters

(P-19078)
VILLAGES GOLF AND COUNTRY
CLUB
Also Called: Villages, The
5000 Cribari Ln, San Jose (95135-1397)
PHONE.....................................408 274-4400
Virginia Fanelli, *CEO*
David Gonzales, *Area Spvr*
Maria Hernandez, *Admin Asst*
Elissa Caruso, *Administration*
Jim White, *Finance Dir*
EMP: 170
SALES (est): 15.5MM **Privately Held**
WEB: www.the-villages.com
SIC: 7997 Country club, membership

(P-19079)
VINTAGE CLUB (PA)
75005 Vintage Dr W, Indian Wells
(92210-7304)
PHONE.....................................760 346-5566
John Buttemiller Broker, *Sales Staff*
Marc D Ray, *COO*
Jennifer Latteri, *Office Mgr*
Kay Gentile, *Controller*
Candice Morgan, *Human Res Dir*
EMP: 50
SQ FT: 86,000
SALES (est): 18.9MM **Privately Held**
WEB: www.thevintageclub.com
SIC: 7997 5813 5812 5941 Country club, membership; bar (drinking places); American restaurant; golf goods & equipment; tennis services & professionals; real estate agents & managers

(P-19080)
VINTAGE CLUB
Vintage Club Tennis Shop
75001 Vintage Dr W, Indian Wells
(92210-7304)
PHONE.....................................760 340-0500
Patricia Sargent, *Manager*
Charles Spillman, *Security Dir*
Steve Cenicola, *General Mgr*
Tom Murphy, *General Mgr*
Michael Tyler, *Purch Mgr*
EMP: 90
SALES (est): 4.7MM
SALES (corp-wide): 18.9MM **Privately Held**
WEB: www.thevintageclub.com
SIC: 7997 Country club, membership
PA: The Vintage Club
75005 Vintage Dr W
Indian Wells CA 92210
760 346-5566

(P-19081)
VIRGINIA COUNTRY CLUB
4602 N Virginia Rd, Long Beach
(90807-1999)
PHONE.....................................562 427-0924
Jamie Mulligan, *CEO*
Susan Ledesma, *Executive*
EMP: 110
SQ FT: 15,000
SALES: 6.8MM **Privately Held**
SIC: 7997 Country club, membership; golf club, membership

(P-19082)
VISALIA COUNTRY CLUB
625 N Ranch St, Visalia (93291-4317)
P.O. Box 3410 (93278-3410)
PHONE.....................................559 734-3733
Steve Beargeon, *Principal*
EMP: 80
SQ FT: 60,000
SALES: 4.5MM **Privately Held**
SIC: 7997 Country club, membership

(P-19083)
VISTA VALLEY COUNTRY CLUB
Also Called: V Vcc Havens
29354 Vista Valley Dr, Vista (92084-2209)
PHONE................................760 758-2800
John Havens, *President*
Marissa Gerlach, *Executive*
Alex Maio, *Executive*
Phil Rodriguez, *General Mgr*
Nani McCumber, *Executive Asst*
EMP: 70
SQ FT: 15,000
SALES (est): 5.5MM **Privately Held**
WEB: www.vistavalley.com
SIC: 7997 5812 7999 Country club, membership; eating places; golf cart, power, rental

(P-19084)
WALSH GROUP INC
Also Called: Sun Oaks Tennis & Fitness
3135 Agassi Ln, Redding (96002-9548)
PHONE................................530 221-4405
Jo Campbell, *Principal*
Jeremiah Walsh, *Principal*
Matthew Perdue, *Personnel*
EMP: 95
SQ FT: 217,800
SALES (est): 378.5K **Privately Held**
SIC: 7997 Tennis club, membership

(P-19085)
WEST HILLS GOLF ASSOCIATES
Also Called: Western Hills Country Club
1800 Carbon Canyon Rd, Chino Hills
(91709-2300)
PHONE................................714 528-6400
Michael Donovan, *Partner*
William Donovan, *Ltd Ptnr*
Ron Lane, *Ltd Ptnr*
EMP: 50
SQ FT: 12,000
SALES (est): 2.1MM **Privately Held**
SIC: 7997 7299 Golf club, membership; banquet hall facilities

(P-19086)
WESTGROUP KONA KAI LLC
Also Called: Kona Kai Resort Hotel
1551 Shelter Island Dr, San Diego
(92106-3102)
PHONE................................619 221-8000
Kathy Little,
EMP: 99
SALES (est): 5.3MM **Privately Held**
SIC: 7997 7011 Membership sports & recreation clubs; resort hotel

(P-19087)
WILSHIRE COUNTRY CLUB
301 N Rossmore Ave, Los Angeles
(90004-2499)
PHONE................................323 934-6050
Jeffrey Ornstein, *CEO*
Norman Branchflower, *President*
Todd Keefer, *Officer*
Mirion Bowers MD, *Vice Pres*
Robert Martin, *Foreman/Supr*
EMP: 94
SQ FT: 50,000
SALES (est): 11MM **Privately Held**
WEB: www.wilshirecc.com
SIC: 7997 5941 5812 Country club, membership; sporting goods & bicycle shops; eating places

(P-19088)
YUBA CITY RACQUET CLUB INC
825 Jones Rd, Yuba City (95991-6124)
PHONE................................530 673-6900
Judie Jacoby, *President*
Terry Townsend, *Maintenance Dir*
▲ EMP: 73
SQ FT: 40,000
SALES (est): 3.1MM **Privately Held**
WEB: www.ycrc.com
SIC: 7997 7991 Tennis club, membership; health club

7999 Amusement & Recreation Svcs, NEC

(P-19089)
29 PALMS ENTERPRISES CORP
Also Called: Spotlight 29 Casino
46200 Harrison Pl, Coachella
(92236-2031)
PHONE................................760 775-5566
Darrel Mike, *President*
Marcia R Martin, *CFO*
Robert Paul, *General Mgr*
Gordon Howe, *MIS Staff*
Stephenie Streiff-Process, *Analyst*
EMP: 600
SQ FT: 70,000
SALES (est): 33.4MM **Privately Held**
WEB: www.spotlight29.net
SIC: 7999 5812 Gambling establishment; eating places

(P-19090)
ADVENTURE CITY INC
1238 S Beach Blvd, Anaheim
(92804-4828)
PHONE................................714 821-3311
Allan Ansdell Jr, *President*
Yvonne Ansdell, *Treasurer*
Barb Karch, *Bookkeeper*
Trina Ansdell, *Human Res Mgr*
EMP: 100
SALES (est): 3MM **Privately Held**
WEB: www.adventurecity.com
SIC: 7999 7996 Tourist attractions, amusement park concessions & rides; amusement parks

(P-19091)
ADVENTURE CONNECTION INC
986 Lotus Rd, Lotus (95651)
PHONE................................530 626-7385
Nathan J Rangel, *President*
EMP: 60
SQ FT: 2,400
SALES (est): 750K **Privately Held**
WEB: www.raftcalifornia.com
SIC: 7999 4725 Rafting tours; tour operators

(P-19092)
ALAMEDA COUNTY AG FAIR ASSN
Also Called: Alameda County Fair
4501 Pleasanton Ave, Pleasanton
(94566-7001)
PHONE................................925 426-7600
Rick Pickering, *CEO*
Randy Magee, *CFO*
Randy Maggie, *CFO*
EMP: 75
SQ FT: 125,000
SALES (est): 22.3MM **Privately Held**
WEB: www.alamedacountyfair.com
SIC: 7999 Agricultural fair

(P-19093)
ALPINE CAMP CONFERENCE CTR INC
415 Clubhouse Dr, Blue Jay (92317)
P.O. Box 155 (92317-0155)
PHONE................................909 337-6287
Kim Polson, *Administration*
Anthony Xepolis, *President*
Joel Rude, *Principal*
Mark Gilliland, *Accountant*
John Gehrig, *Director*
EMP: 68
SALES (est): 1.7MM **Privately Held**
SIC: 7999 7032 Instruction schools, camps & services; youth camps

(P-19094)
AMBASSADOR GAMING INC
Also Called: Key Largo Casino
660 Newport Center Dr # 1050, Newport
Beach (92660-6401)
PHONE................................714 969-8730
Stephen K Bone, *President*
Robert L Mayer Jr, *Treasurer*
EMP: 112

SALES (est): 4.8MM **Privately Held**
WEB: www.keylargocasino.com
SIC: 7999 7993 Gambling machines, operation; gambling establishments operating coin-operated machines; slot machines

(P-19095)
AMBROSE RECREATION & PARK DST
3105 Willow Pass Rd, Bay Point
(94565-3149)
PHONE................................925 458-1601
Travis Stombaugh, *General Mgr*
Gloria Magleby, *Ch of Bd*
Doug Long, *General Mgr*
Veronica Washington, *Planning*
Greg Enholm, *Director*
EMP: 100 EST: 1952
SALES (est): 2.4MM **Privately Held**
SIC: 7999 Recreation services

(P-19096)
ANAHEIM ICE
Also Called: Rinks Anaheim Ice, The
300 W Lincoln Ave, Anaheim (92805-2947)
PHONE................................714 535-7465
Eddie Hawkins, *General Mgr*
Art Trottier, *Vice Pres*
Jill Herzogge, *General Mgr*
EMP: 70
SALES (est): 1.6MM **Privately Held**
SIC: 7999 Ice skating rink operation; skating rink operation services

(P-19097)
ANGELES LOS EQUESTRIAN CENTER
480 W Riverside Dr, Burbank (91506-3209)
PHONE................................818 840-9063
J Albert Garcia, *President*
George Chatigny, *Manager*
EMP: 120
SALES (est): 3.4MM **Privately Held**
SIC: 7999 Riding stable

(P-19098)
APEX PARKS GROUP LLC
Also Called: Upland Valley Fun Center
1500 W 7th St, Upland (91786-6921)
PHONE................................909 981-5251
Richard Towfiegh, *Manager*
EMP: 70
SALES (corp-wide): 39.9MM **Privately Held**
SIC: 7999 Miniature golf course operation
PA: Apex Parks Group, Llc
27061 Aliso Creek Rd # 100
Aliso Viejo CA 92656
949 349-8461

(P-19099)
APEX PARKS GROUP LLC
Also Called: Malibu Castle
27061 Aliso Creek Rd # 100, Aliso Viejo
(92656-5322)
PHONE................................210 341-6663
EMP: 100
SALES (corp-wide): 39.9MM **Privately Held**
SIC: 7999 5599
PA: Apex Parks Group, Llc
27061 Aliso Creek Rd # 100
Aliso Viejo CA 92656
949 349-8461

(P-19100)
ARISE LLC
1033 Van Ness Ave, Fresno (93721-2006)
PHONE................................559 485-0881
Darrell Miers, *CEO*
EMP: 60
SALES (est): 1.9MM **Privately Held**
SIC: 7999 Gambling establishment

(P-19101)
ARIZONA CHANNEL ISLA
300 W 9th St, Oxnard (93030-7060)
PHONE................................480 788-0755
Roger Burt, *CEO*
Abou Dieng, *CFO*
EMP: 75
SQ FT: 60,000
SALES (est): 282.9K **Privately Held**
SIC: 7999 Amusement & recreation

(P-19102)
AROMA SPA & SPORTS LLC
Also Called: Aroma Wilshire Center
3680 Wilshire Blvd # 301, Los Angeles
(90010-2708)
PHONE................................213 387-2111
Byoung G Choi,
Jae Whang, *Executive*
Keejune Huh,
EMP: 60
SALES (est): 1.9MM **Privately Held**
SIC: 7999 7991 Recreation center; health club

(P-19103)
ARTICHOKE JOES INC
Also Called: Artichoke Joe's Casino
659 Huntington Ave, San Bruno
(94066-3608)
PHONE................................650 589-8812
Dennis J Sammut, *CEO*
Helen Sammut, *Corp Secy*
EMP: 330
SALES (est): 15.2MM **Privately Held**
WEB: www.artichokejoes.com
SIC: 7999 5812 5813 Game parlor; eating places; tavern (drinking places)

(P-19104)
ARTISTS STUDIO GALLERY
5504 Crestridge Rd, Rancho Palos Verdes
(90275-4905)
PHONE................................424 206-9902
EMP: 55 **Privately Held**
SIC: 7999 Art gallery, commercial
PA: Artists Studio Gallery Of The Palos
Verdes
550 Deep Valley Dr # 327
Rllng Hls Est CA 90274

(P-19105)
AUBURN OLD TOWN GALLERY
Also Called: Old Town Gallery of Fine Art
218 Washington St Ste A, Auburn
(95603-5048)
PHONE................................530 887-9150
Sonja Hamilton, *President*
Mike Miller,
Marilyn Russell,
EMP: 60
SALES (est): 2.2MM **Privately Held**
WEB: www.auburnoldtowngallery.com
SIC: 7999 5999 Art gallery, commercial; art dealers

(P-19106)
BAY AREA SEATING SERVICE INC
Also Called: Bass Tickets
1855 Gateway Blvd Ste 630, Concord
(94520-3200)
PHONE................................925 671-4000
W Thomas Gimple, *President*
Doug Levenson, *Exec VP*
EMP: 300 EST: 1974
SQ FT: 18,000
SALES (est): 1.7MM
SALES (corp-wide): 194.3MM **Privately Held**
WEB: www.tickets.com
SIC: 7999 Ticket sales office for sporting events, contract
HQ: California Tickets.Com Inc.
555 Anton Blvd Fl 11
Costa Mesa CA 92626
714 327-5400

(P-19107)
BAY CLUB HOLDINGS III LLC
Also Called: Golden Gtwy Tennis & Swim CLB
370 Drumm St, San Francisco
(94111-2010)
PHONE................................415 433-2936
Jim Gerber, *Branch Mgr*
EMP: 80
SALES (corp-wide): 46.3MM **Privately Held**
SIC: 7999 Tennis services & professionals
PA: Bay Club Holdings Iii, Llc
1 Lombard St Lbby
San Francisco CA 94111
415 781-1874

(P-19108)
BEAR VALLEY SKI CO
Also Called: Bear Valley Mountain Resort
2280 State Rte 207, Bear Valley (95223)
P.O. Box 5038 (95223-5038)
PHONE..................................209 753-2301
Tim Bottomley, *CEO*
Barbara Moreci, *Maintence Staff*
EMP: 325
SQ FT: 70,000
SALES (est): 15.1MM
SALES (corp-wide): 84.8MM **Privately Held**
WEB: www.bearvalley.com
SIC: 7999 5941 Recreation services; ski rental concession; ski instruction; skiing equipment
HQ: Skyline Investments Inc
150 King St W Suite 2108
Toronto ON M5H 1
416 368-2565

(P-19109)
BELL GARDENS BICYCLE CLUB INC
Also Called: Bicycle Club Casino
888 Bicycle Casino Dr, Bell Gardens (90201-7617)
PHONE..................................562 806-4646
George Hardie, *President*
Jim Griffo, *President*
George G Hardie, *President*
Christina Bay, *Human Res Dir*
EMP: 1300
SQ FT: 110,000
SALES (est): 35.1MM **Privately Held**
WEB: www.thebicyclecasino.com
SIC: 7999 5812 Card rooms; coffee shop

(P-19110)
BIG 5 SPORTING GOODS CORP
11310 Crenshaw Blvd, Inglewood (90303-2807)
PHONE..................................323 755-2663
EMP: 431 **Publicly Held**
SIC: 7999 5941 5699 5661 Sporting goods rental; sporting goods & bicycle shops; sports apparel; shoe stores
PA: Big 5 Sporting Goods Corp
2525 E El Segundo Blvd
El Segundo CA 90245

(P-19111)
BISHOP PAIUTE GAMING CORP
Also Called: Paiute Palace Casino
2742 N Sierra Hwy, Bishop (93514-2218)
PHONE..................................760 872-6005
Gloriana Bailey, *President*
EMP: 150
SALES (est): 8.3MM **Privately Held**
WEB: www.paiutepalace.com
SIC: 7999 Gambling establishment

(P-19112)
BLACK OAK CASINO
19400 Tuolumne Rd N, Tuolumne (95379-9696)
PHONE..................................209 928-9300
Ron Patel, *General Mgr*
Michael Cox, *Treasurer*
Liane Crawford-Smith, *Exec Dir*
James Hodge, *General Mgr*
James Canon, *Technology*
EMP: 99
SQ FT: 168,000
SALES (est): 8.9MM **Privately Held**
WEB: www.blackoakcasino.com
SIC: 7999 Gambling establishment
PA: Tuolumne Me-Wuk Tribal Council
19595 Mi Wu St
Tuolumne CA 95379
209 928-5300

(P-19113)
BLUE BUS TOURS LLC
Also Called: Grayline of San Francisco
50 Quint St, San Francisco (94124-1424)
PHONE..................................415 353-5310
Raman Fargoni, *President*
EMP: 120 **EST:** 2011
SQ FT: 4,200
SALES: 350K **Privately Held**
SIC: 7999 Tourist attraction, commercial

(P-19114)
BRIAR GOLF LP
Also Called: Cathedral Cyn Golf Tennis CLB
68311 Paseo Real, Cathedral City (92234-6767)
PHONE..................................760 328-6571
Tom Moran, *General Ptnr*
David Flickwir, *General Ptnr*
EMP: 70
SALES (est): 1.4MM **Privately Held**
SIC: 7999 Golf services & professionals

(P-19115)
BUSINESS AND SUPPORT SERVICES
Also Called: Marine Corps Community Svcs
Mccs Bldg 2273 Elrod Ave, San Diego (92145-0001)
P.O. Box 452008 (92145-2008)
PHONE..................................858 577-1061
Mary Bradford, *President*
EMP: 800 **Publicly Held**
WEB: www.mccssc.com
SIC: 7999 9711 Recreation center; Marine Corps;
HQ: Business And Support Services
3044 Catlin Ave
Quantico VA 22134
703 432-0109

(P-19116)
BVK GAMING INC
3466 Broadway St, American Canyon (94503-1263)
P.O. Box 10078 (94503-0078)
PHONE..................................707 644-8853
Brian Altizer, *President*
Von Altizer, *President*
EMP: 90 **EST:** 2005
SALES (est): 785.4K **Privately Held**
SIC: 7999 Card rooms

(P-19117)
CAESARS ENTRTNMENT OPRTING INC
Also Called: Harrah's
777 Harrahs Rincon Way, Valley Center (92082-5343)
PHONE..................................760 751-3100
Janet Deronio, *Branch Mgr*
Janet Beroino, *General Mgr*
Pom Maldonado, *Info Tech Mgr*
Paul Kenyon, *IT/INT Sup*
Gerardo Quiambao, *IT/INT Sup*
EMP: 1400
SALES (corp-wide): 4.8B **Publicly Held**
WEB: www.flamingolv.com
SIC: 7999 7011 Gambling establishment; casino hotel
HQ: Caesars Entertainment Operating Company, Inc.
1 Caesars Palace Dr
Las Vegas NV 89109
702 407-6000

(P-19118)
CAHUILLA CREEK REST & CASINO
Also Called: Cahuilla Creek Casino
52702 Us Highway 371, Anza (92539-8707)
PHONE..................................951 763-1200
Leonardo Pasquarelli, *General Mgr*
Jon Gregory, *General Mgr*
Susan Bellamy, *Mktg Dir*
EMP: 103
SQ FT: 14,000
SALES (est): 8MM **Privately Held**
WEB: www.cahuillacreekcasino.com
SIC: 7999 5812 5813 Gambling establishment; American restaurant; bar (drinking places); tavern (drinking places)

(P-19119)
CAPITOL CASINO
411 N 16th St, Sacramento (95811-0516)
PHONE..................................916 446-0700
Clarke Rosa, *President*
EMP: 150
SQ FT: 7,500
SALES (est): 3.8MM **Privately Held**
WEB: www.capitol-casino.com
SIC: 7999 5813 Card rooms; cocktail lounge

(P-19120)
CATALINA BUSINESS ENTPS INC
635 Crescent Ave, Avalon (90704)
P.O. Box 1919 (90704-1919)
PHONE..................................310 510-1600
Buddy Wilson, *President*
EMP: 50
SALES (corp-wide): 1.7MM **Privately Held**
SIC: 7999 Golf cart, power, rental
PA: Catalina Business Enterprises, Inc.
800 Cresent Ave
Avalon CA 90704
310 510-2550

(P-19121)
CHER-AE HEIGHTS INDIAN CMNTY
Also Called: Cher Ae Heights Casino
27 Scenic Dr, Trinidad (95570-9767)
P.O. Box 610 (95570-0610)
PHONE..................................707 677-3611
Ron Dadouin, *Manager*
EMP: 196 **Privately Held**
WEB: www.trinidadrancheria.com
SIC: 7999 7011 Card rooms; casino hotel
PA: Cher-Ae Heights Indian Community
1 Cher Ae Ln
Trinidad CA 95570
707 677-0211

(P-19122)
CHICKEN RANCH BINGO & CASINO
16929 Chicken Ranch Rd, Jamestown (95327-9779)
P.O. Box 1699 (95327-1699)
PHONE..................................209 984-3000
Lloyd Matheson, *Owner*
Trish Magdaleno, *Human Res Mgr*
EMP: 150
SQ FT: 35,000
SALES: 5.7K **Privately Held**
SIC: 7999 Bingo hall

(P-19123)
CHICO AREA RECREATION & PK DST (PA)
Also Called: Dorothy Johnson Center
545 Vallombrosa Ave, Chico (95926-4037)
PHONE..................................530 895-4711
Mary Cahill, *General Mgr*
Suzanne Bullock, *Executive*
Jennifer Marciales, *Executive Asst*
Olivia Wilson, *Business Mgr*
Heidi Radcliffe, *Finance Asst*
EMP: 135
SQ FT: 27,000
SALES (est): 4.7MM **Privately Held**
WEB: www.chicorec.com
SIC: 7999 8322 Recreation services; individual & family services

(P-19124)
CHOPRA CNTRE FOR WLL-BEING LLC
Also Called: Chopra Center For Wellbeing
2013 Costa Del Mar Rd, Carlsbad (92009-6801)
PHONE..................................760 494-1600
Deepak Chopra, *Principal*
David Simon MD, *Principal*
▲ **EMP:** 51 **EST:** 1996
SALES (est): 4.6MM **Privately Held**
SIC: 7999 8299 7991 Yoga instruction; meditation therapy; spas

(P-19125)
CHRISTIANSEN AMUSEMENTS CORP
1725 S Escondido Blvd E, Escondido (92025-6546)
P.O. Box 997 (92033-0997)
PHONE..................................760 735-8542
Stacey Brown, *President*
William Jacob, *Vice Pres*
Mindy Seltmann, *Vice Pres*
EMP: 70
SALES (est): 2.1MM **Privately Held**
WEB: www.carnivalgame.com
SIC: 7999 Carnival operation; amusement ride

(P-19126)
CHUMASH CASINO RESORT (HQ)
3400 E Highway 246, Santa Ynez (93460-9405)
PHONE..................................805 686-0855
Carol Clearwater, *CFO*
John Featherstone, *Executive*
Mike Hackett, *Exec Dir*
John Martino, *Exec Dir*
William Peters, *General Mgr*
EMP: 168
SQ FT: 29,000
SALES (est): 28.9MM **Privately Held**
WEB: www.chumashcasino.com
SIC: 7999 7011 Gambling establishment; resort hotel

(P-19127)
CITY OF COMMERCE
Also Called: Parks & Recreation
2535 Commerce Way, Commerce (90040-1410)
PHONE..................................323 722-4805
Jim Jimenez, *Director*
EMP: 400 **Privately Held**
SIC: 7999 7991 Recreation center; physical fitness facilities
PA: City Of Commerce
2535 Commerce Way
Commerce CA 90040
323 722-4805

(P-19128)
CITY OF COMPTON
Also Called: William Love Swimming Pool
1108 N Oleander Ave, Compton (90222-4041)
PHONE..................................310 635-3484
Vanessa Little, *Principal*
EMP: 60 **Privately Held**
SIC: 7999 9111 Swimming pool, non-membership; mayors' offices
PA: City Of Compton
205 S Willowbrook Ave
Compton CA 90220
310 605-5500

(P-19129)
CITY OF CORONADO
Also Called: Recreation Dept
1845 Strand Way, Coronado (92118-3005)
PHONE..................................619 522-7342
Linda Rahn, *Director*
EMP: 100 **Privately Held**
WEB: www.coronadoplayhouse.com
SIC: 7999 7997 Swimming pool, non-membership; membership sports & recreation clubs
PA: City Of Coronado
1825 Strand Way
Coronado CA 92118
619 522-7300

(P-19130)
CITY OF FOLSOM
Also Called: Park and Recreation
48 Natoma St, Folsom (95630-2614)
PHONE..................................916 355-7285
Robert Goss, *Director*
EMP: 75 **Privately Held**
WEB: www.folsompd.com
SIC: 7999 Recreation services
PA: City Of Folsom
50 Natoma St
Folsom CA 95630
916 355-7200

(P-19131)
CITY OF FOSTER CITY
Parks & Recreation
650 Shell Blvd, Foster City (94404-2501)
PHONE..................................650 286-3380
Kevin Miller, *Director*
Estelle Gobrera, *Assistant*
EMP: 50 **Privately Held**
WEB: www.fostercitymothersclub.org
SIC: 7999 9111 Recreation services; mayors' offices
PA: City Of Foster City
610 Foster City Blvd
Foster City CA 94404
650 286-3260

(P-19132)
CITY OF GALT
Also Called: Galt Park Recreation
660 Chabolla Ave, Galt (95632)
PHONE...................................209 366-7180
Boyce Jeffries, Director
EMP: 65　Privately Held
WEB: www.ci.galt.ca.us
SIC: 7999　Recreation center
PA: City Of Galt
　　380 Civic Dr
　　Galt CA 95632
　　209 366-7000

(P-19133)
CITY OF INGLEWOOD
Also Called: Edward Vincent Park
700 Warren Ln, Inglewood (90302-3208)
PHONE...................................310 412-5370
James Henry, Manager
EMP: 65　Privately Held
SIC: 7999　9111　Recreation services; may-
　ors' offices
PA: City Of Inglewood
　　1 W Manchester Blvd
　　Inglewood CA 90301
　　310 412-5301

(P-19134)
CITY OF IRVINE
Also Called: Parks-Rcreation-Community
Svcs
6443 Oak Cyn, Irvine (92618-5202)
PHONE...................................949 724-7740
EMP: 63　Privately Held
SIC: 7999　Recreation services
PA: City Of Irvine
　　1 Civic Center Plz
　　Irvine CA 92606
　　949 724-6000

(P-19135)
CITY OF IRVINE
4531 Bryan Ave, Irvine (92620-2600)
PHONE...................................949 724-6728
Deborah Brunn, Manager
EMP: 54　Privately Held
SIC: 7999　Recreation center
PA: City Of Irvine
　　1 Civic Center Plz
　　Irvine CA 92606
　　949 724-6000

(P-19136)
CITY OF MILL VALLEY
Also Called: Mill Valley Parks & Recreation
180 Camino Alto, Mill Valley (94941-4603)
PHONE...................................415 383-1370
Christine Som, Director
EMP: 50　Privately Held
WEB: www.donnadacuti.com
SIC: 7999　9111　Recreation services; may-
　ors' offices
PA: City Of Mill Valley
　　26 Corte Madera Ave
　　Mill Valley CA 94941
　　415 388-4033

(P-19137)
CITY OF MONTEREY PARK
Also Called: City Mnterey Pk Recreation Ctr
320 W Newmark Ave Fl 1, Monterey Park
(91754-2896)
PHONE...................................626 307-1388
Harry Panagiotes, Director
EMP: 100　Privately Held
SIC: 7999　9111　Recreation center; may-
　ors' offices
PA: City Of Monterey Park
　　320 W Newmark Ave
　　Monterey Park CA 91754
　　626 307-1255

(P-19138)
CITY OF OAKLAND
Also Called: Sports Office
250 Frank H Ogawa Plz # 6300, Oakland
(94612-2052)
PHONE...................................510 238-3494
Michael Hammock, Principal
Somjintana R Mossman, Cashier
EMP: 50　Privately Held
WEB: www.cityofbuellton.com
SIC: 7999　Sports instruction, schools &
　camps

PA: City Of Oakland
　　150 Frank H Ogawa Plz # 3332
　　Oakland CA 94612
　　510 238-3280

(P-19139)
CITY OF OAKLAND
Also Called: Oakland Ice Center
519 18th St, Oakland (94612-1511)
PHONE...................................510 268-9000
Dave Fies, General Mgr
Peggy Young, Accountant
EMP: 50　Privately Held
WEB: www.cityofbuellton.com
SIC: 7999　Ice skating rink operation
PA: City Of Oakland
　　150 Frank H Ogawa Plz # 3332
　　Oakland CA 94612
　　510 238-3280

(P-19140)
CITY OF ORANGE
Also Called: Parks Recreation Libraries
230 E Chapman Ave, Orange
(92866-1506)
PHONE...................................714 744-7272
Gary Wann, Director
EMP: 50　Privately Held
WEB: www.cityoforange.org
SIC: 7999　Recreation services
PA: City Of Orange
　　300 E Chapman Ave
　　Orange CA 92866
　　714 744-5500

(P-19141)
CITY OF RICHMOND
Also Called: Convention Center Booking Off
3230 Macdonald Ave Fl 2, Richmond
(94804-3012)
P.O. Box 4046 (94804-0046)
PHONE...................................510 620-6788
Jesse Washington, Director
Sue Hartman, Vice Pres
EMP: 100　Privately Held
WEB: www.kcrt.com
SIC: 7999　Recreation center
PA: City Of Richmond
　　450 Civic Center Plaza
　　Richmond CA 94804
　　510 620-6727

(P-19142)
CITY OF SOUTH LAKE TAHOE
Also Called: Recreation Complex
1180 Rufus Allen Blvd, South Lake Tahoe
(96150-8211)
PHONE...................................530 542-6056
Gary Moore, Superintendent
Dennis Churchill, Supervisor
EMP: 78　Privately Held
WEB: www.cityofslt.com
SIC: 7999　Swimming pool, non-member-
　ship
PA: City Of South Lake Tahoe
　　1901 Airport Rd Ste 210
　　South Lake Tahoe CA 96150
　　530 541-0480

(P-19143)
CITY OF TORRANCE
Also Called: Park Maintenance
20500 Madrona Ave, Torrance
(90503-3692)
PHONE...................................310 781-6901
Robert Carson, General Mgr
EMP: 55　Privately Held
SIC: 7999　Recreation center
PA: City Of Torrance
　　3031 Torrance Blvd
　　Torrance CA 90503
　　310 328-5310

(P-19144)
CITY OF VISTA
Wave Water Park
101 Wave Dr, Vista (92083-5824)
PHONE...................................760 940-9283
Natalie Livingston, Branch Mgr
EMP: 150　Privately Held
WEB: www.cityofvista.com
SIC: 7999　Tourist attractions, amusement
　park concessions & rides

PA: City Of Vista
　　200 Civic Center Dr
　　Vista CA 92084
　　760 726-1340

(P-19145)
CITY OF WOODLAND
Also Called: Charles Brooks Cmnty Swim Ctr
2001 East St, Woodland (95776-5183)
PHONE...................................530 661-5878
Dan Gentry, Director
EMP: 200　Privately Held
WEB: www.ci.woodland.ca.us
SIC: 7999　9111　Swimming pool, non-
　membership; mayors' offices
PA: City Of Woodland
　　300 1st St
　　Woodland CA 95695
　　530 661-5830

(P-19146)
**CONCESSION MANAGEMENT
SVCS INC**
Also Called: C M S Hospitality
6033 W Century Blvd # 890, Los Angeles
(90045-6414)
P.O. Box 180250 (90018-0717)
PHONE...................................310 846-5830
Clarence A Daniels Jr, CEO
EMP: 150
SQ FT: 800
SALES (est): 9.7MM　Privately Held
SIC: 7999　Concession operator

(P-19147)
**CONCESSIONAIRES URBAN
PARK (PA)**
Also Called: Angel Island Co
2150 Main St Ste 5, Red Bluff
(96080-2372)
PHONE...................................530 529-1512
John W Koeberer, CEO
Kris Koeberer, Vice Pres
Pamela Koeberrer Pitts, Vice Pres
William Klair, General Mgr
Michele Silva Lane, Controller
EMP: 300
SQ FT: 2,800
SALES (est): 16.2MM　Privately Held
WEB: www.angelisland.com
SIC: 7999　5941　5812　Beach & water
　sports equipment rental & services; fish-
　ing equipment; snack bar

(P-19148)
**CONCESSIONAIRES URBAN
PARK**
Also Called: Camanche Recreation-North
2000 Camanche Rd Ofc Ofc, Ione
(95640-9420)
PHONE...................................209 763-5121
Chris Cantwell, Branch Mgr
EMP: 50
SALES (corp-wide): 16.2MM　Privately
Held
WEB: www.angelisland.com
SIC: 7999　7032　Beach & water sports
　equipment rental & services; recreational
　camps
PA: Urban Park Concessionaires
　　2150 Main St Ste 5
　　Red Bluff CA 96080
　　530 529-1512

(P-19149)
**CONCESSIONAIRES URBAN
PARK**
Also Called: Camanche Northshore Store
2000 Camanche Rd Ofc Ofc, Ione
(95640-9420)
PHONE...................................209 763-5166
Chris Cantwell, Branch Mgr
EMP: 75
SALES (corp-wide): 16.2MM　Privately
Held
WEB: www.angelisland.com
SIC: 7999　5941　5812　Beach & water
　sports equipment rental & services; fish-
　ing equipment; snack bar
PA: Urban Park Concessionaires
　　2150 Main St Ste 5
　　Red Bluff CA 96080
　　530 529-1512

(P-19150)
**CONCESSIONAIRES URBAN
PARK**
34600 Ardenwood Blvd, Fremont
(94555-3645)
PHONE...................................530 529-1596
Michele Silva Lane, Branch Mgr
EMP: 100
SALES (corp-wide): 16.2MM　Privately
Held
WEB: www.angelisland.com
SIC: 7999　5941　5812　Beach & water
　sports equipment rental & services; fish-
　ing equipment; snack bar
PA: Urban Park Concessionaires
　　2150 Main St Ste 5
　　Red Bluff CA 96080
　　530 529-1512

(P-19151)
**CONCESSIONAIRES URBAN
PARK**
Also Called: Ranch At Little Hills, The
18013 Bollinger Canyon Rd, San Ramon
(94583-1501)
PHONE...................................530 529-1513
Michele Silva Lane, Manager
Richard Bayer, Vice Pres
EMP: 100
SALES (corp-wide): 16.2MM　Privately
Held
WEB: www.angelisland.com
SIC: 7999　5941　5812　Beach & water
　sports equipment rental & services; fish-
　ing equipment; snack bar
PA: Urban Park Concessionaires
　　2150 Main St Ste 5
　　Red Bluff CA 96080
　　530 529-1512

(P-19152)
**COSUMNES COMMUNITY SVCS
DST**
9355 E Stockton Blvd, Elk Grove
(95624-9476)
PHONE...................................916 405-7150
Rod Brewer, President
Rich Lozano, Vice Pres
Jeff Ramos, General Mgr
Orlando Fuentes, Director
Jim Luttrell, Director
EMP: 387　EST: 1985
SQ FT: 10,000
SALES: 60MM　Privately Held
SIC: 7999　Recreation services

(P-19153)
COUNTY OF KERN
Parks & Recreation
500 Cascade Pl, Taft (93268-2641)
P.O. Box 1406 (93268-1406)
PHONE...................................661 763-4246
Les Clark, Superintendent
EMP: 50　Privately Held
WEB: www.kccfc.org
SIC: 7999　Recreation services
PA: County Of Kern
　　1115 Truxtun Ave Rm 505
　　Bakersfield CA 93301
　　661 868-3690

(P-19154)
COUNTY OF RIVERSIDE
Economic Development
82503 Us Highway 111, Indio (92201-5633)
PHONE...................................760 863-8247
Darrell Shippy, Manager
EMP: 60　Privately Held
SIC: 7999　9611　9512　Fair; economic de-
　velopment agency, government; ; land,
　mineral & wildlife conservation;
PA: County Of Riverside
　　4080 Lemon St Fl 11
　　Riverside CA 92501
　　951 955-1110

(P-19155)
**CRESSE MARK SCHOOL OF
BASEBALL**
58 Fulmar Ln, Aliso Viejo (92656-1764)
PHONE...................................714 892-6145
Mark E Cresse, President
Jeff Courvoisier, Exec Dir
EMP: 80

SALES: 1.4MM **Privately Held**
SIC: 7999 Baseball instruction school

(P-19156)
CTOUR HOLIDAY LLC
222 E Huntington Dr # 105, Monrovia
(91016-8006)
PHONE..............................323 261-8811
Charlie Lu, *Mng Member*
EMP: 300 EST: 2016
SALES (est): 1.6MM **Privately Held**
SIC: 7999 Tour & guide services

(P-19157)
DESERT RECREATION DISTRICT
(PA)
45305 Oasis St, Indio (92201-4337)
PHONE..............................760 347-3484
Rudy Acosta, *President*
Laura McGalliard, *Vice Pres*
EMP: 55
SQ FT: 40,000
SALES (est): 4.1MM **Privately Held**
WEB: www.cvrpd.org
SIC: 7999 Recreation center

(P-19158)
DESTINY ARTS CENTER
970 Grace Ave, Oakland (94608-2784)
PHONE..............................510 597-1619
Cristy Johnson, *Exec Dir*
Sarah Crowell, *Exec Dir*
Cristy Johnston-Limon, *Exec Dir*
Nasim Coy, *Opers Staff*
Salim Rollins, *Director*
EMP: 50
SALES: 1.9MM **Privately Held**
WEB: www.destinyarts.org
SIC: 7999 7911 Martial arts school; golf
professionals; dance studio & school

(P-19159)
DISNEY REGIONAL ENTRMT INC
(HQ)
500 S Buena Vista St, Burbank
(91521-0001)
PHONE..............................818 560-1000
Arthur Levitt, *President*
Gary Marcotte, *CFO*
Marc Lange, *Vice Pres*
David Duffey, *Editor*
Allen Sliwa, *Accounts Exec*
EMP: 200
SALES (est): 36.7MM **Publicly Held**
SIC: 7999 5812 5813 Recreation center;
eating places; American restaurant; drink-
ing places; bar (drinking places)

(P-19160)
DOWNTOWN SD VENTURES LLC
Also Called: Bassmnt
20162 Sw Birch St Ste 350, Newport Beach
(92660-0790)
PHONE..............................619 231-9200
Mike Kinsella, *Mng Member*
EMP: 60
SQ FT: 1,500
SALES (est): 1.1MM **Privately Held**
SIC: 7999 Night club, not serving alcoholic
beverages

(P-19161)
DROPZONE WATERPARK
2165 Trumble Rd, Perris (92571-9211)
PHONE..............................951 210-1600
Erica Bice, *Director*
EMP: 150
SALES (est): 164.7K **Privately Held**
SIC: 7999 Recreation services

(P-19162)
EAST BAY BTNCAL
ZOOLOGICAL SOC
Also Called: Oakland Zoo In Knowland Park
9777 Golf Links Rd, Oakland (94605-4925)
P.O. Box 5238 (94605-0238)
PHONE..............................510 632-9525
Joel J Parrott, *CEO*
Steven E Kane, *Ch of Bd*
William L Marchant, *Admin Sec*
EMP: 85
SQ FT: 1,000
SALES: 21.4MM **Privately Held**
SIC: 7999 Zoological garden, commercial

(P-19163)
EAST BAY REGIONAL PARK DST
Also Called: East Bay Regional Park Public
17930 Lake Chabot Rd, Castro Valley
(94546-1950)
PHONE..............................510 881-1833
Timothy Anderson, *Chief*
EMP: 75
SALES (corp-wide): 187.2MM **Privately**
Held
SIC: 7999 Recreation services
PA: East Bay Regional Park District
2950 Peralta Oaks Ct
Oakland CA 94605
888 327-2757

(P-19164)
EAST VALLEY TOURIST DEV
AUTH
Also Called: Fantasy Springs Resort Casino
84245 Indio Springs Dr, Indio (92203-3405)
PHONE..............................760 342-5000
John James, *Ch of Bd*
Angela Roosevelt, *Corp Secy*
Mark Benitez, *Vice Ch Bd*
Brenda Soulliere, *Vice Ch Bd*
Don Casper, *Vice Pres*
EMP: 1200
SQ FT: 94,000
SALES (est): 57.6MM **Privately Held**
WEB: www.fantasyspringsresort.com
SIC: 7999 Gambling establishment; off-
track betting

(P-19165)
EASTBIZ CORPORATION (PA)
Also Called: Shipito
3501 Jack Northrop Ave, Hawthorne
(90250-4444)
PHONE..............................310 212-7134
Jan Vanhara, *President*
Anthony Scalise, *Supervisor*
EMP: 52
SALES (est): 9.3MM **Privately Held**
SIC: 7999 5091 Sporting goods rental;
sporting & recreation goods

(P-19166)
ELK GROVE PARK DISTRICT
8820 Elk Grove Blvd Ste 2, Elk Grove
(95624-1876)
PHONE..............................916 685-9502
Deon Nesson, *Branch Mgr*
EMP: 295 **Privately Held**
SIC: 7999 Recreation services
PA: Elk Grove Park District
499 Biesterfield Rd
Elk Grove Village IL 60007
847 437-9494

(P-19167)
ENCORE INC
Also Called: Encore Gymnstics Dnce Climb-
ing
999 Bancroft Rd, Concord (94518-3911)
P.O. Box 30113, Walnut Creek (94598-
9113)
PHONE..............................925 932-1033
Tamara Gerlach, *President*
Virginia Kelley, *Director*
EMP: 50
SQ FT: 17,000
SALES: 1MM **Privately Held**
SIC: 7999 Gymnastic instruction, non-
membership

(P-19168)
FAIRPLEX ENTERPRISES INC
1101 W Mckinley Ave, Pomona
(91768-1650)
PHONE..............................909 623-3111
James Henwood, *President*
Michelle Demott, *Vice Pres*
Christina Dempsey, *Executive Asst*
Judi Brooks, *Admin Asst*
Marcella Garnica, *Administration*
▲ EMP: 52
SALES (est): 4.8MM
SALES (corp-wide): 23.6MM **Privately**
Held
SIC: 7999 Fair
PA: Los Angeles County Fair Association
1101 W Mckinley Ave
Pomona CA 91768
909 623-3111

(P-19169)
FEATHER RVER RECREATION
PK DST
1875 Feather River Blvd, Oroville
(95965-5701)
PHONE..............................530 533-2011
Vicky Smith, *Chairman*
Apryl Ramage, *Executive*
Shaw Carter, *Director*
Victoria Coots, *Director*
Gary Emberland, *Director*
EMP: 76
SQ FT: 3,000
SALES (est): 1.6MM **Privately Held**
WEB: www.frrpd.com
SIC: 7999 Recreation services

(P-19170)
FESTIVAL FUN PARKS LLC
Also Called: Boomers
4590 Macarthur Blvd # 400, Newport Beach
(92660-2027)
PHONE..............................954 921-1411
EMP: 150 **Privately Held**
SIC: 7999
HQ: Festival Fun Parks, Llc
4590 Macarthur Blvd # 400
Newport Beach CA 92660
949 261-0404

(P-19171)
FESTIVAL FUN PARKS LLC
Also Called: Camelot Park Santa Maria
2250 Preisker Ln, Santa Maria
(93458-9060)
PHONE..............................805 922-1574
Jesse Ghormley, *Manager*
EMP: 160 **Privately Held**
SIC: 7999 7993 7991 Miniature golf
course operation; arcades; physical fit-
ness facilities
HQ: Festival Fun Parks, Llc
4590 Macarthur Blvd # 400
Newport Beach CA 92660
949 261-0404

(P-19172)
FESTIVAL FUN PARKS LLC
Also Called: Boomers
1525 W Vista Way, Vista (92083-4001)
PHONE..............................760 945-9474
Mark Williams, *Manager*
EMP: 85 **Privately Held**
SIC: 7999 Recreation services
HQ: Festival Fun Parks, Llc
4590 Macarthur Blvd # 400
Newport Beach CA 92660
949 261-0404

(P-19173)
FESTIVAL FUN PARKS LLC
Also Called: Palace Park
3405 Michelson Dr, Irvine (92612-1605)
PHONE..............................949 559-8336
Craig Stieglitz, *General Mgr*
EMP: 100 **Privately Held**
SIC: 7999 7996 Tourist attractions,
amusement park concessions & rides;
amusement parks
HQ: Festival Fun Parks, Llc
4590 Macarthur Blvd # 400
Newport Beach CA 92660
949 261-0404

(P-19174)
FESTIVAL OF ARTS LAGUNA
BEACH
650 Laguna Canyon Rd, Laguna Beach
(92651-1899)
PHONE..............................949 494-1145
Fredric Sattler, *CEO*
Bob Moffett, *Bd of Directors*
David Perry, *Vice Pres*
Monica Daebritz, *Office Mgr*
Pat Kollenda, *Admin Sec*
EMP: 51
SQ FT: 6,500
SALES (est): 9.6MM **Privately Held**
SIC: 7999 Festival operation

(P-19175)
FINLEY SWIM CENTER
Also Called: Ridgway
2060 W College Ave, Santa Rosa
(95401-4458)
PHONE..............................707 543-3760
Don Hicks, *Principal*
EMP: 50
SALES (est): 681.5K **Privately Held**
WEB: www.ridgway.com
SIC: 7999 Swimming pool, non-member-
ship

(P-19176)
FOOD & AGRICULTURE CAL
DEPT
Also Called: 32nd District-Orange Cnty Fair
88 Fair Dr, Costa Mesa (92626-6521)
PHONE..............................714 751-3247
Becky Bailey-Findley, *Branch Mgr*
EMP: 70 **Privately Held**
WEB: www.cmab.net
SIC: 7999 9641 6512 Agricultural fair;
regulation of agricultural marketing; ; non-
residential building operators
HQ: Food & Agriculture, California Dept
1220 N St Ste 400
Sacramento CA 95814
-

(P-19177)
GARDEN CITY INC
Also Called: Garden City Casino & Rest
1887 Matrix Blvd, San Jose (95110-2309)
PHONE..............................408 244-3333
Pete V Lunardi III, *CEO*
Eli Reinhard, *President*
Llene Brandon, *CFO*
Kathy Reiner, *CFO*
Frederick Wyle, *Trustee*
EMP: 569 EST: 1974
SQ FT: 22,000
SALES (est): 10.5MM **Privately Held**
SIC: 7999 Card rooms

(P-19178)
GLAD ENTERTAINMENT INC (PA)
Also Called: Blackbeard's Family Fun Center
4055 N Chestnut Ave, Fresno
(93726-4701)
PHONE..............................559 292-9000
Greg Florer, *President*
Don Jackley, *Corp Secy*
Judy Nielsen, *Executive*
EMP: 70
SQ FT: 12,000
SALES (est): 3.4MM **Privately Held**
WEB: www.blackbeardsfresno.com
SIC: 7999 Miniature golf course operation;
baseball batting cage; waterslide opera-
tion; amusement concession

(P-19179)
GOLF & TENNIS PRO SHOP INC
1751 E Bayshore Rd, East Palo Alto
(94303-2523)
PHONE..............................650 600-5200
Dustin Mahoney, *Branch Mgr*
EMP: 55
SALES (corp-wide): 123.1MM **Privately**
Held
SIC: 7999 Tour & guide services
PA: Golf & Tennis Pro Shop, Inc.
1005 Holcomb Woods Pkwy
Roswell GA 30076
770 640-0933

(P-19180)
GREATER VALLEJO
RECREATION DST
395 Amador St, Vallejo (94590-6320)
PHONE..............................707 648-4600
William Pendergast III, *Ch of Bd*
Anthony Kenaston, *Admin Sec*
Rosa Ringseth, *Mktg Dir*
Dana Asbury, *Assistant*
Salvador Nuno, *Supervisor*
EMP: 150 EST: 1944
SQ FT: 5,000
SALES (est): 7.1MM **Privately Held**
WEB: www.gvrd.org
SIC: 7999 Recreation services

(P-19181)
HIGH DESERT PHOENIX
42980 Staffordshire Dr, Lancaster
(93534-6263)
PHONE..................................661 547-5630
Norma Cook, *Principal*
EMP: 50
SALES (est): 316K **Privately Held**
SIC: 7999 Amusement & recreation

(P-19182)
HOPLAND BAND POMO INDIANS INC
Also Called: Casino
13101 Nokomis Rd, Hopland (95449-9793)
PHONE..................................707 744-1395
John O'Neil, *Manager*
EMP: 200
SALES (corp-wide): 17.8MM **Privately Held**
WEB: www.hoplandtribe.com
SIC: 7999 7011 5813 5812 Gambling establishment; casino hotel; drinking places; eating places
PA: Hopland Band Of Pomo Indians Inc.
3000 Shanel Rd
Hopland CA 95449
707 472-2100

(P-19183)
HOUSE OF AIR LLC
926 Mason St, San Francisco
(94129-1602)
PHONE..................................415 345-9675
Paul McGeehan,
Shoshanna Moody, *General Mgr*
David Schaeffer,
EMP: 61 EST: 2009
SALES (est): 1.7MM **Privately Held**
SIC: 7999 Recreation center; trampoline operation

(P-19184)
HOWE COMMUNITY CENTER
2201 Cottage Way, Sacramento
(95825-1022)
PHONE..................................916 927-3802
Jeff Dubchnasky, *General Mgr*
Jeff Dubchansky, *General Mgr*
EMP: 50
SALES (est): 303.8K **Privately Held**
SIC: 7999 Recreation center

(P-19185)
ICE CENTER ENTERPRISES LLC
Also Called: Ice Center, The
10123 N Wolfe Rd Ste 1020, Cupertino
(95014-2585)
P.O. Box 1433, Alameda (94501-0155)
PHONE..................................510 604-8878
Michael Benesh,
Christopher Hathaway, *COO*
Mike Benesh, *Executive*
Chris Hathaway,
EMP: 75
SQ FT: 28,000
SALES (est): 1.7MM **Privately Held**
WEB: www.icecenter.net
SIC: 7999 Ice skating rink operation

(P-19186)
ICE SPECIALTY ENTRMT INC (PA)
Also Called: Iceoplex
409 Santa Monica Blvd E, Santa Monica
(90401-2378)
PHONE..................................310 899-3889
Bradford Becken, *President*
EMP: 140
SQ FT: 1,300
SALES (est): 5MM **Privately Held**
SIC: 7999 Skating rink operation services

(P-19187)
ICE STATION VALENCIA L L C
27745 Smyth Dr, Valencia (91355-4019)
PHONE..................................661 775-8686
Roger Perez, *Principal*
Russell Drinnan, *Facilities Mgr*
EMP: 60
SALES (est): 277.6K **Privately Held**
SIC: 7999 7299 Ice skating rink operation; party planning service

(P-19188)
IGT GLOBAL SOLUTIONS CORP
Also Called: Gtech
10415 Slusher Dr Ste 1, Santa Fe Springs
(90670-7331)
PHONE..................................562 946-9922
Lance Gunn, *Branch Mgr*
EMP: 70 **Privately Held**
WEB: www.gtech.com
SIC: 7999 Lottery operation
HQ: Igt Global Solutions Corporation
10 Memorial Blvd
Providence RI 02903
401 392-1000

(P-19189)
INTERNATIONAL SPT SCIENCE ASSN
Also Called: Issa
1015 Mark Ave, Carpinteria (93013-2912)
PHONE..................................805 745-8111
Sal Aria, *President*
Fred Hatfield, *Partner*
Frank Meile, *Vice Pres*
Mike Stein, *Vice Pres*
Sal Arria, *Principal*
EMP: 50
SQ FT: 10,000
SALES (est): 5.4MM **Privately Held**
SIC: 7999 Physical fitness instruction

(P-19190)
KAIMANU OUTRIGGER CANOE CLUB
13424 Doolittle Dr, San Leandro
(94577-4141)
PHONE..................................510 895-0435
Debbie Green, *President*
EMP: 60 EST: 1977
SALES (est): 2.2MM **Privately Held**
SIC: 7999 Rowboat & canoe rental

(P-19191)
KATHERINE BOUSSON
1015 Palisade St, Hayward (94542-1025)
PHONE..................................510 582-1166
Katherine Bousson, *Owner*
EMP: 85
SQ FT: 1,000
SALES (est): 2.2MM **Privately Held**
WEB: www.palacecardclub.com
SIC: 7999 Card rooms

(P-19192)
KEB KEB MAGIC CLOWN
637 Germaine Dr, Galt (95632-2161)
PHONE..................................916 369-6054
Kevin Keller, *Owner*
EMP: 72
SALES: 10MM **Privately Held**
SIC: 7999 Tennis services & professionals

(P-19193)
KERN RIVER TOURS INC
2712 Mayfair Rd, Lake Isabella
(93240-9643)
P.O. Box 3444 (93240-3444)
PHONE..................................760 379-4616
Kenneth Busheing, *President*
Joseph M Kent, *Corp Secy*
EMP: 70
SQ FT: 2,250
SALES: 500K **Privately Held**
WEB: www.kernrivertours.com
SIC: 7999 Tourist guide

(P-19194)
KINGS CASINO MANAGEMENT CORP
6510 Antelope Rd, Citrus Heights
(95621-1077)
PHONE..................................916 560-4405
Ryan Stone, *CEO*
EMP: 350 EST: 2013
SALES (est): 8.4MM **Privately Held**
SIC: 7999 Card & game services

(P-19195)
LEISURE PLANET
Also Called: Jungle Fun & Adventure
1975 Diamond Blvd, Concord
(94520-5792)
PHONE..................................925 687-4386
Olivier Sermet, *President*
EMP: 130

SQ FT: 15,000
SALES (est): 2.9MM **Privately Held**
WEB: www.junglefunadventure.com
SIC: 7999 5947 Tourist attractions; amusement park concessions & rides; gifts & novelties

(P-19196)
LIVERMORE AREA RCRATION PK DST
71 Trevarno Rd, Livermore (94551-4931)
PHONE..................................925 373-5700
Doug Bell, *Branch Mgr*
EMP: 131
SALES (est): 1MM
SALES (corp-wide): 9.5MM **Privately Held**
SIC: 7999 8211 Recreation services; public elementary & secondary schools
PA: Livermore Area Recreation & Park District
4444 East Ave
Livermore CA 94550
925 373-5700

(P-19197)
LIVERMORE AREA RCRATION PK DST (PA)
4444 East Ave, Livermore (94550-5053)
PHONE..................................925 373-5700
Tim Barry, *General Mgr*
Don Humphrey, *Finance Mgr*
Denise Deprato, *Human Res Mgr*
Maryalice Faltings, *Director*
David Furst, *Director*
EMP: 260 EST: 1947
SQ FT: 71,000
SALES (est): 9.5MM **Privately Held**
WEB: www.larpd.dst.ca.us
SIC: 7999 Recreation services

(P-19198)
LOGITECH ICE AT SAN JOSE
Also Called: Shark's Ice
1500 S 10th St, San Jose (95112-6410)
PHONE..................................408 279-6000
Jon Gustafson, *Vice Pres*
EMP: 50
SQ FT: 150,000
SALES (est): 2.7MM **Privately Held**
WEB: www.logitechice.com
SIC: 7999 5461 Ice skating rink operation; bakeries

(P-19199)
LOS ANGELES COUNTY FAIR ASSN (PA)
Also Called: Fairplex Rv Park
1101 W Mckinley Ave, Pomona
(91768-1639)
PHONE..................................909 623-3111
Ronald Bolding, *Director*
Micheal Seder, *Vice Pres*
Yvonne Tejeda, *General Mgr*
Richard Rodriguez, *Facilities Mgr*
Tammy Roush, *Manager*
EMP: 300
SALES (est): 23.6MM **Privately Held**
SIC: 7999 8412 Fair; museums & art galleries

(P-19200)
LUCKY CHANCES INC
Also Called: Lucky Chances Casino
1700 Hillside Blvd, Colma (94014-2801)
PHONE..................................650 758-2237
Rommel R Medina, *CEO*
Ruell Medina, *President*
Chrystal Lee, *HR Admin*
Kyle Alegrete, *Manager*
Ralph Baude, *Manager*
EMP: 650
SALES (est): 25.7MM **Privately Held**
SIC: 7999 Card rooms

(P-19201)
LYTTON RANCHERIA
Also Called: Casino San Pablo
13255 San Pablo Ave, San Pablo
(94806-3907)
PHONE..................................510 215-7888
Michael Gorczysnski, *General Mgr*
Marcella Taylor, *Executive*
Cathi Hamel, *Principal*
Michael Gorczynski, *General Mgr*

Jeff Dossey, *Info Tech Mgr*
EMP: 547
SALES (est): 20.7MM **Privately Held**
WEB: www.casinosanpablo.com
SIC: 7999 Gambling & lottery services

(P-19202)
MESQUITE GOLF & CNTRY CLB CORP
2700 E Mesquite Ave Ofc, Palm Springs
(92264-5009)
PHONE..................................760 323-9377
Dae H Yoo, *CEO*
Lee Yoong, *Owner*
EMP: 50
SALES (est): 756.9K **Privately Held**
SIC: 7999 5812 Golf driving range; eating places

(P-19203)
MINDFULL BODY
2876 California St, San Francisco
(94115-2545)
PHONE..................................415 931-2639
Roy N Bergmann, *Owner*
Charisse Sharpe, *Human Res Mgr*
EMP: 80
SALES (est): 1.6MM **Privately Held**
SIC: 7999 7299 Yoga instruction; massage parlor

(P-19204)
MOORETOWN RANCHERIA (PA)
Also Called: Feather Falls Casino
1 Alverda Dr, Oroville (95966-9379)
PHONE..................................530 533-3625
Gary Archuleta, *Ch of Bd*
Kayla Lobo, *Treasurer*
Melvin Jackson, *Vice Pres*
Julie McIntosh, *Principal*
Penny Palmer, *Admin Sec*
EMP: 50
SALES (est): 23.5MM **Privately Held**
WEB: www.drumvision.com
SIC: 7999 5993 Gambling establishment; cigar store

(P-19205)
MOUNT SAN JACINTO WIN PK AUTH
Also Called: PALM SPRINGS AERIAL TRAMWAY
1 Tramway Rd, Palm Springs
(92262-1827)
PHONE..................................760 325-1449
Rob Parkins, *President*
Marjorie Dela Cruz, *Vice Pres*
Nancy Nichols, *Vice Pres*
Greg Vogelsang, *Vice Pres*
Marjorie De La Cruz, *HR Admin*
▲ EMP: 64 EST: 1945
SQ FT: 50,000
SALES: 18.8MM **Privately Held**
WEB: www.pstramway.com
SIC: 7999 Aerial tramway or ski lift, amusement or scenic

(P-19206)
MUSEUM OF CHILDRENS ART
Also Called: Mocha
1221 Broadway, Oakland (94612-1837)
PHONE..................................510 465-8770
Karen Ransom, *Director*
Roxanne Padgett, *Exec Dir*
Simon Muturi, *Administration*
Haldun Morgan, *Marketing Staff*
Katie Sammon, *Program Dir*
EMP: 50
SQ FT: 4,800
SALES (est): 844.6K **Privately Held**
WEB: www.mocha.org
SIC: 7999 8412 Art gallery, commercial; instruction schools, camps & services; museum

(P-19207)
NAPA VALLEY WINE TRAIN LLC (HQ)
Also Called: NAPA Valley Railroad Co
1275 Mckinstry St, NAPA (94559-1925)
PHONE..................................707 253-2160
Anthony J Giaccio,
Vincent M De Deminico Jr, *Vice Pres*
Jaspreet Kaur, *Persnl Mgr*
Ragina Garcia, *Cust Svc Dir*

Denise Perkins, *Sales Staff*
▲ EMP: 125
SQ FT: 20,000
SALES (est): 10.1MM **Privately Held**
WEB: www.winetrain.com
SIC: 7999 5812 4011 4119 Scenic railroads for amusement; eating places; railroads, line-haul operating; local passenger transportation

(P-19208)
NEW COLUSA INDIAN BINGO
Also Called: Colusa Casino Resort
3770 State Highway 45, Colusa
(95932-4021)
PHONE..............................530 458-8844
Steve Gonzales, *Principal*
Fred Pina, *Vice Pres*
Dennis Pinney, *Info Tech Mgr*
Ricardo Cardona, *Technology*
Brianna Garcia, *Auditing Mgr*
EMP: 450
SALES (est): 1.7MM **Privately Held**
SIC: 7999 Card & game services

(P-19209)
NORMANDIE CLUB LP
Also Called: Normandie Casino & Showroom
57 Via Malona, Rancho Palos Verdes
(90275-4882)
PHONE..............................310 352-3486
Lawrence F Miller, *Managing Prtnr*
Russel Miller Jr, *General Ptnr*
Greg Miller, *Partner*
Steve Miller, *Partner*
Sandra Holtzmann, *Marketing Mgr*
▲ EMP: 600
SQ FT: 44,000
SALES (est): 21.6MM **Privately Held**
WEB: www.normandiecasino.com
SIC: 7999 5812 Card & game services; eating places

(P-19210)
O A OUTFITTING INC
Also Called: Kern River Outfitters
6602 Wofford Heights Blvd, Bayside
(95524)
P.O. Box 91 (95524-0091)
PHONE..............................707 498-2917
James Ritter, *President*
Robert Volpert, *CEO*
EMP: 55
SALES: 1MM **Privately Held**
SIC: 7999 Recreation services

(P-19211)
O C SAILING CLUB INC
Also Called: Olympic Circle Sailing Club
1 Spinnaker Way, Berkeley (94710-1612)
PHONE..............................510 843-4200
Anthony P Sandberg, *President*
Brian Faltys, *Manager*
EMP: 65
SQ FT: 5,000
SALES (est): 3.4MM **Privately Held**
WEB: www.ocscsailing.com
SIC: 7999 5651 Sailing instruction; pleasure boat rental; family clothing stores

(P-19212)
OCEANSIDE LIFEGUARDS
300 N Coast Hwy, Oceanside
(92054-2824)
PHONE..............................760 435-4500
Ray Duncan, *Manager*
EMP: 73
SALES (est): 774.8K **Privately Held**
WEB: www.ci.oceanside.ca.us
SIC: 7999 Lifeguard service

(P-19213)
PALACE ENTERTAINMENT INC (DH)
4590 Macarthur Blvd # 400, Newport Beach
(92660-2027)
PHONE..............................949 261-0404
Alexander Weber Jr, *CEO*
John Cora, *President*
Russ Owens, *CFO*
Albert Cabuco, *Vice Pres*
Bill Lentz, *Vice Pres*
EMP: 50
SQ FT: 8,000

SALES (est): 82.9MM **Privately Held**
SIC: 7999 7993 Miniature golf course operation; arcades
HQ: Parque De Atracciones Madrid Sa
Calle Parque Atracciones (Casa De Campo), S/N
Madrid 28011
902 345-001

(P-19214)
PARC MANAGEMENT LLC
Also Called: Waterworld USA
1950 Waterworld Pkwy, Concord
(94520-2602)
PHONE..............................925 609-1364
Steve Mayer, *Manager*
EMP: 1984
SALES (corp-wide): 76.1MM **Privately Held**
WEB: www.parcmanagement.com
SIC: 7999 Picnic ground operation
PA: Parc Management, Llc
8649 Baypine Rd Ste 101
Jacksonville FL 32256
904 732-7272

(P-19215)
PARKS AND RECREATION CAL DEPT
Also Called: Camanche Lake
2000 Camanche Rd Ofc, Ione
(95640-9420)
PHONE..............................209 763-5121
Mary Mendence, *Manager*
EMP: 50 **Privately Held**
WEB: www.aprpd.org
SIC: 7999 Recreation center; ping pong parlor
HQ: California Department Of Parks And Recreation
1416 9th St Ste 1041
Sacramento CA 95814
800 777-0369

(P-19216)
PAUL MAURER COMPANY
Also Called: Paul Maurer Shows
16081 Warren Ln, Huntington Beach
(92649-2433)
PHONE..............................714 231-8241
Paul Maurer, *Owner*
EMP: 60
SALES (est): 1MM **Privately Held**
SIC: 7999 Amusement ride

(P-19217)
PIT RIVER TRIBAL COUNCIL
Also Called: Pit River Casino
20265 Tamarack Ave, Burney
(96013-4064)
PHONE..............................530 335-2334
Nathan Schoofield, *Manager*
Gary Dittman, *Accountant*
Mike Avelar, *Manager*
EMP: 54
SALES (corp-wide): 4.5MM **Privately Held**
WEB: www.pitrivercasino.com
SIC: 7999 Card & game services; bingo hall
PA: Pit River Tribal Council
37960 Park Ave
Burney CA 96013
530 335-5487

(P-19218)
PLAYWORKS EDUCATION ENERGIZED (PA)
380 Washington St, Oakland (94607-3800)
PHONE..............................510 893-4180
Jill Vialet, *President*
Elizabeth Cushing, *President*
David Carroll, *CFO*
Phillis Carte, *CFO*
Amanda Casey, *CFO*
EMP: 50
SALES (est): 20.7MM **Privately Held**
WEB: www.sports4kids.org
SIC: 7999 Recreation services

(P-19219)
PYRAMID ENTERPRISES INC (PA)
Also Called: Lake Piru Marina
28368 Constellation Rd # 380, Valencia
(91355-5005)
PHONE..............................661 702-1420
Chester Roberts, *President*
Traci Roberts, *General Mgr*
EMP: 60
SQ FT: 1,300
SALES (est): 6.3MM **Privately Held**
WEB: www.lake-piru.org
SIC: 7999 4493 Beach & water sports equipment rental & services; marinas

(P-19220)
QUECHAN INDIAN TRIBE
Also Called: Quechan Gaming Commission
350 Picacho Rd, Winterhaven
(92283-9769)
P.O. Box 2737, Yuma AZ (85366-2573)
PHONE..............................760 572-2413
Mike Jackson, *President*
Juan Gabriel Leyva, *Comp Spec*
EMP: 300 **Privately Held**
SIC: 7999 5812 Gambling establishment; eating places
PA: Quechan Indian Tribe
350 Picacho Rd
Winterhaven CA 92283
760 572-0213

(P-19221)
RAINBOW CAMP INC
26619 Marigold Ct, Calabasas
(91302-2945)
PHONE..............................310 456-3066
EMP: 50
SALES: 165K **Privately Held**
WEB: www.rainbowcamp.com
SIC: 7999

(P-19222)
RANCHO JURUPA PARK
4800 Crestmore Rd, Riverside
(92509-6839)
PHONE..............................951 684-7032
Paul Franzen, *President*
EMP: 50
SALES (est): 553K **Privately Held**
SIC: 7999 Recreation services

(P-19223)
RANCHO SIMI RECREATION PK DST (PA)
4201 Guardian St, Simi Valley
(93063-3372)
PHONE..............................805 584-4400
Doug Gale, *Administration*
Larry Peterson, *District Mgr*
Theresa Pennington, *Accounting Mgr*
Samuel Cooksey, *Director*
Gene Hostetler, *Director*
EMP: 70 EST: 1961
SQ FT: 1,589
SALES (est): 5.3MM **Privately Held**
WEB: www.rsrpd.org
SIC: 7999 Recreation services

(P-19224)
REDWOOD BRIDGE CLUB
3111 6th Ave, San Diego (92103-5836)
PHONE..............................619 296-4274
Warren Edelson, *President*
Evelyn Flowers, *Vice Pres*
EMP: 80
SALES (est): 28.3K **Privately Held**
WEB: www.redwoodbridgeclub.com
SIC: 7999 Amusement & recreation

(P-19225)
REDWOOD EMPIRE ICE OPRTONS LLC (PA)
Also Called: Snoopy's Galary and Gift Shop
1667 W Steele Ln, Santa Rosa
(95403-2625)
PHONE..............................707 546-7147
Jean F Schulz,
EMP: 80 EST: 1968
SQ FT: 40,000
SALES (est): 2.7MM **Privately Held**
SIC: 7999 5947 5812 Ice skating rink operation; gift shop; coffee shop

(P-19226)
ROLLING HLLS ESTTES TENNIS CLB
Also Called: Rolling Hills Estates City of
25851 Hawthorne Blvd, Rllng HLS Est
(90275)
PHONE..............................310 541-4585
Andy Clark, *Director*
EMP: 50
SALES (est): 417.7K **Privately Held**
WEB: www.ci.rolling-hills-estates.ca.us
SIC: 7999 Tennis courts, outdoor/indoor: non-membership

(P-19227)
ROSEVILLE SPORTWORLD INC
Also Called: Skatetown
1009 Orlando Ave, Roseville (95661-5230)
PHONE..............................916 783-8550
Scott Slavensky, *President*
Althea Slavensky, *Shareholder*
Frank Slavensky, *Shareholder*
Kerry Slavensky, *Corp Secy*
EMP: 83
SQ FT: 61,679
SALES (est): 3.1MM **Privately Held**
SIC: 7999 5941 Ice skating rink operation; skating equipment

(P-19228)
SAC RIVER OUTFITTERS
1403 Edgewood Dr, Redding (96003-9227)
PHONE..............................530 275-3500
Chris King, *Owner*
EMP: 70
SALES (est): 440.3K **Privately Held**
WEB: www.sacriveroutfitters.com
SIC: 7999 Outfitters, recreation

(P-19229)
SAN DIEGO GULLS HOCKEY CLB LLC
7676 Hazard Center Dr, San Diego
(92108-4503)
PHONE..............................619 359-4700
Michael Schulman, *Director*
Steven Brown, *Comms Mgr*
David Desrochers, *Opers Staff*
Andrew Rubinstein, *Sales Mgr*
Mark Kramer, *Marketing Staff*
EMP: 65
SQ FT: 2,000
SALES: 8.5MM **Privately Held**
SIC: 7999 Sports professionals

(P-19230)
SAN FRANCISCO ZOOLOGICAL SOC
1 Zoo Rd, San Francisco (94132-1098)
PHONE..............................415 753-7080
Tanya Peterson, *CEO*
Robert Pedrero, *Chairman*
EMP: 222
SQ FT: 2,000
SALES: 24.2MM **Privately Held**
WEB: www.sfzoo.org
SIC: 7999 7389 Concession operator; fund raising organizations

(P-19231)
SAN MANUEL INDIAN BINGO CASINO (PA)
777 San Manuel Blvd, Highland
(92346-6713)
PHONE..............................909 864-5050
James Ramos, *Chairman*
Becky Spalding, *CFO*
Rebecca Spalding, *CFO*
Peter Watts, *Chief Mktg Ofcr*
Susana Lopez, *Officer*
▲ EMP: 3000
SALES (est): 89.5MM **Privately Held**
SIC: 7999 Bingo hall; card & game services

(P-19232)
SAN MATEO CNTY EXPO FAIR ASSN
Also Called: SAN MATEO COUNTY EXPO CENTER
2495 S Delaware St, San Mateo
(94403-1902)
PHONE..............................650 574-3247
Chris Carpenter, *General Mgr*

P
R
O
D
U
C
T
S

&

S
V
C
S

Charlene King, *Manager*
▲ EMP: 50
SQ FT: 225,000
SALES: 8.9MM **Privately Held**
WEB: www.smexpo.com
SIC: 7999 6512 Exhibition operation; exposition operation; fair; nonresidential building operators

(P-19233)
SANTA CLARA COUNTY OF
Parks & Recreation Dept
298 Garden Hill Dr, Los Gatos (95032-7669)
PHONE..............................408 355-2200
Lisa Killough, *Branch Mgr*
EMP: 140 **Privately Held**
WEB: www.countyairports.org
SIC: 7999 9512 Recreation services; land, mineral & wildlife conservation;
PA: County Of Santa Clara
　3180 Newberry Dr Ste 150
　San Jose CA 95118
　408 299-5105

(P-19234)
SANTA CLARITA CITY OF
Also Called: Cowboy Poetry
23920 Valencia Blvd # 300, Santa Clarita (91355-2175)
PHONE..............................661 284-1423
Ken Pulskamp, *Manager*
Carl Newton,
EMP: 350 **Privately Held**
WEB: www.golfsantaclarita.com
SIC: 7999 Festival operation
PA: Santa Clarita, City Of
　23920 Valencia Blvd # 300
　Santa Clarita CA 91355
　661 259-2489

(P-19235)
SCANDIA SPORTS INC
Also Called: Scandia Family Fun Center
5070 Hillsdale Blvd, Sacramento (95842-3520)
PHONE..............................916 331-5757
Paul Wood, *Manager*
EMP: 50
SALES (corp-wide): 2.4MM **Privately Held**
SIC: 7999 Miniature golf course operation; recreation center; trampoline operation
PA: Scandia Sports, Inc
　1155 S Wanamaker Ave
　Ontario CA 91761
　909 390-3092

(P-19236)
SHASTA LAKE RESORTS LP
Also Called: Jones Valley Resorts
22300 Jones Vly Marina Dr, Redding (96003-7829)
PHONE..............................209 785-3300
David M Smith, *Partner*
Steve Woodward, *Partner*
Water Resorts, *Managing Prtnr*
EMP: 55
SQ FT: 3,500
SALES (est): 3.1MM **Privately Held**
SIC: 7999 4493 5411 Pleasure boat rental; marinas; grocery stores, independent

(P-19237)
SHINGLE SPRNG TRBAL GMING AUTH
Also Called: Red Hawk Casino
1 Red Hawk Pkwy, Placerville (95667-8639)
PHONE..............................530 677-7000
Nicholas Fonseca, *Ch of Bd*
Tyler Bila, *President*
Matthew Morgan, *President*
Tyrone Huff, *CFO*
Evan Smith, *Vice Pres*
EMP: 1200
SQ FT: 278,000
SALES (est): 64MM **Privately Held**
WEB: www.shinglespringsrancheria.com
SIC: 7999 Gambling establishment
PA: Shingle Springs Rancheria
　5168 Honpie Rd
　Placerville CA 95667

(P-19238)
SKATE ENTERPRISES INC
12356 Central Ave, Chino (91710-2601)
PHONE..............................562 924-0911
Jerry Curran, *President*
Robert E Osborne, *Corp Secy*
David O Clark, *Vice Pres*
Robert E Maurer, *Vice Pres*
EMP: 54
SQ FT: 1,200
SALES (est): 2MM **Privately Held**
WEB: www.skateenterprises.com
SIC: 7999 Roller skating rink operation

(P-19239)
SKYHIGH WOODLAND HILLS LLC
Also Called: Sky High Sports
6051 De Soto Ave, Woodland Hills (91367-3707)
PHONE..............................805 484-6300
Ron Rafia, *Branch Mgr*
EMP: 60
SALES (corp-wide): 400K **Privately Held**
SIC: 7999 6512 Art gallery, commercial; nonresidential building operators
PA: Skyhigh Woodland Hills, Llc
　6033 De Soto Ave
　Woodland Hills CA 91367
　818 346-6300

(P-19240)
SPEARMAN CLUBS INC (PA)
Also Called: Laguna Niguel Racquet Club
23500 Clubhouse Dr, Laguna Niguel (92677-2902)
PHONE..............................949 496-2070
Cecil E Spearman Jr, *Ch of Bd*
Mark Spearman, *President*
Steven Spearman, *CFO*
Jean Spearman, *Vice Ch Bd*
Scott Spearman, *Vice Pres*
EMP: 90 EST: 1979
SQ FT: 20,000
SALES (est): 6.4MM **Privately Held**
WEB: www.spearmanclubs.com
SIC: 7999 7991 Tennis club, non-membership; physical fitness clubs with training equipment

(P-19241)
SPLASH SWIM SCHOOL INC
2411 Old Crow Canyon Rd, San Ramon (94583-1240)
PHONE..............................925 838-7946
Elisabeth Claytor, *President*
D Christian Claytor, *Admin Sec*
EMP: 50
SQ FT: 7,310
SALES (est): 2.3MM **Privately Held**
SIC: 7999 Swimming instruction

(P-19242)
SUGAR BOWL CORPORATION
629 Sugar Bowl Rd, Norden (95724)
P.O. Box 5 (95724-0005)
PHONE..............................530 426-9000
Nancy Bechtle, *Ch of Bd*
Warren Haellman, *Shareholder*
Robert H Kautz, *President*
Bonny Bavetta, *CFO*
Dan Kingsley, *Treasurer*
▲ EMP: 100
SQ FT: 30,000
SALES (est): 9.8MM **Privately Held**
SIC: 7999 Ski rental concession

(P-19243)
SYCUAN CASINO
Also Called: Sycuan Resort and Casino
5459 Casino Way, El Cajon (92019)
PHONE..............................619 445-6002
John Denius, *General Mgr*
Javier Murillo, *Senior VP*
Andrew Kerzmann, *Vice Pres*
Juan Baca, *Security Dir*
Marilynn Cormier, *Admin Asst*
EMP: 2000
SQ FT: 236,000
SALES (est): 70.8MM **Privately Held**
SIC: 7999 7997 Gambling establishment; membership sports & recreation clubs

(P-19244)
TICKETWEB LLC
685 Market St Ste 200, San Francisco (94105-4203)
PHONE..............................415 901-0210
Dan Teree, *COO*
Anatoly Rutus, *Senior Engr*
EMP: 50
SALES (est): 1.2MM
SALES (corp-wide): 10.3B **Publicly Held**
WEB: www.ticketweb.com
SIC: 7999
HQ: Ticketmaster L.L.C.
　7060 Hollywood Blvd Fl 4
　Los Angeles CA 90028
　323 441-7336

(P-19245)
TIERRA DEL SOL FOUNDATION
Also Called: Tierra Del Soul
250 W 1st St Ste 120, Claremont (91711-4741)
PHONE..............................909 626-8301
Rebecca Hamm, *Branch Mgr*
EMP: 69
SALES (corp-wide): 11.6MM **Privately Held**
SIC: 7999 5999 Art gallery, commercial; art dealers
PA: Tierra Del Sol Foundation
　9919 Sunland Blvd
　Sunland CA 91040
　818 352-1419

(P-19246)
TONAL SYSTEMS INC
325 Vermont St, San Francisco (94103-5022)
PHONE..............................855 698-6625
Aly Orady, *CEO*
EMP: 65
SALES: 5MM **Privately Held**
SIC: 7999 Physical fitness instruction

(P-19247)
TOP SEED TENNIS ACADEMY INC
23400 Park Sorrento, Calabasas (91302-1743)
PHONE..............................818 222-2782
Steve McAvoy, *President*
EMP: 65 EST: 1996
SALES (est): 1MM **Privately Held**
WEB: www.topseed.us
SIC: 7999 Tennis services & professionals

(P-19248)
TOPGOLF MEDIA LLC (HQ)
100 California St Ste 650, San Francisco (94111-4531)
PHONE..............................214 377-0615
Ken May,
EMP: 79
SALES (est): 237.8K
SALES (corp-wide): 278.2MM **Privately Held**
SIC: 7999 Golf driving range
PA: Topgolf International, Inc.
　8750 N Cntl Expy Ste 1200
　Dallas TX 75231
　214 377-0663

(P-19249)
TRICKS GYMNASTIC INC (PA)
4070 Cavitt Stallman Rd, Granite Bay (95746-9460)
PHONE..............................916 791-4496
Vern Taylor, *President*
Kenny Aldana, *Manager*
EMP: 75
SQ FT: 10,000
SALES (est): 2.6MM **Privately Held**
WEB: www.tricks-gymnastics.com
SIC: 7999 7911 Gymnastic instruction, non-membership; dance instructor & school services

(P-19250)
TRUCKEE DNNER RCREATION PK DST
8924 Donner Pass Rd, Truckee (96161-2996)
PHONE..............................530 582-7720
Steve Randall, *General Mgr*
Kristin York, *Vice Chairman*

Peter Werbel, *Chairman*
Jennifer Boehm, *Office Mgr*
Kevin Murphy, *Admin Sec*
EMP: 100 EST: 1962
SQ FT: 10,000
SALES: 8.7MM **Privately Held**
WEB: www.tdrpd.com
SIC: 7999 Recreation services

(P-19251)
TUMBLEWEED EDUCATIONAL ENTPS
Also Called: Tumbleweed Day Camp
1024 Hanley Ave, Los Angeles (90049-1306)
P.O. Box 49291 (90049-0291)
PHONE..............................310 444-3232
Erin Benfield, *President*
Mike Sagner, *Maintenance Dir*
Anthony Bates, *Director*
Liz Kimmelman, *Director*
Brooks McCall, *Director*
EMP: 160
SQ FT: 6,500
SALES: 9.3MM **Privately Held**
SIC: 7999 4151 Day camp; school buses

(P-19252)
UCD RECREATION HALL
1 Shields Ave, Davis (95616-5200)
PHONE..............................530 752-6071
Jim Rodens, *Director*
George Bruening, *Manager*
EMP: 100
SALES (est): 3.9MM **Privately Held**
WEB: www.primal.ucdavis.edu
SIC: 7999 7997 Recreation center; membership sports & recreation clubs

(P-19253)
UCLA MARINA CENTER
111 Deneve Dr, Los Angeles (90095-0001)
PHONE..............................310 825-3671
Steve Tevenajera, *Branch Mgr*
EMP: 80
SALES (corp-wide): 2.2MM **Privately Held**
SIC: 7999 Recreation services
PA: Marina Ucla Center
　14001 Fiji Way
　Marina Del Rey CA 90292
　310 823-0048

(P-19254)
UNIVERSITY OF PACIFIC
Also Called: Athletic Department
1040 E Stadium Dr, Stockton (95204)
PHONE..............................209 946-2030
Donald Derosa, *President*
EMP: 600
SALES (corp-wide): 418.2MM **Privately Held**
WEB: www.uop.edu
SIC: 7999 8221 Ticket sales office for sporting events, contract; university
PA: University Of The Pacific
　3601 Pacific Ave
　Stockton CA 95211
　209 946-2401

(P-19255)
VALLEY WIDE RECREATION PK DST (PA)
901 W Esplanade Ave, San Jacinto (92582-4501)
P.O. Box 907 (92581-0907)
PHONE..............................951 654-1505
Nick Schouton, *President*
Kenneth Hyatt, *President*
Sam Goepp, *General Mgr*
EMP: 80
SQ FT: 30,000
SALES: 161.4K **Privately Held**
WEB: www.vwrpd.org/index.cfm
SIC: 7999 7996 Recreation services; amusement parks

(P-19256)
VILLAGE CLUB
429 Broadway, Chula Vista (91910-4320)
PHONE..............................619 425-3333
Harvey Souza, *Owner*
EMP: 50
SQ FT: 1,200
SALES (est): 1.7MM **Privately Held**
SIC: 7999 Card rooms

(P-19257)
VOLUME SERVICES INC
Also Called: Centerplate
24 Willie Mays Plz, San Francisco
(94107-2134)
PHONE..................................415 972-1500
Angie Perrilliat, *General Mgr*
EMP: 97
SALES (corp-wide): 139.1MM **Privately Held**
WEB: www.volumeservicesamerica.com
SIC: 7999 Concession operator
HQ: Volume Services, Inc.
2187 Atlantic St Ste 6
Stamford CT 06902

(P-19258)
VOLUME SERVICES INC
5333 Zoo Dr, Los Angeles (90027-1451)
PHONE..................................323 644-6038
Greg Edgar, *Manager*
EMP: 97
SALES (corp-wide): 139.1MM **Privately Held**
WEB: www.volumeservicesamerica.com
SIC: 7999 Concession operator
HQ: Volume Services, Inc.
2187 Atlantic St Ste 6
Stamford CT 06902

(P-19259)
VOLUME SERVICES INC
111 W Harbor Dr, San Diego (92101-7822)
PHONE..................................619 525-5800
EMP: 97
SALES (corp-wide): 139.1MM **Privately Held**
WEB: www.volumeservicesamerica.com
SIC: 7999 Concession operator
HQ: Volume Services, Inc.
2187 Atlantic St Ste 6
Stamford CT 06902

(P-19260)
VOLUME SERVICES INC
Also Called: Centerplate
500 Diamond Dr, Lake Elsinore
(92530-4457)
PHONE..................................951 245-9995
Dan Kreuzer, *Branch Mgr*
EMP: 100
SALES (corp-wide): 139.1MM **Privately Held**
WEB: www.volumeservicesamerica.com
SIC: 7999 Concession operator
HQ: Volume Services, Inc.
2187 Atlantic St Ste 6
Stamford CT 06902

(P-19261)
WEST VALLEY JEWISH CMNTY CTR
22622 Vanowen St, Canoga Park
(91307-2646)
PHONE..................................818 348-0048
Anthony Flores, *Director*
EMP: 60 **EST:** 2000
SALES (est): 879.9K **Privately Held**
SIC: 7999 Recreation center

(P-19262)
WIN-RIVER RESORT & CASINO
2100 Redding Rancheria Rd, Redding
(96001-5530)
PHONE..................................530 243-3377
Redding Rancheria Tribe, *Owner*
Esteban Pizano, *Vice Pres*
Gary Hayward, *General Mgr*
Kim Kinyln, *General Mgr*
Chris De Camp, *Info Tech Mgr*
EMP: 310
SQ FT: 3,000
SALES (est): 10.2MM **Privately Held**
SIC: 7999 Bingo hall

(P-19263)
WINCHESTER MYSTERY HOUSE LLC
525 S Winchester Blvd, San Jose
(95128-2588)
PHONE..................................408 247-2101

Ray K Farris II,
Vakerue Bovone,
Sandy Turner, *Manager*
EMP: 90
SQ FT: 44,000
SALES (est): 5.3MM **Privately Held**
WEB: www.winchestermysteryhouse.com
SIC: 7999 Tourist attraction, commercial

(P-19264)
YOUNG MENS CHRISTIAN ASSO
Also Called: Simi Valley Family YMCA
3200 Cochran St, Simi Valley (93065-2769)
PHONE..................................805 583-5338
Dan Jaeger, *Director*
EMP: 100
SALES (corp-wide): 20.9MM **Privately Held**
SIC: 7999 8351 8641 7997 Recreation center; child day care services; civic social & fraternal associations; membership sports & recreation clubs
PA: Young Men's Christian Association Of Southeast Ventura County
100 E Thousand Oaks Blvd # 107
Thousand Oaks CA 91360
805 497-3081

(P-19265)
ZEPHYR RIVER EXPEDITIONS INC
Also Called: Zephyr White Water Expeditions
22517 Parrotts Ferry Rd, Columbia
(95310-9757)
P.O. Box 510 (95310-0510)
PHONE..................................800 431-3636
Bob Ferguson, *President*
EMP: 60
SQ FT: 2,000
SALES (est): 1.2MM **Privately Held**
WEB: www.zrafting.com
SIC: 7999 Rafting tours

8011 Offices & Clinics Of Doctors Of Medicine

(P-19266)
A & C HEALTH CARE SERVICES INC
Also Called: A & C Convatescent Hospital
33 Mateo Ave, Millbrae (94030-2037)
PHONE..................................650 689-5784
Carlos P Ragudo, *President*
Amparo B Ragudo, *CFO*
EMP: 135
SALES (est): 4.6MM **Privately Held**
SIC: 8011 Clinic, operated by physicians

(P-19267)
ADVANCED SURGERY INSTITUTE LLC
1739 4th St, Santa Rosa (95404-3601)
PHONE..................................707 528-6331
Jeff Simmons, *Principal*
Gian Nhan MD,
EMP: 122
SALES (est): 20.6MM
SALES (corp-wide): 17.6B **Privately Held**
SIC: 8011 Surgeon
HQ: Santa Rosa Memorial Hospital Inc
1165 Montgomery Dr
Santa Rosa CA 95405
707 546-3210

(P-19268)
ADVENTIST HEALTH SYSTEM
Also Called: Adventist Health Cmnty. Care
250 W El Monte Way, Dinuba
(93618-1554)
PHONE..................................559 595-9890
Wayne Ferch, *Branch Mgr*
EMP: 5004 **Privately Held**
SIC: 8011 Offices & clinics of medical doctors
PA: Adventist Health System Sunbelt Healthcare Corporation
900 Hope Way
Altamonte Springs FL 32714

(P-19269)
ADVENTIST HEALTH SYSTEM/WEST
14880 Olympic Dr, Clearlake (95422-9521)
P.O. Box 6710 (95422-6710)
PHONE..................................707 995-4888
Patricia Van Horn, *Manager*
EMP: 115
SALES (corp-wide): 4.1B **Privately Held**
SIC: 8011 Clinic, operated by physicians
PA: Adventist Health System/West
2100 Douglas Blvd
Roseville CA 95661
916 781-2000

(P-19270)
ADVENTIST HEALTH SYSTEM/WEST
Also Called: St Helena Hospital Clearlake
18th Ave Hwy 53, Clearlake (95422)
PHONE..................................707 994-6486
Kendall Fults, *CEO*
Duane Barnes, *Finance*
Becky Holton, *Med Doctor*
EMP: 330
SALES (corp-wide): 4.1B **Privately Held**
WEB: www.sthelenahospital.com
SIC: 8011 Surgeon
PA: Adventist Health System/West
2100 Douglas Blvd
Roseville CA 95661
916 781-2000

(P-19271)
ALL CARE MEDICAL GROUP INC
Also Called: Professional Svcs Med Group
31 Crescent St, Huntington Park (90255)
PHONE..................................408 278-3550
Samuel Rotenberg MD, *Director*
EMP: 85 **EST:** 1946
SQ FT: 33,000
SALES (est): 8MM **Privately Held**
WEB: www.allcaremg.com
SIC: 8011 Physicians' office, including specialists

(P-19272)
ALLEN MEDICAL GROUP INC
14416 Victory Blvd # 211, Van Nuys
(91401-1441)
PHONE..................................818 698-8444
Avionne Petal Allen-Singh, *President*
EMP: 50 **EST:** 2008
SALES: 11MM **Privately Held**
SIC: 8011 Offices & clinics of medical doctors

(P-19273)
ALLIANCE MEDICAL CENTER INC
1381 University St, Healdsburg
(95448-3314)
PHONE..................................707 431-8234
Beatrice Bostick, *CEO*
Jack Neureuter, *CEO*
Deena Trucco, *Human Res Dir*
EMP: 99
SALES: 13.3MM **Privately Held**
WEB: www.alliancemedicalcenter.com
SIC: 8011 Clinic, operated by physicians

(P-19274)
ALLIED ANESTHESIA MED GROUP
400 N Tustin Ave, Santa Ana (92705-3813)
P.O. Box 1628, Orange (92856-0628)
PHONE..................................951 830-9816
George Kanaly, *CEO*
Kaveh Matin, *President*
EMP: 99
SALES (est): 3.3MM **Privately Held**
SIC: 8011 Anesthesiologist

(P-19275)
ALTA VISTA HEALTHCARE AND WELL
9020 Garfield St, Riverside (92503-3903)
PHONE..................................951 688-8200
EMP: 105
SALES (est): 5.5MM **Privately Held**
SIC: 8011

(P-19276)
ALTAMED HEALTH SERVICES CORP
5427 Whittier Blvd, Los Angeles
(90022-4101)
PHONE..................................323 980-4466
Irene Avilar, *Principal*
EMP: 80
SALES (corp-wide): 178.2MM **Privately Held**
WEB: www.altamed.org
SIC: 8011 Clinic, operated by physicians
PA: Altamed Health Services Corporation
2040 Camfield Ave
Commerce CA 90040
323 725-8751

(P-19277)
ALTAMED HEALTH SERVICES CORP
1820 W Lincoln Ave, Anaheim
(92801-6730)
PHONE..................................714 635-0593
EMP: 161
SALES (corp-wide): 178.2MM **Privately Held**
SIC: 8011 Gynecologist
PA: Altamed Health Services Corporation
2040 Camfield Ave
Commerce CA 90040
323 725-8751

(P-19278)
ALTAMED HEALTH SERVICES CORP
9436 Slauson Ave, Pico Rivera
(90660-4748)
PHONE..................................562 949-6069
Gary Ramirez, *Branch Mgr*
EMP: 56
SALES (corp-wide): 178.2MM **Privately Held**
SIC: 8011 Offices & clinics of medical doctors
PA: Altamed Health Services Corporation
2040 Camfield Ave
Commerce CA 90040
323 725-8751

(P-19279)
ALTAMED HEALTH SERVICES CORP (PA)
2040 Camfield Ave, Commerce
(90040-1574)
PHONE..................................323 725-8751
Castulo De La Rocha, *CEO*
Jose U Esparza, *CFO*
Marie S Torres, *Senior VP*
Zoila D Escobar, *Vice Pres*
Laura Ragsdale, *Admin Asst*
EMP: 135
SQ FT: 27,345
SALES: 178.2MM **Privately Held**
WEB: www.altamed.org
SIC: 8011 8099 Gynecologist; pediatrician; radiologist; medical services organization

(P-19280)
ALTAMED HEALTH SERVICES CORP
10418 Valley Blvd Ste B, El Monte
(91731-3600)
PHONE..................................877 462-2582
Juan Esquivez, *Branch Mgr*
EMP: 919
SALES (corp-wide): 178.2MM **Privately Held**
WEB: www.altamed.org
SIC: 8011 Gynecologist
PA: Altamed Health Services Corporation
2040 Camfield Ave
Commerce CA 90040
323 725-8751

(P-19281)
ALTAMED HEALTH SERVICES CORP
Also Called: Indiana Adhc
5425 Pomona Blvd, Los Angeles
(90022-1716)
PHONE..................................323 980-4000
Irma Wisenberg, *Branch Mgr*
EMP: 50

SALES (corp-wide): 178.2MM **Privately Held**
WEB: www.altamed.org
SIC: **8011** 8322 Gynecologist; adult day care center
PA: Altamed Health Services Corporation
2040 Camfield Ave
Commerce CA 90040
323 725-8751

(P-19282)
ALTAMED HEALTH SERVICES CORP
1814 W Lincoln Ave, Anaheim (92801-6730)
PHONE..................................714 780-5690
EMP: 115
SALES (corp-wide): 178.2MM **Privately Held**
SIC: **8011** Gynecologist
PA: Altamed Health Services Corporation
2040 Camfield Ave
Commerce CA 90040
323 725-8751

(P-19283)
ALTURA CENTERS FOR HEALTH
1201 N Cherry St, Tulare (93274-2233)
PHONE..................................559 686-9097
Graciela Soto-Perez, *President*
Dennis Jungwirth, *Executive*
Dawn Wells, *General Mgr*
Amy Azevedo, *Admin Asst*
Manuel Pedroza, *Info Tech Dir*
EMP: 83
SQ FT: 18,000
SALES: 25.6MM **Privately Held**
WEB: www.tchci.com
SIC: **8011** 8021 Clinic, operated by physicians; primary care medical clinic; offices & clinics of dentists

(P-19284)
AMEN CLINICS INC A MED CORP
350 N Wiget Ln Ste 105, Walnut Creek (94598-5960)
PHONE..................................650 416-7830
Daniel G Amen MD, *Owner*
EMP: 50
SALES (est): 1.9MM **Privately Held**
WEB: www.amenclinic.com
SIC: **8011** Psychiatrist

(P-19285)
AMERICAN HEALTH SERVICES LLC
Also Called: Palmdale Med Mental Hlth Svcs
26460 Summit Cir, Santa Clarita (91350-2991)
P.O. Box 801809 (91380-1809)
PHONE..................................661 254-6630
Stan Sharma, *CEO*
Leni Legaspi, *CFO*
Hamir Sinha, *Treasurer*
Sean Sharma, *Vice Pres*
Arlyn Barner, *Admin Sec*
EMP: 110
SALES: 4.9MM **Privately Held**
SIC: **8011** 8361 Offices & clinics of medical doctors; rehabilitation center, residential: health care incidental

(P-19286)
AMIR AHMAD MD
628 California Blvd Ste D, San Luis Obispo (93401-2558)
PHONE..................................805 545-8100
Amir Ahmad, *Owner*
EMP: 80
SALES (est): 825.7K **Privately Held**
SIC: **8011** General & family practice, physician/surgeon

(P-19287)
AMN HEALTHCARE INC (HQ)
12400 High Bluff Dr, San Diego (92130-3077)
PHONE..................................858 792-0711
Susan R Nowakowski, *CEO*
Susan R Salka, *President*
Marcia Faller, *Vice Pres*
Julie Fletcher, *Vice Pres*
Michael Healey, *Vice Pres*
EMP: 168

SALES (est): 249.8MM
SALES (corp-wide): 1.9B **Publicly Held**
WEB: www.amnhealthcare.com
SIC: **8011** Primary care medical clinic
PA: Amn Healthcare Services, Inc.
12400 High Bluff Dr
San Diego CA 92130
866 871-8519

(P-19288)
AMPLA HEALTH
Also Called: Chico Family Health Center
680 Cohasset Rd, Chico (95926-2213)
PHONE..................................530 342-4395
Amalia Bejerano, *Branch Mgr*
EMP: 57
SALES (corp-wide): 50.2MM **Privately Held**
SIC: **8011** Clinic, operated by physicians
PA: Ampla Health
935 Market St
Yuba City CA 95991
530 674-4261

(P-19289)
AMPLA HEALTH
Also Called: Lindhurst Family Health Center
4941 Olivehurst Ave, Olivehurst (95961-4225)
PHONE..................................530 743-4614
Sally Moore, *Branch Mgr*
EMP: 51
SALES (corp-wide): 50.2MM **Privately Held**
SIC: **8011** Health maintenance organization
PA: Ampla Health
935 Market St
Yuba City CA 95991
530 674-4261

(P-19290)
ANAHEIM HARBOR MEDICAL GROUP (PA)
Also Called: Family Urgent Care Center
710 N Euclid St, Anaheim (92801-4122)
PHONE..................................714 533-4511
David L Tsoong MD, *President*
Joseph M Mule MD, *Admin Sec*
Miguel Estrada, *VP Finance*
EMP: 185
SQ FT: 10,000
SALES (est): 8.1MM **Privately Held**
SIC: **8011** Pediatrician; internal medicine, physician/surgeon; orthopedic physician; obstetrician

(P-19291)
ANAHEIM MEDICAL CENTER
1111 W La Palma Ave, Anaheim (92801-2804)
PHONE..................................714 774-1450
Patrick Petre, *Principal*
Cindy Gross, *COO*
Sharon Hoyt, *Lab Dir*
Jeff Deroches, *CIO*
Kathy Doi, *Human Res Dir*
EMP: 62
SALES (est): 6.9MM **Privately Held**
SIC: **8011** Medical centers

(P-19292)
ANAHEIM REGIONAL MEDICAL CTR
Also Called: Ahmc
1111 W La Palma Ave, Anaheim (92801-2804)
PHONE..................................714 999-3847
Patrick Petre, *Branch Mgr*
Sheri Wilhelmi, *Admin Asst*
Joseph Reick, *Project Mgr*
Ricky Eggleston, *Technical Staff*
Lily Hong, *Director*
EMP: 383
SALES (corp-wide): 188.8MM **Privately Held**
SIC: **8011** Medical centers
PA: Anaheim Regional Medical Center
1111 W La Palma Ave
Anaheim CA 92801
714 774-1450

(P-19293)
ANDREW M GOLDEN MD
4647 Zion Ave, San Diego (92120-2507)
PHONE..................................619 528-5342

Andrew Golden, *Principal*
EMP: 51
SALES (est): 4MM **Privately Held**
SIC: **8011** Physicians' office, including specialists

(P-19294)
ANESTHESIA BUSINESS CONS INC
Also Called: Anesthesia Consultants of Cont
1600 Riviera Ave Ste 420, Walnut Creek (94596-7115)
PHONE..................................925 951-1366
Kristina Coster, *Branch Mgr*
Ruth Morton, *Marketing Staff*
Edwin Cheng, *Anesthesiology*
EMP: 80
SALES (corp-wide): 5.1MM **Privately Held**
SIC: **8011** 8741 Anesthesiologist; management services
PA: Anesthesia Business Consultants, Inc.
8905 Sw Nimbus Ave # 300
Beaverton OR 97008
503 372-2740

(P-19295)
ANESTHESIA SERVICE MED GROUP
Also Called: Asmg
3626 Ruffin Rd, San Diego (92123-1810)
P.O. Box 82807 (92138-2807)
PHONE..................................858 277-4767
Peter Raudaskoski, *President*
Thomas R Farrell MD, *President*
EMP: 50
SQ FT: 11,200
SALES (est): 15.7MM **Privately Held**
WEB: www.asmgmd.com
SIC: **8011** Anesthesiologist

(P-19296)
ANKA BEHAVIORAL HEALTH INC
942 Barbara Ln, Pomona (91767-4118)
PHONE..................................909 622-8217
Jacqueline Oyeseso, *Manager*
EMP: 91
SALES (corp-wide): 40.4MM **Privately Held**
SIC: **8011** Group health association
PA: Anka Behavioral Health, Incorporated
1850 Gateway Blvd Ste 900
Concord CA 94520
925 825-4700

(P-19297)
ANNE M KENT MD
500 Superior Ave Ste 310, Newport Beach (92663-3609)
PHONE..................................949 650-7100
Anne Kent, *Principal*
EMP: 60
SALES (est): 307.4K **Privately Held**
SIC: **8011** General & family practice, physician/surgeon

(P-19298)
ANTELOPE VALLEY HOSPITAL INC
1601 W Avenue J Ste 201, Lancaster (93534-2824)
PHONE..................................661 949-1550
Pradeep Damle, *Branch Mgr*
EMP: 56
SALES (corp-wide): 456.8MM **Privately Held**
SIC: **8011** General & family practice, physician/surgeon
PA: Antelope Valley Hospital, Inc.
1600 W Avenue J
Lancaster CA 93534
661 949-5000

(P-19299)
ANTELOPE VALLEY HOSPITAL INC
Ob Clinic
1600 W Avenue J, Lancaster (93534-2894)
PHONE..................................661 726-6180
Vikki Haley, *Principal*
EMP: 167

SALES (corp-wide): 456.8MM **Privately Held**
SIC: **8011** Offices & clinics of medical doctors
PA: Antelope Valley Hospital, Inc.
1600 W Avenue J
Lancaster CA 93534
661 949-5000

(P-19300)
ANTELOPE VALLEY MEDICAL GROUP
44469 10th St W, Lancaster (93534-3324)
PHONE..................................661 945-2783
Karunyan Arul, *Partner*
Donna Acosta, *Manager*
EMP: 50
SALES (est): 1.4MM **Privately Held**
SIC: **8011** Clinic, operated by physicians

(P-19301)
APLA HEALTH & WELLNESS
Also Called: AIDS PROJECT LA
611 S Kingsley Dr, Los Angeles (90005-2319)
PHONE..................................213 201-1546
Craig Thompson, *CEO*
Robyn Goldman, *CFO*
EMP: 56 EST: 2010
SALES: 13.3MM
SALES (corp-wide): 10.3MM **Privately Held**
SIC: **8011** Primary care medical clinic
PA: Aids Project Los Angeles
611 S Kingsley Dr
Los Angeles CA 90005
213 201-1600

(P-19302)
ARBOR MEDICAL GROUP INC (PA)
1502 Marilyn Way, Santa Maria (93454-5945)
PHONE..................................805 614-7591
Gerald Ebner MD, *President*
Margaret Elfering MD, *Vice Pres*
Dennis Shepard MD, *Admin Sec*
EMP: 60
SQ FT: 10,000
SALES (est): 2.2MM **Privately Held**
SIC: **8011** Physicians' office, including specialists

(P-19303)
ARLENE KELLER MD
Also Called: Pacific Interior Medicine
2100 Webster St Ste 423, San Francisco (94115-2380)
PHONE..................................415 923-3598
Arlene Keller, *Principal*
EMP: 50
SALES (est): 1.9MM **Privately Held**
SIC: **8011** General & family practice, physician/surgeon

(P-19304)
ARROYO SECO MEDICAL GROUP (PA)
301 S Fair Oaks Ave # 300, Pasadena (91105-2561)
PHONE..................................626 795-7556
Henry Sideropoulos MD, *President*
Andrew Muller MD, *Vice Pres*
EMP: 65
SQ FT: 9,145
SALES (est): 6.5MM **Privately Held**
WEB: www.arroyoseco.net
SIC: **8011** Internal medicine, physician/surgeon; general & family practice, physician/surgeon

(P-19305)
ARROYO VSTA FMLY HLTH FNDATION (PA)
Also Called: ARROYO VISTA FAMILY HEALTH CEN
6000 N Figueroa St, Los Angeles (90042-4232)
PHONE..................................323 254-5221
Lorraine Estradas, *CEO*
Luisa Fernandez, *Director*
Roger Estrada, *Manager*
Linda Ly, *Manager*
Teresia McCollister, *Manager*
EMP: 160

▲ = Import ▼=Export
◆ =Import/Export

SQ FT: 16,000
SALES: 20.3MM **Privately Held**
SIC: 8011 Primary care medical clinic

(P-19306)
ASIAN HEALTH SERVICES
INC (PA)
270 13th St, Oakland (94612-4801)
PHONE..............................510 986-0601
Sherry Hirota, *Branch Mgr*
EMP: 58
SALES (corp-wide): 42MM **Privately Held**
SIC: 8011 Offices & clinics of medical doctors
PA: Asian Health Services
    101 8th St
    Oakland CA 94607
    510 986-6800

(P-19307)
ASIAN HEALTH SERVICES (PA)
101 8th St, Oakland (94607-4707)
PHONE..............................510 986-6800
Sherry Hirota, *CEO*
Grace Fung, *Executive*
Dong Suh, *Associate Dir*
Daniela Kim, *Director*
Mary Lee, *Manager*
EMP: 147
SQ FT: 30,000
SALES: 42MM **Privately Held**
SIC: 8011 Clinic, operated by physicians

(P-19308)
ASSOCIATED INTERNAL MEDICINE (PA)
350 30th St Ste 320, Oakland
(94609-3425)
PHONE..............................510 465-6700
Dean J Nickles, *President*
▲ EMP: 51
SALES (est): 8.6MM **Privately Held**
WEB: www.aimmg.com
SIC: 8011 Internal medicine, physician/surgeon

(P-19309)
ASSOCIATED PATHOLOGY MED GROUP
1555 Soquel Dr, Santa Cruz (95065-1705)
PHONE..............................831 462-7625
Steve Mc Carthy, *Principal*
EMP: 85
SALES (est): 1.2MM **Privately Held**
SIC: 8011 General & family practice, physician/surgeon

(P-19310)
ASSOCIATED STUDENTS UCLA
Also Called: Ucla Mdcn SC Phrmclgy
650 Chrls Yng S Rm 23 120, Los Angeles
(90095-0001)
PHONE..............................310 825-9451
Michael Phelps, *Principal*
EMP: 800
SALES (corp-wide): 42.7MM **Privately Held**
SIC: 8011 General & family practice, physician/surgeon
PA: Associated Students U.C.L.A.
    308 Westwood Plz
    Los Angeles CA 90095
    310 825-4321

(P-19311)
ASSOCTED GSTRNTRLOGY MED GROUP (PA)
1211 W La Palma Ave, Anaheim
(92801-2815)
PHONE..............................714 778-1300
Michael De Micco MD, *Partner*
Dennis Riff MD, *Partner*
Dennis Riffs, *Pathologist*
EMP: 52
SQ FT: 2,698
SALES (est): 5.4MM **Privately Held**
SIC: 8011 Gastronomist

(P-19312)
AUDREY ADAMS MD
718 University Ave # 211, Los Gatos
(95032-7608)
PHONE..............................408 354-2114
Franklin Chow, *Principal*
Anthony Lin, *Anesthesiology*

EMP: 50
SALES (est): 1.3MM **Privately Held**
SIC: 8011 General & family practice, physician/surgeon

(P-19313)
AXMINSTER MEDICAL GROUP INC (PA)
11539 Hawthorne Blvd Fl 6, Hawthorne
(90250-2325)
PHONE..............................310 670-3255
Raymond Jing MD, *CEO*
Huey-Jer Su MD, *Treasurer*
Spencer H Wenger MD, *Vice Pres*
Stanley E Golden MD, *Admin Sec*
Ron Robinson, *Asst Sec*
EMP: 56
SQ FT: 20,000
SALES (est): 12.2MM **Privately Held**
WEB: www.axminstermedicalgroup.com
SIC: 8011 Internal medicine, physician/surgeon; pediatrician; gynecologist

(P-19314)
BAY AREA PDATRIC MED GROUP INC (PA)
901 Campus Dr Ste 111, Daly City
(94015-4930)
PHONE..............................650 992-4200
James Ferrara MD, *President*
Diane Swabe MD, *Treasurer*
Robert C Zaglin MD, *Vice Pres*
EMP: 70
SQ FT: 1,579
SALES (est): 3MM **Privately Held**
WEB: www.bapmg.com
SIC: 8011 Pediatrician

(P-19315)
BAY AREA SURGICAL MGT LLC
2110 Forest Ave Fl 2, San Jose
(95128-1469)
PHONE..............................408 297-3432
Stephanie Halls,
Katherine Altonaga, *Administration*
Chuck Bonnici, *Business Mgr*
Roy Chua,
Kathy Cardoza, *Receptionist*
EMP: 50
SALES (est): 1.5MM **Privately Held**
SIC: 8011 Surgeon

(P-19316)
BAY IMAGING CONS MED GROUP INC (PA)
175 Lennon Ln Ste 100, Walnut Creek
(94598-2466)
PHONE..............................925 296-7150
Anton C Pogany, *Director*
Keith Tao, *Partner*
Reed Smoller, *Info Tech Dir*
Wendy Patton, *Pediatrics*
Erik Gaensler, *Radiology*
EMP: 85
SQ FT: 4,500
SALES (est): 5.9MM **Privately Held**
SIC: 8011 Radiologist

(P-19317)
BAY MEDICAL MANAGEMENT LLC
2125 Oak Grove Rd Ste 200, Walnut Creek
(94598-2520)
PHONE..............................925 296-7150
Mary Gerard, *Mng Member*
Graciela Paguirigan, *Admin Asst*
Kurtis Kamm, *Technology*
Shannon Wilson, *Marketing Mgr*
Jimmy Cardoza, *Med Doctor*
EMP: 160
SALES (est): 20.9MM **Privately Held**
WEB: www.bmmi.net
SIC: 8011 Radiologist

(P-19318)
BAY VALLEY MEDICAL GROUP INC (PA)
27212 Calaroga Ave, Hayward
(94545-4349)
PHONE..............................510 785-5000
Shelley A Horwitz, *CEO*
Roland J Wong, *Ch of Bd*
Eric S Kohleriter, *President*
Misha Roitshteyn, *Director*
Sheri Task, *Director*

EMP: 93
SQ FT: 28,734
SALES (est): 20.3MM **Privately Held**
WEB: www.bvmed.com
SIC: 8011 Clinic, operated by physicians

(P-19319)
BAYSPRING MEDICAL GROUP A PRO
1199 Bush St Ste 500, San Francisco
(94109-5976)
PHONE..............................415 674-2600
Laurel Dawson, *President*
Marilyn Milkman, *Treasurer*
Susan Rosen, *Vice Pres*
EMP: 50
SALES (est): 3.8MM **Privately Held**
SIC: 8011 General & family practice, physician/surgeon; internal medicine practitioners; obstetrician; gynecologist

(P-19320)
BEAVER MEDICAL CLINIC INC (PA)
1615 Orange Tree Ln, Redlands
(92374-4501)
P.O. Box 10069, San Bernardino (92423-
0069)
PHONE..............................909 793-3311
Robert Klein, *President*
Eric R Fox, *Family Practiti*
James Stewart, *Surgeon*
Paul S Kim, *Anesthesiology*
Jeffrey Lewis, *Anesthesiology*
EMP: 190
SQ FT: 79,212
SALES: 158.4K **Privately Held**
WEB: www.epiclp.com
SIC: 8011 Clinic, operated by physicians

(P-19321)
BEAVER MEDICAL GROUP LP (HQ)
Also Called: Beaver Medical Clinic
7000 Boulder Ave, Highland (92346-3348)
PHONE..............................909 425-3321
John Goodman, *CEO*
James Watson M D, *Partner*
Robert Bourne M D, *Partner*
Robert Rentschler, *Partner*
James Bennett, *MIS Dir*
EMP: 170
SALES (est): 15.7MM **Privately Held**
SIC: 8011 Allergist

(P-19322)
BELVILLE ENTERPRISES INC
Also Called: Ron's Pharmacy Services
6225 Nancy Ridge Dr, San Diego
(92121-2245)
PHONE..............................858 652-6960
Ronald W Belville, *CEO*
EMP: 100
SQ FT: 27,000
SALES (est): 15.5MM **Privately Held**
SIC: 8011 5912 Offices & clinics of medical doctors; drug stores & proprietary stores

(P-19323)
BEVERLY RADIOLOGY MED GROUP (PA)
Also Called: Tower- Imaging Roxanne
465 N Roxbury Dr Ste 101, Beverly Hills
(90210-4230)
PHONE..............................310 975-1500
Howard G Berger MD, *President*
Michael J Krane MD, *Vice Pres*
EMP: 250
SALES (est): 6.4MM **Privately Held**
SIC: 8011 Radiologist

(P-19324)
BORREGO CMNTY HLTH FOUNDATION
2721 Washington, Julian (92036)
P.O. Box 969 (92036-0969)
PHONE..............................760 765-1223
Gina Glenn, *Branch Mgr*
EMP: 265
SALES (corp-wide): 64.3MM **Privately Held**
SIC: 8011 Offices & clinics of medical doctors

PA: Borrego Community Health Foundation
    4343 Yaqui Pass Rd
    Borrego Springs CA 92004
    760 767-5051

(P-19325)
BORREGO CMNTY HLTH FOUNDATION (PA)
Also Called: Borrego Medical Center
4343 Yaqui Pass Rd, Borrego Springs
(92004)
P.O. Box 2369 (92004-2369)
PHONE..............................760 767-5051
Bruce E Smith, *CEO*
Dianna Troncoso, *CFO*
EMP: 140
SQ FT: 8,054
SALES: 64.3MM **Privately Held**
SIC: 8011 Offices & clinics of medical doctors

(P-19326)
BREAST DIAGNOSTIC CENTER
3275 Skypark Dr Ste A, Torrance
(90505-5027)
PHONE..............................310 517-4709
George Gram, *President*
EMP: 50 EST: 2001
SALES (est): 1MM **Privately Held**
SIC: 8011 General & family practice, physician/surgeon

(P-19327)
BRIGHT HEALTH PHYSICIANS (PA)
15725 Whittier Blvd # 500, Whittier
(90603-2350)
PHONE..............................562 947-8478
William H Stimmler MD, *Ch of Bd*
Keith Miyamoto MD, *President*
Don T Eli, *Principal*
Berent Gray MD, *Admin Sec*
EMP: 140
SQ FT: 50,000
SALES (est): 120.5MM **Privately Held**
WEB: www.brightmedical.com
SIC: 8011 Physicians' office, including specialists

(P-19328)
BROOKSIDE COMMUNITY HEALTH CTR
1030 Nevin Ave, Richmond (94801-3122)
PHONE..............................510 215-5001
Norman L Banks, *Director*
EMP: 50
SALES (corp-wide): 7.9MM **Privately Held**
SIC: 8011 Offices & clinics of medical doctors
PA: Brookside Community Health Center
    2023 Vale Rd
    San Pablo CA 94806
    510 215-9092

(P-19329)
BROWN & TOLAND MEDICAL GROUP (PA)
1221 Broadway Ste 700, Oakland
(94612-1898)
P.O. Box 72710 (94612-8910)
PHONE..............................415 972-4162
Joel Klompus, *President*
Deborah Keef, *COO*
Michael Gam, *CFO*
Jackie Bright, *Senior VP*
Nancy Griest, *Senior VP*
EMP: 240
SQ FT: 8,000
SALES (est): 66.6MM **Privately Held**
WEB: www.brownandtoland.com
SIC: 8011 Medical centers

(P-19330)
BROWN & TOLAND MEDICAL GROUP
3905 Sacramento St # 301, San Francisco
(94118-1636)
PHONE..............................415 752-8038
EMP: 148
SALES (corp-wide): 66.6MM **Privately Held**
SIC: 8011 Physicians' office, including specialists

PA: Brown & Toland Medical Group Inc
1221 Broadway Ste 700
Oakland CA 94612
415 972-4162

(P-19331)
BUENA PARK MEDICAL GROUP INC (PA)
6301 Beach Blvd Ste 101, Buena Park (90621-4030)
P.O. Box 277 (90621-0277)
PHONE.............................714 994-5290
Martin Ahn, *CEO*
Edgardo M Gonzalez, *Med Doctor*
Felicia Tran, *Med Doctor*
Bertha Serna, *Manager*
EMP: 100
SQ FT: 20,000
SALES (est): 5.2MM **Privately Held**
SIC: 8011 General & family practice, physician/surgeon

(P-19332)
BUENAVENTURA MEDICAL GROUP (PA)
888 S Hill Rd, Ventura (93003-8400)
PHONE.............................805 477-6000
James Malone, *CEO*
David E Graham, *COO*
David Grahm, *COO*
Kevin Moore, *CFO*
EMP: 350
SQ FT: 27,000
SALES (est): 5.5MM **Privately Held**
SIC: 8011 Clinic, operated by physicians

(P-19333)
BUENAVENTURA MEDICAL GROUP
2601 E Main St Ste 104, Ventura (93003-2801)
PHONE.............................805 477-6220
James Malone, *CEO*
G Dennis Horvath, *Surgeon*
EMP: 100
SALES (corp-wide): 5.5MM **Privately Held**
SIC: 8011 Clinic, operated by physicians
PA: Buenaventura Medical Group Inc
888 S Hill Rd
Ventura CA 93003
805 477-6000

(P-19334)
BUTTE PRIMARY CARE MED GROUP
6585 Clark Rd Ste 200, Paradise (95969-3500)
PHONE.............................530 877-0762
D L Miller MD, *President*
Joseph Lee, *CFO*
Thomas Roth MD, *CFO*
Kenneth Logan MD, *Vice Pres*
Donald Smith MD, *Vice Pres*
EMP: 60
SQ FT: 1,150
SALES (est): 3.1MM **Privately Held**
SIC: 8011 General & family practice, physician/surgeon

(P-19335)
BUTTERWICK DR KIMBERLY JANE MD
9339 Genesee Ave Ste 300, San Diego (92121-2122)
PHONE.............................858 657-1002
Mitchell Goldman, *Owner*
Lillian Wills, *CFO*
EMP: 95
SALES (est): 1.9MM **Privately Held**
SIC: 8011 Physicians' office, including specialists

(P-19336)
C E P
400 N Pepper Ave Ste 107, Colton (92324-1801)
PHONE.............................909 580-1456
Rodney Burger,
EMP: 60
SALES (est): 1.7MM **Privately Held**
SIC: 8011 Offices & clinics of medical doctors

(P-19337)
C/O UC SAN FRANCISCO
1245 16th St Ste 225, Santa Monica (90404-1240)
PHONE.............................310 794-1841
EMP: 92
SALES (corp-wide): 49.8MM **Privately Held**
SIC: 8011 8221 Specialized medical practitioners, except internal; university
PA: C/O Uc San Francisco
1111 Franklin St Fl 12
Oakland CA 94607
858 534-7323

(P-19338)
CALIFORNIA ANESTHESIA ASSO MED
400 N Tustin Ave Ste 400 # 400, Santa Ana (92705-3850)
P.O. Box 3493, Laguna Hills (92654-3493)
PHONE.............................800 888-2186
Kevin Jones, *President*
Alan Ross, *CEO*
EMP: 60
SALES (est): 1.8MM **Privately Held**
SIC: 8011 Anesthesiologist

(P-19339)
CALIFORNIA CANCER ASSCTES
Also Called: Ccare West
7130 N Millbrook Ave, Fresno (93720-3347)
PHONE.............................559 447-4949
Thomas Hackett, *Branch Mgr*
EMP: 80
SALES (corp-wide): 20.7MM **Privately Held**
SIC: 8011 Oncologist; hematologist
PA: California Cancer Associates For Research And Excellence, Inc.
1791 E Fir Ave
Fresno CA 93720
800 456-5860

(P-19340)
CALIFORNIA EYE INSTITUTE
Low Vision Dept St Agnes, Fresno (93720)
PHONE.............................559 449-5000
Kathy Ploszaj, *Administration*
Eye Medical Center, *Shareholder*
Gary R Fogg MD, *Shareholder*
Saint Agnes Hospital, *Shareholder*
Larry R Lawrence MD, *Shareholder*
EMP: 180
SQ FT: 59,000
SALES (est): 9.6MM **Privately Held**
SIC: 8011 Ophthalmologist

(P-19341)
CALIFORNIA FORENSIC MED GROUP
Also Called: CALIFORNIA FORENSIC MEDICAL GROUP INC
200 E Hackett Rd, Modesto (95358-9415)
PHONE.............................209 525-5670
L Cottrel, *Principal*
EMP: 79
SALES (corp-wide): 35.8MM **Privately Held**
SIC: 8011 Primary care medical clinic
PA: California Forensic Medical Group, Incorporated
2511 Garden Rd Ste A160
Monterey CA 93940
831 649-8994

(P-19342)
CALIFORNIA KIDNEY MED GROUP
375 Rolling Oaks Dr # 100, Thousand Oaks (91361-1023)
PHONE.............................805 497-7775
Kant Tucker, *President*
Margie Manwell, *Manager*
EMP: 130
SALES (est): 4.4MM **Privately Held**
SIC: 8011 Offices & clinics of medical doctors

(P-19343)
CALIFRNIA FRNSIC MED GROUP INC
1410 Natividad Rd, Salinas (93906-3102)
PHONE.............................831 755-3886
EMP: 197
SALES (corp-wide): 35.8MM **Privately Held**
SIC: 8011 Primary care medical clinic
PA: California Forensic Medical Group, Incorporated
2511 Garden Rd Ste A160
Monterey CA 93940
831 649-8994

(P-19344)
CALIFRNIA PSYCHTRIC TRNSITIONS
9234n Hinton Ave, Delhi (95315-8200)
P.O. Box 339 (95315-0339)
PHONE.............................209 667-9304
John T Hackett MD, *President*
EMP: 70
SQ FT: 25,000
SALES (est): 4.2MM **Privately Held**
SIC: 8011 Psychiatric clinic

(P-19345)
CAMARENA HEALTH
505 E Almond Ave, Madera (93637-5742)
PHONE.............................559 664-4000
Paulo A Soares, *CEO*
EMP: 86
SALES (corp-wide): 35.7MM **Privately Held**
SIC: 8011 Health maintenance organization
PA: Camarena Health
344 E 6th St
Madera CA 93638
559 664-4000

(P-19346)
CAMARENA HEALTH
49169 Road 426, Oakhurst (93644-8702)
PHONE.............................559 642-6724
Johnny McCrory, *President*
EMP: 86
SALES (corp-wide): 35.7MM **Privately Held**
SIC: 8011 Offices & clinics of medical doctors
PA: Camarena Health
344 E 6th St
Madera CA 93638
559 664-4000

(P-19347)
CARDIC ARITHMIAS
Also Called: Ruder, Michael MD
770 Welch Rd Ste 100, Palo Alto (94304-1505)
PHONE.............................650 617-8100
Michael Ruder, *Partner*
Bruce Benedick, *Med Doctor*
Gregory Engel, *Med Doctor*
Hardwi Mead, *Med Doctor*
Nellis Smith, *Med Doctor*
EMP: 50
SALES (est): 2.2MM **Privately Held**
SIC: 8011 Cardiologist & cardio-vascular specialist

(P-19348)
CARDIOVASCULAR CONSULTANTS HEA
1207 E Herndon Ave, Fresno (93720-3235)
PHONE.............................559 432-4303
Kevin J Boran, *President*
William E Hanks MD, *Treasurer*
Donald Gregory MD, *Admin Sec*
EMP: 67
SQ FT: 17,000
SALES (est): 11.5MM **Privately Held**
SIC: 8011 Cardiologist & cardio-vascular specialist

(P-19349)
CARDIVSCLR MDCL GRP OF STHRN
Also Called: Harold L Karpman MD
414 N Camden Dr Ste 1100, Beverly Hills (90210-4517)
PHONE.............................310 278-3400
Harold L Karpman, *President*
Selvyn B Bleifer MD, *President*
EMP: 50
SALES (est): 952.9K **Privately Held**
SIC: 8011 Cardiologist & cardio-vascular specialist

(P-19350)
CAREMARK RX INC
Also Called: US Family Care
1851 N Riverside Ave, Rialto (92376-8069)
PHONE.............................909 822-1164
Steve Heide, *Administration*
EMP: 70
SALES (corp-wide): 184.7B **Publicly Held**
WEB: www.medpartners.com
SIC: 8011 General & family practice, physician/surgeon; internal medicine, physician/surgeon; obstetrician; gynecologist
HQ: Caremark Rx, Inc.
445 Great Circle Rd
Nashville TN 37228

(P-19351)
CAREMARK RX LLC
Also Called: US Family Care
15576 Main St, Hesperia (92345-3482)
PHONE.............................760 948-6606
Rochelle Steen, *Principal*
EMP: 50
SALES (corp-wide): 184.7B **Publicly Held**
WEB: www.medpartners.com
SIC: 8011 General & family practice, physician/surgeon
HQ: Caremark Rx, Inc.
445 Great Circle Rd
Nashville TN 37228

(P-19352)
CAREMARK RX LLC
Also Called: Mullikin Medical Center
800 Douglas Rd, Stockton (95207-3607)
PHONE.............................209 957-7050
Susan Schofield, *Principal*
EMP: 50
SALES (corp-wide): 184.7B **Publicly Held**
WEB: www.medpartners.com
SIC: 8011
HQ: Caremark Rx, Inc.
445 Great Circle Rd
Nashville TN 37228

(P-19353)
CAREMORE HEALTH PLAN (HQ)
Also Called: Caremore Insurance Services
12900 Park Plaza Dr # 150, Cerritos (90703-9329)
PHONE.............................562 622-2950
Toll Free:.............................888
Leeba R Lessin, *President*
Jason Barker, *President*
John KAO, *President*
Allan Hoops, *CEO*
Vish Sankaran, *COO*
EMP: 81
SALES (est): 38.9MM
SALES (corp-wide): 90B **Publicly Held**
WEB: www.caremore.com
SIC: 8011 6411 Offices & clinics of medical doctors; insurance agents, brokers & service
PA: Anthem, Inc.
120 Monument Cir Ste 200
Indianapolis IN 46204
317 331-1476

(P-19354)
CAREONSITE INC
1805 Arnold Dr, Martinez (94553-4182)
PHONE.............................562 437-0381
EMP: 70
SALES (corp-wide): 12MM **Privately Held**
SIC: 8011 Occupational & industrial specialist, physician/surgeon
PA: Careonsite, Inc.
1250 Pacific Ave
Long Beach CA 90813
562 437-0831

(P-19355)
CAREONSITE INC (PA)
1250 Pacific Ave, Long Beach (90813-3026)
P.O. Box 11389, Carson (90749-1389)
PHONE.............................562 437-0831
Helen Tang, *President*

Brian Tang, *Vice Pres*
Charles B Tang, *Vice Pres*
EMP: 50
SALES: 12MM **Privately Held**
SIC: 8011 Occupational & industrial specialist, physician/surgeon

(P-19356)
CARES COMMUNITY HEALTH
Also Called: Pharmacy At Cares, The
1500 21st St, Sacramento (95811-5216)
PHONE.................916 443-3299
Christy Ward, *CEO*
Richard Soohoo, *Ch of Bd*
Kathleen Marshall, *COO*
Bob Styron, *CFO*
Mark Thomas, *Admin Sec*
EMP: 105
SALES: 22.6MM **Privately Held**
SIC: 8011 8299 Offices & clinics of medical doctors; educational services

(P-19357)
CASSIDY MEDICAL GROUP INC (PA)
145 Thunder Dr, Vista (92083-6010)
PHONE.................760 630-5487
John Bennett, *President*
EMP: 75
SQ FT: 14,495
SALES (est): 5MM **Privately Held**
SIC: 8011 General & family practice, physician/surgeon

(P-19358)
CATHOLIC CHARITIES
2625 Zanker Rd Ste 200, San Jose (95134-2130)
PHONE.................408 468-0100
Connie D Hobson, *Principal*
EMP: 50 **EST:** 2009
SALES (est): 6.3MM **Privately Held**
SIC: 8011 8661 Offices & clinics of medical doctors; Catholic Church

(P-19359)
CEDARS-SINAI MEDICAL CENTER
Also Called: Nephrology
8635 W 3rd St Ste 1195, Los Angeles (90048-6146)
PHONE.................310 824-3664
Larry Froch, *Principal*
Hyung Kim MD, *Assoc Prof*
Elaine Kamil, *Nephrology*
Dechu Puliyanda, *Nephrology*
Robert Frantz, *Cardiovascular*
EMP: 201
SALES (corp-wide): 3.4B **Privately Held**
SIC: 8011 Nephrologist
PA: Cedars-Sinai Medical Center
8700 Beverly Blvd
West Hollywood CA 90048
310 423-3277

(P-19360)
CEDARS-SINAI MEDICAL CENTER
Also Called: Cardiac Noninvasive Laboratory
127 S San Vicente Blvd # 3417, Los Angeles (90048-3311)
PHONE.................310 423-3849
Timothy Henry, *Director*
EMP: 336
SALES (corp-wide): 3.4B **Privately Held**
SIC: 8011 Cardiologist & cardio-vascular specialist
PA: Cedars-Sinai Medical Center
8700 Beverly Blvd
West Hollywood CA 90048
310 423-3277

(P-19361)
CEDARS-SINAI MEDICAL CENTER
8631 W 3rd St Ste 730, Los Angeles (90048-5911)
P.O. Box 48955 (90048-0955)
PHONE.................323 866-8483
Graham Woolf, *Principal*
Steven Edwards, *Manager*
EMP: 5095
SALES (corp-wide): 3.4B **Privately Held**
SIC: 8011 Medical centers

PA: Cedars-Sinai Medical Center
8700 Beverly Blvd
West Hollywood CA 90048
310 423-3277

(P-19362)
CENTER MEDICAL COMPANY
12100 Valley Blvd 109a, El Monte (91732-3100)
P.O. Box 6208 (91734-6208)
PHONE.................626 575-7500
Mohammad Rasekhi, *President*
EMP: 50
SALES (est): 602.9K **Privately Held**
SIC: 8011 Offices & clinics of medical doctors

(P-19363)
CENTRAL ANESTHESIA SERVICE
Also Called: Case Medical Group
3315 Watt Ave, Sacramento (95821-3600)
P.O. Box 660910 (95866-0910)
PHONE.................916 481-6800
David Downs MD, *President*
Vince Isso, *CFO*
Shaunda Barry, *Executive*
Claudia Halkyer, *Hum Res Coord*
Conrad Arnold, *Anesthesiology*
EMP: 80
SALES (est): 12.4MM **Privately Held**
WEB: www.casemedgroup.com
SIC: 8011 Group health association

(P-19364)
CENTRAL CALIFORNIA EAR NOSE
Also Called: Ent Facial Surgery Center
1351 E Spruce Ave, Fresno (93720-3342)
PHONE.................559 432-3724
Marvin Beil MD, *Partner*
Allan Evans MD, *Partner*
Brent Lanier MD, *Partner*
Jerry Moore MD, *Partner*
Oscar Tamez MD, *Partner*
EMP: 50
SQ FT: 24,000
SALES (est): 10.6MM **Privately Held**
SIC: 8011 8049 5999 Eyes, ears, nose & throat specialist: physician/surgeon; audiologist; hearing aids

(P-19365)
CENTRAL CALIFORNIA FACULTY MED (PA)
2625 E Divisadero St, Fresno (93721-1431)
PHONE.................559 453-5200
Karl Van Gundy, *CEO*
Robert A Frediani, *COO*
Randall Stern, *Treasurer*
Joyce Fields-Keene, *Exec Dir*
Jenny Eastman, *Office Mgr*
EMP: 100
SQ FT: 19,053
SALES (est): 54.6MM **Privately Held**
WEB: www.ccfmg.org
SIC: 8011 Medical centers

(P-19366)
CENTRAL CARDIOLOGY MED CLINIC
2901 Sillect Ave Ste 100, Bakersfield (93308-6372)
P.O. Box 1139 (93302-1139)
PHONE.................661 395-0000
Brijesh Bahmbi, *Partner*
Peter Nalos MD, *Partner*
William Nyitray MD, *Partner*
EMP: 120
SALES (est): 23.2MM **Privately Held**
WEB: www.heart24.com
SIC: 8011 Cardiologist & cardio-vascular specialist; medical centers

(P-19367)
CENTRAL VALLEY INDIAN HLTH INC (PA)
2740 Herndon Ave, Clovis (93611-6813)
PHONE.................559 299-2578
Chuck Fowler, *CEO*
Julie Ramsey, *Executive*
Daniel Aguayo, *Exec Dir*
Paul Bains, *Financial Exec*
Gurpal S Bains, *Finance*

PA: Cedars-Sinai Medical Center
8700 Beverly Blvd
West Hollywood CA 90048
310 423-3277

EMP: 74 **EST:** 1974
SQ FT: 14,000
SALES: 18.1MM **Privately Held**
WEB: www.cvih.org
SIC: 8011 8021 8042 8093 Clinic, operated by physicians; dental clinic; offices & clinics of optometrists; substance abuse clinics (outpatient)

(P-19368)
CENTRE CARE MANAGEMENT CO LLC
Also Called: Centre For Health Care
15611 Pomerado Rd Ste 400, Poway (92064-2437)
PHONE.................858 613-6255
Jerome P Brodkin, *Mng Member*
Stephen Shewmake, *Dermatology*
Stuart Graham, *Med Doctor*
Kamen Zakov, *Med Doctor*
David J Carty,
EMP: 200 **EST:** 1997
SALES (est): 8.4MM
SALES (corp-wide): 760.9MM **Privately Held**
SIC: 8011 General & family practice, physician/surgeon
HQ: Arch Health Partners, Inc.
15611 Pomerado Rd Ste 575
Poway CA 92064
858 675-3100

(P-19369)
CENTURY CITY PRIMARY CARE
2080 Century Park E # 1605, Los Angeles (90067-2019)
PHONE.................310 553-3189
Jay S Rudin MD, *Principal*
EMP: 50
SALES (est): 4.8MM **Privately Held**
SIC: 8011 Allergist

(P-19370)
CEP AMERICA LLC
Also Called: Vituity
2100 Powell St Ste 900, Emeryville (94608-1844)
PHONE.................510 350-2691
Theo Koury,
EMP: 90
SALES (est): 4.1MM **Privately Held**
SIC: 8011 Offices & clinics of medical doctors

(P-19371)
CHADWICK CENTER FOR CHILDREN &
3020 Childrens Way, San Diego (92123-4223)
PHONE.................858 966-5814
Charles Wlison, *Principal*
EMP: 50
SALES (est): 2.7MM **Privately Held**
SIC: 8011 Primary care medical clinic

(P-19372)
CHAPA-DE INDIAN HEALTH (PA)
11670 Atwood Rd, Auburn (95603-9522)
PHONE.................530 887-2800
Lisa Davies, *President*
Sierk Haitsma, *CFO*
EMP: 85
SQ FT: 65,000
SALES: 21.2MM **Privately Held**
SIC: 8011 8322 8021 8042 Clinic, operated by physicians; outreach program; multi-service center; dentists' office; orthodontist; offices & clinics of optometrists; dietician

(P-19373)
CHARLIE W SHAEFFER JR MD
Also Called: Eisenhower Desert Crdiolgy Ctr
39000 Bob Hope Dr, Rancho Mirage (92270-3221)
PHONE.................760 346-0642
Charlie Schaeffer MD, *Principal*
Lin Fang, *Cardiology*
Patricia Garcia,
EMP: 61
SALES (est): 2.5MM **Privately Held**
SIC: 8011 General & family practice, physician/surgeon

(P-19374)
CHICO IMMDATE CARE MED CTR INC (PA)
376 Vallombrosa Ave, Chico (95926-3900)
PHONE.................530 891-1676
Bradley M Smith, *CEO*
EMP: 50
SQ FT: 4,000
SALES (est): 7.1MM **Privately Held**
SIC: 8011 Clinic, operated by physicians

(P-19375)
CHILDRENS CLINIC SERVING CHL
701 E 28th St Ste 200, Long Beach (90806-2784)
PHONE.................562 264-4638
Elisa A Nicholas, *CEO*
Jina Lee Lawler, *COO*
Maria Y Chandler, *CFO*
Albert P Ocampo, *CFO*
Knut P Thune, *CFO*
EMP: 320
SQ FT: 24,000
SALES: 30.4MM **Privately Held**
SIC: 8011 Clinic, operated by physicians

(P-19376)
CHILDRENS HEALTHCARE CAL
Also Called: Pediatric Cancer Research
455 S Main St, Orange (92868-3835)
P.O. Box 5700 (92863-5700)
PHONE.................714 997-3000
Kimberly Crite, *CEO*
EMP: 1600 **Privately Held**
SIC: 8011 Pediatrician
PA: Children's Healthcare Of California
1201 W La Veta Ave
Orange CA 92868

(P-19377)
CHILDRENS HOSPITAL LOS (PA)
Also Called: Childrens Hosp La Med Group
6430 W Sunset Blvd # 600, Los Angeles (90028-7909)
PHONE.................323 361-2336
Robert Adler, *President*
Teresa Avila, *Manager*
EMP: 100
SQ FT: 10,000
SALES: 140MM **Privately Held**
SIC: 8011 Pediatrician

(P-19378)
CHILDRENS HOSPITAL LOS ANGELES
Also Called: Santa Monica Outpatient Center
1301 20th St Ste 460, Santa Monica (90404-2090)
PHONE.................310 820-8608
Ronald J Gowey, *President*
EMP: 155
SALES (corp-wide): 1B **Privately Held**
SIC: 8011 Pediatrician
PA: The Childrens Hospital Los Angeles
4650 W Sunset Blvd
Los Angeles CA 90027
323 660-2450

(P-19379)
CHILDRENS HOSPITAL LOS ANGELES
Also Called: Division of Rheumatology
4650 W Sunset Blvd, Los Angeles (90027-6062)
PHONE.................323 361-2119
Andreas O Reiff, *Principal*
Matthew Keefer, *Med Doctor*
EMP: 341
SALES (corp-wide): 1B **Privately Held**
SIC: 8011 Pediatrician
PA: The Childrens Hospital Los Angeles
4650 W Sunset Blvd
Los Angeles CA 90027
323 660-2450

(P-19380)
CHILDRENS SPECIALIST OF SAN D (PA)
Also Called: Childrens Associated Med Group
3020 Childrens Way, San Diego (92123-4223)
PHONE.................858 576-1700

**P
R
O
D
U
C
T
S
&
S
V
C
S**

Michael Segall MD, *President*
Yvonne Gagen, *Finance*
Elizabeth Yu, *Gastroenterlgy*
Allison Dickinson, *Med Doctor*
Laura Barba, *Nurse Practr*
EMP: 352
SALES: 283.3K **Privately Held**
SIC: 8011 Offices & clinics of medical doctors

(P-19381)
CHINO MEDICAL GROUP INC
5475 Walnut Ave, Chino (91710-2699)
PHONE..............................909 591-6446
J A Lira MD, *President*
Fidel F Pinzon MD, *Vice Pres*
Steven Pulverman, *Vice Pres*
Jeffrey R Unger MD, *Vice Pres*
EMP: 100
SQ FT: 36,000
SALES (est): 14.3MM **Privately Held**
WEB: www.chinomedicalgroup.com
SIC: 8011 8031 Clinic, operated by physicians; offices & clinics of osteopathic physicians

(P-19382)
CIRRUS HEALTH II LP
Also Called: Laguna Hills Surgery Center
24331 El Toro Rd Ste 150, Laguna Hills (92637-8818)
PHONE..............................949 855-0562
Kim Wood, *Principal*
EMP: 113
SALES (corp-wide): 12.1MM **Privately Held**
WEB: www.cirrushealth.com
SIC: 8011 Offices & clinics of medical doctors
PA: Cirrus Health Ii, L.P.
2800 E Highway 114 # 300
Trophy Club TX 76262
214 217-0100

(P-19383)
CITRUS VLY HLTH PARTNERS INC
Also Called: Queen of The Valley Campus
1115 S Sunset Ave, West Covina (91790-3940)
PHONE..............................626 962-4011
Debbie Segaram, *Branch Mgr*
EMP: 376 **Privately Held**
SIC: 8011 Medical centers
PA: Citrus Valley Health Partners, Inc.
210 W San Bernardino Rd
Covina CA 91723

(P-19384)
CLINICA MEDICA FAMILIAR
517 N Main St Ste 100, Santa Ana (92701-4684)
PHONE..............................714 541-0870
Ricardo Limon MD, *President*
EMP: 100
SALES (est): 8.9MM **Privately Held**
SIC: 8011 Primary care medical clinic

(P-19385)
CLINICA MSR OSCAR A ROMERO (PA)
123 S Alvarado St, Los Angeles (90057-2201)
PHONE..............................213 989-7700
Carlos Antonio H Vaquerano, *President*
Harsh Gupta, *CFO*
Pablo F Lopez, *Treasurer*
Marcello Villagomez, *Vice Pres*
Jonathan Miranda Canas C, *Admin Sec*
EMP: 52
SALES: 13.6MM **Privately Held**
WEB: www.clinicaromero.com
SIC: 8011 Clinic, operated by physicians

(P-19386)
CLINICA POPULAR MEDICAL GROUP
101 S Rossmore Ave, Los Angeles (90004-3736)
PHONE..............................213 381-7175
Daniel Berdakin MD, *President*
EMP: 50 **EST:** 1977
SQ FT: 7,000

SALES (est): 1.6MM **Privately Held**
SIC: 8011 General & family practice, physician/surgeon

(P-19387)
CLINICA SAGRADO CORAZON
831 S Harbor Blvd, Anaheim (92805-5157)
PHONE..............................714 491-7777
Ivone Alfaro, *Principal*
EMP: 50 **EST:** 2011
SALES (est): 713K **Privately Held**
SIC: 8011 Offices & clinics of medical doctors

(P-19388)
CLINICA SIERRA VISTA (PA)
Also Called: KERN RIVER HEALTH CENTER
1430 Truxtun Ave Ste 400, Bakersfield (93301-5220)
P.O. Box 1559 (93302-1559)
PHONE..............................661 635-3050
Matthew Clark, *Ch of Bd*
Christine Goltz, *COO*
Christine Pence, *COO*
Consuelo E Cantu, *CFO*
Consuelo Contu, *CFO*
EMP: 90 **EST:** 1971
SQ FT: 14,599
SALES: 136.6MM **Privately Held**
WEB: www.clinicasierravista.org
SIC: 8011 Clinic, operated by physicians

(P-19389)
CLINICA SIERRA VISTA
7202 N Millbrook Ave, Fresno (93720-3341)
PHONE..............................559 457-5292
Stephen W Schilling, *Branch Mgr*
EMP: 74
SALES (corp-wide): 136.6MM **Privately Held**
SIC: 8011 Clinic, operated by physicians
PA: Clinica Sierra Vista
1430 Truxtun Ave Ste 400
Bakersfield CA 93301
661 635-3050

(P-19390)
CLINICAS DE SLUD DEL PEBLO INC (PA)
1166 K St, Brawley (92227-2737)
P.O. Box 1279 (92227-1279)
PHONE..............................760 344-9951
Yvonne Bell, *CEO*
Gloria Santillan, *CFO*
Josie Godinez, *Administration*
Felix Leon, *Administration*
Marlene Romero, *Business Mgr*
EMP: 62 **EST:** 1970
SQ FT: 15,251
SALES: 39.6MM **Privately Held**
WEB: www.clinicasdesalud.com
SIC: 8011 8049 Clinic, operated by physicians; gynecologist; nutrition specialist; dental hygienist

(P-19391)
CLINICAS DE SLUD DEL PEBLO INC
Also Called: Betty Jimenez
900 Main St, Brawley (92227-2630)
PHONE..............................760 344-6471
Betty Jimenez, *Branch Mgr*
EMP: 55
SALES (corp-wide): 39.6MM **Privately Held**
WEB: www.clinicasdesalud.com
SIC: 8011 8049 Clinic, operated by physicians; gynecologist; nutrition specialist; dental hygienist
PA: Clinicas De Salud Del Pueblo, Inc.
1166 K St
Brawley CA 92227
760 344-9951

(P-19392)
CO D L PHAM MD
Also Called: Bolsa Medical Group
10362 Bolsa Ave Ste 110, Westminster (92683-6763)
PHONE..............................714 531-2091
Co L Pham MD, *President*
Tuan V Pham, *Family Practiti*
EMP: 50
SALES (est): 7.2MM **Privately Held**
SIC: 8011 Gynecologist

(P-19393)
COASTAL RADIATION ONCOLOGY MED
1240 S Westlake Blvd, Westlake Village (91361-1929)
PHONE..............................805 494-4483
Kimberly Commins, *Director*
Lauren Lovett, *Director*
EMP: 99
SALES (est): 458.8K **Privately Held**
SIC: 8011 Offices & clinics of medical doctors

(P-19394)
COLORADO RIVER MEDICAL CENTER
1401 Bailey Ave, Needles (92363-3198)
PHONE..............................760 326-4531
Steve Lopez, *CEO*
Knaya Tabora, *COO*
Ron Chieffo, *Programmer Anys*
Pam Barrett, *Human Res Dir*
Mary Smith, *Human Res Dir*
EMP: 100
SQ FT: 46,000
SALES: 9.7MM **Privately Held**
SIC: 8011 8062 Clinic, operated by physicians; general medical & surgical hospitals

(P-19395)
COMMUNICARE HEALTH CENTERS
2051 John Jones Rd, Davis (95616-9701)
P.O. Box 1260 (95617-1260)
PHONE..............................530 758-2060
Robin Affrime, *CEO*
Sherry Cauchois, *CFO*
EMP: 200
SALES: 22.9MM **Privately Held**
SIC: 8011 Clinic, operated by physicians

(P-19396)
COMMUNITY HEALTH CENTERS (PA)
150 Tejas Pl, Nipomo (93444-9123)
P.O. Box 430 (93444-0430)
PHONE..............................805 929-3211
Sharon Smith, *CEO*
Denise Stewart, *COO*
Bob Lotwala, *CFO*
Ronald Castle, *Exec Dir*
Erica Guijarro, *Office Mgr*
EMP: 135
SQ FT: 10,000
SALES (est): 22.6MM **Privately Held**
SIC: 8011 8021 Clinic, operated by physicians; dental clinic

(P-19397)
COMMUNITY HEALTH GROUP
2420 Fenton St Ste 100, Chula Vista (91914-3516)
PHONE..............................800 224-7766
Norma A Diaz, *CEO*
Ann Warren, *COO*
William Rice, *CFO*
Patricia Urbina, *Executive*
Arianna Reyna, *Info Tech Mgr*
EMP: 140
SQ FT: 26,000
SALES: 52.1MM **Privately Held**
WEB: www.communityhealthgroup.com
SIC: 8011 Health maintenance organization

(P-19398)
COMMUNITY HEALTH SYSTEMS INC
Also Called: Moreno Valley Family Hlth Ctr
22675 Alessandro Blvd # 1, Moreno Valley (92553-8551)
PHONE..............................951 571-2300
Lori Holeman, *CEO*
Raeisha George, *Human Resources*
Eric Grover, *Family Practiti*
Yolanda Gomez, *Director*
EMP: 130
SALES: 20.8MM **Privately Held**
SIC: 8011 Primary care medical clinic

(P-19399)
COMMUNITY MED GROUP OF RVRSIDE
4444 Magnolia Ave, Riverside (92501-4136)
PHONE..............................951 274-3414
Thomas W Jackson, *President*
Prabu U Dhalla MD, *Vice Pres*
Larry G Ding, *Vice Pres*
Christophe Fleming MD, *Vice Pres*
Thomas Jackson MD, *Vice Pres*
EMP: 106
SQ FT: 27,000
SALES (est): 12MM **Privately Held**
WEB: www.comgri.com
SIC: 8011 Orthopedic physician

(P-19400)
COMMUNITY MEDICAL CENTERS INC
Also Called: Channel Medical Center
701 E Channel St, Stockton (95202-2628)
P.O. Box 779 (95201-0779)
PHONE..............................209 944-4700
Alice Souligen, *Manager*
EMP: 100
SALES (corp-wide): 44.6MM **Privately Held**
SIC: 8011 Medical centers
PA: Community Medical Centers Inc
7210 Murray Dr
Stockton CA 95210
209 373-2800

(P-19401)
COMMUNITY ORTHOPEDIC MEDICAL
26401 Crown Valley Pkwy # 101, Mission Viejo (92691-6302)
PHONE..............................949 348-4000
Kent Adamson, *President*
Sherri Casillas, *Admin Sec*
Edmund Evangelista, *VP Opers*
EMP: 63
SALES (est): 10.1MM **Privately Held**
WEB: www.comg.com
SIC: 8011 Orthopedic physician

(P-19402)
COMPREHENSIVE CMNTY HLTH CTR
5059 York Blvd, Los Angeles (90042-1713)
PHONE..............................323 344-4144
EMP: 50
SALES (est): 78K **Privately Held**
SIC: 8011

(P-19403)
CONGRESS MED SURGERY CTR LLC
800 S Raymond Ave, Pasadena (91105-3229)
PHONE..............................626 396-8100
James A Shankwiler, *President*
Gregory J Adamson,
EMP: 100
SALES (est): 1.4MM **Privately Held**
SIC: 8011 Ambulatory surgical center

(P-19404)
CONRAD A COX
Also Called: Caremore Medical Group
9040 Telegraph Rd, Downey (90240-2393)
PHONE..............................562 927-0033
Conrad A Cox, *Owner*
EMP: 50
SALES (est): 3MM **Privately Held**
SIC: 8011 Gastronomist

(P-19405)
COPTIC CLINICS
3803 W Mission Blvd, Pomona (91766-6823)
PHONE..............................562 900-2692
Henry Kirolos, *Director*
Bishop Serapion, *Exec Dir*
EMP: 99
SALES (est): 1.7MM **Privately Held**
SIC: 8011 8021 Offices & clinics of medical doctors; specialized dental practitioners

(P-19406)
CORIZON HEALTH INC
5325 Broder Blvd, Dublin (94568-3309)
PHONE..............................925 551-6500
Nomali Toman, *Principal*
EMP: 105
SALES (corp-wide): 398.2MM **Privately Held**
SIC: **8011** Dispensery, operated by physicians
HQ: Corizon Health, Inc.
   103 Powell Ct
   Brentwood TN 37027
   800 729-0069

(P-19407)
COUNTY OF ALAMEDA
Also Called: Alameda, County Medical Center
2060 Fairmont Dr, San Leandro (94578-1001)
PHONE..............................510 481-4141
Robert Jones, *Director*
Satira A Dalton, *Director*
EMP: 220 **Privately Held**
WEB: www.co.alameda.ca.us
SIC: **8011** 9431 8361 8093 Psychiatric clinic; mental health agency administration, government; ; residential care; specialty outpatient clinics; psychiatric hospitals
PA: County Of Alameda
   1221 Oak St Ste 555
   Oakland CA 94612
   510 272-6691

(P-19408)
COUNTY OF KERN
Also Called: Admin
1721 Westwind Dr, Bakersfield (93301-3026)
PHONE..............................661 868-8360
Carol Bowman, *Principal*
EMP: 50 **Privately Held**
WEB: www.kccfc.org
SIC: **8011** 9111 Medical centers; county supervisors' & executives' offices
PA: County Of Kern
   1115 Truxtun Ave Rm 505
   Bakersfield CA 93301
   661 868-3690

(P-19409)
COUNTY OF LOS ANGELES
1212 Pico St, San Fernando (91340-3503)
PHONE..............................818 837-6969
Gretchen McGinley, *Principal*
EMP: 123 **Privately Held**
WEB: www.co.la.ca.us
SIC: **8011** 9111 Clinic, operated by physicians; executive offices
PA: County Of Los Angeles
   500 W Temple St Ste 437
   Los Angeles CA 90012
   213 974-1101

(P-19410)
COUNTY OF LOS ANGELES
Also Called: L A County Hospital
1000 W Carson St, Torrance (90502-2004)
PHONE..............................310 222-4220
EMP: 119 **Privately Held**
SIC: **8011** Medical centers
PA: County Of Los Angeles
   500 W Temple St Ste 437
   Los Angeles CA 90012
   213 974-1101

(P-19411)
COUNTY OF LOS ANGELES
Also Called: Health Services, Dept of
1200 N State St, Los Angeles (90033-1029)
PHONE..............................323 226-6221
Vernessa Fountin, *Manager*
Virgina Perz, *CFO*
Victoriano Del Fierro, *IT/INT Sup*
Andy Lin, *Technology*
Arthur Stepanyan, *Analyst*
EMP: 300 **Privately Held**
WEB: www.co.la.ca.us
SIC: **8011** 9431 Medical centers;
PA: County Of Los Angeles
   500 W Temple St Ste 437
   Los Angeles CA 90012
   213 974-1101

(P-19412)
COUNTY OF LOS ANGELES
Also Called: Hudson, H Claude Cmplte Hlth
2829 S Grand Ave, Los Angeles (90007-3304)
PHONE..............................213 744-3677
Michael Mills, *Administration*
EMP: 300 **Privately Held**
WEB: www.co.la.ca.us
SIC: **8011** 9431 8093 Medical centers; administration of public health programs; ; specialty outpatient clinics
PA: County Of Los Angeles
   500 W Temple St Ste 437
   Los Angeles CA 90012
   213 974-1101

(P-19413)
COUNTY OF LOS ANGELES
Also Called: HI Desert Hospital
335 E Avenue I, Lancaster (93535-1916)
PHONE..............................661 948-8581
Abueg Isagani, *Owner*
EMP: 600 **Privately Held**
WEB: www.co.la.ca.us
SIC: **8011** 9431 Medical centers; administration of public health programs;
PA: County Of Los Angeles
   500 W Temple St Ste 437
   Los Angeles CA 90012
   213 974-1101

(P-19414)
COUNTY OF LOS ANGELES
Also Called: Health Services, Dept of
1325 Broad Ave, Wilmington (90744-2604)
PHONE..............................310 518-8800
Dr Jesus Gutierrez, *Director*
EMP: 52 **Privately Held**
WEB: www.co.la.ca.us
SIC: **8011** 9431 Offices & clinics of medical doctors; administration of public health programs;
PA: County Of Los Angeles
   500 W Temple St Ste 437
   Los Angeles CA 90012
   213 974-1101

(P-19415)
COUNTY OF LOS ANGELES
Also Called: Los Angeles County
13300 Van Nuys Blvd, Pacoima (91331-3004)
PHONE..............................818 896-1903
Miriam Sanchez, *Administration*
EMP: 123
SQ FT: 47,532 **Privately Held**
SIC: **8011** Clinic, operated by physicians
PA: County Of Los Angeles
   500 W Temple St Ste 437
   Los Angeles CA 90012
   213 974-1101

(P-19416)
COUNTY OF LOS ANGELES
Also Called: Mental Health Dept of
2600 Redondo Ave 3, Long Beach (90806-2325)
PHONE..............................562 599-9200
Margie Pappas, *Chief*
EMP: 123 **Privately Held**
WEB: www.co.la.ca.us
SIC: **8011** 9431 Offices & clinics of medical doctors; administration of public health programs;
PA: County Of Los Angeles
   500 W Temple St Ste 437
   Los Angeles CA 90012
   213 974-1101

(P-19417)
COUNTY OF MONTEREY
Also Called: Alisal Health Center
559 E Alisal St Ste 201, Salinas (93905-2516)
PHONE..............................831 769-8800
Len Foster, *Director*
EMP: 50 **Privately Held**
WEB: www.montereycountyfarmbureau.org
SIC: **8011** Offices & clinics of medical doctors
PA: County Of Monterey
   168 W Alisal St Fl 2
   Salinas CA 93901
   831 755-5040

(P-19418)
COUNTY OF RIVERSIDE
Also Called: Rubidoux Family Care Center
5256 Mission Blvd, Riverside (92509-4624)
PHONE..............................951 955-0840
Koen Brown, *Exec Dir*
EMP: 84 **Privately Held**
SIC: **8011** Offices & clinics of medical doctors
PA: County Of Riverside
   4080 Lemon St Fl 11
   Riverside CA 92501
   951 955-1110

(P-19419)
COUNTY OF RIVERSIDE
Also Called: Public Social Services
26520 Cactus Ave, Moreno Valley (92555-3927)
PHONE..............................951 486-4000
Donna Matney, *Administration*
EMP: 84 **Privately Held**
SIC: **8011** 9431 Medical centers; mental health agency administration, government;
PA: County Of Riverside
   4080 Lemon St Fl 11
   Riverside CA 92501
   951 955-1110

(P-19420)
COUNTY OF RIVERSIDE
Also Called: Community Health Agency
7140 Indiana Ave, Riverside (92504-4544)
PHONE..............................951 358-6000
Ibrahim Sumarli, *Med Doctor*
Peter Lee, *Associate Dir*
Jessica Orona, *Human Resources*
EMP: 84
SQ FT: 1,276 **Privately Held**
SIC: **8011** 9431 Clinic, operated by physicians; administration of public health programs;
PA: County Of Riverside
   4080 Lemon St Fl 11
   Riverside CA 92501
   951 955-1110

(P-19421)
COUNTY OF RIVERSIDE
Also Called: Community Health Agency
26520 Cactus Ave, Moreno Valley (92555-3927)
PHONE..............................951 486-4000
Jim Watkins, *Principal*
Carol Young, *Admin Sec*
Adolfo Aguilera, *Director*
EMP: 300 **Privately Held**
SIC: **8011** 9431 Medical centers; public health agency administration, government
PA: County Of Riverside
   4080 Lemon St Fl 11
   Riverside CA 92501
   951 955-1110

(P-19422)
COUNTY OF RIVERSIDE
Also Called: Indio Family Care Center
47923 Oasis St Ste A, Indio (92201-9788)
PHONE..............................760 863-8283
Koen Brown, *Exec Dir*
Raymond Kramer, *Family Practiti*
EMP: 84 **Privately Held**
SIC: **8011** Clinic, operated by physicians
PA: County Of Riverside
   4080 Lemon St Fl 11
   Riverside CA 92501
   951 955-1110

(P-19423)
CRIPTS HEALTH CARE
10666 N Torrey Pines Rd, La Jolla (92037-1027)
PHONE..............................858 554-8646
Hubert Greenway MD, *Director*
EMP: 50
SALES (est): 823.2K **Privately Held**
SIC: **8011** Physicians' office, including specialists

(P-19424)
CYPRESS CTR FOR FMLY MEDICINE
10601 Walker St Ste 250, Cypress (90630-4733)
PHONE..............................562 799-4801

Franklin Lowe, *President*
Scott Brunner, *Vice Pres*
Sharon Cooper, *Office Mgr*
Bethany Gray, *Med Doctor*
Jennifer Salsameda, *Nurse*
EMP: 90
SQ FT: 4,200
SALES (est): 6.1MM **Privately Held**
SIC: **8011** Primary care medical clinic; general & family practice, physician/surgeon

(P-19425)
CYPRESS HALTHCARE PARTNERS LLC (PA)
100 Wilson Rd Ste 100 # 100, Monterey (93940-7885)
PHONE..............................831 649-1000
Michael K McMillan,
Anil Melwani, *Technology*
Siomara Barajas, *Accountant*
William Hines,
Clayton Howard, *Manager*
EMP: 250
SQ FT: 8,500
SALES (est): 22.6MM **Privately Held**
WEB: www.doctorsonduty.com
SIC: **8011** Offices & clinics of medical doctors

(P-19426)
DANIEL O MONGIANO MD A PR
Also Called: AV Occupational Medicine
42220 10th St W Ste 109, Lancaster (93534-7075)
PHONE..............................661 951-9195
Daniel Mongiano, *President*
EMP: 50
SALES (est): 3.8MM **Privately Held**
WEB: www.avoccmed.com
SIC: **8011** Physicians' office, including specialists

(P-19427)
DAVID CIVALIER MD INC
Also Called: Redding Medical Group
2510 Airpark Dr Ste 104, Redding (96001-2461)
PHONE..............................530 244-4034
David Civalier MD, *President*
EMP: 50
SALES (est): 4.1MM **Privately Held**
SIC: **8011** General & family practice, physician/surgeon

(P-19428)
DAVIS COMMUNITY CLINIC (PA)
Also Called: Davis Cmnty Clnic Dntl Program
2040 Sutter Pl, Davis (95616-6201)
P.O. Box 1260 (95617-1260)
PHONE..............................530 758-2060
Sherry Cauchois, *Exec Dir*
EMP: 100
SQ FT: 5,000
SALES (est): 4.7MM **Privately Held**
SIC: **8011** Clinic, operated by physicians

(P-19429)
DAVITA MAGAN MANAGEMENT INC (DH)
Also Called: M M C
420 W Rowland St, Covina (91723-2943)
PHONE..............................626 331-6411
Bradley J Rosenberg, *Principal*
Connie Solorza, *Division VP*
Howard Ort MD, *Exec VP*
Miguel Garcia, *Vice Pres*
Tommie Anderson, *Executive*
EMP: 250
SQ FT: 66,000
SALES (est): 32.3MM **Publicly Held**
WEB: www.maganclinic.com
SIC: **8011** Clinic, operated by physicians; urologist; internal medicine, physician/surgeon; ophthalmologist

(P-19430)
DAVITA MAGAN MANAGEMENT INC
330 W Covina Blvd, San Dimas (91773)
PHONE..............................909 592-9712
Beth Nunn, *Human Resources*
EMP: 91 **Publicly Held**
WEB: www.maganclinic.com
SIC: **8011** 8071 Clinic, operated by physicians; medical laboratories

PRODUCTS & SVCS

HQ: Davita Magan Management, Inc.
420 W Rowland St
Covina CA 91723
626 331-6411

(P-19431)
DAVITA MEDICAL MANAGEMENT LLC
Also Called: Healthcare Partners Med Group
2601 Via Campo, Montebello (90640-1807)
PHONE.............................323 720-1144
Sonia Flores, *Branch Mgr*
Maribeth A Ching, *Family Practiti*
Calvin Eng, *Med Doctor*
Allison Taylor, *Manager*
EMP: 100 **Publicly Held**
WEB: www.davidv.com
SIC: **8011** Clinic, operated by physicians
HQ: Davita Medical Management, Llc
2175 Park Pl
El Segundo CA 90245

(P-19432)
DAVITA MEDICAL MANAGEMENT LLC
Also Called: Healthcare Partners Med Group
3144 Santa Anita Ave # 201, El Monte
(91733-1316)
PHONE.............................626 444-0333
Joseph Soto, *Branch Mgr*
Rosalinda Macias, *Admin Sec*
Angelina Espinoza, *Manager*
EMP: 60 **Publicly Held**
WEB: www.davidv.com
SIC: **8011** Clinic, operated by physicians
HQ: Davita Medical Management, Llc
2175 Park Pl
El Segundo CA 90245

(P-19433)
DAVITA MEDICAL MANAGEMENT LLC (HQ)
Also Called: Healthcare Partners Med Group
2175 Park Pl, El Segundo (90245-4705)
PHONE.............................310 354-4200
Robert J Margolis, *CEO*
Marianne Garrity, *President*
Matthew Mazdyasni, *Exec VP*
Paula De Almeida, *Vice Pres*
Suzanne Hansen, *Vice Pres*
EMP: 600
SQ FT: 38,000
SALES (est): 399.7MM **Publicly Held**
WEB: www.davidv.com
SIC: **8011** Group health association

(P-19434)
DEL PUERTO HEALTH CARE DST
Also Called: Del Puerto Health Center
875 E St, Patterson (95363-2670)
P.O. Box 187 (95363-0187)
PHONE.............................209 892-9100
Margo Arnold, *Administration*
Ursula Schroyer, *Human Res Dir*
Jake Schulke, *Education*
Yumi Edwards, *Manager*
EMP: 55
SQ FT: 25,000
SALES (est): 9.3MM **Privately Held**
SIC: **8011** Medical centers

(P-19435)
DESERT CARDIOLOGY CONSULTANTS
Also Called: Desert Cardiology Cons Med G
39000 Bob Hope Dr, Rancho Mirage
(92270-3221)
PHONE.............................760 346-0642
Keenan F Barber MD, *Vice Pres*
Barry Hackshaw, *President*
Merle R Bolton, *Treasurer*
John Nelson, *Officer*
Andrew Frutkin, *Managing Dir*
EMP: 70
SALES (est): 6.6MM **Privately Held**
WEB: www.desertcard.com
SIC: **8011** Internal medicine practitioners;
cardiologist & cardio-vascular specialist;
surgeon

(P-19436)
DESERT MEDICAL GROUP INC (PA)
Also Called: Desert Oasis Healthcare
275 N El Cielo Rd D-402, Palm Springs
(92262-6972)
PHONE.............................760 320-8814
Richard E Merkin MD, *President*
Mark Grant, *Vice Pres*
Tom Rancilio, *Director*
Kristi Vaughn, *Manager*
Yolanda Diaz, *Receptionist Se*
EMP: 240
SQ FT: 13,000
SALES (est): 43.2MM **Privately Held**
WEB: www.oasisipa.com
SIC: **8011** General & family practice, physi-
cian/surgeon; freestanding emergency
medical center

(P-19437)
DESERT MEDICAL GROUP INC
Also Called: Oasis IPA
275 N El Cielo Rd Ste C, Palm Springs
(92262-6972)
PHONE.............................760 323-8657
Tammy Torres, *Manager*
EMP: 250
SALES (corp-wide): 43.2MM **Privately
Held**
WEB: www.oasisipa.com
SIC: **8011** General & family practice, physi-
cian/surgeon
PA: Desert Medical Group, Inc.
275 N El Cielo Rd D-402
Palm Springs CA 92262
760 320-8814

(P-19438)
DESERT ORTHOPDC CENTER A MDCL (PA)
39000 Bob Hope Dr W301, Rancho Mirage
(92270-3221)
PHONE.............................760 568-2684
Ronald Lamb MD, *President*
Robert Murphy MD, *Ch of Bd*
Stephen O Connell MD, *CFO*
James Bell MD, *Vice Pres*
David Friscia, *Vice Pres*
EMP: 98
SQ FT: 23,000
SALES (est): 9.9MM **Privately Held**
SIC: **8011** Orthopedic physician

(P-19439)
DESERT VALLEY MED GROUP INC
12401 Hesperia Rd Ste 9, Victorville
(92395-5844)
PHONE.............................760 245-2474
Paula Perez, *Manager*
EMP: 68
SALES (corp-wide): 51.6MM **Privately
Held**
SIC: **8011** Orthopedic physician
PA: Desert Valley Medical Group, Inc.
16850 Bear Valley Rd
Victorville CA 92395
760 241-8000

(P-19440)
DESERT VALLEY MED GROUP INC (PA)
16850 Bear Valley Rd, Victorville
(92395-5794)
PHONE.............................760 241-8000
Prem Reddy MD, *CEO*
Lex Reddy, *President*
M Mansukhani, *CFO*
Diane Van Velkinburg, *Project Mgr*
Donald W Herrmann, *Med Doctor*
EMP: 300
SQ FT: 15,000
SALES (est): 51.6MM **Privately Held**
WEB: www.dvmc.com
SIC: **8011** Physicians' office, including spe-
cialists

(P-19441)
DIAGNOSTIC AND INTERVENTIO
13160 Mindanao Way # 150, Marina Del
Rey (90292-6358)
PHONE.............................310 574-0400
Robert S Bray Jr, *President*
Keren Reiter, *COO*

Ofelia David, *Accounting Mgr*
EMP: 100
SALES: 35MM **Privately Held**
SIC: **8011** Surgeon

(P-19442)
DIGNITY HEALTH
8120 Timberlake Way # 201, Sacramento
(95823-5412)
PHONE.............................916 667-0000
Daniel Yuen, *Principal*
Ann Engwer, *Program Mgr*
Brent Keane, *Director*
EMP: 193
SALES (corp-wide): 6.7B **Privately Held**
WEB: www.chw.edu
SIC: **8011** Clinic, operated by physicians
PA: Dignity Health
185 Berry St Ste 300
San Francisco CA 94107
415 438-5500

(P-19443)
DIGNITY HEALTH
Also Called: James A Kiley MD
1600 Creekside Dr # 3700, Folsom
(95630-3444)
PHONE.............................916 983-7988
James Kiley, *Partner*
EMP: 60
SALES (corp-wide): 6.7B **Privately Held**
WEB: www.mercycare.net
SIC: **8011** Offices & clinics of medical doc-
tors
PA: Dignity Health
185 Berry St Ste 300
San Francisco CA 94107
415 438-5500

(P-19444)
DIGNITY HEALTH
Also Called: Emergency Physicians Med
Group
8350 Auburn Blvd Ste 200, Citrus Heights
(95610-0396)
PHONE.............................916 536-2420
Art B Wong MD, *Branch Mgr*
Christine Braid, *Family Practiti*
Jennifer Fisher, *Hematology*
EMP: 90
SALES (corp-wide): 6.7B **Privately Held**
WEB: www.chw.edu
SIC: **8011** Offices & clinics of medical doc-
tors
PA: Dignity Health
185 Berry St Ste 300
San Francisco CA 94107
415 438-5500

(P-19445)
DINUBA MEDICAL CLINIC (PA)
Also Called: Dinuba Medical Center
271 N L St, Dinuba (93618-2107)
P.O. Box 367 (93618-0367)
PHONE.............................559 591-1820
John Moore, *Manager*
EMP: 61
SALES (est): 5.3MM **Privately Held**
SIC: **8011** Physicians' office, including spe-
cialists; general & family practice, physi-
cian/surgeon; pediatrician; internal
medicine, physician/surgeon

(P-19446)
DISCOVERY PRACTICE MANAGEMENT
Also Called: Center For Discovery
4136 Ann Arbor Rd, Lakewood
(90712-3817)
PHONE.............................562 425-6404
Craig M Brown, *President*
Robert Weitzman, *CFO*
Cathlin Ongkowidjojo, *Info Tech Mgr*
Jennifer Gorman, *Opers Staff*
EMP: 50
SQ FT: 2,500
SALES (est): 2.3MM **Privately Held**
SIC: **8011** General & family practice, physi-
cian/surgeon

(P-19447)
DOCTORS COMPANY
185 Greenwood Rd, NAPA (94558-7540)
PHONE.............................707 226-0289
M Puebla, *Owner*
Jean Jose, *Producer*

EMP: 90 EST: 2014
SALES (est): 28.2MM **Privately Held**
SIC: **8011** Offices & clinics of medical doc-
tors

(P-19448)
DOS PALOS MEMORIAL HOSP INC
Also Called: Dos Palos Mem Rur Hlth Clinic
2118 Marguerite St, Dos Palos
(93620-2339)
PHONE.............................209 392-6121
Fax: 209 392-8872
EMP: 60
SQ FT: 16,000
SALES (est): 2.7MM **Privately Held**
SIC: **8011** 8051

(P-19449)
DOUGLAS W JACKSON MD
2760 Atlantic Ave, Long Beach
(90806-2755)
PHONE.............................562 424-6666
Douglas W Jackson MD, *Owner*
EMP: 60
SALES (est): 736.1K **Privately Held**
SIC: **8011** General & family practice, physi-
cian/surgeon

(P-19450)
DRUMMOND MEDICAL GROUP INC
Also Called: Indian Wells Vly Surgery Ctr
900 N Heritage Dr Ste A, Ridgecrest
(93555-3196)
PHONE.............................760 446-4571
Douglas E Roberts Jr, *President*
EMP: 120 EST: 1958
SQ FT: 30,000
SALES (est): 6.2MM **Privately Held**
WEB: www.drummondmedical.com
SIC: **8011** General & family practice, physi-
cian/surgeon

(P-19451)
EAST BAY NEPHROLOGY
2089 Vale Rd Ste 32, San Pablo
(94806-3850)
PHONE.............................510 235-1057
Ellen Morrissey, *Principal*
EMP: 50 EST: 2011
SALES (est): 97.7K **Privately Held**
SIC: **8011** Nephrologist

(P-19452)
EBSC LP
Also Called: Surgery Center of Health South
3875 Telegraph Ave, Oakland
(94609-2428)
PHONE.............................510 547-2244
Judy Rich, *Administration*
Allan Horn, *Med Doctor*
EMP: 65
SQ FT: 12,500
SALES (est): 7.8MM **Privately Held**
SIC: **8011** Ambulatory surgical center

(P-19453)
EDEN LABS MED GROUP INC
20103 Lake Chabot Rd, Castro Valley
(94546-5305)
PHONE.............................510 537-1234
John Carney, *President*
Katherine Thomas, *Admin Sec*
Kathy Lawrence, *Nursing Dir*
EMP: 50
SQ FT: 9,000
SALES (est): 3.3MM **Privately Held**
SIC: **8011** Pathologist

(P-19454)
EDINGER MEDICAL GROUP INC (PA)
9900 Talbert Ave 302, Fountain Valley
(92708-5153)
PHONE.............................714 965-2500
Burton F Willis MD, *President*
Bertram N Dias MD, *CFO*
Gary Ahn MD, *Vice Pres*
Stanley W Arnold MD, *Vice Pres*
Matthew C Boone MD, *Vice Pres*
▲ EMP: 101 EST: 1961

SALES (est): 15.4MM **Privately Held**
WEB: www.edingermedicalgroup.com
SIC: 8011 General & family practice, physician/surgeon

(P-19455)
EDWARDS LIFESCIENCES LLC (HQ)
1 Edwards Way, Irvine (92614-5688)
PHONE..............................949 250-2500
Michael A Mussallem, *CEO*
Huimin Wang MD, *President*
Patricia Garvey, *Vice Pres*
John H Kehl Jr, *Vice Pres*
Mark Schreiber, *Vice Pres*
▲ EMP: 1700
SALES (est): 453.6MM
SALES (corp-wide): 3.4B **Publicly Held**
SIC: 8011 Cardiologist & cardio-vascular specialist
PA: Edwards Lifesciences Corp
1 Edwards Way
Irvine CA 92614
949 250-2500

(P-19456)
EL DORADO COUNTY HEALTH DEPT
Also Called: County of El Dorado
931 Spring St, Placerville (95667-4543)
PHONE..............................530 621-6100
Lori Walker, *CFO*
Todd Truka, *Info Tech Mgr*
Lynnan Svensson, *Nursing Dir*
Barry Wasserman, *Program Dir*
Mike Deatherage, *Manager*
EMP: 94
SALES (est): 1.3MM **Privately Held**
SIC: 8011 Primary care medical clinic

(P-19457)
ELDORADO COMMUNITY SERVICE CTR
335 E Manchester Blvd, Inglewood (90301-1814)
PHONE..............................424 227-7971
Stan Sharma, *Principal*
Ararat Alex Yarijanian, *Marketing Staff*
EMP: 99
SALES (est): 996.8K **Privately Held**
SIC: 8011 8049 Physicians' office, including specialists; clinical psychologist

(P-19458)
ELICA HEALTH CENTERS
3701 J St Ste 201, Sacramento (95816-5542)
PHONE..............................916 454-2345
Tamara Miroshniehenko, *Branch Mgr*
Tracy Hernandez, *Admin Asst*
Laton Fuller, *Info Tech Mgr*
EMP: 80
SALES (corp-wide): 13.6MM **Privately Held**
SIC: 8011 Clinic, operated by physicians
PA: Elica Health Centers
1860 Howe Ave Ste 440
Sacramento CA 95825
916 569-8484

(P-19459)
EMERGENCY MED GROUP OF FOLSOM
1650 Creekside Dr, Folsom (95630-3400)
PHONE..............................916 983-7470
Dwight B Stalker, *Principal*
EMP: 80 EST: 2011
SALES (est): 138.6K **Privately Held**
SIC: 8011 Freestanding emergency medical center

(P-19460)
EMERGENT MEDICAL ASSOCIATES (PA)
111 N Sepulveda Blvd # 210, Manhattan Beach (90266-6849)
PHONE..............................310 379-2134
Mark Bell, *Principal*
▲ EMP: 58
SALES (est): 9.6MM **Privately Held**
WEB: www.emergentmed.com
SIC: 8011 Medical centers

(P-19461)
ENLOE MEDICAL CENTER
Also Called: Payroll Dept.
175 W 5th Ave, Chico (95926)
PHONE..............................530 332-7522
Linda Irvine, *Branch Mgr*
EMP: 336
SALES (corp-wide): 528.3MM **Privately Held**
SIC: 8011 Medical centers
PA: Enloe Medical Center
1531 Esplanade
Chico CA 95926
530 332-7300

(P-19462)
ENLOE MEDICAL CENTER
Also Called: Children's Health Center
277 Cohasset Rd, Chico (95926-2242)
PHONE..............................530 332-6000
Dorothy Chinnock, *Branch Mgr*
Lisa Brake, *Office Mgr*
EMP: 403
SALES (corp-wide): 528.3MM **Privately Held**
SIC: 8011 Clinic, operated by physicians
PA: Enloe Medical Center
1531 Esplanade
Chico CA 95926
530 332-7300

(P-19463)
ERIC D FELDMAN MD INC
Also Called: Rehab Associates
2760 Atlantic Ave, Long Beach (90806-2755)
PHONE..............................562 424-6666
Eric D Feldman MD, *President*
EMP: 50
SALES (est): 1.5MM **Privately Held**
SIC: 8011 General & family practice, physician/surgeon

(P-19464)
EYE MEDICAL CLINIC FRESNO INC
Also Called: Eye Medical Center of Fresno
1360 E Herndon Ave # 301, Fresno (93720-3326)
PHONE..............................559 486-5000
Richard H Whitten Jr, *CEO*
George Bertolucci M, *President*
Carolyn Sakauye, *Bd of Directors*
Juanita Esparza, *Office Mgr*
Carmen Mares, *Office Mgr*
EMP: 55
SQ FT: 12,000
SALES (est): 6.8MM **Privately Held**
SIC: 8011 8042 Ophthalmologist; offices & clinics of optometrists

(P-19465)
EYE Q VISION CARE (PA)
7075 N Sharon Ave, Fresno (93720-3329)
PHONE..............................559 486-2000
Scott Bridgeman, *CEO*
Sarah Jaimenez, *Administration*
EMP: 175
SALES (est): 19.3MM **Privately Held**
SIC: 8011 8042 8031 Ophthalmologist; offices & clinics of optometrists; offices & clinics of osteopathic physicians

(P-19466)
FACEY MEDICAL FOUNDATION
27924 Seco Canyon Rd, Santa Clarita (91350-3870)
PHONE..............................661 513-2100
Joan Rhee, *Manager*
Lorna De, *Manager*
EMP: 86
SALES (corp-wide): 197.1MM **Privately Held**
SIC: 8011 Physicians' office, including specialists
PA: Facey Medical Foundation
15451 San Fernando Msn
Mission Hills CA 91345
818 365-9531

(P-19467)
FACEY MEDICAL FOUNDATION
11165 Sepulveda Blvd, Mission Hills (91345-1125)
PHONE..............................818 365-9531
Judy Breen, *Branch Mgr*

Melissa Beaman, *Info Tech Mgr*
Jennifer Decker, *Med Doctor*
Albert C Ko, *Med Doctor*
Kayur H Shah, *Med Doctor*
EMP: 220
SALES (corp-wide): 197.1MM **Privately Held**
SIC: 8011 Physicians' office, including specialists
PA: Facey Medical Foundation
15451 San Fernando Msn
Mission Hills CA 91345
818 365-9531

(P-19468)
FACIAL RECONSTRUCTIVE SURGERY
Also Called: Facial Reconstructive Surg &
1900 University Ave 101e, East Palo Alto (94303-2212)
PHONE..............................650 328-0511
Steven Schendel, *Partner*
Mary Lynn Fouche, *Assistant*
EMP: 50
SALES (est): 3MM **Privately Held**
WEB: www.sleepsurgery.com
SIC: 8011 Plastic surgeon

(P-19469)
FACULTY PHYSCANS SRGEONS LLUSM
11370 Anderson St, Loma Linda (92354-3450)
P.O. Box 945 (92354-0945)
PHONE..............................909 558-4000
Ricardo Peverini, *President*
EMP: 99
SALES (est): 3.9MM **Privately Held**
SIC: 8011 Physicians' office, including specialists

(P-19470)
FAMILY HEALTHCARE NETWORK
Also Called: Porterville Annex
1137 W Poplar Ave, Porterville (93257-5839)
PHONE..............................559 781-7242
EMP: 347
SALES (corp-wide): 114.6MM **Privately Held**
SIC: 8011 Primary care medical clinic
PA: Family Healthcare Network
305 E Center Ave
Visalia CA 93291
559 737-4700

(P-19471)
FAMILY HEALTHCARE NETWORK
33025 159th Rd, Ivanhoe (93235)
PHONE..............................559 798-1877
Yterry Abbott, *Manager*
EMP: 103
SALES (corp-wide): 114.6MM **Privately Held**
SIC: 8011 8021 Physicians' office, including specialists; offices & clinics of dentists
PA: Family Healthcare Network
305 E Center Ave
Visalia CA 93291
559 737-4700

(P-19472)
FAMILY PLG ASSOC MED GROUP (PA)
3050 E Airport Way, Long Beach (90806-2404)
PHONE..............................213 738-7283
Edward C Allred MD, *Principal*
EMP: 52
SQ FT: 14,000
SALES (est): 36.1MM **Privately Held**
WEB: www.fpamg.net
SIC: 8011 Clinic, operated by physicians

(P-19473)
FERTILITY & REPRODUCTIVE
Also Called: F R H I
2581 Samaritan Dr Ste 302, San Jose (95124-4112)
PHONE..............................408 358-2500
G D Adamson MD, *Director*
EMP: 60

SALES (est): 3.5MM
SALES (corp-wide): 12.4B **Privately Held**
SIC: 8011 Fertility specialist, physician
HQ: Palo Alto Medical Foundation For Health Care, Research And Education (Inc)
795 El Camino Real
Palo Alto CA 94301
650 321-4121

(P-19474)
FOOTHILL HEALTH CENTER INC
Also Called: SAN JOSE FOOTHILL FAMILY
2670 S White Rd Ste 200, San Jose (95148-2073)
PHONE..............................408 729-4290
Salvador Chavarin, *CEO*
Shuchung Chang, *Manager*
EMP: 170
SQ FT: 2,200
SALES: 16.8MM **Privately Held**
WEB: www.sjffcc.com
SIC: 8011 Primary care medical clinic

(P-19475)
FRANK D YELIAN MD PC
Also Called: Life Ivf Center
3500 Barranca Pkwy # 300, Irvine (92606-8232)
PHONE..............................949 788-1133
Frank D Yelian, *CEO*
EMP: 50 EST: 2010
SALES: 8MM **Privately Held**
SIC: 8011 Fertility specialist, physician

(P-19476)
FREEMONT RIDEOUT HEALTH GROUP
989 Plumas St, Yuba City (95991-4012)
PHONE..............................530 751-4000
Kevin Woodward, *Principal*
Mary Corralez, *Buyer*
EMP: 72
SALES (corp-wide): 26.9MM **Privately Held**
SIC: 8011 Medical centers
PA: Freemont Rideout Health Group
989 Plumas St
Yuba City CA 95991
530 751-4010

(P-19477)
FREMONT AMBLTORY SRGERY CTR LP
Also Called: Fremont Surgery Center
39350 Civic Center Dr, Fremont (94538-2343)
PHONE..............................510 456-4600
John Mazoros, *General Ptnr*
EMP: 80
SQ FT: 19,000
SALES (est): 15.1MM **Privately Held**
WEB: www.fremontsurgerycenter.com
SIC: 8011 Ambulatory surgical center; surgeon

(P-19478)
FRIEDMAN PROFESSIONAL MGT CO
Also Called: Post Surgical Recovery Center
17752 Beach Blvd Side, Huntington Beach (92647-6838)
PHONE..............................714 842-1426
Kelly Trackman, *President*
Neil Friedman MD, *President*
Madeline Tinkler, *Corp Secy*
Jo Ann Friedman, *Vice Pres*
EMP: 70 EST: 1975
SQ FT: 35,500
SALES (est): 4.1MM **Privately Held**
SIC: 8011

(P-19479)
FRITCH EYE CARE MEDICAL CENTER
9000 Ming Ave Ste L2, Bakersfield (93311-1324)
PHONE..............................661 665-2020
Donald Bradley, *Partner*
Charles D Fritch, *Partner*
H Mohammadi, *Partner*
EMP: 85

SALES (est): 2.1MM
SALES (corp-wide): 2MM **Privately Held**
WEB: www.fritcheyecare.com
SIC: 8011 Eyes, ears, nose & throat specialist: physician/surgeon
PA: Charles D Fritch Md Inc
8501 Brimhall Rd Ste 402
Bakersfield CA 93312
661 665-2020

(P-19480)
GARY LASK
Also Called: U C L A Dermatology
200 Ucla Medical Plz 4, Los Angeles
(90095-8344)
PHONE..........................310 825-0631
Gary Lask, *Principal*
EMP: 60
SALES (est): 3.4MM **Privately Held**
SIC: 8011 Offices & clinics of medical doctors

(P-19481)
GASTROENTEROLOGY DIVISION
Also Called: San Francisco General Hospital
1001 Potrero Ave Ste 1e21, San Francisco
(94110-3518)
PHONE..........................415 206-8823
Amy Akbarian, *Administration*
EMP: 50
SALES (est): 30.3MM **Privately Held**
SIC: 8011 Gastronomist

(P-19482)
GEORGE M RAJACICH MD PC
Also Called: Valley Eye Center Group
14914 Sherman Way, Van Nuys
(91405-2113)
PHONE..........................818 787-2020
George M Rajacich MD, *President*
Dorcas Fikejs, *Office Mgr*
EMP: 50
SQ FT: 12,000
SALES (est): 6.4MM **Privately Held**
SIC: 8011 Ophthalmologist

(P-19483)
GLENDALE EYE MEDICAL GROUP
500 N Cntl Ave Ste 400, Glendale (91203)
PHONE..........................818 956-1010
James M Mc Caffery MD, *President*
EMP: 80
SQ FT: 11,000
SALES (est): 1.9MM **Privately Held**
SIC: 8011 Ophthalmologist

(P-19484)
GLENDALE EYE MEDICAL GROUP (PA)
Also Called: Amsurg
607 N Central Ave Ste 203, Glendale
(91203-1845)
PHONE..........................818 956-1010
Richard Weise, *Partner*
Stephen Chang, *Partner*
Candy Sorgani, *Executive*
Heather McKinney,
EMP: 70
SALES (est): 7.6MM **Privately Held**
SIC: 8011 Physicians' office, including specialists; ophthalmologist

(P-19485)
GOLDEN RAIN FOUNDATION
1661 Golden Rain Rd, Seal Beach
(90740-4999)
P.O. Box 2685 (90740-1685)
PHONE..........................562 493-9581
EMP: 83
SALES (corp-wide): 15MM **Privately Held**
SIC: 8011 Geriatric specialist, physician/surgeon
PA: Rain Golden Foundation
13531 Saint Andrews Dr
Seal Beach CA 90740
562 431-6586

(P-19486)
GOOD SAMARITAN HOSPITAL AUX
1225 Wilshire Blvd, Los Angeles
(90017-1901)
PHONE..........................213 977-2121
Andrew Leeka, *CEO*
Claus Von Zychlin, *COO*
Robert Peroutka, *Med Doctor*
EMP: 1500
SALES: 118.6K **Privately Held**
SIC: 8011 Medical centers

(P-19487)
GOODMAN USA INC
605 W California Ave, Sunnyvale
(94086-4831)
PHONE..........................408 329-5400
Kiminori Toda, *President*
Takaharu Tanaka, *General Mgr*
EMP: 66
SALES (est): 1.2MM **Privately Held**
SIC: 8011 Offices & clinics of medical doctors

(P-19488)
GRAYBILL MEDICAL GROUP INC (PA)
332 S Juniper St Ste 100, Escondido
(92025-4249)
PHONE..........................866 228-2236
Floyd Farley, *CEO*
Marvin V Beddoe, *President*
David Borecky, *CEO*
George A Pleitez, *Vice Pres*
Jackie Craw, *Executive*
EMP: 180
SALES (est): 36.5MM **Privately Held**
SIC: 8011 Physicians' office, including specialists

(P-19489)
HAIDER SPINE CTR MED GROUP INC
6276 River Crest Dr Ste A, Riverside
(92507-0754)
PHONE..........................951 413-0200
Thomas Haider, *President*
David Siambanes, *Principal*
Steve Davila, *Office Mgr*
EMP: 50
SALES (est): 4MM **Privately Held**
SIC: 8011 Orthopedic physician

(P-19490)
HEALTH NET CMNTY SOLUTIONS INC
11971 Foundation Pl, Gold River
(95670-4502)
PHONE..........................800 675-6110
Woodrow Fennell, *Principal*
EMP: 122 **EST:** 2013
SALES (est): 1MM **Publicly Held**
SIC: 8011 Health maintenance organization
HQ: Health Net, Inc.
21650 Oxnard St Fl 25
Woodland Hills CA 91367

(P-19491)
HEALTHCARE PARTNERS LLC
Also Called: Healthcare Partners Med Group
3932 Long Beach Blvd, Long Beach
(90807-2615)
PHONE..........................562 304-2100
Kenny Heine, *Branch Mgr*
EMP: 67 **Publicly Held**
SIC: 8011 Group health association
HQ: Davita Medical Management, Llc
2175 Park Pl
El Segundo CA 90245

(P-19492)
HEALTHCARE PARTNERS LLC
Harriman Jones Medical
2600 Redondo Ave Ste 405, Long Beach
(90806-2330)
PHONE..........................562 988-7000
Jill R Cortese, *Principal*
Dayna Bennett-Pierce, *Vice Pres*
Frank Lopez, *Vice Pres*
Erin Mills, *Vice Pres*
Alexandre Portet, *Vice Pres*

EMP: 405 **Publicly Held**
WEB: www.davidv.com
SIC: 8011 Clinic, operated by physicians
HQ: Davita Medical Management, Llc
2175 Park Pl
El Segundo CA 90245

(P-19493)
HEALTHCARE SYSTEM 2000
9191 Westminster Ave, Garden Grove
(92844-2751)
PHONE..........................714 899-2000
Michael Dao, *Owner*
Quin Rudin, *Principal*
Peter H Vu, *Pediatrics*
Tao Duong, *Cardiovascular*
EMP: 65
SALES (est): 1.6MM **Privately Held**
SIC: 8011 8062 General & family practice, physician/surgeon; general medical & surgical hospitals

(P-19494)
HEALTHPOINTE MEDICAL GROUP INC (PA)
Also Called: Southern Cal Orthopedics
16702 Valley View Ave, La Mirada
(90638-5824)
PHONE..........................714 956-2663
Ismael Silva, *President*
Mickie White, *Office Mgr*
Victoria Callaway, *Office Admin*
James Aviles, *Info Tech Mgr*
Floyd Bender, *Info Tech Mgr*
EMP: 52
SQ FT: 10,000
SALES (est): 13.3MM **Privately Held**
SIC: 8011 Orthopedic physician; sports medicine specialist, physician; surgeon

(P-19495)
HEALTHY BEGINNINGS FRENCH CAMP
Also Called: Women' S Health
500 W Hospital Rd, French Camp
(95231-9693)
P.O. Box 1020, Stockton (95201-3120)
PHONE..........................209 468-6147
Michael Smith, *Principal*
Janet Crawford, *Executive*
EMP: 80
SALES (est): 2.1MM **Privately Held**
SIC: 8011 Offices & clinics of medical doctors

(P-19496)
HEMET VALLEY IMAGING MED GROUP (PA)
Also Called: Professional Medical MGT
3292 E Florida Ave Ste F, Hemet
(92544-4941)
P.O. Box 459 (92546-0459)
PHONE..........................951 925-6537
Frederick E White, *President*
EMP: 65
SQ FT: 12,196
SALES (est): 4.1MM **Privately Held**
SIC: 8011 Radiologist

(P-19497)
HENRY MAYO NEWHALL MEM HOSP
23845 Mcbean Pkwy, Valencia
(91355-2001)
PHONE..........................661 253-8112
EMP: 94 **EST:** 2013
SALES: 245.5MM **Privately Held**
SIC: 8011

(P-19498)
HERALD CHRISTIAN HEALTH CENTER (PA)
8841 Garvey Ave, Rosemead
(91770-3358)
PHONE..........................626 286-8700
David Lee, *CEO*
Carolin Eng, *COO*
Emily Szeto, *CFO*
Seran S Ng,
Kimberly Chow, *Supervisor*
EMP: 80
SQ FT: 11,000

SALES: 6.3MM **Privately Held**
SIC: 8011 8021 Primary care medical clinic; dental clinics & offices

(P-19499)
HERITAGE MEDICAL GROUP (PA)
Also Called: Bakersfield Family Medical Ctr
4580 California Ave, Bakersfield
(93309-1104)
P.O. Box 10749 (93389-0749)
PHONE..........................661 327-4411
Stanley Wohl, *CEO*
Richard Merkin, *Owner*
EMP: 51
SALES (est): 21.4MM **Privately Held**
SIC: 8011 Offices & clinics of medical doctors

(P-19500)
HIGH DESERT MED CORP A MED GRP (PA)
Also Called: Heritage Health Care
43839 15th St W, Lancaster (93534-4756)
P.O. Box 7007 (93539-7007)
PHONE..........................661 945-5984
Richard N Merkin, *CEO*
Clara Hauke, *Records Dir*
Rafael Gonzalez, *Administration*
Kimberly Powell, *Administration*
Saro Arakelians, *Research*
EMP: 120
SQ FT: 25,000
SALES (est): 22.6MM **Privately Held**
WEB: www.regalmed.com
SIC: 8011 Clinic, operated by physicians

(P-19501)
HIGH DSERT PTENT CARE SVCS LLC
17095 Main St, Hesperia (92345-6004)
PHONE..........................760 956-4150
Medhi Izadi,
Ziad R El-Hajjaoui,
Zoheir El-Hajjaoui,
EMP: 53
SQ FT: 9,000
SALES: 5MM **Privately Held**
SIC: 8011 Offices & clinics of medical doctors

(P-19502)
HILARY A BRODIE MD PHD
2521 Stockton Blvd 7200, Sacramento
(95817-2207)
PHONE..........................916 734-3744
Hilary Brodie MD, *Chairman*
EMP: 60
SALES (est): 2.4MM **Privately Held**
SIC: 8011 Ears, nose & throat specialist: physician/surgeon

(P-19503)
HILL PHYSICIANS MED GROUP INC (PA)
2409 Camino Ramon, San Ramon
(94583-4285)
P.O. Box 5080 (94583-0980)
PHONE..........................800 445-5747
Bruce A Bob D, *Chairman*
Steve McDermott, *President*
Harpreet Grewal, *Bd of Directors*
Leslie Plotner, *Executive Asst*
Joanne Rodriguez, *Admin Asst*
EMP: 488
SQ FT: 36,000
SALES: 504.8MM **Privately Held**
SIC: 8011 8031 General & family practice, physician/surgeon; offices & clinics of osteopathic physicians

(P-19504)
HUNTINGTON AMBLTRY SURG CTR
625 S Fair Oaks Ave, Pasadena
(91105-2613)
P.O. Box 840189, Los Angeles (90084-0189)
PHONE..........................626 229-8999
Harry Bowles, *Mng Member*
Bernadette Molino,
James Noble,
Stephen Ralph,
Robin Waldvogel, *Director*
EMP: 50

SALES (est): 4.6MM **Privately Held**
SIC: **8011** Surgeon

(P-19505)
HUNTINGTON BEACH COMMNTY CLINC
Also Called: Huntington Beach Cmnty Clinic
8041 Newman Ave, Huntington Beach
(92647-7034)
PHONE...................................714 847-4222
William Borden, *Ch of Bd*
Al Guidotti, *Ch of Bd*
Jacqueline Cherewick, *President*
T Gregory, *Treasurer*
D Harris, *Vice Pres*
▲ EMP: 120
SQ FT: 3,500
SALES (est): 4.2MM **Privately Held**
WEB: www.cchcoc.org
SIC: **8011** Clinic, operated by physicians

(P-19506)
HUNTINGTON OTPTENT SURGERY CTR
625 S Fair Oaks Ave # 380, Pasadena
(91105-2613)
PHONE...................................626 535-2434
Sandy Bidlack, *Director*
EMP: 55
SQ FT: 12,030
SALES (est): 3.5MM **Privately Held**
SIC: **8011** Ambulatory surgical center; surgeon

(P-19507)
HUNTINGTON REPRODCTVE CTR INC (PA)
Also Called: Hrc Fertility
135 S Rosemead Blvd, Pasadena
(91107-3955)
PHONE...................................626 204-9699
Timothy J McGinley, *CEO*
John Wilcox, *Treasurer*
Jeffrey R Nelson, *Vice Pres*
Tanya Kain, *Administration*
Norman Quan, *Controller*
EMP: 50
SQ FT: 22,394
SALES (est): 20.1MM **Privately Held**
WEB: www.havingbabies.com
SIC: **8011** Fertility specialist, physician

(P-19508)
IGO MEDICAL GROUP A MED CORP (PA)
Also Called: Infertlity Gynclogy Obstetrics
9339 Genesee Ave Ste 220, San Diego
(92121-2196)
PHONE...................................858 455-7520
Benito Villanueva, *President*
Wendy M Buchi, *CEO*
Dr Philip E Young, *CFO*
Steven Hebert, *Bd of Directors*
Dr Stephen Herbert, *Vice Pres*
EMP: 70
SQ FT: 11,500
SALES (est): 8.5MM **Privately Held**
WEB: www.igomed.com
SIC: **8011** Gynecologist; obstetrician; fertility specialist, physician

(P-19509)
IMAGING HLTHCARE SPCALISTS LLC (PA)
150 W Washington St, San Diego
(92103-2005)
PHONE...................................619 295-9729
Thomas D Cleary, *President*
Donielle Sullivan,
EMP: 65
SALES (est): 16.2MM **Privately Held**
SIC: **8011** Radiologist

(P-19510)
INDIAN HLTH CTR SNTA CLARA VLY
1333 Meridian Ave, San Jose
(95125-5212)
PHONE...................................408 445-3400
Sonya M Tetnowski, *CEO*
Barbara Miao, *CFO*
Robert Verette, *Podiatrist*
EMP: 200
SQ FT: 10,000

SALES (est): 24.3MM **Privately Held**
WEB: www.ihcscv.org
SIC: **8011** 8322 Clinic, operated by physicians; individual & family services

(P-19511)
INLAND EYE INST MED GROUP INC (PA)
1900 E Washington St, Colton
(92324-4698)
P.O. Box 1427 (92324-0836)
PHONE...................................909 825-3425
Loren Denler MD, *President*
Harold P Wallar, *Treasurer*
Wayne B Isaeff, *Vice Pres*
Melissa Goins, *Nursing Dir*
EMP: 70
SQ FT: 12,500
SALES (est): 10MM **Privately Held**
SIC: **8011** Ophthalmologist

(P-19512)
INLAND HLTH ORG OF SO CAL (HQ)
1980 Orange Tree Ln # 200, Redlands
(92374-4534)
P.O. Box 10457, San Bernardino (92423-0457)
PHONE...................................909 335-7171
Jeff Winter, *President*
Paula Lamar, *Vice Pres*
EMP: 50
SQ FT: 12,000
SALES (est): 8MM
SALES (corp-wide): 6.7B **Privately Held**
WEB: www.pulliamgroup.com
SIC: **8011** Clinic, operated by physicians
PA: Dignity Health
185 Berry St Ste 300
San Francisco CA 94107
415 438-5500

(P-19513)
INNOVATIVE SLEEP CENTERS INC
Also Called: Mehrdad Razavi
1050 Northgate Dr Ste 250, San Rafael
(94903-2511)
PHONE...................................415 927-4990
Mehrdad Razavi, *CEO*
Mary Quenzer, *CFO*
Diane Taylor, *Opers Staff*
EMP: 65 EST: 2014
SQ FT: 2,000
SALES (est): 1.5MM **Privately Held**
SIC: **8011** Physical medicine, physician/surgeon

(P-19514)
INSITE DIGESTIVE HEALTH CARE
200 Jose Figueres Ave, San Jose
(95116-1500)
PHONE...................................408 471-2222
Margarita Joaquin, *Branch Mgr*
EMP: 153
SALES (corp-wide): 9.2MM **Privately Held**
SIC: **8011** Gastronomist
PA: Insite Digestive Health Care
5525 Etiwanda Ave Ste 110
Tarzana CA 91356
818 437-8105

(P-19515)
IPC HEALTHCARE INC (DH)
Also Called: Intrepid Healthcare Svcs Inc
4605 Lankershim Blvd, North Hollywood
(91602-1818)
PHONE...................................888 447-2362
Adam D Singer, *CEO*
R Jeffrey Taylor, *President*
Richard H Kline III, *CFO*
Kerry E Weiner, *Chief Mktg Ofcr*
Richard G Russell, *Exec VP*
EMP: 86
SALES (est): 624.5MM
SALES (corp-wide): 287.4MM **Privately Held**
WEB: www.ipcm.com
SIC: **8011** Physicians' office, including specialists

HQ: Team Health Holdings, Inc.
265 Brookview Centre Way
Knoxville TN 37919
865 693-1000

(P-19516)
JAMES D TATE MD
Also Called: Tate Neurological Surgery
2888 Eureka Way Ste 200, Redding
(96001-0210)
PHONE...................................530 225-8710
James D Tate MD, *Owner*
Tracey Lattimore, *Office Mgr*
EMP: 62
SALES (est): 2.2MM **Privately Held**
SIC: **8011** Surgeon

(P-19517)
JANET K HARTZLER MD
72057 Dinah Shore Dr D, Rancho Mirage
(92270-1791)
PHONE...................................760 340-3937
Janet Hartzler, *Principal*
Bart Ketover, *Med Doctor*
EMP: 60
SALES (est): 1MM **Privately Held**
SIC: **8011** Ophthalmologist

(P-19518)
JAYASINGHE MEDICAL GROUP INC (PA)
Also Called: Ameri-West Medical Associates
200 S Beach Blvd Ste A2, La Habra
(90631-5181)
PHONE...................................562 267-7000
Walter Jayasinghe MD, *President*
Earla Quisido, *Director*
EMP: 60
SQ FT: 4,000
SALES (est): 2.3MM **Privately Held**
SIC: **8011** Obstetrician; gynecologist

(P-19519)
JERRY S POWELL MD
4501 X St, Sacramento (95817-2229)
PHONE...................................916 734-5959
Jerry S Powell, *Owner*
EMP: 70
SALES (est): 1.9MM **Privately Held**
SIC: **8011** Oncologist

(P-19520)
JOHN M ADAMS JR MD
1301 20th St Ste 150, Santa Monica
(90404-2050)
PHONE...................................310 829-2663
Kevin Airheart MD, *Owner*
Natasha Trentacosta, *Surgeon*
EMP: 60
SALES (est): 938.5K **Privately Held**
SIC: **8011** General & family practice, physician/surgeon

(P-19521)
JOHN MUIR PHYSICIAN NETWORK
Also Called: Alamo Medical Group
1505 Saint Alphonsus Way, Alamo
(94507-1570)
PHONE...................................925 838-4633
Judy Hicklin, *Manager*
EMP: 50
SALES (corp-wide): 322.9MM **Privately Held**
SIC: **8011** Pediatrician; internal medicine, physician/surgeon
PA: John Muir Physician Network
1450 Treat Blvd
Walnut Creek CA 94597
925 296-9700

(P-19522)
JUDY MADRIGAL & ASSOCIATES INC
Also Called: J M A
2000 Alameda De Las Pulga, San Mateo
(94403-1289)
PHONE...................................650 873-3444
Judy Madrigal, *President*
Tammy Attard, *Vice Pres*
EMP: 550

SALES (est): 21.8MM **Privately Held**
WEB: www.judymadrigal.com
SIC: **8011** 8742 Offices & clinics of medical doctors; management consulting services

(P-19523)
KAISER FOUNDATION HOSPITALS
Also Called: Lakeview Medical Offices
411 N Lakeview Ave, Anaheim
(92807-3028)
PHONE...................................714 279-4675
Suzie Characky, *Manager*
EMP: 105
SALES (corp-wide): 94.1B **Privately Held**
SIC: **8011** Offices & clinics of medical doctors
HQ: Kaiser Foundation Hospitals Inc
1 Kaiser Plz
Oakland CA 94612
510 271-6611

(P-19524)
KAISER FOUNDATION HOSPITALS
Also Called: Aliso Viejo Medical Offices
24502 Pacific Park Dr, Aliso Viejo
(92656-3033)
PHONE...................................949 425-3150
Bruce Sogioka, *Branch Mgr*
EMP: 105
SALES (corp-wide): 94.1B **Privately Held**
SIC: **8011** Offices & clinics of medical doctors
HQ: Kaiser Foundation Hospitals Inc
1 Kaiser Plz
Oakland CA 94612
510 271-6611

(P-19525)
KAISER FOUNDATION HOSPITALS
8889 Rio San Diego Dr, San Diego
(92108-1670)
PHONE...................................619 542-7210
Kate Kessler, *Branch Mgr*
Robert Alger, *Vice Pres*
EMP: 55
SALES (corp-wide): 94.1B **Privately Held**
SIC: **8011** Health maintenance organization
HQ: Kaiser Foundation Hospitals Inc
1 Kaiser Plz
Oakland CA 94612
510 271-6611

(P-19526)
KAISER FOUNDATION HOSPITALS
Also Called: Kaiser Permanente Santa
401 Bicentennial Way, Santa Rosa
(95403-2149)
PHONE...................................707 393-4000
Susan Janvirin, *Branch Mgr*
Freida Smith, *Records Dir*
Judy Coffey, *Area Mgr*
Rudy Collins, *Human Res Mgr*
John Fannin, *Buyer*
EMP: 2000
SALES (corp-wide): 94.1B **Privately Held**
WEB: www.kaiserpermanente.org
SIC: **8011** Medical centers
HQ: Kaiser Foundation Hospitals Inc
1 Kaiser Plz
Oakland CA 94612
510 271-6611

(P-19527)
KAISER FOUNDATION HOSPITALS
Also Called: Kaiser Prmnnte Antioch Med Ctr
4501 Sand Creek Rd, Antioch
(94531-8687)
PHONE...................................925 813-6500
Albert L Carver, *Branch Mgr*
EMP: 105
SALES (corp-wide): 94.1B **Privately Held**
SIC: **8011** Internal medicine practitioners
HQ: Kaiser Foundation Hospitals Inc
1 Kaiser Plz
Oakland CA 94612
510 271-6611

(P-19528)
KAISER FOUNDATION HOSPITALS
Also Called: Kaiser Permanente
12100 Euclid St, Garden Grove
(92840-3304)
PHONE..................................714 741-3448
Betty Bohner, *Administration*
Thanh Bui, *Family Practiti*
Joe To, *Family Practiti*
Chris Chang, *Manager*
EMP: 100
SALES (corp-wide): 94.1B **Privately Held**
WEB: www.kaiserpermanente.org
SIC: **8011** Offices & clinics of medical doctors
HQ: Kaiser Foundation Hospitals Inc
1 Kaiser Plz
Oakland CA 94612
510 271-6611

(P-19529)
KAISER FOUNDATION HOSPITALS
Also Called: Oakland Medical Center
3600 Broadway, Oakland (94611-5730)
P.O. Box 12929 (94604-3010)
PHONE..................................510 752-1000
David J Artenburn, *Manager*
Allan Chu, *Accountant*
Douglass Crawford, *Family Practiti*
Michelle A Sallee, *Psychologist*
Richanne Sniezek, *Psychologist*
EMP: 2200
SALES (corp-wide): 94.1B **Privately Held**
WEB: www.kaiserpermanente.org
SIC: **8011** 8062 Medical centers; general medical & surgical hospitals
HQ: Kaiser Foundation Hospitals Inc
1 Kaiser Plz
Oakland CA 94612
510 271-6611

(P-19530)
KAISER FOUNDATION HOSPITALS
Also Called: Kaiser Permanente San
2425 Geary Blvd, San Francisco
(94115-3358)
PHONE..................................415 833-2000
Harry Chima, *Branch Mgr*
Joy Buenviaje, *Financial Exec*
Mitchell Adachi, *Pathologist*
Junming Fang, *Pathologist*
James M Colville Jr, *Surgeon*
EMP: 750
SALES (corp-wide): 94.1B **Privately Held**
WEB: www.kaiserpermanente.org
SIC: **8011** 8062 Medical centers; general medical & surgical hospitals
HQ: Kaiser Foundation Hospitals Inc
1 Kaiser Plz
Oakland CA 94612
510 271-6611

(P-19531)
KAISER FOUNDATION HOSPITALS
Also Called: Kaiser Permanente
1301 California St, Redlands (92374-2910)
PHONE..................................888 750-0036
Cindy Wong, *Director*
Nairy Sarkis, *Family Practiti*
EMP: 52
SALES (corp-wide): 94.1B **Privately Held**
WEB: www.kaiserpermanente.org
SIC: **8011** Offices & clinics of medical doctors
HQ: Kaiser Foundation Hospitals Inc
1 Kaiser Plz
Oakland CA 94612
510 271-6611

(P-19532)
KAISER FOUNDATION HOSPITALS
Also Called: Kaiser Permanente
1900 E Lambert Rd, Brea (92821-4371)
PHONE..................................714 672-5100
David Jeng, *Principal*
Sangeeta L Kumar, *Family Practiti*
Kevin Liao, *Family Practiti*
EMP: 52
SQ FT: 9,240

SALES (corp-wide): 94.1B **Privately Held**
WEB: www.kaiserpermanente.org
SIC: **8011** Offices & clinics of medical doctors
HQ: Kaiser Foundation Hospitals Inc
1 Kaiser Plz
Oakland CA 94612
510 271-6611

(P-19533)
KAISER FOUNDATION HOSPITALS
Also Called: Kaiser Permanente
99 Montecillo Rd, San Rafael
(94903-3308)
PHONE..................................415 444-2000
Patricia Kendall, *Administration*
Brian Bane,
Susan Gess, *Business Dir*
Lori Kennelly, *Office Mgr*
Betty Alfstad, *Admin Asst*
EMP: 1500
SALES (corp-wide): 94.1B **Privately Held**
WEB: www.kaiserpermanente.org
SIC: **8011** 8062 Medical centers; general medical & surgical hospitals
HQ: Kaiser Foundation Hospitals Inc
1 Kaiser Plz
Oakland CA 94612
510 271-6611

(P-19534)
KAISER FOUNDATION HOSPITALS
Also Called: Kaiser Permanente
901 Nevin Ave, Richmond (94801-3143)
PHONE..................................510 307-1500
Debbie Vachau, *Manager*
Deborah Pints, *Records Dir*
Linda Marietta, *Office Mgr*
Debbie Foster, *QA Dir*
Kimberly J Duir, *Family Practiti*
EMP: 400
SALES (corp-wide): 94.1B **Privately Held**
WEB: www.kaiserpermanente.org
SIC: **8011** 8062 Medical centers; general medical & surgical hospitals
HQ: Kaiser Foundation Hospitals Inc
1 Kaiser Plz
Oakland CA 94612
510 271-6611

(P-19535)
KAISER FOUNDATION HOSPITALS
Also Called: Kaiser Permanente West
6041 Cadillac Ave, Los Angeles
(90034-1700)
PHONE..................................323 857-2000
Howard Fullman, *Admin Director*
Todd Sachs,
Ann M Visosky, *Top Exec*
Karen Schellhardt, *Lab Dir*
Maria Masangkay, *Admin Asst*
EMP: 2000
SALES (corp-wide): 94.1B **Privately Held**
WEB: www.kaiserpermanente.org
SIC: **8011** Medical centers
HQ: Kaiser Foundation Hospitals Inc
1 Kaiser Plz
Oakland CA 94612
510 271-6611

(P-19536)
KAISER FOUNDATION HOSPITALS
17284 Slover Ave, Fontana (92337-7584)
PHONE..................................909 609-3800
Gregory Christian, *Branch Mgr*
EMP: 106
SALES (corp-wide): 94.1B **Privately Held**
SIC: **8011** General & family practice, physician/surgeon
HQ: Kaiser Foundation Hospitals Inc
1 Kaiser Plz
Oakland CA 94612
510 271-6611

(P-19537)
KAISER FOUNDATION HOSPITALS
Also Called: Vacaville Medical Center
1 Quality Dr, Vacaville (95688-9494)
PHONE..................................707 624-4000
EMP: 593

SALES (corp-wide): 94.1B **Privately Held**
SIC: **8011** Medical centers
HQ: Kaiser Foundation Hospitals Inc
1 Kaiser Plz
Oakland CA 94612
510 271-6611

(P-19538)
KAISER FOUNDATION HOSPITALS
Also Called: Tracy Medical Offices
2185 W Grant Line Rd, Tracy
(95377-7309)
PHONE..................................209 839-3200
Anale Cunningham, *Branch Mgr*
EMP: 593
SALES (corp-wide): 94.1B **Privately Held**
SIC: **8011** Offices & clinics of medical doctors
HQ: Kaiser Foundation Hospitals Inc
1 Kaiser Plz
Oakland CA 94612
510 271-6611

(P-19539)
KAISER FOUNDATION HOSPITALS
Also Called: Union City Medical Offices
3555 Whipple Rd, Union City (94587-1507)
PHONE..................................510 675-4010
Andrea Wilcox, *President*
EMP: 593
SALES (corp-wide): 94.1B **Privately Held**
SIC: **8011** Offices & clinics of medical doctors
HQ: Kaiser Foundation Hospitals Inc
1 Kaiser Plz
Oakland CA 94612
510 271-6611

(P-19540)
KAISER FOUNDATION HOSPITALS
Also Called: Rancho Cucamonga Medical Offs
10850 Arrow Rte, Rancho Cucamonga
(91730-4833)
PHONE..................................888 750-0036
EMP: 593
SALES (corp-wide): 94.1B **Privately Held**
SIC: **8011** Medical centers
HQ: Kaiser Foundation Hospitals Inc
1 Kaiser Plz
Oakland CA 94612
510 271-6611

(P-19541)
KAISER FOUNDATION HOSPITALS
Also Called: Anaheim Hills Medical Offices
5475 E La Palma Ave, Anaheim
(92807-2075)
PHONE..................................888 988-2800
EMP: 593
SALES (corp-wide): 94.1B **Privately Held**
SIC: **8011** Offices & clinics of medical doctors
HQ: Kaiser Foundation Hospitals Inc
1 Kaiser Plz
Oakland CA 94612
510 271-6611

(P-19542)
KAISER FOUNDATION HOSPITALS
Also Called: Central Medical Offices
3733 San Dimas St, Bakersfield
(93301-1407)
PHONE..................................877 524-7373
EMP: 593
SALES (corp-wide): 94.1B **Privately Held**
SIC: **8011** Offices & clinics of medical doctors
HQ: Kaiser Foundation Hospitals Inc
1 Kaiser Plz
Oakland CA 94612
510 271-6611

(P-19543)
KAISER FOUNDATION HOSPITALS
Also Called: Anaheim Kraemer Medical Offs
3460 E La Palma Ave, Anaheim
(92806-2020)
PHONE..................................888 988-2800

Benjamin Spurgeon, *Neurology*
Tina Lin, *Pediatrics*
EMP: 593
SALES (corp-wide): 94.1B **Privately Held**
SIC: **8011** Offices & clinics of medical doctors
HQ: Kaiser Foundation Hospitals Inc
1 Kaiser Plz
Oakland CA 94612
510 271-6611

(P-19544)
KAISER FOUNDATION HOSPITALS
Also Called: Chester Avenue Medical Offices
2531 Chester Ave, Bakersfield
(93301-2012)
PHONE..................................877 524-7373
Vinh Trang, *Surgeon*
EMP: 593
SALES (corp-wide): 94.1B **Privately Held**
SIC: **8011** Medical centers
HQ: Kaiser Foundation Hospitals Inc
1 Kaiser Plz
Oakland CA 94612
510 271-6611

(P-19545)
KAISER FOUNDATION HOSPITALS
Also Called: Chester Avenue Medical Offs II
2620 Chester Ave, Bakersfield
(93301-2015)
PHONE..................................661 337-7160
EMP: 593
SALES (corp-wide): 94.1B **Privately Held**
SIC: **8011** Offices & clinics of medical doctors
HQ: Kaiser Foundation Hospitals Inc
1 Kaiser Plz
Oakland CA 94612
510 271-6611

(P-19546)
KAISER FOUNDATION HOSPITALS
Also Called: Discovery Plz Med & Admin Offs
1200 Discovery Dr, Bakersfield
(93309-7032)
PHONE..................................877 524-7373
EMP: 593
SALES (corp-wide): 94.1B **Privately Held**
SIC: **8011** Medical centers
HQ: Kaiser Foundation Hospitals Inc
1 Kaiser Plz
Oakland CA 94612
510 271-6611

(P-19547)
KAISER FOUNDATION HOSPITALS
Also Called: Cerritos Medical Office Bldg
10820 183rd St, Cerritos (90703-8010)
PHONE..................................800 823-4040
EMP: 593
SALES (corp-wide): 94.1B **Privately Held**
SIC: **8011** Offices & clinics of medical doctors
HQ: Kaiser Foundation Hospitals Inc
1 Kaiser Plz
Oakland CA 94612
510 271-6611

(P-19548)
KAISER FOUNDATION HOSPITALS
Also Called: Las Posas Road Medical Offices
2620 Las Posas Rd, Camarillo
(93010-3400)
PHONE..................................888 515-3500
EMP: 593
SALES (corp-wide): 94.1B **Privately Held**
SIC: **8011** Offices & clinics of medical doctors
HQ: Kaiser Foundation Hospitals Inc
1 Kaiser Plz
Oakland CA 94612
510 271-6611

(P-19549)
KAISER FOUNDATION HOSPITALS
Also Called: Ming Medical Offices
8800 Ming Ave, Bakersfield (93311-1308)
PHONE..................................877 524-7373

EMP: 593
SALES (corp-wide): 94.1B Privately Held
SIC: 8011 Offices & clinics of medical doctors
HQ: Kaiser Foundation Hospitals Inc
    1 Kaiser Plz
    Oakland CA 94612
    510 271-6611

(P-19550)
KAISER FOUNDATION HOSPITALS
Also Called: Crossroads Medical Offices
12801 Crossroads Pkwy S, City of Industry (91746-3502)
PHONE..................................562 463-4377
EMP: 593
SALES (corp-wide): 94.1B Privately Held
SIC: 8011 Offices & clinics of medical doctors
HQ: Kaiser Foundation Hospitals Inc
    1 Kaiser Plz
    Oakland CA 94612
    510 271-6611

(P-19551)
KAISER FOUNDATION HOSPITALS
Also Called: Orchard Medical Offices
9449 Imperial Hwy, Downey (90242-2814)
PHONE..................................800 823-4040
Leon Randolph, President
EMP: 593
SALES (corp-wide): 94.1B Privately Held
SIC: 8011 Offices & clinics of medical doctors
HQ: Kaiser Foundation Hospitals Inc
    1 Kaiser Plz
    Oakland CA 94612
    510 271-6611

(P-19552)
KAISER FOUNDATION HOSPITALS
Also Called: Palomar Medical Center
2185 Citracado Pkwy, Escondido (92029-4159)
PHONE..................................442 281-5000
EMP: 593
SALES (corp-wide): 94.1B Privately Held
SIC: 8011 Medical centers
HQ: Kaiser Foundation Hospitals Inc
    1 Kaiser Plz
    Oakland CA 94612
    510 271-6611

(P-19553)
KAISER FOUNDATION HOSPITALS
Also Called: Diamond Bar Medical Offices
1336 Bridgegate Dr, Diamond Bar (91765-3955)
PHONE..................................800 780-1277
EMP: 593
SALES (corp-wide): 94.1B Privately Held
SIC: 8011 Medical centers
HQ: Kaiser Foundation Hospitals Inc
    1 Kaiser Plz
    Oakland CA 94612
    510 271-6611

(P-19554)
KAISER FOUNDATION HOSPITALS
Also Called: Palomar Health Downtown Campus
555 E Valley Pkwy, Escondido (92025-3048)
PHONE..................................760 739-3000
EMP: 593
SALES (corp-wide): 94.1B Privately Held
SIC: 8011 Medical centers
HQ: Kaiser Foundation Hospitals Inc
    1 Kaiser Plz
    Oakland CA 94612
    510 271-6611

(P-19555)
KAISER FOUNDATION HOSPITALS
Also Called: Garden Medical Offices
9353 Imperial Hwy, Downey (90242-2812)
PHONE..................................800 823-4040
Glenn Shulman, Osteopathy
EMP: 593

SALES (corp-wide): 94.1B Privately Held
SIC: 8011 Offices & clinics of medical doctors
HQ: Kaiser Foundation Hospitals Inc
    1 Kaiser Plz
    Oakland CA 94612
    510 271-6611

(P-19556)
KAISER FOUNDATION HOSPITALS
Also Called: Fairfield Medical Offices
1550 Gateway Blvd, Fairfield (94533-6901)
PHONE..................................707 427-4000
EMP: 593
SALES (corp-wide): 94.1B Privately Held
SIC: 8011 Offices & clinics of medical doctors
HQ: Kaiser Foundation Hospitals Inc
    1 Kaiser Plz
    Oakland CA 94612
    510 271-6611

(P-19557)
KAISER FOUNDATION HOSPITALS
Also Called: Foothill Ranch Medical Offices
26882 Towne Centre Dr # 1, Foothill Ranch (92610-2862)
PHONE..................................800 922-2000
EMP: 593
SALES (corp-wide): 94.1B Privately Held
SIC: 8011 Medical centers
HQ: Kaiser Foundation Hospitals Inc
    1 Kaiser Plz
    Oakland CA 94612
    510 271-6611

(P-19558)
KAISER FOUNDATION HOSPITALS
Also Called: Fontana Mental Health Offices
9310 Sierra Ave, Fontana (92335-5711)
PHONE..................................866 205-3595
EMP: 593
SALES (corp-wide): 94.1B Privately Held
SIC: 8011 Psychiatrists & psychoanalysts
HQ: Kaiser Foundation Hospitals Inc
    1 Kaiser Plz
    Oakland CA 94612
    510 271-6611

(P-19559)
KAISER FOUNDATION HOSPITALS
Also Called: Folsom Ambulatory Surgery Ctr
285 Palladio Pkwy, Folsom (95630-8741)
PHONE..................................916 986-4178
EMP: 593
SALES (corp-wide): 94.1B Privately Held
SIC: 8011 Ambulatory surgical center
HQ: Kaiser Foundation Hospitals Inc
    1 Kaiser Plz
    Oakland CA 94612
    510 271-6611

(P-19560)
KAISER FOUNDATION HOSPITALS
Also Called: Carson Medical Offices
18600 S Figueroa St, Gardena (90248-4505)
PHONE..................................800 780-1230
EMP: 593
SALES (corp-wide): 94.1B Privately Held
SIC: 8011 Medical centers
HQ: Kaiser Foundation Hospitals Inc
    1 Kaiser Plz
    Oakland CA 94612
    510 271-6611

(P-19561)
KAISER FOUNDATION HOSPITALS
Also Called: Balboa Plaza Admin Offices
10605 Balboa Blvd Ste 330, Granada Hills (91344-6358)
PHONE..................................818 832-7200
Dennis C Benton, Exec Dir
EMP: 593
SALES (corp-wide): 94.1B Privately Held
SIC: 8011 Health maintenance organization

HQ: Kaiser Foundation Hospitals Inc
    1 Kaiser Plz
    Oakland CA 94612
    510 271-6611

(P-19562)
KAISER FOUNDATION HOSPITALS
Also Called: Glendale Orange St Med Offs
501 N Orange St, Glendale (91203-1970)
PHONE..................................800 954-8000
EMP: 593
SALES (corp-wide): 94.1B Privately Held
SIC: 8011 Offices & clinics of medical doctors
HQ: Kaiser Foundation Hospitals Inc
    1 Kaiser Plz
    Oakland CA 94612
    510 271-6611

(P-19563)
KAISER FOUNDATION HOSPITALS
Also Called: Indio Medical Offices
46900 Monroe St, Indio (92201-4827)
PHONE..................................866 984-7483
EMP: 593
SALES (corp-wide): 94.1B Privately Held
SIC: 8011 Medical centers
HQ: Kaiser Foundation Hospitals Inc
    1 Kaiser Plz
    Oakland CA 94612
    510 271-6611

(P-19564)
KAISER FOUNDATION HOSPITALS
Also Called: Rancho San Diego Medical Offs
3875 Avocado Blvd, La Mesa (91941-7303)
PHONE..................................619 528-5000
Indushree Ghosh, Family Practiti
Michael Moreno, Family Practiti
Tracy Santos, Family Practiti
Joanna L Gunn, Med Doctor
EMP: 593
SALES (corp-wide): 94.1B Privately Held
SIC: 8011 Offices & clinics of medical doctors
HQ: Kaiser Foundation Hospitals Inc
    1 Kaiser Plz
    Oakland CA 94612
    510 271-6611

(P-19565)
KAISER FOUNDATION HOSPITALS
Also Called: Lincoln Medical Offices
1900 Dresden Dr, Lincoln (95648-8803)
PHONE..................................916 543-5153
EMP: 593
SALES (corp-wide): 94.1B Privately Held
SIC: 8011 Medical centers
HQ: Kaiser Foundation Hospitals Inc
    1 Kaiser Plz
    Oakland CA 94612
    510 271-6611

(P-19566)
KAISER FOUNDATION HOSPITALS
Also Called: Behavioral Health
44444 20th St W, Lancaster (93534-2714)
PHONE..................................661 951-0070
EMP: 593
SALES (corp-wide): 94.1B Privately Held
SIC: 8011 Psychiatrists & psychoanalysts
HQ: Kaiser Foundation Hospitals Inc
    1 Kaiser Plz
    Oakland CA 94612
    510 271-6611

(P-19567)
KAISER FOUNDATION HOSPITALS
Also Called: Lomita Medical Offices
2081 Palos Verdes Dr N, Lomita (90717-3701)
PHONE..................................310 325-6542
EMP: 593
SALES (corp-wide): 94.1B Privately Held
SIC: 8011 Offices & clinics of medical doctors

HQ: Kaiser Foundation Hospitals Inc
    1 Kaiser Plz
    Oakland CA 94612
    510 271-6611

(P-19568)
KAISER FOUNDATION HOSPITALS
Also Called: Lynwood Medical Offices
3830 Martin Luther King, Lynwood (90262-3625)
PHONE..................................310 604-5700
Sepehr Katiraie MD, CEO
EMP: 593
SALES (corp-wide): 94.1B Privately Held
SIC: 8011 Offices & clinics of medical doctors
HQ: Kaiser Foundation Hospitals Inc
    1 Kaiser Plz
    Oakland CA 94612
    510 271-6611

(P-19569)
KAISER FOUNDATION HOSPITALS
Also Called: Modesto Medical Offices
4601 Dale Rd, Modesto (95356-9718)
PHONE..................................209 735-5000
EMP: 593
SALES (corp-wide): 94.1B Privately Held
SIC: 8011 Medical centers
HQ: Kaiser Foundation Hospitals Inc
    1 Kaiser Plz
    Oakland CA 94612
    510 271-6611

(P-19570)
KAISER FOUNDATION HOSPITALS
Also Called: North Hollywood Medical Offs
5250 Lankershim Blvd, North Hollywood (91601-3186)
PHONE..................................888 778-5000
EMP: 593
SALES (corp-wide): 94.1B Privately Held
SIC: 8011 Offices & clinics of medical doctors
HQ: Kaiser Foundation Hospitals Inc
    1 Kaiser Plz
    Oakland CA 94612
    510 271-6611

(P-19571)
KAISER FOUNDATION HOSPITALS
Also Called: Bangs Avenue Medical Offices
4125 Bangs Ave, Modesto (95356-8713)
PHONE..................................209 735-5000
EMP: 593
SALES (corp-wide): 94.1B Privately Held
SIC: 8011 Offices & clinics of medical doctors
HQ: Kaiser Foundation Hospitals Inc
    1 Kaiser Plz
    Oakland CA 94612
    510 271-6611

(P-19572)
KAISER FOUNDATION HOSPITALS
Also Called: Norwalk Medical Offices
12501 Imperial Hwy, Norwalk (90650-3179)
PHONE..................................562 807-6100
EMP: 593
SALES (corp-wide): 94.1B Privately Held
SIC: 8011 Offices & clinics of medical doctors
HQ: Kaiser Foundation Hospitals Inc
    1 Kaiser Plz
    Oakland CA 94612
    510 271-6611

(P-19573)
KAISER FOUNDATION HOSPITALS
Also Called: Ontario Vineyard Medical Offs
2295 S Vineyard Ave, Ontario (91761-7925)
PHONE..................................909 724-5000
EMP: 593
SALES (corp-wide): 94.1B Privately Held
SIC: 8011 Medical centers

HQ: Kaiser Foundation Hospitals Inc
1 Kaiser Plz
Oakland CA 94612
510 271-6611

(P-19574)
KAISER FOUNDATION HOSPITALS
Also Called: Oxnard 2200 East Gonzales
2200 E Gonzales Rd, Oxnard
(93036-0619)
PHONE..................888 515-3500
EMP: 593
SALES (corp-wide): 94.1B **Privately Held**
SIC: **8011** Offices & clinics of medical doctors
HQ: Kaiser Foundation Hospitals Inc
1 Kaiser Plz
Oakland CA 94612
510 271-6611

(P-19575)
KAISER FOUNDATION HOSPITALS
Also Called: Kaiser Permanente Member Svcs
73733 Fred Waring Dr, Palm Desert
(92260-2589)
PHONE..................800 777-1256
Virginia McLain, *Branch Mgr*
EMP: 593
SALES (corp-wide): 94.1B **Privately Held**
SIC: **8011** Health maintenance organization
HQ: Kaiser Foundation Hospitals Inc
1 Kaiser Plz
Oakland CA 94612
510 271-6611

(P-19576)
KAISER FOUNDATION HOSPITALS
Also Called: Oxnard 2103 East Gonzales Road
2103 E Gonzales Rd, Oxnard
(93036-3757)
PHONE..................805 988-6300
EMP: 593
SALES (corp-wide): 94.1B **Privately Held**
SIC: **8011** Offices & clinics of medical doctors
HQ: Kaiser Foundation Hospitals Inc
1 Kaiser Plz
Oakland CA 94612
510 271-6611

(P-19577)
KAISER FOUNDATION HOSPITALS
Also Called: Pinole Medical Offices
1301 Pinole Valley Rd, Pinole
(94564-1384)
PHONE..................510 243-4000
EMP: 593
SALES (corp-wide): 94.1B **Privately Held**
SIC: **8011** Offices & clinics of medical doctors
HQ: Kaiser Foundation Hospitals Inc
1 Kaiser Plz
Oakland CA 94612
510 271-6611

(P-19578)
KAISER FOUNDATION HOSPITALS
Also Called: Palm Desert Medical Offices
University Park Ctr, Palm Desert (92211)
PHONE..................866 984-7483
EMP: 593
SALES (corp-wide): 19.1B **Privately Held**
SIC: **8011**
PA: Kaiser Foundation Hospitals Inc
1 Kaiser Plz Ste 2600
Oakland CA 94612
510 271-5800

(P-19579)
KAISER FOUNDATION HOSPITALS
Also Called: Canyon Crest Mental Hlth Offs
5225 Canyon Crest Dr, Riverside
(92507-6301)
PHONE..................951 248-4000
EMP: 593

SALES (corp-wide): 94.1B **Privately Held**
SIC: **8011** Psychiatrists & psychoanalysts
HQ: Kaiser Foundation Hospitals Inc
1 Kaiser Plz
Oakland CA 94612
510 271-6611

(P-19580)
KAISER FOUNDATION HOSPITALS
Also Called: Meridian Medical Offices
14305 Meridian Pkwy, Riverside
(92518-3034)
PHONE..................866 984-7483
EMP: 593
SALES (corp-wide): 94.1B **Privately Held**
SIC: **8011** Medical centers
HQ: Kaiser Foundation Hospitals Inc
1 Kaiser Plz
Oakland CA 94612
510 271-6611

(P-19581)
KAISER FOUNDATION HOSPITALS
Also Called: Carmel Valley Medical Offices
3851 Shaw Ridge Rd, San Diego
(92130-2807)
PHONE..................858 847-3500
EMP: 593
SALES (corp-wide): 94.1B **Privately Held**
SIC: **8011** Offices & clinics of medical doctors
HQ: Kaiser Foundation Hospitals Inc
1 Kaiser Plz
Oakland CA 94612
510 271-6611

(P-19582)
KAISER FOUNDATION HOSPITALS
Also Called: Kaiser Permanente Kearny
4510 Viewridge Ave, San Diego
(92123-1637)
PHONE..................858 502-1350
EMP: 593
SALES (corp-wide): 94.1B **Privately Held**
SIC: **8011** Specialized medical practitioners, except internal
HQ: Kaiser Foundation Hospitals Inc
1 Kaiser Plz
Oakland CA 94612
510 271-6611

(P-19583)
KAISER FOUNDATION HOSPITALS
Also Called: Kaiser Permanente San
1000 Franklin Pkwy, San Mateo
(94403-1922)
PHONE..................650 358-7000
David Kvancz, *Vice Pres*
EMP: 593
SALES (corp-wide): 94.1B **Privately Held**
SIC: **8011** Medical centers
HQ: Kaiser Foundation Hospitals Inc
1 Kaiser Plz
Oakland CA 94612
510 271-6611

(P-19584)
KAISER FOUNDATION HOSPITALS
Also Called: Kaiser Permanente San
2500 Merced St, San Leandro
(94577-4201)
PHONE..................510 454-1000
Thomas S Hanenburg, *Senior VP*
Ratnadeep Patel, *Internal Med*
Sachin Gupta, *Cardiovascular*
Aaron Pessl, *Emerg Med Spec*
EMP: 593
SALES (corp-wide): 94.1B **Privately Held**
SIC: **8011** 8062 Medical centers; general medical & surgical hospitals
HQ: Kaiser Foundation Hospitals Inc
1 Kaiser Plz
Oakland CA 94612
510 271-6611

(P-19585)
KAISER FOUNDATION HOSPITALS
Also Called: San Ramon Medical Offices
2300 Camino Ramon, San Ramon
(94583-1354)
PHONE..................925 244-7600
EMP: 593
SALES (corp-wide): 94.1B **Privately Held**
SIC: **8011** Offices & clinics of medical doctors
HQ: Kaiser Foundation Hospitals Inc
1 Kaiser Plz
Oakland CA 94612
510 271-6611

(P-19586)
KAISER FOUNDATION HOSPITALS
Also Called: Harbor Corporate Park
3601 S Harbor Blvd, Santa Ana
(92704-7909)
PHONE..................714 223-2606
EMP: 593
SALES (corp-wide): 94.1B **Privately Held**
SIC: **8011** Psychiatric clinic
HQ: Kaiser Foundation Hospitals Inc
1 Kaiser Plz
Oakland CA 94612
510 271-6611

(P-19587)
KAISER FOUNDATION HOSPITALS
Also Called: Canyon Country Medical Offices
26415 Carl Boyer Dr, Santa Clarita
(91350-5824)
PHONE..................888 778-5000
EMP: 593
SALES (corp-wide): 94.1B **Privately Held**
SIC: **8011** Offices & clinics of medical doctors
HQ: Kaiser Foundation Hospitals Inc
1 Kaiser Plz
Oakland CA 94612
510 271-6611

(P-19588)
KAISER FOUNDATION HOSPITALS
Also Called: Thosand Oaks 145 Hodencamp
145 Hodencamp Rd, Thousand Oaks
(91360-5810)
PHONE..................888 515-3500
EMP: 593
SALES (corp-wide): 94.1B **Privately Held**
SIC: **8011** Offices & clinics of medical doctors
HQ: Kaiser Foundation Hospitals Inc
1 Kaiser Plz
Oakland CA 94612
510 271-6611

(P-19589)
KAISER FOUNDATION HOSPITALS
Also Called: Santa Clara Arques Med Offs
1263 E Arques Ave, Sunnyvale
(94085-4701)
PHONE..................408 851-1000
EMP: 593
SALES (corp-wide): 94.1B **Privately Held**
SIC: **8011** Offices & clinics of medical doctors
HQ: Kaiser Foundation Hospitals Inc
1 Kaiser Plz
Oakland CA 94612
510 271-6611

(P-19590)
KAISER FOUNDATION HOSPITALS
Also Called: Thousand Oaks 322 E Thousand
322 E Thousand Oaks Blvd, Thousand Oaks (91360-5804)
PHONE..................888 515-3500
EMP: 593
SALES (corp-wide): 94.1B **Privately Held**
SIC: **8011** Offices & clinics of medical doctors
HQ: Kaiser Foundation Hospitals Inc
1 Kaiser Plz
Oakland CA 94612
510 271-6611

(P-19591)
KAISER FOUNDATION HOSPITALS
Also Called: Tustin Ranch Medical Offices
2521 Michelle Dr, Tustin (92780-7014)
PHONE..................888 988-2800
EMP: 593
SALES (corp-wide): 94.1B **Privately Held**
SIC: **8011** Offices & clinics of medical doctors
HQ: Kaiser Foundation Hospitals Inc
1 Kaiser Plz
Oakland CA 94612
510 271-6611

(P-19592)
KAISER FOUNDATION HOSPITALS
Also Called: Kaiser Permanente
250 Hospital Pkwy, San Jose (95119-1103)
PHONE..................408 972-7000
Joann Zimmerman, *Branch Mgr*
Armand Bareng, *Administration*
Seema Sidhu, *Obstetrician*
An Kok Lie, *Anesthesiology*
Ann B Von Gehr, *Hematology*
EMP: 650
SALES (corp-wide): 94.1B **Privately Held**
WEB: www.kaiserpermanente.org
SIC: **8011** Medical centers
HQ: Kaiser Foundation Hospitals Inc
1 Kaiser Plz
Oakland CA 94612
510 271-6611

(P-19593)
KAISER FOUNDATION HOSPITALS
Also Called: Kaiser Permanente
1100 Veterans Blvd, Redwood City
(94063-2037)
PHONE..................650 299-2000
Eric Rasmussen, *Manager*
Derrick Taylor,
Dion Bennett, *Info Tech Mgr*
Linda Williams, *Technician*
Ron Cappa, *Engineer*
EMP: 1500
SALES (corp-wide): 94.1B **Privately Held**
WEB: www.kaiserpermanente.org
SIC: **8011** 8062 Medical centers; general medical & surgical hospitals
HQ: Kaiser Foundation Hospitals Inc
1 Kaiser Plz
Oakland CA 94612
510 271-6611

(P-19594)
KAISER FOUNDATION HOSPITALS
Also Called: Kaiser Permanente
1425 S Main St, Walnut Creek
(94596-5318)
PHONE..................925 295-4000
Michael Tully-Cintron, *Branch Mgr*
Paul Fukumae, *Lab Dir*
Andrea Han, *Pharmacy Dir*
Norma Rutherford, *Project Mgr*
Deneen Wohlford, *Mktg Dir*
EMP: 2000
SQ FT: 11,840
SALES (corp-wide): 94.1B **Privately Held**
WEB: www.kaiserpermanente.org
SIC: **8011** Medical centers
HQ: Kaiser Foundation Hospitals Inc
1 Kaiser Plz
Oakland CA 94612
510 271-6611

(P-19595)
KAISER FOUNDATION HOSPITALS
Also Called: Kaiser Permanente
25825 Vermont Ave, Harbor City
(90710-3518)
PHONE..................310 325-5111
Mary A Barnes, *Branch Mgr*
Michael Ward,
Sophia Salazar, *Records Dir*
Michael Kusunoki, *Officer*
Cristeta L Lozon, *Top Exec*
EMP: 1700
SALES (corp-wide): 94.1B **Privately Held**
WEB: www.kaiserpermanente.org
SIC: **8011** Medical centers

HQ: Kaiser Foundation Hospitals Inc
   1 Kaiser Plz
   Oakland CA 94612
   510 271-6611

(P-19596)
KAISER FOUNDATION HOSPITALS
Also Called: Kaiser Permanente San Fran
601 Van Ness Ave Ste 2008, San Francisco (94102-6310)
PHONE..................................415 833-9688
EMP: 105
SALES (corp-wide): 94.1B **Privately Held**
SIC: 8011 Occupational & industrial specialist, physician/surgeon
HQ: Kaiser Foundation Hospitals Inc
   1 Kaiser Plz
   Oakland CA 94612
   510 271-6611

(P-19597)
KAISER FOUNDATION HOSPITALS
Also Called: Kaiser Permanente
9961 Sierra Ave, Fontana (92335-6720)
PHONE..................................909 427-5000
William Meyer, *Principal*
David Young, *Officer*
Jeff Jobe, *Radiology Dir*
Linda Clement, *Admin Asst*
Jesse James, *Engineer*
EMP: 1700
SALES (corp-wide): 94.1B **Privately Held**
WEB: www.kaiserpermanente.org
SIC: 8011 Medical centers
HQ: Kaiser Foundation Hospitals Inc
   1 Kaiser Plz
   Oakland CA 94612
   510 271-6611

(P-19598)
KAISER FOUNDATION HOSPITALS
Also Called: Milpitas Medical Offices
770 E Calaveras Blvd, Milpitas (95035-5491)
PHONE..................................408 945-2900
Ellen Sinclair, *Manager*
Curtis L Mark, *Internal Med*
Quang D Dao, *Pediatrics*
Jason C Chang, *Med Doctor*
Quang Dao, *Med Doctor*
EMP: 50
SALES (corp-wide): 94.1B **Privately Held**
WEB: www.kaiserpermanente.org
SIC: 8011 8062 Medical centers; general medical & surgical hospitals
HQ: Kaiser Foundation Hospitals Inc
   1 Kaiser Plz
   Oakland CA 94612
   510 271-6611

(P-19599)
KAISER FOUNDATION HOSPITALS
Kaiser Permanente
1950 Franklin St, Oakland (94612-5190)
PHONE..................................510 987-1000
Maryanne Williams, *Manager*
Carol Cardinale,
Wade Overgaard, *Vice Pres*
Kathy Weiner, *Managing Dir*
Michele Bottrell, *Program Mgr*
EMP: 793
SALES (corp-wide): 94.1B **Privately Held**
WEB: www.kaiserpermanente.org
SIC: 8011 Health maintenance organization
HQ: Kaiser Foundation Hospitals Inc
   1 Kaiser Plz
   Oakland CA 94612
   510 271-6611

(P-19600)
KAISER FOUNDATION HOSPITALS
Also Called: La Palma Medical Offices
5 Centerpointe Dr, La Palma (90623-1050)
PHONE..................................714 562-3420
Josefina Guzman-Inouye, *Manager*
Wendy Y Leu, *Family Practiti*
Diane V Pham, *Family Practiti*
Ayesha G Munir, *Pediatrics*
Waldo Luciano, *Med Doctor*

EMP: 50
SALES (corp-wide): 94.1B **Privately Held**
WEB: www.kaiserpermanente.org
SIC: 8011 Offices & clinics of medical doctors
HQ: Kaiser Foundation Hospitals Inc
   1 Kaiser Plz
   Oakland CA 94612
   510 271-6611

(P-19601)
KAISER FOUNDATION HOSPITALS
Also Called: Glendale Medical Offices
444 W Glenoaks Blvd, Glendale (91202-2917)
PHONE..................................818 552-3000
Avetis Tashyan, *Branch Mgr*
Kreighton L Chan, *Partner*
Joshua T Fleischman, *Family Practiti*
Ricardo Sistos, *Family Practiti*
Nicolle Thomas, *Family Practiti*
EMP: 50
SALES (corp-wide): 94.1B **Privately Held**
WEB: www.kaiserpermanente.org
SIC: 8011 Medical centers
HQ: Kaiser Foundation Hospitals Inc
   1 Kaiser Plz
   Oakland CA 94612
   510 271-6611

(P-19602)
KAISER FOUNDATION HOSPITALS
Also Called: Kaiser Prmnnte Psadena Med Off
3280 E Foothill Blvd, Pasadena (91107-3103)
P.O. Box 7005 (91109-7005)
PHONE..................................626 440-5639
Ronald Pham, *Family Practiti*
EMP: 50
SALES (corp-wide): 94.1B **Privately Held**
WEB: www.kaiserpermanente.org
SIC: 8011 Medical centers
HQ: Kaiser Foundation Hospitals Inc
   1 Kaiser Plz
   Oakland CA 94612
   510 271-6611

(P-19603)
KAISER FOUNDATION HOSPITALS
Also Called: Yorba Linda Medical Offices
22550 Savi Ranch Pkwy, Yorba Linda (92887-4670)
PHONE..................................714 685-3520
Marie Kohl, *Administration*
Deepti D Gandhi, *Family Practiti*
Lisa Rivera, *Nurse Practr*
EMP: 50
SALES (corp-wide): 94.1B **Privately Held**
WEB: www.kaiserpermanente.org
SIC: 8011 Offices & clinics of medical doctors
HQ: Kaiser Foundation Hospitals Inc
   1 Kaiser Plz
   Oakland CA 94612
   510 271-6611

(P-19604)
KAISER FOUNDATION HOSPITALS
Also Called: Clairemont Medical Offices
7060 Clairemont Mesa Blvd, San Diego (92111-1003)
PHONE..................................858 573-0299
Michael Mellon MD, *Manager*
Ali Aboutaleb, *Family Practiti*
Dennis Andrade, *Family Practiti*
Raymond Berdugo, *Family Practiti*
Mark S Fenster, *Family Practiti*
EMP: 50
SALES (corp-wide): 94.1B **Privately Held**
WEB: www.kaiserpermanente.org
SIC: 8011 Offices & clinics of medical doctors
HQ: Kaiser Foundation Hospitals Inc
   1 Kaiser Plz
   Oakland CA 94612
   510 271-6611

(P-19605)
KAISER FOUNDATION HOSPITALS
Also Called: Escondido Medical Offices
732 N Broadway, Escondido (92025-1897)
PHONE..................................619 528-5000
Han Kim, *Manager*
Roderick T Ang, *Family Practiti*
Gloria Gutierrez, *Med Doctor*
William McKown, *Med Doctor*
Keith Sato,
EMP: 50
SALES (corp-wide): 94.1B **Privately Held**
WEB: www.kaiserpermanente.org
SIC: 8011 Offices & clinics of medical doctors
HQ: Kaiser Foundation Hospitals Inc
   1 Kaiser Plz
   Oakland CA 94612
   510 271-6611

(P-19606)
KAISER FOUNDATION HOSPITALS
Also Called: Davis Medical Offices
1955 Cowell Blvd, Davis (95618-6325)
PHONE..................................530 757-7100
Robert Talkington, *Manager*
EMP: 50
SALES (corp-wide): 94.1B **Privately Held**
WEB: www.kaiserpermanente.org
SIC: 8011 Medical centers
HQ: Kaiser Foundation Hospitals Inc
   1 Kaiser Plz
   Oakland CA 94612
   510 271-6611

(P-19607)
KAISER FOUNDATION HOSPITALS
Also Called: Kaiser Prmnnte Hayward Med Ctr
27400 Hesperian Blvd, Hayward (94545-4235)
PHONE..................................510 678-4000
Cynthia Seay, *Manager*
Eve Newton-Gill, *Volunteer Dir*
Elizabeth Calvet, *Administration*
Roger Mennis, *Administration*
Aruna Koduri, *Pediatrics*
EMP: 1200
SALES (corp-wide): 94.1B **Privately Held**
WEB: www.kaiserpermanente.org
SIC: 8011 Medical centers
HQ: Kaiser Foundation Hospitals Inc
   1 Kaiser Plz
   Oakland CA 94612
   510 271-6611

(P-19608)
KAISER FOUNDATION HOSPITALS
Also Called: Permanentee Medical Group
1001 Riverside Ave, Roseville (95678-5134)
PHONE..................................916 784-4000
Deb Royer, *Manager*
Richard Guy, *Oncology*
EMP: 200
SALES (corp-wide): 94.1B **Privately Held**
WEB: www.kaiserpermanente.org
SIC: 8011 Offices & clinics of medical doctors
HQ: Kaiser Foundation Hospitals Inc
   1 Kaiser Plz
   Oakland CA 94612
   510 271-6611

(P-19609)
KAISER FOUNDATION HOSPITALS
Also Called: Kaiser Perminente
2155 Iron Point Rd, Folsom (95630-8707)
PHONE..................................916 817-5200
Larry Marini, *Manager*
Ryan Pearson, *Family Practiti*
Hamid R Kazerouni Zadeh, *Internal Med*
Robert Madrigal, *Pediatrics*
Trent Wise, *Pediatrics*
EMP: 200
SALES (corp-wide): 94.1B **Privately Held**
WEB: www.kaiserpermanente.org
SIC: 8011 Health maintenance organization

HQ: Kaiser Foundation Hospitals Inc
   1 Kaiser Plz
   Oakland CA 94612
   510 271-6611

(P-19610)
KAISER FOUNDATION HOSPITALS
Also Called: Kaiser Foundation Health Plan
220 E Hacienda Ave, Campbell (95008-6617)
PHONE..................................408 871-6500
Joyce Snowbarger, *Manager*
Sara Murphy, *OB/GYN*
Mimi Hocking, *Director*
EMP: 100
SALES (corp-wide): 94.1B **Privately Held**
WEB: www.kaiser.com
SIC: 8011 8062 Medical centers; general medical & surgical hospitals
HQ: Kaiser Foundation Hospitals Inc
   1 Kaiser Plz
   Oakland CA 94612
   510 271-6611

(P-19611)
KAISER FOUNDATION HOSPITALS
Also Called: Kaiser Permanente
1200 El Camino Real, South San Francisco (94080-3208)
PHONE..................................650 742-2000
Evelyn Chan, *Branch Mgr*
Hamid Motamed,
Laurel Ullrich, *Info Tech Dir*
Brenda Leonard, *Engineer*
Bill Spremich, *Engineer*
EMP: 1500
SALES (corp-wide): 94.1B **Privately Held**
WEB: www.kaiserpermanente.org
SIC: 8011 8062 Medical centers; general medical & surgical hospitals
HQ: Kaiser Foundation Hospitals Inc
   1 Kaiser Plz
   Oakland CA 94612
   510 271-6611

(P-19612)
KAISER FOUNDATION HOSPITALS
Also Called: Kaiser Permanente South
6600 Bruceville Rd, Sacramento (95823-4671)
PHONE..................................916 688-2000
Sarah Krevans, *Branch Mgr*
Joel Weber,
Robert Alvarez, *President*
Kyra Wink, *Engineer*
Kevin Peterson, *Human Res Dir*
EMP: 3600
SALES (corp-wide): 94.1B **Privately Held**
WEB: www.kaiserpermanente.org
SIC: 8011 Medical centers
HQ: Kaiser Foundation Hospitals Inc
   1 Kaiser Plz
   Oakland CA 94612
   510 271-6611

(P-19613)
KAISER FOUNDATION HOSPITALS
Also Called: Kaiser Permanente
39400 Paseo Padre Pkwy, Fremont (94538-2310)
PHONE..................................510 248-3000
Calvin Wheeler, *Manager*
Victoria O'Gorman, *Administration*
Peter H D, *IT/INT Sup*
Phil Wald, *Controller*
Cathy Gibson, *Psychologist*
EMP: 400
SQ FT: 86,710
SALES (corp-wide): 94.1B **Privately Held**
WEB: www.kaiserpermanente.org
SIC: 8011 8062 Medical centers; general medical & surgical hospitals
HQ: Kaiser Foundation Hospitals Inc
   1 Kaiser Plz
   Oakland CA 94612
   510 271-6611

PRODUCTS & SVCS

(P-19614)
KAISER FOUNDATION HOSPITALS
Also Called: Kaiser Permanente
27107 Tourney Rd, Santa Clarita
(91355-1860)
PHONE..............................661 222-2323
Pat Kenney, *Principal*
Carrie Algozine, *Internal Med*
Seth Glickman, *Pediatrics*
Scott Steiglitz, *Med Doctor*
EMP: 52
SQ FT: 70,835
SALES (corp-wide): 94.1B **Privately Held**
WEB: www.kaiserpermanente.org
SIC: **8011** Offices & clinics of medical doctors
HQ: Kaiser Foundation Hospitals Inc
1 Kaiser Plz
Oakland CA 94612
510 271-6611

(P-19615)
KAISER FOUNDATION HOSPITALS
Also Called: Riverside Medical Center
10800 Magnolia Ave, Riverside
(92505-3000)
PHONE..............................951 353-2000
Vita Willett, *Director*
Denise Topliff, *Lab Dir*
Mario Casupanan, *Comp Lab Dir*
Sandhya K Menda, *Obstetrician*
Douglas M Montgomery, *Obstetrician*
EMP: 1000
SALES (corp-wide): 94.1B **Privately Held**
WEB: www.kaiserpermanente.org
SIC: **8011** 8062 Medical centers; general medical & surgical hospitals
HQ: Kaiser Foundation Hospitals Inc
1 Kaiser Plz
Oakland CA 94612
510 271-6611

(P-19616)
KAISER FOUNDATION HOSPITALS
Also Called: Kaiser Permanente San Jose
250 Hospital Pkwy Bldg D, San Jose
(95119-1103)
PHONE..............................408 972-3000
Thomas Hau, *Branch Mgr*
Krammie M Chan, *Radiology Dir*
Patrick W Suen, *Surgeon*
Amir Hadid, *Obstetrician*
Heidi Olander, *Obstetrician*
EMP: 105
SQ FT: 5,976
SALES (corp-wide): 94.1B **Privately Held**
WEB: www.kaiserpermanente.org
SIC: **8011** 8062 General & family practice, physician/surgeon; general medical & surgical hospitals
HQ: Kaiser Foundation Hospitals Inc
1 Kaiser Plz
Oakland CA 94612
510 271-6611

(P-19617)
KAISER FOUNDATION HOSPITALS
Also Called: Kaiser Permanente
2425 Geary Blvd, San Francisco
(94115-3358)
PHONE..............................415 833-2000
Mike Alexander, *Senior VP*
Eugene Lee, *Internal Med*
Roger Flanigan, *Psychiatry*
Monique Schaulis, *Emerg Med Spec*
Karen Lai, *Pharmacist*
EMP: 720
SALES (corp-wide): 94.1B **Privately Held**
WEB: www.kaiserpermanente.org
SIC: **8011** Medical centers
HQ: Kaiser Foundation Hospitals Inc
1 Kaiser Plz
Oakland CA 94612
510 271-6611

(P-19618)
KAISER FOUNDATION HOSPITALS
Also Called: Kaiser Permanente Moreno
27300 Iris Ave, Moreno Valley
(92555-4802)
PHONE..............................951 243-0811
Tom Mc Ciltock, *Manager*
Pamela Gibson, *Lab Dir*
Marisa Cailing, *Technician*
EMP: 400
SALES (corp-wide): 94.1B **Privately Held**
WEB: www.kaiserpermanente.org
SIC: **8011** Medical centers
HQ: Kaiser Foundation Hospitals Inc
1 Kaiser Plz
Oakland CA 94612
510 271-6611

(P-19619)
KAISER FOUNDATION HOSPITALS
Also Called: Kaiser Permanente
110 N La Brea Ave, Inglewood
(90301-1708)
PHONE..............................310 419-3303
Victor Ahaiwe, *President*
Mauricio Flores, *Family Practiti*
Greg D Saccone, *Internal Med*
EMP: 450
SALES (corp-wide): 94.1B **Privately Held**
WEB: www.kaiserpermanente.org
SIC: **8011** Offices & clinics of medical doctors
HQ: Kaiser Foundation Hospitals Inc
1 Kaiser Plz
Oakland CA 94612
510 271-6611

(P-19620)
KAISER FOUNDATION HOSPITALS
Also Called: Kaiser Permanente
7300 N Fresno St, Fresno (93720-2941)
PHONE..............................559 448-4500
Susan Ryan, *Senior VP*
Debbie Oneal, *Director*
EMP: 2000
SALES (corp-wide): 94.1B **Privately Held**
WEB: www.kaiserpermanente.org
SIC: **8011** Medical centers
HQ: Kaiser Foundation Hospitals Inc
1 Kaiser Plz
Oakland CA 94612
510 271-6611

(P-19621)
KAISER FOUNDATION HOSPITALS
Also Called: Carlsbad Medical Offices
6860 Avenida Encinas, Carlsbad
(92011-3201)
PHONE..............................760 931-4228
Phong Nguyen, *Manager*
EMP: 105
SALES (corp-wide): 94.1B **Privately Held**
SIC: **8011** Health maintenance organization
HQ: Kaiser Foundation Hospitals Inc
1 Kaiser Plz
Oakland CA 94612
510 271-6611

(P-19622)
KAISER MED CLINIC
555 Castro St, Mountain View
(94041-2009)
PHONE..............................650 903-2103
Patricia Carpenter MGA, *Manager*
Patricia MGA, *Manager*
EMP: 110
SALES (est): 2.9MM **Privately Held**
SIC: **8011** Clinic, operated by physicians

(P-19623)
KAWEAH DLTA HLTH CARE DST GILD
1014 San Juan Ave, Exeter (93221-1312)
PHONE..............................559 592-7128
EMP: 118
SALES (corp-wide): 537.4MM **Privately Held**
SIC: **8011** Offices & clinics of medical doctors

PA: Kaweah Delta Health Care District
400 W Mineral King Ave
Visalia CA 93291
559 624-2000

(P-19624)
KAWEAH DLTA HLTH CARE DST GILD
1110 S Ben Maddox Way, Visalia
(93292-3643)
PHONE..............................559 624-4800
EMP: 177
SALES (corp-wide): 537.4MM **Privately Held**
SIC: **8011** Medical centers
PA: Kaweah Delta Health Care District
400 W Mineral King Ave
Visalia CA 93291
559 624-2000

(P-19625)
KERLAN-JOBE ORTHOPEDIC CLINIC (PA)
6801 Park Ter Ste 500, Los Angeles
(90045-9212)
PHONE..............................310 665-7200
Ralph A Gambardella, *CEO*
Stephen Lombardo, *Admin Sec*
EMP: 78
SQ FT: 37,000
SALES (est): 13.7MM **Privately Held**
WEB: www.kerlanjobe.com
SIC: **8011** Orthopedic physician

(P-19626)
KERN HEALTH SYSTEMS INC
Also Called: Kern Family Helathcare
9700 Stockdale Hwy, Bakersfield
(93311-3617)
P.O. Box 25003 (93390-5003)
PHONE..............................661 664-5000
Paul Hensler, *Ch of Bd*
Lamberson Philip, *Administration*
Doris Alvarez, *Purch Agent*
Louis Iturriria, *Mktg Dir*
Jenna Campbell, *Marketing Staff*
EMP: 98
SQ FT: 16,000
SALES (est): 19.1MM **Privately Held**
WEB: www.kernfamilyhealthcare.com
SIC: **8011** Clinic, operated by physicians

(P-19627)
KERN RDLGY IMAGING SYSTEMS INC (PA)
2301 Bahamas Dr, Bakersfield
(93309-0663)
PHONE..............................661 326-9600
David P Schale, *CEO*
Jeff Child MD, *Treasurer*
John Gundzik MD, *Vice Pres*
EMP: 180
SQ FT: 20,000
SALES (est): 17.4MM **Privately Held**
SIC: **8011** Radiologist

(P-19628)
LA CLINICA DE LA RAZA INC
1515 Fruitvale Ave, Oakland (94601-2355)
PHONE..............................510 535-6300
Jim Eitel, *Partner*
Maria Hernandez, *COO*
Daniel Ayala, *Vice Pres*
Dan Gilliam, *Technology*
Khalil Carter, *OB/GYN*
EMP: 178
SALES (corp-wide): 102.2MM **Privately Held**
SIC: **8011** 8699 Clinic, operated by physicians; charitable organization
PA: La Clinica De La Raza, Inc.
1450 Fruitvale Ave Fl 3
Oakland CA 94601
510 535-4000

(P-19629)
LA CLINICA DE LA RAZA INC
243 Georgia St, Vallejo (94590-5905)
PHONE..............................707 556-8100
Jane Garcia, *Branch Mgr*
EMP: 276
SALES (corp-wide): 102.2MM **Privately Held**
SIC: **8011** Clinic, operated by physicians

PA: Kaweah Delta Health Care District
400 W Mineral King Ave
Visalia CA 93291
559 624-2000

PA: La Clinica De La Raza, Inc.
1450 Fruitvale Ave Fl 3
Oakland CA 94601
510 535-4000

(P-19630)
LA CLINICA DE LA RAZA INC
Also Called: Mental Health Department
1601 Fruitvale Ave, Oakland (94601-2418)
PHONE..............................510 535-6200
Jane Garcia, *CEO*
Susanna Moore, *Psychiatry*
Monica M Pearson, *Fmly & Gen Dent*
Leslie Preston, *Director*
Lisa Montang, *Assistant*
EMP: 222
SALES (corp-wide): 102.2MM **Privately Held**
SIC: **8011** Clinic, operated by physicians
PA: La Clinica De La Raza, Inc.
1450 Fruitvale Ave Fl 3
Oakland CA 94601
510 535-4000

(P-19631)
LA COUNTY HIGH DESERT HLTH SYS
44900 60th St W, Lancaster (93536-7618)
PHONE..............................661 945-8461
Beryl Brooks, *Exec Dir*
EMP: 400
SALES (est): 11.9MM **Privately Held**
SIC: **8011** 8062 8093 Ambulatory surgical center; hospital, AMA approved residency; specialty outpatient clinics

(P-19632)
LA JOLLA ORTHOPAEDIC
4120 La Jolla Village Dr, La Jolla
(92037-1406)
PHONE..............................858 657-0055
Scott Leggett, *Mng Member*
EMP: 69
SALES (est): 11.3MM **Privately Held**
WEB: www.osclajolla.com
SIC: **8011** Orthopedic physician; surgeon

(P-19633)
LA LASER CENTER PC CPMC
10884 Santa Monica Blvd # 300, Los Angeles (90025-7638)
P.O. Box 16297, Beverly Hills (90209-2297)
PHONE..............................310 446-4400
Mehry Tahery, *Admin Sec*
Keith Guddy, *Accountant*
EMP: 95
SALES (est): 1.3MM **Privately Held**
SIC: **8011** Dermatologist

(P-19634)
LA MAESTRA FAMILY CLINIC INC
165 S 1st St, El Cajon (92019-4795)
PHONE..............................619 280-1105
Marty Straw, *Branch Mgr*
EMP: 100 **Privately Held**
SIC: **8011** Clinic, operated by physicians
PA: La Maestra Family Clinic, Inc.
4060 Fairmount Ave
San Diego CA 92105

(P-19635)
LA MAESTRA FAMILY CLINIC INC
Also Called: La Maestra Community Clinic
4060 Fairmount Ave, San Diego
(92105-1608)
PHONE..............................619 280-4213
Alejanderina Areizaza, *Manager*
EMP: 100 **Privately Held**
SIC: **8011** Clinic, operated by physicians
PA: La Maestra Family Clinic, Inc.
4060 Fairmount Ave
San Diego CA 92105

(P-19636)
LA MAESTRA FAMILY CLINIC INC
4305 University Ave # 120, San Diego
(92105-1645)
PHONE..............................619 501-1235
Liv David, *Branch Mgr*

EMP: 100 **Privately Held**
SIC: **8011** Clinic, operated by physicians
PA: La Maestra Family Clinic, Inc.
    4060 Fairmount Ave
    San Diego CA 92105

(P-19637)
LA MAESTRA FAMILY CLINIC INC (PA)
Also Called: La Maestra Community Hlth Ctrs
4060 Fairmount Ave, San Diego
(92105-1608)
PHONE................................619 584-1612
Zara Marselian, *CEO*
Carlos Hanessian, *Ch of Bd*
Mary David, *CFO*
Alex Pantoja, *CFO*
Samuel Mirelles, *Vice Ch Bd*
EMP: 152
SQ FT: 5,000
SALES: 29.8MM **Privately Held**
SIC: **8011** Clinic, operated by physicians

(P-19638)
LA MESA INTRNL MDC MDCL GR
Also Called: La Mesa Internal Medical Group
5111 Garfield St, La Mesa (91941-5147)
PHONE................................619 460-4050
Donald Patterson, *President*
John Dapolito, *Shareholder*
Dr Kenneth Hanson, *Shareholder*
James Malinak, *Shareholder*
Dr Roger English, *President*
EMP: 50
SQ FT: 10,000
SALES (est): 2.9MM **Privately Held**
SIC: **8011** Internal medicine, physician/surgeon

(P-19639)
LA PEER SURGERY CENTER LLC
Also Called: La Peer Health Systems
8920 Wilshire Blvd # 101, Beverly Hills
(90211-2007)
PHONE................................310 360-9119
Dr Siamak Tabib, *Mng Member*
EMP: 78 EST: 2000
SQ FT: 2,300
SALES: 28.3MM **Privately Held**
SIC: **8011** Surgeon

(P-19640)
LA VIDA MLTISPECIALTY MED CTRS
Also Called: Northeast Community Clinics
1400 S Grand Ave, Los Angeles
(90015-3048)
PHONE................................213 765-7500
Amber Crujillo, *Office Mgr*
Chuca Chidi, *President*
EMP: 60 EST: 2000
SQ FT: 52,000
SALES: 23MM **Privately Held**
SIC: **8011** Offices & clinics of medical doctors

(P-19641)
LANCASTER CRDLGY MED GROUP INC (PA)
Also Called: Physicians Referral Service
43847 Heaton Ave Ste B, Lancaster
(93534-4936)
PHONE................................661 726-3058
Shun K Sunder MD, *President*
E Ekong MD, *Vice Pres*
Kanagarath Sivalingam MD, *Admin Sec*
EMP: 90
SQ FT: 30,000
SALES (est): 4MM **Privately Held**
SIC: **8011** Cardiologist & cardio-vascular specialist

(P-19642)
LARCHMONT RADIOLOGY MED GROUP
Also Called: Westcoast Medial Imaging
2010 Wilshire Blvd # 409, Los Angeles
(90057-3598)
PHONE................................213 483-5953
Stewart A Lapin, *President*
EMP: 55
SQ FT: 4,500

SALES (est): 2.2MM **Privately Held**
SIC: **8011** Radiologist

(P-19643)
LAREN D TAN MD
11234 Anderson St, Loma Linda
(92354-2804)
PHONE................................909 558-4444
Laren Tan, *Principal*
EMP: 89
SALES (est): 2.6MM **Privately Held**
SIC: **8011** Physicians' office, including specialists

(P-19644)
LAS ISLAS FAMILY MED GROUP PC
325 W Chnnel Islands Blvd, Oxnard
(93033-4501)
PHONE................................805 385-8662
Miguel Cervantes, *Director*
EMP: 65
SALES (est): 6MM **Privately Held**
WEB: www.lasislasfamilymedical.com
SIC: **8011** General & family practice, physician/surgeon

(P-19645)
LASSEN MEDICAL GROUP INC (PA)
Also Called: Mercy Medical
2450 Sster Mary Clumba Dr, Red Bluff
(96080-4356)
PHONE................................530 527-0414
Kimberli R Frantz, *President*
Kimberli Frantz, *COO*
Dan Mc Daniel MD, *Treasurer*
Richard Wickenheiser, *Bd of Directors*
Eugene Plett MD, *Admin Sec*
EMP: 57
SALES (est): 12.1MM **Privately Held**
SIC: **8011** 8099 Physicians' office, including specialists; blood related health services

(P-19646)
LELAND STANFORD JUNIOR UNIV
1201 Welch Rd, Stanford (94305-5102)
PHONE................................650 723-7863
William C Mobley, *Principal*
Bruce Phillips, *IT/INT Sup*
EMP: 54
SALES (corp-wide): 5.6B **Privately Held**
SIC: **8011** Radiologist
PA: Leland Stanford Junior University
    450 Serra Mall
    Stanford CA 94305
    650 723-2300

(P-19647)
LELAND STANFORD JUNIOR UNIV
Health Promotion Resource Ctr
211 Quarry Rd N229, Palo Alto
(94304-1416)
PHONE................................650 725-4416
Wes Alles, *Principal*
Sandy Chan, *Manager*
EMP: 54
SALES (corp-wide): 5.6B **Privately Held**
SIC: **8011** 8221 Health maintenance organization; university
PA: Leland Stanford Junior University
    450 Serra Mall
    Stanford CA 94305
    650 723-2300

(P-19648)
LELAND STANFORD JUNIOR UNIV
Also Called: Cowell Student Health Service
870 Campus Dr, Stanford (94305-8508)
PHONE................................650 723-0821
Dr Ira Friedman, *Director*
EMP: 100
SALES (corp-wide): 5.6B **Privately Held**
SIC: **8011** 8031 8221 Medical centers; offices & clinics of osteopathic physicians; university
PA: Leland Stanford Junior University
    450 Serra Mall
    Stanford CA 94305
    650 723-2300

(P-19649)
LES KELLEY FAMILY HEALTH CTR
1920 Colorado Ave, Santa Monica
(90404-3414)
PHONE................................310 319-4700
Michele Bholat, *Director*
Eric Chamers, *Administration*
Benjamin Gilmore, *Med Doctor*
EMP: 60
SALES (est): 2.4MM **Privately Held**
SIC: **8011** Clinic, operated by physicians

(P-19650)
LIFELONG MEDICAL CARE (PA)
Also Called: Over 60 Health Center
2344 6th St, Berkeley (94710-2412)
P.O. Box 11247 (94712-2247)
PHONE................................510 704-6010
Marty A Lynch, *CEO*
Brenda Shipp, *COO*
Rick Clark, *CFO*
EMP: 50
SQ FT: 4,200
SALES (est): 59.1MM **Privately Held**
SIC: **8011** General & family practice, physician/surgeon

(P-19651)
LINDA LOMA UNIV HLTH CARE
Also Called: Loma Linda Faculty Med Group
11370 Anderson St # 2100, Loma Linda
(92354-3450)
P.O. Box 626 (92354-0626)
PHONE................................909 558-2851
Ilene Spencer, *Manager*
Leo Chan-June Jeng, *Pediatrics*
Mary Ann Magoun, *Pediatrics*
EMP: 250 **Privately Held**
SIC: **8011** Offices & clinics of medical doctors
PA: Loma Linda University Health Care
    11175 Campus St
    Loma Linda CA 92350
    -

(P-19652)
LINDA LOMA UNIV HLTH CARE (PA)
11175 Campus St, Loma Linda
(92350-1700)
PHONE................................909 558-4729
Roger Hadley MD, *President*
David B Hinshaw Jr, *Vice Chairman*
Munaf Kadri, *Lab Dir*
Brian Bull MD, *Admin Sec*
EMP: 850
SQ FT: 70,000
SALES: 166.4MM **Privately Held**
SIC: **8011** Offices & clinics of medical doctors

(P-19653)
LINDA LOMA UNIV HLTH CARE
Also Called: Llu Center For Fertility
11370 Anderson St # 3950, Loma Linda
(92354-3450)
P.O. Box 1009 (92354-1009)
PHONE................................909 558-2840
Linda Moore, *Administration*
EMP: 153 **Privately Held**
SIC: **8011** Fertility specialist, physician
PA: Loma Linda University Health Care
    11175 Campus St
    Loma Linda CA 92350
    -

(P-19654)
LINDEN CREST SURGERY CENTER
9735 Wilshire Blvd # 100, Beverly Hills
(90212-2114)
PHONE................................310 601-3900
Christina Niegos, *Principal*
Manuel Unzueta, *Manager*
EMP: 60
SALES (est): 2.9MM **Privately Held**
WEB: www.lindencrestsurgery.com
SIC: **8011** Surgeon

(P-19655)
LIVINGSTON COMMUNITY HEALTH
Also Called: HILMAR HEALTH CENTER
1140 Main St, Livingston (95334-1257)
PHONE................................209 394-7913
Leslie McGowan, *CEO*
Selina Montoya, *CFO*
EMP: 101
SQ FT: 10,623
SALES: 18.1MM **Privately Held**
SIC: **8011** Primary care medical clinic

(P-19656)
LLU ADVNTIST HLTH SCIENCES CTR
Also Called: Risk Management
101 E Redlands Blvd, San Bernardino
(92408-3710)
P.O. Box 1770, Loma Linda (92354-0570)
PHONE................................909 558-4386
Mark Hubbard, *Director*
EMP: 52
SALES (est): 3.4MM **Privately Held**
SIC: **8011** Medical centers

(P-19657)
LODI MEMORIAL HOSP ASSN INC
Also Called: Rehabilitation Center
800 S Lower Sacramento Rd, Lodi
(95242-3635)
PHONE................................209 333-3100
Linda Escobar, *Director*
EMP: 120
SALES (corp-wide): 4.1B **Privately Held**
SIC: **8011** 8069 Specialized medical practitioners, except internal; specialty hospitals, except psychiatric
HQ: Lodi Memorial Hospital Association, Inc.
    975 S Fairmont Ave
    Lodi CA 95240
    209 334-3411

(P-19658)
LOMA LINDA UNIVERSITY
1911 W Park Ave, Redlands (92373-8045)
P.O. Box 1740, Loma Linda (92354-0240)
PHONE................................909 558-6422
Brian Bull, *President*
EMP: 65
SALES: 11.4MM **Privately Held**
SIC: **8011** Pathologist

(P-19659)
LOMA LINDA UNIVERSITY MED CTR
11234 Anderson St, Loma Linda
(92354-2871)
PHONE................................877 558-6248
Jason Peterson, *Manager*
EMP: 8529
SALES (est): 91.9K **Privately Held**
SIC: **8011** Medical centers

(P-19660)
LOS ANGELES CARDIOLOGY ASSOC (PA)
1245 Wilshire Blvd # 703, Los Angeles
(90017-4810)
PHONE................................213 977-0419
David S Cannom MD, *Partner*
Anil K Bhandari MD, *Partner*
Steven Burstein MD, *Partner*
Robert D Lerman MD, *Partner*
Charles Pollick MD, *Partner*
EMP: 100
SQ FT: 12,000
SALES (est): 8.5MM **Privately Held**
SIC: **8011** Cardiologist & cardio-vascular specialist

(P-19661)
LOS ANGELES COUNTY HEALTH SVC
1108 N Oleander Ave, Compton
(90222-4041)
PHONE................................310 763-2244
Lorraine Madison, *Principal*
Rochelle Banks, *Social Worker*
David Gallien, *Supervisor*
EMP: 50

SALES (est): 1.6MM **Privately Held**
SIC: **8011** Clinic, operated by physicians

(P-19662)
LOS ANGELES FREE CLINIC (PA)
Also Called: Saban Community Clinic
8405 Beverly Blvd, Los Angeles
(90048-3401)
PHONE..................323 653-8622
Jeffrey Bujer, CEO
Eric Jung, Treasurer
Denise Martin, Officer
Emanuel Mkrtichian, CIO
Anne Kim, QA Dir
EMP: 300
SQ FT: 26,615
SALES: 17.4MM **Privately Held**
SIC: **8011** Clinic, operated by physicians

(P-19663)
LOS ANGELES FREE CLINIC
8405 Beverly Blvd, Los Angeles
(90048-3401)
PHONE..................323 653-8622
Abbe Land, CEO
Noemi Portillo, Director
EMP: 99
SALES: 32.6K **Privately Held**
SIC: **8011** General & family practice, physician/surgeon

(P-19664)
LUCILE SALTER PACKARD CHIL
Also Called: Bayside Medical Group
5601 Norris Canyon Rd # 230, San Ramon
(94583-5407)
PHONE..................925 277-7550
K C Campion, CEO
EMP: 110
SALES (corp-wide): 1.4B **Privately Held**
SIC: **8011** Pediatrician
PA: Lucile Salter Packard Children's Hospital At Stanford
725 Welch Rd
Palo Alto CA 94304
650 497-8000

(P-19665)
MADISON RADIOLOGY MED GROUP
65 N Madison Ave Ste M250, Pasadena
(91101-2000)
PHONE..................626 793-8189
Terry S Becker, President
Eric Becker, Info Tech Dir
Jeanette Velasco, Manager
EMP: 55
SALES (est): 3.1MM **Privately Held**
SIC: **8011** Radiologist

(P-19666)
MANGROVE MEDICAL GROUP
Also Called: Mangrove Lab & X-Ray
1040 Mangrove Ave, Chico (95926-3509)
PHONE..................530 345-0064
Dewayne E Caviness MD, Partner
Randall E Caviness MD, Partner
Kurt E Johnson MD, Partner
Dean P Smith MD, Partner
Randall S Williams MD, Partner
EMP: 50
SQ FT: 12,000
SALES (est): 7.8MM **Privately Held**
SIC: **8011** General & family practice, physician/surgeon

(P-19667)
MARIN COMMUNITY CLINIC
Also Called: Marin Community Clinics
9 Commercial Blvd Ste 100, Novato
(94949-6137)
PHONE..................415 448-1500
Linda Tavaszi, CEO
Peggy Dracker, COO
David Klinetobe, CFO
Connie Kadera, Officer
John Shen, Exec Dir
EMP: 99
SQ FT: 9,000
SALES: 35.1MM **Privately Held**
SIC: **8011** Primary care medical clinic; clinic, operated by physicians

(P-19668)
MARINOW HARRY MD FACS INC
Also Called: Feiwell, Lawrence MD
3742 Katella Ave Ste 401, Los Alamitos
(90720-3172)
PHONE..................562 430-3561
Korinne Walker, President
Gina Gomez, Supervisor
EMP: 50
SALES (est): 2.4MM **Privately Held**
SIC: **8011** Physicians' office, including specialists

(P-19669)
MARK E JACOBSON M D
1260 N Dutton Ave Ste 230, Santa Rosa
(95401-7161)
PHONE..................707 571-4022
Mark Jacobson MD, President
EMP: 60
SALES (est): 658.3K **Privately Held**
SIC: **8011** Offices & clinics of medical doctors

(P-19670)
MARK H LEIBENHAUT MD
Also Called: Ras
2800 L St Ste 110, Sacramento
(95816-5616)
PHONE..................916 454-6600
Mark H Leibenhaut, Partner
EMP: 50
SALES (est): 1.1MM **Privately Held**
SIC: **8011** Offices & clinics of medical doctors

(P-19671)
MARTECH MEDICAL PRODUCTS INC
565 Clara Nofal Rd, Calexico (92231-9533)
PHONE..................215 256-8833
EMP: 101
SALES (corp-wide): 42.1MM **Privately Held**
SIC: **8011** Offices & clinics of medical doctors
PA: Martech Medical Products, Inc.
1500 Delp Dr
Harleysville PA 19438
215 256-8833

(P-19672)
MARTIN LTHER KING/DREW MED CTR
1670 E 120th St, Los Angeles
(90059-3026)
PHONE..................310 773-4926
Hank Wells, CEO
Linda McAuley, COO
Anthony Gray, CFO
Kate Edmunson, Human Resources
Roger Peeks, Director
EMP: 74
SALES (est): 19MM **Privately Held**
SIC: **8011** Clinic, operated by physicians

(P-19673)
MCHENRY MEDICAL GROUP INC
1541 Florida Ave Ste 200, Modesto
(95350-4438)
PHONE..................209 577-3388
John Porteous, President
Harris M Goodman, Treasurer
EMP: 100
SQ FT: 22,000
SALES (est): 9.8MM **Privately Held**
WEB: www.mchenrymedical.com
SIC: **8011** Internal medicine, physician/surgeon; gastronomist; dermatologist; surgeon

(P-19674)
MD IMAGING INC A PROF MED CORP
Also Called: Women's Imaging Center
2020 Court St, Redding (96001-1822)
PHONE..................530 243-1249
Michael G Davis, CEO
Richard J Slepicka, CFO
Annie Ogden, Administration
David Guerra, Info Tech Mgr
Charlene Cundy, Human Res Mgr
EMP: 100

SALES (est): 20MM **Privately Held**
WEB: www.mdimaging.net
SIC: **8011** Radiologist

(P-19675)
MEDICAL GROUP BVERLY HILLS INC (PA)
Also Called: CEDARS SINAI MEDICAL GROUP
200 N Robertson Blvd, Beverly Hills
(90211-1769)
PHONE..................310 385-3200
Thomas D Gordon, CEO
Antoinette T Hubenette MD, President
Stephen C Deutsch MD, Treasurer
James L Caplan MD, Vice Pres
Mary Claire Lingel, Exec Dir
EMP: 50
SQ FT: 14,500
SALES: 394.7MM **Privately Held**
SIC: **8011** Offices & clinics of medical doctors

(P-19676)
MEDICAL GROUP BVERLY HILLS INC
Also Called: Cedar Sinai Medical Group
250 N Robertson Blvd # 603, Beverly Hills
(90211-1788)
PHONE..................310 247-4646
Tom Gordon, Branch Mgr
Nicholas Szumski, Neurology
John Andrews, Med Doctor
James L Caplan, Med Doctor
EMP: 50
SALES (corp-wide): 394.7MM **Privately Held**
SIC: **8011** Offices & clinics of medical doctors
PA: Medical Group Of Beverly Hills, Inc.
200 N Robertson Blvd
Beverly Hills CA 90211
310 385-3200

(P-19677)
MEDICL IMGNG CTR OF SOUTHRN CA
2811 Wilshire Blvd # 100, Santa Monica
(90403-4803)
PHONE..................310 829-9788
Bradley Jabour MD, President
Nicole Pelissier, COO
EMP: 65
SQ FT: 22,000
SALES (est): 7.4MM **Privately Held**
WEB: www.corbyandcorby.com
SIC: **8011** Radiologist

(P-19678)
MEDNAX INC
23441 Madison St Ste 215, Torrance
(90505-4756)
PHONE..................310 375-7172
EMP: 227 **Publicly Held**
SIC: **8011** General & family practice, physician/surgeon
PA: Mednax, Inc.
1301 Concord Ter
Sunrise FL 33323

(P-19679)
MEDPOINT MANAGEMENT
6400 Canoga Ave Ste 163, Woodland Hills
(91367-2435)
PHONE..................818 702-0100
Sheldon Lewenfuff Preident, Principal
Sheldon Lewenfuf, President
Sheldon Lewenfus, Vice Pres
Karen Marino, Executive Asst
Joy Say, Executive Asst
EMP: 50
SALES (est): 6.9MM **Privately Held**
WEB: www.medpointmanagement.com
SIC: **8011** Health maintenance organization

(P-19680)
MEMOR ORTHO SURGIC GROUP A M
Also Called: Southern California Cen
2760 Atlantic Ave, Long Beach
(90806-2755)
PHONE..................562 424-6666
Peter R Kurzweil, CEO

Douglas W Jackson MD, President
Curtis W Spencer III, Vice Pres
Leang Prum, Office Mgr
David S Morrison MD, Admin Sec
▲ EMP: 70
SQ FT: 12,000
SALES (est): 8.8MM **Privately Held**
SIC: **8011** Orthopedic physician; sports medicine specialist, physician; surgeon; physical medicine, physician/surgeon

(P-19681)
MEMORIAL COUNSELING ASSOC INC
4525 E Atherton St, Long Beach
(90815-3700)
PHONE..................562 961-0155
A Sarkis, President
EMP: 80
SALES (est): 3.4MM **Privately Held**
WEB: www.mcapsych.com
SIC: **8011** **8322** Offices & clinics of medical doctors; general counseling services

(P-19682)
MEMORIAL PROMPTCARE MEDICAL GR (PA)
Also Called: Prompt Care
15464 Goldenwest St, Westminster
(92683-6149)
PHONE..................714 891-9008
Jamie B Lewis MD, President
Kim Salaya, Executive
Andrea Lewis, Admin Sec
Rosemary Donaldson-Ford, Family Practiti
Cynthia Birkhimer, Manager
EMP: 50
SQ FT: 7,400
SALES (est): 3MM **Privately Held**
SIC: **8011** **4119** Physicians' office, including specialists; ambulance service

(P-19683)
MEMORIAL PSYCHIATRIC HLTH SVCS
4525 E Atherton St, Long Beach
(90815-3700)
PHONE..................562 494-9243
Lee Yoseloff, President
Sarkis Gavin MD, Principal
Juliette Gabel, Manager
EMP: 50
SALES (est): 3.2MM **Privately Held**
SIC: **8011** Psychiatrist

(P-19684)
MENDOCINO CMNTY HLTH CLNIC INC (PA)
Also Called: McHc
333 Laws Ave, Ukiah (95482-6540)
PHONE..................707 468-1010
John Pavoni, CEO
Tim Dolan, CFO
Alicia Gordon, Office Mgr
Carolynn Hansen, Human Res Dir
Kelly Clark, Human Resources
EMP: 235
SQ FT: 24,000
SALES: 30.9MM **Privately Held**
WEB: www.mchcinc.org
SIC: **8011** Primary care medical clinic

(P-19685)
MENLO MED CLINIC A MED CORP
1300 Crane St, Menlo Park (94025-4260)
PHONE..................650 498-6500
Ed Kelly, Administration
Nancy Adelman MD, Partner
Gayle S Hunt-Cahan Anp-C, Partner
Katherine A Blenko MD, Partner
Martin Bronk MD, Partner
EMP: 150 EST: 1946
SQ FT: 40,000
SALES (est): 20.7MM **Privately Held**
WEB: www.ucsfstanford.org
SIC: **8011** Clinic, operated by physicians

(P-19686)
MERCY HM SVCS A CAL LTD PARTNR
Also Called: Administrative Office
2175 Rosaline Ave Ste A, Redding
(96001-2549)
PHONE..................530 225-6000

Ronald Cloud, *Branch Mgr*
Steven Bleiweiss, *Ch Pathology*
Arthur Fontaine, *Ch Radiology*
Dwight Martin, *Officer*
Linde Cheema, *Vice Pres*
EMP: 340
SALES (corp-wide): 6.7B **Privately Held**
SIC: 8011 Medical centers
HQ: Mercy Home Services A California Limited Partnership
2175 Rosaline Ave Ste A
Redding CA 96001
530 225-6000

(P-19687)
MERRIDIAN NEURO CARE
18a Journey Ste 200, Aliso Viejo
(92656-5342)
PHONE...................................949 263-6630
Jim Ashby, *Principal*
EMP: 50
SALES (est): 1.6MM **Privately Held**
SIC: 8011 Neurologist

(P-19688)
MICHAEL S DUFFY SR DO INC
1501 5th Ave Ste 100, San Diego
(92101-3251)
PHONE...................................619 461-3717
Brian Gonzales, *CEO*
David Duffy, *CFO*
Michael Duffy, *Principal*
EMP: 95 **EST:** 2011
SALES (est): 439.8K **Privately Held**
SIC: 8011 Offices & clinics of medical doctors

(P-19689)
MICHAEL SD NAGATINI
5400 W Hillsdale Ave, Visalia (93291-8222)
PHONE...................................559 738-7502
Bill Brower, *CEO*
Angelina P Mallari, *Family Practiti*
EMP: 60 **EST:** 2001
SALES (est): 709.1K **Privately Held**
SIC: 8011 Offices & clinics of medical doctors

(P-19690)
MISSION INTERNAL MED GROUP INC
Also Called: Arthur Loussararian MD
26800 Crown Valley Pkwy # 103, Mission Viejo (92691-6389)
PHONE...................................949 364-3570
Arthur Loussararian, *Principal*
EMP: 102
SALES (est): 2.7MM
SALES (corp-wide): 19.8MM **Privately Held**
WEB: www.mimg.com
SIC: 8011 Primary care medical clinic
PA: Mission Internal Medical Group, Inc.
26732 Crown Valley Pkwy # 411
Mission Viejo CA 92691
949 282-1600

(P-19691)
MISSION INTERNAL MED GROUP INC
26800 Crown Valley Pkwy # 103, Mission Viejo (92691-6389)
PHONE...................................949 364-6559
Bruce L Nelson, *Manager*
EMP: 200
SALES (corp-wide): 19.8MM **Privately Held**
WEB: www.mimg.com
SIC: 8011 Internal medicine, physician/surgeon
PA: Mission Internal Medical Group, Inc.
26732 Crown Valley Pkwy # 411
Mission Viejo CA 92691
949 282-1600

(P-19692)
MISSION INTERNAL MED GROUP INC
Also Called: West Coast Physical Therapy
27882 Forbes Rd Ste 110, Laguna Niguel
(92677-1267)
PHONE...................................949 364-3605
Joan Shrum-Brown, *Principal*
EMP: 102

SALES (corp-wide): 19.8MM **Privately Held**
WEB: www.mimg.com
SIC: 8011 8049 Cardiologist & cardio-vascular specialist; physical therapist
PA: Mission Internal Medical Group, Inc.
26732 Crown Valley Pkwy # 411
Mission Viejo CA 92691
949 282-1600

(P-19693)
MISSION NEIGHBORHOOD HLTH CTR (PA)
Also Called: Mission Neighborhood Hlth Ctr
240 Shotwell St, San Francisco
(94110-1323)
PHONE...................................415 552-3870
Brenda Storey, *CEO*
Amelia Martinez, *President*
Patty Caplan, *COO*
Charles Moser, *Trustee*
Francis Allen, *Vice Pres*
EMP: 110
SQ FT: 21,000
SALES: 19.5MM **Privately Held**
WEB: www.mnhc.org
SIC: 8011 Primary care medical clinic

(P-19694)
MISSION PEAK ORTHOPEDICS
5924 Stoneridge Dr # 200, Pleasanton
(94588-2887)
PHONE...................................510 797-3933
Co V Banh, *Principal*
EMP: 65
SALES (est): 113.3K **Privately Held**
SIC: 8011 Orthopedic physician

(P-19695)
MISSION VALLEY HTS SURGERY CTR
Also Called: Amsurg
7485 Mission Valley Rd # 106, San Diego
(92108-4422)
PHONE...................................619 291-3737
William S Adsit MD, *Partner*
Drew A Peterson MD, *Partner*
Kevin Smith MD, *Principal*
Stephanie Gonia, *Administration*
Jocelyn Day, *Business Mgr*
EMP: 59 **EST:** 2001
SQ FT: 14,000
SALES (est): 6.7MM **Privately Held**
WEB: www.mvhsc.com
SIC: 8011 Surgeon

(P-19696)
MOLINA HEALTHCARE INC
790 E Foothill Blvd, Rialto (92376-5269)
PHONE...................................909 546-7116
EMP: 133
SALES (corp-wide): 19.8B **Publicly Held**
SIC: 8011 Health maintenance organization
PA: Molina Healthcare, Inc.
200 Oceangate Ste 100
Long Beach CA 90802
562 435-3666

(P-19697)
MOLINA HEALTHCARE INC (PA)
200 Oceangate Ste 100, Long Beach
(90802-4317)
P.O. Box 22813 (90801-5813)
PHONE...................................562 435-3666
Joseph M Zubretsky, *President*
Dale B Wolf, *Ch of Bd*
Joseph W White, *CFO*
Ronna E Romney, *Vice Ch Bd*
Jeff D Barlow,
EMP: 2800
SALES: 19.8B **Publicly Held**
WEB: www.molinahealthcare.com
SIC: 8011 6324 Health maintenance organization; hospital & medical service plans; health maintenance organization (HMO), insurance only

(P-19698)
MOLINA HEALTHCARE CALIFORNIA
200 Oceangate Ste 100, Long Beach
(90802-4317)
PHONE...................................800 526-8196
EMP: 215

SALES (est): 113.8K
SALES (corp-wide): 19.8B **Publicly Held**
SIC: 8011 Offices & clinics of medical doctors
PA: Molina Healthcare, Inc.
200 Oceangate Ste 100
Long Beach CA 90802
562 435-3666

(P-19699)
MONARCH HEALTHCARE A MEDICAL (HQ)
11 Technology Dr, Irvine (92618-2302)
PHONE...................................949 923-3200
Bartley Asner, *CEO*
Marcie Greene, *CEO*
Marvin Gordon MD, *CFO*
Jay J Cohen MD, *Vice Pres*
Steven Rudy MD, *Vice Pres*
EMP: 79
SQ FT: 75,000
SALES (est): 43.7MM
SALES (corp-wide): 201.1B **Publicly Held**
WEB: www.mhealth.com
SIC: 8011 Group health association
PA: Unitedhealth Group Incorporated
9900 Bren Rd E Ste 300w
Minnetonka MN 55343
952 936-1300

(P-19700)
MONROVIA HEALTH CENTER
330 W Maple Ave, Monrovia (91016-3387)
PHONE...................................626 256-1600
Maxine Liggins, *Director*
EMP: 60
SQ FT: 2,400
SALES (est): 3.6MM **Privately Held**
SIC: 8011 Medical centers

(P-19701)
MONTAGE HEALTH
P.O. Box Hh (93942-6032)
PHONE...................................831 625-4821
Judi Sanderlin, *CEO*
EMP: 2500
SALES (est): 6MM **Privately Held**
SIC: 8011 Health maintenance organization

(P-19702)
MOUNTAIN HLTH & CMNTY SVCS INC (PA)
Also Called: Mountain Empire Fmly Medicine
1388 Buckman Springs Rd, Campo
(91906-2028)
P.O. Box 37 (91906-0037)
PHONE...................................619 478-5311
Judith Shaplin, *Exec Dir*
Amy Weisiger, *CFO*
Kristie Coronado, *Officer*
Amy Arsenault, *Executive Asst*
Amy Finch, *Executive Asst*
EMP: 76
SALES: 9.5MM **Privately Held**
WEB: www.mtnhealth.org
SIC: 8011 8093 Primary care medical clinic; mental health clinic, outpatient

(P-19703)
MUIR ORTHOPEDIC SPECIALISTS
2405 Shadelands Dr # 210, Walnut Creek
(94598-5905)
PHONE...................................925 939-8585
K C Campion, *CEO*
Ramiro Miranda MD, *President*
EMP: 177
SALES: 20MM **Privately Held**
SIC: 8011 Orthopedic physician

(P-19704)
NATIVE AMERICAN HEALTH CTR INC (PA)
2950 International Blvd, Oakland
(94601-2228)
PHONE...................................510 535-4400
Martin Waukazoo, *CEO*
Ana M Oconnor, *COO*
Alan Wong, *CFO*
Dr Joseph Marquis, *Chief Mktg Ofcr*
Natalie Aguilera, *Human Resources*
EMP: 80 **EST:** 1971
SQ FT: 16,000

SALES: 22.3MM **Privately Held**
WEB: www.nativehealth.org
SIC: 8011 8021 8093 Clinic, operated by physicians; dentists' office; mental health clinic, outpatient

(P-19705)
NEIGHBORHOOD HEALTHCARE (PA)
425 N Date St Ste 203, Escondido
(92025-3413)
PHONE...................................760 520-8372
Tracy Ream, *CEO*
Johnny Watson, *President*
Amparo Mahler, *COO*
Lisa Daigle, *CFO*
Richard Marino, *Vice Pres*
EMP: 625
SQ FT: 17,000
SALES: 57.9MM **Privately Held**
SIC: 8011 Clinic, operated by physicians

(P-19706)
NEIGHBORHOOD HEALTHCARE
855 E Madison Ave, El Cajon (92020-3819)
PHONE...................................619 440-2751
Alex Nunez, *Director*
Nishwan Jibri, *Family Practiti*
EMP: 100
SQ FT: 9,198
SALES (corp-wide): 57.9MM **Privately Held**
SIC: 8011 General & family practice, physician/surgeon
PA: Neighborhood Healthcare
425 N Date St Ste 203
Escondido CA 92025
760 520-8372

(P-19707)
NEIGHBORHOOD HEALTHCARE
460 N Elm St, Escondido (92025-3002)
PHONE...................................760 737-2000
Gail Thomsky, *Manager*
EMP: 88
SQ FT: 9,288
SALES (corp-wide): 57.9MM **Privately Held**
SIC: 8011 Clinic, operated by physicians
PA: Neighborhood Healthcare
425 N Date St Ste 203
Escondido CA 92025
760 520-8372

(P-19708)
NEONATAL MEDICAL ASSOC INC
1022 E Tehachapi Dr, Long Beach
(90807-2452)
PHONE...................................562 933-8100
Jose M Perez MD, *President*
EMP: 318
SALES (est): 2.7MM **Publicly Held**
SIC: 8011 Medical centers
PA: Mednax, Inc.
1301 Concord Ter
Sunrise FL 33323

(P-19709)
NEW PORT ORTHOPEDIC INSTITUTE
19582 Beach Blvd Ste 118, Huntington Beach (92648-2996)
PHONE...................................949 722-5071
Alan Beyer MD, *Principal*
EMP: 60
SALES (est): 4.1MM **Privately Held**
SIC: 8011 Orthopedic physician

(P-19710)
NEWPORT BEACH ORTHOPEDIC INST
22 Corporate Plaza Dr, Newport Beach
(92660-7985)
P.O. Box 2597 (92659-1597)
PHONE...................................949 722-7038
Alan Beyer MD, *Owner*
EMP: 79
SALES (est): 4.6MM **Privately Held**
SIC: 8011 Orthopedic physician

(P-19711)
NEWPORT BEACH SURGERY CTR LLC
361 Hospital Rd Ste 124, Newport Beach (92663-3521)
PHONE..........................949 631-0988
John McNutt, *Managing Dir*
Bruce Albert,
Robert Anderson,
Perter Broekelschen, *Mng Member*
Harvey Heinrichs, *Mng Member*
EMP: 120
SQ FT: 10,000
SALES (est): 14.5MM **Privately Held**
WEB: www.nbbrewco.com
SIC: **8011** Surgeon

(P-19712)
NEWPORT FMLY MDCNE/A MED GROUP
Also Called: Campion, Catherine A MD
520 Superior Ave, Newport Beach (92663-3637)
PHONE..........................949 644-1025
Maclyn Somers MD, *Partner*
Catherine A Campion MD, *Partner*
Sheryl L Long MD, *Partner*
William R Somers MD, *Partner*
Benjamin B Wright MD, *Partner*
EMP: 65
SQ FT: 9,000
SALES (est): 5.8MM **Privately Held**
WEB: www.newportfamilymedicine.com
SIC: **8011** General & family practice, physician/surgeon

(P-19713)
NEWPORT HARBOR RADIOLOGY ASSOC
Also Called: Newport Imaging Center
360 San Miguel Dr # 105106, Newport Beach (92660-7853)
PHONE..........................949 721-8191
Hurwitz Robert, *Owner*
EMP: 61
SALES (est): 2.2MM **Privately Held**
SIC: **8011** Radiologist

(P-19714)
NORTH BAY EYE ASSOC A MED CORP
Also Called: North Bay Eye Assoc Med Group
50 Professional Center Dr # 210, Rohnert Park (94928-2173)
PHONE..........................707 206-0849
Christian Kim, *Principal*
Michele Clites, *Human Res Mgr*
Lisa Kaiser, *Human Resources*
EMP: 65
SALES (est): 4.5MM **Privately Held**
SIC: **8011** Ophthalmologist

(P-19715)
NORTH COUNTY HEALTH PRJ INC (PA)
Also Called: North County Services
150 Valpreda Rd Frnt, San Marcos (92069-2944)
PHONE..........................760 736-6755
Irma Cota, *CEO*
Sheila Brown, *Vice Chairman*
Kathy Martinez, *CFO*
Marnel Hernandez, *Nursing Mgr*
Marcela Vargas, *Planning*
EMP: 221 EST: 1973
SQ FT: 69,880
SALES: 72MM **Privately Held**
SIC: **8011** Clinic, operated by physicians

(P-19716)
NORTH COUNTY OB-GYN MED GROUP (PA)
9850 Genesee Ave Ste 600, La Jolla (92037-1207)
PHONE..........................858 453-0753
Allan Silver, *CEO*
EMP: 50
SQ FT: 2,000
SALES (est): 2.1MM **Privately Held**
WEB: www.ncogmedical.com
SIC: **8011** Gynecologist; obstetrician; specialized medical practitioners, except internal

(P-19717)
NORTH STATE RADIOLOGY
Also Called: North State Imaging
1702 Esplanade, Chico (95926-3315)
PHONE..........................530 898-0504
Scot Woolley, *CEO*
Don Hubbard, *CFO*
Chelsi Shaw-Jones, *Administration*
Chris Jones, *Info Tech Mgr*
Thomas Nolan-Gosslin, *Financial Exec*
EMP: 50
SALES (est): 13.6MM **Privately Held**
SIC: **8011** Radiologist

(P-19718)
NORTHCOUNTRY CLINIC
Also Called: Dickinson, Diane MD
785 18th St, Arcata (95521-5683)
PHONE..........................707 822-2481
Herrmann Spetzler, *Administration*
Judy Burns, *Med Doctor*
Sheyenne Spetzler, *Director*
EMP: 55
SQ FT: 10,000
SALES (est): 3.3MM **Privately Held**
WEB: www.northcoastclinics.org
SIC: **8011** Clinic, operated by physicians

(P-19719)
NORTHEAST COMMUNITY CLINIC
3751 S Harvard Blvd, Los Angeles (90018-4546)
PHONE..........................323 373-9400
Emilio Garza, *Principal*
EMP: 80
SALES (corp-wide): 28MM **Privately Held**
WEB: www.lausd.k12.ca.us
SIC: **8011** Offices & clinics of medical doctors
PA: Northeast Community Clinic
    2550 W Main St Ste 301
    Alhambra CA 91801
    626 457-6900

(P-19720)
NORTHEAST VALLEY HEALTH CORP
Also Called: San Fernando Health Center
1600 San Fernando Rd, San Fernando (91340-3115)
PHONE..........................818 365-8086
Beverly Jenkins, *Manager*
Jenori Galicia, *Admin Asst*
Joy Ahrens, *Director*
Amelia Escobedo, *Relations*
EMP: 85
SALES (corp-wide): 89.4MM **Privately Held**
SIC: **8011** Clinic, operated by physicians
PA: Northeast Valley Health Corp
    1172 N Maclay Ave
    San Fernando CA 91340
    818 898-1388

(P-19721)
NORTHEAST VALLEY HEALTH CORP
12756 Van Nuys Blvd, Pacoima (91331-1696)
PHONE..........................818 896-0531
Kathreen Dayanim, *Manager*
Rocio Duque, *Office Mgr*
EMP: 100
SQ FT: 11,645
SALES (corp-wide): 89.4MM **Privately Held**
SIC: **8011** **8071** Clinic, operated by physicians; medical laboratories
PA: Northeast Valley Health Corp
    1172 N Maclay Ave
    San Fernando CA 91340
    818 898-1388

(P-19722)
NORTHEASTERN RUR HLTH CLINICS (PA)
Also Called: Nrhc
1850 Spring Ridge Dr, Susanville (96130-6100)
PHONE..........................530 251-5000
Phil Nowak, *CEO*
Richard Hrezo, *Treasurer*
Pamela Robbins, *Admin Sec*

Don Workman, *Data Proc Exec*
Steven E Braatz, *Med Doctor*
EMP: 65 EST: 1977
SQ FT: 27,000
SALES (est): 12.2MM **Privately Held**
WEB: www.northeasternhealth.org
SIC: **8011** Clinic, operated by physicians

(P-19723)
NORTHERN CALIFORNIA CARDIOLOGY (PA)
Also Called: Ncca Diagnostics Medical Group
5301 F St Ste 117, Sacramento (95819-3220)
PHONE..........................916 733-1788
David Woodruff, *Partner*
Daniel Flamm, *Partner*
Stanley Henjum, *Partner*
Edmond Lee, *Partner*
Harvey Matlof, *Partner*
EMP: 67
SQ FT: 13,000
SALES (est): 3.9MM **Privately Held**
SIC: **8011** Cardiologist & cardio-vascular specialist

(P-19724)
NORTHWEST MEDICAL GROUP INC
Also Called: Good Neighbor Pharmacy
7355 N Palm Ave Ste 100, Fresno (93711-5770)
PHONE..........................559 271-6302
Cecil Bullard MD, *President*
Diane Hubbard, *Shareholder*
Vivian Hernandez MD, *Admin Sec*
Lisa Jelinek, *Administration*
Roman Malley, *Internal Med*
EMP: 75
SQ FT: 5,000
SALES (est): 7.1MM **Privately Held**
SIC: **8011** **5912** Pediatrician; drug stores

(P-19725)
NORTHWEST PHYSICIANS MED GROUP
Also Called: Northwest Medical Pharmacy
7355 N Palm Ave Ste 100, Fresno (93711-5770)
PHONE..........................559 271-6370
David A Wilcox, *Branch Mgr*
EMP: 82
SALES (corp-wide): 4.3MM **Privately Held**
SIC: **8011** Physicians' office, including specialists
PA: Northwest Physicians Medical Group Inc
    7355 N Palm Ave Ste 100
    Fresno CA 93711
    559 271-6300

(P-19726)
OAK GROVE INST FOUNDATION INC (PA)
Also Called: Oak Grove Center
24275 Jefferson Ave, Murrieta (92562-7285)
PHONE..........................951 677-5599
Tamara L Wilson, *CEO*
Barry Soper, *Ch of Bd*
Fe Santiago, *CFO*
EMP: 388
SQ FT: 39,000
SALES: 19MM **Privately Held**
WEB: www.oak-grove.org
SIC: **8011** **8211** **8361** Psychiatric clinic; specialty education; residential care

(P-19727)
OAKS DIAGNOSTICS INC (PA)
Also Called: California Imaging Nework
6310 San Vicente Blvd, Los Angeles (90048-5426)
P.O. Box 5355, Beverly Hills (90209-5355)
PHONE..........................310 855-0035
Ronald Grusd MD, *CEO*
EMP: 60
SQ FT: 9,000
SALES (est): 7MM **Privately Held**
WEB: www.milleniumimaging.com
SIC: **8011** Radiologist

(P-19728)
OCEAN PARK HEALTH CENTER
Also Called: Community Health Netwrk of San
1351 24th Ave, San Francisco (94122-1616)
PHONE..........................415 753-8100
Lisa Golden, *Director*
EMP: 50
SALES (est): 3MM **Privately Held**
SIC: **8011** Offices & clinics of medical doctors

(P-19729)
OCONNOR IMAGING MED GROUP INC
Also Called: Oconnor Hospital
2105 Forest Ave, San Jose (95128-1425)
PHONE..........................408 947-2992
Charles Griffin MD, *President*
Dr Richard Turner, *Vice Pres*
EMP: 60
SQ FT: 2,000
SALES (est): 2.8MM **Privately Held**
SIC: **8011** Radiologist

(P-19730)
OLE HEALTH
1100 Trancas St Ste 300, NAPA (94558-2921)
PHONE..........................707 254-1770
Tanir AMI, *CEO*
Molly Nelson, *CFO*
Susie Duprez, *Accountant*
EMP: 50
SALES: 23.5MM **Privately Held**
WEB: www.clinicole.org
SIC: **8011** General & family practice, physician/surgeon

(P-19731)
OLIVE VIEW-UCLA MEDICAL CENTER (PA)
Also Called: Valley Care Olive View Med Ctr
14445 Olive View Dr, Sylmar (91342-1438)
PHONE..........................818 364-1555
Carolyn Rhee, *CEO*
Cynthia O'Donnell, *Executive*
Chisa Aoyama, *Pathologist*
Barbara Fletcher, *Obstetrician*
EMP: 87
SALES: 357.8MM **Privately Held**
WEB: www.uclasfvp.org
SIC: **8011** Medical centers

(P-19732)
OMNI FAMILY HEALTH (PA)
Also Called: COMMUNITY HEALTH CENTER
4900 California Ave 400b, Bakersfield (93309-7024)
P.O. Box 1060, Shafter (93263-1060)
PHONE..........................661 459-1900
Francisco L Castillon, *CEO*
Milad Khalil, *President*
Diego Martinez, *COO*
Novira Irawan, *CFO*
Linda Oates, *Office Mgr*
EMP: 80 EST: 1978
SQ FT: 14,000
SALES: 66.4MM **Privately Held**
SIC: **8011** Clinic, operated by physicians

(P-19733)
OMNI WOMENS HLTH MED GROUP INC
2550 Merced St, Fresno (93721-1812)
PHONE..........................559 441-4271
Robert Frediani, *Branch Mgr*
EMP: 69
SALES (corp-wide): 12.5MM **Privately Held**
SIC: **8011** Gynecologist
PA: Omni Women's Health Medical Group, Inc.
    3812 N 1st St
    Fresno CA 93726
    559 495-3120

(P-19734)
ON LOK INC
1333 Bush St, San Francisco (94109-5691)
PHONE..........................415 292-8888
Grace LI, *CEO*
May Liu, *Volunteer Dir*

Grace Lee, *COO*
Gary Campanella, *CFO*
Kelly Walsh, *CFO*
EMP: 99
SALES: 7.7MM **Privately Held**
SIC: 8011 Offices & clinics of medical doctors

(P-19735)
ONE MEDICAL GROUP INC (PA)
130 Sutter St Fl 2, San Francisco
(94104-4009)
P.O. Box 779 (94104-0779)
PHONE...................................415 578-3100
Thomas H Lee, *CEO*
Kimber Lockhart, *Vice Pres*
Robin Riske, *Vice Pres*
Michael Sarmiento, *Vice Pres*
Honore Lansen, *Managing Dir*
EMP: 116
SALES (est): 76.9MM **Privately Held**
SIC: 8011 Physical medicine, physician/surgeon

(P-19736)
ONE MEDICAL GROUP INC
3885 24th St, San Francisco (94114-3840)
PHONE...................................415 529-4522
Elizabeth Maier, *Administration*
Russell Alpert, *Family Practiti*
EMP: 53
SALES (corp-wide): 76.9MM **Privately Held**
SIC: 8011 Offices & clinics of medical doctors
PA: One Medical Group, Inc.
    130 Sutter St Fl 2
    San Francisco CA 94104
    415 578-3100

(P-19737)
OPERATION SAMAHAN INC
Also Called: Camino Ruiz Suite 235
10737 Camino Ruiz Ste 235, San Diego
(92126-2375)
PHONE...................................619 477-4451
Dirk Virbel, *CEO*
EMP: 128
SALES (corp-wide): 13.9MM **Privately Held**
SIC: 8011 8021 Clinic, operated by physicians; offices & clinics of dentists
PA: Operation Samahan, Inc.
    1428 Highland Ave
    National City CA 91950
    619 477-4451

(P-19738)
OROVILLE INTERNAL MEDS GROUP
Also Called: Roy C Shannon MD
2721 Olive Hwy Ste 12, Oroville
(95966-6115)
PHONE...................................530 538-3171
Roy Shannon, *President*
EMP: 50
SQ FT: 3,600
SALES (est): 2.9MM **Privately Held**
SIC: 8011 Internal medicine, physician/surgeon; physicians' office, including specialists

(P-19739)
ORTHOPEDIC CONSULTANTS (PA)
16311 Ventura Blvd # 800, Encino
(91436-2140)
PHONE...................................818 788-7343
Lester Cohn, *President*
EMP: 50
SQ FT: 8,300
SALES (est): 3.9MM **Privately Held**
WEB: www.ocmgortho.com
SIC: 8011 Orthopedic physician

(P-19740)
OUTPATNT EYE SRGRY CTR OF DSRT
Also Called: Milauskas Eye Institute
72057 Dinah Shore Dr D1, Rancho Mirage
(92270-1791)
PHONE...................................760 340-3937
Albert T Milauskas, *President*
EMP: 50

SALES (est): 1.1MM **Privately Held**
SIC: 8011 Ambulatory surgical center; ophthalmologist

(P-19741)
PACIFIC EYE ASSOCIATED INC
2100 Webster St Ste 214, San Francisco
(94115-2375)
PHONE...................................415 923-3007
Wayne E Fung MD, *President*
Arthur W Allen Jr, *Vice Pres*
Bee Veeraseati, *General Mgr*
EMP: 60
SQ FT: 8,000
SALES (est): 8.2MM **Privately Held**
SIC: 8011 Ophthalmologist

(P-19742)
PACIFIC INPTIENT MED GROUP INC
9 Jeffrey Ct, Novato (94945-1739)
P.O. Box 573 (94948-0573)
PHONE...................................415 485-8824
Fabiola Cobarrubias, *President*
Christopher M Valentino, *COO*
EMP: 69
SALES (est): 4.5MM **Privately Held**
SIC: 8011 Offices & clinics of medical doctors

(P-19743)
PACIFIC SHORES MED GROUP INC (PA)
1043 Elm Ave Ste 104, Long Beach
(90813-3244)
PHONE...................................562 590-0345
Simon Tchekmedyian, *CEO*
Jonathan Rigutto, *District Mgr*
Cecilia Yeung, *Purchasing*
Helene Au, *Hematology*
Marcy Lebeau, *Med Doctor*
EMP: 100
SQ FT: 3,300
SALES (est): 17.2MM **Privately Held**
WEB: www.pacshoresoncology.com
SIC: 8011 Medical centers; oncologist

(P-19744)
PACKARD CHILDRENS HLTH ALIANCE
Also Called: Pcha
725 Welch Rd, Palo Alto (94304-1601)
PHONE...................................650 497-8000
Kim Robert, *CEO*
Lisa Holbrook, *COO*
Anh-Thu Lewis, *Nurse Practr*
Michael Lipman, *Director*
EMP: 100
SALES: 81.8MM
SALES (corp-wide): 1.4B **Privately Held**
SIC: 8011 Pediatrician; obstetrician; cardiologist & cardio-vascular specialist; gynecologist
PA: Lucile Salter Packard Children's Hospital At Stanford
    725 Welch Rd
    Palo Alto CA 94304
    650 497-8000

(P-19745)
PACKARD MEDICAL GROUP INC
770 Welch Rd, Palo Alto (94304-1511)
PHONE...................................650 724-3637
Tika Martin, *Human Resources*
EMP: 85
SALES (est): 3.1MM **Privately Held**
SIC: 8011 Obstetrician; pediatrician

(P-19746)
PAIN MANAGEMENT SPECIALISTS PC
1551 Bishop St Ste 230, San Luis Obispo
(93401-4661)
PHONE...................................805 544-7246
Borris Pilch MD, *President*
EMP: 50
SALES (est): 950.9K **Privately Held**
SIC: 8011 Specialized medical practitioners, except internal

(P-19747)
PALMDALE CENTER FOR PAIN MGT
819 Auto Center Dr, Palmdale
(93551-4599)
PHONE...................................661 267-6876
Shahin Sadik, *Owner*
EMP: 50
SALES (est): 1.6MM **Privately Held**
SIC: 8011 Specialized medical practitioners, except internal

(P-19748)
PALO ALTO MEDICAL CLINIC
795 El Camino Real, Palo Alto
(94301-2302)
PHONE...................................650 321-4121
John Cooper, *Principal*
David S Leibowitz, *Hematology*
David Leibowitz, *Oncology*
Norman Banks, *Med Doctor*
Robyn Juster, *Med Doctor*
EMP: 50
SALES (est): 5.5MM **Privately Held**
SIC: 8011 Primary care medical clinic

(P-19749)
PALO ALTO MEDICAL FOUNDATION (HQ)
Also Called: Palo Alto Clinic
795 El Camino Real, Palo Alto
(94301-2302)
P.O. Box 254738, Sacramento (95865-4738)
PHONE...................................650 321-4121
Jeff Gerard, *CEO*
David Drucker, *President*
Brian Dumo, *COO*
Null M Null Akhtar, *Officer*
Mara Kook, *Vice Pres*
EMP: 700
SQ FT: 200,000
SALES (est): 156.1MM
SALES (corp-wide): 12.4B **Privately Held**
SIC: 8011 Clinic, operated by physicians
PA: Sutter Health
    2200 River Plaza Dr
    Sacramento CA 95833
    916 733-8800

(P-19750)
PALO ALTO MEDICAL FOUNDATION
Also Called: Los Altos Center
370 Distel Cir, Los Altos (94022-1404)
PHONE...................................650 254-5200
Sandy Greenberg, *Manager*
Margaret Lo, *Family Practiti*
A Sastri H Sukhdeo, *Obstetrician*
Jonathan Albeg, *Med Doctor*
Meagan Jennings, *Med Doctor*
EMP: 60
SQ FT: 32,059
SALES (corp-wide): 12.4B **Privately Held**
SIC: 8011 Pediatrician
HQ: Palo Alto Medical Foundation For Health Care, Research And Education (Inc)
    795 El Camino Real
    Palo Alto CA 94301
    650 321-4121

(P-19751)
PALO ALTO MEDICAL FOUNDATION
Also Called: Steven Rubinstein MD
201 Old San Francisco Rd, Sunnyvale
(94086-6385)
P.O. Box 3496 (94088-3496)
PHONE...................................408 730-4390
Kam Yung, *Branch Mgr*
Inderjeet Uppal, *Family Practiti*
Priya Bhusri, *Internal Med*
Grace Guo, *Internal Med*
Christina Vu, *Pediatrics*
EMP: 62
SALES (corp-wide): 12.4B **Privately Held**
SIC: 8011 Allergist
HQ: Palo Alto Medical Foundation For Health Care, Research And Education (Inc)
    795 El Camino Real
    Palo Alto CA 94301
    650 321-4121

(P-19752)
PALO ALTO MEDICAL FOUNDATION
1085 W El Camino Real, Sunnyvale
(94087-1030)
PHONE...................................408 524-5900
Tom Frick, *President*
Michael Fain,
EMP: 62
SALES (corp-wide): 12.4B **Privately Held**
SIC: 8011 Offices & clinics of medical doctors
HQ: Palo Alto Medical Foundation For Health Care, Research And Education (Inc)
    795 El Camino Real
    Palo Alto CA 94301
    650 321-4121

(P-19753)
PALO ALTO MEDICAL FOUNDATION
701 E El Camino Real, Mountain View
(94040-2833)
PHONE...................................408 739-6000
Richard Slavin, *Branch Mgr*
EMP: 62
SALES (corp-wide): 12.4B **Privately Held**
SIC: 8011 8733 Clinic, operated by physicians; medical research
HQ: Palo Alto Medical Foundation For Health Care, Research And Education (Inc)
    795 El Camino Real
    Palo Alto CA 94301
    650 321-4121

(P-19754)
PAVILION SURGERY CENTER LLC
1140 W La Veta Ave, Orange (92868-4225)
PHONE...................................714 744-8850
David Yomtoob, *Ch of Bd*
EMP: 70
SQ FT: 49,000
SALES (est): 65.5K **Privately Held**
SIC: 8011 Surgeon

(P-19755)
PEACH TREE HEALTHCARE
5730 Packard Ave Ste 500, Marysville
(95901-7119)
PHONE...................................530 749-3242
Thomas Walther, *President*
EMP: 97
SALES: 11.8MM **Privately Held**
SIC: 8011 General & family practice, physician/surgeon

(P-19756)
PEACHWOOD MEDICAL GROUP CLOVIS
275 W Herndon Ave, Clovis (93612-0204)
PHONE...................................559 324-6200
Lee Copeland MD, *President*
Jeffrey Hubbard, *Vice Pres*
Sue Marino, *Administration*
EMP: 70
SQ FT: 33,595
SALES (est): 13.7MM **Privately Held**
SIC: 8011 Primary care medical clinic

(P-19757)
PENINSULA WOMENS HEALTH (PA)
1828 El Camino Real Ste 8, Burlingame
(94010-3103)
P.O. Box 1509, Millbrae (94030-5509)
PHONE...................................650 692-3818
Andrew Jurow MD, *President*
EMP: 50 **EST:** 1952
SQ FT: 2,800
SALES (est): 4.8MM **Privately Held**
WEB: www.peninsulawomenshealth.com
SIC: 8011 Gynecologist; obstetrician

(P-19758)
PEOPLE CREATING SUCCESS INC
380 Arneill Rd, Camarillo (93010-6406)
PHONE...................................805 644-9480
Marie McManus, *Branch Mgr*
EMP: 122

SALES (corp-wide): 12.8MM **Privately Held**
SIC: 8011 Offices & clinics of medical doctors
PA: People Creating Success, Inc.
2585 Teller Rd
Newbury Park CA 91320
805 375-9222

(P-19759)
PERMANENTE MEDICAL GROUP INC
7300 N Fresno St, Fresno (93720-2941)
PHONE..................................559 448-4500
Irene Ann Heetebry, *Principal*
EMP: 63
SALES (corp-wide): 94.1B **Privately Held**
SIC: 8011 Offices & clinics of medical doctors
HQ: The Permanente Medical Group Inc
1950 Franklin St Fl 18th
Oakland CA 94612
866 858-2226

(P-19760)
PERMANENTE MEDICAL GROUP INC
6600 Bruceville Rd, Sacramento (95823-4671)
PHONE..................................916 688-2055
Kevin L Smith, *Branch Mgr*
Hienvu Nguyen, *Podiatrist*
EMP: 58
SALES (corp-wide): 94.1B **Privately Held**
WEB: www.permanente.net
SIC: 8011 Gynecologist
HQ: The Permanente Medical Group Inc
1950 Franklin St Fl 18th
Oakland CA 94612
866 858-2226

(P-19761)
PERMANENTE MEDICAL GROUP INC
901 El Camino Real, San Bruno (94066-3009)
PHONE..................................650 742-2100
Cheryl Halcovich, *Manager*
David J Malit, *Internal Med*
Allen Lew, *Manager*
EMP: 58
SALES (corp-wide): 94.1B **Privately Held**
SIC: 8011 Offices & clinics of medical doctors
HQ: The Permanente Medical Group Inc
1950 Franklin St Fl 18th
Oakland CA 94612
866 858-2226

(P-19762)
PERMANENTE MEDICAL GROUP INC
3558 Round Barn Blvd, Santa Rosa (95403-1780)
PHONE..................................707 393-4000
Pat Henson, *Principal*
Andrew R Goldstein, *Surgeon*
Cortney Harper, *Obstetrician*
Krishneel Lall, *Anesthesiology*
Nicolaj Andersen, *Hematology*
EMP: 58
SALES (corp-wide): 94.1B **Privately Held**
SIC: 8011 Medical centers
HQ: The Permanente Medical Group Inc
1950 Franklin St Fl 18th
Oakland CA 94612
866 858-2226

(P-19763)
PERMANENTE MEDICAL GROUP INC
275 Hospital Pkwy Ste 470, San Jose (95119-1138)
PHONE..................................408 972-6883
Maurice Alfaro, *Director*
EMP: 78
SALES (corp-wide): 94.1B **Privately Held**
SIC: 8011 Offices & clinics of medical doctors
HQ: The Permanente Medical Group Inc
1950 Franklin St Fl 18th
Oakland CA 94612
866 858-2226

(P-19764)
PERMANENTE MEDICAL GROUP INC
200 Muir Rd, Martinez (94553-4614)
PHONE..................................925 372-1000
EMP: 69
SALES (corp-wide): 94.1B **Privately Held**
SIC: 8011 Offices & clinics of medical doctors
HQ: The Permanente Medical Group Inc
1950 Franklin St Fl 18th
Oakland CA 94612
866 858-2226

(P-19765)
PERMANENTE MEDICAL GROUP INC
3779 Piedmont Ave, Oakland (94611-5347)
PHONE..................................510 752-1000
Ellen P Brennan, *Branch Mgr*
Eva Thomas, *Oncology*
EMP: 58
SALES (corp-wide): 94.1B **Privately Held**
SIC: 8011 Medical centers
HQ: The Permanente Medical Group Inc
1950 Franklin St Fl 18th
Oakland CA 94612
866 858-2226

(P-19766)
PERMANENTE MEDICAL GROUP INC
39400 Paseo Padre Pkwy, Fremont (94538-2310)
PHONE..................................510 248-3000
EMP: 78
SALES (corp-wide): 94.1B **Privately Held**
SIC: 8011 Offices & clinics of medical doctors
HQ: The Permanente Medical Group Inc
1950 Franklin St Fl 18th
Oakland CA 94612
866 858-2226

(P-19767)
PERMANENTE MEDICAL GROUP INC
770 E Calaveras Blvd, Milpitas (95035-5491)
PHONE..................................408 945-2900
Bindu Israni, *Branch Mgr*
EMP: 78
SALES (corp-wide): 94.1B **Privately Held**
SIC: 8011 Offices & clinics of medical doctors
HQ: The Permanente Medical Group Inc
1950 Franklin St Fl 18th
Oakland CA 94612
866 858-2226

(P-19768)
PERMANENTE MEDICAL GROUP INC
4501 Sand Creek Rd, Antioch (94531-8687)
PHONE..................................925 813-6149
Kim Daily, *Branch Mgr*
EMP: 78
SALES (corp-wide): 94.1B **Privately Held**
SIC: 8011 Offices & clinics of medical doctors
HQ: The Permanente Medical Group Inc
1950 Franklin St Fl 18th
Oakland CA 94612
866 858-2226

(P-19769)
PERMANENTE MEDICAL GROUP INC
1150 Veterans Blvd, Redwood City (94063-2037)
PHONE..................................650 299-2000
Arlene McCarthy, *Principal*
Ray Powell, *Info Tech Mgr*
Janis Turner, *Project Mgr*
Alvin Mok, *Orthopedist*
Cynthia Y Ng, *Dermatology*
EMP: 78
SALES (corp-wide): 94.1B **Privately Held**
SIC: 8011 Offices & clinics of medical doctors

HQ: The Permanente Medical Group Inc
1950 Franklin St Fl 18th
Oakland CA 94612
866 858-2226

(P-19770)
PERMANENTE MEDICAL GROUP INC
910 Marshall St, Redwood City (94063-2033)
PHONE..................................650 299-2015
Christina Apostolakos, *Director*
EMP: 59
SALES (corp-wide): 94.1B **Privately Held**
SIC: 8011 Medical centers
HQ: The Permanente Medical Group Inc
1950 Franklin St Fl 18th
Oakland CA 94612
866 858-2226

(P-19771)
PERMANENTE MEDICAL GROUP INC
914 Marina Way S, Richmond (94804-3739)
PHONE..................................510 231-5406
C J Bhalla, *Vice Pres*
EMP: 70
SALES (corp-wide): 94.1B **Privately Held**
SIC: 8011 Offices & clinics of medical doctors
HQ: The Permanente Medical Group Inc
1950 Franklin St Fl 18th
Oakland CA 94612
866 858-2226

(P-19772)
PERMANENTE MEDICAL GROUP INC
2500 Merced St, San Leandro (94577-4201)
PHONE..................................510 454-1000
Vijay Tiwari, *Internal Med*
Darlene D Lin, *Urology*
Evelyn J Chow, *Emerg Med Spec*
Robert Fan, *Emerg Med Spec*
Anthony Le, *Emerg Med Spec*
EMP: 63
SALES (corp-wide): 94.1B **Privately Held**
SIC: 8011 Offices & clinics of medical doctors
HQ: The Permanente Medical Group Inc
1950 Franklin St Fl 18th
Oakland CA 94612
866 858-2226

(P-19773)
PERMANENTE MEDICAL GROUP INC
99 Montecillo Rd, San Rafael (94903-3308)
PHONE..................................415 444-2000
EMP: 63
SALES (corp-wide): 94.1B **Privately Held**
SIC: 8011 Offices & clinics of medical doctors
HQ: The Permanente Medical Group Inc
1950 Franklin St Fl 18th
Oakland CA 94612
866 858-2226

(P-19774)
PERMANENTE MEDICAL GROUP INC
320 Lennon Ln, Walnut Creek (94598-2419)
PHONE..................................925 906-2000
Rochelle Benning, *Director*
David Peterson, *Director*
EMP: 63
SALES (corp-wide): 94.1B **Privately Held**
SIC: 8011 Offices & clinics of medical doctors
HQ: The Permanente Medical Group Inc
1950 Franklin St Fl 18th
Oakland CA 94612
866 858-2226

(P-19775)
PERMANENTE MEDICAL GROUP INC
100 Rowland Way Ste 125, Novato (94945-5012)
PHONE..................................415 209-2444
EMP: 69

HQ: The Permanente Medical Group Inc
1950 Franklin St Fl 18th
Oakland CA 94612
866 858-2226

SALES (corp-wide): 94.1B **Privately Held**
SIC: 8011 Offices & clinics of medical doctors
HQ: The Permanente Medical Group Inc
1950 Franklin St Fl 18th
Oakland CA 94612
866 858-2226

(P-19776)
PERMANENTE MEDICAL GROUP INC
97 San Marin Dr, Novato (94945-1100)
PHONE..................................415 899-7400
Willa Jefferson-Stokes, *Manager*
EMP: 100
SALES (corp-wide): 94.1B **Privately Held**
WEB: www.permanente.net
SIC: 8011 Internal medicine practitioners
HQ: The Permanente Medical Group Inc
1950 Franklin St Fl 18th
Oakland CA 94612
866 858-2226

(P-19777)
PERMANENTE MEDICAL GROUP INC
1600 Eureka Rd, Roseville (95661-3027)
PHONE..................................916 784-4000
Craig Green MD, *Director*
EMP: 63
SALES (corp-wide): 94.1B **Privately Held**
SIC: 8011 Offices & clinics of medical doctors
HQ: The Permanente Medical Group Inc
1950 Franklin St Fl 18th
Oakland CA 94612
866 858-2226

(P-19778)
PERMANENTE MEDICAL GROUP INC
1750 2nd St, Berkeley (94710-1705)
PHONE..................................510 559-5338
Dianne Easterwood, *General Mgr*
EMP: 100
SALES (corp-wide): 94.1B **Privately Held**
WEB: www.permanente.net
SIC: 8011 Offices & clinics of medical doctors
HQ: The Permanente Medical Group Inc
1950 Franklin St Fl 18th
Oakland CA 94612
866 858-2226

(P-19779)
PERMANENTE MEDICAL GROUP INC
3900 Lakeville Hwy, Petaluma (94954-5698)
PHONE..................................707 765-3900
Willa Jefferson-Stokes, *Manager*
Michael Matsumoto, *Director*
EMP: 75
SALES (corp-wide): 94.1B **Privately Held**
WEB: www.permanente.net
SIC: 8011 Clinic, operated by physicians
HQ: The Permanente Medical Group Inc
1950 Franklin St Fl 18th
Oakland CA 94612
866 858-2226

(P-19780)
PERMANENTE MEDICAL GROUP INC
3000 Las Positas Rd, Livermore (94551-9627)
PHONE..................................925 243-2600
Stan Combs, *Manager*
EMP: 55
SALES (corp-wide): 94.1B **Privately Held**
WEB: www.permanente.net
SIC: 8011 Offices & clinics of medical doctors
HQ: The Permanente Medical Group Inc
1950 Franklin St Fl 18th
Oakland CA 94612
866 858-2226

(P-19781)
PERMANENTE MEDICAL GROUP INC
1000 Franklin Pkwy, San Mateo (94403-1922)
PHONE..................................650 358-7000
EMP: 69

SALES (corp-wide): 94.1B **Privately Held**
SIC: **8011** Offices & clinics of medical doctors
HQ: The Permanente Medical Group Inc
1950 Franklin St Fl 18th
Oakland CA 94612
866 858-2226

(P-19782)
PERMANENTE MEDICAL GROUP INC
1617 Broadway St, Vallejo (94590-2406)
PHONE......................707 765-3930
Robin E Bjorger, *Branch Mgr*
Christian Lopez Reyes, *Internal Med*
EMP: 58
SALES (corp-wide): 94.1B **Privately Held**
SIC: **8011** Medical centers
HQ: The Permanente Medical Group Inc
1950 Franklin St Fl 18th
Oakland CA 94612
866 858-2226

(P-19783)
PERMANENTE MEDICAL GROUP INC
1800 Harrison St Fl 7th, Oakland (94612-3467)
PHONE......................510 625-6262
Connie Wilson, *Branch Mgr*
EMP: 78
SALES (corp-wide): 94.1B **Privately Held**
SIC: **8011** Offices & clinics of medical doctors
HQ: The Permanente Medical Group Inc
1950 Franklin St Fl 18th
Oakland CA 94612
866 858-2226

(P-19784)
PERMANENTE MEDICAL GROUP INC
235 W Macarthur Blvd, Oakland (94611-5641)
PHONE......................510 752-1190
Marta Perl, *Branch Mgr*
EMP: 58
SALES (corp-wide): 94.1B **Privately Held**
SIC: **8011** Medical centers
HQ: The Permanente Medical Group Inc
1950 Franklin St Fl 18th
Oakland CA 94612
866 858-2226

(P-19785)
PERMANENTE MEDICAL GROUP INC
7373 West Ln, Stockton (95210-3377)
PHONE......................209 476-3737
Michael Coleman, *Principal*
Howard Young, *Director*
EMP: 58
SALES (corp-wide): 94.1B **Privately Held**
SIC: **8011** Medical centers
HQ: The Permanente Medical Group Inc
1950 Franklin St Fl 18th
Oakland CA 94612
866 858-2226

(P-19786)
PERMANENTE MEDICAL GROUP INC
1305 Tommydon St, Stockton (95210-3364)
PHONE......................209 476-2000
Jack Gilliman, *Branch Mgr*
Hymavathy Jasti, *Med Doctor*
EMP: 50
SALES (corp-wide): 94.1B **Privately Held**
WEB: www.permanente.net
SIC: **8011** Offices & clinics of medical doctors
HQ: The Permanente Medical Group Inc
1950 Franklin St Fl 18th
Oakland CA 94612
866 858-2226

(P-19787)
PERMANENTE MEDICAL GROUP INC
10725 International Dr, Rancho Cordova (95670-7967)
PHONE......................916 631-3000
Donald Forrester, *Branch Mgr*
Dennis H Nguyen, *Med Doctor*

Sarah L Truong, *Med Doctor*
EMP: 130
SALES (corp-wide): 94.1B **Privately Held**
WEB: www.permanente.net
SIC: **8011** Offices & clinics of medical doctors
HQ: The Permanente Medical Group Inc
1950 Franklin St Fl 18th
Oakland CA 94612
866 858-2226

(P-19788)
PERMANENTE MEDICAL GROUP INC
395 Hickey Blvd Fl 1, Daly City (94015-2770)
PHONE......................650 301-5860
Jennifer Normoyle, *Branch Mgr*
Betty Lee, *Obstetrician*
Yvonne Ong, *Pediatrics*
Laura Prager, *Pediatrics*
Bertha Saucedo, *Pediatrics*
EMP: 78
SALES (corp-wide): 94.1B **Privately Held**
SIC: **8011** Offices & clinics of medical doctors
HQ: The Permanente Medical Group Inc
1950 Franklin St Fl 18th
Oakland CA 94612
866 858-2226

(P-19789)
PETALUMA HEALTH CENTER INC
1179 N Mcdowell Blvd A, Petaluma (94954-1171)
PHONE......................707 559-7500
Kathryn Powell, *CEO*
Daymon Doss, *COO*
Jane Read, *COO*
Brian Burns, *CFO*
EMP: 325
SALES: 37.9MM **Privately Held**
WEB: www.phealthcenter.org
SIC: **8011** Clinic, operated by physicians

(P-19790)
PETER J WOLK MD
2721 Olive Hwy, Oroville (95966-6115)
PHONE......................530 534-6517
Peter Wolk, *Principal*
EMP: 50 EST: 2001
SALES (est): 719.3K **Privately Held**
SIC: **8011** Offices & clinics of medical doctors

(P-19791)
PIONEER MEDICAL GROUP INC
11411 Brookshire Ave # 108, Downey (90241-5008)
PHONE......................562 862-2775
Gergie Salsky, *Manager*
EMP: 52
SALES (corp-wide): 37.9MM **Privately Held**
SIC: **8011** **5047** Medical centers; medical equipment & supplies
PA: Pioneer Medical Group, Inc.
17777 Center Court Dr N # 400
Cerritos CA 90703
562 597-4181

(P-19792)
PIT RIVER TRIBAL COUNCIL
Also Called: Pit River Health Services
36977 Park Ave, Burney (96013-4067)
PHONE......................530 335-3651
Keith Ratcliff, *Manager*
EMP: 52
SALES (corp-wide): 4.5MM **Privately Held**
WEB: www.pitrivercasino.com
SIC: **8011** **8021** Offices & clinics of medical doctors; offices & clinics of dentists
PA: Pit River Tribal Council
37960 Park Ave
Burney CA 96013
530 335-5487

(P-19793)
PLUMAS DISTRICT HOSPITAL
Also Called: Quincy Family Medicine
1045 Bucks Lake Rd, Quincy (95971-9507)
PHONE......................530 283-0650
Dan Brandes, *Director*
EMP: 120

SALES (corp-wide): 20.4MM **Privately Held**
SIC: **8011** **8062** Clinic, operated by physicians; general medical & surgical hospitals
PA: Plumas District Hospital
1065 Bucks Lake Rd
Quincy CA 95971
530 283-2121

(P-19794)
PRECISION MEDICAL PRODUCTS INC
2217 Plaza Dr, Rocklin (95765-4421)
PHONE......................573 474-9302
Jeremy Perkins, *CEO*
EMP: 99
SALES (est): 835K **Privately Held**
SIC: **8011** Offices & clinics of medical doctors

(P-19795)
PREDICINE INC
3555 Arden Rd, Hayward (94545-3922)
PHONE......................650 300-2188
Shidong Jia, *CEO*
EMP: 50 EST: 2015
SALES (est): 1.2MM **Privately Held**
SIC: **8011** Health maintenance organization

(P-19796)
PRIMARY CRITICAL CARE MEDICAL
620 N Brand Blvd Ste 500, Glendale (91203-4218)
P.O. Box 998, North Hollywood (91603-0998)
PHONE......................818 847-9950
Bruce Gipe MD, *President*
Susan Harris Rn CPA, *CFO*
EMP: 164 EST: 1995
SALES (est): 1.8MM
SALES (corp-wide): 287.4MM **Privately Held**
SIC: **8011**
HQ: Team Health Holdings, Inc.
265 Brookview Centre Way
Knoxville TN 37919
865 693-1000

(P-19797)
PROFESSIONAL HEALTH TECH
Also Called: Cardio Pulmonary Services
8131 Calle Del Cielo, La Jolla (92037-3148)
PHONE......................858 449-1599
Stanley Pappelbaum MD, *President*
Searle Turner MD, *Corp Secy*
EMP: 77 EST: 1976
SALES (est): 7MM **Privately Held**
SIC: **8011** **8399** Cardiologist & cardio-vascular specialist; health systems agency

(P-19798)
PROMED HLTH CARE ADMNISTRATORS
9302 Pttsbrgh Ave Ste 220, Rancho Cucamonga (91730)
PHONE......................909 932-1045
Jeereedi Prasad, *President*
Brian Wederman, *COO*
Karen Harvey, *Executive Asst*
EMP: 75
SALES (est): 3.3MM
SALES (corp-wide): 815.3MM **Privately Held**
SIC: **8011** Offices & clinics of medical doctors
PA: Prospect Medical Holdings, Inc.
3415 S Sepulveda Blvd # 9
Los Angeles CA 90034
310 943-4500

(P-19799)
PROSPECT MEDICAL HOLDINGS INC (PA)
3415 S Sepulveda Blvd # 9, Los Angeles (90034-6060)
PHONE......................310 943-4500
Samuel S Lee, *Ch of Bd*
Mike Heather, *CFO*
David Topper, *Officer*
Linda Hodges, *Exec VP*
Von Crockett, *Vice Pres*

EMP: 100
SQ FT: 7,154
SALES (est): 815.3MM **Privately Held**
WEB: www.prospectmedicalholdings.com
SIC: **8011** Health maintenance organization

(P-19800)
PROVIDENCE HEALTH SYSTEM
15031 Rinaldi St, Mission Hills (91345-1207)
PHONE......................818 898-4530
Terry Carmondy, *Administration*
EMP: 1200
SALES (corp-wide): 17.6B **Privately Held**
SIC: **8011** Offices & clinics of medical doctors
HQ: Providence Health System-Southern California
1801 Lind Ave Sw
Renton WA 98057
425 525-3355

(P-19801)
PROVIDENCE HEALTH SYSTEM
Beach Cties Amblatory Care Ctr
20929 Hawthorne Blvd, Torrance (90503-4611)
PHONE......................310 376-9474
Andy Hoover, *Owner*
EMP: 1200
SALES (corp-wide): 17.6B **Privately Held**
WEB: www.lcmhs.org
SIC: **8011** Ambulatory surgical center
HQ: Providence Health System-Southern California
1801 Lind Ave Sw
Renton WA 98057
425 525-3355

(P-19802)
PSYCHIATRIC CTRS AT SAN DIEGO (PA)
4542 Ruffner St Ste 200, San Diego (92111-2239)
P.O. Box 609001 (92160-9001)
PHONE......................619 528-4600
Sabah Chammas PHD, *President*
Dr Sharon McClure, *Treasurer*
Dr Katherine Dixon, *Vice Pres*
Brian Beck, *Accounting Mgr*
▲ EMP: 68
SQ FT: 2,000
SALES (est): 8.9MM **Privately Held**
WEB: www.psychiatriccenters.com
SIC: **8011** Psychiatrist

(P-19803)
PSYCHIATRIC SOLUTIONS INC
Also Called: Sierra Vista Hospital
8001 Bruceville Rd, Sacramento (95823-2329)
PHONE......................916 288-0300
Mike Zauner, *CEO*
Tammi Brooks, *Director*
EMP: 125
SALES (corp-wide): 10.4B **Publicly Held**
WEB: www.intermountainhospital.com
SIC: **8011** **8063** Psychiatric clinic; psychiatric hospitals
HQ: Psychiatric Solutions, Inc.
6640 Carothers Pkwy # 500
Franklin TN 37067
615 312-5700

(P-19804)
PSYCHIATRIC SOLUTIONS INC
Fremont Hospital
39001 Sundale Dr, Fremont (94538-2005)
PHONE......................510 796-1100
Toll Free:......................888 -
Joan Bettencourt Newman, *Principal*
John Truong, *QA Dir*
EMP: 150
SALES (corp-wide): 10.4B **Publicly Held**
WEB: www.intermountainhospital.com
SIC: **8011** **8093** **8361** **8069** Psychiatric clinic; specialty outpatient clinics; residential care; specialty hospitals, except psychiatric; psychiatric hospitals
HQ: Psychiatric Solutions, Inc.
6640 Carothers Pkwy # 500
Franklin TN 37067
615 312-5700

PRODUCTS & SVCS

(P-19805)
PSYCHIATRIC SOLUTIONS INC
17241 Van Buren Blvd, Riverside
(92504-5942)
PHONE.....................951 789-4405
Joseph McCoy, *Branch Mgr*
EMP: 137
SALES (corp-wide): 10.4B **Publicly Held**
WEB: www.intermountainhospital.com
SIC: 8011 Psychiatric clinic
HQ: Psychiatric Solutions, Inc.
    6640 Carothers Pkwy # 500
    Franklin TN 37067
    615 312-5700

(P-19806)
PUBLIC HEALTH CALIFORNIA DEPT
320 W 4th St Ste 830, Los Angeles
(90013-2348)
PHONE.....................213 620-6160
Donna Mc Callum, *Principal*
EMP: 140 **Privately Held**
SIC: 8011 Clinic, operated by physicians
HQ: California Department Of Public Health
    1615 Capitol Ave
    Sacramento CA 95814

(P-19807)
PUBLIC HEALTH CALIFORNIA DEPT
Also Called: Wic
2400 Wible Rd Ste 14, Bakersfield
(93304-4734)
PHONE.....................661 835-4668
EMP: 140 **Privately Held**
SIC: 8011 Clinic, operated by physicians
HQ: California Department Of Public Health
    1615 Capitol Ave
    Sacramento CA 95814

(P-19808)
PUBLIC HEALTH CALIFORNIA DEPT
Also Called: Genetic Dsase Screening Program
850 Marina Bay Pkwy F175, Richmond
(94804-6403)
PHONE.....................510 412-1502
Melissa Huang, *Manager*
EMP: 140 **Privately Held**
SIC: 8011 9431 Offices & clinics of medical doctors; administration of public health programs;
HQ: California Department Of Public Health
    1615 Capitol Ave
    Sacramento CA 95814

(P-19809)
PULMONARY MEDICINE ASSOC
2801 K St Ste 500, Sacramento
(95816-5119)
PHONE.....................916 733-5040
Geneva Lee, *Manager*
EMP: 54
SALES (corp-wide): 5.5MM **Privately Held**
SIC: 8011 Clinic, operated by physicians
PA: Pulmonary Medicine Associated Medical Group
    1300 Ethan Way Ste 600
    Sacramento CA 95825
    916 482-7623

(P-19810)
QUEENSCARE HEALTH CENTERS
Also Called: Queenscare Fmly Clinics-Eastsd
4816 E 3rd St, Los Angeles (90022-1602)
PHONE.....................323 780-4510
Evelyn Moody, *Manager*
EMP: 77
SALES (corp-wide): 24.4MM **Privately Held**
SIC: 8011 Clinic, operated by physicians
PA: Queenscare Health Centers
    950 S Grand Ave
    Los Angeles CA 90015
    323 669-4301

(P-19811)
QUEENSCARE HEALTH CENTERS
4618 Fountain Ave, Los Angeles
(90029-1977)
PHONE.....................323 644-6180
Guillermo Diaz, *Branch Mgr*
Cynthia Borders, *Director*
EMP: 88
SALES (corp-wide): 24.4MM **Privately Held**
SIC: 8011 Clinic, operated by physicians
PA: Queenscare Health Centers
    950 S Grand Ave
    Los Angeles CA 90015
    323 669-4301

(P-19812)
RADIATION MEDICAL GROUP INC (PA)
9333 Genesee Ave Ste 300, San Diego
(92121-2114)
P.O. Box 33865 (92163-3865)
PHONE.....................619 220-4100
Sara Rosenthal MD, *President*
Donald Fuller MD, *Vice Pres*
Ronald Davis MD, *Admin Sec*
EMP: 50
SQ FT: 2,156
SALES (est): 2.4MM **Privately Held**
WEB: www.rmgmed.com
SIC: 8011 Radiologist

(P-19813)
RADIOLOGY DEPARTMENT CAL HOSP
1338 S Hope St Fl 4, Los Angeles
(90015-2902)
PHONE.....................213 742-5840
Phil Faircharles, *Manager*
EMP: 50 EST: 2001
SQ FT: 88,284
SALES (est): 1MM **Privately Held**
SIC: 8011 Radiologist

(P-19814)
REDDING FAMILY MEDICINE ASSOC
2510 Airpark Dr Ste 201, Redding
(96001-2461)
PHONE.....................530 244-4907
David Civalier MD, *President*
Vance Harris, *Partner*
Jack Kimple, *Partner*
Richard Maples, *Partner*
David Short, *Partner*
EMP: 50
SALES (est): 3.5MM **Privately Held**
WEB: www.reddingaquaticcenter.com
SIC: 8011 General & family practice, physician/surgeon

(P-19815)
REDDING PATHOLOGISTS LAB (PA)
1725 Gold St, Redding (96001-1820)
PHONE.....................530 225-8050
Richard Severance MD, *Partner*
Tikoes Blankenberg MD, *Partner*
Richard O Boyd MD, *Partner*
John P Greaves Jr, *Partner*
William Reuss MD, *Partner*
EMP: 115
SQ FT: 8,000
SALES (est): 10.4MM **Privately Held**
WEB: www.reddingpath.com
SIC: 8011 8071 Pathologist; medical laboratories

(P-19816)
REDWOOD COAST MEDICAL SERVICES (PA)
46900 Ocean Dr, Gualala (95445-8353)
P.O. Box 1100 (95445-1100)
PHONE.....................707 884-1721
Dianne Agee, *Director*
Thomas A Bertolli, *Exec Dir*
EMP: 50 EST: 1977
SQ FT: 5,000
SALES: 6.4MM **Privately Held**
WEB: www.rcms-healthcare.org
SIC: 8011 Clinic, operated by physicians; primary care medical clinic

(P-19817)
REDWOOD REGIONAL MEDICAL GROUP
1165 S Dora St Bldg H, Ukiah
(95482-8325)
PHONE.....................707 463-3636
Jay Joseph, *Branch Mgr*
EMP: 59
SALES (corp-wide): 11.1MM **Privately Held**
SIC: 8011 General & family practice, physician/surgeon
PA: Redwood Regional Medical Group Drug Company, Llc
    990 Sonoma Ave Ste 15
    Santa Rosa CA 95404
    707 525-4080

(P-19818)
REPRODUCTIVE PTNR MED GRP INC (PA)
510 N Prospect Ave # 202, Redondo Beach
(90277-3028)
PHONE.....................310 318-3010
Gabriel Garzo, *Principal*
Billy Yee, *Pathologist*
David R Meldrum, *Director*
EMP: 50
SQ FT: 3,800
SALES (est): 5.8MM **Privately Held**
WEB: www.reproductivepartners.com
SIC: 8011 Fertility specialist, physician; gynecologist

(P-19819)
REPRODUCTIVE SCIENCE CENTER
Also Called: Reproductive Science Ctr Bay
100 Park Pl Ste 200, San Ramon
(94583-4416)
PHONE.....................925 867-1800
Susan Willman, *Principal*
Donald I Galen, *Vice Pres*
Louis Weckstein, *Vice Pres*
Karen Volpe, *Opers Staff*
David Saffan, *Director*
EMP: 75
SALES (est): 5MM **Privately Held**
SIC: 8011 Physicians' office, including specialists

(P-19820)
RESPONSIBLE MED SOLUTIONS CORP
Also Called: Temecula 24 Hour Care
41715 Winchester Rd # 101, Temecula
(92590-4808)
PHONE.....................951 308-0024
Steven J Schutz, *President*
Paul Schutz, *Admin Sec*
Brian Sharp, *Physician Asst*
EMP: 50 EST: 2007
SQ FT: 5,000
SALES: 6.5MM **Privately Held**
SIC: 8011 Freestanding emergency medical center

(P-19821)
RETINAL CONSULTANTS INC (PA)
3939 J St Ste 106, Sacramento
(95819-3631)
PHONE.....................916 454-4861
Neil E Kelly MD, *President*
Arun C Patel, *Shareholder*
Robert T Wendel, *Shareholder*
James W Wells Jr, *Vice Pres*
James Wells, *Vice Pres*
EMP: 55
SALES (est): 11.9MM **Privately Held**
WEB: www.retinamed.com
SIC: 8011 Ophthalmologist

(P-19822)
RIAD ADOUMIE MD
23560 Madison St Ste 110, Torrance
(90505-4709)
PHONE.....................310 373-6864
Riad Adoumie MD, *Owner*
EMP: 60
SALES (est): 1MM **Privately Held**
SIC: 8011 Surgeon

(P-19823)
RICHARD BURNS MD
41637 Margarita Rd # 100, Temecula
(92591-2990)
PHONE.....................951 296-9300
Richard Burns, *Principal*
EMP: 70
SALES (est): 1.6MM **Privately Held**
SIC: 8011 Physicians' office, including specialists

(P-19824)
RICHARD J METZ MD INC
2080 Century Park E # 1609, Los Angeles
(90067-2001)
PHONE.....................310 553-3189
Richard J Metz MD, *President*
Laura A Cavazos, *Office Mgr*
EMP: 50
SALES (est): 2.3MM **Privately Held**
SIC: 8011 Internal medicine, physician/surgeon

(P-19825)
RICHARD SHAMES MD
25 Mitchell Blvd Ste 8, San Rafael
(94903-2013)
PHONE.....................415 388-0456
Elson Haas, *Director*
EMP: 63
SALES (est): 1.2MM **Privately Held**
SIC: 8011 Physicians' office, including specialists

(P-19826)
RIDGECREST REGIONAL HOSPITAL
Also Called: Specialty Center
1011 N China Lake Blvd, Ridgecrest
(93555-3130)
PHONE.....................760 499-7260
EMP: 404
SALES (corp-wide): 106.3MM **Privately Held**
SIC: 8011 Gastronomist
PA: Ridgecrest Regional Hospital
    1081 N China Lake Blvd
    Ridgecrest CA 93555
    760 446-3551

(P-19827)
RIVERSIDE MEDICAL CLINIC INC
7117 Brockton Ave, Riverside
(92506-2658)
PHONE.....................951 683-6370
Judy Carpenter, *Manager*
EMP: 300
SALES (corp-wide): 111.6MM **Privately Held**
SIC: 8011 Clinic, operated by physicians
PA: Riverside Medical Clinic, Inc.
    3660 Arlington Ave
    Riverside CA 92506
    951 683-6370

(P-19828)
RIVERSIDE MEDICAL CLINIC INC (PA)
Also Called: Riverside Med Clnic Ptient Ctr
3660 Arlington Ave, Riverside
(92506-3987)
PHONE.....................951 683-6370
Steven E Larson, *President*
Judy Carpenter, *President*
Susan Marinaro, *COO*
Tony Lazcano, *Vice Pres*
Ruben Muradyan, *Executive*
EMP: 300
SQ FT: 65,000
SALES (est): 111.6MM **Privately Held**
SIC: 8011 Clinic, operated by physicians

(P-19829)
RIVERSIDE-SAN BERNARDINO
Also Called: Soboba Indian Health Clinic
607 Donna Way, San Jacinto (92583-5517)
PHONE.....................951 654-0803
Maria Adams, *Manager*
EMP: 60
SALES (corp-wide): 35.9MM **Privately Held**
SIC: 8011 Clinic, operated by physicians

PA: Riverside-San Bernardino County Indian Health, Inc.
11555 1/2 Potrero Rd
Banning CA 92220
951 849-4761

(P-19830)
ROGER L CRUMLEY MD INC
Also Called: University Head Neck Surgeons
101 City Dr S Bldg 56 5, Orange (92868)
PHONE.................................714 456-5750
Roger L Crumley MD, *President*
EMP: 50
SALES (est): 3.2MM **Privately Held**
SIC: 8011 Surgeon; plastic surgeon

(P-19831)
ROUND VALLEY INDIAN HEALTH CTR
Hwy 162 Biggar Ln, Covelo (95428)
P.O. Box 247 (95428-0247)
PHONE.................................707 983-6182
James Russ, *Director*
EMP: 60 **EST:** 1968
SALES: 4.7MM **Privately Held**
SIC: 8011 8021 Clinic, operated by physicians; dental clinic

(P-19832)
RUSSIAN RIVER HEALTH CENTER
16319 3rd St, Guerneville (95446)
PHONE.................................707 869-2849
Mary Szecsey, *Director*
EMP: 50
SALES (est): 11.4MM **Privately Held**
SIC: 8011 8093 8322 Offices & clinics of medical doctors; mental health clinic, outpatient; individual & family services

(P-19833)
SACRAMENTO EAR NOSE & THROAT (PA)
1111 Expo Blvd Bldg 700, Sacramento (95815-4314)
PHONE.................................916 736-3399
Ernest E Johnson MD, *President*
Kevin Mc Kennan MD, *Treasurer*
Barbara Bennitt, *Office Mgr*
Richard G Areen MD, *Admin Sec*
Eric Salinas, *Info Tech Mgr*
EMP: 55
SQ FT: 12,000
SALES (est): 9.5MM **Privately Held**
SIC: 8011 Ears, nose & throat specialist: physician/surgeon

(P-19834)
SACRAMNTO NTIV AMERCN HLTH CTR
2020 J St, Sacramento (95811-3120)
PHONE.................................916 341-0575
Britta Guerrero, *Exec Dir*
Ricardo Torres, *Ch of Bd*
Lisa McKay, *Admin Dir*
Britta Guerrero, *Exec Dir*
EMP: 119
SQ FT: 39,573
SALES: 9.6MM **Privately Held**
WEB: www.snahc.org
SIC: 8011 Clinic, operated by physicians

(P-19835)
SAINT JHNS HLTH CTR FOUNDATION
Wayne, John Cancer Institute
2200 Santa Monica Blvd, Santa Monica (90404-2312)
PHONE.................................310 315-6111
Donald Mortan, *Director*
EMP: 125
SQ FT: 7,100
SALES (corp-wide): 2.6B **Privately Held**
SIC: 8011 8731 Primary care medical clinic; commercial physical research
HQ: Saint John's Health Center Foundation.
2121 Santa Monica Blvd
Santa Monica CA 90404
310 829-5511

(P-19836)
SALINAS MED MNGT SRVCS ORG INC
Also Called: Salinas Valley Prime Care Med
355 Abbott St Ste 100, Salinas (93901-4484)
PHONE.................................831 751-7070
Gerald W Oehler, *President*
Glen Yoneda, *Treasurer*
Robert Patton, *Vice Pres*
EMP: 70 **EST:** 1997
SQ FT: 6,612
SALES (est): 2.9MM **Privately Held**
SIC: 8011 General & family practice, physician/surgeon

(P-19837)
SALINAS VALLEY MEDICAL CLINIC
236 San Jose St, Salinas (93901-3901)
PHONE.................................831 424-7389
EMP: 371 **EST:** 2017
SALES: 50.5MM
SALES (corp-wide): 494.4MM **Privately Held**
SIC: 8011 Cardiologist & cardio-vascular specialist
PA: Salinas Valley Memorial Healthcare Systems
450 E Romie Ln
Salinas CA 93901
831 757-4333

(P-19838)
SALINAS VALLEY MEMORIAL HLTHCA
5 Lower Ragsdale Dr 102, Monterey (93940)
PHONE.................................831 884-5048
EMP: 329
SALES (corp-wide): 494.4MM **Privately Held**
SIC: 8011 Cardiologist & cardio-vascular specialist
PA: Salinas Valley Memorial Healthcare Systems
450 E Romie Ln
Salinas CA 93901
831 757-4333

(P-19839)
SALUD PARA LA GENTE
Also Called: Salud Para La Gnte Hlth Clinic
195 Aviation Way Ste 200, Watsonville (95076-2059)
PHONE.................................831 728-0222
Dori Rose Inda, *CEO*
Tony Balistreri, *CFO*
Rachel Sandobal, *Business Mgr*
Guillermina Porraz, *Human Res Dir*
Emilio Sanchez, *Facilities Mgr*
EMP: 125
SALES: 27.4MM **Privately Held**
SIC: 8011 Medical centers

(P-19840)
SAN BERNARDINO MED GROUP INC (PA)
1700 N Waterman Ave, San Bernardino (92404-5115)
PHONE.................................909 883-8611
James Malin, *CEO*
Thomas Hellwig, *President*
James W Malin, *CEO*
Louis Francisco MD, *Treasurer*
Paul G Godfrey MD, *Vice Pres*
EMP: 160
SQ FT: 55,000
SALES (est): 25.5MM **Privately Held**
SIC: 8011 General & family practice, physician/surgeon

(P-19841)
SAN DIEGO DIAGNSTC RADLGY MEDI (PA)
8745 Aero Dr Ste 200, San Diego (92123-1774)
P.O. Box 23540 (92193-3540)
PHONE.................................858 565-6328
Patrick H Carey, *President*
Joey Shull, *Financial Exec*
EMP: 80
SQ FT: 8,700

SALES (est): 6.1MM **Privately Held**
WEB: www.sddrmg.com
SIC: 8011 Radiologist

(P-19842)
SAN DIEGO FAMILY CARE (PA)
Also Called: LINDA VISTA HEALTH CARE CENTER
6973 Linda Vista Rd, San Diego (92111-6342)
PHONE.................................858 279-0925
Roberta L Feinberg, *CEO*
Manuel Quintanar, *CFO*
Kevin Gomez, *Administration*
Margarita Caudillo, *Data Proc Staff*
Lauren Woolley, *Psychologist*
EMP: 93
SALES: 24.3MM **Privately Held**
WEB: www.lvhcc.com
SIC: 8011 Clinic, operated by physicians

(P-19843)
SAN DIEGO IMAGING - CHULA VIST (PA)
8745 Aero Dr Ste 200, San Diego (92123-1774)
PHONE.................................858 565-0950
Keth Prince, *Principal*
▲ **EMP:** 53
SALES (est): 4.9MM **Privately Held**
WEB: www.sandiegoimaging.com
SIC: 8011 Radiologist

(P-19844)
SAN DIEGO ORTHOPAEDIC ASSOCIAT
Also Called: S D O A
4060 4th Ave Ste 700, San Diego (92103-2121)
PHONE.................................619 299-8500
Larry Dodge, *President*
William E Bowman MD, *Principal*
EMP: 52 **EST:** 1973
SQ FT: 11,000
SALES (est): 8.2MM **Privately Held**
SIC: 8011 Orthopedic physician; surgeon

(P-19845)
SAN DIEGO PATHOLOGISTS MEDICAL (PA)
7592 Metro Dr Ste 406, San Diego (92108)
PHONE.................................619 297-4012
Carla Stayboldt MD, *President*
Slavek Niewiadomski MD, *Treasurer*
David Francis MD, *Exec VP*
Bruce Robbins MD, *Exec VP*
Nancy L Harrison MD, *Vice Pres*
EMP: 120
SQ FT: 3,500
SALES (est): 8.6MM **Privately Held**
WEB: www.sdpath.com
SIC: 8011 Pathologist

(P-19846)
SAN DIMAS MEDICAL GROUP INC
100 Old River Rd, Bakersfield (93311-8823)
PHONE.................................661 663-4800
Frank Ynostroza MD, *Ch of Bd*
Ken Knutson, *CFO*
Kandi Knudsen, *Executive*
Wendy Crenshaw MD, *Principal*
Philip H Davis MD, *Principal*
EMP: 60
SQ FT: 20,000
SALES (est): 9.8MM **Privately Held**
WEB: www.sandimasmedical.com
SIC: 8011 Obstetrician; gynecologist

(P-19847)
SAN FRANCISCO FERTILITY CTRS
55 Francisco St Ste 300, San Francisco (94133-2113)
PHONE.................................415 834-3000
Carl Herbert, *Med Doctor*
Maryellen Moore, *CEO*
EMP: 74
SALES (est): 5.6MM **Privately Held**
SIC: 8011 Fertility specialist, physician

(P-19848)
SAN GABRIEL AMBULATORY SUGERY
207 S Santa Anita St G16, San Gabriel (91776-1147)
PHONE.................................626 300-5300
Brenda Durgin, *Manager*
EMP: 643
SALES (est): 34.5MM
SALES (corp-wide): 19.3B **Publicly Held**
SIC: 8011 Surgeon
HQ: United Surgical Partners International, Inc.
15305 Dallas Pkwy # 1600
Addison TX 75001
972 713-3500

(P-19849)
SAN JOSE STATE UNIVERSITY
Also Called: Student Health Services
1 Washington Sq, San Jose (95112-3613)
PHONE.................................408 924-1000
Robert J Latta MD, *Director*
Eric Bonesteel, *Officer*
Chris Nordby, *Associate Dir*
Lisa Beltran, *Admin Asst*
Darren Coelho, *Admin Asst*
EMP: 50 **Privately Held**
WEB: www.sjsu.edu
SIC: 8011 8221 9411 Dispensary, operated by physicians; university;
HQ: San Jose State University
1 Washington Sq
San Jose CA 95192
408 924-1000

(P-19850)
SAN LEANDRO SURGERY CENTER LT
15035 E 14th St, San Leandro (94578-1901)
PHONE.................................510 276-2800
Sheila Cook, *Partner*
EMP: 60
SQ FT: 33,000
SALES (est): 6.6MM **Privately Held**
WEB: www.slsurgery.com
SIC: 8011 Surgeon

(P-19851)
SANSUM CLINIC (PA)
470 S Patterson Ave, Santa Barbara (93111-2404)
P.O. Box 1200 (93102-1200)
PHONE.................................805 681-7700
Kurt Ransohoff MD, *President*
Chad Hine, *CFO*
Chris McNamara, *Senior VP*
Paul Jaconette, *Admin Asst*
Antonio Sanchez, *Admin Asst*
EMP: 60
SQ FT: 10,944
SALES: 287.3MM **Privately Held**
WEB: www.sansum.com
SIC: 8011 Clinic, operated by physicians

(P-19852)
SANTA ANA RADIOLOGY CENTER
Also Called: West Coast Radiology Center
1100 N Tustin Ave Ste A, Santa Ana (92705-3509)
PHONE.................................714 835-6055
Tim Chavez, *CEO*
Matt Albers, *Office Mgr*
Susan Dalessandro, *Marketing Staff*
Glenda Romero, *Oncology*
EMP: 60
SQ FT: 15,000
SALES (est): 4.8MM **Privately Held**
SIC: 8011 8071 Radiologist; X-ray laboratory, including dental

(P-19853)
SANTA CLARA COUNTY OF
Also Called: Public Health Dept
976 Lenzen Ave Ste 1800, San Jose (95126-2737)
PHONE.................................408 792-5680
G Dickinson, *Director*
EMP: 75 **Privately Held**
WEB: www.countyairports.org
SIC: 8011 9431 Clinic, operated by physicians; administration of public health programs;

PRODUCTS & SVCS

PA: County Of Santa Clara
3180 Newberry Dr Ste 150
San Jose CA 95118
408 299-5105

(P-19854)
SANTA CLARA VALLEY MEDICAL CTR
2400 Moorpark Ave, San Jose
(95128-2631)
PHONE..........................408 885-6300
EMP: 449 **Privately Held**
SIC: **8011** Medical centers
PA: Santa Clara Valley Medical Center
751 S Bascom Ave
San Jose CA 95128
-

(P-19855)
SANTA CLARITA MEDICAL GROUP
25775 Mcbean Pkwy Ste 209, Valencia
(91355-3703)
PHONE..........................661 255-6802
Kurt Olson, *Branch Mgr*
EMP: 50
SALES (est): 1MM
SALES (corp-wide): 3.3MM **Privately Held**
SIC: **8011** Physicians' office, including specialists
PA: Santa Clarita Medical Group, Inc
1680 S Garfield Ave
Alhambra CA
661 250-0100

(P-19856)
SANTA CRUZ COUNTY OF
Also Called: Watsonville Health Clinic
1430 Freedom Blvd Ste D, Watsonville
(95076-2752)
PHONE..........................831 763-8400
Michelle Violich, *Director*
EMP: 50 **Privately Held**
WEB: www.scsheriff.com
SIC: **8011** 9111 Clinic, operated by physicians; county supervisors' & executives' offices
PA: County Of Santa Cruz
701 Ocean St Rm 520
Santa Cruz CA 95060
831 454-2100

(P-19857)
SANTA CRUZ MEDICAL FOUNDATION (HQ)
2025 Soquel Ave, Santa Cruz
(95062-1323)
PHONE..........................831 458-5537
Larry De Ghetaldi, *Director*
Blanca Rodriguez, *Office Mgr*
Meghan Pursell, *Administration*
Michael Rankin, *Med Doctor*
David A Sofen, *Med Doctor*
EMP: 53
SQ FT: 60,000
SALES (est): 31.6MM
SALES (corp-wide): 12.4B **Privately Held**
WEB: www.sutterhealth.org
SIC: **8011** General & family practice, physician/surgeon
PA: Sutter Health
2200 River Plaza Dr
Sacramento CA 95833
916 733-8800

(P-19858)
SANTA MONICA BAY PHYSICIANS
881 Alma Real Dr Ste 214, Pacific Palisades (90272-3750)
PHONE..........................310 459-2363
Mark R Needham, *President*
EMP: 180
SALES (est): 6.8MM **Privately Held**
SIC: **8011** Physical medicine, physician/surgeon

(P-19859)
SANTA MONICA BAY PHYSICIANS HE (PA)
Also Called: Bay Area Community Med Group
5767 W Century Blvd, Los Angeles
(90045-5631)
PHONE..........................310 417-5900

Eileen McGrath, *President*
Dr Richard Zachrich, *Treasurer*
Dr Steven Seizer, *Vice Pres*
Dr David Cutler, *Admin Sec*
EMP: 85
SALES (est): 14.9MM **Privately Held**
WEB: www.smbp.com
SIC: **8011** Clinic, operated by physicians

(P-19860)
SANTA MONICA ORTHOPEDIC (PA)
2020 Santa Monica Blvd # 230, Santa Monica (90404-2124)
PHONE..........................310 315-2018
Ramin M Modabber MD, *President*
Kevin M Erhardt MD, *Vice Pres*
Kenton S Horacek MD, *Admin Sec*
EMP: 60
SQ FT: 28,242
SALES: 248.9K **Privately Held**
WEB: www.aclprevent.com
SIC: **8011** Orthopedic physician

(P-19861)
SCRIPPS CLINIC CARMEL VALLEY
Also Called: Division Infectious Diseases
10666 N Torrey Pines Rd, La Jolla
(92037-1092)
PHONE..........................858 554-8096
EMP: 271
SALES (corp-wide): 21.9MM **Privately Held**
SIC: **8011**
PA: Scripps Clinic Carmel Valley
3811 Valley Centre Dr
San Diego CA 92130
858 764-3000

(P-19862)
SCRIPPS CLINIC MEDICAL GROUP
10666 N Torrey Pines Rd, La Jolla
(92037-1092)
PHONE..........................858 554-9606
Thomas Waltz, *CEO*
James Collins, *CFO*
Emma Du, *Pathologist*
Edward Kane, *Pathologist*
Anthony Novo,
EMP: 300
SALES (est): 15MM **Privately Held**
SIC: **8011** Physicians' office, including specialists

(P-19863)
SCRIPPS DIALASYS INC (PA)
Also Called: Scripps Dialysis Center
9870 Genesee Ave, La Jolla (92037-1205)
PHONE..........................619 453-9070
John Aalbers, *Principal*
EMP: 50
SQ FT: 10,000
SALES (est): 2.2MM **Privately Held**
SIC: **8011** 8092 Clinic, operated by physicians; kidney dialysis centers

(P-19864)
SCRIPPS HEALTH
Also Called: Scripps Whttier Dbetes Program
10140 Campus Point Dr, San Diego
(92121-1520)
PHONE..........................858 622-9076
Athena Philis-Tsimikas, *Branch Mgr*
Cecile Hozouri, *President*
Jane Specialist, *Executive*
Rodney Sackett, *Senior Engr*
Garay Anna, *Director*
EMP: 60
SALES (corp-wide): 2.9B **Privately Held**
SIC: **8011** Diabetes specialist, physician/surgeon
PA: Scripps Health
10140 Campus Point Dr Ax415
San Diego CA 92121
800 727-4777

(P-19865)
SCRIPPS HEALTH
Also Called: Rancho Clinic Rancho San Diego
10862 Calle Verde, La Mesa (91941-7340)
PHONE..........................619 670-5400
Yvonne Markovitz, *Manager*

Michael Magpile, *Orthopedist*
Michaela Miller, *Internal Med*
Ziad Allos, *Med Doctor*
Erik Gilbertson, *Manager*
EMP: 70
SALES (corp-wide): 2.9B **Privately Held**
WEB: www.scripps.org
SIC: **8011** Clinic, operated by physicians
PA: Scripps Health
10140 Campus Point Dr Ax415
San Diego CA 92121
800 727-4777

(P-19866)
SCRIPPS HEALTH
7910 Frost St Ste 320, San Diego
(92123-2791)
PHONE..........................858 292-4211
Steven F Mosher MD, *Owner*
EMP: 300
SALES (corp-wide): 2.9B **Privately Held**
SIC: **8011** Physicians' office, including specialists
PA: Scripps Health
10140 Campus Point Dr Ax415
San Diego CA 92121
800 727-4777

(P-19867)
SCRIPPS HEALTH
Also Called: Scripps Clinic - Encinatas
310 Santa Fe Dr Ste 200, Encinitas
(92024-5124)
PHONE..........................760 633-6915
Cheryl Suqua, *Administration*
Scott Musinski, *Obstetrician*
EMP: 60
SQ FT: 38,331
SALES (corp-wide): 2.9B **Privately Held**
WEB: www.scripps.org
SIC: **8011** General & family practice, physician/surgeon
PA: Scripps Health
10140 Campus Point Dr Ax415
San Diego CA 92121
800 727-4777

(P-19868)
SCRIPPS HEALTH
488 E Valley Pkwy Ste 411, Escondido
(92025-3380)
PHONE..........................760 806-5700
Kelly A Martinez, *Obstetrician*
EMP: 200
SALES (corp-wide): 2.9B **Privately Held**
SIC: **8011** Offices & clinics of medical doctors
PA: Scripps Health
10140 Campus Point Dr Ax415
San Diego CA 92121
800 727-4777

(P-19869)
SCRIPPS HEALTH
9834 Genesee Ave Ste 311, La Jolla
(92037-1221)
PHONE..........................858 458-5100
Douglas Bolitho, *Plastic Surgeon*
EMP: 264
SALES (corp-wide): 2.9B **Privately Held**
SIC: **8011** Plastic surgeon
PA: Scripps Health
10140 Campus Point Dr Ax415
San Diego CA 92121
800 727-4777

(P-19870)
SCRIPPS HEALTH
9850 Genesee Ave Ste 620, La Jolla
(92037-1217)
PHONE..........................858 626-5200
EMP: 132
SALES (corp-wide): 2.9B **Privately Held**
SIC: **8011** 8059 Offices & clinics of medical doctors; convalescent home
PA: Scripps Health
10140 Campus Point Dr Ax415
San Diego CA 92121
800 727-4777

(P-19871)
SCRIPPS HEALTH
10666 N Torrey Pines Rd, La Jolla
(92037-1027)
PHONE..........................858 554-8892
Larry Harrison, *President*

Quang Nguyen, *Med Doctor*
Lisa Otte, *Director*
Katalin Fejes, *Manager*
EMP: 60
SQ FT: 99,999
SALES (corp-wide): 2.9B **Privately Held**
SIC: **8011** Physicians' office, including specialists
PA: Scripps Health
10140 Campus Point Dr Ax415
San Diego CA 92121
800 727-4777

(P-19872)
SCRIPPS HEALTH
10666 N Torrey Pines Rd, La Jolla
(92037-1027)
PHONE..........................858 554-9489
Allan Saven MD, *Principal*
EMP: 60
SALES (corp-wide): 2.9B **Privately Held**
WEB: www.scripps.org
SIC: **8011** Physicians' office, including specialists
PA: Scripps Health
10140 Campus Point Dr Ax415
San Diego CA 92121
800 727-4777

(P-19873)
SCRIPPS HEALTH
3998 Vista Way Ste E, Oceanside
(92056-4514)
PHONE..........................760 901-5200
John Kroener, *Surgeon*
Maria Murillo, *Obstetrician*
Madeline Rodriguez, *Obstetrician*
EMP: 231
SALES (corp-wide): 2.9B **Privately Held**
SIC: **8011** General & family practice, physician/surgeon
PA: Scripps Health
10140 Campus Point Dr Ax415
San Diego CA 92121
800 727-4777

(P-19874)
SCRIPPS HEALTH
Also Called: Clinic Business
10790 Rancho Bernardo Rd, San Diego
(92127-5705)
PHONE..........................858 784-5888
Breaux Castleman, *President*
Susan Erickson, *Manager*
Chuck Korogi, *Manager*
EMP: 100
SALES (corp-wide): 2.9B **Privately Held**
WEB: www.scripps.org
SIC: **8011** Internal medicine practitioners; specialized medical practitioners, except internal
PA: Scripps Health
10140 Campus Point Dr Ax415
San Diego CA 92121
800 727-4777

(P-19875)
SD SPORTS MDCNE&FMLY HLTH CNTR
6699 Alvarado Rd Ste 2100, San Diego
(92120-5238)
PHONE..........................619 229-3910
Jo Baxter, *Office Mgr*
Michelle Look, *Sports Medicine*
Bill Taylor,
Greg Bourque, *Director*
EMP: 52
SALES (est): 3.7MM **Privately Held**
WEB: www.sandiegosportsmed.com
SIC: **8011** Clinic, operated by physicians

(P-19876)
SENECA HEALTHCARE DISTRICT
Also Called: Seneca Hospital Almanor Clinic
199 Reynolds Rd, Chester (96020)
PHONE..........................530 258-1977
Camille Hovellerdale, *Manager*
Mary Garrett, *Office Mgr*
EMP: 78
SALES (corp-wide): 26.3MM **Privately Held**
SIC: **8011** Clinic, operated by physicians

PA: Seneca Healthcare District
130 Brentwood Dr
Chester CA 96020
530 258-2151

(P-19877)
SEQUOIA SURGICAL CENTER LP
Also Called: Sequoia Surgical Pavilion
2405 Shadelands Dr # 200, Walnut Creek
(94598-5916)
PHONE..................................925 935-6700
Debbie Mack, *General Ptnr*
EMP: 50
SQ FT: 14,750
SALES (est): 5MM
SALES (corp-wide): 1.1B **Publicly Held**
SIC: 8011 Ambulatory surgical center
HQ: National Surgical Hospitals, Inc.
250 S Wacker Dr Ste 500
Chicago IL 60606
312 627-8400

(P-19878)
SERRA COMMUNITY MED CLINIC INC
9375 San Fernando Rd, Sun Valley
(91352-1418)
PHONE..................................818 768-3000
Sadayappa K Durairaj, *CEO*
Karla Pieters, *CFO*
Kumar Soundar, *CFO*
Dr Arnold Jacobs, *Treasurer*
Dr Carlos Jimenez, *Admin Sec*
EMP: 163
SQ FT: 60,000
SALES (est): 18.5MM **Privately Held**
SIC: 8011 Clinic, operated by physicians

(P-19879)
SERRA MEDICAL CLINIC INC
9375 San Fernando Rd, Sun Valley
(91352-1418)
PHONE..................................818 768-3000
S K Durairaj MD, *President*
EMP: 100 **EST:** 1974
SQ FT: 62,000
SALES (est): 3.8MM **Privately Held**
SIC: 8011 Internal medicine, physician/surgeon

(P-19880)
SHARP HEALTHCARE
7910 Frost St Ste 280, San Diego
(92123-2752)
PHONE..................................619 398-2988
Joey Scarafone, *Analyst*
Barry Uhl, *Oncology*
Geoffrey Weinstein, *Oncology*
Phillip Zentner, *Oncology*
Steve Rindsberg, *Pediatrics*
EMP: 131
SALES (corp-wide): 3.4B **Privately Held**
SIC: 8011 Neurologist
PA: Sharp Healthcare
8695 Spectrum Center Blvd
San Diego CA 92123
858 499-4000

(P-19881)
SHARP HEALTHCARE
3575 Euclid Ave, San Diego (92105-2925)
PHONE..................................619 284-1400
Evelyn Fraser, *Nurse*
Marjorie Ethridge, *Director*
EMP: 54
SALES (corp-wide): 3.4B **Privately Held**
SIC: 8011 Physicians' office, including specialists
PA: Sharp Healthcare
8695 Spectrum Center Blvd
San Diego CA 92123
858 499-4000

(P-19882)
SHARP HEALTHCARE
Also Called: Eye Physican Medical Group
225 W Madison Ave Ste 1, El Cajon
(92020-3454)
PHONE..................................619 442-0844
Christopher H Hsu, *Med Doctor*
EMP: 54
SALES (corp-wide): 3.4B **Privately Held**
SIC: 8011 General & family practice, physician/surgeon

PA: Sharp Healthcare
8695 Spectrum Center Blvd
San Diego CA 92123
858 499-4000

(P-19883)
SHARP HEALTHCARE
Also Called: Sharp Rees-Stealy Div
300 Fir St, San Diego (92101-2327)
PHONE..................................619 446-1575
Donna Mills, *Administration*
Eric Giroux, *Partner*
Teresa Harris, *Partner*
Stacey Richard, *Partner*
Marlena Montgomery, *Nursing Mgr*
EMP: 150
SQ FT: 61,608
SALES (corp-wide): 3.4B **Privately Held**
SIC: 8011 Medical centers
PA: Sharp Healthcare
8695 Spectrum Center Blvd
San Diego CA 92123
858 499-4000

(P-19884)
SHARP HEALTHCARE
8901 Activity Rd, San Diego (92126-4427)
PHONE..................................858 653-6100
Joy Stewart, *Director*
EMP: 100
SALES (corp-wide): 3.4B **Privately Held**
SIC: 8011 Offices & clinics of medical doctors
PA: Sharp Healthcare
8695 Spectrum Center Blvd
San Diego CA 92123
858 499-4000

(P-19885)
SHARP HEALTHCARE
2020 Genesee Ave Fl 2, San Diego
(92123-4219)
PHONE..................................858 616-8411
Leticia Rawls, *Principal*
EMP: 100
SQ FT: 33,244
SALES (corp-wide): 3.4B **Privately Held**
SIC: 8011 Clinic, operated by physicians
PA: Sharp Healthcare
8695 Spectrum Center Blvd
San Diego CA 92123
858 499-4000

(P-19886)
SHARP HEALTHCARE
Also Called: Sharp Reece Stealy Med Group
4510 Viewridge Ave, San Diego
(92123-1637)
PHONE..................................800 827-4277
Don Balfour, *Manager*
Joseph Marty, *Business Mgr*
Marguerite Paradis, *Director*
EMP: 70
SALES (corp-wide): 3.4B **Privately Held**
SIC: 8011 Clinic, operated by physicians
PA: Sharp Healthcare
8695 Spectrum Center Blvd
San Diego CA 92123
858 499-4000

(P-19887)
SHARP HEALTHCARE
8860 Center Dr Ste 450, La Mesa
(91942-7001)
PHONE..................................619 460-6200
Scott Musicant, *Branch Mgr*
Barzan Mohedin, *Internal Med*
EMP: 85
SALES (corp-wide): 3.4B **Privately Held**
SIC: 8011 General & family practice, physician/surgeon
PA: Sharp Healthcare
8695 Spectrum Center Blvd
San Diego CA 92123
858 499-4000

(P-19888)
SHARP HEALTHCARE
2020 Genesee Ave, San Diego
(92123-4219)
PHONE..................................858 616-8200
Dawn M Long, *Family Practiti*
EMP: 62
SALES (corp-wide): 3.4B **Privately Held**
SIC: 8011 Medical centers

PA: Sharp Healthcare
8695 Spectrum Center Blvd
San Diego CA 92123
858 499-4000

(P-19889)
SHARPER FUTURE
Also Called: Social Hblttion Rlpse Prvntion
870 Market St Ste 1265, San Francisco
(94102-2917)
PHONE..................................415 297-6767
Thomas Tobin, *Partner*
Mary-Perry Miller, *Partner*
EMP: 56 **EST:** 1995
SALES (est): 1.3MM **Privately Held**
WEB: www.sharperfuture.com
SIC: 8011 Psychiatric clinic

(P-19890)
SHEPARD EYE CENTER
1418 E Main St Ste 110, Santa Maria
(93454-4836)
PHONE..................................805 925-2637
Dennis D Shepard MD, *President*
James T Franta, *Principal*
EMP: 50
SQ FT: 10,000
SALES (est): 4.8MM **Privately Held**
SIC: 8011 Ophthalmologist

(P-19891)
SIERRA PACIFIC ORTHO
1630 E Herndon Ave, Fresno (93720-3391)
PHONE..................................559 256-5200
Joe Clark, *CEO*
Eric C Hanson, *President*
Paramjeet Gill, *Officer*
Jerry Smith, *Sports Medicine*
Jerome Dunklin, *Surgeon*
EMP: 200 **EST:** 2000
SALES (est): 5.1MM **Privately Held**
WEB: www.spoc-ortho.com
SIC: 8011 Orthopedic physician

(P-19892)
SIERRA VIEW DST HOSP LEAG INC (PA)
465 W Putnam Ave, Porterville
(93257-3320)
PHONE..................................559 784-1110
Donna Hefner, *President*
Frederick Young,
Kuldeep Jagpal,
Thomas Maclennan, *Ch Radiology*
Debbie Zebofkey, *Records Dir*
◆ **EMP:** 168 **EST:** 1948
SQ FT: 135,000
SALES: 138.3MM **Privately Held**
WEB: www.sierra-view.com
SIC: 8011 8062 Offices & clinics of medical doctors; general medical & surgical hospitals

(P-19893)
SOBOL PHILIP A MD P C INC
8618 S Sepulveda Blvd # 130, Los Angeles
(90045-4005)
PHONE..................................310 649-5894
Philip A Sobol, *President*
EMP: 50
SALES (est): 2.3MM **Privately Held**
SIC: 8011 Offices & clinics of medical doctors

(P-19894)
SOC PATHOLOGY MEDICAL GROUP
2374 E Pacifica Pl, Rancho Dominguez
(90220-6214)
PHONE..................................310 225-3220
Meredith Peake, *CEO*
Stanette Kennebrew, *Administration*
EMP: 85
SALES: 1MM **Privately Held**
SIC: 8011 Pathologist

(P-19895)
SOLANO REGIONAL MEDICAL GROUP (PA)
1234 Empire St, Fairfield (94533-5711)
PHONE..................................707 426-3911
Edward Levin MD, *President*
George Stock MD, *Treasurer*
Sam Santoro Do, *Vice Pres*
Teresa Wilson, *Director*

EMP: 250
SQ FT: 40,000
SALES (est): 10.1MM **Privately Held**
SIC: 8011 General & family practice, physician/surgeon

(P-19896)
SONOMA COUNTY INDIAN HEALTH PR (PA)
Also Called: Scihp
144 Stony Point Rd, Santa Rosa
(95401-4122)
PHONE..................................707 521-4545
Betty Arterverry, *CEO*
Molin T Malicay, *CEO*
Lori Houston, *Planning*
Dr Don Carlos Stele, *Medical Dir*
EMP: 170
SQ FT: 70,000
SALES: 21.8MM **Privately Held**
SIC: 8011 Clinic, operated by physicians

(P-19897)
SOUTH BAY FAMILY MEDICAL GROUP
Also Called: Mellor, Anna B MD
3105 Lomita Blvd, Torrance (90505-5108)
PHONE..................................310 378-2234
Glenn M Wishon MD, *Partner*
Nancy Griffith MD, *Partner*
George A Joseph MD, *Partner*
Lee G Kissel MD, *Partner*
Joseph Mansen, *Partner*
EMP: 70
SQ FT: 6,400
SALES (est): 3.4MM **Privately Held**
WEB: www.sbfmg.com
SIC: 8011 General & family practice, physician/surgeon

(P-19898)
SOUTH CENTRAL FAMILY HLTH CTR
4425 S Central Ave, Los Angeles
(90011-3629)
PHONE..................................323 908-4200
Richard Veloz, *President*
Paul Ramos, *CFO*
Ruby Raya Morones, *Chief Mktg Ofcr*
Sandra Tatum Green, *Human Res Dir*
EMP: 92
SQ FT: 13,000
SALES: 13.7MM **Privately Held**
WEB: www.scfhc.org
SIC: 8011 Clinic, operated by physicians

(P-19899)
SOUTH COUNTY ORTHOPEDIC SPECIA
Also Called: Moskow, Lonnie J MD
24331 El Toro Rd Ste 200, Laguna Hills
(92637-3116)
PHONE..................................949 586-3200
James Mullen, *President*
Kyle W Coker, *Principal*
Larry M Gursten, *Principal*
Lance R Montgomery, *Principal*
Lonnie J Moskow, *Principal*
EMP: 75
SALES (est): 9.8MM **Privately Held**
WEB: www.scosortho.com
SIC: 8011 Orthopedic physician

(P-19900)
SOUTHERN CA HLTH & RHBLTN PRG
2610 Industry Way Ste A, Lynwood
(90262-4028)
PHONE..................................310 631-8004
Jack M Barbour, *CEO*
Rita Floyd, *President*
EMP: 165
SQ FT: 6,000
SALES (est): 10.4MM **Privately Held**
SIC: 8011 Psychiatric clinic

(P-19901)
SOUTHERN CAL ORTHPD INST LP
375 Rolling Oaks Dr, Thousand Oaks
(91361-1023)
PHONE..................................805 497-7015
David M Auerbach, *Branch Mgr*
Mark Getelman, *Sports Medicine*
David Auerbach, *Surgeon*

EMP: 61
SALES (est): 1.5MM **Privately Held**
SIC: 8011 Orthopedic physician
PA: Southern California Orthopedic Insti-
tute, L.P.
6815 Noble Ave
Van Nuys CA 91405
-

(P-19902)
SOUTHERN CAL ORTHPD INST
LP
Also Called: Satellite Office
6815 Noble Ave Frnt Frnt, Van Nuys
(91405-6515)
PHONE.....................818 901-6600
Patricia McKeever, *Partner*
EMP: 150 **Privately Held**
WEB: www.scoiclasroom.com
SIC: 8011 Orthopedic physician
PA: Southern California Orthopedic Insti-
tute, L.P.
6815 Noble Ave
Van Nuys CA 91405

(P-19903)
SOUTHERN CAL ORTHPD INST
LP
6815 Noble Ave Ste 112, Westlake Village
(91361)
PHONE.....................818 901-6600
Dr Mark Friedman, *Partner*
EMP: 66 **Privately Held**
WEB: www.scoiclasroom.com
SIC: 8011 Orthopedic physician
PA: Southern California Orthopedic Insti-
tute, L.P.
6815 Noble Ave
Van Nuys CA 91405
-

(P-19904)
SOUTHERN CAL ORTHPD INST
LP (PA)
6815 Noble Ave, Van Nuys (91405-3796)
PHONE.....................818 901-6600
Marc J Friedman, *Partner*
Michael Bahk, *Managing Dir*
Tammy Molidor, *Office Mgr*
Susan Nadeau, *Administration*
Carol Weiske, *Administration*
EMP: 135
SALES (est): 30.5MM **Privately Held**
WEB: www.scoiclasroom.com
SIC: 8011 8249 Orthopedic physician;
medical training services

(P-19905)
SOUTHERN CAL PRMNNTE MED
GROUP
6 Willard, Irvine (92604-4694)
PHONE.....................949 262-5780
Debra Dannemeyer, *Administration*
EMP: 100
SALES (corp-wide): 3.5B **Privately Held**
WEB: www.permanente.net
SIC: 8011 Clinic, operated by physicians
PA: Southern California Permanente Med-
ical Group
393 Walnut Dr
Pasadena CA 91107
626 405-5704

(P-19906)
SOUTHERN CAL PRMNNTE MED
GROUP
3501 Stockdale Hwy, Bakersfield
(93309-2150)
PHONE.....................661 398-5085
EMP: 54
SALES (corp-wide): 3.5B **Privately Held**
SIC: 8011 Offices & clinics of medical doc-
tors
PA: Southern California Permanente Med-
ical Group
393 Walnut Dr
Pasadena CA 91107
626 405-5704

(P-19907)
SOUTHERN CAL PRMNNTE MED
GROUP
Also Called: Kaiser Permanente
4647 Zion Ave, San Diego (92120-2507)
PHONE.....................619 528-5000
Terry Belmont, *Principal*
Peter Martin, *Top Exec*
Jane Finley, *Senior VP*
Pamela Reger, *Case Mgmt Dir*
Nancy Hebert, *Finance*
EMP: 53
SALES (corp-wide): 3.5B **Privately Held**
SIC: 8011 Medical centers
PA: Southern California Permanente Med-
ical Group
393 Walnut Dr
Pasadena CA 91107
626 405-5704

(P-19908)
SOUTHERN CAL PRMNNTE MED
GROUP
3830 Martin L King Jr Blv, Lynwood
(90262-3625)
PHONE.....................310 604-5700
EMP: 53
SALES (corp-wide): 3.5B **Privately Held**
SIC: 8011 Medical centers
PA: Southern California Permanente Med-
ical Group
393 Walnut Dr
Pasadena CA 91107
626 405-5704

(P-19909)
SOUTHERN CAL PRMNNTE MED
GROUP
6041 Cadillac Ave, Los Angeles
(90034-1702)
PHONE.....................323 857-2000
Larry Poston, *Director*
Stephanie Leong, *Med Doctor*
Philip Seifer, *Med Doctor*
EMP: 58
SALES (corp-wide): 3.5B **Privately Held**
SIC: 8011 Radiologist
PA: Southern California Permanente Med-
ical Group
393 Walnut Dr
Pasadena CA 91107
626 405-5704

(P-19910)
SOUTHERN CAL PRMNNTE MED
GROUP
25825 Vermont Ave, Harbor City
(90710-3518)
PHONE.....................800 780-1230
EMP: 58
SALES (corp-wide): 3.5B **Privately Held**
WEB: www.permanente.net
SIC: 8011 Offices & clinics of medical doc-
tors
PA: Southern California Permanente Med-
ical Group
393 Walnut Dr
Pasadena CA 91107
626 405-5704

(P-19911)
SOUTHERN CAL PRMNNTE MED
GROUP
4841 Hollywood Blvd, Los Angeles
(90027-5301)
PHONE.....................323 783-5455
Srinivas J Sarma, *Surgeon*
Sumit M Khandhar, *Cardiovascular*
Ramin Shadman, *Cardiovascular*
Colin T Watanabe, *Cardiovascular*
Kevin Y Lin, *Emerg Med Spec*
EMP: 70
SALES (corp-wide): 3.5B **Privately Held**
SIC: 8011 Medical centers
PA: Southern California Permanente Med-
ical Group
393 Walnut Dr
Pasadena CA 91107
626 405-5704

(P-19912)
SOUTHERN CAL PRMNNTE MED
GROUP
Also Called: Orthopedics Department
4760 W Sunset Blvd, Los Angeles
(90027-6063)
PHONE.....................323 783-4893
Dolores Cobbarrubias, *Office Mgr*
EMP: 443
SALES (corp-wide): 3.5B **Privately Held**
SIC: 8011 Orthopedic physician
PA: Southern California Permanente Med-
ical Group
393 Walnut Dr
Pasadena CA 91107
626 405-5704

(P-19913)
SOUTHERN CAL PRMNNTE MED
GROUP
Also Called: S C P M G
789 E Cooley Dr, Colton (92324-4007)
PHONE.....................909 370-2501
EMP: 50
SALES (corp-wide): 3.5B **Privately Held**
WEB: www.permanente.net
SIC: 8011 Offices & clinics of medical doc-
tors
PA: Southern California Permanente Med-
ical Group
393 Walnut Dr
Pasadena CA 91107
626 405-5704

(P-19914)
SOUTHERN CAL PRMNNTE MED
GROUP
18081 Beach Blvd, Huntington Beach
(92648-1304)
PHONE.....................714 841-7293
EMP: 50
SALES (corp-wide): 3.5B **Privately Held**
WEB: www.permanente.net
SIC: 8011 Offices & clinics of medical doc-
tors
PA: Southern California Permanente Med-
ical Group
393 Walnut Dr
Pasadena CA 91107
626 405-5704

(P-19915)
SOUTHERN CAL PRMNNTE MED
GROUP
Also Called: S C P M G
1630 E Main St, El Cajon (92021-5204)
PHONE.....................619 528-5000
Brenda Scott-Mead, *Manager*
EMP: 50
SALES (corp-wide): 3.5B **Privately Held**
WEB: www.permanente.net
SIC: 8011 Medical centers
PA: Southern California Permanente Med-
ical Group
393 Walnut Dr
Pasadena CA 91107
626 405-5704

(P-19916)
SOUTHERN CAL PRMNNTE MED
GROUP
Also Called: S C P M G
411 N Lakeview Ave, Anaheim
(92807-3028)
PHONE.....................714 279-4675
Ryan Williams, *Manager*
Janet Hartmann Jones, *Hematology*
Edward M Nepomuceno, *Med Doctor*
EMP: 50
SALES (corp-wide): 3.5B **Privately Held**
WEB: www.permanente.net
SIC: 8011 Offices & clinics of medical doc-
tors
PA: Southern California Permanente Med-
ical Group
393 Walnut Dr
Pasadena CA 91107
626 405-5704

(P-19917)
SOUTHERN CAL PRMNNTE MED
GROUP
Also Called: S C P M G
30400 Camino Capistrano, San Juan
Capistrano (92675-1300)
PHONE.....................949 234-2139
EMP: 50
SALES (corp-wide): 3.5B **Privately Held**
WEB: www.permanente.net
SIC: 8011 Offices & clinics of medical doc-
tors
PA: Southern California Permanente Med-
ical Group
393 Walnut Dr
Pasadena CA 91107
626 405-5704

(P-19918)
SOUTHERN CAL PRMNNTE MED
GROUP
Also Called: S C P M G
22550 Savi Ranch Pkwy, Yorba Linda
(92887-4670)
PHONE.....................714 685-3520
Kamil Antonios MD, *Manager*
EMP: 50
SALES (corp-wide): 3.5B **Privately Held**
WEB: www.permanente.net
SIC: 8011 Offices & clinics of medical doc-
tors
PA: Southern California Permanente Med-
ical Group
393 Walnut Dr
Pasadena CA 91107
626 405-5704

(P-19919)
SOUTHERN CAL PRMNNTE MED
GROUP
Also Called: S C P M G
1900 E 4th St, Santa Ana (92705-3962)
PHONE.....................714 967-4760
Julie White-Dahlgren, *Branch Mgr*
EMP: 60
SALES (corp-wide): 3.5B **Privately Held**
WEB: www.permanente.net
SIC: 8011 8049 Obstetrician; psychiatric
social worker
PA: Southern California Permanente Med-
ical Group
393 Walnut Dr
Pasadena CA 91107
626 405-5704

(P-19920)
SOUTHERN CAL PRMNNTE MED
GROUP
Also Called: S C P M G
4405 Vandever Ave, San Diego
(92120-3315)
PHONE.....................619 516-6000
Thomas Volle, *Med Doctor*
EMP: 50
SALES (corp-wide): 3.5B **Privately Held**
WEB: www.permanente.net
SIC: 8011 Medical centers
PA: Southern California Permanente Med-
ical Group
393 Walnut Dr
Pasadena CA 91107
626 405-5704

(P-19921)
SOUTHERN CAL PRMNNTE MED
GROUP
Also Called: S C P M G
732 N Broadway, Escondido (92025-1870)
PHONE.....................760 839-7200
Alex Anderson, *Manager*
EMP: 50
SALES (corp-wide): 3.5B **Privately Held**
WEB: www.permanente.net
SIC: 8011 Medical centers
PA: Southern California Permanente Med-
ical Group
393 Walnut Dr
Pasadena CA 91107
626 405-5704

(P-19922)
SOUTHERN CAL PRMNNTE MED GROUP
Also Called: S C P M G
7825 Atlantic Ave, Cudahy (90201-5022)
PHONE....................................323 562-6459
Maria Gonzalez, *Principal*
EMP: 50
SALES (corp-wide): 3.5B **Privately Held**
WEB: www.permanente.net
SIC: 8011 Offices & clinics of medical doctors
PA: Southern California Permanente Medical Group
      393 Walnut Dr
      Pasadena CA 91107
      626 405-5704

(P-19923)
SOUTHERN CAL PRMNNTE MED GROUP
Also Called: S C P M G
21263 Erwin St, Woodland Hills
(91367-3715)
PHONE....................................818 592-3038
Cary Glass, *Branch Mgr*
EMP: 50
SALES (corp-wide): 3.5B **Privately Held**
WEB: www.permanente.net
SIC: 8011 Offices & clinics of medical doctors
PA: Southern California Permanente Medical Group
      393 Walnut Dr
      Pasadena CA 91107
      626 405-5704

(P-19924)
SOUTHERN CAL PRMNNTE MED GROUP
Also Called: S C P M G
27107 Tourney Rd, Santa Clarita
(91355-1860)
PHONE....................................661 222-2150
EMP: 50
SALES (corp-wide): 3.5B **Privately Held**
WEB: www.permanente.net
SIC: 8011 Offices & clinics of medical doctors
PA: Southern California Permanente Medical Group
      393 Walnut Dr
      Pasadena CA 91107
      626 405-5704

(P-19925)
SOUTHERN CAL PRMNNTE MED GROUP
5055 California Ave, Bakersfield
(93309-0701)
PHONE....................................661 334-2020
Geckeley, *Principal*
EMP: 100
SALES (corp-wide): 3.5B **Privately Held**
WEB: www.permanente.net
SIC: 8011 Offices & clinics of medical doctors
PA: Southern California Permanente Medical Group
      393 Walnut Dr
      Pasadena CA 91107
      626 405-5704

(P-19926)
SOUTHERN CAL STONE CTR LLC
Also Called: So Calif Stone Center
5400 Balboa Blvd Ste 111, Encino
(91316-5206)
PHONE....................................818 784-8975
Jerry Garrett MD, *Principal*
James Orecklin MD,
EMP: 56
SALES (est): 4MM **Privately Held**
SIC: 8011 Medical centers

(P-19927)
SOUTHERN INDIAN HEALTH COUNCIL (PA)
4058 Willows Rd, Alpine (91901-1668)
P.O. Box 2128 (91903-2128)
PHONE....................................619 445-1188
Carolina Monsano, *Exec Dir*
Laura Caswell, *COO*

Donna James, *Exec Dir*
Natalie Alvarado, *Human Resources*
Laura Quaha, *Exec Sec*
EMP: 100
SQ FT: 11,000
SALES: 14.6MM **Privately Held**
SIC: 8011 8021 Clinic, operated by physicians; dental clinic

(P-19928)
SOUTHLAND ARTHRITIS OSTEO
949 Calhoun Pl Ste F, Hemet (92543-4403)
PHONE....................................951 672-1866
Chantra V Mehta, *Owner*
Amal Mehta, *Internal Med*
Dharmarajan Ramaswamy, *Director*
EMP: 50 EST: 2011
SALES (est): 860.5K **Privately Held**
SIC: 8011 Rheumatology specialist, physician/surgeon

(P-19929)
SOUTHWESTERN ORTHPD MED CORP
Also Called: Downey Orthopedic Med Group
15901 Hawthorne Blvd, Lawndale
(90260-2655)
P.O. Box 4489, Montebello (90640-9309)
PHONE....................................562 803-0600
Lucy Guttierez, *Branch Mgr*
EMP: 50
SALES (corp-wide): 3.3MM **Privately Held**
SIC: 8011 Orthopedic physician
PA: Southwestern Orthopedic Medical Corporation
      905 S A St
      Oxnard CA 93030
      805 486-4501

(P-19930)
SPALDING SRGCL CTR OF BVRLY HL
Also Called: S&B Surgery Center II
27520 Hawthorne Blvd # 176, Rllng HLS Est (90274-3576)
PHONE....................................949 863-0022
Theordore Goldstrein, *President*
Randy Rosen, *CFO*
EMP: 120
SQ FT: 8,000
SALES (est): 12MM **Privately Held**
WEB: www.snbsurgery.com
SIC: 8011 Surgeon

(P-19931)
SPECIALTY SURG CTR BEVERLY HIL
8670 Wilshire Blvd # 301, Beverly Hills
(90211-2924)
PHONE....................................310 659-6333
David M Alessi, *Principal*
EMP: 72
SALES (est): 321K
SALES (corp-wide): 1.1B **Publicly Held**
SIC: 8011 Ambulatory surgical center
HQ: Surgery Partners, Inc.
      310 Seven Springs Way
      Brentwood TN 37027
      615 234-5900

(P-19932)
SPECIALTY SURGICAL CENTERS
15825 Laguna Canyon Rd # 200, Irvine
(92618-2127)
PHONE....................................949 341-3499
Andrew Brooks MD, *President*
Linda Mansfield, *Director*
Terry Weisman, *Director*
EMP: 50
SALES (est): 7.8MM **Privately Held**
SIC: 8011 Physicians' office, including specialists

(P-19933)
SPECILTY SRGICAL CTR ENCINO LP
16501 Ventura Blvd # 103, Encino
(91436-2007)
PHONE....................................310 659-6333
Andrew Brooks,
EMP: 73

SALES (est): 480K
SALES (corp-wide): 1.1B **Publicly Held**
SIC: 8011 Surgeon
HQ: Surgery Partners, Inc.
      310 Seven Springs Way
      Brentwood TN 37027
      615 234-5900

(P-19934)
SPH-IRVINE LLC
Also Called: Starpoint Surgery Center
18952 Macarthur Blvd # 103, Irvine
(92612-1401)
PHONE....................................949 833-1432
Eric Friedlander, *Mng Member*
EMP: 50
SALES (est): 358.5K **Privately Held**
SIC: 8011 Ambulatory surgical center

(P-19935)
SPINECARE MEDICAL GROUP INC
455 Hickey Blvd Ste 310, Daly City
(94015-2630)
PHONE....................................650 985-7500
Arthur H White MD, *Ch of Bd*
James B Reynolds MD, *President*
Noel D Goldthwaite MD, *Treasurer*
Richard Derby MD, *Vice Pres*
Garrett Kine MD, *Vice Pres*
EMP: 57
SQ FT: 82,000
SALES (est): 7.7MM **Privately Held**
WEB: www.spinecare.com
SIC: 8011 Clinic, operated by physicians; surgeon

(P-19936)
ST FRANCIS MEDICAL CENTER (HQ)
Also Called: Sfmc
3630 E Imperial Hwy, Lynwood
(90262-2609)
P.O. Box 1168, San Carlos (94070-1168)
PHONE....................................310 900-8900
Fax: 310 604-0864
EMP: 168
SALES: 451.1MM
SALES (corp-wide): 225.4MM **Privately Held**
SIC: 8011
PA: Verity Health System Of California, Inc.
      2040 E Mariposa Ave
      El Segundo CA 90245
      650 551-6650

(P-19937)
ST JOSEPH HEALTH SYSTEM
Humboldt Medical Speicialists
2280 Harrison Ave Ste B, Eureka
(95501-3200)
PHONE....................................707 443-9371
William Stiles, *Manager*
EMP: 50
SALES (corp-wide): 17.6B **Privately Held**
SIC: 8011 Internal medicine practitioners; internal medicine, physician/surgeon
HQ: St. Joseph Health System
      3345 Michelson Dr Ste 100
      Irvine CA 92612
      949 381-4000

(P-19938)
ST JOSEPH SURGERY CENTER LP
1800 N California St # 1, Stockton
(95204-6019)
PHONE....................................209 467-6316
Don Wiley, *President*
Annette Aldridge, *Manager*
EMP: 75
SALES (est): 7MM **Privately Held**
SIC: 8011 Surgeon

(P-19939)
ST JUDE HERITAGE MEDICAL GROUP
4300 Rose Dr, Yorba Linda (92886-2026)
PHONE....................................714 528-4211
Lytton Smith MD, *President*
Richard Kenfield MD, *Treasurer*
R S Hall MD, *Vice Pres*
Kenneth Tan MD, *Admin Sec*
Marcia Wilken, *Opers Staff*
EMP: 148

SALES (est): 8.1MM **Privately Held**
SIC: 8011 Clinic, operated by physicians; general & family practice, physician/surgeon

(P-19940)
ST JUDE HOSPITAL
Also Called: St Jude Medical Ctr Purch Dept
101 E Valencia Mesa Dr, Fullerton
(92835-3875)
PHONE....................................714 992-3057
David Saffert, *Director*
Mylinh Bui, *General Mgr*
EMP: 2500
SALES (corp-wide): 17.6B **Privately Held**
WEB: www.stjudemedicalcenter.com
SIC: 8011 Medical centers
HQ: St. Jude Hospital
      101 E Valencia Mesa Dr
      Fullerton CA 92835
      714 871-3280

(P-19941)
ST JUDE HOSPITAL YORBA LINDA
27800 Medical Center Rd, Mission Viejo
(92691-6410)
PHONE....................................949 365-2492
Nicki Levitt, *Manager*
EMP: 50
SALES (corp-wide): 17.6B **Privately Held**
SIC: 8011 General & family practice, physician/surgeon
HQ: St. Jude Hospital Yorba Linda
      200 W Ctr St Promenade
      Anaheim CA 92805
      714 712-3308

(P-19942)
ST JUDE HOSPITAL YORBA LINDA
Also Called: Bristol Park Medical Group
11420 Warner Ave, Fountain Valley
(92708-2529)
PHONE....................................714 665-1797
Helena Rivas, *Manager*
EMP: 200
SALES (corp-wide): 17.6B **Privately Held**
SIC: 8011 8071 Offices & clinics of medical doctors; medical laboratories
HQ: St. Jude Hospital Yorba Linda
      200 W Ctr St Promenade
      Anaheim CA 92805
      714 712-3308

(P-19943)
STANFORD HEALTH CARE PRIMARY
Also Called: Stanford Health Services
211 Quarry Rd Fl 3, Palo Alto (94304-1416)
PHONE....................................650 723-6963
Nancy Morioka, *Principal*
EMP: 75
SALES (est): 3.1MM **Privately Held**
SIC: 8011 General & family practice, physician/surgeon

(P-19944)
STANLEY M KIRKPATRICK MD
Also Called: Childerns Spec of San Deigo
3020 Childrens Way, San Diego
(92123-4223)
PHONE....................................858 966-5855
Stanley M Kirkpatrick MD, *Partner*
Robert Newbury, *Director*
▲ EMP: 50
SALES (est): 2.1MM **Privately Held**
SIC: 8011 Pediatrician

(P-19945)
STANLEY R KLEIN MD FACS INC
23451 Madison St Ste 300, Torrance
(90505-4737)
PHONE....................................310 373-6864
Stanley Klein, *President*
EMP: 50
SALES (est): 3MM **Privately Held**
SIC: 8011 Surgeon

(P-19946)
STEPHEN B MEISEL MD PC
Also Called: Medfocus Radiology Network
2811 Wilshire Blvd # 900, Santa Monica
(90403-4805)
PHONE....................................310 828-8843

PRODUCTS & SVCS

Stephen B Meisel MD, *President*
Karen Byrd, *Opers Staff*
EMP: 50
SQ FT: 20,000
SALES (est): 3MM **Privately Held**
WEB: www.medfocuslogin.net
SIC: 8011 Radiologist

(P-19947)
STEPHEN B MEISEL MD A MED CORP (HQ)
Also Called: Med Focus/California Radiology
2811 Wilshire Blvd # 900, Santa Monica
(90403-4805)
PHONE.....................310 828-8843
Joseph P Delaney, *President*
EMP: 52
SQ FT: 14,000
SALES (est): 5.1MM **Privately Held**
WEB: www.medfocus.net
SIC: 8011 Radiologist

(P-19948)
STEVEN G FOGG MD
1360 E Herndon Ave # 401, Fresno
(93720-3326)
PHONE.....................559 449-5010
Steven G Fogg, *Principal*
EMP: 80
SALES (est): 1.2MM **Privately Held**
SIC: 8011 Ophthalmologist

(P-19949)
STEVEN P ABELOW MD
2311 Lake Tahoe Blvd, South Lake Tahoe
(96150-7129)
PHONE.....................530 544-8033
Steven Abelow MD, *Owner*
EMP: 100
SALES (est): 236.7K **Privately Held**
SIC: 8011 Orthopedic physician; general & family practice, physician/surgeon

(P-19950)
STOCKTON CARDIOLOGY MEDICAL GR
1148 Norman Dr Ste 3, Manteca
(95336-5961)
PHONE.....................209 824-1555
Gina Callegari, *Manager*
EMP: 60
SALES (corp-wide): 12.6MM **Privately Held**
SIC: 8011 Cardiologist & cardio-vascular specialist
PA: Stockton Cardiology Medical Group
Complete Heart Care, Inc
415 E Harding Way Ste D
Stockton CA 95204
209 994-5750

(P-19951)
STOCKTON CARDIOLOGY MEDICAL GR (PA)
415 E Harding Way Ste D, Stockton
(95204-6118)
PHONE.....................209 994-5750
Rajiv Punjya, *President*
Tuan A Pham, *Treasurer*
John A Bouteller, *Vice Pres*
EMP: 50
SQ FT: 6,500
SALES: 12.6MM **Privately Held**
SIC: 8011 Cardiologist & cardio-vascular specialist

(P-19952)
STOCKTON ORTHPD MED GROUP INC
Also Called: Crooks, Jerry C MD
2545 W Hammer Ln, Stockton
(95209-2839)
PHONE.....................209 948-1641
Kevin Mikaelian, *Principal*
Scott Bethune, *Treasurer*
Miklein Kevin MD, *Vice Pres*
EMP: 50
SALES (est): 4.3MM **Privately Held**
WEB: www.stocktonortho.com
SIC: 8011 Orthopedic physician; surgeon

(P-19953)
STUART LOVETT
350 30th St Ste 208, Oakland
(94609-3425)
PHONE.....................510 444-0790
Stuart Lovett, *Owner*
EMP: 51
SALES (est): 444.8K **Privately Held**
SIC: 8011 Obstetrician

(P-19954)
SUN HEALTHCARE GROUP INC (DH)
27442 Portola Pkwy # 200, Foothill Ranch
(92610-2822)
PHONE.....................949 255-7100
George V Hager Jr, *CEO*
Melissa Craig, *President*
Richard Edwards, *Vice Pres*
▲ **EMP:** 300
SALES (est): 730.7MM **Publicly Held**
WEB: www.sunh.com
SIC: 8011 8322 Medical insurance plan; referral service for personal & social problems
HQ: Genesis Healthcare Corporation
101 E State St
Kennett Square PA 19348
610 444-6350

(P-19955)
SURGERY CENTER OF ALTA BATES
Also Called: Herrick Hospital
2001 Dwight Way, Berkeley (94704-2608)
PHONE.....................510 204-4411
Albert Greene, *Branch Mgr*
Andrea Clark, *Manager*
EMP: 50
SQ FT: 6,750
SALES (corp-wide): 12.4B **Privately Held**
WEB: www.altabates.com
SIC: 8011 8051 Medical centers; skilled nursing care facilities
HQ: The Surgery Center Of Alta Bates
Summit Medical Center Llc
2450 Ashby Ave
Berkeley CA 94705
510 204-4444

(P-19956)
SURGERY CENTER OF ALTA BATES
Also Called: Alta Btes Cmprhnsive Cncer Ctr
2001 Dwight Way, Berkeley (94704-2608)
PHONE.....................510 204-1591
Peter H Jessup, *CEO*
Shlomo Leibowich, *Ch Radiology*
Oliver Delarosa, *Security Dir*
Sunil Krishnan, *QA Dir*
Josh Iufer, *Food Svc Dir*
EMP: 82
SALES (corp-wide): 12.4B **Privately Held**
SIC: 8011 Offices & clinics of medical doctors
HQ: The Surgery Center Of Alta Bates
Summit Medical Center Llc
2450 Ashby Ave
Berkeley CA 94705
510 204-4444

(P-19957)
SUTTER GOULD MED FOUNDATION (PA)
600 Coffee Rd, Modesto (95355-4201)
PHONE.....................209 948-5940
David Bradley, *CEO*
E Lewis Cobb, *Obstetrician*
EMP: 50
SALES (est): 15.6MM **Privately Held**
SIC: 8011 Obstetrician

(P-19958)
SUTTER HEALTH
2068 John Jones Rd # 100, Davis
(95616-9711)
PHONE.....................530 747-0389
EMP: 133
SALES (corp-wide): 12.4B **Privately Held**
SIC: 8011 Internal medicine, physician/surgeon
PA: Sutter Health
2200 River Plaza Dr
Sacramento CA 95833
916 733-8800

(P-19959)
SUTTER HEALTH
Also Called: Mamone James M
3 Medical Plaza Dr # 100, Roseville
(95661-3088)
PHONE.....................916 797-4725
Patricia Fone, *Med Doctor*
EMP: 186
SALES (corp-wide): 12.4B **Privately Held**
SIC: 8011 Offices & clinics of medical doctors
PA: Sutter Health
2200 River Plaza Dr
Sacramento CA 95833
916 733-8800

(P-19960)
SUTTER HEALTH
795 El Camino Real, Palo Alto
(94301-2302)
PHONE.....................650 853-2975
Rahul Verma, *Gastroenterlgy*
EMP: 239
SALES (corp-wide): 12.4B **Privately Held**
SIC: 8011 Offices & clinics of medical doctors
PA: Sutter Health
2200 River Plaza Dr
Sacramento CA 95833
916 733-8800

(P-19961)
SUTTER HEALTH
2734 El Camino Real, Santa Clara
(95051-3007)
PHONE.....................408 524-5952
Medina Irene,
EMP: 266
SALES (corp-wide): 12.4B **Privately Held**
SIC: 8011 General & family practice, physician/surgeon
PA: Sutter Health
2200 River Plaza Dr
Sacramento CA 95833
916 733-8800

(P-19962)
SUTTER HEALTH
100 Mission Blvd, Jackson (95642-2536)
PHONE.....................209 223-5445
Melody Eurbe, *Officer*
Pam Spellman, *Materials Mgr*
Nancy Leland, *Director*
EMP: 133
SALES (corp-wide): 12.4B **Privately Held**
SIC: 8011 Cardiologist & cardio-vascular specialist
PA: Sutter Health
2200 River Plaza Dr
Sacramento CA 95833
916 733-8800

(P-19963)
SUTTER HEALTH
8170 Laguna Blvd Ste 210, Elk Grove
(95758-7902)
PHONE.....................916 691-5900
Solomon Yeung, *President*
EMP: 159
SALES (corp-wide): 12.4B **Privately Held**
SIC: 8011 General & family practice, physician/surgeon
PA: Sutter Health
2200 River Plaza Dr
Sacramento CA 95833
916 733-8800

(P-19964)
SUTTER HEALTH
5196 Hill Rd E Ste 300, Lakeport
(95453-6374)
PHONE.....................707 263-6885
Harneet Bath, *Branch Mgr*
EMP: 200
SALES (corp-wide): 12.4B **Privately Held**
SIC: 8011 Offices & clinics of medical doctors
PA: Sutter Health
2200 River Plaza Dr
Sacramento CA 95833
916 733-8800

(P-19965)
SUTTER HEALTH
2725 Capitol Ave, Sacramento
(95816-6004)
PHONE.....................916 262-9400
EMP: 186
SALES (corp-wide): 12.4B **Privately Held**
SIC: 8011 Specialized medical practitioners, except internal
PA: Sutter Health
2200 River Plaza Dr
Sacramento CA 95833
916 733-8800

(P-19966)
SUTTER HEALTH
2725 Capitol Ave Dept 304, Sacramento
(95816-6006)
PHONE.....................916 262-9414
Damon Namvar, *Podiatrist*
EMP: 239
SALES (corp-wide): 12.4B **Privately Held**
SIC: 8011 Offices & clinics of medical doctors
PA: Sutter Health
2200 River Plaza Dr
Sacramento CA 95833
916 733-8800

(P-19967)
SUTTER HEALTH
1500 Expo Pkwy, Sacramento
(95815-4227)
PHONE.....................916 646-8300
EMP: 1000
SALES (corp-wide): 11B **Privately Held**
SIC: 8011 8071
PA: Sutter Health
2200 River Plaza Dr
Sacramento CA 95833
916 286-6670

(P-19968)
SUTTER HEALTH
3875 Telegraph Ave, Oakland
(94609-2428)
PHONE.....................510 547-2244
Aaron Adams, *Branch Mgr*
EMP: 320
SALES (corp-wide): 12.4B **Privately Held**
SIC: 8011 Medical centers
PA: Sutter Health
2200 River Plaza Dr
Sacramento CA 95833
916 733-8800

(P-19969)
SUTTER HEALTH
3000 Telegraph Ave, Oakland
(94609-3218)
PHONE.....................510 869-8777
Stefan Arnold, *Branch Mgr*
Rick Beach, *Manager*
EMP: 133
SALES (corp-wide): 12.4B **Privately Held**
SIC: 8011 Offices & clinics of medical doctors
PA: Sutter Health
2200 River Plaza Dr
Sacramento CA 95833
916 733-8800

(P-19970)
SUTTER HEALTH
475 Pioneer Ave Ste 400, Woodland
(95776-4905)
PHONE.....................530 406-5600
Manuel Diaz, *President*
EMP: 266
SALES (corp-wide): 12.4B **Privately Held**
SIC: 8011 Offices & clinics of medical doctors
PA: Sutter Health
2200 River Plaza Dr
Sacramento CA 95833
916 733-8800

(P-19971)
SUTTER HEALTH
475 Pioneer Ave Ste 100, Woodland
(95776-4905)
PHONE.....................530 406-5600
Judi Monday, *Director*
EMP: 200

▲ = Import ▼=Export
◆ =Import/Export

SALES (corp-wide): 12.4B **Privately Held**
SIC: **8011** Offices & clinics of medical doctors
PA: Sutter Health
2200 River Plaza Dr
Sacramento CA 95833
916 733-8800

(P-19972)
SUTTER HEALTH
3612 Dale Rd, Modesto (95356-0500)
PHONE...................................209 522-0146
EMP: 186
SALES (corp-wide): 12.4B **Privately Held**
SIC: **8011** Offices & clinics of medical doctors
PA: Sutter Health
2200 River Plaza Dr
Sacramento CA 95833
916 733-8800

(P-19973)
SUTTER HEALTH
50 S San Mateo Dr Ste 470, San Mateo (94401-3833)
PHONE...................................650 262-4262
Roger Larsen, *President*
Sherlyn Aronce, *Executive Asst*
Cynthia Rattler, *Admin Asst*
Laurie Rubin, *Admin Asst*
Kenneth Doran, *Database Admin*
EMP: 204
SALES (corp-wide): 12.4B **Privately Held**
SIC: **8011** Orthopedic physician
PA: Sutter Health
2200 River Plaza Dr
Sacramento CA 95833
916 733-8800

(P-19974)
SUTTER HEALTH
25 W Micheltorena St, Santa Barbara (93101-2509)
PHONE...................................805 966-1600
EMP: 213
SALES (corp-wide): 12.4B **Privately Held**
SIC: **8011** Offices & clinics of medical doctors
PA: Sutter Health
2200 River Plaza Dr
Sacramento CA 95833
916 733-8800

(P-19975)
SUTTER HEALTH
999 S Fairmont Ave # 200, Lodi (95240-5100)
PHONE...................................209 334-3333
Carol Nakashima, *Med Doctor*
EMP: 106
SALES (corp-wide): 12.4B **Privately Held**
SIC: **8011** Specialized medical practitioners, except internal
PA: Sutter Health
2200 River Plaza Dr
Sacramento CA 95833
916 733-8800

(P-19976)
SUTTER HEALTH
Also Called: Nguyen, Myhanh MD
325 N Mathilda Ave, Sunnyvale (94085-4207)
PHONE...................................408 733-4380
Connie Conover, *Branch Mgr*
Connie Caraang, *Buyer*
Myhanh Nguyen, *Med Doctor*
April Espaniola, *Supervisor*
EMP: 146
SALES (corp-wide): 12.4B **Privately Held**
SIC: **8011** Occupational & industrial specialist, physician/surgeon
PA: Sutter Health
2200 River Plaza Dr
Sacramento CA 95833
916 733-8800

(P-19977)
SUTTER HEALTH
Also Called: Sutter Pacific Med Foundation
5196 Hill Rd E Ste 300, Lakeport (95453-6374)
PHONE...................................707 263-6885
EMP: 121
SALES (corp-wide): 11B **Privately Held**
SIC: **8011**

PA: Sutter Health
2200 River Plaza Dr
Sacramento CA 95833
916 733-8800

(P-19978)
SUTTER HEALTH
Also Called: Palo Alpo Medical Foudation
795 El Camino Real, Palo Alto (94301-2302)
PHONE...................................650 853-2904
Nan A Link, *Branch Mgr*
EMP: 117
SALES (corp-wide): 12.4B **Privately Held**
SIC: **8011** Offices & clinics of medical doctors
PA: Sutter Health
2200 River Plaza Dr
Sacramento CA 95833
916 733-8800

(P-19979)
SUTTER HEALTH
Also Called: Breast Imaging Center
3161 L St, Sacramento (95816-5234)
PHONE...................................916 451-3344
Jerry Fosselman, *Branch Mgr*
EMP: 100
SALES (corp-wide): 12.4B **Privately Held**
WEB: www.radiological.com
SIC: **8011 8071** Offices & clinics of medical doctors; medical laboratories
PA: Sutter Health
2200 River Plaza Dr
Sacramento CA 95833
916 733-8800

(P-19980)
SUTTER HEALTH
1020 29th St Ste 570b, Sacramento (95816-5173)
PHONE...................................916 453-5955
EMP: 133
SALES (corp-wide): 12.4B **Privately Held**
SIC: **8011** Offices & clinics of medical doctors
PA: Sutter Health
2200 River Plaza Dr
Sacramento CA 95833
916 733-8800

(P-19981)
SUTTER HEALTH
3555 Cesar Chavez, San Francisco (94110-4403)
PHONE...................................415 647-8600
Carol Kunita, *Principal*
Michelle Mayfield, *Human Resources*
Trish Barrett, *Director*
EMP: 109
SALES (corp-wide): 12.4B **Privately Held**
WEB: www.sutterhealth.org
SIC: **8011** Offices & clinics of medical doctors
PA: Sutter Health
2200 River Plaza Dr
Sacramento CA 95833
916 733-8800

(P-19982)
SUTTER HEALTH
969 Plumas St Ste 103116, Yuba City (95991-4011)
PHONE...................................530 749-3585
Aparna Kareti, *Branch Mgr*
EMP: 200
SALES (corp-wide): 12.4B **Privately Held**
WEB: www.sutterhealth.org
SIC: **8011** Medical centers
PA: Sutter Health
2200 River Plaza Dr
Sacramento CA 95833
916 733-8800

(P-19983)
SUTTER HEALTH
Also Called: Sutter Occupational Hlth Svcs
3 Medical Plaza Dr # 100, Roseville (95661-3088)
PHONE...................................916 797-4700
Dave Gladden, *Branch Mgr*
EMP: 60
SALES (corp-wide): 12.4B **Privately Held**
SIC: **8011** Offices & clinics of medical doctors

PA: Sutter Health
2200 River Plaza Dr
Sacramento CA 95833
916 733-8800

(P-19984)
SUTTER HEALTH
2725 Capitol Ave Dept 404, Sacramento (95816-6032)
PHONE...................................916 262-9456
EMP: 152
SALES (corp-wide): 12.4B **Privately Held**
SIC: **8011** Medical centers
PA: Sutter Health
2200 River Plaza Dr
Sacramento CA 95833
916 733-8800

(P-19985)
SUTTER HEALTH AT WORK
Also Called: Sutter Hlth At Work - Natomas
1014 N Market Blvd Ste 20, Sacramento (95834-1986)
PHONE...................................916 565-8607
Judi Monday, *President*
Sally Greene, *Director*
EMP: 75
SALES (est): 2.4MM **Privately Held**
SIC: **8011** General & family practice, physician/surgeon

(P-19986)
SUTTER HLTH SCRMNTO SIERRA REG
Also Called: Sutter West Foundation
2030 Sutter Pl Ste 2000, Davis (95616-6216)
PHONE...................................530 747-5010
Jo Lisa Miller, *Radiology*
EMP: 641
SALES (corp-wide): 12.4B **Privately Held**
SIC: **8011** General & family practice, physician/surgeon
HQ: Sutter Health Sacramento Sierra Region
2200 River Plaza Dr
Sacramento CA 95833
916 733-8800

(P-19987)
SUTTER HLTH SCRMNTO SIERRA REG
Also Called: Sutter Amador Hospital Lab
100 Mission Blvd, Jackson (95642-2536)
PHONE...................................209 223-7540
Margie Souza, *Branch Mgr*
EMP: 1268
SALES (corp-wide): 12.4B **Privately Held**
SIC: **8011** Radiologist
HQ: Sutter Health Sacramento Sierra Region
2200 River Plaza Dr
Sacramento CA 95833
916 733-8800

(P-19988)
SUTTER HLTH SCRMNTO SIERRA REG
Also Called: Sutter Medical Center
475 Pioneer Ave Ste 100, Woodland (95776-4905)
PHONE...................................530 406-5616
Leefeldt Randall, *Branch Mgr*
EMP: 641
SALES (corp-wide): 12.4B **Privately Held**
SIC: **8011** Physicians' office, including specialists
HQ: Sutter Health Sacramento Sierra Region
2200 River Plaza Dr
Sacramento CA 95833
916 733-8800

(P-19989)
SUTTER MED GROUP OF REDWOODS
3883 Airway Dr Ste 202, Santa Rosa (95403-1671)
PHONE...................................707 546-2788
John Dervin MD, *President*
Steven Levenberg, *President*
Sean Gaskie MD, *Treasurer*
Romayne Farrell Fnp, *Admin Sec*
EMP: 62

SALES (est): 5.6MM
SALES (corp-wide): 12.4B **Privately Held**
WEB: www.suttersantarosa.com
SIC: **8011** General & family practice, physician/surgeon
HQ: Sutter Santa Rosa Regional Hospital
30 Mark West Springs Rd
Santa Rosa CA 95403
707 576-4000

(P-19990)
SUTTER N MED GROUP A PROF CORP (PA)
969 Plumas St Ste 205, Yuba City (95991-4011)
PHONE...................................530 749-3661
Robert H Wright Jr, *President*
EMP: 84
SQ FT: 30,096
SALES (est): 3.3MM **Privately Held**
SIC: **8011** Offices & clinics of medical doctors

(P-19991)
SUTTER NORTH MED FOUNDATION (PA)
Also Called: Multi Specialty Group Practice
969 Plumas St, Yuba City (95991-4011)
PHONE...................................530 741-1300
Bruce Tigner, *CEO*
Tom Walther, *COO*
Kelly Danna, *CFO*
Nindya Burhan, *Med Doctor*
Nindya D Burhan, *Director*
EMP: 160
SALES (est): 27.2MM **Privately Held**
WEB: www.snmf.com
SIC: **8011** General & family practice, physician/surgeon; clinic, operated by physicians

(P-19992)
SUTTER NORTH MED FOUNDATION
480 Plumas Blvd, Yuba City (95991-5005)
PHONE...................................530 749-3635
William G Hoffman MD, *Principal*
EMP: 100
SALES (corp-wide): 27.2MM **Privately Held**
WEB: www.snmf.com
SIC: **8011** Offices & clinics of medical doctors
PA: North Sutter Medical Foundation
969 Plumas St
Yuba City CA 95991
530 741-1300

(P-19993)
SUTTER NORTH MED FOUNDATION
Also Called: Home Health Brownsville
16911 Willow Glen Rd, Brownsville (95919)
PHONE...................................530 675-1245
Cindy White, *Branch Mgr*
EMP: 55
SALES (corp-wide): 27.2MM **Privately Held**
WEB: www.snmf.com
SIC: **8011** Offices & clinics of medical doctors
PA: North Sutter Medical Foundation
969 Plumas St
Yuba City CA 95991
530 741-1300

(P-19994)
SUTTER NORTH MED FOUNDATION
Also Called: Suttter North Home Health
400 Plumas Blvd Ste 115, Yuba City (95991-5081)
PHONE...................................530 749-3450
Shelley Sanbury, *Branch Mgr*
Diana Barber, *Accountant*
EMP: 55
SALES (corp-wide): 27.2MM **Privately Held**
WEB: www.snmf.com
SIC: **8011** Offices & clinics of medical doctors
PA: North Sutter Medical Foundation
969 Plumas St
Yuba City CA 95991
530 741-1300

(P-19995)
SUTTER REGIONAL MED FOUNDATION
770 Mason St, Vacaville (95688-4646)
PHONE.................707 454-5800
EMP: 80
SALES (corp-wide): 31.7MM Privately Held
WEB: www.sutterdavis.org
SIC: 8011 Offices & clinics of medical doctors
PA: Sutter Regional Medical Foundation Inc
2702 Low Ct
Fairfield CA 94534
707 427-4900

(P-19996)
SWAMINATHA MAHADEVAN MD
701 Welch Rd Bldg C, Palo Alto (94304)
PHONE.................650 723-6576
Swaminatha Mahadevan, Chairman
EMP: 90
SALES (est): 224.2K Privately Held
SIC: 8011 Freestanding emergency medical center

(P-19997)
SYNERMED
Also Called: Ehs Medical Group
1200 Corp Ctr Dr Ste 200, Monterey Park (91754)
PHONE.................216 406-2845
Cindy Ehnes, CEO
James Mason, President
Cindy Ehne, CEO
Wallis Wong, Software Engr
Paul D Weber, Business Anlyst
EMP: 180
SALES (est): 11MM Privately Held
SIC: 8011 Offices & clinics of medical doctors

(P-19998)
TAMMI R JAMES MD
7273 14th Ave Ste 120b, Sacramento (95820-3500)
PHONE.................916 383-6783
Tammi James, Principal
EMP: 50
SALES (est): 543.9K Privately Held
SIC: 8011 8093 Pediatrician; mental health clinic, outpatient

(P-19999)
TENET HEALTHSYSTEM MEDICAL
414 Cliffside Dr, Danville (94526-4810)
PHONE.................925 275-8303
Phillip Gustafson, Director
EMP: 500
SALES (corp-wide): 19.3B Publicly Held
WEB: www.tenenthealth.com
SIC: 8011 Offices & clinics of medical doctors
HQ: Tenet Healthsystem Medical, Inc.
1445 Ross Ave Ste 1400
Dallas TX 75202
469 893-2000

(P-20000)
TENET HEALTHSYSTEM MEDICAL
Also Called: Lakewood Regional Medical Ctr
3700 South St, Lakewood (90712-1419)
PHONE.................562 531-2550
Carol Mammolite, Branch Mgr
Covina Evans, Controller
Sheri Kollerbohm, Director
William Madrid, Director
Roseann Millward, Director
EMP: 700
SALES (corp-wide): 19.3B Publicly Held
WEB: www.tenenthealth.com
SIC: 8011 8062 Medical centers; general medical & surgical hospitals
HQ: Tenet Healthsystem Medical, Inc.
1445 Ross Ave Ste 1400
Dallas TX 75202
469 893-2000

(P-20001)
TENET HEALTHSYSTEM MEDICAL
Los Alamitos Med Ctr
3751 Katella Ave, Los Alamitos (90720-3113)
PHONE.................805 546-7698
Michelle Finney, Principal
EMP: 625
SALES (corp-wide): 19.3B Publicly Held
WEB: www.tenenthealth.com
SIC: 8011 8062 Offices & clinics of medical doctors; general medical & surgical hospitals
HQ: Tenet Healthsystem Medical, Inc.
1445 Ross Ave Ste 1400
Dallas TX 75202
469 893-2000

(P-20002)
TENET HEALTHSYSTEM MEDICAL
Also Called: Leisure World Pharmacy
1661 Golden Rain Rd, Seal Beach (90740-4907)
P.O. Box 2685 (90740-1685)
PHONE.................562 493-9581
Diana Doyle, Manager
EMP: 60
SALES (corp-wide): 19.3B Publicly Held
WEB: www.tenenthealth.com
SIC: 8011 5912 Offices & clinics of medical doctors; drug stores
HQ: Tenet Healthsystem Medical, Inc.
1445 Ross Ave Ste 1400
Dallas TX 75202
469 893-2000

(P-20003)
TENET HEALTHSYSTEM MEDICAL
1000 S Fremont Ave Unit 1, Alhambra (91803-8801)
PHONE.................626 300-5500
Joy Davis, Director
EMP: 200
SALES (corp-wide): 19.3B Publicly Held
WEB: www.tenenthealth.com
SIC: 8011 Offices & clinics of medical doctors
HQ: Tenet Healthsystem Medical, Inc.
1445 Ross Ave Ste 1400
Dallas TX 75202
469 893-2000

(P-20004)
TENNANT HEALTH SYSTEMS
1000 S Fremont Ave Unit 2, Alhambra (91803-8834)
PHONE.................626 300-3500
Dawn Castro, Director
EMP: 120 EST: 1996
SALES (est): 8.1MM Privately Held
SIC: 8011 8721 Offices & clinics of medical doctors; accounting, auditing & bookkeeping

(P-20005)
THE ORTHOPEDIC INSTITUTE OF
616 Witmer St, Los Angeles (90017-2308)
PHONE.................213 977-2010
Andrew B Leeka, CEO
EMP: 674
SALES: 120.9K
SALES (corp-wide): 319.2MM Privately Held
SIC: 8011 Orthopedic physician
PA: Good Samaritan Hospital
1225 Wilshire Blvd
Los Angeles CA 90017
213 977-2121

(P-20006)
TIBURCIO VASQUEZ HLTH CTR INC (PA)
33255 9th St, Union City (94587-2137)
PHONE.................510 471-5880
David B Vliet, CEO
Luis Arenas, Partner
Yolanda Triana, President
Malou Martinez, CFO
Jesse Robles, Treasurer
EMP: 50
SQ FT: 15,000

SALES: 23.7MM Privately Held
SIC: 8011 Primary care medical clinic

(P-20007)
TIBURCIO VASQUEZ HLTH CTR INC
22331 Mission Blvd, Hayward (94541-3911)
PHONE.................510 471-5907
Malou Martinez, Branch Mgr
EMP: 86
SALES (corp-wide): 23.7MM Privately Held
SIC: 8011 Primary care medical clinic
PA: Tiburcio Vasquez Health Center Incorporated
33255 9th St
Union City CA 94587
510 471-5880

(P-20008)
TORRANCE SURGERY CENTER LP
Also Called: Amsurg
23560 Crenshaw Blvd # 104, Torrance (90505-5233)
PHONE.................310 986-2005
Nick Silvino MD, Partner
Ripu Arora MD, Partner
Marc Colman MD, Partner
Steve Dinsmore MD, Partner
Nelman Low MD, Partner
EMP: 2176 EST: 2001
SQ FT: 6,300
SALES (est): 42.9MM
SALES (corp-wide): 643.1MM Privately Held
WEB: www.natsurgcare.com
SIC: 8011 Surgeon
HQ: Envision Healthcare Corporation
1a Burton Hills Blvd
Nashville TN 37215
615 665-1283

(P-20009)
TOWER HEMATOLOGY ONCOLOGY MEDI
9090 Wilshire Blvd # 200, Beverly Hills (90211-1848)
P.O. Box 5624 (90209-5605)
PHONE.................310 888-8680
Robert W Decker MD, Partner
Leland M Green MD, Partner
Cheryl Elzinga, Vice Pres
Kevin Scher, Managing Dir
Heydi Ellis, Admin Asst
EMP: 75
SQ FT: 13,000
SALES (est): 10MM Privately Held
WEB: www.toweroncology.com
SIC: 8011 Hematologist; oncologist

(P-20010)
TRACY TRUJILLO MD
200 Porter Dr Ste 300, San Ramon (94583-1524)
PHONE.................925 838-6511
Tracy Trujillo, Principal
EMP: 50
SALES (est): 670.9K Privately Held
SIC: 8011 Pediatrician

(P-20011)
TRI CITY ORTHOPEDIC SGY & MDCL
Also Called: Neville Alleyne MD
3905 Waring Rd, Oceanside (92056-4405)
PHONE.................760 724-9000
James Esch, President
Dr Neville Alleyne, Bd of Directors
Dr James Helgager, Bd of Directors
Dr Norman Kane, Bd of Directors
Dr Richard Muir, Bd of Directors
▲ EMP: 50
SQ FT: 10,000
SALES (est): 7.3MM Privately Held
WEB: www.tricityortho.com
SIC: 8011 Orthopedic physician; surgeon

(P-20012)
TRI-CITY HEALTH CENTER (PA)
39500 Liberty St, Fremont (94538-2211)
PHONE.................510 770-8040
Kathleen Lievre, CEO
Amy Hsieh, Planning

Shenita Hurskin, Director
Michael Ellson, Manager
EMP: 148 EST: 1972
SALES: 30.3MM Privately Held
WEB: www.tri-cityhealth.org
SIC: 8011 Offices & clinics of medical doctors

(P-20013)
TUOLUMNE ME-WUK INDIAN
Also Called: Tuolumne Mewuk Indian Health
18880 Cherry Valley Blvd, Tuolumne (95379-9506)
PHONE.................209 928-5400
Christopher Gorsky, Principal
Darla Merlin, Ch of Bd
Tammy Barker, Finance Dir
EMP: 90
SQ FT: 11,000
SALES: 7.8MM Privately Held
SIC: 8011 General & family practice, physician/surgeon

(P-20014)
TWIN CITIES COMMUNITY HOSP INC
1100 Las Tablas Rd, Templeton (93465-9704)
PHONE.................805 434-3500
Mark P Lisa, CEO
Mareeni Stanislaus,
Paul Posmosga, CFO
Daphne Martin, Lab Dir
Mary Shalhoub, Food Svc Dir
EMP: 450
SQ FT: 120,000
SALES: 17.7K
SALES (corp-wide): 19.3B Publicly Held
WEB: www.tenenthealth.com
SIC: 8011 8062 Medical centers; general medical & surgical hospitals
PA: Tenet Healthcare Corporation
1445 Ross Ave Ste 1400
Dallas TX 75202
469 893-2200

(P-20015)
UC DAVIS HEALTH SYSTEM (PA)
4610 X St, Sacramento (95817-2200)
PHONE.................916 734-1000
Katherine Wesnousky, Principal
Claire Pomeroy, Principal
Daniel Slauson, Persnl Mgr
Malathy Kapali, Pathologist
Mohammad Rasool, Manager
EMP: 99
SALES (est): 7.9MM Privately Held
SIC: 8011 Internal medicine practitioners

(P-20016)
UC REGENTS
Also Called: Ucla Nrpsychtric Bhvioral Hlth
300 Medical Plaza, Los Angeles (90095-0001)
PHONE.................310 301-8777
Jody Gaspar, Principal
Lavonte Hickman, Principal
EMP: 99
SALES (est): 4.2MM Privately Held
SIC: 8011 8049 Medical centers; clinical psychologist; speech pathologist; psychiatric social worker; psychotherapist, except M.D.

(P-20017)
UCLA HEALTH SYSTEM
Also Called: Ronald Reagan Building
757 Westwood Plz, Los Angeles (90095-8358)
PHONE.................310 825-9111
Dr David T Feinberg, CEO
EMP: 90
SALES (est): 20.1MM Privately Held
SIC: 8011 Medical centers

(P-20018)
UNITED FAMILY CARE INC (PA)
8110 Mango Ave Ste 104, Fontana (92335-3603)
PHONE.................909 874-1679
Keith Schauermann, President
EMP: 120
SALES (est): 5.7MM Privately Held
WEB: www.unitedfamilycare.com
SIC: 8011 Primary care medical clinic

(P-20019)
UNITED INDIAN HEALTH SVCS INC (PA)
Also Called: Potawot Health Clinic
1600 Weeot Way, Arcata (95521-4734)
PHONE..................................707 825-5000
David Rosen, *CFO*
Julia T Barron, *Physician Asst*
David Tuttle, *Manager*
EMP: 150
SQ FT: 46,304
SALES: 26.7MM **Privately Held**
WEB: www.uihs.org
SIC: **8011** 8021 8031 5912 Clinic, operated by physicians; primary care medical clinic; dental clinics & clinics; offices & clinics of osteopathic physicians; drug stores; mental health clinic, outpatient; community center

(P-20020)
UNITED MEDICAL IMAGING INC
Also Called: Umi of Huntington Beach
16161 Gothard St Ste C, Huntington Beach (92647-3603)
PHONE..................................714 843-6255
EMP: 118 **Privately Held**
SIC: **8011** Offices & clinics of medical doctors
PA: United Medical Imaging, Inc.
   1762 Westwood Blvd # 230
   Los Angeles CA 90024

(P-20021)
UNITED STATES DEPT OF NAVY
8808 Balboa Ave, San Diego (92123-1592)
PHONE..................................619 532-6397
Mike Clark, *Branch Mgr*
EMP: 924 **Publicly Held**
SIC: **8011** Medical centers
HQ: United States Department Of The Navy
   1200 Navy Pentagon
   Washington DC 20350

(P-20022)
UNITED STATES DEPT OF NAVY
34800 Bob Wilson Dr # 409, San Diego (92134-1409)
PHONE..................................619 532-8953
Elizabeth Ferrara, *Principal*
EMP: 924 **Publicly Held**
SIC: **8011** Anesthesiologist
HQ: United States Department Of The Navy
   1200 Navy Pentagon
   Washington DC 20350

(P-20023)
UNITED STATES DEPT OF NAVY
Also Called: Naval Dental Center
2310 Craven St, San Diego (92136-5596)
PHONE..................................619 556-8210
Pete Seder, *Branch Mgr*
Felicia Lamb, *Buyer*
EMP: 300 **Publicly Held**
SIC: **8011** 9711 Health maintenance organization; Navy;
HQ: United States Department Of The Navy
   1200 Navy Pentagon
   Washington DC 20350

(P-20024)
UNITED STATES DEPT OF NAVY
Also Called: US Naval Medical Clinical Lab
162 1st St, Port Hueneme (93043-4316)
PHONE..................................805 982-6392
Sharon West, *Principal*
EMP: 924 **Publicly Held**
SIC: **8011** 9711 Primary care medical clinic; Navy;
HQ: United States Department Of The Navy
   1200 Navy Pentagon
   Washington DC 20350

(P-20025)
UNITED STATES DEPT OF NAVY
Naval Med Ctr Crdiology Clinic
34730 Bob Wilson Dr, San Diego (92134-3098)
PHONE..................................619 532-7400
Ed Doorn, *Manager*
EMP: 924 **Publicly Held**

SIC: **8011** 9711 Cardiologist & cardio-vascular specialist; Navy;
HQ: United States Department Of The Navy
   1200 Navy Pentagon
   Washington DC 20350

(P-20026)
UNITED STATES DEPT OF NAVY
Also Called: Naval Medical Clinic
162 1st St Bldg 1402, Port Hueneme (93043-4316)
PHONE..................................805 982-6370
J F Murray, *Branch Mgr*
EMP: 924 **Publicly Held**
SIC: **8011** 9711 Primary care medical clinic; Navy;
HQ: United States Department Of The Navy
   1200 Navy Pentagon
   Washington DC 20350

(P-20027)
UNITED STATES DEPT OF NAVY
Also Called: Navmedwest
4170 Norman Scott Rd, San Diego (92136-5501)
PHONE..................................619 767-6592
Cdr M Campbell, *Branch Mgr*
Patty Miller, *Director*
EMP: 924 **Publicly Held**
SIC: **8011** Offices & clinics of medical doctors
HQ: United States Department Of The Navy
   1200 Navy Pentagon
   Washington DC 20350

(P-20028)
UNIVERSITY CAL LOS ANGELES
Also Called: Ucla Primary Care Westlake
1250 Avanta Dr Ste 207, Westlake Village (91361)
PHONE..................................805 494-6920
Dina Sarabia, *Branch Mgr*
EMP: 50 **Privately Held**
SIC: **8011** 8221 9411 Primary care medical clinic; university; administration of educational programs;
HQ: University Of California, Los Angeles
   405 Hilgard Ave
   Los Angeles CA 90095

(P-20029)
UNIVERSITY CAL SAN FRANCISCO
Also Called: Ucsf Medical Center
3330 Geary Blvd, San Francisco (94118-3347)
PHONE..................................415 353-3155
Monica Seay, *Branch Mgr*
EMP: 60 **Privately Held**
SIC: **8011** 8221 9411 Medical centers; university; administration of educational programs;
HQ: University Cal San Francisco
   500 Parnassus Ave
   San Francisco CA 94143

(P-20030)
UNIVERSITY CALIFORNIA DAVIS
2315 Stockton Blvd # 6309, Sacramento (95817-2201)
PHONE..................................916 734-2846
Valerie Adame, *Branch Mgr*
Garrett Wong, *Cardiovascular*
EMP: 50 **Privately Held**
SIC: **8011** 8221 9411 Surgeon; university; administration of educational programs;
HQ: University Of California, Davis
   1 Shields Ave
   Davis CA 95616

(P-20031)
UNIVERSITY CALIFORNIA DAVIS
Also Called: Cowell Student Health Center
Student House Ctr, Davis (95616)
PHONE..................................530 752-2300
Dr Michelle Famula, *Director*
EMP: 150 **Privately Held**

WEB: www.ucdavis.edu
SIC: **8011** 8221 9411 Medical centers; university; administration of educational programs;
HQ: University Of California, Davis
   1 Shields Ave
   Davis CA 95616

(P-20032)
UNIVERSITY CALIFORNIA IRVINE
Also Called: Uc Irvine Hlth Rgonal Burn Ctr
101 The City Dr S Bldg 1a, Orange (92868-3201)
PHONE..................................714 456-6170
Howard Federoff, *Vice Chancellor*
Ralph Cygan, *Exec Dir*
Aaron Nisley, *Practice Mgr*
Michael Tran, *Prgrmr*
Wendy Goldberg, *Professor*
EMP: 1757 **Privately Held**
WEB: www.com.uci.edu
SIC: **8011** 8221 9411 Medical centers; university; administration of educational programs;
HQ: University Of California, Irvine
   510 Aldrich Hall
   Irvine CA 92697
   949 824-8343

(P-20033)
UNIVERSITY CALIFORNIA IRVINE
Also Called: UCI Family Health Center
800 N Main St, Santa Ana (92701-3576)
PHONE..................................714 480-2443
Nancy D Hurtado, *Manager*
Ivan Coziahr, *Director*
EMP: 65
SQ FT: 49,361 **Privately Held**
WEB: www.com.uci.edu
SIC: **8011** 8221 9411 Medical centers; university; administration of educational programs;
HQ: University Of California, Irvine
   510 Aldrich Hall
   Irvine CA 92697
   949 824-8343

(P-20034)
UNIVERSITY CALIFORNIA IRVINE
1640 Newport Blvd Ste 340, Costa Mesa (92627-7730)
PHONE..................................949 646-2267
Olivia Reil, *Branch Mgr*
EMP: 50 **Privately Held**
SIC: **8011** 8221 9411 Gynecologist; university; administration of educational programs;
HQ: University Of California, Irvine
   510 Aldrich Hall
   Irvine CA 92697
   949 824-8343

(P-20035)
UNIVERSITY CALIFORNIA BERKELEY
Also Called: University Health Services
2222 Bancroft Way, Berkeley (94720-4301)
PHONE..................................510 642-2000
Diane Liu MD, *Principal*
Karen Patchell, *Officer*
Albert Yuen, *Vice Pres*
David Zusman, *Professor*
Adam Lucas, *Instructor*
EMP: 370 **Privately Held**
WEB: www.law.berkeley.edu
SIC: **8011** 8221 9411 Dispensary, operated by physicians; university; administration of educational programs;
HQ: The University California Berkeley
   200 Clfrnia Hall Spc 1500
   Berkeley CA 94720
   510 642-6000

(P-20036)
UNIVERSITY SOUTHERN CALIFORNIA
Also Called: Usc Student Health Center
849 W 34th St Ste 208, Los Angeles (90089-0079)
PHONE..................................213 743-5339
Dr Steven Gardner, *Principal*

Gilda Bares, *Executive*
EMP: 60
SALES (corp-wide): 2.6B **Privately Held**
WEB: www.usc.edu
SIC: **8011** 8221 Medical centers; university
PA: University Of Southern California
   3720 S Flower St Fl 3
   Los Angeles CA 90089
   213 740-7762

(P-20037)
UROLOGY ASSOC OF CEN CAL
7014 N Whitney Ave Ste A, Fresno (93720-0155)
PHONE..................................559 321-2800
Gilbert Dale MD, *President*
Artin Jibilian MD, *Treasurer*
Irwin S Barg MD, *Vice Pres*
William Schiff MD, *Admin Sec*
Joe Vidal, *Info Tech Dir*
EMP: 90
SQ FT: 28,074
SALES (est): 6.7MM **Privately Held**
WEB: www.fresnosecurity.us
SIC: **8011** Urologist

(P-20038)
US DEPT OF THE AIR FORCE
Also Called: Sgokc
15301 Warren Shingle Rd, Beale Afb (95903-1907)
PHONE..................................530 634-4738
Melvin Antonio, *Branch Mgr*
EMP: 90 **Publicly Held**
WEB: www.af.mil
SIC: **8011** 9711 Pediatrician; Air Force;
HQ: United States Department Of The Air Force
   1000 Air Force Pentagon
   Washington DC 20330

(P-20039)
USC EMERGENCY MEDICINE ASSOC
1200 N State St Ste 1011, Los Angeles (90033-1029)
PHONE..................................323 226-6667
Fax: 323 226-6806
EMP: 80
SALES (est): 3.9MM **Privately Held**
SIC: **8011**

(P-20040)
USC INSTITUTE FOR NEUROIMAGING
Also Called: Usc MARk& Mary Steven Neuro
2001 N Soto St Ste 102, Los Angeles (90032-3675)
PHONE..................................323 442-7246
Arthur Toga, *Director*
EMP: 125
SALES (est): 222.8K **Privately Held**
SIC: **8011** Offices & clinics of medical doctors

(P-20041)
USC SURGEONS INCORPORATED
Also Called: Usc Srgcal Edcatn RES Fndation
1510 San Pablo St Ste 514, Los Angeles (90033-5324)
PHONE..................................323 442-5910
Tom Demeester MD, *President*
Eric Alcorn, *Exec VP*
Albert Yellin MD, *Admin Sec*
Dilip Parekh, *Professor*
EMP: 250
SQ FT: 15,000
SALES (est): 11.1MM **Privately Held**
SIC: **8011** Specialized medical practitioners, except internal

(P-20042)
VALLEY CHILDRENS HEALTHCARE
9300 Valley Childrens Pl, Madera (93636-8761)
PHONE..................................559 353-3000
Todd Suntrapak, *CEO*
Danielle Barry, *Vice Pres*
William Chaltraw, *Vice Pres*
Karen Dahl, *Vice Pres*
David Hodge, *Vice Pres*

PRODUCTS & SVCS

EMP: 2800
SALES: 604.3MM **Privately Held**
SIC: 8011 8069 Physical medicine, physician/surgeon; physicians' office, including specialists; children's hospital

(P-20043)
VALLEY COMMUNITY HEALTHCARE
6801 Coldwater Canyon Ave 1b, North Hollywood (91605-5164)
PHONE...........................818 763-8836
Paula Wilson, *CEO*
Lee Huey, *CFO*
Allaine Herrera, *Controller*
Alfonso Rios, *Director*
EMP: 300
SQ FT: 15,000
SALES: 21.3MM **Privately Held**
WEB: www.valleycommunityclinic.org
SIC: 8011 Clinic, operated by physicians

(P-20044)
VALLEY MEDICAL GROUP OF LOMPOC
Also Called: Bailey, Rollin C MD
136 N 3rd St, Lompoc (93436-7099)
PHONE...........................805 736-1253
William H Gausman Jr, *President*
B J Coughlin MD, *Corp Secy*
Eldon Elam MD, *Vice Pres*
Rollin C Bailey, *Managing Dir*
Thomas E Fritch, *Managing Dir*
EMP: 60 **EST:** 1965
SQ FT: 10,700
SALES (est): 8.3MM **Privately Held**
WEB: www.vmglompoc.com
SIC: 8011 Internal medicine, physician/surgeon; general & family practice, physician/surgeon

(P-20045)
VALLEY OB GYN MEDICAL GROUP
400 N Pepper Ave Fl 6, Colton (92324-1801)
PHONE...........................909 580-6333
Guillermo Valenzuela, *President*
EMP: 50
SALES (est): 4.3MM **Privately Held**
SIC: 8011 Gynecologist

(P-20046)
VALLEYCARE HOSPITAL CORP (DH)
Also Called: Valleycare Health
1111 E Stanley Blvd, Livermore (94550-4115)
PHONE...........................925 447-7000
Marcelina L Feit, *President*
Tracy McClain, *CFO*
Felicia Ziomek, *Officer*
Doreen Maples, *Vice Pres*
Laura Stewart, *Nursing Mgr*
EMP: 68
SALES (est): 62.2MM
SALES (corp-wide): 5.6B **Privately Held**
SIC: 8011 Primary care medical clinic
HQ: The Hospital Committee For The Livermore-Pleasanton Areas
5555 W Las Positas Blvd
Pleasanton CA 94588
925 847-3000

(P-20047)
VAN GROW JACK S MD
1140 W La Veta Ave # 640, Orange (92868-4225)
PHONE...........................714 564-3300
Jack Van Grow, *Partner*
Jack Vangrow, *Partner*
EMP: 50
SALES (est): 723.5K **Privately Held**
WEB: www.ocheart.org
SIC: 8011 Cardiologist & cardio-vascular specialist

(P-20048)
VANTAGE ONCOLOGY LLC (HQ)
1500 Rosecrans Ave # 400, Manhattan Beach (90266-3754)
P.O. Box 10033 (90267-7533)
PHONE...........................310 335-4000
Michael Fiore, *CEO*
Dee Delapp, *President*

Marshal Salomon, *COO*
Brian Rizkallah, *CFO*
Leslie E Botnick, *Chief Mktg Ofcr*
EMP: 300
SQ FT: 150,000
SALES (est): 59.3MM
SALES (corp-wide): 208.3B **Publicly Held**
SIC: 8011 Oncologist
PA: Mckesson Corporation
1 Post St Fl 18
San Francisco CA 94104
415 983-8300

(P-20049)
VENICE FAMILY CLINIC (PA)
604 Rose Ave, Venice (90291-2767)
PHONE...........................310 664-7703
Elizabeth Forer, *CEO*
Gordon Lee, *Treasurer*
Stewart Seradsky, *Treasurer*
Jeffrey E Sinaiko, *Treasurer*
Paula Davis, *Bd of Directors*
EMP: 64
SALES: 41.8MM **Privately Held**
SIC: 8011 Primary care medical clinic

(P-20050)
VENICE FAMILY CLINIC
2509 Pico Blvd, Santa Monica (90405-1828)
PHONE...........................310 392-8636
Elizabeth B Forer, *Principal*
EMP: 176
SALES (corp-wide): 41.8MM **Privately Held**
SIC: 8011 Clinic, operated by physicians
PA: Venice Family Clinic
604 Rose Ave
Venice CA 90291
310 664-7703

(P-20051)
VENTURA COUNTY HEMATOLOGY (PA)
1700 N Rose Ave Ste 320, Oxnard (93030-7648)
PHONE...........................805 485-8709
Kooros Parsa MD, *Partner*
Kevin Cheng, *Partner*
Ann S Kelley MD, *Partner*
Lynn Kong, *Partner*
Rosemary McIntyre, *Partner*
EMP: 50
SALES (est): 3.9MM **Privately Held**
WEB: www.venturaoncology.com
SIC: 8011 Oncologist

(P-20052)
VENTURA COUNTY MEDICAL CENTER
Also Called: Santa Paula Hospital
845 N 10th St Ste 3, Santa Paula (93060-1348)
PHONE...........................805 933-8600
Minako Watabe, *Obstetrician*
EMP: 69
SALES (corp-wide): 371.8MM **Privately Held**
SIC: 8011 Medical centers
PA: Ventura County Medical Center
3291 Loma Vista Rd
Ventura CA 93003
805 652-6000

(P-20053)
VENTURA COUNTY MEDICAL CENTER (PA)
3291 Loma Vista Rd, Ventura (93003-3099)
PHONE...........................805 652-6000
Ronald O'Halloran, *Principal*
George Paul,
Robert McMahan, *Ch Radiology*
Amanda Pyper, *Regional Mgr*
Veronica Gonzalez, *Executive Asst*
EMP: 159
SALES: 371.8MM **Privately Held**
SIC: 8011 Medical centers

(P-20054)
VENTURA COUNTY MEDICAL CENTER
Also Called: Ana Nacapa Surgical Associates
3291 Loma Vista Rd # 343, Ventura (93003-3099)
PHONE...........................805 652-6201
Scott Arnold, *Principal*
Tamir Keshen, *Pediatrics*
EMP: 85
SALES (corp-wide): 371.8MM **Privately Held**
SIC: 8011 Medical centers
PA: Ventura County Medical Center
3291 Loma Vista Rd
Ventura CA 93003
805 652-6000

(P-20055)
VERDUGO HILLS URGENT CARE MG
Also Called: Verdugo Hills Medical Assoc
544 N Glendale Ave, Glendale (91206-3311)
PHONE...........................818 241-4331
Richard A Foullon, *President*
Cynthia Foullon, *Vice Pres*
EMP: 62
SQ FT: 11,000
SALES (est): 4.8MM **Privately Held**
WEB: www.vhma.com
SIC: 8011 Medical centers

(P-20056)
VERITY MEDICAL FOUNDATION (HQ)
Also Called: San Jose Medical Group / MGT
400 Race St, San Jose (95126-3518)
PHONE...........................408 278-3000
Richard Adcock, *CEO*
Ernest Wallerstein, *CEO*
Christine Hoskinson, *CFO*
Arthur Feldman, *Med Doctor*
Mauro Ruffy, *Med Doctor*
EMP: 80
SALES (est): 48.6MM
SALES (corp-wide): 1.2B **Privately Held**
SIC: 8011 8741 Medical centers; management services
PA: Verity Health System Of California, Inc.
2040 E Mariposa Ave
El Segundo CA 90245
650 551-6650

(P-20057)
VETERANS AFFRS LNG BCH HLTHRE
5901 E 7th St, Long Beach (90822-5201)
PHONE...........................562 826-8000
Samar Azawi, *Principal*
Samuel Wilson,
Maria Dacosta, *Lab Dir*
Lela Richardson, *Personnel Assit*
Angel Hernandez, *Buyer*
EMP: 51
SALES (est): 2.2MM **Privately Held**
SIC: 8011 Offices & clinics of medical doctors

(P-20058)
VETERANS HEALTH ADMINISTRATION
Also Called: Mare Island Outpatient Clinic
Walnut Ave Bldg 201, Vallejo (94589)
PHONE...........................707 562-8200
Debra Nathanson, *Manager*
EMP: 264 **Publicly Held**
WEB: www.veterans-ru.org
SIC: 8011 9451 Clinic, operated by physicians; psychiatric clinic;
HQ: Veterans Health Administration
810 Vermont Ave Nw
Washington DC 20420

(P-20059)
VETERANS HEALTH ADMINISTRATION
Also Called: West Los Angeles V A Med Ctr
11301 Wilshire Blvd, Los Angeles (90073-1003)
PHONE...........................310 478-3711
Donna Beiter, *Director*
Michael Choi, *General Mgr*

EMP: 4374 **Publicly Held**
WEB: www.veterans-ru.org
SIC: 8011 9451 Clinic, operated by physicians; psychiatric clinic;
HQ: Veterans Health Administration
810 Vermont Ave Nw
Washington DC 20420

(P-20060)
VETERANS HEALTH ADMINISTRATION
Also Called: San Luis Obispo VA Cboc
1288 Morro St Ste 200, San Luis Obispo (93401-6302)
PHONE...........................805 543-1233
Mark Donaldson, *Branch Mgr*
EMP: 264 **Publicly Held**
SIC: 8011 9451 Clinic, operated by physicians;
HQ: Veterans Health Administration
810 Vermont Ave Nw
Washington DC 20420

(P-20061)
VETERANS HEALTH ADMINISTRATION
Also Called: Sacramento Mental Hlth Clinic
10535 Hospital Way, Mather (95655-4200)
PHONE...........................916 366-5427
Charles Barnett, *Manager*
EMP: 264 **Publicly Held**
WEB: www.veterans-ru.org
SIC: 8011 9451 Clinic, operated by physicians; psychiatric clinic;
HQ: Veterans Health Administration
810 Vermont Ave Nw
Washington DC 20420

(P-20062)
VETERANS HEALTH ADMINISTRATION
Also Called: Central Cal Healthcare Sys
2615 E Clinton Ave, Fresno (93703-2223)
PHONE...........................559 225-6100
Al Perry, *Branch Mgr*
EMP: 800 **Publicly Held**
WEB: www.veterans-ru.org
SIC: 8011 9451 Medical centers; administration of veterans' affairs;
HQ: Veterans Health Administration
810 Vermont Ave Nw
Washington DC 20420

(P-20063)
VETERANS HEALTH ADMINISTRATION
Also Called: Redding V A Outpatient Clinic
351 Hartnell Ave, Redding (96002-1845)
PHONE...........................530 226-7555
Anthony Pineda, *Branch Mgr*
Corsini Templado, *Internal Med*
EMP: 264 **Publicly Held**
WEB: www.veterans-ru.org
SIC: 8011 9451 Clinic, operated by physicians; psychiatric clinic;
HQ: Veterans Health Administration
810 Vermont Ave Nw
Washington DC 20420

(P-20064)
VETERANS HEALTH ADMINISTRATION
Also Called: Palo Alto VA Medical Center
3801 Miranda Ave Bldg 101, Palo Alto (94304-1207)
PHONE...........................650 493-5000
Elizabeth Freeman, *Director*
Josefina Ledezma, *Purch Dir*
EMP: 3500 **Publicly Held**
WEB: www.veterans-ru.org
SIC: 8011 9451 Medical centers;
HQ: Veterans Health Administration
810 Vermont Ave Nw
Washington DC 20420

(P-20065)
VETERANS HEALTH ADMINISTRATION
Also Called: Oakland V A Outpatient Clinic
2221 Martin Luther King J, Oakland
(94612-1318)
PHONE.................................510 267-7820
Dr Elmer Anderson, *Principal*
EMP: 264 Publicly Held
WEB: www.veterans-ru.org
SIC: 8011 9451 Clinic, operated by physicians; psychiatric clinic;
HQ: Veterans Health Administration
810 Vermont Ave Nw
Washington DC 20420

(P-20066)
VETERANS HEALTH ADMINISTRATION
Also Called: San Francisco Vamc
4150 Clement St 6205, San Francisco
(94121-1563)
PHONE.................................415 750-2009
Brian J Kelly, *Manager*
EMP: 85 Publicly Held
WEB: www.veterans-ru.org
SIC: 8011 9451 Medical centers; psychiatric clinic;
HQ: Veterans Health Administration
810 Vermont Ave Nw
Washington DC 20420

(P-20067)
VETERANS HEALTH ADMINISTRATION
Also Called: Chico V A Outpatient Clinic
280 Cohasset Rd, Chico (95926-2210)
PHONE.................................530 879-5000
Sonny Morgan, *Manager*
EMP: 264 Publicly Held
WEB: www.veterans-ru.org
SIC: 8011 9451 Clinic, operated by physicians; psychiatric clinic;
HQ: Veterans Health Administration
810 Vermont Ave Nw
Washington DC 20420

(P-20068)
VETERANS HEALTH ADMINISTRATION
Also Called: Eureka Veterans Clinic
727 E St, Eureka (95501-1854)
PHONE.................................707 442-5335
Phillip Wagner, *Manager*
EMP: 264 Publicly Held
WEB: www.veterans-ru.org
SIC: 8011 9451 Clinic, operated by physicians; psychiatric clinic;
HQ: Veterans Health Administration
810 Vermont Ave Nw
Washington DC 20420

(P-20069)
VETERANS HEALTH ADMINISTRATION
Also Called: Santa Rosa Clinic
3315 Chanate Rd, Santa Rosa
(95404-1736)
PHONE.................................707 570-3800
Donald B Dean, *Manager*
EMP: 264 Publicly Held
WEB: www.veterans-ru.org
SIC: 8011 9451 Clinic, operated by physicians; psychiatric clinic;
HQ: Veterans Health Administration
810 Vermont Ave Nw
Washington DC 20420

(P-20070)
VETERANS HEALTH ADMINISTRATION
Also Called: Chula Vista Veterans Center
835 Third Ave, Chula Vista (91911-1352)
PHONE.................................619 409-1600
Harvey Souza, *Manager*
EMP: 264 Publicly Held
WEB: www.veterans-ru.org
SIC: 8011 9451 Medical centers; psychiatric clinic;

HQ: Veterans Health Administration
810 Vermont Ave Nw
Washington DC 20420

(P-20071)
VETERANS HEALTH ADMINISTRATION
Also Called: Escondido Veterans Center
815 E Pennsylvania Ave, Escondido
(92025-3424)
PHONE.................................760 745-2000
Jamie Switzer, *Principal*
EMP: 264 Publicly Held
WEB: www.veterans-ru.org
SIC: 8011 9451 Medical centers; psychiatric clinic;
HQ: Veterans Health Administration
810 Vermont Ave Nw
Washington DC 20420

(P-20072)
VETERANS HEALTH ADMINISTRATION
Also Called: Oxnard Veterans Center
250 Citrus Grove Ln # 250, Oxnard
(93036-9030)
PHONE.................................805 983-6384
EMP: 263 Publicly Held
SIC: 8011 9451
HQ: Veterans Health Administration
810 Vermont Ave Nw
Washington DC 20420

(P-20073)
VETERANS HEALTH ADMINISTRATION
16111 Plummer St, North Hills
(91343-2036)
PHONE.................................818 895-9311
Mike Domres, *Principal*
EMP: 183 Publicly Held
WEB: www.veterans-ru.org
SIC: 8011 9451 Clinic, operated by physicians;
HQ: Veterans Health Administration
810 Vermont Ave Nw
Washington DC 20420

(P-20074)
VETERANS HEALTH ADMINISTRATION
Also Called: Mission Valley V A
8810 Rio San Diego Dr, San Diego
(92108-1698)
PHONE.................................619 400-5000
EMP: 264 Publicly Held
WEB: www.veterans-ru.org
SIC: 8011 9451 Clinic, operated by physicians; psychiatric clinic;
HQ: Veterans Health Administration
810 Vermont Ave Nw
Washington DC 20420

(P-20075)
VETERANS HEALTH ADMINISTRATION
Also Called: Sepulveda Ambulatory Care
16111 Plummer St, North Hills
(91343-2036)
PHONE.................................818 891-7711
Dolly G Whitehead, *Manager*
EMP: 900 Publicly Held
WEB: www.veterans-ru.org
SIC: 8011 9451 Medical centers; psychiatric clinic;
HQ: Veterans Health Administration
810 Vermont Ave Nw
Washington DC 20420

(P-20076)
VETERANS HEALTH ADMINISTRATION
Also Called: Sacramento V A Medical Center
10535 Hospital Way, Mather (95655-4200)
PHONE.................................916 843-7000
Lawrence Sandlers, *Director*
EMP: 500 Publicly Held
WEB: www.veterans-ru.org

SIC: 8011 9451 Medical centers; administration of veterans' affairs;
HQ: Veterans Health Administration
810 Vermont Ave Nw
Washington DC 20420

(P-20077)
VETERANS HEALTH ADMINISTRATION
Also Called: Livermore VA Medical Center
4951 Arroyo Rd, Livermore (94550-9650)
PHONE.................................925 447-2560
C H Nixon, *Director*
EMP: 450 Publicly Held
WEB: www.veterans-ru.org
SIC: 8011 9451 Medical centers;
HQ: Veterans Health Administration
810 Vermont Ave Nw
Washington DC 20420

(P-20078)
VETERANS HEALTH ADMINISTRATION
Also Called: Loma Linda Healthcare Sys 605
11201 Benton St, Loma Linda
(92357-1000)
PHONE.................................909 825-7084
Debbie Romero, *Branch Mgr*
EMP: 2000 Publicly Held
WEB: www.veterans-ru.org
SIC: 8011 9451 Medical centers; psychiatric clinic;
HQ: Veterans Health Administration
810 Vermont Ave Nw
Washington DC 20420

(P-20079)
VETERANS HEALTH ADMINISTRATION
Also Called: Menlo Park VA Medical Center
795 Willow Rd, Menlo Park (94025-2539)
PHONE.................................650 614-9997
Lisa Freeman, *Director*
EMP: 3000 Publicly Held
WEB: www.veterans-ru.org
SIC: 8011 9451 Medical centers; psychiatric clinic;
HQ: Veterans Health Administration
810 Vermont Ave Nw
Washington DC 20420

(P-20080)
VETERANS HEALTH ADMINISTRATION
Also Called: VA HSR&d Center of Excellence
16111 Plummer St, North Hills
(91343-2036)
PHONE.................................818 895-9449
Lisa Rubenstein, *Branch Mgr*
EMP: 99 Publicly Held
WEB: www.veterans-ru.org
SIC: 8011 9451 Medical centers; administration of veterans' affairs;
HQ: Veterans Health Administration
810 Vermont Ave Nw
Washington DC 20420

(P-20081)
VETERANS HEALTH ADMINISTRATION
Also Called: Anaheim V A Clinic
1801 W Romneya Dr Ste 303, Anaheim
(92801-1825)
PHONE.................................714 780-5400
Teresa Carpenter, *Branch Mgr*
EMP: 183 Publicly Held
WEB: www.veterans-ru.org
SIC: 8011 9451 Clinic, operated by physicians; administration of veterans' affairs;
HQ: Veterans Health Administration
810 Vermont Ave Nw
Washington DC 20420

(P-20082)
VETERANS HEALTH ADMINISTRATION
Also Called: Bakersfield Community Based
1801 Westwind Dr, Bakersfield
(93301-3028)
PHONE.................................661 632-1871
Joan Van Horn, *Manager*
EMP: 50 Publicly Held
WEB: www.veterans-ru.org
SIC: 8011 9451 Clinic, operated by physicians; psychiatric clinic;
HQ: Veterans Health Administration
810 Vermont Ave Nw
Washington DC 20420

(P-20083)
VETERANS HEALTH ADMINISTRATION
Also Called: Los Angles Ambulatory Care Ctr
351 E Temple St, Los Angeles
(90012-3328)
PHONE.................................213 253-2677
Lane Turzan, *General Mgr*
EMP: 190 Publicly Held
WEB: www.veterans-ru.org
SIC: 8011 9451 Medical centers; psychiatric clinic;
HQ: Veterans Health Administration
810 Vermont Ave Nw
Washington DC 20420

(P-20084)
VETERANS HEALTH ADMINISTRATION
Also Called: Bakersfield Vet Center
1110 Golden Valley Fwy, Bakersfield
(93301)
PHONE.................................661 323-8387
Jenney Frank, *Office Mgr*
EMP: 264 Publicly Held
SIC: 8011 9451 Medical centers; psychiatric clinic;
HQ: Veterans Health Administration
810 Vermont Ave Nw
Washington DC 20420

(P-20085)
VETERINARY SURGICAL ASSOCIATES
251 N Amphlett Blvd, San Mateo
(94401-1805)
PHONE.................................650 696-8196
Sharon Ullman, *Manager*
EMP: 60
SALES (est): 736.1K
SALES (corp-wide): 6.1MM **Privately Held**
SIC: 8011 0742 Freestanding emergency medical center; surgeon; veterinarian, animal specialties
PA: Veterinary Surgical Associates
1410 Monu Blvd Ste 100
Concord CA 94520
925 827-1777

(P-20086)
VIA CARE CMNTY HLTH CTR INC
Also Called: Bienvenidos Community Hlth Ctr
507 S Atlantic Blvd, Los Angeles
(90022-2621)
PHONE.................................323 268-9191
Deborah Villar, *CEO*
Joe Gotsill, *CFO*
Denia Garfias, *Pediatrics*
Eduardo Vasquez, *Director*
EMP: 60
SALES: 2MM **Privately Held**
SIC: 8011 Primary care medical clinic

(P-20087)
VINOD KUMAR MD
5020 Commerce Dr, Bakersfield
(93309-0631)
P.O. Box 1351 (93302-1351)
PHONE.................................661 324-4100
Vinod Kumar, *Owner*
EMP: 75
SALES (est): 623K **Privately Held**
SIC: 8011 Cardiologist & cardio-vascular specialist

PRODUCTS & SVCS

(P-20088)
VISALIA MEDICAL CLINIC INC (PA)
Also Called: Multi Specialty Medical Svc
5400 W Hillsdale Ave, Visalia (93291-5140)
PHONE...................................559 733-5222
Richard E Strid, CEO
Ahmad Shahroz, Managing Dir
Gilbert Sunio, Managing Dir
Rebecca Enos, Office Mgr
Richie Choi, Administration
EMP: 299
SQ FT: 70,000
SALES (est): 41.1MM Privately Held
SIC: 8011 8071 Clinic, operated by physicians; medical laboratories

(P-20089)
VISCENT ORTHPD SOLUTIONS LLC (DH)
2885 Loker Ave E, Carlsbad (92010-6626)
PHONE...................................214 501-0180
Brad Lee, Mng Member
EMP: 50
SALES (est): 10.4MM
SALES (corp-wide): 478.8MM Privately Held
SIC: 8011 Orthopedic physician
HQ: Breg, Inc.
　　2885 Loker Ave E
　　Carlsbad CA 92010
　　760 599-3000

(P-20090)
VISION CARE CENTER (PA)
Also Called: Vision Care Center Central Cal
7075 N Sharon Ave, Fresno (93720-3329)
PHONE...................................559 486-2000
Julie Cleeland, CEO
Ralph Hadley Od, President
Michael Herman, CFO
EMP: 82
SQ FT: 18,000
SALES (est): 11MM Privately Held
WEB: www.eyeqvc.com
SIC: 8011 8042 Ophthalmologist; offices & clinics of optometrists

(P-20091)
WATTS HEALTHCARE CORPORATION
700 W Imperial Hwy, Los Angeles (90044-4127)
PHONE...................................323 241-1780
EMP: 162
SALES (corp-wide): 34.1MM Privately Held
SIC: 8011
PA: Watts Healthcare Corporation
　　10300 Compton Ave
　　Los Angeles CA 90002
　　323 568-3059

(P-20092)
WATTS HEALTHCARE CORPORATION (PA)
10300 Compton Ave, Los Angeles (90002-3628)
PHONE...................................323 564-4331
Roderick Seamster, President
Carroll J McNeely, CFO
Victor Cortez, Bd of Directors
Carroll McNeely, Officer
Hara Yohannes, Vice Pres
EMP: 180
SALES (est): 37.3MM Privately Held
WEB: www.wattshealthcare.com
SIC: 8011 Medical centers

(P-20093)
WAVE PLASTIC SURGERY CTR INC
18433 Colima Rd, La Puente (91748-5815)
PHONE...................................626 964-7788
Peter Lee, President
EMP: 346
SALES (corp-wide): 16.1MM Privately Held
SIC: 8011 Plastic surgeon
PA: Wave Plastic Surgery Center Inc.
　　3680 Wilshire Blvd Fl 2
　　Los Angeles CA 90010
　　213 383-4800

(P-20094)
WAYNE R KIDDER
915 Via Los Padres, Santa Barbara (93111-1325)
PHONE...................................805 967-6993
Wayne R Kidder, Owner
EMP: 80
SALES (est): 3.6MM Privately Held
SIC: 8011 Offices & clinics of medical doctors

(P-20095)
WEST COAST CHILDRENS CENTER
545 Ashbury Ave, El Cerrito (94530-3220)
PHONE...................................510 269-9030
Dr Stacey Kath, Exec Dir
Dr Kenneth Parker, Exec Dir
Edwin Calles, Admin Asst
EMP: 50
SALES (est): 11.4MM Privately Held
SIC: 8011 8322 8049 Clinic, operated by physicians; social worker; clinical psychologist

(P-20096)
WEST COUNTY HEALTH CENTERS INC
Also Called: Occidental Area Health Center
16312 3rd St, Guerneville (95446)
P.O. Box 1449 (95446-1449)
PHONE...................................707 869-2849
Mary Szecsey, Exec Dir
John Kornfeld, President
Dwight Cary, Treasurer
Debra Johnson, Vice Pres
EMP: 75
SALES (est): 7.4MM Privately Held
WEB: www.wchealth.org
SIC: 8011 Primary care medical clinic; clinic, operated by physicians

(P-20097)
WEST COVINA MEDICAL CLINIC INC (PA)
1500 W West Covina Pkwy, West Covina (91790-2708)
PHONE...................................626 960-8614
Dr Ziad Dabuni, President
Dr Suntheetha Ali, Treasurer
Dr Shivani Shah, Exec VP
Kathy Wright, Project Mgr
Dr Jose Bautista, Asst Treas
EMP: 225
SQ FT: 50,000
SALES (est): 15.8MM Privately Held
SIC: 8011 Clinic, operated by physicians

(P-20098)
WEST DERMATOLOGY MED MGT INC
400 Newport Center Dr # 702, Newport Beach (92660-7601)
PHONE...................................909 793-3000
J Robert West, President
EMP: 140
SALES (est): 10.7MM Privately Held
SIC: 8011 Dermatologist

(P-20099)
WEST VENTURA FAMILY CARE CTR
Also Called: Rocha, Jill B MD
133 W Santa Clara St, Ventura (93001-2543)
PHONE...................................805 641-5620
Joan E Baumer MD, Owner
Tiffany Chan, Physician Asst
Maricela Marmolejo, Assistant
EMP: 54
SALES (est): 2.4MM Privately Held
SIC: 8011 Medical centers

(P-20100)
WESTERN MED ASSOC MED GROUP (PA)
1595 Soquel Dr Ste 330, Santa Cruz (95065-1722)
PHONE...................................831 475-1111
Robert D Keet MD, Principal
Statish Chandra MD, Principal
Vernon Loverde MD, Principal
EMP: 60

SALES: 7.5MM Privately Held
SIC: 8011 Internal medicine, physician/surgeon

(P-20101)
WHITAKER WELNESS INSTITUTE IN
4321 Birch St Ste 100, Newport Beach (92660-1940)
PHONE...................................949 851-1550
Julian Whitaker, President
Peggy Dace, Manager
EMP: 60
SQ FT: 8,500
SALES (est): 8.1MM Privately Held
WEB: www.whitakerwellness.com
SIC: 8011 Cardiologist & cardio-vascular specialist; diabetes specialist, physician/surgeon

(P-20102)
WHITE MEMORIAL MED GROUP INC (PA)
1701 E Cesar E Chavez Ave # 510, Los Angeles (90033-2464)
P.O. Box 51741 (90051-6041)
PHONE...................................323 987-1300
Alan Lau, President
EMP: 75
SQ FT: 20,000
SALES (est): 7.3MM Privately Held
SIC: 8011 8742 Medical centers; hospital & health services consultant

(P-20103)
WILLIAM H WARDEN III MD
2760 Atlantic Ave, Long Beach (90806-2755)
PHONE...................................562 424-6666
William Warden, Principal
EMP: 75
SALES (est): 978K Privately Held
SIC: 8011 Orthopedic physician

(P-20104)
WILLIAM MCGANN MD
1 Shrader St Ste 650, San Francisco (94117-1036)
PHONE...................................415 221-0665
A Noble MD, President
Alan Noble MD, President
Ray Schmidt, Office Mgr
EMP: 54
SQ FT: 7,000
SALES (est): 1.6MM Privately Held
SIC: 8011 Internal medicine, physician/surgeon; pediatrician

(P-20105)
ZEITER EYE MEDICAL GROUP INC (PA)
255 E Weber Ave, Stockton (95202-2706)
PHONE...................................209 366-0446
John H Zeiter MD, President
Joseph Zeiter MD, CFO
Henry J Zeiter MD, Vice Pres
Erin K McCarthy, Office Mgr
Amanda Marchini, Business Anlyst
EMP: 95
SQ FT: 11,500
SALES (est): 10.5MM Privately Held
WEB: www.zeitereye.com
SIC: 8011 Ophthalmologist

8021 Offices & Clinics Of Dentists

(P-20106)
ACCESS DENTAL PLAN (PA)
Also Called: Access Dental Centers
8890 Cal Center Dr, Sacramento (95826-3200)
PHONE...................................916 922-5000
Reza M Abbaszadeh, President
Teri Abbaszadeh, President
Hideo Kakiuchi, CFO
Laura Shively, Vice Pres
Armando Chavez, Office Mgr
▲ EMP: 70
SQ FT: 4,700
SALES (est): 10.2MM Privately Held
SIC: 8021 Dental clinic

(P-20107)
ADVANCED HM HLTH & HOSPICE INC
Also Called: Advanced Home House
4354 Auburn Blvd, Sacramento (95841-4107)
PHONE...................................916 978-0744
Angela Sehr, CEO
Deb Ryan, Asst Admin
Kathleen Boesch, Director
▲ EMP: 100
SALES (est): 2.2MM Privately Held
SIC: 8021 Group & corporate practice dentists

(P-20108)
AMERICAN DNTL PARTNERS OF CAL
Also Called: Rouche O Edgar DDS
7251 Magnolia Ave, Riverside (92504-3811)
PHONE...................................951 689-5031
Greg Serrao, CEO
EMP: 165
SQ FT: 9,700
SALES (est): 2.8MM Privately Held
SIC: 8021 Dentists' office

(P-20109)
AMPLA HEALTH (PA)
935 Market St, Yuba City (95991-4217)
PHONE...................................530 674-4261
Benjamin Flores, CEO
Hilton Perez, COO
Dale Johnson, CFO
Carlos Peralta, Officer
Daniel Siri, Officer
EMP: 245
SQ FT: 10,200
SALES: 50.2MM Privately Held
SIC: 8021 8011 Dental clinic; health maintenance organization; primary care medical clinic; pediatrician

(P-20110)
ANTHONY P GAROFALO A DENTAL
Also Called: Horizon Dental Grp
742 Broadway, El Cajon (92021-4630)
PHONE...................................619 440-0071
Anthony P Garofalo, President
EMP: 60
SALES (est): 2.6MM Privately Held
WEB: www.horizondentalgroup.com
SIC: 8021 Dentists' office

(P-20111)
BRIGHTER INC
Also Called: Brightercom
501 Santa Monica Blvd # 403, Santa Monica (90401-2431)
PHONE...................................888 230-4413
Jake Winebaum, CEO
Andrew Pease, CFO
Petra Kaur Ljungman, Vice Pres
Eric Angel, Engineer
Scott Oshima, Engineer
EMP: 60
SALES (est): 3.2MM
SALES (corp-wide): 41.6B Publicly Held
SIC: 8021 Dental clinics & offices
PA: Cigna Corporation
　　900 Cottage Grove Rd
　　Bloomfield CT 06002
　　860 226-6000

(P-20112)
BUSINESS AND SUPPORT SERVICES
Camp Pendleton Mc Base, Oceanside (92055)
P.O. Box 555221, Camp Pendleton (92055-5221)
PHONE...................................760 725-5187
EMP: 320 Publicly Held
WEB: www.mccssc.com
SIC: 8021 9711 Offices & clinics of dentists; Marine Corps;
HQ: Business And Support Services
　　3044 Catlin Ave
　　Quantico VA 22134
　　703 432-0109

(P-20113)
CASTLE DENTAL
Also Called: South Gate Dental Group
4433 Tweedy Blvd, South Gate
(90280-6303)
PHONE..............................323 567-1227
Elliott Schlang DDS, *Manager*
EMP: 50
SALES (est): 1.2MM **Privately Held**
SIC: 8021 Specialized dental practitioners

(P-20114)
CHILDRENS HOSPITAL LOS ANGELES
7891 Talbert Ave Ste 103, Huntington
Beach (92648-8613)
PHONE..............................714 841-4990
Richard P Mungo DDS, *President*
Richard Mungo, *Fmly & Gen Dent*
Julie Hines,
Claudia Marquez,
EMP: 341
SQ FT: 100
SALES (corp-wide): 1B **Privately Held**
SIC: 8021 Dentists' office
PA: The Childrens Hospital Los Angeles
4650 W Sunset Blvd
Los Angeles CA 90027
323 660-2450

(P-20115)
DHS MEMBER SERVICES
3833 Atlantic Ave, Long Beach
(90807-3505)
PHONE..............................562 595-5151
Godfrey Pernell, *Principal*
EMP: 50
SALES (est): 675.4K **Privately Held**
SIC: 8021 Dental insurance plan

(P-20116)
ELIAS ELLIOTT LAMPASI FEHN (PA)
7251 Magnolia Ave, Riverside
(92504-3811)
PHONE..............................951 689-5031
Douglass R Gerald, *CEO*
Jay Elliot, *Vice Pres*
Dee Elias, *Admin Sec*
EMP: 59
SALES (est): 4MM **Privately Held**
WEB: www.riversidedentalgroup.com
SIC: 8021 Dentists' office

(P-20117)
INTERDENT INC (HQ)
Also Called: Smile Keepers
9800 S La Cienega Blvd # 800, Inglewood
(90301-4442)
PHONE..............................310 765-2400
Ivar S Chhina, *President*
Scott Bremen, *COO*
Robert W Hill, *CFO*
Matthew Wickesberg, *CFO*
Jeffrey Sulitzer, *Officer*
EMP: 55
SQ FT: 10,000
SALES (est): 111.8MM **Privately Held**
SIC: 8021 Dentists' office
PA: H.I.G. Middle Market Llc
1 Sansome St Fl 37
San Francisco CA 94104
415 439-5500

(P-20118)
INTERDENT SERVICE CORPORATION (DH)
9800 S La Cienega Blvd # 800, Inglewood
(90301-4442)
PHONE..............................310 765-2400
Marshal Salomon, *CEO*
Matthew Wickesberg, *CFO*
Kevin Webb, *Vice Pres*
EMP: 55
SQ FT: 10,000
SALES (est): 52MM
SALES (corp-wide): 111.8MM **Privately Held**
SIC: 8021 Dental clinic
HQ: Interdent, Inc.
9800 S La Cienega Blvd # 800
Inglewood CA 90301
310 765-2400

(P-20119)
JOHN J MAGUIRE DDS
Also Called: Fremont Dental Group
39340 Fremont Blvd, Fremont
(94538-1320)
PHONE..............................213 740-6462
John J Maguire DDS, *Owner*
EMP: 100
SALES (est): 4.6MM **Privately Held**
WEB: www.fremontdentalgroup.com
SIC: 8021 Offices & clinics of dentists

(P-20120)
JOSEPH A FOROOSH DENTAL CORP (PA)
Also Called: Desert Dental Group
12640 Hesperia Rd Ste A, Victorville
(92395-7753)
PHONE..............................760 241-3336
Joseph Foroosh, *Owner*
EMP: 60
SALES (est): 5.9MM **Privately Held**
WEB: www.desertdentalgroup.com
SIC: 8021 Dentists' office

(P-20121)
LA CLINICA DE LA RAZA INC
3050 E 16th St, Oakland (94601-2319)
PHONE..............................510 535-4700
Magnolia Rios, *Office Mgr*
Joan Thompson, *Manager*
EMP: 222
SQ FT: 5,208
SALES (corp-wide): 102.2MM **Privately Held**
SIC: 8021 Dental clinic
PA: La Clinica De La Raza, Inc.
1450 Fruitvale Ave Fl 3
Oakland CA 94601
510 535-4000

(P-20122)
LA CLINICA DE LA RAZA INC
Also Called: Laclinica
337 E Leland Rd, Pittsburg (94565-4911)
PHONE..............................925 431-1250
Viola Lujan, *Branch Mgr*
Zenaida Aguilera, *Officer*
Yassin Janneh, *Manager*
EMP: 230
SALES (corp-wide): 102.2MM **Privately Held**
SIC: 8021 Dental clinic
PA: La Clinica De La Raza, Inc.
1450 Fruitvale Ave Fl 3
Oakland CA 94601
510 535-4000

(P-20123)
LAKE CNTY TRBAL HLTH CNSORTIUM
925 Bevins Ct, Lakeport (95453-9754)
P.O. Box 1950 (95453-1950)
PHONE..............................707 263-8382
Mike Icay, *President*
Crista Ray, *Ch of Bd*
Tanya Michel, *CFO*
Tina Ramos, *Chairman*
Ernesto Padilla, *Exec Dir*
EMP: 80
SQ FT: 10,832
SALES (est): 28.4MM **Privately Held**
WEB: www.lcthc.org
SIC: 8021 Dental clinic

(P-20124)
LAKEWOOD CERRITOS DENTAL CTR
5819 Adenmoor Ave, Lakewood
(90713-1067)
PHONE..............................562 860-0388
Kosmas Pappas DDS, *Owner*
EMP: 100
SQ FT: 5,600
SALES (est): 4.1MM **Privately Held**
WEB: www.doctorlopez.com
SIC: 8021 Dentists' office

(P-20125)
LEONID M GLOSMAN DDS A D
Also Called: Dentalville
7864 Van Nuys Blvd, Panorama City
(91402-6069)
PHONE..............................818 989-2400
EMP: 100

SALES (corp-wide): 2.7MM **Privately Held**
SIC: 8021 Dental clinics & offices
PA: Leonid M. Glosman, D.D.S., A Dental Corporation
833 W Whittier Blvd
Montebello CA 90640
323 266-1000

(P-20126)
LINDHURST DENTAL CLINIC
4941 Olivehurst Ave, Olivehurst
(95961-4225)
PHONE..............................530 743-4614
Sally Moore, *Manager*
EMP: 50
SQ FT: 13,712
SALES (est): 1.5MM **Privately Held**
SIC: 8021 Dental clinic

(P-20127)
MICHAEL P BYKO DDS A PROF CORP (PA)
164 W Hospitality Ln # 14, San Bernardino
(92408-3316)
PHONE..............................909 888-7817
Michael Boyko, *President*
Amy Ferrance, *COO*
Wesley Okumura, *Fmly & Gen Dent*
Heather Dunham, *Manager*
◆ EMP: 60
SQ FT: 3,000
SALES (est): 3.9MM **Privately Held**
SIC: 8021 Dentists' office; orthodontist

(P-20128)
MONTEREY DENTAL GROUP
333 El Dorado St, Monterey (93940-4606)
PHONE..............................831 373-3068
Rick Baldwin, *Principal*
Mark Bayless, *Partner*
Arthur Benoit, *Partner*
S Bhaskar, *Partner*
P Breuleux, *Partner*
EMP: 55
SQ FT: 13,330
SALES (est): 2.2MM **Privately Held**
WEB: www.quantified.com
SIC: 8021 Dentists' office

(P-20129)
MONTEREY PENINSULA DNTL GROUP
333 El Dorado St, Monterey (93940-4645)
PHONE..............................831 373-3068
Ronald Faia, *Partner*
J Mark Baliff, *Partner*
S N Bashcor, *Partner*
John Faia III, *Partner*
Mick Falkel, *Partner*
EMP: 60
SQ FT: 13,000
SALES (est): 3.7MM **Privately Held**
WEB: www.mpdg.com
SIC: 8021 Group & corporate practice dentists; dentists' office

(P-20130)
MY KIDS DENTIST
24635 Madison Ave Ste E, Murrieta
(92562-7556)
PHONE..............................951 600-1062
Theresa Gomez, *Branch Mgr*
EMP: 400
SALES (corp-wide): 4.9MM **Privately Held**
SIC: 8021 Dentists' office
PA: My Kid's Dentist
17000 Red Hill Ave
Irvine CA 92614
909 854-1437

(P-20131)
NORTHERN VLY INDIAN HLTH INC
845 W East Ave, Chico (95926-2002)
PHONE..............................530 896-9400
Maureen Self, *Manager*
EMP: 90
SALES (corp-wide): 35.3MM **Privately Held**
WEB: www.nvih.org
SIC: 8021 8011 Dental clinic; primary care medical clinic

PA: Northern Valley Indian Health, Inc.
207 N Butte St
Willows CA
530 934-9293

(P-20132)
PACIFIC DENTAL SERVICES LLC (PA)
Also Called: Pds
17000 Red Hill Ave, Irvine (92614-5626)
P.O. Box 19723 (92623-9723)
PHONE..............................714 845-8500
Stephen E Thorne IV, *President*
John Barnes, *Partner*
Scott Beck, *Vice Chairman*
Brady Aase, *CFO*
Dan Burke, *Senior VP*
▲ EMP: 300
SQ FT: 40,000
SALES (est): 358.9MM **Privately Held**
WEB: www.pacificdentalservices.com
SIC: 8021 6794 Dental clinic; franchises, selling or licensing

(P-20133)
RANCHO NIGUEL DENTAL GROUP
30140 Town Center Dr, Laguna Niguel
(92677-2037)
PHONE..............................949 249-4180
Steve Krieger, *Partner*
Rodney Boyd, *Partner*
Gary Mar, *Partner*
Hugh Murray, *Partner*
Mary Stay, *Partner*
EMP: 50
SALES (est): 1.8MM **Privately Held**
SIC: 8021 Dental clinic

(P-20134)
SAC HEALTH SYSTEM (PA)
1455 3rd Ave, San Bernardino
(92408-0218)
PHONE..............................909 382-7100
Richard H Hart MD, *President*
George Cencel, *CFO*
Barry Randolph, *Opers Staff*
Donna S Burgess, *Manager*
EMP: 64
SALES (est): 17.2MM **Privately Held**
SIC: 8021 8011 8093 Offices & clinics of dentists; offices & clinics of medical doctors; mental health clinic, outpatient

(P-20135)
SANTA ROSA DENTAL GROUP
1820 Sonoma Ave Ste 80, Santa Rosa
(95405-6617)
PHONE..............................707 545-0944
Allen Barbieri, *Partner*
Perry Bingham, *Partner*
Richard L Blechel, *Partner*
James J Bridges, *Partner*
Ted Degolia, *Partner*
EMP: 64
SQ FT: 8,000
SALES (est): 3MM **Privately Held**
SIC: 8021 Dentists' office

(P-20136)
SCHNIEROW DENTAL CARE
Also Called: Piehl, Joel J DDS
13450 Hawthorne Blvd, Hawthorne
(90250-5806)
PHONE..............................310 377-6453
Burton Schnierow, *President*
EMP: 50
SQ FT: 3,200
SALES (est): 4.9MM **Privately Held**
SIC: 8021 Dentists' office

(P-20137)
SCOTT JACKS DDS INC
Also Called: Adult & Childrens Dental Group
4444 Tweedy Blvd, South Gate
(90280-6392)
PHONE..............................323 564-2444
Scott Jacks, *CEO*
Marsha Jacks, *Admin Sec*
EMP: 111
SQ FT: 9,375
SALES (est): 6.7MM **Privately Held**
SIC: 8021 Dentists' office

P
R
O
D
U
C
T
S
&
S
V
C
S

(P-20138)
ST JOHNS WELL CHILD (PA)
Also Called: SAINT JOHN'S WELL CHILD
CENTER
808 W 58th St, Los Angeles (90037-3632)
PHONE..............................323 541-1600
James J Mangia, *CEO*
Liz Meisler, *CFO*
Phillip Velasco, *Info Tech Dir*
Martin Chao, *Director*
Mario Chavez, *Director*
EMP: 89
SALES: 63.5MM **Privately Held**
WEB: www.wellchild.org
SIC: 8021 8011 Dental clinic; offices &
clinics of medical doctors

(P-20139)
THURSTON MARTIN H DDS MS
11616 Iberia Pl, San Diego (92128-2404)
PHONE..............................858 676-5010
Martin Thurston, *Principal*
Mary E Ordoukhaniam, *Financial Exec*
EMP: 50
SALES (est): 1.1MM **Privately Held**
SIC: 8021 Orthodontist

(P-20140)
**TOIYABE INDIAN HEALTH PRJ
INC (PA)**
250 N See Vee Ln, Bishop (93514-8130)
PHONE..............................760 873-8461
David Lent, *CEO*
Mary Daniel, *CFO*
Michael Franks, *CFO*
Monty Bengochia, *Chairman*
Christie Martindale, *Associate Dir*
EMP: 113
SQ FT: 66,300
SALES: 16.4MM **Privately Held**
WEB: www.toiyabe.us
SIC: 8021 8011 Dental clinic; clinic, oper-
ated by physicians; psychiatric clinic

(P-20141)
U C S F SCHOOL OF DENTISTRY
Also Called: Buchanan Dental Center
100 Buchanan St, San Francisco
(94102-6147)
PHONE..............................415 476-5609
Mark Kirkland DDS, *Administration*
Chui Chan, *Med Doctor*
Mark D Kirkland, *Med Doctor*
Avelino Silva,
Jyoti S Singh,
EMP: 50
SALES (est): 2MM **Privately Held**
SIC: 8021 Dental clinics & offices

(P-20142)
VALLEY OAK DENTAL GROUP
1507 W Yosemite Ave, Manteca
(95337-5182)
PHONE..............................209 823-9341
Marvin Bledsoe, *President*
Bonnie Morehead DDS, *Corp Secy*
Mark Hochhalter DDS, *Vice Pres*
Ron Joseph, *Fmly & Gen Dent*
Bonnie J Morehead, *Fmly & Gen Dent*
EMP: 70
SALES (est): 4.5MM **Privately Held**
SIC: 8021 Dental clinic; specialized dental
practitioners; periodontist; dentists' office

(P-20143)
**VETERANS HEALTH
ADMINISTRATION**
Also Called: Dental
3350 La Jolla Village Dr, San Diego
(92161-0002)
PHONE..............................858 552-7525
EMP: 264 **Publicly Held**
WEB: www.veterans-ru.org
SIC: 8021 9451 Dental clinic;
HQ: Veterans Health Administration
810 Vermont Ave Nw
Washington DC 20420

(P-20144)
**WESTERN DENTAL SERVICES
INC (PA)**
530 S Main St Ste 600, Orange
(92868-4544)
P.O. Box 14227 (92863-1227)
PHONE..............................714 480-3000
Thomas W Erickson, *CEO*
Samuel H Gruenbaum, *President*
Stuart Gray, *COO*
David Joe, *CFO*
Theresa Carrara, *Officer*
EMP: 350
SALES (est): 279.5MM **Privately Held**
WEB: www.westerndental.com
SIC: 8021 Dentists' office

(P-20145)
**WILSHIRE CENTER DENTAL
GROUP**
3932 Wilshire Blvd # 102, Los Angeles
(90010-3334)
PHONE..............................213 386-3336
Gregory Kaplan, *Owner*
EMP: 50
SQ FT: 7,000
SALES (est): 1.8MM **Privately Held**
SIC: 8021 Dental clinic; dental surgeon; or-
thodontist; pedodontist

8031 Offices & Clinics Of Doctors Of Osteopathy

(P-20146)
**ENCOMPASS FMLY PHY MED
GRP INC (PA)**
10225 Austin Dr Ste 103, Spring Valley
(91978-1521)
PHONE..............................619 660-6212
John Dailey, *Director*
Terry Winegar, *President*
Joseph Aiello Do, *Treasurer*
EMP: 60
SQ FT: 700
SALES (est): 4.3MM **Privately Held**
WEB: www.efpmg.com
SIC: 8031 Offices & clinics of osteopathic
physicians

(P-20147)
FACEY MEDICAL FOUNDATION
2655 1st St, Simi Valley (93065-1547)
PHONE..............................805 206-2000
EMP: 157
SALES (corp-wide): 197.1MM **Privately
Held**
SIC: 8031 8011 Offices & clinics of osteo-
pathic physicians; offices & clinics of
medical doctors
PA: Facey Medical Foundation
15451 San Fernando Msn
Mission Hills CA 91345
818 365-9531

(P-20148)
FACEY MEDICAL FOUNDATION
191 S Buena Vista St, Burbank
(91505-4554)
PHONE..............................818 861-7831
Jennifer Sung MD, *Branch Mgr*
EMP: 126
SALES (corp-wide): 197.1MM **Privately
Held**
SIC: 8031 8011 Offices & clinics of osteo-
pathic physicians; offices & clinics of
medical doctors
PA: Facey Medical Foundation
15451 San Fernando Msn
Mission Hills CA 91345
818 365-9531

(P-20149)
FCS MEDICAL CORPORATION
1701 E Cesar E Chavez Ave # 230, Los An-
geles (90033-2464)
PHONE..............................323 317-9200
Mimi House, *Manager*
EMP: 93
SALES (corp-wide): 14MM **Privately
Held**
SIC: 8031 8011 Offices & clinics of osteo-
pathic physicians; offices & clinics of
medical doctors

PA: Fcs Medical Corporation
5823 York Blvd Ste 1
Los Angeles CA 90042
323 255-1575

(P-20150)
SUTTER HEALTH
5150 Hill Rd Ste E, Lakeport (95453-5100)
PHONE..............................707 263-3520
EMP: 249
SALES (est): 87K
SALES (corp-wide): 12.4B **Privately Held**
SIC: 8031 8011 Offices & clinics of osteo-
pathic physicians; offices & clinics of
medical doctors
PA: Sutter Health
2200 River Plaza Dr
Sacramento CA 95833
916 733-8800

(P-20151)
VISTA COMMUNITY CLINIC (PA)
1000 Vale Terrace Dr, Vista (92084-5218)
PHONE..............................760 631-5000
Fernando Sanudo, *CEO*
Michele Lambert, *CFO*
Thomas Van Bui, *Analyst*
Jorge A Gaspar, *Manager*
Steven Gil, *Manager*
EMP: 280
SQ FT: 60,000
SALES: 49.2MM **Privately Held**
WEB: www.vistacommunityclinic.org
SIC: 8031 8011 Offices & clinics of osteo-
pathic physicians; medical centers

(P-20152)
VISTA COMMUNITY CLINIC
134 Grapevine Rd, Vista (92083-4004)
PHONE..............................760 631-5030
Sonia Jimenez, *Branch Mgr*
EMP: 50
SALES (corp-wide): 49.2MM **Privately
Held**
SIC: 8031 8011 Offices & clinics of osteo-
pathic physicians; medical centers
PA: Vista Community Clinic
1000 Vale Terrace Dr
Vista CA 92084
760 631-5000

8041 Offices & Clinics Of Chiropractors

(P-20153)
**CORNERSTONE MEDICAL
GROUP**
1881 Commercenter E # 112, San
Bernardino (92408-3442)
PHONE..............................909 890-4353
Steve Mansker, *CEO*
Michelle Van Dyke, *Treasurer*
Mark C Hamilton DC, *Vice Pres*
EMP: 50
SQ FT: 6,000
SALES (est): 1.7MM **Privately Held**
WEB: www.cornerstonemedical.com
SIC: 8041 Offices & clinics of chiropractors

(P-20154)
**HAYWARD AREA RECREATION
PKDIST**
1099 E St, Hayward (94541-5210)
PHONE..............................510 881-6700
John Gouveia, *General Mgr*
EMP: 100
SALES (corp-wide): 34.9MM **Privately
Held**
SIC: 8041 Offices & clinics of chiropractors
PA: Hayward Area Recreation & Pk.Dist
1099 E St
Hayward CA 94541
510 670-1665

(P-20155)
**LANDMARK HEALTHCARE
SVCS INC (DH)**
1610 Arden Way Ste 280, Sacramento
(95815-4050)
PHONE..............................800 638-4557
Adam Boehler, *CEO*
Christopher Goldsmith, *President*
Carol Devol, *CFO*

EMP: 120
SQ FT: 330,215
SALES (est): 7.8MM
SALES (corp-wide): 100B **Publicly Held**
WEB: www.lmhealthcare.com
SIC: 8041 8049 Offices & clinics of chiro-
practors; acupuncturist
HQ: Carecore National, Llc
400 Buckwalter Place Blvd
Bluffton SC 29910
800 918-8924

(P-20156)
**S CA UNIVERSITY HLTH
SCIENCES**
Also Called: Los Angles Cllege Chiropractic
P.O. Box 1166 (90609-1166)
PHONE..............................562 947-8755
John Scaringe, *Branch Mgr*
EMP: 50
SALES (corp-wide): 24.2MM **Privately
Held**
SIC: 8041 Offices & clinics of chiropractors
PA: Southern California University Of
Health Sciences
16200 Amber Valley Dr
Whittier CA 90604
562 947-8755

8042 Offices & Clinics Of Optometrists

(P-20157)
**FIRSTSIGHT VISION SERVICES
INC (DH)**
1202 Monte Vista Ave # 17, Upland
(91786-8208)
PHONE..............................909 920-5008
Robert K Patton, *President*
Joseph T Heidelman, *CFO*
EMP: 55
SALES (est): 11.7MM
SALES (corp-wide): 1.3B **Publicly Held**
SIC: 8042 Specialized optometrists
HQ: National Vision, Inc.
2435 Commerce Ave # 2200
Duluth GA 30096
770 822-3600

(P-20158)
**LINDEN OPTOMETRY A PROF
CORP**
Also Called: Pasadena Vision
477 E Colorado Blvd, Pasadena
(91101-2024)
PHONE..............................323 681-5678
Allan Linfat, *President*
William J Linden, *Shareholder*
Elianna Samaniego, *Human Res Mgr*
EMP: 100
SALES (est): 7.1MM **Privately Held**
SIC: 8042 Specialized optometrists

(P-20159)
PACIFIC VISION SERVICES INC
1900 E Washington St, Colton
(92324-4614)
PHONE..............................909 824-6090
Christopher Blanton, *President*
EMP: 90
SQ FT: 5,000
SALES (est): 7.4MM **Privately Held**
WEB: www.visioncarebylaser.com
SIC: 8042 Offices & clinics of optometrists

8049 Offices & Clinics Of Health Practitioners, NEC

(P-20160)
A IS FOR APPLE INC
1485 Saratoga Ave Ste 200, San Jose
(95129-4965)
PHONE..............................877 991-0009
Marilyn Freeman, *President*
John Freeman, *Vice Pres*
Chrystala Nikolaou, *Supervisor*
EMP: 113
SALES: 6MM **Privately Held**
SIC: 8049 Speech pathologist

(P-20161)
ADDUS HEALTHCARE INC
2851 Park Marina Dr # 150, Redding (96001-2813)
PHONE.................................530 247-0858
Michele Dugar, *Branch Mgr*
EMP: 80 **Publicly Held**
WEB: www.addus.com
SIC: **8049** 8011 Nurses & other medical assistants; clinic, operated by physicians
HQ: Addus Healthcare, Inc.
2300 Warrenville Rd
Downers Grove IL 60515
630 296-3400

(P-20162)
AMN HEALTHCARE SERVICES INC
Also Called: American Mobile Healthcare
12400 High Bluff Dr # 100, San Diego (92130-3077)
PHONE.................................858 792-0711
Ralph Henderson, *President*
EMP: 750
SALES (corp-wide): 1.9B **Publicly Held**
WEB: www.amnhealthcare.com
SIC: **8049** Physical therapist; nurses & other medical assistants
PA: Amn Healthcare Services, Inc.
12400 High Bluff Dr
San Diego CA 92130
866 871-8519

(P-20163)
APEX HEALTHCARE MED CTR INC (PA)
Also Called: Apex Medical Group Lab
2390 E Florida Ave # 201, Hemet (92544-4707)
PHONE.................................951 765-0700
Kali P Chaudhuri MD, *President*
Surya Reddy MD, *Treasurer*
Herman Mathia MD, *Admin Sec*
EMP: 60
SALES (est): 2.5MM **Privately Held**
SIC: **8049** Physical therapist

(P-20164)
BACCI GLINN PHYSCL THERAPY INC
5533 W Hillsdale Ave A, Visalia (93291-5138)
P.O. Box 7779 (93290-7779)
PHONE.................................559 733-2478
Robert Bacci, *President*
James Glinn, *Vice Pres*
EMP: 50
SALES (est): 3.2MM **Privately Held**
SIC: **8049** Physiotherapist; physical therapist

(P-20165)
BURGER PHYSCL THERAPY SVCS INC (HQ)
Also Called: Burger Physcl Thrapy Rhblttion
1301 E Bidwell St Ste 201, Folsom (95630-3565)
PHONE.................................916 983-5900
Carol Burger, *President*
Elizabeth Johnson, *Human Resources*
Felicia Krieger, *Manager*
EMP: 140
SALES (est): 4.3MM **Privately Held**
SIC: **8049** Physical therapist

(P-20166)
BURGER PHYSICAL THERAPY
1301 E Bidwell St Ste 101, Folsom (95630-3565)
PHONE.................................916 983-5900
Carol K Burger, *President*
EMP: 50
SQ FT: 5,800
SALES (est): 1MM **Privately Held**
SIC: **8049** 8093 Physical therapist; rehabilitation center, outpatient treatment; speech defect clinic
PA: Burger Rehabilitation Systems, Inc.
1301 E Bidwell St Ste 201
Folsom CA 95630

(P-20167)
BURGER RHBLITATION SYSTEMS INC
2101 Stone Blvd Ste 175, West Sacramento (95691-4055)
PHONE.................................916 617-2400
EMP: 71 **Privately Held**
SIC: **8049** Physical therapist
PA: Burger Rehabilitation Systems, Inc.
1301 E Bidwell St Ste 201
Folsom CA 95630

(P-20168)
BURGER RHBLITATION SYSTEMS INC
6614 Mercy Ct Ste C, Fair Oaks (95628-3167)
PHONE.................................916 863-5785
Carol Burger, *Branch Mgr*
Jack Lomba, *Manager*
EMP: 71 **Privately Held**
SIC: **8049** Physical therapist
PA: Burger Rehabilitation Systems, Inc.
1301 E Bidwell St Ste 201
Folsom CA 95630

(P-20169)
BURGER RHBLITATION SYSTEMS INC (PA)
1301 E Bidwell St Ste 201, Folsom (95630-3565)
PHONE.................................800 900-8491
Carol K Burger, *President*
Babak Amali, *Vice Pres*
Eric Burger, *Business Dir*
Carol Burger, *Data Proc Staff*
Joanne Walder,
EMP: 200
SQ FT: 5,000
SALES (est): 12.9MM **Privately Held**
SIC: **8049** Occupational therapist; speech specialist; physical therapist

(P-20170)
CENTER FOR AUTISM & (PA)
21600 Oxnard St Ste 1800, Woodland Hills (91367-7807)
PHONE.................................818 345-2345
Doreen Granpeesheh, *Director*
Mark Keller, *CFO*
Katharine Gutshall, *Admin Mgr*
Aubrey Nigoza, *Admin Mgr*
Alva Powell, *CTO*
EMP: 143
SALES (est): 51.6MM **Privately Held**
WEB: www.centerforautism.com
SIC: **8049** Clinical psychologist

(P-20171)
COMMUNITY THERAPIES
Also Called: Community Therapies Baby Steps
19040 Soledad Canyon Rd, Santa Clarita (91351-3363)
P.O. Box 432, Lancaster (93584-0432)
PHONE.................................661 945-7878
Roy Jensen, *Owner*
EMP: 50 EST: 1996
SALES (est): 474.7K **Privately Held**
WEB: www.babysteps.com
SIC: **8049** Speech therapist

(P-20172)
COMPREHENSIVE AUTISM CTR INC
7839 University Ave # 105, La Mesa (91942-0476)
PHONE.................................951 813-4035
EMP: 67
SALES (corp-wide): 2MM **Privately Held**
SIC: **8049** Physical therapist
PA: Comprehensive Autism Center, Inc.
40485 Mrreta Hot Sprng Rd
Murrieta CA 92563
951 813-4034

(P-20173)
EMPERORS CLG TRDTNL ORNTL MDC
Also Called: Emperor's Clge & Clnc Tradtn
1807 Wilshire Blvd Ste B, Santa Monica (90403-5678)
PHONE.................................310 453-8383
Yun Kim, *President*
Bong Dal Kim, *Shareholder*
Alisa Daniels, *COO*
Marianne Ruane, *Program Mgr*
Sun Kim, *Bookkeeper*
EMP: 90
SQ FT: 10,000
SALES (est): 4.5MM **Privately Held**
SIC: **8049** Acupuncturist

(P-20174)
ENLOE MEDICAL CENTER
Also Called: Enloe Rehabilitation Center
340 W East Ave, Chico (95926-7238)
PHONE.................................530 332-6138
Diane Jones, *Administration*
Les Doll, *Opers Mgr*
Michelle Evans, *Director*
EMP: 100
SQ FT: 61,571
SALES (corp-wide): 528.3MM **Privately Held**
SIC: **8049** Physical therapist
PA: Enloe Medical Center
1531 Esplanade
Chico CA 95926
530 332-7300

(P-20175)
EQUINOX-76TH STREET INC
Also Called: Health Fitness America
1980 Main St Fl 4, Irvine (92614-7200)
PHONE.................................949 975-8400
Ian McFodden, *Manager*
EMP: 300
SALES (corp-wide): 10.6B **Privately Held**
SIC: **8049** 7991 Physical therapist; health club
HQ: Equinox-76th Street, Inc.
895 Broadway Fl 3
New York NY 10003

(P-20176)
FAMILY HEALTHCARE NETWORK
501 N Bridge St, Visalia (93291-5014)
PHONE.................................559 734-1939
Travis Chapin, *Principal*
Ivan Sarria, *Obstetrician*
EMP: 232
SALES (corp-wide): 114.6MM **Privately Held**
SIC: **8049** Acupuncturist
PA: Family Healthcare Network
305 E Center Ave
Visalia CA 93291
559 737-4700

(P-20177)
FORTA (PA)
Also Called: Fortanasce & Associates
671 W Naomi Ave, Arcadia (91007-7502)
P.O. Box 661150 (91066-1150)
PHONE.................................626 446-7027
Michael Fortanasce, *President*
EMP: 60
SQ FT: 10,250
SALES (est): 4.8MM **Privately Held**
WEB: www.fortanasce.com
SIC: **8049** Physiotherapist; physical therapist

(P-20178)
HOLMAN FAMILY COUNSELING INC (PA)
Also Called: Holman Group, The
9451 Corbin Ave Ste 100, Northridge (91324-1662)
PHONE.................................818 704-1444
Ron Holman PHD, *President*
Margaret Dykinga, *Vice Pres*
Linda Holman, *Vice Pres*
EMP: 66
SQ FT: 40,000
SALES (est): 8.4MM **Privately Held**
SIC: **8049** Clinical psychologist

(P-20179)
INLAND EMPIRE THERAPY PROVIDER (PA)
Also Called: Life Enchancing Therapies
1150 N Mountain Ave # 214, Upland (91786-3668)
PHONE.................................909 985-7905
James W Milton, *President*
EMP: 65
SALES (est): 2MM **Privately Held**
SIC: **8049** Physical therapist; speech therapist; occupational therapist

(P-20180)
INLAND VALLEY PARTNERS LLC
Also Called: INLAND VALLEY CARE & REHAB CTR
250 W Artesia St, Pomona (91768-1807)
PHONE.................................909 623-7100
Robert Nelson,
Sylvia Johnson, *Records Dir*
Elizabeth Casey,
Phil Chase,
Susan Chase,
EMP: 250
SALES: 23.6MM **Privately Held**
SIC: **8049** Nurses & other medical assistants

(P-20181)
INSTITUTE FOR APPLIED BEHAVIOR (PA)
Also Called: Iaba
5777 W Century Blvd # 675, Los Angeles (90045-5600)
PHONE.................................310 649-0499
Gary W Lavigna PHD, *President*
▲ EMP: 140
SQ FT: 3,000
SALES (est): 11.9MM **Privately Held**
WEB: www.iaba.com
SIC: **8049** 8741 8093 Clinical psychologist; management services; specialty outpatient clinics

(P-20182)
INSTITUTE FOR APPLIED BEHAVIOR
Also Called: Iaba
2310 E Ponderosa Dr Ste 1, Camarillo (93010-4747)
PHONE.................................805 987-5886
Gary Lavigna, *Director*
EMP: 170
SALES (corp-wide): 11.9MM **Privately Held**
WEB: www.iaba.com
SIC: **8049** 8399 Clinical psychologist; community development groups
PA: Institute For Applied Behavior Analysis, A Psychological Corporation
5777 W Century Blvd # 675
Los Angeles CA 90045
310 649-0499

(P-20183)
INSTITUTE FOR APPLIED BEHAVIOR
Also Called: Institute Applied Bhvior Anlis
19510 Ventura Blvd # 204, Tarzana (91356-2969)
PHONE.................................818 881-1933
Fax: 818 881-1835
EMP: 61
SALES (corp-wide): 17.3MM **Privately Held**
SIC: **8049** 8322 8093
PA: Institute For Applied Behavior Analysis, A Psychological Corporation
5777 W Century Blvd # 675
Los Angeles CA 90045
310 649-0499

(P-20184)
INTERCARE THERAPY INC
4221 Wilshire Blvd 300a, Los Angeles (90010-3537)
PHONE.................................323 866-1880
Naomi Heller, *President*
Eri Heller, *Vice Pres*
EMP: 130

SALES (est): 7.1MM **Privately Held**
SIC: 8049 Psychologist, psychotherapist &
hypnotist; occupational therapist; speech
specialist

(P-20185)
INTERFACE REHAB INC
774 S Placentia Ave # 200, Placentia
(92870-6826)
PHONE..................................714 646-8300
Anant B Desai, *CEO*
Falguni Desai, *Admin Sec*
EMP: 657
SQ FT: 10,000
SALES (est): 31.6MM **Privately Held**
WEB: www.interfacerehab.com
SIC: 8049 Physical therapist; speech spe-
cialist

(P-20186)
INTERGRO REHAB SERVICE
1922 N Broadway, Santa Ana
(92706-2610)
PHONE..................................714 901-4200
Sherrilyn Tong, *President*
Katie Jeffery, *Opers Staff*
EMP: 80
SQ FT: 2,000
SALES (est): 6.7MM **Privately Held**
WEB: www.intergrorehab.com
SIC: 8049 Physical therapist; speech spe-
cialist; occupational therapist

(P-20187)
**INTERSTATE RHBLTATION SVCS
LLC (PA)**
333 E Glenoaks Blvd # 204, Glendale
(91207-2074)
PHONE..................................818 244-5656
James Pietsch, *Owner*
James Peach, *Executive*
Beth Cera-Celo,
Sandy Pietsch,
EMP: 120
SALES (est): 3.9MM **Privately Held**
WEB: www.interstaterehab.com
SIC: 8049 Physical therapist

(P-20188)
LEAD STAFFING CORPORATION
216 S Citrus St Ste 397, West Covina
(91791-2144)
PHONE..................................800 928-5561
Lilian Nyamoita, *CEO*
EMP: 225
SALES (est): 3.5MM **Privately Held**
SIC: 8049 7363 Nurses & other medical
assistants; medical help service

(P-20189)
LOCUMS UNLIMITED LLC
4141 Jutland Dr Ste 305, San Diego
(92117-3658)
PHONE..................................619 550-3763
Sigrid Boring,
Christa Folkers, *Vice Pres*
Gerald Cohen, *Recruiter*
Ian McNeil, *Recruiter*
Emma Nowak, *Opers Staff*
EMP: 420
SALES (est): 43.2K **Privately Held**
SIC: 8049 Nurses & other medical assis-
tants
PA: Aya Healthcare, Inc.
5930 Cornerstone Ct W # 300
San Diego CA 92121

(P-20190)
**MOUNTAIN VIEW PHYSICAL
THERAPY**
Also Called: Inland Hand Therapy & Rehab
299 W Fthill Blvd Ste 200, Upland (91786)
PHONE..................................909 949-6235
Catherine Konn, *President*
EMP: 54
SALES (est): 816.5K **Privately Held**
SIC: 8049 Physical therapist

(P-20191)
OROVILLE HOSPITAL
Also Called: Golden Vly Occpational Therapy
2353 Myers St Ste B, Oroville
(95966-5334)
PHONE..................................530 538-8700
Trish Hopps, *Branch Mgr*

EMP: 55
SALES (corp-wide): 286.9MM **Privately
Held**
SIC: 8049 Physical therapist
PA: Oroville Hospital
2767 Olive Hwy
Oroville CA 95966
530 533-8500

(P-20192)
**PHYSICAL REHABILITATION
NETWRK**
2833 Junction Ave Ste 206, San Jose
(95134-1920)
P.O. Box 612260 (95161-2260)
PHONE..................................408 570-0510
Fax: 408 570-0516
EMP: 50 **Privately Held**
SIC: 8049 8742
PA: Physical Rehabilitation Network
5962 La Place Ct Ste 170
Carlsbad CA 92011

(P-20193)
**PHYSICAL RHBLTATION
NETWRK LLC (PA)**
3025 Corte Del Nogal, Carlsbad (92011)
PHONE..................................760 931-8310
Bruce McDaniel, *CEO*
Galen Danielson, *President*
Craig Rettke, *President*
James Ripp, *President*
Tim Varley, *Vice Pres*
EMP: 75
SALES (est): 51.4MM **Privately Held**
SIC: 8049 8011 8093 Physiotherapist;
sports medicine specialist, physician; re-
habilitation center, outpatient treatment

(P-20194)
**PHYSICAL THERAPY HAND
CTRS INC (PA)**
540 S Andreasen Dr Ste C, Escondido
(92029-1916)
PHONE..................................760 294-9800
David Boutelle, *President*
Barbara J Boutelle, *Vice Pres*
EMP: 69
SALES (est): 4MM **Privately Held**
WEB: www.pthc-pt.com
SIC: 8049 Physiotherapist; physical thera-
pist

(P-20195)
**PHYSICAL THERAPY HAND
CTRS INC**
Also Called: Valley Physical Theraphy
1815 E Valley Pkwy Ste 5, Escondido
(92027-2550)
PHONE..................................760 233-9655
Mike Morasel, *Manager*
EMP: 50
SALES (corp-wide): 4MM **Privately Held**
WEB: www.pthc-pt.com
SIC: 8049 Physical therapist
PA: Physical Therapy & Hand Centers, Inc.
540 S Andreasen Dr Ste C
Escondido CA 92029
760 294-9800

(P-20196)
**POMONA VALLEY HOSPITAL
MED CTR**
Also Called: Pamona Valley Physical Therapy
1775 Monte Vista Ave, Claremont
(91711-2916)
PHONE..................................909 621-7956
Joseph Bomgardner, *Director*
EMP: 70
SALES (corp-wide): 631.3MM **Privately
Held**
WEB: www.pvhmc.org
SIC: 8049 Physical therapist
PA: Pomona Valley Hospital Medical Center
1798 N Garey Ave
Pomona CA 91767
909 865-9500

(P-20197)
R & R PROFESSION
Also Called: R and R Professional Medical
2216 S El Camino Real # 211, Oceanside
(92054-6369)
PHONE..................................760 754-9020

George Hebeler, *President*
Renee Hebeler, *CFO*
Rachel Sterling, *Vice Pres*
EMP: 150
SQ FT: 900
SALES (est): 3.6MM **Privately Held**
SIC: 8049 7363 7361 Nurses, registered
& practical; help supply services; employ-
ment agencies

(P-20198)
R DS FOR HEALTHCARE
Also Called: Body Transformations
1420 W Kettleman Ln N5, Lodi
(95242-4557)
PHONE..................................209 333-2115
Terri Novadinavich, *Owner*
EMP: 50
SALES (est): 1.2MM **Privately Held**
SIC: 8049 Nutrition specialist

(P-20199)
**RANCHO PHYSICAL THERAPY
INC**
277 Rancheros Dr, San Marcos
(92069-2976)
PHONE..................................760 752-1011
James Lin, *Branch Mgr*
EMP: 177
SALES (corp-wide): 15MM **Privately
Held**
SIC: 8049 8011 Physical therapist; offices
& clinics of medical doctors
PA: Rancho Physical Therapy, Inc.
24630 Washington Ave # 200
Murrieta CA 92562
951 696-9353

(P-20200)
**RANCHO PHYSICAL THERAPY
INC (PA)**
24630 Washington Ave # 200, Murrieta
(92562-6177)
PHONE..................................951 696-9353
John Waite, *CEO*
Greg Smith, *Principal*
Pedro Romero, *Phys Thrpy Dir*
Jennifer Orr,
Bill Atkins,
EMP: 230
SALES: 15MM **Privately Held**
SIC: 8049 8093 Physical therapist; respi-
ratory therapy clinic

(P-20201)
**RIVER OAK CENTER FOR
CHILDREN**
9412 Big Horn Blvd Ste 6, Elk Grove
(95758-1101)
PHONE..................................916 226-2800
Laurie Clothier, *Branch Mgr*
EMP: 200
SALES (corp-wide): 17.3MM **Privately
Held**
SIC: 8049 Clinical psychologist
PA: River Oak Center For Children
5445 Laurel Hills Dr
Sacramento CA 95841
916 609-5100

(P-20202)
**SAN LUIS PHYSICAL THERAPY
(PA)**
Also Called: San Luis Sports Physical Therp
1106 Walnut St 110, San Luis Obispo
(93401-2416)
PHONE..................................805 788-0805
Kelly M Sanders, *CEO*
Serena D Roda,
Julie Butler, *Director*
Richard Goldbach, *Director*
Randall Hill, *Director*
EMP: 50 EST: 2000
SALES (est): 3.5MM **Privately Held**
SIC: 8049 7231 Physiotherapist; nutrition-
ist; depilatory salon, electrolysis

(P-20203)
SCRIPPS HEALTH
237 Church Ave, Chula Vista (91910-2702)
PHONE..................................619 862-6600
EMP: 132
SALES (corp-wide): 2.9B **Privately Held**
SIC: 8049 Acupuncturist

PA: Scripps Health
10140 Campus Point Dr Ax415
San Diego CA 92121
800 727-4777

(P-20204)
**SIMI VLY HOSP & HLTH CARE
SVCS (HQ)**
Also Called: Therapy & Rehabilitation Ctrs
2975 Sycamore Dr, Simi Valley
(93065-1201)
PHONE..................................805 955-6000
Margaret Peterson, *President*
Mitchell Solomon,
Caroline Esparza, *President*
Clif Patten, *CFO*
Ann Svolos, *Risk Mgmt Dir*
EMP: 96
SALES: 138.1MM
SALES (corp-wide): 4.1B **Privately Held**
SIC: 8049 Physical therapist
PA: Adventist Health System/West
2100 Douglas Blvd
Roseville CA 95661
916 781-2000

(P-20205)
SUTTER MEDICAL FOUNDATION
1014 N Market Blvd Ste 20, Sacramento
(95834-1986)
PHONE..................................916 924-7764
Judi Monday, *Branch Mgr*
EMP: 519 **Privately Held**
SIC: 8049 8011 Physical therapist; offices
& clinics of medical doctors
PA: Sutter Valley Medical Foundation
2700 Gateway Oaks Dr
Sacramento CA 95833

(P-20206)
**TEXAS HOME HEALTH AMERICA
LP (PA)**
1455 Auto Center Dr # 200, Ontario
(91761-2239)
PHONE..................................972 201-3800
Steve Abshire, *Partner*
Judy Bishop, *Partner*
Mark Lamp, *Partner*
Duff Whitaker, *Partner*
EMP: 100 EST: 1969
SQ FT: 18,000
SALES (est): 119.3MM **Privately Held**
WEB: www.txhha.com
SIC: 8049 Nurses, registered & practical

(P-20207)
**THERAPEUTIC ASSOCIATES
INC**
Also Called: Physical Therapy Unit
Saint Joseph Hospital, Burbank (91505)
PHONE..................................818 843-5111
Julianne Courtney, *Manager*
EMP: 65
SALES (corp-wide): 68.3MM **Privately
Held**
SIC: 8049 Physical therapist
PA: Therapeutic Associates, Inc.
20829 72nd Ave S Ste 710
Kent WA 98032
253 872-6028

(P-20208)
THERAPEUTIC PATHWAYS INC
Also Called: Candle Center The
2775 Cottage Way Ste 8, Sacramento
(95825-1220)
PHONE..................................916 489-1376
Coleen R Sparkman, *Director*
EMP: 70
SALES (corp-wide): 11.9MM **Privately
Held**
SIC: 8049 Clinical psychologist
PA: Therapeutic Pathways, Inc.
1115 14th St
Modesto CA 95354
209 572-2589

(P-20209)
THERAPY FOR KIDS INC
Also Called: Gallagher Pediatric Therapy
233 Orangefair Mall, Fullerton
(92832-3038)
PHONE..................................714 870-6116
Mary K Gallagher, *President*

Gene Riddle, *CFO*
Jessica Alter,
Stacy Cobbs,
Jennifer Leghart, *Manager*
EMP: 50
SALES (est): 2.7MM **Privately Held**
WEB: www.gptkids.com
SIC: 8049 Occupational therapist

(P-20210)
TIMOTHY EVERITT
Also Called: Newbury Park Clinic
1000 Newbury Rd Ste 135, Newbury Park
(91320-6437)
PHONE......................805 214-9933
Timothy Everitt, *Owner*
EMP: 50
SALES (est): 88K **Privately Held**
SIC: 8049 Physical therapist

(P-20211)
**TRI COUNTY REGIONAL
CENTER**
2220 E Gonzales Rd 210a, Oxnard
(93036-8294)
PHONE......................805 485-3177
Gary Feldman, *President*
Sha Azedi, *Director*
EMP: 55
SALES (est): 1.7MM **Privately Held**
WEB: www.garyfeldman.com
SIC: 8049 Psychiatric social worker

(P-20212)
VALLEY NURSES
1450 W 9th St, Pomona (91766-2607)
PHONE......................714 549-2512
Bob Gill, *Owner*
EMP: 65
SALES (est): 2.5MM **Privately Held**
SIC: 8049 7361 Nurses & other medical
assistants; nurses' registry

8051 Skilled Nursing Facilities

(P-20213)
**1000 EXECUTIVE PARKWAY
LLC**
Also Called: Oroville Hosp Post Acute Ctr
1000 Executive Pkwy, Oroville
(95966-5100)
PHONE......................530 533-7335
Tina Nickolas, *Administration*
EMP: 161
SALES: 14.2MM **Privately Held**
SIC: 8051 Mental retardation hospital

(P-20214)
1130 W LA PALMA AVE INC
Also Called: La Palma Nursing Center
4115 E Broadway, Long Beach
(90803-1532)
PHONE......................562 930-0777
Brenda Mandelbaum, *CEO*
Janet Mandelbaum, *Vice Pres*
Joseph Berkowitz, *Administration*
EMP: 90
SALES (est): 1MM **Privately Held**
SIC: 8051 Skilled nursing care facilities

(P-20215)
1135 N LEISURE CT INC
Also Called: Leisure Court Nursing Center
1135 N Leisure Ct, Anaheim (92801-2939)
PHONE......................714 772-1353
Patricia Smith, *Director*
Aura Galindo, *Administration*
EMP: 130 **EST:** 1965
SQ FT: 15,000
SALES (est): 6.1MM **Privately Held**
SIC: 8051 Skilled nursing care facilities

(P-20216)
3067 ORANGE AVENUE LLC
Also Called: Anaheim Crest Nursing Center
3067 W Orange Ave, Anaheim
(92804-3156)
PHONE......................714 827-2440
Alireza Talebi,
Joanna Rabanes, *Human Res Dir*
Jacob Wintner,
EMP: 120

SALES (est): 3.2MM **Privately Held**
SIC: 8051 Skilled nursing care facilities

(P-20217)
A B C D ASSOCIATES
Also Called: Casa Coloma Health Care Center
10410 Coloma Rd, Rancho Cordova
(95670-2108)
PHONE......................916 363-4843
Deborah Portela, *Administration*
Arden Millermon, *Partner*
Betty Millermon, *Partner*
EMP: 106 **EST:** 1975
SQ FT: 37,000
SALES: 9.4MM **Privately Held**
SIC: 8051 8052 Skilled nursing care facilities; intermediate care facilities

(P-20218)
A F V W HEALTH CENTER
17050 Arnold Dr Ofc, Riverside
(92518-2879)
PHONE......................951 697-2025
James Melin, *President*
Charlie Lamb, *President*
Bruce Cameron, *COO*
Ervin Reed, *CFO*
EMP: 270
SALES (est): 2.3MM **Privately Held**
SIC: 8051 Convalescent home with continuous nursing care

(P-20219)
**ACCREDITED NURSING
SERVICES**
Also Called: Accredited Nursing Care
80 S Lake Ave Ste 630, Pasadena
(91101-4971)
PHONE......................626 573-1234
Teresa Salvino, *Manager*
EMP: 80
SALES (corp-wide): 16.8MM **Privately Held**
WEB: www.accreditednursing.com
SIC: 8051 Skilled nursing care facilities
PA: Accredited Nursing Services
17141 Ventura Blvd # 201
Encino CA
818 986-6017

(P-20220)
**AEGIS SENIOR COMMUNITIES
LLC**
Also Called: Aegis Assisted Living
4050 Walnut Ave, Carmichael
(95608-1600)
PHONE......................916 972-1313
Terry Ervin, *Branch Mgr*
EMP: 340
SALES (corp-wide): 122.5MM **Privately Held**
SIC: 8051 Skilled nursing care facilities
PA: Senior Aegis Communities Llc
415 118th Ave Se
Bellevue WA 98005
866 688-5829

(P-20221)
AGEMARK CORPORATION (PA)
25 Avenida De Orinda, Orinda
(94563-2305)
PHONE......................925 257-4671
Richard J Westin, *Ch of Bd*
Jesse A Pittore, *CEO*
James P Tolley, *CFO*
Linda Larkin, *Vice Pres*
Michael Pittore, *Vice Pres*
EMP: 209
SQ FT: 2,100
SALES (est): 13.5MM **Privately Held**
SIC: 8051 Convalescent home with continuous nursing care

(P-20222)
**AHMC GARFIELD MEDICAL CTR
LP**
525 N Garfield Ave, Monterey Park
(91754-1202)
PHONE......................626 573-2222
Patrick Petre, *CEO*
Steve Maekewa, *Partner*
Ericka Smith, *COO*
Helen Razon, *Executive Asst*
Carmen Sendis, *Executive Asst*

EMP: 150
SALES (est): 195.3MM
SALES (corp-wide): 572.3MM **Privately Held**
WEB: www.garfieldmedicalcenter.com
SIC: 8051 8062 Skilled nursing care facilities; general medical & surgical hospitals
PA: Ahmc Healthcare Inc.
1000 S Fremont Ave Unit 6
Alhambra CA 91803
626 943-7526

(P-20223)
AIR FORCE VILLAGE WEST INC
Also Called: VILLAGE WEST HEALTH CENTER
17050 Arnold Dr, Riverside (92518-2806)
PHONE......................951 697-2000
James L Melin, *President*
Ervin Reed, *CFO*
Charles Dalton, *Vice Pres*
EMP: 350
SQ FT: 494,000
SALES: 5.7MM **Privately Held**
WEB: www.afvw.com
SIC: 8051 8052 Convalescent home with continuous nursing care; intermediate care facilities

(P-20224)
**ALAMEDA HLTHCARE &
WELLNSS CTR**
Also Called: Alameda Healthcare Wellness Ctr
430 Willow St, Alameda (94501-6130)
PHONE......................510 523-8857
Sharrod Brooks,
Brenna McDaniel,
Sol Healthcare LLC,
Sol Majer,
EMP: 99
SALES (est): 4.2MM **Privately Held**
SIC: 8051 Convalescent home with continuous nursing care

(P-20225)
**ALAMITOS-BELMONT REHAB
INC**
Also Called: Alamitos Blmont Rhblttion Hosp
3901 E 4th St, Long Beach (90814-1632)
PHONE......................562 434-8421
Darian Dahl, *Administration*
Nancy Graham, *Records Dir*
Raquel Quijano, *Records Dir*
Mark Hall, *Administration*
Arlene Donato, *Human Res Dir*
EMP: 150 **EST:** 1969
SQ FT: 30,000
SALES: 10.5MM **Privately Held**
WEB: www.alamitosbelmont.com
SIC: 8051 Skilled nursing care facilities

(P-20226)
**ALHAMBRA CONVALESCENT
HOSP LLC**
331 Ilene St, Martinez (94553-2631)
PHONE......................925 228-2020
Nina Gilbert, *Administration*
Walter Peters, *Director*
EMP: 60
SALES: 3.2MM **Privately Held**
SIC: 8051 8322 Convalescent home with continuous nursing care; rehabilitation services

(P-20227)
**ALHAMBRA HEALTHCARE &
WELLNESS**
415 S Garfield Ave, Alhambra
(91801-3838)
PHONE......................626 282-3151
Sharrod Brooks, *Partner*
EMP: 99 **EST:** 2012
SALES: 10.4MM **Privately Held**
SIC: 8051 Mental retardation hospital

(P-20228)
ALMAVIA OF SAN FRANCISCO
1 Thomas More Way, San Francisco
(94132-2914)
PHONE......................415 337-1339
Janeane Randolph, *Owner*
EMP: 60
SALES (est): 1.6MM **Privately Held**
SIC: 8051 Convalescent home with continuous nursing care

(P-20229)
AMADA ENTERPRISES INC
Also Called: View Heights Convalescent Hosp
12619 Avalon Blvd, Los Angeles
(90061-2727)
PHONE......................323 757-1881
Shedrick D Jones, *CEO*
John Jones, *Administration*
Ana Chavez, *Facilities Dir*
EMP: 135
SQ FT: 36,600
SALES (est): 6.9MM **Privately Held**
WEB: www.viewheights.com
SIC: 8051 Convalescent home with continuous nursing care

(P-20230)
AMERICAN RETIREMENT CORP
2107 Ocean Ave, Santa Monica
(90405-2299)
PHONE......................310 399-3227
EMP: 112
SALES (corp-wide): 4.7B **Publicly Held**
SIC: 8051 Skilled nursing care facilities
HQ: American Retirement Corporation
111 Westwood Pl Ste 200
Brentwood TN 37027
615 221-2250

(P-20231)
**APPLE VLY CNVALESCENT
HOSP INC**
Also Called: Apple Valley Care & Rehab
1035 Gravenstein Hwy N, Sebastopol
(95472)
PHONE......................707 823-7675
Jeff Barbieri, *Administration*
Garrin Obrien, *Records Dir*
Sharon Conrotto, *Executive*
Sara Reyes, *Office Mgr*
Brett Moore, *Administration*
EMP: 120
SQ FT: 20,000
SALES (est): 8.1MM **Privately Held**
WEB: www.applevalleyrehab.com
SIC: 8051 8322 Convalescent home with continuous nursing care; rehabilitation services

(P-20232)
APPLEWOOD CARE CENTER
1090 Rio Ln, Sacramento (95822-1706)
PHONE......................916 446-2506
Bill Drennen, *Administration*
EMP: 50
SALES (est): 2.7MM
SALES (corp-wide): 9.4MM **Privately Held**
SIC: 8051 Skilled nursing care facilities
PA: Riverside Health Care Corporation
1469 Humboldt Rd Ste 175
Chico CA 95928
530 897-5100

(P-20233)
AQUINAS CORPORATION
Also Called: San Tomas Convalescent Hosp
3580 Payne Ave, San Jose (95117-2925)
PHONE......................408 248-7100
Ken Dunton, *Ch of Bd*
Julita Javier, *President*
EMP: 135 **EST:** 1974
SQ FT: 15,000
SALES (est): 9.9MM **Privately Held**
WEB: www.aquinascorp.com
SIC: 8051 8059 Convalescent home with continuous nursing care; convalescent home

(P-20234)
**ARROWHEAD CONVALESCENT
HOME**
Also Called: Arrowhead Home
4343 N Sierra Way, San Bernardino
(92407-3822)
PHONE......................909 886-4731
Joe Bolton, *President*
Don Popovich, *President*
EMP: 56
SQ FT: 6,000
SALES (est): 3MM **Privately Held**
SIC: 8051 Convalescent home with continuous nursing care

PRODUCTS & SVCS

(P-20235)
ARTESIA HEALTHCARE INC
Also Called: Alameda Care Center
925 W Alameda Ave, Burbank
(91506-2801)
PHONE....................818 843-1771
Lori De Kruif, Administration
EMP: 99
SALES (est): 3MM Privately Held
SIC: 8051 Mental retardation hospital

(P-20236)
ASH HOLDINGS LLC
Also Called: REDLANDS HEALTHCARE
CENTER
1620 W Fern Ave, Redlands (92373-4918)
PHONE....................909 793-2609
Novie Sitanggang, Administration
Scott Clawson, President
Suzette Banks, Info Tech Mgr
EMP: 85
SALES: 9.5MM Privately Held
SIC: 8051 Skilled nursing care facilities

(P-20237)
ASHLEY LTC INC
Also Called: Santa Rosa Convalescent Hosp
446 Arrowood Dr, Santa Rosa
(95407-7503)
PHONE....................707 528-2100
Robert O Benson, President
EMP: 60
SQ FT: 18,000
SALES (est): 3.4MM Privately Held
WEB: www.santarosaconvalescent.com
SIC: 8051 Convalescent home with contin-
uous nursing care

(P-20238)
**ASTORIA CONVALESCENT
HOSPITAL**
Also Called: Astoria Nursing & Rehab Center
14040 Astoria St, Sylmar (91342-2998)
PHONE....................818 367-5881
Grace Mercado, Exec Dir
EMP: 202
SQ FT: 50,000
SALES (est): 4.9MM Privately Held
SIC: 8051 8059 8322 Convalescent home
with continuous nursing care; convales-
cent home; rehabilitation services

(P-20239)
ATHERTON BAPTIST HOMES
214 S Atlantic Blvd, Alhambra
(91801-3298)
PHONE....................626 863-1710
Craig Statton, President
Dennis E McFadden, President
Jackie Pascual, CFO
Dale Torry, Vice Pres
Karlyn Flesch, Executive Asst
EMP: 200
SQ FT: 42,000
SALES: 19.5MM Privately Held
WEB: www.abh.org
SIC: 8051 Convalescent home with contin-
uous nursing care; extended care facility

(P-20240)
**ATLANTIC MEM HEALTHCARE
ASSOC (PA)**
Also Called: ATLANTIC MEMORIAL HEALTH-
CARE C
2750 Atlantic Ave, Long Beach
(90806-2713)
PHONE....................562 424-8101
Jake Rothey, Administration
EMP: 180
SALES: 10.6MM Privately Held
WEB: www.atlanticmemorial.com
SIC: 8051 Convalescent home with contin-
uous nursing care

(P-20241)
AUBURN OAKS CARE CENTER
3400 Bell Rd, Auburn (95603-9241)
PHONE....................650 949-7777
Ellen Kuykendall, President
Kevin Hadfield, Administration
EMP: 99
SALES (est): 3.3MM Privately Held
SIC: 8051 Convalescent home with contin-
uous nursing care

(P-20242)
AVALON CARE CEN
Also Called: Hy-Lond Hlth Care Cnter-Merced
3170 M St, Merced (95348-2403)
PHONE....................209 723-1056
Charles R Kirton,
EMP: 73
SALES (est): 2.2MM
SALES (corp-wide): 648.5MM Privately
Held
SIC: 8051 Skilled nursing care facilities
PA: Avalon Health Care, Inc.
206 N 2100 W Ste 300
Salt Lake City UT 84116
801 596-8844

(P-20243)
AVALON CARE CENTER
Also Called: Mark Twain Conv. Hospital
900 Mountain Ranch Rd, San Andreas
(95249-9713)
PHONE....................209 754-3823
Larry Washington, Administration
EMP: 101
SALES (est): 2.5MM
SALES (corp-wide): 648.5MM Privately
Held
SIC: 8051 Skilled nursing care facilities
PA: Avalon Health Care, Inc.
206 N 2100 W Ste 300
Salt Lake City UT 84116
801 596-8844

(P-20244)
**AVALON CARE CENTER -
MERCED**
Also Called: Franciscan Conv. Hospital
3169 M St, Merced (95348-2404)
PHONE....................209 722-6231
Larry Imperial, Administration
EMP: 74
SALES (est): 2.5MM
SALES (corp-wide): 648.5MM Privately
Held
SIC: 8051 Skilled nursing care facilities
PA: Avalon Health Care, Inc.
206 N 2100 W Ste 300
Salt Lake City UT 84116
801 596-8844

(P-20245)
**AVALON CARE CENTER -
MODESTO**
Also Called: Hy-Lond Hlth Care Cntr-Modesto
1900 Coffee Rd, Modesto (95355-2703)
PHONE....................209 526-1775
Randy Kirton, CEO
Donna Rooney, Officer
Michelle Marquez, Vice Pres
Sheree Clarke, Executive
Michelle Smith, Administration
EMP: 92 EST: 2003
SALES (est): 2.1MM
SALES (corp-wide): 648.5MM Privately
Held
SIC: 8051 Convalescent home with contin-
uous nursing care
PA: Avalon Health Care, Inc.
206 N 2100 W Ste 300
Salt Lake City UT 84116
801 596-8844

(P-20246)
**AVALON CARE CTR -
CHWCHLLA LLC**
Also Called: Chowchilla Conv. Center
1010 Ventura Ave, Chowchilla
(93610-2368)
PHONE....................559 665-4826
EMP: 74
SALES: 4.2MM
SALES (corp-wide): 648.5MM Privately
Held
SIC: 8051 Skilled nursing care facilities
PA: Avalon Health Care, Inc.
206 N 2100 W Ste 300
Salt Lake City UT 84116
801 596-8844

(P-20247)
**AVALON CARE CTR - MADERA
LLC**
Also Called: Avalon Health Care - Madera
1700 Howard Rd, Madera (93637-5131)
PHONE....................559 673-9278

Jim Lundy, Exec Dir
Mary Lee, Social Dir
EMP: 67
SALES (est): 2.4MM Privately Held
SIC: 8051 Convalescent home with contin-
uous nursing care

(P-20248)
**AVALON CARE CTR - MODESTO
LLC**
515 E Orangeburg Ave, Modesto
(95350-5510)
PHONE....................209 529-0516
Darla Lorenzen, Exec Dir
EMP: 65
SALES (est): 3.3MM
SALES (corp-wide): 648.5MM Privately
Held
SIC: 8051 Skilled nursing care facilities
PA: Avalon Health Care, Inc.
206 N 2100 W Ste 300
Salt Lake City UT 84116
801 596-8844

(P-20249)
**AVALON CARE CTR - NEWMAN
LLC**
Also Called: San Luis Care Center
709 N St, Newman (95360-1162)
PHONE....................209 862-2862
David Robinson,
EMP: 60
SALES (est): 1.1MM
SALES (corp-wide): 648.5MM Privately
Held
SIC: 8051 Skilled nursing care facilities
PA: Avalon Health Care, Inc.
206 N 2100 W Ste 300
Salt Lake City UT 84116
801 596-8844

(P-20250)
**AVALON CARE CTR - SONORA
LLC**
Also Called: AVALON HEALTH CARE
GROUP
19929 Greenley Rd, Sonora (95370-5996)
PHONE....................209 533-2500
Faye Lincoln, Vice Pres
EMP: 87
SALES: 19.7MM
SALES (corp-wide): 648.5MM Privately
Held
SIC: 8051 Skilled nursing care facilities
PA: Avalon Health Care, Inc.
206 N 2100 W Ste 300
Salt Lake City UT 84116
801 596-8844

(P-20251)
**AVE MARIA CONVALESCENT
HOSP**
Also Called: Ave Maria Senior Living
1249 Josselyn Canyon Rd, Monterey
(93940-5265)
PHONE....................831 373-1216
Barbara Reid, Exec Dir
Josefina Pimentel, Director
EMP: 62
SALES (est): 2.3MM Privately Held
SIC: 8051 8361 Convalescent home with
continuous nursing care; residential care

(P-20252)
AVENUE H LLC
35253 Avenue H, Yucaipa (92399-5415)
PHONE....................909 795-2476
Carrey Beers, Principal
Covey Christensen, Principal
EMP: 99
SALES (est): 324.2K Privately Held
SIC: 8051 Skilled nursing care facilities

(P-20253)
B-SPRING VALLEY LLC
Also Called: Brighton Place Spring Valley
9009 Campo Rd, Spring Valley
(91977-1112)
PHONE....................619 797-3991
Sharrod Brooks,
EMP: 91
SALES: 7.4MM Privately Held
SIC: 8051 Convalescent home with contin-
uous nursing care

(P-20254)
BAKERSFIELD HEALTHCARE
Also Called: Rehablttion Cntre of Bkrsfield
2211 Mount Vernon Ave, Bakersfield
(93306-3309)
PHONE....................661 872-2121
Sharrod Brooks,
EMP: 99
SALES (est): 2.6MM Privately Held
SIC: 8051 Mental retardation hospital

(P-20255)
BALBOA ENTERPRISES INC
Also Called: Mountain View Healthcare Ctr
2530 Solace Pl, Mountain View
(94040-4309)
PHONE....................650 961-6161
Karl Vitt, President
Sue Andersen, Food Svc Dir
Roland Garcia, Manager
Maria Camacho, Supervisor
EMP: 130
SQ FT: 30,000
SALES (est): 8.8MM Privately Held
WEB: www.mvhealthcare.com
SIC: 8051 Convalescent home with contin-
uous nursing care

(P-20256)
**BAY VIEW RHBILITATION HOSP
LLC**
516 Willow St, Alameda (94501-6132)
PHONE....................510 521-5600
Thomas Chambers, Mng Member
EMP: 99
SALES (est): 4.3MM Privately Held
SIC: 8051 8062 8361 Skilled nursing care
facilities; general medical & surgical hos-
pitals; rehabilitation center, residential:
health care incidental

(P-20257)
BAYSHORE HEALTHCARE INC
Also Called: Bella Vsta Trnstional Care Ctr
3033 Augusta St, San Luis Obispo
(93401-5820)
PHONE....................805 544-5100
Benjamin Flinders, CEO
Paul McLean, CFO
Johannah Tamba, Administration
EMP: 160
SQ FT: 43,000
SALES: 9.4MM Privately Held
SIC: 8051 Convalescent home with contin-
uous nursing care

(P-20258)
BEGROUP
Also Called: Royal Oaks Manor
1763 Royal Oaks Dr Ofc, Duarte
(91010-1989)
PHONE....................626 359-9371
EMP: 79
SALES (corp-wide): 20.3MM Privately
Held
SIC: 8051 Skilled nursing care facilities
PA: Be.Group
516 Burchett St
Glendale CA 91203
818 638-4563

(P-20259)
**BELLA VISTA HEALTHCARE
CENTER**
Also Called: Kf Bella Vista Health Care
933 E Deodar St, Ontario (91764-1309)
PHONE....................909 985-2731
Doug Ason, CEO
EMP: 100
SQ FT: 10,000
SALES (est): 4.6MM Privately Held
SIC: 8051 Skilled nursing care facilities

(P-20260)
**BENT TREE NURSING CENTER
INC**
Also Called: Garden Terrace Health Care Ctr
247 E Bobier Dr, Vista (92084-3026)
PHONE....................760 945-3033
Arch B Gilbert, President
Candy Rowland, Administration
EMP: 200
SQ FT: 57,000
SALES (est): 2.3MM Privately Held
SIC: 8051 Skilled nursing care facilities

(P-20261)
BERKLEY VLY CNVLSCENT HOSP INC
6600 Sepulveda Blvd, Van Nuys (91411-1203)
PHONE................................818 786-0020
Sol Galper, *President*
EMP: 150
SALES: 7.3MM **Privately Held**
SIC: 8051 Convalescent home with continuous nursing care

(P-20262)
BEVERLY WEST HEALTH CARE INC
1020 S Fairfax Ave, Los Angeles (90019-4401)
PHONE................................323 938-2451
Louise Koss, *President*
Glynis Kilpatrick, *Records Dir*
Lydia Cruz, *President*
EMP: 85
SQ FT: 23,848
SALES (est): 3.5MM **Privately Held**
SIC: 8051 Convalescent home with continuous nursing care

(P-20263)
BLYTHE NURSING CARE CENTER
Also Called: CORPRATE OFFICE
285 W Chanslor Way, Blythe (92225-1246)
PHONE................................760 922-8176
Sandra Blessing, *Owner*
David Shellmann, *Administration*
EMP: 64
SQ FT: 12,000
SALES: 3.8MM **Privately Held**
WEB: www.blythenursing.com
SIC: 8051 Convalescent home with continuous nursing care

(P-20264)
BRASWELLS YUCAIPA VALLEY C
35253 Avenue H, Yucaipa (92399-5415)
PHONE................................909 795-2476
James Braswell, *CEO*
EMP: 59
SALES (est): 879K **Privately Held**
SIC: 8051 Convalescent home with continuous nursing care

(P-20265)
BRIARCREST NURSING CENTER INC
5648 Gotham St, Bell (90201-5413)
PHONE................................562 927-2641
Jack Silverman, *President*
Wilson Park, *CFO*
EMP: 110
SALES: 11.7MM **Privately Held**
SIC: 8051 Skilled nursing care facilities

(P-20266)
BRIGHTON GARDENS INC
13101 Hartfield Ave, San Diego (92130-1511)
PHONE................................858 259-2222
Scott Polzin, *Manager*
EMP: 100
SALES (est): 2.5MM **Privately Held**
SIC: 8051 8052 Skilled nursing care facilities; intermediate care facilities

(P-20267)
BRIGHTON HEALTH ALLIANCE (PA)
Also Called: Brighton Place of San Diego
8322 Clairemont Mesa Blvd, San Diego (92111-1317)
PHONE................................619 461-0376
Berry T Crow, *President*
EMP: 83
SQ FT: 20,000
SALES (est): 3.2MM **Privately Held**
SIC: 8051 Convalescent home with continuous nursing care

(P-20268)
BRIGHTON PLACE EAST INC
8625 Lamar St, Spring Valley (91977-2518)
PHONE................................619 461-3222
Guy Reggev, *Administration*

EMP: 62
SQ FT: 11,500
SALES: 5.1MM **Privately Held**
SIC: 8051 Skilled nursing care facilities

(P-20269)
BRIGHTON PLACE SAN DIEGO
1350 Euclid Ave, San Diego (92105-5424)
PHONE................................619 263-2166
Cristin Whittaker, *Exec Dir*
EMP: 150
SQ FT: 12,000
SALES: 11MM **Privately Held**
SIC: 8051 Convalescent home with continuous nursing care

(P-20270)
BROADVIEW INC
Also Called: HIGH HAVEN
4570 Griffin Ave, Los Angeles (90031-1422)
PHONE................................323 221-9174
Micheal Fisher, *Administration*
EMP: 50
SQ FT: 24,000
SALES: 2.2MM **Privately Held**
SIC: 8051 Skilled nursing care facilities

(P-20271)
BROOKDALE LVING CMMUNITIES INC
Also Called: Brookdale Redwood City
485 Woodside Rd Ofc, Redwood City (94061-3890)
PHONE................................650 366-3900
Diane Morton, *Director*
Michelle Merritt, *Marketing Staff*
Shawn Cull, *Director*
EMP: 64
SALES (corp-wide): 4.7B **Publicly Held**
WEB: www.parkplace-spokane.com
SIC: 8051 Skilled nursing care facilities
HQ: Brookdale Living Communities, Inc.
515 N State St Ste 1750
Chicago IL 60654

(P-20272)
BROOKDALE SENIOR LIVING INC
Also Called: Brookdale Elk Grove
6727 Laguna Park Dr, Elk Grove (95758-5069)
PHONE................................916 683-1881
Ricky David, *Exec Dir*
EMP: 51
SALES (corp-wide): 4.7B **Publicly Held**
SIC: 8051 Skilled nursing care facilities
PA: Brookdale Senior Living
111 Westwood Pl Ste 400
Brentwood TN 37027
615 221-2250

(P-20273)
BUENA VENTURA CARE CENTER INC (PA)
1016 S Record Ave, Los Angeles (90023-2533)
PHONE................................323 268-0106
Vernon Aguirre, *Administration*
Steve Keh, *Vice Pres*
EMP: 75
SQ FT: 15,000
SALES: 6.6MM **Privately Held**
SIC: 8051 Convalescent home with continuous nursing care

(P-20274)
BUENA VISTA CARE CENTER INC
1440 S Euclid St, Anaheim (92802-2156)
PHONE................................714 535-7264
Firouzeh Fathi, *Persnl Dir*
EMP: 90
SQ FT: 27,613
SALES (est): 3.8MM **Privately Held**
WEB: www.buenavistacarecenter.com
SIC: 8051 Skilled nursing care facilities

(P-20275)
BURLINGTON CONVALESCENT HOSP (PA)
Also Called: VIEW PARK CONVALESCENT CENTER
845 S Burlington Ave, Los Angeles (90057-4296)
PHONE................................213 381-5585
Jacob Friedman, *President*
Ervin Friedman, *Vice Pres*
Kathleen Becker, *Administration*
EMP: 100
SQ FT: 5,000
SALES: 10.8MM **Privately Held**
SIC: 8051 8059 8052 Skilled nursing care facilities; convalescent home; intermediate care facilities

(P-20276)
BURLINGTON CONVALESCENT HOSP
Also Called: View Park Convalescent Center
3737 Don Felipe Dr, Los Angeles (90008-4210)
PHONE................................323 295-7737
Joe Voltes, *Manager*
Shanae Curl, *Human Res Dir*
EMP: 79
SQ FT: 40,000
SALES (corp-wide): 10.8MM **Privately Held**
SIC: 8051 Skilled nursing care facilities
PA: Burlington Convalescent Hospital
845 S Burlington Ave
Los Angeles CA 90057
213 381-5585

(P-20277)
C J HEALTH SERVICES INC
Also Called: Marina Convalescent Center
38650 Mission Blvd, Fremont (94536-4391)
PHONE................................510 793-3000
Catherine Joseph, *President*
EMP: 100
SQ FT: 5,000
SALES: 3.3MM **Privately Held**
SIC: 8051 Skilled nursing care facilities

(P-20278)
CAL SOUTHERN PRESBT HOMES
Also Called: Buena Vista Manor
802 Buena Vista St, Duarte (91010-1702)
PHONE................................626 359-8141
Judy Phornkein, *Manager*
EMP: 65
SALES (corp-wide): 84.4MM **Privately Held**
WEB: www.scths.com
SIC: 8051 Convalescent home with continuous nursing care
PA: Southern California Presbyterian Homes
516 Burchett St
Glendale CA 91203
818 247-0420

(P-20279)
CAL-COAST HEALTHCARE INC
Also Called: Hillside Care Center
81 Professional Ctr Pkwy, San Rafael (94903-2702)
PHONE................................415 479-5149
Stephen Rodrigues, *Administration*
Richard Martin, *Director*
EMP: 100
SQ FT: 28,000
SALES (est): 4.6MM **Privately Held**
SIC: 8051 Skilled nursing care facilities

(P-20280)
CALDWELL VENTURES LLC
Also Called: Prestige Asstd Lvng in Chico
1351 E Lassen Ave Ofc, Chico (95973-7700)
PHONE................................530 899-0814
Gordon Wiens, *Manager*
EMP: 50
SALES (corp-wide): 4.1MM **Privately Held**
SIC: 8051 Skilled nursing care facilities

PA: Caldwell Ventures, L.L.C.
7700 Ne Parkway Dr # 300
Vancouver WA 98662
360 735-7155

(P-20281)
CALIFORNIA CONVALESCENT HOSPTL
Also Called: Californian-Pasadena
120 Bellefontaine St, Pasadena (91105-3102)
PHONE................................626 793-5114
Luis Pages, *President*
Eva M Casner, *Treasurer*
Clyde L Casner, *Vice Pres*
Nancy Bower, *Administration*
EMP: 100
SQ FT: 30,000
SALES (est): 490.8K **Privately Held**
SIC: 8051 Convalescent home with continuous nursing care

(P-20282)
CALIFORNIA NURSING AND REHAB
Also Called: CALIFORNIA NURSING & REHABILIT
2299 N Indian Ave, Palm Springs (92262-3098)
PHONE................................760 325-2937
Kennon Shea, *Administration*
Victoria Shea, *Treasurer*
Linda Jackson, *Administration*
Shlomo Rechnitz,
EMP: 150
SQ FT: 22,000
SALES: 9.9MM **Privately Held**
SIC: 8051 Skilled nursing care facilities

(P-20283)
CALIMESA OPERATIONS LLC
Also Called: Calimesa Post Acute
13542 2nd St, Yucaipa (92399-5396)
PHONE................................909 795-2421
Jordan Thompson,
Covey Christensen,
EMP: 105 EST: 2015
SALES (est): 740K **Privately Held**
SIC: 8051 Skilled nursing care facilities

(P-20284)
CAMELLIA GARDENS CARE CTR
Also Called: CAMELLIA GARDENS CARE CENTER
1920 N Fair Oaks Ave, Pasadena (91103-1623)
PHONE................................626 798-6777
Pompeyo Rosales, *President*
Arlene Rosales, *Vice Pres*
EMP: 80
SALES: 8.3MM **Privately Held**
WEB: www.arpom.org
SIC: 8051 Convalescent home with continuous nursing care

(P-20285)
CAPISTRANO BEACH EXTENDED
35410 Del Rey, Capistrano Beach (92624-1814)
PHONE................................949 496-5786
Nora Deleon, *Administration*
EMP: 60
SALES (est): 1.8MM **Privately Held**
SIC: 8051 Skilled nursing care facilities

(P-20286)
CARE TECH INC
Also Called: Hill Cress Home
4280 Cypress Dr, San Bernardino (92407-2960)
PHONE................................909 882-2965
Carol Dichman, *Administration*
EMP: 70
SALES (corp-wide): 3.8MM **Privately Held**
SIC: 8051 Skilled nursing care facilities
PA: Care Tech Inc
401 N Central Ave Ste B
Upland CA 91786
909 373-3766

(P-20287)
CARE WITH DIGNITY HEALTHCARE
Also Called: Granite Hlls Convalescent Hosp
1340 E Madison Ave, El Cajon
(92021-8501)
PHONE................................619 447-1020
Lynn Festee, *Manager*
EMP: 100
SALES (corp-wide): 2.7MM **Privately Held**
SIC: 8051 Skilled nursing care facilities
PA: Care With Dignity Healthcare, Inc
8060 Frost St
San Diego CA 92123
858 278-4750

(P-20288)
CARE WITH DIGNITY HEALTHCARE (PA)
Also Called: Care With Dignity Convalescent
8060 Frost St, San Diego (92123-2703)
PHONE................................858 278-4750
Gary D Devoir, *President*
Jeannie Devoir, *Admin Sec*
EMP: 107
SQ FT: 20,000
SALES (est): 2.7MM **Privately Held**
SIC: 8051 Skilled nursing care facilities

(P-20289)
CAREAGE INC
Also Called: Mission De La Casa
2501 Alvin Ave, San Jose (95121-1660)
PHONE................................408 238-9751
Kim Nguyen, *Branch Mgr*
EMP: 50
SALES (corp-wide): 18.6MM **Privately Held**
SIC: 8051 Convalescent home with continuous nursing care
PA: Careage, Inc.
4411 Point Fosdick Dr Nw
Gig Harbor WA 98335
253 853-4457

(P-20290)
CARMICHAEL CARE INC
Also Called: Rosewood Rehabilitation
6041 Fair Oaks Blvd, Carmichael
(95608-4816)
PHONE................................916 483-8103
John L Sorensen, *President*
Donald Laws, *Shareholder*
David Sorensen, *Shareholder*
EMP: 140
SALES (est): 9.2MM **Privately Held**
SIC: 8051 Extended care facility

(P-20291)
CASAVINA FOUNDATION CORP
2501 Alvin Ave, San Jose (95121-1660)
PHONE................................408 238-9751
Ngai Nguyen, *President*
CHI Nguyen, *Admin Sec*
EMP: 187
SALES (est): 5MM **Privately Held**
SIC: 8051 Convalescent home with continuous nursing care

(P-20292)
CASTLE MANOR INC
Also Called: Castle Manor Convalescent Ctr
541 S V Ave, National City (91950-2828)
PHONE................................619 791-7900
Ruth Cheneweth, *President*
J Edwin Cheneweth, *Treasurer*
EMP: 98
SALES: 10.6MM **Privately Held**
SIC: 8051 Skilled nursing care facilities

(P-20293)
CATHEDRAL PIONEER CHURCH HOMES (PA)
Also Called: Pioneer House
415 P St Ofc, Sacramento (95814-5300)
PHONE................................916 442-4906
Calvin Hara, *Administration*
EMP: 96
SQ FT: 52,000
SALES: 3.9K **Privately Held**
SIC: 8051 8699 Skilled nursing care facilities; charitable organization

(P-20294)
CEDAR HOLDINGS LLC
Also Called: HIGHLAND PALMS HEALTH-CARE CENT
7534 Palm Ave, Highland (92346-3736)
PHONE................................909 862-0611
Ryan McCook, *Mng Member*
Carroll Collins, *Office Mgr*
Stephanie Lopez, *Telecom Exec*
Julie Smith, *Info Tech Mgr*
Myrna De Guzman,
EMP: 99
SALES: 10.2MM **Privately Held**
SIC: 8051 Skilled nursing care facilities

(P-20295)
CEDAR OPERATIONS LLC
Also Called: Cedar Mountain Post Acute
11970 4th St, Yucaipa (92399-2720)
PHONE................................909 790-2273
Covey Christensen,
EMP: 140
SALES (est): 108.7K
SALES (corp-wide): 1.2MM **Privately Held**
SIC: 8051 Skilled nursing care facilities
PA: Madison Creek Partners, Llc
701 Palomar Airport Rd
Carlsbad CA
760 518-6418

(P-20296)
CENTER OF REHABILITATION
9021 Knott Ave, Buena Park (90620-4138)
PHONE................................714 826-2330
Peter Madigan, *President*
Robert Nelson, *President*
EMP: 125
SALES (est): 5.5MM **Privately Held**
SIC: 8051 8059 Convalescent home with continuous nursing care; rest home, with health care

(P-20297)
CENTINELA SKILLED NURSING AND
950 S Flower St, Inglewood (90301-4186)
PHONE................................310 674-3216
Nichole Tons, *Vice Pres*
EMP: 99
SQ FT: 6,000
SALES (est): 711.8K **Privately Held**
SIC: 8051 Skilled nursing care facilities

(P-20298)
CENTINELA SKLLD NRSNG & WLLNSS
Also Called: Osage Hlthcare Wellness Centre
1001 S Osage Ave, Inglewood
(90301-4116)
PHONE................................310 674-3216
Chaim Kolodny, *Principal*
EMP: 99
SALES (est): 4.1MM **Privately Held**
SIC: 8051 Convalescent home with continuous nursing care

(P-20299)
CENTRAL GARDENS INC
Also Called: CENTRAL GARDENS CONVALESCENT H
1355 Ellis St, San Francisco (94115-4215)
PHONE................................415 567-2967
Irene Lieberman, *President*
David P Lieberman, *Treasurer*
Michael Lieberman, *Vice Pres*
Cleitus Jones, *Social Dir*
Paula Lieberman, *Admin Sec*
EMP: 136 EST: 1964
SALES: 8MM **Privately Held**
WEB: www.centralgardenssf.com
SIC: 8051 Convalescent home with continuous nursing care

(P-20300)
CENTRAL VLY SPECIALTY HOSP INC
730 17th St, Modesto (95354-1209)
PHONE................................209 248-7700
Gia Smith, *CEO*
Reyle Hutchins, *Analyst*
Chris Lowey, *Case Mgr*
EMP: 93 EST: 2012
SALES: 40.7MM **Privately Held**
SIC: 8051 Skilled nursing care facilities

(P-20301)
CENTURY SKILL CARE
Also Called: Century Skilled Nursing Care
301 Centinela Ave, Inglewood
(90302-3231)
PHONE................................310 672-1012
Oscar Parel, *Exec Dir*
Christopher Arias, *Administration*
Jamshid Niknam, *Director*
EMP: 100
SALES (est): 5.5MM **Privately Held**
SIC: 8051 Skilled nursing care facilities

(P-20302)
CF MERCED LA SIERRA LLC
Also Called: La Sierra Care Center
2424 M St, Merced (95340-2808)
PHONE................................209 723-4224
Carson Day, *President*
Bryan Tanner, *COO*
EMP: 82
SQ FT: 15,000
SALES (est): 29.2MM
SALES (corp-wide): 125.3MM **Privately Held**
WEB: www.countryvillahealth.com
SIC: 8051 Skilled nursing care facilities
PA: Country Villa Service Corp.
2400 E Katella Ave # 800
Anaheim CA 92806
310 574-3733

(P-20303)
CF SAN RAFAEL LLC
81 Professional Ctr Pkwy, San Rafael
(94903-2702)
PHONE................................415 479-5161
Joel Saltzburg, *CFO*
EMP: 99
SALES (est): 4.6MM **Privately Held**
SIC: 8051 Convalescent home with continuous nursing care

(P-20304)
CF WATSONVILLE LLC
Also Called: Watsonville Post Acute Center
525 Auto Center Dr, Watsonville
(95076-3745)
PHONE................................831 724-7505
Doug Easton, *Manager*
Imelda Gil, *Records Dir*
Krista Garcia, *Social Dir*
Angelina Martinez, *Office Mgr*
Leticia Mayotte, *Office Mgr*
EMP: 96
SQ FT: 24,000
SALES (est): 1.9MM **Privately Held**
SIC: 8051 Skilled nursing care facilities

(P-20305)
CF WATSONVILLE EAST LLC
Also Called: Watsonville Nursing Center
535 Auto Center Dr, Watsonville
(95076-3745)
PHONE................................310 574-3733
Joel Saltzburg,
Gordon Buechs, *CFO*
EMP: 99
SALES: 5.1MM **Privately Held**
SIC: 8051 Convalescent home with continuous nursing care

(P-20306)
CF WATSONVILLE WEST LLC
Also Called: Watsonville Post Acute Center
525 Auto Center Dr, Watsonville
(95076-3745)
PHONE................................831 724-7505
Doug Easton, *CEO*
Jacob Wintner, *Manager*
EMP: 96
SQ FT: 24,000
SALES (est): 1.1MM **Privately Held**
SIC: 8051 Skilled nursing care facilities

(P-20307)
CHANDLER CONVALESCENT HOSPITAL
525 S Central Ave, Glendale (91204-2099)
PHONE................................818 240-1610
Richard Statler, *President*
Charles Levine, *President*
Harry Levine, *Vice Pres*
Charles Levin, *Executive*
EMP: 70

(P-20308)
CHAPARRAL FOUNDATION
Also Called: Chaparral House
1309 Allston Way, Berkeley (94702-1920)
PHONE................................510 848-8774
K J Paige, *Administration*
EMP: 90
SQ FT: 21,000
SALES: 6MM **Privately Held**
WEB: www.chaparralhouse.org
SIC: 8051 Convalescent home with continuous nursing care

(P-20309)
CHAPMAN HBR SKLLED NRSING CARE
Also Called: Chapmn-Hrbor Sklled Nrsing Ctr
12232 Chapman Ave, Garden Grove
(92840-3717)
PHONE................................714 971-5517
Lydia Goodell, *President*
Aaron Victor, *President*
EMP: 95
SQ FT: 15,000
SALES (est): 3.3MM **Privately Held**
SIC: 8051 Convalescent home with continuous nursing care

(P-20310)
CHINO VALLEY HEALTHCARE CENTER
2351 S Towne Ave, Pomona (91766-6227)
PHONE................................909 628-1245
Wanita Orkia, *Administration*
EMP: 85 EST: 1995
SQ FT: 17,684
SALES: 11.6MM **Privately Held**
SIC: 8051 Convalescent home with continuous nursing care

(P-20311)
CHOWCHILLA MEM HLTH CARE DST (PA)
1104 Ventura Ave, Chowchilla
(93610-2244)
PHONE................................559 665-3781
Cathy Flores, *Administration*
Leland Decker, *Principal*
EMP: 55
SQ FT: 23,000
SALES: 1.9MM **Privately Held**
SIC: 8051 Skilled nursing care facilities

(P-20312)
CITRUS VALLEY HOSPICE
Also Called: CITRUS VALLEY HOME HEALTH
820 N Phillips Ave, West Covina
(91791-1121)
PHONE................................626 859-2263
Robert Curry, *CEO*
Felipe Dela Riva, *Records Dir*
Stephanie Oliver, *Purchasing*
Larry Bustos, *Opers Staff*
Christine Espinas,
EMP: 100
SQ FT: 16,000
SALES: 9.5MM **Privately Held**
SIC: 8051 8082 Convalescent home with continuous nursing care; home health care services

(P-20313)
CLAIREMONT HEALTHCARE
8060 Frost St, San Diego (92123-2703)
PHONE................................858 278-4750
Sharrod Brooks,
EMP: 99 EST: 2012
SALES: 8.6MM **Privately Held**
SIC: 8051 Mental retardation hospital

(P-20314)
CLARA BALDWIN STOCKER HOME
527 S Valinda Ave, West Covina
(91790-3008)
PHONE................................626 962-7151
Laura Qualls, *Administration*
Barabara Giesa, *Trustee*
Alfred Giese, *Trustee*
Ann Koecritz, *Trustee*

Ann E Koeckritz, *Administration*
EMP: 50
SQ FT: 12,218
SALES: 3.8MM **Privately Held**
SIC: 8051 Skilled nursing care facilities

(P-20315)
CLOISTERS OF LA JOLLA INC
7160 Fay Ave, La Jolla (92037-5511)
PHONE..............................858 459-4361
Kennon S Shea, *President*
Jenna Ramesh, *Exec Dir*
Arvie Mora, *Nursing Dir*
EMP: 75
SQ FT: 5,000
SALES (est): 4.5MM **Privately Held**
SIC: 8051 Convalescent home with contin-
uous nursing care

(P-20316)
CNRC LLC
Also Called: Califrnia Nrsing Rhbltition Ctr
2299 N Indian Ave, Palm Springs (92262)
PHONE..............................760 325-2937
John Black, *Administration*
EMP: 99 EST: 2000
SALES (est): 2.8MM **Privately Held**
SIC: 8051 Skilled nursing care facilities

(P-20317)
**COALINGA DSTNGISHED
CMNTY CARE**
834 Maple Rd, Coalinga (93210-1348)
PHONE..............................559 935-5939
Richard Carter, *CEO*
EMP: 67
SQ FT: 52,000
SALES (est): 1.1MM **Privately Held**
SIC: 8051

(P-20318)
COASTAL HEALTH CARE INC
Also Called: Brentwood Health Care Center
1321 Franklin St, Santa Monica
(90404-2603)
PHONE..............................310 828-5596
John Sorensen, *President*
Tim Paulsen, *Exec VP*
Tanner Mitchell, *General Mgr*
Jessica Kari, *Rector*
Alaya Leyva, *Director*
EMP: 75
SALES (est): 10.9MM **Privately Held**
WEB: www.brentwoodnursing.com
SIC: 8051 Convalescent home with contin-
uous nursing care

(P-20319)
**COLDWATER CARE CENTER
LLC**
Also Called: Sherman Village Hlth Care Ctr
12750 Riverside Dr, North Hollywood
(91607-3319)
PHONE..............................818 766-6105
Brenan Lowery, *Manager*
EMP: 99
SALES: 12.9MM **Privately Held**
SIC: 8051 Convalescent home with contin-
uous nursing care

(P-20320)
**COMMUNITY CARE REHAB CTR
LLC**
Also Called: COMMUNITY CARE & REHA-
BILITATIO
4070 Jurupa Ave, Riverside (92506-2234)
PHONE..............................951 680-6500
Frank Johnson, *CEO*
Irving Bauman, *COO*
Kelly Iasparro, *Vice Pres*
Micah Rhead, *Administration*
EMP: 190
SALES: 16.6MM **Privately Held**
SIC: 8051 Skilled nursing care facilities

(P-20321)
**COMMUNITY CONVALESCENT
CENTER**
9620 Fremont Ave, Montclair (91763-2320)
PHONE..............................909 621-4751
Sim Mndlbum,
EMP: 99
SQ FT: 10,000
SALES (est): 348.7K **Privately Held**
SIC: 8051 Skilled nursing care facilities

(P-20322)
**COMMUNITY CONVALESCENT
HOSPITA**
638 E Colorado Ave, Glendora
(91740-4422)
PHONE..............................626 963-6091
Ledmile Gierowitz, *President*
EMP: 80
SQ FT: 10,000
SALES (est): 1.1MM **Privately Held**
SIC: 8051 Convalescent home with contin-
uous nursing care

(P-20323)
COPPER RIDGE CARE CENTER
Also Called: APPLEWOOD OPERATING
201 Hartnell Ave, Redding (96002-1843)
PHONE..............................530 222-2273
Darrell Thompson, *President*
Dan Gallegos, *Telecom Exec*
EMP: 200
SALES: 16MM **Privately Held**
SIC: 8051 Convalescent home with contin-
uous nursing care

(P-20324)
**CORECARE V A CAL LTD
PARTNR**
Also Called: PARK VISTA AT MORNINGSIDE
2525 Brea Blvd, Fullerton (92835-2787)
PHONE..............................714 256-1000
Gary R Stork, *Principal*
Melody Olmstead, *Controller*
Karrie Castles, *Food Svc Dir*
EMP: 200
SALES: 12.9MM **Privately Held**
SIC: 8051 Convalescent home with contin-
uous nursing care

(P-20325)
**COUNTRY HILLS HEALTH CARE
INC**
1580 Broadway, El Cajon (92021-5124)
PHONE..............................619 441-8745
Glen Larson, *President*
Robert Peacock, *Administration*
Pat Van, *Administration*
Eva Nasser, *Food Svc Dir*
Nita Hansen, *Hlthcr Dir*
EMP: 247
SALES: 27.1MM **Privately Held**
WEB: www.countryhills.com
SIC: 8051 Convalescent home with contin-
uous nursing care

(P-20326)
**COUNTRY OAKS CARE CENTER
INC**
830 E Chapel St, Santa Maria
(93454-4699)
PHONE..............................805 922-6657
John Henning, *President*
Sharon Henning, *Principal*
EMP: 70
SQ FT: 14,000
SALES: 4.4MM **Privately Held**
SIC: 8051 Convalescent home with contin-
uous nursing care

(P-20327)
**COUNTRY OAKS PARTNERS
LLC**
Also Called: Country Oaks Care Center
215 W Pearl St, Pomona (91768-3114)
PHONE..............................909 622-1067
Tanner Person, *Administration*
Kelly Iasparro, *Vice Pres*
William Presnell, *Admin Sec*
EMP: 99 EST: 2008
SQ FT: 10,601
SALES (est): 324.2K **Privately Held**
SIC: 8051 8049 Skilled nursing care facili-
ties; physical therapist

(P-20328)
COUNTRY VILLA IMPERIAL LLC
Also Called: Country Villa Los Feliz
3002 Rowena Ave, Los Angeles
(90039-2005)
PHONE..............................323 666-1544
Stephen E Reissman, *CEO*
Andrea Cuevas, *Social Dir*
Greg Ricco, *Office Mgr*
Luis Rivas, *Maint Spvr*

Emerald Saakyan, *Food Svc Dir*
EMP: 125
SALES (est): 4.7MM **Privately Held**
SIC: 8051 Convalescent home with contin-
uous nursing care

(P-20329)
COUNTRY VILLA SERVICE CORP
1208 S Central Ave, Glendale
(91204-2504)
PHONE..............................818 246-5516
Adam Mitchel, *Administration*
Anna Trejo, *Data Proc Staff*
EMP: 70
SALES (corp-wide): 125.3MM **Privately
Held**
SIC: 8051 Skilled nursing care facilities
PA: Country Villa Service Corp.
2400 E Katella Ave # 800
Anaheim CA 92806
310 574-3733

(P-20330)
COUNTRY VILLA SERVICE CORP
400 W Huntington Dr, Arcadia
(91007-3470)
PHONE..............................626 445-2421
Shelly Andresen, *Principal*
EMP: 70
SALES (corp-wide): 125.3MM **Privately
Held**
SIC: 8051 Skilled nursing care facilities
PA: Country Villa Service Corp.
2400 E Katella Ave # 800
Anaheim CA 92806
310 574-3733

(P-20331)
COUNTRY VILLA SERVICE CORP
3611 E Imperial Hwy, Lynwood
(90262-2608)
PHONE..............................310 537-2500
Jacob Wintner, *Branch Mgr*
EMP: 70
SALES (corp-wide): 125.3MM **Privately
Held**
SIC: 8051 Skilled nursing care facilities
PA: Country Villa Service Corp.
2400 E Katella Ave # 800
Anaheim CA 92806
310 574-3733

(P-20332)
COUNTY OF MODOC
Also Called: Care Wst-Wrner Mtn Nursing Ctr
228 W Mcdowell Ave, Alturas (96101-3934)
PHONE..............................530 233-3416
Bonney Markgrass, *Director*
Dick Steyer, *Exec Dir*
Teresa Jacques, *Director*
EMP: 161 **Privately Held**
WEB: www.modoccounty.us
SIC: 8051 Skilled nursing care facilities
PA: County Of Modoc
202 W 4th St Ste A
Alturas CA 96101
530 233-6400

(P-20333)
COUNTY OF SACRAMENTO
Also Called: Public Health Nursing Service
9616 Micron Ave Ste 750, Sacramento
(95827-2604)
PHONE..............................916 875-0900
Jan Peters, *Director*
EMP: 55 **Privately Held**
WEB: www.sna.com
SIC: 8051 9431 Skilled nursing care facili-
ties; administration of public health pro-
grams;
PA: County Of Sacramento
700 H St Ste 7650
Sacramento CA 95814
916 874-5544

(P-20334)
COURTYARD PLAZA
6951 Lennox Ave, Van Nuys (91405-4034)
PHONE..............................818 780-5005
Donahue G Vanderhider, *Principal*
EMP: 50
SALES (est): 1.4MM **Privately Held**
SIC: 8051 Skilled nursing care facilities

(P-20335)
COVENANT CARE LLC
Also Called: Pacific Coast Manor
1935 Wharf Rd, Capitola (95010-2606)
PHONE..............................831 476-0770
Christine Sims, *Manager*
Diana Bunter, *Director*
EMP: 90
SALES (est): 1.9MM **Privately Held**
WEB: www.willowtreenursingcenter.com
SIC: 8051 Convalescent home with contin-
uous nursing care
HQ: Covenant Care California, Llc
27071 Aliso Creek Rd # 100
Aliso Viejo CA 92656

(P-20336)
**COVENANT CARE CALIFORNIA
LLC**
Also Called: Downey Care Center
13007 Paramount Blvd, Downey
(90242-4329)
PHONE..............................562 923-9301
Marc Brian, *Principal*
Maria Cruz, *Chf Purch Ofc*
EMP: 75 **Privately Held**
WEB: www.willowtreenursingcenter.com
SIC: 8051 Skilled nursing care facilities
HQ: Covenant Care California, Llc
27071 Aliso Creek Rd # 100
Aliso Viejo CA 92656

(P-20337)
**COVENANT CARE CALIFORNIA
LLC**
Also Called: Wagner Heights Nursing &
Rehab
9289 Branstetter Pl, Stockton
(95209-1700)
PHONE..............................209 477-5252
Janey Hargreaves, *Branch Mgr*
Frank Cervantes, *Director*
EMP: 160 **Privately Held**
WEB: www.willowtreenursingcenter.com
SIC: 8051 Skilled nursing care facilities
HQ: Covenant Care California, Llc
27071 Aliso Creek Rd # 100
Aliso Viejo CA 92656

(P-20338)
**COVENANT CARE CALIFORNIA
LLC**
Also Called: Palo Alto Nursing Center
911 Bryant St, Palo Alto (94301-2711)
PHONE..............................415 327-0511
Roland Gandy, *Branch Mgr*
Marina Safro, *Hlthcr Dir*
EMP: 55 **Privately Held**
WEB: www.willowtreenursingcenter.com
SIC: 8051 8059 Skilled nursing care facili-
ties; personal care home, with health care
HQ: Covenant Care California, Llc
27071 Aliso Creek Rd # 100
Aliso Viejo CA 92656

(P-20339)
**COVENANT CARE CALIFORNIA
LLC**
Also Called: Catered Manor
4010 N Virginia Rd, Long Beach
(90807-2627)
PHONE..............................562 426-0394
Jolene Huren, *Executive*
Bryan Soriano, *Social Dir*
Julian Baltazar, *Human Res Dir*
Tracy Davis, *Nursing Dir*
Nora Saulietis, *Director*
EMP: 90 **Privately Held**
WEB: www.willowtreenursingcenter.com
SIC: 8051 8322 Convalescent home with
continuous nursing care; rehabilitation
services
HQ: Covenant Care California, Llc
27071 Aliso Creek Rd # 100
Aliso Viejo CA 92656

(P-20340)
COVENANT CARE CALIFORNIA LLC
Also Called: Mission Skilled Nursing Home
410 N Winchester Blvd, Santa Clara
(95050-6325)
PHONE...............................408 248-3736
Kathleen Glass, *Manager*
EMP: 75 **Privately Held**
WEB: www.willowtreenursingcenter.com
SIC: 8051 Skilled nursing care facilities
HQ: Covenant Care California, Llc
27071 Aliso Creek Rd # 100
Aliso Viejo CA 92656

(P-20341)
COVENANT CARE CALIFORNIA LLC
Also Called: Willow Tree Nursing Center
2124 57th Ave, Oakland (94621-4322)
PHONE...............................510 261-2628
Tony Moya, *Manager*
EMP: 90 **Privately Held**
WEB: www.willowtreenursingcenter.com
SIC: 8051 Skilled nursing care facilities
HQ: Covenant Care California, Llc
27071 Aliso Creek Rd # 100
Aliso Viejo CA 92656

(P-20342)
COVENANT CARE CALIFORNIA LLC
Also Called: Royal Care Skilled Nursing Ctr
2725 Pacific Ave, Long Beach
(90806-2612)
PHONE...............................562 427-7493
Nasreen Pervaiz, *Branch Mgr*
EMP: 90 **Privately Held**
WEB: www.willowtreenursingcenter.com
SIC: 8051 Convalescent home with contin-
uous nursing care
HQ: Covenant Care California, Llc
27071 Aliso Creek Rd # 100
Aliso Viejo CA 92656

(P-20343)
COVENANT CARE CALIFORNIA LLC
Also Called: Shoreline Care Center
5225 S J St, Oxnard (93033-8320)
PHONE...............................805 488-3696
Cindy Poulsen, *Exec Dir*
EMP: 200 **Privately Held**
WEB: www.willowtreenursingcenter.com
SIC: 8051 Skilled nursing care facilities
HQ: Covenant Care California, Llc
27071 Aliso Creek Rd # 100
Aliso Viejo CA 92656

(P-20344)
COVENANT CARE CALIFORNIA LLC
Also Called: Huntington Park Nursing Center
6425 Miles Ave, Huntington Park
(90254-4348)
PHONE...............................323 589-5941
Toni Mazzeo, *Branch Mgr*
Paula Holman, *Purch Agent*
EMP: 140 **Privately Held**
WEB: www.willowtreenursingcenter.com
SIC: 8051 Skilled nursing care facilities
HQ: Covenant Care California, Llc
27071 Aliso Creek Rd # 100
Aliso Viejo CA 92656

(P-20345)
COVENANT CARE CALIFORNIA LLC
Also Called: Pacific Gardens Hlth Care Ctr
577 S Peach Ave, Fresno (93727-3952)
PHONE...............................559 251-8463
Bart Vanderwal, *Branch Mgr*
EMP: 150
SQ FT: 40,000 **Privately Held**
WEB: www.willowtreenursingcenter.com
SIC: 8051 Skilled nursing care facilities

HQ: Covenant Care California, Llc
27071 Aliso Creek Rd # 100
Aliso Viejo CA 92656

(P-20346)
COVENANT CARE CALIFORNIA LLC
Also Called: Capital Transitional Care
6821 24th St, Sacramento (95822-4037)
PHONE...............................916 391-6011
Richard Thorp, *Branch Mgr*
Nathan Wiitala, *Tech/Comp Coord*
EMP: 100 **Privately Held**
WEB: www.willowtreenursingcenter.com
SIC: 8051 Skilled nursing care facilities
HQ: Covenant Care California, Llc
27071 Aliso Creek Rd # 100
Aliso Viejo CA 92656

(P-20347)
COVENANT CARE CALIFORNIA LLC
Also Called: Buena Vista Care Center
160 S Patterson Ave, Santa Barbara
(93111-2006)
PHONE...............................805 964-4871
David Hibarger, *Branch Mgr*
Cynthia Robles, *Executive*
Jaime Mejia, *Office Mgr*
Michael Malloy, *Business Anlyst*
Sergio Zaragoza, *Chf Purch Ofc*
EMP: 150 **Privately Held**
WEB: www.willowtreenursingcenter.com
SIC: 8051 Skilled nursing care facilities
HQ: Covenant Care California, Llc
27071 Aliso Creek Rd # 100
Aliso Viejo CA 92656

(P-20348)
COVENANT CARE CALIFORNIA LLC
Also Called: Turlock Nrsing Rhabilation Ctr
1111 E Tuolumne Rd, Turlock
(95382-1541)
PHONE...............................209 632-3821
Loris Gielczyk, *Principal*
Stephanie Morris, *Director*
EMP: 135 **Privately Held**
WEB: www.willowtreenursingcenter.com
SIC: 8051 Convalescent home with contin-
uous nursing care
HQ: Covenant Care California, Llc
27071 Aliso Creek Rd # 100
Aliso Viejo CA 92656

(P-20349)
COVENANT CARE CALIFORNIA LLC
Also Called: Gilroy Health Care
8170 Murray Ave, Gilroy (95020-4605)
PHONE...............................408 842-9311
Doreen McGary, *Director*
EMP: 150 **Privately Held**
WEB: www.willowtreenursingcenter.com
SIC: 8051 Skilled nursing care facilities
HQ: Covenant Care California, Llc
27071 Aliso Creek Rd # 100
Aliso Viejo CA 92656

(P-20350)
COVENANT CARE CALIFORNIA LLC (HQ)
27071 Aliso Creek Rd # 100, Aliso Viejo
(92656-5325)
PHONE...............................949 349-1200
Robert Levin, *President*
David Mlodecki, *Shareholder*
Mary A Evans, *COO*
Mary Evans, *COO*
Christine Sims, *CFO*
EMP: 50
SQ FT: 10,000
SALES (est): 179.6MM **Privately Held**
WEB: www.willowtreenursingcenter.com
SIC: 8051 Skilled nursing care facilities

(P-20351)
COVENANT CARE CALIFORNIA LLC
Also Called: Valle Vista Convalescent Hosp
1025 W 2nd Ave, Escondido (92025-3839)
PHONE...............................760 745-1288
Kristina Kuizon, *Branch Mgr*
EMP: 50
SQ FT: 15,494 **Privately Held**
WEB: www.willowtreenursingcenter.com
SIC: 8051 Convalescent home with contin-
uous nursing care
HQ: Covenant Care California, Llc
27071 Aliso Creek Rd # 100
Aliso Viejo CA 92656

(P-20352)
COVENANT CARE CALIFORNIA LLC
Also Called: St Edna Sbcute Cnvalescent Ctr
1929 N Fairview St, Santa Ana
(92706-2205)
PHONE...............................714 554-9700
Joshua Torres, *Manager*
Josh Torres, *Exec Dir*
EMP: 125 **Privately Held**
WEB: www.willowtreenursingcenter.com
SIC: 8051 Convalescent home with contin-
uous nursing care
HQ: Covenant Care California, Llc
27071 Aliso Creek Rd # 100
Aliso Viejo CA 92656

(P-20353)
COVENANT CARE CALIFORNIA LLC
Also Called: Los Alts Sub-Acute Rhbltn
809 Fremont Ave, Los Altos (94024-5617)
PHONE...............................650 941-5255
Annie Buerhaus, *Branch Mgr*
Alfred Tenoso, *Maintence Staff*
Leva Bong, *Nurse*
EMP: 200 **Privately Held**
WEB: www.willowtreenursingcenter.com
SIC: 8051 8093 Skilled nursing care facili-
ties; rehabilitation center, outpatient treat-
ment
HQ: Covenant Care California, Llc
27071 Aliso Creek Rd # 100
Aliso Viejo CA 92656

(P-20354)
COVENANT CARE INDIANA INC (DH)
27071 Aliso Creek Rd # 100, Aliso Viejo
(92656-5325)
PHONE...............................949 349-1200
Robert Levin, *President*
Christine Sims, *CFO*
EMP: 52
SALES (est): 12.2MM **Privately Held**
WEB:
www.covingtonmanornursingcenter.com
SIC: 8051 Skilled nursing care facilities

(P-20355)
COVENANT CARE LA JOLLA LLC
Also Called: La Jolla Nrsing Rhbltation Ctr
2552 Torrey Pines Rd # 1, La Jolla
(92037-3432)
PHONE...............................858 453-5810
Lisa Parker, *Administration*
Carol Tiaadwai, *Administration*
Angel Sanchez, *Manager*
EMP: 150
SALES (est): 4.3MM **Privately Held**
WEB: www.willowtreenursingcenter.com
SIC: 8051 Skilled nursing care facilities
HQ: Covenant Care California, Llc
27071 Aliso Creek Rd # 100
Aliso Viejo CA 92656

(P-20356)
COVENTRY COURT HEALTH CENTER
2040 S Euclid St, Anaheim (92802-3111)
PHONE...............................714 636-2800
Saun Dohl, *CEO*
Jeff Deguzman, *Executive*

EMP: 200
SALES: 13MM **Privately Held**
SIC: 8051 Skilled nursing care facilities

(P-20357)
COVIA AFFORDABLE COMMUNITIES
2185 N Calif Blvd Ste 215, Walnut Creek
(94596-3566)
PHONE...............................925 956-7400
Kevin Gerber, *CEO*
Jonathan Casey, *CFO*
EMP: 180
SALES: 2.1MM **Privately Held**
WEB: www.lyttongardens.org
SIC: 8051 Skilled nursing care facilities

(P-20358)
COVINA REHABILITATION CENTER
Also Called: Regency Health Services
261 W Badillo St, Covina (91723-1907)
PHONE...............................626 967-3874
Teresa Dearmond, *Director*
Agnes Maron, *Director*
EMP: 110
SQ FT: 27,800
SALES: 11.3MM **Privately Held**
SIC: 8051 Skilled nursing care facilities

(P-20359)
CREEKSIDE CNVALESCENT HOSP INC
850 Sonoma Ave, Santa Rosa
(95404-4715)
PHONE...............................707 544-7750
Robert Bates, *Administration*
Lawrence R De Beni, *President*
EMP: 160
SQ FT: 44,000
SALES (est): 4.9MM **Privately Held**
SIC: 8051 Convalescent home with contin-
uous nursing care

(P-20360)
CREEKSIDE HEALTHCARE CTR
1900 Church Ln, San Pablo (94806-3708)
PHONE...............................510 235-5514
Dianna Haines, *Administration*
EMP: 50
SALES (est): 437.6K **Privately Held**
SIC: 8051 Extended care facility

(P-20361)
CREEKSIDE REHAB AND BEHAVIORAL
850 Sonoma Ave, Santa Rosa
(95404-4715)
PHONE...............................707 524-7030
Paul Duranczsk, *Administration*
Prema Thekkek, *President*
EMP: 208 EST: 2000
SALES (est): 7.2MM **Privately Held**
SIC: 8051 Convalescent home with contin-
uous nursing care

(P-20362)
CRESTVIEW CNVALESCENT HOSP INC
1471 S Riverside Ave, Rialto (92376-7703)
PHONE...............................909 877-1361
Roy Berglund MD, *President*
EMP: 220
SQ FT: 44,000
SALES (est): 5.7MM **Privately Held**
WEB: www.crestviewcarecenter.com
SIC: 8051 Convalescent home with contin-
uous nursing care

(P-20363)
CROCUS HOLDINGS LLC
Also Called: Roseville Care Center
1161 Cirby Way, Roseville (95661-4421)
PHONE...............................916 782-1238
James Huish,
Ben Tuifua, *Exec Dir*
Myrna De Guzman, *Controller*
Jessica Abney, *Food Svc Dir*
Jack Sanofsky, *Manager*
EMP: 99
SALES: 20.8MM **Privately Held**
SIC: 8051 Convalescent home with contin-
uous nursing care

(P-20364)
CUPERTINO HEALTHCARE
Also Called: Cupertino Hlthcare Wllness Ctr
22590 Voss Ave, Cupertino (95014-2627)
PHONE..............................408 253-9034
Aaron Robin, *Mng Member*
EMP: 99
SALES: 15MM **Privately Held**
SIC: 8051 Convalescent home with continuous nursing care

(P-20365)
DANVILLE LONG-TERM CARE INC
Also Called: Danville Post Acute Rehab
336 Diablo Rd, Danville (94526-3417)
PHONE..............................925 837-4566
John L Sorensen, *President*
Tim Paulsen, *Vice Pres*
Taylor Ellis, *Administration*
EMP: 80
SALES (est): 2.6MM **Privately Held**
SIC: 8051 Convalescent home with continuous nursing care

(P-20366)
DANVILLE VILLAGE SKILLED NURSN
Also Called: Danville Rehsbilitation
336 Diablo Rd, Danville (94526-3417)
PHONE..............................925 837-4566
Spencer Brinton, *Administration*
EMP: 65
SQ FT: 13,760
SALES: 9.4MM **Privately Held**
SIC: 8051 Skilled nursing care facilities

(P-20367)
DAVID ROSS INC
Also Called: Rose Garden Convalescent Ctr
1899 N Raymond Ave, Pasadena
(91103-1733)
PHONE..............................323 684-7673
Arlene Rosales, *Ch of Bd*
Susan Requina, *Nursing Dir*
▲ EMP: 100
SQ FT: 27,000
SALES: 7MM **Privately Held**
SIC: 8051 Skilled nursing care facilities

(P-20368)
DAVID-KLEIS INC
Also Called: Beaumont Care Center
9246 Avenida Miravilla, Cherry Valley
(92223-3835)
PHONE..............................951 845-1166
Jumer Roque, *Administration*
EMP: 110
SQ FT: 20,000
SALES (est): 4.3MM **Privately Held**
SIC: 8051 Convalescent home with continuous nursing care

(P-20369)
DEL AMO GRDNS CNVLSCNT HOSP &
22419 Kent Ave, Torrance (90505-2303)
PHONE..............................310 378-4233
Morris Weiss, *President*
Barry Weiss, *Vice Pres*
Harumi Takeda, *Risk Mgmt Dir*
Daniella Gonzalez, *Office Mgr*
Harry Jacobs, *Admin Sec*
EMP: 92
SQ FT: 21,298
SALES: 8.2MM **Privately Held**
WEB: www.delamogardens.com
SIC: 8051 Convalescent home with continuous nursing care

(P-20370)
DEL RIO HEALTH CARE INC
Also Called: Del Rio Convalescent Center
16016 Rio Florida Dr, Whittier
(90603-1045)
PHONE..............................562 947-5221
Steven Highland, *President*
Mahmood M Moledina, *Treasurer*
EMP: 150
SQ FT: 42,000
SALES (est): 2.6MM **Privately Held**
SIC: 8051 Skilled nursing care facilities

(P-20371)
DEL RIO SANITARIUM INC
Also Called: Del Rio Convalescent
7002 Gage Ave, Bell Gardens
(90201-2014)
PHONE..............................562 927-6586
Joy Thune, *President*
EMP: 150
SALES (est): 8.2MM **Privately Held**
SIC: 8051 Skilled nursing care facilities

(P-20372)
DEL ROSA VILLA INC
2018 Del Rosa Ave, San Bernardino
(92404-5642)
PHONE..............................909 885-3261
Carol Wagner, *Administration*
Thomas S Plott, *President*
Elizabeth Plott, *Corp Secy*
EMP: 85
SQ FT: 20,000
SALES (est): 3.3MM **Privately Held**
SIC: 8051 Convalescent home with continuous nursing care

(P-20373)
DELANO DST SKLLED NRSING FCLTY
1509 Tokay St, Delano (93215-3603)
PHONE..............................661 720-2100
Dennis Karnowski, *Administration*
Janice Calzo, *Business Dir*
Veronica Perez, *Human Res Dir*
Wan Lin, *Nutritionist*
EMP: 115
SQ FT: 30,000
SALES (est): 9.7MM **Privately Held**
SIC: 8051 Skilled nursing care facilities

(P-20374)
DELTA NRSING RHBILITATION HOSP
Also Called: Delta Nrsing Rhabilitation Ctr
514 N Bridge St, Visalia (93291-5015)
PHONE..............................559 625-4003
Mark Fisher, *President*
EMP: 60
SALES (est): 1.7MM **Privately Held**
WEB: www.missioncaregroup.com
SIC: 8051 Convalescent home with continuous nursing care

(P-20375)
DEVELOPMENTAL SVCS CAL DEPT
Also Called: Porterville Developmental Ctr
26501 Avenue 140, Porterville
(93257-9109)
P.O. Box 2000 (93258-2000)
PHONE..............................559 782-2222
Theresa Villeci, *Principal*
Patricia Sutherland, *Director*
EMP: 1800 **Privately Held**
WEB: www.ldc.dds.ca.gov
SIC: 8051 9431 Mental retardation hospital; administration of public health programs;
HQ: California Department Of Developmental Services
1600 9th St
Sacramento CA 95814
916 654-1690

(P-20376)
DEVONSHIRE CARE CENTER LLC
1350 E Devonshire Ave, Hemet
(92544-8629)
P.O. Box 1405, Riverside (92502-1405)
PHONE..............................951 925-2571
Jose Lynch, *Mng Member*
Andrea Abbes, *Mng Member*
EMP: 90
SALES: 8.4MM **Privately Held**
SIC: 8051 Skilled nursing care facilities

(P-20377)
DIGNITY HEALTH
Also Called: Marian Extended Care Cntr
1530 Cypress Way, Santa Maria
(93454-5900)
PHONE..............................805 739-3650
Debbie M Young, *Manager*
Debbie Young, *Director*
Karen Gloyd, *Manager*

EMP: 132
SALES (corp-wide): 6.7B **Privately Held**
WEB: www.chw.edu
SIC: 8051 8082 Skilled nursing care facilities; home health care services
PA: Dignity Health
185 Berry St Ste 300
San Francisco CA 94107
415 438-5500

(P-20378)
DOUGLAS FIR HOLDINGS LLC
Also Called: HUNTINGTON VALLEY HEALTHCARE C
8382 Newman Ave, Huntington Beach
(92647-7038)
PHONE..............................714 842-5551
Brad Truhar, *Administration*
EMP: 145
SALES: 16.8MM **Privately Held**
SIC: 8051 Skilled nursing care facilities

(P-20379)
DOWNEY COMMUNITY HEALTH CENTER
8425 Iowa St, Downey (90241-4929)
P.O. Box 340 (90241-0340)
PHONE..............................562 862-6506
Rich Coberly, *Administration*
Stanley Diller, *Partner*
EMP: 175
SQ FT: 60,000
SALES: 15.1MM **Privately Held**
SIC: 8051 Convalescent home with continuous nursing care

(P-20380)
E W C H INC
1805 West St, Hayward (94545-1932)
PHONE..............................510 783-4811
Ada Lukban, *Administration*
Mark Costa, *Sales Executive*
EMP: 100
SQ FT: 26,000
SALES (est): 1MM **Privately Held**
SIC: 8051 8069 Convalescent home with continuous nursing care; specialty hospitals, except psychiatric

(P-20381)
EARLWOOD LLC
Also Called: Earlwood Convalescent Hospital
20820 Earl St, Torrance (90503-4307)
PHONE..............................310 371-1228
Kevin Thomas, *Administration*
EMP: 75
SALES (est): 1.6MM **Publicly Held**
WEB: www.parkviewnursing.net
SIC: 8051 Skilled nursing care facilities
HQ: Skilled Healthcare, Llc
27442 Portola Pkwy # 200
Foothill Ranch CA 92610
949 282-5800

(P-20382)
EASTERN PLUMAS HEALTH CARE
700 3rd St, Loyalton (96118)
PHONE..............................530 993-1225
G Koortbojian, *Administration*
EMP: 85
SQ FT: 20,000
SALES (est): 5.5MM **Privately Held**
SIC: 8051 Skilled nursing care facilities

(P-20383)
EDEN WEST REHABILITATION
1805 West St, Hayward (94545-1932)
PHONE..............................510 783-4811
Ruth Gildea, *Administration*
EMP: 99
SALES (est): 920.5K **Privately Held**
SIC: 8051 Skilled nursing care facilities

(P-20384)
EDGEWATER CONVALESCENT HOSP
Also Called: Edgewater Skilled Nursing Ctr
2625 E 4th St, Long Beach (90814-1299)
PHONE..............................562 434-0974
Debbie Grani, *President*
Norma Cowles, *Vice Pres*
Charlena Padilla, *Office Mgr*
Jonathan Chapman, *Administration*
Sarah Hall, *Marketing Staff*

EMP: 75 EST: 1954
SQ FT: 18,000
SALES: 9.5MM **Privately Held**
SIC: 8051 Convalescent home with continuous nursing care

(P-20385)
EL CAJON VLY CONVALESCENT CTR
510 E Washington Ave, El Cajon
(92020-5324)
PHONE..............................619 440-1211
Joellen Zayer, *Vice Pres*
Helen Bunn, *President*
EMP: 240
SQ FT: 25,000
SALES (est): 4.3MM **Privately Held**
SIC: 8051 Convalescent home with continuous nursing care

(P-20386)
EL ENCANTO HEALTHCARE & REHAB
Also Called: EL ENCANTO HOME HEALTH CARE
555 El Encanto Rd, City of Industry
(91745-1017)
PHONE..............................626 336-1274
Steve Blackwell, *Administration*
EMP: 212
SQ FT: 70,000
SALES: 13MM **Privately Held**
WEB: www.elencantohealthcare.com
SIC: 8051 Convalescent home with continuous nursing care; mental retardation hospital

(P-20387)
ELDER CARE ALLIANCE SAN RAFAEL
1301 Marina Village Pkwy # 210, Alameda
(94501-1082)
PHONE..............................510 769-2700
Jesse Janteen, *President*
EMP: 75
SALES: 10MM **Privately Held**
SIC: 8051 Convalescent home with continuous nursing care

(P-20388)
ELDORADO CARE CENTER LP
Also Called: Avocado Post Acute
510 E Washington Ave, El Cajon
(92020-5324)
PHONE..............................619 440-1211
Jacob Graff, *Owner*
EMP: 298
SALES (est): 17.2MM **Privately Held**
WEB: www.eldoradocarecenterllc.com
SIC: 8051 8322 Convalescent home with continuous nursing care; adult day care center

(P-20389)
ELIM ALZHEIMERS & REHAB
668 E Bullard Ave, Fresno (93710-5401)
PHONE..............................559 320-2200
Ronald E Howe, *President*
M K Howe, *Admin Sec*
EMP: 95
SQ FT: 28,000
SALES (est): 1.3MM **Privately Held**
SIC: 8051 Skilled nursing care facilities

(P-20390)
ELMS SANITARIUM INC
Also Called: Elms Convalescent Hospital
3247 Windmist Ave, Thousand Oaks
(91362-1151)
PHONE..............................818 240-6720
Aleck Knell, *President*
Lena Knell, *Treasurer*
William Knell, *Vice Pres*
EMP: 60
SQ FT: 11,000
SALES: 3.8MM **Privately Held**
SIC: 8051 Skilled nursing care facilities

(P-20391)
EMERITUS CORPORATION
Also Called: Brookdale Clairemont
5219 Clairemont Mesa Blvd, San Diego
(92117-2206)
PHONE..............................858 292-8044
S Wheeler, *Exec Dir*

EMP: 50
SALES (corp-wide): 4.7B **Publicly Held**
SIC: 8051 Skilled nursing care facilities
HQ: Emeritus Corporation
3131 Elliott Ave Ste 500
Milwaukee WI 53214

(P-20392)
EMPRES FINANCIAL SERVICES LLC
Also Called: Living Centers
1527 Springs Rd, Vallejo (94591-5448)
PHONE...................................707 643-2793
David Hicks, *Manager*
EMP: 61
SALES (corp-wide): 5MM **Privately Held**
SIC: 8051 Skilled nursing care facilities
HQ: Empres Financial Services, Llc
4601 Ne 77th Ave Ste 300
Vancouver WA 98662
360 892-6628

(P-20393)
ENGLISH OAKS CONVALESCENT
Also Called: ENGLISH OAKS CONVALES-
CENT & RE
2633 W Rumble Rd, Modesto
(95350-0154)
PHONE...................................209 577-1001
Terry L Mundy, *President*
Pamela Mundy, *Admin Sec*
EMP: 225
SQ FT: 57,000
SALES: 22.2MM **Privately Held**
SIC: 8051 Convalescent home with contin-
uous nursing care

(P-20394)
ENSIGN CLOVERDALE LLC
Also Called: Cloverdale Healthcare Center
300 Cherry Creek Rd, Cloverdale
(95425-3811)
PHONE...................................707 894-5201
Soon Burnam, *Administration*
Misty Robinson, *Social Dir*
Jill Browne, *Office Mgr*
Adam Willits, *Administration*
Trang Davis, *Human Res Dir*
EMP: 66
SALES: 6.6MM
SALES (corp-wide): 1.8B **Publicly Held**
SIC: 8051 Convalescent home with contin-
uous nursing care
HQ: Northern Pioneer Healthcare, Inc.
27101 Puerta Real
Mission Viejo CA 92691
949 487-9500

(P-20395)
ENSIGN GROUP INC
340 Victoria St, Costa Mesa (92627-1914)
PHONE...................................949 642-0387
Cindy Ramirez, *Director*
EMP: 84
SALES (corp-wide): 1.8B **Publicly Held**
SIC: 8051 Skilled nursing care facilities
PA: The Ensign Group Inc
27101 Puerta Real Ste 450
Mission Viejo CA 92691
949 487-9500

(P-20396)
ENSIGN GROUP INC
Also Called: Panaroma Gardens
9541 Van Nuys Blvd, Panorama City
(91402-1315)
PHONE...................................818 893-6385
Alicia Gamero, *Administration*
Manuel Sanchez, *Chf Purch Ofc*
Belen Herrera, *Hlthcr Dir*
Esperanza Hernandez, *Director*
EMP: 115
SALES (corp-wide): 1.8B **Publicly Held**
WEB: www.theensigngroup.com
SIC: 8051 Convalescent home with contin-
uous nursing care
PA: The Ensign Group Inc
27101 Puerta Real Ste 450
Mission Viejo CA 92691
949 487-9500

(P-20397)
ENSIGN GROUP INC
Also Called: Whittier Hills Health Care Ctr
10426 Bogardus Ave, Whittier
(90603-2642)
PHONE...................................562 947-7817
Lisa Matarazzo, *Administration*
Pat Guevara, *Records Dir*
Robert Gray, *QC Dir*
EMP: 150
SQ FT: 36,316
SALES (corp-wide): 1.8B **Publicly Held**
WEB: www.theensigngroup.com
SIC: 8051 8059 Convalescent home with
continuous nursing care; rest home, with
health care
PA: The Ensign Group Inc
27101 Puerta Real Ste 450
Mission Viejo CA 92691
949 487-9500

(P-20398)
ENSIGN GROUP INC
Also Called: Park View Gardens
3751 Montgomery Dr, Santa Rosa
(95405-5214)
PHONE...................................707 525-1250
Eric Moessing, *Director*
EMP: 110
SALES (corp-wide): 1.8B **Publicly Held**
WEB: www.theensigngroup.com
SIC: 8051 Convalescent home with contin-
uous nursing care
PA: The Ensign Group Inc
27101 Puerta Real Ste 450
Mission Viejo CA 92691
949 487-9500

(P-20399)
ENSIGN GROUP INC
Also Called: Palomar Vista Healthcare Ctr
201 N Fig St, Escondido (92025-3416)
PHONE...................................760 746-0303
William Adams, *Manager*
Pam Campbell, *Executive*
Andrew Rios, *Envir Svcs Dir*
Bobbi Portillo, *Office Mgr*
EMP: 100
SALES (corp-wide): 1.8B **Publicly Held**
WEB: www.theensigngroup.com
SIC: 8051 Convalescent home with contin-
uous nursing care
PA: The Ensign Group Inc
27101 Puerta Real Ste 450
Mission Viejo CA 92691
949 487-9500

(P-20400)
ENSIGN GROUP INC
Also Called: Mission Care Center
4800 Delta Ave, Rosemead (91770-1127)
PHONE...................................626 607-2400
Tin Nelson, *Director*
Sheila Manapat, *Human Res Dir*
EMP: 60
SALES (corp-wide): 1.8B **Publicly Held**
WEB: www.missioncareandrehab.com
SIC: 8051 Skilled nursing care facilities
PA: The Ensign Group Inc
27101 Puerta Real Ste 450
Mission Viejo CA 92691
949 487-9500

(P-20401)
ENSIGN GROUP INC
Also Called: California Mission Inn
8417 Mission Dr, Rosemead (91770-1188)
PHONE...................................626 287-0438
David Gatewood, *Owner*
Gin Lopez, *Exec Dir*
EMP: 237
SALES (corp-wide): 1.8B **Publicly Held**
SIC: 8051 Skilled nursing care facilities
PA: The Ensign Group Inc
27101 Puerta Real Ste 450
Mission Viejo CA 92691
949 487-9500

(P-20402)
ENSIGN PALM I LLC
Also Called: Premier Care Center For Palm
2990 E Ramon Rd, Palm Springs
(92264-7931)
PHONE...................................760 323-2638
Soon Burnam, *Treasurer*
Bryce Campbell, *Records Dir*

Leeron Hever, *Administration*
Misty Edgemon, *Manager*
EMP: 90
SALES (est): 3.2MM **Privately Held**
SIC: 8051 Convalescent home with contin-
uous nursing care

(P-20403)
ENSIGN SERVICES INC
27101 Puerta Real Ste 450, Mission Viejo
(92691-8566)
PHONE...................................949 487-9500
Christopher Christensen, *CEO*
Beverly B Wittekind, *Treasurer*
Chad Keetch, *Admin Sec*
Sue Kelley,
EMP: 90
SALES (est): 8.8MM **Privately Held**
SIC: 8051 Convalescent home with contin-
uous nursing care

(P-20404)
ENSIGN SOUTHLAND LLC
Also Called: Southland Care
27101 Puerta Real Ste 450, Mission Viejo
(92691-8566)
PHONE...................................949 487-9500
Allan Norman,
EMP: 150
SALES (est): 1.3MM
SALES (corp-wide): 1.8B **Publicly Held**
WEB: www.ensigngroup.net
SIC: 8051 Extended care facility
PA: The Ensign Group Inc
27101 Puerta Real Ste 450
Mission Viejo CA 92691
949 487-9500

(P-20405)
EPISCOPAL COMMUNITIES & SERVIC
Also Called: Canterbury, The
5801 Crestridge Rd, Pls Vrds Pnsl
(90275-4961)
PHONE...................................310 544-2204
Consuelo Haire, *Branch Mgr*
EMP: 100
SALES (corp-wide): 36.6MM **Privately
Held**
WEB: www.episcopalhome.org
SIC: 8051 8361 8059 Extended care facil-
ity; home for the aged; personal care
home, with health care
PA: Episcopal Communities & Services For
Seniors
605 E Huntington Dr # 207
Monrovia CA 91016
626 403-5880

(P-20406)
EQUICARE MEDICAL SUPPLY INC
Also Called: Emerald Ter Convalescent Hosp
1154 S Alvarado St, Los Angeles
(90006-4110)
PHONE...................................213 385-1715
Elena Mendoza-Legaspi, *President*
Elena M Mendoza-Legaspi, *President*
Christina Mendoza, *Administration*
EMP: 55
SALES: 3MM **Privately Held**
SIC: 8051 Convalescent home with contin-
uous nursing care

(P-20407)
ESKATON PROPERTIES INC
Also Called: Eskaton Village Care Center
3847 Walnut Ave, Carmichael
(95608-2148)
PHONE...................................916 974-2060
Larry Bahr, *Manager*
EMP: 1000
SALES (corp-wide): 90.6MM **Privately
Held**
SIC: 8051 Skilled nursing care facilities
PA: Eskaton Properties Incorporated
5105 Manzanita Ave Ste A
Carmichael CA 95608
916 334-0810

(P-20408)
ESKATON PROPERTIES INC
Eskaton Manzanita Manor
5318 Manzanita Ave, Carmichael
(95608-0512)
PHONE...................................916 331-8513

Denie Crum, *Administration*
EMP: 100
SALES (corp-wide): 90.6MM **Privately
Held**
SIC: 8051 Extended care facility
PA: Eskaton Properties Incorporated
5105 Manzanita Ave Ste A
Carmichael CA 95608
916 334-0810

(P-20409)
ESKATON PROPERTIES INC
Also Called: Homestead of Fair Oaks
11300 Fair Oaks Blvd, Fair Oaks
(95628-5141)
PHONE...................................916 965-4663
Tom Coffey, *Manager*
EMP: 160
SALES (corp-wide): 90.6MM **Privately
Held**
SIC: 8051 Convalescent home with contin-
uous nursing care
PA: Eskaton Properties Incorporated
5105 Manzanita Ave Ste A
Carmichael CA 95608
916 334-0810

(P-20410)
ESKATON PROPERTIES INC
Also Called: Eskaton Center of Greenhaven
455 Florin Rd, Sacramento (95831-2024)
PHONE...................................916 393-2550
Heather Craig, *Manager*
EMP: 180
SALES (corp-wide): 90.6MM **Privately
Held**
SIC: 8051 Convalescent home with contin-
uous nursing care
PA: Eskaton Properties Incorporated
5105 Manzanita Ave Ste A
Carmichael CA 95608
916 334-0810

(P-20411)
ESKATON PROPERTIES INC (PA)
Also Called: 0epi
5105 Manzanita Ave Ste A, Carmichael
(95608-0523)
PHONE...................................916 334-0810
Todd Murch, *President*
Betsy Donovan, *Senior VP*
Bill Pace, *Senior VP*
Sheri Peifer, *Senior VP*
Charles Garcia, *Vice Pres*
▲ **EMP:** 60
SQ FT: 27,000
SALES: 90.6MM **Privately Held**
SIC: 8051 Skilled nursing care facilities

(P-20412)
ESTRELLA INC
Also Called: Woodruff Convalescent Center
17836 Woodruff Ave, Bellflower
(90706-7029)
PHONE...................................562 925-6418
Liberation De Leon MD, *President*
EMP: 110
SQ FT: 32,000
SALES (est): 7MM **Privately Held**
SIC: 8051 Convalescent home with contin-
uous nursing care

(P-20413)
EUREKA REHAB & WELLNESS CENTER
Also Called: Eureka Rhbltation Wellness Ctr
2353 23rd St, Eureka (95501-3201)
PHONE...................................707 445-3261
Sharrod Brooks, *Partner*
Shlomo Rechnitz, *Partner*
EMP: 98 **EST:** 2011
SALES: 6.3MM **Privately Held**
SIC: 8051 Skilled nursing care facilities

(P-20414)
EVERGREEN AT CHICO LLC
Also Called: Twin Oaks Nrsing Rhblttion Ctr
1200 Springfield Dr, Chico (95928-6340)
PHONE...................................530 342-4885
Barbara Addington, *Manager*
Carla McClintock, *Executive*
EMP: 150

SALES (corp-wide): 102.4MM **Privately Held**
SIC: 8051 8069 Convalescent home with continuous nursing care; specialty hospitals, except psychiatric
PA: Evergreen At Chico, L.L.C.
4601 Ne 77th Ave Ste 300
Vancouver WA 98662
360 892-6472

(P-20415)
EVERGREEN AT LAKEPORT LLC (PA)
Also Called: Evergreen Lkport Hlthcare Ctr
1291 Craig Ave, Lakeport (95453-5704)
PHONE.................................707 263-6382
Steve Hendrickson, *Administration*
Annette A Mott, *Records Dir*
EMP: 100
SQ FT: 36,240
SALES (est): 8.2MM **Privately Held**
SIC: 8051 Convalescent home with continuous nursing care

(P-20416)
EVERGREEN AT LAKEPORT LLC
Also Called: Evergreen Healthcare Center
6212 Tudor Way, Bakersfield (93306-7067)
PHONE.................................661 871-3133
Gloria Melliti, *Executive*
EMP: 125
SALES (corp-wide): 8.2MM **Privately Held**
SIC: 8051 Convalescent home with continuous nursing care
PA: Evergreen At Lakeport Llc
1291 Craig Ave
Lakeport CA 95453
707 263-6382

(P-20417)
EVERGREEN AT OROVILLE LLC
Also Called: Olive Ridge Post Acute Care
1000 Executive Pkwy, Oroville (95966-5100)
PHONE.................................530 533-7335
Dale Patterson,
EMP: 99
SALES (est): 2MM **Privately Held**
SIC: 8051 Mental retardation hospital

(P-20418)
EVERGREEN AT PETALUMA LLC
Also Called: Empres Post Acute Rhbilitation
300 Douglas St, Petaluma (94952-2503)
PHONE.................................707 763-6887
Connie Smith, *Exec Dir*
EMP: 121
SQ FT: 21,965
SALES (est): 4.1MM
SALES (corp-wide): 553.1K **Privately Held**
SIC: 8051 Skilled nursing care facilities
PA: Empres California Healthcare, Llc
4601 Ne 77th Ave Ste 300
Vancouver WA 98662
360 892-6628

(P-20419)
EVERGREEN HEALTH CARE LLC
323 Campus Dr, Arvin (93203-1047)
PHONE.................................661 854-4475
Cody Rasmussen, *Exec Dir*
Sandy Lawrence, *Administration*
Holly Schmunk, *Administration*
Rush Melliti, *Manager*
EMP: 92
SALES: 6.1MM
SALES (corp-wide): 102.4MM **Privately Held**
SIC: 8051 Skilled nursing care facilities
PA: Evergreen At Chico, L.L.C.
4601 Ne 77th Ave Ste 300
Vancouver WA 98662
360 892-6472

(P-20420)
EXTENDED CARE HOSP WESTMINSTER
206 Hospital Cir, Westminster (92683-3910)
PHONE.................................714 891-2769
George Rhodes, *Administration*

Connie Black, *Partner*
Fred Landry, *Partner*
Mark Landry, *Partner*
EMP: 115
SALES (est): 6.7MM **Privately Held**
SIC: 8051 8069 Convalescent home with continuous nursing care; specialty hospitals, except psychiatric

(P-20421)
FAIRFIELD NURSING & REHAB CTR
Also Called: Fairfield Healthcare Center
1255 Travis Blvd, Fairfield (94533-4801)
PHONE.................................707 425-0623
Steve Hendrickson, *Administration*
Joan Wandyke, *Administration*
Patti Turner, *Info Tech Mgr*
EMP: 90
SALES (est): 4.9MM **Privately Held**
SIC: 8051 Convalescent home with continuous nursing care

(P-20422)
FAITH ENTERPRISES INC
545 W Beverly Pl, Tracy (95376-3012)
PHONE.................................209 835-6034
R David Delisle, *President*
EMP: 50
SQ FT: 18,159
SALES (est): 1.4MM **Privately Held**
SIC: 8051 Convalescent home with continuous nursing care

(P-20423)
FALLBROOK SKLLED NRSING FCILTY
325 Potter St, Fallbrook (92028-3068)
PHONE.................................760 728-2330
Larry Payton, *CEO*
Victor Lang, *Facilities Dir*
Jennifer Paul, *Director*
EMP: 95
SALES (est): 5MM **Privately Held**
SIC: 8051 Skilled nursing care facilities

(P-20424)
FAR WEST INC
Also Called: Linwood Grdns Convalescent Ctr
4444 W Meadow Ave, Visalia (93277-1652)
PHONE.................................559 627-1241
Robert Barker, *Manager*
Aaron Burrup, *Administration*
EMP: 70
SALES (corp-wide): 103.7MM **Privately Held**
SIC: 8051 8059 Convalescent home with continuous nursing care; convalescent home
HQ: Far West, Inc
4020 Sierra College Blvd
Rocklin CA 95677
-

(P-20425)
FAR WEST INC
Also Called: South Gate Care Centers
8455 State St, South Gate (90280-2339)
PHONE.................................323 564-7761
James Hagar, *Administration*
EMP: 78
SALES (corp-wide): 103.7MM **Privately Held**
SIC: 8051 8059 Convalescent home with continuous nursing care; convalescent home
HQ: Far West, Inc
4020 Sierra College Blvd
Rocklin CA 95677

(P-20426)
FAR WEST INC
Also Called: Medical Center
467 E Gilbert St, San Bernardino (92404-5318)
PHONE.................................909 884-4781
Frank De Leosa, *Manager*
EMP: 80
SALES (corp-wide): 103.7MM **Privately Held**
SIC: 8051 8059 Convalescent home with continuous nursing care; rest home, with health care

HQ: Far West, Inc
4020 Sierra College Blvd
Rocklin CA 95677

(P-20427)
FERNVIEW CONVALESCENT HOSPITAL
Also Called: Pinegrove Hlthcare Wllness Ctr
126 N San Gabriel Blvd, San Gabriel (91775-2499)
PHONE.................................626 285-3131
Benjamin Garret, *President*
EMP: 72 **EST:** 1964
SQ FT: 38,000
SALES (est): 2.2MM **Privately Held**
SIC: 8051 8322 8399 Convalescent home with continuous nursing care; rehabilitation services; advocacy group

(P-20428)
FIG HOLDINGS LLC
Also Called: GARDEN CITY HEALTHCARE CENTER
1310 W Granger Ave, Modesto (95350-3911)
PHONE.................................209 524-4817
Gary Collins,
Diana Reyes, *Office Mgr*
Christyn Young, *Hlthcr Dir*
Lee Sorensen,
EMP: 100
SQ FT: 23,000
SALES: 14.8MM
SALES (corp-wide): 40.2MM **Privately Held**
SIC: 8051 Convalescent home with continuous nursing care
PA: Plum Healthcare Group, Llc
100 E San Marcos Blvd # 200
San Marcos CA 92069
760 471-0388

(P-20429)
FIVE STAR QUALITY CARE INC
Also Called: Flagship Health Care Center
466 Flagship Rd, Newport Beach (92663-3635)
PHONE.................................949 642-8044
Bonny Christino, *Manager*
EMP: 200 **Publicly Held**
WEB: www.fivestarqualitycare.com
SIC: 8051 Skilled nursing care facilities
PA: Five Star Senior Living Inc.
400 Centre St
Newton MA 02458

(P-20430)
FIVE STAR QUALITY CARE INC
Also Called: Lasaltte Hlth Rhbilitation Ctr
537 E Fulton St, Stockton (95204-2227)
PHONE.................................209 466-2066
Gus Ropalidis, *Administration*
Chris Fenicle, *Financial Exec*
EMP: 150 **Publicly Held**
WEB: www.fivestarqualitycare.com
SIC: 8051 Skilled nursing care facilities
PA: Five Star Senior Living Inc.
400 Centre St
Newton MA 02458

(P-20431)
FIVE STAR QUALITY CARE INC
Also Called: Van Nuys Health Care Center
6835 Hazeltine Ave, Van Nuys (91405-3218)
PHONE.................................818 997-1841
Grace Alberto, *Administration*
EMP: 65 **Publicly Held**
WEB: www.fivestarqualitycare.com
SIC: 8051 Skilled nursing care facilities
PA: Five Star Senior Living Inc.
400 Centre St
Newton MA 02458
-

(P-20432)
FIVE STAR QUALITY CARE INC
Also Called: Thousand Oaks Health Care Ctr
93 W Avnida De Los Arbles, Thousand Oaks (91360)
PHONE.................................805 492-2444
Larisa Machneva, *Administration*
EMP: 130 **Publicly Held**

WEB: www.fivestarqualitycare.com
SIC: 8051 Skilled nursing care facilities
PA: Five Star Senior Living Inc.
400 Centre St
Newton MA 02458
-

(P-20433)
FIVE STAR QUALITY CARE INC
Also Called: Remington Club I & II
16925 Hierba Dr, San Diego (92128-2688)
PHONE.................................858 673-6300
Kristen Crinigan, *Exec Dir*
EMP: 300 **Publicly Held**
WEB: www.fivestarqualitycare.com
SIC: 8051 Skilled nursing care facilities
PA: Five Star Senior Living Inc.
400 Centre St
Newton MA 02458

(P-20434)
FIVE STAR QUALITY CARE INC
Also Called: Somerford Place Fresno
6075 N Marks Ave, Fresno (93711-1600)
PHONE.................................559 446-6226
Kathy Gorman, *Exec Dir*
EMP: 154 **Publicly Held**
WEB: www.fivestarqualitycare.com
SIC: 8051 Skilled nursing care facilities
PA: Five Star Senior Living Inc.
400 Centre St
Newton MA 02458

(P-20435)
FOOTHILL OAKS CARE CENTER INC
3400 Bell Rd, Auburn (95603-9241)
PHONE.................................530 888-6257
Art Whitney, *CEO*
Ellen Kuykendall, *President*
EMP: 90
SALES (est): 1.9MM
SALES (corp-wide): 103.7MM **Privately Held**
WEB: www.villadelrey.com
SIC: 8051 8093 8062 Convalescent home with continuous nursing care; rehabilitation center; outpatient treatment; general medical & surgical hospitals
HQ: Horizon West Healthcare, Inc.
4020 Sierra College Blvd # 190
Rocklin CA 95677
916 624-6230

(P-20436)
FORUM HEALTHCARE CENTER
23600 Via Esplendor, Cupertino (95014-6571)
PHONE.................................650 944-0200
Lynda Kaser, *Administration*
EMP: 245 **EST:** 1998
SALES (est): 6.1MM **Privately Held**
SIC: 8051 8052 Convalescent home with continuous nursing care; intermediate care facilities

(P-20437)
FOUR SEASONS HEALTHCARE
5335 Laurel Canyon Blvd, North Hollywood (91607-2711)
PHONE.................................818 985-1814
Sharrod Brooks, *Partner*
EMP: 99
SALES (est): 3MM **Privately Held**
SIC: 8051 Mental retardation hospital

(P-20438)
FREEDOM VILLAGE HEALTHCARE CTR
Also Called: Rehabworks At Freedom Village
23442 El Toro Rd Bldg 2, Lake Forest (92630-6992)
PHONE.................................949 472-4733
Joel Niblett, *Administration*
Mary Beth Melby, *Records Dir*
Chery Roscamp, *CFO*
Teresa Leleux, *Administration*
Christine Hall, *Controller*
EMP: 100
SALES (est): 5.1MM **Privately Held**
SIC: 8051 8052 Convalescent home with continuous nursing care; intermediate care facilities

(P-20439)
FRENCH PARK CARE CENTER
Also Called: TENET
600 E Washington Ave, Santa Ana
(92701-3843)
P.O. Box 139036, Dallas TX (75313-9036)
PHONE...................714 973-1656
Talmadge Cline, *Administration*
Candise Nomellini, *Marketing Staff*
EMP: 150
SQ FT: 171,000
SALES: 21.9MM
SALES (corp-wide): 19.3B **Publicly Held**
WEB: www.tenethealth.com
SIC: 8051 Convalescent home with continuous nursing care
PA: Tenet Healthcare Corporation
1445 Ross Ave Ste 1400
Dallas TX 75202
469 893-2200

(P-20440)
FRESNO SKILLED NURSING
Also Called: Healthcare Centre of Fresno
1665 M St, Fresno (93721-1121)
PHONE...................559 268-5361
Sharrod Brooks,
EMP: 99
SALES (est): 6.5MM **Privately Held**
SIC: 8051 Mental retardation hospital

(P-20441)
FRONT PORCH COMMUNITIES
Also Called: Kingsley Manor
1055 N Kingsley Dr, Los Angeles
(90029-1207)
PHONE...................323 661-1128
Cindy Gonzales, *Principal*
Abraham Cervantes, *Officer*
Sindy Gonzalez, *Executive*
Emily Ruyes, *Office Mgr*
Nick Padula, *Food Svc Dir*
EMP: 130
SQ FT: 106,521
SALES (corp-wide): 165.1MM **Privately Held**
SIC: 8051 Convalescent home with continuous nursing care
PA: Front Porch Communities And Services - Casa De Manana, Llc
800 N Brand Blvd Fl 19
Glendale CA 91203
818 729-8100

(P-20442)
FRONT PORCH COMMUNITIES & SVCS
Also Called: Apple Valley Care Center
11959 Apple Valley Rd, Apple Valley
(92308-7507)
PHONE...................760 240-5051
Terry Blumer, *Manager*
EMP: 80
SQ FT: 36,151
SALES (corp-wide): 165.1MM **Privately Held**
SIC: 8051 Convalescent home with continuous nursing care
PA: Front Porch Communities And Services - Casa De Manana, Llc
800 N Brand Blvd Fl 19
Glendale CA 91203
818 729-8100

(P-20443)
FRUITVALE LONG TERM CARE LLC
3020 E 15th St, Oakland (94601-2305)
PHONE...................510 261-5613
Kam McGavock,
EMP: 75
SALES (est): 838.7K **Privately Held**
SIC: 8051 Mental retardation hospital

(P-20444)
G AND E HEALTHCARE SVCS LLC
Also Called: Astoria Nursing and Rehab Ctr
14040 Astoria St, Sylmar (91342-2949)
PHONE...................818 367-5881
Grace Mercado, *Administration*
EMP: 194

SALES (est): 633.9K
SALES (corp-wide): 12.2MM **Privately Held**
SIC: 8051 Skilled nursing care facilities
PA: G And E Healthcare Services Llc
14040 Astoria St
Sylmar CA 91342
818 367-5881

(P-20445)
GARDEN CREST CONVALESCE
Also Called: Garden Crest Rtrment Residence
909 Lucile Ave, Los Angeles (90026-1598)
PHONE...................323 663-8281
Paul Barron, *CEO*
Vera Barron, *Vice Pres*
EMP: 90
SQ FT: 30,000
SALES (est): 6.9MM **Privately Held**
WEB: www.gardencrestweb.com
SIC: 8051 8059 8322 Convalescent home with continuous nursing care; convalescent home; old age assistance

(P-20446)
GARDEN VIEW CARE CENTER INC
14475 Garden View Ln, Baldwin Park
(91706-6000)
PHONE...................626 962-7095
John Sorensen, *President*
Jason Roberts, *Administration*
EMP: 80 **EST:** 1990
SALES: 12MM **Privately Held**
WEB: www.gardenviewcarecenter.com
SIC: 8051 Convalescent home with continuous nursing care

(P-20447)
GARDENA FLORES INC
Also Called: Las Flores Convalescent Hosp
14165 Purche Ave, Gardena (90249-2824)
PHONE...................310 323-4570
Keith Fortune, *Director*
Diana Fortune, *Treasurer*
EMP: 90
SQ FT: 10,000
SALES (est): 5MM **Privately Held**
SIC: 8051 Skilled nursing care facilities

(P-20448)
GARFIELD NURSING HOME INC
Also Called: Morton Bakar Center
1100 Marina Village Pkwy # 100, Alameda
(94501-6461)
PHONE...................510 582-7676
Ann Bakar, *CEO*
Robert H Guttman, *President*
Marshall D Langfeld, *CFO*
Ross C Peterson, *Vice Pres*
EMP: 125
SALES (est): 2.1MM
SALES (corp-wide): 201.7MM **Privately Held**
WEB: www.telecarecorp.com
SIC: 8051 Convalescent home with continuous nursing care
PA: Telecare Corporation
1080 Marina Village Pkwy # 100
Alameda CA 94501
510 337-7950

(P-20449)
GEM TRANSITIONAL CARE CENTER
Also Called: Gem Trans Care
716 S Fair Oaks Ave, Pasadena
(91105-2618)
PHONE...................626 737-0560
Rupert Ouano, *Director*
Manuel Dellana, *Administration*
Arnie Claudio, *Facilities Mgr*
EMP: 80
SALES (est): 3.7MM **Privately Held**
SIC: 8051 Convalescent home with continuous nursing care

(P-20450)
GENESIS HEALTHCARE CORPORATION
Also Called: Meadowbrook Bhavioral Hlth Ctr
3951 East Blvd, Los Angeles (90066-4605)
PHONE...................310 391-8266
Michael Mayer, *Branch Mgr*

Ramona Jessop, *Director*
EMP: 85 **Publicly Held**
SIC: 8051 Skilled nursing care facilities
HQ: Genesis Healthcare Corporation
101 E State St
Kennett Square PA 19348
610 444-6350

(P-20451)
GENESIS HEALTHCARE CORPORATION
Also Called: Laurel Park
1425 Laurel Ave, Pomona (91768-2837)
PHONE...................909 622-1069
Gerald Bogard, *Branch Mgr*
Sylvia Roderiguez, *Administration*
EMP: 50 **Publicly Held**
SIC: 8051 Skilled nursing care facilities
HQ: Genesis Healthcare Corporation
101 E State St
Kennett Square PA 19348
610 444-6350

(P-20452)
GENESIS HEALTHCARE CORPORATION
Also Called: Olive Vista, Center
2335 S Towne Ave, Pomona (91766-6227)
PHONE...................909 628-6024
Richard Escontrias, *Branch Mgr*
EMP: 120 **Publicly Held**
SIC: 8051 8361 Convalescent home with continuous nursing care; residential care
HQ: Genesis Healthcare Corporation
101 E State St
Kennett Square PA 19348
610 444-6350

(P-20453)
GEORGIA ATKISON SNF LLC
Also Called: Alliance Nrsing Rhbltation Ctr
3825 Durfee Ave, El Monte (91732-2505)
PHONE...................626 444-2535
Eli Quinones, *Mng Member*
Marissa Marquez, *Bookkeeper*
Ngo Phan, *Director*
EMP: 125
SQ FT: 30,000
SALES (est): 9MM **Privately Held**
WEB: www.alliancenursingrehab.com
SIC: 8051 Skilled nursing care facilities

(P-20454)
GERI CARE INC
Also Called: Harbor Post Accute Care Center
21521 S Vermont Ave, Torrance
(90502-1939)
PHONE...................310 320-0961
Emmanuel David, *President*
EMP: 100 **EST:** 1975
SQ FT: 30,000
SALES (est): 5.9MM **Privately Held**
SIC: 8051 Convalescent home with continuous nursing care

(P-20455)
GLADIOLUS HOLDINGS LLC
Also Called: Pines At Plcrvlle Hlthcare Ctr
1040 Marshall Way, Placerville
(95667-5706)
PHONE...................530 622-3400
Nick Anderson, *President*
Jared Edmunds, *General Mgr*
EMP: 99
SALES: 950K **Privately Held**
SIC: 8051 Convalescent home with continuous nursing care

(P-20456)
GLENDALE HEALTHCARE CENTER
Also Called: Country Villa Glendale
1208 S Central Ave, Glendale
(91204-2504)
PHONE...................818 246-5516
Adam Mitchel, *Administration*
Irene Deanon, *Personnel Exec*
EMP: 70
SALES: 5.5MM **Privately Held**
SIC: 8051 Convalescent home with continuous nursing care

(P-20457)
GLENWOOD CORPORATION
Also Called: Glenwood Care Center
1300 N C St, Oxnard (93030-4006)
PHONE...................805 983-0305
Jerry E Wells, *President*
Frank Chung MD, *Treasurer*
Wallace Tamoyose MD, *Vice Pres*
Harvey Wilson, *Admin Sec*
Dave Merkley, *Administration*
EMP: 70
SQ FT: 30,000
SALES: 12.1MM **Privately Held**
SIC: 8051 Skilled nursing care facilities

(P-20458)
GLENWOOD GARDENS
Also Called: A E W/Careage Ops
350 Calloway Dr Unit A1, Bakersfield
(93312-2966)
PHONE...................661 587-0221
Cindy Boudreaux, *Business Mgr*
EMP: 260
SALES (est): 9.6MM **Privately Held**
SIC: 8051 Skilled nursing care facilities

(P-20459)
GOLDEN CROSS CARE II INC
Also Called: Golden Cross Hlth Care Fresno
1233 A St, Fresno (93706-3299)
PHONE...................559 268-3023
Marlene Z Robertson, *President*
EMP: 70
SALES (est): 2.9MM **Privately Held**
SIC: 8051 Skilled nursing care facilities

(P-20460)
GOLDEN CROSS CARE INC
Also Called: Golden Cross Health Care
1450 N Fair Oaks Ave, Pasadena
(91103-1801)
PHONE...................626 791-1948
Marlene Robertson, *President*
EMP: 160
SQ FT: 30,000
SALES (est): 6.6MM **Privately Held**
SIC: 8051 Skilled nursing care facilities

(P-20461)
GOLDEN LIVING LLC
Also Called: Beverly
1715 S Cedar Ave, Fresno (93702-4331)
PHONE...................559 237-8377
Ed Johnson, *Exec Dir*
EMP: 93
SALES (corp-wide): 7.4MM **Privately Held**
SIC: 8051 8361 8063 8082 Skilled nursing care facilities; residential care; psychiatric hospitals; home health care services
PA: Golden Living Llc
5220 Tennyson Pkwy # 400
Plano TX 75024
972 372-6300

(P-20462)
GOLDEN LIVING LLC
Also Called: Beverly
1306 E Sumner Ave, Fowler (93625-2627)
PHONE...................559 834-2542
Christine Clark, *Branch Mgr*
EMP: 60
SALES (corp-wide): 7.4MM **Privately Held**
SIC: 8051 8082 Skilled nursing care facilities; home health care services
PA: Golden Living Llc
5220 Tennyson Pkwy # 400
Plano TX 75024
972 372-6300

(P-20463)
GOLDEN LIVING LLC
Also Called: Beverly Healthcare
340 Victoria St, Costa Mesa (92627-1914)
P.O. Box 1933, San Marcos (92079-1933)
PHONE...................949 642-0387
David Sedgwick, *Exec Dir*
EMP: 100
SALES (corp-wide): 7.4MM **Privately Held**
WEB: www.nwbeccorp.com
SIC: 8051 Convalescent home with continuous nursing care

▲ = Import ▼=Export
◆ =Import/Export

PA: Golden Living Llc
5220 Tennyson Pkwy # 400
Plano TX 75024
972 372-6300

(P-20464)
GOLDEN LIVING LLC
Also Called: Golden Livingcenter - Chateau
1221 Rosemarie Ln, Stockton
(95207-6703)
PHONE...............................707 546-0471
Susan Morgan, *Manager*
EMP: 100
SALES (corp-wide): 7.4MM **Privately Held**
SIC: **8051** Convalescent home with continuous nursing care
PA: Golden Living Llc
5220 Tennyson Pkwy # 400
Plano TX 75024
972 372-6300

(P-20465)
GOLDEN LIVING LLC
Also Called: Golden Livingctr-Country View
925 N Cornelia Ave, Fresno (93706-1031)
PHONE...............................559 275-4785
Deann Walters, *Manager*
EMP: 93
SALES (corp-wide): 7.4MM **Privately Held**
SIC: **8051 8059** Skilled nursing care facilities; convalescent home
PA: Golden Living Llc
5220 Tennyson Pkwy # 400
Plano TX 75024
972 372-6300

(P-20466)
GOLDEN LIVING LLC
Also Called: Beverly Healthcare
1477 Grove St, San Francisco
(94117-1421)
PHONE...............................415 563-0565
Simon Chen, *Manager*
Sean De Ocampo, *Social Dir*
EMP: 100
SALES (corp-wide): 7.4MM **Privately Held**
WEB: www.nwbeccorp.com
SIC: **8051** Skilled nursing care facilities
PA: Golden Living Llc
5220 Tennyson Pkwy # 400
Plano TX 75024
972 372-6300

(P-20467)
GOLDEN LIVING LLC
Also Called: Golden Lvngcnter - Bakersfield
3601 San Dimas St, Bakersfield
(93301-1405)
PHONE...............................661 323-2894
Will Maloney, *Director*
EMP: 70
SALES (corp-wide): 7.4MM **Privately Held**
SIC: **8051** Skilled nursing care facilities
PA: Golden Living Llc
5220 Tennyson Pkwy # 400
Plano TX 75024
972 372-6300

(P-20468)
GOLDEN LIVING LLC
Also Called: Beverly Healthcare
1300 N C St, Oxnard (93030-4006)
PHONE...............................805 983-0305
David Banks, *Ch of Bd*
EMP: 100
SALES (corp-wide): 7.4MM **Privately Held**
WEB: www.nwbeccorp.com
SIC: **8051** Skilled nursing care facilities
PA: Golden Living Llc
5220 Tennyson Pkwy # 400
Plano TX 75024
972 372-6300

(P-20469)
GOLDEN LIVING LLC
Also Called: Beverly Healthcare
5445 Everglades St, Ventura (93003-6523)
PHONE...............................805 642-1736
Jay Brady, *Branch Mgr*
EMP: 100

SALES (corp-wide): 7.4MM **Privately Held**
WEB: www.nwbeccorp.com
SIC: **8051** Skilled nursing care facilities
PA: Golden Living Llc
5220 Tennyson Pkwy # 400
Plano TX 75024
972 372-6300

(P-20470)
GOLDEN LIVING LLC
Also Called: Beverly Healthcare
950 S Fairmont Ave, Lodi (95240-5131)
PHONE...............................209 368-0693
Beverly Mannon, *Principal*
EMP: 70
SALES (corp-wide): 7.4MM **Privately Held**
WEB: www.nwbeccorp.com
SIC: **8051** Convalescent home with continuous nursing care
PA: Golden Living Llc
5220 Tennyson Pkwy # 400
Plano TX 75024
972 372-6300

(P-20471)
GOLDEN LIVING LLC
Also Called: Golden Lvngcenter - Santa Rosa
4650 Hoen Ave, Santa Rosa (95405-9407)
PHONE...............................707 546-0471
Georgia Otterson, *Exec Dir*
EMP: 100
SALES (corp-wide): 7.4MM **Privately Held**
SIC: **8051 8069** Skilled nursing care facilities; specialty hospitals, except psychiatric
PA: Golden Living Llc
5220 Tennyson Pkwy # 400
Plano TX 75024
972 372-6300

(P-20472)
GOLDEN LIVING LLC
Also Called: Beverly Healthcare
850 S Sunkist Ave, West Covina
(91790-2534)
PHONE...............................626 962-3368
Mary Julienne, *Manager*
EMP: 80
SQ FT: 25,000
SALES (corp-wide): 7.4MM **Privately Held**
WEB: www.nwbeccorp.com
SIC: **8051 8093** Convalescent home with continuous nursing care; rehabilitation center, outpatient treatment
PA: Golden Living Llc
5220 Tennyson Pkwy # 400
Plano TX 75024
972 372-6300

(P-20473)
GOLDEN LIVING LLC
Also Called: Golden Livingcenter - Petaluma
217 Lakeville St Apt 3, Petaluma
(94952-3166)
PHONE...............................707 763-4109
Monica Choperena, *General Mgr*
EMP: 72
SALES (corp-wide): 7.4MM **Privately Held**
SIC: **8051** Skilled nursing care facilities
PA: Golden Living Llc
5220 Tennyson Pkwy # 400
Plano TX 75024
972 372-6300

(P-20474)
GOLDEN LIVING LLC
Also Called: Golden Livingcenter - San Jose
401 Ridge Vista Ave, San Jose
(95127-1501)
PHONE...............................408 923-7232
Almaroos Apapira, *Exec Dir*
EMP: 105
SALES (corp-wide): 7.4MM **Privately Held**
SIC: **8051** Skilled nursing care facilities
PA: Golden Living Llc
5220 Tennyson Pkwy # 400
Plano TX 75024
972 372-6300

(P-20475)
GOLDEN LIVING LLC
Also Called: Beverly Healthcare
35410 Del Rey, Capistrano Beach
(92624-1814)
PHONE...............................949 496-5786
Nora Saulietis, *Administration*
EMP: 60
SALES (corp-wide): 7.4MM **Privately Held**
WEB: www.nwbeccorp.com
SIC: **8051** Extended care facility
PA: Golden Living Llc
5220 Tennyson Pkwy # 400
Plano TX 75024
972 372-6300

(P-20476)
GOLDEN LIVING LLC
3510 E Shields Ave, Fresno (93726-6909)
PHONE...............................559 222-4807
Kara Pappanduros, *Manager*
EMP: 100
SALES (corp-wide): 7.4MM **Privately Held**
WEB: www.nwbeccorp.com
SIC: **8051** Skilled nursing care facilities
PA: Golden Living Llc
5220 Tennyson Pkwy # 400
Plano TX 75024
972 372-6300

(P-20477)
GOLDEN LIVING LLC
Also Called: Golden Livingcenter - Clovis
111 Barstow Ave, Clovis (93612-2225)
PHONE...............................559 299-2591
Michelle Tathem, *Manager*
EMP: 93
SALES (corp-wide): 7.4MM **Privately Held**
SIC: **8051** Convalescent home with continuous nursing care
PA: Golden Living Llc
5220 Tennyson Pkwy # 400
Plano TX 75024
972 372-6300

(P-20478)
GOLDEN LIVING LLC
Also Called: Beverly Healthcare
3672 N 1st St, Fresno (93726-6810)
PHONE...............................559 227-5383
Kristine Clark, *Manager*
EMP: 65
SALES (corp-wide): 7.4MM **Privately Held**
WEB: www.nwbeccorp.com
SIC: **8051** Skilled nursing care facilities
PA: Golden Living Llc
5220 Tennyson Pkwy # 400
Plano TX 75024
972 372-6300

(P-20479)
GOLDEN LIVING LLC
Also Called: Golden Livingcenter - Reedley
1090 E Dinuba Ave, Reedley (93654-3577)
PHONE...............................559 638-3577
Julie Whiteside, *Manager*
EMP: 93
SALES (corp-wide): 7.4MM **Privately Held**
SIC: **8051 8082** Skilled nursing care facilities; home health care services
PA: Golden Living Llc
5220 Tennyson Pkwy # 400
Plano TX 75024
972 372-6300

(P-20480)
GOLDEN LIVING LLC
Also Called: Beverly Healthcare
1900 Coffee Rd, Modesto (95355-2703)
PHONE...............................209 548-0318
Belinda Guzman, *CEO*
Kim Damale, *Vice Pres*
EMP: 108
SALES (corp-wide): 7.4MM **Privately Held**
WEB: www.nwbeccorp.com
SIC: **8051** Skilled nursing care facilities
PA: Golden Living Llc
5220 Tennyson Pkwy # 400
Plano TX 75024
972 372-6300

(P-20481)
GOLDEN LIVING LLC
Also Called: Beverly Healthcare
350 De Soto Dr, Los Gatos (95032-2402)
PHONE...............................408 356-9151
Julie Okada, *Exec Dir*
EMP: 60
SALES (corp-wide): 7.4MM **Privately Held**
WEB: www.nwbeccorp.com
SIC: **8051** Convalescent home with continuous nursing care
PA: Golden Living Llc
5220 Tennyson Pkwy # 400
Plano TX 75024
972 372-6300

(P-20482)
GOLDEN LIVING LLC
Also Called: Golden Livingcenter - Portside
2740 N California St, Stockton
(95204-5529)
PHONE...............................209 466-3522
Judy Thornhill, *Director*
EMP: 100
SALES (corp-wide): 7.4MM **Privately Held**
SIC: **8051** Convalescent home with continuous nursing care
PA: Golden Living Llc
5220 Tennyson Pkwy # 400
Plano TX 75024
972 372-6300

(P-20483)
GOLDEN LIVING LLC
Also Called: Golden Livingcenter
678 2nd St W, Sonoma (95476-6901)
PHONE...............................707 938-1096
Keith Gold, *Administration*
EMP: 72
SALES (corp-wide): 7.4MM **Privately Held**
SIC: **8051** Skilled nursing care facilities
PA: Golden Living Llc
5220 Tennyson Pkwy # 400
Plano TX 75024
972 372-6300

(P-20484)
GOLDEN LIVING LLC
Also Called: Beverly Healthcare
188 Cohasset Ln, Chico (95926-2206)
PHONE...............................530 343-6084
John Crowley, *Administration*
Barbara Juede Santos, *Director*
EMP: 80
SALES (corp-wide): 7.4MM **Privately Held**
WEB: www.nwbeccorp.com
SIC: **8051** Extended care facility
PA: Golden Living Llc
5220 Tennyson Pkwy # 400
Plano TX 75024
972 372-6300

(P-20485)
GOLDEN LIVING LLC
Also Called: Beverly Healthcare
709 N St, Newman (95360-1162)
PHONE...............................209 862-2862
Darla Larinda, *Exec Dir*
EMP: 69
SALES (corp-wide): 7.4MM **Privately Held**
WEB: www.nwbeccorp.com
SIC: **8051** Convalescent home with continuous nursing care
PA: Golden Living Llc
5220 Tennyson Pkwy # 400
Plano TX 75024
972 372-6300

(P-20486)
GOLDEN STATE HABILITATION CONV (PA)
Also Called: Golden State Care Center
1758 Big Dalton Ave, Baldwin Park
(91706-5910)
PHONE...............................626 962-3274
Eden Salceda, *President*
Claudio Hernandez, *Vice Pres*
Emmanual David, *Admin Sec*
EMP: 400

SALES (est): 8.6MM **Privately Held**
SIC: 8051 8361 8052 Convalescent home with continuous nursing care; residential care; intermediate care facilities

(P-20487)
GOLDEN STATE HEALTH CTRS INC (PA)
13347 Ventura Blvd, Sherman Oaks (91423-3979)
PHONE.....................818 385-3200
Martin J Weiss, *CEO*
Ronald Mayer, *CFO*
David B Weiss, *Chairman*
Ronny Mayer, *Executive*
Howard Weiss, *Admin Sec*
EMP: 121
SQ FT: 2,000
SALES: 62.1MM **Privately Held**
WEB: www.goldenstatehealth.com
SIC: 8051 Skilled nursing care facilities

(P-20488)
GOLDEN STATE WEST VALLEY
7057 Shoup Ave, Canoga Park (91307-2335)
PHONE.....................818 348-8422
Susan Henry, *President*
Rose Kasirer, *Admin Sec*
EMP: 110 EST: 1968
SQ FT: 26,937
SALES (est): 3.7MM
SALES (corp-wide): 62.1MM **Privately Held**
WEB: www.goldenstatehealth.com
SIC: 8051 Skilled nursing care facilities
PA: Golden State Health Centers, Inc.
13347 Ventura Blvd
Sherman Oaks CA 91423
818 385-3200

(P-20489)
GOOD SHEPHERD HEALTH CARE CE
1131 Arizona Ave, Santa Monica (90401-2009)
PHONE.....................310 451-4809
Jeong Lee, *CEO*
EMP: 55
SQ FT: 8,136
SALES (est): 2.2MM **Privately Held**
SIC: 8051 Convalescent home with continuous nursing care

(P-20490)
GOODMAN GROUP INC
Also Called: Alamitos Convalescent Hospital
3902 Katella Ave, Los Alamitos (90720-3304)
PHONE.....................562 596-5561
Pradeep Muley, *Exec Dir*
EMP: 65
SALES (corp-wide): 27.7MM **Privately Held**
WEB: www.thepalmsoflargo.com
SIC: 8051 Convalescent home with continuous nursing care facilities
PA: The Goodman Group Inc
1107 Hazeltine Blvd # 200
Chaska MN 55318
952 361-8000

(P-20491)
GRANADA HLLS CONVALESCENT HOSP
Also Called: Granada Hills Care Center
16123 Chatsworth St, Granada Hills (91344-7045)
PHONE.....................818 891-1745
Seid Sadat, *President*
Abraham Birnbaum, *President*
Kim Marconet, *Vice Pres*
EMP: 64 EST: 1963
SQ FT: 96,680
SALES (est): 2MM **Privately Held**
SIC: 8051 Convalescent home with continuous nursing care

(P-20492)
GRANCARE LLC
Also Called: Vale Healthcare Center
13484 San Pablo Ave, San Pablo (94806-3904)
PHONE.....................510 232-5945
Tim Neal, *Principal*
Remy Rhodes, *President*

Kenneth Tabler, *President*
EMP: 277
SALES (corp-wide): 1B **Privately Held**
SIC: 8051 Skilled nursing care facilities
HQ: Grancare Llc
1 Ravinia Dr Ste 1400
Atlanta GA 30346
770 393-0199

(P-20493)
GRAND PARK CONVALESCENT HOSP
2312 W 8th St, Los Angeles (90057-3955)
PHONE.....................213 382-7315
Barry Kohn, *President*
Toby Kohn, *Vice Pres*
EMP: 135
SQ FT: 60,000
SALES (est): 6.3MM **Privately Held**
SIC: 8051 8361 Convalescent home with continuous nursing care; rehabilitation center, residential: health care incidental

(P-20494)
GRAND TERRACE CARE CENTER
Also Called: Sunbridge Care Ctr - Grnd Ter
12000 Mount Vernon Ave, Grand Terrace (92313-5174)
PHONE.....................909 825-5221
Darlene Simonias, *Branch Mgr*
EMP: 53
SALES (corp-wide): 9.2MM **Privately Held**
SIC: 8051 Convalescent home with continuous nursing care
PA: Grand Terrace Care Center
12000 Mount Vernon Ave
Grand Terrace CA 92313
909 825-5221

(P-20495)
GRAND VALLEY HEALTH CARE CTR
13524 Sherman Way, Van Nuys (91405-2830)
PHONE.....................818 786-3470
Janet Mandelbaum, *Mng Member*
Brenda Mandelbaum, *Mng Member*
Mikhael Reyadh, *Director*
EMP: 108
SALES (est): 3.9MM **Privately Held**
SIC: 8051 Skilled nursing care facilities

(P-20496)
GRANITE HILLS HEALTHCARE
1340 E Madison Ave, El Cajon (92021-8501)
PHONE.....................619 447-1020
Sharrod Brooks,
EMP: 99 EST: 2012
SALES (est): 8.9MM **Privately Held**
SIC: 8051 Skilled nursing care facilities

(P-20497)
GRIFFITH PK RHBLTATION CTR LLC
Also Called: Griffith Park Healthcare Ctr
201 Allen Ave, Glendale (91201-2803)
PHONE.....................818 845-8507
Crystal Solorzano,
EMP: 75 EST: 2015
SALES (est): 279.9K **Privately Held**
SIC: 8051 Skilled nursing care facilities

(P-20498)
GROSS CONVALESCENT HOSPITAL
321 W Turner Rd, Lodi (95240-0517)
PHONE.....................209 334-3760
Paul Gross, *Vice Pres*
Elsie Gross, *Corp Secy*
Oscar Gross, *Principal*
EMP: 73
SQ FT: 10,000
SALES (est): 2.8MM **Privately Held**
SIC: 8051 Convalescent home with continuous nursing care

(P-20499)
GUARDIANS OF THE LOS ANGELES
10780 Santa Monica Blvd # 225, Los Angeles (90025-4749)
PHONE.....................310 479-2468
Shannon Slater, *Manager*
EMP: 67
SALES: 595.8K **Privately Held**
SIC: 8051 Skilled nursing care facilities

(P-20500)
GVA ENTERPRISES INC
Also Called: Angels Nursing Center
415 S Union Ave, Los Angeles (90017-1007)
PHONE.....................213 484-0784
Marco Cortes, *Manager*
EMP: 57
SALES (corp-wide): 5.3MM **Privately Held**
SIC: 8051 Skilled nursing care facilities
PA: Gva Enterprises Inc
316 S Westlake Ave
Los Angeles CA 90057
213 484-0510

(P-20501)
H C C S INC
Also Called: Sherwood Healthcare Center
4700 Elvas Ave, Sacramento (95819-2250)
PHONE.....................916 454-5752
David Hilburn, *Director*
John Lund, *Director*
EMP: 70
SALES (est): 2.7MM **Privately Held**
WEB: www.sherwoods.com
SIC: 8051 Convalescent home with continuous nursing care

(P-20502)
HACIENDA REHABILITATION & HEAL (PA)
1440 S State College Blvd 2a, Anaheim (92806-5724)
PHONE.....................714 778-0221
Rex Moore, *President*
Robert L Stotts, *Ch of Bd*
Donna Stotts, *Treasurer*
EMP: 126
SALES (est): 5MM **Privately Held**
SIC: 8051 Skilled nursing care facilities

(P-20503)
HACIENDA REHABILITATION & HEAL
Also Called: Hacienda Health Care
361 E Grangeville Blvd, Hanford (93230-3054)
PHONE.....................559 582-9221
Rex Moore, *Branch Mgr*
EMP: 120
SALES (est): 3.6MM
SALES (corp-wide): 5MM **Privately Held**
SIC: 8051 8069 Convalescent home with continuous nursing care; specialty hospitals, except psychiatric
PA: Hacienda Rehabilitation & Health Care Center, Inc
1440 S State College Blvd 2a
Anaheim CA 92806
714 778-0221

(P-20504)
HANCOCK PK RHBLITATION CTR LLC
505 N La Brea Ave, Los Angeles (90036-2015)
PHONE.....................323 937-4860
Kelly Atkins,
Chris Felfe,
Roland Rapp,
EMP: 135
SALES (est): 3.9MM **Privately Held**
SIC: 8051 Skilled nursing care facilities

(P-20505)
HARBOR GLEN CARE CENTER
1033 E Arrow Hwy, Glendora (91740-6110)
PHONE.....................626 963-7531
Kevin Thomas, *Owner*
EMP: 100 EST: 2000

SALES (est): 2.9MM
SALES (corp-wide): 1.8B **Publicly Held**
WEB: www.theensigngroup.com
SIC: 8051 Convalescent home with continuous nursing care
PA: The Ensign Group Inc
27101 Puerta Real Ste 450
Mission Viejo CA 92691
949 487-9500

(P-20506)
HAWTHORNE HEALTHCARE
11630 Grevillea Ave, Hawthorne (90250-2231)
PHONE.....................310 679-9732
Sharrod Brooks, *Managing Prtnr*
EMP: 99 EST: 2011
SALES (est): 365K **Privately Held**
SIC: 8051 Skilled nursing care facilities

(P-20507)
HB HEALTHCARE ASSOCIATES LLC
Also Called: Sea Cliff Healthcare Center
18811 Florida St, Huntington Beach (92648-1920)
PHONE.....................714 887-0144
Mike Williams,
Jose Lemus, *QC Dir*
Kirk Lindahl, *Director*
EMP: 90
SALES: 16.2MM **Privately Held**
SIC: 8051 Convalescent home with continuous nursing care

(P-20508)
HCR MANORCARE MED SVCS FLA LLC
Also Called: Manorcare Health Services
1975 Tice Valley Blvd, Walnut Creek (94595-2201)
PHONE.....................925 274-1325
Roger Hogan, *Branch Mgr*
Gilbert Castro, *Records Dir*
Jonathan Frank, *Director*
EMP: 125
SQ FT: 53,335
SALES (corp-wide): 3.6B **Publicly Held**
WEB: www.manorcare.com
SIC: 8051 Convalescent home with continuous nursing care
HQ: Hcr Manorcare Medical Services Of Florida, Llc
333 N Summit St Ste 100
Toledo OH 43604
419 252-5500

(P-20509)
HCR MANORCARE MED SVCS FLA LLC
Also Called: Manor Care
11680 Warner Ave, Fountain Valley (92708-2513)
PHONE.....................714 241-9800
Mark Shaffer, *Administration*
EMP: 195
SALES (corp-wide): 3.6B **Publicly Held**
WEB: www.manorcare.com
SIC: 8051 Convalescent home with continuous nursing care
HQ: Hcr Manorcare Medical Services Of Florida, Llc
333 N Summit St Ste 100
Toledo OH 43604
419 252-5500

(P-20510)
HCR MANORCARE MED SVCS FLA LLC
Also Called: Manor Care
7807 Uplands Way, Citrus Heights (95610-7500)
PHONE.....................916 967-2929
Terri Ballesteros, *Principal*
EMP: 180
SALES (corp-wide): 3.6B **Publicly Held**
WEB: www.manorcare.com
SIC: 8051 Convalescent home with continuous nursing care
HQ: Hcr Manorcare Medical Services Of Florida, Llc
333 N Summit St Ste 100
Toledo OH 43604
419 252-5500

(P-20511)
HCR MANORCARE MED SVCS FLA LLC
Also Called: Manorcare Health Svcs Hemet
1717 W Stetson Ave, Hemet (92545-6882)
PHONE..................................951 925-9171
Ron Ellenich, *Branch Mgr*
EMP: 180
SALES (corp-wide): 3.6B **Publicly Held**
WEB: www.manorcare.com
SIC: 8051 Convalescent home with continuous nursing care
HQ: Hcr Manorcare Medical Services Of
    Florida, Llc
    333 N Summit St Ste 100
    Toledo OH 43604
    419 252-5500

(P-20512)
HCR MANORCARE MED SVCS FLA LLC
Also Called: Manor Care
1150 Tilton Dr, Sunnyvale (94087-2440)
PHONE..................................408 735-7200
Arthur Spencer, *Branch Mgr*
EMP: 100
SALES (corp-wide): 3.6B **Publicly Held**
WEB: www.manorcare.com
SIC: 8051 Convalescent home with continuous nursing care
HQ: Hcr Manorcare Medical Services Of
    Florida, Llc
    333 N Summit St Ste 100
    Toledo OH 43604
    419 252-5500

(P-20513)
HCR MANORCARE MED SVCS FLA LLC
Also Called: Manorcare Health Svcs Rossmoor
1226 Rossmoor Pkwy, Walnut Creek
(94595-2538)
PHONE..................................925 975-5000
John Gallick, *Manager*
EMP: 105
SQ FT: 69,382
SALES (corp-wide): 3.6B **Publicly Held**
WEB: www.manorcare.com
SIC: 8051 Convalescent home with continuous nursing care
HQ: Hcr Manorcare Medical Services Of
    Florida, Llc
    333 N Summit St Ste 100
    Toledo OH 43604
    419 252-5500

(P-20514)
HCR MANORCARE MED SVCS FLA LLC
Also Called: Manorcare Hlth Svcs Encinitas
944 Regal Rd, Encinitas (92024-4634)
PHONE..................................760 944-0331
James Elton, *Manager*
EMP: 100
SQ FT: 38,890
SALES (corp-wide): 3.6B **Publicly Held**
SIC: 8051 Convalescent home with continuous nursing care
HQ: Hcr Manorcare Medical Services Of
    Florida, Llc
    333 N Summit St Ste 100
    Toledo OH 43604
    419 252-5500

(P-20515)
HEALTH & REHABILITATION CENTER
Also Called: Mariner
2065 Los Gatos Almaden Rd, San Jose
(95124-5417)
PHONE..................................408 377-9275
James Brende, *Administration*
EMP: 50
SALES (est): 528.3K **Privately Held**
SIC: 8051 Skilled nursing care facilities

(P-20516)
HEALTH CARE INVESTMENTS INC
Also Called: Rosecrans Care Center
1140 W Rosecrans Ave, Gardena
(90247-2664)
PHONE..................................310 323-3194

Pompeyo Rosales, *President*
Gonzalo Delrosario, *Admin Sec*
EMP: 106
SALES: 2.8MM **Privately Held**
SIC: 8051 Skilled nursing care facilities

(P-20517)
HEALTHCARE CTR OF DOWNEY LLC
Also Called: Lakewood Healthcare Center
12023 Lakewood Blvd, Downey
(90242-2635)
PHONE..................................562 869-0978
Vince Hambright, *CEO*
Ken Lehmann,
EMP: 250
SQ FT: 1,076,391
SALES: 21.6MM **Privately Held**
SIC: 8051 Mental retardation hospital

(P-20518)
HEALTHCARE INVESTMENTS II LLC
Also Called: Royal Oaks Care Center
2001 Terra Ln, Arcadia (91007-8142)
PHONE..................................310 638-9377
Pompeyo Rosales, *Mng Member*
Cipriano Bautista Jr, *Administration*
Gonzalo Delrosario Jr,
EMP: 80
SQ FT: 10,000
SALES (est): 4MM **Privately Held**
WEB: www.healthcareinvestment.com
SIC: 8051 Skilled nursing care facilities

(P-20519)
HEALTHCARE MGT SYSTEMS INC (PA)
Also Called: BRADLEY COURT
900 Lane Ave Ste 190, Chula Vista
(91914-4558)
PHONE..................................619 521-9641
Tanya Pontecorvo, *President*
Kevin Cablayan, *CFO*
Erwin Cablayan, *Vice Pres*
EMP: 120
SALES: 3.5MM **Privately Held**
SIC: 8051 Skilled nursing care facilities

(P-20520)
HEALTHCARE MGT SYSTEMS INC
Also Called: Bradley Grdns Convalescent Ctr
980 W 7th St, San Jacinto (92582-3814)
PHONE..................................951 654-9347
Dyan Lewis, *Manager*
EMP: 55
SALES (est): 1.3MM
SALES (corp-wide): 3.5MM **Privately Held**
SIC: 8051 Convalescent home with continuous nursing care
PA: Healthcare Management Systems, Inc.
    900 Lane Ave Ste 190
    Chula Vista CA 91914
    619 521-9641

(P-20521)
HEBREW HOME FOR AGED DISABLED
Also Called: San Franciso Campus For Jewish
302 Silver Ave, San Francisco
(94112-1510)
PHONE..................................415 334-2500
Daniel Ruth, *President*
Kevin T Potter, *CFO*
Matthew Patchell, *Officer*
Ken Dip, *Administration*
Daniel Hoebeke, *Planning*
EMP: 600 EST: 1889
SALES: 112.8MM **Privately Held**
WEB: www.jhsf.org
SIC: 8051 Skilled nursing care facilities

(P-20522)
HELIOS HEALTHCARE LLC
Also Called: El Camino Care Center
2540 Carmichael Way, Carmichael
(95608-5314)
PHONE..................................916 482-0465
Evelyn McGraff, *Administration*
EMP: 140

SALES (corp-wide): 24.2MM **Privately Held**
SIC: 8051 Skilled nursing care facilities
PA: Helios Healthcare, Llc
    520 Capitol Mall Ste 800
    Sacramento CA 95814
    916 471-2241

(P-20523)
HELIOS HEALTHCARE LLC
Also Called: Sunridge Care & Rehabilitation
350 Iris Dr, Salinas (93906-3514)
PHONE..................................831 449-1515
Rachael Bruton, *Administration*
EMP: 150
SALES (corp-wide): 24.2MM **Privately Held**
SIC: 8051 Skilled nursing care facilities
PA: Helios Healthcare, Llc
    520 Capitol Mall Ste 800
    Sacramento CA 95814
    916 471-2241

(P-20524)
HELPING HANDS SANCTUARY OF IDA
Also Called: Lacumbre Senior Living
3880 Via Lucero, Santa Barbara
(93110-1605)
PHONE..................................805 687-6651
Lender Warren, *Manager*
EMP: 130
SALES (corp-wide): 54.6MM **Privately Held**
SIC: 8051 Skilled nursing care facilities
PA: Helping Hands Sanctuary Of Idaho Inc
    4978 Rainbow Ln
    Pocatello ID

(P-20525)
HELPING HANDS SANCTUARY OF IDA
Also Called: Helping Hands of Westminster
240 Hospital Cir, Westminster
(92683-3953)
PHONE..................................714 892-6686
Jon Peralez, *Administration*
Cristina Saril, *Director*
EMP: 100
SQ FT: 24,214
SALES (est): 2.6MM **Privately Held**
SIC: 8051 Skilled nursing care facilities

(P-20526)
HERITAGE HEALTH CARE INC
Also Called: Heritage Gardens Hlth Care Ctr
25271 Barton Rd, Loma Linda
(92354-3013)
PHONE..................................909 796-0216
Stephen Flood, *CEO*
Gregory S Goings, *CEO*
Jim Kilian, *CFO*
EMP: 150
SALES: 11.6MM **Privately Held**
SIC: 8051 8059 Skilled nursing care facilities; rest home, with health care

(P-20527)
HERITAGE MANOR INC
610 N Garfield Ave, Monterey Park
(91754-1103)
PHONE..................................626 573-3141
Janie Campos, *Administration*
Janie Chen, *Administration*
Cathriene Mc Dowell, *Financial Exec*
EMP: 80
SALES: 9.3MM **Privately Held**
SIC: 8051 Skilled nursing care facilities

(P-20528)
HERMAN HEALTH CARE CENTER
2295 Plummer Ave, San Jose
(95125-4767)
PHONE..................................408 269-0701
Jeff Maggard, *Manager*
Erica Covarrubias, *Social Dir*
Sandra Stumps, *Training Spec*
Mandy Sollis, *Mktg Dir*
Mike Bottarini, *Director*
EMP: 99
SALES (est): 3.5MM **Privately Held**
SIC: 8051 Convalescent home with continuous nursing care

(P-20529)
HERMAN SANITARIUM
2295 Plummer Ave, San Jose
(95125-4767)
PHONE..................................408 269-0701
Steve Marcus, *Administration*
Robert Sollis, *President*
EMP: 104
SQ FT: 4,500
SALES (est): 3.4MM **Privately Held**
SIC: 8051 Convalescent home with continuous nursing care

(P-20530)
HIGHLAND PARK SKILLED NURSING
5125 Monte Vista St, Los Angeles
(90042-3931)
PHONE..................................323 254-6125
Shlomo Rechnitz,
Jenny Hwang, *Director*
EMP: 72 EST: 2008
SALES: 6.3MM **Privately Held**
SIC: 8051 Convalescent home with continuous nursing care

(P-20531)
HILLVIEW CONVALESCENT HOSPITAL
530 W Dunne Ave, Morgan Hill
(95037-4823)
PHONE..................................408 779-3633
James Ross, *Owner*
Richard Ross, *Co-Owner*
Steve Ross, *Administration*
EMP: 50
SQ FT: 10,000
SALES: 3.7MM **Privately Held**
SIC: 8051 Convalescent home with continuous nursing care

(P-20532)
HONEY FLOWER HOLDINGS LLC
Also Called: ARLINGTON GARDENS CARE CENTER
3688 Nye Ave, Riverside (92505-1818)
PHONE..................................951 351-2800
Mark Ballif, *Mng Member*
Latasha Woods, *Office Mgr*
Brett Hill, *Administration*
Mariela Villegas, *Social Worker*
Paul Hubbard, *Mng Member*
EMP: 170
SALES: 15.1MM **Privately Held**
SIC: 8051 Convalescent home with continuous nursing care

(P-20533)
HORIZON WEST INC
Also Called: Walnut Whtney Convalecent Hosp
3529 Walnut Ave, Carmichael
(95608-3049)
PHONE..................................916 488-8601
Kathy Spake, *Branch Mgr*
EMP: 130
SALES (corp-wide): 103.7MM **Privately Held**
SIC: 8051 Convalescent home with continuous nursing care
PA: Horizon West, Inc.
    4020 Sierra College Blvd
    Rocklin CA 95677
    916 624-6230

(P-20534)
HORIZON WEST INC
Also Called: Heritage Conalescent Hospital
5255 Hemlock St, Sacramento
(95841-3017)
PHONE..................................916 331-4590
Randy Balecha, *Manager*
EMP: 100
SALES (corp-wide): 103.7MM **Privately Held**
SIC: 8051 8361 8059 Skilled nursing care facilities; residential care; convalescent home
PA: Horizon West, Inc.
    4020 Sierra College Blvd
    Rocklin CA 95677
    916 624-6230

(P-20535)
HORIZON WEST HEALTHCARE INC (HQ)
4020 Sierra College Blvd # 190, Rocklin (95677-3906)
PHONE....................916 624-6230
Martine D Harmon, *CEO*
Dennis Roccaforte, *Corp Secy*
Bernice Schrabeck, *Vice Pres*
EMP: 59
SQ FT: 6,000
SALES (est): 52.6MM
SALES (corp-wide): 103.7MM **Privately Held**
WEB: www.villadelrey.com
SIC: 8051 Convalescent home with continuous nursing care
PA: Horizon West, Inc.
4020 Sierra College Blvd
Rocklin CA 95677
916 624-6230

(P-20536)
HORIZON WEST HEALTHCARE INC
Also Called: Valley View Skilled Nursing
1162 S Dora St, Ukiah (95482-6340)
PHONE....................707 462-1436
Paul Medlin, *Administration*
EMP: 60
SALES (corp-wide): 103.7MM **Privately Held**
WEB: www.villadelrey.com
SIC: 8051 Convalescent home with continuous nursing care
HQ: Horizon West Healthcare, Inc.
4020 Sierra College Blvd # 190
Rocklin CA 95677
916 624-6230

(P-20537)
HOSPICE OF SAN JOAQUIN
3888 Pacific Ave, Stockton (95204-1953)
PHONE....................209 957-3888
Stephen L Guasco, *CEO*
Kerrie Biddle, *CFO*
Melanie Payne, *Officer*
Stephen Guasco, *Exec Dir*
Russ Pate, *Business Mgr*
EMP: 90
SQ FT: 5,000
SALES: 15.1MM **Privately Held**
WEB: www.hospicesj.org
SIC: 8051 8641 Skilled nursing care facilities; social associations

(P-20538)
HOVLID SKILLED NURSING
240 Spruce St, Gridley (95948-2216)
PHONE....................530 846-9065
John Turner, *Director*
EMP: 50
SALES (est): 440.4K **Privately Held**
SIC: 8051 Convalescent home with continuous nursing care

(P-20539)
HUNTINGTON BCH CNVLESCENT HOSP
Also Called: Sea Cliff Health Care
18811 Florida St, Huntington Beach (92648-1920)
PHONE....................714 847-3515
Michael Williams, *Administration*
Evelyn Aranton, *Nursing Dir*
EMP: 300
SALES (est): 8.3MM **Privately Held**
SIC: 8051 Convalescent home with continuous nursing care

(P-20540)
HYDE PARK CONVALESCENT HOSP
6520 West Blvd, Los Angeles (90043-4393)
PHONE....................323 753-1354
Jeff Mendell, *President*
Elaine Wiesel, *Admin Sec*
EMP: 50
SQ FT: 15,258
SALES: 3.4MM **Privately Held**
SIC: 8051 Skilled nursing care facilities

(P-20541)
IMAGINATIVE HORIZONS INC
Also Called: Hillcrest Manor Sanitarium
1889 National City Blvd, National City (91950-5517)
PHONE....................619 477-1176
Gary Byrnes, *President*
Rosella Byrnes, *Treasurer*
Dan Byrnes, *Info Tech Dir*
EMP: 84
SQ FT: 30,000
SALES (est): 6.1MM **Privately Held**
WEB: www.specialized-care.com
SIC: 8051 Skilled nursing care facilities

(P-20542)
INDIO HLTHCARE WLLNESS CTR LLC
Also Called: Desert Springs Healthcare
82262 Valencia Ave, Indio (92201-3120)
PHONE....................760 347-6000
Sharrod Brooks,
EMP: 99 EST: 2010
SALES (est): 3.4MM **Privately Held**
SIC: 8051 Skilled nursing care facilities

(P-20543)
INFINITY CARE OF EAST LA
101 S Fickett St, Los Angeles (90033-4017)
PHONE....................323 261-8108
Dr Bina Kambar, *President*
Rani Magboo, *Executive*
EMP: 98
SALES: 8.4MM **Privately Held**
SIC: 8051 Skilled nursing care facilities

(P-20544)
INLAND CHRISTIAN HOME INC
1950 S Mountain Ave Ofc, Ontario (91762-6709)
PHONE....................909 395-9322
David Stienstra, *President*
Lisa Stueve, *Marketing Staff*
Karen Miedema, *Director*
EMP: 114
SQ FT: 100,000
SALES: 5.2MM **Privately Held**
WEB: www.ichome.org
SIC: 8051 8052 6513 8361 Skilled nursing care facilities; intermediate care facilities; retirement hotel operation; residential care

(P-20545)
INTEGRTED CARE COMMUNITIES INC
Also Called: Inegrated Care Communities
11751 Davis St, Moreno Valley (92557-6316)
PHONE....................951 243-3837
Carl Rowe, *President*
Phillip Saucedo, *CFO*
EMP: 50
SALES (est): 3MM **Privately Held**
WEB: www.icare.bz
SIC: 8051 Skilled nursing care facilities

(P-20546)
INTERCOMMUNITY CARE CENTERS
2626 Grand Ave, Long Beach (90815-1707)
PHONE....................562 427-8915
Russel Boydston, *Branch Mgr*
Rosemary Valentin, *Office Mgr*
Janet Sosky, *Director*
EMP: 120
SQ FT: 32,159
SALES (corp-wide): 7.9MM **Privately Held**
WEB: www.iccare.org
SIC: 8051 Mental retardation hospital
PA: Intercommunity Care Centers Inc
2660 Grand Ave
Long Beach CA
562 426-1368

(P-20547)
J P H CONSULTING INC (PA)
1101 Crenshaw Blvd, Los Angeles (90019-3112)
PHONE....................323 934-5660
Jeoung H Lee, *President*
Greda Bernabe, *CFO*

Jewel Son, *Legal Staff*
Kyle Watanabe, *Director*
EMP: 50
SALES (est): 22.8MM **Privately Held**
SIC: 8051 Skilled nursing care facilities

(P-20548)
J P H CONSULTING INC
4515 Huntington Dr S, Los Angeles (90032-1940)
PHONE....................323 934-5660
EMP: 206
SALES (corp-wide): 22.8MM **Privately Held**
SIC: 8051 Skilled nursing care facilities
PA: J P H Consulting, Inc.
1101 Crenshaw Blvd
Los Angeles CA 90019
323 934-5660

(P-20549)
JEFFREY PINE HOLDINGS LLC
Also Called: Villa Las Plmas Healthcare Ctr
622 S Anza St, El Cajon (92020-6602)
PHONE....................619 442-0544
Myrna De Guzman,
Melinda Astudillo, *Records Dir*
Ellen Livingston, *Vice Pres*
Adriana Bernal, *Social Dir*
Erin Chancler, *General Mgr*
EMP: 99
SALES: 17.4MM **Privately Held**
SIC: 8051 Convalescent home with continuous nursing care

(P-20550)
JOHNRE CARE LLC
461 E Johnston Ave, Hemet (92543-7113)
PHONE....................951 658-6374
Johnny Sicat, *Mng Member*
EMP: 60
SALES (est): 1.9MM **Privately Held**
SIC: 8051 Skilled nursing care facilities

(P-20551)
KARMA INC
Also Called: Manteca Care Rhabilitation Ctr
410 Eastwood Ave, Manteca (95336-3167)
PHONE....................209 239-1222
Antony Thekkek, *President*
Prema Thekkek, *Vice Pres*
EMP: 165
SQ FT: 29,700
SALES (est): 5.9MM
SALES (corp-wide): 12.1MM **Privately Held**
WEB: www.paksn.com
SIC: 8051 Convalescent home with continuous nursing care
PA: Paksn, Inc.
540 W Monte Vista Ave
Vacaville CA 95688
707 449-3400

(P-20552)
KATELLA PROPERTIES
Also Called: Alamitos W Convalescent Hosp
3902 Katella Ave, Los Alamitos (90720-3304)
PHONE....................562 596-5561
Marilyn Gelgincolin, *Director*
Dora Hernandez, *Technology*
Gerardo Tapia, *Maintence Staff*
EMP: 170
SALES (est): 4.7MM
SALES (corp-wide): 4MM **Privately Held**
WEB: www.katellamanor.com
SIC: 8051 Convalescent home with continuous nursing care
PA: Katella Properties
3952 Katella Ave
Los Alamitos CA 90720
562 596-2773

(P-20553)
KIMBERLY CARE CENTER INC
Also Called: SANTA MARIA CARE CENTER
820 W Cook St, Santa Maria (93458-5414)
PHONE....................805 925-8877
Walter Matjasic, *President*
EMP: 75
SQ FT: 20,000
SALES: 3.7MM **Privately Held**
SIC: 8051 Skilled nursing care facilities

(P-20554)
KINDRED HEALTHCARE OPER INC
Also Called: Kindred Nrsing Hlthcre- Bybrry
1800 Adobe St, Concord (94520-2313)
PHONE....................925 692-5886
J Seawell, *Exec Dir*
EMP: 106
SQ FT: 25,780
SALES (corp-wide): 6B **Privately Held**
WEB: www.salemhaven.com
SIC: 8051 Skilled nursing care facilities
HQ: Kindred Healthcare Operating, Llc
680 S 4th St
Louisville KY 40202
502 596-7300

(P-20555)
KINDRED HEALTHCARE OPER INC
4700 Elvas Ave, Sacramento (95819-2250)
PHONE....................916 454-5752
David Hilburn, *Director*
EMP: 75
SALES (corp-wide): 6B **Privately Held**
WEB: www.salemhaven.com
SIC: 8051 Skilled nursing care facilities
HQ: Kindred Healthcare Operating, Llc
680 S 4th St
Louisville KY 40202
502 596-7300

(P-20556)
KINDRED HEALTHCARE OPER INC
Also Called: Kindred Hospital - Brea
875 N Brea Blvd, Brea (92821-2606)
PHONE....................714 529-6842
Donna Hoover, *Administration*
Wendy Ellington, *Pharmacy Dir*
Grace Yang, *Pharmacist*
Steve Aird, *Director*
EMP: 79
SALES (corp-wide): 6B **Privately Held**
WEB: www.salemhaven.com
SIC: 8051 Extended care facility
HQ: Kindred Healthcare Operating, Llc
680 S 4th St
Louisville KY 40202
502 596-7300

(P-20557)
KINDRED HEALTHCARE OPER INC
7534 Palm Ave, Highland (92346-3736)
PHONE....................909 862-0611
Lance Squire, *Administration*
EMP: 161
SALES (corp-wide): 6B **Privately Held**
WEB: www.salemhaven.com
SIC: 8051 8069 Skilled nursing care facilities; specialty hospitals, except psychiatric
HQ: Kindred Healthcare Operating, Llc
680 S 4th St
Louisville KY 40202
502 596-7300

(P-20558)
KINDRED HEALTHCARE OPER INC
Also Called: Kindred Nursng & Healthcare
76 Fenton St, Livermore (94550-4144)
PHONE....................925 443-1800
Canbice Hale, *Branch Mgr*
Nancy Currie, *Director*
EMP: 90
SALES (corp-wide): 6B **Privately Held**
WEB: www.salemhaven.com
SIC: 8051 Skilled nursing care facilities
HQ: Kindred Healthcare Operating, Llc
680 S 4th St
Louisville KY 40202
502 596-7300

(P-20559)
KINDRED HEALTHCARE OPER INC
1586 W San Marcos Blvd, San Marcos (92078-4019)
PHONE....................760 471-2986
Daicel Gasperian, *Manager*
EMP: 130

▲ = Import ▼=Export
◆ =Import/Export

SALES (corp-wide): 6B **Privately Held**
WEB: www.salemhaven.com
SIC: 8051 Skilled nursing care facilities
HQ: Kindred Healthcare Operating, Llc
680 S 4th St
Louisville KY 40202
502 596-7300

(P-20560)
KINDRED HEALTHCARE OPER INC
Also Called: Pacific Coast Care Center
720 E Romie Ln, Salinas (93901-4208)
PHONE..........................831 424-8072
Gerald Hunter, *Administration*
EMP: 165
SALES (corp-wide): 6B **Privately Held**
WEB: www.salemhaven.com
SIC: 8051 Skilled nursing care facilities
HQ: Kindred Healthcare Operating, Llc
680 S 4th St
Louisville KY 40202
502 596-7300

(P-20561)
KINDRED HEALTHCARE OPER INC
Also Called: Kindred Nursing
2121 Pine St, San Francisco (94115-2829)
PHONE..........................415 922-5085
Melissa Jones, *Director*
EMP: 100
SALES (corp-wide): 6B **Privately Held**
WEB: www.salemhaven.com
SIC: 8051 Skilled nursing care facilities
HQ: Kindred Healthcare Operating, Llc
680 S 4th St
Louisville KY 40202
502 596-7300

(P-20562)
KINDRED HEALTHCARE OPERATING
2211 Mount Vernon Ave, Bakersfield (93306-3309)
PHONE..........................661 872-2121
Lori Hay, *Manager*
EMP: 200
SALES (corp-wide): 6B **Privately Held**
WEB: www.salemhaven.com
SIC: 8051 Skilled nursing care facilities
HQ: Kindred Healthcare Operating, Llc
680 S 4th St
Louisville KY 40202
502 596-7300

(P-20563)
KINDRED HEALTHCARE OPERATING
223 Fargo Way, Folsom (95630-2961)
PHONE..........................916 351-9151
Meridith Taylor, *Administration*
EMP: 150
SALES (corp-wide): 6B **Privately Held**
WEB: www.salemhaven.com
SIC: 8051 Skilled nursing care facilities
HQ: Kindred Healthcare Operating, Llc
680 S 4th St
Louisville KY 40202
502 596-7300

(P-20564)
KINDRED NURSING CENTERS W LLC
Also Called: Kindred Transitional Care
516 Willow St, Alameda (94501-6132)
PHONE..........................510 521-5600
Richard Espinosa, *Administration*
Christine Christopher, *Executive*
Tom Wood, *Finance Mgr*
Norbu Sangpo, *Chf Purch Ofc*
Frank Rynig, *Director*
EMP: 99
SALES (corp-wide): 6B **Privately Held**
WEB: www.salemhaven.com
SIC: 8051 Skilled nursing care facilities
HQ: Kindred Nursing Centers West Llc
3128 Boxelder Dr
Cheyenne WY 82001
307 634-7901

(P-20565)
KINDRED NURSING CENTERS W LLC
Also Called: Kindred Transitional Care
2120 Benton Dr, Redding (96003-2151)
PHONE..........................530 243-6317
Michael Sowerby, *Manager*
EMP: 141
SALES (corp-wide): 6B **Privately Held**
WEB: www.salemhaven.com
SIC: 8051 Skilled nursing care facilities
HQ: Kindred Nursing Centers West Llc
3128 Boxelder Dr
Cheyenne WY 82001
307 634-7901

(P-20566)
KINDRED NURSING CENTERS W LLC
Also Called: Kindred Transitional
1517 Knickerbocker Dr, Stockton (95210-3119)
PHONE..........................209 957-4539
Keith Braley, *Administration*
EMP: 112
SALES (corp-wide): 6B **Privately Held**
WEB: www.salemhaven.com
SIC: 8051 Skilled nursing care facilities
HQ: Kindred Nursing Centers West Llc
3128 Boxelder Dr
Cheyenne WY 82001
307 634-7901

(P-20567)
KISSITO HEALTH CASE INC
Also Called: Arbor Vly Nrsing Rhblttion Ctr
1310 W Granger Ave, Modesto (95350-3911)
PHONE..........................209 524-4817
Al Johnson, *Branch Mgr*
EMP: 127
SALES (corp-wide): 61.6MM **Privately Held**
SIC: 8051 8361 Convalescent home with continuous nursing care; rehabilitation center, residential: health care incidental
PA: Kissito Healthcare, Inc.
5228 Valleypointe Pkwy
Roanoke VA 24019
540 265-0322

(P-20568)
KNOLLS CONVALESCENT HOSPITAL (PA)
Also Called: Desert Knlls Convalescent Hosp
16890 Green Tree Blvd, Victorville (92395-5618)
PHONE..........................760 245-5361
Gary L Bechtold, *President*
Fred Bechtold, *Vice Pres*
Larry Bechtold, *Vice Pres*
EMP: 130
SQ FT: 5,421
SALES (est): 8.4MM **Privately Held**
SIC: 8051 8052 Convalescent home with continuous nursing care; intermediate care facilities

(P-20569)
KNOLLS CONVALESCENT HOSPITAL
Also Called: Desert Knolls Convalescent
14973 Hesperia Rd, Victorville (92395-3923)
PHONE..........................760 245-6477
Gary Bechtold, *General Mgr*
EMP: 80
SALES (est): 1.1MM
SALES (corp-wide): 8.4MM **Privately Held**
SIC: 8051 6513 Convalescent home with continuous nursing care; apartment building operators
PA: Knolls Convalescent Hospital Inc
16890 Green Tree Blvd
Victorville CA 92395
760 245-5361

(P-20570)
KSM HEALTHCARE INC
Also Called: DREIER'S NURSING CARE CENTER
1400 W Glenoaks Blvd, Glendale (91201-1911)
PHONE..........................818 242-1183

John Haedrich, *President*
EMP: 76
SQ FT: 40,000
SALES: 4.7MM **Privately Held**
WEB: www.nursing-care.com
SIC: 8051 Skilled nursing care facilities

(P-20571)
KU KYOUNG
Also Called: Eden Villa
19960 Santa Maria Ave, Castro Valley (94546-4220)
P.O. Box 590428 (94546)
PHONE..........................510 582-2765
Kyoung Ku, *Owner*
EMP: 170
SQ FT: 37,157
SALES (est): 3.9MM **Privately Held**
SIC: 8051 1522 Convalescent home with continuous nursing care; residential construction

(P-20572)
LA JOLLA VILLAGE TOWERS 500
8515 Costa Verde Blvd Ofc, San Diego (92122-1152)
PHONE..........................858 646-7700
Steve Brudnick, *Administration*
Vicki Simpson, *Administration*
EMP: 65
SQ FT: 900,000
SALES (est): 1.4MM **Privately Held**
SIC: 8051 Skilled nursing care facilities

(P-20573)
LA PALMA CARE CENTER
Also Called: La Palma Nursing Center
1130 W La Palma Ave, Anaheim (92801-2803)
PHONE..........................714 772-7480
Sim Mandelbaum, *President*
Joseph Berkowitc, *Administration*
EMP: 75
SQ FT: 20,000
SALES (est): 3.5MM **Privately Held**
SIC: 8051 Convalescent home with continuous nursing care

(P-20574)
LAFALTTE RHBILITATION CARE CTR
537 E Fulton St, Stockton (95204-2227)
PHONE..........................209 466-2066
Gus Ropalidas, *Administration*
EMP: 100
SALES (est): 1.1MM **Privately Held**
SIC: 8051 Convalescent home with continuous nursing care

(P-20575)
LAKEWOOD MANOR NORTH INC
831 S Lake St, Los Angeles (90057-4013)
PHONE..........................213 380-9175
Kim C Elliott, *Administration*
EMP: 74 EST: 1971
SQ FT: 23,000
SALES (est): 3.8MM **Privately Held**
SIC: 8051 Skilled nursing care facilities

(P-20576)
LAS VILLAS DEL NORTE
Also Called: Healthcare Group
1325 Las Villas Way, Escondido (92026-1946)
PHONE..........................760 741-1047
John Helpsley, *Director*
EMP: 100
SALES (corp-wide): 3MM **Privately Held**
SIC: 8051 8052 Skilled nursing care facilities; intermediate care facilities
PA: Las Villas Del Norte
416 W Spruce St
Junction City KS 66441
760 741-1046

(P-20577)
LAWNDALE HEALTHCARE & WELLNESS
15100 Prairie Ave, Lawndale (90260-2209)
PHONE..........................310 679-3344
Sharrod Brooks,
EMP: 99 EST: 2011
SALES (est): 6.5MM **Privately Held**
SIC: 8051 Mental retardation hospital

(P-20578)
LIBERTY HEALTHCARE OF OKLAHOMA
Also Called: Regency
4463 San Felipe Rd Ofc, San Jose (95135-1515)
PHONE..........................408 532-7677
Aliyan Montose, *Manager*
EMP: 80 **Privately Held**
SIC: 8051 Skilled nursing care facilities
PA: Liberty Healthcare Of Oklahoma Inc
3073 Horseshoe Dr S # 100
Naples FL 34104

(P-20579)
LIFE CARE CENTERS AMERICA INC
Also Called: Life Care Center of La Habra
1233 W La Habra Blvd, La Habra (90631-5226)
PHONE..........................562 690-0852
Daniel Husband, *Administration*
Therese Allen, *Office Mgr*
EMP: 90
SALES (corp-wide): 119.8MM **Privately Held**
SIC: 8051 Convalescent home with continuous nursing care
PA: Life Care Centers Of America, Inc.
3570 Keith St Nw
Cleveland TN 37312
423 472-9585

(P-20580)
LIFE CARE CENTERS AMERICA INC
11926 La Mirada Blvd, La Mirada (90638-1303)
PHONE..........................562 943-7156
Chris Stottlemyer, *Manager*
Dori Vandenries, *Office Mgr*
EMP: 100
SALES (corp-wide): 119.8MM **Privately Held**
SIC: 8051 Convalescent home with continuous nursing care
PA: Life Care Centers Of America, Inc.
3570 Keith St Nw
Cleveland TN 37312
423 472-9585

(P-20581)
LIFE CARE CENTERS AMERICA INC
Also Called: Mirada Hills Rehb & Conva
12200 La Mirada Blvd, La Mirada (90638-1306)
PHONE..........................562 947-8691
Selina Stewart, *Exec Dir*
Dolores Estrada, *QC Dir*
EMP: 150
SALES (corp-wide): 119.8MM **Privately Held**
SIC: 8051 Skilled nursing care facilities
PA: Life Care Centers Of America, Inc.
3570 Keith St Nw
Cleveland TN 37312
423 472-9585

(P-20582)
LIFE CARE CENTERS AMERICA INC
Also Called: Life Care Center San Gabriel
909 W Santa Anita Ave, San Gabriel (91776-1018)
PHONE..........................626 289-5365
Eunice Fletcher, *Manager*
EMP: 90
SALES (corp-wide): 119.8MM **Privately Held**
SIC: 8051 Convalescent home with continuous nursing care
PA: Life Care Centers Of America, Inc.
3570 Keith St Nw
Cleveland TN 37312
423 472-9585

(P-20583)
LIFE CARE CENTERS AMERICA INC
Also Called: Life Care Centers of Escondido
1980 Felicita Rd, Escondido (92025-5922)
PHONE..........................760 741-6109

PRODUCTS & SVCS

Trent Weaver, *Administration*
EMP: 200
SALES (corp-wide): 119.8MM **Privately Held**
SIC: 8051 Convalescent home with continuous nursing care
PA: Life Care Centers Of America, Inc.
3570 Keith St Nw
Cleveland TN 37312
423 472-9585

(P-20584)
LIFE CARE CENTERS AMERICA INC
Also Called: Lake Forest Nursing Center
25652 Old Trabuco Rd, Lake Forest (92630-2776)
PHONE.....................949 380-9380
Kim Le, *Branch Mgr*
EMP: 200
SALES (corp-wide): 119.8MM **Privately Held**
SIC: 8051 Convalescent home with continuous nursing care
PA: Life Care Centers Of America, Inc.
3570 Keith St Nw
Cleveland TN 37312
423 472-9585

(P-20585)
LIFE CARE CENTERS AMERICA INC
Also Called: Imperial Convalescent
11926 La Mirada Blvd, La Mirada (90638-1303)
PHONE.....................562 943-7156
Ted Stultz, *Manager*
Araseli Bejar, *Hum Res Coord*
EMP: 150
SALES (corp-wide): 119.8MM **Privately Held**
SIC: 8051 8741 Convalescent home with continuous nursing care; management services
PA: Life Care Centers Of America, Inc.
3570 Keith St Nw
Cleveland TN 37312
423 472-9585

(P-20586)
LIFE CARE CENTERS AMERICA INC
Also Called: Life Care Center of Bellflower
16910 Woodruff Ave, Bellflower (90706-6036)
PHONE.....................562 867-1761
Tooren Bel, *Manager*
Ester Del Mundo, *Teacher Per Dir*
Mary Helen Gomez, *Director*
EMP: 100
SALES (corp-wide): 119.8MM **Privately Held**
SIC: 8051 Convalescent home with continuous nursing care
PA: Life Care Centers Of America, Inc.
3570 Keith St Nw
Cleveland TN 37312
423 472-9585

(P-20587)
LIFE CARE CENTERS AMERICA INC
Also Called: Life Care Center of Norwalk
12350 Rosecrans Ave, Norwalk (90650-5064)
PHONE.....................562 921-6624
Steve Ramsdel, *Vice Pres*
EMP: 60
SALES (corp-wide): 119.8MM **Privately Held**
SIC: 8051 Convalescent home with continuous nursing care
PA: Life Care Centers Of America, Inc.
3570 Keith St Nw
Cleveland TN 37312
423 472-9585

(P-20588)
LIFE CARE CENTERS AMERICA INC
27555 Rimrock Rd, Barstow (92311-4230)
PHONE.....................760 252-2515
EMP: 381

SALES (corp-wide): 119.8MM **Privately Held**
SIC: 8051 Convalescent home with continuous nursing care
PA: Life Care Centers Of America, Inc.
3570 Keith St Nw
Cleveland TN 37312
423 472-9585

(P-20589)
LIFE GNERATIONS HEALTHCARE LLC
Also Called: Stanford Court Nursing Center
7800 Parkway Dr, La Mesa (91942-2001)
PHONE.....................619 460-2330
Jim Geddie, *Administration*
EMP: 110
SALES (est): 2.7MM
SALES (corp-wide): 63.1MM **Privately Held**
SIC: 8051 Convalescent home with continuous nursing care
PA: Life Generations Healthcare Llc
6 Hutton Cntre Dr Ste 400
Santa Ana CA 92707
714 241-5600

(P-20590)
LIFECARE SYSTEMS INC
Also Called: Medical Inst of Little Co Mary
4101 Torrance Blvd, Torrance (90503-4607)
PHONE.....................310 540-7676
Karl Carrier, *President*
Henry G Walker, *President*
EMP: 150
SALES: 17.6MM **Privately Held**
SIC: 8051 Skilled nursing care facilities

(P-20591)
LIGHTHOUSE HEALTHCARE CTR LLC
2222 Santa Ana S, Los Angeles (90059-1350)
PHONE.....................323 564-4461
Sharrod Brooks,
EMP: 99
SALES (est): 3MM **Privately Held**
SIC: 8051 Skilled nursing care facilities

(P-20592)
LILY HOLDINGS LLC
Also Called: Oakwood Gardens Care Center
3510 E Shields Ave, Fresno (93726-6909)
PHONE.....................559 222-4807
Ashley Specht,
Ryan Williams, *Administration*
Richard Martin,
EMP: 99
SALES (est): 2MM **Privately Held**
SIC: 8051 Convalescent home with continuous nursing care

(P-20593)
LINDA VISTA MANOR INC
Also Called: Kearny Mesa Convalescent Hosp
7675 Family Cir, San Diego (92111-5304)
PHONE.....................858 278-8121
Richard Hebbel, *President*
Jeanette Hebbel, *Vice Pres*
EMP: 109
SQ FT: 30,000
SALES (est): 7.5MM **Privately Held**
WEB: www.kearnymesaconvalescent.com
SIC: 8051 6411 Skilled nursing care facilities; insurance agents, brokers & service

(P-20594)
LITTLE SISTERS THE POOR OF LA
Also Called: Jeanne Jugan, A Residence
2100 S Western Ave, San Pedro (90732-4389)
PHONE.....................310 548-0625
Margaret McArthy, *President*
Clotilde Jardim, *Treasurer*
Michael Mugan, *Vice Pres*
Victor Salcido, *Human Res Dir*
Holly Blaskiewicz, *Director*
EMP: 100
SQ FT: 145,530

SALES: 7.3MM **Privately Held**
SIC: 8051 8361 8052 Extended care facility; residential care; intermediate care facilities

(P-20595)
LONE TREE CONVALESCENT HOSP
4001 Lone Tree Way, Antioch (94509-6232)
PHONE.....................925 754-0470
Lowell Callaway, *President*
Mark Callaway, *Corp Secy*
Velda C Pierce, *Vice Pres*
EMP: 135 **EST:** 1968
SQ FT: 10,000
SALES (est): 8.6MM **Privately Held**
SIC: 8051 Convalescent home with continuous nursing care

(P-20596)
LONG BEACH CARE CENTER INC
2615 Grand Ave, Long Beach (90815-1708)
PHONE.....................562 426-6141
William A Nelson, *President*
EMP: 108
SQ FT: 43,962
SALES: 14.6MM **Privately Held**
WEB: www.longbeachcarecenter.com
SIC: 8051 Convalescent home with continuous nursing care

(P-20597)
LONGWOOD MANAGEMENT CORP
Also Called: Imperial Crest Healthcare Ctr
11834 Inglewood Ave, Hawthorne (90250-0107)
PHONE.....................310 679-1461
Robert Villalub, *Administration*
Priscilla Quizon, *Office Mgr*
Margie Linder, *Nursing Dir*
Rahul Dhakwadar, *Director*
EMP: 150
SALES (corp-wide): 170MM **Privately Held**
SIC: 8051 Convalescent home with continuous nursing care
PA: Longwood Management Corp.
4032 Wilshire Blvd Fl 6
Los Angeles CA 90010
213 389-6900

(P-20598)
LONGWOOD MANAGEMENT CORP
Also Called: Magnolia Grdns Convalescent HM
17922 San Frnando Msn, Granada Hills (91344-4043)
PHONE.....................818 360-1864
Ojijoji Gervacio, *Principal*
EMP: 100
SALES (corp-wide): 170MM **Privately Held**
SIC: 8051 Convalescent home with continuous nursing care
PA: Longwood Management Corp.
4032 Wilshire Blvd Fl 6
Los Angeles CA 90010
213 389-6900

(P-20599)
LONGWOOD MANAGEMENT CORP
Also Called: Green Acres Lodge
8101 Hill Dr, Rosemead (91770-4169)
PHONE.....................626 280-2293
Karen Fugate, *Administration*
EMP: 60
SALES (corp-wide): 170MM **Privately Held**
SIC: 8051 Convalescent home with continuous nursing care
PA: Longwood Management Corp.
4032 Wilshire Blvd Fl 6
Los Angeles CA 90010
213 389-6900

(P-20600)
LONGWOOD MANAGEMENT CORP
Also Called: San Gabriel Convalescent Ctr
8035 Hill Dr, Rosemead (91770-4116)
PHONE.....................626 280-4820
Gigi Garcia, *Branch Mgr*
EMP: 150
SALES (corp-wide): 170MM **Privately Held**
SIC: 8051 Convalescent home with continuous nursing care
PA: Longwood Management Corp.
4032 Wilshire Blvd Fl 6
Los Angeles CA 90010
213 389-6900

(P-20601)
LONGWOOD MANAGEMENT CORP
Also Called: Crenshaw Nursing
1900 S Longwood Ave, Los Angeles (90016-1408)
PHONE.....................323 933-1560
Gilbert Fimbres, *Manager*
EMP: 50
SALES (corp-wide): 170MM **Privately Held**
SIC: 8051 8052 Convalescent home with continuous nursing care; intermediate care facilities
PA: Longwood Management Corp.
4032 Wilshire Blvd Fl 6
Los Angeles CA 90010
213 389-6900

(P-20602)
LONGWOOD MANOR
Also Called: Longwood Manor Convalescent HM
4853 W Washington Blvd, Los Angeles (90016-1501)
PHONE.....................323 935-1157
Jacob Friedman, *President*
Lea Friedman, *Corp Secy*
Irving Friedman, *Vice Pres*
EMP: 200
SQ FT: 30,000
SALES: 16.3MM **Privately Held**
SIC: 8051 Convalescent home with continuous nursing care

(P-20603)
LOS ANGLES JEWISH HM FOR AGING (PA)
Also Called: Grancell Village
7150 Tampa Ave, Reseda (91335-3700)
PHONE.....................818 774-3000
Andrew Berman, *Ch of Bd*
Jeffrey Glassman, *Vice Chairman*
Molly Forrest, *CEO*
John Graham, *COO*
Larissa Stepanians, *COO*
EMP: 400
SQ FT: 35,000
SALES: 133.3MM **Privately Held**
WEB: www.jha.org
SIC: 8051 8361 Skilled nursing care facilities; residential care

(P-20604)
LOS ANGLES JEWISH HM FOR AGING
Also Called: Eisenberg Village
18855 Victory Blvd, Reseda (91335-6445)
PHONE.....................818 774-3000
Annette Brinnon, *Manager*
Anna Haro, *Human Res Dir*
EMP: 350
SALES (est): 8.5MM
SALES (corp-wide): 133.3MM **Privately Held**
WEB: www.jha.org
SIC: 8051 Convalescent home with continuous nursing care
PA: Los Angeles Jewish Home For The Aging
7150 Tampa Ave
Reseda CA 91335
818 774-3000

(P-20605)
MADERA CONVALESCENT HOSPITAL (PA)
517 S A St, Madera (93638-3896)
PHONE.....................559 673-9228
Arden Bennett, *CEO*
Dennis Albers, *Ch of Bd*
Mathilde Albers, *Corp Secy*
Emile Damia, *Vice Pres*
EMP: 160 EST: 1965
SQ FT: 1,500
SALES (est): 5.6MM **Privately Held**
SIC: 8051 Convalescent home with continuous nursing care

(P-20606)
MADISON CARE CENTER LLC
1391 E Madison Ave, El Cajon (92021-8568)
PHONE.....................619 444-1107
Emmanuel David, *President*
EMP: 100
SALES (est): 1.9MM **Privately Held**
SIC: 8051 Skilled nursing care facilities

(P-20607)
MANNING GARDENS INC
Also Called: Manning Grdns Cnvalescent Hosp
2113 E Manning Ave, Fresno (93725-9681)
PHONE.....................559 834-2586
Cary Hanson, *Administration*
Jacob Kizirian, *President*
Norman Kizirian, *Vice Pres*
EMP: 50 EST: 1962
SQ FT: 15,000
SALES (est): 2.2MM **Privately Held**
SIC: 8051 Skilled nursing care facilities

(P-20608)
MANNING GARDENS CARE CTR INC
2113 E Manning Ave, Fresno (93725-9681)
PHONE.....................559 834-2586
Ronald Kinnersley, *President*
EMP: 82 EST: 2011
SALES (est): 1.7MM **Privately Held**
SIC: 8051 Skilled nursing care facilities

(P-20609)
MARIN CNVLSCENT RHBLTTION HOSP
30 Hacienda Dr, Belvedere Tiburon (94920-1127)
PHONE.....................415 435-4554
Mary Wollam, *President*
Debbie Allen, *Manager*
EMP: 60
SQ FT: 5,000
SALES (est): 3.3MM **Privately Held**
WEB: www.marinconvalescent.com
SIC: 8051 Convalescent home with continuous nursing care

(P-20610)
MARINER HEALTH CARE INC
Also Called: Driftwood Health Care Ctr
4109 Emerald St, Torrance (90503-3105)
PHONE.....................310 371-4628
Jennifer Torgrude, *Manager*
EMP: 100
SALES (corp-wide): 1B **Privately Held**
WEB: www.marinerhealth.com
SIC: 8051 Extended care facility
HQ: Mariner Health Care, Inc.
   1 Ravinia Dr Ste 1500
   Atlanta GA 30346
   678 443-7000

(P-20611)
MARINER HEALTH CARE INC
Also Called: Freemont Health Care Center
39022 Presidio Way, Fremont (94538-1221)
PHONE.....................510 792-3743
Carinagayle Gorospe, *Administration*
Mary Grace Abuan, *Chf Purch Ofc*
EMP: 170
SALES (corp-wide): 1B **Privately Held**
WEB: www.marinerhealth.com
SIC: 8051 Extended care facility
HQ: Mariner Health Care, Inc.
   1 Ravinia Dr Ste 1500
   Atlanta GA 30346
   678 443-7000

(P-20612)
MARINER HEALTH CARE INC
Also Called: Gilroy Health & Rehab Ctr
8170 Murray Ave, Gilroy (95020-4605)
PHONE.....................408 842-9311
Gerald Hunter, *Administration*
Hector Yanez, *Facilities Dir*
EMP: 145
SALES (corp-wide): 1B **Privately Held**
WEB: www.marinerhealth.com
SIC: 8051 Extended care facility
HQ: Mariner Health Care, Inc.
   1 Ravinia Dr Ste 1500
   Atlanta GA 30346
   678 443-7000

(P-20613)
MARINER HEALTH CARE INC
Also Called: Skyline Health Care Center
2065 Forest Ave, San Jose (95128-4807)
PHONE.....................408 298-3950
Richard Park, *Administration*
EMP: 250
SALES (corp-wide): 1B **Privately Held**
SIC: 8051 Extended care facility
HQ: Mariner Health Care, Inc.
   1 Ravinia Dr Ste 1500
   Atlanta GA 30346
   678 443-7000

(P-20614)
MARINER HEALTH CARE INC
7400 24th St, Sacramento (95822-5350)
PHONE.....................916 422-4825
Robert Lorenzo, *Manager*
EMP: 120
SALES (corp-wide): 1B **Privately Held**
WEB: www.marinerhealth.com
SIC: 8051 Extended care facility
HQ: Mariner Health Care, Inc.
   1 Ravinia Dr Ste 1500
   Atlanta GA 30346
   678 443-7000

(P-20615)
MARINER HEALTH CARE INC
Also Called: Vale Healthcare Center
13484 San Pablo Ave, San Pablo (94806-3904)
PHONE.....................510 232-5945
Remy Dise, *Director*
EMP: 210
SALES (corp-wide): 1B **Privately Held**
WEB: www.marinerhealth.com
SIC: 8051 Extended care facility
HQ: Mariner Health Care, Inc.
   1 Ravinia Dr Ste 1500
   Atlanta GA 30346
   678 443-7000

(P-20616)
MARINER HEALTH CARE INC
Also Called: Inglewood Health Care Center
100 S Hillcrest Blvd, Inglewood (90301-1313)
PHONE.....................310 677-9114
Amanda Arevalo, *Administration*
EMP: 128
SALES (corp-wide): 1B **Privately Held**
WEB: www.marinerhealth.com
SIC: 8051 Extended care facility
HQ: Mariner Health Care, Inc.
   1 Ravinia Dr Ste 1500
   Atlanta GA 30346
   678 443-7000

(P-20617)
MARINER HEALTH CARE INC
Also Called: Skyline Health Care Ctr
3032 Rowena Ave, Los Angeles (90039-2005)
PHONE.....................323 665-1185
Kathleen Glass, *Administration*
EMP: 100
SALES (corp-wide): 1B **Privately Held**
WEB: www.marinerhealth.com
SIC: 8051 Extended care facility
HQ: Mariner Health Care, Inc.
   1 Ravinia Dr Ste 1500
   Atlanta GA 30346
   678 443-7000

(P-20618)
MARINER HEALTH CARE INC
Also Called: Driftwood Convalescent Hosp
1850 E 8th St, Davis (95616-2502)
PHONE.....................530 756-1800
David Ormiston, *Principal*
EMP: 150
SALES (corp-wide): 1B **Privately Held**
WEB: www.marinerhealth.com
SIC: 8051 Extended care facility
HQ: Mariner Health Care, Inc.
   1 Ravinia Dr Ste 1500
   Atlanta GA 30346
   678 443-7000

(P-20619)
MARINER HEALTH CARE INC
Also Called: Autumn Hills Convalescent Home
430 N Glendale Ave, Glendale (91206-3309)
PHONE.....................818 246-5677
Jenik Akopian, *Principal*
EMP: 120
SALES (corp-wide): 1B **Privately Held**
WEB: www.marinerhealth.com
SIC: 8051 Extended care facility
HQ: Mariner Health Care, Inc.
   1 Ravinia Dr Ste 1500
   Atlanta GA 30346
   678 443-7000

(P-20620)
MARINER HEALTH CARE INC
675 24th Ave, Santa Cruz (95062-4205)
PHONE.....................831 475-6323
EMP: 85
SALES (corp-wide): 1B **Privately Held**
WEB: www.marinerhealth.com
SIC: 8051 Extended care facility
HQ: Mariner Health Care, Inc.
   1 Ravinia Dr Ste 1500
   Atlanta GA 30346
   678 443-7000

(P-20621)
MARINER HEALTH CARE INC
Also Called: Hayward Hills Health Care Ctr
1768 B St, Hayward (94541-3102)
PHONE.....................510 538-4424
Annamarie Magna, *Branch Mgr*
EMP: 99
SALES (corp-wide): 1B **Privately Held**
WEB: www.marinerhealth.com
SIC: 8051 Extended care facility
HQ: Mariner Health Care, Inc.
   1 Ravinia Dr Ste 1500
   Atlanta GA 30346
   678 443-7000

(P-20622)
MARINER HEALTH CARE INC
Also Called: Driftwood Healthcare Center
19700 Hesperian Blvd, Hayward (94541-4704)
PHONE.....................510 785-2880
Ellen Renner, *Administration*
EMP: 135
SALES (corp-wide): 1B **Privately Held**
WEB: www.marinerhealth.com
SIC: 8051 Extended care facility
HQ: Mariner Health Care, Inc.
   1 Ravinia Dr Ste 1500
   Atlanta GA 30346
   678 443-7000

(P-20623)
MARINER HEALTH CARE INC
Also Called: El Rancho Vista Hlth Care Ctr
8925 Mines Ave, Pico Rivera (90660-3006)
PHONE.....................562 942-7019
Richard Widerynski, *Sales/Mktg Mgr*
EMP: 100
SALES (corp-wide): 1B **Privately Held**
WEB: www.marinerhealth.com
SIC: 8051 Extended care facility
HQ: Mariner Health Care, Inc.
   1 Ravinia Dr Ste 1500
   Atlanta GA 30346
   678 443-7000

(P-20624)
MARINER HEALTH CARE INC
Also Called: Pinedridge Care Ctr
45 Professional Ctr Pkwy, San Rafael (94903-2702)
PHONE.....................415 479-3610
Louise Kalchek, *Director*
Marivic Yumul, *Nursing Dir*
EMP: 70
SALES (corp-wide): 1B **Privately Held**
WEB: www.marinerhealth.com
SIC: 8051 Extended care facility
HQ: Mariner Health Care, Inc.
   1 Ravinia Dr Ste 1500
   Atlanta GA 30346
   678 443-7000

(P-20625)
MARINER HEALTH CARE INC
Also Called: Almaden Health & Rehab Ctr
2065 Los Gatos Almaden Rd, San Jose (95124-5417)
PHONE.....................408 377-9275
Yvette Bonnet, *Branch Mgr*
EMP: 100
SALES (corp-wide): 1B **Privately Held**
WEB: www.marinerhealth.com
SIC: 8051 Extended care facility
HQ: Mariner Health Care, Inc.
   1 Ravinia Dr Ste 1500
   Atlanta GA 30346
   678 443-7000

(P-20626)
MARINER HEALTH CARE INC
Also Called: Excell Care Ctr
3025 High St, Oakland (94619-1807)
PHONE.....................510 261-5200
Elma Conway, *Administration*
EMP: 100
SALES (corp-wide): 1B **Privately Held**
WEB: www.marinerhealth.com
SIC: 8051 Extended care facility
HQ: Mariner Health Care, Inc.
   1 Ravinia Dr Ste 1500
   Atlanta GA 30346
   678 443-7000

(P-20627)
MARINER HEALTH CARE INC
Also Called: La Salette Rehab Convlesc Hos
537 E Fulton St, Stockton (95204-2227)
PHONE.....................209 466-2066
Karol Ford, *Manager*
EMP: 125
SALES (corp-wide): 1B **Privately Held**
WEB: www.marinerhealth.com
SIC: 8051 Extended care facility
HQ: Mariner Health Care, Inc.
   1 Ravinia Dr Ste 1500
   Atlanta GA 30346
   678 443-7000

(P-20628)
MARINER HEALTH CARE INC
Also Called: Windsor Gardens Hea
13000 Victory Blvd, North Hollywood (91606-2926)
PHONE.....................818 985-5990
Dolly Piper, *Manager*
EMP: 100
SALES (corp-wide): 1B **Privately Held**
WEB: www.marinerhealth.com
SIC: 8051 Extended care facility
HQ: Mariner Health Care, Inc.
   1 Ravinia Dr Ste 1500
   Atlanta GA 30346
   678 443-7000

(P-20629)
MARINER HEALTH CARE INC
Also Called: Verdugo Vista Healthcare Ctr
3050 Montrose Ave, La Crescenta (91214-3619)
PHONE.....................818 957-0850
Jeri-Enn Shelton, *Administration*
EMP: 90
SALES (corp-wide): 1B **Privately Held**
WEB: www.marinerhealth.com
SIC: 8051 Extended care facility
HQ: Mariner Health Care, Inc.
   1 Ravinia Dr Ste 1500
   Atlanta GA 30346
   678 443-7000

P R O D U C T S & S V C S

(P-20630)
MARINER HEALTH CARE INC
Also Called: Arden Health & Rehab Ctr
3400 Alta Arden Expy, Sacramento
(95825-2103)
PHONE...................................916 481-5500
John Pritchard, Manager
EMP: 150
SALES (corp-wide): 1B Privately Held
WEB: www.marinerhealth.com
SIC: 8051 8069 Extended care facility;
specialty hospitals, except psychiatric
HQ: Mariner Health Care, Inc.
1 Ravinia Dr Ste 1500
Atlanta GA 30346
678 443-7000

(P-20631)
MARLORA INVESTMENTS LLC
Also Called: MARLORA POST ACCUTE RE-
HABLITAT
3801 E Anaheim St, Long Beach
(90804-4004)
PHONE...................................562 494-3311
Marilyn A Hauser,
Gabriela Patheco, Officer
Cathy Hernandez, Marketing Staff
EMP: 100
SQ FT: 22,118
SALES: 8.6MM Privately Held
SIC: 8051 Convalescent home with contin-
uous nursing care

(P-20632)
**MARY HLTH SCK CNVLSCNT
&NRSNG**
2929 Theresa Dr, Newbury Park
(91320-3136)
PHONE...................................805 498-3644
Jody Rupp, Administration
Sister Purificaion Fererro, CEO
Diane Zimanski, Office Mgr
EMP: 92
SQ FT: 5,000
SALES: 7.2MM Privately Held
SIC: 8051 Convalescent home with contin-
uous nursing care

(P-20633)
**MARYSVLLE NRSING REHAB
CTR LLC**
Also Called: Marysville Care Center
1617 Ramirez St, Marysville (95901-4334)
PHONE...................................530 742-7311
Jim Bursey, Administration
Joseph Palli,
EMP: 90
SALES (est): 4.7MM Privately Held
SIC: 8051 Skilled nursing care facilities

(P-20634)
**MAYWOOD HALTHCARE
WELLNESS CTR**
Also Called: Pine Crest
6025 Pine Ave, Maywood (90270-3108)
PHONE...................................323 560-0720
Emmanuel Bernabe, President
EMP: 50
SALES (est): 4.3MM Privately Held
SIC: 8051 Convalescent home with contin-
uous nursing care

(P-20635)
MEADOW VIEW MANOR INC
396 Dorsey Dr, Grass Valley (95945-5368)
PHONE...................................530 272-2273
Jim Bursey, Administration
EMP: 100
SQ FT: 22,000
SALES (est): 726K
SALES (corp-wide): 103.7MM Privately
Held
WEB: www.villadelrey.com
SIC: 8051 Skilled nursing care facilities
HQ: Horizon West Healthcare, Inc.
4020 Sierra College Blvd # 190
Rocklin CA 95677
916 624-6230

(P-20636)
**MEADOWOOD HLTH
REHABILITATION**
Also Called: Meadowood Care Center
3110 Wagner Heights Rd, Stockton
(95209-4848)
PHONE...................................209 956-3444
Keith Berry, President
Chard Hardcastle, President
Ilona Corpus, Food Svc Dir
EMP: 370
SQ FT: 43,800
SALES (est): 5.8MM Privately Held
SIC: 8051 Skilled nursing care facilities

(P-20637)
**MEDICAL CARE
PROFESSIONALS**
363 El Cmino Real Ste 215, South San
Francisco (94080)
PHONE...................................650 583-9898
Sharon Youngberg, President
EMP: 100
SQ FT: 550
SALES (est): 3.2MM Privately Held
WEB: www.medicalcareprofessionals.com
SIC: 8051 8082 Skilled nursing care facili-
ties; home health care services

(P-20638)
MEDICREST OF CALIFORNIA 1
Also Called: Montclair Mnor Cnvlescent Hosp
5119 Bandera St, Montclair (91763-4410)
PHONE...................................909 626-1294
Melinda Mabini, Administration
EMP: 60
SALES (corp-wide): 103.7MM Privately
Held
SIC: 8051 Convalescent home with contin-
uous nursing care
HQ: Medicrest Of California 1, Inc
4020 Sierra College Blvd
Rocklin CA 95677
916 624-6238

(P-20639)
MEK ESCONDIDO LLC
Also Called: Escondido Post Acute Rehab
421 E Mission Ave, Escondido
(92025-1909)
PHONE...................................760 747-0430
Frank S Diolosa,
EMP: 99
SALES (est): 2.5MM Privately Held
SIC: 8051 Convalescent home with contin-
uous nursing care

(P-20640)
MEK NORWOOD PINES LLC
500 Jessie Ave, Sacramento (95838-2609)
PHONE...................................916 922-7177
Bobby Federico, Manager
EMP: 99
SALES (est): 3.8MM Privately Held
SIC: 8051 Convalescent home with contin-
uous nursing care

(P-20641)
MELON HOLDINGS LLC
Also Called: Marysville Post-Acute
1617 Ramirez St, Marysville (95901-4334)
PHONE...................................530 742-7311
Joseph Cunliffe, Administration
Nicklas Anderson, President
Matt Jackson, President
EMP: 99 EST: 2016
SALES (est): 985.7K Privately Held
SIC: 8051 Convalescent home with contin-
uous nursing care

(P-20642)
**MENTAL HLTH CNVLSCENT
SVCS INC**
Also Called: Lakewood Park Health Center
12023 Lakewood Blvd, Downey
(90242-2635)
PHONE...................................562 869-0978
Daniel C Zilafro, President
Daniel Zilafro, Administration
EMP: 300
SQ FT: 60,000
SALES: 11.4MM Privately Held
SIC: 8051 Skilled nursing care facilities

(P-20643)
**MESA VERDE CONVALESCENT
HOSP**
Also Called: Mesa Verde Prosecute Care
661 Center St, Costa Mesa (92627-2708)
PHONE...................................949 548-5584
Rita Simms, Administration
Edleandro De Lima, Office Mgr
Joseph Munoz, Administration
Joye Tsuchiyama, Administration
EMP: 200
SALES (est): 8.5MM Privately Held
WEB: www.mesaverdehealthcare.com
SIC: 8051 Convalescent home with contin-
uous nursing care

(P-20644)
**MID WILSHIRE HEALTH CARE
CTR**
676 S Bonnie Brae St, Los Angeles
(90057-3710)
PHONE...................................213 483-9921
Jeoung Hie Lee, President
EMP: 60
SQ FT: 17,469
SALES: 4.6MM Privately Held
SIC: 8051 Skilled nursing care facilities

(P-20645)
**MIRAMONTE ENTERPRISES
LLC**
Also Called: San Jacinto Healthcare
275 N San Jacinto St, Hemet (92543-4453)
PHONE...................................951 658-9441
Emmanuel B David, President
EMP: 134
SQ FT: 22,968
SALES (est): 8.4MM Privately Held
SIC: 8051 Skilled nursing care facilities

(P-20646)
**MISSION HILLS HEALTHCARE
INC**
Also Called: MISSION HILLS HEALTHCARE
CENTE
4033 6th Ave, San Diego (92103-2202)
PHONE...................................619 297-4086
Patrick Higgins, CEO
Leah Higgins, President
Kaya Crump, Director
EMP: 92
SQ FT: 25,000
SALES: 7.6MM Privately Held
SIC: 8051 Convalescent home with contin-
uous nursing care

(P-20647)
MISSION MEDICAL ENTPS INC
Also Called: Hanford Nursing Rehabilitation
1007 W Lacey Blvd, Hanford (93230-4331)
PHONE...................................559 582-2871
Mark Fisher, General Mgr
EMP: 120
SALES (corp-wide): 9MM Privately Held
WEB: www.missioncaregroup.com
SIC: 8051 Convalescent home with contin-
uous nursing care
PA: Mission Medical Enterprises, Inc.
1007 W Lacey Blvd
Hanford CA 93230
559 582-2871

(P-20648)
MISSION MEDICAL ENTPS INC
Also Called: Kings Nrsing Rhabilitation Ctr
851 Leslie Ln, Hanford (93230-5643)
PHONE...................................559 582-4414
Mark Fisher, Branch Mgr
EMP: 82
SALES (corp-wide): 9MM Privately Held
SIC: 8051 Skilled nursing care facilities
PA: Mission Medical Enterprises, Inc.
1007 W Lacey Blvd
Hanford CA 93230
559 582-2871

(P-20649)
MJB PARTNERS LLC
Also Called: Pomona Vista Care Center
651 N Main St, Pomona (91768-3110)
PHONE...................................909 623-2481
Frank Johnson,
Kelly Iasparro, Vice Pres
EMP: 62
SQ FT: 8,844

SALES (est): 207.3K Privately Held
SIC: 8051 Skilled nursing care facilities

(P-20650)
MONTECITO RETIREMENT ASSN
Also Called: Casa Dorinda
300 Hot Springs Rd, Santa Barbara
(93108-2037)
PHONE...................................805 969-8011
Robin Drew, CFO
Claudia Bott, Admin Sec
Travis Dunn, Graphic Designe
Alan Blaver, Broker
Jerome Williams, Human Res Dir
EMP: 265
SQ FT: 350,000
SALES: 27.7MM Privately Held
WEB: www.casadorinda.com
SIC: 8051 8052 8361 Skilled nursing care
facilities; personal care facility; rest home,
with health care incidental

(P-20651)
**MONTEREY HEALTHCARE &
WELLNESS**
1267 San Gabriel Blvd, Rosemead
(91770-4237)
PHONE...................................626 280-3220
Shlomo Rechnitz, CEO
Sharrod Brooks, Senior VP
EMP: 90 EST: 2013
SALES (est): 2.4MM Privately Held
SIC: 8051 Mental retardation hospital

(P-20652)
**MONTEREY PINES SKLLD
NURSG FAC**
Also Called: Horizon West
1501 Skyline Dr, Monterey (93940-4110)
PHONE...................................831 373-3716
Gene Sajcich, Administration
EMP: 94
SQ FT: 32,000
SALES (est): 1.9MM
SALES (corp-wide): 103.7MM Privately
Held
WEB: www.villadelrey.com
SIC: 8051 Convalescent home with contin-
uous nursing care
HQ: Horizon West Healthcare, Inc.
4020 Sierra College Blvd # 190
Rocklin CA 95677
916 624-6230

(P-20653)
**MORNINGSIDE CORECARE
ASSOC LP**
2180 Sand Hill Rd Ste 200, Menlo Park
(94025-6949)
PHONE...................................650 854-5600
Justin Wilson, Partner
Carl Wilson, Director
EMP: 200
SALES (est): 2MM Privately Held
SIC: 8051 Skilled nursing care facilities

(P-20654)
**MOUNT RBDOUX
CONVALESCENT HOSP**
Also Called: Plott Family Care Center
6401 33rd St, Riverside (92509-1404)
PHONE...................................951 681-2200
Thomas Plott, President
EMP: 150 EST: 1971
SALES (est): 6.2MM Privately Held
SIC: 8051 8059 Convalescent home with
continuous nursing care; convalescent
home

(P-20655)
**MOUNTAIN VIEW CNVALESCENT
HOSP**
13333 Fenton Ave, Sylmar (91342-3113)
PHONE...................................818 367-1033
Ray Talebi, Owner
EMP: 50
SALES (est): 2.2MM Privately Held
SIC: 8051 Convalescent home with contin-
uous nursing care

(P-20656)
MOYLES CENTRAL VLY HLTH CARE (PA)
999 N M St, Tulare (93274-2019)
PHONE..................................559 688-0288
Ken Moyel III, *President*
EMP: 340
SALES (est): 6.9MM **Privately Held**
WEB: www.portervillecon.com
SIC: 8051 Skilled nursing care facilities

(P-20657)
MOYLES CENTRAL VLY HLTH CARE
Also Called: Porterville Convalescent Hosp
1100 W Morton Ave, Porterville
(93257-1947)
PHONE..................................559 782-1509
James Higbee, *CFO*
EMP: 120
SALES (corp-wide): 6.9MM **Privately Held**
WEB: www.portervillecon.com
SIC: 8051 Convalescent home with continuous nursing care
PA: Moyles Central Valley Health Care Inc
999 N M St
Tulare CA 93274
559 688-0288

(P-20658)
NAPA NURSING CENTER INC
3275 Villa Ln, NAPA (94558-3094)
PHONE..................................707 257-0931
Martine D Harmon, *CEO*
Tim Motooka, *President*
Georgia Ottersos, *Administration*
EMP: 130
SQ FT: 48,000
SALES (est): 5.1MM
SALES (corp-wide): 103.7MM **Privately Held**
WEB: www.napayellowpages.com
SIC: 8051 Convalescent home with continuous nursing care
HQ: Horizon West Healthcare, Inc.
4020 Sierra College Blvd # 190
Rocklin CA 95677
916 624-6230

(P-20659)
NEW COVENANT CARE OF DINUBA
Also Called: NEW COVENANT CARE CENTER OF DI
1730 S College Ave, Dinuba (93618-2812)
PHONE..................................559 591-3300
Gary V Guarisco, *President*
EMP: 100
SQ FT: 26,692
SALES (est): 6.2MM **Privately Held**
SIC: 8051 Skilled nursing care facilities

(P-20660)
NEWPORT SBACUTE HEALTHCARE CTR
Also Called: Milestone Health Care Center
2570 Newport Blvd, Costa Mesa
(92627-1331)
PHONE..................................949 642-1974
Tony Ricci, *President*
EMP: 120
SQ FT: 22,000
SALES (est): 4.6MM **Privately Held**
WEB: www.milestonehealthcare.com
SIC: 8051 Skilled nursing care facilities

(P-20661)
NICE AVENUE LLC
Also Called: Mill Creek Manor
2278 Nice Ave, Mentone (92359-9655)
PHONE..................................909 794-1189
Jason Bell, *Administration*
EMP: 65
SALES (est): 343.1K **Privately Held**
SIC: 8051 Skilled nursing care facilities

(P-20662)
NORTH PT HLTH WELLNESS CTR LLC
Also Called: Northpointe Healthcare Centre
668 E Bullard Ave, Fresno (93710-5401)
PHONE..................................559 320-2200
Stephen Reissman,

Janet Bamper,
Cheryl Petterson,
EMP: 99
SALES (est): 3.7MM **Privately Held**
SIC: 8051 Skilled nursing care facilities

(P-20663)
NORTH SHORE INVESTMENT INC
Also Called: Crescent Cy Convalescent Hosp
1280 Marshall St, Crescent City
(95531-2217)
PHONE..................................707 464-6151
Jeffery Davis, *President*
Crystal Velazquez, *Accountant*
EMP: 100
SQ FT: 35,000
SALES: 5.4MM **Privately Held**
SIC: 8051 Convalescent home with continuous nursing care

(P-20664)
NORTHERN CALIFORNIA PRESBYTERI
Also Called: Sequos-San Frncsco Residential
1400 Geary Blvd, San Francisco
(94109-6561)
PHONE..................................415 922-9700
Michael Daugherty, *Branch Mgr*
Steve Martinez, *Human Res Dir*
Mark Bradley, *Director*
EMP: 277
SALES (corp-wide): 69.3MM **Privately Held**
SIC: 8051 Convalescent home with continuous nursing care
PA: Northern California Presbyterian
Homes And Services, Inc.
1525 Post St
San Francisco CA 94109
415 922-0200

(P-20665)
NORWALK MEADOWS NURSING CTR LP
10625 Leffingwell Rd, Norwalk
(90650-3434)
PHONE..................................562 864-2541
Pnina Graff, *Partner*
Jacob Graff, *Partner*
EMP: 152
SQ FT: 23,632
SALES (est): 9.2MM **Privately Held**
SIC: 8051 Convalescent home with continuous nursing care

(P-20666)
NOVATO HEALTHCARE CENTER LLC
1565 Hill Rd, Novato (94947-4063)
PHONE..................................415 897-6161
Michael J Torgan, *Principal*
Sharrod Brooks,
EMP: 200 EST: 2007
SALES: 18.3MM **Privately Held**
SIC: 8051 Convalescent home with continuous nursing care

(P-20667)
NUEVACARE LLC
2100 Geng Rd Ste 210, Palo Alto
(94303-3307)
PHONE..................................650 396-3596
EMP: 82
SALES (corp-wide): 3.6MM **Privately Held**
SIC: 8051 Skilled nursing care facilities
PA: Nuevacare Llc
1900 S Norfolk St Ste 350
San Mateo CA 94403
650 539-2000

(P-20668)
OAK KNOLL CONVALESCENT CENTER
Also Called: Oaks, The
450 Hayes Ln, Petaluma (94952-4010)
PHONE..................................707 778-8686
Ann Abbott, *President*
Tony Meyers, *CEO*
EMP: 72
SQ FT: 36,000
SALES: 4.9MM **Privately Held**
SIC: 8051 Convalescent home with continuous nursing care

(P-20669)
OAK RIVER REHABILITATION
3300 Franklin St, Anderson (96007-3279)
PHONE..................................530 365-0025
Andy Tanner, *Manager*
Krista Brown, *Executive*
Dan Funk, *Administration*
Tanya Gipson, *Nursing Dir*
Trish Williams, *Manager*
EMP: 150
SQ FT: 3,000
SALES: 19.2MM **Privately Held**
SIC: 8051 Convalescent home with continuous nursing care

(P-20670)
OAKDALE HEIGHTS SENIOR LIVING
3209 Brookside Dr, Bakersfield
(93311-3459)
PHONE..................................661 663-9671
Mike Laudon, *President*
EMP: 50
SALES (est): 1.4MM **Privately Held**
SIC: 8051 Skilled nursing care facilities

(P-20671)
OAKHURST SKILLED NURSING WELLN
Also Called: OAKHURST HEALTHCARE & WELLNESS
40131 Highway 49, Oakhurst (93644-9560)
PHONE..................................559 683-2244
Stepan Sarmazian, *Administration*
EMP: 99
SALES: 5.5MM **Privately Held**
SIC: 8051 Mental retardation hospital

(P-20672)
OAKLAND HEALTHCARE & WELLNESS
Also Called: Akland Healthcare Wellness Ctr
3030 Webster St, Oakland (94609-3411)
PHONE..................................323 330-6572
Sol Majer, *Mng Member*
EMP: 131
SQ FT: 20,000
SALES: 427.9K **Privately Held**
SIC: 8051 Convalescent home with continuous nursing care

(P-20673)
OCADIAN CARE CENTERS LLC
Also Called: Northern Cal Rehabilitation
2801 Eureka Way, Redding (96001-0222)
PHONE..................................530 246-9000
Chris Jones, *Exec Dir*
Debbie Wiechman, *Infect Cntl Dir*
Jody Carter, *Radiology Dir*
Kevin Rainsford, *Director*
EMP: 250
SALES (corp-wide): 4.8MM **Privately Held**
WEB: www.ocadian.com
SIC: 8051 5912 8069 Skilled nursing care facilities; drug stores & proprietary stores; specialty hospitals, except psychiatric
PA: Ocadian Care Centers, Llc
104 Main St
Belvedere Tiburon CA 94920
415 789-5427

(P-20674)
OCADIAN CARE CENTERS LLC
Also Called: Medical Hill Rehabilitation
475 29th St, Oakland (94609-3510)
PHONE..................................510 832-3222
Robert G Peirce, *President*
EMP: 100
SALES (corp-wide): 4.8MM **Privately Held**
WEB: www.ocadian.com
SIC: 8051 Convalescent home with continuous nursing care
PA: Ocadian Care Centers, Llc
104 Main St
Belvedere Tiburon CA 94920
415 789-5427

(P-20675)
OCADIAN CARE CENTERS LLC
Also Called: Greenbrea Care Center
1220 S Eliseo Dr, Greenbrae (94904-2006)
PHONE..................................415 461-9700
Susan Weaver, *Manager*

EMP: 75
SALES (corp-wide): 4.8MM **Privately Held**
WEB: www.ocadian.com
SIC: 8051 8069 8052 Skilled nursing care facilities; specialty hospitals, except psychiatric; intermediate care facilities
PA: Ocadian Care Centers, Llc
104 Main St
Belvedere Tiburon CA 94920
415 789-5427

(P-20676)
OCADIAN CARE CENTERS LLC
1550 Silveira Pkwy, San Rafael
(94903-4879)
PHONE..................................415 499-1000
Linda Creekmoore, *Manager*
EMP: 90
SALES (corp-wide): 4.8MM **Privately Held**
WEB: www.ocadian.com
SIC: 8051 8361 Skilled nursing care facilities; residential care
PA: Ocadian Care Centers, Llc
104 Main St
Belvedere Tiburon CA 94920
415 789-5427

(P-20677)
OCADIAN CARE CENTERS LLC
Also Called: Homewood Care Center
75 N 13th St, San Jose (95112-3439)
PHONE..................................408 295-2665
David Martinez, *Administration*
EMP: 50
SALES (corp-wide): 4.8MM **Privately Held**
WEB: www.ocadian.com
SIC: 8051 Skilled nursing care facilities
PA: Ocadian Care Centers, Llc
104 Main St
Belvedere Tiburon CA 94920
415 789-5427

(P-20678)
ODYSSEY HEALTHCARE INC
525 Cabrillo Park Dr # 150, Santa Ana
(92701-5017)
PHONE..................................714 245-7420
Rodney Dirk Allison, *Principal*
EMP: 52
SALES (corp-wide): 6B **Privately Held**
SIC: 8051
HQ: Odyssey Healthcare, Inc.
7801 Mesquite Bend Dr # 105
Irving TX 75063

(P-20679)
ODYSSEY HEALTHCARE INC
1500 E Hamilton Ave # 212, Campbell
(95008-0809)
PHONE..................................408 626-4868
Elaine Fritz, *Principal*
EMP: 52
SALES (corp-wide): 6B **Privately Held**
SIC: 8051 Extended care facility
HQ: Odyssey Healthcare, Inc.
7801 Mesquite Bend Dr # 105
Irving TX 75063

(P-20680)
OLEANDER HOLDINGS LLC
Also Called: Sacramento Post-Acute
5255 Hemlock St, Sacramento
(95841-3017)
PHONE..................................916 331-4590
James Huish,
Myrna De Guzman, *Controller*
Nick Anderson,
Toby Tilford,
EMP: 99
SALES (est): 1.5MM **Privately Held**
SIC: 8051 Convalescent home with continuous nursing care

(P-20681)
ORANGE HEALTHCARE & WELLNESS
920 W La Veta Ave, Orange (92868-4302)
PHONE..................................714 633-3568
Jonathan Weiss,
Brad Zelden, *Administration*
Slusser Kathy, *Human Resources*

Sharrod Brooks,
Linda Mendoza, *Social Worker*
EMP: 110
SALES (est): 6.5MM **Privately Held**
SIC: 8051 Skilled nursing care facilities

(P-20682)
ORCHARD - POST ACUTE CARE CTR
12385 Washington Blvd, Whittier
(90606-2502)
PHONE......................562 693-7701
Rich Jorgensen, *Principal*
EMP: 1660
SALES: 15.6MM
SALES (corp-wide): 1.8B **Publicly Held**
SIC: 8051 Convalescent home with contin-
uous nursing care
PA: The Ensign Group Inc
27101 Puerta Real Ste 450
Mission Viejo CA 92691
949 487-9500

(P-20683)
OUR LADY OF FATIMA VILLA INC
20400 Srtoga Los Gatos Rd, Saratoga
(95070-5997)
PHONE......................408 741-2950
Bella Mahoney, *Administration*
EMP: 90
SQ FT: 45,123
SALES: 12.5MM **Privately Held**
WEB: www.fatimavilla.org
SIC: 8051 Skilled nursing care facilities

(P-20684)
OXNARD MANOR HEALTHCARE CTR LP
1400 W Gonzales Rd, Oxnard
(93036-3392)
PHONE......................805 983-0324
Steven Rieder, *Ltd Ptnr*
Sharrod Brooks, *Partner*
Bertie Krieger, *Partner*
Grace Catabay, *Education*
Arlene Castaneda, *Hlthcr Dir*
EMP: 99
SALES: 10.1MM **Privately Held**
SIC: 8051 Skilled nursing care facilities

(P-20685)
P R N CONVALESCENT HOSPITAL
Also Called: High Valley Lodge
7912 Topley Ln, Sunland (91040-3336)
PHONE......................818 352-3158
Pauline Albert, *President*
Luis Albert Jr, *Vice Pres*
EMP: 54
SQ FT: 11,712
SALES (est): 2.9MM **Privately Held**
SIC: 8051 Skilled nursing care facilities

(P-20686)
PACIFIC REHABILITATION & WEL
2211 Harrison Ave, Eureka (95501-3214)
PHONE......................707 443-9767
Sharrod Brooks, *Senior VP*
EMP: 65 **EST:** 2011
SQ FT: 20,000
SALES (est): 6.1MM **Privately Held**
SIC: 8051 8322 Mental retardation hospi-
tal; rehabilitation services

(P-20687)
PACIFICA CARE CENTER
Also Called: Pacifica Nursing & Rehab Ctr
385 Esplanade Ave, Pacifica (94044-1882)
PHONE......................650 355-5622
Jacob Beaman, *Administration*
Elizabeth De Guzman, *Records Dir*
Filipina Atienza, *Director*
EMP: 150
SALES: 17MM **Privately Held**
WEB: www.pacifica-rehab.com
SIC: 8051 Convalescent home with contin-
uous nursing care

(P-20688)
PACIFICA LINDA MAR INC
Also Called: Linda Mar Care Center
751 San Pedro Terrace Rd, Pacifica
(94044-4101)
PHONE......................650 359-4800
David Mahrt, *Administration*
Carmen Paz, *Director*
EMP: 85
SQ FT: 10,000
SALES: 5.8MM **Privately Held**
WEB: www.lawgate.byu.edu
SIC: 8051 Convalescent home with contin-
uous nursing care

(P-20689)
PALMCREST GRAND CARE CTR INC
3501 Cedar Ave, Long Beach
(90807-3809)
PHONE......................562 595-4551
William Nelson, *President*
EMP: 99
SALES (est): 5.7MM **Privately Held**
SIC: 8051 Skilled nursing care facilities

(P-20690)
PANORAMA MADOWS NURSING CTR LP
Also Called: Sun-Air Convalescent Hospital
14857 Roscoe Blvd, Panorama City
(91402-4617)
PHONE......................818 894-5707
Glen Bennett, *Administration*
Brenda Mandelbaum, *Treasurer*
Uri Mandelbaum, *Vice Pres*
EMP: 80 **EST:** 1969
SQ FT: 25,000
SALES (est): 5.4MM **Privately Held**
SIC: 8051 Skilled nursing care facilities

(P-20691)
PARA & PALLI INC
Also Called: Los Banos Nursing and Rehab
931 Idaho Ave, Los Banos (93635-3405)
PHONE......................209 826-0790
Joseph Palli, *President*
▲ **EMP:** 65
SQ FT: 1,000
SALES (est): 4.3MM **Privately Held**
SIC: 8051 Skilled nursing care facilities

(P-20692)
PARADISE VLY HLTH CARE CTR INC
2575 E 8th St, National City (91950-2913)
PHONE......................619 470-6700
Kenneth Michael Funk, *President*
Jason Murray, *CEO*
Mark Hancock, *CFO*
EMP: 59
SALES (est): 5.7MM **Privately Held**
SIC: 8051 Skilled nursing care facilities

(P-20693)
PARK CNTL CARE RHBLITATION CTR
2100 Parkside Dr, Fremont (94536-5326)
PHONE......................510 797-5300
Anthony P Thekkek, *President*
Prema Thekkek, *Vice Pres*
EMP: 100
SALES (est): 4.2MM **Privately Held**
SIC: 8051 Skilled nursing care facilities

(P-20694)
PARKSIDE SPECIAL CARE CENTER
444 W Lexington Ave, El Cajon
(92020-4416)
PHONE......................619 442-7744
Edd Long, *Administration*
Julie Bennett, *Executive Asst*
Myrna Pascual, *Assistant*
EMP: 75
SALES (est): 4.7MM **Privately Held**
SIC: 8051 Convalescent home with contin-
uous nursing care

(P-20695)
PARKVIEW JLIAN CNVLESCENT HOSP
1801 Julian Ave, Bakersfield (93304-6419)
PHONE......................661 831-9150

Ligia Denham, *Vice Pres*
EMP: 100
SQ FT: 8,000
SALES: 7.2MM **Privately Held**
WEB: www.parkviewjulian.com
SIC: 8051 Convalescent home with contin-
uous nursing care

(P-20696)
PASADENA HOSPITAL ASSN LTD
Also Called: Huntington Extended Care Ctr
716 S Fair Oaks Ave, Pasadena
(91105-2618)
PHONE......................626 397-3322
Ken Hoff, *Manager*
EMP: 75
SALES (corp-wide): 695.6MM **Privately Held**
WEB: www.huntingtonhospital.com
SIC: 8051 Skilled nursing care facilities
PA: Pasadena Hospital Association, Ltd.
100 W California Blvd
Pasadena CA 91105
626 397-5000

(P-20697)
PASADENA MADOWS NURSING CTR LP
150 Bellefontaine St, Pasadena
(91105-3102)
PHONE......................626 796-1103
Pnina Graff, *Partner*
Khristine Bondoc, *Marketing Mgr*
EMP: 99
SALES (est): 5.6MM **Privately Held**
SIC: 8051 Skilled nursing care facilities

(P-20698)
PATER DIGINTAS INC
Also Called: Carmel Hills Care Center
23795 Holman Hwy, Monterey
(93940-5903)
PHONE......................831 624-1875
Robert Bowersox, *President*
Kim Bowersox, *CFO*
EMP: 90
SQ FT: 30,000
SALES: 11.5MM **Privately Held**
WEB: www.carmelhillscarecenter.com
SIC: 8051 Convalescent home with contin-
uous nursing care

(P-20699)
PAVILION AT SUNNY HILLS
Also Called: Evergreen Fullerton Healthcare
2222 N Harbor Blvd, Fullerton
(92835-2605)
PHONE......................714 992-5701
Shlomo Rechnitz,
Sharrod Brooks, *Senior VP*
Wesley Jones, *Administration*
EMP: 125
SALES (est): 4.2MM **Privately Held**
SIC: 8051 Skilled nursing care facilities

(P-20700)
PINE GROVE HEALTHCARE
126 N San Gabriel Blvd, San Gabriel
(91775-2427)
PHONE......................626 285-3131
Sharrod Brooks, *Partner*
EMP: 99 **EST:** 2012
SALES (est): 3.9MM **Privately Held**
SIC: 8051 Mental retardation hospital

(P-20701)
PINERS NURSING HOME INC
Also Called: Piner's Medical Supply
1800 Pueblo Ave, NAPA (94558-4751)
PHONE......................707 224-7925
Gary Piner, *President*
Starr Piner, *Treasurer*
EMP: 65 **EST:** 1944
SQ FT: 20,000
SALES (est): 5.2MM **Privately Held**
SIC: 8051 4119 5999 Convalescent home
with continuous nursing care; ambulance
service; medical apparatus & supplies

(P-20702)
PITTSBURG CARE CENTER LTD
535 School St, Pittsburg (94565-3937)
PHONE......................925 432-3831
Abby Tiller, *Owner*
Elaine Estrada, *Social Dir*

Terence Tumbale, *Director*
EMP: 50
SQ FT: 20,000
SALES (est): 2.2MM **Privately Held**
SIC: 8051 Extended care facility

(P-20703)
PITTSBURG SKILLED NURSING
535 School St, Pittsburg (94565-3937)
PHONE......................925 808-6540
Allen Leung, *Admin Sec*
EMP: 67
SQ FT: 12,140
SALES (est): 1.3MM **Privately Held**
SIC: 8051 Skilled nursing care facilities

(P-20704)
PLEASANT CARE OF VISTA
247 E Bobier Dr, Vista (92084-3026)
PHONE......................760 945-3033
Thomas Delucia, *Administration*
Diane Thibodeau, *Administration*
EMP: 180
SALES (est): 5.1MM **Privately Held**
SIC: 8051 Skilled nursing care facilities

(P-20705)
PLOTT MANAGEMENT CO
Also Called: Plott Family Home Care
264 E 18th St, San Bernardino
(92404-4708)
PHONE......................909 883-0288
EMP: 88
SALES (est): 3.6MM **Privately Held**
SIC: 8051

(P-20706)
PLUM HEALTHCARE GROUP LLC (PA)
100 E San Marcos Blvd # 200, San Marcos
(92069-2987)
PHONE......................760 471-0388
Toby Tilford, *Principal*
Will Huish, *Exec VP*
Neela Blon, *Social Dir*
Melissa Cottonwood, *Social Dir*
Rick Burke, *Creative Dir*
EMP: 100
SALES (est): 40.2MM **Privately Held**
SIC: 8051 Skilled nursing care facilities

(P-20707)
PLUM HEALTHCARE GROUP LLC
Also Called: White Blossom Care Center
1990 Fruitdale Ave, San Jose
(95128-2709)
PHONE......................408 998-8447
Mark Lamb, *Manager*
Laura Barrientos, *Administration*
Jose Iniguez, *Director*
EMP: 100
SALES (est): 3.5MM
SALES (corp-wide): 40.2MM **Privately Held**
SIC: 8051 Skilled nursing care facilities
PA: Plum Healthcare Group, Llc
100 E San Marcos Blvd # 200
San Marcos CA 92069
760 471-0388

(P-20708)
PLUM HEALTHCARE GROUP LLC
Also Called: Cottonwood Cyn Healthcare Ctr
1391 E Madison Ave, El Cajon
(92021-8568)
PHONE......................619 873-2500
Leticia Guerrero, *Business Mgr*
Linell Serquina, *Records Dir*
EMP: 120
SALES (corp-wide): 40.2MM **Privately Held**
SIC: 8051 8059 Skilled nursing care facili-
ties; nursing home, except skilled & inter-
mediate care facility
PA: Plum Healthcare Group, Llc
100 E San Marcos Blvd # 200
San Marcos CA 92069
760 471-0388

(P-20709)
POINT LOMA CONVALESCENT HOSP
3202 Duke St, San Diego (92110-5401)
PHONE................................619 224-4141
Samuel Horowitz, *Partner*
Joseph Fisch, *General Ptnr*
Reena Horowitz, *General Ptnr*
J Axelrod, *Ltd Ptnr*
B Crow, *Ltd Ptnr*
EMP: 160
SQ FT: 25,402
SALES (est): 7.1MM **Privately Held**
WEB: www.pointlomarehab.com
SIC: 8051 Convalescent home with continuous nursing care

(P-20710)
POINT LOMA RHBLITATION CTR LLC
Also Called: Point Loma Post Acute Care Ctr
3202 Duke St, San Diego (92110-5401)
PHONE................................619 224-4141
Guy Reggev,
Luchie Diwa, *Manager*
EMP: 130
SQ FT: 30,895
SALES (est): 5MM **Privately Held**
SIC: 8051 Skilled nursing care facilities

(P-20711)
POMERADO OPERATIONS LLC
Also Called: Boulder Creek Post Acute
12696 Monte Vista Rd, Poway (92064-2500)
PHONE................................858 487-6242
Covey Christensen, *CEO*
James Gamett, *President*
Leland Bruce, *COO*
Travis Greenwood, *CFO*
EMP: 99
SALES (est): 1.1MM **Privately Held**
SIC: 8051 Convalescent home with continuous nursing care

(P-20712)
PROVIDNCE ALL STS SUBACUTE LLC
1652 Mono Ave, San Leandro (94578-2020)
PHONE................................510 481-3200
Jason Murray, *President*
EMP: 99 EST: 2015
SALES (est): 392.3K **Privately Held**
SIC: 8051 Skilled nursing care facilities

(P-20713)
QUALITY LONG TERM CARE NEV INC
Also Called: Eineridge Care Center
14122 Hubbard St, Sylmar (91342-4712)
PHONE................................818 361-0191
Scott Dale, *Branch Mgr*
EMP: 65 **Privately Held**
SIC: 8051 Skilled nursing care facilities
PA: Quality Long Term Care Of Nevada, Inc.
2800 W Sahara Ave
Las Vegas NV 89102

(P-20714)
R FELLEN INC
Also Called: Sunnyside Convalescent Hosp
2939 S Peach Ave, Fresno (93725-9302)
PHONE................................559 233-6248
Michael Fellen, *President*
Steven Fellen, *Vice Pres*
EMP: 95
SQ FT: 10,000
SALES (est): 7MM **Privately Held**
SIC: 8051 Convalescent home with continuous nursing care

(P-20715)
RAMONA CARE CENTER INC
Also Called: Ramona Nrsing Rhbilitation Ctr
11900 Ramona Blvd, El Monte (91732-2314)
PHONE................................626 442-5721
John Sorensen, *Vice Pres*
Trevor Lords, *Administration*
Jan Stine, *Administration*
Marylyn Schumacher, *Nursing Dir*
EMP: 140

SQ FT: 35,000
SALES: 16.5MM **Privately Held**
SIC: 8051 Convalescent home with continuous nursing care

(P-20716)
RAZAVI CORPORATION
Also Called: Hilldale Habilitation Center
7979 La Mesa Blvd, La Mesa (91942-5565)
PHONE................................619 465-8010
Darius Razavi, *President*
Maria Razavi, *Vice Pres*
▲ EMP: 60
SQ FT: 20,080
SALES (est): 2MM **Privately Held**
SIC: 8051 Convalescent home with continuous nursing care

(P-20717)
REBECCA TERLEY
Also Called: Sunbrdge Care Ctr - Bellflower
9028 Rose St, Bellflower (90706-6418)
PHONE................................562 925-4252
Andrew Ashton, *Exec Dir*
EMP: 53
SALES (est): 966.2K **Privately Held**
SIC: 8051 Skilled nursing care facilities

(P-20718)
RECHE CYN RHBLITATION HLTH CTR
Also Called: Reche Cyn Regional Rehab Ctr
1350 Reche Canyon Rd, Colton (92324-9528)
PHONE................................909 370-4411
Fred Frank, *Administration*
Benjamin Atkins, *CEO*
EMP: 350
SALES (est): 25.9MM **Privately Held**
SIC: 8051 Convalescent home with continuous nursing care

(P-20719)
REGENCY CENTERS LP
40 Main St, Vista (92083-5831)
PHONE................................760 724-9795
Darrell Musick, *Principal*
EMP: 507
SALES (est): 63.4K **Publicly Held**
WEB: www.regencycenters.com
SIC: 8051 Skilled nursing care facilities
HQ: Regency Centers Texas Llc
1 Independent Dr Ste 102
Jacksonville FL 32202
904 598-7000

(P-20720)
REGENCY OAKS CARE CENTER
3850 E Esther St, Long Beach (90804-2009)
PHONE................................562 498-3368
Vince Hambright, *President*
Lori Johnson, *Manager*
EMP: 110
SALES (est): 5.3MM **Privately Held**
SIC: 8051 Convalescent home with continuous nursing care

(P-20721)
REHABLTION CNTRE OF BVRLY HLLS
580 S San Vicente Blvd, Los Angeles (90048-4621)
PHONE................................323 782-1500
Eldon Teper, *President*
EMP: 200
SALES (est): 14.1MM **Privately Held**
SIC: 8051 Convalescent home with continuous nursing care

(P-20722)
RIO HNDO SBCUTE NRSING CTR LLC
Also Called: Rio Hondo Convalescent Hosp
273 E Beverly Blvd, Montebello (90640-3775)
PHONE................................323 838-5915
Alice Enrique, *Administration*
EMP: 150
SALES (est): 9.6MM **Publicly Held**
WEB: www.parkviewnursing.net
SIC: 8051 Skilled nursing care facilities

PA: Genesis Healthcare, Inc.
101 E State St
Kennett Square PA 19348

(P-20723)
RIVER BEND NURSING HOME INC
2215 Oakmont Way, West Sacramento (95691-3022)
PHONE................................916 371-1890
Nell Stamm, *President*
Pat Zarate, *Asst Admin*
EMP: 90
SQ FT: 34,000
SALES (est): 3.6MM **Privately Held**
WEB: www.somersetnursingcenter.com
SIC: 8051 Convalescent home with continuous nursing care

(P-20724)
RIVERA SANITARIUM INC
Also Called: Colonial Gardens Nursing Home
7246 Rosemead Blvd, Pico Rivera (90660-4010)
P.O. Box 2098 (90662-2098)
PHONE................................562 949-2591
Elizabeth Stephens, *President*
Kent Stephens, *Administration*
EMP: 86
SQ FT: 30,000
SALES (est): 4.8MM **Privately Held**
SIC: 8051 Skilled nursing care facilities

(P-20725)
RIVERSIDE CARE INC
Also Called: VALENCIA GARDENS HEALTH CARE CENTER
4301 Caroline Ct, Riverside (92506-2902)
PHONE................................951 683-7111
Ted Holt, *President*
Spencer E Olsen, *Treasurer*
Jenny Ortiz, *Office Mgr*
EMP: 130
SALES: 6.9MM
SALES (corp-wide): 69.3MM **Privately Held**
SIC: 8051 Convalescent home with continuous nursing care
PA: North American Health Care, Inc.
5150 E A Palma Ave 206
Anaheim CA 92807
949 240-2423

(P-20726)
RIVERSIDE EQUITIES LLC
Also Called: MISSION CARE CENTER
8487 Magnolia Ave, Riverside (92504-3222)
PHONE................................951 688-2222
Frank Johnson, *CEO*
Irving Bauman, *COO*
Carey Van Boxtel, *Administration*
EMP: 93
SALES (est): 7.5MM **Privately Held**
SIC: 8051 Mental retardation hospital

(P-20727)
RIVERSIDE HEALTH CARE CORP
1090 Rio Ln, Sacramento (95822-1706)
PHONE................................916 446-2506
Larry Meyer, *Administration*
EMP: 65
SALES (corp-wide): 9.4MM **Privately Held**
SIC: 8051 Skilled nursing care facilities
PA: Riverside Health Care Corporation
1469 Humboldt Rd Ste 175
Chico CA 95928
530 897-5100

(P-20728)
RIVERSIDE SANITARIUM LLC
Also Called: Riverside Bhvral Heathcare Ctr
4580 Palm Ave, Riverside (92501-3950)
PHONE................................951 684-7701
Kim Iola, *Principal*
Barbara O'Connor, *Administration*
EMP: 99
SALES (est): 2.8MM **Privately Held**
SIC: 8051 Skilled nursing care facilities

(P-20729)
RIVIERA NURSING & CONVA
Also Called: Riviera Health Care Center
8203 Telegraph Rd, Pico Rivera (90660-4905)
PHONE................................562 806-2576
Morris Weiss, *President*
Harry Jacobs, *Officer*
Bessie Weiss, *Vice Pres*
Rolan Calungsod, *Office Mgr*
Edie Gonzalez, *Manager*
EMP: 118
SQ FT: 60,000
SALES (est): 6.3MM **Privately Held**
WEB: www.rivierahealthcare.com
SIC: 8051 8059 Convalescent home with continuous nursing care; convalescent home

(P-20730)
ROCKPORT ADM SVCS LLC
4585 N Figueroa St, Los Angeles (90065-3026)
PHONE................................323 223-3441
Rita C Simms, *Administration*
EMP: 87 **Privately Held**
SIC: 8051 Skilled nursing care facilities
PA: Rockport Administrative Services, Llc
5900 Wilshire Blvd # 1600
Los Angeles CA 90036

(P-20731)
ROWLAND CONVALESCENT HOSP INC
Also Called: ROWLAND, THE
330 W Rowland St, Covina (91723-2941)
PHONE................................626 967-2741
Anthony Kalomas, *President*
EMP: 100
SQ FT: 30,000
SALES: 8.3MM **Privately Held**
SIC: 8051 Convalescent home with continuous nursing care

(P-20732)
ROYAL CONVALESCENT HOSPITAL
320 Cattle Call Dr, Brawley (92227-3198)
P.O. Box 1380 (92227-1380)
PHONE................................760 344-5431
Tobias Friedman, *President*
Ida Friedman, *Admin Sec*
Fred Friedman, *Administration*
Tobias Friedman, *Agent*
EMP: 80
SQ FT: 25,000
SALES (est): 1.6MM **Privately Held**
SIC: 8051 Skilled nursing care facilities

(P-20733)
ROYAL TERRACE HEALTHCARE
1340 Highland Ave, Duarte (91010-2520)
PHONE................................626 256-4654
Eloisa Heiser, *Director*
Alma Hechanova, *Director*
Anabell Reyes, *Director*
EMP: 60 EST: 2003
SALES (est): 1.7MM **Privately Held**
SIC: 8051 Skilled nursing care facilities

(P-20734)
S L H C C INC
Also Called: Saylor Lane Healthcare Center
3500 Folsom Blvd, Sacramento (95816-6615)
PHONE................................916 457-6521
Dave Hilburn, *President*
EMP: 50
SALES (est): 2.6MM **Privately Held**
SIC: 8051 Convalescent home with continuous nursing care

(P-20735)
S&F MANAGEMENT COMPANY LLC (PA)
9200 W Sunset Blvd # 700, West Hollywood (90069-3502)
PHONE................................310 385-1090
Lee C Samson,
Harold Walt, *CFO*
Thelma Luna, *Accounting Mgr*
EMP: 100

P R O D U C T S & S V C S

SALES (est): 35.9MM **Privately Held**
WEB: www.snfmgt.com
SIC: 8051 Convalescent home with continuous nursing care

(P-20736)
SACRAMENTO OPERATING CO LP
Also Called: Double Tree Past Acute
7400 24th St, Sacramento (95822-5350)
PHONE.................................916 422-4825
Kenneth Tabler, *Partner*
Cynthia Mitchell,
EMP: 120
SALES (est): 2.7MM **Privately Held**
SIC: 8051 Extended care facility

(P-20737)
SAINT CLAIRES NURSING CTR LLC
6248 66th Ave, Sacramento (95823-2733)
PHONE.................................916 392-4440
Kathryn J Hill, *President*
Michael Maderas, *Administration*
EMP: 124
SALES: 6.5MM **Privately Held**
SIC: 8051 Skilled nursing care facilities

(P-20738)
SAN DIEGO HEBREW HOMES (PA)
Also Called: Leichtag Assisted Living
211 Saxony Rd, Encinitas (92024-2791)
PHONE.................................760 942-2695
Yehudi Gaffen, *Chairman*
Pam Ferris, *President*
Robin Weiner, *CFO*
Brad Blose, *Vice Pres*
Kimberly Fuson, *Vice Pres*
EMP: 180
SQ FT: 219,000
SALES: 20.6MM **Privately Held**
WEB: www.seacrestvillage.com
SIC: 8051 8059 6513 Skilled nursing care facilities; rest home, with health care; retirement hotel operation

(P-20739)
SAN JOSES HEALTHCARE & WELL
Also Called: San Jose Hlthcare Wellness Ctr
75 N 13th St, San Jose (95112-3439)
PHONE.................................408 295-2665
Sole Majer, *Mng Member*
David Martinez, *Financial Exec*
Tess Gintu, *Nursing Dir*
Aaron Robins,
EMP: 90
SALES (est): 6MM **Privately Held**
SIC: 8051 Convalescent home with continuous nursing care

(P-20740)
SAN LEANDRO HEALTHCARE CENTER
368 Juana Ave, San Leandro (94577-4811)
PHONE.................................510 357-4015
Pat Poddatoori, *President*
Marissa Ilagan, *Office Mgr*
EMP: 70
SALES (est): 2.8MM **Privately Held**
SIC: 8051 Convalescent home with continuous nursing care

(P-20741)
SAN MARCOS OPERATING CO LP
Also Called: Village Square Healthcare Ctr
1586 W Square Marcos Blvd, San Marcos (92078)
PHONE.................................760 471-2986
Kristina Kuizon,
EMP: 85
SALES (est): 300.8K **Privately Held**
SIC: 8051 Skilled nursing care facilities

(P-20742)
SAN MATEO HEALTHCARE & WELLNES
Also Called: Burlingame Long Term Care
1100 Trousdale Dr, Burlingame (94010-3207)
PHONE.................................650 692-3758
Sharrod Brooks,

Marcus Weenig, *Manager*
EMP: 99
SALES (est): 6.4MM **Privately Held**
SIC: 8051 Mental retardation hospital

(P-20743)
SAN PABLO HEALTHCARE
13328 San Pablo Ave, San Pablo (94806-3902)
PHONE.................................510 235-3720
Suzette Cheatham, *Mng Member*
Sol Majer,
EMP: 130
SALES (est): 2.7MM **Privately Held**
SIC: 8051 Skilled nursing care facilities

(P-20744)
SAN PEDRO CONVALESCENT HM INC
Also Called: Los Palos Convalescent Hosp
1430 W 6th St, San Pedro (90732-3503)
PHONE.................................310 832-6431
Celia Valdomar, *President*
Edgar Baltazar, *Human Resources*
EMP: 90
SQ FT: 10,000
SALES (est): 5.6MM **Privately Held**
SIC: 8051 Convalescent home with continuous nursing care

(P-20745)
SANDHURST CONVALES GRP LTD A
Also Called: Windsor Garden Conv Ctr Hwthrn
13922 Cerise Ave, Hawthorne (90250-8688)
PHONE.................................310 675-3304
Anne Josafat, *Records Dir*
Donna Henderson, *Administration*
Paryus Patel, *Director*
EMP: 50
SALES (est): 990K **Privately Held**
SIC: 8051 Convalescent home with continuous nursing care

(P-20746)
SANHYD INC
Also Called: Kyakamena Sklled Nrsing Fcilty
2131 Carleton St, Berkeley (94704-3213)
PHONE.................................510 843-2131
Pat Poddatoori, *President*
EMP: 52 **EST:** 1965
SQ FT: 15,000
SALES (est): 2.3MM **Privately Held**
SIC: 8051 Convalescent home with continuous nursing care

(P-20747)
SANTA ANITA CONVALESCENT HOSPI
5522 Gracewood Ave, Temple City (91780)
PHONE.................................626 579-0310
Miriam Weiss, *President*
Jacob Kasirer, *Vice Pres*
Lupe Hinojos, *Office Mgr*
EMP: 150
SQ FT: 88,615
SALES (est): 4.8MM
SALES (corp-wide): 62.1MM **Privately Held**
WEB: www.goldenstatehealth.com
SIC: 8051 Skilled nursing care facilities
PA: Golden State Health Centers, Inc.
13347 Ventura Blvd
Sherman Oaks CA 91423
818 385-3200

(P-20748)
SCRIPPS HEALTH
122 Civic Center Dr # 101, Vista (92084-6040)
PHONE.................................760 806-9263
EMP: 267
SALES (corp-wide): 2.9B **Privately Held**
SIC: 8051 Skilled nursing care facilities
PA: Scripps Health
10140 Campus Point Dr Ax415
San Diego CA 92121
800 727-4777

(P-20749)
SCRIPPS HEALTH
Also Called: Scripps Shared Services
10790 Rancho Bernardo Rd, San Diego (92127-5705)
P.O. Box 85105 (92186-5105)
PHONE.................................858 657-4218
Vickie Tickel, *Director*
Lily Bao, *Programmer Anys*
Winston Carter, *Project Mgr*
Tierre Neal, *Engineer*
Brian Moffit, *Diag Radio*
EMP: 150
SALES (corp-wide): 2.9B **Privately Held**
WEB: www.scripps.org
SIC: 8051 8082 Skilled nursing care facilities; home health care services
PA: Scripps Health
10140 Campus Point Dr Ax415
San Diego CA 92121
800 727-4777

(P-20750)
SEA BREEZE HEALTH CARE INC
Also Called: Beachside Nursing Center
7781 Garfield Ave, Huntington Beach (92648-2026)
PHONE.................................714 847-9671
Tim Paulson, *President*
Renee Scott, *Social Dir*
Nate Beck, *Administration*
ARI Corona, *Payroll Mgr*
Racquel Sierra, *Nursing Dir*
EMP: 132
SQ FT: 14,895
SALES (est): 9.9MM
SALES (corp-wide): 69.3MM **Privately Held**
SIC: 8051 Convalescent home with continuous nursing care
PA: North American Health Care, Inc.
5150 E A Palma Ave 206
Anaheim CA 92807
949 240-2423

(P-20751)
SEACREST CONVALESCENT HOSP INC
1416 W 6th St, San Pedro (90732-3550)
PHONE.................................310 833-3526
Cecelia Valdomar, *President*
Cecelia D Valdomar, *President*
Joy Nacionales, *Admin Sec*
Jose Valdomar, *Director*
EMP: 70
SALES (est): 3.2MM **Privately Held**
SIC: 8051 Convalescent home with continuous nursing care

(P-20752)
SELA HEALTHCARE INC (PA)
Also Called: Holiday Manor Care Center
867 E 11th St, Upland (91786-4867)
PHONE.................................909 985-1981
Philip Weinberger, *CEO*
Marylynn Mahan, *CFO*
EMP: 140
SQ FT: 60,000
SALES (est): 8.5MM **Privately Held**
SIC: 8051 Skilled nursing care facilities

(P-20753)
SERRANO COVALESCENT HOSPITAL
5401 Fountain Ave, Los Angeles (90029-1006)
PHONE.................................323 465-2106
Lydia Cruz, *Manager*
EMP: 80
SALES (est): 1.5MM **Privately Held**
SIC: 8051 Skilled nursing care facilities

(P-20754)
SHADOW HLLS CNVLSCENT HOSP INC
10158 Sunland Blvd, Sunland (91040-1651)
PHONE.................................818 352-4438
Orlando Clarizio Jr, *President*
Dino Clarizio, *Treasurer*
Michale Clarizio, *Admin Sec*
EMP: 67
SQ FT: 13,000

SALES: 3.8MM **Privately Held**
SIC: 8051 Convalescent home with continuous nursing care

(P-20755)
SHADOWBROOK HEALTH CARE INC
1 Gilmore Ln, Oroville (95966-5147)
PHONE.................................530 534-1353
Sharon Jennings, *President*
EMP: 50
SQ FT: 10,100
SALES: 3.4MM
SALES (corp-wide): 9.4MM **Privately Held**
SIC: 8051 Skilled nursing care facilities
PA: Riverside Health Care Corporation
1469 Humboldt Rd Ste 175
Chico CA 95928
530 897-5100

(P-20756)
SHARON CARE CENTER LLC
8167 W 3rd St, Los Angeles (90048-4314)
PHONE.................................323 655-2023
Isaac Shabat, *Exec Dir*
EMP: 108
SALES (est): 1.6MM **Publicly Held**
WEB: www.parkviewnursing.net
SIC: 8051 8059 Skilled nursing care facilities; convalescent home
HQ: Genesis Healthcare Corporation
101 E State St
Kennett Square PA 19348
610 444-6350

(P-20757)
SHARP HEALTHCARE
Also Called: Birch Ptrick Convalescent Cntr
751 Medical Center Ct, Chula Vista (91911-6617)
PHONE.................................858 499-2000
Lily Reyes, *Director*
Zoe Gardner, *Human Res Mgr*
Elaine Montijo, *Buyer*
Sylvia Heffron, *Sales Staff*
Henrietta Chong, *Nurse*
EMP: 140
SALES (corp-wide): 3.4B **Privately Held**
SIC: 8051 Skilled nursing care facilities
PA: Sharp Healthcare
8695 Spectrum Center Blvd
San Diego CA 92123
858 499-4000

(P-20758)
SHATTUCK HEALTH CARE INC
Also Called: Elmwood Care Center
2829 Shattuck Ave, Berkeley (94705-1037)
PHONE.................................510 665-2800
Pat Podatorri, *President*
Terry McGregor, *Vice Pres*
EMP: 97
SQ FT: 34,404
SALES (est): 2.9MM **Privately Held**
SIC: 8051 Convalescent home with continuous nursing care

(P-20759)
SHERWOOD OAKS ENTERPRISES
Also Called: Sherwood Oaks Health Center
130 Dana St, Fort Bragg (95437-4506)
PHONE.................................707 964-6333
Melanie Reding, *President*
Joe Reding, *Treasurer*
EMP: 90 **EST:** 1975
SQ FT: 19,000
SALES (est): 5.1MM **Privately Held**
SIC: 8051 Convalescent home with continuous nursing care

(P-20760)
SHIELDS NURSING CENTERS INC (PA)
606 Alfred Nobel Dr, Hercules (94547-1834)
PHONE.................................510 724-9911
William Shields Jr, *CEO*
EMP: 150
SQ FT: 6,100
SALES (est): 9.6MM **Privately Held**
WEB: www.shieldsnursingcenters.com
SIC: 8051 Convalescent home with continuous nursing care

(P-20761)
SHIELDS NURSING CENTERS INC
3230 Carlson Blvd, El Cerrito (94530-3907)
PHONE..................................510 525-3212
William Shields, *Administration*
EMP: 58
SALES (corp-wide): 9.6MM **Privately Held**
WEB: www.shieldsnursingcenters.com
SIC: 8051 Convalescent home with continuous nursing care
PA: Shields Nursing Centers, Inc.
606 Alfred Nobel Dr
Hercules CA 94547
510 724-9911

(P-20762)
SIERRA CARE REHABILITATION CTR
310 Oak Ridge Dr, Roseville (95661-3420)
PHONE..................................916 782-3188
Alice Mills, *Principal*
Rachelle McCoure, *Admin Asst*
EMP: 90
SALES (est): 1MM **Privately Held**
SIC: 8051 Skilled nursing care facilities

(P-20763)
SIERRA VIEW CARE HOLDINGS LLC
Also Called: Sierra View Care Center
14318 Ohio St, Baldwin Park (91706-2553)
PHONE..................................626 960-1971
Jordan Fishman, *Mng Member*
Irving Bauman, *President*
Matheson Chambers, *Principal*
David Johnson, *Principal*
Eli Marmur, *Principal*
EMP: 99
SALES: 8MM **Privately Held**
SIC: 8051 Skilled nursing care facilities

(P-20764)
SIERRA VIEW HOMES
Also Called: SIERRA VIEW HOMES RESIDENTIAL
1155 E Springfield Ave, Reedley (93654-3225)
PHONE..................................559 637-2256
Vito Genna, *Exec Dir*
Joyce Gregory, *Exec Dir*
Janice Gray, *Office Mgr*
Kecia Friesen, *Admin Asst*
Crystal Rogalsky, *Marketing Staff*
EMP: 140 EST: 1960
SQ FT: 63,600
SALES: 8.6MM **Privately Held**
WEB: www.sierraview.org
SIC: 8051 8059 6513 Skilled nursing care facilities; personal care home, with health care; apartment hotel operation

(P-20765)
SILVERADO SENIOR LIVING INC
Also Called: Beach Cities Memory Care Cmnty
514 N Prospect Ave # 120, Redondo Beach (90277-3036)
PHONE..................................424 257-6418
Thomas V Croal, *CFO*
Daizel Gasperian, *Vice Pres*
Chris Henger, *Exec Dir*
Sara Sanderman, *Administration*
EMP: 88
SALES (corp-wide): 180.3MM **Privately Held**
SIC: 8051 Skilled nursing care facilities
PA: Senior Silverado Living Inc
6400 Oak Cyn Ste 200
Irvine CA 92618
949 240-7200

(P-20766)
SILVERSCREEN HEALTHCARE INC
Also Called: Golden State Colonial Convales
10830 Oxnard St, North Hollywood (91606-5021)
PHONE..................................818 763-8247
Philip Weinberger, *President*
Marylynn Mahan, *CFO*
Klara Elekes, *Admin Sec*
EMP: 58 EST: 1964
SQ FT: 16,477
SALES (est): 2.2MM **Privately Held**
SIC: 8051 8059 Convalescent home with continuous nursing care; convalescent home

(P-20767)
SKILLED HEALTHCARE LLC (DH)
27442 Portola Pkwy # 200, Foothill Ranch (92610-2822)
PHONE..................................949 282-5800
George V Hager Jr,
Richard Edwards, *Vice Pres*
EMP: 58
SQ FT: 22,000
SALES (est): 116MM **Publicly Held**
WEB: www.skilledhealthcare.com
SIC: 8051 6513 5122 Skilled nursing care facilities; retirement hotel operation; drugs, proprietaries & sundries

(P-20768)
SKILLED HEALTHCARE LLC
Also Called: Brier Oak On Sunset Rehab
5154 W Sunset Blvd, Los Angeles (90027-5708)
PHONE..................................323 663-3951
Douglas Lehnhoff, *Exec Dir*
EMP: 100 **Publicly Held**
WEB: www.skilledhealthcare.com
SIC: 8051 8049 8059 Skilled nursing care facilities; physical therapist; personal care home, with health care
HQ: Skilled Healthcare, Llc
27442 Portola Pkwy # 200
Foothill Ranch CA 92610
949 282-5800

(P-20769)
SKYLINE HEALTHCARE & WELLNESS
Also Called: Skyline Healthcare Center
3032 Rowena Ave, Los Angeles (90039-2005)
PHONE..................................323 665-1185
Bernon Aguilar, *Administration*
Sharrod Brooks,
EMP: 99
SALES (est): 4.8MM **Privately Held**
SIC: 8051 Mental retardation hospital

(P-20770)
SLCH INC (PA)
Also Called: Sophia Lyn Convalescent Hosp
1920 N Fair Oaks Ave, Pasadena (91103-1623)
PHONE..................................626 798-0558
Phillip Rosales, *President*
Lolita Asero, *Administration*
EMP: 50
SQ FT: 16,757
SALES: 3.2MM **Privately Held**
WEB: www.slch.com
SIC: 8051 Skilled nursing care facilities

(P-20771)
SOLEDAD CMNTY HLTH CARE DST
Also Called: SOLEDAD MEDICAL GROUP
612 Main St, Soledad (93960-2533)
PHONE..................................831 678-2462
Steven Pritt, *CEO*
Ralph Sarmento, *President*
Rosemary Guidotti, *Admin Sec*
Jack Franscioni, *Director*
EMP: 80
SALES: 30.2K **Privately Held**
WEB: www.schcd.com
SIC: 8051 Skilled nursing care facilities

(P-20772)
SOUTH COAST HEALTH WELLNESS
Also Called: Community Care On Palm
4768 Palm Ave, Riverside (92501-4012)
PHONE..................................951 686-9001
Cheryl B Jumonville, *President*
EMP: 50
SALES (est): 388K **Privately Held**
SIC: 8051 Skilled nursing care facilities

(P-20773)
SOUTHERN INYO HEALTHCARE DST
501 E Locust St, Lone Pine (93545)
PHONE..................................760 876-5501
Lee Barron, *CEO*
EMP: 106
SQ FT: 29,000
SALES (est): 13.9MM **Privately Held**
WEB: www.sihd.org
SIC: 8051 Skilled nursing care facilities

(P-20774)
SPRING VALLEY POST ACUTE LLC
14973 Hesperia Rd, Victorville (92395-3923)
PHONE..................................760 245-6477
David Johnson, *Mng Member*
Matheson Chambers,
Thomas Chambers,
EMP: 200
SALES (est): 4.1MM **Privately Held**
SIC: 8051 Skilled nursing care facilities

(P-20775)
SSC CARMICHAEL OPERATING CO LP
Also Called: Mission Crmchael Halthcare Ctr
3630 Mission Ave, Carmichael (95608-2933)
PHONE..................................916 485-4793
Anne Gilles, *Administration*
Wayne M Sanner, *Partner*
Mary Ruvalcaba, *Director*
EMP: 99
SALES (est): 12.6MM
SALES (corp-wide): 1.3B **Privately Held**
SIC: 8051 Skilled nursing care facilities
PA: Savaseniorcare, Llc
1 Ravinia Dr Ste 1500
Atlanta GA 30346
770 829-5100

(P-20776)
SSC NEWPORT BEACH OPER CO LP
Also Called: Flagship Healthcare Center
466 Flagship Rd, Newport Beach (92663-3635)
PHONE..................................949 642-8044
Scott Harris, *Partner*
Wayne Sanner, *Partner*
Wynn Sims, *Partner*
EMP: 133
SQ FT: 21,903
SALES (est): 3.5MM **Privately Held**
SIC: 8051 Convalescent home with continuous nursing care

(P-20777)
SSC OAKLAND EXCELL OPER CO LP
Also Called: Excell Health Care Center
3025 High St, Oakland (94619-1807)
PHONE..................................510 261-5200
Elma Conway, *Manager*
Wayne M Sanner,
EMP: 99
SALES (est): 1.2MM **Privately Held**
SIC: 8051 Skilled nursing care facilities

(P-20778)
SSC SAN JOSE OPERATING CO LP
Also Called: Courtyard Care Center
340 Northlake Dr, San Jose (95117-1251)
PHONE..................................408 249-0344
Wayne M Sanner,
EMP: 94
SALES (est): 6.3MM
SALES (corp-wide): 1.2B **Privately Held**
SIC: 8051 Skilled nursing care facilities
PA: Savaseniorcare, Llc
1 Ravinia Dr Ste 1500
Atlanta GA 30346
770 829-5100

(P-20779)
ST LUKE HLTHCR & REHAB CTR LL
2321 Newburg Rd, Fortuna (95540-2815)
PHONE..................................707 725-4467
Ted Chigaros,

EMP: 100
SALES: 1,000K **Privately Held**
SIC: 8051 Skilled nursing care facilities

(P-20780)
ST MICHAEL CONVALESCENT HOSP
Also Called: Vintage Estates of Hayward
25919 Gading Rd, Hayward (94544-2798)
PHONE..................................510 782-8424
Sally Rapp, *CEO*
Roland Rapp, *Treasurer*
Cheryl A Rapp, *Principal*
EMP: 99
SQ FT: 6,000
SALES (est): 2.4MM **Privately Held**
WEB: www.vintage-estates.com
SIC: 8051 Skilled nursing care facilities

(P-20781)
STANDARDBEARER INSUR CO LTD
27101 Puerta Real Ste 450, Mission Viejo (92691-8566)
PHONE..................................949 487-9500
EMP: 474
SALES (est): 682.9K
SALES (corp-wide): 1.8B **Publicly Held**
SIC: 8051 Skilled nursing care facilities
PA: The Ensign Group Inc
27101 Puerta Real Ste 450
Mission Viejo CA 92691
949 487-9500

(P-20782)
STJOHN GOD RTIREMENT CARE CTR
2468 S St Andrews Pl, Los Angeles (90018-2042)
PHONE..................................323 731-0641
Michael Bessimer, *Administration*
EMP: 200
SQ FT: 99,392
SALES: 16.5MM **Privately Held**
SIC: 8051 8052 Skilled nursing care facilities; intermediate care facilities

(P-20783)
STONEBROOK CONVALESCENT CENTER
Also Called: Stonebrook Health Care Center
4367 Concord Blvd, Concord (94521-1100)
PHONE..................................925 689-7457
James D Hightower, *President*
EMP: 206
SQ FT: 44,000
SALES (est): 14.1MM **Privately Held**
WEB: www.healthmarkservices.com
SIC: 8051 Convalescent home with continuous nursing care
PA: Healthmark Services Inc
217 Lakewood Rd
Van Buren AR 72956
479 471-9797

(P-20784)
SUN HAVEN CARE INC
Also Called: Terrace View Care Center
201 E Bastanchury Rd, Fullerton (92835-2604)
PHONE..................................714 870-0060
John Sworenson, *CEO*
Brendon Bahl, *Vice Pres*
Renae Rodriguez, *Training Spec*
Bem Lemaster, *Director*
EMP: 60
SALES (est): 3MM **Privately Held**
SIC: 8051 Convalescent home with continuous nursing care

(P-20785)
SUN MAR MANAGEMENT SERVICES
8171 Magnolia Ave, Riverside (92504-3409)
PHONE..................................951 687-3842
Robert Ginn, *Administration*
EMP: 100
SALES (corp-wide): 50.5MM **Privately Held**
WEB: www.extendedcarehospital.com
SIC: 8051 Skilled nursing care facilities

P
R
O
D
U
C
T
S

&

S
V
C
S

PA: Sun Mar Management Services
3050 Saturn St Ste 201
Brea CA 92821
714 577-3880

(P-20786)
SUN VILLA INC
350 N Villa St, Porterville (93257-3211)
PHONE......................559 784-6644
David Green, *Administration*
Salvador Estrada, *Director*
Mark Mann, *Manager*
EMP: 120 EST: 1971
SQ FT: 50,000
SALES (est): 4.7MM **Privately Held**
SIC: 8051 Convalescent home with contin-
uous nursing care

(P-20787)
**SUNBRIDGE BRITTANY REHAB
CENTR**
Also Called: American River Care
3900 Garfield Ave, Carmichael
(95608-6647)
PHONE......................916 484-1393
Andrew Turner, *President*
Carly Migdal, *Social Dir*
Anne Butler, *Administration*
Kristine Perry, *Director*
Sultan Yusufzai, *Director*
EMP: 120
SALES (est): 3.5MM **Publicly Held**
SIC: 8051 8069 Skilled nursing care facili-
ties; specialty hospitals, except psychi-
atric
HQ: Regency Health Services, Inc.
5100 Sun Ave Ne
Albuquerque NM 87109
505 821-3355

(P-20788)
**SUNBRIDGE CARE ENTPS W
INC**
Also Called: Kingsburg Center
1101 Stroud Ave, Kingsburg (93631-1016)
PHONE......................559 897-5881
Ron Kennersly, *Manager*
J Richard Edwards, *Treasurer*
EMP: 100 **Publicly Held**
SIC: 8051 Skilled nursing care facilities
HQ: Sunbridge Care Enterprises West, Inc.
101 Sun Ave Ne
Albuquerque NM 87109
925 988-9100

(P-20789)
**SUNBRIDGE CARE ENTPS W
LLC**
Also Called: Kingsburg Center
1101 Stroud Ave, Kingsburg (93631-1016)
PHONE......................559 897-5881
Ron Kinnersly, *Administration*
EMP: 2729
SALES (est): 10.5MM **Publicly Held**
SIC: 8051 Skilled nursing care facilities
HQ: Genesis Healthcare Llc
101 E State St
Kennett Square PA 19348

(P-20790)
SUNBRIDGE HARBOR VIEW
Also Called: Harbor View Rehabilitation Ctr
490 W 14th St, Long Beach (90813-2943)
PHONE......................562 989-9907
Rick Matros, *President*
Wendy McLearie, *Administration*
EMP: 200
SALES (est): 4.6MM **Publicly Held**
SIC: 8051 8361 Skilled nursing care facili-
ties; residential care
HQ: Regency Health Services, Inc.
5100 Sun Ave Ne
Albuquerque NM 87109
505 821-3355

(P-20791)
SUNBRIDGE HEALTHCARE LLC
Also Called: Sunbridge Elmhaven Care Cen-
ter
6940 Pacific Ave, Stockton (95207-2602)
PHONE......................209 477-4817
Mike Blaufus, *Administration*
Beth Clark, *Office Mgr*
Karen Smith, *Administration*

Richard Gonzales, *Facilities Dir*
Suzie Vargas, *Director*
EMP: 99 **Publicly Held**
SIC: 8051 Convalescent home with contin-
uous nursing care
HQ: Sunbridge Healthcare, Llc
101 Sun Ave Ne
Albuquerque NM 87109
505 821-3355

(P-20792)
**SUNBRIDGE PARADISE
RHBLTTN CTR**
Also Called: Pine View Center
8777 Skyway, Paradise (95969-2110)
PHONE......................530 872-3200
Annie Buerhaus, *Branch Mgr*
EMP: 100 **Publicly Held**
SIC: 8051 8049 Skilled nursing care facili-
ties; speech therapist
HQ: Sunbridge Paradise Rehabilitation
Center, Inc.
101 Sun Ave Ne
Albuquerque NM

(P-20793)
**SUNNYSIDE RHBLTTION
NRSING CTR**
22617 S Vermont Ave, Torrance
(90502-2550)
PHONE......................310 320-4130
Judy Narloda, *President*
Jaime Deutsch, *Vice Pres*
Shane Dahl, *Administration*
EMP: 220
SQ FT: 35,000
SALES (est): 9.3MM **Privately Held**
SIC: 8051 8361 8069 8052 Convalescent
home with continuous nursing care; resi-
dential care; specialty hospitals, except
psychiatric; intermediate care facilities

(P-20794)
**SUNNYVALE HEALTHCARE
CENTER**
Also Called: Sunnyvale Health Care
1291 S Bernardo Ave, Sunnyvale
(94087-2060)
PHONE......................408 245-8070
Hermina Chavez, *CEO*
Maricel De Guzman, *Records Dir*
Vanessa Chavez, *Treasurer*
Mario Chavez, *Vice Pres*
Nathan Roseberry, *Associate Dir*
EMP: 75
SQ FT: 26,679
SALES (est): 4.2MM **Privately Held**
WEB: www.svhcc.com
SIC: 8051 Convalescent home with contin-
uous nursing care

(P-20795)
SUNRISE SENIOR LIVING INC
Also Called: Sunrise At Alta Loma
9519 Baseline Rd, Rancho Cucamonga
(91730-1313)
PHONE......................909 941-3001
Carol Lininger, *Exec Dir*
Luis Rodriquez, *Exec Dir*
Gloria Tafesh, *Marketing Staff*
Billy Davis, *Food Svc Dir*
Jenna Altshule, *Nursing Dir*
EMP: 60
SALES (corp-wide): 4.3B **Publicly Held**
WEB: www.sunrise.com
SIC: 8051 8322 Skilled nursing care facili-
ties; senior citizens' center or association
HQ: Sunrise Senior Living, Llc
7902 Westpark Dr
Mc Lean VA 22102

(P-20796)
SUNRISE SENIOR LIVING INC
Also Called: Brighton Gardens of Sunrise
72201 Country Club Dr, Palm Desert
(92210)
PHONE......................760 340-5999
Ernie Schaffer, *Director*
EMP: 58
SALES (corp-wide): 4.3B **Publicly Held**
WEB: www.sunrise.com
SIC: 8051 8361 Skilled nursing care facili-
ties; residential care

HQ: Sunrise Senior Living, Llc
7902 Westpark Dr
Mc Lean VA 22102

(P-20797)
SUNRISE SENIOR LIVING INC
Also Called: Sunrise of Oakland Hills
1600 Canyon Rd 103, Moraga
(94556-1709)
PHONE......................510 531-7190
Bill Keck, *Branch Mgr*
EMP: 65
SQ FT: 64,421
SALES (corp-wide): 4.3B **Publicly Held**
WEB: www.sunrise.com
SIC: 8051 8361 Skilled nursing care facili-
ties; residential care
HQ: Sunrise Senior Living, Llc
7902 Westpark Dr
Mc Lean VA 22102

(P-20798)
SUNRISE SENIOR LIVING INC
Also Called: Sunrise of Petaluma
815 Wood Sorrel Dr, Petaluma
(94954-6857)
PHONE......................707 776-2885
Carla Sanchez, *Exec Dir*
EMP: 62
SALES (corp-wide): 4.3B **Publicly Held**
WEB: www.sunrise.com
SIC: 8051 8361 Skilled nursing care facili-
ties; residential care
HQ: Sunrise Senior Living, Llc
7902 Westpark Dr
Mc Lean VA 22102

(P-20799)
SUNRISE SENIOR LIVING INC
Also Called: Sunrise Asssted Lving San Mteo
955 S El Camino Real, San Mateo
(94402-2346)
PHONE......................650 558-8555
Andrew Smith, *Manager*
EMP: 65
SALES (corp-wide): 4.3B **Publicly Held**
WEB: www.sunrise.com
SIC: 8051 8361 Skilled nursing care facili-
ties; home for the aged
HQ: Sunrise Senior Living, Llc
7902 Westpark Dr
Mc Lean VA 22102

(P-20800)
SUNRISE SENIOR LIVING INC
3840 Lampson Ave, Seal Beach
(90740-2797)
PHONE......................562 594-5788
Bonnie Christie, *Branch Mgr*
EMP: 58
SALES (corp-wide): 4.3B **Publicly Held**
WEB: www.sunrise.com
SIC: 8051 8361 Skilled nursing care facili-
ties; residential care
HQ: Sunrise Senior Living, Llc
7902 Westpark Dr
Mc Lean VA 22102

(P-20801)
SUNRISE SENIOR LIVING INC
Also Called: Sunrise of Woodland Hills
5501 Newcastle Ave # 130, Encino
(91316-2147)
PHONE......................818 346-9046
Tom Colomaria, *Manager*
EMP: 50
SALES (corp-wide): 4.3B **Publicly Held**
WEB: www.sunrise.com
SIC: 8051 8361 Skilled nursing care facili-
ties; residential care
HQ: Sunrise Senior Living, Llc
7902 Westpark Dr
Mc Lean VA 22102

(P-20802)
SUNRISE SENIOR LIVING INC
Also Called: Sunrise of Palo Alto
201 N Crescent Dr Apt 503, Beverly Hills
(90210-6184)
PHONE......................650 326-1108

Ken Claire, *Branch Mgr*
EMP: 65
SALES (corp-wide): 4.3B **Publicly Held**
WEB: www.sunrise.com
SIC: 8051 8361 Skilled nursing care facili-
ties; residential care
HQ: Sunrise Senior Living, Llc
7902 Westpark Dr
Mc Lean VA 22102

(P-20803)
SUNRISE SENIOR LIVING INC
Also Called: Sunrise At Sterling Canyon
25815 Mcbean Pkwy Ofc, Valencia
(91355-2071)
PHONE......................661 253-3551
Pamela Sellers, *Director*
EMP: 65
SALES (corp-wide): 4.3B **Publicly Held**
WEB: www.sunrise.com
SIC: 8051 8361 Skilled nursing care facili-
ties; home for the aged
HQ: Sunrise Senior Living, Llc
7902 Westpark Dr
Mc Lean VA 22102

(P-20804)
SUNRISE SENIOR LIVING INC
Also Called: Fountains At Sea Bluffs
25421 Sea Bluffs Dr, Dana Point
(92629-2196)
PHONE......................949 234-3000
David Omalley, *Branch Mgr*
EMP: 58
SALES (corp-wide): 4.3B **Publicly Held**
WEB: www.sunrise.com
SIC: 8051 8361 Skilled nursing care facili-
ties; home for the aged
HQ: Sunrise Senior Living, Llc
7902 Westpark Dr
Mc Lean VA 22102

(P-20805)
SUNRISE SENIOR LIVING INC
Also Called: Sunrise of Beverly Hills
201 N Crescent Dr, Beverly Hills
(90210-4898)
PHONE......................310 274-4479
Brandy Velencia, *Manager*
EMP: 58
SALES (corp-wide): 4.3B **Publicly Held**
WEB: www.sunrise.com
SIC: 8051 Skilled nursing care facilities
HQ: Sunrise Senior Living, Llc
7902 Westpark Dr
Mc Lean VA 22102

(P-20806)
SUNRISE SENIOR LIVING INC
Also Called: Sunrise of Playa Vista
5555 Playa Vista Dr, Los Angeles
(90094-2234)
PHONE......................310 437-7178
Wendy McIlnay, *Manager*
EMP: 59
SALES (corp-wide): 4.3B **Publicly Held**
WEB: www.sunrise.com
SIC: 8051 8361 Skilled nursing care facili-
ties; home for the aged
HQ: Sunrise Senior Living, Llc
7902 Westpark Dr
Mc Lean VA 22102

(P-20807)
SUNRISE SENIOR LIVING INC
1601 19th Ave, San Francisco
(94122-3468)
PHONE......................415 664-6264
Jeannie Hung, *Branch Mgr*
EMP: 58
SALES (corp-wide): 4.3B **Publicly Held**
WEB: www.sunrise.com
SIC: 8051 8361 Skilled nursing care facili-
ties; home for the aged
HQ: Sunrise Senior Living, Llc
7902 Westpark Dr
Mc Lean VA 22102

(P-20808)
SUNRISE SENIOR LIVING INC
Also Called: Vintage Silver Creek
4855 San Felipe Rd, San Jose
(95135-1287)
PHONE..................................408 223-1312
Rick Qwaza, *Branch Mgr*
EMP: 58
SALES (corp-wide): 4.3B Publicly Held
WEB: www.sunrise.com
SIC: 8051 8361 Skilled nursing care facili-
ties; home for the aged
HQ: Sunrise Senior Living, Llc
    7902 Westpark Dr
    Mc Lean VA 22102
    -

(P-20809)
SUNRISE SENIOR LIVING INC
Also Called: Villa Valencia Health Care Ctr
24552 Paseo De Valencia, Laguna Hills
(92653-4236)
PHONE..................................949 581-6111
Terry Records, *Chief*
EMP: 58
SALES (corp-wide): 4.3B Publicly Held
WEB: www.sunrise.com
SIC: 8051 8361 Skilled nursing care facili-
ties; home for the aged
HQ: Sunrise Senior Living, Llc
    7902 Westpark Dr
    Mc Lean VA 22102
    -

(P-20810)
SUNRISE SENIOR LIVING INC
Also Called: Sunrise of Carmichael
5451 Fair Oaks Blvd, Carmichael
(95608-5748)
PHONE..................................916 485-4500
EMP: 58
SALES (corp-wide): 4.3B Publicly Held
WEB: www.sunrise.com
SIC: 8051 8361 Skilled nursing care facili-
ties; home for the aged
HQ: Sunrise Senior Living, Llc
    7902 Westpark Dr
    Mc Lean VA 22102
    -

(P-20811)
SUNRISE SENIOR LIVING INC
Also Called: Sunrise of Monterey
1110 Carmelo St, Monterey (93940-4508)
PHONE..................................831 643-2400
Susan Sundell, *Branch Mgr*
EMP: 58
SALES (corp-wide): 4.3B Publicly Held
WEB: www.sunrise.com
SIC: 8051 8361 Skilled nursing care facili-
ties; home for the aged
HQ: Sunrise Senior Living, Llc
    7902 Westpark Dr
    Mc Lean VA 22102
    -

(P-20812)
SUNRISE SENIOR LIVING INC
Also Called: Sunrise of Santa Rosa
3250 Chanate Rd Ofc, Santa Rosa
(95404-1771)
PHONE..................................707 575-7503
Rob Komorowski, *Manager*
EMP: 50
SALES (corp-wide): 4.3B Publicly Held
WEB: www.sunrise.com
SIC: 8051 8361 Skilled nursing care facili-
ties; home for the aged
HQ: Sunrise Senior Living, Llc
    7902 Westpark Dr
    Mc Lean VA 22102
    -

(P-20813)
SUNRISE SENIOR LIVING LLC
Also Called: Sunrise of Danville
1027 Diablo Rd, Danville (94526-1923)
PHONE..................................925 309-4178
Sol Spencer, *Director*
EMP: 80
SALES (corp-wide): 4.3B Publicly Held
WEB: www.sunrise.com
SIC: 8051 Skilled nursing care facilities

HQ: Sunrise Senior Living, Llc
    7902 Westpark Dr
    Mc Lean VA 22102

(P-20814)
SUNRISE SENIOR LIVING LLC
Also Called: Sunrise Assistd Lving of Wlnt
2175 Ygnacio Valley Rd, Walnut Creek
(94598-3385)
PHONE..................................925 932-3500
Kathlyn McParron, *Manager*
EMP: 50
SALES (corp-wide): 4.3B Publicly Held
WEB: www.sunrise.com
SIC: 8051 Skilled nursing care facilities
HQ: Sunrise Senior Living, Llc
    7902 Westpark Dr
    Mc Lean VA 22102
    -

(P-20815)
SUNRISE SENIOR LIVING LLC
17650 Devonshire St, Northridge
(91325-1445)
PHONE..................................818 886-1616
Susan Nasraty, *General Mgr*
EMP: 58
SALES (corp-wide): 4.3B Publicly Held
WEB: www.sunrise.com
SIC: 8051 8361 Skilled nursing care facili-
ties; residential care
HQ: Sunrise Senior Living, Llc
    7902 Westpark Dr
    Mc Lean VA 22102
    -

(P-20816)
SUNRISE SENIOR LIVING LLC
Also Called: Sunrise of Mission Viejo
26151 Country Club Dr, Mission Viejo
(92691-5907)
PHONE..................................949 582-2010
Lynn Piglao, *Director*
EMP: 60
SALES (corp-wide): 4.3B Publicly Held
WEB: www.sunrise.com
SIC: 8051 Skilled nursing care facilities
HQ: Sunrise Senior Living, Llc
    7902 Westpark Dr
    Mc Lean VA 22102
    -

(P-20817)
SUNRISE SENIOR LIVING LLC
Also Called: Sunrise of Hermosa Beach
1837 Pacific Coast Hwy, Hermosa Beach
(90254-3160)
PHONE..................................310 937-0959
Josie Hecht, *Manager*
EMP: 50
SALES (corp-wide): 4.3B Publicly Held
WEB: www.sunrise.com
SIC: 8051 8361 Skilled nursing care facili-
ties; home for the aged
HQ: Sunrise Senior Living, Llc
    7902 Westpark Dr
    Mc Lean VA 22102
    -

(P-20818)
SUNRISE SENIOR LIVING LLC
Also Called: Sunrise At La Costa
7020 Manzanita St, Carlsbad (92011-5123)
PHONE..................................760 930-0060
Euginia Whelch, *Director*
EMP: 100
SALES (corp-wide): 4.3B Publicly Held
WEB: www.sunrise.com
SIC: 8051 8361 Skilled nursing care facili-
ties; home for the aged
HQ: Sunrise Senior Living, Llc
    7902 Westpark Dr
    Mc Lean VA 22102
    -

(P-20819)
SUNRISE SENIOR LIVING LLC
Also Called: Sunrise At Bonita
3302 Bonita Rd, Chula Vista (91910-3207)
PHONE..................................619 470-2220
Gwen Krushensky, *Manager*
EMP: 55

SALES (corp-wide): 4.3B Publicly Held
WEB: www.sunrise.com
SIC: 8051 8361 Skilled nursing care facili-
ties; residential care
HQ: Sunrise Senior Living, Llc
    7902 Westpark Dr
    Mc Lean VA 22102
    -

(P-20820)
SUNRISE SENIOR LIVING LLC
Also Called: Sunrise of Sacramento
345 Munroe St, Sacramento (95825-6459)
PHONE..................................916 486-0200
Lyndee Whaley, *Manager*
EMP: 50
SALES (corp-wide): 4.3B Publicly Held
WEB: www.sunrise.com
SIC: 8051 8361 Skilled nursing care facili-
ties; residential care
HQ: Sunrise Senior Living, Llc
    7902 Westpark Dr
    Mc Lean VA 22102
    -

(P-20821)
SUNRISE SENIOR LIVING LLC
530 Water St Fl 5, Oakland (94607-3532)
PHONE..................................303 410-0500
Shanelle Armas, *Manager*
EMP: 58
SALES (corp-wide): 4.3B Publicly Held
WEB: www.sunrise.com
SIC: 8051 Skilled nursing care facilities
HQ: Sunrise Senior Living, Llc
    7902 Westpark Dr
    Mc Lean VA 22102
    -

(P-20822)
SUNRISE SENIOR LIVING LLC
Also Called: Sunrise of Sunnyvale
633 S Knickerbocker Dr # 263, Sunnyvale
(94087-1034)
PHONE..................................408 749-8600
Tina Bagheri, *Manager*
EMP: 65
SALES (corp-wide): 4.3B Publicly Held
WEB: www.sunrise.com
SIC: 8051 8361 Skilled nursing care facili-
ties; home for the aged
HQ: Sunrise Senior Living, Llc
    7902 Westpark Dr
    Mc Lean VA 22102
    -

(P-20823)
SUNRISE SENIOR LIVING LLC
Also Called: Sunrise of Westlake Village
3101 Townsgate Rd, Westlake Village
(91361-5835)
PHONE..................................805 557-1100
Angela Ling, *Branch Mgr*
EMP: 58
SALES (corp-wide): 4.3B Publicly Held
WEB: www.sunrise.com
SIC: 8051 8361 Skilled nursing care facili-
ties; residential care
HQ: Sunrise Senior Living, Llc
    7902 Westpark Dr
    Mc Lean VA 22102
    -

(P-20824)
SUNRISE SENIOR LIVING LLC
Also Called: Sunrise of Studio City
4610 Coldwater Canyon Ave, Studio City
(91604-1031)
PHONE..................................818 505-8484
Jason Malone, *Manager*
EMP: 58
SALES (corp-wide): 4.3B Publicly Held
WEB: www.sunrise.com
SIC: 8051 8361 Skilled nursing care facili-
ties; residential care
HQ: Sunrise Senior Living, Llc
    7902 Westpark Dr
    Mc Lean VA 22102
    -

(P-20825)
SUNRISE SENIOR LIVING LLC
Also Called: Sunrise of Fresno
7444 N Cedar Ave, Fresno (93720-3636)
PHONE..................................559 325-8170
Jessica Lopez, *Director*

EMP: 70
SALES (corp-wide): 4.3B Publicly Held
WEB: www.sunrise.com
SIC: 8051 8361 Skilled nursing care facili-
ties; residential care
HQ: Sunrise Senior Living, Llc
    7902 Westpark Dr
    Mc Lean VA 22102
    -

(P-20826)
SUNRISE SENIOR LIVING LLC
Also Called: Sunrise of La Palma
5321 La Palma Ave Fl 2, La Palma
(90623-1703)
PHONE..................................714 739-8111
Jennifer Munoz, *Mayor*
EMP: 60
SALES (corp-wide): 4.3B Publicly Held
WEB: www.sunrise.com
SIC: 8051 Skilled nursing care facilities
HQ: Sunrise Senior Living, Llc
    7902 Westpark Dr
    Mc Lean VA 22102
    -

(P-20827)
SUNRISE SENIOR LIVING LLC
Also Called: Sunrise of San Juan Capis-
trano (92675-6722)
31741 Rancho Viejo Rd, San Juan Capis-
trano (92675-6722)
PHONE..................................949 248-8855
Tiffany Calahan, *Manager*
EMP: 58
SALES (corp-wide): 4.3B Publicly Held
WEB: www.sunrise.com
SIC: 8051 8361 Convalescent home with
continuous nursing care; residential care
HQ: Sunrise Senior Living, Llc
    7902 Westpark Dr
    Mc Lean VA 22102
    -

(P-20828)
SUNRISE SENIOR LIVING LLC
Also Called: Sunrise of Palm Springs
1780 E Baristo Rd, Palm Springs
(92262-7114)
PHONE..................................760 322-3444
Lisa Kennedy, *Exec Dir*
EMP: 80
SALES (corp-wide): 4.3B Publicly Held
WEB: www.sunrise.com
SIC: 8051 8361 Skilled nursing care facili-
ties; residential care
HQ: Sunrise Senior Living, Llc
    7902 Westpark Dr
    Mc Lean VA 22102
    -

(P-20829)
SUNRISE SENIOR LIVING LLC
1301 Ralston Ave Ste A, Belmont
(94002-1961)
PHONE..................................650 654-9700
Bradford Liebman, *Branch Mgr*
EMP: 58
SALES (corp-wide): 4.3B Publicly Held
WEB: www.sunrise.com
SIC: 8051 8361 Skilled nursing care facili-
ties; home for the aged
HQ: Sunrise Senior Living, Llc
    7902 Westpark Dr
    Mc Lean VA 22102
    -

(P-20830)
SUNRISE SENIOR LIVING LLC
Also Called: Brighton Gardens of Camarillo
6000 Santa Rosa Rd Ofc, Camarillo
(93012-7121)
PHONE..................................805 388-8086
Stan Main, *Branch Mgr*
EMP: 58
SALES (corp-wide): 4.3B Publicly Held
WEB: www.sunrise.com
SIC: 8051 8361 Convalescent home with
continuous nursing care; home for the
aged
HQ: Sunrise Senior Living, Llc
    7902 Westpark Dr
    Mc Lean VA 22102

PRODUCTS & SVCS

(P-20831)
SUNRISE SENIOR LIVING LLC
Also Called: Sunrise of Hemet
1177 S Palm Ave, Hemet (92543-7817)
PHONE..................................951 929-5988
Kent K Goforth, *Branch Mgr*
EMP: 58
SALES (corp-wide): 4.3B **Publicly Held**
WEB: www.sunrise.com
SIC: 8051 Skilled nursing care facilities
HQ: Sunrise Senior Living, Llc
    7902 Westpark Dr
    Mc Lean VA 22102

(P-20832)
SUNRISE SENIOR LIVING LLC
Also Called: Sunrise of Rocklin
6100 Sierra College Blvd, Rocklin
(95677-3505)
PHONE..................................916 632-3003
Josh Lancaster, *Branch Mgr*
EMP: 59
SALES (corp-wide): 4.3B **Publicly Held**
WEB: www.sunrise.com
SIC: 8051 Skilled nursing care facilities
HQ: Sunrise Senior Living, Llc
    7902 Westpark Dr
    Mc Lean VA 22102
    -

(P-20833)
SUNRISE SENIOR LIVING LLC
Also Called: Fountains At The Carlotta
41505 Carlotta Dr, Palm Desert
(92211-3279)
PHONE..................................760 346-5420
EMP: 58
SALES (corp-wide): 4.3B **Publicly Held**
WEB: www.sunrise.com
SIC: 8051 8361 Skilled nursing care facili-
ties; home for the aged
HQ: Sunrise Senior Living, Llc
    7902 Westpark Dr
    Mc Lean VA 22102
    -

(P-20834)
SUNRISE SENIOR LIVING LLC
Also Called: Sunrise At Raincross Village
5232 Central Ave, Riverside (92504-1825)
PHONE..................................951 785-1200
Christi Steichen, *Branch Mgr*
EMP: 58
SALES (corp-wide): 4.3B **Publicly Held**
WEB: www.sunrise.com
SIC: 8051 8361 Skilled nursing care facili-
ties; home for the aged
HQ: Sunrise Senior Living, Llc
    7902 Westpark Dr
    Mc Lean VA 22102
    -

(P-20835)
SUTTER HEALTH
3707 Schriever Ave, Mather (95655-4202)
PHONE..................................916 454-8200
Sheila Black, *Branch Mgr*
Kerry Johnson, *Network Enginr*
Mark O'Sullivan, *Network Enginr*
Don Reed, *Network Enginr*
Troy Baker, *Engineer*
EMP: 60
SALES (corp-wide): 12.4B **Privately Held**
WEB: www.sutterhealth.org
SIC: 8051 8062 Skilled nursing care facili-
ties; general medical & surgical hospitals
PA: Sutter Health
    2200 River Plaza Dr
    Sacramento CA 95833
    916 733-8800

(P-20836)
**SUTTER VSTING NRSE ASSN
HSPICE**
1651 Alvarado St, San Leandro
(94577-2636)
PHONE..................................510 618-5277
Rosemarie Avery, *Manager*
EMP: 100
SALES (corp-wide): 12.4B **Privately Held**
WEB: www.suttervnaandhospice.com
SIC: 8051 8082 Skilled nursing care facili-
ties; home health care services

HQ: Sutter Visiting Nurse Association &
    Hospice
    1900 Powell St Ste 300
    Emeryville CA 94608
    866 652-9178

(P-20837)
T C H P INC
Also Called: Palm Terrace Care Center
11162 Palm Terrace Ln, Riverside
(92505-2338)
PHONE..................................951 687-7330
Jeremy Jergensen, *Administration*
Mariela Wilson, *Social Dir*
David Gunnell, *Administration*
Ryan Leet, *Administration*
Jane Macharia, *Nursing Dir*
EMP: 75
SALES: 10.9MM
SALES (corp-wide): 69.3MM **Privately
Held**
WEB: www.palmterracecare.com
SIC: 8051 Skilled nursing care facilities
PA: North American Health Care, Inc.
    5150 E A Palma Ave 206
    Anaheim CA 92807
    949 240-2423

(P-20838)
TLC OF BAY AREA INC
Also Called: Valley House Care Center
991 Clyde Ave, Santa Clara (95054-1905)
P.O. Box 607, Indiana PA (15701-0607)
PHONE..................................408 988-7667
Marcy Colkitt, *President*
Merlin Davey, *Exec Dir*
EMP: 51
SALES (est): 5.7MM **Privately Held**
SIC: 8051 Skilled nursing care facilities

(P-20839)
**TORRANCE CARE CENTER
WEST INC**
4333 Torrance Blvd, Torrance
(90503-4401)
PHONE..................................310 370-4561
Vicki P Rollins, *President*
EMP: 180
SALES: 17.8MM **Privately Held**
SIC: 8051 Skilled nursing care facilities

(P-20840)
**TOWN & COUNTRY MANOR OF
THE CH**
555 E Memory Ln Ofc Ofc, Santa Ana
(92706-1708)
PHONE..................................714 547-7581
Dirk De Wolfe, *Administration*
Jeff Leis, *CFO*
Mirissa Brinones, *Executive*
Dirk D Wolfe, *Administration*
Marianne Daniels, *Marketing Staff*
EMP: 210 **EST:** 1975
SQ FT: 208,000
SALES: 18.9MM **Privately Held**
SIC: 8051 8059 8052 Skilled nursing care
facilities; nursing home, except skilled &
intermediate care facility; intermediate
care facilities

(P-20841)
TRINITY HEALTH SYSTEMS
Also Called: Villa Maria Care Center
723 E 9th St, Long Beach (90813-4611)
PHONE..................................562 437-2797
Jordan Fishman, *Administration*
EMP: 57
SALES (corp-wide): 9.1MM **Privately
Held**
SIC: 8051 8059 Convalescent home with
continuous nursing care; nursing home,
except skilled & intermediate care facility
PA: Trinity Health Systems
    14318 Ohio St
    Baldwin Park CA 91706
    626 960-1971

(P-20842)
TRINITY HEALTH SYSTEMS (PA)
Also Called: Villa Maria Care Center
14318 Ohio St, Baldwin Park (91706-2553)
PHONE..................................626 960-1971
Randal Kleis, *President*
EMP: 80
SQ FT: 35,000

SALES (est): 9.1MM **Privately Held**
SIC: 8051 Skilled nursing care facilities

(P-20843)
**TULARE NRSING RHBLITATION
HOSP**
Also Called: Tulare Nrsing Rhbilitation Ctr
680 E Merritt Ave, Tulare (93274-2135)
PHONE..................................559 686-8581
Mark Fisher, *President*
Norm Christianson, *CFO*
Sharon A Fisher, *Admin Sec*
EMP: 125
SALES (est): 3.9MM **Privately Held**
WEB: www.missioncaregroup.com
SIC: 8051 Skilled nursing care facilities

(P-20844)
TWILIGHT HAVEN
1717 S Winery Ave, Fresno (93727-5011)
PHONE..................................559 251-8417
David Viancourt, *Administration*
Linda Perez, *Records Dir*
Kenneth Karle, *President*
Kamaljit Kaur, *Officer*
Robert Herman, *Vice Pres*
EMP: 95 **EST:** 1957
SQ FT: 70,000
SALES: 5.5MM **Privately Held**
WEB: www.twilighthaven.com
SIC: 8051 8052 8361 Convalescent home
with continuous nursing care; personal
care facility; rest home, with health care
incidental

(P-20845)
UNITED COM SERVE
Also Called: FOUNTAINS, THE
1260 Williams Way, Yuba City
(95991-2400)
PHONE..................................530 790-3000
Ryan Dickerson, *President*
Chris Parker, *Administration*
EMP: 100
SQ FT: 40,000
SALES: 15.9MM
SALES (corp-wide): 26.9MM **Privately
Held**
SIC: 8051 Skilled nursing care facilities
PA: Freemont Rideout Health Group
    989 Plumas St
    Yuba City CA 95991
    530 751-4010

(P-20846)
UNITED HEALTH SYSTEMS INC
Also Called: Alderson Convalescent Hospital
124 Walnut St, Woodland (95695-3137)
PHONE..................................530 662-9161
Santiago M S Miguel, *CEO*
Thomas E Mullen, *President*
Lynn Mullen, *Admin Sec*
EMP: 154
SQ FT: 40,000
SALES: 11.3MM **Privately Held**
WEB: www.unitedhealthsystems.com
SIC: 8051 Convalescent home with contin-
uous nursing care

(P-20847)
US SKILLSERVE INC
Also Called: Communty Convlscnt Hosp Mnt-
clr
9620 Fremont Ave, Montclair (91763-2320)
PHONE..................................909 621-4751
Johannes Simanjuntak, *Manager*
EMP: 140
SALES (corp-wide): 74.8MM **Privately
Held**
SIC: 8051 Convalescent home with contin-
uous nursing care
PA: U.S. Skillserve Inc
    4115 E Broadway Ste A
    Long Beach CA 90803
    562 930-0777

(P-20848)
V S N F INC
Also Called: Valley Skilled Nursing Care
2120 Stockton Blvd, Sacramento
(95817-1337)
PHONE..................................916 452-6631
John Sorensen, *President*
EMP: 55
SALES (est): 2MM **Privately Held**
SIC: 8051 Extended care facility

(P-20849)
**VALLEY CAREIDENCE OPCO
LLC**
Also Called: Gateway Post Acute
661 W Poplar Ave, Porterville
(93257-5926)
PHONE..................................559 784-8371
Jason Murray, *CEO*
Mark Hancock, *CFO*
EMP: 75
SALES (est): 231.3K
SALES (corp-wide): 951.8K **Privately
Held**
SIC: 8051 Skilled nursing care facilities
PA: Providence Group Of California, Llc
    140 N Union Ave Ste 320
    Farmington UT 84025
    619 756-6800

(P-20850)
**VALLEY HEALTHCARE CENTER
LLC**
4840 E Tulare Ave, Fresno (93727-3062)
PHONE..................................559 251-7161
George V Hagaer Jr, *CEO*
EMP: 100 **EST:** 2003
SALES (est): 574.4K **Publicly Held**
SIC: 8051 Skilled nursing care facilities
HQ: Genesis Healthcare Llc
    101 E State St
    Kennett Square PA 19348
    -

(P-20851)
**VALLEY HEALTHCARE CENTER
LLC**
4840 E Tulare Ave, Fresno (93727-3062)
PHONE..................................559 251-7161
Leila Malicoat, *Administration*
EMP: 105
SALES (est): 2.1MM **Publicly Held**
SIC: 8051 Skilled nursing care facilities
HQ: Skilled Healthcare, Llc
    27442 Portola Pkwy # 200
    Foothill Ranch CA 92610
    949 282-5800

(P-20852)
**VALLEY VIEW SKLLED NURSING
CTR**
1162 S Dora St, Ukiah (95482-6340)
PHONE..................................707 462-1436
Rosemary Brown, *Administration*
EMP: 58
SALES (est): 1.1MM
SALES (corp-wide): 103.7MM **Privately
Held**
WEB: www.villadelrey.com
SIC: 8051 Convalescent home with contin-
uous nursing care
HQ: Horizon West Healthcare, Inc.
    4020 Sierra College Blvd # 190
    Rocklin CA 95677
    916 624-6230

(P-20853)
**VALLEY VISTA NURSING AND
TRANS**
6120 Vineland Ave, North Hollywood
(91606-4914)
PHONE..................................818 763-6275
Crystal Solorzano,
EMP: 170
SALES (est): 2.1MM **Privately Held**
SIC: 8051 Skilled nursing care facilities

(P-20854)
**VALLEY WEST HEALTH CARE
INC**
Also Called: Valley View Care Center
2649 Topeka St, Riverbank (95367-2248)
PHONE..................................209 869-2569
Terry Bane, *Principal*
EMP: 80
SALES (corp-wide): 4.2MM **Privately
Held**
SIC: 8051 8062 Convalescent home with
continuous nursing care; general medical
& surgical hospitals
PA: Valley West Health Care Inc
    1224 E St
    Williams CA 95987
    530 473-5321

(P-20855)
VAN INN II INC (PA)
25 Avenida De Orinda, Orinda
(94563-2305)
PHONE.............................510 548-6600
Richard J Westin, *Principal*
Jesse Pittore, *Principal*
EMP: 55
SQ FT: 2,000
SALES (est): 696.4K **Privately Held**
SIC: 8051 6513 Skilled nursing care facilities; retirement hotel operation

(P-20856)
VETERANS AFFAIRS CAL DEPT
Also Called: Redding Veterans Home, The
3400 Knighton Rd, Redding (96002-9657)
PHONE.............................530 224-3300
Tim Bouseman, *Administration*
EMP: 200 **Privately Held**
SIC: 8051 Skilled nursing care facilities
HQ: California Department Of Veterans Affairs
1227 O St Ste 105
Sacramento CA 95814
800 952-5626

(P-20857)
VETERANS HOME CAL - FRESNO
2811 W California Ave, Fresno
(93706-2306)
PHONE.............................559 493-4400
Stanley Jones, *Director*
EMP: 99 EST: 2012
SALES (est): 3.7MM **Privately Held**
SIC: 8051 Skilled nursing care facilities

(P-20858)
VICTORIA CARE CENTER
5445 Everglades St, Ventura (93003-6523)
PHONE.............................805 642-1736
Scott Porter, *Exec Dir*
Jay Brady, *President*
EMP: 100
SQ FT: 85,000
SALES: 16.9MM **Privately Held**
WEB: www.victoriacarecenter.com
SIC: 8051 Convalescent home with continuous nursing care
PA: Beverly Health Care Corporation
5445 Everglades St
Ventura CA 93003

(P-20859)
VIENNA CONVALESCENT HOSPITAL
800 S Ham Ln, Lodi (95242-3543)
PHONE.............................209 368-7141
Kenneth Heffel, *President*
Diana Heffel, *Admin Sec*
Jamie Henderson, *Mktg Dir*
David Duncan, *Director*
Alfred Loza, *Supervisor*
EMP: 131
SQ FT: 25,000
SALES: 827MM **Privately Held**
SIC: 8051 Skilled nursing care facilities

(P-20860)
VILLA CONVALESCENT HOSP INC
8965 Magnolia Ave, Riverside
(92503-4432)
PHONE.............................951 689-5788
Jacob Paulson, *Administration*
Spencer E Olsen, *CFO*
EMP: 90 EST: 1971
SQ FT: 25,000
SALES (est): 9.2MM **Privately Held**
WEB: www.villahealthcare.com
SIC: 8051 Convalescent home with continuous nursing care

(P-20861)
VILLA RANCHO BRNO HLTH CR LLC
Also Called: VILLA RANCHO BERNARDO CARE CEN
15720 Bernardo Center Dr, San Diego
(92127-5861)
PHONE.............................858 672-3900
Irving Bauman,
Brank Johnson,

(P-20862)
VILLA SERENA HEALTHCARE CENTER
723 E 9th St, Long Beach (90813-4611)
PHONE.............................562 437-2797
Matt Carp, *President*
EMP: 70
SALES (est): 42K **Privately Held**
SIC: 8051 Skilled nursing care facilities

(P-20863)
VILLAGE PACIFIC MGT GROUP
Also Called: Village At Sydney Creek
1234 Laurel Ln, San Luis Obispo
(93401-5860)
PHONE.............................805 543-2350
Leona Baker, *Manager*
EMP: 55 **Privately Held**
SIC: 8051 Skilled nursing care facilities
PA: Village Pacific Management Group Inc
55 Broad St
San Luis Obispo CA 93405

(P-20864)
VILLAGE PACIFIC MGT GROUP (PA)
Also Called: Village At Sydney Creek
55 Broad St, San Luis Obispo
(93405-1745)
PHONE.............................805 543-2300
Patrick Smith, *Principal*
EMP: 55
SALES (est): 3.8MM **Privately Held**
SIC: 8051 Skilled nursing care facilities

(P-20865)
VILLAGE SQUARE NURSING CENTER
1586 W San Marcos Blvd, San Marcos
(92078-4019)
PHONE.............................760 471-2986
G Wiswell, *Exec Dir*
Gavin Wiswell, *Exec Dir*
Pam Turner, *Administration*
EMP: 140
SALES (est): 10MM **Privately Held**
SIC: 8051 8093 Skilled nursing care facilities; rehabilitation center, outpatient treatment

(P-20866)
VINDRA INC
Also Called: Meadowood Nursing Center
3805 Dexter Ln, Clearlake (95422-8850)
PHONE.............................707 994-7738
Calvin Baker Jr, *President*
Gloria Ghiringhelli, *Office Mgr*
EMP: 100
SQ FT: 30,250
SALES (est): 6.1MM **Privately Held**
SIC: 8051 8069 Convalescent home with continuous nursing care; specialty hospitals, except psychiatric

(P-20867)
VIRGIL SNTRIUM CNVLESCENT HOSP
Also Called: Virgil Convalescent Hospital
975 N Virgil Ave, Los Angeles
(90029-2944)
PHONE.............................323 665-5793
Miriam Weiss, *President*
Lucy Santos, *Records Dir*
Stuart Greenberg, *Administration*
Susan Lopez, *Food Svc Dir*
Adriana Quintero, *Director*
EMP: 150
SALES (est): 5.3MM
SALES (corp-wide): 62.1MM **Privately Held**
WEB: www.goldenstatehealth.com
SIC: 8051 Convalescent home with continuous nursing care
PA: Golden State Health Centers, Inc.
13347 Ventura Blvd
Sherman Oaks CA 91423
818 385-3200

(P-20868)
VISTA COVE CARE CENTER AT LONG
3401 Cedar Ave, Long Beach
(90807-4422)
PHONE.............................562 426-4461
Bonaparte Liu, *Principal*
Sean Brophy, *Principal*
Floyd Rhoades, *Principal*
Marcela Rodriguez, *Principal*
EMP: 99
SALES (est): 4.9MM **Privately Held**
SIC: 8051 Mental retardation hospital

(P-20869)
VISTA COVE CARE CTR - RIALTO
1471 S Riverside Ave, Rialto (92376-7703)
PHONE.............................909 877-1361
Sean William Brophy, *Admin Sec*
EMP: 99
SALES (est): 13.1MM **Privately Held**
SIC: 8051 Skilled nursing care facilities

(P-20870)
VISTA KNOLL INC
2000 Westwood Rd, Vista (92083-5123)
PHONE.............................760 630-2273
Gary R Byrnes, *President*
Gary Byrnes, *President*
Carol Byrnes, *Officer*
Leo Halpins, *Vice Pres*
EMP: 70
SQ FT: 45,000
SALES (est): 2.3MM **Privately Held**
WEB: www.vistaknoll.com
SIC: 8051 Skilled nursing care facilities

(P-20871)
VISTA PACIFICA ENTERPRISES INC (PA)
Also Called: VISTA PACIFICA CONVALESCENT CE
3662 Pacific Ave, Riverside (92509-1923)
PHONE.............................951 682-4833
Cheryl Jumonville, *CEO*
James Braswell, *Shareholder*
Ruth Braswell, *Shareholder*
A L Braswell Jr, *President*
Adelai Alba-Ortega, *CFO*
EMP: 180
SALES (est): 3.7MM **Privately Held**
SIC: 8051 8059 Skilled nursing care facilities; domiciliary care

(P-20872)
VISTA WOODS HEALTH ASSOC LLC
Also Called: Vista Knoll Spclzed Care Fclty
2000 Westwood Rd, Vista (92083-5123)
PHONE.............................760 630-2273
Ron Cook, *Mng Member*
Clay Gardner,
EMP: 130
SALES: 15.2MM
SALES (corp-wide): 1.8B **Publicly Held**
WEB: www.theensigngroup.com
SIC: 8051 Convalescent home with continuous nursing care
PA: The Ensign Group Inc
27101 Puerta Real Ste 450
Mission Viejo CA 92691
949 487-9500

(P-20873)
W H C INC
Also Called: Woodside Healthcare Center
2240 Northrop Ave, Sacramento
(95825-7408)
PHONE.............................916 927-9300
John Lund, *CEO*
Judy Cantrell, *Principal*
Jay Anderson, *Administration*
EMP: 75
SALES (est): 2MM **Privately Held**
SIC: 8051 Convalescent home with continuous nursing care

(P-20874)
WALNUT WHTNEY CNVLESCENT HOSP
3529 Walnut Ave, Carmichael
(95608-3049)
PHONE.............................916 488-8601

Jesse Barrios, *Administration*
Sharon Laidley, *Administration*
EMP: 110
SALES (est): 2.2MM
SALES (corp-wide): 103.7MM **Privately Held**
WEB: www.villadelrey.com
SIC: 8051 Convalescent home with continuous nursing care
HQ: Horizon West Healthcare, Inc.
4020 Sierra College Blvd # 190
Rocklin CA 95677
916 624-6230

(P-20875)
WASHINGTON ENTERPRISES 3 LLC
Also Called: St Andrews Health Care
2300 W Washington Blvd, Los Angeles
(90018-1445)
PHONE.............................323 731-0861
Emmanuel David,
Gloria Fonicer, *Treasurer*
Dolores N Chivi, *Admin Sec*
EMP: 68
SQ FT: 5,000
SALES (est): 2.3MM **Privately Held**
SIC: 8051 Skilled nursing care facilities

(P-20876)
WATERMAN CONVALESCENT HOSPITAL (PA)
Also Called: Mt Rubidoux Convalescent Hosp
1850 N Waterman Ave, San Bernardino
(92404-4895)
PHONE.............................909 882-1215
Thomas Plott, *President*
Elizabeth Plott, *Corp Secy*
Mr Terry Steege, *Account Dir*
EMP: 109
SQ FT: 13,000
SALES (est): 11.1MM **Privately Held**
SIC: 8051 Convalescent home with continuous nursing care

(P-20877)
WATERMARK RTRMENT CMMNTIES INC
Also Called: Fountains At The Carlotta, The
41505 Carlotta Dr, Palm Desert
(92211-3279)
PHONE.............................760 346-5420
EMP: 70 **Privately Held**
SIC: 8051 8052 Skilled nursing care facilities; intermediate care facilities
HQ: Watermark Retirement Communities, Inc.
2020 W Rudasill Rd
Tucson AZ 85704
520 797-4000

(P-20878)
WATERS EDGE INC
Also Called: Waters Edge Nursing Home
2401 Blanding Ave, Alameda (94501-1503)
PHONE.............................510 748-4300
Christian Zimmerman, *President*
John C Zimmerman, *President*
Virginia Zimmerman, *Corp Secy*
Moira Morris, *Executive*
EMP: 110
SQ FT: 24,000
SALES (est): 6.9MM **Privately Held**
SIC: 8051 Skilled nursing care facilities

(P-20879)
WELLS HSE HSPICE FUNDATION INC
245 Cherry Ave, Long Beach (90802-3901)
PHONE.............................714 952-3795
Ronald Morgan, *President*
EMP: 60 EST: 1997
SALES (est): 1.9MM **Privately Held**
WEB: www.wellshousehospice.com
SIC: 8051 Convalescent home with continuous nursing care

(P-20880)
WESCORDON INCORPORATED (PA)
Also Called: Valley Care Center
661 W Poplar Ave, Porterville
(93257-5926)
P.O. Box 3566 (93258-3566)
PHONE.............................559 784-8371

Donald C Smith, *President*
EMP: 150 **EST:** 1948
SQ FT: 14,000
SALES (est): 4.6MM **Privately Held**
SIC: 8051 Convalescent home with continuous nursing care

(P-20881)
WEST ANAHEIM EXTENDED CARE
Also Called: West Anaheim Care Center
645 S Beach Blvd, Anaheim (92804-3102)
PHONE..................714 821-1993
Mark Landry, *Managing Prtnr*
Connie Black, *Partner*
George Rodes, *CFO*
Robert Mills, *Bookkeeper*
Lucy Blanco, *Chf Purch Ofc*
EMP: 125
SQ FT: 39,000
SALES (est): 10.2MM **Privately Held**
SIC: 8051 Convalescent home with continuous nursing care

(P-20882)
WEST CNTINELA VLY CARE CTR INC
Also Called: Centinela Skld Nrng Wlns Cntr
950 S Flower St, Inglewood (90301-4186)
PHONE..................310 674-3216
Koom S Son, *CEO*
Karen Tanedo, *Records Dir*
Nancy Aguillar, *Social Dir*
Faye Sorianosos, *Nursing Dir*
Ruby Heredia, *Hlthcr Dir*
EMP: 99
SALES (est): 5.7MM **Privately Held**
SIC: 8051 Skilled nursing care facilities

(P-20883)
WEST ESCONDIDO HEALTHCARE LLC
Also Called: Palomar Vista Healthcare Ctr
201 N Fig St, Escondido (92025-3416)
PHONE..................760 746-0303
Mike Conrad,
Bobbi J Portillo, *Financial Exec*
Soon Burnam,
David Mayo,
EMP: 95
SALES: 6.8MM **Privately Held**
SIC: 8051 Convalescent home with continuous nursing care

(P-20884)
WESTERN HEALTHCARE MANAGEMENT
Also Called: Western Healthcare Center
1700 E Washington St, Colton (92324-4619)
PHONE..................909 824-1530
Everett Goings, *Owner*
EMP: 102
SALES (est): 3.9MM **Privately Held**
SIC: 8051 Skilled nursing care facilities

(P-20885)
WESTERN SLOPE HEALTH CENTER
Also Called: Western Slope Health Care
3280 Washington St, Placerville (95667-5838)
PHONE..................530 622-6842
Jeff Maggard, *Owner*
Doug Hawkings, *Administration*
EMP: 90
SALES: 12.6MM **Privately Held**
WEB: www.eldoradocounty.org
SIC: 8051 Convalescent home with continuous nursing care

(P-20886)
WESTGATE GARDENS CARE CENTER
4525 W Tulare Ave, Visalia (93277-1560)
PHONE..................559 733-0901
Eric Tolman, *Administration*
Gabby Cervantes, *Records Dir*
Christina Quinones, *Executive*
Jamie Mudford, *Office Mgr*
Margie Relph, *Mktg Dir*
EMP: 127

SALES (corp-wide): 103.7MM **Privately Held**
WEB: www.horizonwest.com
SIC: 8051 Skilled nursing care facilities
HQ: Westgate Gardens Care Center, Inc
4020 Sierra College Blvd # 190
Rocklin CA 95677
916 624-6230

(P-20887)
WESTLAKE HEALTH CARE CENTER
1101 Crenshaw Blvd, Los Angeles (90019-3112)
PHONE..................805 494-1233
Jeoung Lee, *President*
EMP: 250
SALES (est): 9.9MM
SALES (corp-wide): 22.8MM **Privately Held**
SIC: 8051 Skilled nursing care facilities
PA: J P H Consulting, Inc.
1101 Crenshaw Blvd
Los Angeles CA 90019
323 934-5660

(P-20888)
WESTVIEW HEALH CARE CENTER
Also Called: Kerria
12225 Shale Ridge Ln, Auburn (95602-8870)
PHONE..................530 885-7511
Edmund Erapt, *Administration*
EMP: 222
SALES (est): 5.9MM
SALES (corp-wide): 40.2MM **Privately Held**
SIC: 8051 Convalescent home with continuous nursing care
PA: Plum Healthcare Group, Llc
100 E San Marcos Blvd # 200
San Marcos CA 92069
760 471-0388

(P-20889)
WESTVIEW SERVICES INC
Also Called: Westview Cmnty Arts Program
1701 S Euclid St Ste E, Anaheim (92802-2408)
PHONE..................714 956-4199
Britain Semain, *Manager*
EMP: 205
SALES (corp-wide): 16.6MM **Privately Held**
SIC: 8051 8322 Mental retardation hospital; adult day care center
PA: Westview Services, Inc
10522 Katella Ave
Anaheim CA 92804
714 517-6606

(P-20890)
WESTWOOD HEALTHCARE CENTER LP
Also Called: COUNTRY VILLA WESTWOOD NURSING
12121 Santa Monica Blvd, Los Angeles (90025-2515)
PHONE..................310 826-0821
Stephen Reissman, *General Ptnr*
Hillard Torgan, *Partner*
EMP: 75 **EST:** 1970
SQ FT: 18,000
SALES: 8.9MM **Privately Held**
SIC: 8051 Skilled nursing care facilities

(P-20891)
WILD KARMA INC
Also Called: Divine Home Care
400 Estudillo Ave Ste 100, San Leandro (94577-4962)
PHONE..................510 639-9088
Robbin R Beebe, *CEO*
Robin Beebe, *CEO*
EMP: 270 **EST:** 2007
SQ FT: 2,400
SALES (est): 7.5MM **Privately Held**
SIC: 8051 8059 Convalescent home with continuous nursing care; personal care home, with health care

(P-20892)
WILLOW CREEK HEALTHCARE CTR LLC
650 W Alluvial Ave, Clovis (93611-6716)
PHONE..................559 323-6200
George V Hager Jr, *CEO*
EMP: 2335
SALES (est): 5.8MM **Publicly Held**
SIC: 8051 Skilled nursing care facilities
HQ: Genesis Healthcare Llc
101 E State St
Kennett Square PA 19348

(P-20893)
WILLOW CREEK HEALTHCARE CTR LLC
Also Called: Willow Creek Care Center
650 W Alluvial Ave, Clovis (93611-6716)
PHONE..................559 323-6200
Lillian Werntz, *President*
EMP: 99
SALES (est): 1.3MM **Publicly Held**
WEB: www.parkviewnursing.net
SIC: 8051 Convalescent home with continuous nursing care
HQ: Skilled Healthcare, Llc
27442 Portola Pkwy # 200
Foothill Ranch CA 92610
949 282-5800

(P-20894)
WILMON CORPORATION
Also Called: Millers Progressive Care
8951 Granite Hill Dr, Riverside (92509-1104)
PHONE..................951 685-7474
Wilmer W Miller, *President*
Michael Miller, *Executive*
EMP: 65 **EST:** 1962
SQ FT: 16,000
SALES (est): 4.2MM **Privately Held**
SIC: 8051 Skilled nursing care facilities

(P-20895)
WINDFLOWER HOLDINGS LLC
Also Called: Rocky Point Care Center
625 16th St, Lakeport (95453-3501)
PHONE..................707 263-6101
Mark Ballif, *Mng Member*
Paul Hubbard,
EMP: 80
SQ FT: 5,000
SALES: 2.9MM
SALES (corp-wide): 40.2MM **Privately Held**
WEB: www.villadelrey.com
SIC: 8051 Convalescent home with continuous nursing care
PA: Plum Healthcare Group, Llc
100 E San Marcos Blvd # 200
San Marcos CA 92069
760 471-0388

(P-20896)
WINDSOR ANAHEIM HEALTHCARE (PA)
Also Called: Windsor Grdns Cnvlescent Ctr A
3415 W Ball Rd, Anaheim (92804-3708)
PHONE..................714 826-8950
Lee Samson, *President*
Matt Diaz, *Facilities Dir*
EMP: 264
SQ FT: 37,245
SALES (est): 6.2MM **Privately Held**
SIC: 8051 Skilled nursing care facilities

(P-20897)
WINDSOR CONVALESCENT
Also Called: WINDSOR MANOR REHABILITATION CENTER OF CO
3806 Clayton Rd, Concord (94521-2516)
PHONE..................925 689-2266
Lee Samson, *Mng Member*
Melissa Lozano, *Hlthcr Dir*
EMP: 133
SALES: 22.4MM **Privately Held**
SIC: 8051 Convalescent home with continuous nursing care
PA: Lexington Group International, Inc
9200 W Sunset Blvd # 700
West Hollywood CA 90069

(P-20898)
WINDSOR CONVALESCENT
Also Called: Windsor Park Care Ctr Fremont
2400 Parkside Dr, Fremont (94536-5332)
PHONE..................510 793-7222
Lee Samson, *Mng Member*
Melissa Napiza, *Administration*
EMP: 133
SALES (est): 3.7MM **Privately Held**
SIC: 8051 Convalescent home with continuous nursing care
PA: Lexington Group International, Inc
9200 W Sunset Blvd # 700
West Hollywood CA 90069

(P-20899)
WINDSOR CONVALESCENT
Also Called: Windsor Gardens
637 E Romie Ln, Salinas (93901-4205)
PHONE..................831 424-0687
Lee Samson, *Mng Member*
Barbara Hutchison, *Administration*
EMP: 133
SALES (est): 13.5MM **Privately Held**
SIC: 8051 Convalescent home with continuous nursing care
PA: Lexington Group International, Inc
9200 W Sunset Blvd # 700
West Hollywood CA 90069

(P-20900)
WINDSOR GARDENS
Also Called: Windsor Gardens of Long Beach
4333 Torrance Blvd, Torrance (90503-4401)
PHONE..................562 422-9219
Calcin Warren, *Administration*
Christina Saril, *Nursing Dir*
EMP: 100 **Privately Held**
SIC: 8051 Skilled nursing care facilities
PA: Windsor Anaheim Healthcare, Ltd
3415 W Ball Rd
Anaheim CA 92804

(P-20901)
WINDSOR GARDENS
Also Called: Southwest Convalesant
13922 Cerise Ave, Hawthorne (90250-8688)
PHONE..................310 675-3304
Michael Gamet, *Administration*
EMP: 100 **Privately Held**
SIC: 8051 Skilled nursing care facilities
PA: Windsor Anaheim Healthcare, Ltd
3415 W Ball Rd
Anaheim CA 92804

(P-20902)
WINDSOR GARDENS CONVALESCNT
915 Crenshaw Blvd, Los Angeles (90019-1938)
PHONE..................323 937-5466
Nathan Alyeshmerni, *Administration*
Lee Samson, *President*
EMP: 99
SALES: 12.9MM **Privately Held**
SIC: 8051 8742 Convalescent home with continuous nursing care; hospital & health services consultant

(P-20903)
WINDSOR GARDNS HEALTHCARE CNTR
Also Called: WINDSOR GARDENS OF FULLERTON
245 E Wilshire Ave, Fullerton (92832-1935)
PHONE..................714 871-6020
Lee Samson,
Jen Hone, *Administration*
EMP: 133
SALES: 10.7MM **Privately Held**
SIC: 8051 Convalescent home with continuous nursing care
PA: Lexington Group International, Inc
9200 W Sunset Blvd # 700
West Hollywood CA 90069

(P-20904)
WINDSOR HEALTHCARE MANAGEMENT
Also Called: Windsor Gardens Convalescnt
220 E 24th St, National City (91950-6705)
PHONE..................................619 474-6741
Lee Samson, *President*
Faye Bourbeau, *Administration*
EMP: 115
SALES: 8.6MM **Privately Held**
SIC: 8051 Convalescent home with continuous nursing care

(P-20905)
WINDSOR SKYLINE CARE CTR LLC
348 Iris Dr, Salinas (93906-3514)
PHONE..................................831 449-5496
Patricia Roels, *Vice Pres*
Nikki Thomas, *Office Mgr*
EMP: 91
SALES: 8.9MM **Privately Held**
SIC: 8051 Skilled nursing care facilities
PA: S&F Management Company, Llc
9200 W Sunset Blvd # 700
West Hollywood CA 90069

(P-20906)
WINDSOR TWIN PALMS HLTHCARE
Also Called: Windsor Palms Care Ctr Artesia
11900 Artesia Blvd, Artesia (90701-4039)
PHONE..................................562 865-0271
John Ryan, *Administration*
Lee Samson, *Partner*
EMP: 133
SALES (est): 6.8MM **Privately Held**
WEB: www.windsor.com
SIC: 8051 Convalescent home with continuous nursing care
PA: Lexington Group International, Inc
9200 W Sunset Blvd # 700
West Hollywood CA 90069

(P-20907)
WINSOR HOUSE COMPALESSANT
Also Called: Winsor House Convalescent Hosp
101 S Orchard Ave, Vacaville (95688-3635)
PHONE..................................707 448-6458
Prema Thekkek, *President*
Joe Niccoli, *Administration*
Pam Lopez, *Director*
EMP: 77 EST: 1972
SALES (est): 2.1MM **Privately Held**
SIC: 8051 Convalescent home with continuous nursing care

(P-20908)
WINTER CARE CENTER SACRAMENTO
501 Jessie Ave, Sacramento (95838-2608)
PHONE..................................916 922-8855
Ariane Swick, *Administration*
Kay Conley, *Nursing Dir*
EMP: 120
SQ FT: 25,000
SALES (est): 2.6MM **Privately Held**
SIC: 8051 8322 Skilled nursing care facilities; rehabilitation services

(P-20909)
WISH I AH CARE CENTER INC
1665 M St, Fresno (93721-1121)
PHONE..................................559 855-2211
Janice Harshman, *President*
John E Harshman II, *Vice Pres*
EMP: 118
SQ FT: 60,000
SALES (est): 4.9MM **Privately Held**
WEB: www.fmaaa.org
SIC: 8051 Extended care facility

(P-20910)
WISH-I-AH HLTHCRE & WELLNESS
1665 M St, Fresno (93721-1121)
PHONE..................................559 855-2211
Maceo Garcia, *Principal*
EMP: 99

SALES (est): 2.3MM **Privately Held**
SIC: 8051 Skilled nursing care facilities

(P-20911)
WISH-I-AH SKILLED NURSING
Also Called: Wish-Ah Skilled
1665 M St, Fresno (93721-1121)
PHONE..................................949 285-8859
Aaron Robin, *COO*
EMP: 145 EST: 2008
SALES (est): 2.4MM **Privately Held**
SIC: 8051 Skilled nursing care facilities

(P-20912)
YORK HLTHCARE WLLNESS CNTRE LP
6071 York Blvd, Los Angeles (90042-3503)
PHONE..................................323 254-3407
Sharrod Brooks, *Partner*
EMP: 99 EST: 2012
SALES: 10.4MM **Privately Held**
SIC: 8051 Rehabilitation services

(P-20913)
YUBA CITY NURSING & REHAB LLC
1220 Plumas St, Yuba City (95991-3411)
PHONE..................................530 671-0550
Joseph Pallivathucal,
Babu Parayil,
James Paul,
EMP: 75
SALES (est): 4.5MM **Privately Held**
SIC: 8051 Skilled nursing care facilities

8052 Intermediate Care Facilities

(P-20914)
834 W ARROW HIGHWAY LP
4032 Wilshire Blvd # 600, Los Angeles (90010-3405)
PHONE..................................213 355-1024
David Friedman, *Vice Pres*
Scott Hayashi, *Finance*
EMP: 99
SALES (est): 839.6K **Privately Held**
SIC: 8052 Intermediate care facilities

(P-20915)
ALLIANCE FOR HOUSING & HEALING (PA)
Also Called: AID FOR AIDS
825 Colorado Blvd Ste 100, Los Angeles (90041-1741)
PHONE..................................323 344-4885
Terry Goddard, *Exec Dir*
Warren R Wimmer, *President*
EMP: 63
SQ FT: 1,620
SALES: 8.9MM **Privately Held**
SIC: 8052 Personal care facility

(P-20916)
ARCADIA GARDENS MGT CORP
Also Called: Independnt Asstd Lvng & Memory
720 W Camino Real Ave, Arcadia (91007-7839)
PHONE..................................626 574-8571
Julie Chirikian, *President*
David Chirikian, *Vice Pres*
EMP: 100
SQ FT: 120,320
SALES (est): 5.4MM **Privately Held**
SIC: 8052 Intermediate care facilities

(P-20917)
BEST CONSULTING INC
8795 Folsom Blvd Ste 103, Sacramento (95826-3720)
PHONE..................................916 448-2050
Sergio E Pinto, *President*
Danielle Nuzum, *COO*
Jaclyn Shandy-Pinto, *Vice Pres*
EMP: 50
SALES (est): 2.2MM **Privately Held**
SIC: 8052 Home for the mentally retarded, with health care

(P-20918)
CARE INC
15315 Magnolia Blvd # 306, Sherman Oaks (91403-1173)
PHONE..................................818 232-7940
Yue LI, *Principal*
EMP: 50
SALES (est): 1.6MM **Privately Held**
SIC: 8052 Home for the mentally retarded, with health care

(P-20919)
CC-PALO ALTO INC
Also Called: VI At Palo Alto
620 Sand Hill Rd, Palo Alto (94304-2002)
PHONE..................................650 853-5000
Penny Pritzker, *President*
EMP: 225
SALES (est): 11.4MM **Privately Held**
SIC: 8052 8322 8361 Personal care facility; adult day care center; rehabilitation center, residential; health care incidental

(P-20920)
CHARTER HOSPICE INC
1007 E Cooley Dr Ste 100, Colton (92324-3901)
PHONE..................................909 825-2969
Fred Frank, *President*
Meagan Huynh, *Human Res Dir*
Kelli Caudill, *Personnel Assit*
Sabina Del Rosario, *Sales Staff*
EMP: 120
SALES (est): 13.3MM **Privately Held**
SIC: 8052 Personal care facility

(P-20921)
COMMUNITY HOME PARTNERS LLC
Also Called: Pacific Gardens
2384 Pacific Dr, Santa Clara (95051-1458)
PHONE..................................408 985-5252
Maxine Brookner,
EMP: 85
SQ FT: 56,300
SALES: 4MM **Privately Held**
SIC: 8052 Intermediate care facilities

(P-20922)
COMMUNITY HOSPICE INC (PA)
Also Called: C H I
4368 Spyres Way, Modesto (95356-9259)
PHONE..................................209 578-6300
Harold A Peterson III, *CEO*
Rick Dahlseid, *CFO*
Lynis Chaffey, *Exec Dir*
Karen Aiello, *Admin Asst*
Michael Hernandez, *Administration*
EMP: 150
SQ FT: 24,000
SALES: 22.8MM **Privately Held**
SIC: 8052 8069 Personal care facility; specialty hospitals, except psychiatric

(P-20923)
COMMUNITY HOSPICE INC
2201 Euclid Ave, Hughson (95326-9183)
PHONE..................................209 578-6380
Laura Miller, *Administration*
EMP: 50
SALES (corp-wide): 22.8MM **Privately Held**
SIC: 8052 Personal care facility
PA: Community Hospice, Inc.
4368 Spyres Way
Modesto CA 95356
209 578-6300

(P-20924)
CORNERSTONE HEALTHCARE INC
143 Triunfo Canyon Rd # 103, Westlake Village (91361-2514)
PHONE..................................805 777-1133
Andre, *Med Doctor*
EMP: 120
SALES (corp-wide): 1.8B **Publicly Held**
SIC: 8052 Personal care facility
HQ: Cornerstone Healthcare, Inc.
420 E State St Ste 135
Eagle ID 83616

(P-20925)
COUNTY OF ORANGE
405 W 5th St Ofc, Santa Ana (92701-4519)
PHONE..................................714 834-6021
David L Riley, *Director*
EMP: 2500 **Privately Held**
SIC: 8052 Intermediate care facilities
PA: County Of Orange
333 W Santa Ana Blvd 3f
Santa Ana CA 92701
714 834-6200

(P-20926)
COUNTY OF SOLANO
Also Called: Adult Mddlhlth Otptient Clinic
2101 Courage Dr, Fairfield (94533-6717)
PHONE..................................707 784-2080
Rod Kennedy, *Manager*
EMP: 100 **Privately Held**
SIC: 8052 5719 Intermediate care facilities; linens
PA: County Of Solano
675 Texas St Ste 2600
Fairfield CA 94533
707 784-6706

(P-20927)
CYPRESS GARDEN AT CITRUS HTS
7375 Stock Ranch Rd, Citrus Heights (95621-5616)
PHONE..................................916 729-2722
Pepper Bell, *Exec Dir*
Sondra Campbell, *Deputy Dir*
EMP: 50
SALES (est): 1.6MM **Privately Held**
SIC: 8052 Personal care facility

(P-20928)
DEVELOPMENTAL SVCS CAL DEPT
Also Called: Agnews Developmental Center
3500 Zanker Rd, San Jose (95134-2201)
P.O. Box 24165 (95154-4165)
PHONE..................................408 451-6000
Angela Vraanac, *Director*
EMP: 1000 **Privately Held**
WEB: www.ldc.dds.ca.gov
SIC: 8052 9431 Intermediate care facilities;
HQ: California Department Of Developmental Services
1600 9th St
Sacramento CA 95814
916 654-1690

(P-20929)
EMERITUS CORPORATION
2261 Tuolumne St, Vallejo (94589-2560)
PHONE..................................707 552-3336
EMP: 50
SALES (corp-wide): 4.7B **Publicly Held**
SIC: 8052 Personal care facility
HQ: Emeritus Corporation
3131 Elliott Ave Ste 500
Milwaukee WI 53214

(P-20930)
EMERITUS CORPORATION
800 Oregon St, Sonoma (95476-6445)
PHONE..................................707 996-7101
Melon Rivera, *Hlthcr Dir*
EMP: 50
SALES (corp-wide): 4.7B **Publicly Held**
SIC: 8052 8361 Personal care facility; geriatric residential care
HQ: Emeritus Corporation
3131 Elliott Ave Ste 500
Milwaukee WI 53214

(P-20931)
EMERITUS CORPORATION
Also Called: Emeritus At Casa Glendale
426 Piedmont Ave, Glendale (91206-3448)
PHONE..................................818 246-7457
David Wilkens, *Branch Mgr*
EMP: 50
SALES (corp-wide): 4.7B **Publicly Held**
SIC: 8052 Personal care facility
HQ: Emeritus Corporation
3131 Elliott Ave Ste 500
Milwaukee WI 53214

(P-20932)
EMERITUS CORPORATION
Also Called: Emeritus At Villa Colima
19850 Colima Rd, Walnut (91789-3411)
PHONE...........................909 595-5030
Wanda Reynolds, *Branch Mgr*
EMP: 50
SALES (corp-wide): 4.7B **Publicly Held**
SIC: 8052 Personal care facility
HQ: Emeritus Corporation
3131 Elliott Ave Ste 500
Milwaukee WI 53214

(P-20933)
HILLSIDE HOUSE INC
1235 Veronica Springs Rd, Santa Barbara
(93105-4522)
PHONE...........................805 687-4818
Pam Flynt, *Administration*
Michael Williams, *CFO*
Chuck Klein, *Principal*
Peter Troesch, *Principal*
Angela Biancone, *Admin Asst*
EMP: 88 EST: 1945
SQ FT: 24,000
SALES: 4.8MM **Privately Held**
WEB: www.hillsidehousesb.org
SIC: 8052 Home for the mentally retarded,
with health care

(P-20934)
HOFFMAN HOSPICE OF THE VALLEY
8501 Brimhall Rd Bldg 100, Bakersfield
(93312-2327)
PHONE...........................661 410-1010
Beth Hosman, *President*
Darci Nieto, *Human Res Dir*
EMP: 67
SQ FT: 8,500
SALES: 12.8MM **Privately Held**
SIC: 8052 Personal care facility

(P-20935)
HOSPICE AND PALLIATIVE CARE
Also Called: Hospice of The East Bay
2849 Miranda Ave, Alamo (94507-1443)
PHONE...........................925 945-8924
Laura Pakar, *Branch Mgr*
EMP: 75
SALES (corp-wide): 1.5MM **Privately Held**
SIC: 8052 Personal care facility
PA: Hospice And Palliative Care
3470 Buskirk Ave
Concord CA 94523
925 887-5678

(P-20936)
JONBEC CARE INCORPORATED (PA)
1711 Plum Ln, Redlands (92374-2874)
P.O. Box 10788, San Bernardino (92423-0788)
PHONE...........................909 798-4003
Jonathan Joseph, *President*
Cindy Collins, *Treasurer*
Becky Joseph, *Vice Pres*
Oynnie Joseph, *Admin Sec*
Kittie Mann, *Bookkeeper*
EMP: 52
SQ FT: 13,000
SALES: 12.2MM **Privately Held**
SIC: 8052 Home for the mentally retarded,
with health care

(P-20937)
KERN CNTY MNTAL HLTH CHILD SYS
1111 Columbus St Ste 3000, Bakersfield
(93305-1939)
P.O. Box 1000 (93302-1000)
PHONE...........................661 868-8300
James Waterman, *Director*
EMP: 62
SALES (est): 1MM **Privately Held**
SIC: 8052 Home for the mentally retarded,
with health care

(P-20938)
LEISURE CARE LLC
Also Called: Fairwinds-West Hills
8138 Woodlake Ave, Canoga Park
(91304-3500)
PHONE...........................818 713-0900
Pat Luc, *General Mgr*
EMP: 60
SALES (corp-wide): 128.3MM **Privately Held**
WEB: www.leisurecare.com
SIC: 8052 Intermediate care facilities
PA: Leisure Care, Llc
999 3rd Ave Ste 4500
Seattle WA 98104
800 327-3490

(P-20939)
LOS ANGELES CTY RNCH LOS AMGOS
7601 Imperial Hwy, Downey (90242-3456)
PHONE...........................562 385-7111
Jorge Orozco, *CEO*
EMP: 1400
SALES (est): 112.3K **Privately Held**
SIC: 8052 Personal care facility

(P-20940)
MAGNOLIA SPECIAL CARE CENTER
Also Called: Magnolia Post Acute Care
635 S Magnolia Ave, El Cajon
(92020-6012)
PHONE...........................619 442-8826
Kennon S Shea, *President*
Joanne Starkley, *Training Spec*
EMP: 99
SQ FT: 24,088
SALES (est): 4.7MM **Privately Held**
SIC: 8052 8059 8051 Personal care facil-
ity; convalescent home; nursing home,
except skilled & intermediate care facility;
skilled nursing care facilities

(P-20941)
MARYMOUNT VILLA LLC
345 Davis St Ofc, San Leandro
(94577-2795)
PHONE...........................510 895-5007
Jasbir Walia, *Mng Member*
Arjun Bhagat, *Mng Member*
EMP: 65
SALES (est): 2.4MM **Privately Held**
SIC: 8052 8059 Personal care facility;
convalescent home

(P-20942)
MILESTONE HOSPICE
1500 Crenshaw Blvd # 200, Torrance
(90501-2400)
PHONE...........................310 782-1177
Harry Mc Namra, *CEO*
Minda Mc Namra, *Administration*
EMP: 120
SQ FT: 3,800
SALES: 14MM **Privately Held**
SIC: 8052 Personal care facility

(P-20943)
MILESTONES OF DEVELOPMENT INC
1 Florida St, Vallejo (94590-5000)
PHONE...........................707 644-0496
Cynthia Mack, *Director*
Joan Yates, *Ch of Bd*
Faith Ohara, *Admin Sec*
EMP: 55
SQ FT: 7,564
SALES: 5.5MM **Privately Held**
SIC: 8052 Home for the mentally retarded,
with health care

(P-20944)
MOUNTAIN SHADOWS SUPPORT GROUP (PA)
Also Called: MOUNTAIN SHADOWS COM-
MUNITY HOM
2067 W El Norte Pkwy, Escondido
(92026-1899)
PHONE...........................760 743-3714
Richard W Marrs, *President*
Wade Wilde, *Exec Dir*
Toni Albright, *Human Res Dir*
Fred Lindahl,
EMP: 200

SQ FT: 3,000
SALES: 16.7MM **Privately Held**
WEB: www.mtnshadows.org
SIC: 8052 8059 Personal care facility; rest
home, with health care

(P-20945)
MOUNTAIN VALLEY CHILD AND FAMI
24077 State Highway 49, Nevada City
(95959-8519)
PHONE...........................530 265-9057
Daniel Petrie, *CEO*
Richard Milhous, *CFO*
Janet Milhous, *Business Mgr*
Teresa Petrie, *Food Svc Dir*
Kathleen Benson, *Director*
EMP: 220
SQ FT: 22,000
SALES: 11.2MM **Privately Held**
SIC: 8052 8361 Intermediate care facili-
ties; residential care

(P-20946)
MURRIETA GARDENS SENIOR LIVING
18878 E Armstead St, Azusa (91702-4805)
PHONE...........................951 600-7676
Michelle Tehlam, *Director*
EMP: 60
SALES (est): 3MM **Privately Held**
SIC: 8052 Intermediate care facilities

(P-20947)
OPTIMAL HOSPICE FOUNDATION
3200 E 19th St, Signal Hill (90755-1244)
PHONE...........................562 494-7687
EMP: 51
SALES (corp-wide): 300K **Privately Held**
SIC: 8052 Personal care facility
PA: Optimal Hospice Foundation
1315 Boughton Dr
Bakersfield CA 93308
661 410-3000

(P-20948)
QUAIL PARK RETIREMENT VILLAGE
4520 W Cypress Ave, Visalia (93277-1577)
PHONE...........................559 624-3500
Denis Bryant, *Manager*
EMP: 65
SALES (est): 4.1MM **Privately Held**
WEB: www.quail-park.com
SIC: 8052 6513 Intermediate care facili-
ties; apartment building operators

(P-20949)
RANCHO VISTA HEALTH CENTER
200 Grapevine Rd Apt 15, Vista
(92083-4042)
PHONE...........................760 941-1480
Alan Shigley, *Exec Dir*
EMP: 205
SALES (est): 8MM
SALES (corp-wide): 36.5MM **Privately Held**
WEB: www.healthcaregrp.com
SIC: 8052 8051 8361 Intermediate care
facilities; skilled nursing care facilities;
residential care
PA: Activcare Living, Inc.
9619 Chesapeake Dr # 103
San Diego CA 92123
858 565-4424

(P-20950)
RES-CARE INC
611 S Central Ave, Glendale (91204-2008)
PHONE...........................818 637-7727
Michael Sowerby, *Manager*
EMP: 130
SALES (corp-wide): 24.5B **Privately Held**
WEB: www.rescare.com
SIC: 8052 Home for the mentally retarded,
with health care
HQ: Res-Care, Inc.
9901 Linn Station Rd
Louisville KY 40223
502 394-2100

(P-20951)
RES-CARE CALIFORNIA INC
Also Called: Edgewood Center
200 W Paramount St, Azusa (91702-4422)
PHONE...........................626 334-7862
Danny Soto, *Branch Mgr*
Dan Armstrong, *Info Tech Mgr*
Michelle Nelson, *Data Proc Staff*
EMP: 50
SQ FT: 78,991
SALES (corp-wide): 24.5B **Privately Held**
SIC: 8052 Home for the mentally retarded,
with health care
HQ: Res-Care California, Inc.
6170 Purple Hills Dr
San Jose CA 95119

(P-20952)
ROSS VALLEY HOMES INC
Also Called: TAMALPAIS
501 Via Casitas, Greenbrae (94904-1901)
PHONE...........................415 461-2300
David Berg, *CEO*
Don Meninga, *CFO*
Belinda Ong, *Controller*
EMP: 100
SALES: 24.4MM **Privately Held**
WEB: www.rossvalleyhomes.com
SIC: 8052 Personal care facility

(P-20953)
SCOTT STREET SENIOR HOUSING CO
Also Called: RHODA GOLDMAN PLAZA
2180 Post St, San Francisco (94115-6013)
PHONE...........................415 345-5083
Marrianne Nannesthad, *Director*
Ira Kurtz, *Exec Dir*
Candiece Milford, *Managing Dir*
Patricia Afoa, *Administration*
Nicki Pun, *Controller*
EMP: 105
SQ FT: 195,000
SALES: 11.9MM **Privately Held**
WEB: www.rgplaza.org
SIC: 8052 Personal care facility

(P-20954)
SENIOR CARE INC
4960 Mills St, La Mesa (91942-9310)
PHONE...........................619 928-5644
Rhonda Hernandez, *Director*
EMP: 113 **Privately Held**
SIC: 8052 Intermediate care facilities
PA: Senior Care, Inc.
700 N Hurstbourne Pkwy # 200
Louisville KY 40222

(P-20955)
SENIOR CARE INC
3423 Channel Way, San Diego
(92110-5104)
PHONE...........................619 817-8855
Floyd C Weathers, *Owner*
EMP: 113 **Privately Held**
SIC: 8052 Intermediate care facilities
PA: Senior Care, Inc.
700 N Hurstbourne Pkwy # 200
Louisville KY 40222

(P-20956)
SENIOR LIVING SOLUTIONS LLC
1725 S Bascom Ave Apt 105, Campbell
(95008-0676)
PHONE...........................408 385-1835
Daniel P Schneider,
Daniel Schneider,
EMP: 120
SALES (est): 1.9MM **Privately Held**
SIC: 8052 Personal care facility

(P-20957)
SHORELINE S INTERMEDIATE CARE
Also Called: Alameda Care Center
430 Willow St, Alameda (94501-6130)
PHONE...........................510 523-8857
Jack E Easterday, *President*
EMP: 200
SQ FT: 38,000

SALES (est): 5.2MM **Privately Held**
SIC: 8052 8051 Intermediate care facilities; skilled nursing care facilities

(P-20958)
SIERRA HILLS CARE CENTER INC
1139 Cirby Way, Roseville (95661-4421)
PHONE.................................916 782-7007
Ellen L Kuykendall, *President*
Brad Wilcox, *Treasurer*
EMP: 53
SQ FT: 30,000
SALES (est): 1.9MM
SALES (corp-wide): 103.7MM **Privately Held**
WEB: www.villadelrey.com
SIC: 8052 Personal care facility
HQ: Horizon West Healthcare, Inc.
4020 Sierra College Blvd # 190
Rocklin CA 95677
916 624-6230

(P-20959)
SNOWLINE HSPC ELDORADO CNTY
6520 Pleasant Valley Rd, Diamond Springs (95619-9512)
PHONE.................................916 817-2338
Tom Heflin, *President*
William Fisher, *Treasurer*
Mary Newton, *Exec Dir*
Michael Schmidt, *Exec Dir*
Leah Hall, *Admin Sec*
EMP: 140
SQ FT: 8,900
SALES: 8.7MM **Privately Held**
SIC: 8052 Personal care facility

(P-20960)
SNOWLINE HSPICE EL DORADO CNTY
6520 Pleasant Valley Rd, Diamond Springs (95619-9512)
PHONE.................................530 621-7820
Michael Sehmidt, *Exec Dir*
Richard B Esposito, *President*
William Fisher, *Treasurer*
Jon Lehrman, *Vice Pres*
Leah Hall, *Admin Sec*
EMP: 140
SQ FT: 8,900
SALES: 9.7MM **Privately Held**
SIC: 8052 Personal care facility

(P-20961)
SOMERSET SPECIAL CARE CENTER
Also Called: Shea Family Care Somerset
151 Claydelle Ave, El Cajon (92020-4505)
PHONE.................................619 442-0245
Kennon S Shea, *President*
EMP: 56
SALES (est): 4MM **Privately Held**
SIC: 8052 Personal care facility

(P-20962)
SPECIAL HOME NEEDS
1440 Jackson St, Santa Clara (95050-4210)
PHONE.................................408 985-8666
Vivian Ascusion, *President*
EMP: 51
SALES: 500K **Privately Held**
SIC: 8052 Intermediate care facilities

(P-20963)
STRATGIES TO EMPWER PEOPLE INC (PA)
Also Called: Step
2330 Glendale Ln, Sacramento (95825-2455)
PHONE.................................916 679-1527
Jacquine Difoss, *President*
Diana Miller, *Technology*
Claudia Loveless, *Controller*
Lydia Edinborough, *Human Res Mgr*
Tracy Cummins, *Director*
EMP: 53
SALES (est): 14.9MM **Privately Held**
SIC: 8052 Personal care facility

(P-20964)
SUNBRIDGE HEALTHCARE LLC
Also Called: Willows Care Rhabilitation Ctr
320 N Crawford St, Willows (95988-2326)
PHONE.................................530 934-2834
Tina Brey, *Manager*
EMP: 99 **Publicly Held**
WEB: www.innoventurehealthcare.com
SIC: 8052 8051 Intermediate care facilities; skilled nursing care facilities
HQ: Sunbridge Healthcare, Llc
101 Sun Ave Ne
Albuquerque NM 87109
505 821-3355

(P-20965)
SUNBRIDGE HEALTHCARE LLC
Also Called: Harbor View Community Svcs Ctr
850 E Wardlow Rd, Long Beach (90807-4628)
PHONE.................................562 981-9392
Dan Thorne, *Branch Mgr*
EMP: 200 **Publicly Held**
WEB: www.innoventurehealthcare.com
SIC: 8052 8051 Intermediate care facilities; skilled nursing care facilities
HQ: Sunbridge Healthcare, Llc
101 Sun Ave Ne
Albuquerque NM 87109
505 821-3355

(P-20966)
SUNBRIDGE HEALTHCARE LLC
Also Called: Sunbridge Care Ctr For Downey
9300 Telegraph Rd, Downey (90240-2425)
PHONE.................................562 869-2567
Wendy Johnson, *Principal*
EMP: 119 **Publicly Held**
SIC: 8052 8051 Intermediate care facilities; skilled nursing care facilities
HQ: Sunbridge Healthcare, Llc
101 Sun Ave Ne
Albuquerque NM 87109
505 821-3355

(P-20967)
SUNBRIDGE HEALTHCARE LLC
Also Called: San Lndro Care Rhblitation Ctr
14766 Washington Ave, San Leandro (94578-4220)
PHONE.................................510 352-2211
Joe Gengilcore, *Administration*
Danielle Houston, *Human Res Dir*
EMP: 100
SQ FT: 28,635 **Publicly Held**
WEB: www.innoventurehealthcare.com
SIC: 8052 8093 8051 Intermediate care facilities; rehabilitation center, outpatient treatment; skilled nursing care facilities
HQ: Sunbridge Healthcare, Llc
101 Sun Ave Ne
Albuquerque NM 87109
505 821-3355

(P-20968)
SUTTER HEALTH
1651 Alvarado St, San Leandro (94577-2636)
PHONE.................................510 618-5200
EMP: 106
SALES (corp-wide): 12.4B **Privately Held**
SIC: 8052 Personal care facility
PA: Sutter Health
2200 River Plaza Dr
Sacramento CA 95833
916 733-8800

(P-20969)
TUSTIN CARE CENTER CORP
1051 Bryan Ave, Tustin (92780-4419)
PHONE.................................714 832-6780
Jeoung H Lee, *President*
EMP: 60
SALES (est): 3.2MM **Privately Held**
SIC: 8052 Intermediate care facilities

(P-20970)
VITAS HEALTHCARE CORPORATION
333 N Lantana St Ste 124, Camarillo (93010-9007)
PHONE.................................805 437-2100
Rita Peddycoart, *Manager*
EMP: 95

SALES (corp-wide): 1.6B **Publicly Held**
WEB: www.vitasinnovativehospicecare.com
SIC: 8052 Personal care facility
HQ: Vitas Healthcare Corporation
201 S Biscayne Blvd # 400
Miami FL 33131
305 374-4143

(P-20971)
WATTS HEALTH FOUNDATION INC (HQ)
Also Called: Uhp Healthcare
3405 W Imperial Hwy # 304, Inglewood (90303-2219)
PHONE.................................310 424-2220
Dr Clyde W Oden, *President*
Jennifer Stapalding, *CEO*
Dr Darryl Leong, *MIS Dir*
EMP: 400 **EST: 1967**
SALES (est): 19.3MM
SALES (corp-wide): 31.9MM **Privately Held**
WEB: www.sonnytran.com
SIC: 8052 8011 8741 Intermediate care facilities; health maintenance organization; management services
PA: Watts Health Systems, Inc
3405 W Imperial Hwy
Inglewood CA
310 424-2220

(P-20972)
XCITE STEPS CORP
3978 Sorrento Valley Blvd # 100, San Diego (92121-1436)
PHONE.................................858 722-1948
Matthew Winkley, *Principal*
Lindsey Hinzo, *Opers Spvr*
Drew Jeglinski, *Director*
EMP: 140
SALES: 3MM **Privately Held**
SIC: 8052 Home for the mentally retarded, with health care

8059 Nursing & Personal Care Facilities, NEC

(P-20973)
14766 WASH AVE OPERATIONS LLC
14766 Washington Ave, San Leandro (94578-4220)
PHONE.................................510 352-2211
EMP: 552
SALES (est): 293.5K **Publicly Held**
SIC: 8059 Nursing home, except skilled & intermediate care facility
HQ: Sun Healthcare Group, Inc.
27442 Portola Pkwy # 200
Foothill Ranch CA 92610

(P-20974)
8520 WESTERN AVE INC
Also Called: Buena Park Nursing Center
10811 Kiowa Rd Apt 2a, Apple Valley (92308-7989)
PHONE.................................714 828-8222
Sim Mandelbaum, *President*
Brenda Mandelbaum, *Principal*
EMP: 135
SQ FT: 31,474
SALES (est): 7.4MM **Privately Held**
SIC: 8059 8051 Convalescent home; skilled nursing care facilities

(P-20975)
A CORI PARTNERSHIP
Also Called: Casitas Care Center
10626 Balboa Blvd, Granada Hills (91344-6329)
PHONE.................................818 368-2802
Claire Badama, *Partner*
EMP: 90 **EST: 1982**
SALES (est): 2.8MM **Privately Held**
SIC: 8059 8051 Convalescent home; nursing home, except skilled & intermediate care facility; skilled nursing care facilities

(P-20976)
A T ASSOCIATES INC
Also Called: Berkeley Pines Care Center
2223 Ashby Ave, Berkeley (94705-1907)
PHONE.................................510 649-6670
Natalie Montijo, *Director*
EMP: 50
SALES (est): 1.1MM **Privately Held**
SIC: 8059 Personal care home, with health care
PA: A T Associates, Inc
535 School St
Pittsburg CA 94565

(P-20977)
A T ASSOCIATES INC
Also Called: Oakridge Care Center
2919 Fruitvale Ave, Oakland (94602-2108)
PHONE.................................510 261-8564
Abby Tiller, *Manager*
EMP: 100 **Privately Held**
SIC: 8059 8051 Convalescent home; skilled nursing care facilities
PA: A T Associates, Inc
535 School St
Pittsburg CA 94565

(P-20978)
A T ASSOCIATES INC (PA)
535 School St, Pittsburg (94565-3937)
PHONE.................................925 808-6540
Alba F Tiller, *President*
EMP: 75
SALES: 2.5MM **Privately Held**
SIC: 8059 8011 Convalescent home; free-standing emergency medical center

(P-20979)
ACCESS INTEGRATED HEALTHCARE
Also Called: A I H
550 N Brand Blvd Fl 20, Glendale (91203-1900)
PHONE.................................866 460-7465
Manel Sweetmore, *CEO*
James Castro, *Exec VP*
Mendy Fry, *Vice Pres*
Sattar Mir, *General Mgr*
Laszlo Kupan, *General Counsel*
EMP: 51
SALES (est): 273.2K **Privately Held**
SIC: 8059 Nursing home, except skilled & intermediate care facility

(P-20980)
AG FACILITIES OPERATIONS LLC
6380 Wilshire Blvd # 800, Los Angeles (90048-5003)
PHONE.................................323 651-1808
Jacob Winter,
Leo Krieger, *CFO*
Scott Krieger,
EMP: 1000
SALES (est): 8.1MM **Privately Held**
SIC: 8059 Nursing home, except skilled & intermediate care facility

(P-20981)
AG REDLANDS LLC
Also Called: Highland Care Center Redlands
700 E Highland Ave, Redlands (92374-6233)
PHONE.................................909 793-2678
Tyrus Lefler, *Director*
Doug Easton, *CEO*
EMP: 110
SALES (est): 5.5MM **Privately Held**
SIC: 8059 Nursing home, except skilled & intermediate care facility

(P-20982)
AGE ADVANTAGE HM CARE SVCS
5480 Baltimore Dr Ste 214, La Mesa (91942-2066)
PHONE.................................619 449-5900
Daphne Archer, *President*
Joyce Porterfield, *Exec VP*
Ellen Hanson, *Office Mgr*
EMP: 75
SQ FT: 1,200

SALES (est): 2.4MM **Privately Held**
SIC: 8059 Personal care home, with health care

(P-20983)
ALAIDANDREW CORPORATION
1205 8th St, Bakersfield (93304-2123)
PHONE................661 334-2200
Julita A Javier, *President*
EMP: 79
SALES (est): 2MM
SALES (corp-wide): 3.4MM **Privately Held**
SIC: 8059 Convalescent home
PA: Bettec Corporation
3210 W Pico Blvd
Los Angeles CA
323 734-2171

(P-20984)
ALDERWOOD INC
115 Bridge St, San Gabriel (91775-2719)
PHONE................626 289-4439
Ben Garrett, *President*
Eva Mae Casner, *Treasurer*
Christin Garret, *Admin Sec*
Louis Pages, *Administration*
EMP: 90
SALES (est): 5.4MM **Privately Held**
SIC: 8059 Convalescent home

(P-20985)
ALEXANDRIA CARE CENTER LLC
1515 N Alexandria Ave, Los Angeles (90027-5203)
PHONE................323 660-1800
Robert Snukal, *President*
Edwin Evangelista, *Director*
Julio Guzman, *Director*
EMP: 140
SQ FT: 30,000
SALES (est): 9MM **Publicly Held**
WEB: www.parkviewnursing.net
SIC: 8059 8051 Convalescent home; skilled nursing care facilities
PA: Genesis Healthcare, Inc.
101 E State St
Kennett Square PA 19348

(P-20986)
ALTA CARE CENTER LLC
13075 Blackbird St, Garden Grove (92843-2902)
PHONE................714 530-6322
EMP: 118
SALES (est): 788.6K **Publicly Held**
WEB: www.parkviewnursing.net
SIC: 8059 8051 Convalescent home; skilled nursing care facilities
HQ: Skilled Healthcare, Llc
27442 Portola Pkwy # 200
Foothill Ranch CA 92610
949 282-5800

(P-20987)
AMDAL IN-HOME CARE INC (PA)
147 N K St, Tulare (93274-4003)
P.O. Box 1318 (93275-1318)
PHONE................559 686-6611
Deanne Martin Soares, *CEO*
Julian Mack, *Shareholder*
Charles Mack, *Admin Sec*
EMP: 50
SALES (est): 3.5MM **Privately Held**
WEB: www.amdalinhome.com
SIC: 8059 Personal care home, with health care

(P-20988)
AMDAL IN-HOME CARE INC
4848 N 1st St Ste 104, Fresno (93726-0526)
PHONE................559 227-1701
Deanne Martin-Soares, *Manager*
EMP: 55
SALES (corp-wide): 3.5MM **Privately Held**
WEB: www.amdalinhome.com
SIC: 8059 Personal care home, with health care
PA: Amdal In-Home Care, Inc.
147 N K St
Tulare CA 93274
559 686-6611

(P-20989)
AMERICAN BAPTIST HOMES OF WEST
Also Called: Rosewood Retirement Community
1401 New Stine Rd, Bakersfield (93309-3530)
PHONE................661 834-0620
Ellen Renner, *Branch Mgr*
Rebecca Humes, *Records Dir*
Diane Kimbrough, *Social Dir*
Brenda Ocheao, *Office Mgr*
Rowena Lopez, *Nursing Dir*
EMP: 150
SALES (corp-wide): 178.8MM **Privately Held**
WEB: www.abhow.com
SIC: 8059 8052 8051 Rest home, with health care; intermediate care facilities; skilled nursing care facilities
HQ: American Baptist Homes Of The West
6120 Stoneridge Mall Rd # 300
Pleasanton CA 94588
925 924-7100

(P-20990)
AMERICAN BAPTIST HOMES OF WEST
Also Called: Plymouth Village
900 Salem Dr, Redlands (92373-6147)
PHONE................909 793-1233
Keith Kasin, *Branch Mgr*
EMP: 250
SQ FT: 8,000
SALES (corp-wide): 178.8MM **Privately Held**
WEB: www.abhow.com
SIC: 8059 8051 Rest home, with health care; skilled nursing care facilities
HQ: American Baptist Homes Of The West
6120 Stoneridge Mall Rd # 300
Pleasanton CA 94588
925 924-7100

(P-20991)
AMERICAN BAPTIST HOMES OF WEST
Also Called: Pilgrim Haven Retirement Home
373 Pine Ln, Los Altos (94022-1648)
PHONE................650 948-8291
Rae Holt, *Manager*
EMP: 120
SQ FT: 95,130
SALES (corp-wide): 178.8MM **Privately Held**
WEB: www.abhow.com
SIC: 8059 8052 8051 Convalescent home; intermediate care facilities; skilled nursing care facilities
HQ: American Baptist Homes Of The West
6120 Stoneridge Mall Rd # 300
Pleasanton CA 94588
925 924-7100

(P-20992)
AMERICAN BAPTIST HOMES OF WEST
Also Called: Terraces of Los Gatos Agei
800 Blossom Hill Rd Ofc, Los Gatos (95032-3563)
PHONE................408 357-1100
A Candalla, *Exec Dir*
Jonathan Fermin, *Social Dir*
Patty Lopez, *Food Svc Dir*
EMP: 115
SALES (corp-wide): 178.8MM **Privately Held**
WEB: www.abhow.com
SIC: 8059 8052 8051 6513 Rest home, with health care; intermediate care facilities; skilled nursing care facilities; apartment building operators
HQ: American Baptist Homes Of The West
6120 Stoneridge Mall Rd # 300
Pleasanton CA 94588
925 924-7100

(P-20993)
ANTELOPE VLY RETIREMENT HM INC
Also Called: Antelope Vly Convalecent Hosp
44445 15th St W, Lancaster (93534-2801)
PHONE................661 948-7501
Marsha Weldon, *Director*
EMP: 400

(P-20994)
ANTELOPE VLY RETIREMENT HM INC
Also Called: A V Nursing Care Center
44567 15th St W, Lancaster (93534-2803)
PHONE................661 949-5524
Alfred Jones, *Manager*
EMP: 200
SALES (corp-wide): 11.4MM **Privately Held**
SIC: 8059 8051 Convalescent home; skilled nursing care facilities
PA: Antelope Valley Retirement Home, Inc.
44523 15th St W
Lancaster CA 93534
661 949-5584

(P-20995)
ARARAT HOME OF LOS ANGELES
Also Called: Ararat Nursing Facility
15099 Mission Hills Rd, Mission Hills (91345-1102)
PHONE................818 837-1800
M Kebhichien, *Administration*
EMP: 250
SALES (corp-wide): 32.9MM **Privately Held**
SIC: 8059 8051 Nursing home, except skilled & intermediate care facility; skilled nursing care facilities
PA: Ararat Home Of Los Angeles Inc
15105 Mission Hills Rd
Mission Hills CA 91345
818 365-3000

(P-20996)
ARARAT HOME OF LOS ANGELES (PA)
Also Called: ARARAT RESIDENTAIL CARE FACILI
15105 Mission Hills Rd, Mission Hills (91345-1103)
PHONE................818 365-3000
Walter Hekimian, *Administration*
John G Yaldezian, *Chairman*
Violette Alahaidoyan, *Administration*
Rita Noravian, *Administration*
EMP: 330
SALES: 32.9MM **Privately Held**
SIC: 8059 Nursing home, except skilled & intermediate care facility

(P-20997)
ARCADIA CONVALESCENT HOSP INC (PA)
Also Called: Arcadia Health Care Center
1601 S Baldwin Ave, Arcadia (91007-7910)
PHONE................323 681-1504
Orlando Clarizio Jr, *CEO*
Mario Andrade, *Envir Svcs Dir*
EMP: 117
SQ FT: 21,342
SALES (est): 11.5MM **Privately Held**
SIC: 8059 8051 Convalescent home; skilled nursing care facilities

(P-20998)
ARIZONA AND 21ST CORP
Also Called: Berkley East Convalescent Hosp
2021 Arizona Ave, Santa Monica (90404-1335)
PHONE................310 829-5377
Sol Galper, *President*
Steven Galper, *Corp Secy*
EMP: 60 **EST:** 1968
SALES: 17.1MM **Privately Held**
SIC: 8059 Convalescent home

(P-20999)
ARTESIA CHRISTIAN HOME INC
11614 183rd St, Artesia (90701-5506)
PHONE................562 865-5218
Elroy Van Derley, *Exec Dir*
Carol Smidt, *Technology*
EMP: 140

SQ FT: 43,223
SALES: 9.8MM **Privately Held**
SIC: 8059 8052 8051 Convalescent home; intermediate care facilities; skilled nursing care facilities

(P-21000)
ASBURY PK NRSING RHBLTTION CTR
2257 Fair Oaks Blvd, Sacramento (95825-5501)
PHONE................916 649-2000
John Lund, *President*
Austin Brickner, *Manager*
EMP: 130 **EST:** 1997
SQ FT: 30,000
SALES: 10.9MM **Privately Held**
SIC: 8059 Nursing home, except skilled & intermediate care facility

(P-21001)
B & E CONVALESCENT CENTER INC (PA)
Also Called: Gardena Convalescent Center
11627 Telg Rd Ste 200, Santa Fe Springs (90670)
PHONE................562 923-9449
Barry J Weiss, *President*
Esther Weiss, *Treasurer*
EMP: 60
SALES (est): 4.8MM **Privately Held**
WEB: www.gardenaconvalescentcenter.com
SIC: 8059 Convalescent home

(P-21002)
BASSARD CONVALESCENT & MED HM (PA)
Also Called: Bassard Convalscent Home
3269 D St, Hayward (94541-4599)
PHONE................510 537-6700
Prema Thekkek, *President*
Bobby Singh, *Administration*
EMP: 65
SQ FT: 25,000
SALES (est): 1.6MM **Privately Held**
SIC: 8059 Convalescent home

(P-21003)
BEGROUP (PA)
516 Burchett St, Glendale (91203-1014)
PHONE................818 638-4563
John H Cochrane III, *President*
David L Pierce, *CFO*
Daniel S Ogus, *Exec VP*
Michelle Esser, *Vice Pres*
EMP: 59
SALES (est): 20.3MM **Privately Held**
SIC: 8059 Nursing home, except skilled & intermediate care facility

(P-21004)
BELMONT VILLAGE LP
Also Called: Belmont Village At Sabre Sprng
13075 Evening Creek Dr S, San Diego (92128-8101)
PHONE................858 486-5020
Inan Linton, *Manager*
EMP: 85
SALES (corp-wide): 37.6MM **Privately Held**
SIC: 8059 Nursing home, except skilled & intermediate care facility
PA: Belmont Village, L.P.
7660 Woodway Dr Ste 400
Houston TX 77063
713 463-1700

(P-21005)
BEN BENNETT INC (PA)
Also Called: Community Care Rhblitation Ctr
3419 Via Lido 646, Newport Beach (92663-3908)
PHONE................949 209-9712
Bruce Bennett, *President*
▲ **EMP:** 200
SQ FT: 50,000
SALES (est): 9MM **Privately Held**
WEB: www.commcare.org
SIC: 8059 8069 8051 Convalescent home; specialty hospitals, except psychiatric; skilled nursing care facilities

---

(P-21006)
BERKELEY E CONVALESCENT HOSP
Also Called: Berkeley E Convalescent Hosp
2021 Arizona Ave, Santa Monica
(90404-1335)
PHONE.....................310 829-5377
Paul Bartolucce, *President*
Saul Galper, *Corp Secy*
EMP: 150
SQ FT: 10,000
SALES (est): 93.8K **Privately Held**
SIC: 8059 Convalescent home

(P-21007)
BERNARDO HTS HEALTHCARE INC
Also Called: Carmel Mtn Rhab Healthcare Ctr
11895 Avenue Of Industry, San Diego
(92128-3423)
PHONE.....................858 673-0101
Christopher R Christensen, *CEO*
Covey C Christensen, *President*
EMP: 99
SALES (est): 3.9MM
SALES (corp-wide): 1.8B **Publicly Held**
SIC: 8059 8051 8011 Nursing home, except skilled & intermediate care facility; skilled nursing care facilities; clinic, operated by physicians
PA: The Ensign Group Inc
27101 Puerta Real Ste 450
Mission Viejo CA 92691
949 487-9500

(P-21008)
BERRYMAN HEALTH INC
Also Called: Ukiah Convalescent Hospital
1349 S Dora St, Ukiah (95482-6512)
PHONE.....................707 462-8864
Barbara Jimenez, *Principal*
EMP: 63
SALES (corp-wide): 2.4MM **Privately Held**
WEB: www.ukiahconvalescent.com
SIC: 8059 Convalescent home
PA: Berryman Health Inc
615 E Chapman Ave Ste 3
Orange CA

(P-21009)
BETHEL LUTHERAN HOME INC
2280 Dockery Ave, Selma (93662-3898)
PHONE.....................559 896-4900
C Kaylene Steele, *Administration*
EMP: 100 **EST:** 1928
SQ FT: 33,000
SALES (est): 4MM **Privately Held**
SIC: 8059 8051 Domiciliary care; extended care facility

(P-21010)
BETHEL RETIREMENT COMMUNITY
2345 Scenic Dr, Modesto (95355-4574)
PHONE.....................209 577-1901
Tony Musolino, *General Ptnr*
Kenneth Lemmings DDS, *Partner*
Robert Pirtle, *Partner*
Stephen P Thomas, *Partner*
EMP: 100
SQ FT: 120,000
SALES (est): 4.2MM **Privately Held**
WEB: www.bethelretirement.com
SIC: 8059 8361 Nursing home, except skilled & intermediate care facility; home for the aged

(P-21011)
BONNIE BRAE CNVLSCENT HOSP INC (PA)
Also Called: California Convalescent Center
420 S Bonnie Brae St, Los Angeles
(90057-3010)
PHONE.....................213 483-8144
Elma Cayton, *CEO*
Albert Ballo, *Treasurer*
Michelle Cayton, *Administration*
Divina Matabalan-Billing, *Clerk*
EMP: 60 **EST:** 1960
SALES (est): 6.7MM **Privately Held**
SIC: 8059 8051 Convalescent home; skilled nursing care facilities

(P-21012)
BRASWELL COL CARE REDLANDS CA
1618 Laurel Ave, Redlands (92373-4838)
PHONE.....................909 792-6050
James Braswell, *Partner*
EMP: 245 **EST:** 1987
SALES (est): 10.6MM **Privately Held**
SIC: 8059 8051 Rest home, with health care; skilled nursing care facilities

(P-21013)
BRASWELLS VILLA MONTE VISTA
12696 Monte Vista Rd, Poway
(92064-2500)
PHONE.....................858 487-6242
James Braswell, *Partner*
EMP: 160
SALES: 7.3MM **Privately Held**
SIC: 8059 8051 Convalescent home; skilled nursing care facilities

(P-21014)
BRENTWOOD SKILL NURSNG & REHAB
Also Called: Brentwood Sklled Nursng Rhbltn
1795 Walnut St, Red Bluff (96080-3645)
PHONE.....................530 527-2046
Phil Sullivan, *Administration*
Daniel McNeal, *Maint Spvr*
Terri Sullivan, *Nursing Dir*
Stephen Datu, *Director*
Becky Taroli, *Receptionist*
EMP: 66
SQ FT: 1,600
SALES (est): 1.8MM **Privately Held**
SIC: 8059 Convalescent home

(P-21015)
BRIARWOOD HEALTH CARE INC
5901 Lemon Hill Ave, Sacramento
(95824-3231)
PHONE.....................916 383-2741
Sharron Jennings, *President*
EMP: 50
SALES: 3.4MM **Privately Held**
SIC: 8059 Convalescent home

(P-21016)
BRIER OAK ON SUNSET LLC
Also Called: Brier Oak On Sunset Rehab Ctr
8318 S Main St Apt 1, Los Angeles
(90003-2951)
PHONE.....................323 663-3951
Barry Gans, *Manager*
Nenita Brizo, *Records Dir*
Hazel Delacruz, *Marketing Staff*
Cindy Kashiwabara, *Food Svc Dir*
Claudia Velasquez, *Director*
EMP: 120
SALES (est): 406.5K **Publicly Held**
SIC: 8059 8051 Convalescent home; skilled nursing care facilities; rehabilitation center, residential: health care incidental
HQ: Skilled Healthcare, Llc
27442 Portola Pkwy # 200
Foothill Ranch CA 92610
949 282-5800

(P-21017)
BRIGHTON CONVALESCENT CENTER
1836 N Fair Oaks Ave, Pasadena
(91103-1619)
PHONE.....................626 798-9124
Alex Makabuhay, *Administration*
Pat Capello, *Administration*
Rose Wilson, *Systems Mgr*
EMP: 100
SALES: 7.4MM **Privately Held**
SIC: 8059 8051 Convalescent home; skilled nursing care facilities

(P-21018)
BROOKDALE SENIOR LIVING INC
72201 Country Club Dr, Rancho Mirage
(92270-4001)
PHONE.....................760 340-5999
EMP: 98
SALES (corp-wide): 4.7B **Publicly Held**
SIC: 8059 Nursing home, except skilled & intermediate care facility

PA: Brookdale Senior Living
111 Westwood Pl Ste 400
Brentwood TN 37027
615 221-2250

(P-21019)
BROOKDALE SENIOR LIVING INC
72750 Country Club Dr, Rancho Mirage
(92270-4083)
PHONE.....................760 346-7772
EMP: 87
SALES (corp-wide): 4.7B **Publicly Held**
SIC: 8059 6513 Nursing home, except skilled & intermediate care facility; retirement hotel operation
PA: Brookdale Senior Living
111 Westwood Pl Ste 400
Brentwood TN 37027
615 221-2250

(P-21020)
BROOKDALE SENIOR LIVING INC
Also Called: Brookdale Folsom
780 Harrington Way, Folsom (95630-3458)
PHONE.....................916 983-9300
Rhonda Carter, *Manager*
EMP: 65
SALES (corp-wide): 4.7B **Publicly Held**
SIC: 8059 Nursing home, except skilled & intermediate care facility
PA: Brookdale Senior Living
111 Westwood Pl Ste 400
Brentwood TN 37027
615 221-2250

(P-21021)
BROOKDALE SENIOR LIVING INC
Also Called: Brookdale Sunwest
1001 N Lyon Ave, Hemet (92545-1753)
PHONE.....................951 744-9861
T Byington, *Exec Dir*
EMP: 65
SALES (corp-wide): 4.7B **Publicly Held**
SIC: 8059 Nursing home, except skilled & intermediate care facility
PA: Brookdale Senior Living
111 Westwood Pl Ste 400
Brentwood TN 37027
615 221-2250

(P-21022)
BROOKDALE SENIOR LIVING INC
2005 Kellogg Ave, Corona (92879-3111)
PHONE.....................951 808-9387
EMP: 54
SALES (corp-wide): 4.7B **Publicly Held**
SIC: 8059 8093 Nursing home, except skilled & intermediate care facility; mental health clinic, outpatient
PA: Brookdale Senior Living
111 Westwood Pl Ste 400
Brentwood TN 37027
615 221-2250

(P-21023)
BROOKDALE SNIOR LVING CMMNTIES
Also Called: Wynwood At The Palms
25585 Van Leuven St, Loma Linda
(92354-2442)
PHONE.....................909 796-5421
David Tamo, *Manager*
EMP: 60
SALES (corp-wide): 4.7B **Publicly Held**
WEB: www.assisted.com
SIC: 8059 Rest home, with health care
HQ: Brookdale Senior Living Communities, Inc.
6737 W Wa St Ste 2300
Milwaukee WI 53214
414 918-5000

(P-21024)
BUENA VENTURA CARE CENTER INC
Also Called: Leisure Glen Convalescent Ctr
1505 Colby Dr, Glendale (91205-3307)
PHONE.....................818 247-4476
Yolanda Wise, *Administration*
EMP: 80

SALES (corp-wide): 6.6MM **Privately Held**
SIC: 8059 8051 Convalescent home; skilled nursing care facilities
PA: Buena Ventura Care Center Inc
1016 S Record Ave
Los Angeles CA 90023
323 268-0106

(P-21025)
BURLINGAME SENIOR CARE LLC
Also Called: Burlingame Healtcare Center
1100 Trousdale Dr, Burlingame
(94010-3207)
PHONE.....................650 692-3758
Timothy B Cassidy, *Mng Member*
Don Doyle, *Admin Asst*
EMP: 300
SALES (est): 6.1MM **Privately Held**
SIC: 8059 Nursing home, except skilled & intermediate care facility

(P-21026)
BV GENERAL INC
Also Called: Kennedy Care Center
619 N Fairfax Ave, Los Angeles
(90036-1714)
PHONE.....................323 651-0043
James Kargol, *Branch Mgr*
EMP: 70
SALES (corp-wide): 14.4MM **Privately Held**
WEB: www.hmscal.com
SIC: 8059 Rest home, with health care
PA: B.V. General, Inc.
1332 S Glendale Ave
Glendale CA 91205
760 747-0430

(P-21027)
CALIFORNIA CONVALESCENT HOSP
Also Called: Santa Barbara Convalescent Ctr
2225 De La Vina St, Santa Barbara
(93105-3815)
PHONE.....................805 682-1355
Dorothy Shea, *President*
Laurie Shea, *President*
Roger Shea, *Treasurer*
S Laurie Anderson, *Admin Sec*
Kathleen Shea, *Admin Sec*
EMP: 70
SQ FT: 25,000
SALES (est): 6.2MM **Privately Held**
SIC: 8059 Convalescent home

(P-21028)
CALIFORNIA HM FOR THE AGED INC
Also Called: CALIFORNIA ARMENIAN HOME
6720 E Kings Canyon Rd, Fresno
(93727-3603)
PHONE.....................559 251-8414
Ray Wark, *Administration*
EMP: 165 **EST:** 1950
SQ FT: 39,000
SALES: 23.5MM **Privately Held**
SIC: 8059 Convalescent home; nursing home, except skilled & intermediate care facility

(P-21029)
CALIFORNIA VOCATIONS INC
Also Called: Arthur Schawlow Center
1620 Cypress Ln, Paradise (95969-2824)
P.O. Box 538 (95967-0538)
PHONE.....................530 877-0937
Bob Irvine, *Exec Dir*
Richard Welsh, *President*
George Dailey, *Treasurer*
Lisa Nixon, *Officer*
Denise Worth, *Vice Pres*
EMP: 195
SQ FT: 5,700
SALES: 6.8MM **Privately Held**
WEB: www.calvoc.org
SIC: 8059 Home for the mentally retarded, exc. skilled or intermediate

(P-21030)
CALIFRNIA-NEVADA METHDST HOMES
Also Called: Lake Park Retirment Residence
1850 Alice St Ofc, Oakland (94612-4169)
PHONE..................................510 835-5511
Steve Jacobson, *Manager*
Barbara Conlon, *Executive*
EMP: 100
SALES (est): 3.2MM
SALES (corp-wide): 19.6MM **Privately Held**
WEB: www.foresthillmanor.com
SIC: 8059 Rest home, with health care
PA: California-Nevada Methodist Homes
201 19th St Ste 100
Oakland CA 94612
510 893-8989

(P-21031)
CANYON PROPERTIES III LLC
Also Called: Country Manor Health Care
11723 Fenton Ave, Sylmar (91342-6431)
PHONE..................................818 890-0430
Donna Santos, *Administration*
EMP: 99
SALES: 5.1MM **Privately Held**
WEB: www.countrymanorhealthcare.com
SIC: 8059 Nursing & personal care

(P-21032)
CAPITOLA CARE CENTER INC
Also Called: Capitola Manor
1098 38th Ave, Santa Cruz (95062-4416)
PHONE..................................831 477-0329
Adolfo D Calanoc, *President*
Maria Correa, *Manager*
EMP: 100
SQ FT: 10,000
SALES (est): 7.3MM **Privately Held**
SIC: 8059 8051 Convalescent home;
skilled nursing care facilities

(P-21033)
CARE CHOICE HEALTH SYSTEMS INC
Also Called: Care Choice Home Care
338 Via Vera Cruz Ste 120, San Marcos
(92078-2647)
PHONE..................................760 798-4508
Tara Pardo, *CEO*
EMP: 60
SALES (est): 982K **Privately Held**
SIC: 8059 8082 Personal care home, with
health care; home health care services

(P-21034)
CASA DE SANTA FE OF ROCKLIN
3201 Santa Fe Way Apt 1, Rocklin
(95765-5582)
PHONE..................................916 435-8800
Joe Donham, *Administration*
EMP: 80
SALES (est): 3.1MM **Privately Held**
SIC: 8059 Personal care home, with health
care

(P-21035)
CENTRAL COAST CMNTY HLTH CARE
5 Lower Ragsdale Dr # 102, Monterey
(93940-5817)
P.O. Box 2480 (93942-2480)
PHONE..................................831 372-6668
Carol Snow, *President*
EMP: 250
SQ FT: 18,014
SALES (est): 8.9MM **Privately Held**
SIC: 8059 Convalescent home

(P-21036)
CHANCELLOR HLTH CARE CAL I INC (PA)
Also Called: Linda Valley Care Center
25383 Cole St, Loma Linda (92354-3103)
PHONE..................................909 796-0235
Corbin Swafford, *Exec Dir*
Edmond Peters, *Vice Ch Bd*
Ferney Zuluaga, *Exec Dir*
Hoselito Acuna, *Office Mgr*
Dave Green, *Administration*
EMP: 70 EST: 1960
SQ FT: 32,000
SALES (est): 6.2MM **Privately Held**
SIC: 8059 6513 8051 Convalescent
home; nursing home, except skilled & in-
termediate care facility; apartment build-
ing operators; skilled nursing care
facilities

(P-21037)
CHANNING HOUSE
850 Webster St Ofc, Palo Alto
(94301-2859)
PHONE..................................650 327-0950
Melvin Matsumoto, *CEO*
Dr Thomas Fiene, *Trustee*
Carl Braginsky, *Exec Dir*
EMP: 100
SQ FT: 300,000
SALES: 20.3MM **Privately Held**
WEB: www.channinghouse.com
SIC: 8059 Rest home, with health care

(P-21038)
CHASE CARE CENTER INC
1101 Crenshaw Blvd, Los Angeles
(90019-3112)
PHONE..................................323 935-8490
Jeoung H Lee, *President*
John Yoo, *Administration*
EMP: 121
SQ FT: 83,000
SALES (est): 5.6MM **Privately Held**
SIC: 8059 8051 Convalescent home;
skilled nursing care facilities

(P-21039)
COASTAL VIEW HALTHCARE CTR LLC
4904 Telegraph Rd, Ventura (93003-4109)
PHONE..................................805 642-4101
Sim Mandelbaum,
Beverly Bragado, *Administration*
Debbie Smith, *Marketing Staff*
EMP: 96
SALES (est): 4MM **Privately Held**
SIC: 8059 Convalescent home

(P-21040)
COLLWOOD TER STELLAR CARE INC
4518 54th St, San Diego (92115-3527)
PHONE..................................619 287-2920
Chris Cho, *President*
EMP: 90
SALES (est): 3.7MM **Privately Held**
SIC: 8059 Personal care home, with health
care

(P-21041)
COMPASS HEALTH INC
Also Called: Mission View Health Center
1425 Woodside Dr, San Luis Obispo
(93401-5936)
PHONE..................................805 543-0210
Linda Lindsey, *Manager*
EMP: 99 **Privately Held**
SIC: 8059 Nursing home, except skilled &
intermediate care facility
PA: Compass Health, Inc.
200 S 13th St Ste 208
Grover Beach CA 93433

(P-21042)
COMPASS HEALTH INC
Also Called: Bayside Care Center
1405 Teresa Dr, Morro Bay (93442-2458)
PHONE..................................805 772-7372
Harold Carder, *Manager*
Mindi Martin, *Executive*
ERA-Lynn Ridge, *Chf Purch Ofc*
Susy Grills, *Hlthcr Dir*
Nicole Dauphine, *Director*
EMP: 131 **Privately Held**
SIC: 8059 Nursing home, except skilled &
intermediate care facility
PA: Compass Health, Inc.
200 S 13th St Ste 208
Grover Beach CA 93433

(P-21043)
COMPASS HEALTH INC
Also Called: Arroyo Grande Care Center
1212 Farroll Ave, Arroyo Grande
(93420-3718)
PHONE..................................805 489-8137

Harold Carder, *Administration*
Sonja Rogers, *Director*
Joni Nilsby, *Manager*
EMP: 131 **Privately Held**
SIC: 8059 Nursing home, except skilled &
intermediate care facility
PA: Compass Health, Inc.
200 S 13th St Ste 208
Grover Beach CA 93433

(P-21044)
COMPASS HEALTH INC
Also Called: Danish Care Center
10805 El Camino Real, Atascadero
(93422-8868)
PHONE..................................805 466-9254
Mark Woolpert, *President*
Sharon Ray, *Office Mgr*
Linda Lindsay, *Administration*
EMP: 70
SALES (est): 1.9MM **Privately Held**
SIC: 8059 Nursing home, except skilled &
intermediate care facility
PA: Compass Health, Inc.
200 S 13th St Ste 208
Grover Beach CA 93433

(P-21045)
COUNTRY VILLA BLMNT HGHT HLTH
Also Called: BELMONT CONVALESCENT
HOSPITAL
1730 Grand Ave, Long Beach
(90804-2011)
PHONE..................................562 597-8817
Sherry Gradon, *Administration*
EMP: 70
SALES: 11.8MM **Privately Held**
SIC: 8059 Convalescent home

(P-21046)
COUNTRY VILLA EAST LP
Also Called: Country Vlla Nrsing Rhbltation
5916 W Pico Blvd, Los Angeles
(90035-2615)
PHONE..................................323 939-3184
Stephen Reissman, *Partner*
Steve Reissmann, *Partner*
Cindy Amaya, *Social Dir*
Cherrie Villanueva, *VP Human Res*
Tristan Viola, *Human Res Dir*
EMP: 200
SALES (est): 9.2MM **Privately Held**
SIC: 8059 8051 Convalescent home;
skilled nursing care facilities

(P-21047)
COUNTRY VILLA SERVICE CORP
112 E Broadway, San Gabriel
(91776-1805)
PHONE..................................626 285-2165
J Caballero, *Administration*
EMP: 188
SALES (corp-wide): 125.3MM **Privately
Held**
SIC: 8059 Nursing home, except skilled &
intermediate care facility
PA: Country Villa Service Corp.
2400 E Katella Ave # 800
Anaheim CA 92806
310 574-3733

(P-21048)
COUNTRY VILLA TERRACE (PA)
Also Called: Country Vlla Convalescent Hosp
6050 W Pico Blvd, Los Angeles
(90035-2647)
PHONE..................................323 653-3980
Steven Reissman, *President*
Diana Reissman, *Vice Pres*
David Ramin, *Director*
EMP: 75
SQ FT: 6,000
SALES (est): 5.4MM **Privately Held**
SIC: 8059 8361 Convalescent home; resi-
dential care

(P-21049)
COUNTRY VILLA TERRACE
Also Called: Flora Ter Convalescent Hosp
5916 W Pico Blvd, Los Angeles
(90035-2615)
PHONE..................................323 939-3184
Lydia Reyes, *Manager*

EMP: 50
SQ FT: 15,240
SALES (corp-wide): 5.4MM **Privately
Held**
SIC: 8059 Convalescent home
PA: Country Villa Terrace
6050 W Pico Blvd
Los Angeles CA 90035
323 653-3980

(P-21050)
COVENANT CARE CALIFORNIA LLC
Also Called: Vintage Faire Nrsng Rhbltn
3620 Dale Rd Ste B, Modesto
(95356-0598)
PHONE..................................209 521-2094
Julie Abram, *Administration*
Nikki Love, *Social Dir*
EMP: 105 **Privately Held**
WEB: www.willowtreenursingcenter.com
SIC: 8059 8051 Convalescent home;
skilled nursing care facilities
HQ: Covenant Care California, Llc
27071 Aliso Creek Rd # 100
Aliso Viejo CA 92656

(P-21051)
COVENANT RTIREMENT COMMUNITIES
325 Kempton St, Spring Valley
(91977-5810)
PHONE..................................619 479-4790
Thad Rothrock, *Branch Mgr*
EMP: 193
SALES (corp-wide): 3.3MM **Privately
Held**
SIC: 8059 Nursing home, except skilled &
intermediate care facility
HQ: Covenant Retirement Communities
5700 Old Orchard Rd # 100
Skokie IL 60077

(P-21052)
CPCC INC
Also Called: Chatsworth Park Hlth Care Ctr
10610 Owensmouth Ave, Chatsworth
(91311-2151)
PHONE..................................818 882-3200
John Sorensen, *President*
Greg Ethington, *Administration*
Cynthia Cornejo, *Receptionist*
EMP: 99
SALES (est): 4.2MM **Privately Held**
SIC: 8059 8051 Convalescent home;
skilled nursing care facilities

(P-21053)
CRESCENT COURT NURSING HOME
1334 S Ham Ln, Lodi (95242-3903)
PHONE..................................209 367-7400
Kerry Bains, *President*
Terry Jen, *President*
Sharon Jennings, *President*
Bea Halsell, *Principal*
Mary Chow, *Director*
EMP: 50
SQ FT: 5,000
SALES (est): 1.9MM
SALES (corp-wide): 9.4MM **Privately
Held**
SIC: 8059 8052 Convalescent home; in-
termediate care facilities
PA: Riverside Health Care Corporation
1469 Humboldt Rd Ste 175
Chico CA 95928
530 897-5100

(P-21054)
CULVER WEST HEALTH CENTER LLC
4035 Grand View Blvd, Los Angeles
(90066-5211)
PHONE..................................310 390-9506
Harry Jacobs,
EMP: 90
SQ FT: 25,000
SALES (est): 8.1MM **Privately Held**
SIC: 8059 Convalescent home

890   2019 Directory of California
Wholesalers and Services Companies   ▲ = Import ▼=Export
◆ =Import/Export

(P-21055)

CYPRESS GARDENS CONVALESCENT H

9025 Colorado Ave, Riverside (92503-2167)

PHONE......................951 688-3643

Stanley Angermeir, *President*
Edward Erzen, *Vice Pres*
EMP: 115
SALES (est): 5.5MM **Privately Held**
SIC: 8059 8051 Convalescent home; skilled nursing care facilities

(P-21056)

D & C CARE CENTER INC

Also Called: Sunrise Convalescent Hospital
1640 N Fair Oaks Ave, Pasadena (91103-1615)

PHONE......................626 798-1175

Felipe T Chu, *CEO*
June Cayabyab, *Administration*
June Ceayabyab, *Administration*
EMP: 75
SALES (est): 5.9MM **Privately Held**
SIC: 8059 Convalescent home

(P-21057)

D K FORTUNE & ASSOCIATES INC

Also Called: Marina Care Center
5240 Sepulveda Blvd, Culver City (90230-5214)

PHONE......................310 391-7266

Fax: 310 397-4998
EMP: 130
SALES: 9.2MM **Privately Held**
SIC: 8059 8051

(P-21058)

DAVID KING CONVALESCENT HOSP

1340 15th St, Santa Monica (90404-1802)

PHONE......................310 451-9706

Miriam Weiss, *President*
EMP: 99
SQ FT: 62,075
SALES (est): 1MM
SALES (corp-wide): 62.1MM **Privately Held**
WEB: www.goldenstatehealth.com
SIC: 8059 Nursing & personal care
PA: Golden State Health Centers, Inc.
13347 Ventura Blvd
Sherman Oaks CA 91423
818 385-3200

(P-21059)

DIVERSIFIED HEALTH SVCS DEL (PA)

136 Washington Ave, Richmond (94801-3947)

PHONE......................510 231-6200

Garrett Loube, *President*
EMP: 200 **EST:** 1968
SALES (est): 5.3MM **Privately Held**
SIC: 8059 Convalescent home

(P-21060)

EL MONTE CONVALESCENT HOSPITAL

4096 Easy St, El Monte (91731-1054)

PHONE......................626 442-1500

Jesse Telles, *CEO*
Nhu Devera, *Nursing Dir*
David Gu, *Director*
Linda Torres, *Receptionist*
EMP: 75 **EST:** 1964
SQ FT: 21,208
SALES: 5.9MM **Privately Held**
WEB: www.elmonteconvalescent.com
SIC: 8059 Convalescent home

(P-21061)

ELENA VILLA HEALTHCARE CENTER

13226 Studebaker Rd, Norwalk (90650-2532)

PHONE......................562 868-0591

Floyd Loupot, *President*
Everett E Goings, *Vice Pres*
EMP: 90
SQ FT: 24,000

SALES (est): 4.1MM **Privately Held**
SIC: 8059 8051 Convalescent home; skilled nursing care facilities

(P-21062)

EMMANUEL CNVLSCENT HOSP ALMEDA

Also Called: Pleasant Care
508 Westline Dr, Alameda (94501-5847)

PHONE......................510 521-5765

Suzanne Valoppi, *Administration*
EMP: 100
SALES (est): 3.7MM **Privately Held**
SIC: 8059 8051 Convalescent home; skilled nursing care facilities

(P-21063)

EMPRESS CARE CENTER

1299 S Bascom Ave, San Jose (95128-3514)

PHONE......................408 287-0616

Ben Laub, *Director*
Kin Mohamed, *Director*
EMP: 65
SALES (est): 3.4MM **Privately Held**
SIC: 8059 Convalescent home

(P-21064)

ENSIGN WILLITS LLC

Also Called: North Brook Nursing and Rehab
64 Northbrook Way, Willits (95490-3019)

PHONE......................707 459-5592

Matt Rutter, *Principal*
EMP: 60
SALES (est): 1.3MM
SALES (corp-wide): 1.8B **Publicly Held**
SIC: 8059 Nursing home, except skilled & intermediate care facility
HQ: Northern Pioneer Healthcare, Inc.
27101 Puerta Real
Mission Viejo CA 92691
949 487-9500

(P-21065)

FAR WEST INC

Also Called: Westgage Grdn Convalescent Ctr
4525 W Tulare Ave, Visalia (93277-1560)

PHONE......................559 733-0901

Ellen Rioux, *Principal*
EMP: 113
SALES (corp-wide): 103.7MM **Privately Held**
SIC: 8059 8051 Convalescent home; skilled nursing care facilities
HQ: Far West, Inc
4020 Sierra College Blvd
Rocklin CA 95677

(P-21066)

FILLMORE CONVALESCENT CTR LLC

118 B St, Fillmore (93015-1763)

PHONE......................805 524-0083

Fax: 805 524-7260
EMP: 80
SQ FT: 13,800
SALES (est): 4.5MM **Privately Held**
WEB: www.fillmoreconvalescentcenter.com
SIC: 8059 8051

(P-21067)

FOWLER CONVALESCENT HOSPITAL

1306 E Sumner Ave, Fowler (93625-2697)

PHONE......................559 834-2542

Roy Delacerda, *Administration*
EMP: 50
SALES (est): 917.2K **Privately Held**
SIC: 8059 8051 Convalescent home; skilled nursing care facilities

(P-21068)

FRAN-JOM INC

Also Called: Temple City Convalescent Hosp
5101 Tyler Ave, Temple City (91780-3682)

PHONE......................626 443-3028

Gary Elliott, *President*
Bryan Elliott, *Vice Pres*
Frank Elliott, *Vice Pres*
EMP: 60
SQ FT: 15,000
SALES (est): 2.5MM **Privately Held**
SIC: 8059 Convalescent home

(P-21069)

FRONT PORCH COMMUNITIES

Also Called: Walnut Manor Care Center
1401 W Ball Rd, Anaheim (92802-1711)

PHONE......................714 776-7150

Sondra Coughlin, *Manager*
EMP: 159
SALES (corp-wide): 165.1MM **Privately Held**
SIC: 8059 8051 Rest home, with health care; skilled nursing care facilities
PA: Front Porch Communities And Services - Casa De Manana, Llc
800 N Brand Blvd Fl 19
Glendale CA 91203
818 729-8100

(P-21070)

FRONT PORCH COMMUNITIES (PA)

Also Called: Fredericka Manor Care Center
800 N Brand Blvd Fl 19, Glendale (91203-1231)

PHONE......................818 729-8100

Gary Wheeler, *CEO*
Roberta Jacobsen, *President*
Mary Miller, *CFO*
Ed Salvador, *CFO*
Jeff Sianko, *Division VP*
EMP: 100
SQ FT: 20,000
SALES: 165.1MM **Privately Held**
SIC: 8059 8051 Rest home, with health care; skilled nursing care facilities

(P-21071)

FRONT PORCH COMMUNITIES

Also Called: Carlsbad By The Sea
2855 Carlsbad Blvd, Carlsbad (92008-2902)

PHONE......................760 729-4983

Tim Wetzel, *Manager*
Heidi Kvitli, *Director*
EMP: 150
SALES (corp-wide): 165.1MM **Privately Held**
SIC: 8059 Rest home, with health care
PA: Front Porch Communities And Services - Casa De Manana, Llc
800 N Brand Blvd Fl 19
Glendale CA 91203
818 729-8100

(P-21072)

FRONT PORCH COMMUNITIES

Also Called: Claremont Manor
650 Harrison Ave, Claremont (91711-4538)

PHONE......................909 626-1227

Joseph Peduzzi, *Branch Mgr*
Kari Miner, *President*
EMP: 150
SQ FT: 167,053
SALES (corp-wide): 165.1MM **Privately Held**
SIC: 8059 8052 6513 Convalescent home; intermediate care facilities; apartment building operators
PA: Front Porch Communities And Services - Casa De Manana, Llc
800 N Brand Blvd Fl 19
Glendale CA 91203
818 729-8100

(P-21073)

FRONT PORCH COMMUNITIES

Also Called: Fredericka Manor Care Center
111 Third Ave, Chula Vista (91910-1822)

PHONE......................619 427-2777

Loraine Wiencek, *Administration*
Chris Marquand, *General Mgr*
Cindy Ross, *Marketing Staff*
EMP: 178
SALES (corp-wide): 165.1MM **Privately Held**
SIC: 8059 8051 Convalescent home; skilled nursing care facilities
PA: Front Porch Communities And Services - Casa De Manana, Llc
800 N Brand Blvd Fl 19
Glendale CA 91203
818 729-8100

(P-21074)

FRONT PORCH COMMUNITIES & SVCS

Also Called: Lutheran Health Facility
303 N Glenoaks Blvd # 1000, Burbank (91502-1116)

PHONE......................818 729-8100

Bob Moses, *Director*
EMP: 60
SALES (corp-wide): 165.1MM **Privately Held**
SIC: 8059 8011 Rest home, with health care; clinic, operated by physicians
PA: Front Porch Communities And Services - Casa De Manana, Llc
800 N Brand Blvd Fl 19
Glendale CA 91203
818 729-8100

(P-21075)

FRONT PORCH COMMUNITIES & SVCS

Also Called: Southland Lutheran Home
11701 Studebaker Rd, Norwalk (90650-7544)

PHONE......................562 868-9761

Covy Christiansen, *Manager*
EMP: 200
SALES (corp-wide): 165.1MM **Privately Held**
SIC: 8059 8011 8052 8051 Rest home, with health care; geriatric specialist, physician/surgeon; intermediate care facilities; skilled nursing care facilities
PA: Front Porch Communities And Services - Casa De Manana, Llc
800 N Brand Blvd Fl 19
Glendale CA 91203
818 729-8100

(P-21076)

FRONT PRCH CMMUNITIES/SERVICES

3775 Modoc Rd, Santa Barbara (93105-4474)

PHONE......................805 687-0793

Roberta Jacobsen, *Branch Mgr*
Michael Pointer, *Director*
EMP: 250
SQ FT: 68,000
SALES (corp-wide): 165.1MM **Privately Held**
SIC: 8059 8051 Rest home, with health care; skilled nursing care facilities
PA: Front Porch Communities And Services - Casa De Manana, Llc
800 N Brand Blvd Fl 19
Glendale CA 91203
818 729-8100

(P-21077)

FRONT ST INC

Also Called: Front St Residential Care
2115 7th Ave, Santa Cruz (95062-1663)

PHONE......................831 420-0120

Anne Butler, *President*
Peggy Butler, *Vice Pres*
EMP: 115
SALES: 1.1MM **Privately Held**
WEB: www.frontst.com
SIC: 8059 Personal care home, with health care

(P-21078)

GAITHERS FAMILY HOME

1408 S Newcomb St, Porterville (93257-9354)

PHONE......................559 781-0301

Henrietta Gaithers, *President*
EMP: 50
SALES (est): 1.5MM **Privately Held**
SIC: 8059 Home for the mentally retarded, exc. skilled or intermediate

(P-21079)

GARDEN GROVE CONVALES

12882 Shackelford Ln, Garden Grove (92841-5109)

PHONE......................714 638-9470

Aurea Sarigan, *Administration*
Percy Miranda, *Records Dir*
Uri Mandelbaum, *President*
Carol Bercich, *Social Dir*
Letty Vasquez, *Social Dir*
EMP: 125

SQ FT: 6,000
SALES (est): 5MM **Privately Held**
SIC: 8059 8051 Convalescent home;
  skilled nursing care facilities

(P-21080)
GERI-CARE II INC
Also Called: Vermont Care Center
22035 S Vermont Ave, Torrance
(90502-2120)
P.O. Box 6069 (90504-0069)
PHONE..................310 328-0812
Emmanuel David, *President*
Engelica Vivillanueva, *Vice Pres*
EMP: 250
SQ FT: 40,000
SALES: 10.7MM **Privately Held**
SIC: 8059 8051 Convalescent home;
  skilled nursing care facilities

(P-21081)
GHC OF SUNNYVALE LLC
Also Called: CEDAR CREST NURSING &
REHABILITATION CENTER
797 E Fremont Ave, Sunnyvale
(94087-2805)
PHONE..................408 738-4880
Thomas Olds Jr,
EMP: 140 **EST:** 2000
SALES: 12.7MM
SALES (corp-wide): 63.1MM **Privately
Held**
SIC: 8059 8051 Nursing home, except
  skilled & intermediate care facility; skilled
  nursing care facilities
PA: Life Generations Healthcare Llc
  6 Hutton Cntre Dr Ste 400
  Santa Ana CA 92707
  714 241-5600

(P-21082)
**GIBRALTER CONVALESCENT
HOSP**
Also Called: Sunset Manor Convalescent
Hosp
2720 Nevada Ave, El Monte (91733-2318)
PHONE..................626 443-9425
Marcel Morales, *Manager*
EMP: 100
SALES (corp-wide): 828.1MM **Privately
Held**
SIC: 8059 8051 Convalescent home;
  skilled nursing care facilities
PA: Gibralter Convalescent Hospital
  600 E Washington Ave
  Santa Ana CA
  714 550-5380

(P-21083)
GOLDEN CARE INC
Also Called: Valley Manor Convalescent Hosp
6120 Vineland Ave, North Hollywood
(91606-4914)
PHONE..................818 763-6275
Evelyn Del Rosario, *President*
Gonzalo Del Rosario, *Treasurer*
EMP: 80
SQ FT: 32,000
SALES (est): 4.1MM **Privately Held**
SIC: 8059 8361 Convalescent home; resi-
  dential care

(P-21084)
GOLDEN LIVING LLC
Also Called: Beverly Healthcare
9541 Van Nuys Blvd, Panorama City
(91402-1315)
PHONE..................818 893-6385
Christopher Christenson, *Sales/Mktg Mgr*
EMP: 100
SALES (corp-wide): 7.4MM **Privately
Held**
WEB: www.nwbeccorp.com
SIC: 8059 8051 Convalescent home;
  skilled nursing care facilities
PA: Golden Living Llc
  5220 Tennyson Pkwy # 400
  Plano TX 75024
  972 372-6300

(P-21085)
GOLDEN LIVING LLC
Also Called: Beverly Healthcare
2123 Verdugo Blvd, Montrose
(91020-1628)
PHONE..................818 249-3925

Shahid Chaudhry, *Manager*
EMP: 51
SALES (corp-wide): 7.4MM **Privately
Held**
WEB: www.nwbeccorp.com
SIC: 8059 Convalescent home
PA: Golden Living Llc
  5220 Tennyson Pkwy # 400
  Plano TX 75024
  972 372-6300

(P-21086)
GOLDEN LIVING LLC
Also Called: Golden Livingcenter - NAPA
705 Trancas St, NAPA (94558-3014)
PHONE..................707 255-6060
Jerry Wells, *Manager*
EMP: 55
SALES (corp-wide): 7.4MM **Privately
Held**
SIC: 8059 8051 Convalescent home;
  skilled nursing care facilities
PA: Golden Living Llc
  5220 Tennyson Pkwy # 400
  Plano TX 75024
  972 372-6300

(P-21087)
GOLDEN LIVING LLC
Also Called: Beverly Healthcare
19929 Greenley Rd, Sonora (95370-5996)
PHONE..................209 533-2500
Michael Ramstead, *Manager*
EMP: 105
SALES (corp-wide): 7.4MM **Privately
Held**
WEB: www.nwbeccorp.com
SIC: 8059 8051 Convalescent home;
  skilled nursing care facilities
PA: Golden Living Llc
  5220 Tennyson Pkwy # 400
  Plano TX 75024
  972 372-6300

(P-21088)
GOLDEN LIVING LLC
Also Called: Beverly Healthcare
515 E Orangeburg Ave, Modesto
(95350-5510)
PHONE..................209 529-0516
Belinda Guzman, *Exec Dir*
EMP: 76
SALES (corp-wide): 7.4MM **Privately
Held**
WEB: www.nwbeccorp.com
SIC: 8059 Convalescent home
PA: Golden Living Llc
  5220 Tennyson Pkwy # 400
  Plano TX 75024
  972 372-6300

(P-21089)
GOLDEN LIVING LLC
Also Called: Beverly Healthcare
14946 Terreno De Flores, Los Gatos
(95032-2023)
PHONE..................408 356-8136
Richard Gotmaster, *Branch Mgr*
EMP: 70
SALES (corp-wide): 7.4MM **Privately
Held**
WEB: www.nwbeccorp.com
SIC: 8059 Convalescent home
PA: Golden Living Llc
  5220 Tennyson Pkwy # 400
  Plano TX 75024
  972 372-6300

(P-21090)
GOLDEN LIVING LLC
Also Called: Beverly Healthcare
3000 N Gate Rd, Seal Beach (90740-2535)
PHONE..................562 598-2477
Lory Heredia, *Director*
EMP: 80
SALES (corp-wide): 7.4MM **Privately
Held**
WEB: www.nwbeccorp.com
SIC: 8059 8051 8721 Convalescent
  home; skilled nursing care facilities; billing
  & bookkeeping service
PA: Golden Living Llc
  5220 Tennyson Pkwy # 400
  Plano TX 75024
  972 372-6300

(P-21091)
GOLDEN LIVING LLC
Also Called: Beverly Healthcare
1700 Howard Rd, Madera (93637-5131)
PHONE..................559 673-9278
Ken Evans, *Principal*
EMP: 65
SALES (corp-wide): 7.4MM **Privately
Held**
WEB: www.nwbeccorp.com
SIC: 8059 Convalescent home
PA: Golden Living Llc
  5220 Tennyson Pkwy # 400
  Plano TX 75024
  972 372-6300

(P-21092)
GOLDEN LIVING LLC
Also Called: Golden Livingcenter - Redding
1836 Gold St, Redding (96001-1817)
PHONE..................530 241-6756
Pam Eiszele, *Manager*
EMP: 55
SALES (corp-wide): 7.4MM **Privately
Held**
SIC: 8059 8051 Convalescent home;
  skilled nursing care facilities
PA: Golden Living Llc
  5220 Tennyson Pkwy # 400
  Plano TX 75024
  972 372-6300

(P-21093)
GOLDEN LIVING LLC
Also Called: Golden Livingcenter - Fresno
2715 Fresno St, Fresno (93721-1304)
PHONE..................559 486-4433
Debbie Witt, *Manager*
EMP: 55
SALES (corp-wide): 7.4MM **Privately
Held**
SIC: 8059 8051 Convalescent home;
  skilled nursing care facilities
PA: Golden Living Llc
  5220 Tennyson Pkwy # 400
  Plano TX 75024
  972 372-6300

(P-21094)
GOLDEN LIVING LLC
Also Called: Golden Livingcenter - Hyland
3408 E Shields Ave, Fresno (93726-6907)
PHONE..................559 227-4063
Michelle Tatham, *Administration*
EMP: 55
SALES (corp-wide): 7.4MM **Privately
Held**
SIC: 8059 Convalescent home
PA: Golden Living Llc
  5220 Tennyson Pkwy # 400
  Plano TX 75024
  972 372-6300

(P-21095)
GOLDEN LIVING LLC
Also Called: Beverly Healthcare
3169 M St, Merced (95348-2404)
PHONE..................209 722-6231
Mary Imperial, *Manager*
EMP: 70
SALES (corp-wide): 7.4MM **Privately
Held**
WEB: www.nwbeccorp.com
SIC: 8059 Convalescent home
PA: Golden Living Llc
  5220 Tennyson Pkwy # 400
  Plano TX 75024
  972 372-6300

(P-21096)
GOLDEN LIVING LLC
Also Called: Golden Livingcenter - Sanger
2550 9th St, Sanger (93657-2716)
PHONE..................559 875-6501
Leslie Cotham, *Branch Mgr*
EMP: 100
SALES (corp-wide): 7.4MM **Privately
Held**
SIC: 8059 8051 Convalescent home;
  skilled nursing care facilities
PA: Golden Living Llc
  5220 Tennyson Pkwy # 400
  Plano TX 75024
  972 372-6300

(P-21097)
**GOLDEN STATE HEALTH CTRS
INC**
5522 Gracewood Ave, Temple City (91780)
PHONE..................626 579-0310
David Schachter, *Manager*
EMP: 153
SALES (corp-wide): 62.1MM **Privately
Held**
WEB: www.goldenstatehealth.com
SIC: 8059 8051 Convalescent home;
  skilled nursing care facilities
PA: Golden State Health Centers, Inc.
  13347 Ventura Blvd
  Sherman Oaks CA 91423
  818 385-3200

(P-21098)
**GOLDEN STATE HEALTH CTRS
INC**
Also Called: Chatsworth Health & Rehab
21820 Craggy View St, Chatsworth
(91311-2909)
P.O. Box 3909 (91313-3909)
PHONE..................818 882-8233
Emmanuel Ruiz, *Manager*
EMP: 105
SALES (corp-wide): 62.1MM **Privately
Held**
WEB: www.goldenstatehealth.com
SIC: 8059 8051 Convalescent home;
  skilled nursing care facilities
PA: Golden State Health Centers, Inc.
  13347 Ventura Blvd
  Sherman Oaks CA 91423
  818 385-3200

(P-21099)
**GOLDSTAR HLTHCR CNTR OF
CHTSWR**
145 S Fairfax Ave Ste 200, Los Angeles
(90036-2186)
P.O. Box 3909, Chatsworth (91313-3909)
PHONE..................818 882-8233
Miriam Weiss, *President*
David Weiss, *Ch of Bd*
Rose Kasirer, *Vice Pres*
EMP: 147
SQ FT: 26,650
SALES: 7.5MM
SALES (corp-wide): 62.1MM **Privately
Held**
WEB: www.goldenstatehealth.com
SIC: 8059 Convalescent home
PA: Golden State Health Centers, Inc.
  13347 Ventura Blvd
  Sherman Oaks CA 91423
  818 385-3200

(P-21100)
**GRANADA HEALTHCRE &
REHAB CNTR**
2885 Harris St, Eureka (95503-4808)
PHONE..................707 443-1627
Maria Coda,
Ted Chigaros,
EMP: 99
SALES: 950K **Privately Held**
SIC: 8059 Convalescent home

(P-21101)
**GREAT WSTN CNVLESCENT
HOSP INC**
Also Called: Verdugo Vly Convalescent Hosp
2635 Honolulu Ave, Montrose
(91020-1706)
PHONE..................818 248-6856
Ishkhan Khatchadurian, *President*
Barbara Khatchadurian, *Vice Pres*
EMP: 130
SQ FT: 22,000
SALES (est): 3.7MM **Privately Held**
SIC: 8059 8361 8051 Convalescent
  home; residential care; skilled nursing
  care facilities

(P-21102)
**GUARDIAN REHABILITATION
HOSP**
533 S Fairfax Ave, Los Angeles
(90036-3129)
PHONE..................323 930-4815
Uri Mandelbaum, *President*
EMP: 90

SQ FT: 10,000
SALES (est): 5.7MM Privately Held
SIC: 8059 8069 8051 Convalescent home; specialty hospitals, except psychiatric; skilled nursing care facilities

(P-21103)
GVA ENTERPRISES INC (PA)
Also Called: Angels Nursing Center
316 S Westlake Ave, Los Angeles (90057-4500)
PHONE................................213 484-0510
George Rabinowitz, *President*
EMP: 53
SQ FT: 22,578
SALES (est): 5.3MM Privately Held
SIC: 8059 Convalescent home

(P-21104)
HANK FISHER PROPERTIES INC
Also Called: Chateau At River's Edge
641 Feature Dr Apt 233, Sacramento (95825-8331)
PHONE................................916 921-1970
Jeff Hertzig, *Director*
EMP: 92
SALES (est): 3.9MM
SALES (corp-wide): 15.9MM Privately Held
SIC: 8059 8052 Convalescent home; intermediate care facilities
PA: Hank Fisher Properties, Inc.
    641 Fulton Ave Ste 200
    Sacramento CA 95825
    916 485-1441

(P-21105)
HARBOR VILLA CARE CENTER
861 S Harbor Blvd, Anaheim (92805-5157)
PHONE................................714 635-8131
Ramon Martinez, *Administration*
Ana Tigno, *Food Svc Dir*
EMP: 90
SQ FT: 25,000
SALES (est): 2.9MM Privately Held
SIC: 8059 Convalescent home

(P-21106)
HEALTH INFORMATION PARTNERS
4041 Macarthur Blvd # 360, Newport Beach (92660-2512)
P.O. Box 10129 (92658-0129)
PHONE................................949 261-5000
Joseph A Farris, *CEO*
EMP: 125
SALES (est): 7MM Privately Held
WEB: www.hip-inc.com
SIC: 8059 Rest home, with health care

(P-21107)
HELIOS HEALTHCARE LLC
Also Called: Chico Creek Care Rhabilitation
587 Rio Lindo Ave, Chico (95926-1816)
PHONE................................530 345-1306
Carl Lewis, *Manager*
EMP: 170
SQ FT: 51,457
SALES (corp-wide): 24.2MM Privately Held
SIC: 8059 Convalescent home
PA: Helios Healthcare, Llc
    520 Capitol Mall Ste 800
    Sacramento CA 95814
    916 471-2241

(P-21108)
HELIOS HEALTHCARE LLC
Also Called: Windsor Vallejo Care Center
2200 Tuolumne St, Vallejo (94589-2523)
PHONE................................707 644-7401
Laura Curly, *Manager*
EMP: 180
SALES (corp-wide): 24.2MM Privately Held
SIC: 8059 8051 Convalescent home; skilled nursing care facilities
PA: Helios Healthcare, Llc
    520 Capitol Mall Ste 800
    Sacramento CA 95814
    916 471-2241

(P-21109)
HERMITAGE HLTHCR MNKN MNR
400 Circle Dr, Angwin (94508-9806)
PHONE................................410 651-0011
Bonnie Stone,
EMP: 165
SQ FT: 52,000
SALES (est): 1.6MM Privately Held
SIC: 8059 8051 Convalescent home; skilled nursing care facilities

(P-21110)
HILLCREST CARE INC
4280 Cypress Dr, San Bernardino (92407-2960)
PHONE................................909 882-2965
C David Benfield, *President*
EMP: 100 EST: 1977
SALES (est): 4.9MM Privately Held
SIC: 8059 Nursing home, except skilled & intermediate care facility

(P-21111)
HILLCREST CNVALESCENT HOSP INC
3401 Cedar Ave, Long Beach (90807-4422)
PHONE................................323 636-3462
Rosalyn Zisman, *CEO*
Gaby Chacanas, *Treasurer*
EMP: 130
SQ FT: 37,500
SALES (est): 3.3MM Privately Held
SIC: 8059 Convalescent home

(P-21112)
HILLSDALE GROUP LP
Also Called: Sherman Village Hlth Care Ctr
12750 Riverside Dr, North Hollywood (91607-3319)
PHONE................................818 623-2170
Rich Terrell, *Principal*
EMP: 100
SALES (corp-wide): 13.5MM Privately Held
WEB: www.greenhillsretirement.com
SIC: 8059 8051 8093 8011 Convalescent home; skilled nursing care facilities; rehabilitation center, outpatient treatment; clinic, operated by physicians
PA: The Hillsdale Group L P
    1199 Howard Ave Ste 200
    Burlingame CA 94010
    650 348-6783

(P-21113)
HILLSDALE GROUP LP
Also Called: Green Hills Retirement Center
1201 Broadway Ofc, Millbrae (94030-1976)
PHONE................................650 742-9150
Pooja Sadarangani, *Manager*
EMP: 50
SALES (corp-wide): 13.5MM Privately Held
WEB: www.greenhillsretirement.com
SIC: 8059 8051 Nursing home, except skilled & intermediate care facility; skilled nursing care facilities
PA: The Hillsdale Group L P
    1199 Howard Ave Ste 200
    Burlingame CA 94010
    650 348-6783

(P-21114)
HILLSDALE GROUP LP
Also Called: Hayward Convalescent Hospital
1832 B St, Hayward (94541-3140)
PHONE................................510 538-3866
Mark Bornta, *Manager*
EMP: 80
SALES (corp-wide): 13.5MM Privately Held
WEB: www.greenhillsretirement.com
SIC: 8059 8051 Nursing home, except skilled & intermediate care facility; convalescent home with continuous nursing care
PA: The Hillsdale Group L P
    1199 Howard Ave Ste 200
    Burlingame CA 94010
    650 348-6783

(P-21115)
HORIZON WEST HEALTHCARE INC
Also Called: Hilltop Manor
12225 Shale Ridge Ln, Auburn (95602-8870)
PHONE................................530 885-7511
Sheilia Waddell, *Director*
EMP: 180
SALES (corp-wide): 103.7MM Privately Held
WEB: www.villadelrey.com
SIC: 8059 8051 Convalescent home; skilled nursing care facilities
HQ: Horizon West Healthcare, Inc.
    4020 Sierra College Blvd # 190
    Rocklin CA 95677
    916 624-6230

(P-21116)
HUMANGOOD (PA)
Also Called: Terraces At Squaw Peak
6120 Stoneridge Mall Rd, Pleasanton (94588-3296)
PHONE................................602 906-4024
John Cochran, *CEO*
Krispy Collins, *Education*
Munirah Henderson, *Director*
EMP: 52 EST: 1959
SQ FT: 161,000
SALES (est): 178.8MM Privately Held
WEB: www.abhow.com
SIC: 8059 8051 8322 Rest home, with health care; skilled nursing care facilities; old age assistance

(P-21117)
INDEPENDENT QUALITY CARE INC
Also Called: Northgate Convalescent Hosp
40 Professional Ctr Pkwy, San Rafael (94903-2703)
PHONE................................415 479-1230
Theresa D Guzman, *Principal*
Zeke Griffin, *Administration*
Dawn Bright, *Director*
Debra Koonce, *Director*
Linda Pearson, *Director*
EMP: 75
SALES (corp-wide): 11.6MM Privately Held
WEB: www.iqcare.com
SIC: 8059 Convalescent home
PA: Independent Quality Care, Inc
    3 Crow Canyon Ct
    San Ramon CA 94583
    925 855-0881

(P-21118)
INDEPENDENT QUALITY CARE INC (PA)
Also Called: Woodland Lfytte Cnvlscent Hosp
3 Crow Canyon Ct, San Ramon (94583-1619)
PHONE................................925 855-0881
Daniel W Alger, *President*
Jeremy Grimes, *Vice Pres*
▲ EMP: 75
SALES (est): 11.6MM Privately Held
WEB: www.iqcare.com
SIC: 8059 Convalescent home

(P-21119)
INDEPENDENT QUALITY CARE INC
Also Called: McClure Convalescent Hospital
2910 Mcclure St, Oakland (94609-3505)
PHONE................................510 836-3677
Hung-Chee Chan, *Manager*
EMP: 55
SQ FT: 5,000
SALES (corp-wide): 11.6MM Privately Held
WEB: www.iqcare.com
SIC: 8059 Convalescent home
PA: Independent Quality Care, Inc
    3 Crow Canyon Ct
    San Ramon CA 94583
    925 855-0881

(P-21120)
INDEPENDENT QUALITY CARE INC
Also Called: Woodland Lfyett Sklled Nursing
3721 Mt Diablo Blvd, Lafayette (94549-3538)
PHONE................................925 284-5544
Christine Nacion, *Branch Mgr*
EMP: 75
SALES (corp-wide): 11.6MM Privately Held
WEB: www.iqcare.com
SIC: 8059 Convalescent home
PA: Independent Quality Care, Inc
    3 Crow Canyon Ct
    San Ramon CA 94583
    925 855-0881

(P-21121)
INNOVATIVE BUS PARTNERSHIPS
17191 Jasmine St, Victorville (92395-7727)
P.O. Box 3339 (92393-3339)
PHONE................................760 243-2229
Therese Krageness, *President*
EMP: 50
SALES (est): 1MM Privately Held
SIC: 8059 Home for the mentally retarded, exc. skilled or intermediate

(P-21122)
INSTITUTE ON AGING
2100 Embarcadero Ste 101, Oakland (94606-5309)
PHONE................................510 536-3377
EMP: 150 **Privately Held**
SIC: 8059 Convalescent home
PA: Institute On Aging
    3575 Geary Blvd
    San Francisco CA 94118

(P-21123)
KENNEDY CARE CENTER
Also Called: Kennedy Care Ctr Kosher Certif
619 N Fairfax Ave, Los Angeles (90036-1714)
PHONE................................323 651-0043
Alisa Berdnik, *Administration*
EMP: 98 EST: 1968
SQ FT: 25,000
SALES (est): 4.8MM Privately Held
SIC: 8059 Convalescent home

(P-21124)
KF COMMUNITY CARE LLC
Also Called: Community Care Center
2335 Mountain Ave, Duarte (91010-3559)
PHONE................................626 357-3207
Barbara O'Connor, *Administration*
Gordon Buechs, *CFO*
EMP: 170
SQ FT: 11,000
SALES (est): 7.5MM Privately Held
SIC: 8059 Convalescent home

(P-21125)
KF ONTARIO HEALTHCARE LLC
Also Called: Ontario Healthcare Center
1661 S Euclid Ave, Ontario (91762-5826)
PHONE................................909 984-6713
Jacob Wintner, *CEO*
Edward S Shea, *President*
Gordon Buechs, *CFO*
Marcella Allard, *Administration*
EMP: 50
SALES (est): 1.8MM Privately Held
SIC: 8059 8051 Convalescent home; nursing home, except skilled & intermediate care facility; skilled nursing care facilities

(P-21126)
KF SUNRAY LLC
Also Called: Sunray Healthcare Center
3210 W Pico Blvd, Los Angeles (90019-3643)
PHONE................................323 734-2171
Douglas Easton, *Owner*
Daniel Wintner, *General Mgr*
Vandana Desai, *Administration*
EMP: 99
SALES (est): 4.3MM Privately Held
SIC: 8059 Convalescent home

(P-21127)
KINDRED HEALTHCARE OPER INC
Also Called: Saylor Lane Healthcare Center
3500 Folsom Blvd, Sacramento
(95816-6615)
PHONE.....................................916 457-6521
David Hilburn, *Manager*
EMP: 127
SALES (corp-wide): 6B **Privately Held**
WEB: www.salemhaven.com
SIC: 8059 Convalescent home
HQ: Kindred Healthcare Operating, Llc
680 S 4th St
Louisville KY 40202
502 596-7300

(P-21128)
KINDRED HEALTHCARE OPER INC
Also Called: Maywood Acres Health Care Ctr
2641 S C St, Oxnard (93033-4502)
PHONE.....................................805 487-7840
Bonnie Velal, *Manager*
EMP: 100
SALES (corp-wide): 6B **Privately Held**
WEB: www.salemhaven.com
SIC: 8059 8051 Convalescent home;
skilled nursing care facilities
HQ: Kindred Healthcare Operating, Llc
680 S 4th St
Louisville KY 40202
502 596-7300

(P-21129)
KINDRED HEALTHCARE OPERATING
Also Called: Alta Vista Healthcare Center
9020 Garfield St, Riverside (92503-3903)
PHONE.....................................951 688-8200
Jeff Henson, *Director*
EMP: 100
SALES (corp-wide): 6B **Privately Held**
WEB: www.salemhaven.com
SIC: 8059 8051 Nursing home, except
skilled & intermediate care facility; skilled
nursing care facilities
HQ: Kindred Healthcare Operating, Llc
680 S 4th St
Louisville KY 40202
502 596-7300

(P-21130)
KNOLLS WEST POST ACUTE LLC
16890 Green Tree Blvd, Victorville
(92395-5618)
PHONE.....................................760 245-5361
David Johnson, *Mng Member*
Thomas Chambers,
Ryan O'Hara,
EMP: 99
SALES (est): 1.9MM **Privately Held**
SIC: 8059 Nursing home, except skilled &
intermediate care facility

(P-21131)
L C C H ASSOCIATES INC
Also Called: Health Care Group
4311 3rd Ave B, San Diego (92103-1407)
PHONE.....................................858 565-4424
William M Chance, *President*
Renee Barnard, *COO*
Ronald McElloit, *Exec VP*
Rn Case, *Manager*
EMP: 50
SQ FT: 10,000
SALES (est): 2.3MM **Privately Held**
SIC: 8059 Convalescent home

(P-21132)
LA MESA HEALTH CARE CENTER
3780 Massachusetts Ave, La Mesa
(91941-7638)
PHONE.....................................619 465-1313
John Jimenez, *Administration*
Paul Hubbert, *President*
EMP: 130
SQ FT: 22,000
SALES (est): 4.4MM **Privately Held**
SIC: 8059 8051 Convalescent home;
skilled nursing care facilities

(P-21133)
LEE JOHNSON
Also Called: Casa Palmera Care Center
14750 El Camino Real, Del Mar
(92014-4204)
PHONE.....................................858 481-4411
Lee Johnson, *Owner*
Clara Jimenez, *Administration*
▲ EMP: 132
SQ FT: 36,000
SALES (est): 10.7MM **Privately Held**
SIC: 8059 8051 Convalescent home;
skilled nursing care facilities

(P-21134)
LIFE CARE CENTERS AMERICA INC
Also Called: Vista Del Mar Health Centers
304 N Melrose Dr, Vista (92083-4814)
PHONE.....................................760 724-8222
Michael Ramstead, *Branch Mgr*
Nada Elaile, *Food Svc Dir*
EMP: 170
SALES (corp-wide): 119.8MM **Privately Held**
SIC: 8059 8051 Convalescent home;
skilled nursing care facilities
PA: Life Care Centers Of America, Inc.
3570 Keith St Nw
Cleveland TN 37312
423 472-9585

(P-21135)
LIFE GNERATIONS HEALTHCARE LLC
Also Called: Stanford Crt Nrsing Cntr-Sntee
8778 Cuyamaca St, Santee (92071-4255)
PHONE.....................................619 449-5555
Andy Ashton, *Administration*
Carolyn Martinez, *Records Dir*
EMP: 100
SALES (corp-wide): 63.1MM **Privately Held**
SIC: 8059 8051 8049 Convalescent
home; skilled nursing care facilities; phys-
ical therapist
PA: Life Generations Healthcare Llc
6 Hutton Cntre Dr Ste 400
Santa Ana CA 92707
714 241-5600

(P-21136)
LINCOLN GLEN MANOR
Also Called: LINCOLN GLEN SKILLED
NURSING
2671 Plummer Ave Ste A, San Jose
(95125-4877)
PHONE.....................................408 267-1492
Loren Kroeker, *Exec Dir*
Loren H Kroeker, *Executive*
Barbara Filler, *Administration*
Rebecca Turner, *Administration*
Anne Phoenix, *Info Tech Mgr*
EMP: 110
SQ FT: 68,000
SALES (est): 6.7MM **Privately Held**
WEB: www.lgmanor.org
SIC: 8059 Convalescent home

(P-21137)
LOMITA VERDE INC
Also Called: Lomita Care Center
1955 Lomita Blvd, Lomita (90717-1807)
PHONE.....................................310 325-1970
Donald G Laws, *President*
David E Sorenson, *Treasurer*
Wayne Fortin, *Administration*
Roy Ruiz, *Food Svc Dir*
Nabil El Sayad, *Director*
EMP: 60
SALES: 9.9MM **Privately Held**
WEB: www.lomitacare.com
SIC: 8059 8322 Convalescent home; indi-
vidual & family services

(P-21138)
LOMPOC VALLEY MEDICAL CENTER
Also Called: Lompoc Convlsnt Care Ctr
216 N 3rd St, Lompoc (93436-6104)
PHONE.....................................805 736-3466
Judy Smith, *Principal*
EMP: 150

SALES (est): 2.2MM
SALES (corp-wide): 93.2MM **Privately Held**
SIC: 8059 Convalescent home
PA: Lompoc Valley Medical Center
1515 E Ocean Ave
Lompoc CA 93436
805 737-3300

(P-21139)
LONGWOOD MANAGEMENT CORP
Also Called: Sunny View Care Center
2000 W Washington Blvd, Los Angeles
(90018-1637)
PHONE.....................................323 735-5146
Amber Gooden, *Administration*
EMP: 80
SALES (corp-wide): 170MM **Privately Held**
SIC: 8059 Convalescent home
PA: Longwood Management Corp.
4032 Wilshire Blvd Fl 6
Los Angeles CA 90010
213 389-6900

(P-21140)
LONGWOOD MANAGEMENT CORP
Also Called: Broadway Manor Care Center
605 W Broadway, Glendale (91204-1007)
PHONE.....................................818 246-7174
Dolly Piper, *Manager*
EMP: 70
SQ FT: 7,000
SALES (corp-wide): 170MM **Privately Held**
SIC: 8059 8051 Convalescent home;
skilled nursing care facilities
PA: Longwood Management Corp.
4032 Wilshire Blvd Fl 6
Los Angeles CA 90010
213 389-6900

(P-21141)
LONGWOOD MANAGEMENT CORP
Also Called: Western Convelescence
2190 W Adams Blvd, Los Angeles
(90018-2039)
PHONE.....................................323 737-7778
Emma Camanag, *Administration*
EMP: 80
SALES (corp-wide): 170MM **Privately Held**
SIC: 8059 6512 Convalescent home; com-
mercial & industrial building operation
PA: Longwood Management Corp.
4032 Wilshire Blvd Fl 6
Los Angeles CA 90010
213 389-6900

(P-21142)
LONGWOOD MANAGEMENT CORP
Also Called: Aldon Ter Convalsent Hosptial
1240 S Hoover St, Los Angeles
(90006-3606)
PHONE.....................................213 382-8461
John Sicat, *Principal*
EMP: 170
SALES (corp-wide): 170MM **Privately Held**
SIC: 8059 8051 Convalescent home;
skilled nursing care facilities
PA: Longwood Management Corp.
4032 Wilshire Blvd Fl 6
Los Angeles CA 90010
213 389-6900

(P-21143)
LONGWOOD MANAGEMENT CORP
Also Called: Imperial Care Center
11429 Ventura Blvd, Studio City
(91604-3143)
PHONE.....................................818 980-8200
Emma Dellanuoni, *Manager*
Danny Farahmandian, *Director*
EMP: 200
SQ FT: 29,525
SALES (corp-wide): 170MM **Privately Held**
SIC: 8059 8051 Convalescent home;
skilled nursing care facilities

PA: Longwood Management Corp.
4032 Wilshire Blvd Fl 6
Los Angeles CA 90010
213 389-6900

(P-21144)
LONGWOOD MANAGEMENT CORP
Also Called: Live Oak Rehab
537 W Live Oak St, San Gabriel
(91776-1149)
PHONE.....................................626 289-3763
Ranita Phan, *Manager*
EMP: 100
SALES (corp-wide): 170MM **Privately Held**
SIC: 8059 8051 Convalescent home;
skilled nursing care facilities
PA: Longwood Management Corp.
4032 Wilshire Blvd Fl 6
Los Angeles CA 90010
213 389-6900

(P-21145)
LONGWOOD MANAGEMENT CORP
Also Called: Colonial Care Center
1913 E 5th St, Long Beach (90802-2024)
PHONE.....................................562 432-5751
Laura McCuphen, *Manager*
EMP: 150
SALES (corp-wide): 170MM **Privately Held**
SIC: 8059 8051 Convalescent home;
skilled nursing care facilities
PA: Longwood Management Corp.
4032 Wilshire Blvd Fl 6
Los Angeles CA 90010
213 389-6900

(P-21146)
LYNWOOD DEVELOPMENTAL CARE
Also Called: Compton Adult Day Care
14925 S Atlantic Ave, Compton
(90221-3005)
PHONE.....................................310 764-2023
James E Logan, *CEO*
Lavern L Neal, *Treasurer*
EMP: 75
SALES (est): 2.7MM **Privately Held**
SIC: 8059 Personal care home, with health
care

(P-21147)
MADERA CONVALESCENT HOSPITAL
Also Called: Merced Convalescent Hospital
510 W 26th St, Merced (95340-2804)
PHONE.....................................209 723-2911
Dave Yarborough, *Manager*
EMP: 130
SALES (corp-wide): 5.6MM **Privately Held**
SIC: 8059 8051 Convalescent home;
skilled nursing care facilities
PA: Madera Convalescent Hospital, Inc
517 S A St
Madera CA 93638
559 673-9228

(P-21148)
MADERA CONVALESCENT HOSPITAL
Also Called: Auburn Gardens Care Center
260 Racetrack St, Auburn (95603-5422)
PHONE.....................................530 885-7051
Clayton Green, *Administration*
EMP: 78
SALES (est): 402.6K
SALES (corp-wide): 5.6MM **Privately Held**
SIC: 8059 Nursing home, except skilled &
intermediate care facility
PA: Madera Convalescent Hospital, Inc
517 S A St
Madera CA 93638
559 673-9228

(P-21149)
MAGNOLIA RHBLTTION NURSING CTR
Also Called: MAGNOLIA CONVALESCENT HOSPITAL
8133 Magnolia Ave, Riverside (92504-3409)
PHONE..................951 688-4321
Larry Mays, *President*
Grant Edgeson, *Treasurer*
Bennie J Mays, *Vice Pres*
Vanessa Romo, *Executive*
Bobbie N Mays, *Admin Sec*
EMP: 140
SQ FT: 25,000
SALES: 9.4MM **Privately Held**
SIC: 8059 8051 Convalescent home; skilled nursing care facilities

(P-21150)
MANCHSTER MNOR CNVLESCENT HOSP
837 W Manchester Ave, Los Angeles (90044-4913)
PHONE..................323 753-1789
Phadra Johnson-Fenton, *Administration*
Wilisha Jackson, *Office Mgr*
Phadra Fenton, *Administration*
EMP: 65
SQ FT: 10,000
SALES (est): 2.8MM **Privately Held**
WEB: www.manchestermanorch.com
SIC: 8059 Convalescent home

(P-21151)
MARK ONE CORPORATION
Also Called: Ha-Le Aloha Convalescent Hosp
1711 Richland Ave, Ceres (95307-4509)
PHONE..................209 537-4581
Fax: 209 537-0035
EMP: 50
SALES (corp-wide): 12.7MM **Privately Held**
SIC: 8059
PA: Mark One Corporation
812 W Main St
Turlock CA
209 667-2484

(P-21152)
MARLINDA MANAGEMENT INC (PA)
Also Called: Sherwood Guest Home
3351 E Imperial Hwy, Lynwood (90262-3305)
PHONE..................310 638-6691
Martha Lang, *President*
Linda Gassoumis, *CFO*
EMP: 124
SALES (est): 3.8MM **Privately Held**
SIC: 8059 Convalescent home

(P-21153)
MARNA HEALTH SERVICES INC
Also Called: Sillcrest Nursing Home
4280 Cypress Dr, San Bernardino (92407-2960)
PHONE..................909 882-2965
Maria Barrios, *President*
Napoleon Garcia, *Vice Pres*
EMP: 70
SQ FT: 120
SALES (est): 2MM **Privately Held**
SIC: 8059 7389 8049 Personal care home, with health care; ; physical therapist

(P-21154)
MARYCREST MANOR
10664 Saint James Dr, Culver City (90230-5498)
PHONE..................310 838-2778
SIS V Del Carmen, *Administration*
SIS Veronica Del Carmen, *Administration*
EMP: 86
SQ FT: 43,449
SALES: 6.3MM **Privately Held**
SIC: 8059 8051 Convalescent home; skilled nursing care facilities

(P-21155)
MBK SENIOR LIVING LLC
Also Called: Sterling Senior Communities
41780 Btterfield Stage Rd, Temecula (92592-9206)
PHONE..................951 506-5555
Nancy Halleck, *Director*
EMP: 60
SALES (corp-wide): 1.9MM **Privately Held**
SIC: 8059 Rest home, with health care
PA: Senior Mbk Living Llc
895 Dove St Ste 450
Newport Beach CA

(P-21156)
MEDICAL DIAGNOSTIC
Also Called: Bright Caregivers
17682 Beach Blvd Ste 103, Huntington Beach (92647-6812)
PHONE..................714 841-2273
Robert M Soto, *President*
EMP: 62
SQ FT: 1,000
SALES: 2MM **Privately Held**
SIC: 8059 Personal care home, with health care

(P-21157)
MEDICAL INVESTMENT CO
Also Called: Rinaldi Convalescent Hospital
16553 Rinaldi St, Granada Hills (91344-3762)
PHONE..................818 360-1003
Glen Padama, *Principal*
EMP: 175
SQ FT: 25,000
SALES (est): 5.9MM **Privately Held**
SIC: 8059 8051 Convalescent home; skilled nursing care facilities

(P-21158)
MILLBRAE SERRA SANITARIUM
Also Called: Millbrae Srra Cnvalescent Hosp
150 Serra Ave, Millbrae (94030-2629)
P.O. Box 789 (94030-0789)
PHONE..................650 697-8386
Fax: 650 697-3058
EMP: 125
SQ FT: 10,000
SALES: 4.6MM **Privately Held**
SIC: 8059 8051

(P-21159)
MONROVIA CONVALESCENT HOSPITAL
1220 Huntington Dr, Duarte (91010-2477)
PHONE..................626 359-6618
Lydia Cruz, *President*
EMP: 63
SQ FT: 15,000
SALES (est): 1.6MM **Privately Held**
SIC: 8059 Convalescent home

(P-21160)
MONTEREY PK CONVALESCENT HOSP
Also Called: Sun Mar Management Service
416 N Garfield Ave, Monterey Park (91754-1203)
PHONE..................626 280-0280
Irving Bauman, *President*
William Presnell, *Treasurer*
Frank Johnson, *Principal*
Eli Marmur, *Principal*
EMP: 85
SQ FT: 22,000
SALES (est): 3.3MM **Privately Held**
SIC: 8059 8051 Convalescent home; skilled nursing care facilities

(P-21161)
MOYLES HEALTH CARE INC
604 E Merritt Ave, Tulare (93274-2135)
PHONE..................559 686-1601
Kensett J Moyle III, *President*
Kensett J Moyle IV, *Vice Pres*
Mark Harris, *Admin Sec*
EMP: 550
SALES: 3MM **Privately Held**
SIC: 8059 Convalescent home

(P-21162)
MT MIQUEL COVENANT VILLAGE
325 Kempton St, Spring Valley (91977-5810)
PHONE..................619 479-4790
Rich Miller, *Director*
EMP: 241
SQ FT: 316,465
SALES: 18.4MM
SALES (corp-wide): 3.3MM **Privately Held**
SIC: 8059 Rest home, with health care
PA: Covenant Retirement Communities, Inc.
5700 Old Orchard Rd
Skokie IL 60077
773 878-2294

(P-21163)
NEW VISA HEALTH SERVICES INC
3414 Preakness Ct, Fallbrook (92028-9096)
PHONE..................760 723-0053
Robert Craig, *President*
EMP: 500
SALES (est): 3.8MM **Privately Held**
SIC: 8059 Nursing home, except skilled & intermediate care facility

(P-21164)
NEW VISTA HEALTH SERVICES
Also Called: New Vista Pst Act Care Cntr
1516 Sawtelle Blvd, Los Angeles (90025-3207)
PHONE..................310 477-5501
Eugene Tipo, *Administration*
Rizaldo Rickafort, *Administration*
EMP: 150
SALES (corp-wide): 18.9MM **Privately Held**
WEB: www.newvista.us
SIC: 8059 8051 Nursing home, except skilled & intermediate care facility; skilled nursing care facilities
PA: New Vista Health Services, Inc
1987 Vartikian Ave
Clovis CA 93611
559 298-3236

(P-21165)
NEW VISTA HEALTH SERVICES
Also Called: New Vsta Nrsing Rhbltation Ctr
8647 Fenwick St, Sunland (91040-1957)
PHONE..................818 352-1421
Robert Craig, *President*
Alexis Remington-Perez, *Vice Pres*
Jesus Beraza, *Purch Mgr*
EMP: 130
SALES (est): 2.5MM
SALES (corp-wide): 18.9MM **Privately Held**
WEB: www.newvista.us
SIC: 8059 8361 Nursing home, except skilled & intermediate care facility; rehabilitation center, residential: health care incidental
PA: New Vista Health Services, Inc
1987 Vartikian Ave
Clovis CA 93611
559 298-3236

(P-21166)
NORCAL CARE CENTERS INC
Also Called: Antioch Convalescent Hospital
1210 A St, Antioch (94509-2327)
PHONE..................925 757-8787
Thaylene Sunga, *Manager*
EMP: 80
SALES (est): 3.2MM
SALES (corp-wide): 2MM **Privately Held**
SIC: 8059 Nursing home, except skilled & intermediate care facility
PA: Norcal Care Centers Inc
3788 Fairway Dr
Cameron Park CA
530 677-9477

(P-21167)
NORTHERN CA CNGRGTNL RTMT
Also Called: Carmel Valley Manor
8545 Carmel Valley Rd, Carmel (93923-9556)
PHONE..................831 624-1281
Roger D Bolgard, *Ch of Bd*
Jane Ipsen, *CEO*
Richard Boluga, *CFO*
James Valentine, *Administration*
Toni Ford, *Director*
EMP: 162 EST: 1960
SQ FT: 196,800
SALES: 16.8MM **Privately Held**
WEB: www.cvmanor.com
SIC: 8059 Convalescent home

(P-21168)
NORTHERN CALIFORNIA PRESBYTERI
Also Called: Tamal Pais
501 Via Casitas Ofc, Greenbrae (94904-1958)
PHONE..................415 464-1767
EMP: 100
SALES (corp-wide): 69.3MM **Privately Held**
WEB: www.contracostasbdc.com
SIC: 8059 8062 8051 8052 Rest home, with health care; general medical & surgical hospitals; skilled nursing care facilities; intermediate care facilities
PA: Northern California Presbyterian Homes And Services, Inc.
1525 Post St
San Francisco CA 94109
415 922-0200

(P-21169)
NORTHGATE CARE CENTER
40 Professional Ctr Pkwy, San Rafael (94903-2703)
PHONE..................415 479-1230
Jeremy Zrimes, *President*
EMP: 52 EST: 1970
SQ FT: 11,000
SALES (est): 3.3MM
SALES (corp-wide): 11.6MM **Privately Held**
WEB: www.iqcare.com
SIC: 8059 Convalescent home
PA: Independent Quality Care, Inc
3 Crow Canyon Ct
San Ramon CA 94583
925 855-0881

(P-21170)
NOTELLAGE CORPORATION
Also Called: College Vsta Convalescent Hosp
4681 Eagle Rock Blvd, Los Angeles (90041-3036)
PHONE..................323 257-8151
Michael Stifere, *Administration*
EMP: 50
SQ FT: 10,000
SALES (est): 2.3MM **Privately Held**
SIC: 8059 Convalescent home

(P-21171)
OAKVIEW CONVALESCENT HOSPITAL
9166 Tujunga Canyon Blvd, Tujunga (91042-3498)
PHONE..................818 352-4426
Ben Garrett, *President*
Christen Garrett, *Treasurer*
Clyde Casner, *Vice Pres*
Eva Casner, *Admin Sec*
EMP: 50
SALES (est): 1.7MM **Privately Held**
SIC: 8059 Convalescent home

(P-21172)
ODYSSEY HEALTHCARE INC
74350 Country Club Dr, Palm Desert (92260-1608)
PHONE..................760 674-0066
Candice Heldenbrand, *Manager*
EMP: 50
SALES (corp-wide): 6B **Privately Held**
SIC: 8059 Convalescent home

P R O D U C T S & S V C S

HQ: Odyssey Healthcare, Inc.
7801 Mesquite Bend Dr # 105
Irving TX 75063

(P-21173)
OLYMPIA CONVALESCENT HOSPITAL
1100 S Alvarado St, Los Angeles (90006-4110)
PHONE..................213 487-3000
Otto Schwartz, *Administration*
Sam Lidell, *Ltd Ptnr*
Andre Pollak, *Ltd Ptnr*
Marco Cantoreggi, *Director*
EMP: 115
SQ FT: 25,000
SALES (est): 3.9MM **Privately Held**
SIC: 8059 8051 Convalescent home; skilled nursing care facilities

(P-21174)
ON MY OWN INDEPENDENT LIVING
920 1st St W, Sonoma (95476-7417)
PHONE..................707 938-9156
EMP: 60
SALES (est): 427.9K **Privately Held**
SIC: 8059 Nursing & personal care

(P-21175)
ORANGE COUNTY ROYALE CONVLSCNT (PA)
1030 W Warner Ave, Santa Ana (92707-3147)
PHONE..................714 546-6450
Mitchell Kantor, *President*
Harriet Ochoa, *Admin Asst*
Donald Connelly, *Administration*
Mike Pierson, *Administration*
Ignacio Robles, *Maintence Staff*
EMP: 330
SQ FT: 87,000
SALES (est): 18.9MM **Privately Held**
WEB: www.royalehealth.com
SIC: 8059 8051 Convalescent home; skilled nursing care facilities

(P-21176)
ORINDA CONVALESCENT HOSPITAL
11 Altarinda Rd, Orinda (94563-2602)
PHONE..................925 254-6500
David Cronin, *President*
Charles Speers, *Administration*
EMP: 52
SQ FT: 5,000
SALES (est): 3.5MM **Privately Held**
SIC: 8059 Convalescent home

(P-21177)
OUR HOUSE RESIDENTIAL CARE CTR
109 E Central Ave, Madera (93638-3109)
PHONE..................559 674-8670
Carolyn Pipes, *Owner*
EMP: 70
SALES (est): 2.5MM **Privately Held**
SIC: 8059 Rest home, with health care

(P-21178)
PACIFIC GROVE CNVALESCENT HOSP
200 Lighthouse Ave, Pacific Grove (93950-3022)
PHONE..................831 375-2695
John Lund, *Owner*
John P Jones, *Manager*
EMP: 60
SALES (est): 1.2MM **Privately Held**
SIC: 8059 Convalescent home

(P-21179)
PACIFIC HAVEN CONVALESCENT HM
Also Called: Pacific Haven Convalescent HM
12072 Trask Ave, Garden Grove (92843-3881)
PHONE..................714 534-1942
Mike Uranga, *Administration*
Allan Chou, *Director*
EMP: 100

SALES (est): 8.7MM **Privately Held**
SIC: 8059 8051 Convalescent home; skilled nursing care facilities

(P-21180)
PACIFIC HOMES FOUNDATION
303 N Lennox Glenoaks 1000 # 1000, Burbank (91502)
PHONE..................818 729-8106
Gary Wheeler, *CEO*
Mort Swales, *CEO*
EMP: 70 EST: 2001
SALES: 1.8MM **Privately Held**
SIC: 8059 Nursing home, except skilled & intermediate care facility

(P-21181)
PALADIN HOME CARE
555 Pierce St Ste Cml 4, Albany (94706-1078)
PHONE..................510 526-2273
Shaun M Charles, *Principal*
EMP: 50
SALES (est): 431.6K **Privately Held**
SIC: 8059 Personal care home, with health care

(P-21182)
PALM HARBOR RESIDENCY LP
Also Called: Palmcrest North Convalescent
3501 Cedar Ave, Long Beach (90807-3809)
PHONE..................562 595-4551
Leonard Muskin, *General Ptnr*
EMP: 200 EST: 1971
SQ FT: 120,000
SALES: 2.5MM **Privately Held**
SIC: 8059 8052 Convalescent home; intermediate care facilities

(P-21183)
PARAMOUNT CONVALESCENT GROUP
8558 Rosecrans Ave, Paramount (90723-3644)
PHONE..................562 634-6895
Irving Bauman, *President*
Zeny Evaldez, *Manager*
EMP: 65
SQ FT: 12,000
SALES (est): 2.3MM **Privately Held**
SIC: 8059 Nursing home, except skilled & intermediate care facility

(P-21184)
PARK MARINO CONVALESCENT CTR
2585 E Washington Blvd, Pasadena (91107-1446)
PHONE..................626 463-4105
William Kite, *Administration*
EMP: 50 EST: 1966
SALES (est): 828K
SALES (corp-wide): 5.3MM **Privately Held**
SIC: 8059 8051 Convalescent home; skilled nursing care facilities
PA: Diversified Health Services (Del)
136 Washington Ave
Richmond CA 94801
510 231-6200

(P-21185)
PEOPLE CREATING SUCCESS INC (PA)
2585 Teller Rd, Newbury Park (91320-2220)
PHONE..................805 375-9222
Jason Romero, *President*
Angela Buse, *CFO*
EMP: 400
SALES (est): 12.8MM **Privately Held**
SIC: 8059 Personal care home, with health care

(P-21186)
PILGRIM PLACE IN CLAREMONT (PA)
625 Mayflower Rd, Claremont (91711-4240)
PHONE..................909 399-5500
William R Cunitz, *President*
Sue Fairley, *Vice Pres*
Bernard Valek, *Vice Pres*
Joyce Yarborough, *Vice Pres*

Mary Ann Macias, *Director*
EMP: 175
SQ FT: 2,000
SALES: 17.9MM **Privately Held**
WEB: www.pilgrimplace.org
SIC: 8059 8051 8052 Rest home, with health care; skilled nursing care facilities; intermediate care facilities

(P-21187)
PLACERVLLE PNES CNVLSCENT HOSP
1040 Marshall Way, Placerville (95667-5706)
PHONE..................530 622-3400
Jared Edmunds, *Administration*
Laurie Brady, *Nursing Dir*
EMP: 130
SQ FT: 40,000
SALES (est): 2.8MM
SALES (corp-wide): 103.7MM **Privately Held**
WEB: www.villadelrey.com
SIC: 8059 8051 Convalescent home; skilled nursing care facilities
HQ: Horizon West Healthcare, Inc.
4020 Sierra College Blvd # 190
Rocklin CA 95677
916 624-6230

(P-21188)
PLEASANT VIEW CONVALESCENT HOS
22590 Voss Ave, Cupertino (95014-2627)
PHONE..................408 253-9034
Jack Easterday, *President*
Jet Rupisan, *Administration*
EMP: 140
SQ FT: 55,000
SALES (est): 4.5MM **Privately Held**
SIC: 8059 8069 8051 Convalescent home; specialty hospitals, except psychiatric; skilled nursing care facilities

(P-21189)
PORCHLIGHT INC
Also Called: Scan
3800 Kilroy Airport Way, Long Beach (90806-2494)
P.O. Box 22616 (90801-5616)
PHONE..................562 989-5100
Jay Greenberg, *President*
Sue Cameron, *COO*
Michael Lombardi, *Chief Mktg Ofcr*
Christian Zorn, *Vice Pres*
Nancy M Monk, *Risk Mgmt Dir*
EMP: 100
SALES (est): 9.4MM
SALES (corp-wide): 329.7MM **Privately Held**
WEB: www.scanhealthplan.com
SIC: 8059 Personal care home, with health care
PA: Senior Care Action Network Foundation
3800 Kilroy Airport Way
Long Beach CA 90806
562 989-5100

(P-21190)
PRUITTHEALTH INC
Also Called: United Care Homes
1982 Camwood Ave, City of Industry (91748-4044)
PHONE..................626 810-5567
Susana Tubianosa, *Branch Mgr*
EMP: 50
SALES (corp-wide): 387.8MM **Privately Held**
WEB: www.peachtreechristianhospice.com
SIC: 8059 Convalescent home
PA: Pruitthealth, Inc.
1626 Jeurgens Ct
Norcross GA 30093
770 279-6200

(P-21191)
RAFAEL CONVALESCENT HOSPITAL
234 N San Pedro Rd, San Rafael (94903-2858)
PHONE..................415 479-3450
Timothy J Egan, *President*
Michael Egan, *Admin Sec*
EMP: 180
SQ FT: 9,000

SALES (est): 10.6MM **Privately Held**
SIC: 8059 8051 Convalescent home; skilled nursing care facilities

(P-21192)
RCC FACILITY INCORPORATED
Also Called: Rounseville Rehabilitation Ctr
210 40th Street Way, Oakland (94611-5612)
PHONE..................510 658-2041
Jack Easterday, *President*
EMP: 70
SQ FT: 10,000
SALES: 6.7MM **Privately Held**
SIC: 8059 Convalescent home

(P-21193)
REDLANDS CMNTY HOSP FOUNDATION
Also Called: Asistencia Villa
1875 Barton Rd, Redlands (92373-5308)
PHONE..................909 793-1382
Ron Dahlgren, *Manager*
EMP: 101
SALES (corp-wide): 1.1MM **Privately Held**
WEB: www.redlandshospital.com
SIC: 8059 8051 8093 Convalescent home; skilled nursing care facilities; rehabilitation center, outpatient treatment
PA: Redlands Community Hospital Foundation
350 Terracina Blvd
Redlands CA 92373
909 335-5540

(P-21194)
REDWOOD CONVALESCENT HOSPITAL
22103 Redwood Rd, Castro Valley (94546-7173)
PHONE..................510 537-8848
Frank V Kreske MD, *President*
Elizabeth Kreske, *Vice Pres*
EMP: 56
SQ FT: 10,000
SALES (est): 4MM **Privately Held**
SIC: 8059 Convalescent home

(P-21195)
REYNOLDS HEALTH INDUSTRIES
Also Called: Skylight Convalescent Center
1201 Walnut Ave, Long Beach (90813-3822)
PHONE..................562 591-7621
Caul Murayama, *President*
Vicki Reynolds, *Vice Pres*
EMP: 70
SQ FT: 21,000
SALES: 2.1MM **Privately Held**
SIC: 8059 Convalescent home

(P-21196)
RIVER OAK CENTER FOR CHILDREN
5445 Laurel Hills Dr, Sacramento (95841-3105)
PHONE..................916 550-5600
EMP: 94
SALES (corp-wide): 13.5MM **Privately Held**
SIC: 8059 8063
PA: River Oak Center For Children
5445 Laurel Hills Dr
Sacramento CA 95841
916 609-5100

(P-21197)
RIVERSIDE CNVALESCENT HOSP INC (PA)
Also Called: RIVERSIDE CONVALESCENT HOSPIT
375 Cohasset Rd, Chico (95926-2211)
PHONE..................530 343-5595
Gladys Jennings, *President*
Michael Lunsford, *Director*
EMP: 72 EST: 1963
SQ FT: 50,000
SALES: 7.1MM **Privately Held**
SIC: 8059 Convalescent home

▲ = Import ▼=Export
◆ =Import/Export

(P-21198)
RIVERSIDE HEALTH CARE CORP
Also Called: Scenic Circle Care Center
1611 Scenic Dr, Modesto (95355-4907)
PHONE....................................209 523-5667
Jim Dickinson, *Branch Mgr*
EMP: 80
SALES (corp-wide): 9.4MM **Privately Held**
SIC: 8059 Nursing home, except skilled & intermediate care facility
PA: Riverside Health Care Corporation
     1469 Humboldt Rd Ste 175
     Chico CA 95928
     530 897-5100

(P-21199)
RIVERSIDE HEALTH CARE CORP (PA)
1469 Humboldt Rd Ste 175, Chico
(95928-9204)
PHONE....................................530 897-5100
Sharon Jennings Kearns, *CEO*
EMP: 60
SQ FT: 9,000
SALES (est): 9.4MM **Privately Held**
SIC: 8059 Convalescent home

(P-21200)
ROCK CANYON HEALTHCARE INC
Also Called: Riverwalk PST-Cute Rhblitation
27101 Puerta Real Ste 450, Mission Viejo
(92691-8566)
PHONE....................................949 487-9500
Dave Jorgensen, *President*
Soon Burnam, *Treasurer*
Beverly Wittekind, *Admin Sec*
EMP: 415 EST: 2014
SALES (est): 1.9MM
SALES (corp-wide): 1.8B **Publicly Held**
SIC: 8059 Personal care home, with health care
PA: The Ensign Group Inc
     27101 Puerta Real Ste 450
     Mission Viejo CA 92691
     949 487-9500

(P-21201)
SABU ENTERPRISES INC
Also Called: Idle Acres Convalescent Hosp
5044 Buffington Rd, El Monte
(91732-1466)
PHONE....................................626 443-1351
Solomon Silverberg, *President*
Uri Mendelbaum, *Vice Pres*
Barry Silverberg, *Director*
EMP: 50
SQ FT: 17,000
SALES (est): 1.8MM **Privately Held**
SIC: 8059 Convalescent home

(P-21202)
SAN BERNARDINO CARE COMPANY
467 E Gilbert St, San Bernardino
(92404-5318)
PHONE....................................909 884-4781
Jenq Chen, *President*
EMP: 110
SALES (est): 196.3K **Privately Held**
SIC: 8059 Convalescent home

(P-21203)
SAN DIEGO CENTER FOR CHILDREN (PA)
3002 Armstrong St, San Diego
(92111-5702)
PHONE....................................858 277-9550
Moises Baron, *CEO*
EMP: 90
SQ FT: 38,000
SALES: 21.5MM **Privately Held**
WEB: www.centerforchildren.org
SIC: 8059 8361 Personal care home, with health care; residential care

(P-21204)
SAN MARINO MANOR
6812 Oak Ave, San Gabriel (91775-2099)
PHONE....................................626 446-5263
Ruth Jackson, *Administration*
Solomon Silberberg, *Treasurer*

Mike Elbert, *Administration*
Barry Silberberg, *Administration*
EMP: 50
SALES: 3.3MM **Privately Held**
SIC: 8059 Convalescent home

(P-21205)
SECROM INC
Also Called: Carson Senior Assisted Living
345 E Carson St, Carson (90745-2709)
PHONE....................................310 830-4010
Shlomo Rechnitz, *CEO*
EMP: 55
SALES (est): 950.8K **Privately Held**
SIC: 8059 Rest home, with health care

(P-21206)
SHASTA CONVALESCENT CENTER
Also Called: Shasta Convalescent Hospital
3550 Churn Creek Rd, Redding
(96002-2718)
PHONE....................................530 222-3630
Donald Ostrom, *President*
Marlene Ostrom, *Vice Pres*
EMP: 180 EST: 1969
SQ FT: 38,000
SALES (est): 4.2MM **Privately Held**
SIC: 8059 8051 Convalescent home; nursing home, except skilled & intermediate care facility; skilled nursing care facilities

(P-21207)
SIERRA VALLEY REHAB CENTER
301 W Putnam Ave, Porterville
(93257-3429)
PHONE....................................559 784-7375
Steve Brown, *Administration*
Emmanuel B David, *President*
Ramona Villaluz, *Treasurer*
EMP: 170
SQ FT: 26,000
SALES (est): 5.7MM **Privately Held**
SIC: 8059 8051 Convalescent home; skilled nursing care facilities

(P-21208)
SILVERADO SENIOR LIVING INC
Also Called: Bay Area At Home
1301 Ralston Ave Ste A, Belmont
(94002-1961)
PHONE....................................650 226-8017
Constanza Pierre, *Hlthcr Dir*
EMP: 54
SALES (corp-wide): 180.3MM **Privately Held**
SIC: 8059 Personal care home, with health care
PA: Senior Silverado Living Inc
     6400 Oak Cyn Ste 200
     Irvine CA 92618
     949 240-7200

(P-21209)
SILVERADO SENIOR LIVING INC (PA)
6400 Oak Cyn Ste 200, Irvine
(92618-5233)
PHONE....................................949 240-7200
George L Chapman, *CEO*
Rick Barker, *President*
Daizel Gasperian, *President*
Kathy Greene, *President*
Shannon Gutierrez, *President*
EMP: 65 EST: 1996
SQ FT: 65,000
SALES (est): 180.3MM **Privately Held**
WEB: www.silveradosenior.com
SIC: 8059 Personal care home, with health care

(P-21210)
SILVERADO SENIOR LIVING INC
Also Called: Sierra Vista Memory Care Cmnty
125 W Sierra Madre Ave, Azusa
(91702-2023)
P.O. Box 636 (91702-0636)
PHONE....................................626 650-9891
Bida Gwinn, *Manager*
Maria Torres, *Admin Asst*
EMP: 54

SALES (corp-wide): 180.3MM **Privately Held**
WEB: www.silveradosenior.com
SIC: 8059 8051 Personal care home, with health care; skilled nursing care facilities
PA: Senior Silverado Living Inc
     6400 Oak Cyn Ste 200
     Irvine CA 92618
     949 240-7200

(P-21211)
SILVERADO SENIOR LIVING INC
Also Called: Newport Mesa Memory Care Cmnty
350 W Bay St, Costa Mesa (92627-2020)
PHONE....................................949 945-0189
Michelle Egrer, *Administration*
Lee Riggs, *COO*
Raul Parra, *Opers Mgr*
Jamie Langston, *Hlthcr Dir*
EMP: 70
SQ FT: 20,331
SALES (corp-wide): 180.3MM **Privately Held**
WEB: www.silveradosenior.com
SIC: 8059 Personal care home, with health care
PA: Senior Silverado Living Inc
     6400 Oak Cyn Ste 200
     Irvine CA 92618
     949 240-7200

(P-21212)
SILVERADO SENIOR LIVING INC
Also Called: Huntington Memory Care Cmnty
1118 N Stoneman Ave, Alhambra
(91801-1007)
PHONE....................................626 872-3941
Vida Gwin, *Administration*
Tamra Mitchell, *Human Res Dir*
EMP: 50
SALES (corp-wide): 180.3MM **Privately Held**
WEB: www.silveradosenior.com
SIC: 8059 Personal care home, with health care
PA: Senior Silverado Living Inc
     6400 Oak Cyn Ste 200
     Irvine CA 92618
     949 240-7200

(P-21213)
SILVERADO SENIOR LIVING INC
Also Called: Escondido Memory Care Cmnty
1500 Borden Rd, Escondido (92026-2373)
PHONE....................................760 456-5137
Jean Busher, *Administration*
Thomas V Croal, *Technology*
EMP: 91
SQ FT: 33,000
SALES (corp-wide): 180.3MM **Privately Held**
WEB: www.silveradosenior.com
SIC: 8059 Personal care home, with health care
PA: Senior Silverado Living Inc
     6400 Oak Cyn Ste 200
     Irvine CA 92618
     949 240-7200

(P-21214)
SILVERADO SENIOR LIVING INC
Also Called: Encinitas Memory Care Cmnty
335 Saxony Rd, Encinitas (92024-2723)
PHONE....................................760 270-9917
Dina Trester, *Director*
Thomas V Croal, *CFO*
Jolene Farish, *Asst Director*
EMP: 70
SALES (corp-wide): 180.3MM **Privately Held**
WEB: www.silveradosenior.com
SIC: 8059 Personal care home, with health care
PA: Senior Silverado Living Inc
     6400 Oak Cyn Ste 200
     Irvine CA 92618
     949 240-7200

(P-21215)
SILVERADO SENIOR LIVING INC
Also Called: Tustin Hcnda Memory Care Cmnty
240 E 3rd St, Tustin (92780-3623)
PHONE....................................657 888-5752
EMP: 54

SALES (corp-wide): 180.3MM **Privately Held**
WEB: www.silveradosenior.com
SIC: 8059 Personal care home, with health care; skilled nursing care facilities
PA: Senior Silverado Living Inc
     6400 Oak Cyn Ste 200
     Irvine CA 92618
     949 240-7200

(P-21216)
SILVERADO SENIOR LIVING INC
Also Called: Beverly Pl Memory Care Cmnty
330 N Hayworth Ave, Los Angeles
(90048-2702)
PHONE....................................323 984-7313
Beth Medina, *Principal*
Monica Westphaln, *Administration*
EMP: 73
SALES (corp-wide): 180.3MM **Privately Held**
SIC: 8059 Personal care home, with health care
PA: Senior Silverado Living Inc
     6400 Oak Cyn Ste 200
     Irvine CA 92618
     949 240-7200

(P-21217)
SILVERSCREEN HEALTHCARE INC
Also Called: Asistencia Villa Rehab & Care
1875 Barton Rd, Redlands (92373-5308)
PHONE....................................909 793-1382
Philip Weinberger, *CEO*
Marylynn Mahan, *CFO*
Tracey Johns, *Exec Dir*
EMP: 135 EST: 2010
SALES (est): 4.4MM **Privately Held**
SIC: 8059 8322 Convalescent home; rehabilitation services

(P-21218)
SISTERS OF NAZARETH
Also Called: Nazareth House
245 Nova Albion Way, San Rafael
(94903-3539)
PHONE....................................415 479-8282
Sister Rose Hoye, *Principal*
Sister John Berchmans, *Administration*
Alice Lynch, *Administration*
EMP: 91
SALES (est): 3.9MM **Privately Held**
SIC: 8059 8051 Rest home, with health care; skilled nursing care facilities

(P-21219)
SPRINGHILL MANOR REHABILITATIO
Also Called: Spring Hl Mnor Cnvlescent Hosp
355 Joerschke Dr, Grass Valley
(95945-5288)
PHONE....................................530 273-7247
Brian Collier, *Principal*
Patricia Vixie, *Treasurer*
Gregory Vixie, *Vice Pres*
EMP: 50 EST: 1966
SQ FT: 14,000
SALES: 8.5MM **Privately Held**
SIC: 8059 Convalescent home

(P-21220)
SSC PITTSBURG OPERATING CO LP
Also Called: Diamond Ridge Healthcare Ctr
2351 Loveridge Rd, Pittsburg (94565-5117)
PHONE....................................925 427-4444
Wayne M Sanner,
EMP: 2836
SALES: 14MM
SALES (corp-wide): 1.2B **Privately Held**
SIC: 8059 Nursing home, except skilled & intermediate care facility
PA: Savaseniorcare, Llc
     1 Ravinia Dr Ste 1500
     Atlanta GA 30346
     770 829-5100

(P-21221)
ST FRANCIS EXTENDED CARE INC
718 Bartlett Ave, Hayward (94541-3698)
PHONE....................................510 785-3630
Sally Rapp, *President*
Roland Rapp, *Vice Pres*
Elizabeth Gonzalez, *Personnel*

EMP: 67
SQ FT: 13,120
SALES: 5.9MM **Privately Held**
SIC: 8059 Convalescent home

(P-21222)
ST FRANCIS HTS CONVALESCENT
35 Escuela Dr, Daly City (94015-4003)
PHONE..................650 755-9515
Kordel Erickson, *Administration*
Evelyn Goddard, *Principal*
Kathleen Lovato, *Administration*
Glen Gotter, *Director*
EMP: 100 EST: 1967
SQ FT: 12,000
SALES (est): 2.7MM **Privately Held**
WEB: www.sfhouseprices.net
SIC: 8059 8051 Convalescent home;
skilled nursing care facilities

(P-21223)
ST JOHNS RETIREMENT VILLAGE (PA)
Also Called: Stollwood Convalescent Hosp
135 Woodland Ave, Woodland
(95695-2701)
PHONE..................530 662-9674
John Prichard, *Administration*
Theresa Ely, *CFO*
Maryann Adams, *Human Res Dir*
Maryann Frisbee, *Hum Res Coord*
Janet Martinez, *Hlthcr Dir*
EMP: 142 EST: 1964
SALES: 9.7MM **Privately Held**
SIC: 8059 8051 8361 Convalescent
home; convalescent home with continu-
ous nursing care; geriatric residential
care; home for the aged; rest home, with
health care incidental

(P-21224)
STOCKTON EDSON HEALTHCARE CORP
Also Called: GOOD SAMARITAN REHAB
AND CARE
1630 N Edison St, Stockton (95204-5633)
PHONE..................209 948-8762
Emanuel Bernabe, *President*
Gilda Dizon, *Corp Secy*
Sedy Demesa, *Exec VP*
EMP: 100
SQ FT: 4,000
SALES: 8.4MM **Privately Held**
SIC: 8059 8051 Nursing home, except
skilled & intermediate care facility; skilled
nursing care facilities

(P-21225)
SUN MAR NURSING CENTER INC
Also Called: SUN MAR MANAGEMENT
SERVICES
1720 W Orange Ave, Anaheim
(92804-2699)
PHONE..................714 776-1720
Chris William, *Administration*
Blaine Hendrickson, *President*
Bill Presnell, *Corp Secy*
EMP: 75
SQ FT: 10,000
SALES: 8.2MM **Privately Held**
SIC: 8059 Nursing home, except skilled &
intermediate care facility

(P-21226)
SUNNY RETIREMENT HOME
22445 Cupertino Rd, Cupertino
(95014-1052)
PHONE..................408 454-5600
Sally Plank, *Exec Dir*
Jonathan Shaw, *Food Svc Dir*
Bethany Dinh, *Director*
Nelson Rodriguez, *Director*
EMP: 140 EST: 1964
SQ FT: 112,000
SALES: 2.9MM **Privately Held**
WEB: www.sunny4care.com
SIC: 8059 Rest home, with health care

(P-21227)
SYCAMORE PARK CARE CENTER LLC
Also Called: SYCAMORE PARK CONVALES-
CENT HOSPITAL
4585 N Figueroa St, Los Angeles
(90065-3026)
PHONE..................323 223-3441
Robert Snukal, *President*
Consolacion Padama, *Corp Secy*
Manuel Padama, *Vice Pres*
Sheila Snukal, *Vice Pres*
▲ EMP: 80
SQ FT: 20,000
SALES (est): 5.1MM **Publicly Held**
WEB: www.skilledhealthcare.com
SIC: 8059 8051 Convalescent home;
skilled nursing care facilities
PA: Genesis Healthcare, Inc.
101 E State St
Kennett Square PA 19348

(P-21228)
TEMPLE PARK CONVALESCENT HOSP
2411 W Temple St, Los Angeles
(90026-4899)
PHONE..................213 380-2035
Barry Kohn, *President*
Toby Kohn, *Vice Pres*
EMP: 77
SALES (est): 4.2MM **Privately Held**
SIC: 8059 Convalescent home

(P-21229)
TJD LLC
Also Called: Anberry Rehabilitation Hosp
1685 Shaffer Rd, Atwater (95301-4456)
PHONE..................209 357-3420
Donald W Gormly Jr,
Nancy Romero, *Education*
Sara Choudhry, *Nursing Dir*
Jerry Holloway,
EMP: 140
SQ FT: 40,000
SALES: 11.9MM **Privately Held**
WEB: www.anberryhospital.com
SIC: 8059 8051 8093 Nursing home, ex-
cept skilled & intermediate care facility;
convalescent home with continuous nurs-
ing care; rehabilitation center, outpatient
treatment

(P-21230)
TRANQUILITY INCORPORATED
Also Called: San Miguel Villa
1050 San Miguel Rd, Concord
(94518-2094)
PHONE..................925 825-4280
Velda Pierce, *CEO*
EMP: 180
SQ FT: 20,000
SALES: 15.7MM **Privately Held**
SIC: 8059 8051 Convalescent home;
skilled nursing care facilities

(P-21231)
TRINITY HEALTH SYSTEMS
Also Called: Valley Palms Convalescent Hosp
13400 Sherman Way, North Hollywood
(91605-4415)
PHONE..................818 983-0103
Roland Santos, *Manager*
EMP: 100
SALES (corp-wide): 9.1MM **Privately
Held**
SIC: 8059 8051 Convalescent home;
skilled nursing care facilities
PA: Trinity Health Systems
14318 Ohio St
Baldwin Park CA 91706
626 960-1971

(P-21232)
TWO PALMS NURSING CENTER INC (PA)
2637 E Washington Blvd, Pasadena
(91107-1412)
PHONE..................626 798-8991
Marthann Demchuk, *CEO*
EMP: 50
SALES (est): 7.7MM **Privately Held**
SIC: 8059 Convalescent home

(P-21233)
TWO PALMS NURSING CENTER INC
Also Called: Marlinda Imperial Hospital
150 Bellefontaine St, Pasadena
(91105-3102)
PHONE..................626 796-1103
EMP: 85
SQ FT: 28,955
SALES (corp-wide): 7.7MM **Privately
Held**
SIC: 8059 8051 Convalescent home;
skilled nursing care facilities
PA: Two Palms Nursing Center, Inc.
2637 E Washington Blvd
Pasadena CA 91107
626 798-8991

(P-21234)
TWO PALMS NURSING CENTER INC
150 Bellefontaine St, Pasadena
(91105-3102)
PHONE..................323 681-4615
Marthann Demchuk, *Manager*
EMP: 100
SALES (corp-wide): 7.7MM **Privately
Held**
SIC: 8059 8051 Convalescent home;
skilled nursing care facilities
PA: Two Palms Nursing Center, Inc.
2637 E Washington Blvd
Pasadena CA 91107
626 798-8991

(P-21235)
TZIPPY CARE INC
Also Called: Western Convalescent Hospital
2190 W Adams Blvd, Los Angeles
(90018-2039)
PHONE..................323 737-7778
David Friedman, *President*
Ken Lehman, *Corp Secy*
Aaron Friedman, *Vice Pres*
EMP: 95
SALES: 12.8MM **Privately Held**
SIC: 8059 Convalescent home

(P-21236)
UNITED CONVALESCENT FACILITIES
Also Called: University Park Healthcare Ctr
230 E Adams Blvd, Los Angeles
(90011-1426)
PHONE..................626 629-6950
Doug Easton, *Owner*
Deshan Campbell, *Personnel*
EMP: 80
SQ FT: 1,300
SALES: 4MM **Privately Held**
SIC: 8059 Nursing home, except skilled &
intermediate care facility

(P-21237)
UNITED CP/S CHLDRNS FNDN LA
Also Called: Ucp Dronfield North
13272 Dronfield Ave, Sylmar (91342-2961)
PHONE..................818 364-5911
Liz McLaughlin, *Administration*
EMP: 70
SALES (corp-wide): 26.4MM **Privately
Held**
SIC: 8059 Home for the mentally retarded,
exc. skilled or intermediate
PA: United Cerebral Palsy/Spastic Chil-
dren's Foundation Of Los Angeles And
Ventura Counties
6430 Independence Ave
Woodland Hills CA 91367
818 782-2211

(P-21238)
UNITED CP/S CHLDRNS FNDN LA
6430 Independence Ave, Woodland Hills
(91367-2607)
PHONE..................818 782-2211
Mae Stephenson, *General Mgr*
EMP: 70
SALES (corp-wide): 26.4MM **Privately
Held**
SIC: 8059 Personal care home, with health
care

PA: United Cerebral Palsy/Spastic Children's Foundation Of Los Angeles And
Ventura Counties
6430 Independence Ave
Woodland Hills CA 91367
818 782-2211

(P-21239)
UNITED MEDICAL MANAGEMENT INC
Also Called: Valley Healthcare
1680 N Waterman Ave, San Bernardino
(92404-5113)
PHONE..................909 886-5291
Alan Hull, *Administration*
EMP: 125
SQ FT: 30,000
SALES (est): 5.3MM **Privately Held**
WEB: www.healthcare-centers.com
SIC: 8059 8051 8322 Convalescent
home; skilled nursing care facilities; reha-
bilitation services

(P-21240)
UPLAND COMMUNITY CARE INC
Also Called: Upland Rehabilitation Care Ctr
1221 E Arrow Hwy, Upland (91786-4911)
PHONE..................909 985-1903
Owen Hammond, *CEO*
Nora Moscozo, *Human Res Dir*
Beverly Hughes, *Chf Purch Ofc*
EMP: 99
SALES (est): 3MM
SALES (corp-wide): 1.8B **Publicly Held**
SIC: 8059 Convalescent home
PA: The Ensign Group Inc
27101 Puerta Real Ste 450
Mission Viejo CA 92691
949 487-9500

(P-21241)
VACAVLLE CNVALESCENT REHAB CTR
585 Nut Tree Ct, Vacaville (95687-3353)
PHONE..................707 449-8000
Joe Nicolli, *President*
EMP: 120
SQ FT: 38,000
SALES (est): 6MM **Privately Held**
SIC: 8059 Convalescent home

(P-21242)
VALENCIA HEALTH CARE INC
Also Called: Santa Clarita Convalescent HM
23801 Newhall Ave, Newhall (91321-3126)
PHONE..................661 254-2425
Ishkhan Khatchadurian, *President*
Armand Masongsong, *Director*
EMP: 75 EST: 1969
SQ FT: 24,000
SALES: 3.9MM **Privately Held**
SIC: 8059 Convalescent home

(P-21243)
VALLE VSTA CNVLESCENT HOSP INC
1025 W 2nd Ave, Escondido (92025-3839)
PHONE..................760 745-1288
Kristina Kuivon, *CEO*
EMP: 85 EST: 1961
SQ FT: 19,000
SALES (est): 2.7MM **Privately Held**
SIC: 8059 Convalescent home; nursing
home, except skilled & intermediate care
facility
PA: Covenant Care, Llc
27071 Aliso Creek Rd # 100
Aliso Viejo CA 92656

(P-21244)
VALLEY WEST HEALTH CARE INC (PA)
Also Called: Valley West Care Center
1224 E St, Williams (95987)
P.O. Box 1059 (95987-1059)
PHONE..................530 473-5321
Sharon Jennings, *President*
Gladys Jennings, *CFO*
EMP: 95
SQ FT: 32,000
SALES (est): 4.2MM **Privately Held**
SIC: 8059 Convalescent home

▲ = Import ▼=Export
◆ =Import/Export

(P-21245)
VAN NUYS CARE CENTER INC
Also Called: Lake Balboa Care Center
16955 Vanowen St, Van Nuys
(91406-4542)
PHONE..............................818 343-0700
Chad Thornton, *President*
John Thornton, *President*
Wayne A Evans, *Vice Pres*
Ana Rosa Aguilar, *Director*
Paolo Andres, *Director*
EMP: 88
SQ FT: 12,500
SALES (est): 3.9MM **Privately Held**
SIC: 8059 8051 Convalescent home;
skilled nursing care facilities

(P-21246)
VICTORIA POST ACUTE CARE
654 S Anza St, El Cajon (92020-6602)
PHONE..............................619 440-5005
Ed Dove, *Administration*
Michelle Cook, *Executive Asst*
EMP: 150
SALES (est): 6.6MM **Privately Held**
SIC: 8059 8361 Convalescent home; re-
habilitation center, residential: health care
incidental

(P-21247)
VILLA DE LA MAR INC
Also Called: Bel Vista Convalescent Hosp
5001 E Anaheim St, Long Beach
(90804-3214)
PHONE..............................562 494-5001
Allen Anderson, *Principal*
Barbara Danna, *Office Mgr*
EMP: 50
SALES (corp-wide): 4.2MM **Privately
Held**
WEB: www.villadelafontaine.com
SIC: 8059 Convalescent home
PA: Villa De La Mar, Inc
3901 E 4th St
Long Beach CA

(P-21248)
VILLA SIENA
1855 Miramonte Ave 117, Mountain View
(94040-4029)
PHONE..............................650 961-6484
Corrine Bernard, *CEO*
Margaret McDonnell, *Treasurer*
Mary Ellen Barber, *Nursing Dir*
EMP: 68
SQ FT: 40,000
SALES: 204.5K **Privately Held**
WEB: www.villasiena.com
SIC: 8059 Nursing home, except skilled &
intermediate care facility

(P-21249)
**VINCENT HAYLEY
ENTERPRISES**
Also Called: St Vincent Health Care
1810 N Fair Oaks Ave, Pasadena
(91103-1619)
PHONE..............................626 398-8182
Rob Barrett, *President*
Cipriano Baustista, *Administration*
Ashley McGinty, *Hlthcr Dir*
EMP: 75
SALES (est): 6.5MM **Privately Held**
SIC: 8059 Nursing home, except skilled &
intermediate care facility

(P-21250)
VISTA COVE CARE CENTER
250 March St, Santa Paula (93060-2512)
PHONE..............................805 525-7134
Floyd Rhoades, *President*
Bonatarte Liu, *Treasurer*
Sean Brophy, *Admin Sec*
EMP: 100
SALES (est): 4.6MM **Privately Held**
SIC: 8059 Nursing home, except skilled &
intermediate care facility

(P-21251)
**VISTA PACIFICA ENTERPRISES
INC**
Also Called: Vista Pcifica Convalescent Ctr
3662 Pacific Ave, Riverside (92509-1923)
PHONE..............................951 682-4867

Cheryl Jumonville, *Director*
EMP: 200 **Privately Held**
SIC: 8059 Convalescent home
PA: Vista Pacifica Enterprises, Inc.
3662 Pacific Ave
Riverside CA 92509

(P-21252)
VOCH INC
Also Called: Villa Oaks Convalescent Homes
1920 N Fair Oaks Ave, Pasadena
(91103-1623)
PHONE..............................626 798-1111
Pompeyo Rosales, *Owner*
EMP: 60
SQ FT: 16,000
SALES (est): 2.3MM
SALES (corp-wide): 3.2MM **Privately
Held**
WEB: www.slch.com
SIC: 8059 Convalescent home
PA: Slch, Inc
1920 N Fair Oaks Ave
Pasadena CA 91103
626 798-0558

(P-21253)
WEST COAST HOSPITALS INC
Also Called: Valley Convalescent Hospital
919 Freedom Blvd, Watsonville
(95076-3804)
P.O. Box 1242 (95077-1242)
PHONE..............................831 722-3581
Richard Murphy, *Principal*
EMP: 65
SQ FT: 20,000
SALES: 6.5MM **Privately Held**
SIC: 8059 Convalescent home

(P-21254)
WESTMINSTER GARDENS
1420 Santo Domingo Ave, Duarte
(91010-2698)
PHONE..............................626 359-2571
Judy Thorndyke, *Exec Dir*
EMP: 54
SQ FT: 1,306,800
SALES: 6.3MM **Privately Held**
WEB: www.westgardens.org
SIC: 8059 Rest home, with health care;
nursing home, except skilled & intermedi-
ate care facility

(P-21255)
WICORO INC (HQ)
Also Called: COLONIAL MANOR CONVA-
LESCENT HOSPITAL
919 N Sunset Ave, West Covina
(91790-1244)
PHONE..............................626 962-4489
C David Benfield, *President*
Amber Felix, *Manager*
EMP: 50
SQ FT: 15,000
SALES: 3.3MM
SALES (corp-wide): 3.8MM **Privately
Held**
SIC: 8059 Convalescent home
PA: Care Tech Inc
401 N Central Ave Ste B
Upland CA 91786
909 373-3766

(P-21256)
**WILLOW TREE NURSING
CENTER**
Also Called: Willow Tree Convalescent Hosp
2124 57th Ave, Oakland (94621-4322)
PHONE..............................510 261-2628
Preston SOO, *Administration*
Maria Lew, *Nursing Dir*
Breta Conroy, *Director*
EMP: 90 EST: 1976
SQ FT: 18,000
SALES (est): 4.3MM **Privately Held**
SIC: 8059 8052 Convalescent home; in-
termediate care facilities

(P-21257)
**WILSHIRE HEALTH AND CMNTY
SVCS**
Also Called: Wilshire Nursing & Rehab
290 Heather Ct, Templeton (93465-9738)
PHONE..............................805 434-3035
Jack Doria, *Manager*

EMP: 100
SALES (corp-wide): 13MM **Privately
Held**
SIC: 8059 8051 Convalescent home;
skilled nursing care facilities
PA: Wilshire Health And Community Serv-
ices, Inc.
285 South St Ste J
San Luis Obispo CA 93401
805 547-7025

(P-21258)
**WILSHIRE HLTH & CMNTY SVCS
INC**
Also Called: Hawthorne Convalescent Center
11630 Grevillea Ave, Hawthorne
(90250-2231)
PHONE..............................310 679-9732
Theresa Reyes, *Director*
EMP: 100
SALES (corp-wide): 13MM **Privately
Held**
SIC: 8059 8051 Convalescent home;
skilled nursing care facilities
PA: Wilshire Health And Community Serv-
ices, Inc.
285 South St Ste J
San Luis Obispo CA 93401
805 547-7025

(P-21259)
**WILSHIRE HLTH & CMNTY SVCS
INC**
Also Called: Kings Nrsing Rhabilitaion Hosp
851 Leslie Ln, Hanford (93230-5643)
PHONE..............................559 582-4414
Mark Fisher, *Owner*
EMP: 74
SALES (corp-wide): 13MM **Privately
Held**
SIC: 8059 Convalescent home
PA: Wilshire Health And Community Serv-
ices, Inc.
285 South St Ste J
San Luis Obispo CA 93401
805 547-7025

(P-21260)
**WINDSOR GARDENS
HEALTHCARE C**
1628 B St, Hayward (94541-3020)
PHONE..............................510 582-4636
Lee Samson, *CEO*
Celina Tercias, *Chf Purch Ofc*
EMP: 133
SQ FT: 5,000
SALES: 8.8MM **Privately Held**
SIC: 8059 Convalescent home
PA: Lexington Group International, Inc
9200 W Sunset Blvd # 700
West Hollywood CA 90069

(P-21261)
**WINDSOR MONTEREY CARE
CTR LLC**
1575 Skyline Dr, Monterey (93940-4110)
PHONE..............................831 373-2731
Lawrence Feigen,
Cheryl Cartney, *Administration*
Sushila Singh, *Chf Purch Ofc*
EMP: 95
SALES (est): 4.3MM **Privately Held**
SIC: 8059 Nursing home, except skilled &
intermediate care facility

(P-21262)
**WOODLAND CARE CENTER
LLC**
7120 Corbin Ave, Reseda (91335-3618)
PHONE..............................818 881-4540
Ailean Yosmco, *Principal*
EMP: 100
SALES (est): 2.7MM **Publicly Held**
WEB: www.parkviewnursing.net
SIC: 8059 8051 Convalescent home;
skilled nursing care facilities
HQ: Skilled Healthcare, Llc
27442 Portola Pkwy # 200
Foothill Ranch CA 92610
949 282-5800

8062 General Medical &
Surgical Hospitals

(P-21263)
**ADVENTIST HEALTH
CLEARLAKE (HQ)**
Also Called: Saint Helena Hosp Clearlake
15630 18th Ave, Clearlake (95422-9336)
P.O. Box 6710 (95422-6710)
PHONE..............................707 994-6486
David Santos, *CEO*
Carlton Jacobson, *CFO*
Meredith Jobe, *Admin Sec*
Michael Shepherd, *Obstetrician*
Jenny Senff, *Nursing Dir*
EMP: 287
SQ FT: 41,750
SALES: 82.5MM
SALES (corp-wide): 4.1B **Privately Held**
SIC: 8062 8011 Hospital, affiliated with
AMA residency; medical centers
PA: Adventist Health System/West
2100 Douglas Blvd
Roseville CA 95661
916 781-2000

(P-21264)
**ADVENTIST HEALTH SONORA
(HQ)**
Also Called: Sonora Regional Medical Center
1000 Greenley Rd, Sonora (95370-5200)
PHONE..............................209 532-5000
Andrew Jahn, *President*
David Larsen, *CFO*
Gene Scott, *Lab Dir*
Edward Clinite, *Principal*
Jeff Eler, *Principal*
EMP: 712
SQ FT: 60,000
SALES: 249.4MM
SALES (corp-wide): 4.1B **Privately Held**
SIC: 8062 8051 General medical & surgi-
cal hospitals; skilled nursing care facilities
PA: Adventist Health System/West
2100 Douglas Blvd
Roseville CA 95661
916 781-2000

(P-21265)
**ADVENTIST HEALTH
SYSTEM/WEST (PA)**
2100 Douglas Blvd, Roseville
(95661-3898)
P.O. Box 619002 (95661-9002)
PHONE..............................916 781-2000
Robert Carmen, *President*
Carrie Bannister, *President*
Lowell Church, *President*
Roland Fargo, *President*
Michelle Fuentes, *President*
EMP: 350
SQ FT: 55,000
SALES: 4.1B **Privately Held**
SIC: 8062 General medical & surgical hos-
pitals

(P-21266)
**ADVENTIST HEALTH
SYSTEM/WEST**
Also Called: Adventist Hlth Med Foundation
381 Merrill Ave, Glendale (91206-4178)
PHONE..............................818 409-8540
Iris Weil, *CEO*
EMP: 50
SALES (corp-wide): 4.1B **Privately Held**
SIC: 8062 General medical & surgical hos-
pitals
PA: Adventist Health System/West
2100 Douglas Blvd
Roseville CA 95661
916 781-2000

(P-21267)
**ADVENTIST HEALTH
SYSTEM/WEST**
Also Called: Clearlake Family Health Center
15230 Lakeshore Dr, Clearlake
(95422-8107)
PHONE..............................707 995-4500
Ilona Horton, *Director*
EMP: 50

SALES (corp-wide): 4.1B **Privately Held**
SIC: **8062** General medical & surgical hospitals
PA: Adventist Health System/West
2100 Douglas Blvd
Roseville CA 95661
916 781-2000

(P-21268)
ADVENTIST MEDICAL CENTER-SELMA
Also Called: Urgent Care-Selma Dst Hosp
1141 Rose Ave, Selma (93662-3241)
PHONE...................................559 891-1000
Wayne Ferch, *President*
Dave Larsen, *CFO*
Kreby McKague, *CFO*
Lena Madrigal, *Executive*
Michael Aubry, *CIO*
EMP: **339** EST: 1962
SQ FT: 67,000
SALES (est): 31.8MM **Privately Held**
SIC: **8062** 8051 General medical & surgical hospitals; skilled nursing care facilities

(P-21269)
ADVINTIST HLTH CLEARLAKE HOSP
Also Called: St Helena Hospital Clearlake
18th Ave & Hwy 53, Clearlake (95422)
PHONE...................................707 994-6486
Terry Newmeyer, *CEO*
Jeniffer Swenson, *Vice Pres*
EMP: **340**
SQ FT: 62,000
SALES: 65.9MM **Privately Held**
WEB: www.rchea.org
SIC: **8062** General medical & surgical hospitals

(P-21270)
AHM GEMCH INC
Also Called: GREATER EL MONTE COMMUNITY HOSPITAL
1701 Santa Anita Ave, El Monte (91733-3411)
PHONE...................................626 579-7777
Jeffrey Flocken, *CEO*
Patrick Steinhauser, *COO*
Gary Louis, *CFO*
Julie Emery, *Admin Sec*
Pasha Dourseau, *Opers Staff*
EMP: **180**
SQ FT: 71,500
SALES: 50.5MM
SALES (corp-wide): 572.3MM **Privately Held**
WEB: www.greaterelmonte.com
SIC: **8062** General medical & surgical hospitals
PA: Ahmc Healthcare Inc.
1000 S Fremont Ave Unit 6
Alhambra CA 91803
626 943-7526

(P-21271)
AHMC HEALTHCARE
55 S Raymond Ave Ste 105, Alhambra (91801-7101)
PHONE...................................626 570-0612
Jonathan Wu, *Ch of Bd*
Peter Zhou, *Financial Analy*
Mina Holland, *Director*
EMP: **150**
SALES (est): 15.7MM **Privately Held**
SIC: **8062** General medical & surgical hospitals

(P-21272)
AHMC HEALTHCARE INC (PA)
1000 S Fremont Ave Unit 6, Alhambra (91803-8836)
PHONE...................................626 943-7526
Jonathan Wu MD, *CEO*
Judy Saito, *Vice Pres*
Mike Craig, *Radiology Dir*
Sharon Carpenter, *Ch Nursing Ofcr*
Patti Metzger, *Program Mgr*
EMP: **150**
SALES (est): 572.3MM **Privately Held**
SIC: **8062** 8641 General medical & surgical hospitals; civic social & fraternal associations

(P-21273)
AHMC HEALTHCARE INC
1701 Santa Anita Ave, South El Monte (91733-3411)
PHONE...................................626 579-7777
EMP: **645**
SALES (corp-wide): 572.3MM **Privately Held**
SIC: **8062** General medical & surgical hospitals
PA: Ahmc Healthcare Inc.
1000 S Fremont Ave Unit 6
Alhambra CA 91803
626 943-7526

(P-21274)
AHMC WHITTIER HOSP MED CTR LP
9080 Colima Rd, Whittier (90605-1600)
PHONE...................................562 945-3561
Richard Castro, *CEO*
Krystal Reyes, *Admin Asst*
Norma Bridger, *Purch Mgr*
Zenaida Vasquez, *Food Svc Dir*
Brandon Muse, *Internal Med*
EMP: **850**
SQ FT: 16,782
SALES (est): 41.9MM
SALES (corp-wide): 572.3MM **Privately Held**
WEB: www.ahmchealth.com
SIC: **8062** General medical & surgical hospitals
PA: Ahmc Healthcare Inc.
1000 S Fremont Ave Unit 6
Alhambra CA 91803
626 943-7526

(P-21275)
ALAKOR HEALTHCARE LLC
Also Called: Monrovia Memorial Hospital
323 S Heliotrope Ave, Monrovia (91016-2914)
PHONE...................................626 408-9800
Kevin Smith,
Katty Johnson, *Human Res Mgr*
Ron Kupferstein,
Jon Woods,
Dennis Hawkins, *Director*
EMP: **126**
SQ FT: 10,000
SALES: 47.2MM **Privately Held**
SIC: **8062** General medical & surgical hospitals

(P-21276)
ALAMEDA HEALTH SYSTEM (PA)
Also Called: Highland Hosp Hghland Wellness
1411 E 31st St, Oakland (94602-1018)
PHONE...................................510 437-4800
Daniel Boggan Jr, *CEO*
Aldon Harken,
Jason Pokorny, *Volunteer Dir*
Mark S Fratzke, *COO*
David Cox, *CFO*
EMP: **99**
SALES (est): 52.7MM **Privately Held**
SIC: **8062** General medical & surgical hospitals

(P-21277)
ALECTO HEALTHCARE SERVICES LLC (PA)
16310 Bake Pkwy Ste 200, Irvine (92618-4684)
P.O. Box 351209, Los Angeles (90035-9609)
PHONE...................................323 938-3161
John A Calderone, *CEO*
Babur Ozkan, *CFO*
Natalie Tran, *Program Mgr*
Garry Miller, *Engineer*
Karen Knueven, *Chief*
EMP: **900**
SALES (est): 1.1B **Privately Held**
WEB: www.olympiamc.com
SIC: **8062** General medical & surgical hospitals

(P-21278)
ALHAMBRA HOSPITAL MED CTR LP
100 S Raymond Ave, Alhambra (91801-3166)
PHONE...................................626 570-1606
Iris Lai, *Marketing Staff*
Geraldine Thaung,
Christie Hernandez, *Admin Asst*
Juan Rodriquez, *Purchasing*
Sevan Tulgar, *Safety Dir*
EMP: **160** EST: 1920
SQ FT: 200,000
SALES: 81.7MM
SALES (corp-wide): 572.3MM **Privately Held**
SIC: **8062** General medical & surgical hospitals
PA: Ahmc Healthcare Inc.
1000 S Fremont Ave Unit 6
Alhambra CA 91803
626 943-7526

(P-21279)
ALTA HOSPITALS SYSTEM LLC
Also Called: Los Angeles Community Hospital
4081 E Olympic Blvd, Los Angeles (90023-3330)
PHONE...................................323 267-0477
Remy Hart, *Branch Mgr*
Keith Levy, *Administration*
Luz Sanchez, *Administration*
Carlos Mota, *Purch Mgr*
David Guerrero, *Hlthcr Dir*
EMP: **250**
SQ FT: 64,024
SALES (corp-wide): 815.3MM **Privately Held**
SIC: **8062** General medical & surgical hospitals
HQ: Alta Hospitals System, Llc
10780 Santa Monica Blvd # 400
Los Angeles CA 90025
-

(P-21280)
ALTA HOSPITALS SYSTEM LLC
Also Called: Foothill Regional Medical Ctr
14662 Newport Ave, Tustin (92780-6064)
PHONE...................................714 619-7700
EMP: **575**
SALES (corp-wide): 815.3MM **Privately Held**
SIC: **8062** General medical & surgical hospitals
HQ: Alta Hospitals System, Llc
10780 Santa Monica Blvd # 400
Los Angeles CA 90025

(P-21281)
ALTA HOSPITALS SYSTEM LLC (HQ)
10780 Santa Monica Blvd # 400, Los Angeles (90025-7616)
PHONE...................................310 943-4500
Samuel S Lee, *Mng Member*
Lalit Katz, *President*
Lily Runke, *President*
Ralph Uribe, *President*
Becky Levy, *Senior VP*
EMP: **159**
SALES (est): 86.7MM
SALES (corp-wide): 815.3MM **Privately Held**
SIC: **8062** General medical & surgical hospitals
PA: Prospect Medical Holdings, Inc.
3415 S Sepulveda Blvd # 9
Los Angeles CA 90034
310 943-4500

(P-21282)
ALVARADO HOSPITAL LLC (DH)
6655 Alvarado Rd, San Diego (92120-5208)
PHONE...................................619 287-3270
Tracey Tally, *CFO*
Darlene Wetton, *COO*
Natalie Mercille, *Lab Dir*
Tony Sangermano, *Technician*
Robert Kessler, *Facilities Mgr*
EMP: **62**

SALES: 154.2K
SALES (corp-wide): 3.4B **Privately Held**
SIC: **8062** General medical & surgical hospitals

(P-21283)
AMERICAN HOSPITAL MGT CORP (PA)
Also Called: MAD RIVER COMMUNITY HOSPITAL
3800 Janes Rd, Arcata (95521-4742)
P.O. Box 1115 (95518-1115)
PHONE...................................707 822-3621
Allen E Shaw, *President*
Patty Carroll, *Records Dir*
Michael Young, *CFO*
Doug A Shaw, *Vice Pres*
Matt Raczka, *Program Mgr*
EMP: **500**
SQ FT: 60,000
SALES: 66.8MM **Privately Held**
WEB: www.madriverhospital.com
SIC: **8062** General medical & surgical hospitals

(P-21284)
AMI-HTI TARZANA ENCINO JOINT V
Also Called: A M I Encn-Trzana Rgnal Med Ce
18321 Clark St, Tarzana (91356-3501)
PHONE...................................818 881-0800
Dale Surowitz, *Managing Prtnr*
Igor Kozlov, *Pathologist*
Bryan Tzy Young Lin, *Pathologist*
Jo Ann Lewis, *Director*
EMP: **1800**
SQ FT: 180,000
SALES: 14.6MM **Privately Held**
SIC: **8062** General medical & surgical hospitals

(P-21285)
AMISUB (IRVINE REGIONAL HOSPI)
1400 S Douglass Rd # 250, Anaheim (92806-6904)
PHONE...................................949 916-7556
Dan F Ausman, *CEO*
Dr Jack Campion, *Ch of Bd*
Richard Robinson, *Principal*
EMP: **590**
SQ FT: 244,000
SALES (est): 17.9MM **Privately Held**
SIC: **8062** 5912 General medical & surgical hospitals; drug stores

(P-21286)
AMISUB OF CALIFORNIA INC (DH)
18321 Clark St, Tarzana (91356-3501)
PHONE...................................818 881-0800
Dale Surowitz, *CEO*
Don Kreitz, *COO*
Nick Lymberopolous, *CFO*
Edward Gong, *Vice Pres*
EMP: **900** EST: 1979
SQ FT: 180,000
SALES (est): 480K
SALES (corp-wide): 19.3B **Publicly Held**
SIC: **8062** General medical & surgical hospitals
HQ: Tenet Healthsystem Medical, Inc.
1445 Ross Ave Ste 1400
Dallas TX 75202
469 893-2000

(P-21287)
ANAHEIM GLOBAL MEDICAL CENTER
1025 S Anaheim Blvd, Anaheim (92805-5806)
PHONE...................................714 533-6220
Marven E Howard, *CEO*
Lori Nekota, *Pharmacy Dir*
Jason Liu, *Principal*
EMP: **500**
SALES (est): 14MM
SALES (corp-wide): 440.5MM **Privately Held**
SIC: **8062** General medical & surgical hospitals

PA: Kpc Healthcare, Inc.
1301 N Tustin Ave
Santa Ana CA 92705
714 953-3652

(P-21288)
ANAHEIM REGIONAL MEDICAL CTR
Also Called: Cardiac Unit
1111 W La Palma Ave, Anaheim
(92801-2804)
PHONE...............................714 774-1450
EMP: 767
SALES (corp-wide): 188.8MM Privately Held
WEB: www.cardiacunit.com
SIC: 8062 General medical & surgical hospitals
PA: Anaheim Regional Medical Center
1111 W La Palma Ave
Anaheim CA 92801
714 774-1450

(P-21289)
ANTELOPE VALLEY HOSPITAL INC (PA)
Also Called: Antelope Valley Hlth Care Dst
1600 W Avenue J, Lancaster (93534-2894)
P.O. Box 7001 (93539-7001)
PHONE...............................661 949-5000
Michael Wall, President
Patalappa Chandrashekar,
Jennifer Hill, Ch Radiology
Jack Burke, COO
Dennis Empey, CFO
EMP: 1660
SQ FT: 300,000
SALES: 456.8MM Privately Held
WEB: www.avhospital.com
SIC: 8062 General medical & surgical hospitals

(P-21290)
ARCH HEALTH PARTNERS INC (HQ)
15611 Pomerado Rd Ste 575, Poway
(92064-2438)
PHONE...............................858 675-3100
Deanna Kyrimis, CEO
Matt Niedzwiecki, COO
Hugh King, CFO
Vicky Lister, Exec Dir
Kristen Napierskie, Executive Asst
EMP: 92 EST: 2009
SALES: 49.5MM
SALES (corp-wide): 760.9MM Privately Held
SIC: 8062 General medical & surgical hospitals
PA: Palomar Health Technology, Inc.
456 E Grand Ave
Escondido CA 92025
442 281-5000

(P-21291)
ARROWHEAD REGIONAL MEDICAL CTR
Also Called: Armc
400 N Pepper Ave, Colton (92324-1819)
PHONE...............................909 580-1000
Patrick Petre, Director
Theodore Friedman, Lab Dir
Cliff Hiroshige, Pharmacy Dir
Jeanette Pirio, Office Mgr
Mari Craig, Executive Asst
EMP: 2500
SQ FT: 950,000
SALES: 468.9MM Privately Held
SIC: 8062 General medical & surgical hospitals
PA: County Of San Bernardino
385 N Arrowhead Ave
San Bernardino CA 92415
909 387-3841

(P-21292)
AURORA HEALTHCARE INC
Also Called: Aurora Behavioral Hlth Care
11878 Avenue Of Industry, San Diego
(92128-3423)
PHONE...............................858 487-3200
James S Plummer, CEO
EMP: 50

SALES (est): 3.8MM Privately Held
SIC: 8062 General medical & surgical hospitals

(P-21293)
AUXILIARY OF MISSION
27700 Medical Center Rd, Mission Viejo
(92691-6426)
PHONE...............................949 364-1400
Eduardo Jordan, Ch of Bd
Kenn McFarland, President
Vicki J Veal, CEO
Lynette Klett, Human Res Mgr
Gregory Macchio, Anesthesiology
EMP: 54
SALES: 516.9K
SALES (corp-wide): 547.3MM Privately Held
SIC: 8062 General medical & surgical hospitals
PA: Mission Hospital Regional Medical Center Inc
27700 Medical Center Rd
Mission Viejo CA 92691
949 364-1400

(P-21294)
BAKERSFIELD MEMORIAL HOSPITAL
Also Called: Memorial Center
420 34th St, Bakersfield (93301-2237)
P.O. Box 1888 (93303-1888)
PHONE...............................661 327-1792
Jon Van Boening, CEO
Gordon K Foster, Ch of Bd
R Mark R Root, Vice Pres
Jeff Vague, Data Proc Staff
Gary De Risio, Opers Mgr
EMP: 1100
SQ FT: 364,000
SALES: 401.3MM
SALES (corp-wide): 6.7B Privately Held
SIC: 8062 Hospital, affiliated with AMA residency
PA: Dignity Health
185 Berry St Ste 300
San Francisco CA 94107
415 438-5500

(P-21295)
BANNER HEALTH
1800 Spring Ridge Dr, Susanville
(96130-6100)
PHONE...............................530 251-3147
Teena Carver, Officer
Bonnie B Olsen, Officer
Peter S Fine, Branch Mgr
Benjamin Gonzales, Technology
Dan Bandy, Radiology
EMP: 165
SALES (corp-wide): 7.8B Privately Held
WEB: www.bannerhealth.com
SIC: 8062 General medical & surgical hospitals
PA: Banner Health
2901 N Central Ave # 160
Phoenix AZ 85012
602 747-4000

(P-21296)
BANNER LASSEN MEDICAL CENTER
1800 Spring Ridge Dr, Susanville
(96130-6100)
PHONE...............................530 252-2000
Bob Edwards, CEO
Shelby Diede, CFO
Kimberly Hamelton, Radiology Dir
Bob Nix, Business Mgr
Debbie Ingle, Accountant
EMP: 200
SALES: 40.1MM Privately Held
SIC: 8062 8051 General medical & surgical hospitals; skilled nursing care facilities

(P-21297)
BARTON HOSPITAL
2170 South Ave, South Lake Tahoe
(96150-7026)
P.O. Box 9578 (96158-9578)
PHONE...............................530 543-5685
Clint Purvance, CEO
Darcy Wallace, Vice Pres
EMP: 1200 EST: 2014

SALES (est): 107.1K Privately Held
SIC: 8062 General medical & surgical hospitals

(P-21298)
BEAR VLY CMNTY HEALTHCARE DST (PA)
41870 Garstin Dr, Big Bear Lake (92315)
PHONE...............................909 866-6501
Raymond Hino, CEO
Barbara Espinoza, Vice Pres
Donna Nicely, Vice Pres
Shelly Egerer, General Mgr
Christopher Fagan, Admin Sec
EMP: 150
SQ FT: 25,000
SALES: 26.2K Privately Held
SIC: 8062 General medical & surgical hospitals

(P-21299)
BEVERLY COMMUNITY HOSP ASSN
101 E Beverly Blvd # 104, Montebello
(90640-4300)
PHONE...............................323 889-2452
Norma Valdez, Principal
EMP: 327
SALES (corp-wide): 176.9MM Privately Held
SIC: 8062 8011 General medical & surgical hospitals; clinic, operated by physicians
PA: Beverly Community Hospital Association
309 W Beverly Blvd
Montebello CA 90640
323 726-1222

(P-21300)
BEVERLY COMMUNITY HOSP ASSN (PA)
Also Called: Beverly Hospital
309 W Beverly Blvd, Montebello
(90640-4308)
PHONE...............................323 726-1222
Gary Kiff, CEO
Luis Sanchez, President
Larry Pugh, CFO
Renee D Martinez, Treasurer
Wendy Beesley, Senior VP
EMP: 124 EST: 1949
SQ FT: 274,000
SALES: 176.9MM Privately Held
WEB: www.beverly.org
SIC: 8062 General medical & surgical hospitals

(P-21301)
BEVERLY COMMUNITY HOSP ASSN
Also Called: Kelpien Health Care
1920 W Whittier Blvd, Montebello
(90640-4009)
PHONE...............................323 725-1519
Wendy Torres, Manager
EMP: 544
SALES (corp-wide): 176.9MM Privately Held
WEB: www.beverly.org
SIC: 8062 General medical & surgical hospitals
PA: Beverly Community Hospital Association
309 W Beverly Blvd
Montebello CA 90640
323 726-1222

(P-21302)
CALIFORNIA PACIFIC CA
2100 Webster St Ste 516, San Francisco
(94115-2381)
PHONE...............................415 345-0940
Bruce Brent MD, President
Elaine Chow, COO
Richard Francoz MD, Vice Pres
EMP: 50
SQ FT: 3,500
SALES: 3.5MM Privately Held
WEB: www.cpcmg.com
SIC: 8062 General medical & surgical hospitals

(P-21303)
CALIFORNIA PACIFIC MEDICAL CTR
2100 Webster St Ste 115, San Francisco
(94115-2374)
PHONE...............................415 600-1378
Matthew Poland, Principal
Yvette Salas, Office Mgr
Peter Traquina, Research
Michelle Haynes, Osteopathy
EMP: 99
SALES (est): 5.5MM Privately Held
SIC: 8062 General medical & surgical hospitals

(P-21304)
CALIFRNIA HOSP MED CTR FNDTION
1401 S Grand Ave, Los Angeles
(90015-3010)
PHONE...............................213 748-2411
Phillip C Hill, Ch of Bd
Nathan R Nusbaum, President
Margaret R Peterson, President
Harold Newton, COO
Clark Underwood, CFO
▲ EMP: 1500 EST: 1926
SQ FT: 800,000
SALES: 396.8MM
SALES (corp-wide): 6.7B Privately Held
WEB: www.chw.edu
SIC: 8062 Hospital, medical school affiliated with nursing & residency
PA: Dignity Health
185 Berry St Ste 300
San Francisco CA 94107
415 438-5500

(P-21305)
CASA COLINA HOSPITAL AND CENTE (HQ)
Also Called: CASA COLINA CENTERS FOR REHABILITATION
255 E Bonita Ave, Pomona (91767-1933)
P.O. Box 6001 (91769-6001)
PHONE...............................909 596-7733
Felice Loverso, CEO
Steve Norin, Chairman
Randy Blackman, Treasurer
Stephen Graeber, Treasurer
Mary Lou Jensen, Admin Sec
▲ EMP: 500
SQ FT: 90,000
SALES: 53.4MM
SALES (corp-wide): 113.3MM Privately Held
WEB: www.casacolina.org
SIC: 8062 General medical & surgical hospitals
PA: Casa Colina, Inc.
255 E Bonita Ave
Pomona CA 91767
909 596-7733

(P-21306)
CEDARS-SINAI MEDICAL CENTER
Also Called: Health System Medical Network
250 N Robertson Blvd # 101, Beverly Hills
(90211-1788)
PHONE...............................310 385-3400
Tom Gordon, CEO
Rosa Fuentes, Executive
Amy Rutman, Internal Med
Paula Carruthers, Med Doctor
Janet Leis, Manager
EMP: 200
SALES (corp-wide): 3.4B Privately Held
SIC: 8062 8011 General medical & surgical hospitals; offices & clinics of medical doctors
PA: Cedars-Sinai Medical Center
8700 Beverly Blvd
West Hollywood CA 90048
310 423-3277

(P-21307)
CENTRAL VALLEY GENERAL HOSP (HQ)
1025 N Douty St, Hanford (93230-3722)
PHONE...............................559 583-2100
Wayne Ferch, CEO
Douglas Lafferty, COO
Kirby McKague, Vice Pres
Michelle Polen, Terminal Mgr

Richard Tamez, *Hlthcr Dir*
EMP: 400
SQ FT: 96,000
SALES: 109MM
SALES (corp-wide): 4.1B **Privately Held**
SIC: 8062 General medical & surgical hospitals
PA: Adventist Health System/West
2100 Douglas Blvd
Roseville CA 95661
916 781-2000

(P-21308)
CFHS HOLDINGS INC
Also Called: Centinela Frman Rgonal Med Ctr
4650 Lincoln Blvd, Marina Del Rey (90292-6306)
PHONE..............................310 823-8911
EMP: 650
SQ FT: 150,000
SALES (corp-wide): 113.5MM **Privately Held**
SIC: 8062 General medical & surgical hospitals
PA: Cfhs Holdings, Inc.
4650 Lincoln Blvd
Marina Del Rey CA 90292
310 823-8911

(P-21309)
CFHS HOLDINGS INC
Also Called: Centinela Frman Rgonal Med Ctr
4640 Admiralty Way # 650, Marina Del Rey (90292-6667)
PHONE..............................310 448-7800
Bob Bokern, *Principal*
EMP: 1940
SALES (corp-wide): 113.5MM **Privately Held**
SIC: 8062 General medical & surgical hospitals
PA: Cfhs Holdings, Inc.
4650 Lincoln Blvd
Marina Del Rey CA 90292
310 823-8911

(P-21310)
CFHS HOLDINGS INC
Also Called: Centinela Frman Rgonal Med Ctr
555 E Hardy St, Inglewood (90301-4011)
PHONE..............................310 673-4660
Michael Rembis, *Branch Mgr*
EMP: 1200
SALES (corp-wide): 113.5MM **Privately Held**
SIC: 8062 General medical & surgical hospitals
PA: Cfhs Holdings, Inc.
4650 Lincoln Blvd
Marina Del Rey CA 90292
310 823-8911

(P-21311)
CHA HOLLYWOOD MEDICAL CTR LP (PA)
Also Called: Hollywood Presbyterian Med Ctr
1300 N Vermont Ave, Los Angeles (90027-6098)
PHONE..............................213 413-3000
Jeff A Nelson, *CEO*
Galen Gorman, *CFO*
▲ **EMP:** 1500
SQ FT: 900,000
SALES: 288.9MM **Privately Held**
WEB: www.hollywoodpresbyterian.com
SIC: 8062 8351 Hospital, affiliated with AMA residency; child day care services

(P-21312)
CHAPMAN GLOBAL MEDICAL CENTER
Also Called: Chapman Family Health
2601 E Chapman Ave, Orange (92869-3206)
PHONE..............................714 633-0011
Don Kreitz, *CEO*
Lori Firman, *President*
Kenneth K Westbrook, *CEO*
Robert Heinemeier, *CFO*
EMP: 425
SQ FT: 96,000

SALES: 46.3MM
SALES (corp-wide): 440.5MM **Privately Held**
WEB: www.chapmanmedicalcenter.com
SIC: 8062 General medical & surgical hospitals
PA: Kpc Healthcare, Inc.
1301 N Tustin Ave
Santa Ana CA 92705
714 953-3652

(P-21313)
CHHP MANAGEMENT LLC
Also Called: COMMUNITY HOSPITAL OF HUNTINGTON PARK
2623 E Slauson Ave, Huntington Park (90255-2926)
P.O. Box 2729 (90255-8129)
PHONE..............................323 583-1931
Joel Freedman, *Principal*
Mark Bell, *Principal*
Jamie Macpherson, *Principal*
Yolanda Vasquez, *Executive Asst*
EMP: 99 **EST:** 2010
SALES: 49.7MM
SALES (corp-wide): 253.3MM **Privately Held**
SIC: 8062 General medical & surgical hospitals
HQ: Chhp Holdings Ii, Llc
2623 E Slauson Ave
Huntington Park CA 90255
323 583-1931

(P-21314)
CHILDRENS HOSPITAL LOS ANGELES
Also Called: Childrens Laboratory
5359 Balboa Blvd, Encino (91316-2819)
PHONE..............................818 728-4930
Paul Pattengale, *Director*
EMP: 186
SALES (corp-wide): 1B **Privately Held**
SIC: 8062 General medical & surgical hospitals
PA: The Childrens Hospital Los Angeles
4650 W Sunset Blvd
Los Angeles CA 90027
323 660-2450

(P-21315)
CHILDRENS HOSPITAL LOS ANGELES
5000 W Sunset Blvd # 400, Los Angeles (90027-5865)
PHONE..............................323 361-2153
EMP: 248
SALES (corp-wide): 1B **Privately Held**
SIC: 8062 General medical & surgical hospitals
PA: The Childrens Hospital Los Angeles
4650 W Sunset Blvd
Los Angeles CA 90027
323 660-2450

(P-21316)
CHILDRENS HOSPITAL LOS ANGELES
468 E Santa Clara St, Arcadia (91006-7228)
PHONE..............................626 795-7177
Anahit Petrosyan, *Nurse*
EMP: 248
SALES (corp-wide): 1B **Privately Held**
SIC: 8062 General medical & surgical hospitals
PA: The Childrens Hospital Los Angeles
4650 W Sunset Blvd
Los Angeles CA 90027
323 660-2450

(P-21317)
CHILDRENS HOSPITAL LOS ANGELES
Foundation Division
4650 W Sunset Blvd, Los Angeles (90027-6062)
PHONE..............................323 660-2450
Claudia Looney, *Vice Pres*
EMP: 80
SALES (corp-wide): 1B **Privately Held**
SIC: 8062 8641 General medical & surgical hospitals; civic social & fraternal associations

PA: The Childrens Hospital Los Angeles
4650 W Sunset Blvd
Los Angeles CA 90027
323 660-2450

(P-21318)
CHILDRENS HOSPITAL ORANGE CNTY
980 Roosevelt, Irvine (92620-3672)
PHONE..............................949 387-2586
EMP: 1036
SALES (corp-wide): 523.1MM **Privately Held**
SIC: 8062 8099 8082 6321 General medical & surgical hospitals; childbirth preparation clinic; home health care services; accident & health insurance
PA: Children's Hospital Of Orange County
1201 W La Veta Ave
Orange CA 92868
714 997-3000

(P-21319)
CHILDRENS HOSPOTAL & RESEARCH (PA)
Also Called: Ucsf Benioff Chld Hosp Oakland
747 52nd St, Oakland (94609-1809)
PHONE..............................510 428-3000
Bertram Lubin, *President*
Richard Rowe,
Kenneth Henderson, *Records Dir*
Harold Davis, *Ch of Bd*
Kathleen Cain, *CFO*
EMP: 1900
SQ FT: 160,000
SALES: 178.6MM **Privately Held**
SIC: 8062 Hospital, AMA approved residency

(P-21320)
CHINESE HOSPITAL ASSOCIATION (PA)
845 Jackson St, San Francisco (94133-4899)
PHONE..............................415 982-2400
Brenda Yee, *CEO*
Linda Schumacher, *COO*
Thomas Bolger, *CFO*
Stuart Fong, *Risk Mgmt Dir*
Helen Lee, *Systs Prg Mgr*
EMP: 279
SQ FT: 54,000
SALES: 202.7MM **Privately Held**
WEB: www.cchphmo.com
SIC: 8062 General medical & surgical hospitals

(P-21321)
CHINO RDOLOGICAL REGISTRY CORP
6719 Eagle Dr, Chino (91710-6283)
PHONE..............................909 591-6688
Robert A Esquibel, *President*
EMP: 99
SALES: 950K **Privately Held**
SIC: 8062 7361 General medical & surgical hospitals; employment agencies

(P-21322)
CITRUS VALLEY MEDICAL CTR INC (PA)
1115 S Sunset Ave, West Covina (91790-3940)
P.O. Box 6108, Covina (91722-5108)
PHONE..............................626 962-4011
Robert Curry, *President*
Elvia Foulke, *COO*
Roger Sharma, *COO*
Debbie Cooper, *Finance*
Donna Brotman, *Director*
EMP: 1229
SQ FT: 285,000
SALES: 502.7MM **Privately Held**
WEB: www.cvpg.org
SIC: 8062 General medical & surgical hospitals

(P-21323)
CITRUS VALLEY MEDICAL CTR INC
Also Called: Human Resources Department
140 W College St, Covina (91723-2007)
PHONE..............................626 858-8515
Robert H Curry, *Administration*
EMP: 746

SALES (corp-wide): 502.7MM **Privately Held**
SIC: 8062 General medical & surgical hospitals
PA: Citrus Valley Medical Center, Inc.
1115 S Sunset Ave
West Covina CA 91790
626 962-4011

(P-21324)
CITRUS VALLEY MEDICAL CTR INC
Also Called: Queen of The Valley Hospital
1115 S Sunset Ave, West Covina (91790-3940)
PHONE..............................626 963-8411
Robert Curry, *President*
EMP: 2000
SALES (corp-wide): 502.7MM **Privately Held**
WEB: www.cvpg.org
SIC: 8062 General medical & surgical hospitals
PA: Citrus Valley Medical Center, Inc.
1115 S Sunset Ave
West Covina CA 91790
626 962-4011

(P-21325)
CITRUS VALLEY MEDICAL CTR INC
Also Called: Inter Community Hospital
210 W San Bernardino Rd, Covina (91723-1515)
PHONE..............................626 331-7331
Toll Free:..........................877 -
Jim Yoshioka, *President*
Kumari Wickramasinghe, *Pathologist*
EMP: 1000
SALES (corp-wide): 502.7MM **Privately Held**
WEB: www.cvpg.org
SIC: 8062 General medical & surgical hospitals
PA: Citrus Valley Medical Center, Inc.
1115 S Sunset Ave
West Covina CA 91790
626 962-4011

(P-21326)
CITY & COUNTY OF SAN FRANCISCO
Also Called: San Francisco General Hospital
1001 Potrero Ave, San Francisco (94110-3518)
PHONE..............................415 206-8000
Susan Currin, *Principal*
Linda Lee, *Risk Mgmt Dir*
Sue Currin, *Ch Nursing Ofcr*
Sarah Haynes, *Principal*
Jean O'Connel, *Principal*
EMP: 5000 **Privately Held**
SIC: 8062 General medical & surgical hospitals
PA: City & County Of San Francisco
1 Dr Carlton B Goodlett P
San Francisco CA 94102
415 554-7500

(P-21327)
CITY ALAMEDA HEALTH CARE CORP (PA)
Also Called: ALAMEDA HOSPITAL
2070 Clinton Ave, Alameda (94501-4399)
PHONE..............................510 522-3700
Deborah E Stebbins, *CEO*
Roger Rieger, *Executive*
Drue Obertello, *Admin Sec*
Kristen Thorson, *Administration*
Dan Dickenson, *MIS Dir*
EMP: 84 **EST:** 1894
SQ FT: 150,000
SALES: 85.9MM **Privately Held**
WEB: www.alamedahospital.com
SIC: 8062 8051 General medical & surgical hospitals; skilled nursing care facilities

(P-21328)
CITY HOPE NATIONAL MEDICAL CTR
1500 Duarte Rd, Duarte (91010-3012)
PHONE..............................626 256-4673
Michael A Friedman, *CEO*
Robert Stone, *CEO*
Diana Keim, *Assoc VP*

Dan Seyler, *Radiology Dir*
Leonard Chen, *Admin Dir*
EMP: 1900
SALES (est): 860.5MM
SALES (corp-wide): 1.4B **Privately Held**
SIC: 8062 General medical & surgical hospitals
PA: City Of Hope
1500 Duarte Rd
Duarte CA 91010
626 256-4673

(P-21329)
COALINGA REGIONAL MEDICAL CENT
Also Called: Crmc
1191 Phelps Ave, Coalinga (93210-9609)
PHONE...................................559 935-6400
EMP: 230 **EST:** 1947
SQ FT: 60,000
SALES: 20.1MM **Privately Held**
WEB: www.coalingamedicalcenter.com
SIC: 8062 8051 Hospital, affiliated with AMA residency; skilled nursing care facilities

(P-21330)
COAST PLAZA DOCTORS HOSPITAL (PA)
13100 Studebaker Rd, Norwalk (90650-2531)
PHONE...................................562 868-3751
John Ferrelli, *CEO*
Craig B Garner, *CEO*
Mihi Lee, *CFO*
Joel Freedman, *Principal*
EMP: 59
SQ FT: 58,000
SALES (est): 18.7MM **Privately Held**
WEB: www.coastplazahospital.com
SIC: 8062 Hospital, medical school affiliation

(P-21331)
COMMUNITY HLTH ALANCE PASADENA (PA)
Also Called: Chap
1855 N Fair Oaks Ave # 200, Pasadena (91103-1620)
P.O. Box 94873 (91109-4873)
PHONE...................................626 398-6300
Margaret Martinez, *CEO*
Sergio Bautista, *COO*
Marcy Chavez, *Office Mgr*
EMP: 56
SALES: 9.9MM **Privately Held**
SIC: 8062 General medical & surgical hospitals

(P-21332)
COMMUNITY HOSP SAN BERNARDINO (HQ)
1805 Medical Center Dr, San Bernardino (92411-1217)
PHONE...................................909 887-6333
June Collisone, *President*
Ed Sorenson, *CFO*
Dave Evans, *Executive*
Leeann Sanders, *Administration*
Sharon Kerns, *Info Tech Mgr*
EMP: 350
SALES: 244.8MM
SALES (corp-wide): 6.7B **Privately Held**
SIC: 8062 Hospital, affiliated with AMA residency
PA: Dignity Health
185 Berry St Ste 300
San Francisco CA 94107
415 438-5500

(P-21333)
COMMUNITY HOSPITAL LONG BEACH
1760 Termino Ave Ste 105, Long Beach (90804-2157)
PHONE...................................562 494-0600
John Bishop, *CEO*
Krikor Jansian, *President*
Kevin Peterson, *CEO*
Judith Luong, *Program Mgr*
Linda Tatum, *Planning*
EMP: 570

SALES: 5.4K
SALES (corp-wide): 2.2B **Privately Held**
SIC: 8062 Hospital, affiliated with AMA residency
PA: Memorial Health Services
17360 Brookhurst St # 160
Fountain Valley CA 92708
714 377-6748

(P-21334)
COMMUNITY HOSPITALS CENTL CAL (PA)
Also Called: Community Health System
2823 Fresno St, Fresno (93721-1324)
P.O. Box 1232 (93715-1232)
PHONE...................................559 459-6000
Tim A Joslin, *CEO*
Gordon Webster Jr, *Vice Chairman*
Phyllis Baltz, *COO*
Craig S Castro, *COO*
Tracy Kiritani, *CFO*
EMP: 3400
SQ FT: 200,000
SALES (est): 1.6B **Privately Held**
SIC: 8062 8011 8051 General medical & surgical hospitals; ambulatory surgical center; clinic, operated by physicians; extended care facility

(P-21335)
COMMUNITY HOSPITALS CENTL CAL
Also Called: Community Regional Medical Ctr
2823 Fresno St, Fresno (93721-1324)
PHONE...................................559 459-6000
Tim Joslin, *President*
Margaret Breen, *Senior VP*
Linda Wilson, *Admin Asst*
Matthew Joslin, *Administration*
Craig Castro, *CIO*
EMP: 1000
SALES: 1.5B **Privately Held**
SIC: 8062 General medical & surgical hospitals

(P-21336)
COMMUNITY MEDICAL CENTER
Also Called: Clovis Community Living
3003 N Mariposa St, Fresno (93703-1127)
PHONE...................................559 222-7416
Lesi McQuone, *Manager*
Iesha Neal, *Office Mgr*
EMP: 150
SALES (corp-wide): 1.6B **Privately Held**
SIC: 8062 8051
PA: Community Hospitals Of Central California
2823 Fresno St
Fresno CA 93721
559 459-6000

(P-21337)
COMMUNITY MEDICAL CENTER
Also Called: California Cancer Center
7257 N Fresno St, Fresno (93720-2950)
PHONE...................................559 447-4050
Maria Schaffer, *Manager*
Paul Nugent, *Surgeon*
Brent Kane, *Internal Med*
Alec Beach, *Oncology*
Himmat Gill, *Med Doctor*
EMP: 75
SQ FT: 25,044
SALES (corp-wide): 1.6B **Privately Held**
SIC: 8062 8069 General medical & surgical hospitals; cancer hospital
PA: Community Hospitals Of Central California
2823 Fresno St
Fresno CA 93721
559 459-6000

(P-21338)
COMMUNITY MEDICAL CENTERS
Also Called: Alzheimer's Living Center
668 E Bullard Ave, Fresno (93710-5401)
PHONE...................................559 320-2200
Patrick Uribe, *Manager*
Harvey L Edmonds, *Neurology*
EMP: 110
SQ FT: 28,845
SALES (corp-wide): 1.6B **Privately Held**
SIC: 8062 8051 General medical & surgical hospitals; skilled nursing care facilities

PA: Community Hospitals Of Central California
2823 Fresno St
Fresno CA 93721
559 459-6000

(P-21339)
COMMUNITY MEDICAL CENTERS
Also Called: Advanced Medical Imaging
6297 N Fresno St, Fresno (93710-5209)
PHONE...................................559 447-4000
Donna Moora, *Director*
Hans Hildebrandt, *Med Doctor*
EMP: 70
SALES (corp-wide): 1.6B **Privately Held**
SIC: 8062 8011 8093 General medical & surgical hospitals; radiologist; specialty outpatient clinics
PA: Community Hospitals Of Central California
2823 Fresno St
Fresno CA 93721
559 459-6000

(P-21340)
COMMUNITY MEM HSP/SN BENUA
Also Called: Purchasing Department
147 N Brent St, Ventura (93003-2809)
PHONE...................................805 652-5072
Chuck Gray, *Manager*
▲ **EMP:** 99
SALES: 285MM **Privately Held**
WEB: www.cmhhospital.org
SIC: 8062 General medical & surgical hospitals

(P-21341)
COMMUNITY MEMORIAL HEALTH SYS (PA)
Also Called: COMMUNITY MEMORIAL HOSPITAL
147 N Brent St, Ventura (93003-2809)
PHONE...................................805 652-5011
Gary Wilde, *President*
Diane Cornell,
Mary Green, *Records Dir*
Mary Jane Greene, *Records Dir*
Steve Caryer, *President*
▲ **EMP:** 1881
SQ FT: 174,000
SALES: 406.1MM **Privately Held**
SIC: 8062 Hospital, affiliated with AMA residency

(P-21342)
COMMUNITY MEMORIAL HEALTH SYS
Also Called: Ojai Valley Community Hospital
1306 Maricopa Hwy, Ojai (93023-3131)
PHONE...................................805 646-1401
Gary Wilde, *President*
EMP: 120
SALES (corp-wide): 406.1MM **Privately Held**
SIC: 8062 General medical & surgical hospitals
PA: Community Memorial Health System
147 N Brent St
Ventura CA 93003
805 652-5011

(P-21343)
CORCORAN DISTRICT HOSPITAL
1310 Hanna Ave, Corcoran (93212-2314)
P.O. Box 758 (93212-0758)
PHONE...................................559 992-3300
Mike Graville, *CEO*
Jonathan Brain, *CEO*
Alan Macphee, *CFO*
Jess Martinez, *Admin Sec*
Brian Dukes, *Technology*
EMP: 100 **EST:** 1951
SQ FT: 35,000
SALES (est): 7.8MM **Privately Held**
SIC: 8062 General medical & surgical hospitals

(P-21344)
CORRECTONS RHBLTATION CAL DEPT
Also Called: Cdcr Cal Instn For Men Hosp
14901 Central Ave, Chino (91710-9500)
P.O. Box 128 (91708-0128)
PHONE...................................909 597-1821
ME Poulls, *Warden*
Binh L Tran-Lei, *Internal Med*
Maria Salgado, *Case Mgr*
EMP: 179 **Privately Held**
SIC: 8062 9223 General medical & surgical hospitals; house of correction, government;
HQ: California Department Of Corrections & Rehabilitation
1515 S St
Sacramento CA 95811

(P-21345)
COTTAGE CARE CENTER
Also Called: Santa Barbara Cottage Care Ctr
2415 De La Vina St, Santa Barbara (93105-3819)
P.O. Box 689 (93102-0689)
PHONE...................................805 682-7111
Dr Peter Macdougall, *Ch of Bd*
James L Ash, *President*
Reece Duca, *CFO*
EMP: 160
SQ FT: 45,000
SALES: 7.8MM **Privately Held**
SIC: 8062 General medical & surgical hospitals

(P-21346)
COTTAGE HEALTH (PA)
Also Called: Santa Barbara Cottage Hospital
400 W Pueblo St, Santa Barbara (93105-4353)
P.O. Box 689 (93102-0689)
PHONE...................................805 682-7111
Ronald C Werft, *President*
James Benzian, *Ch Radiology*
Steven Fellows, *Exec VP*
Joan Bricher, *Senior VP*
Ronald Biscaro, *Vice Pres*
EMP: 2422
SQ FT: 202,500
SALES (est): 610.4MM **Privately Held**
SIC: 8062 8741 General medical & surgical hospitals; hospital management

(P-21347)
COTTAGE HEALTH
2050 Viborg Rd, Solvang (93463-2220)
PHONE...................................805 688-6432
John Blaustein, *Ch Pathology*
Wende Cappetta, *Vice Pres*
Judy Blokdyk, *Purchasing*
Thomas Reaper, *Med Doctor*
EMP: 171
SALES (est): 3.9MM
SALES (corp-wide): 610.4MM **Privately Held**
SIC: 8062 General medical & surgical hospitals
PA: Cottage Health
400 W Pueblo St
Santa Barbara CA 93105
805 682-7111

(P-21348)
COTTAGE HEALTH SYSTEM
351 S Patterson Ave, Goleta (93111-2403)
PHONE...................................805 967-3411
EMP: 1389
SALES (corp-wide): 610.4MM **Privately Held**
SIC: 8062 General medical & surgical hospitals
PA: Cottage Health
400 W Pueblo St
Santa Barbara CA 93105
805 682-7111

(P-21349)
COUNTY OF CONTRA COSTA
Also Called: Department of Health Services
2500 Alhambra Ave, Martinez (94553-3156)
PHONE...................................925 370-5000
Jeff Smith, *CEO*
Patrick Godley, *CFO*
Anna Roth, *Officer*

P R O D U C T S & S V C S

Jaspreet Benepal, *Nursing Dir*
Steve Tremain, *Director*
EMP: 200 **Privately Held**
WEB: www.cccounty.us
SIC: 8062 9431 General medical & surgi-
cal hospitals; administration of public
health programs;
PA: County Of Contra Costa
625 Court St Ste 100
Martinez CA 94553
925 957-5280

(P-21350)
COUNTY OF KERN
Public Health Dept
1700 Mount Vernon Ave, Bakersfield
(93306-4018)
PHONE..................661 326-2054
Peter Bryan, *CEO*
Debbie Hubbell, *Purch Dir*
EMP: 800 **Privately Held**
WEB: www.kccfc.org
SIC: 8062 9431 General medical & surgi-
cal hospitals; administration of public
health programs;
PA: County Of Kern
1115 Truxtun Ave Rm 505
Bakersfield CA 93301
661 868-3690

(P-21351)
COUNTY OF LOS ANGELES
Health Services, Dept of
14445 Olive View Dr 2b, Sylmar
(91342-1437)
PHONE..................818 364-1555
Melinda Anderson, *CEO*
Richard Tennant, *Associate*
EMP: 200 **Privately Held**
WEB: www.co.la.ca.us
SIC: 8062 9431 General medical & surgi-
cal hospitals;
PA: County Of Los Angeles
500 W Temple St Ste 437
Los Angeles CA 90012
213 974-1101

(P-21352)
COUNTY OF LOS ANGELES
Also Called: Health Services Dept
1000 W Carson St Fl 8 Flr 8, Palos Verdes
Peninsu (90274)
PHONE..................310 222-2401
Miguel Ortiz Marroquin, *CEO*
EMP: 300 **Privately Held**
WEB: www.co.la.ca.us
SIC: 8062 9431 General medical & surgi-
cal hospitals; administration of public
health programs;
PA: County Of Los Angeles
500 W Temple St Ste 437
Los Angeles CA 90012
213 974-1101

(P-21353)
COUNTY OF LOS ANGELES
Also Called: Health Services, Dept of
12025 Wilmington Ave, Los Angeles
(90059)
PHONE..................310 668-4545
Willie T May, *Exec Dir*
EMP: 197 **Privately Held**
WEB: www.co.la.ca.us
SIC: 8062 9431 General medical & surgi-
cal hospitals; administration of public
health programs;
PA: County Of Los Angeles
500 W Temple St Ste 437
Los Angeles CA 90012
213 974-1101

(P-21354)
COUNTY OF LOS ANGELES
Also Called: Health Services Dept
1100 N Mission Rd Rm 236, Los Angeles
(90033-1017)
PHONE..................323 226-6021
Scott Drewgan, *Director*
EMP: 200 **Privately Held**
WEB: www.co.la.ca.us
SIC: 8062 9431 General medical & surgi-
cal hospitals; administration of public
health programs

PA: County Of Los Angeles
500 W Temple St Ste 437
Los Angeles CA 90012
213 974-1101

(P-21355)
COUNTY OF LOS ANGELES
Also Called: Los Angles Cnty Cntl Jail Hosp
450 Bauchet St, Los Angeles (90012-2907)
PHONE..................213 473-6100
Don Knable, *Ch of Bd*
EMP: 278 **Privately Held**
WEB: www.co.la.ca.us
SIC: 8062 9431 General medical & surgi-
cal hospitals;
PA: County Of Los Angeles
500 W Temple St Ste 437
Los Angeles CA 90012
213 974-1101

(P-21356)
COUNTY OF MONTEREY
Also Called: Residncy Prgram Natividad Hosp
1441 Constitution Blvd # 100, Salinas
(93906-3136)
P.O. Box 81611 (93912-1611)
PHONE..................831 755-4201
Dr Gary Gray, *Director*
EMP: 600 **Privately Held**
WEB: www.montereycountyfarmbureau.org
SIC: 8062 General medical & surgical hos-
pitals
PA: County Of Monterey
168 W Alisal St Fl 2
Salinas CA 93901
831 755-5040

(P-21357)
COUNTY OF SAN DIEGO
Also Called: Medical Examiner
9320 Farnham St, San Diego (92123)
PHONE..................858 694-2895
Brian Blackburn, *Branch Mgr*
EMP: 50 **Privately Held**
WEB: www.sdlcc.org
SIC: 8062 9431 General medical & surgi-
cal hospitals;
PA: County Of San Diego
1600 Pacific Hwy Ste 209
San Diego CA 92101
619 531-5880

(P-21358)
COUNTY OF SAN LUIS OBISPO
Also Called: County General Hospital
2180 Johnson Ave, San Luis Obispo
(93401-4558)
PHONE..................805 781-4800
Nancy Rosen, *Manager*
EMP: 275
SQ FT: 4,500 **Privately Held**
SIC: 8062 8721 General medical & surgi-
cal hospitals; accounting, auditing &
bookkeeping
PA: County Of San Luis Obispo
Government Center Rm. 300
San Luis Obispo CA 93408
805 781-5040

(P-21359)
COUNTY OF SONOMA
Also Called: Palm Drive Healthcare District
501 Petaluma Ave, Sebastopol
(95472-4215)
PHONE..................707 823-8511
Shawndra Nimtz, *CEO*
EMP: 200
SQ FT: 3,684 **Privately Held**
WEB: www.sonomacompost.com
SIC: 8062 8051 General medical & surgi-
cal hospitals; skilled nursing care facilities
PA: County Of Sonoma
585 Fiscal Dr 100
Santa Rosa CA 95403
707 565-2431

(P-21360)
COUNTY OF STANISLAUS
Also Called: Stanislaus Medical Center
830 Scenic Dr, Modesto (95350-6131)
P.O. Box 3271 (95353-3271)
PHONE..................209 525-7000
Beverly M Finley, *Manager*
Neil Bronstein, *Executive*
Donna Meyer, *Technology*
EMP: 600

SQ FT: 1,866 **Privately Held**
WEB: www.co.stanislaus.ca.us
SIC: 8062 General medical & surgical hos-
pitals
PA: County Of Stanislaus
1010 10th St Ste 5100
Modesto CA 95354
209 525-6398

(P-21361)
**COVENANT CARE CALIFORNIA
LLC**
Also Called: Grant-Cuesta Nursing Center
1949 Grant Rd, Mountain View
(94040-3217)
PHONE..................650 964-0543
Cheryl Cartney, *Branch Mgr*
EMP: 100 **Privately Held**
WEB: www.willowtreenursingcenter.com
SIC: 8062 8051 8069 General medical &
surgical hospitals; skilled nursing care fa-
cilities; specialty hospitals, except psychi-
atric
HQ: Covenant Care California, Llc
27071 Aliso Creek Rd # 100
Aliso Viejo CA 92656

(P-21362)
**DAMERON HOSPITAL
ASSOCIATION (PA)**
525 W Acacia St, Stockton (95203-2484)
PHONE..................209 944-5550
Lorraine Auerbach, *CEO*
Melanie Parker,
Nicholas Arismendi, *COO*
David Kerrins, *CFO*
Debbie Hill, *Bd of Directors*
EMP: 1003
SQ FT: 136,061
SALES: 190.4MM **Privately Held**
WEB: www.dameronhospital.org
SIC: 8062 General medical & surgical hos-
pitals

(P-21363)
**DEL MAR CONVALESCENT
HOSPITAL**
3136 Del Mar Ave, Rosemead
(91770-2326)
PHONE..................626 288-8353
Walter Chameides, *Principal*
EMP: 60
SALES: 5.9MM **Privately Held**
SIC: 8062 8051 8322 General medical &
surgical hospitals; skilled nursing care fa-
cilities; rehabilitation services

(P-21364)
**DESERT REGIONAL MED CTR
INC (HQ)**
Also Called: Tenet
1150 N Indian Canyon Dr, Palm Springs
(92262-4872)
P.O. Box 2739 (92263-2739)
PHONE..................760 323-6511
Toll Free:..................888 -
Carolyn Caldwell, *CEO*
Robert Rosser, *Ch Pathology*
David Duffner,
Cris Rodriguez, *Records Dir*
Lisa Wilson, *President*
EMP: 1200
SQ FT: 400,000
SALES (est): 518.1MM
SALES (corp-wide): 19.3B **Publicly Held**
SIC: 8062 General medical & surgical hos-
pitals
PA: Tenet Healthcare Corporation
1445 Ross Ave Ste 1400
Dallas TX 75202
469 893-2200

(P-21365)
**DESERT VALLEY HOSPITAL INC
(DH)**
16850 Bear Valley Rd, Victorville
(92395-5794)
PHONE..................760 241-8000
Margaret R Peterson, *CEO*
Roger Krissman, *CFO*
Kristina Woodworth, *Hum Res Coord*
Janeen Johansen, *Director*
▲ **EMP:** 106
SQ FT: 63,000

SALES (est): 140.5MM
SALES (corp-wide): 3.4B **Privately Held**
SIC: 8062 General medical & surgical hos-
pitals

(P-21366)
DIGNITY HEALTH
3215 Prospect Park Dr, Rancho Cordova
(95670-6017)
PHONE..................916 861-1100
Diane Brack, *Branch Mgr*
Julie Chang, *Manager*
EMP: 140
SALES (corp-wide): 6.7B **Privately Held**
WEB: www.chw.edu
SIC: 8062 General medical & surgical hos-
pitals
PA: Dignity Health
185 Berry St Ste 300
San Francisco CA 94107
415 438-5500

(P-21367)
DIGNITY HEALTH
2131 W 3rd St, Los Angeles (90057-1901)
PHONE..................213 484-7111
William Parente, *President*
EMP: 500
SALES (corp-wide): 6.7B **Privately Held**
WEB: www.chw.edu
SIC: 8062 General medical & surgical hos-
pitals
PA: Dignity Health
185 Berry St Ste 300
San Francisco CA 94107
415 438-5500

(P-21368)
DIGNITY HEALTH
1650 Creekside Dr, Folsom (95630-3400)
PHONE..................916 983-7400
Karl L Silberstein, *Manager*
Kathy Watrobski, *Executive*
Sandy Ludwig, *Purch Mgr*
Edna Onodera,
Denise Pimintel,
EMP: 193
SALES (corp-wide): 6.7B **Privately Held**
WEB: www.chw.edu
SIC: 8062 General medical & surgical hos-
pitals
PA: Dignity Health
185 Berry St Ste 300
San Francisco CA 94107
415 438-5500

(P-21369)
DIGNITY HEALTH
Also Called: Marian Regional Medical Center
1400 E Church St, Santa Maria
(93454-5906)
PHONE..................805 739-3000
Charles Cova, *President*
Bruce Ourieff,
Bob Turbow, *Officer*
Karen Mase, *Ch Nursing Ofcr*
Sue Andersen, *General Mgr*
EMP: 400
SALES (corp-wide): 6.7B **Privately Held**
WEB: www.chw.edu
SIC: 8062 8011 General medical & surgi-
cal hospitals; offices & clinics of medical
doctors
PA: Dignity Health
185 Berry St Ste 300
San Francisco CA 94107
415 438-5500

(P-21370)
DIGNITY HEALTH
7601 Hospital Dr Ste 103, Sacramento
(95823-5408)
PHONE..................916 681-1600
Amir Sweha MD, *Branch Mgr*
EMP: 50
SALES (corp-wide): 6.7B **Privately Held**
SIC: 8062 General medical & surgical hos-
pitals
PA: Dignity Health
185 Berry St Ste 300
San Francisco CA 94107
415 438-5500

(P-21371)
DIGNITY HEALTH
Also Called: Mercy San Juan Med Trauma Ctr
6501 Coyle Ave Fl 6, Carmichael
(95608-0306)
PHONE..............................916 537-5151
Donna Utley, *Director*
Debbie Walker, *Admin Asst*
Cynthia Cox, *Analyst*
Jay Conner, *Facilities Mgr*
Peter Skaff, *Neurology*
EMP: 1700
SALES (corp-wide): 6.7B **Privately Held**
WEB: www.mercycare.net
SIC: 8062 General medical & surgical hospitals
PA: Dignity Health
    185 Berry St Ste 300
    San Francisco CA 94107
    415 438-5500

(P-21372)
DIGNITY HEALTH
5051 Verdugo Way Ste 100, Camarillo
(93012-8681)
PHONE..............................805 384-8071
Tom Lowry, *Branch Mgr*
Jason Newmark, *Marketing Staff*
Jocelyn Napod, *Internal Med*
Cynthia Fiacco, *Nurse Practr*
EMP: 452
SALES (corp-wide): 6.7B **Privately Held**
SIC: 8062 General medical & surgical hospitals
PA: Dignity Health
    185 Berry St Ste 300
    San Francisco CA 94107
    415 438-5500

(P-21373)
DIGNITY HEALTH
3400 Data Dr, Rancho Cordova
(95670-7956)
PHONE..............................916 851-2153
Rick Canning, *Principal*
Marian Bell-Holmes, *Human Res Dir*
Daniel Andresen, *Director*
Jim Dieser, *Director*
EMP: 193
SALES (corp-wide): 6.7B **Privately Held**
WEB: www.chw.edu
SIC: 8062 General medical & surgical hospitals
PA: Dignity Health
    185 Berry St Ste 300
    San Francisco CA 94107
    415 438-5500

(P-21374)
DIGNITY HEALTH
Also Called: Arroyo Grande Community Hosp
345 S Halcyon Rd, Arroyo Grande
(93420-3817)
PHONE..............................805 473-7626
Sue Anderson, *CFO*
Montisa Lopez, *Vice Pres*
Christina Squires, *Vice Pres*
Villa Infanto, *Ch Nursing Ofcr*
Tauny Sexton, *Exec Dir*
EMP: 400
SALES (corp-wide): 6.7B **Privately Held**
SIC: 8062 General medical & surgical hospitals
PA: Dignity Health
    185 Berry St Ste 300
    San Francisco CA 94107
    415 438-5500

(P-21375)
DIGNITY HEALTH
1700 Montgomery St # 300, San Francisco
(94111-1021)
PHONE..............................415 438-5500
Parmod Garg, *Finance*
Digna Rodriguez, *Office Admin*
Kara Lewis, *Med Doctor*
Chela Chavez, *Director*
Paula Green, *Manager*
EMP: 474
SALES (corp-wide): 6.7B **Privately Held**
WEB: www.chw.edu
SIC: 8062 General medical & surgical hospitals

PA: Dignity Health
    185 Berry St Ste 300
    San Francisco CA 94107
    415 438-5500

(P-21376)
DIGNITY HEALTH
Also Called: Saint Mary Medical Center
1050 Linden Ave, Long Beach
(90813-3321)
PHONE..............................562 491-9000
Chris Diccio, *Principal*
Ann Marie Levan, *Ch Radiology*
Karen Matthews, *Op Rm Dir*
Yvonne Sison, *Purchasing*
Pamela Martin, *Education*
EMP: 1450
SALES (corp-wide): 6.7B **Privately Held**
WEB: www.chw.edu
SIC: 8062 General medical & surgical hospitals
PA: Dignity Health
    185 Berry St Ste 300
    San Francisco CA 94107
    415 438-5500

(P-21377)
DIGNITY HEALTH (PA)
Also Called: Mercy Hospital
185 Berry St Ste 300, San Francisco
(94107-1773)
PHONE..............................415 438-5500
Lloyd Dean, *President*
Marvin O'Quinn, *COO*
Michael Blaszyk, *CFO*
Lisa Zuckerman, *Treasurer*
Charles Francis, *Sr Exec VP*
▲ **EMP:** 120
SALES (est): 6.7B **Privately Held**
WEB: www.chw.edu
SIC: 8062 General medical & surgical hospitals

(P-21378)
DIGNITY HEALTH
Also Called: California Hospital Med Ctr
1401 S Grand Ave, Los Angeles
(90015-3010)
PHONE..............................213 748-2411
Mark A Meyers, *President*
Thomas Bogaard,
Bruce Swartz, *Vice Pres*
Nicole Kerns, *Administration*
Debbie Gappa, *Business Anlyst*
EMP: 1500
SALES (corp-wide): 6.7B **Privately Held**
WEB: www.chw.edu
SIC: 8062 8741 General medical & surgical hospitals; management services
PA: Dignity Health
    185 Berry St Ste 300
    San Francisco CA 94107
    415 438-5500

(P-21379)
DIGNITY HEALTH
Also Called: Mercy San Juan Medical Center
6501 Coyle Ave, Carmichael (95608-0306)
PHONE..............................916 537-5000
Rian Ivie, *Director*
Jeanne Kim, *Anesthesiology*
Eugene Leyble, *Internal Med*
Nabil Majid, *Internal Med*
Vijay Jethanandani, *Psychiatry*
EMP: 1500
SALES (corp-wide): 6.7B **Privately Held**
WEB: www.mercycare.net
SIC: 8062 8011 General medical & surgical hospitals; offices & clinics of medical doctors
PA: Dignity Health
    185 Berry St Ste 300
    San Francisco CA 94107
    415 438-5500

(P-21380)
DIGNITY HEALTH
Mercy Hospital of Folsom
1650 Creekside Dr, Folsom (95630-3400)
PHONE..............................916 983-7400
Donald Hudson, *President*
Robin Rogness, *Treasurer*
Larry Ames, *Engineer*
Richard Mattern, *Engineer*
Amy Mantell, *Human Res Mgr*
EMP: 400

SALES (corp-wide): 6.7B **Privately Held**
WEB: www.mercycare.net
SIC: 8062 4119 General medical & surgical hospitals; ambulance service
PA: Dignity Health
    185 Berry St Ste 300
    San Francisco CA 94107
    415 438-5500

(P-21381)
DIGNITY HEALTH
Also Called: Mercy Medical Center Redding
2175 Rosaline Ave Ste A, Redding
(96001-2549)
PHONE..............................530 225-6345
Scott Foster, *Branch Mgr*
Mark Korth, *Vice Pres*
Henry Niessink, *Info Tech Dir*
Rodger Page, *Purchasing*
John Coe, *Gnrl Med Prac*
EMP: 193
SALES (corp-wide): 6.7B **Privately Held**
SIC: 8062 General medical & surgical hospitals
PA: Dignity Health
    185 Berry St Ste 300
    San Francisco CA 94107
    415 438-5500

(P-21382)
DIGNITY HEALTH
20 N Cottonwood St, Woodland
(95695-2585)
PHONE..............................530 666-8828
Dawn M Purkey, *Branch Mgr*
Salil Kharat, *Info Tech Dir*
Herb Inscho, *Director*
Dawnese Kindelt, *Director*
Leonard Smith, *Director*
EMP: 187
SALES (corp-wide): 6.7B **Privately Held**
SIC: 8062 General medical & surgical hospitals
PA: Dignity Health
    185 Berry St Ste 300
    San Francisco CA 94107
    415 438-5500

(P-21383)
DIGNITY HEALTH
1555 Soquel Dr, Santa Cruz (95065-1705)
PHONE..............................831 462-7700
Nanette Mickiewicz, *Principal*
Susan Macmillan, *Business Dir*
Lauren Smith, *Chief Engr*
Kevin Keith, *Plant Mgr*
Rita Dean, *Pastor Care Dir*
EMP: 1500
SALES (corp-wide): 6.7B **Privately Held**
WEB: www.chw.edu
SIC: 8062 General medical & surgical hospitals
PA: Dignity Health
    185 Berry St Ste 300
    San Francisco CA 94107
    415 438-5500

(P-21384)
DIGNITY HEALTH
Also Called: Mark Twain St Josephs Hospital
768 Mountain Ranch Rd, San Andreas
(95249-9707)
PHONE..............................209 754-3521
Narlene Cain, *Admin Sec*
Roger Orman, *Med Doctor*
EMP: 193
SALES (corp-wide): 6.7B **Privately Held**
WEB: www.chw.edu
SIC: 8062 General medical & surgical hospitals
PA: Dignity Health
    185 Berry St Ste 300
    San Francisco CA 94107
    415 438-5500

(P-21385)
DIGNITY HEALTH
Also Called: Methodist Hospital Sacramento
7500 Hospital Dr, Sacramento
(95823-5403)
PHONE..............................916 423-5940
William J Hunt, *Principal*
Marian Antona, *Business Anlyst*
Steve Hern, *Engineer*
Lisa Sanders, *Hlthcr Dir*
Andrea Barton, *Director*

EMP: 193
SALES (corp-wide): 6.7B **Privately Held**
WEB: www.chw.edu
SIC: 8062 General medical & surgical hospitals
PA: Dignity Health
    185 Berry St Ste 300
    San Francisco CA 94107
    415 438-5500

(P-21386)
DIGNITY HEALTH
Also Called: Mercy General Hospital Bus Off
4001 J St, Sacramento (95819-3626)
P.O. Box 3008, Rancho Cordova (95741-3008)
PHONE..............................916 453-4545
Thomas Peterson, *Director*
Patsy Freeman, *Officer*
Page West, *Vice Pres*
Julie Lawson, *Med Doctor*
Miguel Rivera, *Med Doctor*
EMP: 1600
SALES (corp-wide): 6.7B **Privately Held**
WEB: www.mercycare.net
SIC: 8062 General medical & surgical hospitals
PA: Dignity Health
    185 Berry St Ste 300
    San Francisco CA 94107
    415 438-5500

(P-21387)
DIGNITY HEALTH
551 Shanley Ct, Bakersfield (93311-1306)
PHONE..............................661 663-6767
Mike Depetro, *Manager*
EMP: 50
SALES (corp-wide): 6.7B **Privately Held**
WEB: www.chw.edu
SIC: 8062 General medical & surgical hospitals
PA: Dignity Health
    185 Berry St Ste 300
    San Francisco CA 94107
    415 438-5500

(P-21388)
DIGNITY HEALTH
Also Called: St. Johns Pleasant Valley Hosp
2309 Antonio Ave, Camarillo (93010-1414)
PHONE..............................805 389-5800
Daniel Herlinger, *Branch Mgr*
Darren Lee, *Officer*
M Eugene Fussell, *Vice Pres*
EMP: 250
SALES (corp-wide): 6.7B **Privately Held**
WEB: www.chw.edu
SIC: 8062 General medical & surgical hospitals
PA: Dignity Health
    185 Berry St Ste 300
    San Francisco CA 94107
    415 438-5500

(P-21389)
DIGNITY HEALTH
Methodist Hospital Sacramento
7500 Hospital Dr, Sacramento
(95823-5403)
PHONE..............................916 423-3000
Timothy Moran, *President*
Michael Earn, *CEO*
Bonnie Jenkins, *CFO*
Stanley C Oppegard, *Administration*
Bonnie Andrade, *QA Dir*
EMP: 990
SQ FT: 1,000
SALES (corp-wide): 6.7B **Privately Held**
WEB: www.mercycare.net
SIC: 8062 8011 General medical & surgical hospitals; clinic, operated by physicians
PA: Dignity Health
    185 Berry St Ste 300
    San Francisco CA 94107
    415 438-5500

(P-21390)
DIGNITY HEALTH
Also Called: Marian West
505 Plaza Dr, Santa Maria (93454-6907)
PHONE..............................805 739-3100
Kathleen Sullivan, *Manager*
Kathy Fuerch,
Daniel Fulton, *Supervisor*

EMP: 1400
SALES (corp-wide): 6.7B **Privately Held**
WEB: www.chw.edu
SIC: 8062 General medical & surgical hospitals
PA: Dignity Health
    185 Berry St Ste 300
    San Francisco CA 94107
    415 438-5500

(P-21391)
DIGNITY HEALTH
Also Called: St Johns Regional Medical Ctr
1600 N Rose Ave, Oxnard (93030-3722)
PHONE..............................805 988-2500
George West, *Vice Pres*
Henry Montes, *Bd of Directors*
Laurie Eberst, *Officer*
Debi Klein, *Vice Pres*
Chris Champlin, *Business Dir*
EMP: 1900
SALES (corp-wide): 6.7B **Privately Held**
SIC: 8062 General medical & surgical hospitals
PA: Dignity Health
    185 Berry St Ste 300
    San Francisco CA 94107
    415 438-5500

(P-21392)
DIGNITY HEALTH
Also Called: St. Mary's Medical Center
450 Stanyan St, San Francisco (94117-1019)
PHONE..............................415 668-1000
Gracia Wiarda, *Director*
Amy Carrillo, *Executive Asst*
Sarah Williams, *Executive Asst*
Reshmi Prasad, *Admin Sec*
Mariam Harris, *Office Spvr*
EMP: 1100
SALES (corp-wide): 6.7B **Privately Held**
SIC: 8062 8322 General medical & surgical hospitals; adult day care center
PA: Dignity Health
    185 Berry St Ste 300
    San Francisco CA 94107
    415 438-5500

(P-21393)
DIGNITY HEALTH
Also Called: Pedi Center
400 Old River Rd, Bakersfield (93311-9781)
P.O. Box 119 (93302-0119)
PHONE..............................661 632-5279
Kirk Douglas, *Branch Mgr*
Kim Horton, *Nursing Dir*
Jerry Hoffman, *Director*
Rey De Claro, *Supervisor*
Rey Declaro, *Supervisor*
EMP: 120
SALES (corp-wide): 6.7B **Privately Held**
WEB: www.chw.edu
SIC: 8062 8099 8011 General medical & surgical hospitals; childbirth preparation clinic; offices & clinics of medical doctors
PA: Dignity Health
    185 Berry St Ste 300
    San Francisco CA 94107
    415 438-5500

(P-21394)
DIGNITY HEALTH
Also Called: Mercy Hospital
2215 Truxtun Ave, Bakersfield (93301-3602)
PHONE..............................661 632-5000
Rodney B Winegarner, *Branch Mgr*
Colleen Goodman, *Lab Dir*
Stacy Close, *Nursing Mgr*
Ken Stonecipher, *Plant Mgr*
Lynn Godat, *Director*
EMP: 474
SALES (corp-wide): 6.7B **Privately Held**
SIC: 8062 General medical & surgical hospitals
PA: Dignity Health
    185 Berry St Ste 300
    San Francisco CA 94107
    415 438-5500

(P-21395)
DIGNITY HEALTH MED FOUNDATION (HQ)
Also Called: Dignity Hlth Med Grp-Dominican
3400 Data Dr, Rancho Cordova (95670-7956)
PHONE..............................916 379-2840
Laurie Schwarctz, *President*
Kristy Kelly, *Vice Pres*
David Herman, *Admin Sec*
Sherry Penlesky, *Admin Asst*
Jennean Rogers, *Admin Asst*
EMP: 200
SQ FT: 45,000
SALES: 570.1MM
SALES (corp-wide): 6.7B **Privately Held**
WEB: www.chwmedicalfoundation.com
SIC: 8062 General medical & surgical hospitals
PA: Dignity Health
    185 Berry St Ste 300
    San Francisco CA 94107
    415 438-5500

(P-21396)
DOCTORS HOSPITAL W COVINA INC
Also Called: WEST COVINA PHYSICAL THERAPY
725 S Orange Ave, West Covina (91790-2614)
PHONE..............................626 338-8481
Pareed Mohamed, *CEO*
Jong Kim MD, *Treasurer*
Akbar Omar MD, *Vice Pres*
Gerald Wallman, *Executive*
Pareed Aliyar MD, *Admin Sec*
EMP: 155
SQ FT: 50,000
SALES: 16MM **Privately Held**
SIC: 8062 8049 General medical & surgical hospitals; physical therapist

(P-21397)
DOCTORS MED CTR MODESTO INC (HQ)
Also Called: TENET
1441 Florida Ave, Modesto (95350-4404)
P.O. Box 139036, Dallas TX (75313-9036)
PHONE..............................209 578-1211
Warren J Kirk, *CEO*
Greg Berry, *CFO*
Jill Fisher, *Admin Asst*
Steve Lauer, *Engineer*
Dan Martin, *Engineer*
EMP: 67
SALES: 587.9MM
SALES (corp-wide): 19.3B **Publicly Held**
SIC: 8062 General medical & surgical hospitals
PA: Tenet Healthcare Corporation
    1445 Ross Ave Ste 1400
    Dallas TX 75202
    469 893-2200

(P-21398)
DOMINICAN HOSPITAL FOUNDATION (HQ)
1555 Soquel Dr, Santa Cruz (95065-1794)
PHONE..............................831 462-7700
Beverly Grova, *CEO*
Chuck Maffia, *President*
Jon Sisk, *President*
Sam Leask, *CEO*
Ted Burke, *Vice Pres*
EMP: 114
SQ FT: 110,000
SALES: 2.9MM
SALES (corp-wide): 6.7B **Privately Held**
SIC: 8062 8051 General medical & surgical hospitals; skilled nursing care facilities
PA: Dignity Health
    185 Berry St Ste 300
    San Francisco CA 94107
    415 438-5500

(P-21399)
EAST VALLEY GLENDORA HOSP LLC
Also Called: East Valley Hospital Med Ctr
150 W Route 66, Glendora (91740-6207)
PHONE..............................626 852-5000
C Joseph Chang, *Ch of Bd*
Jinny Kim, *Business Dir*
Robert Gordon,

EMP: 300
SQ FT: 60,592
SALES: 29.3MM **Privately Held**
WEB: www.evhmc.org
SIC: 8062 General medical & surgical hospitals

(P-21400)
EDEN TOWNSHIP HOSPITAL DST
Also Called: Eden Medical Center
20400 Lake Chabot Rd # 303, Castro Valley (94546-5316)
PHONE..............................510 538-2031
Terry Glubka, *President*
George Weaver, *Foreman/Supr*
Cindy Dove, *Mktg Dir*
Evan Wythe, *Emerg Med Spec*
Lisa King, *Director*
EMP: 968
SQ FT: 190,000
SALES: 334.5MM
SALES (corp-wide): 12.4B **Privately Held**
WEB: www.edenmedcenter.org
SIC: 8062 8011 General medical & surgical hospitals; offices & clinics of medical doctors
PA: Sutter Health
    2200 River Plaza Dr
    Sacramento CA 95833
    916 733-8800

(P-21401)
EISENHOWER MEDICAL CENTER (PA)
39000 Bob Hope Dr, Rancho Mirage (92270-3221)
PHONE..............................760 340-3911
G Aubrey Serfling, *CEO*
Barbara Comess, *Ch Pathology*
Christoph Cantilena,
Kimberly Osborne, *CFO*
Martin J Massiello, *Exec VP*
▲ **EMP:** 2000
SQ FT: 240,000
SALES: 640.2MM **Privately Held**
SIC: 8062 8082 General medical & surgical hospitals; home health care services

(P-21402)
EL CAMINO SURGERY CENTER LLC
2480 Grant Rd Fl 1, Mountain View (94040-4334)
PHONE..............................650 961-1200
Lisa Cooper, *Mng Member*
Marla Marlow, *Mng Member*
Sandy Keating, *Director*
EMP: 70
SQ FT: 16,500
SALES: 15K **Privately Held**
WEB: www.ecsc.com
SIC: 8062 General medical & surgical hospitals

(P-21403)
EL CENTRO REGIONAL MEDICAL CTR (PA)
Also Called: E C R M C
1415 Ross Ave, El Centro (92243-4306)
PHONE..............................760 339-7100
Robert R Frantz, *President*
Jacqueline Lara, *Records Dir*
Barbara Blevins, *President*
Claudia Dubbe, *President*
Kathy Farmer, *CFO*
EMP: 603
SQ FT: 187,044
SALES: 127.8MM **Privately Held**
WEB: www.ecrmc.org
SIC: 8062 General medical & surgical hospitals

(P-21404)
ELADH LP
Also Called: East Los Angeles Doctors Hosp
4060 Whittier Blvd, Los Angeles (90023-2526)
PHONE..............................323 268-5514
Gerald Clute, *CEO*
Hector Hernandez, *Managing Prtnr*
Julie Tarazon, *Executive Asst*
Chris Mancao, *Accountant*
Suzanna Zemer, *Train & Dev Mgr*
EMP: 99

SALES: 72.1MM
SALES (corp-wide): 253.3MM **Privately Held**
SIC: 8062 General medical & surgical hospitals
PA: Avanti Hospitals, Llc
    222 N Splvd Blvd Ste 950
    El Segundo CA 90245
    310 356-0550

(P-21405)
EMANUEL MEDICAL CENTER INC
Also Called: Brandel Manor
1801 N Olive Ave, Turlock (95382-2568)
PHONE..............................209 667-5600
Dawn Sughruel, *Director*
EMP: 160
SQ FT: 58,282
SALES (corp-wide): 19.3B **Publicly Held**
WEB: www.emanuelmedicalcenter.com
SIC: 8062 8051 General medical & surgical hospitals; convalescent home with continuous nursing care
HQ: Emanuel Medical Center, Inc.
    825 Delbon Ave
    Turlock CA 95382
    209 667-4200

(P-21406)
EMANUEL MEDICAL CENTER INC (DH)
825 Delbon Ave, Turlock (95382-2016)
PHONE..............................209 667-4200
Susan Micheletti, *CEO*
Huy Dao,
Ronald Arakelian MD, *Ch Radiology*
Joseph L Higgins, *Ch Radiology*
Beth Walker, *CTO*
EMP: 850
SQ FT: 200,000
SALES: 209.5MM
SALES (corp-wide): 19.3B **Publicly Held**
WEB: www.emanuelmedicalcenter.com
SIC: 8062 General medical & surgical hospitals
HQ: Doctors Medical Center Of Modesto, Inc.
    1441 Florida Ave
    Modesto CA 95350
    209 578-1211

(P-21407)
EMANUEL MEDICAL CENTER INC
Also Called: Turlock Diagnostic Center
2121 Colorado Ave Ste A, Turlock (95382-2012)
PHONE..............................209 664-2520
Michael Iltis, *Manager*
EMP: 103
SALES (corp-wide): 19.3B **Publicly Held**
WEB: www.emanuelmedicalcenter.com
SIC: 8062 8011 General medical & surgical hospitals; medical centers
HQ: Emanuel Medical Center, Inc.
    825 Delbon Ave
    Turlock CA 95382
    209 667-4200

(P-21408)
EMERGENCY MEDICINE SPECIALIST
Also Called: Emsoc
1010 W La Veta Ave # 755, Orange (92868-4306)
PHONE..............................714 543-8911
James Pierog, *Chairman*
Linda J Pierog, *Office Mgr*
David Merin, *Emerg Med Spec*
EMP: 90
SALES (est): 5.8MM **Privately Held**
SIC: 8062 General medical & surgical hospitals

(P-21409)
ENCINO HOSPITAL MEDICAL CENTER
16237 Ventura Blvd, Encino (91436-2272)
PHONE..............................818 995-5000
Bockhi Park, *CEO*
Prem Reddy, *President*
EMP: 400

▲ = Import ▼=Export
◆ =Import/Export

SALES: 52.4MM
SALES (corp-wide): 3.4B **Privately Held**
SIC: 8062 General medical & surgical hospitals
HQ: Prime Healthcare Services Inc
3300 E Guasti Rd Ste 300
Ontario CA 91761

(P-21410)
ENCINO TRZANA REGIONAL MED CTR
16237 Ventura Blvd, Encino (91436-2201)
PHONE..................................818 995-5000
EMP: 450
SALES: 41.7MM **Privately Held**
SIC: 8062

(P-21411)
ENLOE HOSPT-PHYS THRPY
1444 Magnolia Ave, Chico (95926-3227)
PHONE..................................530 891-7300
Brenda Logan, *Director*
EMP: 173
SALES (corp-wide): 4.3MM **Privately Held**
SIC: 8062 General medical & surgical hospitals
PA: Enloe Hospital - Physical Therapy Dept
1600 Esplanade
Chico CA 95926
530 891-7300

(P-21412)
ENLOE MEDICAL CENTER
Also Called: E E G and E P
560 Cohasset Rd, Chico (95926-2281)
PHONE..................................530 332-4111
Joan Lilly, *Principal*
Marcia Nelson, *Administration*
Steven Wahlen, *Oncology*
Brenda Boggs-Hargis, *Director*
Marty Marshall, *Director*
EMP: 53
SALES (corp-wide): 528.3MM **Privately Held**
SIC: 8062 General medical & surgical hospitals
PA: Enloe Medical Center
1531 Esplanade
Chico CA 95926
530 332-7300

(P-21413)
ENLOE MEDICAL CENTER
Also Called: Enloe Outpatient Center
888 Lakeside Vlg Cmns, Chico (95928-3979)
PHONE..................................530 332-6400
Joleen Nixon, *Director*
Kathy Buck, *Director*
EMP: 130
SQ FT: 44,171
SALES (corp-wide): 528.3MM **Privately Held**
SIC: 8062 8093 General medical & surgical hospitals; specialty outpatient clinics
PA: Enloe Medical Center
1531 Esplanade
Chico CA 95926
530 332-7300

(P-21414)
FAMILY MDCINE RSIDENCY PROGRAM
155 N Fresno St Ste 326, Fresno (93701-2302)
PHONE..................................559 499-6450
Ivan Gomez, *Director*
EMP: 60
SALES (est): 871.4K **Privately Held**
SIC: 8062 Hospital, AMA approved residency

(P-21415)
FEATHER RIVER HOSPITAL (PA)
5974 Pentz Rd, Paradise (95969-5593)
PHONE..................................530 877-9361
Wayne Ferch, *CEO*
Tim Gleason,
Dan Gordon, *CFO*
Gloria Santos, *Vice Pres*
Karen Corsen, *Lab Dir*
EMP: 925
SQ FT: 30,000

SALES: 207MM **Privately Held**
SIC: 8062 8051 General medical & surgical hospitals; convalescent home with continuous nursing care

(P-21416)
FEATHER RIVER HOSPITAL
Also Called: Feather River Home Health
6626 Clark Rd Ste P, Paradise (95969-3523)
PHONE..................................530 872-3378
Gregg Quattlevaum, *Manager*
EMP: 60
SALES (corp-wide): 207MM **Privately Held**
SIC: 8062 8082 General medical & surgical hospitals; home health care services
PA: Feather River Hospital
5974 Pentz Rd
Paradise CA 95969
530 877-9361

(P-21417)
FOOTHILL HOSPITAL-MORRIS L JO (PA)
Also Called: FOOTHILL PRESBYTERIAN HOSPITAL
250 S Grand Ave, Glendora (91741-4218)
PHONE..................................626 857-3145
Robert Curry, *President*
Melissa Howard, *Administration*
Diana Zenner, *Administration*
Ed Tronez,
EMP: 400
SQ FT: 104,371
SALES: 110.1MM **Privately Held**
SIC: 8062 Hospital, affiliated with AMA residency

(P-21418)
FOUNTAIN VALLEY REGL HOSPL
17100 Euclid St, Fountain Valley (92708-4043)
P.O. Box 8010 (92728-8010)
PHONE..................................714 966-7200
Kenneth McFarlin, *CEO*
Edward F Littlejohn, *COO*
Ken Jordan, *CFO*
Alex Fink, *Buyer*
Lourdes Salao, *Nursing Dir*
EMP: 1200
SALES (est): 478.1K
SALES (corp-wide): 19.3B **Publicly Held**
WEB: www.tenenthealth.com
SIC: 8062 Hospital, affiliated with AMA residency
HQ: Tenet Healthsystem Medical, Inc.
1445 Ross Ave Ste 1400
Dallas TX 75202
469 893-2000

(P-21419)
FREMONT HOSPITAL
Also Called: Fremont Medical Center
620 J St, Marysville (95901-5413)
PHONE..................................530 751-4000
Thomas P Hayes, *CEO*
Jeanne Martin, *Admin Sec*
EMP: 598
SQ FT: 121,000
SALES (est): 17.8MM
SALES (corp-wide): 26.9MM **Privately Held**
SIC: 8062 General medical & surgical hospitals
PA: Freemont Rideout Health Group
989 Plumas St
Yuba City CA 95991
530 751-4010

(P-21420)
FRENCH HOSP MED CTR FOUNDATION (HQ)
1911 Johnson Ave, San Luis Obispo (93401-4131)
PHONE..................................805 543-5353
Jim Copeland, *Chairman*
Allan Iftiniuk, *President*
Sue Anderson, *CFO*
Mark Soll, *Bd of Directors*
Sandy Mugg, *Risk Mgmt Dir*
EMP: 480
SQ FT: 80,000

SALES: 126.7MM
SALES (corp-wide): 6.7B **Privately Held**
SIC: 8062 Hospital, affiliated with AMA residency
PA: Dignity Health
185 Berry St Ste 300
San Francisco CA 94107
415 438-5500

(P-21421)
FRESNO CMNTY HOSP & MED CTR
Also Called: Clovis Community Medical Ctr
2755 Herndon Ave, Clovis (93611-6800)
PHONE..................................559 324-4000
Phyllis Baltz, *Manager*
Joseph Boado, *Lab Dir*
Angelica Tover, *Human Res Mgr*
Amy Flach, *Mktg Dir*
Paul Luchi, *Food Svc Dir*
EMP: 95
SQ FT: 36,000
SALES (corp-wide): 1.6B **Privately Held**
SIC: 8062 General medical & surgical hospitals
HQ: Fresno Community Hospital And Medical Center
2823 Fresno St
Fresno CA 93721
559 459-6000

(P-21422)
FRESNO CMNTY HOSP & MED CTR (HQ)
2823 Fresno St, Fresno (93721-1324)
P.O. Box 1232 (93715-1232)
PHONE..................................559 459-6000
Phillip Hinton, *President*
Tim A Joslin, *CEO*
William Grigg, *CFO*
Roger Fretwell, *Treasurer*
Mike Kingbury, *Senior VP*
EMP: 3000
SQ FT: 2,469
SALES (est): 1.5B
SALES (corp-wide): 1.6B **Privately Held**
SIC: 8062 General medical & surgical hospitals
PA: Community Hospitals Of Central California
2823 Fresno St
Fresno CA 93721
559 459-6000

(P-21423)
FRESNO HEART HOSPITAL LLC
15 E Audubon Dr, Fresno (93720-1542)
PHONE..................................559 433-8000
Wanda Holderman, *Mng Member*
Tim A Joslin, *CEO*
Patrick Rafferty, *Exec VP*
Peg Breen, *Senior VP*
Mitzi Whigan, *Infect Cntl Dir*
EMP: 330
SQ FT: 140,000
SALES (est): 42.2MM
SALES (corp-wide): 1.6B **Privately Held**
WEB: www.fresnoheart.com
SIC: 8062 General medical & surgical hospitals
PA: Community Hospitals Of Central California
2823 Fresno St
Fresno CA 93721
559 459-6000

(P-21424)
FRESNO SURGERY CENTER LP (PA)
Also Called: Fresno Surgical Hospital
6125 N Fresno St, Fresno (93710-5207)
PHONE..................................559 431-8000
Kristine Kassahn, *CEO*
Bruce Cecil, *CFO*
Paramjeet Gill, *Chairman*
Pamela Hutton, *Vice Pres*
Imelda Daniel, *Lab Dir*
EMP: 213
SQ FT: 32,000
SALES: 74MM **Privately Held**
WEB: www.fresnosurgerycenter.com
SIC: 8062 8011 General medical & surgical hospitals; orthopedic physician; gynecologist; surgeon

(P-21425)
GARDENA HOSPITAL LP
Also Called: MEMORIAL HOSPITAL OF GARDENA
1145 W Redondo Beach Blvd, Gardena (90247-3511)
PHONE..................................310 532-4200
Kathy Wojno, *CEO*
John N Loizeaux-Witte, *Partner*
David Lee, *CFO*
Eileen Ishizu, *Human Res Dir*
Michael Ditommaso, *Facilities Mgr*
EMP: 760
SALES: 132.7MM
SALES (corp-wide): 253.3MM **Privately Held**
SIC: 8062 General medical & surgical hospitals
PA: Avanti Hospitals, Llc
222 N Splvd Blvd Ste 950
El Segundo CA 90245
310 356-0550

(P-21426)
GLENDALE ADVENTIST MEDICAL CTR (HQ)
1509 Wilson Ter, Glendale (91206-4007)
PHONE..................................818 409-8000
Kevin A Roberts, *President*
Irene Bourdon, *President*
Katherine Buckner, *President*
Warren Tetz, *COO*
Kevin Roberts, *Officer*
EMP: 2550
SQ FT: 700,000
SALES: 408.3MM
SALES (corp-wide): 4.1B **Privately Held**
WEB: www.glendaleadventist.com
SIC: 8062 8093 8011 General medical & surgical hospitals; mental health clinic, outpatient; freestanding emergency medical center
PA: Adventist Health System/West
2100 Douglas Blvd
Roseville CA 95661
916 781-2000

(P-21427)
GLENN MEDICAL CENTER INC
1133 W Sycamore St, Willows (95988-2601)
PHONE..................................530 934-4681
William Casey, *CEO*
John Lovrich, *CFO*
Gary Pea, *CFO*
Deborah McMillan, *Executive*
Sam Ruma, *Administration*
EMP: 99
SQ FT: 62,000
SALES: 13.7MM **Privately Held**
SIC: 8062 General medical & surgical hospitals

(P-21428)
GLENOAKS CONVALESCENT HOSP LP
409 W Glenoaks Blvd, Glendale (91202-2916)
PHONE..................................818 240-4300
Elaine Levine, *Partner*
EMP: 85
SQ FT: 22,306
SALES: 4.9MM **Privately Held**
SIC: 8062 General medical & surgical hospitals

(P-21429)
GOLDEN EMPIRE CONVALESCENT HOS
121 Dorsey Dr, Grass Valley (95945-5201)
PHONE..................................530 273-1316
Vicki Young, *Partner*
Chan Sinsaeng, *Social Dir*
Diana Dallago, *Hlthcr Dir*
EMP: 180
SALES (est): 12.9MM **Privately Held**
WEB: www.goldenempiresnf.com
SIC: 8062 General medical & surgical hospitals

PRODUCTS & SVCS

(P-21430)
GOLETA VALLEY COTTAGE HOSPITAL
Also Called: COTTAGE HEALTH SYSTEM
351 S Patterson Ave, Santa Barbara
(93111-2403)
P.O. Box 689 (93102-0689)
PHONE................................805 681-6468
Ronald C Werft, *President*
Michael Trambert, *Ch Radiology*
Robert Knight, *Ch of Bd*
Joan Bricher, *CFO*
Diane Wisby, *Vice Pres*
EMP: 275
SQ FT: 92,273
SALES: 79MM **Privately Held**
SIC: 8062 General medical & surgical hospitals

(P-21431)
GOOD SAMARITAN HOSPITAL
901 Olive Dr, Bakersfield (93308-4144)
P.O. Box 85002 (93380-5002)
PHONE................................661 399-4461
Andrew B Leeka, *CEO*
David Huff, *Partner*
Sakrepatna Manohara, *President*
Anand Manohara, *CEO*
Canesh Acharya, *CFO*
EMP: 400
SQ FT: 49,001
SALES (est): 43.7MM **Privately Held**
SIC: 8062 8063 8069 General medical & surgical hospitals; psychiatric hospitals; specialty hospitals, except psychiatric

(P-21432)
GOOD SAMARITAN HOSPITAL (PA)
1225 Wilshire Blvd, Los Angeles
(90017-1901)
PHONE................................213 977-2121
Andrew B Leeka, *CEO*
Charles Munger, *Ch of Bd*
Alan Ino, *CFO*
John Jaymes, *Officer*
Cynthia Miller, *Officer*
▲ **EMP:** 136
SQ FT: 350,000
SALES: 319.2MM **Privately Held**
SIC: 8062 Hospital, affiliated with AMA residency

(P-21433)
GOOD SAMARITAN HOSPITAL LP (DH)
Also Called: HOSPITAL COPORATION OF AMERICA
2425 Samaritan Dr, San Jose
(95124-3985)
P.O. Box 550, Nashville TN (37202-0550)
PHONE................................408 559-2011
Paul Beaupre, *CEO*
Jordan Herget, *COO*
Lana Arad, *CFO*
Darrel Neuenschwander, *CFO*
Paul Deaupre, *Officer*
EMP: 1200
SALES: 618.4MM **Publicly Held**
WEB: www.goodsamsj.org
SIC: 8062 General medical & surgical hospitals
HQ: Hca Inc.
　　1 Park Plz
　　Nashville TN 37203
　　615 344-9551

(P-21434)
GOOD SAMARITAN HOSPITAL LP
Also Called: Mission Oaks Hospital
15891 Los Gtos Almaden Rd, Los Gatos
(95032-3742)
PHONE................................408 356-4111
Brian Knecht, *COO*
Gary Holmes, *Director*
Elaine Retzer, *Manager*
EMP: 200 **Publicly Held**
WEB: www.goodsamsj.org
SIC: 8062 General medical & surgical hospitals
HQ: Good Samaritan Hospital, L.P.
　　2425 Samaritan Dr
　　San Jose CA 95124
　　408 559-2011

(P-21435)
GORDON LANE CONVALESCENT HOSP
1821 E Chapman Ave, Fullerton
(92831-4102)
PHONE................................714 879-7301
Lee Shannon, *President*
Toni Spencer, *Business Dir*
EMP: 65 **EST:** 1971
SQ FT: 24,180
SALES (est): 5.5MM **Privately Held**
SIC: 8062 8051 General medical & surgical hospitals; skilled nursing care facilities

(P-21436)
GROSSMONT HOSPITAL CORPORATION (HQ)
5555 Grossmont Center Dr, La Mesa
(91942-3077)
PHONE................................619 740-6000
Dan Gross, *CEO*
Tere Trout, *Ch Radiology*
Hoangmy Nguyen, *Pharmacy Dir*
Susan Olsen, *Administration*
Vincent Kater, *Director*
EMP: 1740
SQ FT: 494,000
SALES (est): 133.9MM
SALES (corp-wide): 3.4B **Privately Held**
WEB: www.grossmonthealthcare.com
SIC: 8062 General medical & surgical hospitals
PA: Sharp Healthcare
　　8695 Spectrum Center Blvd
　　San Diego CA 92123
　　858 499-4000

(P-21437)
GROSSMONT HOSPITAL CORPORATION
Also Called: Grossmont Home Hlth & Hospice
8881 Fletcher Pkwy # 105, La Mesa
(91942-3134)
PHONE................................619 667-1900
Jean Cruise, *Manager*
EMP: 150
SALES (corp-wide): 3.4B **Privately Held**
WEB: www.grossmonthealthcare.com
SIC: 8062 8082 General medical & surgical hospitals; home health care services
HQ: Grossmont Hospital Corporation
　　5555 Grossmont Center Dr
　　La Mesa CA 91942
　　619 740-6000

(P-21438)
HANFORD COMMUNITY HOSPITAL (HQ)
Also Called: ADVENTIST HEALTH
115 Mall Dr, Hanford (93230-5786)
P.O. Box 619002, Roseville (95661-9002)
PHONE................................559 582-9000
Scott Reiner, *Chairman*
Lori Ruffner, *Opers Staff*
Stephen M Avalos, *Pathologist*
Michael Crawford, *Pathologist*
Randy Bernabe, *Surgeon*
EMP: 640
SQ FT: 52,060
SALES: 230.4MM
SALES (corp-wide): 4.1B **Privately Held**
WEB: www.hanford.ah.org
SIC: 8062 General medical & surgical hospitals
PA: Adventist Health System/West
　　2100 Douglas Blvd
　　Roseville CA 95661
　　916 781-2000

(P-21439)
HARBOR-CLA MED CTR DEPT SRGERY
1000 W Carson St 25, Torrance
(90502-2004)
PHONE................................310 222-2701
Christian De Virgillo, *Chairman*
Steven Lee, *Principal*
Kyle Mock, *Principal*
Alexander Schwed, *Principal*
EMP: 99
SALES (est): 947.5K **Privately Held**
SIC: 8062 General medical & surgical hospitals

(P-21440)
HARBOR-UCLA MEDICAL CENTER
1000 W Carson St 2, Torrance
(90502-2059)
PHONE................................310 222-2345
Miguel Ortiz, *CEO*
Kim McKenzie, *COO*
Jody Nakasuji, *CFO*
Kevin Dawson, *Vice Pres*
Pattie Soltero Sanchez, *Ch Nursing Ofcr*
EMP: 3000
SALES: 637.4MM **Privately Held**
SIC: 8062 General medical & surgical hospitals

(P-21441)
HAYWARD SISTERS HOSPITAL (HQ)
Also Called: St Rose Hospital
27200 Calaroga Ave, Hayward
(94545-4339)
PHONE................................510 264-4000
Michael Mahoney, *President*
Ken Henkelman, *CFO*
Clifford Tschetter, *Lab Dir*
Sylvia Ventura, *Ch Nursing Ofcr*
Aman Dhuper, *Exec Dir*
EMP: 842
SQ FT: 173,000
SALES: 147.7MM
SALES (corp-wide): 1.1B **Privately Held**
WEB: www.aboutinfectioncontrol.com
SIC: 8062 Hospital, affiliated with AMA residency
PA: Alecto Healthcare Services Llc
　　16310 Bake Pkwy Ste 200
　　Irvine CA 92618
　　323 938-3161

(P-21442)
HCA INC
Also Called: Main Hospital
225 N Jackson Ave, San Jose
(95116-1603)
PHONE................................408 729-2801
Trey Abshier, *COO*
David Hutto, *Op Rm Dir*
Nancy Clark, *Human Res Dir*
Lucy Barousse, *Purchasing*
Bev Mikalonis, *Pub Rel Dir*
EMP: 115 **Publicly Held**
SIC: 8062 General medical & surgical hospitals
HQ: Hca Inc.
　　1 Park Plz
　　Nashville TN 37203
　　615 344-9551

(P-21443)
HCA INC
Also Called: Columbia San Clemente Hospital
654 Camino De Los Mares, San Clemente
(92673-2827)
PHONE................................949 496-1122
Patricia Wolfram, *CEO*
Jamie Coate, *Info Tech Mgr*
EMP: 250 **Publicly Held**
SIC: 8062 General medical & surgical hospitals
HQ: Hca Inc.
　　1 Park Plz
　　Nashville TN 37203
　　615 344-9551

(P-21444)
HEALTH RESOURCES CORP
Also Called: Coastal Community Hospital
2701 S Bristol St, Santa Ana (92704-6201)
PHONE................................714 754-5454
Trevor Fetter, *President*
EMP: 400
SALES (est): 11.6MM
SALES (corp-wide): 440.5MM **Privately Held**
WEB: www.ihhioc.com
SIC: 8062 General medical & surgical hospitals
PA: Kpc Healthcare, Inc.
　　1301 N Tustin Ave
　　Santa Ana CA 92705
　　714 953-3652

(P-21445)
HEALTHCARE BARTON SYSTEM (PA)
2170 South Ave, South Lake Tahoe
(96150-7026)
P.O. Box 9578 (96158-9578)
PHONE................................530 541-3420
John Williams, *CEO*
Dick Derby, *CFO*
Richard Derby, *CFO*
Sharon Bishop, *Branch Mgr*
Jeffrey V Behar, *Med Doctor*
EMP: 554
SQ FT: 112,190
SALES: 179.7MM **Privately Held**
SIC: 8062 General medical & surgical hospitals

(P-21446)
HEALTHCARE BARTON SYSTEM
2170 South Ave, South Lake Tahoe
(96150-7026)
PHONE................................530 543-5685
Sharon Bishop, *Branch Mgr*
EMP: 50
SALES (corp-wide): 179.7MM **Privately Held**
SIC: 8062 General medical & surgical hospitals
PA: Barton Healthcare System
　　2170 South Ave
　　South Lake Tahoe CA 96150
　　530 541-3420

(P-21447)
HEALTHSMART PACIFIC INC (PA)
Also Called: Long Beach Pain Center
180 E Ocean Blvd Ste 650, Long Beach
(90802-4741)
P.O. Box 513565, Los Angeles (90051-3565)
PHONE................................562 595-1911
Michael Ddrobot, *CEO*
Michael D Drobot, *CEO*
Robert Vance, *Security Dir*
Linda Lopez, *Human Resources*
Peter Lomeli, *Facilities Mgr*
EMP: 610
SQ FT: 150,000
SALES (est): 99.5MM **Privately Held**
SIC: 8062 General medical & surgical hospitals

(P-21448)
HENRY MAYO NEWHALL MEM HLTH
Also Called: Henrymayo Newhall Mem Hosp
23845 Mcbean Pkwy, Valencia
(91355-2001)
P.O. Box 55279 (91385-0279)
PHONE................................661 253-8000
Roger Seaver, *President*
Bob Hudson, *Vice Pres*
Terry Stone, *Vice Pres*
Cindy Martin, *Lab Dir*
Larry Kidd, *Ch Nursing Ofcr*
EMP: 1500
SALES: 251.8MM **Privately Held**
SIC: 8062 General medical & surgical hospitals

(P-21449)
HENRY MAYO NEWHALL MEM HOSP (PA)
23845 Mcbean Pkwy, Valencia
(91355-2001)
PHONE................................661 253-8000
Roger E Seaver, *President*
Elizabeth Hopp, *Ch of Bd*
Mimi Baum, *President*
Donald L Kimball, *President*
Debra Weyand, *President*
EMP: 1600
SQ FT: 210,000
SALES: 320MM **Privately Held**
WEB: www.henrymayo.com
SIC: 8062 General medical & surgical hospitals

(P-21450)
HI-DESERT MEM HLTH CARE DST (PA)
Also Called: Hi-Desert Medical Center
6530 Lcontenpa Rd Ste 100, Yucca Valley (92284)
PHONE.............................760 820-9229
Jacqueline Combs, *CEO*
EMP: 70 EST: 1964
SALES: 62.8MM **Privately Held**
WEB: www.carolyager.com
SIC: 8062 General medical & surgical hospitals

(P-21451)
HOAG MEMORIAL HOSPITAL PRESBT (PA)
1 Hoag Dr, Newport Beach (92663-4162)
P.O. Box 6100 (92658-6100)
PHONE.............................949 764-4624
Robert Braithwaite, *CEO*
William Vandalsem, *Ch Radiology*
Steven C Moreau, *COO*
Kris Iyer, *Bd of Directors*
Richard Taketa, *Bd of Directors*
EMP: 3600
SALES: 894MM **Privately Held**
SIC: 8062 General medical & surgical hospitals

(P-21452)
HOAG MEMORIAL HOSPITAL PRESBT
16200 Sand Canyon Ave, Irvine (92618-3714)
PHONE.............................949 764-4624
EMP: 1818 **Privately Held**
SIC: 8062 General medical & surgical hospitals
PA: Hoag Memorial Hospital Presbyterian
1 Hoag Dr
Newport Beach CA 92663

(P-21453)
HOLLYWOOD COMMUNITY HOSPITAL M
Also Called: Hollywood Cmnty Hosp Hollywood
6245 De Longpre Ave, Los Angeles (90028-8253)
PHONE.............................323 462-2271
Robert Starling, *CEO*
Ron Messenger, *President*
Manfred Krukemeyer, *Vice Ch Bd*
Vernon Edwards, *Vice Pres*
Madeline Williams, *Ch Nursing Ofcr*
EMP: 220
SQ FT: 100,000
SALES (est): 54.8MM **Privately Held**
WEB: www.clarenthospital.com
SIC: 8062 Hospital, affiliated with AMA residency

(P-21454)
HOLLYWOOD MEDICAL CENTER LP
Also Called: Hollywood Presbyterian Med Ctr
1300 N Vermont Ave, Los Angeles (90027-6098)
PHONE.............................213 413-3000
Jeff Nelson, *Partner*
EMP: 1250
SALES: 281.2MM **Privately Held**
WEB: www.qahpmc.com
SIC: 8062 General medical & surgical hospitals
PA: Cha Health Systems, Inc
3731 Wilshire Blvd # 850
Los Angeles CA 90010
213 487-3211

(P-21455)
HOSPITAL OF BARSTOW INC
Also Called: Barstow Community Hospital
820 E Mountain View St, Barstow (92311-3004)
PHONE.............................760 256-1761
Kane Dawson, *CEO*
EMP: 215
SQ FT: 54,000

SALES (est): 60.7MM
SALES (corp-wide): 2B **Publicly Held**
WEB: www.barstowhospital.com
SIC: 8062 Hospital, affiliated with AMA residency
PA: Qhccs, Llc
1573 Mallory Ln Ste 100
Brentwood TN 37027
615 221-1400

(P-21456)
HUNTINGTON HOSPITAL
100 W California Blvd, Pasadena (91105-3010)
PHONE.............................626 397-5000
Peter W Corrigan, *Principal*
James Buese,
Bonnie Kass, *Vice Pres*
Jane Liu, *Pharmacist*
John Sato, *Manager*
EMP: 3500 EST: 2011
SALES: 646.5MM **Privately Held**
SIC: 8062 General medical & surgical hospitals

(P-21457)
INDIAN VALLEY HEALTH CARE DIST
Also Called: Indian Valley Hospital
184 Hot Springs Rd, Greenville (95947-9747)
PHONE.............................530 284-7191
Sue Neer, *CEO*
Wick Viswell, *Administration*
EMP: 80
SQ FT: 20,000
SALES (est): 3.2MM **Privately Held**
WEB: www.ivhcd.com
SIC: 8062 General medical & surgical hospitals

(P-21458)
INLAND VLY RGIONAL MED CTR INC (HQ)
36485 Inland Valley Dr, Wildomar (92595-9681)
PHONE.............................951 677-1111
Alan B Miller, *CEO*
Barry Thorfinnson, *CFO*
Ginny Ince, *Nursing Dir*
EMP: 67
SQ FT: 77,000
SALES (est): 54.1MM
SALES (corp-wide): 10.4B **Publicly Held**
SIC: 8062 8011 General medical & surgical hospitals; clinic, operated by physicians
PA: Universal Health Services, Inc.
367 S Gulph Rd
King Of Prussia PA 19406
610 768-3300

(P-21459)
INSTITUTE FOR HEALTH & HEALING
2300 California St # 101, San Francisco (94115-2754)
P.O. Box 7999 (94120-7999)
PHONE.............................415 600-3503
William B Stewart, *Owner*
EMP: 50
SALES (est): 1.3MM **Privately Held**
SIC: 8062 General medical & surgical hospitals

(P-21460)
INTERHEALTH CORP (PA)
Also Called: Pih Health
12401 Washington Blvd, Whittier (90602-1006)
PHONE.............................562 698-0811
Jane Dicus, *Ch of Bd*
Richard Atwood, *Vice Chairman*
Gary Koger, *CFO*
Kenton Woods, *Treasurer*
Ronald Yoshihara, *Vice Pres*
EMP: 1100
SQ FT: 500,000
SALES: 27.7MM **Privately Held**
SIC: 8062 8011 General medical & surgical hospitals; offices & clinics of medical doctors

(P-21461)
JOHN C FREMONT HEALTHCARE DST
Also Called: FREMONT HOSPITAL
5189 Hospital Rd, Mariposa (95338-9524)
P.O. Box 216 (95338-0216)
PHONE.............................209 966-3631
Matthew Matthiessen, *CEO*
Dana Oster, *Bd of Directors*
Bonnie Newman, *Radiology Dir*
Joanne Eskra, *Department Mgr*
Rebecca Swisher, *Education*
EMP: 250
SQ FT: 59,112
SALES: 21.7MM **Privately Held**
SIC: 8062 General medical & surgical hospitals

(P-21462)
JOHN F KENNEDY MEMORIAL HOSP
Also Called: John F Knnedy Mem Hosp Emrgncy
47111 Monroe St, Indio (92201-6799)
PHONE.............................760 347-6191
Gary Honts, *CEO*
Bruce Gottlieb, *Pharmacy Dir*
Sue Smothers, *Admin Sec*
Patrick Allen, *Technology*
Amy Huff, *Recruiter*
EMP: 650
SALES: 125.8MM
SALES (corp-wide): 471MM **Privately Held**
WEB: www.jfkfoundation.org
SIC: 8062 Hospital, affiliated with AMA residency
HQ: St. Luke's Des Peres Episcopal-Presbyterian Hospital
2345 Dougherty Ferry Rd
Saint Louis MO 63122
314 966-9100

(P-21463)
JOHN MUIR HEALTH
5003 Commercial Cir, Concord (94520-1268)
PHONE.............................925 692-5600
Cynthia Liedstrand, *Branch Mgr*
EMP: 775
SALES (corp-wide): 1.8B **Privately Held**
SIC: 8062 General medical & surgical hospitals
PA: John Muir Health
1601 Ygnacio Valley Rd
Walnut Creek CA 94598
925 947-4449

(P-21464)
JOHN MUIR HEALTH
380 Civic Dr Ste 100, Pleasant Hill (94523-1946)
PHONE.............................925 952-2887
EMP: 940
SALES (corp-wide): 1.8B **Privately Held**
SIC: 8062 General medical & surgical hospitals
PA: John Muir Health
1601 Ygnacio Valley Rd
Walnut Creek CA 94598
925 947-4449

(P-21465)
JOHN MUIR HEALTH (PA)
1601 Ygnacio Valley Rd, Walnut Creek (94598-3122)
P.O. Box 9023 (94596-9023)
PHONE.............................925 947-4449
Calvin Knight, *CEO*
Michael S Thomas, *President*
Jane A Willemsen, *President*
Michael Kern, *Chief Mktg Ofcr*
Lori Johnson, *Officer*
EMP: 1600
SQ FT: 5,500
SALES: 1.8B **Privately Held**
WEB: www.johnmuirmtdiablo.com
SIC: 8062 General medical & surgical hospitals

(P-21466)
JOHN MUIR HEALTH
Also Called: Outpatient Rehabilitation Svcs
1981 N Broadway Ste 180, Walnut Creek (94596-3817)
PHONE.............................925 947-5300
Sid Hsu, *Manager*
EMP: 50
SALES (corp-wide): 1.8B **Privately Held**
WEB: www.johnmuirmtdiablo.com
SIC: 8062 8049 8093 General medical & surgical hospitals; clinical psychologist; rehabilitation center, outpatient treatment
PA: John Muir Health
1601 Ygnacio Valley Rd
Walnut Creek CA 94598
925 947-4449

(P-21467)
JOHN MUIR HEALTH
Also Called: John Muir Medical Center
1601 Ygnacio Valley Rd, Walnut Creek (94598-3122)
PHONE.............................925 939-3000
Vicki C Lee, *Administration*
Vivian Wing, *Bd of Directors*
Ken Meehan, *Exec VP*
Lee Huskin, *Vice Pres*
Michael Monaldo, *Vice Pres*
EMP: 775
SALES (corp-wide): 1.8B **Privately Held**
SIC: 8062 General medical & surgical hospitals
PA: John Muir Health
1601 Ygnacio Valley Rd
Walnut Creek CA 94598
925 947-4449

(P-21468)
JOHN MUIR HEALTH
Also Called: John Muir Med Ctr Cncord Cmpus
2540 East St, Concord (94520-1906)
PHONE.............................925 682-8200
Tish Murphy, *Director*
Nancy Boren, *President*
Donna Brackley, *Vice Pres*
Jane Willemsen, *Admin Asst*
Harold Berlin, *Technology*
EMP: 1500
SALES (corp-wide): 1.8B **Privately Held**
SIC: 8062 General medical & surgical hospitals
PA: John Muir Health
1601 Ygnacio Valley Rd
Walnut Creek CA 94598
925 947-4449

(P-21469)
JOHN MUIR PHYSICIAN NETWORK
112 La Casa Via Ste 300, Walnut Creek (94598-3059)
PHONE.............................925 952-2701
EMP: 634
SALES (corp-wide): 322.9MM **Privately Held**
SIC: 8062 General medical & surgical hospitals
PA: John Muir Physician Network
1450 Treat Blvd
Walnut Creek CA 94597
925 296-9700

(P-21470)
JOHN MUIR PHYSICIAN NETWORK
91 Gregory Ln Ste 15, Pleasant Hill (94523-4927)
PHONE.............................925 685-0843
Aileen Mirabel, *Branch Mgr*
EMP: 634
SALES (corp-wide): 322.9MM **Privately Held**
SIC: 8062 General medical & surgical hospitals
PA: John Muir Physician Network
1450 Treat Blvd
Walnut Creek CA 94597
925 296-9700

(P-21471)
JOHN MUIR PHYSICIAN NETWORK
Also Called: Mount Diablo Medical Center
2540 East St, Concord (94520-1906)
PHONE..................925 682-8200
Deborah Kolhede, *Vice Pres*
Sue Ellen Thompson, *Cardiology*
Sue Thompson, *Cardiology*
Eugene Wong, *Director*
EMP: 1500
SALES (corp-wide): 322.9MM **Privately Held**
SIC: **8062** 8011 General medical & surgical hospitals; offices & clinics of medical doctors
PA: John Muir Physician Network
1450 Treat Blvd
Walnut Creek CA 94597
925 296-9700

(P-21472)
JOHN MUIR PHYSICIAN NETWORK (PA)
Also Called: JOHN MUIR MEDICAL CENTER
1450 Treat Blvd, Walnut Creek (94597-2168)
PHONE..................925 296-9700
Cal Knight, *Principal*
Richard Kamrath, *COO*
Laura Kazaglis, *Admin Asst*
Lisa Hudson, *Internal Med*
Moizah Saad, *Internal Med*
EMP: 1601
SQ FT: 83,579
SALES: 322.9MM **Privately Held**
SIC: **8062** 8069 8093 7363 General medical & surgical hospitals; substance abuse hospitals; substance abuse clinics (outpatient); medical help service

(P-21473)
JOHN MUIR PHYSICIAN NETWORK
Also Called: Mt Diablo Medical Center
1601 Ygnacio Valley Rd, Walnut Creek (94598-3122)
PHONE..................925 939-3000
J Kendall Anderson, *President*
Dave Hook, *Exec Dir*
Angela Weberski, *Analyst*
Sandra Rigney, *Nutritionist*
Tom Greely, *Med Doctor*
EMP: 399
SALES (corp-wide): 322.9MM **Privately Held**
SIC: **8062** General medical & surgical hospitals
PA: John Muir Physician Network
1450 Treat Blvd
Walnut Creek CA 94597
925 296-9700

(P-21474)
JOHN MUIR PHYSICIAN NETWORK
Also Called: Mt Diablo Heart Health Center
2720 Grant St, Concord (94520-2294)
PHONE..................925 674-2200
Elizabeth Stalling, *Branch Mgr*
Kelly Beatty, *Principal*
George Melendez, *Technology*
Marty Tarnowski, *Marketing Staff*
Elizabeth Stallings, *Med Doctor*
EMP: 634
SALES (corp-wide): 322.9MM **Privately Held**
SIC: **8062** General medical & surgical hospitals
PA: John Muir Physician Network
1450 Treat Blvd
Walnut Creek CA 94597
925 296-9700

(P-21475)
KAISER FOUNDATION HOSPITALS
Also Called: Barranca Medical Offices
6 Willard, Irvine (92604-4694)
PHONE..................949 262-5780
George Disalvo, *Owner*
Vicki Crowe, *Family Practiti*
Raymond Chung, *Med Doctor*
Alec Does, *Med Doctor*
Thu Tran, *Med Doctor*

EMP: 105
SQ FT: 51,080
SALES (corp-wide): 94.1B **Privately Held**
SIC: **8062** General medical & surgical hospitals
HQ: Kaiser Foundation Hospitals Inc
1 Kaiser Plz
Oakland CA 94612
510 271-6611

(P-21476)
KAISER FOUNDATION HOSPITALS
Also Called: Kaiser Permanente Eye
1680 E Roseville Pkwy, Roseville (95661-3988)
PHONE..................916 746-3937
Daniel Rule, *Branch Mgr*
Don R Robinson, *Psychiatry*
EMP: 105
SALES (corp-wide): 94.1B **Privately Held**
SIC: **8062** General medical & surgical hospitals
HQ: Kaiser Foundation Hospitals Inc
1 Kaiser Plz
Oakland CA 94612
510 271-6611

(P-21477)
KAISER FOUNDATION HOSPITALS
Also Called: Kaiser Permanente
5601 De Soto Ave, Woodland Hills (91367-6701)
PHONE..................818 719-2000
Cathy Casas, *Senior VP*
Michael Wells, *Officer*
Gail Knight, *Executive*
Donna Moore, *Executive*
Michael Tutko, *Security Dir*
EMP: 1200
SALES (corp-wide): 94.1B **Privately Held**
WEB: www.kaiserpermanente.org
SIC: **8062** General medical & surgical hospitals
HQ: Kaiser Foundation Hospitals Inc
1 Kaiser Plz
Oakland CA 94612
510 271-6611

(P-21478)
KAISER FOUNDATION HOSPITALS
Also Called: Kaiser Permanente
43112 15th St W, Lancaster (93534-6219)
PHONE..................661 726-2500
Barbara Fordice, *General Mgr*
Robert Trautman, *Branch Mgr*
Zhongheng Tu, *Family Practiti*
Freddy S Calderon, *Nephrology*
Syed Hasan, *Rheumtlgy Spec*
EMP: 175
SALES (corp-wide): 94.1B **Privately Held**
WEB: www.kaiserpermanente.org
SIC: **8062** Hospital, affiliated with AMA residency
HQ: Kaiser Foundation Hospitals Inc
1 Kaiser Plz
Oakland CA 94612
510 271-6611

(P-21479)
KAISER FOUNDATION HOSPITALS
Also Called: Kaiser Permanente
4867 W Sunset Blvd, Los Angeles (90027-5969)
PHONE..................323 783-4011
Vicken Aharonian, *Med Doctor*
Roy Braganza,
Mary Jo Jenkins, *Records Dir*
Sima Hartounian, *Officer*
Brian Herzberger, *Administration*
EMP: 60
SALES (corp-wide): 94.1B **Privately Held**
WEB: www.kaiserpermanente.org
SIC: **8062** 8099 6321 6324 General medical & surgical hospitals; physical examination service; insurance; health insurance carriers; hospital & medical service plans
HQ: Kaiser Foundation Hospitals Inc
1 Kaiser Plz
Oakland CA 94612
510 271-6611

(P-21480)
KAISER FOUNDATION HOSPITALS
Also Called: Park Shadelands Medical Offs
320 Lennon Ln, Walnut Creek (94598-2419)
PHONE..................925 906-2380
David Nievr, *President*
EMP: 52
SALES (corp-wide): 94.1B **Privately Held**
WEB: www.kaiserpermanente.org
SIC: **8062** 8011 General medical & surgical hospitals; general & family practice, physician/surgeon
HQ: Kaiser Foundation Hospitals Inc
1 Kaiser Plz
Oakland CA 94612
510 271-6611

(P-21481)
KAISER FOUNDATION HOSPITALS
Also Called: Kaiser Permanente
1011 Baldwin Park Blvd, Baldwin Park (91706-5806)
PHONE..................626 851-1011
Linda Margarita Gutierrez, *Principal*
Linda Salazar, *Officer*
Lisa Marcos, *QA Dir*
Shirley Lac, *Project Mgr*
Ivan Alvarents, *Purch Dir*
EMP: 793
SALES (corp-wide): 94.1B **Privately Held**
WEB: www.kaiserpermanente.org
SIC: **8062** General medical & surgical hospitals
HQ: Kaiser Foundation Hospitals Inc
1 Kaiser Plz
Oakland CA 94612
510 271-6611

(P-21482)
KAISER FOUNDATION HOSPITALS
Also Called: Kaiser Prmnente Downey Med Ctr
9333 Imperial Hwy, Downey (90242-2812)
PHONE..................562 657-9000
Gemma Abad, *Branch Mgr*
Jordyn Hall, *Anesthesiology*
Pravin Acharya, *Emerg Med Spec*
Sawrav Mukherjee, *Emerg Med Spec*
Michelle Tomassi, *Emerg Med Spec*
EMP: 410
SALES (corp-wide): 94.1B **Privately Held**
SIC: **8062** General medical & surgical hospitals
HQ: Kaiser Foundation Hospitals Inc
1 Kaiser Plz
Oakland CA 94612
510 271-6611

(P-21483)
KAISER FOUNDATION HOSPITALS (HQ)
Also Called: Kaiser Permanente
1 Kaiser Plz, Oakland (94612-3610)
P.O. Box 12929 (94604-3010)
PHONE..................510 271-6611
Bernard J Tyson, *President*
Kathryn Beiser, *President*
Janet Liang, *President*
Kathy Lancaster, *CFO*
Patrick Courneya, *Exec VP*
▲ EMP: 250 EST: 1948
SQ FT: 90,000
SALES (corp-wide): 94.1B **Privately Held**
WEB: www.kaiserpermanente.org
SIC: **8062** 8011 General medical & surgical hospitals; medical centers
PA: Kaiser Foundation Health Plan, Inc.
1 Kaiser Plz
Oakland CA 94612
510 271-5800

(P-21484)
KAISER FOUNDATION HOSPITALS
Also Called: Kaiser Permanente
9400 Rosecrans Ave, Bellflower (90706-2246)
PHONE..................562 461-3000
James T Heidenreich, *Principal*
Christopher C Lin, *President*
Patrick Wirfel, *President*

Susan Murphy, *Analyst*
Cristina Garcia, *Human Res Dir*
EMP: 2000
SALES (corp-wide): 94.1B **Privately Held**
WEB: www.kaiserpermanente.org
SIC: **8062** General medical & surgical hospitals
HQ: Kaiser Foundation Hospitals Inc
1 Kaiser Plz
Oakland CA 94612
510 271-6611

(P-21485)
KAISER FOUNDATION HOSPITALS
Also Called: Kaiser Permanente
280 W Macarthur Blvd, Oakland (94611-5642)
PHONE..................510 752-1000
Bettie Coles, *Manager*
Kenji Miyaji, *Info Tech Mgr*
Luis Davila, *Opers Mgr*
Miriam E Dunham, *Family Practiti*
Nora Emon, *Family Practiti*
EMP: 708
SALES (corp-wide): 94.1B **Privately Held**
SIC: **8062** General medical & surgical hospitals
HQ: Kaiser Foundation Hospitals Inc
1 Kaiser Plz
Oakland CA 94612
510 271-6611

(P-21486)
KAISER FOUNDATION HOSPITALS
Also Called: Kaiser Permanente
1255 W Arrow Hwy, San Dimas (91773-2340)
PHONE..................909 394-2530
Will Tatum, *Manager*
EMP: 52
SQ FT: 23,801
SALES (corp-wide): 94.1B **Privately Held**
WEB: www.kaiserpermanente.org
SIC: **8062** 8011 General medical & surgical hospitals; general & family practice, physician/surgeon
HQ: Kaiser Foundation Hospitals Inc
1 Kaiser Plz
Oakland CA 94612
510 271-6611

(P-21487)
KAISER FOUNDATION HOSPITALS
Also Called: Kaiser Permanente
4405 Vandever Ave Fl 5, San Diego (92120-3315)
PHONE..................619 528-2583
David Mandler, *Manager*
Scott Greenway, *Surgeon*
Thomas Paluch, *Surgeon*
William Devor, *Neurology*
Aaron Harper, *Pediatrics*
EMP: 52
SALES (corp-wide): 94.1B **Privately Held**
WEB: www.kaiserpermanente.org
SIC: **8062** General medical & surgical hospitals
HQ: Kaiser Foundation Hospitals Inc
1 Kaiser Plz
Oakland CA 94612
510 271-6611

(P-21488)
KAISER FOUNDATION HOSPITALS
Also Called: Kaiser Permanente
13651 Willard St, Panorama City (91402)
PHONE..................818 375-2000
Dev Mahadevan, *Principal*
Suzy Ghadarossin, *Lab Dir*
Michael Flores, *Radiology Dir*
Jane Ryang, *Business Dir*
Kelly Singh, *Opers Staff*
EMP: 3000
SALES (corp-wide): 94.1B **Privately Held**
WEB: www.kaiserpermanente.org
SIC: **8062** General medical & surgical hospitals
HQ: Kaiser Foundation Hospitals Inc
1 Kaiser Plz
Oakland CA 94612
510 271-6611

(P-21489)
KAISER FOUNDATION HOSPITALS
280 Hospital Pkwy, San Jose (95119-1103)
PHONE..................................408 972-6010
Rajan Bhandari, *Branch Mgr*
Alicia Hernandez, *Assistant*
EMP: 267
SALES (corp-wide): 94.1B Privately Held
SIC: 8062 General medical & surgical hospitals
HQ: Kaiser Foundation Hospitals Inc
1 Kaiser Plz
Oakland CA 94612
510 271-6611

(P-21490)
KAISER FOUNDATION HOSPITALS
Also Called: Kaiser Foundation Health Plan
3355 E 26th St, Vernon (90058-4169)
PHONE..................................323 264-4310
Jose Montero, *Principal*
EMP: 75
SALES (corp-wide): 94.1B Privately Held
SIC: 8062 8011 General medical & surgical hospitals; medical centers
HQ: Kaiser Foundation Hospitals Inc
1 Kaiser Plz
Oakland CA 94612
510 271-6611

(P-21491)
KAISER FOUNDATION HOSPITALS
Also Called: San Joaquin Community Hospital
2615 Chester Ave, Bakersfield (93301-2014)
PHONE..................................661 395-3000
EMP: 267
SALES (corp-wide): 94.1B Privately Held
SIC: 8062 General medical & surgical hospitals
HQ: Kaiser Foundation Hospitals Inc
1 Kaiser Plz
Oakland CA 94612
510 271-6611

(P-21492)
KAISER FOUNDATION HOSPITALS
Also Called: Antelope Valley Hospital
1600 W Avenue J, Lancaster (93534-2814)
PHONE..................................661 949-5000
Harriet R Lee, *Administration*
EMP: 267
SALES (corp-wide): 94.1B Privately Held
SIC: 8062 General medical & surgical hospitals
HQ: Kaiser Foundation Hospitals Inc
1 Kaiser Plz
Oakland CA 94612
510 271-6611

(P-21493)
KAISER FOUNDATION HOSPITALS
Also Called: Kaiser Prmanente Internet Svcs
5820 Owens Dr Bldg E-2, Pleasanton (94588-3900)
PHONE..................................925 598-2799
Sarah Threlfall, *Sales Staff*
EMP: 267
SALES (corp-wide): 94.1B Privately Held
SIC: 8062 General medical & surgical hospitals
HQ: Kaiser Foundation Hospitals Inc
1 Kaiser Plz
Oakland CA 94612
510 271-6611

(P-21494)
KAISER FOUNDATION HOSPITALS
Also Called: Kaiser Permanente
1650 Response Rd, Sacramento (95815-4807)
PHONE..................................916 973-5000
Sandra Lee Panora, *Branch Mgr*
Monica Balfour, *Obstetrician*
Andrea B Sherman, *Obstetrician*
SAE H Sohn, *Obstetrician*
Michael Z Sheen, *Internal Med*

EMP: 52
SALES (corp-wide): 94.1B Privately Held
WEB: www.kaiserpermanente.org
SIC: 8062 General medical & surgical hospitals
HQ: Kaiser Foundation Hospitals Inc
1 Kaiser Plz
Oakland CA 94612
510 271-6611

(P-21495)
KAISER FOUNDATION HOSPITALS
10990 San Dego Mission Rd, San Diego (92108-2417)
PHONE..................................619 641-4663
Caroline Bonner, *Director*
Claudia F De Carvalho, *Pharmacist*
Inga X Garmanyan, *Pharmacist*
Christina T Nguyen, *Pharmacist*
Chris J Sando, *Pharmacist*
EMP: 410
SALES (corp-wide): 94.1B Privately Held
WEB: www.kaiserpermanente.org
SIC: 8062 General medical & surgical hospitals
HQ: Kaiser Foundation Hospitals Inc
1 Kaiser Plz
Oakland CA 94612
510 271-6611

(P-21496)
KAISER FOUNDATION HOSPITALS
Also Called: La Mesa Medical Offices
8080 Parkway Dr, La Mesa (91942-2104)
PHONE..................................619 528-5000
Caroline Wu, *Principal*
Lorraine Eubany, *Internal Med*
EMP: 50
SALES (corp-wide): 94.1B Privately Held
WEB: www.kaiserpermanente.org
SIC: 8062 General medical & surgical hospitals
HQ: Kaiser Foundation Hospitals Inc
1 Kaiser Plz
Oakland CA 94612
510 271-6611

(P-21497)
KAISER FOUNDATION HOSPITALS
Also Called: Stockdale Medical Offices
3501 Stockdale Hwy, Bakersfield (93309-2150)
PHONE..................................661 398-5011
KY P Ho, *Principal*
Marvin Campos II, *Family Practiti*
Nooshin Jahangiri, *Med Doctor*
EMP: 50
SALES (corp-wide): 94.1B Privately Held
WEB: www.kaiserpermanente.org
SIC: 8062 General medical & surgical hospitals
HQ: Kaiser Foundation Hospitals Inc
1 Kaiser Plz
Oakland CA 94612
510 271-6611

(P-21498)
KAISER FOUNDATION HOSPITALS
Also Called: Wildomar Medical Offices
36450 Inland Valley Dr # 204, Wildomar (92595-9583)
PHONE..................................951 353-2000
Geoffrey Gomez, *Principal*
Anh T Dinh, *Family Practiti*
EMP: 50
SALES (corp-wide): 94.1B Privately Held
WEB: www.kaiserpermanente.org
SIC: 8062 General medical & surgical hospitals
HQ: Kaiser Foundation Hospitals Inc
1 Kaiser Plz
Oakland CA 94612
510 271-6611

(P-21499)
KAISER FOUNDATION HOSPITALS
Also Called: Bostonia Medical Offices
1630 E Main St, El Cajon (92021-5204)
PHONE..................................619 528-5000
Jennifer Park, *Med Doctor*

EMP: 50
SALES (corp-wide): 94.1B Privately Held
WEB: www.kaiserpermanente.org
SIC: 8062 General medical & surgical hospitals
HQ: Kaiser Foundation Hospitals Inc
1 Kaiser Plz
Oakland CA 94612
510 271-6611

(P-21500)
KAISER FOUNDATION HOSPITALS
Also Called: Cudahy Medical Offices
7825 Atlantic Ave, Cudahy (90201-5022)
PHONE..................................323 562-6400
Karen Warren, *Manager*
Robert L Escalera, *Family Practiti*
Anna Millan, *Family Practiti*
Jorge Ramirez, *Family Practiti*
Rosa Rodriguez, *Family Practiti*
EMP: 100
SALES (corp-wide): 94.1B Privately Held
WEB: www.kaiserpermanente.org
SIC: 8062 General medical & surgical hospitals
HQ: Kaiser Foundation Hospitals Inc
1 Kaiser Plz
Oakland CA 94612
510 271-6611

(P-21501)
KAISER FOUNDATION HOSPITALS
Also Called: El Cajon Medical Offices
250 Travelodge Dr, El Cajon (92020-4126)
PHONE..................................619 528-5000
Carolyn Bonner, *Administration*
Derek Boone, *Analyst*
Katherine A Hartzell, *Obstetrician*
William Ohara, *Osteopathy*
Jeffrey Korn, *Podiatrist*
EMP: 50
SQ FT: 47,486
SALES (corp-wide): 94.1B Privately Held
WEB: www.kaiserpermanente.org
SIC: 8062 General medical & surgical hospitals
HQ: Kaiser Foundation Hospitals Inc
1 Kaiser Plz
Oakland CA 94612
510 271-6611

(P-21502)
KAISER FOUNDATION HOSPITALS
Also Called: Kaiser Permanente
1249 S Sunset Ave, West Covina (91790-3960)
PHONE..................................866 319-4269
Jane Lau, *General Mgr*
Chan Kiet Wong, *Pharmacist*
EMP: 50
SALES (corp-wide): 94.1B Privately Held
WEB: www.kaiserpermanente.org
SIC: 8062 General medical & surgical hospitals
HQ: Kaiser Foundation Hospitals Inc
1 Kaiser Plz
Oakland CA 94612
510 271-6611

(P-21503)
KAISER FOUNDATION HOSPITALS
Also Called: Gardena Medical Offices
15446 S Western Ave, Gardena (90249-4319)
PHONE..................................310 517-2956
Mary Mauch, *Manager*
Agnes E Chen, *Family Practiti*
Raven Copeland, *Family Practiti*
Cristina Y Amaya, *Obstetrician*
Uzma Khan, *Internal Med*
EMP: 50
SQ FT: 114,575
SALES (corp-wide): 94.1B Privately Held
WEB: www.kaiserpermanente.org
SIC: 8062 General medical & surgical hospitals
HQ: Kaiser Foundation Hospitals Inc
1 Kaiser Plz
Oakland CA 94612
510 271-6611

(P-21504)
KAISER FOUNDATION HOSPITALS
Also Called: Erwin Street Medical Offices
21263 Erwin St, Woodland Hills (91367-3715)
PHONE..................................818 592-3100
Karen Kim, *Executive*
Michael Agress, *Med Doctor*
EMP: 50
SQ FT: 28,398
SALES (corp-wide): 94.1B Privately Held
WEB: www.kaiserpermanente.org
SIC: 8062 General medical & surgical hospitals
HQ: Kaiser Foundation Hospitals Inc
1 Kaiser Plz
Oakland CA 94612
510 271-6611

(P-21505)
KAISER FOUNDATION HOSPITALS
Also Called: Petaluma Medical Offices
3900 Lakeville Hwy, Petaluma (94954-5698)
PHONE..................................707 765-3900
Claudia R Viazzoli, *Principal*
Amos Yew, *Psychologist*
Helene M Spivak, *Obstetrician*
Joshua Blume, *Psychiatry*
John Dahmen, *Med Doctor*
EMP: 50
SQ FT: 39,000
SALES (corp-wide): 94.1B Privately Held
WEB: www.kaiserpermanente.org
SIC: 8062 General medical & surgical hospitals
HQ: Kaiser Foundation Hospitals Inc
1 Kaiser Plz
Oakland CA 94612
510 271-6611

(P-21506)
KAISER FOUNDATION HOSPITALS
Also Called: Novato Medical Offices
97 San Marin Dr, Novato (94945-1100)
PHONE..................................415 899-7400
Margaret R Hill, *Principal*
Mary Nelson, *Office Mgr*
Vicki Darrow, *Obstetrician*
Jonathan Delson, *Internal Med*
Katherine Bloom, *Nurse*
EMP: 50
SALES (corp-wide): 94.1B Privately Held
WEB: www.kaiserpermanente.org
SIC: 8062 General medical & surgical hospitals
HQ: Kaiser Foundation Hospitals Inc
1 Kaiser Plz
Oakland CA 94612
510 271-6611

(P-21507)
KAISER FOUNDATION HOSPITALS
Also Called: Permanente Medical Group
555 Castro St Fl 3, Mountain View (94041-2009)
PHONE..................................650 903-3000
Patricia Carpenter, *Director*
Wakako Nomura, *Med Doctor*
John G Poochigian, *Med Doctor*
Gretchen H Rooker,
George Johnson, *Director*
EMP: 200
SALES (corp-wide): 94.1B Privately Held
WEB: www.kaiserpermanente.org
SIC: 8062 Hospital, affiliated with AMA residency
HQ: Kaiser Foundation Hospitals Inc
1 Kaiser Plz
Oakland CA 94612
510 271-6611

(P-21508)
KAISER FOUNDATION HOSPITALS
Also Called: Kaiser Permanente
501 Lennon Ln, Walnut Creek (94598-2414)
PHONE..................................925 906-2000
Christina Robinson, *Principal*
Scott Dambrauckas, *Info Tech Mgr*

(PA)=Parent Co (HQ)=Headquarters (DH)=Div Headquarters
✿ = New Business established in last 2 years

Marianne Agudo, *Analyst*
Richard Soublet, *Persnl Dir*
Uma Desai, *Family Practiti*
EMP: 1000
SALES (corp-wide): 94.1B **Privately Held**
WEB: www.kaiserpermanente.org
SIC: 8062 General medical & surgical hospitals
HQ: Kaiser Foundation Hospitals Inc
1 Kaiser Plz
Oakland CA 94612
510 271-6611

(P-21509)
KAISER FOUNDATION HOSPITALS
Also Called: Kaiser Permanente
7601 Stoneridge Dr, Pleasanton
(94588-4501)
PHONE...................925 847-5000
Linsey Dicks, *Admin Director*
Carl Haupt, *Info Tech Mgr*
Alpesh Patel, *Analyst*
Edith Ang, *Family Practiti*
Marika Issakhanian, *Neurology*
EMP: 350
SALES (corp-wide): 94.1B **Privately Held**
WEB: www.kaiserpermanente.org
SIC: 8062 General medical & surgical hospitals
HQ: Kaiser Foundation Hospitals Inc
1 Kaiser Plz
Oakland CA 94612
510 271-6611

(P-21510)
KAISER FOUNDATION HOSPITALS
Also Called: Kaiser Permanente Division RES
2000 Brdwy, Oakland (94612)
PHONE...................510 891-3400
Joe Shelby MD, *Director*
Louis Dinopoulos, *Executive*
Dennis Hubbard, *Managing Dir*
Mike Dunker, *Program Mgr*
Erika Tallmadge, *Business Anlyst*
EMP: 400
SQ FT: 86,875
SALES (corp-wide): 94.1B **Privately Held**
WEB: www.kaiserpermanente.org
SIC: 8062 General medical & surgical hospitals
HQ: Kaiser Foundation Hospitals Inc
1 Kaiser Plz
Oakland CA 94612
510 271-6611

(P-21511)
KAISER FOUNDATION HOSPITALS
Also Called: Kaiser Permanente
5055 California Ave # 110, Bakersfield
(93309-0701)
P.O. Box 12099 (93389-2099)
PHONE...................661 334-2020
Kevin P Stiles, *Med Doctor*
Leslie Golich, *Director*
Audra Kessler, *Director*
Sandra L Lara, *Accounts Mgr*
EMP: 105
SALES (corp-wide): 94.1B **Privately Held**
SIC: 8062 General medical & surgical hospitals
HQ: Kaiser Foundation Hospitals Inc
1 Kaiser Plz
Oakland CA 94612
510 271-6611

(P-21512)
KAISER FOUNDATION HOSPITALS
Also Called: Kaiser Prmnnte Vallejo Med Ctr
975 Sereno Dr, Vallejo (94589-2441)
PHONE...................707 651-1000
Katie Rickleff, *Principal*
Jeanne Rodriguez, *Admin Asst*
Leland Rudloff, *Buyer*
Pervie McAlpin, *Opers Staff*
Sherry Fung-Sakita, *Family Practiti*
EMP: 2700
SALES (corp-wide): 94.1B **Privately Held**
WEB: www.kaiserpermanente.org
SIC: 8062 General medical & surgical hospitals

HQ: Kaiser Foundation Hospitals Inc
1 Kaiser Plz
Oakland CA 94612
510 271-6611

(P-21513)
KAISER FOUNDATION HOSPITALS
Also Called: Kaiser Permanente
12470 Whittier Blvd, Whittier (90602-1017)
PHONE...................866 340-5974
Beth Lopez, *Principal*
Eddie Kim, *Internal Med*
Zoltan Katona, *Med Doctor*
EMP: 50
SALES (corp-wide): 94.1B **Privately Held**
WEB: www.kaiserpermanente.org
SIC: 8062 General medical & surgical hospitals
HQ: Kaiser Foundation Hospitals Inc
1 Kaiser Plz
Oakland CA 94612
510 271-6611

(P-21514)
KAISER FOUNDATION HOSPITALS
Also Called: Bonita Medical Offices
3955 Bonita Rd, Bonita (91902-1230)
PHONE...................619 409-6405
James Lentz, *Principal*
EMP: 72
SQ FT: 67,760
SALES (corp-wide): 94.1B **Privately Held**
WEB: www.kaiser.com
SIC: 8062 General medical & surgical hospitals
HQ: Kaiser Foundation Hospitals Inc
1 Kaiser Plz
Oakland CA 94612
510 271-6611

(P-21515)
KAISER FOUNDATION HOSPITALS
Also Called: Kaiser Prmnnte Manteca Med Ctr
1777 W Yosemite Ave, Manteca
(95337-5187)
PHONE...................209 825-3700
Anita Kennedy, *COO*
Lisa Dasko, *Controller*
David Finnen, *Supervisor*
EMP: 593
SALES (corp-wide): 94.1B **Privately Held**
SIC: 8062 General medical & surgical hospitals
HQ: Kaiser Foundation Hospitals Inc
1 Kaiser Plz
Oakland CA 94612
510 271-6611

(P-21516)
KAISER FOUNDATION HOSPITALS
Also Called: Kaiser Foundation Health Plan
5755 Cottle Rd, San Jose (95123-3640)
PHONE...................408 972-3376
Donald D Mordecai, *Branch Mgr*
John Bosch, *Managing Dir*
David Emmert, *Psychologist*
Marianne Mandle, *Psychologist*
Susan Imamura, *Psychiatry*
EMP: 99
SALES (corp-wide): 94.1B **Privately Held**
WEB: www.kaiser.com
SIC: 8062 8011 6321 6324 General medical & surgical hospitals; offices & clinics of medical doctors; accident & health insurance; health maintenance organization (HMO), insurance only
HQ: Kaiser Foundation Hospitals Inc
1 Kaiser Plz
Oakland CA 94612
510 271-6611

(P-21517)
KAISER FOUNDATION HOSPITALS
Also Called: Kaiser Permanente San
275 Hospital Pkwy 765a, San Jose
(95119-1106)
PHONE...................408 972-6700
Diana Ochoa, *Branch Mgr*
EMP: 105

SALES (corp-wide): 94.1B **Privately Held**
WEB: www.kaiserpermanente.org
SIC: 8062 8021 General medical & surgical hospitals; offices & clinics of dentists
HQ: Kaiser Foundation Hospitals Inc
1 Kaiser Plz
Oakland CA 94612
510 271-6611

(P-21518)
KAISER FOUNDATION HOSPITALS
Also Called: Kaiser Permanente
1055 E Colo Blvd Ste 100, Pasadena
(91106)
PHONE...................626 440-5659
Jeanine Boudakian, *Branch Mgr*
George Di Salvo, *CFO*
Marc Moreels, *Officer*
Patti Harvey, *Senior VP*
Laurel Junk, *Senior VP*
EMP: 500
SALES (corp-wide): 94.1B **Privately Held**
WEB: www.kaiserpermanente.org
SIC: 8062 General medical & surgical hospitals
HQ: Kaiser Foundation Hospitals Inc
1 Kaiser Plz
Oakland CA 94612
510 271-6611

(P-21519)
KAISER FOUNDATION HOSPITALS
Also Called: Kaiser Permanente
1600 Eureka Rd, Roseville (95661-3027)
PHONE...................916 784-4000
Douglas Freeman, *Branch Mgr*
Vince Golla, *Vice Pres*
Frank Hsieh, *Research*
Larry Perrin, *Engineer*
Richard Welch, *Engineer*
EMP: 2300
SALES (corp-wide): 94.1B **Privately Held**
WEB: www.kaiserpermanente.org
SIC: 8062 General medical & surgical hospitals
HQ: Kaiser Foundation Hospitals Inc
1 Kaiser Plz
Oakland CA 94612
510 271-6611

(P-21520)
KAISER FOUNDATION HOSPITALS
Also Called: Kaiser Foundation Health Plan
4867 W Sunset Blvd, Los Angeles
(90027-5969)
PHONE...................800 954-8000
Joseph Hummel, *Manager*
EMP: 50
SALES (corp-wide): 94.1B **Privately Held**
WEB: www.kaiser.com
SIC: 8062 6324 General medical & surgical hospitals; hospital & medical service plans
HQ: Kaiser Foundation Hospitals Inc
1 Kaiser Plz
Oakland CA 94612
510 271-6611

(P-21521)
KAISER FOUNDATION HOSPITALS
Also Called: Kaiser Foundation Health Plan
7300 N Fresno St, Fresno (93720-2941)
PHONE...................559 448-4500
Jeffrey Collins, *Manager*
Adolfo Alvarez,
Marilyn Kelley, *Info Tech Mgr*
Bill Lyons, *Chief Engr*
Alok Gaur, *Surgeon*
EMP: 2300
SALES (corp-wide): 94.1B **Privately Held**
WEB: www.kaiser.com
SIC: 8062 General medical & surgical hospitals
HQ: Kaiser Foundation Hospitals Inc
1 Kaiser Plz
Oakland CA 94612
510 271-6611

(P-21522)
KAISER FOUNDATION HOSPITALS
Also Called: Kaiser Permanente
250 W San Jose Ave, Claremont
(91711-5295)
PHONE...................888 750-0036
Bell Pacific, *Manager*
EMP: 267
SQ FT: 17,908
SALES (corp-wide): 94.1B **Privately Held**
WEB: www.kaiserpermanente.org
SIC: 8062 General medical & surgical hospitals
HQ: Kaiser Foundation Hospitals Inc
1 Kaiser Plz
Oakland CA 94612
510 271-6611

(P-21523)
KAISER FOUNDATION HOSPITALS
Also Called: Kaiser Permanente Advice
7300 Wyndham Dr, Sacramento
(95823-4913)
PHONE...................916 525-6300
Tony Le, *Manager*
Susan C Doi, *Psychologist*
Arlene R Burton, *Psychiatry*
Jeffrey Rabowsky, *Med Doctor*
Haifeng Yu, *Med Doctor*
EMP: 105
SALES (corp-wide): 94.1B **Privately Held**
SIC: 8062 General medical & surgical hospitals
HQ: Kaiser Foundation Hospitals Inc
1 Kaiser Plz
Oakland CA 94612
510 271-6611

(P-21524)
KAISER FOUNDATION HOSPITALS
Also Called: Kaiser Permanente
7373 West Ln, Stockton (95210-3377)
PHONE...................209 476-3101
Gene Long, *Branch Mgr*
Lulu Esau, *Project Mgr*
EMP: 175
SALES (corp-wide): 94.1B **Privately Held**
WEB: www.kaiserpermanente.org
SIC: 8062 General medical & surgical hospitals
HQ: Kaiser Foundation Hospitals Inc
1 Kaiser Plz
Oakland CA 94612
510 271-6611

(P-21525)
KAISER FOUNDATION HOSPITALS
Also Called: Kaiser Permanente Santa
710 Lawrence Expy, Santa Clara
(95051-5173)
PHONE...................408 851-1000
Ana Herdocia, *Executive Asst*
Stephanie Higgins, *Lab Dir*
Dave Faraone, *Engineer*
Ron Rich, *VP Sales*
Kavitha Pancholy, *Family Practiti*
EMP: 593
SALES (corp-wide): 94.1B **Privately Held**
SIC: 8062 General medical & surgical hospitals
HQ: Kaiser Foundation Hospitals Inc
1 Kaiser Plz
Oakland CA 94612
510 271-6611

(P-21526)
KAISER PERMANENTE
3505 Broadway, Oakland (94611-5798)
PHONE...................510 450-2109
T Raine Bennett, *Med Doctor*
Lawrence H Kushi, *Associate Dir*
Julie Ross, *Project Mgr*
Paul Zimmerman, *Business Mgr*
Martin R Hardlund, *Sales Mgr*
EMP: 72
SALES (est): 3.1MM **Privately Held**
SIC: 8062 General medical & surgical hospitals

(P-21527)
KAWEAH DELTA HEALTH CARE DST
355 Monte Vista Dr, Dinuba (93618-9228)
PHONE.....................559 591-5513
Gary K Herbst, *CFO*
EMP: 236
SALES (corp-wide): 537.4MM **Privately Held**
SIC: 8062 Hospital, AMA approved residency
PA: Kaweah Delta Health Care District
400 W Mineral King Ave
Visalia CA 93291
559 624-2000

(P-21528)
KAWEAH DELTA HEALTH CARE DST (PA)
Also Called: Kaweah Delta Medical Center
400 W Mineral King Ave, Visalia
(93291-6237)
PHONE.....................559 624-2000
Donna Archer, *CEO*
Lindsay K Mann, *CEO*
Gary Herbst, *CFO*
Mark Garfield, *Chief Mktg Ofcr*
Janet Danielson, *Vice Pres*
EMP: 1800
SQ FT: 250,255
SALES: 537.4MM **Privately Held**
SIC: 8062 Hospital, AMA approved residency

(P-21529)
KECK HOSPITAL OF USC
1500 San Pablo St, Los Angeles
(90033-5313)
PHONE.....................800 872-2273
Thomas E Jackiewicz, *CEO*
Mike Fong, *Records Dir*
Rodney B Hanners, *COO*
Kamyar Afshar, *CFO*
James J Uli Jr, *CFO*
▲ **EMP:** 77
SALES (est): 761.1MM **Privately Held**
SIC: 8062 General medical & surgical hospitals

(P-21530)
KEIRO NURSING HOME
2221 Lincoln Park Ave, Los Angeles
(90031-2998)
PHONE.....................323 276-5700
Janie Teshima, *Administration*
EMP: 150
SALES (corp-wide): 16.5MM **Privately Held**
SIC: 8062 8052 8051 General medical & surgical hospitals; intermediate care facilities; skilled nursing care facilities
PA: Keiro Nursing Home
325 S Boyle Ave
Los Angeles CA 90033
323 263-9655

(P-21531)
KENNETH CORP
Also Called: GARDEN GROVE HOSPITAL
12601 Garden Grove Blvd, Garden Grove
(92843-1908)
PHONE.....................714 537-5160
Edward Mirzabegian, *CEO*
Hassan Alkhouli, *Ch of Bd*
Bader Elghussein, *Manager*
EMP: 615
SQ FT: 133,083
SALES: 108.4MM **Privately Held**
SIC: 8062 General medical & surgical hospitals

(P-21532)
KERN COUNTY HOSPITAL AUTHORITY
1700 Mount Vernon Ave, Bakersfield
(93306-4018)
PHONE.....................661 326-2102
Russell Judd, *CEO*
Andrew Cantu, *CFO*
Tyler Whitezell, *VP Admin*
EMP: 1000 **EST:** 1865
SQ FT: 29,800
SALES (est): 647.1K **Privately Held**
SIC: 8062 General medical & surgical hospitals

(P-21533)
KERN VALLEY HOSP FOUNDATION (PA)
6412 Laurel Ave, Lake Isabella
(93240-9529)
P.O. Box 1628 (93240-1628)
PHONE.....................760 379-2681
Clarence Semonious, *President*
Mary Completo, *Treasurer*
Anne Litz, *Vice Pres*
Kay Knight, *Admin Sec*
Sally Partin, *Director*
EMP: 300
SQ FT: 65,000
SALES: 57K **Privately Held**
SIC: 8062 8051 Hospital, affiliated with AMA residency; extended care facility

(P-21534)
KINDRED HEALTHCARE INC
4030 Moorpark Ave Ste 251, San Jose
(95117-1807)
PHONE.....................408 261-6943
EMP: 99
SALES (corp-wide): 6B **Privately Held**
SIC: 8062 8082 General medical & surgical hospitals; home health care services
HQ: Kindred Healthcare, Llc
680 S 4th St
Louisville KY 40202
502 596-7300

(P-21535)
KINDRED HEALTHCARE OPER INC
145 E Dana St, Mountain View
(94041-1507)
PHONE.....................650 962-6000
Rod Wong, *Branch Mgr*
EMP: 219
SALES (corp-wide): 6B **Privately Held**
WEB: www.salemhaven.com
SIC: 8062 General medical & surgical hospitals
HQ: Kindred Healthcare Operating, Llc
680 S 4th St
Louisville KY 40202
502 596-7300

(P-21536)
KINDRED HEALTHCARE OPER INC
Also Called: Kindred Hospital
2800 Benedict Dr, San Leandro
(94577-6840)
PHONE.....................510 357-8300
Wendy Mamoon, *CEO*
Virgil Williams, *Ch Radiology*
Jack Barritt, *Lab Dir*
EMP: 450
SALES (corp-wide): 6B **Privately Held**
WEB: www.salemhaven.com
SIC: 8062 General medical & surgical hospitals
HQ: Kindred Healthcare Operating, Llc
680 S 4th St
Louisville KY 40202
502 596-7300

(P-21537)
KINDRED HEALTHCARE OPER INC
1575 7th Ave, San Francisco (94122-3704)
PHONE.....................415 566-1200
Melissa Jones, *Administration*
EMP: 218
SALES (corp-wide): 6B **Privately Held**
SIC: 8062 General medical & surgical hospitals
HQ: Kindred Healthcare Operating, Llc
680 S 4th St
Louisville KY 40202
502 596-7300

(P-21538)
KINDRED HEALTHCARE OPER INC
Also Called: Ontario Community Hospital
550 N Monterey Ave, Ontario (91764-3318)
PHONE.....................909 391-0333
Peter Adamo, *CEO*
Debi Walker, *Purch Dir*
Michael Williams, *Buyer*
Nancy Hickerson, *Director*
Carol Kirk, *Director*

EMP: 275
SALES (corp-wide): 6B **Privately Held**
WEB: www.salemhaven.com
SIC: 8062 General medical & surgical hospitals
HQ: Kindred Healthcare Operating, Llc
680 S 4th St
Louisville KY 40202
502 596-7300

(P-21539)
KINDRED HEALTHCARE OPERATING
5525 W Slauson Ave, Los Angeles
(90056-1047)
PHONE.....................310 642-0325
Adam Darvish, *Manager*
Nancy Sagaral, *President*
Shawn Matty, *Prgmr*
Alex Nava, *Purch Agent*
Kenny Vega,
EMP: 280
SALES (corp-wide): 6B **Privately Held**
WEB: www.salemhaven.com
SIC: 8062 General medical & surgical hospitals
HQ: Kindred Healthcare Operating, Llc
680 S 4th St
Louisville KY 40202
502 596-7300

(P-21540)
KINDRED HOSPITAL-WESTMINSTER
200 Hospital Cir, Westminster
(92683-3910)
PHONE.....................714 372-3014
Virg Narbutas, *CEO*
Jack Boggess, *COO*
Adam Darvish, *Vice Pres*
Joanne Watanabe, *Data Proc Staff*
Michael Arellano, *Director*
EMP: 400 **EST:** 1957
SQ FT: 107,000
SALES: 74.8MM
SALES (corp-wide): 6B **Privately Held**
WEB: www.khwestminster.com
SIC: 8062 Hospital, affiliated with AMA residency
HQ: Kindred Healthcare, Llc
680 S 4th St
Louisville KY 40202
502 596-7300

(P-21541)
KINDRED NURSING CENTERS W LLC
Also Called: Kindred Nursing and Reha
1601 5th Ave, San Rafael (94901-1808)
PHONE.....................415 456-7170
Richard Espinoza, *Manager*
EMP: 65
SALES (corp-wide): 6B **Privately Held**
WEB: www.salemhaven.com
SIC: 8062 General medical & surgical hospitals
HQ: Kindred Nursing Centers West Llc
3128 Boxelder Dr
Cheyenne WY 82001
307 634-7901

(P-21542)
KND DEVELOPMENT 55 LLC
Also Called: Kindred Hospital - Rancho
10841 White Oak Ave, Rancho Cucamonga
(91730-3817)
PHONE.....................909 581-6400
Miller Debroah, *Director*
Victor Carrasco, *Officer*
Tessie Mancilla, *Human Res Mgr*
Leonard Wolfe, *Director*
EMP: 68 **EST:** 2007
SALES: 45.1MM **Privately Held**
SIC: 8062 General medical & surgical hospitals

(P-21543)
KPC HEALTHCARE INC
2701 S Bristol St, Santa Ana (92704-6201)
PHONE.....................714 800-1919
EMP: 310
SALES (corp-wide): 440.5MM **Privately Held**
SIC: 8062 General medical & surgical hospitals

PA: Kpc Healthcare, Inc.
1301 N Tustin Ave
Santa Ana CA 92705
714 953-3652

(P-21544)
LA PALMA HOSPITAL MEDICAL CTR
Also Called: LA PALMA INTERCOMMUNITY HOSPITAL
7901 Walker St, La Palma (90623-1764)
PHONE.....................714 670-7400
Virg Narbutas, *CEO*
Sami Shoukair, *Chairman*
Marlene Pritchard, *Vice Pres*
Prem Reddy,
Allen Smith,
EMP: 400 **EST:** 1970
SQ FT: 94,000
SALES: 56.9MM
SALES (corp-wide): 3.4B **Privately Held**
SIC: 8062 General medical & surgical hospitals
HQ: Prime Healthcare Services Inc
3300 E Guasti Rd Ste 300
Ontario CA 91761
-

(P-21545)
LAC USC MEDICAL CENTER
Also Called: Los Angeles County Hospital
1200 N State St Rm 5250, Los Angeles
(90033-1083)
P.O. Box 63 (90078-0063)
PHONE.....................323 226-7858
Robert Henderson, *Director*
Michael Siegel, *Principal*
David Lopez, *Admin Asst*
Danny Amaya, *Administration*
Adelaida Dela Cerda, *Pub Rel Dir*
EMP: 198
SALES (est): 59.3MM **Privately Held**
SIC: 8062 6324 General medical & surgical hospitals; hospital & medical service plans

(P-21546)
LAST FRONTIER HEALTHCARE DST
Also Called: MODOC MEDICAL CENTER
228 W Mcdowell Ave, Alturas (96101-3934)
PHONE.....................530 233-5131
Kevin Kramer, *CEO*
Jo Knoch, *CFO*
Diane Hagelthorne, *Human Resources*
EMP: 190
SQ FT: 56,094
SALES: 15.9MM **Privately Held**
WEB: www.modoccounty.us
SIC: 8062 General medical & surgical hospitals

(P-21547)
LELAND STANFORD JUNIOR UNIV
Also Called: Cantor Art Ctr Stanford Univ
328 Lomita Dr, Palo Alto (94305-5006)
PHONE.....................650 723-2997
Jesse Cool, *Manager*
Sara Larsen, *Manager*
EMP: 50
SALES (corp-wide): 5.6B **Privately Held**
SIC: 8062 8069 8221 General medical & surgical hospitals; children's hospital; university
PA: Leland Stanford Junior University
450 Serra Mall
Stanford CA 94305
650 723-2300

(P-21548)
LELAND STANFORD JUNIOR UNIV
Also Called: Stanford Hospitals and Clinics
820 Quarry Rd, Palo Alto (94304-2202)
PHONE.....................650 725-2377
Roy King, *Branch Mgr*
PO Wang, *Psychiatry*
Ricardo Castillo, *Med Doctor*
Norman H Silverman, *Med Doctor*
EMP: 2285
SALES (corp-wide): 5.6B **Privately Held**
SIC: 8062 8221 General medical & surgical hospitals; university

PA: Leland Stanford Junior University
450 Serra Mall
Stanford CA 94305
650 723-2300

(P-21549)
LELAND STANFORD JUNIOR UNIV
Also Called: Stanford Medical Center
2680 Hanover St, Palo Alto (94304-1117)
PHONE..................650 723-4000
Elizabeth Eilers, *Director*
Andy Switky, *Professor*
EMP: 2285
SALES (corp-wide): 5.6B **Privately Held**
SIC: 8062 8221 General medical & surgical hospitals; university
PA: Leland Stanford Junior University
450 Serra Mall
Stanford CA 94305
650 723-2300

(P-21550)
LELAND STANFORD JUNIOR UNIV
Also Called: Stanford University Med Ctr
1000 Welch Rd, Palo Alto (94304-1811)
PHONE..................650 725-4617
Kate Lorig, *Principal*
Chris McMurdo, *Director*
Rudy Arthofer, *Manager*
Cecilia Cadet, *Manager*
Seamus Giffen, *Manager*
EMP: 2285
SALES (corp-wide): 5.6B **Privately Held**
SIC: 8062 8221 Hospital, medical school affiliation; university
PA: Leland Stanford Junior University
450 Serra Mall
Stanford CA 94305
650 723-2300

(P-21551)
LELAND STANFORD JUNIOR UNIV
Also Called: Stanford University
473 Via Ortega, Stanford (94305-4121)
PHONE..................650 725-2386
Richard Luthy, *Branch Mgr*
EMP: 2285
SALES (corp-wide): 5.6B **Privately Held**
SIC: 8062 8069 8221 General medical & surgical hospitals; children's hospital; university
PA: Leland Stanford Junior University
450 Serra Mall
Stanford CA 94305
650 723-2300

(P-21552)
LELAND STANFORD JUNIOR UNIV
Also Called: Stanford University
243 Via Panama St, Stanford (94305-4102)
PHONE..................650 725-6127
Phil Reese, *Branch Mgr*
Michelle Collette, *Technology*
Vijay Gandra, *Director*
EMP: 2285
SALES (corp-wide): 5.6B **Privately Held**
SIC: 8062 8069 8221 General medical & surgical hospitals; children's hospital; university
PA: Leland Stanford Junior University
450 Serra Mall
Stanford CA 94305
650 723-2300

(P-21553)
LELAND STANFORD JUNIOR UNIV
Also Called: Stanford University Medical
300 Pasteur Dr, Stanford (94305-2200)
PHONE..................650 723-4000
Martha Marsh, *Administration*
Jenni Vargas, *President*
Christina Saint Martin, *Vice Pres*
Gregg Zoll, *Planning*
Jonathan Binkley, *Software Engr*
EMP: 6120
SQ FT: 33,503
SALES (corp-wide): 5.6B **Privately Held**
SIC: 8062 8011 8221 General medical & surgical hospitals; offices & clinics of medical doctors; university

PA: Leland Stanford Junior University
450 Serra Mall
Stanford CA 94305
650 723-2300

(P-21554)
LIFEPOINT HEALTH INC
Also Called: Colorado River Medical Center
1401 Bailey Ave, Needles (92363-3103)
PHONE..................760 326-7100
James Arp, *Manager*
EMP: 215
SALES (corp-wide): 6.2B **Publicly Held**
WEB: www.ennisregional.com
SIC: 8062 General medical & surgical hospitals
PA: Lifepoint Health, Inc.
330 Seven Springs Way
Brentwood TN 37027
615 920-7000

(P-21555)
LINDA LOMA UNIV HLTH CARE (HQ)
11370 Anderson St # 3900, Loma Linda (92350-1715)
P.O. Box 2000 (92354-0200)
PHONE..................909 558-2806
Richard Hart, *President*
Rosita Fike, *CEO*
Nelia Wurangian-Caan, *Vice Pres*
Maxine Ullery, *Associate Dir*
Padmini Davamony, *Exec Dir*
EMP: 71
SALES (est): 1.7B
SALES (corp-wide): 301.3MM **Privately Held**
SIC: 8062 8011 8051 5999 Hospital, medical school affiliated with residency; medical centers; extended care facility; convalescent equipment & supplies
PA: Loma Linda University
11060 Anderson St
Loma Linda CA 92350
909 558-4540

(P-21556)
LITTLE COMPANY MARY HOSPITAL
Also Called: Leader Drug Store
4101 Torrance Blvd, Torrance (90503-4664)
PHONE..................310 540-7676
Joseph Zanetta, *CEO*
Elizabeth Zuanich, *CFO*
Traci Smith, *Info Tech Mgr*
Betsy Smith, *Accountant*
▲ **EMP:** 1200
SQ FT: 300,000
SALES (est): 9.4MM
SALES (corp-wide): 17.6B **Privately Held**
WEB: www.lcmhs.org
SIC: 8062 8051 General medical & surgical hospitals; skilled nursing care facilities
HQ: Providence Health System-Southern California
1801 Lind Ave Sw
Renton WA 98057
425 525-3355

(P-21557)
LODI MEMORIAL HOSP ASSN INC (HQ)
975 S Fairmont Ave, Lodi (95240-5118)
P.O. Box 3004 (95241-1908)
PHONE..................209 334-3411
Daniel Wolcott, *CEO*
Roland Simeon,
Nagui N Sorour,
Sarah Beasley, *Volunteer Dir*
Joseph P Harrington, *President*
EMP: 700
SQ FT: 97,057
SALES (est): 120.3MM
SALES (corp-wide): 4.1B **Privately Held**
SIC: 8062 Hospital, affiliated with AMA residency
PA: Adventist Health System/West
2100 Douglas Blvd
Roseville CA 95661
916 781-2000

(P-21558)
LODI MEMORIAL HOSP ASSN INC
Also Called: Conrad Lab, The
1200 W Vine St, Lodi (95240-5136)
PHONE..................209 339-7583
Dave Mack, *Director*
Sue Anderson, *Manager*
Cindy Billups, *Supervisor*
Jackie Vollmer, *Supervisor*
EMP: 50
SALES (corp-wide): 4.1B **Privately Held**
SIC: 8062 General medical & surgical hospitals
HQ: Lodi Memorial Hospital Association, Inc.
975 S Fairmont Ave
Lodi CA 95240
209 334-3411

(P-21559)
LOMA LINDA - INLAND EMPIRE C
Also Called: Llieche
11175 Campus St Csp 11006 11006 Csp, Loma Linda (92354)
PHONE..................909 651-5832
Daniel Giang, *President*
EMP: 141 **EST:** 2013
SALES (est): 1.6MM **Privately Held**
SIC: 8062 Hospital, medical school affiliated with residency

(P-21560)
LOMA LINDA UNIVERSITY MED CTR
Also Called: Craniofacial Department
11370 Anderson St 2100, Loma Linda (92350-1715)
P.O. Box 982 (92354-0982)
PHONE..................909 558-2100
Leonard Bailey MD, *Principal*
Lynne Karman, *Nurse*
Linda Stewart, *Manager*
EMP: 105
SALES (corp-wide): 301.3MM **Privately Held**
WEB: www.llumc.com
SIC: 8062 8221 Hospital, medical school affiliation; university
HQ: Loma Linda University Medical Center
11234 Anderson St
Loma Linda CA 92354
909 558-4000

(P-21561)
LOMA LINDA UNIVERSITY MED CTR (DH)
Also Called: Llumc
11234 Anderson St, Loma Linda (92354-2871)
P.O. Box 2000 (92354-0200)
PHONE..................909 558-4000
Richard H Hart, *Vice Chairman*
David Hinshaw Jr, *Ch Radiology*
James Jesse, *President*
Steven Mohr, *CFO*
Noni Patchett, *Treasurer*
EMP: 4600
SQ FT: 630,000
SALES (est): 1.7B
SALES (corp-wide): 301.3MM **Privately Held**
WEB: www.llumc.com
SIC: 8062 8011 8051 5999 Hospital, medical school affiliated with residency; medical centers; extended care facility; medical apparatus & supplies
HQ: Loma Linda University Health Care
11370 Anderson St # 3900
Loma Linda CA 92350
909 558-2806

(P-21562)
LOMA LINDA UNIVERSITY MED CTR
Also Called: Loma Linda Catering Center
11175 Campus St, Loma Linda (92350-1700)
PHONE..................909 558-8244
Najwa Medina, *Manager*
Barbara Sharp, *Exec Dir*
Brent Boyko, *IT/INT Sup*
David J Michelson, *Neurology*
Edward Tagge, *Pediatrics*

EMP: 100
SALES (corp-wide): 301.3MM **Privately Held**
WEB: www.llumc.com
SIC: 8062 Hospital, medical school affiliation
HQ: Loma Linda University Medical Center
11234 Anderson St
Loma Linda CA 92354
909 558-4000

(P-21563)
LOMA LINDA UNIVERSITY MED CTR
Also Called: Behavioral Medicine Center
1710 Barton Rd, Redlands (92373-5304)
PHONE..................909 558-9275
Ruthita Fike, *Manager*
Edward L Field, *Exec Dir*
Stephanie Hunt- Eicher, *Hlthcr Dir*
Lauren Ball, *Director*
Norie Bencito, *Director*
EMP: 310
SQ FT: 62,476
SALES (corp-wide): 301.3MM **Privately Held**
WEB: www.llumc.com
SIC: 8062 8221 Hospital, medical school affiliation; university
HQ: Loma Linda University Medical Center
11234 Anderson St
Loma Linda CA 92354
909 558-4000

(P-21564)
LOMA LINDA UNIVERSITY MED CTR
Also Called: Loma Linda Pharmacy
11223 Campus St, Loma Linda (92354-3203)
PHONE..................909 558-4216
Bill Robinson, *Manager*
EMP: 200
SALES (corp-wide): 301.3MM **Privately Held**
WEB: www.llumc.com
SIC: 8062 General medical & surgical hospitals
HQ: Loma Linda University Medical Center
11234 Anderson St
Loma Linda CA 92354
909 558-4000

(P-21565)
LOMA LINDA UNIVERSITY MED CTR
Also Called: Loma Linda Community Hospital
25333 Barton Rd, Loma Linda (92350-0210)
PHONE..................909 796-0167
Todd Nelson, *Manager*
Mark Hubbard, *Vice Pres*
Lisa Berry, *Director*
EMP: 172
SQ FT: 79,580
SALES (corp-wide): 301.3MM **Privately Held**
WEB: www.llumc.com
SIC: 8062 General medical & surgical hospitals
HQ: Loma Linda University Medical Center
11234 Anderson St
Loma Linda CA 92354
909 558-4000

(P-21566)
LOMPOC VALLEY MEDICAL CENTER (PA)
Also Called: LOMPOC SKILLED CARE CENTER
1515 E Ocean Ave, Lompoc (93436-7092)
P.O. Box 1058 (93438-1058)
PHONE..................805 737-3300
Jim Raggio, *CEO*
Naishadh Buch, *COO*
Jim White, *Exec VP*
Jayne Scalise, *Principal*
Eric Lykens, *Systs Prg Mgr*
EMP: 675
SQ FT: 150,000
SALES: 93.2MM **Privately Held**
SIC: 8062 8051 Hospital, affiliated with AMA residency; skilled nursing care facilities

(P-21567)
LONG BEACH MEMORIAL MED CTR (HQ)
Also Called: Miller Children's Hospital
2801 Atlantic Ave Fl 2, Long Beach
(90806-1701)
PHONE.....................................562 933-2000
John Bishop, *CEO*
Barry Arbuckle PHD, *President*
Tamra Kaplan, *COO*
Suize Reinsvold, *COO*
Wendy Dorchester,
EMP: 2000
SQ FT: 1,100,000
SALES: 618.7MM
SALES (corp-wide): 2.2B **Privately Held**
WEB: www.longbeachstate.com
SIC: 8062 General medical & surgical hospitals
PA: Memorial Health Services
17360 Brookhurst St # 160
Fountain Valley CA 92708
714 377-6748

(P-21568)
LONGWOOD MANAGEMENT CORP
Also Called: Shea Convalescent Hospital
7716 Pickering Ave, Whittier (90602-2001)
PHONE.....................................562 693-5240
Richard Esconrias, *Manager*
EMP: 100
SALES (corp-wide): 170MM **Privately Held**
SIC: 8062 8051 8011 General medical & surgical hospitals; skilled nursing care facilities; offices & clinics of medical doctors
PA: Longwood Management Corp.
4032 Wilshire Blvd Fl 6
Los Angeles CA 90010
213 389-6900

(P-21569)
LONGWOOD MANAGEMENT CORP
Also Called: Northridge Nursing Center
7836 Reseda Blvd, Reseda (91335-1902)
PHONE.....................................818 881-7414
Deffie Biczi, *General Mgr*
EMP: 80
SALES (corp-wide): 170MM **Privately Held**
SIC: 8062 General medical & surgical hospitals
PA: Longwood Management Corp.
4032 Wilshire Blvd Fl 6
Los Angeles CA 90010
213 389-6900

(P-21570)
LOS ALAMITOS MEDICAL CTR INC (HQ)
3751 Katella Ave, Los Alamitos
(90720-3113)
P.O. Box 533 (90720-0533)
PHONE.....................................714 826-6400
Kent Clayton, *CEO*
Alice Livingood, *President*
Margaret Watkins, *President*
Rosa Espinoza, *Human Res Dir*
Steven Forman, *Persnl Dir*
EMP: 1100
SQ FT: 900
SALES: 210.5MM
SALES (corp-wide): 19.3B **Publicly Held**
SIC: 8062 General medical & surgical hospitals
PA: Tenet Healthcare Corporation
1445 Ross Ave Ste 1400
Dallas TX 75202
469 893-2200

(P-21571)
LOS ROBLES HOSPITAL & MED CTR (DH)
Also Called: HOSPITAL COPORATION OF AMERICA
215 W Janss Rd, Thousand Oaks
(91360-1899)
P.O. Box 550, Nashville TN (37220-0550)
PHONE.....................................805 497-2727
Greg Angle, *CEO*
Barry Klein, *Ch Radiology*
Maureen Nicols, *CEO*
Glenda Cox, *Ch Nursing Ofcr*

Cynthia Johnson, *Ch Nursing Ofcr*
◆ **EMP:** 94
SQ FT: 475
SALES: 474.6MM **Publicly Held**
SIC: 8062 General medical & surgical hospitals
HQ: Hca Inc.
1 Park Plz
Nashville TN 37203
615 344-9551

(P-21572)
MADERA COMMUNITY HOSPITAL
Also Called: Family Health Services Clinic
1210 E Almond Ave Ste A, Madera
(93637-5606)
PHONE.....................................559 675-5530
Robert Kelly, *CEO*
EMP: 209
SALES (corp-wide): 81.3MM **Privately Held**
SIC: 8062 General medical & surgical hospitals
PA: Madera Community Hospital
1250 E Almond Ave
Madera CA 93637
559 675-5555

(P-21573)
MADERA COMMUNITY HOSPITAL
Also Called: Chowchilla Medical Center
285 Hospital Dr, Chowchilla (93610-2041)
PHONE.....................................559 665-3768
Mark J Foote, *CEO*
EMP: 209
SALES (corp-wide): 81.3MM **Privately Held**
SIC: 8062 General medical & surgical hospitals
PA: Madera Community Hospital
1250 E Almond Ave
Madera CA 93637
559 675-5555

(P-21574)
MADERA COMMUNITY HOSPITAL (PA)
Also Called: Mch
1250 E Almond Ave, Madera (93637-5696)
P.O. Box 1328 (93639-1328)
PHONE.....................................559 675-5555
Evan J Rayner, *CEO*
Connie Wise, *Executive Asst*
Alejandra Contreras, *Personnel Assit*
Zafar Sheikh, *Hlthcr Dir*
EMP: 383
SQ FT: 66,300
SALES: 81.3MM **Privately Held**
SIC: 8062 General medical & surgical hospitals

(P-21575)
MAIN STREET SPECIALTY SURGERY
280 S Mn St Ste 100, Orange (92868)
PHONE.....................................714 704-1900
Betty Hoogenban, *Director*
EMP: 92
SALES (est): 13.1MM **Privately Held**
WEB: www.msssc.com
SIC: 8062 General medical & surgical hospitals

(P-21576)
MARIN GENERAL HOSPITAL
250 Bon Air Rd, Kentfield (94904-1784)
P.O. Box 8010, San Rafael (94912-8010)
PHONE.....................................415 925-7000
Lee Domanico, *CEO*
David Bradley, *CEO*
Theresa Daughton, *CFO*
James McManus, *CFO*
Linda Lang, *Executive*
EMP: 1100 **EST:** 1947
SQ FT: 125,000
SALES: 370.9MM
SALES (corp-wide): 23MM **Privately Held**
WEB: www.sutterhealth.org
SIC: 8062 8011 General medical & surgical hospitals; offices & clinics of medical doctors

PA: Marin Healthcare District
100b Drakes Landing Rd
Greenbrae CA 94904
415 464-2090

(P-21577)
MARINA DEL REY HOSPITAL
4650 Lincoln Blvd, Marina Del Rey
(90292-6306)
PHONE.....................................310 823-8911
Sean Fowler, *CEO*
EMP: 601
SQ FT: 117,640
SALES (est): 12.3MM **Privately Held**
SIC: 8062 General medical & surgical hospitals

(P-21578)
MARK TWAIN MEDICAL CENTER (HQ)
Also Called: MARK TWAIN ST JOSEPH'S HOSPITAL
768 Mountain Ranch Rd, San Andreas
(95249-9707)
PHONE.....................................209 754-3521
Craig J Marks, *CEO*
Greg Jordan, *President*
Jacob Lews, *CFO*
Linda Lewis, *Treasurer*
Dean Kelaita, *Bd of Directors*
EMP: 225
SQ FT: 40,000
SALES: 62.8MM
SALES (corp-wide): 6.7B **Privately Held**
SIC: 8062 General medical & surgical hospitals
PA: Dignity Health
185 Berry St Ste 300
San Francisco CA 94107
415 438-5500

(P-21579)
MARK TWAIN MEDICAL CENTER
Also Called: Silver Service
768 Mountain Ranch Rd, San Andreas
(95249-9707)
PHONE.....................................209 754-1487
Mike Lawson, *President*
John Krieg, *Human Res Mgr*
EMP: 300
SALES (corp-wide): 6.7B **Privately Held**
SIC: 8062 8322 General medical & surgical hospitals; geriatric social service
HQ: Mark Twain Medical Center
768 Mountain Ranch Rd
San Andreas CA 95249

(P-21580)
MARSHALL MEDICAL CENTER
1100 Marshall Way, El Dorado Hills
(95762)
PHONE.....................................916 933-2273
EMP: 221
SALES (corp-wide): 238.8MM **Privately Held**
SIC: 8062 General medical & surgical hospitals
PA: Marshall Medical Center
1100 Marshall Way
Placerville CA 95667
530 622-1441

(P-21581)
MARSHALL MEDICAL CENTER (PA)
Also Called: Marshall Hospital
1100 Marshall Way, Placerville
(95667-6533)
P.O. Box 872 (95667-0872)
PHONE.....................................530 622-1441
James Whipple, *CEO*
Shannon Truesdell, *COO*
Laurie Eldridge, *CFO*
Jennifer Baker, *Exec Dir*
Maia Schneider, *Exec Dir*
EMP: 1000
SQ FT: 124,000
SALES: 238.8MM **Privately Held**
SIC: 8062 8071 8082 General medical & surgical hospitals; medical laboratories; X-ray laboratory, including dental; home health care services

(P-21582)
MATER MISERICORDIAE HOSPITAL (PA)
Also Called: MERCY MEDICAL CENTER MERCED
333 Mercy Ave, Merced (95340-8319)
PHONE.....................................209 564-5000
David Dunham, *CEO*
Chuck Kassis, *COO*
Michael Strasser, *CFO*
Cheryl Baijnauth, *Information Mgr*
Paul Feltz, *Marketing Staff*
EMP: 668
SQ FT: 60,000
SALES: 298.8MM **Privately Held**
SIC: 8062 General medical & surgical hospitals

(P-21583)
MCKINLEY PARK CARE CENTER
3700 H St, Sacramento (95816-4611)
PHONE.....................................916 452-3592
Radio Shey, *Administration*
Gary Weemers, *Administration*
EMP: 85
SALES (est): 4.8MM **Privately Held**
SIC: 8062 General medical & surgical hospitals

(P-21584)
MEMORIALCARE SURGICAL CENTER A
Also Called: Orange Coast Ctr For Surgl Cr
18111 Brookhurst St # 3200, Fountain Valley (92708-6728)
PHONE.....................................714 369-1100
Dana Pratt, *CEO*
EMP: 60
SALES (est): 7.9MM **Privately Held**
SIC: 8062 General medical & surgical hospitals

(P-21585)
MENDOCINO COAST DISTRICT HOSP (PA)
700 River Dr, Fort Bragg (95437-5403)
PHONE.....................................707 961-1234
Jonathan Baker, *CEO*
Mark Smith, *CFO*
Patricia Jauregui Darland, *Chairman*
Tom Birdsell, *Treasurer*
Camille Ranker, *Treasurer*
▲ **EMP:** 320
SQ FT: 71,500
SALES: 52.5MM **Privately Held**
SIC: 8062 General medical & surgical hospitals

(P-21586)
MENDOCINO COAST DISTRICT HOSP
Also Called: Mendicino Cast Otptent Surgery
700 River Dr, Fort Bragg (95437-5403)
PHONE.....................................707 961-4736
Jonathan Baker, *Branch Mgr*
EMP: 167
SALES (corp-wide): 52.5MM **Privately Held**
SIC: 8062 8011 General medical & surgical hospitals; surgeon
PA: Mendocino Coast District Hospital
700 River Dr
Fort Bragg CA 95437
707 961-1234

(P-21587)
MERCY HM SVCS A CAL LTD PARTNR
2215 Truxtun Ave, Bakersfield
(93301-3602)
PHONE.....................................661 632-5234
Russel Judd, *President*
EMP: 200
SALES (corp-wide): 6.7B **Privately Held**
WEB: www.mercyhealth.org
SIC: 8062 General medical & surgical hospitals
HQ: Mercy Home Services A California Limited Partnership
2175 Rosaline Ave Ste A
Redding CA 96001
530 225-6000

PRODUCTS & SVCS

(P-21588)
MERCY HM SVCS A CAL LTD PARTNR (HQ)
Also Called: Mercy Medical Center - Redding
2175 Rosaline Ave Ste A, Redding
(96001-2549)
P.O. Box 496009 (96049-6009)
PHONE.....................530 225-6000
George A Govier, *CEO*
Wendy Scott, *Info Tech Mgr*
Alexis Ross, *Analyst*
Denise Little, *Human Res Dir*
Peggy Podliska, *Buyer*
EMP: 700
SQ FT: 250,000
SALES: 446.3MM
SALES (corp-wide): 6.7B **Privately Held**
WEB: www.mercyhealth.org
SIC: 8062 Hospital, affiliated with AMA residency
PA: Dignity Health
185 Berry St Ste 300
San Francisco CA 94107
415 438-5500

(P-21589)
MERCY HM SVCS A CAL LTD PARTNR
914 Pine St, Mount Shasta (96067-2143)
PHONE.....................530 926-6111
Kenneth Platou, *CEO*
Lisa Hubbard, *Med Doctor*
EMP: 340
SALES (corp-wide): 6.7B **Privately Held**
WEB: www.mercyhealth.org
SIC: 8062 General medical & surgical hospitals
HQ: Mercy Home Services A California Limited Partnership
2175 Rosaline Ave Ste A
Redding CA 96001
530 225-6000

(P-21590)
MERCY HM SVCS A CAL LTD PARTNR
Also Called: Mercy General Hospital
4001 J St, Sacramento (95819-3626)
PHONE.....................916 453-4545
Edmundo Castaneda, *President*
Conrad Megia, *Vice Pres*
Joyce Hugo, *Office Admin*
Rod Fuller, *Engineer*
Cynthia Kirch, *VP Human Res*
EMP: 1000
SALES (corp-wide): 6.7B **Privately Held**
WEB: www.mercyhealth.org
SIC: 8062 Hospital, affiliated with AMA residency
HQ: Mercy Home Services A California Limited Partnership
2175 Rosaline Ave Ste A
Redding CA 96001
530 225-6000

(P-21591)
MERCY HM SVCS A CAL LTD PARTNR
Also Called: Mercy Medical Center
2740 M St, Merced (95340-2813)
PHONE.....................209 564-4200
Lisa Wegley, *Manager*
EMP: 340
SALES (corp-wide): 6.7B **Privately Held**
WEB: www.mercyhealth.org
SIC: 8062 General medical & surgical hospitals
HQ: Mercy Home Services A California Limited Partnership
2175 Rosaline Ave Ste A
Redding CA 96001
530 225-6000

(P-21592)
METHODIST HOSP SOUTHERN CAL (PA)
300 W Huntington Dr, Arcadia
(91007-3402)
PHONE.....................626 898-8000
Dan F Ausman, *CEO*
Bridgett Didier, *Records Dir*
Rose Dealba, *Officer*
Clifford R Daniels, *Senior VP*
William E Grigg, *Senior VP*
EMP: 933

SQ FT: 100,000
SALES: 297.3MM **Privately Held**
SIC: 8062 General medical & surgical hospitals

(P-21593)
METHODIST HOSPITAL OF S CA
300 W Huntington Dr, Arcadia
(91007-3402)
P.O. Box 60016 (91066-6016)
PHONE.....................626 574-3755
Dennis Lee, *Principal*
Jason Aranda, *Manager*
EMP: 61
SALES (est): 7.2MM **Privately Held**
SIC: 8062 General medical & surgical hospitals

(P-21594)
MISSION HOSP REGIONAL MED CTR (PA)
27700 Medical Center Rd, Mission Viejo
(92691-6426)
PHONE.....................949 364-1400
Kenn Nicfaralnd, *CEO*
Eileen Haubl, *CFO*
Ed Jordan, *Bd of Directors*
Terry Wooten, *Officer*
Warren Spalding, *Lab Dir*
EMP: 2600
SQ FT: 750,000
SALES: 547.3MM **Privately Held**
WEB: www.drvonmaur.com
SIC: 8062 General medical & surgical hospitals

(P-21595)
MOFFITT H C HOSPITAL
505 Parnassus Ave, San Francisco
(94143-2204)
PHONE.....................415 476-1000
EMP: 148 EST: 2008
SALES (est): 283.3K
SALES (corp-wide): 9.5B **Privately Held**
SIC: 8062
HQ: University Of California, San Francisco
505 Parnassus Ave
San Francisco CA 94143
415 476-9000

(P-21596)
MONTEREY PARK HOSPITAL
Also Called: MONTEREY PARK HOSPITAL
900 S Atlantic Blvd, Monterey Park
(91754-4780)
PHONE.....................626 570-9000
Philip A Cohen, *CEO*
Robert M Dubbs, *President*
Robert W Fleming Jr, *Senior VP*
Minerva Mandujano, *Administration*
Judith Rodriguez, *Recruiter*
EMP: 150
SQ FT: 90,575
SALES: 74.7MM
SALES (corp-wide): 572.3MM **Privately Held**
WEB: www.montereyparkhosp.com
SIC: 8062 General medical & surgical hospitals
PA: Ahmc Healthcare Inc.
1000 S Fremont Ave Unit 6
Alhambra CA 91803
626 943-7526

(P-21597)
MONTEREY PENINSULA HOSPITAL
Also Called: Community Hosp Recovery Ctr
576 Hartnell St Ste 260, Monterey
(93940-2887)
PHONE.....................831 373-0924
Oscar Reyes, *Director*
Wayne Lavengood, *Manager*
EMP: 50
SALES (est): 1.7MM
SALES (corp-wide): 200MM **Privately Held**
SIC: 8062 General medical & surgical hospitals
PA: Montage Health
23625 Holman Hwy
Monterey CA 93940
831 625-4830

(P-21598)
MOTION PICTURE AND TV FUND (PA)
Also Called: Bob Hope Health Center
23388 Mulholland Dr # 200, Woodland Hills
(91364-2733)
P.O. Box 51151, Los Angeles (90051-5451)
PHONE.....................818 876-1777
Robert Beitcher, *CEO*
Bob Pisano, *Ch of Bd*
Jay Roth, *Treasurer*
Scott Kaiser, *Officer*
Mike Spalinger, *Security Dir*
EMP: 688 EST: 1924
SQ FT: 50,000
SALES: 23MM **Privately Held**
WEB: www.mptvfund.com
SIC: 8062 8051 8011 8351 General medical & surgical hospitals; convalescent home with continuous nursing care; medical centers; child day care services; individual & family services; retirement hotel operation

(P-21599)
MOTION PICTURE AND TV FUND
Also Called: Westside Health Center
1950 Sawtelle Blvd # 130, Los Angeles
(90025-7072)
PHONE.....................310 231-3000
Micheal West, *Manager*
Sharon Siefert, *Vice Pres*
Norman Solomon, *Director*
EMP: 66
SALES (corp-wide): 23MM **Privately Held**
SIC: 8062 8011 General medical & surgical hospitals; offices & clinics of medical doctors
PA: Motion Picture And Television Fund
23388 Mulholland Dr # 200
Woodland Hills CA 91364
818 876-1777

(P-21600)
MOUNTAIN COMM HLTH CRE DIST
Also Called: Trinity Hospital
410 N Taylor St, Weaverville (96093)
P.O. Box 1229 (96093-1229)
PHONE.....................530 623-5541
David Yarbrough, *Director*
EMP: 130
SALES (corp-wide): 15.2MM **Privately Held**
SIC: 8062 General medical & surgical hospitals
PA: Mountain Communities Health Care District
60 Easter Ave
Weaverville CA 96093
530 623-5541

(P-21601)
MOUNTAIN COMM HLTH CRE DIST (PA)
Also Called: Trinity Hospital
60 Easter Ave, Weaverville (96093)
P.O. Box 1229 (96093-1229)
PHONE.....................530 623-5541
Aaron Rogers, *CEO*
Jake Odom, *CIO*
Carol Huang, *Director*
EMP: 108
SALES: 15.2MM **Privately Held**
WEB: www.mcmedical.org
SIC: 8062 General medical & surgical hospitals

(P-21602)
MOUNTAIN VIEW CHILD CARE INC (PA)
Also Called: Totally Kids Rhbilitation Hosp
1720 Mountain View Ave, Loma Linda
(92354-1799)
PHONE.....................909 796-6915
Doug Pagett, *CEO*
Cynthia Capetillo, *CFO*
Donald Nydam, *Vice Pres*
Loma Linda, *Principal*
Sun Valley, *Principal*
EMP: 490

SALES (est): 46.3MM **Privately Held**
SIC: 8062 8052 8051 General medical & surgical hospitals; intermediate care facilities; skilled nursing care facilities

(P-21603)
MOUNTAINS COMMUNITY HOSP FNDTN
29101 Hospital Rd, Lake Arrowhead
(92352-9706)
P.O. Box 70 (92352-0070)
PHONE.....................909 336-3651
Don Willerth, *CEO*
EMP: 180
SQ FT: 18,500
SALES: 520.9K **Privately Held**
WEB: www.mchcares.com
SIC: 8062 8051 General medical & surgical hospitals; skilled nursing care facilities

(P-21604)
NATIVIDAD MEDICAL CENTER
Also Called: Occupational Medicine
1441 Constitution Blvd, Salinas
(93906-3100)
PHONE.....................831 755-4111
Gary Gray, *CEO*
EMP: 659
SALES: 211.3MM **Privately Held**
WEB: www.natividad.com
SIC: 8062 8011 8093 General medical & surgical hospitals; offices & clinics of medical doctors; specialty outpatient clinics

(P-21605)
NORTH SONOMA COUNTY HOSP DST
Also Called: Healdsburg District Hospital
1375 University St, Healdsburg
(95448-3382)
PHONE.....................707 431-6500
Evan J Rayner, *CEO*
Regina Novello, *COO*
Dan Hull, *CFO*
Johnny Hargrove, *Vice Pres*
Kristina Holloway, *Executive*
EMP: 171
SALES (est): 37.5MM **Privately Held**
SIC: 8062 General medical & surgical hospitals

(P-21606)
NORTHBAY HEALTHCARE CORP (PA)
Also Called: Northbay Healthcare System
1200 B Gale Wilson Blvd, Fairfield
(94533-3552)
PHONE.....................707 646-5000
Gary J Passama, *President*
Dante Tolbert, *President*
Nicole Brocato, *Vice Pres*
Wayne Gietz, *Vice Pres*
Jerry Simmers, *Lab Dir*
EMP: 114
SQ FT: 24,000
SALES (est): 63.6MM **Privately Held**
SIC: 8062 8011 General medical & surgical hospitals; offices & clinics of medical doctors

(P-21607)
NORTHBAY HEALTHCARE GROUP (PA)
Also Called: Northbay Medical Center
1200 B Gale Wilson Blvd, Fairfield
(94533-3552)
PHONE.....................707 646-5000
Toll Free:.....................888 -
Deborah Sugiyama, *CEO*
Susan Gornall, *Op Rm Dir*
Traci Duncan, *Ch Nursing Ofcr*
Christopher Gamboa, *Technician*
Kathy Halkett, *Technician*
EMP: 1200
SQ FT: 125,000
SALES: 530.8MM **Privately Held**
SIC: 8062 General medical & surgical hospitals

(P-21608)
NORTHERN CALIFORNIA REHAB
2801 Eureka Way, Redding (96001-0222)
PHONE.....................530 246-9000

Brad Hollinger, *Mng Member*
Penny Booth, *Info Tech Dir*
Lisa Stevens, *Opers Staff*
Stephen Marcus,
Ryan Zumalt, *Director*
EMP: 250
SALES: 39.2MM
SALES (corp-wide): 323.5MM **Privately Held**
SIC: 8062 General medical & surgical hospitals
PA: Vibra Healthcare, Llc
4600 Lena Dr Ste 100
Mechanicsburg PA 17055
717 591-5700

(P-21609)
NORTHERN INYO HEALTHCARE DST
Also Called: Northern Inyo Hospital
150 Pioneer Ln, Bishop (93514-2556)
PHONE....................................760 873-5811
Victoria Alexander-Lane, *CEO*
Kelli Huntsinger, *Records Dir*
M C Hubbard, *President*
Peter Watercott, *Treasurer*
Denise Hayden, *Vice Pres*
EMP: 402
SQ FT: 55,000
SALES: 76.2MM **Privately Held**
WEB: www.nih.org
SIC: 8062 General medical & surgical hospitals

(P-21610)
NORWALK COMMUNITY HOSPITAL
13222 Bloomfield Ave, Norwalk (90650-3200)
PHONE....................................562 863-4763
David Topper, *President*
David Herrera, *Vice Pres*
Connor Obrien, *Food Svc Dir*
EMP: 100
SQ FT: 18,935
SALES (est): 11.2MM
SALES (corp-wide): 815.3MM **Privately Held**
SIC: 8062 General medical & surgical hospitals
HQ: Alta Healthcare System Llc
4081 E Olympic Blvd
Los Angeles CA 90023
323 267-0477

(P-21611)
OAK VALLEY HOSPITAL DISTRICT (HQ)
350 S Oak Ave, Oakdale (95361-3519)
PHONE....................................209 847-3011
John McCormick, *CEO*
Bob Wikoff, *Ch of Bd*
Gail Sward, *Vice Ch Bd*
Michael Hendricks, *Info Tech Mgr*
Sherry Arndt, *Legal Exec*
EMP: 325
SQ FT: 55,000
SALES: 66.4MM
SALES (corp-wide): 6.7B **Privately Held**
WEB: www.ovhd.com
SIC: 8062 8051 General medical & surgical hospitals; skilled nursing care facilities
PA: Dignity Health
185 Berry St Ste 300
San Francisco CA 94107
415 438-5500

(P-21612)
OCONNOR HOSPITAL
Also Called: O'Connor Hospital Pedia Center
2039 Forest Ave, San Jose (95128-4817)
P.O. Box 1347, San Carlos (94070-7347)
PHONE....................................408 947-2929
James F Dover, *President*
EMP: 53
SALES (corp-wide): 1.2B **Privately Held**
SIC: 8062 General medical & surgical hospitals
HQ: O'connor Hospital
2105 Forest Ave
San Jose CA 95128
408 947-2500

(P-21613)
OCONNOR HOSPITAL (HQ)
Also Called: O'Connor Wound Care Clinic
2105 Forest Ave, San Jose (95128-1471)
PHONE....................................408 947-2500
Richard Adcock, *CEO*
James F Dover, *CEO*
Dawn Goeringer, *Officer*
David W Carroll, *Senior VP*
Craig Rucker, *Vice Pres*
EMP: 1000
SQ FT: 750,000
SALES (est): 238MM
SALES (corp-wide): 1.2B **Privately Held**
SIC: 8062 General medical & surgical hospitals
PA: Verity Health System Of California, Inc.
2040 E Mariposa Ave
El Segundo CA 90245
650 551-6650

(P-21614)
OLYMPIA HEALTH CARE LLC
Also Called: Olympia Medical Center
5900 W Olympic Blvd, Los Angeles (90036-4671)
PHONE....................................323 938-3161
John A Calderone, *CEO*
Babur Ozkan, *CFO*
Genevieve Angel, *Ch Nursing Ofcr*
Steve Rosenthaul, *Marketing Staff*
Stan Horn, *Facilities Mgr*
EMP: 875 **EST:** 2004
SQ FT: 500,000
SALES (est): 37.7MM
SALES (corp-wide): 1.1B **Privately Held**
SIC: 8062 Hospital, affiliated with AMA residency
PA: Alecto Healthcare Services Llc
16310 Bake Pkwy Ste 200
Irvine CA 92618
323 938-3161

(P-21615)
ORANGE COAST MEMORIAL MED CTR (HQ)
9920 Talbert Ave, Fountain Valley (92708-5153)
PHONE....................................714 378-7000
Toll Free:....................................888   -
Marcia Manker, *President*
Ramin Rabbani,
Richard Wasley, *Ch Radiology*
David Steward, *Records Dir*
Aaron Coley, *CFO*
EMP: 79
SQ FT: 40,361
SALES: 245.8MM
SALES (corp-wide): 2.2B **Privately Held**
SIC: 8062 General medical & surgical hospitals
PA: Memorial Health Services
17360 Brookhurst St # 160
Fountain Valley CA 92708
714 377-6748

(P-21616)
ORANGE COUNTY ROYALE CONVLSCNT
Also Called: Royale Hlth Care Mission Viejo
23228 Madero, Mission Viejo (92691-2706)
PHONE....................................949 458-6346
William Arellanes, *Exec Dir*
Jenny Forkey, *Manager*
EMP: 100
SQ FT: 54,500
SALES (corp-wide): 18.9MM **Privately Held**
WEB: www.royalehealth.com
SIC: 8062 General medical & surgical hospitals
PA: Orange County Royale Convalescent Hospital, Inc.
1030 W Warner Ave
Santa Ana CA 92707
714 546-6450

(P-21617)
ORANGETREE CONVALESCENT HOSP
Also Called: Plott Family Care Centers
4000 Harrison St, Riverside (92503-3599)
PHONE....................................951 785-6060
Elizabeth Plott, *President*
EMP: 120

SALES (est): 9.6MM **Privately Held**
SIC: 8062 8051 General medical & surgical hospitals; skilled nursing care facilities

(P-21618)
ORCHARD HOSPITAL
240 Spruce St, Gridley (95948-2216)
P.O. Box 97 (95948-0097)
PHONE....................................530 846-9000
Wade Sturgeon, *CEO*
Steve Stark, *CEO*
Tracy Atkins, *COO*
Kristina Hessong, *CFO*
Kristina Sanke, *CFO*
EMP: 235
SQ FT: 12,000
SALES: 24.4MM **Privately Held**
SIC: 8062 General medical & surgical hospitals

(P-21619)
OROVILLE HOSPITAL (PA)
2767 Olive Hwy, Oroville (95966-6118)
PHONE....................................530 533-8500
Robert J Wentz, *CEO*
Scott Chapple, *COO*
Ashok Khanchandani, *CFO*
Sultan Chopan, *Trustee*
Matthew Fine, *Chief Mktg Ofcr*
EMP: 1170
SQ FT: 68,133
SALES: 286.9MM **Privately Held**
SIC: 8062 General medical & surgical hospitals

(P-21620)
ORTHOPAEDIC HOSPITAL (PA)
Also Called: Orthopaedic Inst For Children
403 W Adams Blvd, Los Angeles (90007-2664)
P.O. Box 60132 (90060-0132)
PHONE....................................213 742-1000
Anthony A Scaduto, *President*
Diane Moon, *CFO*
Nicholas V McClure, *Bd of Directors*
EMP: 168
SQ FT: 105,000
SALES: 48.7MM **Privately Held**
SIC: 8062 8011 General medical & surgical hospitals; primary care medical clinic

(P-21621)
PACIFIC HEALTH CORPORATION
Also Called: Anaheim General Hospital
3699 Wilshire Blvd # 540, Los Angeles (90010-2723)
PHONE....................................714 619-7797
Fax: 714 761-1295
EMP: 500
SALES (corp-wide): 93MM **Privately Held**
SIC: 8062
HQ: Pacific Health Corporation
14642 Newport Ave
Tustin CA 92780
714 838-9600

(P-21622)
PACIFIC OCCPTNAL MEDICINE SVCS
2776 Pacific Ave, Long Beach (90806-2613)
PHONE....................................562 997-2290
Michael PH, *Principal*
Kathy Gerard, *Principal*
EMP: 50
SALES (est): 753.3K **Privately Held**
SIC: 8062 General medical & surgical hospitals

(P-21623)
PACIFICA OF VALLEY CORPORATION
Also Called: Pacifica Hospital of Valley
9449 San Fernando Rd, Sun Valley (91352-1421)
PHONE....................................818 767-3310
Paul Tuft, *Ch of Bd*
Kathryn Calafato, *CFO*
Ayman Mousa, *Officer*
Ron Stinnett, *Risk Mgmt Dir*
Danny Santos, *Lab Dir*
EMP: 525
SQ FT: 148,020

SALES: 101.8MM **Privately Held**
WEB: www.pacificahospital.com
SIC: 8062 Hospital, affiliated with AMA residency

(P-21624)
PALO ALTO MED FNDTION STA CRUZ
2025 Soquel Ave, Santa Cruz (95062-1323)
PHONE....................................831 458-5670
Larry Beghttaldi, *President*
Howard Salvay MD, *Admin Sec*
Arthur Vedder, *Director*
Pia Zoliniak, *Supervisor*
EMP: 2000
SALES (est): 69.1MM **Privately Held**
SIC: 8062 General medical & surgical hospitals

(P-21625)
PALO VERDE HEALTH CARE DST
Also Called: Palo Verde Hospital
250 N 1st St, Blythe (92225-1702)
PHONE....................................760 922-4115
Sandra J Anaya, *CEO*
Dennis Rutherford, *CFO*
EMP: 180 **EST:** 1938
SALES: 23.8MM **Privately Held**
WEB: www.paloverdehospital.com
SIC: 8062 8069 General medical & surgical hospitals; specialty hospitals, except psychiatric

(P-21626)
PALO VERDE HOSPITAL ASSN
250 N 1st St, Blythe (92225-1702)
PHONE....................................760 922-4115
Sandra J Anaya, *CEO*
Jim Carney, *President*
Larry Blitz, *CEO*
Samuel Burton, *Treasurer*
Beatrice Pinon, *Vice Pres*
EMP: 135
SQ FT: 44,000
SALES (est): 21.2MM **Privately Held**
SIC: 8062 General medical & surgical hospitals

(P-21627)
PALOMAR HEALTH
Also Called: Patient Business Services
555 E Valley Pkwy 6, Escondido (92025-3048)
PHONE....................................858 675-5360
Laurie Rose, *Manager*
Timothy Barlow, *Lab Dir*
Dennis Dechant, *Administration*
Nancy Ventura, *MIS Dir*
Donny Nichols, *Technology*
EMP: 300
SALES (corp-wide): 760.9MM **Privately Held**
WEB: www.sunbridge.com
SIC: 8062 General medical & surgical hospitals
PA: Palomar Health Technology, Inc.
456 E Grand Ave
Escondido CA 92025
442 281-5000

(P-21628)
PALOMAR HEALTH
Also Called: Palomar Medical Center
2185 Citracado Pkwy, Escondido (92029-4159)
PHONE....................................760 739-3000
Michael Covert, *CEO*
Thea McKenzie, *Partner*
Gerald Bracht,
Aria Anvar, *Managing Dir*
Steve Gold, *Admin Asst*
EMP: 1200
SALES (corp-wide): 760.9MM **Privately Held**
WEB: www.sunbridge.com
SIC: 8062 General medical & surgical hospitals
PA: Palomar Health Technology, Inc.
456 E Grand Ave
Escondido CA 92025
442 281-5000

(P-21629)
PALOMAR HEALTH
Also Called: Pomerado Hospital
15615 Pomerado Rd, Poway (92064-2405)
PHONE...........................858 613-4000
Jim Flinn, *Administration*
Timothy Nguyen, *Vice Pres*
Gil Carson, *Administration*
Amanda Macias, *Recruiter*
Cynthia Linder, *Regional*
EMP: 300
SALES (corp-wide): 760.9MM **Privately Held**
WEB: www.sunbridge.com
SIC: 8062 General medical & surgical hospitals
PA: Palomar Health Technology, Inc.
     456 E Grand Ave
     Escondido CA 92025
     442 281-5000

(P-21630)
PALOMAR HEALTH TECHNOLOGY INC (PA)
Also Called: Palomar Medical Center
456 E Grand Ave, Escondido (92025-3319)
PHONE...........................442 281-5000
Dara Czerwonka, *Principal*
Robert McCaulley, *Officer*
Opal Reinbold, *Officer*
Frank Beirne, *Exec VP*
Prudence August, *Vice Pres*
EMP: 180
SQ FT: 66,000
SALES (est): 760.9MM **Privately Held**
WEB: www.sunbridge.com
SIC: 8062 8059 General medical & surgical hospitals; convalescent home

(P-21631)
PAMC LTD (PA)
Also Called: Pamc Health Foundation
531 W College St, Los Angeles (90012-2315)
PHONE...........................213 624-8411
John Edwards, *CEO*
Henry Tran, *Info Tech Mgr*
Pratima Subedee,
Lisa Lui, *Manager*
EMP: 530
SQ FT: 75,600
SALES (est): 56.7MM **Privately Held**
SIC: 8062 General medical & surgical hospitals

(P-21632)
PANORAMA COMMUNITY HOSPITAL
14850 Roscoe Blvd, Panorama City (91402-4618)
PHONE...........................818 787-2222
David Green, *CEO*
Rick Velagarza, *Vice Pres*
EMP: 50
SALES (est): 3.3MM **Privately Held**
SIC: 8062 General medical & surgical hospitals

(P-21633)
PARACELSUS LOS ANGELES COMM
4081 E Olympic Blvd, Los Angeles (90023-3330)
PHONE...........................323 267-0477
Lou Rubino, *Acting CEO*
Omar Ramirez, *COO*
Clyde Nagatani, *Radiology Dir*
Elizabeth Aguilera, *Administration*
Keith Levy, *Analyst*
EMP: 250
SALES: 141.6MM **Privately Held**
SIC: 8062 General medical & surgical hospitals

(P-21634)
PARADISE VALLEY HOSPITAL (PA)
2400 E 4th St, National City (91950-2098)
PHONE...........................619 470-4100
Alan Soderblom, *CEO*
Robert Carmen, *Ch of Bd*
Prem Reddy, *Ch of Bd*
Luin Leon, *CEO*
Bob Beehler, *Vice Pres*
EMP: 925 **EST:** 1904

SQ FT: 230,000
SALES: 120.3MM **Privately Held**
WEB: www.paradisevalleyhospital.org
SIC: 8062 General medical & surgical hospitals

(P-21635)
PARKVIEW CMNTY HOSP MED CTR
3865 Jackson St, Riverside (92503-3919)
PHONE...........................951 354-7404
Norm Martin, *President*
Doug Drumwright, *CEO*
Carlos Carreron, *CFO*
Tom Santos, *Ch Nursing Ofcr*
Jane Wingate, *Ch Nursing Ofcr*
EMP: 1149
SQ FT: 132,651
SALES: 151.9MM **Privately Held**
SIC: 8062 8011 General medical & surgical hospitals; offices & clinics of medical doctors

(P-21636)
PASADENA CYTO PATHOLOGY LAB
Also Called: Huntington Med Pathology Group
100 W Calif Blvd Fl 3, Pasadena (91105-3010)
PHONE...........................626 397-8616
Susan Murakami MD, *President*
Henry Slosser MD, *Vice Pres*
Linan Wang, *Pathologist*
Steve Ralph, *Director*
EMP: 300
SALES (est): 7.3MM **Privately Held**
SIC: 8062 General medical & surgical hospitals

(P-21637)
PASADENA HOSPITAL ASSN LTD (PA)
Also Called: Huntington Memorial Hospital
100 W California Blvd, Pasadena (91105-3010)
P.O. Box 7013 (91109-7013)
PHONE...........................626 397-5000
Lois Matthews, *Chairman*
James Buese,
Paul Ouyang, *Ch of Bd*
Linda Jackson, *President*
Stephen A Ralph, *President*
EMP: 2100
SQ FT: 928,000
SALES: 695.6MM **Privately Held**
WEB: www.huntingtonhospital.com
SIC: 8062 8051 8063 General medical & surgical hospitals; skilled nursing care facilities; psychiatric hospitals

(P-21638)
PATIENTS HOSPITAL
2900 Eureka Way, Redding (96001-0220)
PHONE...........................530 225-8700
James D Tate MD, *President*
Shari Lejsek, *Administration*
Ezra Hemping, *Engineer*
EMP: 80
SALES: 5.9MM **Privately Held**
WEB: www.patientshospital.com
SIC: 8062 General medical & surgical hospitals

(P-21639)
PERMANENTE MEDICAL GROUP INC
Also Called: Laboratory
2425 Geary Blvd, San Francisco (94115-3358)
PHONE...........................415 833-2000
Harry Chima, *Manager*
EMP: 100
SALES (corp-wide): 94.1B **Privately Held**
WEB: www.permanente.net
SIC: 8062 General medical & surgical hospitals
HQ: The Permanente Medical Group Inc
     1950 Franklin St Fl 18th
     Oakland CA 94612
     866 858-2226

(P-21640)
PERRIS VALLEY CMNTY HOSP LLC (PA)
Also Called: Vista Specialty Hosp Riverside
2224 Medical Center Dr, Perris (92571-2638)
PHONE...........................951 436-5000
James Linhares, *Mng Member*
Marc C Ferrell, *Mng Member*
Marc A Furstman, *Mng Member*
ARA Tavitian, *Mng Member*
Lori Garrison, *Director*
EMP: 260
SALES (est): 6.1MM **Privately Held**
SIC: 8062 General medical & surgical hospitals

(P-21641)
PERRIS VALLEY CMNTY HOSP LLC
Also Called: Vista Hospital Riverside
10841 White Oak Ave, Rancho Cucamonga (91730-3817)
PHONE...........................909 581-6400
Edward L Kuntz, *CEO*
EMP: 234 **Privately Held**
SIC: 8062 General medical & surgical hospitals
PA: Perris Valley Community Hospital, Llc
     2224 Medical Center Dr
     Perris CA 92571
     -

(P-21642)
PHYSICIANS FOR HEALTHY HOSPITA (PA)
Also Called: PHH
1117 E Devonshire Ave, Hemet (92543-3083)
PHONE...........................951 652-2811
Kali Chaudhuri, *CEO*
Sreenivasa Nakka, *President*
Ashok Agarwal, *Vice Pres*
Kali Priyo Chaudhuri, *Vice Pres*
Neelam Gupta, *Vice Pres*
EMP: 52 **EST:** 2009
SALES: 150.8MM **Privately Held**
SIC: 8062 General medical & surgical hospitals

(P-21643)
PHYSICIANS FOR HEALTHY HOSPITA
Also Called: Menifee Valley Hospital Center
28400 Mccall Blvd, Sun City (92585-9658)
PHONE...........................951 679-8888
Jeffrey Lang, *CEO*
EMP: 300
SALES (corp-wide): 150.8MM **Privately Held**
SIC: 8062 General medical & surgical hospitals
PA: Physicians For Healthy Hospitals, Inc.
     1117 E Devonshire Ave
     Hemet CA 92543
     951 652-2811

(P-21644)
PHYSICIANS FOR HEALTHY HOSPITA
Also Called: Leland Health Care Services
371 N Weston Pl, Hemet (92543-3006)
PHONE...........................951 652-2811
Carol Wood, *Director*
EMP: 110
SALES (corp-wide): 150.8MM **Privately Held**
SIC: 8062 8051 8059 General medical & surgical hospitals; skilled nursing care facilities; nursing home, except skilled & intermediate care facility
PA: Physicians For Healthy Hospitals, Inc.
     1117 E Devonshire Ave
     Hemet CA 92543
     951 652-2811

(P-21645)
PHYSICIANS FOR HEALTHY HOSPITA
1280 S Buena Vista St, San Jacinto (92583-4604)
PHONE...........................951 652-2811
Tim Murray, *Manager*
EMP: 180

SALES (corp-wide): 150.8MM **Privately Held**
SIC: 8062 General medical & surgical hospitals
PA: Physicians For Healthy Hospitals, Inc.
     1117 E Devonshire Ave
     Hemet CA 92543
     951 652-2811

(P-21646)
PIH HEALTH HOSPITAL - DOWNEY
11500 Brookshire Ave, Downey (90241-4917)
PHONE...........................562 698-0811
James R West, *President*
Bryan Smolskis, *COO*
Greg Williams, *CFO*
Kenton Woods, *Treasurer*
Rosalio Lopez MD, *Senior VP*
EMP: 1150
SQ FT: 225,000
SALES: 126.8MM
SALES (corp-wide): 555.9MM **Privately Held**
SIC: 8062 General medical & surgical hospitals
PA: Pih Health Hospital - Whittier
     12401 Washington Blvd
     Whittier CA 90602
     562 698-0811

(P-21647)
PIH HEALTH HOSPITAL - WHITTI
122 N Primrose Ave Apt A, Monrovia (91016-2162)
PHONE...........................626 357-6876
EMP: 399
SALES (corp-wide): 555.9MM **Privately Held**
SIC: 8062 8011 General medical & surgical hospitals; clinic, operated by physicians
PA: Pih Health Hospital - Whittier
     12401 Washington Blvd
     Whittier CA 90602
     562 698-0811

(P-21648)
PIH HEALTH HOSPITAL - WHITTI
Also Called: Downey Regional Medical Center
11500 Brookshire Ave, Downey (90241-4917)
PHONE...........................562 904-5482
James R West, *CEO*
EMP: 1150
SALES (corp-wide): 555.9MM **Privately Held**
SIC: 8062 8071 General medical & surgical hospitals; medical laboratories
PA: Pih Health Hospital - Whittier
     12401 Washington Blvd
     Whittier CA 90602
     562 698-0811

(P-21649)
PIH HEALTH HOSPITAL - WHITTIER (PA)
Also Called: Pih Home Health Services
12401 Washington Blvd, Whittier (90602-1006)
PHONE...........................562 698-0811
James R West, *CEO*
Mitchell Thomas, *CFO*
Rosalio J Lopez, *Vice Pres*
Monica Lopez, *Comp Lab Dir*
Victoria Deras, *Sales Dir*
EMP: 1900
SQ FT: 500,000
SALES (est): 555.9MM **Privately Held**
SIC: 8062 General medical & surgical hospitals

(P-21650)
PIONEERS MEM HEALTHCARE DST (PA)
Also Called: Pioneers Memorial Hospital
207 W Legion Rd, Brawley (92227-7780)
PHONE...........................760 351-3333
Richard L Mendoza, *CEO*
Daniel Heckathorne, *CFO*
Aracely Smith, *Officer*
Justina Aguirre, *Vice Pres*
Clara Miranda, *Case Mgmt Dir*
EMP: 571

SQ FT: 171,445
SALES: 117.7MM **Privately Held**
WEB: www.pioneersmemorialhospital.com
SIC: 8062 Hospital, affiliated with AMA residency

(P-21651)
PLUMAS DISTRICT HOSPITAL (PA)
1065 Bucks Lake Rd, Quincy (95971-9599)
PHONE.................................530 283-2121
Doug Lafferty, *President*
▲ EMP: 180 EST: 1959
SQ FT: 30,000
SALES: 20.4MM **Privately Held**
SIC: 8062 Hospital, affiliated with AMA residency

(P-21652)
POMONA VALLEY HOSPITAL MED CTR (PA)
Also Called: Pvhmc
1798 N Garey Ave, Pomona (91767-2918)
PHONE.................................909 865-9500
Richard E Yochum, *CEO*
Jasvir Sandhu,
Rosie Rieger, *President*
Cecilia Lopez, *COO*
Kurt Weinmeister, *COO*
EMP: 2121
SQ FT: 362,000
SALES: 631.3MM **Privately Held**
WEB: www.pvhmc.org
SIC: 8062 Hospital, medical school affiliated with residency

(P-21653)
POMONA VALLEY HOSPITAL MED CTR
Also Called: Claremont Outpatient Clinic
1601 Monte Vista Ave, Claremont (91711-2962)
PHONE.................................909 865-9104
Joan Harper, *Manager*
EMP: 728
SALES (corp-wide): 631.3MM **Privately Held**
SIC: 8062 Hospital, medical school affiliated with residency
PA: Pomona Valley Hospital Medical Center
1798 N Garey Ave
Pomona CA 91767
909 865-9500

(P-21654)
POMONA VALLEY HOSPITAL MED CTR
Also Called: Montclair Physical Therapy
1601 Monte Vista Ave # 270, Claremont (91711-2962)
PHONE.................................909 865-9977
Antoinette Fernandez, *Director*
EMP: 728
SALES (corp-wide): 631.3MM **Privately Held**
WEB: www.montclairphysicaltherapy.com
SIC: 8062 Hospital, medical school affiliated with residency
PA: Pomona Valley Hospital Medical Center
1798 N Garey Ave
Pomona CA 91767
909 865-9500

(P-21655)
PRIME HEALTH CARE SVCS GRDN GR
Also Called: Garden Grove Hospital Med Ctr
12601 Garden Grove Blvd, Garden Grove (92843-1908)
PHONE.................................714 537-5160
Mike Sarian, *President*
Kevan Metcalfe, *CEO*
Alan Smith, *CFO*
Sofia Abrina, *Administration*
Eileen Nicodemus, *MIS Dir*
EMP: 500
SALES: 101.8MM **Privately Held**
SIC: 8062 General medical & surgical hospitals

(P-21656)
PRIME HEALTHCARE ANAHEIM LLC
Also Called: WEST ANAHEIM MEDICAL CENTER
3033 W Orange Ave, Anaheim (92804-3156)
PHONE.................................714 827-3000
Virg Narbutas, *CEO*
Kora Guoyavatin, *CFO*
David Lang, *Executive*
Reena Mahadevan, *Engineer*
John Lovrich, *Controller*
EMP: 800 EST: 1963
SQ FT: 180,000
SALES: 123.9MM
SALES (corp-wide): 3.4B **Privately Held**
SIC: 8062 Hospital, affiliated with AMA residency
HQ: Prime Healthcare Services Inc
3300 E Guasti Rd Ste 300
Ontario CA 91761
-

(P-21657)
PRIME HEALTHCARE CENTINELA LLC
Also Called: Centinela Hospital Medical Ctr
555 E Hardy St, Inglewood (90301-4011)
PHONE.................................310 673-4660
Linda Bradley, *CEO*
Kavya Kandula, *Technology*
Barbara Kokolowski, *Director*
Alex Lucero, *Manager*
EMP: 1500
SALES: 259.6MM
SALES (corp-wide): 3.4B **Privately Held**
SIC: 8062 General medical & surgical hospitals
HQ: Prime Healthcare Services Inc
3300 E Guasti Rd Ste 300
Ontario CA 91761

(P-21658)
PRIME HEALTHCARE SERVICES
Also Called: Shasta Regional Med Ctr Srmc
1100 Butte St, Redding (96001-0852)
P.O. Box 491810 (96049-1810)
PHONE.................................530 244-5400
Cyndy Gordon, *CEO*
Solomon Eboigbodin, *Records Dir*
Linda Leaell, *COO*
Edward Price, *Ch Nursing Ofcr*
Tom Salerno, *Safety Dir*
EMP: 850
SALES: 152.3MM
SALES (corp-wide): 3.4B **Privately Held**
SIC: 8062 8011 General medical & surgical hospitals; offices & clinics of medical doctors
HQ: Prime Healthcare Services Inc
3300 E Guasti Rd Ste 300
Ontario CA 91761

(P-21659)
PRIME HEALTHCARE SERVS SH
1450 Liberty St, Redding (96001-0838)
P.O. Box 491810 (96049-1810)
PHONE.................................530 244-5458
Cindy Gordon, *CEO*
EMP: 902
SALES: 50MM **Privately Held**
SIC: 8062 General medical & surgical hospitals

(P-21660)
PRIME HEALTHCARE SVCS II LLC
Also Called: Sherman Oaks Hospital
4929 Van Nuys Blvd, Sherman Oaks (91403-1702)
PHONE.................................818 981-7111
Prem Reddy, *CEO*
John Deady, *CFO*
EMP: 500
SQ FT: 36,000
SALES: 62.4MM
SALES (corp-wide): 3.4B **Privately Held**
SIC: 8062 General medical & surgical hospitals

HQ: Prime Healthcare Services Inc
3300 E Guasti Rd Ste 300
Ontario CA 91761
-

(P-21661)
PRIME HEALTHCARE SVCS III LLC (DH)
Also Called: MONTCLAIR HOSPITAL MEDICAL CENTER
5000 San Bernardino St, Montclair (91763-2326)
PHONE.................................909 625-5411
Jennifer Ramirez, *Exec Sec*
Prem Reddy, *Chairman*
David Chu, *Manager*
EMP: 113
SALES: 55.4MM
SALES (corp-wide): 3.4B **Privately Held**
WEB: www.dhmcm.com
SIC: 8062 General medical & surgical hospitals

(P-21662)
PRIME HEALTHCARE-SAN DIMAS LLC
Also Called: SAN DIMAS COMMUNITY HOSPITAL
1350 W Covina Blvd, San Dimas (91773-3245)
PHONE.................................909 599-6811
Gregory Brentano, *CEO*
Dan Galles, *CFO*
Dora Noriega, *Risk Mgmt Dir*
Roy Guerra, *Facilities Mgr*
EMP: 350
SQ FT: 90,000
SALES: 81.7MM
SALES (corp-wide): 3.4B **Privately Held**
SIC: 8062 General medical & surgical hospitals
HQ: Prime Healthcare Services Inc
3300 E Guasti Rd Ste 300
Ontario CA 91761

(P-21663)
PRIME HLTHCARE HNTNGTON BCH
Also Called: Huntington Beach Hospital
17772 Beach Blvd, Huntington Beach (92647-6819)
PHONE.................................714 843-5000
Prem Reddy, *CEO*
Eileen Fisler, *CEO*
Ravi Alla, *Vice Pres*
Barbara Tenneson, *Ch Nursing Ofcr*
Denise Flaws, *Director*
EMP: 480 EST: 1957
SQ FT: 100,000
SALES (est): 52.5MM
SALES (corp-wide): 3.4B **Privately Held**
WEB: www.hbhospital.com
SIC: 8062 General medical & surgical hospitals
HQ: Prime Healthcare Services Inc
3300 E Guasti Rd Ste 300
Ontario CA 91761
-

(P-21664)
PROMISE HOSP E LOS ANGELES LP
Also Called: Suburban Medical Center
16453 Colorado Ave, Paramount (90723-5011)
PHONE.................................562 531-3110
Michael Kerr, *CEO*
Dennis Talisay,
Jodi Hein, *Principal*
EMP: 265
SALES (est): 27.9MM
SALES (corp-wide): 599.2MM **Privately Held**
SIC: 8062 General medical & surgical hospitals
PA: Promise Healthcare, Inc.
999 W Yamato Rd Ste 300
Boca Raton FL 33431
561 869-3100

(P-21665)
PROVIDENCE HEALTH & SERVICES F
Also Called: Providnce Holy Cross Fundation
501 S Buena Vista St, Burbank (91505-4809)
PHONE.................................818 843-5111
Patricia Modrzejewski, *CEO*
Lee Kanon Alpert, *Chairman*
Ruth Arevalo, *Opers Staff*
Heddy Mondheim, *Pharmacist*
EMP: 2000
SALES: 19.1MM **Privately Held**
SIC: 8062 General medical & surgical hospitals

(P-21666)
PROVIDENCE HEALTH & SERVICES S
Also Called: Providence Little Company of M
1300 W 7th St, San Pedro (90732-3505)
PHONE.................................310 832-3311
EMP: 99
SALES (est): 4.7MM **Privately Held**
SIC: 8062

(P-21667)
PROVIDENCE HEALTH & SVCS - ORE
540 23rd St, Oakland (94612-1724)
PHONE.................................510 444-0839
Tim Zaricznyj, *Director*
EMP: 360
SALES (corp-wide): 17.6B **Privately Held**
WEB: www.providence.org
SIC: 8062 General medical & surgical hospitals
HQ: Providence Health & Services - Oregon
1801 Lind Ave Sw
Renton WA 98057
425 525-3355

(P-21668)
PROVIDENCE HEALTH & SVCS - ORE
Also Called: Providence Holy Cross Med Ctr
15031 Rinaldi St, Mission Hills (91345-1207)
PHONE.................................818 365-8051
David Mast, *Branch Mgr*
Gail Ermer, *Food Svc Dir*
Stanley Cyran, *Dermatology*
Georgia Colkitt, *Director*
Pamela Wegner, *Director*
EMP: 360
SALES (corp-wide): 17.6B **Privately Held**
SIC: 8062 General medical & surgical hospitals
HQ: Providence Health & Services - Oregon
1801 Lind Ave Sw
Renton WA 98057
425 525-3355

(P-21669)
PROVIDENCE HEALTH SYSTEM
Also Called: Providence Holy Cross Med Ctr
15031 Rinaldi St, Mission Hills (91345-1207)
PHONE.................................818 898-4561
Kerry Carmody, *Administration*
EMP: 1000
SALES (corp-wide): 17.6B **Privately Held**
SIC: 8062 8661 General medical & surgical hospitals; Catholic Church
HQ: Providence Health System-Southern California
1801 Lind Ave Sw
Renton WA 98057
425 525-3355

(P-21670)
PROVIDENCE HEALTH SYSTEM
Also Called: San Pedro Peninsula Hospital
1300 W 7th St, San Pedro (90732-3505)
PHONE.................................310 832-3311
Hero Nishi, *Principal*
David Nastri, *Project Mgr*
Kathryn Sprague, *Mktg Dir*
Justin Montoya, *Facilities Mgr*
Mary J Jones, *Nursing Dir*
EMP: 880

PRODUCTS & SVCS

SALES (corp-wide): 17.6B **Privately Held**
SIC: 8062 8051 5912 General medical & surgical hospitals; skilled nursing care facilities; drug stores
HQ: Providence Health System-Southern California
1801 Lind Ave Sw
Renton WA 98057
425 525-3355

(P-21671)
PROVIDENCE HEALTH SYSTEM
Providence St Joseph Med Ctr
501 S Buena Vista St, Burbank
(91505-4809)
PHONE.................818 843-5111
Georgianne Johnson, *COO*
Arnie Schaffer, *CEO*
Kimberly Hernandez, *Director*
EMP: 2000
SALES (corp-wide): 17.6B **Privately Held**
SIC: 8062 General medical & surgical hospitals
HQ: Providence Health System-Southern California
1801 Lind Ave Sw
Renton WA 98057
425 525-3355

(P-21672)
PROVIDENCE HEALTH SYSTEM
Also Called: San Pedro Hospital Pavilion
1322 W 6th St, San Pedro (90732-3501)
PHONE.................310 514-5270
Julie Theiring, *Principal*
EMP: 100
SALES (corp-wide): 17.6B **Privately Held**
SIC: 8062 8051 General medical & surgical hospitals; convalescent home with continuous nursing care
HQ: Providence Health System-Southern California
1801 Lind Ave Sw
Renton WA 98057
425 525-3355

(P-21673)
PROVIDENCE HEALTH SYSTEM
2601 Airport Dr Ste 230, Torrance
(90505-6142)
PHONE.................310 530-3800
Catherine Pearlman, *Branch Mgr*
EMP: 760
SALES (corp-wide): 17.6B **Privately Held**
SIC: 8062 General medical & surgical hospitals
HQ: Providence Health System-Southern California
1801 Lind Ave Sw
Renton WA 98057
425 525-3355

(P-21674)
PROVIDENCE HOLY CROSS (PA)
15031 Rinaldi St, Mission Hills
(91345-1207)
PHONE.................818 365-8051
Lee Kanon Alpert, *Chairman*
June E Drake, *CEO*
Paul Steinke, *CFO*
Cynthia Simmons, *Executive Asst*
Anne-Marie Brody, *Info Tech Dir*
▲ **EMP:** 70 **EST:** 1960
SALES (est): 255.5MM **Privately Held**
SIC: 8062 General medical & surgical hospitals

(P-21675)
PROVIDENCE ST JOHNS HLTH CTR
2121 Santa Monica Blvd, Santa Monica
(90404-2303)
PHONE.................310 829-6562
Marcel Loh, *CEO*
Donald Larsen Jr, *Officer*
Melody Craff, *Vice Pres*
Stuart Prey, *Business Dir*
Ann Dechairo-Marino, *Ch Nursing Ofcr*
EMP: 350
SQ FT: 60,000
SALES (est): 366.7K **Privately Held**
SIC: 8062 General medical & surgical hospitals

(P-21676)
PROVIDENCE TARZANA MEDICAL CTR
18321 Clark St, Tarzana (91356-3501)
PHONE.................818 881-0800
Dale Surowitz, *CEO*
Kathy Evans, *CEO*
Nick Lymberopoulos, *COO*
Bushra Ashfaq, *Assistant*
EMP: 1300
SALES (est): 221.2MM **Privately Held**
SIC: 8062 General medical & surgical hospitals

(P-21677)
QUEEN OF ANGELS HOLLYWOOD PRES
1300 N Vermont Ave, Los Angeles
(90027-6300)
PHONE.................213 413-3000
John Fenton, *President*
EMP: 1200
SALES: 23.7MM **Privately Held**
SIC: 8062 Hospital, affiliated with AMA residency

(P-21678)
QUEEN OF VALLEY HOSPITAL
1115 S Sunset Ave, West Covina
(91790-3940)
PHONE.................626 962-4011
Louis Conyers, *CFO*
Robert Curry, *CEO*
Elvia Foulke, *COO*
Gilbert Furman, *Med Doctor*
Norman Owashi, *Med Doctor*
EMP: 900
SALES (est): 37.5MM **Privately Held**
SIC: 8062 General medical & surgical hospitals

(P-21679)
QUEEN OF VALLEY MEDICAL CENTER (DH)
Also Called: NAPA VALLEY MEDICAL CENTER
1000 Trancas St, NAPA (94558-2906)
PHONE.................707 252-4411
Walt Mickens, *President*
Vincent Morgese, *COO*
Bob Diehl, *CFO*
Don Miller, *CFO*
Mich Riccioni, *CFO*
EMP: 653 **EST:** 1953
SQ FT: 278,500
SALES: 268.1MM
SALES (corp-wide): 17.6B **Privately Held**
SIC: 8062 General medical & surgical hospitals
HQ: St. Joseph Health System
3345 Michelson Dr Ste 100
Irvine CA 92612
949 381-4000

(P-21680)
R M MATOVU MEMORIAL
327 Consuelo Dr, Santa Barbara
(93110-1419)
PHONE.................412 337-5975
Annette Ndagano, *President*
EMP: 50 **EST:** 2016
SALES (est): 286.2K **Privately Held**
SIC: 8062 General medical & surgical hospitals

(P-21681)
RADY CHLD HOSPITAL-SAN DIEGO (HQ)
3020 Childrens Way, San Diego
(92123-4223)
PHONE.................858 576-1700
Donald Kearns, *CEO*
David Frankville,
Amy Durazo, *Officer*
Sarah Cooper, *Vice Pres*
Remmi Molthen, *Nursing Mgr*
EMP: 2000 **EST:** 1952
SQ FT: 276,000
SALES: 522MM
SIC: 8062 General medical & surgical hospitals

(P-21682)
RAMONA REHABILITATION AND POST
485 W Johnston Ave, Hemet (92543-7012)
PHONE.................951 652-0011
Stan Leland, *President*
Heidi Vickers, *Admin Sec*
EMP: 120
SQ FT: 30,000
SALES (est): 7.2MM **Privately Held**
SIC: 8062 8051 General medical & surgical hospitals; convalescent home with continuous nursing care

(P-21683)
RANCHO CCAMONGA CMNTY HOSP LLC
Also Called: Rancho Speciality Hospital
10841 White Oak Ave, Rancho Cucamonga
(91730-3817)
PHONE.................909 581-6400
Marc C Ferrell,
Mark Ferrell,
Vartan Hovsetian,
ARA Tavitian,
EMP: 110
SQ FT: 100,000
SALES (est): 9.5MM **Privately Held**
SIC: 8062 General medical & surgical hospitals

(P-21684)
REDLANDS COMMUNITY HOSPITAL (PA)
350 Terracina Blvd, Redlands
(92373-4897)
PHONE.................909 335-5500
James R Holmes, *CEO*
Alvin Umeda, *Otolaryngology*
Steve Mera, *Med Doctor*
Kerry Rold, *Med Doctor*
Theodore Shankel, *Med Doctor*
EMP: 99
SALES: 174.1MM **Privately Held**
SIC: 8062 General medical & surgical hospitals

(P-21685)
REDWOOD MEMORIAL HOSP FORTUNA (PA)
3300 Renner Dr, Fortuna (95540-3120)
PHONE.................707 725-7327
Thomas McConnell, *CEO*
Bob Branigan, *COO*
Joe Rogers, *COO*
Kevin Clouder, *CFO*
Erik Burman, *Pathologist*
EMP: 150
SQ FT: 65,000
SALES: 55.5MM **Privately Held**
SIC: 8062 Hospital, affiliated with AMA residency

(P-21686)
RIDEOUT MEMORIAL HOSPITAL (HQ)
726 4th St, Marysville (95901-5656)
P.O. Box 2128 (95901-0075)
PHONE.................530 749-4416
Ronald M Sweeney, *Chairman*
Theresa Hamilton, *CEO*
John Cary, *Treasurer*
Lisa Del Pero, *Admin Sec*
EMP: 700
SQ FT: 100,000
SALES: 335MM
SALES (corp-wide): 26.9MM **Privately Held**
SIC: 8062 8082 General medical & surgical hospitals; home health care services
PA: Freemont Rideout Health Group
989 Plumas St
Yuba City CA 95991
530 751-4010

(P-21687)
RIDGECREST REGIONAL HOSPITAL (PA)
Also Called: Southern Sierra Medical Clinic
1081 N China Lake Blvd, Ridgecrest
(93555-3130)
PHONE.................760 446-3551
James A Suver, *CEO*
Donna Kiser, *CFO*

Don Zdeba, *Bd of Directors*
Michelle Lemke, *Risk Mgmt Dir*
Elizabeth Cole, *Admin Sec*
EMP: 96
SQ FT: 80,000
SALES: 106.3MM **Privately Held**
WEB: www.rrh.org
SIC: 8062 General medical & surgical hospitals

(P-21688)
RIVERSIDE CMNTY HLTH SYSTEMS (DH)
Also Called: Riverside Community Hospital
4445 Magnolia Ave Fl 6, Riverside
(92501-4135)
PHONE.................951 788-3000
Partrick Brilliant, *President*
Doug Long, *COO*
Tracey Fernandez, *CFO*
Diane Elkhoury, *Admin Asst*
Barbara Everett, *Internal Med*
EMP: 83
SQ FT: 386,100
SALES: 435.8MM **Publicly Held**
WEB: www.rchc.org
SIC: 8062 8011 General medical & surgical hospitals; offices & clinics of medical doctors
HQ: Hca Inc.
1 Park Plz
Nashville TN 37203
615 344-9551

(P-21689)
RIVERSIDE HEALTHCARE SYSTEM LP
Also Called: Riverside Community Hospital
4445 Magnolia Ave, Riverside
(92501-4135)
PHONE.................951 788-3000
Patrick Brilliant, *Managing Prtnr*
EMP: 1600
SALES (est): 28.7MM **Publicly Held**
SIC: 8062 General medical & surgical hospitals
HQ: Hca Inc.
1 Park Plz
Nashville TN 37203
615 344-9551

(P-21690)
RIVERSIDE UNIVERSITY HEALTH (PA)
Also Called: Riverside Cnty Rgional Med Ctr
4065 County Circle Dr, Riverside
(92503-3410)
PHONE.................951 358-5000
Douglas D Bagley, *CEO*
Ellie Bennett, *COO*
David Runke, *CFO*
Michael Leon, *Info Tech Mgr*
Minqi Hao, *Family Practiti*
EMP: 77
SALES (est): 1.5MM **Privately Held**
SIC: 8062 General medical & surgical hospitals

(P-21691)
RIVERSIDE UNIVERSITY HEALTH
Also Called: Ruhs-Emergency Department
26520 Cactus Ave, Moreno Valley
(92555-3927)
PHONE.................951 486-4000
Bret Powers Do, *Principal*
EMP: 723 **Privately Held**
SIC: 8062 General medical & surgical hospitals
PA: Riverside University Health System Foundation
4065 County Circle Dr
Riverside CA 92503

(P-21692)
SADDLEBACK MEMORIAL MED CTR (HQ)
24451 Health Center Dr # 1, Laguna Hills
(92653-3689)
PHONE.................949 837-4500
Steve Geidt, *CEO*
Daniel Lamont,
Kathleen Sullivan,
Barry Arbuckle, *President*

Adolfo Chanez, *CFO*
EMP: 1020
SQ FT: 195,000
SALES: 349.1MM
SALES (corp-wide): 2.2B **Privately Held**
SIC: 8062 8011 8093 8099 General medical & surgical hospitals; medical centers; diabetes specialist, physician/surgeon; cardiologist & cardio-vascular specialist; pediatrician; rehabilitation center, outpatient treatment; blood related health services; medical laboratories; cancer hospital; maternity hospital; orthopedic hospital
PA: Memorial Health Services
17360 Brookhurst St # 160
Fountain Valley CA 92708
714 377-6748

(P-21693)
SAINT AGNES MEDICAL CENTER (HQ)
1303 E Herndon Ave, Fresno (93720-3309)
PHONE..................559 450-3000
Nancy R Hollingsworth, *CEO*
Tai-PO Tschang, *Ch Pathology*
Tom Anderson,
Michael Martinez, *Vice Chairman*
Andrea Lanier, *Treasurer*
EMP: 1688
SQ FT: 200,000
SALES: 486MM
SALES (corp-wide): 14.7B **Privately Held**
SIC: 8062 General medical & surgical hospitals
PA: Trinity Health Corporation
20555 Victor Pkwy
Livonia MI 48152
734 343-1000

(P-21694)
SAINT FRANCIS MEMORIAL HOSP (HQ)
900 Hyde St, San Francisco (94109-4899)
PHONE..................415 353-6000
Thomas G Hennessy, *CEO*
John G Williams, *President*
Cheryl A Fama Rn, *COO*
Ray Miller, *Pharmacy Dir*
Robert Dureault, *Principal*
EMP: 800
SQ FT: 300,000
SALES: 217.8MM
SALES (corp-wide): 6.7B **Privately Held**
SIC: 8062 General medical & surgical hospitals
PA: Dignity Health
185 Berry St Ste 300
San Francisco CA 94107
415 438-5500

(P-21695)
SAINT JHNS HLTH CTR FOUNDATION
Also Called: St John's Health Centre
2020 Santa Monica Blvd 3rdfl3, Santa Monica (90404-2023)
PHONE..................310 829-8970
Lou Laztin, *CEO*
EMP: 297
SALES (corp-wide): 2.6B **Privately Held**
SIC: 8062 General medical & surgical hospitals
HQ: Saint John's Health Center Foundation.
2121 Santa Monica Blvd
Santa Monica CA 90404
310 829-5511

(P-21696)
SAINT LOUISE HOSPITAL
9400 N Name Uno, Gilroy (95020-3528)
PHONE..................408 848-2000
Jim Dober, *CEO*
Terry Curley, *Vice Pres*
Joanne Allan, *Principal*
Kel Kanady, *Marketing Mgr*
Diane Sanchez, *Obstetrician*
EMP: 500
SALES: 90.6MM **Privately Held**
SIC: 8062 General medical & surgical hospitals

(P-21697)
SALINAS VALLEY MEMORIAL HLTHCA
440 E Romie Ln, Salinas (93901-4017)
PHONE..................831 759-3236
Lea Graff, *Pathologist*
EMP: 274
SALES (corp-wide): 494.4MM **Privately Held**
SIC: 8062 General medical & surgical hospitals
PA: Salinas Valley Memorial Healthcare Systems
450 E Romie Ln
Salinas CA 93901
831 757-4333

(P-21698)
SALINAS VALLEY MEMORIAL HLTHCA (PA)
Also Called: Salinas Valley Memorial Hosp
450 E Romie Ln, Salinas (93901-4029)
P.O. Box 4760 (93912-4760)
PHONE..................831 757-4333
Pete Delgado, *President*
Khanh Ngo,
Paul Steinberg,
Henry Ornelas, *COO*
Agustine Lopez, *CFO*
▲ **EMP:** 85
SQ FT: 187,942
SALES: 494.4MM **Privately Held**
SIC: 8062 Hospital, affiliated with AMA residency

(P-21699)
SALINAS VALLEY MEMORIAL HLTHCA
Also Called: Salinas Urgent Care
558 Abbott St, Salinas (93901-4326)
PHONE..................831 755-7880
Angela Mendez, *Office Mgr*
Karina A Rusk, *Corp Comm Staff*
Joseph D Zakar, *Pharmacist*
Deborah Avilez, *Manager*
Linda K Roquemore, *Manager*
EMP: 329
SALES (corp-wide): 494.4MM **Privately Held**
WEB: www.salinasurgentcare.com
SIC: 8062 General medical & surgical hospitals
PA: Salinas Valley Memorial Healthcare Systems
450 E Romie Ln
Salinas CA 93901
831 757-4333

(P-21700)
SAN ANTONIO COMMUNITY HOSPITAL
Also Called: Rancho San Antonio Medical Ctr
7777 Milliken Ave Ste A, Rancho Cucamonga (91730-7489)
PHONE..................909 948-8000
Jullian Doxon, *Director*
EMP: 50
SALES (corp-wide): 316.1MM **Privately Held**
WEB: www.sach.com
SIC: 8062 General medical & surgical hospitals
PA: San Antonio Regional Hospital
999 San Bernardino Rd
Upland CA 91786
909 985-2811

(P-21701)
SAN ANTONIO REGIONAL HOSPITAL (PA)
999 San Bernardino Rd, Upland (91786-4920)
PHONE..................909 985-2811
Jim Milhiser, *Chairman*
Carlos Canizales,
Mike Segura,
Ian F Sandy,
Peter Yoo, *Ch Radiology*
▲ **EMP:** 1900 **EST:** 1906
SQ FT: 349,000
SALES: 316.1MM **Privately Held**
WEB: www.sach.com
SIC: 8062 5912 General medical & surgical hospitals; drug stores & proprietary stores

(P-21702)
SAN BENITO HEALTH CARE DST (PA)
Also Called: Hazel Hawkins Memorial Hosp
911 Sunset Dr Ste A, Hollister (95023-5608)
PHONE..................831 637-5711
Ken Underwood, *CEO*
Beth Ivy, *President*
Mark Robinson, *CFO*
Lynn Gomez, *Vice Pres*
Lois Owens, *Vice Pres*
▲ **EMP:** 270
SQ FT: 42,000
SALES (est): 110.9MM **Privately Held**
WEB: www.hazelhawkins.com
SIC: 8062 8051 8059 General medical & surgical hospitals; skilled nursing care facilities; convalescent home

(P-21703)
SAN CLEMENTE MEDICAL CTR LLC
Also Called: Saddleback Memorial Hospital
654 Camino De Los Mares, San Clemente (92673-2827)
PHONE..................949 496-1122
Ronald McGee,
William Van Derreis,
Gus Gialamas MD,
Kurt Miller MD,
Pat Wolfram,
EMP: 300
SQ FT: 65,000
SALES (est): 20.2MM **Privately Held**
SIC: 8062 8011 General medical & surgical hospitals; offices & clinics of medical doctors

(P-21704)
SAN GBRIEL VLY MED CTR FNDTION
438 W Las Tunas Dr, San Gabriel (91776-1216)
P.O. Box 1507 (91778-1507)
PHONE..................626 289-5454
Thomas Mone, *CEO*
Harold Way, *CFO*
Richard Polver, *Treasurer*
Edward Shuey, *Admin Sec*
He Chang, *Med Doctor*
EMP: 850
SQ FT: 42,000
SALES: 2.5K
SALES (corp-wide): 6.7B **Privately Held**
WEB: www.sgvmc.com
SIC: 8062 General medical & surgical hospitals
PA: Dignity Health
185 Berry St Ste 300
San Francisco CA 94107
415 438-5500

(P-21705)
SAN GORGONIO MEMORIAL HOSPITAL (PA)
600 N Highland Sprng Ave, Banning (92220-3046)
PHONE..................951 845-1121
Steven Barron, *CEO*
Devin Borna,
Hillary Falconer, *President*
Dave Recupero, *CFO*
Dorothy Ellis, *Chairman*
EMP: 250
SQ FT: 76,000
SALES: 56.1MM **Privately Held**
WEB: www.sgmh.org
SIC: 8062 Hospital, affiliated with AMA residency

(P-21706)
SAN JOAQUIN COMMUNITY HOSPITAL (PA)
2615 Chester Ave, Bakersfield (93301-2014)
PHONE..................661 395-3000
Sharlet Briggs, *President*
Kathy Szura,
Mike Lukens, *CFO*
Sam Itani, *Vice Pres*
Jack Houston, *Human Res Dir*
EMP: 850 **EST:** 1910
SQ FT: 137,000

SALES: 368.6MM **Privately Held**
SIC: 8062 8011 General medical & surgical hospitals; offices & clinics of medical doctors

(P-21707)
SAN JOAQUIN GENERAL HOSPITAL
Also Called: Healthcare Services
500 W Hospital Rd, French Camp (95231-9693)
PHONE..................209 468-6000
David Colberson, *CEO*
Ronald Kruetner, *CFO*
EMP: 1300
SALES: 313MM **Privately Held**
SIC: 8062 General medical & surgical hospitals

(P-21708)
SAN JOAQUIN GENERAL HOSPITAL
500 W Hospital Rd, French Camp (95231-9693)
P.O. Box 1020, Stockton (95201-3120)
PHONE..................209 468-6000
Sheker Itemi, *Principal*
Ramesh Dharawat,
James Pucelik,
Deborah Kolhede, *COO*
Michael P Dacoco, *Lab Dir*
EMP: 154
SALES (est): 56.9MM **Privately Held**
SIC: 8062 General medical & surgical hospitals

(P-21709)
SAN JOSE MEDICAL SYSTEMS LP
Also Called: Regional Medical Ctr San Jose
225 N Jackson Ave, San Jose (95116-1603)
PHONE..................408 259-5000
Mike Johnson, *Partner*
Veeral Shah, *Officer*
Darrel Odell, *MIS Dir*
Kenneth Smith, *Nutritionist*
Todd Maxwell, *Director*
EMP: 1200
SQ FT: 203,685
SALES: 446.9MM **Publicly Held**
SIC: 8062 General medical & surgical hospitals
HQ: Hca Inc.
1 Park Plz
Nashville TN 37203
615 344-9551

(P-21710)
SAN LEANDRO HOSPITAL LP
13855 E 14th St, San Leandro (94578-2600)
PHONE..................510 357-6500
Ronnie Bayduza, *CEO*
Janay Defer, *Administration*
EMP: 475
SALES: 13.7K **Privately Held**
WEB: www.triadhospitals.com
SIC: 8062 8361 General medical & surgical hospitals; residential care
PA: Alameda Health System
1411 E 31st St
Oakland CA 94602

(P-21711)
SAN MIGUEL HOSPITAL ASSN
Also Called: Hillside Hospital
1940 El Cajon Blvd, San Diego (92104-1005)
PHONE..................619 297-2251
Kenneth R Dillard, *President*
Rupert Graves MD, *Ch of Bd*
Edwin Yorbe MD, *Corp Secy*
John Ingersoll, *Vice Ch Bd*
EMP: 248
SQ FT: 100,000
SALES: 31.8MM **Privately Held**
SIC: 8062 General medical & surgical hospitals

P
R
O
D
U
C
T
S

&

S
V
C
S

(P-21712)
SAN RAMON REGIONAL MED CTR LLC
6001 Norris Canyon Rd, San Ramon (94583-5400)
PHONE..............................925 275-9200
Shawn Dewers,
Kimi Miyamura, *Volunteer Dir*
Laz Vasquez, *Buyer*
Steve Barnum, *Opers Staff*
Nancy Schemel, *Opers Staff*
EMP: 600 EST: 1983
SALES (est): 195.5K
SALES (corp-wide): 19.3B **Publicly Held**
WEB: www.tenethealth.com
SIC: 8062 8093 General medical & surgical hospitals; rehabilitation center, outpatient treatment
PA: Tenet Healthcare Corporation
1445 Ross Ave Ste 1400
Dallas TX 75202
469 893-2200

(P-21713)
SAN VICENTE HOSPITAL
6000 San Vicente Blvd, Los Angeles (90036-4404)
PHONE..............................323 930-1040
Gill Tepper, *President*
John Fenton, *CEO*
EMP: 100
SALES: 699.4K **Privately Held**
SIC: 8062 General medical & surgical hospitals

(P-21714)
SANTA BARBARA COTTAGE HOSPITAL
Pathology Department
400 W Pueblo St, Santa Barbara (93105-4353)
P.O. Box 689 (93102-0689)
PHONE..............................805 569-7367
Ron Werdt, *President*
EMP: 575
SALES (corp-wide): 646.4MM **Privately Held**
WEB:
www.santabarbaracottagehospital.com
SIC: 8062 General medical & surgical hospitals
PA: Santa Barbara Cottage Hospital
400 W Pueblo St
Santa Barbara CA 93105
805 682-7111

(P-21715)
SANTA BARBARA COTTAGE HOSPITAL (PA)
Also Called: Cottage Hospital Childrens Ctr
400 W Pueblo St, Santa Barbara (93105-4353)
P.O. Box 689 (93102-0689)
PHONE..............................805 682-7111
Gretchen Milligan, *Chairman*
Patricia Dooley, *Volunteer Dir*
Ronald C Werft, *President*
Steven Fellows, *Exec VP*
Sharon Lutz, *Vice Pres*
EMP: 60
SQ FT: 485,874
SALES: 646.4MM **Privately Held**
SIC: 8062 Hospital, AMA approved residency

(P-21716)
SANTA BARBARA COTTAGE HOSPITAL
Also Called: Santa Barbara Cnty Social Svcs
2125 Centerpointe Pkwy, Santa Maria (93455-1337)
PHONE..............................805 346-7135
Charlene Chase, *Director*
EMP: 210
SALES (corp-wide): 646.4MM **Privately Held**
SIC: 8062 General medical & surgical hospitals
PA: Santa Barbara Cottage Hospital
400 W Pueblo St
Santa Barbara CA 93105
805 682-7111

(P-21717)
SANTA CLARA COUNTY OF
Also Called: Santa Clara Valley Health & Ho
2325 Enborg Ln Ste 380, San Jose (95128-2649)
PHONE..............................408 885-6818
Kim Roberts, *Finance*
EMP: 50 **Privately Held**
WEB: www.countyairports.org
SIC: 8062 9431 9311 Hospital, medical school affiliated with nursing & residency; administration of public health programs; ; finance, taxation & monetary policy;
PA: County Of Santa Clara
3180 Newberry Dr Ste 150
San Jose CA 95118
408 299-5105

(P-21718)
SANTA CLARA VALLEY MEDICAL CTR (PA)
Also Called: SCVMC
751 S Bascom Ave, San Jose (95128-2699)
PHONE..............................408 885-5000
Paul E Lorenz, *CEO*
Joy Alexiou, *Planning*
Dave Manson, *Human Res Dir*
Dave Gord, *Facilities Mgr*
Dawn Darbonne, *Pathologist*
EMP: 289
SALES: 490.9MM **Privately Held**
SIC: 8062 6324 General medical & surgical hospitals; hospital & medical service plans

(P-21719)
SANTA ROSA MEMORIAL HOSPITAL (DH)
Also Called: SJHS SONOMA COUNTY
1165 Montgomery Dr, Santa Rosa (95405-4897)
P.O. Box 522 (95402-0522)
PHONE..............................707 546-3210
Todd Salnas, *CEO*
Mich Riccioni, *CFO*
Gary Greensweig, *Vice Pres*
Gary Shaw, *Radiology Dir*
Kathrine Hardin, *Ch Nursing Ofcr*
EMP: 1500 EST: 1948
SQ FT: 163,692
SALES: 518MM
SALES (corp-wide): 17.6B **Privately Held**
WEB: www.stjosephhealth.org
SIC: 8062 General medical & surgical hospitals
HQ: St. Joseph Health System
3345 Michelson Dr Ste 100
Irvine CA 92612
949 381-4000

(P-21720)
SANTA ROSA SURGERY CENTER LP
Also Called: Sutter Health
1111 Sonoma Ave Ste 214, Santa Rosa (95405-4833)
PHONE..............................707 575-5831
Dan Peterson, *Administration*
Jiries Mogannam, *Principal*
EMP: 75
SQ FT: 8,000
SALES (est): 5.3MM **Privately Held**
WEB: www.srsurgerycenter.com
SIC: 8062 General medical & surgical hospitals

(P-21721)
SANTA TERESA CONV HOSPITAL
9140 Verner St, Pico Rivera (90660-2741)
PHONE..............................562 948-1961
Nick Cardenas, *Director*
EMP: 85
SALES (est): 1.3MM **Privately Held**
SIC: 8062 5912 General medical & surgical hospitals; drug stores & proprietary stores

(P-21722)
SANTA TERESITA INC (PA)
Also Called: Manor At Santa Teresita Hosp
819 Buena Vista St, Duarte (91010-1703)
PHONE..............................626 359-3243
Sister Mary Clare Mancini, *CEO*

EMP: 278
SQ FT: 232,165
SALES: 13.2MM **Privately Held**
WEB: www.santa-teresita.org
SIC: 8062 8051 General medical & surgical hospitals; skilled nursing care facilities

(P-21723)
SANTA YNEZ VALLEY COTTAGE HOSP
2050 Viborg Rd, Solvang (93463-2220)
P.O. Box 689, Santa Barbara (93102-0689)
PHONE..............................805 688-6431
Ron Werft, *President*
Wende Cappetta, *Vice Pres*
June Martin, *Administration*
Carla Long, *Director*
Madeline Lozono, *Manager*
EMP: 75 EST: 1962
SQ FT: 30,000
SALES: 19.4MM **Privately Held**
WEB: www.cottagehealthsystem.org
SIC: 8062 General medical & surgical hospitals

(P-21724)
SCHMIDT PHYLLIS MD CORPORATION
711 W College St, Los Angeles (90012-1163)
PHONE..............................213 613-1163
Phyllis Schmidt MD, *President*
EMP: 600
SALES (est): 4.5MM **Privately Held**
SIC: 8062 General medical & surgical hospitals

(P-21725)
SCRIPPS CLINIC
12395 El Camino Real, San Diego (92130-3082)
P.O. Box 2469, La Jolla (92038-2469)
PHONE..............................858 794-1250
Chris Van Gorder, *CEO*
James Collins, *President*
Dr Hubert Greenway, *CEO*
EMP: 116 EST: 1999
SALES (est): 20.3MM **Privately Held**
SIC: 8062 General medical & surgical hospitals

(P-21726)
SCRIPPS HEALTH
Also Called: Scripps Ambulatory Surgery Ctr
320 Santa Fe Dr Ste 310, Encinitas (92024-5140)
PHONE..............................760 753-8413
Donna Danley, *Principal*
Roy Kaplan, *Rheumtlgy Spec*
Roy Avalos, *Med Doctor*
EMP: 60
SALES (corp-wide): 2.9B **Privately Held**
SIC: 8062 General medical & surgical hospitals
PA: Scripps Health
10140 Campus Point Dr Ax415
San Diego CA 92121
800 727-4777

(P-21727)
SCRIPPS HEALTH
Also Called: Scripps Mercy Hospital
4077 5th Ave, San Diego (92103-2105)
PHONE..............................619 294-8111
Jacqueline Saucier, *Director*
Michael Tobin, *Ch Radiology*
Chris Nicholson, *Lab Dir*
Nadeen Hosein, *Endocrinology*
Laura Chia, *Internal Med*
EMP: 99
SALES (corp-wide): 2.9B **Privately Held**
WEB: www.scripps.org
SIC: 8062 General medical & surgical hospitals
PA: Scripps Health
10140 Campus Point Dr Ax415
San Diego CA 92121
800 727-4777

(P-21728)
SCRIPPS HEALTH
Also Called: Scripps Rancho Bernardo
15004 Innovation Dr, San Diego (92128-3491)
PHONE..............................858 271-9770
Melody Stewart, *Administration*

Rodger Casillan, *Lab Dir*
Beth Serrano, *Admin Asst*
Michael D Lee, *Family Practiti*
Mark D Shalauta, *Family Practiti*
EMP: 259
SALES (corp-wide): 2.9B **Privately Held**
WEB: www.scripps.org
SIC: 8062 General medical & surgical hospitals
PA: Scripps Health
10140 Campus Point Dr Ax415
San Diego CA 92121
800 727-4777

(P-21729)
SCRIPPS HEALTH
477 N El Camino Real A208, Encinitas (92024-1328)
PHONE..............................760 479-3900
Stacey Lin, *Family Practiti*
EMP: 165
SALES (corp-wide): 2.9B **Privately Held**
SIC: 8062 General medical & surgical hospitals
PA: Scripps Health
10140 Campus Point Dr Ax415
San Diego CA 92121
800 727-4777

(P-21730)
SCRIPPS HEALTH
Also Called: Scripps Mem Hosp - Encinatas
354 Santa Fe Dr, Encinitas (92024-5142)
P.O. Box 230817 (92023-0817)
PHONE..............................760 753-6501
Rebecca Ropchan, *Branch Mgr*
Rajgopal Ujwala,
Alice Dang, *Bd of Directors*
Lisa Blair, *Officer*
Andrew Trzebiatowski, *Officer*
EMP: 250
SALES (corp-wide): 2.9B **Privately Held**
WEB: www.scripps.org
SIC: 8062 5912 General medical & surgical hospitals; drug stores
PA: Scripps Health
10140 Campus Point Dr Ax415
San Diego CA 92121
800 727-4777

(P-21731)
SCRIPPS HEALTH
Also Called: Scripps Mercy Hospitals
435 H St, Chula Vista (91910-4307)
PHONE..............................619 691-7000
Pott Hoff, *COO*
Juan Tovar MD, *Vice Chairman*
Todd Hoff, *COO*
Jim Mulvey, *Senior VP*
Virginia Gonzales, *Programmer Anys*
EMP: 1000
SALES (corp-wide): 2.9B **Privately Held**
WEB: www.scripps.org
SIC: 8062 General medical & surgical hospitals
PA: Scripps Health
10140 Campus Point Dr Ax415
San Diego CA 92121
800 727-4777

(P-21732)
SCRIPPS HEALTH (PA)
10140 Campus Point Dr Ax415, San Diego (92121-1520)
PHONE..............................800 727-4777
Chris D Van Gorder, *President*
Carrie Cushman, *Volunteer Dir*
Richard K Rothberger, *CFO*
Mary J Anderson, *Trustee*
Jan Coughlin, *Officer*
EMP: 2514
SQ FT: 95,000
SALES (est): 2.9B **Privately Held**
WEB: www.scripps.org
SIC: 8062 8049 8042 8043 General medical & surgical hospitals; physical therapist; psychologist, psychotherapist & hypnotist; offices & clinics of optometrists; offices & clinics of podiatrists

(P-21733)
SCRIPPS HEALTH
Also Called: Scripps Green Hospital
10666 N Torrey Pines Rd, La Jolla (92037-1027)
PHONE..............................858 455-9100

Robin Brown, *Branch Mgr*
Barry Zamost,
Alison Edinger, *Bd of Directors*
Johannes Otter, *Admin Dir*
Curtiss Stinis, *Branch Mgr*
EMP: 326
SALES (corp-wide): 2.9B **Privately Held**
WEB: www.scripps.org
SIC: 8062 General medical & surgical hospitals
PA: Scripps Health
    10140 Campus Point Dr Ax415
    San Diego CA 92121
    800 727-4777

(P-21734)
SCRIPPS HEALTH
Also Called: Scripps Mercy Hospital
4077 Fifth Ave, San Diego (92103-2105)
PHONE 619 294-8111
Medical Records, *Manager*
Janmar Ramirez, *Technology*
Alexandra Salazar, *Analyst*
Kristy Jaques, *QC Mgr*
Victoria Tsai, *Internal Med*
EMP: 300
SQ FT: 3,062
SALES (corp-wide): 2.9B **Privately Held**
WEB: www.scripps.org
SIC: 8062 General medical & surgical hospitals
PA: Scripps Health
    10140 Campus Point Dr Ax415
    San Diego CA 92121
    800 727-4777

(P-21735)
SCRIPPS HEALTH
Also Called: Scripps Torrey Pines
10666 N Torrey Pines Rd, La Jolla
(92037-1027)
PHONE 800 727-4777
Larry Harrison, *Manager*
Ben Jarboe, *Administration*
Fisseha Genet, *Nurse*
Lofgren Nancie,
Grace Baldo,
EMP: 200
SALES (corp-wide): 2.9B **Privately Held**
WEB: www.scripps.org
SIC: 8062 General medical & surgical hospitals
PA: Scripps Health
    10140 Campus Point Dr Ax415
    San Diego CA 92121
    800 727-4777

(P-21736)
SCRIPPS HEALTH
Also Called: Scripps Mem Hospital-La Jolla
9888 Genesee Ave, La Jolla (92037-1205)
PHONE 858 626-6150
James Bruffey, *Branch Mgr*
Greg Martin, *Sr Ntwrk Engine*
Jeff Mitchell, *Data Proc Dir*
Karen Lyon, *Technology*
Alece Hon, *Analyst*
EMP: 326
SALES (corp-wide): 2.9B **Privately Held**
SIC: 8062 General medical & surgical hospitals
PA: Scripps Health
    10140 Campus Point Dr Ax415
    San Diego CA 92121
    800 727-4777

(P-21737)
SCRIPPS HEALTH
Also Called: Scripps Mem Hosp - La Jolla
9888 Genesee Ave, La Jolla (92037-1205)
PHONE 858 626-4123
Gary Fybel, *CEO*
Mary Doyle, *Ch Nursing Ofcr*
Marilou Donica, *Admin Sec*
Larry Juarez, *Admin Sec*
Pat Meyers, *Admin Sec*
EMP: 200
SALES (corp-wide): 2.9B **Privately Held**
WEB: www.scripps.org
SIC: 8062 General medical & surgical hospitals
PA: Scripps Health
    10140 Campus Point Dr Ax415
    San Diego CA 92121
    800 727-4777

(P-21738)
SCRIPPS MEMORIAL HOSPITALS
9834 Genesee Ave Ste 328, La Jolla
(92037-1216)
PHONE 858 450-4481
Kathleen A Bulley, *Principal*
Brad Pfeifer, *Program Mgr*
Janet Kruse, *Executive Asst*
Mielle Schwartz, *Executive Asst*
Stephanie Whittington, *Executive Asst*
EMP: 54
SALES (est): 7.7MM **Privately Held**
SIC: 8062 General medical & surgical hospitals

(P-21739)
SCRIPPS MERCY HOSPITAL
4077 5th Ave Mer35, San Diego
(92103-2105)
PHONE 619 294-8111
Andrew C Ping, *Principal*
Nina Galvan, *CFO*
Seth Krosner, *Exec VP*
Gayle Sandhu, *Risk Mgmt Dir*
George Ochoa, *Radiology Dir*
EMP: 77
SALES: 750.4MM **Privately Held**
SIC: 8062 General medical & surgical hospitals

(P-21740)
SENECA HEALTHCARE DISTRICT (PA)
130 Brentwood Dr, Chester (96020)
P.O. Box 737 (96020-0737)
PHONE 530 258-2151
Linda Wagner, *CEO*
David Slusher Jr, *President*
Cheryl Darnell, *CFO*
William Howe, *Treasurer*
Bob Caton, *Vice Pres*
EMP: 130
SQ FT: 12,417
SALES: 26.3MM **Privately Held**
SIC: 8062 General medical & surgical hospitals

(P-21741)
SEQUOIA HEALTH SERVICES (HQ)
Also Called: SEQUOIA HOSPITAL
170 Alameda De Las Pulgas, Redwood City
(94062-2751)
PHONE 650 369-5811
Glenna Vaskellas, *Administration*
Kathleen Kane, *Executive*
Mary Tasker, *Admin Asst*
Krissy Mangiola, *Administration*
Debi Simon, *Safety Dir*
EMP: 81
SQ FT: 350,000
SALES: 258.7MM
SALES (corp-wide): 6.7B **Privately Held**
WEB: www.sequoiahealthcaredistrict.com
SIC: 8062 General medical & surgical hospitals
PA: Dignity Health
    185 Berry St Ste 300
    San Francisco CA 94107
    415 438-5500

(P-21742)
SETON MEDICAL CENTER (HQ)
1900 Sullivan Ave, Daly City (94015-2229)
PHONE 650 992-4000
Mark S Fratzke, *President*
Christopher Yoo, *Ch Radiology*
Mark Okashima, *Financial Exec*
Deborah Jones, *Purch Dir*
Antoinette L Rowin, *Education*
EMP: 1099
SQ FT: 400,000
SALES (est): 213.3MM
SALES (corp-wide): 1.2B **Privately Held**
WEB: www.sportsmedshop.com
SIC: 8062 8051 General medical & surgical hospitals; skilled nursing care facilities
PA: Verity Health System Of California, Inc.
    2040 E Mariposa Ave
    El Segundo CA 90245
    650 551-6650

(P-21743)
SETON MEDICAL CENTER
Also Called: Seton Medical Center Coastside
600 Marine Blvd, Moss Beach
(94038-9641)
PHONE 650 563-7100
Judy Cook, *Director*
Ron Viray, *Analyst*
Robert Telfer MD, *Med Doctor*
Marifi Dizon, *Director*
EMP: 160
SALES (corp-wide): 1.2B **Privately Held**
WEB: www.sportsmedshop.com
SIC: 8062 5812 8051 General medical & surgical hospitals; eating places; skilled nursing care facilities
HQ: Seton Medical Center
    1900 Sullivan Ave
    Daly City CA 94015
    650 992-4000

(P-21744)
SETON MEDICAL CENTER
West Bay HM Hlth & Cmnty Svcs
1784 Sullivan Ave Ste 200, Daly City
(94015-2067)
PHONE 650 992-4000
Fax: 650 991-4146
EMP: 60
SALES (corp-wide): 225.4MM **Privately Held**
SIC: 8062 7361 8082
HQ: Seton Medical Center
    1900 Sullivan Ave
    Daly City CA 94015
    650 992-4000

(P-21745)
SHARP CHULA VISTA MEDICAL CTR
Also Called: Sharp Chula Vista Medical Ctr
751 Medical Center Ct, Chula Vista
(91911-6617)
PHONE 619 502-5800
Chris Boyd, *CEO*
Michael Murphy, *President*
Rick King, *CFO*
Vennie Henderson, *General Mgr*
Andrew Moyers, *Admin Asst*
EMP: 1600
SQ FT: 270,205
SALES: 367.2MM
SALES (corp-wide): 3.4B **Privately Held**
SIC: 8062 General medical & surgical hospitals
PA: Sharp Healthcare
    8695 Spectrum Center Blvd
    San Diego CA 92123
    858 499-4000

(P-21746)
SHARP CHULA VISTA MEDICAL CTR
8695 Spectrum Center Blvd, San Diego
(92123-1489)
PHONE 858 499-5150
Chris Boyd, *CEO*
Dolly Delarosa, *Admin Asst*
Lori Moody, *Recruiter*
Kimberly Castillo, *Director*
Jorge Martinez, *Manager*
EMP: 99
SALES: 407.7MM **Privately Held**
SIC: 8062 General medical & surgical hospitals

(P-21747)
SHARP HEALTHCARE
Also Called: Sharp Rees-Stealy
8008 Frost St Ste 106, San Diego
(92123-4229)
PHONE 858 939-5434
Lori Allshouse, *Training Spec*
Alfred Saleh, *Oncology*
Carola Romero, *Physician Asst*
Larry Cousins, *Med Doctor*
Bertha Ramirez,
EMP: 54
SALES (corp-wide): 3.4B **Privately Held**
SIC: 8062 General medical & surgical hospitals
PA: Sharp Healthcare
    8695 Spectrum Center Blvd
    San Diego CA 92123
    858 499-4000

(P-21748)
SHARP HEALTHCARE (PA)
Also Called: Sharp Rees-Stealy Pharmacy
8695 Spectrum Center Blvd, San Diego
(92123-1489)
PHONE 858 499-4000
Michael Murphy, *President*
Lance Altenau,
Keith Kortman, *Ch Radiology*
Ann Pumpian, *CFO*
James Brown, *Treasurer*
EMP: 760
SQ FT: 15,700
SALES: 3.4B **Privately Held**
SIC: 8062 8741 6324 General medical & surgical hospitals; hospital management; nursing & personal care facility management; hospital & medical service plans

(P-21749)
SHARP HEALTHCARE
Also Called: Sharp Health Care
3554 Ruffin Rd Ste Soca, San Diego
(92123-2596)
PHONE 858 627-5152
Alison Fleury, *Finance Other*
EMP: 150
SALES (corp-wide): 3.4B **Privately Held**
SIC: 8062 General medical & surgical hospitals
PA: Sharp Healthcare
    8695 Spectrum Center Blvd
    San Diego CA 92123
    858 499-4000

(P-21750)
SHARP HEALTHCARE
Also Called: Sharp Mission Park Medical Ctr
130 Cedar Rd, Vista (92083-5102)
PHONE 760 806-5600
Meredith Acosta, *Branch Mgr*
EMP: 59
SALES (corp-wide): 3.4B **Privately Held**
SIC: 8062 General medical & surgical hospitals
PA: Sharp Healthcare
    8695 Spectrum Center Blvd
    San Diego CA 92123
    858 499-4000

(P-21751)
SHARP HEALTHCARE
10670 Wexford St, San Diego
(92131-3940)
PHONE 858 621-4010
Susan Horton, *Branch Mgr*
EMP: 59
SALES (corp-wide): 3.4B **Privately Held**
SIC: 8062 General medical & surgical hospitals
PA: Sharp Healthcare
    8695 Spectrum Center Blvd
    San Diego CA 92123
    858 499-4000

(P-21752)
SHARP MARY BIRCH H
3003 Health Center Dr, San Diego
(92123-2700)
PHONE 858 939-3400
Trisha Khaleghi, *CEO*
Susan Sachs, *Pharmacy Dir*
Samantha Heddy, *Admin Sec*
John S Lee, *Pathologist*
Henrik Manassarians, *Neurology*
EMP: 73
SALES (est): 13.8MM **Privately Held**
SIC: 8062 General medical & surgical hospitals

(P-21753)
SHARP MEMORIAL HOSPITAL (HQ)
Also Called: SHARP REES-STEALY PHARMACY
7901 Frost St, San Diego (92123-2701)
PHONE 858 939-3636
Tim Smith, *CEO*
Cheryl Balderas, *Lab Dir*
Mario Grozdanovic, *Network Mgr*
Mark Freed, *Programmer Anys*
Dan Bannister, *Analyst*
▲ **EMP:** 3000 **EST:** 1957

P R O D U C T S & S V C S

SALES: 1.1B
SALES (corp-wide): 3.4B **Privately Held**
SIC: 8062 General medical & surgical hospitals
PA: Sharp Healthcare
8695 Spectrum Center Blvd
San Diego CA 92123
858 499-4000

(P-21754)
SHERMAN OAKS HEALTH SYSTEM
4929 Van Nuys Blvd, Sherman Oaks (91403-1702)
PHONE 818 981-7111
David Levinsohn, *CEO*
EMP: 51
SALES: 341.2K **Privately Held**
SIC: 8062 General medical & surgical hospitals

(P-21755)
SIERRA VIEW LOCAL HOSPITAL DST
Also Called: Sierra View District Hospital
283 Pearson Dr, Porterville (93257-3353)
PHONE 559 781-7877
Dennis Coleman, *Branch Mgr*
EMP: 432
SALES (corp-wide): 138.3MM **Privately Held**
SIC: 8062 General medical & surgical hospitals
PA: Sierra View District Hospital League, Inc.
465 W Putnam Ave
Porterville CA 93257
559 784-1110

(P-21756)
SIERRA VISTA HOSPITAL INC (HQ)
Also Called: Sierra Vista Regional Med Ctr
1010 Murray Ave, San Luis Obispo (93405-8801)
P.O. Box 1367 (93406-1367)
PHONE 805 546-7600
Joseph Deschryver, *CEO*
Candace Markwith, *President*
Ikenna Mmeje, *COO*
Richard Phillips, *CFO*
Rollie Pirkl, *CFO*
EMP: 575
SQ FT: 138,690
SALES: 150MM
SALES (corp-wide): 19.3B **Publicly Held**
WEB: www.rasloweb.com
SIC: 8062 General medical & surgical hospitals
PA: Tenet Healthcare Corporation
1445 Ross Ave Ste 1400
Dallas TX 75202
469 893-2200

(P-21757)
SISKIYOU HOSPITAL INC
Also Called: Fairchild Medical Center
444 Bruce St, Yreka (96097-3450)
PHONE 530 842-4121
Dwayne Jones, *CEO*
Kathy Severson, *Records Dir*
Marcus Issoglio, *President*
Jonathon C Andrus, *CEO*
Joann Farmento, *COO*
EMP: 450
SALES: 81.7MM **Privately Held**
WEB: www.fairchildmed.org
SIC: 8062 General medical & surgical hospitals

(P-21758)
SOMA SURGICENTER
1580 Valencia St, San Francisco (94110-4423)
PHONE 415 641-6889
Mary Sherman, *Manager*
EMP: 50
SALES (est): 543.5K **Privately Held**
SIC: 8062 General medical & surgical hospitals

(P-21759)
SONOMA VALLEY HEALTH CARE DST (PA)
Also Called: SONOMA VALLEY HOSPITAL
347 Andrieux St, Sonoma (95476-6811)
PHONE 707 935-5000
Carl Gerlach, *CEO*
Timothy Noakes, *CFO*
Courtney McMahon, *Infect Cntl Dir*
Chris Kutza, *Business Dir*
Vivian Woodall, *Executive Asst*
EMP: 450
SQ FT: 115,000
SALES: 56.5MM **Privately Held**
WEB: www.svh.com
SIC: 8062 General medical & surgical hospitals

(P-21760)
SOUTHERN CAL HALTHCARE SYS INC
Also Called: Southern Cal Hosp At Culver Cy
3828 Delmas Ter, Culver City (90232-2713)
PHONE 310 836-7000
EMP: 968 **Privately Held**
SIC: 8062 General medical & surgical hospitals
PA: Southern California Healthcare System, Inc.
3415 S Sepulveda Blvd # 9
Los Angeles CA 90034

(P-21761)
SOUTHERN CAL PRMNNTE MED GROUP
26415 Carl Boyer Dr, Santa Clarita (91350-5824)
PHONE 661 290-3100
EMP: 78
SALES (corp-wide): 3.5B **Privately Held**
SIC: 8062 General medical & surgical hospitals
PA: Southern California Permanente Medical Group
393 Walnut Dr
Pasadena CA 91107
626 405-5704

(P-21762)
SOUTHERN CAL PRMNNTE MED GROUP
Also Called: S C P M G
9961 Sierra Ave, Fontana (92335-6720)
PHONE 909 427-5000
Gerald McCall, *Branch Mgr*
George Kable, *Director*
Kathleen Sager, *Director*
EMP: 50
SALES (corp-wide): 3.5B **Privately Held**
WEB: www.permanente.net
SIC: 8062 General medical & surgical hospitals
PA: Southern California Permanente Medical Group
393 Walnut Dr
Pasadena CA 91107
626 405-5704

(P-21763)
SOUTHERN CAL SPCIALTY CARE INC
Also Called: Kindred Hospital La Mirata
845 N Lark Ellen Ave, West Covina (91791-1069)
PHONE 626 339-5451
Nenda Estudillo, *Director*
Victor Reyes, *Director*
EMP: 100
SQ FT: 34,082
SALES (corp-wide): 6B **Privately Held**
SIC: 8062 General medical & surgical hospitals
HQ: Southern California Specialty Care, Inc.
14900 Imperial Hwy
La Mirada CA 90638

(P-21764)
SOUTHERN CAL SPCIALTY CARE INC
1901 College Ave, Santa Ana (92706-2334)
PHONE 714 564-7800
Morgan Topper, *CEO*
Diana Hanyak, *Administration*
Elaine Pardee, *Director*
EMP: 162
SALES (corp-wide): 6B **Privately Held**
SIC: 8062 General medical & surgical hospitals
HQ: Southern California Specialty Care, Inc.
14900 Imperial Hwy
La Mirada CA 90638

(P-21765)
SOUTHERN CAL SPCIALTY CARE INC (DH)
Also Called: Kindred Hospital La Mirada
14900 Imperial Hwy, La Mirada (90638-2172)
PHONE 562 944-1900
Ty Richardson, *President*
George Burkley, *COO*
Robin Rapp, *COO*
Judie Sheldon, *Ch Credit Ofcr*
Susan Hung, *Admin Asst*
EMP: 100
SQ FT: 74,074
SALES: 109.3MM
SALES (corp-wide): 6B **Privately Held**
SIC: 8062 General medical & surgical hospitals
HQ: Specialty Healthcare Services, Inc
680 S 4th St
Louisville KY 40202
502 596-7300

(P-21766)
SOUTHERN HMBLDT CMNTY DST HOSP
Also Called: Southern Humboldt Cmnty Clinic
733 Cedar St, Garberville (95542-3201)
PHONE 707 923-3921
Deborah Scaife, *President*
Guy Vitello, *Facilities Mgr*
Barbara Hayes, *Nurse Practr*
Marie Brown, *Supervisor*
EMP: 95
SQ FT: 17,000
SALES (est): 6.1MM **Privately Held**
SIC: 8062 General medical & surgical hospitals

(P-21767)
SOUTHERN HUMBOLDT COMM HLTH CR
733 Cedar St, Garberville (95542-3201)
PHONE 707 923-3925
Matt Rees, *CEO*
Kent Sown, *COO*
Paul Eves, *CFO*
Vanessa King,
Margo Acuna, *Manager*
EMP: 85 **EST:** 2001
SALES (est): 323.2K **Privately Held**
SIC: 8062 General medical & surgical hospitals

(P-21768)
SOUTHERN MNTEREY CNTY MEM HOSP (PA)
Also Called: George L Mee Memorial Hospital
300 Canal St, King City (93930-3431)
PHONE 831 385-6000
Lex T Smith, *CEO*
Susan Childers, *CFO*
Jim Keller, *Vice Pres*
Christina Zaro, *Vice Pres*
Vijay Diesh, *Pharmacy Dir*
EMP: 495
SQ FT: 5,000
SALES: 65.3MM **Privately Held**
WEB: www.meememorial.com
SIC: 8062 Hospital, affiliated with AMA residency

(P-21769)
SOUTHERN MNTEREY CNTY MEM HOSP
467 El Camino Real, Greenfield (93927-4915)
PHONE 831 674-0112
Camille Sanz, *Director*
EMP: 146
SALES (corp-wide): 65.3MM **Privately Held**
SIC: 8062 Hospital, affiliated with AMA residency
PA: Southern Monterey County Memorial Hospital Inc
300 Canal St
King City CA 93930
831 385-6000

(P-21770)
SOUTHERN MONO HEALTHCARE DST
Also Called: Mammoth Hospital
85 Sierra Park Rd, Mammoth Lakes (93546-2073)
P.O. Box 660 (93546-0660)
PHONE 760 934-3311
Helen Shepherd, *Chairman*
Gary Myers, *CEO*
Stephen Swisher M D, *Treasurer*
Christy Mc Millan, *Director*
EMP: 350
SQ FT: 20,000
SALES: 67.7MM **Privately Held**
SIC: 8062 General medical & surgical hospitals

(P-21771)
SOUTHWEST HEALTHCARE SYS AUX
Also Called: Business Department
38977 Sky Canyon Dr # 200, Murrieta (92563-2681)
PHONE 800 404-6627
Paula Dalbeck, *Controller*
EMP: 50
SALES (corp-wide): 10.4B **Publicly Held**
SIC: 8062 General medical & surgical hospitals
HQ: Southwest Healthcare System Auxiliary
25500 Medical Center Dr
Murrieta CA 92562

(P-21772)
SOUTHWEST HEALTHCARE SYS AUX (HQ)
Also Called: Rancho Springs Medical Center
25500 Medical Center Dr, Murrieta (92562-5965)
PHONE 951 696-6000
Brad Neet, *CEO*
Diane Moon, *CFO*
Barry Thorfenson, *CFO*
Anne Marie Watkins, *Ch Nursing Ofcr*
Nikole Devries, *QA Dir*
▲ **EMP:** 450
SALES: 51.1K
SALES (corp-wide): 10.4B **Publicly Held**
SIC: 8062 8051 8059 4119 General medical & surgical hospitals; skilled nursing care facilities; convalescent home; ambulance service
PA: Universal Health Services, Inc.
367 S Gulph Rd
King Of Prussia PA 19406
610 768-3300

(P-21773)
SRM ALLIANCE HOSPITAL SERVICES (PA)
Also Called: Petaluma Valley Hospital
400 N Mcdowell Blvd, Petaluma (94954-2339)
PHONE 707 778-1111
Deborah A Proctor, *President*
Jane Reed, *Vice Pres*
Katy Hillenmeyer, *Executive*
Ryan Ackerman, *Admin Asst*
Gary Toavs, *Chief Engr*
EMP: 400
SQ FT: 50,000
SALES: 89.2MM **Privately Held**
SIC: 8062 General medical & surgical hospitals

(P-21774)
ST ELIZABETH COMMUNITY HOSP (HQ)
2550 Sister Mary Clumba Dr, Red Bluff (96080-4327)
PHONE...............530 529-7760
Todd Smith, *CEO*
Charlene Almocera, *Records Dir*
John Halfhide, *President*
Dena Platz, *Human Res Dir*
Tammy Fuller, *Mktg Dir*
EMP: 89 EST: 1901
SQ FT: 98,000
SALES: 95.6MM
SALES (corp-wide): 6.7B **Privately Held**
SIC: 8062 6513 General medical & surgical hospitals; retirement hotel operation
PA: Dignity Health
185 Berry St Ste 300
San Francisco CA 94107
415 438-5500

(P-21775)
ST HELENA HOSPITAL (PA)
Also Called: Deer Park Pharmacy
10 Woodland Rd, Saint Helena (94574-9554)
PHONE...............707 963-1882
Steven Herber, *CEO*
Whie OH,
Timothy J Kares, *CFO*
Edward McDonald, *CFO*
Edward Buck McDonald, *Senior VP*
EMP: 750
SQ FT: 200,000
SALES: 214.6MM **Privately Held**
WEB: www.sthelenahospital.com
SIC: 8062 8063 General medical & surgical hospitals; psychiatric hospitals

(P-21776)
ST JOSEPH HEALTH SYSTEM
101 E Valencia Mesa Dr, Fullerton (92835-3809)
PHONE...............714 992-3000
Deborah Proctor, *Principal*
Robert Morten, *Ch Radiology*
Karen Mihelic, *Exec Dir*
Dennis Giordano, *Area Mgr*
Janice Mullis, *Admin Asst*
EMP: 65
SALES (est): 3.9MM **Privately Held**
SIC: 8062 General medical & surgical hospitals

(P-21777)
ST JOSEPH HEALTH SYSTEM
Also Called: Petaluma Valley Hospital
400 N Mcdowell Blvd Fl 1, Petaluma (94954-2339)
PHONE...............707 778-2505
Hollis Belwaey, *Manager*
Brenda McMillin, *Director*
EMP: 50
SALES (corp-wide): 17.6B **Privately Held**
SIC: 8062 General medical & surgical hospitals
HQ: St. Joseph Health System
3345 Michelson Dr Ste 100
Irvine CA 92612
949 381-4000

(P-21778)
ST JOSEPH HERITAGE MED GROUP (PA)
Also Called: Yorba Park Medical Group
2212 E 4th St Ste 201, Santa Ana (92705-3872)
PHONE...............714 633-1011
Charles Foster, *President*
C R Burke, *CFO*
Dennis Long MD, *Treasurer*
Marc Bennette MD, *Vice Pres*
Joseph Brown MD, *Vice Pres*
▲ EMP: 134
SQ FT: 58,000
SALES (est): 16.2MM **Privately Held**
WEB: www.sjhmg.org
SIC: 8062 General medical & surgical hospitals

(P-21779)
ST JOSEPH HOSPITAL (PA)
2700 Dolbeer St, Eureka (95501-4799)
PHONE...............707 445-8121

Toll Free:...............888 -
Joseph Mark, *CEO*
David O'Brien, *President*
Terry Conrad, *CFO*
Andrew Rybolt, *CFO*
Donald Baird, *Bd of Directors*
▲ EMP: 79 EST: 1920
SQ FT: 125,000
SALES: 248.2MM **Privately Held**
WEB: www.meyerinsure.com
SIC: 8062 General medical & surgical hospitals

(P-21780)
ST JOSEPH HOSPITAL
Also Called: Neurosurgery
2752 Harrison Ave Ste A, Eureka (95501-4738)
PHONE...............707 268-0190
Maureen Lawlor, *Manager*
EMP: 674
SALES (corp-wide): 248.2MM **Privately Held**
SIC: 8062 General medical & surgical hospitals
PA: St. Joseph Hospital
2700 Dolbeer St
Eureka CA 95501
707 445-8121

(P-21781)
ST JOSEPH HOSPITAL OF EUREKA
2700 Dolbeer St, Eureka (95501-4736)
P.O. Box 5600, Orange (92863-5600)
PHONE...............707 445-8121
Megan Zagone, *Pathologist*
EMP: 970 EST: 2011
SALES: 268.6MM
SALES (corp-wide): 17.6B **Privately Held**
SIC: 8062 General medical & surgical hospitals
HQ: St. Joseph Hospital Of Orange
1100 W Stewart Dr
Orange CA 92868
714 633-9111

(P-21782)
ST JOSEPH HOSPITAL OF ORANGE (DH)
1100 W Stewart Dr, Orange (92868-3891)
P.O. Box 5600 (92863-5600)
PHONE...............714 633-9111
Larry K Ainsworth, *President*
Linda Youkhan, *Partner*
Tina Nycroft, *CFO*
Jim Cora, *Chairman*
Warren D Johnson, *Vice Ch Bd*
EMP: 2100 EST: 1929
SQ FT: 448,000
SALES: 655MM
SALES (corp-wide): 17.6B **Privately Held**
SIC: 8062 General medical & surgical hospitals
HQ: St. Joseph Health System
3345 Michelson Dr Ste 100
Irvine CA 92612
949 381-4000

(P-21783)
ST JOSEPH HOSPITAL OF ORANGE
Also Called: Renal Center
1100 W Stewart Dr, Orange (92868-3891)
P.O. Box 5600 (92863-5600)
PHONE...............714 771-8037
Mary McKenzie, *Director*
EMP: 100
SALES (corp-wide): 17.6B **Privately Held**
SIC: 8062 General medical & surgical hospitals
HQ: St. Joseph Hospital Of Orange
1100 W Stewart Dr
Orange CA 92868
714 633-9111

(P-21784)
ST JOSEPHS MED CTR STOCKTON
1800 N California St, Stockton (95204-6019)
P.O. Box 213008 (95213-9008)
PHONE...............209 943-2000
Donald J Wiley, *President*
Lindsay Bureaux, *Director*

EMP: 2366
SALES: 4.2MM
SALES (corp-wide): 6.7B **Privately Held**
WEB: www.chw.edu
SIC: 8062 General medical & surgical hospitals
PA: Dignity Health
185 Berry St Ste 300
San Francisco CA 94107
415 438-5500

(P-21785)
ST JOSEPHS MEDICAL CENTER
1800 N California St, Stockton (95204-6019)
P.O. Box 213008 (95213-9008)
PHONE...............209 943-2000
Donald J Wiley, *President*
Dr Susan McDonald, *Vice Pres*
Terry Spring, *Vice Pres*
Kathy Tohrnan, *Vice Pres*
Rae Charos, *Executive*
EMP: 150
SQ FT: 18,000
SALES: 478MM
SALES (corp-wide): 6.7B **Privately Held**
WEB: www.chw.edu
SIC: 8062 General medical & surgical hospitals
PA: Dignity Health
185 Berry St Ste 300
San Francisco CA 94107
415 438-5500

(P-21786)
ST JUDE HOSPITAL (DH)
Also Called: ST JUDE MEDICAL CENTER
101 E Valencia Mesa Dr, Fullerton (92835-3875)
PHONE...............714 871-3280
Robert Fraschetti, *President*
Patrick L Fitzgibbons, *Ch Pathology*
Pamela Frey, *Records Dir*
Doreen Dann, *CEO*
Lee Penrose, *CEO*
▲ EMP: 2582
SQ FT: 190,000
SALES: 544MM
SALES (corp-wide): 17.6B **Privately Held**
WEB: www.stjudemedicalcenter.com
SIC: 8062 General medical & surgical hospitals
HQ: St. Joseph Health System
3345 Michelson Dr Ste 100
Irvine CA 92612
949 381-4000

(P-21787)
ST MARY MEDICAL CENTER (HQ)
Also Called: ST MARY'S SCHOOL OF NURSING
1050 Linden Ave, Long Beach (90813-3321)
P.O. Box 887 (90801-0887)
PHONE...............562 491-9000
Trammie McMann, *CEO*
Alan Garrett, *CEO*
Tammie McMann, *CEO*
Stephen Dunn, *Lab Dir*
Ed S Engessers, *Finance Other*
EMP: 1929
SQ FT: 700,000
SALES: 254.7MM
SALES (corp-wide): 6.7B **Privately Held**
SIC: 8062 Hospital, medical school affiliated with nursing & residency
PA: Dignity Health
185 Berry St Ste 300
San Francisco CA 94107
415 438-5500

(P-21788)
ST MARY MEDICAL CENTER (PA)
18300 Us Highway 18, Apple Valley (92307-2206)
PHONE...............760 242-2311
Alan H Garrett, *President*
Kelly Linden, *COO*
Marilyn Drone, *CFO*
Tracey Fernandez, *CFO*
Diana Carloni - O'Malley, *Trustee*
EMP: 1350
SQ FT: 92,000

SALES: 333.5MM **Privately Held**
WEB: www.stmaryapplevalley.com
SIC: 8062 General medical & surgical hospitals

(P-21789)
ST MARYS MED CTR FOUNDATION
Also Called: MERCY HOSPITAL
450 Stanyan St, San Francisco (94117-1019)
PHONE...............415 668-1000
Ken Steele, *President*
James Wentz, *CFO*
Dee Mostofi, *Marketing Staff*
Natalia Petrosova, *Anesthesiology*
EMP: 1067 EST: 1983
SALES: 3.7MM
SALES (corp-wide): 6.7B **Privately Held**
WEB: www.chw.edu
SIC: 8062 Hospital, professional nursing school
PA: Dignity Health
185 Berry St Ste 300
San Francisco CA 94107
415 438-5500

(P-21790)
STANFORD HEALTH CARE
Also Called: Quality Management
300 Pasteur Dr, Stanford (94305-2200)
PHONE...............650 723-4000
Raksha Patel, *Bd of Directors*
Jane Shannahan, *VP Bus Dvlpt*
Thomas Bruynell, *Lab Dir*
Judy Kaufman, *Associate Dir*
Michael Brown, *Pharmacy Dir*
EMP: 2523
SALES (corp-wide): 5.6B **Privately Held**
SIC: 8062 8099 Hospital, medical school affiliated with residency; childbirth preparation clinic
HQ: Stanford Health Care
300 Pasteur Dr
Stanford CA 94305
650 723-4000

(P-21791)
STANFORD HEALTH CARE
Also Called: Stanford Cancer Center S Bay
2589 Samaritan Dr, San Jose (95124-4102)
PHONE...............408 426-4900
Patrick Swift, *Med Doctor*
EMP: 2523
SALES (corp-wide): 5.6B **Privately Held**
SIC: 8062 Hospital, medical school affiliated with residency
HQ: Stanford Health Care
300 Pasteur Dr
Stanford CA 94305
650 723-4000

(P-21792)
STANFORD HEALTH CARE (HQ)
Also Called: Stanford Medical Center
300 Pasteur Dr, Stanford (94305-2200)
PHONE...............650 723-4000
David Entwistle, *CEO*
Barbara Clemons, *President*
Quinn L McKenna, *COO*
Tracey Lewis Taylor, *COO*
David Connor, *CFO*
▲ EMP: 4050
SALES: 4.4B
SALES (corp-wide): 5.6B **Privately Held**
WEB: www.stanfordmedicalcenter.com
SIC: 8062 Hospital, medical school affiliated with residency
PA: Leland Stanford Junior University
450 Serra Mall
Stanford CA 94305
650 723-2300

(P-21793)
STANFORD HEALTH CARE
Also Called: Shc Reference Laboratory
3375 Hillview Ave, Palo Alto (94304-1204)
PHONE...............650 736-7844
Edward Gwin, *Business Anlyst*
Martha Aragon, *Director*
John Christopher, *Manager*
Lisa Furtado, *Manager*
EMP: 2523

SALES (corp-wide): 5.6B **Privately Held**
SIC: 8062 General medical & surgical hospitals
HQ: Stanford Health Care
300 Pasteur Dr
Stanford CA 94305
650 723-4000

(P-21794)
STANFORD HOSPITAL AND CLINICS
1510 Page Mill Rd Ste 2, Palo Alto (94304-1133)
PHONE..................650 213-8360
Martha Marsh, *President*
Kim Lopez, *Technology*
Bassam Kadry, *Anesthesiology*
Vivianne Tawfik, *Anesthesiology*
EMP: 2523
SALES (corp-wide): 5.6B **Privately Held**
SIC: 8062 Hospital, medical school affiliated with residency
HQ: Stanford Health Care
300 Pasteur Dr
Stanford CA 94305
650 723-4000

(P-21795)
STANISLAUS SURGICAL HOSP LLC (PA)
Also Called: Stanislaus Surgical Center
1421 Oakdale Rd, Modesto (95355-3356)
PHONE..................209 572-2700
Douglas V Johnson, *CEO*
Leslie Konkin,
Timothy J Noakes, *Mng Member*
EMP: 230
SQ FT: 50,000
SALES: 24MM **Privately Held**
WEB: www.stanislaussurgical.com
SIC: 8062 General medical & surgical hospitals

(P-21796)
SURGERY CENTER OF ALTA BATES (HQ)
Also Called: Alta Bates Summit Medical Ctr
2450 Ashby Ave, Berkeley (94705-2067)
PHONE..................510 204-4444
Warren Kirk, *President*
Robert Petrina, *CFO*
Larry Perucca, *Engineer*
Joseph V Mersol, *Radiology*
Michael W Tsang, *Cardiovascular*
EMP: 653
SQ FT: 749,000
SALES (est): 411.7MM
SALES (corp-wide): 12.4B **Privately Held**
WEB: www.altabates.com
SIC: 8062 General medical & surgical hospitals
PA: Sutter Health
2200 River Plaza Dr
Sacramento CA 95833
916 733-8800

(P-21797)
SURPRISE VALLEY HEALTH CARE DI
741 N Main St, Cedarville (96104)
P.O. Box 246 (96104-0246)
PHONE..................530 279-6111
EMP: 72
SQ FT: 13,330
SALES: 3.9MM **Privately Held**
SIC: 8062 General medical & surgical hospitals

(P-21798)
SUTTER AMADOR HOSPITAL (HQ)
Also Called: SUTTER C H S
200 Mission Blvd, Jackson (95642-2564)
PHONE..................209 223-7500
Anne Platt, *CEO*
Denise Sammons, *Officer*
Beverly Revels, *Human Res Mgr*
Doug Archer, *Recruiter*
Kim Vagt, *Nutritionist*
EMP: 385
SALES: 80.9MM
SALES (corp-wide): 12.4B **Privately Held**
WEB: www.sutteramador.com
SIC: 8062 General medical & surgical hospitals

PA: Sutter Health
2200 River Plaza Dr
Sacramento CA 95833
916 733-8800

(P-21799)
SUTTER BAY HOSPITALS (HQ)
Also Called: California Pacific Medical Ctr
633 Folsom St Fl 5, San Francisco (94107-3623)
P.O. Box 7999 (94120-7999)
PHONE..................415 600-6000
Jeff Gerard, *CEO*
Martin Brotman, *President*
Jamey Schmidt, *Admin Asst*
Cecilia Thomas, *Prgrmr*
Douglas Wong, *Marketing Staff*
EMP: 2578
SALES: 1.5B
SALES (corp-wide): 12.4B **Privately Held**
WEB: www.cpmc.org
SIC: 8062 General medical & surgical hospitals
PA: Sutter Health
2200 River Plaza Dr
Sacramento CA 95833
916 733-8800

(P-21800)
SUTTER CENTRAL VLY HOSPITALS (HQ)
Also Called: Memorial Medical Center
1700 Coffee Rd, Modesto (95355-2803)
P.O. Box 942 (95353-0942)
PHONE..................209 526-4500
James Conforti, *CEO*
John Talieh,
Todd Smith, *Ch of Bd*
David P Benn, *CEO*
Sutter Pat Fry, *CEO*
EMP: 112 **EST:** 1947
SQ FT: 180,000
SALES: 772MM
SALES (corp-wide): 12.4B **Privately Held**
WEB: www.memorialmedicalcenter.org
SIC: 8062 General medical & surgical hospitals
PA: Sutter Health
2200 River Plaza Dr
Sacramento CA 95833
916 733-8800

(P-21801)
SUTTER COAST HOSPITAL (HQ)
800 E Washington Blvd, Crescent City (95531-8359)
PHONE..................707 464-8511
Eugene Suksi, *President*
Jim Strong, *CFO*
Debra Faulk, *Systems Mgr*
Erik Burman, *Gnrl Med Prac*
Wendi Workinger, *Radiology*
▲ **EMP:** 250
SQ FT: 70,000
SALES: 75MM
SALES (corp-wide): 12.4B **Privately Held**
WEB: www.suttercoast.com
SIC: 8062 General medical & surgical hospitals
PA: Sutter Health
2200 River Plaza Dr
Sacramento CA 95833
916 733-8800

(P-21802)
SUTTER DELTA MEDICAL CTR AUX
3901 Lone Tree Way, Antioch (94509-6200)
P.O. Box 3225 (94531-3225)
PHONE..................925 779-7200
Linda Lee Rovai, *President*
Ken Hammer, *COO*
Linda Horn, *Administration*
Janice Falzano, *Finance*
Phil Gardiner, *Human Resources*
EMP: 53
SQ FT: 150,000
SALES (est): 9.9MM **Privately Held**
WEB: www.sutterdelta.com
SIC: 8062 8082 8093 8069 General medical & surgical hospitals; home health care services; specialty outpatient clinics; orthopedic hospital

(P-21803)
SUTTER HEALTH
1625 Stockton Blvd # 207, Sacramento (95816-7092)
PHONE..................916 733-1025
Brenda Batchelder, *Partner*
EMP: 239
SALES (corp-wide): 12.4B **Privately Held**
SIC: 8062 General medical & surgical hospitals
PA: Sutter Health
2200 River Plaza Dr
Sacramento CA 95833
916 733-8800

(P-21804)
SUTTER HEALTH
Also Called: Cpmc
P.O. Box 7999 (94120-7999)
PHONE..................415 600-7034
Kathy Blankenship, *Vice Pres*
Suzann Samet, *Supervisor*
EMP: 266
SALES (corp-wide): 12.4B **Privately Held**
SIC: 8062 8051 8011 6513 General medical & surgical hospitals; skilled nursing care facilities; offices & clinics of medical doctors; retirement hotel operation
PA: Sutter Health
2200 River Plaza Dr
Sacramento CA 95833
916 733-8800

(P-21805)
SUTTER HEALTH
1020 29th St Ste 600, Sacramento (95816-5126)
PHONE..................916 733-9588
EMP: 159
SALES (corp-wide): 12.4B **Privately Held**
SIC: 8062 General medical & surgical hospitals
PA: Sutter Health
2200 River Plaza Dr
Sacramento CA 95833
916 733-8800

(P-21806)
SUTTER HEALTH
2000 Sutter Pl, Davis (95616-6201)
PHONE..................530 757-5111
Tom Carlson, *Manager*
EMP: 319
SALES (corp-wide): 12.4B **Privately Held**
SIC: 8062 General medical & surgical hospitals
PA: Sutter Health
2200 River Plaza Dr
Sacramento CA 95833
916 733-8800

(P-21807)
SUTTER HEALTH
Also Called: Sutter Med Group of Redwoods
510 Doyle Park Dr, Santa Rosa (95405-4570)
PHONE..................707 526-1800
Norma Driscoll Johns, *Branch Mgr*
EMP: 159
SALES (corp-wide): 12.4B **Privately Held**
SIC: 8062 General medical & surgical hospitals
PA: Sutter Health
2200 River Plaza Dr
Sacramento CA 95833
916 733-8800

(P-21808)
SUTTER HEALTH
3901 Lone Tree Way, Antioch (94509-6200)
PHONE..................925 779-7273
Tim Bouslog, *Purch Mgr*
Theresa Mostasisa,
Melinda Mata, *Director*
Stephanie Davis, *Manager*
EMP: 691
SALES (corp-wide): 12.4B **Privately Held**
SIC: 8062 General medical & surgical hospitals
PA: Sutter Health
2200 River Plaza Dr
Sacramento CA 95833
916 733-8800

(P-21809)
SUTTER HEALTH
3468 California St, San Francisco (94118-1837)
PHONE..................415 345-0100
Steven Goldman, *Med Doctor*
Dong Hwang, *Med Doctor*
EMP: 266
SALES (corp-wide): 12.4B **Privately Held**
SIC: 8062 General medical & surgical hospitals
PA: Sutter Health
2200 River Plaza Dr
Sacramento CA 95833
916 733-8800

(P-21810)
SUTTER HEALTH
1335 S Fairmont Ave, Lodi (95240-5520)
PHONE..................209 366-2007
EMP: 133
SALES (corp-wide): 12.4B **Privately Held**
SIC: 8062 General medical & surgical hospitals
PA: Sutter Health
2200 River Plaza Dr
Sacramento CA 95833
916 733-8800

(P-21811)
SUTTER HEALTH
595 Buckingham Way # 515, San Francisco (94132-1909)
P.O. Box 320427 (94132-0427)
PHONE..................415 731-6300
EMP: 133
SALES (corp-wide): 12.4B **Privately Held**
SIC: 8062 General medical & surgical hospitals
PA: Sutter Health
2200 River Plaza Dr
Sacramento CA 95833
916 733-8800

(P-21812)
SUTTER HEALTH
Also Called: Sutter Pacific Med Foundation
1375 Sutter St, San Francisco (94109-5438)
PHONE..................415 600-0110
EMP: 213
SALES (corp-wide): 12.4B **Privately Held**
SIC: 8062 General medical & surgical hospitals
PA: Sutter Health
2200 River Plaza Dr
Sacramento CA 95833
916 733-8800

(P-21813)
SUTTER HEALTH
3 Medical Plaza Dr # 100, Roseville (95661-3088)
PHONE..................916 797-4715
Carla Ellis,
EMP: 186
SALES (corp-wide): 12.4B **Privately Held**
SIC: 8062 General medical & surgical hospitals
PA: Sutter Health
2200 River Plaza Dr
Sacramento CA 95833
916 733-8800

(P-21814)
SUTTER HEALTH
2030 Sutter Pl Ste 1000, Davis (95616-6215)
PHONE..................530 750-5904
Lydia Lindsay, *Branch Mgr*
EMP: 159
SALES (corp-wide): 12.4B **Privately Held**
SIC: 8062 General medical & surgical hospitals
PA: Sutter Health
2200 River Plaza Dr
Sacramento CA 95833
916 733-8800

(P-21815)
SUTTER HEALTH
110 Stony Point Rd # 200, Santa Rosa (95401-4118)
PHONE..................707 535-5600
Pam Carroll, *Manager*
EMP: 159

SALES (corp-wide): 12.4B **Privately Held**
SIC: 8062 General medical & surgical hospitals
PA: Sutter Health
  2200 River Plaza Dr
  Sacramento CA 95833
  916 733-8800

(P-21816)
SUTTER HEALTH
Also Called: Sutter Alhambra Surgery Center
8170 Laguna Blvd Ste 103, Elk Grove
(95758-7902)
PHONE..............................916 455-8137
EMP: 213
SALES (corp-wide): 12.4B **Privately Held**
SIC: 8062 General medical & surgical hospitals
PA: Sutter Health
  2200 River Plaza Dr
  Sacramento CA 95833
  916 733-8800

(P-21817)
SUTTER HEALTH
2340 Clay St Rm 121, San Francisco
(94115-1932)
P.O. Box 7999 (94120-7999)
PHONE..............................415 600-1020
Blair Parker, *Officer*
Warren Browner, *Vice Pres*
Abe Dosi, *Vice Pres*
Chris Riley, *Sr Ntwrk Engine*
Peter Gasper, *Research*
EMP: 585
SALES (corp-wide): 12.4B **Privately Held**
SIC: 8062 General medical & surgical hospitals
PA: Sutter Health
  2200 River Plaza Dr
  Sacramento CA 95833
  916 733-8800

(P-21818)
SUTTER HEALTH
2880 Gateway Oaks Dr # 220, Sacramento
(95833-4332)
PHONE..............................916 566-4819
Vicki Flemming, *Branch Mgr*
Kristin Maxim, *Project Mgr*
Amanda Peterson, *Sr Project Mgr*
Troy Franklin, *Manager*
Robert Stephens, *Manager*
EMP: 239
SALES (corp-wide): 12.4B **Privately Held**
SIC: 8062 General medical & surgical hospitals
PA: Sutter Health
  2200 River Plaza Dr
  Sacramento CA 95833
  916 733-8800

(P-21819)
SUTTER HEALTH
Also Called: Sutter Elk Grove Surgery Ctr
8200 Laguna Blvd, Elk Grove
(95758-7956)
PHONE..............................916 544-5423
EMP: 532
SALES (corp-wide): 12.4B **Privately Held**
SIC: 8062 General medical & surgical hospitals
PA: Sutter Health
  2200 River Plaza Dr
  Sacramento CA 95833
  916 733-8800

(P-21820)
SUTTER HEALTH
1375 Sutter St Ste 208, San Francisco
(94109-5465)
PHONE..............................415 600-0140
EMP: 159
SALES (corp-wide): 12.4B **Privately Held**
SIC: 8062 General medical & surgical hospitals
PA: Sutter Health
  2200 River Plaza Dr
  Sacramento CA 95833
  916 733-8800

(P-21821)
SUTTER HEALTH
2015 Steiner St Fl 1, San Francisco
(94115-2627)
PHONE..............................415 600-4280

Dorothy Coleman-Riese MD, *President*
Elizabeth Peralta, *Surgeon*
Vanessa Dumont, *Nurse Practr*
EMP: 983
SALES (corp-wide): 12.4B **Privately Held**
SIC: 8062 General medical & surgical hospitals
PA: Sutter Health
  2200 River Plaza Dr
  Sacramento CA 95833
  916 733-8800

(P-21822)
SUTTER HEALTH
100 Rowland Way Ste 210, Novato
(94945-5041)
PHONE..............................415 897-8495
Vicki Del, *Branch Mgr*
Sherie Hickman, *Administration*
EMP: 146
SALES (corp-wide): 12.4B **Privately Held**
SIC: 8062 General medical & surgical hospitals
PA: Sutter Health
  2200 River Plaza Dr
  Sacramento CA 95833
  916 733-8800

(P-21823)
SUTTER HEALTH
Also Called: Sutter Medical Center
2825 Capitol Ave, Sacramento
(95816-6039)
PHONE..............................916 887-0000
Tory Starr, *Vice Pres*
Greg Walaitis, *Exec Dir*
Carlos Jamis-Dow, *Managing Dir*
Andrew Pete, *Regional Mgr*
Mike Goetz, *Network Enginr*
EMP: 372
SALES (corp-wide): 12.4B **Privately Held**
SIC: 8062 General medical & surgical hospitals
PA: Sutter Health
  2200 River Plaza Dr
  Sacramento CA 95833
  916 733-8800

(P-21824)
SUTTER HEALTH (PA)
Also Called: Sutter C H S
2200 River Plaza Dr, Sacramento
(95833-4134)
PHONE..............................916 733-8800
Patrick Fry, *President*
Jim Gray, *Ch of Bd*
Steve O'Brien, *CEO*
Robert D Reed, *CFO*
Gordon Hunt MD, *Officer*
EMP: 900
SALES: 12.4B **Privately Held**
WEB: www.sutterhealth.org
SIC: 8062 8051 8011 6513 General medical & surgical hospitals; skilled nursing care facilities; offices & clinics of medical doctors; retirement hotel operation

(P-21825)
SUTTER HEALTH
600 Coffee Rd, Modesto (95355-4201)
PHONE..............................209 524-1211
Laurie Scott, *Principal*
James Mott, *Technology*
Johanna Dailey, *Buyer*
Audrey Gilbert, *Buyer*
Dawn Bongatti, *Opers Spvr*
EMP: 200
SALES (corp-wide): 12.4B **Privately Held**
WEB: www.sutterhealth.org
SIC: 8062 General medical & surgical hospitals
PA: Sutter Health
  2200 River Plaza Dr
  Sacramento CA 95833
  916 733-8800

(P-21826)
SUTTER HEALTH
2516 E Whitmore Ave, Ceres (95307-2645)
PHONE..............................209 538-1733
EMP: 133
SALES (corp-wide): 12.4B **Privately Held**
SIC: 8062 General medical & surgical hospitals

PA: Sutter Health
  2200 River Plaza Dr
  Sacramento CA 95833
  916 733-8800

(P-21827)
SUTTER HEALTH
8170 Laguna Blvd Ste 220, Elk Grove
(95758-7902)
PHONE..............................916 691-5900
Kim Caldwell, *Manager*
EMP: 262
SALES (corp-wide): 12.4B **Privately Held**
SIC: 8062 General medical & surgical hospitals
PA: Sutter Health
  2200 River Plaza Dr
  Sacramento CA 95833
  916 733-8800

(P-21828)
SUTTER HEALTH
Also Called: Biomedical Engineering Center
5151 F St, Sacramento (95819-3223)
PHONE..............................916 733-8133
Jon Rice, *Engrg Dir*
Angela Nerghes, *Pharmacy Dir*
Christine Aasen, *Office Mgr*
Julia Daniels, *Admin Asst*
Kathy Seymour, *Admin Asst*
EMP: 60
SALES (corp-wide): 12.4B **Privately Held**
WEB: www.sutterhealth.org
SIC: 8062 General medical & surgical hospitals
PA: Sutter Health
  2200 River Plaza Dr
  Sacramento CA 95833
  916 733-8800

(P-21829)
SUTTER HEALTH
2880 Soquel Ave Ste 10, Santa Cruz
(95062-1423)
PHONE..............................831 477-3600
Kathleen McNupp, *Manager*
Mary Mahone, *Opers Staff*
EMP: 50
SALES (corp-wide): 12.4B **Privately Held**
WEB: www.sutterhealth.org
SIC: 8062 General medical & surgical hospitals
PA: Sutter Health
  2200 River Plaza Dr
  Sacramento CA 95833
  916 733-8800

(P-21830)
SUTTER HEALTH
Also Called: Sutter Pacific Med Foundation
4702 Hoen Ave, Santa Rosa (95405-7824)
PHONE..............................707 545-2255
Dorothy Coleman, *Med Doctor*
EMP: 292
SALES (corp-wide): 12.4B **Privately Held**
SIC: 8062 General medical & surgical hospitals
PA: Sutter Health
  2200 River Plaza Dr
  Sacramento CA 95833
  916 733-8800

(P-21831)
SUTTER HEALTH
Also Called: Eden Medical Center
P.O. Box 160100 (95816-0100)
PHONE..............................916 731-5672
EMP: 117
SALES (corp-wide): 12.4B **Privately Held**
WEB: www.sutterhealth.org
SIC: 8062 General medical & surgical hospitals
PA: Sutter Health
  2200 River Plaza Dr
  Sacramento CA 95833
  916 733-8800

(P-21832)
SUTTER HEALTH
2449 Summerfield Rd, Santa Rosa
(95405-7815)
PHONE..............................707 523-7253
EMP: 213
SALES (corp-wide): 12.4B **Privately Held**
SIC: 8062 General medical & surgical hospitals

PA: Sutter Health
  2200 River Plaza Dr
  Sacramento CA 95833
  916 733-8800

(P-21833)
SUTTER HEALTH
8318 Ferguson Ave, Sacramento
(95828-0902)
PHONE..............................916 454-6747
Angie Parisi, *Manager*
EMP: 478
SALES (corp-wide): 12.4B **Privately Held**
SIC: 8062 General medical & surgical hospitals
PA: Sutter Health
  2200 River Plaza Dr
  Sacramento CA 95833
  916 733-8800

(P-21834)
SUTTER HEALTH
Also Called: Shuler, Kurt MD
2030 Sutter Pl Ste 1300, Davis
(95616-6215)
PHONE..............................530 750-5888
EMP: 133
SALES (corp-wide): 12.4B **Privately Held**
SIC: 8062 General medical & surgical hospitals
PA: Sutter Health
  2200 River Plaza Dr
  Sacramento CA 95833
  916 733-8800

(P-21835)
SUTTER HEALTH
100 Rowland Way, Novato (94945-5011)
PHONE..............................415 602-5380
Bill Davis, *CEO*
EMP: 133
SALES (corp-wide): 12.4B **Privately Held**
SIC: 8062 General medical & surgical hospitals
PA: Sutter Health
  2200 River Plaza Dr
  Sacramento CA 95833
  916 733-8800

(P-21836)
**SUTTER HLTH SCRMNTO
SIERRA REG (HQ)**
Also Called: Sutter Memorial Hospital
2200 River Plaza Dr, Sacramento
(95833-4134)
P.O. Box 160727 (95816-0727)
PHONE..............................916 733-8800
Patrick E Fry, *CEO*
Darling Lones, *President*
Debbie Ball, *Practice Mgr*
Mark McDaniel, *Engineer*
Suzanne Hopkins, *Corp Comm Staff*
▲ **EMP:** 300 **EST:** 1935
SQ FT: 20,000
SALES: 1.8B
SALES (corp-wide): 12.4B **Privately Held**
SIC: 8062 8063 8052 General medical & surgical hospitals; psychiatric hospitals; intermediate care facilities
PA: Sutter Health
  2200 River Plaza Dr
  Sacramento CA 95833
  916 733-8800

(P-21837)
**SUTTER HLTH SCRMNTO
SIERRA REG**
Also Called: Sutter Davis Hospital
2000 Sutter Pl, Davis (95616-6201)
P.O. Box 1617 (95617-1617)
PHONE..............................530 756-6440
Janet Wagner, *Branch Mgr*
David Rosas, *President*
Stella Henthorn, *Nursing Mgr*
Jill Antonides, *Pub Rel Dir*
Abram Levin, *Emerg Med Spec*
EMP: 350
SALES (corp-wide): 12.4B **Privately Held**
SIC: 8062 8011 General medical & surgical hospitals; offices & clinics of medical doctors
HQ: Sutter Health Sacramento Sierra Region
  2200 River Plaza Dr
  Sacramento CA 95833
  916 733-8800

(P-21838)
SUTTER HLTH SCRMNTO SIERRA REG
Also Called: Sutter Memorial Hospital
5151 F St, Sacramento (95819-3223)
P.O. Box 160727 (95816-0727)
PHONE..................916 454-2222
Richard Foohoo, *Administration*
John Culver, *QA Dir*
Jim Kubota, *Finance Mgr*
Myra Malkiewicz, *Financial Analy*
Karen Kiyomura,
EMP: 310
SALES (corp-wide): 12.4B **Privately Held**
SIC: 8062 8011 General medical & surgical hospitals; offices & clinics of medical doctors
HQ: Sutter Health Sacramento Sierra Region
2200 River Plaza Dr
Sacramento CA 95833
916 733-8800

(P-21839)
SUTTER HLTH SCRMNTO SIERRA REG
Also Called: Sutter Roseville Medical Ctr
1 Medical Plaza Dr, Roseville (95661-3037)
PHONE..................916 781-1000
Patrick Grady, *Manager*
Tiffany Ortega, *Manager*
EMP: 1180
SALES (corp-wide): 12.4B **Privately Held**
SIC: 8062 General medical & surgical hospitals
HQ: Sutter Health Sacramento Sierra Region
2200 River Plaza Dr
Sacramento CA 95833
916 733-8800

(P-21840)
SUTTER HLTH SCRMNTO SIERRA REG
Also Called: Sutter Medical Center
2800 L St, Sacramento (95816-5616)
P.O. Box 160727 (95816-0727)
PHONE..................916 733-3095
Sarah Krevans, *Branch Mgr*
Mike Boyce, *Engineer*
EMP: 2500
SALES (corp-wide): 12.4B **Privately Held**
SIC: 8062 General medical & surgical hospitals
HQ: Sutter Health Sacramento Sierra Region
2200 River Plaza Dr
Sacramento CA 95833
916 733-8800

(P-21841)
SUTTER LAKESIDE HOSPITAL (HQ)
Also Called: SUTTER C H S
5176 Hill Rd E, Lakeport (95453-6357)
PHONE..................707 262-5000
Siri Nelson, *CEO*
Bob Anderson, *CFO*
Kelly Mather, *Administration*
Diane J Pege, *Internal Med*
Jill Minudri, *Pharmacist*
EMP: 340 **EST:** 1945
SQ FT: 26,000
SALES: 80MM
SALES (corp-wide): 12.4B **Privately Held**
SIC: 8062 General medical & surgical hospitals
PA: Sutter Health
2200 River Plaza Dr
Sacramento CA 95833
916 733-8800

(P-21842)
SUTTER MATERNITY & SURGERY CTR
2900 Chanticleer Ave, Santa Cruz (95065-1816)
PHONE..................831 477-2200
Larry De Ghetaldi, *CEO*
Richard Nichols, *Administration*
Mark Riley, *Mktg Dir*
Mark S Isaacson, *Anesthesiology*
Michael Wieland, *Director*
EMP: 225

SALES: 74.4MM **Privately Held**
SIC: 8062 General medical & surgical hospitals

(P-21843)
SUTTER ROSEVILLE MEDICAL CTR
1 Medical Plaza Dr, Roseville (95661-3037)
PHONE..................916 781-1000
Patrick Brady, *CEO*
Julie Fralick, *Human Res Mgr*
Alex Alba, *Hematology*
Sivakumar Reddy, *Hematology*
Napoleon Bernardo, *Med Doctor*
EMP: 1700
SALES: 669.3MM **Privately Held**
SIC: 8062 General medical & surgical hospitals

(P-21844)
SUTTER RSVLLE MED CTR FNDATION
1 Medical Plaza Dr, Roseville (95661-3037)
PHONE..................916 781-1000
Patricia Marquez, *President*
Claudine McLaughlin, *Buyer*
Syed A Ahmed, *Internal Med*
Karrie N Berg, *Internal Med*
Christopher Pease, *Internal Med*
EMP: 2000
SALES: 2.6MM **Privately Held**
SIC: 8062 General medical & surgical hospitals

(P-21845)
SUTTER SOLANO MEDICAL CENTER (HQ)
Also Called: SUTTER C H S
300 Hospital Dr, Vallejo (94589-2594)
PHONE..................707 554-4444
Mary A Hayes, *Principal*
Brett Moore, *CFO*
Robert Butler, *Project Mgr*
Angie Hammons, *Manager*
Carol Berry, *Assistant*
EMP: 542
SQ FT: 94,000
SALES: 181.5MM
SALES (corp-wide): 12.4B **Privately Held**
WEB: www.suttersolano.org
SIC: 8062 General medical & surgical hospitals
PA: Sutter Health
2200 River Plaza Dr
Sacramento CA 95833
916 733-8800

(P-21846)
SUTTER SURGICAL HOSPITAL N VLY
455 Plumas Blvd, Yuba City (95991-5074)
PHONE..................530 749-5700
Toni Morris, *Principal*
EMP: 121 **EST:** 2010
SALES (est): 14.8MM
SALES (corp-wide): 1.1B **Publicly Held**
SIC: 8062 General medical & surgical hospitals
HQ: National Surgical Hospitals, Inc.
250 S Wacker Dr Ste 500
Chicago IL 60606
312 627-8400

(P-21847)
SUTTER VALLEY MED FOUNDATION (PA)
Also Called: Sutter Health
2700 Gateway Oaks Dr, Sacramento (95833-4337)
PHONE..................916 887-7122
Tom Blinn, *CEO*
Tanya Hughes, *Project Mgr*
Gloria Alvarez, *Marketing Staff*
Suzanne Suzuki, *Marketing Staff*
Jack Breezee, *Nutritionist*
EMP: 700
SALES (est): 119.3MM **Privately Held**
SIC: 8062 Hospital, AMA approved residency

(P-21848)
SUTTER WEST BAY HOSPITALS (HQ)
Also Called: SUTTER C H S
180 Rowland Way, Novato (94945-5009)
P.O. Box 1108 (94948-1108)
PHONE..................415 209-1300
Brian Alexander, *CEO*
David Bradley, *President*
Timothy C Gee, *Emerg Med Spec*
Marc Tatarian, *Director*
▲ **EMP:** 329 **EST:** 1952
SQ FT: 50,000
SALES: 68MM
SALES (corp-wide): 12.4B **Privately Held**
WEB: www.sutterhealth.org
SIC: 8062 General medical & surgical hospitals
PA: Sutter Health
2200 River Plaza Dr
Sacramento CA 95833
916 733-8800

(P-21849)
TAHOE FOREST HOSPITAL DISTRICT
Also Called: Tahoe Workx
10956 Donner Paca Rd, Truckee (96161)
PHONE..................530 582-3277
Ricardo Fergazo, *Director*
Ted Owens, *Pub Rel Dir*
John Swanson, *Med Doctor*
Grace Waymire, *Supervisor*
EMP: 111
SALES (est): 5MM
SALES (corp-wide): 157.2MM **Privately Held**
SIC: 8062 8071 General medical & surgical hospitals; X-ray laboratory, including dental
PA: Tahoe Forest Hospital District
10121 Pine Ave
Truckee CA 96161
530 587-6011

(P-21850)
TAHOE FOREST HOSPITAL DISTRICT (PA)
10121 Pine Ave, Truckee (96161-4856)
P.O. Box 759 (96160-0759)
PHONE..................530 587-6011
Robert Schapper, *CEO*
Jeff Dodd,
David Kitts,
Thomas Specht,
Tad Laird, *Ch Radiology*
EMP: 600 **EST:** 1952
SQ FT: 120,000
SALES: 157.2MM **Privately Held**
WEB: www.tfhd.com
SIC: 8062 General medical & surgical hospitals

(P-21851)
TENET HEALTH SYSTEMS NORRIS
Also Called: Kenneth Norris Cancer Hospital
1441 Eastlake Ave, Los Angeles (90089-1019)
PHONE..................323 865-3000
Scott Evans, *CEO*
Strawn Steele, *CFO*
Isaac Asante, *Research*
Manuella Santa Cruz, *Nurse*
Ellen Whalen, *Nursing Dir*
EMP: 352
SQ FT: 175,000
SALES: 179.2MM **Privately Held**
SIC: 8062 General medical & surgical hospitals

(P-21852)
TENET HEALTHSYSTEM MEDICAL
13032 Earlham St, Santa Ana (92705-2113)
PHONE..................714 966-8191
Tim Smith, *CEO*
EMP: 1500
SALES (corp-wide): 19.3B **Publicly Held**
WEB: www.tenenthealth.com
SIC: 8062 General medical & surgical hospitals

HQ: Tenet Healthsystem Medical, Inc.
1445 Ross Ave Ste 1400
Dallas TX 75202
469 893-2000

(P-21853)
TENET HEALTHSYSTEM MEDICAL
16331 Arthur St, Cerritos (90703-2128)
PHONE..................562 531-2550
John R Nickens, *Principal*
EMP: 509
SALES (corp-wide): 19.3B **Publicly Held**
WEB: www.tenenthealth.com
SIC: 8062 8011 General medical & surgical hospitals; offices & clinics of medical doctors
HQ: Tenet Healthsystem Medical, Inc.
1445 Ross Ave Ste 1400
Dallas TX 75202
469 893-2000

(P-21854)
TENET HEALTHSYSTEM MEDICAL
Also Called: Tenet Health System Hospital
1205 E North St, Manteca (95336-4932)
PHONE..................209 823-3111
Brenden Panzarello, *Branch Mgr*
Debra Garcia, *Records Dir*
Melissa Dejohn, *Officer*
Shawn Collins, *Recruiter*
Brittany Bellmer, *Pharmacist*
EMP: 474
SALES (corp-wide): 19.3B **Publicly Held**
SIC: 8062 General medical & surgical hospitals
HQ: Tenet Healthsystem Medical, Inc.
1445 Ross Ave Ste 1400
Dallas TX 75202
469 893-2000

(P-21855)
TENET HEALTHSYSTEM MEDICAL
Also Called: Irvine Regional Hospital
1400 S Duglaca Rd Ste 250, Anaheim (92806)
PHONE..................714 428-6800
Donald Lorack, *CEO*
EMP: 509
SALES (corp-wide): 19.3B **Publicly Held**
WEB: www.tenethealth.com
SIC: 8062 General medical & surgical hospitals
HQ: Tenet Healthsystem Medical, Inc.
1445 Ross Ave Ste 1400
Dallas TX 75202
469 893-2000

(P-21856)
TENET HEALTHSYSTEM MEDICAL
Cnty HSP/Rhb Ctr/Ls GTS-Srtg
815 Pollard Rd, Los Gatos (95032-1438)
PHONE..................408 378-6131
Toll Free:..................888 -
Gary Honts, *CEO*
EMP: 750
SALES (corp-wide): 19.3B **Publicly Held**
WEB: www.tenenthealth.com
SIC: 8062 8011 General medical & surgical hospitals; offices & clinics of medical doctors
HQ: Tenet Healthsystem Medical, Inc.
1445 Ross Ave Ste 1400
Dallas TX 75202
469 893-2000

(P-21857)
THOUSAND OAKS SURGICAL HOSP LP
401 Rolling Oaks Dr, Thousand Oaks (91361-1050)
PHONE..................805 777-7750
Micheal Bass, *Partner*
Marissa Mc Arthur, *Exec Sec*
EMP: 100
SQ FT: 50,000
SALES (est): 13.9MM **Privately Held**
WEB: www.toshospital.com
SIC: 8062 General medical & surgical hospitals

▲ = Import ▼=Export
◆ =Import/Export

(P-21858)

TORRANCE HEALTH ASSN INC (PA)

Also Called: Torrance Memorial Medical Ctr
3330 Lomita Blvd, Torrance (90505-5002)
P.O. Box 13717 (90503-0717)
PHONE..................................310 325-9110
Craig Leach, *CEO*
Bill Larson, *CFO*
Sally Eberhard, *Senior VP*
John McNamara, *Senior VP*
Bernadette Reid, *Vice Pres*
EMP: 3000
SQ FT: 180,000
SALES: 138.2MM **Privately Held**
SIC: 8062 General medical & surgical hospitals

(P-21859)

TORRANCE MEMORIAL MEDICAL CTR (HQ)

Also Called: PHYSICIAN OFFICE SUPPORT SERVI
3330 Lomita Blvd, Torrance (90505-5002)
P.O. Box 13717 (90503-0717)
PHONE..................................310 325-9110
Craig Leach, *President*
John McNamara, *Vice Pres*
Eric Milefchik, *Infectious Dis*
Behzad Noorian, *Infectious Dis*
Mark V Ancheta, *Anesthesiology*
EMP: 1500
SALES: 164.8MM
SALES (corp-wide): 138.2MM **Privately Held**
WEB: www.torrancememorial.org
SIC: 8062 Hospital, affiliated with AMA residency
PA: Torrance Health Association, Inc.
　　3330 Lomita Blvd
　　Torrance CA 90505
　　310 325-9110

(P-21860)

TRACY SUTTER COMMUNITY HOSP

1420 N Tracy Blvd, Tracy (95376-3451)
PHONE..................................209 835-1500
David Thompson, *President*
Traci Robles, *Admin Sec*
Eric Dalton, *Administration*
Karen Geyer, *Technology*
Jenny Ford, *Purch Mgr*
▲ **EMP:** 400
SQ FT: 80,000
SALES (est): 54.9MM
SALES (corp-wide): 12.4B **Privately Held**
WEB: www.suttertracy.org
SIC: 8062 8051 8011 General medical & surgical hospitals; skilled nursing care facilities; offices & clinics of medical doctors
PA: Sutter Health
　　2200 River Plaza Dr
　　Sacramento CA 95833
　　916 733-8800

(P-21861)

TRI-CITY HOSPITAL DISTRICT (PA)

Also Called: Tri-City Medical Center
4002 Vista Way, Oceanside (92056-4506)
PHONE..................................760 724-8411
Larry Schallock, *Chairman*
Casey Fatch, *CEO*
Robert Wardwell, *CFO*
Rosemarie V Reno, *Treasurer*
David Bennett, *Chief Mktg Ofcr*
EMP: 2100
SQ FT: 50,000
SALES: 319.2MM **Privately Held**
WEB: www.tcmccareers.com
SIC: 8062 General medical & surgical hospitals

(P-21862)

TULARE LOCAL HEALTH CARE DST

Also Called: Tulare Home Care
869 N Cherry St, Tulare (93274-2207)
PHONE..................................559 685-3462
Shawn Bolouki, *CEO*
Filomina Santos, *Records Dir*
Sherrie Bell, *President*
Fred Capozello, *CFO*
Steven Debuskey, *Vice Pres*

EMP: 700
SQ FT: 140,000
SALES (est): 79.4MM **Privately Held**
SIC: 8062 General medical & surgical hospitals

(P-21863)

U C MED HUMN RSRCES APLCAT SVC

Also Called: U C Health Systems
2730 Stockton Blvd # 21002500, Sacramento (95817-2217)
PHONE..................................916 734-5916
Gloria Alvardo, *Director*
John Gubbels, *Manager*
EMP: 75
SALES (est): 1.8MM **Privately Held**
SIC: 8062 General medical & surgical hospitals

(P-21864)

UCLA HEALTHCARE

1821 Wilshire Blvd Fl 6, Santa Monica (90403-5618)
PHONE..................................310 319-4560
Tami Dennis, *Exec Dir*
EMP: 77
SALES (est): 150.4K **Privately Held**
SIC: 8062 9411 General medical & surgical hospitals; administration of educational programs;
HQ: University Of California, Los Angeles
　　405 Hilgard Ave
　　Los Angeles CA 90095

(P-21865)

UHS-CORONA INC (HQ)

Also Called: Corona Regional Med Ctr Hosp
800 S Main St, Corona (92882-3420)
PHONE..................................951 737-4343
Marvin Pember, *CEO*
Alan B Miller, *President*
Ken Rivers, *CEO*
Kevan Metcalf, *Principal*
Teresa Lindsey, *Sales Mgr*
▲ **EMP:** 900
SALES: 169.5MM
SALES (corp-wide): 10.4B **Publicly Held**
SIC: 8062 General medical & surgical hospitals
PA: Universal Health Services, Inc.
　　367 S Gulph Rd
　　King Of Prussia PA 19406
　　610 768-3300

(P-21866)

UKIAH ADVENTIST HOSPITAL (HQ)

Also Called: Ukiah Valley Medical Center
275 Hospital Dr, Ukiah (95482-4531)
PHONE..................................707 462-3111
Terry Burns, *President*
David Debooy,
Rod Granger, *CFO*
Jeremy Mann, *Bd of Directors*
Debra McEntee, *Network Engnr*
EMP: 500 **EST:** 1967
SQ FT: 50,000
SALES: 148MM
SALES (corp-wide): 4.1B **Privately Held**
SIC: 8062 General medical & surgical hospitals
PA: Adventist Health System/West
　　2100 Douglas Blvd
　　Roseville CA 95661
　　916 781-2000

(P-21867)

UKIAH ADVENTIST HOSPITAL

1120 S Dora St, Ukiah (95482-6340)
PHONE..................................707 462-3111
Val Gene Devitt, *Branch Mgr*
EMP: 150
SQ FT: 43,500
SALES (corp-wide): 4.1B **Privately Held**
SIC: 8062 General medical & surgical hospitals
HQ: Ukiah Adventist Hospital
　　275 Hospital Dr
　　Ukiah CA 95482
　　707 462-3111

(P-21868)

UNITED STATES DEPT OF NAVY

Also Called: Navy Hospital
937 Vista Pl, Lemoore (93245)
PHONE..................................559 998-4201
Clinton Butler, *Exec Dir*
D V Nostrand, *Director*
EMP: 711 **Publicly Held**
SIC: 8062 9711 General medical & surgical hospitals; Navy;
HQ: United States Department Of The Navy
　　1200 Navy Pentagon
　　Washington DC 20350

(P-21869)

UNITED STATES DEPT OF NAVY

Also Called: Naval Hospital Lemoore
Bldg 937 Franklin Ave, Lemoore (93246-0001)
PHONE..................................559 998-4481
Stephen Mandia, *Director*
Joshua Brawner, *Technician*
EMP: 600 **Publicly Held**
SIC: 8062 9711 General medical & surgical hospitals; Navy;
HQ: United States Department Of The Navy
　　1200 Navy Pentagon
　　Washington DC 20350

(P-21870)

UNITED STATES DEPT OF NAVY

Also Called: Naval Medical Center
34800 Bob Wilson Dr, San Diego (92134-1098)
PHONE..................................619 532-6400
Esther Lynn, *Branch Mgr*
Michael Vasquez, *Administration*
Ronald Miller, *Info Tech Mgr*
Joseph Carney, *Orthopedist*
J Williams Sparks, *Anesthesiology*
EMP: 4250 **Publicly Held**
SIC: 8062 9711 General medical & surgical hospitals; Navy;
HQ: United States Department Of The Navy
　　1200 Navy Pentagon
　　Washington DC 20350

(P-21871)

UNITED STATES DEPT OF NAVY

Us Naval Hosp Bldg 1145, Twentynine Palms (92278)
PHONE..................................760 830-2190
Mark Bowman,
EMP: 500 **Publicly Held**
SIC: 8062 9711 General medical & surgical hospitals; Navy;
HQ: United States Department Of The Navy
　　1200 Navy Pentagon
　　Washington DC 20350

(P-21872)

UNITED STATES DEPT OF NAVY

Also Called: Daps Naval Hosp
937 Franklin Blvd, Lemoore (93246-4700)
PHONE..................................559 998-2894
Maryalice Morro, *Principal*
EMP: 400 **Publicly Held**
SIC: 8062 General medical & surgical hospitals
HQ: United States Department Of The Navy
　　1200 Navy Pentagon
　　Washington DC 20350

(P-21873)

UNIVERS OF CALIF SAN DIEGO HS

200 W Arbor Dr 8201, San Diego (92103-1911)
PHONE..................................619 543-3713
Tom McAsee, *Principal*
Margarita Baggett, *CEO*
Duncan Campbell, *COO*
Angela Sciao, *Chief Mktg Ofcr*
EMP: 3281
SALES (est): 121.4MM **Privately Held**
SIC: 8062 General medical & surgical hospitals

(P-21874)

UNIVERSITY CAL LOS ANGELES

Also Called: Ucla Medical Center
200 Ucla Medical Plz, Los Angeles (90095-8344)
PHONE..................................310 825-0640
Evelyn Cederbaum, *Branch Mgr*
EMP: 2056 **Privately Held**
WEB: www.ucla.edu
SIC: 8062 8221 9411 General medical & surgical hospitals; university; administration of educational programs;
HQ: University Of California, Los Angeles
　　405 Hilgard Ave
　　Los Angeles CA 90095

(P-21875)

UNIVERSITY CAL LOS ANGELES

Also Called: Ucla Medical Center
14445 Olive View Dr, Sylmar (91342-1437)
PHONE..................................818 364-1555
Dr Dennis Cope, *Branch Mgr*
EMP: 3000 **Privately Held**
WEB: www.ucla.edu
SIC: 8062 8221 9411 General medical & surgical hospitals; university; administration of educational programs;
HQ: University Of California, Los Angeles
　　405 Hilgard Ave
　　Los Angeles CA 90095

(P-21876)

UNIVERSITY CAL LOS ANGELES

Also Called: Santa Monica Ucla Medical Ctr
1225 15th St, Santa Monica (90404-1101)
PHONE..................................310 319-4000
Susan Colley, *Principal*
EMP: 1111
SQ FT: 7,350 **Privately Held**
WEB: www.ucla.edu
SIC: 8062 8221 9411 General medical & surgical hospitals; university; administration of educational programs;
HQ: University Of California, Los Angeles
　　405 Hilgard Ave
　　Los Angeles CA 90095

(P-21877)

UNIVERSITY CAL LOS ANGELES

Also Called: Ronald Reagan Ucla Medical Ctr
757 Westwood Plz, Los Angeles (90095-8358)
PHONE..................................310 825-9111
Tatiana Orloff, *Branch Mgr*
Mohammed Mahbouba, *Officer*
Andrew Cink, *Network Engnr*
Gary Satou, *Cardiology*
Gale Henke, *Director*
EMP: 2056 **Privately Held**
SIC: 8062 8221 9411 General medical & surgical hospitals; university; administration of educational programs;
HQ: University Of California, Los Angeles
　　405 Hilgard Ave
　　Los Angeles CA 90095

(P-21878)

UNIVERSITY CAL SAN DIEGO

Also Called: Medical Center
200 W Arbor Dr Frnt, San Diego (92103-9000)
PHONE..................................619 543-6654
Richard Likeweg, *Manager*
Jennifer Atkins, *Officer*
Julie Thomas, *Program Mgr*
Sophia Davidson, *Admin Asst*
Jennifer Hickman, *Admin Asst*
EMP: 4000 **Privately Held**
WEB: www.medicine.ucsd.edu
SIC: 8062 8221 9411 General medical & surgical hospitals; university; administration of educational programs;
HQ: University Of California, San Diego
　　9500 Gilman Dr
　　La Jolla CA 92093
　　858 534-2230

(P-21879)
UNIVERSITY CAL SAN DIEGO
Also Called: Ucsd Thornton Hospital
9300 Campus Point Dr, La Jolla
(92037-1300)
PHONE....................858 657-7000
Paul Hensler, *Director*
Gary Hagney, *Pharmacy Dir*
Evelyn Tecoma, *Neurology*
Mary Hackim, *Director*
EMP: 500 **Privately Held**
WEB: www.medicine.ucsd.edu
SIC: 8062 8221 9411 General medical &
surgical hospitals; university; administra-
tion of educational programs;
HQ: University Of California, San Diego
9500 Gilman Dr
La Jolla CA 92093
858 534-2230

(P-21880)
UNIVERSITY CAL SAN FRANCISCO
Ucsf Langley Porter
401 Parnassus Ave, San Francisco
(94143-2211)
PHONE....................415 476-7000
Craig Van Dyke, *Manager*
Tim Greer, *Info Tech Mgr*
Ann Saggio, *Data Proc Staff*
Mark D Eisner, *Med Doctor*
Descartes LI, *Med Doctor*
EMP: 1000 **Privately Held**
WEB: www.uchastings.edu
SIC: 8062 8221 9411 General medical &
surgical hospitals; university; administra-
tion of educational programs;
HQ: University Cal San Francisco
500 Parnassus Ave
San Francisco CA 94143

(P-21881)
UNIVERSITY CAL SAN FRANCISCO
Also Called: Department of Urology
400 Parnassus Ave A633, San Francisco
(94143-2202)
P.O. Box 738 (94104-0738)
PHONE....................415 476-1611
Christine McDevitt, *Manager*
Yam Srey, *Analyst*
Cynthia Lee, *Teacher*
EMP: 50 **Privately Held**
WEB: www.uchastings.edu
SIC: 8062 8221 9411 General medical &
surgical hospitals; university; administra-
tion of educational programs;
HQ: University Cal San Francisco
500 Parnassus Ave
San Francisco CA 94143

(P-21882)
UNIVERSITY CAL SAN FRANCISCO
Also Called: Ucsf Medical Center At Mt Zion
1600 Divisadero St, San Francisco
(94143-3010)
PHONE....................415 567-6600
Mark Laret, *Manager*
Laurel Bray-Hanin, *Executive*
Cynthia Hammond, *Radiology Dir*
Stig Kreps, *Program Mgr*
Edmon Obiniana, *Office Mgr*
EMP: 360 **Privately Held**
WEB: www.uchastings.edu
SIC: 8062 8221 9411 General medical &
surgical hospitals; university;
HQ: University Cal San Francisco
500 Parnassus Ave
San Francisco CA 94143

(P-21883)
UNIVERSITY CALIFORNIA DAVIS
Also Called: Medical Centre
4400 V St, Sacramento (95817-1445)
PHONE....................916 734-3141
Dr William Ellis, *Principal*
Claudia Greco, *Pathologist*
EMP: 3575 **Privately Held**
WEB: www.ucdavis.edu

SIC: 8062 8221 9411 General medical &
surgical hospitals; university; administration of educational programs;
HQ: University Of California, Davis
1 Shields Ave
Davis CA 95616

(P-21884)
UNIVERSITY CALIFORNIA DAVIS
Also Called: Uc Davis Medical Center
2450 48th St Ste 2401, Sacramento
(95817-1538)
PHONE....................916 734-2011
Mauda Butte, *Principal*
Madeleine Silva, *Project Mgr*
Bryan Green, *Director*
EMP: 3575 **Privately Held**
SIC: 8062 8221 9411 General medical &
surgical hospitals; university; administra-
tion of educational programs;
HQ: University Of California, Davis
1 Shields Ave
Davis CA 95616

(P-21885)
UNIVERSITY CALIFORNIA DAVIS
Also Called: Department of Ane
4150 V St Ste 1200, Sacramento
(95817-1460)
PHONE....................916 734-5113
Karen Anderson, *Manager*
Cynthia Adedipe, *Executive*
Pia Anette Hof, *Anesthesiology*
EMP: 3575 **Privately Held**
SIC: 8062 8221 9411 General medical &
surgical hospitals; university; administra-
tion of educational programs;
HQ: University Of California, Davis
1 Shields Ave
Davis CA 95616

(P-21886)
UNIVERSITY CALIFORNIA IRVINE
Also Called: Uc Irvine Medical Center
101 The City Dr S, Orange (92868-3201)
PHONE....................714 456-6011
Mary Piccione, *Exec Dir*
Janet Shigei, *Admin Dir*
Jesus Lopez, *Department Mgr*
Thomas Wen, *Administration*
Kim Ritorto, *Network Enginr*
EMP: 3000 **Privately Held**
WEB: www.com.uci.edu
SIC: 8062 8221 9411 General medical &
surgical hospitals; university;
HQ: University Of California, Irvine
510 Aldrich Hall
Irvine CA 92697
949 824-8343

(P-21887)
UNIVERSITY CALIFORNIA IRVINE
Also Called: Irvine Medical Center
200 S Manchester Ave # 400, Orange
(92868-3220)
PHONE....................714 456-5558
Joy Grosse, *Director*
EMP: 4000 **Privately Held**
WEB: www.com.uci.edu
SIC: 8062 8221 9411 General medical &
surgical hospitals; university; administra-
tion of educational programs;
HQ: University Of California, Irvine
510 Aldrich Hall
Irvine CA 92697
949 824-8343

(P-21888)
UNIVERSITY SOUTHERN CALIFORNIA
Also Called: Usc University Hospital
1500 San Pablo St, Los Angeles
(90033-5313)
PHONE....................323 442-8500
Paul Vivano, *Director*
Shawn Sheffield, *Officer*
Jay Santa Ana, *Lab Dir*
Melinda Mendoza, *Executive Asst*

Alejandro Sanchez, *Administration*
EMP: 875
SALES (corp-wide): 2.6B **Privately Held**
WEB: www.tenenthealth.com
SIC: 8062 8011 General medical & surgi-
cal hospitals; offices & clinics of medical
doctors
PA: University Of Southern California
3720 S Flower St Fl 3
Los Angeles CA 90089
213 740-7762

(P-21889)
US DEPT OF THE AIR FORCE
Also Called: 9th Medical Group
15301 Warren Shingle Rd, Marysville
(95903-1907)
PHONE....................530 634-4839
Melvin Antonio, *Branch Mgr*
EMP: 400 **Publicly Held**
WEB: www.af.mil
SIC: 8062 9711 General medical & surgi-
cal hospitals; Air Force;
HQ: United States Department Of The Air
Force
1000 Air Force Pentagon
Washington DC 20330

(P-21890)
USC CARE MEDICAL GROUP INC
Also Called: Cardiology Department
1510 San Pablo St Ste 649, Los Angeles
(90033-5404)
PHONE....................323 442-5100
Varma Rohit, *President*
Vivian MO, *CEO*
Angel Padilla, *Office Mgr*
Glenn Ehresmann, *Rheumtlgy Spec*
EMP: 80 EST: 1995
SALES (est): 7.8MM **Privately Held**
SIC: 8062 Hospital, medical school affili-
ated with nursing & residency

(P-21891)
USC VERDUGO HILLS HOSPITAL LLC
1812 Verdugo Blvd, Glendale
(91208-1407)
PHONE....................818 790-7100
Paul Craig, *CEO*
Hack Lash, *CFO*
Tracy Valenzuela, *Program Mgr*
Andrew Brown, *Buyer*
Chandnish Ahluwalia, *Pathologist*
EMP: 750
SQ FT: 45,000
SALES (est): 57.7MM
SALES (corp-wide): 2.6B **Privately Held**
SIC: 8062 Hospital, affiliated with AMA res-
idency
PA: University Of Southern California
3720 S Flower St Fl 3
Los Angeles CA 90089
213 740-7762

(P-21892)
USC VRDUGO HLLS HOSP FUNDATION (PA)
1812 Verdugo Blvd, Glendale
(91208-1407)
PHONE....................800 872-2273
Armand Dorian, *Principal*
Debbie L Walsh, *President*
Paul Craig, *CEO*
Donna Tasker, *Admin Sec*
John Blaha, *Technology*
EMP: 446
SQ FT: 225,000
SALES (est): 67.6MM **Privately Held**
SIC: 8062 General medical & surgical hos-
pitals

(P-21893)
VALLEY CHILDRENS HOSPITAL
Also Called: Charlie Mitchell Chld Clinic
9300 Valley Childrens Pl, Madera
(93636-8762)
PHONE....................559 353-6425
Annette Humphrys, *Manager*
Danny Davis, *Exec Dir*
Jeffrey Lefors, *Exec Dir*
Mike Gengozian, *Info Tech Dir*
Sandra Blaylock, *Info Tech Mgr*
EMP: 226

SALES (corp-wide): 518.1MM **Privately Held**
SIC: 8062 General medical & surgical hospitals
PA: Valley Children's Hospital
9300 Valley Childrens Pl
Madera CA 93636
559 353-3000

(P-21894)
VALLEY CHILDRENS HOSPITAL (PA)
9300 Valley Childrens Pl, Madera
(93636-8762)
PHONE....................559 353-3000
Todd Sunterapak, *President*
Timothy Hansen,
Jessie Hudgins, *COO*
Michele Waldrin, *CFO*
David Krause, *Bd of Directors*
EMP: 1500 EST: 1949
SQ FT: 300,000
SALES (est): 518.1MM **Privately Held**
SIC: 8062 General medical & surgical hos-
pitals

(P-21895)
VALLEY HOSPITAL MEDICAL CENTER (HQ)
Also Called: CALEX
18300 Roscoe Blvd, Northridge
(91325-4105)
PHONE....................818 885-8500
Patrick Hawthorne, *President*
Stephen Farnum,
Nana N Deeb, *Radiology Dir*
Pam Alfenito, *Admin Sec*
Ed Lopez, *CTO*
EMP: 400
SQ FT: 300,000
SALES: 403.2MM
SALES (corp-wide): 6.7B **Privately Held**
WEB: www.northridgemg.com
SIC: 8062 General medical & surgical hos-
pitals
PA: Dignity Health
185 Berry St Ste 300
San Francisco CA 94107
415 438-5500

(P-21896)
VALLEY PRESBYTERIAN HOSPITAL
Also Called: V P H
15107 Vanowen St, Van Nuys
(91405-4597)
PHONE....................818 782-6600
Gustavo Valdespino, *CEO*
Janice Klostermeier, *CFO*
Bill Wilson, *CFO*
Jose Claudio, *Officer*
Clyde Wesp, *Officer*
EMP: 1600
SQ FT: 400,000
SALES: 319.5MM **Privately Held**
SIC: 8062 General medical & surgical hos-
pitals

(P-21897)
VERITAS HEALTH SERVICES INC
Also Called: CHINO VALLEY MEDICAL CEN-
TER
5451 Walnut Ave, Chino (91710-2609)
PHONE....................909 464-8600
Prem Reddy, *CEO*
Irv E Edwards, *President*
Nicholas Valadez, *Buyer*
David J Gonzales, *Family Practiti*
Jacob Jensen, *Podiatrist*
EMP: 600 EST: 2000
SALES: 95.3MM
SALES (corp-wide): 3.4B **Privately Held**
WEB: www.cvmc.com
SIC: 8062 General medical & surgical hos-
pitals
HQ: Prime Healthcare Services Inc
3300 E Guasti Rd Ste 300
Ontario CA 91761

(P-21898)
VERITY HEALTH SYSTEM CAL INC
Also Called: St Francis Medical Center
203 Redwood Shores Pkwy, Redwood City
(94065-1198)
PHONE..................................310 900-8900
Fax: 626 744-3686
EMP: 300
SALES (corp-wide): 225.4MM **Privately Held**
SIC: 8062
PA: Verity Health System Of California, Inc.
2040 E Mariposa Ave
El Segundo CA 90245
650 551-6650

(P-21899)
VERITY HEALTH SYSTEM CAL INC
Also Called: Paryroll Department
203 Redwood Shores Pkwy # 700, Redwood City (94065-1198)
PHONE..................................650 551-6507
EMP: 200
SALES (corp-wide): 225.4MM **Privately Held**
SIC: 8062 8721
PA: Verity Health System Of California, Inc.
2040 E Mariposa Ave
El Segundo CA 90245
650 551-6650

(P-21900)
VERITY HEALTH SYSTEM CAL INC
Also Called: St. Louise Regional Hospital
9400 N Name Uno, Gilroy (95020-3528)
PHONE..................................408 848-2000
David Carl, Ch Pathology
Alma Vandenraadt, Software Dev
Patty S See-Bald, Nurse
EMP: 87
SALES (corp-wide): 1.2B **Privately Held**
SIC: 8062 General medical & surgical hospitals
PA: Verity Health System Of California, Inc.
2040 E Mariposa Ave
El Segundo CA 90245
650 551-6650

(P-21901)
VERITY HEALTH SYSTEM CAL INC
3680 E Imperial Hwy # 306, Lynwood
(90262-2659)
PHONE..................................310 900-2000
EMP: 100
SALES (corp-wide): 225.4MM **Privately Held**
SIC: 8062
PA: Verity Health System Of California, Inc.
2040 E Mariposa Ave
El Segundo CA 90245
650 551-6650

(P-21902)
VERITY HEALTH SYSTEM CAL INC
Also Called: St. Francis Medical Center
3630 E Imperial Hwy, Lynwood
(90262-2609)
PHONE..................................310 900-8900
Gerald Kozai, Manager
Kim Deese, Ch Nursing Ofcr
Kelly Eckhardt, Human Resources
Catherine Naiman, Director
Diane Premeau, Director
EMP: 760
SALES (corp-wide): 1.2B **Privately Held**
SIC: 8062 8011 General medical & surgical hospitals; medical centers
PA: Verity Health System Of California, Inc.
2040 E Mariposa Ave
El Segundo CA 90245
650 551-6650

(P-21903)
VETERANS HEALTH ADMINISTRATION
Also Called: VA Hospital
2615 E Clinton Ave, Fresno (93703-2223)
PHONE..................................559 225-6100
Rhonda Aday, CFO

EMP: 961 **Publicly Held**
SIC: 8062 9451 General medical & surgical hospitals;
HQ: Veterans Health Administration
810 Vermont Ave Nw
Washington DC 20420

(P-21904)
VIBRA HEALTHCARE LLC
1315 Shaw Ave Ste 102, Clovis
(93612-3963)
PHONE..................................559 325-5601
Scott Mooneyham, Branch Mgr
EMP: 71
SALES (corp-wide): 323.5MM **Privately Held**
SIC: 8062 General medical & surgical hospitals
PA: Vibra Healthcare, Llc
4600 Lena Dr Ste 100
Mechanicsburg PA 17055
717 591-5700

(P-21905)
VIBRA HEALTHCARE LLC
Also Called: Vibra Hospital Northern Cal
2801 Eureka Way, Redding (96001-0222)
PHONE..................................530 246-9000
Ross Domke, Business Dir
Amber Howell, Director
EMP: 95
SALES (corp-wide): 323.5MM **Privately Held**
SIC: 8062 General medical & surgical hospitals
PA: Vibra Healthcare, Llc
4600 Lena Dr Ste 100
Mechanicsburg PA 17055
717 591-5700

(P-21906)
VIBRA HEALTHCARE LLC
7173 N Sharon Ave, Fresno (93720-3329)
PHONE..................................559 436-3600
Mary Jacobson, Principal
EMP: 71
SALES (corp-wide): 323.5MM **Privately Held**
SIC: 8062 General medical & surgical hospitals
PA: Vibra Healthcare, Llc
4600 Lena Dr Ste 100
Mechanicsburg PA 17055
717 591-5700

(P-21907)
VIBRA HEALTHCARE LLC
Also Called: Vibra Hospital of San Diego
555 Washington St, San Diego
(92103-2289)
PHONE..................................619 260-8300
Meeta Jones, CEO
EMP: 141
SALES (corp-wide): 323.5MM **Privately Held**
WEB: www.vibrahealthcare.com
SIC: 8062 8069 8322 General medical & surgical hospitals; specialty hospitals, except psychiatric; rehabilitation services
PA: Vibra Healthcare, Llc
4600 Lena Dr Ste 100
Mechanicsburg PA 17055
717 591-5700

(P-21908)
VIBRA HOSP SAN BERNARDINO LLC
Also Called: Ballard Rehabilitation Hosp
1760 W 16th St, San Bernardino
(92411-1160)
PHONE..................................909 473-1233
Brad Hollinger, Mng Member
Stacey Hedrick, Partner
EMP: 185
SQ FT: 55,000
SALES: 22MM **Privately Held**
SIC: 8062 General medical & surgical hospitals

(P-21909)
VIBRA HOSPITAL SACRAMENTO LLC
330 Montrose Dr, Folsom (95630-2720)
PHONE..................................916 351-9151
Janet Biedrone, CEO

Brad E Hollinger, Mng Member
EMP: 246
SQ FT: 22,000
SALES (est): 16.7MM
SALES (corp-wide): 323.5MM **Privately Held**
SIC: 8062 General medical & surgical hospitals
PA: Vibra Healthcare, Llc
4600 Lena Dr Ste 100
Mechanicsburg PA 17055
717 591-5700

(P-21910)
VIBRA HOSPITAL SAN DIEGO LLC
555 Washington St, San Diego
(92103-2289)
PHONE..................................619 260-8300
Martha Heubach, CEO
Joe Leppert, Officer
Brian Deitz, Pharmacy Dir
Leath Smith, Engineer
Tania Khalique, Human Res Dir
EMP: 57
SALES (est): 9.7MM **Privately Held**
SIC: 8062 General medical & surgical hospitals

(P-21911)
VISTA SPECIALTY HOSP CAL LP
Also Called: Vista Hospital San Gabriel Vly
14148 Francisquito Ave, Baldwin Park
(91706-6120)
PHONE..................................626 388-2700
Marc C Ferrell, Partner
Rick Rezkalla, Director
EMP: 200
SQ FT: 44,400
SALES (est): 8.6MM **Privately Held**
WEB: www.vistahealthcare.net
SIC: 8062 General medical & surgical hospitals

(P-21912)
WASHINGTON OUTPATIENT
Also Called: Washington Otpent Surgery Ctr
2299 Mowry Ave Fl 1, Fremont
(94538-1621)
PHONE..................................510 791-5374
Gary Charland, Partner
Martha Garcia, Accounting Mgr
Kimberly Hartz,
Neil Marks,
David A Larson, Director
EMP: 97
SQ FT: 18,000
SALES (est): 13.9MM **Privately Held**
WEB: www.washosc.com
SIC: 8062 General medical & surgical hospitals

(P-21913)
WASHINGTON TOWNSHIP
2000 Mowry Ave, Fremont (94538-1716)
PHONE..................................510 797-3342
Nancy Farber, CEO
Diane Watters, Records Dir
Chris Henry, CFO
Cathy Messman, Treasurer
John Engers, Officer
EMP: 1600
SQ FT: 250,000
SALES: 507MM **Privately Held**
SIC: 8062 General medical & surgical hospitals

(P-21914)
WEST SIDE DISTRICT HOSPITAL
Also Called: Skilled Nursing Facility
110 E North St, Taft (93268-3606)
PHONE..................................805 763-4211
Morgan Clayton, Ch of Bd
John Ruffner, Administration
EMP: 155
SQ FT: 30,000
SALES (est): 6.4MM **Privately Held**
WEB: www.chw.com
SIC: 8062 8051 8011 General medical & surgical hospitals; skilled nursing care facilities; offices & clinics of medical doctors

(P-21915)
WESTERN MEDICAL CENTER AUX (HQ)
Also Called: Western Med Center-Santa Ana
1301 N Tustin Ave, Santa Ana
(92705-8619)
PHONE..................................714 835-3555
Dan Brothman, CEO
Patricia Stites, CEO
EMP: 200
SALES (est): 122.9MM
SALES (corp-wide): 440.5MM **Privately Held**
WEB: www.westernmedanaheim.com
SIC: 8062 General medical & surgical hospitals
PA: Kpc Healthcare, Inc.
1301 N Tustin Ave
Santa Ana CA 92705
714 953-3652

(P-21916)
WHITE MEMORIAL MEDICAL CENTER (HQ)
Also Called: Cecilla Gonzalez De Al Hoya CA
1720 E Cesar E Chavez Ave, Los Angeles
(90033-2414)
PHONE..................................323 268-5000
Beth D Zachary, CEO
Mark J Newmyer, President
John G Raffoul, CEO
Terri Day, CFO
Mara C Bryant, Vice Pres
EMP: 1200 EST: 1913
SQ FT: 454,000
SALES: 465.6MM
SALES (corp-wide): 4.1B **Privately Held**
WEB: www.whitememorial.com
SIC: 8062 General medical & surgical hospitals
PA: Adventist Health System/West
2100 Douglas Blvd
Roseville CA 95661
916 781-2000

(P-21917)
WHITTIER HOSPITAL MED CTR INC
9080 Colima Rd, Whittier (90605-1600)
PHONE..................................562 945-3561
Richard Castro, CEO
Priscilla Baah, Internal Med
Jay Geldhof, Director
EMP: 180
SQ FT: 144,000
SALES (est): 33.5MM
SALES (corp-wide): 572.3MM **Privately Held**
SIC: 8062 General medical & surgical hospitals
PA: Ahmc Healthcare Inc.
1000 S Fremont Ave Unit 6
Alhambra CA 91803
626 943-7526

(P-21918)
WILLITS HOSPITAL INC
Also Called: Howard Frank R Memorial Hosp
1 Marcela Dr, Willits (95490-5769)
PHONE..................................707 459-6801
Rich Bockmann, CEO
Diane Moratti, Records Dir
Carlton Jacobsen, CFO
Karen Scott, Vice Pres
Karen Scott Vpres, Vice Pres
EMP: 283
SQ FT: 27,000
SALES: 63.3MM **Privately Held**
WEB: www.howardhospital.com
SIC: 8062 General medical & surgical hospitals

(P-21919)
WOODLAND HEALTHCARE
2660 W Covell Blvd, Davis (95616-5645)
PHONE..................................530 756-2364
Kevin Mould, Branch Mgr
Philip M Laughlin MD, Med Doctor
Kevin S Mould MD, Med Doctor
EMP: 63
SALES (corp-wide): 6.7B **Privately Held**
SIC: 8062 8011 General medical & surgical hospitals; offices & clinics of medical doctors

PRODUCTS & SVCS

HQ: Woodland Healthcare
1325 Cottonwood St
Woodland CA 95695
530 662-3961

(P-21920)
WOODLAND HEALTHCARE
1207 Fairchild Ct, Woodland (95695-4321)
PHONE..................530 668-2600
Bill Hunt, *Principal*
Tara Newhall, *Clerk*
EMP: 150
SALES (corp-wide): 6.7B **Privately Held**
WEB: www.woodlandhealthcare.com
SIC: 8062 8011 General medical & surgical hospitals; offices & clinics of medical doctors
HQ: Woodland Healthcare
1325 Cottonwood St
Woodland CA 95695
530 662-3961

8063 Psychiatric Hospitals

(P-21921)
7TH AVENUE CENTER LLC
1171 7th Ave, Santa Cruz (95062-2714)
PHONE..................831 476-1700
Ann Butler,
Tami Toop, *Office Mgr*
Diana Cornell, *Bookkeeper*
EMP: 92
SALES (est): 4.7MM **Privately Held**
WEB: www.insuranceneighborhood.com
SIC: 8063 8361 8011 Psychiatric hospitals; residential care; offices & clinics of medical doctors

(P-21922)
ALTA HOLLYWOOD COMMUNITY HSPTL
14433 Emelita St, Van Nuys (91401-4213)
PHONE..................818 787-1511
Irving Loube, *President*
Claude Lowen, *Corp Secy*
EMP: 115
SQ FT: 34,192
SALES (est): 4.8MM **Privately Held**
SIC: 8063 Psychiatric hospitals

(P-21923)
AURORA BEHAVIORAL HEALTH
1287 Fulton Rd, Santa Rosa (95401-4923)
PHONE..................707 800-7700
Susan Rose, *CEO*
EMP: 75 EST: 2000
SQ FT: 50,000
SALES (est): 6.2MM
SALES (corp-wide): 5.8B **Publicly Held**
SIC: 8063 Psychiatric hospitals
HQ: Aurora Behavioral Healthcare Llc
4238 Green River Rd
Corona CA 92880
951 549-8032

(P-21924)
AURORA BEHAVIORAL HEALTH CARE
Also Called: MAGELLAN HEALTH
11878 Avenue Of Industry, San Diego (92128-3423)
PHONE..................858 487-3200
Jim Plummer, *CEO*
Jane Jones, *CFO*
Veronica Herrera, *Executive*
Michael Ross, *Business Dir*
Susan Writer, *Human Resources*
EMP: 150
SQ FT: 50,000
SALES: 29MM
SALES (corp-wide): 5.8B **Publicly Held**
WEB: www.aurorabehavioral.com
SIC: 8063 8069 Psychiatric hospitals; drug addiction rehabilitation hospital
PA: Magellan Health, Inc.
4800 N Scottsdale Rd # 4400
Scottsdale AZ 85251
602 572-6050

(P-21925)
AURORA LAS ENCINAS LLC
Also Called: Aurora Las Encinas Hospital
2900 E Del Mar Blvd, Pasadena (91107-4375)
PHONE..................626 795-9901
James Wilcox,
Brenda Nocon Rn,
EMP: 236
SQ FT: 132,000
SALES (est): 23.5MM **Publicly Held**
WEB: www.lasencinashospital.com
SIC: 8063 8069 Hospital for the mentally ill; alcoholism rehabilitation hospital
HQ: Hca Inc.
1 Park Plz
Nashville TN 37203
615 344-9551

(P-21926)
BAYVIEW HOSPITAL AND MENTAL
330 Moss St, Chula Vista (91911-2005)
PHONE..................619 426-6311
Robert Bourseau, *Principal*
EMP: 250
SALES (est): 16.3MM **Privately Held**
SIC: 8063 Psychiatric hospitals

(P-21927)
BEACON HEALTHCARE SERVICES
Also Called: Newport Bay Hospital
1501 E 16th St, Newport Beach (92663-5924)
PHONE..................949 650-9750
James E Parkhurst, *President*
EMP: 60
SALES: 10.3MM **Privately Held**
WEB: www.newportbayhospital.com
SIC: 8063 Psychiatric hospitals

(P-21928)
BEHAVIORAL H BAKERSFIELD
5201 White Ln, Bakersfield (93309-6200)
PHONE..................661 398-1800
Ganesh Acharya, *CEO*
Amber Smithson, *Mktg Dir*
Sergio Herrera, *Food Svc Dir*
Brian Nelson, *Hlthcr Dir*
EMP: 235
SALES (est): 799.4K **Privately Held**
SIC: 8063 8011 Psychiatric hospitals; medical centers

(P-21929)
BEHAVIORAL HEALTH RESOURCES
Also Called: KNOLLWOOD PSYCHIATRIC CENTER
5900 Brockton Ave, Riverside (92506-1862)
PHONE..................951 275-8400
Robert B Summerour, *President*
Karen Jerotz, *CFO*
EMP: 175
SALES: 7MM **Privately Held**
SIC: 8063 Psychiatric hospitals

(P-21930)
BH-SD OPCO LLC
7050 Parkway Dr, La Mesa (91942-1535)
PHONE..................619 465-4411
Patrick Ziemer, *CEO*
Chad Engbrecht, *CFO*
James Adamson,
EMP: 99 EST: 2014
SALES (est): 1.6MM **Privately Held**
SIC: 8063 Psychiatric hospitals

(P-21931)
CALIFRNIA DEPT STATE HOSPITALS
Also Called: Coalinga State Hospital
24511 W Jayne Ave, Coalinga (93210-9503)
P.O. Box 5000 (93210-5000)
PHONE..................559 935-4300
Tom Voss, *Director*
EMP: 300 **Privately Held**
SIC: 8063 9431 Psychiatric hospitals; mental health agency administration, government;

HQ: California Department Of State Hospitals
1600 9th St Ste 350
Sacramento CA 95814

(P-21932)
CALIFRNIA DEPT STATE HOSPITALS
Also Called: Fairview Developmental Center
2501 Harbor Blvd, Costa Mesa (92626-6143)
PHONE..................714 957-5000
Michael Hatton, *Principal*
EMP: 1500 **Privately Held**
SIC: 8063 9431 Hospital for the mentally ill; mental health agency administration, government;
HQ: California Department Of State Hospitals
1600 9th St Ste 350
Sacramento CA 95814

(P-21933)
CALIFRNIA DEPT STATE HOSPITALS
Also Called: NAPA State Hospital
2100 Napa Vallejo Hwy, NAPA (94558-6234)
PHONE..................707 253-5000
Sidney Herndon, *Branch Mgr*
Carol A Kuchmak, *Med Doctor*
Beverly De Chavez,
Margie Van Dam,
EMP: 2500 **Privately Held**
SIC: 8063 9431 8361 Hospital for the mentally ill; mental health agency administration, government; ; residential care
HQ: California Department Of State Hospitals
1600 9th St Ste 350
Sacramento CA 95814

(P-21934)
CALIFRNIA DEPT STATE HOSPITALS
Also Called: Patton State Hospital
3102 E Highland Ave, Patton (92369-7813)
PHONE..................909 425-7000
Bruce Parks, *Director*
Chinh Pham, *Med Doctor*
EMP: 2000 **Privately Held**
SIC: 8063 9431 Hospital for the mentally ill; mental health agency administration, government;
HQ: California Department Of State Hospitals
1600 9th St Ste 350
Sacramento CA 95814

(P-21935)
CALIFRNIA DEPT STATE HOSPITALS
Also Called: Atascadero State Hospital
10333 El Camino Real, Atascadero (93422-5808)
P.O. Box 7001 (93423-7001)
PHONE..................805 468-2000
John De Morales, *Branch Mgr*
EMP: 1600 **Privately Held**
SIC: 8063 9431 8062 Hospital for the mentally ill; mental health agency administration, government; ; general medical & surgical hospitals
HQ: California Department Of State Hospitals
1600 9th St Ste 350
Sacramento CA 95814

(P-21936)
CALIFRONIA DEPARTMENT OF STATE
10333 El Camino Real, Atascadero (93422-5808)
PHONE..................805 468-2501
Peter Sotello,
Christopher Stuiber, *Partner*
Faith Jewell,
EMP: 1953 EST: 1954
SALES (est): 42.4MM **Privately Held**
SIC: 8063 Psychiatric hospitals

(P-21937)
CANYON RIDGE HOSPITAL INC
Also Called: UHS
5353 G St, Chino (91710-5250)
PHONE..................909 590-3700
Peggy Minnick, *CEO*
George Wilcox, *Manager*
EMP: 150
SALES (est): 19.1MM
SALES (corp-wide): 10.4B **Publicly Held**
WEB: www.intermountainhospital.com
SIC: 8063 8093 Hospital for the mentally ill; mental health clinic, outpatient
HQ: Psychiatric Solutions, Inc.
6640 Carothers Pkwy # 500
Franklin TN 37067
615 312-5700

(P-21938)
CATASYS INC (PA)
11601 Wilshire Blvd # 1100, Los Angeles (90025-1747)
PHONE..................310 444-4300
Terren S Peizer, *Ch of Bd*
Richard A Anderson, *President*
Christopher Shirley, *CFO*
Richard Berman, *Bd of Directors*
Marc Cummins, *Bd of Directors*
EMP: 90
SQ FT: 9,120
SALES: 7.7MM **Publicly Held**
WEB: www.hythiam.com
SIC: 8063 Psychiatric hospitals

(P-21939)
CHARTER BEHAVIORAL HEALTH SYST
Also Called: Charter Oak Hospital
1161 E Covina Blvd, Covina (91724-1523)
PHONE..................626 966-1632
Todd Smith, *CEO*
Janet Ray Perkins, *Officer*
Christine De La Paz, *Human Res Dir*
Martha Rojas, *Food Svc Dir*
Crescent Real Estate Funding L,
EMP: 100
SALES (est): 7.8MM **Privately Held**
SIC: 8063 Psychiatric hospitals

(P-21940)
CHLB LLC
Also Called: College Medical Center
2776 Pacific Ave, Long Beach (90806-2613)
PHONE..................562 997-2000
Joe Avelino, *CEO*
Rod Bell, *CFO*
Roderick Bell, *CFO*
Betty Jackson, *Office Mgr*
Gregory Dixon, *Info Tech Dir*
EMP: 74
SALES (est): 14.1MM **Privately Held**
SIC: 8063 Psychiatric hospitals
PA: College Health Enterprises
11627 Telg Rd Ste 200
Santa Fe Springs CA 90670

(P-21941)
COLLEGE HOSPITAL INC (PA)
Also Called: College Hospital Cerritos
10802 College Pl, Cerritos (90703-1579)
PHONE..................562 924-9581
Stephen A Witt, *President*
Bessie Weiss, *Corp Secy*
EMP: 700
SQ FT: 60,000
SALES: 70.3MM **Privately Held**
WEB: www.collegehospitals.com
SIC: 8063 Hospital for the mentally ill

(P-21942)
COUNTY OF EL DORADO
Also Called: Psychiatric Health Facility
935b Spring St, Placerville (95667-4523)
PHONE..................530 621-6210
Kathlen Burne, *Branch Mgr*
EMP: 76 **Privately Held**
WEB: www.filmtahoe.com
SIC: 8063 9111 Psychiatric hospitals; executive offices
PA: County Of El Dorado
330 Fair Ln
Placerville CA 95667
530 621-5830

(P-21943)
COUNTY OF SAN DIEGO
Also Called: Health & Human Services
3853 Rosecrans St, San Diego
(92110-3115)
PHONE..................................619 692-8200
Karen Hogan, *CEO*
Lynne Prizzia, *Technology*
Randall Krogman, *Manager*
Shelley Rieth, *Manager*
EMP: 350 **Privately Held**
WEB: www.sdlcc.org
SIC: 8063 9431 Psychiatric hospitals; administration of public health programs;
PA: County Of San Diego
1600 Pacific Hwy Ste 209
San Diego CA 92101
619 531-5880

(P-21944)
COUNTY OF SONOMA
Department Mental Health Svcs
3322 Chanate Rd, Santa Rosa
(95404-1708)
PHONE..................................707 565-4850
Marcus Crosdowny, *Director*
Cynthia Pilgrim, *Psychiatry*
Randye Royston,
Steve Parsons, *Director*
EMP: 63 **Privately Held**
WEB: www.sonomacompost.com
SIC: 8063 Hospital for the mentally ill
PA: County Of Sonoma
585 Fiscal Dr 100
Santa Rosa CA 95403
707 565-2431

(P-21945)
**CRESTWOOD BEHAVIORAL
HLTH INC**
Also Called: 112 Modesto Snf
1400 Celeste Dr, Modesto (95355-5041)
PHONE..................................209 526-8050
Lauri Blaufus, *Branch Mgr*
EMP: 200
SQ FT: 56,538
SALES (corp-wide): 171.2MM **Privately
Held**
WEB: www.dreamcatch.us
SIC: 8063 Psychiatric hospitals
PA: Crestwood Behavioral Health, Inc.
520 Capitol Mall Ste 800
Sacramento CA 95814
510 651-1244

(P-21946)
**CRESTWOOD BEHAVIORAL
HLTH INC**
Also Called: 106 Sacramento Mhrc
2600 Stockton Blvd, Sacramento
(95817-2210)
PHONE..................................916 452-1431
Cindy Mataraso, *Administration*
EMP: 120
SALES (corp-wide): 171.2MM **Privately
Held**
WEB: www.dreamcatch.us
SIC: 8063 8361 Hospital for the mentally
ill; residential care
PA: Crestwood Behavioral Health, Inc.
520 Capitol Mall Ste 800
Sacramento CA 95814
510 651-1244

(P-21947)
**CRESTWOOD BEHAVIORAL
HLTH INC**
Also Called: 145 Fresno Bridge
153 N U St, Fresno (93701-2438)
PHONE..................................559 445-9094
Giang T Nguyen, *Principal*
EMP: 89
SALES (corp-wide): 171.2MM **Privately
Held**
SIC: 8063 Psychiatric hospitals
PA: Crestwood Behavioral Health, Inc.
520 Capitol Mall Ste 800
Sacramento CA 95814
510 651-1244

(P-21948)
**CRESTWOOD BEHAVIORAL
HLTH INC**
Also Called: Our House
2201 Tuolumne St, Vallejo (94589-2524)
PHONE..................................707 558-1777
Gail McDonald, *Branch Mgr*
EMP: 55
SALES (corp-wide): 171.2MM **Privately
Held**
SIC: 8063 8011 Psychiatric hospitals; offices & clinics of medical doctors
PA: Crestwood Behavioral Health, Inc.
520 Capitol Mall Ste 800
Sacramento CA 95814
510 651-1244

(P-21949)
**CRESTWOOD BEHAVIORAL
HLTH INC**
Also Called: 111 Vallejo IMD
115 Oddstad Dr, Vallejo (94589-2520)
PHONE..................................707 552-0215
Minda Bunggay, *Administration*
EMP: 89
SALES (corp-wide): 171.2MM **Privately
Held**
SIC: 8063 Psychiatric hospitals
PA: Crestwood Behavioral Health, Inc.
520 Capitol Mall Ste 800
Sacramento CA 95814
510 651-1244

(P-21950)
**CRESTWOOD BEHAVIORAL
HLTH INC**
Also Called: 153 American River PHF
4741 Engle Rd, Carmichael (95608-2223)
PHONE..................................916 977-0949
EMP: 89
SALES (corp-wide): 171.2MM **Privately
Held**
SIC: 8063 Psychiatric hospitals
PA: Crestwood Behavioral Health, Inc.
520 Capitol Mall Ste 800
Sacramento CA 95814
510 651-1244

(P-21951)
**CRESTWOOD BEHAVIORAL
HLTH INC**
Also Called: 144 Pleasant Hill The Pathway
550 Patterson Blvd, Pleasant Hill
(94523-4155)
PHONE..................................925 938-8050
Cynthia Mathraso, *Branch Mgr*
EMP: 89
SALES (corp-wide): 171.2MM **Privately
Held**
SIC: 8063 Psychiatric hospitals
PA: Crestwood Behavioral Health, Inc.
520 Capitol Mall Ste 800
Sacramento CA 95814
510 651-1244

(P-21952)
DEANCO HEALTHCARE LLC
Also Called: Mission Community Hospital
14850 Roscoe Blvd, Panorama City
(91402-4618)
PHONE..................................818 787-2222
James Theiring,
Dianne Wagner, *COO*
Craig Garner, *Officer*
Brian Padveen, *Vice Pres*
Joe Magpantay, *Lab Dir*
EMP: 700
SALES (est): 80.9MM **Privately Held**
SIC: 8063 Psychiatric hospitals

(P-21953)
DEL AMO HOSPITAL INC
Also Called: UHS
23700 Camino Del Sol, Torrance
(90505-5000)
P.O. Box 61558, King of Prussia PA
(19406-0958)
PHONE..................................310 530-1151
Lisa Moncen, *CEO*
Alan B Miller, *Ch of Bd*
Kirk E Gorman, *Treasurer*
Sidney Miller, *Exec VP*
Samuel Armenta, *Info Tech Dir*
EMP: 300
SQ FT: 88,000

SALES: 42.9MM
SALES (corp-wide): 10.4B **Publicly Held**
WEB: www.uhsinc.com
SIC: 8063 Psychiatric hospitals
PA: Universal Health Services, Inc.
367 S Gulph Rd
King Of Prussia PA 19406
610 768-3300

(P-21954)
**GATEWAYS HOSP MENTAL
HLTH CTR**
340 N Madison Ave, Los Angeles
(90004-3504)
PHONE..................................323 644-2026
Mara Pelsman, *Branch Mgr*
Richard Ciasca, *Psychiatry*
EMP: 92
SALES (corp-wide): 26.3MM **Privately
Held**
SIC: 8063 Hospital for the mentally ill
PA: Gateway's Hospital And Mental Health
Center Inc
1891 Effie St
Los Angeles CA 90026
323 644-2000

(P-21955)
**GATEWAYS HOSP MENTAL
HLTH CTR (PA)**
1891 Effie St, Los Angeles (90026-1711)
PHONE..................................323 644-2000
Mara Pelsman, *CEO*
Jeff Emery, *CFO*
Joshua Ly, *Pharmacy Dir*
Sara Garza, *Nursing Mgr*
Pam Goodman, *Admin Asst*
EMP: 150 EST: 1953
SQ FT: 40,000
SALES: 26.3MM **Privately Held**
WEB: www.gatewayshospital.org
SIC: 8063 8093 Hospital for the mentally
ill; mental health clinic, outpatient

(P-21956)
**GOLDEN STATE HEALTH CTRS
INC**
Also Called: Sylmar Hlth Rehabilitation Ctr
12220 Foothill Blvd, Sylmar (91342-6001)
PHONE..................................818 834-5082
Cherlyn Hawkins, *Manager*
Michael Freeman, *Manager*
EMP: 250
SALES (corp-wide): 62.1MM **Privately
Held**
WEB: www.goldenstatehealth.com
SIC: 8063 8069 Psychiatric hospitals; specialty hospitals, except psychiatric
PA: Golden State Health Centers, Inc.
13347 Ventura Blvd
Sherman Oaks CA 91423
818 385-3200

(P-21957)
HELIX HEALTHCARE INC
Also Called: Alvarado Parkway Institute
7050 Parkway Dr, La Mesa (91942-1535)
PHONE..................................619 465-4411
Roy Rodriguez, *CEO*
Robert Sanders, *Shareholder*
Megan Monrgomery -West, *COO*
Mohammed Bari, *Vice Pres*
Andrew Noorollah, *Exec Dir*
EMP: 310
SQ FT: 37,354
SALES (est): 40MM **Privately Held**
WEB: www.alvaradoparkwayinstitute.com
SIC: 8063 Hospital for the mentally ill

(P-21958)
**JOHN MUIR BEHAVIORAL HLTH
CTR**
2740 Grant St, Concord (94520-2265)
PHONE..................................925 674-4100
Elizabeth Stallings, *COO*
Amanda Tucker, *Persnl Dir*
Cindy Bolter, *Opers Staff*
Nagui Achamallah, *Med Doctor*
EMP: 165
SQ FT: 40,000
SALES (est): 15.8MM **Privately Held**
SIC: 8063 8051 Psychiatric hospitals;
skilled nursing care facilities

(P-21959)
**KAISER FOUNDATION
HOSPITALS**
Also Called: Kaiser Mental Health Center
765 W College St, Los Angeles
(90012-1181)
PHONE..................................213 580-7200
Kurt Hastings, *Manager*
EMP: 200
SQ FT: 66,697
SALES (corp-wide): 94.1B **Privately Held**
WEB: www.kaiserpermanente.org
SIC: 8063 Psychiatric hospitals
HQ: Kaiser Foundation Hospitals Inc
1 Kaiser Plz
Oakland CA 94612
510 271-6611

(P-21960)
**KEDREN COMMUNITY HLTH CTR
INC (PA)**
Also Called: Kedren Acute Psychia Hospit An
4211 Avalon Blvd, Los Angeles
(90011-5622)
PHONE..................................323 233-0425
John Griffith, *President*
Robert Lawson, *Treasurer*
Lupe Ross, *Admin Sec*
Maria Dia, *Administration*
Earle Charles, *CIO*
EMP: 400
SQ FT: 144,000
SALES: 35.8MM **Privately Held**
WEB: www.kedren.com
SIC: 8063 8093 Hospital for the mentally
ill; specialty outpatient clinics

(P-21961)
**KNOLLWOOD PSYCHIATRIC
AND CHEM**
Also Called: Knollwood Center
5900 Brockton Ave, Riverside
(92506-1862)
PHONE..................................951 275-8400
Robert B Summerour, *President*
Byron Defour, *Shareholder*
EMP: 100
SQ FT: 50,000
SALES (est): 6.3MM **Privately Held**
SIC: 8063 Psychiatric hospitals

(P-21962)
**LANDMARK MEDICAL
SERVICES INC**
Also Called: Landmark Medical Center
2030 N Garey Ave, Pomona (91767-2722)
PHONE..................................909 593-2585
Rose Horsman, *President*
EMP: 100
SQ FT: 27,500
SALES (est): 7.6MM **Privately Held**
SIC: 8063 Hospital for the mentally ill

(P-21963)
LINDEN CENTER
Also Called: LINDEN CENTER BUSINESS
OFC
816 N Fairfax Ave, Los Angeles
(90046-7208)
P.O. Box 57366 (90057-0366)
PHONE..................................213 251-8226
Fax: 213 251-8238
EMP: 80
SQ FT: 6,000
SALES: 236.8K **Privately Held**
WEB: www.lindencenter.com
SIC: 8063

(P-21964)
**MADERA CONVALESCENT
HOSPITAL**
1255 B St, Merced (95341-6345)
PHONE..................................209 723-8814
Jerry Allgood, *Principal*
EMP: 80
SALES (corp-wide): 5.6MM **Privately
Held**
SIC: 8063 Psychiatric hospitals
PA: Madera Convalescent Hospital, Inc
517 S A St
Madera CA 93638
559 673-9228

PRODUCTS & SVCS

(P-21965)
MARIN COUNTY SART PROGRAM
Also Called: Canyon Manor Residential Treat
655 Canyon Rd, Novato (94947-4331)
P.O. Box 865 (94948-0865)
PHONE..............................415 892-1628
Donald Harris, President
Ben Lan, Corp Secy
EMP: 100
SQ FT: 15,000
SALES (est): 2.4MM Privately Held
SIC: 8063 8361 8069 Hospital for the mentally ill; residential care; specialty hospitals, except psychiatric

(P-21966)
MENTAL HEALTH CALIFORNIA DEPT
Also Called: Vacaville Psychiatric Program
1600 California Dr, Vacaville (95696)
P.O. Box 2297 (95696-8297)
PHONE..............................707 449-6504
Victor Brewer, Director
EMP: 283 Privately Held
SIC: 8063 9431 Hospital for the mentally ill; mental health agency administration, government;
HQ: California Department Of State Hospitals
1600 9th St Ste 350
Sacramento CA 95814

(P-21967)
NORTHERN VLY INDIAN HLTH INC
175 W Court St, Woodland (95695-2913)
PHONE..............................530 661-4400
EMP: 52
SALES (est): 82.2K
SALES (corp-wide): 35.3MM Privately Held
SIC: 8063 Psychiatric hospitals
PA: Northern Valley Indian Health, Inc.
207 N Butte St
Willows CA
530 934-9293

(P-21968)
OASIS MENTAL HEALTH TRTMNT CTR
47915 Oasis St, Indio (92201-6950)
PHONE..............................760 863-8609
Mary Jane Gross, President
EMP: 103 EST: 1995
SALES (est): 2.5MM Privately Held
SIC: 8063 Hospital for the mentally ill

(P-21969)
PSYCHIATRIC SOLUTIONS INC
Heritage Oaks Hospital
4250 Auburn Blvd, Sacramento (95841-4100)
PHONE..............................916 489-3336
Shawn Silva, CEO
Brent Turner, Exec VP
Tammy Vanella, Executive Asst
Dana Ashcroft, Human Res Dir
EMP: 135
SALES (corp-wide): 10.4B Publicly Held
WEB: www.intermountainhospital.com
SIC: 8063 Psychiatric hospitals
HQ: Psychiatric Solutions, Inc.
6640 Carothers Pkwy # 500
Franklin TN 37067
615 312-5700

(P-21970)
SAGE BEHAVIOR SERVICES INC
505 E Commonwealth Ave, Fullerton (92832-4009)
PHONE..............................714 773-0077
Tammy Heo, Director
Cindy Hebert, Director
Kareem A Khouri, Director
EMP: 60
SQ FT: 6,000
SALES (est): 3.2MM Privately Held
SIC: 8063 Psychiatric hospitals

(P-21971)
SAN GBRIEL VLY CNVLESCENT HOSP
Also Called: Pennmar
3938 Cogswell Rd, El Monte (91732-2404)
PHONE..............................626 401-1557
Dori Dimla, Administration
Carmen Fletcher, Records Dir
Mitchel Kantor, President
Dory Dimla, Executive
EMP: 65
SALES: 5MM Privately Held
WEB: www.pennmar.com
SIC: 8063 Psychiatric hospitals

(P-21972)
SHARP MEMORIAL HOSPITAL
Also Called: Sharp Mesa Vista Hospital
7850 Vista Hill Ave, San Diego (92123-2717)
PHONE..............................858 278-4110
Carolyn Mason, Director
Linda Carson, Volunteer Dir
Karen Ross, Office Mgr
Loralie Woods, Education
Jeff Sugar, Med Doctor
EMP: 190
SALES (corp-wide): 3.4B Privately Held
SIC: 8063 8069 8093 Psychiatric hospitals; substance abuse hospitals; specialty outpatient clinics
HQ: Sharp Memorial Hospital
7901 Frost St
San Diego CA 92123
858 939-3636

(P-21973)
STAR VIEW ADOLESCENT CENTER
4025 W 226th St, Torrance (90505-2340)
PHONE..............................310 373-4556
Mary Jane Gross, President
Deidra Kearns, Manager
EMP: 80 EST: 1996
SALES (est): 5.4MM Privately Held
SIC: 8063 Psychiatric hospitals

(P-21974)
SYLMAR HLTH REHABILITATION CTR
Also Called: Sylmar Hlth Rehabilitation Ctr
12220 Foothill Blvd, Sylmar (91342-6001)
PHONE..............................818 834-5082
Marty Weiss, President
Cherlyn Brintnell, Administration
EMP: 200 EST: 1969
SALES (est): 8.4MM
SALES (corp-wide): 62.1MM Privately Held
WEB: www.goldenstatehealth.com
SIC: 8063 Psychiatric hospitals
PA: Golden State Health Centers, Inc.
13347 Ventura Blvd
Sherman Oaks CA 91423
818 385-3200

(P-21975)
TELECARE CORPORATION
275 Baker St, Costa Mesa (92626-4566)
PHONE..............................714 361-6760
Anne Bakar, Branch Mgr
EMP: 61
SALES (corp-wide): 201.7MM Privately Held
SIC: 8063 Psychiatric hospitals
PA: Telecare Corporation
1080 Marina Village Pkwy # 100
Alameda CA 94501
510 337-7950

(P-21976)
TELECARE CORPORATION
Also Called: Willow Rock Center
2050 Fairmont Dr, San Leandro (94578-1001)
PHONE..............................510 895-5502
Peter Zucker, Branch Mgr
EMP: 60
SALES (corp-wide): 201.7MM Privately Held
SIC: 8063 Psychiatric hospitals
PA: Telecare Corporation
1080 Marina Village Pkwy # 100
Alameda CA 94501
510 337-7950

(P-21977)
TELECARE CORPORATION
16460 Victor St, Victorville (92395-3918)
PHONE..............................760 245-8837
Clarissa Dodd, Branch Mgr
EMP: 60
SALES (corp-wide): 201.7MM Privately Held
SIC: 8063 8093 Psychiatric hospitals; mental health clinic, outpatient
PA: Telecare Corporation
1080 Marina Village Pkwy # 100
Alameda CA 94501
510 337-7950

(P-21978)
TELECARE CORPORATION
1675 Morena Blvd Ste 100, San Diego (92110-3703)
PHONE..............................619 275-8000
Tara Booth, Administration
EMP: 60
SALES (corp-wide): 201.7MM Privately Held
SIC: 8063 Psychiatric hospitals
PA: Telecare Corporation
1080 Marina Village Pkwy # 100
Alameda CA 94501
510 337-7950

(P-21979)
TELECARE CORPORATION (PA)
1080 Marina Village Pkwy # 100, Alameda (94501-1078)
PHONE..............................510 337-7950
Anne L Bakar, President
Marshall Langfeld, CFO
Anita Barnas, Senior VP
Faithe Richie, Senior VP
Steve Wilson, Senior VP
EMP: 50
SQ FT: 15,000
SALES (est): 201.7MM Privately Held
WEB: www.telecarecorp.com
SIC: 8063 8011 Psychiatric hospitals; health maintenance organization

(P-21980)
TELECARE CORPORATION
Also Called: La Casa Mhrc
6060 N Paramount Blvd, Long Beach (90805-3711)
PHONE..............................562 630-8672
Anne Bakar, CEO
EMP: 99
SALES (est): 5.7MM
SALES (corp-wide): 201.7MM Privately Held
SIC: 8063 Psychiatric hospitals
PA: Telecare Corporation
1080 Marina Village Pkwy # 100
Alameda CA 94501
510 337-7950

(P-21981)
TELECARE CORPORATION
Also Called: La Casa Mental Health Center
6060 N Paramount Blvd, Long Beach (90805-3711)
PHONE..............................562 634-9534
David Effron, Branch Mgr
EMP: 230
SALES (corp-wide): 201.7MM Privately Held
WEB: www.telecarecorp.com
SIC: 8063 8011 Psychiatric hospitals; health maintenance organization
PA: Telecare Corporation
1080 Marina Village Pkwy # 100
Alameda CA 94501
510 337-7950

(P-21982)
TELECARE CORPORATION
Also Called: Garfield Nuerobehavioral Ctr
1451 28th Ave, Oakland (94601-1632)
PHONE..............................510 261-9191
Alonzo Clemens, Director
EMP: 110
SQ FT: 2,117
SALES (corp-wide): 201.7MM Privately Held
WEB: www.telecarecorp.com
SIC: 8063 8011 Psychiatric hospitals; health maintenance organization

PA: Telecare Corporation
1080 Marina Village Pkwy # 100
Alameda CA 94501
510 337-7950

(P-21983)
TELECARE CORPORATION
Also Called: Morton Bakar Center
494 Blossom Way, Hayward (94541-1948)
PHONE..............................510 582-7676
Mary Thrower, Branch Mgr
EMP: 125
SALES (corp-wide): 201.7MM Privately Held
WEB: www.telecarecorp.com
SIC: 8063 8011 Psychiatric hospitals; health maintenance organization
PA: Telecare Corporation
1080 Marina Village Pkwy # 100
Alameda CA 94501
510 337-7950

(P-21984)
TELECARE CORPORATION
Also Called: Villa Fairmont Mental Hlth Ctr
15200 Foothill Blvd, San Leandro (94578-1013)
PHONE..............................510 352-9690
Regina Scott, Manager
EMP: 132
SALES (corp-wide): 201.7MM Privately Held
WEB: www.telecarecorp.com
SIC: 8063 8011 Psychiatric hospitals; health maintenance organization
PA: Telecare Corporation
1080 Marina Village Pkwy # 100
Alameda CA 94501
510 337-7950

(P-21985)
TELECARE CORPORATION
Also Called: San Diego Choices
3851 Rosecrans St, San Diego (92110-3115)
PHONE..............................619 692-8225
Scherry Messic, Branch Mgr
EMP: 58
SALES (corp-wide): 201.7MM Privately Held
WEB: www.telecarecorp.com
SIC: 8063 8011 Psychiatric hospitals; health maintenance organization
PA: Telecare Corporation
1080 Marina Village Pkwy # 100
Alameda CA 94501
510 337-7950

(P-21986)
TELECARE CORPORATION
Also Called: Los Posadas Service Center
1756 S Lewis Rd, Camarillo (93012-8520)
PHONE..............................805 383-3669
Tim Kuehnel, Manager
EMP: 55
SALES (corp-wide): 201.7MM Privately Held
WEB: www.telecarecorp.com
SIC: 8063 8011 Psychiatric hospitals; health maintenance organization
PA: Telecare Corporation
1080 Marina Village Pkwy # 100
Alameda CA 94501
510 337-7950

(P-21987)
TELECARE CORPORATION
Also Called: Cordilleras Mental Health Ctr
200 Edmonds Rd, Redwood City (94062-3813)
PHONE..............................650 367-1890
Bill Kruse, Branch Mgr
EMP: 123
SALES (corp-wide): 201.7MM Privately Held
WEB: www.telecarecorp.com
SIC: 8063 8011 Psychiatric hospitals; health maintenance organization
PA: Telecare Corporation
1080 Marina Village Pkwy # 100
Alameda CA 94501
510 337-7950

▲ = Import ▼=Export
◆ =Import/Export

(P-21988)
TELECARE CORPORATION
Also Called: Cresta Loma
1080 Marina Village Pkwy # 100, Alameda
(94501-1078)
PHONE.....................................510 337-7950
Becky Clark, *Branch Mgr*
EMP: 101
SQ FT: 44,000
SALES (corp-wide): 201.7MM **Privately Held**
WEB: www.telecarecorp.com
SIC: 8063 8011 Psychiatric hospitals; health maintenance organization
PA: Telecare Corporation
   1080 Marina Village Pkwy # 100
   Alameda CA 94501
   510 337-7950

(P-21989)
TELECARE CORPORATION
Also Called: La Paz Geropsychiatric Center
8835 Vans St, Paramount (90723-4656)
PHONE.....................................562 633-5111
Rich Widerynski, *Administration*
Faye Bernardo, *Director*
Cynthia Lopez, *Director*
Kiana Moten, *Director*
EMP: 150
SALES (corp-wide): 201.7MM **Privately Held**
WEB: www.telecarecorp.com
SIC: 8063 8011 Psychiatric hospitals; health maintenance organization
PA: Telecare Corporation
   1080 Marina Village Pkwy # 100
   Alameda CA 94501
   510 337-7950

(P-21990)
TELECARE CORPORATION
Also Called: Telecare Fsp
300 Harbor Blvd E, Belmont (94002-4018)
PHONE.....................................650 817-9070
Kevin Jones, *Administration*
EMP: 60
SALES (corp-wide): 201.7MM **Privately Held**
SIC: 8063 8621 Psychiatric hospitals; health association
PA: Telecare Corporation
   1080 Marina Village Pkwy # 100
   Alameda CA 94501
   510 337-7950

(P-21991)
TELECARE CORPORATION
Also Called: Heritage Psychiatric Health
2633 E 27th St, Oakland (94601-1912)
PHONE.....................................510 535-5115
Patty Espeseth, *Branch Mgr*
EMP: 120
SALES (corp-wide): 201.7MM **Privately Held**
WEB: www.telecarecorp.com
SIC: 8063 8011 Psychiatric hospitals; health maintenance organization
PA: Telecare Corporation
   1080 Marina Village Pkwy # 100
   Alameda CA 94501
   510 337-7950

(P-21992)
TENET HEALTHSYSTEM MEDICAL
330 Moss St, Chula Vista (91911-2005)
PHONE.....................................619 426-6310
EMP: 150
SALES (corp-wide): 11.1B **Publicly Held**
SIC: 8063
HQ: Tenet Healthsystem Medical, Inc
   1445 Ross Ave Ste 1400
   Dallas TX 75202
   469 893-2000

(P-21993)
VISTA BEHAVIORAL HEALTH INC
Also Called: Pacific Grove Hospital
5900 Brockton Ave, Riverside
(92506-1862)
PHONE.....................................800 992-0901
Nelson Smith, *CEO*
EMP: 67 **EST:** 2015

SALES (est): 2.6MM **Publicly Held**
SIC: 8063 Psychiatric hospitals
PA: Acadia Healthcare Company, Inc.
   6100 Tower Cir Ste 1000
   Franklin TN 37067

8069 Specialty Hospitals, Except Psychiatric

(P-21994)
1125 SIR FRANCIS DRAKE BOULEVA
Also Called: Kentfield Rehabilation Hosp
1125 Sir Francis Drake Bl, Kentfield
(94904-1418)
PHONE.....................................415 456-9680
Brad Hollinger,
James Boatman, *CFO*
Denise Mace, *Radiology Dir*
Deborah Doherty, *Exec Dir*
Anucheat Chea, *Infectious Dis*
EMP: 250
SALES (est): 44.2MM **Privately Held**
WEB: www.kentfieldrehab.com
SIC: 8069 Children's hospital

(P-21995)
ANAHEIM REGIONAL MEDICAL CTR (PA)
1111 W La Palma Ave, Anaheim
(92801-2804)
PHONE.....................................714 774-1450
Patrick Petre, *CEO*
Deborah Webber, *COO*
Fred Drewette, *CFO*
Phyllis Snyder, *Ch Nursing Ofcr*
Jeff Deroches, *CIO*
EMP: 50
SALES (est): 188.8MM **Privately Held**
SIC: 8069 8062 Children's hospital; general medical & surgical hospitals

(P-21996)
ASIAN AMERCN RECOVERY SVCS INC
Also Called: Place Asian Amrcn Rcovery Svcs
1340 Tully Rd Ste 304, San Jose
(95122-3055)
PHONE.....................................408 271-3900
Jeff Mori, *Exec Dir*
EMP: 125
SALES (corp-wide): 6MM **Privately Held**
WEB: www.aars-inc.org
SIC: 8069 Drug addiction rehabilitation hospital
PA: Asian American Recovery Services, Inc.
   1115 Mission Rd 2
   South San Francisco CA 94080
   650 243-4888

(P-21997)
BARLOW GROUP (PA)
Also Called: Barlow Respiratory Hospital
2000 Stadium Way, Los Angeles
(90026-2606)
PHONE.....................................213 250-4200
Margaret W Crane, *CEO*
EMP: 250
SALES: 3.4MM **Privately Held**
SIC: 8069 7389 8733 Specialty hospitals, except psychiatric; fund raising organizations; medical research

(P-21998)
BARLOW RESPIRATORY HOSPITAL (PA)
2000 Stadium Way, Los Angeles
(90026-2606)
PHONE.....................................213 250-4200
Margaret W Crane, *CEO*
Edward Engesser, *CFO*
Maggie LI, *Pharmacist*
EMP: 250 **EST:** 1902
SQ FT: 80,000
SALES: 55.2MM **Privately Held**
SIC: 8069 Specialty hospitals, except psychiatric

(P-21999)
BETTY FORD CENTER (HQ)
39000 Bob Hope Dr, Rancho Mirage
(92270-3297)
P.O. Box 1560 (92270-1056)
PHONE.....................................760 773-4100
Mark Mishek, *President*
James Blaha, *CFO*
Greg Fisher, *Officer*
Briar Geraci, *Vice Pres*
Charlene Montgomery, *Vice Pres*
EMP: 250
SALES: 38.3MM
SALES (corp-wide): 175.2MM **Privately Held**
SIC: 8069 Drug addiction rehabilitation hospital
PA: Hazelden Betty Ford Foundation
   15251 Pleasant Valley Rd
   Center City MN 55012
   651 213-4000

(P-22000)
CALIFORNIA HISPANIC COM
9033 Washington Blvd, Pico Rivera
(90660-3839)
PHONE.....................................562 942-9625
Samuel Campbell, *Director*
EMP: 123
SALES (corp-wide): 12.3MM **Privately Held**
SIC: 8069 Alcoholism rehabilitation hospital
PA: California Hispanic Commission On Alcohol And Drug Abuse Inc
   9942 13th St
   Garden Grove CA 92844
   916 443-5473

(P-22001)
CAMP RECOVERY CENTERS LP
Also Called: Azure Acres
2264 Green Hill Rd, Sebastopol
(95472-9034)
PHONE.....................................707 823-3385
Shannon Clay, *Administration*
EMP: 4046 **Privately Held**
WEB: www.azureacres.com
SIC: 8069 8361 Substance abuse hospitals; rehabilitation center, residential: health care incidental
PA: The Camp Recovery Centers L P
   6100 Tower Cir Ste 1000
   Franklin TN 37067

(P-22002)
CBEST INC
11620 Wilshire Blvd # 450, Los Angeles
(90025-1779)
PHONE.....................................310 445-2378
Bahador, *President*
EMP: 80 **EST:** 2011
SALES (est): 710.5K **Privately Held**
SIC: 8069 Children's hospital

(P-22003)
CENTER FOR DSCOVERY ADOLOSCENT
4136 Ann Arbor Rd, Lakewood
(90712-3817)
PHONE.....................................562 425-6404
Craig Brown, *Director*
Greg Corbin, *COO*
EMP: 50
SALES (est): 640.4K **Privately Held**
SIC: 8069 Drug addiction rehabilitation hospital

(P-22004)
CHILDRENS HEALTHCARE CAL (PA)
1201 W La Veta Ave, Orange (92868-4203)
PHONE.....................................714 997-3000
Kimberly C Cripe, *President*
Thomas Brotherton, *COO*
Kerri Ruppert, *CFO*
Maria Minon MD, *Vice Pres*
Ashley Loera, *Associate Dir*
EMP: 1800
SALES: 548.7MM **Privately Held**
SIC: 8069 Children's hospital

(P-22005)
CHILDRENS HOSPITAL LOS ANGELES (PA)
4650 W Sunset Blvd, Los Angeles
(90027-6062)
PHONE.....................................323 660-2450
Richard Cordova, *President*
Lannie Tonnu, *CFO*
Thomas E Larkin, *Trustee*
Owen Lei, *Officer*
Anna Weiser, *Assoc VP*
▲ **EMP:** 98 **EST:** 1901
SQ FT: 750,000
SALES: 1B **Privately Held**
SIC: 8069 8062 Children's hospital; general medical & surgical hospitals

(P-22006)
CHILDRENS HOSPITAL LOS ANGELES
800 N Brand Blvd, Glendale (91203-1245)
PHONE.....................................323 361-2215
EMP: 217
SALES (corp-wide): 1B **Privately Held**
SIC: 8069 8093 Children's hospital; specialty outpatient clinics
PA: The Childrens Hospital Los Angeles
   4650 W Sunset Blvd
   Los Angeles CA 90027
   323 660-2450

(P-22007)
CHILDRENS HOSPITAL LOS ANGELES
Also Called: Chidren's Hospital Center
4661 W Sunset Blvd, Los Angeles
(90027-6042)
PHONE.....................................323 361-5702
Nikita Tripuraneni, *Principal*
EMP: 160
SALES (corp-wide): 1B **Privately Held**
SIC: 8069 Children's hospital
PA: The Childrens Hospital Los Angeles
   4650 W Sunset Blvd
   Los Angeles CA 90027
   323 660-2450

(P-22008)
CHILDRENS HOSPITAL ORANGE CNTY (PA)
Also Called: Choc
1201 W La Veta Ave, Orange (92868-4203)
PHONE.....................................714 997-3000
Kimberly Cripe, *President*
L Kenneth Heuler DDS, *Ch of Bd*
Sally Gallagher, *President*
Cathy Mc Donnell, *Officer*
Cathy McDonnell, *Officer*
EMP: 84 **EST:** 1950
SQ FT: 328,200
SALES: 523.1MM **Privately Held**
SIC: 8069 Children's hospital

(P-22009)
CHILDRENS HOSPITAL ORANGE CNTY
Also Called: Choc Mission
455 S Main St, Orange (92868-3835)
PHONE.....................................949 365-2416
Kerri Ruppert Schiller, *Principal*
Kerri Schiller, *Officer*
Susan Burrows, *Vice Pres*
James Fabella, *Vice Pres*
Patricia Faiman, *Vice Pres*
EMP: 255
SALES (corp-wide): 523.1MM **Privately Held**
SIC: 8069 Children's hospital
PA: Children's Hospital Of Orange County
   1201 W La Veta Ave
   Orange CA 92868
   714 997-3000

(P-22010)
CITY OF SAN DIEGO
Also Called: Park and Recreation
202 C St Ms37c, San Diego (92101-3860)
PHONE.....................................619 533-6518
Albert Cuevas, *Administration*
EMP: 99
SALES (est): 486.2K **Privately Held**
SIC: 8069 Specialty hospitals, except psychiatric

(P-22011)
COUNTY OF LOS ANGELES
Also Called: Health Services, Dept of
30500 Arrastre Canyon Rd, Acton
(93510-2160)
P.O. Box 25 (93510-0025)
PHONE......................661 223-8700
Suzanna Kassinger, *Administration*
Liz Martinez, *Officer*
EMP: 100 **Privately Held**
WEB: www.co.la.ca.us
SIC: **8069** 9431 8361 Alcoholism rehabilitation hospital; administration of public health programs; ; residential care
PA: County Of Los Angeles
500 W Temple St Ste 437
Los Angeles CA 90012
213 974-1101

(P-22012)
COUNTY OF LOS ANGELES
515 E 6th St, Los Angeles (90021-1009)
PHONE......................213 974-7284
Maria Lopez, *Manager*
EMP: 1000 **Privately Held**
WEB: www.co.la.ca.us
SIC: **8069** 9111 Tuberculosis hospital; executive offices
PA: County Of Los Angeles
500 W Temple St Ste 437
Los Angeles CA 90012
213 974-1101

(P-22013)
COUNTY OF LOS ANGELES
Also Called: Department of Health Services
1240 N Mission Rd, Los Angeles
(90033-1019)
PHONE......................323 226-3468
Barbara Oliver, *Exec Dir*
EMP: 1000 **Privately Held**
WEB: www.co.la.ca.us
SIC: **8069** 9431 8062 Specialty hospitals, except psychiatric; administration of public health programs; ; general medical & surgical hospitals
PA: County Of Los Angeles
500 W Temple St Ste 437
Los Angeles CA 90012
213 974-1101

(P-22014)
CRC HEALTH CORPORATION (DH)
20400 Stevens Creek Blvd # 600, Cupertino (95014-2296)
PHONE......................877 272-8668
Jerome E Rhodes, *CEO*
R Andrew Eckert, *Ch of Bd*
Leanne M Stewart, *CFO*
Philip L Herschman, *Officer*
Pamela B Burke, *Senior VP*
EMP: 80
SALES: 452.2MM **Publicly Held**
WEB: www.crchealth.com
SIC: **8069** 8099 8322 8093 Drug addiction rehabilitation hospital; medical services organization; general counseling services; substance abuse clinics (outpatient)
HQ: Crc Health Group, Inc.
20400 Stev Creek Blvd 6 Flr 6
Cupertino CA 95014
877 272-8668

(P-22015)
CRESTWOOD BEHAVIORAL HLTH INC
Also Called: 137 Bakersfield Bridge
6744 Eucalyptus Dr, Bakersfield
(93306-6053)
PHONE......................661 363-6711
Lori Blackburn, *Branch Mgr*
EMP: 200
SALES (corp-wide): 171.2MM **Privately Held**
SIC: **8069** Specialty hospitals, except psychiatric
PA: Crestwood Behavioral Health, Inc.
520 Capitol Mall Ste 800
Sacramento CA 95814
510 651-1244

(P-22016)
DANIEL LORIA NOVARTIS
4560 Horton St, Emeryville (94608-2916)
PHONE......................510 655-8729
Daniel Loria Novartis, *Principal*
David Bell, *Exec VP*
Michael F Smith, *Vice Pres*
Nancy N Dougherty, *Associate Dir*
Trisha Fazio, *Associate Dir*
EMP: 156
SALES (est): 10.5MM **Privately Held**
SIC: **8069** Eye, ear, nose & throat hospital

(P-22017)
DESERT REGIONAL MED CTR INC
Also Called: Tenet
1695 N Sunrise Way, Palm Springs
(92262-3701)
PHONE......................760 323-6640
Truman Gates, *Manager*
EMP: 190
SALES (corp-wide): 19.3B **Publicly Held**
SIC: **8069** 8082 Specialty hospitals, except psychiatric; home health care services
HQ: Desert Regional Medical Center, Inc.
1150 N Indian Canyon Dr
Palm Springs CA 92262
760 323-6511

(P-22018)
DOCTORS HOSPITAL MANTECA INC
1205 E North St, Manteca (95336-4900)
PHONE......................209 823-3111
Nicholas Tejeda, *CEO*
Mark Lisa, *President*
Katherine Medeiros, *President*
Tracy Roman, *CFO*
Tammie Helm, *Admin Asst*
EMP: 400 EST: 2001
SALES: 90.8MM
SALES (corp-wide): 19.3B **Publicly Held**
SIC: **8069** Specialty hospitals, except psychiatric
PA: Tenet Healthcare Corporation
1445 Ross Ave Ste 1400
Dallas TX 75202
469 893-2200

(P-22019)
EL CAMINO HOSPITAL
Also Called: Occupational Health Services
625 Ellis St Ste 100, Mountain View
(94043-2225)
PHONE......................650 988-4825
Todd Blancept, *Manager*
Erica Rosen, *Med Doctor*
EMP: 217
SALES (corp-wide): 930.5MM **Privately Held**
SIC: **8069** Alcoholism rehabilitation hospital
PA: El Camino Hospital
2500 Grant Rd
Mountain View CA 94040
408 224-6660

(P-22020)
ENCOMPASS HEALTH CORPORATION
Also Called: HealthSouth
3875 Telegraph Ave, Oakland
(94609-2428)
PHONE......................510 547-2244
Ann Banchero, *Branch Mgr*
EMP: 55
SALES (corp-wide): 3.9B **Publicly Held**
WEB: www.healthsouth.com
SIC: **8069** Orthopedic hospital
PA: Encompass Health Corporation
9001 Liberty Pkwy
Birmingham AL 35242
205 967-7116

(P-22021)
EXODUS RECOVERY CTR AT BROTMAN (PA)
3828 Delmas Ter, Culver City (90232-2713)
PHONE......................310 253-9494
Luana Murphy, *Principal*
Mitch Kayle, *Case Mgr*
EMP: 59

SALES (est): 2.8MM **Privately Held**
SIC: **8069** Drug addiction rehabilitation hospital

(P-22022)
GUAVA HOLDINGS LLC
Also Called: Yuba City Post-Acute
1220 Plumas St, Yuba City (95991-3411)
PHONE......................530 671-0550
Toby Tilford, *President*
Dustin Murray, *Administration*
Nicklas Anderson, *Manager*
Naveed Hakim, *Manager*
EMP: 50 EST: 2017
SALES (est): 747.1K **Privately Held**
SIC: **8069** Geriatric hospital

(P-22023)
HEALTHCARE CENTRE OF FRESNO
1665 M St, Fresno (93721-1121)
PHONE......................559 268-5361
Lucille Epperson, *Administration*
Charles J Enoch, *Partner*
Joyce S Lopez, *Partner*
Laverne E Masten, *Partner*
Barbara H Rose, *Partner*
EMP: 163
SQ FT: 87,000
SALES (est): 4.6MM **Privately Held**
SIC: **8069** 8051 Specialty hospitals, except psychiatric; convalescent home with continuous nursing care

(P-22024)
HORIZON WEST HEALTHCARE INC
Also Called: Roseville Convalescent Hosp
1161 Cirby Way, Roseville (95661-4421)
PHONE......................916 782-1238
James Paul, *Manager*
EMP: 150
SALES (corp-wide): 103.7MM **Privately Held**
WEB: www.villadelrey.com
SIC: **8069** 8051 Specialty hospitals, except psychiatric; skilled nursing care facilities
HQ: Horizon West Healthcare, Inc.
4020 Sierra College Blvd # 190
Rocklin CA 95677
916 624-6230

(P-22025)
HOSPITAL OF COMMUNITY (HQ)
23625 Holman Hwy, Monterey
(93940-5902)
P.O. Box Hh (93942-6032)
PHONE......................831 624-5311
Steven J Packer, *President*
Laura Zehm, *CFO*
David Benjamin, *Treasurer*
Steven X Cabrales, *Vice Pres*
Terril Lowe, *Vice Pres*
EMP: 1500
SQ FT: 550,000
SALES: 526.9MM
SALES (corp-wide): 200MM **Privately Held**
SIC: **8069** 8011 Geriatric hospital; hematologist
PA: Montage Health
23625 Holman Hwy
Monterey CA 93940
831 625-4830

(P-22026)
INSIGHT HEALTH CORP (DH)
Also Called: Insight Imaging
23725 Birtcher Dr Ste 200, Lake Forest
(92630-1772)
PHONE......................877 566-6500
Bob Baumgartner, *CEO*
Rick Long, *CEO*
Darren Wight, *Train & Dev Mgr*
EMP: 50
SQ FT: 12,300
SALES (est): 12.3MM
SALES (corp-wide): 52.7MM **Privately Held**
SIC: **8069** 8071 8011 7352 Specialty hospitals, except psychiatric; medical laboratories; clinic, operated by physicians; medical equipment rental; home health care services; medical & hospital equipment

(P-22027)
KINDRED HEALTHCARE OPER INC
1940 El Cajon Blvd, San Diego
(92104-1005)
PHONE......................502 596-7300
Susan Baley, *CEO*
Elvia Martinez, *Nursing Dir*
Samuel Clark, *Director*
Diana Nawrocki, *Director*
Judith Vincent, *Director*
EMP: 222
SALES (corp-wide): 6B **Privately Held**
WEB: www.salemhaven.com
SIC: **8069** Specialty hospitals, except psychiatric
HQ: Kindred Healthcare Operating, Llc
680 S 4th St
Louisville KY 40202
502 596-7300

(P-22028)
KINDRED HEALTHCARE OPERATING
Also Called: Hillhaven Convalescent Hosp
1609 Trousdale Dr, Burlingame
(94010-4520)
PHONE......................650 697-1865
Jan Clemons, *Administration*
EMP: 500
SALES (corp-wide): 6B **Privately Held**
WEB: www.salemhaven.com
SIC: **8069** Specialty hospitals, except psychiatric
HQ: Kindred Healthcare Operating, Llc
680 S 4th St
Louisville KY 40202
502 596-7300

(P-22029)
LIGHTBRIDGE HOSPICE LLC
Also Called: Lightbrdge Hspice Plltive Care
6155 Cornerstone Ct E, San Diego
(92121-4736)
PHONE......................858 458-2992
Jill Mendlen, *CEO*
Pamela Hough, *Senior VP*
Cindy Hutchinson, *Vice Pres*
Nan Johnson, *Vice Pres*
Maria Danilychev, *Associate Dir*
EMP: 90
SALES: 130.2K **Privately Held**
WEB: www.lightbridgehospice.com
SIC: **8069** Specialty hospitals, except psychiatric

(P-22030)
LUCILE PACKARD CHILDRENS HOSP
730 Welch Rd Ste B, Palo Alto
(94304-1504)
PHONE......................650 321-2545
Christophe Dawes, *CEO*
EMP: 57
SALES (est): 8.4MM **Privately Held**
SIC: **8069** Children's hospital

(P-22031)
LUCILE PACKARD CHILDRENS HOSP
1520 Page Mill Rd, Palo Alto (94304-1125)
PHONE......................650 736-4089
Anita Brewer, *Director*
Christopher Longhurst, *Officer*
Tony Loosli, *Sr Ntwrk Engine*
Harinder Singh, *Manager*
EMP: 50
SALES (est): 8.2MM **Privately Held**
SIC: **8069** Children's hospital

(P-22032)
LUCILE SALTER PACKARD CHIL (PA)
725 Welch Rd, Palo Alto (94304-1601)
PHONE......................650 497-8000
Christopher Dawes, *President*
Robert Rouse, *Ch of Bd*
Timothy W Carmack, *CFO*
Les Lifter, *Chief Mktg Ofcr*
Greg Souza, *Officer*
▲ EMP: 120
SALES: 1.4B **Privately Held**
SIC: **8069** 8082 5912 Children's hospital; home health care services; drug stores & proprietary stores

(P-22033)
LUCILE SALTER PACKARD CHIL
300 Pasteur Dr, Stanford (94305-2200)
PHONE..................................650 723-5791
Jeff Driver, *Principal*
EMP: 176
SALES (corp-wide): 1.4B **Privately Held**
SIC: 8069 Children's hospital
PA: Lucile Salter Packard Children's Hospital At Stanford
725 Welch Rd
Palo Alto CA 94304
650 497-8000

(P-22034)
MARINE CORPS UNITED STATES
Also Called: Camp Pendleton Hospital
Camp Pendleton, Oceanside (92055)
P.O. Box 555191, Camp Pendleton (92055-5191)
PHONE..................................760 725-1304
Richard R Jeffries, *Manager*
EMP: 1000 **Publicly Held**
WEB: www.usmc.mil
SIC: 8069 9711 Specialty hospitals, except psychiatric; Marine Corps;
HQ: United States Marine Corps
Pentagon Rm 4b544
Washington DC 20380

(P-22035)
MATRIX INSTITUTE ON ADDICTIONS (PA)
1849 Sawtelle Blvd # 670, Los Angeles (90025-7082)
PHONE..................................310 478-6006
Jeanne Obert, *Chairman*
Jeremy Martinez, *Exec Dir*
Michael McCann MA, *Admin Sec*
Richard Hibbs, *Finance*
Dan George, *Opers Staff*
EMP: 60
SQ FT: 6,000
SALES: 4.4MM **Privately Held**
WEB: www.matrixinstitute.org
SIC: 8069 Drug addiction rehabilitation hospital

(P-22036)
MONROE OPERATIONS LLC
Also Called: Newport Academy
811 N Ranch Wood Trl, Orange (92869-2305)
PHONE..................................714 288-0872
Jamison Monroe Jr, *Mng Member*
Jim Monroe,
EMP: 177
SALES (est): 2.4MM **Privately Held**
SIC: 8069 Drug addiction rehabilitation hospital; children's hospital

(P-22037)
NEW BRIDGE FOUNDATION INC
1820 Scenic Ave, Berkeley (94709-1395)
PHONE..................................510 548-7270
Kosta Markakis, *Exec Dir*
EMP: 73
SQ FT: 3,000
SALES (est): 6.2MM **Privately Held**
SIC: 8069 Drug addiction rehabilitation hospital

(P-22038)
POMONA VALLEY HOSPITAL MED CTR
Also Called: Pamona Vallley Hospital
1798 N Garey Ave, Pomona (91767-2918)
PHONE..................................909 865-9700
Dee Ann Gibs, *Director*
EMP: 200
SALES (corp-wide): 631.3MM **Privately Held**
WEB: www.pvhmc.org
SIC: 8069 Maternity hospital
PA: Pomona Valley Hospital Medical Center
1798 N Garey Ave
Pomona CA 91767
909 865-9500

(P-22039)
PROGRESSIVE SUB-ACUTE CARE
Also Called: Sub-Acute Saratoga Hospital
13425 Sousa Ln, Saratoga (95070-4637)
PHONE..................................408 378-8875
Michael Zarcone, *President*
Elio Amaya, *Food Svc Dir*
EMP: 130
SQ FT: 10,000
SALES (est): 14.5MM **Privately Held**
WEB: www.subacutesaratoga.com
SIC: 8069 Children's hospital

(P-22040)
RADY CHILDRENS HOSP & HLTH CTR (PA)
3020 Childrens Way, San Diego (92123-4223)
PHONE..................................858 576-1700
Donald B Kearns, *President*
Christopher E Dory, *Ch Radiology*
Dorothy O'Hagan, *Records Dir*
Nicholas Holmes, *COO*
Roger G Roux, *CFO*
EMP: 1700
SALES: 1.2B **Privately Held**
SIC: 8069 Children's hospital

(P-22041)
RADY CHLD HOSPITAL-SAN DIEGO
8001 Frost St, San Diego (92123-2746)
PHONE..................................858 966-6795
Lynn M Dubenko, *Principal*
Olivia Hsin, *Psychologist*
EMP: 1025 **Privately Held**
SIC: 8069 Children's hospital
HQ: Rady Children's Hospital-San Diego
3020 Childrens Way
San Diego CA 92123
858 576-1700

(P-22042)
RECOVERY PLACE INC
5000 E Spring St Ste 650, Long Beach (90815-5205)
PHONE..................................954 200-8308
John Cates, *President*
EMP: 100
SALES (est): 7.9MM **Privately Held**
SIC: 8069 Drug addiction rehabilitation hospital

(P-22043)
SALINAS VALLEY MEMORIAL HLTHCA
Also Called: Svmc Precision Orthopedics
611 Abbott St Ste 101, Salinas (93901-4391)
PHONE..................................831 757-3041
EMP: 438
SALES (corp-wide): 494.4MM **Privately Held**
SIC: 8069 Orthopedic hospital
PA: Salinas Valley Memorial Healthcare Systems
450 E Romie Ln
Salinas CA 93901
831 757-4333

(P-22044)
SEQUOIA REGIONAL CANCER CENTER
602 W Willow Ave, Visalia (93291-6102)
PHONE..................................559 624-3000
Toni M Boniske, *Admin Dir*
Cindy Vasquez, *Receptionist*
EMP: 118
SALES (est): 4.9MM
SALES (corp-wide): 537.4MM **Privately Held**
SIC: 8069 Cancer hospital
PA: Kaweah Delta Health Care District
400 W Mineral King Ave
Visalia CA 93291
559 624-2000

(P-22045)
SHARP MCDONALD CENTER
7989 Linda Vista Rd, San Diego (92111-5106)
PHONE..................................858 637-6920
Michael Murphy, *President*

Daniel L Gross, *Exec VP*
EMP: 800
SALES (est): 39.7MM
SALES (corp-wide): 3.4B **Privately Held**
SIC: 8069 Drug addiction rehabilitation hospital
PA: Sharp Healthcare
8695 Spectrum Center Blvd
San Diego CA 92123
858 499-4000

(P-22046)
SHIELDS FOR FAMILIES (PA)
11601 S Western Ave, Los Angeles (90047-5006)
P.O. Box 59129 (90059-0129)
PHONE..................................323 242-5000
Kathryn S Icenhower, *CEO*
Xylina Bean, *President*
Norma Mtume, *CFO*
Gerald Phillips, *Chairman*
Susan Haynes, *Treasurer*
EMP: 82
SALES: 20.3MM **Privately Held**
SIC: 8069 Drug addiction rehabilitation hospital

(P-22047)
SHRINERS HSPITALS FOR CHILDREN
Also Called: Shriner's Hospital
3160 Geneva St, Los Angeles (90020-1117)
PHONE..................................213 388-3151
Terence Cunningham, *Principal*
G Frank Labonte, *Administration*
Karen Lopez, *Human Res Dir*
Laura Allen, *Human Res Mgr*
Maria Rivas, *Education*
EMP: 300 **Privately Held**
SIC: 8069 8062 Children's hospital; general medical & surgical hospitals
HQ: Shriners Hospitals For Children
12502 Usf Pine Dr
Tampa FL 33612
813 972-2250

(P-22048)
SHRINERS HSPITALS FOR CHILDREN
2425 Stockton Blvd, Sacramento (95817-2215)
PHONE..................................916 453-2050
Margaret Bryan, *Administration*
Sophie Taylor, *Director*
Robert Tolbert, *Manager*
EMP: 500 **Privately Held**
SIC: 8069 Children's hospital
HQ: Shriners Hospitals For Children
12502 Usf Pine Dr
Tampa FL 33612
813 972-2250

(P-22049)
SHRINERS HSPITALS FOR CHILDREN
2425 Stockton Blvd, Sacramento (95817-2215)
PHONE..................................916 453-2000
Margaret B Brian, *Director*
Margaret Bryan, *Administration*
Star Deppe, *Administration*
Allan Johnson, *Quality Imp Dir*
John Bevel, *Info Tech Mgr*
EMP: 400 **Privately Held**
SIC: 8069 8062 Specialty hospitals, except psychiatric; general medical & surgical hospitals
HQ: Shriners Hospitals For Children
12502 Usf Pine Dr
Tampa FL 33612
813 972-2250

(P-22050)
SOCIAL SCIENCE SERVICE CENTER
Also Called: Cedar House Rehabilitation Ctr
18612 Santa Ana Ave, Bloomington (92316-2636)
PHONE..................................909 421-7120
Daniel Gakgolla, *CEO*
Allen Eisenman, *Admin Sec*
Enrique Gonzalez, *Manager*
EMP: 63
SQ FT: 29,000

SALES (est): 3.5MM **Privately Held**
WEB: www.cedarhouse.org
SIC: 8069 8322 Substance abuse hospitals; individual & family services

(P-22051)
SPECIAL NEEDS NETWORK
4401 Crenshaw Blvd # 215, Los Angeles (90043-1200)
PHONE..................................323 291-7100
Julia Djeke, *President*
Shamya Ullah, *Bd of Directors*
Edguin Castellanos, *Officer*
Daniel Fausto, *Comms Dir*
Marcos Aguilar, *Administration*
EMP: 50 EST: 2013
SALES: 2.8MM **Privately Held**
SIC: 8069 Children's hospital

(P-22052)
SUBACUTE CHLD HOSP CAL INC
Also Called: Childrens Rcvery Ctr Nthrn Cal
3777 S Bascom Ave, Campbell (95008-7320)
PHONE..................................408 558-3644
Micahel Zarcone, *CEO*
Julie Harris, *Director*
EMP: 80
SQ FT: 17,000
SALES (est): 8.4MM **Privately Held**
SIC: 8069 Children's hospital

(P-22053)
SURE HAVEN INC
Also Called: Sure Haven Addiction Treatment
1730 Pomona Ave Ste 3, Costa Mesa (92627-3628)
PHONE..................................949 467-9213
Steve Fennelly, *CEO*
Tanisha Porreca, *COO*
Elizabeth Perry, *Vice Pres*
Mark Shandrow, *Vice Pres*
EMP: 550 EST: 2010
SQ FT: 7,500
SALES (est): 47.7MM **Privately Held**
SIC: 8069 Alcoholism rehabilitation hospital

(P-22054)
TENET HEALTHSYSTEM MEDICAL
Also Called: Placentia Linda Hospital
1301 N Rose Dr, Placentia (92870-3802)
PHONE..................................714 993-2000
Kent Clayton, *CEO*
Ann Marie Watkins, *Ch Nursing Ofcr*
Mary Ann Railey, *Planning*
Freddie Sanchez, *MIS Dir*
Lena Laroco, *Director*
EMP: 400
SALES (corp-wide): 19.3B **Publicly Held**
WEB: www.tenethealth.com
SIC: 8069 8011 8062 Specialty hospitals, except psychiatric; offices & clinics of medical doctors; general medical & surgical hospitals
HQ: Tenet Healthsystem Medical, Inc.
1445 Ross Ave Ste 1400
Dallas TX 75202
469 893-2000

(P-22055)
THERAPEUTIC ASSOCIATES INC
Also Called: Providence St Joseph Med Ctr
181 S Buena Vista St, Burbank (91505-4504)
PHONE..................................818 748-4900
EMP: 87
SALES (corp-wide): 68.3MM **Privately Held**
SIC: 8069 Cancer hospital
PA: Therapeutic Associates, Inc.
20829 72nd Ave S Ste 710
Kent WA 98032
253 872-6028

(P-22056)
UNITED CEREBRAL PALSY ASSOCIAT
Also Called: United Cerebral Palsy Assn San
333 W Benjamin Holt Dr # 1, Stockton (95207-3906)
PHONE..................................209 956-0295

Ray Call, *CEO*
Leslie Heier, *COO*
Lillian Callangan, *Finance*
EMP: 137
SALES (est): 3.5MM **Privately Held**
SIC: 8069 8322 Chronic disease hospital;
individual & family services

(P-22057)
WATERMAN CONVALESCENT HOSPITAL
Mt Rubidoux Convalescent Hosp
6401 33rd St, Riverside (92509-1404)
PHONE..................................951 681-2200
Magda Williams, *Director*
EMP: 130
SALES (corp-wide): 11.1MM **Privately Held**
SIC: 8069 8051 Specialty hospitals, except psychiatric; skilled nursing care facilities
PA: Waterman Convalescent Hospital, Inc
1850 N Waterman Ave
San Bernardino CA 92404
909 882-1215

8071 Medical Laboratories

(P-22058)
ALLIANCE HEALTHCARE SVCS INC (DH)
18201 Von Karman Ave, Irvine
(92612-1000)
P.O. Box 19532 (92623-9532)
PHONE..................................949 242-5300
Percy C Tomlinson, *CEO*
Rhonda A Longmore-Grund, *CFO*
Richard W Johns,
Howard Aihara, *Exec VP*
Laurie R Miller, *Exec VP*
EMP: 250
SALES: 505.5MM **Privately Held**
WEB: www.mvhs.org
SIC: 8071 Ultrasound laboratory
HQ: Thaihot Investment Company Us Limited
18201 Von Karman Ave
Irvine CA 92612
949 242-5300

(P-22059)
AMBRY GENETICS CORPORATION (DH)
15 Argonaut, Aliso Viejo (92656-1423)
P.O. Box 55064, Irvine (92619-5064)
PHONE..................................949 900-5500
Charles Lm Dunlop, *President*
Ardy Arianpour, *President*
Linh H Le, *COO*
Jessica Rios, *COO*
Charles Caporale, *CFO*
EMP: 85
SQ FT: 20,000
SALES (est): 17.8MM
SALES (corp-wide): 9.6B **Privately Held**
WEB: www.ambrygen.com
SIC: 8071 Medical laboratories
HQ: Konica Minolta Healthcare Americas, Inc.
411 Newark Pompton Tpke
Wayne NJ 07470
973 633-1500

(P-22060)
AMEN CLINICS INC A MED CORP (PA)
Also Called: Mindworks Press
3150 Bristol St Ste 400, Costa Mesa
(92626-3054)
PHONE..................................888 564-2700
Daniel Amen, *President*
Catherine J Hanlon, *Administration*
Amy Hernandez, *Controller*
Cherri P Myers, *Physician Asst*
▲ **EMP:** 50
SALES (est): 9.5MM **Privately Held**
WEB: www.amenclinics.com
SIC: 8071 Neurological laboratory

(P-22061)
ASCEND CLINICAL LLC (PA)
1400 Industrial Way, Redwood City
(94063-1101)
PHONE..................................650 780-5500

Paul F Beyer, *CEO*
Jeffrey Vizethann, *President*
Patricia Hunsader, *COO*
Olivier Gindraux, *CFO*
Martin Blair, *Vice Pres*
▲ **EMP:** 72
SALES (est): 13.6MM **Privately Held**
WEB: www.satellitelabs.com
SIC: 8071 Blood analysis laboratory

(P-22062)
BIO-REFERENCE LABORATORIES INC
2605 Winchester Blvd, Campbell
(95008-5379)
PHONE..................................408 341-8600
Sally Howlett, *Vice Pres*
EMP: 150
SALES (corp-wide): 1B **Publicly Held**
SIC: 8071 Testing laboratories
HQ: Bio-Reference Laboratories, Inc.
481 Edward H Ross Dr
Elmwood Park NJ 07407
201 791-2600

(P-22063)
BIOTHERANOSTICS INC (PA)
9640 Towne Centre Dr # 200, San Diego
(92121-1986)
P.O. Box 749249, Los Angeles (90074-9249)
PHONE..................................877 886-6739
Gail Sloan, *CFO*
Don Hardison, *CEO*
Mary J Mullen, *Officer*
Macey Johnson, *Vice Pres*
Karla Kelly, *Admin Sec*
EMP: 55
SALES (est): 7.8MM **Privately Held**
WEB: www.aviaradx.com
SIC: 8071 2835 Medical laboratories; in vitro diagnostics

(P-22064)
CAP DIAGNOSTICS LLC
Also Called: Pathnostics
17661 Cowan, Irvine (92614-6031)
PHONE..................................714 966-1221
David A Baunoch,
Matt Tate, *Vice Pres*
EMP: 59
SALES (est): 9.4MM **Privately Held**
SIC: 8071 Medical laboratories

(P-22065)
CARDIODX INC
600 Saginaw Dr, Redwood City
(94063-4751)
PHONE..................................650 475-2788
Khush F Mehta, *President*
Timothy Henn, *CFO*
David Levison, *Officer*
Mark Monane, *Officer*
Mark Willig, *Vice Pres*
EMP: 146
SQ FT: 33,000
SALES: 7.9MM **Privately Held**
WEB: www.cardiodx.com
SIC: 8071 2834 Medical laboratories; drugs acting on the cardiovascular system, except diagnostic

(P-22066)
CAREDX INC (PA)
3260 Bayshore Blvd, Brisbane
(94005-1021)
PHONE..................................415 287-2300
Peter Maag, *President*
Michael D Goldberg, *Ch of Bd*
Mitchell J Nelles, *COO*
Michael Bell, *CFO*
George Bickerstaff, *Bd of Directors*
EMP: 129
SQ FT: 46,000
SALES: 48.3MM **Publicly Held**
SIC: 8071 8733 Medical laboratories; non-commercial research organizations

(P-22067)
CENTRAL REFERENCE LAB INC (PA)
Also Called: Diamond Reference Laboratory
1470 Valley Vista Dr # 100, Pomona
(91765-3903)
PHONE..................................909 861-6966
Morteza Rajaee, *Vice Pres*

Abbas Rajaee, *President*
EMP: 110
SQ FT: 6,000
SALES: 15MM **Privately Held**
SIC: 8071 Medical laboratories

(P-22068)
CLARIENT DIAGNOSTIC SVCS INC
31 Columbia, Aliso Viejo (92656-1460)
PHONE..................................888 443-3310
Cindy Collins, *CEO*
Renika Seghal, *CFO*
Michael Brown, *Vice Pres*
Mark Machulcz, *Vice Pres*
EMP: 313
SALES (est): 1.7MM
SALES (corp-wide): 258.6MM **Publicly Held**
SIC: 8071 Testing laboratories
HQ: Clarient, Inc.
31 Columbia
Aliso Viejo CA 92656
949 445-7300

(P-22069)
CONSOLDTED MED BO-ANALYSIS INC (PA)
Also Called: Cmb Laboratory
10700 Walker St, Cypress (90630-4703)
P.O. Box 2369 (90630-1869)
PHONE..................................714 657-7369
Chin Kuo Fan, *President*
Gloria Fan, *Shareholder*
CAM Chinh Fan, *Senior VP*
Michelle Fan, *Vice Pres*
Irene Zacharczuk, *Lab Dir*
EMP: 100
SQ FT: 11,000
SALES: 12MM **Privately Held**
SIC: 8071 Testing laboratories

(P-22070)
CONSOLDTED MED BO-ANALYSIS INC
7631 Wyoming St Ste 105a, Westminster
(92683-3904)
PHONE..................................714 657-7389
Chin Kuo Fan, *President*
David Tran, *Manager*
EMP: 51
SALES (corp-wide): 12MM **Privately Held**
SIC: 8071 Testing laboratories
PA: Consolidated Medical Bio-Analysis, Inc.
10700 Walker St
Cypress CA 90630
714 657-7369

(P-22071)
CONSOLDTED MED BO-ANALYSIS INC
12665 Garden Grove Blvd, Garden Grove
(92843-1901)
PHONE..................................714 467-0240
Chin Kuo Fan, *Owner*
EMP: 51
SALES (corp-wide): 12MM **Privately Held**
SIC: 8071 Medical laboratories
PA: Consolidated Medical Bio-Analysis, Inc.
10700 Walker St
Cypress CA 90630
714 657-7369

(P-22072)
COUNSYL INC
180 Kimball Way, South San Francisco
(94080-6218)
PHONE..................................888 268-6795
Ramji Srinivasan, *CEO*
Joel Jung, *CFO*
Noah Nasser, *Ch Credit Ofcr*
Eric A Evans, *Officer*
James Goldberg, *Officer*
EMP: 281
SALES: 96.3MM **Publicly Held**
WEB: www.counsyl.com
SIC: 8071 Medical laboratories
PA: Myriad Genetics, Inc.
320 S Wakara Way
Salt Lake City UT 84108

(P-22073)
COUNTY OF ORANGE
Also Called: Health Care Agency
1729 W 17th St, Santa Ana (92706-2316)
PHONE..................................714 834-8385
Richard Alexander, *Director*
Lydia Mikhail, *Lab Dir*
EMP: 50 **Privately Held**
SIC: 8071 9431 Medical laboratories; administration of public health programs;
PA: County Of Orange
333 W Santa Ana Blvd 3f
Santa Ana CA 92701
714 834-6200

(P-22074)
COUNTY OF SAN BERNARDINO
Arrowhead Regional Medical Ctr
400 N Pepper Ave, Colton (92324-1801)
PHONE..................................909 580-1000
Toll Free:..................................877 -
June Griffith, *CEO*
Patrick Petre, *CEO*
Joseph Davis, *Osteopathy*
EMP: 210 **Privately Held**
SIC: 8071 9431 Medical laboratories; administration of public health programs;
PA: County Of San Bernardino
385 N Arrowhead Ave
San Bernardino CA 92415
909 387-3841

(P-22075)
DEPARTMENT HEALTH CARE SVCS
Also Called: Microbial Diseases Laboratory
850 Marina Bay Pkwy, Richmond
(94804-6403)
PHONE..................................510 412-3700
Michael Janda, *Branch Mgr*
EMP: 70 **Privately Held**
WEB: www.calsurv.org
SIC: 8071 9431 Medical laboratories; administration of public health programs;
HQ: Department Of Health Care Services
1501 Capitol Ave
Sacramento CA 95814

(P-22076)
DIAZYME LABORATORIES INC
12889 Gregg Ct, Poway (92064-6833)
PHONE..................................858 455-4754
Chong Yuan PHD, *Managing Dir*
Sandra Alguera, *Purchasing*
Douglas Borses, *Sales Dir*
Olivia Vu,
EMP: 90
SALES (est): 2.1MM **Privately Held**
SIC: 8071 Medical laboratories

(P-22077)
DIGNITY HEALTH
Health Care Lab
2102 N California St, Stockton
(95204-6031)
PHONE..................................209 467-6430
Terry Bryan, *Director*
EMP: 115
SQ FT: 2,944
SALES (corp-wide): 6.7B **Privately Held**
WEB: www.chw.edu
SIC: 8071 Testing laboratories
PA: Dignity Health
185 Berry St Ste 300
San Francisco CA 94107
415 438-5500

(P-22078)
DIGNITY HEALTH
Also Called: Mercy General Hospital
4001 J St, Sacramento (95819-3626)
PHONE..................................916 453-4453
Tom Peterson, *President*
Danielle Minkstein, *Administration*
EMP: 2000
SALES (corp-wide): 6.7B **Privately Held**
WEB: www.mercycare.net
SIC: 8071 X-ray laboratory, including dental
PA: Dignity Health
185 Berry St Ste 300
San Francisco CA 94107
415 438-5500

(P-22079)
DR SYSTEMS INC
Also Called: Dominator Radiology Systems
10140 Mesa Rim Rd, San Diego
(92121-2914)
PHONE..............................858 625-3344
Justin Dearborn, *President*
Charles Zuckerman, *CFO*
EMP: 205
SQ FT: 42,250
SALES (est): 17.3MM
SALES (corp-wide): 79.1B **Publicly Held**
WEB: www.dominator.com
SIC: 8071 Testing laboratories
HQ: Merge Healthcare Incorporated
 900 Walnut Ridge Dr
 Hartland WI 53029
 262 367-0700

(P-22080)
DUAL DIAGNOSIS TRTMNT CTR INC
Also Called: Sovereign Health of California
12832 Short Ave, Los Angeles
(90066-6421)
PHONE..............................424 289-9031
EMP: 102
SALES (corp-wide): 84.5MM **Privately Held**
SIC: 8071 Medical laboratories
PA: Dual Diagnosis Treatment Center, Inc.
 1211 Puerta Del Sol # 200
 San Clemente CA 92673
 949 276-5553

(P-22081)
EL CAMINO HOSPITAL
Evergreen Dialisist
2240 Tully Rd, San Jose (95122-1347)
PHONE..............................650 940-7000
Chu Nuyen, *Manager*
EMP: 174
SALES (corp-wide): 930.5MM **Privately Held**
SIC: 8071 Medical laboratories
PA: El Camino Hospital
 2500 Grant Rd
 Mountain View CA 94040
 408 224-6660

(P-22082)
ENDOCRINE SCIENCES INC
Also Called: Esoterix Ctr For Clncal Trails
4301 Lost Hills Rd, Calabasas
(91301-5358)
PHONE..............................818 880-8040
Darrel Mayes, *CEO*
Dennis Griffin, *President*
EMP: 125 EST: 1972
SQ FT: 35,000
SALES (est): 6.6MM **Publicly Held**
WEB: www.esoterix.com
SIC: 8071 2869 Medical laboratories; industrial organic chemicals
HQ: Esoterix Inc
 4509 Freidrich Ln Ste 100
 Austin TX 78744
 512 225-1100

(P-22083)
EPIC SCIENCES INC
9381 Judicial Dr Ste 200, San Diego
(92121-3832)
PHONE..............................858 356-6610
Murali K Prahalad, *President*
Michael Rodriguez, *CFO*
Katherine Atkinson, *Ch Credit Ofcr*
Chris Bernard, *Officer*
Elena Antonova, *Vice Pres*
EMP: 80
SALES (est): 14.2MM **Privately Held**
SIC: 8071 Blood analysis laboratory

(P-22084)
EXAGEN DIAGNOSTICS INC
1221 Liberty Way Ste A, Vista
(92081-8368)
PHONE..............................505 272-7966
Robert Mignatti, *President*
EMP: 64
SALES (corp-wide): 13.6MM **Privately Held**
SIC: 8071 Medical laboratories

PA: Exagen Diagnostics, Inc.
 1261 Liberty Way Ste C
 Vista CA 92081
 760 560-1501

(P-22085)
FOCUS DIAGNOSTICS INC
11331 Valley View St # 150, Cypress
(90630-5300)
PHONE..............................714 220-1900
John Hurrell PHD, *President*
Anh Ha, *Research*
Michelle Tabb, *Research*
Susan Vogeli, *Technical Staff*
Mario Guillen, *Purchasing*
EMP: 400
SQ FT: 36,000
SALES (est): 3.3MM
SALES (corp-wide): 7.7B **Publicly Held**
WEB: www.focusdx.com
SIC: 8071 Testing laboratories
PA: Quest Diagnostics Incorporated
 500 Plaza Dr Ste G
 Secaucus NJ 07094
 973 520-2700

(P-22086)
FOCUS TECHNOLOGIES HOLDING CO
10703 Progress Way, Cypress
(90630-4714)
PHONE..............................800 838-4548
Charles C Harwood, *President*
Edward Caffrey, *Vice Pres*
Don Mooney, *Vice Pres*
Laurence R McCarthy, *CTO*
Aruna Seth, *Finance Mgr*
EMP: 454
SQ FT: 28,000
SALES (est): 6.7MM **Privately Held**
WEB: www.focustechnologies.com
SIC: 8071 3826 Testing laboratories; analytical instruments

(P-22087)
GARDEN GROVE ADVANCED IMAGING
1510 Cotner Ave, Los Angeles
(90025-3303)
PHONE..............................310 445-2800
EMP: 209
SALES (est): 1.1MM **Publicly Held**
SIC: 8071 Medical laboratories
HQ: Radnet Management, Inc.
 1510 Cotner Ave
 Los Angeles CA 90025
 310 445-2800

(P-22088)
GENMARK DIAGNOSTICS INC (PA)
5964 La Place Ct Ste 100, Carlsbad
(92008-8829)
PHONE..............................760 448-4300
Hany Massarany, *President*
James Fox, *Ch of Bd*
Scott Mendel, *CFO*
Daryl Faulkner, *Bd of Directors*
Michael Kagnoff, *Bd of Directors*
EMP: 135
SQ FT: 53,000
SALES: 52.5MM **Publicly Held**
SIC: 8071 Medical laboratories

(P-22089)
GENOMEDX BIOSCIENCES CORP
10355 Science Center Dr # 240, San Diego
(92121-1158)
PHONE..............................888 975-4540
Doug Dolginow, *CEO*
Elai Davicioni, *President*
William Kachioff, *CFO*
EMP: 100 EST: 2012
SQ FT: 15,000
SALES: 7.3MM **Privately Held**
SIC: 8071 Biological laboratory
PA: Genomedx Biosciences Inc
 1038 Homer St
 Vancouver BC V6B 2
 888 975-4540

(P-22090)
GENOMIC HEALTH INC (PA)
301 Penobscot Dr, Redwood City
(94063-4700)
PHONE..............................650 556-9300
Kimberly J Popovits, *Ch of Bd*
Frederic Pla, *COO*
G Bradley Cole, *CFO*
Phillip Febbo, *Chief Mktg Ofcr*
Jason W Radford,
EMP: 142
SQ FT: 180,700
SALES: 340.7MM **Publicly Held**
WEB: www.genomichealth.com
SIC: 8071 8731 Medical laboratories; biotechnical research, commercial

(P-22091)
GENOMIC HEALTH INC
101 University Ave, Palo Alto (94301-1638)
PHONE..............................650 269-0545
EMP: 385
SALES (corp-wide): 340.7MM **Publicly Held**
SIC: 8071 Medical laboratories
PA: Genomic Health, Inc.
 301 Penobscot Dr
 Redwood City CA 94063
 650 556-9300

(P-22092)
GENOMIC HEALTH INC
101 Galveston Dr, Redwood City
(94063-4734)
PHONE..............................650 556-9300
Kimberly Popovits, *CEO*
Sabine Lang, *Associate Dir*
Julie Elliot, *Marketing Staff*
Bonnie Cheng, *Director*
Keith Gran, *Director*
EMP: 336
SALES (corp-wide): 340.7MM **Publicly Held**
SIC: 8071 8731 Medical laboratories; commercial physical research
PA: Genomic Health, Inc.
 301 Penobscot Dr
 Redwood City CA 94063
 650 556-9300

(P-22093)
GENOPTIX INC (PA)
Also Called: Genoptix Medical Laboratory
2131 Faraday Ave, Carlsbad (92008-7252)
PHONE..............................760 268-6200
Joseph M Limber, *CEO*
Mark Spring, *CFO*
Hutan Hashemi, *Associate Dir*
Wen Wu, *Research*
Christopher Leonardi, *Marketing Staff*
EMP: 144
SQ FT: 116,000
SALES (est): 51.5MM **Privately Held**
WEB: www.genoptix.com
SIC: 8071 Medical laboratories

(P-22094)
GENOPTIX INC
Also Called: Genoptix Mdcial Lab A Novartis
2110 Rutherford Rd, Carlsbad
(92008-7328)
PHONE..............................760 268-6200
Christian Itin, *Manager*
Kristen Tuba, *Info Tech Mgr*
Nick Sanna, *Business Mgr*
Burt De Mill, *VP Sales*
Sam Cruz, *Accounts Mgr*
EMP: 260
SALES (corp-wide): 51.5MM **Privately Held**
SIC: 8071 Testing laboratories
PA: Genoptix, Inc.
 2131 Faraday Ave
 Carlsbad CA 92008
 760 268-6200

(P-22095)
GRIFOLS DIAGNSTC SOLUTIONS INC (HQ)
4560 Horton St, Emeryville (94608-2916)
PHONE..............................323 225-2221
David Bell, *Exec VP*
Sergio Molina, *Vice Pres*
Dennis Cody, *Senior Engr*
Marco Tamagno, *VP Finance*
Shubhi Sharma, *Analyst*

EMP: 168
SALES (est): 171.8MM
SALES (corp-wide): 696.8MM **Privately Held**
SIC: 8071 Testing laboratories; biological laboratory; blood analysis laboratory; pathological laboratory
PA: Grifols Sa
 Calle Jesus I Maria 6
 Barcelona 08022
 935 710-196

(P-22096)
GUARDANT HEALTH INC
505 Penobscot Dr, Redwood City
(94063-4737)
PHONE..............................855 698-8887
Helmy Eltoukhy, *CEO*
Amirali Talasaz, *Ch of Bd*
Derek Bertocci, *CFO*
Richard Lanman, *Chief Mktg Ofcr*
Michael Wiley,
EMP: 275
SQ FT: 114,000
SALES: 49.8MM **Privately Held**
SIC: 8071 Medical laboratories

(P-22097)
IDEXX REFERENCE LABS INC
1370 Reynolds Ave Ste 109, Irvine
(92614-5545)
PHONE..............................949 477-2840
Carlos Vasquez, *Manager*
EMP: 50
SALES (corp-wide): 1.9B **Publicly Held**
SIC: 8071 Testing laboratories
HQ: Idexx Reference Laboratories, Inc.
 1 Idexx Dr
 Westbrook ME 04092
 207 556-0300

(P-22098)
IDEXX REFERENCE LABS INC
2825 Kovr Dr, West Sacramento
(95605-1600)
PHONE..............................916 372-4200
Lewis Knight, *Branch Mgr*
William Flaherty, *Opers Staff*
Vera Yang, *Manager*
Dave Fisher, *Regional*
EMP: 175
SALES (corp-wide): 1.9B **Publicly Held**
SIC: 8071 Testing laboratories
HQ: Idexx Reference Laboratories, Inc.
 1 Idexx Dr
 Westbrook ME 04092
 207 556-0300

(P-22099)
KAISER MANTECA MEDICAL OFFICE
1721 W Yosemite Ave, Manteca
(95337-5130)
PHONE..............................209 825-3700
Melanie Hatchel, *Owner*
EMP: 115 EST: 1998
SALES (est): 4.7MM **Privately Held**
SIC: 8071 Medical laboratories

(P-22100)
KAISER RADIOLOGY
7300 N Fresno St, Fresno (93720-2941)
PHONE..............................559 448-5541
Quemars Ahmadi, *Manager*
Mary Cooper, *Manager*
EMP: 80 EST: 1986
SALES (est): 4.6MM **Privately Held**
SIC: 8071 X-ray laboratory, including dental

(P-22101)
KAN-DI-KI LLC (PA)
Also Called: Diagnostic Labs & Rdlgy
2820 N Ontario St, Burbank (91504-2015)
PHONE..............................818 549-1880
Mark Parrish, *CEO*
Maiker Gomez, *Technology*
Julie Ravin, *VP Human Res*
Zachary Reyes, *Radiology*
Kelly McCullum,
EMP: 129
SQ FT: 7,000
SALES (est): 62.8MM **Privately Held**
SIC: 8071 Testing laboratories; X-ray laboratory, including dental

PRODUCTS & SVCS

(P-22102)
LABORATORY CORPORATION AMERICA
14901 Rinaldi St Ste 203, Mission Hills (91345-1251)
PHONE.................818 361-7089
Paul Rodriguez, *Manager*
EMP: 84 **Publicly Held**
SIC: 8071 Medical laboratories
HQ: Laboratory Corporation Of America
358 S Main St Ste 458
Burlington NC 27215
336 229-1127

(P-22103)
LABORATORY CORPORATION AMERICA
10930 Bigge St, San Leandro (94577-1121)
PHONE.................510 635-4555
Kimberly Williams, *Branch Mgr*
David Wilson, *Director*
Pu Fung, *Manager*
EMP: 84 **Publicly Held**
SIC: 8071 Testing laboratories
HQ: Laboratory Corporation Of America
358 S Main St Ste 458
Burlington NC 27215
336 229-1127

(P-22104)
LATARA ENTERPRISE INC (PA)
Also Called: Foundation Laboratory
1716 W Holt Ave, Pomona (91768-3333)
PHONE.................909 623-9301
Stepan Vartanian, *CEO*
Michelle Lewis, *CFO*
ARA Vartanian, *Treasurer*
Lala Vartanian, *Exec VP*
Esther Boyamyan, *Human Resources*
EMP: 120
SQ FT: 19,000
SALES (est): 13.4MM **Privately Held**
WEB: www.foundationlaboratory.com
SIC: 8071 Pathological laboratory

(P-22105)
LATARA ENTERPRISE INC
9610 Stockdale Hwy, Bakersfield (93311-3625)
PHONE.................661 665-9780
Rosie Chavez, *Manager*
EMP: 62
SALES (corp-wide): 13.4MM **Privately Held**
SIC: 8071 Testing laboratories
PA: Latara Enterprise, Inc.
1716 W Holt Ave
Pomona CA 91768
909 623-9301

(P-22106)
LATARA ENTERPRISE INC
705 E Virginia Way Ste D, Barstow (92311-3955)
PHONE.................760 256-3450
Susan Reese, *Manager*
EMP: 62
SALES (corp-wide): 13.4MM **Privately Held**
SIC: 8071 Testing laboratories
PA: Latara Enterprise, Inc.
1716 W Holt Ave
Pomona CA 91768
909 623-9301

(P-22107)
LAWRENCE BERKELEY NATIONAL LAB
1 Cyclotron Rd 50-4133, Berkeley (94720-8099)
PHONE.................510 486-5111
Michael Witherell, *Director*
Donald J Depaolo, *Director*
▲ EMP: 4636
SALES (est): 206.1MM **Publicly Held**
SIC: 8071 Biological laboratory
HQ: United States Department Of Energy
Berkeley Office
1 Cyclotron Rd
Berkeley CA 94720
510 486-5784

(P-22108)
MAGNETIC IMAGING AFFILATES
5730 Telegraph Ave, Oakland (94609-1710)
PHONE.................510 204-1820
Stefan Arnold, *Director*
EMP: 55
SQ FT: 3,500
SALES (est): 2.4MM **Privately Held**
SIC: 8071 Medical laboratories

(P-22109)
MAX MRI IMAGING INC (PA)
17530 Ventura Blvd # 105, Encino (91316-3883)
PHONE.................818 382-2220
Rafi Hedvat, *Principal*
Javad Ahmadian, *President*
Cecilia Saldana, *Manager*
EMP: 50
SQ FT: 10,000
SALES (est): 5MM **Privately Held**
WEB: www.maxmriimaging.com
SIC: 8071 X-ray laboratory, including dental

(P-22110)
MAX/MR IMAGING INC
17530 Ventura Blvd # 105, Encino (91316-3883)
PHONE.................818 382-2220
Javad Ahmadian, *President*
Rafi Hedvat, *CFO*
Majid Ahmadian, *Vice Pres*
Laura Melendez, *Administration*
Alfredo Flores, *Technology*
EMP: 100
SALES (est): 2.8MM **Privately Held**
SIC: 8071 X-ray laboratory, including dental

(P-22111)
MID RCKLAND IMGING PRTNERS INC (HQ)
1510 Cotner Ave, Los Angeles (90025-3303)
PHONE.................310 445-2800
Howard G Berger, *CEO*
▲ EMP: 50
SQ FT: 1,000
SALES (est): 8.3MM **Publicly Held**
SIC: 8071 Ultrasound laboratory; X-ray laboratory, including dental; neurological laboratory

(P-22112)
MOSS LANDING MARINE LABS
8272 Moss Landing Rd, Moss Landing (95039-9647)
PHONE.................831 771-4400
James Harvey, *Director*
Jason Taylor, *President*
Toni R Fitzwater, *Exec Dir*
Sandy Yarbrough, *Admin Asst*
April Guimaraes, *Technician*
EMP: 150
SALES (est): 13.6MM **Privately Held**
WEB: www.mlml.calstate.edu
SIC: 8071 Biological laboratory

(P-22113)
MUIR LABS
Also Called: Muirlab
1601 Ygnacio Valley Rd, Walnut Creek (94598-3122)
PHONE.................925 947-3335
Pat Morgan, *Director*
Jim Manus, *Manager*
EMP: 400
SALES (est): 5MM **Privately Held**
SIC: 8071 Medical laboratories

(P-22114)
NATERA INC (PA)
201 Industrial Rd Ste 410, San Carlos (94070-2396)
PHONE.................650 249-9090
Matthew Rabinowitz, *Ch of Bd*
Steve Chapman, *COO*
Michael Brophy, *CFO*
Jonathan Sheena, *CTO*
EMP: 215
SQ FT: 113,000
SALES: 210.9MM **Publicly Held**
SIC: 8071 2835 Testing laboratories; in vitro diagnostics

(P-22115)
NATIONAL GENETICS INSTITUTE
2440 S Sepulveda Blvd # 235, Los Angeles (90064-1748)
PHONE.................310 996-6610
Mike Aicher, *CEO*
EMP: 169 **Publicly Held**
SIC: 8071 Testing laboratories
HQ: National Genetics Institute
2440 S Sepulveda Blvd # 235
Los Angeles CA 90064
-

(P-22116)
NEWPORT DIAGNOSTIC CENTER INC (PA)
Also Called: Newport Radio Surgery Center
1605 Avocado Ave, Newport Beach (92660-7725)
PHONE.................949 760-3025
Hazem H Chehabi, *President*
Nader Morcos, *Vice Pres*
Brian Olson, *Exec Dir*
Gregg Stempson, *Info Tech Dir*
Brigit Lieb, *Tech/Comp Coord*
EMP: 60
SQ FT: 26,000
SALES (est): 7.7MM **Privately Held**
SIC: 8071 Testing laboratories

(P-22117)
NICHOLS INST REFERENCE LABS (DH)
33608 Ortega Hwy, San Juan Capistrano (92675-2042)
PHONE.................949 728-4000
Douglas Harrington, *President*
Charles Olson, *CFO*
Jolene Kahn, *Treasurer*
Michael O'Gorman, *Vice Pres*
Murugan R Pandian, *Vice Pres*
EMP: 525
SQ FT: 240,000
SALES (est): 10.8MM
SALES (corp-wide): 7.7B **Publicly Held**
SIC: 8071 Testing laboratories
HQ: Quest Diagnostics Nichols Institute
33608 Ortega Hwy
San Juan Capistrano CA 92675
949 728-4000

(P-22118)
OPTICS LABORATORY INC
9480 Telstar Ave Ste 3, El Monte (91731-2988)
PHONE.................626 350-1926
Patricia Chiu, *CEO*
Shawn Ko, *Chairman*
Wilson Wong, *Technology*
George Lin, *Business Mgr*
Sweety Wijaya, *Assistant VP*
▲ EMP: 60
SQ FT: 7,500
SALES (est): 3.3MM **Privately Held**
WEB: www.opticslab.com
SIC: 8071 Testing laboratories

(P-22119)
PENNISULA PTHLOGISTS MED GROUP
Also Called: Peninsula Pathology Associates
393 E Grand Ave Ste I, South San Francisco (94080-6233)
PHONE.................650 616-2940
Leonard A Valentino MD, *President*
Judy Alonzo, *President*
Carolyn Katzen MD, *Treasurer*
Jay A Guichard MD, *Vice Pres*
Martha S Hales, *Admin Sec*
EMP: 60
SALES (est): 3.7MM **Privately Held**
SIC: 8071 Pathological laboratory

(P-22120)
PENTRON CLINICAL TECH LLC
1717 W Collins Ave, Orange (92867-5422)
PHONE.................203 265-7397
EMP: 85
SALES (est): 2.3MM
SALES (corp-wide): 16.8MM **Privately Held**
SIC: 8071

PA: Pentron Corporation
53 N Plains Industrial Rd
Wallingford CT 06492
203 265-7397

(P-22121)
PHIFACTOR TECHNOLOGIES LLC
6415 Surfside Way, Malibu (90265-3627)
PHONE.................424 234-9494
Heiko Schmidt, *CEO*
EMP: 60
SQ FT: 2,700
SALES: 6.5MM **Privately Held**
SIC: 8071 3841 8731 Medical laboratories; diagnostic apparatus, medical; biotechnical research, commercial

(P-22122)
PHYSICIANS AUTOMATED LAB INC (DH)
Also Called: Central Coast Pathology Lab
820 34th St Ste 102, Bakersfield (93301-1933)
P.O. Box 1536 (93302-1536)
PHONE.................661 325-0744
Ken Botta, *CEO*
William R Schmalhorst MD, *President*
Bruce Smith, *CEO*
Joyce Hulen, *Admin Sec*
Mimi Breslin, *Finance Dir*
EMP: 69
SQ FT: 63,000
SALES (est): 27.1MM **Privately Held**
SIC: 8071 Medical laboratories

(P-22123)
POLYPEPTIDE LABORATORIES INC (DH)
365 Maple Ave, Torrance (90503-2602)
PHONE.................310 782-3569
Jane Salik, *President*
Tim Culbreth, *Vice Pres*
Nagana Goud, *Vice Pres*
Michael Verlander, *Vice Pres*
Brant Zell, *Vice Pres*
▲ EMP: 90
SQ FT: 19,200
SALES (est): 12.8MM **Privately Held**
WEB: www.polypeptide.com
SIC: 8071 8731 Medical laboratories; biotechnical research, commercial
HQ: Polypeptide Laboratories Holding (Ppl) Ab
Soldattorpsv 5
Limhamn 216 1
403 662-00

(P-22124)
PRECISION TOXICOLOGY LLC
4215 Sorrento Valley Blvd, San Diego (92121-1408)
PHONE.................800 635-6901
Jason Hansen, *CEO*
Miguel Gallego, *COO*
Kenton Whitfield, *CFO*
EMP: 60
SALES (est): 7.5MM
SALES (corp-wide): 79.5MM **Privately Held**
SIC: 8071 Testing laboratories
PA: Belhealth Investment Partners, Llc
126 E 56th St Fl 23
New York NY 10022
347 308-7011

(P-22125)
PRIMEX CLINICAL LABS INC (PA)
16742 Stagg St Ste 120, Van Nuys (91406-1641)
PHONE.................818 779-0496
Oshin Hartoonian, *President*
Erik Avaniss-Aghajano, *Vice Pres*
ARA Hartoonian, *Vice Pres*
Andre Aslanian, *Info Tech Dir*
Ed Mekhitarian, *Technology*
EMP: 80
SQ FT: 3,000
SALES (est): 13MM **Privately Held**
WEB: www.primexlab.com
SIC: 8071 Blood analysis laboratory

(P-22126)
PROGENITY INC (PA)
Also Called: Amdx Laboratory Sciences
4330 La Jolla Village Dr # 200, San Diego
(92122-6201)
P.O. Box 674425, Detroit MI (48267-4425)
PHONE..................................760 494-1555
Harry Stylli, *CEO*
Jeni Rein, *Executive Asst*
Don Goss, *Software Dev*
Robert Manikowski, *Software Dev*
Mark Saur, *Software Engr*
EMP: 145 **EST:** 2002
SALES (est): 39.3MM **Privately Held**
WEB: www.amdxlabs.com
SIC: 8071 8731 Blood analysis laboratory;
biotechnical research, commercial

(P-22127)
PROOVE MEDICAL LABS INC
15326 Elton Pkwy, Irvine (92618)
PHONE..................................949 427-5303
Brian Meshkin, *CEO*
Sean Roddi, *COO*
Russell Skibsted, *CFO*
EMP: 175
SQ FT: 71,000
SALES: 201MM **Privately Held**
SIC: 8071 Biological laboratory

(P-22128)
**QUEST DGNSTICS CLNCAL
LABS INC**
2369 Bering Dr, San Jose (95131-1125)
PHONE..................................408 975-1015
Dennis Hogle, *Manager*
EMP: 320
SALES (corp-wide): 7.7B **Publicly Held**
WEB: www.questcentrallab.com
SIC: 8071 Testing laboratories
HQ: Quest Diagnostics Clinical Laborato-
ries, Inc.
1201 S Collegeville Rd
Collegeville PA 19426
610 454-6000

(P-22129)
**QUEST DGNSTICS CLNCAL
LABS INC**
26081 Avenue Hall 150, Valencia
(91355-1241)
PHONE..................................661 964-6582
Dennis Hogle, *Branch Mgr*
John Nelson, *Project Leader*
EMP: 350
SQ FT: 40,000
SALES (corp-wide): 7.7B **Publicly Held**
WEB: www.questcentrallab.com
SIC: 8071 Medical laboratories
HQ: Quest Diagnostics Clinical Laborato-
ries, Inc.
1201 S Collegeville Rd
Collegeville PA 19426
610 454-6000

(P-22130)
**QUEST DIAGNOSTICS
INCORPORATED**
401 Gregory Ln Ste 146, Pleasant Hill
(94523-2836)
PHONE..................................925 687-2514
Claire McCrossen, *Manager*
EMP: 450
SALES (corp-wide): 7.7B **Publicly Held**
WEB: www.questdiagnostics.com
SIC: 8071 Testing laboratories
PA: Quest Diagnostics Incorporated
500 Plaza Dr Ste G
Secaucus NJ 07094
973 520-2700

(P-22131)
**QUEST DIAGNOSTICS
INCORPORATED**
33608 Ortega Hwy, Mission Viejo
(92675-2042)
PHONE..................................949 728-4235
Jon Nakamoto, *Manager*
EMP: 500
SALES (corp-wide): 7.7B **Publicly Held**
WEB: www.questdiagnostics.com
SIC: 8071 Testing laboratories

PA: Quest Diagnostics Incorporated
500 Plaza Dr Ste G
Secaucus NJ 07094
973 520-2700

(P-22132)
**QUEST DIAGNOSTICS
INCORPORATED**
1275 E Spruce Ave Ste 102, Fresno
(93720-3372)
PHONE..................................559 438-2893
Jeff Owens, *Manager*
EMP: 60
SALES (corp-wide): 7.7B **Publicly Held**
WEB: www.questdiagnostics.com
SIC: 8071 Medical laboratories
PA: Quest Diagnostics Incorporated
500 Plaza Dr Ste G
Secaucus NJ 07094
973 520-2700

(P-22133)
RADNET INC (PA)
1510 Cotner Ave, Los Angeles
(90025-3303)
PHONE..................................310 445-2800
Howard G Berger, *Ch of Bd*
Mark D Stolper, *CFO*
Lawrence Levitt, *Bd of Directors*
Jeffrey L Linden, *Exec VP*
Michael M Murdock, *Exec VP*
EMP: 150
SQ FT: 21,500
SALES: 922.1MM **Publicly Held**
WEB: www.radnetonline.com
SIC: 8071 Ultrasound laboratory

(P-22134)
REDDING PATHOLOGISTS LAB
2036 Railroad Ave, Redding (96001-1801)
PHONE..................................530 225-8050
EMP: 55
SALES (corp-wide): 11.6MM **Privately
Held**
SIC: 8071
PA: Redding Pathologists Laboratory
1725 Gold St
Redding CA 96001
530 225-8050

(P-22135)
**REDWOOD REGIONAL MEDICAL
GROUP (PA)**
Also Called: Redwood Regional Oncology Ctr
990 Sonoma Ave Ste 15, Santa Rosa
(95404-4813)
PHONE..................................707 525-4080
Mike Smith, *CFO*
Allan P Fishbein,
David A Keefer,
EMP: 70
SQ FT: 20,000
SALES (est): 12.3MM **Privately Held**
WEB: www.rrmginc.com
SIC: 8071 8011 X-ray laboratory, including
dental; radiologist

(P-22136)
**REDWOOD TOXICOLOGY LAB
INC**
3650 Westwind Blvd, Santa Rosa
(95403-1066)
P.O. Box 5680 (95402-5680)
PHONE..................................707 577-7958
Albert Berger, *CEO*
Wayne Ross, *Shareholder*
Alber Berger, *CEO*
Barry Chapman, *CFO*
Brian Krawchuk, *Technician*
▲ **EMP:** 120
SQ FT: 23,000
SALES (est): 19.8MM
SALES (corp-wide): 27.3B **Publicly Held**
WEB: www.redwoodtoxicology.com
SIC: 8071 8734 Testing laboratories; test-
ing laboratories
HQ: Alere Inc.
51 Sawyer Rd Ste 200
Waltham MA 02453
781 647-3900

(P-22137)
**RHEUMATOLOGY DIAGNOSTICS
LAB**
Also Called: Rdl Reference Laboratory
10755 Venice Blvd, Los Angeles
(90034-6214)
P.O. Box 34020 (90034-0020)
PHONE..................................310 253-5455
Morris Robert I, *President*
Laura Lehrhoff, *COO*
Allan Metzger MD, *Vice Pres*
Phillip Stepanik, *Safety Dir*
Barbara RAO, *Director*
EMP: 60
SQ FT: 33,000
SALES (est): 7.7MM **Privately Held**
WEB: www.rdlinc.com
SIC: 8071 Pathological laboratory

(P-22138)
**SADDLEBACK MEMORIAL MED
CTR**
Also Called: Saddleback Mem Med Lab Svcs
24411 Health Center Dr, Laguna Hills
(92653-3651)
PHONE..................................949 452-3405
Cheryl Dilbeck, *Manager*
EMP: 150
SALES (corp-wide): 2.2B **Privately Held**
SIC: 8071 Medical laboratories
HQ: Saddleback Memorial Medical Center
24451 Health Center Dr # 1
Laguna Hills CA 92653
949 837-4500

(P-22139)
SAMARITAN IMAGING CENTER
1245 Wilshire Blvd # 205, Los Angeles
(90017-4812)
PHONE..................................213 977-2140
Andrew B Leeka, *CEO*
EMP: 658
SALES: 3.8MM
SALES (corp-wide): 319.2MM **Privately
Held**
SIC: 8071 Medical laboratories
PA: Good Samaritan Hospital
1225 Wilshire Blvd
Los Angeles CA 90017
213 977-2121

(P-22140)
SANTA BARBRA CTTGE HSPTL
Respiratory Care
400 W Pueblo St, Santa Barbara
(93105-4353)
PHONE..................................805 569-7224
Dr Phillip Michael, *Director*
EMP: 303
SALES (corp-wide): 646.4MM **Privately
Held**
SIC: 8071 Medical laboratories
PA: Santa Barbara Cottage Hospital
400 W Pueblo St
Santa Barbara CA 93105
805 682-7111

(P-22141)
**SANTA MNICA WLSHIRE IMGING
LLC**
Also Called: Tower St John Imaging
5455 Wilshire Blvd, Los Angeles
(90036-4201)
PHONE..................................323 549-3055
Gerald Roth MD,
EMP: 50
SALES (est): 5MM **Privately Held**
SIC: 8071 X-ray laboratory, including den-
tal

(P-22142)
**SANTA ROSA RADIOLOGY MED
GROUP (PA)**
121 Sotoyome St, Santa Rosa
(95405-4871)
PHONE..................................707 546-4062
Kim Miranda, *CFO*
EMP: 50
SQ FT: 20,000
SALES (est): 4.4MM **Privately Held**
WEB: www.wyominglobbyist.com
SIC: 8071 8011 X-ray laboratory, including
dental; radiologist

(P-22143)
**SCANTIBODIES CLINICAL LAB
INC**
9236 Abraham Way, Santee (92071-5611)
PHONE..................................866 249-1212
Thomas L Cantor, *President*
Denise Ly, *Info Tech Mgr*
Karen Rodriguez, *Accountant*
EMP: 50
SALES (est): 2.4MM
SALES (corp-wide): 97.2MM **Privately
Held**
SIC: 8071 Testing laboratories
PA: Scantibodies Laboratory, Inc.
9336 Abraham Way
Santee CA 92071
619 258-9300

(P-22144)
**SCHRYVER MED SLS & MKTG
LLC**
526 Mccormick St, San Leandro
(94577-1108)
PHONE..................................303 371-0073
Todd Hubbard, *Manager*
EMP: 120 **Privately Held**
SIC: 8071 Medical laboratories
PA: Schryver Medical Sales And Marketing,
Llc
12075 E 45th Ave Ste 600
Denver CO 80239
-

(P-22145)
**SCHRYVER MED SLS & MKTG
LLC**
1845 N Case St, Orange (92865-4234)
PHONE..................................303 459-8160
Jose Silva, *Branch Mgr*
EMP: 91 **Privately Held**
SIC: 8071 Ultrasound laboratory; X-ray
laboratory, including dental
PA: Schryver Medical Sales And Marketing,
Llc
12075 E 45th Ave Ste 600
Denver CO 80239

(P-22146)
**SCHRYVER MED SLS & MKTG
LLC**
310 N Cluff Ave Ste 212, Lodi
(95240-0764)
PHONE..................................303 459-8150
Marc Martin, *Branch Mgr*
EMP: 91 **Privately Held**
SIC: 8071 Ultrasound laboratory; X-ray
laboratory, including dental
PA: Schryver Medical Sales And Marketing,
Llc
12075 E 45th Ave Ste 600
Denver CO 80239

(P-22147)
**SEQUENOM CENTER FOR
MOLECULAR**
Also Called: Sequenom Laboratories
3595 John Hopkins Ct, San Diego
(92121-1121)
PHONE..................................858 202-9051
Jeffrey D Linton, *Admin Sec*
Carolyn D Beaver, *Treasurer*
Daniel Grosu, *Vice Pres*
◆ **EMP:** 400
SALES: 89.7MM **Publicly Held**
WEB: www.sequenom.com
SIC: 8071 Medical laboratories
HQ: Sequenom, Inc.
3595 John Hopkins Ct
San Diego CA 92121

(P-22148)
**SPECIALTY LABORATORIES
INC (DH)**
Also Called: Quest Diagn Nichols Inst Valen
27027 Tourney Rd, Valencia (91355-5386)
PHONE..................................661 799-6543
R Keith Laughman, *President*
Vicki Difrancesco, *Vice Pres*
Lupe Garza, *Admin Sec*
Nicole Larkins, *Administration*
Michael Bond, *Info Tech Mgr*

PRODUCTS & SVCS

▲ EMP: 633 EST: 1975
SALES (est): 20.9MM
SALES (corp-wide): 7.7B **Publicly Held**
WEB: www.specialtylabs.com
SIC: 8071 Testing laboratories
HQ: Ameripath, Inc.
   7111 Fairway Dr Ste 101
   Palm Beach Gardens FL 33418
   561 712-6200

(P-22149)
SPRING BIOSCIENCE CORP
4300 Hacienda Dr, Pleasanton
(94588-2722)
PHONE.....................925 474-8463
Meghan Lehrkamp, *Manager*
EMP: 785
SALES (est): 4.1MM
SALES (corp-wide): 53.9B **Privately Held**
WEB: www.springbio.com
SIC: 8071 Medical laboratories
HQ: Ventana Medical Systems, Inc.
   1910 E Innovation Park Dr
   Oro Valley AZ 85755
   520 887-2155

(P-22150)
SUTTER HEALTH
2001 Dwight Way, Berkeley (94704-2608)
PHONE.....................510 204-1591
EMP: 239
SALES (corp-wide): 12.4B **Privately Held**
SIC: 8071 Medical laboratories
PA: Sutter Health
   2200 River Plaza Dr
   Sacramento CA 95833
   916 733-8800

(P-22151)
SUTTER HEALTH
Also Called: Roseville Imaging
1640 E Roseville Pkwy, Roseville
(95661-3902)
PHONE.....................916 784-2277
Jerry Fosselman, *Manager*
EMP: 85
SALES (corp-wide): 12.4B **Privately Held**
WEB: www.radiological.com
SIC: 8071 8011 Medical laboratories; specialized medical practitioners, except internal
PA: Sutter Health
   2200 River Plaza Dr
   Sacramento CA 95833
   916 733-8800

(P-22152)
TRUXTUN RADIOLOGY MED GROUP LP
3940 San Dimas St, Bakersfield
(93301-1458)
PHONE.....................661 325-6200
Girish Patel, *General Ptnr*
Joan Brandehoff, *Shareholder*
EMP: 150
SALES (est): 1.8MM **Privately Held**
SIC: 8071 X-ray laboratory, including dental

(P-22153)
UNCHAINED LABS (PA)
Also Called: Optim
6870 Koll Center Pkwy # 20, Pleasanton
(94566-3176)
PHONE.....................925 587-9800
Tim Harness, *CEO*
Jason Novi, *COO*
Terry Salyer, *Ch Credit Ofcr*
Will Lachnit, *Vice Pres*
Scott Lockard, *Vice Pres*
EMP: 140
SALES (est): 42.3MM **Privately Held**
SIC: 8071 Medical laboratories

(P-22154)
UNILAB CORPORATION (HQ)
Also Called: Quest Diagnostics
8401 Fallbrook Ave, West Hills
(91304-3226)
PHONE.....................818 737-6000
Surya Mohapatra, *CEO*
Robert Moverley, *Managing Dir*
Anthony Gouveia, *Controller*
Alexis Pacheco, *Training Spec*
Lee Hilbourne, *Med Doctor*
EMP: 400

SALES (est): 553.2MM
SALES (corp-wide): 7.7B **Publicly Held**
WEB: www.unilab.com
SIC: 8071 Testing laboratories
PA: Quest Diagnostics Incorporated
   500 Plaza Dr Ste G
   Secaucus NJ 07094
   973 520-2700

(P-22155)
UNILAB CORPORATION
6475 Camden Ave Ste 104, San Jose
(95120-2847)
PHONE.....................408 927-8331
Ian Brotchie, *President*
EMP: 300
SALES (corp-wide): 7.7B **Publicly Held**
WEB: www.unilab.com
SIC: 8071 Testing laboratories
HQ: Unilab Corporation
   8401 Fallbrook Ave
   West Hills CA 91304
   818 737-6000

(P-22156)
VALLEY RADIOLOGY CONSULTANTS (PA)
6185 Paseo Del Norte # 110, Carlsbad
(92011-1152)
PHONE.....................619 797-8248
Allen Nalbandian, *President*
Raymond Sung, *Treasurer*
Marcus Van Demetrie, *Admin Sec*
EMP: 52
SALES (est): 9.6MM **Privately Held**
WEB: www.valleyrad.com
SIC: 8071 8011 X-ray laboratory, including dental; radiologist

(P-22157)
VALLEY TOXICOLOGY SERVICE INC
Also Called: Valtox Laboratories
2401 Port St, West Sacramento
(95691-3501)
P.O. Box 427 (95691-0427)
PHONE.....................916 371-5440
Jon Knapp, *President*
Carol Knapp, *Admin Sec*
EMP: 70 EST: 1970
SQ FT: 7,000
SALES (est): 2.6MM **Privately Held**
WEB: www.valtox.com
SIC: 8071 Bacteriological laboratory

(P-22158)
VERACYTE INC
6000 Shoreline Ct Ste 300, South San Francisco (94080-7606)
PHONE.....................650 243-6300
Bonnie H Anderson, *Ch of Bd*
Christopher M Hall, *President*
Keith Kennedy, *CFO*
Mike Rosenbluth, *Vice Pres*
Severin Gose, *Associate Dir*
EMP: 246
SQ FT: 59,000
SALES: 71.9MM **Privately Held**
SIC: 8071 8733 2835 Medical laboratories; medical research; cytology & histology diagnostic agents

(P-22159)
WEST PACIFIC MEDICAL LAB LLC (PA)
10200 Pioneer Blvd # 500, Santa Fe Springs (90670-6008)
PHONE.....................818 773-9771
Martin Borish, *President*
Manny Jaime, *President*
EMP: 76 EST: 2009
SALES (est): 24.1MM **Privately Held**
SIC: 8071 Medical laboratories

(P-22160)
WHITEFIELD MEDICAL LAB INC (PA)
Also Called: Whitefield Medical Lab & Rdlgy
764 Indigo Ct Ste A, Pomona (91767-2269)
PHONE.....................909 625-2114
Jatin Laxpati, *President*
Shaila Laxpati, *Treasurer*
EMP: 50
SQ FT: 7,000

SALES (est): 5.9MM **Privately Held**
SIC: 8071 Medical laboratories

8072 Dental Laboratories

(P-22161)
ADVANCED DENTAL IMAGING LLC
4028 Via Laguna, Santa Barbara
(93110-2116)
PHONE.....................805 687-5571
Kathleen S Cox,
EMP: 50
SALES (est): 3.5MM **Privately Held**
WEB: www.adisb.com
SIC: 8072 Dental laboratories

(P-22162)
CALIFORNIA DENTAL ARTS LLC
20421 Pacifica Dr, Cupertino (95014-3013)
PHONE.....................408 255-1020
Leon Frangadakis, *Mng Member*
Steve Pavlidakis, *Planning*
Jesus Rubio, *Technician*
Jan Martz, *Controller*
Lonnie Fountain, *Marketing Mgr*
EMP: 58
SQ FT: 4,000
SALES (est): 5.7MM **Privately Held**
WEB: www.caldentalarts.com
SIC: 8072 Crown & bridge production

(P-22163)
CANEW INC
22135 Roscoe Blvd, Canoga Park
(91304-3885)
PHONE.....................818 703-5100
Dan Materdomini, *President*
Zhanna Radinsky, *CFO*
EMP: 120
SQ FT: 22,000
SALES (est): 12.5MM **Privately Held**
WEB: www.davincilab.com
SIC: 8072 5047 Crown & bridge production; dental equipment & supplies

(P-22164)
CONTINENTAL DNTL CERAMICS INC
1873 Western Way, Torrance (90501-1124)
PHONE.....................310 618-8821
Jerry Doviack, *President*
Krystina Doviack, *Corp Secy*
EMP: 50
SQ FT: 12,000
SALES (est): 4.9MM **Privately Held**
SIC: 8072 Crown & bridge production

(P-22165)
DLH DAVINCI LLC
22135 Roscoe Blvd Ste 101, West Hills
(91304-3857)
PHONE.....................818 703-5100
EMP: 65
SALES (est): 294.8K **Privately Held**
SIC: 8072

(P-22166)
DURA METRICS INC (PA)
816 Piner Rd, Santa Rosa (95403-2019)
P.O. Box 873 (95402-0873)
PHONE.....................707 546-5138
Michael Kulwiec, *President*
EMP: 68 EST: 1968
SQ FT: 7,500
SALES (est): 4.7MM **Privately Held**
SIC: 8072 Dental laboratories

(P-22167)
EURODENT INC
9310 Topanga Canyon Blvd # 200,
Chatsworth (91311-5713)
PHONE.....................818 832-1325
Adam Adamonis, *President*
V J Lyons, *Vice Pres*
Chris Lalli, *Corp Comm Staff*
EMP: 60
SQ FT: 1,800
SALES (est): 4.1MM **Privately Held**
WEB: www.eurodentlab.com
SIC: 8072 Crown & bridge production

(P-22168)
G & H DENTAL ARTS INC (PA)
Also Called: G&H Dental Arts Cushman Dental
4212 Artesia Blvd, Torrance (90504-3106)
PHONE.....................310 214-8007
Glen Yamamoto, *President*
Kiichi Yamamoto, *Vice Pres*
Emiko Onda, *Accountant*
Brian Smith, *Sales Staff*
▲ EMP: 79
SQ FT: 4,500
SALES: 10MM **Privately Held**
WEB: www.gandhdental.com
SIC: 8072 Crown & bridge production

(P-22169)
JAMES R GLIDEWELL DENTAL
Also Called: Bdl Prosthetics
2181 Dupont Dr, Irvine (92612-1301)
PHONE.....................800 411-9723
Robert Rosen, *Branch Mgr*
EMP: 1000
SALES (corp-wide): 252.9MM **Privately Held**
SIC: 8072 Crown & bridge production
PA: James R. Glidewell, Dental Ceramics, Inc.
   4141 Macarthur Blvd
   Newport Beach CA 92660
   949 440-2600

(P-22170)
JAMES R GLIDEWELL DENTAL (PA)
Also Called: Glidewell Laboratories
4141 Macarthur Blvd, Newport Beach
(92660-2015)
PHONE.....................949 440-2600
James R Glidewell, *CEO*
Greg Minzenmayer, *COO*
Sasaki Glenn, *CFO*
Rob Grice, *CFO*
Glenn Sasaki, *CFO*
▲ EMP: 1100 EST: 1969
SQ FT: 72,000
SALES (est): 252.9MM **Privately Held**
WEB: www.glidewelldental.com
SIC: 8072 Crown & bridge production

(P-22171)
KEATING DENTAL ARTS INC
16881 Hale Ave Ste A, Irvine (92606-5068)
PHONE.....................949 955-2100
Shaun Keating, *President*
EMP: 105
SQ FT: 26,000
SALES: 13MM **Privately Held**
WEB: www.keatingdentalarts.com
SIC: 8072 Crown & bridge production

(P-22172)
PALOMAR HEALTH
Also Called: Pomerado Hospital
15615 Pomerado Rd, Poway (92064-2405)
PHONE.....................858 613-4000
David Parrot, *Administration*
Kim Jackson, *Records Dir*
Mark Miller, *Technology*
Robert Kozel, *Engineer*
Michael Stillwell, *Pharmacist*
EMP: 100
SALES (corp-wide): 760.9MM **Privately Held**
WEB: www.sunbridge.com
SIC: 8072 Dental laboratories
PA: Palomar Health Technology, Inc.
   456 E Grand Ave
   Escondido CA 92025
   442 281-5000

(P-22173)
POSCA BROTHERS DENTAL LAB
641 W Willow St, Long Beach
(90806-2832)
PHONE.....................562 427-1811
Alex Posca, *President*
Yanette Posca, *Corp Secy*
Angel Jorge Posca, *Vice Pres*
Greg Muro, *General Mgr*
▲ EMP: 55 EST: 1965
SQ FT: 5,000

SALES (est): 7.2MM **Privately Held**
WEB: www.poscabrothers.com
SIC: 8072 3843 Dental laboratories; teeth,
artificial (not made in dental laboratories)

(P-22174)
TRIDENT LABS LLC
Also Called: Trident Dental Labratories
12000 Aviation Blvd, Hawthorne
(90250-3438)
PHONE..........................310 915-9121
Laurence K Fishman, *President*
Richard B Mc Donald, *CFO*
Veronica Fitzgerald, *Executive Asst*
▲ EMP: 125
SQ FT: 16,000
SALES (est): 15.1MM
SALES (corp-wide): 140.4MM **Privately
Held**
WEB: www.tridentlab.com
SIC: 8072 Crown & bridge production
PA: Gdc Holdings, Inc.
11601 Kew Gardens Ave # 200
Palm Beach Gardens FL 33410
763 398-0654

8082 Home Health Care

(P-22175)
24HR HOMECARE LLC (PA)
300 N Pacific Coast Hwy # 1065, El Se-
gundo (90245-4490)
PHONE..........................310 906-3683
Sonia Aouriri, *Principal*
EMP: 54
SALES (est): 10MM **Privately Held**
SIC: 8082 Home health care services

(P-22176)
A & A HOME CARE SERVICES
7756 Cntry Clb Dr Bldg A, Palm Springs
(92263)
PHONE..........................760 416-6769
Suzanne O Armstrong, *Owner*
EMP: 60
SALES (est): 588.7K **Privately Held**
SIC: 8082 7299 Home health care serv-
ices; personal financial services; personal
shopping service

(P-22177)
A BETTER LIFE TOGETHER INC
3322 Sweetwater Springs B, Spring Valley
(91977-3142)
PHONE..........................619 741-1548
Kim Wilson, *Principal*
Kimberly Mills, *Owner*
EMP: 90
SALES (est): 2.6MM **Privately Held**
SIC: 8082 Visiting nurse service

(P-22178)
**A BETTER SOLUTION IN HOME
CARE**
1409 N 2nd St, El Cajon (92021-3436)
PHONE..........................619 447-1528
Lillia Smith Pratt, *Branch Mgr*
EMP: 183
SALES (corp-wide): 7.6MM **Privately
Held**
SIC: 8082 Home health care services
PA: A Better Solution In Home Care, Inc
3636 Camino Del Rio N # 100
San Diego CA 92108
619 585-9011

(P-22179)
**A CAOS MEDICAL
CORPORATION**
2655 Camino Del R, San Diego (92108)
PHONE..........................800 362-2731
Angel Iscovich, *President*
EMP: 99
SALES (est): 371.5K **Privately Held**
SIC: 8082 Home health care services

(P-22180)
A CAREGIVER LLC
31520 Rr Cyn Rd Ste A, Canyon Lake
(92587-9499)
PHONE..........................951 676-4190
EMP: 50
SALES (est): 841.8K **Privately Held**
SIC: 8082

(P-22181)
A PLUS IN HOME CARE
Also Called: A Plus Mini Market
5150 N 6th St Ste 111, Fresno
(93710-7505)
PHONE..........................559 224-9442
Lyle Fester, *President*
EMP: 53
SALES: 1MM **Privately Held**
SIC: 8082 Home health care services

(P-22182)
A-1 HOSPICE CARE INC
217 E Alameda Ave Ste 306, Burbank
(91502-2621)
PHONE..........................818 237-2700
Femi Samuel, *CFO*
EMP: 65
SQ FT: 2,800
SALES (est): 239.3K **Privately Held**
SIC: 8082 Home health care services

(P-22183)
ABC HOME HEALTH CARE LLC
5090 Shoreham Pl Ste 209, San Diego
(92122-5935)
PHONE..........................858 455-5000
Joseph Monteforte, *Exec Dir*
Hamid Alebrahim, *Mng Member*
Hamideh F Panabi, *Mng Member*
EMP: 125
SALES: 1.1MM **Privately Held**
WEB: www.abchomehealthcare.com
SIC: 8082 7371 Home health care serv-
ices; computer software development &
applications

(P-22184)
ABLE HANDS INC
18780 Amar Rd Ste 207, Walnut
(91789-4559)
PHONE..........................626 965-2233
Salvador L Abiera, *President*
Cynthia Magtoto, *CFO*
EMP: 100
SALES (est): 1.7MM **Privately Held**
SIC: 8082 Home health care services

(P-22185)
**ABOVE HLTH HM CARE
SLTIONS LLC**
960 S Peregrine Pl, Anaheim (92806-4727)
PHONE..........................714 585-2185
Jesselle Macis, *
EMP: 53 EST: 2011
SALES (est): 467.9K **Privately Held**
SIC: 8082 Home health care services

(P-22186)
ACCENTCARE INC
5050 Mrphy Knyan Rd St200, San Diego
(92123)
PHONE..........................858 576-7410
EMP: 1587
SALES (corp-wide): 423.9MM **Privately
Held**
SIC: 8082 7389 Home health care serv-
ices;
PA: Accentcare, Inc.
17855 Dallas Pkwy
Dallas TX 75287
800 834-3059

(P-22187)
**ACCENTCARE HM HLTH
SCRMNTO INC**
2880 Sunrise Blvd Ste 218, Rancho Cor-
dova (95742-6101)
PHONE..........................916 852-5888
Karin Stark, *President*
Rochelle Ward, *Vice Pres*
EMP: 55
SQ FT: 10,000
SALES (est): 1.5MM
SALES (corp-wide): 423.9MM **Privately
Held**
SIC: 8082 Visiting nurse service
HQ: Accentcare Home Health, Inc.
135 Technology Dr Ste 150
Irvine CA 92618

(P-22188)
ACCENTCARE HOME HEALTH
2344 S 2nd St Ste A, El Centro
(92243-5606)
PHONE..........................760 352-4022
Melanie Ihler, *CEO*
EMP: 50
SALES (est): 925.5K
SALES (corp-wide): 423.9MM **Privately
Held**
WEB: www.accentcare.com
SIC: 8082 Home health care services
HQ: Accentcare Home Health, Inc.
135 Technology Dr Ste 150
Irvine CA 92618

(P-22189)
**ACCENTCARE HOME HEALTH
CAL INC**
Also Called: Sunplus HM Care - Pleasant HI
2300 Contra Costa Blvd # 125, Pleasant
Hill (94523-3918)
PHONE..........................925 356-6066
Francine Cummings, *Administration*
EMP: 84
SALES (corp-wide): 423.9MM **Privately
Held**
WEB: www.dhsi.com
SIC: 8082 Visiting nurse service
HQ: Accentcare Home Health Of California,
Inc.
17855 Dallas Pkwy
Dallas TX 75287
-

(P-22190)
**ACCENTCARE HOME HEALTH
CAL INC**
15455 San Fernando Ste, Mission Hills
(91345)
PHONE..........................818 528-8855
Patricia Haynes, *Administration*
Annette Van As, *Administration*
EMP: 50
SALES (corp-wide): 423.9MM **Privately
Held**
WEB: www.dhsi.com
SIC: 8082 8051 Home health care serv-
ices; skilled nursing care facilities
HQ: Accentcare Home Health Of California,
Inc.
17855 Dallas Pkwy
Dallas TX 75287
-

(P-22191)
**ACCENTCARE HOME HEALTH
CAL INC**
Also Called: Sunplus Home Care - Ontario
1455 Auto Center Dr # 200, Ontario
(91761-2239)
PHONE..........................909 605-7000
Sharon Guller, *Branch Mgr*
EMP: 58
SALES (corp-wide): 423.9MM **Privately
Held**
WEB: www.dhsi.com
SIC: 8082 8051 Home health care serv-
ices; skilled nursing care facilities
HQ: Accentcare Home Health Of California,
Inc.
17855 Dallas Pkwy
Dallas TX 75287
-

(P-22192)
**ACCENTCARE HOME HEALTH
CAL INC**
Also Called: Sunplus Home Care - San Diego
5050 Murphy Canyon Rd # 200, San Diego
(92123-4441)
PHONE..........................858 576-7410
Joan Laforteza, *Manager*
EMP: 184
SQ FT: 4,000
SALES (corp-wide): 423.9MM **Privately
Held**
WEB: www.dhsi.com
SIC: 8082 Visiting nurse service
HQ: Accentcare Home Health Of California,
Inc.
17855 Dallas Pkwy
Dallas TX 75287

(P-22193)
**ACCENTCARE HOME HEALTH
CAL INC**
Also Called: Sunplus HM Hlth - Newport Bch
3636 Birch St Ste 195, Newport Beach
(92660-2644)
PHONE..........................949 250-0133
Mary Lynn, *Manager*
EMP: 56
SALES (corp-wide): 423.9MM **Privately
Held**
WEB: www.dhsi.com
SIC: 8082 8051 Home health care serv-
ices; skilled nursing care facilities
HQ: Accentcare Home Health Of California,
Inc.
17855 Dallas Pkwy
Dallas TX 75287

(P-22194)
**ACCREDITED NURSING
SERVICES**
Also Called: Accredited Nursing Care
950 S Coast Dr Ste 215, Costa Mesa
(92626-7850)
PHONE..........................714 973-1234
Meryll Jones, *Manager*
EMP: 65
SALES (corp-wide): 16.8MM **Privately
Held**
WEB: www.accreditednursing.com
SIC: 8082 Home health care services
PA: Accredited Nursing Services
17141 Ventura Blvd # 201
Encino CA
818 986-6017

(P-22195)
ACCUMEN INC (PA)
5414 Oberlin Dr Ste 200, San Diego
(92121-4745)
PHONE..........................858 777-8160
Jeff Osborne, *President*
Jim Bredy, *COO*
John Adams, *CFO*
Jarrod Panza, *Exec VP*
Xaver Douwes, *Vice Pres*
EMP: 57
SALES (est): 9MM **Privately Held**
SIC: 8082 Home health care services

(P-22196)
ACT HOME HEALTH INC
12431 Lewis St Ste 101, Garden Grove
(92840-4653)
PHONE..........................714 560-0800
Catherine Johnston, *President*
EMP: 60
SQ FT: 2,500
SALES (est): 2.8MM **Privately Held**
WEB: www.acthh.com
SIC: 8082 Visiting nurse service

(P-22197)
**ACTION HOME NURSING
SERVICES**
561 Torero Way, El Dorado Hills
(95762-3541)
PHONE..........................530 756-2600
J Karen Hahn, *President*
Steven Weishaar, *Vice Pres*
EMP: 70
SALES (est): 2.5MM **Privately Held**
WEB: www.actionhomenursing.com
SIC: 8082 Visiting nurse service

(P-22198)
ADDUS HEALTHCARE INC
817 Coffee Rd Ste B1, Modesto
(95355-4241)
PHONE..........................209 526-8451
Linda Stinson, *Branch Mgr*
EMP: 100 **Publicly Held**
WEB: www.addus.com
SIC: 8082 Home health care services
HQ: Addus Healthcare, Inc.
2300 Warrenville Rd
Downers Grove IL 60515
630 296-3400

(P-22199)
ADDUS HEALTHCARE INC
936 Mangrove Ave, Chico (95926-3950)
PHONE..........................530 566-0405

P
R
O
D
U
C
T
S

&

S
V
C
S

Mary Gorman, *Manager*
Sandra Kester, *Director*
EMP: 50 Publicly Held
WEB: www.addus.com
SIC: 8082 Home health care services
HQ: Addus Healthcare, Inc.
2300 Warrenville Rd
Downers Grove IL 60515
630 296-3400

(P-22200)
ADDUS HEALTHCARE INC
1730 S Amphlett Blvd, San Mateo
(94402-2707)
PHONE..................650 638-7943
Nancy Kline, *Manager*
EMP: 495 Publicly Held
WEB: www.addus.com
SIC: 8082 Home health care services
HQ: Addus Healthcare, Inc.
2300 Warrenville Rd
Downers Grove IL 60515
630 296-3400

(P-22201)
ADIA LLC
3625 Del Amo Blvd Ste 225, Torrance
(90503-1696)
PHONE..................310 370-0555
Pamela Penson, *Mng Member*
EMP: 70
SALES (est): 2.1MM **Privately Held**
SIC: 8082 Home health care services

(P-22202)
ADMIRAL HOME HEALTH INC
4010 Watson Plaza Dr # 140, Lakewood
(90712-4047)
PHONE..................562 421-0777
Josie Jones, *President*
Danilo Bautista, *Vice Pres*
EMP: 70
SQ FT: 5,900
SALES (est): 3.4MM **Privately Held**
WEB: www.admiralhomehealth.com
SIC: 8082 Visiting nurse service

(P-22203)
ADVANCE HEALTH SOLUTIONS LLC
7825 Fay Ave Ste 200, La Jolla
(92037-4270)
PHONE..................858 876-0136
F Chubak,
Maryam Navaie,
EMP: 60 EST: 2008
SALES (est): 787.5K **Privately Held**
SIC: 8082 Home health care services

(P-22204)
ADVANCED HOME HEALTH INC
4354 Auburn Blvd, Sacramento
(95841-4107)
PHONE..................916 978-0744
Angela Sehr, *President*
Angie Macadangdang, *Principal*
Charity Edwards, *Office Mgr*
Cindy Patrick, *Admin Asst*
Carolyn Beddow, *Human Res Mgr*
EMP: 75
SQ FT: 4,000
SALES (est): 4.4MM **Privately Held**
SIC: 8082 8621 Visiting nurse service;
nursing association

(P-22205)
AEGIS SENIOR COMMUNITIES LLC
Also Called: Aegis Gardens
36281 Fremont Blvd, Fremont
(94536-3509)
PHONE..................510 739-0909
Emily Poon, *Manager*
EMP: 50
SALES (corp-wide): 122.5MM **Privately Held**
WEB: www.aegisal.com
SIC: 8082 8051 Home health care services; skilled nursing care facilities
PA: Senior Aegis Communities Llc
415 118th Ave Se
Bellevue WA 98005
866 688-5829

(P-22206)
AEGIS SENIOR COMMUNITIES LLC
Also Called: Aegis Living
1660 Oak Park Blvd, Pleasant Hill
(94523-4422)
PHONE..................925 588-7030
Fax: 925 939-2785
EMP: 70
SALES (corp-wide): 138.5MM **Privately Held**
SIC: 8082 8051
PA: Senior Aegis Communities Llc
415 118th Ave Se
Bellevue WA 98005
866 688-5829

(P-22207)
AEGIS SENIOR COMMUNITIES LLC
Also Called: Aegis Assisted Living
125 Heather Ter, Aptos (95003-3825)
PHONE..................831 684-2700
Janice Ibaio, *Manager*
EMP: 50
SALES (corp-wide): 122.5MM **Privately Held**
WEB: www.aegisal.com
SIC: 8082 8051 Home health care services; skilled nursing care facilities
PA: Senior Aegis Communities Llc
415 118th Ave Se
Bellevue WA 98005
866 688-5829

(P-22208)
AEGIS SENIOR COMMUNITIES LLC
Also Called: Aegis of Granada Hills
10801 Lindley Ave, Granada Hills
(91344-4441)
PHONE..................818 363-3373
Bill Phelps, *Branch Mgr*
EMP: 80
SALES (corp-wide): 122.5MM **Privately Held**
WEB: www.aegisal.com
SIC: 8082 8052 8051 8361 Home health care services; intermediate care facilities; skilled nursing care facilities; residential care
PA: Senior Aegis Communities Llc
415 118th Ave Se
Bellevue WA 98005
866 688-5829

(P-22209)
AGAPE IN HOME CARE INC
4800 District Blvd Ste A, Bakersfield
(93313-2325)
PHONE..................661 835-0364
Sandra Oxford, *President*
EMP: 50
SALES (est): 1.2MM **Privately Held**
SIC: 8082 Home health care services

(P-22210)
ALEGRECARE INC
1375 Sutter St Ste 110, San Francisco
(94109-5465)
PHONE..................415 974-3530
Charles Symes II, *President*
Corie Moyers, *Client Mgr*
Joanne Foy, *Director*
EMP: 400 EST: 2014
SALES (est): 6MM **Privately Held**
SIC: 8082 Home health care services

(P-22211)
ALL SEASONS HOMECARE
262 E Hamilton Ave Ste C, Campbell
(95008-0238)
PHONE..................408 378-0900
Lou Anne Mowry, *Owner*
Christina Sater, *Director*
EMP: 80
SALES (est): 1.1MM
SALES (corp-wide): 131.8K **Privately Held**
SIC: 8082 Home health care services
PA: All Seasons Homecare
5653 Stoneridge Dr # 110
Pleasanton CA 94588
650 368-4040

(P-22212)
ALL VALLEY HOME HLTH CARE INC
Also Called: All Valley Home Care
3665 Ruffin Rd Ste 103, San Diego
(92123-1871)
PHONE..................619 276-8001
Glen Amador, *President*
Michael Drake, *Regional Mgr*
EMP: 100
SQ FT: 2,500
SALES (est): 1.6MM **Privately Held**
SIC: 8082 Home health care services

(P-22213)
ALLIANCE HOSPITAL SERVICES
Also Called: Mills-Peninsula Health HM Care
100 S San Mateo Dr, San Mateo
(94401-3805)
PHONE..................650 697-6900
Sheila Schubert, *Branch Mgr*
EMP: 50
SALES (corp-wide): 7.5MM **Privately Held**
WEB: www.hospitalconsort.org
SIC: 8082 Home health care services
PA: Alliance Hospital Services, Inc
309 Lennon Ln Ste 200
Walnut Creek CA 94598
925 304-1107

(P-22214)
ALLIED PROF NURSING CARE
2345 W Fthlls Blvd Ste 14, Upland (91786)
PHONE..................909 949-1066
Michael Gutierrez, *President*
Karen Gutierrez, *Administration*
EMP: 80 EST: 1996
SALES: 1MM **Privately Held**
SIC: 8082 Visiting nurse service

(P-22215)
ALWAYS HOME NURSING SVC INC
7777 Greenback Ln Ste 208, Citrus Heights
(95610-5800)
PHONE..................916 989-6420
Nancy Giachino, *President*
Janice Simcoe, *Business Mgr*
EMP: 200
SALES (est): 7.8MM **Privately Held**
SIC: 8082 Visiting nurse service

(P-22216)
ALWAYS THERE LIVE IN CARE LLC
7121 Magnolia Ave, Riverside
(92504-3805)
PHONE..................888 606-8880
Anntwonette Howard, *President*
Anntwonette Bonner, *President*
EMP: 72
SALES: 190K **Privately Held**
SIC: 8082 7389 Home health care services;

(P-22217)
ALZHEIMERS CARE SINCE 1983
Also Called: Garden, The
3730 S Greenville St, Santa Ana
(92704-7092)
PHONE..................714 641-0959
Violet Lazarescu, *Administration*
EMP: 50
SALES (est): 477.3K **Privately Held**
SIC: 8082 Home health care services

(P-22218)
AMBIENTE ENTERPRISES INC
Also Called: Home Instead Senior Care
73726 Alessandro Dr # 203, Palm Desert
(92260-3640)
PHONE..................760 674-1905
Rob Costello, *President*
EMP: 120
SQ FT: 2,600
SALES: 1.5MM **Privately Held**
SIC: 8082 Home health care services

(P-22219)
AMERICAN CAREQUEST INC (PA)
819 Cowan Rd Ste C, Burlingame
(94010-1220)
PHONE..................415 885-3324

Margarita Riskin, *President*
Eric Levsky, *Admin Sec*
EMP: 80
SQ FT: 1,100
SALES (est): 3.4MM **Privately Held**
WEB: www.americancarequest.com
SIC: 8082 5047 Home health care services; medical & hospital equipment

(P-22220)
AMERICAN PRIVATE DUTY INC
Also Called: American Untd HM Care Crp-Priv
13111 Ventura Blvd # 100, Studio City
(91604-2218)
PHONE..................818 386-6358
Ann Koshy, *President*
EMP: 80
SALES (est): 3.7MM **Privately Held**
WEB: www.americanprivateduty.com
SIC: 8082 Visiting nurse service

(P-22221)
AMERICAN SPCLTY HLTH GROUP INC (HQ)
10221 Wateridge Cir # 201, San Diego
(92121-2702)
PHONE..................858 754-2000
George T Devries, *CEO*
Robert White, *COO*
William M Comer Jr, *CFO*
Kevin E Kujawa, *Exec VP*
R Douglas Metz, *Exec VP*
▲ **EMP: 378**
SQ FT: 148,000
SALES (est): 144.5MM **Privately Held**
WEB: www.ashbenefits.com
SIC: 8082 Home health care services

(P-22222)
ANGEL CARE HOME HEALTH INC
850 Colorado Blvd Ste 103, Los Angeles
(90041-1733)
PHONE..................818 248-8811
Vivian A Kono, *President*
EMP: 50
SQ FT: 1,700
SALES: 3MM **Privately Held**
SIC: 8082 Home health care services

(P-22223)
ANGELES HOME HEALTH CARE INC
3701 Wilshire Blvd # 900, Los Angeles
(90010-2871)
PHONE..................213 487-5131
Rita L Doll, *CEO*
EMP: 125
SALES (est): 3.5MM
SALES (corp-wide): 1.8B **Publicly Held**
SIC: 8082 Visiting nurse service
HQ: Cornerstone Healthcare, Inc.
420 E State St Ste 135
Eagle ID 83616

(P-22224)
ANGELS IN MOTION LLC
Also Called: Visiting Angels
4091 Riverside Dr Ste 111, Chino
(91710-3195)
PHONE..................909 590-9102
Dominique Alvarez, *Mng Member*
EMP: 70 EST: 2010
SALES (est): 1.6MM **Privately Held**
SIC: 8082 Home health care services

(P-22225)
APEXCARE INC (PA)
1418 Howe Ave Ste B, Sacramento
(95825-3230)
PHONE..................916 924-9111
Kenneth Wang, *President*
EMP: 2000
SALES (est): 17.4MM **Privately Held**
SIC: 8082 Home health care services

(P-22226)
APRIA HEALTHCARE GROUP INC (HQ)
26220 Enterprise Ct, Lake Forest
(92630-8405)
PHONE..................949 639-2000
John G Figueroa, *Ch of Bd*

Debra L Morris, *CFO*
Peter A Reynolds, *CFO*
Nichola Denney, *Exec VP*
William Guidetti, *Exec VP*
◆ **EMP:** 75
SQ FT: 100,000
SALES (est): 2.4B **Privately Held**
WEB: www.respimed.com
SIC: 8082 Home health care services

(P-22227)
APRIA HEALTHCARE LLC
815 Marlborough Ave # 200, Riverside
(92507-2175)
PHONE.................................951 320-1100
Diana Castro, *Manager*
Diana Santos, *Admin Sec*
EMP: 83 **Privately Held**
WEB: www.apria.com
SIC: 8082 Home health care services
HQ: Apria Healthcare Llc
26220 Enterprise Ct
Lake Forest CA 92630
949 639-2163

(P-22228)
APRIA HEALTHCARE LLC
2476 Verna Ct, San Leandro (94577-4223)
PHONE.................................510 346-4000
Carl Caldwell, *Branch Mgr*
Jodi Roberts, *Sales Executive*
EMP: 66 **Privately Held**
WEB: www.apria.com
SIC: 8082 Home health care services
HQ: Apria Healthcare Llc
26220 Enterprise Ct
Lake Forest CA 92630
949 639-2163

(P-22229)
ARCADIA HEALTH SERVICES INC
1400 Florida Ave Ste 206, Modesto
(95350-4445)
PHONE.................................209 572-7650
Corie Moyers, *Manager*
EMP: 100 **Publicly Held**
SIC: 8082 Home health care services
HQ: Arcadia Health Services, Inc.
20750 Civic Center Dr # 100
Southfield MI 48076
866 224-7541

(P-22230)
ASHLEY HOME CARE SERVICES LLC
200 Spectrum Center Dr # 300, Irvine
(92618-5004)
P.O. Box 25321, Overland Park KS (66225-5321)
PHONE.................................323 286-2831
Lance Ashley, *Mng Member*
EMP: 50
SQ FT: 65,672
SALES (est): 2.5MM **Privately Held**
SIC: 8082 Home health care services

(P-22231)
ASIST INC
1974 N Gateway Blvd # 102, Fresno
(93727-1632)
PHONE.................................559 251-7701
Amy Anne Sequeira, *Director*
Amy Sequeira, *Director*
EMP: 75 **EST:** 1999
SALES (est): 1.4MM **Privately Held**
SIC: 8082 Home health care services

(P-22232)
ATTENDANT CARE REFERRALS INC
2801 Ocean Park Blvd # 192, Santa Monica
(90405-2905)
PHONE.................................310 399-2904
Gail Shaffer, *President*
EMP: 85
SALES (est): 1MM **Privately Held**
WEB: www.tlcacr.com
SIC: 8082 Visiting nurse service

(P-22233)
AVIDA CAREGIVERS INC
11500 W Olympic Blvd # 400, Los Angeles
(90064-1525)
PHONE.................................323 498-1500

Chanel N Devlin, *CEO*
Samuel Bradley, *President*
EMP: 855 **EST:** 2014
SALES (est): 428.7K **Privately Held**
SIC: 8082 Home health care services

(P-22234)
BAYWOOD COURT (PA)
Also Called: Baywood Court Retirement Ctr
21966 Dolores St Apt 279, Castro Valley
(94546-6973)
PHONE.................................510 733-2102
Kelly Wiest, *Exec Dir*
EMP: 92
SALES (est): 19.3MM **Privately Held**
WEB: www.baywoodcourt.org
SIC: 8082 8051 6513 Home health care
services; skilled nursing care facilities; retirement hotel operation

(P-22235)
BEAR FLAG MARKETING CORP
Also Called: At Home Caregivers
7599 Redwood Blvd Ste 200, Novato
(94945-7706)
PHONE.................................415 899-8466
Peter L Rubens, *CEO*
EMP: 117
SQ FT: 1,200
SALES (est): 3.4MM **Privately Held**
WEB: www.bearflagmarketing.com
SIC: 8082 Home health care services

(P-22236)
BLIZE HEALTHCARE CAL INC
750 Alfred Nobel Dr # 202, Hercules
(94547-1837)
PHONE.................................800 343-2549
Ukeje Elendu, *President*
Blessing Elendu, *COO*
EMP: 100
SQ FT: 3,700
SALES (est): 7MM **Privately Held**
SIC: 8082 Home health care services

(P-22237)
BLUEBRIDGE PROFESSIONAL SVCS
Also Called: Comfort Keepers
420 W Baseline Rd Ste D, Claremont
(91711-1621)
PHONE.................................909 625-6151
Michael Craig II, *CEO*
EMP: 68
SALES (est): 352.3K **Privately Held**
SIC: 8082 Home health care services

(P-22238)
BRADEN PARTNERS LP A CALIF (HQ)
Also Called: Pacific Pulmonary Services Co
1304 Sthpint Blvd Ste 130, Petaluma
(94954)
PHONE.................................415 893-1518
Jane Thomas, *CEO*
Tsutomu Igawa, *Ch of Bd*
Travis Avila, *Vice Pres*
Timothy Hall, *Program Mgr*
Ali Khan, *Administration*
▲ **EMP:** 65
SALES (est): 68.9MM **Privately Held**
SIC: 8082 Home health care services

(P-22239)
BRANLYN PROMINENCE INC
Also Called: Home Instead Senior Care
13334 Amargosa Rd, Victorville
(92392-8504)
PHONE.................................760 843-5655
Chris Parmelee, *General Mgr*
EMP: 130
SQ FT: 1,800 **Privately Held**
SIC: 8082 Home health care services
PA: Branlyn Prominence, Inc.
9213 Archibald Ave
Rancho Cucamonga CA 91730

(P-22240)
BRANLYN PROMINENCE INC (PA)
Also Called: Home Instead Senior Care
9213 Archibald Ave, Rancho Cucamonga
(91730-5207)
PHONE.................................909 476-9030

Brandi Johnson, *CEO*
Lynda Patriquin, *Vice Pres*
EMP: 100
SALES (est): 9.1MM **Privately Held**
SIC: 8082 Home health care services

(P-22241)
BRIGHT EXPECTATIONS INC
8175 Limonite Ave Ste C, Riverside
(92509-6121)
PHONE.................................951 360-2070
Charley Cox, *President*
EMP: 50
SQ FT: 1,000
SALES (est): 2.1MM **Privately Held**
SIC: 8082 Home health care services

(P-22242)
BRITTNEY HOUSE
5401 E Centralia St, Long Beach
(90808-1494)
PHONE.................................562 421-4717
Major Chief, *Owner*
EMP: 72
SALES (est): 295K **Privately Held**
SIC: 8082 8051 Home health care services; skilled nursing care facilities

(P-22243)
BURDETTE DE COCK INC
Also Called: Home Instead Senior Care
3625 Del Amo Blvd Ste 105, Torrance
(90503-1698)
PHONE.................................310 542-0563
Denise De Cock, *President*
EMP: 110
SALES (est): 4.4MM **Privately Held**
SIC: 8082 Home health care services

(P-22244)
BUTTE HOME HEALTH INC
Also Called: BUTTE HOME HEALTH & HOSPICE
10 Constitution Dr, Chico (95973-4903)
P.O. Box 5171 (95927-5171)
PHONE.................................530 895-0462
Brooke Quilici, *President*
Mike Quilici, *Vice Pres*
EMP: 105
SQ FT: 7,100
SALES (est): 6.7MM **Privately Held**
WEB: www.buttehomehealth.com
SIC: 8082 Visiting nurse service

(P-22245)
CALIFORNIA HOME CARE INC
3078 El Cajon Blvd, San Diego
(92104-1322)
PHONE.................................619 521-5858
Margarette Borg, *President*
EMP: 350
SALES (est): 10.3MM **Privately Held**
WEB: www.cahomecare.com
SIC: 8082 Home health care services

(P-22246)
CAMBRIAN HOMECARE INC
15401 Anacapa Rd Ste 2, Victorville
(92392-2466)
PHONE.................................760 955-2250
EMP: 60 **Privately Held**
SIC: 8082 Home health care services
PA: Cambrian Homecare Inc
5199 E Pacific Coast Hwy
Long Beach CA 90804

(P-22247)
CARE OPTIONS MANAGEMENT PLANS
7000 Village Pkwy Ste A, Dublin
(94568-2413)
PHONE.................................925 551-3227
Joanne McCarley, *Branch Mgr*
EMP: 77 **Privately Held**
SIC: 8082 Home health care services
PA: Care Options Management Plans And
Supportive Services, Llc
1020 Market St
Redding CA 96001

(P-22248)
CARE OPTIONS MANAGEMENT PLANS (PA)
Also Called: C.O.M.P.A.S.S.
1020 Market St, Redding (96001-0512)
P.O. Box 993753 (96099-3753)
PHONE.................................530 242-8580
Sadie Hess, *Mng Member*
Eric Hess,
Joanne McCarley, *Mng Member*
▲ **EMP:** 63
SALES (est): 8.5MM **Privately Held**
WEB: www.compasscares.com
SIC: 8082 Home health care services

(P-22249)
CARE PLUS HOME CARE INC
22931 Triton Way Ste 133, Laguna Hills
(92653-1237)
PHONE.................................949 716-2273
Carl Buffa, *President*
Maria Buffa, *Admin Sec*
Margarita Souders, *Manager*
EMP: 250
SALES (est): 4.5MM **Privately Held**
SIC: 8082 Home health care services

(P-22250)
CARE PLUS NURSING SERVICES INC
Also Called: Care Plus Home Health
22931 Triton Way Ste 236, Laguna Hills
(92653-1237)
PHONE.................................949 600-7194
Carl Buffa, *President*
Maria Buffa, *Vice Pres*
Deby Welty, *Office Mgr*
Sharon Henry, *Administration*
Kyle Moffett, *Administration*
EMP: 160
SALES (est): 3.8MM **Privately Held**
SIC: 8082 8051 Visiting nurse service;
skilled nursing care facilities

(P-22251)
CARE SOLUTION ASSOCIATES LLC
179 Contractors Ave, Livermore
(94551-8856)
PHONE.................................925 443-1000
Keith Beck, *Exec Dir*
EMP: 100
SALES (est): 275K **Privately Held**
SIC: 8082 Home health care services

(P-22252)
CARE UNLIMITED HEALTH SYSTEMS
1025 W Arrow Hwy Ste 105, Glendora
(91740-5407)
PHONE.................................626 332-3767
Carol Weatherburns, *Owner*
EMP: 75 **EST:** 1999
SALES (est): 1.9MM **Privately Held**
SIC: 8082 Home health care services

(P-22253)
CAREABILITY HEALTH SVCS CORP
Also Called: All For You Home Care
1329 Howe Ave Ste 100, Sacramento
(95825-3363)
PHONE.................................916 479-8554
Daniel Gourley, *Director*
EMP: 65
SALES: 950K **Privately Held**
SIC: 8082 Home health care services

(P-22254)
CARESOUTH HOME HEALTH SVCS LLC
815 Pollard Rd, Los Gatos (95032-1438)
PHONE.................................408 378-6131
Carol Parker, *Branch Mgr*
EMP: 50 **Privately Held**
SIC: 8082 Home health care services
HQ: Caresouth Home Health Services, Llc
1 10th St Ste 500
Augusta GA 30901

P R O D U C T S & S V C S

(P-22255)
CARING COMPANIONS HOME
Also Called: Caring Cmpanions Referral Agcy
116 Las Lunas St, Hemet (92543-4028)
PHONE..................................951 765-1441
Deanna Hosick, *President*
EMP: 80
SQ FT: 700
SALES (est): 3.7MM **Privately Held**
SIC: 8082 Home health care services

(P-22256)
CARLTON SENIOR LIVING
Also Called: Senior Assisted Living Comm Ch
175 Cleaveland Rd, Pleasant Hill
(94523-3875)
PHONE..................................925 935-1001
Jeffrey Dillon, *Manager*
EMP: 65
SALES (corp-wide): 29.6MM **Privately Held**
SIC: 8082 Home health care services
PA: Senior Carlton Living Inc
4005 Port Chicago Hwy # 120
Concord CA 94520
925 338-2434

(P-22257)
CASTRO VALLEY HEALTH INC
Also Called: Cvh Home Health Services
2410 Camino Ramon Ste 331, San Ramon
(94583-4324)
PHONE..................................510 690-1930
Mark R Parinas, *CEO*
Isobel Parinas, *CFO*
Sara Pfeffer, *Manager*
Priyanka Khole, *Consultant*
EMP: 200
SALES: 3MM **Privately Held**
WEB: www.parinashouse.com
SIC: 8082 Visiting nurse service

(P-22258)
CASWELL BAY INC
Also Called: Hillendale Home Care
1777 N Calif Blvd Ste 210, Walnut Creek
(94596-4150)
PHONE..................................925 933-8181
Bridget Waller, *President*
Weldon Waller, *Corp Secy*
Elizabeth Waller, *Opers Mgr*
EMP: 60
SQ FT: 1,100
SALES (est): 2.3MM **Privately Held**
WEB: www.hillendale.net
SIC: 8082 Home health care services

(P-22259)
CENTRAL COAST CMNTY HLTH CARE
Also Called: Central Cast Vsting Nurse Assn
40 Ragsdale Dr Ste 150, Monterey
(93940-5790)
P.O. Box 2480 (93942-2480)
PHONE..................................831 648-4200
Norma J Harlacher, *President*
EMP: 350
SALES (est): 7.7MM **Privately Held**
SIC: 8082 Home health care services

(P-22260)
CENTRAL COAST VNA & HOSPICE (PA)
5 Lower Ragsdale Dr 102, Monterey
(93940)
P.O. Box 2480 (93942-2480)
PHONE..................................831 372-6668
Carol Snow, *CEO*
Gayle McConnell, *President*
Steven A Johnson, *CEO*
James Graber, *CFO*
Cynthia Peck, *Vice Pres*
EMP: 175
SALES: 31.3MM **Privately Held**
SIC: 8082 Visiting nurse service

(P-22261)
CENTRAL COAST VNA & HOSPICE
45 Plaza Cir, Salinas (93901-2902)
PHONE..................................831 758-8243
Raul Perez, *Manager*
EMP: 75

SALES (corp-wide): 31.3MM **Privately Held**
SIC: 8082 Visiting nurse service
PA: Central Coast Vna & Hospice, Inc
5 Lower Ragsdle Dr 102
Monterey CA 93940
831 372-6668

(P-22262)
CENTRAL HEALTH PLAN CAL INC
1055 Park View Dr Ste 355, Covina
(91724-3745)
PHONE..................................626 938-7120
Sam Kam, *President*
EMP: 3064
SQ FT: 16,144
SALES (est): 18.6MM
SALES (corp-wide): 572.3MM **Privately Held**
SIC: 8082 Home health care services
PA: Ahmc Healthcare Inc.
1000 S Fremont Ave Unit 6
Alhambra CA 91803
626 943-7526

(P-22263)
CHAROLAIS CARE V INC
Also Called: San Francisco Bay
1426 Fillmore St Ste 207, San Francisco
(94115-4164)
PHONE..................................415 921-5038
Jim Everton, *CEO*
EMP: 100 EST: 2008
SALES (est): 1.1MM
SALES (corp-wide): 27MM **Privately Held**
SIC: 8082 Home health care services
PA: B.R.P. Health Management Systems, Inc.
275 S 5th Ave Lowr Level
Pocatello ID 83201
208 233-4673

(P-22264)
CK FRANCHISING INC (DH)
Also Called: Comfort Keepers
1 Park Plz Ste 300, Irvine (92614-2510)
PHONE..................................800 498-8144
Sarosh Mistry, *CEO*
Joann Cottengim, *Vice Pres*
Tim Purcey, *Vice Pres*
Sherry Johnson, *Branch Mgr*
Don True, *Branch Mgr*
EMP: 76
SQ FT: 11,160
SALES (est): 12.1MM
SALES (corp-wide): 139.1MM **Privately Held**
SIC: 8082 Visiting nurse service
HQ: Sodexo, Inc.
9801 Washingtonian Blvd # 1
Gaithersburg MD 20878
301 987-4000

(P-22265)
COASTAL CMNTY SENIOR CARE LLC
Also Called: Home Instead Senior Care
5500 E Atherton St # 216, Long Beach
(90815-4016)
PHONE..................................562 596-4884
Donald Pierce, *Mng Member*
EMP: 140
SQ FT: 2,300
SALES (est): 959.8K **Privately Held**
SIC: 8082 Home health care services

(P-22266)
COLLABRIA CARE
414 S Jefferson St, NAPA (94559-4515)
PHONE..................................707 258-9080
Linda Gibson, *President*
Mark Maltun, *Finance Dir*
EMP: 90
SALES: 15.1MM **Privately Held**
WEB: www.hospiceofnapa.org
SIC: 8082 Home health care services

(P-22267)
COLONIAL HOME CARE SVCS INC
326 W Katella Ave Ste F, Orange
(92867-4756)
PHONE..................................714 289-7220

Catherina Bertaina, *President*
Trevor O'Neil, *Administration*
EMP: 180
SQ FT: 1,200
SALES: 2.5MM **Privately Held**
WEB: www.colonialhomecareservices.com
SIC: 8082 Home health care services

(P-22268)
COMMUNITY CAREGIVERS INC
80 Garden Ct Ste 105, Monterey
(93940-5367)
PHONE..................................831 645-1434
Norris Blockhus, *Controller*
EMP: 72
SALES: 950K **Privately Held**
SIC: 8082 Home health care services

(P-22269)
COMMUNITY HEALTH NETWORK LLC
25102 Jefferson Ave Ste B, Murrieta
(92562-1708)
PHONE..................................951 265-8281
Greg Maasberg, *Mng Member*
EMP: 55
SALES (est): 355K **Privately Held**
SIC: 8082 Home health care services

(P-22270)
COMPANION HOME HLTH & HOSPICE
Also Called: Companion Hospice
2041 W Orangewood Ave B, Orange
(92868-1902)
PHONE..................................714 560-8177
Michael Uranga, *President*
Chris Vallandigham, *COO*
Eleonor Phillips, *Manager*
EMP: 95
SALES (est): 12.3MM **Privately Held**
WEB: www.companionhospice.com
SIC: 8082 Visiting nurse service

(P-22271)
COMPANION HOSPICE AND
6133 Bristol Parkday 11 # 110, Culver City
(90230)
PHONE..................................310 338-1257
Elo Sahagian,
Eleonor Phillips, *Manager*
EMP: 99
SQ FT: 2,000
SALES (est): 229.3K **Privately Held**
SIC: 8082 Home health care services

(P-22272)
COMPANION HOSPICE CARE LLC
8130 Florence Ave Ste 200, Downey
(90240-3977)
PHONE..................................562 944-2711
Michael A Uranga, *CEO*
Chris Vallandigham, *COO*
EMP: 125
SQ FT: 5,000
SALES (est): 5MM **Privately Held**
SIC: 8082 Home health care services

(P-22273)
COMPANION HOSPICE LLC
8130 Florence Ave Ste 200, Downey
(90240-3977)
PHONE..................................562 944-2711
EMP: 99
SALES (est): 229.3K **Privately Held**
SIC: 8082 Home health care services

(P-22274)
COMPETENT CARE INC
Also Called: Competent Care HM Hlth Nursing
2900 Bristol St Ste D107, Costa Mesa
(92626-5940)
PHONE..................................714 545-4818
Lynett Laroche, *President*
EMP: 70
SALES (est): 1.2MM **Privately Held**
WEB: www.competentcare.com
SIC: 8082 7299 Visiting nurse service; information services, consumer

(P-22275)
COMPPARTNERS INC
333 City Blvd W Ste 1500, Orange
(92868-5913)
PHONE..................................949 253-3111
Bruce Carlin, *CEO*
Bernard J Mansheim, *Chief Mktg Ofcr*
Eleanor Marciniak, *CTO*
Mary Mata,
Joyce Ho, *Director*
EMP: 70
SQ FT: 15,000
SALES (est): 2.5MM **Privately Held**
WEB: www.comppartners.com
SIC: 8082 Home health care services

(P-22276)
COMPREHENSIVE COMMUNITY HEALTH
801 S Chevy Chase Dr, Glendale
(91205-4431)
PHONE..................................818 265-2264
Grace Javellana, *CFO*
EMP: 50
SALES: 23.9MM **Privately Held**
SIC: 8082 Home health care services

(P-22277)
CORNERSTONE FAMILY SVCS LLC
Also Called: Comfort Keepers - 509
1748 W Katella Ave # 207, Orange
(92867-3437)
PHONE..................................714 744-3800
Christopher Gamble, *Managing Prtnr*
EMP: 55
SALES (est): 163.5K **Privately Held**
SIC: 8082 Home health care services

(P-22278)
CORNERSTONE HOSPICE CAL LLC
1461 E Cooley Dr Ste 220, Colton
(92324-3921)
PHONE..................................909 872-8100
Blaine Whitson, *President*
Erick Kerner, *Vice Pres*
EMP: 60
SALES (est): 3.8MM **Publicly Held**
WEB: www.cornerstonehospice.net
SIC: 8082 Visiting nurse service
PA: Genesis Healthcare, Inc.
101 E State St
Kennett Square PA 19348

(P-22279)
COSMOPRO WEST INC
15773 Gateway Cir, Tustin (92780-6470)
PHONE..................................714 258-8301
Antoine Macoule, *President*
◆ EMP: 50
SALES (est): 1.4MM **Privately Held**
SIC: 8082 Home health care services

(P-22280)
CPH HOSPITAL MANAGEMENT LLC
Also Called: Coast Plaza Hospital
13100 Studebaker Rd, Norwalk
(90650-2531)
PHONE..................................562 838-3751
James Paul Macpherson,
EMP: 781
SALES (est): 6.2MM
SALES (corp-wide): 253.3MM **Privately Held**
SIC: 8082 Home health care services
PA: Avanti Hospitals, Llc
222 N Splvd Blvd Ste 950
El Segundo CA 90245
310 356-0550

(P-22281)
CRESCENT HEALTHCARE INC (DH)
11980 Telg Rd Ste 100, Santa Fe Springs
(90670)
PHONE..................................714 520-6300
Paul Mastrapa, *CEO*
Virginia Havai, *President*
David Zelaskowski, *President*
William P Forster, *CFO*
Pamela Bowen, *CIO*

EMP: 150
SQ FT: 26,000
SALES (est): 22.1MM
SALES (corp-wide): 131.5B **Publicly Held**
WEB: www.crescenthealthcare.com
SIC: **8082** Home health care services
HQ: Walgreen Co.
200 Wilmot Rd
Deerfield IL 60015
847 315-2500

(P-22282)
CUSTOMCARE HOME HLTH SVCS INC
9826 Bond Rd Ste A, Elk Grove
(95624-9419)
PHONE..........................916 714-1155
Audrey Acosta, *CEO*
EMP: 70
SALES (est): 1.5MM **Privately Held**
SIC: **8082** 7361 Home health care services; nurses' registry

(P-22283)
DELTA-T GROUP INC
4420 Hotel Circle Ct # 205, San Diego
(92108-3423)
PHONE..........................619 543-0556
EMP: 534 **Privately Held**
SIC: **8082** Home health care services
PA: Delta-T Group, Inc.
950 E Haverford Rd # 200
Bryn Mawr PA 19010

(P-22284)
DIGNITY HEALTH
Also Called: Marian Hospital Homecare
1054 E Grand Ave Ste A, Arroyo Grande
(93420-2527)
PHONE..........................805 489-4261
Mike Cornaire, *Manager*
Linda Patrick, *Admin Asst*
Elva Nava, *Director*
EMP: 73
SALES (corp-wide): 6.7B **Privately Held**
WEB: www.chw.edu
SIC: **8082** Home health care services
PA: Dignity Health
185 Berry St Ste 300
San Francisco CA 94107
415 438-5500

(P-22285)
DIGNITY HEALTH
Also Called: Marian Home Care and Hospice
124 S College Dr, Santa Maria
(93454-5325)
PHONE..........................805 739-3830
Toll Free:..........................877
Cathy Sullivan, *Administration*
Kathleen Sullivan, *Vice Pres*
EMP: 120
SALES (corp-wide): 6.7B **Privately Held**
WEB: www.chw.edu
SIC: **8082** Home health care services
PA: Dignity Health
185 Berry St Ste 300
San Francisco CA 94107
415 438-5500

(P-22286)
DIGNITY HEALTH
Home Health Dept of St Joseph
2333 W March Ln Ste B, Stockton
(95207-5272)
PHONE..........................209 943-4663
EMP: 50
SALES (corp-wide): 10.4B **Privately Held**
SIC: **8082**
PA: Dignity Health
185 Berry St Ste 300
San Francisco CA 94107
415 438-5500

(P-22287)
DUNN & BERGER INC
Also Called: Accredited Nursing Care
5955 De Soto Ave Ste 160, Woodland Hills
(91367-5101)
PHONE..........................818 986-1234
Barry Berger, *President*
EMP: 500
SALES (est): 11.7MM **Privately Held**
SIC: **8082** Home health care services

(P-22288)
DYNAMIC HOME CARE SERVICE INC (PA)
14260 Ventura Blvd # 301, Sherman Oaks
(91423-2734)
PHONE..........................818 981-4446
Nissan Pardo, *CEO*
Carol Silver, *President*
Jeff Friedman, *Sales Staff*
Marilyn Flick, *Manager*
EMP: 200
SALES (est): 6MM **Privately Held**
WEB: www.dynamicnursing.com
SIC: **8082** Visiting nurse service

(P-22289)
E R G HOME HEALTH PROVIDER
11700 South St Ste 200, Artesia
(90701-6619)
PHONE..........................562 403-1070
Fax: 562 403-1068
EMP: 60
SALES (est): 2.2MM **Privately Held**
SIC: **8082**

(P-22290)
EL CAMINO HOSPITAL AUXILIARY
2500 Grant Rd, Mountain View
(94040-4378)
P.O. Box 7025 (94039-7025)
PHONE..........................650 940-7214
Linda Heider, *President*
EMP: 600
SQ FT: 2,000
SALES: 104.3K
SALES (corp-wide): 930.5MM **Privately Held**
SIC: **8082** Home health care services
PA: El Camino Hospital
2500 Grant Rd
Mountain View CA 94040
408 224-6660

(P-22291)
ELIZABETH HOSPICE INC (PA)
500 La Terraza Blvd # 130, Escondido
(92025-3876)
PHONE..........................760 737-2050
Jan Jones, *President*
Laura Miller, *President*
Andrea Goodwin, *COO*
Kiprian Skavinski, *CFO*
Michelle Goldbach, *Regional Mgr*
EMP: 250
SQ FT: 14,000
SALES: 33.9MM **Privately Held**
WEB: www.elizabethhospice.org
SIC: **8082** Home health care services

(P-22292)
EMINENCE HOME HEALTH CARE INC
16921 Parthenia St # 301, Northridge
(91343-4559)
PHONE..........................818 830-7113
Oscar Parel, *CEO*
EMP: 50
SALES (est): 2.6MM **Privately Held**
SIC: **8082** Home health care services

(P-22293)
ENLOE MEDICAL CENTER
Also Called: Enloe Homecare Services
1390 E Lassen Ave, Chico (95973-7823)
PHONE..........................530 332-6050
Leslie Gunghl, *Director*
EMP: 300
SALES (corp-wide): 528.3MM **Privately Held**
SIC: **8082** Home health care services
PA: Enloe Medical Center
1531 Esplanade
Chico CA 95926
530 332-7300

(P-22294)
EXCEL HOME HEALTH INC
5575 Lake Park Way # 220, La Mesa
(91942-1664)
PHONE..........................619 460-6622
SRI Gopal, *President*
Anidta Krishnan, *Vice Pres*
Sonia Silva, *Sls & Mktg Exec*
Crystal Kays,

EMP: 50
SALES: 600K **Privately Held**
WEB: www.excelhomehealth.com
SIC: **8082** Visiting nurse service

(P-22295)
EXPERIENCED HOME CARE REGISTRY
110 Civic Center Dr # 206, Vista
(92084-6037)
PHONE..........................760 724-0880
Deborah W Dahlin, *Owner*
EMP: 60
SALES (est): 1.3MM **Privately Held**
SIC: **8082** Home health care services

(P-22296)
FAITH JONES & ASSOCIATES INC (PA)
Also Called: Aall Care In Home Services
7801 Mission Center Ct # 106, San Diego
(92108-1314)
PHONE..........................619 297-9601
Faith Jones, *President*
Norman Jones, *CFO*
EMP: 90
SQ FT: 1,200
SALES (est): 5.2MM **Privately Held**
WEB: www.aallcare.com
SIC: **8082** Home health care services

(P-22297)
FAR EAST HOME CARE INC
3407 W 6th St Ste 710, Los Angeles
(90020-2554)
PHONE..........................949 673-3100
Rosendo Labadlabad, *President*
Emma Obut, *Manager*
EMP: 110
SALES (est): 2.5MM **Privately Held**
WEB: www.fareasthomecare.com
SIC: **8082** 8322 Home health care services; individual & family services

(P-22298)
FIRSTAT NURSING SERVICES INC
411 Camino Del Rio S # 100, San Diego
(92108-3508)
PHONE..........................619 220-7600
Linnea Goodrich, *Owner*
Kathleen Tickle, *President*
EMP: 105
SQ FT: 1,800
SALES (est): 2.8MM **Privately Held**
SIC: **8082** Visiting nurse service

(P-22299)
FIVE STAR QUALITY CARE INC
Also Called: Somerford Place Stockton
3530 Deer Park Dr, Stockton (95219-2350)
PHONE..........................209 951-6500
Leslie Anderson, *Manager*
EMP: 50 **Publicly Held**
WEB: www.fivestarqualitycare.com
SIC: **8082** Home health care services
PA: Five Star Senior Living Inc.
400 Centre St
Newton MA 02458

(P-22300)
FOUNDERS HEALTHCARE LLC
Also Called: Lifecare Solutions
170 N Daisy Ave, Pasadena (91107-3465)
PHONE..........................626 683-5401
Rene Moreno, *Principal*
EMP: 57
SALES (corp-wide): 731.6MM **Privately Held**
SIC: **8082** Home health care services
HQ: Founders Healthcare, L.L.C.
4601 E Hilton Ave Ste 100
Phoenix AZ 85034
800 636-2123

(P-22301)
GLENDALE ADVENTIST MEDICAL CTR
Also Called: Adventist Health Homecare Svcs
281 Harvey Dr Unit B, Glendale
(91206-4112)
PHONE..........................818 409-8379
Bruce Nelson, *Med Doctor*
EMP: 50

SALES (corp-wide): 4.1B **Privately Held**
SIC: **8082** Home health care services
HQ: Glendale Adventist Medical Center Inc
1509 Wilson Ter
Glendale CA 91206
818 409-8000

(P-22302)
GLOBAL MED SERVICES INC
Also Called: East West
11818 South St Ste 201a, Cerritos
(90703-6831)
PHONE..........................562 207-6970
Kwang Chang, *President*
▲ EMP: 600
SQ FT: 22,250
SALES (est): 10MM **Privately Held**
SIC: **8082** Home health care services

(P-22303)
GOLDEN LIVING LLC
Also Called: Golden Livingcenter - Galt
144 F St, Galt (95632-1833)
PHONE..........................209 745-1537
Brigitte Coleman, *Administration*
EMP: 90
SALES (corp-wide): 7.4MM **Privately Held**
SIC: **8082** 8051 Home health care services; skilled nursing care facilities
PA: Golden Living Llc
5220 Tennyson Pkwy # 400
Plano TX 75024
972 372-6300

(P-22304)
GOLDEN LIVING LLC
Also Called: California Healthcare
6700 Sepulveda Blvd, Van Nuys
(91411-1248)
PHONE..........................805 494-4949
Jerry Catama, *Exec Dir*
EMP: 100
SALES (corp-wide): 7.4MM **Privately Held**
WEB: www.nwbecorp.com
SIC: **8082** Home health care services
PA: Golden Living Llc
5220 Tennyson Pkwy # 400
Plano TX 75024
972 372-6300

(P-22305)
GOLDEN LIVING LLC
Also Called: Beverly
1131 N China Lake Blvd, Ridgecrest
(93555-3131)
PHONE..........................760 446-3591
Steven Rodriguez, *Exec Dir*
EMP: 100
SALES (corp-wide): 7.4MM **Privately Held**
WEB: www.nwbecorp.com
SIC: **8082** 8051 Home health care services; skilled nursing care facilities
PA: Golden Living Llc
5220 Tennyson Pkwy # 400
Plano TX 75024
972 372-6300

(P-22306)
GOOD WORKS LLC
Also Called: Right At Home
1250 E Walnut St Ste 220, Pasadena
(91106-5118)
PHONE..........................626 584-8130
Renee Concialdi, *Mng Member*
Joseph A Concialdi,
EMP: 65
SQ FT: 1,300
SALES: 2.5MM **Privately Held**
SIC: **8082** Home health care services

(P-22307)
GRANDCARE HEALTH SERVICES LLC (PA)
2555 E Colorado Blvd Fl 4, Pasadena
(91107-6620)
PHONE..........................866 554-2447
EMP: 150
SALES (est): 4.2MM **Privately Held**
SIC: **8082** Home health care services

(P-22308)
GREATER SOUTH BAY AREA HM HLTH
Also Called: Greater South Bay Home Health
18726 S Wstn Ave Ste 409, Gardena (90248)
PHONE......................310 329-4835
Lilia Ramos, *President*
EMP: 50
SALES (est): 2.6MM **Privately Held**
WEB: www.gsbhh.com
SIC: 8082 Home health care services

(P-22309)
H & K ABOUAF CORPORATION
9100 S Sepulveda Blvd # 1, Los Angeles (90045-4814)
PHONE......................310 393-1282
Hadas Abouaf, *CEO*
Jeffrey Taylor, *CFO*
EMP: 65
SALES: 950K **Privately Held**
SIC: 8082 Home health care services

(P-22310)
HARMONY HOME HEALTH LLC
Also Called: Harmony Homecare
2500 Ranch Rd Ste 104, Placerville (95667-9181)
PHONE......................916 933-9777
Jennifer Jarrett, *Mng Member*
Patrick Philbrick, *Executive*
EMP: 70
SALES: 500K **Privately Held**
SIC: 8082 Home health care services

(P-22311)
HCS HOLDCO LLC (DH)
27071 Aliso Creek Rd # 100, Aliso Viejo (92656-5327)
PHONE......................949 349-1200
Robert Levin, *President*
EMP: 219
SALES (est): 5.1MM **Privately Held**
SIC: 8082 Home health care services

(P-22312)
HEALTH BY DESIGN
3029 La Via Way, Sacramento (95825-1818)
PHONE......................916 974-3322
Peg Cannon, *President*
▲ EMP: 50
SQ FT: 1,200
SALES (est): 1.6MM **Privately Held**
WEB: www.healthbydesign.net
SIC: 8082 Visiting nurse service

(P-22313)
HEALTH ENTPS LF LONG PLAN
Also Called: Health Entps Life-Long Plans
5805 Sepulveda Blvd, Van Nuys (91411-2546)
PHONE......................818 654-0330
Johnathan Istrin, *President*
EMP: 500
SQ FT: 4,000
SALES (est): 6MM **Privately Held**
SIC: 8082 Home health care services

(P-22314)
HEALTH SOURCE STAFFING INC
438 Camino, San Diego (92108)
PHONE......................619 220-8044
Lloyd Enke, *CEO*
Renee Freitas, *Vice Pres*
EMP: 60
SQ FT: 1,000
SALES (est): 2.1MM **Privately Held**
SIC: 8082 Oxygen tent service

(P-22315)
HEALTHCARE CALIFORNIA
6327 N Fresno St Ste 104, Fresno (93710-5236)
PHONE......................559 243-9990
Harry G Harris, *President*
Bevan S Nugent, *COO*
June Webb, *Director*
EMP: 70
SALES (est): 3.3MM **Privately Held**
SIC: 8082 Home health care services

(P-22316)
HEALTHCARE PATHWAYS MANAGEMENT
5 Mandeville Ct, Monterey (93940-5745)
PHONE......................831 373-1111
Duncan McCarter, *President*
Elizabeth Johnson Rn, *COO*
Maribeth Long, *Director*
EMP: 99
SQ FT: 250
SALES (est): 1.2MM **Privately Held**
WEB: www.advantacarehpm.com
SIC: 8082 Home health care services

(P-22317)
HELP UNLMTED PERSONNEL SVC INC
319 E Carrillo St Ste 102, Santa Barbara (93101-7453)
PHONE......................805 962-4646
Leanna McNealy, *Manager*
EMP: 150 **Privately Held**
SIC: 8082 7363 Visiting nurse service; medical help service
PA: Help Unlimited Personnel Service, Inc.
1957 Eastman Ave
Ventura CA 93003
-

(P-22318)
HERITAGE SENIOR CARE INC
15428 Civic Dr Ste 345, Victorville (92392-2383)
PHONE......................800 562-2734
EMP: 67 **Privately Held**
SIC: 8082 8322 Home health care services; individual & family services
PA: Heritage Senior Care, Inc.
2755 Jefferson St Ste 101
Carlsbad CA 92008

(P-22319)
HIRED HAND HOME CARE
2901 Cleveland Ave # 203, Santa Rosa (95403-2785)
PHONE......................707 575-4700
Lynn Winter, *Owner*
EMP: 200 EST: 2007
SALES (est): 1MM **Privately Held**
SIC: 8082 Visiting nurse service

(P-22320)
HIS PASSION INC
Also Called: Senior Helpers South Coast
17195 Newhope St Ste 201, Fountain Valley (92708-4211)
PHONE......................800 760-6389
George Miller, *President*
Dawn Miller, *Vice Pres*
EMP: 50
SALES: 896.4K **Privately Held**
SIC: 8082 Home health care services

(P-22321)
HOLLYWOOD HEALTH SYSTEM INC
Also Called: Hollywood Home Health Services
4640 Lankershim Blvd # 100, North Hollywood (91602-1845)
PHONE......................323 662-3731
Siranush Manukyan, *CEO*
EMP: 99
SALES (est): 3.6MM **Privately Held**
SIC: 8082 Home health care services

(P-22322)
HOME CARE OF AMERICA INC
Also Called: Home Care America-San Marino
1122 E Green St 10, Pasadena (91106-2500)
PHONE......................626 309-7696
Nymia Cucueco, *President*
EMP: 75
SQ FT: 1,600
SALES (est): 3.4MM **Privately Held**
WEB: www.americani.org
SIC: 8082 Visiting nurse service

(P-22323)
HOME HEALTH CARE MANAGEMENT (PA)
1398 Ridgewood Dr, Chico (95973-7801)
PHONE......................530 343-0727

Barbara Hanna, *President*
Terry Gordon, *Vice Pres*
Julie Lehmann, *General Mgr*
Amicie Zimmerman, *VP Human Res*
Sherri-Lynn Messier,
EMP: 100
SQ FT: 27,007
SALES (est): 4.9MM **Privately Held**
SIC: 8082 8322 Visiting nurse service; general counseling services

(P-22324)
HOME HELPERS SAN MATEO COUNTY
655 Miramontes St, Half Moon Bay (94019-1945)
PHONE......................650 532-3122
Peggy Milne, *Owner*
EMP: 60
SALES (est): 311.7K **Privately Held**
SIC: 8082 Home health care services

(P-22325)
HOME INSTEAD SENIOR CARE
9665 Gran Rdge Dr Ste 250, San Diego (92123)
PHONE......................858 277-3722
Robert Perez, *President*
Jessica Perez, *Vice Pres*
EMP: 60 EST: 1997
SQ FT: 900
SALES (est): 3.1MM **Privately Held**
SIC: 8082 Home health care services

(P-22326)
HOME INSTEAD SENIOR CARE
11160 Sun Center Dr, Rancho Cordova (95670-6121)
PHONE......................916 920-2273
Scott Shaw, *Owner*
EMP: 60
SALES (est): 1.5MM **Privately Held**
WEB: www.scottshaw.com
SIC: 8082 Home health care services

(P-22327)
HOME INSTEAD SENIOR CARE
1720 E Los Angeles Ave H, Simi Valley (93065-2080)
PHONE......................805 577-0926
Don Reed, *Owner*
EMP: 175 EST: 1997
SALES (est): 5.1MM **Privately Held**
SIC: 8082 Home health care services

(P-22328)
HOME INSTEAD SENIOR CARE
5360 Jackson Dr Ste 120, La Mesa (91942-6003)
PHONE......................619 460-6222
Leslie Bojorquez, *President*
Steve Bojorquez, *CFO*
EMP: 50
SQ FT: 1,500
SALES (est): 1.2MM **Privately Held**
SIC: 8082 Home health care services

(P-22329)
HOME INSTEAD SENIOR CARE
405 Court St, Woodland (95695-3421)
PHONE......................707 678-2005
Thomas Suharik, *President*
EMP: 50
SALES (est): 988.3K **Privately Held**
SIC: 8082 Home health care services

(P-22330)
HOME INSTEAD SENIOR CARE
26 Carmello Rd, Walnut Creek (94597-3402)
PHONE......................510 686-9940
Ron Macarthur, *President*
Renee Macarthur, *CFO*
EMP: 100
SALES (est): 2.2MM **Privately Held**
SIC: 8082 Home health care services

(P-22331)
HOME INSTEAD SENIOR CARE
28570 Marguerite Pkwy # 221, Mission Viejo (92692-3733)
PHONE......................949 347-6767
Jim Efzlinger, *Managing Prtnr*
Fred Wollman, *Managing Prtnr*
Joe Sanders, *Principal*
EMP: 50

SALES (est): 1.9MM **Privately Held**
SIC: 8082 8322 Home health care services; senior citizens' center or association

(P-22332)
HOMECARE PROFESSIONALS INC
1849 Willow Pass Rd # 305, Concord (94520-2524)
PHONE......................925 215-1214
Andrew Howard, *Principal*
Juliana Williams, *Director*
EMP: 80 EST: 2005
SQ FT: 1,200
SALES (est): 270.1K **Privately Held**
SIC: 8082 Home health care services

(P-22333)
HOSPICE & HOME HEALTH OF E BAY
Also Called: Pathways
333 Hegenberger Rd # 700, Oakland (94621-1420)
PHONE......................510 632-4390
Barbara Burgess, *President*
Donna Lopez, *Vice Pres*
EMP: 200
SQ FT: 10,000
SALES (est): 3.3MM **Privately Held**
WEB: www.pathwayshealth.org
SIC: 8082 Home health care services

(P-22334)
HOSPICE BY BAY (PA)
Also Called: Hospice of Marin
17 E Sir Francis Drake Bl, Larkspur (94939-1708)
PHONE......................415 927-2273
Kitty Whitaker, *CEO*
Mary Taverna, *President*
Denis Viscek, *CFO*
Dennis A Gilardi, *Chairman*
Michael R Dailey, *Treasurer*
EMP: 220
SQ FT: 8,000
SALES (est): 57.6MM **Privately Held**
SIC: 8082 Home health care services

(P-22335)
HOSPICE CHEERS
625 Fair Oaks Ave Ste 229, South Pasadena (91030-2697)
PHONE......................626 799-2727
David Friedman, *President*
Vivian Allen, *Opers Staff*
EMP: 95
SALES (est): 1.2MM **Privately Held**
SIC: 8082 Home health care services

(P-22336)
HOSPICE OF FOOTHILLS (PA)
11270 Rough And Ready Hwy, Grass Valley (95945-8530)
PHONE......................530 272-5739
Vanessa Bengston, *Director*
Sue Hodge, *Exec Dir*
EMP: 95
SQ FT: 5,000
SALES: 8.1MM **Privately Held**
WEB: www.hospiceofthefoothills.org
SIC: 8082 Visiting nurse service

(P-22337)
HOSPICE OF SANTA CRUZ COUNTY (PA)
Also Called: HOSPICE CARING PROJECT
940 Disc Dr, Scotts Valley (95066-4544)
PHONE......................831 430-3000
Michael Milward, *CEO*
Judi Humble, *Officer*
Ann Pomper, *Exec Dir*
Nancy Houseman, *Financial Exec*
Kim Bartley, *Human Resources*
EMP: 110
SQ FT: 2,300
SALES: 21MM **Privately Held**
WEB: www.hospicesantacruz.org
SIC: 8082 Home health care services

948   2019 Directory of California
Wholesalers and Services Companies   ▲ = Import ▼=Export
◆ =Import/Export

(P-22338)
HOSPICE OF SANTA CRUZ COUNTY
Also Called: Hospice Caring Project
65 Neilson St Ste 121, Watsonville
(95076-2491)
PHONE.................................831 430-3000
Michael Milward, *CEO*
EMP: 60
SALES (corp-wide): 21MM **Privately Held**
SIC: 8082 Home health care services
PA: Hospice Of Santa Cruz County
940 Disc Dr
Scotts Valley CA 95066
831 430-3000

(P-22339)
HUMAN TOUCH HOME HEALTH
3629 N Sepulveda Blvd, Manhattan Beach
(90266-3632)
PHONE.................................424 247-8165
Kameria Ahmed Ibrahim, *Principal*
Sada Kelisa, *Financial Exec*
EMP: 120
SALES: 950K **Privately Held**
SIC: 8082 Home health care services

(P-22340)
HUNTINGTON CARE LLC
Also Called: Huntington Care, Inc.
2555 E Colo Blvd Ste 400h, Pasadena
(91107)
PHONE.................................877 405-6990
Carlo Stepanians, *CEO*
Sergio Varela, *President*
EMP: 350
SALES (est): 3.8MM
SALES (corp-wide): 4.2MM **Privately Held**
SIC: 8082 Home health care services
PA: Grandcare Health Services Llc
2555 E Colorado Blvd Fl 4
Pasadena CA 91107
866 554-2447

(P-22341)
IN HOME HEALTH INC
Also Called: Home Health Plus
2005 De La Cruz Blvd # 271, Santa Clara
(95050-3031)
PHONE.................................408 986-8160
Cheryl Bartin, *Manager*
EMP: 132
SALES (corp-wide): 32.2MM **Privately Held**
SIC: 8082 Visiting nurse service
PA: In Home Health, Inc.
333 N Summit St
Toledo OH
419 252-5500

(P-22342)
IN HOME HEALTH INC
Also Called: Home Health Plus
1000 Lakes Dr Ste 200, West Covina
(91790-2927)
PHONE.................................419 254-7841
Wendy Myers, *Director*
EMP: 60
SALES (corp-wide): 32.2MM **Privately Held**
SIC: 8082 Home health care services
PA: In Home Health, Inc.
333 N Summit St
Toledo OH
419 252-5500

(P-22343)
INFINITE HOME HEALTH INC
22151 Ventura Blvd # 102, Woodland Hills
(91364-1666)
PHONE.................................818 888-7772
Taimoor Bidari, *President*
EMP: 60
SQ FT: 4,000
SALES: 4.5MM **Privately Held**
SIC: 8082 Home health care services

(P-22344)
INTEGRITY HEALTHCARE SERVICES
425 W 5th Ave Ste 101, Escondido
(92025-4843)
PHONE.................................760 432-9811

Wendy Olayvar, *President*
EMP: 70 **Privately Held**
SIC: 8082 Home health care services
PA: Integrity Healthcare Services Inc
5625 Ruffin Rd Ste 225
San Diego CA 92123

(P-22345)
INTERHEALTH SERVICES INC (HQ)
Also Called: Presbyterian Inter Cmnty Hosp
12401 Washington Blvd, Whittier
(90602-1006)
PHONE.................................562 698-0811
Daniel F Adams, *President*
Jim West, *President*
Gary Koger, *CFO*
Peggy Chulack, *Admin Sec*
EMP: 53
SQ FT: 1,000
SALES (est): 7.6MM
SALES (corp-wide): 27.7MM **Privately Held**
SIC: 8082 8062 Home health care services; general medical & surgical hospitals
PA: Interhealth Corp.
12401 Washington Blvd
Whittier CA 90602
562 698-0811

(P-22346)
INTERIM ASSISTED CARE OF NORT
Also Called: Interim Services
373 Smile Pl, Redding (96001-3637)
PHONE.................................530 722-1530
Robert Seawright, *President*
EMP: 99
SALES (est): 1.4MM **Privately Held**
SIC: 8082 Home health care services

(P-22347)
INTERIM HLTHCARE NTHRN CAL INC (PA)
1647 Court St, Redding (96001-1737)
PHONE.................................530 221-1300
Robert Seawright, *President*
Renee Rand, *Admin Sec*
EMP: 350
SQ FT: 4,000
SALES (est): 9.4MM **Privately Held**
SIC: 8082 Home health care services

(P-22348)
KAISER FOUNDATION HOSPITAL
4501 Broadway, Oakland (94611-4615)
PHONE.................................510 752-6295
Kirs Holm, *Director*
EMP: 50
SALES (est): 211.9K **Privately Held**
SIC: 8082 Home health care services

(P-22349)
KAISER FOUNDATION HOSPITALS
Also Called: Kaiser Permanente
50 Great Oaks Blvd, San Jose
(95119-1381)
PHONE.................................408 361-2100
Ellie Farahabadi, *Consultant*
EMP: 793
SALES (corp-wide): 94.1B **Privately Held**
SIC: 8082 8011 Home health care services; health maintenance organization
HQ: Kaiser Foundation Hospitals Inc
1 Kaiser Plz
Oakland CA 94612
510 271-6611

(P-22350)
KEARN ALTERNATIVE CARE INC (PA)
2029 21st St, Bakersfield (93301-4219)
PHONE.................................661 631-2036
Jean Schamblin, *President*
J R Doty, *Admin Sec*
EMP: 300
SALES (est): 5.6MM **Privately Held**
SIC: 8082 Visiting nurse service

(P-22351)
KERN ALTERNATIVE CARE INC
2029 21st St, Bakersfield (93301-4219)
PHONE.................................661 631-2036
Jeanne Schamblin, *President*
Leo Schamblin, *Vice Pres*
EMP: 160
SQ FT: 1,800
SALES (est): 6.3MM **Privately Held**
SIC: 8082 Visiting nurse service

(P-22352)
KIDS OVERCOMING LLC
40029 St Ste 204, Oakland (94609)
PHONE.................................415 748-8052
Anne Swinney, *Mng Member*
Matt McAlear,
EMP: 75
SALES (est): 1.3MM **Privately Held**
SIC: 8082 Home health care services

(P-22353)
KIND HOMECARE INC
3705 Haven Ave Ste 104, Menlo Park
(94025-1011)
PHONE.................................888 885-5463
Aida Bruun, *CEO*
EMP: 99
SALES (est): 277.5K **Privately Held**
SIC: 8082 7389 Home health care services; nurses' registry

(P-22354)
KISSITO HEALTH CARE INC
Also Called: Bay Point Healthcare Center
442 Sunset Blvd, Hayward (94541-3832)
PHONE.................................510 582-8311
Bob Ewing, *Manager*
EMP: 100
SALES (corp-wide): 61.6MM **Privately Held**
SIC: 8082 8051 8052 Home health care services; skilled nursing care facilities; intermediate care facilities
PA: Kissito Healthcare, Inc.
5228 Valleypointe Pkwy
Roanoke VA 24019
540 265-0322

(P-22355)
KISSITO HEALTH CASE INC
Also Called: Willow Pass Healthcare Center
3318 Willow Pass Rd, Concord
(94519-2316)
PHONE.................................925 689-9222
Fax: 925 689-3412
EMP: 100
SALES (corp-wide): 62.4MM **Privately Held**
SIC: 8082 8051
PA: Kissito Health Care, Inc.
5228 Valleypointe Pkwy
Roanoke VA 24019
540 265-0322

(P-22356)
KISSITO HEALTH CASE INC
Also Called: San Leandro Healthcare Center
368 Juana Ave, San Leandro (94577-4811)
PHONE.................................510 357-4015
Vinny Poddapoori, *Administration*
EMP: 80
SALES (corp-wide): 61.6MM **Privately Held**
SIC: 8082 8051 Home health care services; skilled nursing care facilities
PA: Kissito Healthcare, Inc.
5228 Valleypointe Pkwy
Roanoke VA 24019
540 265-0322

(P-22357)
LANDMARK HEALTH LLC
7755 Center Ave Ste 630, Huntington
Beach (92647-9152)
PHONE.................................253 394-2566
Adam Boehler,
Christopher Goldsmith, *President*
Brandon Kerns, *CFO*
EMP: 294 EST: 2013
SALES (est): 802.5K **Privately Held**
SIC: 8082 Home health care services

(P-22358)
LIVHOME INC (PA)
5670 Wilshire Blvd # 500, Los Angeles
(90036-5682)
PHONE.................................800 807-5854
Toll Free:.................................877 -
Mike Nicholson, *Ch of Bd*
Cody D Legler, *Officer*
Kevin Poirier, *Vice Pres*
Leslie Saller, *Office Mgr*
Nancy Kavin, *Technology*
EMP: 1299
SQ FT: 7,454
SALES (est): 49.3MM **Privately Held**
SIC: 8082 Home health care services

(P-22359)
LOMA LINDA UNIVERSITY MED CTR
Loma Linda Home Health Care
11265 Mountain View Ave E, Loma Linda
(92354-3863)
P.O. Box 2000 (92354-0200)
PHONE.................................909 558-3096
Jan Huckins, *Director*
EMP: 120
SALES (corp-wide): 301.3MM **Privately Held**
WEB: www.llumc.org
SIC: 8082 7361 Home health care services; nurses' registry
HQ: Loma Linda University Medical Center
11234 Anderson St
Loma Linda CA 92354
909 558-4000

(P-22360)
LOVELY LIVING HOMECARE
112 Harvard Ave, Claremont (91711-4716)
PHONE.................................909 625-7999
Lee Rodriguez, *President*
EMP: 65
SALES (est): 632.2K **Privately Held**
SIC: 8082 Home health care services

(P-22361)
LUMINA HEALTHCARE LLC (PA)
Also Called: Lumina At Home
5220 Pacific Concourse Dr, Los Angeles
(90045-6277)
PHONE.................................888 958-6462
Mary Ellen Hardin, *President*
Robert C Mathuny, *Vice Pres*
EMP: 55
SALES: 8MM **Privately Held**
SIC: 8082 Home health care services

(P-22362)
MANAGED HOMECARE INC
2520 Redhill Ave, Santa Ana (92705-5542)
PHONE.................................951 341-0782
David Ross, *Administration*
EMP: 50
SQ FT: 1,910
SALES (est): 1.9MM **Privately Held**
SIC: 8082 Home health care services

(P-22363)
MATCHED CAREGIVERS INC
Also Called: Matched Care Gvrs Cntns Care
1800 El Camino Real Ste B, Atherton
(94027-4103)
PHONE.................................408 560-2382
Kathryn Janz, *President*
Christina Martinez, *Associate Dir*
Christina Mendez, *Associate Dir*
EMP: 130
SQ FT: 2,000
SALES (est): 2.2MM **Privately Held**
SIC: 8082 Home health care services

(P-22364)
MAXIM HEALTHCARE SERVICES INC
Also Called: Los Angles Homecare Pediatrics
4221 Wilshire Blvd # 130, Los Angeles
(90010-3538)
PHONE.................................323 937-9410
Jeff Poitras, *Manager*
EMP: 250
SALES (corp-wide): 1.5B **Privately Held**
WEB: www.maximstaffing.com
SIC: 8082 Home health care services

P
R
O
D
U
C
T
S
&
S
V
C
S

PA: Maxim Healthcare Services, Inc.
7227 Lee Deforest Dr
Columbia MD 21046
410 910-1500

(P-22365)
MAXIMUS INC
3130 Kilgore Rd Ste 100, Rancho Cordova
(95670-6298)
PHONE....................................916 364-6610
Bob Britton, *Principal*
Greg Hanzelka, *Technology*
Ankur Jaswal, *Analyst*
Michelle D'Mello, *Senior Mgr*
Himanshu Arora, *Manager*
EMP: 80
SALES (corp-wide): 2.4B **Publicly Held**
SIC: 8082 Home health care services
PA: Maximus, Inc.
1891 Metro Center Dr
Reston VA 20190
703 251-8500

(P-22366)
MERCY HM SVCS A CAL LTD
PARTNR
1544 Market St, Redding (96001-1023)
P.O. Box 496009 (96049-6009)
PHONE....................................530 245-4070
Ginger White, *Director*
EMP: 80
SALES (corp-wide): 6.7B **Privately Held**
WEB: www.mercyhealth.org
SIC: 8082 Visiting nurse service
HQ: Mercy Home Services A California Limited Partnership
2175 Rosaline Ave Ste A
Redding CA 96001
530 225-6000

(P-22367)
MIRACLE HOME HEALTH
AGENCY
13146 Mungo Ct, Rancho Cucamonga
(91739-9157)
PHONE....................................562 653-0668
Bernice Osunwa, *President*
EMP: 50
SALES (est): 889.2K **Privately Held**
SIC: 8082 Home health care services

(P-22368)
MOMS ORANGE COUNTY
1128 W Santa Ana Blvd, Santa Ana
(92703-3833)
PHONE....................................714 972-2610
Pamela Pimentel Rn, *Exec Dir*
EMP: 50
SALES: 5.4MM **Privately Held**
WEB: www.oc-moms.org
SIC: 8082 Home health care services

(P-22369)
MONTE NIDO RESIDENTIAL CTR
LLC (PA)
Also Called: Monte Nido & Affiliates
23815 Stuart Ranch Rd, Malibu
(90265-4861)
PHONE....................................310 457-9958
Carolyn Costin, *President*
EMP: 68
SALES (est): 60MM **Privately Held**
SIC: 8082 Home health care services

(P-22370)
MSJ HEALTHCARE LLC
Also Called: Grandcare Home Health Services
2555 E Colorado Blvd Fl 4, Pasadena
(91107-6620)
PHONE....................................818 244-8446
Sergio Varela, *President*
Jay Pamintuan, *Vice Pres*
Douglas Saylor, *Marketing Staff*
Nurmina Banaag, *Director*
Dr David Bell, *Director*
EMP: 50
SQ FT: 4,800
SALES (est): 1.6MM **Privately Held**
SIC: 8082 Home health care services

(P-22371)
MY CHOICE INHOME CARE LLC
31610 Rr Cyn Rd Ste 4, Canyon Lake
(92587-9454)
PHONE....................................951 244-8770
Julie Zimmerer,
EMP: 87
SALES: 480K **Privately Held**
SIC: 8082 Home health care services

(P-22372)
NO ORDINARY MOMENTS INC
16742 Gothard St Ste 115, Huntington
Beach (92647-4564)
PHONE....................................714 848-3800
Luis Pena, *President*
EMP: 250
SALES (est): 4.7MM **Privately Held**
SIC: 8082 8322 Home health care services; emergency social services

(P-22373)
NORTH COAST HOME CARE
INC
Also Called: Homewatch Caregivers
5731 Palmer Way Ste F, Carlsbad
(92010-7247)
PHONE....................................760 260-8700
Tanya Finnerty, *President*
Michael Finnerty, *Admin Sec*
EMP: 70
SQ FT: 1,000
SALES: 1MM **Privately Held**
SIC: 8082 Home health care services

(P-22374)
NORTHERN CALIFORNIA HLTH
CARE
Also Called: Arcadia Healthcare
16201 Plateau Cir, Redding (96001-9720)
PHONE....................................530 223-2332
Tim Araiza, *President*
EMP: 60
SALES (est): 1.1MM **Privately Held**
WEB: www.norcalarcadia.com
SIC: 8082 Home health care services

(P-22375)
NURSES TUCH HM HLTH
PRVDER INC
135 S Jackson St Ste 100, Glendale
(91205-4917)
PHONE....................................818 500-4877
Evangeline Ursua, *President*
EMP: 50
SALES (est): 483.7K **Privately Held**
SIC: 8082 Home health care services

(P-22376)
NURSING & REHAB AT HOME
1660 S Amphlett Blvd # 112, San Mateo
(94402-2507)
PHONE....................................650 286-4272
Lorna Beukema, *President*
EMP: 54
SQ FT: 3,000
SALES (est): 3MM **Privately Held**
WEB: www.rehabathome.org
SIC: 8082 Home health care services

(P-22377)
OAK HILL CAPITAL PARTNERS
LP
2775 Sand Hill Rd Ste 220, Menlo Park
(94025-7085)
PHONE....................................650 234-0500
Steven B Gruber, *President*
EMP: 859
SALES (corp-wide): 2.9B **Privately Held**
SIC: 8082 Home health care services
PA: Oak Hill Capital Partners, L.P.
65 E 55th St Fl 32
New York NY 10022
212 527-8400

(P-22378)
ODYSSEY HEALTHCARE INC
9444 Balboa Ave Ste 290, San Diego
(92123-4901)
PHONE....................................858 565-2499
Diana Thompson, *Manager*
EMP: 70
SALES (corp-wide): 6B **Privately Held**
SIC: 8082 Home health care services

HQ: Odyssey Healthcare, Inc.
7801 Mesquite Bend Dr # 105
Irving TX 75063

(P-22379)
ODYSSEY HEALTHCARE INC
17290 Jasmine St Ste 104, Victorville
(92395-8300)
PHONE....................................760 241-7044
Jodi Schmidt, *Branch Mgr*
EMP: 53
SALES (corp-wide): 6B **Privately Held**
SIC: 8082 Home health care services
HQ: Odyssey Healthcare, Inc.
7801 Mesquite Bend Dr # 105
Irving TX 75063

(P-22380)
ONEBODY INC
Also Called: Consensus Health
2000 Powell St Ste 555, Emeryville
(94608-1838)
P.O. Box 6219, Moraga (94570-6219)
PHONE....................................510 285-2000
Kendall Lockhart, *Ch of Bd*
Susan M Rowe, *CFO*
EMP: 60 **EST:** 1996
SALES (est): 2.2MM **Privately Held**
SIC: 8082 Home health care services

(P-22381)
ONTARIO HEALTH EDUCATN CO
INC
3130 Sedona Ct, Ontario (91764-6554)
PHONE....................................951 817-8553
David Pyle, *President*
EMP: 50 **EST:** 2008
SALES (est): 510.6K **Privately Held**
SIC: 8082 Home health care services

(P-22382)
OPTIMAL HEALTH SERVICES
INC
1315 Boughton Dr, Bakersfield
(93308-1613)
PHONE....................................661 393-4483
Doug Clary, *President*
Sarah Shelbourne, *CFO*
Patrick Loschke, *Vice Pres*
Mary Conarroe, *Vice Pres*
Shelly Hutsell,
EMP: 81
SALES (est): 7.4MM **Privately Held**
SIC: 8082 Visiting nurse service

(P-22383)
OPTIMAL HOSPICE
FOUNDATION
Also Called: Optimal Hospice Care
1675 Chester Ave Ste 401, Bakersfield
(93301-5225)
PHONE....................................661 716-4000
Doug Clary, *CEO*
EMP: 133
SALES (corp-wide): 300K **Privately Held**
SIC: 8082 Visiting nurse service
PA: Optimal Hospice Foundation
1315 Boughton Dr
Bakersfield CA 93308
661 410-3000

(P-22384)
OPTION CARE HOME CARE INC
9401 Chivers Ave, Sun Valley
(91352-2655)
PHONE....................................818 351-3000
Jon Pyshny, *Branch Mgr*
EMP: 55
SALES (corp-wide): 131.5B **Publicly**
Held
SIC: 8082 Home health care services
HQ: Option Care Home Care, Inc.
1417 Lake Cook Rd Ste 100
Deerfield IL 60015

(P-22385)
OUR WATCH
Also Called: Assistance In Home Care
12832 Valley View St # 211, Garden Grove
(92845-2524)
PHONE....................................714 897-1022
Ramona Streit, *Principal*

EMP: 52
SALES (est): 1.9MM **Privately Held**
SIC: 8082

(P-22386)
PACIFIC CARE INC
Also Called: Pro Care 2000 Home Health
Care
1903 Redondo Ave, Long Beach
(90755-1226)
PHONE....................................562 494-6500
Michael Siller, *President*
Steve Liss, *Vice Pres*
Mike Bladuka MD, *Medical Dir*
EMP: 60
SALES: 1.2MM **Privately Held**
SIC: 8082 Visiting nurse service

(P-22387)
PACIFIC COAST SERVICES INC
Also Called: Pacific Homecare Services
3202 W March Ln Ste D, Stockton
(95219-2351)
PHONE....................................209 956-2532
Leticia Robles, *President*
EMP: 550
SQ FT: 2,000
SALES: 3.5MM **Privately Held**
SIC: 8082 Visiting nurse service

(P-22388)
PACIFIC PALMS HEALTHCARE
LLC
Empress Rehabilitation Center
1020 Termino Ave, Long Beach
(90804-4123)
PHONE....................................562 433-6791
Emmanuel B David, *Branch Mgr*
EMP: 51
SALES (corp-wide): 991.5K **Privately**
Held
SIC: 8082 Home health care services
PA: Pacific Palms Healthcare, Llc
1020 Termino Ave
Long Beach CA 90804
562 433-6791

(P-22389)
PARADISE VALLEY HOSPITAL
Also Called: West Health Care
180 Otay Lakes Rd Ste 100, Bonita
(91902-2464)
PHONE....................................619 472-7474
Connie Mayo, *Director*
EMP: 80
SALES (corp-wide): 120.3MM **Privately**
Held
WEB: www.paradisevalleyhospital.org
SIC: 8082 Home health care services
PA: Paradise Valley Hospital
2400 E 4th St
National City CA 91950
619 470-4100

(P-22390)
PATHFINDER HEALTH INC
10051 Lampson Ave, Garden Grove
(92840-4716)
PHONE....................................714 636-5649
Avelina Cumbis, *President*
EMP: 150
SALES (est): 3.4MM **Privately Held**
SIC: 8082 Visiting nurse service

(P-22391)
PEACEFUL HEARTS HOME
CARE INC
387 Magnolia Ave Ste 103, Corona
(92879-3308)
PHONE....................................951 541-9343
Brian McKee, *President*
EMP: 55
SALES (est): 1.1MM **Privately Held**
SIC: 8082 Home health care services

(P-22392)
PEGASUS HOME HEALTH CARE
A CA
Also Called: Pegasus Home Health Services
132 N Artsakh St, Glendale (91206-4094)
PHONE....................................818 551-1932
Pamela Spiszman, *President*
Kimberly D Moss, *Vice Pres*
▼**EMP:** 80
SQ FT: 2,800

▲ = Import ▼=Export
◆ =Import/Export

SALES (est): 3.8MM **Privately Held**
SIC: **8082** Visiting nurse service

(P-22393)
PEOPLES CARE INC
13901 Amargosa Rd Ste 101, Victorville
(92392-2409)
PHONE......................760 962-1900
Stacey Minwalla, *Owner*
EMP: 195
SALES (corp-wide): 42.3MM **Privately Held**
SIC: **8082** Home health care services
PA: People's Care Inc.
13920 City Center Dr # 230
Chino Hills CA 91709
855 773-6753

(P-22394)
PERSONLZED HMCARE HMMAKER AGCY
4700 Northgate Blvd, Sacramento
(95834-1128)
PHONE......................916 979-4975
Celso Avaricio II, *CEO*
Pat Mitchell, *Program Dir*
EMP: 100
SQ FT: 900
SALES (est): 403K **Privately Held**
SIC: **8082** Home health care services

(P-22395)
PHYSICIANS CHOICE HM HLTH INC
3220 Sepulveda Blvd # 100, Torrance
(90505-8160)
PHONE......................310 793-1616
Shari Sunada, *President*
EMP: 50
SQ FT: 2,500
SALES: 3.5MM **Privately Held**
SIC: **8082** Home health care services

(P-22396)
POLARIS HOME CARE LLC
830 Stewart Dr Ste 214, Sunnyvale
(94085-4513)
PHONE......................408 400-7020
Gregory Kemper, *Principal*
EMP: 55
SALES (est): 351.8K **Privately Held**
SIC: **8082** Home health care services

(P-22397)
PREMIER MANAGEMENT COMPANY
Also Called: Jacob Health Care Center
4075 54th St, San Diego (92105-2301)
PHONE......................619 582-5168
Guy Reggeb, *Manager*
EMP: 50 **Privately Held**
SIC: **8082** 8051 Home health care services; skilled nursing care facilities
PA: Premier Management Company
1141 S Beverly Dr Fl 3
Los Angeles CA 90035

(P-22398)
PROVIDENCE HEALTH SYSTEM
Also Called: Trinity Home Care
4101 Torrance Blvd, Torrance
(90503-4607)
PHONE......................310 370-5895
EMP: 200
SALES (corp-wide): 17.6B **Privately Held**
SIC: **8082** 8051
HQ: Providence Health System-Southern
California
1801 Lind Ave Sw
Renton WA 98057
425 525-3355

(P-22399)
PW JADE LLC
Also Called: Right At Home
1825 4th St, Santa Rosa (95404-3202)
PHONE......................707 843-5192
Robert Brohmer, *Principal*
EMP: 60
SALES (est): 664K **Privately Held**
SIC: **8082** Home health care services

(P-22400)
QUALITY IN-HMECARE SPECIALISTS
1166 Broadway Ste T, Placerville
(95667-5745)
PHONE......................530 303-3477
Pete Messimore, *CEO*
Arlene Secondo, *Treasurer*
Gloria Tingley, *Principal*
EMP: 99
SQ FT: 597
SALES (est): 2.3MM **Privately Held**
WEB: www.qualityinhomecare.com
SIC: **8082** Visiting nurse service

(P-22401)
RAINBOW HOME CARE SERVICES
1560 Brookhollow Dr # 100, Santa Ana
(92705-5411)
PHONE......................714 544-8070
Barbara Hedges, *CEO*
EMP: 55
SALES (est): 2.8MM **Privately Held**
WEB: www.rainbowhomecareservices.com
SIC: **8082** Home health care services

(P-22402)
RAMONA COMMUNITY SERVICES CORP (HQ)
Also Called: Ramona Vna & Hospice
890 W Stetson Ave Ste A, Hemet
(92543-7311)
PHONE......................951 658-9288
Patricia McBe, *Branch Mgr*
Patrick Searl, *Ch of Bd*
Carol Wood, *CEO*
Lauien Mahieu, *COO*
John Brudin, *Treasurer*
EMP: 195
SQ FT: 14,000
SALES (est): 9.2MM
SALES (corp-wide): 12.4MM **Privately Held**
WEB: www.ramonavna.org
SIC: **8082** Visiting nurse service
PA: Kpc Group Llc
6800 Indiana Ave Ste 130
Riverside CA 92506
951 782-8812

(P-22403)
RELIABLE CAREGIVERS INC
1700 California St # 400, San Francisco
(94109-0429)
PHONE......................415 436-0100
Linda Leary, *President*
Susan Anastasio, *Business Dir*
Keith Trottier, *Admin Asst*
Bobbie Joe Keating, *Finance Dir*
Bobbie Keating, *Finance*
EMP: 120
SALES: 3MM **Privately Held**
WEB: www.reliablecaregivers.net
SIC: **8082** Home health care services

(P-22404)
RES-CARE INC
Also Called: Socal Home Care-Givers Svcs
17291 Irvine Blvd Ste 150, Tustin
(92780-2900)
PHONE......................800 707-8781
Babli Dusttrama, *Branch Mgr*
EMP: 100
SALES (corp-wide): 24.5B **Privately Held**
SIC: **8082** Home health care services
HQ: Res-Care, Inc.
9901 Linn Station Rd
Louisville KY 40223
502 394-2100

(P-22405)
RIGHT AT HOME
Also Called: Sierra West Home Care
3435 Ocean Park Blvd # 110, Santa Monica
(90405-3318)
PHONE......................310 313-0600
Timothy Petlin, *Principal*
EMP: 75 **EST:** 2011
SALES: 1.2MM **Privately Held**
SIC: **8082** Home health care services

(P-22406)
RIGHT CHOICE IN-HOME CARE INC
7104 Owensmouth Ave, Canoga Park
(91303-2007)
PHONE......................818 836-6001
Don Lucas, *Director*
Linda Weinberg, *President*
EMP: 680
SQ FT: 1,800
SALES (est): 10.5MM **Privately Held**
SIC: **8082** Home health care services

(P-22407)
ROBERTS & ASSOCIATES INC
Also Called: Visiting Angels Riverside Cnty
8175 Limonite Ave Ste A1, Riverside
(92509-6121)
PHONE......................951 727-4357
Joan Roberts, *President*
Robert Roberts, *Treasurer*
Benita Roberts, *Vice Pres*
EMP: 55
SQ FT: 400
SALES (est): 1.9MM **Privately Held**
SIC: **8082** Home health care services

(P-22408)
S B C SENIOR CARE INC
Also Called: Home Instead Senior Care
101 W Anapamu St Ste C, Santa Barbara
(93101-3140)
PHONE......................805 560-6995
Susan Johnson, *Owner*
EMP: 75
SALES (est): 1.4MM **Privately Held**
SIC: **8082** Home health care services

(P-22409)
SAFELY HOME
Also Called: Home Instead Senior Care
461 Tennessee St Ste O, Redlands
(92373-8161)
PHONE......................909 370-0343
Neva Labate, *President*
EMP: 54
SQ FT: 1,000
SALES (est): 178K **Privately Held**
SIC: **8082** Home health care services

(P-22410)
SAN DIEGO HOSPICE
Also Called: San Diego Hospice & Institute
2400 Historic Decatur Rd # 107, San Diego
(92106-6158)
PHONE......................619 688-1600
Fax: 619 688-1599
EMP: 600
SALES (corp-wide): 9.8MM **Privately Held**
SIC: **8082**
PA: San Diego Hospice & Palliative Care
Corporation
4311 3rd Ave
San Diego CA 92103
619 688-1600

(P-22411)
SANSUM CLINIC
Also Called: Community Home Health Agency
509 E Montecito St # 200, Santa Barbara
(93103-3259)
PHONE......................805 682-6507
Melanie Thompson, *Director*
EMP: 50
SALES (corp-wide): 287.3MM **Privately Held**
WEB: www.sansum.com
SIC: **8082** Home health care services
PA: Sansum Clinic
470 S Patterson Ave
Santa Barbara CA 93111
805 681-7700

(P-22412)
SCRIPPS HEALTH
3811 Valley Centre Dr, San Diego
(92130-3318)
PHONE......................858 764-3000
Robert B Sarnoff MD, *President*
Gail E Sowa, *Obstetrician*
Dimitri Sherev, *Cardiology*
Julie Gollin, *Internal Med*
Kirsten Starr, *Internal Med*
EMP: 333

SALES (corp-wide): 2.9B **Privately Held**
SIC: **8082** Home health care services
PA: Scripps Health
10140 Campus Point Dr Ax415
San Diego CA 92121
800 727-4777

(P-22413)
SELECT HOME CARE
2393 Townsgate Rd Ste 100, Westlake Village (91361-2513)
PHONE......................805 777-3855
Dylan Hull, *CEO*
Scott Witt, *Managing Prtnr*
Jamie Rodriguez, *Client Mgr*
EMP: 100
SALES (est): 2.8MM **Privately Held**
SIC: **8082** Home health care services

(P-22414)
SERACADA
Also Called: Home Instead Senior Care
709 E Lavender Way, Azusa (91702-6294)
PHONE......................626 486-0800
Ada Wong, *President*
EMP: 50
SALES: 350K **Privately Held**
SIC: **8082** Home health care services

(P-22415)
SERVING SENIORS LLC
2764 Rogue River Cir, West Sacramento
(95691-4922)
PHONE......................916 372-9640
Priyanka Bansal, *Mng Member*
EMP: 70
SALES (est): 482.5K **Privately Held**
SIC: **8082** Home health care services

(P-22416)
SHARP HEALTHCARE
Also Called: Sharp Home Care
8080 Dagget St Ste 200, San Diego
(92111-2333)
PHONE......................858 541-4850
Dan Gross, *Manager*
Suzanne Johnson, *Vice Pres*
Ray Kelley, *Purchasing*
Shawn Meade,
EMP: 66
SALES (corp-wide): 3.4B **Privately Held**
SIC: **8082** Home health care services
PA: Sharp Healthcare
8695 Spectrum Center Blvd
San Diego CA 92123
858 499-4000

(P-22417)
SHERPAUL CORPORATION
Also Called: Home Instead Senior Care
901 Hacienda Dr Ste B, Vista
(92081-6498)
PHONE......................760 639-6472
Sherry Dziuban, *President*
Paul Dziuban, *Vice Pres*
EMP: 54
SQ FT: 951
SALES (est): 2.1MM **Privately Held**
SIC: **8082** Home health care services

(P-22418)
SIERRA NEVADA MEMORIAL HM CARE
Also Called: Sierra Nevada Home Care
1020 Mccourtney Rd Ste A, Grass Valley
(95949-7453)
P.O. Box 1029 (95945-1029)
PHONE......................530 274-6350
Sharon Turner, *Director*
EMP: 90
SQ FT: 6,200
SALES: 3.7MM
SALES (corp-wide): 6.7B **Privately Held**
WEB: www.snhc.org
SIC: **8082** 7361 Home health care services; nurses' registry
PA: Dignity Health
185 Berry St Ste 300
San Francisco CA 94107
415 438-5500

(P-22419)
SILVERADO BELLINGHAM LLC
6400 Oak Cyn Ste 200, Irvine
(92618-5233)
PHONE......................949 240-7200

Loren Shook, *CEO*
EMP: 80 **EST:** 2015
SALES (est): 202.9K **Privately Held**
SIC: 8082 Home health care services

(P-22420)
SMITH RESIDENTIAL CARE FCILTY (PA)
318 E 4th St, Hanford (93230-5125)
P.O. Box 1093 (93232-1093)
PHONE..................................559 584-8451
Catherine Smith, *Owner*
EMP: 70
SALES (est): 2MM **Privately Held**
SIC: 8082 Home health care services

(P-22421)
SOUTH BAY SENIOR SERVICES INC
Also Called: Homewatch Caregivers
8929 S Sepulveda Blvd # 314, Los Angeles (90045-3616)
PHONE..................................310 338-8558
Richard Williams, *President*
Patricia Greaney, *Admin Sec*
EMP: 77
SQ FT: 700
SALES (est): 1.6MM **Privately Held**
WEB: www.homewatchcaregivers.com/los-angeles
SIC: 8082 Visiting nurse service

(P-22422)
SOUTH BAY SENIOR SOLUTIONS INC
Also Called: Home Instead Senior Care
1660 Hamilton Ave Ste 204, San Jose (95125-5434)
PHONE..................................408 370-6360
Brian Jackson, *President*
EMP: 65 **EST:** 1996
SQ FT: 1,500
SALES (est): 2.7MM **Privately Held**
SIC: 8082 Home health care services

(P-22423)
ST JOSEPH COMMUNITY HOME CARE
7400 Shoreline Dr Ste 4, Stockton (95219-5498)
PHONE..................................209 478-9547
Carol Harpman, *Director*
EMP: 75
SALES (est): 2.5MM **Privately Held**
SIC: 8082 Home health care services

(P-22424)
ST JOSEPH HEALTH PER CARE SVCS
1315 Corona Pointe Ct, Corona (92879-1785)
PHONE..................................800 365-1110
Greg Henderson, *Principal*
EMP: 99
SALES (corp-wide): 2.7MM **Privately Held**
SIC: 8082 Home health care services
PA: St Joseph Health Personal Care Services
200 W Center St Promenade
Anaheim CA 92805
714 712-7100

(P-22425)
ST JOSEPH HOME HEALTH NETWORK (DH)
200 W Center St Promenade, Anaheim (92805-3960)
PHONE..................................714 712-9500
Linda Glomp, *Director*
Vincent Castaldo, *CFO*
Dina Montalvo, *Manager*
Clara Seal, *Supervisor*
EMP: 93 **EST:** 1982
SQ FT: 25,000
SALES (est): 27.5MM
SALES (corp-wide): 17.6B **Privately Held**
SIC: 8082 Home health care services
HQ: St Joseph Health System
3345 Michelson Dr Ste 100
Irvine CA 92612
949 381-4000

(P-22426)
ST JOSEPH HOME HEALTH NETWORK
Also Called: Saint Joseph Hlth Sys HM Hlth
200 W Center St Promenade, Anaheim (92805-3960)
PHONE..................................714 712-9559
Kris Kowlaski, *Director*
Anne Jahnsen, *Business Anlyst*
Sheree Simpson, *Analyst*
Connie Zappone,
EMP: 50
SALES (corp-wide): 17.6B **Privately Held**
SIC: 8082 Visiting nurse service
HQ: St Joseph Home Health Network
200 W Center St Promenade
Anaheim CA 92805
714 712-9500

(P-22427)
STAFFING SPECIALISTS INTL
Also Called: Staffing Home Care
2598 Olympic Dr, San Bruno (94066-1251)
PHONE..................................650 737-0777
Tina Desuasido, *Owner*
EMP: 50
SALES (est): 842.8K **Privately Held**
SIC: 8082 Home health care services

(P-22428)
SUCCESS HEALTHCARE 1 LLC (PA)
Also Called: Silver Lake Medical Center
1711 W Temple St, Los Angeles (90026-5421)
PHONE..................................213 989-6100
Peter R Baronoff,
Brian Dunn, *CEO*
Jamie Yoo, *COO*
James Hopwood, *CFO*
George Watkins, *CFO*
EMP: 700
SALES (est): 43.9MM **Privately Held**
SIC: 8082 Home health care services

(P-22429)
SUTTER VSTING NRSE ASSN HSPICE
1625 Van Ness Ave, San Francisco (94109-3370)
PHONE..................................415 600-6200
Cindy Brown, *Manager*
EMP: 80
SALES (corp-wide): 12.4B **Privately Held**
SIC: 8082 8049 7361 Visiting nurse service; nurses & other medical assistants; nurses' registry
HQ: Sutter Visiting Nurse Association & Hospice
1900 Powell St Ste 300
Emeryville CA 94608
866 652-9178

(P-22430)
SUTTER VSTING NRSE ASSN HSPICE (HQ)
Also Called: Vnahnc
1900 Powell St Ste 300, Emeryville (94608-1815)
P.O. Box 22250, Salt Lake City UT (84122-0250)
PHONE..................................866 652-9178
Marcia Reissig, *CEO*
Maryellen Rota, *COO*
Gregg Davis, *CFO*
Tim Larkin, *Manager*
EMP: 50
SQ FT: 24,000
SALES: 171MM
SALES (corp-wide): 12.4B **Privately Held**
WEB: www.suttervnaandhospice.com
SIC: 8082 Visiting nurse service
PA: Sutter Health
2200 River Plaza Dr
Sacramento CA 95833
916 733-8800

(P-22431)
SUTTER VSTING NRSE ASSN HSPICE
Also Called: Sutter Vsiting Nurse Assn Hosp
5099 Commercial Cir # 20594520, Concord (94520-1291)
PHONE..................................925 677-4250
Windi Heaton, *Manager*

EMP: 100
SALES (corp-wide): 12.4B **Privately Held**
SIC: 8082 Visiting nurse service
HQ: Sutter Visiting Nurse Association & Hospice
1900 Powell St Ste 300
Emeryville CA 94608
866 652-9178

(P-22432)
TA-KAI HOME CARE INC
22349 La Palma Ave # 105, Yorba Linda (92887-3809)
PHONE..................................714 393-4586
Brian Nakamura, *Principal*
EMP: 69
SALES (est): 437.4K **Privately Held**
SIC: 8082 Home health care services

(P-22433)
TENDER HOME HEALTHCARE INC
Also Called: Home Instead Senior Care
3550 Wilshire Blvd # 700, Los Angeles (90010-2428)
PHONE..................................323 466-2345
Ben Jarakunnel, *President*
EMP: 80
SALES (est): 1.9MM **Privately Held**
SIC: 8082 Home health care services

(P-22434)
TENET HEALTHSYSTEM MEDICAL
Also Called: Redding Medical Home Care
475 Knollcrest Dr, Redding (96002-0101)
P.O. Box 494130 (96049-4130)
PHONE..................................530 222-1992
Judith Moroney, *Manager*
EMP: 60
SALES (corp-wide): 19.3B **Publicly Held**
WEB: www.tenenthealth.com
SIC: 8082 Home health care services
HQ: Tenet Healthsystem Medical, Inc.
1445 Ross Ave Ste 1400
Dallas TX 75202
469 893-2000

(P-22435)
THERAPY IN YOUR HOME O TP TS
147 Vista Del Monte, Los Gatos (95030-6335)
PHONE..................................408 358-0201
Julie Groves, *Owner*
EMP: 51
SALES (est): 1.4MM **Privately Held**
WEB: www.therapyinyourhome.net
SIC: 8082 Home health care services

(P-22436)
THOM SHARON & G ENTERPRISES
Also Called: Home Helpers
2620 Larkspur Ln Ste N, Redding (96002-1043)
PHONE..................................530 226-8350
Sharon Clark, *President*
EMP: 50
SQ FT: 750
SALES (est): 1.4MM **Privately Held**
SIC: 8082 Home health care services

(P-22437)
THRIVE SUPPORT SERVICES INC
900 Court St, Martinez (94553-1731)
PHONE..................................925 682-2273
Eric Partridge, *President*
EMP: 50 **EST:** 2009
SALES (est): 2MM **Privately Held**
SIC: 8082 Home health care services

(P-22438)
TRI-CITY HOME CARE SERVICES
2095 W Vista Way Ste 220, Vista (92083-6029)
PHONE..................................760 940-5800
Vernon Petelle, *Director*
Barbara Beckman, *Exec Dir*
EMP: 140
SALES (est): 4.1MM **Privately Held**
SIC: 8082 Home health care services

(P-22439)
TRINITY HOME HEALTH SVCS INC
Also Called: Saint Agnes HM Hlth & Hospice
6729 N Willow Ave Ste 103, Fresno (93710-5952)
PHONE..................................559 450-5112
B Smart, *Exec Dir*
Erin Denholm, *President*
Barbara Sears, *Principal*
EMP: 90
SALES (corp-wide): 14.7B **Privately Held**
SIC: 8082 8093 Visiting nurse service; rehabilitation center, outpatient treatment
HQ: Trinity Home Health Services
17410 College Pkwy # 150
Livonia MI 48152
734 542-8200

(P-22440)
TRINITYCARE LLC (PA)
Also Called: Trinity Care & Nutria
13030 Alondra Blvd, Cerritos (90703-2246)
PHONE..................................818 709-4221
Peggy Chris,
EMP: 60
SALES (est): 1.9MM **Privately Held**
SIC: 8082 Home health care services

(P-22441)
UCLA HEALTH SYSTEM AUXILIARY
10920 Wilshire Blvd, Los Angeles (90024-6502)
PHONE..................................310 267-4327
David T Feinberg, *President*
Patricia Kapur, *Exec VP*
Patty Cuen, *Exec Dir*
Beki Heffler, *Director*
EMP: 11154 **EST:** 1981
SALES (est): 185.6MM **Privately Held**
SIC: 8082 Home health care services

(P-22442)
UNIVERSAL HOME CARE INC
151 N San Vicente Blvd, Beverly Hills (90211-2323)
PHONE..................................323 653-9222
Marina Greenberg, *CEO*
Stephen Shapiro MD, *Vice Pres*
Svetlana Razhavsky, *Office Mgr*
Roy Eisenberg, *Sales Executive*
Bonnie Siegal, *Director*
EMP: 200
SALES (est): 5.6MM **Privately Held**
SIC: 8082 Home health care services

(P-22443)
VINA HOLDINGS INC
13800 Arizona St, Westminster (92683-3951)
PHONE..................................714 622-5334
Cuong Nguyen, *President*
EMP: 80 **EST:** 2015
SALES (est): 395.4K **Privately Held**
SIC: 8082 Home health care services

(P-22444)
VISITING CARE & COMPANIONS INC
Also Called: PERSONAL CARE SERVICES
509 E Montecito St # 200, Santa Barbara (93103-3293)
PHONE..................................805 690-6202
Lynda Panner, *CEO*
Karen Wallace, *CFO*
EMP: 84
SALES: 2.8MM **Privately Held**
SIC: 8082 Visiting nurse service

(P-22445)
VISITING NRSE ASSN ORANGE CNTY (PA)
Also Called: Vna Home Health Systems
2520 Redhill Ave, Santa Ana (92705-5542)
PHONE..................................949 263-4700
Jeneane A Brian, *President*
Joan Randall, *COO*
▼ **EMP:** 55
SQ FT: 30,000
SALES: 2MM **Privately Held**
WEB: www.vnahhs.com
SIC: 8082 Home health care services

(P-22446)
VISITING NURSE ASSOCI
Also Called: Vna Private Duty Care
150 W 1st St Ste 176, Claremont
(91711-4739)
P.O. Box 1208 (91711-1208)
PHONE..................................909 621-3961
Marsha Fox, *Director*
EMP: 100 EST: 1984
SALES: 2.8MM **Privately Held**
SIC: 8082 Visiting nurse service

(P-22447)
VISITING NURSE ASSOCIATION
Also Called: Center Coast Home Help Care
5 Lower Ragsdle Dr 102, Monterey
(93940)
P.O. Box 2480 (93942-2480)
PHONE..................................831 385-1014
Carol Snow, *President*
Gayle McConnell, *CFO*
Gena Gett, *Director*
EMP: 80
SALES (est): 823.2K **Privately Held**
SIC: 8082 Visiting nurse service

(P-22448)
**VISITNG NURSE ASSN INLND
CNT (PA)**
Also Called: Vnaic
6235 River Crest Dr Ste L, Riverside
(92507-0758)
P.O. Box 1649 (92502-1649)
PHONE..................................951 413-1200
Mike A Rusnak, *President*
Gerrard Gier, *Info Tech Dir*
Mary Reed, *Info Tech Mgr*
Jennifer Rock, *Graphic Designe*
Nancy Kendrick, *Opers Staff*
EMP: 720
SQ FT: 12,000
SALES: 56.8MM **Privately Held**
SIC: 8082 Visiting nurse service

(P-22449)
**VISITNG NURSE ASSN INLND
CNT**
42600 Cook St Ste 202, Palm Desert
(92211-5143)
PHONE..................................760 346-3982
Anne Tyer, *Director*
EMP: 130
SALES (corp-wide): 56.8MM **Privately
Held**
SIC: 8082 8621 Visiting nurse service;
nursing association
PA: Visiting Nurse Association Of The In-
land Counties
6235 River Crest Dr Ste L
Riverside CA 92507
951 413-1200

(P-22450)
**VISTA HOME HEALTH SERVICE
INC**
343 E Palmdale Blvd Ste 4, Palmdale
(93550-7138)
PHONE..................................818 701-1877
Alma A Jastia, *President*
EMP: 57
SALES (est): 2.2MM **Privately Held**
WEB: www.vistahomehealth.com
SIC: 8082 Visiting nurse service

(P-22451)
VITAS HEALTHCARE CORP CAL
Also Called: Vitas Innovative Hospice Care
670 N Mccarthy Blcvd 220, Milpitas
(95035)
PHONE..................................408 964-6800
Roslyn Stenson, *Branch Mgr*
EMP: 80
SALES (corp-wide): 1.6B **Publicly Held**
WEB: www.vitasinnovativehospicecare.com
SIC: 8082 Home health care services
HQ: Vitas Healthcare Corporation Of Cali-
fornia
7888 Mission Grove Pkwy S
Riverside CA 92508
305 374-4143

(P-22452)
VITAS HEALTHCARE CORP CAL
2710 Gateway Oaks Dr # 100, Sacramento
(95833-3505)
PHONE..................................916 925-7010
Sharon Rostoker, *Principal*
EMP: 95
SALES (corp-wide): 1.6B **Publicly Held**
WEB: www.vitasinnovativehospicecare.com
SIC: 8082 Home health care services
HQ: Vitas Healthcare Corporation Of Cali-
fornia
7888 Mission Grove Pkwy S
Riverside CA 92508
305 374-4143

(P-22453)
VITAS HEALTHCARE CORP CAL
355 Lennon Ln Ste 150, Walnut Creek
(94598-2475)
PHONE..................................925 930-9373
Shirley Blethen, *Branch Mgr*
Nicholas Chastain, *Human Resources*
EMP: 95
SALES (corp-wide): 1.6B **Publicly Held**
WEB: www.vitasinnovativehospicecare.com
SIC: 8082 Home health care services
HQ: Vitas Healthcare Corporation Of Cali-
fornia
7888 Mission Grove Pkwy S
Riverside CA 92508
305 374-4143

(P-22454)
VITAS HEALTHCARE CORP CAL
Also Called: Vitas Innovative Hospice Care
7888 Mission Grove Pkwy S, Riverside
(92508-5089)
PHONE..................................909 386-6000
Karen Bennett, *Manager*
EMP: 170
SALES (corp-wide): 1.6B **Publicly Held**
WEB: www.vitasinnovativehospicecare.com
SIC: 8082 8011 Home health care serv-
ices; physical medicine, physician/sur-
geon
HQ: Vitas Healthcare Corporation Of Cali-
fornia
7888 Mission Grove Pkwy S
Riverside CA 92508
305 374-4143

(P-22455)
VITAS HEALTHCARE CORP CAL
1343 N Grand Ave Ste 100, Covina
(91724-4043)
PHONE..................................626 918-2273
Thomas E Combs, *Owner*
Susan Patterson, *Executive*
Darren Le, *Technology*
Bruce Schlecter, *Director*
EMP: 80
SALES (corp-wide): 1.6B **Publicly Held**
WEB: www.vitasinnovativehospicecare.com
SIC: 8082 Home health care services
HQ: Vitas Healthcare Corporation Of Cali-
fornia
7888 Mission Grove Pkwy S
Riverside CA 92508
305 374-4143

(P-22456)
VITAS HEALTHCARE CORP CAL
990 W 190th St Ste 550, Torrance
(90502-1046)
PHONE..................................310 324-2273
Marie Hagerty, *Principal*
EMP: 70
SALES (corp-wide): 1.6B **Publicly Held**
WEB: www.vitasinnovativehospicecare.com
SIC: 8082 Home health care services
HQ: Vitas Healthcare Corporation Of Cali-
fornia
7888 Mission Grove Pkwy S
Riverside CA 92508
305 374-4143

(P-22457)
VITAS HEALTHCARE CORP CAL
Also Called: Vitas Innovative Hospice Care
9655 Gran Rdge Dr Ste 300, San Diego
(92123)
PHONE..................................619 680-4400
Judy Brenton, *Branch Mgr*
EMP: 95

SALES (corp-wide): 1.6B **Publicly Held**
WEB: www.vitasinnovativehospicecare.com
SIC: 8082 Home health care services
HQ: Vitas Healthcare Corporation Of Cali-
fornia
7888 Mission Grove Pkwy S
Riverside CA 92508
305 374-4143

(P-22458)
VITAS HEALTHCARE CORP CAL
Also Called: Vitas Innovative Hospice Care
16830 Ventura Blvd # 315, Encino
(91436-1723)
PHONE..................................818 760-2273
Susie Fishenfeld, *Branch Mgr*
Albert Hoston, *Technology*
EMP: 60
SALES (corp-wide): 1.6B **Publicly Held**
WEB: www.vitasinnovativehospicecare.com
SIC: 8082 Home health care services
HQ: Vitas Healthcare Corporation Of Cali-
fornia
7888 Mission Grove Pkwy S
Riverside CA 92508
305 374-4143

(P-22459)
VN HOME HEALTH CARE LP
2528 Qume Dr Ste 7, San Jose
(95131-1836)
PHONE..................................408 998-0550
Ngai Nguyen, *Principal*
EMP: 62
SALES (est): 1.6MM **Privately Held**
SIC: 8082 Home health care services

(P-22460)
**VNA HOSPICE & PLLATVE CRE
S CA**
Also Called: V N A & Hospice Southern Calif
412 E Vanderbilt Way, San Bernardino
(92408-3552)
PHONE..................................909 384-0737
Toll Free:..................................888 -
Marsha Fox, *President*
EMP: 150
SQ FT: 3,230
SALES (corp-wide): 40.1MM **Privately
Held**
WEB: www.vnasocal.org
SIC: 8082 Visiting nurse service
PA: Vna Hospice And Palliative Care Of
Southern California
412 E Vanderbilt Way
San Bernardino CA 92408
909 624-3574

(P-22461)
**VNA HOSPICE & PLLATVE CRE
S CA (PA)**
Also Called: Vna Private Duty Care
412 E Vanderbilt Way, San Bernardino
(92408-3552)
P.O. Box 908, Claremont (91711-0908)
PHONE..................................909 624-3574
Marsha Fox, *President*
Cindy Cameron, *CFO*
Patty Meinhardt, *Business Mgr*
Valerie Hogman, *Human Res Dir*
Linda Adams, *Marketing Staff*
EMP: 122
SALES: 40.1MM **Privately Held**
SIC: 8082 Visiting nurse service

(P-22462)
WAY COOL HOMECARE INC
Also Called: Comfort Keepers
900 N Cuyamaca St Ste 201, El Cajon
(92020-1865)
PHONE..................................619 444-3200
Moura A Everhart, *President*
Benjamin Everhart, *Treasurer*
EMP: 50
SQ FT: 1,650
SALES: 1.4MM **Privately Held**
SIC: 8082 Home health care services

(P-22463)
WELL BEING GROUP INC
7075 N Howard St Ste 102, Fresno
(93720-2922)
PHONE..................................559 432-3737
Mark Dyson, *President*
EMP: 80

SALES (est): 1.3MM **Privately Held**
SIC: 8082 Home health care services

(P-22464)
**WILLOW PASS HLTH CARE CTR
INC**
3318 Willow Pass Rd, Concord
(94519-2316)
PHONE..................................925 689-9222
Pratap Poddatoori, *CEO*
EMP: 100
SALES (est): 168.3K **Privately Held**
SIC: 8082 8051 Home health care serv-
ices; skilled nursing care facilities
PA: Hycare, Inc.
524 Callan Ave
San Leandro CA 94577

(P-22465)
YOLO HOSPICE INC (PA)
1909 Galileo Ct Ste A, Davis (95618-4890)
P.O. Box 1014 (95617-1014)
PHONE..................................530 758-5566
Doug Jena, *Exec Dir*
EMP: 60
SALES: 7.3MM **Privately Held**
WEB: www.yolohospice.org
SIC: 8082 8322 Home health care serv-
ices; individual & family services

8092 Kidney Dialysis Centers

(P-22466)
**BIO-MDCAL APPLICATIONS CAL
INC**
Also Called: FMC Dialysis Svcs Bellflower
10116 Rosecrans Ave, Bellflower
(90706-2564)
PHONE..................................562 920-2070
Nelly McPhail, *Administration*
EMP: 52
SALES (corp-wide): 20.9B **Privately Held**
WEB: www.fresenius.org
SIC: 8092 Kidney dialysis centers
HQ: Bio-Medical Applications Of California,
Inc.
920 Winter St
Waltham MA 02451
-

(P-22467)
**BIO-MDCAL APPLICATIONS CAL
INC**
Also Called: BMA San Gabriel
1801 W Valley Blvd # 102, Alhambra
(91803-2300)
PHONE..................................626 457-9002
Monique Hartell, *Manager*
EMP: 50
SALES (corp-wide): 20.9B **Privately Held**
SIC: 8092 Kidney dialysis centers
HQ: Bio-Medical Applications Of California,
Inc.
920 Winter St
Waltham MA 02451

(P-22468)
**BIO-MDCAL APPLICATIONS CAL
INC**
Also Called: FMC Dialysis Svcs Riverside
3470 La Sierra Ave Ste E, Riverside
(92503-5223)
PHONE..................................951 343-7700
Gina Harper, *Manager*
EMP: 52
SALES (corp-wide): 20.9B **Privately Held**
SIC: 8092 Kidney dialysis centers
HQ: Bio-Medical Applications Of California,
Inc.
920 Winter St
Waltham MA 02451

(P-22469)
**BIO-MDICAL APPLICATIONS RI
INC**
Also Called: Fresenius Medical Care
3636 N 1st St Ste 144, Fresno
(93726-6818)
PHONE..................................559 221-6311

PRODUCTS & SVCS

Monique Hartell, *Manager*
EMP: 53
SALES (corp-wide): 20.9B **Privately Held**
SIC: 8092 Kidney dialysis centers
HQ: Bio-Medical Applications Of Rhode Island, Inc.
    920 Winter St Ste A
    Waltham MA 02451
    781 699-9000

(P-22470)
DAVITA INC
15271 Laguna Canyon Rd, Irvine
(92618-3146)
PHONE....................949 930-4400
Viki Anderson, *Branch Mgr*
Patricia Ruiz, *Admin Asst*
Chad Luminarias, *Technician*
Michael Staffieri, *Finance*
Dakota Lafee, *Analyst*
EMP: 270 **Publicly Held**
WEB: www.davita.com
SIC: 8092 Kidney dialysis centers
PA: Davita Inc.
    2000 16th St
    Denver CO 80202

(P-22471)
DAVITA INC
601 Hawaii St, El Segundo (90245-4814)
PHONE....................310 536-2400
Larry Buckelew, *Principal*
Jenny Carrillo, *Managing Prtnr*
Bill Myers, *Vice Pres*
Edward Stahel, *Vice Pres*
Philipp Stephanus, *Vice Pres*
EMP: 87 **Publicly Held**
SIC: 8092 Kidney dialysis centers
PA: Davita Inc.
    2000 16th St
    Denver CO 80202

(P-22472)
DIALYSIS CENTERS VENTURA CNTY
4567 Telephone Rd Ste 101, Ventura
(93003-5665)
PHONE....................805 658-9211
Laura Norkinson, *Manager*
EMP: 67
SQ FT: 6,000
SALES (est): 1.4MM **Privately Held**
SIC: 8092 Kidney dialysis centers

(P-22473)
DIALYSIS CLINIC INC
1771 Stockton Blvd # 200, Sacramento
(95816-7040)
PHONE....................916 453-0803
Cecelia Cronk, *Manager*
EMP: 50
SALES (corp-wide): 736.2MM **Privately Held**
WEB: www.dciinc.org
SIC: 8092 Kidney dialysis centers
PA: Dialysis Clinic, Inc.
    1633 Church St Ste 500
    Nashville TN 37203
    615 327-3061

(P-22474)
DVA RENAL HEALTHCARE INC
Also Called: Saddleback Dialysis
23141 Plaza Pointe Dr, Laguna Hills
(92653-1425)
PHONE....................949 588-9211
Remy Obrt, *Branch Mgr*
EMP: 75 **Publicly Held**
WEB: www.us.gambro.com
SIC: 8092 Kidney dialysis centers
HQ: Dva Renal Healthcare, Inc.
    2000 16th St
    Denver CO 80202
    253 258-9501

(P-22475)
EL CAMINO HOSPITAL
Also Called: Camino Dialysis Svcs Oak 110
2505 Hospital Dr Ste 1, Mountain View
(94040-4127)
PHONE....................650 940-7310
George Ting, *Director*
Kaitlyn McChesney,
Stephanie Foster, *Assistant*

Rachel Melia, *Consultant*
EMP: 75
SALES (corp-wide): 930.5MM **Privately Held**
SIC: 8092 Kidney dialysis centers
PA: El Camino Hospital
    2500 Grant Rd
    Mountain View CA 94040
    408 224-6660

(P-22476)
FRESENIUS MED CARE LONG BEACH
Also Called: BMA Long Beach
440 W Ocean Blvd, Long Beach
(90802-4518)
PHONE....................562 432-4444
Monique Hartell, *Manager*
EMP: 50
SALES (corp-wide): 20.9B **Privately Held**
WEB: www.fresenius.org
SIC: 8092 Kidney dialysis centers
HQ: Fresenius Medical Care Long Beach, Llc
    920 Winter St
    Waltham MA 02451
    781 699-9000

(P-22477)
HEMODIALYSIS INC (PA)
Also Called: Glentrans
710 W Wilson Ave, Glendale (91203-2409)
PHONE....................818 500-8736
John R Depalma, *President*
EMP: 200
SQ FT: 1,500
SALES (est): 10.4MM **Privately Held**
SIC: 8092 Kidney dialysis centers

(P-22478)
HEMODIALYSIS INC
14901 Rinaldi St Ste 100, Mission Hills
(91345-1253)
PHONE....................818 365-6961
John R Depalma, *Branch Mgr*
EMP: 50
SALES (est): 553.4K
SALES (corp-wide): 10.4MM **Privately Held**
SIC: 8092 Kidney dialysis centers
PA: Hemodialysis, Inc.
    710 W Wilson Ave
    Glendale CA 91203
    818 500-8736

(P-22479)
INTERCOMMUNITY DIALYSIS SVCS
Also Called: Intercommunity Dialysis Center
12455 Washington Blvd, Whittier
(90602-1006)
P.O. Box 11065 (90603-0065)
PHONE....................562 696-1841
Riad Darwish, *Administration*
Evelyn Sandoval, *Principal*
Dr John Shaib, *Principal*
EMP: 50
SQ FT: 7,400
SALES (est): 3.8MM **Privately Held**
SIC: 8092 8011 Kidney dialysis centers; clinic, operated by physicians

(P-22480)
JAMBOOR MEDICAL CORPORATION
Also Called: Desert Cities Dialysis
12675 Hesperia Rd, Victorville
(92395-5878)
PHONE....................760 241-8063
Jay Shankar, *President*
Saguna Jayashankar, *Admin Sec*
EMP: 65
SQ FT: 7,000
SALES (est): 5.8MM **Privately Held**
SIC: 8092 Kidney dialysis centers

(P-22481)
KIDNEY CENTER INC
Also Called: Kidney Dialysis Center Verdugo
50 Moreland Rd, Simi Valley (93065-1659)
P.O. Box 940838 (93094-0838)
PHONE....................805 433-7777
Kant Tucker MD, *CEO*
Rajesh Thakkar, *President*
Ushakant Thakkar, *President*

Sandip Thakkar, *Exec VP*
Leena Thakkar, *Director*
EMP: 200
SQ FT: 10,000
SALES (est): 14.6MM **Privately Held**
SIC: 8092 Kidney dialysis centers

(P-22482)
LOS ALMTOS HMODIALYSIS CTR INC
Also Called: Los Alamitos Hemo Dialysis Ctr
3810 Katella Ave, Los Alamitos
(90720-3302)
PHONE....................562 426-8881
Maher A Azer, *President*
EMP: 60
SQ FT: 15,000
SALES (est): 4.2MM **Privately Held**
WEB: www.dialysisflorence.com
SIC: 8092 Kidney dialysis centers

(P-22483)
MOHAN DIALYSIS CENTER INDUSTRY
15757 E Valley Blvd, City of Industry
(91744-3900)
PHONE....................626 333-3801
Krishna Mohan, *Director*
Ana Mohan, *Admin Sec*
Eva Avila, *Administration*
EMP: 70
SALES: 5MM **Privately Held**
SIC: 8092 Kidney dialysis centers

(P-22484)
MOHAN DIALYSIS CTR OF COVINA
Also Called: Mdcc
158 W College St, Covina (91723-2007)
PHONE....................626 859-2522
Dr Krishna Mohan, *Director*
▲ **EMP:** 70
SQ FT: 5,500
SALES (est): 5MM **Privately Held**
WEB: www.mdcc.com
SIC: 8092 Kidney dialysis centers

(P-22485)
RENAL TREATMENT CTRS - CAL INC
Also Called: Brea Dialysis Center
595 Tamarack Ave Ste A, Brea
(92821-3125)
PHONE....................714 990-0110
Agnes Henry, *Branch Mgr*
EMP: 70 **Publicly Held**
WEB: www.davita.com
SIC: 8092 Kidney dialysis centers
HQ: Renal Treatment Centers - California, Inc.
    2000 16th St
    Denver CO 80202
    303 405-2100

(P-22486)
RENAL TREATMENT CTRS - CAL INC
Also Called: Davita Dialysis
15271 Laguna Canyon Rd, Irvine
(92618-3146)
PHONE....................949 930-6882
Kent Thiry, *CEO*
Christian Orem, *Info Tech Mgr*
Edna McCoy, *Manager*
EMP: 99
SALES (est): 3.1MM **Privately Held**
SIC: 8092 Kidney dialysis centers

(P-22487)
RIVERSIDE DIALYSIS CENTER
4361 Latham St Ste 100, Riverside
(92501-1767)
PHONE....................951 682-2700
Linda Sherman, *Principal*
▲ **EMP:** 50
SALES (est): 1.1MM **Privately Held**
SIC: 8092 Kidney dialysis centers

(P-22488)
SATELLITE HEALTHCARE INC
Also Called: Satellite Dialysis
3500 Coffee Rd Ste 21, Modesto
(95355-1315)
PHONE....................209 578-0691
Susie Phillips, *Branch Mgr*

Janet Luker, *Admin Sec*
EMP: 60
SALES (corp-wide): 188.9MM **Privately Held**
WEB: www.satellitehealth.com
SIC: 8092 8011 Kidney dialysis centers; offices & clinics of medical doctors
PA: Satellite Healthcare, Inc.
    300 Santana Row Ste 300 # 300
    San Jose CA 95128
    650 404-3600

(P-22489)
SATELLITE HEALTHCARE INC (PA)
Also Called: Satellite Dialysis Centers
300 Santana Row Ste 300 # 300, San Jose
(95128-2424)
PHONE....................650 404-3600
Rick J Barnett, *President*
Norman S Coplon, *Ch of Bd*
Charlene Boyer, *President*
Dave Carter, *COO*
Susan Del Bene, *Officer*
EMP: 75
SQ FT: 12,000
SALES: 188.9MM **Privately Held**
WEB: www.satellitehealth.com
SIC: 8092 Kidney dialysis centers

(P-22490)
SATELLITE HEALTHCARE INC
2121 Alexian Dr Ste 118, San Jose
(95116-1905)
PHONE....................408 258-8720
Mark Carlston, *Manager*
EMP: 80
SALES (corp-wide): 188.9MM **Privately Held**
WEB: www.satellitehealth.com
SIC: 8092 8011 Kidney dialysis centers; clinic, operated by physicians
PA: Satellite Healthcare, Inc.
    300 Santana Row Ste 300 # 300
    San Jose CA 95128
    650 404-3600

(P-22491)
TOTAL RENAL CARE INC
Also Called: TRC Pleasanton Dialysis Cntr
5720 Stoneridge Mall Rd # 160, Pleasanton
(94588-2828)
PHONE....................925 737-0120
Connie Edwards, *Administration*
Kari Everson, *Admin Sec*
EMP: 50 **Publicly Held**
WEB: www.davita.com
SIC: 8092 Kidney dialysis centers
HQ: Total Renal Care, Inc.
    2000 16th St
    Denver CO 80202
    303 405-2100

(P-22492)
TOTAL RENAL CARE INC
15271 Laguna Canyon Rd, Irvine
(92618-3146)
PHONE....................949 930-6882
Kent Thiry, *President*
Jennifer Werner, *Info Tech Mgr*
EMP: 99
SALES (est): 1.4MM **Publicly Held**
SIC: 8092 Kidney dialysis centers
PA: Davita Inc.
    2000 16th St
    Denver CO 80202

(P-22493)
TOTAL RENAL CARE INC
Also Called: Carquinez Dialysis
125 Corporate Pl Ste C, Vallejo
(94590-6968)
PHONE....................707 556-3637
Agnes Brabek, *CEO*
EMP: 600 **Publicly Held**
WEB: www.davita.com
SIC: 8092 Kidney dialysis centers
HQ: Total Renal Care, Inc.
    2000 16th St
    Denver CO 80202
    303 405-2100

2019 Directory of California
Wholesalers and Services Companies

▲ = Import ▼=Export
◆ =Import/Export

(P-22494)
TOTAL RENAL CARE INC
Also Called: Davita Hesperia Dialysis Ctr
14135 Main St Ste 501, Hesperia
(92345-8097)
PHONE..................................760 947-7405
EMP: 60
SALES (corp-wide): 12.8B **Publicly Held**
SIC: 8092
HQ: Total Renal Care, Inc.
601 Hawaii St
El Segundo CA 80202
310 536-2400

8093 Specialty Outpatient Facilities, NEC

(P-22495)
21ST CENTURY HEALTH CLUB (PA)
680a E Cotati Ave, Cotati (94931-4092)
PHONE..................................707 795-0400
John Ford, *President*
Dr Robert Gardner, *Treasurer*
Frank Ford, *Vice Pres*
Elizabeth Gardner, *Admin Sec*
David Chasin, *Manager*
▲ EMP: 70
SQ FT: 20,000
SALES (est): 3.1MM **Privately Held**
SIC: 8093 7991 Rehabilitation center, outpatient treatment; health club

(P-22496)
ADDICTION RES & TRTMNT INC
433 Turk St, San Francisco (94102-3329)
PHONE..................................415 928-7800
Teresa Fleming, *Branch Mgr*
EMP: 56 **Privately Held**
SIC: 8093 Drug clinic, outpatient
PA: Addiction Research And Treatment, Inc.
1145 Market St Fl 10
San Francisco CA 94103
-

(P-22497)
AEGIS TREATMENT CENTERS LLC (PA)
7246 Remmet Ave, Canoga Park
(91303-1531)
PHONE..................................818 206-0360
Alex Dodd, *CEO*
James Ferguson, *Accounting Mgr*
David Devine, *Controller*
Jovan Blake, *Recruiter*
Anna Raghavan, *Recruiter*
EMP: 50
SALES (est): 10.1MM **Privately Held**
SIC: 8093 Rehabilitation center, outpatient treatment

(P-22498)
AGENDIA INC
22 Morgan, Irvine (92618-2022)
PHONE..................................949 540-6300
Mark R Straley, *CEO*
Glen Fredenberg, *CFO*
Kurt Schmidt, *CFO*
Peter C Wulff, *CFO*
M William Audeh, *Chief Mktg Ofcr*
EMP: 107 EST: 2008
SALES: 18.7MM
SALES (corp-wide): 31.3MM **Privately Held**
SIC: 8093 Drug clinic, outpatient
PA: Agendia N.V.
Science Park 406
Amsterdam
204 621-500

(P-22499)
ALCOHOL DRG PROGRAM YOLO CNTY
137 N Cottonwood St Ste 1, Woodland
(95695-6646)
PHONE..................................530 666-8650
Karen Gerbasi, *Exec Dir*
EMP: 50 EST: 2001
SALES (est): 1.5MM **Privately Held**
SIC: 8093 Specialty outpatient clinics

(P-22500)
ALGOS INC A MEDICAL CORP (PA)
Also Called: Pasadena Rehabilitation Inst
224 N Fair Oaks Ave, Pasadena
(91103-3618)
PHONE..................................626 696-1400
Clayton Varga, *President*
Matt Talbot, *COO*
Robert Castaneda, *CFO*
Gerri Summe, *CFO*
Andrew G Seltzer, *Anesthesiology*
EMP: 60
SQ FT: 8,000
SALES (est): 7.3MM **Privately Held**
WEB: www.thebigmd.com
SIC: 8093 8049 8011 Rehabilitation center, outpatient treatment; physical therapist; specialized medical practitioners, except internal

(P-22501)
ALLIANT EDUCATIONAL FOUNDATION
5130 E Clinton Way, Fresno (93727-2014)
PHONE..................................559 456-2777
Jennifer Wilson, *Branch Mgr*
EMP: 200
SALES (corp-wide): 71.7MM **Privately Held**
SIC: 8093 8221 Mental health clinic, outpatient; university
PA: Alliant International University, Inc.
10455 Pomerado Rd
San Diego CA 92131
415 955-2000

(P-22502)
ALPINE CONVALESCENT CENTER INC
Also Called: Alpine Special Treatment Ctr
2120 Alpine Blvd, Alpine (91901-2113)
PHONE..................................619 659-3120
Michael E Doyle, *CEO*
Kristine Tiernan, *Psychologist*
EMP: 100
SQ FT: 15,000
SALES (est): 7.1MM **Privately Held**
WEB: www.astci.com
SIC: 8093 Rehabilitation center, outpatient treatment; mental health clinic, outpatient

(P-22503)
AMANECER CMNTY COUNSELING SVC
1200 Wilshire Blvd # 200, Los Angeles
(90017-1908)
PHONE..................................213 481-7464
Tim Ryder, *Exec Dir*
Frank Chargualaf, *CFO*
Linda Sanner, *CFO*
Teddie Valenzuela, *Officer*
Laura Gonzalez, *Executive Asst*
EMP: 100 EST: 1975
SALES: 9.1MM **Privately Held**
WEB: www.ccsla.org
SIC: 8093 Mental health clinic, outpatient

(P-22504)
ANKA BEHAVIORAL HEALTH INC (PA)
1850 Gateway Blvd Ste 900, Concord
(94520-8418)
PHONE..................................925 825-4700
Chris Withrow, *CEO*
Yolanda Braxton, *President*
Naja W Boyd, *COO*
Marty Giffin, *Senior VP*
Karen Wise, *Senior VP*
EMP: 168
SALES: 40.4MM **Privately Held**
SIC: 8093 Mental health clinic, outpatient

(P-22505)
ARC - IMPERIAL VALLEY
340 E 1st St, Calexico (92231-2732)
PHONE..................................760 768-1944
Alex King, *Principal*
Ramon Aguirre, *Transportation*
EMP: 58

SALES (corp-wide): 10.8MM **Privately Held**
SIC: 8093 4783 2051 5812 Rehabilitation center, outpatient treatment; packing goods for shipping; bakery: wholesale or wholesale/retail combined; delicatessen (eating places); caterers
PA: Arc - Imperial Valley
298 E Ross Ave
El Centro CA 92243
760 352-0180

(P-22506)
ARC OF VENTURA COUNTY INC
Also Called: ARC Community Enrichment
210 Canada St, Ojai (93023-2523)
PHONE..................................805 650-8611
Lisa Emery, *Manager*
EMP: 60
SALES (corp-wide): 13.2MM **Privately Held**
SIC: 8093 8322 Rehabilitation center, outpatient treatment; social services for the handicapped
PA: The Arc Of Ventura County Inc
5103 Walker St
Ventura CA 93003
805 650-8611

(P-22507)
ARC OF VENTURA COUNTY INC
4277 Transport St Ste F, Ventura
(93003-5657)
PHONE..................................805 644-0880
Alisa Mahrer, *Manager*
EMP: 192
SALES (corp-wide): 13.2MM **Privately Held**
SIC: 8093 8361 8322 8331 Rehabilitation center, outpatient treatment; residential care; individual & family services; sheltered workshop
PA: The Arc Of Ventura County Inc
5103 Walker St
Ventura CA 93003
805 650-8611

(P-22508)
ASIAN COMMUNITY MENTAL HLTH BD
Also Called: Asian Cmnty Mlth Svcs
310 8th St Ste 201, Oakland (94607-6527)
PHONE..................................510 869-6000
Lawrence Fong, *President*
John Fong, *Treasurer*
Betty Hong, *Vice Pres*
Sharon Sue, *Admin Sec*
Albert Gaw, *Psychiatry*
EMP: 95
SALES: 6MM **Privately Held**
WEB: www.acmhs.org
SIC: 8093 Mental health clinic, outpatient

(P-22509)
AXIS COMMUNITY HEALTH INC
4361 Railroad Ave, Pleasanton
(94566-6611)
PHONE..................................925 462-1755
Sue Compton, *CEO*
Christina McFadden, *COO*
Joe Flarity, *CFO*
Kanwar Singh, *CFO*
Sonia Cross, *Officer*
EMP: 99 EST: 1972
SALES: 12.2MM **Privately Held**
WEB: www.axishealth.org
SIC: 8093 Mental health clinic, outpatient

(P-22510)
BAART BEHAVIORAL HLTH SVCS INC
433 Turk St, San Francisco (94102-3329)
PHONE..................................415 928-7800
Teresa Fleming, *Branch Mgr*
EMP: 56
SALES (corp-wide): 6.4MM **Privately Held**
SIC: 8093 Substance abuse clinics (outpatient)
HQ: Baart Behavioral Health Services, Inc.
1145 Market St Fl 10
San Francisco CA 94103
415 552-7914

(P-22511)
BAART COMMUNITY HEALTHCARE
433 Turk St, San Francisco (94102-3329)
PHONE..................................415 928-7800
Teresa Fleming, *Branch Mgr*
EMP: 56
SALES (corp-wide): 4.4MM **Privately Held**
SIC: 8093 Drug clinic, outpatient
PA: Baart Community Healthcare
1145 Market St Fl 10
San Francisco CA 94103
415 863-3883

(P-22512)
BAKER PLACES INC
101 Gough St, San Francisco
(94102-5903)
PHONE..................................415 503-3137
EMP: 134
SALES (corp-wide): 12.5MM **Privately Held**
SIC: 8093 Substance abuse clinics (outpatient)
PA: Baker Places, Inc.
1000 Brannan St Ste 401
San Francisco CA 94103
415 864-4655

(P-22513)
BASQUEZ TIBURCIO HEALTH CENTER
33255 9th St, Union City (94587-2137)
PHONE..................................510 471-5907
Jose J Garcia, *CEO*
EMP: 160
SALES (est): 1.4MM **Privately Held**
SIC: 8093 Specialty outpatient clinics

(P-22514)
BRIDGES AT SN PDRO PNNSLA HSPT
1300 W 7th St Fl 4, San Pedro
(90732-3505)
PHONE..................................310 514-5359
Vivian Harvey, *Director*
EMP: 55
SALES (est): 804.6K **Privately Held**
SIC: 8093 Mental health clinic, outpatient

(P-22515)
CAMINAR
Also Called: Jobs Plus
376 Rio Lindo Ave, Chico (95926-1914)
PHONE..................................530 343-4421
Tracy Watkins, *Branch Mgr*
Charles Huggins, *CEO*
EMP: 65
SALES (corp-wide): 18.6MM **Privately Held**
SIC: 8093 Mental health clinic, outpatient
PA: Caminar
2600 S El Camino Real # 200
San Mateo CA 94403
650 372-4080

(P-22516)
CAMP RECOVERY CENTERS LLP
3192 Glen Canyon Rd, Santa Cruz
(95066-4916)
P.O. Box 66569, Scotts Valley (95067-6569)
PHONE..................................831 438-1868
Page Bottom, *Exec Dir*
Steve Hanusa, *Director*
EMP: 100
SALES (est): 2.5MM **Privately Held**
WEB: www.camprecovery.com
SIC: 8093 Rehabilitation center, outpatient treatment

(P-22517)
CARLSBAD SURGERY CENTER LLC
6121 Paseo Del Norte # 100, Carlsbad
(92011-1161)
PHONE..................................760 448-2488
David W Douglas, *Mng Member*
EMP: 50
SALES (est): 5.4MM **Privately Held**
SIC: 8093 Specialty outpatient clinics

(P-22518)
CARNAHAN OCCUPATIONAL THERAPY
116 E College Ave Ste G, Lompoc
(93436-5331)
PHONE....................805 737-1604
Juanita Carnahan, *Owner*
EMP: 50
SALES (est): 800.8K **Privately Held**
WEB: www.carnahantherapy.com
SIC: 8093 Rehabilitation center, outpatient treatment

(P-22519)
CASA COLIN COMPREHENSIVE
255 E Bonita Ave, Pomona (91767-1923)
PHONE....................909 596-7733
Felice Loverso, *CEO*
Susan Stanley, *Vice Pres*
Ross Lessons, *MIS Dir*
Ross Lesins, *Telecomm Mgr*
EMP: 150
SQ FT: 35,000
SALES: 2.8MM **Privately Held**
SIC: 8093 Rehabilitation center, outpatient treatment

(P-22520)
CASTLE FAMILY HEALTH CTRS INC (PA)
3605 Hospital Rd Ste H, Atwater
(95301-5173)
PHONE....................209 381-2000
Edward H Lujano, *CEO*
Bill Able, *CFO*
Fily Cale, *Executive Asst*
David Thompson, *Info Tech Dir*
Madelyn Finister, *Analyst*
EMP: 99
SALES: 19MM **Privately Held**
SIC: 8093 Specialty outpatient clinics

(P-22521)
CENTER FOR ATISM RLTED DSRDERS
106 Discovery, Irvine (92618-3131)
PHONE....................949 203-8872
EMP: 50 EST: 2016
SALES (est): 41.5K **Privately Held**
SIC: 8093 Mental health clinic, outpatient

(P-22522)
CENTER FOR AUTSM RSRCH EVLTN
Also Called: Cares
10174 Old Grove Rd, San Diego
(92131-1652)
PHONE....................858 444-8823
Olanderia Brown, *Manager*
EMP: 140 EST: 2007
SALES (est): 4.4MM
SALES (corp-wide): 29.6MM **Privately Held**
SIC: 8093 Specialty outpatient clinics
PA: Fred Finch Youth Center
3800 Coolidge Ave
Oakland CA 94602
510 773-6669

(P-22523)
CENTRAL VALLEY CLINIC INC
Also Called: Sants Clair Alcohol Meth Prog
2425 Enborg Ln, San Jose (95128-2648)
PHONE....................408 885-5400
Robert Garner, *Director*
EMP: 50 EST: 1985
SALES (est): 991.4K **Privately Held**
SIC: 8093 Drug clinic, outpatient

(P-22524)
CENTRAL VLY REGIONAL CTR INC
5441 W Cypress Ave, Visalia (93277-8341)
PHONE....................559 738-2200
Lorraine Bortes, *General Mgr*
Ed Araim, *Technology*
EMP: 120
SALES (est): 1.1MM
SALES (corp-wide): 277.3MM **Privately Held**
SIC: 8093 8399 Mental health clinic, outpatient; social service information exchange

PA: Central Valley Regional Center, Inc.
4615 N Marty Ave
Fresno CA
559 276-4300

(P-22525)
CENTRE FOR NEURO SKILLS (PA)
5215 Ashe Rd, Bakersfield (93313-2069)
PHONE....................661 872-3408
Mark J Ashley, *CEO*
Roslyn Hart, *Exec Dir*
EMP: 168
SQ FT: 14,000
SALES: 320.2K **Privately Held**
SIC: 8093 Rehabilitation center, outpatient treatment

(P-22526)
CENTRO DE SALUD DE LA (PA)
Also Called: San Ysidro Health Center
4004 Beyer Blvd, San Ysidro (92173-2007)
PHONE....................619 428-4463
Kevin Mattson, *CEO*
M Gutierrez, *President*
Maria Carriedo-Cenice, *Vice Pres*
Ana Melgoza, *Vice Pres*
Alicia Rodriguez, *Vice Pres*
EMP: 80
SQ FT: 2,000
SALES: 87.1MM **Privately Held**
SIC: 8093 8011 Specialty outpatient clinics; offices & clinics of medical doctors

(P-22527)
CHILD AND FAMILY GUIDANCE CTR
Also Called: Valley Child Guidance Clinic
310 E Plmdle Blvd G, Palmdale (93550)
PHONE....................661 265-8627
Joelle Hunnewell, *Director*
Deborah Hansen, *Prgrmr*
Rocio Cabrales, *Director*
EMP: 72
SALES (corp-wide): 29.1MM **Privately Held**
WEB: www.childguidance.org
SIC: 8093 Mental health clinic, outpatient
PA: Child And Family Guidance Center
9650 Zelzah Ave
Northridge CA 91325
818 739-5140

(P-22528)
CHILD AND FAMILY GUIDANCE CTR (PA)
Also Called: Northpoint Day Treatment Sch
9650 Zelzah Ave, Northridge (91325-2003)
PHONE....................818 739-5140
Roy Marshall, *Exec Dir*
Russell Jones, *Ch of Bd*
Robert Garcia, *President*
Ronald Call, *Treasurer*
Stephen J Howard PHD, *Vice Pres*
EMP: 200
SQ FT: 35,000
SALES: 29.1MM **Privately Held**
WEB: www.childguidance.org
SIC: 8093 Mental health clinic, outpatient

(P-22529)
CHILD AND FAMILY GUIDANCE CTR
Also Called: Family Stress Center
8550 Balboa Blvd Ste 150, Northridge
(91325-3579)
PHONE....................818 830-0200
Jessica Card, *Director*
EMP: 50
SALES (corp-wide): 29.1MM **Privately Held**
WEB: www.childguidance.org
SIC: 8093 8322 Mental health clinic, outpatient; general counseling services
PA: Child And Family Guidance Center
9650 Zelzah Ave
Northridge CA 91325
818 739-5140

(P-22530)
CHOICE IN AGING (PA)
Also Called: Mt Diablo Center
490 Golf Club Rd, Pleasant Hill
(94523-1553)
PHONE....................925 682-6330

Debbie Toth, *CEO*
Wisal Khoury, *Financial Exec*
Jeaneen McPherson, *Finance*
Bonnie Price, *Human Resources*
Danielle Lopez, *Nurse*
EMP: 85
SQ FT: 24,335
SALES: 4.5MM **Privately Held**
WEB: www.rsnc-centers.org
SIC: 8093 8331 Rehabilitation center, outpatient treatment; vocational rehabilitation agency

(P-22531)
CHOICE MEDICAL GROUP INC
2322 Butano Dr Ste 205, Sacramento
(95825-0657)
PHONE....................916 483-2885
Lisa Vaughn, *General Mgr*
Laurie Luiza, *Treasurer*
EMP: 70
SALES (est): 1.4MM **Privately Held**
SIC: 8093 Abortion clinic

(P-22532)
CLINIC INC (PA)
Also Called: To Help Everyone Health & Weln
3834 S Western Ave, Los Angeles
(90062-1104)
PHONE....................323 730-1920
Jamesina E Henderson, *Exec Dir*
Tatyana Klochko, *CFO*
Rise K Phillips, *Technology*
Lilian Alvarez, *Human Res Dir*
Kimmella Collins, *Facilities Mgr*
EMP: 63
SQ FT: 26,000
SALES: 12.6MM **Privately Held**
WEB: www.theclinicinc.org
SIC: 8093 Specialty outpatient clinics

(P-22533)
CLINICAS DEL CAMINO REAL INC
Also Called: Dental Office
650 Meta St, Oxnard (93030-7182)
PHONE....................805 487-5351
Patricia Andrade, *General Mgr*
EMP: 73
SALES (corp-wide): 97.9MM **Privately Held**
SIC: 8093 8011 Specialty outpatient clinics; ambulatory surgical center
PA: Clinicas Del Camino Real, Inc.
200 S Wells Rd Ste 200 # 200
Ventura CA 93004
805 647-6322

(P-22534)
CLINICAS DEL CAMINO REAL INC (PA)
200 S Wells Rd Ste 200 # 200, Ventura
(93004-1377)
P.O. Box 1270, Camarillo (93011-1270)
PHONE....................805 647-6322
Roberto S Juarez, *CEO*
Chris Velasco, *CFO*
Gagan Pawar, *Family Practiti*
Hideto Saito, *Family Practiti*
Zoheir Kassem, *Psychiatry*
EMP: 230
SQ FT: 4,000
SALES: 97.9MM **Privately Held**
SIC: 8093 Specialty outpatient clinics

(P-22535)
COMMUNITY ACTION MARIN
Also Called: Community Action Marine
1108 Tamalpais Ave, San Rafael
(94901-3247)
PHONE....................415 459-6330
Michael Payne, *President*
EMP: 212
SALES (corp-wide): 14.8MM **Privately Held**
SIC: 8093 Mental health clinic, outpatient
PA: Community Action Marin
555 Northgate Dr Ste 100
San Rafael CA 94903
415 485-1489

(P-22536)
COMMUNITY FAMILY GUIDANCE CTR (PA)
10929 South St Ste 208b, Cerritos
(90703-5391)
PHONE....................562 865-6444
Richard Murase, *President*
Lesley Watkins, *CFO*
Patricia Taylor PH, *Training Dir*
Patricia M Taylor, *Psychologist*
Lindsay Rosser, *Med Doctor*
EMP: 65
SALES: 34.8K **Privately Held**
WEB: www.cfgconline.com
SIC: 8093 Mental health clinic, outpatient

(P-22537)
COMMUNITY MEDICAL CENTERS INC (PA)
7210 Murray Dr, Stockton (95210-3339)
P.O. Box 779 (95201-0779)
PHONE....................209 373-2800
Kathleen Marshall, *CEO*
Art Feagles, *CFO*
Maria Flores, *Executive*
Benjamin Morrison, *Associate Dir*
Michael Kirkpatrick, *General Mgr*
EMP: 90 EST: 1978
SQ FT: 14,000
SALES: 44.6MM **Privately Held**
SIC: 8093 8011 Specialty outpatient clinics; offices & clinics of medical doctors

(P-22538)
CONSOLIDATED TRIBAL HEALTH PRJ
6991 N State St, Redwood Valley
(95470-9629)
P.O. Box 387, Calpella (95418-0387)
PHONE....................707 485-5115
Michael Knight, *Chairman*
George Provencher, *Treasurer*
Debra Ramirez, *Principal*
Donna Schuler, *Admin Sec*
EMP: 65
SALES: 9.5MM **Privately Held**
WEB: www.cthp.org
SIC: 8093 Mental health clinic, outpatient

(P-22539)
CORRECTONS RHBLTATION CAL DEPT
Also Called: Cdcr - California Men's Colony
Hwy 1 N, San Luis Obispo (93409-0001)
P.O. Box 8101 (93403-8101)
PHONE....................805 547-7900
John Marshall, *Warden*
EMP: 2000 **Privately Held**
SIC: 8093 9223 Specialty outpatient clinics;
HQ: California Department Of Corrections
& Rehabilitation
1515 S St
Sacramento CA 95811

(P-22540)
COUNTY OF BUTTE
Also Called: Butte County Mental Hlth Svcs
107 Parmac Rd Ste 4, Chico (95926-2298)
PHONE....................530 891-2850
Bradford Luz PHD, *Director*
EMP: 400 **Privately Held**
WEB: www.bcihsspa.org
SIC: 8093 9111 Substance abuse clinics (outpatient); county supervisors' & executives' offices
PA: County Of Butte
25 County Center Dr # 125
Oroville CA 95965
530 538-7701

(P-22541)
COUNTY OF CONTRA COSTA
Also Called: Department of Health Services
1420 Willow Pass Rd # 140, Concord
(94520-5823)
PHONE....................925 646-5480
John Allen, *Director*
EMP: 50 **Privately Held**
WEB: www.cccounty.us
SIC: 8093 9431 Mental health clinic, outpatient; administration of public health programs;

PA: County Of Contra Costa
625 Court St Ste 100
Martinez CA 94553
925 957-5280

(P-22542)
COUNTY OF FRESNO
Also Called: Department Behavioral Health
4417 E Inyo St Bldg 333, Fresno
(93702-2977)
PHONE..................................559 600-4600
Sean Patterson, *Business Mgr*
EMP: 99 EST: 1872
SQ FT: 4,000
SALES (est): 562.3K **Privately Held**
SIC: 8093 Mental health clinic, outpatient

(P-22543)
COUNTY OF GLENN
Also Called: Department of Mental Health
242 N Villa Ave, Willows (95988-2641)
PHONE..................................530 934-6582
Scott Gruentl, *Director*
Robert L Zadra, *Med Doctor*
EMP: 75 **Privately Held**
WEB: www.countyofglen.net
SIC: 8093 9111 Mental health clinic, outpatient; county supervisors' & executives' offices
PA: County Of Glenn
516 W Sycamore St Fl 2
Willows CA 95988
530 934-6410

(P-22544)
COUNTY OF HUMBOLDT
Also Called: Humboldt County Mental Health
720 Wood St, Eureka (95501-4413)
PHONE..................................707 476-4054
Cindy Moore, *Manager*
EMP: 120 **Privately Held**
SIC: 8093 9111 8063 Mental health clinic, outpatient; county supervisors' & executives' offices; psychiatric hospitals
PA: County Of Humboldt
825 5th St
Eureka CA 95501
707 268-2543

(P-22545)
COUNTY OF IMPERIAL
Also Called: Imperial County Mental Health
202 N 8th St, El Centro (92243-2302)
PHONE..................................760 482-4120
Rudy Lopez, *Director*
Anna Welzein, *Human Res Dir*
EMP: 100 **Privately Held**
WEB: www.imperialcounty.net
SIC: 8093 9111 Mental health clinic, outpatient; county supervisors' & executives' offices
PA: County Of Imperial
940 W Main St Ste 208
El Centro CA 92243
760 482-4556

(P-22546)
COUNTY OF LOS ANGELES
Also Called: Health Services, Dept of
7601 Imperial Hwy, Downey (90242-3456)
PHONE..................................562 401-7088
Valeria Orange, *Director*
Aries Limbaga, *Ch Nursing Ofcr*
EMP: 1400 **Privately Held**
WEB: www.co.la.ca.us
SIC: 8093 9431 Rehabilitation center, outpatient treatment;
PA: County Of Los Angeles
500 W Temple St Ste 437
Los Angeles CA 90012
213 974-1101

(P-22547)
COUNTY OF LOS ANGELES
Also Called: Health Services, Dept of
5205 Melrose Ave, Los Angeles
(90038-3144)
PHONE..................................323 769-7800
Rosa Pinon, *Branch Mgr*
EMP: 100 **Privately Held**
WEB: www.co.la.ca.us
SIC: 8093 9431 Family planning & birth control clinics; administration of public health programs;

PA: County Of Los Angeles
500 W Temple St Ste 437
Los Angeles CA 90012
213 974-1101

(P-22548)
COUNTY OF LOS ANGELES
Also Called: Mental Health Dept of
17707 Studebaker Rd, Artesia
(90703-2640)
PHONE..................................562 402-0688
Latisha Guvman, *Manager*
EMP: 50 **Privately Held**
WEB: www.co.la.ca.us
SIC: 8093 9431 Specialty outpatient clinics; administration of public health programs;
PA: County Of Los Angeles
500 W Temple St Ste 437
Los Angeles CA 90012
213 974-1101

(P-22549)
COUNTY OF LOS ANGELES
Also Called: Antelope Valley Health Center
335 E Avenue K6 Ste B, Lancaster
(93535-4645)
PHONE..................................661 524-2005
Mary Nolan, *Manager*
EMP: 59 **Privately Held**
SIC: 8093 Family planning clinic
PA: County Of Los Angeles
500 W Temple St Ste 437
Los Angeles CA 90012
213 974-1101

(P-22550)
COUNTY OF MARIN
Also Called: Community Mental Health Clinic
250 Bon Air Rd, Greenbrae (94904-1702)
P.O. Box 2728, San Rafael (94912-2728)
PHONE..................................415 448-1500
Bruce Gurganus, *Director*
Jack Liebster, *Planning Mgr*
Aude Foisy, *Admin Sec*
Tammy Taylor, *Planning*
Rachel Warner, *Planning*
EMP: 100 **Privately Held**
SIC: 8093 9111 Mental health clinic, outpatient; county supervisors' & executives' offices
PA: County Of Marin
3501 Civic Center Dr # 258
San Rafael CA 94903
415 473-6358

(P-22551)
COUNTY OF MENDOCINO
Also Called: County of Medocina Dept of Mnt
860a N Bush St, Ukiah (95482-3919)
PHONE..................................707 463-4396
Anna Mahoney, *Manager*
EMP: 200 **Privately Held**
WEB: www.mcdss.org
SIC: 8093 9111
PA: County Of Mendocino
501 Low Gap Rd Rm 1010
Ukiah CA 95482
707 463-4441

(P-22552)
COUNTY OF NAPA
Also Called: Health Department
2261 Elm St, NAPA (94559-3721)
PHONE..................................707 253-4461
Bruce Heid, *Manager*
Richard J Forde, *Psychiatry*
EMP: 260 **Privately Held**
WEB: www.billkeller.com
SIC: 8093 9111 Specialty outpatient clinics; county supervisors' & executives' offices
PA: County Of Napa
1195 Third St Ste 310
Napa CA 94559
707 253-4421

(P-22553)
COUNTY OF PLACER
Also Called: Health & Human Services
11584 B Ave, Auburn (95603-2605)
PHONE..................................530 889-7215
Robert Long, *Systems Mgr*
Mark Rideout, *Architect*
EMP: 75
SQ FT: 1,100 **Privately Held**

WEB: www.ssvems.com
SIC: 8093 9431 Specialty outpatient clinics; administration of public health programs;
PA: County Of Placer
2986 Richardson Dr
Auburn CA 95603
530 889-4200

(P-22554)
COUNTY OF SAN JOAQUIN
Also Called: Mental Health Services
1212 N California St, Stockton
(95202-1552)
PHONE..................................209 468-8750
Bruce Hopperstead, *Principal*
EMP: 300 **Privately Held**
WEB: www.sjclawlib.org
SIC: 8093 9111 8361 Mental health clinic, outpatient; county supervisors' & executives' offices; residential care
PA: County Of San Joaquin
44 N San Joaquin St # 640
Stockton CA 95202
209 468-3203

(P-22555)
COUNTY OF SAN LUIS OBISPO
Also Called: Community Mental Health Svcs
2178 Johnson Ave, San Luis Obispo
(93401-4535)
PHONE..................................805 781-4700
Tom Omalley, *Principal*
EMP: 250 **Privately Held**
SIC: 8093 Mental health clinic, outpatient
PA: County Of San Luis Obispo
Government Center Rm. 300
San Luis Obispo CA 93408
805 781-5040

(P-22556)
COUNTY OF SAN MATEO
Also Called: Health System
150 W 20th Ave, San Mateo (94403-1341)
PHONE..................................650 372-8540
Sonia Celmira Lucana, *Principal*
EMP: 100 **Privately Held**
WEB: www.ci.sanmateo.ca.us
SIC: 8093 9431 Mental health clinic, outpatient;
PA: County Of San Mateo
400 County Ctr
Redwood City CA 94063
650 363-4123

(P-22557)
COUNTY OF SANTA BARBARA ALCOHO
Also Called: Admhs
300 N San Antonio Rd, Santa Barbara
(93110-1316)
PHONE..................................805 681-4093
Al Rodriguez, *Principal*
EMP: 90
SALES (est): 2.2MM **Privately Held**
SIC: 8093 Alcohol clinic, outpatient

(P-22558)
COUNTY OF SISKIYOU
Also Called: Behavioral Health Services
1107 Ream Ave, Mount Shasta
(96067-9768)
PHONE..................................530 918-7200
Hap Stemm, *Manager*
Arden Carr, *Hlthcr Dir*
EMP: 60 **Privately Held**
WEB: www.siskiyoucounty.org
SIC: 8093 9111 Specialty outpatient clinics; county supervisors' & executives' offices
PA: County Of Siskiyou
311 4th St Rm 108
Yreka CA 96097
530 841-4100

(P-22559)
COUNTY OF STANISLAUS
Also Called: Stanisluas County Mental Hlth
800 Scenic Dr Bldg B, Modesto
(95350-6131)
PHONE..................................209 525-7423
Dennise Han, *Director*
EMP: 200 **Privately Held**
WEB: www.co.stanislaus.ca.us
SIC: 8093 Specialty outpatient clinics

PA: County Of Stanislaus
1010 10th St Ste 5100
Modesto CA 95354
209 525-6398

(P-22560)
COUNTY OF SUTTER
Also Called: Sutter Yuba Mental Health Svcs
1965 Live Oak Blvd, Yuba City
(95991-8850)
P.O. Box 1520 (95992-1520)
PHONE..................................530 822-7250
Joann Hoss, *Director*
EMP: 200 **Privately Held**
WEB: www.co.yuba.ca.us
SIC: 8093 9431 Mental health clinic, outpatient; mental health agency administration, government;
PA: County Of Sutter
1160 Civic Center Blvd A
Yuba City CA 95993
530 822-7100

(P-22561)
COUNTY OF YOLO
Also Called: Dept of Mental Health
292 W Beamer St, Woodland (95695-2511)
PHONE..................................530 666-8630
Kim Suderman, *Director*
EMP: 80 **Privately Held**
WEB: www.yctd.org
SIC: 8093 9111 Mental health clinic, outpatient; county supervisors' & executives' offices
PA: County Of Yolo
625 Court St Ste 102
Woodland CA 95695
530 666-8114

(P-22562)
CRASH INC SHORT TERM I
4161 Marlborough Ave, San Diego
(92105-1412)
PHONE..................................619 282-7274
Sue Dolby, *Exec Dir*
EMP: 50
SALES (est): 869.7K **Privately Held**
SIC: 8093 Substance abuse clinics (outpatient)

(P-22563)
CRC HEALTH CORPORATE
Also Called: Recovery Solutions Santa Ana
2101 E 1st St, Santa Ana (92705-4007)
PHONE..................................714 542-3581
Tfu Bach Tran, *Manager*
EMP: 60 **Publicly Held**
SIC: 8093 Drug clinic, outpatient
HQ: Crc Health Corporate
20400 Stevens
Cupertino CA 95014
408 367-0044

(P-22564)
CRC HEALTH CORPORATE (DH)
Also Called: Willamette Valley Trtmnt Ctr
20400 Stevens, Cupertino (95014)
PHONE..................................408 367-0044
R Andrew Eckert, *CEO*
Kevin Hogge, *CFO*
Gary Fisher, *Chief Mktg Ofcr*
Pamela B Burke, *Vice Pres*
James Hudak, *Vice Pres*
EMP: 60
SALES (est): 55.7MM **Publicly Held**
SIC: 8093 Substance abuse clinics (outpatient)
HQ: Crc Health Corporation
20400 Stevens Creek Blvd # 600
Cupertino CA 95014
877 272-8668

(P-22565)
DEL AMO DIAGNOSTIC CENTER
Also Called: Little Mary Amblatory Care Ctr
3531 Fashion Way, Torrance (90503-4807)
PHONE..................................310 316-2424
Steve Magennis, *Director*
EMP: 50
SQ FT: 25,000
SALES (est): 2.8MM **Privately Held**
SIC: 8093 8011 Specialty outpatient clinics; clinic, operated by physicians

P R O D U C T S & S V C S

(P-22566)
DELTA HLTH CARE MGT SVCS CORP (PA)
4662 Precissi Ln Ste 200, Stockton (95207-6225)
P.O. Box 550 (95201-0550)
PHONE................................209 444-8300
Irwin Staller, *Director*
EMP: 75 **EST:** 1968
SQ FT: 4,800
SALES: 3MM **Privately Held**
WEB: www.deltahealthcare.org
SIC: 8093 8322 Family planning clinic; individual & family services

(P-22567)
DEVEREUX FOUNDATION
Also Called: Devereux California Center
7055 Seaway Dr, Goleta (93117-4358)
P.O. Box 6784, Santa Barbara (93160-6784)
PHONE................................805 968-2525
Amy Evans, *Principal*
EMP: 400
SALES (corp-wide): 460.5MM **Privately Held**
SIC: 8093 Mental health clinic, outpatient
PA: Devereux Foundation
444 Devereux Dr
Villanova PA 19085
610 520-3000

(P-22568)
DRUG & ALCOHOL SERVICES OF
2180 Johnson Ave Ste A, San Luis Obispo (93401-4558)
PHONE................................805 781-4275
Paul Hyman, *Director*
Michael Stevens, *Executive*
Jeff Hamm, *Director*
EMP: 80
SALES (est): 1.6MM **Privately Held**
SIC: 8093 Rehabilitation center, outpatient treatment

(P-22569)
DRUG ABUSE ALTERNATIVES CENTER
Also Called: Redwood Empire Addctons Prgram
2403 Prof Dr Ste 103, Santa Rosa (95403)
PHONE................................707 571-2233
Sushana Taylor, *President*
EMP: 50
SALES (corp-wide): 5.9MM **Privately Held**
WEB: www.daacinfo.org
SIC: 8093 Drug clinic, outpatient
PA: Drug Abuse Alternatives Center
2403 Prof Dr Ste 102
Santa Rosa CA 95403
707 544-3295

(P-22570)
DUAL DIAGNOSIS TRTMNT CTR INC (PA)
Also Called: Sovereign Health of California
1211 Puerta Del Sol # 200, San Clemente (92673-6342)
PHONE................................949 276-5553
Tonmoy Sharma, *CEO*
Rishi Barkataki, *President*
Kevin Gallagher, *CFO*
Nidhi Grover, *Executive*
Lise Stevens, *Comms Mgr*
EMP: 168
SALES (est): 84.5MM **Privately Held**
SIC: 8093 Mental health clinic, outpatient

(P-22571)
DUAL DIAGNOSIS TRTMNT CTR INC
6167 Bristol Pkwy, Culver City (90230-6610)
PHONE................................424 207-2220
Marissa Maldonado, *Branch Mgr*
EMP: 152
SALES (corp-wide): 84.5MM **Privately Held**
SIC: 8093 Mental health clinic, outpatient
PA: Dual Diagnosis Treatment Center, Inc.
1211 Puerta Del Sol # 200
San Clemente CA 92673
949 276-5553

(P-22572)
EAST LOS ANGELES MENTAL HLTH
1436 Goodrich Blvd, Commerce (90022-5111)
PHONE................................323 725-1337
Alfredo Lavios, *President*
Jungyeol OH, *Nurse Practr*
EMP: 60
SALES (est): 895.8K **Privately Held**
SIC: 8093 Mental health clinic, outpatient

(P-22573)
EAST VALLEY CMNTY HLTH CTR INC (PA)
420 S Glendora Ave, West Covina (91790-3001)
PHONE................................626 919-3402
Alicia Mardini, *CEO*
Sophia Shavira, *Ch of Bd*
Alicia Thomas, *CEO*
EMP: 65
SQ FT: 24,000
SALES: 18.7MM **Privately Held**
SIC: 8093 Family planning clinic

(P-22574)
ELEMENTS BEHAVIORAL HEALTH INC (PA)
5000 Arprt Plz Dr Ste 100, Long Beach (90815)
PHONE................................562 741-6470
David Sack, *CEO*
Rob Mahan, *CFO*
Elissa Weisberger-Cohen, *VP Human Res*
Pat Connors, *Director*
Robin Mastroni, *Director*
EMP: 112
SALES (est): 54.8MM **Privately Held**
SIC: 8093 8049 Substance abuse clinics (outpatient); nutrition specialist

(P-22575)
ENCOMPASS HEALTH CORPORATION
Also Called: HealthSouth
14851 Yorba St, Tustin (92780-2925)
PHONE................................714 832-9200
Cathline Smith, *Branch Mgr*
Ladonna Butler, *Nursing Dir*
Jovita Bejinez, *Manager*
Deborah Christiaan, *Manager*
EMP: 200
SALES (corp-wide): 3.9B **Publicly Held**
WEB: www.healthsouth.com
SIC: 8093 Rehabilitation center, outpatient treatment
PA: Encompass Health Corporation
9001 Liberty Pkwy
Birmingham AL 35242
205 967-7116

(P-22576)
EXODUS RECOVERY INC (PA)
9808 Venice Blvd Ste 700, Culver City (90232-6824)
PHONE................................310 945-3350
Luana Murphy, *President*
Leeann Skorohod, *President*
Lezlie Murch, *Senior VP*
Grace Lee, *Vice Pres*
Kathy Shoemaker, *Vice Pres*
EMP: 84
SALES: 4MM **Privately Held**
SIC: 8093 Mental health clinic, outpatient

(P-22577)
FAMILY HLTH CTRS SAN DIEGO INC (PA)
823 Gateway Center Way, San Diego (92102-4541)
PHONE................................619 515-2303
Fran Butler-Cohen, *President*
SAI Vulchi, *Business Anlyst*
James Grubbs MBA, *Analyst*
Lori Smith,
Michael King, *Director*
EMP: 65 **EST:** 1972
SQ FT: 32,000
SALES: 147.1MM **Privately Held**
SIC: 8093 Mental health clinic, outpatient

(P-22578)
FAMILY PATHS INC (PA)
Also Called: CHILD ABUSE PREVENTION
1727 M L King Jr Way, Oakland (94612-1327)
PHONE................................510 893-9230
Lyda Mata, *CFO*
Danielle Sellers, *Treasurer*
Barbra Silver, *Exec Dir*
Kimberly Porter, *Program Mgr*
Shay Black, *Administration*
EMP: 70
SQ FT: 2,300
SALES: 5.3MM **Privately Held**
WEB: www.psshelps.org
SIC: 8093 Mental health clinic, outpatient

(P-22579)
GARDNER FAMILY CARE CORP
160 E Virginia St Ste 280, San Jose (95112-5817)
PHONE................................408 935-3906
Reymundo Estinoza, *CEO*
Frania Coria, *COO*
Ignacio Perez, *CFO*
EMP: 190
SALES: 19.4MM **Privately Held**
SIC: 8093 Mental health clinic, outpatient

(P-22580)
GARDNER FAMILY HLTH NETWRK INC (PA)
1621 Gold St, Alviso (95002)
PHONE................................408 200-2291
Reymundo C Espinoza, *CEO*
EMP: 50 **EST:** 1968
SALES (est): 14.2MM **Privately Held**
SIC: 8093 Mental health clinic, outpatient

(P-22581)
GENESIS HEALTHCARE PARTNERS PC
Also Called: Integrated Medical Specialists
2466 1st Ave Ste B, San Diego (92101-1408)
P.O. Box 33865 (92163-3865)
PHONE................................619 230-0400
Edward S Cohen, *CEO*
EMP: 113
SALES (corp-wide): 13.3MM **Privately Held**
SIC: 8093 Specialty outpatient clinics
PA: Genesis Healthcare Partners, P.C.
3444 Kearny Villa Rd
San Diego CA 92123
858 810-7200

(P-22582)
GENESIS HEALTHCARE PARTNERS PC (PA)
3444 Kearny Villa Rd, San Diego (92123-1959)
P.O. Box 33865 (92163-3865)
PHONE................................858 810-7200
Edward Cohen, *CEO*
Kellie Golshan, *CFO*
Chauntay Cross, *Office Mgr*
Alexis Harding, *Executive Asst*
Tim Erickson, *Info Tech Mgr*
EMP: 175
SQ FT: 15,000
SALES (est): 13.3MM **Privately Held**
SIC: 8093 Rehabilitation center, outpatient treatment

(P-22583)
GHC OF LOMPOC LLC
Also Called: Lompoc Skilled Nursing & Rehab
1428 W North Ave, Lompoc (93436-3961)
PHONE................................805 735-4010
Thomas Olds,
Lois Mastrocola,
EMP: 250
SALES (est): 8.1MM
SALES (corp-wide): 63.1MM **Privately Held**
SIC: 8093 Rehabilitation center, outpatient treatment
PA: Life Generations Healthcare Llc
6 Hutton Cntre Dr Ste 400
Santa Ana CA 92707
714 241-5600

(P-22584)
GOLDEN VALLEY HEALTH CENTERS (PA)
737 W Childs Ave, Merced (95341-6805)
PHONE................................209 383-1848
Tony Weber, *CEO*
Rebecca Cabrera-Reyes, *President*
Lue Thao, *CFO*
Lisa Swenson, *Officer*
David Simenson, *Associate Dir*
EMP: 850
SQ FT: 23,000
SALES: 102.5MM **Privately Held**
SIC: 8093 Specialty outpatient clinics

(P-22585)
GOLDEN VALLEY HEALTH CENTERS
Also Called: Women's Health Center
797 W Childs Ave, Merced (95341-6805)
PHONE................................209 383-5871
Pierre Scales, *Branch Mgr*
George Alkhouri, *Med Doctor*
EMP: 100
SALES (corp-wide): 102.5MM **Privately Held**
SIC: 8093 8011 Specialty outpatient clinics; clinic, operated by physicians
PA: Golden Valley Health Centers
737 W Childs Ave
Merced CA 95341
209 383-1848

(P-22586)
GRASSHOPPER HOUSE LLC
Also Called: Passages
6428 Meadows Ct, Malibu (90265-4492)
PHONE................................310 589-2880
Chris Prentiss,
Pax Prentiss,
EMP: 105
SQ FT: 16,000
SALES (est): 10.5MM **Privately Held**
WEB: www.passagesmalibu.com
SIC: 8093 Substance abuse clinics (outpatient)

(P-22587)
GREATER SACRAMENTO SUR
Also Called: Greater Sacramento Surgery Ctr
2288 Auburn Blvd Ste 201, Sacramento (95821-1620)
PHONE................................916 929-7229
Marvin Kamras, *Partner*
EMP: 60
SQ FT: 15,000
SALES (est): 7.6MM **Privately Held**
SIC: 8093 8011 Specialty outpatient clinics; ambulatory surgical center

(P-22588)
GREATER VALLEY MEDICAL GROUP (PA)
11600 Indian Hills Rd # 300, Mission Hills (91345-1225)
PHONE................................818 838-4500
Don Rebhun MD, *President*
Howard Sawyer MD, *Corp Secy*
Mohyi Soleiman MD, *Vice Pres*
EMP: 255
SALES (est): 6.2MM **Privately Held**
SIC: 8093 Specialty outpatient clinics

(P-22589)
GUIDANCE CENTER (PA)
1301 Pine Ave, Long Beach (90813-3124)
PHONE................................562 595-1159
David Stotler, *President*
Rev Paul Lance, *Admin Sec*
EMP: 125
SQ FT: 11,000
SALES: 14.2MM **Privately Held**
WEB: www.tcgclb.org
SIC: 8093 8322 Mental health clinic, outpatient; child related social services

(P-22590)
HEALTHFIRST MEDICAL GROUP INC (PA)
13440 Imperial Hwy, Santa Fe Springs (90670-4820)
PHONE................................562 949-9328
Ronald Crowell, *President*
Monica Malone, *Marketing Staff*
Gregory O D, *Med Doctor*

Lilian Gonzalez,
Andrea Ramos, *Manager*
EMP: 50
SALES (est): 4.5MM **Privately Held**
SIC: 8093 Rehabilitation center, outpatient
treatment

(P-22591)
HELP GROUP WEST (PA)
13130 Burbank Blvd, Sherman Oaks
(91401-6000)
PHONE..................................818 781-0360
Barbara Firestone, *President*
Michael Love, *CFO*
Susan Berman PH, *Exec VP*
EMP: 200
SQ FT: 100,000
SALES: 19.3MM **Privately Held**
SIC: 8093 Speech defect clinic

(P-22592)
HENRIETTA WEILL MEMORIAL CHILD (PA)
3628 Stockdale Hwy, Bakersfield
(93309-2153)
PHONE..................................661 322-1021
Blake Smith, *President*
Lindsey West, *Treasurer*
Candy Coats, *Executive*
David Camara, *Exec Dir*
Paula Abbott, *Administration*
EMP: 70
SQ FT: 16,000
SALES: 7.1MM **Privately Held**
SIC: 8093 Specialty outpatient clinics

(P-22593)
HILLVIEW MENTAL HEALTH CENTER
12450 Van Nuys Blvd # 200, Pacoima
(91331-1391)
PHONE..................................818 896-1161
Eva S McCraven, *President*
Carl C Mc Craven, *Treasurer*
Julie E Jones, *Vice Pres*
Beth K Meltzer, *Vice Pres*
Myron Cohen, *Admin Sec*
EMP: 80
SQ FT: 17,600
SALES: 10.4MM **Privately Held**
SIC: 8093 Mental health clinic, outpatient

(P-22594)
HOLLYWOOD MENTAL HEALTH CENTER
1224 Vine St, Los Angeles (90038-1612)
PHONE..................................323 769-6100
Barbara Engleman, *President*
EMP: 65
SALES (est): 1.8MM **Privately Held**
SIC: 8093 Mental health clinic, outpatient

(P-22595)
HOPE OF VALLEY MISSION
19379 Soledad Canyon Rd, Santa Clarita
(91351-2630)
PHONE..................................661 673-5951
EMP: 50
SALES (est): 351.7K **Privately Held**
SIC: 8093 Rehabilitation center, outpatient
treatment

(P-22596)
HOSPICE OF HUMBOLDT INC (PA)
3327 Timber Fall Ct, Eureka (95503-4894)
PHONE..................................707 445-8443
Marylee Bytheriver, *Director*
Gay Miller, *President*
Neal Ewald, *Treasurer*
Ann Richmond PHD, *Vice Pres*
Joe Rogers, *Exec Dir*
EMP: 80
SQ FT: 1,000
SALES: 7.5MM **Privately Held**
WEB: www.hospiceofhumboldt.org
SIC: 8093 8082 Specialty outpatient clin-
ics; home health care services

(P-22597)
I P S SERVICES INC
627 E Foothill Blvd, San Dimas
(91773-1208)
PHONE..................................909 305-0250
Robert Hernandez, *CEO*

David Nickel, *Shareholder*
EMP: 60
SALES (est): 4.3MM **Privately Held**
SIC: 8093 Mental health clinic, outpatient

(P-22598)
IMPERIAL COUNTY BEHAVIORAL HLT
2695 S 4th St, El Centro (92243-6012)
PHONE..................................760 482-2149
Michael Horn, *Director*
Mary Esquer, *Program Mgr*
Franciso Ortiz, *Senior Mgr*
EMP: 50
SALES (est): 738.6K **Privately Held**
SIC: 8093 Substance abuse clinics (outpa-
tient); mental health clinic, outpatient

(P-22599)
KAISER FOUNDATION HOSPITALS
Also Called: Kaiser Permanente
710 S Broadway, Walnut Creek
(94596-5294)
PHONE..................................925 295-4145
Vikki Antonelli, *Manager*
Ryan E Kolakoski, *Psychologist*
EMP: 793
SALES (corp-wide): 94.1B **Privately Held**
WEB: www.kaiserpermanente.org
SIC: 8093 Mental health clinic, outpatient
HQ: Kaiser Foundation Hospitals Inc
1 Kaiser Plz
Oakland CA 94612
510 271-6611

(P-22600)
KAISER FOUNDATION HOSPITALS
Also Called: Oak Street Physical Therapy
2040 Pacific Coast Hwy, Lomita
(90717-2660)
PHONE..................................424 251-7000
EMP: 192
SALES (corp-wide): 94.1B **Privately Held**
SIC: 8093 Rehabilitation center, outpatient
treatment
HQ: Kaiser Foundation Hospitals Inc
1 Kaiser Plz
Oakland CA 94612
510 271-6611

(P-22601)
KAISER FOUNDATION HOSPITALS
Also Called: Positive Choice Wellness Ctr
7035 Convoy Ct, San Diego (92111-1016)
PHONE..................................858 573-0090
EMP: 192
SALES (corp-wide): 94.1B **Privately Held**
SIC: 8093 Weight loss clinic, with medical
staff
HQ: Kaiser Foundation Hospitals Inc
1 Kaiser Plz
Oakland CA 94612
510 271-6611

(P-22602)
KAISER FOUNDATION HOSPITALS
Also Called: Health Educatn Psychiatry Offs
5105 W Goldleaf Cir, Los Angeles
(90056-1269)
PHONE..................................323 298-3300
Natasha Elliott, *Branch Mgr*
EMP: 200
SALES (corp-wide): 94.1B **Privately Held**
SIC: 8093 Specialty outpatient clinics
HQ: Kaiser Foundation Hospitals Inc
1 Kaiser Plz
Oakland CA 94612
510 271-6611

(P-22603)
KAISER FOUNDATION HOSPITALS
Also Called: Kaiser Permanente
3400 Delta Fair Blvd, Antioch (94509-4004)
PHONE..................................925 779-5000
Dan Sonnier, *Manager*
Kara King, *Obstetrician*
Gulshan S Panjwani, *Internal Med*
Syed Qadri, *Internal Med*
Zhihong Zhong, *Internal Med*
EMP: 200

SQ FT: 47,307
SALES (corp-wide): 94.1B **Privately Held**
WEB: www.kaiserpermanente.org
SIC: 8093 8011 8062 Specialty outpatient
clinics; general & family practice, physi-
cian/surgeon; general medical & surgical
hospitals
HQ: Kaiser Foundation Hospitals Inc
1 Kaiser Plz
Oakland CA 94612
510 271-6611

(P-22604)
KAISER FOUNDATION HOSPITALS
Also Called: Kaiser Permanente
23621 Main St, Carson (90745-5743)
PHONE..................................310 513-6707
Lora Griffin, *Branch Mgr*
Ann La Fever, *Executive*
EMP: 60
SALES (corp-wide): 94.1B **Privately Held**
WEB: www.kaiserpermanente.org
SIC: 8093 8062 Specialty outpatient clin-
ics; general medical & surgical hospitals
HQ: Kaiser Foundation Hospitals Inc
1 Kaiser Plz
Oakland CA 94612
510 271-6611

(P-22605)
KEITH T KUSUNIS MD
Also Called: Family Health Center
91767 N Orange Grv Ave, Pomona (91767)
PHONE..................................909 469-9494
Keith T Kusunas, *Principal*
Keith T Kusunis, *President*
EMP: 65
SALES (est): 627.6K **Privately Held**
SIC: 8093 Family planning clinic

(P-22606)
KIMA W MEDICAL CENTER
535 Airport Rd, Hoopa (95546-9615)
PHONE..................................530 625-4114
Emmit Chase, *CEO*
Dennis Jones, *COO*
Jessica Mosier, *General Mgr*
EMP: 80
SQ FT: 11,000
SALES: 6.5MM **Privately Held**
SIC: 8093 8399 Specialty outpatient clin-
ics; health systems agency

(P-22607)
KINDRED NURSING CENTERS W LLC
Also Called: Kindred Transitional Care
1359 Pine St, San Francisco (94109-4807)
PHONE..................................415 673-8405
Joseph L Landenwich,
Richard E Chapman,
EMP: 200
SALES (est): 222.6K
SALES (corp-wide): 6B **Privately Held**
SIC: 8093 Rehabilitation center, outpatient
treatment
HQ: Kindred Healthcare Operating, Llc
680 S 4th St
Louisville KY 40202
502 596-7300

(P-22608)
KINGS VIEW
Also Called: Mental Hlth Svcs For Kngs Cnty
289 E 8th St, Hanford (93230-3935)
PHONE..................................559 582-9307
Brenda Johnson Hill, *Principal*
EMP: 100
SALES (corp-wide): 26.8MM **Privately
Held**
SIC: 8093 Mental health clinic, outpatient
PA: Kings View
7170 N Fincl Dr Ste 110
Fresno CA 93720
559 256-0100

(P-22609)
KINGSVIEW CORP
Also Called: Tuolomne Cnty Bhvrl Hlth
2 S Green St, Sonora (95370-4618)
PHONE..................................209 533-6245
Jack Tanebaum, *Exec Dir*
EMP: 63
SALES (est): 846.5K **Privately Held**
SIC: 8093 Mental health clinic, outpatient

(P-22610)
LATINO COMMISSION ON ALCOHOL (PA)
1001 Sneath Ln Ste 307, San Bruno
(94066-2349)
PHONE..................................650 244-1444
Debra Camarillo, *Principal*
EMP: 50
SALES: 2.6MM **Privately Held**
SIC: 8093 8361 Mental health clinic, out-
patient; home for the mentally retarded

(P-22611)
LEARNING SERVICES CORPORATION
2335 Bear Valley Pkwy, Escondido
(92027-3854)
PHONE..................................760 746-3223
Sharon Brown, *Manager*
EMP: 50
SALES (corp-wide): 17.9MM **Privately
Held**
WEB: www.learningservices.com
SIC: 8093 Rehabilitation center, outpatient
treatment
PA: Learning Services Corporation
131 Langley Dr Ste B
Lawrenceville GA 30046
470 235-4700

(P-22612)
LEARNING SERVICES CORPORATION
Also Called: Learning Services Northern Cal
10855 De Bruin Way, Gilroy (95020-9315)
PHONE..................................408 848-4379
Kayree Fhreeve, *Director*
EMP: 50
SALES (corp-wide): 17.9MM **Privately
Held**
WEB: www.learningservices.com
SIC: 8093 Rehabilitation center, outpatient
treatment
PA: Learning Services Corporation
131 Langley Dr Ste B
Lawrenceville GA 30046
470 235-4700

(P-22613)
LINCOLN (PA)
1266 14th St, Oakland (94607-2205)
PHONE..................................510 273-4700
Christine Stoner-Mertz, *CEO*
Nancy L Oakley, *COO*
Enrico Hernandez, *CFO*
Rico Hernandez, *CFO*
Allison Becwar, *Principal*
EMP: 83
SQ FT: 40,000
SALES: 17.3MM **Privately Held**
WEB: www.lincolncc.org
SIC: 8093 8361 8049 Mental health clinic,
outpatient; orphanage; psychiatric social
worker

(P-22614)
LOS ANGELES CENTER FOR ALCOHOL (PA)
11015 Bloomfield Ave, Santa Fe Springs
(90670-4601)
P.O. Box 3205 (90670-0205)
PHONE..................................562 906-2676
Brenda Wiewel, *Exec Dir*
Liana Sanchez, *Program Mgr*
Lawrence Fernandez, *Manager*
EMP: 65
SQ FT: 20,000
SALES: 7.3MM **Privately Held**
WEB: www.lacada.com
SIC: 8093 8069 8299 Alcohol clinic, out-
patient; detoxification center, outpatient;
drug clinic, outpatient; alcoholism rehabili-
tation hospital; drug addiction rehabilita-
tion hospital; educational services

(P-22615)
LOS ANGELES UNIFIED SCHOOL DST
Also Called: Mental Health Dept
6651 Balboa Blvd, Van Nuys (91406-5529)
PHONE..................................818 997-2640
Gil Palacio, *Director*
EMP: 300

SALES (corp-wide): 3.8B **Privately Held**
WEB: www.lausd.k12.ca.us
SIC: 8093 Mental health clinic, outpatient
PA: Los Angeles Unified School District
333 S Beaudry Ave Ste 209
Los Angeles CA 90017
213 241-1000

(P-22616)
MADERA CNTY BHVIORAL HLTH SVCS
209 E 7th St, Madera (93638-3780)
P.O. Box 1288 (93639-1288)
PHONE.................................559 673-3508
Dennis Koch, *President*
EMP: 126 EST: 2010
SQ FT: 25,000
SALES: 17MM **Privately Held**
SIC: 8093 Specialty outpatient clinics

(P-22617)
MCALISTER INSTITUTE FOR TREAT (PA)
1400 N Johnson Ave # 101, El Cajon (92020-1650)
PHONE.................................619 442-0277
Jeanne Mc Alister, *President*
Steve Hubbard, *Vice Pres*
EMP: 130
SQ FT: 9,000
SALES: 14.1MM **Privately Held**
WEB: www.mcalisterinstitute.org
SIC: 8093 Drug clinic, outpatient

(P-22618)
MCALISTER INSTITUTE FOR TREAT
3923 Waring Rd, Oceanside (92056-4457)
PHONE.................................760 726-4451
EMP: 59
SALES (corp-wide): 14.1MM **Privately Held**
SIC: 8093 Drug clinic, outpatient
PA: Mcalister Institute For Treatment & Education, Inc.
1400 N Johnson Ave # 101
El Cajon CA 92020
619 442-0277

(P-22619)
MENDOCINO COAST CLINICS INC
205 South St, Fort Bragg (95437-5540)
PHONE.................................707 964-1251
Paula Cohen, *Exec Dir*
Jeff Warner, *Chairman*
Richard Moon, *Treasurer*
Claudia Boudreau, *Admin Sec*
▲ EMP: 93
SQ FT: 5,000
SALES: 7MM **Privately Held**
WEB: www.mendocinocoastclinics.org
SIC: 8093 Family planning & birth control clinics

(P-22620)
MFI RECOVERY CENTER (PA)
5870 Arlington Ave # 103, Riverside (92504-2037)
PHONE.................................951 683-6596
Craig Lamdon, *Exec Dir*
Darcy McNaboe, *Vice Pres*
Denise Arellano, *Accounting Mgr*
Julio Ibarra, *Psychologist*
Kimberly Arnett, *Director*
EMP: 125
SQ FT: 864
SALES: 11MM **Privately Held**
WEB: www.mfirecovery.com
SIC: 8093 8322 Alcohol clinic, outpatient; family counseling services

(P-22621)
NATIONAL THERAPEUTIC SVCS INC (PA)
Also Called: Joshua House
3822 Campus Dr Ste 100, Newport Beach (92660-2636)
PHONE.................................866 311-0003
Michael Neatherton, *President*
Paul Alexander, *COO*
Ray Pacini, *CFO*
John Mumm, *Controller*
Tib Albach, *Program Dir*
EMP: 94

SALES (est): 13.6MM **Privately Held**
SIC: 8093 Alcohol clinic, outpatient

(P-22622)
NATIONL MEDCL ASSN COMP HEALTH
3177 Ocean View Blvd, San Diego (92113-1432)
PHONE.................................619 231-9300
Shirleen Freeman, *Director*
EMP: 60
SALES (corp-wide): 3.7MM **Privately Held**
WEB: www.nmasandiego.org
SIC: 8093 Specialty outpatient clinics
PA: National Medical Association Comprehensive Health Center
1275 30th St
San Diego CA 92154
619 231-3200

(P-22623)
NEVADA COUNTY BEHAVIORAL HLTH
500 Crown Point Cir # 120, Grass Valley (95945-9561)
PHONE.................................530 265-1450
Michael Heggarty, *Director*
Jill Blake, *Director*
EMP: 50
SQ FT: 22,168
SALES (est): 2.3MM **Privately Held**
SIC: 8093 Mental health clinic, outpatient

(P-22624)
NORTH COAST SURGERY CENTER
3903 Waring Rd, Oceanside (92056-4405)
PHONE.................................760 940-0997
Dr Bruce Hochman, *Partner*
EMP: 79
SQ FT: 11,000
SALES (est): 4.5MM **Privately Held**
SIC: 8093 Specialty outpatient clinics

(P-22625)
OPEN DOOR COMMUNITY HLTH CTRS
Also Called: Humboldt Open Door Clinic
770 10th St, Arcata (95521-6210)
PHONE.................................707 826-8610
Hermann Spetzler, *Branch Mgr*
EMP: 72 **Privately Held**
WEB: www.opendoorhealth.com
SIC: 8093 8011 Smoking clinic; offices & clinics of medical doctors
PA: Open Door Community Health Centers
670 9th St Ste 203cfo
Arcata CA 95521

(P-22626)
OPEN DOOR COMMUNITY HLTH CTRS (PA)
670 9th St Ste 203cfo, Arcata (95521-6248)
PHONE.................................707 826-8642
Sydney Fisher Larsen, *CEO*
EMP: 70
SQ FT: 18,000
SALES: 57.5MM **Privately Held**
WEB: www.opendoorhealth.com
SIC: 8093 Smoking clinic

(P-22627)
OPTIONS FAMILY OF SERVICES
5755 Valentina Ave, Atascadero (93422-3532)
PHONE.................................805 462-8544
EMP: 50
SQ FT: 576
SALES (corp-wide): 5.6MM **Privately Held**
SIC: 8093
PA: Options Family Of Services, Inc
800 Quintana Rd Ste 2c
Morro Bay CA 93442
805 772-6066

(P-22628)
OPYA INC
1720 S Amphlett Blvd # 110, San Mateo (94402-2702)
PHONE.................................650 931-6300
Jonathan Wright, *CEO*

Keiko Ikeda, *COO*
Suchi Deshpande, *Vice Pres*
Monica Tabora, *Admin Asst*
EMP: 55 EST: 2017
SALES (est): 79.7K **Privately Held**
SIC: 8093 8049 7371 Specialty outpatient clinics; speech therapist; computer software development & applications

(P-22629)
ORENDA CENTER
1430 Neotomas Ave, Santa Rosa (95405-7575)
PHONE.................................707 565-7450
Diane Madrigal, *Director*
EMP: 60
SALES (est): 873.5K **Privately Held**
SIC: 8093 Rehabilitation center, outpatient treatment

(P-22630)
PACIFIC CLINICS
11721 Telegraph Rd Ste A, Santa Fe Springs (90670-6835)
PHONE.................................562 949-8455
Sharon Corey, *Director*
EMP: 65
SALES (corp-wide): 91.3MM **Privately Held**
SIC: 8093 Mental health clinic, outpatient
PA: Pacific Clinics Foundation.
800 S Santa Anita Ave
Arcadia CA 91006
626 254-5000

(P-22631)
PACIFIC FRNSIC PSYCHLOGY ASSOC
9261 Folsom Blvd Ste 300, Sacramento (95826-2559)
PHONE.................................925 253-3111
Tom Tobin, *CEO*
EMP: 75
SALES (est): 520.7K **Privately Held**
SIC: 8093 Mental health clinic, outpatient

(P-22632)
PARAGON HEALTH & REHAB CT
1090 E Dinuba Ave, Reedley (93654-3577)
PHONE.................................559 638-3578
EMP: 50 EST: 2005
SALES (est): 2.3MM **Privately Held**
SIC: 8093

(P-22633)
PARENTHOOD OF PLANNED
1140 Sonoma Ave Ste 3, Santa Rosa (95405-4817)
PHONE.................................707 527-7656
EMP: 51
SALES (corp-wide): 63.3MM **Privately Held**
SIC: 8093 Family planning & birth control clinics
PA: Planned Parenthood Of San Diego And Riverside Counties
1075 Camino Del Rio S # 100
San Diego CA 92108
619 881-4500

(P-22634)
PARENTHOOD OF PLANNED (PA)
1075 Camino Del Rio S # 100, San Diego (92108-3539)
PHONE.................................619 881-4500
Darrah Johnson, *CEO*
Len Dodson, *CFO*
Nora Vargas, *Vice Pres*
David Priver, *Managing Dir*
Ann Elise Ryder, *Controller*
EMP: 100
SQ FT: 24,000
SALES: 63.3MM **Privately Held**
WEB: www.planned.org
SIC: 8093 Family planning clinic; family planning & birth control clinics

(P-22635)
PARENTHOOD OF PLANNED
12900 Frederick St Ste C, Moreno Valley (92553-5266)
PHONE.................................951 222-3101
Theresa Gonzales, *Director*
EMP: 61

SALES (corp-wide): 63.3MM **Privately Held**
SIC: 8093 Family planning & birth control clinics
PA: Planned Parenthood Of San Diego And Riverside Counties
1075 Camino Del Rio S # 100
San Diego CA 92108
619 881-4500

(P-22636)
PARENTHOOD OF PLANNED
2935 Bechelli Ln, Redding (96002-1905)
PHONE.................................530 351-7100
EMP: 51
SALES (corp-wide): 63.3MM **Privately Held**
SIC: 8093 Family planning clinic
PA: Planned Parenthood Of San Diego And Riverside Counties
1075 Camino Del Rio S # 100
San Diego CA 92108
619 881-4500

(P-22637)
PASADENA CHILD DEV ASSOC INC
620 N Lake Ave, Pasadena (91101-1220)
PHONE.................................626 793-7350
Diane Cullinane MD, *Principal*
Tanya Robles, *Admin Asst*
Claudia Salinas, *Finance Asst*
Julia Scheibmeir, *Director*
Juliet McNeil, *Receptionist*
EMP: 80
SALES: 3.8MM **Privately Held**
SIC: 8093 Mental health clinic, outpatient

(P-22638)
PATHWAY SOCIETY
102 S 11th St, San Jose (95112-2132)
PHONE.................................408 244-1834
Joanne Buckley, *Exec Dir*
EMP: 50
SALES (corp-wide): 7.3MM **Privately Held**
WEB: www.pathwayinc.com
SIC: 8093 Drug clinic, outpatient; rehabilitation center, outpatient treatment
PA: Pathway Society, Inc.
1659 Scott Blvd Ste 210
Santa Clara CA 95050
408 244-1834

(P-22639)
PEDIATRIC & FAMILY MEDICAL CTR
Also Called: Eisner Pediatric Fmly Med Ctr
1530 S Olive St, Los Angeles (90015-3023)
PHONE.................................213 342-3325
Carl Coan, *CEO*
Edward Matthews III, *Ch of Bd*
Kevin Rossi, *Ch of Bd*
Herb Schultz, *President*
Carl Edward Coan, *CEO*
EMP: 160
SQ FT: 21,000
SALES: 25.4MM **Privately Held**
SIC: 8093 Specialty outpatient clinics

(P-22640)
PEDIATRIC PHYSICAL REHAB CLNC
Also Called: Physical/Occupational Therapy
9300 Valley Childrens Pl, Madera (93636-8761)
PHONE.................................559 353-6130
Carol Kurushima, *Manager*
EMP: 50
SALES (est): 1.8MM **Privately Held**
SIC: 8093 Rehabilitation center, outpatient treatment

(P-22641)
PEDIATRIC THERAPY NETWORK
1815 W 213th St Ste 100, Torrance (90501-2852)
PHONE.................................310 328-0276
Zoe Mailloux, *Exec Dir*
Tom Gosney, *CFO*
John Wilkerson, *Treasurer*
Heather McGuire, *Comms Mgr*
Gina Coleman, *Exec Dir*
EMP: 100

SQ FT: 20,000
SALES: 9.5MM **Privately Held**
WEB: www.pediatrictherapy.com
SIC: 8093 Rehabilitation center, outpatient treatment

(P-22642)
PLACER COUNTY- ADULT SYS CARE
11533 C Ave, Auburn (95603-2703)
PHONE..................................530 886-2974
Maureen F Bauman, *Director*
EMP: 99
SALES (est): 1.1MM **Privately Held**
SIC: 8093 Specialty outpatient clinics

(P-22643)
PLANNED PARENTHOOD FEDERATION
601 W 19th St Ste B, Costa Mesa
(92627-5060)
PHONE..................................949 548-8830
EMP: 73
SALES (corp-wide): 196.8MM **Privately Held**
SIC: 8093 8011 Family planning clinic; clinic, operated by physicians
PA: Planned Parenthood Federation Of America, Inc.
123 William St Fl 10
New York NY 10038
212 541-7800

(P-22644)
PLANNED PARENTHOOD FEDERATION
555 Capitol Mall Ste 510, Sacramento
(95814-4581)
PHONE..................................916 446-5247
Ana Sandoval, *Director*
EMP: 63
SALES (corp-wide): 196.8MM **Privately Held**
SIC: 8093 Family planning & birth control clinics
PA: Planned Parenthood Federation Of America, Inc.
123 William St Fl 10
New York NY 10038
212 541-7800

(P-22645)
PLANNED PARENTHOOD LOS ANGELES (PA)
400 W 30th St, Los Angeles (90007-3320)
PHONE..................................213 284-3200
Sue Dunlap, *President*
Mark Kimura, *CFO*
Adrianne Black, *Vice Pres*
Amanda Novak, *Executive*
Oscar Cerrillo, *IT/INT Sup*
EMP: 80
SQ FT: 30,000
SALES: 63.9MM **Privately Held**
WEB: www.plannedparenthood.org
SIC: 8093 Family planning clinic; birth control clinic

(P-22646)
PLANNED PARENTHOOD MAR MONTE (PA)
Also Called: Region Dev & Affairs Off
316 N Main St Ste 100, Salinas
(93901-2844)
PHONE..................................831 373-1709
Linda Williams, *CEO*
Irene Floyd, *Principal*
Josephine Ramrus, *Admin Sec*
EMP: 63
SALES (est): 2.2MM **Privately Held**
SIC: 8093 Family planning clinic

(P-22647)
PLANNED PARENTHOOD/ORANGE AND (PA)
700 S Tustin St Fl 1, Orange (92866-3425)
PHONE..................................714 633-6373
Alexis McGill Johnson, *Chairman*
Cecile Richards, *President*
Jon Dunn, *CEO*
Betha Schnelle, *COO*
Claudia Palomares, *Executive*
EMP: 250

(P-22648)
PLANNED PRNTHOD SHST-DBLO INC (PA)
Also Called: Planned Parenthood Shasta-Paci
2185 Pacheco St, Concord (94520-2309)
PHONE..................................925 676-0300
Heather Estes, *CEO*
Cecile Richards, *President*
Shelley Sella, *Med Doctor*
EMP: 50
SQ FT: 5,500
SALES (est): 26.9MM **Privately Held**
SIC: 8093 Family planning & birth control clinics

(P-22649)
PLANNED PRNTHOOD CAL CNTL CAST (PA)
518 Garden St, Santa Barbara
(93101-1606)
PHONE..................................805 963-2445
Cheryl Rollings, *Exec Dir*
Jenna Tosh, *Exec Dir*
Jennifer Navarro, *Administration*
EMP: 54
SQ FT: 9,000
SALES (est): 20.7MM **Privately Held**
SIC: 8093 Birth control clinic

(P-22650)
PLANNED PRNTHOOD MAR MONTE INC
1691 The Alameda, San Jose
(95126-2203)
PHONE..................................408 287-7529
Linda Williams, *CEO*
EMP: 150
SALES (corp-wide): 111.7MM **Privately Held**
SIC: 8093 Family planning clinic
PA: Planned Parenthood Mar Monte, Inc.
1691 The Alameda
San Jose CA 95126
408 287-7532

(P-22651)
PLANNED PRNTHOOD MAR MONTE INC (PA)
1691 The Alameda, San Jose
(95126-2203)
PHONE..................................408 287-7532
Linda T Williams, *President*
John Giambruno, *CFO*
Jeanne Ewy, *Vice Pres*
Alison Gaulden, *Vice Pres*
Rosemary Kamei, *Vice Pres*
EMP: 58
SQ FT: 41,000
SALES: 111.7MM **Privately Held**
SIC: 8093 Family planning clinic

(P-22652)
PLANNED PRNTHOOD MAR MONTE INC
26302 La Paz Rd 200, Mission Viejo
(92691-5313)
PHONE..................................949 768-3643
EMP: 64
SALES (corp-wide): 111.7MM **Privately Held**
SIC: 8093 8011 Family planning & birth control clinics; clinic, operated by physicians
PA: Planned Parenthood Mar Monte, Inc.
1691 The Alameda
San Jose CA 95126
408 287-7532

(P-22653)
PLEASANTVIEW INDUSTRIES INC
27921 Urbandale Ave, Saugus
(91350-1916)
PHONE..................................661 296-6700
Gerald Howard, *Director*
Del Duyer, *President*
Gerry Howard, *Exec Dir*
Jennifer Zimmerman, *Administration*
EMP: 77 **EST:** 1969

SQ FT: 5,500
SALES: 717.6K **Privately Held**
WEB: www.pleasantviewindustries.org
SIC: 8093 Rehabilitation center, outpatient treatment

(P-22654)
PRINCIPLES INC (PA)
Also Called: Impact DRG Alcohol Trtmnt Ctr
1680 N Fair Oaks Ave, Pasadena
(91103-1642)
P.O. Box 93607 (91109-3607)
PHONE..................................323 681-2575
James M Stillwell, *CEO*
Lois Gonzales, *Controller*
Mark Paquet, *Ch Admin Ofcr*
Patty Fiendel, *Manager*
Jim Stillwell, *Manager*
EMP: 51
SQ FT: 40,000
SALES: 10MM **Privately Held**
WEB: www.mcdpartners.com
SIC: 8093 Rehabilitation center, outpatient treatment

(P-22655)
PROVIDENCE SERVICE CORPORATION
1021 4th St, Taft (93268-2433)
PHONE..................................661 765-7025
Courtney Morris, *Branch Mgr*
EMP: 50
SALES (corp-wide): 1.6B **Publicly Held**
SIC: 8093 Mental health clinic, outpatient
PA: Providence Service Corporation
700 Canal St Ste 3
Stamford CT 06902
203 307-2800

(P-22656)
PROVIDENCE SPEECH HEARING CTR
Also Called: Word and Brown Hearing Ctr
1301 W Providence Ave, Orange
(92868-3892)
PHONE..................................714 639-4990
Linda Smith, *CEO*
Bill Ross, *President*
Jack Shradder, *Treasurer*
Margaret A Inman PH, *Founder*
Jerry O'Connor, *Exec VP*
EMP: 50
SQ FT: 15,000
SALES: 12.9MM **Privately Held**
WEB: www.pshc.org
SIC: 8093 Speech defect clinic

(P-22657)
PSYCHIATRIC SOLUTIONS INC
Also Called: B H C Alhambra Hospital
4619 Rosemead Blvd, Rosemead
(91770-1478)
P.O. Box 369 (91770-0369)
PHONE..................................626 286-1191
Margaret Minnick, *Manager*
Ray Castillo, *Director*
Ashley Bullock, *Coordinator*
EMP: 200
SALES (corp-wide): 10.4B **Publicly Held**
WEB: www.intermountainhospital.com
SIC: 8093 8011 8361 8063 Mental health clinic, outpatient; psychiatric clinic; residential care; hospital for the mentally ill
HQ: Psychiatric Solutions, Inc.
6640 Carothers Pkwy # 500
Franklin TN 37067
615 312-5700

(P-22658)
PYRAMID ALTERNATIVES INC (PA)
480 Manor Pl, Pacifica (94044)
PHONE..................................650 355-8787
Linda Malone, *Exec Dir*
EMP: 50 **EST:** 1974
SQ FT: 5,000
SALES: 1.6MM **Privately Held**
WEB: www.pyramidalternatives.org
SIC: 8093 8322 Mental health clinic, outpatient; individual & family services; child related social services; family counseling services; general counseling services

(P-22659)
REACH PROJECT (PA)
1915 D St, Antioch (94509-2571)
PHONE..................................925 754-3673
Mickey Marchetti, *Exec Dir*
EMP: 83
SALES: 775.9K **Privately Held**
SIC: 8093 8322 Specialty outpatient clinics; individual & family services

(P-22660)
REHABLTATION INST SOUTHERN CAL (PA)
Also Called: Rehabilitation Inst Orange Cnty
1800 E La Veta Ave, Orange (92866-2902)
PHONE..................................714 633-7400
Praim S Singh, *Director*
Randy Holdeman, *Officer*
Katherine Meyer, *Mktg Dir*
Lisa Jenks, *Director*
Jason Leavell, *Assistant*
EMP: 155
SQ FT: 75,000
SALES: 8.3MM **Privately Held**
WEB: www.rio-rehab.com
SIC: 8093 Rehabilitation center, outpatient treatment

(P-22661)
RICHMOND AREA MLT-SERVICES INC
720 Sacramento St, San Francisco
(94108-2535)
PHONE..................................415 392-4453
Kavoos Bassiri, *CEO*
Ken Choi, *CFO*
EMP: 99
SALES (est): 4.9MM **Privately Held**
SIC: 8093 Mental health clinic, outpatient

(P-22662)
RICHMOND AREA MLT-SERVICES INC
3120 Mission St, San Francisco
(94110-4504)
PHONE..................................415 800-0699
Kavoos Bassiri, *CEO*
Ken Choi, *CFO*
EMP: 99
SALES (est): 4.9MM **Privately Held**
SIC: 8093 Mental health clinic, outpatient

(P-22663)
RICHMOND AREA MLT-SERVICES INC
1375 Mission St, San Francisco
(94103-2621)
PHONE..................................415 689-5662
Kavoos Bassiri, *CEO*
Kenneth Choi, *CFO*
EMP: 99
SALES (est): 770.4K **Privately Held**
SIC: 8093 Mental health clinic, outpatient

(P-22664)
RICHMOND AREA MLT-SERVICES INC
1282 Market St, San Francisco
(94102-4801)
PHONE..................................415 579-3021
Kenneth Choi, *CFO*
EMP: 61
SALES (corp-wide): 19.7MM **Privately Held**
SIC: 8093 Mental health clinic, outpatient
PA: Richmond Area Multi-Services, Inc.
639 14th Ave
San Francisco CA 94118
415 800-0699

(P-22665)
RICHMOND AREA MLT-SERVICES INC (PA)
639 14th Ave, San Francisco (94118-3502)
PHONE..................................415 800-0699
Kavoos Bassiri, *CEO*
Lenore Williams, *CFO*
Natalie Quan, *Admin Asst*
Michael Leyva, *Psychologist*
Anna Zozulinsky, *Psychologist*
EMP: 76
SQ FT: 8,400

P R O D U C T S & S V C S

SALES: 19.7MM **Privately Held**
WEB: www.ramsinc.org
SIC: 8093 Mental health clinic, outpatient

(P-22666)
RIVER OAK CENTER FOR CHILDREN (PA)
5445 Laurel Hills Dr, Sacramento (95841-3105)
PHONE.................................916 609-5100
Laurie Clothier, *CEO*
EMP: 140
SQ FT: 26,000
SALES: 17.3MM **Privately Held**
SIC: 8093 8699 Mental health clinic, outpatient; charitable organization

(P-22667)
RIVERSIDE-SAN BERNARDINO (PA)
11555 1/2 Potrero Rd, Banning (92220-6946)
PHONE.................................951 849-4761
Jackie Wisespirit, *President*
Brandie Miranda, *Treasurer*
Bill Thomsen, *Officer*
Charles Castello, *Vice Pres*
Joe Becerra, *Office Admin*
EMP: 100
SQ FT: 5,200
SALES: 35.9MM **Privately Held**
SIC: 8093 8011 Specialty outpatient clinics; offices & clinics of medical doctors

(P-22668)
SAFE HARBOR TREATMENT CEN
722 Superba Ave, Venice (90291-3869)
PHONE.................................949 645-1026
Maggie Grisham, *Director*
Christine Aubele, *Opers Mgr*
EMP: 50
SALES (est): 1.5MM **Privately Held**
SIC: 8093 Alcohol clinic, outpatient

(P-22669)
SALVATION ARMY
200 19th St, Bakersfield (93301-4904)
PHONE.................................661 325-8626
Michael Gomes, *Branch Mgr*
EMP: 79
SALES (corp-wide): 4.3B **Privately Held**
WEB: www.salvationarmy.usawest.org
SIC: 8093 Substance abuse clinics (outpatient)
HQ: The Salvation Army
180 E Ocean Blvd Ste 500
Long Beach CA 90802
562 491-8464

(P-22670)
SALVATION ARMY
1247 S Wilson Way, Stockton (95205-7096)
PHONE.................................209 466-3871
Dale Brockelman, *Manager*
EMP: 82
SALES (corp-wide): 4.3B **Privately Held**
WEB: www.salvationarmy.usawest.org
SIC: 8093 Rehabilitation center, outpatient treatment
HQ: The Salvation Army
180 E Ocean Blvd Ste 500
Long Beach CA 90802
562 491-8464

(P-22671)
SAN FERNANDO CITY OF INC
10605 Balboa Blvd Ste 100, Granada Hills (91344-6367)
PHONE.................................818 832-2400
Wendi Tovey, *Branch Mgr*
EMP: 100 **Privately Held**
SIC: 8093 9111 Mental health clinic, outpatient; county supervisors' & executives' offices
PA: San Fernando, City Of Inc
117 N Macneil St
San Fernando CA 91340
818 898-1201

(P-22672)
SAN FERNANDO VALLEY COMMUNITY (PA)
16360 Roscoe Blvd Fl 2, Van Nuys (91406-1219)
PHONE.................................818 901-4830
Ian Hunter PHD, *President*
Emily Chen, *CFO*
Bonnie Roth, *Exec Dir*
Christina Giles, *Program Mgr*
Denise Richman, *Admin Sec*
EMP: 450
SQ FT: 13,000
SALES: 40.1MM **Privately Held**
SIC: 8093 Substance abuse clinics (outpatient); mental health clinic, outpatient

(P-22673)
SAN FRANCISCO CITY CLINIC
356 7th St, San Francisco (94103-4030)
PHONE.................................415 487-5500
Jeffrey Klausner, *Director*
Wendy Wolf, *Deputy Dir*
Susan Philip, *Director*
EMP: 80
SQ FT: 2,500
SALES (est): 3.6MM **Privately Held**
WEB: www.cityclinic.net
SIC: 8093 Birth control clinic

(P-22674)
SAN GORGONIO MEMORIAL HOSPITAL
Also Called: Behavioral Health Center
1751 N Sunrise Way Ste G, Palm Springs (92262-3408)
PHONE.................................760 656-2251
Carole Dozier, *Director*
EMP: 100
SALES (corp-wide): 56.1MM **Privately Held**
SIC: 8093 Mental health clinic, outpatient
PA: San Gorgonio Memorial Hospital
600 N Highland Sprng Ave
Banning CA 92220
951 845-1121

(P-22675)
SAN JOAQUIN VALLEY REHABILI (HQ)
7173 N Sharon Ave, Fresno (93720-3329)
PHONE.................................559 436-3600
Edward C Palacios, *Partner*
Shaina Shaikh, *Pharmacy Dir*
Kelly Rudolph, *QA Dir*
Diane Kisling, *Accountant*
Mark Rakis, *Opers Mgr*
EMP: 275
SALES: 35MM
SALES (corp-wide): 323.5MM **Privately Held**
WEB: www.sjvrehab.com
SIC: 8093 Rehabilitation center, outpatient treatment
PA: Vibra Healthcare, Llc
4600 Lena Dr Ste 100
Mechanicsburg PA 17055
717 591-5700

(P-22676)
SAN MATEO CNTY PUB HLTH CLINIC
380 90th St, Daly City (94015-1807)
PHONE.................................650 301-8600
Cathy Lehmkuhl, *Director*
Denise R Gonzalez, *Internal Med*
EMP: 50
SALES (est): 1.1MM **Privately Held**
WEB: www.sanmateolafco.org
SIC: 8093 Birth control clinic

(P-22677)
SARAH ELIZABETH TREUSDELL
921 W Avenue J Ste C, Lancaster (93534-3443)
PHONE.................................661 949-0131
S E Treusdell, *Principal*
Sarah Elizabeth Treusdell, *Principal*
EMP: 50
SALES (est): 124.3K **Privately Held**
SIC: 8093 Mental health clinic, outpatient

(P-22678)
SCRIPPS HEALTH
Also Called: Scripps Del Mar
3811 Valley Centre Dr, San Diego (92130-3318)
PHONE.................................858 794-0160
Melody Stewart, *Manager*
EMP: 250
SALES (corp-wide): 2.9B **Privately Held**
WEB: www.scripps.org
SIC: 8093 Specialty outpatient clinics
PA: Scripps Health
10140 Campus Point Dr Ax415
San Diego CA 92121
800 727-4777

(P-22679)
SKIN HEALTH EXPERTS MEDIC
Also Called: Kate Summerville
144 S Beverly Dr Ste 500, Beverly Hills (90212-3023)
PHONE.................................310 623-6869
Michelle Taylor, *CEO*
Laura Shaff, *CFO*
EMP: 70
SALES (est): 956.9K **Privately Held**
SIC: 8093 Specialty outpatient clinics

(P-22680)
SMILE HOUSING CORPORATION
800 Quintana Rd Ste 2c, Morro Bay (93442-2300)
P.O. Box 877 (93443-0877)
PHONE.................................805 772-6066
Debbie Bertrando, *CEO*
Jennifer Gaalswyk, *CFO*
EMP: 99 **EST:** 2008
SALES: 99.8K **Privately Held**
SIC: 8093 Specialty outpatient clinics

(P-22681)
SOUTH BAYLO UNIVERSITY
Also Called: South Baylo Acupuncture Clinic
2727 W 6th St, Los Angeles (90057-3111)
PHONE.................................213 387-2414
David J Park, *President*
Mimi Park, *Officer*
Kee H Park, *Site Mgr*
EMP: 136
SALES (corp-wide): 6.8MM **Privately Held**
SIC: 8093 8221 8049
PA: South Baylo University
1126 N Brookhurst St
Anaheim CA 92801
714 533-1495

(P-22682)
SOUTH CNTL HEATLH & REHAB PROG
Also Called: Barbour & Floyd Medical Assoc
2620 Industry Way, Lynwood (90262-4024)
PHONE.................................310 667-4070
Jack M Barbour, *Principal*
EMP: 53 **Privately Held**
SIC: 8093 Rehabilitation center, outpatient treatment
PA: South Central Health & Rehabilitation Program
2610 Industry Way Ste A
Lynwood CA 90262
-

(P-22683)
SOUTH CNTL HEATLH & REHAB PROG
Also Called: Scharp's Oasis House
5201 S Vermont Ave, Los Angeles (90037-3527)
PHONE.................................323 751-2677
Jack Barbour, *Director*
EMP: 100 **Privately Held**
SIC: 8093 Mental health clinic, outpatient
PA: South Central Health & Rehabilitation Program
2610 Industry Way Ste A
Lynwood CA 90262
-

(P-22684)
SOUTHERN CALIFORNIA ALCOHOL AN (PA)
11500 Paramount Blvd, Downey (90241-4530)
PHONE.................................562 923-4545

Lynne Appel, *CEO*
Gary Munger, *Ch of Bd*
Marsie Alford, *CFO*
Judith Edwards, *Treasurer*
Leon Emerson, *Treasurer*
EMP: 60 **EST:** 1972
SALES: 9.3MM **Privately Held**
SIC: 8093 Specialty outpatient clinics

(P-22685)
SOUTHWEST CORRECTIONAL MEDICAL
Also Called: Correctional Medical Grp
2511 Garden Rd Ste A160, Monterey (93940-5377)
PHONE.................................831 641-3298
Kip Hallman, *CEO*
Elaine Hustedt, *COO*
Don Myll, *CFO*
Dan Hustedt,
EMP: 60 **EST:** 2014
SQ FT: 12,000
SALES: 1.1MM
SALES (corp-wide): 16.9MM **Privately Held**
SIC: 8093 Mental health clinic, outpatient
HQ: Correctional Medical Group Companies, Inc.
3911 Sorrento Valley Blvd # 130
San Diego CA 92121
831 649-8994

(P-22686)
SPENCER RECOVERY CENTERS INC (PA)
1316 S Coast Hwy, Laguna Beach (92651-3118)
P.O. Box 9296 (92652-7261)
PHONE.................................949 376-3705
Chris Spencer, *President*
Cindy Spencer, *Admin Sec*
Melissa Mounie, *Admin Asst*
EMP: 53
SQ FT: 2,000
SALES (est): 5.8MM **Privately Held**
WEB: www.spencerrecovery.com
SIC: 8093 Alcohol clinic, outpatient; substance abuse clinics (outpatient)

(P-22687)
SPIRIT OF WOMAN OF CALIFORNIA
327 W Belmont Ave, Fresno (93728-2801)
PHONE.................................559 233-4353
Candis Bazley, *Administration*
James Betts, *Chairman*
Dallas Nuemann, *Treasurer*
Audrey Riley, *Principal*
Jennette Williams, *Principal*
EMP: 52
SALES: 1.6MM **Privately Held**
WEB: www.spiritofwomanunlimited.com
SIC: 8093 Substance abuse clinics (outpatient)

(P-22688)
STRATEGIES FOR CHANGE (PA)
4343 Williamsbourgh Dr, Sacramento (95823-2006)
PHONE.................................916 395-3552
Bobby J Davis, *Exec Dir*
B J Davis, *Exec Dir*
Sue Strausser, *Info Tech Mgr*
EMP: 60
SQ FT: 8,000
SALES: 2.8MM **Privately Held**
SIC: 8093 Substance abuse clinics (outpatient)

(P-22689)
SUBACUTE TRTMNT ADOLESCNT REHA (PA)
Also Called: Stars
545 Estudillo Ave, San Leandro (94577-4611)
PHONE.................................510 352-9200
Peter Zucker, *President*
John Weller, *CFO*
Kent Dunlap, *Senior VP*
EMP: 77
SQ FT: 7,442

SALES: 3.9MM **Privately Held**
SIC: **8093** 8051 Mental health clinic, outpatient; substance abuse clinics (outpatient); drug clinic, outpatient; rehabilitation center, outpatient treatment; mental retardation hospital

(P-22690)
SUTTER HEALTH
Also Called: Sutter Auburn Faith Hospital
11775 Education St # 201, Auburn
(95602-2453)
PHONE.....................530 888-4500
Mitch Hanna, *CEO*
Nancy Turner, *Executive*
Lynda Dasaro, *Human Res Dir*
Yvette Martinez, *Hum Res Coord*
Ingrid Metzler, *Internal Med*
EMP: 650
SQ FT: 7,584
SALES (corp-wide): 12.4B **Privately Held**
WEB: www.sutterhealth.org
SIC: **8093** 8062 8011 Rehabilitation center, outpatient treatment; general medical & surgical hospitals; hospital, medical school affiliated with nursing & residency; freestanding emergency medical center
PA: Sutter Health
2200 River Plaza Dr
Sacramento CA 95833
916 733-8800

(P-22691)
TARZANA TREATMENT CENTERS INC
422 W Rancho Vista Blvd C280, Palmdale
(93551-3793)
PHONE.....................818 654-3815
Albert Senella, *President*
EMP: 115
SALES (corp-wide): 49.1MM **Privately Held**
SIC: **8093** Substance abuse clinics (outpatient)
PA: Tarzana Treatment Centers, Inc.
18646 Oxnard St
Tarzana CA 91356
818 996-1051

(P-22692)
TARZANA TREATMENT CENTERS INC (PA)
18646 Oxnard St, Tarzana (91356-1411)
PHONE.....................818 996-1051
Albert Senella, *President*
Sylvia Cadena, *CFO*
Bobbi Sloan, *Corp Secy*
Kathy Nguyen, *Admin Asst*
Rochelle Price, *Admin Asst*
EMP: 160
SQ FT: 14,000
SALES: 49.1MM **Privately Held**
WEB: www.tarzanatc.com
SIC: **8093** 8322 8063 Mental health clinic, outpatient; individual & family services; psychiatric hospitals

(P-22693)
TARZANA TREATMENT CENTERS INC
Also Called: Tarzana Trtmnt Ctrs LNG Bch O
5190 Atlantic Ave, Lakewood (90805-6510)
PHONE.....................562 428-4111
EMP: 138
SALES (corp-wide): 49.1MM **Privately Held**
SIC: **8093** 8299 Substance abuse clinics (outpatient); airline training
PA: Tarzana Treatment Centers, Inc.
18646 Oxnard St
Tarzana CA 91356
818 996-1051

(P-22694)
TARZANA TREATMENT CENTERS INC
2101 Magnolia Ave, Long Beach
(90806-4521)
PHONE.....................562 218-1868
Angela Knox, *Branch Mgr*
Devin Smith, *Technician*
EMP: 50
SQ FT: 11,482

SALES (corp-wide): 49.1MM **Privately Held**
WEB: www.tarzanatc.com
SIC: **8093** Substance abuse clinics (outpatient)
PA: Tarzana Treatment Centers, Inc.
18646 Oxnard St
Tarzana CA 91356
818 996-1051

(P-22695)
TARZANA TREATMENT CENTERS INC
Also Called: Tarzana Treatment Ctr
44447 10th St W, Lancaster (93534-3324)
PHONE.....................661 726-2630
Theresa Scott, *Director*
Marcus Nelson, *Info Tech Mgr*
Jennifer Poillot, *Manager*
Teque Geer, *Supervisor*
EMP: 70
SALES (corp-wide): 49.1MM **Privately Held**
WEB: www.tarzanatc.com
SIC: **8093** 8069 8011 Drug clinic, outpatient; drug addiction rehabilitation hospital; clinic, operated by physicians
PA: Tarzana Treatment Centers, Inc.
18646 Oxnard St
Tarzana CA 91356
818 996-1051

(P-22696)
TELECARE LA STEP DOWN
4335 Atlantic Ave, Long Beach
(90807-2803)
PHONE.....................562 216-4900
Mariela Gorosito, *Branch Mgr*
EMP: 50
SALES (est): 483.4K **Privately Held**
SIC: **8093** Mental health clinic, outpatient

(P-22697)
TELECARE LAS POSADAS
1756 S Lewis Rd, Camarillo (93012-8520)
PHONE.....................805 383-3669
Larry Berent, *Principal*
EMP: 60
SALES (est): 141.1K **Privately Held**
SIC: **8093** 8082 Mental health clinic, outpatient; home health care services

(P-22698)
TRANSITIONS - MENTAL HLTH ASSN
117 W Tunnell St, Santa Maria
(93458-4096)
PHONE.....................805 614-4940
Frank Ricceri, *Principal*
EMP: 64 **Privately Held**
SIC: **8093** 8049 Mental health clinic, outpatient; psychologist, psychotherapist & hypnotist
PA: Transitions - Mental Health Association
784 High St
San Luis Obispo CA 93401

(P-22699)
TRANSITIONS - MENTAL HLTH ASSN
Also Called: Lompoc Act
401 E Cypress Ave, Lompoc (93436-6806)
PHONE.....................805 865-1940
Frank S Ricceri, *President*
EMP: 64 **Privately Held**
SIC: **8093** Mental health clinic, outpatient
PA: Transitions - Mental Health Association
784 High St
San Luis Obispo CA 93401

(P-22700)
TRI CITY MENTAL HEALTH CENTER
1900 Royalty Dr, Pomona (91767-3032)
PHONE.....................909 784-3200
Debbie Johnson, *Branch Mgr*
EMP: 60
SALES (corp-wide): 6.2MM **Privately Held**
SIC: **8093** 8322 Mental health clinic, outpatient; individual & family services

PA: Tri City Mental Health Center
2008 N Garey Ave Ste 2c
Pomona CA 91767
909 623-6131

(P-22701)
TULE RIVER INDIAN HLTH CTR INC
380 N Reservation Rd, Porterville
(93257-9673)
P.O. Box 768 (93258-0768)
PHONE.....................559 784-2316
Zahid Sheikh, *CEO*
Casey Carrillo, *CFO*
EMP: 65
SQ FT: 15,000
SALES: 10.5MM **Privately Held**
SIC: **8093** Specialty outpatient clinics

(P-22702)
TURN BEHAVIORAL HLTH SVCS INC (PA)
9465 Farnham St, San Diego
(92123-1308)
PHONE.....................858 573-2600
Kimberly Bond, *CEO*
Stacy Maxa, *CFO*
Michael Hawkey, *Senior VP*
Ron Stark, *Vice Pres*
Laura L Whitehouse, *Vice Pres*
EMP: 70
SQ FT: 18,000
SALES: 77.3MM **Privately Held**
WEB: www.mhsinc.org
SIC: **8093** Mental health clinic, outpatient

(P-22703)
TURN BEHAVIORAL HLTH SVCS INC
Also Called: MHS
2550 W Clinton Ave, Fresno (93705-4201)
PHONE.....................559 264-7521
Kimberly R Bond, *President*
EMP: 53
SALES (corp-wide): 77.3MM **Privately Held**
SIC: **8093** 8011 Mental health clinic, outpatient; medical centers
PA: Turn Behavioral Health Services, Inc.
9465 Farnham St
San Diego CA 92123
858 573-2600

(P-22704)
UHS-CORONA INC
Also Called: Corona Regional Medical Center
730 Magnolia Ave, Corona (92879-3117)
PHONE.....................951 736-7200
Pat Sanders, *Director*
David Aguirre, *Marketing Staff*
EMP: 200
SALES (corp-wide): 10.4B **Publicly Held**
SIC: **8093** 8062 8069 8051 Rehabilitation center, outpatient treatment; general medical & surgical hospitals; specialty hospitals, except psychiatric; skilled nursing care facilities
HQ: Uhs-Corona, Inc.
800 S Main St
Corona CA 92882
951 737-4343

(P-22705)
UNITED HEALTH CTRS SAN JOAQUIN (PA)
650 S Zediker Ave Bldg 3, Parlier
(93648-2667)
P.O. Box 790 (93648-0790)
PHONE.....................559 646-6618
Colleen Curtis, *CEO*
Justin Preas, *COO*
Robert Shankerman, *Principal*
Maria Quinones, *Human Res Dir*
Peter Lopez, *Personnel*
EMP: 412
SQ FT: 7,500
SALES: 71MM **Privately Held**
WEB: www.unitedhealthcenters.org
SIC: **8093** Specialty outpatient clinics

(P-22706)
UNITED HEALTH CTRS SAN JOAQUIN
Also Called: Orange Cove Health Center
445 11th St, Orange Cove (93646-2211)
P.O. Box 427 (93646-0427)
PHONE.....................559 626-4031
Lynee Wilder, *Manager*
EMP: 51
SQ FT: 14,623
SALES (corp-wide): 71MM **Privately Held**
SIC: **8093** Family planning clinic
PA: United Health Centers Of The San Joaquin Valley
650 S Zediker Ave Bldg 3
Parlier CA 93648
559 646-6618

(P-22707)
UNIVERSAL CARE INC (PA)
Also Called: Smile Wide Dental
19762 Macarthur Blvd # 100, Irvine
(92612-2425)
PHONE.....................562 424-6200
Howard E Davis, *CEO*
Mark Gunter, *CFO*
Jay Davis, *Vice Pres*
Jeffrey Davis, *Admin Sec*
EMP: 350
SQ FT: 73,000
SALES (est): 23.4MM **Privately Held**
WEB: www.universalcare.com
SIC: **8093** Specialty outpatient clinics

(P-22708)
UPLIFT FAMILY SERVICES
Also Called: Emq Familiesfirst
499 Loma Alta Ave, Los Gatos
(95030-6227)
PHONE.....................408 379-3790
Cynthia Goodman, *Branch Mgr*
EMP: 100
SALES (corp-wide): 93.6MM **Privately Held**
SIC: **8093** 8063 8011 Mental health clinic, outpatient; hospital for the mentally ill; offices & clinics of medical doctors
PA: Uplift Family Services
251 Llewellyn Ave
Campbell CA 95008
408 379-3790

(P-22709)
VERDUGO MENTAL HEALTH
1540 E Colorado St, Glendale
(91205-1514)
PHONE.....................818 244-7257
Jeff Smith, *Exec Dir*
Karo Povolitis, *Ch of Bd*
David Igler, *Vice Ch Bd*
Lois Neil, *Vice Pres*
Richard Slavett, *Admin Sec*
EMP: 64 **EST:** 1957
SALES (est): 2.1MM **Privately Held**
WEB: www.vmhc.org
SIC: **8093** Mental health clinic, outpatient

(P-22710)
VETERINARY PRACTICE ASSOC INC
Also Called: Veterinary Specialty Hospital
10435 Sorrento Valley Rd, San Diego
(92121-1607)
PHONE.....................949 833-9020
Keith P Richter, *CEO*
Gilbert Velasquez, *Administration*
Laura Stokking, *Dermatology*
Courtney Zwahlen, *Oncology*
EMP: 150
SQ FT: 26,280
SALES: 18MM **Privately Held**
SIC: **8093** Specialty outpatient clinics

(P-22711)
VIBRANTCARE OUTPATIENT REHAB (PA)
2270 Douglas Blvd Ste 216, Roseville
(95661-4239)
PHONE.....................916 782-1212
David Smith, *President*
Roberto Saavedra, *Administration*
Brandon Brown, *Opers Staff*
Kari Kockler, *Opers Staff*
Alice Veley, *Assistant*

P R O D U C T S & S V C S

EMP: 65
SALES (est): 23.8MM **Privately Held**
SIC: 8093 Rehabilitation center, outpatient treatment

(P-22712)
VICTOR CMNTY SUPPORT SVCS INC (PA)
1360 E Lassen Ave, Chico (95973-7823)
PHONE.................................530 893-0758
Douglas Scott, *CEO*
Lenny Verser, *CFO*
Rebecca Reed, *Internal Med*
Lindsay Doss, *Manager*
EMP: 402
SQ FT: 4,500
SALES: 37.7MM **Privately Held**
SIC: 8093 Mental health clinic, outpatient

(P-22713)
VISIONS UNLIMITED (PA)
6833 Stockton Blvd # 485, Sacramento (95823-2372)
PHONE.................................916 394-0800
Roleda Bates, *CEO*
EMP: 104
SQ FT: 20,000
SALES: 3.6MM **Privately Held**
WEB: www.vuinc.org
SIC: 8093 Mental health clinic, outpatient

(P-22714)
WELLSPACE HEALTH (PA)
Also Called: Effort, The
1820 J St, Sacramento (95811-3010)
PHONE.................................916 325-5556
Robert Caulk, *CEO*
Jonathan Porteus, *President*
Chue Vang, *Analyst*
EMP: 56
SQ FT: 12,500
SALES (est): 13.5MM **Privately Held**
WEB: www.theeffort.com
SIC: 8093 Mental health clinic, outpatient; alcohol clinic, outpatient; rehabilitation center, outpatient treatment

(P-22715)
WEST OAKLAND HEALTH COUNCIL (PA)
Also Called: West Oakland Health Center
700 Adeline St, Oakland (94607-2608)
PHONE.................................510 835-9610
Benjamin Pettus, *CEO*
EMP: 145
SQ FT: 26,000
SALES (est): 23MM **Privately Held**
SIC: 8093 8021 8011 Mental health clinic, outpatient; drug clinic, outpatient; dental clinic; offices & clinics of medical doctors

(P-22716)
WESTCOAST CHILDRENS CLINIC
3301 E 12th St Ste 259, Oakland (94601-2940)
PHONE.................................510 269-9030
Stacy Anne Katz, *Exec Dir*
Eric Kelly, *COO*
Jeff Wands, *CFO*
Mariana Ordaz, *Admin Asst*
Michael Schrecker, *Network Mgr*
EMP: 140
SALES: 14.4MM **Privately Held**
SIC: 8093 Mental health clinic, outpatient

(P-22717)
WINDSOR RDGE RHBLTTION CTR LLC
350 Iris Dr, Salinas (93906-3514)
PHONE.................................831 449-1515
Lee C Samson,
Lawrence E Feigen,
EMP: 99
SALES: 13.4MM **Privately Held**
SIC: 8093 Rehabilitation center, outpatient treatment

(P-22718)
WOMEN HEALTH CENTER (PA)
1469 Humboldt Rd Ste 200, Chico (95928-9203)
PHONE.................................530 891-1917
Shauna Heckert, *Exec Dir*
Kimberly Edmunds, *Manager*

EMP: 75
SALES (est): 1.9MM **Privately Held**
SIC: 8093 Specialty outpatient clinics

(P-22719)
WORKING WITH AUTISM
16530 Ventura Blvd # 310, Encino (91436-4598)
PHONE.................................818 501-4240
Jennifer Sabin, *Director*
Paul Craig, *Director*
Hilya Delband, *Director*
John-Paul Prakash, *Director*
Traci Oberg, *Supervisor*
EMP: 100
SALES (est): 4.9MM **Privately Held**
WEB: www.workingwithautism.com
SIC: 8093 Mental health clinic, outpatient

8099 Health & Allied Svcs, NEC

(P-22720)
1LIFE HEALTHCARE INC
Also Called: One Medical Group
130 Sutter St Fl 2, San Francisco (94104-4009)
P.O. Box 779 (94104-0779)
PHONE.................................415 644-5265
Thomas H Lee MD, *President*
Paul Kirincich, *CFO*
Michael Swartzburg, *Vice Pres*
Melissa Costa, *Admin Asst*
Anneka Huntley, *Manager*
EMP: 98
SQ FT: 11,500
SALES (est): 10.5MM **Privately Held**
WEB: www.1life.com
SIC: 8099 Medical services organization

(P-22721)
24 HOUR FITNESS USA INC
6345 Commerce Blvd, Rohnert Park (94928-2403)
PHONE.................................707 536-0048
John-Paul Scirica, *Manager*
EMP: 50
SALES (corp-wide): 535.4MM **Privately Held**
SIC: 8099 7991 Nutrition services; health club
HQ: 24 Hour Fitness Usa, Inc.
    12647 Alcosta Blvd # 500
    San Ramon CA 94583
    925 543-3100

(P-22722)
24 HOUR FITNESS USA INC
1903 W Empire Ave, Burbank (91504-3433)
PHONE.................................818 531-0257
EMP: 50
SALES (corp-wide): 535.4MM **Privately Held**
SIC: 8099 7991 Nutrition services; physical fitness clubs with training equipment
HQ: 24 Hour Fitness Usa, Inc.
    12647 Alcosta Blvd # 500
    San Ramon CA 94583
    925 543-3100

(P-22723)
24 HOUR FITNESS USA INC
1870 Harbor Blvd Ste 124, Costa Mesa (92627-5023)
PHONE.................................949 610-0651
EMP: 50
SALES (corp-wide): 535.4MM **Privately Held**
SIC: 8099 7991 Nutrition services; physical fitness clubs with training equipment
HQ: 24 Hour Fitness Usa, Inc.
    12647 Alcosta Blvd # 500
    San Ramon CA 94583
    925 543-3100

(P-22724)
AHMC HEALTHCARE INC
500 E Main St, Alhambra (91801-3961)
PHONE.................................626 248-3452
Claudia Ang, *Nurse*
EMP: 968

SALES (corp-wide): 572.3MM **Privately Held**
SIC: 8099 8062 Blood bank; general medical & surgical hospitals
PA: Ahmc Healthcare Inc.
    1000 S Fremont Ave Unit 6
    Alhambra CA 91803
    626 943-7526

(P-22725)
ALIGNMENT HEALTHCARE USA LLC (PA)
1100 W Town And Country R, Orange (92868-4698)
PHONE.................................844 310-2247
John KAO, *CEO*
David Jarboe, *President*
Matt Malin, *President*
Matthew Malin, *President*
Scott Powers, *President*
EMP: 95
SALES (est): 9.6MM **Privately Held**
SIC: 8099 8011 Blood related health services; physical medicine, physician/surgeon

(P-22726)
ALTAMED HEALTH SERVICES CORP
10454 Valley Blvd, El Monte (91731-2444)
PHONE.................................323 889-7847
EMP: 138
SALES (corp-wide): 178.2MM **Privately Held**
SIC: 8099 Childbirth preparation clinic
PA: Altamed Health Services Corporation
    2040 Camfield Ave
    Commerce CA 90040
    323 725-8751

(P-22727)
ALTAMED HEALTH SERVICES CORP
Also Called: Slauson Plaza Med Group
9436 Slauson Ave, Pico Rivera (90660-4748)
PHONE.................................562 949-8717
Alfredo Nunez, *Branch Mgr*
Anh Le, *Gnrl Med Prac*
Marlo Herrera, *Physician Asst*
Elsa Amezquita, *Nursing Dir*
EMP: 60
SALES (corp-wide): 178.2MM **Privately Held**
WEB: www.altamed.org
SIC: 8099 8011 Medical services organization; clinic, operated by physicians
PA: Altamed Health Services Corporation
    2040 Camfield Ave
    Commerce CA 90040
    323 725-8751

(P-22728)
AMERICAN HLTHCARE ADM SVCS INC
Also Called: American Health Care
3850 Atherton Rd, Rocklin (95765-3700)
PHONE.................................916 773-7227
Lance Aizen, *CEO*
Christine Lee, *Ch Credit Ofcr*
EMP: 490
SQ FT: 8,000
SALES (est): 21.3MM **Privately Held**
WEB: www.americanhealthcare.com
SIC: 8099 Medical services organization

(P-22729)
AMERICAN INDIAN HEALTH & SVCS
4141 State St Ste B11, Santa Barbara (93110-1898)
PHONE.................................805 681-7356
Scott Black, *Exec Dir*
Merin McCabe-Black, *Vice Pres*
Martha Vasquez, *Admin Asst*
Hollanda A Leon, *Family Practiti*
Allison Chin, *Fmly & Gen Dent*
EMP: 50
SQ FT: 4,000
SALES: 9.1MM **Privately Held**
SIC: 8099 Health screening service

(P-22730)
AMERICAN NATIONAL RED CROSS
6230 Claremont Ave, Oakland (94618-1324)
PHONE.................................510 594-5100
Jay Winkenbach, *CEO*
Patricia Lari, *Personnel Exec*
EMP: 165
SQ FT: 42,714
SALES (corp-wide): 2.5B **Privately Held**
WEB: www.redcross.org
SIC: 8099 Blood related health services
PA: The American National Red Cross
    430 17th St Nw
    Washington DC 20006
    202 737-8300

(P-22731)
AMERICAN NATIONAL RED CROSS
100 Red Cross Cir, Pomona (91768-2580)
PHONE.................................909 859-7006
Joan Manning, *General Mgr*
Dan D'Angelo, *Associate Dir*
Janelle Brown, *Administration*
Ben Vigna, *Analyst*
EMP: 1200
SALES (corp-wide): 2.5B **Privately Held**
WEB: www.redcross.org
SIC: 8099 Blood donor station
PA: The American National Red Cross
    430 17th St Nw
    Washington DC 20006
    202 737-8300

(P-22732)
ANKA BEHAVIORAL HEALTH INC
458 Almond Dr, Lodi (95240-7823)
PHONE.................................209 982-4697
EMP: 91
SALES (corp-wide): 40.4MM **Privately Held**
SIC: 8099 Childbirth preparation clinic
PA: Anka Behavioral Health, Incorporated
    1850 Gateway Blvd Ste 900
    Concord CA 94520
    925 825-4700

(P-22733)
ANKA BEHAVIORAL HEALTH INC
7515 Willow Way, Citrus Heights (95610-2936)
PHONE.................................916 722-3700
EMP: 91
SALES (corp-wide): 40.4MM **Privately Held**
SIC: 8099 Childbirth preparation clinic
PA: Anka Behavioral Health, Incorporated
    1850 Gateway Blvd Ste 900
    Concord CA 94520
    925 825-4700

(P-22734)
ANKA BEHAVIORAL HEALTH INC
Also Called: Casa Fremont
5149 Winston Ct, Fremont (94536-6523)
PHONE.................................510 494-1567
Wayne Thurston, *Director*
EMP: 69
SALES (corp-wide): 40.4MM **Privately Held**
SIC: 8099 Childbirth preparation clinic
PA: Anka Behavioral Health, Incorporated
    1850 Gateway Blvd Ste 900
    Concord CA 94520
    925 825-4700

(P-22735)
APRIA HEALTHCARE LLC
Also Called: Distribution Warehouse
1680 Tide Ct Ste B, Woodland (95776-6237)
PHONE.................................530 669-6441
Dan Starck, *Branch Mgr*
EMP: 60 **Privately Held**
WEB: www.respimed.com
SIC: 8099 Blood related health services
HQ: Apria Healthcare Llc
    26220 Enterprise Ct
    Lake Forest CA 92630
    949 639-2163

(P-22736)
APRIA HEALTHCARE LLC
220 Scttsvlle Blvd Bldg A, Jackson (95642)
PHONE..................................209 223-7727
Lawrence Mastrovich, *Principal*
EMP: 180 **Privately Held**
WEB: www.respimed.com
SIC: **8099** Blood related health services
HQ: Apria Healthcare Llc
26220 Enterprise Ct
Lake Forest CA 92630
949 639-2163

(P-22737)
APRIA HEALTHCARE LLC
26220 Enterprise Ct, Lake Forest
(92630-8405)
PHONE..................................949 639-2000
Jill Pusser, *President*
Luz Espinoza, *Branch Mgr*
David Bullivant, *Sr Software Eng*
Benjamin R Garcia, *Buyer*
Stephanie Christianson, *Opers Staff*
EMP: 173 **Privately Held**
SIC: **8099** Blood related health services
HQ: Apria Healthcare Llc
26220 Enterprise Ct
Lake Forest CA 92630
949 639-2163

(P-22738)
ARBORMED INC (PA)
725 W Town And Country Rd, Orange
(92868-4703)
PHONE..................................714 689-1500
Charles Morf, *President*
William Shaw, *CFO*
Scott Everson, *Vice Pres*
Karen Isaacs, *Human Res Dir*
EMP: 175
SQ FT: 11,000
SALES (est): 3.1MM **Privately Held**
WEB: www.arbormed.com
SIC: **8099** 8742 Medical services organization; management consulting services

(P-22739)
ATLAS LIFT TECH INC
210 Porter Dr Ste 300, San Ramon
(94583-1525)
PHONE..................................415 283-1804
Eric Race, *President*
Wendy McCollom, *CFO*
Jillian Einck, *Executive Asst*
Alvin Huggins, *Controller*
Bz Petroff, *Human Res Dir*
EMP: 150
SALES (est): 8.7MM **Privately Held**
SIC: **8099** Health screening service

(P-22740)
BAKERSFIELD FAMILY MED GROUP
5601 Auburn St Unit A, Bakersfield
(93306-2977)
PHONE..................................661 846-3605
EMP: 66
SALES (corp-wide): 26.9MM **Privately Held**
SIC: **8099** Childbirth preparation clinic
PA: Bakersfield Family Medical Group, Inc
4580 California Ave
Bakersfield CA 93309
661 327-4411

(P-22741)
BEHAVIORAL HEALTH WORKS INC
1301 E Orangewood Ave, Anaheim
(92805-6807)
PHONE..................................800 249-1266
Dr Robert Douk, *CEO*
Montgomery Lim, *Director*
EMP: 99 EST: 2011
SALES (est): 209.7K **Privately Held**
SIC: **8099** Blood related health services

(P-22742)
BIO-MED SERVICES INC
Also Called: Prime Healthcare Services
3300 E Guasti Rd, Ontario (91761-8655)
PHONE..................................909 235-4400
Prem Reddy, *CEO*
EMP: 85

SALES (est): 869.3K
SALES (corp-wide): 3.4B **Privately Held**
SIC: **8099** Medical services organization
HQ: Prime Healthcare Services Inc
3300 E Guasti Rd Ste 300
Ontario CA 91761
-

(P-22743)
BIOMAT USA INC
2410 Lillyvale Ave, Los Angeles
(90032-3514)
PHONE..................................310 772-7777
Barry Plost, *Manager*
EMP: 975
SALES (corp-wide): 696.8MM **Privately Held**
SIC: **8099** Plasmapherous center; blood bank
HQ: Biomat Usa, Inc.
2410 Lillyvale Ave
Los Angeles CA 90032
323 225-2221

(P-22744)
BIOMAT USA INC (DH)
2410 Lillyvale Ave, Los Angeles
(90032-3514)
PHONE..................................323 225-2221
Gregory Rich, *CEO*
Max Debrouwer, *CFO*
Shinji Wada, *Exec VP*
David Bell, *Vice Pres*
Denisse Avila, *Technician*
▲ EMP: 50
SQ FT: 20,000
SALES (est): 162.4MM
SALES (corp-wide): 696.8MM **Privately Held**
SIC: **8099** Plasmapherous center; blood bank
HQ: Grifols Shared Services North America, Inc.
2410 Lillyvale Ave
Los Angeles CA 90032
323 225-2221

(P-22745)
BIOMAT USA INC
246 Bernard St, Bakersfield (93305-3541)
PHONE..................................661 863-0621
Gustavo Castellanos, *Manager*
EMP: 62
SALES (corp-wide): 696.8MM **Privately Held**
SIC: **8099** Blood bank
HQ: Biomat Usa, Inc.
2410 Lillyvale Ave
Los Angeles CA 90032
323 225-2221

(P-22746)
BLOOD BANK OF REDWOODS (PA)
Also Called: Blood Center of The Pacific
3505 Industrial Dr, Santa Rosa
(95403-2064)
PHONE..................................707 545-1222
Cathy Bryan, *Administration*
EMP: 110
SQ FT: 13,540
SALES (est): 10.1MM **Privately Held**
WEB: www.bbr.org
SIC: **8099** Blood bank

(P-22747)
BLOOD BANK OF SAN BERNARDINO A (PA)
Also Called: Lifestream
384 W Orange Show Rd, San Bernardino
(92408-2028)
P.O. Box 1429 (92402-1429)
PHONE..................................909 885-6503
Frederick B Axelrod, *CEO*
Robert Albee, *Vice Pres*
Joseph Dunn, *Vice Pres*
Steven Favero, *Vice Pres*
Susan Marquez, *Vice Pres*
EMP: 280
SQ FT: 50,000
SALES: 66.5MM **Privately Held**
WEB: www.bbsrc.org
SIC: **8099** Blood bank; blood donor station

(P-22748)
BLOOD CENTERS OF PACIFIC (PA)
Also Called: Shasta Blood Center
270 Masonic Ave, San Francisco
(94118-4496)
PHONE..................................415 567-6400
Nora Hirschler, *President*
Lage Anderson, *Treasurer*
Kent Corley, *Trustee*
Angelina Lee, *Officer*
Sylvia Turner, *Admin Asst*
EMP: 120
SQ FT: 67,000
SALES: 59.7MM **Privately Held**
SIC: **8099** Blood bank

(P-22749)
BLOOD CENTERS OF PACIFIC
Also Called: NAPA Solano Cmnty Blood Ctr
1325 Gateway Blvd Ste C1, Fairfield
(94533-6919)
PHONE..................................707 428-6001
Lana Dyson, *Manager*
EMP: 50
SALES (corp-wide): 59.7MM **Privately Held**
SIC: **8099** Blood bank
PA: Blood Centers Of The Pacific
270 Masonic Ave
San Francisco CA 94118
415 567-6400

(P-22750)
BLOODSOURCE INC (PA)
10536 Peter A Mccuen Blvd, Mather
(95655-4128)
PHONE..................................916 456-1500
Michael J Fuller, *CEO*
Jim Eldridge, *CFO*
Dirk Johnson, *Vice Pres*
EMP: 325
SQ FT: 105,000
SALES: 85MM **Privately Held**
WEB: www.bloodsource.org
SIC: **8099** Blood bank

(P-22751)
BLOODSOURCE INC
382 E Yosemite Ave, Merced (95340-9100)
PHONE..................................209 724-0428
Jaime Suarez, *Manager*
EMP: 54
SALES (corp-wide): 85MM **Privately Held**
SIC: **8099** Blood bank
PA: Bloodsource, Inc.
10536 Peter A Mccuen Blvd
Mather CA 95655
916 456-1500

(P-22752)
BLOODSOURCE INC
3099 Fair Oaks Blvd, Sacramento
(95864-5613)
PHONE..................................916 488-1701
Whitney Karen, *Branch Mgr*
EMP: 50
SALES (corp-wide): 85MM **Privately Held**
SIC: **8099** Blood bank
PA: Bloodsource, Inc.
10536 Peter A Mccuen Blvd
Mather CA 95655
916 456-1500

(P-22753)
CALIFORNIA CRYOBANK INC
Also Called: Califrnia Cryobank Lf Sciences
611 Gateway Blvd Ste 820, South San
Francisco (94080)
PHONE..................................650 635-1420
EMP: 300
SALES (corp-wide): 16.1MM **Privately Held**
SIC: **8099** Blood bank
PA: California Cryobank, Inc.
11915 La Grange Ave
Los Angeles CA 90025
310 443-5244

(P-22754)
CALIFORNIA CRYOBANK INC (PA)
11915 La Grange Ave, Los Angeles
(90025-5213)
PHONE..................................310 443-5244
Charles A Sims, *CEO*
Lorraine Kirby, *Owner*
Pamela Richardson, *President*
Don Fish, *Lab Dir*
Dave Moss, *Info Tech Dir*
EMP: 75
SQ FT: 21,300
SALES (est): 14.6MM **Privately Held**
WEB: www.cryobank.com
SIC: **8099** Sperm bank

(P-22755)
CALIFORNIA FORENSIC MED GROUP
2801 Meadow Lark Dr, San Diego
(92123-2709)
PHONE..................................858 694-4690
Penny Looper, *General Mgr*
EMP: 70
SALES (corp-wide): 35.8MM **Privately Held**
WEB: www.cfmg.com
SIC: **8099** 9223 Medical services organization; jail, government
PA: California Forensic Medical Group, Incorporated
2511 Garden Rd Ste A160
Monterey CA 93940
831 649-8994

(P-22756)
CALIFORNIA FORENSIC MED GROUP
800 S Victoria Ave, Ventura (93009-0001)
PHONE..................................805 654-3343
Elaine Hustedt, *Vice Pres*
EMP: 100
SALES (corp-wide): 35.8MM **Privately Held**
WEB: www.cfmg.com
SIC: **8099** Medical services organization
PA: California Forensic Medical Group, Incorporated
2511 Garden Rd Ste A160
Monterey CA 93940
831 649-8994

(P-22757)
CARE 1ST HEALTH PLAN (PA)
601 Potrero Grande Dr # 2, Monterey Park
(91755-7444)
PHONE..................................323 889-6638
Maureen Tyson, *President*
Michael Lasconia, *President*
Carol Thornton, *President*
Anna Tran, *CEO*
Janet Jan, *CFO*
EMP: 165
SALES (est): 30.4MM **Privately Held**
WEB: www.care1st.com
SIC: **8099** Blood related health services

(P-22758)
CAREFUSION CORPORATION
1100 Bird Center Dr, Palm Springs
(92262-8000)
PHONE..................................760 778-7200
Carol Zilm, *President*
Emilio Salgado, *QC Mgr*
EMP: 66
SALES (corp-wide): 12B **Publicly Held**
SIC: **8099** Medical services organization
HQ: Carefusion Corporation
3750 Torrey View Ct
San Diego CA 92130

(P-22759)
CENTER FOR BETTER HEALTH AND
1520 Nutmeg Pl Ste 220, Costa Mesa
(92626-2597)
PHONE..................................714 751-8110
Evan S Marlowe, *Med Doctor*
EMP: 53
SALES (est): 6.5MM **Privately Held**
SIC: **8099** 8011 5734 Health screening service; medical centers; computer software & accessories

P
R
O
D
U
C
T
S

&

S
V
C
S

(P-22760)
CENTER TO PROMOTE HEALTHCARE A (PA)
Also Called: SOCIAL INTEREST SOLUTIONS
1951 Webster St Fl 2, Oakland (94612-2909)
PHONE..................510 834-1300
John Caterham, *President*
Lucy Streett, *General Mgr*
James Holdsworth, *Info Tech Mgr*
CHI Huynh, *Info Tech Mgr*
Immanuel Udaiyar, *Software Dev*
EMP: 58
SQ FT: 6,000
SALES: 26.6MM **Privately Held**
SIC: 8099 Medical services organization

(P-22761)
CENTRAL CALIFORNIA BLOOD CTR
Also Called: Ccbc Reference Lab
4343 W Herndon Ave, Fresno (93722-3794)
PHONE..................559 389-5433
Kenneth Benell, *Branch Mgr*
EMP: 98
SALES (corp-wide): 21.6MM **Privately Held**
SIC: 8099 8071
PA: Central California Blood Center
4343 W Herndon Ave
Fresno CA 93722
559 389-5433

(P-22762)
CENTRAL CALIFORNIA BLOOD CTR
8094 N Cedar Ave, Fresno (93720-1817)
PHONE..................559 324-1211
Dean Eller, *Branch Mgr*
EMP: 98
SALES (corp-wide): 21.6MM **Privately Held**
SIC: 8099 Blood bank
PA: Central California Blood Center
4343 W Herndon Ave
Fresno CA 93722
559 389-5433

(P-22763)
CENTRAL CALIFORNIA BLOOD CTR (PA)
4343 W Herndon Ave, Fresno (93722-3794)
PHONE..................559 389-5433
Dean Eller, *President*
Jerry Harder, *CFO*
Doane Stewart, *Executive*
Saiyed Iqbal, *Info Tech Dir*
Shanel Jackson, *Info Tech Mgr*
EMP: 180
SQ FT: 53,000
SALES: 21.6MM **Privately Held**
WEB: www.cencalblood.org
SIC: 8099 Blood bank

(P-22764)
CENTRAL CALIFORNIA FACULTY MED
1085 W Minnesota Ave, Turlock (95382-0827)
PHONE..................209 620-6937
Jason Elliot, *Branch Mgr*
EMP: 262
SALES (corp-wide): 54.6MM **Privately Held**
SIC: 8099 Blood related health services
PA: Central California Faculty Medical Group, Inc.
2625 E Divisadero St
Fresno CA 93721
559 453-5200

(P-22765)
CHICO CSU
400 W 1st St, Chico (95929-0001)
PHONE..................530 898-3917
James Holloway, *Principal*
Rob White, *Planning*
Mike Wood, *Prgrmr*
K Aiken, *Marketing Staff*
Melanie Connor, *Council Mbr*
EMP: 61

SALES (est): 4MM **Privately Held**
SIC: 8099 Health & allied services

(P-22766)
CHIRON CORPORATION
4560 Horton St, Emeryville (94608-2916)
PHONE..................510 655-8730
Edward E Penhoet, *President*
Steve Litster, *Engineer*
EMP: 72
SALES (est): 70.9MM
SALES (corp-wide): 39.8B **Privately Held**
WEB: www.chiron.com
SIC: 8099 Blood related health services
HQ: Novartis Vaccines And Diagnostics, Inc.
475 Green Oaks Pkwy
Holly Springs NC 27540
617 871-7000

(P-22767)
CITRUS VLY HLTH PARTNERS INC
1325 N Grand Ave Ste 300, Covina (91724-4046)
PHONE..................626 732-3100
Carol Eaton, *Principal*
EMP: 1127 **Privately Held**
SIC: 8099 Blood related health services
PA: Citrus Valley Health Partners, Inc.
210 W San Bernardino Rd
Covina CA 91723

(P-22768)
CLINICA SIERRA VISTA
1430 Truxtun Ave Ste 300, Bakersfield (93301-5220)
PHONE..................661 326-6490
Steve Shilling, *Director*
EMP: 50
SALES (corp-wide): 136.6MM **Privately Held**
SIC: 8099 Childbirth preparation clinic
PA: Clinica Sierra Vista
1430 Truxtun Ave Ste 400
Bakersfield CA 93301
661 635-3050

(P-22769)
COMMUNITY BLOOD BANK INC
70025 Highway 111 Ste 101, Rancho Mirage (92270-2935)
PHONE..................760 773-4190
Robert E Albee, *President*
Michelle Shanahan,
EMP: 61 **EST:** 1972
SQ FT: 8,000
SALES: 80.9K **Privately Held**
SIC: 8099 Blood bank

(P-22770)
COUNTY OF GLENN
Also Called: Glenn County Health Svcs Agcy
247 N Villa Ave, Willows (95988-2607)
PHONE..................530 934-6582
Scott Gruendl, *Director*
EMP: 100 **Privately Held**
WEB: www.countyofglen.net
SIC: 8099 9111 Medical services organization; county supervisors' & executives' offices
PA: County Of Glenn
516 W Sycamore St Fl 2
Willows CA 95988
530 934-6410

(P-22771)
COUNTY OF IMPERIAL
Also Called: Public Health Department
935 Broadway Ave, El Centro (92243-2349)
PHONE..................760 482-4441
Evon Smith, *Director*
Holly Maag, *Lab Dir*
EMP: 134 **Privately Held**
WEB: www.imperialcounty.net
SIC: 8099 9111 Health screening service; county supervisors' & executives' offices
PA: County Of Imperial
940 W Main St Ste 208
El Centro CA 92243
760 482-4556

(P-22772)
COUNTY OF LOS ANGELES
Also Called: Countywide Childrens Case MGT
600 S Commwl Ave Fl 2 Flr 2, Los Angeles (90005)
PHONE..................213 739-2360
Bryan Mershon, *Branch Mgr*
EMP: 85 **Privately Held**
SIC: 8099 Blood related health services
PA: County Of Los Angeles
500 W Temple St Ste 437
Los Angeles CA 90012
213 974-1101

(P-22773)
COUNTY OF LOS ANGELES
Also Called: Compton Family Mhc Fsp
546 W Compton Blvd, Compton (90220-3011)
PHONE..................310 885-2100
Phillip Mobley, *Manager*
EMP: 85 **Privately Held**
SIC: 8099 Blood related health services
PA: County Of Los Angeles
500 W Temple St Ste 437
Los Angeles CA 90012
213 974-1101

(P-22774)
COUNTY OF LOS ANGELES
921 E Compton Blvd, Compton (90221-3303)
PHONE..................310 668-6845
Marvin Southard, *Branch Mgr*
EMP: 85 **Privately Held**
SIC: 8099 Blood related health services
PA: County Of Los Angeles
500 W Temple St Ste 437
Los Angeles CA 90012
213 974-1101

(P-22775)
COUNTY OF LOS ANGELES
Also Called: Specilzed Foster Care Pasadena
532 E Colorado Blvd Fl 8, Pasadena (91101-2044)
PHONE..................626 229-3825
Jonathan E Sherin, *Director*
EMP: 85 **Privately Held**
SIC: 8099 Blood related health services
PA: County Of Los Angeles
500 W Temple St Ste 437
Los Angeles CA 90012
213 974-1101

(P-22776)
COUNTY OF LOS ANGELES
Also Called: Department of Health
3530 Wilshire Blvd Fl 9, Los Angeles (90010-2344)
PHONE..................213 351-7800
Michelle Parra PHD, *Manager*
Eloisa Gonzalez, *Info Tech Dir*
Montgomery Messex, *Deputy Dir*
EMP: 70 **Privately Held**
WEB: www.co.la.ca.us
SIC: 8099 9431 Medical services organization; administration of public health programs;
PA: County Of Los Angeles
500 W Temple St Ste 437
Los Angeles CA 90012
213 974-1101

(P-22777)
COUNTY OF LOS ANGELES
Also Called: Los Angeles County Pub Works
5525 Imperial Hwy, South Gate (90280-7417)
PHONE..................562 861-0316
Phil Doudar, *Manager*
EMP: 100 **Privately Held**
WEB: www.co.la.ca.us
SIC: 8099 9111 Blood related health services; executive offices
PA: County Of Los Angeles
500 W Temple St Ste 437
Los Angeles CA 90012
213 974-1101

(P-22778)
COUNTY OF LOS ANGELES
313 N Figueroa St, Los Angeles (90012-2602)
PHONE..................213 240-7780

Valerie Orange, *Branch Mgr*
EMP: 85 **Privately Held**
WEB: www.co.la.ca.us
SIC: 8099 9431 Physical examination & testing services; health statistics center, government
PA: County Of Los Angeles
500 W Temple St Ste 437
Los Angeles CA 90012
213 974-1101

(P-22779)
COUNTY OF RIVERSIDE DEPARTMENT
554 S Paseo Dorotea, Palm Springs (92264-1445)
PHONE..................760 320-1048
EMP: 76
SALES (corp-wide): 3.6MM **Privately Held**
SIC: 8099 Childbirth preparation clinic
PA: The County Of Riverside Department Of Public Health Auxialiary
4065 County Circle Dr
Riverside CA 92503
951 358-5000

(P-22780)
COUNTY OF SAN DIEGO
Also Called: Medical Examiner Forensic Ctr
5570 Overland Ave Ste 101, San Diego (92123-1215)
PHONE..................619 531-4521
Glenn Wagner, *Chief Mktg Ofcr*
EMP: 60 **Privately Held**
WEB: www.sdlcc.org
SIC: 8099 Medical services organization
PA: County Of San Diego
1600 Pacific Hwy Ste 209
San Diego CA 92101
619 531-5880

(P-22781)
CRC HEALTH GROUP INC (HQ)
20400 Stev Creek Blvd 6 Flr 6, Cupertino (95014)
PHONE..................877 272-8668
Jerome E Rhodes, *CEO*
Leanne M Stewart, *CFO*
Philip L Herschman, *Officer*
Kathleen Sylvia, *Exec VP*
John Peloquin, *Vice Pres*
▲ **EMP:** 65
SALES (est): 452.2MM **Publicly Held**
SIC: 8099 Medical services organization

(P-22782)
DELTA BLOOD BANK
1900 W Orangeburg Ave, Modesto (95350-3740)
PHONE..................209 943-3830
Dr Benjamin Spindler, *Principal*
EMP: 100
SQ FT: 6,239
SALES (corp-wide): 2.5B **Privately Held**
SIC: 8099 7389 Blood bank; personal service agents, brokers & bureaus
HQ: Delta Blood Bank
65 N Commerce St
Stockton CA 95202
800 244-6794

(P-22783)
DELTA BLOOD BANK (HQ)
65 N Commerce St, Stockton (95202-2318)
P.O. Box 800 (95201-0800)
PHONE..................800 244-6794
Benjamin Spindler, *CEO*
Robert Lawrence, *Ch of Bd*
Alfonso Figueroa, *CFO*
◆ **EMP:** 85
SQ FT: 30,000
SALES: 3.1MM
SALES (corp-wide): 2.5B **Privately Held**
SIC: 8099 Blood bank
PA: The American National Red Cross
430 17th St Nw
Washington DC 20006
202 737-8300

(P-22784)
DIGNITY HEALTH MED FOUNDATION
6615 Valley Hi Dr, Sacramento (95823-7076)
PHONE...................916 681-6300
Douglas Locke, *Branch Mgr*
Kristina Freas, *Director*
EMP: 76
SALES (corp-wide): 6.7B **Privately Held**
SIC: 8099 8011 Medical services organization; eyes, ears, nose & throat specialist: physician/surgeon
HQ: Dignity Health Medical Foundation
3400 Data Dr
Rancho Cordova CA 95670

(P-22785)
DIGNITY HEALTH MED FOUNDATION
Also Called: Dignity Health Medical Grp
1667 Dominican Way # 134, Santa Cruz (95065-1518)
PHONE...................831 475-8834
George Lenzi, *CFO*
EMP: 95
SALES (corp-wide): 6.7B **Privately Held**
SIC: 8099 Medical rescue squad
HQ: Dignity Health Medical Foundation
3400 Data Dr
Rancho Cordova CA 95670

(P-22786)
DIGNITY HEALTH MED FOUNDATION
Also Called: Dignity Hlth Med Grp-Dominican
9515 Soquel Dr Ste 100, Aptos (95003-4136)
PHONE...................831 535-1560
Cristina Lingo, *General Mgr*
EMP: 95
SALES (corp-wide): 6.7B **Privately Held**
SIC: 8099 Medical services organization
HQ: Dignity Health Medical Foundation
3400 Data Dr
Rancho Cordova CA 95670

(P-22787)
DIGNITY HEALTH MED FOUNDATION
Also Called: Dignity Hlth Med Grp-Dominican
3400 Data Dr, Rancho Cordova (95670-7956)
PHONE...................916 379-2840
Laurie Schwartcz, *President*
EMP: 900
SQ FT: 45,000
SALES (corp-wide): 6.7B **Privately Held**
SIC: 8099 Medical services organization
HQ: Dignity Health Medical Foundation
3400 Data Dr
Rancho Cordova CA 95670

(P-22788)
DIGNITY HEALTH MED FOUNDATION
2110 Prfcional Dr Ste 120, Roseville (95661)
PHONE...................916 787-0404
A Alan White, *Principal*
EMP: 76
SALES (corp-wide): 6.7B **Privately Held**
SIC: 8099 8071 8011 Medical services organization; medical laboratories; radiologist
HQ: Dignity Health Medical Foundation
3400 Data Dr
Rancho Cordova CA 95670

(P-22789)
DIRECT FLOW MEDICAL INC (PA)
3945 Freedom Cir Ste 560, Santa Clara (95054-1269)
PHONE...................707 576-0420
Daniel Lemaitre, *President*
David R Elizondo, *COO*
David Boyle, *CFO*
Alexis Wagle, *Buyer*

David Pozzi, *Director*
EMP: 78
SALES (est): 18.1MM **Privately Held**
WEB: www.directflowmedical.com
SIC: 8099 Medical services organization

(P-22790)
DIVERSIFIED CLINICAL SERVICES
4225 E La Palma Ave, Anaheim (92807-1815)
PHONE...................714 579-8400
James R Sechrist, *Ch of Bd*
EMP: 85
SQ FT: 74,000
SALES (est): 1.1MM **Privately Held**
SIC: 8099 Medical services organization

(P-22791)
DONOR NETWORK WEST (PA)
12667 Alcosta Blvd # 500, San Ramon (94583-4427)
PHONE...................925 480-3100
Cynthia D Siljestrom, *CEO*
Sandra Mejia, *CFO*
Nikole Neidlinger, *Bd of Directors*
Jt Mason, *Senior VP*
Mark Borer, *Vice Pres*
EMP: 121
SQ FT: 41,039
SALES: 81.3MM **Privately Held**
SIC: 8099 Medical services organization

(P-22792)
DONOR NETWORK WEST
Also Called: Ctdn - Redding
5800 Airport Rd Ste B, Redding (96002-9359)
PHONE...................510 418-0336
EMP: 78
SALES (corp-wide): 81.3MM **Privately Held**
SIC: 8099 Medical services organization
PA: Donor Network West
12667 Alcosta Blvd # 500
San Ramon CA 94583
925 480-3100

(P-22793)
DUAL DIAGNOSIS TRTMNT CTR INC
Also Called: Sovereign Health
69640 Highway 111, Rancho Mirage (92270-2868)
PHONE...................949 324-4531
Tonmoy Sharma, *Branch Mgr*
EMP: 178
SALES (corp-wide): 84.5MM **Privately Held**
SIC: 8099 Childbirth preparation clinic
PA: Dual Diagnosis Treatment Center, Inc.
1211 Puerta Del Sol # 200
San Clemente CA 92673
949 276-5553

(P-22794)
EAST BAY FOUNDATION GRAD MED
1411 E 31st St, Oakland (94602-1018)
P.O. Box 309, Concord (94522-0309)
PHONE...................510 437-4197
Theresa Azevedo, *Exec Dir*
Alden Harken, *Ch of Bd*
EMP: 54
SALES: 4.1MM **Privately Held**
SIC: 8099 Medical services organization

(P-22795)
EASTER SEAL SOC SUPERIOR CAL (PA)
Also Called: Easter Seals Main Office
3205 Hurley Way, Sacramento (95864-3853)
PHONE...................916 485-6711
Gary T Kasai, *President*
Sue Harris, *General Mgr*
EMP: 200
SQ FT: 28,500
SALES: 11.6MM **Privately Held**
WEB: www.essuperior.org
SIC: 8099 8093 Medical services organization; rehabilitation center, outpatient treatment

(P-22796)
EASTERN PLUMAS HEALTH CARE (PA)
Also Called: Eastern Plumas Hospital
500 1st Ave, Portola (96122-9406)
PHONE...................530 832-4277
Milind D D, *Cardiology*
Virginia Luhring, *President*
Tom Hayes, *CEO*
Jeri Nelson, *CFO*
Terri Becky, *CIO*
EMP: 161 EST: 1992
SQ FT: 18,500
SALES: 52.8K **Privately Held**
SIC: 8099 8011 8322 Medical services organization; primary care medical clinic; rehabilitation services

(P-22797)
EASY CARE MSO LLC
3900 Kilroy Airport Way # 110, Long Beach (90806-6811)
PHONE...................562 676-9600
Michelle Bui, *President*
EMP: 270
SALES (est): 244K
SALES (corp-wide): 19.8B **Publicly Held**
SIC: 8099 Medical services organization
PA: Molina Healthcare, Inc.
200 Oceangate Ste 100
Long Beach CA 90802
562 435-3666

(P-22798)
EHEALTHWIRECOM INC
2450 Venture Oaks Way # 100, Sacramento (95833-3292)
PHONE...................916 924-8092
Yousry Mekhamer, *Chairman*
Sue Barnes, *Personnel Exec*
EMP: 250
SQ FT: 17,000
SALES (est): 2.8MM **Privately Held**
WEB: www.ehealthline.com
SIC: 8099 Health screening service

(P-22799)
ELIZABETH GLASER PEDIA
16130 Ventura Blvd # 250, Encino (91436-2503)
PHONE...................310 231-0400
Charles Lyons, *Branch Mgr*
EMP: 875
SALES (corp-wide): 126MM **Privately Held**
SIC: 8099 Medical services organization
PA: Elizabeth Glaser Pediatric Aids Foundation
1140 Conn Ave Nw Ste 200
Washington DC 20036
202 296-9165

(P-22800)
EPOCRATES INC (HQ)
50 Hawthorne St, San Francisco (94105-3902)
PHONE...................650 227-1700
Rob Cosinuke, *President*
Meredith Aucker, *President*
Murat Erdem, *President*
Patti Paczkowski, *President*
Howard Schargel, *President*
EMP: 50
SQ FT: 59,000
SALES (est): 19MM
SALES (corp-wide): 1.2B **Publicly Held**
WEB: www.epocrates.com
SIC: 8099 Health screening service
PA: Athenahealth, Inc.
311 Arsenal St Ste 14
Watertown MA 02472
617 402-1000

(P-22801)
EVOLENT HEALTH INC
1 Kearny St Ste 300, San Francisco (94108-5549)
PHONE...................571 389-6000
EMP: 466
SALES (corp-wide): 434.9MM **Publicly Held**
SIC: 8099 Medical services organization
PA: Evolent Health, Inc.
800 N Glebe Rd Ste 500
Arlington VA 22203
571 389-6000

(P-22802)
EXAMONE WORLD WIDE INC
7480 Mission Valley Rd # 101, San Diego (92108-4433)
PHONE...................619 299-3926
EMP: 100
SALES (corp-wide): 7.7B **Publicly Held**
SIC: 8099 Physical examination service, insurance
HQ: Examone World Wide, Inc.
10101 Renner Blvd
Lenexa KS 66219
913 888-1770

(P-22803)
FACEY MEDICAL FOUNDATION (PA)
15451 San Fernando Msn, Mission Hills (91345-1368)
P.O. Box 9601 (91346-9601)
PHONE...................818 365-9531
Bill Gill, *CEO*
Jim Corwin, *CFO*
Janna Boyer, *Executive*
Cheryl Dee, *Executive*
Robert Reaves, *Administration*
EMP: 170
SQ FT: 306,000
SALES: 197.1MM **Privately Held**
WEB: www.facey.com
SIC: 8099 Medical services organization

(P-22804)
FACEY MEDICAL FOUNDATION
11211 Sepulveda Blvd, Mission Hills (91345-1115)
PHONE...................818 837-5677
Cathy Hawes, *Branch Mgr*
Cornelia De Licona MD, *Med Doctor*
EMP: 200
SALES (corp-wide): 197.1MM **Privately Held**
SIC: 8099 8042 8011 Medical services organization; offices & clinics of optometrists; offices & clinics of medical doctors
PA: Facey Medical Foundation
15451 San Fernando Msn
Mission Hills CA 91345
818 365-9531

(P-22805)
FACEY MEDICAL FOUNDATION
Also Called: Facey Medical Group
17909 Soledad Canyon Rd, Santa Clarita (91387-3210)
PHONE...................661 250-5225
Leslie Holland, *Branch Mgr*
Khai Kim T Tram, *Director*
EMP: 60
SALES (corp-wide): 197.1MM **Privately Held**
SIC: 8099 8011 Medical services organization; offices & clinics of medical doctors
PA: Facey Medical Foundation
15451 San Fernando Msn
Mission Hills CA 91345
818 365-9531

(P-22806)
FACEY MEDICAL FOUNDATION
Also Called: Marshall, Spector MD
1237 E Main St, San Gabriel (91776)
PHONE...................626 576-0800
Ana Ventura, *Manager*
EMP: 86
SALES (corp-wide): 197.1MM **Privately Held**
SIC: 8099 8011 Medical services organization; pediatrician
PA: Facey Medical Foundation
15451 San Fernando Msn
Mission Hills CA 91345
818 365-9531

(P-22807)
GLENHAVEN HEALTHCARE LLC
212 W Chevy Chase Dr, Glendale (91204-2318)
PHONE...................818 240-6720
Matthew Karp, *Principal*
Gretta Bernabe, *Principal*
EMP: 68
SALES (est): 800.4K **Privately Held**
SIC: 8099 Health & allied services

P R O D U C T S & S V C S

(P-22808)
GLENVIEW ASSISTED LIVING LLP
1950 Calle Barcelona, Carlsbad (92009-8401)
PHONE...................760 704-6800
Justin Wilson, *Partner*
EMP: 50
SALES (est): 976.9K **Privately Held**
SIC: 8099 8361 8052 Health & allied services; residential care; intermediate care facilities

(P-22809)
GLOBAL MEDDATA INC
735 Industrial Rd Ste 203, San Carlos (94070-3315)
PHONE...................650 369-9734
Raj Patel, *CEO*
Naina Khatri, *Director*
EMP: 62
SQ FT: 3,200
SALES (est): 1.3MM **Privately Held**
WEB: www.globalmeddata.net
SIC: 8099 7374 Medical services organization; data processing & preparation

(P-22810)
HALO UNLIMTED INC
Also Called: Infant Hring Scrning Spcalists
1867 California Ave # 101, Corona (92881-7281)
P.O. Box 77010 (92877-0100)
PHONE...................714 692-2270
Martha Hawkins, *President*
EMP: 54
SQ FT: 7,500
SALES (est): 4.5MM **Privately Held**
SIC: 8099 Hearing testing service

(P-22811)
HARBOR HEALTH SYSTEMS LLC
3501 Jamboree Rd Ste 3000, Newport Beach (92660-2904)
PHONE...................949 273-7020
Gregory Moore, *CEO*
James W Dolan, *CEO*
EMP: 68 EST: 2001
SALES (est): 3MM **Privately Held**
SIC: 8099 7372 Blood related health services; business oriented computer software
PA: One Call Medical, Inc.
841 Prudential Dr Ste 900
Jacksonville FL 32207

(P-22812)
HEALTHCARE PARTNERS LLC
1236 N Magnolia Ave, Anaheim (92801-2607)
PHONE...................714 995-1000
Kathy Porter, *Admin Asst*
Shu Wu, *Family Practiti*
EMP: 60 **Publicly Held**
SIC: 8099 8011 Medical services organization; offices & clinics of medical doctors
HQ: Davita Medical Management, Llc
2175 Park Pl
El Segundo CA 90245

(P-22813)
HEALTHCARE PARTNERS LLC
Also Called: Family Health Program
4910 Airport Plaza Dr, Long Beach (90815-1264)
PHONE...................562 429-2473
Rhonda Luster, *Director*
EMP: 100 **Publicly Held**
SIC: 8099 8011 Medical services organization; clinic, operated by physicians
HQ: Davita Medical Management, Llc
2175 Park Pl
El Segundo CA 90245

(P-22814)
HEALTHCARE PARTNERS LLC
3501 S Harbor Blvd # 100, Santa Ana (92704-6919)
PHONE...................714 964-6229
Francis Gale, *Manager*
EMP: 50 **Publicly Held**

SIC: 8099 Blood related health services
HQ: Davita Medical Management, Llc
2175 Park Pl
El Segundo CA 90245

(P-22815)
HEMACARE CORPORATION (PA)
15350 Sherman Way, Van Nuys (91406-4203)
PHONE...................818 986-3883
Pete Van Der Wal, *President*
Anna Stock, *COO*
Lisa Bacerra, *CFO*
Robert Chilton, *CFO*
Viktor Mohacsy, *CFO*
EMP: 104 EST: 1978
SQ FT: 19,600
SALES (est): 15.8MM **Publicly Held**
WEB: www.hemacare.com
SIC: 8099 5122 Blood related health services; blood bank; blood donor station; blood plasma

(P-22816)
HENRY MAYO NEWHALL MEM HOSP
Also Called: Santa Clarita Health Care Ctr
23845 Mcbean Pkwy, Santa Clarita (91355-2001)
PHONE...................661 253-8227
David R Tumilty, *Principal*
EMP: 467
SALES (corp-wide): 320MM **Privately Held**
WEB: www.henrymayo.com
SIC: 8099 Childbirth preparation clinic
PA: Henry Mayo Newhall Memorial Hospital
23845 Mcbean Pkwy
Valencia CA 91355
661 253-8000

(P-22817)
HERITAGE MEDICAL GROUP
12370 Hesperia Rd Ste 6, Victorville (92395-4787)
PHONE...................760 956-1286
Stanley Wohl, *Branch Mgr*
Merlin Aalborg, *Officer*
EMP: 237 **Privately Held**
SIC: 8099 Blood related health services
PA: Heritage Medical Group
4580 California Ave
Bakersfield CA 93309

(P-22818)
HORIZONS ADULT DAY HEALTH CARE
1035 Harbison Ave, National City (91950-3919)
PHONE...................619 474-1822
Marina Murashova, *President*
Russ Kraus, *CFO*
EMP: 75
SALES (est): 2.7MM **Privately Held**
SIC: 8099 Blood related health services

(P-22819)
HOUCHIN BLOOD SERVICES (PA)
11515 Bolthouse Dr, Bakersfield (93311-8822)
PHONE...................661 323-4222
Greg Gallion, *CEO*
Walter Heisey, *President*
Joe Engel, *Vice Pres*
EMP: 70
SQ FT: 6,000
SALES: 8.6MM **Privately Held**
SIC: 8099 Blood bank

(P-22820)
HOUCHIN BLOOD SERVICES
11515 Bolthouse Dr, Bakersfield (93311-8822)
PHONE...................661 327-8541
Greg Gallion, *Branch Mgr*
EMP: 60
SALES (corp-wide): 8.6MM **Privately Held**
WEB: www.hcbb.com
SIC: 8099

PA: Houchin Blood Services
11515 Bolthouse Dr
Bakersfield CA 93311
661 323-4222

(P-22821)
IN SHAPE HEALTH CLUB
14601 Valley Center Dr, Victorville (92395-4216)
PHONE...................760 381-1200
Derrick Johnson, *General Mgr*
EMP: 50 EST: 2014
SALES (est): 229.7K **Privately Held**
SIC: 8099 7991 Health & allied services; health club

(P-22822)
INCARE DME
15446 Sherman Way Apt 319, Van Nuys (91406-4254)
PHONE...................818 582-1016
Natasha Larson, *Owner*
EMP: 99
SALES (est): 721.7K **Privately Held**
SIC: 8099 Health & allied services

(P-22823)
INLAND BHAVIORAL HLTH SVCS INC (PA)
1963 N E St, San Bernardino (92405-3919)
PHONE...................909 881-6146
Temetry Ann Lindsey, *President*
Vernon Bragg Jr, *Ch of Bd*
John Wilson, *COO*
Peter Demel, *CFO*
Rachel Jones, *Administration*
EMP: 68
SQ FT: 13,500
SALES: 9.7MM **Privately Held**
WEB: www.ibhealth.org
SIC: 8099 8093 Medical services organization; drug clinic, outpatient; alcohol clinic, outpatient

(P-22824)
INSTITUTE FOR BHVORAL HLTH INC
1905 Bus Ctr Dr S Ste 100, San Bernardino (92408)
PHONE...................909 289-1041
Azadeh K Jebelli, *President*
EMP: 265
SALES (est): 264.4K **Privately Held**
SIC: 8099 Childbirth preparation clinic

(P-22825)
INTEGRATED BEHAVIORAL HLTH INC
3070 Bristol St Ste 350, Costa Mesa (92626-7825)
P.O. Box 30018, Laguna Niguel (92607-0018)
PHONE...................714 442-4150
Tom H Yankoff, *Chairman*
Jonathan Bosanac, *President*
David Sockel, *Ch Credit Ofcr*
Edward M Bosanac, *Admin Sec*
EMP: 54
SQ FT: 11,000
SALES (est): 4.8MM **Privately Held**
WEB: www.ibhworklife.com
SIC: 8099 Health screening service

(P-22826)
JWCH INSTITUTE INC
14371 Clark Ave, Bellflower (90706-2901)
PHONE...................562 867-7999
Alvaro Ballesteros, *Branch Mgr*
EMP: 78
SALES (corp-wide): 33.9MM **Privately Held**
SIC: 8099 Blood related health services
PA: Jwch Institute, Inc.
5650 Jillson St
Commerce CA 90040
323 477-1171

(P-22827)
KAISER FOUNDATION HOSPITALS
Also Called: Kaiser Foundation Health Plan
2055 Kellogg Ave, Corona (92879-3111)
PHONE...................866 984-7483
Ruth Jasse, *Administration*
Richard Liu, *Family Practiti*

Christine Duong, *Internal Med*
EMP: 99
SALES (corp-wide): 94.1B **Privately Held**
WEB: www.kaiser.com
SIC: 8099 Childbirth preparation clinic
HQ: Kaiser Foundation Hospitals Inc
1 Kaiser Plz
Oakland CA 94612
510 271-6611

(P-22828)
KAWEAH DLTA HLTH CARE DST GILD
4945 W Cypress Ave, Visalia (93277-1592)
PHONE...................559 624-3100
Robert Havard, *President*
EMP: 236
SALES (corp-wide): 537.4MM **Privately Held**
SIC: 8099 Childbirth preparation clinic
PA: Kaweah Delta Health Care District
400 W Mineral King Ave
Visalia CA 93291
559 624-2000

(P-22829)
KAWEAH DLTA HLTH CARE DST GILD
1014 San Juan Ave Ste A, Exeter (93221-1312)
PHONE...................559 592-7300
EMP: 236
SALES (corp-wide): 537.4MM **Privately Held**
SIC: 8099 Childbirth preparation clinic
PA: Kaweah Delta Health Care District
400 W Mineral King Ave
Visalia CA 93291
559 624-2000

(P-22830)
KIDANGO INC
730 Empey Way, San Jose (95128-4705)
PHONE...................408 297-9044
Stacey Gray, *Manager*
EMP: 95
SALES (corp-wide): 26MM **Privately Held**
SIC: 8099 Blood related health services
PA: Kidango, Inc.
44000 Old Warm Sprng Blvd
Fremont CA 94538
510 897-6900

(P-22831)
KIMCO STAFFING SERVICES INC
1801 Oakland Blvd Ste 220, Walnut Creek (94596-7033)
PHONE...................925 256-3132
EMP: 1162
SALES (corp-wide): 135.7MM **Privately Held**
SIC: 8099 Medical services organization
PA: Kimco Staffing Services, Inc.
17872 Cowan
Irvine CA 92614
949 331-1199

(P-22832)
LEGACY HEALTHCARE CENTER LLC
1570 N Fair Oaks Ave, Pasadena (91103-1822)
PHONE...................626 798-0558
Raphael Oscherowitz, *Principal*
Dov Jacobs, *Principal*
EMP: 90
SALES (est): 885.1K **Privately Held**
SIC: 8099 Health & allied services

(P-22833)
LELAND STANFORD JUNIOR UNIV
Stanford Blood Center
3373 Hillview Ave, Palo Alto (94304-1204)
PHONE...................650 723-5548
Edgar Engleman, *Director*
Deba Hiraki, *Med Doctor*
Monica Ochoa, *Manager*
Renee Gipson, *Supervisor*
EMP: 200
SALES (corp-wide): 5.6B **Privately Held**
SIC: 8099 8221 Blood bank; university

PA: Leland Stanford Junior University
450 Serra Mall
Stanford CA 94305
650 723-2300

(P-22834)
LIFE LINE SCREENING AMER LTD
2854 Casitas Ave, Altadena (91001-4960)
PHONE..................................626 797-9774
EMP: 330 **Privately Held**
SIC: 8099 Health screening service
PA: Life Line Screening Of America Ltd.
6150 Oak Tree Blvd
Independence OH 44131

(P-22835)
LONG BEACH BEHAVIORAL HEALTH U
3200 Long Beach Blvd, Long Beach
(90807-5062)
PHONE..................................310 221-6336
Yvonne Lozano, *Principal*
EMP: 60
SALES (est): 210.7K **Privately Held**
SIC: 8099 Health & allied services

(P-22836)
LOS ANGELES CNTY DEV SVC FNDTN
Also Called: Frank D Lanterman Regional Ctr
3303 Wilshire Blvd # 700, Los Angeles
(90010-1704)
PHONE..................................213 383-1300
Dianne Anand, *Exec Dir*
Frank Lara, *Bd of Directors*
Patrick Aulicino, *Associate Dir*
Tammy Simmons, *Technology*
Marcus Smith, *Technology*
EMP: 180
SQ FT: 80,000
SALES: 147.3MM **Privately Held**
SIC: 8099 8322 8093 Medical services
organization; individual & family services;
mental health clinic, outpatient

(P-22837)
MCKESSON PTENT CARE SLTONS INC (HQ)
Also Called: National Rehab
9235 Activity Rd Ste 105, San Diego
(92126-4440)
P.O. Box 1135, Coraopolis PA (15108-
6135)
PHONE..................................412 507-0077
Heather Edmunds, *President*
John Blood, *Corp Secy*
Bill Cornman, *Marketing Mgr*
Christine Hartz, *Marketing Mgr*
Julian Gordon, *Regl Sales Mgr*
EMP: 65
SQ FT: 26,500
SALES (est): 10.3MM
SALES (corp-wide): 208.3B **Publicly Held**
SIC: 8099 5047 Medical services organi-
zation; medical equipment & supplies
PA: Mckesson Corporation
1 Post St Fl 18
San Francisco CA 94104
415 983-8300

(P-22838)
MEDASEND BIOMEDICAL INC (PA)
1402 Daisy Ave, Long Beach (90813-1521)
PHONE..................................800 200-3581
Steve Grand, *CEO*
Stephanie Harrison, *Vice Pres*
EMP: 150
SQ FT: 10,000
SALES: 5MM **Privately Held**
SIC: 8099 4953 Health screening service;
hazardous waste collection & disposal

(P-22839)
MEDISCAN DIAGNOSTIC SVCS LLC
Also Called: Mediscan Staffing Services
21050 Califa Ste 100, Woodland Hills
(91367-5103)
PHONE..................................818 758-4224
Val Serebryany, *President*
EMP: 100

SALES (est): 3.9MM
SALES (corp-wide): 865MM **Publicly Held**
WEB: www.mediscan.net
SIC: 8099 Medical services organization
HQ: Mediscan Nursing Staffing, Llc
21050 Califa St Ste 100
Woodland Hills CA 91367
818 758-8680

(P-22840)
MERCY FOUNDATION NORTH
2625 Edith Ave Ste E, Redding
(96001-3040)
PHONE..................................530 247-3424
Jeanine Hedman, *President*
Alisa Johnson, *Officer*
EMP: 60
SALES: 2.4MM **Privately Held**
SIC: 8099 Medical services organization

(P-22841)
MOLINA HEALTHCARE INC
9275 Sky Park Ct Ste 400, San Diego
(92123-4386)
PHONE..................................858 614-1580
Lisa Ferrari, *Manager*
Connie Robertson, *Vice Pres*
Lisa Baird, *Program Mgr*
Carla Cook, *Program Mgr*
Crystal Moran, *Program Mgr*
EMP: 376
SALES (corp-wide): 19.8B **Publicly Held**
SIC: 8099 Blood related health services
PA: Molina Healthcare, Inc.
200 Oceangate Ste 100
Long Beach CA 90802
562 435-3666

(P-22842)
MOLINA HEALTHCARE INC
1 Golden Shore, Long Beach (90802-4202)
PHONE..................................562 435-3666
Sriram Bharadwaj, *Branch Mgr*
Robert Gordon, *President*
Rajan Jain, *President*
Robert Osburn, *Officer*
Khaled Ghaly, *Assoc VP*
EMP: 378
SALES (corp-wide): 19.8B **Publicly Held**
SIC: 8099 Blood related health services
PA: Molina Healthcare, Inc.
200 Oceangate Ste 100
Long Beach CA 90802
562 435-3666

(P-22843)
MORRISON MGT SPECIALISTS INC
Also Called: Morrison MGT Specialists
2823 Fresno St, Fresno (93721-1324)
PHONE..................................559 459-6449
EMP: 200
SALES (corp-wide): 27.3B **Privately Held**
SIC: 8099
HQ: Morrison Management Specialists, Inc.
5801 Pachtree Dunwoody Rd
Atlanta GA 30350

(P-22844)
NATIONAL ORGANIZATION OF
18663 Ventura Blvd, Tarzana (91356-4162)
PHONE..................................800 489-0210
Amonra Elohim, *President*
EMP: 150 **EST:** 1999
SALES (est): 9.3MM **Privately Held**
SIC: 8099 Blood related health services

(P-22845)
NATURAL HEALTH TRENDS CORP
609 Deep Valley Dr # 390, Rllng HLS Est
(90274-3629)
PHONE..................................310 541-0888
EMP: 56
SALES (corp-wide): 197.5MM **Publicly Held**
SIC: 8099 Blood related health services
PA: Natural Health Trends Corp.
609 Deep Valley Dr # 395
Rllng Hls Est CA 90274
310 541-0888

(P-22846)
NEIGHBORHOOD HEALTHCARE
41840 Enterprise Cir N, Temecula
(92590-5654)
PHONE..................................951 225-6400
EMP: 88
SALES (corp-wide): 57.9MM **Privately Held**
SIC: 8099 Childbirth preparation clinic
PA: Neighborhood Healthcare
425 N Date St Ste 203
Escondido CA 92025
760 520-8372

(P-22847)
NEW MEDISCAN II LLC
Also Called: Mediscan Staffing Services
21050 Califa St 100, Woodland Hills
(91367-5103)
PHONE..................................866 758-4224
Val Serebryany, *President*
EMP: 100
SQ FT: 7,500
SALES (est): 3.3MM
SALES (corp-wide): 865MM **Publicly Held**
WEB: www.mediscan.net
SIC: 8099 Medical services organization
HQ: Mediscan Nursing Staffing, Llc
21050 Califa St Ste 100
Woodland Hills CA 91367
818 758-8680

(P-22848)
NORTHEAST VALLEY HEALTH CORP
7107 Remmet Ave, Canoga Park
(91303-2016)
PHONE..................................818 340-3570
Gary Morris, *Branch Mgr*
EMP: 77
SALES (corp-wide): 89.4MM **Privately Held**
SIC: 8099 Blood related health services
PA: Northeast Valley Health Corp
1172 N Maclay Ave
San Fernando CA 91340
818 898-1388

(P-22849)
NORTHEAST VALLEY HEALTH CORP
7223 Fair Ave, Sun Valley (91352-4964)
PHONE..................................818 432-4400
Sarah Schwartz, *Physician Asst*
EMP: 92
SALES (corp-wide): 89.4MM **Privately Held**
SIC: 8099 Childbirth preparation clinic
PA: Northeast Valley Health Corp
1172 N Maclay Ave
San Fernando CA 91340
818 898-1388

(P-22850)
OCCUPNL URGNT CARE HLTH SYST
Also Called: Ouch Systems
750 Riverpoint Dr, West Sacramento
(95605-1625)
PHONE..................................916 374-4600
James C Smith, *President*
Joseph Whitters, *CFO*
Dan Brunner, *Exec VP*
EMP: 380
SALES (est): 4.9MM **Privately Held**
WEB: www.ouchsystems.com
SIC: 8099 Medical services organization

(P-22851)
OCEANSIDE HLTHCARE STFFING INC
Also Called: R and R Prof Hlthcare Staffing
2216 El Camino Rela 211, Santa Clarita
(91350)
PHONE..................................213 503-5649
Andy Gibbs, *President*
EMP: 140
SALES: 2.2MM **Privately Held**
SIC: 8099 Childbirth preparation clinic

(P-22852)
ONELEGACY
221 S Figueroa St Ste 500, Los Angeles
(90012-2526)
PHONE..................................213 229-5600
Diane Marshallgreen, *Principal*
EMP: 124
SALES (corp-wide): 88.6MM **Privately Held**
SIC: 8099 8062 Organ bank; general
medical & surgical hospitals
PA: Onelegacy
221 S Figueroa St Ste 500
Los Angeles CA 90012
213 625-0665

(P-22853)
ONELEGACY (PA)
221 S Figueroa St Ste 500, Los Angeles
(90012-2526)
PHONE..................................213 625-0665
Thomas D Mone, *CEO*
Robert Mendez, *President*
Matthew Crump, *Vice Pres*
Rachel Grayczyk, *Executive Asst*
Lutfi Freij, *Administration*
EMP: 60
SALES: 88.6MM **Privately Held**
SIC: 8099 Organ bank

(P-22854)
ONSITE HEALTH INC (PA)
85 Argonaut Ste 220, Aliso Viejo
(92656-4105)
PHONE..................................949 305-2253
Ernest Blackwelder, *CEO*
David Joe, *Principal*
EMP: 69
SALES (est): 400MM **Privately Held**
SIC: 8099 Medical services organization

(P-22855)
ONTARIO MONTCLAR SCH DIST FOOD
1525 S Bon View Ave, Ontario
(91761-4408)
PHONE..................................909 930-6360
James Hammon, *Principal*
Sara Maragni, *Director*
EMP: 120
SALES (est): 3.2MM **Privately Held**
SIC: 8099 Nutrition services

(P-22856)
PANCREATIC CANCR ACTN NETWRK I (PA)
Also Called: Pancan
1500 Rosecrans Ave # 200, Manhattan
Beach (90266-3763)
PHONE..................................310 725-0025
Julie Fleshman, *President*
Elaine Matteucci, *Partner*
Jeanne Weaver Ruesch, *Ch of Bd*
Abigail Winston, *CFO*
Megan Gordon Don, *Vice Pres*
EMP: 130
SALES: 32.6MM **Privately Held**
WEB: www.pancan.com
SIC: 8099 8399 Medical services organi-
zation; social service information ex-
change

(P-22857)
PATHWAYS HOME HEALTH
395 Oyster Point Blvd # 128, South San
Francisco (94080-1928)
PHONE..................................650 634-0133
Mary Dias, *Manager*
EMP: 50
SALES (est): 352.3K **Privately Held**
SIC: 8099 Health & allied services

(P-22858)
PERMANENTE MEDICAL GROUP INC (DH)
1950 Franklin St Fl 18th, Oakland
(94612-5118)
PHONE..................................866 858-2226
Robert M Pearl, *CEO*
Gerard C Bajada, *CFO*
Pat Conolly, *Exec Dir*
Rhoda Wynn, *Med Doctor*
Elaine Schow, *Nurse*
EMP: 500 **EST:** 1945
SQ FT: 10,000

PRODUCTS & SVCS

SALES (est): 805.2MM
SALES (corp-wide): 94.1B **Privately Held**
WEB: www.permanente.net
SIC: 8099 Medical services organization
HQ: Kaiser Foundation Hospitals Inc
1 Kaiser Plz
Oakland CA 94612
510 271-6611

(P-22859)
PIONEER MEDICAL GROUP INC
16510 Bloomfield Ave, Cerritos (90703-2115)
PHONE..................562 229-0902
Tanya Lee-Jordan, *Manager*
Marilyn Kamerer, *Human Res Mgr*
EMP: 78
SALES (corp-wide): 37.9MM **Privately Held**
SIC: 8099 Blood related health services
PA: Pioneer Medical Group, Inc.
17777 Center Court Dr N # 400
Cerritos CA 90703
562 597-4181

(P-22860)
PIT RIVER HEALTH SERVICE INC (PA)
36977 Park Ave, Burney (96013-4067)
PHONE..................530 335-3651
Glenna Moore, *Exec Dir*
Jeremy Wheeler, *General Mgr*
Inder Wadhwa, *Administration*
Richard Johnston, *Info Tech Mgr*
EMP: 57
SALES: 5.6MM **Privately Held**
SIC: 8099 Medical services organization

(P-22861)
PLASMA COLLECTION CENTERS INC
2410 Lillyvale Ave, Los Angeles (90032-3514)
PHONE..................323 441-7720
David Bell, *Ch of Bd*
Shinji Wada, *President*
EMP: 200
SALES (est): 16.6MM **Privately Held**
SIC: 8099 Blood related health services

(P-22862)
PPONEXT INC
1501 Hughes Way Ste 400, Long Beach (90810-1881)
PHONE..................888 446-6098
Barbara E Rodin PHD, *President*
EMP: 300 **EST:** 1999
SALES (est): 2MM
SALES (corp-wide): 3.7B **Publicly Held**
WEB: www.pponext.com
SIC: 8099 Medical services organization
HQ: Beech Street Corporation
25550 Commercentre Dr # 200
Lake Forest CA 92630
949 672-1000

(P-22863)
PUBLIC HLTH FNDATION ENTPS INC
12781 Schabarum Ave, Irwindale (91706-6807)
PHONE..................626 856-6600
Eliose Jenks, *Branch Mgr*
Kiran Saluja, *Principal*
EMP: 133
SALES (corp-wide): 97.5MM **Privately Held**
SIC: 8099 Blood related health services
PA: Public Health Foundation Enterprises, Inc.
13300 Crssrds Pkwy N
City Of Industry CA 91746
800 201-7320

(P-22864)
PUBLIC HLTH FNDATION ENTPS INC
8666 Whittier Blvd, Pico Rivera (90660-2655)
PHONE..................562 801-2323
Nicolle Fevere, *Principal*
EMP: 133
SALES (corp-wide): 97.5MM **Privately Held**
SIC: 8099 Blood related health services

PA: Public Health Foundation Enterprises, Inc.
13300 Crssrds Pkwy N
City Of Industry CA 91746
800 201-7320

(P-22865)
PUBLIC HLTH FNDATION ENTPS INC
1649 W Washington Blvd, Los Angeles (90007-1116)
PHONE..................323 733-9381
Eloise Jenks, *President*
EMP: 178
SALES (corp-wide): 97.5MM **Privately Held**
SIC: 8099 Blood related health services
PA: Public Health Foundation Enterprises, Inc.
13300 Crssrds Pkwy N
City Of Industry CA 91746
800 201-7320

(P-22866)
PUBLIC HLTH FNDATION ENTPS INC
Also Called: Wic
12781 Shama Rd, El Monte (91732)
PHONE..................626 856-6618
Juan Chong, *Branch Mgr*
EMP: 222
SALES (corp-wide): 97.5MM **Privately Held**
SIC: 8099 Blood related health services
PA: Public Health Foundation Enterprises, Inc.
13300 Crssrds Pkwy N
City Of Industry CA 91746
800 201-7320

(P-22867)
QTC MANAGEMENT INC (DH)
924 Overland Ct, San Dimas (91773-1742)
PHONE..................800 260-1515
Stephanie Hill, *CEO*
Tony Buratti, *Vice Pres*
Ryan Shelton, *Regional Mgr*
Dee Garcia, *Office Mgr*
Buddy Lunati, *Office Mgr*
▼ **EMP:** 160
SQ FT: 20,000
SALES (est): 61.6MM
SALES (corp-wide): 10.1B **Publicly Held**
SIC: 8099 Medical services organization
HQ: Qtc Holdings Inc.
700 N Frederick Ave
Gaithersburg MD 20879
301 240-4000

(P-22868)
QTC MDCAL GROUP INC A MED CORP
21700 Copley Dr Ste 200, Diamond Bar (91765-2219)
PHONE..................800 260-1515
Brant Kim, *CEO*
Tracy Schenk, *Associate Dir*
EMP: 1000
SALES (est): 546.4K **Privately Held**
SIC: 8099 Physical examination & testing services

(P-22869)
REDDING RANCHERIA
Also Called: Redding Ranch Indian Hlth CL
1441 Liberty St, Redding (96001-0811)
PHONE..................530 224-2700
Ron Sissan, *Director*
EMP: 65
SALES (corp-wide): 36.5MM **Privately Held**
WEB: www.redding-rancheria.com
SIC: 8099 Medical services organization
PA: Redding Rancheria
2000 Redding Rancheria Rd
Redding CA 96001
530 225-8979

(P-22870)
RESCUE MISSION ALLIANCE
125 S Harrison Ave, Oxnard (93030-6038)
PHONE..................805 201-4341
Carol Roberg, *Principal*
EMP: 50

SALES (est): 1.2MM
SALES (corp-wide): 26.5MM **Privately Held**
WEB: www.erescuemission.com
SIC: 8099 Health & allied services
PA: Rescue Mission Alliance
315 N A St
Oxnard CA 93030
805 487-1234

(P-22871)
SAINT AGNES MED PROVIDERS INC
1379 E Herndon Ave, Fresno (93720-3309)
PHONE..................559 435-2630
David J Cavagnaro MD, *Partner*
EMP: 69
SALES (corp-wide): 4.7MM **Privately Held**
SIC: 8099 Childbirth preparation clinic
PA: Saint Agnes Medical Providers, Inc.
1105 E Spruce Ave Ste 201
Fresno CA 93720
559 450-7200

(P-22872)
SAINT-JOSEPH HOME HEALTH
1525 Mccarthy Blvd # 208, Milpitas (95035-7452)
PHONE..................408 244-5488
Daryl Velasco, *Principal*
EMP: 50
SALES (est): 1.4MM **Privately Held**
SIC: 8099 Medical services organization

(P-22873)
SAN BERNARDINO CITY UNF SCHOOL
Also Called: Nutrition Services
1257 Northpark Blvd, San Bernardino (92407-2946)
PHONE..................909 881-8000
Adrian Robles, *Branch Mgr*
EMP: 65
SALES (corp-wide): 469.2MM **Privately Held**
WEB: www.sbcusd.k12.ca.us
SIC: 8099 8211 Nutrition services; elementary school
PA: San Bernardino City Unified School District
777 N F St
San Bernardino CA 92410
909 381-1100

(P-22874)
SAN DIEGO BLOOD BANK (PA)
Also Called: San Diego Blood Bnk Foundation
3636 Gtwy Ctr Ave Ste 100, San Diego (92102-4508)
PHONE..................619 296-6393
Ramona Walker, *CEO*
Marge Lorang, *Bd of Directors*
Michele Brown, *Officer*
Richard Dickson, *Vice Pres*
Doris Tyler, *Vice Pres*
▲ **EMP:** 163
SQ FT: 132,000
SALES: 39MM **Privately Held**
SIC: 8099 8071 Blood bank; medical laboratories

(P-22875)
SAN DIEGO BLOOD BANK
776 Arnele Ave, El Cajon (92020-2502)
PHONE..................619 441-1804
Ramona Walker, *Branch Mgr*
EMP: 202
SALES (corp-wide): 39MM **Privately Held**
SIC: 8099 Blood bank
PA: San Diego Blood Bank
3636 Gtwy Ctr Ave Ste 100
San Diego CA 92102
619 296-6393

(P-22876)
SAN DIEGO COASTL MED GROUP INC
2201 Mission Ave, Oceanside (92058-2313)
PHONE..................760 901-5259
Meredith Acosta, *Principal*
Mary Beth Casement, *Pediatrics*

EMP: 132
SALES (est): 962.3K
SALES (corp-wide): 2.9B **Privately Held**
SIC: 8099 Health & allied services
PA: Scripps Health
10140 Campus Point Dr Ax415
San Diego CA 92121
800 727-4777

(P-22877)
SAN DIEGO FAMILY CARE
4290 Polk Ave, San Diego (92105-1524)
PHONE..................619 563-0250
EMP: 114
SALES (corp-wide): 24.3MM **Privately Held**
SIC: 8099 Childbirth preparation clinic
PA: San Diego Family Care
6973 Linda Vista Rd
San Diego CA 92111
858 279-0925

(P-22878)
SAN MATEO HEALTH COMMISSION
Also Called: Health Plan of San Mateo
801 Gateway Blvd Ste 100, South San Francisco (94080-7408)
PHONE..................650 616-0050
Maya Altman, *CEO*
Ron Robinson, *CFO*
Rion Manning, *Marketing Staff*
Jimmy Holman, *Manager*
EMP: 211
SQ FT: 58,758
SALES (est): 17.2MM **Privately Held**
WEB: www.hpsm.org
SIC: 8099 Physical examination service, insurance

(P-22879)
SANTA ANA UNIFIED SCHOOL DST
Also Called: Nutririon Services
1749 Carnegie Ave, Santa Ana (92705-5525)
PHONE..................714 431-1900
Mark Chavez, *Director*
EMP: 100
SQ FT: 30,295
SALES (corp-wide): 771.7MM **Privately Held**
WEB: www.santaanaeducation.com
SIC: 8099 Nutrition services
PA: Santa Ana Unified School District Public Facilities Corporation
1601 E Chestnut Ave
Santa Ana CA 92701
714 558-5501

(P-22880)
SANTA BARBARA COUNTY OF
Also Called: Public Health Dept
345 Camino Del Remedio, Santa Barbara (93110-1332)
PHONE..................805 681-5100
Tekashi Wada, *Director*
EMP: 60 **Privately Held**
WEB: www.sbcountyhr.org
SIC: 8099 9431 Medical services organization; administration of public health programs
PA: County Of Santa Barbara
105 E Anapamu St Rm 406
Santa Barbara CA 93101
805 568-3400

(P-22881)
SANTA CLARA VALLEY MEDICAL CTR
2220 Moorpark Ave, San Jose (95128-2613)
PHONE..................408 885-5730
EMP: 599 **Privately Held**
SIC: 8099 Childbirth preparation clinic
PA: Santa Clara Valley Medical Center
751 S Bascom Ave
San Jose CA 95128

(P-22882)
SCRIPPS HEALTH
7565 Mission Valley Rd # 200, San Diego (92108-4431)
PHONE..................619 245-2350

Sevil Brahme, *Branch Mgr*
Aleksandr M Itkin, *Dermatology*
EMP: 364
SALES (corp-wide): 2.9B **Privately Held**
SIC: 8099 Blood related health services
PA: Scripps Health
    10140 Campus Point Dr Ax415
    San Diego CA 92121
    800 727-4777

(P-22883)
SEA VIEW MEDICAL GROUP INC
1901 Solar Dr Ste 265, Oxnard
(93036-2692)
PHONE..................805 373-5781
Dr Gary Prossfett, *Director*
Dr Yacoob Mall, *Treasurer*
Dr Richard Brand, *Admin Sec*
Veronica Vasquez, *Director*
EMP: 80
SQ FT: 6,000
SALES (est): 1.5MM
SALES (corp-wide): 96.2MM **Privately Held**
WEB: www.hserve.com
SIC: 8099 Medical services organization
HQ: Change Healthcare Practice Management Solutions Group, Inc.
    7 Parkway Ctr Ste 400
    Pittsburgh PA 15220
    -

(P-22884)
SIERRA VISTA FAMILY MEDICAL
1227 E Los Angeles Ave, Simi Valley
(93065-2871)
PHONE..................805 582-4000
EMP: 80 **EST:** 2009
SALES (est): 2.6MM **Privately Held**
SIC: 8099

(P-22885)
SIGNET ARMORLITE INC (DH)
5803 Newton Dr Ste A, Carlsbad
(92008-7380)
P.O. Box 3309, Carol Stream IL (60132-3309)
PHONE..................760 744-4000
Brad Staley, *President*
Bruno Salvadori, *Ch of Bd*
Lauri Crawford, *Exec VP*
Edward P Derosa, *Exec VP*
M Kathryn Bernard, *Vice Pres*
▲ **EMP:** 400
SQ FT: 138,000
SALES: 76MM **Privately Held**
WEB: www.signetarmorlite.com
SIC: 8099 Eye banks
HQ: Essilor Of America, Inc.
    13555 N Stemmons Fwy
    Dallas TX 75234
    214 496-4000

(P-22886)
SOBALIVING LLC
22669 Pacific Coast Hwy, Malibu
(90265-5036)
PHONE..................800 595-3803
Gregory Hannley, *President*
EMP: 50
SALES (est): 4.1MM **Privately Held**
SIC: 8099 Health & allied services

(P-22887)
SOUTH CNTY CMNTY HLTH CTR INC (PA)
Also Called: Ravenswood Family Health Ctr
1885 Bay Rd, East Palo Alto (94303-1312)
PHONE..................650 330-7407
Wayne Yost, *CFO*
Lisa Chamberlain, *Bd of Directors*
Laila Gulzar, *Officer*
Luisa Buada, *Exec Dir*
Isabel Quinonez, *Admin Sec*
EMP: 70
SALES: 23.3MM **Privately Held**
SIC: 8099 Medical services organization

(P-22888)
SOUTHERN CAL PRMNNTE MED GROUP
23781 Maquina, Mission Viejo
(92691-2716)
PHONE..................949 376-8619

EMP: 354
SALES (corp-wide): 3.5B **Privately Held**
SIC: 8099 Blood related health services
PA: Southern California Permanente Medical Group
    393 Walnut Dr
    Pasadena CA 91107
    626 405-5704

(P-22889)
STAR OF CALIFORNIA
299 W Hillcrest Dr, Thousand Oaks
(91360-4264)
PHONE..................805 379-1401
Doug Moes, *Branch Mgr*
Keegan Tangeman, *Director*
EMP: 56 **Privately Held**
SIC: 8099 Medical services organization
PA: Star Of California, A Professional Psychological Corporation
    4880 Market St
    Ventura CA 93003

(P-22890)
STAR OF CALIFORNIA
8834 Morro Rd, Atascadero (93422-3953)
PHONE..................805 466-1638
EMP: 195 **Privately Held**
SIC: 8099 Medical services organization
PA: Star Of California, A Professional Psychological Corporation
    4880 Market St
    Ventura CA 93003

(P-22891)
STAR OF CALIFORNIA (PA)
4880 Market St, Ventura (93003-7783)
PHONE..................805 644-7823
Doug Moes, *President*
Doug Wright, *CFO*
Quy Neel, *Office Admin*
Steve Yeager, *Info Tech Mgr*
Jodi Turner, *Opers Mgr*
EMP: 110
SQ FT: 6,640
SALES (est): 5.3MM **Privately Held**
SIC: 8099 Medical services organization

(P-22892)
SUTTER HEALTH
2950 Collier Canyon Rd, Livermore
(94551-9224)
PHONE..................925 371-3800
Ronald D Workman, *Branch Mgr*
EMP: 80
SALES (corp-wide): 12.4B **Privately Held**
SIC: 8099 Blood related health services
PA: Sutter Health
    2200 River Plaza Dr
    Sacramento CA 95833
    916 733-8800

(P-22893)
SUTTER HLTH SCRMNTO SIERRA REG
701 Howe Ave Ste F20, Sacramento
(95825-4681)
PHONE..................916 733-7080
Mary Ashuckian, *Branch Mgr*
Samuel Warnke, *Admin Asst*
Gregory Graves, *Director*
Barbara Berry, *Manager*
EMP: 1265
SALES (corp-wide): 12.4B **Privately Held**
SIC: 8099 Blood related health services
HQ: Sutter Health Sacramento Sierra Region
    2200 River Plaza Dr
    Sacramento CA 95833
    916 733-8800

(P-22894)
TELEMEDICINE CORP
8920 Wilshire Blvd # 310, Beverly Hills
(90211-2007)
PHONE..................888 472-2853
David Woroboff, *CEO*
George Willard, *COO*
EMP: 50
SQ FT: 2,000
SALES (est): 400K **Privately Held**
SIC: 8099 Childbirth preparation clinic

(P-22895)
TENDERLOIN HOUSING CLINIC INC
472 Turk St, San Francisco (94102-3330)
PHONE..................415 771-2427
Randall Shaw, *Branch Mgr*
Colleen Carrigan, *Sales Dir*
Reina Cristales, *Case Mgr*
Simone Sims, *Case Mgr*
EMP: 226 **Privately Held**
SIC: 8099 Blood related health services
PA: Tenderloin Housing Clinic, Inc.
    126 Hyde St
    San Francisco CA 94102

(P-22896)
TRIANIM HEALTH SERVICES INC
27201 Tourney Rd Ste 115, Valencia
(91355-1801)
PHONE..................818 362-6882
Gary Winkler, *Buyer*
Jennifer Jasinski, *Purchasing*
Karen Hickman, *Buyer*
Keith Ainsco, *Opers Staff*
John Chiles, *Mktg Dir*
EMP: 52
SALES (est): 3.7MM **Privately Held**
SIC: 8099 Health & allied services

(P-22897)
UCSD HEALTHCARE
355 Dickinson St 340, San Diego
(92103-2075)
P.O. Box 33268 (92163-3268)
PHONE..................858 657-7105
Stephen Crawford, *Principal*
EMP: 92
SALES (est): 11.4MM **Privately Held**
SIC: 8099 Health & allied services

(P-22898)
UNIFIED INV PROGRAMS INC (PA)
Also Called: Palm Grove Health Care
2368 Torrance Blvd # 200, Torrance
(90501-2500)
PHONE..................310 782-1878
Cynthia Schein, *Owner*
Emmanuel B David, *President*
EMP: 70
SALES (est): 1.7MM **Privately Held**
SIC: 8099 8051 Medical services organization; skilled nursing care facilities

(P-22899)
UNIVERSITY CAL IRVINE MED CENT
208 Giotto, Irvine (92614-8573)
PHONE..................714 456-5678
Glenn Levine, *Principal*
Shellie Nazarenus, *President*
Robin Cook, *Executive Asst*
Jennifer Wilkens, *Executive Asst*
Janet Ko, *Administration*
EMP: 281
SALES (est): 10.9MM **Privately Held**
SIC: 8099 Health & allied services

(P-22900)
VITALANT
Also Called: Blood Systems
111 Review Way, Hayward (94544-1224)
PHONE..................510 785-9554
EMP: 168
SALES (corp-wide): 11.7B **Privately Held**
SIC: 8099 Blood bank
PA: Vitalant
    6210 E Oak St
    Scottsdale AZ 85257
    480 675-5600

(P-22901)
VITALANT
Also Called: United Blood Services Ventura
4119 Broad St Ste 100, San Luis Obispo
(93401-7965)
PHONE..................805 543-1077
Vicki Finson, *Exec Dir*
EMP: 90
SALES (corp-wide): 11.7B **Privately Held**
SIC: 8099 Blood bank

PA: Vitalant
    6210 E Oak St
    Scottsdale AZ 85257
    480 675-5600

(P-22902)
VITALANT
Also Called: Tri-Counties Blood Bank
4119 Broad St Ste 100, San Luis Obispo
(93401-7965)
PHONE..................831 751-1993
Vicky Finson, *Director*
EMP: 80
SALES (corp-wide): 11.7B **Privately Held**
SIC: 8099 Blood bank
PA: Vitalant
    6210 E Oak St
    Scottsdale AZ 85257
    480 675-5600

8111 Legal Svcs

(P-22903)
A BUCHALTER PROFESSIONAL CORP (PA)
1000 Wilshire Blvd # 1500, Los Angeles
(90017-2457)
PHONE..................213 891-0700
Adam Bass, *CEO*
Daniel Slate, *Shareholder*
Venus Bernardo, *President*
Steven Chu, *President*
Alison Melanson, *President*
EMP: 209
SQ FT: 84,000
SALES (est): 51.9MM **Privately Held**
SIC: 8111 General practice law office

(P-22904)
AARON DOWLING INCORPORATED
8080 N Palm Ave Ste 300, Fresno
(93711-5797)
P.O. Box 28902 (93729-8902)
PHONE..................559 432-4500
Larry B Lindenau, *CEO*
Ronald Henderson, *Partner*
Leigh Burnside, *Shareholder*
Michael Dowling, *Shareholder*
Donald Fischbach, *Shareholder*
EMP: 80
SQ FT: 16,000
SALES (est): 13.2MM **Privately Held**
SIC: 8111 Corporate, partnership & business law

(P-22905)
ADELSON TESTAN BRUNDO NOVEL (PA)
31330 Oak Crest Dr, Westlake Village
(91361-4632)
PHONE..................805 604-1816
Steven Testan, *President*
Lilly Shyu, *CFO*
Judy Robertson, *Executive Asst*
Bryan Montalbon, *Info Tech Dir*
Dennis Bonnilla, *Info Tech Mgr*
EMP: 50
SQ FT: 17,900
SALES (est): 57.7MM **Privately Held**
SIC: 8111 Labor & employment law

(P-22906)
AKIN GUMP STRAUSS
2029 Century Park E # 2400, Los Angeles
(90067-3010)
PHONE..................310 229-1000
David Allen, *Managing Prtnr*
Yvonne Shawver, *President*
Eric Kurtz, *Info Tech Mgr*
Quinton McKenna, *Technology*
Mary Eklund, *Marketing Staff*
EMP: 100
SALES (corp-wide): 260MM **Privately Held**
WEB: www.akingump.com
SIC: 8111 General practice law office
PA: Akin, Gump, Strauss, Hauer, & Feld Llp
    1333 New Hampshire Ave Nw # 400
    Washington DC 20036
    202 887-4000

(P-22907)
AKIN GUMP STRAUSS HAUER & FEL
580 California St # 1500, San Francisco (94104-1000)
PHONE.....................415 765-9500
Karen Kubin, *Branch Mgr*
Eric G Ruehe, *Associate*
EMP: 131
SALES (corp-wide): 260MM **Privately Held**
WEB: www.akingump.net
SIC: 8111 General practice law office
PA: Akin, Gump, Strauss, Hauer, & Feld Llp
1333 New Hampshire Ave Nw # 400
Washington DC 20036
202 887-4000

(P-22908)
ALDRIDGE PITE LLP
4375 Jutland Dr Ste 200, San Diego (92117-3600)
P.O. Box 17935 (92177-7923)
PHONE.....................858 750-7700
Benton Christina C, *Associate*
EMP: 170
SALES (corp-wide): 61.7MM **Privately Held**
SIC: 8111 Real estate law
PA: Aldridge Pite Llp
3575 Piedmont Rd Ne 15-500
Atlanta GA 30305
404 994-7400

(P-22909)
ALLEN MATKINS LECK GMBLE
3 Embarcadero Ctr # 1200, San Francisco (94111-4015)
PHONE.....................415 837-1515
Richard C Mallory, *Partner*
Jerry Neuman, *Partner*
EMP: 80
SALES (corp-wide): 64.6MM **Privately Held**
WEB: www.allenmatkins.com
SIC: 8111 Real estate law
PA: Allen Matkins Leck Gamble Mallory & Natsis Llp
865 S Figueroa St # 2800
Los Angeles CA 90017
213 622-5555

(P-22910)
ALLEN MATKINS LECK GMBLE (PA)
865 S Figueroa St # 2800, Los Angeles (90017-2543)
PHONE.....................213 622-5555
David L Osias, *Managing Prtnr*
Frederick L Allen, *Partner*
Keith Paul Bishop, *Partner*
Raymond M Buddie, *Partner*
Jeffrey Chine, *Partner*
EMP: 300
SQ FT: 40,000
SALES (est): 64.6MM **Privately Held**
WEB: www.allenmatkins.com
SIC: 8111 General practice law office; labor & employment law; corporate, partnership & business law; real estate law

(P-22911)
ALLEN MATKINS LECK GMBLE
1900 Main St Fl 5, Irvine (92614-7321)
PHONE.....................949 553-1313
Drew Emmel, *Senior Partner*
Julie Arden, *President*
Allen Matkins, *General Counsel*
Paul Nash, *Associate*
EMP: 100
SALES (est): 8.6MM
SALES (corp-wide): 64.6MM **Privately Held**
WEB: www.allenmatkins.com
SIC: 8111 General practice law office
PA: Allen Matkins Leck Gamble Mallory & Natsis Llp
865 S Figueroa St # 2800
Los Angeles CA 90017
213 622-5555

(P-22912)
ALSTON & BIRD LLP
333 S Hope St Ste 1600, Los Angeles (90071-1410)
PHONE.....................213 626-8830
Wayne Mitchell, *Branch Mgr*
Cynthia Ambriz, *Admin Sec*
Kathleen Hill, *Planning*
Charles Ostrowski, *Info Tech Mgr*
Martha S Doty, *Counsel*
EMP: 165
SALES (corp-wide): 781.8MM **Privately Held**
SIC: 8111 General practice attorney, lawyer
PA: Alston & Bird Llp
1201 W Peachtree St Nw # 4000
Atlanta GA 30309
404 881-7000

(P-22913)
ALSTON & BIRD LLP
2815 Towngate Rd Ste 200, Westlake Village (91361-3091)
PHONE.....................202 239-3673
Michael D Bradbury, *Principal*
EMP: 294
SALES (corp-wide): 781.8MM **Privately Held**
SIC: 8111 General practice attorney, lawyer
PA: Alston & Bird Llp
1201 W Peachtree St Nw # 4000
Atlanta GA 30309
404 881-7000

(P-22914)
ALVARADOSMITH A PROF CORP (PA)
1 Macarthur Pl Ste 200, Santa Ana (92707-5941)
PHONE.....................714 852-6800
Ruben A Smith, *CEO*
Kevin Day, *Shareholder*
Jonathan Werner, *Shareholder*
Thomas Zeigler, *Shareholder*
Julia Evans, *President*
EMP: 110
SALES (est): 16.9MM **Privately Held**
SIC: 8111 General practice law office

(P-22915)
ANDATHA INTERNATIONAL INC (PA)
Also Called: Evolve Discovery
611 Mission St Fl 4, San Francisco (94105-3535)
PHONE.....................415 398-8600
Andrew F Jimenez, *President*
Shamir B Colloff, *CTO*
Wendy Lee, *Financial Analy*
EMP: 70
SQ FT: 3,500
SALES (est): 30.1MM **Privately Held**
SIC: 8111 Legal services

(P-22916)
ANDERSON MCPHARLIN CONNERS LLP (PA)
Also Called: AMC&
707 Wilshire Blvd # 4000, Los Angeles (90017-3623)
PHONE.....................213 688-0080
David T Dibiase, *Partner*
Mark E Aronson, *Partner*
Carleton R Burch, *Partner*
Colleen A Dziel, *Partner*
Jesse S Hernandez, *Partner*
EMP: 54
SQ FT: 23,000
SALES (est): 12.3MM **Privately Held**
WEB: www.amclaw.com
SIC: 8111 General practice attorney, lawyer

(P-22917)
ARCHER NORRIS A PROF LAW CORP (PA)
2033 N Main St Ste 800, Walnut Creek (94596-3759)
P.O. Box 8035 (94596-8035)
PHONE.....................925 930-6000
Douglas C Strauss, *Partner*
Eugene C Blackard Jr, *Partner*
W Eric Blumhardt, *Partner*

Kathy Jay, *President*
Richard E Norris, *Admin Sec*
EMP: 138
SQ FT: 43,254
SALES: 41.5MM **Privately Held**
SIC: 8111 General practice law office

(P-22918)
ARENT FOX LLP
555 W 5th St Ste 4800, Los Angeles (90013-1065)
PHONE.....................213 629-7400
Robert O'Brien, *Partner*
Elliott Kroll, *Partner*
Richard Newman, *Partner*
Andrew Ross, *Partner*
Peter Unger, *Partner*
EMP: 115
SALES (corp-wide): 143.2MM **Privately Held**
SIC: 8111 General practice attorney, lawyer
PA: Arent Fox Llp
1717 K St Nw Ste B1
Washington DC 20006
202 857-6000

(P-22919)
ARNOLD & PORTER LLP
3 Embarcadero Ctr Fl 7, San Francisco (94111-4078)
PHONE.....................818 788-8081
Elizabeth Respess, *Exec Dir*
Deborah G Douglas, *Manager*
EMP: 350
SALES (corp-wide): 356.6MM **Privately Held**
SIC: 8111 Corporate, partnership & business law
PA: Arnold & Porter Kaye Scholer Llp
601 Massachusetts Ave Nw
Washington DC 20001
202 942-5000

(P-22920)
ARNOLD & PORTER PC
3 Embarcadero Ctr Fl 7, San Francisco (94111-4078)
PHONE.....................415 434-1600
Lawrence Rabkin, *Ch of Bd*
Alina Austin, *President*
Judy Lord, *President*
Michelle Johnson, *Exec Dir*
Michelle L Johnson, *Exec Dir*
EMP: 350
SQ FT: 70,000
SALES (est): 26.1MM **Privately Held**
WEB: www.hrice.com
SIC: 8111 Corporate, partnership & business law

(P-22921)
ARNOLD PORTER KAYE SCHOLER LLP
3000 El Camino Real 2-500, Palo Alto (94306-2125)
PHONE.....................650 319-4500
Aurel Iderstine, *Manager*
EMP: 68
SALES (corp-wide): 356.6MM **Privately Held**
SIC: 8111 General practice law office
PA: Arnold & Porter Kaye Scholer Llp
601 Massachusetts Ave Nw
Washington DC 20001
202 942-5000

(P-22922)
ARNOLD PORTER KAYE SCHOLER LLP
1999 Avenue Of The Stars # 1600, Los Angeles (90067-4616)
PHONE.....................310 788-1000
Aurel Van Iderstine, *Branch Mgr*
Rhonda Trotter, *Managing Prtnr*
Aurel V Iderstine, *Branch Mgr*
Ruth Vega,
EMP: 128
SALES (corp-wide): 356.6MM **Privately Held**
SIC: 8111 General practice law office
PA: Arnold & Porter Kaye Scholer Llp
601 Massachusetts Ave Nw
Washington DC 20001
202 942-5000

(P-22923)
ARTIANO SHINOFF ABED (PA)
Also Called: Law Offices of James F. Holtz
16935 W Bernardo Dr # 114, San Diego (92127-1634)
PHONE.....................619 232-3122
Shari Randall, *Administration*
Robert E Gallagher, *Admin Sec*
James F Holtz,
Robert R Templeton Jr,
EMP: 51
SALES (est): 7.7MM **Privately Held**
WEB: www.stutzlawfirm.com
SIC: 8111 General practice attorney, lawyer

(P-22924)
ATKINSON AND LY RD & RM LW (PA)
Also Called: Atkinson Andelson Loya
12800 Center Court Dr S # 300, Cerritos (90703-9363)
PHONE.....................562 653-3200
James C Romo, *CEO*
Edward Ho, *Partner*
Sherry G Gordon, *Managing Prtnr*
Steven Atkinson, *President*
Steven Andelson, *Vice Pres*
EMP: 150
SALES (est): 39.9MM **Privately Held**
SIC: 8111 General practice attorney, lawyer

(P-22925)
BAKER KEENER & NAHRA
Also Called: Baker Keener & Nahra
633 W 5th St Ste 5500, Los Angeles (90071-2014)
PHONE.....................213 241-0900
Robert Baker, *Partner*
Patricia Aguayo, *President*
EMP: 50
SQ FT: 18,000
SALES (est): 9.9MM **Privately Held**
WEB: www.bknlawyers.com
SIC: 8111 Malpractice & negligence law

(P-22926)
BAKER & HOSTETLER LLP
11601 Wilshire Blvd Fl 14, Los Angeles (90025-1750)
PHONE.....................310 820-8800
John F Cermak Jr, *Partner*
Cathryn Rowley, *Partner*
Bob Lofton,
Teresa R Tracy,
Scott Koller, *Counsel*
EMP: 76
SALES (corp-wide): 313.3MM **Privately Held**
SIC: 8111 General practice attorney, lawyer; bankruptcy law; labor & employment law; real estate law
PA: Baker & Hostetler Llp
127 Public Sq Ste 2000
Cleveland OH 44114
216 621-0200

(P-22927)
BAKER & MCKENZIE LLP
2 Embarcadero Ctr # 1100, San Francisco (94111-3911)
PHONE.....................415 576-3000
Peter Engstrom, *Manager*
Bartley Baer, *Partner*
Edward D Burmeister, *Partner*
Robin Chesler, *Partner*
Peter Denwood, *Partner*
EMP: 120
SALES (corp-wide): 783.7MM **Privately Held**
SIC: 8111 Administrative & government law; corporate, partnership & business law
PA: Baker & Mckenzie Llp
300 E Randolph St # 5000
Chicago IL 60601
312 861-8000

(P-22928)
BAKER & MCKENZIE LLP
660 Hansen Way Ste 1, Palo Alto (94304-1045)
PHONE.....................650 856-2400
Peter Engstrom, *Branch Mgr*
Jon Appleton, *Partner*

Bartley Baer, *Partner*
Michael Bumbaca, *Partner*
Robin Chesler, *Partner*
EMP: 60
SALES (corp-wide): 783.7MM **Privately Held**
SIC: 8111 8011 General practice law office; medical centers
PA: Baker & Mckenzie Llp
300 E Randolph St # 5000
Chicago IL 60601
312 861-8000

(P-22929)
BAKER MNOCK JENSEN A PROF CORP
Also Called: Baker Mnock Jnsen Attys At Law
5260 N Palm Ave Ste 421, Fresno
(93704-2217)
PHONE...................559 432-5400
Bob Smittcamp, *CEO*
Donald P Fishbach, *Senior Partner*
Douglas B Jensen, *Senior Partner*
Kendall Manock, *Senior Partner*
David Camenson, *Vice Pres*
EMP: 110 EST: 1904
SQ FT: 30,000
SALES (est): 13MM **Privately Held**
WEB: www.bmj-law.com
SIC: 8111 General practice law office

(P-22930)
BALLARD ROSENBERG GOLPER SAV (PA)
15760 Ventura Blvd # 1800, Encino
(91436-3000)
PHONE...................818 508-3700
John Golper,
Richard Rosenberg, *Executive*
Karen Thomson, *Admin Sec*
Marlene Aposhian, *Administration*
Elsa Baauelos, *Counsel*
EMP: 51
SQ FT: 21,000
SALES: 9.4MM **Privately Held**
WEB: www.brgslaw.com
SIC: 8111 Labor & employment law; general practice attorney, lawyer

(P-22931)
BALLARD SPAHR LLP
2029 Century Park E # 800, Los Angeles
(90067-2909)
PHONE...................424 204-4400
Alan Petlak, *Branch Mgr*
Irma Williams, *Marketing Mgr*
Anne Stowell, *Accounts Exec*
Jose Flores, *Supervisor*
EMP: 76
SALES (corp-wide): 276.8MM **Privately Held**
SIC: 8111 General practice attorney, lawyer
PA: Ballard Spahr Llp
1735 Market St Fl 51
Philadelphia PA 19103
215 665-8500

(P-22932)
BANKRUPTCY MGT SOLUTIONS INC (PA)
Also Called: B M S
5 Peters Canyon Rd # 200, Irvine
(92606-1404)
PHONE...................949 222-1212
Steve Moore, *CEO*
Melinda Teter, *Vice Pres*
Cory Clemmons, *CTO*
Neha Sharma, *Software Engr*
Tan Nguyen, *Asst Controller*
EMP: 62
SALES (est): 21.1MM **Privately Held**
SIC: 8111 Bankruptcy referee

(P-22933)
BARGER & WOLEN LLP
275 Battery St Ste 480, San Francisco
(94111-3309)
PHONE...................415 434-2800
Linda Kiel, *Branch Mgr*
Margarita Fernandez, *President*
Victor Levit, *COO*
EMP: 50

SALES (corp-wide): 19.3MM **Privately Held**
WEB: www.bargerwolen.com
SIC: 8111 General practice law office
PA: Barger & Wolen Llp
633 W 5th St Ste 5000
Los Angeles CA
213 680-2800

(P-22934)
BARNES & THORNBURG LLP
2029 Century Park E # 300, Los Angeles
(90067-2904)
PHONE...................310 284-3880
Paul J Laurin, *Partner*
Scott Witlin, *Partner*
Andrea Augustine, *Admin Sec*
Cherie Hunt, *Admin Sec*
Kendra Lounsberry, *Associate*
EMP: 113
SALES (corp-wide): 167.8MM **Privately Held**
SIC: 8111 General practice attorney, lawyer
PA: Barnes & Thornburg Llp
11 S Meridian St Ste 1313
Indianapolis IN 46204
317 236-1313

(P-22935)
BARRETT BUSINESS SERVICES INC
Also Called: B B S I
8880 Rio San Diego Dr # 800, San Diego
(92108-1634)
PHONE...................858 314-1100
Milan Todorovic, *Branch Mgr*
EMP: 5003
SALES (corp-wide): 920.4MM **Publicly Held**
SIC: 8111 Legal services
PA: Barrett Business Services Inc
8100 Ne Parkway Dr # 200
Vancouver WA 98662
360 828-0700

(P-22936)
BARRY BISHOP
6001 Shellmound St # 875, Emeryville
(94608-1957)
PHONE...................510 596-0888
Nelson C Barry Sr, *President*
Nelson C Barry III, *Vice Pres*
Jeffrey N Haney, *Vice Pres*
Fredric W Trester, *Vice Pres*
Rebecca B Ahern, *Admin Sec*
EMP: 60 EST: 1917
SQ FT: 14,000
SALES (est): 7.1MM **Privately Held**
WEB: www.bbhhr.com
SIC: 8111 General practice law office

(P-22937)
BARTHOLOMEW BARRY & ASSOCIATES
701 N Brand Blvd Ste 800, Glendale
(91203-3279)
PHONE...................818 543-4000
EMP: 73
SALES (est): 3.7MM **Privately Held**
SIC: 8111

(P-22938)
BARTKO ZANKEL TARRANT & MIL
1 Embarcadero Ctr Ste 800, San Francisco
(94111-3629)
PHONE...................415 956-1900
Richard T Tarrant, *President*
Martin I Zankel, *Chairman*
Charles Miller, *Vice Pres*
John Bartko, *Principal*
Holly Adams, *Counsel*
EMP: 80 EST: 1975
SQ FT: 18,000
SALES (est): 11.3MM **Privately Held**
WEB: www.bztm.com
SIC: 8111 Corporate, partnership & business law; real estate law; bankruptcy law

(P-22939)
BERDING & WEIL LLP (PA)
2175 N Calif Blvd Ste 500, Walnut Creek
(94596-7336)
PHONE...................925 838-2090

Tyler Berding, *Partner*
Terri Nocco, *President*
David M Austin,
Cori L Barton,
Scott W Barton,
EMP: 75
SQ FT: 20,000
SALES (est): 18.9MM **Privately Held**
WEB: www.bwclassaction.com
SIC: 8111 General practice law office; general practice attorney, lawyer

(P-22940)
BERG WLLIAM L ATTORNEY AT LAW (PA)
Also Called: Berg Injury Lawyers
2440 Santa Clara Ave, Alameda
(94501-4537)
PHONE...................510 523-3200
William L Berg, *Owner*
Cathy Froncek, *COO*
Linda Thomas, *Office Mgr*
Bobbie Rocha, *Human Resources*
William Ginsburg, *Litigation*
EMP: 53
SALES (est): 6MM **Privately Held**
SIC: 8111 Criminal law; specialized law offices, attorneys

(P-22941)
BERGER KAHN (PA)
Also Called: Simon and Gladstone A Prof
4551 Glencoe Ave Ste 245, Marina Del Rey
(90292-7925)
PHONE...................310 578-6800
Craig Simon, *Owner*
Ron Alberts, *Partner*
Jason Wallach, *Partner*
Mike Aiken, *Principal*
Arthur I Willner, *Principal*
EMP: 70 EST: 1928
SQ FT: 22,250
SALES (est): 18MM **Privately Held**
WEB: www.bergerkahn.com
SIC: 8111 General practice attorney, lawyer

(P-22942)
BERGER KAHN
2 Park Plz Ste 650, Irvine (92614-2519)
PHONE...................310 821-9000
Craig S Simon, *Manager*
Craig Simon, *Managing Prtnr*
Pam Daubert, *Admin Sec*
Jess Block, *Mktg Dir*
Julia Mouser,
EMP: 50
SALES (est): 5.1MM
SALES (corp-wide): 18MM **Privately Held**
WEB: www.bergerkahn.com
SIC: 8111 General practice attorney, lawyer
PA: Berger Kahn
4551 Glencoe Ave Ste 245
Marina Del Rey CA 90292
310 578-6800

(P-22943)
BERRY & BERRY LAW FIRM
475 14th St Ste 550, Oakland
(94612-1938)
PHONE...................510 250-0200
Phillip S Berry, *President*
Vicky Inayama, *Executive*
EMP: 75
SALES (est): 8.7MM **Privately Held**
SIC: 8111 General practice attorney, lawyer

(P-22944)
BEST BEST & KRIEGER LLP (PA)
Also Called: BB&k
3390 University Ave # 500, Riverside
(92501-3369)
P.O. Box 1028 (92502-1028)
PHONE...................951 686-1450
Eric L Garner, *Managing Prtnr*
Jason M Ackerman, *Partner*
Franklin C Adams, *Partner*
Franklin Adams, *Partner*
Clark Alsop, *Partner*
EMP: 188 EST: 1891
SQ FT: 57,000

SALES (est): 63.7MM **Privately Held**
WEB: www.bbklaw.com
SIC: 8111 General practice attorney, lawyer

(P-22945)
BEST BEST & KRIEGER LLP
18101 Von Karman Ave # 1000, Irvine
(92612-0164)
PHONE...................949 263-2600
Monica Elmar, *Branch Mgr*
EMP: 50
SALES (corp-wide): 63.7MM **Privately Held**
SIC: 8111 General practice attorney, lawyer
PA: Best Best & Krieger Llp
3390 University Ave # 500
Riverside CA 92501
951 686-1450

(P-22946)
BET TZEDEK
3250 Wilshire Blvd Fl 13, Los Angeles
(90010-1601)
PHONE...................323 939-0506
Jessie Kornberg, *President*
Stanley Kandel, *President*
Harry Rimalower, *Vice Chairman*
David Bubis, *President*
Isabela Garcia, *President*
EMP: 51
SALES: 9MM **Privately Held**
SIC: 8111 Legal aid service

(P-22947)
BIRD MRLLA BXER WLPERT A PROF
1875 Century Park E Fl 23, Los Angeles
(90067-2337)
PHONE...................310 201-2100
Vincent Marella, *Partner*
Terry Bird, *Partner*
Joel Boxer, *Partner*
Dorothy Wolpert, *Partner*
Sandy Palmieri, *President*
EMP: 60
SALES: 6MM **Privately Held**
WEB: www.bmbwlaw.com
SIC: 8111 General practice law office

(P-22948)
BLANK ROME LLP
2029 Century Park E Fl 6, Los Angeles
(90067-2901)
PHONE...................424 239-3400
William Small, *Branch Mgr*
Danielle Garcia, *Counsel*
Kevin Omalley, *Associate*
EMP: 91
SALES (corp-wide): 152.9MM **Privately Held**
SIC: 8111 General practice attorney, lawyer
PA: Blank Rome Llp
1 Logan Sq
Philadelphia PA 19103
215 569-5500

(P-22949)
BLOOM DAVID LAW OFFICES OF
3530 Wilshire Blvd # 1300, Los Angeles
(90010-2318)
PHONE...................323 938-5248
David Bloom, *Owner*
EMP: 50 EST: 1974
SALES (est): 2.9MM **Privately Held**
SIC: 8111 General practice law office

(P-22950)
BLOOM HERGOTT DIEMER COOK LLC
Also Called: Bloom, Jacob A
150 S Rodeo Dr Fl 3, Beverly Hills
(90212-2410)
PHONE...................310 859-6800
Jacob A Bloom, *Partner*
Lawrence H Graves, *Partner*
Candice S Hansen, *Partner*
Allen Hergott, *Partner*
Tina J Kahn, *Partner*
EMP: 52
SALES (est): 6.6MM **Privately Held**
SIC: 8111 General practice law office

P R O D U C T S & S V C S

(P-22951)
BMC GROUP INC
Also Called: Bankruptcy Management Cons
300 N Cntntl Blvd Ste 570, El Segundo
(90245)
PHONE..............................310 321-5555
Shawn Allen, *President*
EMP: 100 **Privately Held**
SIC: 8111 Bankruptcy referee
PA: The Bmc Group Inc
720 3rd Ave Fl 23
Seattle WA 98104

(P-22952)
BOHM LAW GROUP INC (PA)
4600 Northgate Blvd # 210, Sacramento
(95834-1133)
PHONE..............................916 927-5574
Lawrance Bohm, *CEO*
EMP: 50
SALES (est): 5.7MM **Privately Held**
SIC: 8111 General practice law office

(P-22953)
BONNE BRIDGE MUELL OKEEF & (PA)
3699 Wilsh Boule Fl 10 Flr 10, Los Angeles
(90010)
PHONE..............................213 480-1900
David J O'Keefe, *President*
George Peterson, *Corp Secy*
James D Nichols, *Vice Pres*
Kris Marse, *Exec Sec*
EMP: 100
SQ FT: 48,000
SALES (est): 20.3MM **Privately Held**
SIC: 8111 General practice attorney,
lawyer

(P-22954)
BOORNAZIAN JENSEN & GARTHE A
555 12th St, Oakland (94607-4046)
PHONE..............................510 834-4350
David Garthe, *Principal*
Denise Agan, *President*
Brenda Bruessard, *President*
Leslie Hassberg, *President*
Charles Eisner, *CFO*
EMP: 60
SQ FT: 18,500
SALES (est): 7.7MM **Privately Held**
WEB: www.bjg.com
SIC: 8111 General practice attorney,
lawyer

(P-22955)
BOWLES & VERNA
2121 N Calif Blvd Ste 875, Walnut Creek
(94596-7335)
PHONE..............................925 935-3300
Richard Bowles, *Partner*
Richard Ergo, *Partner*
Kp Dean Harper, *Partner*
Mary Sullivan, *Partner*
Michael Verna, *Partner*
EMP: 50
SQ FT: 15,000
SALES (est): 6.8MM **Privately Held**
WEB: www.bv-law.com
SIC: 8111 Corporate, partnership & business law

(P-22956)
BOWMAN AND BROOKE LLP
Also Called: Bowman & Brooke-Attys
970 W 190th St Ste 700, Torrance
(90502-1091)
PHONE..............................310 768-3068
Mark Berry, *Manager*
Rosy Cervantes, *Legal Staff*
Anthony Parascandola, *Counsel*
Marcelo Lee, *Associate*
Autumn Lewis, *Associate*
EMP: 84
SALES (corp-wide): 55.7MM **Privately Held**
WEB: www.bowmanandbrooke.com
SIC: 8111 General practice law office
PA: Bowman And Brooke Llp
150 S 5th St Ste 3000
Minneapolis MN 55402
612 339-8682

(P-22957)
BRADFORD & BARTHEL LLP (PA)
2518 River Plaza Dr, Sacramento
(95833-3673)
PHONE..............................916 569-0790
Donald R Barthel, *Partner*
Tom Bradford, *Partner*
Melissa Gorski, *President*
Fritzie Gumalo, *President*
Arna Hines, *President*
EMP: 150
SALES: 37MM **Privately Held**
SIC: 8111 General practice law office

(P-22958)
BRADY VORWERCK RYDR & CSPNO (PA)
19200 Von Karman Ave, Irvine
(92612-8553)
PHONE..............................480 456-9888
James Brady, *CEO*
Robert Ryder, *Principal*
Gregg Vorwerck, *Principal*
EMP: 75
SALES (est): 8.9MM **Privately Held**
SIC: 8111 Legal services

(P-22959)
BRAYTON PURCELL APC (PA)
222 Rush Landing Rd, Novato
(94945-2469)
P.O. Box 6169 (94948-6169)
PHONE..............................415 898-1555
Alan Richard Brayton, *CEO*
Shawna Mahoney, *President*
Kim Beary, *CFO*
Rzsheridan Sheridan, *Executive*
Mike Molakides, *Administration*
EMP: 250
SQ FT: 40,000
SALES (est): 34.8MM **Privately Held**
WEB: www.asbestosnetwork.com
SIC: 8111 General practice attorney,
lawyer

(P-22960)
BREMER WHYTE BROWN OMEARA LLP (PA)
Also Called: Bremer Whyte Brown Omeara
20320 Sw Birch St Ste 200, Newport Beach
(92660-1791)
PHONE..............................949 221-1000
Keith Bremer, *Partner*
Nicole Whyte, *Partner*
Shawn Reutter, *President*
Brenda Newkirk, *General Mgr*
Eric Alden, *Associate*
EMP: 50
SQ FT: 6,000
SALES (est): 16.7MM **Privately Held**
SIC: 8111 Specialized legal services

(P-22961)
BRYAN CAVE LIGHTON PAISNER LLP
333 Market St Fl 25, San Francisco
(94105-2126)
PHONE..............................415 675-3400
Alicia Kuhn, *Manager*
Terri Parafina, *President*
Mary McHugh, *Manager*
EMP: 50
SALES (corp-wide): 446.5MM **Privately Held**
SIC: 8111 General practice attorney,
lawyer
PA: Bryan Cave Leighton Paisner Llp
1 Metropolitan Sq
Saint Louis MO 63102
314 259-2000

(P-22962)
BRYAN CAVE LIGHTON PAISNER LLP
3161 Michelson Dr # 1500, Irvine
(92612-4400)
PHONE..............................949 223-7000
Ren Hayhurst, *Manager*
Ren Hayhurft, *Partner*
EMP: 56
SALES (corp-wide): 446.5MM **Privately Held**
SIC: 8111 General practice attorney,
lawyer

PA: Bryan Cave Leighton Paisner Llp
1 Metropolitan Sq
Saint Louis MO 63102
314 259-2000

(P-22963)
BRYAN CAVE LIGHTON PAISNER LLP
120 Broadway Ste 300, Santa Monica
(90401-2386)
PHONE..............................310 576-2100
Louise Caplan, *Administration*
Leslie Asaraf, *President*
Nicole J Simonian, *Technical Staff*
Samuel Garcia, *Manager*
Nancy Neiman, *Manager*
EMP: 130
SALES (corp-wide): 446.5MM **Privately Held**
SIC: 8111 General practice attorney,
lawyer
PA: Bryan Cave Leighton Paisner Llp
1 Metropolitan Sq
Saint Louis MO 63102
314 259-2000

(P-22964)
BUCHALTER NEMER A PROF CORP
Also Called: BUCHALTER NEMER, A PROFESSIONAL CORPORATION
18400 Von Karman Ave # 800, Irvine
(92612-0514)
PHONE..............................714 549-5150
Tammy Curtis, *Manager*
Mitchell Olejko, *Shareholder*
Philip Schroeder, *Shareholder*
EMP: 60
SALES (corp-wide): 51.9MM **Privately Held**
SIC: 8111 Legal services
PA: A Buchalter Professional Corporation
1000 Wilshire Blvd # 1500
Los Angeles CA 90017
213 891-0700

(P-22965)
BURKE WILLIAMS & SORENSEN LLP (PA)
444 S Flower St Ste 2400, Los Angeles
(90071-2953)
PHONE..............................213 236-0600
John J Welsh, *Managing Prtnr*
James T Bradshaw Jr, *Partner*
Harold Bridges, *Partner*
Steven J Dawson, *Partner*
Leland C Dolley, *Partner*
EMP: 90
SQ FT: 51,000
SALES (est): 24.9MM **Privately Held**
WEB: www.bwslaw.com
SIC: 8111 General practice law office

(P-22966)
BURNHAM BROWN A PROF CORP
Also Called: Burnham & Brown
1901 Harrison St Ste 1100, Oakland
(94612-3648)
P.O. Box 119 (94604-0119)
PHONE..............................510 444-6800
Gregory D Brown, *President*
Cathy Arias, *Partner*
Thomas Downey, *Partner*
Michael Johnson, *Partner*
John Verber, *Managing Prtnr*
EMP: 120 EST: 1899
SQ FT: 50,000
SALES (est): 18.6MM **Privately Held**
WEB: www.burnhambrown.com
SIC: 8111 General practice law office

(P-22967)
C T CORPORATION SYSTEM
2875 Michelle Ste 100, Irvine (92606-1024)
PHONE..............................925 287-9801
Despina Shields, *Regional Mgr*
EMP: 60
SALES (corp-wide): 5.2B **Privately Held**
WEB: www.ctadvantage.com
SIC: 8111 5999 7375 Legal services; telephone equipment & systems; information retrieval services

HQ: C T Corporation System
111 8th Ave Fl 13
New York NY 10011
212 894-8940

(P-22968)
CALL & JENSEN APC
610 Nwport Ctr Dr Ste 700, Newport Beach
(92660)
PHONE..............................949 717-3000
Wayne W Call, *President*
Jon Jensen, *Administration*
Gina Miller, *Administration*
Carrie Daly, *Legal Staff*
Katie Dominick, *Legal Staff*
EMP: 50
SALES (est): 7.7MM **Privately Held**
SIC: 8111 General practice attorney,
lawyer

(P-22969)
CARR & FERRELL
120 Constitution Dr, Menlo Park
(94025-1107)
PHONE..............................650 812-3400
Wininger Aaron, *Principal*
Robert P Pacheco, *Controller*
Joel Samson, *Patent Law*
Sarah Ferguson, *Director*
Ron Rohde, *Associate*
EMP: 72 EST: 2010
SALES (est): 3.4MM **Privately Held**
SIC: 8111 Legal services

(P-22970)
CARR & FERRELL LLP (PA)
120 Constitution Dr, Menlo Park
(94025-1107)
PHONE..............................650 812-3400
Barry Carr, *Partner*
John S Ferrell, *General Ptnr*
Stuart Clark, *Partner*
Jill E Fishbein, *Partner*
Jefferson F Scher, *Partner*
EMP: 68
SALES (est): 9.5MM **Privately Held**
WEB: www.carr-ferrell.com
SIC: 8111 General practice attorney,
lawyer; corporate, partnership & business
law; patent, trademark & copyright law;
labor & employment law

(P-22971)
CARR MC CLELLAN INGERSOLL THOM (PA)
Also Called: Carr, McClellan
216 Park Rd, Burlingame (94010-4200)
P.O. Box 513 (94011-0513)
PHONE..............................650 342-9600
Mark A Cassanego, *President*
Tracy Francis, *President*
Vanessa Hodam, *President*
Darsy Meghinasso, *President*
Steven D Anderson, *CFO*
EMP: 65
SQ FT: 19,000
SALES (est): 10.7MM **Privately Held**
WEB: www.cmithlaw.com
SIC: 8111 General practice attorney,
lawyer

(P-22972)
CARROLL BURDICK MC DONOUGH LLP (PA)
275 Battery St Ste 2600, San Francisco
(94111-3358)
PHONE..............................415 989-5900
Angela Bradstreet, *Partner*
Doris Alexander, *Exec Dir*
Marcelino Nogueiro, *Analyst*
Mary Holland, *Human Res Dir*
Carmen Tapia, *Legal Staff*
EMP: 142
SQ FT: 50,000
SALES (est): 22.7MM **Privately Held**
WEB: www.cbmlaw.com
SIC: 8111 General practice attorney,
lawyer

(P-22973)
CARSON KURTZMAN CONSULTANTS (DH)
Also Called: K C C
2335 Alaska Ave, El Segundo
(90245-4808)
PHONE.................................310 823-9000
Jon A Orr,
James Le Transitions, *Exec VP*
Justin Hughes, *Vice Pres*
Daniel Marotto, *Vice Pres*
Kurt Whittaker, *Business Anlyst*
EMP: 180
SQ FT: 46,000
SALES (est): 20.5MM **Privately Held**
WEB: www.kccllc.com
SIC: 8111 Specialized legal services

(P-22974)
CHILDRENS LAW CENTER CAL (PA)
101 Centre Plaza Dr, Monterey Park
(91754-2155)
PHONE.................................323 980-8700
Leslie Starr Heimov, *CEO*
David Estep, *Director*
Debra Lopez, *Supervisor*
EMP: 122
SALES: 30.7MM **Privately Held**
SIC: 8111 Legal aid service

(P-22975)
CHODOROW DE CASTRO WEST
10960 Wilshire Blvd # 1400, Los Angeles
(90024-3717)
PHONE.................................310 478-2541
Hugo Decastro, *President*
Hilton Chodorow,
Buddy Epstein,
Henry Reitzenstein,
EMP: 65
SQ FT: 19,400
SALES (est): 10.2MM **Privately Held**
WEB: www.dwclaw.com
SIC: 8111 General practice law office

(P-22976)
CITY & COUNTY OF SAN FRANCISCO
Also Called: City Attorney
1 Carlton B Goodlett Pl # 234, San Francisco (94102-4604)
PHONE.................................415 554-4700
Dennis Herrera, *Principal*
EMP: 250 **Privately Held**
SIC: 8111 9222 General practice attorney, lawyer; legal counsel & prosecution; ;
PA: City & County Of San Francisco
    1 Dr Carlton B Goodlett P
    San Francisco CA 94102
    415 554-7500

(P-22977)
CITY & COUNTY OF SAN FRANCISCO
Also Called: District Attorney's Office
850 Bryant St Ste 600, San Francisco
(94103-4613)
PHONE.................................415 553-1752
Kamala Harris, *Manager*
EMP: 130 **Privately Held**
SIC: 8111 9222 Legal services; legal counsel & prosecution; ;
PA: City & County Of San Francisco
    1 Dr Carlton B Goodlett P
    San Francisco CA 94102
    415 554-7500

(P-22978)
CITY OF LONG BEACH
Also Called: Long Beach Cty Flt Svc Ofc
2600 Temple Ave, Long Beach
(90806-2209)
PHONE.................................562 570-5423
Dennis Hill, *Principal*
EMP: 67 **Privately Held**
WEB: www.polb.us
SIC: 8111 Legal services
PA: City Of Long Beach
    333 W Ocean Blvd Fl 10
    Long Beach CA 90802
    562 570-6450

(P-22979)
CITY OF LONG BEACH
Also Called: City Attorneys Office
333 W Ocean Blvd Lbby, Long Beach
(90802-4664)
PHONE.................................562 570-6919
Karen Brandt, *Manager*
Rajan Hoyle, *District Mgr*
Jennifer Kumiyama, *Office Mgr*
EMP: 67 **Privately Held**
WEB: www.polb.us
SIC: 8111 9111 General practice attorney, lawyer; mayors' offices
PA: City Of Long Beach
    333 W Ocean Blvd Fl 10
    Long Beach CA 90802
    562 570-6450

(P-22980)
CITY OF LOS ANGELES
Also Called: City Los Angeles General Svcs
111 E 1st St Ste 401, Los Angeles
(90012-3678)
PHONE.................................213 978-4049
Len Appledaum, *Chief Acct*
Gail Brown, *Info Tech Mgr*
Adrine Issavy, *Prgrmr*
Victor Yee, *Finance*
Charles Huang, *Analyst*
EMP: 200 **Privately Held**
WEB: www.lacity.org
SIC: 8111 Legal services
PA: City Of Los Angeles
    200 N Spring St Ste 303
    Los Angeles CA 90012
    213 978-0600

(P-22981)
CITY OF LOS ANGELES
Also Called: City Attorney
200 N Main St Ste 800, Los Angeles
(90012-4133)
PHONE.................................213 978-8100
Mike Feuer, *General Mgr*
Rich Llewellyn, *Persnl Dir*
Frank Mateljan, *Manager*
Michiko Reyes, *Manager*
EMP: 800 **Privately Held**
WEB: www.lacity.org
SIC: 8111 9222 Legal services; legal counsel & prosecution;
PA: City Of Los Angeles
    200 N Spring St Ste 303
    Los Angeles CA 90012
    213 978-0600

(P-22982)
CLIFFORD & BROWN A PROF CORP
1430 Truxtun Ave Ste 900, Bakersfield
(93301-5226)
PHONE.................................661 322-6023
Steven Clifford, *President*
Arnold Anchordoquy, *Treasurer*
Michael O'Dell, *Executive*
Jim Brown, *Principal*
Bob Harding, *Admin Sec*
EMP: 51
SQ FT: 100,000
SALES: 2.5MM **Privately Held**
WEB: www.clifford-law.com
SIC: 8111 General practice law office

(P-22983)
CLYDE & CO US LLP
101 2nd St 24, San Francisco
(94105-3665)
PHONE.................................415 365-9800
Rhonda Jenkins, *Principal*
Cathy Christ, *Admin Mgr*
Chriszayda Escobar, *Office Admin*
Michael Burns, *Technology*
Debra O'Connor, *Human Resources*
EMP: 55
SALES (corp-wide): 637.8MM **Privately Held**
SIC: 8111 General practice attorney, lawyer
HQ: Clyde & Co Us Llp
    405 Lexington Ave
    New York NY 10174

(P-22984)
COBLENTZ PATCH DUFFY BASS LLP
1 Montgomery St Ste 3000, San Francisco
(94104-5500)
PHONE.................................510 655-4598
Michael Meyers, *Partner*
William Coblentz, *Senior Partner*
Paul Escobosa, *Partner*
Susan Jamison, *Partner*
Jeffrey B Knowles, *Partner*
EMP: 100
SQ FT: 30,000
SALES (est): 22.8MM **Privately Held**
WEB: www.cpdb.com
SIC: 8111 General practice attorney, lawyer

(P-22985)
COLLINS CLLINS MUIR STWART LLP
1100 El Centro St Frnt, South Pasadena
(91030-5213)
PHONE.................................626 243-1100
John Collins, *Partner*
Samuel J Muir, *Partner*
Brian Stewart, *Partner*
Laurey Carpenter, *President*
Chelsea Reyes, *President*
EMP: 50
SQ FT: 20,000
SALES (est): 7.5MM **Privately Held**
SIC: 8111 General practice attorney, lawyer

(P-22986)
COMMUNITY ACTION PARTNERSHIP
1152 E Grand Ave, Arroyo Grande
(93420-2583)
PHONE.................................805 489-4026
Raye Flemming, *Branch Mgr*
EMP: 249
SALES (corp-wide): 57.3MM **Privately Held**
SIC: 8111 General practice law office
PA: Community Action Partnership Of San Luis Obispo County, Inc.
    1030 Southwood Dr
    San Luis Obispo CA 93401
    805 544-4355

(P-22987)
COMPEX LEGAL SERVICES INC (PA)
325 Maple Ave, Torrance (90503-2602)
PHONE.................................310 782-1801
Arvind Korde, *CEO*
Nitin Mehta, *Chairman*
Anthony Bazurto, *Senior VP*
Margaret Guevara, *Vice Pres*
Humildad Pasimio, *Vice Pres*
EMP: 120
SQ FT: 47,740
SALES (est): 84.7MM **Privately Held**
WEB: www.compexlegal.com
SIC: 8111 7338 7334 Specialized legal services; secretarial & court reporting; photocopying & duplicating services

(P-22988)
COOKSEY TOOLEN GAGE DUFFY (PA)
535 Anton Blvd Fl 10, Costa Mesa
(92626-1947)
PHONE.................................714 431-1100
David Cooksey, *President*
Robert L Toolen, *Vice Pres*
Richard C Buck,
Leroy E Einspahr,
Kim Patterson Gage,
EMP: 54
SALES (est): 14.1MM **Privately Held**
WEB: www.cookseylaw.com
SIC: 8111 General practice law office

(P-22989)
COOLEY LLP
Also Called: Cooley Godward Kronish
101 California St Fl 5, San Francisco
(94111-5800)
PHONE.................................415 693-2000
Lee Benton, *Partner*
Olton Rensch, *Comp Tech*
Natalie Kaup, *Analyst*

Jonie Kondracki, *Opers Mgr*
Wesley Riddle, *Corp Comm Staff*
EMP: 100
SALES (corp-wide): 187.7MM **Privately Held**
WEB: www.cooley.com
SIC: 8111 Specialized law offices, attorneys
PA: Cooley Llp
    3175 Hanover St
    Palo Alto CA 94304
    650 843-5000

(P-22990)
COOLEY LLP (PA)
3175 Hanover St, Palo Alto (94304-1130)
PHONE.................................650 843-5000
Joe Conroy, *Managing Prtnr*
Tom Reicher -, *Partner*
Kenneth J Adelson, *Partner*
Mike Attanasio, *Partner*
Andrew Basile, *Partner*
EMP: 300
SALES (est): 187.7MM **Privately Held**
WEB: www.cooley.com
SIC: 8111 Corporate, partnership & business law

(P-22991)
COOLEY LLP
4 Palo Alto Sq, Palo Alto (94306-2122)
PHONE.................................650 843-5124
Chris Johnston, *Branch Mgr*
Mercedes Milana, *President*
Iris Wong, *President*
EMP: 143
SALES (corp-wide): 187.7MM **Privately Held**
SIC: 8111 General practice attorney, lawyer
PA: Cooley Llp
    3175 Hanover St
    Palo Alto CA 94304
    650 843-5000

(P-22992)
COOLEY LLP
4401 Eastgate Mall, San Diego
(92121-1909)
PHONE.................................858 550-6000
Fred Muto, *Partner*
Christopher J Kearns, *Partner*
Patricia Nicholls, *Admin Sec*
Lisa St John, *Personnel Exec*
David L Crawford, *Associate*
EMP: 150
SALES (corp-wide): 187.7MM **Privately Held**
WEB: www.cooley.com
SIC: 8111 General practice law office
PA: Cooley Llp
    3175 Hanover St
    Palo Alto CA 94304
    650 843-5000

(P-22993)
COOPER WHITE & COOPER LLP (PA)
201 California St Fl 17, San Francisco
(94111-5002)
PHONE.................................415 433-1900
Mark P Schreiber, *Partner*
Walter Hansell, *Partner*
Keith Howard, *Partner*
Peter Sibley, *Partner*
Jed Solomon, *Partner*
EMP: 120
SQ FT: 44,000
SALES (est): 22.3MM **Privately Held**
WEB: www.cwclaw.com
SIC: 8111 General practice law office

(P-22994)
COUNTY OF FRESNO
Also Called: Superior Court Unit
1130 O St, Fresno (93724-2201)
PHONE.................................559 600-3420
Rick Chavez, *Manager*
EMP: 96 **Privately Held**
WEB: www.first5fresno.org
SIC: 8111 9199 Divorce & family law;
PA: County Of Fresno
    2420 Mariposa St
    Fresno CA 93721
    559 600-1710

P R O D U C T S & S V C S

(P-22995)
COUNTY OF FRESNO
Also Called: Public Defender's Office
2220 Tulare St Ste 300, Fresno
(93721-2130)
PHONE.....................559 600-3546
Kenneth Taniguchi, *Branch Mgr*
Douglas Feinberg, *Counsel*
EMP: 96 **Privately Held**
WEB: www.first5fresno.org
SIC: 8111 9222 Specialized law offices, attorneys; public defenders' offices;
PA: County Of Fresno
2420 Mariposa St
Fresno CA 93721
559 600-1710

(P-22996)
COUNTY OF KERN
1215 Truxtun Ave Fl 4, Bakersfield
(93301-4619)
PHONE.....................661 868-2000
William Fawns, *Branch Mgr*
EMP: 95 **Privately Held**
SIC: 8111 Legal services
PA: County Of Kern
1115 Truxtun Ave Rm 505
Bakersfield CA 93301
661 868-3690

(P-22997)
COUNTY OF LOS ANGELES
Also Called: Public Defenders Office
1601 Eastlake Ave Ste 4, Los Angeles
(90033-1009)
PHONE.....................323 226-8998
Ron Brown, *Principal*
EMP: 214 **Privately Held**
SIC: 8111 Legal services
PA: County Of Los Angeles
500 W Temple St Ste 437
Los Angeles CA 90012
213 974-1101

(P-22998)
COUNTY OF LOS ANGELES
300 S Park Ave Ste 770, Pomona
(91766-1557)
PHONE.....................909 620-3330
EMP: 214 **Privately Held**
SIC: 8111 General practice attorney,
lawyer
PA: County Of Los Angeles
500 W Temple St Ste 437
Los Angeles CA 90012
213 974-1101

(P-22999)
COUNTY OF LOS ANGELES
Also Called: District Attorney
200 W Compton Blvd # 700, Compton
(90220-6676)
PHONE.....................310 603-7483
Julie Sulman, *Manager*
EMP: 110 **Privately Held**
WEB: www.co.la.ca.us
SIC: 8111 9222 Legal services; District Attorneys' offices;
PA: County Of Los Angeles
500 W Temple St Ste 437
Los Angeles CA 90012
213 974-1101

(P-23000)
COUNTY OF LOS ANGELES
Also Called: Public Defender Administration
210 W Temple St Fl 19, Los Angeles
(90012-3231)
PHONE.....................213 974-2811
Ronald Brown, *Branch Mgr*
EMP: 200 **Privately Held**
WEB: www.co.la.ca.us
SIC: 8111 9222 Legal services; public defenders' offices;
PA: County Of Los Angeles
500 W Temple St Ste 437
Los Angeles CA 90012
213 974-1101

(P-23001)
COUNTY OF LOS ANGELES
Also Called: Public Defender
200 W Compton Blvd Fl 8, Compton
(90220-6676)
PHONE.....................310 603-7271
John Brock, *Manager*

EMP: 214 **Privately Held**
WEB: www.co.la.ca.us
SIC: 8111 9222 Legal services; public defenders' offices;
PA: County Of Los Angeles
500 W Temple St Ste 437
Los Angeles CA 90012
213 974-1101

(P-23002)
COUNTY OF LOS ANGELES
Also Called: Court House
20221 Hamilton Ave, Torrance
(90502-1321)
PHONE.....................310 222-3552
Charles Mandel, *Branch Mgr*
EMP: 214 **Privately Held**
SIC: 8111 General practice attorney,
lawyer
PA: County Of Los Angeles
500 W Temple St Ste 437
Los Angeles CA 90012
213 974-1101

(P-23003)
COUNTY OF LOS ANGELES
Also Called: District Attorney
6230 Sylmar Ave Ste 201, Van Nuys
(91401-2731)
PHONE.....................818 374-2406
Nancy Lidamore, *Director*
EMP: 60 **Privately Held**
WEB: www.co.la.ca.us
SIC: 8111 9222 General practice attorney,
lawyer; District Attorneys' offices;
PA: County Of Los Angeles
500 W Temple St Ste 437
Los Angeles CA 90012
213 974-1101

(P-23004)
COUNTY OF ORANGE
Also Called: Public Defender
1440 N Harbor Blvd # 400, Fullerton
(92835-4127)
PHONE.....................714 626-3700
Sharon Petrosino, *Manager*
EMP: 50 **Privately Held**
SIC: 8111 9222 Legal services; public defenders' offices;
PA: County Of Orange
333 W Santa Ana Blvd 3f
Santa Ana CA 92701
714 834-6200

(P-23005)
COUNTY OF RIVERSIDE
Also Called: Public Defender- Main Office
4075 Main St, Riverside (92501-3701)
PHONE.....................951 955-6000
Gary Windom, *Administration*
Barbara Plate, *Supervisor*
EMP: 200 **Privately Held**
SIC: 8111 9222 Legal services; public defenders' offices;
PA: County Of Riverside
4080 Lemon St Fl 11
Riverside CA 92501
951 955-1110

(P-23006)
COUNTY OF SACRAMENTO
Also Called: Public Defender's Office
700 H St Ste 270, Sacramento
(95814-1289)
PHONE.....................916 874-5411
Paulino G Duran, *Director*
EMP: 170 **Privately Held**
WEB: www.sna.com
SIC: 8111 9222 Legal services; public defenders' offices;
PA: County Of Sacramento
700 H St Ste 7650
Sacramento CA 95814
916 874-5544

(P-23007)
COUNTY OF SAN DIEGO
District Attorney
330 W Broadway Ste 1020, San Diego
(92101-3827)
PHONE.....................619 531-4040
Steven Silva, *Admin Sec*
Anne Calle, *Officer*
Wilson Tang, *Technology*
Barbara Medina, *Media Spec*

Karen Stanfill, *Legal Staff*
EMP: 93 **Privately Held**
WEB: www.sdlcc.org
SIC: 8111 9222 Specialized legal services;
District Attorneys' offices
PA: County Of San Diego
1600 Pacific Hwy Ste 209
San Diego CA 92101
619 531-5880

(P-23008)
COUNTY OF SHASTA
Also Called: Dist Attorney's Office
1355 West St, Redding (96001-1652)
PHONE.....................530 245-6300
Gerald Benito, *Principal*
EMP: 85 **Privately Held**
WEB: www.rsdnmp.org
SIC: 8111 Legal services
PA: County Of Shasta
1450 Court St Ste 308a
Redding CA 96001
530 225-5561

(P-23009)
COUNTY OF SONOMA
Also Called: District Attorney
600 Administration Dr 212j, Santa Rosa
(95403-2825)
PHONE.....................707 565-2209
Jill R Ravitch, *Branch Mgr*
Jill Ravitch, *Branch Mgr*
Desiree Henley, *Technician*
EMP: 120 **Privately Held**
WEB: www.sonomacompost.com
SIC: 8111 9111 Legal services; county supervisors' & executives' offices
PA: County Of Sonoma
585 Fiscal Dr 100
Santa Rosa CA 95403
707 565-2431

(P-23010)
COVINGTON & BURLING LLP
333 Twin Dolphin Dr # 700, Redwood City
(94065-1418)
PHONE.....................650 632-4700
Kurt G Calia, *Manager*
EMP: 115
SALES (corp-wide): 234.2MM **Privately Held**
SIC: 8111 General practice law office
PA: Covington & Burling Llp
1 City Center 850 Tenth
Washington DC 20001
202 662-6000

(P-23011)
COVINGTON & BURLING LLP
1 Front St Fl 35, San Francisco
(94111-5323)
PHONE.....................415 591-6000
Jim Snipes, *Partner*
George M Chester Jr, *Partner*
Jason Smith, *Info Tech Mgr*
Wendy L Feng, *Counsel*
Stephen Humenik, *Counsel*
EMP: 50
SALES (corp-wide): 234.2MM **Privately Held**
SIC: 8111 General practice law office
PA: Covington & Burling Llp
1 City Center 850 Tenth
Washington DC 20001
202 662-6000

(P-23012)
COVINGTON & BURLING LLP
1999 Avenue Of The Stars # 3500, Los Angeles (90067-4643)
PHONE.....................424 332-4800
Michelle Liffman, *Manager*
Raymond Smith, *Info Tech Dir*
Teresa Park, *Manager*
EMP: 311
SALES (corp-wide): 234.2MM **Privately Held**
SIC: 8111 General practice law office
PA: Covington & Burling Llp
1 City Center 850 Tenth
Washington DC 20001
202 662-6000

(P-23013)
COX CASTLE & NICHOLSON LLP (PA)
Also Called: Cox Castle
2029 Cntury Nicholson Llp, Los Angeles
(90067)
PHONE.....................310 284-2200
Gary A Glick, *Partner*
Lindsey H Barr, *Partner*
Robin L Bennett, *Partner*
Kenneth B Bley, *Partner*
Erica A Bose, *Partner*
EMP: 165
SQ FT: 60,000
SALES (est): 98MM **Privately Held**
SIC: 8111 General practice attorney,
lawyer

(P-23014)
CROWELL & MORING LLP
275 Battery St Ste 2200, San Francisco
(94111-3337)
PHONE.....................415 986-2800
Dawn Tonya, *Branch Mgr*
Joanne Richardson, *President*
Cristina Solorio, *President*
Anita Stephen, *Administration*
Hammad Alam, *Associate*
EMP: 60
SALES (corp-wide): 126.6MM **Privately Held**
SIC: 8111 General practice attorney,
lawyer
PA: Crowell & Moring Llp
1001 Penn Ave Nw Fl 10
Washington DC 20004
202 624-2500

(P-23015)
CROWELL & MORING LLP
3 Park Plz Ste 2000, Irvine (92614-2591)
PHONE.....................949 263-8400
Daniel Sasse, *Manager*
Karen A Gibbs, *Partner*
Steven P Rice, *Partner*
Donald E Sovie, *Partner*
John Oliverio, *CFO*
EMP: 50
SALES (corp-wide): 126.6MM **Privately Held**
WEB: www.crowell.com
SIC: 8111 Specialized law offices, attorneys
PA: Crowell & Moring Llp
1001 Penn Ave Nw Fl 10
Washington DC 20004
202 624-2500

(P-23016)
CUNEO BLACK WARD MISSLER A LAW
Also Called: Cuneo, Black, Ward & Missler
700 University Ave # 110, Sacramento
(95825-6722)
P.O. Box 276650 (95827-6650)
PHONE.....................916 363-8822
John Black, *President*
Jim Cuneo, *Partner*
Jim Missler, *Partner*
James Missler, *Shareholder*
Alan Jong, *CFO*
EMP: 50
SQ FT: 13,000
SALES (est): 5.8MM **Privately Held**
WEB: www.cbwmlaw.com
SIC: 8111 General practice law office

(P-23017)
CURTIS LEGAL GROUP A PROFESSI
1300 K St Fl 2, Modesto (95354-0928)
P.O. Box 3030 (95353-3030)
PHONE.....................209 521-1800
Ralph S Curtis, *Partner*
Tracy Thomas, *Financial Exec*
Connie Gonzalez, *Controller*
Amy Hahn, *Legal Staff*
Andrew Mendlin, *Director*
EMP: 50
SQ FT: 18,000
SALES (est): 6MM **Privately Held**
SIC: 8111 General practice attorney,
lawyer

(P-23018)
DALEY & HEFT ATTORNEYS
462 Stevens Ave Ste 201, Solana Beach
(92075-2099)
PHONE..........................858 755-5666
Dennis W Daley, *Partner*
Robert Brockman Jr, *Partner*
Mitchell D Dean, *Partner*
Robert Heft, *Partner*
Neal Meyers, *Partner*
EMP: 50
SALES (est): 8.2MM **Privately Held**
WEB: www.daleyheft.com
SIC: 8111 General practice law office

(P-23019)
DAMRELL NELSON SCHRIMP PALL
Also Called: Schrimp, Roger Attorney
703 W F St, Oakdale (95361-3736)
PHONE..........................209 848-3500
Roger Schrimp, *Branch Mgr*
EMP: 50
SALES (corp-wide): 4.5MM **Privately Held**
SIC: 8111 General practice law office
PA: Damrell, Nelson, Schrimp, Pallios,
Pacher, Silva Pc
1601 I St Ste 500
Modesto CA 95354
209 526-3500

(P-23020)
DANIEL ROBERT KNOWLTON
68368 Madrid Rd, Cathedral City
(92234-4836)
PHONE..........................760 265-5293
Daniel R Knowlton, *Owner*
EMP: 73 **EST:** 2010
SALES (est): 182.5K **Privately Held**
SIC: 8111 Legal services

(P-23021)
DANNING GILL DAMND KOLLITZ LLP
1900 Avenue Of The Stars # 11, Los Angeles (90067-4301)
PHONE..........................310 277-0077
David A Gill, *Partner*
Richard K Diamond, *Partner*
Howard Kollitz, *Partner*
David M Poitras, *Partner*
Eric P Israel PC, *Partner*
EMP: 70
SALES (est): 8.7MM **Privately Held**
WEB: www.dgdk.com
SIC: 8111 General practice law office

(P-23022)
DANNIS WLVER KLLEY A PROF CORP (PA)
275 Battery St Ste 1150, San Francisco
(94111-3333)
PHONE..........................415 543-4111
Gregory Dannis, *President*
A'Ree Hewitt, *President*
David Miller, *Vice Pres*
Nia Freeman, *Associate*
EMP: 70
SQ FT: 14,000
SALES (est): 8.3MM **Privately Held**
WEB: www.mbdlaw.com
SIC: 8111 General practice attorney,
lawyer

(P-23023)
DAVID DARROCH
300 Lakeside Dr Fl 24, Oakland
(94612-3534)
PHONE..........................510 835-9100
H James Wulfsberg, *Ch of Bd*
Charles W Reese, *President*
EMP: 60
SQ FT: 34,000
SALES (est): 4.5MM **Privately Held**
WEB: www.wulfslaw.com
SIC: 8111 General practice attorney,
lawyer

(P-23024)
DAVIS WRIGHT TREMAINE LLP
505 Montgomery St Ste 800, San Francisco
(94111-6533)
PHONE..........................415 276-6500
Jeff Gray, *Partner*

Gerald Hinkley, *Partner*
Michael Labianca, *Partner*
Paul Leboffe, *Partner*
Gregory Miller, *Partner*
EMP: 75
SALES (corp-wide): 98.4MM **Privately Held**
WEB: www.dwt.com
SIC: 8111 Legal services
PA: Davis Wright Tremaine Llp
1201 3rd Ave Ste 2200
Seattle WA 98101
206 622-3150

(P-23025)
DAVIS WRIGHT TREMAINE LLP
865 S Figueroa St # 2400, Los Angeles
(90017-2566)
PHONE..........................213 633-6800
Mary Haas, *Partner*
EMP: 90
SALES (corp-wide): 98.4MM **Privately Held**
WEB: www.dwt.com
SIC: 8111 General practice law office
PA: Davis Wright Tremaine Llp
1201 3rd Ave Ste 2200
Seattle WA 98101
206 622-3150

(P-23026)
DECHERT LLP
650 Town Center Dr # 700, Costa Mesa
(92626-7122)
PHONE..........................949 442-6000
Robert Roberton, *Mng Member*
Jane Portillo, *President*
EMP: 210
SALES (corp-wide): 296.8MM **Privately Held**
SIC: 8111 General practice law office
PA: Dechert Llp
2929 Arch St Ste 400
Philadelphia PA 19104
202 261-3300

(P-23027)
DECHERT LLP
633 W 5th St Ste 3700, Los Angeles
(90071-2013)
PHONE..........................213 489-1357
EMP: 210
SALES (corp-wide): 296.8MM **Privately Held**
SIC: 8111 Corporate, partnership & business law
PA: Dechert Llp
2929 Arch St Ste 400
Philadelphia PA 19104
202 261-3300

(P-23028)
DECHERT LLP
1 Bush St Ste 1600, San Francisco
(94104-4422)
PHONE..........................415 262-4500
John Randal, *Office Mgr*
Allison H Fumai, *Partner*
David Linder, *Partner*
Virgen M Laureano, *President*
Martill Seymour, *President*
EMP: 50
SALES (corp-wide): 296.8MM **Privately Held**
SIC: 8111 8748 General practice law office; business consulting
PA: Dechert Llp
2929 Arch St Ste 400
Philadelphia PA 19104
202 261-3300

(P-23029)
DEMLER ARMSTRONG & ROWLAND LLP
4500 E Pacific Cst Hwy # 400, Long Beach
(90804-3293)
PHONE..........................562 597-0029
Robert Armstrong, *Partner*
Sean Beatty, *Partner*
Edison Demler, *Partner*
Terry Rowland, *Partner*
EMP: 50
SQ FT: 13,500
SALES (est): 6.7MM **Privately Held**
WEB: www.darlaw.com
SIC: 8111 General practice law office

(P-23030)
DENTONS US LLP
1530 Page Mill Rd Ste 200, Palo Alto
(94304-1140)
PHONE..........................650 798-0300
Joe Borski, *Director*
Quincy Smith, *Counsel*
EMP: 65
SALES (corp-wide): 466MM **Privately Held**
SIC: 8111 General practice attorney,
lawyer
PA: Dentons Us Llp
233 S Wacker Dr Ste 5900
Chicago IL 60606
312 876-8000

(P-23031)
DENTONS US LLP
4675 Macarthur Ct # 1250, Newport Beach
(92660-8803)
PHONE..........................949 732-3700
Roger Rushing, *Owner*
Jess Bressi, *Partner*
EMP: 104
SALES (corp-wide): 466MM **Privately Held**
SIC: 8111 Legal services
PA: Dentons Us Llp
233 S Wacker Dr Ste 5900
Chicago IL 60606
312 876-8000

(P-23032)
DENTONS US LLP
750 B St Ste 3300, San Diego
(92101-8188)
PHONE..........................619 595-5400
Douglas Farry, *Director*
EMP: 51
SALES (corp-wide): 466MM **Privately Held**
WEB: www.mckennalong.com
SIC: 8111 Legal services
PA: Dentons Us Llp
233 S Wacker Dr Ste 5900
Chicago IL 60606
312 876-8000

(P-23033)
DENTONS US LLP
4655 Executive Dr Ste 700, San Diego
(92121-3128)
PHONE..........................619 236-1414
Nancy Scott, *Technology*
Kathy Caudillo, *Manager*
EMP: 350
SALES (corp-wide): 466MM **Privately Held**
SIC: 8111 General practice law office
PA: Dentons Us Llp
233 S Wacker Dr Ste 5900
Chicago IL 60606
312 876-8000

(P-23034)
DENTONS US LLP
1 Market Plz Fl 24, San Francisco
(94105-1102)
PHONE..........................415 882-5000
Paul Glad, *Branch Mgr*
Janice Castillo, *President*
Donald McKeever, *Technical Staff*
Margaret Wong, *Accounting Mgr*
D W Kallstrom,
EMP: 120
SALES (corp-wide): 466MM **Privately Held**
WEB: www.sonnenschein.com
SIC: 8111 General practice law office
PA: Dentons Us Llp
233 S Wacker Dr Ste 5900
Chicago IL 60606
312 876-8000

(P-23035)
DENTONS US LLP
601 S Figueroa St # 2500, Los Angeles
(90017-5704)
PHONE..........................213 623-9300
Edwin Reeser, *General Mgr*
Michael Lubic, *Partner*
John Walker, *Partner*
Sharon Atkinson, *Officer*
Paterson Lee,
EMP: 150

SALES (corp-wide): 466MM **Privately Held**
WEB: www.sonnenschein.com
SIC: 8111 General practice attorney,
lawyer
PA: Dentons Us Llp
233 S Wacker Dr Ste 5900
Chicago IL 60606
312 876-8000

(P-23036)
DENTONS US LLP
300 S Grand Ave Fl 14, Los Angeles
(90071-3124)
PHONE..........................213 688-1000
Janice Moor, *Administration*
Ned Black, *IT/INT Sup*
Michael T Kavanaugh, *Manager*
Benjie Zosa, *Supervisor*
EMP: 104
SALES (corp-wide): 466MM **Privately Held**
SIC: 8111 General practice attorney,
lawyer
PA: Dentons Us Llp
233 S Wacker Dr Ste 5900
Chicago IL 60606
312 876-8000

(P-23037)
DICKENSON PEATMAN & FOGARTY A (PA)
1455 1st St Ste 301, NAPA (94559-2822)
PHONE..........................707 252-7122
Rodeo Ocampo, *Office Mgr*
Elizabeth Mayhew, *Trust Officer*
Melvin Cheah, *Network Mgr*
Linda Hovis, *Accountant*
Scott Zaleski, *Controller*
EMP: 50
SQ FT: 3,000
SALES (est): 6.6MM **Privately Held**
WEB: www.dpfnapa.com
SIC: 8111 General practice attorney,
lawyer; general practice law office

(P-23038)
DIEPENBROCK ELKIN LLP
500 Capitol Mall Ste 650, Sacramento
(95814-4739)
PHONE..........................916 492-5000
Bradley Elkin, *President*
Michael V Brady, *Shareholder*
John Diepenbrock, *Shareholder*
Serena Albaeck, *President*
Michael Brady, *Chairman*
EMP: 56
SQ FT: 20,000
SALES: 15MM **Privately Held**
WEB: www.diepenbrock.com
SIC: 8111 General practice law office

(P-23039)
DIETZ GLMOR CHAZEN A PROF CORP (PA)
7071 Convoy Ct Ste 300, San Diego
(92111-1023)
PHONE..........................858 565-0269
William Dietz, *Principal*
Avery G Chazen, *Principal*
Michael Dofflemyre, *Principal*
Mark R Gilmor, *Principal*
Zachary Yarian, *Associate*
EMP: 50
SALES (est): 13.9MM **Privately Held**
SIC: 8111 Specialized law offices, attorneys

(P-23040)
DISABILITY GROUP INC
1014 23rd St, Santa Monica (90403-4520)
PHONE..........................310 829-5100
Ronald D Miller, *President*
EMP: 258
SALES (est): 15.2MM **Privately Held**
SIC: 8111 Specialized law offices, attorneys

(P-23041)
DISABILITY RIGHTS CALIFORNIA
350 S Bixel St, Los Angeles (90017-1418)
PHONE..........................213 213-8000
Kathy Blakemore, *President*
EMP: 76

SALES (corp-wide): 23.7MM **Privately Held**
SIC: 8111 Legal services
PA: Disability Rights California
1831 K St
Sacramento CA 95811
916 488-9950

(P-23042)
DISABILITY RIGHTS CALIFORNIA (PA)
Also Called: D R C
1831 K St, Sacramento (95811-4114)
PHONE................................916 488-9950
Izetta Jackson, *President*
Herb Anderson, *CFO*
Diana Lynn Nelson, *CFO*
Catherine Blakemore, *Exec Dir*
Diana Honig, *Admin Sec*
EMP: 55
SQ FT: 8,500
SALES: 23.7MM **Privately Held**
SIC: 8111 Legal services

(P-23043)
DISCOVERREADY LLC
27200 Tourney Rd Ste 450, Valencia
(91355-4992)
PHONE................................661 284-6401
Phil Richard, *Branch Mgr*
Kiefer Lance, *Vice Pres*
Jeff Knight, *Software Dev*
Norm Rippon, *Technology*
EMP: 70
SALES (corp-wide): 36.6MM **Privately Held**
SIC: 8111 Legal services
HQ: Discoverready Llc
200 S College St Fl 10
Charlotte NC 28202
980 939-7516

(P-23044)
DLA PIPER LLP (US)
550 S Hope St Ste 2400, Los Angeles
(90071-2618)
PHONE................................213 330-7700
Betty Shumener, *Principal*
Joan Lancaster, *Admin Sec*
Paul Wallis, *Controller*
Stephanie Cooley, *Marketing Mgr*
Annelies Verlinden,
EMP: 305
SALES (corp-wide): 493.7MM **Privately Held**
SIC: 8111 Corporate, partnership & business law
HQ: Dla Piper Llp (Us)
6225 Smith Ave Ste 200
Baltimore MD 21209
410 580-3000

(P-23045)
DLA PIPER LLP (US)
2000 University Ave # 100, East Palo Alto
(94303-2215)
PHONE................................650 833-2000
Francis Burch Jr, *CEO*
Carol Buss,
Elisabeth Eisner,
Michelle Harbottle,
Stacy Snowman,
EMP: 300
SALES (corp-wide): 493.7MM **Privately Held**
SIC: 8111 General practice attorney, lawyer
HQ: Dla Piper Llp (Us)
6225 Smith Ave Ste 200
Baltimore MD 21209
410 580-3000

(P-23046)
DLA PIPER LLP (US)
2000 Avenue Of The Stars 400n, Los Angeles (90067-4735)
PHONE................................310 595-3000
Ronnie Decesare, *Branch Mgr*
Verne Patane, *Legal Staff*
Susan N Acquista, *Associate*
Anthony Portelli, *Associate*
EMP: 100
SALES (corp-wide): 493.7MM **Privately Held**
SIC: 8111 General practice attorney, lawyer

(P-23047)
DLA PIPER LLP (US)
2000 University Ave # 100, East Palo Alto
(94303-2215)
PHONE................................650 833-2000
Rusty Conner, *Partner*
Eugene T Liipfert,
EMP: 400
SALES (corp-wide): 493.7MM **Privately Held**
SIC: 8111 General practice law office
HQ: Dla Piper Llp (Us)
6225 Smith Ave Ste 200
Baltimore MD 21209
410 580-3000

(P-23048)
DLA PIPER LLP (US)
401 B St Ste 1700, San Diego
(92101-4297)
PHONE................................619 699-2700
Steven Draeger, *Branch Mgr*
EMP: 250
SALES (corp-wide): 493.7MM **Privately Held**
SIC: 8111 General practice attorney, lawyer
HQ: Dla Piper Llp (Us)
6225 Smith Ave Ste 200
Baltimore MD 21209
410 580-3000

(P-23049)
DLA PIPER LLP (US)
4365 Executive Dr # 1100, San Diego
(92121-2123)
PHONE................................858 677-1400
Gary O'Malley, *Partner*
Jeffrey Baglio, *COO*
Carla Hoffman, *Office Admin*
Mitzi Barnes, *Admin Sec*
Cheryl Dearden, *Admin Sec*
EMP: 100
SALES (corp-wide): 493.7MM **Privately Held**
SIC: 8111 General practice attorney, lawyer
HQ: Dla Piper Llp (Us)
6225 Smith Ave Ste 200
Baltimore MD 21209
410 580-3000

(P-23050)
DOMINGUEZ FIRM INC
Also Called: Law Offices Juan J. Dominguez
3250 Wilshire Blvd # 1200, Los Angeles
(90010-1600)
PHONE................................213 388-7788
Juan J Dominguez, *President*
EMP: 100
SQ FT: 5,000
SALES (est): 7.6MM **Privately Held**
WEB: www.juanjdominguez.com
SIC: 8111 General practice attorney, lawyer; general practice law office

(P-23051)
DONAHUE GALLAGER WOODS LLP (PA)
1999 Harrison St Ste 2500, Oakland
(94612-4705)
PHONE................................415 381-4161
Lawrence K Rockwell, *Partner*
George J Barron, *Partner*
John J Coppinger, *Partner*
Michael J Dalton, *Partner*
Eric W Doney, *Partner*
EMP: 75 EST: 1918
SQ FT: 20,827
SALES (est): 7MM **Privately Held**
WEB: www.donahue.com
SIC: 8111 General practice attorney, lawyer

(P-23052)
DOWNEY BRAND LLP (PA)
621 Capitol Mall Fl 18, Sacramento
(95814-4731)
PHONE................................916 444-1000
Dale A Stern, *Managing Prtnr*
David R E Aladjem, *Partner*

Rhonda Cate Canby, *Partner*
Julie A Carter, *Partner*
Thomas N Cooper, *Partner*
EMP: 207 EST: 1926
SALES (est): 38.5MM **Privately Held**
WEB: www.dbsr.com
SIC: 8111 General practice attorney, lawyer

(P-23053)
DREYER BBICH BCCOLA CLLHAM LLP
20 Bicentennial Cir, Sacramento
(95826-2802)
PHONE................................916 379-3500
Roger A Dreyer, *Managing Prtnr*
Joseph J Babich, *Partner*
Robert A Buccola, *Partner*
William Callaham, *Partner*
Debbie Hunter, *Office Mgr*
EMP: 70
SQ FT: 5,000
SALES (est): 7.7MM **Privately Held**
WEB: www.dbbc.com
SIC: 8111 General practice attorney, lawyer

(P-23054)
DRINKER BIDDLE & REATH LLP
1800 Century Park E # 1400, Los Angeles
(90067-1517)
PHONE................................310 229-1282
Heather Abrigo, *Counsel*
EMP: 170
SALES (corp-wide): 291.3MM **Privately Held**
SIC: 8111 Specialized law offices, attorneys
PA: Drinker, Biddle & Reath Llp
1 Logan Sq Ste 2000
Philadelphia PA 19103
215 988-2700

(P-23055)
DRINKER BIDDLE & REATH LLP
4 Embarcadero Ctr Lbby, San Francisco
(94111-4174)
PHONE................................415 591-7500
Debra Krueger, *Principal*
Gail Guglielmo, *Personnel Assit*
Matthew Smith, *Associate*
EMP: 170
SALES (corp-wide): 291.3MM **Privately Held**
SIC: 8111 Specialized law offices, attorneys
PA: Drinker, Biddle & Reath Llp
1 Logan Sq Ste 2000
Philadelphia PA 19103
215 988-2700

(P-23056)
DUANE MORRIS LLP
1 Market Plz Ste 2200, San Francisco
(94105-1127)
PHONE................................415 957-3000
Leslye Olson, *Manager*
Glenn Manishin, *Partner*
Beth Coffey, *President*
Barry L Bunshoft, *Counsel*
Joseph M Burton, *Manager*
EMP: 150
SALES (corp-wide): 300MM **Privately Held**
WEB: www.duanemorris.com
SIC: 8111 General practice attorney, lawyer
PA: Duane Morris Llp
30 S 17th St Fl 5
Philadelphia PA 19103
215 979-1000

(P-23057)
DUCKOR SPRADLING METZGER
101 W Broadway Ste 1700, San Diego
(92101-8289)
PHONE................................619 209-3000
Michael J Duckor, *President*
Scott Metzger, *Shareholder*
Jill Osmars, *Shareholder*
Gary J Spradling, *Vice Ch Bd*
Sarah O'Brien, *Executive*
EMP: 70
SQ FT: 25,000

SALES (est): 8.5MM **Privately Held**
WEB: www.dsm-law.com
SIC: 8111 General practice law office

(P-23058)
DYKEMA GOSSETT PLLC
333 S Grand Ave Ste 2100, Los Angeles
(90071-1525)
PHONE................................213 457-1800
Caroline Acossano, *Manager*
David Newman, *Analyst*
Nancy Adams, *Sales Executive*
Jason Grinnell, *Counsel*
E L Horton, *Counsel*
EMP: 60
SALES (corp-wide): 136.9MM **Privately Held**
SIC: 8111 General practice law office
PA: Dykema Gossett P.L.L.C.
400 Renaissance Ctr
Detroit MI 48243
313 568-6800

(P-23059)
EILEEN NOTTOLI
Also Called: Allen Matkins
3 Embarcadero Ctr # 1200, San Francisco
(94111-4003)
PHONE................................415 837-1515
EMP: 75 EST: 2013
SALES (est): 1.7MM **Privately Held**
SIC: 8111

(P-23060)
ENGSTROM LIPSCOMB AND LACK A (PA)
10100 Santa Monica Blvd # 1200, Los Angeles (90067-4113)
PHONE................................310 552-3800
Paul Engstrom, *President*
Lee G Lipscomb, *Vice Pres*
Walter J Lack, *Admin Sec*
EMP: 70 EST: 1974
SQ FT: 22,000
SALES (est): 13.6MM **Privately Held**
WEB: www.elllaw.com
SIC: 8111 General practice law office

(P-23061)
EPSTEIN BECKER & GREEN PC
1875 Century Park E # 500, Los Angeles
(90067-2337)
PHONE................................310 556-8861
Sandy Siciliano, *Manager*
Ellie Cook, *Admin Sec*
Joy Ingoglia, *Admin Sec*
Alan B Dickson,
William O Stein,
EMP: 60
SALES (corp-wide): 106.9MM **Privately Held**
SIC: 8111 General practice attorney, lawyer
PA: Epstein Becker & Green, P.C.
250 Park Ave Fl 12
New York NY 10177
212 351-4500

(P-23062)
ERICKSEN ARBUTHNOT KILDUFF (PA)
570 Lennon Ln, Walnut Creek
(94598-2415)
PHONE................................925 947-1702
Douglas Kilduff, *President*
Sharon Hightower, *Senior Partner*
Robert M Arbuthnot, *President*
Douglas M Kilduff, *Treasurer*
Julia F Day, *Vice Pres*
EMP: 90
SALES (est): 11.8MM **Privately Held**
SIC: 8111 General practice attorney, lawyer

(P-23063)
FEDERAL DFENDERS SAN DIEGO INC (PA)
225 Broadway Ste 900, San Diego
(92101-5030)
PHONE................................619 234-8467
Jami Ferrara, *CEO*
Shereen J Charlick, *Principal*
Linda Acosta, *CTO*
Lou Soldinger, *Financial Exec*
Maria Acuna, *Human Res Dir*

EMP: 75
SALES: 23.1MM **Privately Held**
SIC: **8111** General practice law office

(P-23064)
FENWICK & WEST LLP (PA)
801 California St, Mountain View
(94041-1990)
PHONE.............................650 988-8500
Gordon K Davidson, *General Ptnr*
Michael R Blum, *Partner*
Darren E Donnelly, *Partner*
Dan Dorosin, *Partner*
Stephen D Gillespie, *Partner*
EMP: 375 EST: 1971
SALES (est): 80MM **Privately Held**
SIC: **8111** General practice attorney,
lawyer; patent, trademark & copyright law;
taxation law

(P-23065)
FENWICK & WEST LLP
555 California St # 1200, San Francisco
(94104-1515)
PHONE.............................415 875-2300
Kacey Leonis, *Office Mgr*
Madison Kaiser, *President*
Chris Howland, *Legal Staff*
Michael Zwerin, *Director*
Adam Lewin, *Associate*
EMP: 120
SALES (corp-wide): 80MM **Privately
Held**
SIC: **8111** General practice attorney,
lawyer; patent, trademark & copyright law;
taxation law
PA: Fenwick & West Llp
801 California St
Mountain View CA 94041
650 988-8500

(P-23066)
FIRM A CHUGH PROFESSIONAL CORP
15925 Carmenita Rd, Cerritos
(90703-2206)
PHONE.............................562 229-1220
Navneet Singh Chugh, *Principal*
EMP: 73 EST: 2011
SALES (est): 10.5MM **Privately Held**
SIC: **8111** General practice law office

(P-23067)
FIRM A CHUGH PROFESSIONAL CORP
4800 Great America Pkwy # 310, Santa
Clara (95054-1227)
PHONE.............................408 970-0100
Navneet Chugh, *Manager*
EMP: 50
SALES (corp-wide): 20.7MM **Privately
Held**
WEB: www.chugh.com
SIC: **8111** General practice law office
PA: Chugh Firm, The A Professional Corpo-
ration
15925 Carmenita Rd
Cerritos CA 90703
562 229-1220

(P-23068)
FIRST LEGAL SUPPORT SVCS LLC (PA)
1517 Beverly Blvd, Los Angeles
(90026-5704)
PHONE.............................213 250-1111
Elisha Gilboa, *Mng Member*
Nia Troup, *Vice Pres*
Bryan Blair, *Executive*
Tony Levey, *Regional Mgr*
Brian Malouf, *Regional Mgr*
EMP: 54
SQ FT: 3,000
SALES (est): 13.7MM **Privately Held**
WEB: www.firstlegalsupport.com
SIC: **8111** Legal aid service

(P-23069)
FISH & RICHARDSON PC
500 Arguello St Ste 500 # 500, Redwood
City (94063-1568)
PHONE.............................650 839-5070
Peter Devlin, *President*
Lori Cox, *President*
Leeanne Martin, *Executive*

Cecilia Acosta, *Admin Sec*
Yvonne Mills, *Financial Exec*
EMP: 100
SALES (corp-wide): 90.9MM **Privately
Held**
WEB: www.fr.com
SIC: **8111** General practice attorney,
lawyer
PA: Fish & Richardson P.C.
1 Marina Park Dr Ste 1700
Boston MA 02210
617 542-5070

(P-23070)
FISH & RICHARDSON PC
12390 El Camino Real, San Diego
(92130-3162)
PHONE.............................858 678-5070
Cindy Winters, *Manager*
Carol Cameron, *President*
Susan Rodriguez, *Admin Asst*
Jenifer Potter, *Project Mgr*
Rudy Cobian, *Technology*
EMP: 150
SALES (corp-wide): 90.9MM **Privately
Held**
WEB: www.fr.com
SIC: **8111** General practice law office
PA: Fish & Richardson P.C.
1 Marina Park Dr Ste 1700
Boston MA 02210
617 542-5070

(P-23071)
FISHER & PHILLIPS LLP
2050 Main St Ste 1000, Irvine
(92614-8240)
PHONE.............................949 851-2424
James McDonald, *Partner*
Connie Jedrzejewski, *Admin Asst*
Edward Patten, *Info Tech Mgr*
Philip Azzara, *Associate*
Seth E Ort, *Associate*
EMP: 53
SALES (corp-wide): 171.2MM **Privately
Held**
WEB: www.laborlawyers.com
SIC: **8111** General practice attorney,
lawyer; general practice law office
PA: Fisher & Phillips Llp
1075 Peachtree St Ne # 3500
Atlanta GA 30309
404 231-1400

(P-23072)
FITZGRALD ABBOTT BEARDSLEY LLP
1221 Broadway Fl 21, Oakland
(94612-1837)
P.O. Box 12867 (94604-2867)
PHONE.............................510 451-3300
Michael S Word, *Managing Prtnr*
Susan Von,
EMP: 71
SQ FT: 20,000
SALES (est): 9MM **Privately Held**
WEB: www.fablaw.com
SIC: **8111** General practice law office

(P-23073)
FLOYD SKEREN & KELLY LLP (PA)
Also Called: FS&k
101 Moody Ct Ste 200, Thousand Oaks
(91360-6068)
PHONE.............................818 206-9222
Thomas M Skeren Jr, *President*
Matthew Sherman, *Business Dir*
Todd Kelly, *Principal*
Thomas Skeren, *Principal*
Cecily Coco, *Legal Staff*
EMP: 74
SALES (est): 24.8MM **Privately Held**
SIC: **8111** General practice law office

(P-23074)
FOLEY & LARDNER LLP
975 Page Mill Rd, Palo Alto (94304-1013)
PHONE.............................650 856-3700
Susan Lamont, *Manager*
Brenda Allen-Johnson, *President*
Jane Barr, *President*
Monique Blakey, *President*
Deborah Collins, *President*
EMP: 121

SALES (corp-wide): 454.8MM **Privately
Held**
SIC: **8111** General practice attorney,
lawyer
PA: Foley & Lardner Llp
777 E Wisconsin Ave # 3800
Milwaukee WI 53202
414 271-2400

(P-23075)
FOLEY & LARDNER LLP
555 California St # 1700, San Francisco
(94104-1503)
PHONE.............................415 434-4484
Eileen Ridley, *Managing Prtnr*
Nancy Geenen, *Partner*
EMP: 80
SQ FT: 3,000
SALES (corp-wide): 454.8MM **Privately
Held**
WEB: www.foley.com
SIC: **8111** General practice attorney,
lawyer
PA: Foley & Lardner Llp
777 E Wisconsin Ave # 3800
Milwaukee WI 53202
414 271-2400

(P-23076)
FOLEY & LARDNER LLP
555 S Flower St Ste 3300, Los Angeles
(90071-2418)
PHONE.............................213 972-4500
Sergiy Sivochek, *Branch Mgr*
Deborah Felianco, *Executive*
Debbie Wasson, *Administration*
Jeffery Atkin, *Associate*
Adam Hepworth, *Associate*
EMP: 125
SALES (corp-wide): 454.8MM **Privately
Held**
SIC: **8111** Corporate, partnership & busi-
ness law
PA: Foley & Lardner Llp
777 E Wisconsin Ave # 3800
Milwaukee WI 53202
414 271-2400

(P-23077)
FOLEY & LARDNER LLP
3579 Vly Cntre Dr Ste 300, San Diego
(92130)
PHONE.............................858 847-6700
Greg Moser, *Partner*
Steven Millendorf, *Associate*
EMP: 70
SALES (corp-wide): 454.8MM **Privately
Held**
WEB: www.foley.com
SIC: **8111** General practice law office
PA: Foley & Lardner Llp
777 E Wisconsin Ave # 3800
Milwaukee WI 53202
414 271-2400

(P-23078)
FONDA & FRAZER LLP (PA)
1925 Century Park E # 1360, Los Angeles
(90067-2710)
PHONE.............................310 553-3320
Peter M Fonda, *Partner*
Pamela A Benben, *Partner*
Todd E Croutch, *Partner*
Stephen C Fraser, *Partner*
Alexander M Watson, *Partner*
EMP: 60
SQ FT: 11,000
SALES (est): 3.3MM **Privately Held**
WEB: www.fondafraserlaw.com
SIC: **8111** Criminal law

(P-23079)
FORD MOTOR COMPANY
3 Glen Bell Way Ste 200, Irvine
(92618-3392)
PHONE.............................949 341-5800
Michael O'Driscoll, *President*
Scott Gerald, *Business Anlyst*
Henry Ford, *Sales Mgr*
Ulrich John, *Sales Staff*
Adrianne Larouche, *Sales Staff*
EMP: 450

SALES (corp-wide): 156.7B **Publicly
Held**
WEB: www.ford.com
SIC: **8111** **7549** Corporate, partnership &
business law; automotive customizing
services, non-factory basis
PA: Ford Motor Company
1 American Rd
Dearborn MI 48126
313 322-3000

(P-23080)
FRAGOMEN DEL REY BERNSE
11238 El Camino Real # 100, San Diego
(92130-2653)
PHONE.............................858 793-1600
Gary Perl, *Partner*
EMP: 60
SALES (corp-wide): 248.8MM **Privately
Held**
SIC: **8111** General practice law office
PA: Fragomen, Del Rey, Bernsen & Loewy,
Llp
90 Matawan Rd
Matawan NJ 07747
732 862-5000

(P-23081)
FRAGOMEN DEL REY BERNSE
11150 W Olympic Blvd # 1000, Los Angeles
(90064-1827)
PHONE.............................310 820-3322
Peter Loewy, *Principal*
Shelly Song, *Associate*
EMP: 50
SALES (corp-wide): 248.8MM **Privately
Held**
SIC: **8111** General practice law office
PA: Fragomen, Del Rey, Bernsen & Loewy,
Llp
90 Matawan Rd
Matawan NJ 07747
732 862-5000

(P-23082)
FRAGOMEN DEL REY BERNSE
18401 Von Karman Ave # 255, Irvine
(92612-1596)
PHONE.............................949 660-3504
EMP: 81
SALES (corp-wide): 248.2MM **Privately
Held**
SIC: **8111**
PA: Fragomen, Del Rey, Bernsen & Loewy,
Llp
90 Matawan Rd
Matawan NJ 07747
732 862-5000

(P-23083)
FRAGOMEN DEL REY BERNSE
2121 Tasman Dr, Santa Clara
(95054-1027)
PHONE.............................408 919-0600
Cynthia Lang, *Branch Mgr*
Geri Soutar, *Human Resources*
Lan Nguyen, *Manager*
Margaret Espinal, *Associate*
Da N Rowan, *Associate*
EMP: 81
SALES (corp-wide): 248.2MM **Privately
Held**
SIC: **8111** General practice attorney,
lawyer
PA: Fragomen, Del Rey, Bernsen & Loewy,
Llp
90 Matawan Rd
Matawan NJ 07747
732 862-5000

(P-23084)
FRANCISCO EMILIO ASSOC LAW OFF
17532 Von Karman Ave, Irvine
(92614-6279)
PHONE.............................949 474-2222
Emilio Francisco, *President*
EMP: 100
SALES (est): 3.7MM **Privately Held**
SIC: **8111** General practice attorney,
lawyer

(P-23085)
FRANDZEL SHARE ROBINS BLOOM LC
1000 Wilshire Blvd # 1900, Los Angeles (90017-2427)
PHONE..................323 852-1000
Steve N Bloom, *President*
Patricia Trendacosta, *COO*
Thomas Robins, *Vice Pres*
EMP: 55
SQ FT: 40,000
SALES (est): 7.7MM **Privately Held**
WEB: www.frandzel.com
SIC: 8111 General practice attorney, lawyer; general practice law office

(P-23086)
FREEMAN FREEMAN & SMILEY (PA)
Also Called: Freeman Freeman & Smiley LLP
1888 Century Park E Fl 19, Los Angeles (90067-1723)
PHONE..................310 398-6100
Bruce M Smiley, *Principal*
Jill Draffin, *Partner*
Douglas K Freeman, *Partner*
Elyse Henry, *President*
Fred J Marcus, *Principal*
EMP: 94
SQ FT: 25,000
SALES (est): 17.3MM **Privately Held**
WEB: www.ffslaw.com
SIC: 8111 General practice law office; general practice attorney, lawyer

(P-23087)
FULWIDER AND PATTON LLP
6100 Center Dr Ste 1200, Los Angeles (90045-9203)
PHONE..................310 824-5555
Richard A Bardin, *Managing Prtnr*
Scott Hansen, *Partner*
Katherine McDaniel, *Partner*
David Pitman, *Partner*
EMP: 100
SQ FT: 48,000
SALES (est): 12.5MM **Privately Held**
SIC: 8111 General practice attorney, lawyer

(P-23088)
GALLOWAY LUCCHESE EVERSON
2300 Contra Costa Blvd, Walnut Creek (94596)
PHONE..................925 930-9090
G Patrick Galloway, *President*
David R Lucchese, *Vice Pres*
Diana Dempsey, *Admin Asst*
Carrie Hughes, *Admin Asst*
Jeannette Avila, *Legal Staff*
EMP: 50
SQ FT: 13,700
SALES (est): 5.5MM **Privately Held**
WEB: www.glattys.com
SIC: 8111 General practice law office

(P-23089)
GAW VAN MALE SMITH MYERS
1411 Oliver Rd Ste 300, Fairfield (94534-3433)
PHONE..................707 425-1250
Scott Reynolds, *Manager*
EMP: 62
SALES (corp-wide): 8.7MM **Privately Held**
WEB: www.gvmsmm.com
SIC: 8111 General practice attorney, lawyer
PA: Gaw, Van Male, Smith, Myers & Miroglio A Professional Corp
1000 Main St Ste 300
Napa CA 94559
707 469-7100

(P-23090)
GIBBS GIDEN LOCHER
1880 Century Park E # 1200, Los Angeles (90067-1621)
PHONE..................310 552-3400
Richard J Wittbrodt, *Principal*
A Walker, *President*
Kenneth C Gibbs, *Principal*
Joseph M Giden, *Principal*
William D Locher, *Principal*

EMP: 70
SQ FT: 27,000
SALES (est): 10.7MM **Privately Held**
WEB: www.gglt.com
SIC: 8111 General practice attorney, lawyer

(P-23091)
GIBSON DUNN & CRUTCHER LLP
1881 Page Mill Rd, Palo Alto (94304-1146)
PHONE..................650 849-5300
Russel Hansel, *Managing Prtnr*
Paul J Collins, *Partner*
H Mark Lyon, *Partner*
Ruby Pitt, *Admin Asst*
Dave Goodell, *Info Tech Mgr*
EMP: 60
SALES (corp-wide): 305.4MM **Privately Held**
WEB: www.gibsondunn.com
SIC: 8111 General practice law office
PA: Gibson, Dunn & Crutcher Llp
333 S Grand Ave Ste 4600
Los Angeles CA 90071
213 229-7000

(P-23092)
GIBSON DUNN & CRUTCHER LLP
3161 Michelson Dr # 1200, Irvine (92612-4412)
PHONE..................949 451-3800
Karen Kubani, *Branch Mgr*
Alba Cabriales, *President*
Kathleen Taylor, *President*
Celine Chow, *Office Admin*
Donna Luca, *Admin Sec*
EMP: 200
SALES (corp-wide): 305.4MM **Privately Held**
WEB: www.gibsondunn.com
SIC: 8111 General practice law office
PA: Gibson, Dunn & Crutcher Llp
333 S Grand Ave Ste 4600
Los Angeles CA 90071
213 229-7000

(P-23093)
GIBSON DUNN & CRUTCHER LLP (PA)
333 S Grand Ave Ste 4600, Los Angeles (90071-1512)
PHONE..................213 229-7000
Kenneth M Doran, *Managing Prtnr*
Nicholas Aleksander, *Partner*
Peter Alexiadis, *Partner*
Lisa A Alfaro, *Partner*
Lisa Alfaro, *Partner*
EMP: 500
SQ FT: 250,000
SALES (est): 305.4MM **Privately Held**
WEB: www.gibsondunn.com
SIC: 8111 General practice law office

(P-23094)
GIBSON DUNN & CRUTCHER LLP
2029 Century Park E # 4000, Los Angeles (90067-3026)
PHONE..................310 552-8500
Julie Denton, *General Mgr*
William Stinehart Jr, *Partner*
EMP: 65
SALES (corp-wide): 305.4MM **Privately Held**
WEB: www.gibsondunn.com
SIC: 8111 General practice law office
PA: Gibson, Dunn & Crutcher Llp
333 S Grand Ave Ste 4600
Los Angeles CA 90071
213 229-7000

(P-23095)
GIBSON DUNN & CRUTCHER LLP
555 Mission St Ste 3000, San Francisco (94105-0921)
PHONE..................415 393-8200
Mike Saad, *Manager*
Kathrin Sears, *Partner*
Kevin Yeh, *Finance Mgr*
Vanessa Bratcher, *Manager*
Vanessa Fitzpatrick, *Manager*
EMP: 101

SALES (corp-wide): 305.4MM **Privately Held**
WEB: www.gibsondunn.com
SIC: 8111 General practice law office
PA: Gibson, Dunn & Crutcher Llp
333 S Grand Ave Ste 4600
Los Angeles CA 90071
213 229-7000

(P-23096)
GILBERT KLLY CRWLEY JNNETT LLP (PA)
550 S Hope St Ste 2200, Los Angeles (90017-2631)
PHONE..................213 615-7000
Jon H Tisdale, *Managing Prtnr*
Paul Bigley, *Partner*
Timothy Kenna, *Partner*
Arthur J Mc Keon III, *Partner*
Lisa Braham, *President*
EMP: 75
SQ FT: 30,000
SALES (est): 12.9MM **Privately Held**
WEB: www.gilbertkelly.com
SIC: 8111 General practice law office

(P-23097)
GIPSON HOFFMAN & PANCIONE A
1901 Avenue Of The Stars # 1100, Los Angeles (90067-6002)
PHONE..................310 556-4660
Lawrence R Barnett, *President*
Richard P Solomon, *Partner*
Kenneth I Sidle, *President*
Robert E Gipson, *Vice Pres*
Robert H Steinberg, *Vice Pres*
EMP: 70
SQ FT: 27,000
SALES (est): 9.8MM **Privately Held**
WEB: www.ghplaw.com
SIC: 8111 General practice attorney, lawyer; corporate, partnership & business law; bankruptcy law

(P-23098)
GIRARDI & KEESE (PA)
1126 Wilshire Blvd, Los Angeles (90017-1904)
PHONE..................213 977-0211
Thomas V Girardi, *Partner*
Robert M Keese, *Partner*
Elizabeth Escobedo, *President*
Shelby Fujioka, *President*
Graham B Lippsmith, *Asbestos Litgtn*
EMP: 100
SQ FT: 5,000
SALES (est): 16.2MM **Privately Held**
WEB: www.girardikeese.com
SIC: 8111 General practice attorney, lawyer

(P-23099)
GLASER WEIL FINK JACOBS (PA)
10250 Constellation Blvd # 1900, Los Angeles (90067-6229)
PHONE..................310 553-3000
Terry Christensen, *Managing Prtnr*
Barry E Fink, *Partner*
Patricia L Glaser, *Partner*
John Mason, *Partner*
George Wall, *Partner*
EMP: 160
SQ FT: 76,000
SALES (est): 34.4MM **Privately Held**
SIC: 8111 General practice law office

(P-23100)
GLASPY & GLASPY A PROF CORP
100 Pringle Ave Ste 750, Walnut Creek (94596-7330)
P.O. Box 8104 (94596-8104)
PHONE..................408 279-8844
David M Glaspy, *President*
Thomas C Glaspy, *Vice Pres*
Stephanie Payne, *Manager*
EMP: 50
SALES (est): 4.1MM **Privately Held**
WEB: www.glaspy.com
SIC: 8111 Corporate, partnership & business law

(P-23101)
GLOBAL USA GREEN CARD
201 Spear St Ste 1100, San Francisco (94105-6164)
PHONE..................415 915-4151
Eran Druker, *VP Opers*
EMP: 60 EST: 2016
SALES (est): 1MM **Privately Held**
SIC: 8111 Immigration & naturalization law

(P-23102)
GOODWIN PROCTER LLP
601 S Figueroa St # 4100, Los Angeles (90017-5710)
PHONE..................213 426-2500
Dean Pappas, *Managing Prtnr*
EMP: 60
SALES (corp-wide): 340.8MM **Privately Held**
SIC: 8111 General practice attorney, lawyer
PA: Goodwin Procter Llp
100 Northern Ave
Boston MA 02210
617 570-1000

(P-23103)
GORDON EDELSTEIN KREPACK GR
Also Called: Gordon Edelstein & Krepack
3580 Wilshire Blvd # 1800, Los Angeles (90010-2530)
PHONE..................213 739-7000
Roger L Gordon, *Partner*
Mark Edelstein, *Partner*
Richard Felton, *Partner*
Irwin Goldstein, *Partner*
Larry Goldstein, *Partner*
EMP: 50
SALES (est): 9.7MM **Privately Held**
WEB: www.geklaw.com
SIC: 8111 Legal services

(P-23104)
GORDON REES SCLLY MNSKHANI LLP
655 University Ave # 200, Sacramento (95825-6707)
PHONE..................916 830-6900
Kathleen M Rhoads, *Managing Prtnr*
Kara Keister, *Counsel*
Sara Moore, *Associate*
EMP: 94
SALES (corp-wide): 174.4MM **Privately Held**
SIC: 8111 Specialized law offices, attorneys
PA: Rees Gordon Scully Mansukhani Llp
275 Battery St Ste 2000
San Francisco CA 94111
415 986-5900

(P-23105)
GORDON REES SCLLY MNSKHANI LLP
2211 Michelson Dr, Irvine (92612-1384)
PHONE..................949 255-6950
Douglas Smith, *Office Mgr*
Sandra Avants, *President*
Steve Holub, *Office Mgr*
Tara Martin, *Counsel*
EMP: 80
SALES (corp-wide): 174.4MM **Privately Held**
SIC: 8111 Specialized law offices, attorneys
PA: Rees Gordon Scully Mansukhani Llp
275 Battery St Ste 2000
San Francisco CA 94111
415 986-5900

(P-23106)
GORDON REES SCLLY MNSKHANI LLP (PA)
275 Battery St Ste 2000, San Francisco (94111-3361)
PHONE..................415 986-5900
Dion N Cominos, *Partner*
Jorge J Perez, *Partner*
Stephen E Ronk, *Partner*
Peter Siachos, *Partner*
Marc Thirkell, *Partner*
EMP: 325
SQ FT: 57,500

SALES (est): 174.4MM **Privately Held**
WEB: www.gordonrees.com
SIC: 8111 Corporate, partnership & business law

(P-23107)
GORDON REES SCLLY MNSKHANI LLP
633 W 5th St Fl 52, Los Angeles (90071-2086)
PHONE..........................213 576-5000
Scott Sirlin, *Owner*
Ronald Giller, *Managing Prtnr*
Dina Cordero, *President*
Wendy Fletcher, *President*
Mila Owen, *President*
EMP: 79
SALES (corp-wide): 174.4MM **Privately Held**
SIC: 8111 Specialized law offices, attorneys
PA: Rees Gordon Scully Mansukhani Llp
275 Battery St Ste 2000
San Francisco CA 94111
415 986-5900

(P-23108)
GORDON REES SCLLY MNSKHANI LLP
101 W Broadway Ste 1600, San Diego (92101-8217)
PHONE..........................619 696-6700
Gary Zacher, *Managing Prtnr*
Roger Mansukhani, *COO*
Dawn Lodico, *Administration*
Mark Saxon, *Administration*
Susan Orona, *Marketing Staff*
EMP: 100
SQ FT: 7,000
SALES (corp-wide): 174.4MM **Privately Held**
WEB: www.gordonrees.com
SIC: 8111 Specialized law offices, attorneys
PA: Rees Gordon Scully Mansukhani Llp
275 Battery St Ste 2000
San Francisco CA 94111
415 986-5900

(P-23109)
GORDON REES SCLLY MNSKHANI LLP
101 W Broadway Ste 2000, San Diego (92101-8221)
PHONE..........................415 986-5900
Craig Hill, *Manager*
Heather Wadsworth, *Legal Staff*
Andrew Jacob, *Counsel*
Brooke Anderson, *Associate*
Bradley S Hagadorn, *Associate*
EMP: 90
SALES (corp-wide): 174.4MM **Privately Held**
WEB: www.gordonrees.com
SIC: 8111 Specialized law offices, attorneys
PA: Rees Gordon Scully Mansukhani Llp
275 Battery St Ste 2000
San Francisco CA 94111
415 986-5900

(P-23110)
GREEN GLUSK FIELD CLAMA & MACH
1900 Avenue Of The Stars 21f, Los Angeles (90067-4301)
PHONE..........................310 553-3610
Jonathan R Fitzgarrald, *Principal*
ARI B Brumer, *Partner*
Ricardo P Cestero, *Partner*
Stephen Claman, *Partner*
Bert Fields, *Partner*
EMP: 200
SQ FT: 80,000
SALES (est): 32.1MM **Privately Held**
SIC: 8111 General practice attorney, lawyer

(P-23111)
GREENBERG TRAURIG LLP
4 Embarcadero Ctr # 3000, San Francisco (94111-5983)
PHONE..........................415 655-1300
Evan S Nadel, *Branch Mgr*
Alison Gathright, *Shareholder*

Howard Holderness, *Shareholder*
Leslie Katz, *Shareholder*
Brad Marsh, *Shareholder*
EMP: 98
SALES (corp-wide): 458.4MM **Privately Held**
SIC: 8111 General practice attorney, lawyer
HQ: Greenberg Traurig, Llp
200 Park Ave Fl 438
New York NY 10166
-

(P-23112)
GREENBERG TRAURIG LLP
1840 Century Park E # 1900, Los Angeles (90067-2121)
PHONE..........................310 586-7708
Richard Rowan, *Branch Mgr*
Tom ARA, *Shareholder*
Vincent Chieffo, *Shareholder*
Matthew Gershman, *Shareholder*
Jeffrey Joyner, *Shareholder*
EMP: 76
SALES (corp-wide): 458.4MM **Privately Held**
SIC: 8111 General practice attorney, lawyer
HQ: Greenberg Traurig, Llp
200 Park Ave Fl 438
New York NY 10166

(P-23113)
GREENBERG TRAURIG LLP
1900 University Ave Fl 5, East Palo Alto (94303-2283)
PHONE..........................650 328-8500
Lance Joseph, *Branch Mgr*
Vivek Chavan, *Shareholder*
Cindy Hamilton, *Shareholder*
David Oppenheim, *Shareholder*
Stephen Pepper, *Shareholder*
EMP: 73
SALES (corp-wide): 458.4MM **Privately Held**
SIC: 8111 General practice attorney, lawyer
HQ: Greenberg Traurig, Llp
200 Park Ave Fl 438
New York NY 10166
-

(P-23114)
GREENBERG TRAURIG LLP
3161 Michelson Dr # 1000, Irvine (92612-4410)
PHONE..........................949 732-6500
Ray Lee, *Managing Prtnr*
Bruce Fischer, *Shareholder*
Craig Glorioso, *Shareholder*
Jeffrey Joy, *Shareholder*
Raymond Lee, *Shareholder*
EMP: 70
SALES (corp-wide): 458.4MM **Privately Held**
SIC: 8111 General practice attorney, lawyer
HQ: Greenberg Traurig, Llp
200 Park Ave Fl 438
New York NY 10166

(P-23115)
GREENE RDVSKY MALONEY SHARE LP
4 Embarcadero Ctr # 4000, San Francisco (94111-4106)
PHONE..........................415 981-1400
Mark Hennigh, *Managing Prtnr*
Richard Green, *Senior Partner*
James Abrams, *Partner*
Thomas Feldstein, *Partner*
James Fotenos, *Partner*
EMP: 69
SQ FT: 18,800
SALES (est): 7.6MM **Privately Held**
WEB: www.grmslaw.com
SIC: 8111 Specialized law offices, attorneys; corporate, partnership & business law; real estate law; taxation law

(P-23116)
GRESHAM SAVAGE NOLAN & TILDEN (PA)
550 E Hospitality Ln # 300, San Bernardino (92408-4205)
PHONE..........................619 794-0050
Mark A Ostoich, *President*
Bob Ritter, *Partner*
Christie Bowman, *President*
Tom Jacobsen, *COO*
Robert Ritter, *CFO*
EMP: 53
SQ FT: 16,500
SALES (est): 11.8MM **Privately Held**
SIC: 8111 General practice law office

(P-23117)
GUNDERSON DETTMER STOUGH VILLE (PA)
550 Allerton St, Redwood City (94063-1524)
PHONE..........................650 321-2400
Robert Gunderson, *Partner*
Darrin Brown, *Partner*
Colin Chapman, *Partner*
Dan O Connor, *Partner*
Joshua Cook, *Partner*
EMP: 125
SALES (est): 28.1MM **Privately Held**
WEB: www.gdsvfh.com
SIC: 8111 General practice law office

(P-23118)
HAHN & HAHN LLP
301 E Colo Blvd Ste 900, Pasadena (91101)
PHONE..........................626 796-9123
Karl Swaidan, *Managing Prtnr*
Gene E Gregg Jr, *Partner*
R Scott Jenkins, *Partner*
Kristianne Kerns, *Partner*
Natasha Zaharov, *Partner*
EMP: 80
SQ FT: 15,175
SALES (est): 9.7MM **Privately Held**
WEB: www.hahnlawyers.com
SIC: 8111 General practice attorney, lawyer

(P-23119)
HAIGHT BROWN & BONESTEEL LLP (PA)
555 S Flower St Ste 4500, Los Angeles (90071-2441)
PHONE..........................213 542-8000
S Christian Stouder, *Managing Prtnr*
Anthony Forde, *COO*
Carolyn Harper, *CFO*
Monique Lopez, *Admin Sec*
Marie Wolfe, *Info Tech Mgr*
EMP: 80
SQ FT: 36,265
SALES (est): 25.4MM **Privately Held**
WEB: www.hbblaw.com
SIC: 8111 General practice law office

(P-23120)
HANNA BROPHY MAC LEAN MC ALE (PA)
1956 Webster St Ste 450, Oakland (94612-2930)
PHONE..........................510 839-1180
Leslie Tuxhorn, *Managing Prtnr*
Joseph Nisim, *Partner*
Barbara Wood, *Partner*
EMP: 50
SQ FT: 10,000
SALES (est): 43.8MM **Privately Held**
WEB: www.hannabrophy.com
SIC: 8111 General practice law office

(P-23121)
HANSON BRIDGETT LLP
500 Capitol Mall Ste 1500, Sacramento (95814-4740)
PHONE..........................916 442-3333
Terrie Rasica, *Office Mgr*
Marie Coleman, *Admin Sec*
Shelby Smith, *Admin Sec*
EMP: 50
SALES (corp-wide): 49.3MM **Privately Held**
SIC: 8111 General practice attorney, lawyer

PA: Hanson Bridgett Llp
425 Market St Fl 26
San Francisco CA 94105
415 543-2055

(P-23122)
HANSON BRIDGETT LLP (PA)
425 Market St Fl 26, San Francisco (94105-2532)
PHONE..........................415 543-2055
Andrew G Giacomini,
Lawrence Cirelli, *Partner*
Batya Forsyth, *Partner*
Lisa Dal Gallo, *Partner*
Theodore A Hellman, *Partner*
EMP: 263
SQ FT: 79,120
SALES (est): 49.3MM **Privately Held**
WEB: www.hansonbridgett.com
SIC: 8111 General practice attorney, lawyer

(P-23123)
HARRIS STOCKWELL (PA)
3580 Wilshire Blvd Fl 19, Los Angeles (90010-2532)
PHONE..........................310 277-6669
Steven I Harris, *CEO*
Steven Harris, *CFO*
Anne Bobchick, *Vice Pres*
Jamie Fox, *Vice Pres*
Richard Green, *Vice Pres*
EMP: 50 EST: 1970
SALES (est): 18.3MM **Privately Held**
SIC: 8111 General practice attorney, lawyer

(P-23124)
HART KING COLDREN A PROF CORP
4 Hutton Cntre Dr Ste 900, Santa Ana (92707)
PHONE..........................714 432-8700
Robert S Coldren, *President*
Gary R King, *Treasurer*
William R Hart, *Admin Sec*
William Hart, *CTO*
Russ Harmon, *Technology*
EMP: 60 EST: 1982
SQ FT: 20,000
SALES (est): 9.2MM **Privately Held**
WEB: www.hkclaw.com
SIC: 8111 General practice attorney, lawyer

(P-23125)
HASSARD BONNINGTON LLP (PA)
Also Called: H B
275 Battery St Ste 1600, San Francisco (94111-3993)
PHONE..........................415 288-9800
James M Goodman, *General Ptnr*
Phillip F Ward, *Partner*
Peter Mallon, *Officer*
EMP: 59
SALES (est): 12.3MM **Privately Held**
WEB: www.hassard.com
SIC: 8111 General practice law office

(P-23126)
HAYNES AND BOONE LLP
525 University Ave # 400, Palo Alto (94301-1903)
PHONE..........................650 687-8800
Laurie Armstrong, *Manager*
EMP: 91
SALES (corp-wide): 192.9MM **Privately Held**
SIC: 8111 General practice attorney, lawyer
PA: Haynes And Boone, Llp
2323 Victory Ave Ste 700
Dallas TX 75219
214 651-5000

(P-23127)
HEIGHT BROWN AND BONESTEEL
555 S Flower St Ste 4500, Los Angeles (90071-2441)
PHONE..........................213 241-0900
Christian Stouder, *Managing Prtnr*
EMP: 60

SALES (est): 1.8MM **Privately Held**
SIC: 8111 Legal services

(P-23128)
HEMAR ROUSSO & HEALD L L P
Also Called: Hemar & Rousso Attys At Law
15910 Ventura Blvd # 1201, Encino
(91436-2829)
PHONE..............................818 501-3800
Richard P Hemar, *Managing Prtnr*
Daniel E Heald, *Partner*
Martin J Rousso, *Partner*
Tammy Dunn, *President*
Mary Rousso, *Office Admin*
EMP: 50
SQ FT: 10,000
SALES (est): 5.4MM **Privately Held**
WEB: www.hemar-rousso.com
SIC: 8111 General practice law office

(P-23129)
HIGGS FLETCHER & MACK LLP
Also Called: Goproto
401 W A St Ste 2600, San Diego
(92101-7913)
PHONE..............................619 236-1551
John Morrell, *General Ptnr*
Anna F Roppo, *Partner*
Phillip C Samouis, *Partner*
Therese P Ketteringham, *Vice Pres*
David R Catalino,
EMP: 150
SQ FT: 45,000
SALES (est): 26MM **Privately Held**
WEB: www.higgslaw.com
SIC: 8111 General practice attorney,
lawyer

(P-23130)
HILL FARRER & BURRILL
Also Called: One California Plaza
300 S Grand Ave Fl 37, Los Angeles
(90071-3147)
PHONE..............................213 620-0460
Scott Gilmore, *Partner*
Steven W Bacon, *Partner*
Julia L Birkel, *Partner*
William M Bitting, *Partner*
Michael S Blanton, *Partner*
EMP: 100
SQ FT: 32,000
SALES (est): 16MM **Privately Held**
WEB: www.hillfarrer.com
SIC: 8111 General practice law office

(P-23131)
HINSHAW & CULBERTSON LLP
633 W 5th St Ste 4700, Los Angeles
(90071-2043)
PHONE..............................213 680-2800
Jenny Bernal, *Administration*
Katherine Cheng, *Associate*
EMP: 51
SALES (corp-wide): 200MM **Privately
Held**
SIC: 8111 General practice law office
PA: Hinshaw & Culbertson Llp
151 N Franklin St # 2500
Chicago IL 60606
312 704-3000

(P-23132)
**HIRSCHFELD KRAEMER LLP
(PA)**
505 Montgomery St Fl 13, San Francisco
(94111-2551)
PHONE..............................415 835-9000
Richard Curiale, *Partner*
Birmingham Montgomery,
EMP: 50
SALES (est): 6.4MM **Privately Held**
WEB: www.employmentlawalliance.com
SIC: 8111 General practice law office

(P-23133)
HOLLAND & KNIGHT LLP
400 S Hope St Ste 800, Los Angeles
(90071-2809)
PHONE..............................213 896-2400
Maita Prout, *Manager*
Angelica Rivera, *Admin Sec*
Jimmy Davila, *Technology*
Rishi Maragh, *Technology*
Katie Sapolu, *Technology*
EMP: 100

SALES (corp-wide): 100MM **Privately
Held**
WEB: www.hollandandknight.com
SIC: 8111 General practice attorney,
lawyer
PA: Holland & Knight Llp
524 Grand Regency Blvd
Brandon FL 33510
813 901-4200

(P-23134)
HOLLAND & KNIGHT LLP
Also Called: Haight Gdnr Holland & Knight
50 California St Ste 2800, San Francisco
(94111-4726)
PHONE..............................415 743-6900
Erik Dale, *Manager*
Donald Walden, *Records Dir*
Scott Abrams, *Partner*
Matthew Vafidis, *Partner*
Trisha Rich, *COO*
EMP: 50
SALES (corp-wide): 100MM **Privately
Held**
WEB: www.hollandandknight.com
SIC: 8111 General practice law office
PA: Holland & Knight Llp
524 Grand Regency Blvd
Brandon FL 33510
813 901-4200

(P-23135)
**HOLLINS SCHECHTER A PROF
CORP**
1851 E 1st St Ste 600, Santa Ana
(92705-4049)
PHONE..............................714 558-9119
Andrew S Hollins, *President*
Bruce L Schechter, *Vice Pres*
Jennifer Tusko, *Finance*
Kathleen K Carter, *Manager*
EMP: 60 **EST:** 1978
SQ FT: 15,000
SALES (est): 4.3MM **Privately Held**
WEB: www.hollins-law.com
SIC: 8111 General practice attorney,
lawyer

(P-23136)
**HOPKINS & CARLEY A LAW
CORP (PA)**
70 S 1st St, San Jose (95113-2406)
P.O. Box 1469 (95109-1469)
PHONE..............................408 286-9800
William S Klein, *Principal*
Candice Allen, *President*
Elena Amaro, *President*
Toni Antonio, *President*
Edwina Feguis, *President*
EMP: 80
SQ FT: 33,000
SALES (est): 18.1MM **Privately Held**
WEB: www.hopkinscarley.com
SIC: 8111 Corporate, partnership & busi-
ness law; divorce & family law; environ-
mental law; real estate law

(P-23137)
HUESTON HENNIGAN LLP
523 W 6th St Ste 400, Los Angeles
(90014-1208)
PHONE..............................213 788-4340
Marshall A Camp, *Partner*
Douglas J Dixon, *Partner*
Alexander C D Giza, *Partner*
Brian J Hennigan, *Partner*
John C Hueston, *Partner*
EMP: 80
SQ FT: 25,000
SALES (est): 387.6K **Privately Held**
SIC: 8111 General practice attorney,
lawyer

(P-23138)
**HUNT ORTMANN PALFFY
NIEVES**
301 N Lake Ave Fl 7, Pasadena
(91101-5118)
PHONE..............................626 440-5200
Dale A Ortmann, *Co-Founder*
Kevin Brody, *Shareholder*
Thomas Palffy, *Treasurer*
Gordon Hunt, *Principal*
Laurence Lubka, *Principal*
EMP: 50
SQ FT: 18,000

SALES (est): 7.7MM **Privately Held**
SIC: 8111 General practice law office

(P-23139)
HUNTON ANDREWS KURTH LLP
50 California St Ste 1700, San Francisco
(94111-4604)
PHONE..............................415 975-3700
Fraser McAlpine, *Partner*
Fraser A McAlpine, *Managing Prtnr*
H Elmore, *Associate*
EMP: 94
SALES (corp-wide): 290.6MM **Privately
Held**
SIC: 8111 General practice attorney,
lawyer
PA: Hunton Andrews Kurth Llp
951 E Byrd St
Richmond VA 23219
804 788-8200

(P-23140)
HUNTON ANDREWS KURTH LLP
550 S Hope St Ste 2000, Los Angeles
(90071-2631)
PHONE..............................213 532-2000
Wally Martinez, *Managing Prtnr*
Roland M Juarez, *Partner*
Ann M Mortimer, *Managing Prtnr*
Becky MA, *Office Admin*
Julio Matamoros, *Info Tech Mgr*
EMP: 91
SALES (corp-wide): 290.6MM **Privately
Held**
SIC: 8111 General practice attorney,
lawyer
PA: Hunton Andrews Kurth Llp
951 E Byrd St
Richmond VA 23219
804 788-8200

(P-23141)
IMMERSION MEDICAL INC
50 Rio Robles, San Jose (95134-1806)
PHONE..............................408 467-1900
Shum Mukherjee, *CFO*
Guna Raja, *Technology*
Bryan Liu, *Sales Dir*
Chris Hayden, *Manager*
EMP: 85 **EST:** 1995
SALES (est): 5.1MM **Publicly Held**
WEB: www.immersion.com
SIC: 8111 5047 Patent, trademark & copy-
right law; instruments, surgical & medical
PA: Immersion Corporation
50 Rio Robles
San Jose CA 95134

(P-23142)
IRELL & MANELLA LLP (PA)
1800 Avenue Of The Stars # 900, Los An-
geles (90067-4276)
PHONE..............................310 277-1010
Elliot Brown, *Managing Prtnr*
Gregory Klein, *Partner*
David Siegel, *Partner*
Cindy Altenfelder, *Admin Sec*
Kent Jones, *Admin Sec*
EMP: 400
SQ FT: 154,000
SALES: 34.6K **Privately Held**
WEB: www.irell.com
SIC: 8111 General practice law office

(P-23143)
IRELL & MANELLA LLP
840 Nwport Ctr Dr Ste 400, Newport Beach
(92660)
PHONE..............................949 760-0991
Nancy Adams, *Manager*
Daniel Lefler, *Partner*
Sherman Richard,
Robert W Stedman,
EMP: 100
SALES (corp-wide): 34.6K **Privately Held**
WEB: www.irell.com
SIC: 8111 General practice attorney,
lawyer
PA: Irell & Manella Llp
1800 Avenue Of The Stars # 900
Los Angeles CA 90067
310 277-1010

(P-23144)
IRELL & MANELLA LLP
1800 Avenue Of The Stars # 900, Los An-
geles (90067-4276)
PHONE..............................213 620-1555
Ed Cauffman, *Partner*
EMP: 500
SALES (corp-wide): 34.6K **Privately Held**
WEB: www.irell.com
SIC: 8111 General practice law office
PA: Irell & Manella Llp
1800 Avenue Of The Stars # 900
Los Angeles CA 90067
310 277-1010

(P-23145)
IRON LAW INC (PA)
663 S Rancho Santa Fe Rd, San Marcos
(92078-3973)
PHONE..............................844 476-6529
Jesse Wagner, *CEO*
EMP: 80 **EST:** 2015
SQ FT: 500
SALES (est): 4.5MM **Privately Held**
SIC: 8111 General practice law office

(P-23146)
**IVIE MCNEILL WYATT A PROF
LAW**
444 S Flower St Ste 1800, Los Angeles
(90071-2919)
PHONE..............................213 489-0028
Robert H Mc Neill Jr, *President*
Rickey Ivie, *Vice Pres*
Keith Wyatt, *Admin Sec*
Antonio Kizzie, *Associate*
Marie Maurice, *Associate*
EMP: 50
SALES (est): 7.1MM **Privately Held**
WEB: www.imwlaw.com
SIC: 8111 General practice attorney,
lawyer

(P-23147)
**JACKOWAY TYREMAN
WERTHEIMER AU**
1925 Century Park E Fl 2, Los Angeles
(90067-2701)
PHONE..............................310 553-0305
Barry Hirsch, *President*
EMP: 100
SQ FT: 3,000
SALES (est): 13.3MM **Privately Held**
SIC: 8111 General practice law office

(P-23148)
**JACKSON DEMARCO TIDUS
PETER (PA)**
2030 Main St Ste 1200, Irvine
(92614-7256)
P.O. Box 19703 (92623-9703)
PHONE..............................949 752-8585
M Alim Malik, *CEO*
James Demarco, *President*
Thomas D Peckenpaugh, *President*
Ruth Mijuskovic, *CEO*
Andrew V Leitch,
EMP: 82
SQ FT: 23,000
SALES (est): 11.9MM **Privately Held**
SIC: 8111 General practice law office

(P-23149)
**JEFFER MNGELS BTLR
MTCHELL LLP (PA)**
Also Called: Jmbm
1900 Avenue Of The Stars, Los Angeles
(90067-4301)
PHONE..............................310 203-8080
Bruce P Jeffer, *Managing Prtnr*
James R Butler Jr, *Partner*
Dan E Chambers, *Partner*
Jennifer A Irrgang, *Partner*
Robert E Mangels, *Partner*
EMP: 230
SALES (est): 47.3MM **Privately Held**
WEB: www.jmbm.com
SIC: 8111 General practice attorney,
lawyer

(P-23150)
JEFFER MNGELS BTLR MTCHELL LLP
2 Embarcadero Ctr Fl 5, San Francisco (94111-3813)
PHONE...............................415 398-8080
Richard Rogan, *Manager*
Scott Castro, *Partner*
Nicolas De Lancie, *Partner*
Nicolas Delancie, *Partner*
Michael Hassen, *Partner*
EMP: 65
SALES (corp-wide): 47.3MM **Privately Held**
WEB: www.jmbm.com
SIC: 8111 General practice attorney, lawyer
PA: Jeffer, Mangels, Butler & Mitchell, Llp
1900 Avenue Of The Stars
Los Angeles CA 90067
310 203-8080

(P-23151)
JOHN F DMINGUE ATTORNEY AT LAW
10 Almaden Blvd Ste 1100, San Jose (95113-2270)
PHONE...............................408 591-5180
John F Domingue, *Owner*
EMP: 150
SALES (est): 2.7MM **Privately Held**
SIC: 8111 Labor & employment law; general practice law office

(P-23152)
JOHNSON LA FOLLETTE
2677 N Main St Ste 901, Santa Ana (92705-6632)
PHONE...............................714 558-7008
Dennis Ames, *Managing Prtnr*
Staci Orange, *President*
Odell Steven,
Scott Foley, *Associate*
EMP: 65
SALES (corp-wide): 17.9MM **Privately Held**
WEB: www.ljdfa.com
SIC: 8111 General practice law office
PA: La Follette, Johnson, De Haas,
865 S Figueroa St # 3200
Los Angeles CA 90017
213 426-3600

(P-23153)
JONES DAY LIMITED PARTNERSHIP
4655 Executive Dr # 1500, San Diego (92121-3134)
PHONE...............................858 314-1200
Gerga Dow Lamaire, *Mng Member*
Jayne McCullough, *Admin Sec*
Jordan B Arakawa, *Associate*
Cameron Reese, *Associate*
EMP: 60
SALES (corp-wide): 833.4MM **Privately Held**
SIC: 8111 Legal services
PA: Jones Day Limited Partnership
901 Lakeside Ave E Ste 2
Cleveland OH 44114
216 586-3939

(P-23154)
JONES DAY LIMITED PARTNERSHIP
3161 Michelson Dr Ste 800, Irvine (92612-4408)
PHONE...............................949 851-3939
R J Grabowski, *General Mgr*
Thomas R Malcolm, *Partner*
Cher Schuerman, *Admin Sec*
Lisa Girdlestone, *Legal Staff*
Dulcie D Brand, *Manager*
EMP: 85
SQ FT: 22,500
SALES (corp-wide): 833.4MM **Privately Held**
SIC: 8111 General practice law office
PA: Jones Day Limited Partnership
901 Lakeside Ave E Ste 2
Cleveland OH 44114
216 586-3939

(P-23155)
JONES DAY LIMITED PARTNERSHIP
1755 Embarcadero Rd # 101, Palo Alto (94303-3340)
PHONE...............................650 739-3955
Shawn Farrell, *Manager*
Behrooz Shariati, *Partner*
Bob Clarkson, *Managing Prtnr*
Peters Jackie, *Office Mgr*
Sylvie Anacker, *Executive Asst*
EMP: 100
SALES (corp-wide): 833.4MM **Privately Held**
SIC: 8111 General practice attorney, lawyer
PA: Jones Day Limited Partnership
901 Lakeside Ave E Ste 2
Cleveland OH 44114
216 586-3939

(P-23156)
JOSEPH C SANSONE COMPANY (PA)
Also Called: Tobin Lucks
21300 Victory Blvd # 300, Woodland Hills (91367-2525)
P.O. Box 4502 (91365-4502)
PHONE...............................818 226-3400
Irvin Lucks, *Managing Prtnr*
Edwin Lucks, *Partner*
Donald Tobin, *Partner*
Eliel Duarte, *Admin Asst*
Maria Hernandez, *Admin Asst*
EMP: 97
SALES (est): 23.5MM **Privately Held**
SIC: 8111 General practice law office

(P-23157)
K&L GATES LLP
55 2nd St Ste 1700, San Francisco (94105-3493)
PHONE...............................415 882-8200
Bob Schweda, *Manager*
Polly A Dinkel, *Partner*
EMP: 70
SALES (corp-wide): 496MM **Privately Held**
WEB: www.klxtra.com
SIC: 8111 General practice attorney, lawyer
PA: K&L Gates Llp
210 6th Ave Ste 1100
Pittsburgh PA 15222
412 355-6500

(P-23158)
K&L GATES LLP
10100 Santa Monica Blvd # 700, Los Angeles (90067-4003)
PHONE...............................310 552-5000
Karen Doyle, *Manager*
Jeryl A Bowers, *Partner*
Frederick J Ufkes, *Partner*
Roslyn Pitts, *President*
Derek Christopher, *Analyst*
EMP: 50
SALES (corp-wide): 496MM **Privately Held**
WEB: www.klxtra.com
SIC: 8111 General practice law office
PA: K&L Gates Llp
210 6th Ave Ste 1100
Pittsburgh PA 15222
412 355-6500

(P-23159)
K&L GATES LLP
4 Embarcadero Ctr Lbby 10, San Francisco (94111-4124)
PHONE...............................415 249-1000
Patsy Pressley, *Administration*
Laurence A Goldberg, *Partner*
Mark D Perlow, *Partner*
EMP: 100
SALES (corp-wide): 496MM **Privately Held**
SIC: 8111 Corporate, partnership & business law
PA: K&L Gates Llp
210 6th Ave Ste 1100
Pittsburgh PA 15222
412 355-6500

(P-23160)
KASDAN SMNDS RILEY VAUGHAN LLP (PA)
19900 Macarthur Blvd # 850, Irvine (92612-8422)
PHONE...............................949 851-9000
Kenneth Kasdan, *Partner*
EMP: 56
SQ FT: 20,000
SALES (est): 11.1MM **Privately Held**
SIC: 8111 General practice law office

(P-23161)
KATTEN MUCHIN ROSENMAN LLP
515 S Flower St, Los Angeles (90071-2201)
PHONE...............................310 788-4498
Susan Taylor, *Branch Mgr*
EMP: 175
SALES (corp-wide): 302.7MM **Privately Held**
SIC: 8111 General practice law office
PA: Katten Muchin Rosenman Llp
525 W Monroe St Ste 1900
Chicago IL 60661
312 902-5200

(P-23162)
KATTEN MUCHIN ROSENMAN LLP
1999 Harrison St Ste 700, Oakland (94612-4704)
PHONE...............................415 360-5444
Shannon Broome, *Branch Mgr*
Michael Rubin, *Accounting Mgr*
EMP: 175
SALES (corp-wide): 302.7MM **Privately Held**
SIC: 8111 General practice law office
PA: Katten Muchin Rosenman Llp
525 W Monroe St Ste 1900
Chicago IL 60661
312 902-5200

(P-23163)
KATTEN MUCHIN ROSENMAN LLP
2029 Century Park E # 2600, Los Angeles (90067-3012)
PHONE...............................310 788-4400
Tanya Russell, *Branch Mgr*
Jonathan Baum, *Partner*
Steve Cochran, *Partner*
Stacey Knight, *Partner*
Eric Kuwana, *Partner*
EMP: 150
SALES (corp-wide): 302.7MM **Privately Held**
WEB: www.kattenlaw.com
SIC: 8111 General practice law office
PA: Katten Muchin Rosenman Llp
525 W Monroe St Ste 1900
Chicago IL 60661
312 902-5200

(P-23164)
KAWELA ONE LLC
3000 El Camino Real, Palo Alto (94306-2100)
PHONE...............................650 843-5000
Cooley Godward, *Principal*
EMP: 79
SALES (est): 7.5MM **Privately Held**
SIC: 8111 Specialized law offices, attorneys

(P-23165)
KAZAN MCCLAIN SATTERLEY &
55 Harrison St Ste 400, Oakland (94607-3858)
PHONE...............................877 995-6372
Steven Kazan, *Partner*
Denise Abrams, *Partner*
Justin Bosl, *Partner*
Denyse Clancy, *Partner*
Gordon Greenwood, *Partner*
EMP: 108
SALES (est): 11.6MM **Privately Held**
SIC: 8111 General practice law office

(P-23166)
KEESAL YOUNG LOGAN A PROF CORP (PA)
400 Oceangate Ste 1400, Long Beach (90802-4325)
PHONE...............................562 436-2000
Samuel A Keesal Jr, *CEO*
Robert Stemler, *Shareholder*
Racquel Sullivan, *President*
J Stephen Young, *Corp Secy*
Chris Almaraz, *Technology*
EMP: 90
SQ FT: 65,000
SALES (est): 846.7K **Privately Held**
WEB: www.kyl.com
SIC: 8111 General practice law office

(P-23167)
KEKER AND VAN NEST LLP
633 Battery St Bsmt 91, San Francisco (94111-1899)
PHONE...............................415 391-5400
John W Keker,
Bryant Cavers, *President*
Susan Cole, *President*
DOT D Fox, *President*
Sandy Giminez, *President*
EMP: 100
SQ FT: 70,000
SALES (est): 20.5MM **Privately Held**
WEB: www.kvn.com
SIC: 8111 Criminal law; specialized law offices, attorneys

(P-23168)
KELLEY DRYE & WARREN LLP
10100 Santa Monica Blvd, Los Angeles (90067-4003)
PHONE...............................310 712-6100
Ken Kow, *Branch Mgr*
EMP: 210
SALES (corp-wide): 183.8MM **Privately Held**
SIC: 8111 General practice law office
PA: Kelley Drye & Warren Llp
101 Park Ave Fl 30
New York NY 10178
212 808-7800

(P-23169)
KILPATRICK TWNSEND STCKTON LLP
2175 N California Blvd, Walnut Creek (94596-3579)
PHONE...............................925 472-5000
Harold Williams, *Branch Mgr*
Lisa Flanagan, *Associate*
EMP: 103
SALES (corp-wide): 263.8MM **Privately Held**
SIC: 8111 General practice attorney, lawyer
PA: Kilpatrick Townsend & Stockton Llp
1100 Peachtree St Ne
Atlanta GA 30309
404 815-6500

(P-23170)
KIMBALL TIREY & ST JOHN LLP (PA)
7676 Hazard Center Dr # 900, San Diego (92108-4515)
PHONE...............................619 234-1690
Theodore C Kimball, *Partner*
Maria Wampler, *President*
Machelle Lozano, *Vice Pres*
Leslie Mason, *Principal*
Lauren Bloodworth, *Administration*
EMP: 70
SQ FT: 6,000
SALES (est): 22MM **Privately Held**
SIC: 8111 General practice attorney, lawyer

(P-23171)
KING & SPALDING LLP
101 2nd St Ste 2300, San Francisco (94105-3664)
PHONE...............................415 318-1200
Donald Zimmer, *Partner*
Missy Heinz, *Partner*
Gracy Alexander, *President*
Elvetra Cossie, *President*
Sharon Holberg, *President*
EMP: 296

SALES (corp-wide): 421.4MM **Privately Held**
SIC: **8111** General practice law office
PA: King & Spalding Llp
1180 Peachtree St
Atlanta GA 30309
404 572-4600

(P-23172)
KING HLMES PTRNO BERLINER LLP
1900 Avenue Of The Stars # 25, Los Angeles (90067-4301)
PHONE.................310 282-8989
Howard King, *Partner*
Keith Holmes, *Partner*
Peter Paterno, *Partner*
Lori Soriano, *Partner*
Aurora Gomez, *President*
EMP: 50
SALES (est): 7.6MM **Privately Held**
WEB: www.khpblaw.com
SIC: **8111** General practice attorney, lawyer

(P-23173)
KIRKLAND & ELLIS LLP
3330 Hillview Ave, Palo Alto (94304-1059)
PHONE.................650 852-9131
Alex Kaufman, *Branch Mgr*
Ted M Frankel, *Partner*
Francine Davis, *President*
Christian Cooley, *CFO*
Francisco Jacoby-Rivera, *Associate Dir*
EMP: 510
SALES (corp-wide): 506.8MM **Privately Held**
SIC: **8111** Real estate law; specialized law offices, attorneys
PA: Kirkland & Ellis Llp
300 N La Salle Dr # 2400
Chicago IL 60654
312 862-2000

(P-23174)
KIRKLAND & ELLIS LLP
555 California St # 2700, San Francisco (94104-1603)
PHONE.................415 439-1400
Caroline Recht, *Manager*
Mark Nomellini, *Partner*
Paullet Delong, *President*
Josephine Isvoranu, *President*
Bao Nguyen, *Executive*
EMP: 200
SALES (corp-wide): 506.8MM **Privately Held**
WEB: www.kirkland.com
SIC: **8111** General practice law office
PA: Kirkland & Ellis Llp
300 N La Salle Dr # 2400
Chicago IL 60654
312 862-2000

(P-23175)
KLEIN DENATALE GOLDNER ET AL (PA)
Also Called: Klein Denatale Goldner Cooper
4550 California Ave Fl 2, Bakersfield (93309-7012)
P.O. Box 11172 (93389-1172)
PHONE.................661 401-7755
Anthony J Klein, *Partner*
Anthony Klein, *Senior Partner*
Jennifer A Adams, *Partner*
Hagop T Bedoyan, *Partner*
David J Cooper, *Partner*
EMP: 83
SQ FT: 25,000
SALES (est): 21.4MM **Privately Held**
SIC: **8111** General practice law office

(P-23176)
KLEIN-TESTAN-BRUNDO
1851 E 1st St Ste 100, Santa Ana (92705-4036)
PHONE.................714 245-8888
Jeffrey Adelson, *Partner*
EMP: 50
SALES (est): 282.2K **Privately Held**
SIC: **8111** Labor & employment law

(P-23177)
KNOBBE MARTENS OLSON BEAR LLP (PA)
2040 Main St Fl 14, Irvine (92614-8214)
PHONE.................949 760-0404
Steven J Nataupsky, *Managing Prtnr*
Michelle Armond, *Partner*
William B Bunker, *Partner*
Drew S Hamilton, *Partner*
Ned Israelsen, *Partner*
EMP: 350
SQ FT: 120,000
SALES (est): 120.4MM **Privately Held**
WEB: www.knobbe.com
SIC: **8111** General practice law office

(P-23178)
KNOX ATTORNEY SERVICE INC (PA)
Also Called: Knox Services
2250 4th Ave Ste 200, San Diego (92101-2124)
PHONE.................619 233-9700
Steve Knox, *President*
Robert Porambo, *CFO*
Marilyn Menard, *Executive*
Danny Marin, *Office Mgr*
Jack Kwiatkowski, *Info Tech Mgr*
EMP: 227 EST: 1973
SQ FT: 165,929
SALES (est): 39.3MM **Privately Held**
WEB: www.knoxservices.com
SIC: **8111** Legal aid service

(P-23179)
KOELLER NBKER CRLSON HLUCK LLP (PA)
3 Park Plz Ste 1500, Irvine (92614-8558)
PHONE.................949 864-3400
Keith Koeller, *Managing Prtnr*
Bob Carlson, *Managing Prtnr*
William Haluck, *Managing Prtnr*
Bill Nebeker, *Managing Prtnr*
Dale Langley, *Office Mgr*
EMP: 56
SALES (est): 16.2MM **Privately Held**
SIC: **8111** General practice law office

(P-23180)
KRONICK MOSKOVITZ TIEDEMANN (PA)
400 Capitol Mall Fl 27, Sacramento (95814-4416)
PHONE.................916 321-4500
Robert Murphy, *Chairman*
Michael A Grob, *President*
Bruce A Scheidt, *CEO*
Rick Fowler, *COO*
Kren A Sluiter, *CFO*
EMP: 93
SQ FT: 35,781
SALES (est): 20.8MM **Privately Held**
WEB: www.kmtg.com
SIC: **8111** General practice law office

(P-23181)
LA FOLLETTE JOHNSON DE HAAS (PA)
865 S Figueroa St # 3200, Los Angeles (90017-5431)
PHONE.................213 426-3600
Daren T Johnson, *President*
Jeff Erickson, *Managing Prtnr*
Donald Fesler, *Shareholder*
Mark Stewart, *Shareholder*
Haydee Chun, *President*
EMP: 105
SALES (est): 17.9MM **Privately Held**
WEB: www.ljdfa.com
SIC: **8111** General practice law office

(P-23182)
LADAS & PARRY LLP
5670 Wilshire Blvd # 2100, Los Angeles (90036-5606)
PHONE.................323 934-2300
Richard P Berg, *Partner*
Louis Pezzullo, *Executive*
Marc Trachtenberg, *Administration*
Daifei Zhang, *Associate*
EMP: 50
SALES (corp-wide): 25.1MM **Privately Held**
WEB: www.ladas.com
SIC: **8111** General practice law office

PA: Ladas & Parry Llp
1040 Ave Of The Amrcs 5
New York NY 10018
212 246-8959

(P-23183)
LANG RICHERT & PATCH
Also Called: Attorneys At Law
5200 N Palm Ave Ste 401, Fresno (93704-2227)
P.O. Box 40012 (93755-4012)
PHONE.................559 228-6700
Val W Saldana, *President*
Robert Patch, *President*
Douglas Griffin, *CFO*
Rene La Streto II, *Vice Pres*
Victoria Salisch, *Admin Sec*
EMP: 50 EST: 1962
SQ FT: 17,500
SALES (est): 7.1MM **Privately Held**
WEB: www.lrplaw.net
SIC: **8111** General practice law office

(P-23184)
LATHAM & WATKINS LLP
140 Scott Dr, Menlo Park (94025-1008)
PHONE.................650 328-4600
Ora Fisher, *Branch Mgr*
Kirsten Germeraad, *Practice Mgr*
Alan Mendelson, *Assistant*
Gabriel Bell, *Associate*
Jennifer N Cadet, *Associate*
EMP: 180
SALES (corp-wide): 678.8MM **Privately Held**
WEB: www.lw.com
SIC: **8111** Corporate, partnership & business law
PA: Latham & Watkins Llp
355 S Grand Ave Ste 1000
Los Angeles CA 90071
213 485-1234

(P-23185)
LATHAM & WATKINS LLP
1722 Skyhill Way, Santa Ana (92705-2585)
PHONE.................714 755-8288
Perry Viscouty, *Partner*
EMP: 323
SALES (corp-wide): 678.8MM **Privately Held**
SIC: **8111** Legal services
PA: Latham & Watkins Llp
355 S Grand Ave Ste 1000
Los Angeles CA 90071
213 485-1234

(P-23186)
LATHAM & WATKINS LLP
111 Univrsl Hllywd 257, Universal City (91608-1054)
PHONE.................818 753-5000
EMP: 323
SALES (corp-wide): 678.8MM **Privately Held**
SIC: **8111** Legal services
PA: Latham & Watkins Llp
355 S Grand Ave Ste 1000
Los Angeles CA 90071
213 485-1234

(P-23187)
LATHAM & WATKINS LLP (PA)
355 S Grand Ave Ste 1000, Los Angeles (90071-3419)
PHONE.................213 485-1234
Robert Dell, *Managing Prtnr*
Christopher J Allen, *Partner*
James P Beaubien, *Partner*
Joseph A Bevash, *Partner*
Jos Luis Blanco, *Partner*
EMP: 570 EST: 1934
SALES (est): 678.8MM **Privately Held**
WEB: www.lw.com
SIC: **8111** General practice attorney, lawyer

(P-23188)
LATHAM & WATKINS LLP
555 W 5th St Ste 800, Los Angeles (90013-1021)
PHONE.................213 891-7108
Carol Mindzak, *President*
Wayne Gustafson, *Risk Mgmt Dir*
Elisa Carlucci, *Admin Sec*
Marie D'Egidio, *Admin Sec*

Adriane Harper, *Admin Sec*
EMP: 74
SALES (corp-wide): 678.8MM **Privately Held**
SIC: **8111** General practice attorney, lawyer
PA: Latham & Watkins Llp
355 S Grand Ave Ste 1000
Los Angeles CA 90071
213 485-1234

(P-23189)
LATHAM & WATKINS LLP
650 Town Center Dr # 2000, Costa Mesa (92626-7135)
PHONE.................714 540-1235
Shayne Kennedy, *Managing Prtnr*
Scott Shean, *Managing Prtnr*
Mary Newman, *President*
Nancy Eberhart, *Administration*
Bror Andringa, *Info Tech Mgr*
EMP: 175
SALES (corp-wide): 678.8MM **Privately Held**
WEB: www.lw.com
SIC: **8111** General practice law office
PA: Latham & Watkins Llp
355 S Grand Ave Ste 1000
Los Angeles CA 90071
213 485-1234

(P-23190)
LATHAM & WATKINS LLP
520 S Grand Ave Ste 200, Los Angeles (90071-2655)
PHONE.................213 891-1200
Leanne Black, *Director*
Rene Mendoza, *Admin Asst*
Anthony Ojeda, *Administration*
Farhan Aziz, *Auditing Mgr*
Amy Xu, *Accountant*
EMP: 200
SALES (corp-wide): 678.8MM **Privately Held**
SIC: **8111** Specialized legal services
PA: Latham & Watkins Llp
355 S Grand Ave Ste 1000
Los Angeles CA 90071
213 485-1234

(P-23191)
LATHAM & WATKINS LLP
505 Montgomery St # 1900, San Francisco (94111-2562)
PHONE.................415 391-0600
Scott Haber, *Managing Prtnr*
Kenneth Blohm, *Partner*
Lisa Loef, *Office Admin*
Sean McGlamery, *Admin Asst*
Ruby Ordonio, *Admin Asst*
EMP: 240
SALES (corp-wide): 678.8MM **Privately Held**
WEB: www.lw.com
SIC: **8111** General practice law office
PA: Latham & Watkins Llp
355 S Grand Ave Ste 1000
Los Angeles CA 90071
213 485-1234

(P-23192)
LATHROP & GAGE LLP
1888 Century Park E # 1000, Los Angeles (90067-1714)
PHONE.................310 789-4600
John Schaffer, *Branch Mgr*
EMP: 70
SALES (corp-wide): 134.4MM **Privately Held**
SIC: **8111** General practice law office; general practice attorney, lawyer
PA: Lathrop & Gage Llp
2345 Grand Blvd Ste 2200
Kansas City MO 64108
816 292-2000

(P-23193)
LAUGHLIN FALBO LEVY MORESI LLP (PA)
555 12th St Ste 1900, Oakland (94607-4098)
PHONE.................510 628-0496
John Geyer, *Managing Prtnr*
John Bennett Jr, *Partner*
Phillip J Klein, *Partner*
James Wesolowski, *Partner*

Kevin Calegari, *Managing Prtnr*
EMP: 76
SQ FT: 25,000
SALES (est): 37.7MM **Privately Held**
SIC: 8111 Labor & employment law

(P-23194)
LAW OFFICES BERGLUND & JOHNSON (PA)
Also Called: Berglund & Johnson Law Office
21550 Oxnard St Ste 900, Woodland Hills
(91367-7144)
PHONE..............................951 276-4783
David W Berglund, *Partner*
Daniel W Johnson, *Partner*
EMP: 56
SALES (est): 4MM **Privately Held**
WEB: www.bjslawfirm.com
SIC: 8111 General practice law office

(P-23195)
LAW OFFICES OF THOMAS W
14286 Danielson St # 103, Poway
(92064-8819)
P.O. Box 503230, San Diego (92150-3230)
PHONE..............................858 883-2000
Thomas W Rutledge, *President*
Allison R Rutledge, *Exec VP*
Laurie Rauh, *Accounting Mgr*
Ace Blackburn, *General Counsel*
EMP: 135
SQ FT: 6,000
SALES (est): 12.8MM **Privately Held**
SIC: 8111 Legal services

(P-23196)
LEE HONG DEGERMAN KANG
3501 Jamboree Rd Ste 6000, Newport
Beach (92660-2960)
PHONE..............................949 250-9954
Melissa Well, *Principal*
EMP: 60
SALES (corp-wide): 6.8MM **Privately Held**
SIC: 8111 Specialized law offices, attorneys
PA: Lee, Hong, Degerman, Kang & Waimey, A Professional Corporation
660 S Figueroa St # 2300
Los Angeles CA 90017
213 623-2221

(P-23197)
LEGAL AID SOCIETY OF SAN DIEGO (PA)
110 S Euclid Ave, San Diego (92114-3796)
PHONE..............................619 263-1872
Gregory Knoll, *Director*
Russ Rasmassen, *Ch of Bd*
EMP: 50
SQ FT: 10,000
SALES: 18.7MM **Privately Held**
SIC: 8111 Legal aid service

(P-23198)
LEGAL RECOVERY LAW OFFICES INC
5030 Camino De La Siesta # 340, San
Diego (92108-3118)
P.O. Box 84060 (92138-4060)
PHONE..............................619 275-4001
Mark Walsh, *President*
Andrew Rundquist, *Admin Sec*
EMP: 70
SQ FT: 2,500
SALES (est): 9.1MM **Privately Held**
WEB: www.lrlo.com
SIC: 8111 General practice law office

(P-23199)
LEGAL SOLUTIONS HOLDINGS INC
Also Called: Getmedlegal
955 Overland Ct Ste 200, San Dimas
(91773-1747)
PHONE..............................800 244-3495
Greg Webber, *CEO*
Kenneth Gleockler, *CFO*
Keahi Kakugawa, *Principal*
EMP: 237
SALES: 29.3MM **Privately Held**
SIC: 8111 Legal services

(P-23200)
LEGALLY YOURS LLC
750 N Diamond Bar Blvd # 224, Diamond
Bar (91765-1023)
PHONE..............................909 396-7200
Andrea Dubois, *Mng Member*
John Dickson,
EMP: 123
SQ FT: 2,200
SALES (est): 9.9MM **Privately Held**
SIC: 8111 Legal services

(P-23201)
LEGALMATCHCOM (PA)
395 Oyster Point Blvd, South San Francisco (94080-1928)
PHONE..............................415 946-0800
Randy Wells, *CEO*
Robert Proden, *Associate Dir*
Kasey Acosta, *Office Mgr*
Neal Carmichael, *VP Sales*
Ernesto Garcia, *Marketing Mgr*
EMP: 50
SQ FT: 25,000
SALES (est): 6.3MM **Privately Held**
WEB: www.legalmatch.com
SIC: 8111 General practice attorney, lawyer

(P-23202)
LEGALZOOMCOM INC (DH)
101 N Brand Blvd Fl 11, Glendale
(91203-2638)
PHONE..............................323 962-8600
John Suh, *CEO*
Elizabeth Yoon, *Partner*
Edward Hartman, *Shareholder*
Robert Shapiro, *Shareholder*
Brian Liu, *Ch of Bd*
EMP: 300
SQ FT: 17,000
SALES (est): 11.9MM
SALES (corp-wide): 69.9MM **Privately Held**
WEB: www.legalzoom.com
SIC: 8111 Legal services
HQ: Permira Advisers Llc
320 Park Ave Fl 28
New York NY 10022
212 386-7480

(P-23203)
LEVIN AND SIMES
353 Sacramento St # 2000, San Francisco
(94111-3620)
PHONE..............................415 426-3000
William A Levin, *Mng Member*
Martha-Alice Berman, *Principal*
EMP: 50
SQ FT: 10,000
SALES (est): 4.7MM **Privately Held**
SIC: 8111 Labor & employment law

(P-23204)
LEWIS BRSBOIS BSGARD SMITH LLP
633 W 5th St Ste 4000, Los Angeles
(90071-2074)
PHONE..............................213 250-1800
EMP: 97
SALES (corp-wide): 239.5MM **Privately Held**
SIC: 8111 General practice law office
PA: Lewis Brisbois Bisgaard & Smith Llp
633 W 5th St Ste 4000
Los Angeles CA 90071
213 250-1800

(P-23205)
LEWIS BRSBOIS BSGARD SMITH LLP
28765 Single Oak Dr Ste 1, Temecula
(92590-3661)
PHONE..............................951 252-6150
Robert F Lewis, *Managing Prtnr*
EMP: 97
SALES (corp-wide): 239.5MM **Privately Held**
SIC: 8111 General practice law office
PA: Lewis Brisbois Bisgaard & Smith Llp
633 W 5th St Ste 4000
Los Angeles CA 90071
213 250-1800

(P-23206)
LEWIS BRSBOIS BSGARD SMITH LLP (PA)
633 W 5th St Ste 4000, Los Angeles
(90071-2074)
PHONE..............................213 250-1800
Robert F Lewis, *Managing Prtnr*
Christopher P Bisgaard, *Partner*
Roy M Brisbois, *Partner*
Heather Jensen, *Partner*
Jeff Bash, *Managing Prtnr*
EMP: 650
SQ FT: 80,000
SALES (est): 239.5MM **Privately Held**
WEB: www.lbbslaw.com
SIC: 8111 General practice law office

(P-23207)
LEWIS BRSBOIS BSGARD SMITH LLP
701 B St Ste 1900, San Diego
(92101-8198)
PHONE..............................619 233-1006
Susan O' Brien, *Systems Mgr*
Sherry Bernal, *President*
Christine Jordan, *President*
Missy Palka, *President*
Martha Villavicenzio, *President*
EMP: 100
SALES (corp-wide): 239.5MM **Privately Held**
WEB: www.lbbslaw.com
SIC: 8111 General practice law office
PA: Lewis Brisbois Bisgaard & Smith Llp
633 W 5th St Ste 4000
Los Angeles CA 90071
213 250-1800

(P-23208)
LEWIS BRSBOIS BSGARD SMITH LLP
650 Town Center Dr # 1400, Costa Mesa
(92626-1989)
PHONE..............................714 545-6015
Shawn Derfer, *Manager*
Lee A Wood, *Partner*
Steve T Gubner, *Partner*
Christine E Howson,
Madonna Hultman,
EMP: 60
SALES (corp-wide): 239.5MM **Privately Held**
WEB: www.lbbslaw.com
SIC: 8111 General practice law office
PA: Lewis Brisbois Bisgaard & Smith Llp
633 W 5th St Ste 4000
Los Angeles CA 90071
213 250-1800

(P-23209)
LEWIS BRSBOIS BSGARD SMITH LLP
333 Bush St, San Francisco (94104-2806)
PHONE..............................415 362-2580
Cindy Aiello, *Manager*
Kathryn L Anderson, *Partner*
Jeffrey Bairey, *Partner*
Donald E Brier, *Partner*
Peter Dixon, *Partner*
EMP: 150
SALES (corp-wide): 239.5MM **Privately Held**
WEB: www.lbbslaw.com
SIC: 8111 General practice law office
PA: Lewis Brisbois Bisgaard & Smith Llp
633 W 5th St Ste 4000
Los Angeles CA 90071
213 250-1800

(P-23210)
LEWIS BRSBOIS BSGARD SMITH LLP
650 E Hospitality Ln # 600, San Bernardino
(92408-3535)
PHONE..............................909 387-1130
John Lowenthal, *Manager*
EMP: 50
SQ FT: 6,203
SALES (corp-wide): 239.5MM **Privately Held**
WEB: www.lbbslaw.com
SIC: 8111 General practice law office

PA: Lewis Brisbois Bisgaard & Smith Llp
633 W 5th St Ste 4000
Los Angeles CA 90071
213 250-1800

(P-23211)
LEWIS MARENSTEIN WICKE SHERWIN
20750 Ventura Blvd # 400, Woodland Hills
(91364-2390)
PHONE..............................818 703-6000
Michael B Lewis, *Partner*
Alan B Marenstein, *Partner*
Robert Sherwin, *Partner*
Thomas Wicke, *Partner*
Kal Borisov, *Info Tech Mgr*
EMP: 50 **EST:** 1971
SQ FT: 15,000
SALES (est): 5.9MM **Privately Held**
WEB: www.lmwslaw.com
SIC: 8111 General practice law office

(P-23212)
LEWIS P C JACKSON
50 California St Ste 900, San Francisco
(94111-4615)
PHONE..............................415 394-9400
Gloria Kennard, *Administration*
Robert Pattison, *Managing Prtnr*
Wolfgang Timm, *MIS Dir*
John Bartkowiak, *Legal Staff*
Joanna L Brooks, *Associate*
EMP: 50
SALES (corp-wide): 277.6MM **Privately Held**
WEB: www.jacksonlewis.com
SIC: 8111 Legal services
PA: Lewis P C Jackson
1133 Weschester Ave
White Plains NY 10604
914 872-8060

(P-23213)
LEWIS P C JACKSON
725 S Figueroa St # 2500, Los Angeles
(90017-5408)
PHONE..............................213 689-0404
Wendy Sweet, *Manager*
Valerie Barnard, *CFO*
Josh Sable,
Arthur Escalante, *Legal Staff*
Sarah Ritter, *Legal Staff*
EMP: 100
SQ FT: 2,000
SALES (corp-wide): 277.6MM **Privately Held**
WEB: www.jacksonlewis.com
SIC: 8111 General practice law office
PA: Lewis P C Jackson
1133 Weschester Ave
White Plains NY 10604
914 872-8060

(P-23214)
LFK LAW
9595 Wilshire Blvd, Beverly Hills
(90212-2512)
PHONE..............................310 300-8464
Louis Fkmontcho, *CFO*
EMP: 55
SALES (est): 823.2K **Privately Held**
SIC: 8111 Legal services

(P-23215)
LIEFF CABRASER HEIMANN & (PA)
275 Battery St Ste 2800, San Francisco
(94111-3314)
PHONE..............................415 788-0245
Robert L Lieff, *Partner*
William Bernstein, *Partner*
Elizabeth J Cabraser, *Partner*
James M Finberg, *Partner*
Richard M Heimann, *Partner*
EMP: 120
SQ FT: 42,592
SALES (est): 23.2MM **Privately Held**
SIC: 8111 Antitrust & trade regulation law; environmental law; labor & employment law; securities law

(P-23216)
LINER LLP
Also Called: Liner Law
1100 Glendon Ave 14th, Los Angeles
(90024-3503)
PHONE..................................310 500-3500
Stuart A Liner, *Managing Prtnr*
Najwa Batarse, *Human Res Mgr*
Cheryleigh Bullock, *Legal Staff*
Laura Ettleson, *Legal Staff*
Andrea Heller, *Legal Staff*
EMP: 104 **EST:** 1996
SQ FT: 21,000
SALES (est): 527.4K
SALES (corp-wide): 493.7MM **Privately
Held**
SIC: 8111 Legal services
HQ: Dla Piper Llp (Us)
6225 Smith Ave Ste 200
Baltimore MD 21209
410 580-3000

(P-23217)
LITTLER MENDELSON PC (PA)
333 Bush St Fl 34, San Francisco
(94104-2874)
P.O. Box 45547 (94145-0547)
PHONE..................................415 433-1940
Thomas J Bender, *CEO*
John A Berg, *Shareholder*
Amber Isom-Thompson, *Shareholder*
Latoi Mayo, *Shareholder*
Renata Neeser, *Shareholder*
EMP: 500
SQ FT: 85,000
SALES (est): 342.9MM **Privately Held**
SIC: 8111 General practice law office

(P-23218)
LLP DOWNEY BRAND
621 Capitol Mall Fl 18, Sacramento
(95814-4731)
PHONE..................................775 329-5900
Jeffrey Hartman, *Owner*
EMP: 77
SALES (corp-wide): 38.5MM **Privately
Held**
SIC: 8111 General practice attorney,
lawyer
PA: Downey Brand Llp
621 Capitol Mall Fl 18
Sacramento CA 95814
916 444-1000

(P-23219)
LLP LOCKE LORD
101 Montgomery St # 1950, San Francisco
(94104-4151)
PHONE..................................415 318-8800
Matthew Blackburn, *Branch Mgr*
EMP: 161
SALES (corp-wide): 308.8MM **Privately
Held**
SIC: 8111 General practice attorney,
lawyer
PA: Locke Lord Llp
2200 Ross Ave Ste 2800
Dallas TX 75201
214 740-8000

(P-23220)
LLP LOCKE LORD
300 S Grand Ave Ste 2600, Los Angeles
(90071-3194)
PHONE..................................213 485-1500
Marilyn Loreta, *Administration*
EMP: 161
SALES (corp-wide): 308.8MM **Privately
Held**
SIC: 8111 Corporate, partnership & busi-
ness law; general practice law office
PA: Locke Lord Llp
2200 Ross Ave Ste 2800
Dallas TX 75201
214 740-8000

(P-23221)
LLP LOCKE LORD
660 Nwport Ctr Dr Ste 900, Newport Beach
(92660)
PHONE..................................949 423-2100
Jon-Paul Lapointe, *Branch Mgr*
EMP: 87
SALES (corp-wide): 308.8MM **Privately
Held**
SIC: 8111 General practice law office

PA: Locke Lord Llp
2200 Ross Ave Ste 2800
Dallas TX 75201
214 740-8000

(P-23222)
LLP MAYER BROWN
2 Palo Alto Sq Ste 300, Palo Alto
(94306-2122)
PHONE..................................650 331-2000
Martin Collins, *Branch Mgr*
EMP: 679
SALES (corp-wide): 707.3MM **Privately
Held**
SIC: 8111 General practice attorney,
lawyer
PA: Mayer Brown Llp
71 S Wacker Dr Ste 1000
Chicago IL 60606
312 782-0600

(P-23223)
LLP MAYER BROWN
Also Called: Mayer Brown & Platt
350 S Grand Ave Ste 2500, Los Angeles
(90071-3486)
PHONE..................................213 229-9500
Jim Tancula, *Manager*
David B Bolstad, *Partner*
Pierre Vogelenzang, *Partner*
Brian Neale, *Info Tech Mgr*
L Eatman,
EMP: 130
SALES (corp-wide): 707.3MM **Privately
Held**
SIC: 8111 General practice law office
PA: Mayer Brown Llp
71 S Wacker Dr Ste 1000
Chicago IL 60606
312 782-0600

(P-23224)
LLP ROBINS KAPLAN
2049 Century Park E # 3400, Los Angeles
(90067-3208)
PHONE..................................310 552-0130
Roman Silberfeld, *Manager*
David Bocan,
EMP: 78
SALES (corp-wide): 117.5MM **Privately
Held**
WEB: www.rkmc.com
SIC: 8111 General practice attorney,
lawyer
PA: Llp Robins Kaplan
800 Lasalle Ave Ste 2800
Minneapolis MN 55402
612 349-8500

(P-23225)
LOEB & LOEB LLP (PA)
10100 Santa Monica Blvd # 2200, Los An-
geles (90067-4120)
PHONE..................................310 282-2000
Barry I Slotnick, *Chairman*
Kenneth B Anderson, *Partner*
Daniel D Frohling, *Partner*
Douglas N Masters, *Partner*
Mickey Mayerson, *Partner*
EMP: 134
SALES (est): 56.7MM **Privately Held**
WEB: www.loeb.com
SIC: 8111 General practice law office

(P-23226)
LOEWS CORPORATION
4000 Coronado Bay Rd, Coronado
(92118-3290)
PHONE..................................619 424-4000
Kathleen Cochran, *General Mgr*
Zanna Liedike, *Info Tech Mgr*
Theresa Lu, *Asst Director*
EMP: 400
SALES (corp-wide): 13.7B **Publicly Held**
WEB: www.loews.com
SIC: 8111 General practice law office
PA: Loews Corporation
667 Madison Ave Fl 7
New York NY 10065
212 521-2000

(P-23227)
LONG & LEVIT LLP
465 California St Ste 500, San Francisco
(94104-1814)
PHONE..................................415 397-2222

Joseph McMonigle, *Managing Prtnr*
Jessica R Macgregor, *Partner*
Robert Kwong, *Info Tech Dir*
Luzia Ebnoether, *Financial Exec*
Shane Cahill, *Sr Associate*
EMP: 50
SQ FT: 48,500
SALES (est): 8.2MM **Privately Held**
WEB: www.longlevit.com
SIC: 8111 Corporate, partnership & busi-
ness law; taxation law; environmental law

(P-23228)
**LORBER GREENFIELD &
POLITO LLP (PA)**
13985 Stowe Dr, Poway (92064-6887)
PHONE..................................858 486-6757
Bruce Lorber, *Partner*
Joyia Greenfield, *Partner*
Cherrie Harris, *Partner*
Jill Ann Herman, *Partner*
Thomas Olsen, *Partner*
EMP: 62 **EST:** 1980
SQ FT: 20,000
SALES (est): 19.4MM **Privately Held**
SIC: 8111 General practice law office

(P-23229)
**LOUIE ALMEIDA & SETTLER
(PA)**
303 N Glenoaks Blvd # 400, Burbank
(91502-1116)
PHONE..................................818 461-9559
Peter Louie, *Partner*
David Stettler, *Senior Partner*
Donald Leiber, *Partner*
EMP: 54
SALES (est): 4.8MM **Privately Held**
SIC: 8111 General practice law office

(P-23230)
**LOW BALL & LYNCH A PROF
CORP (PA)**
505 Montgomery St Fl 7, San Francisco
(94111-6522)
PHONE..................................415 981-6630
Steven D Werth, *President*
Mark Hazelwood, *Treasurer*
Raymont Coates, *Principal*
Linda Meyer, *Admin Sec*
Tom Losavio,
EMP: 72
SQ FT: 20,000
SALES (est): 10.3MM **Privately Held**
SIC: 8111 General practice law office

(P-23231)
LOWENSTEIN SANDLER LLP
390 Lytton Ave, Palo Alto (94301-1432)
PHONE..................................650 433-5800
Stephen Dermer, *Counsel*
James O'Grady, *Counsel*
Rahul Shekher, *Associate*
Tracy Snow, *Associate*
EMP: 50
SALES (corp-wide): 119.8MM **Privately
Held**
SIC: 8111 General practice law office
PA: Lowenstein Sandler Llp
1 Lowenstein Dr
Roseland NJ 07068
973 597-2500

(P-23232)
LOZANO SMITH LLP
7404 N Spalding Ave, Fresno
(93720-3370)
PHONE..................................559 431-5600
Andrew Garcia, *Exec Dir*
Carlita C Romero, *Exec Dir*
Mariela Cantoriano, *Admin Sec*
Melissa Gonzales, *Admin Sec*
Jennifer Ha, *Admin Sec*
EMP: 167
SALES: 30K **Privately Held**
SIC: 8111 Legal services

(P-23233)
**LOZANO SMITH A PROF CORP
(PA)**
7404 N Spalding Ave, Fresno
(93720-3370)
PHONE..................................559 431-5600
Gregory A Wedner, *CEO*
Tina Cobabe, *President*

Lou Lozano, *President*
Krista Steiner, *President*
Peter Fagen, *Treasurer*
EMP: 54
SALES (est): 21.2MM **Privately Held**
SIC: 8111 Corporate, partnership & busi-
ness law

(P-23234)
**LYNBERG & WATKINS A PROF
CORP (PA)**
Also Called: Lynberg & Watkins Attys At Law
1150 S Olive St Fl 18, Los Angeles
(90015-3989)
PHONE..................................213 624-8700
Norman J Watkins, *President*
Charles A Lynberg, *President*
Randall J Peters, *CEO*
Aracely Estrada, *Administration*
Serj Daniel, *Clerk*
EMP: 50
SQ FT: 32,108
SALES (est): 13.8MM **Privately Held**
WEB: www.lynberg.com
SIC: 8111 General practice law office

(P-23235)
**LYNCH GILARDI & GRUMMER
LLP**
170 Columbus Ave Fl 5, San Francisco
(94133-5128)
PHONE..................................415 397-2800
Robert Lynch, *Managing Prtnr*
Dwane Grummer, *Managing Prtnr*
William A Bogdan,
James E Sell,
Kenneth F Vierra Jr,
EMP: 50
SQ FT: 4,000
SALES (est): 5.4MM **Privately Held**
WEB: www.lgglaw.com
SIC: 8111 Malpractice & negligence law;
product liability law; corporate, partner-
ship & business law

(P-23236)
**MALCOLM & CISNEROS A LAW
CORP**
Also Called: Malcolm Cisneros
2112 Business Center Dr # 200, Irvine
(92612-7135)
PHONE..................................949 252-1039
William Malcolm, *CEO*
Roman Cisneros, *COO*
Arturo Cisneros, *CFO*
EMP: 110
SALES (est): 16.3MM **Privately Held**
WEB: www.malcolmcisneros.com
SIC: 8111 General practice law office

(P-23237)
**MANATT PHELPS & PHILLIPS
LLP**
695 Town Center Dr # 1400, Costa Mesa
(92626-7223)
PHONE..................................714 371-2500
Shierley Hands, *Manager*
John Grosvenor, *Partner*
Tracey Dunn, *President*
Viral Mehta, *Associate*
EMP: 50
SALES (corp-wide): 180.9MM **Privately
Held**
WEB: www.manatt.com
SIC: 8111 General practice attorney,
lawyer
PA: Manatt, Phelps & Phillips, Llp
11355 W Olympic Blvd Fl 2
Los Angeles CA 90064
310 312-4000

(P-23238)
**MANNING KASS ELLROD RAM
TRESTR (PA)**
801 S Figueroa St Fl 15, Los Angeles
(90017-5504)
PHONE..................................213 624-6900
Steven D Manning, *Managing Prtnr*
Demetrius Roman, *Info Tech Mgr*
Robert Santos, *Facilities Mgr*
Eugene Egan, *Legal Staff*
Anthony Ellrod, *Legal Staff*
EMP: 150

SALES (est): 35.8MM **Privately Held**
WEB: www.mmker.com
SIC: **8111** General practice attorney, lawyer

(P-23239)
MATHENY SARS LINKERT JAIME LLP
3638 American River Dr, Sacramento (95864-5901)
PHONE..................................916 978-3434
Richard S Linkert, *Partner*
Matthew C Jamie, *Partner*
Douglas A Sears, *Partner*
Jack Klauschie, *Principal*
EMP: 52
SQ FT: 12,000
SALES (est): 5.7MM **Privately Held**
WEB: www.msll.com
SIC: **8111** General practice law office

(P-23240)
MAYNARD COOPER & GALE PC
600 Montgomery St # 2600, San Francisco (94111-2728)
PHONE..................................415 704-7433
Mila Dunn, *Corp Counsel*
EMP: 117
SALES (corp-wide): 57.9MM **Privately Held**
SIC: **8111** Specialized law offices, attorneys; general practice attorney, lawyer
PA: Maynard, Cooper & Gale, P.C.
1901 6th Ave N Ste 2400
Birmingham AL 35203
205 254-1000

(P-23241)
MC NAMARA DODGE NEY BEATT (PA)
3480 Buskirk Ave Ste 250, Pleasant Hill (94523-7310)
PHONE..................................925 939-5330
Richard Dodge, *Partner*
Thomas G Beatty, *Partner*
Guy Borges, *Partner*
Roger Brothers, *Partner*
Michael J Ney, *Partner*
EMP: 70 EST: 1965
SQ FT: 9,500
SALES (est): 8.6MM **Privately Held**
WEB: www.mcnamaralaw.com
SIC: **8111** Specialized law offices, attorneys; malpractice & negligence law

(P-23242)
MCCORMICK BARSTOW SHEPPRD WAYT (PA)
Also Called: McCormick Barstow
7647 N Fresno St, Fresno (93720-2578)
P.O. Box 28912 (93729-8912)
PHONE..................................559 433-1300
Jeffrey M Reid, *Managing Prtnr*
Anil Pai, *Records Dir*
Kenneth A Baldwin, *Partner*
Michael F Ball, *Partner*
Todd W Baxter, *Partner*
EMP: 123
SQ FT: 67,000
SALES (est): 31.2MM **Privately Held**
WEB: www.mbswc.com
SIC: **8111** Antitrust & trade regulation law; corporate, partnership & business law; bankruptcy law

(P-23243)
MCDERMOTT WILL & EMERY LLP INC
2049 Century Park E Fl 38, Los Angeles (90067-3101)
PHONE..................................310 277-4110
Joan Schulman, *Partner*
Margaret Dalmada, *Admin Sec*
Richard K Simon, *Partner*
Christine P Johnson, *Associate*
Anna Park, *Associate*
EMP: 140
SALES (corp-wide): 1.2B **Privately Held**
WEB: www.europe.mwe.com
SIC: **8111** General practice law office
PA: Mcdermott Will & Emery Llp Inc.
444 W Lake St Ste 4000
Chicago IL 60606
312 372-2000

(P-23244)
MCDERMOTT WILL & EMERY LLP INC
4 Park Plz Ste 1700, Irvine (92614-2559)
PHONE..................................949 757-7165
Vicki Lowenstein, *Systems Mgr*
Matthew Amaya, *Network Enginr*
Susan Manriquez, *Corp Counsel*
Todd Mobley,
EMP: 70
SALES (corp-wide): 1.2B **Privately Held**
WEB: www.europe.mwe.com
SIC: **8111** General practice law office
PA: Mcdermott Will & Emery Llp Inc.
444 W Lake St Ste 4000
Chicago IL 60606
312 372-2000

(P-23245)
MCGUIREWOODS LLP
1800 Century Park E Fl 8, Los Angeles (90067-1501)
PHONE..................................310 315-8200
Richard Grant, *Managing Prtnr*
Thomas Becket, *Vice Pres*
Teri Tingen, *Admin Asst*
Bonnie Dann, *Legal Staff*
Charlotte Snyder, *Legal Staff*
EMP: 92
SALES (corp-wide): 347.5MM **Privately Held**
SIC: **8111** General practice attorney, lawyer
PA: Mcguirewoods Llp
800 E Canal St
Richmond VA 23219
804 775-1000

(P-23246)
MCKOOL SMITH HENNIGAN
300 S Grand Ave Ste 2900, Los Angeles (90071-3139)
PHONE..................................213 694-1200
J Michael Hennigan, *Partner*
Bruce Bennett, *Partner*
James W Mercer, *Partner*
Jim Bergman, *MIS Dir*
Bruce Mac Leod,
EMP: 90
SQ FT: 35,000
SALES (est): 11.4MM **Privately Held**
WEB: www.hbdlawyers.com
SIC: **8111** Legal services

(P-23247)
MCMANIS FAULKNER A PROF CORP
50 W San Fernando St # 1000, San Jose (95113-2415)
PHONE..................................408 279-8700
James McManis, *President*
Sharon Kirsch, *President*
Carlos Nunez, *President*
William Faulkner, *Admin Sec*
Alvin Margallo, *Technology*
EMP: 50
SALES (est): 7.9MM **Privately Held**
WEB: www.mfmlaw.com
SIC: **8111** General practice attorney, lawyer

(P-23248)
MED-LEGAL LLC
4401 Atlantic Ave, Long Beach (90807-2218)
PHONE..................................626 653-1600
Victor Landero, *COO*
EMP: 116
SALES (corp-wide): 14.3MM **Privately Held**
SIC: **8111** Legal aid service
PA: Med-Legal, Llc
955 Overland Ct Ste 200
San Dimas CA 91773
626 653-5160

(P-23249)
MELMET STEVEN J LAW OFC
2912 Daimler St, Santa Ana (92705-5811)
PHONE..................................949 263-1000
Steven J Melmet, *President*
Nancy Salzman,
EMP: 70

SALES: 10MM **Privately Held**
WEB: www.melmetlaw.com
SIC: **8111** **6531** General practice law office; debt collection law; escrow agent, real estate

(P-23250)
MEXICAN AMERICAN LEGAL DEFENSE (PA)
Also Called: MALDEF
634 S Spring St Ste 1100, Los Angeles (90014-1974)
PHONE..................................213 629-2512
Thomas A Saenz, *President*
Jonhatan Aragon, *President*
Ann Tallman, *President*
Joseph Stern, *Chairman*
Yonny Aguilar, *Admin Asst*
EMP: 84
SQ FT: 20,000
SALES: 8.8MM **Privately Held**
WEB: www.maldef.org
SIC: **8111** Legal aid service

(P-23251)
MEYERS NAVE RIBACK SILVER & (PA)
555 12th St Ste 1500, Oakland (94607-4095)
PHONE..................................510 351-4300
David W Skinner, *CEO*
Jo Barrington, *President*
Terry Bremer, *President*
Sandra Chao, *President*
Anabelle Cotapos, *President*
EMP: 107
SQ FT: 28,678
SALES (est): 19.3MM **Privately Held**
WEB: www.meyersnave.com
SIC: **8111** Specialized law offices, attorneys

(P-23252)
MICHAEL SULLIVAN & ASSOC LLP
400 Continental Blvd # 250, El Segundo (90245-5076)
P.O. Box 85059, San Diego (92186-5059)
PHONE..................................310 337-4480
Michael W Sullivan, *Partner*
Dee Demarest, *Supervisor*
Zaneta Crayton, *Associate*
EMP: 147
SALES: 22.6MM **Privately Held**
SIC: **8111** General practice attorney, lawyer

(P-23253)
MILLER STARR & REGALIA A PRO (PA)
1331 N Calif Blvd Ste 500, Walnut Creek (94596-4599)
P.O. Box 8177 (94596-8177)
PHONE..................................925 935-9400
Anthony M Leones, *CEO*
Richard Carlson, *Principal*
Margot Canapa, *Controller*
Shari Santos, *Legal Staff*
Jamie Dierks, *Manager*
EMP: 90
SQ FT: 30,000
SALES (est): 12.7MM **Privately Held**
WEB: www.msandr.com
SIC: **8111** General practice law office

(P-23254)
MILLER & ASSOCIATES LLP
2530 Wilshire Blvd Fl 1, Santa Monica (90403-4664)
PHONE..................................310 315-1100
Ronald Miller, *Partner*
W Ashington Ttorney,
Angela Lumzy Jones,
EMP: 60
SALES: 11.1MM **Privately Held**
WEB: www.criminallawyer.net
SIC: **8111** General practice attorney, lawyer

(P-23255)
MINAMI TAMAKI LLP
360 Post St Fl 8, San Francisco (94108-4911)
PHONE..................................415 788-9000
Dale Minami, *Co-Owner*

Minette Kwok, *Partner*
Jack Lee, *Partner*
Donald K Tamaki, *Partner*
Brad Yamauchi, *Partner*
EMP: 50
SQ FT: 4,500
SALES: 10MM **Privately Held**
WEB: www.mltsf.com
SIC: **8111** General practice attorney, lawyer

(P-23256)
MINTZ LEVIN COHN FERRIS GL
3580 Carmel Mountain Rd # 300, San Diego (92130-6768)
PHONE..................................858 314-1500
Natalie K Schiller, *Technical Staff*
Dawn Saunders, *Counsel*
Randy Jones,
Ched Dipasupil, *Assistant*
Diane Johnson, *Assistant*
EMP: 100
SALES (corp-wide): 216.7MM **Privately Held**
SIC: **8111** General practice law office
PA: Mintz, Levin, Cohn, Ferris, Glovsky And Popeo, P.C.
1 Financial Ctr Fl 39
Boston MA 02111
617 348-4951

(P-23257)
MITCHELL SILBERBERG KNUPP LLP (PA)
11377 W Olympic Blvd Fl 2, Los Angeles (90064-1683)
PHONE..................................310 312-2000
Jeffrey K Eisen, *Principal*
Thomas P Lambert, *Managing Prtnr*
Kevin E Gaut, *COO*
Doug Gold, *Chief Mktg Ofcr*
Jerry Kaufman, *Exec Dir*
EMP: 108
SALES: 27.7K **Privately Held**
WEB: www.msk.com
SIC: **8111** General practice law office; real estate law; taxation law; labor & employment law

(P-23258)
ML PRIOR INC
955 Berrand Ct Ste 200, San Dimas (91773)
PHONE..................................626 653-5160
Stephen Schneider, *President*
Warren Schneider, *CEO*
Cathy Gonzalez, *Administration*
Gabriela Guzman, *Manager*
Anthony Martinez, *Manager*
EMP: 135
SQ FT: 31,770
SALES (est): 13.1MM **Privately Held**
SIC: **8111** Legal services

(P-23259)
MOORE LAW GROUP A PROF CORP
3710 S Susan St Ste 210, Santa Ana (92704-6956)
PHONE..................................714 431-2000
Harvey Moore, *President*
Donnie Pangburn, *Treasurer*
Angela Dawson, *Info Tech Mgr*
Connie Kopp, *Manager*
Sheila Shahriyarpour, *Associate*
EMP: 65 EST: 2008
SALES (est): 8.3MM **Privately Held**
SIC: **8111** General practice law office

(P-23260)
MORGAN LEWIS & BOCKIUS LLP
1 Market St Ste 500, San Francisco (94105-1306)
PHONE..................................415 393-2000
Donn Pickett, *Partner*
Dale Barnes, *Partner*
Michael Begert, *Partner*
Charles Crompton, *Partner*
Anne Deibert, *Partner*
EMP: 696 EST: 1880

SALES (est): 83.4MM
SALES (corp-wide): 752MM **Privately Held**
SIC: **8111** General practice law office
PA: Morgan, Lewis & Bockius Llp
　1701 Market St Ste Con
　Philadelphia PA 19103
　215 963-5000

(P-23261)
MORGAN LEWIS & BOCKIUS LLP
1400 Page Mill Rd, Palo Alto (94304-1124)
PHONE..................650 843-4000
Thomas Kellerman, *Partner*
Alexandre Bailly, *Partner*
Rekha Chudasama, *President*
Kathleen Gregory, *President*
Stephen Cheong, *Associate Dir*
EMP: 75
SALES (corp-wide): 752MM **Privately Held**
WEB: www.envinfo.com
SIC: **8111** General practice law office
PA: Morgan, Lewis & Bockius Llp
　1701 Market St Ste Con
　Philadelphia PA 19103
　215 963-5000

(P-23262)
MORGAN LEWIS & BOCKIUS LLP
600 Anton Blvd Ste 1800, Costa Mesa (92626-7653)
PHONE..................949 399-7000
Anne M Brafford, *Branch Mgr*
Randy Wood, *Associate*
EMP: 181
SALES (corp-wide): 752MM **Privately Held**
SIC: **8111** General practice attorney, lawyer
PA: Morgan, Lewis & Bockius Llp
　1701 Market St Ste Con
　Philadelphia PA 19103
　215 963-5000

(P-23263)
MORGAN LEWIS & BOCKIUS LLP
300 S Grand Ave Ste 2200, Los Angeles (90071-3132)
PHONE..................213 612-2500
John F Hartigan, *Managing Prtnr*
Matthew Hogan, *Partner*
J Jack, *Partner*
Michael Jack, *Partner*
Gary C Moss, *Partner*
EMP: 200
SALES (corp-wide): 752MM **Privately Held**
WEB: www.envinfo.com
SIC: **8111** General practice law office
PA: Morgan, Lewis & Bockius Llp
　1701 Market St Ste Con
　Philadelphia PA 19103
　215 963-5000

(P-23264)
MORGAN LEWIS & BOCKIUS LLP
1 Market Plz Lbby 1 # 1, San Francisco (94105-1002)
PHONE..................415 442-1000
Erika Smith, *Officer*
EMP: 300
SALES (corp-wide): 752MM **Privately Held**
WEB: www.envinfo.com
SIC: **8111** General practice law office
PA: Morgan, Lewis & Bockius Llp
　1701 Market St Ste Con
　Philadelphia PA 19103
　215 963-5000

(P-23265)
MORGAN LEWIS & BOCKIUS LLP
Also Called: Burton P Scott
300 S Grand Ave Ste 2200, Los Angeles (90071-3132)
PHONE..................213 612-2500
Neeraj Arora, *Counsel*
Richard Riordan, *Counsel*
Luis Blanco, *Manager*

Emily Calmeyer, *Associate*
Jason W Capps, *Associate*
EMP: 110
SALES (corp-wide): 752MM **Privately Held**
SIC: **8111** General practice law office
PA: Morgan, Lewis & Bockius Llp
　1701 Market St Ste Con
　Philadelphia PA 19103
　215 963-5000

(P-23266)
MORRIS POLICH & PURDY LLP (PA)
1055 W 7th St Ste 2400, Los Angeles (90017-2550)
PHONE..................213 891-9100
Theodore D Levin, *Partner*
Jeff Barron, *Partner*
William M Betley, *Partner*
Anthony Brazil, *Partner*
James Chantland, *Partner*
EMP: 100
SQ FT: 40,000
SALES (est): 27.7MM **Privately Held**
WEB: www.mpplaw.com
SIC: **8111** General practice attorney, lawyer

(P-23267)
MORRISON & FOERSTER LLP
12531 High Bluff Dr # 100, San Diego (92130-3014)
PHONE..................858 720-5100
Mark Zebrowski, *Managing Prtnr*
James J Mullen, *Managing Prtnr*
Jenkin Clark, *President*
Rajka K Hayden, *Regional Mgr*
Julie B Lucas, *Accounting Mgr*
EMP: 125
SALES (corp-wide): 900MM **Privately Held**
SIC: **8111** General practice law office
PA: Morrison & Foerster Llp
　425 Market St Fl 30
　San Francisco CA 94105
　415 268-7000

(P-23268)
MORRISON & FOERSTER LLP
Also Called: Morrison & Foerster - Library
755 Page Mill Rd Ste A100, Palo Alto (94304-1061)
PHONE..................650 813-5600
Alan Cope Johnston, *Managing Prtnr*
Michael Carlson, *Partner*
Gerald Dodson, *Partner*
Tyler M Dylan, *Partner*
Suzanne S Graeser, *Partner*
EMP: 277
SALES (corp-wide): 900MM **Privately Held**
SIC: **8111** General practice law office
PA: Morrison & Foerster Llp
　425 Market St Fl 30
　San Francisco CA 94105
　415 268-7000

(P-23269)
MORRISON & FOERSTER LLP
425 Market St Fl 32, San Francisco (94105-2467)
P.O. Box 8130, Walnut Creek (94596)
PHONE..................925 295-3300
David A Gold, *Managing Prtnr*
R Clark Morrison, *Partner*
EMP: 50
SALES (corp-wide): 900MM **Privately Held**
SIC: **8111** General practice law office
PA: Morrison & Foerster Llp
　425 Market St Fl 30
　San Francisco CA 94105
　415 268-7000

(P-23270)
MORRISON & FOERSTER LLP
707 Wilshire Blvd # 6000, Los Angeles (90017-3501)
PHONE..................213 892-5200
Gregory Koltun, *Managing Prtnr*
John W Alden Jr, *Partner*
Mark T Gillett, *Partner*
Dan Marmalefsky, *Partner*
A Max Olson, *Partner*
EMP: 250

SALES (corp-wide): 900MM **Privately Held**
SIC: **8111** General practice law office
PA: Morrison & Foerster Llp
　425 Market St Fl 30
　San Francisco CA 94105
　415 268-7000

(P-23271)
MORRISON & FOERSTER LLP (PA)
Also Called: Mofo
425 Market St Fl 30, San Francisco (94105-2482)
PHONE..................415 268-7000
Larren Nashelsky, *Chairman*
Jay Baris, *Partner*
Paul T Friedman, *Partner*
Greg Giammittorio, *Partner*
Craig D Martin, *Partner*
EMP: 400 EST: 2000
SALES (est): 900MM **Privately Held**
SIC: **8111** General practice attorney, lawyer

(P-23272)
MORRISON & FOERSTER LLP
Also Called: Marketing Department
425 Market St Fl 32, San Francisco (94105-2467)
PHONE..................415 268-7178
Roland Brandel, *Branch Mgr*
EMP: 143
SALES (corp-wide): 900MM **Privately Held**
SIC: **8111** Legal services
PA: Morrison & Foerster Llp
　425 Market St Fl 30
　San Francisco CA 94105
　415 268-7000

(P-23273)
MULLEN & HENZELL LLP
112 E Victoria St, Santa Barbara (93101-2068)
P.O. Box 789 (93102-0789)
PHONE..................805 966-1501
Dennis W Reilly, *Mng Member*
Brittany Boon, *President*
Erin Costigan, *President*
Lea Hanna, *President*
Nicole Herrera, *President*
EMP: 50 EST: 1931
SQ FT: 15,000
SALES (est): 7.3MM **Privately Held**
WEB: www.mullenlaw.com
SIC: **8111** Real estate law; will, estate & trust law; general practice attorney, lawyer

(P-23274)
MUNGER TOLLES & OLSON LLP
350 S Grand Ave Fl 50, Los Angeles (90071-3426)
PHONE..................213 683-9100
Sandra Seville-Jones, *Partner*
Thomas B Edwards, *Exec Dir*
EMP: 108
SALES (est): 30.4MM **Privately Held**
SIC: **8111** Corporate, partnership & business law; specialized law offices, attorneys

(P-23275)
MUNGER TOLLES OLSON FOUNDATION (PA)
350 S Grand Ave 50, Los Angeles (90071-3406)
PHONE..................213 683-9100
O'Malley M Miller, *CEO*
Robert Johnson, *President*
Larry Kleinberg, *CFO*
Mark Helm, *Vice Pres*
Steven B Weisburd, *Vice Pres*
EMP: 420
SQ FT: 100,000
SALES (est): 26.1MM **Privately Held**
WEB: www.mto.com
SIC: **8111** General practice attorney, lawyer

(P-23276)
MUNGER TOLLES OLSON FOUNDATION
560 Mission St Fl 27, San Francisco (94105-3089)
PHONE..................415 512-4000
Kim Coates, *Branch Mgr*
EMP: 50
SALES (est): 6MM
SALES (corp-wide): 26.1MM **Privately Held**
WEB: www.mto.com
SIC: **8111** Specialized law offices, attorneys
PA: Munger Tolles & Olson Foundation
　350 S Grand Ave 50
　Los Angeles CA 90071
　213 683-9100

(P-23277)
MURCHISON & CUMMING LLP (PA)
Also Called: M & C
801 S Grand Ave Ste 900, Los Angeles (90017-4624)
PHONE..................213 623-7400
Friedrich W Seitz, *Partner*
Edmund G Farrell, *Senior Partner*
Guy R Gruppie, *Senior Partner*
Jean M Lawler, *Senior Partner*
Michael Lawler, *Senior Partner*
EMP: 100
SQ FT: 30,000
SALES (est): 20.1MM **Privately Held**
WEB: www.murchison-cumming.com
SIC: **8111** General practice law office

(P-23278)
MURPHY (PA)
88 Kearny St Fl 10, San Francisco (94108-5524)
PHONE..................415 788-1900
Michael P Bradley, *President*
William S Kronenberg, *Partner*
Gena James, *President*
Gregory A Bastian, *Vice Pres*
John H Feeney, *Vice Pres*
EMP: 53 EST: 1978
SALES (est): 18.5MM **Privately Held**
WEB: www.mpbf.com
SIC: **8111** General practice law office

(P-23279)
MURTAUGH MYER NLSON TRGLIA LLP
2603 Main St Ste 900, Irvine (92614-4270)
P.O. Box 19627 (92623-9627)
PHONE..................949 794-4000
Michael J Nelson, *Managing Prtnr*
Harry A Halkowich, *Partner*
Mark S Himmelstein, *Partner*
Robert T Lemen, *Partner*
James A Murphy IV, *Partner*
EMP: 60
SALES (est): 7MM **Privately Held**
WEB: www.mmnt.com
SIC: **8111** General practice law office

(P-23280)
MUSICK PEELER & GARRETT LLP (PA)
624 S Grand Ave Ste 2000, Los Angeles (90017-3321)
PHONE..................213 629-7600
R Joseph De Briyn, *Managing Prtnr*
Peter J Diedrich, *Partner*
Edward Landrey, *Partner*
Wayne Littlefied, *Partner*
Gary Overstreet, *Partner*
EMP: 168
SQ FT: 100,000
SALES (est): 38.2MM **Privately Held**
WEB: www.mpgweb.com
SIC: **8111** General practice law office; taxation law; corporate, partnership & business law; labor & employment law

(P-23281)
NATIONWIDE LEGAL LLC (PA)
Also Called: Headquarters
1609 James M Wood Blvd, Los Angeles (90015-1005)
P.O. Box 15012 (90015-0012)
PHONE..................213 249-9999
Tony Davoodi, *CEO*

Joe Caamal, *COO*
Louis Nelson, *Exec VP*
Michael Lazcano, *Senior VP*
Hector Velazquez, *Branch Mgr*
EMP: 58
SALES (est): 39.2MM **Privately Held**
SIC: 8111 General practice attorney, lawyer

(P-23282)
NED E DUNPHY
4550 California Ave Fl 2, Bakersfield (93309-7012)
P.O. Box 11172 (93389-1172)
PHONE..................................661 395-1000
Ned E Dunphy, *Partner*
EMP: 56
SALES (est): 1.9MM **Privately Held**
SIC: 8111 General practice attorney, lawyer

(P-23283)
NEIL DYMOTT FRANK MCFALL
Also Called: Neil Dymott Perkins Brown
110 W A St, San Diego (92101-3711)
PHONE..................................619 238-1712
Michael I Neil, *President*
Teresa Anderson, *President*
Robert Frank, *Vice Pres*
Mona McKee, *Admin Sec*
Jose Trueba, *Info Tech Mgr*
EMP: 108
SQ FT: 15,000
SALES (est): 11.9MM **Privately Held**
WEB: www.neil-dymott.com
SIC: 8111 General practice law office

(P-23284)
NEWMEYER & DILLION LLP (PA)
895 Dove St Fl 5, Newport Beach (92660-2999)
PHONE..................................949 854-7000
Gregory L Dillion, *Partner*
Michael S Cucchissi, *Partner*
Joseph A Ferrentino, *Partner*
John A O Hara, *Partner*
Jon J Janecek, *Partner*
EMP: 115
SQ FT: 52,000
SALES (est): 35.7MM **Privately Held**
WEB: www.newmeyeranddillion.com
SIC: 8111 General practice law office

(P-23285)
NICOLAIDES FINK THORPE MICHAEL
101 Montgomery St # 2300, San Francisco (94104-4131)
PHONE..................................415 745-3778
Sarah Thorpe, *Senior Partner*
Jodi Green, *Associate*
Seth Manfredi, *Associate*
EMP: 60
SALES (est): 3.2MM **Privately Held**
SIC: 8111 Legal services

(P-23286)
NICOLE PTTRSON CRT RPRTING LLC
545 E Alluvial Ave # 109, Fresno (93720-2826)
PHONE..................................559 400-2407
Nicole Patterso, *President*
Nicole Patterson, *President*
EMP: 50
SALES (est): 1.5MM **Privately Held**
SIC: 8111 7338 Legal services; court reporting service

(P-23287)
NIXON PEABODY LLP
1 Embarcadero Ctr Fl 18, San Francisco (94111-3716)
PHONE..................................415 984-8200
Gina Hrens, *Manager*
Rosie Mangin, *President*
David Valencia, *Technology*
Domenico C Perrella, *Manager*
Stacy M Boven, *Associate*
EMP: 150
SALES (corp-wide): 236.3MM **Privately Held**
SIC: 8111 Specialized law offices, attorneys; antitrust & trade regulation law; environmental law; labor & employment law

PA: Nixon Peabody Llp
1300 Clinton Sq
Rochester NY 14604
585 263-1000

(P-23288)
NIXON PEABODY LLP
555 W 5th St Fl 30, Los Angeles (90013-1048)
PHONE..................................213 629-6000
Steph Levy, *Managing Prtnr*
Alexandra Busto, *Associate*
Kate M Ferrara, *Associate*
Eric R Ideta, *Associate*
Gretchen Sherwood, *Associate*
EMP: 85
SALES (corp-wide): 236.3MM **Privately Held**
SIC: 8111 General practice law office
PA: Nixon Peabody Llp
1300 Clinton Sq
Rochester NY 14604
585 263-1000

(P-23289)
NOLAND HAMERLY ETIENNE (PA)
333 Salinas St, Salinas (93901-2751)
PHONE..................................831 372-7525
Myron Etienne, *President*
Lloyd W Lowerly Jr, *Shareholder*
Mike Masuda, *Shareholder*
Werner Meyenberg, *Shareholder*
Terry O' Connor, *Shareholder*
EMP: 50
SQ FT: 10,000
SALES (est): 3.6MM **Privately Held**
WEB: www.nheh.com
SIC: 8111 General practice law office

(P-23290)
NORDMAN CORMANY HAIR & COMPTON
1000 Town Center Dr Fl 6, Oxnard (93036-1132)
P.O. Box 9100 (93031-9100)
PHONE..................................805 485-1000
Tammian Cook, *CEO*
Marc L Charney, *Partner*
Robert L Compton, *Partner*
Glenn J Dickinson, *Partner*
Randall H George, *Partner*
EMP: 115
SQ FT: 35,000
SALES (est): 10.6MM **Privately Held**
WEB: www.nchc.com
SIC: 8111 General practice law office

(P-23291)
NOSSAMAN LLP (PA)
777 S Figueroa St # 3400, Los Angeles (90017-5834)
PHONE..................................213 612-7800
E George Joseph, *Managing Prtnr*
Thomas Dover, *Partner*
Barbara Virga, *Bd of Directors*
Beth Cassioli, *Admin Sec*
Joyce Chen, *Admin Sec*
EMP: 74 EST: 1944
SQ FT: 20,000
SALES (est): 52.6MM **Privately Held**
WEB: www.nossaman.com
SIC: 8111 General practice attorney, lawyer

(P-23292)
NOSSAMAN LLP
1925 Palomar Oaks Way # 220, Carlsbad (92008-6526)
PHONE..................................760 918-0500
EMP: 76
SALES (corp-wide): 52.6MM **Privately Held**
SIC: 8111 Legal services
PA: Nossaman Llp
777 S Figueroa St # 3400
Los Angeles CA 90017
213 612-7800

(P-23293)
NOSSAMAN LLP
Also Called: Bagley, William T
50 California St Ste 3400, San Francisco (94111-4799)
PHONE..................................415 398-3600
Susan Eres, *Manager*

Barney Allison,
Martin A Mattes,
Cheryl Harmon, *Manager*
EMP: 50
SALES (corp-wide): 52.6MM **Privately Held**
WEB: www.nossaman.com
SIC: 8111 General practice law office
PA: Nossaman Llp
777 S Figueroa St # 3400
Los Angeles CA 90017
213 612-7800

(P-23294)
NOSSAMAN LLP
18101 Von Karman Ave # 1800, Irvine (92612-0177)
PHONE..................................949 833-7800
George Joseph, *Partner*
Kathryn Bell-Taylor, *Admin Sec*
Robin Golder, *Admin Sec*
Karyn McIvor, *Admin Sec*
Patricia Cooper, *Admin Asst*
EMP: 50
SALES (corp-wide): 52.6MM **Privately Held**
WEB: www.nossaman.com
SIC: 8111 General practice attorney, lawyer
PA: Nossaman Llp
777 S Figueroa St # 3400
Los Angeles CA 90017
213 612-7800

(P-23295)
OGLETREE DEAKINS NASH SMOAK
1 Market St Ste 1300, San Francisco (94105-1497)
PHONE..................................415 442-4810
Patrick Sum, *Chairman*
Dawn Collins, *Shareholder*
Jack Sholkoff, *Shareholder*
Eileen Lewis, *Legal Staff*
Kevin Bland, *Manager*
EMP: 90
SALES (corp-wide): 317.4MM **Privately Held**
SIC: 8111 General practice law office
PA: Ogletree, Deakins, Nash, Smoak & Stewart, P.C.
300 N Main St Ste 500
Greenville SC 29601
864 271-1300

(P-23296)
OMELVENY & MYERS LLP (PA)
400 S Hope St Fl 19, Los Angeles (90071-2831)
PHONE..................................213 430-6000
Arthur B Culvahouse Jr, *Mng Member*
Larry Sussman, *Managing Prtnr*
Brett J Williamson, *Managing Prtnr*
Cathy Hagen, *Bd of Directors*
Christopher Brearton,
EMP: 850 **EST:** 1885
SQ FT: 250,000
SALES (est): 320.6MM **Privately Held**
SIC: 8111 General practice law office

(P-23297)
OMELVENY & MYERS LLP
610 Nwport Ctr Dr Fl 17 Flr 17, Newport Beach (92660)
PHONE..................................949 760-9600
Elizabeth L McKeen, *Manager*
Terrence R Allen, *Partner*
Richard Jones,
EMP: 130
SALES (corp-wide): 320.6MM **Privately Held**
SIC: 8111 General practice law office
PA: O'melveny & Myers Llp
400 S Hope St Fl 19
Los Angeles CA 90071
213 430-6000

(P-23298)
OMELVENY & MYERS LLP
1999 Avenue Of The Stars # 600, Los Angeles (90067-6035)
PHONE..................................310 553-6700
Jodi Yamada, *Manager*
EMP: 225

SALES (corp-wide): 320.6MM **Privately Held**
SIC: 8111 General practice attorney, lawyer; general practice law office
PA: O'melveny & Myers Llp
400 S Hope St Fl 19
Los Angeles CA 90071
213 430-6000

(P-23299)
OMELVENY & MYERS LLP
2765 Sand Hill Rd, Menlo Park (94025-7098)
PHONE..................................650 473-2600
Tina Schinick, *Branch Mgr*
EMP: 201
SALES (corp-wide): 320.6MM **Privately Held**
SIC: 8111 General practice law office
PA: O'melveny & Myers Llp
400 S Hope St Fl 19
Los Angeles CA 90071
213 430-6000

(P-23300)
OMELVENY & MYERS LLP
2 Embarcadero Ctr Fl 28, San Francisco (94111-3823)
PHONE..................................415 984-8700
Luann Simmons, *Manager*
Debra Belaga, *Partner*
William Franklin Birchfield, *Partner*
Claire Philipott,
Glen Underwood, *Manager*
EMP: 175
SALES (corp-wide): 320.6MM **Privately Held**
SIC: 8111 General practice law office
PA: O'melveny & Myers Llp
400 S Hope St Fl 19
Los Angeles CA 90071
213 430-6000

(P-23301)
ORRICK HRRINGTON SUTCLIFFE LLP (PA)
405 Howard St, San Francisco (94105-2625)
PHONE..................................415 773-5700
Ralph H Baxter Jr, *CEO*
Martin Bartlam, *Partner*
Peter A Bicks, *Partner*
Benedikt Burger, *Partner*
Neel Chatterjee, *Partner*
EMP: 148
SQ FT: 146,000
SALES (est): 299.7MM **Privately Held**
WEB: www.orrick.com
SIC: 8111 General practice law office

(P-23302)
ORRICK HRRINGTON SUTCLIFFE LLP
1000 Marsh Rd, Menlo Park (94025-1015)
PHONE..................................650 614-7400
Don Keller, *Branch Mgr*
Jacob M Heath, *Associate*
Diana Rutowski, *Associate*
Stacey E Stillman, *Associate*
EMP: 160
SALES (corp-wide): 299.7MM **Privately Held**
SIC: 8111 General practice attorney, lawyer
PA: Orrick, Herrington & Sutcliffe, Llp
405 Howard St
San Francisco CA 94105
415 773-5700

(P-23303)
ORRICK HRRINGTON SUTCLIFFE LLP
1020 Marsh Rd, Menlo Park (94025-1015)
PHONE..................................650 614-7454
Barbara Whiteley, *Branch Mgr*
Peter Cohen, *Partner*
Christopher R Ottenweller,
EMP: 152
SALES (corp-wide): 299.7MM **Privately Held**
WEB: www.orrick.com
SIC: 8111 General practice attorney, lawyer

P R O D U C T S & S V C S

PA: Orrick, Herrington & Sutcliffe, Llp
405 Howard St
San Francisco CA 94105
415 773-5700

(P-23304)
ORRICK HRRINGTON SUTCLIFFE LLP
777 S Figueroa St # 3200, Los Angeles (90017-5800)
PHONE..................213 629-2020
Delores Hamilton, *Branch Mgr*
William Oxley, *Partner*
Daniel Tyukody Jr, *Partner*
Jerry J Walsh, *Partner*
Ramon Galvan,
EMP: 118
SALES (corp-wide): 299.7MM **Privately Held**
WEB: www.orrick.com
SIC: 8111 General practice attorney, lawyer
PA: Orrick, Herrington & Sutcliffe, Llp
405 Howard St
San Francisco CA 94105
415 773-5700

(P-23305)
ORRICK HRRINGTON SUTCLIFFE LLP
400 Capitol Mall Ste 3000, Sacramento (95814-4497)
PHONE..................916 447-9200
Betty Neal,
Virginia Magan, *Partner*
John Myers,
EMP: 67
SQ FT: 19,336
SALES (corp-wide): 299.7MM **Privately Held**
WEB: www.orrick.com
SIC: 8111 General practice attorney, lawyer
PA: Orrick, Herrington & Sutcliffe, Llp
405 Howard St
San Francisco CA 94105
415 773-5700

(P-23306)
PACHULSKI STANG ZEHL JONES LLP (PA)
Also Called: Pszyjw
10100 Santa Monica Blvd # 1100, Los Angeles (90067-4003)
PHONE..................310 277-6910
Richard M Pachulski, *President*
Diane Potts, *President*
Tanya Thompson, *President*
Dean A Ziehl, *Vice Pres*
James I Stang, *Admin Sec*
EMP: 90
SQ FT: 21,000
SALES (est): 39MM **Privately Held**
WEB: www.pszyj.com
SIC: 8111 General practice law office

(P-23307)
PACIFIC LEGAL FOUNDATION (PA)
930 G St, Sacramento (95814-1802)
PHONE..................916 419-7111
Robert K Best, *President*
John C Harris, *Ch of Bd*
Robin L Rivett, *President*
Todd Gaziano, *Exec Dir*
Patricia Castillo, *Admin Sec*
EMP: 55
SQ FT: 14,000
SALES (est): 13.3MM **Privately Held**
SIC: 8111 General practice law office

(P-23308)
PALUMBO LAWYERS LLP (PA)
15635 Alton Pkwy Ste 300, Irvine (92618-7332)
PHONE..................949 442-0300
Diane O Palumbo, *Partner*
Jay Bergstrom, *Partner*
Julia Bergstrom, *Partner*
Diane Palumbo, *Managing Prtnr*
Melissa Forbes, *Office Mgr*
EMP: 54
SQ FT: 13,258

SALES (est): 7.5MM **Privately Held**
WEB: www.palumbolawyers.com
SIC: 8111 General practice attorney, lawyer

(P-23309)
PARASEC INCORPORATED (PA)
2804 Gateway Oaks Dr # 100, Sacramento (95833-4346)
P.O. Box 160568 (95816-0568)
PHONE..................916 576-7000
Matthew Marzucco, *President*
Barbara Geiger, *Vice Pres*
Lynn Conner, *Principal*
Jessica Sierras, *Opers Mgr*
Ian Sierchio, *Sales Mgr*
EMP: 53
SQ FT: 24,000
SALES (est): 21.7MM **Privately Held**
WEB: www.parasec.com
SIC: 8111 Specialized legal services

(P-23310)
PARKER MILLIKEN CLARK OHAR
555 S Flower St Fl 30, Los Angeles (90071-2440)
PHONE..................818 784-8087
Larry Ivanjack, *President*
Brent Cheney, *Shareholder*
Gary Ganchrow, *Shareholder*
Gary Meyer, *Shareholder*
Richard D Robbins, *President*
EMP: 70 EST: 1914
SQ FT: 25,000
SALES (est): 9.1MM **Privately Held**
WEB: www.pmcos.com
SIC: 8111 General practice law office

(P-23311)
PARKER STANBURY LLP (PA)
444 S Flower St Ste 1900, Los Angeles (90071-2909)
PHONE..................619 528-1259
Robert Lo Presti, *Partner*
Graham J Baldwin, *Partner*
John D Barrett Jr, *Partner*
John W Dannhausen, *Partner*
Douglas M Degrade, *Partner*
EMP: 60 EST: 1922
SQ FT: 17,152
SALES (est): 12.7MM **Privately Held**
WEB: www.parkstan.com
SIC: 8111 General practice law office

(P-23312)
PATENAUDE & FELIX A PROF CORP (PA)
4545 Murphy Canyon Rd # 3, San Diego (92123-4363)
PHONE..................858 244-7600
Raymond Patenaude, *Partner*
Patrick Felix, *Partner*
Neal Prasad, *COO*
Jeff Dillon, *CFO*
EMP: 57
SQ FT: 30,000
SALES (est): 20.4MM **Privately Held**
WEB: www.pandf.us
SIC: 8111 General practice attorney, lawyer

(P-23313)
PATTERSON RITNER LOCKWOOD (PA)
620 N Brand Blvd Fl 3, Glendale (91203-4221)
PHONE..................818 241-8001
William F Ritner, *Partner*
Harold H Gartner III, *Partner*
John A Jurich, *Partner*
Clyde E Lockwood, *Partner*
James McGahan, *Partner*
EMP: 90 EST: 1968
SQ FT: 16,000
SALES (est): 5.4MM **Privately Held**
WEB: www.pattersonritner.com
SIC: 8111 General practice law office

(P-23314)
PAUL HASTINGS LLP
695 Town Center Dr # 120, Costa Mesa (92626-7216)
PHONE..................714 668-6200
Marilyn Radley, *Partner*

EMP: 100
SALES (corp-wide): 334MM **Privately Held**
SIC: 8111 General practice law office
PA: Paul Hastings Llp
515 S Flower St Fl 25
Los Angeles CA 90071
213 683-6000

(P-23315)
PAUL HASTINGS LLP
695 Town Center Dr # 120, Costa Mesa (92626-7216)
PHONE..................714 668-6200
Marilyn Radley, *Managing Prtnr*
Douglas A Schaaf, *Partner*
Peter J Tennyson, *Partner*
Craig Davis, *Business Mgr*
Stephen D Coke,
EMP: 200
SALES (corp-wide): 334MM **Privately Held**
SIC: 8111 General practice law office
PA: Paul Hastings Llp
515 S Flower St Fl 25
Los Angeles CA 90071
213 683-6000

(P-23316)
PAUL HASTINGS LLP (PA)
515 S Flower St Fl 25, Los Angeles (90071-2228)
PHONE..................213 683-6000
Greg Nitzkowski, *Mng Member*
George W Abele, *Partner*
Jesse H Austin, *Partner*
Dino T Barajas, *Partner*
Tollie Besson, *Partner*
EMP: 148
SQ FT: 209,000
SALES (est): 334MM **Privately Held**
SIC: 8111 General practice law office

(P-23317)
PAUL HASTINGS LLP
4747 Executive Dr # 1200, San Diego (92121-3095)
PHONE..................858 458-3000
Craig Price, *Administration*
Anita Patel, *Executive*
Todd Schneider, *Executive*
EMP: 100
SALES (corp-wide): 334MM **Privately Held**
SIC: 8111 General practice law office
PA: Paul Hastings Llp
515 S Flower St Fl 25
Los Angeles CA 90071
213 683-6000

(P-23318)
PAUL HASTINGS LLP
101 California St, San Francisco (94111-5802)
PHONE..................415 856-7000
Dennis Dehrens, *Administration*
Lane D Barrasso, *Associate*
Kelly R Winslow, *Associate*
EMP: 168
SALES (corp-wide): 334MM **Privately Held**
SIC: 8111 General practice law office
PA: Paul Hastings Llp
515 S Flower St Fl 25
Los Angeles CA 90071
213 683-6000

(P-23319)
PAUL HASTINGS LLP
1117 California Ave, Palo Alto (94304-1106)
PHONE..................650 320-1800
Paul Janofsky, *Branch Mgr*
Tom Wisialowski, *Manager*
EMP: 179
SALES (corp-wide): 334MM **Privately Held**
SIC: 8111 General practice law office
PA: Paul Hastings Llp
515 S Flower St Fl 25
Los Angeles CA 90071
213 683-6000

(P-23320)
PAYNE & FEARS LLP (PA)
4 Park Plz Ste 1100, Irvine (92614-8550)
PHONE..................949 851-1101

James L Payne, *Partner*
Jeffrey Brown, *Partner*
Daniel Fears, *Partner*
Eric Fohlgren, *Partner*
Karen Frankudakis, *Partner*
EMP: 68
SQ FT: 22,000
SALES (est): 18.3MM **Privately Held**
SIC: 8111 Corporate, partnership & business law; labor & employment law

(P-23321)
PEARLMAN BORSKA & WAX LLP (PA)
15910 Ventura Blvd Fl 18, Encino (91436-2819)
PHONE..................818 501-4343
Barry S Pearlman, *Partner*
Elliot F Borska, *Partner*
Dean Brown, *Partner*
Steven H Wax, *Partner*
Carol Ellison, *CFO*
EMP: 60
SQ FT: 4,000
SALES: 13.3MM **Privately Held**
WEB: www.4pbw.com
SIC: 8111 General practice law office

(P-23322)
PERKINS COIE LLP
3150 Porter Dr, Palo Alto (94304-1212)
PHONE..................415 725-1313
Edward West, *Manager*
Christian Lee, *Associate*
EMP: 70
SALES (corp-wide): 316MM **Privately Held**
WEB: www.perkinscoie.com
SIC: 8111 General practice attorney, lawyer
PA: Perkins Coie Llp
1201 3rd Ave Ste 4900
Seattle WA 98101
206 359-8000

(P-23323)
PERKINS COIE LLP
1620 26th St Ste 600s, Santa Monica (90404-4013)
PHONE..................310 788-9900
Sally Cano, *Manager*
Mark E Birnbaum, *Partner*
Shawn Henry, *Opers Mgr*
Donald E Karl,
EMP: 75
SALES (corp-wide): 316MM **Privately Held**
WEB: www.perkinscoie.com
SIC: 8111 General practice attorney, lawyer
PA: Perkins Coie Llp
1201 3rd Ave Ste 4900
Seattle WA 98101
206 359-8000

(P-23324)
PERKINS COIE LLP
505 Howard St Ste 1000, San Francisco (94105-3222)
PHONE..................415 344-7000
John Rossiter, *Principal*
Laurel Heicher, *Executive Asst*
Marie Cooper, *Counsel*
Deborah Gutfeld, *Counsel*
Wing Liang, *Counsel*
EMP: 50
SALES (corp-wide): 316MM **Privately Held**
WEB: www.perkinscoie.com
SIC: 8111 General practice attorney, lawyer
PA: Perkins Coie Llp
1201 3rd Ave Ste 4900
Seattle WA 98101
206 359-8000

(P-23325)
PERONA LANGER BECK A PROF CORP
300 E San Antonio Dr, Long Beach (90807-2002)
PHONE..................562 426-6155
James T Perona, *President*
Major A Langer, *CFO*
Ronald Beck, *Admin Sec*
EMP: 100 EST: 1966

SQ FT: 18,000
SALES (est): 11.3MM **Privately Held**
WEB: www.fightforyou.com
SIC: 8111 General practice law office

(P-23326)
PETTI KOHN INGRASSIA & L PR CO

11622 El Camino Real, San Diego (92130-2049)
PHONE..................310 649-5772
Andrew N Kohn, *President*
Jeff Miyamoto, *Shareholder*
John Durant, *COO*
Thomas S Ingrassia, *CFO*
Douglas Pettit, *Vice Pres*
EMP: 66
SALES (est): 7.3MM **Privately Held**
SIC: 8111 General practice law office

(P-23327)
PHILLIPS & ASSOC LAW OFFS PC

1300 Clay St Ste 600, Oakland (94612-1427)
PHONE..................510 464-8040
P Knudsen, *Branch Mgr*
EMP: 76 **Privately Held**
SIC: 8111 General practice law office
PA: Phillips & Associates Law Offices Pc
3101 N Central Ave # 1500
Phoenix AZ 85012

(P-23328)
PILLSBURY WINTHROP SHAW

4 Embarcadero Ctr # 2100, San Francisco (94111-4128)
PHONE..................415 983-1000
Jeffrey M Vesely, *General Ptnr*
Kathleen Hilton, *Director*
Caitlin B Stulberg, *Associate*
EMP: 194
SALES (corp-wide): 313MM **Privately Held**
SIC: 8111 Legal services
PA: Pillsbury Winthrop Shaw Pittman Llp
1540 Broadway Fl 9
New York NY 10036
212 858-1000

(P-23329)
PILLSBURY WINTHROP SHAW

725 S Figueroa St # 2900, Los Angeles (90017-5429)
PHONE..................213 488-7100
Melissa Burton, *Administration*
Catherine D Meyer,
EMP: 150
SALES (corp-wide): 313MM **Privately Held**
SIC: 8111 General practice law office
PA: Pillsbury Winthrop Shaw Pittman Llp
1540 Broadway Fl 9
New York NY 10036
212 858-1000

(P-23330)
PILLSBURY WINTHROP SHAW

29 Eucalyptus Rd, Berkeley (94705-2801)
PHONE..................415 983-1865
Thomas Loran, *Branch Mgr*
EMP: 143
SALES (corp-wide): 313MM **Privately Held**
SIC: 8111 Legal services
PA: Pillsbury Winthrop Shaw Pittman Llp
1540 Broadway Fl 9
New York NY 10036
212 858-1000

(P-23331)
PILLSBURY WINTHROP SHAW

50 Fremont St Ste 522, San Francisco (94105-2232)
P.O. Box 7880 (94120-7880)
PHONE..................415 983-1075
Jeffrey M Vesely, *Partner*
Catherine Schmitz, *President*
Miriam Ben-Natan, *Administration*
Yury Lafontaine, *Technology*
Toni Rembe, *CPA*
EMP: 300
SALES (corp-wide): 313MM **Privately Held**
SIC: 8111 General practice law office

PA: Pillsbury Winthrop Shaw Pittman Llp
1540 Broadway Fl 9
New York NY 10036
212 858-1000

(P-23332)
PILLSBURY WINTHROP SHAW

2550 Hanover St, Palo Alto (94304-1115)
PHONE..................650 233-4500
Kathie Pieri, *Manager*
Hall Trish, *President*
Maria Cho, *Associate*
EMP: 200
SALES (corp-wide): 313MM **Privately Held**
SIC: 8111 General practice law office
PA: Pillsbury Winthrop Shaw Pittman Llp
1540 Broadway Fl 9
New York NY 10036
212 858-1000

(P-23333)
PIRCHER NICHOLS & MEEKS (PA)

1925 Century Park E # 1700, Los Angeles (90067-2740)
PHONE..................310 201-0132
Gary Laughlin, *Senior Partner*
Stevens Carey, *Partner*
Eugene Leone, *Partner*
Leo Pircher, *Partner*
Helen Brooks, *President*
EMP: 95
SQ FT: 35,000
SALES (est): 19MM **Privately Held**
WEB: www.pircher.
SIC: 8111 General practice law office

(P-23334)
POLLARD CRNERT CRWFORD STEVENS

35 N Lake Ave Ste 500, Pasadena (91101-4195)
PHONE..................626 793-4440
Michael Pollard, *Principal*
Janice Okanishi, *Legal Staff*
EMP: 50
SALES (est): 4MM **Privately Held**
SIC: 8111 General practice attorney, lawyer

(P-23335)
POLSINELLI PC

Also Called: Polsinelli LLP
2049 Century Park E, Los Angeles (90067-3101)
PHONE..................310 556-1801
Norma Ayala, *Administration*
EMP: 70
SALES (corp-wide): 222.8MM **Privately Held**
SIC: 8111 General practice attorney, lawyer
PA: Polsinelli Pc
900 W 48th Pl Ste 900 # 900
Kansas City MO 64112
816 753-1000

(P-23336)
PRICE ASSOCIATES

Also Called: Price, Stuart
15760 Ventura Blvd # 1100, Encino (91436-3044)
PHONE..................818 995-9216
Stuart Price, *Owner*
Karen Tahler, *Opers Staff*
EMP: 50
SALES (est): 2.7MM **Privately Held**
SIC: 8111 General practice law office

(P-23337)
PRICE LAW GROUP A PROF CORP (PA)

15760 Ventura Blvd # 1100, Encino (91436-3044)
PHONE..................818 995-4540
Stuart M Price, *President*
EMP: 115
SQ FT: 15,000
SALES (est): 13.4MM **Privately Held**
SIC: 8111 Bankruptcy law; debt collection law

(P-23338)
PRICE POSTEL AND PARMA LLP

200 E Carrillo St Ste 400, Santa Barbara (93101-2190)
P.O. Box 99 (93102-0099)
PHONE..................805 962-0011
Terry J Schwartz, *Partner*
Lonni Meanley Collins, *Partner*
James H Hurley Jr, *Partner*
Shereef Moharram, *Partner*
Gerald S Thede, *Partner*
EMP: 60
SQ FT: 5,000
SALES (est): 8.6MM **Privately Held**
WEB: www.ppplaw.com
SIC: 8111 General practice law office

(P-23339)
PRINDLE DECKER & AMARO LLP (PA)

310 Golden Shore Fl 4, Long Beach (90802-4232)
PHONE..................562 436-3946
R Joseph Decker, *Partner*
Michael Amaro, *Partner*
Kenneth Prindle, *Partner*
Greg Fox, *Technology*
Tina McGuire, *Finance*
EMP: 85
SALES (est): 8.7MM **Privately Held**
SIC: 8111 General practice attorney, lawyer

(P-23340)
PRISON INDUSTRY AUTHORITY-PIA

1 Kings Way, Avenal (93204-9708)
PHONE..................559 386-6060
EMP: 60
SALES (est): 8.9MM **Privately Held**
SIC: 8111 Legal services

(P-23341)
PROBER & RAPHAEL A LAW CORP

Also Called: Prober & Raphael, ALC
20750 Ventura Blvd # 100, Woodland Hills (91364-2338)
P.O. Box 4365 (91365-4365)
PHONE..................818 227-0100
Dean R Prober, *President*
Lee Raphael, *Managing Prtnr*
Barbara Scott, *President*
Lee S Raphael, *Principal*
Dean Prober, *General Mgr*
EMP: 70
SALES (est): 8.3MM **Privately Held**
SIC: 8111 General practice law office

(P-23342)
PROSKAUER ROSE LLP

Also Called: Scott J Witlin Atty
2049 Century Park E # 3200, Los Angeles (90067-3206)
PHONE..................310 557-2900
Alan Jaffe, *President*
EMP: 60
SALES (corp-wide): 260.6MM **Privately Held**
SIC: 8111 General practice attorney, lawyer
PA: Proskauer Rose Llp
11 Times Sq Fl 17
New York NY 10036
212 969-3000

(P-23343)
PUBLIC COUNSEL

610 S Ardmore Ave, Los Angeles (90005-2322)
PHONE..................213 385-2977
Margaret Morrow, *President*
Madaline Kleiner, *Ch of Bd*
Gabriela Metcalfe-Smith, *Manager*
Erika Luna, *Receptionist*
EMP: 94 EST: 1970
SQ FT: 12,000
SALES: 13MM **Privately Held**
SIC: 8111 Specialized law offices, attorneys

(P-23344)
QUINN EMANUEL URQUHART

50 California St Ste 2200, San Francisco (94111-4788)
PHONE..................415 875-6600
Charles K Verhoeven, *Managing Prtnr*
Karen Beck, *Admin Sec*
Eric Gebhardt, *Administration*
Leonard Tingin, *Technology*
Juan Barron, *Cust Mgr*
EMP: 50
SALES (corp-wide): 199.2MM **Privately Held**
SIC: 8111 Specialized law offices, attorneys
PA: Quinn Emanuel Urquhart & Sullivan, Llp
865 S Figueroa St Fl 10
Los Angeles CA 90017
213 443-3000

(P-23345)
QUINN EMANUEL URQUHART

555 Twin Dolphin Dr Fl 5, Redwood City (94065-2129)
PHONE..................650 801-5000
Claude M Stern, *Managing Prtnr*
Chad Okada, *IT/INT Sup*
Maryann Bramhall, *Recruiter*
Rachel Herrick, *Counsel*
Jennifer Bauer, *Associate*
EMP: 80
SALES (corp-wide): 199.2MM **Privately Held**
SIC: 8111 Specialized law offices, attorneys
PA: Quinn Emanuel Urquhart & Sullivan, Llp
865 S Figueroa St Fl 10
Los Angeles CA 90017
213 443-3000

(P-23346)
QUINN EMANUEL URQUHART (PA)

865 S Figueroa St Fl 10, Los Angeles (90017-5003)
PHONE..................213 443-3000
John B Quinn, *Partner*
Adam Abensohn, *Partner*
Anthony Alden, *Partner*
Wayne Alexander, *Partner*
Steven Anderson, *Partner*
EMP: 366
SALES (est): 199.2MM **Privately Held**
SIC: 8111 General practice law office

(P-23347)
RAINES LAW GROUP LLP

9720 Wilshire Blvd Fl 5, Beverly Hills (90212-2014)
PHONE..................310 440-4100
Andrew Raines, *General Ptnr*
Robert Pardo, *Partner*
Megan Bulow, *Accounting Mgr*
EMP: 50
SALES (est): 1.2MM **Privately Held**
SIC: 8111 General practice law office

(P-23348)
REED SMITH LLP

2 Embarcadero Ctr Fl 20, San Francisco (94111-3922)
PHONE..................415 659-5964
Janette Davis, *Manager*
Adaline J Hilgard, *Counsel*
Christine M Morgan, *Counsel*
EMP: 70
SALES (corp-wide): 335.4MM **Privately Held**
SIC: 8111 General practice law office
PA: Reed Smith Llp
225 5th Ave Ste 1200
Pittsburgh PA 15222
412 288-3131

(P-23349)
REED SMITH LLP

355 S Grand Ave Ste 2900, Los Angeles (90071-1514)
PHONE..................213 457-8000
Peter Kennedy, *Partner*
Patty Carr, *President*
Socorro Dominguez, *President*
Charlie Koster, *President*
Sonia Martinez, *President*

EMP: 158
SALES (corp-wide): 335.4MM **Privately Held**
WEB: www.reedsmith.com
SIC: 8111 General practice attorney, lawyer
PA: Reed Smith Llp
225 5th Ave Ste 1200
Pittsburgh PA 15222
412 288-3131

(P-23350)
REED SMITH LLP
101 2nd St Ste 1800, San Francisco (94105-3659)
PHONE............................415 543-8700
Bettie B Epstein, *Partner*
Sandi Brooks, *President*
Nancy Schulein, *President*
Danny Silva, *Admin Sec*
Donna Fagan, *Manager*
EMP: 158
SALES (corp-wide): 335.4MM **Privately Held**
WEB: www.reedsmith.com
SIC: 8111 Legal services
PA: Reed Smith Llp
225 5th Ave Ste 1200
Pittsburgh PA 15222
412 288-3131

(P-23351)
REED SMITH LLP
2 Embarcadero Ctr Fl 21, San Francisco (94111-3995)
PHONE............................415 543-8700
David A Thompson, *Partner*
Gloria Sandoval, *President*
EMP: 143
SALES (corp-wide): 335.4MM **Privately Held**
WEB: www.reedsmith.com
SIC: 8111 Legal services
PA: Reed Smith Llp
225 5th Ave Ste 1200
Pittsburgh PA 15222
412 288-3131

(P-23352)
REID & HELLY
3880 Lemon St Fl 5, Riverside (92501-3667)
P.O. Box 1300 (92502-1300)
PHONE............................951 682-1771
Michael Kerbs, *Partner*
EMP: 60
SALES (est): 3.4MM **Privately Held**
SIC: 8111 General practice law office

(P-23353)
REPUBLIC DOCUMENT MANAGEMENT (PA)
660 N Diamond Bar Blvd # 258, Diamond Bar (91765-1058)
PHONE............................909 718-1421
Daniel Lopez, *President*
Barbara Callan, *Treasurer*
Robert Callan, *Exec VP*
Maria Lopez, *Admin Sec*
Todd McDonald, *Opers Mgr*
EMP: 72
SQ FT: 4,714
SALES (est): 4.8MM **Privately Held**
WEB: www.republicdm.net
SIC: 8111 Legal services

(P-23354)
RICHARDS WATSON & GERSHON PC (PA)
Also Called: RW&g
355 S Grand Ave Fl 40, Los Angeles (90071-1560)
PHONE............................213 626-8484
Laurence S Wiener, *CEO*
Terence Boga, *Shareholder*
Robert Ceccon, *Shareholder*
Bruce Galloway, *Shareholder*
Jim G Grayson, *Shareholder*
EMP: 125
SQ FT: 45,000
SALES (est): 17.3MM **Privately Held**
WEB: www.rwglaw.com
SIC: 8111 General practice law office

(P-23355)
ROBBINS GELLER RUDMAN DOWD LLP (PA)
655 W Broadway Ste 1900, San Diego (92101-8498)
PHONE............................619 231-1058
Michael J Dowd, *Partner*
Jonathan E Behar, *Partner*
Christopher M Burke, *Partner*
James Deguelle, *Partner*
Amber L Eck, *Partner*
EMP: 300
SQ FT: 135,000
SALES (est): 64.7MM **Privately Held**
WEB: www.lcsr.com
SIC: 8111 Corporate, partnership & business law; specialized law offices, attorneys

(P-23356)
ROBINSN CLGNE RSN SHPR DVS INC
620 Nwport Ctr Dr Ste 700, San Diego (92101)
PHONE............................619 338-4060
Mark P Robinson, *Principal*
Allan F Davis,
EMP: 60
SALES (corp-wide): 8.5MM **Privately Held**
SIC: 8111 General practice attorney, lawyer
PA: Robinson Calcagnie Robinson Shapiro Davis, Inc.
19 Corporate Plaza Dr
Newport Beach CA 92660
949 720-1288

(P-23357)
ROBINSON AND WOOD INC
Also Called: Bautista, Jennifer L
160 W Santa Clara St # 1000, San Jose (95113-1000)
PHONE............................408 298-7120
Archie Robinson, *President*
Bonnie Ross, *COO*
Hugh Lennon, *Corp Secy*
Joseph Balestrieri, *Vice Pres*
Arthur Casey, *Vice Pres*
EMP: 60
SQ FT: 23,000
SALES (est): 7.5MM **Privately Held**
WEB: www.robinsonwood.com
SIC: 8111 General practice law office

(P-23358)
RONALD J LEMIEUX ASSOC LAW OFF
4195 N Viking Way Ste E, Long Beach (90808-1470)
PHONE............................562 375-0095
Ronald J Lemieux, *President*
EMP: 60
SALES (est): 5.1MM **Privately Held**
SIC: 8111 Specialized law offices, attorneys

(P-23359)
ROPERS MAJESKI KOHN BENTLEY (PA)
Also Called: Ropers Majeski Kohn & Bentley
1001 Marshall St Fl 3, Redwood City (94063-2054)
PHONE............................650 364-8200
Jesshill E Love, *CEO*
Anthony CHI-Hung, *Partner*
Anthony Grande, *Partner*
Geoffrey Heineman, *Partner*
Eugene J Majeski, *Partner*
EMP: 81
SQ FT: 69,000
SALES (est): 41.5MM **Privately Held**
WEB: www.ropers.com
SIC: 8111 General practice law office

(P-23360)
ROPES & GRAY LLP
3 Embarcadero Ctr Ste 300, San Francisco (94111-4006)
PHONE............................415 315-6300
Adam Trott, *Branch Mgr*
Jeff Murray, *Network Enginr*
Edward Baer, *Counsel*
Kyle Bassman, *Associate*
Haley N Bavasi, *Associate*

EMP: 410
SALES (corp-wide): 383.6MM **Privately Held**
SIC: 8111 General practice law office
PA: Ropes & Gray Llp
Prudential Tower 800 Boys
Boston MA 02199
617 951-7000

(P-23361)
ROPES & GRAY LLP
1900 University Ave # 600, East Palo Alto (94303-2299)
PHONE............................650 617-4000
Kitty Dowgert, *Branch Mgr*
Eric Wright, *Partner*
Debra Rubin, *Admin Asst*
Jonathan Safran, *Analyst*
Joe Ramos, *Payroll Mgr*
EMP: 63
SALES (corp-wide): 383.6MM **Privately Held**
SIC: 8111 General practice law office
PA: Ropes & Gray Llp
Prudential Tower 800 Boys
Boston MA 02199
617 951-7000

(P-23362)
ROSSI HAMERSLOUGH REISHCHL &
1960 The Alameda Ste 200, San Jose (95126-1451)
PHONE............................408 244-4570
Sam Chuck, *President*
Molly Edgar, *Legal Staff*
Carmen Mendez, *Legal Staff*
EMP: 54
SALES (est): 4.9MM **Privately Held**
SIC: 8111 Real estate law

(P-23363)
RUTAN & TUCKER LLP (PA)
611 Anton Blvd Ste 1400, Costa Mesa (92626-1931)
P.O. Box 1950 (92628-1950)
PHONE............................714 641-5100
Richard Boden, *Mng Member*
William F Meehan, *Partner*
Tony Malkani, *CFO*
Dana Ross, *Mktg Coord*
Cecilia Solorzano, *Legal Staff*
EMP: 141
SQ FT: 90,000
SALES: 82MM **Privately Held**
WEB: www.rutan.com
SIC: 8111 General practice law office

(P-23364)
SALTZBURG RAY & BERGMAN LLP
12121 Wilshire Blvd # 600, Los Angeles (90025-1188)
PHONE............................310 481-6700
David Ray, *Partner*
Alan Bergman, *Partner*
Genise Reiter, *Partner*
Henley Saltzburg, *Partner*
Aaron Rosenberg, *President*
EMP: 124
SQ FT: 15,000
SALES (est): 12.9MM **Privately Held**
WEB: www.srblaw.com
SIC: 8111 7389 General practice attorney, lawyer; courier or messenger service

(P-23365)
SAN BERNARDINO CALIFORNIA CITY (PA)
290 N D St, San Bernardino (92401-1734)
PHONE............................909 384-7272
R Carey Davis, *Mayor*
Palupe Iosefa, *Treasurer*
David Kennedy, *Treasurer*
Erica Lithen, *Officer*
Helen Mielke, *Officer*
EMP: 352
SALES (est): 160MM **Privately Held**
SIC: 8111 Administrative & government law

(P-23366)
SANTA BARBARA COUNTY OF
Also Called: District Attorney
312 E Cook St Ste D, Santa Maria (93454-5162)
PHONE............................805 346-7540
Joyce Bedley, *Principal*
EMP: 50 **Privately Held**
WEB: www.sbcountyhr.org
SIC: 8111 9222 General practice attorney, lawyer; District Attorneys' offices;
PA: County Of Santa Barbara
105 E Anapamu St Rm 406
Santa Barbara CA 93101
805 568-3400

(P-23367)
SANTA CLARA COUNTY OF
Also Called: District Attorney's Office
3180 Newberry Dr Ste 150, San Jose (95118-1566)
PHONE............................408 792-2704
George Doorley, *Manager*
EMP: 600 **Privately Held**
WEB: www.countyairports.org
SIC: 8111 Legal services
PA: County Of Santa Clara
3180 Newberry Dr Ste 150
San Jose CA 95118
408 299-5105

(P-23368)
SCOTT A PORTER PROF CORP
350 University Ave # 200, Sacramento (95825-6581)
P.O. Box 255428 (95865-5428)
PHONE............................916 929-1481
Sherrie Cork, *Office Mgr*
Tom Bailey, *Partner*
Tim Blaine, *Partner*
Craig Caldwell, *Partner*
Carl Calnero, *Partner*
EMP: 85
SQ FT: 22,000
SALES (est): 12.9MM **Privately Held**
WEB: www.pswdlaw.com
SIC: 8111 General practice attorney, lawyer; general practice law office

(P-23369)
SEAN P OCONNOR
Also Called: D'Angelo, Michael L
1900 Main St Ste 700, Irvine (92614-7328)
PHONE............................949 851-7323
Michael L D'Angelo, *Principal*
EMP: 80
SALES (est): 2.4MM **Privately Held**
SIC: 8111 General practice attorney, lawyer

(P-23370)
SELTZER CAPLAN MCMAHON (PA)
750 B St Ste 2100, San Diego (92101-8177)
PHONE............................619 685-3003
Robert Caplan, *Shareholder*
Brian Katusian, *Shareholder*
Brian Seltzer, *COO*
James Dawe, *CFO*
Neal P Panish, *Treasurer*
EMP: 173
SQ FT: 78,000
SALES (est): 22.7MM **Privately Held**
WEB: www.scmv.com
SIC: 8111 General practice attorney, lawyer

(P-23371)
SEVERSON & WERSON A PROF CORP
1 Embarcadero Ctr Fl 26, San Francisco (94111-3745)
PHONE............................415 398-3344
James B Werson, *Ch of Bd*
Donald Read, *Partner*
Veronica Appleberry, *President*
Sylvia Coleman, *President*
Emily Rhea, *President*
EMP: 100
SQ FT: 40,000
SALES: 19.3MM **Privately Held**
WEB: www.severson.com
SIC: 8111 Labor & employment law; corporate, partnership & business law

(P-23372)
SEYFARTH SHAW LLP
333 S Hope St Ste 3900, Los Angeles
(90071-3043)
PHONE...............................213 270-9600
Arthur Wood IV, *Branch Mgr*
Hilary White, *Office Mgr*
Christine Kim, *Associate*
Brian Long, *Associate*
Navid More, *Associate*
EMP: 125
SALES (corp-wide): 98.4MM **Privately Held**
SIC: 8111 General practice attorney, lawyer
PA: Seyfarth Shaw Llp
233 S Wacker Dr Ste 8000
Chicago IL 60606
312 460-5000

(P-23373)
SEYFARTH SHAW LLP
2029 Century Park E # 3400, Los Angeles
(90067-3020)
PHONE...............................310 277-7200
Sandy Abrahamian, *Branch Mgr*
David Kadue, *Partner*
Fern Jenkins, *President*
Jennifer Malcho, *Office Admin*
James Aguilera, *Admin Sec*
EMP: 200
SALES (corp-wide): 98.4MM **Privately Held**
WEB: www.seyfarth.com
SIC: 8111 General practice law office
PA: Seyfarth Shaw Llp
233 S Wacker Dr Ste 8000
Chicago IL 60606
312 460-5000

(P-23374)
SEYFARTH SHAW LLP
560 Mission St Fl 31, San Francisco
(94105-2930)
PHONE...............................415 397-2823
William Dritsas, *Principal*
Constance Hughes, *Admin Asst*
Patricia H Cullison,
Michael Stevens, *Sr Associate*
Elaine Baarde, *Supervisor*
EMP: 100
SALES (corp-wide): 98.4MM **Privately Held**
WEB: www.seyfarth.com
SIC: 8111 General practice law office
PA: Seyfarth Shaw Llp
233 S Wacker Dr Ste 8000
Chicago IL 60606
312 460-5000

(P-23375)
SHARTSIS FRIESE LLP
1 Maritime Plz Fl 18, San Francisco
(94111-3508)
PHONE...............................415 421-6500
Arthur J Shartsis, *Partner*
Derek Boswell, *Partner*
Zesara Chan, *Partner*
Frank Cialone, *Partner*
Paul Feasby, *Partner*
EMP: 120
SQ FT: 47,709
SALES (est): 19.4MM **Privately Held**
WEB: www.sflaw.com
SIC: 8111 Patent, trademark & copyright law; taxation law; will, estate & trust law; real estate law

(P-23376)
SHEKINAH INC
7755 Center Ave Ste 1000, Huntington Beach (92647-3090)
PHONE...............................714 475-5460
Cecilia Trent, *President*
James Trent, *CFO*
David Vasquez Sr, *Vice Pres*
Scott Cass, *Director*
Dana Kowprowski, *Director*
EMP: 50
SQ FT: 2,400
SALES (est): 1.9MM **Privately Held**
SIC: 8111 Debt collection law

(P-23377)
SHEPPARD MULLIN RICHTER (PA)
Also Called: Sheppard Mullin
333 S Hope St Fl 43, Los Angeles
(90071-1422)
PHONE...............................213 620-1780
Guy N Halgren, *Partner*
Charles Barker, *Partner*
Robert Beall, *Partner*
Lawrence Braun, *Partner*
Justine M Casey, *Partner*
EMP: 370
SQ FT: 52,820
SALES (est): 230.7MM **Privately Held**
WEB: www.smrh.com
SIC: 8111 General practice law office

(P-23378)
SHEPPARD MULLIN RICHTER
12275 El Camino R Ste 200, San Diego
(92130)
PHONE...............................619 338-6500
EMP: 84
SALES (corp-wide): 200.4MM **Privately Held**
SIC: 8111
PA: Sheppard, Mullin, Richter & Hampton, Llp
333 S Hope St Fl 43
Los Angeles CA 90071
202 218-0000

(P-23379)
SHEPPARD MULLIN RICHTER
4 Embarcadero Ctr # 1700, San Francisco
(94111-4158)
PHONE...............................415 434-9100
Aline Pearl, *Office Admin*
Phipp Atkins-Pattensen, *Partner*
Julie Ebert, *Partner*
Douglas R Hart, *Partner*
Betsey McDaniel, *Partner*
EMP: 62
SALES (corp-wide): 230.7MM **Privately Held**
SIC: 8111 Corporate, partnership & business law; general practice law office
PA: Sheppard, Mullin, Richter & Hampton, Llp
333 S Hope St Fl 43
Los Angeles CA 90071
213 620-1780

(P-23380)
SHEPPARD MULLIN RICHTER
1901 Avenue Of The Stars # 1600, Los Angeles (90067-6055)
PHONE...............................310 228-3700
Sherry Wilson, *Administration*
David Garcia, *Partner*
Cristina Ongsing, *Admin Sec*
Brian Kay, *Analyst*
Vivian Katapodis, *Legal Staff*
EMP: 61
SALES (corp-wide): 230.7MM **Privately Held**
SIC: 8111 General practice law office
PA: Sheppard, Mullin, Richter & Hampton, Llp
333 S Hope St Fl 43
Los Angeles CA 90071
213 620-1780

(P-23381)
SHEPPARD MULLIN RICHTER
650 Town Center Dr Fl 4, Costa Mesa
(92626-1993)
PHONE...............................714 513-5100
Sheila Cantrell, *Office Admin*
Finley Taylor, *Partner*
Carole Dubienny, *President*
Tina Hammer, *President*
EMP: 100
SALES (corp-wide): 230.7MM **Privately Held**
SIC: 8111 General practice law office
PA: Sheppard, Mullin, Richter & Hampton, Llp
333 S Hope St Fl 43
Los Angeles CA 90071
213 620-1780

(P-23382)
SHERIFFS OFFICES
Also Called: Inyo Sheriff Office
550 S Clay St, Independence (93526)
PHONE...............................760 878-0383
Dan Lucas, *Principal*
William Lutze, *Principal*
EMP: 60 **EST:** 2001
SALES (est): 2.5MM **Privately Held**
SIC: 8111 General practice law office

(P-23383)
SHOOK HARDY & BACON LLP
1 Montgomery St Ste 2700, San Francisco
(94104-5527)
PHONE...............................415 544-1900
Shannon Spangler, *Managing Prtnr*
Matthew Vanis, *Associate*
EMP: 60
SALES (corp-wide): 310MM **Privately Held**
WEB: www.shb.com
SIC: 8111 General practice law office
PA: Shook, Hardy & Bacon L.L.P.
2555 Grand Blvd
Kansas City MO 64108
816 474-6550

(P-23384)
SIDEMAN & BANCROFT LLP
1 Embarcadero Ctr Ste 860, San Francisco
(94111-3645)
PHONE...............................415 392-1960
Jeffrey Hallam, *General Ptnr*
Kelly P McCarthy, *Partner*
Hilary Pierce, *Partner*
Melissa Burks, *President*
Mary Eslava, *President*
EMP: 95
SALES (est): 17.3MM **Privately Held**
SIC: 8111 General practice law office

(P-23385)
SIDLEY AUSTIN LLP
1001 Page Mill Rd Bldg 1, Palo Alto
(94304-1006)
PHONE...............................650 565-7000
Dorce Zimmermann, *Branch Mgr*
Matthew J Dolan, *Associate*
Christopher P Masterson, *Associate*
Dorna Moini, *Associate*
Nathan B Wenk, *Associate*
EMP: 85
SALES (corp-wide): 566.8MM **Privately Held**
SIC: 8111 General practice attorney, lawyer
PA: Sidley Austin Llp
1 S Dearborn St Ste 900
Chicago IL 60603
312 853-7000

(P-23386)
SIDLEY AUSTIN LLP
1001 Page Mill Rd Bldg 1, Palo Alto
(94304-1006)
PHONE...............................650 565-7000
Martin A Wellington, *Partner*
EMP: 295
SALES (corp-wide): 566.8MM **Privately Held**
SIC: 8111 Legal services
PA: Sidley Austin Llp
1 S Dearborn St Ste 900
Chicago IL 60603
312 853-7000

(P-23387)
SILVER FREDMAN A PROF LAW CORP
2029 Century Park E # 1900, Los Angeles
(90067-2901)
PHONE...............................310 556-2356
Perry Silver, *President*
Andrew B Kaplan, *Partner*
Neil Freedman, *Admin Sec*
EMP: 50
SQ FT: 21,500
SALES (est): 3.4MM **Privately Held**
WEB: www.silver-freedman.com
SIC: 8111 General practice law office

(P-23388)
SIMPSON DELMORE AND GREENE LLP (PA)
600 W Broadway Ste 400, San Diego
(92101-3352)
PHONE...............................619 515-1194
Paul Delmore, *Partner*
Terence Greene, *Partner*
John Simpson, *Partner*
Lizbeth Alonso, *President*
Kris Boggis, *Admin Sec*
EMP: 50
SQ FT: 20,000
SALES (est): 5.8MM **Privately Held**
WEB: www.sdgllp.com
SIC: 8111 General practice law office

(P-23389)
SIMPSON THACHER & BARTLETT LLP
2475 Hanover St, Palo Alto (94304-1155)
PHONE...............................650 251-5000
Richard Capelouto, *Manager*
Rachel Goodman, *President*
Teresa Firoozye, *Admin Asst*
Paul Barrus, *Info Tech Mgr*
Misael Amador, *Technology*
EMP: 120
SALES (corp-wide): 908.1K **Privately Held**
WEB: www.stblaw.com
SIC: 8111 Corporate, partnership & business law
PA: Simpson Thacher & Bartlett Llp
425 Lexington Ave Fl 15
New York NY 10017
212 455-2000

(P-23390)
SKADDEN ARPS SLATE MEAGHER & F
300 S Grand Ave Ste 3400, Los Angeles
(90071-3137)
PHONE...............................213 687-5000
Rand S April, *Partner*
Michael Beinus, *Partner*
Kenneth J Betts, *Partner*
Meryl K Chae, *Partner*
Kristine Dunn, *Partner*
EMP: 250
SALES (corp-wide): 625.6MM **Privately Held**
SIC: 8111 General practice attorney, lawyer
PA: Skadden, Arps, Slate, Meagher & Flom Llp
4 Times Sq Fl 24
New York NY 10036
212 735-3000

(P-23391)
SMS TRANSPORTATION
18516 S Broadway, Gardena (90248-4615)
PHONE...............................310 527-9200
John W Harris, *Principal*
Terrell Guess, *Office Mgr*
EMP: 100
SALES (est): 8MM **Privately Held**
SIC: 8111 Legal services

(P-23392)
SNELL & WILMER LLP
600 Anton Blvd Ste 1400, Costa Mesa
(92626-7689)
PHONE...............................714 427-7000
Andrea Bryant, *Principal*
Alexander L Conti, *Partner*
Frank Cronin, *Partner*
Christy D Joseph, *Partner*
Louise Mishler, *President*
EMP: 160
SQ FT: 3,000
SALES (corp-wide): 101.7MM **Privately Held**
SIC: 8111 General practice law office; specialized law offices, attorneys
PA: Snell & Wilmer L.L.P.
400 E Van Buren St Fl 10
Phoenix AZ 85004
602 382-6000

(P-23393)
SOBEL ROSS H LAW OFFICES
Also Called: Sobel, Ross Howell
1875 Century Park E, Los Angeles
(90067-2337)
PHONE..............................310 788-8995
Ross H Sobel, *Owner*
EMP: 50
SALES (est): 2.1MM **Privately Held**
SIC: 8111 Legal services

(P-23394)
SOLOMON WARD SDNWURM SMITH LLP
401 B St Ste 1200, San Diego
(92101-4295)
PHONE..............................619 231-0303
Herbert Solomon, *Partner*
Lawrence Kaplan, *Partner*
Richard E McCarthy, *Partner*
Richard L Seidenwurm, *Partner*
Jeffrey H Silberman, *Partner*
EMP: 60
SQ FT: 17,000
SALES (est): 9.5MM **Privately Held**
WEB: www.swsslaw.com
SIC: 8111 General practice attorney, lawyer

(P-23395)
SQUIRE PATTON BOGGS (US) LLP
555 S Flower St Ste 3100, Los Angeles
(90071-2255)
PHONE..............................213 624-2500
Chris M Amantea, *Manager*
Brandi Hann, *Office Admin*
Marilyn Stimson, *Executive Asst*
James Burton, *Technology*
Alan Jenkins, *Technology*
EMP: 60
SALES (corp-wide): 294.4MM **Privately Held**
WEB: www.squiresandersdempsey.com
SIC: 8111 General practice law office
PA: Squire Patton Boggs (Us) Llp
4900 Key Tower 127 Pub Sq
Cleveland OH 44114
216 479-8500

(P-23396)
SQUIRE PATTON BOGGS (US) LLP
275 Battery St Ste 2600, San Francisco
(94111-3356)
PHONE..............................415 954-0334
Thomas H Woofter, *Manager*
Joan Klaassen, *Office Admin*
Mary Padilla, *Admin Sec*
Carrie Takahata, *Admin Sec*
Ani Kantarci, *Business Mgr*
EMP: 120
SALES (corp-wide): 294.4MM **Privately Held**
WEB: www.squiresandersdempsey.com
SIC: 8111 General practice law office
PA: Squire Patton Boggs (Us) Llp
4900 Key Tower 127 Pub Sq
Cleveland OH 44114
216 479-8500

(P-23397)
STEELE CIS LLC
1 Sansome St Ste 3500, San Francisco
(94104-4436)
PHONE..............................415 692-5000
Ken Kurtz, *President*
Mehak Waraich, *Project Mgr*
Rojer Du, *Analyst*
EMP: 350
SALES (est): 27MM **Privately Held**
SIC: 8111 Legal services

(P-23398)
STEIN & LUBIN LLP
600 Montgomery St Fl 14, San Francisco
(94111-2716)
PHONE..............................415 981-0550
Mark Lubin, *Partner*
Ellen A Cirangle, *Partner*
Robert S Stein, *Partner*
Eyleen Nadolny, *President*
Sabrina Stewart, *President*
EMP: 50

SALES (est): 7.7MM **Privately Held**
WEB: www.steinlubin.com
SIC: 8111 General practice law office

(P-23399)
STEPTOE & JOHNSON LLP
633 W 5th St Fl 7, Los Angeles
(90071-3503)
PHONE..............................213 439-9400
Leslie Graine, *Administration*
Beth Gibson, *Executive Asst*
Phyllis Lee, *Executive Asst*
Carmen Markarian, *Admin Sec*
Marsha Kendall, *Administration*
EMP: 50
SALES (corp-wide): 356MM **Privately Held**
WEB: www.steptoe.com
SIC: 8111 General practice law office
PA: Steptoe & Johnson Llp
1330 Connecticut Ave Nw
Washington DC 20036
202 429-3000

(P-23400)
STRADLING YOCCA CARLSON & RAUT (PA)
660 Newport Center Dr # 1600, Newport
Beach (92660-6458)
PHONE..............................949 725-4000
John F Cannon, *Principal*
Bruce Feuchter, *Partner*
Sean Absher, *Shareholder*
Jason Anderson, *Shareholder*
Ryan Azlein, *Shareholder*
EMP: 200
SQ FT: 64,000
SALES (est): 40.6MM **Privately Held**
WEB: www.sycr.com
SIC: 8111 General practice law office

(P-23401)
STRADLING YOCCA CARLSON & RAUT
500 Capitol Mall, Sacramento
(95814-4737)
PHONE..............................916 449-2350
Kevin Civale, *Manager*
EMP: 108
SALES (corp-wide): 40.6MM **Privately Held**
SIC: 8111 General practice law office
PA: Stradling Yocca Carlson & Rauth A Professional Corp
660 Newport Center Dr # 1600
Newport Beach CA 92660
949 725-4000

(P-23402)
STROOCK & STROOCK & LAVAN LLP
2029 Century Park E # 1800, Los Angeles
(90067-3086)
PHONE..............................310 556-5800
Diane Cohen, *Branch Mgr*
Howard Lavin, *Partner*
Jin Wee, *Administration*
Margaret Jones, *Librarian*
Richard Acosta, *Manager*
EMP: 150
SALES (corp-wide): 102.3MM **Privately Held**
SIC: 8111 General practice law office
PA: Stroock & Stroock & Lavan Llp
180 Maiden Ln Fl 17
New York NY 10038
212 806-5400

(P-23403)
STUTMAN TRSTER GLATT PROF CORP
Also Called: Stutman Treister Glatt Prof Co
1901 Avenue Of The Ste 200, Los Angeles
(90067)
PHONE..............................310 228-5600
Scott H Yun, *CEO*
Charles D Axelrod, *Vice Pres*
Michael H Goldstein, *Vice Pres*
Robert A Greenfield, *Vice Pres*
Robert Greenfield, *Vice Pres*
EMP: 75
SQ FT: 40,000
SALES (est): 465.4K **Privately Held**
WEB: www.stutman.com
SIC: 8111 General practice law office

(P-23404)
SULLIVAN & CROMWELL LLP
1888 Century Park E # 2100, Los Angeles
(90067-1725)
PHONE..............................310 712-6600
Laura Henry, *Manager*
Adam S Paris, *Partner*
Michael H Steinberg, *Partner*
Konstantin Technau, *Partner*
Liana Tucker, *President*
EMP: 65
SALES (corp-wide): 396.8MM **Privately Held**
SIC: 8111 Specialized law offices, attorneys
PA: Sullivan & Cromwell Llp
125 Broad St Fl 35
New York NY 10004
212 558-4000

(P-23405)
SYNNEXXUS LLC
20251 Sw Acacia St # 200, Newport Beach
(92660-1716)
PHONE..............................714 933-4500
Frank Nese, *Mng Member*
EMP: 50
SALES (est): 3MM **Privately Held**
SIC: 8111 Legal services

(P-23406)
TERIS-BAY AREA LLC
2455 Faber Pl Ste 200, Palo Alto
(94303-3316)
PHONE..............................650 213-9922
Stefan Wikstrom, *CEO*
Kip Hauser, *COO*
Darisa Hill, *Controller*
EMP: 99
SALES (est): 3.8MM **Privately Held**
SIC: 8111 Legal services

(P-23407)
THARPE & HOWELL (PA)
15250 Ventura Blvd Fl 9, Sherman Oaks
(91403-3221)
PHONE..............................714 437-4900
John Maile, *Managing Prtnr*
Todd R Howell, *Partner*
Timothy D Lake, *Partner*
Christopher S Maile, *Partner*
Christopher P Ruiz, *Partner*
EMP: 83
SQ FT: 13,500
SALES (est): 11MM **Privately Held**
WEB: www.tharpe-howell.com
SIC: 8111 General practice law office

(P-23408)
THOMPSON & COLEGATE LLP
3610 14th St Lowr, Riverside (92501-3852)
P.O. Box 1299 (92502-1299)
PHONE..............................951 682-5550
John W Marshall, *Partner*
John A Boyd, *Partner*
Donald G Grant, *Partner*
J E Holmes III, *Partner*
Michael J Marlatt, *Partner*
EMP: 50 EST: 1920
SQ FT: 28,500
SALES: 4.9MM **Privately Held**
WEB: www.tclaw.net
SIC: 8111 General practice attorney, lawyer

(P-23409)
THOMPSON COBURN LLP
2029 Century Park E # 1900, Los Angeles
(90067-3005)
PHONE..............................310 282-2500
EMP: 304
SALES (corp-wide): 139.2MM **Privately Held**
SIC: 8111 General practice law office
PA: Thompson Coburn Llp
505 N 7th St Ste 2700
Saint Louis MO 63101
314 552-6000

(P-23410)
THORSNES BARTOLOTTA & MCGUIRE
2550 5th Ave Ste 1100, San Diego
(92103-6694)
PHONE..............................619 236-9363
Mickey McGuire, *Partner*

Vincent Bartolotta, *Partner*
Mitchell Golub, *Partner*
Darel Mazzerlla, *Partner*
Kevin Quinn, *Partner*
EMP: 67
SQ FT: 20,000
SALES (est): 10.5MM **Privately Held**
WEB: www.tbmlawyers.com
SIC: 8111 General practice law office

(P-23411)
TRESSLER LLP
2 Park Plz Ste 1050, Irvine (92614-8521)
PHONE..............................949 336-1200
Katherine Liner, *Owner*
Ryan Luther, *Associate*
EMP: 69
SALES (corp-wide): 41.6MM **Privately Held**
SIC: 8111 Specialized law offices, attorneys
PA: Tressler Llp
233 S Wacker Dr Fl 22
Chicago IL 60606
312 627-4000

(P-23412)
TROPE AND TROPE LLP
Also Called: Trope & Trope
12121 Wilshire Blvd # 801, Los Angeles
(90025-1164)
PHONE..............................323 879-2726
Sorrell Trope, *Partner*
EMP: 57
SALES (est): 7.7MM **Privately Held**
SIC: 8111 Divorce & family law

(P-23413)
TROUTMAN SANDERS LLP
11682 El Camino Real # 400, San Diego
(92130-2092)
PHONE..............................858 509-6000
Michael J Whitton, *Branch Mgr*
Michael Whitton, *Managing Prtnr*
Roy Bell, *Counsel*
Christopher M Franich, *Associate*
EMP: 88
SALES (corp-wide): 337.2MM **Privately Held**
SIC: 8111 General practice attorney, lawyer
PA: Troutman Sanders Llp
600 Peachtree St Ne Ste 3
Atlanta GA 30308
404 885-3000

(P-23414)
TROUTMAN SANDERS LLP
580 California St # 1100, San Francisco
(94104-1000)
PHONE..............................415 477-5700
EMP: 82
SALES (corp-wide): 337.2MM **Privately Held**
SIC: 8111 General practice attorney, lawyer
PA: Troutman Sanders Llp
600 Peachtree St Ne Ste 3
Atlanta GA 30308
404 885-3000

(P-23415)
TROYGOULD PC
1801 Century Park E # 1600, Los Angeles
(90067-2367)
PHONE..............................310 553-4441
Sanford J Hillsberg, *Principal*
Diane Gordon, *Exec Dir*
EMP: 80
SQ FT: 24,000
SALES (est): 12.6MM **Privately Held**
WEB: www.troygould.com
SIC: 8111 General practice law office

(P-23416)
TUCKER ELLIS LLP
1000 Wilshire Blvd # 1800, Los Angeles
(90017-2457)
PHONE..............................213 430-3400
William Weech, *Administration*
Karen Scheel, *President*
Rebecca Gutierrez, *Associate*
EMP: 54

▲ = Import ▼=Export
◆ =Import/Export

SALES (est): 2.4MM
SALES (corp-wide): 49.1MM **Privately Held**
WEB: www.tuckerellis.com
SIC: 8111 General practice attorney, lawyer
PA: Tucker Ellis Llp
950 Main Ave Ste 1100
Cleveland OH 44113
216 592-5000

(P-23417)
TYLER PALMIERI WIENER
1900 Main St Ste 700, Irvine (92614-7328)
P.O. Box 19712 (92623-9712)
PHONE..............................949 851-9400
James E Wilhelm, *Partner*
Mike Greene, *Partner*
Robert Ihrke, *Partner*
David Parr, *Partner*
L Richard Rawls, *Partner*
EMP: 100
SQ FT: 34,000
SALES (est): 16.6MM **Privately Held**
SIC: 8111 General practice law office

(P-23418)
UNISOURCE DISCOVERY LLC (PA)
625 The City Dr S Ste 303, Orange (92868-4984)
PHONE..............................888 248-0020
Steven Cerasale,
Jennifer Hews, *Vice Pres*
EMP: 60
SALES (est): 8.3MM **Privately Held**
WEB: www.unisourcediscovery.com
SIC: 8111 Legal services

(P-23419)
UNITED STATES ATTORNEYS
300 N Los Angeles St Lbby, Los Angeles (90012-3336)
PHONE..............................213 894-2400
Leon Wheidman, *Chief*
EMP: 101 **Publicly Held**
WEB: www.mvpdallas.com
SIC: 8111 9222 Legal services; United States attorneys' offices;
HQ: United States Attorneys, Executive Office For
175 N St Ne Fl 6
Washington DC 20002

(P-23420)
VEATCH CARLSON GROGAN & NELSON
1055 Wilshire Blvd Fl 11, Los Angeles (90017-2431)
PHONE..............................213 381-2861
Jim Galloway, *Partner*
David Failer, *Partner*
Juana Guevara, *President*
Cyril Czajkowskyj, *Executive*
Phillip M Borini, *Exec Dir*
EMP: 100
SALES (est): 6.2MM **Privately Held**
WEB: www.veatchfirm.com
SIC: 8111 General practice law office

(P-23421)
VINSON & ELKINS LLP
1841 Page Mill Rd Fl 2, Palo Alto (94304-1255)
PHONE..............................650 617-8400
EMP: 198
SALES (corp-wide): 420.7MM **Privately Held**
SIC: 8111 General practice attorney, lawyer
PA: Vinson & Elkins L.L.P.
1001 Fannin St Ste 2500
Houston TX 77002
713 758-2222

(P-23422)
VINSON & ELKINS LLP
555 Mission St Ste 2000, San Francisco (94105-0923)
PHONE..............................415 979-6900
EMP: 198
SALES (corp-wide): 420.7MM **Privately Held**
SIC: 8111 Legal services

PA: Vinson & Elkins L.L.P.
1001 Fannin St Ste 2500
Houston TX 77002
713 758-2222

(P-23423)
WADE & LOWE A PROF CORP (PA)
3200 Inland Empire Blvd # 160, Ontario (91764-5575)
PHONE..............................909 483-6700
Richard W Miller, *CEO*
William R Lowe, *President*
Randolph W Even, *Treasurer*
Edwin Brown, *Vice Pres*
Bradley M Bush, *Vice Pres*
EMP: 100
SQ FT: 7,000
SALES (est): 7.7MM **Privately Held**
WEB: www.evencrandall.com
SIC: 8111 General practice law office

(P-23424)
WALKUP MELODIA KELLY
Also Called: Walkup Law Office
650 California St Fl 26, San Francisco (94108-2615)
PHONE..............................415 981-7210
Paul W Melodia, *President*
Kirsten Benzien, *President*
Lily Connors, *President*
Kevin Domecus, *Treasurer*
Jefferey Holl, *Vice Pres*
EMP: 50
SQ FT: 30,000
SALES (est): 8.1MM **Privately Held**
WEB: www.walkuplawoffice.com
SIC: 8111 Labor & employment law; malpractice & negligence law

(P-23425)
WALSWRTH FRNKLIN BEVINS MCCALL (PA)
Also Called: Walsworth Franklin & Bevins
1 City Blvd W Ste 500, Orange (92868-3677)
PHONE..............................714 634-2522
Jeffrey P Walsworth, *Partner*
Ronald H Bevins Jr, *Partner*
Ian P Dillon, *Partner*
Ferdie F Franklin, *Partner*
Daniel R Jacobs, *Partner*
EMP: 55
SQ FT: 2,800
SALES (est): 16.1MM **Privately Held**
SIC: 8111 General practice law office

(P-23426)
WARREN DRYE KELLEY
10100 Santa Monica Blvd # 1050, Los Angeles (90067-4003)
PHONE..............................310 712-6100
Andrew White, *Managing Prtnr*
Michael O'Connor, *Managing Prtnr*
EMP: 60
SALES (est): 5.8MM **Privately Held**
SIC: 8111 General practice law office

(P-23427)
WASSERMAN COMDEN & CASSELMAN (PA)
5567 Reseda Blvd Ste 330, Tarzana (91356-2699)
P.O. Box 7033 (91357-7033)
PHONE..............................323 872-0995
Steve Wasserman, *Partner*
David B Casselman, *Partner*
Leonard J Comden, *Partner*
Clifford H Pearson, *Partner*
EMP: 96
SQ FT: 15,000
SALES (est): 11.2MM **Privately Held**
WEB: www.wcclaw.com
SIC: 8111 General practice law office

(P-23428)
WEIL GOTSHAL & MANGES LLP
201 Redwood Shors Pkwy, Redwood City (94065)
PHONE..............................650 802-3000
Craig Adas, *Managing Prtnr*
Rod J Howard, *Partner*
Kyle C Krpata, *Partner*
Curtis L MO, *Partner*
Gerilyn Ward, *Office Admin*

EMP: 180
SALES (corp-wide): 358.6MM **Privately Held**
WEB: www.weil.com
SIC: 8111 General practice law office
PA: Weil, Gotshal & Manges Llp
767 5th Ave Fl Conc1
New York NY 10153
212 310-8000

(P-23429)
WEINBERG ROGER & RESENFELD (PA)
1001 Marina Village Pkwy # 200, Alameda (94501-6480)
PHONE..............................510 337-1001
Stewart Weinberg, *President*
Kristina Hillman, *Shareholder*
Emily Rich, *Shareholder*
David Rosenfeld, *Shareholder*
Antonio Ruiz, *Shareholder*
EMP: 69 **EST:** 1964
SQ FT: 12,000
SALES (est): 10.5MM **Privately Held**
WEB: www.unioncounsel.net
SIC: 8111 General practice law office

(P-23430)
WEINTRAUB TOBIN CHEDIAK
9665 Wilshire Blvd # 900, Beverly Hills (90212-2315)
PHONE..............................310 858-7888
Marvin Gelfand, *Partner*
EMP: 50 **Privately Held**
SIC: 8111 General practice law office
PA: Weintraub Tobin Chediak Coleman Grodin Law Corporation
400 Capitol Mall Fl 11
Sacramento CA 95814

(P-23431)
WEINTRAUB TOBIN CHEDIAK (PA)
400 Capitol Mall Fl 11, Sacramento (95814-4434)
PHONE..............................916 558-6000
Michael Kvarme, *CEO*
Thadd A Blizzard, *Partner*
Karen L Boon, *Partner*
Kelly L Borelli, *Partner*
Gary L Bradus, *Partner*
EMP: 50
SQ FT: 44,900
SALES (est): 20.8MM **Privately Held**
WEB: www.weintraub.com
SIC: 8111 General practice law office

(P-23432)
WEITZ & LUXENBERG PC
1880 Century Park E # 700, Los Angeles (90067-1618)
PHONE..............................310 247-0921
Perry Weitz, *Branch Mgr*
EMP: 68
SALES (corp-wide): 76.8MM **Privately Held**
SIC: 8111 General practice attorney, lawyer
PA: Weitz & Luxenberg, P.C.
700 Broadway Lbby A
New York NY 10003
212 558-5500

(P-23433)
WENDEL ROSEN BLACK & DEAN LLP (PA)
1111 Broadway Fl 24, Oakland (94607-4139)
PHONE..............................510 834-6600
Howard Lance, *Managing Prtnr*
C Gregg Ankenman, *Partner*
Mark S Bostic, *Partner*
Elizabeth Burke-Dreyfuss, *Partner*
Joan M Cambray, *Partner*
EMP: 77
SQ FT: 40,000
SALES (est): 20.2MM **Privately Held**
WEB: www.wendel.com
SIC: 8111 General practice attorney, lawyer

(P-23434)
WHITE & CASE LLP
555 S Flower St Ste 2700, Los Angeles (90071-2433)
PHONE..............................213 687-9655
Betty Archer, *Manager*
Jon Bowden, *Partner*
Jacquelyn Maclennan, *Partner*
Reyes Tello, *Partner*
Anthony Wong, *Partner*
EMP: 115
SALES (corp-wide): 487.4MM **Privately Held**
SIC: 8111 General practice attorney, lawyer
PA: White & Case Llp
1221 Avenue Of The Americ
New York NY 10020
212 819-8200

(P-23435)
WILMER CUTLER PICK HALE DORR
350 S Grand Ave Ste 2100, Los Angeles (90071-3409)
PHONE..............................213 443-5300
Mark Flanagan, *Partner*
David C Marcus, *Partner*
Andrew Margolis, *Office Admin*
EMP: 247
SALES (corp-wide): 98.4MM **Privately Held**
SIC: 8111 Specialized law offices, attorneys
PA: Wilmer Cutler Pickering Hale And Dorr Llp
1875 Pennsylvania Ave Nw
Washington DC 20006
202 663-6000

(P-23436)
WILNER KLEIN SIEGEL
9601 Wilshire Blvd # 700, Beverly Hills (90210-5213)
PHONE..............................310 550-4595
Sam Wilner, *Partner*
Walter Klein, *Partner*
Lynn Siegel, *Partner*
EMP: 50
SALES (est): 2.1MM **Privately Held**
SIC: 8111 Legal services

(P-23437)
WILSON ELSER MOSKOWITZ
555 S Flower St Ste 2900, Los Angeles (90071-2407)
PHONE..............................213 443-5100
Patrick M Kelly, *Manager*
Martin K Deniston, *Partner*
Richard Klein, *Partner*
Ruben Silva, *Director*
Patrick Kelly, *Manager*
EMP: 62
SALES (corp-wide): 351.9MM **Privately Held**
SIC: 8111 General practice law office
PA: Wilson, Elser, Moskowitz, Edelman & Dicker Llp
150 E 42nd St Fl 23
New York NY 10017
212 490-3000

(P-23438)
WILSON SONSINI GOODRICH & ROSA
12235 El Camino Real # 200, San Diego (92130-3002)
PHONE..............................858 350-2300
Tina Drews, *Office Mgr*
Monica Huettl, *President*
Trina Slama, *Executive Asst*
Scott Burkette, *Associate*
Uri Greenwald MD, *Associate*
EMP: 120
SALES (corp-wide): 98.4MM **Privately Held**
SIC: 8111 General practice attorney, lawyer
PA: Wilson Sonsini Goodrich & Rosati, Professional Corporation
650 Page Mill Rd
Palo Alto CA 94304
650 493-9300

(P-23439)
WILSON SONSINI GOODRICH & ROSA (PA)
650 Page Mill Rd, Palo Alto (94304-1001)
PHONE...................................650 493-9300
Steven E Bochner, *CEO*
James A Diboise, *Partner*
Jack Sheridan, *Partner*
Effie Toshav, *Partner*
Douglas Clark, *Managing Prtnr*
EMP: 1300 **EST:** 1961
SQ FT: 184,000
SALES (est): 98.4MM **Privately Held**
WEB: www.rsklaw.com
SIC: 8111 Corporate, partnership & business law

(P-23440)
WILSON SONSINI GOODRICH & ROSA
1 Market Plz Fl 33, San Francisco (94105-1196)
PHONE...................................415 947-2000
Peter Mostow, *Partner*
Debra Jones, *Admin Asst*
Anthony Lee, *Technology*
Usha Smerdon,
Andrew Kirkpatrick, *Associate*
EMP: 60
SALES (est): 3.5MM
SALES (corp-wide): 98.4MM **Privately Held**
WEB: www.rsklaw.com
SIC: 8111 Corporate, partnership & business law
PA: Wilson Sonsini Goodrich & Rosati, Professional Corporation
650 Page Mill Rd
Palo Alto CA 94304
650 493-9300

(P-23441)
WILSON TURNER KOSMO LLP
550 W C St Ste 1050, San Diego (92101-3532)
PHONE...................................619 236-9600
Claudette G Wilson, *Partner*
Frederick W Kosmo Jr, *Partner*
Joe Devos, *Administration*
Barbara Boxer,
Wilson Kosmo,
EMP: 54
SQ FT: 20,000
SALES (est): 11.4MM **Privately Held**
WEB: www.wilsonturnerkosmo.com/
SIC: 8111 General practice law office

(P-23442)
WINGERT GREBING BRUBAKER & JUS
600 W Broadway Ste 1200, San Diego (92101-3314)
PHONE...................................619 232-8151
Stephen Grebing, *Partner*
Michael Anello, *Partner*
Alan Brubaker, *Partner*
James Goodwin, *Partner*
Charles Grebing, *Partner*
EMP: 100
SALES (est): 11.2MM **Privately Held**
WEB: www.wingertlaw.com
SIC: 8111 General practice attorney, lawyer

(P-23443)
WINSTON & STRAWN LLP
Also Called: Silicon Valley Office
275 Middlefield Rd # 205, Menlo Park (94025-3597)
PHONE...................................650 858-6500
Tom Fitzgerald, *Partner*
EMP: 411
SALES (corp-wide): 280.9MM **Privately Held**
SIC: 8111 Patent, trademark & copyright law
PA: Winston & Strawn Llp
35 W Wacker Dr Ste 4200
Chicago IL 60601
312 558-5600

(P-23444)
WOLF FIRM A LAW CORPORATION
2955 Main St Ste 200, Irvine (92614-2528)
PHONE...................................949 720-9200
Alan S Wolf, *President*
Brenda Britten, *Trustee*
Darlene Clark, *Officer*
Scott Jackson, *Exec VP*
Danielle Farmer, *Admin Asst*
EMP: 60
SALES (est): 8.8MM **Privately Held**
WEB: www.wolffirm.com
SIC: 8111 General practice law office; specialized law offices, attorneys

(P-23445)
WOMBLE BOND DICKINSON (US) LLP
1841 Page Mill Rd Fl 2, Palo Alto (94304-1255)
PHONE...................................408 720-8300
Karen Wilson, *Director*
Bill Holbrow, *Partner*
Paul Mendonsa, *Partner*
Gregory Caldwell, *Managing Prtnr*
Diane Robson, *Executive*
EMP: 120
SALES (corp-wide): 254.8MM **Privately Held**
WEB: www.bstz.com
SIC: 8111 General practice law office
PA: Womble Bond Dickinson (Us) Llp
1 W 4th St
Winston Salem NC 27101
336 721-3600

(P-23446)
WOOD SMITH HENNING BERMAN LLP (PA)
Also Called: WSH&b
10960 Wilshire Blvd Fl 18, Los Angeles (90024-3804)
PHONE...................................310 481-7600
David Wood, *Partner*
Tracy Abatemarco, *Partner*
Daniel Berman, *Partner*
Robert Hellner, *Partner*
Steven Henning, *Partner*
EMP: 50
SQ FT: 24,500
SALES (est): 39.2MM **Privately Held**
WEB: www.wshblaw.com
SIC: 8111 General practice law office

(P-23447)
WOODRUFF SPRADLIN & SMART
555 Anton Blvd Ste 1200, Costa Mesa (92626-7670)
PHONE...................................714 558-7000
Ken Smart, *President*
Joseph Forbath, *Shareholder*
Thomas L Woodruff, *Treasurer*
Lois E Jeffrey, *Vice Pres*
Daniel K Spradlin, *Vice Pres*
EMP: 62
SALES (est): 10.3MM **Privately Held**
WEB: www.wss-law.com
SIC: 8111 General practice attorney, lawyer

(P-23448)
WRIGHT FINLAY & ZAK LLP
4665 Macarthur Ct Ste 200, Newport Beach (92660-1811)
PHONE...................................949 477-5050
Robin P Wright, *Managing Prtnr*
Robert Finley, *Partner*
Dana Nitz, *Partner*
Jonathan Zak, *Partner*
Gretchen Grant, *Admin Sec*
EMP: 60
SALES (est): 10.6MM **Privately Held**
WEB: www.wrightlegal.net
SIC: 8111 Corporate, partnership & business law

(P-23449)
YUKEVICH / CVANAUGH A LAW CORP (PA)
355 S Grand Ave Fl 15, Los Angeles (90071-3180)
PHONE...................................213 362-7777
James J Yukevich, *Managing Prtnr*

Alexander Calfo, *Principal*
Todd Cavanaugh, *Principal*
Vivian Powers, *Office Admin*
Tom Szeto, *Info Tech Mgr*
EMP: 65
SALES (est): 10.8MM **Privately Held**
WEB: www.asonnettlaw.com
SIC: 8111 General practice law office

(P-23450)
ZELLE HOFMANN VOELBEL MASN LLP
44 Montgomery St Ste 3400, San Francisco (94104-4807)
PHONE...................................415 693-0700
Dan Mason, *Manager*
Elizabeth Kniffen, *Associate*
EMP: 50
SALES (corp-wide): 24MM **Privately Held**
WEB: www.zelle.com
SIC: 8111 General practice law office
PA: Zelle Llp
500 Washington Ave S # 4000
Minneapolis MN 55415
612 339-2020

(P-23451)
ZIFFREN B B F G-L S&C FND
1801 Century Park W, Los Angeles (90067-6409)
PHONE...................................310 552-3388
Kenneth Ziffren, *Owner*
Sheri Tooley, *Officer*
John G Branca, *Principal*
Harry M Brittenham, *Principal*
Steven Burkow, *Principal*
EMP: 103
SQ FT: 33,000
SALES (est): 16.4MM **Privately Held**
WEB: www.ziffrenlaw.com
SIC: 8111 General practice law office

(P-23452)
ZWICKER & ASSOCIATES PC
1320 Willow Paca Rd 730, Concord (94520)
PHONE...................................925 689-7070
Dawn Valverde, *Human Res Mgr*
Jonathan Espinola, *VP Opers*
EMP: 225
SALES (corp-wide): 94.2MM **Privately Held**
SIC: 8111 General practice attorney, lawyer
PA: Zwicker & Associates, P.C.
80 Minuteman Rd
Andover MA 01810
978 686-2255

8322 Individual & Family Social Svcs

(P-23453)
A PLUS SENIOR CARE INC
4701 Arrow Hwy, Montclair (91763-1229)
PHONE...................................909 989-2563
Gahta Lutfi, *Owner*
EMP: 50
SALES (est): 370.9K **Privately Held**
SIC: 8322 Senior citizens' center or association

(P-23454)
A TOUCH OF KINDNESS
353 1/2 N La Brea Ave, Los Angeles (90036-2517)
P.O. Box 481270 (90048-9761)
PHONE...................................323 997-6500
Yona Landau, *Director*
EMP: 75
SALES (est): 1.1MM **Privately Held**
WEB: www.atouchofkindness.com
SIC: 8322 Public welfare center

(P-23455)
ABILITIES UNITED (PA)
525 E Charleston Rd, Palo Alto (94306-4247)
PHONE...................................650 494-0550
Charlie Weidanz, *CEO*
Jane Machin, *CFO*
Rod Linhares, *Vice Pres*
Tim Harper, *Admin Sec*

Linda Roberts, *Human Res Dir*
EMP: 120
SQ FT: 4,000
SALES: 6.4MM **Privately Held**
WEB: www.c-a-r.org
SIC: 8322 8361 Multi-service center; residential care

(P-23456)
ABILITYFIRST
Also Called: LL Frank Work Center
3812 S Grand Ave, Los Angeles (90037-1336)
PHONE...................................213 748-7309
Fennie Washington, *Director*
EMP: 80
SQ FT: 15,854
SALES (corp-wide): 14.3MM **Privately Held**
WEB: www.abilityfirst.com
SIC: 8322 8093 Association for the handicapped; rehabilitation center, outpatient treatment
PA: Abilityfirst
1300 E Green St
Pasadena CA 91106
626 396-1010

(P-23457)
ABODE SERVICES (PA)
40849 Fremont Blvd, Fremont (94538-4306)
PHONE...................................510 657-7409
Louis Chicoine, *Exec Dir*
Catherine Vu, *Accountant*
Carol Guterman, *Hum Res Coord*
Paula Cartwright, *Opers Mgr*
Joy Corbett, *Property Mgr*
EMP: 70
SALES: 30MM **Privately Held**
WEB: www.tricityhomeless.org
SIC: 8322 Social service center

(P-23458)
ABRAZAR INC
Also Called: ABRAZAR ELDERLY ASSISTANCE
7101 Wyoming St, Westminster (92683-3811)
PHONE...................................714 893-3581
Gloria Reyes, *CEO*
Mario Ortega, *COO*
EMP: 80
SALES: 7.7MM **Privately Held**
WEB: www.abrazarinc.com
SIC: 8322 Social service center

(P-23459)
ADMINSTRTIVE OFFICE OF US CRTS
Also Called: United States Fdral Prbatn
280 S 1st St, San Jose (95113-3002)
PHONE...................................408 535-5200
Sue Rossi, *Office Mgr*
EMP: 69 **Publicly Held**
WEB: www.ao.uscourts.gov
SIC: 8322 Probation office
HQ: The United States Courts Administrative Office Of
1 Columbus Cir Ne
Washington DC 20544
202 502-3800

(P-23460)
ADMINSTRTIVE OFFICE OF US CRTS
Also Called: United States Probation Office
101 W Broadway Ste 700, San Diego (92101-8208)
PHONE...................................619 557-6650
Kennith O Young, *Director*
EMP: 200 **Publicly Held**
WEB: www.ao.uscourts.gov
SIC: 8322 9211 Individual & family services; courts
HQ: The United States Courts Administrative Office Of
1 Columbus Cir Ne
Washington DC 20544
202 502-3800

(P-23461)
AFRICAN AMERICAN UNITY CENTER
Also Called: A A U C
944 W 53rd St, Los Angeles (90037-3643)
PHONE..................................323 789-7300
Charisse Bermond, *Exec Dir*
Will Harris, *Principal*
Elondra Jackson, *Principal*
EMP: 62
SALES: 683.8K **Privately Held**
SIC: 8322 8331 Social service center; job training & vocational rehabilitation services

(P-23462)
AGE CONCERNS INC
2650 Camino Del Rio N # 203, San Diego (92108-1621)
PHONE..................................619 544-1622
Ed Petrivelli, *Exec Dir*
Laura Spitler-Hansen, *President*
EMP: 295
SQ FT: 2,700
SALES (est): 1.9MM
SALES (corp-wide): 49.3MM **Privately Held**
SIC: 8322 8082 7361 Geriatric social service; home health care services; nurses' registry
PA: Livhome, Inc.
5670 Wilshire Blvd # 500
Los Angeles CA 90036
800 807-5854

(P-23463)
AGE WELL SENIOR SERVICES INC (PA)
24461 Ridge Route Dr # 220, Laguna Hills (92653-1686)
PHONE..................................949 855-8033
Steve Moyer, *Acting CEO*
Marlene Bridge, *President*
Dan Du Bois, *Treasurer*
Marilyn Ditty, *General Mgr*
Ray Chicoine, *Admin Sec*
EMP: 70
SQ FT: 10,000
SALES: 5.7MM **Privately Held**
WEB: www.southcountyseniors.org
SIC: 8322 Senior citizens' center or association

(P-23464)
AIDS PROJECT LOS ANGELES (PA)
Also Called: AIDS PROJECT LA
611 S Kingsley Dr, Los Angeles (90005-2319)
PHONE..................................213 201-1600
Craig E Thompson, *CEO*
Robyn Goldman, *CFO*
EMP: 90
SALES: 10.3MM **Privately Held**
SIC: 8322 Social service center

(P-23465)
AIDS SVCS FNDATION ORANGE CNTY
Also Called: AIDS WALK ORANGE COUNTY
17982 Sky Park Cir Ste J, Irvine (92614-6482)
PHONE..................................949 809-5700
Alan Witchey, *Exec Dir*
EMP: 66
SQ FT: 16,051
SALES: 8.9MM **Privately Held**
SIC: 8322 8011 Social service center; clinic, operated by physicians

(P-23466)
ALAMEDA CNTY CMNTY FD BNK INC
7900 Edgewater Dr, Oakland (94621-2004)
P.O. Box 2599 (94614-0599)
PHONE..................................510 635-3663
Suzan Bateson, *President*
EMP: 70
SQ FT: 118,000
SALES: 16.5MM **Privately Held**
WEB: www.accfb.org
SIC: 8322 Social service center

(P-23467)
ALL CARE SERVICES INC
17671 Irvine Blvd Ste 110, Tustin (92780-3128)
PHONE..................................714 669-1148
Lynn Stevens, *Director*
Kenneth E Stevens, *Administration*
EMP: 100
SALES: 2.5MM **Privately Held**
WEB: www.allcareservices.com
SIC: 8322 Old age assistance

(P-23468)
ALPHA PROJECT FOR HOMELESS (PA)
3737 5th Ave Ste 203, San Diego (92103-4217)
PHONE..................................619 542-1877
Bob McElroy, *President*
Amy Gonyeau, *COO*
Jan Norby, *CFO*
Kyla Winters, *Principal*
Robert Mullins, *Bookkeeper*
EMP: 70
SQ FT: 5,000
SALES: 6.9MM **Privately Held**
SIC: 8322 Community center

(P-23469)
ALTA CAL REGIONAL CTR INC
950 Tharp Rd Ste 202, Yuba City (95993-8345)
PHONE..................................530 674-3070
Terry Rhoades, *Manager*
EMP: 300
SALES (corp-wide): 383.5MM **Privately Held**
WEB: www.altaregional.org
SIC: 8322 8699 General counseling services; charitable organization
PA: Alta California Regional Center, Inc.
2241 Harvard St Ste 100
Sacramento CA 95815
916 978-6400

(P-23470)
ALTA LOMA ASSISTED LIVING LLC
Also Called: Sunlit Gardens
9428 19th St, Murrieta (92562)
PHONE..................................909 481-2600
Ernest Hix, *Mng Member*
Sharon Hix,
EMP: 66
SALES (est): 1.3MM **Privately Held**
SIC: 8322 Old age assistance

(P-23471)
ALZHEIMERS GREATER LOS ANGELES
4221 Wilshire Blvd # 400, Los Angeles (90010-3512)
PHONE..................................323 938-3379
Heather Cooper Ortner, *President*
Debra Cherry, *Exec VP*
John Seiber, *Vice Pres*
Matthew Wolf, *Mng Member*
EMP: 58
SALES: 5.5MM **Privately Held**
SIC: 8322 Geriatric social service

(P-23472)
AMERICAN CARE GIVERS WESTWOOD
947 Tiverton Ave Ste 533, Los Angeles (90024-3012)
PHONE..................................310 208-8005
Vicky London, *President*
Denise London, *CFO*
David London, *Vice Pres*
EMP: 60
SALES (est): 1.1MM **Privately Held**
WEB: www.americancaregivers.com
SIC: 8322 Geriatric social service

(P-23473)
AMERICAN CORRECTIVE COUNSELING
Also Called: Accs
180 Avenida La Pata # 200, San Clemente (92673-6300)
PHONE..................................949 369-6210
Michael C Schreck, *President*
Mike Wilhelms, *CFO*

Brett Stohlton, *Exec VP*
EMP: 297
SQ FT: 2,000
SALES (est): 4.8MM **Privately Held**
SIC: 8322 General counseling services
PA: Accs Corp
180 Avenida La Pata # 200
San Clemente CA 92673

(P-23474)
AMERICAN NATIONAL RED CROSS
601 N Golden Circle Dr, Santa Ana (92705-3902)
P.O. Box 11364 (92711-1364)
PHONE..................................714 481-5300
Stanley Perdue, *Branch Mgr*
EMP: 50
SQ FT: 30,092
SALES (corp-wide): 2.5B **Privately Held**
WEB: www.redcross.org
SIC: 8322 Individual & family services
PA: The American National Red Cross
430 17th St Nw
Washington DC 20006
202 737-8300

(P-23475)
AMERICAN NATIONAL RED CROSS
1663 Market St, San Francisco (94103-1238)
PHONE..................................415 427-8134
Harold Brooks, *Manager*
EMP: 120
SALES (corp-wide): 2.5B **Privately Held**
WEB: www.redcross.org
SIC: 8322 Social service center
PA: The American National Red Cross
430 17th St Nw
Washington DC 20006
202 737-8300

(P-23476)
AMERICAN NATIONAL RED CROSS
Also Called: American Red Cross
1300 Alberta Way, Concord (94521-3705)
PHONE..................................925 603-7400
Harold Brooks, *Principal*
EMP: 50
SQ FT: 4,765
SALES (corp-wide): 2.5B **Privately Held**
SIC: 8322 Individual & family services
HQ: The American National Red Cross
8550 Arlington Blvd # 100
Fairfax VA 22031
703 584-8400

(P-23477)
AMERICAN NATIONAL RED CROSS
3950 Calle Fortunada, San Diego (92123-1827)
PHONE..................................858 309-1200
Dodie Rotherham, *CEO*
EMP: 90
SALES (corp-wide): 2.5B **Privately Held**
WEB: www.redcross.org
SIC: 8322 Social service center
PA: The American National Red Cross
430 17th St Nw
Washington DC 20006
202 737-8300

(P-23478)
AMERICAN RED CROSS
11355 Ohio Ave, Los Angeles (90025-3266)
PHONE..................................310 445-9900
Enrique Rivera, *Office Mgr*
Brian Kilb, *Partner*
EMP: 100
SALES (corp-wide): 2.5B **Privately Held**
WEB: www.redcross.org
SIC: 8322 Individual & family services
PA: The American National Red Cross
430 17th St Nw
Washington DC 20006
202 737-8300

(P-23479)
AMERICAN RED CROSS LA CHAPTER (PA)
11355 Ohio Ave, Los Angeles (90025-3266)
PHONE..................................310 445-9900
Roger Dixon, *CEO*
Kirk Richard Hyde, *Ch of Bd*
Scott J Olmsted, *Ch of Bd*
Michelle McCarthy, *CFO*
Thomas E Stephenson, *CFO*
EMP: 376
SQ FT: 5,000
SALES (est): 16.6MM **Privately Held**
SIC: 8322 Social service center

(P-23480)
AMERICAN WHT MSSN IN STHRN
7212 Orangethorpe Ave 7a, Buena Park (90621-3341)
P.O. Box 1400, Cypress (90630-6400)
PHONE..................................714 522-4599
Young Lee, *Owner*
EMP: 100
SALES (est): 1MM **Privately Held**
SIC: 8322 Temporary relief service

(P-23481)
ANTELOPE VALLEY FOUNDATION
Also Called: DAYSTAR FOUNDATION
646 W Lancaster Blvd # 109, Lancaster (93534-3154)
PHONE..................................661 945-7290
Steven Sultan, *President*
Dorothy Edgar, *CEO*
Linda Harris, *Sales Executive*
EMP: 50
SQ FT: 11,000
SALES: 2MM **Privately Held**
SIC: 8322 5999 Individual & family services; technical aids for the handicapped

(P-23482)
ANTELOPE VLY DOM VLNCE COUNCIL (PA)
Also Called: VALLEY OASIS SHELTER
43434 Sahuayo St, Lancaster (93535-4659)
P.O. Box 2980 (93539-2980)
PHONE..................................661 723-7772
Carol Crabson, *Exec Dir*
Darryl Kniss, *CFO*
Lorraine Hines, *Program Mgr*
Toni Severino, *Accountant*
EMP: 52
SQ FT: 16,500
SALES: 6.6MM **Privately Held**
SIC: 8322 8361 Individual & family services; halfway group home, persons with social or personal problems

(P-23483)
ARC - IMPERIAL VALLEY (PA)
298 E Ross Ave, El Centro (92243-9303)
P.O. Box 1828 (92244-1828)
PHONE..................................760 352-0180
Arturo Santos, *CEO*
Poli Flores, *President*
Lorie Weaver, *Human Res Dir*
Laura Sperber,
Tina Snyder, *Director*
EMP: 158
SQ FT: 22,000
SALES: 10.8MM **Privately Held**
SIC: 8322 4729 8361 Adult day care center; carpool/vanpool arrangement; home for the mentally handicapped

(P-23484)
ARC OF ALAMEDA COUNTY (PA)
14700 Doolittle Dr, San Leandro (94577-6619)
PHONE..................................510 357-3569
Ron Luter, *Exec Dir*
Sandie Craven, *Admin Sec*
Angie Tam, *Technology*
Nancy Freeman, *Accountant*
Mary Foster, *Program Dir*
▲ **EMP:** 135 **EST:** 1969
SQ FT: 66,000
SALES: 6.5MM **Privately Held**
WEB: www.tiw-alameda.com
SIC: 8322 Association for the handicapped

(P-23485)
ARC OF BUTTE COUNTY (PA)
2030 Park Ave, Chico (95928-6701)
P.O. Box 3697 (95927-3697)
PHONE..........................530 891-5865
Courtney Casey, *CEO*
Michael McGinnis, *CEO*
Jean Campbell, *Treasurer*
Nelson Corwin, *Associate Dir*
Tom Leonardi, *Associate Dir*
EMP: 200
SQ FT: 12,268
SALES: 6.1MM **Privately Held**
WEB: www.arcbutte.org
SIC: 8322 Individual & family services

(P-23486)
ARC STARLIGHT CENTER
Also Called: ARC of San Diego
1280 Nolan Ave, Chula Vista (91911-3738)
PHONE..........................619 427-7524
Terri Thorn, *Director*
EMP: 70
SALES (est): 1.6MM **Privately Held**
SIC: 8322 Social services for the handicapped

(P-23487)
ARGONAUT KENSINGTON ASSOCIATES
Also Called: Kensington Place
1580 Geary Rd Ofc, Walnut Creek (94597-2786)
PHONE..........................925 943-1121
Richard Fordiani, *Partner*
James Houston, *Partner*
EMP: 60
SALES (est): 2.9MM **Privately Held**
SIC: 8322 Senior citizens' center or association

(P-23488)
ARMENIAN AMRCN CUNCIL ON AGING
Also Called: ARMENIAN-AMERICAN COUN-CIL ON A
407 E Colorado St, Glendale (91205-1604)
PHONE..........................818 241-8690
Mardiros Edgarian, *Director*
Minas Dersarkissian, *Treasurer*
EMP: 50
SQ FT: 5,600
SALES: 47.7K **Privately Held**
SIC: 8322 Individual & family services

(P-23489)
ARROYO DEVELOPMENTAL SERVICES
1839 Potrero Grande Dr, Monterey Park (91755-5847)
PHONE..........................626 307-2240
Robert Wark, *President*
Federico Nicoletti, *Human Res Mgr*
EMP: 60
SQ FT: 1,232
SALES (est): 1.5MM **Privately Held**
SIC: 8322 Individual & family services

(P-23490)
ARTS AND SERVICES FOR DISABLED
3626 E Pacific Coast Hwy, Long Beach (90804-2015)
PHONE..........................562 377-0302
Kay Hagen, *Director*
EMP: 50
SALES: 2.6MM **Privately Held**
SIC: 8322 Association for the handicapped

(P-23491)
ASANA INTEGRATED MEDICAL GROUP
26135 Mureau Rd Ste 101, Calabasas (91302-3125)
PHONE..........................888 212-7545
Nitin Nanda, *Principal*
EMP: 85
SALES (est): 2.1MM
SALES (corp-wide): 287.4MM **Privately Held**
SIC: 8322 General counseling services

HQ: Ipc Healthcare, Inc.
4605 Lankershim Blvd
North Hollywood CA 91602
888 447-2362

(P-23492)
ASIAN AMERCN RECOVERY SVCS INC (PA)
1115 Mission Rd 2, South San Francisco (94080-1302)
PHONE..........................650 243-4888
Tony Doug, *Exec Dir*
EMP: 160
SALES (est): 6MM **Privately Held**
WEB: www.aars-inc.org
SIC: 8322 8069 General counseling services; substance abuse counseling; drug addiction rehabilitation hospital

(P-23493)
ASIAN COMMUNITY CENTER OF SAC (PA)
Also Called: ACC Senior Services
7334 Park City Dr, Sacramento (95831-3865)
PHONE..........................916 394-6399
William Yee, *President*
King Gee, *CFO*
Teresa Greenman, *Officer*
Jean Shiomoto, *Vice Pres*
Judi Keen, *Admin Sec*
EMP: 150
SALES: 24.3MM **Privately Held**
WEB: www.accsv.org
SIC: 8322 8059 Community center; nursing home, except skilled & intermediate care facility

(P-23494)
ASPEN YOUTH INC
17777 Center Court Dr N # 300, Cerritos (90703-9320)
PHONE..........................562 567-5507
Elliot A Sainer, *Exec Dir*
EMP: 69
SALES (est): 471.8K **Publicly Held**
SIC: 8322 Individual & family services
HQ: Aspen Education Group, Inc.
17777 Center Court Dr N # 300
Cerritos CA 90703
562 467-5500

(P-23495)
ASPIRANET
Also Called: Excell Center, The
2513 Youngstown Rd, Turlock (95380-9707)
PHONE..........................209 667-0327
Christopher Essary, *Principal*
EMP: 60
SALES (corp-wide): 59MM **Privately Held**
WEB: www.verosantes.com
SIC: 8322 8361 Child related social services; residential care
PA: Aspiranet
400 Oyster Point Blvd # 501
South San Francisco CA 94080
650 866-4080

(P-23496)
ASSISTA HLTHCARE PRFSSNALS LLC
Also Called: Assita In-Home Care
2006 Pioneer Ct, San Mateo (94403-1720)
PHONE..........................650 393-4293
Bernadette Galvan-Torrejon, *CEO*
Ernie Torrejon, *CFO*
EMP: 115 EST: 2010
SQ FT: 1,065
SALES (est): 1MM **Privately Held**
SIC: 8322 Old age assistance

(P-23497)
ASSOCIATED STUDENTS INC (PA)
Also Called: ASSICIATED STUDENTS
University Un Bldg 65, San Luis Obispo (93407)
PHONE..........................805 756-1281
Richard Johnson, *Director*
Dwayne Brummett, *Business Mgr*
EMP: 70
SQ FT: 110,000

SALES: 12.7MM **Privately Held**
SIC: 8322 8221 Multi-service center; colleges universities & professional schools

(P-23498)
ATKINSON YOUTH SERVICES INC
4253 Balsam St, Sacramento (95838-2801)
PHONE..........................916 927-1863
Jim Atkinson, *Branch Mgr*
EMP: 64 **Privately Held**
SIC: 8322 Youth center
PA: Atkinson Youth Services Incorporated
1906 El Camino Ave
Sacramento CA 95815

(P-23499)
AUTISM OTRACH SOUTHERN CAL LLC
3110 Cmino Del Rio S 30, San Diego (92108)
PHONE..........................619 795-9925
Abigail R Bun, *Mng Member*
Abigail R Bunt,
EMP: 75
SALES: 4MM **Privately Held**
SIC: 8322 Individual & family services

(P-23500)
AVALON A CERRITOS
11000 New Falcon Way Ofc # 177, Cerritos (90703-1553)
PHONE..........................562 865-9500
Laura Trujillo, *Director*
EMP: 50
SALES (est): 2.6MM **Privately Held**
SIC: 8322 Senior citizens' center or association

(P-23501)
AVENIDAS (PA)
Also Called: Avenidas Senior Hlth Day Hlth
4000 Middlefield Rd Ste I, Palo Alto (94303-4761)
PHONE..........................650 289-5400
Lisa Hendrickson, *President*
Sue Campbell, *Treasurer*
Maureen Breen, *Vice Pres*
Morien Breen, *Vice Pres*
Mary Hohensee, *Vice Pres*
EMP: 60
SQ FT: 25,000
SALES: 6.5MM **Privately Held**
WEB: www.avenidas.org
SIC: 8322 Senior citizens' center or association

(P-23502)
BAY AREA COMMUNITY SVCS INC (PA)
Also Called: East Bay Transitional Homes
390 40th St, Oakland (94609-2633)
PHONE..........................510 613-0330
Jamie Almanza, *CEO*
David Stoloff, *Chairman*
Asha Koshy, *Program Mgr*
Chris Llorente, *Program Mgr*
Jennifer Rodway, *Program Mgr*
EMP: 50
SQ FT: 1,000
SALES: 13MM **Privately Held**
WEB: www.bayareacs.org
SIC: 8322 Senior citizens' center or association

(P-23503)
BAY AREA SENIOR SERVICES INC
Also Called: Peninsula Regent, The
1 Baldwin Ave Ofc, San Mateo (94401-3837)
PHONE..........................650 579-5500
M Mannstab, *Exec Dir*
EMP: 140
SALES (corp-wide): 23.8MM **Privately Held**
WEB: www.peninsularegent.com
SIC: 8322 Senior citizens' center or association
HQ: Bay Area Senior Services Inc
1 Hawthorne St Ste 400
San Francisco CA 94105
415 989-1111

(P-23504)
BEACON HEALTH OPTIONS INC
10805 Holder St Ste 300, Cypress (90630-5147)
PHONE..........................714 763-2405
Steve Rockowitz, *Principal*
Teri Darcy, *Manager*
EMP: 111
SALES (corp-wide): 501.8MM **Privately Held**
SIC: 8322 Individual & family services
HQ: Beacon Health Options, Inc.
200 State St Ste 302
Boston MA 02109
757 459-5100

(P-23505)
BEHAVIORAL HEALTH SERVICES INC (PA)
15519 Crenshaw Blvd, Gardena (90249-4525)
PHONE..........................310 679-9031
Henry Van Oudheudsen, *CEO*
Lawrence T Gentile, *President*
Andy Worrell, *CFO*
Juan Pena, *Opers Mgr*
Theresa L Cannon, *Agent*
EMP: 50
SQ FT: 35,000
SALES: 21MM **Privately Held**
SIC: 8322 Substance abuse counseling; alcoholism counseling, nontreatment; drug abuse counselor, nontreatment; senior citizens' center or association

(P-23506)
BEHAVIORAL HEALTH SERVICES INC
Also Called: Redgate Memorial Hospital
1775 Chestnut Ave, Long Beach (90813-1674)
PHONE..........................562 599-4194
Robert Worrell, *Director*
EMP: 65
SQ FT: 21,780
SALES (corp-wide): 21MM **Privately Held**
SIC: 8322 8069 Substance abuse counseling; alcoholism rehabilitation hospital
PA: Behavioral Health Services, Inc.
15519 Crenshaw Blvd
Gardena CA 90249
310 679-9031

(P-23507)
BEHAVIORAL HEALTH SERVICES INC
Also Called: American Recovery Center
2180 Valley Blvd, Pomona (91768-3325)
PHONE..........................909 865-2336
Booker Blebsoe, *Administration*
Son Hong J Le, *Director*
EMP: 100
SQ FT: 40,868
SALES (corp-wide): 21MM **Privately Held**
SIC: 8322 8093 8361 Drug abuse counselor, nontreatment; specialty outpatient clinics; residential care
PA: Behavioral Health Services, Inc.
15519 Crenshaw Blvd
Gardena CA 90249
310 679-9031

(P-23508)
BEHAVIORAL LEARNING CENTER INC
28245 Avenue Crocker # 220, Valencia (91355-0940)
PHONE..........................661 254-7086
Jody Stiegemeyer, *President*
Shanna Benveniste, *Program Mgr*
Danielle Sheehy, *Admin Sec*
Kim Loth, *Administration*
EMP: 99 EST: 2007
SQ FT: 4,000
SALES (est): 3.8MM **Privately Held**
SIC: 8322 Child related social services

(P-23509)
BEHAVORAL AUTISM THERAPIES LLC (PA)
2930 Inland Empire Blvd, Ontario (91764-4802)
PHONE..........................909 483-5000

Mia Humphreys, *Mng Member*
Larry M Humphreys, *Principal*
Larry Humphreys,
Chris Wong, *Assistant*
EMP: 250
SQ FT: 2,000
SALES (est): 4.7MM **Privately Held**
SIC: 8322 Individual & family services

(P-23510)
BERNARD OSHER MARIN JEWISH COM
Also Called: J C C
200 N San Pedro Rd, San Rafael (94903-4213)
PHONE..................................415 444-8000
Marty Friedman, *President*
Michael Baumstein, *COO*
George Mann, *CFO*
Mark Goodman, *Treasurer*
Deborah Stadtner, *Vice Pres*
EMP: 200
SQ FT: 90,000
SALES: 12.7MM **Privately Held**
SIC: 8322 Community center

(P-23511)
BETTER WAY SERVICES
5329 Office Center Ct # 100, Bakersfield (93309-7425)
PHONE..................................661 326-6444
Jim Kirkendole, *President*
EMP: 100 EST: 2000
SQ FT: 4,000
SALES (est): 3MM **Privately Held**
SIC: 8322 Individual & family services

(P-23512)
BIENVENIDOS CHILDRENS CENTER (PA)
Also Called: BIENVENIDOS FAMILY SERV-ICES
501 S Atlantic Blvd, Los Angeles (90022-2621)
PHONE..................................213 785-5906
Ritchie L Geisel, *CEO*
Michael Still, *CFO*
EMP: 250
SQ FT: 11,000
SALES: 15.1MM **Privately Held**
WEB: www.bienvenidos.org
SIC: 8322 Child related social services

(P-23513)
BILL WILSON CENTER (PA)
3490 The Alameda, Santa Clara (95050-4333)
PHONE..................................408 243-0222
Sparky Harlan, *CEO*
Kirsten Mc Keraghan, *Program Mgr*
Judy Whittier, *Commissioner*
EMP: 87
SQ FT: 19,000
SALES: 16.5MM **Privately Held**
SIC: 8322 General counseling services

(P-23514)
BIRTH CHOICE OF SAN MARCO
277 S Rancho Santa Fe Rd, San Marcos (92078-2343)
PHONE..................................760 744-1313
Rose Mary Brown, *Director*
EMP: 60
SALES (est): 503.9K **Privately Held**
SIC: 8322 Individual & family services

(P-23515)
BONITA HOUSE INC
6333 Telg Ave Ste 102, Oakland (94609)
PHONE..................................510 923-0180
Rick Crispino, *Exec Dir*
Allegra Count, *Opers Mgr*
Amanda Ollis, *Program Dir*
EMP: 76
SQ FT: 4,000
SALES: 6.4MM **Privately Held**
SIC: 8322 Association for the handicapped

(P-23516)
BOYS & GIRLS CLUB SILICON VLY
518 Valley Way, Milpitas (95035-4106)
PHONE..................................408 957-9685
Dana Fraticelli, *Exec Dir*
EMP: 51

SALES: 3.1MM **Privately Held**
WEB: www.bgclub.org
SIC: 8322 Youth center

(P-23517)
BRAILLE INSTITUTE AMERICA INC (PA)
741 N Vermont Ave, Los Angeles (90029-3594)
PHONE..................................323 663-1111
Lester M Sussman, *Ch of Bd*
Peter Mindnich, *President*
Les Stocker, *President*
Rezaur Rahman, *Vice Pres*
Henry Chang, *Executive*
EMP: 208 EST: 1919
SQ FT: 167,079
SALES: 34MM **Privately Held**
SIC: 8322 8231 2731 2759 Individual & family services; specialized libraries; text-books: publishing & printing; commercial printing

(P-23518)
BREAKOUT PRISON OUTREACH
Also Called: California Youth Outreach
1560 Berger Dr, San Jose (95112-2703)
P.O. Box 8671, Fresno (93747-8671)
PHONE..................................408 702-2405
Anthony Ortiz, *President*
Kurt Foreman, *Treasurer*
Sandra Martinez, *Admin Sec*
Mark Riddle, *Accountant*
Christina Yee, *Assistant*
EMP: 72
SQ FT: 1,800
SALES (est): 4.5MM **Privately Held**
SIC: 8322 Youth center

(P-23519)
BRIGHTER BEGINNINGS (PA)
3478 Buskirk Ave Ste 105, Pleasant Hill (94523-4345)
PHONE..................................510 903-7503
Barbara B McCullough, *CEO*
Liz Nickels, *Director*
EMP: 60
SALES: 5.4MM **Privately Held**
WEB: www.brighter-beginnings.org
SIC: 8322 8011 8093 Individual & family services; primary care medical clinic; mental health clinic; outpatient

(P-23520)
BUCKELEW PROGRAMS (PA)
555 Northgate Dr Ste 100, San Rafael (94903-3696)
PHONE..................................415 457-6964
Tamara Player, *CEO*
EMP: 150 EST: 1970
SQ FT: 3,000
SALES: 13.1MM **Privately Held**
WEB: www.buckelew.org
SIC: 8322 Social services for the handi-capped

(P-23521)
BUILDING OPPORTUNITIES (PA)
Also Called: B O S S
1918 University Ave 2a, Berkeley (94704-3263)
PHONE..................................510 649-1930
Donald Frazier, *CEO*
Robert Barrer, *Principal*
Qassim A Moon, *Director*
Timothy Smith, *Director*
EMP: 110
SALES: 6.2MM **Privately Held**
WEB: www.self-sufficiency.org
SIC: 8322 Emergency shelters; emergency social services; general counseling serv-ices

(P-23522)
CALIFORNIA CHILD CARE RESOURC
Also Called: Infant/Toddler Consort
5232 Claremont Ave, Oakland (94618-1033)
PHONE..................................510 658-0381
Betty Cohen, *Exec Dir*
EMP: 50

SALES (est): 287.8K
SALES (corp-wide): 3.5MM **Privately Held**
WEB: www.rrnetwork.org
SIC: 8322 Referral service for personal & social problems
PA: California Child Care Resource & Re-ferral Network
1182 Market St Ste 300
San Francisco CA 94102
415 882-0234

(P-23523)
CALIFORNIA CHILD CARE RESOURCE (PA)
1182 Market St Ste 300, San Francisco (94102-4919)
PHONE..................................415 882-0234
Linda Asato, *Exec Dir*
Tom Calhoun, *CFO*
Lena Bilik, *Executive Asst*
Patricia Siegel, *Director*
Disa Lindgren, *Regional*
EMP: 71
SQ FT: 4,000
SALES: 3.5MM **Privately Held**
WEB: www.rrnetwork.org
SIC: 8322 Child related social services; re-ferral service for personal & social prob-lems

(P-23524)
CALIFORNIA PEDIATRIC FMLY SVCS
Also Called: ABLE
326 E Foothill Blvd, Azusa (91702-2515)
PHONE..................................626 812-0055
Louise Vanzee PHD, *President*
Faviola Acevedo, *Manager*
EMP: 75
SQ FT: 2,417
SALES: 228.3K **Privately Held**
WEB: www.cal-peds.com
SIC: 8322 Family counseling services

(P-23525)
CAN-DO
Also Called: Compass Actn Netwk Dirct Outcm
578 Washington Blvd 39o, Marina Del Rey (90292-5442)
PHONE..................................646 228-7049
Eric Klein, *Director*
EMP: 60
SALES (est): 539.1K **Privately Held**
SIC: 8322 Disaster service

(P-23526)
CARE 4 U LLC
22726 Eccles St, West Hills (91304-3324)
P.O. Box 10297, Canoga Park (91309-1297)
PHONE..................................818 593-7911
Ralph Stokes,
Orli Almog,
EMP: 56
SALES: 225K **Privately Held**
SIC: 8322 Social service center

(P-23527)
CARESCOPE LLC
1455 Response Rd Ste 120, Sacramento (95815-4848)
P.O. Box 2121 (95812-2121)
PHONE..................................916 780-1384
Okja Sim,
Frank Sim, *General Mgr*
EMP: 60
SALES (est): 814.2K **Privately Held**
SIC: 8322 Senior citizens' center or associ-ation

(P-23528)
CARMICHAEL RECREATION & PK DST
5750 Grant Ave, Carmichael (95608-3779)
PHONE..................................916 485-5322
Ronald D Cuppy, *Administration*
EMP: 170
SALES (est): 6.4MM **Privately Held**
WEB: www.carmichaelpark.com
SIC: 8322 Community center

(P-23529)
CASA COLINA INC (PA)
Also Called: Casa Colina Hospital & Ctr
255 E Bonita Ave, Pomona (91767-1933)
PHONE..................................909 596-7733
Felice L Loverso, *CEO*
Debrah Schaultz, *Records Dir*
Donald Driftmier, *Bd of Directors*
Stephanie Bradhurst, *Chief Mktg Ofcr*
Susan Stanley, *Vice Pres*
EMP: 800 EST: 1981
SALES: 113.3MM **Privately Held**
SIC: 8322 8011 Rehabilitation services; ambulatory surgical center

(P-23530)
CASA PACIFICA CENTERS (PA)
1722 S Lewis Rd, Camarillo (93012-8520)
PHONE..................................805 482-3260
Steven E Elson, *CEO*
Felice Ginsberg, *CFO*
Michael Redard, *CFO*
Michelle Maye, *Bd of Directors*
Lynne Gibbons, *Admin Mgr*
EMP: 175
SQ FT: 63,000
SALES: 29.5MM **Privately Held**
WEB: www.casapacifica.org
SIC: 8322 8361 8211 Child related social services; residential care for children; specialty education

(P-23531)
CASPAR COMMUNITY
15051 Caspar Rd, Caspar (95420-0114)
P.O. Box 84 (95420)
PHONE..................................707 964-4997
Judy Parbell, *President*
Rochelle Elkan, *Treasurer*
Maryflannery Kaurt, *Treasurer*
Dalen Anderson, *Admin Sec*
EMP: 50
SALES: 126.3K **Privately Held**
SIC: 8322 Community center

(P-23532)
CATHOLIC CHARITIES DIOCESE (PA)
1106 N El Dorado St, Stockton (95202-1332)
PHONE..................................209 444-5900
Elvira Ramirez, *Exec Dir*
Carmen Thompkins, *Admin Asst*
Nai Sosongkham, *Case Mgr*
EMP: 100
SQ FT: 3,600
SALES: 4.4MM **Privately Held**
WEB: www.catholiccharitiesstk.org
SIC: 8322 Social service center; old age assistance; association for the handi-capped

(P-23533)
CATHOLIC CHARITIES DIOCESE SAN
Also Called: Refugee Resettlement
4575 Mission Gorge Pl A, San Diego (92120-4106)
PHONE..................................619 287-9454
Robert Moser, *Director*
EMP: 50
SALES (corp-wide): 15.4MM **Privately Held**
SIC: 8322 Refugee service
PA: Catholic Charities, Diocese Of San Diego
3888 Paducah Dr
San Diego CA 92117
619 323-2841

(P-23534)
CATHOLIC CHARITIES OF LA INC
21600 Hart St, Canoga Park (91303)
PHONE..................................818 883-6015
EMP: 50
SALES (corp-wide): 29MM **Privately Held**
SIC: 8322
PA: Catholic Charities Of Los Angeles, Inc.
1531 James M Wood Blvd
Los Angeles CA 90015
213 251-3400

(P-23535)
CATHOLIC CHARITIES OF LA INC
1400 James M Wood Blvd, Los Angeles (90015-1210)
P.O. Box 15095 (90015-0095)
PHONE..............................213 251-3400
James E Bathker, *Branch Mgr*
EMP: 71
SALES (corp-wide): 34.2MM **Privately Held**
SIC: 8322 Social service center
PA: Catholic Charities Of Los Angeles, Inc.
1531 James M Wood Blvd
Los Angeles CA 90015
213 251-3400

(P-23536)
CATHOLIC CHARITIES OF SANTA CL (PA)
2625 Zanker Rd Ste 200, San Jose (95134-2130)
PHONE..............................408 468-0100
Gregory Kepferle, *CEO*
Wanda Hale, *Program Mgr*
SOO Poumele, *Program Mgr*
Milena Milivojevic, *Administration*
Don Ngo, *Info Tech Mgr*
EMP: 200
SQ FT: 50,000
SALES: 30.6MM **Privately Held**
SIC: 8322 Social service center

(P-23537)
CATHOLIC CHARITIES OF SANTA CL
303 N Ventura Ave Ste A, Ventura (93001-1961)
PHONE..............................805 643-4694
Robert Batdazian, *Director*
EMP: 60
SALES (corp-wide): 30.6MM **Privately Held**
SIC: 8322 Family counseling services
PA: Catholic Charities Of Santa Clara County
2625 Zanker Rd Ste 200
San Jose CA 95134
408 468-0100

(P-23538)
CATHOLIC CHARITIES OF THE DIOC (PA)
Also Called: CATHOLIC CHARITIES OF EAST BAY
433 Jefferson St, Oakland (94607-3592)
PHONE..............................510 768-3100
Chuck Fernandez, *Exec Dir*
Solomon Belette, *Exec Dir*
EMP: 90
SQ FT: 10,376
SALES: 6.8MM **Privately Held**
SIC: 8322 8661 Social service center; religious organizations

(P-23539)
CATHOLIC CHRTS CYO ARCHDIOCS
810 Avenue D, San Francisco (94130-2002)
PHONE..............................415 743-0017
Nella Goncalves, *Principal*
EMP: 61
SALES (corp-wide): 39.6MM **Privately Held**
SIC: 8322 Social service center
PA: Catholic Charities Cyo Of The Archdiocese Of San Francisco
990 Eddy St
San Francisco CA 94109
415 972-1200

(P-23540)
CATHOLIC CHRTS CYO ARCHDIOCS
Also Called: Leland House
141 Leland Ave, San Francisco (94134-2847)
PHONE..............................415 405-2000
Paul Raia, *Exec Dir*
Jose Cartagena, *Program Mgr*
EMP: 61

SALES (corp-wide): 39.6MM **Privately Held**
SIC: 8322 Child guidance agency
PA: Catholic Charities Cyo Of The Archdiocese Of San Francisco
990 Eddy St
San Francisco CA 94109
415 972-1200

(P-23541)
CATHOLIC CHRTS CYO ARCHDIOCS
1111 Junipero Serra Blvd, San Francisco (94132-2653)
PHONE..............................415 334-5550
Jeffrey Bialik V, *Principal*
EMP: 61
SALES (corp-wide): 39.6MM **Privately Held**
SIC: 8322 Social service center
PA: Catholic Charities Cyo Of The Archdiocese Of San Francisco
990 Eddy St
San Francisco CA 94109
415 972-1200

(P-23542)
CATHOLIC CHRTS CYO ARCHDIOCS
Also Called: Derek Silva Community
20 Franklin St, San Francisco (94102-6000)
PHONE..............................415 553-8700
Theresa Flores, *Principal*
Erwin Barrios, *Case Mgr*
EMP: 61
SALES (corp-wide): 39.6MM **Privately Held**
SIC: 8322 Child guidance agency
PA: Catholic Charities Cyo Of The Archdiocese Of San Francisco
990 Eddy St
San Francisco CA 94109
415 972-1200

(P-23543)
CATHOLIC CHRTS CYO ARCHDIOCS (PA)
990 Eddy St, San Francisco (94109-7713)
PHONE..............................415 972-1200
Jeffrey V Bialik, *CEO*
Keith Spindle, *CFO*
Cailan Franz, *Comms Dir*
Kathie Autumn, *Exec Dir*
Jeff Bialik, *Exec Dir*
EMP: 56 EST: 1907
SALES: 39.6MM **Privately Held**
SIC: 8322 Child guidance agency; senior citizens' center or association; family service agency; rehabilitation services

(P-23544)
CATHOLIC CHRTS CYO ARCHDIOCS
1 Saint Vincents Dr, San Rafael (94903-1504)
PHONE..............................415 507-2000
Chuck Fernandez, *Branch Mgr*
EMP: 300
SALES (corp-wide): 39.6MM **Privately Held**
SIC: 8322 8641 Child related social services; civic social & fraternal associations
PA: Catholic Charities Cyo Of The Archdiocese Of San Francisco
990 Eddy St
San Francisco CA 94109
415 972-1200

(P-23545)
CAVIAR INC (HQ)
Also Called: Try Caviar
220 Montgomery St Ste 370, San Francisco (94104-3436)
PHONE..............................888 978-5619
Jason Wang, *CEO*
EMP: 70
SALES (est): 1.2MM **Publicly Held**
SIC: 8322 4813 Meal delivery program;

(P-23546)
CENTER CNSLNG EDCTN & CRISIS
Also Called: Valley Community Health Center
4361 Railroad Ave, Pleasanton (94566-6611)
PHONE..............................925 462-1755
Ronald Greenspane, *Exec Dir*
EMP: 73
SALES (est): 866.6K **Privately Held**
SIC: 8322 General counseling services

(P-23547)
CENTER FOR IND LIVING INC (PA)
2490 Mariner Square Loop # 210, Alameda (94501-1024)
PHONE..............................510 841-4776
Beatrice Burgess, *Exec Dir*
Henry Leng, *President*
Gail Bergunde, *CFO*
Stuart James, *Exec Dir*
Kimberlee Carr, *Planning*
EMP: 55 EST: 1972
SQ FT: 10,291
SALES: 2MM **Privately Held**
WEB: www.cilberkeley.org
SIC: 8322 Social service center

(P-23548)
CENTER FOR INDVDUAL AND FAM TH
840 W Town And Country Rd, Orange (92868-4712)
PHONE..............................714 558-9266
Jim Masteller, *Director*
EMP: 55
SALES (est): 692.2K **Privately Held**
SIC: 8322 Family (marriage) counseling

(P-23549)
CENTER FOR LEARNING AND
Also Called: Class
424 Peninsula Ave, San Mateo (94401-1653)
PHONE..............................800 538-8365
Denise Pollard, *CEO*
Krista Katusha, *Business Mgr*
Deborah Holtzclaw, *Manager*
EMP: 400
SALES (est): 36.8K **Privately Held**
SIC: 8322 Family counseling services

(P-23550)
CENTER POINT INC (PA)
135 Paul Dr, San Rafael (94903-2023)
PHONE..............................415 492-4444
Sushma D Taylor PHD, *Exec Dir*
Ramin Behravan, *Vice Pres*
John Challis, *Vice Pres*
Marc Hering, *Vice Pres*
Winston Williams, *Finance*
EMP: 90
SQ FT: 7,750
SALES: 29.9MM **Privately Held**
SIC: 8322 Social service center

(P-23551)
CENTRAL VALLEY AUTISM PROJECT
3425 Coffee Rd Ste C2, Modesto (95355-1582)
PHONE..............................209 521-4791
Gina Pallotta, *Director*
EMP: 80 EST: 2000
SALES (est): 3.6MM **Privately Held**
SIC: 8322 Social service center

(P-23552)
CENTRAL VLY CHLD SVCS NETWRK
1911 N Helm Ave, Fresno (93727-1614)
PHONE..............................559 456-1100
Jane Martin, *Exec Dir*
Irene Alvarado, *Admin Asst*
Esperanza Napoles, *Project Mgr*
Ofelia Gonzalez, *Pub Rel Dir*
Marisela Sosa, *Manager*
EMP: 60
SQ FT: 15,000
SALES: 12.2MM **Privately Held**
WEB: www.cvcsn.org
SIC: 8322 Social service center

(P-23553)
CENTRL TERRITRL SALVATION ARMY
10200 Pioneer Rd, Tustin (92782-1417)
PHONE..............................714 832-7100
Nigel Cross, *Director*
Carmen Magdaleno, *Director*
Rosalinda Littlejohn, *Manager*
EMP: 60
SALES (corp-wide): 4.3B **Privately Held**
WEB: www.salarmychicago.org
SIC: 8322 8661 8699 Social service center; religious organizations; charitable organization
HQ: Central Territorial Of The Salvation Army
5550 Prairie Stone Pkwy # 130
Hoffman Estates IL 60192
847 294-2000

(P-23554)
CENTRO DE SALUD DE LA
1420 E Plaza Blvd Ste E4, National City (91950-3636)
PHONE..............................619 477-0165
Marie Mulhall, *Principal*
EMP: 57
SALES (corp-wide): 87.1MM **Privately Held**
SIC: 8322 Individual & family services
PA: Centro De Salud De La Comunidad De San Ysidro, Inc.
4004 Beyer Blvd
San Ysidro CA 92173
619 428-4463

(P-23555)
CHILD & FAMILY CENTER
21545 Centre Pointe Pkwy, Santa Clarita (91350-2947)
PHONE..............................661 259-9439
Joan Aschoff, *CEO*
Cindy Palomares, *Partner*
Victor Chavira, *Exec VP*
Bert Paras, *Vice Pres*
Jane Soto, *Exec Dir*
EMP: 120
SQ FT: 26,581
SALES: 10.5MM **Privately Held**
SIC: 8322 8099 8093 8049 Family counseling services; childbirth preparation clinic; mental health clinic, outpatient; clinical psychologist

(P-23556)
CHILD ABUSE LSTENING MEDIATION
Also Called: C A L M
1236 Chapala St, Santa Barbara (93101-3116)
PHONE..............................805 965-2376
Anna M Kokotovic, *Exec Dir*
Mireya Hernandez, *Info Tech Mgr*
Rachel Hopsicker, *Psychologist*
Jessica Adams, *Director*
Scott Whiteley, *Director*
EMP: 50 EST: 1971
SALES: 7MM **Privately Held**
WEB: www.calm4kids.org
SIC: 8322 Crisis intervention center; general counseling services

(P-23557)
CHILD CARE COORDINATING COUNSI
330 Twin Dolphin Dr # 119, Redwood City (94065-1454)
PHONE..............................650 517-1400
Jan Stokley, *Exec Dir*
EMP: 50
SALES: 8.9MM **Privately Held**
WEB: www.thecouncil.net
SIC: 8322 Referral service for personal & social problems

(P-23558)
CHILD CARE RESOURCE CENTER INC (PA)
20001 Prairie St, Chatsworth (91311-6508)
PHONE..............................818 717-1000
Michael Olenick, *CEO*
Casey Quinn, *CFO*
Denise Trinh, *CFO*
Ellen Cervantes, *Vice Pres*
Rick Robertss, *Vice Pres*

EMP: 130 EST: 1976
SALES: 111.3MM **Privately Held**
SIC: **8322** Child related social services

(P-23559)
CHILD CARE RESOURCE CENTER INC
20001 Prairie St, Chatsworth (91311-6508)
PHONE.................................661 255-2474
Michael Olenick, *CEO*
EMP: 500
SALES (corp-wide): 111.3MM **Privately Held**
SIC: **8322** Child related social services
PA: Child Care Resource Center, Inc.
20001 Prairie St
Chatsworth CA 91311
818 717-1000

(P-23560)
CHILD CARE RESOURCE CENTER INC
250 Grand Cypress Ave # 601, Palmdale (93551-3675)
PHONE.................................661 723-3246
Ann Bubont, *Principal*
EMP: 50
SALES (corp-wide): 111.3MM **Privately Held**
SIC: **8322** Child related social services
PA: Child Care Resource Center, Inc.
20001 Prairie St
Chatsworth CA 91311
818 717-1000

(P-23561)
CHILD DEVELOPMENT INSTITUTE
Also Called: CDI
6340 Variel Ave Ste A, Woodland Hills (91367-2514)
PHONE.................................818 888-4559
Joan Samaltese, *Exec Dir*
Peter Bowers, *CFO*
Dana Kalek, *Program Mgr*
Laura Counts, *Comp Spec*
Tessa Graham, *Director*
EMP: 50
SALES: 3.8MM **Privately Held**
WEB: www.childdevelopmentinstitute.org
SIC: **8322** Child related social services

(P-23562)
CHILD DEVELOPMENT RESOURCES OF (PA)
Also Called: C D R
221 Ventura Blvd, Oxnard (93036-0277)
PHONE.................................805 485-7878
Jack Hinojosa, *Associate Dir*
Alex Solis, *Technician*
Alec Hairabedian, *Controller*
Amneh Qaralleh, *Teacher*
Suzanne Godinez, *Manager*
EMP: 200
SQ FT: 67,007
SALES: 36.2MM **Privately Held**
SIC: **8322** Child guidance agency

(P-23563)
CHILD SUPPORT SVCS CAL DEPT (DH)
11120 International Dr, Rancho Cordova (95670-6096)
P.O. Box 419064 (95741-9064)
PHONE.................................916 464-5000
Jan Sturla, *Director*
EMP: 52
SALES (est): 24.3MM **Privately Held**
SIC: **8322** 9441 Individual & family services; administration of social & manpower programs;

(P-23564)
CHILDNET YOUTH & FMLY SVCS INC (PA)
4155 Outer Traffic Cir, Long Beach (90804-2111)
P.O. Box 4550 (90804-0550)
PHONE.................................562 498-5500
Kathy L Hughes, *CEO*
Kathy Hughes, *COO*
Allan Greenberg, *CFO*
Ana Barraza, *Exec Dir*
Shirley Herrera, *Office Mgr*
EMP: 250

SQ FT: 16,073
SALES: 23.8MM **Privately Held**
WEB: www.childnet.net
SIC: **8322** Child related social services

(P-23565)
CHILDRENS ANGELCARE AID INTL
4535 58th St, San Diego (92115-3711)
PHONE.................................619 795-6234
Michael Challgren, *Chairman*
T P Grosser, *President*
Wayne Peimann, *Vice Pres*
EMP: 200
SQ FT: 2,500
SALES: 5.5MM **Privately Held**
SIC: **8322** Individual & family services

(P-23566)
CHILDRENS CRISIS CNTR STANISLS
1244 Fiori Ave, Modesto (95350-5503)
P.O. Box 1062 (95353-1062)
PHONE.................................209 577-4413
Colleen Garcia, *Exec Dir*
Dale Muratore, *CFO*
Brenda McDonald, *Director*
EMP: 100 EST: 1980
SALES: 3.4MM **Privately Held**
SIC: **8322** Social service center; crisis center

(P-23567)
CHILDRENS CUNCIL SAN FRANCISCO (PA)
445 Church St, San Francisco (94114-1720)
PHONE.................................415 343-3378
Sandee Blechman, *Exec Dir*
Jennifer Holderness, *Bd of Directors*
Marlina Chan, *Department Mgr*
Betty Somocurcio-Leon, *Opers Mgr*
Wendy Bear, *Deputy Dir*
EMP: 110
SALES: 85.9MM **Privately Held**
SIC: **8322** 8351 Youth center; child day care services

(P-23568)
CHILDRENS INST LOS ANGELES
679 S New Hampshire Ave, Los Angeles (90005-1355)
PHONE.................................213 383-2765
Mary Emmons, *Branch Mgr*
EMP: 650
SALES (corp-wide): 696.7K **Privately Held**
SIC: **8322** Social service center
PA: Children's Institute Of Los Angeles
2121 W Temple St
Los Angeles CA 90026
213 385-5100

(P-23569)
CHILDRENS INSTITUTE INC (PA)
2121 W Temple St, Los Angeles (90026-4915)
PHONE.................................213 385-5100
Martine Singer, *CEO*
Elvia Ayala, *Partner*
Shahram Aminian, *President*
Julie Young, *Bd of Directors*
Dr Steve Ambrose, *Senior VP*
EMP: 290 EST: 1906
SQ FT: 18,000
SALES: 66.8MM **Privately Held**
SIC: **8322** Child related social services

(P-23570)
CHILDRENS PROTECTIVE SERVICES
5730 Packard Ave, Marysville (95901-7118)
P.O. Box 2320 (95901-0082)
PHONE.................................530 749-6311
EMP: 60
SALES (est): 492.9K **Privately Held**
WEB: www.childrensprotectiveservices.com
SIC: **8322**

(P-23571)
CHILDRENS SERVICES
Also Called: Colusa City Office Education
345 5th St Ste A, Colusa (95932-2445)
PHONE.................................530 458-0300
Rick Perym, *Director*
Theresa Hawk, *Administration*
EMP: 90
SALES (est): 4.1MM **Privately Held**
SIC: **8322** Children's aid society

(P-23572)
CHRISTIAN COUNSELING CENTERS
3880 S Bascom Ave Ste 202, San Jose (95124-2675)
PHONE.................................408 559-1115
Margeret Greig, *Director*
EMP: 56
SALES (corp-wide): 2.4MM **Privately Held**
SIC: **8322** General counseling services
PA: Christian Counseling Centers, Inc
1161 Cherry St Ste P
San Carlos CA 94070
650 570-7273

(P-23573)
CITY & COUNTY OF SAN FRANCISCO
Also Called: Adult Probation Department
850 Bryant St Ste 200, San Francisco (94103-4614)
PHONE.................................415 553-1706
Karen Fletcher, *Branch Mgr*
Dan Mauer, *Exec Dir*
EMP: 150 **Privately Held**
SIC: **8322** 9221 Probation office; ;
PA: City & County Of San Francisco
1 Dr Carlton B Goodlett P
San Francisco CA 94102
415 554-7500

(P-23574)
CITY & COUNTY OF SAN FRANCISCO
Also Called: Sheriff's Dept
375 Woodside Ave 1, San Francisco (94127-1221)
PHONE.................................415 753-7561
Janete Shalwitz, *Branch Mgr*
EMP: 93 **Privately Held**
SIC: **8322** 9441 Child related social services; administration of social & manpower programs
PA: City & County Of San Francisco
1 Dr Carlton B Goodlett P
San Francisco CA 94102
415 554-7500

(P-23575)
CITY IMPACT INC
555 S A St Ste 175, Oxnard (93030-8115)
P.O. Box 5678 (93031-5678)
PHONE.................................805 983-3636
Betty Alvarez Ham, *President*
Pamela Darcy, *Vice Pres*
Tina Quolas, *Bookkeeper*
Elizabeth Mattox, *Program Dir*
Dustin Oltman, *Director*
EMP: 55
SALES: 1MM **Privately Held**
WEB: www.cityimpact.com
SIC: **8322** Family (marriage) counseling

(P-23576)
CITY OF BAKERSFIELD
Rabobank Arena Theater & Conve
1001 Truxtun Ave, Bakersfield (93301-4714)
PHONE.................................661 852-7300
John Dorman, *General Mgr*
Jon Dorman, *General Mgr*
Chris Hartzell, *Technology*
Deslund Grimes, *Opers Mgr*
Sam Williams, *Sales Mgr*
EMP: 110 **Privately Held**
WEB: www.bakersfieldfire.us
SIC: **8322** 9111 6512 Community center; mayors' offices; nonresidential building operators
PA: City Of Bakersfield
1600 Truxtun Ave Fl 5th
Bakersfield CA 93301
661 326-3000

(P-23577)
CITY OF BELL
Also Called: Dept of Community Services
6330 Pine Ave, Bell (90201-1221)
PHONE.................................323 773-1596
Annett Peretz, *Director*
Jose Garcia, *Supervisor*
EMP: 100 **Privately Held**
SIC: **8322** 9111 Community center; mayors' offices
PA: City Of Bell
6330 Pine Ave
Bell CA 90201
323 588-6211

(P-23578)
CITY OF CARSON
Also Called: Carson Community Center
3 Civic Plaza Dr, Carson (90745-2231)
PHONE.................................310 835-0212
Zenora Bellard, *Director*
EMP: 53 **Privately Held**
SIC: **8322** 9111 7299 5812 Community center; mayors' offices; banquet hall facilities; caterers
PA: City Of Carson
701 E Carson St
Carson CA 90745
310 830-7600

(P-23579)
CITY OF IRVINE
Also Called: Lakeview Senior Center
20 Lake Rd, Irvine (92604-4567)
PHONE.................................949 724-6900
Ed Kaleikini, *Superintendent*
EMP: 72 **Privately Held**
SIC: **8322** Senior citizens' center or association
PA: City Of Irvine
1 Civic Center Plz
Irvine CA 92606
949 724-6000

(P-23580)
CITY OF LA HABRA
Also Called: Community Services Department
101 W La Habra Blvd, La Habra (90631-5401)
P.O. Box 337 (90633-0337)
PHONE.................................562 905-9708
Sal Failla, *Director*
EMP: 50 **Privately Held**
SIC: **8322** Community center
PA: City Of La Habra
110 E La Habra Blvd
La Habra CA 90631
562 383-4053

(P-23581)
CITY OF MOORPARK
Also Called: Moorpark Active Adult Center
799 Moorpark Ave, Moorpark (93021-1155)
PHONE.................................805 517-6261
Steven Kueny, *CEO*
EMP: 60 **Privately Held**
SIC: **8322** Senior citizens' center or association
PA: City Of Moorpark
799 Moorpark Ave
Moorpark CA 93021
805 517-6200

(P-23582)
CITY OF OAKLAND
Also Called: Human Services Dept
150 Frank H Ogawa Plz # 3332, Oakland (94612-2021)
PHONE.................................510 238-6796
Andrea Youngdahl, *Director*
EMP: 300 **Privately Held**
WEB: www.cityofbuellton.com
SIC: **8322** 9441 Individual & family services; administration of social & manpower programs
PA: City Of Oakland
150 Frank H Ogawa Plz # 3332
Oakland CA 94612
510 238-3280

(P-23583)
CITY OF ORANGE
230 E Chapman Ave, Orange (92866-1506)
PHONE.................................714 744-7264
Bonnie Hagen, *Director*

P
R
O
D
U
C
T
S

&

S
V
C
S

EMP: 75 **Privately Held**
WEB: www.cityoforange.org
SIC: 8322 9111 Community center; mayors' offices
PA: City Of Orange
300 E Chapman Ave
Orange CA 92866
714 744-5500

(P-23584)
CITY OF OXNARD
Also Called: Senior Services
350 N C St, Oxnard (93030-4646)
PHONE....................805 385-8019
Jocelyn Peterson, *Director*
EMP: 99 **Privately Held**
WEB: www.oxnardtourism.com
SIC: 8322 9111 Senior citizens' center or association; mayors' offices
PA: City Of Oxnard
300 W 3rd St Uppr Fl4
Oxnard CA 93030
805 385-7803

(P-23585)
CITY OF VACAVILLE
1100 Alamo Dr, Vacaville (95687-5606)
PHONE....................707 449-6122
Carry Walker, *Manager*
Kristina McClellin, *Manager*
EMP: 80 **Privately Held**
WEB: www.lenaugustine.com
SIC: 8322 Community center
PA: City Of Vacaville
650 Merchant St
Vacaville CA 95688
707 449-5100

(P-23586)
CITY OF WHITTIER
Also Called: Whittier City Community Svcs
7630 Washington Ave, Whittier (90602-1733)
PHONE....................562 567-9446
Fran Shields, *Director*
EMP: 100 **Privately Held**
WEB: www.whittierpd.org
SIC: 8322 Community center
PA: City Of Whittier
13230 Penn St
Whittier CA 90602
562 567-9999

(P-23587)
CLARE FOUNDATION INC (PA)
909 Pico Blvd, Santa Monica (90405-1326)
PHONE....................310 314-6200
Nicholas Vrataric, *Exec Dir*
William Blatt, *President*
EMP: 75
SQ FT: 1,162
SALES: 7.4MM **Privately Held**
SIC: 8322 Self-help organization

(P-23588)
CLARE FOUNDATION INC
Also Called: Dui Program
1871 9th St, Santa Monica (90404-4501)
PHONE....................310 314-6200
Nicholas Vrataric, *Exec Dir*
EMP: 60
SALES (corp-wide): 7.4MM **Privately Held**
SIC: 8322 Substance abuse counseling
PA: Clare Foundation, Inc.
909 Pico Blvd
Santa Monica CA 90405
310 314-6200

(P-23589)
CLINICA SIERRA VISTA
3727 N 1st St Ste 106, Fresno (93726-5628)
PHONE....................559 457-6900
Stephen W Schilling, *CEO*
Sheila Marsh, *Family Practiti*
EMP: 86
SALES (corp-wide): 136.6MM **Privately Held**
SIC: 8322 Community center
PA: Clinica Sierra Vista
1430 Truxtun Ave Ste 400
Bakersfield CA 93301
661 635-3050

(P-23590)
COACHELLA VLY RESCUE MISSION
Also Called: CVRM
82873 Via Venecia, Indio (92201-6971)
PHONE....................760 347-3512
Floyd Rhoades, *Ch of Bd*
Pete Del Rio, *Vice Chairman*
Joseph Hayes, *Treasurer*
Jim Parrish, *Vice Ch Bd*
Linda Garland, *Executive*
EMP: 50
SQ FT: 43,000
SALES: 7.3MM **Privately Held**
WEB: www.cvrm.org
SIC: 8322 8661 Social service center; non-church religious organizations

(P-23591)
COALITION FOR FAMILY HARMONY
1030 N Ventura Rd, Oxnard (93030-3855)
PHONE....................805 983-6014
Cherie Douval, *President*
Alma Plazola, *Office Admin*
Laura Dunlap, *Admin Asst*
EMP: 75
SQ FT: 20,000
SALES: 2.3MM **Privately Held**
SIC: 8322 Emergency shelters

(P-23592)
COLUSA CNTY SBSTNCE ABUSE SVCS
Also Called: Colusa County Behavioral Hlth
162 E Carson St Ste A, Colusa (95932-2880)
PHONE....................530 458-0520
Terrance Rooney, *Director*
Jack Joiner, *Deputy Dir*
Gerardo S Toribio, *Psychiatry*
EMP: 52
SALES (est): 1.4MM **Privately Held**
SIC: 8322 Substance abuse counseling

(P-23593)
COMMONWEAL
451 Mesa Rd, Bolinas (94924)
P.O. Box 316 (94924-0316)
PHONE....................415 868-0970
Michael Lerner, *President*
Michael Lerner PHD, *President*
Susan Braun, *Director*
Amber Faur, *Manager*
EMP: 58
SQ FT: 10,800
SALES: 4.5MM **Privately Held**
WEB: www.commonweal.org
SIC: 8322 Social service center; refugee service

(P-23594)
COMMUNITY ACCESS NETWORK
2275 S Main St Ste 201, Corona (92882-5303)
PHONE....................951 279-1333
Rafik Philobos, *President*
Karen Shah, *Vice Pres*
Magaly Sevillano, *Admin Sec*
EMP: 60
SQ FT: 10,000
SALES: 5.1MM **Privately Held**
WEB: www.canffa.org
SIC: 8322 8361 Social service center; family counseling services; residential care

(P-23595)
COMMUNITY ACTION PARTNERSHI (PA)
Also Called: Oc Food Bank
11870 Monarch St, Garden Grove (92841-2113)
PHONE....................714 897-6670
Gregory C Scott, *CEO*
Jennifer Obregon, *Finance Mgr*
Caroline Coleman, *Exec Sec*
EMP: 95
SQ FT: 86,300
SALES: 22.2MM **Privately Held**
WEB: www.capoc.org
SIC: 8322 Individual & family services

(P-23596)
COMMUNITY ACTION PARTNERSHIP
3970 Short St, San Luis Obispo (93401-7567)
PHONE....................805 541-4122
EMP: 333
SALES (corp-wide): 57.3MM **Privately Held**
SIC: 8322 Individual & family services
PA: Community Action Partnership Of San Luis Obispo County, Inc.
1030 Southwood Dr
San Luis Obispo CA 93401
805 544-4355

(P-23597)
COMMUNITY ACTION PARTNERSHIP (PA)
1030 Southwood Dr, San Luis Obispo (93401-5813)
PHONE....................805 544-4355
Anita Robinson, *Ch of Bd*
Frances I Coughlin, *President*
Joan Limov, *CFO*
Rob Garcia, *Treasurer*
Missey Hobson, *Corp Secy*
EMP: 72
SQ FT: 20,000
SALES: 57.3MM **Privately Held**
SIC: 8322 Child related social services

(P-23598)
COMMUNITY ACTION PARTNR KERN
217 W Kern Ave, Mc Farland (93250-1360)
PHONE....................661 792-1066
EMP: 66
SALES (corp-wide): 63.1MM **Privately Held**
SIC: 8322 Individual & family services
PA: Community Action Partnership Of Kern
5005 Business Park N
Bakersfield CA 93309
661 336-5236

(P-23599)
COMMUNITY ACTION PARTNR KERN (PA)
5005 Business Park N, Bakersfield (93309-1651)
PHONE....................661 336-5236
Jeremy Tobias, *Exec Dir*
Pam Pritchard, *Officer*
Glen Ephrom, *Program Mgr*
Lois Hannible, *Program Mgr*
Angelica Nelson, *Program Mgr*
EMP: 50
SQ FT: 14,500
SALES: 63.1MM **Privately Held**
WEB: www.capk.org
SIC: 8322 Social service center; senior citizens' center or association; child guidance agency; public welfare center

(P-23600)
COMMUNITY BRIDGES
Also Called: Golden Age Nutrition Program
114 E 5th St, Watsonville (95076-4309)
PHONE....................831 724-2024
Valerie Rivera, *Principal*
EMP: 104
SALES (corp-wide): 14.4MM **Privately Held**
WEB: www.cbridges.org
SIC: 8322 Senior citizens' center or association
PA: Community Bridges
519 Main St
Watsonville CA 95076
831 688-8840

(P-23601)
COMMUNITY CARE ADHC INC
Also Called: Consultants For Adhc
9917 Las Tunas Dr, Temple City (91780-2211)
PHONE....................626 614-8999
Behrooz Sumekh, *President*
EMP: 60 **EST:** 2001
SALES (est): 2.2MM **Privately Held**
SIC: 8322 Adult day care center

(P-23602)
COMMUNITY CARE MANAGEMENT CORP (PA)
Also Called: MULTIPURPOSE SENIOR SERVICES P
301 S State St, Ukiah (95482-4906)
PHONE....................707 468-9347
Rachel Robison, *Exec Dir*
EMP: 50
SQ FT: 5,000
SALES: 3MM **Privately Held**
WEB: www.communitycare707.com
SIC: 8322 Social service center

(P-23603)
COMMUNITY GATEPATH
Also Called: IMPACT BUSINESS SERVICE
350 Twin Dolphin Dr # 123, Redwood City (94065-1457)
PHONE....................650 259-8500
Sheryl Young, *CEO*
EMP: 120
SQ FT: 25,000
SALES: 13.6MM **Privately Held**
WEB: www.communitygatepath.com
SIC: 8322 Social services for the handicapped

(P-23604)
COMMUNITY HEALTH CTRS CNTRL (PA)
2050 S Blosser Rd, Santa Maria (93458-7310)
PHONE....................805 346-3900
Ronald E Castle, *CEO*
Gail Tutino, *Technology*
Satish Raj, *Med Doctor*
Maria Jauregui-Garcia, *Director*
Kathleen Macmahon, *Director*
EMP: 54
SALES: 91MM **Privately Held**
SIC: 8322 Community center

(P-23605)
COMMUNITY HOUSING OPTIONS
Also Called: CHOICESS
348 E Foothill Blvd, Arcadia (91006-2542)
PHONE....................626 359-3300
Joseph Donofrio, *Director*
Lydia Del Rio, *Office Mgr*
EMP: 100
SQ FT: 850
SALES: 1.9MM **Privately Held**
WEB: www.choicess.com
SIC: 8322 Social services for the handicapped

(P-23606)
COMMUNITY HUMAN SERVICES (PA)
2560 Garden Rd Ste 201b, Monterey (93940-5338)
P.O. Box 3076 (93942-3076)
PHONE....................831 658-3811
Robin McCrae, *Exec Dir*
EMP: 120
SALES: 4.5MM **Privately Held**
WEB: www.chservices.org
SIC: 8322 Social service center; old age assistance

(P-23607)
COMMUNITY INTEGRATED WORK PROG
Also Called: Community Intgrted Work Prgram
1875 Whipple Rd, Hayward (94544-7834)
PHONE....................510 487-9768
Cathi Vaughns, *Manager*
EMP: 50
SALES (corp-wide): 52.2MM **Privately Held**
SIC: 8322 Individual & family services
PA: Community Integrated Work Program, Inc.
2219 Buchanan Rd Ste 3
Antioch CA 94509
925 776-1040

(P-23608)
COMMUNITY INTERFACE SERVICES
2621 Roosevelt St Ste 100, Carlsbad
(92008-1660)
PHONE...................................760 729-3866
Rose M Hanson, *President*
Rojane Lindkvist, *Treasurer*
Shawn Lloyd, *Technical Staff*
Pamela Oakes, *Director*
Christine Sheppard, *Director*
EMP: 100
SALES: 9.3MM **Privately Held**
WEB: www.communityinterfaceservices.org
SIC: 8322 Individual & family services

(P-23609)
COMMUNITY SUPPORT OPTIONS INC
1401 Poso Dr, Wasco (93280-2584)
P.O. Box 8018 (93280-8108)
PHONE...................................661 758-5331
John Stockton, *CEO*
Anna Poggi, *President*
Ben Goosen, *Treasurer*
Jose Hernandez, *Vice Pres*
Violet Ratzlass, *Admin Sec*
EMP: 102
SQ FT: 9,000
SALES: 5.9MM **Privately Held**
SIC: 8322 Association for the handicapped

(P-23610)
COMMUNITY SLNS FOR CHLDRN FMLS (PA)
9015 Murray Ave Ste 100, Gilroy
(95020-3617)
P.O. Box 546, Morgan Hill (95038-0546)
PHONE...................................408 779-2113
Erin O'Brien, *CEO*
Lynn Magruder, *Administration*
Susan Peng, *Controller*
Anita Wilson, *Director*
Priscilla Chavez, *Case Mgr*
EMP: 185
SALES: 19.4MM **Privately Held**
SIC: 8322 Social service center; family counseling services

(P-23611)
COMPASS FAMILY SERVICES
Also Called: Compass Connecting Point
37 Grove St, San Francisco (94102-4702)
PHONE...................................415 644-0504
Erica Kisch, *Principal*
Kay Manansala, *Executive Asst*
Kevin Pelaez, *Producer*
Antonio Zamora, *Marketing Staff*
Linda Scales, *Rector*
EMP: 109
SALES: 10.7MM **Privately Held**
SIC: 8322 Individual & family services

(P-23612)
COMPASS FAMILY SERVICES
626 Polk St, San Francisco (94102-3328)
PHONE...................................415 644-0504
Erica Kisch, *Exec Dir*
EMP: 87
SALES: 10.7MM **Privately Held**
SIC: 8322 Family (marriage) counseling

(P-23613)
COMPASS FAMILY SERVICES
Also Called: COMPASS CLARA HOUSE
111 Page St, San Francisco (94102-5892)
PHONE...................................415 644-0504
Erica Kisch, *Exec Dir*
EMP: 87
SALES: 10.7MM **Privately Held**
SIC: 8322 Individual & family services

(P-23614)
COMPREHENSIVE YOUTH SER
Also Called: C Y S
4545 N West Ave Ste 101, Fresno
(93705-0946)
PHONE...................................559 229-3561
Captain Mike Reid, *President*
Sylvia Kim, *Treasurer*
Kevin Torosian, *Vice Pres*
Sheryl Noel, *Admin Sec*
Jim Pryce, *Opers Spvr*
EMP: 90
SQ FT: 9,000

SALES: 4.7MM **Privately Held**
WEB: www.cys.com
SIC: 8322 Child related social services

(P-23615)
CONCERTO HEALTHCARE INC (PA)
85 Enterprise Ste 200, Aliso Viejo
(92656-2614)
PHONE...................................949 537-3400
Alec Cunningham, *CEO*
Chrissie Cooper, *COO*
Dawn Gilbert, *CFO*
Norris Vivatrat, *Chief Mktg Ofcr*
Julie M Webb-Hopkins, *Officer*
EMP: 118 **EST:** 2004
SALES (est): 25.3MM **Privately Held**
SIC: 8322 Adult day care center

(P-23616)
CONSULTNTS IN EDCTL PER SKILLS (PA)
Also Called: Ceps
5825 Auburn Blvd Ste 1, Sacramento
(95841-2977)
P.O. Box 417010 (95841-7010)
PHONE...................................916 348-1890
Patricia Vollenweider, *Exec Dir*
EMP: 56 **EST:** 1995
SALES: 1.4MM **Privately Held**
SIC: 8322 General counseling services

(P-23617)
CORNELL CORRECTIONS CAL INC (DH)
1811 Knoll Dr, Ventura (93003-7321)
PHONE...................................805 644-8700
David M Cornell, *Ch of Bd*
Tom Jenkens, *President*
Steven W Logan, *President*
Brian E Bergeron, *CFO*
Marvin H Wiebe, *Senior VP*
EMP: 255
SQ FT: 4,100
SALES (est): 5.8MM
SALES (corp-wide): 2.2B **Privately Held**
SIC: 8322 Rehabilitation services

(P-23618)
CORRECTONS RHBLTATION CAL DEPT
Also Called: Parole Unit Office
930 3rd St Ste 100, Eureka (95501-0554)
PHONE...................................707 445-6520
Ray Hilburn, *Manager*
Purvis Alexander, *Manager*
EMP: 73 **Privately Held**
SIC: 8322 Parole office; offender self-help agency
HQ: California Department Of Corrections & Rehabilitation
1515 S St
Sacramento CA 95811
-

(P-23619)
CORRECTONS RHBLTATION CAL DEPT
Also Called: San Bernardino Parole Unit 14
303 W 5th St, San Bernardino
(92401-1306)
PHONE...................................909 806-3516
Michael Passmore, *Administration*
EMP: 60 **Privately Held**
SIC: 8322 9223 Parole office; offender self-help agency; correctional institutions;
HQ: California Department Of Corrections & Rehabilitation
1515 S St
Sacramento CA 95811

(P-23620)
COUNCIL ON AGING - S CALI INC
2 Executive Cir Ste 175, Irvine
(92614-6773)
PHONE...................................714 479-0107
Lisa Wright Jenkins, *CEO*
Joanne Buenaventura, *General Mgr*
Sara Yu, *Manager*
EMP: 83
SALES: 4.4MM **Privately Held**
SIC: 8322 Senior citizens' center or associ-

(P-23621)
COUNCIL ON AGING SVCS FOR SRS (PA)
30 Kawana Springs Rd, Santa Rosa
(95404-6309)
PHONE...................................707 525-0143
Shirlee Zane, *Exec Dir*
Mare O'Cannel, *CFO*
Michael Randall, *Treasurer*
Zachary Carroll, *Director*
EMP: 103
SQ FT: 6,500
SALES: 4.3MM **Privately Held**
WEB: www.councilonaging.com
SIC: 8322 Senior citizens' center or association; adult day care center; meal delivery program; social service center

(P-23622)
COUNTRY VILLA RANCHO
39950 Vista Del Sol, Rancho Mirage
(92270-3206)
PHONE...................................760 340-0053
Scott Gillis, *Administration*
EMP: 200
SALES (est): 11.4MM **Privately Held**
SIC: 8322 Rehabilitation services

(P-23623)
COUNTRY VILLA SERVICE CORP
3000 N Gate Rd, Seal Beach (90740-2535)
PHONE...................................562 598-2477
Jennifer Rose, *Branch Mgr*
Maria Cody, *Office Mgr*
Rose Posadas, *Nursing Dir*
EMP: 82
SALES (corp-wide): 125.3MM **Privately Held**
SIC: 8322 8011 Rehabilitation services; medical centers
PA: Country Villa Service Corp.
2400 E Katella Ave # 800
Anaheim CA 92806
310 574-3733

(P-23624)
COUNTRY VILLA SERVICE CORP
Also Called: Cntry Vlla Merced Hlthcre Cntr
510 W 26th St, Merced (95340-2804)
PHONE...................................209 723-2911
Joel Saltzburg, *CEO*
EMP: 82
SALES (corp-wide): 125.3MM **Privately Held**
SIC: 8322 8051 Rehabilitation services; skilled nursing care facilities
PA: Country Villa Service Corp.
2400 E Katella Ave # 800
Anaheim CA 92806
310 574-3733

(P-23625)
COUNTY MONTEREY SOCIAL SVCS
Also Called: County of Monterey Social Svcs
1281 Broadway Ave, Seaside
(93955-4925)
PHONE...................................831 899-8001
Loma Livernois, *Manager*
EMP: 65
SALES (est): 1.4MM **Privately Held**
SIC: 8322 Social service center

(P-23626)
COUNTY OF BUTTE
Also Called: Butte County Probation
42 County Center Dr, Oroville
(95965-3335)
PHONE...................................530 538-7661
John Wardell, *Chief*
Patrick Boatman, *Officer*
Rob Freitas, *Info Tech Mgr*
EMP: 130 **Privately Held**
WEB: www.bcihsspa.org
SIC: 8322 Probation office
PA: County Of Butte
25 County Center Dr # 125
Oroville CA 95965
530 538-7701

(P-23627)
COUNTY OF BUTTE
25 County Center Dr Ste 110, Oroville
(95965-3316)
PHONE...................................530 538-7721

EMP: 300 **Privately Held**
SIC: 8322 Probation office
PA: County Of Butte
25 County Center Dr # 125
Oroville CA 95965
530 538-7701

(P-23628)
COUNTY OF BUTTE
5910 Clark Rd Ste W, Paradise
(95969-4860)
PHONE...................................530 872-6328
Mac McAll, *Manager*
EMP: 300 **Privately Held**
WEB: www.bcihsspa.org
SIC: 8322 Children's aid society
PA: County Of Butte
25 County Center Dr # 125
Oroville CA 95965
530 538-7701

(P-23629)
COUNTY OF BUTTE
Also Called: Welfare Administration
202 Mira Loma Dr, Oroville (95965-3500)
P.O. Box 1649 (95965-1649)
PHONE...................................530 538-7572
Cathy Grams, *Director*
EMP: 570 **Privately Held**
WEB: www.bcihsspa.org
SIC: 8322 9111 Individual & family services; county supervisors' & executives' offices
PA: County Of Butte
25 County Center Dr # 125
Oroville CA 95965
530 538-7701

(P-23630)
COUNTY OF BUTTE
Also Called: Welfare Dept Warehouse
205 Mira Loma Dr, Oroville (95965-3582)
P.O. Box 1649 (95965-1649)
PHONE...................................530 538-6802
Art Howe, *Superintendent*
Rosalie Sanz, *Program Mgr*
EMP: 500 **Privately Held**
WEB: www.bcihsspa.org
SIC: 8322 9111 Individual & family services; county supervisors' & executives' offices
PA: County Of Butte
25 County Center Dr # 125
Oroville CA 95965
530 538-7701

(P-23631)
COUNTY OF BUTTE
Also Called: Butte County Employment Center
78 Table Mountain Blvd, Oroville
(95965-3578)
P.O. Box 1649 (95965-1649)
PHONE...................................530 538-7711
Cathy Grams, *Branch Mgr*
EMP: 570 **Privately Held**
WEB: www.bcihsspa.org
SIC: 8322 9111 Public welfare center; county supervisors' & executives' offices
PA: County Of Butte
25 County Center Dr # 125
Oroville CA 95965
530 538-7701

(P-23632)
COUNTY OF CALAVERAS
Also Called: Road Dept
891 Mountain Ranch Rd, San Andreas
(95249-9713)
PHONE...................................209 754-6402
Rob Houghton, *Director*
EMP: 80 **Privately Held**
WEB: www.ccsolidwaste.org
SIC: 8322 Public welfare center
PA: County Of Calaveras
891 Mountain Ranch Rd
San Andreas CA 95249
209 754-6303

(P-23633)
COUNTY OF CONTRA COSTA
50 Douglas Dr Ste 200, Martinez
(94553-8500)
PHONE...................................925 313-4000
Lionel Chatman, *Chief*
EMP: 150 **Privately Held**

SIC: 8322 9441 Probation office; parole office; administration of social & manpower programs
PA: County Of Contra Costa
625 Court St Ste 100
Martinez CA 94553
925 957-5280

(P-23634)
COUNTY OF CONTRA COSTA
Also Called: Child Support Svcs
50 Douglas Dr Ste 100, Martinez
(94553-8500)
PHONE..............................866 901-3212
Linda Dippel, *Director*
EMP: 200 Privately Held
SIC: 8322 9441 Individual & family services;
PA: County Of Contra Costa
625 Court St Ste 100
Martinez CA 94553
925 957-5280

(P-23635)
COUNTY OF CONTRA COSTA
Also Called: Employment & Human Services
40 Douglas Dr, Martinez (94553-4068)
PHONE..............................925 313-1500
Danna Fabella, *Director*
EMP: 200 Privately Held
SIC: 8322 9441 Individual & family services; administration of social & manpower programs;
PA: County Of Contra Costa
625 Court St Ste 100
Martinez CA 94553
925 957-5280

(P-23636)
COUNTY OF EL DORADO
Also Called: Edc Probation
3974 Durock Rd Ste 205, Shingle Springs
(95682-8568)
PHONE..............................530 621-5625
Joseph Warchol, *Chief*
Stephanie Clark, *Officer*
Christina Nygard, *Technician*
EMP: 109 Privately Held
WEB: www.filmtahoe.com
SIC: 8322 Probation office
PA: County Of El Dorado
330 Fair Ln
Placerville CA 95667
530 621-5830

(P-23637)
COUNTY OF EL DORADO
Also Called: Department of Social Services
3057 Briw Rd Ste A, Placerville
(95667-5335)
PHONE..............................530 642-7130
Glen Helland, *Director*
EMP: 85 Privately Held
WEB: www.filmtahoe.com
SIC: 8322 9111 Individual & family services; executive offices
PA: County Of El Dorado
330 Fair Ln
Placerville CA 95667
530 621-5830

(P-23638)
COUNTY OF FRESNO
Also Called: Probation Department
2212 N Winery Ave Ste 122, Fresno
(93703-2896)
PHONE..............................559 600-3800
Rick Chavez, *Manager*
EMP: 59 Privately Held
SIC: 8322 9441 Probation office;
PA: County Of Fresno
2420 Mariposa St
Fresno CA 93721
559 600-1710

(P-23639)
COUNTY OF FRESNO
Also Called: Probation Department
333 W Pontiac Way, Clovis (93612-5613)
P.O. Box 453, Fresno (93709-0453)
PHONE..............................559 600-5127
Rick Chavez, *Manager*
Daniel Moore, *Info Tech Mgr*
EMP: 100 Privately Held
WEB: www.first5fresno.org
SIC: 8322 9441 Probation office;

(P-23640)
COUNTY OF FRESNO
Probation Department
3333 E American Ave Ste B, Fresno
(93725-9248)
PHONE..............................559 600-3996
Rick Chavez, *Manager*
EMP: 130 Privately Held
WEB: www.first5fresno.org
SIC: 8322 9441 Probation office; administration of social & manpower programs;
PA: County Of Fresno
2420 Mariposa St
Fresno CA 93721
559 600-1710

(P-23641)
COUNTY OF FRESNO
P.O. Box 352 (93708-0352)
PHONE..............................559 488-3275
EMP: 168 Privately Held
SIC: 8322 9199 Probation office;
PA: County Of Fresno
2420 Mariposa St
Fresno CA 93721
559 600-1710

(P-23642)
COUNTY OF GLENN
525 W Sycamore St Ste A1, Willows
(95988-2748)
P.O. Box 366 (95988-0366)
PHONE..............................530 934-6453
Robert Chittenden, *Branch Mgr*
Linda Durrer, *Persnl Dir*
Dwight Foltz, *Supervisor*
EMP: 97 Privately Held
SIC: 8322 Social service center
PA: County Of Glenn
516 W Sycamore St Fl 2
Willows CA 95988
530 934-6410

(P-23643)
COUNTY OF GLENN
Also Called: Glenn County Humn Resorce Agcy
420 E Laurel St, Willows (95988-3115)
P.O. Box 611 (95988-0611)
PHONE..............................530 934-6514
Kim Gaghagen, *Principal*
David Allee, *Program Mgr*
EMP: 250 Privately Held
WEB: www.countyofglen.net
SIC: 8322 9111 Individual & family services; county supervisors' & executives' offices
PA: County Of Glenn
516 W Sycamore St Fl 2
Willows CA 95988
530 934-6410

(P-23644)
COUNTY OF HUMBOLDT
Also Called: Dept of Social Services
929 Koster St, Eureka (95501-0106)
PHONE..............................707 445-6180
John Frank, *Branch Mgr*
EMP: 300 Privately Held
SIC: 8322 9441 Social service center; administration of social & manpower programs;
PA: County Of Humboldt
825 5th St
Eureka CA 95501
707 268-2543

(P-23645)
COUNTY OF IMPERIAL
Also Called: Imperial County Probation Off
324 Applestille Rd, El Centro (92243-9661)
PHONE..............................760 336-3581
Micheal Kelly, *Director*
Benny Benavidez, *General Mgr*
Gloria Brambila, *General Mgr*
Debbie Angulo, *Business Mgr*
EMP: 150 Privately Held
WEB: www.imperialcounty.net
SIC: 8322 9111 Individual & family services; county supervisors' & executives' offices

PA: County Of Imperial
940 W Main St Ste 208
El Centro CA 92243
760 482-4556

(P-23646)
COUNTY OF KERN
Also Called: Probation Dept-Juvenile
2005 Ridge Rd, Bakersfield (93305-4123)
P.O. Box 3309 (93385-3309)
PHONE..............................661 868-4100
John R Roberts, *Chief*
EMP: 600 Privately Held
WEB: www.kccfc.org
SIC: 8322 9111 Probation office; county supervisors' & executives' offices;
PA: County Of Kern
1115 Truxtun Ave Rm 505
Bakersfield CA 93301
661 868-3690

(P-23647)
COUNTY OF KERN
Also Called: Aging & Adult Services
2014 Calloway Dr, Bakersfield
(93312-2729)
PHONE..............................661 392-2010
Grace Bradbury, *Manager*
EMP: 61 Privately Held
WEB: www.kccfc.org
SIC: 8322 9441 Community center; administration of social & manpower programs;
PA: County Of Kern
1115 Truxtun Ave Rm 505
Bakersfield CA 93301
661 868-3690

(P-23648)
COUNTY OF KERN
2001 28th St Ste C, Bakersfield
(93301-1924)
PHONE..............................661 336-6800
Lewis Verna, *Exec Dir*
EMP: 61 Privately Held
SIC: 8322 Probation office
PA: County Of Kern
1115 Truxtun Ave Rm 505
Bakersfield CA 93301
661 868-3690

(P-23649)
COUNTY OF KERN
Also Called: Aging & Adult Services
5357 Truxtun Ave, Taft (93268)
PHONE..............................661 763-1535
Connie Redfield, *Director*
EMP: 61 Privately Held
WEB: www.kccfc.org
SIC: 8322 9441 Senior citizens' center or association; administration of social & manpower programs;
PA: County Of Kern
1115 Truxtun Ave Rm 505
Bakersfield CA 93301
661 868-3690

(P-23650)
COUNTY OF KERN
Also Called: Human Services Dept
1816 Cecil Ave, Delano (93215-1520)
P.O. Box 339 (93216-0339)
PHONE..............................661 721-5134
Donalda Salsbery, *Director*
EMP: 60 Privately Held
WEB: www.kccfc.org
SIC: 8322 9441 Public welfare center; administration of social & manpower programs;
PA: County Of Kern
1115 Truxtun Ave Rm 505
Bakersfield CA 93301
661 868-3690

(P-23651)
COUNTY OF KERN
Also Called: Aging & Adult Services
6601 Niles Senior St, Bakersfield (93306)
PHONE..............................661 363-8910
Lavita Greenly, *Branch Mgr*
EMP: 61 Privately Held
WEB: www.kccfc.org
SIC: 8322 9441 Senior citizens' center or association; administration of social & manpower programs;

PA: County Of Kern
1115 Truxtun Ave Rm 505
Bakersfield CA 93301
661 868-3690

(P-23652)
COUNTY OF KINGS
Also Called: Kings County Probation Dept.
1424 Forum Dr, Hanford (93230-5900)
PHONE..............................559 852-4316
Dorothy Van Den Berg, *Chief*
Art Perez, *Purch Agent*
Angela Amith, *Exec Sec*
Jeff Taber, *Director*
EMP: 160 Privately Held
WEB: www.countyofkings.com
SIC: 8322 Probation office
PA: County Of Kings
1400 W Lacey Blvd
Hanford CA 93230
559 582-0326

(P-23653)
COUNTY OF LOS ANGELES
Also Called: Probation Department
300 E Walnut St Dept 200, Pasadena
(91101-1584)
PHONE..............................626 356-5281
Diana Cunningham, *Principal*
EMP: 135 Privately Held
WEB: www.co.la.ca.us
SIC: 8322 9199 Probation office;
PA: County Of Los Angeles
500 W Temple St Ste 437
Los Angeles CA 90012
213 974-1101

(P-23654)
COUNTY OF LOS ANGELES
Also Called: County Probation
11234 Valley Blvd Ste 103, El Monte
(91731-3239)
PHONE..............................626 575-4059
Kwadwo Akosah, *Principal*
EMP: 140 Privately Held
SIC: 8322 Probation office
PA: County Of Los Angeles
500 W Temple St Ste 437
Los Angeles CA 90012
213 974-1101

(P-23655)
COUNTY OF LOS ANGELES
Also Called: Probation Department
5300 W Avenue I, Lancaster (93536-8312)
PHONE..............................661 940-4181
Willie Doyle, *Director*
EMP: 300 Privately Held
WEB: www.co.la.ca.us
SIC: 8322 9223 Probation office; correctional institutions;
PA: County Of Los Angeles
500 W Temple St Ste 437
Los Angeles CA 90012
213 974-1101

(P-23656)
COUNTY OF LOS ANGELES
7601 Imperial Hwy, Downey (90242-3456)
PHONE..............................562 401-9413
Lily Atalla, *Branch Mgr*
Eric Werner, *Manager*
EMP: 137 Privately Held
SIC: 8322 Individual & family services
PA: County Of Los Angeles
500 W Temple St Ste 437
Los Angeles CA 90012
213 974-1101

(P-23657)
COUNTY OF LOS ANGELES
Also Called: Child Support Services
5770 S Eastern Ave Fl 4th, Commerce
(90040-2948)
PHONE..............................323 889-3405
Steven Golightly, *Manager*
EMP: 300 Privately Held
WEB: www.co.la.ca.us
SIC: 8322 9441 Child related social services; administration of social & manpower programs;
PA: County Of Los Angeles
500 W Temple St Ste 437
Los Angeles CA 90012
213 974-1101

(P-23658)
COUNTY OF LOS ANGELES
Also Called: Social Services, Dept of
349 E Avenue K6 Ste B, Lancaster
(93535-4546)
PHONE.................................661 723-4051
Joyce Ward, *Principal*
EMP: 175 **Privately Held**
WEB: www.co.la.ca.us
SIC: 8322 9441 Administration of social &
manpower programs; parole office
PA: County Of Los Angeles
500 W Temple St Ste 437
Los Angeles CA 90012
213 974-1101

(P-23659)
COUNTY OF LOS ANGELES
Also Called: Children & Family Svcs Dept
10355 Slusher Dr, Santa Fe Springs
(90670-7353)
PHONE.................................562 903-5000
Barbara Betlem, *Director*
EMP: 350 **Privately Held**
WEB: www.co.la.ca.us
SIC: 8322 9441 Child related social serv-
ices;
PA: County Of Los Angeles
500 W Temple St Ste 437
Los Angeles CA 90012
213 974-1101

(P-23660)
COUNTY OF LOS ANGELES
Also Called: Dept Children and Family Svcs
4060 Watson Plaza Dr, Lakewood
(90712-4033)
PHONE.................................562 497-3500
Joy Russell, *Administration*
EMP: 500 **Privately Held**
WEB: www.co.la.ca.us
SIC: 8322 9111 Children's aid society; ex-
ecutive offices
PA: County Of Los Angeles
500 W Temple St Ste 437
Los Angeles CA 90012
213 974-1101

(P-23661)
COUNTY OF LOS ANGELES
1000 Corp Ctr Dr Ste 200b, Monterey Park
(91754)
PHONE.................................323 265-1804
Renee Watkinson, *Branch Mgr*
EMP: 137 **Privately Held**
SIC: 8322 Individual & family services
PA: County Of Los Angeles
500 W Temple St Ste 437
Los Angeles CA 90012
213 974-1101

(P-23662)
COUNTY OF LOS ANGELES
Also Called: Community & Senior Svcs
777 W Jackman St, Lancaster
(93534-2419)
PHONE.................................661 948-2320
Nusun Muhamad, *Manager*
EMP: 135 **Privately Held**
WEB: www.co.la.ca.us
SIC: 8322 9441 Senior citizens' center or
association; administration of social &
manpower programs;
PA: County Of Los Angeles
500 W Temple St Ste 437
Los Angeles CA 90012
213 974-1101

(P-23663)
COUNTY OF LOS ANGELES
210 W Temple St Fl 18, Los Angeles
(90012-3229)
PHONE.................................818 374-2161
EMP: 140 **Privately Held**
SIC: 8322 Probation office
PA: County Of Los Angeles
500 W Temple St Ste 437
Los Angeles CA 90012
213 974-1101

(P-23664)
COUNTY OF LOS ANGELES
Also Called: Probation Dept
320 W Temple St Ste 1101, Los Angeles
(90012-3289)
PHONE.................................213 974-9331

Mike Verilla, *Director*
EMP: 170 **Privately Held**
WEB: www.co.la.ca.us
SIC: 8322 9223 8093 Probation office;
correctional institutions; ; mental health
clinic, outpatient
PA: County Of Los Angeles
500 W Temple St Ste 437
Los Angeles CA 90012
213 974-1101

(P-23665)
COUNTY OF LOS ANGELES
Also Called: La County Probation
8240 Broadway Ave, Whittier (90606-3120)
PHONE.................................562 908-3119
Donna Rose, *Manager*
EMP: 102 **Privately Held**
WEB: www.co.la.ca.us
SIC: 8322 9111 Probation office; county
supervisors' & executives' offices
PA: County Of Los Angeles
500 W Temple St Ste 437
Los Angeles CA 90012
213 974-1101

(P-23666)
COUNTY OF LOS ANGELES
Also Called: Florence Office
1740 E Gage Ave, Los Angeles
(90001-1814)
PHONE.................................323 586-7263
Olga Miranda, *Director*
EMP: 255 **Privately Held**
WEB: www.co.la.ca.us
SIC: 8322 9441 Aid to families with de-
pendent children (AFDC); administration
of social & manpower programs;
PA: County Of Los Angeles
500 W Temple St Ste 437
Los Angeles CA 90012
213 974-1101

(P-23667)
COUNTY OF LOS ANGELES
Also Called: Probation Department
1601 Eastlake Ave, Los Angeles
(90033-1009)
PHONE.................................323 226-8511
Taula Heath, *Director*
EMP: 135 **Privately Held**
WEB: www.co.la.ca.us
SIC: 8322 Probation office; parole office
PA: County Of Los Angeles
500 W Temple St Ste 437
Los Angeles CA 90012
213 974-1101

(P-23668)
COUNTY OF LOS ANGELES
Also Called: Children & Family Svcs Dept
425 Shatto Pl, Los Angeles (90020-1712)
PHONE.................................213 351-5600
Jackie Contreras, *Director*
EMP: 100 **Privately Held**
WEB: www.co.la.ca.us
SIC: 8322 9441 Child related social serv-
ices; administration of social & manpower
programs;
PA: County Of Los Angeles
500 W Temple St Ste 437
Los Angeles CA 90012
213 974-1101

(P-23669)
COUNTY OF LOS ANGELES
5445 Whittier Blvd Fl 400, Los Angeles
(90022-4125)
PHONE.................................323 727-1639
Minhha Ngyuen, *Branch Mgr*
EMP: 140 **Privately Held**
SIC: 8322 Senior citizens' center or associ-
ation
PA: County Of Los Angeles
500 W Temple St Ste 437
Los Angeles CA 90012
213 974-1101

(P-23670)
COUNTY OF LOS ANGELES
Also Called: Department of Social Services
530 12th St Fl 1, Paso Robles
(93446-2201)
PHONE.................................805 237-3110
Michelle Chambers, *Manager*
EMP: 140 **Privately Held**

SIC: 8322 Social service center
PA: County Of Los Angeles
500 W Temple St Ste 437
Los Angeles CA 90012
213 974-1101

(P-23671)
COUNTY OF LOS ANGELES
Also Called: Public Social Services
2707 S Grand Ave, Los Angeles
(90007-3300)
PHONE.................................213 744-5601
Petra Gonzalez, *Director*
EMP: 430 **Privately Held**
WEB: www.co.la.ca.us
SIC: 8322 9441 Individual & family serv-
ices; administration of social & manpower
programs;
PA: County Of Los Angeles
500 W Temple St Ste 437
Los Angeles CA 90012
213 974-1101

(P-23672)
COUNTY OF LOS ANGELES
Also Called: San Fernando Valley Interfaith
14555 Osborne St Ofc, Van Nuys
(91402-1821)
PHONE.................................818 362-6437
Estella Lyons, *Chairman*
EMP: 135 **Privately Held**
WEB: www.co.la.ca.us
SIC: 8322 9441 Geriatric social service;
administration of social & manpower pro-
grams;
PA: County Of Los Angeles
500 W Temple St Ste 437
Los Angeles CA 90012
213 974-1101

(P-23673)
COUNTY OF LOS ANGELES
Also Called: Health Services, Dept of
17171 Gale Ave, City of Industry
(91745-1822)
PHONE.................................626 854-4987
Althea Shirley, *Director*
EMP: 200 **Privately Held**
WEB: www.co.la.ca.us
SIC: 8322 9431 Public welfare center; ad-
ministration of public health programs;
PA: County Of Los Angeles
500 W Temple St Ste 437
Los Angeles CA 90012
213 974-1101

(P-23674)
COUNTY OF LOS ANGELES
Also Called: County Los Angles Prbtion Dept
1660 W Mission Blvd, Pomona
(91766-1200)
PHONE.................................909 469-4500
Lorraine Hubbard-Johns, *Manager*
EMP: 100 **Privately Held**
WEB: www.co.la.ca.us
SIC: 8322 9223 Probation office; correc-
tional institutions;
PA: County Of Los Angeles
500 W Temple St Ste 437
Los Angeles CA 90012
213 974-1101

(P-23675)
COUNTY OF LOS ANGELES
Also Called: Probation Dept
1725 Main St Rm 125, Santa Monica
(90401-3267)
PHONE.................................310 266-3711
Ernest P Gonzalez, *Branch Mgr*
Curtis McClendon, *Exec Dir*
Glenda Dunn, *Sales Executive*
EMP: 65 **Privately Held**
WEB: www.co.la.ca.us
SIC: 8322 9223 Probation office; correc-
tional institutions;
PA: County Of Los Angeles
500 W Temple St Ste 437
Los Angeles CA 90012
213 974-1101

(P-23676)
COUNTY OF LOS ANGELES
Also Called: Probation Dept
14414 Delano St, Van Nuys (91401-2703)
PHONE.................................818 374-2000
Ed Johnson, *Director*

EMP: 100 **Privately Held**
WEB: www.co.la.ca.us
SIC: 8322 9223 Probation office; correc-
tional institutions;
PA: County Of Los Angeles
500 W Temple St Ste 437
Los Angeles CA 90012
213 974-1101

(P-23677)
COUNTY OF LOS ANGELES
Also Called: Mental Health Dept of
330 E Live Oak Ave, Arcadia (91006-5617)
PHONE.................................626 821-5858
Len Tower, *Director*
EMP: 50 **Privately Held**
WEB: www.co.la.ca.us
SIC: 8322 9431 Crisis center; mental
health agency administration, govern-
ment;
PA: County Of Los Angeles
500 W Temple St Ste 437
Los Angeles CA 90012
213 974-1101

(P-23678)
COUNTY OF LOS ANGELES
Also Called: Probation Dept
4849 Civic Center Way, Los Angeles
(90022-1679)
PHONE.................................323 780-2185
Debbie Nelson, *Director*
EMP: 80 **Privately Held**
WEB: www.co.la.ca.us
SIC: 8322 9223 Probation office; correc-
tional institutions;
PA: County Of Los Angeles
500 W Temple St Ste 437
Los Angeles CA 90012
213 974-1101

(P-23679)
COUNTY OF LOS ANGELES
Also Called: Public Social Services
12727 Norwalk Blvd, Norwalk
(90650-3145)
PHONE.................................562 807-7860
Tony Iniguez, *Director*
EMP: 250 **Privately Held**
WEB: www.co.la.ca.us
SIC: 8322 9441 Individual & family serv-
ices; administration of social & manpower
programs;
PA: County Of Los Angeles
500 W Temple St Ste 437
Los Angeles CA 90012
213 974-1101

(P-23680)
COUNTY OF LOS ANGELES
Also Called: Department Children Fmly Svcs
501 Shatto Pl Ste 301, Los Angeles
(90020-1749)
PHONE.................................213 351-7257
Bill Browning, *Director*
EMP: 700 **Privately Held**
WEB: www.co.la.ca.us
SIC: 8322 9111 Senior citizens' center or
association; executive offices
PA: County Of Los Angeles
500 W Temple St Ste 437
Los Angeles CA 90012
213 974-1101

(P-23681)
COUNTY OF LOS ANGELES
Also Called: Probation Dept
8526 Grape St, Los Angeles (90001-4134)
PHONE.................................323 586-6469
Mark Garcia, *Director*
EMP: 60 **Privately Held**
WEB: www.co.la.ca.us
SIC: 8322 9223 Probation office; correc-
tional institutions;
PA: County Of Los Angeles
500 W Temple St Ste 437
Los Angeles CA 90012
213 974-1101

(P-23682)
COUNTY OF LOS ANGELES
Also Called: Probation Dept
200 W Compton Blvd # 300, Compton
(90220-6676)
PHONE.................................310 603-7311
Peggy May, *Director*

PRODUCTS & SVCS

EMP: 140 **Privately Held**
WEB: www.co.la.ca.us
SIC: **8322** 9223 Probation office; correctional institutions;
PA: County Of Los Angeles
500 W Temple St Ste 437
Los Angeles CA 90012
213 974-1101

(P-23683)
COUNTY OF LOS ANGELES
Also Called: Probation Dept
199 N Euclid Ave, Pasadena (91101-1757)
PHONE..................................626 356-5281
Steve Yoder, *Director*
EMP: 71 **Privately Held**
WEB: www.co.la.ca.us
SIC: **8322** 9223 Probation office; correctional institutions;
PA: County Of Los Angeles
500 W Temple St Ste 437
Los Angeles CA 90012
213 974-1101

(P-23684)
COUNTY OF LOS ANGELES
Also Called: Probation Department
9150 Imperial Hwy, Downey (90242-2835)
PHONE..................................562 940-2476
Robert Taedler, *Chief*
EMP: 500 **Privately Held**
WEB: www.co.la.ca.us
SIC: **8322** 9223 Probation office; correctional institutions;
PA: County Of Los Angeles
500 W Temple St Ste 437
Los Angeles CA 90012
213 974-1101

(P-23685)
COUNTY OF LOS ANGELES
Also Called: Dpss
3307 N Glenoaks Blvd, Burbank
(91504-2011)
PHONE..................................818 557-4164
Pamar Amirian, *Manager*
EMP: 135 **Privately Held**
WEB: www.co.la.ca.us
SIC: **8322** Emergency social services
PA: County Of Los Angeles
500 W Temple St Ste 437
Los Angeles CA 90012
213 974-1101

(P-23686)
COUNTY OF LOS ANGELES
200 W Woodward Ave, Alhambra
(91801-3459)
PHONE..................................626 308-5542
Roger Fernandez, *Branch Mgr*
EMP: 135 **Privately Held**
WEB: www.co.la.ca.us
SIC: **8322** 9111 Probation office; county supervisors' & executives' offices
PA: County Of Los Angeles
500 W Temple St Ste 437
Los Angeles CA 90012
213 974-1101

(P-23687)
COUNTY OF LOS ANGELES
427 Encinal Canyon Rd, Malibu
(90265-2404)
PHONE..................................818 889-1353
Greg Levy, *Manager*
EMP: 140 **Privately Held**
WEB: www.co.la.ca.us
SIC: **8322** 9111 Probation office; county supervisors' & executives' offices
PA: County Of Los Angeles
500 W Temple St Ste 437
Los Angeles CA 90012
213 974-1101

(P-23688)
COUNTY OF LOS ANGELES
Also Called: Madera County Probation Dept
209 W Yosemite Ave, Madera
(93637-3534)
PHONE..................................559 675-7739
Linda Nash, *Manager*
EMP: 140 **Privately Held**
SIC: **8322** Individual & family services

PA: County Of Los Angeles
500 W Temple St Ste 437
Los Angeles CA 90012
213 974-1101

(P-23689)
COUNTY OF MARIN
Also Called: Marin City Library
164 Donahue St, Sausalito (94965-1250)
PHONE..................................415 332-6158
EMP: 300 **Privately Held**
SIC: **8322** Community center
PA: County Of Marin
3501 Civic Center Dr # 258
San Rafael CA 94903
415 473-6358

(P-23690)
COUNTY OF MARIN
Also Called: Marin County Welfare Dept
120 N Redwood Dr, San Rafael
(94903-1941)
P.O. Box 4160 (94913-4160)
PHONE..................................415 499-6970
Jane Chopson, *Director*
EMP: 300 **Privately Held**
SIC: **8322** 9441 Public welfare center; administration of social & manpower programs;
PA: County Of Marin
3501 Civic Center Dr # 258
San Rafael CA 94903
415 473-6358

(P-23691)
COUNTY OF MENDOCINO
Also Called: Social Services, Department of
737 S State St, Ukiah (95482-5815)
P.O. Box 8508 (95482-8508)
PHONE..................................707 463-2437
Alison Glassey, *Administration*
EMP: 300 **Privately Held**
WEB: www.mcdss.org
SIC: **8322** Individual & family services
PA: County Of Mendocino
501 Low Gap Rd Rm 1010
Ukiah CA 95482
707 463-4441

(P-23692)
COUNTY OF MODOC
Also Called: Department of Social Services
120 N Main St, Alturas (96101-4045)
PHONE..................................530 233-6501
Pauline Cravens, *Branch Mgr*
Sarah K Holshouser, *Exec Dir*
EMP: 52 **Privately Held**
SIC: **8322** Social service center
PA: County Of Modoc
202 W 4th St Ste A
Alturas CA 96101
530 233-6400

(P-23693)
COUNTY OF MODOC
Also Called: Modoc County ADM Svcs
204 S Court St Ste 6, Alturas (96101-4138)
PHONE..................................530 233-6400
Michael Maxwell, *Branch Mgr*
EMP: 99 **Privately Held**
WEB: www.modoccounty.us
SIC: **8322** 9111 Individual & family services; county supervisors' & executives' offices
PA: County Of Modoc
202 W 4th St Ste A
Alturas CA 96101
530 233-6400

(P-23694)
COUNTY OF MONTEREY
Department Social & Employment
1000 S Main St Ste 216, Salinas
(93901-2390)
PHONE..................................831 755-8500
Elliot Robinson, *Director*
Andrew Heald, *Officer*
EMP: 600 **Privately Held**
WEB: www.montereycountyfarmbureau.org
SIC: **8322** Social service center; county supervisors' & executives' offices
PA: County Of Monterey
168 W Alisal St Fl 2
Salinas CA 93901
831 755-5040

(P-23695)
COUNTY OF NAPA
Also Called: NAPA Auto Parts
650 Imperial Way Ste 101, NAPA
(94559-1344)
PHONE..................................707 253-4625
Randy Snowden, *Director*
David Morrison, *Planning*
Lisa Soder, *Asst Treas*
Julia Shackford, *Buyer*
Shanna Murray, *Opers Staff*
EMP: 450 **Privately Held**
WEB: www.billkeller.com
SIC: **8322** Geriatric social service
PA: County Of Napa
1195 Third St Ste 310
Napa CA 94559
707 253-4421

(P-23696)
COUNTY OF NAPA
Also Called: NAPA County Juvenile Probation
212 Walnut St, NAPA (94559-3703)
PHONE..................................707 253-4361
Mary Butler, *Director*
EMP: 50
SQ FT: 122,839 **Privately Held**
WEB: www.billkeller.com
SIC: **8322** 9111 Probation office; county supervisors' & executives' offices
PA: County Of Napa
1195 Third St Ste 310
Napa CA 94559
707 253-4421

(P-23697)
COUNTY OF ORANGE
Also Called: District Attorney
8141 13th St, Westminster (92683-4576)
PHONE..................................714 896-7188
Gary Tackett, *Branch Mgr*
EMP: 56 **Privately Held**
SIC: **8322** 9211 Substance abuse counseling; courts
PA: County Of Orange
333 W Santa Ana Blvd 3f
Santa Ana CA 92701
714 834-6200

(P-23698)
COUNTY OF ORANGE
Also Called: Probation Dept
1535 E Orangewood Ave, Anaheim
(92805-6824)
PHONE..................................714 937-4500
Lalaw Reagan, *Manager*
EMP: 100 **Privately Held**
SIC: **8322** 9111 Probation office; executive offices
PA: County Of Orange
333 W Santa Ana Blvd 3f
Santa Ana CA 92701
714 834-6200

(P-23699)
COUNTY OF ORANGE
Also Called: Probation Dept
14180 Beach Blvd Ste 120, Westminster
(92683-4452)
PHONE..................................714 896-7500
Mac Jenkins, *Director*
EMP: 58 **Privately Held**
SIC: **8322** 9223 Probation office; correctional institutions;
PA: County Of Orange
333 W Santa Ana Blvd 3f
Santa Ana CA 92701
714 834-6200

(P-23700)
COUNTY OF ORANGE
Also Called: Children & Family Serivces
800 N Eckhoff St Bldg 121, Orange
(92868-1008)
P.O. Box 14101 (92863-1501)
PHONE..................................714 704-8000
Michael Riley, *Director*
EMP: 150 **Privately Held**
SIC: **8322** 9441 Children's aid society; administration of social & manpower programs;
PA: County Of Orange
333 W Santa Ana Blvd 3f
Santa Ana CA 92701
714 834-6200

(P-23701)
COUNTY OF ORANGE
Also Called: Social Services Agency
2020 W Walnut St, Santa Ana
(92703-4315)
P.O. Box 1943 (92702-1943)
PHONE..................................714 834-8899
Terry Row, *Branch Mgr*
EMP: 56 **Privately Held**
SIC: **8322** 9441 Social service center; public welfare administration: non-operating, government;
PA: County Of Orange
333 W Santa Ana Blvd 3f
Santa Ana CA 92701
714 834-6200

(P-23702)
COUNTY OF ORANGE
Also Called: Social Services Agency
341 The City Dr S, Orange (92868-3205)
PHONE..................................714 935-6435
Linda Perring, *Director*
EMP: 56 **Privately Held**
SIC: **8322** 9441 Social service center; administration of social & manpower programs;
PA: County Of Orange
333 W Santa Ana Blvd 3f
Santa Ana CA 92701
714 834-6200

(P-23703)
COUNTY OF PLACER
Also Called: Health & Human Services
379 Nevada St, Auburn (95603-3722)
PHONE..................................530 886-1870
Don Ferretti, *Manager*
EMP: 58 **Privately Held**
WEB: www.ssvems.com
SIC: **8322** 9441 8231 Senior citizens' center or association; administration of social & manpower programs; ; public library
PA: County Of Placer
2986 Richardson Dr
Auburn CA 95603
530 889-4200

(P-23704)
COUNTY OF PLACER
Also Called: Mental Hlth Sbstnce Abuse Svcs
11512 B Ave, Auburn (95603-2605)
PHONE..................................530 823-4300
Maureen Bauman, *Director*
EMP: 150 **Privately Held**
WEB: www.ssvems.com
SIC: **8322** 9431 Substance abuse counseling; mental health agency administration, government;
PA: County Of Placer
2986 Richardson Dr
Auburn CA 95603
530 889-4200

(P-23705)
COUNTY OF PLACER
Also Called: Probation Dept
2929 Richardson Dr Ste B, Auburn
(95603-2615)
PHONE..................................530 889-7900
Stephen G Pecor, *Principal*
EMP: 120 **Privately Held**
WEB: www.ssvems.com
SIC: **8322** 9221 Probation office; parole office; police protection
PA: County Of Placer
2986 Richardson Dr
Auburn CA 95603
530 889-4200

(P-23706)
COUNTY OF RIVERSIDE
Also Called: Public Social Service
3178 Hamner Ave, Norco (92860-1936)
PHONE..................................951 272-5400
Sherri Feldt, *Manager*
EMP: 50 **Privately Held**
SIC: **8322** 9441 Individual & family services; public welfare administration: non-operating, government;
PA: County Of Riverside
4080 Lemon St Fl 11
Riverside CA 92501
951 955-1110

(P-23707)
COUNTY OF RIVERSIDE
2560 N Perris Blvd Ste N1, Perris
(92571-3251)
PHONE...................................951 443-2262
Kevin Jeffries, *Branch Mgr*
EMP: 99 **Privately Held**
SIC: 8322 Probation office
PA: County Of Riverside
4080 Lemon St Fl 11
Riverside CA 92501
951 955-1110

(P-23708)
COUNTY OF RIVERSIDE
Also Called: Public Social Services
1400 W Minthorn St, Lake Elsinore
(92530-2808)
PHONE...................................951 245-3060
Mary Thoman, *Principal*
EMP: 99 **Privately Held**
SIC: 8322 9441 Individual & family serv-
ices; administration of social & manpower
programs;
PA: County Of Riverside
4080 Lemon St Fl 11
Riverside CA 92501
951 955-1110

(P-23709)
COUNTY OF RIVERSIDE
43264 Business Park Dr # 102, Temecula
(92590-3646)
PHONE...................................951 600-6500
Virginia Hedberg, *Branch Mgr*
EMP: 99 **Privately Held**
SIC: 8322 Public welfare center
PA: County Of Riverside
4080 Lemon St Fl 11
Riverside CA 92501
951 955-1110

(P-23710)
COUNTY OF RIVERSIDE
Also Called: Economic Development Dept
1325 Spruce St Ste 100, Riverside
(92507-0503)
PHONE...................................951 955-3100
Loren Sims, *Office Mgr*
Heidi Marshall, *Asst Director*
Janet Purchase, *Manager*
EMP: 106 **Privately Held**
SIC: 8322 9441 Individual & family serv-
ices; administration of social & manpower
programs;
PA: County Of Riverside
4080 Lemon St Fl 11
Riverside CA 92501
951 955-1110

(P-23711)
COUNTY OF RIVERSIDE
Also Called: Public Social Services
1400 W Minthorn St, Lake Elsinore
(92530-2808)
PHONE...................................951 245-3100
Tom Barnidge, *Manager*
EMP: 99 **Privately Held**
SIC: 8322 9199 Individual & family serv-
ices; general government administration;
PA: County Of Riverside
4080 Lemon St Fl 11
Riverside CA 92501
951 955-1110

(P-23712)
COUNTY OF RIVERSIDE
4168 12th St, Riverside (92501-3409)
PHONE...................................951 275-8783
Yab Cordinator, *Principal*
EMP: 99 **Privately Held**
SIC: 8322 Youth center
PA: County Of Riverside
4080 Lemon St Fl 11
Riverside CA 92501
951 955-1110

(P-23713)
COUNTY OF RIVERSIDE
Also Called: Office On Aging, ADRC Of River
6296 River Crest Dr Ste K, Riverside
(92507-0738)
PHONE...................................951 697-4699
Edward Walsh, *Director*
EMP: 80 **Privately Held**

SIC: 8322 9441 Geriatric social service;
administration of social & manpower programs;
PA: County Of Riverside
4080 Lemon St Fl 11
Riverside CA 92501
951 955-1110

(P-23714)
COUNTY OF RIVERSIDE
Also Called: Riverside Cnty Probation Dept
3960 Orange St Ste 500, Riverside
(92501-3644)
P.O. Box 833 (92502-0833)
PHONE...................................951 955-0905
Michelina Iybar, *Supervisor*
Julie Terrell, *Manager*
EMP: 875 **Privately Held**
SIC: 8322 Probation office
PA: County Of Riverside
4080 Lemon St Fl 11
Riverside CA 92501
951 955-1110

(P-23715)
COUNTY OF RIVERSIDE
Also Called: Van Horn Youth Center
10000 County Farm Rd, Riverside
(92503-3508)
PHONE...................................951 358-4415
Pam Cronk, *Principal*
EMP: 99 **Privately Held**
SIC: 8322 9223 Youth center; correctional
institutions;
PA: County Of Riverside
4080 Lemon St Fl 11
Riverside CA 92501
951 955-1110

(P-23716)
COUNTY OF SACRAMENTO
Also Called: Health and Human Services
9750 Bus Park Dr Ste 104, Sacramento
(95827-1716)
P.O. Box 5140 (95817-0140)
PHONE...................................916 875-4467
Mindy Yamasaki, *Branch Mgr*
EMP: 135 **Privately Held**
WEB: www.sna.com
SIC: 8322 9441 Old age assistance; ad-
ministration of social & human resources;
PA: County Of Sacramento
700 H St Ste 7650
Sacramento CA 95814
916 874-5544

(P-23717)
COUNTY OF SAN BERNARDINO
Also Called: Human Services Systems
412 W Hospitality Ln Fl 2, San Bernardino
(92415-0913)
PHONE...................................909 891-3300
Mae Harns-Oglesby, *Director*
EMP: 70 **Privately Held**
SIC: 8322 9441 Adoption services; admin-
istration of social & manpower programs;
PA: County Of San Bernardino
385 N Arrowhead Ave
San Bernardino CA 92415
909 387-3841

(P-23718)
COUNTY OF SAN BERNARDINO
Also Called: Probation Dept
8303 Haven Ave, Rancho Cucamonga
(91730-3848)
PHONE...................................909 945-4000
Wes Krause, *Branch Mgr*
Tracy Reece, *Manager*
EMP: 70 **Privately Held**
SIC: 8322 9441 Probation office; adminis-
tration of social & manpower programs;
PA: County Of San Bernardino
385 N Arrowhead Ave
San Bernardino CA 92415
909 387-3841

(P-23719)
COUNTY OF SAN BERNARDINO
Also Called: Aging & Adult Services
17270 Bear Valley Rd # 108, Victorville
(92395-7751)
PHONE...................................760 843-5100
EMP: 51 **Privately Held**
SIC: 8322 9441

PA: County Of San Bernardino
385 N Arrowhead Ave
San Bernardino CA 92415
909 387-5455

(P-23720)
COUNTY OF SAN BERNARDINO
Also Called: Transitional Assistance Dept
56357 Pima Trl, Yucca Valley (92284-3607)
PHONE...................................760 228-5234
John Michealson, *Director*
EMP: 70 **Privately Held**
SIC: 8322 9441 Individual & family serv-
ices; administration of social & manpower
programs;
PA: County Of San Bernardino
385 N Arrowhead Ave
San Bernardino CA 92415
909 387-3841

(P-23721)
COUNTY OF SAN DIEGO
Also Called: Health & Human Services
6950 Levant St, San Diego (92111-6010)
PHONE...................................858 694-5141
Debra Zanders-Willis, *Director*
Valesha Bullock, *Manager*
EMP: 82 **Privately Held**
WEB: www.sdlcc.org
SIC: 8322 9441 Adoption services; admin-
istration of social & manpower programs;
PA: County Of San Diego
1600 Pacific Hwy Ste 209
San Diego CA 92101
619 531-5880

(P-23722)
COUNTY OF SAN DIEGO
Also Called: Health & Human Services
130 E Alvarado St, Fallbrook (92028-2048)
PHONE...................................866 262-9881
Carol Schier, *Branch Mgr*
EMP: 82 **Privately Held**
WEB: www.sdlcc.org
SIC: 8322 Parole office
PA: County Of San Diego
1600 Pacific Hwy Ste 209
San Diego CA 92101
619 531-5880

(P-23723)
COUNTY OF SAN DIEGO
Also Called: Health and Human Service Agcy
5560 Overland Ave Ste 310, San Diego
(92123-1204)
PHONE...................................858 495-5537
Pamela B Smith, *Manager*
Ellen Schmeding, *Principal*
Kristen Smith, *Administration*
EMP: 70 **Privately Held**
WEB: www.sdlcc.org
SIC: 8322 9441 Individual & family serv-
ices; administration of social & manpower
programs;
PA: County Of San Diego
1600 Pacific Hwy Ste 209
San Diego CA 92101
619 531-5880

(P-23724)
COUNTY OF SAN DIEGO
Also Called: Probation Dept
330 W Broadway Ste 1100, San Diego
(92101-3827)
P.O. Box 23596 (92193-3596)
PHONE...................................619 515-8202
Don Blevins, *Director*
Julie Martin-Sexauer, *General Mgr*
Ana Desntigo, *Counsel*
Linda Pena, *Manager*
EMP: 82 **Privately Held**
WEB: www.sdlcc.org
SIC: 8322 9431 Probation office; parole
office; administration of public health pro-
grams
PA: County Of San Diego
1600 Pacific Hwy Ste 209
San Diego CA 92101
619 531-5880

(P-23725)
COUNTY OF SAN DIEGO
Also Called: Health & Human Services
1320 Union Plaza Ct, Oceanside
(92054-5659)
PHONE...................................760 754-3456

June Hercog, *Administration*
EMP: 160 **Privately Held**
WEB: www.sdlcc.org
SIC: 8322 9441 Parole office;
PA: County Of San Diego
1600 Pacific Hwy Ste 209
San Diego CA 92101
619 531-5880

(P-23726)
COUNTY OF SAN DIEGO
Also Called: Parks & Recreation Dept
8735 Jamacha Blvd, Spring Valley
(91977-5632)
PHONE...................................619 479-1832
Renell Nailon, *Director*
EMP: 75 **Privately Held**
WEB: www.sdlcc.org
SIC: 8322 9512 Individual & family serv-
ices; recreational program administration,
government;
PA: County Of San Diego
1600 Pacific Hwy Ste 209
San Diego CA 92101
619 531-5880

(P-23727)
COUNTY OF SAN DIEGO
Also Called: Health and Human Services
Agcy
3255 Camino Del Rio S, San Diego
(92108-3806)
PHONE...................................619 563-2765
Delia Mateo, *Principal*
EMP: 74 **Privately Held**
SIC: 8322 Individual & family services
PA: County Of San Diego
1600 Pacific Hwy Ste 209
San Diego CA 92101
619 531-5880

(P-23728)
COUNTY OF SAN DIEGO
Also Called: Health and Human Services
4588 Market St, San Diego (92102-4764)
PHONE...................................619 236-8725
Deborah Lester, *Branch Mgr*
EMP: 150 **Privately Held**
WEB: www.sdlcc.org
SIC: 8322 9441 Individual & family serv-
ices; administration of public health pro-
grams
PA: County Of San Diego
1600 Pacific Hwy Ste 209
San Diego CA 92101
619 531-5880

(P-23729)
COUNTY OF SAN JOAQUIN
Also Called: Dept of Child Support
826 N California St, Stockton (95202-1820)
PHONE...................................209 468-2601
Judy Grimes, *Branch Mgr*
EMP: 400
SQ FT: 1,005 **Privately Held**
WEB: www.sjclawlib.org
SIC: 8322 9441 Child related social serv-
ices; public welfare administration: non-
operating, government
PA: County Of San Joaquin
44 N San Joaquin St # 640
Stockton CA 95202
209 468-3203

(P-23730)
COUNTY OF SAN JOAQUIN
Also Called: San Joaquin County Adult Svcs
24 S Hunter St Ste 201, Stockton
(95202-3231)
PHONE...................................209 468-4100
Dave Newaj, *CEO*
Paul Rinaldo, *Officer*
EMP: 78 **Privately Held**
SIC: 8322 Probation office
PA: County Of San Joaquin
44 N San Joaquin St # 640
Stockton CA 95202
209 468-3203

(P-23731)
COUNTY OF SAN JOAQUIN
Also Called: Mary Grahams Childrens Shelter
500 W Hospital Rd, French Camp
(95231-9693)
P.O. Box 201056, Stockton (95201-3006)
PHONE...................................209 468-6966

Brian Woods, *Director*
EMP: 75 Privately Held
WEB: www.sjclawlib.org
SIC: 8322 9512 Child related social services; land conservation agencies
PA: County Of San Joaquin
44 N San Joaquin St # 640
Stockton CA 95202
209 468-3203

(P-23732)
COUNTY OF SAN LUIS OBISPO
Also Called: Department of Social Services
3433 S Higuera St, San Luis Obispo (93401-7301)
PHONE......................805 781-5437
Lee Collins, *Director*
Brian Aunger, *Exec Dir*
Tracy Schiro, *Asst Director*
EMP: 108 Privately Held
SIC: 8322 Child related social services
PA: County Of San Luis Obispo
Government Center Rm. 300
San Luis Obispo CA 93408
805 781-5040

(P-23733)
COUNTY OF SAN LUIS OBISPO
Also Called: Dept of Social Services Dss
3433 S Higuera St, San Luis Obispo (93401-7301)
P.O. Box 8119 (93403-8119)
PHONE......................805 781-1864
Leland Collins, *Director*
EMP: 450 Privately Held
SIC: 8322 Individual & family services
PA: County Of San Luis Obispo
Government Center Rm. 300
San Luis Obispo CA 93408
805 781-5040

(P-23734)
COUNTY OF SAN MATEO
Also Called: Probation Department
680 Warren St, Redwood City (94063-1522)
PHONE......................650 599-7336
Michael J Stauffer, *Manager*
EMP: 130 Privately Held
WEB: www.ci.sanmateo.ca.us
SIC: 8322 9223 Probation office;
PA: County Of San Mateo
400 County Ctr
Redwood City CA 94063
650 363-4123

(P-23735)
COUNTY OF SAN MATEO
Also Called: Probation Department
222 Paul Scannell Dr, San Mateo (94402-4061)
PHONE......................650 312-5327
Stuart Forrest, *Chief*
EMP: 250 Privately Held
WEB: www.ci.sanmateo.ca.us
SIC: 8322 9223 Probation office; parole office;
PA: County Of San Mateo
400 County Ctr
Redwood City CA 94063
650 363-4123

(P-23736)
COUNTY OF SAN MATEO
Also Called: Probation Department
222 Paul Scannell Dr Fl 2, San Mateo (94402-4061)
PHONE......................650 312-8887
Stewart Forest, *Manager*
EMP: 400 Privately Held
WEB: www.ci.sanmateo.ca.us
SIC: 8322 9199 Probation office; general government administration;
PA: County Of San Mateo
400 County Ctr
Redwood City CA 94063
650 363-4123

(P-23737)
COUNTY OF SAN MATEO
Also Called: Probation Department
2277 University Ave, East Palo Alto (94303-1717)
PHONE......................650 853-3139
Robert Hoover, *Manager*
EMP: 51 Privately Held

WEB: www.ci.sanmateo.ca.us
SIC: 8322 9223 Probation office; parole office;
PA: County Of San Mateo
400 County Ctr
Redwood City CA 94063
650 363-4123

(P-23738)
COUNTY OF SAN MATEO
Child Support Services Dept
555 County Ctr Fl 2, Redwood City (94063-1665)
PHONE......................650 363-1910
Kim Cagno, *Director*
EMP: 80 Privately Held
WEB: www.ci.sanmateo.ca.us
SIC: 8322 9441 Child related social services;
PA: County Of San Mateo
400 County Ctr
Redwood City CA 94063
650 363-4123

(P-23739)
COUNTY OF SAN MATEO
Also Called: Human Services Agency
400 Harbor Blvd Bldg B, Belmont (94002-4047)
PHONE......................650 802-6470
Beverly Beasley Johnson, *Manager*
Ricardo Villarin, *Network Analyst*
EMP: 150 Privately Held
WEB: www.ci.sanmateo.ca.us
SIC: 8322 9441 Adoption services; administration of social & manpower programs;
PA: County Of San Mateo
400 County Ctr
Redwood City CA 94063
650 363-4123

(P-23740)
COUNTY OF SAN MATEO
Also Called: Probation Department
222 Paul Scannell Dr, San Mateo (94402-4061)
PHONE......................650 312-8803
John Keene, *Branch Mgr*
EMP: 200 Privately Held
WEB: www.ci.sanmateo.ca.us
SIC: 8322 9199 Probation office; general government administration;
PA: County Of San Mateo
400 County Ctr
Redwood City CA 94063
650 363-4123

(P-23741)
COUNTY OF SAN MATEO
Also Called: Probation Department
400 County Ctr Fl 5, Redwood City (94063-1662)
P.O. Box 441 (94064-0441)
PHONE......................650 363-4244
John Keene, *Chairman*
Jody Dimauro, *Manager*
EMP: 143 Privately Held
SIC: 8322 9223 Probation office;
PA: County Of San Mateo
400 County Ctr
Redwood City CA 94063
650 363-4123

(P-23742)
COUNTY OF SHASTA
Also Called: Children's Protective Services
1313 Yuba St, Redding (96001-1012)
PHONE......................530 225-5554
Dianna Wagner, *Director*
EMP: 75 Privately Held
WEB: www.rsdnmp.org
SIC: 8322 Children's aid society
PA: County Of Shasta
1450 Court St Ste 308a
Redding CA 96001
530 225-5561

(P-23743)
COUNTY OF SISKIYOU
Also Called: Human Services Department
818 S Main St, Yreka (96097-3321)
PHONE......................530 841-2700
Nadine Dellabitta, *Director*
EMP: 60 Privately Held
WEB: www.siskiyoucounty.org
SIC: 8322 Individual & family services

PA: County Of Siskiyou
311 4th St Rm 108
Yreka CA 96097
530 841-4100

(P-23744)
COUNTY OF SOLANO
Also Called: Health and Social Services
275 Beck Ave, Fairfield (94533-6804)
PHONE......................707 784-8400
Patrick Dulerte, *Director*
Rich Randall, *Business Anlyst*
EMP: 56 Privately Held
SIC: 8322 Individual & family services
PA: County Of Solano
675 Texas St Ste 2600
Fairfield CA 94533
707 784-6706

(P-23745)
COUNTY OF SOLANO
Also Called: Solano County Probation Dept
475 Union Ave, Fairfield (94533-6319)
PHONE......................707 784-7600
Isabelle Voight, *Principal*
Donna Vestal, *Analyst*
EMP: 237 Privately Held
SIC: 8322 Rehabilitation services
PA: County Of Solano
675 Texas St Ste 2600
Fairfield CA 94533
707 784-6706

(P-23746)
COUNTY OF SONOMA
2300 County Center Dr B100, Santa Rosa (95403-3013)
PHONE......................707 527-2641
Peter Boomer, *Branch Mgr*
Robert Kambak, *Architect*
EMP: 60 Privately Held
WEB: www.sonomacompost.com
SIC: 8322 Child related social services
PA: County Of Sonoma
585 Fiscal Dr 100
Santa Rosa CA 95403
707 565-2431

(P-23747)
COUNTY OF STANISLAUS
Also Called: Community Services
830 Scenic Dr, Modesto (95350-6131)
PHONE......................209 558-8828
Nancy Fisher, *Superintendent*
EMP: 75 Privately Held
WEB: www.co.stanislaus.ca.us
SIC: 8322 Youth self-help agency
PA: County Of Stanislaus
1010 10th St Ste 5100
Modesto CA 95354
209 525-6398

(P-23748)
COUNTY OF STANISLAUS
801 11th St, Modesto (95354-2348)
PHONE......................209 567-4120
Delia Basquez, *Branch Mgr*
EMP: 110 Privately Held
SIC: 8322 Probation office
PA: County Of Stanislaus
1010 10th St Ste 5100
Modesto CA 95354
209 525-6398

(P-23749)
COUNTY OF STANISLAUS
108 Campus Way, Modesto (95350-5803)
PHONE......................209 558-7377
Elaine Emory, *Manager*
EMP: 110 Privately Held
SIC: 8322 Individual & family services
PA: County Of Stanislaus
1010 10th St Ste 5100
Modesto CA 95354
209 525-6398

(P-23750)
COUNTY OF STANISLAUS
Also Called: Dcss
251 E Hackett Rd, Modesto (95358-9800)
P.O. Box 4189 (95352-4189)
PHONE......................209 558-9675
Tamara Thomas, *Branch Mgr*
EMP: 223 Privately Held
WEB: www.modairport.com
SIC: 8322 Family counseling services

PA: County Of Stanislaus
1010 10th St Ste 5100
Modesto CA 95354
209 525-6398

(P-23751)
COUNTY OF STANISLAUS
Also Called: Family Support Division
108 Campus Way, Modesto (95350-5803)
P.O. Box 4189 (95352-4189)
PHONE......................209 558-2500
Joan Kingman, *Branch Mgr*
EMP: 95 Privately Held
WEB: www.co.stanislaus.ca.us
SIC: 8322 Child related social services
PA: County Of Stanislaus
1010 10th St Ste 5100
Modesto CA 95354
209 525-6398

(P-23752)
COUNTY OF TEHAMA
Also Called: Mental Health Services
1860 Walnut St, Red Bluff (96080-3611)
P.O. Box 400 (96080-0400)
PHONE......................530 527-5631
Valerie Lucero, *Director*
EMP: 200 Privately Held
SIC: 8322 9111 Social service center; county supervisors' & executives' offices
PA: The County Of Tehama
20639 Walnut St
Red Bluff CA 96080
530 527-4655

(P-23753)
COUNTY OF TEHAMA
Also Called: Probation
1840 Walnut St, Red Bluff (96080-3611)
P.O. Box 99 (96080-0099)
PHONE......................530 527-4052
David Finch, *Branch Mgr*
Ashley Jennings, *Admin Sec*
EMP: 70 Privately Held
SIC: 8322 9111 Probation office; county supervisors' & executives' offices
PA: The County Of Tehama
20639 Walnut St
Red Bluff CA 96080
530 527-4655

(P-23754)
COUNTY OF TUOLUMNE
Also Called: Welfare Department
20075 Cedar Rd N, Sonora (95370-5900)
PHONE......................209 533-5711
Kent Skellenger, *Director*
Ann Connolly, *Director*
EMP: 110 Privately Held
WEB: www.tuolumne.courts.ca.gov
SIC: 8322 Social service center
PA: County Of Tuolumne
2 S Green St
Sonora CA 95370
209 533-5521

(P-23755)
COUNTY OF VENTURA
Also Called: County Ventura Human Resources
800 S Victoria Ave, Ventura (93009-0003)
PHONE......................805 654-2561
Jodi Lee Prior, *Branch Mgr*
Manny Ramos, *Officer*
Leah Velador, *Officer*
Wendy Hibner, *Med Doctor*
Joey Carmona, *Supervisor*
EMP: 104 Privately Held
WEB: www.vcoe.org
SIC: 8322 9441 Individual & family services; administration of social & human resources
PA: County Of Ventura
800 S Victoria Ave
Ventura CA 93009
805 654-2644

(P-23756)
COUNTY OF VENTURA
Also Called: Foster Care Licensing & Svc
4651 Telephone Rd Ste 300, Ventura (93003-8779)
PHONE......................805 654-3456
Ellen Mastright, *Branch Mgr*
Jenny Medrano, *Admin Asst*
Armand Paez, *Human Res Mgr*

Ken Sewell, *Deputy Dir*
Gina Garcia, *Supervisor*
EMP: 90 **Privately Held**
WEB: www.vcoe.org
SIC: 8322 9111 Hotline; executive offices
PA: County Of Ventura
800 S Victoria Ave
Ventura CA 93009
805 654-2644

(P-23757)
COUNTY OF VENTURA
1400 Vanguard Dr Fl 2nd, Oxnard
(93033-2402)
PHONE..............................805 385-8654
Bonita Kraft, *Branch Mgr*
EMP: 104 **Privately Held**
SIC: 8322 Probation office
PA: County Of Ventura
800 S Victoria Ave
Ventura CA 93009
805 654-2644

(P-23758)
COUNTY OF VENTURA
Also Called: Medical Center
3291 Loma Vista Rd, Ventura
(93003-3099)
PHONE..............................805 652-6000
Michael Powers, *Manager*
Mike Maloy, *Administration*
Laura Jordan, *Family Practiti*
Kenneth Parola, *Family Practiti*
Maria Villasenor, *Family Practiti*
EMP: 600 **Privately Held**
WEB: www.vcoe.org
SIC: 8322 9431 Individual & family services; administration of public health programs;
PA: County Of Ventura
800 S Victoria Ave
Ventura CA 93009
805 654-2644

(P-23759)
COUNTY OF VENTURA
Also Called: Department Child Support Svcs
5171 Verdugo Way, Camarillo
(93012-8603)
PHONE..............................805 654-5529
Stanley Trom, *Director*
EMP: 273 **Privately Held**
WEB: www.vcoe.org
SIC: 8322 9431 Individual & family services; child health program administration, government
PA: County Of Ventura
800 S Victoria Ave
Ventura CA 93009
805 654-2644

(P-23760)
COUNTY OF YUBA
Also Called: Yuba County Probation Dept
215 5th St Ste 154, Marysville
(95901-5737)
PHONE..............................530 749-7550
Jim Arnold, *Director*
Dawn Wells, *General Mgr*
EMP: 183 **Privately Held**
SIC: 8322 9199 Probation office;
PA: County Of Yuba
915 8th St Ste 109
Marysville CA 95901
530 749-7575

(P-23761)
COUNTY SANDIEGO DEPT CHLDSPPRT
3666 Krny Vlla Rd Ste 100, San Diego
(92123)
PHONE..............................619 578-6660
Jeff Grissom, *Director*
EMP: 500
SALES (est): 201.2K **Privately Held**
SIC: 8322 Individual & family services

(P-23762)
CRESTWOOD BEHAVIORAL HLTH INC
Also Called: 115 Bakersfield Mhrc
6700 Eucalyptus Dr Ste A, Bakersfield
(93306-6076)
PHONE..............................661 363-8127
Ronda Banclive, *Director*
Deleon Delphina, *Exec Dir*

EMP: 75
SALES (corp-wide): 171.2MM **Privately Held**
WEB: www.crestwoodbehavioralhealth.com
SIC: 8322 8011 Rehabilitation services; psychiatric clinic
PA: Crestwood Behavioral Health, Inc.
520 Capitol Mall Ste 800
Sacramento CA 95814
510 651-1244

(P-23763)
CRUCIBLE
1260 7th St, Oakland (94607-2150)
PHONE..............................510 444-0919
Steven Young, *President*
Michael Sturtz, *Exec Dir*
Jan Schlesinger, *Mktg Dir*
Byrd Pappas, *Manager*
EMP: 100
SQ FT: 46,980
SALES: 2.9MM **Privately Held**
WEB: www.thecrucible.org
SIC: 8322 8331 Outreach program; skill training center

(P-23764)
CRYSTAL STAIRS INC (PA)
5110 W Goldleaf Cir # 150, Los Angeles
(90056-1287)
PHONE..............................323 299-8998
Jackie B Majors, *CEO*
Dianna Torres, *Ch of Bd*
Dr Karen Hill-Scott, *President*
Javier La Fianza, *COO*
Robert Trujillo, *Treasurer*
EMP: 330
SQ FT: 83,000
SALES: 132.2MM **Privately Held**
WEB: www.crystalstairs.com
SIC: 8322 Social service center

(P-23765)
DACARE INC (PA)
Also Called: Dayout Brawley
643 Main St, Brawley (92227-2547)
PHONE..............................760 344-4654
Elizabeth Machado, *CEO*
EMP: 55
SALES (est): 3MM **Privately Held**
WEB: www.daycare.com
SIC: 8322 Adult day care center

(P-23766)
DDSO INC (PA)
5051 47th Ave, Sacramento (95824-4036)
PHONE..............................916 456-5166
Yvonne Soto, *Acting CEO*
Jon Hutchison, *Ch of Bd*
Ann Larson, *Ch of Bd*
Jennifer Bonacorso, *CFO*
Trish Williams, *Sales Executive*
EMP: 99
SQ FT: 36,000
SALES: 4.4MM **Privately Held**
WEB: www.ddso.org
SIC: 8322 Community center

(P-23767)
DESERT AIDS PROJECT (PA)
Also Called: Get Tested Coachella Valley
1695 N Sunrise Way Bldg 1, Palm Springs
(92262-3702)
P.O. Box 2890 (92263-2890)
PHONE..............................760 323-2118
David Brinkman, *CEO*
Mary Park, *CFO*
Matt Farokmanesh, *IT/INT Sup*
Steven Scheibel, *Director*
Kimberly Tollison, *Manager*
EMP: 65
SQ FT: 46,050
SALES: 33.6MM **Privately Held**
WEB: www.desertaidsproject.org
SIC: 8322 5932 8011 General counseling services; used merchandise stores; clinic, operated by physicians

(P-23768)
DESERTARC
Also Called: DESERT VALLEY INDUSTRIES
73255 Country Club Dr, Palm Desert
(92260-2309)
PHONE..............................760 346-1611
Lori Serfling, *Treasurer*
Robert Anzalone, *President*

Robin Keagen, *CFO*
Robin Keegan, *CFO*
Jay Chesterton, *Treasurer*
EMP: 75 **EST:** 1959
SQ FT: 12,000
SALES: 14.1MM **Privately Held**
WEB: www.desertarc.org
SIC: 8322 Association for the handicapped; social services for the handicapped

(P-23769)
DEVELOP DISABILITIES SVC ORG
Also Called: Community Integration Program
2331 Saint Marks Way G1, Sacramento
(95864-0626)
PHONE..............................916 973-1951
Yvonne Soto, *CEO*
Amy Nishimura, *CEO*
Susan Burger, *Deputy Dir*
EMP: 75
SALES (est): 897K **Privately Held**
SIC: 8322 Association for the handicapped; social services for the handicapped

(P-23770)
DIAMOND LEARNING CENTER INC
1620 W Fairmont Ave, Fresno
(93705-0323)
PHONE..............................559 241-0580
Jamie Delacerda, *President*
Daniel F Delacerda, *Vice Pres*
Cheryl Martinez, *Associate Dir*
Kelly Pesenti, *Associate Dir*
Isaac Jimenez, *Transptn Dir*
EMP: 53
SALES (est): 221.5K **Privately Held**
SIC: 8322 Adult day care center

(P-23771)
DIDI HIRSCH PSYCHIATRIC SVC (PA)
Also Called: Didi Hirsch Community Mental
4760 Sepulveda Blvd, Culver City
(90230-4820)
PHONE..............................310 390-6612
Michael Wierwille, *Chairman*
Kita S Curry, *President*
Martin Frank, *Treasurer*
Andrew Rubin, *Admin Sec*
John McGann, *VP Finance*
EMP: 150 **EST:** 1944
SQ FT: 35,000
SALES: 45.4MM **Privately Held**
SIC: 8322 8093 Family counseling services; mental health clinic, outpatient

(P-23772)
DISTRICT COUNCIL DC (PA)
Also Called: St Vincent De Paul
9235 San Leandro St, Oakland
(94603-1237)
PHONE..............................510 638-7600
Vaughn Donaghue, *Exec Dir*
EMP: 100
SQ FT: 40,000
SALES: 7.4MM **Privately Held**
SIC: 8322 5932 Individual & family services; used merchandise stores

(P-23773)
DIVERSE JOURNEYS INC (PA)
525 S Douglas St Ste 210, El Segundo
(90245-4827)
PHONE..............................310 643-7403
Amanda Gerhart, *President*
Laura Broderrick, *Director*
EMP: 98
SQ FT: 2,000
SALES (est): 3.1MM **Privately Held**
SIC: 8322 Social services for the handicapped

(P-23774)
DREW CHILD DEV CORP INC (PA)
1770 E 118th St, Los Angeles
(90059-2518)
PHONE..............................323 249-2950
Michael Jackson, *President*
James Hays, *CEO*
EMP: 150

SALES: 21MM **Privately Held**
SIC: 8322 Child guidance agency

(P-23775)
DRUG ABUSE ALTERNATIVES CENTER (PA)
2403 Prof Dr Ste 102, Santa Rosa (95403)
PHONE..............................707 544-3295
EMP: 130 **EST:** 1969
SQ FT: 9,216
SALES: 5.9MM **Privately Held**
WEB: www.daacinfo.org
SIC: 8322 Individual & family services

(P-23776)
EAST BAY ASIAN YOUTH CENTER
2025 E 12th St, Oakland (94606-4925)
PHONE..............................510 533-1092
Gianna Tran, *President*
EMP: 50
SALES (corp-wide): 5.1MM **Privately Held**
WEB: www.ebayc.org
SIC: 8322 Youth center
PA: East Bay Asian Youth Center
2025 E 12th St
Oakland CA 94606
510 533-1092

(P-23777)
EAST L A REMARKABLE CITIZENS (PA)
Also Called: EL ARCA
3839 Selig Pl, Los Angeles (90031-3143)
PHONE..............................323 223-3079
Carlos Madrid, *Exec Dir*
John Menchaca, *Vice Pres*
Miriam Alarcon, *Human Resources*
Luis Ramirez, *Program Dir*
EMP: 85
SQ FT: 23,360
SALES: 5.1MM **Privately Held**
WEB: www.elarca.com
SIC: 8322 Social services for the handicapped

(P-23778)
EASTER SEALS CENTRAL CAL
9010 Soquel Dr, Aptos (95003-4082)
PHONE..............................831 684-2166
Bruce Hinman, *President*
Donna Alvarez, *Executive*
Anne Bourdeau, *Assistant*
EMP: 300
SALES: 2.7MM **Privately Held**
SIC: 8322 Social service center

(P-23779)
EASTERN LOS ANGELES RE (PA)
1000 S Fremont Ave # 40, Alhambra
(91803-8873)
P.O. Box 7916 (91802-7916)
PHONE..............................626 299-4700
Gloria Wong, *Exec Dir*
Theresa Chen, *Bd of Directors*
Felicitas Navera, *Bd of Directors*
Ana Young, *Admin Sec*
Ping Chen, *Administration*
EMP: 287
SQ FT: 31,704
SALES: 196.3MM **Privately Held**
WEB: www.elarc.org
SIC: 8322 Association for the handicapped

(P-23780)
EASTERN STAR HOMES CALIFORNIA (PA)
Also Called: EASTERN STAR PROFESSIONAL BUIL
16850 Bastanchury Rd, Yorba Linda
(92886-1608)
PHONE..............................714 986-2380
Norma Stillwell, *President*
Danna Willoughby, *President*
EMP: 57
SQ FT: 15,604
SALES: 3.5MM **Privately Held**
SIC: 8322 Geriatric social service

P R O D U C T S & S V C S

(P-23781)
EGGLESTON YOUTH CENTERS INC (PA)
13001 Ramona Blvd Ste E, Irwindale (91706-3752)
P.O. Box 638, Baldwin Park (91706-0638)
PHONE..................626 480-8107
Clarence Brown, *Exec Dir*
April Mitchell, *President*
Don Gutierrez, *Administration*
EMP: 90
SQ FT: 7,616
SALES: 8MM **Privately Held**
SIC: 8322 Social service center; youth center

(P-23782)
EL CAMINO CHILDREN & FMLY SVCS
9900 Lakewood Blvd # 104, Downey (90240-4038)
PHONE..................562 364-1258
Jorge Gutierrez, *CEO*
Robert Donin, *Chairman*
John Rojas, *Vice Pres*
David Sanchez, *Admin Sec*
EMP: 50
SQ FT: 3,000
SALES: 68.2K **Privately Held**
WEB: www.eccafs.org
SIC: 8322 Family counseling services

(P-23783)
EL CAMINO HOSPITAL
1503 Grant Rd Ste 120, Mountain View (94040-3293)
PHONE..................650 988-7444
Vicki Chryssos, *Exec Dir*
Mirella Nguyen, *Manager*
EMP: 173
SALES (corp-wide): 930.5MM **Privately Held**
SIC: 8322 Social worker
PA: El Camino Hospital
2500 Grant Rd
Mountain View CA 94040
408 224-6660

(P-23784)
EL CONCILIO SAN MATEO CNTY INC
Also Called: HISPANIC CONCILIO OF SAN MATEO
3180 Middlefield Rd, Redwood City (94063-3762)
PHONE..................650 373-1080
Ortensia Lopez, *President*
EMP: 50
SALES: 2.1MM **Privately Held**
WEB: www.el-concilio.com
SIC: 8322 Social service center

(P-23785)
EL NIDO FAMILY CENTERS (PA)
10200 Sepulveda Blvd # 350, Mission Hills (91345-3318)
PHONE..................818 830-3646
Liz Herrera, *Director*
Denise Lopez, *Associate*
EMP: 130
SQ FT: 3,650
SALES (est): 8.3MM **Privately Held**
WEB: www.elnidofamilycenters.org
SIC: 8322 Social service center

(P-23786)
ELDER OPTIONS (PA)
82 Main St, Placerville (95667-5506)
P.O. Box 2113 (95667-2113)
PHONE..................530 626-6939
Carol Heape, *Owner*
Betty Flagg, *Administration*
Tabatha Owens, *Manager*
John Carlstrom, *Supervisor*
EMP: 50
SALES (est): 2.5MM **Privately Held**
SIC: 8322 Senior citizens' center or association; geriatric social service

(P-23787)
ENCOMPASS COMMUNITY SERVICES
Also Called: Headstart
225 Westridge Dr, Watsonville (95076-4168)
P.O. Box 927 (95077-0927)
PHONE..................831 724-3885
Gloria Martinez, *Branch Mgr*
EMP: 300
SALES (corp-wide): 29.3MM **Privately Held**
SIC: 8322 8351 Individual & family services; head start center, except in conjunction with school
PA: Encompass Community Services
380 Encinal St Ste 200
Santa Cruz CA 95060
831 427-9670

(P-23788)
EPISCOPAL COMM SVC SAN FRAN (PA)
Also Called: Ecs
165 8th St Fl 3, San Francisco (94103-2726)
PHONE..................415 487-3300
Kenneth J Reggio, *Exec Dir*
Sedge Dienst, *President*
Peter Mc Coy, *CEO*
Alan Fox, *Treasurer*
Andrea Clay, *Vice Pres*
EMP: 200
SQ FT: 12,000
SALES: 21.3MM **Privately Held**
WEB: www.ecs-sf.org
SIC: 8322 Emergency shelters

(P-23789)
EPISCOPAL COMMUNITY
Also Called: Ecs South Bay Head Start
1261 Third Ave Ste B, Chula Vista (91911-3262)
PHONE..................619 228-2800
Buffy Boyer, *Director*
Gene Merlino, *Director*
EMP: 60
SALES (est): 760.2K **Privately Held**
SIC: 8322 8741 Community center; management services

(P-23790)
ETNA POLICE ACTIVITIES LEAGUE
448 Main St, Etna (96027)
PHONE..................530 467-3400
Josh Short, *President*
Autumn Kistler, *Director*
EMP: 200
SALES: 12.9K **Privately Held**
SIC: 8322 Community center

(P-23791)
EXCEPTNAL PRENTS UNLIMITED INC
Also Called: E P U
4440 N 1st St, Fresno (93726-2304)
PHONE..................559 229-2000
Marion Karian, *Exec Dir*
Ellen Knapp, *Exec Dir*
Kim Majors, *Human Res Dir*
Daryl Hitchcock, *Director*
Cindy Stoops, *Manager*
EMP: 100
SQ FT: 24,000
SALES: 7MM **Privately Held**
WEB: www.exceptionalparents.org
SIC: 8322 Family counseling services

(P-23792)
FAMILY & CHILDREN SERVICES
375 Cambridge Ave, Palo Alto (94306-1613)
PHONE..................650 326-6576
Jim Welsh, *President*
Cassie Blume, *Executive*
Howard Lagoze, *General Mgr*
Maryanne McGlothlin, *General Mgr*
Fish Williams, *Finance*
EMP: 100
SQ FT: 6,000
SALES: 9.4MM **Privately Held**
SIC: 8322 Child related social services

(P-23793)
FAMILY ASSESSMENT CNSLNG EDCTN
1651 E 4th St Ste 128, Santa Ana (92701-5141)
PHONE..................714 447-9024
Mary O Harris, *Branch Mgr*
EMP: 50
SALES (est): 301.7K **Privately Held**
SIC: 8322 Family counseling services; general counseling services
PA: Family Assessment Counseling Education Services
2601 E Chapman Ave # 114
Fullerton CA 92831
-

(P-23794)
FAMILY BRIDGES INC
168 11th St, Oakland (94607-4841)
PHONE..................510 839-2270
Corinne Jan, *Exec Dir*
Susanna Ng-Lee, *Vice Pres*
Mary Marshall, *Admin Sec*
Vienna Gao, *Admin Asst*
Amy Yiu, *Administration*
EMP: 126
SQ FT: 5,000
SALES: 6.9MM **Privately Held**
WEB: www.familybridges.net
SIC: 8322 8641 Social service center; civic social & fraternal associations

(P-23795)
FAMILY CIRCLE INC
Also Called: Oxnard Family Circle Adhc
2100 Outlet Center Dr # 380, Oxnard (93036-0612)
PHONE..................805 385-4180
Inna Berger, *CEO*
Katy Krul, *CFO*
Dina Treglia, *Accounts Mgr*
EMP: 56
SQ FT: 12,000
SALES: 3.3MM **Privately Held**
WEB: www.familycircle.com
SIC: 8322 Adult day care center

(P-23796)
FAMILY RESOURCE & REFERRAL CTR
509 W Weber Ave Ste 101, Stockton (95203-3107)
PHONE..................209 948-1553
Fax: 209 948-3554
EMP: 100
SALES (est): 28.6MM **Privately Held**
SIC: 8322

(P-23797)
FAMILY SERVICE AGENCY
Also Called: FSA
101 S B St Ste A, Lompoc (93436-6933)
PHONE..................805 735-4376
Stephanie Wilson, *Co-President*
Lisa Brabo, *Exec Dir*
EMP: 50
SALES (est): 541.3K **Privately Held**
SIC: 8322 8011 Social service center; health maintenance organization

(P-23798)
FAMILY SERVICES TULARE COUNTY
815 W Oak Ave, Visalia (93291-6033)
PHONE..................559 732-1970
Caity Meader, *Exec Dir*
EMP: 85
SQ FT: 2,000
SALES: 4.2MM **Privately Held**
SIC: 8322 Family counseling services; social service center

(P-23799)
FAMILY SUPPORT SERVICES (PA)
401 Grand Ave Ste 500, Oakland (94610-5097)
PHONE..................510 834-2443
Lou Fox, *Director*
EMP: 58
SALES: 5.2MM **Privately Held**
WEB: www.fssba-oak.org
SIC: 8322 Social service center

(P-23800)
FAMILY SVC AGCY SANTA BARBARA
123 W Gutierrez St, Santa Barbara (93101-3424)
PHONE..................805 965-1001
Denise Cicourel, *Administration*
Colleen Breen, *Manager*
EMP: 100
SALES: 5.3MM **Privately Held**
WEB: www.fsacares.org
SIC: 8322 Family (marriage) counseling

(P-23801)
FAMILY SVCS AGCY MARIN CNTY (PA)
Also Called: Family Service Agency
555 Northgate Dr, San Rafael (94903-3680)
PHONE..................415 491-5700
Margret Hallett, *Director*
EMP: 82
SALES (est): 2MM **Privately Held**
SIC: 8322 Family (marriage) counseling

(P-23802)
FAMILY YMCA OF DESERT
42575 Valley Dr, Palm Desert (92210)
PHONE..................760 423-5860
Rosemary Wagner, *Branch Mgr*
EMP: 57
SALES (corp-wide): 7.3MM **Privately Held**
SIC: 8322 Individual & family services
PA: Family Ymca Of The Desert
43930 San Pablo Ave
Palm Desert CA 92260
760 469-4521

(P-23803)
FAR NORTHERN COORDINATING COUN
Also Called: Regional Center
1377 E Lassen Ave, Chico (95973-7824)
PHONE..................530 895-8633
Laura Larson, *Director*
Ivor Thomas, *Analyst*
EMP: 75
SALES (corp-wide): 127MM **Privately Held**
SIC: 8322 8399 Social services for the handicapped; health & welfare council
PA: Far Northern Coordinating Council On Developmental Disabilities
1900 Churn Creek Rd # 114
Redding CA 96002
530 222-4791

(P-23804)
FAR NORTHERN COORDINATING COUN (PA)
Also Called: Far Northern Regional Center
1900 Churn Creek Rd # 114, Redding (96002-0292)
P.O. Box 492418 (96049-2418)
PHONE..................530 222-4791
Laura L Larson, *Exec Dir*
Cynthia Presidio, *COO*
Michael Mintline, *CFO*
Lauren Leisz, *Admin Asst*
Laura Larson, *Director*
EMP: 100
SALES: 127MM **Privately Held**
SIC: 8322 Association for the handicapped; social services for the handicapped

(P-23805)
FHAR FMLY HSING ADULT RSOURCES
205 W 20th Ave, San Mateo (94403-1302)
PHONE..................650 573-3341
Dave Carson, *President*
Phil Surdel, *Director*
EMP: 90
SALES (est): 1.3MM **Privately Held**
WEB: www.fhar.org
SIC: 8322 Social service center

(P-23806)
FIREFIGHTER CANCER SUPPORT NTW
3460 Fletcher Ave, El Monte (91731-3002)
PHONE..................866 994-3276

Dan Crow, *President*
Jeffrey Howe, *Treasurer*
Holden Leon, *Director*
Jeff Strawn, *Director*
Steve Westcott, *Director*
EMP: 50
SALES: 228.2K **Privately Held**
SIC: 8322 Social service center

(P-23807)
FIRST PLACE FOR YOUTH (PA)
426 17th St Ste 100, Oakland
(94612-2814)
PHONE..................510 272-0979
Sam Cobbs, *Exec Dir*
EMP: 50 **EST:** 1999
SALES: 19.2MM **Privately Held**
SIC: 8322 Youth center

(P-23808)
FOUNDATION FOR EARLY CHILDHOOD (PA)
3360 Flair Dr Ste 100, El Monte
(91731-2833)
PHONE..................626 572-5107
Sharyn Muhammad-Beeker, *CEO*
Jaleh Hazian, *Administration*
EMP: 65 **EST:** 1965
SALES: 11.5MM **Privately Held**
SIC: 8322 Child guidance agency

(P-23809)
FRESH LIFELINES FOR YOUTH INC
568 Valley Way, Milpitas (95035-4106)
PHONE..................408 263-2630
Christa Gannon, *CEO*
EMP: 57
SALES (est): 215.8K **Privately Held**
SIC: 8322 Child guidance agency

(P-23810)
FRESNO CNTY ECONOMIC OPPORTUNT
Also Called: Fresno Eoc
1900 Mariposa Mall # 300, Fresno
(93721-2514)
PHONE..................559 263-1000
Bryan Angus, *CEO*
EMP: 1200
SALES (corp-wide): 102.6MM **Privately Held**
SIC: 8322 Social service center
PA: Fresno County Economic Opportunities Commission
1920 Mariposa Mall # 300
Fresno CA 93721
559 263-1010

(P-23811)
FRESNO CNTY ECONOMIC OPPORTUNT (PA)
Also Called: FRESNO EOC
1920 Mariposa Mall # 300, Fresno
(93721-2504)
PHONE..................559 263-1010
Brian Angus, *CEO*
Vongsavanh Mouanoutoua, *President*
Salam Nalia, *CFO*
Marina Magdaleno, *Treasurer*
Alyssa Collins, *Human Res Mgr*
EMP: 600 **EST:** 1965
SQ FT: 115,312
SALES: 102.6MM **Privately Held**
SIC: 8322 8399 Social service center; community development groups

(P-23812)
FRESNO CNTY ECONOMIC OPPORTUNT
3120 W Nielsen Ave # 102, Fresno
(93706-1139)
PHONE..................559 485-3733
George Egewa, *Manager*
EMP: 100
SALES (corp-wide): 102.6MM **Privately Held**
SIC: 8322 Individual & family services
PA: Fresno County Economic Opportunities Commission
1920 Mariposa Mall # 300
Fresno CA 93721
559 263-1010

(P-23813)
FRESNO RESCUE MISSION INC (PA)
263 G St, Fresno (93706-3452)
P.O. Box 470, West Yellowstone MT
(59758-0470)
PHONE..................559 268-0839
Larry Arce, *CEO*
Rob Cravy, *COO*
John Avila, *Bd of Directors*
Rory F Cantando, *Bd of Directors*
Jarrod C Martinez, *Bd of Directors*
EMP: 50
SQ FT: 29,000
SALES: 5.6MM **Privately Held**
WEB: www.fresnorescuemission.org
SIC: 8322 Emergency shelters; child related social services

(P-23814)
FRIENDLY VALLEY RECRTL ASSN
Also Called: FRIENDLY VILLAGE COMMUNITY ASS
19345 Avenue Of The Oaks, Santa Clarita
(91321-1406)
PHONE..................661 252-3223
Debbie Makaryk, *Manager*
Ruth Gauthier, *President*
EMP: 50
SQ FT: 1,500
SALES: 2.1MM **Privately Held**
SIC: 8322 Senior citizens' center or association

(P-23815)
FRIENDS CHBAD LBVTCH SAN DIEGO (PA)
Also Called: Chabad House
6115 Montezuma Rd, San Diego
(92115-1429)
PHONE..................619 265-7700
Rabbi Yonah Fradkin, *President*
Yonah Fradkin, *President*
EMP: 50
SALES (est): 1.9MM **Privately Held**
SIC: 8322 8211 Individual & family services; elementary & secondary schools

(P-23816)
FRIENDS OF FAMILY
16861 Parthenia St, Northridge
(91343-4539)
PHONE..................818 988-4430
Susan Kaplan, *Exec Dir*
Traci Williams, *Division Mgr*
Brenda Hillhouse, *Director*
EMP: 50 **EST:** 1972
SQ FT: 5,500
SALES: 2.2MM **Privately Held**
WEB: www.fofca.org
SIC: 8322 Family counseling services

(P-23817)
FRIENDS OUTSIDE
7272 Murray Dr, Stockton (95210-3339)
P.O. Box 4085 (95204-0085)
PHONE..................209 955-0701
Gretchen Newby, *Exec Dir*
EMP: 130
SQ FT: 7,800
SALES: 4.2MM **Privately Held**
WEB: www.friendsoutside.org
SIC: 8322 Social service center

(P-23818)
FULL SPECTRUM SERVICES INC
Also Called: Community Actv Rhbltn & Emplym
1570 S Railroad Ave, Crescent City
(95531-6821)
P.O. Box 592 (95531-0592)
PHONE..................707 465-1460
Michael Roach, *President*
EMP: 50
SALES (est): 31.8K **Privately Held**
SIC: 8322 Individual & family services

(P-23819)
FUTURES EXPLORED
Also Called: Nifty Thrift
2380 Salvio St Ste 302, Concord
(94520-2193)
P.O. Box 418 (94522-0418)
PHONE..................925 332-7183

Will Stanford, *Director*
Dina Gibson, *Principal*
Angelique Goldberg, *Principal*
Heather Hackett, *Principal*
Dienne Kelly, *Principal*
EMP: 60
SQ FT: 1,740
SALES: 10.9MM **Privately Held**
WEB: www.futures-explored.org
SIC: 8322 Association for the handicapped

(P-23820)
G & L PENASQUITOS INC
Also Called: Arbors, The
10584 Rancho Carmel Dr, San Diego
(92128-3629)
PHONE..................858 538-0802
Gary Penovich, *Exec Dir*
Tiffany Yin, *Exec Dir*
EMP: 65
SQ FT: 48,685
SALES (est): 2.3MM
SALES (corp-wide): 297.8MM **Privately Held**
WEB: www.glrealty.com
SIC: 8322 Individual & family services
PA: G&L Realty Corp, Llc
439 N Bedford Dr
Beverly Hills CA 90210
310 273-9930

(P-23821)
GIARRETTO INSTITUTE
Also Called: Parents United
232 E Gish Rd, San Jose (95112-4706)
PHONE..................408 453-7616
Jerry Doyle, *CEO*
EMP: 50
SALES (est): 711K **Privately Held**
SIC: 8322 Individual & family services

(P-23822)
GOLDEN GATE REGIONAL CTR INC (PA)
1355 Market St Ste 220, San Francisco
(94103-1314)
PHONE..................415 546-9222
Ron Fell, *CEO*
Chris Rognier, *CFO*
Eric Zigman, *Bd of Directors*
Judy Leonard, *Executive Asst*
Erika Bolden, *Admin Asst*
EMP: 210 **EST:** 1966
SQ FT: 16,901
SALES: 243MM **Privately Held**
SIC: 8322 Referral service for personal & social problems; outreach program

(P-23823)
GOLDEN GATE REGIONAL CTR INC
3130 La Selva St Ste 202, San Mateo
(94403-2191)
PHONE..................650 574-9232
David Beuerman, *General Mgr*
EMP: 65
SALES (corp-wide): 243MM **Privately Held**
SIC: 8322 Social services for the handicapped
PA: Golden Gate Regional Center, Inc.
1355 Market St Ste 220
San Francisco CA 94103
415 546-9222

(P-23824)
GOLDEN LIVING LLC
Also Called: Beverly Healthcare
24100 Monroe Ave, Murrieta (92562-9507)
PHONE..................951 600-4640
Doug Lendoff, *Manager*
EMP: 100
SALES (corp-wide): 7.4MM **Privately Held**
WEB: www.nwbeccorp.com
SIC: 8322 Rehabilitation services
PA: Golden Living Llc
5220 Tennyson Pkwy # 400
Plano TX 75024
972 372-6300

(P-23825)
GOOD SAMARITAN SHELTER
245 Inger Dr Ste 103b, Santa Maria
(93454-8669)
PHONE..................805 346-8185

Sylvia Barnard, *Director*
Alexis Nshamamba, *COO*
Kirsten Cahoon, *Manager*
EMP: 60
SQ FT: 2,400
SALES: 5.4MM **Privately Held**
SIC: 8322 Emergency shelters

(P-23826)
GREATER LOS ANGELES AGENCY
2239 Norwalk Ave, Los Angeles (90041)
PHONE..................323 478-8000
Patricia Hughes, *CEO*
EMP: 70
SALES: 7.1MM **Privately Held**
SIC: 8322 Social service center

(P-23827)
H E L P INC
53 S 6th St, Banning (92220-4809)
PHONE..................951 922-2305
Al Silva, *President*
Bruce Kuhn, *Vice Pres*
Nancy Guthrie, *Admin Sec*
EMP: 85
SQ FT: 3,000
SALES (est): 273.3K **Privately Held**
SIC: 8322 Individual & family services

(P-23828)
HALLMARK REHABILITATION GP LLC
27442 Portola Pkwy # 200, El Toro
(92610-2822)
PHONE..................949 282-5900
Jose Lynch,
Jimmy Sims,
Mark Whartley,
Laurie Thomas, *Mng Member*
EMP: 1200
SQ FT: 10,000
SALES (est): 21.9MM **Privately Held**
WEB: www.hallmarkrehabinc.com
SIC: 8322 Rehabilitation services

(P-23829)
HAMILTON FAMILIES
1631 Hayes St, San Francisco
(94117-1326)
PHONE..................415 409-2100
Rosa Caspaneda, *Director*
Patricia Babiraz, *Administration*
Rosa Castaneda, *Finance*
Jack Fagan, *Deputy Dir*
EMP: 65
SALES: 8.8MM **Privately Held**
WEB: www.hamiltonfamilycenter.org
SIC: 8322 Emergency shelters

(P-23830)
HANFORD JOINT UN HIGH SCHL DST
Also Called: Hanford Adult School
905 Campus Dr, Hanford (93230-3552)
PHONE..................559 583-5905
Heather Keran, *Principal*
EMP: 56
SALES (corp-wide): 48.8MM **Privately Held**
SIC: 8322 Adult day care center
PA: Hanford Joint Union High School District
823 W Lacey Blvd
Hanford CA 93230
559 583-5901

(P-23831)
HATHAWAY RESOURCE CENTER
5701 S Eastrn Ave Ste 550, Los Angeles
(90040)
PHONE..................323 837-0838
Many Galledos, *Branch Mgr*
EMP: 50
SALES (corp-wide): 2.6MM **Privately Held**
SIC: 8322 Family counseling services
PA: Hathaway Resource Center
840 N Avenue 66
Los Angeles CA 90042
323 257-9600

PRODUCTS & SVCS

(P-23832)

HEALTH SOUTH TUSTIN REHAB HOSP
14851 Yorba St, Tustin (92780-2925)
PHONE..............................714 832-9200
Paula Redman, *Controller*
Ben Zavala, *Engineer*
Lee Fallon, *Marketing Staff*
EMP: 140
SQ FT: 90,000
SALES (est): 2.4MM
SALES (corp-wide): 3.9B **Publicly Held**
WEB: www.healthsouth.com
SIC: 8322 8069 Rehabilitation services; specialty hospitals, except psychiatric
PA: Encompass Health Corporation
9001 Liberty Pkwy
Birmingham AL 35242
205 967-7116

(P-23833)

HEALTHRIGHT 360
Also Called: Prototypes Women's Center
845 E Arrow Hwy, Pomona (91767-2535)
PHONE..............................909 624-1233
April Wilson, *Vice Pres*
EMP: 100
SALES (corp-wide): 96.1MM **Privately Held**
SIC: 8322 8069 General counseling services; drug addiction rehabilitation hospital
PA: Healthright 360
1563 Mission St Fl 1
San Francisco CA 94103
415 762-3700

(P-23834)

HELP AT HOME INC
4535 Mcuri Flat Rd Ste 2h, Placerville (95667)
PHONE..............................916 933-9050
Marie Harlow, *Director*
EMP: 65
SALES: 1.2MM **Privately Held**
WEB: www.milner-fenwick.com
SIC: 8322 8082 Senior citizens' center or association; home health care services

(P-23835)

HELP FOR THE HURTING INC
Also Called: Helping Hands Pantry
2205 S Artesia St, San Bernardino (92408-3906)
P.O. Box 1224, Redlands (92373-0401)
PHONE..............................909 796-4222
Paul Dickau, *Exec Dir*
EMP: 90 EST: 2009
SALES: 1.6MM **Privately Held**
SIC: 8322 Social service center

(P-23836)

HELP HOSPITALIZED VETERANS II
36585 Penfield Ln, Winchester (92596-9672)
PHONE..............................951 926-4500
Mike Lynch, *Exec Dir*
EMP: 65 EST: 1971
SQ FT: 25,000
SALES: 31MM **Privately Held**
WEB: www.hhv.org
SIC: 8322 Individual & family services

(P-23837)

HELPLINE YOUTH COUNSELING (PA)
14181 Telegraph Rd, Whittier (90604-2554)
PHONE..............................562 273-0722
Deepak Nanda, *Ch of Bd*
Jacques Welche C P A, *Treasurer*
Jeffrey Fleischer, *Executive*
Jeff Farber, *Exec Dir*
Pam Van Alstyne, *Admin Sec*
EMP: 50
SQ FT: 9,000
SALES: 4.1MM **Privately Held**
WEB: www.vfnet.com
SIC: 8322 Family (marriage) counseling; social service center

(P-23838)

HIGH ROAD PROGRAM (PA)
250 N Westlake Blvd # 210, Westlake Village (91362-7009)
PHONE..............................805 497-8800
Robert T Dorris Jr, *President*
Bill McVay, *CEO*
EMP: 62
SQ FT: 2,000
SALES: 3MM **Privately Held**
WEB: www.highroadprogram.org
SIC: 8322 Social service center

(P-23839)

HINDS HOSPICE (PA)
2490 W Shaw Ave Ste 100a, Fresno (93711-3305)
PHONE..............................559 674-0407
Nancy Hinds, *Exec Dir*
Lynne Pietz, *Exec Dir*
Rosa Butler, *Admin Asst*
Bev Robinson, *Finance*
James Majors, *Director*
EMP: 170
SALES: 17.9MM **Privately Held**
SIC: 8322 Individual & family services

(P-23840)

HOMEBOY INDUSTRIES (PA)
Also Called: HOMEBOY BAKERY
130 Bruno St, Los Angeles (90012-1815)
PHONE..............................323 526-1254
Greg Boyle, *Exec Dir*
John Brady, *Ch of Bd*
Jack Faherty, *CFO*
Andrew Platts, *Info Tech Dir*
Chris Evenson, *Controller*
EMP: 300
SQ FT: 3,690
SALES: 14.4MM **Privately Held**
SIC: 8322 Rehabilitation services; social service center

(P-23841)

HOMEBRIDGE INC
Also Called: IHSS Consortium, The
1035 Market St Ste L1, San Francisco (94103-1666)
PHONE..............................415 255-2079
Gay Kaplan, *Principal*
Margaret Baran, *Principal*
Mark Burns, *Principal*
Debra J Dolch, *Principal*
Andrew Gaines, *Exec Dir*
EMP: 500
SALES: 26.7MM **Privately Held**
SIC: 8322 Homemakers' service

(P-23842)

HOMEFRST SVCS SANTA CLARA CNTY
Also Called: EHC LIFEBUILDERS
507 Valley Way, Milpitas (95035-4105)
PHONE..............................408 539-2100
Jennifer Niklaus, *CEO*
Rene Ramirez, *COO*
Mary Zavala, *Officer*
Loann Roe, *Director*
Ophelia Howeth, *Case Mgr*
EMP: 115
SALES: 12.2MM **Privately Held**
SIC: 8322 Individual & family services

(P-23843)

HOMELESS PRENATAL PROGRAM
33 Middle Point Rd, San Francisco (94124-4439)
PHONE..............................415 546-6756
Martha Ryan, *Director*
Laura Springer, *Human Res Mgr*
Roberta Goodman, *Opers Staff*
Sonia Batres, *VP Mktg*
Vivian Harris, *VP Mktg*
EMP: 50
SALES: 8MM **Privately Held**
WEB: www.homelessprenatal.org
SIC: 8322 Social service center

(P-23844)

HOPE OF VALLEY RESCUE MISSION
11076 Norris Ave, Pacoima (91331-2468)
P.O. Box 7609, Mission Hills (91346-7609)
PHONE..............................818 392-0020
Ken Craft, *President*
Michael Klausman, *Ch of Bd*
David Faustina, *COO*
Chris Delaplane, *Treasurer*
Jin Pak, *Bd of Directors*

EMP: 54
SQ FT: 22,000
SALES: 3.2MM **Privately Held**
SIC: 8322 Emergency shelters

(P-23845)

HUCKLEBERRY YOUTH PROGRAMS INC (PA)
3310 Geary Blvd, San Francisco (94118-3324)
PHONE..............................415 668-2622
Bruce Fisher, *Exec Dir*
Jenn Chen, *General Mgr*
Daniel Throop, *Info Tech Mgr*
Elizabeth Ascher, *Research*
Brooke Tao, *Asst Director*
EMP: 72 EST: 1967
SQ FT: 2,000
SALES: 5.9MM **Privately Held**
SIC: 8322 Youth center

(P-23846)

HUMAN OPTIONS INC
1901 Newport Blvd Ste 240, Costa Mesa (92627-2294)
PHONE..............................949 757-3635
Maricela Rios, *Branch Mgr*
Heather Brown, *Human Res Mgr*
Jessica Reynaga, *Education*
Claudia Flores, *Supervisor*
EMP: 50 **Privately Held**
SIC: 8322 Individual & family services
PA: Human Options, Inc
5540 Trabuco Rd Ste 100
Irvine CA 92620

(P-23847)

HUMAN OPTIONS INC (PA)
5540 Trabuco Rd Ste 100, Irvine (92620-5745)
P.O. Box 53745 (92619-3745)
PHONE..............................949 737-5242
Maricela Rios, *Officer*
Gael Libby, *Volunteer Dir*
Vivian Clecak, *Exec Dir*
Kathy Elflein, *Admin Asst*
Gregory Gebhardt, *Finance*
EMP: 65
SALES: 5.1MM **Privately Held**
SIC: 8322 Family counseling services

(P-23848)

HUMBOLDT COMMNTY ACCSS RESRC
Also Called: Baybridge Employment Services
1707 E St Ste 2, Eureka (95501-7621)
PHONE..............................707 443-7077
Ross Jantz, *Principal*
EMP: 56
SALES (corp-wide): 4.2MM **Privately Held**
WEB: www.thestudioonline.net
SIC: 8322 Referral service for personal & social problems
PA: Humboldt Community Access And Resource Center
1707 E St Ste 2
Eureka CA 95501
707 443-7077

(P-23849)

HUMBOLDT SENIOR RESOURCE CTR (PA)
1910 California St, Eureka (95501-2899)
PHONE..............................707 443-9747
Joyce Hayes, *Exec Dir*
Claudia Padilla, *Information Mgr*
Rene Arche, *Marketing Staff*
Tina Taylor, *Food Svc Dir*
EMP: 110
SQ FT: 14,000
SALES: 12.7MM **Privately Held**
SIC: 8322 8741 Senior citizens' center or association; management services

(P-23850)

HUNTINGTON PK POLICE LEAGUE
Also Called: HUNTINGTON PARK POLICE DEPARTM
6542 Miles Ave, Huntington Park (90255-4318)
PHONE..............................323 584-6254
Paul Wadley, *President*

Jorge Cisneros, *President*
Lily Garcia, *Administration*
EMP: 75
SALES: 6.9K **Privately Held**
SIC: 8322 Outreach program

(P-23851)

IDEAL PROGRAM SERVICES INC
3970 W Martin Luther King, Los Angeles (90008-1732)
PHONE..............................323 296-2255
Omolara Okunubi, *CEO*
Karla Melgar, *Director*
Teresa Mc Dougal, *Supervisor*
EMP: 71
SQ FT: 8,880
SALES (est): 1.7MM **Privately Held**
WEB: www.idealprogram.com
SIC: 8322 5999 Social services for the handicapped; technical aids for the handicapped

(P-23852)

IN2VISION PROGRAMS LLC
13601 Whittier Blvd, Whittier (90605-1902)
PHONE..............................562 789-8888
Maria Del Carmen Torres, *Mng Member*
Cesar Torres, *Mng Member*
EMP: 51
SALES (est): 1.9MM **Privately Held**
SIC: 8322 Social services for the handicapped

(P-23853)

INCLUSION SERVICES LLC
13225 Philadelphia St E, Whittier (90601-4321)
PHONE..............................562 945-2000
Cesar Torres, *Mng Member*
Flor Ulloa, *Human Res Mgr*
Israel Ibenez, *Mng Member*
EMP: 103
SQ FT: 1,200
SALES (est): 6.4MM **Privately Held**
SIC: 8322 8331 Social services for the handicapped; skill training center

(P-23854)

INDEPENDENT OPTIONS
Also Called: Harbor Village II
2532 Santa Catalina Dr # 104, Costa Mesa (92626-6880)
PHONE..............................714 434-1175
Dennis Mattson, *Owner*
EMP: 100
SALES (est): 1.6MM **Privately Held**
SIC: 8322 8361 Social services for the handicapped; residential care

(P-23855)

INDIVIDUALS NOW
Also Called: SOCIAL ADVOCATES FOR YOUTH
2447 Summerfield Rd, Santa Rosa (95405-7815)
PHONE..............................707 544-3299
Matt Martin, *CEO*
Katrina Thurman, *COO*
Dave Koressel, *CFO*
Cat Cvengros, *Officer*
Paul Margolis, *Director*
EMP: 55
SALES: 8.4MM **Privately Held**
SIC: 8322 Child guidance agency; youth center

(P-23856)

INLAND VALLEY DRUG & ALCOHOL (PA)
Also Called: ADMINISTRATIVE OFFICES
1260 E Arrow Hwy, Upland (91786-4982)
PHONE..............................909 932-1069
Tina Hughes, *CEO*
Ellen Davis, *Executive*
Stacy Blackstone, *Exec Dir*
Laurie Figueroa, *Finance*
EMP: 65
SALES: 6.3MM **Privately Held**
WEB: www.ivdars.org
SIC: 8322 Alcoholism counseling, nontreatment

▲ = Import ▼=Export
◆ =Import/Export

(P-23857)
INSIDE OUTDOORS FOUNDATION
8755 Santiago Canyon Rd, Silverado
(92676-9758)
P.O. Box 9050, Costa Mesa (92628-9050)
PHONE....................714 708-3885
Manny Kiesser, *President*
Lori Kiesser, *Manager*
Stephanie Smith, *Manager*
EMP: 200
SQ FT: 3,000
SALES: 364.4K **Privately Held**
SIC: 8322 Outreach program

(P-23858)
INSTITUTE ON AGING
Also Called: Irene Swindell's Adult Day Car
3698 California St, San Francisco
(94118-1702)
PHONE....................415 600-2690
Cindy Kauffman, *Administration*
EMP: 100 **Privately Held**
SIC: 8322 Individual & family services
PA: Institute On Aging
   3575 Geary Blvd
   San Francisco CA 94118
-

(P-23859)
INSTITUTE ON AGING (PA)
Also Called: ADULT DAY CARE CENTER
3575 Geary Blvd, San Francisco
(94118-3212)
PHONE....................415 750-4101
J Thomas Briody, *President*
Cindy Kaufmann, *COO*
Roxana Tsougarakis, *CFO*
Ruth Kasle, *Chief Mktg Ofcr*
Shabana Siegel, *Vice Pres*
EMP: 100
SQ FT: 10,000
SALES: 38.9MM **Privately Held**
SIC: 8322 Geriatric social service

(P-23860)
INTERCOMMUNITY CHILD
10155 Colima Rd, Whittier (90603-2042)
PHONE....................562 692-0383
Charlene Dimas, *CEO*
EMP: 70
SALES (est): 655.1K **Privately Held**
SIC: 8322 Child related social services

(P-23861)
INTERFACE COMMUNITY (PA)
Also Called: INTERFACE CHILDREN FAMILY SERV
4001 Mission Oaks Blvd, Camarillo
(93012-5121)
PHONE....................805 485-6114
Charles T Watson, *President*
Dale Stoeber, *CFO*
Terryl Miller,
Erik Sternad, *Exec Dir*
Gayle Pedroza, *Accountant*
EMP: 96
SQ FT: 3,000
SALES: 8.5MM **Privately Held**
WEB: www.icfs.org
SIC: 8322 Family service agency

(P-23862)
INTERFAITH COMMUNITY SVCS INC
550 W Washington Ave B, Escondido
(92025-1643)
PHONE....................760 489-6380
Greg Anglea, *Exec Dir*
Amber Zinsky, *Principal*
Joe Stemmler, *Finance*
EMP: 100
SQ FT: 23,000
SALES: 12.6MM **Privately Held**
WEB: www.interfaithservices.org
SIC: 8322 Social service center

(P-23863)
INTERNATIONAL INST LOS ANGELES (PA)
3845 Selig Pl, Los Angeles (90031-3143)
PHONE....................323 224-3800
E Stephen Voss, *President*
Susan Eckert, *VP Admin*
Sandra Rosas, *VP Finance*

Jo Quach, *Education*
Lilian Alba, *Director*
EMP: 52 **EST:** 1935
SQ FT: 18,000
SALES: 15.5MM **Privately Held**
WEB: www.iilosangeles.org
SIC: 8322 Family service agency

(P-23864)
INTERNATIONAL MEDICAL CORPS (PA)
12400 Wilshire Blvd # 1500, Los Angeles
(90025-1030)
PHONE....................310 826-7800
Nancy Aossey, *President*
Ons Alkhadra, *Sr Corp Ofcr*
Camille Blackman, *Officer*
Janet Gatimu, *Officer*
Ryan Haliday, *Officer*
EMP: 92
SALES: 130.1MM **Privately Held**
WEB: www.imc-la.com
SIC: 8322 Disaster service

(P-23865)
INTERNTNAL RSCUE COMMITTEE INC
5348 University Ave # 205, San Diego
(92105-8025)
PHONE....................619 641-7510
Roisin Wisneski, *Branch Mgr*
Farah A Banna, *Education*
Joseph Jok, *Case Mgr*
Kasra Movahedi, *Manager*
EMP: 63
SALES (corp-wide): 753.5MM **Privately Held**
SIC: 8322 Social service center
PA: International Rescue Committee, Inc.
   122 E 42nd St
   New York NY 10168
   212 551-3000

(P-23866)
INTERPRSNAL DVLPMNTAL FCLTTORS
Also Called: IDS
891 Worcester Ave Apt 3, Pasadena
(91104-4258)
PHONE....................626 793-8967
Dorothea A Bradley, *CEO*
EMP: 71
SALES (est): 567.8K **Privately Held**
SIC: 8322 Association for the handicapped; meal delivery program

(P-23867)
ISLAMIC RELIEF USA
6131 Orangethorpe Ave # 450, Buena Park
(90620-4903)
PHONE....................714 676-1300
Abed Ayoub, *Branch Mgr*
Magda Motawi, *Officer*
Mohammad Abdelmagd, *Principal*
Ahmed El-Bendary, *Principal*
Almas Talib, *Principal*
EMP: 70 **Privately Held**
SIC: 8322 Community center
PA: Islamic Relief Usa
   3655 Wheeler Ave
   Alexandria VA 22304
-

(P-23868)
J GELT CORPORATION
Also Called: Casa Pacifica Adult Day H
1424 30th St Ste C, San Diego
(92154-3417)
PHONE....................619 424-8181
Luba Vaisman, *President*
Tatyana Cohen, *Assistant VP*
EMP: 50
SQ FT: 15,000
SALES: 3.4MM **Privately Held**
SIC: 8322 Adult day care center

(P-23869)
JACOBS CSHMAN SAN DIEGO FD BNK
9850 Distribution Ave, San Diego
(92121-2320)
PHONE....................858 527-1419
James Floros, *President*
Casey Castillo, *CFO*
Vanessa Moore, *Vice Pres*

Vanessa Ruiz, *Vice Pres*
Liz Sheahan, *Vice Pres*
EMP: 50
SALES: 41.2MM **Privately Held**
SIC: 8322 Social service center

(P-23870)
JAMISON CHILDRENS HOME
1010 Shalimar Dr, Bakersfield
(93306-5633)
P.O. Box 511 (93302-0511)
PHONE....................661 334-3500
Carl Guilford, *Director*
EMP: 60
SALES (est): 721.3K **Privately Held**
SIC: 8322 Individual & family services

(P-23871)
JANUS OF SANTA CRUZ
200 7th Ave Ste 150, Santa Cruz
(95062-4669)
PHONE....................831 462-1060
Rod Libbey, *Exec Dir*
Lorraine Shuler, *Human Res Dir*
Jaime Campos, *Director*
Christine Bassi, *Manager*
EMP: 100 **EST:** 1976
SALES: 7.4MM **Privately Held**
WEB: www.janussc.org
SIC: 8322 Rehabilitation services

(P-23872)
JEWISH COMMUNITY CTR LONG BCH
Also Called: ALPERT JEWISH COMMUNITY CENTRE
3801 E Willow St, Long Beach
(90815-1734)
PHONE....................562 426-7601
Gordon Lentzner, *President*
Winston Abigail, *CFO*
Brooke Anderson, *Admin Asst*
Herlina Fraher, *Accountant*
Rick Arciniaga, *Controller*
EMP: 150
SQ FT: 90,000
SALES: 5.9MM **Privately Held**
SIC: 8322 Community center

(P-23873)
JEWISH FAMILY AND CHLD SVCS (PA)
Also Called: CLEANERIFIC
2150 Post St, San Francisco (94115-3508)
P.O. Box 159004 (94115-9004)
PHONE....................415 449-1200
Anita Friedman, *Exec Dir*
Nan Toder, *Partner*
Michael R Zent, *CEO*
Marga Dusedau, *CFO*
Javier Favela, *CFO*
EMP: 500
SALES: 37.8MM **Privately Held**
SIC: 8322 Family service agency

(P-23874)
JEWISH FAMILY SVC LOS ANGELES
Also Called: Valley Stre Frnt Jwsh Fmly Svc
12821 Victory Blvd, North Hollywood
(91606-3012)
PHONE....................818 984-0276
Karen Leaf, *Director*
EMP: 72
SALES (corp-wide): 2.4MM **Privately Held**
WEB: www.jewishla.com
SIC: 8322 5331 Social service center; variety stores
PA: Jewish Family Service Of Los Angeles
   3580 Wilshire Blvd
   Los Angeles CA 90010
   323 761-8800

(P-23875)
JEWISH FAMILY SVC LOS ANGELES
Senior Citizens Center
330 N Fairfax Ave, Los Angeles
(90036-2109)
PHONE....................323 937-5900
Doreen Klee, *Owner*
EMP: 50

SALES (corp-wide): 2.4MM **Privately Held**
WEB: www.jewishla.com
SIC: 8322 Old age assistance
PA: Jewish Family Service Of Los Angeles
   3580 Wilshire Blvd
   Los Angeles CA 90010
   323 761-8800

(P-23876)
JEWISH FAMILY SVC SAN DIEGO (PA)
8804 Balboa Ave, San Diego (92123-1506)
PHONE....................858 637-3000
Michael Hopkins, *CEO*
Felicia Mandelbaum, *President*
Karen Luton, *Office Mgr*
Jennifer Turner, *Executive Asst*
Celeste Grant, *Admin Asst*
EMP: 100
SQ FT: 25,000
SALES: 15.8MM **Privately Held**
SIC: 8322 Family (marriage) counseling; family counseling services

(P-23877)
JEWISH FMLY & CMNTY SVCS E BAY (PA)
Also Called: JFCS/EAST BAY
2484 Shattuck Ave Ste 210, Berkeley
(94704-2076)
PHONE....................510 704-7475
AVI Rose, *Exec Dir*
Barbara Nelson, *Director*
EMP: 63
SALES: 6.5MM **Privately Held**
SIC: 8322 8049 Senior citizens' center or association; psychologist, psychotherapist & hypnotist

(P-23878)
JON K TAKATA CORPORATION (PA)
Also Called: Restoration Management Company
4142 Point Eden Way, Hayward
(94545-3703)
PHONE....................510 315-5400
Jon Takata, *President*
EMP: 70
SQ FT: 100,000
SALES (est): 38.1MM **Privately Held**
WEB: www.restorationmanagement.com
SIC: 8322 1799 4959 Disaster service; asbestos removal & encapsulation; environmental cleanup services

(P-23879)
JONI AND FRIENDS (PA)
30009 Ladyface Ct, Agoura (91301-2583)
PHONE....................818 707-5664
Joni E Tada, *CEO*
Billy Burnett, *Exec VP*
Douglas Mazza, *Exec VP*
EMP: 84
SQ FT: 30,000
SALES: 24.9MM **Privately Held**
SIC: 8322 Association for the handicapped

(P-23880)
KAINOS HOME & TRAINING CTR
Also Called: Kainos Work Activity Ctr
2761 Fair Oaks Ave Ste A, Redwood City
(94063-3540)
PHONE....................650 361-1355
Christen Rodgers, *Manager*
Kristen Uthman, *Program Mgr*
EMP: 50
SALES (corp-wide): 5.2MM **Privately Held**
WEB: www.kainosusa.org
SIC: 8322 Individual & family services
PA: Kainos Home & Training Center For Developmentally Disabled Adults
   3631 Jefferson Ave
   Redwood City CA
   650 363-2423

(P-23881)
KEDREN COMMUNITY HLTH CTR INC
3800 S Figueroa St, Los Angeles
(90037-1206)
PHONE....................323 524-0634
John Griffith, *President*

PRODUCTS & SVCS

EMP: 153
SALES (corp-wide): 35.8MM **Privately Held**
SIC: 8322 Community center
PA: Kedren Community Health Center, Inc.
4211 Avalon Blvd
Los Angeles CA 90011
323 233-0425

(P-23882)
KINGS COMMUNITY ACTION O (PA)
Also Called: Kcao
1130 N 11th Ave, Hanford (93230-3608)
PHONE..........................559 582-4386
David Droker, *Exec Dir*
EMP: 77
SQ FT: 15,000
SALES: 17.2MM **Privately Held**
SIC: 8322 8399 Individual & family services; antipoverty board

(P-23883)
KINGS REHABILITATION CENTER (PA)
490 E Hanford Armona Rd, Hanford (93230-6129)
P.O. Box 719 (93232-0719)
PHONE..........................559 582-9234
Carol Rogers, *Marketing Staff*
Sherrie Martin, *Executive*
Steve Mendoza, *Exec Dir*
Carol Ropers, *Agent*
EMP: 64
SQ FT: 13,000
SALES: 8.3MM **Privately Held**
WEB: www.kingsrehab.com
SIC: 8322 8361 Rehabilitation services; rehabilitation center, residential: health care incidental

(P-23884)
KINSHIP CENTER
Also Called: Seneca Family of Agency
18302 Irvine Blvd Ste 300, Tustin (92780-3437)
PHONE..........................714 979-2365
Josie Romehiod, *Director*
EMP: 100
SALES (corp-wide): 5.5MM **Privately Held**
SIC: 8322 8093 Adoption services; mental health clinic, outpatient
PA: Kinship Center
124 River Rd
Salinas CA 93908
831 455-9965

(P-23885)
KOREAN COMMUNITY SERVICES INC
Also Called: Kc Services
8633 Knott Ave, Buena Park (90620-3852)
PHONE..........................714 527-6561
Ellen Ahn, *Exec Dir*
Kay Ahn, *CFO*
EMP: 50
SALES (est): 2.2MM **Privately Held**
SIC: 8322 8069 Social service center; drug addiction rehabilitation hospital

(P-23886)
KOREAN HEALTH EDUCATION (PA)
Also Called: Kheir
3727 W 6th St Ste 210, Los Angeles (90020-5108)
PHONE..........................213 427-4000
Erin K Pak, *CEO*
Neyadhish Chakma, *Vice Pres*
Mina Turan, *Assistant*
EMP: 59
SQ FT: 800
SALES: 5.6MM **Privately Held**
SIC: 8322 8011 Individual & family services; offices & clinics of medical doctors

(P-23887)
KOREATOWN YOUTH AND CMNTY CTR (PA)
Also Called: KYCC
3727 W 6th St Ste 300, Los Angeles (90020-5108)
PHONE..........................213 365-7400
John Ho Song, *Exec Dir*

Glesteree Blades, *Human Res Mgr*
Yun Pak, *Opers Spvr*
Mihae Jung, *Education*
Rumee Chung, *Psychologist*
EMP: 74
SALES: 6.3MM **Privately Held**
SIC: 8322 8211 8641 Youth center; elementary & secondary schools; environmental protection organization

(P-23888)
LA ASOCIACION NACIONAL PRO PER
Also Called: National Assn For Hispanic
1452 W Temple St Ste 100, Los Angeles (90026-5649)
PHONE..........................213 202-5900
Zecia Soto, *Principal*
EMP: 350
SALES (est): 1.5MM
SALES (corp-wide): 14.4MM **Privately Held**
SIC: 8322 7361 8611 Social service center; employment agencies; business associations
PA: La Asociacion Nacional Pro Personas Mayores
234 E Colo Blvd Ste 300
Pasadena CA 91101
626 564-1988

(P-23889)
LA ASOCIACION NACIONAL PRO PER (PA)
Also Called: NAT'L ASSN FOR HISPANIC ELDERL
234 E Colo Blvd Ste 300, Pasadena (91101)
PHONE..........................626 564-1988
Carmela G Lacayo, *President*
Maria Ramirez, *Ch of Bd*
Carole Kracer, *Treasurer*
Therese Grenier, *Admin Sec*
EMP: 1330
SQ FT: 11,000
SALES: 14.4MM **Privately Held**
SIC: 8322 Social service center

(P-23890)
LA FAMILIA COUNSELING CENTER
5523 34th St, Sacramento (95820-4725)
PHONE..........................916 452-3601
Rachell R Rios, *Exec Dir*
Rachel Rios, *Exec Dir*
EMP: 60
SALES: 3.2MM **Privately Held**
WEB: www.lafcc.com
SIC: 8322 Social service center

(P-23891)
LAURAS HOUSE
999 Corporate Dr Ste 225, Mission Viejo (92694-2156)
PHONE..........................949 361-3775
Margaret Bayston, *Exec Dir*
Sandra Condello, *Principal*
Andrea McCauister, *Director*
EMP: 56
SALES: 3.8MM **Privately Held**
WEB: www.laurashouse.net
SIC: 8322 Crisis center

(P-23892)
LEGACY AND NURSING REHAB
1790 Muir Rd, Martinez (94553-4718)
PHONE..........................925 228-8383
Dipa Gupta, *Owner*
Thomas Joseph, *Principal*
Camilo Jarquin, *Office Mgr*
Burnadett Joseph, *Admin Asst*
Irene Llona, *Corp Comm Staff*
EMP: 90
SALES (est): 1.9MM **Privately Held**
SIC: 8322 Senior citizens' center or association

(P-23893)
LIFE OPTONS VCTNAL RSOURCE CTR (PA)
Also Called: LOVARC
116 N I St, Lompoc (93436-6721)
PHONE..........................805 735-3428
William Reardon, *Exec Dir*
Elen Vanderhoof, *CFO*

▲ **EMP:** 130
SQ FT: 2,000
SALES: 6MM **Privately Held**
WEB: www.lovarc.com
SIC: 8322 Social service center

(P-23894)
LIFE STEPS FOUNDATION INC
Also Called: Lsf Central Cal Adult Svcs
1431 Pomeroy Rd, Arroyo Grande (93420-5943)
PHONE..........................805 474-8431
EMP: 225
SALES (corp-wide): 3.9MM **Privately Held**
SIC: 8322 Social service center
PA: Life Steps Foundation, Inc.
5757 W Century Blvd # 880
Los Angeles CA 90045
310 410-8190

(P-23895)
LIFE STEPS FOUNDATION INC
500 E 4th St, Long Beach (90802-2501)
PHONE..........................562 436-0751
Kristine Engels, *Director*
Robert Turner, *Manager*
EMP: 70
SALES (corp-wide): 3.9MM **Privately Held**
WEB: www.lifestepsfoundation.org
SIC: 8322 8399 Social service center; community development groups
PA: Life Steps Foundation, Inc.
5757 W Century Blvd # 880
Los Angeles CA 90045
310 410-8190

(P-23896)
LIFE STEPS FOUNDATION INC
1107 Johnson Ave, San Luis Obispo (93401-3303)
PHONE..........................805 549-0150
Virginia Franco, *Branch Mgr*
EMP: 80
SALES (corp-wide): 3.9MM **Privately Held**
WEB: www.lifestepsfoundation.org
SIC: 8322 Social service center
PA: Life Steps Foundation, Inc.
5757 W Century Blvd # 880
Los Angeles CA 90045
310 410-8190

(P-23897)
LIFEHOUSE INC (PA)
899 Northgate Dr Ste 500, San Rafael (94903-3667)
PHONE..........................415 472-2373
Nancy Dow Moody, *CEO*
Carol Loughlin, *Administration*
Trice Padecky, *Administration*
Viola Morris, *Finance Dir*
Natalia Andryushina, *Accountant*
EMP: 85 **EST:** 1957
SALES: 12MM **Privately Held**
WEB: www.lifehouseagency.org
SIC: 8322 8361 Social services for the handicapped; general counseling services; self-help organization; residential care for the handicapped

(P-23898)
LIFEMOVES (PA)
181 Constitution Dr, Menlo Park (94025-1106)
PHONE..........................650 685-5880
Bruce Ives, *Principal*
Craig Garber, *CFO*
Lorena Collins, *Assoc VP*
Anne Jarchow, *Vice Pres*
Dwight Powery, *Vice Pres*
EMP: 50
SALES: 24MM **Privately Held**
SIC: 8322 Social service center

(P-23899)
LIFESTYLES SENIOR HOUSING MAN
Also Called: Meadows Senior Living, The
9325 E Stockton Blvd, Elk Grove (95624-1282)
PHONE..........................916 714-3755
Dan Carsel, *Manager*
EMP: 60 **Privately Held**

SIC: 8322 8052 Geriatric social service; intermediate care facilities
PA: Lifestyles Senior Housing Managers Llc
7600 Ne 41st St Ste 330
Vancouver WA 98662

(P-23900)
LIGHTHOUSE LIVING SERVICES (PA)
3600 Power Inn Rd Ste H, Sacramento (95826-3826)
P.O. Box 660905 (95866-0905)
PHONE..........................916 454-4381
Tabias Cowan, *President*
EMP: 53
SQ FT: 4,500
SALES (est): 2.8MM **Privately Held**
WEB: www.lighthouseils.com
SIC: 8322 Social service center

(P-23901)
LITTLE TOKYO SERVICE CENTER (PA)
Also Called: A3M CO
231 E 3rd St Ste G106, Los Angeles (90013-1493)
PHONE..........................213 473-3003
D Matsubayashi, *Exec Dir*
Dave Uyehara, *Treasurer*
Bill Watanabe, *Exec Dir*
William Watanabe, *Exec Dir*
Michi Lew, *Executive Asst*
EMP: 120
SQ FT: 3,000
SALES: 329.6K **Privately Held**
WEB: www.asianmarrow.org
SIC: 8322 General counseling services

(P-23902)
LOS ANGELES REGIONAL FOOD BANK
1734 E 41st St, Vernon (90058-1502)
PHONE..........................323 234-3030
Michael Flood, *President*
Cece Forrester, *President*
Edward McCarthy, *COO*
Czarina Luna, *CFO*
Cassandra Barron, *Executive Asst*
EMP: 120
SQ FT: 100,000
SALES: 90.2MM **Privately Held**
SIC: 8322 Meal delivery program

(P-23903)
LOS ANGELES SEC NATIONAL (PA)
Also Called: NCJW LA
543 N Fairfax Ave, Los Angeles (90036-1715)
PHONE..........................323 651-2930
Hillary Sullivan, *Exec Dir*
Shelli Dodell, *President*
EMP: 50 **EST:** 1909
SALES: 2.2MM **Privately Held**
WEB: www.ncjwla.org
SIC: 8322 Multi-service center

(P-23904)
LOS ANGELES UNIFIED SCHOOL DST
1157 S Berendo St, Los Angeles (90006-3301)
PHONE..........................213 739-5600
EMP: 130
SALES (corp-wide): 3.8B **Privately Held**
SIC: 8322 Individual & family services
PA: Los Angeles Unified School District
333 S Beaudry Ave Ste 209
Los Angeles CA 90017
213 241-1000

(P-23905)
LOS ANGELES UNIFIED SCHOOL DST
Also Called: Westchester Emerson Cmnty
8810 Emerson Ave, Los Angeles (90045-3609)
PHONE..........................310 258-2000
Patricia Colby, *Principal*
EMP: 150
SALES (corp-wide): 3.8B **Privately Held**
WEB: www.lausd.k12.ca.us
SIC: 8322 Adult day care center

PA: Los Angeles Unified School District
333 S Beaudry Ave Ste 209
Los Angeles CA 90017
213 241-1000

(P-23906)
LOS ANGELES UNIFIED SCHOOL DST
Also Called: Marine Avenue Adult Center
1468 N Marine Ave, Wilmington
(90744-2046)
PHONE..................................310 518-1128
Lanny Nelms, *Principal*
EMP: 109
SALES (corp-wide): 3.8B **Privately Held**
WEB: www.lausd.k12.ca.us
SIC: 8322 Adult day care center
PA: Los Angeles Unified School District
333 S Beaudry Ave Ste 209
Los Angeles CA 90017
213 241-1000

(P-23907)
LOS ANGLES CHILD GDANCE CLINIC (PA)
3031 S Vermont Ave, Los Angeles
(90007-3033)
PHONE..................................323 373-2400
Elizabeth Pfromm, *President*
John R Liebman, *Treasurer*
Teresa Leingang, *Vice Pres*
Tiffany T Rodriguez, *Vice Pres*
Cynthia Equihva, *Admin Asst*
EMP: 110
SALES: 18.6MM **Privately Held**
WEB: www.lacgc.net
SIC: 8322 Child guidance agency

(P-23908)
LYDIA C GONZALEZ
1400 Veterans Blvd, Redwood City
(94063-2612)
PHONE..................................650 299-4707
EMP: 50
SALES (est): 1.9MM **Privately Held**
SIC: 8322

(P-23909)
MANCHESTER BAND POMO INDIANS
Also Called: Manchester Point Arena
24 Mamie Laiwa Dr, Point Arena (95468)
P.O. Box 623 (95468-0623)
PHONE..................................707 882-2788
Christina Dukatz, *CEO*
Nelson Pinola, *Chairman*
EMP: 96
SALES: 1.6MM **Privately Held**
SIC: 8322 Individual & family services

(P-23910)
MARIN SNIOR CRDNTING CNCIL INC
Also Called: WHISTLESTOP
930 Tamalpais Ave, San Rafael
(94901-3325)
PHONE..................................415 454-0964
Linda Compton, *CEO*
Joe O'Haire, *CEO*
Edward Fox, *Director*
EMP: 94
SQ FT: 12,000
SALES: 12.4MM **Privately Held**
WEB: www.thewhistlestop.org
SIC: 8322 Senior citizens' center or association

(P-23911)
MARTHAS VILLAGE & KITCHEN
83791 Date Ave, Indio (92201-4737)
PHONE..................................760 347-4741
Joe Carol, *President*
Matthew Packard, *Vice Pres*
Claudia Castorena, *Director*
Gloria Gomez, *Director*
EMP: 65
SALES: 3.8MM **Privately Held**
SIC: 8322 Social service center

(P-23912)
MARTIS CAMP CLUB
7951 Fleur Du Lac Ct, Truckee
(96161-4261)
PHONE..................................530 550-6000
Mark Johnson, *President*

Carla Yeager, *Treasurer*
Julie Akers, *Admin Asst*
Liz Curtiss, *Director*
Paul Hamill, *Director*
EMP: 300
SQ FT: 80,000
SALES: 17MM **Privately Held**
SIC: 8322 Community center

(P-23913)
MD P FOUNDATION INC
Also Called: MARTIN DE PORRES HOUSE
225 Potrero Ave, San Francisco
(94103-4814)
PHONE..................................415 552-0240
Charles Engelstein, *President*
EMP: 200
SQ FT: 7,000
SALES: 261.6K **Privately Held**
WEB: www.mdpfoundation.com
SIC: 8322 Individual & family services

(P-23914)
MEADOWBROOK SENIOR LIVING
5217 Chesebro Rd, Agoura Hills
(91301-2212)
PHONE..................................818 991-3544
Isaac Chernoesky, *Director*
EMP: 80
SALES (est): 1MM **Privately Held**
SIC: 8322 Old age assistance

(P-23915)
MEALS ON WHEELS DIABLO REGION (PA)
1300 Civic Dr Fl 1, Walnut Creek
(94596-4398)
PHONE..................................925 937-8311
Elaine Clark, *Exec Dir*
EMP: 55
SQ FT: 5,500
SALES: 2.3MM **Privately Held**
SIC: 8322 Meal delivery program; family counseling services; geriatric social service; social services for the handicapped

(P-23916)
MEALS ON WHEELS-THE HEALTH TR
1400 Parkmoor Ave Ste 230, San Jose
(95126-3798)
PHONE..................................408 961-9870
Gary Allen, *President*
EMP: 50
SALES (est): 997.6K **Privately Held**
SIC: 8322 Meal delivery program

(P-23917)
MEALS ON WHELS SAN FRNCSCO INC
1375 Fairfax Ave, San Francisco
(94124-1735)
PHONE..................................415 920-1111
Ashley McCumber, *Bd of Directors*
Anne Quaintance, *Principal*
EMP: 50
SQ FT: 19,330
SALES: 21.5MM **Privately Held**
WEB: www.mowsf.org
SIC: 8322 Meal delivery program

(P-23918)
MEALS-ON-WHEELS GRTR SN DIEGO (PA)
Also Called: MEALS ON WHEELS
2254 San Diego Ave # 200, San Diego
(92110-2944)
PHONE..................................619 260-6110
Debbie Case, *President*
Darlyne Baddour, *Ch of Bd*
Matt Topper, *CFO*
Matthew Topper, *CFO*
Barb Fiorina, *Director*
EMP: 84
SQ FT: 3,565
SALES: 4.4MM **Privately Held**
SIC: 8322 Meal delivery program; senior citizens' center or association

(P-23919)
MENTAL HEALTH AMER LOS ANGELES
Also Called: Village Integrated Svc Agcy
456 Elm Ave, Long Beach (90802-2426)
PHONE..................................562 437-6717
Leslie Giambone, *Exec Dir*
Mark R D, *Psychiatry*
EMP: 74
SQ FT: 25,129
SALES (corp-wide): 14.2MM **Privately Held**
WEB: www.myfrontdoor.org
SIC: 8322 Social service center
PA: Mental Health America Of Los Angeles
200 Pine Ave Ste 400
Long Beach CA 90802
562 285-1330

(P-23920)
MEXICAN AMRCN ALCOHOLISM PROGR (PA)
Also Called: MAAP
4241 Florin Rd Ste 110, Sacramento
(95823-2535)
PHONE..................................916 394-2320
Paul Cruz, *President*
EMP: 62
SALES: 2.3MM **Privately Held**
WEB: www.maap.com
SIC: 8322 Alcoholism counseling, nontreatment

(P-23921)
MEXICAN AMRCN OPRTNTY FNDATION (PA)
Also Called: MAOF
401 N Garfield Ave, Montebello
(90640-2901)
P.O. Box 4602 (90640-9311)
PHONE..................................323 890-9600
Martin Vasquez Castro, *President*
Carlos J Viramontes, *Principal*
EMP: 100
SQ FT: 25,000
SALES: 73.3MM **Privately Held**
SIC: 8322 Social service center

(P-23922)
MEXICAN AMRCN OPRTNTY FNDATION
Also Called: Maof Commerce
5657 E Washington Blvd, Commerce
(90040-1405)
PHONE..................................323 890-1555
Martin Castro, *President*
EMP: 60
SALES (corp-wide): 73.3MM **Privately Held**
SIC: 8322 Social service center
PA: Mexican American Opportunity Foundation
401 N Garfield Ave
Montebello CA 90640
323 890-9600

(P-23923)
MHN GOVERNMENT SERVICES LLC
2370 Kerner Blvd, San Rafael
(94901-5546)
PHONE..................................916 294-4941
Billy Maynard, *President*
John Crocker, *Director*
EMP: 189
SQ FT: 67,000
SALES (est): 4.2MM **Publicly Held**
WEB: www.mhn.com
SIC: 8322 Individual & family services
HQ: Health Net, Inc.
21650 Oxnard St Fl 25
Woodland Hills CA 91367

(P-23924)
MILESTONES ADULT DEV CTR
1 Florida St, Vallejo (94590-5000)
PHONE..................................707 644-0464
Terry Rowland, *General Mgr*
Steve Mack, *Administration*
John Yates, *Administration*
EMP: 90
SALES (est): 1.3MM **Privately Held**
SIC: 8322 Adult day care center

(P-23925)
MINORITY AIDS PROJECT INC
5147 W Jefferson Blvd, Los Angeles
(90016-3836)
PHONE..................................323 936-4949
Victor McKamie, *Exec Dir*
Riki Smith, *Manager*
EMP: 55
SQ FT: 3,500
SALES: 1.5MM **Privately Held**
WEB: www.map-usa.org
SIC: 8322 Individual & family services

(P-23926)
MOGANNAM AND WHALEN MED CORP (PA)
1000 S Hope St Ste 101, Los Angeles
(90015-4057)
PHONE..................................213 622-6010
Paul Mogannam, *President*
Sean Whalen, *Vice Pres*
Iris Chen, *Manager*
EMP: 50
SQ FT: 5,322
SALES (est): 12.2MM **Privately Held**
SIC: 8322 Rehabilitation services

(P-23927)
MONO NATION
58288 Road 225, North Fork (93643-9428)
P.O. Box 1377 (93643-1377)
PHONE..................................559 877-2450
Kendrick Sherman, *Principal*
EMP: 65
SALES: 40.2K **Privately Held**
SIC: 8322 Individual & family services

(P-23928)
MUTUAL ASSIST NETWORK DEL PASO (PA)
811 Grand Ave Ste A, Sacramento
(95838-3466)
PHONE..................................916 927-7694
Richard Dana, *Exec Dir*
Lio Saephan, *Executive*
Nou Vang, *Financial Exec*
EMP: 50
SALES: 1.9MM **Privately Held**
WEB: www.mutualassistance.org
SIC: 8322 Individual & family services

(P-23929)
NATIONAL CENTER ON DEAFNESS
18111 Nordhoff St, Northridge
(91330-0001)
PHONE..................................818 677-2054
Meri C Pearson, *Director*
Dean Meri C Pearson, *Pastor*
EMP: 80 **EST:** 2001
SALES (est): 994.9K **Privately Held**
SIC: 8322 Social services for the handicapped

(P-23930)
NEIGHBORHOOD HOUSE ASSOCIATION (PA)
Also Called: N H A
5660 Copley Dr, San Diego (92111-7902)
PHONE..................................858 715-2642
Rudolph A Johnson III, *CEO*
Joseph Maull, *Officer*
Sheryl White, *Vice Pres*
Elizabeth Ferrusca, *Admin Mgr*
Charles E Wilson, *Executive Asst*
EMP: 500 **EST:** 1914
SQ FT: 60,000
SALES: 86.7MM **Privately Held**
WEB: www.sandiegofoodbank.org
SIC: 8322 Neighborhood center

(P-23931)
NEIGHBORHOOD HOUSE ASSOCIATION
Also Called: Naht Care At
4425 Federal Blvd Ste 24, San Diego
(92102-2500)
PHONE..................................619 527-1287
Frank Andrews, *Principal*
EMP: 50
SALES (corp-wide): 86.7MM **Privately Held**
WEB: www.sandiegofoodbank.org
SIC: 8322 Neighborhood center

PRODUCTS & SVCS

PA: The Neighborhood House Association
5660 Copley Dr
San Diego CA 92111
858 715-2642

(P-23932)
NEIGHBORHOOD HOUSE ASSOCIATION
Also Called: Neighborhood Hse Assoc Fmily
841 S 41st St, San Diego (92113-1899)
PHONE...............................619 263-7761
Ellen Brown, *Manager*
Jean Smith, *Office Spvr*
EMP: 100
SALES (corp-wide): 86.7MM **Privately Held**
WEB: www.sandiegofoodbank.org
SIC: 8322 8399 Neighborhood center; community development groups
PA: The Neighborhood House Association
5660 Copley Dr
San Diego CA 92111
858 715-2642

(P-23933)
NEW BRIDGE FOUNDATION INC
2323 Hearst Ave, Berkeley (94709-1319)
PHONE...............................510 548-7270
Kosta Markakis, *CEO*
Jenny Knowles, *CFO*
Sara Khabiri, *Internal Med*
EMP: 65
SALES: 6.1MM **Privately Held**
WEB: www.newbridgefoundation.org
SIC: 8322 Rehabilitation services

(P-23934)
NEW DIRECTIONS INC (PA)
Also Called: New Directions For Veterans
11303 Wilshire Blvd, Los Angeles (90025-5069)
P.O. Box 25536 (90025-0536)
PHONE...............................310 914-4045
Edgar H Howell, *CEO*
Usha Murthy, *CFO*
Susan Michael, *Officer*
Tony Reinis, *Exec Dir*
Duane Byrdsong, *Program Mgr*
EMP: 80
SQ FT: 60,000
SALES: 6.6MM **Privately Held**
SIC: 8322 Substance abuse counseling

(P-23935)
NEW ECONOMICS FOR WOMEN (PA)
303 Loma Dr, Los Angeles (90017-1103)
PHONE...............................213 483-2060
Maggie Cervantes, *Exec Dir*
Liz Garcia, *Admin Asst*
Edith Martinez, *Project Mgr*
Michelle Reyes, *Personnel Assit*
Andrea Osorio, *Director*
EMP: 70
SQ FT: 25,000
SALES: 3.7MM **Privately Held**
WEB: www.neweconomicsforwomen.org
SIC: 8322 Settlement house

(P-23936)
NEW HAVEN YOUTH FMLY SVCS INC
P.O. Box 1199 (92085-1199)
PHONE...............................760 630-4060
EMP: 108
SALES (corp-wide): 8.2MM **Privately Held**
SIC: 8322 Family counseling services
PA: New Haven Youth And Family Services, Inc.
216 W Los Angeles Dr
Vista CA

(P-23937)
NEW IMAGE EMRGNCY SHLTR (PA)
1008 E 59th St, Los Angeles (90001-1010)
PHONE...............................562 983-7289
Brenda K Wilson, *Exec Dir*
Linda Moran, *Director*
EMP: 118
SALES: 151.5K **Privately Held**
SIC: 8322 Emergency shelters

(P-23938)
NEW START HOME HEALTH CARE INC
21515 Vanowen St Ste 205, Canoga Park (91303-2715)
PHONE...............................818 665-7898
Mary Williams, *CEO*
John Eckels, *Manager*
EMP: 200
SQ FT: 2,000
SALES (est): 6.5MM **Privately Held**
SIC: 8322 8082 Social services for the handicapped; home health care services

(P-23939)
NEXCARE COLLABORATIVE (PA)
15477 Ventura Blvd, Sherman Oaks (91403-3006)
PHONE...............................818 907-0322
Pejman Salimpour, *President*
Ralph Salimpour MD, *Corp Secy*
Pedram Salimpour MD, *Exec VP*
EMP: 50
SQ FT: 15,000
SALES (est): 6.7MM **Privately Held**
WEB: www.carenex.com
SIC: 8322 Child related social services

(P-23940)
NO BARRIERS
479 Mason St Ste 325, Vacaville (95688-4592)
PHONE...............................707 451-1947
Joe Zavala, *President*
EMP: 75
SALES (est): 619.1K **Privately Held**
SIC: 8322 Social services for the handicapped

(P-23941)
NORTHCOAST CHILDRENS SERVICES
730 Hwy 96, Willow Creek (95573)
P.O. Box 149 (95573-0149)
PHONE...............................530 629-2283
Jamie Mackenzie, *Director*
EMP: 62
SALES (corp-wide): 9.1MM **Privately Held**
SIC: 8322 Individual & family services
PA: Northcoast Children's Services Inc
1266 9th St
Arcata CA 95521
707 822-7206

(P-23942)
NORTHEAST VALLEY HEALTH CORP (PA)
1172 N Maclay Ave, San Fernando (91340-1328)
PHONE...............................818 898-1388
Kimberly Wyard, *CEO*
Vince Avila, *CFO*
Patricia Moraga, *CFO*
Nelson Wong, *Chairman*
Antonio Lugo, *Treasurer*
EMP: 75 **EST:** 1971
SALES: 89.4MM **Privately Held**
SIC: 8322 Community center

(P-23943)
NORTHERN CAL YUTH FMLY PRGRAMS (PA)
2577 California Park Dr, Chico (95928-4166)
PHONE...............................530 893-2316
Eric James, *Asst Director*
Ralph Ward, *Director*
EMP: 86
SQ FT: 6,000
SALES: 7MM **Privately Held**
SIC: 8322 Child related social services

(P-23944)
NORTHERN CALIFORNIA INALLIANCE
411 4th St, Wheatland (95692-9467)
PHONE...............................530 633-9695
EMP: 120
SALES (corp-wide): 17.2MM **Privately Held**
SIC: 8322 Association for the handicapped

PA: Northern California Inalliance
6950 21st Ave
Sacramento CA 95820
916 381-1300

(P-23945)
NORTHERN CALIFORNIA INALLIANCE (PA)
6950 21st Ave, Sacramento (95820-5948)
PHONE...............................916 381-1300
Richard Royse, *Exec Dir*
Chris Brailsford, *CFO*
Andrea Croom, *Director*
Margaret De Guzman, *Case Mgr*
EMP: 190 **EST:** 1968
SQ FT: 20,000
SALES: 17.2MM **Privately Held**
WEB: www.inallianceinc.com
SIC: 8322 Individual & family services

(P-23946)
NORTHERN VALLEY CATHOLIC SOCIA
2400 Washington Ave, Redding (96001-2802)
PHONE...............................530 241-0552
Jan Maurer Watkins, *CEO*
Don C Chapman, *CEO*
January Giles, *Program Mgr*
Virgie Limones, *Technician*
Kathy Lytle, *Accountant*
EMP: 151
SALES: 10.2MM **Privately Held**
SIC: 8322 Outreach program

(P-23947)
NUEVO AMNECER LATINO CHLD SVCS (PA)
5400 Pomona Blvd, Los Angeles (90022-1717)
PHONE...............................323 720-9951
Norma Duque-Acosta, *President*
EMP: 65
SQ FT: 2,600
SALES: 10.6MM **Privately Held**
SIC: 8322 Individual & family services

(P-23948)
OCEAN PARK COMMUNITY CENTER
Daybreak
1751 Cloverfield Blvd, Santa Monica (90404-4007)
PHONE...............................310 450-0650
Anya Booker, *Director*
Kimberly Krieger, *Manager*
EMP: 76
SALES (corp-wide): 13.5MM **Privately Held**
SIC: 8322 Community center
PA: Ocean Park Community Center
1453 16th St
Santa Monica CA 90404
310 264-6646

(P-23949)
OLDER ADULTS CARE MANAGEMENT (PA)
881 Fremont Ave Ste A2, Los Altos (94024-5637)
PHONE...............................650 329-1411
Cherry Jackson, *Director*
Jim Wilde, *Supervisor*
EMP: 180
SQ FT: 2,000
SALES (est): 4.4MM **Privately Held**
SIC: 8322 8741 8082 Geriatric social service; general counseling services; management services; home health care services

(P-23950)
ONEGENERATION (PA)
17400 Victory Blvd, Van Nuys (91406-5349)
PHONE...............................818 708-6625
Lawrence Gordon, *Exec Dir*
Jodi Jacobsen, *Human Res Mgr*
Brian Arthur, *Director*
Dolores Freeman, *Director*
Amber Fuellenbach, *Director*
EMP: 80

SALES (est): 3.5MM **Privately Held**
WEB: www.onegeneration.net
SIC: 8322 Senior citizens' center or association

(P-23951)
OPARC
355 S Lemon Ave Ste J, Walnut (91789-2739)
PHONE...............................909 598-8055
Tom Randall, *Branch Mgr*
EMP: 53
SALES (corp-wide): 13MM **Privately Held**
SIC: 8322 8051 8049 Association for the handicapped; mental retardation hospital; psychologist, psychotherapist & hypnotist
PA: Oparc
9029 Vernon Ave
Montclair CA 91763
909 982-4090

(P-23952)
ORANGE COUNTY CHILD ABUSE
Also Called: Welcome Baby
2390 E Orangewood Ave # 300, Anaheim (92806-6138)
PHONE...............................714 543-4333
Scott Trotter, *Exec Dir*
Stephanie Enano, *Principal*
EMP: 99
SALES: 7.4MM **Privately Held**
SIC: 8322 Child related social services

(P-23953)
ORANGEWOOD FOUNDATION
1575 E 17th St, Santa Ana (92705-8506)
PHONE...............................714 619-0200
Chris Simonsen, *CEO*
John Luker, *CFO*
Bob Theemling, *Officer*
Lupe Barrera, *Executive Asst*
Linda Levshin, *Info Tech Mgr*
EMP: 85
SQ FT: 22,340
SALES: 12.8MM **Privately Held**
WEB: www.orangewoodfoundation.org
SIC: 8322 Individual & family services

(P-23954)
OSHMAN FAMILY JEWISH CMNTY CTR
3921 Fabian Way, Palo Alto (94303-4606)
PHONE...............................650 223-8700
Alan Sataloff, *Exec Dir*
Haim Hovav, *CFO*
Paul Raczynski, *Info Tech Dir*
EMP: 200
SALES: 26.8MM **Privately Held**
SIC: 8322 Community center

(P-23955)
PACIFIC ASIAN CONSORTM EMPLYMN
Also Called: Pace Administrator To Work
1055 Wilshire Blvd # 1475, Los Angeles (90017-2431)
PHONE...............................213 989-3228
Kerry Doi, *Branch Mgr*
EMP: 100
SALES (corp-wide): 22.8MM **Privately Held**
SIC: 8322 Individual & family services
PA: Pacific Asian Consortium In Employment
1055 Wilshire Blvd Ste 14
Los Angeles CA 90017
213 353-3982

(P-23956)
PACIFIC CLINICS FOUNDATION
855 N Orange Grove Blvd, Pasadena (91103-3333)
PHONE...............................626 796-3453
EMP: 52
SALES (corp-wide): 91.3MM **Privately Held**
SIC: 8322 Youth center
PA: Pacific Clinics Foundation.
800 S Santa Anita Ave
Arcadia CA 91006
626 254-5000

▲ = Import ▼=Export
◆ =Import/Export

(P-23957)
PAJARO VALLEY PREVNTN & STUDEN
335 E Lake Ave, Watsonville (95076-4826)
PHONE..................................831 728-6445
Jenny Sarmiento, *CEO*
Linda Perez, *Exec Dir*
EMP: 65
SALES: 2.6MM **Privately Held**
SIC: 8322 Alcoholism counseling, nontreatment; drug abuse counselor, nontreatment

(P-23958)
PARADISE OAKS YOUTH SERVICES
Also Called: Hoffmann House
7806 Uplands Way A, Citrus Heights (95610-7567)
PHONE..................................916 725-7182
EMP: 65 **Privately Held**
WEB: www.hoffmannhouse.com
SIC: 8322 Youth center
PA: Paradise Oaks Youth Services, Inc
     7806 Uplands Way Ste A
     Citrus Heights CA 95610
     -

(P-23959)
PARTNERS AND ADVOCATES
Also Called: Parca
800 Airport Blvd Ste 320, Burlingame (94010-1919)
PHONE..................................650 312-0730
Diana Conti, *Exec Dir*
Suzanne Hinton, *Human Res Dir*
Brad Pence, *Sales Mgr*
Lori B Milburn, *Corp Comm Staff*
Joseph Fenerty, *Anesthesiology*
EMP: 86 EST: 1952
SALES: 2.6MM **Privately Held**
WEB: www.parca.org
SIC: 8322 Association for the handicapped

(P-23960)
PARTNERS FOR COMMUNITY ACCESS
708 Gilman St, Berkeley (94710-1333)
PHONE..................................510 558-6700
Rosalee Shubert, *Principal*
EMP: 60
SALES (est): 875.3K **Privately Held**
SIC: 8322 Social service center

(P-23961)
PASADENA CHILD DEVELOPMENT ASS
620 N Lake Ave, Pasadena (91101-1220)
PHONE..................................626 793-7350
Diane Cullinane, *Owner*
Mimi Winer, *Co-Owner*
EMP: 70 EST: 1997
SALES (est): 981.6K **Privately Held**
WEB: www.pasadenachilddevelopment.org
SIC: 8322 Individual & family services

(P-23962)
PATHWAY INC
287 W Orange Show Ln, San Bernardino (92408-2037)
PHONE..................................909 890-1070
Robert McGuire, *President*
Joyce Hampton, *President*
EMP: 100
SQ FT: 2,300
SALES (est): 3.1MM **Privately Held**
SIC: 8322 5999 Social services for the handicapped; technical aids for the handicapped

(P-23963)
PATHWAY TO CHOICES INC
751 Belmont Way, Pinole (94564-2661)
PHONE..................................510 724-9044
Juan Velasquez, *President*
EMP: 52
SALES (est): 2.2MM **Privately Held**
SIC: 8322 General counseling services

(P-23964)
PATHWAYS LA (PA)
3325 Wilshire Blvd # 1100, Los Angeles (90010-1703)
PHONE..................................213 427-2700
Karen Park, *President*

Carla Buck, *Vice Pres*
Les Guttman, *Principal*
Duane Dennis, *Exec Dir*
Linda Vuont, *Finance*
EMP: 50
SQ FT: 24,000
SALES: 20.6MM **Privately Held**
WEB: www.pathwaysla.org
SIC: 8322 Child related social services

(P-23965)
PENINSULA FAMILY SERVICE
Also Called: Leo J Ryan Child Care Ctr
1200 Miller Ave, South San Francisco (94080-1221)
PHONE..................................650 952-6848
Liliya Sergiyemko, *Branch Mgr*
EMP: 55
SALES (est): 588.6K
SALES (corp-wide): 12.7MM **Privately Held**
WEB: www.familyserviceagency.org
SIC: 8322 8351 Family (marriage) counseling; child day care services
PA: Peninsula Family Service
     24 2nd Ave
     San Mateo CA 94401
     650 403-4300

(P-23966)
PENINSULA JEWISH COMMUNITY CTR
800 Foster City Blvd, Foster City (94404-2228)
PHONE..................................650 212-7522
Paul Gedulig, *CEO*
Fred Weiner, *CFO*
EMP: 200
SALES: 18.7MM **Privately Held**
SIC: 8322 Community center

(P-23967)
PENINSULA VOLUNTEERS INC (PA)
Also Called: ROSENER HOUSE
800 Middle Ave, Menlo Park (94025-5198)
PHONE..................................650 326-0665
Peter Olsen, *Exec Dir*
Michelle Knapik, *Exec Dir*
Joe Christian, *Controller*
Sarah Schachter, *Social Worker*
Pennie Lundberg, *Director*
EMP: 50 EST: 1947
SQ FT: 25,000
SALES: 4.2MM **Privately Held**
WEB: www.penvol.org
SIC: 8322 Adult day care center

(P-23968)
PEOPLE ASSISTING HOMELESS
Also Called: P A T H
340 N Madison Ave, Los Angeles (90004-3504)
PHONE..................................323 644-2216
Joel John Roberts, *President*
Micaela Reyes, *Manager*
EMP: 167
SALES: 35.3MM **Privately Held**
WEB: www.epath.org
SIC: 8322 Social service center

(P-23969)
PEOPLE CREATING SUCCESS INC
1607 E Palmdale Blvd H, Palmdale (93550-7801)
PHONE..................................661 225-9700
Robert Donery, *Branch Mgr*
EMP: 91
SALES (corp-wide): 12.8MM **Privately Held**
SIC: 8322 Individual & family services
PA: People Creating Success, Inc.
     2585 Teller Rd
     Newbury Park CA 91320
     805 375-9222

(P-23970)
PHFE WIC PROGRAM
12871 Schabarum Ave, Irwindale (91706)
PHONE..................................626 856-6650
Eloise Jenks, *Director*
Shelly Lewis Mm Rd, *Opers Staff*
EMP: 120

SALES (est): 2.8MM **Privately Held**
SIC: 8322 Individual & family services

(P-23971)
PINOLE SENIOR CENTER
2500 Charles St, Pinole (94564-1301)
PHONE..................................510 724-9800
Janette Bilbas, *Director*
Jonathan Torres, *Administration*
EMP: 58
SALES (est): 838.2K **Privately Held**
SIC: 8322 Senior citizens' center or association
PA: City Of Pinole
     2131 Pear St
     Pinole CA 94564
     510 724-9000

(P-23972)
PLAN-IT LIFE INC
5729 Vista Del Caballero, Riverside (92509-6423)
P.O. Box 2994, Corona (92878-2994)
PHONE..................................951 742-7561
Sheila McLean, *CEO*
Nyron McLean, *CFO*
Carl Sampson MD, *Vice Pres*
EMP: 56
SQ FT: 2,800
SALES: 2.3MM **Privately Held**
SIC: 8322 Substance abuse counseling

(P-23973)
PLUMAS RURAL SERVICES
711 E Main St, Quincy (95971-9722)
PHONE..................................530 283-2725
Michele Pillar, *Exec Dir*
EMP: 90
SQ FT: 6,000
SALES: 4.5MM **Privately Held**
WEB: www.plumasruralservices.org
SIC: 8322 Drug abuse counselor, nontreatment

(P-23974)
POMEROY RCRTION RHBLTATION CTR (PA)
Also Called: R C H
207 Skyline Blvd, San Francisco (94132-1025)
PHONE..................................415 665-4100
John McCue, *Exec Dir*
Lorraine Scullion, *Plan/Corp Dev D*
Henry Woo, *Exec Dir*
Lesley Steele, *Administration*
Loida Dantes, *Accountant*
EMP: 180
SQ FT: 22,000
SALES: 9.1MM **Privately Held**
WEB: www.janetpomeroy.org
SIC: 8322 Social services for the handicapped

(P-23975)
POSITIVE OPTION FAMILY SERVICE (PA)
Also Called: WELLSPRING
2400 Glendale Ln Ste H, Sacramento (95825-2431)
P.O. Box 202, Citrus Heights (95611-0202)
PHONE..................................916 973-2838
Joseph B Kovill, *CEO*
EMP: 60
SALES: 1.3MM **Privately Held**
SIC: 8322 8211 Adoption services; elementary & secondary schools

(P-23976)
PRECISION HOME CARE LLC
2450 Venture Oaks Way # 225, Sacramento (95833-4225)
PHONE..................................916 749-4051
John Alves, *Mng Member*
Jonathan Bliss, *Mng Member*
Chris Simmons, *Mng Member*
EMP: 56
SALES (est): 127.4K **Privately Held**
SIC: 8322 8361 Old age assistance; residential care

(P-23977)
PROJECT OPEN HAND (PA)
730 Polk St Fl 3, San Francisco (94109-7813)
PHONE..................................415 292-3400
Mark Ryle, *CEO*

Terri Brennan, *Exec Dir*
Teresa Ballete, *Controller*
EMP: 96
SQ FT: 50,000
SALES: 9.7MM **Privately Held**
WEB: www.openhand.org
SIC: 8322 Meal delivery program

(P-23978)
PROTOTYPES CENTERS FOR INNOV
1000 N Alameda St Ste 390, Los Angeles (90012-1804)
PHONE..................................213 542-3838
Cassandra Loch, *President*
Eli Veitzer, *COO*
Maryann Fraser, *Exec VP*
Dylan Grattidge, *Info Tech Dir*
Vivian Easton, *Manager*
EMP: 250
SQ FT: 8,400
SALES: 20.1MM **Privately Held**
SIC: 8322 General counseling services

(P-23979)
R L SAFETY INC
2157 Cherrystone Dr, San Jose (95128-1217)
PHONE..................................408 557-0887
Brent Rapport, *President*
Loisa Rapport, *Vice Pres*
EMP: 50
SALES (est): 718.3K **Privately Held**
SIC: 8322 8099 7389 Emergency social services; blood related health services;

(P-23980)
RANCHO LOS AMIGOS NATIONA
Also Called: Information Management Svcs
7601 Imperial Hwy, Downey (90242-3456)
PHONE..................................562 401-7111
EMP: 364 **Privately Held**
SIC: 8322 Individual & family services
PA: Rancho Los Amigos National Rehabilitation Center
     7601 Imperial Hwy
     Downey CA 90242

(P-23981)
RANCHO LOS AMIGOS NATIONA
Also Called: Professional Staffing Associat
7601 Imperial Hwy, Downey (90242-3456)
PHONE..................................562 401-7111
Consuelo Diaz, *CEO*
Sara Mulroy, *Lab Dir*
EMP: 729 **Privately Held**
WEB: www.co.la.ca.us
SIC: 8322 Individual & family services
PA: Rancho Los Amigos National Rehabilitation Center
     7601 Imperial Hwy
     Downey CA 90242
     -

(P-23982)
RANCHO LOS AMIGOS NATIONA
12852 Erickson Ave, Downey (90242-4004)
PHONE..................................562 401-7266
EMP: 273 **Privately Held**
SIC: 8322 Individual & family services
PA: Rancho Los Amigos National Rehabilitation Center
     7601 Imperial Hwy
     Downey CA 90242
     -

(P-23983)
RANCHO LOS AMIGOS NATIONA (PA)
7601 Imperial Hwy, Downey (90242-3456)
PHONE..................................562 401-7111
Jorge R Orozco, *CEO*
Benjamin Ovando Sr, *COO*
Robin Bayus, *CFO*
Shawn Phipps, *Officer*
Michelle Sterling, *Ch Nursing Ofcr*
EMP: 84
SALES (est): 74.1MM **Privately Held**
SIC: 8322 Rehabilitation services

(P-23984)
READING PARTNERS
600 Valley Way, Milpitas (95035-4138)
PHONE..................................408 945-5720

Michael Lombardo, *Exec Dir*
Diana Martin, *Program Mgr*
EMP: 91
SALES (corp-wide): 23.5MM **Privately Held**
SIC: 8322 Individual & family services
PA: Reading Partners
180 Grand Ave Ste 800
Oakland CA 94612
510 444-9800

(P-23985)
REDWOOD COAST REGIONAL (PA)
Also Called: REDWOOD COAST REGIONAL CENTER
1116 Airport Park Blvd, Ukiah (95482-7431)
PHONE..................707 462-3832
Mike Ring, *Administration*
Pamela Jensen, *Bd of Directors*
Mary Yates, *Bd of Directors*
Clay Jones, *Exec Dir*
Dina Petterson, *Admin Asst*
EMP: 79
SQ FT: 6,600
SALES: 107.8MM **Privately Held**
WEB: www.redwoodcoastrc.org
SIC: 8322 Social services for the handicapped

(P-23986)
REDWOOD COAST REGIONAL
Also Called: Redwood Coast Regional Center
525 2nd St Ste 300, Eureka (95501-0488)
PHONE..................707 445-0893
Clay Jones, *Director*
Cindy Claus-John, *Manager*
EMP: 50
SALES (est): 1.8MM
SALES (corp-wide): 107.8MM **Privately Held**
WEB: www.redwoodcoastrc.org
SIC: 8322 8699 Social services for the handicapped; personal interest organization
PA: Redwood Coast Developmental Services Corporation
1116 Airport Park Blvd
Ukiah CA 95482
707 462-3832

(P-23987)
REDWOOD COAST SENIORS INC
Also Called: SENIOR NUTRITION
490 N Harold St, Fort Bragg (95437-3331)
PHONE..................707 964-0443
Joseph Curren, *Exec Dir*
EMP: 60
SALES: 993.8K **Privately Held**
SIC: 8322 Senior citizens' center or association

(P-23988)
REDWOOD COMMUNITY SERVICES (PA)
631 S Orchard Ave, Ukiah (95482-5011)
P.O. Box 2077 (95482-2077)
PHONE..................707 467-2000
Camille Shraeder, *Exec Dir*
Lynn Sallee, *CFO*
Michele Mix, *Office Mgr*
Lancy Armstrong, *Admin Sec*
Randy Anderson, *Social Worker*
EMP: 165
SALES: 10.8MM **Privately Held**
SIC: 8322 Family service agency

(P-23989)
REGIONAL CENTER OF E BAY INC
7677 Oakport St Ste 300, Oakland (94621-1933)
PHONE..................510 383-1200
Jim Burton, *Director*
Cynthia Cindy, *Administration*
Raelena Anderson, *Case Mgr*
Dorothy Mueller, *Case Mgr*
Elizabeth Rosas, *Case Mgr*
EMP: 250 **EST:** 1975
SQ FT: 26,000
SALES: 311.1MM **Privately Held**
SIC: 8322 Social services for the handicapped

(P-23990)
REHABILITATION CALIFORNIA DEPT
Also Called: Los Angeles South Bay Dst Off
4300 Long Beach Blvd # 200, Long Beach (90807-2011)
PHONE..................562 422-8325
Brenda Brent, *Manager*
EMP: 50 **Privately Held**
WEB: www.carehab.org
SIC: 8322 9431 Rehabilitation services; administration of public health programs
HQ: California Department Of Rehabilitation
721 Capitol Mall Fl 6
Sacramento CA 95814

(P-23991)
RESCUE CHILDREN INC
Also Called: CRAYCROFT YOUTH CENTER
335 G St, Fresno (93706-3422)
P.O. Box 1422 (93716-1422)
PHONE..................559 268-1123
Fax: 559 268-3465
EMP: 50
SALES: 1.3MM **Privately Held**
SIC: 8322

(P-23992)
RESOURCE CONNECTION OF AMADOR (PA)
Also Called: Resource Connection, The
444 E Saint Charles St, San Andreas (95249-9658)
P.O. Box 919 (95249-0919)
PHONE..................209 754-3114
Linda Foster, *Ch of Bd*
Amber Shelton, *Principal*
Kelli Fraguero, *Admin Dir*
Beverly Stewart, *Human Res Dir*
Catherine C Bourland, *Director*
EMP: 56
SALES: 7.7MM **Privately Held**
WEB: www.theresourceconnection.net
SIC: 8322 Individual & family services

(P-23993)
RESOURCE CONNECTION OF AMADOR
Also Called: W I C
430 Sutter Hill Rd, Sutter Creek (95685-4149)
PHONE..................209 223-7685
Damian Wolin, *President*
EMP: 64
SALES (corp-wide): 7.7MM **Privately Held**
SIC: 8322 Social service center
PA: The Resource Connection Of Amador And Calaveras Counties Incorporated
444 E Saint Charles St
San Andreas CA 95249
209 754-3114

(P-23994)
RESOURCE RFRRAL CHILD CARE DEV
1225 Gill Ave, Madera (93637-5234)
PHONE..................559 673-9173
Mary Jane Nabors, *Director*
EMP: 50
SALES (est): 392.2K **Privately Held**
SIC: 8322 Individual & family services

(P-23995)
REUTLINGER COMMUNITY
Also Called: REUTLINGER COMMUNITY FOR JEWIS
4000 Camino Tassajara, Danville (94506-4711)
PHONE..................925 964-2062
Jay Zimmer, *CEO*
EMP: 160
SALES: 17.7MM **Privately Held**
WEB: www.rcjl.org
SIC: 8322 Individual & family services

(P-23996)
RICHMOND DST NEIGHBORHOOD CTR (PA)
741 30th Ave, San Francisco (94121-3519)
PHONE..................415 751-6600
Michelle Cusano, *Exec Dir*

Michelle Jacques-Menegaz, *Program Mgr*
Megan Han, *Human Res Mgr*
Chris Antipa, *Sales Staff*
Oliver Hack, *Director*
EMP: 80
SALES: 4.3MM **Privately Held**
WEB: www.rdnc.org
SIC: 8322 Community center; outreach program

(P-23997)
RICHMOND RESCUE MISSION (PA)
Also Called: BAY AREA RESCUE MISSION
2114 Macdonald Ave, Richmond (94801-3311)
P.O. Box 1112 (94802-0112)
PHONE..................510 215-4555
John M Anderson, *President*
Tim Hammack, *Vice Pres*
Woody Tausend, *Vice Pres*
Sabrina Gilliam, *Instructor*
Sherwin Harris, *Director*
EMP: 52
SQ FT: 80,000
SALES: 10.6MM **Privately Held**
SIC: 8322 Emergency shelters

(P-23998)
RIO HONDO EDUCATION CONSORTIUM
Also Called: LEARN
7200 Greenleaf Ave # 300, Whittier (90602-1383)
PHONE..................562 945-0150
Robert Arellanes, *CEO*
Brenda Carrillo, *Officer*
Carolina Arce, *Principal*
Robert Bell, *Principal*
Linda Contreras, *Principal*
EMP: 150
SALES: 2.5MM **Privately Held**
WEB: www.riohondoec.org
SIC: 8322 Individual & family services

(P-23999)
RURAL CMNTY ASSISTANCE CORP (PA)
Also Called: RCAC
3120 Freeboard Dr Ste 201, West Sacramento (95691-5039)
PHONE..................916 447-2854
Stan Keasling, *CEO*
Kevin McCumber, *CFO*
Linda Petta, *Manager*
EMP: 60 **EST:** 1978
SALES: 19MM **Privately Held**
SIC: 8322 6111 Individual & family services; federal & federally sponsored credit agencies

(P-24000)
RUTH BARAJAS
Also Called: Bacr
965 Mission St Ste 520, San Francisco (94103-2959)
PHONE..................415 977-6949
Ruth Barajas, *Administration*
Andrea Juarez, *Associate Dir*
EMP: 50
SALES (est): 754K **Privately Held**
WEB: www.chalk.org
SIC: 8322 Youth center

(P-24001)
SACRAMENTO AREA EMERG HOUSING (PA)
Also Called: Next Move
2925 34th St, Sacramento (95817-3113)
PHONE..................916 454-2120
Bonnie K Hyer, *Exec Dir*
EMP: 50
SQ FT: 4,200
SALES: 3.8MM **Privately Held**
SIC: 8322 Social service center

(P-24002)
SACRAMENTO CHINESE COMMUNITY S
420 I St Ste 5, Sacramento (95814-2319)
PHONE..................916 442-4228
Henry Kloczkowski, *Exec Dir*
Oscar Bermudez, *Program Mgr*
David Constancio, *Program Mgr*
Andrea Cunningham, *Program Mgr*

Anna Houston, *Program Mgr*
EMP: 200
SQ FT: 2,000
SALES: 6.3MM **Privately Held**
SIC: 8322 8699 8611 Social service center; charitable organization; community affairs & services

(P-24003)
SACRAMENTO COUNTY OFF EDUCATN
Also Called: Probation Department
9750 Bus Park Dr Ste 220, Sacramento (95827-1716)
PHONE..................916 875-0300
Lee Seale, *Director*
EMP: 50 **Privately Held**
WEB: www.sna.com
SIC: 8322 9199 Probation office;
PA: Sacramento County Office Of Education
10474 Mather Blvd
Mather CA 95655

(P-24004)
SACRAMENTO LOAVES & FISHES (PA)
1351 N C St Ste 22, Sacramento (95811-0608)
P.O. Box 2161 (95812-2161)
PHONE..................916 446-0874
Libby Hernandez, *Director*
Chris Delany, *Vice Pres*
Libby Fernandez, *Exec Dir*
Noel Kammermann, *Exec Dir*
Bryan Gross, *Program Dir*
EMP: 55
SALES: 5.9MM **Privately Held**
SIC: 8322 Social service center

(P-24005)
SALVATION ARMY (HQ)
180 E Ocean Blvd Ste 500, Long Beach (90802-4708)
P.O. Box 93002 (90809-3002)
PHONE..................562 491-8464
James M Knaggs, *Principal*
Commissioner Carolyn R Knaggs, *President*
Susan Lawrence, *Exec Dir*
Raymond Ellington, *Managing Dir*
Commissioner James M Knaggs, *Commander*
EMP: 140
SALES (est): 169.1MM
SALES (corp-wide): 4.3B **Privately Held**
WEB: www.salvationarmy.usawest.org
SIC: 8322 Individual & family services
PA: The Salvation Army National Corporation
615 Slaters Ln
Alexandria VA 22314
703 684-5500

(P-24006)
SALVATION ARMY
2737 W Sunset Blvd, Los Angeles (90026-2181)
PHONE..................213 484-0772
Ana Aguirre, *Director*
EMP: 50
SALES (corp-wide): 4.3B **Privately Held**
WEB: www.salvationarmy.usawest.org
SIC: 8322 Refugee service
HQ: The Salvation Army
180 E Ocean Blvd Ste 500
Long Beach CA 90802
562 491-8464

(P-24007)
SALVATION ARMY GLDEN STATE DIV (PA)
832 Folsom St Fl 6, San Francisco (94107-1142)
P.O. Box 193465 (94119-3465)
PHONE..................415 553-3500
Steve Smith, *Principal*
EMP: 80
SALES (est): 6.9MM **Privately Held**
SIC: 8322 8741 Social service center; administrative management

(P-24008)
SALVATION ARMY RESIDENCES INC
900 James M Wood Blvd, Los Angeles (90015-1356)
PHONE.....................213 553-3273
Paul Bollwahn, *Director*
EMP: 100
SALES (corp-wide): 4.3B **Privately Held**
WEB: www.salvationarmy.usawest.org
SIC: 8322 Individual & family services
HQ: The Salvation Army
180 E Ocean Blvd Ste 500
Long Beach CA 90802
562 491-8464

(P-24009)
SAMARITAN VILLAGE INC
7700 Fox Rd, Hughson (95326-9100)
P.O. Box 444, Yuba City (95992-0444)
PHONE.....................209 883-3212
Daniel Aguilar, *CEO*
Victor Savage, *CEO*
EMP: 115
SALES: 60K **Privately Held**
SIC: 8322 Adult day care center

(P-24010)
SAN ANDREAS REGIONAL CENTER (PA)
6203 San Ignacio Ave # 110, San Jose (95119-1358)
P.O. Box 50002 (95150-0002)
PHONE.....................408 374-9960
Mary Lu Gonzalez, *CEO*
Greg Hoffman, *CFO*
Yoshiharu Kuroiwa, *CFO*
Lisa Lopez, *Vice Pres*
Jamie Nguyen, *District Mgr*
EMP: 174
SQ FT: 29,000
SALES: 310.1MM **Privately Held**
SIC: 8322 Association for the handicapped

(P-24011)
SAN DIEGO LESBIAN GAY BISEXU
Also Called: CENTER, THE
3909 Centre St, San Diego (92103-3410)
P.O. Box 3357 (92163-1357)
PHONE.....................619 692-2077
Delores Jacobs, *Exec Dir*
Connor Maddocks, *Facilities Mgr*
Ricardo Gallego, *Director*
EMP: 50
SQ FT: 15,490
SALES: 7MM **Privately Held**
WEB: www.thecentersd.org
SIC: 8322 Community center

(P-24012)
SAN DIEGO YOUTH SERVICES INC (PA)
Also Called: S D Y S
3255 Wing St Ste 550, San Diego (92110-4641)
P.O. Box 80756 (92138-0756)
PHONE.....................619 221-8600
Walter Philips, *Exec Dir*
Indie Landrum, *Partner*
Angie Tran, *CFO*
Steven Jella, *Exec Dir*
Walter Phillips, *Exec Dir*
EMP: 55
SQ FT: 5,634
SALES: 15MM **Privately Held**
SIC: 8322 Youth center

(P-24013)
SAN DIEGO-IMPERIAL
Also Called: San Diego Regional Ctr For Dev
2727 Hoover Ave, National City (91950-6602)
PHONE.....................619 336-6600
Judy Borchert, *Manager*
Michael Rath, *Program Mgr*
EMP: 54
SALES (corp-wide): 337.1MM **Privately Held**
WEB: www.sdrc.org
SIC: 8322 Social service center

PA: San Diego-Imperial Counties Developmental Services, Inc.
4355 Ruffin Rd Ste 220
San Diego CA 92123
858 576-2996

(P-24014)
SAN DIEGO-IMPERIAL COUNTIES DE (PA)
4355 Ruffin Rd Ste 220, San Diego (92123-4308)
PHONE.....................858 576-2996
Carlos Flores, *Exec Dir*
Edward Kenney, *CFO*
Judy Wallace Patton, *Treasurer*
Mark Gates, *Program Mgr*
Darlene Jean, *Program Mgr*
EMP: 474
SQ FT: 62,000
SALES: 337.1MM **Privately Held**
WEB: www.sdrc.org
SIC: 8322 Social services for the handicapped

(P-24015)
SAN DIEGO-IMPERIAL COUNTIES DE
Also Called: Developmentally Research Ctr
1370 W Sn Mrcos Blvd # 100, San Marcos (92078-1601)
PHONE.....................760 736-1200
Nina Garrett, *Director*
EMP: 70
SALES (est): 542K
SALES (corp-wide): 337.1MM **Privately Held**
WEB: www.sdrc.org
SIC: 8322 Social services for the handicapped
PA: San Diego-Imperial Counties Developmental Services, Inc.
4355 Ruffin Rd Ste 220
San Diego CA 92123
858 576-2996

(P-24016)
SAN FRANCISCO CITY & COUNTY
Also Called: San Francisco Public Schools
1520 Oakdale Ave, San Francisco (94124-2323)
PHONE.....................415 695-5660
David Hollands, *Branch Mgr*
EMP: 93 **Privately Held**
SIC: 8322 Child related social services
PA: City & County Of San Francisco
1 Dr Carlton B Goodlett P
San Francisco CA 94102
415 554-7500

(P-24017)
SAN FRANCISCO AIDS FOUNDATION (PA)
1035 Market St Ste 400, San Francisco (94103-1665)
PHONE.....................415 487-3000
Joe Hollendoner, *CEO*
Jody Schaffer, *Volunteer Dir*
Elizabeth Pesch, *CFO*
Liz Pesch, *CFO*
Robert Grant, *Chief Mktg Ofcr*
EMP: 100
SQ FT: 45,000
SALES: 29.9MM **Privately Held**
WEB: www.sfaf.org
SIC: 8322 Social service center

(P-24018)
SAN FRANCISCO CITY & COUNTY
Also Called: Child Support Services
617 Mission St, San Francisco (94105-3503)
PHONE.....................415 356-2700
Christine Anderson, *Manager*
Lupe Arreola, *Officer*
Romulus Asenloo, *Officer*
Yossef Azim, *Officer*
Karen Fletcher, *Officer*
EMP: 93 **Privately Held**
SIC: 8322 9441 Individual & family services; administration of social & manpower programs; ;

PA: City & County Of San Francisco
1 Dr Carlton B Goodlett P
San Francisco CA 94102
415 554-7500

(P-24019)
SAN FRANCISCO CITY & COUNTY
Also Called: Family Support Bureau
617 Mission St, San Francisco (94105-3503)
PHONE.....................415 356-2700
EMP: 93 **Privately Held**
SIC: 8322 9441 Individual & family services; administration of social & manpower programs
PA: City & County Of San Francisco
1 Dr Carlton B Goodlett P
San Francisco CA 94102
415 554-7500

(P-24020)
SAN FRANCISCO FOOD BANK
Also Called: SF-MARIN FOOD BANK
900 Pennsylvania Ave, San Francisco (94107-3498)
PHONE.....................415 282-1900
Paul Ash, *Exec Dir*
Leslie Bacho, *COO*
Michael Braude, *CFO*
EMP: 80
SQ FT: 55,000
SALES: 96.3MM **Privately Held**
WEB: www.sffb.org
SIC: 8322 Social service center

(P-24021)
SAN FRANCISCO PARTCLR CNCL SCT
525 5th St, San Francisco (94107-1012)
PHONE.....................415 255-3525
EMP: 85
SALES (corp-wide): 6.5MM **Privately Held**
SIC: 8322 Individual & family services
PA: The San Francisco Particular Council Of The Society Of St Vincent De Paul
1175 Howard St
San Francisco CA 94103
415 552-2943

(P-24022)
SAN GABRIEL CHILDRENS CTR INC (PA)
2200 E Route 66 Ste 100, Glendora (91740-4662)
PHONE.....................626 859-2089
Porfirio Rincon, *President*
David K Gaffiend, *CFO*
Janet Lester, *Director*
EMP: 100
SQ FT: 7,500
SALES: 5.8MM **Privately Held**
WEB: www.sangabrielchild.com
SIC: 8322 8361 Child related social services; children's home

(P-24023)
SAN GABRIEL/POMONA VALLEYS
Also Called: SAN GABRIEL/POMONA REGIONAL CE
75 Rancho Camino Dr, Pomona (91766-4728)
PHONE.....................909 620-7722
R Keith Penman, *Exec Dir*
John Hunt, *CFO*
Aaron Christian, *Client Mgr*
Carol Tomblin, *Director*
EMP: 323
SQ FT: 100,000
SALES: 234.2MM **Privately Held**
SIC: 8322 Social service center

(P-24024)
SAN JOAQUIN CNTY AGING & COMMU
102 S San Joaquin St, Stockton (95202-3213)
P.O. Box 201056 (95201-3006)
PHONE.....................209 468-9455
Michael Miller, *Director*
Kirsten Yeh, *Analyst*
EMP: 120

SALES: 10MM **Privately Held**
SIC: 8322 Individual & family services

(P-24025)
SANTA BARBARA COUNTY OF
Also Called: Probation Dept
117 E Carrillo St, Santa Barbara (93101-2110)
PHONE.....................805 882-3700
Beverly Taylor, *Chief*
EMP: 400 **Privately Held**
WEB: www.sbcountyhr.org
SIC: 8322 Probation office; parole office
PA: County Of Santa Barbara
105 E Anapamu St Rm 406
Santa Barbara CA 93101
805 568-3400

(P-24026)
SANTA BARBARA COUNTY OF
Also Called: Probation Dept
1410 S Broadway Ste L, Santa Maria (93454-6971)
PHONE.....................805 614-1550
Brian Carroll, *Branch Mgr*
EMP: 122 **Privately Held**
WEB: www.sbcountyhr.org
SIC: 8322 9223 Child related social services; parole office; correctional institutions;
PA: County Of Santa Barbara
105 E Anapamu St Rm 406
Santa Barbara CA 93101
805 568-3400

(P-24027)
SANTA BARBARA COUNTY OF
Also Called: Social Services Dept
1100 W Laurel Ave, Lompoc (93436-5155)
PHONE.....................805 737-7080
Beverly Littlejohn, *Director*
EMP: 122 **Privately Held**
WEB: www.sbcountyhr.org
SIC: 8322 9441 Public welfare center; administration of social & manpower programs;
PA: County Of Santa Barbara
105 E Anapamu St Rm 406
Santa Barbara CA 93101
805 568-3400

(P-24028)
SANTA BARBARA COUNTY OF
Also Called: Probation Dept
429 N San Antonio Rd, Santa Barbara (93110-1399)
PHONE.....................805 884-1600
Scott Whiteley, *Manager*
EMP: 70 **Privately Held**
WEB: www.sbcountyhr.org
SIC: 8322 9223 Child related social services; correctional institutions;
PA: County Of Santa Barbara
105 E Anapamu St Rm 406
Santa Barbara CA 93101
805 568-3400

(P-24029)
SANTA BARBARA COUNTY OF
Also Called: Human Resources
4 E Carrillo St, Santa Barbara (93101-2707)
PHONE.....................866 901-3212
Karin Roser, *Branch Mgr*
EMP: 122 **Privately Held**
WEB: www.sbcountyhr.org
SIC: 8322 9441 Individual & family services; administration of social & manpower programs;
PA: County Of Santa Barbara
105 E Anapamu St Rm 406
Santa Barbara CA 93101
805 568-3400

(P-24030)
SANTA CLARA COUNTY OF
Also Called: Adult Probation Department
2314 N 1st St, San Jose (95131-1011)
PHONE.....................408 435-2000
Karen Fletcher, *Chief*
EMP: 100 **Privately Held**
SIC: 8322 Probation office
PA: County Of Santa Clara
3180 Newberry Dr Ste 150
San Jose CA 95118
408 299-5105

P R O D U C T S & S V C S

(P-24031)
SANTA CLARA COUNTY OF
Also Called: Probation Dept
2314 N 1st St, San Jose (95131-1011)
PHONE.....................................408 435-2111
Sheila Mitchel, *Director*
EMP: 200 **Privately Held**
WEB: www.countyairports.org
SIC: 8322 9441 Probation office; parole office; administration of social & manpower programs
PA: County Of Santa Clara
　3180 Newberry Dr Ste 150
　San Jose CA 95118
　408 299-5105

(P-24032)
SANTA CLARITA VLLY CMMTT AGING
Also Called: SANTA CLARITA VALLEY SENIOR CE
22900 Market St, Santa Clarita (91321-3608)
PHONE.....................................661 259-9444
Brad Berens, *Director*
Jeff Pollard, *President*
Greg Kory, *CFO*
Don Kimball, *Vice Pres*
EMP: 65
SQ FT: 10,000
SALES: 3.4MM **Privately Held**
WEB: www.scvseniorcenter.org
SIC: 8322 Senior citizens' center or association

(P-24033)
SANTA ROSA COMMUNITY HLTH CTRS (PA)
3569 Round Barn Cir, Santa Rosa (95403-5781)
PHONE.....................................707 547-2222
Naomi Fuchs, *CEO*
EMP: 110 EST: 1996
SALES: 63.7MM **Privately Held**
WEB: www.swhealthcenter.org
SIC: 8322 Individual & family services

(P-24034)
SANTEE SENIOR RETIREMENT COM
Also Called: Pointe At Lantern Crest, The
400 Lantern Crest Way, Santee (92071-4633)
PHONE.....................................619 955-0901
Kaan Ciftci, *Exec Dir*
EMP: 104 **Privately Held**
SIC: 8322 Senior citizens' center or association
PA: Santee Senior Retirement Communities, Llc
　8510 Railroad Ave
　Santee CA 92071
　-

(P-24035)
SANTEE SYSTEMS SERVICES II
229 E Gage Ave, Los Angeles (90003-1533)
PHONE.....................................323 445-0044
Veronica Santee, *CEO*
EMP: 99
SALES (est): 699.6K **Privately Held**
SIC: 8322 Child related social services

(P-24036)
SECOND CHANCE INC (PA)
Also Called: NEWARK CRISIS CENTER
6330 Thornton Ave Ste B, Newark (94560-3734)
P.O. Box 643 (94560-0643)
PHONE.....................................510 792-4357
Jimmy Rogers, *Director*
Tracie Long, *Executive*
Mark McConville, *Exec Dir*
John Balentine, *Office Mgr*
Ron Erlantson, *CTO*
EMP: 50
SQ FT: 10,000
SALES: 2.7MM **Privately Held**
WEB: www.secondchanceinc.com
SIC: 8322 Crisis intervention center

(P-24037)
SECOND HARVEST FOOD
8014 Marine Way, Irvine (92618-2235)
PHONE.....................................949 653-2900
Joe Schoeningh, *Owner*
EMP: 56 EST: 2008
SALES: 53.1MM **Privately Held**
SIC: 8322 Social service center

(P-24038)
SECOND HARVEST FOOD BANK (PA)
750 Curtner Ave, San Jose (95125-2118)
PHONE.....................................408 266-8866
Kathryn Jackson, *CEO*
Pat Ybarra, *Director*
EMP: 50 EST: 1974
SQ FT: 65,000
SALES: 127.6MM **Privately Held**
SIC: 8322 Meal delivery program

(P-24039)
SELF-HELP FOR ELDERLY
777 Stockton St Ste 110, San Francisco (94108-2372)
PHONE.....................................415 391-3843
EMP: 57
SALES (corp-wide): 20.5MM **Privately Held**
SIC: 8322 Senior citizens' center or association
PA: Self-Help For The Elderly
　731 Sansome St Ste 100
　San Francisco CA 94111
　415 677-7600

(P-24040)
SELF-HELP FOR ELDERLY (PA)
Also Called: San Francisco Residential Care
731 Sansome St Ste 100, San Francisco (94111-1735)
PHONE.....................................415 677-7600
Anni Chung, *President*
Janie Kaung, *Vice Chairman*
William Schulte, *Chairman*
Gerald Lee, *Treasurer*
Linda Wang, *Admin Sec*
EMP: 145
SALES: 20.5MM **Privately Held**
WEB: www.selfhelpelderly.org
SIC: 8322 8361 8082 Senior citizens' center or association; residential care; home health care services

(P-24041)
SELF-HELP FOR ELDERLY
940 S Stelling Rd, Cupertino (95014-4269)
PHONE.....................................408 873-1183
Nhi Hua, *Branch Mgr*
EMP: 57
SALES (corp-wide): 20.5MM **Privately Held**
SIC: 8322 Senior citizens' center or association
PA: Self-Help For The Elderly
　731 Sansome St Ste 100
　San Francisco CA 94111
　415 677-7600

(P-24042)
SELMA PORTUGUESE AZORIAN ASSN
1245 Nebraska Ave, Selma (93662-9738)
P.O. Box 734 (93662-0734)
PHONE.....................................559 896-2508
Louis Cardoza, *President*
EMP: 50
SALES: 70.8K **Privately Held**
SIC: 8322 5813 Community center; drinking places

(P-24043)
SENECA FAMILY OF AGENCIES
Also Called: Seneca Center
40950 Chapel Way, Fremont (94538-4236)
PHONE.....................................510 226-6180
Jessica Stryczek, *Principal*
EMP: 100
SALES (corp-wide): 110.9MM **Privately Held**
WEB: www.senecacenter.org
SIC: 8322 8211 8361 Social service center; elementary & secondary schools; home for the emotionally disturbed

PA: Seneca Family Of Agencies
15942 Foothill Blvd
San Leandro CA 94578
510 317-1444

(P-24044)
SENIOR COMPANIONS AT HOME
650 El Camino Real Ste E, Redwood City (94063-1345)
P.O. Box 5715 (94063-0715)
PHONE.....................................650 364-1265
Jovie Magbanua, *Director*
EMP: 50
SALES (est): 1.4MM **Privately Held**
SIC: 8322 Senior citizens' center or association

(P-24045)
SEQUOIA ADRC LP
Also Called: Sequoia Alchol DRG Rcovery Ctr
650 Main St, Redwood City (94063-1922)
PHONE.....................................650 364-5504
Barry Rosan, *Exec Dir*
EMP: 60
SALES (est): 1.6MM **Privately Held**
SIC: 8322 Rehabilitation services

(P-24046)
SEQUOIA SENIOR SOLUTIONS INC
825 S Main St, Lakeport (95453-5510)
PHONE.....................................707 263-3070
Stanton C Lawson, *Branch Mgr*
EMP: 87
SALES (corp-wide): 9.5MM **Privately Held**
SIC: 8322 Adult day care center
PA: Sequoia Senior Solutions, Inc.
　1372 N Mcdowell Blvd S
　Petaluma CA 94954
　707 763-6600

(P-24047)
SEQUOIA SENIOR SOLUTIONS INC
205 W Clay St, Ukiah (95482-5452)
PHONE.....................................707 621-9235
Stanton C Lawson, *Branch Mgr*
EMP: 87
SALES (corp-wide): 9.5MM **Privately Held**
SIC: 8322 Adult day care center
PA: Sequoia Senior Solutions, Inc.
　1372 N Mcdowell Blvd S
　Petaluma CA 94954
　707 763-6600

(P-24048)
SERVING SENIORS (PA)
525 14th St Ste 200, San Diego (92101-7556)
PHONE.....................................619 235-6572
Paul Downey, *CEO*
Dustin Dunbar, *Info Tech Mgr*
Lori Berg, *Bookkeeper*
Kathy Parker, *VP Opers*
Rick Roark, *Sales Mgr*
EMP: 60 EST: 1973
SQ FT: 11,121
SALES: 6.2MM **Privately Held**
WEB: www.servingseniors.org
SIC: 8322 Senior citizens' center or association

(P-24049)
SHELTER INC (PA)
1333 Willow Pass Rd # 206, Concord (94520-7931)
P.O. Box 5368 (94524-0368)
PHONE.....................................925 335-0698
John Eckstrom, *CEO*
Karri Edgers, *COO*
Carol Vicens, *Office Mgr*
Victoria Lopez, *Executive Asst*
Teresa Schow, *Admin Sec*
EMP: 62
SQ FT: 7,000
SALES: 11.6MM **Privately Held**
WEB: www.shelterincofccc.org
SIC: 8322 Emergency social services

(P-24050)
SIERRA FOREVER FAMILIES
Also Called: SFF
8928 Volunteer Ln Ste 100, Sacramento (95826-3238)
PHONE.....................................916 368-5114
Bob Herne, *Exec Dir*
Linda Merrill, *Officer*
Val Marchus, *Exec Dir*
Jennifer Jacobsen, *Finance*
Suzanne Skrabo, *Manager*
EMP: 68
SALES: 6.4MM **Privately Held**
SIC: 8322 Adoption services

(P-24051)
SNB CORPORATION
Also Called: Avalon Malibu
30765 Pacific, Malibu (90265)
PHONE.....................................310 457-9111
Hillary Berens, *CEO*
Alan Bond, *CFO*
Jenny Hirsch, *Human Res Mgr*
EMP: 142
SALES (est): 359.4K
SALES (corp-wide): 3MM **Privately Held**
SIC: 8322 Rehabilitation services
PA: New Vista Behavioral Health, Llc
　1901 Newport Blvd Ste 204
　Costa Mesa CA 92627
　888 316-3665

(P-24052)
SOCIAL ADVOCATES FOR Y
4275 El Cajon Blvd # 101, San Diego (92105-1293)
PHONE.....................................619 283-9624
Nancy G Hornberger, *CEO*
EMP: 202
SALES (corp-wide): 19MM **Privately Held**
SIC: 8322 Social worker
PA: Social Advocates For Youth, San Diego, Inc.
　8755 Aero Dr Ste 100
　San Diego CA 92123
　858 565-4148

(P-24053)
SOCIAL ADVOCATES FOR YOUTH (PA)
105 N Lincoln St, Santa Maria (93458-4319)
PHONE.....................................805 928-1707
William Rogers, *Director*
Judy Nishimori, *Director*
EMP: 50
SQ FT: 3,470
SALES: 2.6MM **Privately Held**
SIC: 8322 Children's aid society; family (marriage) counseling

(P-24054)
SOLANO COUNTY MENTAL HEALTH
Also Called: Exodus Recovery
9808 Venice Blvd Ste 700, Culver City (90232-6824)
PHONE.....................................707 428-1131
Camille Dullathan, *Director*
EMP: 50
SALES (est): 1.3MM **Privately Held**
SIC: 8322 Emergency social services

(P-24055)
SOURCEWISE
2115 The Alameda, San Jose (95126-1141)
PHONE.....................................408 350-3200
Stephen M Schmoll, *Director*
Altamirano Manuel, *COO*
Kimberly Marlar, *CFO*
Nolan Feliciano, *Director*
Crystal Shafiabady, *Director*
EMP: 100
SQ FT: 10,000
SALES: 10.8MM **Privately Held**
WEB: www.scccoa.org
SIC: 8322 Senior citizens' center or association; old age assistance

(P-24056)

SOUTH ASIAN HELP REFERRAL AGCY

Also Called: Sahara
17100 Pioneer Blvd # 260, Artesia
(90701-2776)
PHONE...................................562 402-4132
EMP: 50
SALES: 914.4K **Privately Held**
SIC: 8322

(P-24057)

SOUTH BAY COMMUNITY SERVICES

430 F St, Chula Vista (91910-3711)
PHONE...................................619 420-3620
Kathryn Lembo, *Exec Dir*
Helena Sabala, *Director*
EMP: 200
SQ FT: 2,900
SALES: 27.3MM **Privately Held**
WEB:
www.southbaycommunityservices.org
SIC: 8322 Social service center

(P-24058)

SOUTH BAY CTR FOR COUNSELING

Also Called: SOUTH BAY CENTER FOR
COMMUNITY
540 N Marine Ave, Wilmington
(90744-5528)
PHONE...................................310 414-2090
Colleen Mooney, *Exec Dir*
Brenda Aldaba, *Managing Dir*
Cathy Cesarz, *Division Mgr*
Gina Lomibao-Budnick, *Info Tech Mgr*
Greg Mooney, *Mktg Dir*
EMP: 90
SALES: 6.4MM **Privately Held**
WEB: www.sbaycenter.com
SIC: 8322 General counseling services

(P-24059)

SOUTH COAST CHILDRENS SOC INC

24950 Redlands Blvd, Loma Linda
(92354-4032)
PHONE...................................909 478-3377
EMP: 225
SALES (corp-wide): 30MM **Privately Held**
SIC: 8322 Social service center; rehabilitation services; community center
PA: South Coast Children's Society, Inc.
27261 Las Ramblas Ste 220
Mission Viejo CA 92691
714 966-8650

(P-24060)

SOUTH COAST CHILDRENS SOC INC

11780 Central Ave, Chino (91710-6498)
PHONE...................................909 364-9788
EMP: 135
SALES (corp-wide): 30MM **Privately Held**
SIC: 8322
PA: South Coast Children's Society, Inc.
27261 Las Ramblas Ste 220
Mission Viejo CA 92691
714 966-8650

(P-24061)

SOUTHEAST AREA SOCIAL SERVICES

10400 Pioneer Blvd Ste 8, Santa Fe
Springs (90670-3728)
PHONE...................................562 946-2237
Kirk Kain, *Director*
EMP: 50
SALES (est): 255.2K **Privately Held**
SIC: 8322 Social service center

(P-24062)

SOUTHGATE RECREATION & PK DST

Also Called: Rizal Community Center
7320 Florin Mall Dr, Sacramento
(95823-3255)
PHONE...................................916 421-7275
Jeremy Yee, *Manager*
EMP: 50

SALES (corp-wide): 7.9MM **Privately Held**
SIC: 8322 Community center
PA: Southgate Recreation & Park District
6000 Orange Ave
Sacramento CA 95823
916 428-1171

(P-24063)

SPANISH TRILS GIRL SCOUT CNCIL

5007 Center St, Chino (91710-3409)
PHONE...................................909 627-2609
Bervely Fowler, *Owner*
EMP: 50
SALES (est): 389.4K **Privately Held**
SIC: 8322 Youth center

(P-24064)

SPECTRUM COMMUNITY SERVICES (PA)

2617 Barrington Ct, Hayward (94545-1100)
PHONE...................................510 881-0300
Lara Calvert, *Exec Dir*
Debora Darden, *CFO*
Kamny Wong, *General Mgr*
Michael Dangler, *Opers Mgr*
Mark Smith, *Manager*
EMP: 56
SALES: 5MM **Privately Held**
SIC: 8322 Senior citizens' center or association

(P-24065)

SPIRITUAL DIRECTION

164 San Luis Ave, San Bruno
(94066-5507)
P.O. Box 1454, Millbrae (94030-5454)
PHONE...................................650 952-9456
Ariosto Coelho, *Owner*
EMP: 50
SALES (est): 447.7K **Privately Held**
WEB: www.spiritualdirection.com
SIC: 8322 General counseling services

(P-24066)

ST ANTHONY FOUNDATION (PA)

150 Golden Gate Ave, San Francisco
(94102-3810)
PHONE...................................415 241-2600
John Hardin, *Exec Dir*
Barry J Stenger, *Exec Dir*
Jeanne Zarka Brooks, *Director*
EMP: 50
SQ FT: 45,000
SALES (est): 12.7MM **Privately Held**
WEB: www.stanthonysf.com
SIC: 8322 Social service center

(P-24067)

ST BARNABAS SENIOR CENTER OF L

Also Called: SAINT BARNABAS SENIOR
SERVICES
675 S Carondelet St, Los Angeles
(90057-3309)
PHONE...................................213 388-4444
Rigo Sabareo, *President*
Nick Dumicreseu, *Treasurer*
John Kotick, *Vice Pres*
Jina Provencio, *Admin Asst*
Lani Garcia, *Accountant*
EMP: 61
SQ FT: 27,000
SALES: 6.2MM **Privately Held**
SIC: 8322 Senior citizens' center or association

(P-24068)

ST JOSEPH CENTER

Also Called: SAINT JOSEPH CENTER VOLUNTEER
204 Hampton Dr, Venice (90291-8633)
PHONE...................................310 396-6468
Felecia Adams, *Vice Pres*
John McGann, *CFO*
VA Lecia Adams Kellum, *Exec Dir*
Maia Eaglin, *Program Mgr*
Stanley Elicia, *Program Mgr*
EMP: 85
SQ FT: 32,000

SALES: 24.6MM **Privately Held**
SIC: 8322 8331 8351 Social service center; child related social services; temporary relief service; job training services; vocational rehabilitation agency; child day care services

(P-24069)

ST JOSEPH HOSPICE

Also Called: Saint Joseph Hlth Sys Hospice
200 W Center St Promenade, Anaheim
(92805-3960)
PHONE...................................714 712-7100
Linda Glomp, *Director*
Ron Nagano, *CFO*
Maire Blaistell, *Director*
EMP: 80 EST: 1994
SQ FT: 3,000
SALES (est): 2.2MM
SALES (corp-wide): 17.6B **Privately Held**
WEB: www.stjosephhospice.com
SIC: 8322 8063 Geriatric social service; psychiatric hospitals
HQ: St Joseph Home Health Network
200 W Center St Promenade
Anaheim CA 92805
714 712-9500

(P-24070)

ST VNCENT DE PAUL BLTMORE INC

3100 Norris Ave, Sacramento
(95821-4023)
PHONE...................................916 485-3482
EMP: 125
SALES (corp-wide): 22.2MM **Privately Held**
SIC: 8322 Social service center
PA: St. Vincent De Paul Of Baltimore, Inc.
2305 N Charles St Ste 300
Baltimore MD 21218
410 662-0500

(P-24071)

STANFORD UNIV MED CTR AUX

Also Called: STANFORD LINEAR ACCELERATOR CE
300 Pasteur Dr, Stanford (94305-2200)
P.O. Box 20410, Palo Alto (94309-0410)
PHONE...................................650 723-6636
Mary Dahlquist, *CEO*
Sarah Clark, *President*
P Joanne Cornbleet, *Pathologist*
Robert V Rouse, *Pathologist*
EMP: 400
SALES: 21.4K
SALES (corp-wide): 5.6B **Privately Held**
SIC: 8322 Adult day care center
PA: Leland Stanford Junior University
450 Serra Mall
Stanford CA 94305
650 723-2300

(P-24072)

STANISLAUS COUNTY POLICE

1325 Beverly Dr, Modesto (95351-2313)
PHONE...................................209 529-9121
Alfredo Guerra, *Exec Dir*
Vicki Bauman, *President*
Bret Silveira, *Deputy Dir*
Thania Jimenez, *Supervisor*
Julio Madrigal, *Supervisor*
EMP: 144
SALES: 2MM **Privately Held**
SIC: 8322 Social service center

(P-24073)

STAR INC

Also Called: Enrichment Program
4145 Delmar Ave Ste 1, Rocklin
(95677-4041)
PHONE...................................916 632-8407
Cindy Daniels, *Administration*
Jestine Attaran, *Technology*
EMP: 150 EST: 1999
SALES (est): 3.7MM **Privately Held**
WEB: www.starsacramento.org
SIC: 8322 Individual & family services

(P-24074)

STAR VIEW CHLDRN FMLY SRVCS

1085 W Victoria St, Compton (90220-5817)
PHONE...................................310 868-5379
Paul Stansbury, *CEO*
Kent Dunlap, *Vice Pres*

Maryjane Gross, *Admin Sec*
Ontson Placide, *Director*
EMP: 99
SALES (est): 2.5MM **Privately Held**
SIC: 8322 Family counseling services

(P-24075)

STARVISTA

610 Elm St Ste 212, San Carlos
(94070-3070)
PHONE...................................650 591-9623
Michael GRB, *CEO*
Lexie Munevar, *Partner*
Dianette Washer, *CFO*
Alison Proctor, *Treasurer*
Elayne Pace, *Bd of Directors*
EMP: 118
SQ FT: 7,200
SALES: 12.3MM **Privately Held**
SIC: 8322 Substance abuse counseling

(P-24076)

STEPHOUSE RECOVERY CENTER

Also Called: Step House Recovery
10529 Slater Ave, Fountain Valley
(92708-4841)
PHONE...................................714 394-3494
George J Vilagut, *CEO*
Alvin Nguyen, *Bookkeeper*
Sara Ferrer, *Marketing Staff*
Glen Goldstein, *Marketing Staff*
Eric Peterson, *Marketing Staff*
EMP: 70
SALES: 8MM **Privately Held**
SIC: 8322 General counseling services

(P-24077)

SUN BASKET INC (PA)

1170 Olinder Ct, San Jose (95122-2619)
PHONE...................................408 669-4418
Adam Zbar, *CEO*
Don Barnett, *COO*
Stuart Huizinga, *CFO*
Isobel Jones, *General Counsel*
EMP: 200
SALES (est): 100MM **Privately Held**
SIC: 8322 Meal delivery program

(P-24078)

SUNNY CAL ADHC INC

8450 Valley Blvd Ste 121b, Rosemead
(91770-1681)
PHONE...................................626 307-7772
Tony Leung, *President*
EMP: 60
SALES (est): 1MM **Privately Held**
SIC: 8322 Adult day care center

(P-24079)

SUNRISE FOOD MINISTRY

5901 San Juan Ave, Citrus Heights
(95610-6508)
PHONE...................................916 965-5431
Fred Chirstensen, *President*
EMP: 60
SALES: 89K **Privately Held**
SIC: 8322 Individual & family services

(P-24080)

SUPREME COURT UNITED STATES

Also Called: US Probation
101 W Broadway Ste 700, San Diego
(92101-8208)
PHONE...................................619 557-7149
Kenneth Young, *Chief*
EMP: 157 **Publicly Held**
WEB: www.supremecourtus.gov
SIC: 8322 Probation office; offender rehabilitation agency
HQ: Supreme Court, United States
1 1st St Ne
Washington DC 20543
202 479-3000

(P-24081)

SUTTER HLTH RHABILITATION SVCS

Also Called: Sutter Medical Ctr Sacramento
2801 L St Fl 3, Sacramento (95816-5615)
P.O. Box 160727 (95816-0727)
PHONE...................................916 733-3040
Lisa Drewslucero, *Manager*
Yuhwan Hong, *Surg-Orthopdc*

EMP: 70
SALES (est): 7.5MM **Privately Held**
SIC: 8322 Rehabilitation services

(P-24082)
SUTTER HLTH SCRMNTO SIERRA REG
Also Called: Sutter Senior Care
1234 U St, Sacramento (95818-1433)
PHONE................916 446-3100
Janet Tedesco, *Branch Mgr*
EMP: 57
SALES (corp-wide): 12.4B **Privately Held**
SIC: 8322 Senior citizens' center or association
HQ: Sutter Health Sacramento Sierra Region
2200 River Plaza Dr
Sacramento CA 95833
916 733-8800

(P-24083)
TEEN CHALLENGE NORWESTCAL NEV
Also Called: SOUTHBAY TEEN CHALLENGE
390 Mathew St, Santa Clara (95050-3114)
P.O. Box 24309, San Jose (95154-4309)
PHONE................408 703-2001
Dana Rowe, *Director*
EMP: 100
SALES: 1.3MM **Privately Held**
SIC: 8322 Social service center

(P-24084)
TERKENSHA ASSOCIATES INC
Also Called: NORTH AREA COMMUNITY MENTAL HE
811 Grand Ave Ste D, Sacramento (95838-3466)
PHONE................916 922-9868
William Benda, *Director*
William Moss, *President*
EMP: 52 **EST:** 1980
SALES: 3.6MM **Privately Held**
SIC: 8322 General counseling services

(P-24085)
TERRA NOVA COUNSELING (PA)
5750 Sunrise Blvd Ste 100, Citrus Heights (95610-7639)
PHONE................916 344-0249
Mary Stroube, *Exec Dir*
Donna McClure, *HR Admin*
EMP: 80
SQ FT: 4,789
SALES: 3.3MM **Privately Held**
WEB: www.after.org
SIC: 8322 Alcoholism counseling, nontreatment; drug abuse counselor, nontreatment; family (marriage) counseling; family counseling services

(P-24086)
TESSIE CLVLAND CMNTY SVCS CORP
Also Called: Tccsc
8019 Compton Ave Ste 219, Los Angeles (90001-3409)
PHONE................323 586-7333
Forescee Hogan-Rowles, *CEO*
Tyrone Ingram, *President*
Carolyn Chadwick, *CFO*
Moses Chadwick, *Exec Dir*
Sylvia Ramirez, *General Mgr*
EMP: 100
SALES: 12MM **Privately Held**
WEB: www.tccsc.org
SIC: 8322 Child related social services

(P-24087)
TIFFANYS LIU
9465 Wilshire Blvd, Beverly Hills (90212-2612)
PHONE................415 644-0846
Liu Tiffanys, *Owner*
EMP: 57
SALES: 6MM **Privately Held**
SIC: 8322 8742 Individual & family services; management consulting services

(P-24088)
TLCS INC
650 Howe Ave Ste 400, Sacramento (95825-4732)
PHONE................916 441-0123

Michael Lazar, *Exec Dir*
Leslie Mitchell, *Vice Pres*
EMP: 100
SQ FT: 1,868
SALES: 9.9MM **Privately Held**
SIC: 8322 Social service center

(P-24089)
TOOLWORKS INC
3075 Adeline St Ste 230, Berkeley (94703-2578)
PHONE................510 649-1322
Steve Crabiel, *Branch Mgr*
EMP: 407
SALES (corp-wide): 13.1MM **Privately Held**
SIC: 8322 Individual & family services
PA: Toolworks Inc
25 Kearny St Ste 400
San Francisco CA 94108
415 733-0990

(P-24090)
TOWARD MAXIMUM INDEPENDENCE (PA)
Also Called: T M I
4740 Murphy Canyon Rd # 300, San Diego (92123-4385)
PHONE................858 467-0600
Kerby Wohlander, *Director*
Jessie Campbell, *Exec Dir*
Rachel Harris, *Exec Dir*
Mary Carrington, *Division Mgr*
Cat Ferrero, *Division Mgr*
EMP: 190
SQ FT: 5,700
SALES: 11.2MM **Privately Held**
SIC: 8322 Social services for the handicapped

(P-24091)
TPD DELL DIOS
1817 Avenida Del Diablo, Escondido (92029-3112)
PHONE................760 741-2888
D Williams, *Exec Dir*
Donald Williams, *Exec Dir*
EMP: 50
SALES (est): 650K **Privately Held**
SIC: 8322 Old age assistance

(P-24092)
TRACY INTERFAITH MINISTRIES
311 W Grant Line Rd, Tracy (95376-2547)
P.O. Box 404 (95378-0404)
PHONE................209 836-5424
Darlene Quinn, *Exec Dir*
Lamar Stephenson, *Chairman*
Bob Weinberg, *Treasurer*
Robert Weinberg, *Treasurer*
Marie White, *Manager*
EMP: 65
SALES: 316.3K **Privately Held**
SIC: 8322 Social service center

(P-24093)
TRAINING TOWARD SELF RELIANCE
Also Called: TTSR
1446 Ethan Way 101, Sacramento (95825-2214)
PHONE................916 442-8877
Nancy Chance, *Director*
EMP: 50
SALES: 1MM **Privately Held**
WEB: www.ttsr.org
SIC: 8322 Social services for the handicapped

(P-24094)
TRANSITIONS - MENTAL HLTH ASSN (PA)
Also Called: SLO TRANSITIONS
784 High St, San Luis Obispo (93401-5243)
P.O. Box 15408 (93406-5408)
PHONE................805 540-6500
Jill B White, *Exec Dir*
Marci Johnson, *Finance Mgr*
Kim Banks, *Human Res Dir*
EMP: 60
SQ FT: 8,000

SALES: 13.2MM **Privately Held**
WEB: www.t-mha.org
SIC: 8322 Social services for the handicapped

(P-24095)
TRI COUNTY RESPITE CARE SVC
Also Called: RESPITE SERVICE
1215 Plumas St Ste 1600, Yuba City (95991-3456)
P.O. Box 1296 (95992-1296)
PHONE................530 755-3500
Diane Rose, *Director*
Joy Scott, *Principal*
EMP: 56
SALES: 1.2MM **Privately Held**
SIC: 8322 Individual & family services

(P-24096)
TRI-COUNTIES ASSOCIATION F (PA)
Also Called: TRI-COUNTIES REGIONAL CENTER
520 E Montecito St, Santa Barbara (93103-3278)
PHONE................805 962-7881
Bob Cobbs, *President*
Omar Noorzad, *Exec Dir*
EMP: 240
SQ FT: 16,000
SALES: 293.2MM **Privately Held**
SIC: 8322 Association for the handicapped

(P-24097)
TUPAZ DAY CARE SERVICES INC
3015 Union Ave, San Jose (95124-2006)
PHONE................408 377-1622
Rosario Tupaz, *President*
Beebe Tupaz, *Vice Pres*
EMP: 75
SALES: 2.9MM **Privately Held**
SIC: 8322 Adult day care center

(P-24098)
TURNING POINT CENTRAL CAL INC
Also Called: Visalia Youth Services
711 N Court St, Visalia (93291-3638)
PHONE................559 627-1490
Jose Ochoa, *Branch Mgr*
EMP: 50
SALES (corp-wide): 56.7MM **Privately Held**
SIC: 8322 8093 Individual & family services; mental health clinic, outpatient
PA: Turning Point Of Central California, Inc.
615 S Atwood St
Visalia CA 93277
559 732-8086

(P-24099)
UCSF AIDS HEALTH PROJECT
1930 Market St, San Francisco (94102-6228)
PHONE................415 476-6445
Jim Dilley, *President*
Joanna Rinaldi, *Director*
Lori Thoemmes, *Director*
EMP: 80 **EST:** 1985
SALES (est): 2.6MM **Privately Held**
SIC: 8322 Social service center

(P-24100)
UNION PAN ASIAN COMMUNITIES (PA)
Also Called: Upac
1031 25th St, San Diego (92102-2194)
PHONE................619 232-6454
Margaret Iwanaga-Penrose, *Director*
Koji Fukumura, *Vice Chairman*
EMP: 58
SQ FT: 14,000
SALES: 8.1MM **Privately Held**
WEB: www.upacsd.com
SIC: 8322 Social service center

(P-24101)
UNITED CEREBRAL PALSY ASSOC
980 Roosevelt Ste 100, Irvine (92620-3670)
PHONE................949 333-6400

Deborah Levy, *President*
Megan Feist, *Pathologist*
EMP: 130
SQ FT: 5,000
SALES: 5.2MM **Privately Held**
SIC: 8322 Association for the handicapped

(P-24102)
UNITED CP/S CHLDRNS FNDN LA
2170 N Westlake Blvd 22, Westlake Village (91362-5122)
PHONE................805 494-1141
Steve Bird, *Administration*
EMP: 50
SALES (corp-wide): 26.4MM **Privately Held**
SIC: 8322 Association for the handicapped
PA: United Cerebral Palsy/Spastic Children's Foundation Of Los Angeles And Ventura Counties
6430 Independence Ave
Woodland Hills CA 91367
818 782-2211

(P-24103)
UNITED CP/S CHLDRNS FNDN LA
2628 Brighton Ave, Los Angeles (90018-2752)
PHONE................323 737-0303
Nicole Seaton, *Director*
EMP: 71
SALES (corp-wide): 26.4MM **Privately Held**
SIC: 8322 Association for the handicapped
PA: United Cerebral Palsy/Spastic Children's Foundation Of Los Angeles And Ventura Counties
6430 Independence Ave
Woodland Hills CA 91367
818 782-2211

(P-24104)
UNITED FAMILIES INC (PA)
1561 S 4th St, El Centro (92243-4560)
PHONE................760 336-8922
Bertha Franco, *Exec Dir*
Gabreilla Gonzalez, *Executive*
Magda Franco, *Program Dir*
EMP: 80
SALES: 6.4MM **Privately Held**
SIC: 8322 Child guidance agency

(P-24105)
UNITED WAY OF BAY AREA (PA)
Also Called: UNITED WAY, THE
550 Kearny St Ste 1000, San Francisco (94108-2524)
PHONE................415 808-4300
Anne Wilson, *CEO*
Michael Scanlon, *Chairman*
Moses Awe, *Treasurer*
John Schaver, *Vice Pres*
Susan Sutherland, *Vice Pres*
EMP: 77 **EST:** 1923
SQ FT: 40,000
SALES: 12.5MM **Privately Held**
WEB: www.uwba.org
SIC: 8322 8399 Individual & family services; fund raising organization, non-fee basis

(P-24106)
VALLEY CMNTY COUNSELING SVCS (PA)
6707 Embarcadero Dr, Stockton (95219-3382)
PHONE................209 956-4240
David Love, *Exec Dir*
Sue Sutherland, *General Mgr*
Shana Lucchessi, *Bookkeeper*
Bonnie Bramer, *Director*
EMP: 93
SALES: 6.6MM **Privately Held**
SIC: 8322 General counseling services; substance abuse counseling; referral service for personal & social problems

(P-24107)
VALLEY MTN REGIONAL CTR INC (PA)
702 N Aurora St, Stockton (95202-2200)
P.O. Box 692290 (95269-2290)
PHONE................209 473-0951

Paul Billodeau, *CEO*
Debra Roth, *CFO*
Cindy Jimenez, *Executive*
Julie Dediego, *Program Mgr*
Wanda Farinelli, *Program Mgr*
EMP: 160
SQ FT: 63,000
SALES: 159.8MM **Privately Held**
SIC: 8322 Multi-service center

(P-24108)
VALLEY OAKS RESIDENTIAL
10623 E Highway 120, Manteca
(95336-9715)
P.O. Box 1358 (95336-1146)
PHONE...............................209 239-3244
Mario Duenas, *President*
Gregg Potts, *Director*
EMP: 60
SQ FT: 1,700
SALES: 3MM **Privately Held**
SIC: 8322 Individual & family services

(P-24109)
VENTURA CNTY COUNCIL ON AGING
4917 S Rose Ave, Oxnard (93033-7803)
P.O. Box 2429 (93034-2429)
PHONE...............................805 986-1424
Tom Carlisle, *CEO*
EMP: 60
SQ FT: 15,000
SALES: 46.7K **Privately Held**
SIC: 8322 Senior citizens' center or association

(P-24110)
VINTAGE SENIOR MANAGEMENT INC
2721 W Willow St, Burbank (91505-4544)
PHONE...............................818 954-9500
Brian Flornes, *Branch Mgr*
EMP: 517 **Privately Held**
SIC: 8322 Geriatric social service
PA: Senior Vintage Management Inc
23 Corporate Plaza Dr # 190
Newport Beach CA 92660

(P-24111)
VISALIA UNIFIED SCHOOL DST
Also Called: Office of Nutritional Services
801 N Mooney Blvd, Visalia (93291-3230)
PHONE...............................559 730-7871
Regina Ocampo, *Director*
Angela Sanchez, *Administration*
EMP: 180
SALES (corp-wide): 338MM **Privately Held**
SIC: 8322 8621 Individual & family services; health association
PA: Visalia Unified School District
5000 W Cypress Ave
Visalia CA 93277
559 730-7529

(P-24112)
VISTA CARE GROUP LLC (PA)
Also Called: Vista Gardens
1863 Devon Pl, Vista (92084-7624)
PHONE...............................760 295-3900
Avelen Delgado, *Administration*
Harry Crowell, *Chairman*
Joe Balbas,
EMP: 83
SALES (est): 4.7MM **Privately Held**
SIC: 8322 Senior citizens' center or association

(P-24113)
VISTA HILL FOUNDATION
4125 Alpha St, San Diego (92113-4553)
PHONE...............................619 266-0166
EMP: 85
SALES (corp-wide): 28.2MM **Privately Held**
SIC: 8322 8051 Geriatric social service; skilled nursing care facilities
PA: Vista Hill Foundation
8910 Clairemont Mesa Blvd
San Diego CA 92123
585 514-5100

(P-24114)
VOLUNTEERS OF AMER LOS ANGELES
11512 Valerio St, North Hollywood
(91605-3976)
PHONE...............................818 764-8722
EMP: 166
SALES (corp-wide): 87.5MM **Privately Held**
SIC: 8322 Social service center
PA: Volunteers Of America Of Los Angeles
3600 Wilshire Blvd # 1500
Los Angeles CA 90010
213 389-1500

(P-24115)
VOLUNTEERS OF AMER LOS ANGELES
10896 Lehigh Ave, Pacoima (91331-2584)
PHONE...............................818 834-9097
Paloma Cisneros, *Manager*
EMP: 133
SALES (corp-wide): 87.5MM **Privately Held**
SIC: 8322 Individual & family services
PA: Volunteers Of America Of Los Angeles
3600 Wilshire Blvd # 1500
Los Angeles CA 90010
213 389-1500

(P-24116)
VOLUNTEERS OF AMER LOS ANGELES
522 N Dangler Ave, Los Angeles
(90022-1218)
PHONE...............................323 780-3770
EMP: 133
SALES (corp-wide): 87.5MM **Privately Held**
SIC: 8322 Social service center
PA: Volunteers Of America Of Los Angeles
3600 Wilshire Blvd # 1500
Los Angeles CA 90010
213 389-1500

(P-24117)
VOLUNTEERS OF AMER LOS ANGELES
1760 W Cameron Ave # 104, West Covina
(91790-2739)
PHONE...............................626 337-9878
EMP: 133
SALES (corp-wide): 87.5MM **Privately Held**
SIC: 8322 Social service center
PA: Volunteers Of America Of Los Angeles
3600 Wilshire Blvd # 1500
Los Angeles CA 90010
213 389-1500

(P-24118)
VOLUNTEERS OF AMER LOS ANGELES
25141 Avenida Rondel, Valencia
(91355-3205)
PHONE...............................661 290-2829
EMP: 100
SALES (corp-wide): 87.5MM **Privately Held**
SIC: 8322 Social service center
PA: Volunteers Of America Of Los Angeles
3600 Wilshire Blvd # 1500
Los Angeles CA 90010
213 389-1500

(P-24119)
VOLUNTEERS OF AMER LOS ANGELES
10819 Plainview Ave, Tujunga
(91042-1633)
PHONE...............................818 352-5974
EMP: 166
SALES (corp-wide): 87.5MM **Privately Held**
SIC: 8322 Social service center
PA: Volunteers Of America Of Los Angeles
3600 Wilshire Blvd # 1500
Los Angeles CA 90010
213 389-1500

(P-24120)
VOLUNTEERS OF AMER LOS ANGELES
2100 N Broadway Ste 300, Santa Ana
(92706-2624)
PHONE...............................714 426-9834
EMP: 100
SALES (corp-wide): 87.5MM **Privately Held**
SIC: 8322 Individual & family services
PA: Volunteers Of America Of Los Angeles
3600 Wilshire Blvd # 1500
Los Angeles CA 90010
213 389-1500

(P-24121)
VOLUNTEERS OF AMER LOS ANGELES
6724 Tujunga Ave, North Hollywood
(91606-1910)
PHONE...............................818 769-3617
EMP: 133
SALES (corp-wide): 87.5MM **Privately Held**
SIC: 8322 Individual & family services
PA: Volunteers Of America Of Los Angeles
3600 Wilshire Blvd # 1500
Los Angeles CA 90010
213 389-1500

(P-24122)
VOLUNTEERS OF AMER LOS ANGELES
Also Called: Maud Booth Family Center
11243 Kittridge St, North Hollywood
(91606-2605)
PHONE...............................818 506-0597
Felix Cruz, *Manager*
EMP: 50
SALES (corp-wide): 87.5MM **Privately Held**
WEB: www.voala.org
SIC: 8322 Social service center
PA: Volunteers Of America Of Los Angeles
3600 Wilshire Blvd # 1500
Los Angeles CA 90010
213 389-1500

(P-24123)
VOLUNTEERS OF AMER LOS ANGELES
12550 Van Nuys Blvd, Pacoima
(91331-1354)
PHONE...............................818 834-8957
Leticia Aguirre, *Principal*
EMP: 199
SALES (corp-wide): 87.5MM **Privately Held**
WEB: www.voa.org
SIC: 8322 Individual & family services
PA: Volunteers Of America Of Los Angeles
3600 Wilshire Blvd # 1500
Los Angeles CA 90010
213 389-1500

(P-24124)
VOLUNTEERS OF AMERICA INC
10626 Schirra Ave, Mather (95655-4121)
PHONE...............................609 877-2665
EMP: 101
SALES (corp-wide): 315.2MM **Privately Held**
SIC: 8322 Individual & family services
PA: Volunteers Of America, Inc.
1660 Duke St Ste 100
Alexandria VA 22314
703 341-5000

(P-24125)
VOLUNTEERS OF AMERICA GREATER
672 13th St Ste 100, Oakland
(94612-1280)
PHONE...............................510 663-4546
EMP: 107
SALES (corp-wide): 20.5MM **Privately Held**
SIC: 8322 Individual & family services
PA: Volunteers Of America Northern California And Northern Nevada, Inc.
3434 Marconi Ave Ste A
Sacramento CA 95821
916 265-3400

(P-24126)
VOLUNTEERS OF AMERICA GREATER (PA)
3434 Marconi Ave Ste A, Sacramento
(95821-6242)
PHONE...............................916 265-3400
Leo McFarland, *CEO*
Joel Rusco, *CFO*
Rachele Burton, *Officer*
Rachel Laurie, *Senior VP*
Amani Sawires, *Vice Pres*
EMP: 90
SALES (est): 20.5MM **Privately Held**
WEB: www.voa.org
SIC: 8322 Social service center

(P-24127)
WATCH RESOURCES INC (PA)
Also Called: T.C.A.H
12801 Cabezut Rd, Sonora (95370-5938)
PHONE...............................209 533-0510
Christine Daily, *Exec Dir*
Jeff Rains, *President*
Eric Carlson, *Treasurer*
Bruce Chan, *Treasurer*
Jason Land, *Vice Pres*
EMP: 55
SQ FT: 7,200
SALES: 3.1MM **Privately Held**
SIC: 8322 0782 7349 4783 Association for the handicapped; landscape contractors; janitorial service, contract basis; packing & crating; mailing & messenger services

(P-24128)
WATTS LABOR COMMUNITY ACTION
Also Called: Wlcac
958 E 108th St, Los Angeles (90059-1008)
PHONE...............................323 563-5639
Timothy Watkins, *CEO*
EMP: 190
SALES (corp-wide): 15.3MM **Privately Held**
SIC: 8322 7299 Social service center; handyman service
PA: Watts Labor Community Action Committee
10950 S Central Ave
Los Angeles CA 90059
323 563-5639

(P-24129)
WAYMAKERS (PA)
1221 E Dyer Rd Ste 120, Santa Ana
(92705-5634)
PHONE...............................714 492-1010
Margot R Carlson, *Exec Dir*
Jeff Cadieux, *Treasurer*
Margot Carlson, *Exec Dir*
Ronnetta Johnson, *Exec Dir*
Lita Mercado, *General Mgr*
EMP: 60
SQ FT: 16,000
SALES: 15.3MM **Privately Held**
SIC: 8322 Social service center

(P-24130)
WEINGART CENTER ASSOCIATION
Also Called: Weingart Center For Homeless
566 S San Pedro St, Los Angeles
(90013-2102)
PHONE...............................213 622-6359
Kevin Murray, *President*
Warren Loui, *Partner*
Tonja Boykin, *COO*
Sonny Santa Ines, *CFO*
Jeffrey Catania, *Vice Pres*
EMP: 150
SQ FT: 175,000
SALES: 14.2MM **Privately Held**
SIC: 8322 Emergency social services

(P-24131)
WEST COUNTRA COSTA YOUTH SVCS (PA)
263 S 20th St, Richmond (94804-2709)
PHONE...............................510 412-5647
John Ziesenhenne, *President*
EMP: 55
SALES: 3.2MM **Privately Held**
SIC: 8322 Youth center

P
R
O
D
U
C
T
S

&

S
V
C
S

(P-24132)
WESTVIEW SERVICES INC
Also Called: Day Star Educational Center
626 W Commonwealth Ave, Fullerton
(92832-1725)
PHONE.................................714 879-3980
Gener Garcia, *Manager*
EMP: 88
SQ FT: 4,419
SALES (corp-wide): 16.6MM **Privately Held**
SIC: **8322** Adult day care center
PA: Westview Services, Inc
    10522 Katella Ave
    Anaheim CA 92804
    714 517-6606

(P-24133)
WILLITS SENIORS INC
1501 Baechtel Rd, Willits (95490-4516)
PHONE.................................707 459-6826
Allyn Noneman, *Director*
EMP: 57
SQ FT: 4,000
SALES: 1MM **Privately Held**
SIC: **8322** Senior citizens' center or association

(P-24134)
WOMEN INFANT & CHILDREN
Also Called: Nutrition Service Division
2525 Grand Ave, Long Beach
(90815-1765)
PHONE.................................562 570-4228
Judy Ogunji, *Director*
EMP: 55
SALES (est): 663.3K **Privately Held**
SIC: **8322** Individual & family services

(P-24135)
WOMENS CENTER-YOUTH FMLY SVCS (PA)
620 N San Joaquin St, Stockton
(95202-2030)
PHONE.................................209 941-2611
Joelle Gomez, *CEO*
Elizabeth Bifhay, *Principal*
Kimberly Miller, *Administration*
EMP: 111
SALES: 4.2MM **Privately Held**
SIC: **8322** Child related social services

(P-24136)
WOMENS LAW CENTER
950 W 17th St Ste D, Santa Ana
(92706-3573)
PHONE.................................714 667-1038
Richard C Gilbert, *Owner*
EMP: 100
SALES (est): 1.1MM **Privately Held**
SIC: **8322** Adoption services

(P-24137)
YOUNG MENS CHRSTN ASSN OF LA
Also Called: Downey YMCA
11531 Downey Ave, Downey (90241-4936)
PHONE.................................562 862-4201
George Saikali, *Exec Dir*
Beth Crawford, *Exec Dir*
EMP: 150
SALES (corp-wide): 105.9MM **Privately Held**
SIC: **8322** 7997 Social service center; membership sports & recreation clubs
PA: Young Men's Christian Association Of Metropolitan Los Angeles
    625 S New Hampshire Ave
    Los Angeles CA 90005
    213 351-2256

(P-24138)
YOUTH FOR CHANGE
2400 Washington Ave, Redding
(96001-2802)
PHONE.................................530 605-1520
EMP: 68 **Privately Held**
SIC: **8322** Youth center
PA: Youth For Change
    5538 Skyway
    Paradise CA 95969

(P-24139)
YOUTH FOR CHANGE (PA)
Also Called: Paradise Ridge Fmly Resources
5538 Skyway, Paradise (95969-4932)
P.O. Box 1476 (95967-1476)
PHONE.................................530 877-8187
Dennis Cargile, *Principal*
Janet Goodson, *Partner*
Andy Martinez, *CFO*
Michele Peterson, *Chairman*
Alan White, *Chairman*
EMP: 115
SQ FT: 5,000
SALES: 13.8MM **Privately Held**
SIC: **8322** Youth center

(P-24140)
YOUTH FOR CHANGE
2185 Baldwin Ave, Oroville (95966-5312)
PHONE.................................530 538-8347
Bobby Jones, *Branch Mgr*
EMP: 68 **Privately Held**
SIC: **8322** Youth center
PA: Youth For Change
    5538 Skyway
    Paradise CA 95969

(P-24141)
YUBA COMMUNITY COLLEGE DST
Also Called: Beale Air Force Base Outreach
2088 N Beale Rd, Marysville (95901-7605)
PHONE.................................530 788-0973
Patrick Meleski, *Technology*
Kate Hodge, *Human Resources*
Wendy Duck, *Manager*
EMP: 99
SALES (corp-wide): 18.1MM **Privately Held**
SIC: **8322** Outreach program
PA: Yuba Community College District
    425 Plumas Blvd Ste 200
    Yuba City CA 95991
    530 741-8949

(P-24142)
YUE FENG INC
145 S Fairfax Ave, Los Angeles
(90036-2166)
PHONE.................................310 253-9795
Cheng Chen, *President*
EMP: 72
SQ FT: 8,500
SALES: 7MM **Privately Held**
SIC: **8322** Individual & family services

(P-24143)
YWCA CONTRA COSTA/SACRAMENTO (PA)
1320 Arnold Dr Ste 170, Martinez
(94553-6537)
PHONE.................................925 372-4213
Nancy Atkinson, *CEO*
Pamela Mitchell, *Controller*
Annette Hee Jimenez, *Director*
EMP: 60
SQ FT: 8,000
SALES: 2.9MM **Privately Held**
SIC: **8322** 8641 8351 Individual & family services; community membership club; child day care services

---

8331 Job Training & Vocational Rehabilitation Svcs

(P-24144)
ABILITY COUNTS INC (PA)
775 Trademark Cir Ste 101, Corona
(92879-2084)
PHONE.................................951 734-6595
Joyce Hearn, *CEO*
EMP: 100
SQ FT: 28,000
SALES: 6.7MM **Privately Held**
WEB: www.abilitycounts.org
SIC: **8331** Sheltered workshop

(P-24145)
APPRENTICE & JOURNEYMEN TRN TR
Also Called: Compton Training Center
7850 Haskell Ave, Van Nuys (91406-1907)
PHONE.................................323 636-9871
Micheal Hazard, *Exec Dir*
EMP: 99
SALES: 13.8MM **Privately Held**
SIC: **8331** Job training services

(P-24146)
ARC FRESNO/MADERA COUNTIES (PA)
4490 E Ashlan Ave, Fresno (93726-2647)
PHONE.................................559 226-6268
Lori Rmirez, *CEO*
Carolyn Wallace, *President*
Mike Takechi, *Treasurer*
Peter Mersino, *Vice Pres*
Alan Lagunoff, *Admin Sec*
EMP: 52
SALES: 11.1MM **Privately Held**
SIC: **8331** Job training services

(P-24147)
ARC LOS ANGLES ORANGE COUNTIES (PA)
Also Called: SOUTHEAST INDUSTRIES
12049 Woodruff Ave, Downey
(90241-5669)
PHONE.................................562 803-1556
Kevin Mac Donald, *Exec Dir*
EMP: 94
SQ FT: 9,800
SALES: 3.8MM **Privately Held**
SIC: **8331** 5932 Skill training center; vocational training agency; used merchandise stores

(P-24148)
ARC MID-CITIES INC
14208 Towne Ave, Los Angeles
(90061-2653)
PHONE.................................310 329-9272
Lena Cole Dennis, *President*
John Wagner, *Exec Dir*
Joe Avalos, *Program Mgr*
Nathan Hood, *Info Tech Dir*
Bedsog Jugo, *Human Res Mgr*
EMP: 160
SALES (est): 6.6MM **Privately Held**
WEB: www.arcmidcities.org
SIC: **8331** 8322 Job training services; individual & family services

(P-24149)
ARC OF ALAMEDA COUNTY
Also Called: Walpert Center
1101 Walpert St, Hayward (94541-6705)
PHONE.................................510 582-8151
Renee Tuddel, *Manager*
EMP: 110
SQ FT: 2,000
SALES (corp-wide): 6.5MM **Privately Held**
WEB: www.tiw-alameda.com
SIC: **8331** Sheltered workshop
PA: The Arc Of Alameda County
    14700 Doolittle Dr
    San Leandro CA 94577
    510 357-3569

(P-24150)
ARC SAN FRANCISCO (PA)
1500 Howard St, San Francisco
(94103-2525)
PHONE.................................415 255-7200
Timothy Hornbecker, *Exec Dir*
Kirsten Mellor, *CEO*
Brian Wagman, *CFO*
Dan Cousins, *Director*
Allan S Fox, *Director*
EMP: 156
SQ FT: 30,000
SALES: 10.2MM **Privately Held**
WEB: www.thearcsanfrancisco.org
SIC: **8331** 8361 7361 Job training services; vocational rehabilitation agency; home for the mentally handicapped; employment agencies

(P-24151)
ARRIBA JUNTOS (PA)
1850 Mission St, San Francisco
(94103-3502)
PHONE.................................415 487-3240
Dalila Ohumada, *Director*
EMP: 62 EST: 1965
SQ FT: 10,000
SALES: 8.8MM **Privately Held**
WEB: www.arribajuntos.org
SIC: **8331** Community service employment training program

(P-24152)
ASIAN REHABILITATION SVC INC (PA)
7009 Washington Ave, Whittier
(90602-1416)
PHONE.................................562 632-1141
Si Ho, *Exec Dir*
Ruben Dugay, *Project Mgr*
EMP: 62
SQ FT: 28,000
SALES: 3.4MM **Privately Held**
WEB: www.asianrehab.org
SIC: **8331** Vocational rehabilitation agency

(P-24153)
ASSOC FOR RETARDED CITIZENS
Also Called: School of Hope
796 E 6th St, San Bernardino
(92410-4532)
PHONE.................................909 884-6484
Kris Oxnevad, *Director*
EMP: 55 EST: 1952
SALES: 963.1K **Privately Held**
WEB: www.schoolofhope.com
SIC: **8331** 5399 Job training & vocational rehabilitation services; surplus & salvage goods

(P-24154)
ASSOCIATION FOR RETARDED (PA)
Also Called: Hillside Enterprises
4519 E Stearns St, Long Beach
(90815-2540)
PHONE.................................562 597-7716
Harry A Van Loon, *Director*
EMP: 81
SQ FT: 35,000
SALES: 4.8MM **Privately Held**
SIC: **8331** Sheltered workshop

(P-24155)
BAKERSFIELD ASSC RRTD CTZNS
2240 S Union Ave, Bakersfield
(93307-4158)
PHONE.................................661 834-2272
Jim Baldwin, *President*
EMP: 210
SQ FT: 30,000
SALES (est): 10.8MM **Privately Held**
SIC: **8331** Sheltered workshop; skill training center; work experience center

(P-24156)
BENEFITVISION INC
5550 Topanga Canyon Blvd # 180, Woodland Hills (91367-6478)
PHONE.................................818 348-3100
Terry Fuzue, *Branch Mgr*
EMP: 58
SALES (corp-wide): 20MM **Privately Held**
SIC: **8331** Job training & vocational rehabilitation services
PA: Benefitvision, Inc.
    4522 Rfd
    Long Grove IL 60047
    877 737-5526

(P-24157)
BLANCHARDCOACHINGCOM INC
125 State Pl, Escondido (92029-1323)
PHONE.................................760 489-5005
Kenneth S Blanchard, *President*
Tom McKee, *CEO*
Randy Redwitz, *CFO*
Natalie Halabuk, *Executive*
EMP: 300 EST: 1979

SALES (est): 6.3MM **Privately Held**
SIC: **8331** Job training & vocational rehabilitation services

(P-24158)
BUFFINI & COMPANY (PA)
6349 Palomar Oaks Ct, Carlsbad
(92011-1428)
PHONE..............................760 827-2100
Brian Buffini, *Ch of Bd*
Jim Polzin, *CFO*
Beverly Buffini, *Treasurer*
Lori Martinez, *Vice Pres*
Brian Wildermuth, *Vice Pres*
EMP: 182
SALES (est): 18.7MM **Privately Held**
WEB: www.buffiniandcompany.com
SIC: **8331** Job training services

(P-24159)
BUILD REHABILITATION INDS (PA)
12432 Foothill Blvd, Sylmar (91342-6004)
PHONE..............................818 485-8560
Matthew Lynch, *President*
Isabel Boniface, *COO*
Cynthia Kolke, *Marketing Staff*
Amina Kamoun, *Program Dir*
Patti Cooper, *Director*
EMP: 90 EST: 1967
SQ FT: 15,500
SALES: 5.7MM **Privately Held**
WEB: www.buildworksource.com
SIC: **8331** Vocational rehabilitation agency

(P-24160)
CALIDAD INDUSTRIES INC
1301 30th Ave, Oakland (94601-2208)
PHONE..............................510 534-6666
Robert Taylor, *CEO*
James Caponigro, *CEO*
Patrick Schmalz, *CFO*
EMP: 52
SQ FT: 35,000
SALES: 6.2MM
SALES (corp-wide): 24.5MM **Privately Held**
WEB: www.eastbaygoodwill.org
SIC: **8331** Vocational training agency
PA: Goodwill Industries Of The Greater
East Bay, Inc.
1301 30th Ave
Oakland CA 94601
510 698-7200

(P-24161)
CALIFORNIA HUMAN DEV CORP (PA)
Also Called: Anthony Soto Emplyment Trining
3315 Airway Dr, Santa Rosa (95403-2005)
PHONE..............................707 523-1155
Miguel Mejia, *Chairman*
Christopher Paige, *CEO*
Doris Unsod, *Treasurer*
Hector Brambila, *Admin Sec*
Peter Anderson, *Graphic Designe*
EMP: 140
SQ FT: 15,000
SALES: 12.6MM **Privately Held**
SIC: **8331** 7361 8399 7374 Job training services; placement agencies; community development groups; calculating service (computer)

(P-24162)
CAMBLE CENTER
Also Called: Self-Aid Workshop
6512 San Fernando Rd, Glendale (91201-2109)
PHONE..............................818 242-2434
Wendy Jacoby, *President*
EMP: 100 EST: 1958
SQ FT: 8,000
SALES: 2.1MM **Privately Held**
SIC: **8331** 5947 8322 7389 Job training & vocational rehabilitation services; gift, novelty & souvenir shop; individual & family services; packaging & labeling services; mailing service; recycling, waste materials

(P-24163)
CAREER TRANSITION CENTER
Also Called: Workforce Development Bureau
3447 Atlantic Ave 100, Long Beach (90807-4513)
PHONE..............................562 570-9675
Brian Rogers, *Director*
EMP: 135
SALES (est): 3MM **Privately Held**
SIC: **8331** Job training services

(P-24164)
CENTER FOR EMPLOYMENT TRAINING (PA)
Also Called: C E T
701 Vine St, San Jose (95110-2940)
PHONE..............................408 287-7924
Hermelinda Sapien, *CEO*
Mohammad Aryanpour, *CFO*
Greg Adams, *Bd of Directors*
Deborah A Raimondo, *Officer*
Suyin Rodriguez, *Officer*
EMP: 70
SQ FT: 120,000
SALES: 31.4MM **Privately Held**
SIC: **8331** 9721 Vocational training agency; immigration services, government

(P-24165)
CENTRAL VALLEY OPRTNTY CTR INC (PA)
Also Called: Cvoc
6838 Bridget Ct, Winton (95388)
P.O. Box 1389 (95388-1389)
PHONE..............................209 357-0062
Ernie Flores, *Exec Dir*
Don Curiel-Ruth, *Info Tech Mgr*
Maria Romero, *Software Dev*
Ofelia Reynoso, *Persnl Dir*
EMP: 110
SQ FT: 27,000
SALES (est): 5.9MM **Privately Held**
SIC: **8331** Vocational training agency

(P-24166)
CHINATOWN SERVICE CENTER (PA)
767 N Hill St Ste 200b, Los Angeles (90012-2365)
PHONE..............................213 808-1700
Karen Elizabeth Blakeney, *CEO*
Peter Ng, *President*
Gloria Tang, *Treasurer*
Henry Kwong, *Admin Sec*
Lawrence Lue, *Director*
EMP: 120
SQ FT: 20,000
SALES: 7.5MM **Privately Held**
WEB: www.cscla.org
SIC: **8331** 8322 8011 Job counseling; family (marriage) counseling; clinic, operated by physicians

(P-24167)
COMMUNITY CATALYSTS CALIFORNIA
935 W San Marcos Blvd # 103, San Marcos (92078-1142)
PHONE..............................760 471-3700
EMP: 50 **Privately Held**
SIC: **8331** Job training & vocational rehabilitation services
PA: Community Catalysts Of California
3750 Convoy St Ste 306
San Diego CA 92111

(P-24168)
COMMUNITY INTEGRATED WORK PROG
Also Called: Cwip
4623 W Jacquelyn Ave, Fresno (93722-6413)
PHONE..............................559 276-8564
Louis Leon, *Director*
EMP: 50
SALES (corp-wide): 52.2MM **Privately Held**
SIC: **8331** Vocational training agency
PA: Community Integrated Work Program, Inc.
2219 Buchanan Rd Ste 3
Antioch CA 94509
925 776-1040

(P-24169)
COMPRHNSIVE TRNING SYSTEMS INC
497 11th St Ste 4, Imperial Beach (91932-1661)
PHONE..............................619 424-6650
Linda Blairforth, *President*
EMP: 50
SQ FT: 8,300
SALES: 475.1K **Privately Held**
WEB: www.ctsjobs.org
SIC: **8331** Job training & vocational rehabilitation services

(P-24170)
CONSERVATION CORPS LONG BEACH
340 Nieto Ave, Long Beach (90814-1845)
PHONE..............................562 986-1249
Samara Ashley, *Principal*
Mike Bassett, *CEO*
John Dunay, *CFO*
Mario R Beas, *Admin Sec*
Kedrin Hopkins, *Project Dir*
EMP: 165
SQ FT: 10,000
SALES: 2.9MM **Privately Held**
WEB: www.cclb-corps.org
SIC: **8331** 8322 Community service employment training program; individual & family services

(P-24171)
CONTRA COSTA ARC
Also Called: Commercial Spport Svcs Antioch
2505 W 10th St, Antioch (94509-1374)
PHONE..............................925 755-4925
David Duart, *Manager*
EMP: 70
SQ FT: 7,992
SALES (corp-wide): 19.2MM **Privately Held**
WEB: www.ccarealtors.com
SIC: **8331** 7389 Skill training center; packaging & labeling services
PA: Contra Costa Arc
1340 Arnold Dr Ste 127
Martinez CA 94553
925 646-4690

(P-24172)
CORPORATION OF THE PRESIDENT
Also Called: Deseret Industries
3000 Auburn Blvd Ste B, Sacramento (95821-1831)
PHONE..............................916 482-1480
Jack P McKinney, *Manager*
Jack McKinney, *Manager*
EMP: 100
SALES (corp-wide): 3.9B **Privately Held**
WEB: www.lds.org
SIC: **8331** 5932 Sheltered workshop; used merchandise stores
PA: Corporation Of The President Of The Church Of Jesus Christ Of Latter-Day Saints
50 E North Temple
Salt Lake City UT 84150
801 240-1000

(P-24173)
COUNTY OF ALAMEDA
Private Industry Council
24100 Amador St Ste 130, Hayward (94544-1287)
PHONE..............................510 670-5700
Kirill Elistratov, *Manager*
EMP: 50 **Privately Held**
WEB: www.co.alameda.ca.us
SIC: **8331** 9411 Job training services; administration of educational programs;
PA: County Of Alameda
1221 Oak St Ste 555
Oakland CA 94612
510 272-6691

(P-24174)
COUNTY OF MERCED
Also Called: Workforce Investment- Admin
1205 W 18th St, Merced (95340-4513)
PHONE..............................209 724-2000
Andrea P Baker, *Director*
EMP: 110 **Privately Held**
WEB: www.mercednccp-hcp.net

SIC: **8331** 9441 Job training services; administration of social & manpower programs;
PA: County Of Merced
2222 M St
Merced CA 95340
209 385-7511

(P-24175)
COUNTY OF RIVERSIDE
Also Called: Economic Development
3403 10th St Ste 500, Riverside (92501-3658)
P.O. Box 553 (92502-0553)
PHONE..............................951 955-3100
Selicia Slournoy, *Director*
EMP: 97 **Privately Held**
SIC: **8331** 9441 Skill training center; administration of social & manpower programs;
PA: County Of Riverside
4080 Lemon St Fl 11
Riverside CA 92501
951 955-1110

(P-24176)
COUNTY OF SAN JOAQUIN
San Joaquin County
56 S Lincoln St, Stockton (95203-3100)
PHONE..............................209 468-3500
EMP: 200 **Privately Held**
SIC: **8331** 9111
PA: County Of San Joaquin
44 N San Joaquin St # 640
Stockton CA 95202
209 468-3203

(P-24177)
COUNTY OF STANISLAUS
Also Called: Alliance Work Net
251 E Hackett Rd Ste 2, Modesto (95358-9800)
P.O. Box 3389 (95353-3389)
PHONE..............................209 558-2100
Khristy Santos, *Director*
EMP: 150 **Privately Held**
WEB: www.co.stanislaus.ca.us
SIC: **8331** Job training & vocational rehabilitation services
PA: County Of Stanislaus
1010 10th St Ste 5100
Modesto CA 95354
209 525-6398

(P-24178)
DEL NORTE WORKFORCE CENTER
Also Called: Real Human Svcs & Workforce
875 5th St Ste 12, Crescent City (95531-4000)
PHONE..............................707 464-8347
Cindy Salatnay, *Director*
EMP: 50
SALES (est): 409.9K **Privately Held**
SIC: **8331** Job training services

(P-24179)
DEVELOPMENTAL SVCS CAL DEPT
Also Called: Fairview Developmental Center
2501 Harbor Blvd, Costa Mesa (92626-6143)
PHONE..............................714 957-5151
Bill Wilson, *Exec Dir*
EMP: 1500 **Privately Held**
WEB: www.ldc.dds.ca.gov
SIC: **8331** 9431 8361 Job training & vocational rehabilitation services; administration of public health programs; ; residential care
HQ: California Department Of Developmental Services
1600 9th St
Sacramento CA 95814
916 654-1690

(P-24180)
EDEN AREA REGNL OCCUPATIONAL P
Also Called: Eden Area Rop School
26316 Hesperian Blvd, Hayward (94545-2458)
PHONE..............................510 293-2900
Cyril Bonanno, *Exec Dir*
EMP: 90

PRODUCTS & SVCS

SQ FT: 74,000
SALES (est): 5.9MM **Privately Held**
WEB: www.edenrop.com
SIC: **8331** 8249 Vocational training agency; skill training center; vocational schools

(P-24181)
EMPLOYMENT & COMMUNITY OPTIONS
5050 Murphy Canyon Rd # 220, San Diego (92123-4441)
PHONE................................858 565-9870
Nancy Batterman, *President*
Richard Gutierrez, *CFO*
Alaina Purcell, *Executive*
Lindsay Arvanitis, *Program Mgr*
Michelle Bozman, *Program Mgr*
EMP: 250
SQ FT: 6,000
SALES: 14.1MM **Privately Held**
SIC: **8331** Job training & vocational rehabilitation services

(P-24182)
EXCEPTIONAL CHLD FOUNDATION (PA)
Also Called: PAR SERVICES
5350 Machado Ln, Culver City (90230-8800)
PHONE................................310 204-3300
Scott Bowling, *President*
Denise Orme, *CFO*
Shirley Bianca, *Executive*
Marcus Carter, *Human Resources*
Leonela Gonzalez, *Human Resources*
EMP: 120 EST: 1946
SQ FT: 45,000
SALES: 40.9MM **Privately Held**
WEB: www.ecf-la.org
SIC: **8331** Vocational training agency; vocational rehabilitation agency

(P-24183)
EXCEPTIONAL CHLD FOUNDATION
Also Called: Par Services
5350 Machado Ln, Culver City (90230-8800)
PHONE................................310 204-3300
Scott Bowling, *President*
EMP: 240
SALES (corp-wide): 40.9MM **Privately Held**
WEB: www.ecf-la.org
SIC: **8331** 8351 8699 8322 Vocational training agency; child day care services; charitable organization; individual & family services
PA: Exceptional Children's Foundation
5350 Machado Ln
Culver City CA 90230
310 204-3300

(P-24184)
FONTANA RESOURCES AT WORK
Also Called: INDUSTRIAL SUPPORT SYSTEMS
8608 Live Oak Ave, Fontana (92335-3172)
P.O. Box 848 (92334-0848)
PHONE................................909 428-3833
Ulric Jones, *CFO*
Carole Graham, *Vice Pres*
Sylvia Anderson, *Exec Dir*
EMP: 140
SQ FT: 22,600
SALES: 2MM **Privately Held**
SIC: **8331** 3444 Vocational rehabilitation agency; sheet metalwork

(P-24185)
GLENN CNTY HUMN RESOURCE AGCY
Also Called: Colusa, Glenn, Trinity Communt
420 E Laurel St, Willows (95988-3115)
PHONE................................530 934-6510
Kim W Gaghagen, *Director*
Betty Skala, *Deputy Dir*
EMP: 130
SALES (est): 2.9MM **Privately Held**
SIC: **8331** 8322 Job training services; emergency social services

(P-24186)
GOODWILL INDS ORANGE CNTY CAL
2910 W Garry Ave, Santa Ana (92704-6510)
PHONE................................714 754-7808
EMP: 110
SALES (corp-wide): 126.7MM **Privately Held**
SIC: **8331**
PA: Goodwill Industries Of Orange County, California
410 N Fairview St
Santa Ana CA 92703
714 547-6308

(P-24187)
GOODWILL INDS S CENTL CAL
1115 Olive Dr, Bakersfield (93308-4141)
PHONE................................661 377-0191
Debbie Stwart, *Principal*
EMP: 50
SALES (corp-wide): 15.1MM **Privately Held**
SIC: **8331** Vocational rehabilitation agency
PA: Goodwill Industries Of South Central California
4901 Stine Rd
Bakersfield CA 93313
661 837-0595

(P-24188)
GOODWILL INDUSTRS OF SAN FRANC
1270 Oddstad Dr, Redwood City (94063-2606)
PHONE................................650 556-9709
EMP: 55
SALES (corp-wide): 36.8MM **Privately Held**
SIC: **8331** Vocational rehabilitation agency
PA: Goodwill Industries Of San Francisco, San Mateo, And Marin Counties, Inc.
295 Bay St
San Francisco CA 94133
415 575-2101

(P-24189)
HEARTLAND OPPORTUNITY CTR INC (PA)
4567 N Marty Ave, Fresno (93722-7810)
PHONE................................559 674-4521
Kristy L Anderson, *CEO*
Maria Alvarado, *CFO*
EMP: 63
SQ FT: 6,000
SALES: 2.2MM **Privately Held**
WEB: www.heartlandopportunity.com
SIC: **8331** Vocational rehabilitation agency

(P-24190)
HOPE SERVICES
19055 Portola Dr, Salinas (93908-1212)
PHONE................................831 455-4940
Greg Dinsmore, *Manager*
EMP: 65
SALES (corp-wide): 40.3MM **Privately Held**
SIC: **8331** Vocational rehabilitation agency
PA: Hope Services
30 Las Colinas Ln
San Jose CA 95119
408 284-2850

(P-24191)
HOPE SERVICES (PA)
30 Las Colinas Ln, San Jose (95119-1212)
PHONE................................408 284-2850
John C Christensen, *CEO*
Fred Gawlick, *President*
Ray Abe, *CFO*
Ric Lnd, *CFO*
Rex Zimmerman, *Vice Pres*
EMP: 50
SQ FT: 29,400
SALES: 40.3MM **Privately Held**
SIC: **8331** Vocational rehabilitation agency

(P-24192)
HOWARD TRAINING CENTER (PA)
1424 Stonum Rd, Modesto (95351-5197)
PHONE................................209 538-2431
Claudia K Miller, *Exec Dir*
Tony Thornton, *Vice Pres*

Carla Strong, *Exec Dir*
Marisol Moreno, *Program Mgr*
Kristi Rush, *Program Mgr*
EMP: 100
SQ FT: 10,000
SALES: 6MM **Privately Held**
SIC: **8331** Skill training center

(P-24193)
ICI ENTERPRISES INC
790 E Willow St Ste 150, Long Beach (90806-2719)
PHONE................................562 989-7715
Robert Nelson, *Principal*
EMP: 100
SALES: 8MM **Privately Held**
SIC: **8331** Job training services

(P-24194)
INCLUSIVE CMNTY RESOURCES LLC
2855 Telegraph Ave Ste LI, Berkeley (94705-1168)
PHONE................................510 981-8115
Julie Steinbaugh,
Michael Steinbaugh,
Shana Ring, *Clerk*
EMP: 120
SQ FT: 4,800
SALES (est): 4.1MM **Privately Held**
SIC: **8331** Community service employment training program

(P-24195)
INSTITUTE FOR EDUCTL THERAPY
1007 University Ave, Berkeley (94710-2113)
PHONE................................831 457-1207
Karen Rotstein, *CIO*
Arianna Rosenthal, *Marketing Staff*
EMP: 50 **Privately Held**
WEB: www.baumancollege.com
SIC: **8331** 8249 Vocational training agency; vocational schools
PA: Institute For Educational Therapy
10151 Main St Ste 128
Penngrove CA

(P-24196)
JEWIS VOCATIONAL & COUNSELING
225 Bush St Ste 400, San Francisco (94104-4252)
PHONE................................415 391-3600
Abby Snay, *Exec Dir*
Nathanael Montgomery, *Chief Mktg Ofcr*
Jamie Austin, *Vice Pres*
Matti Paksula, *CTO*
Juha Suuraho, *Software Dev*
EMP: 70
SQ FT: 8,000
SALES: 9.9MM **Privately Held**
WEB: www.jvs.org
SIC: **8331** Job counseling; job training services

(P-24197)
JEWISH VOCATIONAL SERVICES (PA)
Also Called: JVSLA
6505 Wilshire Blvd # 200, Los Angeles (90048-4957)
PHONE................................323 761-8888
Vivian B Seigel, *CEO*
Claudia Finkel, *COO*
Olwen Brown, *CFO*
Zoya Kavutskaya, *Info Tech Dir*
Karen Schneider, *Project Mgr*
EMP: 50
SQ FT: 11,000
SALES: 16.8MM **Privately Held**
SIC: **8331** Vocational rehabilitation agency

(P-24198)
KINGS VIEW
100 Airpark Rd, Atwater (95301-9535)
P.O. Box 774 (95301-0774)
PHONE................................209 357-0321
Sam Kalember, *Branch Mgr*
EMP: 50

SALES (corp-wide): 26.8MM **Privately Held**
SIC: **8331** Sheltered workshop; work experience center
PA: Kings View
7170 N Fincl Dr Ste 110
Fresno CA 93720
559 256-0100

(P-24199)
LAW CROSSING (PA)
175 S Lake Ave Unit 200, Pasadena (91101-2629)
PHONE................................626 243-1801
A Harrison Barnes, *President*
Mihir Sheth, *CTO*
Dennis Archer,
EMP: 65
SALES (est): 1.2MM **Privately Held**
WEB: www.lawcrossing.com
SIC: **8331** Job counseling

(P-24200)
LINCOLN TRAINING CENTER AND RE
2643 Loma Ave, South El Monte (91733-1478)
PHONE................................626 442-0621
Judith Angelo, *CEO*
David Nelson, *Vice Chairman*
Eric Brown, *Chairman*
Melissa Rus, *Program Mgr*
David Dunham, *General Mgr*
EMP: 85
SQ FT: 30,000
SALES: 18.6MM **Privately Held**
WEB: www.lincolntc.com
SIC: **8331** Vocational rehabilitation agency

(P-24201)
LOS ANGELES JOB CORPS
1020 S Olive St, Los Angeles (90015-1602)
PHONE................................213 748-0135
Fred Williams, *Director*
EMP: 197
SALES (est): 5.1MM **Privately Held**
SIC: **8331** Job training services

(P-24202)
LOS ANGELES UNIFIED SCHOOL DST
Also Called: North Valley Occupational Ctr
11450 Sharp Ave, Mission Hills (91345-1232)
PHONE................................818 365-9645
Rosario Galvan, *Principal*
Donald Gaskin, *Principal*
Gloria Martinez, *Principal*
EMP: 250
SALES (corp-wide): 3.8B **Privately Held**
WEB: www.lausd.k12.ca.us
SIC: **8331** 8211 Job training & vocational rehabilitation services; elementary & secondary schools
PA: Los Angeles Unified School District
333 S Beaudry Ave Ste 209
Los Angeles CA 90017
213 241-1000

(P-24203)
MARRIOTT FOUNDATION FOR PEOPLE
Also Called: Bridges From School To Work
344 Thomas L Berkley Way, Oakland (94612-3577)
PHONE................................510 834-4700
Anthea Charles, *Director*
EMP: 80
SALES: 20K **Privately Held**
SIC: **8331** Job training & vocational rehabilitation services

(P-24204)
METROPOLITAN AREA ADVISORY COM (PA)
Also Called: M A A C Project
1355 Third Ave, Chula Vista (91911-4302)
PHONE................................619 426-3595
Arnulfo Manriquez, *CEO*
Antonio Pizano, *President*
Austin Foye, *CFO*
EMP: 100
SQ FT: 820,000

SALES: 44.3MM **Privately Held**
SIC: 8331 8351 8748 Job training services; head start center, except in conjunction with school; energy conservation consultant

(P-24205)
METROPOLITAN AREA ADVISORY COM
Also Called: Maac Project Cwbh
1102 Cesar E Chavez Pkwy, San Diego (92113-2108)
PHONE.....................619 255-7284
Vicky Rodriguez, *Branch Mgr*
EMP: 350
SALES (corp-wide): 44.3MM **Privately Held**
SIC: 8331 Job training services
PA: Metropolitan Area Advisory Committee On Anti-Poverty Of San Diego County, Inc.
1355 Third Ave
Chula Vista CA 91911
619 426-3595

(P-24206)
METROPOLITAN AREA ADVISORY COM
Also Called: Maac Project
1355 Third Ave, Chula Vista (91911-4302)
PHONE.....................619 420-8981
Michael Finneran, *Manager*
EMP: 122
SALES (corp-wide): 44.3MM **Privately Held**
SIC: 8331 8011 Job training services; offices & clinics of medical doctors
PA: Metropolitan Area Advisory Committee On Anti-Poverty Of San Diego County, Inc.
1355 Third Ave
Chula Vista CA 91911
619 426-3595

(P-24207)
MID CITIES ASSN RETARDED CTZNS (PA)
Also Called: HUB-LIMITED WORKSHOP
14208 Towne Ave, Los Angeles (90061-2653)
PHONE.....................310 537-4510
John Wagoner, *Exec Dir*
EMP: 60
SALES: 7.2MM **Privately Held**
SIC: 8331 Sheltered workshop

(P-24208)
NAPA VALLEY PSI INC
651 Trabajo Ln, NAPA (94559-4258)
P.O. Box 600 (94559-0600)
PHONE.....................707 255-0177
Jeanne Fauquet, *President*
Rick Wood, *General Mgr*
Lea Ronald, *Director*
Carin Lawrence, *Manager*
EMP: 80
SQ FT: 43,800
SALES: 718.7K **Privately Held**
SIC: 8331 2521 2511 Vocational rehabilitation agency; filing cabinets (boxes), office: wood; wood household furniture

(P-24209)
NATIONAL MENTOR INC
Also Called: First Step Ind Living Program
9166 Anaheim Pl Ste 200, Rancho Cucamonga (91730-8547)
PHONE.....................909 483-2505
Gregory Torres, *President*
Nancy Bargmann, *Vice Pres*
EMP: 80
SALES (corp-wide): 1.4B **Publicly Held**
SIC: 8331 Job training & vocational rehabilitation services
HQ: National Mentor, Inc.
313 Congress St Fl 5
Boston MA 02210
617 790-4800

(P-24210)
NINTH HOUSE INC
Also Called: Ninth House Network
1 Montgomery St Ste 2200, San Francisco (94104-5501)
PHONE.....................612 339-0927

Robert Rozek, *CEO*
Jonathan Kuai, *Admin Sec*
EMP: 50
SQ FT: 6,000
SALES (est): 2MM
SALES (corp-wide): 1.8B **Publicly Held**
WEB: www.9h.net
SIC: 8331 Job training & vocational rehabilitation services
HQ: Korn Ferry Hay Group, Inc.
33 S 6th St Ste 4900
Minneapolis MN 55402
612 339-0927

(P-24211)
NORTH BAY DEVELOPMENTAL (PA)
Also Called: North Bay Regional Center
10 Executive Ct Ste A, NAPA (94558-6267)
P.O. Box 3360 (94558-0295)
PHONE.....................707 256-1224
Toll Free:.....................888 -
Nancy Gardner, *Exec Dir*
EMP: 100
SALES: 157.1MM **Privately Held**
WEB: www.nbrc.net
SIC: 8331 8322 Job training services; individual & family services

(P-24212)
OAKLAND PRIVATE INDUSTRY COUNC
268 Grand Ave, Oakland (94610-4724)
PHONE.....................510 768-4400
Gay Plair Cobb, *President*
EMP: 64
SALES: 7.1MM **Privately Held**
SIC: 8331 Community service employment training program; job training services

(P-24213)
OPARC (PA)
Also Called: DIVERSIFIED INDUSTRIES
9029 Vernon Ave, Montclair (91763-2000)
PHONE.....................909 982-4090
Ronald P Wolff, *President*
Gregory Mathes, *Officer*
Sonia Borja, *Vice Pres*
Rodney Turner, *Program Mgr*
Jennifer Senee, *Opers Mgr*
EMP: 50
SQ FT: 350,000
SALES: 13MM **Privately Held**
WEB: www.oparc.org
SIC: 8331 8322 Job training & vocational rehabilitation services; individual & family services

(P-24214)
ORANGE CNTY CONSERVATION CORPS
1853 N Raymond Ave, Anaheim (92801-1117)
PHONE.....................714 451-1301
Dick Dittmar, *President*
Peggy Dougherty, *Treasurer*
Max Carter, *Exec Dir*
EMP: 100
SQ FT: 10,000
SALES: 4.4MM **Privately Held**
SIC: 8331 Job training & vocational rehabilitation services

(P-24215)
OWL COMPANIES (PA)
2465 Campus Dr, Irvine (92612-1502)
PHONE.....................949 797-2000
Gregory J Burden, *CEO*
Stephen Seastrom, *Treasurer*
Eric Perea, *Vice Pres*
Nichole Degidio, *Human Res Mgr*
EMP: 1389
SQ FT: 22,800
SALES (est): 42.7MM **Privately Held**
WEB: www.owlcompanies.com
SIC: 8331 6519 4911 Job training & vocational rehabilitation services; real property lessors; generation, electric power

(P-24216)
OWL EDUCATION AND TRAINING
2465 Campus Dr, Irvine (92612-1502)
PHONE.....................949 797-2000
Gregory J Burden, *President*

Stephen Seastrom, *Corp Secy*
EMP: 1380
SQ FT: 22,800
SALES (est): 5.3MM
SALES (corp-wide): 42.7MM **Privately Held**
WEB: www.owlcompanies.com
SIC: 8331 Job training & vocational rehabilitation services
PA: Owl Companies
2465 Campus Dr
Irvine CA 92612
949 797-2000

(P-24217)
PACIFIC ASIAN CONSORTM EMPLYMN (PA)
Also Called: P A C E
1055 Wilshire Blvd Ste 14, Los Angeles (90017-2431)
PHONE.....................213 353-3982
Kerry N Doi, *Exec Dir*
Heidy Aguirre, *Admin Asst*
Myriah Ogas, *Site Mgr*
Rachelle Arizmendi, *Mayor*
Anush Arakelyan, *Education*
EMP: 130 **EST:** 1976
SQ FT: 20,000
SALES: 22.8MM **Privately Held**
SIC: 8331 8322 7361 1521 Community service employment training program; individual & family services; labor contractors (employment agency); new construction, single-family houses

(P-24218)
PATHPOINT
11491 Los Osos Valley Rd, San Luis Obispo (93405-6428)
PHONE.....................805 782-8890
Aline Graham, *Director*
EMP: 100
SALES (corp-wide): 22.8MM **Privately Held**
SIC: 8331 Skill training center; vocational rehabilitation agency
PA: Pathpoint
315 W Haley St Ste 102
Santa Barbara CA 93101
805 966-3310

(P-24219)
POMONA VALLEY WORKSHOP (PA)
4650 Brooks St, Montclair (91763-4797)
PHONE.....................909 624-3555
Karen Jones, *Exec Dir*
Sharon Varga, *Vice Pres*
Mitch Gariador, *Administration*
Stephanie Benjamin, *Sales Staff*
Carol Martinez, *Director*
EMP: 70
SQ FT: 34,000
SALES: 5.5MM **Privately Held**
SIC: 8331 Job training services

(P-24220)
PRIDE INDUSTRIES
Also Called: Auburn Pride
13080 Earhart Ave, Auburn (95602-9536)
PHONE.....................530 888-0331
Vic Wursten, *Branch Mgr*
EMP: 180
SQ FT: 5,000
SALES (corp-wide): 290.6MM **Privately Held**
SIC: 8331 Sheltered workshop
PA: Pride Industries
10030 Foothills Blvd
Roseville CA 95747
916 788-2100

(P-24221)
PRIDE INDUSTRIES
12451 Loma Rica Dr, Grass Valley (95945-9059)
PHONE.....................530 477-1832
Kathy Gardinier, *Branch Mgr*
EMP: 72
SQ FT: 16,290
SALES (corp-wide): 290.6MM **Privately Held**
SIC: 8331 7389 7331 Sheltered workshop; packaging & labeling services; mailing service

PA: Pride Industries
10030 Foothills Blvd
Roseville CA 95747
916 788-2100

(P-24222)
PRIDE INDUSTRIES
3608 Madison Ave Ste 43, North Highlands (95660-5002)
PHONE.....................916 334-5415
Vicki Coyle, *Branch Mgr*
EMP: 57
SQ FT: 2,500
SALES (corp-wide): 290.6MM **Privately Held**
SIC: 8331 Sheltered workshop
PA: Pride Industries
10030 Foothills Blvd
Roseville CA 95747
916 788-2100

(P-24223)
PROGRSSIVE EMPLOYMENT CONCEPTS (PA)
6060 Sunrise Vista Dr # 1875, Citrus Heights (95610-7053)
PHONE.....................916 723-3112
Carole Watilo, *President*
Robert Black, *Treasurer*
Debbie Bates, *Bd of Directors*
Mark Savickas, *Bd of Directors*
Joann Pingree, *Admin Sec*
EMP: 62
SQ FT: 1,500
SALES: 2.5MM **Privately Held**
SIC: 8331 Job training & vocational rehabilitation services

(P-24224)
SACRAMENTO EMPLOYEMENT & TRAIN
Also Called: Set A Head Start Westside
925 Del Paso Blvd Ste 100, Sacramento (95815-3568)
PHONE.....................916 263-3800
Kathy Kossick, *Exec Dir*
EMP: 250 **Privately Held**
SIC: 8331 8351 Job training services; head start center, except in conjunction with school
PA: Sacramento Employment & Training Agency
925 Del Paso Blvd Ste 100
Sacramento CA 95815

(P-24225)
SACRAMENTO EMPLOYEMENT & TRAIN (PA)
Also Called: Seta
925 Del Paso Blvd Ste 100, Sacramento (95815-3568)
PHONE.....................916 263-3800
Kathy Kossick, *Exec Dir*
John Allen, *Human Resources*
Lin Morgan, *Marketing Staff*
Simone Paurley, *Marketing Staff*
Victor Bonanno, *Supervisor*
EMP: 250
SQ FT: 30,000
SALES (est): 19.9MM **Privately Held**
WEB: www.seta.net
SIC: 8331 7361 8351 Job training services; employment agencies; child day care services

(P-24226)
SAN GABRIEL VLY TRAINING CTR (PA)
Also Called: PRODUCTION FACILITIES UNLIMITE
400 S Covina Blvd, La Puente (91746-2212)
PHONE.....................626 330-3185
Randy Hyatt, *Exec Dir*
Mary Ryan Indenbaum, *President*
Robert Darragh, *Treasurer*
Shirley Roland, *Admin Sec*
EMP: 75 **EST:** 1962
SQ FT: 6,400
SALES: 5.1MM **Privately Held**
WEB: www.sgvtc.org
SIC: 8331 7389 Vocational rehabilitation agency; packaging & labeling services

(P-24227)
SAN JOSE CONSERVATION CORPS
2650 Senter Rd, San Jose (95111-1121)
PHONE..................................408 283-7171
Bob Hennessy, *CEO*
Mary Bravo, *Program Mgr*
Scott Curtis, *Teacher*
Erin Krueger, *Director*
EMP: 150
SQ FT: 1,800
SALES: 7.2MM **Privately Held**
WEB: www.sjcccharterschool.org
SIC: 8331 Community service employment
　training program; job counseling

(P-24228)
SANTA ANITA FAMILY YOUNG
501 S Mountain Ave, Monrovia
(91016-3655)
PHONE..................................626 359-9244
Patrice Reinhand, *Ch of Bd*
Damian Colaluca, *CEO*
EMP: 60 EST: 1999
SALES: 1.8MM **Privately Held**
WEB: www.safymca.org
SIC: 8331 Community service employment
　training program

(P-24229)
SISKIYOU OPPORTUNITY CENTER (PA)
Also Called: YREKA EMPLOYMENT SERV-
ICES
1516 S Mount Shasta Blvd, Mount Shasta
(96067-2700)
PHONE..................................530 926-4698
Daniel Chianello, *Director*
EMP: 120
SQ FT: 4,820
SALES: 1.8MM **Privately Held**
WEB: www.siskiyouopportunitycenter.org
SIC: 8331 Job counseling

(P-24230)
SKILLS CENTER INC (PA)
220 Lincoln St, Santa Cruz (95060-4351)
PHONE..................................831 421-9900
John Christensen, *President*
EMP: 70
SQ FT: 9,500
SALES (est): 440.9K **Privately Held**
SIC: 8331 Vocational rehabilitation agency

(P-24231)
SOUTH BAY REGL PUBLIC SAFETY T
Also Called: Sbrpstc
560 Bailey Ave, San Jose (95141-1004)
PHONE..................................408 270-6494
Steve Cushing, *President*
Gregg Giusiana, *Vice Pres*
Mike Lombardo, *Vice Pres*
Linda Vaughn, *Vice Pres*
Mable Rodeo, *Executive*
EMP: 50
SALES (est): 3.1MM **Privately Held**
WEB: www.theacademy.ca.gov
SIC: 8331 Job training services

(P-24232)
SPECIAL SERVICE FOR GROUPS INC (PA)
Also Called: SSG ADMINISTRATIVE OF-
FICES
905 E 8th St Unit 1, Los Angeles
(90021-1853)
PHONE..................................213 368-1888
Herbert K Hatanaka, *CEO*
Donna Wong, *Vice Pres*
Jason Gonzalez, *Associate Dir*
Yvonne Suarez, *Program Mgr*
Stuart H Kessler, *Executive Asst*
EMP: 625
SALES: 60.6MM **Privately Held**
WEB: www.ssgmain.org
SIC: 8331 8093 8399 Vocational rehabili-
　tation agency; mental health clinic, outpa-
　tient; advocacy group

(P-24233)
ST MADELEINE SOPHIES CENTER
2119 E Madison Ave, El Cajon
(92019-1111)
PHONE..................................619 442-5129
Debra Turner, *Director*
Roberta Melgarejo, *Accounting Mgr*
Martha Diobilda, *Accountant*
Neil Fullerton, *Marketing Staff*
David Silva, *Maintence Staff*
EMP: 70
SQ FT: 13,092
SALES: 9.4MM **Privately Held**
WEB: www.stmsc.org
SIC: 8331 Vocational training agency

(P-24234)
STEPPING STN GRWTH CTR FR CHLD
Also Called: Boatworks
311 Macarthur Blvd, San Leandro
(94577-2110)
PHONE..................................510 568-3331
Paula Champagne, *President*
Monte Cohen, *Director*
EMP: 85
SALES: 2.5MM **Privately Held**
WEB: www.steppingstonesgrowth.org
SIC: 8331 8211 8351 Skill training center;
　private special education school; child
　day care services

(P-24235)
SUCCESS STRATEGIES INST INC
Also Called: Tom Ferry Your Coach
6 Executive Cir Ste 250, Irvine
(92614-6732)
PHONE..................................949 721-6808
Thomas Ferry, *President*
Joe Belmonte, *Vice Pres*
Anthony Belmonte, *Social Dir*
Maria Mines, *Executive Asst*
Ruby Sabile, *Executive Asst*
EMP: 70
SALES (est): 6.4MM **Privately Held**
WEB: www.yourcoach.com
SIC: 8331 Job training & vocational reha-
　bilitation services

(P-24236)
THE FOR VALLEY RESOURCE CENTER (PA)
1285 N Santa Fe St, Hemet (92543-1823)
PHONE..................................951 766-8659
Lee Trisler, *CEO*
Valerie Patterson, *Accounting Mgr*
Stephanie Pfaff, *Accounting Mgr*
Darlene Noon, *Human Resources*
Mary Morse, *Director*
EMP: 50
SQ FT: 80,000
SALES: 9MM **Privately Held**
SIC: 8331 2389 Vocational training
　agency; apparel for handicapped

(P-24237)
THE FOR WORK TRAINING CENTER
1811 Kusel Rd, Oroville (95966-9528)
PHONE..................................530 534-1112
Dave Ennes, *Manager*
Michelle Ely, *Director*
EMP: 50
SALES (corp-wide): 10.8MM **Privately
Held**
WEB: www.wtcinc.org
SIC: 8331 Job training & vocational reha-
　bilitation services
PA: Work Training Center For The Handi-
　capped, Inc.
　2255 Fair St
　Chico CA 95928
　530 343-7994

(P-24238)
TOOLWORKS INC (PA)
25 Kearny St Ste 400, San Francisco
(94108-5518)
PHONE..................................415 733-0990
Steve Crabiel, *Exec Dir*
Mike Oxley, *Project Mgr*
Matthew Powell, *Human Res Dir*
Theresa Stroud, *Human Res Dir*

Terry Goodwin, *Director*
EMP: 63
SQ FT: 3,500
SALES: 13.1MM **Privately Held**
WEB: www.toolworks.org
SIC: 8331 Vocational rehabilitation agency

(P-24239)
TULARE CTY TRNG CTR HNDCPD
Also Called: ABLE INDUSTRIES
8929 W Goshen Ave, Visalia (93291-7969)
PHONE..................................559 651-3683
Wende Ayers, *Exec Dir*
Bill Little, *Financial Exec*
Connie Gallego, *Manager*
EMP: 52
SQ FT: 75,000
SALES: 4.7MM **Privately Held**
WEB: www.ableindustries.org
SIC: 8331 Community service employment
　training program; job counseling

(P-24240)
UCP WORK INC (PA)
Also Called: W O R K
5320 Carpinteria Ave G, Carpinteria
(93013-2107)
PHONE..................................805 566-9000
Kathy Webb, *Exec Dir*
EMP: 200
SQ FT: 2,000
SALES: 9.3MM **Privately Held**
SIC: 8331 Vocational rehabilitation agency;
　vocational training agency

(P-24241)
UKIAH VLY ASSN FOR HBILITATION (PA)
Also Called: Mayacama Industries
990 S Dora St, Ukiah (95482-5754)
P.O. Box 689 (95482-0689)
PHONE..................................707 468-8824
Pamela Jensen, *Exec Dir*
Janeen Saunders, *Director*
EMP: 60
SALES: 2.3MM **Privately Held**
WEB: www.uvah.org
SIC: 8331 8361 Sheltered workshop; resi-
　dential care

(P-24242)
UNYEWAY INC (PA)
Also Called: R T C NURSERY
2330 Main St Ste E, Ramona
(92065-2595)
PHONE..................................760 789-5960
Carrie Hancock, *Exec Dir*
Kim E Metli, *Exec Dir*
Kimberly Kelley, *Director*
EMP: 100
SQ FT: 6,200
SALES: 4.9MM **Privately Held**
SIC: 8331 Skill training center

(P-24243)
UNYEWAY INC
11440 Riverside Dr Ste D, Lakeside
(92040-2731)
PHONE..................................619 562-6330
Carrie Hancock, *Branch Mgr*
Christina Graff, *Opers Mgr*
EMP: 52
SALES (est): 1.4MM
SALES (corp-wide): 4.9MM **Privately
Held**
SIC: 8331 8322 Skill training center; family
　counseling services
PA: Unyeway, Inc
　2330 Main St Ste E
　Ramona CA 92065
　760 789-5960

(P-24244)
URBAN CORPS OF SAN DIEGO
3127 Jefferson St, San Diego
(92110-4422)
P.O. Box 80156 (92138-0156)
PHONE..................................619 235-6884
Sam Duran, *CEO*
Michael Sterns, *Chairman*
EMP: 132
SQ FT: 25,000
SALES: 3.2MM **Privately Held**
WEB: www.urbancorpsd.org
SIC: 8331 Work experience center

(P-24245)
VALLEY LIGHT INDUSTRIES INC
5360 Irwindale Ave, Baldwin Park
(91706-2086)
PHONE..................................626 337-6200
Andrew M Altman, *CEO*
Pamela Hayes, *President*
Johnny Camacho, *Technology*
Julie Garcia, *Finance Mgr*
Penny Wiegand, *Director*
EMP: 250
SQ FT: 14,220
SALES: 3.6MM **Privately Held**
WEB: www.valleylightind.org
SIC: 8331 Job training & vocational reha-
　bilitation services

(P-24246)
VOCATIONAL IMPRV PROGRAM INC (PA)
9210 Rochester Ave, Rancho Cucamonga
(91730-5521)
PHONE..................................909 483-5924
Wendy A Rogina, *CEO*
Christopher J McArdle, *Treasurer*
Rick Rogina, *Vice Pres*
M Stephen Cho, *Admin Sec*
EMP: 175
SQ FT: 23,000
SALES: 14.9MM **Privately Held**
WEB: www.vipsolutions.com
SIC: 8331 Vocational rehabilitation agency

(P-24247)
VOCATIONAL VISIONS
26041 Pala, Mission Viejo (92691-2705)
PHONE..................................949 837-7280
Joan McKinney, *CEO*
Kathryn Hebel, *Exec Dir*
EMP: 170 EST: 1975
SQ FT: 17,000
SALES: 7.7MM **Privately Held**
WEB: www.vocationalvisions.org
SIC: 8331 Sheltered workshop

(P-24248)
VTC ENTERPRISES (PA)
2445 A St, Santa Maria (93455-1401)
P.O. Box 1187 (93456-1187)
PHONE..................................805 928-5000
Jason Telander, *CEO*
Dr Mark Malangko, *President*
Lisa Walker, *CFO*
Henry M Grennan, *Treasurer*
Cole Kinney, *Admin Sec*
EMP: 330 EST: 1962
SQ FT: 21,093
SALES: 11.2MM **Privately Held**
WEB: www.vtc-sm.org
SIC: 8331 Vocational rehabilitation agency

(P-24249)
WESTVIEW SERVICES INC
Also Called: Starlight Educational Center
9421 Edinger Ave, Westminster
(92683-7426)
PHONE..................................714 418-2090
Lourdis Painter, *Principal*
EMP: 70
SQ FT: 3,775
SALES (corp-wide): 16.6MM **Privately
Held**
SIC: 8331 8244 Community service em-
　ployment training program; business &
　secretarial schools
PA: Westview Services, Inc
　10522 Katella Ave
　Anaheim CA 92804
　714 517-6606

(P-24250)
WOMENS TRNSTNAL LIVING CTR INC
Also Called: WTLC
P.O. Box 916 (92836-0916)
PHONE..................................714 992-1939
Angelique Tsontos, *CEO*
Mark Lee, *Director*
EMP: 50
SALES: 2MM **Privately Held**
SIC: 8331 Sheltered workshop

(P-24251)
WORK2FUTURE FOUNDATION
Also Called: Work2future - Yuth Training Ctr
2072 Lucretia Ave, San Jose (95122-3305)
PHONE..............................408 794-1234
EMP: 243
SALES (corp-wide): 3.5MM **Privately Held**
SIC: 8331 Skill training center
PA: Work2future Foundation
1601 Foxworthy Ave
San Jose CA 95118
408 794-1100

(P-24252)
WORK2FUTURE FOUNDATION
Also Called: North San Jose Job Center
1901 Zanker Rd, San Jose (95112-4217)
PHONE..............................408 216-6202
EMP: 146
SALES (corp-wide): 3.5MM **Privately Held**
SIC: 8331 Job training services
PA: Work2future Foundation
1601 Foxworthy Ave
San Jose CA 95118
408 794-1100

(P-24253)
WORK2FUTURE FOUNDATION
Also Called: Work2future - Gilroy Job Ctr
379 Tomkins Ct, Gilroy (95020-3631)
PHONE..............................408 758-3477
EMP: 146
SALES (corp-wide): 3.5MM **Privately Held**
SIC: 8331 Skill training center
PA: Work2future Foundation
1601 Foxworthy Ave
San Jose CA 95118
408 794-1100

(P-24254)
XQAWESOME INC
20 Mason Ln, Ladera Ranch (92694-0325)
PHONE..............................949 929-9622
Bonnie Jean Bradley, *CEO*
EMP: 183
SALES (est): 1.3MM **Privately Held**
SIC: 8331 8742 7389 Job training services; marketing consulting services;

8351 Child Day Care Svcs

(P-24255)
4 CS COUNCIL
2515 N 1st St, San Jose (95131-1003)
PHONE..............................408 487-0747
Alfredo Villasenor, *Principal*
EMP: 110
SQ FT: 6,100
SALES (est): 4.9MM **Privately Held**
SIC: 8351 Child day care services

(P-24256)
ABRAHAM JSHA HSCHL DY SCHL WST
27400 Canwood St, Agoura (91301-2462)
PHONE..............................818 707-2365
Bruce Friedman, *CEO*
Suzan Huntington, *Director*
EMP: 62
SALES: 2MM **Privately Held**
SIC: 8351 Group day care center

(P-24257)
ACHIEVER CHRISTIAN PRE-SCHL &
540 Sands Dr, San Jose (95125-6233)
PHONE..............................408 264-2345
Julie Brown, *Principal*
EMP: 50
SALES (est): 677.6K **Privately Held**
SIC: 8351 8211 Montessori child development center; private elementary & secondary schools; private elementary school

(P-24258)
ACTION DAY NRSERIES PRMRY PLUS
18720 Bucknall Rd, Saratoga (95070-4106)
PHONE..............................408 370-0350
Tracy Sarge, *Director*
Sharon Lecznar, *Exec Dir*
EMP: 51
SALES (corp-wide): 6.4MM **Privately Held**
WEB: www.actiondayprimaryplus.com
SIC: 8351 Preschool center
PA: Action Day Nurseries & Primary Plus, Inc
3030 Moorpark Ave Bldg D
San Jose CA 95128
408 247-6972

(P-24259)
ACTION DAY NRSERIES PRMRY PLUS
2148 Lincoln Ave, San Jose (95125-3540)
PHONE..............................408 266-8952
Carol Freitas, *Manager*
Jerri Aguilar, *Education*
Paula Schroeder, *Director*
EMP: 50
SALES (corp-wide): 6.4MM **Privately Held**
WEB: www.actiondayprimaryplus.com
SIC: 8351 Preschool center
PA: Action Day Nurseries & Primary Plus, Inc
3030 Moorpark Ave Bldg D
San Jose CA 95128
408 247-6972

(P-24260)
ADAMS LEARNING CENTER
Also Called: Adams Early Childhood Lrng Ctr
50800 Desert Club Dr, La Quinta (92253-2982)
PHONE..............................760 777-4260
Maria Moore, *Director*
EMP: 50
SALES (est): 511.9K **Privately Held**
SIC: 8351 Preschool center

(P-24261)
ADESTE PROGRAM COMPANY
1531 James M Wood Blvd, Los Angeles (90015-1112)
PHONE..............................213 251-3551
Gregory Cox, *Exec Dir*
Elvia Martinez, *Administration*
Armine Lalaine, *Director*
EMP: 400
SALES (est): 2.9MM **Privately Held**
SIC: 8351 Child day care services

(P-24262)
ALA COSTA CENTER PROGRAM FOR (PA)
1300 Rose St, Berkeley (94702-1108)
PHONE..............................510 527-2550
Michael Pereira, *Director*
Ron Halog, *Exec Dir*
EMP: 52 EST: 1973
SALES: 1.7MM **Privately Held**
WEB: www.alacostacenter.org
SIC: 8351 Child day care services

(P-24263)
ALAMEDA FAMILY SERVICES
2325 Clement Ave, Alameda (94501-7063)
PHONE..............................510 629-6300
Irene Kudarauskas, *Exec Dir*
Bruce Kariya, *VP Finance*
Marjorie Ball, *Facilities Mgr*
Jen Wu, *Program Dir*
Susan Ono, *Supervisor*
EMP: 100
SALES (est): 5.7MM **Privately Held**
WEB: www.alamedafs.org
SIC: 8351 8322 Head start center, except in conjunction with school; youth self-help agency; offender rehabilitation agency; child guidance agency; general counseling services

(P-24264)
ASSOCIATED STUDENTS CDC
460 S 8th St, San Jose (95112-3835)
PHONE..............................408 924-6988

Maria Davis, *Director*
Sheryl Vargas, *Exec Dir*
EMP: 60
SALES (est): 628K **Privately Held**
SIC: 8351 Child day care services

(P-24265)
BELMONT OAKS ACADEMY
2200 Carlmont Dr, Belmont (94002-3310)
PHONE..............................650 593-6175
Pamela Clarke, *President*
Joanna Reames, *Director*
EMP: 63
SALES (est): 2.2MM **Privately Held**
SIC: 8351 8211 Preschool center; private elementary school

(P-24266)
BERMUDA DUNES LEARNING CTR INC
42115 Yucca Ln, Bermuda Dunes (92203-8111)
PHONE..............................760 772-7127
Gayle Clark, *President*
EMP: 50
SALES (est): 1.4MM **Privately Held**
SIC: 8351 Preschool center

(P-24267)
BLIND CHILDRENS LRNG CTR INC
18542 Vanderlip Ave Ste B, Santa Ana (92705-8201)
PHONE..............................714 573-8888
Kathy Buehler, *Exec Dir*
Denise Grajek, *Administration*
Rebecca Shields, *Administration*
EMP: 50
SQ FT: 18,824
SALES: 2.8MM **Privately Held**
WEB: www.blindkids.org
SIC: 8351 8211 Child day care services; private special education school

(P-24268)
BRIGHT HORIZONS CHLD CTRS LLC
Also Called: Camp Amgen
1 Amgen Center Dr, Thousand Oaks (91320-1730)
PHONE..............................805 447-6793
Kelly Travis, *Director*
EMP: 170
SALES (corp-wide): 1.7B **Publicly Held**
WEB: www.atlantaga.ncr.com
SIC: 8351 Child day care services
HQ: Bright Horizons Children's Centers Llc
200 Talcott Ave
Watertown MA 02472
617 673-8000

(P-24269)
BRIGHT HORIZONS CHLD CTRS LLC
Also Called: Sisco Family Connection
800 Barber Ln, Milpitas (95035-7926)
PHONE..............................408 853-2196
Janice Inman, *Exec Dir*
EMP: 120
SALES (corp-wide): 1.7B **Publicly Held**
WEB: www.atlantaga.ncr.com
SIC: 8351 Child day care services
HQ: Bright Horizons Children's Centers Llc
200 Talcott Ave
Watertown MA 02472
617 673-8000

(P-24270)
BUSINESS AND SUPPORT SERVICES
Also Called: Browne Child Development Ctr
Santa Jancinto Rd 20286, Oceanside (92054)
PHONE..............................760 725-2817
Maria Langlie, *Director*
EMP: 50 **Publicly Held**
WEB: www.mccssc.com
SIC: 8351 9711 Child day care services; Marine Corps
HQ: Business And Support Services
3044 Catlin Ave
Quantico VA 22134
703 432-0109

(P-24271)
CABRILLO COLLEGE CHILDREN CTR
6500 Soquel Dr, Aptos (95003-3198)
PHONE..............................831 479-6352
Erick Hoffman, *Director*
EMP: 70
SALES (est): 555.8K **Privately Held**
SIC: 8351 8221 Child day care services; colleges universities & professional schools

(P-24272)
CALVARY BAPTIST CH LOS GATOS
Also Called: Calvary Infant Care Center
16330 Los Gatos Blvd, Los Gatos (95032-4520)
PHONE..............................408 356-5126
Bob Thomas, *Principal*
EMP: 80
SALES (corp-wide): 4.5MM **Privately Held**
WEB: www.calvarylosgatos.org
SIC: 8351 Preschool center
PA: Calvary Baptist Church Of Los Gatos
16330 Los Gatos Blvd # 408
Los Gatos CA 95032
408 358-8871

(P-24273)
CALVARY CHURCH SANTA ANA INC
1010 N Tustin Ave, Santa Ana (92705-3598)
PHONE..............................714 973-4800
Dr D J Mitchell, *Sr Pastor*
EMP: 160
SQ FT: 133,000
SALES: 10.9MM **Privately Held**
SIC: 8351 8661 Nursery school; miscellaneous denomination church

(P-24274)
CAROLYN E WYLIE CENTER
4164 Brockton Ave Ste A, Riverside (92501-3400)
PHONE..............................951 683-5193
Melody Amaral, *CEO*
Lisa M Dryan, *Director*
EMP: 100
SQ FT: 3,000
SALES: 3.4MM **Privately Held**
SIC: 8351 Child day care services

(P-24275)
CENTRAL STATE PRE-SCHOOL
2310 Aldergrove Ave, Escondido (92029-1935)
PHONE..............................760 432-2499
Susan Chambers, *Principal*
EMP: 50
SALES (est): 615.5K **Privately Held**
SIC: 8351 Child day care services

(P-24276)
CHALLENGER SCHOOLS
4949 Harwood Rd, San Jose (95124-5209)
PHONE..............................408 723-0111
Josh McKay, *Principal*
Chris Wood, *IT/INT Sup*
Brad Bowden, *Teacher*
Ryan Baker, *Director*
Cassie Breckenridge, *Director*
EMP: 61
SALES (corp-wide): 109.8MM **Privately Held**
SIC: 8351 8211 Preschool center; private elementary school
PA: Challenger Schools
9424 S 300 W
Sandy UT 84070
801 569-2700

(P-24277)
CHALLENGER SCHOOLS
4949 Harwood Rd, San Jose (95124-5209)
PHONE..............................408 266-7073
Edward Gonzalez, *Principal*
EMP: 50
SALES (corp-wide): 109.8MM **Privately Held**
SIC: 8351 Preschool center

PA: Challenger Schools
9424 S 300 W
Sandy UT 84070
801 569-2700

(P-24278)
CHANGING TIDES FAMILY SERVICES (PA)
2259 Myrtle Ave, Eureka (95501-3325)
PHONE.................................707 444-8293
Carol A Hill, *Exec Dir*
Kerry Venegas, *Exec Dir*
Donna Michaud, *Deputy Dir*
Jeanine Canedo-Moncrief, *Director*
Melia Porter, *Manager*
EMP: 168
SQ FT: 2,500
SALES: 10MM **Privately Held**
SIC: 8351 8322 Head start center, except in conjunction with school; child related social services

(P-24279)
CHARLES DREW UNIV MDCINE SCNCE
Also Called: Head Start Program
135 W Victoria St, Long Beach (90805-2162)
PHONE.................................310 605-0164
Linda Rahman, *Director*
EMP: 210
SALES (corp-wide): 54.7MM **Privately Held**
WEB: www.cdrewu.edu
SIC: 8351 8221 Preschool center; university
PA: Charles Drew University Of Medicine And Science
1731 E 120th St
Los Angeles CA 90059
323 563-4800

(P-24280)
CHILD ACTION INC (PA)
9800 Old Winery Pl, Sacramento (95827-1700)
PHONE.................................916 369-4460
Tracey Strack, *Controller*
Jaci White, *Director*
EMP: 301
SQ FT: 140,000
SALES: 52.6MM **Privately Held**
SIC: 8351 Head start center, except in conjunction with school

(P-24281)
CHILD DAY SCHOOL (PA)
1049 Stuart St, Lafayette (94549-4013)
PHONE.................................925 284-7092
R Ann Whitehead, *Owner*
EMP: 80
SQ FT: 5,000
SALES (est): 1.2MM **Privately Held**
WEB: www.tcdschools.com
SIC: 8351 8211 Preschool center; kindergarten

(P-24282)
CHILD DEVELOPMENT ASSOC INC (PA)
180 Otay Lakes Rd Ste 310, Bonita (91902-2442)
PHONE.................................619 427-4411
Richard Richardson, *President*
Jorge Hernandez, *Treasurer*
EMP: 144
SQ FT: 6,000
SALES: 87.6MM **Privately Held**
WEB: www.cdasandiego.com
SIC: 8351 8322 Preschool center; child related social services

(P-24283)
CHILD DEVELOPMENT CENTER
309 N Rios Ave, Solana Beach (92075-1241)
PHONE.................................858 794-7160
Susan Blackwood, *Director*
Frank Glasson, *Director*
EMP: 50 **EST:** 1980
SALES (est): 1.9MM **Privately Held**
SIC: 8351 Child day care services

(P-24284)
CHILD DEVELOPMENT INCORPORATED (PA)
Also Called: Child Development Centers
350 Woodview Ave, Morgan Hill (95037-8104)
PHONE.................................408 556-7300
Vernon A Plaskett, *CEO*
EMP: 50
SALES: 28MM **Privately Held**
SIC: 8351 Child day care services

(P-24285)
CHILD DEVELOPMENT INCORPORATED
Also Called: Alderwood Child Development
2005 Knollcrest, Irvine (92603-1600)
PHONE.................................949 725-0961
John Dominguez, *Branch Mgr*
EMP: 518
SALES (corp-wide): 28MM **Privately Held**
SIC: 8351 Child day care services
PA: Child Development Incorporated
350 Woodview Ave
Morgan Hill CA 95037
408 556-7300

(P-24286)
CHILD DEVELOPMENT INCORPORATED
Also Called: Turtle Rock Cdc
5151 Amalfi Dr, Irvine (92603-3443)
PHONE.................................949 854-5060
Mindy Ho, *Director*
EMP: 621
SALES (corp-wide): 28MM **Privately Held**
SIC: 8351 Child day care services
PA: Child Development Incorporated
350 Woodview Ave
Morgan Hill CA 95037
408 556-7300

(P-24287)
CHILD EDUCATIONAL CENTER
Also Called: CEC
140 Foothill Blvd, La Canada (91011-3727)
PHONE.................................818 354-3418
Elyssa Nelson, *Director*
EMP: 100
SALES: 8MM **Privately Held**
SIC: 8351 Child day care services

(P-24288)
CHILD FAMILY & CMNTY SVCS INC
32980 Alvarado Niles Rd # 856, Union City (94587-3186)
PHONE.................................510 796-9512
Karen Deshayes, *Exec Dir*
John Anthony Borsella, *Finance Dir*
Catherine Clennen Seymour, *Business Mgr*
Cynthia Esquivel-Delgado, *Human Res Mgr*
Rosalba Tutakhil, *Director*
EMP: 140
SQ FT: 20,000
SALES: 15.7MM **Privately Held**
SIC: 8351 Preschool center

(P-24289)
CHILD START INC (PA)
439 Devlin Rd, NAPA (94558-6274)
PHONE.................................707 252-8931
Deborah Peralez, *Exec Dir*
Robert Stalker, *Chairman*
Debbie Peralez, *Exec Dir*
Marian Owen, *Technician*
Bob De Luca, *Opers Mgr*
EMP: 200 **EST:** 1965
SQ FT: 13,000
SALES: 12.5MM **Privately Held**
WEB: www.childstartinc.org
SIC: 8351 Preschool center

(P-24290)
CHILDREN OF RAINBOW INC (PA)
4890 Logan Ave, San Diego (92113-3004)
PHONE.................................619 615-0652
Gale R Walker, *President*
EMP: 101
SQ FT: 8,500

SALES (est): 3.6MM **Privately Held**
WEB: www.childrenoftherainbow.com
SIC: 8351 Group day care center

(P-24291)
CHILDREN OF THE RAINBOW HEAD
4890 Logan Ave, San Diego (92113-3004)
PHONE.................................619 266-7311
Gale Walker, *Mng Member*
Kursat Misirlioglu,
EMP: 185
SALES: 6.8MM **Privately Held**
SIC: 8351 Child day care services

(P-24292)
CHILDRENS DAY SCHOOL
333 Dolores St, San Francisco (94110-1006)
PHONE.................................415 861-5432
Rick Ackerly, *Director*
Terry Hall, *Info Tech Dir*
Melissa Vainio, *Database Admin*
Jhony Gon, *Technician*
Tim Hathaway, *Accountant*
EMP: 50
SQ FT: 22,050
SALES: 14.7MM **Privately Held**
WEB: www.cds-sf.org
SIC: 8351 8211 Preschool center; elementary & secondary schools

(P-24293)
CHILDRENS HOSPITAL ORANGE CNTY
500 Superior Ave, Newport Beach (92663-3657)
PHONE.................................949 631-2062
EMP: 1036
SALES (corp-wide): 523.1MM **Privately Held**
SIC: 8351 Child day care services
PA: Children's Hospital Of Orange County
1201 W La Veta Ave
Orange CA 92868
714 997-3000

(P-24294)
CHOICES FOR CHILDREN (PA)
111 N Market St Ste 700, San Jose (95113-1108)
PHONE.................................408 297-3295
Vivian Cooper, *Owner*
EMP: 52
SALES (est): 800.7K **Privately Held**
SIC: 8351 Preschool center

(P-24295)
CHRISTIAN KIRKWOOD SCHOOLS (PA)
10822 Brookshire Ave, Downey (90241-3822)
PHONE.................................562 862-4251
William J Kirkwood, *President*
Connie Kirkwood, *Corp Secy*
EMP: 55
SQ FT: 7,000
SALES: 1.7MM **Privately Held**
WEB: www.downeychildcarecenter.com
SIC: 8351 8211 Preschool center; elementary school

(P-24296)
CITY OF PACIFICA-VALLEMAR
170 Santa Maria Ave, Pacifica (94044-2506)
PHONE.................................650 738-7466
Scott Leslie, *Director*
Steven Rhodes, *Manager*
EMP: 55
SALES (est): 413.5K **Privately Held**
SIC: 8351 Preschool center

(P-24297)
COLLEGE OPERATIONS LLC
1730 S College Ave, Dinuba (93618-2812)
PHONE.................................559 353-0576
Travis Greenwood, *CFO*
EMP: 50
SALES (est): 586.8K **Privately Held**
SIC: 8351 Nursery school

(P-24298)
COLTON JOINT UNIFIED SCHL DST
Also Called: San Salvador Pre-School
471 Agua Mansa Rd, Colton (92324-3325)
PHONE.................................909 876-4240
Karen Gladue, *Principal*
EMP: 100
SALES (corp-wide): 297.1MM **Privately Held**
WEB: www.colton.k12.ca.us
SIC: 8351 8211
PA: Colton Joint Unified School District
1212 Valencia Dr
Colton CA 92324
909 580-5000

(P-24299)
COMMUNITY ACTION PARTNR KERN
Also Called: Sunrise Villa Ctr Head Start
1600 Poplar Ave, Wasco (93280-3405)
PHONE.................................661 758-0129
Yolanda Gonzales, *Director*
EMP: 88
SALES (corp-wide): 63.1MM **Privately Held**
SIC: 8351 Head start center, except in conjunction with school
PA: Community Action Partnership Of Kern
5005 Business Park N
Bakersfield CA 93309
661 336-5236

(P-24300)
COMMUNITY ACTION PRTNRSHP (PA)
1225 Gill Ave, Madera (93637-5234)
PHONE.................................559 673-9173
Mattie Mendez, *Exec Dir*
Linda L Wright, *CEO*
Donna Tooley, *CFO*
Melisa Dasilva, *General Mgr*
James Chandler, *Accountant*
EMP: 200
SQ FT: 18,000
SALES: 25MM **Privately Held**
WEB: www.maderacap.org
SIC: 8351 Head start center, except in conjunction with school

(P-24301)
COMMUNITY CHLD CRE CNCL SONOMA (PA)
Also Called: 4 Cs
131a Stony Cir Ste 300, Santa Rosa (95401-9507)
PHONE.................................707 522-1413
Mary A Doan, *Exec Dir*
EMP: 75
SALES (est): 1.9MM **Privately Held**
WEB: www.sonoma4cs.org
SIC: 8351 Group day care center

(P-24302)
COMMUNITY DEV INST HEAD START
12988 Bowron Rd, Poway (92064-5790)
PHONE.................................858 668-2985
EMP: 60
SALES (corp-wide): 67.2MM **Privately Held**
SIC: 8351 Head start center, except in conjunction with school
PA: Community Development Institute Head Start
10065 E Harvard Ave # 700
Denver CO 80231
720 747-5100

(P-24303)
COMPASS FAMILY SERVICES
37 Grove St, San Francisco (94102-4702)
PHONE.................................415 644-0504
Eirca Kisch, *Director*
Carrie Hook, *CFO*
EMP: 85
SALES: 9.2MM **Privately Held**
SIC: 8351 Child day care services

(P-24304)
COMPASS FAMILY SERVICES
Also Called: Compass Children's Center
144 Leavenworth St, San Francisco
(94102-3806)
PHONE....................................415 644-0504
Mary McNamara, *Director*
Erica Kisch, *Exec Dir*
Helen Meier, *Director*
EMP: 87
SQ FT: 12,143
SALES: 950K **Privately Held**
SIC: 8351 Child day care services

(P-24305)
COMPREHENSIVE CHILD DEV INC
Also Called: Comprehensive Child Dev Ctr
769 W 3rd St, San Pedro (90731-2425)
PHONE....................................310 514-4998
Mona Maamoun, *Director*
EMP: 58
SALES (corp-wide): 10.5MM **Privately Held**
SIC: 8351 Preschool center
PA: Comprehensive Child Development, Inc.
2545 Pacific Ave
Long Beach CA 90806
562 427-8834

(P-24306)
CONEJO VALLEY UNIFIED SCHL DST
Also Called: Conejo Vly Nghborhood For Lrng
100 S Conejo School Rd, Thousand Oaks
(91362-2908)
PHONE....................................805 496-9035
Jeffrey Baarstad PHD, *Superintendent*
EMP: 96
SALES (corp-wide): 225.2MM **Privately Held**
SIC: 8351 Child day care services
PA: Conejo Valley Unified School District
1400 E Janss Rd
Thousand Oaks CA 91362
805 497-9511

(P-24307)
COUNTY OF SAN BERNARDINO
Also Called: Preschool Service
385 N Arrowhead Ave, San Bernardino
(92415-0103)
PHONE....................................909 387-5455
Robyn Johnson, *Manager*
Adel Nizami, *Admin Asst*
Mike Dooley, *Analyst*
EMP: 100 **Privately Held**
SIC: 8351 Head start center, except in conjunction with school
PA: County Of San Bernardino
385 N Arrowhead Ave
San Bernardino CA 92415
909 387-3841

(P-24308)
COUNTY OF SAN BERNARDINO
Also Called: Human Services Systems
250 S Lena Rd, San Bernardino
(92415-0461)
PHONE....................................909 387-2363
Ron Griffin, *Director*
Carl Herzberg, *Programmer Anys*
EMP: 67
SQ FT: 934 **Privately Held**
SIC: 8351 9411 8741 Head start center, except in conjunction with school; preschool center; administration of educational programs; ; management services
PA: County Of San Bernardino
385 N Arrowhead Ave
San Bernardino CA 92415
909 387-3841

(P-24309)
COUNTY OF SAN BERNARDINO
Also Called: Highland Head Start
26887 5th St, Highland (92346-4178)
PHONE....................................909 425-0785
Lisa Simmons, *Branch Mgr*
EMP: 50 **Privately Held**
SIC: 8351 Head start center, except in conjunction with school

PA: County Of San Bernardino
385 N Arrowhead Ave
San Bernardino CA 92415
909 387-3841

(P-24310)
COUNTY OF SHASTA
Also Called: Monte Vista School
43 Hilltop Dr, Redding (96003-2807)
PHONE....................................530 225-2999
Sharon Simpson, *Principal*
EMP: 50 **Privately Held**
WEB: www.rsdnmp.org
SIC: 8351 Preschool center
PA: County Of Shasta
1450 Court St Ste 308a
Redding CA 96001
530 225-5561

(P-24311)
COUNTY OF VENTURA
Also Called: Ventura Cnty Human Srvce
300 W 9th St, Oxnard (93030-7014)
PHONE....................................805 240-2701
David Weinreich, *Manager*
EMP: 50 **Privately Held**
WEB: www.vcoe.org
SIC: 8351 9431 Child day care services; child health program administration, government
PA: County Of Ventura
800 S Victoria Ave
Ventura CA 93009
805 654-2644

(P-24312)
CREATIVE CHILD CARE INC (PA)
4719 Quail Lakes Dr G-237, Stockton
(95207-5267)
PHONE....................................209 941-9100
Debbie Eison, *President*
Loretta Young, *Human Res Dir*
Janice Marengo, *Human Res Mgr*
Dora Adafom, *Supervisor*
EMP: 340
SALES: 15.3MM **Privately Held**
SIC: 8351 Preschool center

(P-24313)
DESER SANDS UNIFI SCHOO DISTR
Also Called: Early Childhood Education
47950 Dune Palms Rd, La Quinta
(92253-4000)
PHONE....................................760 777-4200
Debra Loukatos, *Principal*
EMP: 74
SALES (corp-wide): 403.6MM **Privately Held**
SIC: 8351 Preschool center
PA: Desert Sands Unified School District
School Building Corporation
47950 Dune Palms Rd
La Quinta CA 92253
760 771-8567

(P-24314)
DIANNE ADAIR DAY CARE CENTERS (PA)
1862 Bailey Rd, Concord (94521-1349)
PHONE....................................925 429-3232
Todd Porter, *CEO*
Brian Carbine, *CFO*
EMP: 100
SALES (est): 4.7MM **Privately Held**
SIC: 8351 Group day care center

(P-24315)
DIGNITY HEALTH
2301 Ashe Rd, Bakersfield (93309-4301)
P.O. Box 119 (93302-0119)
PHONE....................................661 832-8300
Sharon Brown, *Director*
EMP: 60
SALES (corp-wide): 6.7B **Privately Held**
WEB: www.chw.edu
SIC: 8351 Child day care services
PA: Dignity Health
185 Berry St Ste 300
San Francisco CA 94107
415 438-5500

(P-24316)
E CENTER
1506 Starr Dr, Yuba City (95993-2602)
PHONE....................................530 634-1200
Kulraj Samra, *CEO*
Tom Wagner, *Exec Dir*
Amanda Rhyne, *Administration*
Janice Stout, *CTO*
EMP: 150
SQ FT: 4,000
SALES: 21.7MM **Privately Held**
SIC: 8351 Head start center, except in conjunction with school

(P-24317)
EDUCATION CALIFORNIA DEPT
Also Called: Califrnia Schl For Deaf Frmont
39350 Gallaudet Dr, Fremont (94538-2308)
PHONE....................................510 794-3666
David Eberwein, *Principal*
EMP: 450 **Privately Held**
WEB: www.csb-cde.ca.gov
SIC: 8351 9411 Preschool center;
HQ: California Department Of Education
1430 N St Ste 3217
Sacramento CA 95814

(P-24318)
ENRICHMENT EDUCTL EXPERIENCES
4400 Coldwater Canyon Ave # 300, Studio City (91604-5053)
PHONE....................................818 989-7509
Nancy Simpson, *President*
EMP: 55
SALES (est): 844.4K **Privately Held**
SIC: 8351 Child day care services

(P-24319)
ENVIRONMENTS FOR LEARNING INC (PA)
Also Called: Montessori On The Lake
24291 Muirlands Blvd, Lake Forest
(92630-3001)
PHONE....................................949 855-5630
Sara Smith, *President*
EMP: 79
SALES (est): 2.6MM **Privately Held**
SIC: 8351 8211 Montessori child development center; preparatory school; private combined elementary & secondary school

(P-24320)
FAMILY CARE NETWORK INC (PA)
1255 Kendall Rd, San Luis Obispo
(93401-8750)
PHONE....................................805 503-6240
James Robert, *CEO*
Megan Yoder, *Volunteer Dir*
Celia Sotelo, *Partner*
Jonathan Nibbio, *COO*
Bobbie Boyer, *CFO*
EMP: 71
SQ FT: 2,600
SALES: 14.3MM **Privately Held**
SIC: 8351 Child day care services

(P-24321)
FIRST BAPTIST HEAD START
3890 Railroad Ave, Pittsburg (94565-6540)
PHONE....................................925 473-2000
Arika Spencer-Brown, *Exec Dir*
Linda Anderson, *Marketing Staff*
Monica De Leon, *Assistant*
EMP: 87
SALES (est): 2.5MM **Privately Held**
WEB: www.firstbaptistheadstart.org
SIC: 8351 Head start center, except in conjunction with school

(P-24322)
FIRST EVANG LUTHERAN CH & SCHL
2900 W Carson St, Torrance (90503-6005)
PHONE....................................310 320-9920
Elizabeth Kebschull, *Principal*
Kristine Olson, *Principal*
EMP: 100
SQ FT: 50,232
SALES (est): 4.3MM **Privately Held**
SIC: 8351 Preschool center

(P-24323)
GALT JOINT UNION SCHOOL DST
Also Called: Fairsite Preschool
902 Caroline Ave, Galt (95632-2003)
PHONE....................................209 745-1546
Donna Whitlock, *Principal*
Karen Schauer, *Superintendent*
EMP: 50 **Privately Held**
SIC: 8351 Preschool center
PA: Galt Joint Union School District
1018 C St Ste 210
Galt CA 95632

(P-24324)
GARDEN GROVE UNIFIED SCHL DST
Also Called: Carver Preschool
8371 Orangewood Ave, Garden Grove
(92841-1517)
PHONE....................................714 663-6437
Sharon Hazelleaf, *Principal*
EMP: 71
SALES (corp-wide): 602MM **Privately Held**
SIC: 8351 Preschool center
PA: Garden Grove Unified School District
10331 Stanford Ave
Garden Grove CA 92840
714 663-6000

(P-24325)
GLENN COUNTY OFFICE EDUCATION
Also Called: Child & Family Services
676 E Walker St Fl 2, Orland (95963-2203)
PHONE....................................530 865-1145
Tracey Quarne, *Superintendent*
Deana-Marie Berry, *Info Tech Mgr*
EMP: 81
SALES: 4.4MM **Privately Held**
SIC: 8351 8322 Child day care services; family counseling services

(P-24326)
HARMONIUM INC (PA)
Also Called: CITY ARTS ACADEMY
9245 Activity Rd Ste 200, San Diego
(92126-2383)
PHONE....................................858 684-3080
Rosa Ana Lozada, *CEO*
Melinda Mallie, *CFO*
Carole Steele, *Officer*
Rosana Lozada, *Executive Asst*
Miguel Ortega, *Admin Asst*
EMP: 150
SALES: 7.7MM **Privately Held**
SIC: 8351 Preschool center

(P-24327)
HEAD START CHILD DEV CNCIL INC
2105 N Tracy Blvd, Tracy (95376-2424)
PHONE....................................209 832-7844
Mary Rosenquist, *Branch Mgr*
EMP: 214
SALES (corp-wide): 20MM **Privately Held**
SIC: 8351 Child day care services
PA: Head Start Child Development, Council, Inc.
5361 N Pershing Ave Ste A
Stockton CA 95207

(P-24328)
IMMANUEL BAPTIST CRUCH
Also Called: Immanuel Baptist Day School
28355 Baseline St, Highland (92346-5008)
PHONE....................................909 862-6641
Rob Zinn, *Pastor*
Kimberly Drake, *Exec Dir*
EMP: 65
SALES (est): 2.8MM **Privately Held**
WEB: www.ibchighland.org
SIC: 8351 8661 Preschool center; Baptist Church

(P-24329)
INGLEWOOD UNIFIED SCHOOL DST
Also Called: Inglewood Child Dev Ctr
401 S Inglewood Ave, Inglewood
(90301-2599)
PHONE..................310 419-2691
Linda Anderson, *Principal*
EMP: 80
SALES (corp-wide): 150.1MM **Privately Held**
WEB: www.payne.inglewood.k12.ca.us
SIC: 8351 8211 Child day care services; public elementary school
PA: Inglewood Unified School District
401 S Inglewood Ave
Inglewood CA 90301
310 419-2700

(P-24330)
INSTITUTE FOR HUMN SOCIAL DEV (PA)
Also Called: San Mateo Head Start Program
155 Bovet Rd Ste 300, San Mateo
(94402-3142)
PHONE..................650 871-5613
Amy Liew, *Director*
Angel Barrios, *Exec Dir*
Madelene Gallego, *Technology*
Vanessa Chavez, *Manager*
EMP: 59
SQ FT: 6,000
SALES: 9.9MM **Privately Held**
SIC: 8351 Head start center, except in conjunction with school

(P-24331)
KID IQ 24 HR CHILDCARE
Also Called: Child Care
4451 E Sierra Madre Ave, Fresno
(93726-1158)
PHONE..................310 492-3037
Jotasha Taylor, *Exec VP*
EMP: 99
SALES (est): 432.5K **Privately Held**
SIC: 8351 Preschool center

(P-24332)
KIDANGO INC
4700 Calaveras Ave, Fremont
(94538-1124)
PHONE..................510 494-9601
MAI Ton, *Branch Mgr*
EMP: 72
SALES (corp-wide): 26MM **Privately Held**
SIC: 8351 Child day care services
PA: Kidango, Inc.
44000 Old Warm Sprng Blvd
Fremont CA 94538
510 897-6900

(P-24333)
KIDS KLUB CARE CENTERS INC (PA)
Also Called: Kids Klub Pasadena
380 S Raymond Ave, Pasadena
(91105-2608)
PHONE..................626 795-2501
Michael Wojciechowski, *President*
Bambi Wojciechowski, *Chairman*
EMP: 60
SQ FT: 7,800
SALES (est): 4.9MM **Privately Held**
SIC: 8351 Preschool center

(P-24334)
KIDS N THINGS INC (PA)
4221 Cochran St, Simi Valley (93063-2349)
PHONE..................805 522-1011
Shirley Blaskl, *President*
Lawrence Blasko, *Treasurer*
EMP: 75
SQ FT: 5,000
SALES (est): 2MM **Privately Held**
SIC: 8351 Nursery school; preschool center

(P-24335)
KINDERCARE EDUCATION LLC
3280 Crow Canyon Rd, San Ramon
(94583-1304)
PHONE..................925 824-0267
Thomas Jamison, *Manager*
EMP: 85

SALES (corp-wide): 1.2B **Privately Held**
WEB: www.knowledgelearning.com
SIC: 8351 Group day care center
PA: Kindercare Education Llc
650 Ne Holladay St # 1400
Portland OR 97232
503 872-1300

(P-24336)
KINDERCARE LEARNING CTRS LLC
Also Called: Belmont Shores Kindercare
5251 E Las Lomas St, Long Beach
(90815-4206)
PHONE..................562 961-8882
Bernice Gonzalez, *Director*
Alicia Syfers, *Exec Dir*
Theresa Kappermeyer, *Director*
Tanea Robinson, *Manager*
Vangie Robles, *Manager*
EMP: 80
SALES (corp-wide): 1.2B **Privately Held**
WEB: www.kindercare.com
SIC: 8351 Group day care center
HQ: Kindercare Learning Centers, Llc
650 Ne Holladay St # 1400
Portland OR 97232
503 872-1300

(P-24337)
LAKE ELSINORE UNIFIED SCHL DST
Also Called: Ortega High School
565 Chaney St, Lake Elsinore
(92530-2722)
PHONE..................951 253-7091
Frieda Brands, *Principal*
EMP: 58
SALES (corp-wide): 255.2MM **Privately Held**
SIC: 8351 Head start center, except in conjunction with school
PA: Lake Elsinore Unified School District
545 Chaney St
Lake Elsinore CA 92530
951 253-7000

(P-24338)
LINDA BEACH COOP PRE-SCHOOL
400 Highland Ave, Piedmont (94611-4043)
PHONE..................510 547-4432
Barbara Ulbrich, *Director*
Parents Co-Op, *Principal*
EMP: 50
SALES: 176.5K **Privately Held**
SIC: 8351 Preschool center

(P-24339)
LINDAMOOD-BELL LRNG PROCESSES (PA)
406 Higuera St Ste 120, San Luis Obispo
(93401-6131)
PHONE..................805 541-3836
Nanci Bell, *President*
Holly Aaron, *Partner*
Patricia Lindamood, *Treasurer*
Rod Bell, *Officer*
Ellen Lathrop, *Officer*
EMP: 200
SQ FT: 8,000
SALES (est): 38.2MM **Privately Held**
WEB: www.lblp.com
SIC: 8351 Head start center, except in conjunction with school; preschool center

(P-24340)
LITTLE CITIZENS SCHOOLS INC
4256 S Western Ave, Los Angeles
(90062-1645)
PHONE..................323 732-1212
Doris Evans, *President*
Roy Evans, *Corp Secy*
EMP: 100
SQ FT: 5,000
SALES (est): 2MM **Privately Held**
SIC: 8351 8211 Preschool center; elementary school

(P-24341)
LONG BEACH DAY NURSERY
3965 N Bellflower Blvd, Long Beach
(90808-1902)
PHONE..................562 421-1488
Margareth McMahon, *Director*

EMP: 50
SALES (est): 537.9K
SALES (corp-wide): 2.8MM **Privately Held**
WEB: www.lbdn.org
SIC: 8351 Preschool center
PA: Long Beach Day Nursery
1548 Chestnut Ave
Long Beach CA 90813
562 421-1488

(P-24342)
LOS ANGELES UNIFIED SCHOOL DST
Also Called: Queen Anne Early Education Ctr
1212 Queen Anne Pl, Los Angeles
(90019-6819)
PHONE..................323 939-7322
Salvador Rodriguez, *Principal*
EMP: 60
SALES (corp-wide): 3.8B **Privately Held**
WEB: www.lausd.k12.ca.us
SIC: 8351 Preschool center
PA: Los Angeles Unified School District
333 S Beaudry Ave Ste 209
Los Angeles CA 90017
213 241-1000

(P-24343)
LOS ANGLES UNIVERSAL PRESCHOOL
Also Called: Child360
515 S Figueroa St Ste 900, Los Angeles
(90071-3309)
PHONE..................213 416-1200
William Sperling, *CEO*
Elsa Luna, *CFO*
David Crippens, *Bd of Directors*
Dawn Kurtz, *Officer*
Clare Shephard, *Officer*
EMP: 200
SQ FT: 12,000
SALES: 76.2MM **Privately Held**
WEB: www.laup.net
SIC: 8351 Preschool center

(P-24344)
MARIN HORIZON SCHOOL INC
305 Montford Ave, Mill Valley (94941-3370)
PHONE..................415 388-8408
Rosalind Hamar, *Exec Dir*
EMP: 50
SQ FT: 20,000
SALES: 10.9MM **Privately Held**
WEB: www.marinhorizon.org
SIC: 8351 8211 Montessori child development center; private elementary school

(P-24345)
MARYVALE DAY CARE CENTER
Also Called: Maryvale Edcatn Fmly Rsrce Ctr
2502 Huntington Dr, Duarte (91010-2221)
PHONE..................626 357-1514
Steve Gunther, *Director*
EMP: 124
SALES (corp-wide): 21.9MM **Privately Held**
SIC: 8351 Preschool center
PA: Maryvale Day Care Center
7600 Graves Ave
Rosemead CA 91770
626 280-6511

(P-24346)
MARYVALE DAY CARE CENTER (PA)
Also Called: MARYVALE EDUCATIONAL DAY CARE
7600 Graves Ave, Rosemead
(91770-3414)
P.O. Box 1039 (91770-1000)
PHONE..................626 280-6511
Steve Gunpher, *President*
Renee Chan, *Vice Pres*
Olga Diaz, *Vice Pres*
Ike Kerhulas, *Vice Pres*
Christina Moore, *Vice Pres*
EMP: 200
SALES: 21.9MM **Privately Held**
WEB: www.maryvale-ca.org
SIC: 8351 8361 Child day care services; residential care for children

(P-24347)
MCCUSKER ENTERPRISES INC
Also Called: Kids World Preschool
29879 Santiago Rd, Temecula
(92592-3004)
PHONE..................951 699-9777
John McCusker, *President*
Kris Dean McCusker, *Vice Pres*
EMP: 70 **EST:** 1976
SQ FT: 6,000
SALES (est): 2.1MM **Privately Held**
SIC: 8351 8211 Preschool center; private elementary school

(P-24348)
MERCIES HOME (PA)
910 S Real Rd, Bakersfield (93309-4132)
PHONE..................661 832-3424
Mercedes Penarejo, *Owner*
EMP: 50
SQ FT: 2,300
SALES (est): 1.7MM **Privately Held**
SIC: 8351 8361 Group day care center; home for the mentally handicapped

(P-24349)
MEXICAN AMRCN OPRTNTY FNDATION
2650 Zoe Ave Fl 3, Huntington Park
(90255-4198)
PHONE..................323 588-7320
Lisa Viveros, *Branch Mgr*
EMP: 50
SALES (corp-wide): 73.3MM **Privately Held**
SIC: 8351 Head start center, except in conjunction with school
PA: Mexican American Opportunity Foundation
401 N Garfield Ave
Montebello CA 90640
323 890-9600

(P-24350)
MONTESSORI LEARNING COMMONS (PA)
Also Called: Elk Grove Montessori School
1123 D St, Sacramento (95814-0809)
PHONE..................916 444-7786
Norman Lorenz, *President*
Edward Condon, *CFO*
EMP: 100
SQ FT: 3,500
SALES (est): 1MM **Privately Held**
SIC: 8351 Montessori child development center

(P-24351)
MOUNTAIN VIEW CHILD CARE INC
Also Called: Totally Kids Spcalty Hlth Care
10716 La Tuna Canyon Rd, Sun Valley
(91352-2130)
PHONE..................818 252-5863
Michelle Nydam, *Branch Mgr*
EMP: 150 **Privately Held**
SIC: 8351 Child day care services
PA: Mountain View Child Care, Inc.
1720 Mountain View Ave
Loma Linda CA 92354

(P-24352)
NEIGHBORHOOD HOUSE ASSOCIATION
4111 Home Ave Ste F, San Diego
(92105-5200)
PHONE..................619 262-8199
Michelle Tylor, *Exec Dir*
EMP: 80
SALES (corp-wide): 86.7MM **Privately Held**
SIC: 8351 Head start center, except in conjunction with school
PA: The Neighborhood House Association
5660 Copley Dr
San Diego CA 92111
858 715-2642

(P-24353)
NORTH COAST PRESBYTERIAN CH
1831 S El Camino Real, Encinitas (92024-4913)
PHONE...................760 753-2535
Daniel Foley, *Business Mgr*
Tricia Langowski, *Finance Mgr*
Hunter Benson, *Pastor*
Jonathan Kerhoulas, *Pastor*
Donald Seltzer, *Pastor*
EMP: 70
SALES (est): 1.9MM Privately Held
WEB: www.ncpcinfo.com
SIC: **8351 8661** Preschool center; Presbyterian Church

(P-24354)
NORTH WEST LEARNING CENTER
3485 W Ashcroft Ave, Fresno (93722-4249)
PHONE...................559 228-3057
Rosemary Avalos, *Director*
Alvis Bytel, *Exec Dir*
EMP: 50
SALES (est): 481.7K Privately Held
SIC: **8351** Child day care services

(P-24355)
NURTURING TOTS INC
3784 Winford Dr, Tarzana (91356-5811)
PHONE...................818 996-1602
Eugene Cobuzzi, *Owner*
Linda Cobuzzi, *President*
Debra Dinielli, *President*
EMP: 60
SALES (est): 156.9K Privately Held
SIC: **8351** Child day care services

(P-24356)
OFFICE OF CHILD DEVELOPMENT
10800 Farragut Dr, Culver City (90230-4107)
PHONE...................310 842-4230
Audrey Stephens, *Director*
Audrey Jones, *Director*
Audrey Stevens, *Director*
EMP: 80
SALES (est): 505.5K Privately Held
SIC: **8351** Preschool center

(P-24357)
OLIVE KNOLLS CHRISTIAN SCHOOL
6201 Fruitvale Ave, Bakersfield (93308-2706)
PHONE...................661 393-3566
Wendy Nayes, *Director*
Jabo Baldwin, *Teacher*
Shirley Friberg, *Director*
Theron Friberg, *Director*
EMP: 60
SALES (est): 1.8MM Privately Held
WEB: www.okcs.org
SIC: **8351 8661** Child day care services; religious organizations

(P-24358)
OLYMPUS ADHC INC
Also Called: Olympus Adult Day Hlthcare Ctr
11613 Washington Pl, Los Angeles (90066-5013)
PHONE...................310 572-7272
Boris Frigman, *President*
EMP: 50
SALES (est): 1MM Privately Held
SIC: **8351** Group day care center

(P-24359)
OPTIONS FOR LEARNING
Also Called: State Preschool
2001 Elm St, Alhambra (91803-2905)
PHONE...................626 308-2411
EMP: 75
SALES (corp-wide): 81.7MM Privately Held
SIC: **8351** Group day care center
PA: Options For Learning
885 S Village Oaks Dr # 12
Covina CA 91724
626 967-7848

(P-24360)
ORANGE CHILDREN & PARENTS
Also Called: O C P T
1063 N Glassell St, Orange (92867-5602)
PHONE...................714 639-4000
Robyn Class, *Exec Dir*
Stephanie Ignatius, *Finance*
Maria Encalada, *Accountant*
Kathleen Lim-Valle, *Supervisor*
EMP: 58
SALES: 3.7MM Privately Held
SIC: **8351** Preschool center

(P-24361)
ORANGE CNTY SPRNTNDENT SCHOOLS
Also Called: Lindburgh Child Development
220 23rd St, Costa Mesa (92627-1810)
PHONE...................949 650-2506
Elivira Frescas, *Director*
EMP: 60
SALES (corp-wide): 284.9MM Privately Held
WEB: www.ocprob.com
SIC: **8351** Preschool center
PA: Orange County Superintendent Of Schools
200 Kalmus Dr
Costa Mesa CA 92626
714 966-4000

(P-24362)
ORANGE COUNTY HEAD START (PA)
2501 Pullman St Ste 100, Santa Ana (92705-5515)
P.O. Box 9269, Fountain Valley (92728-9269)
PHONE...................714 241-8920
Colleen Versteeg, *Exec Dir*
Loyal Sharp, *Finance Dir*
Lillian Beltran, *Teacher*
EMP: 75
SQ FT: 20,000
SALES: 37MM Privately Held
SIC: **8351** Preschool center; head start center, except in conjunction with school

(P-24363)
ORANGE COUNTY HEAD START
9200 W Pacific Pl, Anaheim (92804-6387)
PHONE...................714 761-4967
Colleen Versteeg, *Director*
EMP: 136
SALES (corp-wide): 37MM Privately Held
SIC: **8351** Head start center, except in conjunction with school
PA: Orange County Head Start
2501 Pullman St Ste 100
Santa Ana CA 92705
714 241-8920

(P-24364)
PALCARE INC
945 California Dr, Burlingame (94010-3605)
PHONE...................650 340-1289
Pettis Perry, *Exec Dir*
EMP: 50
SQ FT: 12,000
SALES: 3.5MM Privately Held
WEB: www.palcare.org
SIC: **8351** Preschool center

(P-24365)
PALO ALTO COMMUNITY CHILD CARE
890 Escondido Rd, Stanford (94305-7101)
PHONE...................650 855-9828
Gary Prehn, *Principal*
EMP: 65
SALES (corp-wide): 9.6MM Privately Held
SIC: **8351** Child day care services
PA: Palo Alto Community Child Care Inc
3990 Ventura Ct
Palo Alto CA
650 493-5990

(P-24366)
PARA LOS NINOS
845 E 6th St, Los Angeles (90021-1026)
PHONE...................213 623-3942
Tim Gray, *CEO*

EMP: 113
SALES (corp-wide): 31.7MM Privately Held
SIC: **8351** Preschool center
PA: Para Los Ninos
5000 Hollywood Blvd
Los Angeles CA 90027
213 250-4800

(P-24367)
PENINSULA FAMILY SERVICE (PA)
24 2nd Ave, San Mateo (94401-3828)
PHONE...................650 403-4300
Judy Swanson, *CEO*
Laurie Wishard, *President*
Arne Croce, *CEO*
Kimberly Hines, *Vice Pres*
Chanel Paulson, *Facilities Mgr*
EMP: 265 EST: 1950
SALES: 12.7MM Privately Held
WEB: www.familyserviceagency.org
SIC: **8351 8322** Group day care center; family (marriage) counseling

(P-24368)
PEOPLES CARE INC
7355 Greenleaf Ave, Whittier (90602-1621)
PHONE...................562 320-0174
Torres Cesaer, *Principal*
EMP: 152
SALES (corp-wide): 42.3MM Privately Held
SIC: **8351** Child day care services
PA: People's Care Inc.
13920 City Center Dr # 230
Chino Hills CA 91709
855 773-6753

(P-24369)
PLAZA DE LA RAZA CHILD DEVELOP
225 N Avenue 25, Los Angeles (90031-1794)
PHONE...................323 224-1788
EMP: 93
SALES (corp-wide): 21MM Privately Held
SIC: **8351** Head start center, except in conjunction with school
PA: Plaza De La Raza Child Development Services, Inc.
13300 Crssrds Pkwy N 44
La Puente CA 91746
562 776-1301

(P-24370)
PLAZA DE LA RAZA CHILD DEVELOP
6411 Norwalk Blvd, Whittier (90606-1502)
PHONE...................562 695-1070
Adriana Gonzalez, *President*
EMP: 93
SALES (corp-wide): 21MM Privately Held
SIC: **8351** Head start center, except in conjunction with school
PA: Plaza De La Raza Child Development Services, Inc.
13300 Crssrds Pkwy N 44
La Puente CA 91746
562 776-1301

(P-24371)
PLAZA DE LA RAZA CHILD DEVELOP (PA)
13300 Crssrds Pkwy N 44, La Puente (91746)
PHONE...................562 776-1301
Anthony Rendon, *Exec Dir*
Rosalina Fine, *Director*
EMP: 72
SALES: 21MM Privately Held
SIC: **8351** Head start center, except in conjunction with school

(P-24372)
PRECIOUS ENTERPRISES INC
Also Called: Clement Preschool
14130 Douglass Ln, Saratoga (95070-5536)
PHONE...................408 265-2226
Faz Ulla, *Owner*
Shahana Shah, *Co-Owner*
Husna Ulla, *Co-Owner*

Nilu Ulla, *Co-Owner*
EMP: 62
SQ FT: 7,500
SALES (est): 1.1MM Privately Held
WEB: www.preschools.indiaedu.com
SIC: **8351** Preschool center

(P-24373)
PRESTIGE PRESCHOOLS INC (PA)
3795 La Crescenta Ave # 200, Glendale (91208-1057)
PHONE...................818 957-1170
Steven L Bush, *Principal*
EMP: 51
SALES (est): 7.2MM Privately Held
SIC: **8351** Preschool center

(P-24374)
QUALITY CHILDRENS SERVICES (PA)
6108 Innovation Way, Carlsbad (92009-1728)
P.O. Box 234203, Encinitas (92023-4203)
PHONE...................760 942-3433
Amory Ramirez, *President*
EMP: 150
SQ FT: 3,500
SALES: 9MM Privately Held
SIC: **8351** Group day care center

(P-24375)
SAINT JHNS HLTH CTR FOUNDATION
Also Called: Saint Johns Child Fmly Dev Ctr
2121 Santa Monica Blvd, Santa Monica (90404-2303)
PHONE...................310 829-5511
Robert Klein, *Principal*
EMP: 70
SQ FT: 26,032
SALES (corp-wide): 2.6B Privately Held
SIC: **8351** Child day care services
HQ: Saint John's Health Center Foundation.
2121 Santa Monica Blvd
Santa Monica CA 90404
310 829-5511

(P-24376)
SAN BERNARDINO CITY UNF SCHOOL
Also Called: Allred Child Developement Ctr
303 S K St, San Bernardino (92410-2416)
PHONE...................909 388-6307
Latashia Kelly, *Director*
EMP: 100
SALES (corp-wide): 469.2MM Privately Held
WEB: www.sbcusd.k12.ca.us
SIC: **8351** Child day care services
PA: San Bernardino City Unified School District
777 N F St
San Bernardino CA 92410
909 381-1100

(P-24377)
SAN MARCOS UNIFIED SCHOOL DST
255 Pico Ave Ste 250, San Marcos (92069-3712)
PHONE...................760 752-1252
Pamella Mc Coy, *Manager*
Henry Voros, *Asst Supt*
EMP: 100
SALES (corp-wide): 250.3MM Privately Held
WEB: www.smusd.k12.ca.us
SIC: **8351** Child day care services
PA: San Marcos Unified School District
255 Pico Ave Ste 250
San Marcos CA 92069
760 744-4776

(P-24378)
SANTA CRUZ MONTESSORI SCHOOL
Also Called: SCMS
6230 Soquel Dr, Aptos (95003-3118)
PHONE...................831 476-1646
Kathleen Ann Rideout, *CEO*
EMP: 50

SALES: 6.2MM **Privately Held**
WEB: www.savmait.com
SIC: **8351** 8211 Preschool center; private
elementary & secondary schools; private
elementary school; private junior high
school

(P-24379)
SANTA MONICA CITY OF
Also Called: Child Development Office, The
2802 4th St, Santa Monica (90405-4308)
PHONE..............................310 399-5865
Alice Chung, *Director*
EMP: 60 **Privately Held**
WEB: www.santamonicapd.org
SIC: **8351** Child day care services
PA: City Of Santa Monica
1685 Main St
Santa Monica CA 90401
310 458-8411

(P-24380)
**SHASTA COUNTY HEAD START
CHILD (PA)**
375 Lake Blvd Ste 100, Redding
(96003-2557)
PHONE..............................530 241-1036
Carla Clark, *Exec Dir*
EMP: 50
SQ FT: 5,000
SALES: 11.5MM **Privately Held**
SIC: **8351** Head start center, except in con-
junction with school

(P-24381)
**SIERRA CSCADE FMLY
OPPRTNITIES (PA)**
Also Called: Head Start
424 N Mill Creek Rd, Quincy (95971-9678)
PHONE..............................530 283-1242
Brenda Poteete, *Director*
EMP: 101
SQ FT: 2,600
SALES: 3.3MM **Privately Held**
SIC: **8351** Head start center, except in con-
junction with school

(P-24382)
**SJB CHILD DEVELOPMENT
CENTERS (PA)**
Also Called: SICK CHILD CARE CENTER,
THE
1400 Parkmoor Ave Ste 220, San Jose
(95126-3798)
PHONE..............................408 538-0200
Victor Hassan, *CEO*
Kent Williams, *Principal*
Sheryll Ebbs, *Director*
EMP: 110 EST: 1971
SQ FT: 12,840
SALES: 6.1MM **Privately Held**
SIC: **8351** Preschool center

(P-24383)
**SOLANO FAMILY & CHLD
COUNCIL**
Also Called: SOLANO FAMILY & CHIL-
DREN'S SER
421 Executive Ct N, Fairfield (94534-4019)
PHONE..............................707 863-3950
Kathryn Lago, *Exec Dir*
EMP: 74 EST: 1978
SALES: 18.5MM **Privately Held**
WEB: www.solanosfcs.org
SIC: **8351** Child day care services

(P-24384)
**SOUTH MARKET CHILD CARE
INC**
790 Folsom St, San Francisco
(94107-1276)
PHONE..............................415 820-3500
Noushin Mofakham, *Director*
EMP: 54
SALES (corp-wide): 3.3MM **Privately
Held**
SIC: **8351** Montessori child development
center
PA: South Of Market Child Care, Inc.
790 Folsom St
San Francisco CA 94107
415 820-3500

(P-24385)
**ST ANDREWS CHILDREN
CENTER**
4400 Barranca Pkwy, Irvine (92604-4739)
PHONE..............................949 651-0198
Carolyn Jones, *Director*
EMP: 50
SALES (est): 1.4MM **Privately Held**
SIC: **8351** Preschool center

(P-24386)
STATE PRESCHOOL
Also Called: Martin Lthr Kng Chldr Ctr
950 El Pueblo Ave, Pittsburg (94565-4116)
PHONE..............................925 473-4380
Karan Latimer, *Director*
EMP: 50
SALES (est): 354.7K **Privately Held**
SIC: **8351** Preschool center

(P-24387)
STRATFORD SCHOOL INC
220 Kensington Way, Los Gatos
(95032-4028)
PHONE..............................408 371-3020
Esperanza Hernandez, *Principal*
EMP: 53
SALES (corp-wide): 7.9MM **Privately
Held**
SIC: **8351** 8211 Preschool center;
preparatory school
PA: Stratford School, Inc.
870 N California Ave
Palo Alto CA 94303
650 493-1151

(P-24388)
STRATFORD SCHOOL INC (PA)
870 N California Ave, Palo Alto
(94303-3631)
PHONE..............................650 493-1151
Matthew Wulfstat, *CEO*
Joseph Wagner, *President*
Courtney Welch, *Administration*
Celia Schiffner, *Controller*
Kimberly Alexander, *Teacher*
EMP: 50
SALES (est): 7.9MM **Privately Held**
SIC: **8351** 8211 Preschool center; private
elementary school

(P-24389)
STUDENTS OF ASSOCIATED
Also Called: Csus Children's Center
6000 J St, Sacramento (95819-2605)
PHONE..............................916 278-6216
Denise Wessels, *Director*
EMP: 80
SALES (corp-wide): 10.1MM **Privately
Held**
SIC: **8351** Child day care services
PA: Associated Students Of California State
University, Sacramento
6000 J St
Sacramento CA
916 278-7917

(P-24390)
**TAFT COLLEGE CHILDREN
CENTER**
29 Emmons Park Dr, Taft (93268-2317)
PHONE..............................661 763-7850
Genevieve Garcia, *Director*
Leslie Braggo, *Director*
EMP: 50
SALES (est): 853.4K **Privately Held**
SIC: **8351** Child day care services

(P-24391)
THINK TOGETHER
202 E Airport Dr Ste 200, San Bernardino
(92408-3429)
PHONE..............................909 723-1400
EMP: 503
SALES (corp-wide): 47.1MM **Privately
Held**
SIC: **8351** Child day care services
PA: Think Together
2101 E 4th St Ste 200b
Santa Ana CA 92705
714 543-3807

(P-24392)
THINK TOGETHER
800 S Barranca Ave # 120, Covina
(91723-3680)
PHONE..............................626 373-2311
Tom Lopez, *Branch Mgr*
EMP: 704
SALES (corp-wide): 47.1MM **Privately
Held**
SIC: **8351** Child day care services
PA: Think Together
2101 E 4th St Ste 200b
Santa Ana CA 92705
714 543-3807

(P-24393)
THINK TOGETHER
22620 Goldencrest Dr # 104, Moreno Valley
(92553-9032)
PHONE..............................951 571-9944
EMP: 503
SALES (corp-wide): 47.1MM **Privately
Held**
SIC: **8351** Child day care services
PA: Think Together
2101 E 4th St Ste 200b
Santa Ana CA 92705
714 543-3807

(P-24394)
TOM SAWYER CAMPS INC
Also Called: T.S.c
707 W Woodbury Rd Ste F, Altadena
(91001-5386)
PHONE..............................626 794-1156
Sarah Horner Fish, *CEO*
Michael H Horner, *President*
Sally Horner, *Vice Pres*
Katie Enney, *Program Dir*
Eric Ikari, *Director*
EMP: 120
SQ FT: 4,000
SALES (est): 5.4MM **Privately Held**
WEB: www.daycampjobs.com
SIC: **8351** Child day care services

(P-24395)
**TULARE CNTY CHLD CARE
HOME EDU**
7000 W Doe Ave Ste C, Visalia
(93291-8623)
PHONE..............................559 651-0247
Senaida Garcia, *Director*
EMP: 68
SALES (est): 2.6MM **Privately Held**
SIC: **8351** Head start center, except in con-
junction with school

(P-24396)
VANDENBERG AFB CHILD CARE
Summersill Bldg 11613, Lompoc (93437)
PHONE..............................805 606-1555
Verna D Brown, *Director*
EMP: 50
SALES (est): 1.2MM **Privately Held**
SIC: **8351** Child day care services

(P-24397)
**WE CARE DAY CARE & PRE
SCHOOL**
Also Called: West Valley Christian Academy
1790 Sequoia Blvd, Tracy (95376-4329)
PHONE..............................209 832-4072
Tim Smith, *Administration*
EMP: 60 EST: 1996
SALES (est): 1.4MM **Privately Held**
SIC: **8351** Preschool center

(P-24398)
WEST VALLEY FAMILY YMCA
Also Called: Vanalden Ave School
18810 Vanowen St, Reseda (91335-5213)
PHONE..............................818 774-2840
Greg Koubek, *Director*
Stacy Childress, *Principal*
Shane Ruffin, *Principal*
Tim Oconnor, *Director*
EMP: 125
SALES (est): 2.1MM **Privately Held**
SIC: **8351** 8322 Child day care services;
youth center

(P-24399)
**WESTSIDE CHILDRENS CENTER
INC**
5721 W Slauson Ave # 140, Culver City
(90230-6554)
PHONE..............................310 846-4100
Heather Carrigan, *CEO*
Richard Klein, *CFO*
EMP: 92
SQ FT: 18,000
SALES: 8.2MM **Privately Held**
SIC: **8351** 8322 Child day care services;
child related social services

(P-24400)
WU YEE CHILDRENS SERVICES
880 Clay St, San Francisco (94108-1611)
PHONE..............................415 677-0100
Alyson Suzeuki, *Program Dir*
Jimmy Ngo, *Analyst*
Donna Dizon, *Manager*
EMP: 68
SALES (corp-wide): 20.4MM **Privately
Held**
WEB: www.wuyee.org
SIC: **8351** 8322 Group day care center; in-
dividual & family services
PA: Wu Yee Children's Services
827 Broadway
San Francisco CA 94133
415 230-7504

(P-24401)
**YESHIVA RAU ISACSOHN
ACADEMY**
Also Called: Yeshivath Torath Emeth Acad-
emy
540 N La Brea Ave, Los Angeles
(90036-2016)
PHONE..............................323 549-3170
Marc Chopp, *Administration*
Charles Abbott, *Ch of Bd*
Morris Weiss, *President*
Rabbi Berish Goldenberg, *Corp Secy*
EMP: 120
SALES (est): 4MM **Privately Held**
SIC: **8351** 8211 Preschool center; nursery
school; elementary school

(P-24402)
**YOUNG MENS CHRSTN ASSN
OF LA**
Also Called: East Valley Family YMCA Dcc
5142 Tujunga Ave, North Hollywood
(91601-3742)
PHONE..............................818 763-5126
Debbie Lozano, *Director*
EMP: 90
SQ FT: 11,260
SALES (corp-wide): 105.9MM **Privately
Held**
SIC: **8351** 8322 Group day care center;
youth center
PA: Young Men's Christian Association Of
Metropolitan Los Angeles
625 S New Hampshire Ave
Los Angeles CA 90005
213 351-2256

(P-24403)
**YOUNG MNS CHRSTN ASSN OF
E BAY**
Also Called: YMCA Pre School Hillview
3800 Clark Rd, Richmond (94803-3145)
PHONE..............................510 223-7070
EMP: 963
SALES (corp-wide): 27.5MM **Privately
Held**
SIC: **8351** Child day care services
PA: Young Men's Christian Association Of
The East Bay
2330 Broadway
Oakland CA 94612
510 549-4515

(P-24404)
**YOUNG MNS CHRSTN ASSN OF
E BAY**
Also Called: Y M C A
2241 Russell St, Berkeley (94705-1029)
PHONE..............................510 644-6290
Fran Gallati, *President*
EMP: 1927

▲ = Import ▼=Export
◆ =Import/Export

SALES (corp-wide): 27.5MM **Privately Held**
SIC: **8351** Child day care services
PA: Young Men's Christian Association Of
The East Bay
2330 Broadway
Oakland CA 94612
510 549-4515

8361 Residential Care

(P-24405)
ABILTY FIRST
3770 E Willow St, Long Beach
(90815-1731)
PHONE..................562 426-6161
Lori Ganbmi, *President*
EMP: 60
SALES (est): 605K **Privately Held**
SIC: **8361** Residential care

(P-24406)
ACTS FOR CHILDREN (PA)
Also Called: A C T S
18136 Jurupa Ave, Bloomington
(92316-3009)
P.O. Box 848, Colton (92324-0848)
PHONE..................909 877-5499
Ike Kerhulas, *President*
EMP: 55
SALES: 608.9K **Privately Held**
SIC: **8361** Residential care

(P-24407)
ADVENT GROUP MINISTRIES INC
90 Great Oaks Blvd # 108, San Jose
(95119-1314)
PHONE..................408 281-0708
Jeff Davis, *Ch of Bd*
Mark Miller, *Exec Dir*
EMP: 63
SQ FT: 4,400
SALES: 3.3MM **Privately Held**
WEB: www.adventgm.com
SIC: **8361** Children's home

(P-24408)
AEGIS ASSSTED LIVING PRPTS LLC
Also Called: Aegis of Fremont
3850 Walnut Ave 228, Fremont
(94538-2263)
PHONE..................510 739-1515
Dave Peper, *General Mgr*
Barb Wilson, *Nurse*
EMP: 50
SALES (corp-wide): 122.5MM **Privately Held**
SIC: **8361** Residential care
HQ: Aegis Assisted Living Properties, Llc
220 Concourse Blvd
Santa Rosa CA 95403
707 535-3200

(P-24409)
AEGIS ASSSTED LIVING PRPTS LLC
Also Called: Aegis At Shadowridge
1440 S Melrose Dr, Oceanside
(92056-5394)
PHONE..................760 806-3600
Gregory Case, *Manager*
EMP: 65
SALES (corp-wide): 122.5MM **Privately Held**
SIC: **8361** Home for the aged
HQ: Aegis Assisted Living Properties, Llc
220 Concourse Blvd
Santa Rosa CA 95403
707 535-3200

(P-24410)
AEGIS OF CARMICHAEL
4050 Walnut Ave, Carmichael
(95608-1600)
PHONE..................916 972-1313
Dwane Clark, *President*
Jerry Myer, *COO*
EMP: 60 **EST**: 1999
SALES (est): 2.1MM **Privately Held**
SIC: **8361** Home for the aged

(P-24411)
AEGIS SENIOR COMMUNITIES LLC
Also Called: Aegis of Laguna Niguel
32170 Niguel Rd, Laguna Niguel
(92677-4264)
PHONE..................949 496-8080
Pamela Kerr, *Exec Dir*
EMP: 50
SALES (corp-wide): 122.5MM **Privately Held**
WEB: www.aegisal.com
SIC: **8361** Residential care
PA: Senior Aegis Communities Llc
415 118th Ave Se
Bellevue WA 98005
866 688-5829

(P-24412)
AGEIS LIVING
Also Called: Aegis of San Francisco
2280 Gellert Blvd, South San Francisco
(94080-5411)
PHONE..................650 952-6100
Wayne Clark, *President*
EMP: 50 **EST**: 2010
SALES (est): 808.6K **Privately Held**
SIC: **8361** Residential care

(P-24413)
ALLEN SPEES FAMILY HOMES
524 W Roberts Ave, Fresno (93704-1832)
PHONE..................559 432-3664
Sue Allen, *Partner*
Terry Spees, *Partner*
EMP: 50
SALES (est): 1.2MM **Privately Held**
SIC: **8361** Residential care

(P-24414)
ALTCARE CEDAR CREEK LLC
Also Called: Cedar Creek Alzhimers Dementia
868 Ensenada Ave, Berkeley (94707-1850)
PHONE..................510 527-7282
Terry Carson, *CEO*
Cole Smith,
EMP: 55
SALES (est): 975.3K **Privately Held**
SIC: **8361** Residential care

(P-24415)
AMERICAN BAPTIST HOMES OF WEST
Also Called: San Joaquin Gardens
5555 N Fresno St, Fresno (93710-6006)
PHONE..................559 439-4770
Keli Swales, *Branch Mgr*
Binder Singh, *Nursing Dir*
Joseph Fronteras, *Director*
EMP: 203
SALES (corp-wide): 178.8MM **Privately Held**
WEB: www.abhow.com
SIC: **8361 8051** Home for the aged; skilled
nursing care facilities
HQ: American Baptist Homes Of The West
6120 Stoneridge Mall Rd # 300
Pleasanton CA 94588
925 924-7100

(P-24416)
AMERICAN BAPTIST HOMES OF WEST
Also Called: Piedmont Gardens
110 41st St Ofc, Oakland (94611-5219)
PHONE..................510 654-7172
Reginald Nyles, *Branch Mgr*
Timi Tessaro, *Records Dir*
Roxann King, *Education*
Jeremy Thomas, *Food Svc Dir*
Tony Hobbs, *Director*
EMP: 220
SALES (corp-wide): 178.8MM **Privately Held**
WEB: www.abhow.com
SIC: **8361** Home for the aged
HQ: American Baptist Homes Of The West
6120 Stoneridge Mall Rd # 300
Pleasanton CA 94588
925 924-7100

(P-24417)
ANGEL VIEW INC
Also Called: Angel View Resale Store
454 N Indian Canyon Dr, Palm Springs
(92262-6018)
PHONE..................760 322-2440
Tracy Powers, *General Mgr*
EMP: 50
SALES (corp-wide): 24.9MM **Privately Held**
SIC: **8361** Rehabilitation center, residential: health care incidental
PA: Angel View, Inc.
12379 Miracle Hill Rd
Desert Hot Springs CA 92240
760 329-6471

(P-24418)
ARC INDUSTRIES
5143 Cochran St Ste 93063, Simi Valley
(93063-3064)
PHONE..................805 520-0399
Larry Rice, *Manager*
EMP: 57
SALES (est): 682.5K **Privately Held**
SIC: **8361 8999** Rehabilitation center, residential: health care incidental; services

(P-24419)
ARDCORE SENIOR LIVING
Also Called: Canyon Hills Club
525 S Anaheim Hills Rd, Anaheim
(92807-4721)
PHONE..................714 974-2226
J Bert Sprenger, *Manager*
EMP: 70
SALES (est): 1.8MM
SALES (corp-wide): 17.8B **Privately Held**
SIC: **8361 6513** Home for the aged; apartment building operators
PA: Obayashi Corporation
2-15-2, Konan
Minato-Ku TKY 108-0
357 691-111

(P-24420)
ASPIRANET
Also Called: Sunset Neighborhood Beacon Ctr
3925 Noriega St, San Francisco
(94122-3935)
PHONE..................415 759-3690
Ruby LI, *Manager*
EMP: 58
SALES (corp-wide): 59MM **Privately Held**
WEB: www.verosantes.com
SIC: **8361 8322** Residential care; individual & family services
PA: Aspiranet
400 Oyster Point Blvd # 501
South San Francisco CA 94080
650 866-4080

(P-24421)
ASPIRANET
151 E Canal Dr, Turlock (95380-3901)
PHONE..................209 669-2582
Sharon Salaiz, *Manager*
EMP: 58
SALES (corp-wide): 59MM **Privately Held**
SIC: **8361** Group foster home
PA: Aspiranet
400 Oyster Point Blvd # 501
South San Francisco CA 94080
650 866-4080

(P-24422)
ATKINSON YOUTH SERVICES INC (PA)
1906 El Camino Ave, Sacramento
(95815-2818)
P.O. Box 2755, Carmichael (95609-2755)
PHONE..................916 257-0637
Jim Atkinson, *Exec Dir*
EMP: 100
SQ FT: 2,000
SALES: 4.2MM **Privately Held**
WEB: www.atkinsonyouthservices.com
SIC: **8361** Group foster home

(P-24423)
ATRIA SENIOR LIVING INC
Also Called: Atria Park Pacific Palisades
15441 W Sunset Blvd, Pacific Palisades
(90272-3525)
PHONE..................310 573-9545
Elisa Brown, *Director*
EMP: 60
SQ FT: 27,513
SALES (corp-wide): 3.5B **Publicly Held**
WEB: www.sunrise.com
SIC: **8361** Residential care
HQ: Atria Senior Living Inc.
300 E Market St Ste 100
Louisville KY 40202
-

(P-24424)
ATRIA SENIOR LIVING INC
Also Called: Atria Grand Oaks
22032 Arrowhead Ln, Lake Forest
(92630-2301)
PHONE..................805 370-5400
Evan Granucci, *Branch Mgr*
EMP: 70
SALES (corp-wide): 3.5B **Publicly Held**
SIC: **8361** Home for the aged
HQ: Atria Senior Living Inc.
300 E Market St Ste 100
Louisville KY 40202

(P-24425)
ATRIA SENIOR LIVING GROUP INC
Also Called: Villa Las Posas
24 Las Posas Rd, Camarillo (93010-2780)
PHONE..................805 482-9771
Cyntia Drachenberg, *Director*
EMP: 63 **Privately Held**
WEB: www.atriacom.com
SIC: **8361** Home for the aged
PA: Atria Senior Living Group Inc
300 E Market St Ste 100
Louisville KY 40202

(P-24426)
ATRIA SENIOR LIVING GROUP INC
Also Called: Chateau San Juan
32353 San Juan Creek Rd, San Juan
Capistrano (92675-4254)
PHONE..................949 661-1220
Del Woytek, *Manager*
George Gonzalez, *Food Svc Dir*
Laura Garcia, *Director*
EMP: 109 **Privately Held**
WEB: www.atriacom.com
SIC: **8361** Home for the aged
PA: Atria Senior Living Group Inc
300 E Market St Ste 100
Louisville KY 40202

(P-24427)
ATRIA SENIOR LIVING GROUP INC
Also Called: Montego Heights Lodge
1400 Montego, Walnut Creek
(94598-2950)
PHONE..................925 938-6611
Kathy Moore, *Manager*
Cameron Johnson, *Vice Pres*
Melissa Dunn, *Business Dir*
Cyndi Schrock, *Business Dir*
Deborah Suarez, *Business Dir*
EMP: 55 **Privately Held**
WEB: www.atriacom.com
SIC: **8361** Residential care
PA: Atria Senior Living Group Inc
300 E Market St Ste 100
Louisville KY 40202

(P-24428)
ATRIA SENIOR LIVING GROUP INC
Also Called: Willow Glen Villa
1660 Gaton Dr Ofc, San Jose
(95125-4599)
PHONE..................408 266-1660
Laurie Becker, *Exec Dir*
EMP: 63 **Privately Held**
WEB: www.atriacom.com

SIC: **8361** Residential care
PA: Atria Senior Living Group Inc
300 E Market St Ste 100
Louisville KY 40202

(P-24429)
ATRIA SENIOR LIVING GROUP INC
Also Called: Tamalpais Creek
853 Tamalpais Ave Ofc, Novato
(94947-3052)
PHONE.....................415 892-0944
Jason Englehorn, *Exec Dir*
Lori Gutierrez, *Office Mgr*
EMP: 50 **Privately Held**
WEB: www.atriacom.com
SIC: **8361** Home for the aged
PA: Atria Senior Living Group Inc
300 E Market St Ste 100
Louisville KY 40202
-

(P-24430)
ATRIA SENIOR LIVING GROUP INC
Also Called: El Camino Gardens
2426 Garfield Ave Ofc, Carmichael
(95608-5199)
PHONE.....................916 488-5722
Maryann Peterson, *Director*
Ingrid Weber, *Director*
EMP: 70 **Privately Held**
WEB: www.atriacom.com
SIC: **8361** Residential care
PA: Atria Senior Living Group Inc
300 E Market St Ste 100
Louisville KY 40202

(P-24431)
ATRIA SENIOR LIVING GROUP INC
44600 Monterey Ave Ofc, Palm Desert
(92260-3328)
PHONE.....................760 341-0890
Jim Dunning, *Exec Dir*
James Dunning, *Director*
Mary Hilsabeck, *Director*
Usbaldo Martinez, *Director*
EMP: 75 **Privately Held**
WEB: www.atriacom.com
SIC: **8361** Home for the aged
PA: Atria Senior Living Group Inc
300 E Market St Ste 100
Louisville KY 40202

(P-24432)
AVALON AT NEWPORT LLC
Also Called: Avalon At Newport Beach
393 Hospital Rd, Newport Beach
(92663-3501)
PHONE.....................949 631-3555
Fran Lacas, *Administration*
EMP: 93
SQ FT: 4,562
SALES (corp-wide): 4.2MM **Privately Held**
SIC: **8361** Residential care
PA: Avalon At Newport, Llc
23 Corporate Plaza Dr # 190
Newport Beach CA 92660
949 719-4082

(P-24433)
AVALON GOLDEN GATE LLC
Also Called: Vintage Golden Gate
1601 19th Ave Apt 122, San Francisco
(94122-3469)
PHONE.....................415 664-6264
Eric K Davidson, *Principal*
Vicki R Clark,
Brian J Flornes,
EMP: 77
SALES (est): 5MM **Privately Held**
SIC: **8361** Geriatric residential care

(P-24434)
BAKER PLACES INC (PA)
1000 Brannan St Ste 401, San Francisco
(94103-4888)
PHONE.....................415 864-4655
Jonathan Vernick, *President*
Judith Stevenson, *CFO*

EMP: 200 EST: 1969
SQ FT: 3,000
SALES: 12.5MM **Privately Held**
SIC: **8361** Halfway group home, persons with social or personal problems

(P-24435)
BETHESDA LTHRAN CMMUNITIES INC
5440 W Wren Ave, Visalia (93291-9142)
PHONE.....................559 636-6300
EMP: 57
SALES (corp-wide): 126.8MM **Privately Held**
SIC: **8361** Home for destitute men & women
PA: Bethesda Lutheran Communities, Inc.
600 Hoffmann Dr
Watertown WI 53094
920 261-3050

(P-24436)
BEYER PARK VILLAS LLC
3529 Forest Glenn Dr, Modesto
(95355-1360)
PHONE.....................209 236-1900
Bill Schilz,
Clarence Becker,
Donald Cefaloni,
Harold Johnson,
Nicole Rodriguez,
EMP: 75
SQ FT: 59,000
SALES (est): 3.2MM **Privately Held**
SIC: **8361** Home for the aged

(P-24437)
BHO LLC
5801 Sun Lakes Blvd, Banning
(92220-6507)
PHONE.....................951 845-2220
Terry Raisio,
EMP: 50
SALES (est): 973K **Privately Held**
SIC: **8361** Geriatric residential care

(P-24438)
BOYS REPUBLIC (PA)
Also Called: GIRLS REPUBLIC
1907 Boys Republic Dr, Chino Hills
(91709-5447)
PHONE.....................909 902-6690
Dennis Slattery, *CEO*
Timothy J Kay, *President*
Robert Key, *Vice Pres*
Jeff Seymour, *Vice Pres*
Nadine Bosen, *Admin Sec*
EMP: 150
SQ FT: 173,000
SALES: 13.2MM **Privately Held**
SIC: **8361** Group foster home

(P-24439)
BRETHREN HILLCREST HOMES
2705 Mountain View Dr Ofc, La Verne
(91750-4398)
PHONE.....................909 593-4917
Matthew Neeley, *President*
Barbara Feliciano, *CFO*
Christine Carrasco, *Admin Asst*
Scott Frederick, *Human Res Dir*
Mike Townsend, *Mktg Dir*
EMP: 230
SQ FT: 34,000
SALES: 26.7MM **Privately Held**
WEB: www.livingathillcrest.org
SIC: **8361** **8059** **8051** Rest home, with health care incidental; nursing home, except skilled & intermediate care facility; extended care facility

(P-24440)
BRITTANY HOUSE LLC
5401 E Centralia St, Long Beach
(90808-1452)
PHONE.....................562 421-4717
Colleen Rosatti, *Exec Dir*
EMP: 100
SQ FT: 43,018
SALES (est): 3.2MM
SALES (corp-wide): 36.5MM **Privately Held**
WEB: www.healthcaregrp.com
SIC: **8361** Home for the aged

PA: Activcare Living, Inc.
9619 Chesapeake Dr # 103
San Diego CA 92123
858 565-4424

(P-24441)
BROOKDALE LVING CMMUNITIES INC
Also Called: Atrium of San Jose
1009 Blossom River Way, San Jose
(95123-6304)
PHONE.....................408 445-7770
Michele Merritt, *Exec Dir*
Cynthia King, *Vice Pres*
Sam Ganepour, *Admin Sec*
EMP: 110
SALES (corp-wide): 4.7B **Publicly Held**
WEB: www.parkplace-spokane.com
SIC: **8361** Geriatric residential care
HQ: Brookdale Living Communities, Inc.
515 N State St Ste 1750
Chicago IL 60654
-

(P-24442)
BROOKDALE SENIOR LIVING INC
285 W Central Ave, Brea (92821-3374)
PHONE.....................714 671-7898
Steve Ilten, *Executive*
EMP: 65
SALES (corp-wide): 4.7B **Publicly Held**
SIC: **8361** Residential care
PA: Brookdale Senior Living
111 Westwood Pl Ste 400
Brentwood TN 37027
615 221-2250

(P-24443)
BROOKDALE SENIOR LIVING INC
355 W Grant Line Rd Ofc, Tracy
(95376-2586)
PHONE.....................209 835-1000
EMP: 65
SALES (corp-wide): 4.7B **Publicly Held**
SIC: **8361** Home for the aged
PA: Brookdale Senior Living
111 Westwood Pl Ste 400
Brentwood TN 37027
615 221-2250

(P-24444)
BROTHER BENNO FOUNDATION INC (PA)
Also Called: BROTHER BENNO'S FOUNDATION
970 Vine St Apt 209, Oceanside
(92054-4279)
P.O. Box 308 (92049-0308)
PHONE.....................760 439-1244
Harold Kutler, *President*
Daniel Boone Jr, *Treasurer*
EMP: 82
SQ FT: 5,000
SALES: 3.7MM **Privately Held**
WEB: www.brotherbennos.org
SIC: **8361** **8322** Residential care; individual & family services

(P-24445)
CAL SOUTHERN PRESBT HOMES
Also Called: White Sands of La Jolla Clinic
7450 Olivetas Ave Ofc, La Jolla
(92037-4900)
PHONE.....................858 454-4201
Wendy Matalon, *Branch Mgr*
EMP: 165
SALES (corp-wide): 84.4MM **Privately Held**
WEB: www.scths.com
SIC: **8361** Home for the aged; skilled nursing care facilities
PA: Southern California Presbyterian Homes
516 Burchett St
Glendale CA 91203
818 247-0420

(P-24446)
CAL SOUTHERN PRESBT HOMES
Also Called: Redwood Senior Homes & Svcs
710 W 13th Ave, Escondido (92025-5511)
PHONE.....................760 747-4306
Gary Boriero, *Manager*
EMP: 161
SQ FT: 8,552
SALES (corp-wide): 84.4MM **Privately Held**
WEB: www.scths.com
SIC: **8361** Home for the aged
PA: Southern California Presbyterian Homes
516 Burchett St
Glendale CA 91203
818 247-0420

(P-24447)
CAL SOUTHERN PRESBT HOMES
Also Called: Redwood Town Court
500 E Valley Pkwy Ofc, Escondido
(92025-3073)
PHONE.....................760 737-5110
Les Curtis, *Manager*
EMP: 89
SALES (corp-wide): 84.4MM **Privately Held**
WEB: www.scths.com
SIC: **8361** Home for the aged
PA: Southern California Presbyterian Homes
516 Burchett St
Glendale CA 91203
818 247-0420

(P-24448)
CALIFORNIA FRIENDS HOMES
Also Called: QUAKER GARDENS
12151 Dale Ave, Stanton (90680-3889)
PHONE.....................714 530-9100
Randy Brown, *CEO*
Gina Kolb, *Exec Dir*
Dixie Mathers, *Exec Dir*
Glenda Hementiza, *Managing Dir*
Claudia Acosta, *Food Svc Dir*
EMP: 315
SQ FT: 10,000
SALES: 16.4MM **Privately Held**
WEB: www.quakergardens.com
SIC: **8361** **8051** Home for the aged; convalescent home with continuous nursing care

(P-24449)
CALIFORNIA PEO HOME
Also Called: Marguerite Gardens
849 Foothill Blvd Ste 8, La Canada Flintridge (91011-3368)
PHONE.....................626 300-0400
Bessie Ang, *Principal*
Lenita Castillo, *Nursing Dir*
Johee Lee, *Manager*
Joohee Lee, *Manager*
Debra Mecka, *Manager*
EMP: 95
SQ FT: 77,343
SALES: 4.3MM **Privately Held**
SIC: **8361** Home for the aged

(P-24450)
CALIFRNIA-NEVADA METHDST HOMES (PA)
Also Called: FOREST HILL MANOR
201 19th St Ste 100, Oakland
(94612-4258)
PHONE.....................510 893-8989
Robert E Hubbard, *CEO*
Robert Leeper, *Vice Pres*
Loretta Heden, *Admin Sec*
EMP: 217 EST: 1954
SQ FT: 6,000
SALES: 19.6MM **Privately Held**
WEB: www.foresthillmanor.com
SIC: **8361** **8051** Geriatric residential care; convalescent home with continuous nursing care

(P-24451)
CARE ASSOCIATES INC
Also Called: Helen Evans Home For Children
15125 Gale Ave, Hacienda Heights
(91745-1407)
PHONE.........................626 330-4048
Paula De Lisio, *President*
EMP: 60 EST: 1998
SQ FT: 9,698
SALES: 2.7MM **Privately Held**
SIC: 8361 Children's home; home for the
mentally retarded

(P-24452)
CARLTON SENIOR LIVING INC
1075 Fulton Ave, Sacramento
(95825-4275)
PHONE.........................916 971-4800
Timothy Macdonald, *Branch Mgr*
EMP: 144
SALES (corp-wide): 29.6MM **Privately
Held**
SIC: 8361 8052 8051 Residential care; in-
termediate care facilities; skilled nursing
care facilities
PA: Senior Carlton Living Inc
4005 Port Chicago Hwy # 120
Concord CA 94520
925 338-2434

(P-24453)
CARSON SENIOR ASSISTED
LIVING
345 E Carson St, Carson (90745-2709)
PHONE.........................310 830-4010
Fax: 310 830-0264
EMP: 75
SALES (est): 3.3MM **Privately Held**
SIC: 8361

(P-24454)
CASA DE AMPARO (PA)
325 Buena Creek Rd, San Marcos
(92069-9679)
PHONE.........................760 754-5500
Sharon Delphenich, *Exec Dir*
Celeste Lampro, *Volunteer Dir*
Debbie Slattery, *Treasurer*
Tamara Fleck-Myers, *Exec Dir*
Tawny Grant, *Program Mgr*
EMP: 80
SQ FT: 25,000
SALES: 9.7MM **Privately Held**
WEB: www.casadeamparo.org
SIC: 8361 8351 Residential care; child
day care services

(P-24455)
CASA DE LAS CAMPANAS INC
(PA)
18655 W Bernardo Dr # 489, San Diego
(92127-3099)
PHONE.........................858 451-9152
Jill Sorenson, *Exec Dir*
David Johnson, *CFO*
Robert L Reeves, *Chairman*
Maria Rivera, *Officer*
Alecia Dimario, *Administration*
EMP: 132
SQ FT: 709,627
SALES: 37.4MM **Privately Held**
SIC: 8361 8052 8051 6513 Home for the
aged; intermediate care facilities; skilled
nursing care facilities; apartment building
operators

(P-24456)
CASA-PACIFICA INC
Also Called: Freedom Properties
2200 W Acacia Ave Ofc, Hemet
(92545-3737)
PHONE.........................951 658-3369
Mary Ann Casino, *Director*
Suzanne Kaye, *Marketing Staff*
EMP: 300
SALES (corp-wide): 18.7MM **Privately
Held**
WEB: www.fmcwest.com
SIC: 8361 8059 Geriatric residential care;
rest home, with health care
PA: Casa-Pacifica, Inc
23442 El Toro Rd
San Juan Capistrano CA 92675
949 489-0430

(P-24457)
CASA-PACIFICA INC
Also Called: Freedom Properties Village
2400 W Acacia Ave, Hemet (92545-3743)
PHONE.........................951 766-5116
Valeria Machain, *General Mgr*
Oscar Ponce, *Director*
EMP: 100
SALES (corp-wide): 18.7MM **Privately
Held**
WEB: www.fmcwest.com
SIC: 8361 8052 8051 6513 Home for the
aged; intermediate care facilities; skilled
nursing care facilities; apartment building
operators
PA: Casa-Pacifica, Inc
23442 El Toro Rd
San Juan Capistrano CA 92675
949 489-0430

(P-24458)
CASABLANCA ALZHEIMERS
RESID
Also Called: Casablanca Alzheimer's Care
158 Rockaway Rd, Oak View (93022-9306)
PHONE.........................805 649-5143
Nilson Froula, *President*
Laurie Froula, *Partner*
EMP: 60
SQ FT: 12,000
SALES (est): 2.8MM **Privately Held**
SIC: 8361 Rest home, with health care in-
cidental

(P-24459)
CENTINELA VALLEY CARE
CENTER
950 S Flower St, Inglewood (90301-4186)
PHONE.........................310 674-3216
William A Nelson, *President*
EMP: 200
SALES (est): 5MM **Privately Held**
SIC: 8361 8059 Home for the aged; con-
valescent home

(P-24460)
CENTRAL CAL NIKKEI
FOUNDATION
Also Called: VINTAGE GARDENS
540 S Peach Ave, Fresno (93727-3957)
PHONE.........................559 237-4006
Melvin K Renge, *President*
Louis Gebbia, *Exec Dir*
Floyd Green, *Director*
EMP: 52 EST: 1989
SALES: 2.9MM **Privately Held**
SIC: 8361 Residential care

(P-24461)
CHAMBERLAINS CHILDREN
CTR INC
1850 Cienega Rd, Hollister (95023-5516)
P.O. Box 1269 (95024-1269)
PHONE.........................831 636-2121
Robert Freiri, *Exec Dir*
EMP: 60
SALES: 2.9MM **Privately Held**
WEB: www.chamberlaincc.org
SIC: 8361 Residential care for children

(P-24462)
CHARLEE FAMILY CARE
136 E Sixth St, Beaumont (92223-2146)
PHONE.........................951 845-3588
Richard E Rios, *Principal*
Diane Eldred, *CFO*
EMP: 79
SALES: 3.4MM **Privately Held**
SIC: 8361 Residential care

(P-24463)
CHILDHELP INC
Also Called: Child Help Head Start Center
14700 Manzanita Rd, Beaumont
(92223-3026)
P.O. Box 247 (92223-0247)
PHONE.........................951 845-6737
Klara Pakozdi, *Manager*
Diana Correa, *Exec Dir*
EMP: 165
SALES (corp-wide): 36.6MM **Privately
Held**
WEB: www.childhelpusa.com
SIC: 8361 Children's home

PA: Childhelp, Inc.
4350 E Camelback Rd F250
Phoenix AZ 85018
480 922-8212

(P-24464)
CHILDNET YOUTH & FMLY SVCS
INC
Also Called: Behavioral Health Svcs Dept
5150 E Pacific Cst Hwy # 100, Long Beach
(90804-3312)
PHONE.........................562 492-9983
Cathy Hughes, *CEO*
EMP: 65
SALES (corp-wide): 23.8MM **Privately
Held**
WEB: www.childnet.net
SIC: 8361 8322 Juvenile correctional facil-
ities; family counseling services
PA: Childnet Youth And Family Services,
Inc.
4155 Outer Traffic Cir
Long Beach CA 90804
562 498-5500

(P-24465)
CHILDRENS BUREAU
SOUTHERN CAL (PA)
1910 Magnolia Ave, Los Angeles
(90007-1220)
PHONE.........................213 342-0100
Alex Morales, *President*
Sona Chandwani, *CFO*
Ron Brown, *Officer*
Stephanie Enano, *Associate Dir*
Rolando Salvador, *Facilities Mgr*
EMP: 107 EST: 1904
SQ FT: 43,000
SALES: 30.6MM **Privately Held**
SIC: 8361 Residential care for children

(P-24466)
CHILDRENS HOME OF
STOCKTON
430 N Pilgrim St, Stockton (95205-4428)
PHONE.........................209 466-0853
Michael Dutra, *Principal*
EMP: 90
SQ FT: 10,000
SALES: 8.6MM **Privately Held**
WEB: www.chsstk.com
SIC: 8361 8211 Children's home; private
combined elementary & secondary school

(P-24467)
CHILDRENS HOME SOUTHERN
CAL (PA)
22455 Victory Blvd, West Hills
(91307-3729)
PHONE.........................818 592-2960
Jorge Marquez, *Exec Dir*
EMP: 50
SALES: 4MM **Privately Held**
SIC: 8361 Home for the emotionally dis-
turbed

(P-24468)
CHILDRENS RECVG HM
SACRAMENTO
3555 Auburn Blvd, Sacramento
(95821-2071)
PHONE.........................916 482-2370
David Ballard, *CEO*
Rich Bryan, *CFO*
Patricia Santiago, *Manager*
Stephanie Kvasager, *Supervisor*
EMP: 160
SQ FT: 26,000
SALES: 10.2MM **Privately Held**
WEB: www.crhkids.org
SIC: 8361 Children's home

(P-24469)
CHILDRENS VLG OF SONOMA
CNTY
1321 Lia Ln, Santa Rosa (95404-8087)
P.O. Box 2025 (95405-0025)
PHONE.........................707 566-7044
A Utarid, *Exec Dir*
Anjana Utarid, *Principal*
EMP: 50
SALES: 1MM **Privately Held**
SIC: 8361 Group foster home

(P-24470)
CHURCH OF VLY RTRMENT
HMES INC
Also Called: VALLEY VILLAGE
390 N Winchester Blvd, Santa Clara
(95050-6563)
PHONE.........................408 241-7750
Martha Ayala, *President*
Angela Garcia, *Supervisor*
EMP: 52
SALES: 5.2MM **Privately Held**
SIC: 8361 Home for the aged

(P-24471)
CLAREMONT HOUSE
INCORPORATED
Also Called: Claremont Retirement MGT
4500 Gilbert St, Oakland (94611-4657)
PHONE.........................510 658-9266
Douglas R Gill, *President*
Justin Gill, *Exec Dir*
EMP: 75
SALES: 6MM **Privately Held**
SIC: 8361 Home for the aged

(P-24472)
CLIFF VIEW TERRACE INC
Also Called: Mission Terrace
623 W Junipero St, Santa Barbara
(93105-4213)
PHONE.........................805 682-7443
Eve Murphy, *Manager*
EMP: 100
SALES (corp-wide): 13MM **Privately
Held**
SIC: 8361 8051 Home for the aged; con-
valescent home with continuous nursing
care
PA: Cliff View Terrace Inc
1020 Cliff Dr
Santa Barbara CA 93109
805 963-7556

(P-24473)
COMMUNITY HOUSING INC
Also Called: Lytton Garden II
437 Webster St, Palo Alto (94301-1242)
PHONE.........................650 328-3300
Gery Yearout, *President*
Jonathan Casey, *Vice Pres*
EMP: 50
SALES (est): 7.3MM **Privately Held**
SIC: 8361 Home for the aged

(P-24474)
CONGREGATION OF POOR
SISTERS
Also Called: Nazareth House
2121 N 1st St, Fresno (93703-2301)
PHONE.........................559 237-3444
Sister Rose, *Director*
Leah Santos, *Executive*
Frances Delatorre, *Education*
Kevin Nguyen, *Director*
EMP: 84
SQ FT: 58,644
SALES (corp-wide): 4.2MM **Privately
Held**
SIC: 8361 Home for the aged
PA: Nazareth House
169-175 Hammersmith Road
London W6 8D
208 748-3549

(P-24475)
CONTRA COSTA ARC
Also Called: Commercial Support Services
1420 Regatta Blvd, Richmond
(94804-4579)
PHONE.........................510 233-7303
Betty Jo Dubois, *Director*
EMP: 90
SALES (corp-wide): 19.2MM **Privately
Held**
WEB: www.ccarealtors.com
SIC: 8361 Home for the mentally retarded
PA: Contra Costa Arc
1340 Arnold Dr Ste 127
Martinez CA 94553
925 646-4690

P
R
O
D
U
C
T
S

&

S
V
C
S

(P-24476)
CORECARE I I I
Also Called: Morningside of Fullerton
800 Morningside Dr, Fullerton
(92835-3597)
PHONE..............................714 256-8000
Carl Wilkins, *Administration*
EMP: 130
SQ FT: 24,000
SALES (est): 6.9MM **Privately Held**
WEB: www.msfpv.com
SIC: 8361 8052 Home for the aged; intermediate care facilities

(P-24477)
COUNSELING AND RESEARCH ASSOC (PA)
Also Called: MASADA HOMES
108 W Victoria St, Gardena (90248-3523)
P.O. Box 47001 (90247-6801)
PHONE..............................310 715-2020
George Igi, *Chief Mktg Ofcr*
Bernard Smith, *COO*
Richard Coleman, *Executive*
Luis Maimoni, *Internal Med*
John McCullough, *Director*
EMP: 220
SQ FT: 2,500
SALES: 15.9MM **Privately Held**
SIC: 8361 Children's home

(P-24478)
COUNSELING AND RESEARCH ASSOC
Also Called: Masada Homes Foster Fmly Agcy
314 E Avenue K4, Lancaster (93535-4689)
PHONE..............................661 726-5500
Rick Colman, *Branch Mgr*
EMP: 74
SALES (corp-wide): 15.9MM **Privately Held**
SIC: 8361 Children's home
PA: Counseling And Research Associates
108 W Victoria St
Gardena CA 90248
310 715-2020

(P-24479)
COUNTY OF LOS ANGELES
1605 Eastlake Ave, Los Angeles
(90033-1009)
PHONE..............................323 226-8611
Richard Shumsky, *Manager*
EMP: 62 **Privately Held**
WEB: www.co.la.ca.us
SIC: 8361 9111 Juvenile correctional facilities; executive offices
PA: County Of Los Angeles
500 W Temple St Ste 437
Los Angeles CA 90012
213 974-1101

(P-24480)
COUNTY OF LOS ANGELES
Also Called: San Fernando Juvenile Hall
16350 Filbert St, Sylmar (91342-1002)
PHONE..............................818 364-2011
Dan Torres, *Superintendent*
EMP: 69 **Privately Held**
WEB: www.co.la.ca.us
SIC: 8361 9223 8093 Juvenile correctional home; correctional institutions; ; mental health clinic, outpatient
PA: County Of Los Angeles
500 W Temple St Ste 437
Los Angeles CA 90012
213 974-1101

(P-24481)
COUNTY OF LOS ANGELES
4024 Durfee Ave Rm 225, El Monte
(91732-2510)
PHONE..............................626 455-4700
Michael Mills, *Manager*
EMP: 62 **Privately Held**
WEB: www.co.la.ca.us
SIC: 8361 9111 Juvenile correctional home; county supervisors' & executives' offices
PA: County Of Los Angeles
500 W Temple St Ste 437
Los Angeles CA 90012
213 974-1101

(P-24482)
COUNTY OF RIVERSIDE
Also Called: Juvenile Hall
47 665 Oasis St, Indio (92201)
PHONE..............................760 863-7600
Rick Quinata, *Director*
EMP: 100 **Privately Held**
SIC: 8361 9441 Juvenile correctional home; administration of social & manpower programs
PA: County Of Riverside
4080 Lemon St Fl 11
Riverside CA 92501
951 955-1110

(P-24483)
COUNTY OF SAN BERNARDINO
Also Called: Children Services
860 E Gilbert St, San Bernardino
(92415-0002)
PHONE..............................909 387-0535
Allyson Williams, *Manager*
EMP: 60 **Privately Held**
SIC: 8361 9441 Juvenile correctional facilities; rest home, with health care incidental; administration of social & manpower programs
PA: County Of San Bernardino
385 N Arrowhead Ave
San Bernardino CA 92415
909 387-3841

(P-24484)
COURTYARDS AT PINE CREEK INC
1081 Mohr Ln, Concord (94518-3757)
PHONE..............................925 798-3900
Patricia Mead, *Executive*
Kirt Hamburg, *President*
EMP: 50
SALES (est): 2.2MM **Privately Held**
SIC: 8361 Residential care

(P-24485)
COVENANT HOUSE CALIFORNIA
Also Called: CHC
1325 N Western Ave, Los Angeles
(90027-5615)
PHONE..............................323 461-3131
Luz Juan, *CEO*
Luz Buan, *Officer*
Alana Weinroth, *Officer*
George Lozano, *Principal*
Patrick S McCabe, *Exec Dir*
EMP: 150
SQ FT: 16,000
SALES: 10.3MM **Privately Held**
WEB: www.covenanthousecalifornia.net
SIC: 8361 Children's home

(P-24486)
COVENANT RTIREMENT COMMUNITIES
Also Called: Covenant Village of Turlock
2125 N Olive Ave Ofc, Turlock
(95382-1947)
PHONE..............................209 632-9976
Dwayne Gabrielson, *Administration*
EMP: 130
SALES (corp-wide): 3.3MM **Privately Held**
SIC: 8361 8052 8051 Rest home, with health care incidental; intermediate care facilities; skilled nursing care facilities
HQ: Covenant Retirement Communities
5700 Old Orchard Rd # 100
Skokie IL 60077

(P-24487)
COVIA COMMUNITIES
Also Called: St Paul's Towers
100 Bay Pl Ofc, Oakland (94610-4422)
PHONE..............................510 835-4700
Christopher Iechien, *Exec Dir*
Tristan Piper, *Hlthcr Dir*
Rob Anzilotti, *Director*
EMP: 180
SALES (corp-wide): 135.9MM **Privately Held**
SIC: 8361 8052 8051 Home for the aged; intermediate care facilities; skilled nursing care facilities

PA: Covia Communities
2185 N Calif Blvd Ste 215
Walnut Creek CA 94596
925 956-7400

(P-24488)
COVIA COMMUNITIES
Also Called: Canterbury Woods
651 Sinex Ave, Pacific Grove (93950-4253)
PHONE..............................831 373-3111
Norma Brenbella, *Director*
Stella McNish, *Human Res Dir*
Rowena Perez, *Education*
Tammy Brooks, *Hlthcr Dir*
Geozen Snaer, *Director*
EMP: 90
SALES (corp-wide): 135.9MM **Privately Held**
SIC: 8361 Home for the aged
PA: Covia Communities
2185 N Calif Blvd Ste 215
Walnut Creek CA 94596
925 956-7400

(P-24489)
COVIA COMMUNITIES
Also Called: Spring Lake Village
5555 Montgomery Dr, Santa Rosa
(95409-8846)
P.O. Box 1105, Boyes Hot Springs (95416-1105)
PHONE..............................707 538-8400
Sharon York, *Exec Dir*
Renee Hayward, *Social Dir*
Sharon Eldridge, *Administration*
Liz Green, *Director*
EMP: 300
SALES (corp-wide): 135.9MM **Privately Held**
SIC: 8361 6531 8052 8051 Home for the aged; real estate managers; intermediate care facilities; skilled nursing care facilities
PA: Covia Communities
2185 N Calif Blvd Ste 215
Walnut Creek CA 94596
925 956-7400

(P-24490)
COVIA COMMUNITIES
Also Called: San Francisco Towers
1661 Pine St Apt 911, San Francisco
(94109-0410)
PHONE..............................415 776-0500
Donna Teandler, *Branch Mgr*
EMP: 139
SALES (corp-wide): 135.9MM **Privately Held**
SIC: 8361 8052 8051 Home for the aged; intermediate care facilities; skilled nursing care facilities
PA: Covia Communities
2185 N Calif Blvd Ste 215
Walnut Creek CA 94596
925 956-7400

(P-24491)
CREATIVE ALTERNATIVES
2855 Geer Rd Ste A, Turlock (95382-1133)
PHONE..............................209 668-9361
Stephanie Biddle, *CEO*
EMP: 220
SQ FT: 40,000
SALES: 16MM **Privately Held**
SIC: 8361 8211 8322 Children's home; private special education school; child related social services

(P-24492)
CREATIVE LIVING OPTIONS INC
2945 Ramco St Ste 120, West Sacramento
(95691-5998)
PHONE..............................916 372-2102
Joan Schmidt, *CEO*
Mary Anne Delaney, *Finance Dir*
EMP: 115
SALES: 3MM **Privately Held**
WEB: www.creativelivingoptions.com
SIC: 8361 Home for the physically handicapped

(P-24493)
CRESTWOOD BEHAVIORAL HLTH INC
Also Called: 107 San Jose Mhrc
1425 Fruitdale Ave, San Jose
(95128-3234)
PHONE..............................408 275-1067
John Suggs, *Branch Mgr*
Dancey Conger, *VP Finance*
EMP: 85
SALES (corp-wide): 171.2MM **Privately Held**
WEB: www.dreamcatch.us
SIC: 8361 8063 7389 Halfway group home, persons with social or personal problems; psychiatric hospitals; personal service agents, brokers & bureaus
PA: Crestwood Behavioral Health, Inc.
520 Capitol Mall Ste 800
Sacramento CA 95814
510 651-1244

(P-24494)
CRESTWOOD BEHAVIORAL HLTH INC
Also Called: 120 Fremont Snf
3062 Churn Creek Rd, Redding
(96002-2124)
PHONE..............................530 221-0976
Nicoletta Groff, *Administration*
EMP: 80
SQ FT: 15,000
SALES (corp-wide): 171.2MM **Privately Held**
WEB: www.dreamcatch.us
SIC: 8361 8051 Halfway group home, persons with social or personal problems; skilled nursing care facilities
PA: Crestwood Behavioral Health, Inc.
520 Capitol Mall Ste 800
Sacramento CA 95814
510 651-1244

(P-24495)
CRESTWOOD BEHAVIORAL HLTH INC
Also Called: 134 Alameda Snf
4303 Stevenson Blvd, Fremont
(94538-2645)
PHONE..............................510 651-1244
Leeann Labrie, *Administration*
EMP: 150
SQ FT: 33,790
SALES (corp-wide): 171.2MM **Privately Held**
WEB: www.dreamcatch.us
SIC: 8361 8069 Halfway group home, persons with social or personal problems; specialty hospitals, except psychiatric
PA: Crestwood Behavioral Health, Inc.
520 Capitol Mall Ste 800
Sacramento CA 95814
510 651-1244

(P-24496)
CRESTWOOD BEHAVIORAL HLTH INC
Also Called: 152 Vallejo Rcfe
115 Oddstad Dr, Vallejo (94589-2520)
PHONE..............................707 552-0215
Minda Bunnggay, *Manager*
Rebecca Best, *Director*
EMP: 150
SALES (corp-wide): 171.2MM **Privately Held**
WEB: www.dreamcatch.us
SIC: 8361 8063 8051 Halfway group home, persons with social or personal problems; psychiatric hospitals; skilled nursing care facilities
PA: Crestwood Behavioral Health, Inc.
520 Capitol Mall Ste 800
Sacramento CA 95814
510 651-1244

(P-24497)
CRESTWOOD BEHAVIORAL HLTH INC
Also Called: 120 Fremont Snf
2171 Mowry Ave, Fremont (94538-1717)
PHONE..............................510 793-8383
Janet Timble, *Superintendent*
EMP: 100
SQ FT: 10,000

SALES (corp-wide): 171.2MM **Privately Held**
WEB: www.dreamcatch.us
SIC: **8361** 8063 8052 8069 Halfway group home, persons with social or personal problems; psychiatric hospitals; intermediate care facilities; specialty hospitals, except psychiatric
PA: Crestwood Behavioral Health, Inc.
520 Capitol Mall Ste 800
Sacramento CA 95814
510 651-1244

(P-24498)
CRI-HELP INC (PA)
Also Called: CRI HELP DRUG REHABILITATION
11027 Burbank Blvd, North Hollywood (91601-2431)
P.O. Box 899 (91603-0899)
PHONE.................................818 985-8323
Jack Bernstein, *President*
Markus Sola, *Ch of Bd*
Anthony Edmonson, *Corp Secy*
Kim Long, *Program Mgr*
Shirley Salguero, *Project Mgr*
EMP: 101
SQ FT: 40,000
SALES: 6.8MM **Privately Held**
WEB: www.cri-help.org
SIC: **8361** 8069 Rehabilitation center, residential: health care incidental; drug addiction rehabilitation hospital

(P-24499)
CROWN COVE SENIOR CARE CMNTY
3901 E Coast Hwy Ofc, Corona Del Mar (92625-5504)
PHONE.................................949 760-2800
Sanford Fleschman, *Exec Dir*
EMP: 70
SALES (est): 2.7MM **Privately Held**
SIC: **8361** Residential care

(P-24500)
DAVID AND MARGARET HOME INC
Also Called: DAVID & MARGARET YOUTH AND FAM
1350 3rd St, La Verne (91750-5299)
PHONE.................................909 596-5921
Arun Tolia, *President*
Cindy Walkenbach, *President*
Timothy Evans, *Treasurer*
Sabina Sullivan, *Vice Pres*
Charles C Rich, *Exec Dir*
EMP: 240
SQ FT: 40,000
SALES: 15.7MM **Privately Held**
WEB: www.dmhome.org
SIC: **8361** 8322 Home for the emotionally disturbed; individual & family services

(P-24501)
DAYBREAK CARE CENTER (PA)
9040 Sunland Blvd, Sun Valley (91352-2049)
PHONE.................................818 504-6154
Robert Nydam, *President*
Linda Nydam, *CFO*
EMP: 50
SALES (est): 5.2MM **Privately Held**
SIC: **8361** Residential care for the handicapped

(P-24502)
DELANCEY STREET FOUNDATION (PA)
Also Called: Delancey Street Coach Service
600 The Embarcadero, San Francisco (94107-2116)
PHONE.................................415 957-9800
Mimi Silbert, *President*
Jerry Raymond, *Treasurer*
Jeri Raymond, *Accounting Mgr*
EMP: 400 EST: 1971
SQ FT: 325,000
SALES (est): 50.8MM **Privately Held**
SIC: **8361** 5199 8322 4212 Rehabilitation center, residential: health care incidental; advertising specialties; individual & family services; moving services; eating places; caterers

(P-24503)
DESERT MANOR CARE CENTER LP
8515 Cholla Ave, Yucca Valley (92284-4247)
PHONE.................................760 365-0717
Rich Thomas, *CFO*
Sylvia Sanchez-Figueroa, *Administration*
EMP: 70 EST: 2008
SALES: 3.4MM **Privately Held**
SIC: **8361** 8059 8051 Home for the aged; nursing home, except skilled & intermediate care facility; skilled nursing care facilities

(P-24504)
DEVELOPMENTAL SVCS CONTINUUM
7944 Golden Ave, Lemon Grove (91945-1810)
PHONE.................................619 460-7333
Elaine Lewis, *President*
Cecelia Ramsey, *Exec Dir*
EMP: 75
SALES: 2.9MM **Privately Held**
SIC: **8361** Group foster home

(P-24505)
DIVERSIFIED HEALTH SVCS DEL
Also Called: Terraces At Par Marino
2585 E Washington Blvd, Pasadena (91107-1446)
PHONE.................................626 798-6753
Maru Cohen, *Director*
EMP: 50
SALES (corp-wide): 5.3MM **Privately Held**
SIC: **8361** 8059 Home for the aged; convalescent home
PA: Diversified Health Services (Del)
136 Washington Ave
Richmond CA 94801
510 231-6200

(P-24506)
DOMINICAN HOSPITAL FOUNDATION
Also Called: Dominican Rehab Services
610 Frederick St, Santa Cruz (95062-2203)
PHONE.................................831 457-7057
Debbie Hite, *Branch Mgr*
EMP: 200
SALES (corp-wide): 6.7B **Privately Held**
SIC: **8361** 8093 Rehabilitation center, residential: health care incidental; rehabilitation center, outpatient treatment
HQ: Dominican Hospital Foundation
1555 Soquel Dr
Santa Cruz CA 95065
831 462-7700

(P-24507)
DREAM HOME CARE INC
3939 Atlantic Ave Ste 213, Long Beach (90807-3535)
PHONE.................................562 595-9021
Cora Manalang, *CEO*
Reynaldo David, *COO*
Hazel Manalang, *CFO*
Maricris Ocampo, *Admin Asst*
EMP: 60
SALES: 2.4MM **Privately Held**
SIC: **8361** Group foster home

(P-24508)
DREAMCTCHERS EMPWERMENT NETWRK (PA)
Also Called: CRESTWOOD BEHAVIORAL HEALTH
7590 Shoreline Dr Ste B, Stockton (95219-5455)
P.O. Box 7877 (95267-0877)
PHONE.................................209 478-5291
Maria Stefanou, *Manager*
George Lytal, *President*
Lori Blackburn, *Treasurer*
EMP: 590 EST: 1970
SQ FT: 1,500
SALES: 1.4MM **Privately Held**
WEB: www.dreamcatch.us
SIC: **8361** Halfway group home, persons with social or personal problems

(P-24509)
DREAMCTCHERS EMPWERMENT NETWRK
Also Called: Rosewood Convalescent Hospital
1911 Oak Park Blvd, Pleasant Hill (94523-4601)
PHONE.................................925 935-6630
Maggie Yousess, *Administration*
EMP: 111
SALES (corp-wide): 1.4MM **Privately Held**
WEB: www.dreamcatch.us
SIC: **8361** 8051 8059 Halfway group home, persons with social or personal problems; skilled nursing care facilities; convalescent home
PA: Dreamcatchers Empowerment Network
7590 Shoreline Dr Ste B
Stockton CA 95219
209 478-5291

(P-24510)
DREAMCTCHERS EMPWERMENT NETWRK
Elmhaven Convelescent Hospital
6940 Pacific Ave, Stockton (95207-2602)
PHONE.................................209 477-4817
Mike Blaufus, *Principal*
EMP: 100
SALES (corp-wide): 1.4MM **Privately Held**
WEB: www.dreamcatch.us
SIC: **8361** 8051 8052 Halfway group home, persons with social or personal problems; skilled nursing care facilities; intermediate care facilities
PA: Dreamcatchers Empowerment Network
7590 Shoreline Dr Ste B
Stockton CA 95219
209 478-5291

(P-24511)
E & S RSIDENTIAL CARE SVCS LLC
6083 N Marks Ave, Fresno (93711-1600)
PHONE.................................559 275-3555
Stephanie Hendricks, *Mng Member*
Eddie Gilbert, *Mng Member*
EMP: 100
SALES (est): 8.1MM **Privately Held**
SIC: **8361** Residential care for the handicapped

(P-24512)
E R I T INC (PA)
251 Airport Rd, Oceanside (92058-1201)
PHONE.................................760 433-6024
Cheryl Kilmer, *Exec Dir*
William E Mara, *Asst Director*
EMP: 85
SQ FT: 15,000
SALES: 17.1MM **Privately Held**
WEB: www.teriinc.org
SIC: **8361** Home for the mentally retarded

(P-24513)
E R I T INC
Also Called: Our Way
251 Airport Rd, Oceanside (92058-1201)
PHONE.................................760 721-1706
Cheryl Kilmer, *Principal*
EMP: 250
SALES (corp-wide): 17.1MM **Privately Held**
WEB: www.teriinc.org
SIC: **8361** Home for the mentally retarded
PA: E R I T Inc
251 Airport Rd
Oceanside CA 92058
760 433-6024

(P-24514)
EDGEWOOD CTR FOR CHILDRENS (PA)
1801 Vicente St, San Francisco (94116-2923)
PHONE.................................415 681-3211
Lynn Dolce, *CEO*
Anita Adams, *Partner*
Ginger Mendola, *Partner*
Julia Timmons, *Partner*
Larry Holguin, *Principal*
EMP: 320 EST: 1850
SQ FT: 100,000

SALES: 30.5MM **Privately Held**
WEB: www.edgewoodcenter.org
SIC: **8361** 8211 8322 8093 Home for the emotionally disturbed; specialty education; child related social services; specialty outpatient clinics

(P-24515)
EES RESIDENTIAL GROUP HOMES
5369 Camden Ave Ste 280, San Jose (95124-5856)
PHONE.................................408 265-8780
Richard Shanley, *Exec Dir*
Edward Eldefonso, *Ch of Bd*
EMP: 55
SALES: 1.3MM **Privately Held**
SIC: **8361** 8322 Juvenile correctional facilities; child related social services

(P-24516)
ELDER CARE ALLIANCE CAMARILLO
Also Called: ALMA VIA OF CAMARILLO
1301 Marina Village Pkwy # 210, Alameda (94501-1049)
PHONE.................................510 769-2700
Jesse Jantzen, *CEO*
Jerry Cooper, *Director*
EMP: 60
SALES: 5.7MM **Privately Held**
SIC: **8361** Home for the aged

(P-24517)
ENCOMPASS HEALTH CORPORATION
Also Called: HealthSouth
5001 Commerce Dr, Bakersfield (93309-0648)
PHONE.................................661 323-5500
Rosa Arriola, *Manager*
Robert Mosesian, *Controller*
Lori Brackett, *Human Res Dir*
Kathy Szura, *Nursing Dir*
EMP: 200
SALES (corp-wide): 3.9B **Publicly Held**
WEB: www.healthsouth.com
SIC: **8361** 8069 Rehabilitation center, residential: health care incidental; specialty hospitals, except psychiatric
PA: Encompass Health Corporation
9001 Liberty Pkwy
Birmingham AL 35242
205 967-7116

(P-24518)
ENSIGN GROUP INC
1405 E Main St, Santa Maria (93454-4801)
PHONE.................................805 925-8713
Shawn Taylor, *Branch Mgr*
EMP: 237
SALES (corp-wide): 1.8B **Publicly Held**
SIC: **8361** 6513 Geriatric residential care; retirement hotel operation
PA: The Ensign Group Inc
27101 Puerta Real Ste 450
Mission Viejo CA 92691
949 487-9500

(P-24519)
EPISCOPAL SENIOR COMMUNITIES
Also Called: Los Gatos Meadows
110 Wood Rd Ofc, Los Gatos (95030-6799)
PHONE.................................408 354-0211
Tina Heany, *Exec Dir*
Jan McAnelly, *Social Dir*
Cheryl Wilson, *Office Mgr*
Annie Tseng, *Food Svc Dir*
Alex Gerasimov, *Director*
EMP: 120
SALES (corp-wide): 135.9MM **Privately Held**
SIC: **8361** Home for the aged
PA: Covia Communities
2185 N Calif Blvd Ste 215
Walnut Creek CA 94596
925 956-7400

(P-24520)
ESKATON
11390 Coloma Rd Ofc, Gold River (95670-6324)
PHONE.................................916 852-7900

PRODUCTS & SVCS

Tonae Hasik, *Manager*
David Van Reusen, *Administration*
Mark Stull, *Director*
Merari Garcia, *Manager*
EMP: 60
SALES (est): 1.6MM
SALES (corp-wide): 4.3MM **Privately Held**
SIC: 8361 Residential care
PA: Eskaton
5105 Manzanita Ave Ste D
Carmichael CA 95608
916 334-0296

(P-24521)
ESKATON LODGE
22 Cadillac Dr Apt 301, Sacramento
(95825-5413)
PHONE..........................916 789-0326
Vicky Cross, *Director*
Stephanie Watson, *Principal*
Nathan Hayduk, *Hlthcr Dir*
EMP: 50
SALES (est): 1.4MM **Privately Held**
SIC: 8361 Home for the aged

(P-24522)
ESKATON PROPERTIES INC
Also Called: Eskaton Village Roseville
1650 Eskaton Loop, Roseville
(95747-5180)
PHONE..........................916 334-0810
Vicki Cross, *Manager*
Daisy Absalon,
EMP: 60
SALES (corp-wide): 90.6MM **Privately Held**
SIC: 8361 Home for the aged
PA: Eskaton Properties Incorporated
5105 Manzanita Ave Ste A
Carmichael CA 95608
916 334-0810

(P-24523)
ESKATON PROPERTIES INC
Also Called: Eskaton Village Charmichael
3939 Walnut Ave Unit 399, Carmichael
(95608-7333)
PHONE..........................916 974-2000
Betsy Donovan, *Exec Dir*
Tristin C Benjamin, *Director*
EMP: 200
SALES (corp-wide): 90.6MM **Privately Held**
SIC: 8361 Home for the aged
PA: Eskaton Properties Incorporated
5105 Manzanita Ave Ste A
Carmichael CA 95608
916 334-0810

(P-24524)
EVANGELICAL COVENANT CHURCH
Also Called: Mount Miguel Covenant Village
325 Kempton St, Spring Valley
(91977-5810)
PHONE..........................619 931-1114
Thad Rothrock, *Exec Dir*
EMP: 100 **Privately Held**
WEB: www.npcts.edu
SIC: 8361 Rest home, with health care incidental
HQ: The Evangelical Covenant Church
8303 W Higgins Rd Fl 1
Chicago IL 60631
773 907-3303

(P-24525)
EVANGELICAL COVENANT CHURCH
Also Called: Samarkand Retirement Community
2550 Treasure Dr, Santa Barbara
(93105-4148)
PHONE..........................805 687-0701
Kenneth D Noreen, *Administration*
EMP: 200 **Privately Held**
WEB: www.npcts.edu
SIC: 8361 8059 Home for the aged; rest home, with health care
HQ: The Evangelical Covenant Church
8303 W Higgins Rd Fl 1
Chicago IL 60631
773 907-3303

(P-24526)
EVOLVE GROWTH INITIATIVES LLC
Also Called: Evolve Treatment Centers
820 Moraga Dr, Los Angeles (90049-1632)
PHONE..........................424 281-5000
Menachem Baron, *CEO*
EMP: 50
SQ FT: 1,700
SALES (est): 1MM **Privately Held**
SIC: 8361 8093 Rehabilitation center, residential: health care incidental; mental health clinic, outpatient

(P-24527)
FERREES GROUP HOME INC
878 Highland Home Rd, Banning
(92220-1244)
PHONE..........................951 849-1927
Philip Anthony Ferrees, *Director*
EMP: 60
SALES: 1.5MM **Privately Held**
SIC: 8361 Group foster home

(P-24528)
FIVE ACRES-THE BOYS & GIRLS &
760 Mountain View St, Altadena
(91001-4996)
PHONE..........................626 798-6793
Chanel W Boutakidis, *CEO*
Daniel Braun, *CFO*
Jennifer Berger, *Officer*
Chanel Boutakidis, *Exec Dir*
Robert A Ketch, *Exec Dir*
EMP: 419
SQ FT: 70,000
SALES (est): 24.8MM **Privately Held**
SIC: 8361 8322 8211 Children's home; public welfare center; public combined elementary & secondary school

(P-24529)
FIVE STAR QUALITY CARE INC
Also Called: Somerford Place Encinitas
1350 S El Camino Real, Encinitas
(92024-4904)
PHONE..........................760 479-1818
Terry Records, *Manager*
EMP: 50 **Publicly Held**
WEB: www.fivestarqualitycare.com
SIC: 8361 Residential care
PA: Five Star Senior Living Inc.
400 Centre St
Newton MA 02458

(P-24530)
FLORENCE CRITTENTON SERVICES
Also Called: CRITTENTON SERVICES FOR CHILDR
801 E Chapman Ave Ste 203, Fullerton
(92831-3846)
P.O. Box 9 (92836-0009)
PHONE..........................714 680-9000
Joyce Capelle, *CEO*
Fritz Czypull, *CFO*
Denise Cunningham, *Officer*
Audrey Fisher-Price, *Vice Pres*
Cesar Salgado, *Vice Pres*
EMP: 320
SALES: 32.5MM **Privately Held**
SIC: 8361 Residential care for children; home for the emotionally disturbed

(P-24531)
FORD STREET PROJECT INC
139 Ford St, Ukiah (95482-4011)
PHONE..........................707 462-1934
Jacque Williams, *President*
Katrina Hill, *General Mgr*
Clover Martin, *General Mgr*
Jacqueline Williams, *Info Tech Mgr*
Laura Alexander, *Psychologist*
EMP: 120
SALES: 3.4MM **Privately Held**
WEB: www.fordstreet.org
SIC: 8361 Rehabilitation center, residential: health care incidental

(P-24532)
FOREMOST OPERATIONS LLC
Also Called: Foremost Terrace Room
17581 Sultana St, Hesperia (92345-6552)
PHONE..........................760 244-5579
Ben Vangala, *Owner*
Leonard M Crites, *President*
EMP: 50
SALES (est): 1.7MM **Privately Held**
SIC: 8361 6531 Residential care; rental agent, real estate

(P-24533)
FOUNTAINWOOD RESIDENTIAL CARE
8773 Oak Ave, Orangevale (95662-2410)
PHONE..........................916 988-2200
Robert Spince, *President*
EMP: 80
SALES (est): 3MM **Privately Held**
WEB: www.fountainwood.org
SIC: 8361 8059 Home for the aged; convalescent home

(P-24534)
FREDERICKA MANOR
183 Third Ave, Chula Vista (91910-1822)
PHONE..........................619 422-9271
Robert Anderson, *Principal*
Gloria Delrio, *Hum Res Coord*
EMP: 60
SALES (est): 4.4MM **Privately Held**
SIC: 8361 6513 Home for the aged; apartment building operators

(P-24535)
FRESNO HERITAGE PARTNERS
Also Called: Somerford Place
6075 N Marks Ave, Fresno (93711-1600)
PHONE..........................559 446-6226
Sharol Hutchison, *Exec Dir*
Fresno Surgery Center, *General Ptnr*
EMP: 50
SQ FT: 26,166
SALES (est): 1.5MM **Privately Held**
SIC: 8361 Home for the aged

(P-24536)
FRONT PORCH COMMUNITIES & SVCS
Also Called: Villa Gardens
842 E Villa St, Pasadena (91101-1259)
PHONE..........................626 796-8162
Jeff Sianko, *CEO*
Kathleen Vanderveen, *Executive*
Craig Sumner, *Sales Mgr*
EMP: 192
SALES (corp-wide): 165.1MM **Privately Held**
SIC: 8361 Geriatric residential care
PA: Front Porch Communities And Services - Casa De Manana, Llc
800 N Brand Blvd Fl 19
Glendale CA 91203
818 729-8100

(P-24537)
FUTURO INFANTIL HISPANO FFA
2227 E Garvey Ave N, West Covina
(91791-1500)
PHONE..........................626 339-1824
Oma Velasco-Rodrigues, *President*
Jose Tejeda, *Finance Mgr*
Robert Quintana, *Supervisor*
EMP: 50
SALES: 5.5MM **Privately Held**
SIC: 8361 Group foster home

(P-24538)
GATE THREE HEALTHCARE LLC
Also Called: Palm Ter Hlth Care Rhblitation
24962 Calle Aragon, Laguna Hills
(92637-3883)
PHONE..........................949 770-3348
Soon Burnam,
EMP: 120
SALES: 13.4MM **Privately Held**
SIC: 8361 Rehabilitation center, residential: health care incidental

(P-24539)
GATEWAY CTR OF MONTEREY CNTY (PA)
850 Congress Ave, Pacific Grove
(93950-4811)
PHONE..........................831 372-8002
Kathleen Adanson, *President*
Duane Burnell, *Exec Dir*
Stephanie Lyon, *Exec Dir*
Rosie Dias, *Admin Asst*
Siauro Katoa, *Admin Asst*
EMP: 65
SQ FT: 33,000
SALES: 4.7MM **Privately Held**
WEB: www.gatewaycenter.org
SIC: 8361 Home for the mentally handicapped

(P-24540)
GOLDEN LIVING LLC
Also Called: Beverly Healthcare
5555 Prospect Rd Ofc, San Jose
(95129-4897)
PHONE..........................408 255-5555
Ron Anderson, *Manager*
EMP: 50
SALES (corp-wide): 7.4MM **Privately Held**
WEB: www.nwbeccorp.com
SIC: 8361 Geriatric residential care
PA: Golden Living Llc
5220 Tennyson Pkwy # 400
Plano TX 75024
972 372-6300

(P-24541)
GOLDEN POND LP
Also Called: Golden Pond Retirement Cmnty
3415 Mayhew Rd Ofc, Sacramento
(95827-3107)
PHONE..........................916 369-8967
Doug Gill, *Partner*
Paul Mason, *Partner*
Dana McManus, *Partner*
Brian Walgenbach, *Partner*
Jessica Ramirez, *Office Mgr*
EMP: 50
SALES (est): 3.2MM **Privately Held**
SIC: 8361 6513 Home for the aged; apartment building operators

(P-24542)
GOOD SHEPHERD LUTHERAN HM OF W (PA)
Also Called: Good Shepherd Communities
119 N Main St, Porterville (93257-3713)
PHONE..........................559 791-2000
David Geske, *CEO*
EMP: 60
SQ FT: 6,000
SALES (est): 15.9MM **Privately Held**
SIC: 8361 Residential care for the handicapped

(P-24543)
GRASS VALLEY LLC
Also Called: Quail Ridge Senior Living
150 Sutton Way Ofc, Grass Valley
(95945-4104)
PHONE..........................530 272-1055
Mark E Nicol,
EMP: 60
SALES (est): 2.5MM **Privately Held**
WEB: www.quailridgeseniorliving.com
SIC: 8361 Geriatric residential care

(P-24544)
GREENRIDGE SENIOR CARE
2150 Pyramid Dr, El Sobrante
(94803-3220)
PHONE..........................510 758-9600
Linda Joseph, *Director*
EMP: 110
SALES (est): 3.7MM **Privately Held**
SIC: 8361 Geriatric residential care; home for the aged

(P-24545)
HALL WINDSOR
1415 James M Wood Blvd, Los Angeles
(90015-1209)
PHONE..........................213 383-1547
Michael Bolong, *Owner*
Windsor Hall, *Owner*
EMP: 80

SALES (est): 1.5MM **Privately Held**
WEB: www.windsorhall.com
SIC: **8361** Residential care

(P-24546)
HAMBURGER HOME (PA)
Also Called: Aviva Center
7120 Franklin Ave, Los Angeles
(90046-3002)
PHONE..................................323 876-0550
Regina Bette, *President*
EMP: 90
SQ FT: 25,000
SALES: 18.8MM **Privately Held**
SIC: **8361** Children's home

(P-24547)
HAMBURGER HOME
5900 Sepulvda Blvd, Van Nuys
(91411-2511)
PHONE..................................818 980-3200
Jamerson Jeffrey, *Branch Mgr*
EMP: 103
SALES (corp-wide): 18.8MM **Privately Held**
SIC: **8361** Children's home
PA: Hamburger Home
7120 Franklin Ave
Los Angeles CA 90046
323 876-0550

(P-24548)
HANK FISHER PROPERTIES INC
Also Called: Chateau On Capitol Avenue, The
2701 Capitol Ave, Sacramento
(95816-6036)
PHONE..................................916 447-4444
Nancy Fisher, *Branch Mgr*
EMP: 112
SALES (corp-wide): 15.9MM **Privately Held**
SIC: **8361** Geriatric residential care
PA: Hank Fisher Properties, Inc.
641 Fulton Ave Ste 200
Sacramento CA 95825
916 485-1441

(P-24549)
HARBOR HEALTH CARE INC
16917 Clark Ave, Bellflower (90706-5703)
PHONE..................................562 866-7054
Cheryl Hutchins, *President*
EMP: 200
SALES (est): 9.7MM **Privately Held**
WEB: www.harborhealthcare.org
SIC: **8361** Home for the mentally handicapped

(P-24550)
HARVEST MANAGEMENT SUB LLC
Also Called: Las Brisas
1299 Briarwood Dr, San Luis Obispo
(93401-5965)
PHONE..................................805 543-0187
David Dolan, *Branch Mgr*
EMP: 5004
SALES (corp-wide): 450.1MM **Privately Held**
SIC: **8361** Rest home, with health care incidental
PA: Harvest Management Sub Llc
480 N Orlando Ave Ste 236
Winter Park FL 32789
503 370-7070

(P-24551)
HATHAWAY-SYCAMORES CHLD FAM SV
Also Called: Hathaway Children and Family
12502 Van Nuys Blvd # 120, Pacoima
(91331-1321)
PHONE..................................818 897-1766
Muriel Gaudin, *Manager*
Charity Wang, *Vice Pres*
Cherrie Rodriguez, *Admin Asst*
Khoa Kieu, *Engineer*
Veronica Munoz, *Analyst*
EMP: 60
SALES (corp-wide): 51.8MM **Privately Held**
SIC: **8361** Home for the emotionally disturbed

PA: Hathaway-Sycamores Child And Family Services
100 W Walnut St Ste 375
Pasadena CA 91124
626 395-7100

(P-24552)
HATHAWAY-SYCAMORES CHLD FAM SV
840 N Avenue 66, Los Angeles
(90042-1508)
PHONE..................................323 257-9600
Jim Cheney, *President*
EMP: 54
SALES (corp-wide): 51.8MM **Privately Held**
SIC: **8361** 8093 Home for the emotionally disturbed; mental health clinic, outpatient
PA: Hathaway-Sycamores Child And Family Services
100 W Walnut St Ste 375
Pasadena CA 91124
626 395-7100

(P-24553)
HATHAWAY-SYCAMORES CHLD FAM SV
44738 Sierra Hwy, Lancaster (93534-3225)
PHONE..................................661 942-5749
Debbie Manners, *Exec VP*
EMP: 421
SALES (corp-wide): 51.8MM **Privately Held**
SIC: **8361** Home for the mentally handicapped
PA: Hathaway-Sycamores Child And Family Services
100 W Walnut St
Pasadena CA 91124
626 844-1677

(P-24554)
HATHAWAY-SYCAMORES CHLD FAM SV
3741 Stocker St Ste 101, View Park
(90008-5150)
PHONE..................................323 733-0322
Debbie Manners, *Branch Mgr*
EMP: 60
SALES (corp-wide): 51.8MM **Privately Held**
SIC: **8361** Home for the emotionally disturbed
PA: Hathaway-Sycamores Child And Family Services
100 W Walnut St
Pasadena CA 91124
626 844-1677

(P-24555)
HATHAWAY-SYCAMORES CHLD FAM SV (PA)
100 W Walnut St Ste 375, Pasadena
(91124-0001)
PHONE..................................626 395-7100
Michael Galper, *Ch of Bd*
Tracy Hall, *Partner*
Sandra Tudor, *Partner*
William Martone, *President*
Leticia Verduzco-Tom, *President*
EMP: 65
SQ FT: 75,175
SALES: 51.8MM **Privately Held**
SIC: **8361** 8093 Home for the emotionally disturbed; mental health clinic, outpatient

(P-24556)
HAYNES FAMILY PROGRAMS INC
Also Called: Leroy Haynes Center
233 Baseline Rd, La Verne (91750-2353)
P.O. Box 400 (91750-0400)
PHONE..................................909 593-2581
Daniel Maydeck, *President*
Tony Williams, *CFO*
Frank Linebaugh, *Senior VP*
Kristine Gutierrez, *Human Res Mgr*
Jane Woods, *Professor*
EMP: 225
SQ FT: 72,466
SALES: 19.1MM **Privately Held**
WEB: www.leroyhaynes.org
SIC: **8361** 8211 8099 Boys' Towns; specialty education; medical services organization

(P-24557)
HEALTHCARE GROUP
Also Called: Grossmont Grdns Rtrement Cmnty
5480 Marengo Ave Ste 619, La Mesa
(91942-2408)
PHONE..................................619 463-0281
Mary Shepherd, *Exec Dir*
EMP: 235
SQ FT: 5,000
SALES (est): 9.3MM **Privately Held**
SIC: **8361** 8052 8051 Residential care; intermediate care facilities; skilled nursing care facilities

(P-24558)
HEALTHVIEW INC (PA)
Also Called: Harbor View House
921 S Beacon St, San Pedro (90731-3740)
P.O. Box 1860 (90733-1860)
PHONE..................................310 547-3341
Jeff Smith, *CEO*
Susan Major, *Principal*
Susan Martinez, *Manager*
EMP: 135
SQ FT: 110,000
SALES: 5MM **Privately Held**
WEB: www.hvi.com
SIC: **8361** 8052 Home for the mentally handicapped; rehabilitation center, residential: health care incidental; home for the mentally retarded, with health care

(P-24559)
HEALTHVIEW INC
Also Called: Lifecare Health
12750 Center Court Dr S # 410, Cerritos
(90703-8581)
PHONE..................................562 468-0136
Denise Stanton, *Branch Mgr*
EMP: 50
SALES (est): 474.7K
SALES (corp-wide): 5MM **Privately Held**
WEB: www.hvi.com
SIC: **8361** 8082 Home for the mentally handicapped; home health care services
PA: Healthview, Inc.
921 S Beacon St
San Pedro CA 90731
310 547-3341

(P-24560)
HELPING HEARTS FOUNDATION INC
3050 Fite Cir Ste 108, Sacramento
(95827-1808)
PHONE..................................916 368-7200
James Borgmeyer, *President*
Stephanie Garcia, *Vice Pres*
Marsha Vacca, *Manager*
EMP: 55
SALES: 1.3MM **Privately Held**
SIC: **8361** Residential care

(P-24561)
HESPERIA SENIOR LIVING LLC
17581 Sultana St, Hesperia (92345-6552)
PHONE..................................760 244-5579
Wesley Brown,
Greg Anderson,
Cipriano Bautista,
EMP: 75
SALES: 2.7MM **Privately Held**
SIC: **8361** Residential care

(P-24562)
HILLSIDES
940 Avenue 64, Pasadena (91105-2711)
PHONE..................................323 254-2274
Joseph M Costa, *CEO*
Ryan Herren, *CFO*
Amy Cousineau, *Psychologist*
Blanca Gutierrez, *Social Worker*
EMP: 460 EST: 1913
SQ FT: 18,217
SALES: 32.3MM **Privately Held**
SIC: **8361** Home for the emotionally disturbed

(P-24563)
HILLVIEW ACRES
Also Called: Hillview Acres Childrens Home
23091 Mill Creek Dr, Laguna Hills
(92653-1258)
PHONE..................................714 694-2828
Noah McMahon, *Chairman*

Ronald Storm, *President*
Eric Carter, *Corp Secy*
EMP: 75 EST: 1929
SQ FT: 39,989
SALES: 3.5MM **Privately Held**
WEB: www.hillview.org
SIC: **8361** Children's home

(P-24564)
HOLLENBECK PALMS
Also Called: Hollenbeck Home For The Aged
24431 Lyons Ave Apt 336, Newhall
(91321-2360)
PHONE..................................323 263-6195
William G Heideman Jr, *President*
Morris Shockley, *Vice Pres*
John Shively, *Chief Engr*
Johnny Young, *Controller*
Peggy Heideman, *Pub Rel Dir*
EMP: 170
SALES: 17.7MM **Privately Held**
WEB: www.hollenbeckhome.com
SIC: **8361** Halfway group home, persons with social or personal problems

(P-24565)
HOME GUIDING HANDS CORPORATION (PA)
1908 Friendship Dr Ste A, El Cajon
(92020-1154)
PHONE..................................619 938-2850
Mark Klaus, *CEO*
Jan Adams, *Officer*
Edward Hershey, *Vice Pres*
Debra Kudar, *Vice Pres*
Carol A Fitzgibbons, *Exec Dir*
EMP: 266 EST: 1961
SALES (est): 19.3MM **Privately Held**
WEB: www.guidinghands.org
SIC: **8361** 8052 Residential care for the handicapped; intermediate care facilities

(P-24566)
HOPE HSE FOR MLTPLE HNDICAPPED (PA)
Also Called: Schmitt House
4215 Peck Rd, El Monte (91732-2198)
PHONE..................................626 443-1313
D Bernstein, *Exec Dir*
David Bernstein, *Exec Dir*
Dorothy Gonzalez, *Exec Dir*
Mary Guardado, *Admin Sec*
Patty Fraijo, *Comptroller*
EMP: 150
SQ FT: 15,000
SALES (est): 5.3MM **Privately Held**
SIC: **8361** Residential care for the handicapped; rest home, with health care incidental

(P-24567)
HR MISSION COMMONS FC 5183
10 Terracina Blvd, Redlands (92373-4808)
PHONE..................................909 793-8691
Patty Van Dyk, *Principal*
EMP: 88
SALES (est): 3.1MM **Privately Held**
SIC: **8361** Residential care

(P-24568)
INDEPENDENT OPTIONS INC
8555 Aero Dr, San Diego (92123-1743)
PHONE..................................858 598-5260
EMP: 127
SALES (corp-wide): 16MM **Privately Held**
SIC: **8361** Home for the mentally handicapped
PA: Independent Options, Inc
391 Corporate Terrace Cir # 102
Corona CA 92879
951 279-2585

(P-24569)
JEWISH HOME FOR THE AGING OF O
Also Called: HERITAGE POINTE
27356 Bellogente, Mission Viejo
(92691-6341)
PHONE..................................949 364-0010
David Zarnow, *Vice Pres*
Brad Plose, *President*
Ira Victor, *Vice Pres*
Rena Loveless, *Administration*
EMP: 120

SQ FT: 88,928
SALES: 10.8MM **Privately Held**
SIC: 8361 Home for the aged

(P-24570)
KIDS FIRST FOUNDATION
1025 Service Pl Ste 103, Vista
(92084-7271)
PHONE..................................760 631-7550
Ihab Shahawi, *CEO*
EMP: 165
SALES: 6.7MM **Privately Held**
SIC: 8361 Residential care

(P-24571)
KIDS FIRST FOUNDATION
993 S Santa Fe Ave Ste C, Vista
(92083-6995)
PHONE..................................760 631-7550
Ihab Shahawi, *CEO*
EMP: 99
SALES (est): 1.7MM **Privately Held**
SIC: 8361 Residential care

(P-24572)
KNOLLS WEST ENTERPRISE
Also Called: Knolls West Residential Care
16890 Green Tree Blvd, Victorville
(92395-5618)
PHONE..................................760 245-0107
Larry Bechtold, *Partner*
Fred Bechtold, *Partner*
Gary Bechtold, *Partner*
EMP: 100
SQ FT: 44,000
SALES (est): 4.4MM
SALES (corp-wide): 8.4MM **Privately Held**
WEB: www.desertknollsconvhospital.com
SIC: 8361 Geriatric residential care
PA: Knolls Convalescent Hospital Inc
16890 Green Tree Blvd
Victorville CA 92395
760 245-5361

(P-24573)
LA HABRA VILLA
220 Newport Center Dr # 11, Newport
Beach (92660-7506)
PHONE..................................714 529-1697
David Tsoong, *Partner*
Herbert Tarlow MD, *Partner*
EMP: 54
SQ FT: 100,000
SALES (est): 2.7MM **Privately Held**
SIC: 8361 Home for the aged

(P-24574)
LAMP INC
Also Called: Lamp Community
2116 Arlington Ave Lbby, Los Angeles
(90018-1365)
PHONE..................................213 488-9559
Donna Gallup, *CEO*
Kim Carson, *Finance Dir*
EMP: 110
SQ FT: 4,500
SALES: 11.6MM **Privately Held**
SIC: 8361 Residential care for the handi-
capped

(P-24575)
**LASSEN HSE ASSISTED LIVING
LLC**
705 Luther Rd, Red Bluff (96080-4265)
PHONE..................................530 529-2900
Eric Jacobsen,
EMP: 50
SALES: 1.2MM **Privately Held**
SIC: 8361 Geriatric residential care

(P-24576)
LE BLEU CHATEAU INC
Also Called: Bleu Chateau Assisted Living
1900 Grismer Ave, Burbank (91504-4405)
PHONE..................................818 843-3141
Madeline Rosenberg, *President*
Ramon Parado, *President*
Robert Rosenberg, *Vice Pres*
EMP: 50
SALES (est): 1.4MM **Privately Held**
WEB: www.lebleuchateau.com
SIC: 8361 Home for the aged

(P-24577)
LEISURE CARE LLC
Also Called: Nohl Ranch Inn
380 S Anaheim Hills Rd, Anaheim
(92807-4026)
PHONE..................................714 974-1616
Wanda Reynolds, *Branch Mgr*
EMP: 50
SQ FT: 82,222
SALES (corp-wide): 128.3MM **Privately
Held**
WEB: www.leisurecare.com
SIC: 8361 8051 Residential care; skilled
nursing care facilities
PA: Leisure Care, Llc
999 3rd Ave Ste 4500
Seattle WA 98104
800 327-3490

(P-24578)
LEISURE CARE LLC
Also Called: Fairwinds Woodward Park
9525 N Fort Washington Rd, Fresno
(93730-0662)
PHONE..................................559 434-1237
Coint Folwer, *Branch Mgr*
EMP: 100
SALES (corp-wide): 128.3MM **Privately
Held**
WEB: www.leisurecare.com
SIC: 8361 Residential care
PA: Leisure Care, Llc
999 3rd Ave Ste 4500
Seattle WA 98104
800 327-3490

(P-24579)
LINCOLN CHILD CENTER INC
Also Called: Hope Contra Costa
51 Marina Blvd, Pittsburg (94565-2068)
PHONE..................................925 521-1270
Allison Staulcup, *Principal*
EMP: 70
SALES (corp-wide): 17.3MM **Privately
Held**
SIC: 8361 Home for the mentally handi-
capped
PA: Lincoln
1266 14th St
Oakland CA 94607
510 273-4700

(P-24580)
LITTLE PEOPLES
39514 Brookside Ave, Cherry Valley
(92223-4602)
P.O. Box 248, Beaumont (92223-0248)
PHONE..................................951 849-1959
C S Jay Kidogo, *President*
EMP: 60
SALES: 2.8MM **Privately Held**
WEB: www.littlepeoples.com
SIC: 8361

(P-24581)
LITTLE PEOPLES WORLD INC
39514 Brookside Ave, Cherry Valley
(92223-4602)
PHONE..................................951 845-8367
Nadene Daniels, *CEO*
C S J Kidogo, *Exec Dir*
EMP: 50
SALES (est): 2.5MM **Privately Held**
SIC: 8361 Residential care for children

(P-24582)
LITTLE SISTERS OF POOR
Also Called: ST ANNE'S HOME
300 Lake St, San Francisco (94118-1397)
PHONE..................................415 751-6510
Patricia Metzgar, *President*
Margaret Lennon, *Executive*
Andrew Millan, *Training Spec*
EMP: 107
SQ FT: 110,000
SALES: 6.8MM **Privately Held**
SIC: 8361 8661 Home for the aged; reli-
gious organizations

(P-24583)
**LONGWOOD MANAGEMENT
CORP**
Also Called: Parkers Retirement Residence
9925 La Alameda Ave, Fountain Valley
(92708-3548)
PHONE..................................714 962-5531

Stephanie Radu, *Manager*
EMP: 65
SALES (corp-wide): 170MM **Privately
Held**
SIC: 8361 8059 Residential care; rest
home, with health care
PA: Longwood Management Corp.
4032 Wilshire Blvd Fl 6
Los Angeles CA 90010
213 389-6900

(P-24584)
**LOS ANGELES MISSION INC
(PA)**
303 E 5th St, Los Angeles (90013-1505)
PHONE..................................213 629-1227
Herb Smith, *President*
Steve Kennedy, *CFO*
EMP: 77
SQ FT: 155,000
SALES: 13.7MM **Privately Held**
SIC: 8361 Home for destitute men &
women; rehabilitation center, residential:
health care incidental

(P-24585)
**LOS ANGELES ORPHAN
ASYLUM INC**
7600 Graves Ave, Rosemead
(91770-3414)
PHONE..................................323 283-9311
Sister Linda A Cahill, *Director*
EMP: 122
SQ FT: 25,000
SALES: 3.5MM **Privately Held**
SIC: 8361 Orphanage

(P-24586)
**LOS ANGELES ORPHANS HOME
SOC (HQ)**
815 N El Centro Ave, Los Angeles
(90038-3805)
PHONE..................................323 463-2119
Darrell Evora, *President*
Genevieve Morgan, *Psychologist*
Shaghayegh Nourian, *Psychologist*
EMP: 192
SQ FT: 45,000
SALES (est): 2.9MM
SALES (corp-wide): 93.6MM **Privately
Held**
SIC: 8361 Residential care for children
PA: Uplift Family Services
251 Llewellyn Ave
Campbell CA 95008
408 379-3790

(P-24587)
**LOS ANGELES RESIDENTIAL
COMM F**
29890 Bouquet Canyon Rd, Santa Clarita
(91390-5111)
PHONE..................................661 296-8636
Kathy Sturky, *Exec Dir*
Larry Sallows, *CFO*
Maureen Medeiros, *Office Mgr*
Arleen Almsted, *Admin Asst*
Petrina Lesko, *Administration*
EMP: 85
SQ FT: 5,000
SALES (est): 2.4MM **Privately Held**
WEB: www.larcfoundation.org
SIC: 8361 8322 8051 Home for the men-
tally handicapped; individual & family
services; skilled nursing care facilities

(P-24588)
LOS PRIETOS BOYS CAMP
3900 Paradise Rd, Santa Barbara
(93105-9734)
PHONE..................................805 692-1750
Patricia Stewart, *Director*
EMP: 60
SALES (est): 930.1K **Privately Held**
SIC: 8361 Juvenile correctional facilities

(P-24589)
**LOYALTON AT RANCHO
SOLANO**
3350 Cherry Hills Ct Ofc, Fairfield
(94534-7885)
PHONE..................................707 425-3588
Kimberly Kent, *Exec Dir*
Dorothy King, *Manager*
EMP: 60

SALES (est): 1.6MM **Privately Held**
SIC: 8361 Residential care

(P-24590)
MAGNOLIA OF MILLBRAE INC
201 Chadbourne Ave, Millbrae
(94030-2570)
PHONE..................................650 697-7700
Vincent Muzzi, *President*
EMP: 93 EST: 1986
SALES (est): 5.8MM **Privately Held**
WEB: www.themagnolia.com
SIC: 8361 Home for the aged

(P-24591)
MARY AND FRIENDS
1101 Farrington Dr, La Habra (90631-2510)
PHONE..................................562 691-1575
Eric Rico, *CEO*
Christine Rico, *President*
EMP: 120
SALES (est): 3MM **Privately Held**
SIC: 8361 Residential care for the handi-
capped

(P-24592)
MARYVALE
7600 Graves Ave, Rosemead
(91770-3414)
P.O. Box 1039 (91770-1000)
PHONE..................................626 280-6510
Steve Gunter, *CEO*
EMP: 53 EST: 2011
SALES: 22.8MM **Privately Held**
SIC: 8361 8322 Residential care for chil-
dren; public welfare center

(P-24593)
**MASONIC HOMES OF
CALIFORNIA (PA)**
1111 California St, San Francisco
(94108-2252)
PHONE..................................415 776-7000
David R Doan, *President*
Timothy A Wood, *CFO*
Dave Doan, *Treasurer*
Allan Casalou, *Vice Pres*
Andrew Uehling, *Vice Pres*
EMP: 375
SQ FT: 8,000
SALES: 54.8MM **Privately Held**
WEB: www.mhcuc.org
SIC: 8361 Children's home

(P-24594)
**MASONIC HOMES OF
CALIFORNIA**
Also Called: Masonic Home For Adults
34400 Mission Blvd, Union City
(94587-3604)
PHONE..................................510 441-3700
Gilbert Smart, *Branch Mgr*
Manny Gallardo, *Executive*
Dixie U Reeve, *Administration*
EMP: 350
SALES (corp-wide): 54.8MM **Privately
Held**
WEB: www.mhcuc.org
SIC: 8361 8051 Rest home, with health
care incidental; skilled nursing care facili-
ties
PA: Masonic Homes Of California Inc
1111 California St
San Francisco CA 94108
415 776-7000

(P-24595)
**MASONIC HOMES OF
CALIFORNIA**
3823 N Reeder Ave, Covina (91724)
PHONE..................................626 251-2200
John Howle, *Manager*
Christina Drislane, *CTO*
EMP: 100
SALES (corp-wide): 54.8MM **Privately
Held**
WEB: www.mhcuc.org
SIC: 8361 Children's home
PA: Masonic Homes Of California Inc
1111 California St
San Francisco CA 94108
415 776-7000

▲ = Import ▼=Export
◆ =Import/Export

(P-24596)
MCKINLEY CHILDRENS CENTER INC (PA)
762 Cypress St, San Dimas (91773-3505)
PHONE..................................909 599-1227
Anil Vadatary, *CEO*
Michael Frazer, *CFO*
Chris Murray, *Officer*
Paulette Duncan, *Executive*
Julio Arizaga, *Administration*
EMP: 190
SQ FT: 8,055
SALES: 19.3MM **Privately Held**
WEB: www.mckinleycc.org
SIC: 8361 8211 Boys' Towns; private elementary & secondary schools

(P-24597)
MEADOWBROOK CONVALESCENT HOSP
461 E Johnston Ave, Hemet (92543-7195)
PHONE..................................951 658-2293
Bridgette Grimaldi, *President*
EMP: 78 **EST:** 1955
SALES: 2.8MM **Privately Held**
SIC: 8361 8051 Rest home, with health care incidental; convalescent home with continuous nursing care

(P-24598)
MEADOWBROOK VILLAGE CHRISTIAN
100 Holland Gln, Escondido (92026-1354)
PHONE..................................760 746-2500
Jacob Bronwer, *President*
Mark Memmelaar, *Exec Dir*
Sarah Rogh, *Manager*
EMP: 109
SALES: 4.8MM **Privately Held**
SIC: 8361 Home for the aged

(P-24599)
MERCY RETIREMENT AND CARE CTR
3431 Foothill Blvd, Oakland (94601-3199)
PHONE..................................510 534-8540
Jesse Jantzen, *CEO*
Asha Kooliyadan, *Hlthcr Dir*
EMP: 160
SQ FT: 125,000
SALES: 23.9MM **Privately Held**
SIC: 8361 8051 Home for the aged; skilled nursing care facilities

(P-24600)
MGH CORPORATION
Also Called: Mitchells Group Home
1202 W 101st St, Los Angeles (90044-1802)
PHONE..................................323 754-1408
Hazel Mitchell, *President*
Stephnie Weathersby, *Vice Pres*
EMP: 50
SALES (est): 3MM **Privately Held**
SIC: 8361 Geriatric residential care

(P-24601)
MISSION HILLS POST ACUTE CARE
Also Called: Cloisters Mssion Hills Hosp HM
3680 Reynard Way, San Diego (92103-3847)
PHONE..................................619 297-4484
Kennon S Shea, *President*
Sandra Comstock, *Records Dir*
Matt Scott, *Administration*
Joanne Starkley, *Education*
Cindy Martinez, *Director*
EMP: 92
SQ FT: 16,920
SALES (est): 5.2MM **Privately Held**
SIC: 8361 8051 Rehabilitation center, residential: health care incidental; skilled nursing care facilities

(P-24602)
MISSION HILLS SENIOR LIVING
34560 Bob Hope Dr, Rancho Mirage (92270-1727)
PHONE..................................760 770-7737
Roland Gandy, *Exec Dir*
EMP: 62
SALES (est): 1.2MM **Privately Held**
SIC: 8361 Geriatric residential care

(P-24603)
MISSION VILLA LLC
995 E Market St, Daly City (94014-2168)
PHONE..................................650 756-1995
Jeannie Lawler, *Director*
EMP: 50
SALES (est): 2.2MM **Privately Held**
WEB: www.missionvillage.org
SIC: 8361 Home for the aged

(P-24604)
MISSION VLLA ALZHMERS RSIDENCE
3333 S Bascom Ave, Campbell (95008-7005)
PHONE..................................408 559-8301
Jeanie Lalor, *Administration*
EMP: 50
SQ FT: 14,535
SALES (est): 1.1MM **Privately Held**
SIC: 8361 Residential care

(P-24605)
MONARCH PLACE PIEDMONT LLC
4500 Gilbert St, Oakland (94611-4657)
PHONE..................................510 658-9266
Frank J Haffner II, *Mng Member*
EMP: 125
SALES (est): 3.7MM **Privately Held**
SIC: 8361 Home for the aged

(P-24606)
MONTE NIDO RESIDENTIAL CTR LLC
Also Called: Monte Nido & Affiliates
514 Live Oak Circle Dr, Calabasas (91302-2139)
PHONE..................................818 457-9958
EMP: 222
SALES (corp-wide): 60MM **Privately Held**
SIC: 8361 Residential care
PA: Monte Nido Residential Center, Llc
23815 Stuart Ranch Rd
Malibu CA 90265
310 457-9958

(P-24607)
MONTE VISTA GROVE HOMES
2889 San Pasqual St, Pasadena (91107-5364)
PHONE..................................626 796-6135
M Helen Baatz, *Exec Dir*
Kim Houser, *CFO*
Debbie Herbert, *Exec Dir*
Nancy Lain, *Office Mgr*
Jacqueline Choi, *Human Res Dir*
EMP: 85
SQ FT: 12,000
SALES: 9.3MM **Privately Held**
SIC: 8361 Home for the aged

(P-24608)
MOTHER LODE REHABILIT
Also Called: MORE WORKSHOP
399 Placerville Dr, Placerville (95667-3912)
PHONE..................................530 622-4848
Susie Davies, *Exec Dir*
David Eggerton, *Exec Dir*
EMP: 150
SQ FT: 20,000
SALES: 3.3MM **Privately Held**
SIC: 8361 8322 Rehabilitation center, residential: health care incidental; individual & family services

(P-24609)
NEW BTHNY RSDNTL CRE&SKLLD
1441 Berkeley Dr, Los Banos (93635-9599)
PHONE..................................209 827-8933
Lucinda Fonseca, *Exec Dir*
EMP: 80
SALES (est): 2.2MM **Privately Held**
SIC: 8361 Home for the aged

(P-24610)
NEW WAY LLC
1130 Burnett Ave Ste G, Concord (94520-5610)
PHONE..................................925 688-1520
Lupe Henry, *Mng Member*
Steve Zolno, *Mng Member*

EMP: 80
SALES (est): 3.3MM **Privately Held**
SIC: 8361 Residential care for the handicapped

(P-24611)
NINOS LATINO UNIDOS FSA
10016 Pioneer Blvd # 123, Santa Fe Springs (90670-3245)
PHONE..................................562 801-5454
Fahir Milian, *President*
Gurith Torres, *Corp Secy*
Luis I Mendes, *Administration*
EMP: 60
SALES: 6.8MM **Privately Held**
WEB: www.nlu.org
SIC: 8361 8322 Group foster home; individual & family services

(P-24612)
NORTHERN CA RETIREDD OFCRS
Also Called: Paradise Valley Estates
2600 Estates Dr, Fairfield (94533-9711)
PHONE..................................707 432-1200
James G Mertz, *CEO*
Debra Murphy, *CFO*
Neil Calhoun, *Officer*
Sharon M Dominik, *Executive*
Sarena Brown, *Admin Asst*
EMP: 225
SALES: 31.2MM **Privately Held**
WEB: www.pvestates.com
SIC: 8361 Home for the aged

(P-24613)
NURSECORE MANAGEMENT SVCS LLC
1010 S Broadway, Santa Maria (93454-6600)
PHONE..................................805 938-7660
Veronica Aburto, *Branch Mgr*
EMP: 700 **Privately Held**
SIC: 8361 8082 8049 7361 Residential care; home health care services; nurses & other medical assistants; nurses' registry
PA: Nursecore Management Services, Llc
2201 Brookhollow Plaza Dr # 450
Arlington TX 76006

(P-24614)
ODD FELLOW-REBEKAH CHLD HM CAL (PA)
Also Called: REBEKAH CHILDREN'S SERVICES
290 I O O F Ave, Gilroy (95020-5204)
PHONE..................................408 846-2100
Nancy Johnson, *CEO*
Christophe Rebboah, *CEO*
Scott Olson, *Info Tech Mgr*
Debbie Swanson, *Accounting Mgr*
Angela Wimmer, *Accountant*
EMP: 173
SQ FT: 46,000
SALES: 19MM **Privately Held**
SIC: 8361 8093 Home for the emotionally disturbed; mental health clinic, outpatient

(P-24615)
ODD FELLOW-REBEKAH CHLD HM CAL
Also Called: Rebekah Children's Services
1260 S Main St Ste 101, Salinas (93901-2292)
PHONE..................................831 775-0348
Jorge Montes, *Branch Mgr*
EMP: 72
SALES (corp-wide): 19MM **Privately Held**
SIC: 8361 8093 Home for the emotionally disturbed; mental health clinic, outpatient
PA: Odd Fellow-Rebekah Children's Home Of California
290 I O O F Ave
Gilroy CA 95020
408 846-2100

(P-24616)
ODD FELLOWS HOME CALIFORNIA
Also Called: Saratoga Retirement Community
14500 Fruitvale Ave # 3000, Saratoga (95070-6169)
PHONE..................................408 741-7100
Cathy Schumacher, *Administration*
EMP: 275 **EST:** 1853
SALES: 48.7MM **Privately Held**
SIC: 8361 8051 Home for the aged; skilled nursing care facilities

(P-24617)
OLIVE CREST
73700 Dinah Shore Dr # 101, Palm Desert (92211-0815)
PHONE..................................760 341-8507
Angela Allenn, *Branch Mgr*
EMP: 77
SALES (corp-wide): 49.3MM **Privately Held**
SIC: 8361 Group foster home
PA: Olive Crest
2130 E 4th St Ste 200
Santa Ana CA 92705
714 543-5437

(P-24618)
OLIVE CREST
Also Called: Olive Crest Op
917 Pine Ave, Long Beach (90813-4325)
PHONE..................................562 216-8841
Donald Verleur, *Branch Mgr*
EMP: 77
SALES (corp-wide): 49.3MM **Privately Held**
SIC: 8361 Home for the emotionally disturbed
PA: Olive Crest
2130 E 4th St Ste 200
Santa Ana CA 92705
714 543-5437

(P-24619)
OLIVE CREST (PA)
2130 E 4th St Ste 200, Santa Ana (92705-3818)
PHONE..................................714 543-5437
Donald A Verleur, *CEO*
Patricia Barker, *Partner*
Dailene Coad, *Partner*
Cheryl Robinson, *Partner*
Lois Verleur, *Vice Pres*
EMP: 500
SQ FT: 40,000
SALES: 49.3MM **Privately Held**
WEB: www.olivecrest.net
SIC: 8361 8322 Home for the emotionally disturbed; individual & family services

(P-24620)
OMNITRANS INC
Also Called: Omnitrans Access
234 S I St, San Bernardino (92410-2408)
PHONE..................................909 383-1680
Brian Niemann, *Principal*
EMP: 351
SALES (corp-wide): 13.6MM **Privately Held**
SIC: 8361 Home for the physically handicapped
PA: Omnitrans, Inc.
1700 W 5th St
San Bernardino CA 92411
909 379-7100

(P-24621)
P MONTEREY LP
Also Called: Park Lane, The
200 Glenwood Cir Ste A50, Monterey (93940-6748)
PHONE..................................831 250-6159
Deepak Israni, *Principal*
EMP: 70
SALES (est): 3.1MM **Privately Held**
SIC: 8361 Residential care

PRODUCTS & SVCS

(P-24622)
PACIFIC LODGE YOUTH SERVICES
Also Called: Pacific Lodge Boy's Home
4900 Serrania Ave, Woodland Hills
(91364-3301)
P.O. Box 308 (91365-0308)
PHONE..............................818 347-1577
Leslie King, *Ch of Bd*
Lisa Alegria, *CEO*
Hazel Benavides, *Cust Mgr*
Svetlana Mseryan, *Manager*
Joel Hernandez, *Supervisor*
EMP: 110
SQ FT: 22,634
SALES: 4.9MM **Privately Held**
WEB: www.plys.org
SIC: 8361 Residential care

(P-24623)
PACIFIC RETIREMENT SVCS INC
Also Called: University Retirement Cmnty
1515 Shasta Dr Ofc, Davis (95616-6695)
PHONE..............................530 753-1450
Mark Blazer, *Exec Dir*
Kimberly Carston, *Marketing Staff*
Judi Del Ponte, *Marketing Staff*
EMP: 170 **Privately Held**
WEB: www.prsmedia.com
SIC: 8361 Home for the aged
PA: Pacific Retirement Services, Inc.
　　1 W Main St Ste 303
　　Medford OR 97501

(P-24624)
PALADIN EASTSIDE SERVICES INC
111 S Grfield Ave Ste 101, Montebello
(90640)
PHONE..............................323 890-0180
Octavio Delgado, *President*
Lolita David, *CFO*
EMP: 100
SQ FT: 1,800
SALES (est): 3.6MM **Privately Held**
SIC: 8361 Residential care

(P-24625)
PALM GRDNS RSDNTIAL CARE FCLTY
240 Palm Ave, Woodland (95695-2844)
PHONE..............................530 661-0574
Sue Farrow, *President*
EMP: 50
SALES (est): 2.8MM **Privately Held**
SIC: 8361 8322 Geriatric residential care;
　individual & family services

(P-24626)
PALO ALTO COMMONS
4075 El Camino Way, Palo Alto
(94306-4005)
PHONE..............................650 320-8626
William Reller, *Partner*
Carolyn Reller, *Partner*
EMP: 85
SQ FT: 80,000
SALES (est): 6MM **Privately Held**
WEB: www.paloaltocommons.com
SIC: 8361 8052 Home for the aged; inter-
　mediate care facilities

(P-24627)
PASADENA CHLD TRAINING SOC
Also Called: Sycamores School
2933 El Nido Dr, Altadena (91001-4529)
PHONE..............................626 798-0853
William P Martone, *Exec Dir*
EMP: 192
SQ FT: 24,658
SALES (corp-wide): 12.8MM **Privately Held**
WEB: www.sycamores.com
SIC: 8361 8322 Home for the emotionally
　disturbed; individual & family services
PA: Pasadena Children's Training Society
　　210 S De Lacey Ave # 110
　　Pasadena CA 91105
　　626 395-7100

(P-24628)
PEOPLE SERVICES INC (PA)
Also Called: KONOCTI TRANSPORTATION SERVICE
4195 Lakeshore Blvd, Lakeport
(95453-6411)
PHONE..............................707 263-3810
F Ilene Dumont, *Exec Dir*
EMP: 88
SQ FT: 13,125
SALES: 3.9MM **Privately Held**
WEB: www.peopleservices.org
SIC: 8361 Self-help group home

(P-24629)
PEPPERMINT RIDGE (PA)
825 Magnolia Ave, Corona (92879-3129)
PHONE..............................951 273-7320
Danette McCarnes, *Exec Dir*
Susan Glenn, *Treasurer*
Elizabeth Muller, *Agent*
EMP: 83
SQ FT: 25,000
SALES: 7.5MM **Privately Held**
WEB: www.peppermintridge.org
SIC: 8361 8322 Residential care for the
　handicapped; individual & family services

(P-24630)
PHOENIX HOUSE ORANGE COUNTY
1207 E Fruit St, Santa Ana (92701-4296)
PHONE..............................714 953-9373
Pouria Abbassi, *CEO*
Elena Ksendzov, *CFO*
Stephen Donowitz, *Vice Pres*
EMP: 67
SALES (est): 2.2MM
SALES (corp-wide): 12.5MM **Privately Held**
SIC: 8361 Rehabilitation center, residen-
　tial: health care incidental
HQ: Phoenix Houses Of California, Inc
　　11600 Eldridge Ave
　　Sylmar CA 91342
　　818 896-1121

(P-24631)
PHOENIX HOUSES LOS ANGELES INC
Also Called: PHOENIX HSE FNDTN, INC. & AF
11600 Eldridge Ave, Lake View Terrace
(91342-6506)
PHONE..............................818 686-3000
Winifred Wechsler, *President*
Jordan Zipkin, *Med Doctor*
Maja Trochimczyk PHD, *Director*
EMP: 99
SALES: 11.3MM
SALES (corp-wide): 12.5MM **Privately Held**
SIC: 8361 Rehabilitation center, residen-
　tial: health care incidental
HQ: Phoenix Houses Of California, Inc
　　11600 Eldridge Ave
　　Sylmar CA 91342
　　818 896-1121

(P-24632)
POOR SISTERS OF NAZARETH OF SA
Also Called: Nazareth House
6333 Rancho Mission Rd, San Diego
(92108-2001)
PHONE..............................619 563-0480
Sister Margaret Spence, *Administration*
Barbara-Anne Crowley, *Exec Dir*
EMP: 75
SALES (est): 5.6MM **Privately Held**
WEB: www.nazarethhouse.com
SIC: 8361 8051 Geriatric residential care;
　skilled nursing care facilities

(P-24633)
PRIMROSE ALZHEIMERS LIVING (PA)
726 College Ave, Santa Rosa
(95404-4107)
PHONE..............................707 568-4355
John Wotring, *President*
EMP: 50
SALES (est): 4.6MM **Privately Held**
WEB: www.primrosealz.com
SIC: 8361 Home for the aged

(P-24634)
PRIMROSE ALZHEIMERS LIVING
2080 Guerneville Rd, Santa Rosa
(95403-4117)
PHONE..............................707 578-8360
John J Wortring, *Manager*
Vicky Southwells, *Marketing Staff*
Dan Obrien,
Ericka Wotring, *Manager*
EMP: 50
SALES (est): 1.1MM
SALES (corp-wide): 4.6MM **Privately Held**
WEB: www.primrosealz.com
SIC: 8361 Home for the aged
PA: Primrose Alzheimer's Living Inc
　　726 College Ave
　　Santa Rosa CA 95404
　　707 568-4355

(P-24635)
PRIMROSE ALZHEIMERS LIVING
Also Called: Primrose Sacramento
7707 Rush River Dr, Sacramento
(95831-5229)
PHONE..............................916 392-3510
John Wotring, *Exec Dir*
EMP: 65
SALES (corp-wide): 4.6MM **Privately Held**
WEB: www.primrosealz.com
SIC: 8361 8099 Home for the aged; med-
　ical services organization
PA: Primrose Alzheimer's Living Inc
　　726 College Ave
　　Santa Rosa CA 95404
　　707 568-4355

(P-24636)
PROGRESS HOUSE INC (PA)
2844 Coloma St Ste A&B, Placerville
(95667-4406)
P.O. Box 1666 (95667-1666)
PHONE..............................530 626-9240
Barbara Vermilyea, *Exec Dir*
Kristina Harris, *Program Mgr*
EMP: 55
SQ FT: 6,184
SALES: 2.5MM **Privately Held**
WEB: www.progresshouseinc.org
SIC: 8361 Rehabilitation center, residen-
　tial: health care incidental

(P-24637)
PROMESA BEHAVIORAL HEALTH
2815 G St, Merced (95340-2133)
PHONE..............................209 725-3114
Lisa Weigant, *Branch Mgr*
EMP: 51 **Privately Held**
SIC: 8361 Group foster home
PA: Promesa Behavioral Health
　　7120 N Marks Ave
　　Fresno CA 93711

(P-24638)
PROMESA BEHAVIORAL HEALTH (PA)
7120 N Marks Ave, Fresno (93711-0268)
PHONE..............................559 439-5437
Lisa Weigant, *CEO*
Carol Scroggins, *Agent*
EMP: 150
SALES: 8.1MM **Privately Held**
SIC: 8361 Residential care

(P-24639)
PSYNERGY PROGRAMS INC
18225 Hale Ave, Morgan Hill (95037-3547)
PHONE..............................408 776-0422
Christopher Zubaite, *President*
Arturo Uribe, *COO*
Michael S Weinstein, *CFO*
Michael Weinstein, *CFO*
L Jean Edwards, *Ch Credit Ofcr*
EMP: 55
SALES (est): 5.3MM **Privately Held**
SIC: 8361 Residential care

(P-24640)
RAISER SENIOR SERVICES LLC
Also Called: Stratford
601 Laurel Ave Apt 903, San Mateo
(94401-4164)
PHONE..............................650 342-4106
Jennifer Raiser, *President*
Phillip Raiser, *Vice Pres*
EMP: 75
SQ FT: 184,000
SALES (est): 2.5MM **Privately Held**
SIC: 8361 Rest home, with health care in-
　cidental

(P-24641)
RANCHO DE SUS NINOS INC
Also Called: HIS KIDS RANCH
P.O. Box 360 (91963-0360)
PHONE..............................619 661-9232
Steve Horner, *Director*
EMP: 60
SALES: 2MM **Privately Held**
SIC: 8361 Orphanage

(P-24642)
RANCHO SAN ANTONIO BOYS HM INC (PA)
21000 Plummer St, Chatsworth
(91311-4903)
PHONE..............................818 882-6400
Brother John Crowe, *CEO*
Nicholas Rizzo, *Finance Dir*
EMP: 100 EST: 1933
SALES: 2MM **Privately Held**
SIC: 8361 Boys' Towns

(P-24643)
RANCHO SAN ANTONIO RETIREMENT
Also Called: Forum At Rancho San Antonio
23500 Cristo Rey Dr, Cupertino
(95014-6503)
PHONE..............................650 265-2637
Ken Fullmore, *Exec Dir*
EMP: 302
SALES (est): 17.9MM **Privately Held**
SIC: 8361 8051 Rest home, with health
　care incidental; skilled nursing care facili-
　ties

(P-24644)
REDWOOD ELDERLINK SCPH
Also Called: Redwood Elderlink & Homelink
710 W 13th Ave, Escondido (92025-5511)
PHONE..............................760 480-1030
Kurt Norden, *Director*
Dan Johnson, *President*
Tom Vedvick, *Chairman*
Fran Hillebrecht, *Treasurer*
Doug Best, *Admin Sec*
EMP: 450
SQ FT: 200,000
SALES (est): 6.5MM
SALES (corp-wide): 84.4MM **Privately Held**
WEB: www.redwoodelderlink.com
SIC: 8361 8742 Home for the aged; com-
　pensation & benefits planning consultant
PA: Southern California Presbyterian
　　Homes
　　516 Burchett St
　　Glendale CA 91203
　　818 247-0420

(P-24645)
REGENCY PARK SENIOR LIVING INC
Also Called: Regency Park Oak Knoll
255 S Oak Knoll Ave, Pasadena
(91101-2992)
PHONE..............................626 396-4911
Fax: 626 584-5719
EMP: 62
SALES (corp-wide): 10.6MM **Privately Held**
SIC: 8361
PA: Regency Park Senior Living, Inc.
　　150 S Los Robles Ave # 480
　　Pasadena CA 91101
　　626 773-8800

(P-24646)
REGENT ASSISTED LIVING INC
Also Called: Regent Senior Living W Covina
150 S Grand Ave Ofc, West Covina
(91791-2355)
PHONE..............................626 332-3344
Lorena Arechiga, *Manager*
EMP: 60 **Privately Held**
WEB: www.regentassistedliving.com
SIC: 8361 Residential care
PA: Regent Assisted Living, Inc.
121 Sw Morrison St # 950
Portland OR 97204

(P-24647)
REGENT ASSISTED LIVING INC
Also Called: Regent At Laurel Springs
8100 Westwold Dr Ofc, Bakersfield
(93311-3471)
PHONE..............................661 663-8400
Janice Calco, *Manager*
EMP: 50 **Privately Held**
WEB: www.regentassistedliving.com
SIC: 8361 Residential care
PA: Regent Assisted Living, Inc.
121 Sw Morrison St # 950
Portland OR 97204

(P-24648)
REGENT ASSISTED LIVING INC
Also Called: Regent Court
2325 St Pauls Way, Modesto (95355-3309)
PHONE..............................209 491-0800
Karen Schemper, *Manager*
EMP: 53 **Privately Held**
WEB: www.regentassistedliving.com
SIC: 8361 Residential care
PA: Regent Assisted Living, Inc.
121 Sw Morrison St # 950
Portland OR 97204

(P-24649)
REGENT ASSISTED LIVING INC
Also Called: Sunshine Villa Assisted Living
80 Front St, Santa Cruz (95060-5098)
PHONE..............................831 459-8400
Deann Daniel, *Manager*
EMP: 80 **Privately Held**
WEB: www.regentassistedliving.com
SIC: 8361 8052 Geriatric residential care;
intermediate care facilities
PA: Regent Assisted Living, Inc.
121 Sw Morrison St # 950
Portland OR 97204

(P-24650)
REGENT ASSISTED LIVING INC
Also Called: Orchard Park
675 W Alluvial Ave Ofc, Clovis
(93611-4403)
PHONE..............................559 325-8400
Debbie Aramian, *Manager*
EMP: 80 **Privately Held**
WEB: www.regentassistedliving.com
SIC: 8361 8052 Residential care; interme-
diate care facilities
PA: Regent Assisted Living, Inc.
121 Sw Morrison St # 950
Portland OR 97204

(P-24651)
RETIREMENT HOUSING FOUNDATION
Also Called: Auburn Ravine Terrace
750 Auburn Ravine Rd, Auburn
(95603-3820)
PHONE..............................530 823-6131
Robert Mauer, *General Mgr*
EMP: 104
SQ FT: 9,756
SALES (corp-wide): 37.3MM **Privately
Held**
WEB: www.bixbyknollstowers.com
SIC: 8361 Residential care
PA: Retirement Housing Foundation Inc
911 N Studebaker Rd # 100
Long Beach CA 90815
562 257-5100

(P-24652)
RETIREMENT LF CARE COMMUNITIES
Also Called: Carlton Plaza of Fremont
3800 Walnut Ave Apt 401, Fremont
(94538-2273)
PHONE..............................510 505-0555
Stephanie Brice, *Exec Dir*
Melanie Bazan, *Director*
EMP: 64
SQ FT: 104,000
SALES (est): 2.5MM **Privately Held**
SIC: 8361 6513 Home for the aged; retire-
ment hotel operation

(P-24653)
RHF PLYMOUTH TOWER
3401 Lemon St Ofc, Riverside
(92501-2817)
PHONE..............................951 248-0456
Wes Jones, *Administration*
EMP: 65
SALES (est): 2.4MM **Privately Held**
WEB: www.bixbyknollstowers.com
SIC: 8361 Residential care

(P-24654)
RITE OF PASS ATHL TRAI CENT
10400 Fricot City Rd, San Andreas
(95249-9642)
PHONE..............................209 736-4500
Ken Dukek, *Manager*
Tod Gathings, *Officer*
Matthew Gosting, *Info Tech Dir*
Marie Culpepper, *Business Mgr*
Patrick Heath, *Accountant*
EMP: 103 **Privately Held**
SIC: 8361 Residential care for children
PA: Rite Of Passage Adolescent Treatment
Centers And Schools, Inc.
2560 Business Pkwy Ste B
Minden NV 89423

(P-24655)
ROBERT C HAMILTON
Also Called: Bel Vista Convalescent Hosp
1760 N Fair Oaks Ave, Pasadena
(91103-1617)
PHONE..............................626 794-4103
Robert C Hamilton, *Owner*
Ann Hamilton, *Owner*
EMP: 70
SQ FT: 2,230
SALES (est): 767.5K **Privately Held**
SIC: 8361 Children's boarding home

(P-24656)
ROSEMARY CHILDRENS SERVICES (PA)
36 S Kinneloa Ave 200, Pasadena
(91107-3853)
PHONE..............................626 844-3033
Greg Wessels, *Exec Dir*
Sungo Wang, *President*
Lynn Lu, *Vice Pres*
Veronica Fuentes, *Admin Sec*
Lesley Evangelista, *Finance Dir*
EMP: 150
SQ FT: 9,000
SALES: 11.6MM **Privately Held**
WEB: www.rosemarychildren.org
SIC: 8361 Home for the emotionally dis-
turbed

(P-24657)
SACRAMENTO CHILDRENS HOME
1217 Del Paso Blvd Ste B, Sacramento
(95815-3660)
PHONE..............................916 927-5059
Roy Alexander, *CEO*
EMP: 62
SALES (corp-wide): 14.9MM **Privately
Held**
SIC: 8361 Children's home
PA: Sacramento Childrens Home
2750 Sutterville Rd
Sacramento CA 95820
916 452-3981

(P-24658)
SACRAMENTO CHILDRENS HOME (PA)
2750 Sutterville Rd, Sacramento
(95820-1093)
PHONE..............................916 452-3981
Roy Alexander, *CEO*
Julia Chubb, *CFO*
Rebecca Clark, *Executive Asst*
Tammy Davis, *VP Human Res*
Laurel Sunderman, *Marketing Staff*
EMP: 125 **EST:** 1867
SQ FT: 15,500
SALES: 14.9MM **Privately Held**
WEB: www.donatetocharity.com
SIC: 8361 Children's home

(P-24659)
SAFE REFUGE
Also Called: SOBRIETY HOUSE
1041 Redondo Ave, Long Beach
(90804-3928)
PHONE..............................562 987-5722
Kathryn Romo, *Exec Dir*
EMP: 80
SQ FT: 2,300
SALES: 4.4MM **Privately Held**
WEB: www.safinc.org
SIC: 8361 Rehabilitation center, residen-
tial: health care incidental

(P-24660)
SAINT JOSEPH HOME CARE NETWORK
1165 Montgomery Dr, Santa Rosa
(95405-4801)
PHONE..............................707 206-9124
Shirley Sleeker, *Administration*
Robert Stanley, *Manager*
EMP: 80
SALES: 11.3MM **Privately Held**
SIC: 8361 Home for the aged

(P-24661)
SALEM CHRISTIAN HOMES INC (PA)
6921 Edison Ave Ste A, Chino
(91710-9058)
PHONE..............................909 614-0575
Roderick McLeish, *Principal*
Bert V Dam, *Treasurer*
Ray Hommes, *Admin Sec*
EMP: 150 **EST:** 1960
SQ FT: 31,400
SALES: 7.1MM **Privately Held**
WEB: www.salemchristianhomes.org
SIC: 8361 Home for the mentally handi-
capped; home for the physically handi-
capped

(P-24662)
SALVATION ARMY
2799 Health Center Dr, San Diego
(92123-2708)
PHONE..............................858 279-1100
James Knaggs, *President*
David Hudson, *Vice Pres*
Michael Woodruff, *Admin Sec*
EMP: 79
SALES (est): 2.2MM **Privately Held**
SIC: 8361 8322 Self-help group home;
emergency shelters

(P-24663)
SALVATION ARMY
154 Oshaughnessy Blvd, San Francisco
(94127-1718)
PHONE..............................415 643-8000
Larry Nakashima, *Principal*
EMP: 100
SALES (corp-wide): 4.3B **Privately Held**
WEB: www.salvationarmy.usawest.org
SIC: 8361 Rehabilitation center, residen-
tial: health care incidental
HQ: The Salvation Army
180 E Ocean Blvd Ste 500
Long Beach CA 90802
562 491-8464

(P-24664)
SAN CLEMENTE VILLAS BY SEA
660 Camino De Los Mares, San Clemente
(92673-1800)
PHONE..............................949 489-3400
Paul J Brazeau,

Jan McAlister, *Exec Dir*
Paul Brazeau, *Marketing Mgr*
Salvador Caballero, *Food Svc Dir*
EMP: 80
SALES (est): 4.8MM **Privately Held**
SIC: 8361 Home for the aged

(P-24665)
SAN FRANCISCO LADIES PROTECTI
Also Called: Heritage, The
3400 Laguna St, San Francisco
(94123-2271)
PHONE..............................415 931-3136
Marla Hastings, *Exec Dir*
Connie Tiret, *Executive*
Audrey Mahoney, *Recruiter*
Debbie Natoli, *Sales Staff*
Raygenia Stewart, *Nursing Dir*
EMP: 100 **EST:** 1853
SQ FT: 15,000
SALES: 15.8MM **Privately Held**
SIC: 8361 Home for the aged

(P-24666)
SAN GABRIEL CHILDRENS CTR INC
4740 N Grand Ave, Covina (91724-2005)
PHONE..............................626 859-2089
Peter Rincon, *Manager*
EMP: 70 **Privately Held**
WEB: www.sangabrielchild.com
SIC: 8361 8322 Children's home; crisis in-
tervention center
PA: San Gabriel Children's Center, Inc.
2200 E Route 66 Ste 100
Glendora CA 91740

(P-24667)
SANTA CLARA COUNTY OF
Also Called: Probation Dept-Juvenile Div
19050 Malaguerra Ave, Morgan Hill
(95037-9032)
PHONE..............................408 201-7600
Nick Berchard, *Manager*
EMP: 70 **Privately Held**
WEB: www.countyairports.org
SIC: 8361 9223 Juvenile correctional
home; correctional institutions;
PA: County Of Santa Clara
3180 Newberry Dr Ste 150
San Jose CA 95118
408 299-5105

(P-24668)
SEASONS
200 W Whittier Blvd, La Habra
(90631-3877)
PHONE..............................562 691-1200
Phil Smith, *Director*
Sherry Burmmer, *Director*
EMP: 80
SALES (est): 3.1MM **Privately Held**
SIC: 8361 Residential care

(P-24669)
SEAVIEW HLTHCRE & REHAB CTR LL
6400 Purdue Dr, Eureka (95503-7095)
PHONE..............................707 443-5668
Ted Chigaros, *Vice Pres*
EMP: 99
SALES (est): 3.2MM **Privately Held**
WEB: www.seaviewfoundation.org
SIC: 8361 Rehabilitation center, residen-
tial: health care incidental

(P-24670)
SENIOR KEIRO HEALTH CARE
Also Called: Japanese Retirement Home
325 S Boyle Ave, Los Angeles
(90033-3812)
PHONE..............................323 263-9651
Shawn Miyake, *CEO*
George Aratani, *President*
Rev David Shigekawa, *Treasurer*
Christina Tatsugawa, *Technology*
EMP: 90
SQ FT: 50,000
SALES: 7.7MM **Privately Held**
SIC: 8361 Home for the aged

(P-24671)
SENIOR RESOURCE GROUP LLC
Also Called: La Vida Del Mar Associates
850 Del Mar Downs Rd # 338, Solana Beach (92075-2725)
PHONE..................................858 519-0890
Terry Oquest, *Manager*
EMP: 50
SALES (corp-wide): 94.1MM **Privately Held**
WEB: www.srgseniorliving.com
SIC: **8361** Residential care
PA: Senior Resource Group, Llc
500 Stevens Ave Ste 100
Solana Beach CA 92075
858 792-9300

(P-24672)
SHALEV SENIOR LIVING
6245 Matilija Ave, Van Nuys (91401-2923)
PHONE..................................818 780-4808
Mia Levi, *Principal*
EMP: 50
SALES (est): 1.1MM **Privately Held**
SIC: **8361** Geriatric residential care

(P-24673)
SIERRA OAKS SENIOR LIVING
1520 Collyer Dr, Redding (96003-9535)
PHONE..................................530 241-5100
Sue Becker, *Director*
EMP: 60
SALES (est): 2MM **Privately Held**
SIC: **8361** Home for the aged

(P-24674)
SILVERADO SENIOR LIVING HOLDIN
6400 Oak Cyn Ste 200, Irvine (92618-5233)
PHONE..................................949 240-7200
Loren B Shook, *CEO*
EMP: 4000
SALES (est): 5.9MM **Privately Held**
SIC: **8361** Home for the aged

(P-24675)
SIPPI ANNE RIVERSIDE RANCH LLP
Also Called: Anne Sppi Clnic Riverside Rnch
18200 Highway 178, Bakersfield (93306-9510)
PHONE..................................661 871-9697
Michael Rosberg, *Owner*
Suzaane Rajlal, *Administration*
EMP: 50
SALES (est): 2MM **Privately Held**
SIC: **8361** Residential care

(P-24676)
SISTERS OF NZARETH LOS ANGELES
3333 Manning Ave, Los Angeles (90064-4804)
PHONE..................................310 839-2361
Margarette Brody, *Administration*
Denise Thibault, *Exec Dir*
EMP: 100
SQ FT: 62,558
SALES: 5.9MM **Privately Held**
WEB: www.nazarethhousela.org
SIC: **8361** Home for the aged

(P-24677)
SKY PARK GARDENS ASSISTED
5510 Sky Pkwy Ofc, Sacramento (95823-2282)
PHONE..................................916 422-5650
Habib Bokhari, *Owner*
EMP: 55
SALES (est): 1.2MM **Privately Held**
SIC: **8361** Residential care

(P-24678)
SOCIAL VOCATIONAL SERVICES INC
1401 Fulton St Ste 510, Fresno (93721-1644)
PHONE..................................559 443-7119
EMP: 74

SALES (corp-wide): 93.5MM **Privately Held**
SIC: **8361** Rehabilitation center, residential; health care incidental
PA: Social Vocational Services, Inc.
3555 Torrance Blvd
Torrance CA 90503
310 944-3303

(P-24679)
SOLHEIM LUTHERAN HOME
2236 Merton Ave, Los Angeles (90041-1915)
PHONE..................................323 257-7518
James Graunke, *Principal*
Alberta Looney, *Records Dir*
Antonio Davila, *CFO*
Norma Heaton, *Exec Dir*
Kari Stenberg, *Admin Asst*
EMP: 185 **EST:** 1923
SQ FT: 82,591
SALES: 12.7MM **Privately Held**
WEB: www.solheimlh.org
SIC: **8361** Home for the aged

(P-24680)
SONOMA CNTY IND LIVING SKILLS
Also Called: Scils
1799 Pepper Rd, Petaluma (94952-9616)
PHONE..................................707 765-8444
Sean Dirworth, *Director*
EMP: 60 **EST:** 1958
SQ FT: 1,100
SALES: 1MM **Privately Held**
SIC: **8361** 8322 Home for the mentally handicapped; individual & family services

(P-24681)
SONORA RETIREMENT CENTER INC
Also Called: Skyline Place
12877 Sylva Ln Ofc, Sonora (95370-6965)
PHONE..................................209 588-0373
Mark Weisner, *President*
EMP: 50
SQ FT: 56,000
SALES (est): 2.9MM **Privately Held**
SIC: **8361** Home for the aged

(P-24682)
SPRINGHUSE MANOR CARE HLTH SVC
285 W Central Ave Ofc, Brea (92821-7518)
PHONE..................................714 671-7898
Larry Roseth, *Exec Dir*
EMP: 60
SALES (est): 1MM **Privately Held**
SIC: **8361** Residential care

(P-24683)
ST ANNES MATERNITY HOME
155 N Occidental Blvd, Los Angeles (90026-4641)
PHONE..................................213 381-2931
Tony Walker, *President*
EMP: 158
SQ FT: 100,000
SALES: 24.5MM **Privately Held**
SIC: **8361** Rehabilitation center, residential; health care incidental

(P-24684)
ST PAULS EPISCOPAL HOME INC
2635 2nd Ave Ofc, San Diego (92103-6597)
PHONE..................................619 239-2097
EMP: 53
SALES (corp-wide): 19.1MM **Privately Held**
SIC: **8361** Home for the aged
PA: St. Paul's Episcopal Home, Inc.
328 Maple St
San Diego CA 92103
619 239-6900

(P-24685)
ST PAULS EPISCOPAL HOME INC
Saint Pauls Health Care Center
235 Nutmeg St, San Diego (92103-6201)
PHONE..................................619 239-8687
Ben Geske, *Manager*
EMP: 65

SQ FT: 1,100
SALES (corp-wide): 19.1MM **Privately Held**
SIC: **8361** 8051 Rest home, with health care incidental; skilled nursing care facilities
PA: St. Paul's Episcopal Home, Inc.
328 Maple St
San Diego CA 92103
619 239-6900

(P-24686)
ST PAULS EPISCOPAL HOME INC
Also Called: St Paul's Villa
2700 E 4th St, National City (91950-3006)
PHONE..................................619 232-2996
Cheryl Wilson, *Director*
EMP: 65
SALES (corp-wide): 19.1MM **Privately Held**
SIC: **8361** Home for the aged
PA: St. Paul's Episcopal Home, Inc.
328 Maple St
San Diego CA 92103
619 239-6900

(P-24687)
STOCKTON CONGREGATIONAL HOME
Also Called: Plymouth Square
1319 N Madison St Ofc, Stockton (95202-1001)
PHONE..................................209 466-4341
Peter Peabody, *Vice Pres*
Stuart Hartman, *Principal*
EMP: 84
SALES: 3.3MM **Privately Held**
SIC: **8361** Home for the aged

(P-24688)
SUMMER HOUSE INC (PA)
206 5th St, Woodland (95695-3505)
P.O. Box 1724 (95776-1724)
PHONE..................................530 662-8493
Erin Plankryan, *Exec Dir*
Dale Campbell, *Exec Dir*
EMP: 54
SQ FT: 6,500
SALES: 1.6MM **Privately Held**
SIC: **8361** 8059 8322 Residential care for the handicapped; home for the mentally retarded; home for the mentally retarded, exc. skilled or intermediate; social services for the handicapped

(P-24689)
SUMMERVILLE AT HAZEL CREEK LLC
Also Called: Hazel Creek Assisted Living
6125 Hazel Ave, Orangevale (95662-4558)
PHONE..................................916 988-7901
Lonnie Irvine, *President*
EMP: 1724
SALES (est): 14.1MM
SALES (corp-wide): 4.7B **Publicly Held**
SIC: **8361** Home for the aged
HQ: Emeritus Corporation
3131 Elliott Ave Ste 500
Milwaukee WI 53214

(P-24690)
SUMMITVIEW CHILD TREATMENT CTR
5036 Sunrey Rd, Placerville (95667-9529)
PHONE..................................530 644-2412
Carla Wills, *Exec Dir*
Anna Gleason, *Director*
Paul Sunseri, *Director*
EMP: 50
SQ FT: 1,480
SALES (est): 5.2MM **Privately Held**
SIC: **8361** Halfway group home, persons with social or personal problems

(P-24691)
SUN CITY RHF HOUSING INC
Also Called: SUN CITY GARDENS
28500 Bradley Rd, Sun City (92586-3029)
PHONE..................................951 679-2391
Trudi Hendrix, *Administration*
EMP: 69

SALES: 4.5MM **Privately Held**
WEB: www.bixbyknollstowers.com
SIC: **8361** Residential care

(P-24692)
SUNHARBOR MANAGEMENT LLC
Also Called: The Valley Inn
708 E 5th St, Holtville (92250-1514)
PHONE..................................760 356-1262
Gary Rust,
Fred Harder,
John Harder,
Elaine Rust,
Bruce Thorne,
EMP: 50
SALES (est): 1.2MM **Privately Held**
SIC: **8361** Residential care

(P-24693)
SUNNYSIDE GARDENS
1025 Carson Dr, Sunnyvale (94086-5800)
PHONE..................................408 730-4070
Anna Ready, *Director*
Jann Acevedo, *Manager*
EMP: 72
SALES (est): 2.4MM **Privately Held**
SIC: **8361** Geriatric residential care

(P-24694)
SUNRISE OF PETALUMA
815 Wood Sorrel Dr, Petaluma (94954-6857)
PHONE..................................707 776-2885
Erin Carlson, *Director*
EMP: 70
SALES (est): 1.4MM **Privately Held**
SIC: **8361** Geriatric residential care

(P-24695)
TEMPLE GARDEN HOMES INC
5746 Loma Ave, Temple City (91780-2452)
PHONE..................................626 286-6408
Florencia Pilpa, *President*
EMP: 50
SALES (est): 2.3MM **Privately Held**
SIC: **8361** Home for the mentally handicapped

(P-24696)
TERRACES RETIREMENT COMMUNITY
Also Called: Lodge Inn and Health Center
2850 Sierra Sunrise Ter, Chico (95928-8401)
PHONE..................................530 894-1010
Cheryl Haury, *CEO*
Cerel Havority, *President*
Heidi Hukill, *CFO*
Grace Mejia, *Principal*
EMP: 166
SQ FT: 1,000
SALES (est): 2.7MM **Privately Held**
WEB: www.theterraceschico.com
SIC: **8361** 8051 Home for the aged; skilled nursing care facilities

(P-24697)
THE REDWOODS A CMNTY SENIORS
Also Called: Redwoods, The
40 Camino Alto Ofc, Mill Valley (94941-2997)
PHONE..................................415 383-2741
Barbara Solomon, *CEO*
Susan Badger, *COO*
Alan Kern, *CFO*
Ron Bruno, *Human Resources*
Glenn Stepp, *Opers Mgr*
EMP: 140
SQ FT: 140,000
SALES: 19.9MM **Privately Held**
WEB: www.redwoodsoft.com
SIC: **8361** Home for the aged

(P-24698)
TIERRA DEL SOL FOUNDATION (PA)
9919 Sunland Blvd, Sunland (91040-1599)
PHONE..................................818 352-1419
Steve Miller, *Exec Dir*
Anne M Rosenstein, *CFO*
Kevin Lehmann, *Program Mgr*
Ingrid Mares, *Program Mgr*
Sergio Uribe, *Program Mgr*

▲ = Import ▼=Export
◆ =Import/Export

EMP: 200
SQ FT: 20,000
SALES: 11.6MM **Privately Held**
WEB: www.tierradelsol.org
SIC: **8361** 8211 8322 Home for the mentally handicapped; home for the physically handicapped; public special education school; individual & family services

(P-24699)
TLC CHILD & FAMILY SERVICES (PA)
1800 Gravenstein Hwy N, Sebastopol (95472-2607)
P.O. Box 2079 (95473-2079)
PHONE..................................707 823-7300
James E Galsterer, *Exec Dir*
Aleia Coate, *President*
Jens Oetiker, *Treasurer*
John Heide, *Bd of Directors*
Margaret Healy, *Exec VP*
EMP: 104
SQ FT: 15,000
SALES: 8.2MM **Privately Held**
WEB: www.tlc4kids.org
SIC: **8361** 8211 Children's home; private special education school

(P-24700)
TRINITY YOUTH SERVICES (PA)
201 N Indian Hill Blvd # 201, Claremont (91711-4668)
P.O. Box 1210 (91711-1210)
PHONE..................................909 980-4755
John Neiuber, *CEO*
Aris Alexandre, *President*
Nathan Mitakides, *President*
Fr Paul O'Callaghan, *Treasurer*
Gary Vrinos, *Vice Pres*
EMP: 60
SQ FT: 7,600
SALES: 19.2MM **Privately Held**
WEB: www.trinitycfs.org
SIC: **8361** Halfway home for delinquents & offenders

(P-24701)
TURNING POINT CMNTY PROGRAMS
Also Called: Turning Point I S A
4600 47th Ave Ste 111, Sacramento (95824-3923)
PHONE..................................916 393-1222
Andre Lavaly, *Branch Mgr*
Russell F Lim, *Psychiatry*
Ron Gilbert, *Director*
EMP: 72
SALES (corp-wide): 33MM **Privately Held**
SIC: **8361** Residential care
PA: Turning Point Community Programs
10850 Gold Center Dr # 325
Rancho Cordova CA 95670
916 364-8395

(P-24702)
TUTERA GROUP INC
Also Called: Kit Carson Nursing & Rehab
811 Court St, Jackson (95642-2131)
PHONE..................................209 223-2231
Shawn Moody, *Manager*
EMP: 100
SALES (corp-wide): 12.6MM **Privately Held**
WEB: www.tutera.com
SIC: **8361** Rest home, with health care incidental
PA: Tutera Group Inc.
7611 State Line Rd # 301
Kansas City MO 64114
816 444-0900

(P-24703)
UNITED CP/S CHLDRNS FNDN LA
11051 Old Snta Susna Pass, Chatsworth (91311-1206)
PHONE..................................818 998-8755
Rick Macdonough, *Administration*
EMP: 135
SQ FT: 20,019
SALES (corp-wide): 26.4MM **Privately Held**
SIC: **8361** 8322 Rehabilitation center, residential: health care incidental; individual & family services

PA: United Cerebral Palsy/Spastic Children's Foundation Of Los Angeles And Ventura Counties
6430 Independence Ave
Woodland Hills CA 91367
818 782-2211

(P-24704)
UPLIFT FAMILY SERVICES (PA)
Also Called: Emq Familiesfirst
251 Llewellyn Ave, Campbell (95008-1940)
PHONE..................................408 379-3790
Darrell Evora, *CEO*
Julie Martinez, *Partner*
R Donald McNeil, *Ch of Bd*
Ellen Ammerman, *CFO*
Jason D Gurahoo, *CFO*
EMP: 60
SQ FT: 65,000
SALES: 93.6MM **Privately Held**
SIC: **8361** Home for the emotionally disturbed

(P-24705)
VALLEY MTN REGIONAL CTR INC
1620 Cummins Dr, Modesto (95358-6414)
PHONE..................................209 529-2626
Richard Jacobs, *Branch Mgr*
EMP: 70
SALES (corp-wide): 159.8MM **Privately Held**
SIC: **8361** Residential care for the handicapped
PA: Valley Mountain Regional Center, Inc.
702 N Aurora St
Stockton CA 95202
209 473-0951

(P-24706)
VALLEY PINTE NURSING REHAB CTR
20090 Stanton Ave, Castro Valley (94546-5203)
PHONE..................................510 538-8464
Daniel Wittman, *Administration*
EMP: 50
SQ FT: 7,500
SALES (est): 5MM **Privately Held**
SIC: **8361** Rehabilitation center, residential: health care incidental

(P-24707)
VALLEY TEEN RANCH
2610 W Shaw Ln Ste 105, Fresno (93711-2775)
PHONE..................................559 437-1144
Connie Clendenan, *Exec Dir*
Legion Escobar, *Tech/Comp Coord*
Jennifer Moore, *Social Worker*
EMP: 76
SQ FT: 9,996
SALES: 4.3MM **Privately Held**
WEB: www.valleyteenranch.org
SIC: **8361** 8322 Group foster home; individual & family services

(P-24708)
VALLEY VILLAGE (PA)
20830 Sherman Way, Winnetka (91306-2707)
PHONE..................................818 587-9450
Debra Donovan, *CEO*
Rebecca Holik, *Director*
EMP: 75 EST: 1973
SQ FT: 14,000
SALES: 16.8MM **Privately Held**
WEB: www.vvc.org
SIC: **8361** Home for the mentally retarded

(P-24709)
VASINDAS AROUND THE CLOCK CARE
Also Called: Around The Clock Home Care
5251 Office Park Dr # 403, Bakersfield (93309-0695)
PHONE..................................661 395-5820
Mary Vasinda, *President*
John Vasinda, *Vice Pres*
Cassandra Ortiz, *Program Dir*
EMP: 50 EST: 1996
SALES: 1.5MM **Privately Held**
SIC: **8361** Geriatric residential care

(P-24710)
VICTOR TREATMENT CENTERS INC
Also Called: Regional Youth Svcs N Vly Schl
9150 E Hwy 12, Victor (95253)
P.O. Box 680 (95253-0680)
PHONE..................................209 340-7900
David Baker, *President*
EMP: 127
SALES (corp-wide): 25MM **Privately Held**
WEB: www.victor.org
SIC: **8361** Rehabilitation center, residential: health care incidental
PA: Victor Treatment Centers, Inc.
1360 E Lassen Ave
Chico CA 95973
530 893-0758

(P-24711)
VICTOR TREATMENT CENTERS INC
Also Called: Willow Creek Treatment Center
341 Irwin Ln, Santa Rosa (95401-5603)
PHONE..................................707 360-1509
Gala Goodwin, *Branch Mgr*
EMP: 130
SQ FT: 3,060
SALES (corp-wide): 25MM **Privately Held**
WEB: www.victor.org
SIC: **8361** Home for the emotionally disturbed
PA: Victor Treatment Centers, Inc.
1360 E Lassen Ave
Chico CA 95973
530 893-0758

(P-24712)
VILLAGE AT GRANITE BAY
8550 Barton Rd, Granite Bay (95746-8843)
PHONE..................................916 789-0326
EMP: 68
SALES (est): 579K **Privately Held**
SIC: **8361**

(P-24713)
VILLAGE AT NORTHRIDGE
9222 Corbin Ave, Northridge (91324-2409)
PHONE..................................818 514-4497
EMP: 159
SALES (est): 1.2MM
SALES (corp-wide): 94.1MM **Privately Held**
SIC: **8361** Home for the aged
PA: Senior Resource Group, Llc
500 Stevens Ave Ste 100
Solana Beach CA 92075
858 792-9300

(P-24714)
VILLAS DE CARLSBAD LTD A CALI (PA)
Also Called: Las Villas De Carlsbad
9619 Chesapeake Dr # 103, San Diego (92123-1368)
PHONE..................................858 565-4424
Jack Rowe, *Partner*
William M Chance, *Partner*
Ronald J McElliott, *Partner*
Daniel A Moriarty, *Partner*
EMP: 120
SQ FT: 3,200
SALES (est): 2.6MM **Privately Held**
SIC: **8361** Home for the aged

(P-24715)
VILLAS DE CARLSBAD LTD A CALI
Also Called: Las Villas De Carlsbad
1088 Laguna Dr, Carlsbad (92008-1858)
PHONE..................................760 434-7116
Jack Rowe, *Owner*
John Villarin, *Records Dir*
Kimberly Kooy, *QC Dir*
Charles Bloom, *Director*
EMP: 50
SALES (est): 1.8MM
SALES (corp-wide): 2.6MM **Privately Held**
SIC: **8361** Home for the aged

PA: Villas De Carlsbad Ltd, A California Limited Partnership
9619 Chesapeake Dr # 103
San Diego CA 92123
858 565-4424

(P-24716)
VISTA DEL MAR CHILD FMLY SVCS
1533 Euclid St, Santa Monica (90404-3306)
PHONE..................................310 836-1223
Louis Josephson, *Branch Mgr*
EMP: 413
SALES (corp-wide): 45.5MM **Privately Held**
SIC: **8361** Home for the mentally handicapped
PA: Vista Del Mar Child And Family Services
3200 Motor Ave
Los Angeles CA 90034
310 202-0669

(P-24717)
WATERS EDGE LODGE
801 Island Dr Apt 267, Alameda (94502-6765)
PHONE..................................510 769-6264
Christian Zimmerman, *Partner*
John Zimmerman, *Partner*
EMP: 50
SALES (est): 2.9MM **Privately Held**
WEB: www.watersedgelodge.com
SIC: **8361** Home for the aged

(P-24718)
WESTCARE CALIFORNIA INC (HQ)
1900 N Gateway Blvd 100, Fresno (93727-1622)
PHONE..................................559 251-4800
Richard Steinberg, *President*
Jenifer Nolan, *President*
Sean Jenkins, *Vice Pres*
Shawn Jenkins, *Vice Pres*
Maurice Lee, *Vice Pres*
EMP: 54 EST: 1973
SALES (est): 10MM
SALES (corp-wide): 10.1MM **Privately Held**
SIC: **8361** 8093 Rehabilitation center, residential: health care incidental; specialty outpatient clinics
PA: Westcare Foundation, Inc.
1711 Whitney Mesa Dr # 100
Henderson NV 89014
702 385-3330

(P-24719)
WESTERN LIVING CONCEPTS INC (PA)
Also Called: Timber Ridge At Eureka
2740 Timber Ridge Ln Ofc, Eureka (95503-4867)
PHONE..................................707 443-3000
Erica Farnum, *Exec Dir*
Andrew Roberts, *Director*
EMP: 50
SALES (est): 3.3MM **Privately Held**
SIC: **8361** Home for the aged

(P-24720)
WESTLIVING MANAGEMENT LLC (PA)
5800 Armada Dr Ste 100, Carlsbad (92008-4611)
PHONE..................................760 602-5850
John Rimbach,
Kimberly Holmes, *Vice Pres*
Ana Fejerang, *Human Res Dir*
Kathy Naber-Jordan, *Opers Dir*
Kelly East, *Opers Staff*
EMP: 51
SALES (est): 3.7MM **Privately Held**
SIC: **8361** Geriatric residential care

(P-24721)
WESTMONT LIVING INC
Also Called: Terraces of Roseville, The
707 Sunrise Ave, Roseville (95661-4524)
PHONE..................................916 786-3277
Andrew Plant, *President*
Deborah Taylor, *Exec Dir*
EMP: 326

SALES (corp-wide): 37.3MM **Privately Held**
SIC: **8361** Home for the aged
PA: Westmont Living, Inc.
7660 Fay Ave Ste N
La Jolla CA 92037
858 456-1233

(P-24722)
WESTMONT LIVING INC (PA)
7660 Fay Ave Ste N, La Jolla (92037-4875)
PHONE..........................858 456-1233
Michael O Rourke, *CEO*
Susie Stangroom, *Shareholder*
Andrew Plant, *President*
Leo McKinley, *CFO*
Jennie Edwards, *Accountant*
EMP: 135
SALES (est) 37.3MM **Privately Held**
SIC: **8361** Home for the aged

(P-24723)
WHITE RABBIT PARTNERS INC
9000 W Sunset Blvd # 1500, West Holly-
wood (90069-5815)
PHONE..........................310 975-1450
Andrew William Spanswick, *CEO*
EMP: 150 EST: 2009
SALES (est) 3.5MM **Privately Held**
SIC: **8361** Residential care

(P-24724)
WILLOW SPRNGS ALZHMRS SPCL CR
191 Churn Creek Rd, Redding
(96003-3044)
PHONE..........................530 242-0654
Jerry Erwin, *Partner*
EMP: 50
SALES (est) 2.1MM **Privately Held**
SIC: **8361** **8099** Rehabilitation center, resi-
dential: health care incidental; blood re-
lated health services

(P-24725)
WILSHIRE HEALTH AND CMNTY SVCS
Also Called: Heritage House
903 Carmen Dr, Camarillo (93010-4527)
PHONE..........................805 484-2777
Heather Frankel, *Director*
EMP: 60
SALES (corp-wide): 13MM **Privately Held**
SIC: **8361** Home for the aged
PA: Wilshire Health And Community Serv-
ices, Inc.
285 South St Ste J
San Luis Obispo CA 93401
805 547-7025

(P-24726)
YOUTH HOMES INCORPORATED
Also Called: Anderson House
1159 Everett Ct, Concord (94518-1714)
P.O. Box 5759, Walnut Creek (94596-
1759)
PHONE..........................925 933-2627
Stuart McCoullough, *Exec Dir*
Jeffrey Sliemers, *Director*
EMP: 55
SALES (corp-wide): 7.7MM **Privately Held**
WEB: www.youthhomes.org
SIC: **8361** Home for the emotionally dis-
turbed
PA: Youth Homes Incorporated
3480 Buskirk Ave Ste 210
Pleasant Hill CA 94523
925 933-2627

8399 Social Services, NEC

(P-24727)
A BETTER WAY INC (PA)
3200 Adeline St, Berkeley (94703-2407)
PHONE..........................510 601-0203
Shahnaz Mazandarani, *Exec Dir*
Anita Inman, *Office Mgr*
Jonathan Trejo, *Admin Asst*
Tiffany Lawless, *Personnel Assit*
Jessie Cohen, *Opers Spvr*
EMP: 150

SALES: 8.7MM **Privately Held**
SIC: **8399** Community development groups

(P-24728)
A COMMUNITY FOR PEACE
6060 Sunrise Vista Dr # 2340, Citrus
Heights (95610-7057)
PHONE..........................916 728-5613
Carole Ching, *President*
EMP: 51
SALES: 836.8K **Privately Held**
SIC: **8399** Advocacy group

(P-24729)
ADVANCED MEDICAL PLACEMENT
Also Called: Leadhealthstaff
18425 Burbank Blvd # 508, Tarzana
(91356-6692)
PHONE..........................818 996-9812
Labanyendu Pattanaik, *President*
Chris Speer, *Info Tech Dir*
Todd Suk, *Info Tech Dir*
Chalinee Menchaya, *Payroll Mgr*
Todd Sukpatratham, *Manager*
EMP: 120
SQ FT: 1,400
SALES: 2MM **Privately Held**
SIC: **8399** Health systems agency

(P-24730)
ALTA HEALTHCARE SYSTEM LLC
Also Called: Van Nuys Community Hospital
14433 Emelita St, Van Nuys (91401-4213)
PHONE..........................818 787-1511
Tony Lozano, *Branch Mgr*
Rebecca Levy, *CFO*
Joseph Pipes, *Food Svc Dir*
Creg Parks, *Director*
Aimee Tolentino, *Director*
EMP: 250
SALES (corp-wide): 815.3MM **Privately Held**
SIC: **8399** **8063** Health systems agency;
psychiatric hospitals
HQ: Alta Healthcare System Llc
4081 E Olympic Blvd
Los Angeles CA 90023
323 267-0477

(P-24731)
ALTA HEALTHCARE SYSTEM LLC (HQ)
4081 E Olympic Blvd, Los Angeles
(90023-3330)
PHONE..........................323 267-0477
David Topper, *Mng Member*
Mellisa Ramirez, *Human Res Mgr*
Sam Lee,
Mark Blevins, *Manager*
EMP: 250 EST: 1998
SALES (est): 20.5MM
SALES (corp-wide): 815.3MM **Privately Held**
SIC: **8399** Health systems agency
PA: Prospect Medical Holdings, Inc.
3415 S Sepulveda Blvd # 9
Los Angeles CA 90034
310 943-4500

(P-24732)
AMADOR TLMNE CMNTY ACTION AGCY (PA)
Also Called: Atcaa
10590 State Highway 88, Jackson
(95642-9470)
PHONE..........................209 296-2785
Shelly Hance, *Exec Dir*
Patty Cunningham, *Deputy Dir*
EMP: 150
SALES (est): 11MM **Privately Held**
SIC: **8399** Community action agency

(P-24733)
AMADOR TLMNE CMNTY ACTION AGCY
Also Called: Aatcaa Headstart
427 Highway 49, Sonora (95370-5666)
PHONE..........................209 533-1397
Shelly Hance, *Exec Dir*
EMP: 50
SALES (est): 1.3MM
SALES (corp-wide): 11MM **Privately Held**
SIC: **8399** Community action agency

PA: Amador Tuolumne Community Action
Agency
10590 State Highway 88
Jackson CA 95642
209 296-2785

(P-24734)
AMADOR-TOLUMNE CMNTY RESOURCES
Also Called: Atcr
10590 State Highway 88, Jackson
(95642-9470)
PHONE..........................209 223-1485
Shelly Hance, *Exec Dir*
EMP: 99
SALES: 1MM **Privately Held**
SIC: **8399** Community action agency

(P-24735)
AMERICAN CANCER SOC CAL DIV
Also Called: Discovery Shop
1103 Branham Ln, San Jose (95118-3702)
PHONE..........................408 265-5535
Wendy Huge, *Branch Mgr*
EMP: 50
SALES (corp-wide): 38.2MM **Privately Held**
SIC: **8399** Social service information ex-
change
PA: American Cancer Society California Di-
vision, Inc
1001 Marina Village Pkwy
Alameda CA 94501
510 893-7900

(P-24736)
AMERICAN RED CROSS SAN DIEGO (PA)
3950 Calle Fortunada, San Diego
(92123-1827)
PHONE..........................858 309-1200
Joe Craver, *CEO*
EMP: 90
SALES (est): 9.6MM **Privately Held**
SIC: **8399** Council for social agency

(P-24737)
ARC OF SAN DIEGO (PA)
Also Called: ARC ENTERPRISES
3030 Market St, San Diego (92102-3230)
PHONE..........................619 685-1175
David W Schneider, *CEO*
Anthony J Desalis, *COO*
Chad Lyle, *CFO*
Mary Yumul, *Senior VP*
Jennifer Bates Navarra, *Vice Pres*
▲ EMP: 2000
SQ FT: 55,093
SALES: 33.9MM **Privately Held**
WEB: www.arc-sd.com
SIC: **8399** **8351** **8361** **8322** Advocacy
group; child day care services; home for
the mentally retarded; individual & family
services

(P-24738)
ARC OF SAN DIEGO
Also Called: ARC - SD E Cnty Training Ctrs
1855 John Towers Ave, El Cajon
(92020-1116)
PHONE..........................619 448-2415
Millie Oveross, *Manager*
EMP: 175
SALES (est): 1.2MM
SALES (corp-wide): 33.9MM **Privately Held**
WEB: www.arc-sd.com
SIC: **8399** **8361** Advocacy group; home for
the physically handicapped
PA: The Arc Of San Diego
3030 Market St
San Diego CA 92102
619 685-1175

(P-24739)
ASIAN PCF HLTH CARE VENTR INC (PA)
4216 Fountain Ave, Los Angeles
(90029-2256)
PHONE..........................323 644-3880
Kazue Shibata, *CEO*
Nardo Beltran, *CFO*
Raymond Ho, *Executive*
Lorali Delos Reyes, *Principal*

San Kim, *Technology*
EMP: 104
SQ FT: 1,800
SALES: 16.2MM **Privately Held**
WEB: www.realyc.com
SIC: **8399** Health systems agency

(P-24740)
ASSISTANCE LEAGUE FOOTHILL COM
Also Called: SAN ANTONIO COMMUNITY
HOSPITAL
8555 Archibald Ave 8593, Rancho Cuca-
monga (91730-4633)
P.O. Box 927, Upland (91785-0927)
PHONE..........................909 987-2813
Esther Mott, *Treasurer*
Sandy Kimball, *Treasurer*
Linda Melmeth, *Director*
EMP: 167
SQ FT: 10,000
SALES: 506.7K **Privately Held**
SIC: **8399** Fund raising organization, non-
fee basis

(P-24741)
ASSISTANCE LEAGUE OF REDLANDS
Also Called: ASSISTANCE LEAGUE THRIFT
SHOP
506 W Colton Ave, Redlands (92374-3054)
PHONE..........................909 792-2675
Madelene Handy, *President*
Sandy Arsenault, *Treasurer*
Beth Goodrich, *Manager*
EMP: 150
SALES: 593.9K **Privately Held**
WEB: www.assistanceleague.org
SIC: **8399** **5932** Advocacy group; clothing,
secondhand

(P-24742)
ASSOCIATED STUDENTS UCLA (PA)
Also Called: Ucla Bookstore
308 Westwood Plz, Los Angeles
(90095-8355)
PHONE..........................310 825-4321
Robert Williams, *Principal*
Rich Delia, *CFO*
Moises Roman, *Bd of Directors*
Samantha West, *Associate Dir*
Alex Flores, *Social Dir*
EMP: 500
SQ FT: 200,000
SALES: 42.7MM **Privately Held**
SIC: **8399** **5942** Council for social agency;
book stores

(P-24743)
ASSOCIATED STUDENTS UCLA
924 Westwood Blvd, Los Angeles
(90024-2910)
PHONE..........................310 794-0242
Roseanna P Malone, *Branch Mgr*
EMP: 139
SALES (corp-wide): 42.7MM **Privately Held**
SIC: **8399** Council for social agency
PA: Associated Students U.C.L.A.
308 Westwood Plz
Los Angeles CA 90095
310 825-4321

(P-24744)
BASIC OCCPATIONAL TRAINING CTR
Also Called: Basic Occpational Training Ctr
1323 Jet Way, Perris (92571-7466)
PHONE..........................951 657-8028
Richard Yodites, *President*
Mitzies Yodites, *Exec Dir*
EMP: 154 EST: 1994
SQ FT: 12,000
SALES: 6.5MM **Privately Held**
SIC: **8399** Community development groups

(P-24745)
BEACH CITIES HEALTH DISTRICT
514 N Prospect Ave Fl 3, Redondo Beach
(90277-3036)
PHONE..........................310 318-7939
Susan Burden, *CEO*
Steve Groom, *CFO*

EMP: 108
SQ FT: 3,156
SALES (est): 9.8MM **Privately Held**
SIC: 8399 Health systems agency

(P-24746)
CALIFORNIA ENDOWMENT (PA)
1000 N Alameda St, Los Angeles
(90012-1804)
PHONE..................................800 449-4149
Robert K Ross, *President*
Robert Alaniz, *President*
Dan C Deleon, *CFO*
Ruth Wernig, *Ch Invest Ofcr*
Cecilia Echeverr A, *Officer*
EMP: 80
SQ FT: 110,000
SALES: 201.1MM **Privately Held**
SIC: 8399 Fund raising organization, non-fee basis

(P-24747)
CALIFORNIA RURAL INDIAN HEALTH
1020 Sun Down Way, Roseville
(95661-4473)
PHONE..................................916 437-0104
James Crouch, *Exec Dir*
Jason C Lopez, *CFO*
Laura Rambeau-Lawson, *Treasurer*
Susan Dahl, *Officer*
Mark Lebeau, *Exec Dir*
EMP: 80
SQ FT: 18,627
SALES: 53.6MM **Privately Held**
WEB: www.crihb.org
SIC: 8399 Health & welfare council

(P-24748)
CALIFRNIA ATISM FOUNDATION INC (PA)
4075 Lakeside Dr, Richmond (94806-1937)
PHONE..................................510 758-0433
John Rockefeller, *Principal*
John D Rockefeller, *CEO*
Don Johnson, *CFO*
Xiaoming Lou, *Principal*
Monique Hatcher, *Admin Asst*
EMP: 250
SQ FT: 4,400
SALES: 7.3MM **Privately Held**
SIC: 8399 Community development groups

(P-24749)
CANCER FEDERATION INC (PA)
711 W Ramsey St, Banning (92220-4941)
P.O. Box 1298 (92220-0009)
PHONE..................................951 849-4325
John Steinbacher, *Trust Officer*
Karen Alene, *Administration*
EMP: 200
SALES: 580K **Privately Held**
WEB: www.cancerfed.com
SIC: 8399 8011 Social service information exchange; offices & clinics of medical doctors

(P-24750)
CAPC INC
Also Called: COMMUNITY ADVOCATE FOR PEOPLE'
7200 Greenleaf Ave # 170, Whittier
(90602-1391)
PHONE..................................562 693-8826
Carolyn Reggio, *Exec Dir*
Paul Velasco, *President*
Cheryl Turner, *Treasurer*
Maria Segovia, *Admin Sec*
Itzel Ayala, *Director*
EMP: 150
SALES: 3.9MM **Privately Held**
SIC: 8399 Advocacy group

(P-24751)
CEMENT MASON HEALTH & WELFARE
220 Campus Ln, Suisun City (94534-1497)
PHONE..................................707 864-3300
Marvin Johnson, *Manager*
EMP: 100 **EST:** 1963
SQ FT: 43,000
SALES: 25.7MM **Privately Held**
WEB: www.norcalcementmasons.org
SIC: 8399 6282 Fund raising organization, non-fee basis; investment advice

(P-24752)
CITY OF POMONA
Also Called: Welfare Dept
2040 W Holt Ave Fl 2, Pomona
(91768-3307)
PHONE..................................909 397-5506
John Minato, *Director*
EMP: 400
SQ FT: 3,455 **Privately Held**
SIC: 8399 Social service information exchange
PA: Pomona, City Of (Inc)
585 E Holt Ave
Pomona CA 91767
909 620-2051

(P-24753)
COLUSA INDIAN CMNTY COUNCIL
Also Called: Colusa Casino
3740 Highway 45, Colusa (95932-4030)
PHONE..................................530 458-6572
Laurie Costa, *Director*
EMP: 650 **Privately Held**
WEB: www.colusacasino.com
SIC: 8399 7991 Community development groups; health club
PA: Colusa Indian Community Council
3730 State Highway 45 B
Colusa CA 95932
530 458-8231

(P-24754)
COMMUNICATION SVC FOR DEAF INC
Also Called: Community Services For Deaf
81 W March Ln, Stockton (95207-5723)
PHONE..................................209 475-5000
Rhasan Waser, *Manager*
EMP: 50
SALES (corp-wide): 31.5MM **Privately Held**
WEB: www.relaysd.com
SIC: 8399 Social service information exchange
PA: Communication Service For The Deaf, Inc.
2028 E B White 240-5250
Austin TX 78741
844 222-0002

(P-24755)
COMMUNITY ACTION COMMSN SANTA
4545 10th St, Guadalupe (93434-1421)
PHONE..................................805 343-0615
Fran Forman, *Exec Dir*
EMP: 122
SALES (corp-wide): 22.1MM **Privately Held**
SIC: 8399 Community action agency
PA: Community Action Commission Of Santa Barbara County
5638 Hollister Ave # 230
Goleta CA 93117
805 964-8857

(P-24756)
COMMUNITY ACTION COMMSN SANTA
1890 Sandalwood Dr, Santa Maria
(93455-2846)
PHONE..................................805 614-0786
Miriam Angel, *Manager*
EMP: 400
SALES (corp-wide): 22.1MM **Privately Held**
WEB: www.cacsb.com
SIC: 8399 8322 Community action agency; individual & family services
PA: Community Action Commission Of Santa Barbara County
5638 Hollister Ave # 230
Goleta CA 93117
805 964-8857

(P-24757)
COMMUNITY ACTION COMMSN SANTA (PA)
Also Called: C A C
5638 Hollister Ave # 230, Goleta
(93117-3474)
PHONE..................................805 964-8857
Fran Forman, *President*
Linda Wilkes, *Regional Mgr*

Kc Adornetto, *General Mgr*
Elizabeth Fry, *General Mgr*
Mark Navarro, *Accountant*
EMP: 50
SALES: 22.1MM **Privately Held**
WEB: www.cacsb.com
SIC: 8399 Community action agency

(P-24758)
COMMUNITY ACTION COMMSN SANTA
201 W Chapel St, Santa Maria
(93458-4303)
PHONE..................................805 922-2243
Maggie Espinosa, *Manager*
EMP: 60
SALES (corp-wide): 22.1MM **Privately Held**
WEB: www.cacsb.com
SIC: 8399 Community action agency
PA: Community Action Commission Of Santa Barbara County
5638 Hollister Ave # 230
Goleta CA 93117
805 964-8857

(P-24759)
COMMUNITY ACTION PARTNERSHIP O
141 Stony Cir Ste 210, Santa Rosa
(95401-4142)
PHONE..................................707 544-0120
Oscar Chavez, *President*
Karen Erickson, *Vice Pres*
Mary Watts, *Prgrmr*
Herman Hernandez, *Corp Comm Staff*
Marlyn Garcia, *Asst Director*
EMP: 226
SQ FT: 18,000
SALES: 11.4MM **Privately Held**
WEB: www.fhosc.org
SIC: 8399 Antipoverty board; community action agency

(P-24760)
COMMUNITY ACTION PARTNR KERN
7998 Alicante Ave, Lamont (93241-1744)
PHONE..................................661 845-3901
Maryann Mooney, *Manager*
EMP: 88
SALES (corp-wide): 63.1MM **Privately Held**
SIC: 8399 Community action agency
PA: Community Action Partnership Of Kern
5005 Business Park N
Bakersfield CA 93309
661 336-5236

(P-24761)
COMMUNITY ACTION PARTNR KERN
2400 Truxtun Ave, Bakersfield
(93301-3405)
PHONE..................................661 336-0317
EMP: 66
SALES (corp-wide): 63.1MM **Privately Held**
SIC: 8399 8351 Community action agency; preschool center
PA: Community Action Partnership Of Kern
5005 Business Park N
Bakersfield CA 93309
661 336-5236

(P-24762)
COMMUNITY ACTION PARTNR KERN
814 N Norma St, Ridgecrest (93555-3509)
PHONE..................................760 371-1469
Maria Harley, *Branch Mgr*
EMP: 110
SALES (corp-wide): 63.1MM **Privately Held**
SIC: 8399 8351 Community action agency; child day care services
PA: Community Action Partnership Of Kern
5005 Business Park N
Bakersfield CA 93309
661 336-5236

(P-24763)
COMMUNITY ACTION PARTNR KERN
4404 Pioneer Dr, Bakersfield (93306-5730)
PHONE..................................661 366-5953
Marie Galaviz, *Branch Mgr*
EMP: 66
SALES (corp-wide): 63.1MM **Privately Held**
SIC: 8399 Community action agency
PA: Community Action Partnership Of Kern
5005 Business Park N
Bakersfield CA 93309
661 336-5236

(P-24764)
COMMUNITY ACTION PRTNSHIP SB C
Also Called: Capsbc
696 S Tippecanoe Ave, San Bernardino
(92408-2607)
PHONE..................................909 723-1500
Patricia L Nickols, *CEO*
Joanne Gilbert, *Ch of Bd*
Socorro Enriquez, *Vice Chairman*
Richard Schmidt, *CFO*
Ammie Hines, *Treasurer*
EMP: 88
SALES: 24.2MM **Privately Held**
SIC: 8399 8699 Community action agency; charitable organization

(P-24765)
COMMUNITY PARTNERS (PA)
1000 N Alameda St Ste 240, Los Angeles
(90012-1804)
PHONE..................................213 346-3200
Paul Vandeventer, *President*
Gary Erickson, *Ch of Bd*
Janet Elliott, *CFO*
Eric V Ibarra, *Exec Dir*
Alfred Carrillo, *Controller*
EMP: 75
SALES: 41.7MM **Privately Held**
WEB: www.communitypartners.org
SIC: 8399 Social service information exchange

(P-24766)
COUNTY OF DEL NORTE
Also Called: Health and Human Service
880 Northcrest Dr, Crescent City
(95531-2313)
PHONE..................................707 464-3191
Gary Blatnick, *Director*
Warren Rehwaldt, *Director*
Jocelyn Woodral, *Supervisor*
EMP: 120 **Privately Held**
SIC: 8399 Health systems agency
PA: County Of Del Norte
981 H St Ste 200
Crescent City CA 95531
707 464-7204

(P-24767)
COUNTY OF KERN
Also Called: Human Services Dept
100 E California Ave, Bakersfield
(93307-1031)
P.O. Box 511 (93302-0511)
PHONE..................................661 631-6346
Kathleen Irvine, *Director*
EMP: 800 **Privately Held**
WEB: www.kccfc.org
SIC: 8399 9199 Health & welfare council; general government administration
PA: County Of Kern
1115 Truxtun Ave Rm 505
Bakersfield CA 93301
661 868-3690

(P-24768)
COUNTY OF LOS ANGELES
Also Called: Health Services, Dept of
5555 Ferguson Dr, Commerce
(90022-5164)
PHONE..................................323 869-7063
Angie Toyota, *Manager*
Elda Borjas, *Manager*
EMP: 75 **Privately Held**
WEB: www.co.la.ca.us
SIC: 8399 9431 Health systems agency; administration of public health programs;

P R O D U C T S & S V C S

(PA)=Parent Co (HQ)=Headquarters (DH)=Div Headquarters
✿ = New Business established in last 2 years

2019 Directory of California
Wholesalers and Services Companies

1049

PA: County Of Los Angeles
500 W Temple St Ste 437
Los Angeles CA 90012
213 974-1101

(P-24769)
COUNTY OF LOS ANGELES
Also Called: Department Public Social Svcs
8130 Atlantic Ave, Cudahy (90201-5804)
PHONE.....................323 560-5001
Lilia Erviti, *Director*
EMP: 220 **Privately Held**
SIC: 8399 Community development groups
PA: County Of Los Angeles
500 W Temple St Ste 437
Los Angeles CA 90012
213 974-1101

(P-24770)
COUNTY OF MONTEREY
Also Called: Health Department
1270 Natividad Rd, Salinas (93906-3144)
PHONE.....................831 755-4500
Len Foster, *Manager*
EMP: 50 **Privately Held**
WEB: www.montereycountyfarmbureau.org
SIC: 8399 9111 Health & welfare council;
county supervisors' & executives' offices
PA: County Of Monterey
168 W Alisal St Fl 2
Salinas CA 93901
831 755-5040

(P-24771)
COUNTY OF RIVERSIDE
Also Called: Community Health Agency
4065 County Circle Dr, Riverside
(92503-3410)
P.O. Box 7600 (92513-7600)
PHONE.....................951 358-5306
Gary Feldman, *Director*
EMP: 400 **Privately Held**
SIC: 8399 9511 Health systems agency;
PA: County Of Riverside
4080 Lemon St Fl 11
Riverside CA 92501
951 955-1110

(P-24772)
COUNTY OF SAN JOAQUIN
Also Called: Neighborhood Preservation Div
1810 E Hazelton Ave, Stockton
(95205-6232)
PHONE.....................209 468-3021
Carrie Sullivan, *Director*
EMP: 60 **Privately Held**
WEB: www.sjclawlib.org
SIC: 8399 9441 Community development
groups; public welfare administration:
non-operating, government
PA: County Of San Joaquin
44 N San Joaquin St # 640
Stockton CA 95202
209 468-3203

(P-24773)
COUNTY OF STANISLAUS
Also Called: Behavioral Hlth Recovery Svcs
800 Scenic Dr, Modesto (95350-6131)
PHONE.....................209 525-6225
Denise C Hunt, *Director*
Rudy Duran, *Manager*
EMP: 99 **Privately Held**
WEB: www.co.stanislaus.ca.us
SIC: 8399 Health & welfare council
PA: County Of Stanislaus
1010 10th St Ste 5100
Modesto CA 95354
209 525-6398

(P-24774)
DESERT AREA RESOURCES TRAINING
Also Called: Early Childhood Services
201 E Ridgecrest Blvd, Ridgecrest
(93555-3919)
PHONE.....................760 375-8494
Fax: 760 375-1288
EMP: 70
SALES (est): 619.4K **Privately Held**
SIC: 8399

(P-24775)
DREW HEALTH FOUNDATION
1191 Runnymede St, East Palo Alto
(94303-1331)
P.O. Box 50997, Palo Alto (94303-0678)
PHONE.....................650 328-1619
Myrtle Walker, *President*
Ora Johnson, *Manager*
EMP: 50
SQ FT: 84,000
SALES: 152.5K **Privately Held**
SIC: 8399 Health & welfare council; health
systems agency

(P-24776)
EAST BAY COMMUNITY FOUNDATION
Also Called: E B C F
200 Frank H Ogawa Plz, Oakland
(94612-2005)
PHONE.....................510 836-3223
Nichole Taylor, *President*
Karen Stevenson, *President*
EMP: 55
SQ FT: 15,500
SALES: 25.8MM **Privately Held**
WEB: www.eastbaycf.org
SIC: 8399 Community development groups

(P-24777)
EASTER SEALS SOUTHERN CAL INC
710 W Broadway, Glendale (91204-1010)
PHONE.....................818 551-0128
Gloria Acosta, *Director*
EMP: 80
SALES (corp-wide): 179.7MM **Privately Held**
WEB: www.essc.org
SIC: 8399 8322 Fund raising organization,
non-fee basis; individual & family services
PA: Easter Seals Southern California, Inc.
1063 Mcgaw Ave Ste 100
Irvine CA 92614
714 834-1111

(P-24778)
EASTER SEALS SOUTHERN CAL INC
Also Called: Easter Seal Society
340 E Avenue I Ste 101, Lancaster
(93535-1941)
PHONE.....................661 723-3414
Paula Pompa-Craven, *Director*
EMP: 50
SALES (corp-wide): 179.7MM **Privately Held**
WEB: www.essc.org
SIC: 8399 8322 Fund raising organization,
non-fee basis; individual & family services
PA: Easter Seals Southern California, Inc.
1063 Mcgaw Ave Ste 100
Irvine CA 92614
714 834-1111

(P-24779)
EL SEGUNDO EDUCTL FOUNDATION
641 Sheldon St, El Segundo (90245-3036)
PHONE.....................310 615-2650
Duane Conover, *President*
Alex Abad, *Vice Chairman*
Geoff Yantz, *Superintendent*
EMP: 300
SALES: 1.9MM **Privately Held**
SIC: 8399 Fund raising organization, non-
fee basis

(P-24780)
ESSENTIAL ACCESS HEALTH (PA)
Also Called: Cfhc
3600 Wilshire Blvd # 600, Los Angeles
(90010-2603)
PHONE.....................213 386-5614
Julie Rabinovitz, *President*
Diane Chamberlain, *COO*
Ama Fulcher, *CFO*
Nomsa Khalfani, *Senior VP*
Brenda Flores, *Vice Pres*
EMP: 81 **EST:** 1968
SQ FT: 18,000

SALES: 26.4MM **Privately Held**
SIC: 8399 8011 8099 Fund raising organization, non-fee basis; primary care medical clinic; medical services organization

(P-24781)
ETHIOPIAN WORLD FEDERATION
422 E 41st St, Los Angeles (90011-2906)
PHONE.....................323 844-1826
Enoch Nack, *Principal*
EMP: 50
SALES (est): 991.9K **Privately Held**
SIC: 8399 Social services

(P-24782)
FRIENDS FITZGERALD MAR RESERVE
Also Called: F F M L R
200 Nevada Ave, Moss Beach (94038)
PHONE.....................650 728-3584
Mary Wolfe, *Admin Sec*
Mary Delong, *President*
EMP: 70
SALES (est): 798.2K **Privately Held**
WEB: www.fitzgeraldreserve.org
SIC: 8399 Social service information ex-
change

(P-24783)
FRIENDS OF THE LOS ANGELES
8405 Beverly Blvd, Los Angeles
(90048-3401)
PHONE.....................323 653-0440
EMP: 200
SALES: 2.2MM **Privately Held**
SIC: 8399

(P-24784)
GOLD COUNTRY HEALTH CENTER INC (PA)
4301 Golden Center Dr, Placerville
(95667-6260)
PHONE.....................530 621-1100
Suzanne Valoppi, *Administration*
Angela Chuculate, *Director*
EMP: 130
SQ FT: 57,000
SALES (est): 8.2MM **Privately Held**
SIC: 8399 Health & welfare council

(P-24785)
GREATER LOS ANGELES ZOO ASSN
Also Called: Glaza
5333 Zoo Dr, Los Angeles (90027-1451)
PHONE.....................323 644-4200
Connie M Morgan, *President*
Jeb Bonner, *CFO*
Robert N Ruth, *Treasurer*
Eugenia Vasels, *Vice Pres*
Genie Vasels, *Vice Pres*
EMP: 100
SQ FT: 8,200
SALES: 16.8MM **Privately Held**
SIC: 8399 7999 Fund raising organization,
non-fee basis; concession operator

(P-24786)
HABITAT FOR HUMANITY OF GREATE
8739 Artesia Blvd, Bellflower (90706-6330)
PHONE.....................310 323-4663
Erin Garrity Rank, *President*
Mark Van Lue, *COO*
Gia Stokes, *CFO*
Veronica Garcia, *Vice Pres*
Alison Treleaven J, *Vice Pres*
EMP: 50
SALES: 23.2MM **Privately Held**
WEB: www.habitatla.org
SIC: 8399 Fund raising organization, non-
fee basis

(P-24787)
HARBOR DEVELOPMENTAL DISABILIT
Also Called: Harbor Regional Center
21231 Hawthorne Blvd, Torrance
(90503-5501)
P.O. Box 2930 (90509-2930)
PHONE.....................310 540-1711
Judy Wada, *CFO*
Liz Cohen-Zeboulon, *Program Mgr*

Pablo Ibanez, *Program Mgr*
Tonantzin Martinez, *Program Mgr*
Patricia Piceno, *Program Mgr*
EMP: 225
SQ FT: 60,000
SALES: 173.6MM **Privately Held**
SIC: 8399 Council for social agency

(P-24788)
HEALTH ADVOCATES LLC
14721 Califa St, Van Nuys (91411-3107)
PHONE.....................818 995-9500
Al Leibovic, *Mng Member*
William Russell, *CFO*
Nuria Morales, *Human Res Mgr*
Tamla Roberts, *Marketing Staff*
Aaron Leibovic, *Mng Member*
EMP: 371
SQ FT: 40,900
SALES (est): 16.2MM **Privately Held**
SIC: 8399 Advocacy group

(P-24789)
HOSPITAL ASSN SOUTHERN CAL (PA)
Also Called: Hasc
515 S Figueroa St # 1300, Los Angeles
(90071-3301)
PHONE.....................213 347-2002
Jim Barber, *CEO*
Roger Seaver, *Ch of Bd*
Isela Rivas, *President*
Scott Toomey, *CFO*
Martin Gallegos, *Senior VP*
EMP: 58
SQ FT: 30,000
SALES (est): 8.3MM **Privately Held**
WEB: www.reddinet.com
SIC: 8399 Advocacy group

(P-24790)
IAS ADMINISTRATIONS INC
1311 N New Hampshire Ave, Los Angeles
(90027-6001)
PHONE.....................323 953-3490
Deborah Fraser, *President*
Mislav Raos, *Treasurer*
Terence Macmahon, *Admin Sec*
EMP: 65
SALES (est): 2.9MM **Privately Held**
SIC: 8399 7997 8999 8743 Fund raising
organization, non-fee basis; country club,
membership; writing for publication; pro-
motion service

(P-24791)
INYO MONO ADVCTS FR CMMNTY ACT (PA)
Also Called: I M A C A
137 E South St, Bishop (93514-3545)
P.O. Box 845 (93515-0845)
PHONE.....................760 873-8557
Lynn Bethel, *Exec Dir*
EMP: 70
SALES: 3MM **Privately Held**
WEB: www.imaca.net
SIC: 8399 Community action agency

(P-24792)
JAPANESE CMNTY YOUTH COUNCIL (PA)
Also Called: CHIBI CHAN PRESCHOOL
2012 Pine St, San Francisco (94115-2899)
PHONE.....................415 202-7905
John Osaki, *Exec Dir*
Julie Matsueda, *Executive*
Patricia Justafort, *Associate Dir*
Jon Osaki, *Exec Dir*
Derrick Lee, *Office Admin*
EMP: 75
SQ FT: 4,000
SALES: 12.6MM **Privately Held**
SIC: 8399 Community development groups

(P-24793)
JEWISH COMMUNITY FEDRTN SAN FR (PA)
121 Steuart St Fl 7, San Francisco
(94105-1280)
PHONE.....................415 777-0411
Jennifer Gorvitz, *CEO*
Bill Powers, *CFO*
Carol Weitz, *Vice Pres*
Hallie Baron, *Associate Dir*
Carole-Anne Elliott, *Executive Asst*

EMP: 70
SQ FT: 50,000
SALES: 147.2MM **Privately Held**
SIC: 8399 Fund raising organization, non-fee basis

(P-24794)
KCRW FOUNDATION INC
Also Called: KCRW FM RADIO
1900 Pico Blvd, Santa Monica (90405-1628)
PHONE...............................310 450-5183
Jennifer Ferro, *CEO*
Herbert Roney, *Treasurer*
Tom Wertheimer, *Treasurer*
Alexandra Fernandez, *Officer*
Warren Olney, *Social Dir*
EMP: 51
SQ FT: 4,000
SALES: 23.6MM **Privately Held**
SIC: 8399 Fund raising organization, non-fee basis

(P-24795)
KERN REGIONAL CENTER (PA)
3200 N Sillect Ave, Bakersfield (93308-6333)
P.O. Box 2536 (93303-2536)
PHONE...............................661 327-8531
Michal Clark, *Exec Dir*
Duane Law, *CEO*
Jerry Bowman, *CFO*
John Gusman, *CFO*
Laura Hughes, *Client Mgr*
EMP: 178 **EST:** 1971
SQ FT: 33,000
SALES: 169.9MM **Privately Held**
SIC: 8399 Social service information exchange

(P-24796)
KEVIN HOLUBOWSKI LLC
7462 Denrock Ave, Los Angeles (90045-1022)
PHONE...............................310 908-6542
Kevin Holubowski,
EMP: 103
SALES (est): 466.1K **Privately Held**
SIC: 8399 Social services

(P-24797)
KEYSTONE NPS LLC (DH)
Also Called: Keystone Schools-Ramona
11980 Mount Vernon Ave, Grand Terrace (92313-5172)
PHONE...............................909 633-6354
Alfredo Alvarado, *Principal*
Don Whitfield, *CFO*
Martha Petrey, *Exec VP*
EMP: 100
SALES (est): 14.8MM
SALES (corp-wide): 10.4B **Publicly Held**
SIC: 8399 Advocacy group
HQ: Children's Comprehensive Services, Inc.
3401 West End Ave Ste 400
Nashville TN 37203
615 250-0000

(P-24798)
KIPP FOUNDATION
135 Main St Ste 1700, San Francisco (94105-1850)
PHONE...............................415 399-1556
Richard Barth, *CEO*
Jack Chorowsky, *COO*
Tarun Bhatia, *CFO*
Tina Sachs, *CFO*
Amy Hager, *Executive Asst*
EMP: 110
SQ FT: 10,000
SALES: 77.1MM **Privately Held**
SIC: 8399 Fund raising organization, non-fee basis

(P-24799)
LAKE ARROWHEAD CMNTY SVCS DST
6727 Arrowhead Lake Rd, Hesperia (92345-9343)
P.O. Box 700, Lake Arrowhead (92352-0700)
PHONE...............................909 337-6395
Bob Bobki, *Branch Mgr*
EMP: 50

SALES (corp-wide): 13.9MM **Privately Held**
WEB: www.lakearrowheadcsd.com
SIC: 8399 Advocacy group
PA: Lake Arrowhead Community Services District
28200 Highway 189
Lake Arrowhead CA 92352
909 336-1359

(P-24800)
LAWRENCE FAMILY JEWISH COMMU (PA)
4126 Executive Dr, La Jolla (92037-1348)
PHONE...............................858 362-1144
Craig Schluss, *President*
David Wax, *President*
Nancy Johnson, *CFO*
Katharine Wardle, *CFO*
Darren Schwartz, *Officer*
EMP: 150 **EST:** 1945
SALES: 10.3MM **Privately Held**
WEB: www.lfjcc.com
SIC: 8399 8351 Community development groups; child day care services

(P-24801)
LIFESPAN INC
Also Called: Lifespan Care Management Agcy
600 Frederick St, Santa Cruz (95062-2203)
PHONE...............................831 469-4900
Pamela Goodman, *President*
Pam Goodman, *President*
Becky Peters, *Sales Associate*
Dixie Mitchell, *Manager*
EMP: 90
SALES (est): 3.3MM **Privately Held**
WEB: www.lifespancare.com
SIC: 8399 8082 Health systems agency; home health care services

(P-24802)
LONG BEACH CMNTY ACTION PARTNR
Also Called: Long Beach Cap
117 W Victoria St, Long Beach (90805-2162)
PHONE...............................562 216-4600
Darrick Simpson, *Exec Dir*
Janet McCarthy, *Ch of Bd*
Mary Sramek, *Treasurer*
Marissa Semense, *Officer*
Baty Amit, *Principal*
EMP: 110
SQ FT: 10,000
SALES: 5.8MM **Privately Held**
WEB: www.lbcaa.com
SIC: 8399 Antipoverty board; community action agency

(P-24803)
LOS ANGELES LGBT CENTER (PA)
Also Called: L.A. Gay & Lesbian Center
1625 Schrader Blvd, Los Angeles (90028-6213)
P.O. Box 2988 (90078-2988)
PHONE...............................323 993-7618
Lorri L Jean, *CEO*
Michael Holtzman, *CFO*
Mike Holtzman, *CFO*
Jim Key, *Officer*
Simon Costello, *Associate Dir*
EMP: 148
SQ FT: 45,000
SALES: 91.6MM **Privately Held**
WEB: www.lagaycenter.org
SIC: 8399 Community development groups

(P-24804)
MAGNOLIA EDUCTL RES FOUNDATION (PA)
Also Called: MAGNOLIA SCIENCE ACADEMY
250 E 1st St Ste 1500, Los Angeles (90012-3831)
PHONE...............................714 892-5066
Dr Suleyman Bahceci, *CEO*
Mekan Muhammedov, *CEO*
Maria Huezo, *Office Mgr*
Veronica Romero, *Office Mgr*
Albert Nguyen, *Info Tech Mgr*
EMP: 84

SALES: 7.6MM **Privately Held**
SIC: 8399 Fund raising organization, non-fee basis

(P-24805)
MCKINLEY HOME FOUNDATION
762 Cypress St, San Dimas (91773-3505)
PHONE...............................909 599-1227
Victor Liotta, *President*
Mario Gallegos, *Officer*
Beatriz Mendoza, *Assistant*
Jackie Girgis, *Supervisor*
EMP: 100
SQ FT: 8,055
SALES: 1.7MM **Privately Held**
SIC: 8399 6519 Fund raising organization, non-fee basis; landholding office

(P-24806)
MIRAMNTE HIGH SCHL PARENTS CLB
750 Moraga Way, Orinda (94563-4330)
PHONE...............................925 280-3965
Raul Zamora, *Principal*
Catherine Corn, *President*
Dr Craig Dennis, *Treasurer*
Dixie Mohan, *Vice Pres*
Mark Uhrenholt, *Principal*
EMP: 130
SALES: 453.4K **Privately Held**
SIC: 8399 Fund raising organization, non-fee basis

(P-24807)
MISSION OAKS RECREATION PK DST
3344 Mission Ave, Carmichael (95608-3111)
PHONE...............................916 488-2810
Daniel Barton, *Administration*
Lisa Paredes, *Office Admin*
Cindy Paredes-Banvill, *Director*
Ken Matsumoto, *Supervisor*
Terri McAdam, *Supervisor*
EMP: 89
SQ FT: 1,500
SALES (est): 493.1K **Privately Held**
SIC: 8399 Social services

(P-24808)
MOMENTUM FOR MENTAL HEALTH
Also Called: Maccarthy House
2001 The Alameda, San Jose (95126-1136)
PHONE...............................408 261-7777
Paul S Taylor, *CEO*
Flo Laflamme, *Info Tech Mgr*
Irene Chuang, *Psychiatry*
EMP: 100
SALES (corp-wide): 36.8MM **Privately Held**
WEB: www.alliance4care.org
SIC: 8399 8093 8322 Health systems agency; specialty outpatient clinics; individual & family services
PA: Momentum For Mental Health
438 N White Rd
San Jose CA 95127
408 254-6828

(P-24809)
MORALE WELFARE RECREATION FUND
4260 Gigling Rd, Seaside (93955)
PHONE...............................831 242-6631
Bob Emanuel, *President*
EMP: 200
SALES (est): 1.5MM **Privately Held**
SIC: 8399 Fund raising organization, non-fee basis

(P-24810)
MT HAMILTON GRANGE
2840 Aborn Rd, San Jose (95135-2001)
P.O. Box 731060 (95173-1060)
PHONE...............................408 513-5528
Douglas Krause, *Principal*
EMP: 100
SALES: 74.3K **Privately Held**
SIC: 8399 Fund raising organization, non-fee basis

(P-24811)
NATIONAL MENTOR INC
Also Called: California Mentor
2131 Mars Ct, Bakersfield (93308-6830)
PHONE...............................661 387-1000
EMP: 50
SALES (corp-wide): 1.4B **Publicly Held**
SIC: 8399 Social service information exchange
HQ: National Mentor, Inc.
313 Congress St Fl 5
Boston MA 02210
617 790-4800

(P-24812)
NEW ADVANCES FOR PEOPLE DISABI
Also Called: Center For Achievement Center
1120 21st St, Bakersfield (93301-4613)
PHONE...............................661 327-0188
Linda Waninger, *Manager*
EMP: 60
SALES (corp-wide): 7.3MM **Privately Held**
SIC: 8399 Community development groups
PA: New Advances For People With Disabilities
2601 F St
Bakersfield CA 93301
661 395-1361

(P-24813)
NEW VISTA BEHAVIORAL HEALTH
1901 Newport Blvd Ste 200, Costa Mesa (92627-2293)
PHONE...............................949 284-0095
Jennifer Hale, *Controller*
EMP: 99
SALES (est): 311.1K **Privately Held**
SIC: 8399 Social services

(P-24814)
NEXT DOOR SLTONS TO DOM VLENCE
234 E Gish Rd Ste 200, San Jose (95112-4724)
PHONE...............................408 279-2962
Kathleen Krenek, *Exec Dir*
Wayne Mascia, *President*
Chris Holt, *Technology*
Susan McInnis, *Finance*
Colsaria Henderson, *Director*
EMP: 80
SQ FT: 4,100
SALES: 3MM **Privately Held**
WEB: www.nextdoor.org
SIC: 8399 8322 Advocacy group; social change association; individual & family services

(P-24815)
NEXTDOORCOM INC
875 Stevenson St Ste 100, San Francisco (94103-0906)
PHONE...............................415 236-0000
Nirav Tolia, *CEO*
Flora Hsu, *Partner*
Amos Stoltzfus, *Partner*
Prakash Janakiraman, *Vice Pres*
Sarah Leary, *Vice Pres*
EMP: 100 **EST:** 2011
SALES (est): 9.4MM **Privately Held**
SIC: 8399 2741 7371 Social service information exchange; miscellaneous publishing; computer software development & applications

(P-24816)
NORTHERN CALIFORNIA INSTITUTE
Also Called: Ncire
4150 Clement St, San Francisco (94121-1563)
PHONE...............................415 750-6954
Robert Obana, *Exec Dir*
Paul Volberding, *Bd of Directors*
Karen Steeber, *Director*
EMP: 300
SQ FT: 1,650
SALES: 43.4MM **Privately Held**
SIC: 8399 8741 Fund raising organization, non-fee basis; management services

(P-24817)
ON THE MOVE
780 Lincoln Ave, NAPA (94558-5110)
PHONE......................707 251-9432
Leslie Medine, *Exec Dir*
Diana Gordon, *CFO*
Alissa Gentille, *Exec Dir*
Lauren Biehle, *Program Dir*
EMP: 50
SALES: 4.1MM **Privately Held**
SIC: 8399 Social services

(P-24818)
PENNY LANE CENTERS (PA)
15305 Rayen St, North Hills (91343-5117)
P.O. Box 2548 (91393-2548)
PHONE......................818 892-3423
Arthur Barr, *President*
Ivelise Markovits, *Exec Dir*
Sandra Dominguez-Cerri, *Comp Spec*
Lee Overson, *Technology*
Rosana La Fianza, *Opers Staff*
EMP: 275
SQ FT: 7,000
SALES: 56.2MM **Privately Held**
WEB: www.pennylane.org
SIC: 8399 Social service information exchange

(P-24819)
PENNY LANE CENTERS
15317 Rayen St, North Hills (91343-5198)
PHONE......................818 892-3423
Ivelise Markovits, *Branch Mgr*
Donna Bailey, *Project Mgr*
David Serrano, *Recruiter*
Leticia Perez, *Clerk*
EMP: 166
SALES (corp-wide): 56.2MM **Privately Held**
SIC: 8399 Social service information exchange
PA: Penny Lane Centers
15305 Rayen St
North Hills CA 91343
818 892-3423

(P-24820)
PENNY LANE CENTERS
Valley High School
15317 Rayen St, North Hills (91343-5198)
PHONE......................818 892-3423
Shawn Welch, *Principal*
EMP: 170
SALES (corp-wide): 56.2MM **Privately Held**
WEB: www.pennylane.org
SIC: 8399 Social service information exchange
PA: Penny Lane Centers
15305 Rayen St
North Hills CA 91343
818 892-3423

(P-24821)
PENNY LANE CENTERS
10330 Pioneer Blvd # 290, Santa Fe Springs (90670-8279)
PHONE......................562 903-4135
Lily Amezqua, *Manager*
EMP: 170
SALES (corp-wide): 56.2MM **Privately Held**
SIC: 8399 Social service information exchange
PA: Penny Lane Centers
15305 Rayen St
North Hills CA 91343
818 892-3423

(P-24822)
PENNY LANE CENTERS
15331 Rayen St, North Hills (91343)
PHONE......................818 892-3423
Ivelise Markovits, *Branch Mgr*
EMP: 170
SALES (corp-wide): 56.2MM **Privately Held**
WEB: www.pennylane.org
SIC: 8399 Social service information exchange
PA: Penny Lane Centers
15305 Rayen St
North Hills CA 91343
818 892-3423

(P-24823)
PENNY LANE CENTERS
15302 Rayen St, North Hills (91343-5118)
PHONE......................818 892-1112
Evy Markovits, *Manager*
EMP: 170
SALES (corp-wide): 56.2MM **Privately Held**
SIC: 8399 Social service information exchange
PA: Penny Lane Centers
15305 Rayen St
North Hills CA 91343
818 892-3423

(P-24824)
PENNY LANE CENTERS
15256 Acre St, North Hills (91343-5256)
PHONE......................818 892-3423
EMP: 170
SALES (corp-wide): 56.2MM **Privately Held**
SIC: 8399 Social service information exchange
PA: Penny Lane Centers
15305 Rayen St
North Hills CA 91343
818 892-3423

(P-24825)
PENNY LANE CENTERS
1020 E Palmdale Blvd, Palmdale (93550-4756)
PHONE......................818 892-3423
Daniel K Rothenberg, *Psychologist*
EMP: 170
SALES (corp-wide): 56.2MM **Privately Held**
SIC: 8399 Social service information exchange
PA: Penny Lane Centers
15305 Rayen St
North Hills CA 91343
818 892-3423

(P-24826)
PENNY LANE CENTERS
2450 S Atl Blvd Ste 101, Commerce (90040)
PHONE......................323 318-9960
Rosana La Fianza, *Branch Mgr*
Martha Millan, *Principal*
Mike Morellino, *Office Mgr*
Lynda Kennedy, *Manager*
EMP: 170
SALES (corp-wide): 56.2MM **Privately Held**
SIC: 8399 Health & welfare council
PA: Penny Lane Centers
15305 Rayen St
North Hills CA 91343
818 892-3423

(P-24827)
PENNY LANE CENTERS
43520 Division St, Lancaster (93535-4089)
PHONE......................661 274-0770
James Ocon, *President*
EMP: 170
SALES (corp-wide): 56.2MM **Privately Held**
SIC: 8399 Social service information exchange
PA: Penny Lane Centers
15305 Rayen St
North Hills CA 91343
818 892-3423

(P-24828)
PEOPLE COORDINATED SERVICES (PA)
Also Called: SENIOR NUTRITION PROGRAM
1221 S Western Ave, Los Angeles (90006-3107)
PHONE......................323 735-1231
Donna Watson, *Exec Dir*
EMP: 90
SQ FT: 10,000
SALES: 4.7MM **Privately Held**
WEB: www.pcs-socal.org
SIC: 8399 Health & welfare council

(P-24829)
REACH OUT WEST END
1126 W Foothill Blvd # 250, Upland (91786-3786)
PHONE......................909 982-8641
Diana Fox, *Director*
Philip Chu,
Julie Duarte, *Manager*
EMP: 60
SQ FT: 12,232
SALES: 3.6MM **Privately Held**
SIC: 8399 Social change association

(P-24830)
REACHING FOR INDEPENDENCE INC
609 14th St, Fortuna (95540-2464)
PHONE......................707 725-9010
Jeffrey Pockett, *Exec Dir*
EMP: 66 **EST:** 2008
SALES: 1.8MM **Privately Held**
SIC: 8399 Community development groups

(P-24831)
RIO HONDO COMMUNITY DEV CORP
11706 Ramona Blvd Ste 107, El Monte (91732-2300)
PHONE......................626 401-2784
Donna L Duncan, *President*
EMP: 57
SALES: 335K **Privately Held**
SIC: 8399 Community development groups

(P-24832)
ROMAN CTHLIC BSHP OF SNTA ROSA
987 Airway Ct, Santa Rosa (95403-2048)
P.O. Box 4900 (95402-4900)
PHONE......................707 528-8712
Len Marabella, *Branch Mgr*
Marla A Gullickson CP, *Treasurer*
Angie Moeller, *Principal*
EMP: 110
SALES (corp-wide): 8.8MM **Privately Held**
SIC: 8399 Social service information exchange
PA: Roman Catholic Bishop Of Santa Rosa, The
985 Airway Ct
Santa Rosa CA 95403
707 545-7610

(P-24833)
ROSE & KINDEL GRAYLING
1414 K St Ste 220, Sacramento (95814-3967)
PHONE......................916 441-1034
Carl London, *CEO*
EMP: 200
SQ FT: 4,000
SALES (est): 2.7MM **Privately Held**
SIC: 8399 Advocacy group

(P-24834)
SAFE HARBOR INTL RELIEF
30615 Avnida De Las Flres, Rancho Santa Margari (92688)
P.O. Box 80820, Rcho STA Marg (92688-0820)
PHONE......................949 858-6786
Gary Kusunoki, *CEO*
David Kruckenberg, *Principal*
EMP: 50
SALES: 146K **Privately Held**
SIC: 8399 Social services

(P-24835)
SAINT JUSTIN EDUCATION FU
Also Called: IN TOUCH LEADERSHIP PROJECT
2415 Shoredale Ave, Los Angeles (90031-1120)
P.O. Box 27790 (90027-0790)
PHONE......................323 221-3400
Gary Krauss, *CEO*
EMP: 51 **EST:** 1992
SALES: 444.2K **Privately Held**
SIC: 8399 Fund raising organization, non-fee basis

(P-24836)
SALVATION ARMY
3755 N Freeway Blvd, Sacramento (95834-1926)
P.O. Box 348000 (95834-8000)
PHONE......................916 563-3700
Mjr Frank Brown, *Principal*
Dianne Jiminez, *Officer*
Austin Nevers, *Admin Asst*
Mysti Birks, *Asst Director*
Chris Cramer, *Director*
EMP: 75
SALES (corp-wide): 4.3B **Privately Held**
WEB: www.salvationarmy.usawest.org
SIC: 8399 Advocacy group
HQ: The Salvation Army
180 E Ocean Blvd Ste 500
Long Beach CA 90802
562 491-8464

(P-24837)
SAN DIEGO RESCUE MISSION INC (PA)
Also Called: City Rescue Mission
120 Elm St, San Diego (92101-2602)
P.O. Box 80427 (92138-0427)
PHONE......................619 819-1880
Herb Johnson, *CEO*
Kimberly K Elliott, *Bd of Directors*
Dena Williams, *Senior VP*
C Greg Helton, *Vice Pres*
Shari Finney Houser, *Vice Pres*
EMP: 92
SQ FT: 98,000
SALES: 17.7MM **Privately Held**
WEB: www.sdrescue.org
SIC: 8399 5932 8322 Social change association; used merchandise stores; emergency shelters

(P-24838)
SAN FRNCSCO ECON OPRTNTY CNCIL
1426 Fillmore St Ste 301, San Francisco (94115-4164)
PHONE......................415 749-3798
Nathaniel Mason, *Exec Dir*
EMP: 110 **EST:** 1964
SALES: 6MM **Privately Held**
SIC: 8399 Health & welfare council

(P-24839)
SAN FRNNDO VLY INTRFITH CUNCIL
8956 Vanalden Ave, Northridge (91324-3753)
PHONE......................818 885-5220
EMP: 102
SALES (corp-wide): 4.1MM **Privately Held**
SIC: 8399 Council for social agency
PA: San Fernando Valley Interfaith Council, Inc
4505 Las Virgenes Rd
Calabasas CA 91302
818 880-4842

(P-24840)
SILICON VLY EDUCATN FOUNDATION
1400 Parkmoor Ave Ste 200, San Jose (95126-3798)
PHONE......................408 790-9400
Muhammed Chaudhry, *CEO*
Joanne Chin, *Purchasing*
Salma Ferdowsi, *Opers Staff*
Magana Rigo, *Marketing Mgr*
EMP: 1000
SALES: 2.6MM **Privately Held**
WEB: www.fmsd.k12.ca.us
SIC: 8399 Fund raising organization, non-fee basis

(P-24841)
SIX RIVERS PLANNED PARENTHOOD
3225 Timber Fall Ct, Eureka (95503-4892)
P.O. Box 97, Cutten (95534-0097)
PHONE......................707 442-5700
Denise Danden Boss, *CEO*
EMP: 75
SQ FT: 3,900
SALES: 3.6MM **Privately Held**
SIC: 8399 8322 Community development groups; individual & family services

(P-24842)
SOUTH CENTRAL LOS (PA)
Also Called: Sclarc
2500 S Western Ave, Los Angeles
(90018-2609)
PHONE...................213 744-7000
Dexter Henderson, *CEO*
Roy Doronila, *COO*
Alireza Hoveyda, *Consultant*
EMP: 235
SQ FT: 110,470
SALES: 232.7MM **Privately Held**
WEB: www.sclarc.org
SIC: 8399 Health & welfare council

(P-24843)
SOUTHLAND INTEGRATED SVCS INC (PA)
Also Called: VIETNAMESE COMMUNITY OF ORANGE
1618 W 1st St, Santa Ana (92703-3614)
PHONE...................714 558-6009
Tricia Nguyen, *CEO*
EMP: 70
SALES: 4MM **Privately Held**
WEB: www.vietnam-minnesota.org
SIC: 8399 8322 8351 8011 Community development groups; senior citizens' center or association; social service center; preschool center; primary care medical clinic; mental health clinic, outpatient

(P-24844)
SPECIAL SERVICE FOR GROUPS INC
Also Called: Occupational Therapy Training
19401 S Vt Ave Ste A200, Torrance
(90502-4418)
PHONE...................310 323-6887
Sarah Bream, *Branch Mgr*
EMP: 60
SALES (corp-wide): 60.6MM **Privately Held**
SIC: 8399 8322 Community action agency; individual & family services
PA: Special Service For Groups, Inc.
905 E 8th St Unit 1
Los Angeles CA 90021
213 368-1888

(P-24845)
SPECIAL SERVICE FOR GROUPS INC
470 E 3rd St Ste D, Los Angeles
(90013-1630)
PHONE...................213 620-5713
EMP: 65
SALES (est): 424.5K
SALES (corp-wide): 60.6MM **Privately Held**
SIC: 8399 Community action agency
PA: Special Service For Groups, Inc.
905 E 8th St Unit 1
Los Angeles CA 90021
213 368-1888

(P-24846)
STANFORD YOUTH SOLUTIONS (PA)
Also Called: STANFORD & LATHROP MEMORIAL HO
8912 Volunteer Ln, Sacramento
(95826-3221)
PHONE...................916 344-0199
Jovina Neves, *CFO*
Craig Hettrich, *Bd of Directors*
Laura Heintz, *Principal*
Erik Sternad, *Exec Dir*
Kimberly Woods-Burch, *Human Res Dir*
EMP: 85
SQ FT: 30,000
SALES: 11.5MM **Privately Held**
SIC: 8399 Community development groups

(P-24847)
TEHACHAPI VLY HEALTHCARE DST (PA)
305 S Robinson St, Tehachapi
(93561-1726)
P.O. Box 669 (93581-0669)
PHONE...................661 750-4848
Eugene Suksi, *CEO*
Chet Beedle, *CFO*
Allen Burgess, *Principal*
Bridget Thomason, *Controller*

Elizabeth McGehee,
EMP: 123
SQ FT: 18,000
SALES (est): 299.1K **Privately Held**
SIC: 8399 Health systems agency

(P-24848)
TEMPLO CALVARIO CMNTY DEV CORP
2501 W 5th St, Santa Ana (92703-1816)
PHONE...................714 543-3711
Eleazar De Leon, *President*
Beatriz Santana, *Treasurer*
Linda Decker, *Admin Sec*
EMP: 60
SQ FT: 9,000
SALES: 5.2MM **Privately Held**
SIC: 8399 Community action agency

(P-24849)
TIDES INC (PA)
Also Called: Tides Shared Spaces
1014 Torney Ave Ste 1, San Francisco
(94129-1756)
P.O. Box 29198 (94129-0198)
PHONE...................415 561-6400
Melissa Bradley, *CEO*
Nick Hodges, *COO*
China Brotsky, *Vice Pres*
EMP: 110
SQ FT: 180,000
SALES (est): 2.9MM **Privately Held**
SIC: 8399 Community development groups

(P-24850)
TIDES NETWORK
The Prsdio 1014 Trney Ave, San Francisco
(94129)
P.O. Box 29198 (94129-0198)
PHONE...................415 561-6400
Gary Schwartz, *CEO*
Judith Hill, *CFO*
Kim Sarnecki, *Director*
EMP: 80
SALES: 13.9MM **Privately Held**
SIC: 8399 Community development groups

(P-24851)
UNITED CEREBRAL PALSY ASSOC OF
Also Called: RIDE ON TRANSPORTATION
3620 Sacramento Dr # 201, San Luis Obispo (93401-7215)
PHONE...................805 543-2039
Mark Shaffer, *Exec Dir*
Chelo Lund, *CFO*
EMP: 100
SQ FT: 1,600
SALES: 6MM **Privately Held**
WEB: www.ucp-oc.org
SIC: 8399 Fund raising organization, non-fee basis

(P-24852)
UNITED CRBRL PLSY OF CNTRL CA (PA)
Also Called: U C P-UNITED CEREBAL PALSY ASS
4224 N Cedar Ave, Fresno (93726-3731)
PHONE...................559 221-8272
Mark Lanier, *President*
Carol Kloninger, *Vice Pres*
Jamie Marrash, *Exec Dir*
Bonnie Peterson, *Admin Sec*
Grace Bracamonte, *Director*
EMP: 50
SQ FT: 15,000
SALES: 5.3MM **Privately Held**
WEB: www.mcvalleycup.com
SIC: 8399 Fund raising organization, non-fee basis

(P-24853)
UNITED WAY INC
44907 10th St W, Lancaster (93534-2313)
PHONE...................661 874-4288
EMP: 120
SALES (corp-wide): 67MM **Privately Held**
SIC: 8399 Fund raising organization, non-fee basis
PA: United Way, Inc.
1150 S Olive St Ste T500
Los Angeles CA 90015
213 808-6220

(P-24854)
UNITED WAY INC (PA)
Also Called: UNITED WAY OF GREATER LOS ANGE
1150 S Olive St Ste T500, Los Angeles
(90015-2482)
PHONE...................213 808-6220
Caroline W Nahas, *Ch of Bd*
Elise Buik, *President*
Les Brockhurst, *Vice Pres*
Alicia Lara, *Vice Pres*
Mae Tuck, *Vice Pres*
▲ **EMP:** 95
SQ FT: 40,000
SALES: 67MM **Privately Held**
WEB: www.unitedwayla.org
SIC: 8399 Fund raising organization, non-fee basis; United Fund councils; health & welfare council

(P-24855)
VALLEY CAN
921 11th St Ste 220, Sacramento
(95814-2842)
PHONE...................916 273-4890
Carla Musser, *President*
EMP: 50
SALES: 5.5MM **Privately Held**
SIC: 8399 Advocacy group

(P-24856)
VALLEY RSRCE CTR FOR RETARDED
Also Called: Exceed
1285 N Santa Fe St, Hemet (92543-1823)
PHONE...................951 766-8659
Lee Trisler, *Exec Dir*
EMP: 99
SALES (est): 464.6K **Privately Held**
SIC: 8399 Community development groups

(P-24857)
WATSON CARTON
4178 Ross Ave, San Jose (95124-3728)
PHONE...................408 979-9618
Peter Frietman, *CEO*
EMP: 63
SALES (est): 693.7K **Privately Held**
SIC: 8399 Community development groups

(P-24858)
WEST VALLEY AREA SQUAD CLUB
Also Called: Highway Patrol
5825 De Soto Ave, Woodland Hills
(91367-5202)
PHONE...................818 888-0980
Brian Denike, *President*
Oscar Loza, *Officer*
Daniel Olivas, *Officer*
Orrin Heitmann, *Vice Pres*
Samantha Ruiz, *Technician*
EMP: 104
SALES (est): 1.3MM **Privately Held**
SIC: 8399 Fund raising organization, non-fee basis

(P-24859)
WESTSIDE JEWISH CMNTY CTR INC (PA)
5870 W Olympic Blvd, Los Angeles
(90036-4657)
PHONE...................323 938-2531
Brian Greene, *Exec Dir*
Oscar Yglesias, *Facilities Dir*
Rachel Flader, *Teacher*
Edana Appel, *Director*
ARI Cohen, *Director*
EMP: 200
SQ FT: 150,000
SALES: 3.4MM **Privately Held**
SIC: 8399 8641 8322 Community development groups; civic social & fraternal associations; individual & family services

(P-24860)
WESTSIDE LODGE
120 Page St, San Francisco (94102-5811)
PHONE...................415 864-1515
Jonathan Dernick, *President*
EMP: 50
SALES (est): 369.5K **Privately Held**
SIC: 8399 Community development groups

(P-24861)
X PRIZE FOUNDATION INC
800 Crprate Pinte Ste 350, Culver City
(90230)
PHONE...................310 741-4880
Robert Weiss, *President*
Paul Rappoport, *COO*
Gillian Sheldon, *Officer*
Francis B Land, *Vice Pres*
Winona Dorris, *Director*
EMP: 50
SQ FT: 17,705
SALES: 39.4MM **Privately Held**
SIC: 8399 Fund raising organization, non-fee basis

(P-24862)
YUBA CITY UNIFIED SCHOOL
Also Called: Ycusd
750 N Palora Ave, Yuba City (95991-3627)
PHONE...................530 822-7601
Steven Scriven, *President*
Lonetta Riley, *Vice Pres*
Robert Shemwell, *General Mgr*
Steve Otoole, *MIS Dir*
Nancy Aaberg, *Superintendent*
EMP: 2000
SALES (est): 23.2MM **Privately Held**
SIC: 8399 Fund raising organization, non-fee basis

8412 Museums & Art Galleries

(P-24863)
ANAHEIM ARTS COUNCIL
P.O. Box 1364 (92815-1364)
PHONE...................714 868-6094
Charlotte Brady, *Owner*
EMP: 200 EST: 1977
SALES: 52.5K **Privately Held**
WEB: www.anaheimartscouncil.com
SIC: 8412 Museum

(P-24864)
ARMAND HAMMER MUSEUM
10899 Wilshire Blvd, Los Angeles
(90024-4343)
PHONE...................310 443-7000
Ann Philbin, *Education*
Justin Glasson, *Officer*
Mitch Marr, *Senior Mgr*
Margie Hill, *Manager*
Hannah Howe, *Manager*
▲ **EMP:** 101
SQ FT: 20,000
SALES: 85MM **Privately Held**
SIC: 8412 Museum

(P-24865)
ASIAN ART MUSEUM FOUND SAN FRA
Also Called: ASIAN ART MEUSUEM OF SF
200 Larkin St, San Francisco (94102-4734)
PHONE...................415 581-3500
Anthony Sun, *CEO*
Akiko Yamazaki, *President*
Timothy F Kahn, *Treasurer*
Nancy Sackson,
Robert L Duffy, *Vice Pres*
▲ **EMP:** 140
SALES: 31.4MM **Privately Held**
SIC: 8412 Arts or science center

(P-24866)
AUTRY MUSEUM OF AMERICAN WEST
4700 Western Heritage Way, Los Angeles
(90027-1462)
PHONE...................323 667-2000
Richard West, *Principal*
Robert Caragher, *Vice Pres*
Maren Dougherty, *Vice Pres*
Susan Harlow, *Vice Pres*
Lois Hauser, *Manager*
EMP: 140
SQ FT: 144,000
SALES: 33.9MM **Privately Held**
SIC: 8412 5947 5812 6512 Museum; gift shop; cafeteria; theater building, ownership & operation

---

(P-24867)
CALIFRNIA SCNCE CTR FOUNDATION
700 Exposition Park Dr, Los Angeles (90037-1254)
PHONE..................213 744-2545
Jeffrey N Rudolph, *President*
Cynthia Pygin, *CFO*
Erica Guzman, *Accountant*
EMP: 260
SALES: 37.7MM **Privately Held**
WEB: www.casciencectr.com
SIC: 8412 7832 5947 Museum; motion picture theaters, except drive-in; gifts & novelties

(P-24868)
CHARLES W BOWERS MUSEUM CORP
2002 N Main St, Santa Ana (92706-2731)
PHONE..................714 567-3600
Peter C Keller, *President*
Thuy Nguyen, *CFO*
Jennifer Alvarado, *Director*
▲ EMP: 72
SALES: 6.2MM **Privately Held**
SIC: 8412 Museum

(P-24869)
CHILDRENS CREATIVITY MUSEUM
221 4th St, San Francisco (94103-3116)
PHONE..................415 820-3320
Adrienne Pon, *CEO*
Laney Whitcanack, *Ch of Bd*
MAI MAI Wythes, *Chairman*
John Gonzalez, *Treasurer*
Michael Nobleza, *Exec Dir*
EMP: 65
SALES: 2.1MM **Privately Held**
WEB: www.zeum.com
SIC: 8412 5947 Museum; gift shop

(P-24870)
CHILDRENS MUSEUM OF DESERT
Also Called: CHILDREN'S DISCOVERY MUSEUM
71701 Gerald Ford Dr, Rancho Mirage (92270-1934)
PHONE..................760 321-0602
Betty Barker, *Chairman*
Lee Vanderbeck, *Director*
EMP: 50
SQ FT: 18,000
SALES: 986.6K **Privately Held**
WEB: www.cdmod.org
SIC: 8412 Museum

(P-24871)
CITY & COUNTY OF SAN FRANCISCO
Also Called: Asian Art Museum
200 Larkin St, San Francisco (94102-4734)
PHONE..................415 581-3500
Emily Sano, *Director*
Nancy Brennan, *Officer*
Calen McEldowney, *Security Dir*
Kevin Conley, *Info Tech Dir*
Sheng Moua, *Graphic Designe*
EMP: 60 **Privately Held**
SIC: 8412 9199 Museum; general government administration; ;
PA: City & County Of San Francisco
1 Dr Carlton B Goodlett P
San Francisco CA 94102
415 554-7500

(P-24872)
CITY OF FREMONT
Also Called: Ardenwood Farm
34600 Ardenwood Blvd, Fremont (94555-3645)
P.O. Box 5006 (94537-5006)
PHONE..................510 791-4196
Randy Hees, *Manager*
EMP: 105
SQ FT: 72,576 **Privately Held**
WEB: www.ci.fremont.ca.us
SIC: 8412 9111 Historical society; mayors' offices
PA: City Of Fremont
3300 Capitol Ave
Fremont CA 94538
510 284-4000

(P-24873)
CITY OF LOS ANGELES
Also Called: Parks & Recreation Dept
2800 E Observatory Ave, Los Angeles (90027-1255)
PHONE..................213 473-0800
Edwin C Krupp, *Director*
EMP: 200 **Privately Held**
WEB: www.lacity.org
SIC: 8412 9532 Museum; urban & community development
PA: City Of Los Angeles
200 N Spring St Ste 303
Los Angeles CA 90012
213 978-0600

(P-24874)
COMPUTER HISTORY MUSEUM
1401 N Shoreline Blvd, Mountain View (94043-1311)
PHONE..................650 810-1010
John C Hollar, *President*
Cate Robbins, *COO*
George Holmes, *Vice Pres*
Gary Matsushita, *Vice Pres*
Lauren Silver, *Vice Pres*
▲ EMP: 52
SQ FT: 111,670
SALES: 13.1MM **Privately Held**
SIC: 8412 Museum

(P-24875)
CORPORTION OF FINE ARTS MSEUMS
Also Called: Fine Arts Mseums San Francisco
75 Tea Garden Dr, San Francisco (94118-4501)
PHONE..................415 750-3600
Harry S Parker III, *Principal*
EMP: 51 **Privately Held**
SIC: 8412 Museum
PA: Corporation Of The Fine Arts Museums
50 Hagiwara Tea Garden Dr
San Francisco CA 94118

(P-24876)
CORPORTION OF FINE ARTS MSEUMS
Also Called: Palace of The Legion Honor
50 Hagiwara Tea Garden Dr, San Francisco (94118-4502)
PHONE..................415 750-3600
John Duchanan, *Manager*
EMP: 200 **Privately Held**
SIC: 8412 Museum
PA: Corporation Of The Fine Arts Museums
50 Hagiwara Tea Garden Dr
San Francisco CA 94118
-

(P-24877)
CORPORTION OF FINE ARTS MSEUMS
Also Called: M H Deyoung Memorial
50 Golden Gate Pk Hgiwara, San Francisco (94118)
PHONE..................415 750-3600
Debbie Albuquerque, *Branch Mgr*
EMP: 125 **Privately Held**
SIC: 8412 Museum
PA: Corporation Of The Fine Arts Museums
50 Hagiwara Tea Garden Dr
San Francisco CA 94118

(P-24878)
CORPORTION OF FINE ARTS MSEUMS (PA)
Also Called: Deyoung Museum
50 Hagiwara Tea Garden Dr, San Francisco (94118-4502)
PHONE..................415 750-3600
Michelle Gutierrez, *CFO*
Cynthia Inaba, *CFO*
Ken Garcia, *Comms Dir*
Skot Jonz, *Admin Asst*
Erica Wong, *Design Engr*
▲ EMP: 129
SQ FT: 300,000
SALES: 64.5MM **Privately Held**
SIC: 8412 Museum

(P-24879)
COUNTY OF LOS ANGELES
Also Called: Administration
5905 Wilshire Blvd, Los Angeles (90036-4504)
PHONE..................323 857-6000
Andrea L Rich, *President*
EMP: 100 **Privately Held**
WEB: www.co.la.ca.us
SIC: 8412 9411 Art gallery, noncommercial; administration of educational programs;
PA: County Of Los Angeles
500 W Temple St Ste 437
Los Angeles CA 90012
213 974-1101

(P-24880)
DESERT ARTS CENTER
Also Called: DAC
550 N Palm Canyon Dr, Palm Springs (92262-5526)
P.O. Box 2813 (92263-2813)
PHONE..................760 323-7973
Adele Hill, *President*
EMP: 90
SALES: 160.6K **Privately Held**
SIC: 8412 Art gallery, noncommercial

(P-24881)
DUBLIN HSTRCAL PRSRVATION ASSN
7172 Regional St Pmb 316, Dublin (94568-2324)
PHONE..................925 785-2898
Steven Minniear, *President*
EMP: 100
SALES: 6K **Privately Held**
SIC: 8412 Museum

(P-24882)
EASTERN CALIFORNIA MUSEUM (PA)
155 N Grant St, Independence (93526)
PHONE..................760 878-0292
Margaret Mairs, *Ch of Bd*
Leah Kirk, *Treasurer*
Del Hubbs, *Vice Ch Bd*
Kelly Reade, *Analyst*
John Klusmire, *Director*
EMP: 350
SQ FT: 3,200
SALES (est): 1.6MM **Privately Held**
SIC: 8412 Museum

(P-24883)
ETIWANDA HISTORICAL SOCIETY
7150 Etiwanda Ave, Rancho Cucamonga (91739-9758)
P.O. Box 63 (91739-0063)
PHONE..................909 899-8432
Jan Sutton, *President*
EMP: 99
SALES (est): 3.9MM **Privately Held**
SIC: 8412 Historical society

(P-24884)
EXPLORATORIUM (PA)
17 Pier Ste 100, San Francisco (94111-1455)
PHONE..................415 528-4462
Chris Flink, *Exec Dir*
Roberta Katz, *Ch of Bd*
Laura Zander, *COO*
Josie Haspel, *Treasurer*
Chris Hirano, *Sr Corp Ofcr*
▲ EMP: 401
SQ FT: 200,000
SALES: 65.1MM **Privately Held**
WEB: www.exploratorium.org
SIC: 8412 Museum

(P-24885)
HISTORICAL SOC CENTINELA VLY
7634 Midfield Ave, Los Angeles (90045-3234)
PHONE..................310 649-6272
Leonard Utter, *President*
Claydine Burt, *Vice Pres*
EMP: 300
SALES (est): 1.8MM **Privately Held**
SIC: 8412 Historical society

(P-24886)
KIDSPACE A PRTICIPATORY MUSEUM
480 N Arroyo Blvd, Pasadena (91103-3269)
PHONE..................626 449-9144
Jane Popovich, *President*
Mark McKinley, *Treasurer*
Chris Morphy, *Vice Pres*
Stephen H Baumann, *Exec Dir*
Tracy Bechtold, *Exec Dir*
EMP: 83
SALES: 4.4MM **Privately Held**
WEB: www.kidspacemuseum.org
SIC: 8412 Museum

(P-24887)
LINDSAY WILDLIFE MUSEUM
1931 1st Ave, Walnut Creek (94597-2540)
PHONE..................925 935-1978
Kramer Klabau, *President*
John Kikuchi, *President*
Loren Behr, *Exec Dir*
Norma Bishop, *Exec Dir*
Dana Eder, *Opers Mgr*
EMP: 90 EST: 1955
SQ FT: 28,000
SALES: 2.2MM **Privately Held**
WEB: www.wildlife-museum.org
SIC: 8412 Museum

(P-24888)
LONG BCH MUSEUM ART FOUNDATION
2300 E Ocean Blvd, Long Beach (90803-2442)
PHONE..................562 439-2119
Ronald B Nelson, *Director*
Ron Nelson, *Exec Dir*
Ronald C Nelson, *Director*
Matt Harms, *Manager*
Lisa Marsh, *Advisor*
▲ EMP: 62
SQ FT: 24,000
SALES: 997.5K **Privately Held**
WEB: www.lbma.org
SIC: 8412 Museum

(P-24889)
LOS ANGELES CNTY MSEUM OF ART
Also Called: Lacma
5905 Wilshire Blvd, Los Angeles (90036-4504)
PHONE..................323 857-6000
Michael Govan, *CEO*
Ann Rowland, *CFO*
Alison Edelstein, *Officer*
Mark Mitchell, *Officer*
Rachel Zelaya, *Officer*
▲ EMP: 94
SALES (est): 9MM **Privately Held**
SIC: 8412 Museum

(P-24890)
MEXICAN HERITG CTR GALLERY INC
111 S Sutter St, Stockton (95202-3220)
P.O. Box 77985 (95267-1285)
PHONE..................209 969-9306
Gracie Madrid, *President*
EMP: 75
SQ FT: 6,799
SALES: 41.4K **Privately Held**
SIC: 8412 Museums & art galleries

(P-24891)
MUSEUM ASSOCIATES
Also Called: LA COUNTY MUSEUM OF ART
5905 Wilshire Blvd, Los Angeles (90036-4504)
PHONE..................323 857-6172
Michael Gavin, *CEO*
Diana Vesga, *COO*
Mark Mitchell, *Officer*
Ernesto Portillo, *Social Dir*
Amber Thai, *Admin Asst*
EMP: 400
SALES: 189.4MM **Privately Held**
SIC: 8412 Museum

(P-24892)
MUSEUM CNTMPRARY ART SAN DIEGO (PA)
Also Called: McAsd
700 Prospect St, La Jolla (92037-4228)
PHONE................................858 454-3541
Hugh M Davies, *CEO*
Kathlene J Gusel, *Admin Asst*
Anneka Van Dongen, *Accountant*
▼ EMP: 70
SQ FT: 45,200
SALES: 8.1MM **Privately Held**
SIC: 8412 Museum

(P-24893)
MUSEUM OF CONTEMPORARY ART (PA)
250 S Grand Ave, Los Angeles (90012-3021)
PHONE................................213 626-6222
Charles Young, *CEO*
Jeffrey Deitch, *CEO*
Michael Harrison, *Officer*
Jean Lee, *Executive Asst*
Stephanie Morgan, *Asst Director*
▲ EMP: 150
SQ FT: 100,000
SALES (est): 44.1MM **Privately Held**
SIC: 8412 Museum

(P-24894)
MUSEUM OF LATIN AMERICAN ART
628 Alamitos Ave, Long Beach (90802-1513)
PHONE................................562 437-1689
Robert M Gumbiner, *Chairman*
Jessica Salazar, *President*
Mike Deovlet, *Corp Secy*
Wendy Celaya, *Assoc VP*
Lee Gumbiner, *Vice Pres*
▲ EMP: 50
SQ FT: 30,000
SALES: 2.5MM **Privately Held**
SIC: 8412 Arts or science center; museum

(P-24895)
NATURAL HISTORY MUSEUM OF LOS
900 Exposition Blvd, Los Angeles (90007-4057)
PHONE................................213 763-3442
EMP: 300
SALES: 54MM **Privately Held**
SIC: 8412

(P-24896)
NORTON SIMON MUSEUM
411 W Colorado Blvd, Pasadena (91105-1825)
PHONE................................626 449-6840
Ronald H Dykhuizen, *Principal*
Jennifer J Simon, *Ch of Bd*
Walter W Timoshuk, *Treasurer*
Harry Savage, *Vice Pres*
Robert Walker, *Vice Pres*
▲ EMP: 100
SQ FT: 70,000
SALES: 9.4MM **Privately Held**
WEB: www.nortonsimon.org
SIC: 8412 Museum

(P-24897)
OAKLAND MUSEUM OF CALIFORNIA
1000 Oak St, Oakland (94607-4892)
PHONE................................510 318-8400
Lori Fogarty, *CEO*
Lori G Fogarty, *CEO*
Johanna Jones, *Associate Dir*
Michael Silverman, *Associate Dir*
Cynthia Taylor, *Associate Dir*
EMP: 100
SQ FT: 150,000
SALES: 23.5MM **Privately Held**
SIC: 8412 Historical society; museum

(P-24898)
PALM SPRINGS ART MUSEUM INC
101 N Museum Dr, Palm Springs (92262-5659)
P.O. Box 2310 (92263-2310)
PHONE................................760 322-4800

Donna Macmillan, *Ch of Bd*
Elizabeth Armstrong, *Exec Dir*
Alicia Gregory, *Executive Asst*
Lucy Debardeleban, *Controller*
Alicia Thomas, *Human Res Dir*
▲ EMP: 96
SQ FT: 75,000
SALES: 10.5MM **Privately Held**
WEB: www.psmuseum.org
SIC: 8412 Museum

(P-24899)
PARKS AND RECREATION CAL DEPT
Also Called: Malibu Lagoon Museum
23200 Pacific Coast Hwy, Malibu (90265-4937)
P.O. Box 291 (90265-0291)
PHONE................................310 456-8432
Sandra Mitchell, *Branch Mgr*
EMP: 80 **Privately Held**
WEB: www.californiastatepark.com
SIC: 8412 9512 Museum; land, mineral & wildlife conservation;
HQ: California Department Of Parks And Recreation
1416 9th St Ste 1041
Sacramento CA 95814
800 777-0369

(P-24900)
REUBEN H FLEET SCIENCE CENTER
1875 El Prado, San Diego (92101-1625)
P.O. Box 33303 (92163-3303)
PHONE................................619 238-1233
Gary Thomas Phillips, *CEO*
Craig A Blower, *COO*
Jeffrey Kirsch, *Exec Dir*
EMP: 105
SQ FT: 93,500
SALES: 7.7MM **Privately Held**
WEB: www.rhfleet.org
SIC: 8412 Museum

(P-24901)
RONALD REAGAN PRESIDENTIAL
Also Called: Ronald Reagan Presdntl Library
40 Presidential Dr # 200, Simi Valley (93065-0600)
PHONE................................805 522-2977
Glenn Baker, *CFO*
Mike Shahin, *Treasurer*
Melissa Giller, *Comms Dir*
John Heubusch, *Exec Dir*
Katherine Hicks, *Executive Asst*
EMP: 70
SQ FT: 225,000
SALES: 34.9MM **Privately Held**
WEB: www.reaganfoundation.org
SIC: 8412 8231 5947 8399 Museum; public library; gifts & novelties; community development groups; fund raising organization, non-fee basis

(P-24902)
SAN DEGO SOC OF NTURAL HISTORY
Also Called: San Dego Ntural History Museum
1788 El Prado, San Diego (92101-1624)
P.O. Box 121390 (92112-1390)
PHONE................................619 232-3821
Michael W Hager, *CEO*
George Gonyer, *COO*
Susan Loveall, *Vice Pres*
▲ EMP: 70 EST: 1874
SQ FT: 60,000
SALES: 14.5MM **Privately Held**
WEB: www.sdnhm.org
SIC: 8412 5047 Museum; dental equipment & supplies

(P-24903)
SAN DIEGO AEROSPACE MUSEUM
335 Kenney St, El Cajon (92020-1249)
PHONE................................619 258-1221
Jeff Eads, *Manager*
EMP: 60
SALES (est): 491.8K **Privately Held**
WEB: www.sdasm.org
SIC: 8412 Museum

(P-24904)
SAN DIEGO ARCFT CARIER MUSEUM
910 N Harbor Dr, San Diego (92101-5811)
PHONE................................619 544-9600
Theresa Randall, *President*
Jon Lynch, *Pub Rel Mgr*
EMP: 150
SALES: 21.9MM **Privately Held**
WEB: www.midway.org
SIC: 8412 Museum

(P-24905)
SAN DIEGO MUSEUM OF ART
1450 El Prado, San Diego (92101-1618)
P.O. Box 122107 (92112-2107)
PHONE................................619 696-1971
Philip Tom Gildred, *CEO*
Dieter Fenkart-Froesch, *COO*
Sarah Hilliard, *Publications*
Roxanna Velasquez, *Director*
Lilli-Mari Andresen, *Manager*
▲ EMP: 82
SQ FT: 96,278
SALES: 7.9MM **Privately Held**
WEB: www.sdmart.org
SIC: 8412 Museum

(P-24906)
SAN FRANCISCO MERITIME N H P
Fort Myson Ctr Bldg E265, San Francisco (94123)
PHONE................................415 561-7000
Craig Kenkel, *Superintendent*
EMP: 80
SALES (est): 535K **Privately Held**
SIC: 8412 Museum

(P-24907)
SAN FRANCISCO MUSEUM MODRN ART (PA)
Also Called: Sfmoma Museum Store
151 3rd St, San Francisco (94103-3107)
PHONE................................415 357-4035
Robert J Fisher, *President*
Diana Nelson, *Vice Chairman*
Dennis Wong, *Vice Chairman*
Charles R Schwab, *Chairman*
Dennis J Wong, *Treasurer*
▲ EMP: 363
SQ FT: 225,000
SALES (est): 75.8MM **Privately Held**
WEB: www.sfmoma.org
SIC: 8412 5942 Museum; book stores

(P-24908)
SAN FRNCSCO MRTIME NAT PK ASSN (PA)
Fort Mason Fl 2 Bldg E, San Francisco (94123)
P.O. Box 470310 (94147-0310)
PHONE................................415 561-6662
John Tregenza, *CEO*
Bill Parker, *Treasurer*
Ted Regan, *Exec Dir*
Troy Arnold, *Development*
EMP: 50
SQ FT: 2,500
SALES: 2.7MM **Privately Held**
WEB: www.sanbrunosuper8.com
SIC: 8412 8299 8699 Museum; educational services; charitable organization

(P-24909)
SAN JOSE CHLD DISCOVERY MUSEUM
180 Woz Way, San Jose (95110-2722)
PHONE................................408 298-5437
William Sullivan, *CEO*
Patience Davidson, *Executive*
Rachelle Campos, *Exec Dir*
Marilee Jennings, *Exec Dir*
Brittany Waxman, *Executive Asst*
EMP: 85
SQ FT: 52,000
SALES: 8.5MM **Privately Held**
SIC: 8412 Museum

(P-24910)
SAN JOSE MUSEUM OF ART ASSN
110 S Market St, San Jose (95113-2383)
PHONE................................408 271-6840

Daniel Keegan, *Director*
▲ EMP: 70 EST: 1969
SQ FT: 80,000
SALES: 4.5MM **Privately Held**
WEB: www.sjmusart.org
SIC: 8412 5942 5947 Museum; book stores; gift shop

(P-24911)
SANTA BARBARA MUSEUM
2559 Puesta Del Sol, Santa Barbara (93105-2936)
PHONE................................805 682-4711
Luke Swetland, *CEO*
Palmer Jackson Jr, *President*
Diane Wondolowski, *CFO*
Diane Wondowloski, *CFO*
Carolyn Chandler, *Vice Pres*
EMP: 95 EST: 1916
SALES: 11.6MM **Privately Held**
WEB: www.sbnature.org
SIC: 8412 Museum

(P-24912)
SANTA BARBARA MUSEUM OF ART (PA)
Also Called: Fine Arts Museum
1130 State St, Santa Barbara (93101-2746)
PHONE................................805 963-4364
Larry J Feinberg, *CEO*
James Owen, *President*
Diane Wondolowski, *President*
Larry Feinberg, *CEO*
James Hutchinson, *CFO*
▲ EMP: 60
SQ FT: 50,000
SALES: 6.6MM **Privately Held**
WEB: www.sbmuseart.org
SIC: 8412 Museum

(P-24913)
SKIRBALL CULTURAL CENTER
2701 N Sepulveda Blvd, Los Angeles (90049-6833)
PHONE................................310 440-4500
Uri D Herscher, *President*
▲ EMP: 150
SQ FT: 65,000
SALES: 25.4MM **Privately Held**
SIC: 8412 Museum

(P-24914)
SOUTHWESTERN ARTISTS ASSN
1770 Vlg Pl Gallery 23 23 Gallery, San Diego (92101)
PHONE................................619 232-3522
Geln White, *President*
John Davis,
EMP: 50
SALES (est): 386.3K **Privately Held**
SIC: 8412 Art gallery

(P-24915)
STANSBURY HM PRESERVATION ASSN
307 W 5th St, Chico (95928-5505)
P.O. Box 3262 (95927-3262)
PHONE................................530 895-3848
EMP: 50
SQ FT: 3,500
SALES (est): 786.2K **Privately Held**
SIC: 8412

(P-24916)
TECH MUSEUM OF INNOVATION (PA)
201 S Market St, San Jose (95113-2008)
PHONE................................408 795-6116
Peter Friess, *CEO*
Christopher Digiorgio, *Ch of Bd*
Tim Ritchie, *President*
Naresh Kapahi, *CFO*
Bill Bailor, *Vice Pres*
◆ EMP: 88
SQ FT: 130,000
SALES: 19.9MM **Privately Held**
SIC: 8412 Arts or science center; museum

(P-24917)
TECH MUSEUM OF INNOVATION
145 W San Carlos St, San Jose (95113-2006)
PHONE................................408 795-6168

Bill Bailor, *Director*
Rachel Wilner, *Vice Pres*
Pete Adams, *Safety Mgr*
EMP: 76
SALES (corp-wide): 19.9MM **Privately Held**
SIC: 8412 Arts or science center
PA: The Tech Museum Of Innovation
201 S Market St
San Jose CA 95113
408 795-6116

(P-24918)
THE FOR CALIFO CENTE
340 N Escondido Blvd, Escondido
(92025-2600)
PHONE..................................760 839-4138
Vicky Basehore, *President*
Jason Danio, *Office Mgr*
Nancy Harper, *Office Mgr*
Gary Poor, *Finance*
Vanessa Garcia, *Human Res Dir*
EMP: 185
SALES: 5.1MM **Privately Held**
WEB: www.artcenter.org
SIC: 8412 5999 Arts or science center; art
dealers

(P-24919)
TURTLE BAY EXPLORATION PARK
1335 Arboretum Dr Ste A, Redding
(96003-3628)
PHONE..................................530 243-4282
John C Peterson, *President*
Maggie Redmon, *COO*
Stephen Gaston, *Chairman*
Mike Warren, *Bd of Directors*
Judy Lalouche, *Vice Pres*
EMP: 50
SALES: 2.9MM **Privately Held**
SIC: 8412 Museum

(P-24920)
WALT DISNEY FAMILY MUSEUM
104 Montgomery St, San Francisco
(94129-1718)
PHONE..................................415 345-6800
Ronald W Miller, *President*
Jennifer Miller-Goff, *Corp Secy*
Joanna Miller, *Vice Pres*
Carla Flores, *Social Dir*
Kirsten Komoroske, *Exec Dir*
EMP: 60
SALES: 11.4MM **Privately Held**
SIC: 8412 Museum

(P-24921)
WEST ANTLOPE VLY HSTORICAL SOC
45026 11th St W, Lancaster (93534-2206)
PHONE..................................661 945-5369
Milt Stark, *Vice Pres*
David Earl, *President*
EMP: 98
SALES (est): 565.3K **Privately Held**
SIC: 8412 Historical society

8422 Arboreta, Botanical & Zoological Gardens

(P-24922)
AQUARIUM OF PACIFIC
310 Golden Shore Ste 300, Long Beach
(90802-4240)
PHONE..................................562 590-3100
Jerry R Schubel, *Branch Mgr*
EMP: 56 **Privately Held**
SIC: 8422 Aquarium
PA: Aquarium Of The Pacific
100 Aquarium Way
Long Beach CA 90802

(P-24923)
AQUARIUM OF PACIFIC (PA)
100 Aquarium Way, Long Beach
(90802-8126)
PHONE..................................562 590-3100
Jerry R Schubel, *President*
Anthony Brown, *CFO*
Cecile Fisher, *Vice Pres*
Perry Hampton, *Vice Pres*
Kathryn Nirschl, *Vice Pres*

▲ EMP: 300
SQ FT: 10,000
SALES (est): 34.6MM **Privately Held**
SIC: 8422 Aquarium

(P-24924)
BAYORG
Also Called: AQUARIUM OF THE BAY, THE
Embarcadero At Beach St, San Francisco
(94133)
PHONE..................................415 623-5300
John Frawley, *President*
Bobbi Evans, *CFO*
Christopher Low, *Director*
EMP: 99
SALES: 10.2MM **Privately Held**
SIC: 8422 Aquarium

(P-24925)
BIRCH AQUARIUM AT SCRIPPS
Also Called: Scripps Aquarium
2300 Expedition Way, La Jolla (92037)
PHONE..................................858 534-4109
Nigella Hillgarth, *Director*
Patrick Helbling, *Opers Dir*
EMP: 50
SALES (est): 2MM **Privately Held**
SIC: 8422 8412 Aquarium; museum

(P-24926)
CALIFORNIA ACADEMY SCIENCES (PA)
55 Music Concourse Dr, San Francisco
(94118-4503)
PHONE..................................415 379-8000
John Hafernik, *President*
Alison Brown, *CFO*
Mike McGee, *CFO*
Jonathan Foley, *Managing Dir*
Elizabeth Babcock, *Admin Sec*
EMP: 655 EST: 1853
SQ FT: 410,000
SALES: 83.5MM **Privately Held**
SIC: 8422 2721 8412 Aquarium; periodi-
cals: publishing only; museums & art gal-
leries

(P-24927)
CITY OF SAN JOSE
Also Called: Visitor Services & Facilities
1300 Senter Rd, San Jose (95112-2520)
PHONE..................................408 794-6400
Randy Adams, *Supervisor*
EMP: 60 **Privately Held**
WEB: www.csjfinance.org
SIC: 8422 9512 Zoological garden, non-
commercial; recreational program admin-
istration, government;
PA: City Of San Jose
200 E Santa Clara St
San Jose CA 95113
408 535-3500

(P-24928)
FILOLI CENTER
Also Called: FILOLI GARDEN SHOP
86 Canada Rd, Woodside (94062-4144)
PHONE..................................650 364-8300
Cynthia D'Agosta, *CEO*
Pamela Smith, *President*
Wesley Thompson, *Officer*
Julie Lovell, *Social Dir*
Robert Walker, *Principal*
EMP: 60
SQ FT: 1,000
SALES: 6.4MM **Privately Held**
SIC: 8422 Botanical garden

(P-24929)
FRESNOS CHAFFEE ZOO CORP
894 W Belmont Ave, Fresno (93728-2807)
PHONE..................................559 498-5910
Scott Barton, *CEO*
Brian Goldman, *CFO*
Pam Wheelen, *Manager*
Whitney Horn, *Relations*
William Lemaster, *Relations*
◆ EMP: 121
SALES: 15.4MM **Privately Held**
WEB: www.fresnochaffeezoo.com
SIC: 8422 Animal & reptile exhibit

(P-24930)
LIVING DESERT
47900 Portola Ave, Palm Desert
(92260-6156)
PHONE..................................760 346-5694
Allen Monroe, *CEO*
Terrie Correll, *COO*
Bill Powers, *Bd of Directors*
Kathy Lambert, *Officer*
Wendy Enright, *Admin Asst*
EMP: 124
SQ FT: 1,700
SALES: 26.1MM **Privately Held**
WEB: www.livingdesert.org
SIC: 8422 5947 Aquariums & zoological
gardens; botanical garden; gift shop

(P-24931)
LOS ANGLES ARBRETUM FOUNDATION
301 N Baldwin Ave, Arcadia (91007-2697)
PHONE..................................626 821-3222
Richard Schulhof, *CEO*
Jennifer Williams, *Principal*
EMP: 65
SALES: 2.3MM **Privately Held**
SIC: 8422 Arboretum

(P-24932)
MONTALVO ASSOCIATION
Also Called: VILLA MONTALVO
15400 Montalvo Rd, Saratoga
(95070-6327)
P.O. Box 158 (95071-0158)
PHONE..................................408 961-5800
Angela McConnell, *Exec Dir*
EMP: 65
SQ FT: 13,000
SALES: 4.4MM **Privately Held**
WEB: www.villamontalvo.org
SIC: 8422 8412 Arboretum; art gallery,
noncommercial

(P-24933)
MONTEREY BAY AQAR FOUNDATION (PA)
886 Cannery Row, Monterey (93940-1023)
PHONE..................................831 648-4800
Peter Bing, *Ch of Bd*
Susan Wagner, *Volunteer Dir*
Julie E Packard, *CEO*
Edward Prohaska, *CFO*
James Bonovich, *Officer*
EMP: 168
SQ FT: 326,000
SALES: 85.1MM **Privately Held**
WEB: www.montereyaquarium.org
SIC: 8422 Aquarium

(P-24934)
RANCHO SANTA ANA BOTANIC GRDN
1500 N College Ave, Claremont
(91711-3157)
PHONE..................................909 625-8767
Clement Hamilton, *Exec Dir*
Richard Grant, *Chairman*
Sonja Evensen, *Vice Pres*
Lucinda McDade, *Exec Dir*
Phil Majors, *Information Mgr*
EMP: 52
SQ FT: 30,000
SALES: 5.1MM **Privately Held**
WEB: www.rsabg.org
SIC: 8422 Botanical garden

(P-24935)
SACRAMENTO ZOOLOGICAL SOCIETY
3930 W Land Park Dr, Sacramento
(95822-1123)
PHONE..................................916 808-5888
Mary Healy, *Exec Dir*
EMP: 50
SALES: 7MM **Privately Held**
WEB: www.saczoo.com
SIC: 8422 Arboreta & botanical or zoologi-
cal gardens

(P-24936)
SANTA BRBARA ZLGCAL FOUNDATION
500 Ninos Dr, Santa Barbara (93103-3759)
PHONE..................................805 962-1673

Yul Vanek, *CEO*
Fred Clough, *President*
Nancy McToldridge, *COO*
Carol Bedford, *CFO*
Eldon Shiffman, *Treasurer*
▲ EMP: 130
SQ FT: 1,200
SALES (est): 10.1MM **Privately Held**
WEB: www.santabarbarazoo.org
SIC: 8422 Zoological garden, noncommer-
cial

(P-24937)
ZOOLOGICAL SOCIETY SAN DIEGO (PA)
Also Called: World Famous San Diego Zoo
2920 Zoo Dr, San Diego (92101-1646)
P.O. Box 120551 (92112-0551)
PHONE..................................619 231-1515
Douglas G Myers, *Exec Dir*
Richard B Gulley, *President*
Paula S Brock, *CFO*
Frank Alexander, *Treasurer*
Allison Alberts, *Officer*
◆ EMP: 1500
SALES: 274.6MM **Privately Held**
WEB: www.sdzoo.com
SIC: 8422 5812 5947 Aquarium; eating
places; gift shop

(P-24938)
ZOOLOGICAL SOCIETY SAN DIEGO
Also Called: San Diego Wild Animal Park
15500 San Pasqual Vly Rd, Escondido
(92027-7017)
PHONE..................................760 747-8702
Robert McClure, *Manager*
Tracy Bareno, *Food Svc Dir*
EMP: 800
SALES (corp-wide): 274.6MM **Privately Held**
WEB: www.sdzoo.com
SIC: 8422 7999 Animal & reptile exhibit;
tourist attraction, commercial
PA: Zoological Society Of San Diego
2920 Zoo Dr
San Diego CA 92101
619 231-1515

(P-24939)
ZOOLOGICAL SOCIETY SAN DIEGO
Also Called: San Diego Zoo
2920 Zoo Dr, San Diego (92101-1646)
P.O. Box 120551 (92112-0551)
PHONE..................................619 744-3325
Richard Farrar, *Director*
Sara Graef, *Executive Asst*
EMP: 1200
SALES (corp-wide): 274.6MM **Privately Held**
WEB: www.sdzoo.com
SIC: 8422 Arboreta & botanical or zoologi-
cal gardens
PA: Zoological Society Of San Diego
2920 Zoo Dr
San Diego CA 92101
619 231-1515

8611 Business Associations

(P-24940)
AEROVIRONMENT INC
900 Innovators Way, Simi Valley (93065)
PHONE..................................805 581-2187
John Grabowsky, *Branch Mgr*
Joel Dispenza, *Information Mgr*
Sean Kirkhuff, *Engineer*
John Kim, *Senior Buyer*
Christine Casillas, *Buyer*
EMP: 150
SALES (corp-wide): 271MM **Publicly Held**
WEB: www.avinc.com
SIC: 8611 Manufacturers' institute
PA: Aerovironment, Inc.
800 Royal Oaks Dr Ste 210
Monrovia CA 91016
626 357-9983

(P-24941)
ALL STATE ASSOCIATION INC
11487 San Fernando Rd, San Fernando
(91340-3406)
PHONE..............................877 425-2558
Alfred Megrabyan, *President*
Steve Avetyan, *CEO*
Armen Karibyan, *COO*
George Alazyan, *Broker*
Jack Karol, *Opers Mgr*
EMP: 250
SALES (est): 120MM **Privately Held**
SIC: 8611 Trade associations

(P-24942)
**ALMOND BOARD OF
CALIFORNIA**
1150 9th St Ste 1500, Modesto
(95354-0845)
PHONE..............................209 549-8262
Richard Waycott, *CEO*
Julie Adams, *Director*
EMP: 50
SQ FT: 10,000
SALES: 73MM **Privately Held**
WEB: www.almondboard.com
SIC: 8611 Trade associations

(P-24943)
**ASOCIACON DE BOMBEROS
DEL ESTA**
1100 Calle Del Cerro 52d, San Clemente
(92672-6022)
PHONE..............................949 355-4249
Marco Olmos, *Principal*
EMP: 99
SALES (est): 812.4K **Privately Held**
SIC: 8611 Business associations

(P-24944)
**BAY MEADOWS RACING
ASSOCIATION**
2600 S Delaware St, San Mateo
(94403-1904)
P.O. Box 1490 (94401-0872)
PHONE..............................650 573-4500
Fax: 650 573-4677
EMP: 200
SALES (est): 4.5MM **Privately Held**
WEB: www.baymeadows.com
SIC: 8611

(P-24945)
BERES CONSULTING
Also Called: PCA
470 S Bentley Ave, Los Angeles
(90049-3513)
P.O. Box 252008 (90025-8908)
PHONE..............................310 476-9941
John Gleason, *President*
EMP: 80
SALES (est): 1.5MM **Privately Held**
SIC: 8611 Trade associations

(P-24946)
C A H H S
1215 K St Ste 800, Sacramento
(95814-3946)
PHONE..............................916 552-7507
Duane Dauner, *President*
EMP: 65
SALES (est): 597.7K **Privately Held**
WEB: www.calhospital.org
SIC: 8611 Trade associations

(P-24947)
**CALIFORNIA ASSN REALTORS
INC (PA)**
525 S Virgil Ave, Los Angeles
(90020-1403)
PHONE..............................213 739-8200
Joel S Singer, *CEO*
Lefrancis Arnold, *CEO*
Joel S Singer, *CEO*
Don Flyn, *CFO*
Don Faught, *Treasurer*
EMP: 110 **EST:** 1907
SQ FT: 52,000
SALES: 33.4MM **Privately Held**
SIC: 8611 8742 Real Estate Board; real
estate consultant

(P-24948)
**CALIFORNIA CERTIFIED
ORGANIC**
Also Called: CCOF CERTIFICATION SERV-
ICES
2155 Delaware Ave Ste 150, Santa Cruz
(95060-5732)
PHONE..............................831 423-2263
Cathy Calfo, *Exec Dir*
Phil Larocca, *Principal*
Jody Biergiel, *Exec Dir*
Rachel Witte, *General Mgr*
James Marquez, *Info Tech Dir*
EMP: 58
SALES: 3.5MM **Privately Held**
SIC: 8611 Trade associations

(P-24949)
**CALIFORNIA CHAMBER
COMMERCE (PA)**
Also Called: Cal Chamber
1215 K St Ste 1400, Sacramento
(95814-3953)
P.O. Box 1736 (95812-1736)
PHONE..............................916 444-6670
Allan Zaremberg, *President*
Lawrence M Dicke, *CFO*
Jeanne Cain, *Exec VP*
Dave Kilby, *Exec VP*
EMP: 65
SQ FT: 26,000
SALES: 24.6MM **Privately Held**
WEB: www.calchamber.com
SIC: 8611 Chamber of Commerce

(P-24950)
**CALIFORNIA GOLF
ASSOCIATION**
3200 Lopez Rd, Pebble Beach
(93953-2900)
PHONE..............................831 625-4653
Bob Scarpitto, *President*
EMP: 55
SALES: 152.2K **Privately Held**
SIC: 8611 Merchants' association

(P-24951)
**CALIFORNIA SCHOOL BOARDS
ASSN**
Also Called: Csba
3251 Beacon Blvd, West Sacramento
(95691-3531)
PHONE..............................800 266-3382
Vernon M Billy, *CEO*
Cindy Marks, *President*
Stephen Pogemiller, *CFO*
Jesus Holguin, *Vice Pres*
Scott Plotkin, *Exec Dir*
EMP: 100
SQ FT: 15,000
SALES: 15MM **Privately Held**
WEB: www.csba.org
SIC: 8611 Business associations

(P-24952)
CWS UTILITY SERVICES CORP
1720 N 1st St, San Jose (95112-4508)
PHONE..............................408 367-8200
Robert W Foye, *Principal*
EMP: 413
SALES (est): 6.5MM
SALES (corp-wide): 666.8MM **Publicly
Held**
WEB: www.calwater.com
SIC: 8611 Public utility association
PA: California Water Service Group
1720 N 1st St
San Jose CA 95112
408 367-8200

(P-24953)
**DOWNTOWN SAN DIEGO
PARTNR INC (PA)**
401 B St Ste 100, San Diego (92101-4224)
PHONE..............................619 234-0201
Chris Mitchell, *President*
Christina Chadwick, *Vice Pres*
John Hanley, *Vice Pres*
Daniel Reeves, *Vice Pres*
Lindsay Thomas, *Vice Pres*
EMP: 56
SQ FT: 3,500
SALES: 9.1MM **Privately Held**
WEB: www.downtown-digital.com
SIC: 8611 Business associations

(P-24954)
**DOWNTOWN SAN DIEGO
PARTNR INC**
1111 6th Ave Ste 101, San Diego
(92101-5230)
PHONE..............................619 234-8900
Ryan Loofbourrow, *Manager*
Lindsay Thomas, *Vice Pres*
EMP: 55
SQ FT: 10,480
SALES (corp-wide): 9.1MM **Privately
Held**
WEB: www.downtown-digital.com
SIC: 8611 Business associations
PA: Downtown San Diego Partnership, Inc.
401 B St Ste 100
San Diego CA 92101
619 234-0201

(P-24955)
ELECTRA OWNERS ASSOC
700 W E St, San Diego (92101-5984)
PHONE..............................619 236-3310
J E Martin, *Principal*
EMP: 150
SALES (est): 5.4MM
SALES (corp-wide): 71.8MM **Privately
Held**
SIC: 8611 Business associations
PA: Action Property Management, Inc.
2603 Main St Ste 500
Irvine CA 92614
949 450-0202

(P-24956)
**ELK GROVE ADULT CMNTY
TRAINING**
8810 Elk Grove Blvd, Elk Grove
(95624-1811)
PHONE..............................916 431-3162
Larry Sherrill, *CEO*
Gary Lawson, *Exec Dir*
Rebecca Brubaker, *Director*
EMP: 54
SALES (est): 3.4MM **Privately Held**
WEB: www.egact.org
SIC: 8611 Community affairs & services

(P-24957)
FIRE AND POLICE
4645 E Anaheim St, Long Beach
(90804-3122)
PHONE..............................562 961-0066
Patrick Ahern, *CEO*
Kevin Davis, *Director*
EMP: 50
SALES (est): 935.6K **Privately Held**
SIC: 8611 Community affairs & services

(P-24958)
**FOUNDTION FOR CAL CMNTY
CLLGES (PA)**
1102 Q St Ste 4800, Sacramento
(95811-6539)
PHONE..............................916 325-4300
Keetha Mills, *CEO*
John O'Sullivan, *CFO*
Mark Carlock, *Vice Pres*
Melissa Conner, *Vice Pres*
Joseph Quintana, *Vice Pres*
EMP: 250
SQ FT: 10,000
SALES: 38.5MM **Privately Held**
SIC: 8611 Business associations

(P-24959)
GOLDEN BEAR REST ASSN LLC
760 2nd St, San Francisco (94107-2012)
PHONE..............................415 227-8660
Peter W Osborne, *Mng Member*
Peter Osbourne,
EMP: 50
SALES (est): 1.5MM **Privately Held**
SIC: 8611 Merchants' association

(P-24960)
**HAPPY CAMP CHAMBER
COMMERCE**
35 Davis Rd, Happy Camp (96039)
PHONE..............................530 493-2900
James Buchner, *President*
Rosemary Boren, *Treasurer*
Roberta Cullum, *Vice Pres*
EMP: 50

SALES (est): 836K **Privately Held**
SIC: 8611 Chamber of Commerce

(P-24961)
**IAPMO RESEARCH AND
TESTING INC (HQ)**
Also Called: International Assn of Plmbing
5001 E Philadelphia St, Ontario
(91761-2816)
PHONE..............................909 472-4100
G P Russ Chaney, *Exec Dir*
Shahin Moinian, *Surgery Dir*
Neil Bogatz, *General Counsel*
Jeff Ortiz, *Editor*
EMP: 57 **EST:** 1994
SALES: 32.8MM
SALES (corp-wide): 33.7MM **Privately
Held**
SIC: 8611 Contractors' association
PA: International Association Of Plumbing
And Mechanical Officials, A Non-Profit
Corporation
4755 E Philadelphia St
Ontario CA 91761
909 472-4100

(P-24962)
INDIAN HEALTH COUNCIL (PA)
50100 Golsh Rd, Valley Center
(92082-5338)
P.O. Box 406, Pauma Valley (92061-0406)
PHONE..............................760 749-1410
Orvin Hanson, *CEO*
Bill Gallagher, *CFO*
Gina Rothermel, *Officer*
Donna Calac-Dusek, *Assoc VP*
Robert Schostag, *Pharmacy Dir*
EMP: 88
SALES: 22.5MM **Privately Held**
SIC: 8611 Business associations

(P-24963)
**INTERNATIONAL ASSOC OF
PLMBNG (PA)**
Also Called: Iapmo
4755 E Philadelphia St, Ontario
(91761-2810)
PHONE..............................909 472-4100
GP Russ Chaney, *CEO*
Gary Hile, *Corp Secy*
Lee Mercer, *Exec VP*
John Hadi, *Vice Pres*
Tina Marian, *Vice Pres*
▲ **EMP:** 51 **EST:** 1926
SQ FT: 65,000
SALES (est): 33.7MM **Privately Held**
SIC: 8611 Contractors' association

(P-24964)
L W ROTH INSURANCE AGENCY
Also Called: National Association For Self
6060 Sunrise Vista Dr, Citrus Heights
(95610-7053)
PHONE..............................916 721-6273
L W Roth, *Owner*
EMP: 100 **EST:** 1981
SALES (est): 1MM **Privately Held**
SIC: 8611 Regulatory associations

(P-24965)
LASSENS ALI LEADS CLUB (PA)
Also Called: Lassen's, Ali Success System
2644 Madison St, Carlsbad (92008-1721)
P.O. Box 278, Cardiff By The Sea (92007-
0278)
PHONE..............................760 434-3761
Lisa Bentson, *Owner*
EMP: 56
SQ FT: 2,200
SALES (est): 1MM **Privately Held**
WEB: www.leadsclub.com
SIC: 8611 Trade associations

(P-24966)
**LOS ANGLES AREA CHMBER
CMMERCE**
350 S Bixel St, Los Angeles (90017-1418)
PHONE..............................213 580-7500
Maria S Salinas, *President*
Gary Toebben, *President*
David Eads, *COO*
Benjamin Stilp, *CFO*
Alma Salazar, *Vice Pres*
EMP: 85

SALES: 6.7MM **Privately Held**
SIC: 8611 Chamber of Commerce

(P-24967)
MENS APPAREL GUILD IN CAL INC
Also Called: Magic International
2901 28th St Ste 100, Santa Monica (90405-2975)
PHONE..........................310 857-7500
Joe Loggia, *President*
Manny Rodriguez, *Vice Pres*
Lorelyn Eaves, *Exec Dir*
Robert Ehlers, *Exec Dir*
Barbara Goode, *Exec Dir*
EMP: 100 EST: 1932
SALES (est): 2.7MM
SALES (corp-wide): 1B **Privately Held**
WEB: www.magiconline.com
SIC: 8611 Manufacturers' institute
HQ: Advanstar Communications Inc.
2501 Colorado Ave Ste 280
Santa Monica CA 90404
310 857-7500

(P-24968)
MERCY HOUSE LIVING CENTERS
Also Called: Mercy Hse Trnstnal Living Ctrs
807 N Garfield St, Santa Ana (92701-3821)
P.O. Box 1905 (92702-1905)
PHONE..........................714 836-7188
Larry Haynes, *Exec Dir*
Jerome Karcher, *Ch of Bd*
Carrie Delaurie, *Director*
EMP: 109
SQ FT: 19,000
SALES (est): 6.1MM **Privately Held**
WEB: www.mercyhouse.net
SIC: 8611 Community affairs & services

(P-24969)
MOTION PICTURE ASSN AMER INC (PA)
15301 Ventura Blvd Bldg E, Sherman Oaks (91403-5885)
PHONE..........................818 995-6600
Christopher J Dodd, *CEO*
Steven Fabrizio, *Exec VP*
Jim C Williams, *Senior VP*
Melissa Patack, *Principal*
EMP: 120 EST: 1922
SQ FT: 74,000
SALES (est): 19.2MM **Privately Held**
SIC: 8611 6512 Trade associations; commercial & industrial building operation

(P-24970)
NATIONAL ASSN MUS MRCHANTS INC
Also Called: Namm
5790 Armada Dr, Carlsbad (92008-4608)
PHONE..........................760 438-8001
Joe Lamond, *President*
Neil Lilien, *CFO*
Larry Manley, *CFO*
Larry Morton, *Treasurer*
Dominique Agnew, *Associate Dir*
EMP: 62
SQ FT: 38,000
SALES: 24.4MM **Privately Held**
WEB: www.namm.com
SIC: 8611 Trade associations

(P-24971)
NORTHERN MONO CHAMBER COMMERCE
115281 Us Highway 395, Topaz (96133-9127)
PHONE..........................530 208-6078
Pam Hamick, *President*
Dianne Evans, *Corp Secy*
Mary Dayhoff, *Vice Pres*
Susan Robbins, *Admin Sec*
EMP: 50
SALES (est): 1.7MM **Privately Held**
SIC: 8611 Chamber of Commerce

(P-24972)
PGANDE
10901 E Highway 120, Manteca (95336-8920)
PHONE..........................209 942-1745
R Nick Jordan, *Principal*
EMP: 50

SALES (est): 569K **Privately Held**
SIC: 8611 Public utility association

(P-24973)
PRINTING INDS ASSN SUTHERN CAL
5800 S Eastrn Ave Ste 400, Commerce (90040)
P.O. Box 910936, Los Angeles (90091-0936)
PHONE..........................323 728-9500
Robert Lindgren, *President*
EMP: 75
SQ FT: 14,000
SALES: 2.8MM **Privately Held**
SIC: 8611 Merchants' association

(P-24974)
PROJECT CONCERN INTERNATIONAL (PA)
Also Called: PCI
5151 Murphy Canyon Rd # 320, San Diego (92123-4339)
PHONE..........................858 279-9690
Carrie Hessler-Radelet, *President*
George Guimaraes, *CEO*
Mark O Donnell, *COO*
Kote Lomidze, *CFO*
Janine Schooley, *Senior VP*
EMP: 88
SQ FT: 12,000
SALES: 65.6MM **Privately Held**
WEB: www.projectconcern.org
SIC: 8611 Business associations

(P-24975)
PUBLIC POLICY INSTITUTE CAL (PA)
Also Called: Ppic
500 Washington St Ste 600, San Francisco (94111-2907)
PHONE..........................415 291-4400
David Lyon, *President*
Robert E Obana, *CFO*
Andy Grose, *Principal*
Jelena Jezdimirovic, *Research*
Brandon Martin, *Research*
EMP: 73
SQ FT: 105,044
SALES: 12.7MM **Privately Held**
WEB: www.ppic.org
SIC: 8611 8732 Business associations; commercial nonphysical research

(P-24976)
SACRAMENTO HARNESS ASSOCIATION
1600 Exposition Blvd, Sacramento (95815-5104)
PHONE..........................916 239-4040
Ralph Scurfield, *President*
Chris Schick, *Manager*
EMP: 90
SALES (est): 1.3MM **Privately Held**
WEB: www.sacharness.com
SIC: 8611 Merchants' association

(P-24977)
SAN BERNARDINO CALIFORNIA CITY
Also Called: City Hall Pblc Wrks Eng Dpt
300 N D St Fl 3, San Bernardino (92418-0001)
PHONE..........................909 384-5111
James Funt, *Manager*
EMP: 70
SALES (corp-wide): 160MM **Privately Held**
SIC: 8611 Chamber of Commerce
PA: California City Of San Bernardino
290 N D St
San Bernardino CA 92401
909 384-7272

(P-24978)
SAN DIEGO ASSN GOVERNMENTS (PA)
Also Called: Regional Transportation Comm
401 B St Ste 800, San Diego (92101-4231)
PHONE..........................619 699-1900
Jack Dale, *Chairman*
Don Higginson, *Principal*
Jim Janney, *Principal*
Gary L Gallegos, *Exec Dir*
Coleen A Clementson, *Program Mgr*

EMP: 320
SQ FT: 20,000
SALES: 222.5MM **Privately Held**
WEB: www.gonctd.com
SIC: 8611 Business associations

(P-24979)
SAN JOSE SILICON VALLEY CHAM
Also Called: Chamberpac
101 W Santa Clara St, San Jose (95113-1760)
PHONE..........................408 291-5250
Patricia Dando, *President*
EMP: 61 EST: 1874
SALES: 2.4MM **Privately Held**
SIC: 8611 Chamber of Commerce

(P-24980)
SATICOY LEMON ASSOCIATION
600 E 3rd St, Oxnard (93030-6001)
P.O. Box 46, Santa Paula (93061-0046)
PHONE..........................805 654-6543
Kevin Colvard, *Plant Mgr*
EMP: 130
SALES (corp-wide): 171MM **Privately Held**
SIC: 8611 Growers' associations
PA: Saticoy Lemon Association
103 N Peck Rd
Santa Paula CA 93060
805 654-6500

(P-24981)
SEMI (PA)
673 S Milpitas Blvd, Milpitas (95035-5446)
PHONE..........................408 943-6900
Dennis P McGuirk, *President*
Masahiko Hamajima, *President*
Eric Tien, *President*
Richard Salsman, *CFO*
Douglas Neugold, *Chairman*
EMP: 133 EST: 1970
SALES: 41.7MM **Privately Held**
WEB: www.semi.org
SIC: 8611 Trade associations

(P-24982)
SISTERS OF SOUL (SOS) YOUTH
937 Via Lata Ste 400, Colton (92324-3958)
PHONE..........................909 533-4889
Angela Beal, *CEO*
EMP: 55
SQ FT: 2,800
SALES: 200K **Privately Held**
SIC: 8611 8322 Community affairs & services; general counseling services

(P-24983)
SOUTHERN CALIFORNIA GOLF ASSN (PA)
3740 Cahuenga Blvd, North Hollywood (91604-3502)
P.O. Box 7186 (91615-0186)
PHONE..........................818 980-3630
Ken Bien, *President*
Keenan Barber, *Treasurer*
Al Frank, *Vice Pres*
Jonathan Coe, *Comms Mgr*
Tom Lindgren, *Principal*
EMP: 72
SQ FT: 15,000
SALES: 7MM **Privately Held**
WEB: www.scga.org
SIC: 8611 7992 Trade associations; public golf courses

(P-24984)
SPECIALTY EQUIPMENT MKT ASSN (PA)
Also Called: Sema
1575 Valley Vista Dr, Diamond Bar (91765-3914)
PHONE..........................909 396-0289
Christopher J Kersting, *President*
Linda Czarkowski, *VP Admin*
Zack Krelle, *Research*
David Puentes, *Manager*
Leslie Reed, *Clerk*
EMP: 70
SQ FT: 23,000
SALES: 40.5MM **Privately Held**
WEB: www.enjoythedrive.com
SIC: 8611 Trade associations

(P-24985)
STREAMLINE SHIPPERS ASSN INC (PA)
6279 E Slauson Ave # 303, Commerce (90040-3040)
PHONE..........................323 271-3800
Robert Brown, *President*
Ray Camero, *Corp Secy*
Connie Ibarra, *Human Res Dir*
Clay Camero, *Sales Dir*
◆ EMP: 127
SALES (est): 10.8MM **Privately Held**
WEB: www.streamlineshippers.com
SIC: 8611 Shipping & steamship company association

(P-24986)
SURPLUS LINE ASSOCIATION CAL
12667 Alcosta Blvd # 450, San Ramon (94583-4427)
PHONE..........................415 434-4900
Ted Pierce, *Exec Dir*
Susan Bryant, *Vice Pres*
Mike Caturegli, *General Mgr*
Amanda Archuleta, *Admin Asst*
Patricia McAuley, *Data Proc Staff*
EMP: 65
SQ FT: 8,400
SALES: 11.9MM **Privately Held**
SIC: 8611 Trade associations

(P-24987)
UNITED AGRIBUSINESS LEAGUE (PA)
Also Called: U A L
54 Corporate Park, Irvine (92606-5105)
PHONE..........................800 223-4590
William C Goodrich, *President*
Kirti Mutatkar, *CFO*
Clare M Einsmann, *Exec VP*
Donna Bares, *Vice Pres*
EMP: 50
SQ FT: 14,099
SALES: 45.2MM **Privately Held**
WEB: www.ual.org
SIC: 8611 Growers' associations

(P-24988)
US LINES LLC (DH)
3501 Jamboree Rd Ste 300, Newport Beach (92660-2936)
PHONE..........................714 751-3333
Ed Aldridge, *President*
Thomas Aldridge, *Vice Pres*
Timothy Dillon, *Vice Pres*
John Ohle, *Vice Pres*
Lynn Nguyen, *Administration*
EMP: 75
SALES (est): 34.9MM **Privately Held**
WEB: www.uslines.com
SIC: 8611 Shipping & steamship company association
HQ: Cma Cgm
Tour Cma Cgm
Marseille
488 919-000

(P-24989)
VALIANT INTEGRATED SERVICES
9333 Balboa Ave, San Diego (92123-1515)
PHONE..........................858 277-6780
Michael Manser, *President*
Gregory Stone, *President*
Carrie Thomas, *General Mgr*
EMP: 280
SQ FT: 6,800
SALES (est): 4.3MM
SALES (corp-wide): 435.1MM **Privately Held**
WEB: www.omegatraining.com
SIC: 8611 8742 Contractors' association; training & development consultant
PA: Nova Global Supply And Services Llc
205 Van Buren St Ste 310
Herndon VA 20170
703 462-7750

▲ = Import ▼=Export
◆ =Import/Export

(P-24990)
WATER RESOURCES CONTROL BD CAL
Also Called: San Diego Region
2375 Northside Dr Ste 100, San Diego (92108-2700)
PHONE..................................619 521-3010
David Gibson, *Exec Dir*
EMP: 90 **Privately Held**
WEB: www.rb3.swrcb.ca.gov
SIC: **8611** Regulatory associations
HQ: Water Resources Control Board, California
1001 I St
Sacramento CA 95814
-

(P-24991)
WESTERN GROWERS ASSOCIATION (PA)
Also Called: W G A
15525 Sand Canyon Ave, Irvine (92618-3114)
P.O. Box 57089 (92619-7089)
PHONE..................................949 863-1000
Tom A Nassif, *CEO*
Steve Patricio, *Ch of Bd*
Lori Duquette, *Officer*
Matt McInerney, *Exec VP*
Dave Puglia, *Senior VP*
EMP: 150
SQ FT: 35,000
SALES: 7.9MM **Privately Held**
WEB: www.wga.com
SIC: **8611** 8111 Growers' associations; legal services

8621 Professional Membership Organizations

(P-24992)
ACADEMY MPIC ARTS & SCIENCES (PA)
8949 Wilshire Blvd, Beverly Hills (90211-1907)
PHONE..................................310 247-3000
Dawn Hudson, *CEO*
Bruce Younger, *Volunteer Dir*
Andy Horn, *CFO*
Albino Radman, *Officer*
Bruce Davis, *Exec Dir*
EMP: 100
SQ FT: 35,000
SALES: 123.6MM **Privately Held**
SIC: **8621** 7819 8611 Professional membership organizations; services allied to motion pictures; business associations

(P-24993)
ACADEMY TV ARTS & SCIENCES
Also Called: TELEVISION ACADEMY
5220 Lankershim Blvd, North Hollywood (91601-3141)
PHONE..................................818 754-2800
Maury McImtyre, *President*
EMP: 60
SALES: 4.7MM **Privately Held**
SIC: **8621** Professional membership organizations

(P-24994)
AMERICAN ACADEMY OF OPTHALMLGY (PA)
655 Beach St Fl 1, San Francisco (94109-1346)
P.O. Box 7424 (94120-7424)
PHONE..................................415 561-8500
David W Parke II, *CEO*
Keith Carter, *President*
Jill Boyett, *CFO*
Vicky Loni, *CFO*
Cathy Cohen, *Vice Pres*
EMP: 160
SQ FT: 66,000
SALES: 61.6MM **Privately Held**
WEB: www.aao.org
SIC: **8621** Medical field-related associations

(P-24995)
AMERICAN HEART ASSOCIATION INC
Also Called: Western States Affiliate
816 S Figueroa St, Los Angeles (90017-2516)
PHONE..................................213 291-7000
Cass Wheeler, *Branch Mgr*
EMP: 50
SALES (corp-wide): 780.2MM **Privately Held**
WEB: www.americanheart.org
SIC: **8621** Professional membership organizations
PA: American Heart Association, Inc.
7272 Greenville Ave
Dallas TX 75231
214 373-6300

(P-24996)
ARMED FORCES OFFICIALS ASSN
14532 Penasquitos Dr, San Diego (92129-1606)
PHONE..................................858 672-1438
Paul Bardsley, *Treasurer*
Robert Cauffman, *President*
Robery Kauffman, *President*
Clarence Langston, *Vice Pres*
Donald Robinson, *Admin Sec*
EMP: 50
SALES (est): 1.3MM **Privately Held**
SIC: **8621** Education & teacher association

(P-24997)
ARTISTS OF RIVER TOWN
56 Highlands Blvd, Oroville (95966-3643)
PHONE..................................530 534-7690
Dawn Bozine, *President*
Carmen Hironimus, *President*
Bee Boyd, *Treasurer*
Karen Comvey, *Admin Sec*
EMP: 76
SALES (est): 4.5MM **Privately Held**
WEB: www.global411.net
SIC: **8621** Professional membership organizations

(P-24998)
BAR ASSCATION OF SAN FRANCISCO (PA)
301 Battery St Fl 3, San Francisco (94111-3237)
PHONE..................................415 982-1600
James Donato, *President*
Jonathan Bond, *CFO*
Dan Burkhardt, *Exec Dir*
Kelly Cohen, *Admin Asst*
Samantha Silver, *Admin Asst*
EMP: 85
SQ FT: 23,600
SALES: 6.8MM **Privately Held**
SIC: **8621** Bar association

(P-24999)
BEVERLY HILLS POLC OFCRS ASSOC
464 N Rexford Dr, Beverly Hills (90210-4873)
P.O. Box 301 (90213-0301)
PHONE..................................310 288-1755
Joe Chirillo, *President*
EMP: 100
SALES: 399.5K **Privately Held**
SIC: **8621** 8742 Professional membership organizations; management consulting services

(P-25000)
CALIFORNIA ASSOCIATION O (PA)
Also Called: California Hospital Assn Cha
1215 K St Ste 800, Sacramento (95814-3946)
PHONE..................................916 443-7401
Carmela Coyle, *President*
Jennifer Davenport, *President*
Lois M Suder, *COO*
Lois Suder, *COO*
Dietmar Grellmann, *Senior VP*
EMP: 74
SQ FT: 30,000
SALES: 34MM **Privately Held**
SIC: **8621** 8011 Health association; group health association

(P-25001)
CALIFORNIA DENTAL ASSOCIATION (PA)
1201 K St Fl 14, Sacramento (95814-3925)
P.O. Box 13749 (95853-3749)
PHONE..................................916 443-0505
Peter A Dubois, *CEO*
Dennis Kalebjian, *President*
Carol Summerhayes, *President*
Cynthia Schneider, *CFO*
Gary Pilkington, *Director*
EMP: 120 EST: 1873
SQ FT: 28,932
SALES: 21.4MM **Privately Held**
WEB: www.sbvcds.org
SIC: **8621** Dental association

(P-25002)
CALIFORNIA HEALTH BENEFIT EXCH
Also Called: California Health Insur Exch
1601 Exposition Blvd, Sacramento (95815-5103)
PHONE..................................916 228-8210
Peter V Lee, *CEO*
Desi Malone, *Manager*
Desiree Hayhurst Malone, *Manager*
EMP: 99
SALES (est): 12.8MM **Privately Held**
SIC: **8621** Health association

(P-25003)
CALIFORNIA MEDICAL ASSOCIATION (PA)
Also Called: C M A
1201 J St Ste 200, Sacramento (95814-2949)
PHONE..................................916 444-5532
Dustin Corcoren, *CEO*
Lance Lewis, *COO*
Nick Birtcil, *Vice Pres*
Janus Norman, *Vice Pres*
Jennifer Williams, *Executive Asst*
EMP: 77 EST: 1856
SQ FT: 48,960
SALES (est): 2MM **Privately Held**
WEB: www.cmanet.org
SIC: **8621** Professional membership organizations

(P-25004)
CALIFORNIA NURSES ASSOCIATION (PA)
Also Called: NATIONAL NURSES UNITED
155 Grand Ave Ste 115, Oakland (94612-3758)
PHONE..................................510 273-2200
Rose Anne Demoro, *CEO*
Deborah Burger, *President*
Nikki Dones, *Admin Sec*
Mike Griffing, *Director*
EMP: 100
SQ FT: 36,000
SALES: 28.1MM **Privately Held**
WEB: www.calnurse.org
SIC: **8621** Nursing association

(P-25005)
CALIFORNIA TEACHERS ASSN
222 Judy Dr, Kelsey (95667-3325)
PHONE..................................530 622-8013
George Sabato, *Admin Sec*
EMP: 65
SALES (corp-wide): 187.1MM **Privately Held**
WEB: www.cntaonline.org
SIC: **8621** Education & teacher association
PA: California Teachers Association
1705 Murchison Dr
Burlingame CA 94010
650 697-1400

(P-25006)
CALIFORNIA TEACHERS ASSN (PA)
1705 Murchison Dr, Burlingame (94010-4583)
P.O. Box 921 (94011-0921)
PHONE..................................650 697-1400
Carolyn Doggett, *Exec Dir*
Debbie Baker, *Exec Dir*
Ingrid Williams, *Admin Sec*
Jeffrey Hugo, *Technology*
Gregory Gee, *Technical Staff*
EMP: 210

SALES: 187.1MM **Privately Held**
WEB: www.cntaonline.org
SIC: **8621** 8631 Education & teacher association; labor unions & similar labor organizations

(P-25007)
CALIFRNIA CPA EDCATN FUNDATION
1800 Gateway Dr Ste 200, San Mateo (94404-4072)
PHONE..................................800 922-5272
Loretta Doon, *CEO*
EMP: 60 EST: 1966
SQ FT: 8,071
SALES: 11MM **Privately Held**
SIC: **8621** Professional membership organizations

(P-25008)
CAPITAL INVSTMNTS VNTURES CORP (PA)
Also Called: Civco
30151 Tomas, Rcho STA Marg (92688-2125)
PHONE..................................949 858-0647
Drew Richardson, *President*
Brian Cronin, *Ch of Bd*
Gary Prenovost, *CFO*
Marjorie Kelso, *Human Resources*
Lauren Richardson, *Human Resources*
EMP: 195
SQ FT: 95,000
SALES (est): 33.2MM **Privately Held**
SIC: **8621** 4724 Professional membership organizations; travel agencies

(P-25009)
CITY & COUNTY OF SAN FRANCISCO
Public Works Dept Bureau Arch
30 Van Ness Ave Ste 4100, San Francisco (94102-6034)
PHONE..................................415 557-4713
Gary Hoy, *Principal*
Natalie Sierra, *Engineer*
EMP: 75 **Privately Held**
SIC: **8621** 9199 Architect association; general government administration; ;
PA: City & County Of San Francisco
1 Dr Carlton B Goodlett P
San Francisco CA 94102
415 554-7500

(P-25010)
CITY OF IRVINE
Also Called: Irvine Police Department
1 Civic Center Plz, Irvine (92606-5208)
PHONE..................................949 724-7101
David Maggard, *President*
EMP: 81 **Privately Held**
SIC: **8621** Professional membership organizations
PA: City Of Irvine
1 Civic Center Plz
Irvine CA 92606
949 724-6000

(P-25011)
COMMUNITY CLINICS HLTH NETWRK
Also Called: Hqp
3710 Ruffin Rd, San Diego (92123-1812)
PHONE..................................619 542-4300
Henry Tuttle, *CEO*
Deborah McEntee, *Human Resources*
Christy Rosenberg, *Director*
EMP: 50
SALES: 5.5MM
SALES (corp-wide): 35.6MM **Privately Held**
SIC: **8621** Medical field-related associations
PA: Council Of Community Clinics
3710 Ruffin Rd
San Diego CA 92123
619 542-4300

(P-25012)
COOPERTIVE AMRCN PHYSCIANS INC (PA)
Also Called: Cap-Mpt
333 S Hope St Fl 8, Los Angeles (90071-3001)
PHONE..................................213 473-8600

James Weidner, CEO
Cindy Belcher, COO
John Donaldson, CFO
Hammon P Acuna, Senior VP
Nancy Brusegaard Johnson, Senior VP
EMP: 100
SALES (est): 15.2MM Privately Held
WEB: www.cap-mpt.com
SIC: 8621 Medical field-related associations

(P-25013)
COUNTY LAKE HEALTH SERVICES
Also Called: Public Health Di
922 Bevins Ct, Lakeport (95453-9754)
PHONE............................707 263-1090
Denise Pomeroy, Director
Karen Tait, Officer
Carla Ritz, Exec Dir
Geoff Hasz, Info Tech Dir
Susan Bennett, Accountant
EMP: 90 EST: 1950
SALES (est): 2.5MM Privately Held
SIC: 8621 Health association

(P-25014)
COUNTY OF FRESNO
Also Called: Assessor-Recorder's Office
2281 Tulare St Ste 201, Fresno
(93721-2139)
P.O. Box 1146 (93715-1146)
PHONE............................559 600-3534
Paul Dictos, Manager
EMP: 166 Privately Held
WEB: www.first5fresno.org
SIC: 8621 9441 Accounting association;
PA: County Of Fresno
2420 Mariposa St
Fresno CA 93721
559 600-1710

(P-25015)
COUNTY OF LOS ANGELES
313 N Figueroa St Fl 9, Los Angeles
(90012-2602)
PHONE............................213 240-8412
Thomas L Garthwaite, Branch Mgr
Aguilar Aida, Admin Asst
Mike Agostinelli, Info Tech Mgr
Day Al, Manager
Kathleen Dinsmore, Manager
EMP: 863 Privately Held
WEB: www.co.la.ca.us
SIC: 8621 9431 Professional membership
organizations; prenatal (maternity) health
program administration, govt.
PA: County Of Los Angeles
500 W Temple St Ste 437
Los Angeles CA 90012
213 974-1101

(P-25016)
GLEN BEVERLY LABORATORIES INC
Also Called: Inc J-Network
7711 Center Ave Ste 100, Huntington
Beach (92647-3070)
PHONE............................714 848-5777
Akira Kodama, CEO
Mitsuhiro Eguchi, Vice Pres
Jackie Yashiro, Office Mgr
Takashi Egawa, Purch Mgr
Mariko Nakahara, Manager
EMP: 60
SALES (est): 2.1MM Privately Held
SIC: 8621 Professional membership organizations

(P-25017)
HEALTH TRUST (PA)
3180 Newberry Dr Ste 200, San Jose
(95118-1566)
PHONE............................408 513-8700
Frederick J Ferrer, CEO
Robert Humphreys, Partner
Gary Allen, President
Todd Hansen J D, COO
Todd Hansen, COO
EMP: 81 EST: 1960
SALES: 15.2MM Privately Held
SIC: 8621 8299 Health association; educational services

(P-25018)
HERITAGE PROVIDER NETWORK INC (PA)
8510 Balboa Blvd Ste 285, Northridge
(91325-5804)
PHONE............................818 654-3461
Richard N Merkin, President
Kevin J Conroy, Partner
A D Villani, COO
Jaya Kurian, CFO
Scott Bae, Senior VP
EMP: 714
SALES (est): 46.4MM Privately Held
WEB: www.hcmgadmin.com
SIC: 8621 Medical field-related associations

(P-25019)
HUMAN SERVICES ASSOCIATION (PA)
6800 Florence Ave, Bell (90201-4957)
PHONE............................562 806-5400
Susanne Sundberg, Principal
Darren Dunaway, Associate Dir
Daniel Suh, Network Analyst
Celia Marquez, VP Mktg
Rosie Ramos, Senior Mgr
EMP: 75
SQ FT: 10,000
SALES (est): 15.8MM Privately Held
WEB: www.hsala.org
SIC: 8621 Nursing association

(P-25020)
INDYNE
300 W Point Ave, El Granada (94018)
PHONE............................805 606-0664
C Donald Bishop, President
Bob Miller, CFO
EMP: 99
SALES: 950K Privately Held
SIC: 8621 Professional membership organizations

(P-25021)
INTERNAL MDCINE RSDNCY AFFAIRS
Also Called: EC Davis Health Services
4150 V St Ste 3116, Sacramento
(95817-1460)
PHONE............................916 734-7080
Kristi Threlkeld, Manager
Mark Henderson, Director
EMP: 85
SALES (est): 5.8MM Privately Held
SIC: 8621 Health association

(P-25022)
JEWISH FAMILY SVC LOS ANGELES (PA)
Also Called: Jewish Free Loan Association
3580 Wilshire Blvd, Los Angeles
(90010-2501)
PHONE............................323 761-8800
Paul Castro, CEO
Tran Maggard, CFO
Todd Sosna, Senior VP
Teresa Trinidad, Program Mgr
Robert Rome, Office Mgr
EMP: 50
SQ FT: 7,600
SALES: 2.4MM Privately Held
WEB: www.jewishla.com
SIC: 8621 Professional membership organizations

(P-25023)
LEIGHTON GROUP INC
75450 Gerald Ford Dr, Palm Desert
(92211-6022)
PHONE............................760 776-4192
EMP: 105
SALES (corp-wide): 30.7MM Privately Held
SIC: 8621 Professional membership organizations
PA: Leighton Group, Inc.
17781 Cowan
Irvine CA 92614
949 477-4040

(P-25024)
LEXISNEXIS COURTLINK INC
2101 K St, Sacramento (95816-4920)
PHONE............................425 974-5000

Michele Vivona, President
EMP: 160
SQ FT: 40,000
SALES (est): 4.3MM
SALES (corp-wide): 9.7B Privately Held
SIC: 8621 Professional membership organizations
HQ: Relx Inc.
230 Park Ave Ste 700
New York NY 10169
212 309-8100

(P-25025)
LOS ANGELES COUNTY BAR ASSN (PA)
Also Called: Los Angeles Lawyer Magazine
1055 W 7th St Ste 2700, Los Angeles
(90017-2553)
P.O. Box 55020 (90055-2020)
PHONE............................213 627-2727
Paul R Kiesel, President
James P Drummy, Bd of Directors
Kevin Mahoney, Bd of Directors
Sally Suchil, Exec Dir
Ron Deaton, General Mgr
EMP: 85 EST: 1878
SQ FT: 25,000
SALES (est): 11.7MM Privately Held
WEB: www.lacba.org
SIC: 8621 Bar association

(P-25026)
MARIANNE FROSTIG CENTER (PA)
971 N Altadena Dr, Pasadena
(91107-1870)
PHONE............................626 791-1255
Bennett Ross PHD, CEO
Dean Conklin, Exec Dir
Rick Benavides, Administration
Kaye Sergeant, Finance Dir
Giovanni Delgado, Finance
EMP: 50 EST: 1948
SQ FT: 33,000
SALES: 4.6MM Privately Held
WEB: www.frostig.org
SIC: 8621 Education & teacher association

(P-25027)
MEDIMPACT HLTHCARE SYSTEMS INC (HQ)
10181 Scripps Gateway Ct, San Diego
(92131-5152)
PHONE............................858 566-2727
Frederick Howe, Ch of Bd
James Gollaher, CFO
Jeanine Mc Bride, Vice Pres
Jeanine McBride, Vice Pres
Nancy Radtke, Vice Pres
EMP: 595
SQ FT: 100,000
SALES: 16MM Privately Held
WEB: www.medegram.com
SIC: 8621 Medical field-related associations

(P-25028)
MITHUN INC
660 Market St Ste 300, San Francisco
(94104-5012)
PHONE............................415 956-0688
David W Goldberg, Branch Mgr
Marna Abrams, Marketing Mgr
Brad Fanta, Marketing Mgr
Erik Hagen, Associate
EMP: 61
SALES (corp-wide): 20.5MM Privately Held
SIC: 8621 Architect association
PA: Mithun, Inc.
1201 Alaskan Way Ste 200
Seattle WA 98101
206 971-3423

(P-25029)
NATIONAL NOTARY ASSOCIATION
Also Called: Nna Services
9350 De Soto Ave, Chatsworth
(91311-4926)
PHONE............................818 739-4071
Milton G Valera, Chairman
Thomas A Heymann, CEO
Robert Clarke, CFO
Deborah M Thaw, Exec VP

Debbie Valera, Exec VP
EMP: 204
SQ FT: 55,000
SALES (est): 32MM Privately Held
SIC: 8621 Professional membership organizations

(P-25030)
NNA SERVICES
9350 De Soto Ave, Chatsworth
(91311-4926)
PHONE............................818 739-4071
Thomas Heymann, CEO
Robert Clarke, CFO
Milt Valera, Chairman
Bill Anderson, Vice Pres
EMP: 205
SQ FT: 55,000
SALES (est): 1.4MM Privately Held
SIC: 8621 Professional membership organizations

(P-25031)
NORWALK LA MIRADA UNIF
Also Called: Association of CA Schl Admnstr
15135 Escalona Rd, La Mirada
(90638-4601)
PHONE............................714 521-0970
Bonita Cadra-Lytle, Branch Mgr
EMP: 61
SALES (corp-wide): 262.2MM Privately Held
SIC: 8621 Professional membership organizations
PA: Norwalk La Mirada Unified School District
12820 Pioneer Blvd
Norwalk CA 90650
562 868-0431

(P-25032)
ORANGE COUNTY ASSOCIATION (PA)
Also Called: Mental Health Assn Orange Cnty
822 W Town And Country Rd, Orange
(92868-4712)
PHONE............................714 547-7559
Margaret Riley, President
Trisha McDaniel, CFO
Jeff Thrash, Exec Dir
Annie McKnight, Human Res Dir
Thao Pham,
EMP: 53
SQ FT: 3,000
SALES: 6.5MM Privately Held
WEB: www.mhaoc.org
SIC: 8621 Professional membership organizations

(P-25033)
ORANGE COUNTY HEALTH AUTH
505 City Pkwy W, Orange (92868-2924)
PHONE............................714 246-8500
Richard Chambers, CEO
Michael Schrader, CEO
Ladan Khamseh, COO
Kim Cunningham, Officer
Richard Helmer, Officer
EMP: 432
SQ FT: 200,000
SALES (est): 92.6MM Privately Held
SIC: 8621 Professional membership organizations

(P-25034)
ORANGE COUNTY HEALTH CARE AGCY
405 W 5th St Ste 700, Santa Ana
(92701-4534)
PHONE............................714 568-5683
Jenny Qian, Principal
Leslie Sorrells, Manager
EMP: 99
SALES (est): 10.3MM Privately Held
SIC: 8621 Health association

(P-25035)
PADI AMERICAS INC
30151 Tomas, Rcho STA Marg
(92688-2125)
P.O. Box 7005 (92688-7005)
PHONE............................949 858-7234
Drew Richardson, Principal
Gary Prenovost, CFO

Al Hornsby, *Vice Pres*
Roberto Raffaeli, *Vice Pres*
Mark P Spiers, *Vice Pres*
EMP: 200
SQ FT: 96,000
SALES (est): 31.3MM
SALES (corp-wide): 33.2MM **Privately Held**
WEB: www.padi.com
SIC: 8621 Education & teacher association
HQ: Padi Worldwide Corp.
30151 Tomas
Rcho Sta Marg CA 92688
949 858-7234

(P-25036)
PLACER CO BAR ASSOCIATION (PA)
P.O. Box 4598 (95604-4598)
PHONE...................................916 557-9181
David G Cohen, *Principal*
EMP: 284
SALES: 43.2K **Privately Held**
SIC: 8621 Bar association

(P-25037)
POMONA COMMUNITY HEALTH CENTER
Also Called: PARKTREE COMMUNITY HEALTH CENT
1450 E Holt Ave, Pomona (91767-5822)
PHONE...................................909 630-7927
Ellen Silver, *CEO*
Carmen Ibarra, *Exec Dir*
EMP: 60
SALES: 7.1MM **Privately Held**
SIC: 8621 Health association

(P-25038)
REGAL MEDICAL GROUP INC (PA)
Also Called: Heritage California Aco
8510 Balboa Blvd Ste 275, Northridge (91325-5809)
PHONE...................................818 654-3400
Richard N Merkin, *CEO*
Jim Haggard, *President*
Alan Rojas, *Technical Staff*
EMP: 89
SALES (est): 28.9MM **Privately Held**
SIC: 8621 Medical field-related associations

(P-25039)
SALU BEAUTY INC
Also Called: Salu.net
11344 Coloma Rd Ste 725, Gold River (95670-4464)
PHONE...................................916 475-1400
Jim O Steeb, *President*
Steve Brown, *COO*
John V Crisan, *CFO*
Jim Fisher, *Exec Dir*
Imelda Martinez, *Business Anlyst*
EMP: 55
SALES (est): 8.1MM
SALES (corp-wide): 972MM **Privately Held**
SIC: 8621 5961 Health association; general merchandise, mail order
HQ: The Hut.Com Limited
1-2 The Stables
Northwich CW9 7
160 633-8197

(P-25040)
SAN FRANCISCO HEALTH AUTHORITY (PA)
Also Called: Hsf Programme
50 Beale St Fl 12, San Francisco (94105-1813)
P.O. Box 194247 (94119-4247)
PHONE...................................415 615-4407
John Grgurina Jr, *CEO*
Philip Hartman, *President*
James Glauber, *Chief Mktg Ofcr*
Nina Maruyama, *Officer*
Lisa Ghotbi, *Pharmacy Dir*
EMP: 99
SQ FT: 26,000
SALES (est): 27.1MM **Privately Held**
WEB: www.sfhp.org
SIC: 8621 Health association

(P-25041)
SHARP COMMUNITY MEDICAL GROUP
Also Called: Scmg
8695 Spectrum Center Blvd, San Diego (92123-1489)
PHONE...................................858 499-4525
Kenneth Roth, *President*
Eden Keh, *Business Mgr*
Manuel Deleon, *Analyst*
Leanne Gilliland, *Analyst*
Ryan Kulinski, *Training Spec*
EMP: 200
SALES (est): 12.8MM
SALES (corp-wide): 3.4B **Privately Held**
WEB: www.scmg.com
SIC: 8621 Professional membership organizations
PA: Sharp Healthcare
8695 Spectrum Center Blvd
San Diego CA 92123
858 499-4000

(P-25042)
ST BALDRICKS FOUNDATION INC (PA)
1333 S Mayflower Ave, Monrovia (91016-4066)
PHONE...................................626 792-8247
Charles M Chamness, *Ch of Bd*
Kathleen Ruddy, *Exec Dir*
Matthew Wallace, *Administration*
Danette Ocaranza, *Human Res Dir*
Susan Mona, *Marketing Staff*
EMP: 60
SALES: 37.9MM **Privately Held**
SIC: 8621 Health association

(P-25043)
ST VINCENT SENIOR CITIZN NUTR (PA)
2131 W 3rd St, Los Angeles (90057-1901)
PHONE...................................213 484-7775
Sister A Marie Quinn, *President*
Alice Marie Quinn, *President*
EMP: 71
SALES: 7.1MM **Privately Held**
SIC: 8621 Professional membership organizations

(P-25044)
STATE BAR OF CALIFORNIA (PA)
180 Howard St Fl Grnd, San Francisco (94105-6155)
PHONE...................................415 538-2000
Bill Hebert, *President*
Peggy Van Horn, *CFO*
EMP: 296
SQ FT: 72,000
SALES (est): 78.3MM **Privately Held**
SIC: 8621 Bar association

(P-25045)
STATE BAR OF CALIFORNIA
845 S Figueroa St, Los Angeles (90017-2515)
PHONE...................................213 765-1000
Judy Johnson, *Director*
EMP: 277
SALES (corp-wide): 78.3MM **Privately Held**
SIC: 8621 Bar association
PA: State Bar Of California
180 Howard St Fl Grnd
San Francisco CA 94105
415 538-2000

(P-25046)
TRI-COUNTIES ASSOCIATION F
1234 Fairway Dr A, Santa Maria (93455-1406)
PHONE...................................805 922-4640
EMP: 136
SALES (corp-wide): 293.2MM **Privately Held**
SIC: 8621 Professional membership organizations
PA: Tri-Counties Association For The Developmentally Disabled, Inc.
520 E Montecito St
Santa Barbara CA 93103
805 962-7881

(P-25047)
TRUCK UNDERWRITERS ASSOCIATION (DH)
4680 Wilshire Blvd, Los Angeles (90010-3807)
P.O. Box 2478 (90051-0478)
PHONE...................................323 932-3200
Leonard H Gelfand, *President*
Gerald Faulwell, *Vice Pres*
Martin Feinstein, *Vice Pres*
Jason Katz, *Vice Pres*
John Lynch, *Vice Pres*
EMP: 1767
SALES (est): 81.5MM
SALES (corp-wide): 65.1B **Privately Held**
SIC: 8621 Professional membership organizations
HQ: Farmers Group, Inc.
6301 Owensmouth Ave
Woodland Hills CA 91367
323 932-3200

(P-25048)
UNITED CEREBRAL PALSY ASSOC (PA)
Also Called: Cerebral Palsy Assn San Joaqui
333 W Benjamin Holt Dr # 1, Stockton (95207-3906)
PHONE...................................209 956-0290
Ray All, *Exec Dir*
EMP: 175
SQ FT: 15,000
SALES (est): 5.6MM **Privately Held**
WEB: www.ucpsj.org
SIC: 8621 Professional membership organizations

(P-25049)
UPWORK GLOBAL INC
441 Logue Ave, Mountain View (94043-4018)
PHONE...................................650 316-7500
Stephane Kasriel, *CEO*
Brian Kinion, *CFO*
Brian Levey, *Officer*
Hayden Brown, *Vice Pres*
Stratis Karamanlakis, *CTO*
EMP: 50
SQ FT: 16,000
SALES (est): 6MM
SALES (corp-wide): 202.5MM **Publicly Held**
SIC: 8621 7371 2741 Professional membership organizations; computer software development & applications; miscellaneous publishing
PA: Upwork Inc.
441 Logue Ave
Mountain View CA 94043
650 316-7500

(P-25050)
VISITING NURSE & HOSPICE CARE (PA)
Also Called: Visiting Nurse & Hospice Care
509 E Montecito St # 200, Santa Barbara (93103-3293)
PHONE...................................805 965-5555
Lynda Tanner, *CEO*
Karen M Wallace, *CFO*
Michelle Martinich, *Chairman*
Mary Pritchard, *Treasurer*
Rick Keith, *Exec Dir*
EMP: 130
SQ FT: 13,765
SALES: 24.8MM **Privately Held**
WEB: www.sbvna.org
SIC: 8621 Nursing association

(P-25051)
VISITING NURSE ASSOCIATION OF (DH)
2880 Soquel Ave Ste 10, Santa Cruz (95062-1423)
PHONE...................................831 477-2600
Bella Hughes, *Exec Dir*
EMP: 100
SQ FT: 19,000
SALES (est): 6MM
SALES (corp-wide): 12.4B **Privately Held**
SIC: 8621 Professional membership organizations

HQ: Palo Alto Medical Foundation For Health Care, Research And Education (Inc)
795 El Camino Real
Palo Alto CA 94301
650 321-4121

(P-25052)
VISTA HILL FOUNDATION (PA)
8910 Clairemont Mesa Blvd, San Diego (92123-1104)
PHONE...................................585 514-5100
Robert Dean, *President*
Belle Nunley, *Vice Pres*
Elizabeth McInnis, *Nursing Dir*
Susan Schulte, *Director*
Latisha Hill, *Case Mgr*
EMP: 50
SQ FT: 16,802
SALES: 28.2MM **Privately Held**
SIC: 8621 8741 Medical field-related associations; management services

8631 Labor Unions & Similar Organizations

(P-25053)
ALPHA CONNECTION GROUP HOME
Also Called: ALPHA CONNECTION YOUTH FAMILY
22675 Anoka Rd, Apple Valley (92308-5436)
PHONE...................................760 247-6370
Juanita Wilson, *President*
Barron Wilson, *Vice Pres*
Evonnda Hull, *Administration*
EMP: 70
SALES: 2.6MM **Privately Held**
SIC: 8631 Labor unions & similar labor organizations

(P-25054)
ASSOCIATIONS OF UNITED NURSES (PA)
Also Called: UNAC/UHCP
955 Overland Ct Ste 150, San Dimas (91773-1740)
PHONE...................................909 599-8622
Ken Deitz, *President*
Jettie Deden-Castillo, *Treasurer*
Denise Duncan, *Vice Pres*
Graciela Velazquez, *Vice Pres*
Charmaine Morales, *Admin Sec*
EMP: 63
SALES: 8.8MM **Privately Held**
SIC: 8631 Employees' association

(P-25055)
BUENA PARK POLICE ASSOCIATION
6650 Beach Blvd, Buena Park (90621-2905)
PHONE...................................714 562-3901
Sgt Steven Martinez, *President*
Dana Patton, *Officer*
Sgt Frank Nunes, *Vice Pres*
Charlene Magruder, *Admin Sec*
EMP: 90
SALES: 107.9K **Privately Held**
SIC: 8631 Employees' association

(P-25056)
CALIFORNIA CORRECTNL PEACE OFC (PA)
Also Called: CCPOA
755 Riverpoint Dr, West Sacramento (95605-1673)
PHONE...................................916 372-6060
Chuck Alexander, *President*
James Martin, *Treasurer*
Charles Alexander, *Vice Pres*
Perry Speth, *Admin Sec*
Amber Hollingsworth, *Admin Asst*
EMP: 86 **EST:** 1957
SQ FT: 32,000
SALES: 29.3MM **Privately Held**
WEB: www.ccpoa.org
SIC: 8631 8111 Labor union; legal services

(P-25057)
CALIFORNIA SCHL EMPLOYEES ASSN (PA)
Also Called: Csea
2045 Lundy Ave, San Jose (95131-1865)
PHONE....................408 473-1000
Allan Clark, *President*
Michael Bilbrey, *Vice Pres*
Ben Valdepena, *Vice Pres*
Bud Dougherty, *Exec Dir*
EMP: 180
SQ FT: 65,000
SALES: 65.6MM **Privately Held**
WEB: www.csea.com
SIC: 8631 Labor union

(P-25058)
CALIFRNIA STATE EMPLOYEES ASSN (PA)
Also Called: CSEA
1108 O St Ste 405, Sacramento (95814-5746)
PHONE....................916 444-8134
Dave Hart, *President*
Debbie Cotton, *CFO*
Dave Okunura, *Treasurer*
Lee King, *General Mgr*
Alex Velasco, *Technician*
EMP: 270
SQ FT: 30,000
SALES: 5.3MM **Privately Held**
SIC: 8631 Labor unions & similar labor organizations

(P-25059)
COUNTY OF LOS ANGELES
Also Called: Carson Gang Diversion Team
21356 Avalon Blvd, Carson (90745-2213)
PHONE....................310 847-4018
EMP: 226 **Privately Held**
SIC: 8631
PA: County Of Los Angeles
500 W Temple St Ste 375
Los Angeles CA 90012
213 974-1101

(P-25060)
HAYWARD POLICE OFFICERS ASSN
300 W Winton Ave, Hayward (94544-1137)
PHONE....................510 293-7207
Julie Kirkland, *Principal*
EMP: 75
SALES: 404.9K **Privately Held**
SIC: 8631 Labor union

(P-25061)
INTERNATIONAL ALLIANCE THEA
Also Called: Local 442
P.O. Box 413 (93102-0413)
PHONE....................805 898-0442
Gary Hilton, *Principal*
EMP: 60
SALES (est): 75.9K **Privately Held**
SIC: 8631 Labor union

(P-25062)
INTERNATIONAL ASSOC OF MACHINI
Also Called: NFFE-IAM 2152
1303 S Highway 95, Needles (92363-4217)
PHONE....................760 326-7048
Elaine Downing, *President*
Remijio Chavez, *Vice Pres*
EMP: 50
SALES: 68.2K **Privately Held**
SIC: 8631 Labor union

(P-25063)
INTERNATIONAL BRTHRHD OF ELCTR (PA)
Also Called: AFL-CIO #1245
30 Orange Tree Cir, Vacaville (95687-3105)
PHONE....................707 452-2700
Ed Mallory, *President*
James McCulley, *Vice Pres*
Michael J Davis,
Kathy Tindall,
EMP: 64
SALES: 27.8MM **Privately Held**
WEB: www.ibew1245.com
SIC: 8631 Labor union

(P-25064)
INTERNATIONAL LONGSHOREMENS
Also Called: LONGSHOREMEN'S & WARE-HOUSEMENS
22 N Union St, Stockton (95205-4915)
PHONE....................209 464-1827
Marc Cuavas, *President*
Dennis Brueckner, *President*
Lee Flood, *Vice Pres*
Frank Aeonis, *Admin Sec*
EMP: 81 EST: 1934
SQ FT: 1,000
SALES: 218.6K **Privately Held**
SIC: 8631 Trade union; labor union

(P-25065)
INTERNTIONAL UN OPER ENGINEERS
Local 12
150 Corson St, Pasadena (91103-3839)
P.O. Box 7109 (91109-7209)
PHONE....................626 792-2519
William C Waggoner, *Manager*
EMP: 50
SQ FT: 32,534
SALES (corp-wide): 57.9MM **Privately Held**
WEB: www.iuoestateunit12.org
SIC: 8631 Labor union
PA: International Union Of Operating Engineers
1121 L St Ste 401
Sacramento CA 95814
916 444-6880

(P-25066)
INTERNTIONAL UN OPER ENGINEERS (PA)
1121 L St Ste 401, Sacramento (95814-3969)
PHONE....................916 444-6880
Tim Neep, *Director*
EMP: 67 EST: 1939
SALES (est): 57.9MM **Privately Held**
WEB: www.iuoestateunit12.org
SIC: 8631 Labor union

(P-25067)
IUOE STTONARY ENGINEERS LCL 39
Also Called: Iuoe Local 39
1620 N Market Blvd, Sacramento (95834-1958)
PHONE....................916 928-0399
Tony De Marco, *President*
Jerry Kalmar, *Vice Pres*
EMP: 50
SALES (est): 295.6K **Privately Held**
SIC: 8631 Labor union

(P-25068)
LABORERS FUNDS ADMINISTRATIVE (PA)
Also Called: Laborers Trust Funds Nthrn Cal
220 Campus Ln, Fairfield (94534-1498)
PHONE....................707 864-2800
Edward Smith, *Admin Sec*
Leo Ferrer, *Purch Dir*
Monica Martin, *Purch Agent*
Edwin Embery, *Director*
EMP: 110
SQ FT: 43,000
SALES (est): 13.7MM **Privately Held**
SIC: 8631 Labor unions & similar labor organizations

(P-25069)
LOS ANGLES CNTY EMPLOYEES ASSN
Also Called: Service Employee Intl Un
1545 Wilshire Blvd, Los Angeles (90017-4501)
PHONE....................213 368-8660
Annelle Grajeda, *President*
Kathleen Austria, *Treasurer*
Bob Schoonover, *Vice Pres*
Annette Jeffrief, *Admin Sec*
EMP: 60
SQ FT: 40,000
SALES (est): 6.9MM **Privately Held**
WEB: www.local660.org
SIC: 8631 Labor union

(P-25070)
MILLMENS LOCAL 1496
6190 N Cecelia Ave, Fresno (93722-3204)
PHONE....................559 275-8676
Norman Avila, *President*
EMP: 50
SALES: 800.7K **Privately Held**
SIC: 8631 Labor unions & similar labor organizations

(P-25071)
NATIONAL ASSN LTR CARRIERS
Also Called: National Assn Ltr Crrers BR 52
4251 S Higuera St, San Luis Obispo (93401-7700)
PHONE....................805 543-7329
Edward L Somogyi, *Branch Mgr*
EMP: 300
SALES (corp-wide): 1.4B **Privately Held**
SIC: 8631 Labor union
PA: National Association Of Letter Carriers
100 Indana Ave Nw Ste 709
Washington DC 20001
202 393-4695

(P-25072)
NATIONAL ASSN LTR CARRIERS
2310 Mason St Fl 4, San Francisco (94133-1800)
PHONE....................415 362-0214
John Beaumont, *Manager*
Karen Eshabarr, *Exec VP*
EMP: 300
SALES (corp-wide): 1.4B **Privately Held**
WEB: www.nalc.org
SIC: 8631 Labor union
PA: National Association Of Letter Carriers
100 Indana Ave Nw Ste 709
Washington DC 20001
202 393-4695

(P-25073)
PORT OF LONG BCH EMPLOYEES CLB
4801 Airport Plaza Dr, Long Beach (90815-1263)
P.O. Box 570 (90801-0570)
PHONE....................562 590-4102
Paul McArthy, *CEO*
Glenn Farren, *Opers Staff*
Richard Steinke, *Director*
EMP: 400
SALES (est): 40.2MM **Privately Held**
SIC: 8631 4499 Employees' association; marine salvaging & surveying services

(P-25074)
SAG-AFTRA FOUNDATION
5757 Wilshire Blvd Ph 1, Los Angeles (90036-3681)
PHONE....................323 549-6708
Cyd Wilson, *Exec Dir*
Ann Martzell, *Office Mgr*
Rochelle Rose, *Prgrmr*
Marlena Campbell, *Accounting Mgr*
EMP: 50
SALES (est): 8MM **Privately Held**
SIC: 8631 Labor union

(P-25075)
SAN BRNRDINO PUB EMPLYEES ASSN
Also Called: SBPEA
433 N Sierra Way, San Bernardino (92410-4831)
P.O. Box 432 (92402-0432)
PHONE....................909 386-1260
Paula Ready, *President*
EMP: 50
SQ FT: 20,000
SALES: 6.3MM **Privately Held**
WEB: www.sbpea.com
SIC: 8631 Employees' association

(P-25076)
SAN DIEGO COUNTY EMPLOYEES RET
2275 Rio Bonito Way # 100, San Diego (92108-1685)
PHONE....................619 515-6800
Brian White, *CEO*
Karen Johanson, *Associate*
EMP: 90
SALES (est): 7.3MM **Privately Held**
SIC: 8631 Employees' association

(P-25077)
SEIU LOCAL 2015
2910 Beverly Blvd, Los Angeles (90057-1012)
PHONE....................213 985-0384
Laphonza Butler, *President*
Dereck Smith, *COO*
Malcolm Glover, *Controller*
EMP: 210
SALES: 76.9MM **Privately Held**
SIC: 8631 Labor union

(P-25078)
SEIU LOCAL 721
1545 Wilshire Blvd # 100, Los Angeles (90017-4510)
PHONE....................213 368-8660
Annelle Grajeda, *Owner*
EMP: 55
SALES (est): 5.2MM **Privately Held**
SIC: 8631 Labor unions & similar labor organizations

(P-25079)
SEIU UNITED HEALTHCARE WORKERS (PA)
560 Thomas L Berkley Way, Oakland (94612-1602)
PHONE....................510 251-1250
Dave Regan, *President*
Lee Farrell, *President*
Edgard Tajina, *CFO*
Eliseo Medina, *Trustee*
Debbie M Schneider, *Trustee*
EMP: 140
SQ FT: 33,000
SALES: 107.3MM **Privately Held**
WEB: www.seiu-uhw.org
SIC: 8631 Labor union

(P-25080)
SEIU UNITED HEALTHCARE WORKERS
Also Called: Seiu Uhw-West
5480 Ferguson Dr, Commerce (90022-5119)
PHONE....................323 734-8399
Liza Leyva, *Director*
EMP: 50
SALES (corp-wide): 107.3MM **Privately Held**
SIC: 8631 Labor union
PA: Seiu United Healthcare Workers-West Local 2005
560 Thomas L Berkley Way
Oakland CA 94612
510 251-1250

(P-25081)
SERVICE WORKERS LOCAL 715 (PA)
Also Called: Service Employees Intl Union
2302 Zanker Rd, San Jose (95131-1115)
PHONE....................408 678-3300
Rosemary Romo, *President*
Kristina Sermersheim, *Exec Sec*
EMP: 60
SQ FT: 1,000
SALES: 2.1MM **Privately Held**
WEB: www.seiu715.org
SIC: 8631 8621 Labor union; professional membership organizations

(P-25082)
SOUTHWEST RGNAL CNCIL CRPNTERS (PA)
533 S Fremont Ave Fl 10, Los Angeles (90071-1712)
PHONE....................213 385-1457
Jacky Barnett, *President*
Mike McCarron, *President*
Hal Jensen, *Vice Pres*
Jim Bernsen, *Admin Sec*
EMP: 50
SQ FT: 4,000
SALES (est): 27.5MM **Privately Held**
SIC: 8631 Labor union

(P-25083)
SUGAR WORKERS LOCAL 1
641 Loring Ave, Crockett (94525-1233)
PHONE....................510 787-1676
Ed Cummings, *President*
Surinder M Bhanot, *President*
EMP: 330

SQ FT: 5,000
SALES: 237.8K **Privately Held**
SIC: 8631 Labor union

(P-25084)
TEMPORARY STAFFING UNION
19800 Macarthur Blvd, Irvine (92612-2421)
PHONE..................................714 728-5186
Veronica Lake, *CEO*
Fe Santos, *President*
EMP: 4000
SQ FT: 1,500
SALES: 100K **Privately Held**
SIC: 8631 Labor union

(P-25085)
TURLOCK IRRIGATION DISTRICT (PA)
333 E Canal Dr, Turlock (95380-3946)
P.O. Box 949 (95381-0949)
PHONE..................................209 883-8222
Joe Alamo, *President*
Calvin Curtin, *Officer*
Willie Manuel, *Planning*
Ken Nold, *Planning*
Susan Carmichael, *Technician*
EMP: 250
SQ FT: 20,000
SALES (est): 52.2MM **Privately Held**
WEB: www.tid.com
SIC: 8631 Employees' association

(P-25086)
UNITED FARM WORKERS AMERICA (PA)
29700 Wdford Tehachapi Rd, Keene (93531)
P.O. Box 62 (93531-0062)
PHONE..................................661 822-5571
Arturo Rodriguez, *President*
Liz Villarino, *CFO*
Tanis Ybarra, *Corp Secy*
Irv Hershenbaum, *Vice Pres*
Jose Ibarra, *Accounting Mgr*
EMP: 110
SQ FT: 5,000
SALES: 7.2MM **Privately Held**
WEB: www.ufw.org
SIC: 8631 Labor union

(P-25087)
UNITED FOOD AND COMMERCIAL (PA)
Also Called: Ufcw Local 770
630 Shatto Pl Ste 300, Los Angeles (90005-1372)
P.O. Box 770 (90078-0770)
PHONE..................................213 487-7070
Ricardo F Icaza, *President*
Rodney Diamond, *Corp Secy*
John Grant, *Vice Pres*
Lisa Lee, *Comms Mgr*
Johnny Fung, *Controller*
EMP: 60
SALES (est): 19MM **Privately Held**
SIC: 8631 Labor union

(P-25088)
UNITED TEACHERS-LOS ANGELES
Also Called: U T L A
3303 Wilshire Blvd Fl 10, Los Angeles (90010-1794)
PHONE..................................213 487-5560
Aj Duffy, *President*
David Goldberg, *Treasurer*
David Goldburg, *Treasurer*
Joshua Pechthalt, *Vice Pres*
Ana Valencia, *Vice Pres*
EMP: 72
SQ FT: 144,000
SALES: 40.9MM **Privately Held**
WEB: www.utla.net
SIC: 8631 Collective bargaining unit

(P-25089)
WRITERS GUILD AMERICA WEST INC
7000 W 3rd St, Los Angeles (90048-4321)
PHONE..................................323 951-4000
David Young, *CEO*
Paul Kent, *COO*
Theresa F Savino, *COO*
Elias Davis, *Corp Secy*
Kymberly Jackson, *Senior VP*

EMP: 160 EST: 1954
SQ FT: 67,000
SALES: 32.3MM **Privately Held**
WEB: www.wga.org
SIC: 8631 Labor union

8641 Civic, Social & Fraternal Associations

(P-25090)
ACTION PROPERTY MANAGEMENT INC
530 S Hewitt St, Los Angeles (90013-2286)
PHONE..................................800 400-2284
Mary Moore, *Branch Mgr*
EMP: 120
SALES (corp-wide): 71.8MM **Privately Held**
SIC: 8641 Homeowners' association
PA: Action Property Management, Inc.
    2603 Main St Ste 500
    Irvine CA 92614
    949 450-0202

(P-25091)
AMERICAN LEGION AMBULANCE SVC
Also Called: AMERICAN LEGION HALL
11350 American Legion Dr, Sutter Creek (95685)
PHONE..................................209 223-2963
Al Lennox, *General Mgr*
EMP: 70
SQ FT: 800
SALES: 8.2MM **Privately Held**
SIC: 8641 Veterans' organization

(P-25092)
ARTHRTIS FUNDATION PCF REG INC
800 W 6th St Ste 1250, Los Angeles (90017-2721)
PHONE..................................323 954-5760
EMP: 50
SALES: 12.5MM **Privately Held**
SIC: 8641

(P-25093)
ASSOCIATED STUDENTS CALIFORNI
800 N State College Blvd, Fullerton (92831-3547)
P.O. Box 6828 (92834-6828)
PHONE..................................657 278-2468
Fred Sanchez, *Exec Dir*
Amir Dabirian, *President*
Peter Nwosu, *Assoc VP*
Bill Barrett, *Vice Pres*
Owen Holmes, *Vice Pres*
EMP: 51 EST: 1975
SQ FT: 117,000
SALES: 15.1MM **Privately Held**
SIC: 8641 University club

(P-25094)
ASSOCIATED STUDENTS CALIFORNIA
Also Called: A S I
1212 N Bellflower Blvd # 220, Long Beach (90815-4148)
PHONE..................................562 985-4994
Richard Haller, *Exec Dir*
EMP: 260 EST: 1956
SQ FT: 184,000
SALES: 15.1MM **Privately Held**
SIC: 8641 University club

(P-25095)
ASSOCIATED STUDENTS STANFORD (PA)
Also Called: A S S U
201 Tresidder Un, Stanford (94305)
PHONE..................................650 723-4331
Linda Whitcomb, *Director*
Alice Willoughby, *Principal*
EMP: 63
SALES: 1.4MM **Privately Held**
SIC: 8641 University club

(P-25096)
BALANCE4KIDS
4500 Soquel Dr, Soquel (95073-2122)
PHONE..................................831 464-8669
Victoria George, *Director*
Shannon Crane, *Treasurer*
Mary Willis, *Director*
EMP: 92
SALES: 3.5MM **Privately Held**
SIC: 8641 Youth organizations

(P-25097)
BAYVIEW HUNTERS POINT Y M C A
Also Called: YMCA
1601 Lane St, San Francisco (94124-2732)
PHONE..................................415 822-7728
Cheryl Smith-Thornton, *Exec Dir*
EMP: 64
SALES (est): 2.5MM **Privately Held**
SIC: 8641 7991 8351 7032 Youth organizations; physical fitness facilities; child day care services; youth camps; individual & family services

(P-25098)
BEAR VALLEY SPRINGS ASSN
29541 Rollingoak Dr, Tehachapi (93561-7133)
PHONE..................................661 821-5537
Todd Lander, *President*
Terry Quinn, *President*
Larry Thompson, *Treasurer*
Tim Hawkins, *Vice Pres*
EMP: 200
SQ FT: 2,000
SALES: 6.9MM **Privately Held**
WEB: www.bearinfo.com
SIC: 8641 Homeowners' association

(P-25099)
BEL-AIR BAY CLUB LTD
16801 Pacific Coast Hwy, Pacific Palisades (90272-3399)
PHONE..................................310 230-4700
William Howard, *CEO*
Shannon Griffin, *Executive*
Roberto Portillo, *Executive*
Judye Parent, *Admin Mgr*
Bill Howard, *General Mgr*
EMP: 200
SQ FT: 7,500
SALES (est): 10.2MM **Privately Held**
WEB: www.belairbayclub.com
SIC: 8641 Social club, membership

(P-25100)
BODEGA HARBOUR HOMEOWNERS ASSN
Also Called: Bodega Harbour Golf Links
21301 Heron Dr, Bodega Bay (94923-9401)
P.O. Box 368 (94923-0368)
PHONE..................................707 875-3519
Judith A Steeves, *Admin Mgr*
Anna Taylor, *General Mgr*
Brett Fox, *Maint Spvr*
EMP: 65
SQ FT: 10,000
SALES (est): 3MM **Privately Held**
SIC: 8641 5812 5813 7997 Homeowners' association; American restaurant; bars & lounges; yacht club, membership

(P-25101)
BOHEMIAN CLUB (PA)
Also Called: BOHEMIAN GROVE
624 Taylor St, San Francisco (94102-1075)
PHONE..................................415 885-2440
Robert L Spence, *CEO*
Matt Ogerio, *General Mgr*
Jennifer Robertson, *Human Res Dir*
Jessica Eftink, *Manager*
EMP: 105 EST: 1872
SQ FT: 20,000
SALES: 9.3MM **Privately Held**
WEB: www.bc-owl.org
SIC: 8641 Social club, membership

(P-25102)
BOY SCOUTS OF AMERICA (PA)
2333 Scout Way, Los Angeles (90026-4995)
PHONE..................................213 353-9879
Cash Sutton, *President*

Larry Forbes, *CFO*
EMP: 74
SALES: 5.9MM **Privately Held**
SIC: 8641 Boy Scout organization

(P-25103)
BOYS & GIRLS CLUB OF TRACY (PA)
753 W Lowell Ave, Tracy (95376-2935)
PHONE..................................209 832-2582
Kelly Wilson, *President*
EMP: 50
SQ FT: 15,000
SALES: 1.9MM **Privately Held**
SIC: 8641 Boy Scout organization; youth organizations

(P-25104)
BOYS & GIRLS CLUB SIMI VLY INC
2850 Lemon Dr, Simi Valley (93063-2193)
PHONE..................................805 527-4437
Linda White, *CEO*
Beth Welden, *Finance*
James Lucas, *Opers Mgr*
Earle Okamoto, *Program Dir*
Sandee Covone, *Asst Director*
EMP: 50
SALES: 2.5MM **Privately Held**
WEB: www.bgcsimi.com
SIC: 8641 Youth organizations

(P-25105)
BOYS & GIRLS CLUBS CENT SONOMA
1400 N Dutton Ave Ste 14, Santa Rosa (95401-7120)
PHONE..................................707 528-7977
Jennifer Weiss, *Exec Dir*
Dawn Holman, *Administration*
Margaret Forbes, *Business Mgr*
Shannon Baron, *Director*
EMP: 187
SALES: 7.5MM **Privately Held**
SIC: 8641 Youth organizations

(P-25106)
BOYS & GIRLS CLUBS OF MARIN A
1400 N Dutton Ave Ste 23, Santa Rosa (95401-4644)
PHONE..................................707 769-5322
David Solo, *President*
EMP: 56
SQ FT: 11,000
SALES: 2.5MM **Privately Held**
WEB: www.petalumabgc.org
SIC: 8641 Youth organizations

(P-25107)
BOYS & GIRLS CLUBS OF N VLY
601 Wall St, Chico (95928-5626)
PHONE..................................530 899-0335
Rashell Brobst, *Exec VP*
Lisa Spiegler, *Director*
EMP: 80
SQ FT: 14,000
SALES: 2.5MM **Privately Held**
SIC: 8641 Boy Scout organization; youth organizations

(P-25108)
BOYS AND GIRLS CLUBS OF THE LA (PA)
Also Called: BOYS & GIRLS CLUB OF SAN PEDRO
1200 S Cabrillo Ave, San Pedro (90731-4011)
PHONE..................................310 833-1322
Mike Lansing, *Exec Dir*
Robert Nizich, *President*
Dennis Lane, *Treasurer*
Joseph Rich, *Vice Pres*
John Robinson, *Vice Pres*
EMP: 56
SQ FT: 26,083
SALES: 7MM **Privately Held**
WEB: www.bgclaharbor.org
SIC: 8641 Youth organizations

(P-25109)
BOYS AND GIRLS CLUBS OF THE LA
Also Called: Dana Middle Schl Bys Girls CLB
1501 S Cabrillo Ave, San Pedro
(90731-4617)
PHONE...................310 833-1322
Mike Lansing, *Branch Mgr*
EMP: 99
SALES (corp-wide): 7MM **Privately Held**
SIC: 8641 Youth organizations
PA: Boys And Girls Clubs Of The Los Angeles Harbor
1200 S Cabrillo Ave
San Pedro CA 90731
310 833-1322

(P-25110)
BOYS AND GIRLS CLUBS OF THE LA
Also Called: Wilmington Schll Bys & Grls CL
1700 Gulf Ave, Wilmington (90744-1311)
PHONE...................310 833-1322
Mike Lansing, *Branch Mgr*
EMP: 99
SALES (corp-wide): 7MM **Privately Held**
SIC: 8641 Youth organizations
PA: Boys And Girls Clubs Of The Los Angeles Harbor
1200 S Cabrillo Ave
San Pedro CA 90731
310 833-1322

(P-25111)
BOYS GIRLS CLB HUNTINGTON VLY (PA)
16582 Brookhurst St, Fountain Valley
(92708-2353)
PHONE...................714 531-2582
Tanya Hoxsie, *President*
Kim Nguyen, *Finance*
Sem Ibrahim, *Athletic Dir*
Sharanjit Dhaliwal, *Program Dir*
Diana Kacic, *Program Dir*
EMP: 89
SALES: 7.2MM **Privately Held**
SIC: 8641 Youth organizations

(P-25112)
BOYS GIRLS CLB IMPERIAL BEACH
847 Encina Ave, Imperial Beach
(91932-2135)
P.O. Box 520 (91933-0520)
PHONE...................619 424-2266
Ken Blinsman, *Director*
Mark Nagles, *President*
Stephanie Ortega, *Director*
EMP: 100
SALES (est): 3.1MM **Privately Held**
SIC: 8641 5812 Civic social & fraternal associations; eating places

(P-25113)
BOYS GIRLS CLUBS OF KERN CNTY
Also Called: Boy's & Girls Club Bakersfield
801 Niles St, Bakersfield (93305-4419)
PHONE...................661 325-3730
Zane Smith, *Exec Dir*
Ed Kuhn, *President*
Murry Tragish, *President*
Craig Stickler, *Treasurer*
Bill Campbell, *Vice Pres*
EMP: 100
SALES: 5.8MM **Privately Held**
SIC: 8641 8322 Boy Scout organization; individual & family services

(P-25114)
BOYS GRLS CLB SNTA MONICA INC
Also Called: Boys Girls Clubs Santa Monica
1220 Lincoln Blvd, Santa Monica
(90401-1704)
PHONE...................310 361-8500
Aaron Young, *Director*
Jessica Rubecindo, *Volunteer Dir*
Amy Donohue, *Vice Pres*
Nadia Fellows, *Director*
Karina Garcia, *Director*
EMP: 83
SQ FT: 6,000

SALES: 3.6MM **Privately Held**
WEB: www.smbgc.org
SIC: 8641 7997 Youth organizations; membership sports & recreation clubs

(P-25115)
BOYS GRLS CLUBS GRDN GROVE INC
Also Called: Girls and Boys Club Grdn Grove
13645 Clinton St, Garden Grove
(92843-4110)
PHONE...................714 537-8833
Evelyn Matua, *Branch Mgr*
EMP: 169
SALES (corp-wide): 11.5MM **Privately Held**
SIC: 8641 Youth organizations
PA: Boys & Girls Clubs Of Garden Grove, Inc.
10540 Chapman Ave
Garden Grove CA 92840
714 530-0430

(P-25116)
BOYS GRLS CLUBS OF SAN DEGUITO (PA)
Also Called: BOYS & GIRLS CLUBS OF SAN DIEG
533 Lomas Santa Fe Dr, Solana Beach
(92075-1323)
PHONE...................858 755-9371
Alex Barrera, *President*
James Watkins, *Vice Chairman*
Andy Brosche, *COO*
Rose Mary Eller, *Treasurer*
Marineke Vandervort, *Exec Dir*
EMP: 100 EST: 1966
SQ FT: 25,000
SALES: 6MM **Privately Held**
WEB: www.bgcsdto.org
SIC: 8641 Youth organizations

(P-25117)
BOYS GRLS CLUBS OF SQUOIAS INC
1003 San Juan Rd, Exeter (93221-1342)
PHONE...................559 592-4074
Joe Engelbrecht, *Officer*
Galen Quenzer, *COO*
Jerry Petty, *Info Tech Dir*
Maria Almanza, *Site Mgr*
Yamileth Martinez, *Opers Mgr*
EMP: 62
SQ FT: 2,600
SALES (est): 2.4MM **Privately Held**
SIC: 8641 Youth organizations

(P-25118)
BOYSCOUT OF AMERICA
Also Called: BOY SCOUTS OF AMERICA
10 Highland Way, Piedmont (94611-4095)
PHONE...................510 547-4493
Josephine Hazelett, *Exec Dir*
EMP: 78
SALES: 630.3K **Privately Held**
WEB: www.piedmontbsa.org
SIC: 8641 Boy Scout organization

(P-25119)
BRIDGES CLUB AT RANCHO SA
18550 Seven Bridges Rd, Rancho Santa Fe
(92091-0216)
P.O. Box 1322 (92067-1322)
PHONE...................858 759-7200
Tom Martin, *President*
EMP: 140
SALES: 4MM **Privately Held**
SIC: 8641 Social club, membership

(P-25120)
BUNKER HILL CLUB INC
Also Called: City Club On Bunker Hill
555 S Flower St Ste 5100, Los Angeles
(90071-2400)
PHONE...................213 620-9662
Isaias Ledesma, *Manager*
EMP: 72
SQ FT: 16,874
SALES (est): 1.5MM
SALES (corp-wide): 477MM **Privately Held**
WEB: www.remington-gc.com
SIC: 8641 Bars & restaurants, members only

HQ: Clubcorp Usa, Inc.
3030 Lyndon B Johnson Fwy
Dallas TX 75234
972 243-6191

(P-25121)
CALI CALMECAC LANGUAGE ACADEMY
9491 Starr Rd, Windsor (95492-9460)
PHONE...................707 837-7747
Jeanne Acuna, *Principal*
Sharon Ferrer, *Vice Pres*
EMP: 60
SALES: 117.5K **Privately Held**
SIC: 8641 8211 Parent-teachers' association; elementary & secondary schools

(P-25122)
CALIFORNIA CLUB
538 S Flower St, Los Angeles
(90071-2548)
PHONE...................213 622-1391
Robert C Baker, *CEO*
Mark Emerson, *Controller*
Dindo Galanto, *Marketing Staff*
Raj Raghavan, *Director*
Andrew Rosenfield, *Manager*
EMP: 185 EST: 1888
SALES: 15.5MM **Privately Held**
SIC: 8641 7041 Business persons club; bars & restaurants, members only; residence club, organization

(P-25123)
CALIFORNIA CLUB OF CA
1750 Clay St, San Francisco (94109-3613)
PHONE...................415 474-3516
Eleanor Leith, *President*
Isabelle Brown, *Vice Pres*
EMP: 72
SALES (est): 1MM **Privately Held**
SIC: 8641 7922 Social club, membership; community theater production

(P-25124)
CALIFRNIA HLTH CARE FOUNDATION (PA)
1438 Webster St Ste 400, Oakland
(94612-3228)
PHONE...................510 891-3963
Mark D Smith, *President*
Craig Ziegler, *CFO*
EMP: 60
SALES: 16.6MM **Privately Held**
WEB: www.chcf.org
SIC: 8641 Civic social & fraternal associations

(P-25125)
CAMP FIRE USA LONG BEACH CNCL
7070 E Carson St, Long Beach
(90808-2353)
PHONE...................562 421-2725
Shirlee Jackert, *Exec Dir*
Georgia Stewart, *Director*
EMP: 50
SALES: 2.1MM **Privately Held**
WEB: www.campfirelb.org
SIC: 8641 Youth organizations

(P-25126)
CAMP ROYANEH BOY SCOUT
P.O. Box 39 (95421-0039)
PHONE...................707 632-5291
Stanley Andrew, *Principal*
Jim Schiechl, *Director*
EMP: 60
SALES (est): 644.7K **Privately Held**
SIC: 8641 Boy Scout organization

(P-25127)
CANYON LK PROPERTY OWNERS ASSN
31512 Railroad Canyon Rd, Canyon Lake
(92587-9400)
PHONE...................951 244-6841
Carl Armburst, *President*
Marty Gibson, *Treasurer*
Tiffany Cribbs, *Comms Mgr*
Clint Warrell, *General Mgr*
Ron Phipps, *Controller*
EMP: 93 EST: 1968
SQ FT: 18,000

SALES (est): 8.2MM **Privately Held**
SIC: 8641 Homeowners' association

(P-25128)
CARLSBAD INN VACTN CONDO OWNRS
3001 Carlsbad Blvd, Carlsbad
(92008-2964)
PHONE...................760 434-7542
David Brown, *President*
Joe Spirito, *President*
Tim Stripe, *Co-President*
Eric Segal, *Director*
EMP: 68
SQ FT: 130,000
SALES: 3.5MM **Privately Held**
WEB: www.carlsbadinn.com
SIC: 8641 Homeowners' association

(P-25129)
CENTRAL VLY YNG MNS CHRN ASSOC
Also Called: Central Valley YMCA
4045 N Fresno St Ste 101, Fresno
(93726-4099)
PHONE...................559 225-9191
Jeff Teliha, *President*
EMP: 50 EST: 1886
SQ FT: 50,000
SALES: 371.5K **Privately Held**
SIC: 8641 7991 8351 7032 Youth organizations; physical fitness facilities; child day care services; youth camps; individual & family services

(P-25130)
CHANNEL ISLANDS YOUNG MENS CH
Also Called: Lompoc Family YMCA
201 W College Ave, Lompoc (93436-4415)
PHONE...................805 736-3483
Dan Powell, *Branch Mgr*
EMP: 51
SALES (corp-wide): 18.6MM **Privately Held**
WEB: www.ciymca.org
SIC: 8641 7991 8351 7032 Youth organizations; physical fitness facilities; child day care services; youth camps; individual & family services
PA: Channel Islands Young Men's Christian Association
105 E Carrillo St
Santa Barbara CA 93101
805 569-1103

(P-25131)
CHANNEL ISLANDS YOUNG MENS CH
Also Called: Camarillo Family YMCA
3111 Village Park Dr, Camarillo (93012)
PHONE...................805 484-0423
Marge Castellano, *Director*
Mackenzie Hopkins, *Director*
EMP: 85
SALES (corp-wide): 18.6MM **Privately Held**
WEB: www.ciymca.org
SIC: 8641 7991 8351 7032 Youth organizations; physical fitness facilities; child day care services; youth camps; individual & family services
PA: Channel Islands Young Men's Christian Association
105 E Carrillo St
Santa Barbara CA 93101
805 569-1103

(P-25132)
CHANNEL ISLANDS YOUNG MENS CH
Also Called: Santa Barbara Family YMCA
36 Hitchcock Way, Santa Barbara
(93105-3102)
PHONE...................805 687-7727
Tim Hardy, *Branch Mgr*
EMP: 139
SALES (corp-wide): 18.6MM **Privately Held**
WEB: www.ciymca.org
SIC: 8641 7991 8351 7032 Youth organizations; physical fitness facilities; child day care services; youth camps; individual & family services

PA: Channel Islands Young Men's Christian
Association
105 E Carrillo St
Santa Barbara CA 93101
805 569-1103

(P-25133)
CHANNEL ISLANDS YOUNG MENS CH
Also Called: Montecito Family YMCA
591 Santa Rosa Ln, Santa Barbara
(93108-2145)
PHONE.................................805 969-3288
Yvonne Rubio, *Director*
Martin Cramer, *Director*
EMP: 73
SALES (corp-wide): 18.6MM **Privately Held**
WEB: www.ciymca.org
SIC: 8641 7991 8351 7032 Youth organizations; physical fitness facilities; child day care services; youth camps; individual & family services
PA: Channel Islands Young Men's Christian
Association
105 E Carrillo St
Santa Barbara CA 93101
805 569-1103

(P-25134)
CHANNEL ISLANDS YOUNG MENS CH
Also Called: Ventura Family YMCA
3760 Telegraph Rd, Ventura (93003-3421)
PHONE.................................805 484-0423
Sarah Abrams, *Director*
Lori West, *Office Mgr*
Amy Bailey, *Director*
EMP: 144
SALES (corp-wide): 18.6MM **Privately Held**
WEB: www.ciymca.org
SIC: 8641 7991 8351 7032 Youth organizations; physical fitness facilities; child day care services; youth camps; individual & family services
PA: Channel Islands Young Men's Christian
Association
105 E Carrillo St
Santa Barbara CA 93101
805 569-1103

(P-25135)
CHANNEL ISLANDS YOUNG MENS CH
Also Called: Stuart C. Gildred Family YMCA
900 N Refugio Rd, Santa Ynez
(93460-9314)
PHONE.................................805 686-2037
Paula Parisotto, *Branch Mgr*
EMP: 80
SALES (corp-wide): 18.6MM **Privately Held**
WEB: www.ciymca.org
SIC: 8641 7991 8351 7032 Youth organizations; physical fitness facilities; child day care services; youth camps; individual & family services
PA: Channel Islands Young Men's Christian
Association
105 E Carrillo St
Santa Barbara CA 93101
805 569-1103

(P-25136)
CHATEAU LAKE SAN MARCOS HOMEOW
1502 Circa Del Lago, San Marcos
(92078-7201)
PHONE.................................760 471-0083
Chris Arvanitis, *President*
EMP: 75
SQ FT: 240,000
SALES: 3MM **Privately Held**
SIC: 8641 Homeowners' association

(P-25137)
CHICO CSU RESEARCH FOUNDATION
25 Main St Unit 203, Chico (95928-5388)
PHONE.................................530 898-6811
Jessica Bourne, *Exec Dir*
EMP: 2000
SQ FT: 15,000

SALES (est): 41MM **Privately Held**
SIC: 8641 Civic social & fraternal associations

(P-25138)
CHINESE CNSLD BENEVOLENT ASSN
843 Stockton St, San Francisco
(94108-2120)
PHONE.................................415 982-6000
Thomas Ng, *Exec Dir*
EMP: 55
SALES: 43.2K **Privately Held**
SIC: 8641 Community membership club

(P-25139)
COMMUNITY ACTION BRD OF SNT CR
406 Main St Ste 202, Watsonville
(95076-4639)
PHONE.................................831 724-0206
Elena Dela Garza, *Director*
Helen Ewan, *CEO*
EMP: 50
SALES (corp-wide): 3MM **Privately Held**
SIC: 8641 Civic social & fraternal associations
PA: Community Action Board Of Santa
Cruz County Inc
406 Main St Ste 207
Watsonville CA 95076
831 763-2147

(P-25140)
COMMUNITY BUILD INC (PA)
4305 Degnan Blvd Ste 102, Los Angeles
(90008-4949)
PHONE.................................323 290-6560
Brenda Shockley, *President*
Kim Ramsey, *COO*
EMP: 59
SQ FT: 2,400
SALES: 3.5MM **Privately Held**
SIC: 8641 8699 Youth organizations; charitable organization

(P-25141)
CONEJO VALLEY UNIFIED SCHL DST
620 Velarde Dr, Thousand Oaks
(91360-1331)
PHONE.................................805 492-3531
EMP: 120
SALES (corp-wide): 225.2MM **Privately Held**
SIC: 8641 Parent-teachers' association
PA: Conejo Valley Unified School District
1400 E Janss Rd
Thousand Oaks CA 91362
805 497-9511

(P-25142)
CONTEMPRARY HSTRICAL VHCL ASSN
430 Oak View Dr, Vacaville (95688-4224)
PHONE.................................707 448-7266
Eric V Beeby, *Principal*
EMP: 90
SALES (est): 579K **Privately Held**
SIC: 8641 Civic social & fraternal associations

(P-25143)
COUNTY OF SHASTA
Also Called: Shasta Cattle Women
19897 Gas Point Rd, Cottonwood
(96022-9115)
P.O. Box 1491 (96022-1491)
PHONE.................................530 347-6276
Diane Montagner, *President*
EMP: 80 **Privately Held**
WEB: www.rsdnmp.org
SIC: 8641 Civic social & fraternal associations
PA: County Of Shasta
1450 Court St Ste 308a
Redding CA 96001
530 225-5561

(P-25144)
COWELL HOMEOWNERS ASSOCIATION (PA)
Also Called: Walnut Country
4498 Lawson Ct, Concord (94521-4410)
PHONE.................................925 825-0250

Rhinan Harris, *General Mgr*
Michael Demeo, *President*
EMP: 64 **EST:** 1972
SQ FT: 2,300
SALES (est): 1.1MM **Privately Held**
WEB: www.walnutcountry.com
SIC: 8641 8351 Homeowners' association; child day care services

(P-25145)
CRENSHAW YMCA
3820 Santa Rosalia Dr, Los Angeles
(90008-2516)
PHONE.................................323 290-9113
EMP: 70
SALES: 2MM **Privately Held**
SIC: 8641 7991 8351 7032

(P-25146)
CRESCENTA-CANADA YMCA (PA)
Also Called: YMCA Crescenta-Canada
1930 Foothill Blvd, La Canada
(91011-1933)
PHONE.................................818 790-0123
Larry Hall, *CEO*
Ken Gorvetzian, *Ch of Bd*
EMP: 280 **EST:** 1953
SALES (est): 5.2MM **Privately Held**
SIC: 8641 7991 8351 7032 Youth organizations; physical fitness facilities; child day care services; youth camps; individual & family services

(P-25147)
CRESCENTA-CANADA YMCA
Also Called: Learning Tree Pre-School
6840 Foothill Blvd, Tujunga (91042-2711)
PHONE.................................818 352-3255
Kathi Brink, *Branch Mgr*
EMP: 50
SALES (est): 355.8K
SALES (corp-wide): 5.2MM **Privately Held**
SIC: 8641 7991 8351 7032 Youth organizations; physical fitness facilities; child day care services; youth camps; individual & family services
PA: Crescenta-Canada Ymca
1930 Foothill Blvd
La Canada CA 91011
818 790-0123

(P-25148)
CYPRESS COLLEGE FOUNDATION
9200 Valley View Ave, Whittier
(90603-1957)
PHONE.................................714 484-7128
Raul Alvarez, *Principal*
EMP: 62
SALES: 723K **Privately Held**
SIC: 8641 Civic social & fraternal associations

(P-25149)
CYPRESS EDUCATION FOUNDATION
9470 Moody St, Cypress (90630-2919)
PHONE.................................714 220-6900
William D Eller, *CEO*
EMP: 51
SALES: 547.6K **Privately Held**
WEB: www.cypressmonterey.com
SIC: 8641 Educator's association

(P-25150)
D A V INDUSTRIES
1049 Elkelton Blvd, Spring Valley
(91977-4720)
PHONE.................................619 337-9244
William D Mudd, *President*
Donald Pouliot, *CFO*
Bernard Bandish, *Vice Pres*
Clifford Caldwell, *Admin Sec*
EMP: 100
SQ FT: 8,000
SALES: 7.6MM **Privately Held**
WEB: www.davindustries.com
SIC: 8641 5932 Veterans' organization; clothing, secondhand

(P-25151)
DESERT PRNCESS HOMEOWNERS ASSN
Also Called: Desert Princess Hoa
28555 Landau Blvd, Cathedral City
(92234-3508)
PHONE.................................760 322-1907
Mario Gonzales, *CEO*
Tom Adamo, *President*
Marilyn J White, *CEO*
Mark McLaughlin, *Treasurer*
EMP: 100
SQ FT: 3,000
SALES (est): 4.3MM **Privately Held**
WEB: www.desertprincesscc.com
SIC: 8641 Homeowners' association

(P-25152)
DISABLED AMRCN VTRANS DEPT CAL (PA)
Also Called: DAB
13733 Rosecrans Ave, Santa Fe Springs
(90670-5026)
PHONE.................................562 404-1266
Daniel Contreras, *CEO*
Larry Polzin, *Chairman*
Antonette Santson, *Administration*
EMP: 72
SQ FT: 2,500
SALES: 1.8MM **Privately Held**
SIC: 8641 Veterans' organization

(P-25153)
EAST PALO ALTO Y M C A
550 Bell St, East Palo Alto (94303-1701)
PHONE.................................650 328-9622
Robert Huges, *Director*
EMP: 50 **EST:** 1994
SALES (est): 292.5K **Privately Held**
SIC: 8641 7991 8351 7032 Youth organizations; physical fitness facilities; child day care services; youth camps; individual & family services

(P-25154)
EMBARCADERO HOMES ASSN INC
Lincoln Sq Condos, Stockton (95207)
P.O. Box 7003 (95267-0003)
PHONE.................................954 776-2611
Kathy Dharnidharka, *President*
Charles Klass, *Treasurer*
Edmund Weiss, *Bd of Directors*
Cheri Margie, *Vice Pres*
Donna Zuckerman, *Admin Sec*
EMP: 73
SALES (est): 675.4K **Privately Held**
SIC: 8641 Homeowners' association

(P-25155)
EMERSON ELEMENTARY
720 E Cypress Ave, Burbank (91501-1812)
PHONE.................................818 558-5419
Linda Acuff, *Principal*
EMP: 65
SALES: 31.8K **Privately Held**
SIC: 8641 Parent-teachers' association

(P-25156)
FORT WASHINGTON PARENT ASSOC
Also Called: FT. WASHINGTON ELEM.
960 E Teague Ave, Fresno (93720-1704)
PHONE.................................559 327-6600
Melanie Hashimoto, *Principal*
Paula Prince, *Librarian*
EMP: 55
SALES: 40K **Privately Held**
SIC: 8641 Parent-teachers' association

(P-25157)
FOUNDTION FOR HISPANIC EDUCATN (PA)
14271 Story Rd, San Jose (95127-3823)
P.O. Box 730453 (95173-0453)
PHONE.................................408 585-5022
Edward Alvarez, *CEO*
John Ramirez, *Vice Pres*
Nancy Bergner, *Controller*
Elizabeth Barragan, *Corp Comm Staff*
Rafael Escalante, *Director*
EMP: 65
SQ FT: 60

SALES: 15.5MM **Privately Held**
SIC: 8641 Civic social & fraternal associations

(P-25158)
FRIENDS SANTA CRUZ STATE PARKS
1543 Pacific Ave Ste 206, Santa Cruz (95060-3962)
PHONE.................831 429-1840
Bonny Hawley, Exec Dir
EMP: 80
SALES: 5.3MM **Privately Held**
SIC: 8641 Environmental protection organization

(P-25159)
GENERAL GEORGE W SLINEY BASHA
Also Called: China Brma India Veterans Assn
4839 Rio Vista Ave, San Jose (95129-1009)
PHONE.................408 296-3423
Robert E Burke, Treasurer
EMP: 75
SALES (est): 2.8MM **Privately Held**
SIC: 8641 Veterans' organization

(P-25160)
GEOSYNTEC CONSULTANTS INC
2100 Main St Ste 150, Huntington Beach (92648-2460)
PHONE.................714 969-0800
Bert Palmer, Manager
Misty Yanok, Info Tech Mgr
Eric Smalstig, Project Engr
Samantha Fox, Engineer
Susan Bright, Manager
EMP: 55
SALES (corp-wide): 204.7MM **Privately Held**
SIC: 8641 8711 Environmental protection organization; engineering services
PA: Geosyntec Consultants, Inc.
900 Broken Sound Pkwy Nw
Boca Raton FL 33487
561 995-0900

(P-25161)
GIRL SCOUTS HEART CENTRAL CAL
6601 Elvas Ave, Sacramento (95819-4339)
PHONE.................916 452-9181
Linda Farley, CEO
Kerry Koyasako, Vice Pres
Morgan Bauer, Manager
Dede Clark, Manager
EMP: 127
SALES: 8.8MM **Privately Held**
SIC: 8641 Girl Scout organization

(P-25162)
GIRL SCOUTS NORTHERN CAL (PA)
1650 Harbor Bay Pkwy # 100, Alameda (94502-3012)
PHONE.................510 562-8470
Marina Park, CEO
Robin Macgillivray, President
Bruce Morrow, COO
Diana Bell, Vice Pres
Ellen Richey, Vice Pres
EMP: 70
SQ FT: 17,000
SALES: 19.6MM **Privately Held**
SIC: 8641 Girl Scout organization

(P-25163)
GIRL SCTS SN DIEGO-IMPRL CNCL (PA)
1231 Upas St, San Diego (92103-5127)
PHONE.................619 610-0751
Jo Dee C Jacob, CEO
Anne Bader, Business Anlyst
Danielle Russell, Sales Mgr
Mindy Guevara, Sales Staff
Tanya Robinson, Sales Staff
EMP: 112
SQ FT: 7,926
SALES: 11MM **Privately Held**
SIC: 8641 Girl Scout organization

(P-25164)
GIRL SCUTS GREATER LOS ANGELES (PA)
801 S Grand Ave Ste 300, Los Angeles (90017-4621)
PHONE.................626 677-2200
Lise L Luttgens, CEO
Sylvia Rosenberger, COO
EMP: 155
SQ FT: 7,600
SALES: 20.9MM **Privately Held**
WEB: www.gsmwvc.org
SIC: 8641 Girl Scout organization

(P-25165)
GIRL SCUTS SAN GRGONIO COUNCIL (PA)
1751 Plum Ln, Redlands (92374-4505)
PHONE.................909 307-6555
Cynthia Harnisch-Breunig, CEO
EMP: 60
SALES: 7.7MM **Privately Held**
SIC: 8641 Girl Scout organization

(P-25166)
GLENWOOD VILLAGE CMNTY ASSN
Also Called: Seabreeze Management Comp
26840 Aliso Viejo Pkwy # 100, Aliso Viejo (92656-2624)
PHONE.................949 855-1800
Susan Larson, President
Annette Chong, Manager
EMP: 55
SALES (est): 482K **Privately Held**
SIC: 8641 Homeowners' association

(P-25167)
GOLD HILL GRANGE NO 326
1514 5th St, Lincoln (95648-1511)
PHONE.................916 645-3605
Ron Smith, Director
EMP: 75
SALES (est): 687.4K **Privately Held**
SIC: 8641 Fraternal associations

(P-25168)
GOLDEN RAIN FOUNDATION
800 Rockview Dr, Walnut Creek (94595-3002)
PHONE.................925 988-7800
Warren Thurlow Salmons, Branch Mgr
Marie Gray, Receptionist
EMP: 284
SQ FT: 24,100
SALES (corp-wide): 26.4MM **Privately Held**
WEB: www.rossmoornews.com
SIC: 8641 Civic social & fraternal associations
PA: Golden Rain Foundation Of Walnut Creek
1001 Golden Rain Rd
Walnut Creek CA 94595
925 988-7700

(P-25169)
GORDON BETTY MOORE FOUNDATION
1661 Page Mill Rd, Palo Alto (94304-1209)
PHONE.................650 213-3000
Steve McCormick, President
Marion Adeney, Officer
Meaghan Campbell, Officer
Marina Campos, Officer
Janet Coffey, Officer
EMP: 89
SALES (est): 4.4MM **Privately Held**
SIC: 8641 Civic social & fraternal associations

(P-25170)
GROSSMONT-CUYAMACA COMMUNITY
Also Called: Gcccd Auxiliary
8800 Grossmont College Dr, El Cajon (92020-1765)
PHONE.................619 644-7684
Stanley Schroeder, Exec Dir
Sue Rearic, CFO
Sally Cox, Info Tech Mgr
Jamail Carter, Human Res Dir
Shari Waters, Manager
EMP: 86

SQ FT: 1,000
SALES (est): 9.8MM **Privately Held**
SIC: 8641 Educator's association

(P-25171)
HACIENDA INVOLVED PARENT STAFF
1290 Kimberly Dr, San Jose (95118-1536)
PHONE.................408 535-6259
Melissa Mohammed, Principal
EMP: 55
SALES: 272.2K **Privately Held**
SIC: 8641 Parent-teachers' association

(P-25172)
HENTREL GREATHOUSE FOUNDATION
127 S 1st Ave, Barstow (92311-2827)
PHONE.................302 513-4056
David Taylor, President
EMP: 68
SQ FT: 15,000
SALES (est): 74.3K **Privately Held**
SIC: 8641 Civic social & fraternal associations

(P-25173)
HIDDEN VALLEY LAKE ASSOCIATION (PA)
Also Called: Hidden Valley Golf Course
18174 Hidden Valley Rd, Hidden Valley Lake (95467-8690)
PHONE.................707 987-3146
Wililam E Waite, CEO
EMP: 71
SQ FT: 1,000
SALES (est): 6.7MM **Privately Held**
WEB: www.hvla.com
SIC: 8641 7997 5813 Homeowners' association; golf club, membership; swimming club, membership; bar (drinking places)

(P-25174)
HORIZONS 4 CONDOMINIUMS INC
Also Called: Horizon For Hmwners Asscations
2113 Meridan Blvd, Mammoth Lakes (93546)
P.O. Box 175 (93546-0175)
PHONE.................760 934-6779
Fax: 760 934-4224
EMP: 92
SALES (est): 1.1MM **Privately Held**
SIC: 8641

(P-25175)
INSTITUTE FOR WILDLIFE STUDIES (PA)
835 3rd St, Eureka (95501-0511)
P.O. Box 1104, Arcata (95518-1104)
PHONE.................707 822-4258
David K Garcelon, President
Dick Johnson, General Mgr
Dj Wainman, Manager
EMP: 50
SQ FT: 2,300
SALES: 4MM **Privately Held**
WEB: www.iws.org
SIC: 8641 Environmental protection organization

(P-25176)
JEFFERSON CALIFORNIA CONGRESS
6225 El Camino Real, Carlsbad (92009-1604)
PHONE.................760 331-5500
Chad Lund, Principal
EMP: 65
SALES: 88.7K **Privately Held**
SIC: 8641 Parent-teachers' association

(P-25177)
JEWISH CMNTY FNDN OF (PA)
6505 Wilshire Blvd, Los Angeles (90048-4906)
PHONE.................323 761-8700
Richard V Sandler, Ch of Bd
J Sanderson, President
Jack Klein, COO
Ivan Wolkind, CFO
Leslie E Bider, Chairman
EMP: 263

SQ FT: 100,000
SALES: 47.7MM **Privately Held**
SIC: 8641 8661 Community membership club; religious organizations

(P-25178)
JONATHAN CLUB (PA)
545 S Figueroa St, Los Angeles (90071-1793)
PHONE.................213 624-0881
Gregory J Dumas, President
Randolph P Sinnott, CEO
Hollis Cheek, CFO
Plato Skouras, CFO
Paige Rodgers, Officer
EMP: 300 **EST:** 1895
SQ FT: 230,276
SALES: 39.4MM **Privately Held**
WEB: www.jc.org
SIC: 8641 Social club, membership

(P-25179)
KIWANIS INTERNATIONAL INC
Also Called: North Modesto Kiwanis Club
3201 Canterbury Ct, Modesto (95350-1419)
PHONE.................209 578-1448
Robert Dunbar, Principal
EMP: 80
SALES (corp-wide): 22.4MM **Privately Held**
WEB: www.kfne.org
SIC: 8641 Civic associations
PA: Kiwanis International, Inc.
3636 Woodview Trce
Indianapolis IN 46268
317 875-8755

(P-25180)
KNIGHTS OF COLUMBUS
2211 Shamrock Dr, Campbell (95008-6210)
PHONE.................408 371-1531
Steve Duffy, Principal
EMP: 220
SQ FT: 3,024
SALES (corp-wide): 2.2B **Privately Held**
WEB: www.kofc.org
SIC: 8641 Fraternal associations
PA: Knights Of Columbus
1 Columbus Plz Ste 1700
New Haven CT 06510
203 752-4000

(P-25181)
KNIGHTS OF COLUMBUS
1344 Magnolia Dr, Santa Paula (93060-1112)
PHONE.................805 525-7810
Frank Arpuelles, President
EMP: 150
SALES (corp-wide): 2.2B **Privately Held**
WEB: www.kofc.org
SIC: 8641 Fraternal associations
PA: Knights Of Columbus
1 Columbus Plz Ste 1700
New Haven CT 06510
203 752-4000

(P-25182)
LA MESA LIONS CLUB
4387 Summit Dr, La Mesa (91941-7842)
P.O. Box 1441 (91944-1441)
PHONE.................619 469-9988
Howard C Linke, Admin Sec
EMP: 60
SALES: 34K **Privately Held**
SIC: 8641 Civic associations

(P-25183)
LA PUERTA
560 4th Ave, San Diego (92101-6905)
PHONE.................619 696-3466
Darren Morre, Owner
Darren Moore, Owner
EMP: 50
SALES (est): 973.7K **Privately Held**
SIC: 8641 Bars & restaurants, members only

(P-25184)
LACOLINA JR HIGH CA CONGRESS O
4025 Foothill Rd, Santa Barbara (93110-1209)
PHONE.................805 967-4506

Cristine Gallagher, *President*
EMP: 55
SALES (est): 355.1K **Privately Held**
SIC: 8641 Civic social & fraternal associations

(P-25185)
LAKE FOREST LI MASTER HOMEOWN
Also Called: SUN & SAIL CLUB
24752 Toledo Ln, Lake Forest
(92630-2318)
PHONE..................949 586-0860
Sonny Morper, *President*
Jim Richert, *President*
Ted Brackez, *Principal*
Terri Graham, *Principal*
Ken Hedge, *Principal*
EMP: 80 **EST:** 1971
SQ FT: 9,000
SALES: 4.3MM **Privately Held**
WEB: www.lf2.org
SIC: 8641 Homeowners' association

(P-25186)
LAKE MISSION VIEJO ASSOCIATION
22555 Olympiad Rd, Mission Viejo
(92692-1118)
PHONE..................949 770-1313
Fred Mellenbruch, *President*
Sid Wittenberg, *Treasurer*
Jane Chadburn, *Vice Pres*
Sen Jeff Miklaus, *Vice Pres*
Kevin Frabotta, *General Mgr*
EMP: 90
SQ FT: 7,400
SALES: 6.7MM **Privately Held**
WEB: www.lakemissionviejo.org
SIC: 8641 Homeowners' association

(P-25187)
LAKE OF THE PINES ASSOCIATION
Also Called: LAKE OF THE PINES HOME-OWNERS
11665 Lakeshore N, Auburn (95602-8325)
PHONE..................530 268-1141
Edwin Vitrano, *General Mgr*
Donna Lowenthal, *Controller*
Robert A Broyer, *Agent*
EMP: 50
SALES: 7.2MM **Privately Held**
WEB: www.lop.org
SIC: 8641 Homeowners' association

(P-25188)
LAKE WILDWOOD ASSOCIATION
Also Called: LAKE WILDWOOD GOLF COURSE.
11255 Cottontail Way, Penn Valley
(95946-9409)
PHONE..................530 432-1152
Tom Cross, *CEO*
Debbie Casey, *General Mgr*
Meredith Martin, *Administration*
Robert Whiteaker, *Finance Mgr*
William Haushalter, *Director*
EMP: 120
SQ FT: 10,000
SALES: 9.1MM **Privately Held**
SIC: 8641 7997 Homeowners' association; golf club, membership

(P-25189)
LEISURE VILLAGE ASSOCIATION
200 Leisure Village Dr, Camarillo
(93012-6802)
PHONE..................805 484-2861
Robert Scheaffer, *General Mgr*
EMP: 100
SQ FT: 6,000
SALES (est): 3.5MM **Privately Held**
SIC: 8641 Homeowners' association

(P-25190)
LELAND STANFORD JUNIOR UNIV
Also Called: Stanford Alumni Association
326 Galvez St, Stanford (94305-6105)
PHONE..................650 723-2021
Howard Wolf, *Branch Mgr*
EMP: 250

SALES (corp-wide): 5.6B **Privately Held**
SIC: 8641 8221 Alumni association; university
PA: Leland Stanford Junior University
450 Serra Mall
Stanford CA 94305
650 723-2300

(P-25191)
LOMA LINDA VET ASSOCIATION FOR
Also Called: L L V A R E
710 Brookside Ave Ste 2, Redlands
(92373-5181)
P.O. Box 10849, San Bernardino (92423-0849)
PHONE..................909 583-6250
Alan Jacobson, *President*
David Buxbaum, *Treasurer*
Gayle Lee, *Executive*
Colin Rasmussen, *Exec Dir*
Gayle Rundberg, *Exec Dir*
EMP: 60
SQ FT: 44,000
SALES: 3.4MM **Privately Held**
WEB: www.llvare.org
SIC: 8641 Veterans' organization

(P-25192)
LOMA RIVIERA COMMUNITY ASSN
9610 Waples St, San Diego (92121-2955)
PHONE..................619 224-1313
Dale Bredon, *President*
Anne Wagner, *President*
EMP: 100
SQ FT: 300
SALES (est): 3.7MM **Privately Held**
SIC: 8641 Homeowners' association

(P-25193)
LOS ANGELES AIRPORT PEACE OFFC
Also Called: LAAPOA
6080 Center Dr Fl 6, Los Angeles
(90045-9205)
PHONE..................310 242-5218
Marshall E McClain, *President*
Rodney Rouzan, *Treasurer*
Andrei Soto, *Treasurer*
Julius Levy, *Vice Pres*
Richard Andrade, *Admin Sec*
EMP: 425
SQ FT: 500
SALES: 990.6K **Privately Held**
SIC: 8641 Civic social & fraternal associations

(P-25194)
LOS ANGELES UNIFIED SCHOOL DST
Also Called: YMCA Metro La-52nd St School
816 W 51st St, Los Angeles (90037-3603)
PHONE..................323 753-3175
Beverly Crosby, *Principal*
Katie Gaspard, *Principal*
EMP: 200
SALES (corp-wide): 3.8B **Privately Held**
WEB: www.lausd.k12.ca.us
SIC: 8641 7991 8351 7032 Youth organizations; physical fitness facilities; child day care services; youth camps; individual & family services
PA: Los Angeles Unified School District
333 S Beaudry Ave Ste 209
Los Angeles CA 90017
213 241-1000

(P-25195)
MADE IN USA FOUNDATION INC
11950 San Vicente Blvd # 220, Los Angeles
(90049-5013)
PHONE..................310 623-3872
Joel Joseph, *President*
EMP: 50
SALES: 1.1MM **Privately Held**
SIC: 8641 Civic social & fraternal associations

(P-25196)
MARAVILLA FOUNDATION (PA)
5729 Union Pacific Ave, Commerce
(90022-5134)
PHONE..................323 721-4162
Alex M Sotomayor, *CEO*

Tristen Sotomayor, *COO*
George Ross, *CFO*
Deo Tinana, *CFO*
Paul Lopez, *Chairman*
EMP: 65
SQ FT: 30,000
SALES (est): 7.4MM **Privately Held**
SIC: 8641 Civic associations

(P-25197)
MARINES MEMORIAL ASSOCIATION
Also Called: MARINES' MEMORIAL CLUB & HOTEL
609 Sutter St, San Francisco (94102-1081)
PHONE..................415 673-6672
James M Myatt, *President*
Ruby Wu, *CFO*
Bethany Meyer, *Executive*
Michael Allen, *General Mgr*
Michael Allen, *General Mgr*
EMP: 148 **EST:** 1946
SQ FT: 160,062
SALES: 15.4MM **Privately Held**
WEB: www.marineclub.com
SIC: 8641 7011 5921 5813 Veterans' organization; hotels; liquor stores; bar (drinking places); eating places

(P-25198)
MIDNIGHT MISSION (PA)
601 S San Pedro St, Los Angeles
(90014-2415)
PHONE..................213 624-9258
R Stephen Doan, *Chairman*
Larry Adamson, *President*
Charles Cross, *CFO*
Glenn D Woody, *CFO*
Clancy Imislund, *Managing Dir*
EMP: 69 **EST:** 1914
SQ FT: 11,550
SALES: 2.8MM **Privately Held**
WEB: www.midnightmission.org
SIC: 8641 8322 Civic social & fraternal associations; individual & family services

(P-25199)
MILKEN FAMILY FOUNDATION
1250 4th St Fl 1, Santa Monica
(90401-1418)
PHONE..................310 570-4800
Lowell J Milken, *President*
Susan Fox, *CFO*
Mariano Guzm N, *Trustee*
Bonnie Somers, *Vice Pres*
Sonia Lowman, *Comms Dir*
EMP: 200
SALES: 27.8MM **Privately Held**
WEB: www.mff.org
SIC: 8641 Civic social & fraternal associations

(P-25200)
MONTECITO FIRE PROTECTION DST
595 San Ysidro Rd, Santa Barbara
(93108-2124)
PHONE..................805 969-7762
Chip Hickman, *Fire Chief*
Joyce Reed, *Admin Asst*
Todd Edwards, *Chief*
Stephen Hickman, *Fire Chief*
Kevin Wallace, *Fire Chief*
EMP: 50
SALES (est): 2.1MM **Privately Held**
SIC: 8641 9224 Civic social & fraternal associations; fire protection

(P-25201)
MOOSE INTERNATIONAL INC
Also Called: Moose Family Center 545
2470 El Rancho Dr, Santa Cruz
(95060-1106)
P.O. Box 66292, Scotts Valley (95067-6292)
PHONE..................831 438-1817
Perry James, *Administration*
EMP: 208
SQ FT: 2,800
SALES (corp-wide): 48.4MM **Privately Held**
WEB: www.thalist.com
SIC: 8641 Fraternal associations

PA: Moose International, Incorporated
155 S International Dr
Mooseheart IL 60539
630 859-2000

(P-25202)
MORNINGSIDE COMMUNITY ASSN
82 Mayfair Dr, Rancho Mirage
(92270-2562)
PHONE..................760 328-3323
M Abdelnour, *General Mgr*
Michelle Abdelnour, *General Mgr*
EMP: 73
SQ FT: 3,500
SALES (est): 2.5MM **Privately Held**
SIC: 8641 Homeowners' association

(P-25203)
MRCA FIRE DIVISION
1670 Las Virgenes Cyn Rd, Calabasas
(91302-1920)
PHONE..................818 880-4752
Ken Nelson, *COO*
Jakub Slovacek, *Officer*
EMP: 50
SALES (est): 467K **Privately Held**
SIC: 8641 Environmental protection organization

(P-25204)
MXB BATTERY OPERATIONS LP
Also Called: Battery The
717 Battery St, San Francisco
(94111-1515)
PHONE..................415 230-8000
Steven Flowers, *Exec Dir*
Christophe Tassan, *Director*
Cheryl Fleming, *Manager*
EMP: 100
SALES (corp-wide): 1.2MM **Privately Held**
SIC: 8641 Social club, membership
PA: Mxb Battery Operations, Lp
387 Tehama St
San Francisco CA 94103
415 896-9200

(P-25205)
NAPA SUNRISE ROTARY CLUB INC
Also Called: ROTARY CLUB OF NAPA SUNRISE OF
P.O. Box 5324 (94581-0324)
PHONE..................707 257-9564
William Jabin, *Treasurer*
EMP: 80
SALES: 166.6K **Privately Held**
SIC: 8641 Community membership club

(P-25206)
NATURAL RSRCES DEF COUNCIL INC
1314 2nd St, Santa Monica (90401-1103)
PHONE..................310 434-2300
Frances Beinecke, *Exec Dir*
Rene Leni, *Office Admin*
Robert Norris, *Info Tech Dir*
Carl Zichella, *Director*
Gayle Petersen, *Manager*
EMP: 70
SQ FT: 10,558
SALES (corp-wide): 155.1MM **Privately Held**
WEB: www.savebiogems.org
SIC: 8641 Environmental protection organization
PA: Natural Resources Defense Council Inc.
40 W 20th St
New York NY 10011
212 727-2700

(P-25207)
OLYMPIC CLUB (PA)
524 Post St, San Francisco (94102-1295)
PHONE..................415 345-5100
John M Jack, *CEO*
Andrew Collins, *Vice Pres*
Traci Mysliwiec, *Comms Mgr*
Jay Bedsworth, *Principal*
Patrick Merritt, *General Mgr*
EMP: 450 **EST:** 1879
SQ FT: 160,000

SALES: 48.3MM **Privately Held**
WEB: www.ocrugby.com
SIC: **8641** 7997 5812 Civic social & fraternal associations; golf club, membership; health food restaurant

(P-25208)
ORANGE COUNTY CNCL BSA (PA)
1211 E Dyer Rd Ste 100, Santa Ana (92705-5670)
PHONE................714 546-4990
Les Baron, *President*
Robert Neal, *Ch of Bd*
Jeffrie A Herrmann, *President*
Larry Behm, *Principal*
Jan Borja, *Admin Sec*
EMP: 80
SALES: 9.1MM **Privately Held**
WEB: www.ocbsa.com
SIC: **8641** Boy Scout organization

(P-25209)
ORTEGA ELEMENTARY PTO
1283 Terra Nova Blvd, Pacifica (94044-4341)
PHONE................650 738-6670
Jannel Jones, *President*
EMP: 75
SALES (est): 189.2K **Privately Held**
SIC: **8641** Parent-teachers' association

(P-25210)
PACIFIC UNION CLUB
1000 California St, San Francisco (94108-2280)
PHONE................415 775-1234
Thomas Gaston, *General Mgr*
EMP: 62
SQ FT: 54,000
SALES: 10.2MM **Privately Held**
WEB: www.pacificunionclub.com
SIC: **8641** Social club, membership

(P-25211)
PALISADES OPTIMIST FOUNDATION
15312 Whitfield Ave, Pacific Palisades (90272-2547)
PHONE................310 454-4111
Harold Vicau, *Treasurer*
EMP: 71
SALES (est): 2.1MM **Privately Held**
SIC: **8641** Social associations

(P-25212)
PALM DESERT GREENS ASSOCIATION
73750 Country Club Dr, Palm Desert (92260-8663)
PHONE................760 346-8005
Roberta Hollingsworth, *General Mgr*
Ken Dobson, *President*
Mal Sinclair, *Treasurer*
EMP: 75 EST: 1971
SQ FT: 12,400
SALES: 7MM **Privately Held**
SIC: **8641** Homeowners' association

(P-25213)
PALO ALTO FAMILY Y M C A
3412 Ross Rd, Palo Alto (94303-4411)
PHONE................650 856-9622
Scott Glissmeyer, *Manager*
John Logan, *CEO*
EMP: 50
SALES (est): 589.3K **Privately Held**
SIC: **8641** 7991 8351 7032 Youth organizations; physical fitness facilities; child day care services; youth camps; individual & family services

(P-25214)
PARENTHOOD OF PLANNED
1650 Valencia St, San Francisco (94110-5013)
PHONE................415 821-1282
EMP: 51
SALES (corp-wide): 63.3MM **Privately Held**
SIC: **8641** 8322 8093 8049 Civic social & fraternal associations; referral service for personal & social problems; family planning clinic; acupuncturist

PA: Planned Parenthood Of San Diego And Riverside Counties
1075 Camino Del Rio S # 100
San Diego CA 92108
619 881-4500

(P-25215)
PESCADERO CONSERVATION ALIANCE
4100 Cabrillo Hwy, Pescadero (94060-9724)
P.O. Box 873 (94060-0873)
PHONE................650 879-1441
John Wade, *Director*
Randy Bennett, *President*
Jack Olsen, *Admin Sec*
Bert Fewss, *Director*
EMP: 50
SALES: 13.2K **Privately Held**
WEB: www.gazos.org
SIC: **8641** Environmental protection organization

(P-25216)
PINE MOUNTAIN LAKE ASSOCIATION (PA)
19228 Pine Mountain Dr, Groveland (95321-9581)
PHONE................209 962-4080
Brian Sweeney, *President*
Dana Chavarria, *Treasurer*
Ian Morcott, *Vice Pres*
Joe Powell, *General Mgr*
Jerry Dickson, *Admin Sec*
EMP: 130
SQ FT: 20,000
SALES: 9.8MM **Privately Held**
SIC: **8641** Homeowners' association

(P-25217)
PROGRESS FOUNDATION
52 Dore St, San Francisco (94103-3828)
PHONE................415 553-3100
Steven Fields, *Exec Dir*
EMP: 57
SALES (corp-wide): 20.8MM **Privately Held**
SIC: **8641** Civic social & fraternal associations
PA: Progress Foundation
368 Fell St
San Francisco CA 94102
415 861-0828

(P-25218)
PTA CA CNGRSS OF PARNTS TCHRS
3030 N Hesperian St, Santa Ana (92706-1151)
PHONE................714 836-2700
Kim Podd, *Exec Dir*
EMP: 95
SALES (est): 349.6K **Privately Held**
SIC: **8641** Parent-teachers' association

(P-25219)
PTA CA CONGRESS OF PARENTS
Also Called: Serrania Charter Elementary
5014 Serrania Ave, Woodland Hills (91364-3303)
PHONE................818 340-6700
Theresa C Wedaa, *Principal*
Luis Alvoredo, *Principal*
EMP: 50
SALES (est): 112.2K **Privately Held**
SIC: **8641** Parent-teachers' association

(P-25220)
PTA CALIFORNIA CONG P A S ELEM
5280 Irene Way, Livermore (94550-3508)
PHONE................925 606-4700
Denise Mathanson, *Principal*
EMP: 50
SALES (est): 77.9K **Privately Held**
SIC: **8641** Parent-teachers' association

(P-25221)
PTA CALIFORNIA CONGRESS OF PAR
21514 Halldale Ave, Torrance (90501-3016)
PHONE................310 328-3100

Deborah Evers-Allen, *Principal*
EMP: 80
SALES (est): 358.3K **Privately Held**
SIC: **8641** Parent-teachers' association

(P-25222)
PTAC CARMEL VALLEY MID SCHOOL
3800 Mykonos Ln, San Diego (92130-3572)
PHONE................858 481-8221
Laurie Brady, *Principal*
Adam Camacho, *Asst Principal*
EMP: 85
SALES (est): 77K **Privately Held**
SIC: **8641** Parent-teachers' association

(P-25223)
PTAC RAIL RANCH ELEM SCHOOL
25030 Via Santee, Murrieta (92563-5020)
PHONE................951 696-1404
Hunter Wethers, *Principal*
EMP: 60
SALES: 22.8K **Privately Held**
SIC: **8641** Parent-teachers' association

(P-25224)
PUBLIC HLTH FNDATION ENTPS INC
277 S Atlantic Blvd, Los Angeles (90022-1734)
PHONE................323 263-0262
Laurie Hill, *Principal*
EMP: 133
SALES (corp-wide): 97.5MM **Privately Held**
SIC: **8641** Civic social & fraternal associations
PA: Public Health Foundation Enterprises, Inc.
13300 Crssrds Pkwy N
City Of Industry CA 91746
800 201-7320

(P-25225)
PUBLIC HLTH FNDATION ENTPS INC
Also Called: Wic
1640 W Carson St Ste G, Torrance (90501-3877)
PHONE................310 320-5215
EMP: 133
SALES (corp-wide): 97.5MM **Privately Held**
SIC: **8641** Civic social & fraternal associations
PA: Public Health Foundation Enterprises, Inc.
13300 Crssrds Pkwy N
City Of Industry CA 91746
800 201-7320

(P-25226)
PUBLIC HLTH FNDATION ENTPS INC (PA)
Also Called: Heluna Health
13300 Crssrds Pkwy N, City of Industry (91746)
PHONE................800 201-7320
Blain Cutler, *President*
Eric Ramanathan, *Ch of Bd*
Devecchio Finley, *Vice Chairman*
Gerald D Jensen, *President*
Michael R Gomez, *CEO*
EMP: 1437
SQ FT: 25,000
SALES: 97.5MM **Privately Held**
SIC: **8641** Civic social & fraternal associations

(P-25227)
READING AND BEYOND
4670 E Butler Ave, Fresno (93702-4608)
PHONE................559 840-1068
Luis Santana, *President*
Alicia Pearce, *Executive Asst*
Nzong Xiong, *Corp Comm Staff*
Nikki Newsome, *Director*
EMP: 74
SALES: 6.1MM **Privately Held**
SIC: **8641** Youth organizations

(P-25228)
ROSARY ACADEMY PARENT COUNCIL
1340 N Acacia Ave, Fullerton (92831-1202)
PHONE................714 879-6302
Patty Weller, *President*
Kathryn Hennigan, *Principal*
EMP: 72
SALES (est): 3.1MM **Privately Held**
SIC: **8641** Parent-teachers' association

(P-25229)
ROTARY INTERNATIONAL
Also Called: Rotary Club
9839 Meadowlark Way, Palo Cedro (96073-8750)
PHONE................530 547-5272
Bill Evans, *Admin Sec*
EMP: 62
SALES (corp-wide): 355.9MM **Privately Held**
WEB: www.rotary5340.org
SIC: **8641**
PA: Rotary International
1 Rotary Ctr
Evanston IL 60201
847 866-3000

(P-25230)
RRUFF-ROCKLIN RESIDENTS UNITE
3031 St, Rocklin (95765)
PHONE................415 806-2778
Victoria Curtis, *Principal*
EMP: 50
SALES (est): 234.3K **Privately Held**
SIC: **8641** Veterans' organization

(P-25231)
SAA SIERRA PROGRAMS LLC
Also Called: Stanford Sierra Camp & Lodge
130 Fallen Leaf Rd, South Lake Tahoe (96150-6165)
P.O. Box 10618 (96158-3618)
PHONE................530 541-1244
David Bunnett, *Project Mgr*
Antja Thompson, *Asst Director*
Nancy Marzocco, *Director*
EMP: 90
SALES (est): 1.7MM
SALES (corp-wide): 5.6B **Privately Held**
SIC: **8641** Civic associations
PA: Leland Stanford Junior University
450 Serra Mall
Stanford CA 94305
650 723-2300

(P-25232)
SACRAMENTO CY UNIFIED SCHL DST (PA)
5735 47th Ave, Sacramento (95824-4528)
P.O. Box 246870 (95824-6870)
PHONE................916 643-7400
Jose Banda, *Superintendent*
Tom Barrinson, *CFO*
Jorge Aguilar, *Superintendent*
EMP: 300 EST: 1854
SQ FT: 45,000
SALES: 625.2MM **Privately Held**
WEB: www.sachigh.org
SIC: **8641** Veterans' organization; environmental protection organization; Boy Scout organization

(P-25233)
SACROMENTO EDUCTN READNG LIONS
10461 Old Plza Vlle 130, Sacramento (95827)
PHONE................916 228-2219
Alice Furry, *Director*
EMP: 50
SALES (est): 786.9K **Privately Held**
SIC: **8641** Civic associations

(P-25234)
SAN DIEGO COUNTRY ESTATES ASSN
Also Called: San Vicente Inn & Golf Club
24157 San Vicente Rd, Ramona (92065-4166)
PHONE................760 789-3788
Jim Piva, *President*
Dusty Brown, *Treasurer*

Juli Elliott, *Finance Mgr*
Garry Williams, *Maintence Staff*
Janelle Morrow,
EMP: 147
SQ FT: 14,000
SALES (est): 11.6MM **Privately Held**
WEB: www.sdcea.net
SIC: 8641 7997 7992 7011 Homeowners'
association; membership sports & recre-
ation clubs; tennis club, membership; golf
club, membership; boating & swimming
clubs; public golf courses; vacation
lodges; restaurant, family: independent;
bar (drinking places)

(P-25235)
SAN DIEGO-IMPERIAL COUNCIL (PA)
1207 Upas St, San Diego (92103-5127)
PHONE.................................619 294-3806
Terry Trout, *Manager*
EMP: 50 **EST:** 1930
SQ FT: 10,000
SALES: 5.1MM **Privately Held**
SIC: 8641 5699 5941 Boy Scout organi-
zation; uniforms; camping & backpacking
equipment

(P-25236)
SAN FRANCISCO BAY AREA COUNCL
1001 Davis St, San Leandro (94577-1514)
PHONE.................................510 577-9000
Kenneth Mehlhorn, *CEO*
EMP: 62 **EST:** 2008
SALES: 5.7MM **Privately Held**
SIC: 8641 Boy Scout organization

(P-25237)
SAN MARCOS KIDS HELPNG KIDS FN
Also Called: Kid Helping Kids
4750 Hollister Ave, Santa Barbara
(93110-1921)
PHONE.................................800 659-6411
James Devries, *President*
Marley Miller, *COO*
Jacob Iuele, *CFO*
Chris Newton, *Director*
EMP: 147 **EST:** 2002
SALES: 229.5K **Privately Held**
SIC: 8641 Youth organizations

(P-25238)
SAN PABLO LODGE 43
342 Georgia St, Vallejo (94590-5907)
PHONE.................................707 642-1391
Al Hieb, *President*
EMP: 80
SALES (est): 957.4K **Privately Held**
SIC: 8641 Civic social & fraternal associa-
tions

(P-25239)
SANTA CLARA VNGARD BOOSTER CLB
1795 Space Park Dr, Santa Clara
(95054-3436)
PHONE.................................408 727-5532
Jeff Fiedler, *CEO*
Marc Hebert, *President*
Richard Lesher, *Treasurer*
Marie Bienkowski, *Vice Pres*
Linda Garbarino, *Admin Sec*
EMP: 50 **EST:** 1967
SQ FT: 21,000
SALES: 4.2MM **Privately Held**
WEB: www.scvanguard.com
SIC: 8641 Youth organizations

(P-25240)
SANTA MARIA VALLEY YMCA
3400 Skyway Dr, Santa Maria
(93455-2504)
PHONE.................................805 937-8521
Shannon Seifert, *Director*
Dave Wright, *Treasurer*
Kevin James, *Admin Sec*
Andrea Gallardo, *Director*
Diane Majewski, *Director*
EMP: 120
SQ FT: 22,000

SALES: 2.5MM **Privately Held**
WEB: www.smvymca.org
SIC: 8641 7991 8351 7032 Youth organizations; physical fitness facilities; child
day care services; youth camps; individual & family services

(P-25241)
SANTA MNICA MNTINS TRILS CNCIL
24735 Mulholland Hwy, Woodland Hills
(91302-2327)
P.O. Box 345, Agoura Hills (91376-0345)
PHONE.................................818 222-4531
Ruth Gerson, *President*
Anita Sneddon, *Treasurer*
Linda Palmer, *Vice Pres*
Georgia Farinella, *Admin Sec*
EMP: 100
SALES (est): 1.1MM **Privately Held**
WEB: www.smmtc.org
SIC: 8641 Environmental protection organ-
ization

(P-25242)
SAVE OUR SUNOL
2934 Kilkare Rd, Sunol (94586-9428)
PHONE.................................925 862-2263
Patricia Stillman, *President*
Lois Throop, *Treasurer*
Neil Davies, *Vice Pres*
Andrew Turnvull, *Admin Sec*
EMP: 100
SALES (est): 1MM **Privately Held**
WEB: www.sunol.net
SIC: 8641 Environmental protection organ-
ization

(P-25243)
SCIOTS TRACT ASSOCIATION
937 Chestnut Ln, Davis (95616-2411)
PHONE.................................530 753-5219
Robert Monty, *Vice Pres*
Beverly Monty, *Admin Sec*
EMP: 80
SALES (est): 802.2K **Privately Held**
SIC: 8641 Social club, membership

(P-25244)
SCORPION ATHC BOOSTER CLB INC
300 E Esplanade Dr # 250, Oxnard
(93036-1238)
PHONE.................................805 482-2005
Bob Graham, *CEO*
Martin Marietta, *Treasurer*
EMP: 50 **EST:** 2011
SALES: 280.1K **Privately Held**
SIC: 8641 Booster club

(P-25245)
SCRIPPS HEALTH
10010 Campus Point Dr, San Diego
(92121-1518)
PHONE.................................858 678-6966
Chris Van Gorder, *President*
Jaimie Bottorf, *Human Resources*
EMP: 165
SALES (corp-wide): 2.9B **Privately Held**
SIC: 8641 Civic social & fraternal associa-
tions
PA: Scripps Health
10140 Campus Point Dr Ax415
San Diego CA 92121
800 727-4777

(P-25246)
SCRIPPS HEALTH
9850 Genesee Ave Ste 900, La Jolla
(92037-1220)
PHONE.................................858 452-1279
EMP: 200
SALES (corp-wide): 2.9B **Privately Held**
SIC: 8641 Civic social & fraternal associa-
tions
PA: Scripps Health
10140 Campus Point Dr Ax415
San Diego CA 92121
800 727-4777

(P-25247)
SELF HELP ENTERPRISES (PA)
Also Called: S H E
8445 W Elowin Ct, Visalia (93291-9262)
P.O. Box 6520 (93290-6520)
PHONE.................................559 651-1000

Thomas Collishaw, *President*
Kathy Long-Tence, *CFO*
Kristin Ainley, *Admin Asst*
EMP: 75
SQ FT: 15,000
SALES: 29.1MM **Privately Held**
SIC: 8641 Dwelling-related associations

(P-25248)
SIERRA CLUB (PA)
Also Called: Sierra Club Books
2101 Webster St Ste 1300, Oakland
(94612-3546)
PHONE.................................415 977-5500
Robin Mann, *President*
Craig Lubow, *Vice Chairman*
Ginny Quick, *CFO*
Donna Buell, *Treasurer*
Allison Chin, *Treasurer*
EMP: 175 **EST:** 1892
SQ FT: 43,500
SALES: 98.1MM **Privately Held**
WEB: www.youngboglelaw.com
SIC: 8641 8399 Environmental protection
organization; advocacy group

(P-25249)
SIERRA MASONIC ASSOCIATION
Also Called: Sierra Lodge 788
2166 Hwy 49, Oakhurst (93644)
P.O. Box 805 (93644-0805)
PHONE.................................559 683-7713
William Bastian, *Admin Sec*
EMP: 78
SALES (est): 724.8K **Privately Held**
SIC: 8641 Civic associations

(P-25250)
SILICON VLY CMNTY FOUNDATION
Also Called: Svcf
2440 W El Camin, Mountain View (94040)
PHONE.................................650 450-5400
Emmett Carson, *CEO*
Lianne Araki, *President*
Vera Bennett, *CFO*
Lisa Alvarez, *Officer*
Lisa Barr, *Officer*
EMP: 120 **EST:** 2006
SALES (est): 12.1MM **Privately Held**
SIC: 8641 Civic social & fraternal associa-
tions

(P-25251)
SILVER LAKES ASSOCIATION
Also Called: Homeowners Association
15273 Orchard Hill Ln, Helendale (92342)
P.O. Box 179 (92342-0179)
PHONE.................................760 245-1606
Michael Bennett, *General Mgr*
Denise Hammer, *Executive Asst*
Patty Arringdale, *Clerk*
EMP: 90
SQ FT: 3,000
SALES (est): 5MM **Privately Held**
WEB: www.silverlakesassociation.com
SIC: 8641 Homeowners' association

(P-25252)
SONOMA VALLEY WOMANS CLUB
574 1st St E, Sonoma (95476-6753)
PHONE.................................707 938-8313
Carmella A Greco, *Principal*
EMP: 70
SQ FT: 3,216
SALES: 56.8K **Privately Held**
SIC: 8641 Civic associations

(P-25253)
SPYGLASS HILL COMMUNITY ASSN
39 Argonaut Ste 100, Aliso Viejo
(92656-4152)
P.O. Box 57063, Irvine (92619-7063)
PHONE.................................949 855-1800
Susan Larson, *President*
EMP: 50
SALES: 497.4K **Privately Held**
SIC: 8641 Homeowners' association

(P-25254)
SUN CITY PALM DSERT CMNTY ASSN (PA)
Also Called: Palm Desert Community Assn
38180 Del Webb Blvd, Palm Desert
(92211-1256)
PHONE.................................760 200-2100
Helen McEnerney, *President*
EMP: 80
SQ FT: 4,000
SALES: 7.7MM **Privately Held**
SIC: 8641 7992 7997 Dwelling-related as-
sociations; public golf courses; country
club, membership

(P-25255)
SUN LAKES CNTRY CLUB HMEOWNRS
850 Country Club Dr, Banning
(92220-5306)
PHONE.................................951 845-2135
Tim Taylor, *Manager*
EMP: 100
SALES: 23.3K **Privately Held**
SIC: 8641 Homeowners' association

(P-25256)
SUTTER CLUB INC
1220 9th St, Sacramento (95814-4897)
PHONE.................................916 442-0456
Tom Narozonick, *General Mgr*
EMP: 75
SQ FT: 45,000
SALES: 4.1MM **Privately Held**
WEB: www.sutterclub.com
SIC: 8641 Social club, membership

(P-25257)
SUTTER HEALTH
1301 Mission St, Santa Cruz (95060-3530)
PHONE.................................831 458-6310
Roger A Larsen, *President*
Anna R Matelski, *Executive Asst*
Kelley Davis, *Administration*
Dana Lesher, *Project Mgr*
Gregory Johnson, *Engineer*
EMP: 133
SALES (corp-wide): 12.4B **Privately Held**
SIC: 8641 Civic social & fraternal associa-
tions
PA: Sutter Health
2200 River Plaza Dr
Sacramento CA 95833
916 733-8800

(P-25258)
SUTTER HEALTH
2950 Research Park Dr, Soquel
(95073-2000)
PHONE.................................831 458-6272
EMP: 319
SALES (corp-wide): 12.4B **Privately Held**
SIC: 8641 Civic social & fraternal associa-
tions
PA: Sutter Health
2200 River Plaza Dr
Sacramento CA 95833
916 733-8800

(P-25259)
SUTTER HEALTH
520 W I St, Los Banos (93635-3419)
PHONE.................................209 827-4866
Lena Reza, *Office Mgr*
EMP: 133
SALES (corp-wide): 12.4B **Privately Held**
SIC: 8641 Civic social & fraternal associa-
tions
PA: Sutter Health
2200 River Plaza Dr
Sacramento CA 95833
916 733-8800

(P-25260)
SUTTER HEALTH
Also Called: Gyneclgic Onclogy Plvic Srgery
360 Dardanelli Ln Ste 2d, Los Gatos
(95032-1421)
PHONE.................................408 523-3900
EMP: 186
SALES (corp-wide): 12.4B **Privately Held**
SIC: 8641 Civic social & fraternal associa-
tions

PA: Sutter Health
2200 River Plaza Dr
Sacramento CA 95833
916 733-8800

(P-25261)
SUTTER HEALTH
2880 Soquel Ave, Santa Cruz
(95062-1423)
PHONE...................831 458-5500
Kathleen McNupp, *Branch Mgr*
EMP: 159
SALES (corp-wide): 12.4B **Privately Held**
SIC: 8641 Civic social & fraternal associations
PA: Sutter Health
2200 River Plaza Dr
Sacramento CA 95833
916 733-8800

(P-25262)
SUTTER HEALTH
1025 Atlantic Ave Ste 100, Alameda
(94501-1187)
PHONE...................916 286-6665
J Sexton, *Pediatrics*
EMP: 159
SALES (corp-wide): 12.4B **Privately Held**
SIC: 8641 Civic social & fraternal associations
PA: Sutter Health
2200 River Plaza Dr
Sacramento CA 95833
916 733-8800

(P-25263)
SUTTER HEALTH
Also Called: Smf Clinical Lab
2715 K St Ste A, Sacramento
(95816-5128)
PHONE...................916 551-9550
EMP: 266
SALES (corp-wide): 12.4B **Privately Held**
SIC: 8641 Civic social & fraternal associations
PA: Sutter Health
2200 River Plaza Dr
Sacramento CA 95833
916 733-8800

(P-25264)
TABLE COMMUNITY FOUDATION
3201 W Benjamin Holt Dr, Stockton
(95219-3741)
PHONE...................209 951-1753
Tyronne Gross Jr, *President*
EMP: 92
SALES (est): 361.7K **Privately Held**
SIC: 8641 Youth organizations

(P-25265)
TAMARACK BCH CONDO OWNERS ASSN
3200 Carlsbad Blvd, Carlsbad
(92008-3101)
PHONE...................760 729-3500
Connie Bloem, *President*
EMP: 50
SQ FT: 2,000
SALES (est): 857K **Privately Held**
SIC: 8641 Homeowners' association

(P-25266)
TECHSOUP GLOBAL (PA)
Also Called: Tech Soup
435 Brannan St Ste 100, San Francisco
(94107-1780)
PHONE...................800 659-3579
Rebecca Masisak, *CEO*
Geri Doran, *COO*
James Hebert, *CFO*
Marnie Webb, *Co-CEO*
Karen Coppock, *Vice Pres*
EMP: 108
SALES: 30.5MM **Privately Held**
WEB: www.techsoup.org
SIC: 8641 Social associations

(P-25267)
TEMPLE CITY YOUTH DEV FUND
6415 N Muscatel Ave, San Gabriel
(91775-1845)
PHONE...................626 548-5085
Kathy Perini, *Principal*
EMP: 68

SALES (est): 758.1K **Privately Held**
SIC: 8641 Youth organizations

(P-25268)
THEAT AND ARTS FOUND OF SAN DI
Also Called: LA JOLLA PLAYHOUSE
2910 La Jolla Village Dr, La Jolla
(92093-5100)
P.O. Box 12039 (92039-2039)
PHONE...................858 623-3366
Jeffrey Ressler, *Chairman*
Steven Libman, *President*
Michael L Eagle, *CEO*
Lynelle Lynch, *Chairman*
Tim Scott, *Chairman*
EMP: 250
SQ FT: 1,440
SALES: 16.3MM **Privately Held**
WEB: www.lajollaplayhouse.com
SIC: 8641 7922 Civic associations; theatrical producers & services

(P-25269)
TIERRA DEL ORO GIRL SCOUT CNSL
6601 Elvas Ave, Sacramento (95819-4339)
PHONE...................916 452-9174
Pamela Saltenberger, *Exec Dir*
EMP: 84
SQ FT: 12,200
SALES: 8.1MM **Privately Held**
WEB: www.tdogs.org
SIC: 8641 Girl Scout organization

(P-25270)
TWAIN HARTE HORSEMEN
23580 View Ln, Columbia (95310)
P.O. Box 1326, Twain Harte (95383-1326)
PHONE...................209 601-5585
Scott Lewis, *President*
EMP: 99
SALES: 12.3K **Privately Held**
SIC: 8641 Civic social & fraternal associations

(P-25271)
UNITED STATES MARINES YOUTH FD
90 La Venta Dr, Santa Barbara
(93110-1716)
PHONE...................805 967-7990
EMP: 54
SALES (corp-wide): 105.9K **Privately Held**
WEB: www.usmc.mil
SIC: 8641 Veterans' organization
PA: Marine Corps League
3619 Jefferson Davis Hwy # 115
Stafford VA 22554
703 207-9588

(P-25272)
UNIVERSITY STUDENT UNION OF CA
18111 Nordhoff St, Northridge
(91330-0001)
PHONE...................818 677-2251
Debra Hammond, *Exec Dir*
Joseph Illuminate, *Associate Dir*
EMP: 450
SQ FT: 350,000
SALES: 15.2MM **Privately Held**
SIC: 8641 Civic social & fraternal associations

(P-25273)
VALLEY HUNT CLUB
520 S Orange Grove Blvd, Pasadena
(91105-1799)
PHONE...................626 793-7134
David Mole, *CEO*
Donald F Crumrine, *COO*
Bill Roemer, *Controller*
Tayde Lomas, *Human Res Dir*
David Gieselman, *Purch Dir*
EMP: 85
SQ FT: 40,000
SALES: 8.8MM **Privately Held**
WEB: www.valleyhuntclub.com
SIC: 8641 Social club, membership

(P-25274)
VENTURA COUNTY FIRE DEPARTMENT
165 Durley Ave, Camarillo (93010-8586)
PHONE...................805 389-9710
Mark Lorensen, *Fire Chief*
Bob Michels, *Department Mgr*
EMP: 50
SALES (est): 1.6MM **Privately Held**
SIC: 8641 Civic social & fraternal associations

(P-25275)
VENTURA COUNTY OFFICE EDUCATN
1379 Oakridge Ct, Thousand Oaks
(91362-1923)
PHONE...................805 495-7037
EMP: 77 **Privately Held**
SIC: 8641
PA: Ventura County Office Of Education
5189 Verdugo Way
Camarillo CA 93012
805 383-1900

(P-25276)
VETERANS MEDICAL RESEARCH FUND
3350 La Jolla Village Dr, San Diego
(92161-0002)
PHONE...................858 642-3080
Kerstin B Lynam, *CEO*
Barabara Dovenbarger, *CFO*
Maria Sittmann, *Officer*
Simmaly Phommasane, *Purchasing*
EMP: 250
SALES: 19.9MM **Privately Held**
WEB: www.vapop.ucsd.edu
SIC: 8641 Civic social & fraternal associations

(P-25277)
VFW POST 6476
1789 N 8th St, Colton (92324-1303)
PHONE...................909 754-3828
Joe Quioz, *Principal*
EMP: 130
SALES (est): 540K **Privately Held**
SIC: 8641 Veterans' organization

(P-25278)
VICTOR VALLEY MOOSE LODGE NO
10230 E Ave, Hesperia (92345-7615)
P.O. Box 402277 (92340-2277)
PHONE...................760 244-1808
Douglas Padua, *President*
EMP: 140
SQ FT: 9,500
SALES (est): 185.9K **Privately Held**
SIC: 8641 7041 Civic associations; fraternities & sororities

(P-25279)
VIETNAM VETERANS OF SAN DIEGO (PA)
Also Called: Veterans Village of San Diego
4141 Pacific Hwy, San Diego (92110-2030)
PHONE...................619 497-0142
Phil Landis, *President*
Andre Simpson, *COO*
Harry Guess, *CFO*
EMP: 65
SQ FT: 35,719
SALES: 10.6MM **Privately Held**
WEB: www.vvsd.net
SIC: 8641 Veterans' organization

(P-25280)
VIETNMS-MRCAN YUTH ALANCE CORP
Also Called: Vaya
7968 Arjons Dr Ste 109, San Diego
(92126-6362)
P.O. Box 711912 (92171-1912)
PHONE...................619 320-8292
Hien Nguyen, *President*
Roy Valdez, *Area Mgr*
Peter Turnbull, *Project Mgr*
Dave Bain, *Accounts Mgr*
EMP: 50
SALES: 101K **Privately Held**
SIC: 8641 Civic social & fraternal associations

(P-25281)
VILLA BALBOA COMMUNITY ASSOC
22 Mauchly, Irvine (92618-2306)
P.O. Box 4708 (92616-4708)
PHONE...................949 450-1515
Janice Walley, *President*
Frank Jenes, *President*
EMP: 65
SALES (est): 797.3K **Privately Held**
SIC: 8641 Homeowners' association

(P-25282)
VILLA MARIN HOMEOWNERS ASSN
Also Called: Villa Mrin Rtrement Residences
100 Thorndale Dr, San Rafael
(94903-4599)
PHONE...................415 499-8711
Danel Walker, *CEO*
Dan Walker, *CEO*
EMP: 170
SQ FT: 500,000
SALES: 11.7MM **Privately Held**
SIC: 8641 8051 8059 Homeowners' association; skilled nursing care facilities; personal care home, with health care

(P-25283)
VINTAGE CLUB MASTER ASSN INC
75001 Vintage Dr W, Indian Wells
(92210-7304)
PHONE...................760 340-0500
Art Allen, *Exec Dir*
Red Scott, *President*
EMP: 60
SALES: 3MM **Privately Held**
SIC: 8641 Homeowners' association

(P-25284)
WEST END YUNG MNS CHRISTN ASSN
Also Called: Upland Ymca-Valencia
1150 E Foothill Blvd, Upland (91786-4012)
PHONE...................909 946-6120
Leeann Faucett, *Branch Mgr*
EMP: 59
SALES (corp-wide): 3.5MM **Privately Held**
WEB: www.westendymca.org
SIC: 8641 7991 8351 7032 Youth organizations; physical fitness facilities; child day care services; youth camps; individual & family services
PA: West End Young Men's Christian Association Inc
10970 Arrow Rte Ste 106
Rancho Cucamonga CA 91730
909 481-0722

(P-25285)
WEST END YUNG MNS CHRISTN ASSN
Also Called: Rancho Cucamonga Family YMCA
11200 Baseline Rd, Rancho Cucamonga
(91701-5338)
P.O. Box 248 (91729-0248)
PHONE...................909 477-2780
Dianna Lee-Mitchell, *Director*
EMP: 80
SALES (corp-wide): 3.5MM **Privately Held**
WEB: www.westendymca.org
SIC: 8641 7991 8351 7032 Youth organizations; physical fitness facilities; child day care services; youth camps; individual & family services
PA: West End Young Men's Christian Association Inc
10970 Arrow Rte Ste 106
Rancho Cucamonga CA 91730
909 481-0722

(P-25286)
WOODBRIDGE VILLAGE ASSOCIATION
31 Creek Rd, Irvine (92604-4793)
PHONE...................949 786-1800
Kevin Chudy, *Exec Dir*
Bertha Rivera, *Admin Sec*
Matthew Sills, *Pub Rel Mgr*
Santiago Arteaga, *Maintence Staff*

Anne Sheldon,
EMP: 65
SQ FT: 15,000
SALES: 10MM **Privately Held**
WEB: www.wva.org
SIC: 8641 Homeowners' association

(P-25287)
WOODLAND SWIM TEAM BOSTERS CLB
155 West St, Woodland (95695-3162)
P.O. Box 763 (95776-0763)
PHONE..................................530 662-9783
EMP: 60
SALES: 125.2K **Privately Held**
SIC: 8641

(P-25288)
Y W C A OF SONOMA COUNTY
Also Called: YWCA
811 3rd St Ste 100, Santa Rosa (95404-4541)
P.O. Box 3506 (95402-3506)
PHONE..................................707 546-9922
Madeline O'Connell, *Exec Dir*
Julie Lafranchi, *General Mgr*
Jennifer Lake, *General Mgr*
Doreen Lorinczi, *Director*
Madeleine K Oconnell, *Director*
EMP: 50
SALES: 2.2MM **Privately Held**
SIC: 8641 7991 8351 7032 Youth organizations; physical fitness facilities; child day care services; youth camps; individual & family services

(P-25289)
YMCA OF EAST VALLEY (PA)
500 E Citrus Ave, Redlands (92373-5285)
PHONE..................................909 798-9622
Darwin Barnett, *CEO*
Ken Stein, *CEO*
Doug Thorne, *CFO*
Perry Mecate, *Vice Pres*
Carmen Barney, *Director*
EMP: 125 EST: 1887
SQ FT: 100,000
SALES: 12.8MM **Privately Held**
WEB: www.ymcaofredlands.com
SIC: 8641 Youth organizations

(P-25290)
YMCA OF EAST VALLEY
Also Called: San Bernardino Family YMCA
808 E 21st St, San Bernardino (92404-4874)
PHONE..................................909 881-9622
Bill Blank, *Director*
EMP: 50
SALES (corp-wide): 12.8MM **Privately Held**
WEB: www.ymcaofredlands.com
SIC: 8641 7991 8351 7032 Youth organizations; physical fitness facilities; child day care services; youth camps; individual & family services
PA: Ymca Of The East Valley
    500 E Citrus Ave
    Redlands CA 92373
    909 798-9622

(P-25291)
YMCA OF EAST VALLEY
7793 Central Ave, Highland (92346-4106)
PHONE..................................909 425-9622
Ursula Walsh, *Branch Mgr*
EMP: 50
SALES (corp-wide): 12.8MM **Privately Held**
WEB: www.ymcaofredlands.com
SIC: 8641 7991 8351 7032 Youth organizations; physical fitness facilities; child day care services; youth camps; individual & family services
PA: Ymca Of The East Valley
    500 E Citrus Ave
    Redlands CA 92373
    909 798-9622

(P-25292)
YMCA OF NORTH ORANGE COUNTY
Also Called: North Orange Cnty Fmly Y M C A
2000 Youth Way, Fullerton (92835-3878)
PHONE..................................714 879-9622
Jim Lapak, *Exec Dir*

Claire Akenna, *Manager*
EMP: 85
SQ FT: 10,000
SALES (est): 1.1MM **Privately Held**
SIC: 8641 7991 8351 7032 Youth organizations; physical fitness facilities; child day care services; youth camps; individual & family services

(P-25293)
YMCA OF SAN DIEGO COUNTY
Also Called: Y M C A Childcare Resource Ser
1310 Union Plaza Ct # 200, Oceanside (92054-5604)
PHONE..................................760 754-6042
Job Moraido, *Branch Mgr*
EMP: 76
SALES (corp-wide): 170.6MM **Privately Held**
WEB: www.ymcacrs.org
SIC: 8641 7991 8351 7032 Youth organizations; physical fitness facilities; child day care services; youth camps; individual & family services
PA: Ymca Of San Diego County
    3708 Ruffin Rd
    San Diego CA 92123
    858 292-9622

(P-25294)
YMCA OF SAN DIEGO COUNTY
Also Called: La Jolla YMCA
8355 Cliffridge Ave, La Jolla (92037-2107)
PHONE..................................858 453-3483
Sam Wurtzbacher, *Director*
EMP: 200
SALES (corp-wide): 170.6MM **Privately Held**
WEB: www.ymcacrs.org
SIC: 8641 8351 7997 Youth organizations; child day care services; membership sports & recreation clubs
PA: Ymca Of San Diego County
    3708 Ruffin Rd
    San Diego CA 92123
    858 292-9622

(P-25295)
YMCA OF SAN DIEGO COUNTY (PA)
Also Called: Y, THE
3708 Ruffin Rd, San Diego (92123-1812)
PHONE..................................858 292-9622
Baron Herdelin Doherty, *CEO*
Charmaine Carter, *CFO*
John Merritt, *Senior VP*
EMP: 143
SQ FT: 19,600
SALES: 170.6MM **Privately Held**
WEB: www.ymcacrs.org
SIC: 8641 Youth organizations

(P-25296)
YMCA OF SAN DIEGO COUNTY
Also Called: Pelomar Family YMCA
1050 N Broadway, Escondido (92026-3044)
PHONE..................................760 745-7490
Alfredo Velasco, *Manager*
Arlene Shaffer, *Manager*
EMP: 500
SALES (corp-wide): 170.6MM **Privately Held**
WEB: www.ymcacrs.org
SIC: 8641 7991 8351 7032 Youth organizations; physical fitness facilities; child day care services; youth camps; individual & family services
PA: Ymca Of San Diego County
    3708 Ruffin Rd
    San Diego CA 92123
    858 292-9622

(P-25297)
YMCA OF SAN DIEGO COUNTY
8881 Dallas St, La Mesa (91942-3297)
PHONE..................................619 464-1323
Steve Rowe, *Exec Dir*
EMP: 76
SALES (corp-wide): 170.6MM **Privately Held**
WEB: www.ymcacrs.org
SIC: 8641 7991 8351 7032 Youth organizations; physical fitness facilities; child day care services; youth camps; individual & family services

PA: Ymca Of San Diego County
    3708 Ruffin Rd
    San Diego CA 92123
    858 292-9622

(P-25298)
YMCA OF SAN DIEGO COUNTY
Also Called: Magdalena Ecke Family YMCA
200 Saxony Rd, Encinitas (92024-2720)
PHONE..................................858 292-4034
Susan J Cocke, *Branch Mgr*
EMP: 76
SALES (corp-wide): 170.6MM **Privately Held**
WEB: www.ymcacrs.org
SIC: 8641 8351 8322 7997 Youth organizations; child day care services; youth center; membership sports & recreation clubs
PA: Ymca Of San Diego County
    3708 Ruffin Rd
    San Diego CA 92123
    858 292-9622

(P-25299)
YMCA OF SAN DIEGO COUNTY
Also Called: YMCA Youth & Family Services
2927 Meade Ave, San Diego (92116-4251)
PHONE..................................619 281-8313
Cesar Marcano, *Exec Dir*
EMP: 72
SALES (corp-wide): 170.6MM **Privately Held**
SIC: 8641 7991 8351 7032 Youth organizations; physical fitness facilities; child day care services; youth camps; individual & family services
PA: Ymca Of San Diego County
    3708 Ruffin Rd
    San Diego CA 92123
    858 292-9622

(P-25300)
YMCA OF SAN DIEGO COUNTY
Also Called: Peninsula Family YMCA Sunshine
2150 Beryl St Ste 18, San Diego (92109-3617)
PHONE..................................619 226-8888
Andrea Sanchez, *Director*
EMP: 75
SQ FT: 3,500
SALES (corp-wide): 170.6MM **Privately Held**
WEB: www.ymcacrs.org
SIC: 8641 8322 Youth organizations; individual & family services
PA: Ymca Of San Diego County
    3708 Ruffin Rd
    San Diego CA 92123
    858 292-9622

(P-25301)
YMCA OF SAN DIEGO COUNTY
Also Called: YMCA Child Care Resource Svcs
3333 Camino Del Rio S # 400, San Diego (92108-3808)
PHONE..................................619 521-3055
Debbie Macdonald, *Director*
EMP: 180
SALES (corp-wide): 170.6MM **Privately Held**
WEB: www.ymcacrs.org
SIC: 8641 7991 8351 7032 Youth organizations; physical fitness facilities; child day care services; youth camps; individual & family services
PA: Ymca Of San Diego County
    3708 Ruffin Rd
    San Diego CA 92123
    858 292-9622

(P-25302)
YMCA OF SAN DIEGO COUNTY
Also Called: YMCA Overnight Camp
4761 Pine Hills Rd, Julian (92036)
P.O. Box 2440 (92036-2440)
PHONE..................................760 765-0642
Thomas Madeyski, *Exec Dir*
EMP: 50

PA: Ymca Of San Diego County
    3708 Ruffin Rd
    San Diego CA 92123
    858 292-9622

SALES (corp-wide): 170.6MM **Privately Held**
WEB: www.ymcacrs.org
SIC: 8641 7991 8351 7032 Youth organizations; physical fitness facilities; child day care services; youth camps; individual & family services
PA: Ymca Of San Diego County
    3708 Ruffin Rd
    San Diego CA 92123
    858 292-9622

(P-25303)
YMCA OF SAN DIEGO COUNTY
Also Called: Mission Valley YMCA
5505 Friars Rd, San Diego (92110-2682)
PHONE..................................619 298-3576
Dick Webster, *Manager*
EMP: 200
SALES (corp-wide): 170.6MM **Privately Held**
WEB: www.ymcacrs.org
SIC: 8641 7997 Youth organizations; membership sports & recreation clubs
PA: Ymca Of San Diego County
    3708 Ruffin Rd
    San Diego CA 92123
    858 292-9622

(P-25304)
YMCA OF SAN DIEGO COUNTY
Also Called: Cameron Family YMCA
10123 Hoffman Ln, Santee (92071-5295)
PHONE..................................619 449-9622
Steve Rowe, *Branch Mgr*
EMP: 100
SQ FT: 32,970
SALES (corp-wide): 170.6MM **Privately Held**
WEB: www.ymcacrs.org
SIC: 8641 8322 Youth organizations; individual & family services
PA: Ymca Of San Diego County
    3708 Ruffin Rd
    San Diego CA 92123
    858 292-9622

(P-25305)
YMCA OF SAN DIEGO COUNTY
Also Called: Joe & Mary Mottino YMCA
4701 Mesa Dr, Oceanside (92056-6568)
PHONE..................................760 758-0808
Jeff Guzzardo, *Branch Mgr*
Kate Winzenburg, *Sales Executive*
Gary Wegener, *Director*
Brent Ayers, *Manager*
EMP: 100
SALES (corp-wide): 170.6MM **Privately Held**
WEB: www.ymcacrs.org
SIC: 8641 8322 Youth organizations; individual & family services
PA: Ymca Of San Diego County
    3708 Ruffin Rd
    San Diego CA 92123
    858 292-9622

(P-25306)
YMCA OF SAN DIEGO COUNTY
Also Called: Santa Margarita YMCA Garrison
333 Garrison St, Oceanside (92054-4700)
PHONE..................................760 757-8270
Margie Oliver, *Branch Mgr*
EMP: 76
SALES (corp-wide): 170.6MM **Privately Held**
WEB: www.ymcacrs.org
SIC: 8641 7991 8351 7032 Youth organizations; physical fitness facilities; child day care services; youth camps; individual & family services
PA: Ymca Of San Diego County
    3708 Ruffin Rd
    San Diego CA 92123
    858 292-9622

(P-25307)
YMCA OF SAN DIEGO COUNTY
50 Fourth Ave, Chula Vista (91910-1767)
PHONE..................................619 422-8068
Sheri Greene, *Manager*
EMP: 76
SQ FT: 2,832

PRODUCTS & SVCS

SALES (corp-wide): 170.6MM **Privately Held**
WEB: www.ymcacrs.org
SIC: 8641 7991 8351 7032 Youth organizations; physical fitness facilities; child day care services; youth camps; individual & family services
PA: Ymca Of San Diego County
　　3708 Ruffin Rd
　　San Diego CA 92123
　　858 292-9622

(P-25308)
YMCA OF SAN JOAQUIN COUNTY
2105 W March Ln Ste 1, Stockton (95207-6422)
PHONE...................................209 472-9622
Russ Hayward, *CEO*
Rich Good, *Exec Dir*
Sam Prak, *Finance*
EMP: 70
SQ FT: 2,000
SALES: 3.1MM **Privately Held**
WEB: www.ymcasjc.org
SIC: 8641 Social club, membership; youth organizations

(P-25309)
YMCA OF SILICON VALLEY (PA)
80 Saratoga Ave, Santa Clara (95051-7303)
PHONE...................................408 351-6400
Kathy Riggins, *President*
Ed Barrantes, *CFO*
Stan Chinchen, *Bd of Directors*
PA Mdavis, *Bd of Directors*
Doreen Hassan, *Associate Dir*
EMP: 60 EST: 1867
SQ FT: 5,000
SALES: 74.7MM **Privately Held**
WEB: www.scvymca.org
SIC: 8641 7991 8351 7032 Youth organizations; physical fitness facilities; child day care services; youth camps; individual & family services

(P-25310)
YMCA OF SILICON VALLEY
1922 The Alameda Ste 300, San Jose (95126-1430)
PHONE...................................650 493-9622
EMP: 300
SALES (corp-wide): 74.7MM **Privately Held**
SIC: 8641 7991 8351 7032 Youth organizations; physical fitness facilities; child day care services; youth camps; individual & family services
PA: Ymca Of Silicon Valley
　　80 Saratoga Ave
　　Santa Clara CA 95051
　　408 351-6400

(P-25311)
YMCA OF SILICON VALLEY
Also Called: Central Branch YMCA
1717 The Alameda, San Jose (95126-1794)
PHONE...................................408 298-1717
Barbara Cardinez, *Manager*
EMP: 150
SQ FT: 52,715
SALES (corp-wide): 74.7MM **Privately Held**
WEB: www.scvymca.org
SIC: 8641 8351 8322 7997 Youth organizations; child day care services; individual & family services; membership sports & recreation clubs; physical fitness facilities
PA: Ymca Of Silicon Valley
　　80 Saratoga Ave
　　Santa Clara CA 95051
　　408 351-6400

(P-25312)
YMCA OF SILICON VALLEY
Also Called: El Camino YMCA
2400 Grant Rd, Mountain View (94040-4324)
PHONE...................................650 969-9622
Elaine Glissmeyer, *Director*
EMP: 300

SALES (corp-wide): 74.7MM **Privately Held**
SIC: 8641 7991 8351 7032 Youth organizations; physical fitness facilities; child day care services; youth camps; individual & family services
PA: Ymca Of Silicon Valley
　　80 Saratoga Ave
　　Santa Clara CA 95051
　　408 351-6400

(P-25313)
YMCA OF SILICON VALLEY
Also Called: YMCA of Santa Clara Valley
5632 Santa Teresa Blvd, San Jose (95123-2698)
PHONE...................................408 226-9622
Rick Valdez, *Exec Dir*
EMP: 60
SALES (corp-wide): 74.7MM **Privately Held**
WEB: www.scvymca.org
SIC: 8641 7991 8351 7032 Youth organizations; physical fitness facilities; child day care services; youth camps; individual & family services
PA: Ymca Of Silicon Valley
　　80 Saratoga Ave
　　Santa Clara CA 95051
　　408 351-6400

(P-25314)
YMCA OF THE MID-PENINSULA INC
1922 The Alameda Ste 300, San Jose (95126-1430)
PHONE...................................650 493-9622
Kathy Riggins, *CEO*
Elizabeth Jordan, *COO*
Ron Fior, *Treasurer*
Jim Sandstrom, *Admin Sec*
EMP: 300
SQ FT: 6,000
SALES (est): 1.2MM **Privately Held**
SIC: 8641 7991 8351 7032 Youth organizations; physical fitness facilities; child day care services; youth camps; individual & family services

(P-25315)
YMCA YOUTH & FAMILY SERVICES
4080 Centre St Ste 203, San Diego (92103-2657)
PHONE...................................619 543-9850
Laura Mustari, *Principal*
EMP: 64
SALES (est): 1.1MM **Privately Held**
SIC: 8641 7991 8351 7032 Youth organizations; physical fitness facilities; child day care services; youth camps; individual & family services

(P-25316)
YOSEMITE LAKES OWNERS ASSN
30250 Yosemite Springs Pk, Coarsegold (93614-9369)
PHONE...................................559 658-7466
Steve Payne, *General Mgr*
John Nino, *Info Tech Mgr*
Corey Johnson, *Facilities Mgr*
Tammie Damore, *Manager*
Kim Fischer, *Manager*
EMP: 70 EST: 1970
SQ FT: 10,000
SALES (est): 2.8MM **Privately Held**
WEB: www.yloa.org
SIC: 8641 Homeowners' association

(P-25317)
YOUNG MENS CHRISTIAN (PA)
Also Called: YMCA
321 E Magnolia Blvd, Burbank (91502-1132)
PHONE...................................818 845-8551
JC Holt, *CEO*
EMP: 100
SQ FT: 47,000
SALES: 5.3MM **Privately Held**
SIC: 8641 7991 8351 7032 Youth organizations; physical fitness facilities; child day care services; youth camps; individual & family services

(P-25318)
YOUNG MENS CHRISTIAN ASSNSF
Also Called: Presido YMCA
63 Funston Ave, San Francisco (94129-1110)
PHONE...................................415 447-9622
Robert Sindelar, *Exec Dir*
Sean Dries, *Director*
EMP: 86
SALES (corp-wide): 82.8MM **Privately Held**
SIC: 8641 7999 Youth organizations; tennis services & professionals
PA: Young Men's Christian Association Of San Francisco
　　50 California St Ste 650
　　San Francisco CA 94111
　　415 777-9622

(P-25319)
YOUNG MENS CHRISTIAN ASSNSF
Also Called: YMCA Youth & Family Service
1115 3rd St, San Rafael (94901-3017)
PHONE...................................415 459-9622
Don Carney, *Director*
EMP: 200
SALES (corp-wide): 82.8MM **Privately Held**
SIC: 8641 7991 8351 7032 Youth organizations; physical fitness facilities; child day care services; youth camps; individual & family services
PA: Young Men's Christian Association Of San Francisco
　　50 California St Ste 650
　　San Francisco CA 94111
　　415 777-9622

(P-25320)
YOUNG MENS CHRISTIAN ASSO
4031 N Moorpark Rd, Thousand Oaks (91360-2660)
PHONE...................................805 523-7613
Kelly Dulek, *Director*
EMP: 100
SALES (corp-wide): 20.9MM **Privately Held**
SIC: 8641 7997 8351 Civic social & fraternal associations; membership sports & recreation clubs; child day care services
PA: Young Men's Christian Association Of Southeast Ventura County
　　100 E Thousand Oaks Blvd # 107
　　Thousand Oaks CA 91360
　　805 497-3081

(P-25321)
YOUNG MENS CHRISTIAN ASSOC SF
Also Called: Argonne YMCA After School
680 18th Ave, San Francisco (94121-3823)
PHONE...................................415 831-4093
Robin Sharp, *Manager*
EMP: 86
SALES (corp-wide): 82.8MM **Privately Held**
SIC: 8641 7991 8351 7032 Youth organizations; physical fitness facilities; child day care services; youth camps; individual & family services
PA: Young Men's Christian Association Of San Francisco
　　50 California St Ste 650
　　San Francisco CA 94111
　　415 777-9622

(P-25322)
YOUNG MENS CHRISTIAN ASSOC SF
Also Called: Presidio Community YMCA
57 Post St, San Francisco (94104-5003)
PHONE...................................415 447-9602
EMP: 86
SALES (corp-wide): 82.8MM **Privately Held**
SIC: 8641 7999 Youth organizations; swimming instruction
PA: Young Men's Christian Association Of San Francisco
　　50 California St Ste 650
　　San Francisco CA 94111
　　415 777-9622

(P-25323)
YOUNG MENS CHRISTIAN ASSOC SF
Also Called: Peninsula YMCA
1877 S Grant St, San Mateo (94402-2647)
PHONE...................................650 286-9622
Rachel Del Monte, *Manager*
Patrizia Guiotto, *Principal*
EMP: 200
SALES (corp-wide): 82.8MM **Privately Held**
SIC: 8641 7991 8351 Youth organizations; physical fitness facilities; child day care services
PA: Young Men's Christian Association Of San Francisco
　　50 California St Ste 650
　　San Francisco CA 94111
　　415 777-9622

(P-25324)
YOUNG MENS CHRISTIAN ASSOC SF (PA)
Also Called: YMCA OF SAN FRANCISCO
50 California St Ste 650, San Francisco (94111-4607)
PHONE...................................415 777-9622
Charles M Collins, *President*
Kathy Cheng, *CFO*
Rachel Del Monte, *Branch Mgr*
Linda Griffith, *Admin Sec*
Sarah Millett, *Admin Asst*
EMP: 50
SQ FT: 10,000
SALES: 82.8MM **Privately Held**
SIC: 8641 7991 8351 7032 Youth organizations; physical fitness facilities; child day care services; youth camps; individual & family services

(P-25325)
YOUNG MENS CHRISTIAN ASSOC SF
Also Called: Richmond District YMCA
360 18th Ave, San Francisco (94121-2317)
PHONE...................................415 666-9622
Tiffany Patterson, *Branch Mgr*
EMP: 80
SALES (corp-wide): 82.8MM **Privately Held**
SIC: 8641 7991 8351 7032 Youth organizations; physical fitness facilities; child day care services; youth camps; individual & family services
PA: Young Men's Christian Association Of San Francisco
　　50 California St Ste 650
　　San Francisco CA 94111
　　415 777-9622

(P-25326)
YOUNG MENS CHRISTIAN ASSOC SF
Also Called: YMCA
169 Steuart St, San Francisco (94105-1206)
PHONE...................................415 957-9622
Larry Bush, *Branch Mgr*
EMP: 100
SQ FT: 54,186
SALES (corp-wide): 82.8MM **Privately Held**
SIC: 8641 7991 8351 7032 Youth organizations; physical fitness facilities; child day care services; youth camps; individual & family services
PA: Young Men's Christian Association Of San Francisco
　　50 California St Ste 650
　　San Francisco CA 94111
　　415 777-9622

(P-25327)
YOUNG MENS CHRISTIAN ASSOC SF
Also Called: Shih Yu-Lang Central YMCA
246 Eddy St, San Francisco (94102-2716)
PHONE...................................415 885-0460
Carmela Gold, *Exec Dir*
EMP: 100

SALES (corp-wide): 82.8MM **Privately Held**

SIC: **8641** 7997 8322 7999 Youth organizations; membership sports & recreation clubs; senior citizens' center or association; swimming instruction; aerobic dance & exercise classes; hotels

PA: Young Men's Christian Association Of San Francisco
50 California St Ste 650
San Francisco CA 94111
415 777-9622

(P-25328)
YOUNG MENS CHRISTIAN ASSOC SF
Also Called: YMCA Richmond Afterschool Ctr
4545 Anza St, San Francisco (94121-2621)
PHONE..................................415 752-0790
Kevin Lee, *Manager*
EMP: 86
SALES (corp-wide): 82.8MM **Privately Held**
SIC: **8641** 7991 8351 7032 Youth organizations; physical fitness facilities; child day care services; youth camps; individual & family services
PA: Young Men's Christian Association Of San Francisco
50 California St Ste 650
San Francisco CA 94111
415 777-9622

(P-25329)
YOUNG MENS CHRISTIAN ASSOC SF
3 Hamilton Landing # 140, Novato (94949-8248)
PHONE..................................415 883-9622
Jayne Blote, *Branch Mgr*
Maria C Reyes, *Controller*
EMP: 88
SALES (corp-wide): 82.8MM **Privately Held**
SIC: **8641** 7991 8351 7032
PA: Young Men's Christian Association Of San Francisco
50 California St Ste 650
San Francisco CA 94111
415 777-9622

(P-25330)
YOUNG MENS CHRISTIAN ASSOC SF
Also Called: Ymcasf
1500 Los Gamos Dr, San Rafael (94903-1841)
PHONE..................................415 492-9622
Luann Jackman, *Exec Dir*
Jolson Nakamura,
EMP: 300
SALES (corp-wide): 82.8MM **Privately Held**
SIC: **8641** 8351 7991 Community membership club; child day care services; physical fitness facilities
PA: Young Men's Christian Association Of San Francisco
50 California St Ste 650
San Francisco CA 94111
415 777-9622

(P-25331)
YOUNG MENS CHRISTIAN ASSOCIAT
Also Called: Downtown Community Dev YMCA
525 E 7th St, Long Beach (90813-4559)
PHONE..................................562 624-2376
EMP: 99
SALES: 3.3MM **Privately Held**
SIC: **8641** 7991 8351 7032

(P-25332)
YOUNG MENS CHRISTN ASSN ORANGE
2241 E Palmyra Ave, Orange (92869-4636)
PHONE..................................714 771-1287
Dolores Marikian, *CEO*
Hope Altman, *Director*
Liz Martinez, *Director*
EMP: 60
SQ FT: 6,500
SALES: 753.9K **Privately Held**
SIC: **8641** Youth organizations

(P-25333)
YOUNG MENS CHRSTN ASSC GR L B
Also Called: Lakewood Y M C A Gymnastics
4116 South St, Lakewood (90712-1005)
PHONE..................................562 272-4884
Rick Carlson, *Branch Mgr*
EMP: 89
SALES (corp-wide): 20MM **Privately Held**
WEB: www.lbymca.org
SIC: **8641** 7991 8351 7032 Youth organizations; physical fitness facilities; child day care services; youth camps; individual & family services
PA: Young Men's Christian Association Of Greater Long Beach
3605 Lngbach Blvd Ste 210
Long Beach CA 90807
562 279-1700

(P-25334)
YOUNG MENS CHRSTN ASSC GR L B
Also Called: Los Altos YMCA
1720 N Bellflower Blvd, Long Beach (90815-4011)
PHONE..................................562 596-3394
Sierra Lahera, *Director*
EMP: 500
SQ FT: 9,740
SALES (corp-wide): 20MM **Privately Held**
WEB: www.lbymca.org
SIC: **8641** 7991 8351 7032 Youth organizations; physical fitness facilities; child day care services; youth camps; individual & family services
PA: Young Men's Christian Association Of Greater Long Beach
3605 Lngbach Blvd Ste 210
Long Beach CA 90807
562 279-1700

(P-25335)
YOUNG MENS CHRSTN ASSC GR L B
Also Called: Y M C A Los Cerritos
15530 Woodruff Ave, Bellflower (90706-4014)
PHONE..................................562 925-1292
Michele Janssen, *Director*
EMP: 80
SQ FT: 6,190
SALES (corp-wide): 20MM **Privately Held**
WEB: www.lbymca.org
SIC: **8641** 8351 Community membership club; child day care services
PA: Young Men's Christian Association Of Greater Long Beach
3605 Lngbach Blvd Ste 210
Long Beach CA 90807
562 279-1700

(P-25336)
YOUNG MENS CHRSTN ASSC GR L B
Also Called: Weingart-Lakewood Family YMCA
5835 Carson St, Lakewood (90713-3056)
PHONE..................................562 425-7431
Chanelle Collo, *Director*
EMP: 125
SALES (corp-wide): 20MM **Privately Held**
WEB: www.lbymca.org
SIC: **8641** 7991 8351 7032 Youth organizations; physical fitness facilities; child day care services; youth camps; individual & family services
PA: Young Men's Christian Association Of Greater Long Beach
3605 Lngbach Blvd Ste 210
Long Beach CA 90807
562 279-1700

(P-25337)
YOUNG MENS CHRSTN ASSC GR L B
Also Called: Fairfield Family YMCA
4949 Atlantic Ave, Long Beach (90805-6505)
PHONE..................................562 423-0491
Ricky Grober, *Director*

EMP: 60
SALES (corp-wide): 20MM **Privately Held**
WEB: www.lbymca.org
SIC: **8641** 8351 8322 Youth organizations; child day care services; youth center

PA: Young Men's Christian Association Of Greater Long Beach
3605 Lngbach Blvd Ste 210
Long Beach CA 90807
562 279-1700

(P-25338)
YOUNG MENS CHRSTN ASSC GR L B
Also Called: YMCA Glb Grant
4949 Atlantic Ave, Long Beach (90805-6505)
PHONE..................................562 423-0491
Katherine Tarlecky, *Director*
EMP: 89
SALES (corp-wide): 20MM **Privately Held**
WEB: www.lbymca.org
SIC: **8641** 8351 Youth organizations; child day care services
PA: Young Men's Christian Association Of Greater Long Beach
3605 Lngbach Blvd Ste 210
Long Beach CA 90807
562 279-1700

(P-25339)
YOUNG MENS CHRSTN ASSC GR L B
Also Called: Y M C A The
6125 Coke Ave, Long Beach (90805-3925)
PHONE..................................562 633-0106
Lyle Yballe, *Branch Mgr*
EMP: 89
SALES (corp-wide): 20MM **Privately Held**
WEB: www.lbymca.org
SIC: **8641** 7999 8351 Youth organizations; recreation center; group day care center
PA: Young Men's Christian Association Of Greater Long Beach
3605 Lngbach Blvd Ste 210
Long Beach CA 90807
562 279-1700

(P-25340)
YOUNG MENS CHRSTN ASSN OF LA
Also Called: Mid-Valley Y M C A
6901 Lennox Ave, Van Nuys (91405-4002)
PHONE..................................818 989-3800
Wendy Sunders, *Exec Dir*
EMP: 50
SQ FT: 37,223
SALES (corp-wide): 105.9MM **Privately Held**
SIC: **8641** 7991 8351 7032 Youth organizations; physical fitness facilities; child day care services; youth camps; individual & family services
PA: Young Men's Christian Association Of Metropolitan Los Angeles
625 S New Hampshire Ave
Los Angeles CA 90005
213 351-2256

(P-25341)
YOUNG MENS CHRSTN ASSN OF LA
Also Called: South Pasadena San Marino YMCA
1605 Garfield Ave, South Pasadena (91030-4968)
PHONE..................................626 799-9119
Sue Marasco, *Director*
EMP: 65
SQ FT: 23,031
SALES (corp-wide): 105.9MM **Privately Held**
SIC: **8641** 7991 8351 7032 Youth organizations; physical fitness facilities; child day care services; youth camps; individual & family services

PA: Young Men's Christian Association Of Metropolitan Los Angeles
625 S New Hampshire Ave
Los Angeles CA 90005
213 351-2256

(P-25342)
YOUNG MENS CHRSTN ASSN OF LA (PA)
Also Called: YMCA
625 S New Hampshire Ave, Los Angeles (90005-1342)
PHONE..................................213 351-2256
Alan Hostrup, *President*
W J Ellison, *Ch of Bd*
Dan Cooper, *CFO*
Dana Lipman, *Officer*
Rick Politte, *Exec Dir*
EMP: 70
SQ FT: 16,000
SALES: 105.9MM **Privately Held**
SIC: **8641** Youth organizations

(P-25343)
YOUNG MENS CHRSTN ASSN OF LA
Also Called: YMCA of Westchester
8015 S Sepulveda Blvd, Los Angeles (90045-2940)
PHONE..................................310 216-9036
Patricia De Frelice, *Exec Dir*
EMP: 50
SALES (corp-wide): 105.9MM **Privately Held**
SIC: **8641** 8322 Youth organizations; individual & family services
PA: Young Men's Christian Association Of Metropolitan Los Angeles
625 S New Hampshire Ave
Los Angeles CA 90005
213 351-2256

(P-25344)
YOUNG MENS CHRSTN ASSN OF LA
Also Called: YMCA Metro La Summit Park
26147 Mcbean Pkwy, Valencia (91355-2015)
PHONE..................................661 253-3593
Brian Thorn, *Exec Dir*
EMP: 130
SQ FT: 13,124
SALES (corp-wide): 105.9MM **Privately Held**
SIC: **8641** 7991 8351 7032 Youth organizations; physical fitness facilities; child day care services; youth camps; individual & family services
PA: Young Men's Christian Association Of Metropolitan Los Angeles
625 S New Hampshire Ave
Los Angeles CA 90005
213 351-2256

(P-25345)
YOUNG MENS CHRSTN ASSN OF LA
Also Called: National Fitness Testing
1553 N Shrader Blvd, Los Angeles (90028)
PHONE..................................323 467-4161
Rosa Najera, *Branch Mgr*
EMP: 150
SALES (corp-wide): 105.9MM **Privately Held**
SIC: **8641** Youth organizations
PA: Young Men's Christian Association Of Metropolitan Los Angeles
625 S New Hampshire Ave
Los Angeles CA 90005
213 351-2256

(P-25346)
YOUNG MENS CHRSTN ASSN OF LA
Also Called: Downey Family Y M C A
11531 Downey Ave, Downey (90241-4936)
PHONE..................................562 862-4201
George Saikali, *Director*
EMP: 100
SALES (corp-wide): 105.9MM **Privately Held**
SIC: **8641** 7991 8351 7032 Youth organizations; physical fitness facilities; child day care services; youth camps; individual & family services

PA: Young Men's Christian Association Of
Metropolitan Los Angeles
625 S New Hampshire Ave
Los Angeles CA 90005
213 351-2256

(P-25347)
**YOUNG MENS CHRSTN ASSN
OF LA**
Also Called: Ketchum YMCA
401 S Hope St, Los Angeles (90071-1903)
PHONE..................................213 624-2348
Laurie Goganzer, *Director*
EMP: 100
SALES (corp-wide): 105.9MM **Privately
Held**
SIC: 8641 8322 Youth organizations;
youth center
PA: Young Men's Christian Association Of
Metropolitan Los Angeles
625 S New Hampshire Ave
Los Angeles CA 90005
213 351-2256

(P-25348)
**YOUNG MENS CHRSTN ASSN
OF LA**
Also Called: Young Mens Christian Assn
1605 Garfield Ave, South Pasadena
(91030-4968)
PHONE..................................323 682-2147
Sue Marasco, *Manager*
EMP: 75
SALES (corp-wide): 105.9MM **Privately
Held**
SIC: 8641 7991 8351 7032 Youth organi-
zations; physical fitness facilities; child
day care services; youth camps; individ-
ual & family services
PA: Young Men's Christian Association Of
Metropolitan Los Angeles
625 S New Hampshire Ave
Los Angeles CA 90005
213 351-2256

(P-25349)
**YOUNG MENS CHRSTN ASSN
ORANGE**
2300 University Dr, Newport Beach
(92660-3313)
PHONE..................................949 642-9990
Joy Hyde, *General Mgr*
EMP: 65
SQ FT: 17,976
SALES (corp-wide): 36.3MM **Privately
Held**
WEB: www.ymcaoc.com
SIC: 8641 7991 Youth organizations;
physical fitness facilities
PA: Young Men's Christian Association Of
Orange County
13821 Newport Ave Ste 200
Tustin CA 92780
714 549-9622

(P-25350)
**YOUNG MENS CHRSTN ASSN
ORANGE**
Also Called: YMCA
2000 Youth Way, Fullerton (92835-3812)
PHONE..................................714 879-9622
Clare McKenna, *Director*
EMP: 60
SALES (corp-wide): 36.3MM **Privately
Held**
WEB: www.ymcaoc.com
SIC: 8641 8322 7991 Youth organiza-
tions; individual & family services; athletic
club & gymnasiums; membership
PA: Young Men's Christian Association Of
Orange County
13821 Newport Ave Ste 200
Tustin CA 92780
714 549-9622

(P-25351)
**YOUNG MENS CHRSTN ASSN
ORANGE**
Also Called: Saddle Back Valley YMCA
27341 Trabuco Cir, Mission Viejo
(92692-1939)
PHONE..................................949 859-9622
Mary J Goodrick, *Exec Dir*
EMP: 100

SALES (corp-wide): 36.3MM **Privately
Held**
WEB: www.ymcaoc.com
SIC: 8641 7991 8351 7032 Youth organi-
zations; physical fitness facilities; child
day care services; youth camps; individ-
ual & family services
PA: Young Men's Christian Association Of
Orange County
13821 Newport Ave Ste 200
Tustin CA 92780
714 549-9622

(P-25352)
**YOUNG MENS CHRSTN ASSOC
GNDL**
Also Called: Glendale YMCA Swim School
140 N Louise St, Glendale (91206-4226)
PHONE..................................818 484-8256
Tom Tyler, *CEO*
Catherine Gharapetian, *Athletic Dir*
Ryan Nekota, *Director*
Mineh Petrosian, *Director*
Jodi Reneaud, *Director*
EMP: 86 **EST:** 1924
SQ FT: 15,000
SALES: 3.8MM **Privately Held**
WEB: www.glenymca.org
SIC: 8641 Youth organizations

(P-25353)
**YOUNG MNS CHRSTN ASSN OF
E BAY**
Also Called: Urban Services YMCA
3265 Market St, Oakland (94608-4332)
PHONE..................................510 654-9622
Chris Chatmon, *Exec Dir*
Tenika Derbigny, *Admin Asst*
EMP: 72
SALES (corp-wide): 27.5MM **Privately
Held**
SIC: 8641 7991 8351 7032 Youth organi-
zations; physical fitness facilities; child
day care services; youth camps; individ-
ual & family services
PA: Young Men's Christian Association Of
The East Bay
2330 Broadway
Oakland CA 94612
510 549-4515

(P-25354)
**YOUNG MNS CHRSTN ASSN OF
E BAY**
350 Civic Dr, Pleasant Hill (94523-1921)
PHONE..................................925 687-8900
M Saenz, *Exec Dir*
Michael Saenz, *Director*
EMP: 62
SALES (corp-wide): 27.5MM **Privately
Held**
SIC: 8641 Youth organizations
PA: Young Men's Christian Association Of
The East Bay
2330 Broadway
Oakland CA 94612
510 549-4515

(P-25355)
**YOUNG MNS CHRSTN ASSN OF
E BAY**
Also Called: Berkeley Albany YMCA
1705 Thornwood Dr, Concord
(94521-1915)
PHONE..................................925 609-7971
EMP: 1285
SALES (corp-wide): 27.5MM **Privately
Held**
SIC: 8641 Youth organizations
PA: Young Men's Christian Association Of
The East Bay
2330 Broadway
Oakland CA 94612
510 549-4515

(P-25356)
**YOUNG MNS CHRSTN ASSN OF
E BAY**
Also Called: YMCA of East Bay
2350 Broadway, Oakland (94612-2415)
PHONE..................................510 451-8039
Fran Gallati, *President*
EMP: 852

SALES (corp-wide): 27.5MM **Privately
Held**
WEB: www.ymcaoc.com
SIC: 8641 7991 8351 7032 Youth organi-
zations; physical fitness facilities; child
day care services; youth camps; individ-
ual & family services
PA: Young Men's Christian Association Of
Orange County
13821 Newport Ave Ste 200
Tustin CA 92780
714 549-9622

(P-25357)
**YOUNG MNS CHRSTN ASSN OF
E BAY**
Also Called: Emery Marina
4727 San Pablo Ave, Emeryville
(94608-3035)
PHONE..................................510 601-8674
Henry Der, *Branch Mgr*
EMP: 68
SALES (corp-wide): 27.5MM **Privately
Held**
SIC: 8641 7991 8351 7032 Youth organi-
zations; physical fitness facilities; child
day care services; youth camps; individ-
ual & family services
PA: Young Men's Christian Association Of
The East Bay
2330 Broadway
Oakland CA 94612
510 549-4515

(P-25358)
**YOUNG MNS CHRSTN ASSN OF
E BAY**
Also Called: Y M C A Metro Clinic
2111 Mrtn Lthr King Jr Wa, Berkeley
(94704-1108)
PHONE..................................510 486-8400
Larry Bush, *Manager*
EMP: 63
SALES (corp-wide): 27.5MM **Privately
Held**
SIC: 8641 7991 8351 7032 Youth organi-
zations; physical fitness facilities; child
day care services; youth camps; individ-
ual & family services
PA: Young Men's Christian Association Of
The East Bay
2330 Broadway
Oakland CA 94612
510 549-4515

(P-25359)
**YOUNG MNS CHRSTN ASSN OF
E BAY**
Also Called: YMCA Head Start
2009 10th St, Berkeley (94710-2119)
PHONE..................................510 848-9092
Pamela Shaw, *Director*
Toni Browne-Mccree, *Associate Dir*
EMP: 70
SALES (corp-wide): 27.5MM **Privately
Held**
SIC: 8641 7991 8351 7032 Youth organi-
zations; physical fitness facilities; child
day care services; youth camps; individ-
ual & family services
PA: Young Men's Christian Association Of
The East Bay
2330 Broadway
Oakland CA 94612
510 549-4515

(P-25360)
**YOUNG MNS CHRSTN ASSN OF
E BAY**
Also Called: Downtown Berkeley YMCA
2001 Allston Way, Berkeley (94704-1417)
PHONE..................................510 848-9622
Fran Gallati, *Exec Dir*
Sebastian De Rosa, *Director*
Kristine Nachand, *Director*
EMP: 130
SQ FT: 70,135
SALES (corp-wide): 27.5MM **Privately
Held**
SIC: 8641 7991 8351 7032 Youth organi-
zations; physical fitness facilities; child
day care services; youth camps; individ-
ual & family services

PA: Young Men's Christian Association Of
The East Bay
2330 Broadway
Oakland CA 94612
510 549-4515

(P-25361)
**YOUNG MNS CHRSTN ASSN OF
E BAY**
Also Called: Kids' Club YMCA Oxford School
1130 Oxford St, Berkeley (94707-2624)
PHONE..................................510 526-2146
Stephanie Hochman, *Branch Mgr*
EMP: 63
SALES (corp-wide): 27.5MM **Privately
Held**
SIC: 8641 7991 8351 7032 Youth organi-
zations; physical fitness facilities; child
day care services; youth camps; individ-
ual & family services
PA: Young Men's Christian Association Of
The East Bay
2330 Broadway
Oakland CA 94612
510 549-4515

(P-25362)
**YOUNG MNS CHRSTN ASSN OF
E BAY**
Also Called: Coronado YMCA
263 S 20th St, Richmond (94804-2709)
PHONE..................................510 412-5647
Don Lau, *Branch Mgr*
EMP: 325
SQ FT: 16,338
SALES (corp-wide): 27.5MM **Privately
Held**
SIC: 8641 Youth organizations; recreation
association
PA: Young Men's Christian Association Of
The East Bay
2330 Broadway
Oakland CA 94612
510 549-4515

(P-25363)
**YOUNG MNS CHRSTN ASSN OF
E BAY**
Also Called: Hilltop Family YMCA
4300 Lakeside Dr, Richmond (94806-5717)
PHONE..................................510 222-9622
Linda Cook, *Branch Mgr*
EMP: 125
SALES (corp-wide): 27.5MM **Privately
Held**
SIC: 8641 Youth organizations; recreation
association
PA: Young Men's Christian Association Of
The East Bay
2330 Broadway
Oakland CA 94612
510 549-4515

(P-25364)
**YOUNG MNS CHRSTN ASSN OF
E BAY**
2001 Allston Way, Berkeley (94704-1417)
PHONE..................................510 848-6800
Peter Gerharz, *Branch Mgr*
EMP: 62
SALES (corp-wide): 27.5MM **Privately
Held**
SIC: 8641 7991 8351 7032 Youth organi-
zations; physical fitness facilities; child
day care services; youth camps; individ-
ual & family services
PA: Young Men's Christian Association Of
The East Bay
2330 Broadway
Oakland CA 94612
510 549-4515

(P-25365)
**YOUNG MNS CHRSTN ASSN OF
E BAY**
1422 San Pablo Ave, Berkeley
(94702-1024)
PHONE..................................510 559-2090
Larry Bush, *Branch Mgr*
EMP: 68

SALES (corp-wide): 27.5MM **Privately Held**
SIC: **8641** 8322 8351 Youth organizations; individual & family services; head start center, except in conjunction with school
PA: Young Men's Christian Association Of The East Bay
2330 Broadway
Oakland CA 94612
510 549-4515

(P-25366)
YOUNG WOMENS CHRISTIAN ASSOC
2501 W Vernon Ave, Los Angeles (90008-3927)
PHONE.................................323 295-4280
Gloria Rice, *Accounting Mgr*
EMP: 182
SALES (corp-wide): 29.3MM **Privately Held**
SIC: **8641** Youth organizations
PA: Young Women's Christian Association Of Greater Los Angeles, California
1020 S Olive St Fl 7
Los Angeles CA 90015
213 365-2991

(P-25367)
YOUNG WOMENS CHRISTIAN ASSOCI
Also Called: YWCA SILICON VALLEY
375 S 3rd St, San Jose (95112-3649)
PHONE.................................408 295-4011
Keri Procunier McLain, *President*
Tanis Crosby, *CEO*
Lorraine Michelle, *Officer*
Sue Barnes, *Principal*
Adriana Caldera, *Principal*
EMP: 83
SALES: 8.2MM **Privately Held**
WEB: www.ywca-sv.org
SIC: **8641** 8322 Community membership club; individual & family services

(P-25368)
YUEN SOO BENEVOLENT ASSN
119 Chung Wah Ln, Stockton (95202-3221)
PHONE.................................209 464-3048
Maw L Louie, *President*
Kim Fong, *Vice Pres*
EMP: 250
SALES: 32.1K **Privately Held**
SIC: **8641** Dwelling-related associations

8651 Political Organizations

(P-25369)
CALIFRNIA LEAG CNSRVTION VTERS (PA)
350 Frank H Ogawa Plz # 1100, Oakland (94612-2006)
PHONE.................................510 271-0900
Sarah Rose, *Director*
EMP: 55 EST: 1971
SQ FT: 3,500
SALES: 1.5MM **Privately Held**
SIC: **8651** Political organizations

(P-25370)
COUNTY OF ORANGE
Also Called: Registrar of Voters
1300 S Grand Ave Ste C, Santa Ana (92705-4434)
P.O. Box 11298 (92711-1298)
PHONE.................................714 567-7500
Neal Kelly, *Director*
Jim Lehmann, *Executive*
EMP: 50 **Privately Held**
SIC: **8651** 9199 Political campaign organization; general government administration;
PA: County Of Orange
333 W Santa Ana Blvd 3f
Santa Ana CA 92701
714 834-6200

(P-25371)
LEAGUE OF WMEN VOTERS WHITTIER
10011 Melgar Dr, Whittier (90603-1458)
PHONE.................................562 947-5818
Margo Reeg, *Treasurer*
EMP: 50
SALES (est): 1.3MM **Privately Held**
SIC: **8651** Political organizations

(P-25372)
PEACE ACTION WEST (PA)
2201 Broadway Ste 321, Oakland (94612-3044)
PHONE.................................510 830-3600
Eric See, *Finance Dir*
Jonathan Rainwater, *Exec Dir*
Peter Deccy, *Director*
Jonathan Ritter, *Director*
Joe Cicero, *Manager*
EMP: 50
SQ FT: 1,600
SALES: 999.6K **Privately Held**
SIC: **8651** Political action committee

8699 Membership Organizations, NEC

(P-25373)
AAUW ACTION FUND INC
P.O. Box 1239 (94401-0816)
PHONE.................................650 574-9160
Lowla Ghompson, *President*
EMP: 100
SALES (corp-wide): 226.2K **Privately Held**
SIC: **8699** Personal interest organization
PA: Aauw Action Fund, Inc.
1310 L St Nw Ste 1000
Washington DC 20005
202 785-7700

(P-25374)
AFFINITY DEVELOPMENT GROUP INC
Also Called: A D G
10251 Vista Sorrento Pkwy # 300, San Diego (92121-3774)
PHONE.................................858 643-9324
Jeff Skeen, *President*
Gary Drean, *COO*
Greg Siebenthal, *CFO*
Eric Campbell, *Officer*
Mark Stcyr, *Vice Pres*
EMP: 120
SQ FT: 46,000
SALES (est): 13.1MM **Privately Held**
WEB: www.affinitydev.com
SIC: **8699** Automobile owners' association

(P-25375)
AGUA CLNTE BAND CHILLA INDIANS (PA)
5401 Dinah Shore Dr, Palm Springs (92264-5970)
PHONE.................................760 699-6800
Jeff L Grubbe, *Chairman*
Victoria Harvey, *COO*
Vincent Gonzales III, *Corp Secy*
Larry N Olinger, *Principal*
Kari Smith, *Exec Dir*
EMP: 149
SALES (est): 200.2MM **Privately Held**
SIC: **8699** 6552 7999 Reading rooms & other cultural organizations; subdividers & developers; tour & guide services

(P-25376)
ALL SOUTH BAY CENTRAL OFFICE
1411 Marcelina Ave, Torrance (90501-3210)
PHONE.................................310 618-1180
Liza Ferguson, *Manager*
EMP: 80
SALES: 85K **Privately Held**
WEB: www.southbayaa.org
SIC: **8699** Charitable organization

(P-25377)
ALLIANCE FC
Also Called: INLAND EMPIRE SURF SOCCER CLUB
3496 Little League Dr, San Bernardino (92407)
P.O. Box 90211 (92427-1211)
PHONE.................................909 784-0005
Bryan Young, *President*
Taisha Wick, *Treasurer*
Brian Jensen, *Vice Pres*
Rodney Nelson, *Vice Pres*
Donna Hurst, *Admin Sec*
EMP: 50
SALES: 1.2MM **Privately Held**
SIC: **8699** Personal interest organization

(P-25378)
ALLIANCE MEMBER SERVICES INC
333 Front St Ste 200, Santa Cruz (95060-4533)
P.O. Box 8507 (95061-8507)
PHONE.................................831 459-0980
Pamela Davis, *President*
EMP: 63
SQ FT: 25,000
SALES: 12.3MM **Privately Held**
SIC: **8699** Charitable organization

(P-25379)
AMERICAN AUTOMOBILE ASSCTN
Also Called: AAA
1982 Pleasant Valley Ave A, Oakland (94611-4250)
P.O. Box 23392 (94623-0392)
PHONE.................................510 350-2042
Annette Kwan, *Branch Mgr*
EMP: 191
SALES (corp-wide): 907.9MM **Privately Held**
SIC: **8699** 6331 6311 Automobile owners' association; automobile insurance; life insurance carriers
PA: American Automobile Association Of Northern California, Nevada & Utah
1900 Powell St Ste 1200
Emeryville CA 94608
800 922-8228

(P-25380)
AMERICAN AUTOMOBILE ASSCTN
Also Called: Csaa Travel Agency
1277 Treat Blvd Ste 1000, Walnut Creek (94597-8863)
PHONE.................................510 596-3669
EMP: 400
SALES (corp-wide): 907.9MM **Privately Held**
SIC: **8699** Automobile owners' association
PA: American Automobile Association Of Northern California, Nevada & Utah
1900 Powell St Ste 1200
Emeryville CA 94608
800 922-8228

(P-25381)
AMERICAN AUTOMOBILE ASSCTN
Also Called: Csaa Travel Agency
3116 W March Ln Ste 100, Stockton (95219-2374)
PHONE.................................209 952-4100
Jim Owens, *Manager*
EMP: 50
SALES (corp-wide): 907.9MM **Privately Held**
WEB: www.californiastateautomobileassociation.c
SIC: **8699** Automobile owners' association
PA: American Automobile Association Of Northern California, Nevada & Utah
1900 Powell St Ste 1200
Emeryville CA 94608
800 922-8228

(P-25382)
ASSOCIATED STUDENTS SAN DIEGO (PA)
Also Called: MISSION BAY AQUATIC CENTER
5500 Campanile Dr, San Diego (92182-0001)
PHONE.................................619 594-0234
Christina Brown, *Exec Dir*
Jamie Ballard, *Relations*
Ashley Quintero, *Relations*
EMP: 1120
SALES: 27.9MM **Privately Held**
SIC: **8699** Automobile owners' association

(P-25383)
AUTOMOBILE CLUB SOUTHERN CAL
Also Called: AAA
15503 Ventura Blvd # 150, Encino (91436-3115)
PHONE.................................818 997-6230
Jim Okun, *Branch Mgr*
EMP: 50
SALES (corp-wide): 7.2B **Privately Held**
SIC: **8699** 4724 6331 Automobile owners' association; travel agencies; fire, marine & casualty insurance
PA: Automobile Club Of Southern California
2601 S Figueroa St
Los Angeles CA 90007
213 741-3686

(P-25384)
AUTOMOBILE CLUB SOUTHERN CAL
Also Called: AAA
23001 Hawthorne Blvd, Torrance (90505-3702)
P.O. Box 4298 (90510-4298)
PHONE.................................310 325-3111
Bud Hudson, *Branch Mgr*
EMP: 60
SQ FT: 34,720
SALES (corp-wide): 7.2B **Privately Held**
SIC: **8699** Automobile owners' association
PA: Automobile Club Of Southern California
2601 S Figueroa St
Los Angeles CA 90007
213 741-3686

(P-25385)
AUTOMOBILE CLUB SOUTHERN CAL
Also Called: AAA
1501 S Victoria Ave, Ventura (93003-6539)
P.O. Box 3618 (93006-3618)
PHONE.................................805 644-7171
Sigmund Grant, *Manager*
EMP: 70
SALES (corp-wide): 7.2B **Privately Held**
SIC: **8699** 4724 6331 Automobile owners' association; travel agencies; fire, marine & casualty insurance
PA: Automobile Club Of Southern California
2601 S Figueroa St
Los Angeles CA 90007
213 741-3686

(P-25386)
AUTOMOBILE CLUB SOUTHERN CAL
Also Called: AAA
1301s S Grand Ave, Glendora (91740-5040)
PHONE.................................626 963-8531
Connie Stelzer, *Manager*
EMP: 50
SQ FT: 8,261
SALES (corp-wide): 7.2B **Privately Held**
SIC: **8699** Automobile owners' association
PA: Automobile Club Of Southern California
2601 S Figueroa St
Los Angeles CA 90007
213 741-3686

(P-25387)
AUTOMOBILE CLUB SOUTHERN CAL
Also Called: AAA
1500 Commercial Way, Bakersfield (93309-0625)
PHONE.................................661 327-4661
Jeff Goldsmith, *Branch Mgr*

Chere Smith, *Manager*
EMP: 50
SALES (corp-wide): 7.2B **Privately Held**
SIC: 8699 Automobile owners' association
PA: Automobile Club Of Southern California
2601 S Figueroa St
Los Angeles CA 90007
213 741-3686

(P-25388)
AUTOMOBILE CLUB SOUTHERN CAL
Also Called: AAA
9440 Reseda Blvd, Northridge
(91324-6014)
PHONE...............................818 993-1616
Freedom Homes, *Branch Mgr*
EMP: 54
SQ FT: 15,624
SALES (corp-wide): 7.2B **Privately Held**
SIC: 8699 Automobile owners' association
PA: Automobile Club Of Southern California
2601 S Figueroa St
Los Angeles CA 90007
213 741-3686

(P-25389)
AUTOMOBILE CLUB SOUTHERN CAL
Also Called: AAA
22708 Victory Blvd, Woodland Hills
(91367-1697)
PHONE...............................818 883-2660
Glenn Lumley, *Branch Mgr*
EMP: 50
SQ FT: 15,624
SALES (corp-wide): 7.2B **Privately Held**
SIC: 8699 4724 6331 Automobile owners'
association; travel agencies; fire, marine
& casualty insurance
PA: Automobile Club Of Southern California
2601 S Figueroa St
Los Angeles CA 90007
213 741-3686

(P-25390)
AUTOMOBILE CLUB SOUTHERN CAL
3700 Central Ave, Riverside (92506-2421)
P.O. Box 2217 (92516-2217)
PHONE...............................951 684-4250
Richard Meyer, *Branch Mgr*
Anwar Othman, *Sr Corp Ofcr*
EMP: 80
SALES (corp-wide): 7.2B **Privately Held**
SIC: 8699 Automobile owners' association
PA: Automobile Club Of Southern California
2601 S Figueroa St
Los Angeles CA 90007
213 741-3686

(P-25391)
AUTOMOBILE CLUB SOUTHERN CAL
Also Called: A A A Automobile Club So Cal
25181 Paseo De Alicia, Laguna Hills
(92653-4614)
PHONE...............................949 951-1400
Cindy Raymond, *Manager*
EMP: 50
SQ FT: 13,948
SALES (corp-wide): 7.2B **Privately Held**
SIC: 8699 Automobile owners' association
PA: Automobile Club Of Southern California
2601 S Figueroa St
Los Angeles CA 90007
213 741-3686

(P-25392)
AUTOMOBILE CLUB SOUTHERN CAL
2488 Foothill Blvd Ste A, La Verne
(91750-3062)
PHONE...............................909 392-1444
Bob Barron, *Manager*
EMP: 108
SALES (corp-wide): 7.2B **Privately Held**
SIC: 8699 Automobile owners' association
PA: Automobile Club Of Southern California
2601 S Figueroa St
Los Angeles CA 90007
213 741-3686

(P-25393)
AUTOMOBILE CLUB SOUTHERN CAL
19201 Bear Valley Rd C, Apple Valley
(92308-2704)
PHONE...............................760 247-4110
EMP: 108
SALES (corp-wide): 7.2B **Privately Held**
SIC: 8699 Automobile owners' association
PA: Automobile Club Of Southern California
2601 S Figueroa St
Los Angeles CA 90007
213 741-3686

(P-25394)
AUTOMOBILE CLUB SOUTHERN CAL
Also Called: AAA
8765 Fletcher Pkwy, La Mesa
(91942-3200)
PHONE...............................619 464-7001
Marria Porter, *Manager*
Ruth Myers, *Human Resources*
EMP: 75
SQ FT: 42,441
SALES (corp-wide): 7.2B **Privately Held**
SIC: 8699 Automobile owners' association
PA: Automobile Club Of Southern California
2601 S Figueroa St
Los Angeles CA 90007
213 741-3686

(P-25395)
AUTOMOTIVE SERVICE COUNCIL
10813 Airport Dr, El Cajon (92020-1202)
PHONE...............................800 810-4272
Steve Vanlandingham, *President*
EMP: 90
SALES: 42.4K **Privately Held**
SIC: 8699 Automobile owners' association

(P-25396)
BAYVIEW HUNTERS POINT FOUNDATI (PA)
Also Called: BVHP
150 Executive Park Blvd, San Francisco
(94134-3303)
PHONE...............................415 468-5100
Jacob K Moody, *Exec Dir*
Lillian Shine, *Deputy Dir*
EMP: 81
SQ FT: 3,700
SALES: 8.1MM **Privately Held**
SIC: 8699 8641 Animal humane society;
youth organizations

(P-25397)
BEAD SOCIETY
Also Called: Bead Society , The
1454 Valley High Ave, Thousand Oaks
(91362-1906)
P.O. Box 1456, Culver City (90232-1456)
PHONE...............................805 495-2550
Adel Boehm-Mabe, *President*
Adel B Mabe, *President*
Joan Eppen, *CFO*
EMP: 250
SALES: 36.9K **Privately Held**
SIC: 8699 Personal interest organization

(P-25398)
BERKELEY CLINIC AUXUILLARY
Also Called: TURNABOUT SHOP
10052 San Pablo Ave, El Cerrito
(94530-3927)
PHONE...............................510 525-7844
Barbara Coleman, *President*
Vl Galardo, *President*
Peggy Eanaman, *Chairman*
Kay Jevons, *Chairman*
Dorothy Zwoyer, *Treasurer*
EMP: 60
SQ FT: 1,800
SALES: 84.4K **Privately Held**
SIC: 8699 5932 Charitable organization;
used merchandise stores

(P-25399)
BEST FRIENDS ANIMAL SOCIETY
15321 Brand Blvd, Mission Hills
(91345-1438)
PHONE...............................818 643-3989

Marc Peralta, *Manager*
EMP: 360
SALES (corp-wide): 87.1MM **Privately Held**
SIC: 8699 Animal humane society
PA: Best Friends Animal Society
5001 Angel Canyon Rd
Kanab UT 84741
435 644-2001

(P-25400)
BRIARPATCH COOP NEV CNTY INC
Also Called: Briarpatch Coop-Community Mkt
290 Sierra College Dr A, Grass Valley
(95945-5762)
PHONE...............................530 272-5333
Christopher Maher, *CEO*
EMP: 180 EST: 1976
SALES (est): 14.5MM **Privately Held**
WEB: www.briarpatchcoop.com
SIC: 8699 Food co-operative

(P-25401)
BUTTE COUNTY OFFICE EDUCATION
1859 Bird St, Oroville (95965-4854)
PHONE...............................530 532-5786
Don McNelis, *Superintendent*
EMP: 400
SALES (corp-wide): 28.4MM **Privately Held**
SIC: 8699 Charitable organization
PA: Butte County Office Of Education
1859 Bird St
Oroville CA 95965
530 532-5650

(P-25402)
CAL POLY POMONA FOUNDATION INC (PA)
3801 W Temple Ave Bldg 55, Pomona
(91768-2557)
PHONE...............................909 869-2950
J Michael Ortiz, *Chairman*
Sarah Lorenzen, *Ch of Bd*
David Karacozoff, *CEO*
Jonna Lewis, *CFO*
Dr Whinney Dong, *Corp Secy*
EMP: 2200
SQ FT: 27,000
SALES (est): 76.1MM **Privately Held**
WEB: www.kelloggwest.org
SIC: 8699 Charitable organization

(P-25403)
CALIF STAT UNIV FRES FOUN
5370 N Chestnut Ave, Fresno (93725)
PHONE...............................559 278-0850
Linda Alatorre, *Branch Mgr*
Lynn Hemink, *Finance*
David Doleoske, *Director*
EMP: 229
SALES (corp-wide): 76.9MM **Privately Held**
WEB: www.auxiliary.com
SIC: 8699 Amateur sports promotion
PA: California State University, Fresno
Foundation
4910 N Chestnut Ave
Fresno CA 93726
559 278-0850

(P-25404)
CALIFRNIA YUTH SOCCER ASSN INC
1040 Serpentine Ln # 206, Pleasanton
(94566-4754)
PHONE...............................925 426-5437
John Murphy, *Chairman*
Melinda Rainville, *Vice Chairman*
Ilona Montoya, *CFO*
Dino Reali, *Director*
EMP: 87
SALES: 4.5MM **Privately Held**
WEB: www.cysanorth.org
SIC: 8699 Personal interest organization

(P-25405)
CARE 2
203 Redwood Shores Pkwy # 230, Red-
wood City (94065-6106)
PHONE...............................650 622-0860
Randy Paynter, *Principal*
EMP: 56

SALES (est): 1.1MM **Privately Held**
SIC: 8699 Charitable organization

(P-25406)
CASAS - COMPREHENSIVE
5151 Murphy Canyon Rd # 220, San Diego
(92123-4440)
PHONE...............................858 292-2900
Robert S Muir, *Director*
Jennifer Suarez, *Social Dir*
Dick Stiles, *Exec Dir*
Anthony Castle, *Software Dev*
Virginia Posey, *Research*
EMP: 55
SALES: 5.7MM **Privately Held**
SIC: 8699 Charitable organization

(P-25407)
CATHEDRAL CENTER OF ST PAUL
Also Called: Cathedral Bookstore
840 Echo Park Ave, Los Angeles
(90026-4209)
P.O. Box 512164 (90051-0164)
PHONE...............................213 482-2040
Bishop Jon Bruno,
Peter Mann, *Treasurer*
Janet Wild, *Admin Sec*
EMP: 75 EST: 1898
SALES (est): 3.5MM **Privately Held**
WEB: www.cathedralbookstore.com
SIC: 8699 5942 Charitable organization;
books, religious

(P-25408)
CCNA VONS ATHLETES FOR LIFE
Also Called: AFL
10670 6th St Ste 113, Rancho Cucamonga
(91730-5912)
PHONE...............................805 453-2499
Greg Bell, *President*
EMP: 60
SALES (est): 235.4K **Privately Held**
SIC: 8699 7389 Athletic organizations;
fund raising organizations

(P-25409)
CITY IMPACT
230 Jones St Fl 1, San Francisco
(94102-2619)
PHONE...............................415 292-1770
Christian Huang, *Exec Dir*
Lisa Dieker, *Manager*
EMP: 50
SALES (est): 203.6K **Privately Held**
SIC: 8699 Charitable organization

(P-25410)
CITY OF BALDWIN PARK
14403 Pacific Ave, Baldwin Park
(91706-4297)
PHONE...............................626 960-1955
Mark Dunning Harvey, *Branch Mgr*
Darryl Kosaka, *Manager*
Elizabeth Pereida, *Supervisor*
EMP: 96 **Privately Held**
SIC: 8699 Athletic organizations
PA: City Of Baldwin Park
14403 Pacific Ave
Baldwin Park CA 91706
626 960-1955

(P-25411)
CITY OF LOS ANGELES
Also Called: Department of Cultural Affairs
201 N Figueroa St # 1400, Los Angeles
(90012-2623)
PHONE...............................213 202-5500
Karen Constine, *General Mgr*
Helen Santella, *Controller*
EMP: 64 **Privately Held**
WEB: www.lacity.org
SIC: 8699 9512 Literary, film or cultural
club; recreational program administration,
government
PA: City Of Los Angeles
200 N Spring St Ste 303
Los Angeles CA 90012
213 978-0600

(P-25412)
COUNTY OF MONTEREY
Also Called: Monterey County Sheriffs Dept
1414 Natividad Rd, Salinas (93906-3102)
PHONE...............................831 755-3700

Mike Kanalakis, *Sheriff*
EMP: 474 Privately Held
WEB: www.montereycountyfarmbureau.org
SIC: 8699 Personal interest organization
PA: County Of Monterey
168 W Alisal St Fl 2
Salinas CA 93901
831 755-5040

(P-25413)
COUNTY OF RIVERSIDE DEPARTMENT (PA)
4065 County Circle Dr, Riverside (92503-3410)
P.O. Box 7600 (92513-7600)
PHONE..................................951 358-5000
Susan Harrington, *Director*
Socorro Manzanilla, *Administration*
EMP: 99
SALES (est): 3.6MM Privately Held
WEB: www.rivcoph.org
SIC: 8699 Charitable organization

(P-25414)
CROCKER ART MUSEUM ASSOCIATION
Also Called: Crocker Art Museum
216 O St, Sacramento (95814-5324)
PHONE..................................916 808-7000
Lial Jones, *CEO*
EMP: 66 EST: 1875
SQ FT: 150,000
SALES: 7MM Privately Held
WEB: www.crockerartmuseum.org
SIC: 8699 5942 8412 Art council; book stores; museum

(P-25415)
DEATH VALLEY 49ERS INC
1442 Carson Ave, Clovis (93611-6906)
P.O. Box 997, Kernville (93238-0997)
PHONE..................................559 297-5691
Bill Pool, *President*
Edtytat Pool, *Treasurer*
Richard Gering, *Vice Pres*
Marv Jensen, *Vice Pres*
EMP: 80 EST: 1949
SALES: 78.9K Privately Held
WEB: www.deathvalley49ers.org
SIC: 8699 Charitable organization

(P-25416)
DELTA RESCUE INC
P.O. Box 9, Glendale (91209-0009)
PHONE..................................661 269-4010
Leo Grillo, *President*
EMP: 60
SALES (est): 1MM Privately Held
SIC: 8699 Animal humane society

(P-25417)
DFA OF CALIFORNIA
6100 Wilson Landing Rd, Chico (95973-8902)
PHONE..................................530 345-5077
Marie Cowan, *Branch Mgr*
EMP: 166
SALES (corp-wide): 9.7MM Privately Held
SIC: 8699 Athletic organizations
PA: Dfa Of California
710 Striker Ave
Sacramento CA 95834
916 561-5900

(P-25418)
EARTH ISLAND INSTITUTE INC
2150 Allston Way Ste 460, Berkeley (94704-1375)
PHONE..................................510 859-9100
Michael Mitrani, *CEO*
John A Knox, *Principal*
David Phillips, *Exec Dir*
Anisha Desai, *Director*
Mona Shomali, *Director*
EMP: 76
SQ FT: 4,400
SALES: 11.2MM Privately Held
WEB: www.earthisland.org
SIC: 8699 8748 8641 Charitable organization; business consulting; environmental protection organization

(P-25419)
EMPLOYMENT TRAINING ACADEMY
4045 Coronado Ave, Stockton (95204-2311)
PHONE..................................209 475-1529
Stacie J Rodriguez, *Administration*
EMP: 50
SALES (est): 232.2K Privately Held
SIC: 8699 Charitable organization

(P-25420)
EXCEL ACADEMY
1200 Quail St Ste 175, Newport Beach (92660-2707)
PHONE..................................949 387-7822
Heidi Gasca, *Director*
EMP: 90
SALES (est): 202.2K Privately Held
SIC: 8699 Charitable organization

(P-25421)
FAMILY SERVICES
807 W Oak Ave, Visalia (93291-6033)
PHONE..................................559 741-7310
Kaitey Meader, *Director*
Susan Munter, *Deputy Dir*
EMP: 50
SALES (est): 1.9MM Privately Held
SIC: 8699 Charitable organization

(P-25422)
FARMS OF AMADOR
12200b Airport Rd, Jackson (95642-9527)
PHONE..................................209 257-0112
Sean Kriletich, *Principal*
EMP: 99
SALES (est): 2.6MM Privately Held
SIC: 8699 Membership organizations

(P-25423)
FREMONT CANDLE LIGHTERS
Also Called: CANDLE LIGHTERS THE
39261 Fremont Hub, Fremont (94538)
P.O. Box 174 (94537-0174)
PHONE..................................510 796-0595
Claire Douglas, *President*
EMP: 110
SALES: 68.2K Privately Held
SIC: 8699 Charitable organization

(P-25424)
GOODWILL INDS SAN DIEGO CNTY
3841 Plaza Dr Ste 902, Oceanside (92056-4649)
PHONE..................................760 806-7670
Tim Hurley, *Manager*
EMP: 268
SALES (corp-wide): 55.4MM Privately Held
SIC: 8699 8331 5932 Charitable organization; vocational rehabilitation agency; used merchandise stores
PA: Goodwill Industries Of San Diego County
3663 Rosecrans St
San Diego CA 92110
619 225-2200

(P-25425)
GOODWILL INDUSTRIES OF SACRAME
8031 Watt Ave, Sacramento (95843-9793)
PHONE..................................916 331-0237
EMP: 50
SALES (corp-wide): 67.9MM Privately Held
SIC: 8699 8331 5932 Charitable organization; vocational rehabilitation agency; used merchandise stores
PA: Goodwill Industries Of Sacramento Valley & Northern Nevada, Inc.
8001 Folsom Blvd
Sacramento CA 95826
916 395-9000

(P-25426)
HALO
4916 Chism Way, Antioch (94531-8148)
P.O. Box 2011 (94531-2011)
PHONE..................................925 473-4642
Karen Kops, *President*
Linda Mills, *Admin Sec*
EMP: 50

SALES (est): 624.8K Privately Held
SIC: 8699 Animal humane society

(P-25427)
HELEN WOODWARD ANIMAL CENTER (PA)
6461 El Apajo, Rancho Santa Fe (92067)
PHONE..................................858 756-4117
Michael A Arms, *President*
Laurie Doyle, *Volunteer Dir*
Bryce Rhoades, *Ch of Bd*
Renee Resko, *Vice Pres*
Marcie Grube, *Admin Asst*
EMP: 100
SQ FT: 45,000
SALES: 12.2MM Privately Held
WEB: www.sddac.com
SIC: 8699 Animal humane society

(P-25428)
HEWLETT WLLIAM FLORA FNDATION
Also Called: HEWLETT FOUNDATION
2121 Sand Hill Rd, Menlo Park (94025-6909)
PHONE..................................650 234-4500
Paul Brest, *President*
Charlene Cooper, *CFO*
Norma Altshuler, *Officer*
Amy Arbreton, *Officer*
Joseph Asunka, *Officer*
EMP: 60
SALES: 317.4MM Privately Held
SIC: 8699 Charitable organization

(P-25429)
HOPLAND BAND POMO INDIANS INC (PA)
3000 Shanel Rd, Hopland (95449-9809)
PHONE..................................707 472-2100
Romen Carrillo, *President*
Rachel Whetstone, *CFO*
EMP: 84
SQ FT: 3,800
SALES (est): 17.8MM Privately Held
WEB: www.hoplandtribe.com
SIC: 8699 Personal interest organization

(P-25430)
HUMANE SOCIETY SILICON VALLEY
Also Called: PET POURRI
901 Ames Ave, Milpitas (95035-6326)
PHONE..................................408 262-2133
Carol Novello, *CEO*
Christine B Arnold, *Exec Dir*
EMP: 80
SQ FT: 3,000
SALES: 13.4MM Privately Held
SIC: 8699 Animal humane society

(P-25431)
HUMANE SOCIETY SONOMA COUNTY (PA)
Also Called: HUMANE SOCIETY AND S P C A OF
5345 Highway 12, Santa Rosa (95407-6401)
PHONE..................................707 542-0882
W Welling, *Exec Dir*
Mark Penn, *President*
Evelyn Mitchell, *Treasurer*
Wendy Welling, *Exec Dir*
Ronni Berg, *Admin Sec*
EMP: 60 EST: 1931
SQ FT: 1,242
SALES: 5MM Privately Held
WEB: www.hsscpets.org
SIC: 8699 Animal humane society

(P-25432)
INLAND EMPIRE CHAPTER-ASSN OF
4200 Concours Ste 360, Ontario (91764-4982)
PHONE..................................512 478-9000
EMP: 82
SALES: 4.1K Privately Held
SIC: 8699

(P-25433)
INLAND VALLEY BUSINESS AND COM
Also Called: IVBCF
40335 Winchester Rd, Temecula (92591-5500)
PHONE..................................951 378-5316
Steve Matley, *President*
Steve Matly, *President*
Dena Lansford, *Treasurer*
Wendy Johnson, *Bd of Directors*
Hans R Monod De Froideville, *Vice Pres*
EMP: 80
SALES: 31.3K Privately Held
SIC: 8699 Charitable organization

(P-25434)
IRVINE COMPANY LLC
Also Called: Oak Creek Golf Club
1 Golf Club Dr, Irvine (92618-5210)
PHONE..................................949 653-5300
John McCook, *Manager*
John Mc Cook, *Director*
Lorrie De Bellis, *Manager*
EMP: 70
SALES (corp-wide): 2.2B Privately Held
WEB: www.irvineco.com
SIC: 8699 Professional golf association
PA: The Irvine Company Llc
550 Newport Center Dr # 160
Newport Beach CA 92660
949 720-2000

(P-25435)
KNIGHTS OF COLUMBUS
871 Founders Ln, Milpitas (95035-3345)
PHONE..................................408 262-6609
Wm Poehlman Jr, *Owner*
EMP: 80
SALES (est): 2.6MM Privately Held
SIC: 8699 Charitable organization

(P-25436)
LAUGH FACTORY INC
151 S Pine Ave, Long Beach (90802-4536)
PHONE..................................562 495-2844
Ivy Schember, *General Mgr*
EMP: 97
SALES (corp-wide): 10MM Privately Held
SIC: 8699 5813 Athletic organizations; night clubs
PA: Laugh Factory, Inc.
8001 W Sunset Blvd
Los Angeles CA 90046
323 848-2800

(P-25437)
LAVA BEDS NATIONAL MONUMENTS
Also Called: U S GOVERNMENT
1 Indian Wells Hqtrs, Tulelake (96134-8216)
P.O. Box 1240 (96134-1240)
PHONE..................................530 667-2282
Fax: 530 667-3299
EMP: 50 EST: 1963
SALES: 55.2K Publicly Held
SIC: 8699 8412
PA: Government Of The United States
1600 Pennsylvania Ave Nw
Washington DC 20500
202 456-1414

(P-25438)
LAWRENCE LIVERMORE NA
7000 East Ave, Livermore (94550-9698)
P.O. Box 808 (94551-0808)
PHONE..................................925 422-1100
Renee Bryer, *CEO*
Mila Shapovalov, *Admin Asst*
Fred Fritsch, *Comp Scientist*
Charles Tong,
Annie Kersting, *Director*
EMP: 5000
SALES (est): 52.6MM Privately Held
SIC: 8699 Charitable organization

(P-25439)
LINCOLN CHILD CENTER
1266 14th St, Oakland (94607-2205)
PHONE..................................510 531-3111
C Stoner-Mertz, *President*
Christine Stoner-Mertz, *President*
EMP: 200

(PA)=Parent Co (HQ)=Headquarters (DH)=Div Headquarters
✪ = New Business established in last 2 years

2019 Directory of California
Wholesalers and Services Companies

1077

P R O D U C T S & S V C S

SQ FT: 300
SALES: 19.8MM **Privately Held**
SIC: **8699** Charitable organization

(P-25440)
LOS ANGELES MEM COLISEUM COMM
Also Called: La Sports Arena
3911 S Figueroa St, Los Angeles (90037-1207)
PHONE..................213 747-7111
Don Knabe, *President*
Gregory Hellmold, *CFO*
John Sandbrook, *Administration*
EMP: 500
SQ FT: 2,000
SALES (est): 13.4MM **Privately Held**
SIC: **8699** Athletic organizations

(P-25441)
LOS ANGELES POLICE COMMAND
100 W 1st St, Los Angeles (90012-4112)
P.O. Box 53188 (90053-0188)
PHONE..................877 275-5273
Deborah A Gonzales, *Principal*
EMP: 296
SALES: 258K **Privately Held**
SIC: **8699** Charitable organization

(P-25442)
MARIN HUMANE SOCIETY
171 Bel Marin Keys Blvd, Novato (94949-6183)
PHONE..................415 883-4621
Suzanne Golt, *Exec Dir*
Marilyn Castellblanch, *CFO*
EMP: 91
SQ FT: 42,500
SALES: 8.4MM **Privately Held**
WEB: www.marinhumanesociety.com
SIC: **8699** Animal humane society

(P-25443)
MENLO PARK-ATHERTON EDUCATION (PA)
181 Encinal Ave, Atherton (94027-3102)
P.O. Box 584, Menlo Park (94026-0584)
PHONE..................650 325-0100
Ghysels Maurice, *Superintendent*
EMP: 59
SALES: 4.3MM **Privately Held**
SIC: **8699** Charitable organization

(P-25444)
MISSION HOSPICE & HM CARE INC (PA)
1670 S Amphlett Blvd # 300, San Mateo (94402-2534)
PHONE..................650 554-1000
Dwight Wilson, *Exec Dir*
Alex Ignacio, *Officer*
Carol Gray, *Branch Mgr*
Ashton Fulwood, *Technology*
Irene Nasol, *Finance*
EMP: 160
SALES: 21.3MM **Privately Held**
WEB: www.missionhospice.org
SIC: **8699** Charitable organization

(P-25445)
NATIONAL COUNCIL NEGRO WOMEN
Also Called: Golden Gate Section
784 Cole St, San Francisco (94117-3912)
PHONE..................415 564-4153
Catherine J Bradford, *President*
EMP: 99
SALES: 25K **Privately Held**
WEB: www.co.rappahannock.comm-rev.state.va.us
SIC: **8699** Membership organizations

(P-25446)
NATUREBRIDGE
1033 Fort Cronkhite, Sausalito (94965-2609)
PHONE..................415 332-5771
EMP: 65 **Privately Held**
SIC: **8699** Charitable organization
PA: Naturebridge
28 Geary St Ste 650
San Francisco CA 94108

(P-25447)
ONEOC (PA)
Also Called: VOLUNTEER CENTER ORANGE COUNTY
1901 E 4th St Ste 100, Santa Ana (92705-3918)
PHONE..................714 953-5757
Daniel McQuaid, *President*
Ursula Walsh, *Volunteer Dir*
Tim Strauch, *COO*
Darlene Walencewicz, *Executive Asst*
Marci Tillison, *Financial Analy*
EMP: 79 EST: 1958
SQ FT: 7,500
SALES: 11.5MM **Privately Held**
WEB: www.volunteercenter.org
SIC: **8699** 8399 Charitable organization; community development groups

(P-25448)
ORCUTT LIONS CLUB
126 S Broadway St, Orcutt (93455-4607)
PHONE..................805 937-0158
Tom Hughes, *Chairman*
EMP: 56
SQ FT: 2,880
SALES (est): 39.9K **Privately Held**
SIC: **8699** 8641 5813 Personal interest organization; civic associations; drinking places

(P-25449)
ORGANZTION AMRCN KDALY EDCTORS
10801 National Blvd # 590, Los Angeles (90064-4139)
PHONE..................310 441-3555
Roger D Chittum Esq, *Principal*
EMP: 50
SALES: 755.1K **Privately Held**
SIC: **8699** Charitable organization

(P-25450)
PASADENA HUMANE SOCIETY
361 S Raymond Ave, Pasadena (91105-2687)
PHONE..................626 792-7151
Steven R Mc Nall, *President*
Elizabeth Campo, *Vice Pres*
Kristina Lamas, *Vice Pres*
Ruthie Hughes, *Controller*
Eda Chan, *Bookkeeper*
EMP: 70
SQ FT: 26,000
SALES: 15.4MM **Privately Held**
WEB: www.phsspca.org
SIC: **8699** 0752 Animal humane society; animal specialty services

(P-25451)
PETS UNLIMITED
2343 Fillmore St, San Francisco (94115-1812)
PHONE..................415 563-6700
Suzanne Troxel, *President*
Theresa L Smith, *CFO*
Sally Wortman, *Vice Pres*
Nan Vinton-Zimmerma, *Executive*
Chris Lundy,
EMP: 110
SALES (est): 7.7MM **Privately Held**
WEB: www.petsunlimited.org
SIC: **8699** Animal humane society

(P-25452)
POINT REYES BIRD OBSERVATOR
Also Called: Point Blue Cnservation Science
3820 Cypress Dr Ste 11, Petaluma (94954-6964)
P.O. Box 69, Bolinas (94924-0069)
PHONE..................415 868-0371
Allie Cohen, *CEO*
Grant Ballard, *Officer*
Ellie Cohen, *Exec Dir*
Russell Bradley, *Senior Mgr*
Wendell Gilgert, *Director*
EMP: 86 EST: 2011
SQ FT: 20,000
SALES (est): 2.9MM **Privately Held**
SIC: **8699** Charitable organization

(P-25453)
RACELEGAL COM
Also Called: CENTER FOR INJURY PREVENTION
315 Fourth Ave, Chula Vista (91910-3801)
P.O. Box 600943, San Diego (92160-0943)
PHONE..................619 265-8159
Charles Chris, *Chairman*
EMP: 50
SALES: 289.5K **Privately Held**
WEB: www.racelegal.com
SIC: **8699** Charitable organization

(P-25454)
RESCUE MISSION ALLIANCE (PA)
Also Called: MISSION BARGAIN CENTER
315 N A St, Oxnard (93030-4901)
P.O. Box 5545 (93031-5545)
PHONE..................805 487-1234
Gary Gray, *President*
Alan Clother, *President*
David Chittenden, *CFO*
Jim Ownes, *Chairman*
Andy Stay, *Treasurer*
EMP: 77
SQ FT: 30,000
SALES: 26.5MM **Privately Held**
WEB: www.erescuemission.com
SIC: **8699** Charitable organization

(P-25455)
SAN DIEGO FAMILY HOUSING LLC
3360 Murray Ridge Rd, San Diego (92123-2264)
PHONE..................858 874-8100
Carol Klepper, *Managing Prtnr*
Tom Vogt, *Mng Member*
EMP: 350
SALES (est): 15.4MM **Privately Held**
SIC: **8699** Charitable organization

(P-25456)
SAN DIEGO HUMANE SOC & SPCA
5500 Gaines St, San Diego (92110-2572)
PHONE..................619 299-7012
Gary L Weitzman, *President*
Kim Shannon, *COO*
Kristin Macdonald, *CFO*
Kelly Riseley, *CFO*
Renee Harris, *Exec VP*
EMP: 65
SQ FT: 44,500
SALES: 25.8MM **Privately Held**
WEB: www.sdhumane.org
SIC: **8699** Animal humane society

(P-25457)
SAN FRANCISCO BAY AR TRAN ASSN
915 San Antonio Ave, Alameda (94501-3959)
PHONE..................510 501-5318
Jahan Byrne, *President*
Monte Boscovich, *Treasurer*
EMP: 150
SALES: 85.5K **Privately Held**
SIC: **8699** 7389 Athletic organizations; fund raising organizations

(P-25458)
SAN JOAQUIN VALLEY INTERGRP
Also Called: Sjvi
6048 E Cimarron Ave, Fresno (93727-6810)
P.O. Box 8302 (93747-8302)
PHONE..................559 856-0559
Marjorie J Donovan, *Ch of Bd*
EMP: 50
SALES (est): 258.4K **Privately Held**
SIC: **8699** Charitable organization

(P-25459)
SANKARA EYE FOUNDATION USA
1900 Mccarthy Blvd # 302, Milpitas (95035-7440)
PHONE..................408 456-0555
Krishan Murlidharan, *Chairman*
Anil Lal, *Bd of Directors*
EMP: 50 EST: 1998

SALES: 10.1MM **Privately Held**
WEB: www.giftofvision.org
SIC: **8699** 7929 Personal interest organization; entertainers & entertainment groups

(P-25460)
SANTA ANA POLICE OFFICERS ASSN
1607 N Sycamore St, Santa Ana (92701-2352)
PHONE..................714 836-1211
Mark R Nichols, *President*
Alan Berg, *Officer*
Camillo Kim, *Info Tech Mgr*
Debbie Knight, *Programmer Anys*
Alvaro Castellon, *Finance Mgr*
EMP: 600
SQ FT: 10,157
SALES: 116.5K **Privately Held**
SIC: **8699** Athletic organizations

(P-25461)
SANTA MONICA BAY WOMENS CLUB
1210 4th St, Santa Monica (90401-1304)
PHONE..................310 395-1308
Darlene Bahr, *President*
Jessica Hankey, *Admin Sec*
EMP: 50
SQ FT: 12,226
SALES: 232.3K **Privately Held**
SIC: **8699** 6732 Charitable organization; trusts: educational, religious, etc.

(P-25462)
SJSU FOUNDATION
210 N 4th St Ste 300, San Jose (95112-5569)
PHONE..................408 924-1410
Mary Sidney, *COO*
EMP: 750
SALES (est): 6.9MM **Privately Held**
WEB: www.foundation.sjsu.edu
SIC: **8699** Charitable organization

(P-25463)
SKOLL FOUNDATION
250 University Ave Lbby, Palo Alto (94301-1725)
PHONE..................650 331-1031
Jeffrey S Skoll, *Owner*
Richard Fahey, *COO*
Sally Farhat, *Officer*
Renee Kaplan, *Officer*
Suzana Grego, *Comms Dir*
EMP: 50
SALES: 13.9MM **Privately Held**
SIC: **8699** Charitable organization

(P-25464)
SOCIETY FOR SAN FRANCISCO
201 Alabama St, San Francisco (94103-4217)
PHONE..................415 554-3000
Katherine Brown, *Ch of Bd*
Jane McHugh-Smith, *President*
Terrell Duff, *COO*
David Tateosian, *Treasurer*
Eric Roberts, *Vice Ch Bd*
EMP: 200 EST: 1868
SQ FT: 57,000
SALES: 34.5MM **Privately Held**
WEB: www.sfspca.org
SIC: **8699** Animal humane society

(P-25465)
SOCIETY OF ST VINCENT (PA)
2272 San Pablo Ave, Oakland (94612-1321)
PHONE..................510 638-7600
Blase Bova, *Exec Dir*
Ron Dean, *Principal*
Christine Comella, *Director*
EMP: 80
SALES: 7.8MM **Privately Held**
SIC: **8699** Charitable organization

(P-25466)
SOCIETY OF ST VINCENT DE (PA)
Also Called: St Vincent De Paul of La
210 N Avenue 21, Los Angeles (90031-1713)
PHONE..................323 224-6280

David Fields, *Exec Dir*
David Garcia, *Exec Dir*
Susana Santana, *Exec Dir*
Anthony Terrazas, *Sales Executive*
EMP: 77
SQ FT: 108,000
SALES: 11.4MM **Privately Held**
SIC: 8699 Charitable organization

(P-25467)
SOROPTOMIST INTL TAHOE SIERRA
3050 Lake Tahoe Blvd, South Lake Tahoe (96150-7810)
P.O. Box 18727 (96151-8727)
PHONE..............................530 573-1657
Lydia Rogers, *President*
EMP: 50
SALES: 71.1K **Privately Held**
SIC: 8699 Charitable organization

(P-25468)
SOUTH BAY HISTORICAL RR SOC
1005 Railroad Ave, Santa Clara (95050-4319)
PHONE..............................408 243-3969
Robert Dolci, *President*
Steven Costa, *Bd of Directors*
EMP: 50
SALES: 82.4K **Privately Held**
WEB: www.sbhrs.org
SIC: 8699 8412 Personal interest organization; museum

(P-25469)
SOUTHERN CAL BLLDOG RESCUE INC
2219 N Spurgeon St, Santa Ana (92706-2962)
PHONE..............................714 381-7691
Gilbertt Van Der Marliere, *President*
EMP: 50 **EST:** 2008
SALES: 300K **Privately Held**
SIC: 8699 Animal humane society

(P-25470)
ST VINCENT DE PAUL VLG INC
Also Called: Joan Kroc Center
28225 Driza, Mission Viejo (92692-1305)
PHONE..............................619 233-8500
Richard Swain, *Principal*
EMP: 150 **Privately Held**
WEB: www.neighbor.org
SIC: 8699 Charitable organization
PA: St. Vincent De Paul Village, Inc.
3350 E St
San Diego CA 92102

(P-25471)
STEP UP ON SECOND STREET INC (PA)
1328 2nd St Ofc, Santa Monica (90401-1123)
PHONE..............................310 394-6889
Todd Lipka, *CEO*
Barbara Bloom, *COO*
Kim Carson, *CFO*
EMP: 60
SQ FT: 7,500
SALES: 9.6MM **Privately Held**
SIC: 8699 Personal interest organization

(P-25472)
STUDENT UN SAN JOSE STATE UNIV
Also Called: Student Union Building
211 S. 9th Street, San Jose (95192-0001)
PHONE..............................408 924-6405
Terry Gregory, *Manager*
EMP: 60
SALES (corp-wide): 8.3MM **Privately Held**
SIC: 8699 Personal interest organization
PA: Student Union Of San Jose State University
1 Washington Sq
San Jose CA
408 924-6315

(P-25473)
THE DAVID LCILE PCKARD FNDTION
300 2nd St, Los Altos (94022-3694)
PHONE..............................650 917-7167
Carol S Larson, *President*
Katy Lnp, *Principal*
Julie Packard, *Principal*
Edwin Van Bronkhorst, *Manager*
EMP: 85
SALES: 283MM **Privately Held**
SIC: 8699 Personal interest organization

(P-25474)
THE FOR SACRAMENTO SOCIETY
Also Called: SSPCA
6201 Florin Perkins Rd, Sacramento (95828-1012)
PHONE..............................916 383-7387
Maryann Subbotin, *Director*
Kenn Altine, *COO*
Dawn Foster, *Marketing Staff*
Lydia Caronna-Craig, *Manager*
Kristi Maryman, *Manager*
EMP: 76
SQ FT: 40,000
SALES: 5.8MM **Privately Held**
WEB: www.sspca.org
SIC: 8699 Animal humane society

(P-25475)
TORRANCE AMATEUR RDO ASSN INC
Also Called: Tara
2162 248th St, Lomita (90717-1608)
PHONE..............................310 245-0989
Charles Galbasin, *Principal*
Kenneth Edwards, *Principal*
Bruce Fauver, *Principal*
Shelly Fauver, *Principal*
Kathleen Galbasin, *Principal*
EMP: 50
SALES (est): 193K **Privately Held**
SIC: 8699 Membership organizations

(P-25476)
UCP WORK INC
2040 Alameda Padre Serra, Santa Barbara (93103-1760)
PHONE..............................805 962-6699
Jeffrey Cowen, *Branch Mgr*
EMP: 135
SALES (corp-wide): 9.3MM **Privately Held**
SIC: 8699 Charitable organization
PA: Ucp Work, Inc.
5320 Carpinteria Ave G
Carpinteria CA 93013
805 566-9000

(P-25477)
UNITED CEREBRAL PALSY ASSN SAN (PA)
8525 Gibbs Dr Ste 209, San Diego (92123-1765)
PHONE..............................858 495-3155
David Carrucci, *Exec Dir*
James O'Leary, *President*
Daniel Alessio, *Treasurer*
David Carucci, *Exec Dir*
Joy Cole, *Technology*
EMP: 120 **EST:** 1958
SALES: 3.3MM **Privately Held**
WEB: www.readystamps.com
SIC: 8699 Charitable organization

(P-25478)
USA TRAVEL SERVICES LLC
714 Washington Blvd, Marina Del Rey (90292-5543)
PHONE..............................207 899-8803
Julian Brand,
EMP: 800
SALES (est): 1MM **Privately Held**
SIC: 8699 Travel club

(P-25479)
USC SHOAH FNDN INST FOR VISUAL
650 W 35th St Ste 114, Los Angeles (90089-0033)
PHONE..............................213 740-6001
Linda Sturm, *Executive Asst*

Linda Sturmm, *Executive Asst*
EMP: 100
SALES (est): 2.5MM **Privately Held**
WEB: www.vhf.org
SIC: 8699 Historical club

(P-25480)
VICKIE LOBELLO
Also Called: Saint Baldricks Foundation
1333 S Mayflower Ave 40, Simi Valley (93063)
PHONE..............................805 750-2327
Kathleen Ruddy, *CEO*
EMP: 65 **EST:** 2010
SALES (est): 2.3MM **Privately Held**
SIC: 8699 Charitable organization

(P-25481)
VICTORIA PLACE COMMUNITY ASSN
195 N Euclid Ave, Upland (91786-6055)
PHONE..............................909 981-4131
John Melcher, *President*
EMP: 75 **EST:** 2008
SALES (est): 57.8K **Privately Held**
SIC: 8699 Membership organizations

(P-25482)
WALNUT VALLEY UNIFIED SCHL DST
Child Care Program
880 S Lemon Ave, Walnut (91789-2931)
PHONE..............................909 595-1261
Josephine Jones, *Director*
Helen Hall, *President*
EMP: 67
SALES (corp-wide): 162.2MM **Privately Held**
SIC: 8699 8351 Charitable organization; child day care services
PA: Walnut Valley Unified School District
880 S Lemon Ave
Walnut CA 91789
909 595-1261

(P-25483)
WENMAT INC
Also Called: Signature Athletic Club The
6001 Fair Oaks Blvd, Carmichael (95608-4816)
PHONE..............................916 485-0714
Edward Orta, *Branch Mgr*
EMP: 100
SALES (corp-wide): 5MM **Privately Held**
WEB: www.wenmat.com
SIC: 8699 Athletic organizations
PA: Wenmat, Inc.
6001 Fair Oaks Blvd
Carmichael CA 95608
916 485-0714

(P-25484)
WIKIMEDIA FOUNDATION INC
1 Montgomery St Ste 1600, San Francisco (94104-5516)
PHONE..............................415 839-6885
Katherine Maher, *Exec Dir*
V Ronique Kessler, *COO*
Jaime Villagomez, *CFO*
Katy Love, *Officer*
Lisa Seitz-Gruwell, *Officer*
EMP: 240
SALES: 89.9MM **Privately Held**
SIC: 8699 6732 Charitable organization; trusts: educational, religious, etc.

(P-25485)
WILDLIFE WAYSTATION
14831 Lttle Tjunga Cyn Rd, Sylmar (91342-5906)
PHONE..............................818 899-5201
Martine Colette, *President*
Susan Hartland, *Exec Dir*
Allison Delgado, *Office Mgr*
Peggy Summers, *Admin Sec*
Stacey Holman, *Bookkeeper*
EMP: 50
SQ FT: 800
SALES: 2.5MM **Privately Held**
WEB: www.wildlifewaystation.org
SIC: 8699 Animal humane society

(P-25486)
WISDOM UNIVERSITY
35 Miller Ave, Mill Valley (94941-1903)
PHONE..............................415 259-7122

Rhonda Britten, *Principal*
Judith Yost, *Dean*
EMP: 51
SALES: 659.6K **Privately Held**
SIC: 8699 Charitable organization

(P-25487)
WORLD VISION INTERNATIONAL (HQ)
Also Called: Vision Fund International
800 W Chestnut Ave, Monrovia (91016-3198)
PHONE..............................626 303-8811
Dean Hirsch, *President*
Valdir Steuernagel, *Ch of Bd*
Kevin Jenkins, *President*
Maya Assaf, *Officer*
David Baroi, *Officer*
EMP: 196
SQ FT: 94,000
SALES (est): 42.6MM
SALES (corp-wide): 1B **Privately Held**
SIC: 8699 Charitable organization
PA: World Vision Inc.
34834 Weyerhaeuser Way S
Federal Way WA 98001
253 815-1000

(P-25488)
YMCA OF SILICON VALLEY
Also Called: Southwest YMCA
13500 Quito Rd, Saratoga (95070-4749)
PHONE..............................408 370-1877
Maria Drake, *Exec Dir*
EMP: 116
SALES (corp-wide): 74.7MM **Privately Held**
WEB: www.scvymca.org
SIC: 8699 8641 Personal interest organization; youth organizations
PA: Ymca Of Silicon Valley
80 Saratoga Ave
Santa Clara CA 95051
408 351-6400

(P-25489)
YOUR MAN TOURS INC
100 N Pacific Coast Hwy # 1700, El Segundo (90245-5662)
PHONE..............................513 772-4411
Jerrey Fuque, *President*
Katja Jahn, *Manager*
EMP: 90
SALES (corp-wide): 21.8B **Privately Held**
WEB: www.ymtvacations.com
SIC: 8699 Travel club
HQ: Your Man Tours, Inc.
100 N Pacific Coast Hwy # 1700
El Segundo CA 90245
310 649-3820

8711 Engineering Services

(P-25490)
7 LAYERS INC
15 Musick, Irvine (92618-1638)
PHONE..............................949 716-6512
Hans Jrgen Meckelburg, *CEO*
Fernando Rodriguez, *COO*
Don Newton, *Vice Pres*
Dana Nguyen, *Manager*
EMP: 59 **EST:** 1999
SQ FT: 20,000
SALES (est): 15.1MM
SALES (corp-wide): 316.4MM **Privately Held**
WEB: www.7layers.com
SIC: 8711 Consulting engineer
HQ: 7layers Gmbh
Borsigstr. 11
Ratingen 40880
210 274-90

(P-25491)
A P H TECHNOLOGICAL CONSULTING
2500 E Colo Blvd Ste 300, Pasadena (91107)
PHONE..............................626 796-0331
Steve Rodgers, *President*
EMP: 50
SQ FT: 5,000
SALES (est): 2.5MM **Privately Held**
SIC: 8711 Consulting engineer

PRODUCTS & SVCS

(P-25492)
A URSGI-BMDC JOINT VENTURE
4225 Executive Sq # 1600, La Jolla
(92037-9122)
PHONE..............................858 812-9292
Martin Koffel, *CEO*
Burns McDonnell Engineering, *Principal*
Leo Handfelt, *General Mgr*
Patricia Samora, *Engineer*
EMP: 70
SALES (est): 2.7MM **Privately Held**
SIC: 8711 Engineering services

(P-25493)
A-C ELECTRIC COMPANY
Also Called: Automated Ctrl Technical Svcs
315 30th St, Bakersfield (93301-2511)
P.O. Box 81376 (93380-1376)
PHONE..............................661 633-5368
Dave Morton, *VP Opers*
Rusty Stone, *Division Mgr*
Baron Alexander, *General Mgr*
Daren Alexander, *General Mgr*
Chris Clark, *Project Mgr*
EMP: 60
SALES (est): 6.2MM
SALES (corp-wide): 66.6MM **Privately Held**
SIC: 8711 Engineering services
PA: A-C Electric Company
2921 Hanger Way
Bakersfield CA 93308
661 410-0000

(P-25494)
ABBOOD ZEYAD
Also Called: Nafithat Alsharq
7914 La Mesa Blvd Apt 6, La Mesa
(91942-5056)
PHONE..............................619 212-2820
Zeyad Abbood, *Owner*
EMP: 50
SALES (est): 810.9K **Privately Held**
SIC: 8711 0761 1731 1623 Electrical or
electronic engineering; crew leaders, farm
labor; contracting services; electric power
systems contractors; electric power line
construction; excavation & grading, building construction

(P-25495)
ABLE SERVICES INC
868 Folsom St, San Francisco
(94107-1123)
PHONE..............................800 461-9577
Paul Saccone, *CEO*
Mark Kelly, *President*
Ellen Dietrich, *Opers Staff*
Aldo Magana, *Manager*
EMP: 100
SALES (est): 14.8MM **Privately Held**
SIC: 8711 7349 Engineering services;
building maintenance, except repairs

(P-25496)
ABS CONSULTING INC
Also Called: ABS Group
300 Commerce Ste 200, Irvine
(92602-1305)
PHONE..............................714 734-4242
Doug Frazier, *CEO*
Peter Yanev, *President*
Jim Johnson, *COO*
George Reitter, *CFO*
William R Fuller, *Vice Pres*
EMP: 100
SQ FT: 16,700
SALES (est): 8.7MM
SALES (corp-wide): 980.6MM **Privately Held**
SIC: 8711 8742 Consulting engineer;
management consulting services
HQ: Abs Group Of Companies, Inc.
16855 Northchase Dr
Houston TX 77060

(P-25497)
ACCEL BIOTECH LLC
103 Cooper Ct, Los Gatos (95032-7604)
PHONE..............................408 354-1700
Tracy Macneal, *Mng Member*
Sarah Fischer, *Admin Asst*
Joe Bacon, *Sr Software Eng*
David Boone, *Project Mgr*
Brady Boone, *Electrical Engi*

EMP: 68
SALES (est): 5.8MM **Privately Held**
SIC: 8711 Mechanical engineering; con-
sulting engineer; electrical or electronic
engineering
PA: Ximedica, Llc
55 Dupont Dr
Providence RI 02907
-

(P-25498)
ACETECH CONSTRUCTION INC
3699 Wilshire Blvd # 655, Los Angeles
(90010-2742)
PHONE..............................213 637-4702
Chong Lee, *President*
EMP: 50
SALES: 10MM **Privately Held**
SIC: 8711 Building construction consultant

(P-25499)
ACL CONSTRUCTION COMPANY INC
207 W State St, Ontario (91762-4360)
P.O. Box 1929, Chino Hills (91709-0065)
PHONE..............................909 391-4477
Jonathan Jordan, *President*
EMP: 50
SQ FT: 800
SALES: 5MM **Privately Held**
SIC: 8711 Engineering services

(P-25500)
ACRONICS SYSTEMS INC
2102 Commerce Dr, San Jose
(95131-1804)
PHONE..............................408 432-0888
Kim Tran, *CEO*
Tri Nguyen, *Vice Pres*
Long Tran, *Design Engr*
Michael Nguyen, *Project Mgr*
Jessica Tran, *Accountant*
EMP: 110
SQ FT: 16,000
SALES (est): 15.9MM **Privately Held**
WEB: www.acronics.com
SIC: 8711 7373 Electrical or electronic en-
gineering; systems engineering, computer
related

(P-25501)
ADAMS STREETER CIVIL ENGINEERS
15 Corporate Park, Irvine (92606-5109)
PHONE..............................949 474-2330
Jan A Adams, *President*
Deborah Chang, *CFO*
Felix Gonzalez-Pe, *Vice Pres*
Randal Streeter, *Vice Pres*
Nick Streeter-Pe, *Vice Pres*
EMP: 57
SQ FT: 14,000
SALES (est): 6.5MM **Privately Held**
SIC: 8711 Civil engineering

(P-25502)
ADKISON ENGINEERS INC
Also Called: Adkan Engineers
6879 Airport Dr, Riverside (92504-1903)
PHONE..............................951 688-0241
Ed Adkison, *President*
Jerry Snell, *Exec VP*
Charissa Leach, *Vice Pres*
Chrissa Leach, *Vice Pres*
Yasmir Quintero, *Administration*
EMP: 52
SALES (est): 7.8MM **Privately Held**
WEB: www.adkan.com
SIC: 8711 8713 Civil engineering; survey-
ing services

(P-25503)
ADTEK ENGINEERING SERVICE
2090 N Tustin Ave Ste 160, Santa Ana
(92705-7868)
P.O. Box 325, Tustin (92781-0325)
PHONE..............................800 451-0782
Joel R Spellacy, *President*
EMP: 75 EST: 1974
SALES (est): 8.7MM **Privately Held**
WEB: www.adtekjobs.com
SIC: 8711 7361 Consulting engineer; em-
ployment agencies

(P-25504)
ADVANTEDGE TECHNOLOGY INC
271 Market St Ste 15, Port Hueneme
(93041-3219)
PHONE..............................805 488-0405
Tim Edward Huggins, *CEO*
Tim Huggins, *Exec Dir*
Kevin Bradley, *Program Mgr*
Bruce Underwood, *Administration*
David Benham, *Senior Engr*
EMP: 60
SQ FT: 2,000
SALES (est): 14.3MM **Privately Held**
WEB: www.advantedgetechnology.com
SIC: 8711 Engineering services

(P-25505)
AECOM (PA)
1999 Avenue Of The Stars # 2600, Los An-
geles (90067-6033)
PHONE..............................213 593-8000
Michael S Burke, *Ch of Bd*
Richard Silos, *President*
Randall A Wotring, *COO*
W Troy Rudd, *CFO*
Daniel R Tishman, *Vice Ch Bd*
EMP: 148
SQ FT: 31,500
SALES: 20.1B **Publicly Held**
SIC: 8711 8712 Engineering services; ar-
chitectural engineering

(P-25506)
AECOM C&E INC
Also Called: Aecom Environment
1220 Avenida Acaso, Camarillo
(93012-8750)
PHONE..............................805 388-3775
Rick Simon, *Manager*
Tiina Couture, *Project Mgr*
Rachel Fish, *Manager*
EMP: 100
SALES (corp-wide): 20.1B **Publicly Held**
SIC: 8711 Engineering services
HQ: Aecom C&E, Inc
250 Apollo Dr
Chelmsford MA 01824
978 905-2100

(P-25507)
AECOM E&C HOLDINGS INC (DH)
1999 Avenue Of The Stars, Los Angeles
(90067-6022)
PHONE..............................213 593-8000
Robert W Zaist, *CEO*
Gary V Jandegian, *President*
H Thomas Hicks, *CFO*
Judy L Rodgers, *Treasurer*
Joseph Masters, *Vice Pres*
EMP: 108
SALES (est): 5B
SALES (corp-wide): 20.1B **Publicly Held**
SIC: 8711 1611 1629 1623 Engineering
services; general contractor, highway &
street construction; dams, waterways,
docks & other marine construction; indus-
trial plant construction; power plant construction; pipeline construction; industrial
buildings, new construction; bridge con-
struction; tunnel construction; highway
construction, elevated
HQ: Urs Holdings, Inc.
600 Montgomery St Fl 25
San Francisco CA 94111
415 774-2700

(P-25508)
AECOM ENERGY & CNSTR INC
Also Called: Washington Group
16711 Knott Ave, La Mirada (90638-6013)
PHONE..............................714 228-4300
Nancy Delvon, *Branch Mgr*
EMP: 120
SALES (corp-wide): 20.1B **Publicly Held**
WEB: www.wgint.com
SIC: 8711 Engineering services
HQ: Aecom Energy & Construction, Inc.
1999 Avenue Of The Stars
Los Angeles CA 90067
213 593-8100

(P-25509)
AECOM GLOBAL II LLC
1320 S Simpson Cir, Anaheim
(92806-5531)
PHONE..............................415 774-2700
Bill Prior, *Branch Mgr*
EMP: 73
SALES (corp-wide): 20.1B **Publicly Held**
SIC: 8711 Engineering services
HQ: Aecom Global Ii, Llc
1999 Avenue Of The Stars
Los Angeles CA 90067
213 593-8100

(P-25510)
AECOM GLOBAL II LLC
130 Robin Hill Rd Ste 100, Goleta
(93117-3153)
PHONE..............................805 692-0600
Tim Cohen, *Senior Partner*
Julie Doane Allmon, *Project Mgr*
Paul Svacina, *Engineer*
Richard Rosenbaum, *Safety Mgr*
EMP: 74
SALES (corp-wide): 20.1B **Publicly Held**
SIC: 8711 Consulting engineer
HQ: Aecom Global Ii, Llc
1999 Avenue Of The Stars
Los Angeles CA 90067
213 593-8100

(P-25511)
AECOM GLOBAL II LLC (HQ)
1999 Avenue Of The Stars, Los Angeles
(90067-6022)
PHONE..............................213 593-8100
Michael Burke, *Mng Member*
Tommy Bell, *President*
Rick L Randall, *President*
Jean Demianenko, *Manager*
EMP: 65
SALES (est): 10.8B
SALES (corp-wide): 20.1B **Publicly Held**
SIC: 8711 8712 8741 Engineering serv-
ices; consulting engineer; architectural
engineering; construction management
PA: Aecom
1999 Avenue Of The Stars # 2600
Los Angeles CA 90067
213 593-8000

(P-25512)
AECOM GLOBAL II LLC
2870 Gateway Oaks Dr # 150, Sacramento
(95833-3577)
PHONE..............................916 679-2000
Sujan Punyamurthuai, *General Mgr*
EMP: 300
SALES (corp-wide): 20.1B **Publicly Held**
SIC: 8711 Consulting engineer
HQ: Aecom Global Ii, Llc
1999 Avenue Of The Stars
Los Angeles CA 90067
213 593-8100

(P-25513)
AECOM GLOBAL II LLC
600 Montgomery St, San Francisco
(94111-2702)
PHONE..............................415 774-2700
Hugh Blackwood, *Vice Pres*
Octavian Cana, *Vice Pres*
Alan Ebner, *Vice Pres*
Seth Finkel, *Vice Pres*
David Geller, *Vice Pres*
EMP: 83
SALES (corp-wide): 20.1B **Publicly Held**
SIC: 8711 Engineering services
HQ: Aecom Global Ii, Llc
1999 Avenue Of The Stars
Los Angeles CA 90067
213 593-8100

(P-25514)
AECOM GLOBAL II LLC
74 C St, Herlong (96113-7400)
P.O. Box 30 (96113-0030)
PHONE..............................530 827-2406
Mike Rhodes, *Branch Mgr*
EMP: 73
SALES (corp-wide): 20.1B **Publicly Held**
SIC: 8711 Engineering services
HQ: Aecom Global Ii, Llc
1999 Avenue Of The Stars
Los Angeles CA 90067
213 593-8100

(P-25515)
AECOM GLOBAL II LLC
5168 E Dakota Ave, Fresno (93727-7404)
PHONE.............................559 347-5669
Erik Newlander, *Branch Mgr*
EMP: 105
SALES (corp-wide): 20.1B **Publicly Held**
SIC: 8711 Aviation &/or aeronautical engineering
HQ: Aecom Global Ii, Llc
1999 Avenue Of The Stars
Los Angeles CA 90067
213 593-8100

(P-25516)
AECOM TECHNICAL SERVICES INC
1333 Broadway Ste 800, Oakland (94612-1924)
PHONE.............................510 834-4304
David Dickinson, *President*
EMP: 180
SALES (corp-wide): 20.1B **Publicly Held**
WEB: www.earthtech.com
SIC: 8711 8742 Engineering services; transportation consultant
HQ: Aecom Technical Services, Inc.
300 S Grand Ave Ste 1100
Los Angeles CA 90071
213 593-8000

(P-25517)
AECOM TECHNICAL SERVICES INC
901 Via Piemonte Ste 400, Ontario (91764-6597)
PHONE.............................909 554-5000
Brian Weith, *Manager*
EMP: 65
SQ FT: 15,000
SALES (corp-wide): 20.1B **Publicly Held**
WEB: www.earthtech.com
SIC: 8711 8748 Engineering services; environmental consultant
HQ: Aecom Technical Services, Inc.
300 S Grand Ave Ste 1100
Los Angeles CA 90071
213 593-8000

(P-25518)
AECOM TECHNICAL SERVICES INC
401 W A St Ste 1200, San Diego (92101-7905)
PHONE.............................619 610-7600
Richard Leja, *Manager*
EMP: 60
SALES (corp-wide): 20.1B **Publicly Held**
WEB: www.earthtech.com
SIC: 8711 8748 8641 Consulting engineer; environmental consultant; environmental protection organization
HQ: Aecom Technical Services, Inc.
300 S Grand Ave Ste 1100
Los Angeles CA 90071
213 593-8000

(P-25519)
AECOM TECHNOLOGY CORPORATION
2020 L St Ste 400, Sacramento (95811-4267)
PHONE.............................916 414-5800
Colleen Johnston, *Branch Mgr*
EMP: 66
SALES (corp-wide): 20.1B **Publicly Held**
SIC: 8711 Consulting engineer
PA: Aecom
1999 Avenue Of The Stars # 2600
Los Angeles CA 90067
213 593-8000

(P-25520)
AECOM-TSE JOINT VENTURE
300 Lakeside Dr Ste 400, Oakland (94612-3534)
PHONE.............................510 285-6639
Simon Kim, *Vice Pres*
Etty Mercurio, *Administration*
Paul Van Der Wel, *Administration*
EMP: 99 EST: 2017
SQ FT: 150,000
SALES (est): 1.5MM **Privately Held**
SIC: 8711 Engineering services

(P-25521)
AEROVIRONMENT INC
900 Enchanted Way, Simi Valley (93065-0906)
PHONE.............................626 357-9983
Erica Jenkins, *COO*
Calvin Au, *Program Mgr*
Natalie Halvorson, *Program Mgr*
Richard Childress, *CIO*
Ben Bent, *Info Tech Mgr*
EMP: 55
SALES (corp-wide): 271MM **Publicly Held**
SIC: 8711 3694 3721 Engineering services; energy conservation engineering; battery charging alternators & generators; gliders (aircraft)
PA: Aerovironment, Inc.
800 Royal Oaks Dr Ste 210
Monrovia CA 91016
626 357-9983

(P-25522)
AFFORDABLE ENGRG SVCS INC
1455 Frazee Rd Ste 860, San Diego (92108-4309)
PHONE.............................973 890-8915
Jason Kamdar, *Branch Mgr*
EMP: 91
SALES (corp-wide): 39.9MM **Privately Held**
SIC: 8711 Consulting engineer
PA: Affordable Engineering Services, Inc.
1455 Frazee Rd Ste 860
San Diego CA 92108
619 522-9800

(P-25523)
ALAMEDA CORRIDOR ENGRG TEAM
1 Civic Plaza Dr Ste 600, Carson (90745-7980)
PHONE.............................310 816-0460
Rachel Vandenberg, *Admin Mgr*
Moffatt Nichol Engineers, *Partner*
Daniel Mann Johnson and Menden, *Partner*
East Los Angeles Community UNI, *Partner*
EMP: 65
SALES (est): 3.6MM **Privately Held**
WEB: www.trenchteam.com
SIC: 8711 Engineering services

(P-25524)
ALBERT A WEBB ASSOCIATES (PA)
3788 Mccray St, Riverside (92506-2927)
PHONE.............................951 686-1070
A Hubert Webb, *Chairman*
Matt Webb, *President*
Scott Webb, *CFO*
MO Faghihi, *Senior VP*
Roger D Prend Pe, *Senior VP*
EMP: 127
SQ FT: 20,000
SALES (est): 27.8MM **Privately Held**
WEB: www.webbassociates.com
SIC: 8711 Civil engineering

(P-25525)
ALFA TECH CNSLTING ENGNERS INC (PA)
Also Called: Alfa Tech Consulting Entps
1321 Ridder Park Dr 50, San Jose (95131-2306)
PHONE.............................408 487-1200
Jeff Fini, *Ch of Bd*
Saied Nazeri, *Managing Prtnr*
Bryan Burkhart, *Executive*
Zach Wilson, *Managing Dir*
Susanne Dixon, *Office Mgr*
EMP: 86
SQ FT: 22,000
SALES (est): 22.2MM **Privately Held**
WEB: www.atcginc.net
SIC: 8711 Consulting engineer

(P-25526)
ALION SCIENCE AND TECH CORP
266 E Scott St, Port Hueneme (93041-2918)
PHONE.............................805 488-8761
Christopher Learned, *Manager*
Jon Gallero, *Electrical Engi*
Chris Learned, *Engineer*

EMP: 57
SQ FT: 1,000
SALES (corp-wide): 838.9MM **Privately Held**
SIC: 8711 8731 Engineering services; commercial physical research; commercial physical research
PA: Alion Science And Technology Corporation
1750 Tysons Blvd Ste 1300
Mc Lean VA 22102
703 918-4480

(P-25527)
ALLANA BUICK & BERS INC (PA)
990 Commercial St Ste 200, Palo Alto (94303-4930)
PHONE.............................650 543-5600
Karim Allana, *CEO*
Karim P Allana, *CEO*
Eugene Buick, *COO*
John Kelleher, *CFO*
Gerson Bers, *Vice Pres*
EMP: 91
SALES (est): 19.1MM **Privately Held**
WEB: www.abbae.com
SIC: 8711 Engineering services

(P-25528)
ALTA VISTA SOLUTIONS
3260 Blume Dr Ste 500, Richmond (94806-5715)
PHONE.............................510 594-0510
Mazen A Wahbeh, *CEO*
Patrick S Lowry, *President*
EMP: 120
SALES (est): 19.8MM **Privately Held**
SIC: 8711 Consulting engineer

(P-25529)
AMEC FSTER WHELER E C SVCS INC
250 E Rincon St Ste 204, Corona (92879-1363)
PHONE.............................951 273-7400
Thomas Cheahan, *Vice Pres*
EMP: 113
SALES (corp-wide): 6.7B **Privately Held**
SIC: 8711 Engineering services
HQ: Amec Foster Wheeler E&C Services, Inc.
1979 Lkeside Pkwy Ste 400
Tucker GA 30084

(P-25530)
AMERICAN ELECTRONIC WARFARE AS
16766 Bernardo Center Dr, San Diego (92128-2545)
PHONE.............................858 524-6119
EMP: 125
SALES (corp-wide): 56.5MM **Privately Held**
SIC: 8711 Electrical or electronic engineering
PA: American Electronic Warfare Associates, Incorporated
44427 Airport Rd Ste 200
California MD 20619
301 863-7102

(P-25531)
AMERICAN GNC CORPORATION
888 E Easy St, Simi Valley (93065-1812)
PHONE.............................805 582-0582
Dr Ching-Fang Lin, *President*
Traci Ho, *Engineer*
Rebecca Lin, *Manager*
EMP: 50
SQ FT: 30,000
SALES (est): 5MM **Privately Held**
WEB: www.americangnc.com
SIC: 8711 Engineering services

(P-25532)
AMERICAN PRIDE GEN ENGRG INC
529 W 4th Ave Ste B, Escondido (92025-4037)
PHONE.............................760 736-4056
James H Hatter, *CEO*
Barry Blanchard, *Vice Pres*
Bubba Riggins, *Administration*

EMP: 50
SQ FT: 3,000
SALES (est): 7.3MM **Privately Held**
SIC: 8711 Engineering services

(P-25533)
AMERICAN TECH SERVICE
1761 3rd St Ste 105, Norco (92860-2679)
PHONE.............................951 372-9664
Alen Petrossin, *President*
EMP: 60
SALES (est): 6.4MM **Privately Held**
SIC: 8711 Engineering services

(P-25534)
AMERICAN TECHNICAL SVCS INC
9520 Topanga Canyon Blvd, Chatsworth (91311-4045)
PHONE.............................818 590-7784
Alen Petrossian, *President*
EMP: 70
SQ FT: 2,040
SALES (est): 3.7MM **Privately Held**
WEB: www.americantechnicalservices.net
SIC: 8711 Consulting engineer

(P-25535)
AMG HUNTINGTON BEACH LLC
Also Called: Notthoff Engineering
5416 Argosy Ave, Huntington Beach (92649-1039)
PHONE.............................714 894-9802
David L Patterson, *CEO*
J Ross Feeney, *COO*
Robert Taylor, *Exec VP*
Kelley Kaller, *Vice Pres*
John Nicklos, *Vice Pres*
EMP: 50
SALES (est): 11.1MM **Privately Held**
SIC: 8711 Engineering services
HQ: Aerospace Manufacturing Group Inc
5401 Business Dr
Huntington Beach CA 92649
714 373-4300

(P-25536)
ANATEC INTERNATIONAL INC (HQ)
2950 E Birch St, Brea (92821-6246)
PHONE.............................949 498-3350
Blaine Curtis, *President*
EMP: 60
SQ FT: 12,000
SALES (est): 28.2MM
SALES (corp-wide): 2.2B **Publicly Held**
WEB: www.anatectexas.com
SIC: 8711 Consulting engineer
PA: Curtiss-Wright Corporation
130 Harbour Place Dr # 300
Davidson NC 28036
704 869-4600

(P-25537)
APEX MACHINE WORKS INC
2118 Wilshire Blvd # 258, Santa Monica (90403-5704)
PHONE.............................310 393-5987
EMP: 100
SALES (est): 3.3MM **Privately Held**
SIC: 8711

(P-25538)
APPLIED COMPANIES
28020 Avenue Stanford, Santa Clarita (91355-1105)
P.O. Box 802078 (91380-2078)
PHONE.............................661 257-0090
Mary Elizabeth Klinger, *CEO*
Joseph Klinger, *Vice Pres*
Nayeem Khawaja, *Program Mgr*
Steve Stanley, *Opers Staff*
Sheila Garcia, *Clerk*
EMP: 50
SQ FT: 58,000
SALES (est): 10.3MM **Privately Held**
WEB: www.appliedcompanies.net
SIC: 8711 3585 3443 3621 Mechanical engineering; ice making machinery; cylinders, pressure: metal plate; motors & generators

(P-25539)
APPLIED GEOKINETICS
77 Bunsen, Irvine (92618-4218)
PHONE.............................949 502-5353

PRODUCTS & SVCS

Glenn Tofani, *President*
Felicity Meek, *CFO*
Berge Basmadjian, *Executive*
Felicity Meeks, *Executive*
Melita Murphy, *Admin Asst*
EMP: 65
SALES (est): 9.3MM **Privately Held**
WEB: www.appliedgeokinetics.com
SIC: 8711 Consulting engineer

(P-25540)
APTIM CORP
4005 Port Chicago Hwy, Concord
(94520-1180)
PHONE....................925 288-2011
Karen Cracken, *Branch Mgr*
EMP: 502
SALES (corp-wide): 2B **Privately Held**
SIC: 8711 Engineering services
HQ: Aptim Corp.
10001 Woodloch Forest Dr # 450
The Woodlands TX 77380
832 823-2700

(P-25541)
APTIM CORP
18100 Von Karman Ave, Irvine
(92612-0169)
PHONE....................949 261-6441
Richard Fowler, *Branch Mgr*
EMP: 63
SALES (corp-wide): 2B **Privately Held**
SIC: 8711 Pollution control engineering
HQ: Aptim Corp.
10001 Woodloch Forest Dr # 450
The Woodlands TX 77380
832 823-2700

(P-25542)
AQUATIC DESIGNING INC
4801 West End Rd, Arcata (95521-9242)
PHONE....................707 822-4629
Paula E Crowley, *President*
EMP: 50
SALES (est): 1.3MM **Privately Held**
SIC: 8711 Engineering services

(P-25543)
ARCHITRENDS INC
Also Called: ATI
3860 Blackhawk Rd Ste 160, Danville
(94506-4615)
PHONE....................925 648-8800
Robert Desautels, *President*
Paul Didonato, *Vice Pres*
EMP: 70
SQ FT: 3,500
SALES (est): 4MM **Privately Held**
WEB: www.architrends.com
SIC: 8711 8741 Structural engineering;
construction management

(P-25544)
ARIA GROUP INCORPORATED
17395 Daimler St, Irvine (92614-5510)
PHONE....................949 475-2915
Clive Hawkins, *President*
Charles Taylor, *Exec VP*
EMP: 70
SQ FT: 45,489
SALES (est): 12.7MM **Privately Held**
WEB: www.getbedbugs.com
SIC: 8711 Consulting engineer

(P-25545)
ARINC INCORPORATED
4553 Glencoe Ave Ste 100, Marina Del Rey
(90292-7917)
PHONE....................310 301-9040
John Belcher, *CEO*
Pascal Mermoz, *Technology*
EMP: 100 **Publicly Held**
SIC: 8711 Aviation &/or aeronautical engineering
HQ: Arinc Incorporated
2551 Riva Rd
Annapolis MD 21401
410 266-4000

(P-25546)
ARQ LLC
3002 Dow Ave Ste 416, Tustin
(92780-7236)
PHONE....................888 384-0971
Kunal Hinduja, *Mng Member*
Arjun Dua, *CFO*

David Pandoria, *Vice Pres*
Kamal Sadarangani, *Vice Pres*
Jawan Salman, *Vice Pres*
EMP: 85
SALES (est): 21MM **Privately Held**
SIC: 8711 Electrical or electronic engineering

(P-25547)
ARTIMISA & CO
220 Forest Knoll Ln, Quincy (95971-9350)
P.O. Box 3585 (95971-3585)
PHONE....................530 283-3700
Chris D Kennedy, *President*
EMP: 54
SALES (est): 2.4MM **Privately Held**
WEB: www.mainecoon.com
SIC: 8711 Engineering services

(P-25548)
ARUP NORTH AMERICA LIMITED
12777 W Jefferson Blvd, Los Angeles
(90066-7048)
PHONE....................310 578-4182
Tony Panossian, *Branch Mgr*
Dudley Calle, *Office Admin*
Gabrielle Gallagher, *Administration*
Ekaterina Frolov, *Technician*
Joshua Wetzig, *Electrical Engi*
EMP: 101 **Privately Held**
SIC: 8711 Engineering services
HQ: Arup North America Limited
560 Mission St Fl 7
San Francisco CA 94105
415 957-9445

(P-25549)
ARUP NORTH AMERICA LIMITED (DH)
560 Mission St Fl 7, San Francisco
(94105-0915)
PHONE....................415 957-9445
Mahadev Ramen, *President*
Andrew Howard, *Vice Pres*
James Quiter, *Vice Pres*
Anita Daniel, *Executive Asst*
Frances Martinez, *Executive Asst*
EMP: 200
SALES (est): 84.4MM **Privately Held**
SIC: 8711 Engineering services

(P-25550)
ATA ENGINEERING INC (PA)
13290 Evening Creek Dr S # 250, San
Diego (92128-4695)
PHONE....................858 480-2000
Mary Baker, *President*
William Cherom, *CFO*
Paul A Blelloch, *Vice Pres*
Ralph Brillhart, *Vice Pres*
Tricia Sur, *Vice Pres*
EMP: 60
SQ FT: 50,215
SALES: 34.5MM **Privately Held**
WEB: www.ata-e.com
SIC: 8711 Consulting engineer

(P-25551)
ATHICON
6310 San Vicente Blvd, Los Angeles
(90048-5426)
PHONE....................213 454-0662
Victoria Lozada, *Manager*
EMP: 50 EST: 2017 **Privately Held**
SIC: 8711 Engineering services

(P-25552)
ATKINS NORTH AMERICA INC
9275 Sky Park Ct Ste 200, San Diego
(92123-4905)
PHONE....................858 874-1810
Marc Cavallero, *Branch Mgr*
EMP: 100
SALES (corp-wide): 7.3B **Privately Held**
WEB: www.cargillmt.com
SIC: 8711 Consulting engineer
HQ: Atkins North America, Inc.
4030 W Boy Scout Blvd
Tampa FL 33607
813 282-7275

(P-25553)
AUGUSTINE CONSULTING INC (PA)
24560 Silver Cloud Ct # 102, Monterey
(93940-6560)
PHONE....................831 920-1754
Cary Christopher Augustine, *CEO*
Henry Kinnison, *President*
Pete Arsenault, *COO*
Daryl Thies, *Vice Pres*
Mike Gordon, *Program Mgr*
EMP: 98
SALES: 20MM **Privately Held**
SIC: 8711 Engineering services

(P-25554)
AUSENCO PSI LLC (HQ)
1320 Willow Pass Rd # 300, Concord
(94520-5241)
PHONE....................925 939-4420
Ed Meka, *President*
Andrew Fletcher, *Treasurer*
Delbert Boyle, *Senior VP*
Craig Allen, *Admin Sec*
Kenneth Bennert, *Finance Mgr*
EMP: 80
SALES (est): 12.1MM
SALES (corp-wide): 6.7MM **Privately Held**
SIC: 8711 Engineering services
PA: Ausenco Usa Inc.
1320 Willow Pass Rd
Concord CA 94520
925 939-4420

(P-25555)
AUSENCO USA INC (PA)
1320 Willow Pass Rd, Concord
(94520-5232)
PHONE....................925 939-4420
Zimi Meka, *President*
Simon Cmrlec, *President*
Ed Meka, *President*
Craig Allen, *CFO*
Nick Bell, *Exec VP*
EMP: 80 EST: 2010
SALES (est): 6.7MM **Privately Held**
SIC: 8711 Engineering services

(P-25556)
AUSGAR TECHNOLOGIES INC
10721 Treena St, San Diego (92131-1016)
PHONE....................855 428-7427
Jonathan Dien, *President*
Cretia Bowman, *Vice Pres*
EMP: 115
SQ FT: 16,000
SALES (est): 18.4MM **Privately Held**
SIC: 8711 7371 7373 7379 Consulting
engineer; custom computer programming
services; computer integrated systems
design; computer related consulting services; testing laboratories

(P-25557)
AZTEC ENGINEERING GROUP INC
2151 Michelson Dr Ste 100, Irvine
(92612-1311)
PHONE....................951 471-6190
Robert L Lemke Jr Pe, *Branch Mgr*
EMP: 61 **Privately Held**
SIC: 8711 Consulting engineer
PA: Aztec Engineering Group, Inc.
4561 E Mcdowell Rd
Phoenix AZ 85008

(P-25558)
B&C TRANSIT INC (PA)
Also Called: B & C
1924 Franklin St Ste 200, Oakland
(94612-2913)
PHONE....................510 483-3560
Alberto Fernandez, *President*
Tanya Powell, *CFO*
Steven Falk, *Vice Pres*
Jerome S Furman, *Vice Pres*
Richard Riggio, *Vice Pres*
EMP: 70
SQ FT: 25,000
SALES (est): 21.1MM **Privately Held**
SIC: 8711 Electrical or electronic engineering

(P-25559)
BARA INFOWARE INC (PA)
Also Called: Bara Construction
4115 Blackhawk Plaza Cir, Danville
(94506-4901)
PHONE....................925 790-0130
Elina Singh, *President*
Menginder Singh, *Vice Pres*
Kajal Kapoor, *Business Anlyst*
Reet Inder, *Business Mgr*
EMP: 59
SQ FT: 600
SALES: 6.6MM **Privately Held**
SIC: 8711 1542 Engineering services;
custom builders, non-residential

(P-25560)
BEACON WEST ENERGY GROUP LLC
1145 Eugenia Pl Ste 101, Carpinteria
(93013-1970)
PHONE....................805 816-2790
Larry Huskins, *Mng Member*
Christer Peltonen,
Keith Wenal,
Michael Wracher,
EMP: 55
SQ FT: 5,000
SALES: 3MM **Privately Held**
SIC: 8711 Engineering services

(P-25561)
BECHTEL ENERGY CORPORATION
50 Beale St Bsmt 1, San Francisco
(94105-1819)
P.O. Box 193965 (94119-3965)
PHONE....................415 768-1234
R P Bechtel, *Chairman*
G C Proctor, *Senior VP*
J D Carter, *Director*
A Zaccaria, *Director*
EMP: 1588
SQ FT: 300,000
SALES (est): 46.5MM
SALES (corp-wide): 10.4B **Privately Held**
SIC: 8711 8741 Construction & civil engineering; construction management
HQ: Bechtel Power Corporation
50 Beale St Bsmt 2
San Francisco CA 94105
415 768-1234

(P-25562)
BECHTEL ENTERPRISES HOLDINGS (HQ)
50 Beale St Ste 2200, San Francisco
(94105-1827)
P.O. Box 193965 (94119-3965)
PHONE....................415 768-1234
Riley P Bechtel, *Ch of Bd*
V P Unruh, *President*
Marcia B Burkey, *CFO*
H J Haynes, *Vice Ch Bd*
C W Hull, *Vice Ch Bd*
EMP: 85
SQ FT: 300,000
SALES (est): 6.4MM
SALES (corp-wide): 10.4B **Privately Held**
SIC: 8711 Engineering services
PA: Bechtel Group, Inc.
50 Beale St Bsmt 1
San Francisco CA 94105
415 768-1234

(P-25563)
BECHTEL GLOBAL ENERGY INC
50 Beale St Bsmt 1, San Francisco
(94105-1819)
PHONE....................415 768-1234
Riley Bechtel, *Ch of Bd*
Peter A Dawson, *Senior VP*
Judith A Miller, *Director*
A Zaccaria, *Director*
EMP: 4013
SALES (est): 68.2K
SALES (corp-wide): 10.4B **Privately Held**
SIC: 8711 1629 8742 Civil engineering;
industrial plant construction; power plant
construction; construction project management consultant

HQ: Bechtel Corporation
12011 Sunset Hills Rd # 110
Reston VA 20190
571 392-6300

(P-25564)
BECHTEL INTL SYSTEMS INC (DH)
50 Beale St, San Francisco (94105-1813)
PHONE...................................415 768-1234
P A Dawson, *Director*
Jason Orcutt, *Administration*
W N Dudley, *Director*
EMP: 87
SALES: 64.5MM
SALES (corp-wide): 10.4B **Privately Held**
SIC: 8711 1629 8742 Civil engineering;
industrial plant construction; construction
project management consultant
HQ: Bechtel National, Inc.
12011 Sunset Hills Rd
Reston VA 20190
571 392-6300

(P-25565)
BEDON CONSTRUCTION INC
27989 Holland Rd, Menifee (92584-9703)
PHONE...................................951 246-9005
Don Parker, *President*
Marti Manser, *Manager*
EMP: 68
SQ FT: 2,000
SALES (est): 7.9MM **Privately Held**
WEB: www.bedonconstruction.com
SIC: 8711 Construction & civil engineering

(P-25566)
BIGGS CARDOSA ASSOCIATES INC (PA)
865 The Alameda, San Jose (95126-3133)
PHONE...................................408 296-5515
Steven A Biggs, *President*
Mark Cardosa, *Vice Pres*
Carrie Bibolet, *Admin Asst*
Yvonne Mac, *Admin Asst*
Matt Frechette, *Research*
EMP: 70
SQ FT: 7,237
SALES (est): 12.8MM **Privately Held**
SIC: 8711 Structural engineering

(P-25567)
BKF ENGINEERS (PA)
255 Shoreline Dr Ste 200, Redwood City
(94065-1428)
PHONE...................................650 482-6300
David Lavelle, *President*
Maureen Nevin, *CFO*
Max Keech, *Corp Secy*
Todd Adair, *Vice Pres*
Dave Evans, *Vice Pres*
EMP: 250 EST: 1915
SQ FT: 18,155
SALES (est): 68.1MM **Privately Held**
SIC: 8711 8713 Civil engineering; survey-
ing services

(P-25568)
BLACK & VEATCH CORPORATION
5 Peters Canyon Rd # 300, Irvine
(92606-1793)
PHONE...................................913 458-2000
Steve Foellmi, *Vice Pres*
Jacob Holden, *Engineer*
Robert Kaessner, *Engineer*
EMP: 50
SALES (corp-wide): 3.3B **Privately Held**
WEB: www.bv.com
SIC: 8711 Consulting engineer
HQ: Black & Veatch Corporation
11401 Lamar Ave
Overland Park KS 66211
913 458-2000

(P-25569)
BLAIR ENGINEERING INC (PA)
Also Called: Blair, Church & Flynn
451 Clovis Ave Ste 200, Clovis
(93612-1376)
PHONE...................................559 326-1400
David Mowry, *CEO*
Adam Holt, *CFO*
Jeffrey Brians, *Vice Pres*
Karl Kienow, *Vice Pres*

EMP: 95
SQ FT: 15,000
SALES (est): 13.3MM **Privately Held**
WEB: www.bcf-engr.com
SIC: 8711 8713 Civil engineering; consult-
ing engineer; surveying services

(P-25570)
BMT SCIENTIFIC MARINE SVCS INC (HQ)
955 Borra Pl Ste 100, Escondido
(92029-2011)
PHONE...................................760 737-3505
Thomas L Johnson, *President*
Andy Brown, *President*
Cynthia Ballard, *CFO*
Rod Edwards, *Vice Pres*
R Peter Johnson, *Vice Pres*
EMP: 65
SQ FT: 25,000
SALES (est): 23.7MM
SALES (corp-wide): 221.1MM **Privately Held**
WEB: www.scimar.com
SIC: 8711 Marine engineering
PA: Bmt Group Limited
Goodrich House
Teddington MIDDX TW11
208 943-5544

(P-25571)
BOEING COMPANY
329 Bernardo Ave, Mountain View
(94043-5225)
PHONE...................................650 316-3732
Samuel Tricoli, *Manager*
EMP: 500
SALES (corp-wide): 93.3B **Publicly Held**
SIC: 8711 3812 Engineering services;
radar systems & equipment
PA: The Boeing Company
100 N Riverside Plz
Chicago IL 60606
312 544-2000

(P-25572)
BOEING COMPANY
5800 Woolsey Canyon Rd, Canoga Park
(91304-1148)
PHONE...................................818 466-8800
Philip Condit, *Branch Mgr*
EMP: 50
SALES (corp-wide): 93.3B **Publicly Held**
SIC: 8711 8748 Engineering services;
safety training service
PA: The Boeing Company
100 N Riverside Plz
Chicago IL 60606
312 544-2000

(P-25573)
BOOZ ALLEN HAMILTON INC
2250 E Imperial Hwy # 540, El Segundo
(90245-3547)
PHONE...................................310 524-1557
Loren Caddick, *Manager*
Christine Jana, *Facilities Mgr*
EMP: 60 **Publicly Held**
WEB: www.arinc.com
SIC: 8711 Engineering services
HQ: Booz Allen Hamilton Inc.
8283 Greensboro Dr # 700
Mc Lean VA 22102
703 902-5000

(P-25574)
BOYLE ENGINEERING CORPORATION (HQ)
999 W Town And Country Rd, Orange
(92868-4713)
PHONE...................................949 476-3300
Phil Petrocelli, *President*
Keith T Campbell, *President*
Jon S Holmgren, *CFO*
Salvatore D'Angelo, *Vice Pres*
David W Huchel, *Admin Sec*
EMP: 100 EST: 1945
SQ FT: 50,000
SALES (est): 59.9MM
SALES (corp-wide): 20.1B **Publicly Held**
WEB: www.boyleengineering.com
SIC: 8711 8712 Engineering services; ar-
chitectural engineering

PA: Aecom
1999 Avenue Of The Stars # 2600
Los Angeles CA 90067
213 593-8000

(P-25575)
BOYLE ENGINEERING CORPORATION
999 W Town And Country Rd, Orange
(92868-4713)
P.O. Box 7350, Newport Beach (92658-
7350)
PHONE...................................714 543-5274
EMP: 80
SALES (corp-wide): 8.3B **Publicly Held**
SIC: 8711 8712
HQ: Boyle Engineering Corporation
999 W Town And Country Rd
Orange CA 92868
949 476-3300

(P-25576)
BRADY GCE II
2655 Camino, San Diego (92108)
PHONE...................................858 496-0500
Marisol Canales, *Principal*
Richard Brady, *Principal*
Jon Owens, *Principal*
EMP: 99 EST: 2013
SQ FT: 20,000
SALES (est): 2.7MM **Privately Held**
SIC: 8711 1542 1623 8744 Civil engi-
neering; commercial & office building,
new construction; water & sewer line con-
struction;

(P-25577)
BRINDERSON LP (HQ)
19000 Macarthur Blvd # 800, Irvine
(92612-1461)
PHONE...................................714 466-7100
Gary Wilson, *Principal*
Billy Short, *Exec VP*
Gary French, *Program Mgr*
Bob Lawvey, *Program Mgr*
Daniel Weir, *Project Mgr*
EMP: 150
SQ FT: 30,000
SALES (est): 395.8MM
SALES (corp-wide): 1.3B **Publicly Held**
SIC: 8711 1629 Engineering services;
dams, waterways, docks & other marine
construction
PA: Aegion Corporation
17988 Edison Ave
Chesterfield MO 63005
636 530-8000

(P-25578)
BRINDERSON LP
19000 Macarthur Blvd # 800, Irvine
(92612-1461)
PHONE...................................714 466-7100
Allan Updyke, *President*
Jon Rodriguez, *CFO*
EMP: 60
SALES (est): 2.5MM
SALES (corp-wide): 1.3B **Publicly Held**
SIC: 8711
HQ: Energy & Mining Holding Company Llc
17988 Edison Ave
Chesterfield MO 63005
636 530-8000

(P-25579)
BROSAMER & WALL INC
1777 Oakland Blvd Ste 300, Walnut Creek
(94596-4063)
PHONE...................................925 932-7900
Robert Brosamer, *Ch of Bd*
Charles Wall, *Vice Ch Bd*
EMP: 140 EST: 2012
SQ FT: 13,000
SALES: 60.6MM **Privately Held**
SIC: 8711 Engineering services

(P-25580)
BROWN AND CALDWELL (PA)
201 N Civic Dr Ste 115, Walnut Creek
(94596-3865)
P.O. Box 8045 (94596-1220)
PHONE...................................925 937-9010
Craig Goehring, *CEO*
Richard D' Amanto, *President*
James Miller, *Vice Ch Bd*
Cindy Paulson, *Officer*

Dan Davis, *Vice Pres*
EMP: 131
SQ FT: 24,000
SALES (est): 540.3MM **Privately Held**
SIC: 8711 Civil engineering; sanitary engi-
neers; consulting engineer

(P-25581)
BROWN AND CALDWELL
1590 Drew Ave Ste 210, Davis
(95618-7848)
PHONE...................................530 747-0650
Dave Zuber, *Manager*
EMP: 80
SQ FT: 4,000
SALES (corp-wide): 540.3MM **Privately Held**
SIC: 8711 Consulting engineer
PA: Brown And Caldwell
201 N Civic Dr Ste 115
Walnut Creek CA 94596
925 937-9010

(P-25582)
BROWN AND CALDWELL
9665 Chesapeake Dr # 201, San Diego
(92123-1367)
PHONE...................................858 514-8822
George Khoury, *Vice Pres*
Victor Occiano, *Vice Pres*
Shea Petry, *Project Mgr*
Billy Chu, *Engineer*
Jason Gornall, *Engineer*
EMP: 56
SALES (corp-wide): 540.3MM **Privately Held**
SIC: 8711 Civil engineering; sanitary engi-
neers; consulting engineer
PA: Brown And Caldwell
201 N Civic Dr Ste 115
Walnut Creek CA 94596
925 937-9010

(P-25583)
BSK ASSOCIATES
Also Called: B S K Analytical Laboratories
1414 Stanislaus St, Fresno (93706-1623)
PHONE...................................559 497-2888
Jeff Koelewyn, *Director*
EMP: 60
SQ FT: 6,316
SALES (corp-wide): 50.3MM **Privately Held**
WEB: www.bskinc.com
SIC: 8711 8734 Professional engineer;
testing laboratories
PA: Bsk Associates
550 W Locust Ave
Fresno CA 93650
559 497-2880

(P-25584)
BURNS & MCDONNELL INC
140 S State College Blvd, Brea
(92821-5807)
PHONE...................................714 256-1595
Ken Gerling, *Branch Mgr*
Jamie Hoffman, *Assistant*
EMP: 80
SALES (corp-wide): 2.3B **Privately Held**
SIC: 8711 Engineering services
PA: Burns & Mcdonnell, Inc.
9400 Ward Pkwy
Kansas City MO 64114
816 333-9400

(P-25585)
BUTLER AMERICA LLC (HQ)
3820 State St Ste B, Santa Barbara
(93105-3182)
PHONE...................................805 880-1965
Christine Ciocca, *President*
Robert Olson, *CEO*
Stephen Morrison, *CFO*
Bharani K Aroll, *Vice Pres*
James Elsner, *Vice Pres*
EMP: 1000
SQ FT: 160,000
SALES (est): 98.4MM
SALES (est): 37.4MM **Privately Held**
SIC: 8711 8748 7361 Engineering serv-
ices; telecommunications consultant;
labor contractors (employment agency)

PA: Butler America Holdings, Inc.
3820 State St Ste B
Santa Barbara CA 93105
805 880-1978

(P-25586)
C D LYON CONSTRUCTION INC (PA)
380 W Stanley Ave, Ventura (93001-1350)
P.O. Box 1456 (93002-1456)
PHONE..........................805 653-0173
Christopher D Lyon, *CEO*
Debra C Lyon, *Corp Secy*
Vincent Torres, *Opers Mgr*
Chuck Ludaescher, *Advisor*
Jon Alvarado, *Supervisor*
EMP: 80
SALES (est): 23.5MM **Privately Held**
WEB: www.cdlyon.com
SIC: 8711 Petroleum engineering

(P-25587)
CALIFORNIA ENVMTL SYSTEMS INC
12265 Locksley Ln, Auburn (95602-2055)
PHONE..........................530 820-3693
Carter Pierce, *Principal*
Jeanette Pierce, *Controller*
EMP: 70 **EST:** 2011
SQ FT: 10,000
SALES: 6MM **Privately Held**
SIC: 8711 Engineering services

(P-25588)
CALNEV PIPE LINE LLC
1100 W Town And Cntry Rd, Orange (92868-4600)
PHONE..........................714 560-4400
Richard Kinder,
EMP: 200
SALES: 59.2MM **Publicly Held**
WEB: www.kindermorgan.com
SIC: 8711 Energy conservation engineering
HQ: Kinder Morgan Energy Partners, L.P.
1001 La St Ste 1000
Houston TX 77002
713 369-9000

(P-25589)
CAMBRIDGE DESIGN PARTNR INC
228 Hamilton Ave Fl 3, Palo Alto (94301-2583)
PHONE..........................650 387-7812
Matt Schumann, *CEO*
Dominique Freeman, *Admin Sec*
EMP: 85 **EST:** 2015
SALES (est): 1.6MM **Privately Held**
SIC: 8711 8742 7379 Engineering services; management consulting services; business consultant; business planning & organizing services; marketing consulting services; computer related consulting services; data processing consultant

(P-25590)
CAPITAL ENGINEERING CONS INC (PA)
11020 Sun Center Dr # 100, Rancho Cordova (95670-6287)
PHONE..........................916 851-3500
Lowell E Shields, *President*
Thomas Duval, *Treasurer*
John Lionakis, *Vice Pres*
Michael Risch, *MIS Staff*
EMP: 66
SQ FT: 6,800
SALES: 7.6MM **Privately Held**
WEB: www.capital-engineering.com
SIC: 8711 Mechanical engineering

(P-25591)
CARLILEMACY INC
15 3rd St, Santa Rosa (95401-6204)
PHONE..........................707 542-6451
David Hanson, *President*
Mark Hale, *Treasurer*
Curtis Nichols, *Vice Pres*
Bruce Jarvis, *Admin Sec*
Curt Nichols, *Engineer*
EMP: 50
SQ FT: 10,000

SALES (est): 6.8MM **Privately Held**
WEB: www.carlilemacy.com
SIC: 8711 Civil engineering

(P-25592)
CARLSON BARBEE & GIBSON INC
2633 Camino Ramon Ste 350, San Ramon (94583-9139)
PHONE..........................925 866-0322
David Carlson, *President*
Grant Gibson, *Vice Pres*
Michael Barbee, *Admin Sec*
Christopher Quibol, *Admin Asst*
Carrol Rickard, *Admin Asst*
EMP: 100
SQ FT: 6,800
SALES (est): 14.3MM **Privately Held**
WEB: www.cbandg.com
SIC: 8711 Civil engineering

(P-25593)
CAROLLO ENGINEERS INC (PA)
2700 Ygnacio Valley Rd # 300, Walnut Creek (94598-3466)
PHONE..........................925 932-1710
Balakrishnan Narayanan, *President*
Gary Meyerhofer, *Partner*
Rick D Wheadon, *Treasurer*
Laura Baumberger, *Assoc VP*
John Briones, *Assoc VP*
EMP: 100
SQ FT: 20,000
SALES (est): 196.5MM **Privately Held**
SIC: 8711 Consulting engineer

(P-25594)
CAROLLO ENGINEERS INC
3100 S Harbor Blvd # 200, Santa Ana (92704-6823)
PHONE..........................714 540-4300
Mary Lee, *Manager*
Ash K Wason, *Partner*
Toby Weissert, *Partner*
C B Hagar, *Principal*
John S Heckler, *Principal*
EMP: 90
SALES (corp-wide): 196.5MM **Privately Held**
SIC: 8711 Consulting engineer
PA: Carollo Engineers, Inc.
2700 Ygnacio Valley Rd # 300
Walnut Creek CA 94598
925 932-1710

(P-25595)
CAROLLO ENGINEERS INC
701 Palomar Airport Rd, Carlsbad (92011-1027)
PHONE..........................858 505-1020
Gary Deis, *Manager*
EMP: 110
SALES (corp-wide): 196.5MM **Privately Held**
SIC: 8711 Consulting engineer
PA: Carollo Engineers, Inc.
2700 Ygnacio Valley Rd # 300
Walnut Creek CA 94598
925 932-1710

(P-25596)
CBS BROADCASTING INC
7800 Beverly Blvd, Los Angeles (90036-2112)
PHONE..........................323 575-2345
Michael Klausman, *Senior VP*
Garen Vandebeek, *Senior VP*
Pete Ely, *Vice Pres*
Al Colini, *Engineer*
Dana Kwiatkowski, *Engineer*
EMP: 90
SALES (corp-wide): 13.7B **Publicly Held**
SIC: 8711 Engineering services
HQ: Cbs Broadcasting Inc.
51 W 52nd St
New York NY 10019
212 975-4321

(P-25597)
CDI MARINE COMPANY LLC
694 Moss St, Chula Vista (91911-1616)
PHONE..........................619 407-4010
M S Karlovic, *CEO*
Stephen Karlovic, *CEO*
EMP: 50

SALES (corp-wide): 172.3MM **Privately Held**
SIC: 8711 Engineering services
HQ: Cdi Marine Company, Llc
4600 Village Ave
Norfolk VA 23502
757 763-6666

(P-25598)
CDM SMITH INC
46 Discovery Ste 250, Irvine (92618-3133)
PHONE..........................949 752-5452
Steve Brewer, *Manager*
R B Chalmers, *Principal*
Jeffrey Hilger, *Manager*
EMP: 72
SALES (corp-wide): 1.1B **Privately Held**
WEB: www.cdm.com
SIC: 8711 Consulting engineer
PA: Cdm Smith Inc
75 State St Ste 701
Boston MA 02109
617 452-6000

(P-25599)
CDM SMITH INC
Also Called: Camp Dresser & McKee
703 Palomar Airport Rd # 300, Carlsbad (92011-1043)
PHONE..........................760 438-7755
Kelly Burn-Roy, *Director*
Kellene Burn-Roy, *Vice Pres*
Keith London, *Principal*
Tony Arce, *General Mgr*
Jason Yoshimura, *Project Mgr*
EMP: 60
SALES (corp-wide): 1.1B **Privately Held**
WEB: www.cdm.com
SIC: 8711 Sanitary engineers
PA: Cdm Smith Inc
75 State St Ste 701
Boston MA 02109
617 452-6000

(P-25600)
CDM SMITH INC
2300 Clayton Rd Ste 950, Concord (94520-2196)
PHONE..........................617 452-6000
Randall Smith, *Manager*
Ian Lo, *Project Mgr*
John Mooney, *Technology*
John Mariano, *Electrical Engi*
John Wondolleck, *Sr Project Mgr*
EMP: 80
SALES (corp-wide): 1.1B **Privately Held**
WEB: www.cdm.com
SIC: 8711 Consulting engineer
PA: Cdm Smith Inc
75 State St Ste 701
Boston MA 02109
617 452-6000

(P-25601)
CE2 KLEINFELDER JV
7901 Stoneridge Dr # 315, Pleasanton (94588-3677)
PHONE..........................925 463-7301
Clyde Wong, *Principal*
Thomas Berry, *Admin Asst*
EMP: 72
SQ FT: 300
SALES (est): 3.3MM **Privately Held**
SIC: 8711 8748 Consulting engineer; energy conservation engineering; systems analysis & engineering consulting services

(P-25602)
CECOS
Also Called: Csfe
3502 Goodspeed St Ste 1, Port Hueneme (93043-4335)
PHONE..........................805 982-5400
Peter Sanders,
EMP: 50
SALES (est): 2.4MM **Privately Held**
WEB: www.cecos.com
SIC: 8711 Civil engineering

(P-25603)
CEM BUILDERS INC
Also Called: Dirtmarket , The
37 S 4th St, Campbell (95008-2943)
PHONE..........................408 395-1490
David Rossi, *CEO*

Lesley Matheson, *President*
Nathan Stanley, *Vice Pres*
EMP: 50
SQ FT: 3,000
SALES: 2MM **Privately Held**
WEB: www.dirtmarket.com
SIC: 8711 5093 Engineering services; scrap & waste materials

(P-25604)
CH2M HILL INC
2525 Airpark Dr, Redding (96001-2443)
PHONE..........................530 243-5832
Ed Christopherson, *Manager*
Anthony Cugliat, *President*
Hank Halbach, *Program Mgr*
Mike Cooper, *Dept Chairman*
Bill Fox, *Dept Chairman*
EMP: 220
SALES (corp-wide): 10B **Publicly Held**
SIC: 8711 Consulting engineer
HQ: Ch2m Hill, Inc.
9191 S Jamaica St
Englewood CO 80112
303 771-0900

(P-25605)
CH2M HILL INC
2485 Natomas Park Dr # 600, Sacramento (95833-2975)
PHONE..........................916 920-0300
J Hartley, *Branch Mgr*
EMP: 1200
SALES (corp-wide): 10B **Publicly Held**
SIC: 8711 Engineering services
HQ: Ch2m Hill, Inc.
9191 S Jamaica St
Englewood CO 80112
303 771-0900

(P-25606)
CH2M HILL INC
155 Grand Ave Ste 800, Oakland (94612-3767)
P.O. Box 12681 (94604-2681)
PHONE..........................510 604-4144
Robert Keyes, *Manager*
Mark Aikawa, *Vice Pres*
Ana Demorest, *Project Mgr*
Julie Eakins, *Project Mgr*
Ryanne Truex, *Engineer*
EMP: 200
SALES (corp-wide): 10B **Publicly Held**
SIC: 8711 Consulting engineer; civil engineering
HQ: Ch2m Hill, Inc.
9191 S Jamaica St
Englewood CO 80112
303 771-0900

(P-25607)
CHADUXTT JV
1230 Columbia St Ste 1000, San Diego (92101-8588)
PHONE..........................619 525-7188
Michael J Wanta, *President*
Ed Philemonof, *Principal*
EMP: 83
SALES (est): 4.5MM **Privately Held**
SIC: 8711 Consulting engineer

(P-25608)
CHEVRON ENERGY TECHNOLOGY CO (HQ)
100 Chevron Way, Richmond (94801-2016)
PHONE..........................510 242-5059
R William Potter, *Principal*
EMP: 72
SALES (est): 24.9MM
SALES (corp-wide): 141.7B **Publicly Held**
WEB: www.chevrontexaco.com
SIC: 8711 Engineering services
PA: Chevron Corporation
6001 Bollinger Canyon Rd
San Ramon CA 94583
925 842-1000

(P-25609)
CIERRA WIRELESS
2738 Loker Ave W Ste A, Carlsbad (92010-6629)
PHONE..........................760 476-8700
Jason Collinhower, *President*
EMP: 110

SALES (est): 4.2MM **Privately Held**
WEB: www.sierrawireless.com
SIC: **8711** 4813 Engineering services;

(P-25610)
CITY OF DALY CITY
Also Called: Public Works Engineering Div
333 90th St Fl 1, Daly City (94015-1808)
PHONE...................................650 991-8064
John Fuller, *Director*
EMP: 70 **Privately Held**
WEB: www.dalycity.org
SIC: **8711** 9111 Engineering services;
mayors' offices
PA: City Of Daly City
333 90th St
Daly City CA 94015
650 991-8000

(P-25611)
CITY OF GLENDALE
Also Called: Engineering Public Works
633 E Broadway Ste 205, Glendale
(91206-4310)
PHONE...................................818 548-3945
Lou Le Blanc, *Director*
EMP: 60 **Privately Held**
WEB: www.glendaleca.com
SIC: **8711** 9511 Engineering services; air,
water & solid waste management;
PA: City Of Glendale
141 N Glendale Ave Fl 2
Glendale CA 91206
818 548-2085

(P-25612)
CITY OF LOS ANGELES
Also Called: Public Works Dept
600 S Spring St Unit 200, Los Angeles
(90014-1979)
PHONE...................................213 978-0259
Deborah Weignard, *Branch Mgr*
EMP: 1000 **Privately Held**
WEB: www.lacity.org
SIC: **8711** 9532 Mechanical engineering;
electrical or electronic engineering; urban
& community development;
PA: City Of Los Angeles
200 N Spring St Ste 303
Los Angeles CA 90012
213 978-0600

(P-25613)
CITY OF LOS ANGELES
6262 Van Nuys Blvd # 451, Van Nuys
(91401-2793)
PHONE...................................818 756-8022
Michael Kantor, *Branch Mgr*
Claudia Rodriguez, *Bd of Directors*
EMP: 508 **Privately Held**
WEB: www.lacity.org
SIC: **8711** 9224 Fire protection engineer-
ing; fire protection
PA: City Of Los Angeles
200 N Spring St Ste 303
Los Angeles CA 90012
213 978-0600

(P-25614)
CITY OF SAN DIEGO
9573 Chesapeake Dr, San Diego
(92123-1304)
PHONE...................................858 627-3210
Hossein Ruhi, *Branch Mgr*
EMP: 250 **Privately Held**
SIC: **8711** Engineering services
PA: City Of San Diego
202 C St
San Diego CA 92101
619 236-6330

(P-25615)
CITY OF VACAVILLE
Also Called: Public Works Office
650 Merchant St, Vacaville (95688-6992)
PHONE...................................707 449-5170
Dale Pfeiffer, *Manager*
James Loomis, *Engineer*
EMP: 400 **Privately Held**
WEB: www.lenaugustine.com
SIC: **8711** Engineering services
PA: City Of Vacaville
650 Merchant St
Vacaville CA 95688
707 449-5100

(P-25616)
CITY OF WOODLAND
Also Called: Public Works Department
42929 County Road 24, Woodland
(95776-9111)
PHONE...................................530 661-5961
Gary Wagner, *Director*
EMP: 75 **Privately Held**
WEB: www.ci.woodland.ca.us
SIC: **8711** 8748 Engineering services; city
planning
PA: City Of Woodland
300 1st St
Woodland CA 95695
530 661-5830

(P-25617)
CLARK RICHARDSON AND BISKUP
Also Called: C.R. B Cnsulting Engineers Inc
3207 Grey Hawk Ct Ste 150, Carlsbad
(92010-6668)
PHONE...................................760 496-3714
EMP: 51
SALES (corp-wide): 128MM **Privately
Held**
SIC: **8711** Consulting engineer
PA: Clark, Richardson And Biskup Consult-
ing Engineers, Inc.
1251 Nw Briarcliff Pkwy # 500
Kansas City MO 64116
816 880-9800

(P-25618)
COLUMBUS TECH & SVCS INC (PA)
1960 E Grand Ave, El Segundo
(90245-5099)
PHONE...................................310 356-5600
Ajay Handa, *CEO*
Reva Handa, *President*
Bill Bennett, *Finance*
Kim Girard,
Scott Crawford, *Director*
EMP: 385
SQ FT: 5,303
SALES: 67MM **Privately Held**
WEB: www.columbususa.com
SIC: **8711** Consulting engineer

(P-25619)
COMPREHENSIVE ENVIRO
1615 Murray Canyon Rd, San Diego
(92108-4314)
PHONE...................................619 294-9400
EMP: 50
SALES (est): 1.5MM **Privately Held**
SIC: **8711**

(P-25620)
CONNEXSYS ENGINEERING INC
1320 Willow Pass Rd # 500, Concord
(94520-5269)
PHONE...................................510 243-2050
Flavio Santini, *CEO*
Franklin L Baker, *COO*
Leonard George, *COO*
Carol Avila, *Executive*
Paul Chavez, *Info Tech Mgr*
EMP: 50
SQ FT: 10,000
SALES (est): 11.5MM
SALES (corp-wide): 13.1MM **Privately
Held**
WEB: www.connexsysinc.com
SIC: **8711** Consulting engineer
PA: Versa Engineering & Technology, Inc.
1320 Willow Pass Rd # 500
Concord CA 94520
925 405-4505

(P-25621)
CONSTRUCTION TSTG & ENGRG INC (PA)
1441 Montiel Rd Ste 115, Escondido
(92026-2239)
PHONE...................................760 746-4955
Thomas Gaeto, *CEO*
Rodney Ballard, *Vice Pres*
EMP: 60
SQ FT: 4,800
SALES (est): 21.1MM **Privately Held**
SIC: **8711** Construction & civil engineering

(P-25622)
CONTINENTAL GRAPHICS CORP
Also Called: Continental Data Graphics
2401 E Wardlow Rd, Long Beach
(90807-5309)
PHONE...................................714 503-4200
Steve Meade, *Manager*
Cathy Barnard, *Vice Pres*
Gary Beyer, *Vice Pres*
Jose Madrid, *Vice Pres*
Reza Arabashahi, *IT/INT Sup*
EMP: 1080
SALES (corp-wide): 93.3B **Publicly Held**
WEB: www.cdgnow.com
SIC: **8711** Engineering services
HQ: Continental Graphics Corporation
4060 N Lakewood Blvd
Long Beach CA 90808
714 503-4200

(P-25623)
COOPER VALI & ASSOCIATES INC (DH)
1850 Gateway Blvd Ste 100, Concord
(94520-8447)
PHONE...................................510 446-8301
Gary Bedey, *CEO*
Hank Doll, *President*
John Collins, *COO*
Marian Ross, *CFO*
Agnes Weber, *Officer*
EMP: 80
SQ FT: 3,000
SALES (est): 33.7MM
SALES (corp-wide): 165.4MM **Privately
Held**
SIC: **8711** Construction & civil engineering;
building construction consultant
HQ: Trc Companies, Inc.
650 Suffolk St
Lowell MA 01854
978 970-5600

(P-25624)
CORA CONSTRUCTORS INC
Also Called: General Contractor
75140 Saint Charles Pl A, Palm Desert
(92211-9044)
PHONE...................................760 674-3201
Dennis Stockton, *CEO*
Kevin Huculak, *Project Mgr*
EMP: 50
SQ FT: 2,500
SALES (est): 11.3MM **Privately Held**
WEB: www.coraconstructors.com
SIC: **8711** Building construction consultant

(P-25625)
COUNTY ENGINEERS ASSN CAL
120 Round Ct, Petaluma (94952-4720)
PHONE...................................707 762-3492
EMP: 58
SALES: 353.7K **Privately Held**
SIC: **8711**

(P-25626)
COUNTY OF LOS ANGELES
Also Called: Engineering Division
44933 Fern Ave, Lancaster (93534-2461)
PHONE...................................661 723-6088
Bert Perry, *Branch Mgr*
EMP: 130 **Privately Held**
WEB: www.co.la.ca.us
SIC: **8711** 9111 Engineering services; ex-
ecutive offices
PA: County Of Los Angeles
500 W Temple St Ste 437
Los Angeles CA 90012
213 974-1101

(P-25627)
COUNTY OF LOS ANGELES
Public Works, Dept of
14747 Ramona Blvd, Baldwin Park
(91706-3435)
PHONE...................................626 337-1277
William Wolfer, *Branch Mgr*
EMP: 130 **Privately Held**
WEB: www.co.la.ca.us
SIC: **8711** 9199 Engineering services;
general government administration;
PA: County Of Los Angeles
500 W Temple St Ste 437
Los Angeles CA 90012
213 974-1101

(P-25628)
COUNTY OF MARIN
Also Called: Department of Public Works
1600 Los Gamos Dr Ste 200, San Rafael
(94903-1807)
P.O. Box 4186 (94913-4186)
PHONE...................................415 499-7877
Mehdi Sadjadi, *Director*
EMP: 200 **Privately Held**
SIC: **8711** 1611 7349 6552 Civil engineering; highway & street construction;
building maintenance services; subdividers & developers; automotive & apparel trimmings
PA: County Of Marin
3501 Civic Center Dr # 258
San Rafael CA 94903
415 473-6358

(P-25629)
COUNTY OF PLACER
Also Called: Public Works Dept
3091 County Center Dr # 220, Auburn
(95603-2614)
PHONE...................................530 889-7500
Ken Grehm, *Director*
EMP: 150 **Privately Held**
WEB: www.ssvems.com
SIC: **8711** 9511 Structural engineering;
PA: County Of Placer
2986 Richardson Dr
Auburn CA 95603
530 889-4200

(P-25630)
COUNTY OF SAN LUIS OBISPO
Also Called: County Government
Government Center Rm 207, San Luis
Obispo (93408-0001)
PHONE...................................805 781-5258
Tim Nanson, *Branch Mgr*
EMP: 170 **Privately Held**
SIC: **8711** Engineering services
PA: County Of San Luis Obispo
Government Center Rm. 300
San Luis Obispo CA 93408
805 781-5040

(P-25631)
CROWN ENERGY SERVICES INC
Also Called: Able Services
611 Gateway Blvd, South San Francisco
(94080-7015)
PHONE...................................415 546-6534
EMP: 1791 **Privately Held**
SIC: **8711** Engineering services
PA: Crown Energy Services, Inc.
868 Folsom St
San Francisco CA 94107

(P-25632)
CSG CONSULTANTS INC (PA)
550 Pilgrim Dr, Foster City (94404-1253)
PHONE...................................650 522-2500
Cyrus Kianpour, *CEO*
Dave Gottlieb, *CFO*
Khoa Duong, *Vice Pres*
Bradley Donohue, *Admin Sec*
Nourdin Khayata, *Admin Sec*
EMP: 50
SQ FT: 16,000
SALES: 28.3MM **Privately Held**
SIC: **8711** Engineering services

(P-25633)
CUBIC GLOBAL DEFENSE INC
2280 Historic Decatur Rd # 200, San Diego
(92106-6133)
PHONE...................................858 277-8760
Bill Toti, *President*
James Perez, *Officer*
Angela Hartley, *Admin Sec*
EMP: 95
SALES (est): 6.8MM **Privately Held**
SIC: **8711** Engineering services

(P-25634)
CURTISS-WRIGHT CONTROLS (DH)
Also Called: Avionics & Electronics
28965 Avenue Penn, Valencia
(91355-4185)
PHONE...................................626 851-3100

Thomas P Quinly, *CEO*
John Kuperhand, *President*
Tony Sozutek, *Treasurer*
Anabele Cloud, *Admin Sec*
EMP: 69 **EST:** 1978
SQ FT: 27,000
SALES (est): 29.2MM
SALES (corp-wide): 2.2B **Publicly Held**
WEB: www.autronics.com
SIC: 8711 Engineering services
HQ: Curtiss-Wright Controls, Inc.
15801 Brixham Hill Ave # 200
Charlotte NC 28277
704 869-4600

(P-25635)
CURTISS-WRIGHT CONTROLS
28965 Avenue Penn, Santa Clarita
(91355-4185)
PHONE..................661 257-4430
Val Zarov, *Branch Mgr*
EMP: 109
SALES (corp-wide): 2.2B **Publicly Held**
SIC: 8711 Engineering services
HQ: Curtiss-Wright Controls Electronic Systems, Inc.
28965 Avenue Penn
Santa Clarita CA 91355
661 702-1494

(P-25636)
CURTISS-WRIGHT CONTROLS (DH)
28965 Avenue Penn, Santa Clarita
(91355-4185)
PHONE..................661 702-1494
Thomas P Quinly, *CEO*
David Dietz, *President*
David Zirkelbach, *Engineer*
Sara Franke, *Manager*
EMP: 172
SQ FT: 18,700
SALES (est): 51.5MM
SALES (corp-wide): 2.2B **Publicly Held**
WEB: www.cwcembedded.com
SIC: 8711 8731 3769 3625 Consulting engineer; commercial physical research; guided missile & space vehicle parts & auxiliary equipment; relays & industrial controls
HQ: Curtiss-Wright Controls, Inc.
15801 Brixham Hill Ave # 200
Charlotte NC 28277
704 869-4600

(P-25637)
D & K ENGINEERING (PA)
15890 Bernardo Center Dr, San Diego
(92127-2320)
PHONE..................858 451-8999
Scott M Dennis, *CEO*
George Kaplinsky, *President*
Alex Kunczynski, *President*
Jody Zevenbergen, *CFO*
Diane Law, *Vice Pres*
▲ **EMP:** 148
SQ FT: 60,000
SALES (est): 154.7MM **Privately Held**
WEB: www.dkengineering.com
SIC: 8711 3824 Acoustical engineering; mechanical & electromechanical counters & devices

(P-25638)
D A WOOD CONSTRUCTION INC
601 Albers Rd, Modesto (95357-1015)
P.O. Box 1810, Empire (95319-1810)
PHONE..................209 491-4970
Danny Wood, *President*
Kristine Wood, *Admin Sec*
Kimmer Leonard, *Superintendent*
EMP: 56
SQ FT: 960
SALES (est): 9.6MM **Privately Held**
WEB: www.dawoodinc.com
SIC: 8711 Construction & civil engineering

(P-25639)
DAVID EVANS AND ASSOCIATES INC
4141 Inland Empire Blvd # 250, Ontario
(91764-5003)
PHONE..................909 481-5750
Cliff Simental, *Branch Mgr*
EMP: 50

SALES (corp-wide): 129.9MM **Privately Held**
WEB: www.deainc.com
SIC: 8711 Civil engineering
PA: David Evans And Associates, Inc.
2100 Sw River Pkwy
Portland OR 97201
503 223-6663

(P-25640)
DAVID EVANS ENTERPRISES INC
201 S Figueroa St Ste 240, Los Angeles
(90012-2543)
PHONE..................213 337-3680
Adriana Klooth, *Engineer*
EMP: 748
SALES (corp-wide): 28MM **Privately Held**
SIC: 8711 7389 Consulting engineer; design services
PA: David Evans Enterprises, Inc.
2100 Sw River Pkwy
Portland OR 97201
503 223-6663

(P-25641)
DEGENKOLB ENGINEERS (PA)
375 Beale St Ste 500, San Francisco
(94105-2177)
PHONE..................415 392-6952
Stacy Bartoletti, *CEO*
Chris Poland, *Ch of Bd*
Robert Beggs, *CFO*
David Bonneville, *Principal*
James O Malley, *Admin Sec*
EMP: 165
SQ FT: 22,800
SALES (est): 24.6MM **Privately Held**
WEB: www.degenkolb.com
SIC: 8711 Structural engineering; consulting engineer

(P-25642)
DEVELOPMENT RESOURCE CONS INC (PA)
160 S Old Springs Rd # 210, Anaheim
(92808-1260)
PHONE..................714 685-6860
Lawrence Gates, *President*
Megan Shamy, *Design Engr*
Wayne Pena, *Project Mgr*
Cory Mack, *Project Engr*
Homer Maniago, *Project Engr*
EMP: 90
SQ FT: 12,000
SALES (est): 11.7MM **Privately Held**
SIC: 8711 Civil engineering

(P-25643)
DEX CORPORATION
Also Called: Data Exchange
3600 Via Pescador, Camarillo
(93012-5051)
PHONE..................805 388-1711
Sheldon Malchiconfqs, *CEO*
Rajiv Duggal, *Director*
EMP: 150
SQ FT: 100,000
SALES (est): 6.4MM **Privately Held**
SIC: 8711 5065 Engineering services; electronic parts

(P-25644)
DIVERGENT TECHNOLOGIES INC
19601 Hamilton Ave, Torrance
(90502-1309)
PHONE..................310 339-1186
Kevin Czinger, *President*
Broc Tenhouten, *COO*
Kira Khodskaya, *CFO*
EMP: 97
SALES (est): 928.5K **Privately Held**
SIC: 8711 Mechanical engineering

(P-25645)
DMS FACILITY SERVICES LLC
5735 Krny Vlla Rd Ste 108, San Diego
(92123)
PHONE..................858 560-4191
John Harris, *Branch Mgr*
EMP: 150 **Privately Held**
WEB: www.dmsfacilityservices.com

SIC: 8711 7349 0781 Engineering services; janitorial service, contract basis; landscape services
PA: Dms Facility Services, Llc
1040 Arroyo Dr
South Pasadena CA 91030
-

(P-25646)
DOKKEN ENGINEERING (PA)
110 Blue Ravine Rd # 200, Folsom
(95630-4711)
PHONE..................916 858-0642
Richard Dokken, *CEO*
Richard Liptak, *President*
Bradley Dokken, *CFO*
Cathy Chan, *Admin Sec*
Brad Dokken, *Engineer*
EMP: 70
SQ FT: 12,931
SALES: 21.9MM **Privately Held**
WEB: www.dokkenengineering.com
SIC: 8711 8741 Civil engineering; construction management

(P-25647)
DUDEK (PA)
605 3rd St, Encinitas (92024-3513)
PHONE..................760 942-5147
Frank J Dudek, *Ch of Bd*
Joe Monaco, *President*
Dave Carter, *CFO*
June Collins, *Vice Pres*
Kasey Harvey, *Project Engr*
EMP: 100
SQ FT: 50,000
SALES (est): 55.1MM **Privately Held**
SIC: 8711 8748 Civil engineering; environmental consultant

(P-25648)
DUDEK
605 3rd St, Encinitas (92024-3513)
PHONE..................760 942-5147
Kim Tessada, *Branch Mgr*
EMP: 285
SALES (corp-wide): 55.1MM **Privately Held**
SIC: 8711 Engineering services
PA: Dudek
605 3rd St
Encinitas CA 92024
760 942-5147

(P-25649)
DZYNE TECHNOLOGIES INC
11 Vanderbilt, Irvine (92618-2011)
PHONE..................703 454-0704
Thomas Strat, *CEO*
David Sammons, *CFO*
Shane Frasier, *Sr Software Eng*
Adam Thurn, *Engineer*
Joshua Neff, *Accountant*
EMP: 50 **EST:** 2013
SALES (est): 6.4MM **Privately Held**
SIC: 8711 Mechanical engineering; aviation &/or aeronautical engineering

(P-25650)
E2 CONSULTING ENGINEERS INC
1900 Powell St Ste 250, Emeryville
(94608-1807)
PHONE..................510 652-1164
Matthew Rindiera, *Office Mgr*
EMP: 300
SALES (corp-wide): 40MM **Privately Held**
SIC: 8711 Consulting engineer
PA: E2 Consulting Engineers, Inc.
450 E 17th Ave Unit 200
Denver CO 80203
303 232-9800

(P-25651)
EARTH SYSTEMS SOUTHWEST (HQ)
79811 Country Club Dr B, Bermuda Dunes
(92203-1290)
PHONE..................760 345-1588
Mark Spykerman, *President*
Jerol Brown, *Corp Secy*
Scot Stormo, *Senior VP*
Mark Houghton, *Vice Pres*
Lutz Kunze, *Vice Pres*
EMP: 59 **EST:** 1998

SQ FT: 6,750
SALES: 3.2MM
SALES (corp-wide): 20.5MM **Privately Held**
WEB: www.earthsystems.com
SIC: 8711 8734 8748 7389 Engineering services; testing laboratories; soil analysis; environmental consultant; building inspection service
PA: Earth Systems, Inc.
720 Aerovista Pl Ste A
San Luis Obispo CA 93401
805 781-0112

(P-25652)
EDO LLC
Edo Technical Svcs Operations
3500 Willow Ln, Thousand Oaks
(91361-4921)
PHONE..................914 641-2000
Thomas J Gardiner, *General Mgr*
Sam Gasowski, *Counsel*
EMP: 140
SALES (corp-wide): 6.1B **Publicly Held**
WEB: www.nycedo.com
SIC: 8711 3728 Engineering services; aircraft training equipment
HQ: Edo Llc
1500 New Horizons Blvd
Amityville NY 11701
631 630-4000

(P-25653)
EFS WEST
28472 Constellation Rd, Valencia
(91355-5081)
PHONE..................661 705-8200
Arthur Babcock, *CEO*
Robert Golden, *President*
Dante Jumanan, *Vice Pres*
Tom Soper, *Vice Pres*
Jay Persaud, *Project Mgr*
EMP: 50
SQ FT: 41,000
SALES (est): 9.7MM **Privately Held**
SIC: 8711 Engineering services

(P-25654)
EICHLEAY ENGINEERS INC
1390 Willow Pass Rd # 360, Concord
(94520-7936)
P.O. Box 238, Oakdale PA (15071-0238)
PHONE..................925 689-7000
Theodore W Nelson Jr, *President*
Robert C Grier, *Senior VP*
Steven A Bachenheimer, *Vice Pres*
David A De Mario, *Vice Pres*
Denny E Lajevic-Augustine, *Vice Pres*
EMP: 493 **EST:** 1923
SQ FT: 100,000
SALES (est): 28.6MM **Privately Held**
SIC: 8711 Consulting engineer

(P-25655)
EICHLEAY INC
3780 Kilroy Airport Way # 440, Long Beach
(90806-2498)
PHONE..................562 256-8600
Lori M Lofstrom, *Branch Mgr*
EMP: 150
SALES (corp-wide): 42.2MM **Privately Held**
SIC: 8711 Consulting engineer
PA: Eichleay Inc
1390 Willow Pass Rd # 600
Concord CA 94520
925 689-7000

(P-25656)
EICHLEAY INC (PA)
1390 Willow Pass Rd # 600, Concord
(94520-5200)
PHONE..................925 689-7000
George F Eichleay Jr, *President*
Steven S Chan, *Project Engr*
Tom McClure, *Safety Dir*
EMP: 150
SQ FT: 17,000
SALES (est): 42.2MM **Privately Held**
WEB: www.eichleay.com
SIC: 8711 Consulting engineer

(P-25657)
ELECTROSONIC INC (DH)
3320 N San Fernando Blvd, Burbank
(91504-2530)
PHONE..............................818 333-3600
James Bowie, *President*
Scott Meyer, *CFO*
David Mitchell, *Admin Sec*
◆ **EMP:** 150
SALES (est): 42.7MM
SALES (corp-wide): 436.3K **Privately
Held**
WEB: www.mediasonic.com
SIC: 8711 7359 7812 Engineering services; audio-visual equipment & supply rental; audio-visual program production
HQ: Electrosonic Limited
　　Hawley Mill
　　Dartford DA2 7
　　132 222-2211

(P-25658)
EMBEE PROCESSING LLC
Also Called: Embee Processing, Inc.
2136 S Hathaway St, Santa Ana
(92705-5248)
PHONE..............................714 546-9842
Michael Coburn, *CEO*
Scott Chrisman, *CFO*
Jim Pintarelli, *Vice Pres*
Leslie Zimmer, *Vice Pres*
Mitch Tanner, *General Mgr*
EMP: 385 **EST:** 1947
SQ FT: 100,000
SALES (est): 56.6MM **Privately Held**
WEB: www.embee.com
SIC: 8711 3398 3479 8734 Aviation &/or aeronautical engineering; shot peening (treating steel to reduce fatigue); coating of metals & formed products; metallurgical testing laboratory
HQ: All Metals Processing Of Orange County, Llc
　　8401 Standustrial St
　　Stanton CA 90680
　　714 828-8238

(P-25659)
EMERY SMITH LABORATORIES INC
Also Called: Inspection and Testing
1195 N Tustin Ave, Anaheim (92807-1736)
PHONE..............................714 238-6133
Mark Lastufka, *Manager*
EMP: 99
SALES (est): 5.3MM **Privately Held**
SIC: 8711 8071 Engineering services; testing laboratories

(P-25660)
ENCORE SEMI INC
9444 Waples St Ste 150, San Diego
(92121-2941)
PHONE..............................858 225-4993
Olivier Lauvray, *President*
EMP: 67
SALES (est): 11.2MM **Privately Held**
SIC: 8711 Electrical or electronic engineering

(P-25661)
ENERCON SERVICES INC
364 Pacific St, San Luis Obispo
(93401-3847)
PHONE..............................805 242-0600
EMP: 59
SALES (corp-wide): 231.7MM **Privately
Held**
SIC: 8711 Consulting engineer
PA: Enercon Services, Inc.
　　500 Townpark Ln Nw
　　Kennesaw GA 30144
　　770 919-1930

(P-25662)
ENERTIS SOLAR INC
1750 Montgomery St # 127, San Francisco
(94111-1000)
PHONE..............................415 400-5271
Jose Galindo, *President*
Inaki Herrero, *General Mgr*
EMP: 50
SALES (est): 2.8MM **Privately Held**
SIC: 8711 Consulting engineer

(P-25663)
ENGIE SERVICES US INC (HQ)
500 12th St Ste 300, Oakland
(94607-4087)
PHONE..............................844 678-3772
John Mahoney, *CEO*
Ryan Blair, *President*
John Sullivan, *CFO*
Mark Emerson, *Chief Mktg Ofcr*
Brad Boerger, *Vice Pres*
EMP: 60
SQ FT: 17,250
SALES (est): 759.5K
SALES (corp-wide): 24.2B **Privately Held**
SIC: 8711 Energy conservation engineering
PA: Engie
　　1 Place Samuel De Champlain
　　Courbevoie
　　144 220-000

(P-25664)
ENGILITY LLC
Also Called: Titan Pulse Sciences Division
2700 Merced St, San Leandro
(94577-5602)
PHONE..............................510 357-4610
David Price, *Manager*
EMP: 125 **Publicly Held**
SIC: 8711 Consulting engineer
HQ: Engility Llc
　　4803 Stonecroft Blvd
　　Chantilly VA 20151
　　703 708-1400

(P-25665)
ENGILITY LLC
Also Called: Command & Control Systems
7580 Metro Dr Ste 207, San Diego (92108)
PHONE..............................858 552-9500
Mike Lawson, *Branch Mgr*
EMP: 202 **Publicly Held**
SIC: 8711 Consulting engineer
HQ: Engility Llc
　　4803 Stonecroft Blvd
　　Chantilly VA 20151
　　703 708-1400

(P-25666)
ENGILITY LLC
200 W Los Angeles Ave, Simi Valley
(93065-1650)
PHONE..............................703 633-8300
Sewanee Johnson, *Branch Mgr*
Anthony Smeraglinolo, *CEO*
EMP: 3937 **Publicly Held**
SIC: 8711 Engineering services
HQ: Engility Llc
　　4803 Stonecroft Blvd
　　Chantilly VA 20151
　　703 708-1400

(P-25667)
ENGINRING SFTWR SYS SLTONS INC (PA)
Also Called: E S 3
550 W C St Ste 1630, San Diego
(92101-3569)
PHONE..............................619 338-0380
Teri Sgammato, *President*
Chuck Dahms, *CFO*
Daniele Pelessone, *CFO*
Doug Wiser, *Officer*
Clint Forrest, *Principal*
EMP: 80
SQ FT: 8,000
SALES (est): 46.8MM **Privately Held**
WEB: www.es3inc.com
SIC: 8711 Engineering services

(P-25668)
ENGLEKIRK INSTITUTIONAL INC (PA)
888 S Figueroa St Ste 180, Los Angeles
(90017-5307)
PHONE..............................323 733-2640
Tom Sabol, *President*
EMP: 50
SQ FT: 12,000
SALES (est): 6.9MM **Privately Held**
SIC: 8711 Engineering services

(P-25669)
ENGLEKIRK STRUCTURAL ENGINEERS (PA)
888 S Figueroa St # 1800, Los Angeles
(90017-5449)
PHONE..............................323 733-6673
Tom Sabol, *President*
Christopher Rosien, *CFO*
EMP: 50
SALES (est): 6.5MM **Privately Held**
SIC: 8711 Structural engineering

(P-25670)
ENVIRONMENTAL CHEMICAL CORP (PA)
Also Called: Ecc
1240 Bayshore Hwy, Burlingame
(94010-1805)
PHONE..............................650 347-1555
Manjiv Vohra, *President*
Paul Sabharwal, *Shareholder*
Tom Delmastro, *Treasurer*
August Ochabauer, *Vice Pres*
Rick Ebel, *General Mgr*
EMP: 75
SQ FT: 21,000
SALES (est): 149.6MM **Privately Held**
WEB: www.ecc.net
SIC: 8711 1542 8744 Engineering services; commercial & office building contractors;

(P-25671)
EPRISOLUTIONS INC
Also Called: Epri Csg
3412 Hillview Ave, Palo Alto (94304-1395)
PHONE..............................650 855-8900
Philip Curtis, *President*
Roger Ailshie, *Treasurer*
Walter Bak, *Vice Pres*
Dale Eldridge, *Marketing Staff*
EMP: 80
SQ FT: 20,000
SALES (est): 8.4MM **Privately Held**
WEB: www.eprictcenter.com
SIC: 8711 Engineering services

(P-25672)
EPSILON MISSION SOLUTIONS INC
9242 Lightwave Ave # 100, San Diego
(92123-6402)
PHONE..............................619 702-1700
Alan Stewart, *CFO*
Robin Nordberg, *Vice Pres*
EMP: 99
SALES (est): 4.3MM **Privately Held**
SIC: 8711 Electrical or electronic engineering

(P-25673)
EPSILON SYSTEMS SOLUTIONS INC
Also Called: Rugged Engineered Pdts Sector
5482 Complex St Ste 109, San Diego
(92123-1125)
PHONE..............................619 702-1700
Roy Erickson, *Branch Mgr*
EMP: 115
SALES (corp-wide): 110MM **Privately
Held**
SIC: 8711 Electrical or electronic engineering
PA: Epsilon Systems Solutions, Inc.
　　9242 Lightwave Ave # 100
　　San Diego CA 92123
　　619 702-1700

(P-25674)
EPSILON SYSTEMS SOLUTIONS INC (PA)
9242 Lightwave Ave # 100, San Diego
(92123-6402)
PHONE..............................619 702-1700
Bryan Min, *CEO*
Stuart Teshima, *CFO*
Joe Quinn, *Exec VP*
Jim Blasko, *Vice Pres*
Jeff Giglio, *Vice Pres*
EMP: 100
SQ FT: 16,000
SALES: 110MM **Privately Held**
WEB: www.epsilonsystems.com
SIC: 8711 Engineering services

(P-25675)
ERM-WEST INC (DH)
Also Called: Environmental Resources MGT
1277 Treat Blvd Ste 500, Walnut Creek
(94597-7989)
PHONE..............................925 946-0455
Tim Strawn, *President*
Kevin P King, *Partner*
Denise Toombs, *Partner*
John Kinsella, *Vice Pres*
John Cavanaugh, *General Mgr*
EMP: 72
SQ FT: 19,455
SALES: 166.3MM
SALES (corp-wide): 250.4K **Privately
Held**
SIC: 8711 8742 Consulting engineer; management consulting services
HQ: Erm North America, Inc.
　　75 Valley Stream Pkwy
　　Malvern PA 19355
　　484 913-0300

(P-25676)
ES ENGINEERING SERVICES LLC
1 Park Plz Ste 1000, Irvine (92614-8507)
PHONE..............................949 988-3500
EMP: 70
SALES (est): 1MM
SALES (corp-wide): 179.4MM **Privately
Held**
SIC: 8711 Engineering services
PA: Montrose Environmental Group, Inc.
　　1 Park Plz Ste 1000
　　Irvine CA 92614
　　949 988-3500

(P-25677)
EXP US SERVICES INC
5670 Oberlin Dr, San Diego (92121-1721)
PHONE..............................858 597-0555
Paul Gibson, *Branch Mgr*
EMP: 70
SALES (corp-wide): 478MM **Privately
Held**
SIC: 8711 Consulting engineer
HQ: Exp U.S. Services Inc.
　　205 N Mich Aveste 3600
　　Chicago IL 60601
　　312 616-0000

(P-25678)
EXPONENT INC (PA)
149 Commonwealth Dr, Menlo Park
(94025-1133)
PHONE..............................650 326-9400
Toll Free:..............................888
Catherine Corrigan, *President*
Michael R Gaulke, *Ch of Bd*
Richard L Schlenker Jr, *CFO*
Paul Johnston, *Chairman*
Jason Hertzberg, *Vice Pres*
EMP: 148
SQ FT: 153,738
SALES: 347.8MM **Publicly Held**
SIC: 8711 8742 8999 Consulting engineer; management consulting services; scientific consulting

(P-25679)
EXYTE US INC
Also Called: Mw U.S.
1453 Mission St Fl 2, San Francisco
(94103-2560)
PHONE..............................415 621-1199
Mike Hammarstedt, *Manager*
EMP: 50 **Privately Held**
SIC: 8711 8712 Mechanical engineering; electrical or electronic engineering; consulting engineer; architectural engineering
HQ: Exyte U.S., Inc.
　　201 Fuller Rd Ste 400
　　Albany NY 12203
　　518 266-3400

(P-25680)
FARADAY&FUTURE INC
Also Called: Faraday & Future
18455 S Figueroa St, Gardena
(90248-4503)
PHONE..............................424 276-7616
Chaoying Deng, *CEO*
Nick Sampson, *Senior VP*
Alan Cherry, *Vice Pres*
Dag Reckhorn, *Vice Pres*

PRODUCTS & SVCS

Jeff Risher, *Vice Pres*
EMP: 1500 **EST:** 2014
SALES (est): 1MM **Privately Held**
SIC: 8711 7389 6282 Engineering services; design, commercial & industrial; investment advisory service

(P-25681)
FBA INC (PA)
1675 Sabre St, Hayward (94545-1013)
PHONE.................510 265-1888
Waldi Naja, *President*
Jennifer Cassity, *Project Engr*
Chris Bane, *Engineer*
Amir K Kazemi, *Manager*
EMP: 50
SALES (est): 3.2MM **Privately Held**
WEB: www.fbaengineers.com
SIC: 8711 Electrical or electronic engineering

(P-25682)
FEHR & PEERS (PA)
100 Pringle Ave Ste 600, Walnut Creek (94596-3582)
PHONE.................925 977-3200
Matthew Henry, *CEO*
Marion Donnelly, *CFO*
Steven Brown, *Vice Pres*
Alan Telford, *Vice Pres*
Christine Shields, *Branch Mgr*
EMP: 60
SQ FT: 16,000
SALES (est): 55.1MM **Privately Held**
SIC: 8711 Consulting engineer

(P-25683)
FICCADENTI & WAGGONER CONSUL (PA)
16969 Von Karman Ave # 240, Irvine (92606-4944)
PHONE.................949 474-0502
Seb Ficcadenti, *President*
Michael Waggoner, *Vice Pres*
Sayola Elmohtaseb, *Business Dir*
Maggie De Guzman, *Admin Asst*
Sarah Fung, *Design Engr*
EMP: 52
SALES (est): 8.2MM **Privately Held**
WEB: www.fwcse.com
SIC: 8711 Structural engineering

(P-25684)
FLINTCO PACIFIC INC
401 Derek Pl, Roseville (95678-7153)
PHONE.................916 757-1000
John R Bates, *CEO*
David P Parkes, *President*
EMP: 80
SALES (est): 8.1MM
SALES (corp-wide): 1.5B **Privately Held**
SIC: 8711 Building construction consultant
HQ: Flintco, Llc
1624 W 21st St
Tulsa OK 74107
918 587-8451

(P-25685)
FLUOR CORPORATION
Also Called: Trs Staffing Solutions
3 Polaris Way, Aliso Viejo (92656-5338)
PHONE.................949 349-2000
Tim Kirk, *Principal*
Win Moore, *Vice Pres*
David Parker, *Exec Dir*
Maryann Mayshaw, *Executive Asst*
James Cleary, *Info Tech Dir*
EMP: 99
SALES (corp-wide): 19.5B **Publicly Held**
SIC: 8711 7363 Engineering services; help supply services
PA: Fluor Corporation
6700 Las Colinas Blvd
Irving TX 75039
469 398-7000

(P-25686)
FLUOR ENTERPRISES INC
5600 Cottle Rd, San Jose (95123-3696)
PHONE.................408 256-0853
Barry Subotkin, *Branch Mgr*
EMP: 60
SALES (corp-wide): 19.5B **Publicly Held**
SIC: 8711 1799 Building construction consultant; decontamination services

HQ: Fluor Enterprises, Inc.
6700 Las Colinas Blvd
Irving TX 75039
469 398-7000

(P-25687)
FLUOR ENTERPRISES INC
9701 Jeronimo Rd, Irvine (92618-2076)
PHONE.................949 349-2000
Philip J Carroll Jr, *Principal*
Marcia Hamilton, *Training Spec*
Reuben Barrows, *Director*
Richard Dionne, *Manager*
EMP: 100
SALES (corp-wide): 19.5B **Publicly Held**
SIC: 8711 Consulting engineer
HQ: Fluor Enterprises, Inc.
6700 Las Colinas Blvd
Irving TX 75039
469 398-7000

(P-25688)
FLUOR PLANT SERVICES INTL INC
Also Called: Fluor Daniel
1 Enterprise, Aliso Viejo (92656-2606)
PHONE.................949 349-2000
D Michael Steuert, *CFO*
Rhonda Talley, *Administration*
Charles Womack, *Administration*
Gina Hruby, *Info Tech Dir*
John Viggiano, *Info Tech Dir*
EMP: 79
SALES (est): 16.5MM
SALES (corp-wide): 19.5B **Publicly Held**
SIC: 8711 Engineering services
PA: Fluor Corporation
6700 Las Colinas Blvd
Irving TX 75039
469 398-7000

(P-25689)
FLUORAMEC LLC (HQ)
1 Enterprise, Aliso Viejo (92656-2606)
PHONE.................949 349-2000
Michelle Bell, *Director*
EMP: 50
SALES (est): 25.2MM
SALES (corp-wide): 19.5B **Publicly Held**
SIC: 8711 Engineering services
PA: Fluor Corporation
6700 Las Colinas Blvd
Irving TX 75039
469 398-7000

(P-25690)
FORD MOTOR LAND DEV CORP
3 Glen Bell Way Ste 100, Irvine (92618-3390)
PHONE.................949 242-6606
Dan Werbin, *Exec Dir*
Tony Varlesi, *Technology*
EMP: 500
SALES (corp-wide): 156.7B **Publicly Held**
WEB: www.fordcreditpr.com
SIC: 8711 Engineering services
HQ: Ford Motor Land Development Corporation
330 Town Center Dr # 1100
Dearborn MI 48126
313 323-3100

(P-25691)
FORWARD SLOPE INCORPORATED
Also Called: Forward Slope.
2020 Camino Del Rio N, San Diego (92108-1541)
PHONE.................619 299-4400
Carlos Persichetti, *President*
Kevin Noonan, *Vice Pres*
EMP: 80
SALES (est): 12.7MM **Privately Held**
WEB: www.forwardslope.com
SIC: 8711 7371 7389 Consulting engineer; software programming applications; financial services

(P-25692)
FRANK M BOOTH INC (PA)
Also Called: Valley Sheet Metal Co
222 3rd St, Marysville (95901-5948)
P.O. Box 5 (95901-0001)
PHONE.................530 742-7134
Lawrence R Booth, *President*

Richard Gabel, *CFO*
Kathy Kerrisk, *Admin Asst*
Tom Curato, *Project Mgr*
Todd Hoover, *Project Mgr*
EMP: 200
SQ FT: 75,000
SALES (est): 71.4MM **Privately Held**
WEB: www.frankbooth.com
SIC: 8711 Mechanical engineering

(P-25693)
FTI CONSULTING INC
350 S Grand Ave Ste 3000, Los Angeles (90071-3424)
PHONE.................213 689-1200
Stewart Kahn, *President*
Ruth Haile, *Exec Dir*
Emily Kirsch, *Sales Staff*
EMP: 80
SALES (corp-wide): 1.8B **Publicly Held**
SIC: 8711 8748 8742 Consulting engineer; business consulting; management consulting services
PA: Fti Consulting, Inc.
555 12th St Nw Ste 3
Washington DC 20004
202 312-9100

(P-25694)
FUGRO USA LAND INC
1777 Botelho Dr Ste 262, Walnut Creek (94596-5132)
PHONE.................925 256-6070
Osman El Manchawi, *Manager*
EMP: 50
SALES (corp-wide): 36.1K **Privately Held**
SIC: 8711 Engineering services
HQ: Fugro Usa Land, Inc
6100 Hillcroft St Ste 100
Houston TX 77081
713 369-5400

(P-25695)
FUJITSU ELECTRONICS AMER INC (DH)
Also Called: F E A
1250 E Arques Ave, Sunnyvale (94085-5401)
PHONE.................408 737-5600
Shinichi Machida, *President*
Irene Mason, *Assoc VP*
Victor Kan, *Exec VP*
Doug Saylor, *Senior VP*
Dan Callaghan, *Vice Pres*
EMP: 84
SQ FT: 49,000
SALES (est): 23.1MM
SALES (corp-wide): 38.4B **Privately Held**
WEB: www.fma.fujitsu.com
SIC: 8711 5065 Engineering services; electronic parts & equipment
HQ: Fujitsu Electronics Inc.
2-100-45, Shin-Yokohama, Kohoku-Ku
Yokohama KNG 222-0
454 738-030

(P-25696)
FUSCOE ENGINEERING INC (PA)
16795 Von Karman Ave # 100, Irvine (92606-4974)
PHONE.................949 474-1960
Patrick Fuscoe, *President*
EMP: 85
SQ FT: 16,000
SALES (est): 23.8MM **Privately Held**
WEB: www.fuscoe.com
SIC: 8711 Civil engineering

(P-25697)
G2 SOFTWARE SYSTEMS INC
4025 Hancock St Ste 105, San Diego (92110-5167)
PHONE.................619 222-8025
Georgia D Griffiths, *CEO*
Bill Long, *CFO*
William Long, *CFO*
Michelle Krencik, *Executive*
Dennis Ahern, *Sr Software Eng*
EMP: 140
SQ FT: 4,000
SALES (est): 34.2MM **Privately Held**
SIC: 8711 Engineering services

(P-25698)
GARCIA JUAREZ CONSTRUCTION INC (PA)
6801 Atlantic Ave, Long Beach (90805-1413)
P.O. Box 309, Brea (92822-0309)
PHONE.................951 657-3535
Jim Jackson, *CEO*
EMP: 64
SALES (est): 5.1MM **Privately Held**
SIC: 8711 Engineering services

(P-25699)
GARRAD HASSAN AMERICA INC (DH)
Also Called: GL
9665 Chesapeake Dr # 435, San Diego (92123-1378)
PHONE.................858 836-3370
Carole Barbeau, *CEO*
EMP: 70
SQ FT: 1,380
SALES (est): 13MM **Privately Held**
SIC: 8711 Consulting engineer

(P-25700)
GARRETT J GENTRY GEN ENGRG INC
1297 W 9th St, Upland (91786-5706)
PHONE.................909 693-3391
Garrett J Gentry, *President*
Bryan Copping, *Admin Sec*
EMP: 85 **EST:** 2013
SALES (est): 30MM **Privately Held**
SIC: 8711 Acoustical engineering

(P-25701)
GAS TRANSMISSION SYSTEMS INC
Also Called: GTS
130 Amber Grove Dr # 134, Chico (95973-5880)
PHONE.................530 893-6711
Katie Clapp, *President*
Kathleen B Clapp, *President*
Bill Blastic, *Vice Pres*
Robert Gross, *Vice Pres*
Bob Lipscomb, *Vice Pres*
EMP: 220
SQ FT: 4,500
SALES (est): 29.7MM **Privately Held**
WEB: www.gtsinc.us
SIC: 8711 Professional engineer

(P-25702)
GATAN INC (HQ)
5794 W Las Positas Blvd, Pleasanton (94588-4083)
PHONE.................925 463-0200
Benjamin Wood, *President*
Ed Morrissey, *Treasurer*
Jack Buhsmer, *Vice Pres*
Robert Buchanan, *Principal*
David B Liner, *Admin Sec*
EMP: 55
SQ FT: 30,000
SALES (est): 44.4MM
SALES (corp-wide): 4.6B **Publicly Held**
SIC: 8711 3826 Designing: ship, boat, machine & product; analytical optical instruments
PA: Roper Technologies, Inc.
6901 Prof Pkwy E Ste 200
Sarasota FL 34240
941 556-2601

(P-25703)
GDA TECHNOLOGIES INC (HQ)
25 Metro Dr Fl 3, San Jose (95110-1316)
PHONE.................408 753-1191
Isaac Sundarajan, *CEO*
Gopa Periyadan, *Exec VP*
Gopakumar K Periyadan, *Vice Pres*
Ravi Thummarukudy, *Vice Pres*
Sandeep Mohan Kumar, *Sales Mgr*
EMP: 100
SALES (est): 24.4MM **Privately Held**
WEB: www.gdatech.com
SIC: 8711 Electrical or electronic engineering
PA: Larsen And Toubro Limited
L&T House, Ballard Estate
Mumbai MH
226 752-5656

(P-25704)
GEI CONSULTANTS INC
2868 Prospect Park Dr # 400, Rancho Cordova (95670-6065)
PHONE.................................916 631-4500
Frank Leathers, *President*
Jasmine Gerber, *Mktg Coord*
EMP: 60
SALES (corp-wide): 165.7MM **Privately Held**
WEB: www.geiconsultants.com
SIC: 8711 Engineering services
PA: Gei Consultants, Inc.
400 Unicorn Park Dr Ste 8
Woburn MA 01801
781 721-4000

(P-25705)
GENERAL DYNAMICS ADVANCED INFO
General Dynamics Adv Info Sys
100 Ferguson Dr, Mountain View (94043-5239)
P.O. Box 7188 (94039)
PHONE.................................650 966-2000
John Stewart, *Branch Mgr*
Rich Riveron, *Program Mgr*
Dave Lukens, *Technical Mgr*
Gregory Samsonoff, *Engineer*
Jonathan M Sorek, *Engineer*
EMP: 4000
SALES (corp-wide): 30.9B **Publicly Held**
SIC: 8711 8731 Engineering services; commercial physical research
HQ: General Dynamics Mission Systems, Inc.
12450 Fair Lakes Cir # 200
Fairfax VA 22033
703 263-2800

(P-25706)
GENERAL ELECTRIC COMPANY
2120 Diamond Blvd Ste 100, Concord (94520-5720)
PHONE.................................925 602-5950
Malcolm Jepson, *Principal*
EMP: 100
SALES (corp-wide): 122B **Publicly Held**
SIC: 8711 7629 Engineering services; electrical repair shops
PA: General Electric Company
41 Farnsworth St
Boston MA 02210
617 443-3000

(P-25707)
GENERAL SERVICES CAL DEPT
Also Called: Telecommunications Division
601 Sequoia Pacific Blvd, Sacramento (95811-0231)
PHONE.................................916 657-9960
Wendell McCullough, *Branch Mgr*
EMP: 500 **Privately Held**
WEB: www.4c.net
SIC: 8711 9199 Electrical or electronic engineering; general government administration;
HQ: California Department Of General Services
707 3rd St
West Sacramento CA 95605

(P-25708)
GENERAL SERVICES CAL DEPT
Telecommunications Division
601 Sequoia Pacific Blvd, Sacramento (95811-0231)
PHONE.................................916 657-9903
Wendell McCullough, *Director*
EMP: 450 **Privately Held**
WEB: www.4c.net
SIC: 8711 9199 Electrical or electronic engineering; general government administration;
HQ: California Department Of General Services
707 3rd St
West Sacramento CA 95605

(P-25709)
GEOCON INCORPORATED
6960 Flanders Dr, San Diego (92121-3992)
PHONE.................................858 558-6900
Michael Chapin, *CEO*

William Lydon, *CFO*
EMP: 54
SALES: 8MM **Privately Held**
SIC: 8711 Consulting engineer

(P-25710)
GEORGE G SHARP INC
1065 Bay Blvd Ste D, Chula Vista (91911-1626)
PHONE.................................619 425-4211
Joseph Aven, *Manager*
Joe Kuftack, *Manager*
EMP: 75
SALES (corp-wide): 55.6MM **Privately Held**
WEB: www.ggsharp.com
SIC: 8711 Consulting engineer
PA: George G. Sharp, Inc.
160 Broadway
New York NY 10038
212 732-2800

(P-25711)
GEOSYNTEC CONSULTANTS INC
Also Called: Geo Mmi Engineering
1111 Broadway Fl 6th, Oakland (94607-4139)
PHONE.................................510 836-3034
Pat Lucia, *Branch Mgr*
R J Dunn, *Principal*
Patrick Lucia, *Principal*
Holly Van Norman, *Admin Asst*
Syed Rehan, *Senior Engr*
EMP: 50
SALES (corp-wide): 204.7MM **Privately Held**
SIC: 8711 8748 Consulting engineer; environmental consultant
PA: Geosyntec Consultants, Inc.
900 Broken Sound Pkwy Nw
Boca Raton FL 33487
561 995-0900

(P-25712)
GHD INC
718 3rd St, Eureka (95501-0504)
P.O. Box 1010 (95502-1010)
PHONE.................................707 443-8326
Steve Allen, *Principal*
Steve Cox, *Vice Pres*
Wayne McFarland, *Manager*
EMP: 50 **Privately Held**
SIC: 8711 Engineering services
HQ: Ghd Inc.
4747 N 22nd St Ste 200
Phoenix AZ 85016
602 216-7200

(P-25713)
GHD INC
2235 Mercury Way Ste 150, Santa Rosa (95407-5470)
PHONE.................................707 523-1010
Alex Culick, *Principal*
Lloyd B Darnell II, *Principal*
Laura Bryan, *Administration*
Peggy Dezurik, *Info Tech Mgr*
Mary Grace Pawson, *Project Mgr*
EMP: 100 **Privately Held**
WEB: www.sjoeng.com
SIC: 8711 Consulting engineer
HQ: Ghd Inc.
4747 N 22nd St Ste 200
Phoenix AZ 85016
602 216-7200

(P-25714)
GILBANE FEDERAL (DH)
1655 Grant St Fl 12, Concord (94520-2600)
PHONE.................................925 946-3100
Sarabjit Singh, *CEO*
Jon Verlinde, *Senior VP*
EMP: 110
SALES (est): 172.4MM
SALES (corp-wide): 4.9B **Privately Held**
WEB: www.itsi.com
SIC: 8711 8748 Building construction consultant; environmental consultant
HQ: Gilbane Building Company
7 Jackson Walkway Ste 2
Providence RI 02903
401 456-5800

(P-25715)
GLENN A RICK ENGRG & DEV CO (PA)
Also Called: Rick Engineering Company
5620 Friars Rd, San Diego (92110-2513)
PHONE.................................619 291-0708
Roger Ball, *Principal*
William B Rick, *President*
Deborah B Ragione, *CFO*
Bruce Paton, *Bd of Directors*
Dennis C Bowling, *Vice Pres*
EMP: 212 **EST:** 1955
SQ FT: 50,000
SALES (est): 52.9MM **Privately Held**
SIC: 8711 Civil engineering

(P-25716)
GLOBAL SOLUTIONS INTEGRATION
Also Called: Gsico
26632 Towne Centre Dr # 300, Foothill Ranch (92610-2813)
PHONE.................................949 307-1849
Cel Esmundi, *President*
EMP: 75
SQ FT: 3,000
SALES (est): 13.5MM **Privately Held**
SIC: 8711 Engineering services

(P-25717)
GPA TECHNOLOGIES INC
2368 Eastman Ave Ste 8, Ventura (93003-5770)
PHONE.................................805 643-7878
Michael Vaswani, *President*
Dan Powell, *Senior Engr*
Christine Hill, *Controller*
Jeremy Johnson, *Supervisor*
EMP: 55
SQ FT: 6,580
SALES (est): 8.6MM **Privately Held**
WEB: www.gpatech.com
SIC: 8711 Consulting engineer

(P-25718)
GRADIENT ENGINEERS INC
Also Called: Leighton & Associates
17781 Cowan Ste 140, Irvine (92614-6009)
PHONE.................................949 477-0555
Terry Brennan, *Chairman*
Kris Lutton, *President*
Tom Mills, *Vice Pres*
EMP: 70
SALES (est): 3.7MM
SALES (corp-wide): 30.7MM **Privately Held**
WEB: www.gradientengineers.com
SIC: 8711 8744 Engineering services;
PA: Leighton Group, Inc.
17781 Cowan
Irvine CA 92614
949 477-4040

(P-25719)
GULFSTREAM AEROSPACE CORP GA
4150 E Donald Douglas Dr, Long Beach (90808-1725)
PHONE.................................562 420-1818
Barry Russell, *Vice Pres*
Michelle Oliver, *Partner*
Jay Caukin, *Planning*
Joan Caterino, *Software Dev*
Will Jarvis, *Technology*
EMP: 800
SALES (corp-wide): 30.9B **Publicly Held**
WEB: www.gdavservices.net
SIC: 8711 3721 Engineering services; aircraft
HQ: Gulfstream Aerospace Corporation (Georgia)
500 Gulfstream Rd
Savannah GA 31408
912 965-3000

(P-25720)
H M H ENGINEERS
1570 Oakland Rd, San Jose (95131-2430)
PHONE.................................408 487-2200
William J Wagner, *President*
Tom Armstrong, *Vice Pres*
EMP: 54 **EST:** 1976
SALES (est): 8.5MM **Privately Held**
SIC: 8711 8713 Consulting engineer; surveying services

(P-25721)
HARRIS & ASSOCIATES INC
22 Executive Park Ste 200, Irvine (92614-2704)
PHONE.................................949 655-3900
Jeff Cooper, *Branch Mgr*
Randall Berry, *Project Engr*
EMP: 60
SALES (corp-wide): 72.4MM **Privately Held**
WEB: www.harris-assoc.com
SIC: 8711 8712 Construction & civil engineering; civil engineering; sanitary engineers; architectural engineering
PA: Harris & Associates, Inc.
1401 Wllw Pca Rd 500
Concord CA 94520
925 827-4900

(P-25722)
HARRIS & ASSOCIATES INC (PA)
Also Called: Harris & Associates Cnstr MGT
1401 Wllw Pca Rd 500, Concord (94520)
PHONE.................................925 827-4900
Lisa Larrabee, *CEO*
Carl Harris, *Ch of Bd*
Guy Erickson, *President*
Gary Yagade, *President*
Ehab Gerges, *COO*
EMP: 104
SQ FT: 23,000
SALES (est): 72.4MM **Privately Held**
WEB: www.harris-assoc.com
SIC: 8711 8712 Construction & civil engineering; civil engineering; sanitary engineers; architectural engineering

(P-25723)
HARRIS CORPORATION
1400 S Shamrock Ave, Monrovia (91016-4267)
PHONE.................................626 584-4527
Pat Carr, *Branch Mgr*
EMP: 299
SALES (corp-wide): 6.1B **Publicly Held**
WEB: www.ittind.com
SIC: 8711 Electrical or electronic engineering
PA: Harris Corporation
1025 W Nasa Blvd
Melbourne FL 32919
321 727-9100

(P-25724)
HDR ARCHITECTURE INC
Also Called: H D R
350 S Grand Ave Ste 2900, Los Angeles (90071-3406)
PHONE.................................626 584-1700
Al Korth, *Manager*
EMP: 100
SQ FT: 5,905
SALES (corp-wide): 2.3B **Privately Held**
SIC: 8711 8712 Designing: ship, boat, machine & product; architectural services
HQ: Hdr Architecture, Inc.
1917 S 67th St
Omaha NE 68106
402 399-1000

(P-25725)
HDR ARCHITECTURE INC
201 California St # 1500, San Francisco (94111-5002)
PHONE.................................415 546-4242
Bill Brinkman, *Director*
EMP: 55
SALES (corp-wide): 2.3B **Privately Held**
SIC: 8711 8712 Designing: ship, boat, machine & product; architectural services
HQ: Hdr Architecture, Inc.
1917 S 67th St
Omaha NE 68106
402 399-1000

(P-25726)
HDR ENGINEERING INC
3230 El Camino Real # 200, Irvine (92602-1333)
PHONE.................................714 730-2300
William Bennet, *Manager*
EMP: 150
SALES (corp-wide): 2.3B **Privately Held**
SIC: 8711 8742 Engineering services; management consulting services

HQ: Hdr Engineering, Inc.
1917 S 67th St
Omaha NE 68106
402 399-1000

(P-25727)
HDR ENGINEERING INC
401 B St Ste 1110, San Diego
(92101-4271)
PHONE.............................619 231-4865
Melissa Kiscoan, *Branch Mgr*
EMP: 100
SALES (corp-wide): 2.3B Privately Held
SIC: 8711 Consulting engineer
HQ: Hdr Engineering, Inc.
1917 S 67th St
Omaha NE 68106
402 399-1000

(P-25728)
HDR ENGINEERING INC
100 Pringle Ave Ste 400, Walnut Creek
(94596-7326)
PHONE.............................925 974-2500
Zuraile Wilson, *Principal*
EMP: 70
SALES (corp-wide): 2.3B Privately Held
SIC: 8711 8742 Engineering services;
construction project management consult-
ant
HQ: Hdr Engineering, Inc.
1917 S 67th St
Omaha NE 68106
402 399-1000

(P-25729)
HDR ENGINEERING INC
Also Called: Hydro Power Service
2379 Gateway Oaks Dr # 200, Sacramento
(95833-4238)
PHONE.............................916 564-4214
EMP: 74
SALES (corp-wide): 2.3B Privately Held
SIC: 8711
HQ: Hdr Engineering, Inc.
8404 Indian Hills Dr
Omaha NE 68106
402 399-1000

(P-25730)
HDR ENGINEERING INC
431 W Baseline Rd, Claremont
(91711-1608)
PHONE.............................909 626-0967
Graham E Bell, *Branch Mgr*
EMP: 56
SALES (corp-wide): 2.3B Privately Held
SIC: 8711 Engineering services
HQ: Hdr Engineering, Inc.
1917 S 67th St
Omaha NE 68106
402 399-1000

(P-25731)
HDR/CARDNO ENTRIX JOINT
VENTR
2365 Iron Point Rd # 300, Folsom
(95630-8711)
PHONE.............................916 817-4700
Dave Lecureux, *Senior VP*
EMP: 99
SALES (est): 2.6MM Privately Held
SIC: 8711 Engineering services

(P-25732)
HENKEL CORPORATION
Also Called: Aerospace Material Division
2850 Willow Pass Rd, Bay Point
(94565-3237)
P.O. Box 312 (94565-0031)
PHONE.............................925 458-8086
Dennis Cardoza, *General Mgr*
Cherri Dykstra, *Technician*
Manette Gebhardt, *Project Mgr*
Rosen Angelov, *Technology*
Peter Naye, *Engineer*
EMP: 170
SQ FT: 6,325
SALES (corp-wide): 23.6B Privately Held
SIC: 8711 Engineering services
HQ: Henkel Us Operations Corporation
1 Henkel Way
Rocky Hill CT 06067
860 571-5100

(P-25733)
HENWOOD ENERGY SERVICES
INC (DH)
2379 Gateway Oaks Dr # 110, Sacramento
(95833-4239)
PHONE.............................916 955-6031
Mark Henwood, *President*
David Branchcomb, *Vice Pres*
EMP: 118
SALES (est): 8.4MM
SALES (corp-wide): 34.3B Privately Held
WEB: www.globalenergydecisions.com
SIC: 8711 Consulting engineer
HQ: Global Energy Decisions Llc
1495 Canyon Blvd Ste 100
Boulder CO 80302
720 221-5700

(P-25734)
HNTB CORPORATION
601 W 5th St Ste 1000, Los Angeles
(90071-2028)
PHONE.............................213 403-1000
Lanson Nichols, *Vice Pres*
Bill Marek, *Engineer*
Jim Pun, *Sr Project Mgr*
Peter Bruno, *Manager*
EMP: 56
SALES (corp-wide): 48.1MM Privately
Held
WEB: www.hntb.com
SIC: 8711 Consulting engineer
HQ: Hntb Corporation
715 Kirk Dr
Kansas City MO 64105
816 472-1201

(P-25735)
HNTB CORPORATION
200 Sandpointe Ave # 200, Santa Ana
(92707-8797)
PHONE.............................714 460-1600
Andres Ocon, *Branch Mgr*
EMP: 57
SALES (corp-wide): 48.1MM Privately
Held
WEB: www.hntb.com
SIC: 8711 Consulting engineer
HQ: Hntb Corporation
715 Kirk Dr
Kansas City MO 64105
816 472-1201

(P-25736)
HNTB CORPORATION
36 Executive Park Ste 200, Irvine
(92614-4717)
PHONE.............................949 460-1700
Ron Hartje, *Branch Mgr*
EMP: 54
SALES (corp-wide): 48.1MM Privately
Held
SIC: 8711 8712 Consulting engineer; ar-
chitectural services
HQ: Hntb Corporation
715 Kirk Dr
Kansas City MO 64105
816 472-1201

(P-25737)
HNTB GERWICK WATER
SOLUTIONS
200 Sandpointe Ave, Santa Ana
(92707-5751)
PHONE.............................714 460-1600
Larry Davis, *Partner*
Dale Berner, *Partner*
EMP: 150
SALES (est): 3.7MM Privately Held
SIC: 8711 8712 Consulting engineer; ar-
chitectural services

(P-25738)
HOLDREGE KULL CONSULTIMG
ENGR
48 Bellarmine Ct Ste 40, Chico
(95928-7261)
PHONE.............................530 894-2487
Tom Hodrege, *President*
Shane Cummings, *Manager*
EMP: 70
SALES (est): 4.2MM Privately Held
SIC: 8711 Consulting engineer

(P-25739)
HOLMES & NARVER INC (HQ)
999 W Town And Country Rd, Orange
(92868-4713)
P.O. Box 6240 (92863-6240)
PHONE.............................714 567-2400
Danny Seal, *CEO*
Raymond Landy, *President*
Dennis Deslatte, *CFO*
Tina Clugston, *Principal*
EMP: 250 EST: 1933
SQ FT: 100,000
SALES (est): 18.3MM
SALES (corp-wide): 20.1B Publicly Held
SIC: 8711 8742 8741 1542 Engineering
services; training & development consult-
ant; construction management; nonresi-
dential construction
PA: Aecom
1999 Avenue Of The Stars # 2600
Los Angeles CA 90067
213 593-8000

(P-25740)
HUNSAKER & ASSOC IRVINE
INC (PA)
3 Hughes, Irvine (92618-2021)
PHONE.............................949 583-1010
Richard Hunsaker, *CEO*
Douglas Snyder, *President*
Chuck Cater, *Vice Pres*
Kamal Karam, *Vice Pres*
Doug Staley, *Vice Pres*
EMP: 100
SQ FT: 27,000
SALES (est): 52.1MM Privately Held
WEB: www.hunsaker.com
SIC: 8711 8713 Civil engineering; survey-
ing services

(P-25741)
ICI SERVICES CORPORATION
1000 Town Center Dr # 225, Oxnard
(93036-1155)
PHONE.............................805 988-3210
Vicki Ervin, *Branch Mgr*
EMP: 320
SALES (corp-wide): 84.7MM Privately
Held
SIC: 8711 Professional engineer
PA: Ici Services Corporation
500 Viking Dr Ste 400
Virginia Beach VA 23452
757 340-6970

(P-25742)
INDUS TECHNOLOGY INC
2243 San Diego Ave # 200, San Diego
(92110-2069)
PHONE.............................619 299-2555
James B Lasswell, *President*
Rebecca Spane, *CFO*
Will Nevilles, *Senior VP*
Anthony Lopez, *Vice Pres*
Eric Macgregor, *Vice Pres*
EMP: 230
SQ FT: 12,000
SALES (est): 31.9MM Privately Held
WEB: www.industechnology.com
SIC: 8711 Engineering services

(P-25743)
INFINITE TECHNOLOGIES INC
(PA)
1264 Hawks Flight Ct # 210, El Dorado Hills
(95762-9349)
PHONE.............................916 987-3261
John A Runnberg, *CEO*
Michael P Whittle, *President*
Esel Mendoza, *Programmer Anys*
Cheryl Glazer, *Business Anlyst*
Casey Talbot, *Engineer*
EMP: 68
SQ FT: 3,450
SALES (est): 9MM Privately Held
WEB: www.infintech.com
SIC: 8711 7371 7379 Engineering serv-
ices; custom computer programming
services; computer related maintenance
services

(P-25744)
INFORMATION SYSTEMS LABS
INC (PA)
12900 Brookprinter Pl # 800, Poway
(92064-8802)
PHONE.............................858 535-9680
Richard G Miller, *CEO*
William Gang, *COO*
Peter Kuebler, *CFO*
David Honey, *Vice Pres*
James Meyer, *Vice Pres*
EMP: 50
SQ FT: 31,000
SALES (est): 28.2MM Privately Held
WEB: www.islinc.com
SIC: 8711 Electrical or electronic engineer-
ing

(P-25745)
INFRASTRUCTURE ENGRG
CORP
301 Mission Ave Ste 202, Oceanside
(92054-2591)
PHONE.............................760 529-0795
Preston Lewis, *President*
EMP: 50
SALES (est): 2.7MM Privately Held
WEB: www.iecorporation.com
SIC: 8711 Civil engineering

(P-25746)
INGENIUM TECHNOLOGIES
CORP
5665 Oberlin Dr Ste 202, San Diego
(92121-1739)
PHONE.............................858 227-4422
Duane Wingate, *Principal*
EMP: 87
SALES (corp-wide): 19.8MM Privately
Held
SIC: 8711 Consulting engineer
PA: Ingenium Technologies Corp.
4216 Maray Dr
Rockford IL 61107
815 399-8803

(P-25747)
INNOVATIVE ENGRG SYSTEMS
INC (PA)
Also Called: Ies Engineering
8800 Crippen St, Bakersfield (93311-9686)
P.O. Box 20610 (93390-0610)
PHONE.............................661 381-7800
David Wolfer, *President*
Steve Johnson, *Division Mgr*
Bill Shipp, *Division Mgr*
Jordan Stockton, *Division Mgr*
Patricia Kincheloe, *Admin Asst*
EMP: 100
SQ FT: 20,000
SALES: 26.3MM Privately Held
SIC: 8711 1731 Engineering services;
electrical work

(P-25748)
INSPIRIA INC (PA)
Also Called: Audiovisions
25741 Atl Ocn Dr Ste A, Lake Forest
(92630-8864)
PHONE.............................949 206-0606
Mark Hoffenberg, *President*
Ted Taylor, *Vice Pres*
Bob Walpert, *Executive*
John Salow, *Info Tech Mgr*
Todd Leiter, *Prgrmr*
EMP: 64
SQ FT: 20,000
SALES (est): 13.1MM Privately Held
WEB: www.avisions.com
SIC: 8711 Electrical or electronic engineer-
ing

(P-25749)
INTELLIGENT AUTOMATION
CORP
Also Called: I A C
13475 Danielson St # 100, Poway
(92064-8855)
PHONE.............................858 679-4140
Jeffery A Goodrich, *President*
Thomas W Brotherton, *Ch of Bd*
Paul J Grabill, *Vice Pres*
William A Lawler, *Admin Sec*
EMP: 50
SQ FT: 7,000

SALES (est): 3.9MM
SALES (corp-wide): 40.5B **Publicly Held**
WEB: www.iac-online.com
SIC: 8711 Engineering services
PA: Honeywell International Inc.
    115 Tabor Rd
    Morris Plains NJ 07950
    973 455-2000

(P-25750)
INTERACT PMTI INC (PA)
260 Maple Ct Ste 210, Ventura
(93003-3566)
PHONE..............................805 658-5600
Tom Kennedy, *President*
Val Lerma, *Engineer*
Daniel Weissberg, *Controller*
Uliana Micovic, *Manager*
Vicky Johnoson Moore, *Manager*
EMP: 62
SQ FT: 6,000
SALES (est): 5.1MM **Privately Held**
WEB: www.interactpmti.com
SIC: 8711 Consulting engineer

(P-25751)
INTERNATIONAL DESIGN SERVICES
2437 Micheltorena St, Los Angeles
(90039-2531)
PHONE..............................323 662-3963
Zigmas Tanaka, *Ch of Bd*
Betty Tanaka, *President*
Steve Murray, *Exec Dir*
EMP: 57
SQ FT: 3,600
SALES (est): 2.8MM **Privately Held**
SIC: 8711 Consulting engineer

(P-25752)
IQA SOLUTIONS INC
4089 E Conant St, Long Beach
(90808-1777)
PHONE..............................562 420-1000
Mohsem H Hashemi, *CEO*
Andrew Stasio, *Vice Pres*
EMP: 62
SQ FT: 8,500
SALES: 6.8MM **Privately Held**
WEB: www.iqasolutions.com
SIC: 8711 Mechanical engineering

(P-25753)
JACOBS ATCS FEMA A JOINT VENTR
155 N Lake Ave Fl 5, Pasadena
(91101-1849)
PHONE..............................571 218-1115
Ed Pogreba, *Vice Pres*
EMP: 99
SALES (est): 1.3MM **Privately Held**
SIC: 8711 8712 8748 8741 Engineering
    services; architectural services; business
    consulting; management services

(P-25754)
JACOBS CIVIL INC
1500 Hughes Way Ste B400, Long Beach
(90810-1882)
PHONE..............................310 847-2500
EMP: 78
SALES (corp-wide): 10B **Publicly Held**
SIC: 8711 Consulting engineer
HQ: Jacobs Civil Inc.
    501 N Broadway Ste 185
    Saint Louis MO

(P-25755)
JACOBS ENGINEERING COMPANY
1111 S Arroyo Pkwy, Pasadena
(91105-3254)
P.O. Box 7084 (91109-7084)
PHONE..............................626 449-2171
Noel G Watson, *CEO*
C L Martin, *President*
Chris McEnery, *Manager*
EMP: 4000
SALES (est): 98.4MM
SALES (corp-wide): 10B **Publicly Held**
WEB: www.jacobs.com
SIC: 8711 1629 Engineering services;
    chemical plant & refinery construction

PA: Jacobs Engineering Group Inc.
    1999 Bryan St Ste 1200
    Dallas TX 75201
    214 583-8500

(P-25756)
JACOBS ENGINEERING GROUP INC
2600 Michelson Dr Ste 500, Irvine
(92612-6506)
PHONE..............................949 224-7585
Dan Grubb, *Branch Mgr*
Jason Blackburn, *Info Tech Dir*
Sarah Borton, *Technology*
Vic Montellano, *Electrical Engi*
Thomas Freed, *Engineer*
EMP: 88
SALES (corp-wide): 10B **Publicly Held**
WEB: www.jacobs.com
SIC: 8711 Consulting engineer
PA: Jacobs Engineering Group Inc.
    1999 Bryan St Ste 1200
    Dallas TX 75201
    214 583-8500

(P-25757)
JACOBS ENGINEERING GROUP INC
37528 Morning Cir, Palmdale (93550-2578)
PHONE..............................661 275-5685
EMP: 93
SALES (corp-wide): 10B **Publicly Held**
SIC: 8711 Aviation &/or aeronautical engi-
    neering
PA: Jacobs Engineering Group Inc.
    1999 Bryan St Ste 1200
    Dallas TX 75201
    214 583-8500

(P-25758)
JACOBS ENGINEERING GROUP INC
2300 Clayton Rd, Concord (94520-2100)
PHONE..............................925 356-3900
EMP: 92
SALES (corp-wide): 12.7B **Publicly Held**
SIC: 8711
PA: Jacobs Engineering Group Inc.
    155 N Lake Ave
    Pasadena CA 75201
    626 578-3500

(P-25759)
JACOBS ENGINEERING GROUP INC
1500 Hughes Way Ste B400, Long Beach
(90810-1882)
PHONE..............................310 847-2500
Janet Van Peursem, *Project Engr*
Rick Breytspraak, *Engineer*
Jason Gardner, *Engineer*
Tom Gipe, *Engineer*
Chris Shadley, *Business Mgr*
EMP: 91
SALES (corp-wide): 10B **Publicly Held**
SIC: 8711 Consulting engineer
PA: Jacobs Engineering Group Inc.
    1999 Bryan St Ste 1200
    Dallas TX 75201
    214 583-8500

(P-25760)
JACOBS ENGINEERING GROUP INC
3257 E Guasti Rd Ste 130, Ontario
(91761-1237)
PHONE..............................909 974-2700
Chao Chen, *Manager*
Jim Hamlin, *Business Mgr*
James Hoyt, *Manager*
EMP: 88
SALES (corp-wide): 10B **Publicly Held**
SIC: 8711 Consulting engineer
PA: Jacobs Engineering Group Inc.
    1999 Bryan St Ste 1200
    Dallas TX 75201
    214 583-8500

(P-25761)
JACOBS ENGINEERING GROUP INC
95 S Market St Ste 300, San Jose
(95113-2350)
PHONE..............................408 995-3257
Chris R Bartos, *Branch Mgr*

EMP: 88
SALES (corp-wide): 10B **Publicly Held**
WEB: www.jacobs.com
SIC: 8711 Consulting engineer
PA: Jacobs Engineering Group Inc.
    1999 Bryan St Ste 1200
    Dallas TX 75201
    214 583-8500

(P-25762)
JACOBS ENGINEERING GROUP INC
1000 Wilshire Blvd # 2100, Los Angeles
(90017-2417)
PHONE..............................213 362-4336
Bruce Russell, *Branch Mgr*
Norma Teran, *Admin Asst*
Mani Iravani, *Engineer*
Jeff Sedlak, *Director*
Ron Siecke, *Director*
EMP: 250
SALES (corp-wide): 10B **Publicly Held**
SIC: 8711 Consulting engineer
PA: Jacobs Engineering Group Inc.
    1999 Bryan St Ste 1200
    Dallas TX 75201
    214 583-8500

(P-25763)
JACOBS ENGINEERING INC (HQ)
155 N Lake Ave, Pasadena (91101-1849)
P.O. Box 7084 (91109-7084)
PHONE..............................626 578-3500
Craig L Martin, *CEO*
James Dulle, *Vice Pres*
David Syphard, *Vice Pres*
Wayne Modugno, *Program Mgr*
Sandy Barnett, *Admin Mgr*
EMP: 89
SALES (est): 159.4MM
SALES (corp-wide): 10B **Publicly Held**
SIC: 8711 Consulting engineer
PA: Jacobs Engineering Group Inc.
    1999 Bryan St Ste 1200
    Dallas TX 75201
    214 583-8500

(P-25764)
JACOBS INTERNATIONAL LTD INC
155 N Lake Ave, Pasadena (91101-1849)
P.O. Box 7084 (91109-7084)
PHONE..............................626 578-3500
Craig Martin, *President*
John W Prosser Jr, *Treasurer*
Curtis Fisher, *Vice Pres*
Jeff Sanders, *Vice Pres*
Valerie Coltart, *Admin Mgr*
EMP: 300
SQ FT: 120,000
SALES: 85MM
SALES (corp-wide): 10B **Publicly Held**
SIC: 8711 Engineering services
PA: Jacobs Engineering Group Inc.
    1999 Bryan St Ste 1200
    Dallas TX 75201
    214 583-8500

(P-25765)
JACOBS PROJECT MANAGEMENT CO
2600 Michelson Dr Ste 500, Irvine
(92612-6506)
PHONE..............................949 224-7695
Les Steinberger, *Manager*
Frank Joyce, *Contract Mgr*
EMP: 99
SALES: 950K
SALES (corp-wide): 10B **Publicly Held**
SIC: 8711 Engineering services
PA: Jacobs Engineering Group Inc.
    1999 Bryan St Ste 1200
    Dallas TX 75201
    214 583-8500

(P-25766)
JACOBS TECHNOLOGY INC
1550 N Norma St, Ridgecrest
(93555-2556)
PHONE..............................760 446-7084
Chuck Schroeder, *Branch Mgr*
Jean Helm, *Director*
EMP: 100

SALES (corp-wide): 10B **Publicly Held**
SIC: 8711 Engineering services
HQ: Jacobs Technology Inc.
    600 William Northern Blvd
    Tullahoma TN 37388
    931 455-6400

(P-25767)
JACOBS TECHNOLOGY INC
Ames Division
M S 213 15, Mountain View (94035)
PHONE..............................650 604-5946
Ron Marmol, *Vice Pres*
EMP: 50
SALES (corp-wide): 10B **Publicly Held**
SIC: 8711 Aviation &/or aeronautical engi-
    neering
HQ: Jacobs Technology Inc.
    600 William Northern Blvd
    Tullahoma TN 37388
    931 455-6400

(P-25768)
JACOBS TECHNOLOGY INC
1550 N Norma St, Ridgecrest
(93555-2556)
PHONE..............................760 446-1549
Penny Hersley, *Manager*
EMP: 150
SALES (corp-wide): 10B **Publicly Held**
SIC: 8711 Aviation &/or aeronautical engi-
    neering
HQ: Jacobs Technology Inc.
    600 William Northern Blvd
    Tullahoma TN 37388
    931 455-6400

(P-25769)
JAS PACIFIC
201 N Euclid Ave Ste A, Upland
(91786-8308)
P.O. Box 2 (91785-0002)
PHONE..............................909 605-7777
Jason Addison Smith, *CEO*
Addison Smith, *CEO*
Harley J Jenkins, *Manager*
EMP: 110 **EST:** 1992
SALES (est): 7.7MM **Privately Held**
WEB: www.jaspacific.com
SIC: 8711 Engineering services

(P-25770)
JOHNSON CONTROLS INC
2226 Northpoint Pkwy, Santa Rosa
(95407-7398)
PHONE..............................707 546-3042
Glen Nold, *Branch Mgr*
EMP: 82 **Privately Held**
SIC: 8711 7623 Heating & ventilation engi-
    neering; air conditioning repair
HQ: Johnson Controls, Inc.
    5757 N Green Bay Ave
    Milwaukee WI 53209
    414 524-1200

(P-25771)
JSL TECHNOLOGIES INC
1701 Pacific Ave Ste 270, Oxnard
(93033-1887)
PHONE..............................805 985-7700
Joseph T Black III, *President*
Ben Fujikawa, *Exec VP*
Jed Williams, *Exec VP*
EMP: 79
SQ FT: 9,150
SALES (est): 7.5MM **Privately Held**
SIC: 8711 Consulting engineer

(P-25772)
JT3 LLC
190 S Wolfe Ave Bldg 1260, Edwards
(93524-6501)
PHONE..............................661 277-4900
James Tedeschi, *Manager*
EMP: 900
SALES (corp-wide): 150MM **Privately
Held**
WEB: www.jt3.com
SIC: 8711 Engineering services
PA: Jt3, L.L.C.
    821 Grier Dr
    Las Vegas NV 89119
    704 492-2181

(P-25773)
K&B ELECTRIC LLC
Also Called: K&B Engineering
290 Corporate Terrace Cir # 200, Corona
(92879-6033)
PHONE..................................951 808-9501
Sandee Gibbs, *Mng Member*
Trey Gibbs
EMP: 158
SALES (est): 2.6MM **Privately Held**
SIC: 8711 Engineering services

(P-25774)
K&B ENGINEERING
290 Corporate Terrace Cir, Corona
(92879-6033)
PHONE..................................951 808-9501
Trey Gibbs, *Owner*
Connie Moreno, *Admin Asst*
Candice Chavez, *Planning*
Alan Domnisse, *Project Mgr*
Desi Romo, *Project Mgr*
EMP: 200
SALES (est): 23.7MM **Privately Held**
SIC: 8711 Civil engineering

(P-25775)
KAISER GROUP HOLDINGS INC
Also Called: Earthtech
2101 Webster St Ste 1000, Oakland
(94612-3060)
PHONE..................................510 419-6000
EMP: 90
SALES (corp-wide): 527.4MM **Publicly Held**
SIC: 8711
PA: Kaiser Group Holdings, Inc.
9300 Lee Hwy
Fairfax VA 22031
703 934-3000

(P-25776)
KBRWYLE TECH SOLUTIONS LLC
Honeywell
850 E Main St, Barstow (92311-2347)
PHONE..................................760 255-8322
Tom Millard, *Manager*
EMP: 200 **Publicly Held**
WEB: www.honeywell-tsi.com
SIC: 8711 Pollution control engineering
HQ: Kbrwyle Technology Solutions, Llc
7000 Columbia Gateway Dr # 100
Columbia MD 21046
410 964-7000

(P-25777)
KENNEDY/JENKS CONSULTANTS INC (PA)
303 2nd St Ste 300s, San Francisco
(94107-3632)
PHONE..................................415 243-2150
Gary Carlton, *Chairman*
Keith A London, *President*
Patrick J Courtney, *CFO*
Lynn Takaichi, *Chairman*
John Rayner, *Vice Pres*
EMP: 100
SQ FT: 45,000
SALES (est): 120.1MM **Privately Held**
SIC: 8711 Consulting engineer

(P-25778)
KEVCOMP INC
Also Called: Kevcomp Engineering
4300 Long Beach Blvd # 720, Long Beach
(90807-2019)
PHONE..................................562 423-3028
Kevin Ngo, *President*
Mike T Diep, *CEO*
Dennis Romano, *Human Res Mgr*
Tien Le, *Manager*
Vince Costantino, *Accounts Exec*
EMP: 80
SQ FT: 1,500
SALES (est): 7.5MM **Privately Held**
WEB: www.kevcomp.com
SIC: 8711 7379 Engineering services;
computer related consulting services

(P-25779)
KIER & WRIGHT CIVIL ENGRS&SRVY (PA)
Also Called: Kier Wrght Cvil Engneers Survy
3350 Scott Blvd Bldg 22, Santa Clara
(95054-3106)
PHONE..................................408 727-6665
Anthony McCants, *President*
Gene Golobic, *Vice Pres*
David Readler, *Vice Pres*
Barry Schmitt, *Vice Pres*
Ted Wilson, *Vice Pres*
EMP: 70
SQ FT: 5,000
SALES (est): 12.1MM **Privately Held**
WEB: www.kierwright.com
SIC: 8711 8713 Civil engineering; survey-
ing services

(P-25780)
KIMLEY-HORN AND ASSOCIATES INC
401 B St Ste 600, San Diego (92101-4218)
PHONE..................................619 234-9411
James Roberts, *Manager*
EMP: 60
SALES (corp-wide): 579.2MM **Privately Held**
WEB: www.itscareers.com
SIC: 8711 Consulting engineer
HQ: Kimley-Horn And Associates, Inc.
421 Fayetteville St # 600
Raleigh NC 27601
919 677-2000

(P-25781)
KINEMETRICS INC (DH)
222 Vista Ave, Pasadena (91107-3295)
PHONE..................................626 795-2220
Tadashi Jimbo, *CEO*
Michelle Harrington, *Treasurer*
Melvin Lund, *Exec VP*
Ogie Kuraica, *Vice Pres*
Ian Standley, *Vice Pres*
EMP: 59
SQ FT: 50,000
SALES (est): 22.6MM
SALES (corp-wide): 410.1MM **Privately Held**
WEB: www.kinemetrics.com
SIC: 8711 3829 Engineering services;
seismographs

(P-25782)
KLEINFELDER INC (HQ)
550 W C St Ste 1200, San Diego
(92101-3532)
P.O. Box 51958, Los Angeles (90051-6258)
PHONE..................................619 831-4600
George Pierson, *CEO*
John Murphy, *CFO*
Rita Fordiani, *Vice Pres*
Deborah Butera, *Admin Sec*
Laura Anderson, *Administration*
EMP: 160
SQ FT: 5,000
SALES: 175.4MM
SALES (corp-wide): 249.4MM **Privately Held**
WEB: www.kleinfelder.com
SIC: 8711 8712 Consulting engineer; ar-
chitectural engineering
PA: The Kleinfelder Group Inc
550 W C St Ste 1200
San Diego CA 92101
619 831-4600

(P-25783)
KLEINFELDER INC
5125 N Gates Ave Ste 102, Fresno
(93722-6414)
PHONE..................................559 486-0750
Walt Placata, *Manager*
David Pearson, *Project Engr*
EMP: 60
SALES (corp-wide): 249.4MM **Privately Held**
WEB: www.kleinfelder.com
SIC: 8711 8734 8731 Consulting engi-
neer; testing laboratories; commercial
physical research
HQ: Kleinfelder, Inc.
550 W C St Ste 1200
San Diego CA 92101
619 831-4600

(P-25784)
KLEINFELDER INC
6700 Koll Center Pkwy # 120, Pleasanton
(94566-7032)
PHONE..................................925 484-1700
Mike Majchrzak, *Manager*
Chris Dacey, *Lab Dir*
EMP: 60
SALES (corp-wide): 249.4MM **Privately Held**
WEB: www.kleinfelder.com
SIC: 8711 8742 8734 8748 Consulting
engineer; management consulting serv-
ices; testing laboratories; environmental
consultant
HQ: Kleinfelder, Inc.
550 W C St Ste 1200
San Diego CA 92101
619 831-4600

(P-25785)
KLEINFELDER INC
2882 Prospect Park Dr # 200, Rancho Cor-
dova (95670-6058)
PHONE..................................916 366-1701
Mark Cannolly, *Manager*
Qassim Siddiqyar, *CTO*
Maria Boden, *Human Res Mgr*
Nancy Walker, *Opers Staff*
Bruce Ross, *Sr Project Mgr*
EMP: 90
SALES (corp-wide): 249.4MM **Privately Held**
WEB: www.kleinfelder.com
SIC: 8711 Consulting engineer
HQ: Kleinfelder, Inc.
550 W C St Ste 1200
San Diego CA 92101
619 831-4600

(P-25786)
KOCH-ARMSTRONG GENERAL ENGRG
15315 Olde Highway 80, El Cajon
(92021-2408)
P.O. Box 1190, Lakeside (92040-0906)
PHONE..................................619 561-2005
Monte J Koch, *CEO*
Christopher Armstrong, *Vice Pres*
EMP: 65
SALES (est): 9.2MM **Privately Held**
WEB: www.koch-armstrong.com
SIC: 8711 Building construction consultant

(P-25787)
KPFF INC
Also Called: K P F F Consulting Engineers
700 S Flower St Ste 2100, Los Angeles
(90017-4208)
PHONE..................................310 665-1536
John Gavan, *Manager*
EMP: 114
SALES (corp-wide): 162.3MM **Privately Held**
WEB: www.kpff.com
SIC: 8711 Consulting engineer
PA: Kpff, Inc.
1601 5th Ave Ste 1600
Seattle WA 98101
206 622-5822

(P-25788)
KPFF INC
400 Oceangate Ste 500, Long Beach
(90802-4392)
PHONE..................................562 437-9100
Todd Graham, *Branch Mgr*
Harry George, *Administration*
EMP: 71
SALES (corp-wide): 162.3MM **Privately Held**
SIC: 8711 Structural engineering
PA: Kpff, Inc.
1601 5th Ave Ste 1600
Seattle WA 98101
206 622-5822

(P-25789)
KPFF INC
Also Called: Kpff Consulting Engineers
45 Fremont St Fl 28, San Francisco
(94105-2209)
PHONE..................................415 989-1004
Marc Press, *Manager*
EMP: 56

SALES (corp-wide): 162.3MM **Privately Held**
WEB: www.kpff.com
SIC: 8711 Consulting engineer
PA: Kpff, Inc.
1601 5th Ave Ste 1600
Seattle WA 98101
206 622-5822

(P-25790)
KSI ENGINEERING INC
6205 District Blvd, Bakersfield
(93313-2141)
PHONE..................................661 617-1700
Kevin Small, *President*
Glenda Sue Small, *Corp Secy*
Matthew Bouchard, *Manager*
EMP: 50
SQ FT: 7,000
SALES: 6.5MM **Privately Held**
WEB: www.dcck.com
SIC: 8711 Electrical or electronic engineer-
ing

(P-25791)
L3 MARIPRO INC
Also Called: L-3 Communications Maripro Inc
1522 Cook Pl, Goleta (93117-3124)
PHONE..................................805 683-3881
Dan Chabot, *Vice Pres*
Peter Yinger, *Business Anlyst*
EMP: 90
SQ FT: 100,000
SALES (est): 4.1MM
SALES (corp-wide): 9.5B **Publicly Held**
WEB: www.nautronix.com
SIC: 8711 Marine engineering
PA: L3 Technologies, Inc.
600 3rd Ave Fl 34
New York NY 10016
212 697-1111

(P-25792)
LACO ASSOCIATES (PA)
21 W 4th St, Eureka (95501-0216)
P.O. Box 1023 (95502-1023)
PHONE..................................707 443-5054
Leonard Osborne, *President*
Frank Bickner, *Bd of Directors*
David Lindberg, *Vice Pres*
Madison Green, *Admin Mgr*
Rod Wilburn, *Department Mgr*
EMP: 50
SQ FT: 6,000
SALES (est): 8MM **Privately Held**
WEB: www.lacoassociates.us
SIC: 8711 8999 0711 Structural engineer-
ing; mechanical engineering; building
construction consultant; civil engineering;
geological consultant; soil testing services

(P-25793)
LANWAVE TECHNOLOGY INC
20111 Stevens Creek Blvd # 260, Cupertino
(95014-2399)
PHONE..................................408 253-3883
Kenneth Chan, *President*
Alan Chan, *CFO*
EMP: 53
SQ FT: 3,000
SALES (est): 2.3MM **Privately Held**
WEB: www.lanwave.com
SIC: 8711 Consulting engineer

(P-25794)
LEE & RO INC (PA)
1199 Fullerton Rd, City of Industry
(91748-1232)
PHONE..................................626 912-3391
Myong Ro, *CEO*
Gregory Holmes, *CFO*
Dhiru Patel, *Vice Pres*
Charles Ro, *Vice Pres*
EMP: 50 EST: 1979
SQ FT: 19,000
SALES: 9.6MM **Privately Held**
WEB: www.lee-ro.com
SIC: 8711 Civil engineering; mechanical
engineering; sanitary engineers

(P-25795)
LEIDOS ENGINEERING LLC
590 W Central Ave Ste I, Brea
(92821-3019)
PHONE..................................714 257-6400
Sherif Philobos, *Branch Mgr*

EMP: 54
SALES (corp-wide): 10.1B **Publicly Held**
SIC: 8711 Consulting engineer
HQ: Leidos Engineering, Llc
11951 Freedom Dr
Reston VA 20190
571 526-6000

(P-25796)
LEIDOS ENGINEERING LLC
4161 Campus Point Ct E, San Diego
(92121-1513)
PHONE...............................858 826-6000
David Bernal, *Branch Mgr*
Kristen McBride, *Software Engr*
Jeremy Davidson, *Engineer*
Shalini Gupta, *Engineer*
Alban Weber, *Engineer*
EMP: 54
SALES (corp-wide): 10.1B **Publicly Held**
SIC: 8711 Engineering services
HQ: Leidos Engineering, Llc
11951 Freedom Dr
Reston VA 20190
571 526-6000

(P-25797)
LINQUEST CORPORATION (PA)
5140 W Goldleaf Cir # 400, Los Angeles
(90056-1299)
PHONE...............................323 924-1600
Leon Biederman, *President*
F Scott Stowe, *COO*
Matthew C Lyons, *CFO*
Dan Vernon, *Assoc VP*
Patrick Talty, *Vice Pres*
EMP: 200
SQ FT: 20,000
SALES (est): 79.2MM **Privately Held**
WEB: www.linquest.com
SIC: 8711 Aviation &/or aeronautical engineering

(P-25798)
LIONAKIS
20371 Irvine Ave Ste 120, Newport Beach
(92660-0119)
PHONE...............................949 955-1919
Jeffrey Gill, *Principal*
EMP: 156
SALES (corp-wide): 45.6MM **Privately Held**
WEB: www.lbdg.com
SIC: 8711 7389 Civil engineering; design, commercial & industrial
PA: Lionakis
1919 19th St
Sacramento CA 95811
916 558-1901

(P-25799)
LIONAKIS (PA)
1919 19th St, Sacramento (95811-6714)
PHONE...............................916 558-1901
Tim Fry, *President*
Nick Docous, *Vice Pres*
Sue Johnson, *Executive*
Maynard Feist, *Social Dir*
Valerie Hoffman, *Social Dir*
EMP: 150 EST: 1909
SQ FT: 38,000
SALES (est): 45.6MM **Privately Held**
WEB: www.lbdg.com
SIC: 8711 7389 8712 Engineering services; interior design services; architectural services

(P-25800)
LOCKHEED MARTIN CORPORATION
255 California St Ste 400, San Francisco
(94111-4921)
PHONE...............................415 402-0406
Marc Mansour, *Manager*
Brett Clair, *Engineer*
Thomas Logue, *Engineer*
EMP: 232 **Publicly Held**
WEB: www.lockheedmartin.com
SIC: 8711 3721 Aviation &/or aeronautical engineering; aircraft
PA: Lockheed Martin Corporation
6801 Rockledge Dr
Bethesda MD 20817

(P-25801)
LOS ANGELES ENGINEERING INC
633 N Barranca Ave, Covina (91723-1229)
PHONE...............................626 869-1400
Henry Angus O'Brien, *President*
Aaron O'Brien, *COO*
Beth Ballard, *CFO*
EMP: 110
SQ FT: 33,000
SALES (est): 37.3MM **Privately Held**
WEB: www.laeng.net
SIC: 8711 1622 Construction & civil engineering; bridge, tunnel & elevated highway

(P-25802)
LUND CONSTRUCTION CO
5302 Roseville Rd, North Highlands
(95660-5000)
PHONE...............................916 344-5800
Jerry A Lund, *President*
Alta M Lund, *Treasurer*
Jeff Lund, *Vice Pres*
Kevin Lund, *Vice Pres*
EMP: 130 EST: 1959
SQ FT: 7,500
SALES (est): 38.5MM **Privately Held**
SIC: 8711 1794 1623 4212 Construction & civil engineering; excavation & grading; building construction; underground utilities contractor; hazardous waste transport

(P-25803)
LUNDSTROM & ASSOCIATES INC
4804 Sunrise Hills Dr, El Cajon
(92020-8259)
PHONE...............................619 641-5900
Jeffrey R Lundstrom, *President*
Bill Lundstrom, *Vice Pres*
EMP: 50
SALES (est): 4.1MM **Privately Held**
SIC: 8711 Civil engineering; consulting engineer

(P-25804)
M-E ENGINEERS INC
600 Wilshire Blvd # 1200, Los Angeles
(90017-3200)
PHONE...............................310 842-8700
Akira Hiruma, *General Mgr*
EMP: 65
SALES (corp-wide): 39.6MM **Privately Held**
WEB: www.meengineers.com
SIC: 8711 Consulting engineer
PA: M-E Engineers, Inc.
14143 Denver West Pkwy # 300
Lakewood CO 80401
303 421-6655

(P-25805)
MACDONALD MOTT GROUP INC
3699 Crenshaw Blvd, Los Angeles
(90016-4849)
PHONE...............................323 903-4100
EMP: 70
SALES (corp-wide): 507.4MM **Privately Held**
SIC: 8711 Consulting engineer
PA: Macdonald Mott Group Inc
111 Wood Ave S Ste 5
Iselin NJ 08830
973 379-3400

(P-25806)
MACDONALD MOTT GROUP INC
12647 Alcosta Blvd, San Ramon
(94583-4439)
PHONE...............................925 469-8010
Tony Purdon, *Branch Mgr*
Craig Velasquez, *Treasurer*
Melanie Graham, *Executive*
EMP: 75
SALES (corp-wide): 507.4MM **Privately Held**
WEB: www.hatchmott.com
SIC: 8711 Engineering services
PA: Macdonald Mott Group Inc
111 Wood Ave S Ste 5
Iselin NJ 08830
973 379-3400

(P-25807)
MACDONALD MOTT LLC
3103 N 1st St Bldg B, San Jose
(95134-1934)
PHONE...............................408 321-5900
EMP: 64
SALES (corp-wide): 507.4MM **Privately Held**
SIC: 8711 Engineering services
HQ: Macdonald Mott Llc
12647 Alcosta Blvd
San Ramon CA 94583

(P-25808)
MACDONALD MOTT LLC
Also Called: Railroad Technology
2495 Natomas Park Dr # 530, Sacramento
(95833-2935)
PHONE...............................916 399-0580
Cara Stromm, *Office Mgr*
EMP: 64
SALES (corp-wide): 507.4MM **Privately Held**
SIC: 8711 Consulting engineer
HQ: Macdonald Mott Llc
12647 Alcosta Blvd
San Ramon CA 94583

(P-25809)
MACKAY SMPS CVIL ENGINEERS INC (PA)
5142 Franklin Dr Ste C, Pleasanton
(94588-3368)
PHONE...............................925 416-1790
James C Ray, *President*
Bob Chan, *Vice Pres*
John F Kuzia, *Admin Sec*
EMP: 62 EST: 1953
SALES (est): 8.8MM **Privately Held**
WEB: www.msce.com
SIC: 8711 Civil engineering

(P-25810)
MANGAN INC (PA)
3901 Via Oro Ave, Long Beach
(90810-1800)
PHONE...............................310 835-8080
Richard D Mangan, *Principal*
Amin Solehjou, *CEO*
Russell Seward, *CFO*
Brian Cooper, *Bd of Directors*
Jeremy Lucas, *Associate Dir*
EMP: 90
SQ FT: 15,000
SALES (est): 49.4MM **Privately Held**
WEB: www.mangan.com
SIC: 8711 Engineering services

(P-25811)
MARQUES PIPELINE INC
7225 26th St, Sacramento (95834)
PHONE...............................916 923-3434
Jeremy R Jaeger, *CEO*
Jeremy Jaeger, *President*
Dennis Loosli, *Vice Pres*
Kate Ruelas, *Office Mgr*
Garrett Davis, *Project Engr*
EMP: 50
SQ FT: 2,000
SALES (est): 12.7MM **Privately Held**
WEB: www.marquespipeline.com
SIC: 8711 Engineering services

(P-25812)
MARTIN ASSOCIATES GROUP INC (PA)
Also Called: Martin, John A & Associates
950 S Grand Ave Fl 4, Los Angeles
(90015-1436)
PHONE...............................213 483-6490
John A Martin Jr, *CEO*
Barry Schindler, *Vice Pres*
EMP: 63
SQ FT: 70,000
SALES (est): 52MM **Privately Held**
WEB: www.johnmartin.com
SIC: 8711 Structural engineering

(P-25813)
MAZDA RESEARCH & DEV OF N AMER
1421 Reynolds Ave, Irvine (92614-5531)
PHONE...............................949 852-8898

Kelvin Hiraishi, *Manager*
Evon Burkhouse, *Manager*
EMP: 100
SQ FT: 127,000
SALES (est): 5.7MM
SALES (corp-wide): 32.6B **Privately Held**
WEB: www.mazdamotorsports.com
SIC: 8711 Designing: ship, boat, machine & product
HQ: Mazda Motor Of America, Inc.
200 Spectrum Center Dr
Irvine CA 92618
949 727-1990

(P-25814)
MAZZETTI INC (PA)
Also Called: Mazzetti GBA
220 Montgomery St Ste 650, San Francisco
(94104-3491)
PHONE...............................415 362-3266
Walt Vernon, *CEO*
Darryl Wandry, *CFO*
Lisa Sombart, *Principal*
Christine Nagayama, *Office Mgr*
Winna MEI, *Executive Asst*
EMP: 50
SQ FT: 17,700
SALES (est): 51.1MM **Privately Held**
WEB: www.mazzetti.com
SIC: 8711 Electrical or electronic engineering; mechanical engineering; consulting engineer

(P-25815)
MDR INC
Also Called: Accu-Bore Directional Drilling
511 E Channel Rd, Benicia (94510-1158)
P.O. Box 639 (94510-0639)
PHONE...............................707 750-5376
Michael Robirds, *President*
EMP: 90
SALES (est): 26MM **Privately Held**
SIC: 8711 Construction & civil engineering

(P-25816)
MDS CONSULTING (PA)
17320 Red Hill Ave # 350, Irvine
(92614-5644)
PHONE...............................949 251-8821
Stanley C Morse, *Chairman*
Jerry R Schultz, *Co-Owner*
Ed Lenth, *Vice Pres*
Jenny Richard, *Executive Asst*
Dario Bran, *Project Mgr*
EMP: 91 EST: 1976
SQ FT: 8,837
SALES (est): 10.5MM **Privately Held**
WEB: www.mdsconsulting.net
SIC: 8711 Civil engineering

(P-25817)
MEC INTERNATIONAL LLC
1515 Tessa Ave, Sacramento
(95815-1812)
PHONE...............................415 866-4497
Franz Campero, *President*
EMP: 200 EST: 2014
SALES (est): 5.9MM **Privately Held**
SIC: 8711 Consulting engineer

(P-25818)
MGGB INC
Also Called: Alltech Services
10841 Noel St Ste 110, Los Alamitos
(90720-6701)
P.O. Box 1065, Sunset Beach (90742-1065)
PHONE...............................714 226-0520
Miles D Sleeth, *CEO*
Phil Gentile, *Director*
Dan Jakary, *Director*
EMP: 114
SQ FT: 3,900
SALES (est): 8.5MM **Privately Held**
SIC: 8711 8748 Pollution control engineering; construction & civil engineering; environmental consultant

(P-25819)
MICHAEL BAKER JR INC
5051 Verdugo Way Ste 300, Camarillo
(93012-8683)
PHONE...............................805 383-3373
Kurt Bergman, *CEO*
Chad Havens, *Manager*
Louis Levner, *Assistant VP*

EMP: 99
SALES (est): 2.7MM Privately Held
SIC: 8711 Engineering services

(P-25820)
MICHAEL BAKER INTL INC
1 Kaiser Plz Ste 1150, Oakland
(94612-3601)
PHONE...................510 879-0950
Mike Conrad, Branch Mgr
EMP: 140
SALES (corp-wide): 592.9MM Privately Held
SIC: 8711 Engineering services
HQ: Baker Michael Intl Inc
500 Grant St Ste 5400
Pittsburgh PA 15219
412 269-6300

(P-25821)
MICHAEL BAKER INTL INC
40810 County Center Dr # 100, Temecula
(92591-6053)
PHONE...................951 676-8042
William Green, Vice Pres
EMP: 60
SALES (corp-wide): 592.9MM Privately Held
WEB: www.rbf.com
SIC: 8711 8713 Civil engineering; surveying services
HQ: Baker Michael International Inc
14725 Alton Pkwy
Irvine CA 92618
949 472-3505

(P-25822)
MICHAEL CARDELLINI
Also Called: Thornton and Thomasetti
650 California St Fl 14, San Francisco
(94108-2792)
PHONE...................415 243-8400
Michael Cardellini, Principal
EMP: 50 EST: 2015
SALES (est): 86K Privately Held
SIC: 8711 Engineering services

(P-25823)
**MILLENNIUM ENGRG
INTEGRATION**
350 N Akron Rd, Moffett Field (94035)
PHONE...................703 413-7750
Rick Maurer, Branch Mgr
EMP: 99
SALES (corp-wide): 125.9MM Privately Held
SIC: 8711 Engineering services
PA: Millennium Engineering And Integration Co.
1400 Crystal Dr Ste 800
Arlington VA 22202
703 413-7750

(P-25824)
MILLSAP DEGNAN & ASSOC INC
4280 Redwood Hwy Ste 10, San Rafael
(94903-2600)
PHONE...................415 472-4244
Steve Millsap, CEO
Doug Degnan, President
Mike Millsap, Manager
EMP: 60
SALES (est): 5.6MM Privately Held
WEB: www.millsapdegnan.com
SIC: 8711 1522 1771 Engineering services; residential construction; concrete work

(P-25825)
MISTRAS GROUP INC
Also Called: Mistras Impro
21215 Kratzmeyer Rd A, Bakersfield
(93314)
PHONE...................661 829-1192
Jorky Kidwell, General Mgr
EMP: 70 Publicly Held
SIC: 8711 Consulting engineer
PA: Mistras Group, Inc.
195 Clarksville Rd Ste 2
Princeton Junction NJ 08550

(P-25826)
MISTRAS GROUP INC
8427 Atlantic Ave, Cudahy (90201-5809)
PHONE...................323 583-1653

Victor Altomare, General Mgr
EMP: 58 Publicly Held
SIC: 8711 Engineering services
PA: Mistras Group, Inc.
195 Clarksville Rd Ste 2
Princeton Junction NJ 08550

(P-25827)
MNS ENGINEERS INC (PA)
201 N Calle Cesar, Santa Barbara (93103)
PHONE...................805 692-6921
James A Salvito, CEO
Shawn Kowalewski, President
Mark E Reinhardt, CFO
Gregory A Chelini, Vice Pres
Jeffrey L Edwards, Vice Pres
EMP: 94 EST: 1962
SQ FT: 7,000
SALES (est): 18.9MM Privately Held
WEB: www.mnsengineers.com
SIC: 8711 8713 Civil engineering; surveying services

(P-25828)
MOBILENET SERVICES INC (PA)
18 Morgan Ste 200, Irvine (92618-2074)
PHONE...................949 951-4444
Richard Grant, President
Eugene Powell, Vice Pres
Kellie Ohr, Office Admin
Alicia Arroyo, Technical Mgr
Earl Melendres, Engineer
EMP: 180
SQ FT: 17,500
SALES (est): 46.9MM Privately Held
WEB: www.mobilenetservices.net
SIC: 8711 4813 Engineering services; telephone communication, except radio

(P-25829)
MOFFATT & NICHOL
2185 N Calif Blvd Ste 500, Walnut Creek
(94596-3543)
PHONE...................925 944-5411
Robin Rhodes, Manager
EMP: 50
SQ FT: 150,000
SALES (corp-wide): 137.5MM Privately Held
SIC: 8711 Civil engineering
PA: Moffatt & Nichol
3780 Kilroy Arprt Way
Long Beach CA 90806
562 590-6500

(P-25830)
MOFFATT & NICHOL
Also Called: Branch
2185 N Calif Blvd Ste 500, Walnut Creek
(94596-3543)
PHONE...................510 645-1238
Rick Rhode, Branch Mgr
EMP: 50
SALES (corp-wide): 137.5MM Privately Held
WEB: www.moffattnichol.com
SIC: 8711 Consulting engineer
PA: Moffatt & Nichol
3780 Kilroy Arprt Way
Long Beach CA 90806
562 590-6500

(P-25831)
MOFFATT & NICHOL
3780 Kilroy Arprt Way # 600, Long Beach
(90806-2457)
PHONE...................562 426-9551
Mike McCarthy, Manager
Eric Nichol, CEO
EMP: 55
SALES (corp-wide): 137.5MM Privately Held
WEB: www.moffattnichol.com
SIC: 8711 Consulting engineer
PA: Moffatt & Nichol
3780 Kilroy Arprt Way
Long Beach CA 90806
562 590-6500

(P-25832)
MOOG INC
2581 Leghorn St, Mountain View
(94043-1613)
PHONE...................650 210-9000
Christopher Head, CEO

Joseph Maly, Associate
EMP: 57
SALES (corp-wide): 2.7B Publicly Held
SIC: 8711 Engineering services
PA: Moog Inc.
400 Jamison Rd
Elma NY 14059
716 652-2000

(P-25833)
MORTON & PITALO INC (PA)
75 Iron Point Cir Ste 120, Folsom
(95630-8813)
PHONE...................916 984-7621
Eddie Kho, President
Gregory J Bardini, Vice Pres
Christopher J Gorges, Vice Pres
Renee Brandt, Admin Asst
Craig Kendall, Project Mgr
EMP: 64
SQ FT: 5,200
SALES (est): 11.7MM Privately Held
WEB: www.mpengr.com
SIC: 8711 Civil engineering

(P-25834)
MULTAX SYSTEMS INC (PA)
2512 Artesia Blvd 300c, Redondo Beach
(90278-3277)
PHONE...................310 379-8398
Randolph Heinesh, President
EMP: 250 EST: 1981
SQ FT: 1,400
SALES (est): 10.9MM Privately Held
WEB: www.multax.net
SIC: 8711 7371 Engineering services; software programming applications

(P-25835)
MULTIPOINT WIRELESS LLC
2549 Eastbluff Dr Ste 474, Newport Beach
(92660-3500)
PHONE...................714 262-4172
Rick Luch, CEO
Rob Brownjohn, CFO
Ilaha Omar, Vice Pres
EMP: 50
SALES (est): 5.9MM Privately Held
WEB: www.multipointllc.com
SIC: 8711 Engineering services

(P-25836)
MVE INC (PA)
Also Called: M V E
1117 L St, Modesto (95354-0833)
PHONE...................209 526-4214
Kirk Delamare, CEO
Catherine De La Mare, Vice Pres
Sean Tobin, Vice Pres
Michael Lagenour, Info Tech Mgr
EMP: 62
SQ FT: 10,000
SALES (est): 8MM Privately Held
WEB: www.mve.net
SIC: 8711 8713 Civil engineering; surveying services

(P-25837)
MWH AMERICAS INC
437 2nd St, Solvang (93463-2763)
PHONE...................805 683-2409
EMP: 77
SALES (corp-wide): 1.5B Privately Held
SIC: 8711
HQ: Mwh Americas, Inc.
370 Interlocken Blvd
Broomfield CO 80021
303 410-4000

(P-25838)
MWH AMERICAS INC
M W H Laboratories
750 Royal Oaks Dr Ste 100, Monrovia
(91016-6359)
PHONE...................626 386-1100
Mona Alteri, Managing Dir
Andrew Eiche, Executive
Ryan Chang, Director
EMP: 129
SALES (corp-wide): 4B Privately Held
WEB: www.mw.com
SIC: 8711 Engineering services
HQ: Mwh Americas, Inc.
370 Interlocken Blvd
Broomfield CO 80021
303 410-4000

(P-25839)
MWH AMERICAS INC
44 Montgomery St Ste 1400, San Francisco
(94104-4717)
PHONE...................415 430-1800
Janell Cook, Branch Mgr
Jim Loucks, Senior Mgr
Peter Donalek, Manager
Vivian Cho, Associate
EMP: 74
SALES (corp-wide): 4B Privately Held
WEB: www.mwh-inc.com
SIC: 8711 Consulting engineer
HQ: Mwh Americas, Inc.
370 Interlocken Blvd
Broomfield CO 80021
303 410-4000

(P-25840)
MWH AMERICAS INC
618 Michillinda Ave # 200, Arcadia
(91007-6342)
PHONE...................626 796-9141
Ellen Seymour, Branch Mgr
Don Bassett, Senior VP
Bob Armstrong, Vice Pres
Gary Baker, Vice Pres
James Borchardt, Vice Pres
EMP: 74
SALES (corp-wide): 4B Privately Held
SIC: 8711 Consulting engineer
HQ: Mwh Americas, Inc.
370 Interlocken Blvd
Broomfield CO 80021
303 410-4000

(P-25841)
NATIONAL SECURITY TECH LLC
Also Called: Bechtel
161 S Vasco Rd Ste A, Livermore
(94551-5131)
PHONE...................925 960-2500
Gary Still, Branch Mgr
Dan Wagner, COO
Kevin Leader, CFO
Amy S Thompson, Admin Asst
Brian Ward, CTO
EMP: 80
SALES (corp-wide): 565.3MM Privately Held
SIC: 8711 1629 Civil engineering; industrial plant construction
PA: National Security Technologies, Llc
2621 Losee Rd
North Las Vegas NV 89030
702 295-1000

(P-25842)
**NATIONAL TECHNICAL
SYSTEMS INC**
Also Called: NTS Silicon Valley
41039 Boyce Rd, Fremont (94538-2434)
PHONE...................510 578-3500
Anuj Kumar, Branch Mgr
EMP: 50
SALES (corp-wide): 273.9MM Privately Held
SIC: 8711 8748 Consulting engineer; testing services
HQ: Nts Technical Systems
24007 Ventura Blvd # 200
Calabasas CA 91302
818 591-0776

(P-25843)
**NATIONAL TELECONSULTANTS
INC**
550 N Brand Blvd Fl 17, Glendale
(91203-1944)
PHONE...................818 265-4400
Eliot P Graham, Mng Member
Chuck Phelan, Managing Prtnr
Peter Adamiak, President
Rich Hill, President
Charles C Phelan, Exec VP
EMP: 108
SQ FT: 35,400
SALES (est): 22.1MM Privately Held
WEB: www.ntc.com
SIC: 8711 Electrical or electronic engineering

(P-25844)
NAVAL FAC ENG CMMD SW WRKNG CA
1220 Pacific Hwy, San Diego (92132-5190)
PHONE.................................619 532-1158
Shahraam Plaseied, *Principal*
Capt Darius Banaji, *COO*
Mark Johnson, *Engineer*
Nancy Wright, *Accountant*
EMP: 99
SQ FT: 4,000
SALES (est): 5.9MM **Privately Held**
SIC: 8711 1623 8744 Pollution control engineering; civil engineering; underground utilities contractor; base maintenance (providing personnel on continuing basis)

(P-25845)
NEW ENGLAND SHTMTL WORKS INC
2731 S Cherry Ave, Fresno (93706-5423)
P.O. Box 11158 (93771-1158)
PHONE.................................559 268-7375
Michael Hensley, *CEO*
Charles Franks, *CIO*
Trish Persicone, *Human Res Mgr*
Roger Coppole, *Purch Mgr*
Matt Grabowski, *Sales Mgr*
EMP: 150 **EST:** 1920
SQ FT: 43,000
SALES (est): 33.9MM **Privately Held**
WEB: www.nesmw.com
SIC: 8711 8741 1542 Engineering services; construction management; commercial & office building, new construction; commercial & office buildings, renovation & repair; hospital construction; school building construction

(P-25846)
NMI INDUSTRIAL HOLDINGS INC
8503 Weyand Ave, Sacramento (95828-2610)
PHONE.................................916 635-7030
Majid Rahimian, *President*
Javad Rahimian, *CFO*
Steve Mathias, *General Mgr*
William Woodson, *Info Tech Mgr*
Todd Krevitsky, *Technology*
EMP: 90
SALES (est): 7.9MM **Privately Held**
SIC: 8711 1799 Construction & civil engineering; building site preparation

(P-25847)
NOVARIANT INC (PA)
Also Called: Autofarm
46610 Landing Pkwy, Fremont (94538-6420)
PHONE.................................510 933-4800
Dave Vaughn, *President*
Mike Manning, *CFO*
Mark Bittner, *Vice Pres*
Dennis Connor, *Vice Pres*
Husam Kal, *Vice Pres*
EMP: 60
SQ FT: 20,000
SALES (est): 20MM **Privately Held**
WEB: www.novariant.com
SIC: 8711 Engineering services

(P-25848)
NOVO ENGINEERING INC (PA)
1350 Specialty Dr Ste A, Vista (92081-8565)
PHONE.................................760 598-6686
Dan Kline, *CEO*
Rajan Ramaswamy, *President*
Dave Peterson, *Vice Pres*
EMP: 60
SQ FT: 18,000
SALES (est): 16.8MM **Privately Held**
WEB: www.novoengineering.com
SIC: 8711 Consulting engineer

(P-25849)
NV5 INC (DH)
Also Called: Nolte Associates
2525 Natomas Park Dr # 300, Sacramento (95833-2933)
PHONE.................................916 641-9100
Dickerson Wright, *CEO*
Robert Van Uffelen, *Director*
Dennis Mc Donnell, *Manager*

EMP: 80
SQ FT: 27,000
SALES (est): 66.7MM
SALES (corp-wide): 333MM **Publicly Held**
WEB: www.nolte.com
SIC: 8711 Civil engineering

(P-25850)
NV5 INC
Also Called: Nolte, George S & Associates
15092 Avenue Of Science # 200, San Diego (92128-3404)
PHONE.................................858 385-0500
Scott Lyle, *Sr Project Mgr*
EMP: 200
SALES (corp-wide): 333MM **Publicly Held**
WEB: www.nolte.com
SIC: 8711 8713 Civil engineering; surveying services
HQ: Nv5, Inc.
    2525 Natomas Park Dr # 300
    Sacramento CA 95833
    916 641-9100

(P-25851)
NV5 INC
2495 Natomas Park Dr # 300, Sacramento (95833-2935)
PHONE.................................916 641-9100
Steve Hiatt, *Vice Pres*
EMP: 72
SALES (corp-wide): 333MM **Publicly Held**
WEB: www.nolte.com
SIC: 8711 8713 Civil engineering; surveying services
HQ: Nv5, Inc.
    2525 Natomas Park Dr # 300
    Sacramento CA 95833
    916 641-9100

(P-25852)
OC ENGINEERING
300 N Flower St, Santa Ana (92703-5001)
PHONE.................................714 667-3212
Ignacio G Ochoa, *Principal*
EMP: 99
SALES (est): 3.1MM **Privately Held**
SIC: 8711 Engineering services

(P-25853)
ONCORE MANUFACTURING LLC (HQ)
Also Called: Neo Tech
9340 Owensmouth Ave, Chatsworth (91311-6915)
PHONE.................................818 734-6500
Sudesh Arora, *President*
Kunal Sharma, *COO*
Laura Siegal, *CFO*
John Lowrey,
David Lane, *CTO*
EMP: 700
SALES (est): 206.9MM
SALES (corp-wide): 1.2B **Privately Held**
WEB: www.oncorems.com
SIC: 8711 3672 Electrical or electronic engineering; printed circuit boards
PA: Natel Engineering Company Inc
    9340 Owensmouth Ave
    Chatsworth CA 91311
    818 734-6523

(P-25854)
OPERATING ENGINEERS LOCA
325 Digital Dr, Morgan Hill (95037-2878)
PHONE.................................408 782-9803
Lisa Kunkel, *Branch Mgr*
EMP: 208
SALES (corp-wide): 186.7K **Privately Held**
SIC: 8711 Engineering services
PA: Operating Engineers Local Union No. 3
    Scholarship Foundation
    1620 S Loop Rd
    Alameda CA 94502
    510 748-7400

(P-25855)
OPTIMUM INC (PA)
17890 Valley Blvd Ste A, Bloomington (92316-1981)
PHONE.................................909 990-0767
Ivan Iordanov Atanassov, *CEO*

Christopher Giordano, *Vice Pres*
EMP: 50
SALES (est): 11.5MM **Privately Held**
SIC: 8711 1623 Engineering services; underground utilities contractor

(P-25856)
P & D CONSULTANTS INC (HQ)
999 W Town And Country Rd, Orange (92868-4713)
P.O. Box 5367 (92863-5367)
PHONE.................................714 835-4447
John L Kinley, *President*
EMP: 50
SQ FT: 23,000
SALES (est): 11.6MM
SALES (corp-wide): 20.1B **Publicly Held**
SIC: 8711 8742 Civil engineering; planning consultant
PA: Aecom
    1999 Avenue Of The Stars # 2600
    Los Angeles CA 90067
    213 593-8000

(P-25857)
P2S INC
Also Called: P2s Engineering
5000 E Spring St Ste 800, Long Beach (90815-5247)
PHONE.................................562 497-2999
Kevin L Peterson, *CEO*
Kent Peterson, *COO*
Marie Nissen, *Officer*
Jagjit Singh, *Principal*
Kirk Anglin, *Program Mgr*
EMP: 209
SQ FT: 42,700
SALES (est): 18.4MM **Privately Held**
WEB: www.p2seng.com
SIC: 8711 8741 Consulting engineer; construction management

(P-25858)
PACIFIC AIRWORKS GROUP LLC
255 S Leland Norton Way, San Bernardino (92408-0103)
PHONE.................................909 815-7012
Jose L Gonzalez,
Jose Gonzalez,
Dale Stix,
EMP: 84
SQ FT: 15,000
SALES (est): 3.2MM **Privately Held**
SIC: 8711 7699 Aviation &/or aeronautical engineering; aircraft & heavy equipment repair services

(P-25859)
PACIFIC CIVIL & STRL CONS LLC
7415 Greenhaven Dr # 100, Sacramento (95831-5167)
PHONE.................................916 421-1000
Fred Huang, *Partner*
EMP: 50
SALES (est): 5MM **Privately Held**
SIC: 8711 Engineering services

(P-25860)
PACIFIC HYDROTECH CORPORATION
314 E 3rd St, Perris (92570-2225)
PHONE.................................951 943-8803
J Kirk Harns, *President*
Sean Finnegan, *Vice Pres*
Joselito Guintu, *Vice Pres*
Dale McKay, *Vice Pres*
Bobby Owens, *Vice Pres*
EMP: 135
SQ FT: 1,500
SALES (est): 37.2MM **Privately Held**
WEB: www.pachydro.com
SIC: 8711 Construction & civil engineering

(P-25861)
PACIFIC MARINE DEV CORP
Also Called: Internavia
11956 Bernardo Plaza Dr, San Diego (92128-2538)
PHONE.................................760 593-9138
George Pappas, *CEO*
George Peppard, *President*
Tom Wilkins, *Vice Pres*
EMP: 50
SQ FT: 6,000

SALES (est): 1.7MM **Privately Held**
SIC: 8711 Engineering services

(P-25862)
PACIFICA SERVICES INC
106 S Mentor Ave Ste 200, Pasadena (91106-2931)
PHONE.................................626 405-0131
Ernest M Camacho, *President*
Stephen Caropino, *CFO*
Toby Bautista, *Officer*
EMP: 84 **EST:** 1979
SQ FT: 15,000
SALES (est): 14.1MM **Privately Held**
WEB: www.pacificaservices.com
SIC: 8711 7629 8741 Civil engineering; electronic equipment repair; construction management

(P-25863)
PADRE ASSOCIATES INC
3500 Coffee Rd Ste B, Bakersfield (93308-5001)
PHONE.................................661 829-2686
EMP: 57 **Privately Held**
SIC: 8711 Consulting engineer
PA: Padre Associates, Inc.
    1861 Knoll Dr
    Ventura CA 93003

(P-25864)
PANASONIC AVIONICS CORPORATION
26211 Enterprise Way, Lake Forest (92630-8402)
PHONE.................................949 472-2376
Paul Margis, *President*
Charles Ogilvie, *Exec Dir*
Mike Ramos, *Engineer*
Satyajeet Chowdhary, *Manager*
Eduardo Martinez, *Manager*
EMP: 86
SALES (corp-wide): 74.9B **Privately Held**
SIC: 8711 Aviation &/or aeronautical engineering
HQ: Panasonic Avionics Corporation
    26200 Enterprise Way
    Lake Forest CA 92630

(P-25865)
PANASONIC AVIONICS CORPORATION (DH)
26200 Enterprise Way, Lake Forest (92630-8400)
PHONE.................................949 672-2000
Paul Margis, *CEO*
Yasu Enokido, *President*
David Chung, *Treasurer*
Kevin Cooper, *Vice Pres*
Susan Hall, *Vice Pres*
▲ **EMP:** 400
SQ FT: 20,000
SALES (est): 601.2MM
SALES (corp-wide): 74.9B **Privately Held**
SIC: 8711 Aviation &/or aeronautical engineering
HQ: Panasonic Corporation Of North America
    2 Riverfront Plz Ste 200
    Newark NJ 07102
    201 348-7000

(P-25866)
PARSONS ENGRG SCIENCE INC (DH)
100 W Walnut St, Pasadena (91124-0001)
P.O. Box 88954, Chicago IL (60695-1954)
PHONE.................................626 440-2000
Charles Harrington, *CEO*
Mary Ann Hopkins, *President*
Curtis A Bower, *Exec VP*
Nicholas L Presecan, *Senior VP*
Gary L Stone, *Senior VP*
EMP: 500
SALES (est): 170.4MM
SALES (corp-wide): 3.1B **Privately Held**
SIC: 8711 Consulting engineer
HQ: Parsons Government Services Inc.
    100 W Walnut St
    Pasadena CA 91124
    626 440-2000

(P-25867)
PARSONS GOVERNMENT SVCS INC (HQ)
100 W Walnut St, Pasadena (91124-0001)
PHONE..........................626 440-2000
Charles L Harrington, *Ch of Bd*
Carey A Smith, *President*
Marc Radin, *Senior VP*
Jerry Oliver, *Vice Pres*
Gary L Stone, *Vice Pres*
EMP: 500 EST: 1930
SQ FT: 900,000
SALES (est): 752.5MM
SALES (corp-wide): 3.1B **Privately Held**
SIC: 8711 Consulting engineer
PA: The Parsons Corporation
100 W Walnut St
Pasadena CA 91124
626 440-2000

(P-25868)
PARSONS GOVERNMENT SVCS INC
2000 Marina Vista Ave, Martinez (94553-1301)
PHONE..........................925 313-3217
Dean Lunsford, *Manager*
EMP: 75
SALES (corp-wide): 3.1B **Privately Held**
SIC: 8711 Engineering services
HQ: Parsons Government Services Inc.
100 W Walnut St
Pasadena CA 91124
626 440-2000

(P-25869)
PARSONS GOVERNMENT SVCS INC
525 B St Ste 1600, San Diego (92101-4413)
PHONE..........................619 685-0085
Christopher Bush, *Vice Pres*
Carey Smith, *President*
EMP: 301
SALES (corp-wide): 3.1B **Privately Held**
SIC: 8711 Engineering services
HQ: Parsons Government Services Inc.
100 W Walnut St
Pasadena CA 91124
626 440-2000

(P-25870)
PARSONS SERVICES COMPANY
100 W Walnut St, Pasadena (91124-0001)
PHONE..........................626 440-2000
Geoge L Ball, *Principal*
EMP: 797
SALES (est): 79.7MM **Privately Held**
SIC: 8711 Construction & civil engineering

(P-25871)
PARSONS TECHNICAL SERVICES INC
100 W Walnut St, Pasadena (91124-0001)
PHONE..........................626 440-3998
Mary Ann Hopkins, *President*
EMP: 99
SALES (est): 8.1MM
SALES (corp-wide): 3.1B **Privately Held**
SIC: 8711 Engineering services
PA: The Parsons Corporation
100 W Walnut St
Pasadena CA 91124
626 440-2000

(P-25872)
PARSONS WTR INFRASTRUCTURE INC
100 W Walnut St, Pasadena (91124-0001)
PHONE..........................626 440-7000
Virginia Grebbien, *CEO*
Anthony F Leketa, *President*
Christian Alexander, *Accounts Mgr*
EMP: 1522
SQ FT: 1,220,000
SALES (est): 75.4MM
SALES (corp-wide): 3.1B **Privately Held**
SIC: 8711 Consulting engineer
PA: The Parsons Corporation
100 W Walnut St
Pasadena CA 91124
626 440-2000

(P-25873)
PARTNER ASSESSMENT CORPORATION (PA)
Also Called: Partner Engineering & Science
2154 Torrance Blvd # 200, Torrance (90501-2609)
PHONE..........................800 419-4923
Joseph P Derhake, *President*
Megan Cisco, *Partner*
Dillon Deloss, *Partner*
Donald Knox, *Partner*
Dana Derhake, *Shareholder*
EMP: 138
SQ FT: 10,000
SALES (est): 95.5MM **Privately Held**
WEB: www.partneresi.com
SIC: 8711 Consulting engineer

(P-25874)
PERRY & SHAW INC
9029 Park Plaza Dr # 104, La Mesa (91942-3450)
PHONE..........................619 390-6500
Michael Shaw, *President*
Harold Perry, *Vice Pres*
EMP: 85 EST: 1995
SALES (est): 48.5MM **Privately Held**
WEB: www.perry-shaw.com
SIC: 8711 Engineering services

(P-25875)
PHG ENGINEERING SERVICES LLC
180 N Rverview Dr Ste 165, Anaheim (92808)
PHONE..........................714 283-8288
Francis L Price,
Steve Kosto, *Engineer*
EMP: 100
SALES (est): 1.4MM **Privately Held**
SIC: 8711 Engineering services

(P-25876)
POWER ENGINEERS INCORPORATED
731 E Ball Rd Ste 100, Anaheim (92805-5951)
PHONE..........................714 507-2700
Douglas M Sharpe, *Branch Mgr*
EMP: 51
SALES (corp-wide): 460.2MM **Privately Held**
SIC: 8711 Engineering services
PA: Power Engineers, Incorporated
3940 Glenbrook Dr
Hailey ID 83333
208 788-3456

(P-25877)
POWER ENGINEERS INCORPORATED
218 Loreto Ct, Martinez (94553-3551)
P.O. Box 2037 (94553-0203)
PHONE..........................925 372-9284
EMP: 52
SALES (corp-wide): 298.6MM **Privately Held**
SIC: 8711
PA: Power Engineers, Incorporated
3940 Glenbrook Dr
Hailey ID 83333
208 788-3456

(P-25878)
PREDICATE LOGIC INC (PA)
6498 Weathers Pl Ste 200, San Diego (92121-3915)
PHONE..........................858 715-0100
Mary J Lawler, *CEO*
Steve Keller, *Vice Pres*
James M Lawler, *Vice Pres*
EMP: 70
SQ FT: 4,126
SALES (est): 8.6MM **Privately Held**
WEB: www.tychometrics.com
SIC: 8711 Engineering services

(P-25879)
PSOMAS
1075 Crkside Rdg Dr # 200, Roseville (95678-3504)
PHONE..........................916 788-8122
Paul Enneking, *Manager*
EMP: 140

SALES (corp-wide): 95.2MM **Privately Held**
SIC: 8711 8713 Civil engineering; surveying services
PA: Psomas
555 S Flower St Ste 4300
Los Angeles CA 90071
213 223-1400

(P-25880)
PTSI MANAGED SERVICES INC
100 W Walnut St, Pasadena (91124-0001)
PHONE..........................626 440-3118
Mary Ann Hopkins, *President*
EMP: 99 EST: 1983
SALES (est): 5.7MM **Privately Held**
SIC: 8711 Engineering services

(P-25881)
QUAD KNOPF INC (PA)
901 E Main St, Visalia (93292-6546)
P.O. Box 3699 (93278-3699)
PHONE..........................559 733-0440
Michael Knopf, *President*
Janel Freeman, *CFO*
EMP: 50
SQ FT: 11,000
SALES (est): 15.1MM **Privately Held**
WEB: www.quadknopf.com
SIC: 8711 8712 Civil engineering; consulting engineer; architectural services

(P-25882)
QUARTUS ENGINEERING INC (PA)
9689 Towne Centre Dr, San Diego (92121-1964)
PHONE..........................858 875-6000
Mark Stabb, *Principal*
Doug Botos, *CEO*
Chris Flanigan, *Vice Pres*
Jeff Frantz, *Vice Pres*
Valerie Dixon, *Office Mgr*
EMP: 69 EST: 1997
SQ FT: 3,100
SALES (est): 28.1MM **Privately Held**
WEB: www.quartus.com
SIC: 8711 Mechanical engineering

(P-25883)
R AND L LOPEZ ASSOCIATES INC (PA)
Also Called: Lopez & Associates Engineers
3649 Tyler Ave, El Monte (91731-2505)
PHONE..........................626 336-9655
Lourdes P Lopez, *President*
Remberto Lopez, *Vice Pres*
EMP: 80
SQ FT: 2,700
SALES (est): 5.8MM **Privately Held**
SIC: 8711 Consulting engineer

(P-25884)
R G VANDERWEIL ENGINEERS LLP
3760 Kilroy Airport Way # 230, Long Beach (90806-2455)
PHONE..........................562 256-8623
Jeff Duncan, *Principal*
EMP: 110
SALES (corp-wide): 68.8MM **Privately Held**
SIC: 8711 Consulting engineer
PA: R. G. Vanderweil Engineers, Llp
274 Summer St Fl 2
Boston MA 02210
617 423-7423

(P-25885)
R JOY INC
Also Called: Richard Joy Engineering
1584 Wolf Meadows Ln, Portola (96122-7080)
PHONE..........................530 832-5760
Richard Joy, *Owner*
Benjamin Joy, *Vice Pres*
Rick Joy, *General Mgr*
EMP: 100
SALES (est): 1.7MM **Privately Held**
SIC: 8711 Engineering services

(P-25886)
R M A GROUP INC (PA)
Also Called: RMA Group
12130 Santa Margarita Ct, Rancho Cucamonga (91730-6138)
PHONE..........................909 980-6096
Edward Duane Lyon, *Chairman*
Slawek Dymerski, *President*
Ed Lyon, *President*
Sue Lyon, *Corp Secy*
Gregg Arnold, *Business Dir*
EMP: 70
SQ FT: 9,600
SALES (est): 23.9MM **Privately Held**
WEB: www.rmagrp.com
SIC: 8711 Engineering services

(P-25887)
RAILPROS INC (PA)
1 Ada Ste 200, Irvine (92618-5341)
PHONE..........................714 734-8765
Eric Hankinson, *President*
Johnny Johnson, *Vice Pres*
Doug Sawyer, *Vice Pres*
EMP: 54 EST: 2000
SQ FT: 1,200
SALES (est): 13.2MM **Privately Held**
WEB: www.railpros.com
SIC: 8711 Civil engineering

(P-25888)
RAMSGATE ENGINEERING INC
2331 Cepheus Ct, Bakersfield (93308-6944)
P.O. Box 20068 (93390-0068)
PHONE..........................661 392-0050
Donald C Nelson, *President*
EMP: 95
SALES (est): 12MM **Privately Held**
SIC: 8711 Consulting engineer

(P-25889)
RANGE GENERATION NEXT LLC
Also Called: Rgnext
105 13th St Bldg 6525, Vandenberg Afb (93437-5209)
PHONE..........................310 647-9438
Tom Kennedy, *CEO*
Donna Mc Cullough, *Manager*
Donna McCullough, *Manager*
EMP: 99
SQ FT: 100
SALES (est): 3.9MM **Privately Held**
SIC: 8711 Engineering services

(P-25890)
RAYTHEON COMPANY
9985 Pcf Hts Blvd Ste 200, San Diego (92121)
PHONE..........................858 455-9741
Thomas Peppers, *Technical Staff*
Sonya Vitali, *VP Opers*
EMP: 187
SALES (corp-wide): 25.3B **Publicly Held**
SIC: 8711 8733 5045 Aviation &/or aeronautical engineering; scientific research agency; computer software
PA: Raytheon Company
870 Winter St
Waltham MA 02451
781 522-3000

(P-25891)
RAYTHEON COMPANY
2000 E El Segundo Blvd, El Segundo (90245-4501)
PHONE..........................310 647-9438
Donna McCullough, *Branch Mgr*
EMP: 220
SALES (corp-wide): 25.3B **Publicly Held**
SIC: 8711 Electrical or electronic engineering
PA: Raytheon Company
870 Winter St
Waltham MA 02451
781 522-3000

(P-25892)
REAUME AND ASSOCIATES INC
Also Called: Reaume, E M & Associates
11527 W Washington Blvd, Los Angeles (90066-5913)
PHONE..........................310 398-5768
John Wilmer, *President*
Allen John Wilmer, *Vice Pres*
EMP: 80

SQ FT: 1,500
SALES: 1.1MM **Privately Held**
SIC: 8711 Consulting engineer

(P-25893)
RIALTO BIOENERGY FACILITY LLC
5780 Fleet St Ste 310, Carlsbad (92008-4714)
PHONE..................................760 436-8870
Rakesh Dewan, *CEO*
Arun Sharma, *President*
EMP: 250 EST: 2013
SQ FT: 12,937
SALES (est): 5.6MM **Privately Held**
PA: Anaergia Inc
4210 South Service Rd
Burlington ON L7L 4
905 766-3333

(P-25894)
RIVER CY GEOPROFESSIONALS INC
Also Called: Wallace-Kuhl & Associates
3050 Industrial Blvd, West Sacramento (95691-3470)
PHONE..................................916 372-1434
David R Gius, *President*
Andrew Wallace, *CFO*
EMP: 56
SALES (est): 5.7MM **Privately Held**
SIC: 8711 Engineering services

(P-25895)
ROBERT CONSL ENGLEKIRK STRCTRL (PA)
2116 Arlington Ave Lbby, Los Angeles (90018-1365)
PHONE..................................323 733-6673
Robert E Englekirk, *President*
Solveig Jensen, *Treasurer*
EMP: 55 EST: 1969
SQ FT: 12,000
SALES (est): 4.3MM **Privately Held**
SIC: 8711 Structural engineering

(P-25896)
ROQUE DEVELOPMENT AND INV
Also Called: Rdi Engineering
227 E Pomona Blvd Ste B, Monterey Park (91755-7226)
PHONE..................................626 427-9077
Hector Mendoza Jr, *CEO*
Jason Roque, *Real Est Agnt*
EMP: 99
SQ FT: 5,000
SALES (est): 6.8MM **Privately Held**
SIC: 8711 Civil engineering

(P-25897)
ROSS F CARROLL INC
8873 Warnerville Rd, Oakdale (95361-9411)
P.O. Box 1308 (95361-1308)
PHONE..................................209 848-5959
Sean Carroll, *President*
Sheila M Carroll, *Corp Secy*
John Negele, *VP Opers*
EMP: 50
SALES (est): 9.3MM **Privately Held**
WEB: www.rossfcarrollinc.com
SIC: 8711 Engineering services

(P-25898)
RWC ENTERPRISES INC
Also Called: Professional Construction Svcs
9130 Santa Anita Ave, Rancho Cucamonga (91730-6143)
PHONE..................................909 373-4100
Robert William Casey, *President*
Lori Casey, *Admin Sec*
Frank Heaton, *Project Mgr*
EMP: 50
SQ FT: 16,000
SALES (est): 7.3MM **Privately Held**
SIC: 8711 0781 Civil engineering; landscape counseling services

(P-25899)
SAALEX CORP (PA)
Also Called: Saalex Solutions
811 Camarillo Springs Rd A, Camarillo (93012-9465)
PHONE..................................805 482-1070
Travis Mack, *President*
Jim Brenner, *COO*
Stephen E Andersen, *Exec VP*
Dennis Meehan, *Program Mgr*
Daniel Olson, *Administration*
EMP: 106
SQ FT: 7,000
SALES: 36.5MM **Privately Held**
SIC: 8711 7379 Consulting engineer; computer related consulting services

(P-25900)
SAIFUL/BOUQUET CON STRU ENG (PA)
155 N Lake Ave Fl 6, Pasadena (91101-1849)
PHONE..................................626 304-2616
Saiful Islam, *CEO*
Tom Bouquet, *CFO*
Y K Low, *Admin Sec*
Timothy Townsend, *Info Tech Dir*
Carlos Buenrostro, *Project Engr*
EMP: 53 EST: 1997
SQ FT: 25,000
SALES (est): 10.5MM **Privately Held**
WEB: www.sbise.com
SIC: 8711 Structural engineering

(P-25901)
SALAS OBRIEN ENGINEERS INC (PA)
305 S 11th St, San Jose (95112-2218)
PHONE..................................408 282-1500
Paul Silva, *CEO*
Scott Coward, *President*
Carl Salas, *Principal*
John Salas, *Principal*
John Palermo, *Electrical Engi*
EMP: 50
SQ FT: 10,000
SALES (est): 21MM **Privately Held**
WEB: www.salasobrien.com
SIC: 8711 Consulting engineer

(P-25902)
SAN DIEGO COMPOSITES INC
9220 Activity Rd Ste 100, San Diego (92126-4420)
PHONE..................................858 751-0450
Rob Kolozs, *President*
Christine Benzie, *Vice Pres*
Carl Sloan, *Vice Pres*
Josh M Moore, *Managing Dir*
Robert Kolozs, *General Mgr*
EMP: 70
SQ FT: 70,000
SALES: 19MM
SALES (corp-wide): 30.3MM **Privately Held**
WEB: www.sdcomposites.com
SIC: 8711 8734 3761 3764 Consulting engineer; testing laboratories; guided missiles & space vehicles; guided missile & space vehicle propulsion unit parts
PA: Ac&A Enterprises Holdings, Llc
25692 Atlantic Ocean Dr
Lake Forest CA 92630
949 716-3511

(P-25903)
SAN DIEGO TESTING ENGINEERS
Also Called: Testing Engineers San Diego
7895 Convoy Ct Ste 18, San Diego (92111-1215)
PHONE..................................858 715-5800
Mark Baron, *President*
Dickerson Wright, *CEO*
EMP: 94
SQ FT: 13,000
SALES (est): 5.5MM **Privately Held**
WEB: www.uslaboratories.com
SIC: 8711 8734 8742 Engineering services; testing laboratories; construction project management consultant

(P-25904)
SC WRIGHT CONSTRUCTION INC
3838 Camino Del Rio Nth S, San Diego (92108)
P.O. Box 3250, La Mesa (91944-3250)
PHONE..................................619 698-6909
Steven C Wright, *President*
Laurie Beckham, *Admin Asst*
Jim Barker, *Human Res Mgr*
Tracie Maxwell, *Opers Staff*
Lane Bustos, *Consultant*
EMP: 400
SALES (est): 28.6MM **Privately Held**
WEB: www.scwright.com
SIC: 8711 Building construction consultant

(P-25905)
SCHILLING ROBOTICS LLC
Also Called: Manufacturing Facility
201 Cousteau Pl, Davis (95618-5412)
PHONE..................................530 753-6718
Tyler Schilling, *Manager*
Sally Larocca, *Vice Pres*
Scott Callori, *Admin Asst*
Christine Smith, *HR Admin*
Steve Cohan, *Director*
EMP: 100
SALES (corp-wide): 15B **Privately Held**
SIC: 8711 3593 Engineering services; fluid power cylinders & actuators
HQ: Schilling Robotics, Llc
260 Cousteau Pl Ste 200
Davis CA 95618
530 753-6718

(P-25906)
SCICON TECHNOLOGIES CORP (PA)
27525 Newhall Ranch Rd # 2, Valencia (91355-4003)
PHONE..................................661 295-8630
Thomas J Bulger, *President*
Marie Bulger, *Admin Sec*
Randy Doyle, *Info Tech Mgr*
Mitch Greenwood, *Info Tech Mgr*
Omar Pacheco, *Info Tech Mgr*
EMP: 65
SQ FT: 25,000
SALES (est): 10.5MM **Privately Held**
WEB: www.scicontech.com
SIC: 8711 3999 Mechanical engineering; models, except toy

(P-25907)
SCICON TECHNOLOGIES CORP
1300 Quail St Ste 208, Newport Beach (92660-2710)
PHONE..................................949 252-1341
Tom Bulger, *Manager*
Matthew Titner, *Manager*
EMP: 60
SALES (corp-wide): 10.5MM **Privately Held**
WEB: www.scicontech.com
SIC: 8711 Engineering services
PA: Scicon Technologies Corp
27525 Newhall Ranch Rd # 2
Valencia CA 91355
661 295-8630

(P-25908)
SERCO INC
9350 Waxie Way Ste 400, San Diego (92123-1056)
PHONE..................................858 569-8979
Kent Brown, *Branch Mgr*
Tom Tibbitts, *Project Dir*
Olen Hanf, *Purchasing*
EMP: 132
SALES (corp-wide): 3.9B **Privately Held**
WEB: www.serco.com
SIC: 8711 Engineering services
HQ: Serco Inc.
12930 Worldgate Dr # 600
Herndon VA 20170

(P-25909)
SHLEMMER+ALGAZE+ASSOCI (PA)
Also Called: Shlemmer and Algaze Associates
18201 Von Karman Ave # 120, Irvine (92612-1174)
PHONE..................................949 724-8958
Richard Shlemmer, *Principal*
Nelson Algaze, *CEO*
EMP: 92 EST: 1967
SQ FT: 5,000
SALES (est): 8.9MM **Privately Held**
WEB: www.skaia.com
SIC: 8711 Engineering services

(P-25910)
SHN CONSULTING ENGIN (PA)
Also Called: Shn Cnslting Engnrs-Geologists
812 W Wabash Ave, Eureka (95501-2138)
PHONE..................................707 441-8855
Kenneth Jeffrey Nelson, *President*
Tom Herman, *Regional Mgr*
Tony Williams, *IT/INT Sup*
Erik Nielsen, *Project Mgr*
Daniel Graber, *Research*
EMP: 60
SQ FT: 14,000
SALES (est): 14.9MM **Privately Held**
WEB: www.shn-engr.com
SIC: 8711 8999 Consulting engineer; geological consultant

(P-25911)
SIA ENGINEERING (USA) INC
7001 W Imperial Hwy, Los Angeles (90045-6313)
PHONE..................................310 693-7108
Cheng Hian Tan, *CEO*
Chiuyen Tseng, *CFO*
EMP: 51
SALES (est): 8.6MM **Privately Held**
SIC: 8711 Engineering services

(P-25912)
SIEMENS AG
685 E Middlefield Rd, Mountain View (94043-4045)
PHONE..................................650 969-9112
Faid Bolorforfh, *CEO*
Marty Munoz, *Telecomm Dir*
Justin Harvey, *Admin Sec*
Richard Nandkeshwar, *Info Tech Mgr*
Sandhya Patel, *Software Engr*
EMP: 250
SALES (est): 3MM **Privately Held**
SIC: 8711 8721 8742 Engineering services; accounting, auditing & bookkeeping; marketing consulting services

(P-25913)
SIERRA LOBO INC
465 N Halstead St Ste 130, Pasadena (91107-3144)
PHONE..................................626 510-6340
EMP: 126 **Privately Held**
SIC: 8711 Engineering services
PA: Sierra Lobo, Inc.
102 Pinnacle Dr
Fremont OH 43420

(P-25914)
SIERRA NEVADA CORPORATION
985 University Ave Ste 4, Los Gatos (95032-7639)
PHONE..................................408 395-2004
Michael Weiland, *Branch Mgr*
Eren Ozmen, *President*
Fatih Ozmen, *CEO*
Deborah Sipos, *Technology*
EMP: 123
SALES (corp-wide): 1.5B **Privately Held**
SIC: 8711 Engineering services
PA: Sierra Nevada Corporation
444 Salomon Cir
Sparks NV 89434
775 331-0222

(P-25915)
SIMPSON GUMPERTZ & HEGER INC
100 Pine St Ste 1600, San Francisco (94111-5202)
PHONE..................................415 495-3700

John Sumnchit, *Systems Mgr*
Dr Rene W Luff, *Principal*
Mike Tang, *Info Tech Mgr*
Xiu LI, *Engineer*
EMP: 90
SALES (corp-wide): 96.6MM **Privately Held**
WEB: www.sgh.com
SIC: 8711 8741 Consulting engineer; construction management
PA: Simpson Gumpertz & Heger Inc.
41 Seyon St Ste 500
Waltham MA 02453
781 907-9000

(P-25916)
SIMPSON GUMPERTZ & HEGER INC
500 12th St, Oakland (94607-4076)
PHONE....................510 835-0705
EMP: 114
SALES (corp-wide): 96.6MM **Privately Held**
SIC: 8711 Consulting engineer
PA: Simpson Gumpertz & Heger Inc.
41 Seyon St Ste 500
Waltham MA 02453
781 907-9000

(P-25917)
SOLOPOINT SOLUTIONS INC
150 Paularino Ave Ste 282, Costa Mesa (92626-3302)
PHONE....................714 708-3639
Dinh Le, *Branch Mgr*
EMP: 53
SALES (corp-wide): 8.8MM **Privately Held**
SIC: 8711 Consulting engineer
PA: Solopoint Solutions, Inc.
3350 Scott Blvd Bldg 2
Santa Clara CA 95054
408 246-5945

(P-25918)
SOLUTE (PA)
Also Called: Solute Consulting
1660 Hotel Cir N Ste 600, San Diego (92108-2806)
PHONE....................619 224-2810
John Lyons, *CEO*
EMP: 80
SQ FT: 7,000
SALES (est): 15.5MM **Privately Held**
WEB: www.solute.us
SIC: 8711 Civil engineering

(P-25919)
SONIC INDUSTRIES INC
Also Called: Airframer R
20030 Normandie Ave, Torrance (90502-1210)
PHONE....................310 532-8382
Steven Scott Stil, *CEO*
▲ **EMP:** 150
SQ FT: 65,000
SALES (est): 28.7MM
SALES (corp-wide): 674.9MM **Publicly Held**
SIC: 8711 7699 Machine tool design; aviation propeller & blade repair
HQ: Roller Bearing Company Of America, Inc.
102 Willenbrock Rd
Oxford CT 06478
203 267-7001

(P-25920)
SPEC SERVICES INC
10540 Talbert Ave 100e, Fountain Valley (92708-6051)
PHONE....................714 963-8077
Chris Smart, *Manager*
EMP: 100
SALES (corp-wide): 61.3MM **Privately Held**
SIC: 8711 Consulting engineer
PA: Spec Services, Inc.
10540 Talbert Ave 100e
Fountain Valley CA 92708
714 963-8077

(P-25921)
SPEC SERVICES INC (PA)
10540 Talbert Ave 100e, Fountain Valley (92708-6051)
PHONE....................714 963-8077
Kim R Henry, *President*
Dan Letcher, *CFO*
Charles Lake, *Vice Pres*
Chuck Lake, *Vice Pres*
Jazmin Gonzalez, *Admin Asst*
EMP: 190
SQ FT: 16,000
SALES (est): 61.3MM **Privately Held**
WEB: www.specservices.com
SIC: 8711 Consulting engineer

(P-25922)
SPIRAL TECHNOLOGY INC
229 E Avenue K8 Ste 105, Lancaster (93535-4517)
PHONE....................661 723-3148
Archie L Moore, *President*
Steve McCarter, *Ch of Bd*
Daniel Hare, *COO*
Barbara Moore, *Officer*
Robyn Barton, *General Mgr*
EMP: 56
SQ FT: 4,984
SALES (est): 8.9MM **Privately Held**
WEB: www.spiraltechinc.com
SIC: 8711 Industrial engineers

(P-25923)
SSC CONSTRUCTION INC
4195 Chino Hills Pkwy, Chino Hills (91709-2618)
PHONE....................951 278-1177
Gregory E Larkin, *CEO*
Neil Nehmens, *Senior VP*
EMP: 200
SALES (est): 33.4MM **Privately Held**
WEB: www.sscconstruction.com
SIC: 8711 Engineering services

(P-25924)
SSL ROBOTICS LLC (DH)
Also Called: Mda US Systems LLC
1250 Lincoln Ave Ste 100, Pasadena (91103-2466)
PHONE....................626 296-1373
Daniel Friedmann,
Mohammad Manki, *Principal*
Michael Johnson, *Chief Engr*
Mike Adams, *Manager*
EMP: 54
SALES (est): 43.7MM
SALES (corp-wide): 581.1MM **Publicly Held**
SIC: 8711 8731 Aviation &/or aeronautical engineering; commercial physical research
HQ: Maxar Technologies Ltd
200 Burrard St Suite 1570
Vancouver BC V6C 3
604 974-5275

(P-25925)
SSL ROBOTICS LLC
1250 Lincoln Ave Ste 100, Pasadena (91103-2466)
PHONE....................626 296-1373
Mohammad Manki, *Branch Mgr*
Jill Staats, *HR Admin*
Keith Vanbuskirk, *Deputy Dir*
EMP: 65
SALES (corp-wide): 581.1MM **Publicly Held**
SIC: 8711 8731 Aviation &/or aeronautical engineering; commercial physical research
HQ: Ssl Robotics Llc
1250 Lincoln Ave Ste 100
Pasadena CA 91103
626 296-1373

(P-25926)
SSL ROBOTICS LLC
4398 Corporate Center Dr, Los Alamitos (90720-2537)
PHONE....................626 296-1373
Ted Cheng, *General Mgr*
EMP: 150
SALES (corp-wide): 581.1MM **Publicly Held**
SIC: 8711 Aviation &/or aeronautical engineering

HQ: Ssl Robotics Llc
1250 Lincoln Ave Ste 100
Pasadena CA 91103
626 296-1373

(P-25927)
STANTEC ARCH & ENGRG PC
38 Technology Dr Ste 100, Irvine (92618-5312)
PHONE....................949 923-6000
Lori Van Dermark, *Marketing Staff*
EMP: 117
SALES (corp-wide): 4B **Privately Held**
SIC: 8711 8712 Engineering services; architectural services
HQ: Stantec Architecture And Engineering P.C.
311 Summer St
Boston MA 02210

(P-25928)
STANTEC ARCH & ENGRG PC
100 California St # 1000, San Francisco (94111-4505)
PHONE....................415 882-9500
Lori Van Dermark, *Marketing Staff*
EMP: 100
SALES (corp-wide): 4B **Privately Held**
SIC: 8711 8712 Engineering services; architectural services
HQ: Stantec Architecture And Engineering P.C.
311 Summer St
Boston MA 02210

(P-25929)
STANTEC ARCHITECTURE INC
100 California St # 1000, San Francisco (94111-4505)
PHONE....................415 882-9500
Michael Gambucci, *CEO*
Annie Coull, *Vice Pres*
Lori Van Dermark, *Marketing Staff*
Rachel Ginsberg, *Librarian*
Robert Shurell, *Manager*
EMP: 96
SALES (corp-wide): 4B **Privately Held**
SIC: 8711 8712 Engineering services; architectural services
HQ: Stantec Architecture Inc.
224 S Michigan Ave # 1400
Chicago IL 60604
336 714-7413

(P-25930)
STANTEC CONSULTING SVCS INC
1340 Treat Blvd Ste 525, Walnut Creek (94597-7984)
PHONE....................925 627-4500
Stacey Robinson, *Office Mgr*
William Caplin, *Vice Pres*
Janet Sheldon, *Vice Pres*
EMP: 170
SALES (corp-wide): 4B **Privately Held**
WEB: www.mw.com
SIC: 8711 Engineering services
HQ: Stantec Consulting Services Inc.
475 5th Ave Fl 12
New York NY 10017
212 352-5160

(P-25931)
STANTEC CONSULTING SVCS INC
300 N Lake Ave Ste 400, Pasadena (91101-4169)
PHONE....................626 796-9141
Paul Boulos, *Branch Mgr*
Lori Van Dermark, *Agent*
EMP: 79
SALES (corp-wide): 4B **Privately Held**
WEB: www.mw.com
SIC: 8711 Engineering services
HQ: Stantec Consulting Services Inc.
475 5th Ave Fl 12
New York NY 10017
212 352-5160

(P-25932)
STANTEC CONSULTING SVCS INC
3301 C St Ste 1900, Sacramento (95816-3394)
PHONE....................916 924-8844
Mike Watson, *Manager*
Marilyn Summers, *Executive*
Joe Niland, *Principal*
EMP: 50
SALES (corp-wide): 4B **Privately Held**
WEB: www.mw.com
SIC: 8711 Consulting engineer
HQ: Stantec Consulting Services Inc.
475 5th Ave Fl 12
New York NY 10017
212 352-5160

(P-25933)
STANTEC CONSULTING SVCS INC
100 California St # 1000, San Francisco (94111-4505)
PHONE....................415 882-9500
Nicole Collins, *Manager*
David Tagaloa, *Vice Pres*
Todd Tierney, *Vice Pres*
Jason Flory, *Technology*
Lori Van Dermark, *Marketing Staff*
EMP: 96
SALES (corp-wide): 4B **Privately Held**
WEB: www.keithco.com
SIC: 8711 8712 Engineering services; architectural services
HQ: Stantec Consulting Services Inc.
475 5th Ave Fl 12
New York NY 10017
212 352-5160

(P-25934)
STRUCTURAL INTEGRITY ASSOC INC (PA)
5215 Hellyer Ave Ste 210, San Jose (95138-1079)
PHONE....................408 978-8200
David Stager, *CFO*
Laney H Bisbee, *CEO*
Celestine De Leon, *Accountant*
Eric Elder, *Advisor*
EMP: 65
SQ FT: 17,000
SALES: 72MM **Privately Held**
SIC: 8711 Consulting engineer

(P-25935)
STURGEON SON GRADING & PAV INC
Also Called: Sturgeon Services Intl
6516 Cat Canyon Rd, Santa Maria (93454-9605)
PHONE....................805 938-0618
Fax: 805 938-0894
EMP: 114
SALES (corp-wide): 56.7MM **Privately Held**
SIC: 8711 1794
PA: Sturgeon & Son Grading & Paving, Inc.
3511 Gilmore Ave
Bakersfield CA 93308
661 322-4408

(P-25936)
SYSKA & HENNESSY ENGINEERS INC
800 Crprate Pinte Ste 200, Culver City (90230)
PHONE....................310 312-0200
Gary A Brennen, *President*
Ann Banning-Wright, *Vice Pres*
Jennifer Crawford, *Principal*
EMP: 99
SALES (est): 9.3MM **Privately Held**
SIC: 8711 Engineering services

(P-25937)
SYSTEMS APPLICATION & TECH INC
Also Called: Sa-Tech
1000 Town Center Dr # 110, Oxnard (93036-1100)
P.O. Box 25, Port Hueneme (93044-0025)
PHONE....................805 487-7373
Geoff Dezavala, *Senior VP*
EMP: 80

SALES (corp-wide): 67.1MM **Privately Held**
WEB: www.sa-techinc.com
SIC: **8711** Consulting engineer
PA: Systems Application & Technologies, Inc.
1101 Merc Ln Ste 200
Largo MD 20774
301 322-8880

(P-25938)
SYZYGY TECHNOLOGIES INC
1272 Calpella Ct, Chula Vista
(91913-1426)
P.O. Box 1422, Solana Beach (92075-7422)
PHONE..............................619 297-0970
Santos Discar, *President*
EMP: 60
SALES: 2.3MM **Privately Held**
SIC: **8711** **7371** Engineering services; computer software development

(P-25939)
T Y LIN INTERNATIONAL (HQ)
345 California St Fl 23, San Francisco
(94104-2646)
PHONE..............................415 291-3700
Alvaro J Piedrahita, *President*
Robert A Peterson, *CFO*
Man Chung Tang, *Chairman*
Veronica Fennie, *Officer*
Michael Fitzpatrick, *Assoc VP*
EMP: 84
SQ FT: 18,000
SALES (est): 122MM
SALES (corp-wide): 155.9MM **Privately Held**
WEB: www.tyli.com
SIC: **8711** Consulting engineer
PA: T.Y. Lin International Group
345 California St Fl 23
San Francisco CA 94104
415 291-3700

(P-25940)
TALENTSCALE LLC
31805 Temecula Pkwy 204, Temecula
(92592-8203)
PHONE..............................951 744-0053
Douglas Poldrugo, *President*
Steve Santich, *President*
Richard Nester, *Vice Pres*
Kristin Wolfram, *Administration*
Nathan Ogden, *Accounts Mgr*
EMP: 83
SALES (est): 8.3MM
SALES (corp-wide): 12.2MM **Privately Held**
SIC: **8711** Engineering services
PA: Scst, Inc.
6280 Riverdale St
San Diego CA 92120
619 280-4321

(P-25941)
TED JACOB ENGRG GROUP INC (PA)
1763 Broadway, Oakland (94612-2105)
PHONE..............................510 763-4880
Ted Jacob, *President*
Shad Shabbas, *CFO*
EMP: 100
SQ FT: 12,000
SALES: 15MM **Privately Held**
WEB: www.tjeg.com
SIC: **8711** Mechanical engineering; electrical or electronic engineering

(P-25942)
TEECOM
1333 Broadway Ste 601, Oakland
(94612-1906)
PHONE..............................510 337-2800
David Marks, *CEO*
Jerry Dreiling, *CFO*
Samuel Fajner, *Vice Pres*
Christina De La Cruz, *Executive Asst*
Andrew Gonzales, *Design Engr*
EMP: 87
SQ FT: 12,600
SALES (est): 3.1MM **Privately Held**
WEB: www.teecom.com
SIC: **8711** Consulting engineer

(P-25943)
TEPA EC LLC (PA)
1022 South St, Orland (95963-1671)
PHONE..............................719 596-8114
Ken Harris,
EMP: 60
SALES (est): 5.7MM **Privately Held**
WEB: www.tepainc.com
SIC: **8711** Consulting engineer

(P-25944)
TERO TEK INTERNATIONAL INC (PA)
1408 S Lexington St, Delano (93215-9783)
P.O. Box 310 (93216-0310)
PHONE..............................661 725-1135
William R Aldrich, *President*
Jerry Doss, *Vice Pres*
Lee E Brown, *Director*
Lee Brown, *Director*
James C Josephson, *Director*
EMP: 51
SQ FT: 120
SALES: 365.8K **Privately Held**
SIC: **8711** Engineering services

(P-25945)
TETER LLP (PA)
7535 N Palm Ave Ste 201, Fresno
(93711-5504)
PHONE..............................559 437-0887
Glen Teter, *Partner*
Clay Davis, *Partner*
Byron Dietrich, *Partner*
Paul Halajian, *Partner*
Jamie Hickman, *Partner*
EMP: 50
SALES (est): 9.7MM **Privately Held**
WEB: www.tetercon.com
SIC: **8711** **8712** Structural engineering; architectural services

(P-25946)
TETRA TECH INC
17885 Von Karman Ave # 500, Irvine
(92614-5227)
PHONE..............................949 263-0846
Jack Chicca, *Branch Mgr*
EMP: 85
SALES (corp-wide): 2.7B **Publicly Held**
SIC: **8711** Consulting engineer
PA: Tetra Tech, Inc.
3475 E Foothill Blvd
Pasadena CA 91107
626 351-4664

(P-25947)
TETRA TECH INC
Also Called: Tetra Tech Engrg & Arch Svcs
17885 Von Karman Ave # 500, Irvine
(92614-5227)
PHONE..............................949 809-5000
Steve Tedesco, *Branch Mgr*
EMP: 91
SALES (corp-wide): 2.7B **Publicly Held**
SIC: **8711** Civil engineering
PA: Tetra Tech, Inc.
3475 E Foothill Blvd
Pasadena CA 91107
626 351-4664

(P-25948)
TETRA TECH BAS INC (HQ)
Also Called: B A S
1360 Valley Vista Dr, Diamond Bar
(91765-3910)
PHONE..............................909 860-7777
Bryan A Stirrat, *President*
Ira Snyder, *CFO*
Jeanne Stirrat, *Admin Sec*
EMP: 65
SQ FT: 20,000
SALES (est): 11.2MM
SALES (corp-wide): 2.7B **Publicly Held**
WEB: www.bas.com
SIC: **8711** Civil engineering; pollution control engineering
PA: Tetra Tech, Inc.
3475 E Foothill Blvd
Pasadena CA 91107
626 351-4664

(P-25949)
TETRA TECH TECHNICAL SERVICES
3475 E Foothill Blvd Fl 3, Pasadena
(91107-6024)
PHONE..............................626 351-4664
Dan Batrack, *CEO*
EMP: 244
SALES (est): 14.8MM
SALES (corp-wide): 2.7B **Publicly Held**
WEB: www.tetratech.com
SIC: **8711** Consulting engineer
PA: Tetra Tech, Inc.
3475 E Foothill Blvd
Pasadena CA 91107
626 351-4664

(P-25950)
TGCON INC (HQ)
50 Contractors St, Livermore (94551-4863)
PHONE..............................925 449-5764
William L Gates, *President*
John Copriviza, *President*
Brian L Gates, *COO*
Scott Blaine, *CFO*
Brian Gates, *Exec VP*
EMP: 71
SQ FT: 25,000
SALES (est): 55.2MM
SALES (corp-wide): 203MM **Privately Held**
WEB: www.topgradeconstruction.com
SIC: **8711** Construction & civil engineering
PA: Goodfellow Bros. Llc
135 N Wenatchee Ave
Wenatchee WA 98801
509 667-9095

(P-25951)
THERMASOURCE LLC (PA)
150 Post St Ste 400, San Francisco
(94108-4716)
PHONE..............................707 523-2960
Richard Chow, *CEO*
Louis Capuano Jr, *President*
Gerald Hamblin, *COO*
Christopher T Schofield, *CFO*
Linda Capuano, *Treasurer*
EMP: 59
SALES (est): 33.1MM **Privately Held**
WEB: www.thermasource.com
SIC: **8711** Consulting engineer

(P-25952)
THOMAS MARK & COMPANY INC (PA)
2290 N 1st St Ste 304, San Jose
(95131-2017)
PHONE..............................408 453-5373
Mike Lohman, *President*
Robert A Himes, *President*
Richard K Tanaka, *Chairman*
Sasha D Dansky, *Principal*
David E Ross, *Principal*
EMP: 50
SQ FT: 10,600
SALES (est): 30.3MM **Privately Held**
WEB: www.markthomas.com
SIC: **8711** **8713** Consulting engineer; surveying services

(P-25953)
THORNTON TOMASETTI INC
650 California St Fl 14, San Francisco
(94108-2792)
PHONE..............................415 365-6900
Joseph R Sutton, *Office Mgr*
Cristina Medina, *Office Mgr*
EMP: 60
SALES (corp-wide): 239.5MM **Privately Held**
SIC: **8711** Structural engineering
PA: Thornton Tomasetti, Inc.
51 Madison Ave Fl 19
New York NY 10010
917 661-7800

(P-25954)
TJ CROSS ENGINEERS INC
200 New Stine Rd Ste 270, Bakersfield
(93309-2658)
PHONE..............................661 831-8782
Timothy Couch, *Principal*
Kent Halley, *Principal*
Stuart Heisler, *Principal*

Chuck Soderstrom, *Principal*
Lisa Wong, *Principal*
EMP: 130
SQ FT: 22,000
SALES (est): 15MM
SALES (corp-wide): 3.1B **Privately Held**
WEB: www.tjcross.com
SIC: **8711** Consulting engineer
PA: The Parsons Corporation
100 W Walnut St
Pasadena CA 91124
626 440-2000

(P-25955)
TMX ENGINEERING LLC
2141 S Standard Ave, Santa Ana
(92707-3034)
PHONE..............................714 641-5884
Eric Clack, *Principal*
EMP: 70
SALES (est): 2.2MM **Privately Held**
SIC: **8711** Engineering services

(P-25956)
TOYON RESEARCH CORPORATION (PA)
6800 Cortona Dr, Goleta (93117-3139)
PHONE..............................805 968-6787
Joel R Garbarino, *Ch of Bd*
Tom Geyer, *Vice Pres*
Michael Grace, *Vice Pres*
Ryan Strader, *Vice Pres*
Joy Romero, *Executive Asst*
EMP: 84 EST: 1980
SQ FT: 16,000
SALES: 32.7MM **Privately Held**
WEB: www.toyon.com
SIC: **8711** **7371** Electrical or electronic engineering; custom computer programming services

(P-25957)
TRANDES CORP
4250 Pacific Hwy Ste 209, San Diego
(92110-3222)
PHONE..............................619 398-0464
Rollin Cross, *Program Mgr*
Paul Anderson, *Engineer*
EMP: 121
SALES (corp-wide): 13.7MM **Privately Held**
WEB: www.trandes.com
SIC: **8711** **7378** **7371** Consulting engineer; computer maintenance & repair; custom computer programming services
PA: Trandes Corp.
4601 Presidents Dr # 360
Lanham MD 20706
301 459-0200

(P-25958)
TREADWELL & ROLLO INC (DH)
555 Montgomery St # 1300, San Francisco
(94111-2561)
PHONE..............................415 955-9040
Philip Ttringale, *Director*
Philip G Smith, *Exec VP*
Maria G Flessas, *Vice Pres*
Patrick B Hubbard, *Vice Pres*
Richard D Rodgers, *Vice Pres*
EMP: 50
SQ FT: 12,500
SALES (est): 10.9MM
SALES (corp-wide): 177.9MM **Privately Held**
WEB: www.treadwellrollo.com
SIC: **8711** Consulting engineer
HQ: Langan Engineering And Environmental Services, Inc.
300 Kimball Dr
Parsippany NJ 07054
973 560-4900

(P-25959)
TRIAD HOMES ASSOC
Also Called: Triad-Holmes Associates
873 N Main St Ste 150, Bishop
(93514-2479)
PHONE..............................760 873-4273
Thomas Platz, *President*
EMP: 60
SQ FT: 800

PRODUCTS & SVCS

SALES (est): 5MM
SALES (corp-wide): 5.1MM **Privately Held**
SIC: **8711** 8713 6552 Civil engineering; surveying services; subdividers & developers
PA: Holmes Triad Associates
549 Old Mmmoth Rd Ste 202
Mammoth Lakes CA
760 934-7588

(P-25960)
TRUST AUTOMATION INC
143 Suburban Rd Ste 100, San Luis Obispo (93401-1102)
PHONE...................805 544-0761
Ty Safreno, *CEO*
Brett Keegan, *COO*
Trudie Safreno, *CFO*
Chuck Kass, *Exec VP*
Dave Rennie, *Vice Pres*
EMP: 65
SQ FT: 50,000
SALES (est): 16.2MM **Privately Held**
WEB: www.trustautomation.com
SIC: **8711** 3812 3731 3621 Machine tool design; antennas, radar or communications; submersible marine robots, manned or unmanned; generators for gas-electric or oil-electric vehicles; automation & robotics consultant

(P-25961)
TTG ENGINEERS
222 S Harbor Blvd Ste 800, Anaheim (92805-3715)
PHONE...................714 490-5555
Albert Chiu, *Branch Mgr*
EMP: 55
SALES (corp-wide): 54.8MM **Privately Held**
WEB: www.tmadengineers.com
SIC: **8711** Consulting engineer
PA: Ttg Engineers
300 N Lake Ave Fl 14
Pasadena CA 91101
626 463-2800

(P-25962)
TTG ENGINEERS (PA)
Also Called: Mbe
300 N Lake Ave Fl 14, Pasadena (91101-4164)
PHONE...................626 463-2800
Zareh Astourian, *President*
Stephen Boase, *CFO*
Ed Gharabans, *Vice Pres*
Sunil Patel, *Vice Pres*
Ron Sheldon, *Vice Pres*
EMP: 160
SQ FT: 16,000
SALES (est): 54.8MM **Privately Held**
WEB: www.tmadengineers.com
SIC: **8711** Consulting engineer

(P-25963)
TY LIN INTERNATIONAL GROUP (PA)
345 California St Fl 23, San Francisco (94104-2646)
PHONE...................415 291-3700
Robert A Peterson, *President*
EMP: 109 EST: 1961
SQ FT: 34,000
SALES (est): 155.9MM **Privately Held**
SIC: **8711** Consulting engineer

(P-25964)
U S ARMY CORPS OF ENGINEERS
1645 Riverbank Rd, West Sacramento (95605-1743)
PHONE...................916 557-7491
EMP: 66 **Publicly Held**
SIC: **8711** 9199 Engineering services; general government administration
HQ: U S Army Corps Of Engineers
441 G St Nw
Washington DC 20314
202 761-0001

(P-25965)
U S ARMY CORPS OF ENGINEERS
2194 Ascot Ave, Rio Linda (95673-5337)
PHONE...................916 649-0133
EMP: 65 **Publicly Held**
SIC: **8711** 9711 Engineering services; Army;
HQ: U S Army Corps Of Engineers
441 G St Nw
Washington DC 20314
202 761-0001

(P-25966)
U S ARMY CORPS OF ENGINEERS
3900 Roseville Rd, North Highlands (95660-5707)
PHONE...................916 925-7001
Ed Fager, *Branch Mgr*
EMP: 66 **Publicly Held**
SIC: **8711** Engineering services
HQ: U S Army Corps Of Engineers
441 G St Nw
Washington DC 20314
202 761-0001

(P-25967)
U S ARMY CORPS OF ENGINEERS
2100 Bridgeway, Sausalito (94965-1753)
PHONE...................415 289-3067
Linda Holm, *Manager*
EMP: 65 **Publicly Held**
SIC: **8711** Engineering services
HQ: U S Army Corps Of Engineers
441 G St Nw
Washington DC 20314
202 761-0001

(P-25968)
UCI CONSTRUCTION INC
3900 Fruitvale Ave, Bakersfield (93308-5114)
PHONE...................661 587-0192
David Krugh, *Manager*
EMP: 98
SALES (est): 17.7MM **Privately Held**
SIC: **8711** 1521 Professional engineer; new construction, single-family houses

(P-25969)
UNITED INFRSTRCTURE PRJCTS INC
Also Called: Uiprojects
1041 W 18th St Ste B104, Costa Mesa (92627-4583)
PHONE...................949 310-0092
Wail Sadiq, *General Mgr*
Brian Poyant, *Vice Pres*
Zulfa Sadiq, *Director*
EMP: 99
SALES: 950K **Privately Held**
WEB: www.uiprojects.net
SIC: **8711** 1542 Engineering services; custom builders, non-residential

(P-25970)
UNIVERSAL GENERAL BUILDERS
871 Industrial Rd Ste A, San Carlos (94070-3389)
PHONE...................650 591-3104
EMP: 99
SALES (est): 2.6MM **Privately Held**
SIC: **8711** Building construction consultant

(P-25971)
UNIVERSAL SPACE LINES INC
Also Called: Usl
1501 Quail St Ste 102, Newport Beach (92660-2739)
PHONE...................215 328-9130
David Wopschall, *CFO*
EMP: 60
SALES (est): 5.5MM **Privately Held**
SIC: **8711** 8731 Aviation &/or aeronautical engineering; industrial laboratory, except testing

(P-25972)
URS GROUP INC
300 Lakeside Dr Ste 400, Oakland (94612-3534)
PHONE...................510 893-3600
Louise Armstrong, *Manager*
Adam Krpan, *Info Tech Mgr*
Robert Michna, *Project Mgr*
Ivan Wong, *Project Engr*
Robert K Green, *Engineer*
EMP: 200
SALES (corp-wide): 20.1B **Publicly Held**
SIC: **8711** 4953 Engineering services; refuse systems
HQ: Urs Group, Inc.
300 S Grand Ave Ste 1100
Los Angeles CA 90071
213 593-8000

(P-25973)
URS GROUP INC
300 Lakeside Dr Ste 400, Oakland (94612-3534)
PHONE...................415 896-5858
Simon Kim, *Branch Mgr*
Debra Sanders, *Vice Pres*
Margaret Fitzpatrick, *Administration*
Tonya Pullins, *Sr Project Mgr*
Shrujal Amin, *Manager*
EMP: 100
SALES (corp-wide): 20.1B **Publicly Held**
SIC: **8711** 8712 8741 Consulting engineer; architectural engineering; construction management
HQ: Urs Group, Inc.
300 S Grand Ave Ste 1100
Los Angeles CA 90071
213 593-8000

(P-25974)
URS GROUP INC
915 Wilshire Blvd Ste 700, Los Angeles (90017-3436)
P.O. Box 116183, Atlanta GA (30368-6183)
PHONE...................213 996-2200
Paul Ryan, *Manager*
Peapully Krishna, *Vice Pres*
Matthew Lankenau, *Vice Pres*
Carla Willis, *Project Dir*
Kenon Donaville, *HR Admin*
EMP: 99
SALES (corp-wide): 20.1B **Publicly Held**
SIC: **8711** 8712 8741 Consulting engineer; architectural engineering; construction management
HQ: Urs Group, Inc.
300 S Grand Ave Ste 1100
Los Angeles CA 90071
213 593-8000

(P-25975)
URS GROUP INC
901 Via Piemonte Ste 500, Ontario (91764-8502)
PHONE...................909 980-4000
Brian Winne, *Branch Mgr*
Brian Wynne, *Vice Pres*
Bill Obraitis, *Project Mgr*
EMP: 69
SALES (corp-wide): 20.1B **Publicly Held**
SIC: **8711** 8712 8741 Consulting engineer; architectural engineering; construction management
HQ: Urs Group, Inc.
300 S Grand Ave Ste 1100
Los Angeles CA 90071
213 593-8000

(P-25976)
URS GROUP INC
915 Wilshire Blvd Ste 700, Los Angeles (90017-3436)
P.O. Box 116183, Atlanta GA (30368-6183)
PHONE...................213 996-2200
Shahram Bahbagu, *Branch Mgr*
EMP: 100
SALES (corp-wide): 20.1B **Publicly Held**
SIC: **8711** Engineering services
HQ: Urs Group, Inc.
300 S Grand Ave Ste 1100
Los Angeles CA 90071
213 593-8000

(P-25977)
URS GROUP INC
2300 Clayton Rd Ste 1400, Concord (94520-2173)
PHONE...................925 446-3800
Sam Capps, *Branch Mgr*
EMP: 69
SALES (corp-wide): 20.1B **Publicly Held**
SIC: **8711** 8712 8741 Consulting engineer; architectural engineering; construction management
HQ: Urs Group, Inc.
300 S Grand Ave Ste 1100
Los Angeles CA 90071
213 593-8000

(P-25978)
URS GROUP INC
130 Robin Hill Rd Ste 100, Santa Barbara (93117-3153)
PHONE...................805 964-6010
Timothy Cohen, *Manager*
Matt O'Brien, *President*
EMP: 80
SQ FT: 29,621
SALES (corp-wide): 20.1B **Publicly Held**
SIC: **8711** Engineering services
HQ: Urs Group, Inc.
300 S Grand Ave Ste 1100
Los Angeles CA 90071
213 593-8000

(P-25979)
URS GROUP INC
2020 L St Ste 400, Sacramento (95811-4267)
PHONE...................916 679-2000
Gary Horton, *Manager*
Stuart Freeman, *Manager*
EMP: 64
SALES (corp-wide): 20.1B **Publicly Held**
SIC: **8711** 8712 8741 Architectural engineering; construction management; consulting engineer
HQ: Urs Group, Inc.
300 S Grand Ave Ste 1100
Los Angeles CA 90071
213 593-8000

(P-25980)
URS GROUP INC
100 W San Fernando St # 200, San Jose (95113-2219)
PHONE...................408 297-9585
William Hadaya, *Branch Mgr*
Rick Moreland, *Project Mgr*
Ramsey Hissen, *Sr Project Mgr*
Millette Litzinger, *Sr Project Mgr*
EMP: 55
SALES (corp-wide): 20.1B **Publicly Held**
SIC: **8711** Engineering services
HQ: Urs Group, Inc.
300 S Grand Ave Ste 1100
Los Angeles CA 90071
213 593-8000

(P-25981)
URS GROUP INC
300 Lakeside Dr Ste 400, Oakland (94612-3596)
PHONE...................415 896-5858
Rob Robinson, *Branch Mgr*
EMP: 69
SALES (corp-wide): 20.1B **Publicly Held**
SIC: **8711** Engineering services
HQ: Urs Group, Inc.
300 S Grand Ave Ste 1100
Los Angeles CA 90071
213 593-8000

(P-25982)
URS HOLDINGS INC (DH)
600 Montgomery St Fl 25, San Francisco (94111-2724)
PHONE...................415 774-2700
Thomas W Bishop, *CEO*
Martin M Koffel, *Ch of Bd*
Karen Lamoreaux, *Administration*
Judith Nichols, *Contract Mgr*
Carol Frieda Brandenburg-Smith, *Asst Sec*
EMP: 470

SALES (est): 5B
SALES (corp-wide): 20.1B **Publicly Held**
SIC: 8711 7389 6531 8249 Consulting engineer; financial services; real estate agents & managers; aviation school; aircraft maintenance & repair services
HQ: Aecom Global Ii, Llc
1999 Avenue Of The Stars
Los Angeles CA 90067
213 593-8100

(P-25983)
URS-GEI JOINT VENTURE
1333 Broadway Ste 800, Oakland (94612-1924)
PHONE...................510 874-3051
Said Salah-Mars, *Principal*
EMP: 50
SALES (est): 2.1MM **Privately Held**
SIC: 8711 Engineering services

(P-25984)
US ARMY CORPS OF ENGINEERS
1325 J St Frnt, Sacramento (95814-2922)
PHONE...................916 557-7490
Thomas Chapman, *Director*
EMP: 800 **Publicly Held**
WEB: www.sac.usace.army.mil
SIC: 8711 9711 Engineering services; Army;
HQ: U S Army Corps Of Engineers
441 G St Nw
Washington DC 20314
202 761-0001

(P-25985)
US ARMY CORPS OF ENGINEERS
915 Wilshire Blvd Ste 930, Los Angeles (90017-3489)
PHONE...................213 452-3967
Col Richard Thompson, *Manager*
Col R Thompson, *Manager*
EMP: 650 **Publicly Held**
WEB: www.sac.usace.army.mil
SIC: 8711 9711 Engineering services; Army;
HQ: U S Army Corps Of Engineers
441 G St Nw
Washington DC 20314
202 761-0001

(P-25986)
US INTERACTIVE DELAWARE (PA)
1270 Oakmead Pkwy Ste 318, Sunnyvale (94085-4044)
PHONE...................408 863-7500
Sunil Mathur, *CEO*
Tom Morris, *President*
Rashmi Srivastava, *Treasurer*
Kekin Dand, *Administration*
EMP: 150
SALES (est): 7.4MM **Privately Held**
WEB: www.usinteractive.com
SIC: 8711 Consulting engineer

(P-25987)
VANDORPE CHOU ASSOCIATES INC
Also Called: VCA Engineering
1845 W Orangewood Ave # 210, Orange (92868-2096)
PHONE...................714 978-9780
Daniel T Van Dorpe, *President*
Neil Evans, *Shareholder*
David Byrnes, *CFO*
Margaret Van Dorpe, *Corp Secy*
Mark Van Gaale, *Vice Pres*
EMP: 50 EST: 1979
SQ FT: 3,000
SALES (est): 7.9MM **Privately Held**
WEB: www.vcaengineers.com
SIC: 8711 Civil engineering; structural engineering

(P-25988)
VECTOR RESOURCES INC
Also Called: Vector USA
9808 Waples St, San Diego (92121-2921)
PHONE...................858 546-1014
Debra Treece, *Branch Mgr*
EMP: 50

SALES (corp-wide): 76.4MM **Privately Held**
SIC: 8711 Consulting engineer
PA: Vector Resources, Inc.
3530 Voyager St
Torrance CA 90503
310 436-1000

(P-25989)
VELOCITEL RF INC
2415 Campus Dr Ste 200, Irvine (92612-8530)
PHONE...................949 809-4999
EMP: 200
SALES (est): 6.1MM
SALES (corp-wide): 648MM **Privately Held**
SIC: 8711
PA: Velocitel, Inc.
1033 Skokie Blvd Ste 320
Northbrook IL 27616
224 757-0001

(P-25990)
VERSA ENGINEERING & TECH INC (PA)
1320 Willow Pass Rd # 500, Concord (94520-5269)
PHONE...................925 405-4505
Fred Fong, *President*
Flavio Santini, *Chairman*
Tom Nollie, *Principal*
Chris Towles, *Project Engr*
Charles Waitman, *Sr Consultant*
EMP: 55
SALES (est): 13.1MM **Privately Held**
SIC: 8711 Consulting engineer

(P-25991)
VSA & ASSOCIATES INC (PA)
Also Called: Health Care Resource Group
6571 Altura Blvd Ste 100, Buena Park (90620-1020)
PHONE...................562 698-2468
Mahabir S Atwal, *President*
Vicky Sumnogum, *Vice Pres*
Kaunenaka Jain, *Manager*
EMP: 61
SQ FT: 12,000
SALES (est): 5.4MM **Privately Held**
WEB: www.vsaassociates.com
SIC: 8711 8742 Acoustical engineering; business planning & organizing services

(P-25992)
VT MILCOM INC
1660 Logan Ave Ste 2, San Diego (92113-1044)
PHONE...................619 424-9024
Brian Upthegrove, *Branch Mgr*
EMP: 100
SALES (corp-wide): 1.4B **Privately Held**
WEB: www.milcom-systems.com
SIC: 8711 Engineering services
HQ: Vt Milcom Inc.
448 Viking Dr Ste 350
Virginia Beach VA 23452
757 463-2800

(P-25993)
W M LYLES CO
2810 Unicorn Rd, Bakersfield (93308-6853)
PHONE...................661 387-1600
Mike Burson, *President*
EMP: 50
SALES (est): 3.9MM
SALES (corp-wide): 33.7MM **Privately Held**
WEB: www.wmlyles.com
SIC: 8711 1623 Engineering services; pipeline construction
HQ: W. M. Lyles Co.
1210 W Olive Ave
Fresno CA 93728
559 441-1900

(P-25994)
WALLACE-KUHL INVESTMENTS LLC (PA)
3050 Industrial Blvd, West Sacramento (95691-3470)
P.O. Box 1137 (95691-1137)
PHONE...................916 372-1434
Douglas J Kuhl,
Thomas S Wallace,

EMP: 100
SQ FT: 11,300
SALES (est): 9.6MM **Privately Held**
WEB: www.wallace-kuhl.com
SIC: 8711 8748 Civil engineering; business consulting

(P-25995)
WATLOW ELECTRIC MFG CO
6781 Via Del Oro, San Jose (95119-1360)
PHONE...................408 776-6646
EMP: 85
SALES (corp-wide): 586.7MM **Privately Held**
SIC: 8711 Engineering services
PA: Watlow Electric Manufacturing Company
12001 Lackland Rd
Saint Louis MO 63146
314 878-4600

(P-25996)
WEST YOST & ASSOCIATES INC (PA)
2020 Res Pk Dr Ste 100, Davis (95618)
PHONE...................530 756-5905
Charles Duncan, *President*
Bruce West, *President*
Steven R Dalrymple, *Corp Secy*
Kyle Rhorer, *Vice Pres*
Jim Yost, *Vice Pres*
EMP: 76
SQ FT: 25,000
SALES (est): 26.7MM **Privately Held**
WEB: www.westyost.com
SIC: 8711 Civil engineering

(P-25997)
WESTWIND ENGINEERING INC
553 N Pcfc Cst Hwy B179, Redondo Beach (90277)
PHONE...................310 831-3454
Mary Anne Graves, *CEO*
Carl Graves, *Founder*
EMP: 175 EST: 1992
SQ FT: 2,400
SALES: 13MM **Privately Held**
SIC: 8711 7363 Engineering services; temporary help service

(P-25998)
WESTWIND ENGINEERING INC
553 N Pcf Coastte B179 B, Redondo Beach (90277)
PHONE...................310 831-3454
EMP: 70
SALES (est): 2.7MM **Privately Held**
SIC: 8711

(P-25999)
WILLDAN ENGINEERING
2401 E Katella Ave # 300, Anaheim (92806-5909)
PHONE...................714 978-8200
Lisa Penna, *Manager*
EMP: 86
SALES (corp-wide): 273.3MM **Publicly Held**
WEB: www.willdan.com
SIC: 8711 8742 Civil engineering; business planning & organizing services
HQ: Willdan Engineering
2401 E Katella Ave # 300
Anaheim CA 92806
714 978-8200

(P-26000)
WILLDAN GROUP INC (PA)
2401 E Katella Ave # 300, Anaheim (92806-5909)
PHONE...................800 424-9144
Thomas D Brisbin, *Ch of Bd*
Michael A Bieber, *President*
Daniel Chow, *COO*
Stacy B McLaughlin, *CFO*
Stacy McLaughlin, *CFO*
EMP: 82
SQ FT: 18,000
SALES: 273.3MM **Publicly Held**
WEB: www.willdangroup.com
SIC: 8711 8748 Civil engineering; consulting engineer; urban planning & consulting services

(P-26001)
WILLIAM E HEINSELMAN
3303 Luyung Dr, Rancho Cordova (95742-6860)
PHONE...................916 920-0220
William E Heinselman, *Owner*
EMP: 50
SALES: 10MM **Privately Held**
SIC: 8711 Sanitary engineers

(P-26002)
WINZLER & KELLY
2235 Mercury Way Ste 150, Santa Rosa (95407-5470)
PHONE...................707 523-1010
Theodore B Whiton, *Sales & Mktg St*
Iver Skavdal, *General Mgr*
Alex Culick, *Manager*
EMP: 95
SQ FT: 7,000
SALES (corp-wide): 1.2MM **Privately Held**
WEB: www.sjoeng.com
SIC: 8711 8748 8742 Consulting engineer; environmental consultant; industrial hygiene consultant
PA: Winzler & Kelly
2235 Mercury Way Ste 150
Santa Rosa CA 95407
707 523-1010

(P-26003)
WOOD ENVIRONMENT &
121 Innovation Dr Ste 200, Irvine (92617-3094)
PHONE...................949 642-0245
Jay River, *President*
EMP: 95
SALES (corp-wide): 6.7B **Privately Held**
SIC: 8711 Engineering services
HQ: Wood Environment & Infrastructure Solutions, Inc.
1105 Lakewood Pkwy # 300
Alpharetta GA 30009
770 360-0600

(P-26004)
WOOD ENVIRONMENT &
180 Grand Ave Fl 11, Oakland (94612-3741)
PHONE...................510 663-4100
Susan Gallardo, *Branch Mgr*
Calvin Hardcastle, *Vice Pres*
Thomas Jones, *Info Tech Dir*
Khalil Abusaba, *Sr Associate*
EMP: 150
SALES (corp-wide): 6.7B **Privately Held**
SIC: 8711 8999 8744 Consulting engineer; pollution control engineering; earth science services; facilities support services
HQ: Wood Environment & Infrastructure Solutions, Inc.
1105 Lakewood Pkwy # 300
Alpharetta GA 30009
770 360-0600

(P-26005)
WOOD ENVIRONMENT &
6001 Rickenbacker Rd, Commerce (90040-3031)
PHONE...................323 889-5300
Bruce Corkel, *Branch Mgr*
EMP: 85
SQ FT: 30,000
SALES (corp-wide): 6.7B **Privately Held**
SIC: 8711 8748 Consulting engineer; environmental consultant
HQ: Wood Environment & Infrastructure Solutions, Inc.
1105 Lakewood Pkwy # 300
Alpharetta GA 30009
770 360-0600

(P-26006)
WOOD RODGERS INC (PA)
3301 C St Ste 100b, Sacramento (95816-3350)
PHONE...................916 341-7760
Mark Rodgers, *President*
Martin Rodriguez, *Officer*
Steve Balbierz, *Vice Pres*
Gerardo Calvillo, *Vice Pres*
Shyamal Chowdhury, *Vice Pres*
EMP: 120 EST: 1996
SQ FT: 5,500

SALES (est): 44.5MM **Privately Held**
WEB: www.woodrodgers.com
SIC: 8711 Civil engineering

(P-26007)
WORLEYPARSONS GROUP INC
181 W Huntington Dr 100, Monrovia
(91016-3456)
PHONE..................................626 803-9000
Chris Ashton, *Branch Mgr*
EMP: 253
SALES (corp-wide): 3.8B **Privately Held**
SIC: 8711 Engineering services
HQ: Worleyparsons Group Inc.
575 N Dairy Ashford Rd # 200
Houston TX 77079
713 407-5000

(P-26008)
WORLEYPARSONS GROUP INC
721 Charles E Young Dr S, Los Angeles
(90095-8342)
PHONE..................................610 855-2000
Christopher L Parker, *CEO*
EMP: 329
SALES (corp-wide): 3.8B **Privately Held**
SIC: 8711 Acoustical engineering
HQ: Worleyparsons Group Inc.
575 N Dairy Ashford Rd # 200
Houston TX 77079
713 407-5000

(P-26009)
WORLEYPARSONS GROUP INC
100 W Walnut, Pasadena (91101)
PHONE..................................626 440-7000
Antonio V Dy, *Principal*
EMP: 253
SALES (corp-wide): 3.6B **Privately Held**
SIC: 8711 8742 Designing: ship, boat, machine & product; construction project management consultant
HQ: Worleyparsons Group Inc.
575 N Dairy Ashford Rd # 200
Houston TX 77079
713 407-5000

(P-26010)
WSP USA BUILDINGS INC
405 Howard St Ste 500, San Francisco
(94105-2928)
PHONE..................................415 398-3833
Randy J Meyers, *Branch Mgr*
Tom Smith, *Bd of Directors*
Michael Mangione, *Exec VP*
Joseph Delpozzo, *Senior VP*
Patricia McCaffery, *Senior VP*
EMP: 120
SALES (corp-wide): 5.4B **Privately Held**
WEB: www.flackandkurtz.com
SIC: 8711 8748 Consulting engineer; telecommunications consultant
HQ: Wsp Usa Buildings Inc.
1 Penn Plz W34ths
New York NY 10119
602 254-0561

(P-26011)
WSP USA INC
1100 W Town And Cntry 2, Orange
(92868-4600)
PHONE..................................714 973-4880
Charline Talmer, *General Mgr*
Gregory A Kelly, *President*
Mark Briggs, *Vice Pres*
Sarah Bradfield, *Electrical Engi*
Lynn Pham, *Payroll Mgr*
EMP: 100
SALES (corp-wide): 5.4B **Privately Held**
SIC: 8711 Consulting engineer
HQ: Wsp Usa Inc.
1 Penn Plz Ste 200
New York NY 10119
212 465-5000

(P-26012)
WSP USA INC
444 S Flower St Ste 800, Los Angeles
(90071-2962)
PHONE..................................212 465-5000
Carl Enson, *General Mgr*
Gregory A Kelly, *President*
Shawn Simpson, *Administration*
Isanower Jesiah, *Manager*
EMP: 50

SALES (corp-wide): 5.4B **Privately Held**
SIC: 8711 Consulting engineer
HQ: Wsp Usa Inc.
1 Penn Plz Ste 200
New York NY 10119
212 465-5000

(P-26013)
WSP USA INC
425 Market St Fl 17, San Francisco
(94105-2425)
PHONE..................................415 243-4600
Stuart Sunshine, *Branch Mgr*
Gregory A Kelly, *President*
Jim Bourgart, *Vice Pres*
Robert Stromsted, *Vice Pres*
Teresa Carroll, *Admin Asst*
EMP: 180
SALES (corp-wide): 5.4B **Privately Held**
SIC: 8711 Consulting engineer
HQ: Wsp Usa Inc.
1 Penn Plz Ste 200
New York NY 10119
212 465-5000

(P-26014)
WSP USA INC
451 E Vanderbilt Way # 200, San
Bernardino (92408-3614)
PHONE..................................909 888-1106
Danika Bragg, *Branch Mgr*
Gregory A Kelly, *President*
Basem Muallem, *Vice Pres*
EMP: 70
SQ FT: 10,000
SALES (corp-wide): 5.4B **Privately Held**
SIC: 8711 Consulting engineer
HQ: Wsp Usa Inc.
1 Penn Plz Ste 200
New York NY 10119
212 465-5000

(P-26015)
YUPANA INC
5039 Commercial Cir Ste J, Concord
(94520-1445)
PHONE..................................925 482-0657
John McWeeny,
John McWeeney, *Engrg Dir*
Onur Yildirim, *Technical Staff*
Chris Craighead, *Foreman/Supr*
EMP: 50
SALES (est): 4.9MM **Privately Held**
SIC: 8711 Engineering services

8712 Architectural Services

(P-26016)
5 DESIGN INC
Also Called: 5design
1024 N Orange Dr Ste 215, Los Angeles
(90038-2348)
PHONE..................................323 308-3558
Stan Hathaway, *President*
Michael Ellis, *Treasurer*
Arthur Benedetti Jr, *Vice Pres*
Tim Magill, *Admin Sec*
EMP: 76
SALES: 12MM **Privately Held**
WEB: www.5plusdesign.com
SIC: 8712 Architectural engineering

(P-26017)
A SMMW CALIFORNIA CORPORATION
Also Called: Simon Mrtn-Vgue Wnklstein Mris
185 Berry St Ste 5100, San Francisco
(94107-1772)
PHONE..................................415 546-0400
Cathy Simon, *President*
Karen Alschuler, *Chairman*
John Long, *Vice Pres*
Prakash Pinto, *Vice Pres*
Evan Rose, *Vice Pres*
EMP: 60
SQ FT: 16,200
SALES: 10MM **Privately Held**
WEB: www.smmw.com
SIC: 8712 Architectural services

(P-26018)
AECOM
1023 E Avenue J10, Lancaster
(93535-4417)
PHONE..................................661 266-0802
EMP: 120
SALES (corp-wide): 20.1B **Publicly Held**
SIC: 8712 Architectural engineering
PA: Aecom
1999 Avenue Of The Stars # 2600
Los Angeles CA 90067
213 593-8000

(P-26019)
AECOM SERVICES INC (HQ)
Also Called: Aecom Design
300 S Grand Ave Fl 2, Los Angeles
(90071-3470)
PHONE..................................213 593-8000
Michael S Burke, *CEO*
Raymond Landy, *President*
Jane Chmielinski, *COO*
Deborah Klem, *CFO*
Richard G Newman, *Chairman*
EMP: 250 EST: 1946
SALES (est): 1.7B
SALES (corp-wide): 20.1B **Publicly Held**
WEB: www.dmjmhn.com
SIC: 8712 8741 8711 Architectural services; management services; engineering services
PA: Aecom
1999 Avenue Of The Stars # 2600
Los Angeles CA 90067
213 593-8000

(P-26020)
AEDIS ARCHITECTS (PA)
Also Called: Aedis Architech and Planning
387 S 1st St Ste 300, San Jose
(95113-2890)
PHONE..................................949 496-6191
Thang Do, *Owner*
Margot Kenney, *Business Dir*
Deedee Mendez, *Admin Asst*
Pascal Najem, *Admin Asst*
Eric Moss, *Info Tech Mgr*
EMP: 50
SALES (est): 8.7MM **Privately Held**
WEB: www.aedisgroup.com
SIC: 8712 Architectural engineering

(P-26021)
AEWESTJV
363 5th Ave Ste 202, San Diego
(92101-6965)
PHONE..................................619 233-1023
Ralph Joseph Roesling, *Principal*
EMP: 50
SALES (est): 1.2MM **Privately Held**
SIC: 8712 Architectural engineering

(P-26022)
ALTOON PARTNERS LLP (PA)
Also Called: Altoon Porter
617 W 7th St Ste 400, Los Angeles
(90017-3889)
PHONE..................................213 225-1900
Ronald A Altoon, *Partner*
James Auld, *Partner*
Gary Dempster, *Partner*
William Sebring, *Partner*
Leslie Young, *Partner*
EMP: 70
SQ FT: 20,000
SALES (est): 9.2MM **Privately Held**
WEB: www.altoonporter.com
SIC: 8712 Architectural engineering

(P-26023)
ARCHITECTS ORANGE
144 N Orange St, Orange (92866-1400)
PHONE..................................714 639-9860
Jack Selman, *Senior Partner*
RC Alley III, *Partner*
Jim Dietze, *Partner*
Darrel Hebenstreit, *Partner*
Hugh Rose, *Partner*
EMP: 200 EST: 1973
SQ FT: 10,000
SALES (est): 34.9MM **Privately Held**
WEB: www.architectsorange.com
SIC: 8712 Architectural engineering

(P-26024)
ATC SERVICES INC
999 W Town And Country Rd, Orange
(92868-4713)
PHONE..................................213 593-8100
Richard Erickson, *Manager*
Ray Landy, *President*
EMP: 400
SALES (est): 52.8K
SALES (corp-wide): 20.1B **Publicly Held**
SIC: 8712 Architectural services
PA: Aecom
1999 Avenue Of The Stars # 2600
Los Angeles CA 90067
213 593-8000

(P-26025)
AUSTIN VEUM RBBINS PRTNERS INC (PA)
501 W Broadway Ste A, San Diego
(92101-3562)
PHONE..................................619 231-1960
Douglas H Austin, *CEO*
Chris Vium, *President*
Doreen Austin, *CFO*
Jeffrey Parshalle, *Vice Pres*
Randy Robbins, *Vice Pres*
EMP: 83
SQ FT: 12,500
SALES (est): 5.3MM **Privately Held**
SIC: 8712 Architectural services

(P-26026)
BAR ARCHITECTS
901 Battery St Ste 300, San Francisco
(94111-1350)
PHONE..................................415 293-5700
Robert Hunter, *President*
Earl Wilson, *Principal*
Erik Moriel, *Administration*
Liza Bass, *Human Res Dir*
Geo Coelho, *Marketing Staff*
EMP: 80
SQ FT: 13,500
SALES (est): 11.3MM **Privately Held**
WEB: www.bararch.com
SIC: 8712 Architectural engineering

(P-26027)
BASSENIAN/LAGONI ARCHITECTS
2031 Orchard Dr Ste 100, Newport Beach
(92660-0753)
PHONE..................................949 553-9100
Aram Bassenian, *CEO*
Carl Lagoni, *President*
Lee R Rogaliner, *CFO*
Lee Rogaliner, *CFO*
Hans Anderle, *Assoc VP*
EMP: 65
SQ FT: 22,800
SALES (est): 10.7MM **Privately Held**
WEB: www.bassenianlagoni.com
SIC: 8712 Architectural engineering

(P-26028)
CALLISON LLC
1453 3rd Street Promenade # 400, Santa
Monica (90401-3428)
PHONE..................................310 394-8460
Mackey Deasy, *Director*
EMP: 205
SALES (est): 6.5MM **Privately Held**
SIC: 8712 Architectural services
PA: Callison Llc
1420 5th Ave Ste 2400
Seattle WA 98101

(P-26029)
CALLISONRTKL INC
818 W 7th St Ste 300, Los Angeles
(90017-3426)
PHONE..................................213 627-7373
EMP: 140
SALES (corp-wide): 2.5B **Privately Held**
SIC: 8712
HQ: Callisonrtkl Inc
901 S Bond St
Baltimore MD 21231
410 528-8600

(P-26030)
CALLISONRTKL INC
333 S Hope St Ste C200, Los Angeles
(90071-3005)
PHONE................................213 633-6000
Barbara Proano, *Branch Mgr*
Angela Acosta, *Assoc VP*
EMP: 143
SALES (corp-wide): 2.8B **Privately Held**
WEB: www.rtkl.com
SIC: 8712 Architectural engineering
HQ: Callisonrtkl Inc.
    901 S Bond St
    Baltimore MD 21231
    410 537-6000

(P-26031)
CARRIER JOHNSON (PA)
Also Called: Culture
1301 3rd Ave, San Diego (92101-4012)
PHONE................................619 236-9462
Gordon Carrier, *President*
Michael Johnson, *Vice Pres*
EMP: 99
SQ FT: 13,000
SALES (est): 16.9MM **Privately Held**
WEB: www.carrierjohnson.com
SIC: 8712 7389 Architectural engineering;
    interior design services

(P-26032)
CGL COMPANIES LLC
2485 Natomas Park Dr # 300, Sacramento
(95833-2937)
PHONE................................916 678-7890
Robert Glass, *Exec VP*
Donald Boan, *Controller*
EMP: 70 **EST:** 2017
SALES (est): 1.3MM **Privately Held**
SIC: 8712 Architectural services

(P-26033)
CH2M HILL INC
2485 Natomas Park Dr # 600, Sacramento
(95833-2975)
PHONE................................916 920-0300
Craig Eldrich, *Branch Mgr*
Dan Johnson, *Info Tech Mgr*
Geoffrey Lytle, *Info Tech Mgr*
Ed Maechler, *Systs Prg Mgr*
Cindy Erickson, *Project Mgr*
EMP: 50
SALES (corp-wide): 10B **Publicly Held**
SIC: 8712 Architectural services
HQ: Ch2m Hill, Inc.
    9191 S Jamaica St
    Englewood CO 80112
    303 771-0900

(P-26034)
CH2M HILL INC
1737 N 1st St Ste 300, San Jose
(95112-4585)
PHONE................................408 436-4936
Mark Janay, *Finance Other*
Michael Alonzo, *Project Mgr*
James Isles, *Project Mgr*
Steve Long, *Project Mgr*
David Volz, *Electrical Engi*
EMP: 50
SALES (corp-wide): 10B **Publicly Held**
SIC: 8712 8711 1622 1611 Architectural
    services; engineering services; bridge,
    tunnel & elevated highway; highway &
    street construction
HQ: Ch2m Hill, Inc.
    9191 S Jamaica St
    Englewood CO 80112
    303 771-0900

(P-26035)
CHONG PARTNERS ARCHITECHER INC
901 Market St Ste 600, San Francisco
(94103-1740)
PHONE................................613 995-8210
Gordon H Chong, *President*
David A Englund, *CFO*
John Woolston, *Assistant*
EMP: 125
SQ FT: 16,000
SALES: 4.2MM **Privately Held**
SIC: 8712 Architectural services

(P-26036)
CITY OF FREMONT
Also Called: Building & Safety Department
39550 Liberty St, Fremont (94538-2211)
P.O. Box 5006 (94537-5006)
PHONE................................510 494-4460
Neil Hawkins, *General Mgr*
EMP: 150 **Privately Held**
WEB: www.ci.fremont.ca.us
SIC: 8712 Architectural services
PA: City Of Fremont
    3300 Capitol Ave
    Fremont CA 94538
    510 284-4000

(P-26037)
CITY OF LOS ANGELES
Also Called: Architecture Division
1149 S Broadway Ste 800, Los Angeles
(90015-2237)
PHONE................................213 485-4282
Mahmood Karimzadeh, *Manager*
Terry Wesdy, *Analyst*
EMP: 65 **Privately Held**
WEB: www.lacity.org
SIC: 8712 Architectural engineering
PA: City Of Los Angeles
    200 N Spring St Ste 303
    Los Angeles CA 90012
    213 978-0600

(P-26038)
COACT DESIGNWORKS
801 T St, Sacramento (95811-7028)
PHONE................................916 930-5900
Pat Derickson, *President*
Kelly Reynolds, *Vice Pres*
Charlotte Deni, *Marketing Staff*
Chris Garcia, *Education*
Mitch Bjorgum, *Director*
EMP: 50
SQ FT: 12,800
SALES: 9MM **Privately Held**
WEB: www.skwaia.com
SIC: 8712 Architectural engineering

(P-26039)
CUNINGHAM GROUP ARCH INC
Also Called: Cuningham Group, The
8665 Hayden Pl, Culver City (90232-2901)
PHONE................................310 895-2200
John Cuiter, *President*
EMP: 50
SALES (corp-wide): 32MM **Privately Held**
WEB: www.cuningham.com
SIC: 8712 Architectural engineering
PA: Cuningham Group Architecture, Inc.
    201 Se Main St Ste 325
    Minneapolis MN 55414
    612 379-3400

(P-26040)
DAHLIN GROUP INC (PA)
5865 Owens Dr, Pleasanton (94588-3942)
PHONE................................925 251-7200
Nancy K Keenan, *President*
Karl Danielson, *Vice Pres*
Charles Meyer, *Vice Pres*
Harrison Pierson, *Vice Pres*
John Thatch, *Vice Pres*
EMP: 60
SQ FT: 300,000
SALES (est): 17.5MM **Privately Held**
WEB: www.dahlingroup.com
SIC: 8712 Architectural engineering

(P-26041)
DARDEN ARCHITECTS INC
6790 N West Ave Ste 104, Fresno
(93711-4306)
PHONE................................559 448-8051
Martin Dietz, *President*
EMP: 75 **EST:** 1959
SQ FT: 5,000
SALES (est): 12.6MM **Privately Held**
SIC: 8712 7389 Architectural engineering;
    interior designer

(P-26042)
DES ARCHITECTS + ENGINEERS INC
399 Bradford St Ste 300, Redwood City
(94063-1585)
P.O. Box 3599 (94064-3599)
PHONE................................650 364-6453

Thomas Gilman, *President*
Stephen D Mincey, *CFO*
Craig Ivancovich, *Corp Secy*
Brandi Reyes, *Executive*
Jessica Langford, *Admin Asst*
EMP: 115
SQ FT: 35,000
SALES (est): 18.4MM **Privately Held**
WEB: www.des-ae.com
SIC: 8712 8711 Architectural engineering;
    engineering services

(P-26043)
DG ARCHITECTS INC (PA)
Also Called: Dga Plnning L Arch L Interiors
550 Ellis St, Mountain View (94043-2236)
PHONE................................650 943-1660
Randall Dowler, *President*
Nancy Escano, *Treasurer*
Tania Saunders, *Office Admin*
Trey Post, *Planning*
Warren Young, *Project Mgr*
EMP: 78
SQ FT: 15,000
SALES (est): 12.2MM **Privately Held**
WEB: www.dga-mv.com
SIC: 8712 Architectural engineering

(P-26044)
DLR GROUP INC
700 S Flower St Fl 22, Los Angeles
(90017-4209)
PHONE................................626 796-8230
EMP: 150
SALES (corp-wide): 109.7MM **Privately Held**
SIC: 8712 Architectural services
HQ: Dlr Group Inc.
    700 Suth Flwr St Fl 22 Flr 22
    Los Angeles CA 90017
    213 800-9400

(P-26045)
DLR GROUP INC (HQ)
700 Suth Flwr St Fl 22 Flr 22, Los Angeles
(90017)
PHONE................................213 800-9400
Adrian O Cohen, *President*
Dennis Wiederholt, *Treasurer*
Jon P Anderson, *Vice Pres*
Jon Anderson, *Vice Pres*
Brian Arial, *Vice Pres*
EMP: 140 **EST:** 1997
SALES (est): 16.5MM
SALES (corp-wide): 109.7MM **Privately Held**
SIC: 8712 8711 Architectural services; en-
    gineering services; mechanical engineer-
    ing
PA: Dlr Holding Company
    6457 Frances St Ste 200
    Omaha NE
    402 393-4100

(P-26046)
GEHRY PARTNERS LLP
12541 Beatrice St, Los Angeles
(90066-7001)
PHONE................................310 482-3000
Frank Gehry, *Partner*
Brian Aamoth, *Partner*
John Bowers, *Partner*
Anand Devarajan, *Partner*
Berta Gehry, *Partner*
EMP: 130
SQ FT: 12,100
SALES (est): 13.9MM **Privately Held**
SIC: 8712 Architectural services

(P-26047)
GENERAL SERVICES CAL DEPT
Also Called: Division of State Architect
1515 Clay St Ste 1201, Oakland
(94612-1474)
PHONE................................510 622-3101
Lee Roy Tam, *Manager*
EMP: 60 **Privately Held**
WEB: www.4c.net
SIC: 8712 9199 Architectural services;
    general government administration;
HQ: California Department Of General
    Services
    707 3rd St
    West Sacramento CA 95605
    -

(P-26048)
GENERAL SERVICES CAL DEPT
Also Called: Division of State Architect
700 N Alameda St Ste 500, Los Angeles
(90012-3352)
PHONE................................213 897-3995
Sharqat Ullah, *Manager*
EMP: 55 **Privately Held**
WEB: www.4c.net
SIC: 8712 9199 Architectural services;
    general government administration;
HQ: California Department Of General
    Services
    707 3rd St
    West Sacramento CA 95605
    -

(P-26049)
GKK CORPORATION
1775 Hancock St Ste 150, San Diego
(92110-2039)
PHONE................................619 398-0215
EMP: 59 **Privately Held**
SIC: 8712 Architectural engineering
PA: Gkk Corporation
    2355 Main St Ste 220
    Irvine CA 92614

(P-26050)
GKK CORPORATION (PA)
Also Called: Gkkworks
2355 Main St Ste 220, Irvine (92614-4251)
PHONE................................949 250-1500
Praful Kulkarni, *President*
Sam Porter, *CFO*
David Hunt, *Vice Pres*
Leslie Long, *Office Mgr*
Albert Quesada, *Project Mgr*
EMP: 85
SQ FT: 11,000
SALES: 117.5MM **Privately Held**
SIC: 8712 8711 Architectural engineering;
    building construction consultant

(P-26051)
GONZALEZ/GOODALE ARCHITECTS
Also Called: Chcg Architects
135 W Green St Ste 200, Pasadena
(91105-4131)
PHONE................................626 568-1428
Armando L Gonzalez, *CEO*
Ali Barar, *Principal*
Harry Drake, *Principal*
John Ferguson, *Principal*
David Goodale, *Principal*
EMP: 52
SQ FT: 8,000
SALES: 9.8MM **Privately Held**
WEB: www.gonzalezgoodale.com
SIC: 8712 7389 Architectural engineering;
    interior designer

(P-26052)
GOULD EVANS P C
95 Brady St, San Francisco (94103-1241)
PHONE................................415 503-1411
Robert M Baum, *Administration*
Holly Kan, *Associate*
EMP: 75
SALES (corp-wide): 9.7MM **Privately Held**
SIC: 8712 Architectural engineering
PA: Gould Evans, P C
    4041 Mill St Ste A
    Kansas City MO 64111
    816 931-6655

(P-26053)
GRUEN ASSOCIATES
Also Called: Gruen Assoc Archtects Planners
6330 San Vicente Blvd # 200, Los Angeles
(90048-5441)
PHONE................................323 937-4270
Ki Suh Park, *Partner*
Michael A Enomoto, *Partner*
Larry Schlossberg, *Partner*
Michael Enomoto, *Managing Prtnr*
Brian Gruen, *General Mgr*
EMP: 75 **EST:** 1947
SQ FT: 14,000
SALES (est): 11.5MM **Privately Held**
WEB: www.gruenassociates.com
SIC: 8712 Architectural engineering

(P-26054)
HAMMEL GREEN & ABRAHAMSON INC
Also Called: Hga Architects and Engineers
1200 R St Ste 100, Sacramento
(95811-5807)
PHONE.............................916 787-5100
Brent Forslin, *Director*
EMP: 65
SALES (corp-wide): 142.8MM **Privately Held**
WEB: www.hga.com
SIC: 8712 8711 Architectural engineering; engineering services
PA: Hammel, Green And Abrahamson, Inc.
  420 N 5th St Ste 100
  Minneapolis MN 55401
  612 758-4000

(P-26055)
HARLEY ELLIS DEVEREAUX CORP
417 Montgomery St Ste 400, San Francisco
(94104-1111)
PHONE.............................415 981-2345
Lee Vandekerchove, *President*
EMP: 64
SALES (corp-wide): 43.5MM **Privately Held**
SIC: 8712 Architectural engineering
PA: Harley Ellis Devereaux Corp
  26913 Nrthwstrn Hwy 200
  Southfield MI 48033
  248 262-1500

(P-26056)
HDR ENVIRONMENTAL OPE
8690 Balboa Ave Ste 200, San Diego
(92123-6507)
PHONE.............................858 712-8400
Dean Gipson, *Branch Mgr*
EMP: 70
SALES (corp-wide): 2.3B **Privately Held**
SIC: 8712 8711 8748 8999 Architectural services; engineering services; business consulting; communication services
HQ: Hdr Environmental, Operations And Construction, Inc.
  1917 S 67th St
  Omaha NE 68106

(P-26057)
HELLMUTH OBATA & KASSABAUM INC (DH)
Also Called: H O K
1 Bush St Ste 200, San Francisco
(94104-4404)
PHONE.............................415 243-0555
Patrick Macleamy, *CEO*
William Hellmuth, *President*
Lisa Green, *Treasurer*
Thomas Robson, *Officer*
Steve Riley, *Vice Pres*
EMP: 193
SALES (est): 54.8MM
SALES (corp-wide): 274.2MM **Privately Held**
SIC: 8712 8711 8742 7389 Architectural engineering; engineering services; management consulting services; interior design services; landscape architects

(P-26058)
HELLMUTH OBATA & KASSABAUM INC
9530 Jefferson Blvd, Culver City
(90232-2918)
PHONE.............................310 838-9555
Jeff Mayer, *Manager*
Peter Mosanyi,
Michael Thoma, *Associate*
EMP: 50
SALES (corp-wide): 274.2MM **Privately Held**
SIC: 8712 8711 Architectural engineering; engineering services
HQ: Hellmuth, Obata & Kassabaum, Inc.
  1 Bush St Ste 200
  San Francisco CA 94104

(P-26059)
HFS CONCEPTS 4 INC
3229 E Spring St Ste 330, Long Beach
(90806-2486)
PHONE.............................562 424-1720
John Mamer, *President*
EMP: 50
SQ FT: 11,000
SALES (est): 3.6MM **Privately Held**
SIC: 8712 7389 Architectural services; interior designer

(P-26060)
HKS INC
10880 Wilshire Blvd Fl 1850, Los Angeles
(90024-4101)
PHONE.............................310 788-7700
Scott Hunter, *Branch Mgr*
EMP: 70
SALES (corp-wide): 405.8MM **Privately Held**
SIC: 8712 Architectural services
PA: Hks, Inc.
  350 N Saint Paul St # 100
  Dallas TX 75201
  214 969-5599

(P-26061)
HKS ARCHITECTS INC
500 Howard St Fl 4, San Francisco
(94105-3040)
PHONE.............................415 356-3800
Kirk Teske, *COO*
EMP: 50
SALES (est): 197.8K **Privately Held**
SIC: 8712 Architectural services

(P-26062)
HMC GROUP (PA)
Also Called: HMC Architects
3546 Concours, Ontario (91764-5584)
PHONE.............................909 989-9979
Brian Staton, *CEO*
Randal Peterson, *President*
Beverly Prior, *President*
Robert J Kain, *Chairman*
John Nichols, *Data Proc Staff*
EMP: 165
SQ FT: 58,000
SALES (est): 66.6MM **Privately Held**
WEB: www.hmcarchitects.com
SIC: 8712 Architectural engineering

(P-26063)
HMC GROUP
2930 Inland Empire Blvd # 100, Ontario
(91764-4802)
PHONE.............................909 980-8058
Lauie L McCoy, *Manager*
EMP: 56
SALES (corp-wide): 66.6MM **Privately Held**
SIC: 8712 Architectural engineering
PA: Hmc Group
  3546 Concours
  Ontario CA 91764
  909 989-9979

(P-26064)
HNTB-GERWICK JV
1300 Clay St Fl 7, Oakland (94612-1425)
PHONE.............................510 839-8972
Dale Berner, *Partner*
EMP: 70
SALES (est): 2.7MM **Privately Held**
SIC: 8712 8711 8742 8741 Architectural services; engineering services; business planning & organizing services; construction management

(P-26065)
HOK GROUP INC
1 Bush St Ste 200, San Francisco
(94104-4404)
PHONE.............................415 243-0555
Russ Drinker, *Branch Mgr*
EMP: 233
SALES (corp-wide): 274.2MM **Privately Held**
SIC: 8712 8742 8711 Architectural engineering; planning consultant; engineering services
PA: Hok Group, Inc
  10 S Broadway Ste 200
  Saint Louis MO 63102
  314 421-2000

(P-26066)
HOK GROUP INC
9530 Jefferson Blvd, Culver City
(90232-2918)
PHONE.............................310 838-9555
John L Conley, *Branch Mgr*
Sharon Burton, *Principal*
Ethel Lazaro, *Accountant*
Natalie Noel, *Personnel Assit*
Yousef Abougabal, *Associate*
EMP: 150
SALES (corp-wide): 274.2MM **Privately Held**
SIC: 8712 Architectural engineering
PA: Hok Group, Inc
  10 S Broadway Ste 200
  Saint Louis MO 63102
  314 421-2000

(P-26067)
HORNBERGER WORSTELL ASSOC INC
Also Called: Hornberger, Mark R
170 Maiden Ln Ste 600, San Francisco
(94108-5334)
PHONE.............................415 391-1080
Mark Hornberger, *President*
Francine Larose, *CFO*
Jack Worstell, *Exec VP*
John Davis, *Senior VP*
Edward Beltran, *Marketing Staff*
EMP: 50
SALES (est): 8MM **Privately Held**
WEB: www.hornbergerworstell.com
SIC: 8712 Architectural engineering

(P-26068)
HOSPITLITY FCSED SOLUTIONS INC
3229 E Spring St Ste 200, Long Beach
(90806-2472)
PHONE.............................562 424-1720
Chien An Lee, *Chairman*
John Mamer, *President*
John W Wong, *CEO*
Ron Chaney, *Senior VP*
David Chen, *Vice Pres*
EMP: 100
SALES (est): 15.6MM **Privately Held**
WEB: www.concepts4inc.com
SIC: 8712 Architectural services

(P-26069)
HUNTSMAN ARCHITECTURAL GROUP (PA)
50 California St Fl 7, San Francisco
(94111-4624)
PHONE.............................415 394-1212
Sascha Wagner, *President*
Daniel Huntsman, *President*
Susan Williams, *Senior VP*
Linda H Parker, *Vice Pres*
Keith Turner, *Vice Pres*
EMP: 65
SQ FT: 19,000
SALES (est): 14.9MM **Privately Held**
WEB: www.huntsmanag.com
SIC: 8712 Architectural engineering

(P-26070)
JACK P SELMAN
144 N Orange St, Orange (92866-1413)
PHONE.............................714 639-9860
Jack P Selman, *Partner*
R C Alley, *Partner*
Ed Cadavona, *Partner*
Jim Dietze, *Partner*
Darrel Hidenstreit, *Partner*
EMP: 80
SQ FT: 800
SALES (est): 4.3MM **Privately Held**
SIC: 8712 Architectural services

(P-26071)
JEFFREY ROME & ASSOCIATES
131 Innovation Dr Ste 100, Irvine
(92617-3072)
PHONE.............................949 760-3929
Jeffery Rome, *President*
Matt Bradford, *Project Mgr*
Harold Crouch, *Project Mgr*
Zac Noguera, *Project Mgr*
Randal Williams, *Project Mgr*
EMP: 60

SALES (est): 3.4MM **Privately Held**
SIC: 8712 Architectural engineering

(P-26072)
JOHNSON FAIN INC
1201 N Broadway, Los Angeles
(90012-1407)
PHONE.............................323 224-6000
William H Fain Jr, *Co-President*
Scott Johnson, *Partner*
R Scott Johnson, *Co-President*
Natalie Egnatchik, *Executive Asst*
Sherry Miller, *Admin Sec*
EMP: 80
SQ FT: 26,000
SALES (est): 11.7MM **Privately Held**
WEB: www.johnsonfain.com
SIC: 8712 7389 Architectural engineering; interior design services

(P-26073)
KAA DESIGN GROUP INC
4201 Redwood Ave, Los Angeles
(90066-5605)
PHONE.............................310 821-1400
Grant Kirkpatrick, *President*
Michael McGowan, *Sr Project Mgr*
Dan Murphy, *Sr Project Mgr*
David Vazquez, *Architect*
Cecilia McLaren, *Receptionist*
EMP: 55
SQ FT: 2,520
SALES (est): 6.7MM **Privately Held**
WEB: www.kaa-architects.com
SIC: 8712 Architectural engineering

(P-26074)
KFA LLP
1625 Olympic Blvd, Santa Monica
(90404-3822)
PHONE.............................310 399-7975
Jonathan Watts, *Partner*
John Arnold, *Partner*
Lise Bornstein, *Partner*
Barbara Flammang, *Partner*
Wade Killefer, *Partner*
EMP: 58 EST: 2016
SALES (est): 1.3MM **Privately Held**
SIC: 8712 Architectural services

(P-26075)
KMD ARCHITECTS (PA)
417 Montgomery St Ste 200, San Francisco
(94104-1107)
PHONE.............................415 398-5191
Paul Ryan Stevens, *CEO*
Robert Matthew, *Ch of Bd*
Kavinder Singh, *President*
Roy Latka, *Executive*
James Diaz, *Admin Sec*
▲ EMP: 95
SQ FT: 35,000
SALES (est): 22.1MM **Privately Held**
SIC: 8712 Architectural services

(P-26076)
KTGY GROUP INC
1814 Franklin St Ste 400, Oakland
(94612-3461)
PHONE.............................510 463-2097
Tricia Esser, *CEO*
EMP: 50
SALES (corp-wide): 74.7MM **Privately Held**
SIC: 8712 Architectural engineering
PA: Ktgy Group, Inc.
  17911 Von Karman Ave # 250
  Irvine CA 92614
  949 851-2133

(P-26077)
KTGY GROUP INC (PA)
17911 Von Karman Ave # 250, Irvine
(92614-4243)
PHONE.............................949 851-2133
Tricia Esser, *CEO*
Stan Braden, *President*
Brittney Choisnet, *CFO*
Michael Kingsley, *Vice Pres*
Sara Fernandez, *Plan/Corp Dev D*
EMP: 70
SQ FT: 21,000
SALES: 74.7MM **Privately Held**
SIC: 8712 Architectural services

(P-26078)
KTGY GROUP INC
12555 W Jefferson Blvd # 100, Los Angeles
(90066-7032)
PHONE..........................310 394-2625
Stan Braden, *Branch Mgr*
Lara M McKissick, *Purch Mgr*
EMP: 50
SALES (corp-wide): 74.7MM **Privately Held**
SIC: 8712 Architectural engineering
PA: Ktgy Group, Inc.
17911 Von Karman Ave # 250
Irvine CA 92614
949 851-2133

(P-26079)
LANGDON WILSON INTERNATIONAL (PA)
Also Called: Langdon Wilson Arch Plg Intrors
1055 Wilshire Blvd # 1500, Los Angeles
(90017-5633)
PHONE..........................213 250-1186
Asad Khan, *President*
John Patrick Allen, *Vice Pres*
Ziad Khan, *Project Mgr*
Maggie McCain, *Accounting Mgr*
Xochitl Rodriguez, *Human Resources*
EMP: 50
SQ FT: 11,000
SALES (est): 5.7MM **Privately Held**
WEB: www.lw-oc.com
SIC: 8712 Architectural engineering

(P-26080)
LEE BURKHART LIU INC (PA)
5510 Lincoln Blvd Ste 250, Playa Vista
(90094-3008)
PHONE..........................310 829-2249
Kenneth Lee, *President*
Erich Burkart, *Principal*
Ken Liu, *Principal*
EMP: 75
SQ FT: 11,000
SALES (est): 9.9MM **Privately Held**
WEB: www.lblarch.com
SIC: 8712 Architectural engineering

(P-26081)
LEO A DALY COMPANY
Also Called: Leo Daly Company
550 S Hope St Ste 2700, Los Angeles
(90071-2675)
PHONE..........................213 627-9300
Brian A Kite, *Branch Mgr*
Michael Walden, *Vice Pres*
Leah Jurilla, *Marketing Mgr*
Edmund Buch, *Architect*
Bruce E Konschuh, *Architect*
EMP: 60
SALES (corp-wide): 113.5MM **Privately Held**
SIC: 8712 8742 8711 Architectural engi-
neering; planning consultant; consulting
engineer
PA: Leo A. Daly Company
8600 Indian Hills Dr
Omaha NE 68114
808 521-8889

(P-26082)
LEO A DALY COMPANY
550 S Hope St Ste 2700, Los Angeles
(90071-2675)
PHONE..........................213 533-8855
Leo A Daly, *Branch Mgr*
EMP: 62
SALES (corp-wide): 113.5MM **Privately Held**
SIC: 8712 Architectural engineering
PA: Leo A. Daly Company
8600 Indian Hills Dr
Omaha NE 68114
808 521-8889

(P-26083)
LEO A DALY COMPANY
Also Called: Leo A Daly Company
2150 River Plaza Dr, Sacramento
(95833-3883)
PHONE..........................916 564-3259
EMP: 63
SALES (corp-wide): 113.5MM **Privately Held**
SIC: 8712 Architectural engineering

PA: Leo A. Daly Company
8600 Indian Hills Dr
Omaha NE 68114
808 521-8889

(P-26084)
LPA INC (PA)
5161 California Ave # 100, Irvine
(92617-3086)
PHONE..........................949 261-1001
Wendy Rogers, *CEO*
Dan Heinfeld, *President*
Charles Pruitt, *CFO*
James Kelly, *Vice Pres*
David Gilmore, *Admin Mgr*
EMP: 180
SQ FT: 33,700
SALES (est): 42.5MM **Privately Held**
WEB: www.lpainc.com
SIC: 8712 8711 0781 Architectural engi-
neering; engineering services; landscape
counseling & planning

(P-26085)
LPA INC
60 S Market St Ste 150, San Jose
(95113-2368)
PHONE..........................408 780-7200
EMP: 110
SALES (corp-wide): 42.5MM **Privately Held**
SIC: 8712 Architectural services
PA: Lpa, Inc.
5161 California Ave # 100
Irvine CA 92617
949 261-1001

(P-26086)
LPAS INC
2484 Natomas Park Dr # 100, Sacramento
(95833-2928)
PHONE..........................916 443-0335
Theressa Page, *Owner*
Ron Metzker, *Vice Pres*
Heidi Stauffer, *Controller*
Ken Bauer, *Associate*
EMP: 60 EST: 1975
SQ FT: 12,000
SALES (est): 8MM **Privately Held**
WEB: www.lpasacramento.com
SIC: 8712 Architectural engineering

(P-26087)
M ARTHUR GENSLER JR ASSOC INC
225 W Santa Clara St, San Jose
(95113-1723)
PHONE..........................408 885-8100
Kevin Schaeffer, *Branch Mgr*
EMP: 50
SALES (corp-wide): 1.2B **Privately Held**
SIC: 8712 Architectural services
PA: M. Arthur Gensler Jr. & Associates, Inc.
45 Fremont St Ste 1500
San Francisco CA 94105
415 433-3700

(P-26088)
M ARTHUR GENSLER JR ASSOC INC (PA)
45 Fremont St Ste 1500, San Francisco
(94105-2214)
PHONE..........................415 433-3700
Andy Cohen, *Co-CEO*
Robin Klehr Avia, *Ch of Bd*
Walter Hunt, *Vice Chairman*
Linda Havard, *CFO*
Diane Hoskins, *Co-CEO*
EMP: 360 EST: 1965
SQ FT: 57,000
SALES: 1.2B **Privately Held**
SIC: 8712 Architectural services

(P-26089)
M ARTHUR GENSLER JR ASSOC INC
2101 Webster St Ste 2000, Oakland
(94612-3032)
PHONE..........................510 625-7400
EMP: 207
SALES (corp-wide): 915.3MM **Privately Held**
SIC: 8712

PA: M. Arthur Gensler Jr. & Associates, Inc.
2 Harrison St Fl 4
San Francisco CA 94105
415 433-3700

(P-26090)
M ARTHUR GENSLER JR ASSOC INC
Also Called: Gensler and Associates
500 S Figueroa St, Los Angeles
(90071-1705)
PHONE..........................213 927-3600
Rob Jernigan, *Branch Mgr*
James R Baker, *Managing Dir*
Samuel Barry, *Sales Staff*
AIA David Fridlund, *Sr Associate*
William Jenkinson, *Sr Associate*
EMP: 249
SALES (corp-wide): 1.2B **Privately Held**
SIC: 8712 7389 Architectural engineering;
design, commercial & industrial
PA: M. Arthur Gensler Jr. & Associates, Inc.
45 Fremont St Ste 1500
San Francisco CA 94105
415 433-3700

(P-26091)
M ARTHUR GENSLER JR ASSOC INC
4675 Macarthur Ct Ste 100, Newport Beach
(92660-8811)
PHONE..........................949 863-9434
Kim Graham, *Branch Mgr*
Richard T Fleming, *Architect*
EMP: 69
SALES (corp-wide): 1.2B **Privately Held**
SIC: 8712 Architectural services
PA: M. Arthur Gensler Jr. & Associates, Inc.
45 Fremont St Ste 1500
San Francisco CA 94105
415 433-3700

(P-26092)
MARMOL RADZINER
12210 Nebraska Ave, Los Angeles
(90025-3620)
PHONE..........................310 826-6222
Ron Radziner, *CEO*
Leo Marmol, *President*
Scott Tran, *Info Tech Dir*
Colton Cross, *Project Mgr*
Andrew Parks, *Project Mgr*
EMP: 70
SQ FT: 6,500
SALES (est): 13.7MM **Privately Held**
WEB: www.marmol-radziner.com
SIC: 8712 1521 1542 Architectural engi-
neering; general remodeling, single-family
houses; new construction, single-family
houses; commercial & office building, new
construction; commercial & office build-
ings, renovation & repair

(P-26093)
MARTIN AC PARTNERS INC
444 S Flower St Ste 1200, Los Angeles
(90071-2977)
PHONE..........................213 683-1900
Robert Newsom, *President*
Christopher C Martin, *CEO*
David C Martin, *Principal*
EMP: 116 EST: 1906
SALES (est): 19.7MM **Privately Held**
SIC: 8712 Architectural services

(P-26094)
MARTIN ATI-AC INC (PA)
Also Called: ATI Architects & Engineers
4750 Willow Rd Ste 250, Pleasanton
(94588-2962)
PHONE..........................925 648-8800
Paul Didonato, *President*
Olliver Santos, *CFO*
Bruce Gillings, *Vice Pres*
Gmichael Goldsworthy, *Vice Pres*
Jennifer Pagach, *Executive*
EMP: 74
SQ FT: 14,000
SALES (est): 12MM **Privately Held**
WEB: www.atiengineering.com
SIC: 8712 8711 Architectural engineering;
structural engineering

(P-26095)
MBH ARCHITECTS INC
960 Atlantic Ave, Alameda (94501-1086)
PHONE..........................510 865-8663
Dennis Heath, *President*
Clay Fry, *Treasurer*
Joseph Smart, *Vice Pres*
John McNulty, *Principal*
Allen Antoine, *Administration*
EMP: 210
SQ FT: 55,000
SALES (est): 40.2MM **Privately Held**
WEB: www.mbharch.com
SIC: 8712 Architectural services

(P-26096)
MORPHOSIS ARCHITECTS
3440 Wesley St, Culver City (90232-2328)
PHONE..........................310 453-2247
Thom Mayne, *President*
Blythe Allison Mayne, *Vice Pres*
EMP: 62 EST: 1975
SQ FT: 10,000
SALES: 14.2MM **Privately Held**
WEB: www.morphosis.net
SIC: 8712 Architectural engineering

(P-26097)
MVE + PARTNERS INC (PA)
1900 Main St Ste 800, Irvine (92614-7318)
PHONE..........................949 809-3388
Carl F McLarand, *CEO*
Tim Beuchat, *Partner*
Kristine Calixto, *Partner*
Leila Fontaine, *Partner*
Lori Ichisaka, *Partner*
EMP: 60
SQ FT: 22,000
SALES (est): 13.3MM **Privately Held**
WEB: www.mve-architects.com
SIC: 8712 Architectural engineering

(P-26098)
NADEL INC (PA)
1990 S Bundy Dr Ste 400, Los Angeles
(90025-5243)
PHONE..........................310 826-2100
Herbert Nadel, *CEO*
David Jacobson, *Vice Pres*
Dale Yonkin, *Exec Dir*
Susan Adams, *Executive Asst*
Mario Gonzalez, *Project Mgr*
EMP: 55
SQ FT: 29,000
SALES (est): 11MM **Privately Held**
SIC: 8712 Architectural engineering

(P-26099)
NBBJ LP
523 W 6th St Ste 300, Los Angeles
(90014-1227)
PHONE..........................213 243-3333
Brenda Clark, *Manager*
EMP: 50
SALES (corp-wide): 118.9MM **Privately Held**
SIC: 8712 7389 Architectural services; in-
terior design services
PA: Nbbj Lp
223 Yale Ave N
Seattle WA 98109
206 223-5555

(P-26100)
NEWMA GARRIS GILMO + PARTNE I
3100 Bristol St Ste 400, Costa Mesa
(92626-7333)
PHONE..........................949 756-0818
Kevin Newman, *Chairman*
Donald J Meeks, *President*
Jacob Lesic, *Project Mgr*
Jeffrey Marquez, *Project Mgr*
Marianne Peffer, *Accounting Mgr*
EMP: 70 EST: 1974
SQ FT: 7,000
SALES (est): 7.7MM **Privately Held**
WEB: www.nggpartners.com
SIC: 8712 Architectural engineering

(P-26101)
NICHOLS MELBURG ROSSETTO ASSOC (PA)
Also Called: Nmr Design
300 Knollcrest Dr, Redding (96002-0104)
PHONE..................530 222-3300
Gene Nichols, *President*
Dan Rossetto, *Treasurer*
Kyle Matti, *Architect*
EMP: 50
SQ FT: 4,000
SALES (est): 7.9MM **Privately Held**
SIC: 8712 8711 Architectural engineering; structural engineering

(P-26102)
OEL/HHH INC
1833 Victory Blvd, Glendale (91201-2557)
PHONE..................818 246-6050
Fax: 818 240-0430
EMP: 80 EST: 1978
SQ FT: 20,000
SALES (est): 4.5MM **Privately Held**
WEB: www.lhaarchitects.com
SIC: 8712

(P-26103)
RATCLIFF ARCHITECTS
5856 Doyle St, Emeryville (94608-2520)
PHONE..................510 899-6400
Dan Wetherell, *President*
Scott Haney, *COO*
David Dersch, *CFO*
Joseph Nicola, *Business Dir*
Alfred Jacobs, *Practice Mgr*
EMP: 58
SQ FT: 20,000
SALES (est): 11.7MM **Privately Held**
WEB: www.ratcliffarch.com
SIC: 8712 Architectural engineering

(P-26104)
RBB ARCHITECTS INC (PA)
10980 Wilshire Blvd, Los Angeles (90024-3944)
PHONE..................310 479-1473
Joseph A Balbona, *CEO*
Deneys Purcell, *President*
Tarmo Pellon, *Sr Corp Ofcr*
Kevin Boots, *Senior VP*
Arthur E Border, *Senior VP*
EMP: 54
SQ FT: 15,837
SALES (est): 9.1MM **Privately Held**
WEB: www.rbbinc.com
SIC: 8712 Architectural engineering

(P-26105)
RDC-S111 INC (PA)
Also Called: Perkowitz & Ruth Architects
245 E 3rd St, Long Beach (90802)
PHONE..................562 628-8000
Simon Perkowitz, *President*
Steven J Ruth, *Vice Pres*
Renee Barot, *Business Dir*
Miguel Avila, *Project Mgr*
Danelle R Plunkett, *Human Res Dir*
EMP: 86
SALES (est): 21.5MM **Privately Held**
SIC: 8712 Architectural engineering

(P-26106)
RRM DESIGN GROUP (PA)
3765 S Higuera St Ste 102, San Luis Obispo (93401-1577)
PHONE..................805 439-0442
Victor Montgomery, *Ch of Bd*
John Wilbanks, *President*
Keith Gurnee, *Senior VP*
Erik P Justesen, *Principal*
EMP: 99
SQ FT: 23,000
SALES (est): 20.5MM **Privately Held**
WEB: www.rrmdesign.com
SIC: 8712 Architectural engineering

(P-26107)
SKIDMORE OWINGS & MERRILL LLP
1 Front St Ste 2500, San Francisco (94111-5332)
PHONE..................415 981-1555
Gene Schnair, *Partner*
Craig W Hartman, *Partner*
John Kriken, *Partner*

Danielle McGuire, *Project Mgr*
EMP: 240
SALES (corp-wide): 117.2MM **Privately Held**
SIC: 8712 Architectural engineering
PA: Skidmore, Owings & Merrill Llp
224 S Michigan Ave # 1000
Chicago IL 60604
312 554-9090

(P-26108)
SKIDMORE OWINGS & MERRILL LLP
10100 Santa Monica Blvd, Beverly Hills (90210)
PHONE..................310 651-9924
Michael Mann, *Manager*
EMP: 228
SALES (corp-wide): 117.2MM **Privately Held**
SIC: 8712 Architectural engineering
PA: Skidmore, Owings & Merrill Llp
224 S Michigan Ave # 1000
Chicago IL 60604
312 554-9090

(P-26109)
SKIDMORE OWINGS & MERRILL LLP
555 W 5th St Fl 30, Los Angeles (90013-1048)
PHONE..................213 996-8366
Jeffrey McCarthy, *Partner*
EMP: 228
SALES (corp-wide): 117.2MM **Privately Held**
SIC: 8712 Architectural engineering
PA: Skidmore, Owings & Merrill Llp
224 S Michigan Ave # 1000
Chicago IL 60604
312 554-9090

(P-26110)
SMITHGROUP INC
301 Battery St, San Francisco (94111-3236)
PHONE..................415 227-0100
Marleen Tavassoli, *Office Mgr*
EMP: 100
SALES (corp-wide): 256.6MM **Privately Held**
SIC: 8712 Architectural engineering
HQ: Smithgroup, Inc.
1700 New York Ave Nw # 100
Washington DC 20006
602 265-2200

(P-26111)
SMITHGROUP INC
Also Called: Smithgroupjjr
301 Battery St Fl 7, San Francisco (94111-3237)
PHONE..................313 442-8351
Michael Medici, *President*
EMP: 146
SALES (corp-wide): 256.6MM **Privately Held**
WEB: www.dc.smithgroup.com
SIC: 8712 Architectural engineering
HQ: Smithgroup, Inc.
1700 New York Ave Nw # 100
Washington DC 20006
602 265-2200

(P-26112)
STANTEC ARCHITECTURE INC
38 Technology Dr, Irvine (92618-5310)
PHONE..................949 923-6000
Eric Nielsen, *Vice Pres*
Cherri Stolz, *Human Res Mgr*
Therese Patron, *Senior Buyer*
Marika Harris, *Purch Agent*
Lori Van Dermark, *Marketing Staff*
EMP: 117
SALES (corp-wide): 4B **Privately Held**
SIC: 8712 8711 4111 Architectural services; engineering services; local & suburban transit
HQ: Stantec Architecture Inc.
224 S Michigan Ave # 1400
Chicago IL 60604
336 714-7413

(P-26113)
STANTEC ARCHITECTURE INC
300 N Lake Ave Ste 400, Pasadena (91101-4169)
PHONE..................626 796-9141
Simon Bluestone, *Branch Mgr*
EMP: 88
SALES (corp-wide): 4B **Privately Held**
SIC: 8712 Architectural services
HQ: Stantec Architecture Inc.
224 S Michigan Ave # 1400
Chicago IL 60604
336 714-7413

(P-26114)
STANTEC CONSULTING SVCS INC
3875 Atherton Rd, Rocklin (95765-3716)
PHONE..................916 773-8100
Charles Bunker, *Manager*
Shawn Labanowski, *Senior Engr*
Lori Van Dermark, *Marketing Staff*
EMP: 60
SALES (corp-wide): 4B **Privately Held**
SIC: 8712 8711 Architectural services; engineering services
HQ: Stantec Consulting Services Inc.
475 5th Ave Fl 12
New York NY 10017
212 352-5160

(P-26115)
STANTEC CONSULTING SVCS INC
38 Technology Dr Ste 100, Irvine (92618-5312)
PHONE..................949 923-6000
Bob Gomes, *Manager*
Annette Dimaggio, *Administration*
Susan Reid, *Project Engr*
Lori Van Dermark, *Marketing Staff*
EMP: 117
SALES (corp-wide): 4B **Privately Held**
WEB: www.keithco.com
SIC: 8712 8711 Architectural services; engineering services
HQ: Stantec Consulting Services Inc.
475 5th Ave Fl 12
New York NY 10017
212 352-5160

(P-26116)
STEINBERG ARCHITECTS (PA)
Also Called: Steinberg Group Architects
125 S Market St Ste 110, San Jose (95113-2210)
PHONE..................408 295-5446
David Hart, *President*
Robert Steinberg, *Ch of Bd*
Hong Chen, *COO*
Isaac Zamora, *CFO*
Ernest Yamana, *Treasurer*
EMP: 91 EST: 1953
SQ FT: 14,000
SALES (est): 15MM **Privately Held**
WEB: www.tsgarch.com
SIC: 8712 Architectural engineering

(P-26117)
STV ARCHITECTS INC
1055 W 7th St Ste 3150, Los Angeles (90017-2556)
PHONE..................213 482-9444
Wagih Andraos, *Manager*
EMP: 60
SALES (corp-wide): 301MM **Privately Held**
WEB: www.stvinc.com
SIC: 8712 8742 8711 Architectural engineering; transportation consultant; consulting engineer
HQ: Stv Architects Inc
205 W Welsh Dr
Douglassville PA 19518
610 385-8200

(P-26118)
WALTER J CONN & ASSOCIATES
Also Called: Charleston Company
800 W 6th St Ste 600, Los Angeles (90017-2709)
PHONE..................213 683-0500
Walter J Conn, *Partner*
Sally K Conn, *Partner*

EMP: 60
SALES (est): 6.7MM **Privately Held**
WEB: www.charlestoncompany.com
SIC: 8712 Architectural services

(P-26119)
WARE MALCOMB (PA)
10 Edelman, Irvine (92618-4312)
PHONE..................949 660-9128
Lawrence R Armstrong, *CEO*
Tobin Sloane, *CFO*
Jay Todisco, *Exec VP*
Kenneth Wink, *Exec VP*
Matthew Brady, *Vice Pres*
EMP: 137
SQ FT: 22,000
SALES (est): 90.3MM **Privately Held**
SIC: 8712 7336 8711 7389 Architectural engineering; commercial art & graphic design; civil engineering; interior design services; design, commercial & industrial

(P-26120)
WD PARTNERS INC
16808 Armstrong Ave # 100, Irvine (92606-8278)
PHONE..................949 753-7676
Christopher Doerschlag, *President*
EMP: 50
SALES (est): 2.3MM **Privately Held**
SIC: 8712 Architectural engineering

(P-26121)
WILL PERKINS INC
617 W 7th St Fl 12, Los Angeles (90017-3807)
PHONE..................213 270-8400
Gabriella Bullock, *Principal*
Phyllis Dubinsky, *Principal*
Shawn Bullock, *Human Res Mgr*
Merv Burnett, *Sr Associate*
EMP: 129
SALES (corp-wide): 552MM **Privately Held**
SIC: 8712 Architectural services
HQ: Will Perkins Inc
1250 24th St Nw Ste 800
Washington DC 20037

(P-26122)
WILL PERKINS INC
2 Bryant St Ste 300, San Francisco (94105-1641)
PHONE..................415 856-3000
Russ Drinker, *Branch Mgr*
Tyrone Marshall, *Manager*
EMP: 60
SALES (corp-wide): 552MM **Privately Held**
SIC: 8712 Architectural services
HQ: Will Perkins Inc
1250 24th St Nw Ste 800
Washington DC 20037

(P-26123)
WILLIAM HZMLHLCH ARCHTECTS INC
2850 Redhill Ave Ste 200, Santa Ana (92705-5543)
PHONE..................949 250-0607
William Hezmalhalch, *CEO*
Katrina Chase, *Planning*
Brian Crooker, *Info Tech Mgr*
Jeffrey Chouinard, *Project Mgr*
Jorge Garcia, *Project Mgr*
EMP: 75
SALES (est): 14MM **Privately Held**
SIC: 8712 Architectural engineering

(P-26124)
WIMBERLY ALLISON TONG GOO INC
Also Called: Watg
300 Spectrum Center Dr # 500, Irvine (92618-4925)
PHONE..................949 574-8500
Monica Cuervo, *Managing Dir*
EMP: 100
SQ FT: 63
SALES (est): 5.4MM
SALES (corp-wide): 39.1MM **Privately Held**
SIC: 8712 Architectural services

▲ = Import ▼=Export
◆ =Import/Export

PA: Wimberly Allison Tong & Goo, Inc.
700 Bishop St Ste 800
Honolulu HI 96813
808 521-8888

(P-26125)
ZIMMER GUNSUL
Also Called: Zimmer Gnsul Frsca Partnr Amer
515 S Flower St Ste 3700, Los Angeles
(90071-2221)
PHONE..........................213 617-1901
Rachel Morris, *Manager*
Nicholas Awori, *Partner*
Brett Meyer, *Partner*
Rachell J Morris, *Executive*
Nolan Lienhart, *Planning*
EMP: 63
SALES (corp-wide): 67MM **Privately Held**
SIC: 8712 7389 Architectural services; interior designer
PA: Zimmer Gunsul Frasca Architects Llp
1223 Sw Washington St # 200
Portland OR 97205
503 224-3860

8713 Surveying Services

(P-26126)
ADVANCED DCUMENT SOLUTIONS INC (PA)
24307 Magic Mountain Pkwy, Valencia
(91355-3402)
PHONE..........................661 251-0337
Michael Hawley, *President*
Michael Brown, *CFO*
EMP: 50
SALES (est): 2.9MM **Privately Held**
WEB: www.adocsolution.com
SIC: 8713 5045 ; computer software

(P-26127)
ANDREGG GEOMATICS
11661 Blocker Dr Ste 200, Auburn
(95603-4649)
PHONE..........................530 885-7072
Dennis Meyer, *President*
Mark Bardakjian, *COO*
Christine Johnson, *Admin Sec*
Michelle Bengston, *Controller*
EMP: 65
SALES: 4.5MM **Privately Held**
WEB: www.andregg.com
SIC: 8713 Surveying services

(P-26128)
CANNON CORPORATION (PA)
1050 Southwood Dr, San Luis Obispo
(93401-5813)
PHONE..........................805 544-7407
Michael F Cannon, *CEO*
Steve Tomasetti, *CFO*
John Evans, *Vice Pres*
Daniel Hutchinson, *Vice Pres*
Liz Jaeger, *Business Dir*
EMP: 60
SQ FT: 4,200
SALES (est): 17.5MM **Privately Held**
WEB: www.cannoncorp.us
SIC: 8713 8711 1611 Surveying services; civil engineering; highway & street construction

(P-26129)
F3 AND ASSOCIATES INC (PA)
701 E H St, Benicia (94510-3567)
P.O. Box 5099, Petaluma (94955-5099)
PHONE..........................707 748-4300
Fred Feickert, *President*
Gene Feickert, *Partner*
Sean Finn, *Partner*
EMP: 70
SALES: 13MM **Privately Held**
WEB: www.f3-inc.com
SIC: 8713 Surveying services

(P-26130)
HUITT - ZOLLARS INC
2603 Main St Ste 400, Irvine (92614-4250)
PHONE..........................949 988-5815
Mark Harlinger, *Manager*
Remi Candaele, *Engineer*
EMP: 50

SALES (corp-wide): 65.9MM **Privately Held**
WEB: www.huitt-zollars.com
SIC: 8713 8711 Surveying services; consulting engineer
PA: Huitt - Zollars, Inc.
1717 Mckinney Ave # 1400
Dallas TX 75202
214 871-3311

(P-26131)
KIER & WRIGHT CIVIL ENGRS&SRVY
2850 Collier Canyon Rd, Livermore
(94551-9201)
PHONE..........................925 245-8788
Tony McCants, *Manager*
EMP: 50
SALES (est): 6.6MM
SALES (corp-wide): 12.1MM **Privately Held**
WEB: www.kierwright.com
SIC: 8713 8711 Surveying services; civil engineering
PA: Kier & Wright Civil Engineers & Surveyors Inc
3350 Scott Blvd Bldg 22
Santa Clara CA 95054
408 727-6665

(P-26132)
PSOMAS
Also Called: Bonterra Psomas
3 Hutton Cntre Dr Ste 200, Santa Ana
(92707)
PHONE..........................714 751-7373
Ryan McLean, *Manager*
Joan Kelly, *Vice Pres*
EMP: 125
SALES (corp-wide): 95.2MM **Privately Held**
SIC: 8713 8711 Surveying services; consulting engineer
PA: Psomas
555 S Flower St Ste 4300
Los Angeles CA 90071
213 223-1400

(P-26133)
PSOMAS
14369 Park Ave Ste 101b, Victorville
(92392-2392)
PHONE..........................760 843-5700
John Thornton, *Vice Pres*
Steve Gregerson, *Vice Pres*
Ken Stram, *Vice Pres*
EMP: 50
SALES (corp-wide): 95.2MM **Privately Held**
SIC: 8713 8711 Surveying services; construction & civil engineering
PA: Psomas
555 S Flower St Ste 4300
Los Angeles CA 90071
213 223-1400

(P-26134)
PSOMAS (PA)
555 S Flower St Ste 4300, Los Angeles
(90071-2405)
PHONE..........................213 223-1400
Ryan McLean, *President*
Reuben Tolentino, *Vice Pres*
Sean P Vargas, *Vice Pres*
Vinh Huynh, *Administration*
Antonio Perez, *Administration*
EMP: 125
SQ FT: 30,000
SALES (est): 95.2MM **Privately Held**
SIC: 8713 8711 Surveying services; engineering services

(P-26135)
SANDIS CIVIL ENGINEERS (PA)
1700 Winchester Blvd, Campbell
(95008-1163)
P.O. Box 640, Mountain View (94042-0640)
PHONE..........................408 636-0900
Ken Olcott, *President*
Tony Brubaker, *Treasurer*
Jeff Setera, *Vice Pres*
Nicole Nagatani, *Office Mgr*
Carly Kalkoffen, *Admin Asst*
EMP: 61 **EST:** 1965
SQ FT: 12,000

SALES (est): 15MM **Privately Held**
SIC: 8713 8711 Surveying services; civil engineering

(P-26136)
STANTEC CONSULTING SVCS INC
111 E Victoria St, Santa Barbara
(93101-2018)
PHONE..........................805 963-9532
Lori Van Dermark, *Marketing Staff*
EMP: 55
SALES (corp-wide): 4B **Privately Held**
WEB: www.penfieldsmith.com
SIC: 8713 Surveying services
HQ: Stantec Consulting Services Inc.
475 5th Ave Fl 12
New York NY 10017
212 352-5160

(P-26137)
STANTEC ENERGY & RESOURCES INC (DH)
5500 Ming Ave Ste 300, Bakersfield
(93309-4627)
PHONE..........................661 396-3770
Robert Gomes, *President*
Richard Allen, *COO*
Daniel Lefaivre, *Treasurer*
Kirk Morrison, *Exec VP*
Paul Alpern, *Senior VP*
EMP: 182 **EST:** 2015
SALES (est): 9.8MM
SALES (corp-wide): 4B **Privately Held**
SIC: 8713 Surveying services
HQ: Stantec Holdings (Delaware) Iii Inc.
5500 Ming Ave Ste 300
Bakersfield CA 93309
661 396-3770

8721 Accounting, Auditing & Bookkeeping Svcs

(P-26138)
AAA ACCOUNTING SERVICES
2 Enterprise Apt 1211, Aliso Viejo
(92656-7128)
PHONE..........................949 791-7368
Frazier Shayla, *CEO*
EMP: 99
SALES (est): 1.8MM **Privately Held**
SIC: 8721 Auditing services

(P-26139)
ABBOTT STRINGHAM AN
1530 Meridian Ave 2, San Jose
(95125-5350)
PHONE..........................408 377-8700
Morgan Lynch, *President*
Ray Scheaffer, *President*
Franceen Borrillo, *Principal*
Bill Melton, *Principal*
Todd Robinson, *Principal*
EMP: 60
SALES (est): 6.7MM **Privately Held**
WEB: www.aslcpa.com
SIC: 8721 Accounting services, except auditing; certified public accountant

(P-26140)
ACCOUNTANTS 4 CONTRACT
235 Montgomery St Ste 630, San Francisco
(94104-2922)
PHONE..........................415 781-8644
Daniel M Maisler, *CEO*
EMP: 80
SQ FT: 2,300
SALES (est): 7.2MM **Privately Held**
SIC: 8721 Accounting, auditing & bookkeeping

(P-26141)
ACCRETIVE SOLUTIONS INC (HQ)
17101 Armstrong Ave # 100, Irvine
(92614-5742)
PHONE..........................312 994-4600
Kerry Barrett, *CEO*
Jonathan Rosenthal, *Ch of Bd*
Joann Lilek, *CFO*
Richard A Moran, *Vice Ch Bd*
Mike Reinecke, *Exec VP*
EMP: 1000

SALES (est): 34.2MM **Publicly Held**
SIC: 8721 Accounting, auditing & bookkeeping

(P-26142)
AGRI VALLEY SERVICES
1532 N West Ave, Fresno (93728-1306)
PHONE..........................559 253-0104
Carmalee Kossaras, *Owner*
EMP: 100
SALES (est): 2.7MM **Privately Held**
SIC: 8721 7363 Payroll accounting service; labor resource services

(P-26143)
ARMANDO C IBARRA CPA
371 E St, Chula Vista (91910-2615)
PHONE..........................619 422-1348
Armando C Ibarra Sr, *President*
Oscar Ibarra, *Corp Secy*
Armando C Ibarra Jr, *Vice Pres*
Greetings Ibarra, *CPA*
EMP: 60
SALES (est): 2.2MM **Privately Held**
SIC: 8721 7291 Accounting services, except auditing; tax return preparation services

(P-26144)
ARMANINO LLP
11766 Wilshire Blvd Fl 9, Los Angeles
(90025-6548)
PHONE..........................310 478-4148
EMP: 150
SALES (corp-wide): 77.8MM **Privately Held**
SIC: 8721 Certified public accountant
PA: Armanino Llp
12657 Alcosta Blvd # 500
San Ramon CA 94583
925 790-2600

(P-26145)
ARMANINO LLP (PA)
12657 Alcosta Blvd # 500, San Ramon
(94583-4406)
PHONE..........................925 790-2600
Andy Armanino, *Managing Prtnr*
Linda Antonelli, *Partner*
Esther Ratterree, *Partner*
Terri Temkin, *Auditing Mgr*
Bill Brause, *Auditor*
EMP: 160
SQ FT: 5,500
SALES (est): 77.8MM **Privately Held**
WEB: www.amllp.com
SIC: 8721 8742 Certified public accountant; management consulting services

(P-26146)
BARTLETT PRINGLE & WOLF LLP
1123 Chapala St Ste 300, Santa Barbara
(93101-3163)
PHONE..........................805 564-2103
Robert Maloy, *General Ptnr*
Mike Woods, *Managing Prtnr*
Tina Benavides, *Executive Asst*
Karin Durflinger, *Executive Asst*
Stacey Foley, *Auditing Mgr*
EMP: 50
SALES (est): 5.2MM **Privately Held**
SIC: 8721 Certified public accountant

(P-26147)
BDO USA LLP
1 Bush St Fl 18, San Francisco
(94104-4424)
PHONE..........................415 397-7900
Doug Hart, *Managing Prtnr*
Terry Lloyd, *Partner*
Peter Meeks, *Partner*
Suzanna Musick, *Partner*
EMP: 150
SQ FT: 1,500
SALES (corp-wide): 1.2B **Privately Held**
WEB: www.bdo.com
SIC: 8721 Accounting, auditing & bookkeeping
PA: Bdo Usa, Llp
330 N Wabash Ave Ste 3200
Chicago IL 60611
312 240-1236

(P-26148)
BDO USA LLP
3570 Carmel Mountain Rd # 400, San Diego (92130-6767)
PHONE....................858 404-9200
Lee Duran, *Managing Prtnr*
Pamela Holden, *Director*
EMP: 78
SALES (corp-wide): 1.2B **Privately Held**
SIC: 8721 Certified public accountant
PA: Bdo Usa, Llp
    330 N Wabash Ave Ste 3200
    Chicago IL 60611
    312 240-1236

(P-26149)
BDO USA LLP
300 Park Ave Ste 900, San Jose (95110-2839)
PHONE....................408 278-0220
Elliot Binder, *Managing Prtnr*
EMP: 60
SALES (corp-wide): 1.2B **Privately Held**
WEB: www.bdo.com
SIC: 8721 Certified public accountant
PA: Bdo Usa, Llp
    330 N Wabash Ave Ste 3200
    Chicago IL 60611
    312 240-1236

(P-26150)
BDO USA LLP
600 Anton Blvd Ste 500, Costa Mesa (92626-7167)
PHONE....................714 957-3200
Kristen McCarthy, *Managing Prtnr*
Alan Whiley, *Sr Associate*
EMP: 65
SALES (corp-wide): 1.2B **Privately Held**
WEB: www.bdo.com
SIC: 8721 Accounting, auditing & bookkeeping
PA: Bdo Usa, Llp
    330 N Wabash Ave Ste 3200
    Chicago IL 60611
    312 240-1236

(P-26151)
BMS PARENT INC (PA)
1220 Dewey Way Ste F, Upland (91786-1101)
PHONE....................909 981-2341
John Wallace, *CEO*
Barbara Gillet, *Vice Pres*
EMP: 68
SQ FT: 9,000
SALES (est): 12MM **Privately Held**
WEB: www.bmsreimbursement.com
SIC: 8721 5045 Billing & bookkeeping service; computer software

(P-26152)
BROWN ARMSTRONG ACCNTANCY CORP
Also Called: Brown Armstrong Cpas
4200 Truxtun Ave Ste 300, Bakersfield (93309-0668)
PHONE....................661 324-4971
Andrew J Paulden, *President*
Benjamin P Reyes, *Corp Secy*
Christina M Thornburgh, *Corp Secy*
Burton H Armstrong, *Vice Pres*
Diana H Branthoover, *Vice Pres*
EMP: 65
SQ FT: 30,000
SALES (est): 8MM **Privately Held**
WEB: www.bacpas.com
SIC: 8721 Accounting services, except auditing

(P-26153)
BURR PILGER MAYER
110 Stony Point Rd # 210, Santa Rosa (95401-4118)
PHONE....................707 544-4078
Carolyn Amster, *Principal*
Daniel Bachrach, *Manager*
Cris Passaro, *Manager*
EMP: 63
SALES (corp-wide): 49.6MM **Privately Held**
SIC: 8721 Certified public accountant
PA: Mayer Pilger Burr
    600 California St Fl 6
    San Francisco CA 94108
    415 421-5757

(P-26154)
BURR PILGER MAYER (PA)
600 California St Fl 6, San Francisco (94108-2733)
PHONE....................415 421-5757
James Wallace, *CEO*
Robert Houston, *Shareholder*
Diana Borova, *Officer*
Pat Karmin, *Office Mgr*
Jeannie Benton, *Admin Asst*
EMP: 110
SQ FT: 20,824
SALES (est): 49.6MM **Privately Held**
SIC: 8721 Certified public accountant

(P-26155)
BURR PILGER MAYER INC
60 S Market St Ste 800, San Jose (95113-2340)
PHONE....................408 961-6355
Mark Loveless, *Manager*
Brenda Espinosa, *QC Mgr*
EMP: 50
SALES (corp-wide): 49.6MM **Privately Held**
SIC: 8721 Certified public accountant
PA: Mayer Pilger Burr
    600 California St Fl 6
    San Francisco CA 94108
    415 421-5757

(P-26156)
BURR PILGER MAYER INC
2000 University Ave, East Palo Alto (94303-2214)
PHONE....................650 855-6800
Mark Loveless, *Branch Mgr*
EMP: 50
SALES (corp-wide): 49.6MM **Privately Held**
SIC: 8721 Certified public accountant
PA: Mayer Pilger Burr
    600 California St Fl 6
    San Francisco CA 94108
    415 421-5757

(P-26157)
C D PAYROLL INC
2300 W Empire Ave, Burbank (91504-3341)
PHONE....................818 848-1562
Ed Spietel, *President*
Ed Spiegel, *President*
EMP: 60
SQ FT: 12,000
SALES (est): 2.8MM
SALES (corp-wide): 63.9MM **Privately Held**
SIC: 8721 Payroll accounting service
PA: Cast & Crew Payroll, Llc
    2300 W Empire Ave # 500
    Burbank CA 91504
    818 848-6022

(P-26158)
CALSTARS
915 L St Fl 7, Sacramento (95814-3705)
PHONE....................916 445-0211
Freda Luan-Dun, *Co-Owner*
Chris Cox, *Director*
EMP: 50
SALES (est): 1.3MM **Privately Held**
SIC: 8721 Accounting, auditing & bookkeeping

(P-26159)
CAST & CREW PAYROLL LLC (PA)
Also Called: Cast and Crew Entrmt Svcs
2300 W Empire Ave # 500, Burbank (91504-5399)
PHONE....................818 848-6022
Eric Belcher, *President*
Shardell Cavaliere, *President*
Sally Knutson, *CFO*
Andrew Patterson, *CTO*
EMP: 195
SQ FT: 12,000
SALES (est): 63.9MM **Privately Held**
SIC: 8721 Payroll accounting service

(P-26160)
CBIZ MAYOR HOFFMAN MECHAN (PA)
10616 Scripps Summit Ct, San Diego (92131-3966)
PHONE....................858 795-2000
Paul Nation, *President*
David Diamond, *Principal*
Robert Gellman, *Principal*
Steve Hermes, *Principal*
Greg Smith, *Principal*
EMP: 93 EST: 1976
SALES (est): 4.3MM **Privately Held**
WEB: www.nshd.com
SIC: 8721 8742 Certified public accountant; financial consultant

(P-26161)
CBIZMHM LLC
Also Called: Cks Business Services
5060 California Ave # 800, Bakersfield (93309-0728)
PHONE....................661 325-7500
Mark Luttrell, *President*
Dan Sprayberry, *Vice Pres*
Martin Goni, *Accountant*
EMP: 50
SALES (est): 3.6MM **Publicly Held**
SIC: 8721 Certified public accountant
PA: Cbiz, Inc.
    6050 Oak Tree Blvd # 500
    Cleveland OH 44131

(P-26162)
CERIDIAN LLC
1515 W 190th St Ste 100, Gardena (90248-4913)
PHONE....................310 719-7400
Chris Byers, *Branch Mgr*
Mary Berg, *Executive Asst*
Tiffany Hall, *Recruiter*
Steve Dougherty, *Accounts Exec*
Ramona Little, *Accounts Exec*
EMP: 60 **Privately Held**
WEB: www.ceridian.com
SIC: 8721 Payroll accounting service
HQ: Ceridian Llc
    3311 E Old Shakopee Rd
    Minneapolis MN 55425
    952 853-8100

(P-26163)
CERIDIAN TAX SERVICE INC
17390 Brookhurst St # 100, Fountain Valley (92708-3704)
P.O. Box 20805 (92728-0805)
PHONE....................714 963-1311
Webster Hill, *General Mgr*
Joshua Duston, *Engineer*
Bryan Odenwald, *Director*
Addie Brunskow, *Manager*
Diane Haskell, *Manager*
EMP: 300
SQ FT: 130,000
SALES (est): 20.3MM **Privately Held**
WEB: www.ceridian.com
SIC: 8721 Payroll accounting service
HQ: Ceridian Llc
    3311 E Old Shakopee Rd
    Minneapolis MN 55425
    952 853-8100

(P-26164)
CFGI LLC
600 California St Fl 14, San Francisco (94108-2709)
PHONE....................415 670-9041
Greg Lynch, *Manager*
EMP: 128
SALES (corp-wide): 9.7MM **Privately Held**
SIC: 8721 7291 Accounting, auditing & bookkeeping; tax return preparation services
PA: Cfgi, Llc
    99 High St Ste 3001
    Boston MA 02110
    617 531-8270

(P-26165)
CITY OF BERKELEY
Also Called: Police Department
2180 Milvia St, Berkeley (94704-1122)
PHONE....................510 981-6750
Doug Hambleton, *Chief*

EMP: 1500 **Privately Held**
WEB: www.berkeleycamps.com
SIC: 8721 Auditing services
PA: City Of Berkeley
    2120 Milvia St
    Berkeley CA 94704
    510 981-7300

(P-26166)
CLIFTONLARSONALLEN LLP
925 Highland Pointe Dr # 450, Roseville (95678-5427)
PHONE....................916 784-7800
EMP: 300
SALES (corp-wide): 755.1MM **Privately Held**
SIC: 8721 Certified public accountant
PA: Cliftonlarsonallen Llp
    220 S 6th St Ste 300
    Minneapolis MN 55402
    612 376-4500

(P-26167)
CLIFTONLARSONALLEN LLP
2210 E Route 66 Ste 100, Glendora (91740-4676)
PHONE....................626 857-7300
EMP: 55
SALES (corp-wide): 755.1MM **Privately Held**
SIC: 8721 Certified public accountant
PA: Cliftonlarsonallen Llp
    220 S 6th St Ste 300
    Minneapolis MN 55402
    612 376-4500

(P-26168)
CLIFTONLARSONALLEN LLP
Also Called: Nsbn
1925 Century Park E Fl 16, Los Angeles (90067-2701)
PHONE....................310 273-2501
Randy Wells, *Branch Mgr*
EMP: 91
SALES (corp-wide): 755.1MM **Privately Held**
SIC: 8721 Accounting services, except auditing
PA: Cliftonlarsonallen Llp
    220 S 6th St Ste 300
    Minneapolis MN 55402
    612 376-4500

(P-26169)
COHNREZNICK LLP
21600 Oxnard St Ste 700, Woodland Hills (91367-4900)
PHONE....................818 205-2600
Cott Sachs, *Office Mgr*
EMP: 59
SALES (corp-wide): 435.9MM **Privately Held**
SIC: 8721 Certified public accountant
PA: Cohnreznick Llp
    1301 Avenue Of The Americ
    New York NY 10019
    212 297-0400

(P-26170)
COHNREZNICK LLP
11755 Wilshire Blvd # 1700, Los Angeles (90025-1506)
PHONE....................310 477-3722
Thomas J Marino, *Branch Mgr*
EMP: 50
SALES (corp-wide): 435.9MM **Privately Held**
SIC: 8721 Certified public accountant
PA: Cohnreznick Llp
    1301 Avenue Of The Americ
    New York NY 10019
    212 297-0400

(P-26171)
COLLABRUS INC
Also Called: M Squared Consulting
111 Sutter St Ste 900, San Francisco (94104-4523)
PHONE....................415 288-1826
Alex Todd, *CEO*
Russel Orelowitz, *CFO*
EMP: 240
SQ FT: 8,000

SALES (est): 13.8MM
SALES (corp-wide): 43.3MM **Privately Held**
WEB: www.collabrusinc.com
SIC: 8721 Billing & bookkeeping service
HQ: M Squared Consulting, Inc.
    111 Sutter St Ste 900
    San Francisco CA 94104
    415 391-1038

(P-26172)
CONSIDINE & CONSIDINE AN ACCO
8989 Rio San Diego Dr # 250, San Diego
(92108-1646)
PHONE..................................619 231-1977
Perry S Wright, *CEO*
Timothy Considine, *President*
Jerry Hotz, *Treasurer*
Michael Boardman, *Vice Pres*
Don Bonk, *Vice Pres*
EMP: 80
SQ FT: 20,000
SALES (est): 8.1MM **Privately Held**
WEB: www.cccpa.com
SIC: 8721 Certified public accountant

(P-26173)
COUNTY OF LOS ANGELES
Also Called: Internal Services Department
1100 N Eastern Ave, Los Angeles
(90063-3200)
PHONE..................................323 267-2136
Scott Minnix, *Director*
EMP: 1800 **Privately Held**
SIC: 8721 Accounting, auditing & bookkeeping
PA: County Of Los Angeles
    500 W Temple St Ste 437
    Los Angeles CA 90012
    213 974-1101

(P-26174)
COUNTY OF SAN BERNARDINO
Also Called: Auditor Controller Department
222 W Hospitality Ln, San Bernardino
(92415-0013)
PHONE..................................909 386-8818
Larry Walker, *Principal*
A B Brand, *Controller*
EMP: 200
SQ FT: 12,700 **Privately Held**
SIC: 8721 9311 Auditing services; finance,
    taxation & monetary policy;
PA: County Of San Bernardino
    385 N Arrowhead Ave
    San Bernardino CA 92415
    909 387-3841

(P-26175)
COUNTY OF VENTURA
Auditor /controller
800 S Victoria Ave 1540, Ventura
(93009-0003)
PHONE..................................805 654-3152
Christine Cohens, *Manager*
EMP: 61 **Privately Held**
WEB: www.vcoe.org
SIC: 8721 9311 Auditing services; controllers' office, government;
PA: County Of Ventura
    800 S Victoria Ave
    Ventura CA 93009
    805 654-2644

(P-26176)
CROWE LLP
15233 Ventura Blvd Fl 9, Sherman Oaks
(91403-2250)
PHONE..................................818 501-5200
Ray Calvey, *Manager*
Mark Taylor, *Executive*
Jeffrey Fishel, *Managing Dir*
Charles Shureen, *Tax Mgr*
Sue Tomlinson, *CPA*
EMP: 120
SALES (corp-wide): 883.5MM **Privately Held**
SIC: 8721 Certified public accountant
PA: Crowe Llp
    225 W Wacker Ste 2600
    Chicago IL 60606
    312 899-7000

(P-26177)
DELOITTE & TOUCHE LLP
555 W 5th St Ste 2700, Los Angeles
(90013-1024)
PHONE..................................213 688-0800
Byron David, *Branch Mgr*
David N Bowen, *Partner*
Gary Smith, *Partner*
Terry Feit, *Admin Asst*
Maria Quintans, *Admin Asst*
EMP: 1000
SALES (corp-wide): 6.6B **Privately Held**
WEB: www.deloitte.com
SIC: 8721 Accounting services, except auditing
HQ: Deloitte & Touche Llp
    30 Rockefeller Plz # 4350
    New York NY 10112
    212 492-4000

(P-26178)
DELOITTE & TOUCHE LLP
655 W Broadway Ste 700, San Diego
(92101-8480)
PHONE..................................619 232-6500
Cathy Jennings, *Manager*
Theresa Drew, *Managing Prtnr*
Russell Gold, *Managing Prtnr*
Corey Litteken, *Exec VP*
Michelle Pham, *Technology*
EMP: 200
SALES (corp-wide): 6.6B **Privately Held**
WEB: www.deloitte.com
SIC: 8721 7291 Accounting, auditing & bookkeeping; tax return preparation services
HQ: Deloitte & Touche Llp
    30 Rockefeller Plz # 4350
    New York NY 10112
    212 492-4000

(P-26179)
DELOITTE & TOUCHE LLP
695 Town Center Dr # 1200, Costa Mesa
(92626-7188)
PHONE..................................714 436-7419
Bob Grant, *Director*
Jeffrey D Egertson, *Partner*
Scott Ferguson, *Partner*
Vito Francone, *Partner*
Curtis Hildt, *Partner*
EMP: 700
SALES (corp-wide): 6.6B **Privately Held**
WEB: www.deloitte.com
SIC: 8721 7291 Accounting services, except auditing; tax return preparation services
HQ: Deloitte & Touche Llp
    30 Rockefeller Plz # 4350
    New York NY 10112
    212 492-4000

(P-26180)
DELOITTE & TOUCHE LLP
555 Mission St Ste 1400, San Francisco
(94105-0942)
PHONE..................................415 783-4000
Mark Edmonds, *Branch Mgr*
Mike Deverell, *Principal*
David Gully, *Principal*
Mack Schwing, *Principal*
EMP: 350
SALES (corp-wide): 6.6B **Privately Held**
WEB: www.deloitte.com
SIC: 8721 Accounting services, except auditing
HQ: Deloitte & Touche Llp
    30 Rockefeller Plz # 4350
    New York NY 10112
    212 492-4000

(P-26181)
DELOITTE & TOUCHE LLP
225 W Santa Clara St # 600, San Jose
(95113-1728)
PHONE..................................408 704-4000
Jonathan Tharmapalan, *Manager*
EMP: 450
SALES (corp-wide): 6.6B **Privately Held**
WEB: www.deloitte.com
SIC: 8721 8742 6282 Certified public accountant; management consulting services; investment advice

HQ: Deloitte & Touche Llp
    30 Rockefeller Plz # 4350
    New York NY 10112
    212 492-4000

(P-26182)
DELOITTE & TOUCHE LLP
5250 N Palm Ave Ste 300, Fresno
(93704-2200)
PHONE..................................559 449-6300
Nada Barrett, *Branch Mgr*
Alicia Sierra, *Auditor*
Maria Torre, *Training Spec*
Tyler Thalken, *Assistant*
Vincent Paganetti, *Consultant*
EMP: 70
SALES (corp-wide): 6.6B **Privately Held**
WEB: www.deloitte.com
SIC: 8721 Certified public accountant
HQ: Deloitte & Touche Llp
    30 Rockefeller Plz # 4350
    New York NY 10112
    212 492-4000

(P-26183)
DELOITTE & TOUCHE LLP
6210 Stoneridge Mall Rd, Pleasanton
(94588-3268)
PHONE..................................415 782-4020
EMP: 244
SALES (corp-wide): 6.6B **Privately Held**
SIC: 8721 Certified public accountant
HQ: Deloitte & Touche Llp
    30 Rockefeller Plz # 4350
    New York NY 10112
    212 492-4000

(P-26184)
DELOITTE & TOUCHE LLP
555 W 5th St Ste 2700, Los Angeles
(90013-1024)
PHONE..................................213 688-0800
EMP: 244
SALES (corp-wide): 12.3B **Privately Held**
SIC: 8721
HQ: Deloitte & Touche Llp
    30 Rockefeller Plz # 4350
    New York NY 10112
    212 492-4000

(P-26185)
DELOITTE TAX LLP
555 Mission St Ste 1400, San Francisco
(94105-0942)
PHONE..................................415 783-4000
Mark Edmunds, *Branch Mgr*
Carolyn Andrews, *Partner*
Douglas Hansen, *Partner*
Edward Harrison, *Partner*
Lyn Nicholson, *Admin Asst*
EMP: 294
SALES (corp-wide): 6.6B **Privately Held**
SIC: 8721 Auditing services; certified public accountant
HQ: Deloitte Tax Llp
    30 Rockefeller Plz
    New York NY 10112
    212 492-4000

(P-26186)
DELOITTE TAX LLP
225 W Santa Clara St # 600, San Jose
(95113-1728)
PHONE..................................408 704-4000
Garrett Herbert, *Partner*
Tom Dong, *Partner*
Dennis Fox, *Business Dir*
David Skvarna, *Managing Dir*
Prashanthi Gundu, *Admin Sec*
EMP: 294
SALES (corp-wide): 6.6B **Privately Held**
SIC: 8721 Auditing services; certified public accountant
HQ: Deloitte Tax Llp
    30 Rockefeller Plz
    New York NY 10112
    212 492-4000

(P-26187)
ECONA CORP
1344 Paizay Pl Unit 732, Chula Vista
(91913-3972)
P.O. Box 296, Alpine (91903-0296)
PHONE..................................619 722-6555
Branden B Moss, *CEO*
EMP: 50 EST: 2013

SALES (est): 1.8MM **Privately Held**
SIC: 8721 7389 Payroll accounting service;

(P-26188)
EDWARD E STRAINE CPA
1760 Creekside Oaks Dr, Sacramento
(95833-3632)
PHONE..................................916 646-6464
Edward E Straine, *Principal*
EMP: 60
SALES (est): 1.7MM **Privately Held**
SIC: 8721 Certified public accountant

(P-26189)
EGO INC
Also Called: Emergency Groups Office
444 E Huntington Dr # 300, Arcadia
(91006-6203)
PHONE..................................626 447-0296
Andrea Brault, *President*
Del Brault, *President*
Jane Brault, *Treasurer*
James Blakeman, *Senior VP*
Kevin Curran, *Recruiter*
EMP: 150
SQ FT: 8,500
SALES (est): 16.6MM **Privately Held**
SIC: 8721 Billing & bookkeeping service

(P-26190)
ENTERTAINMENT PARTNERS (PA)
2835 N Naomi St, Burbank (91504-2000)
PHONE..................................818 955-6000
Mark Goldstein, *CEO*
George Vaughan, *CFO*
Joseph Chianese, *Exec VP*
Ron Cogan, *Vice Pres*
Ginger Galloway, *Vice Pres*
EMP: 320
SQ FT: 38,000
SALES (est): 53.3MM **Privately Held**
WEB: www.epservices.com
SIC: 8721 Payroll accounting service

(P-26191)
ERNST & YOUNG LLP
Also Called: Ey
725 S Figueroa St Ste 200, Los Angeles
(90017-5403)
PHONE..................................213 977-3200
Jeff Kaufman, *Manager*
James Wang, *Partner*
Kevin Thoeng, *Technology*
Andrew Mokhov, *CPA*
Amy Cerna, *Personnel Assit*
EMP: 1000
SALES (corp-wide): 4.8B **Privately Held**
WEB: www.ey.com
SIC: 8721 8742 7291 Certified public accountant; auditing services; business consultant; management information systems consultant; tax return preparation services
PA: Ernst & Young Llp
    5 Times Sq Fl Conlv1
    New York NY 10036
    212 773-3000

(P-26192)
ERNST & YOUNG LLP
Also Called: Ey
200 N Pacific Coast Hwy # 2, El Segundo
(90245-4340)
PHONE..................................310 725-1764
Kristen Schmitt, *Branch Mgr*
EMP: 228
SALES (corp-wide): 4.8B **Privately Held**
SIC: 8721 Certified public accountant
PA: Ernst & Young Llp
    5 Times Sq Fl Conlv1
    New York NY 10036
    212 773-3000

(P-26193)
ERNST & YOUNG LLP
Also Called: Ey
560 Mission St Ste 1600, San Francisco
(94105-2990)
PHONE..................................415 894-8000
Michael Strachan, *Manager*
Gregory Martin, *Partner*
Eric Owiesny, *Partner*
Charles Reinhard, *Partner*
Monica Fox, *Business Dir*
EMP: 100

PRODUCTS & SVCS

SALES (corp-wide): 4.8B **Privately Held**
WEB: www.ey.com
SIC: 8721 8742 Accounting services, except auditing; management consulting services
PA: Ernst & Young Llp
5 Times Sq Fl Conlv1
New York NY 10036
212 773-3000

(P-26194)
ERNST & YOUNG LLP
Also Called: Ey
1451 California Ave, Palo Alto
(94304-1109)
PHONE..................650 496-1600
Alex Turco, *Branch Mgr*
Adam Barrow, *Auditor*
EMP: 230
SALES (corp-wide): 4.8B **Privately Held**
SIC: 8721 Certified public accountant
PA: Ernst & Young Llp
5 Times Sq Fl Conlv1
New York NY 10036
212 773-3000

(P-26195)
ERNST & YOUNG LLP
Also Called: Ey
303 Almaden Blvd Ste 1000, San Jose
(95110-2723)
PHONE..................408 947-5500
Teri Shaffer, *Partner*
Edwin Carrasquillo, *Partner*
Joseph E Hogan, *Partner*
Brian Outland, *Partner*
Dave Price, *Partner*
EMP: 650
SALES (corp-wide): 4.8B **Privately Held**
WEB: www.ey.com
SIC: 8721 8742 Certified public accountant; auditing services; business consultant; management information systems consultant
PA: Ernst & Young Llp
5 Times Sq Fl Conlv1
New York NY 10036
212 773-3000

(P-26196)
ERNST & YOUNG LLP
Also Called: Ey
4370 La Jolla Village Dr # 500, San Diego
(92122-1251)
PHONE..................858 535-7200
Michael J Hartnett, *Manager*
Riju Parakh, *Manager*
EMP: 135
SALES (corp-wide): 4.8B **Privately Held**
WEB: www.ey.com
SIC: 8721 8742 7291 Certified public accountant; auditing services; business consultant; management information systems consultant; tax return preparation services
PA: Ernst & Young Llp
5 Times Sq Fl Conlv1
New York NY 10036
212 773-3000

(P-26197)
ERNST & YOUNG LLP
Also Called: Ey
18101 Von Karman Ave # 1700, Irvine
(92612-1012)
PHONE..................949 794-2300
Linda Minx, *Office Mgr*
Chris Abston, *Partner*
Kathy Dagestino, *Partner*
Mike Denning, *Partner*
John F Fritz, *Partner*
EMP: 450
SALES (corp-wide): 4.8B **Privately Held**
WEB: www.ey.com
SIC: 8721 8742 Certified public accountant; auditing services; business consultant; management information systems consultant
PA: Ernst & Young Llp
5 Times Sq Fl Conlv1
New York NY 10036
212 773-3000

(P-26198)
ERNST & YOUNG LLP
Also Called: Ey
18006 Sky Park Cir # 106, Irvine
(92614-6406)
PHONE..................949 838-3300
Ted Esau, *Principal*
EMP: 228
SALES (corp-wide): 4.8B **Privately Held**
WEB: www.ey.com
SIC: 8721 Certified public accountant
PA: Ernst & Young Llp
5 Times Sq Fl Conlv1
New York NY 10036
212 773-3000

(P-26199)
ERNST & YOUNG LLP
Also Called: Ey
2931 Townsgate Rd Ste 100, Westlake Village (91361-5874)
PHONE..................805 778-7000
Brian Ladin, *Branch Mgr*
Glen Day, *Director*
EMP: 80
SALES (corp-wide): 4.8B **Privately Held**
WEB: www.ey.com
SIC: 8721 8742 8748 Certified public accountant; auditing services; business consultant; management information systems consultant; business consulting
PA: Ernst & Young Llp
5 Times Sq Fl Conlv1
New York NY 10036
212 773-3000

(P-26200)
ERNST & YOUNG LLP
Also Called: Ey
275 Shoreline Dr Ste 600, Redwood City
(94065-1493)
PHONE..................650 802-4500
Donna Frazer, *Branch Mgr*
Karen Birkmyre, *Info Tech Mgr*
Sunil Bhat, *Consultant*
EMP: 250
SALES (corp-wide): 4.8B **Privately Held**
WEB: www.ey.com
SIC: 8721 8742 Certified public accountant; auditing services; business consultant; management information systems consultant
PA: Ernst & Young Llp
5 Times Sq Fl Conlv1
New York NY 10036
212 773-3000

(P-26201)
ERNST & YOUNG LLP
Also Called: Ey
2901 Douglas Blvd Ste 300, Roseville
(95661-4247)
PHONE..................916 218-1900
Craig Pickett, *Manager*
EMP: 228
SALES (corp-wide): 4.8B **Privately Held**
WEB: www.ey.com
SIC: 8721 Certified public accountant; auditing services
PA: Ernst & Young Llp
5 Times Sq Fl Conlv1
New York NY 10036
212 773-3000

(P-26202)
ERNST & YOUNG LLP
Also Called: Ey
4301 Hacienda Dr Ste 450, Pleasanton
(94588-2791)
PHONE..................925 734-6388
Karen Amato, *Manager*
EMP: 228
SALES (corp-wide): 4.8B **Privately Held**
WEB: www.ey.com
SIC: 8721 Certified public accountant; auditing services
PA: Ernst & Young Llp
5 Times Sq Fl Conlv1
New York NY 10036
212 773-3000

(P-26203)
ERNST & YOUNG LLP
560 Mission St Ste 1600, San Francisco
(94105-0911)
PHONE..................415 894-8000
EMP: 700

SALES (corp-wide): 3B **Privately Held**
SIC: 8721
PA: Ernst & Young Llp
5 Times Sq Fl Conlv1
New York NY 10036
212 773-3000

(P-26204)
FILM PAYROLL SERVICES INC (PA)
Also Called: Quantos Payroll
500 S Sepulveda Blvd Fl 4, Los Angeles
(90049-3550)
PHONE..................310 440-9600
Gregory Pickert, *CEO*
EMP: 100
SQ FT: 5,000
SALES (est): 7.9MM **Privately Held**
SIC: 8721 Payroll accounting service

(P-26205)
FRANK RIMERMAN & CO LLP
1 Embarcadero Ctr # 2410, San Francisco
(94111-3628)
PHONE..................415 439-1144
Bryan Polster, *Managing Prtnr*
Robert Hoffman, *CPA*
Elaine Leung, *CPA*
Anne Macdonald, *CPA*
Karen Valladao, *CPA*
EMP: 62
SALES (corp-wide): 27.7MM **Privately Held**
SIC: 8721 Certified public accountant
PA: Frank, Rimerman & Co. Llp
1801 Page Mill Rd Ste 100
Palo Alto CA
650 845-8100

(P-26206)
GRANT THORNTON LLP
101 California St # 2700, San Francisco
(94111-5830)
PHONE..................415 986-3900
Jeff Pera, *Manager*
Laura Scheflow, *Director*
Orus Dearman, *Manager*
EMP: 70
SALES (corp-wide): 65MM **Privately Held**
WEB: www.gt.com
SIC: 8721 Accounting services, except auditing
HQ: Grant Thornton Llp
171 N Clark St Ste 200
Chicago IL 60601
312 856-0200

(P-26207)
GRANT THORNTON LLP
1000 Wilshire Blvd # 300, Los Angeles
(90017-2457)
PHONE..................213 627-1717
Mark Bagaason, *Manager*
Jim Hayden, *Principal*
Joe A Monti, *Principal*
EMP: 50
SALES (corp-wide): 65MM **Privately Held**
WEB: www.gt.com
SIC: 8721 8742 7291 Accounting services, except auditing; auditing services; management consulting services; tax return preparation services
HQ: Grant Thornton Llp
171 N Clark St Ste 200
Chicago IL 60601
312 856-0200

(P-26208)
GRANT THORNTON LLP
10 Almaden Blvd Ste 800, San Jose
(95113-2016)
PHONE..................408 275-9000
Harry Smith, *Branch Mgr*
Gary J Gemoll, *Managing Prtnr*
Bill Heppner, *Principal*
EMP: 50
SALES (corp-wide): 65MM **Privately Held**
WEB: www.gt.com
SIC: 8721 Certified public accountant
HQ: Grant Thornton Llp
171 N Clark St Ste 200
Chicago IL 60601
312 856-0200

(P-26209)
GRANT THORNTON LLP
515 S Flower St Ste 700, Los Angeles
(90071-2209)
PHONE..................213 627-1717
Don Dahl, *Manager*
Kevin La Roche, *Auditor*
EMP: 99
SALES (corp-wide): 65MM **Privately Held**
WEB: www.gt.com
SIC: 8721 Auditing services
HQ: Grant Thornton Llp
171 N Clark St Ste 200
Chicago IL 60601
312 856-0200

(P-26210)
GRANT THORNTON LLP
12220 El Camino Real, San Diego
(92130-2091)
PHONE..................858 704-8000
Don Williams,
Justin Fiore, *Manager*
EMP: 113
SALES (corp-wide): 65MM **Privately Held**
WEB: www.gt.com
SIC: 8721 Auditing services
HQ: Grant Thornton Llp
171 N Clark St Ste 200
Chicago IL 60601
312 856-0200

(P-26211)
GREEN HASSON & JANKS LLP
10990 Wilshire Blvd Fl 16, Los Angeles
(90024-3925)
PHONE..................310 873-1600
Leon Janks, *Partner*
William Cline, *CFO*
Melissa Rodriguez, *Executive Asst*
Drew Holoubek, *Manager*
EMP: 120
SQ FT: 22,000
SALES (est): 17.8MM **Privately Held**
WEB: www.ghjadvisors.com
SIC: 8721 Certified public accountant

(P-26212)
GROBSTEIN HORWATH & CO
Also Called: Grobstein, Horwath & Company
15233 Ventura Blvd Fl 9, Van Nuys
(91403-2250)
PHONE..................818 501-5200
Michael Grobstein, *Partner*
David Agler, *Partner*
Michael Fenstein, *Partner*
David Gottlieb, *Partner*
Jerry Levine, *Partner*
EMP: 70 **EST:** 1969
SQ FT: 11,000
SALES (est): 4.1MM **Privately Held**
WEB: www.horwathcal.com
SIC: 8721 Certified public accountant

(P-26213)
GURSEY SCHNEIDER & CO LLC (PA)
1888 Century Park E # 900, Los Angeles
(90067-1735)
PHONE..................310 552-0960
Stephan H Wasserman,
Hanieh Novian, *Executive Asst*
Rudy Fuentes, *Admin Asst*
Cameron Roberson, *Admin Asst*
Molly Warren, *Admin Asst*
EMP: 62
SQ FT: 12,000
SALES (est): 17.2MM **Privately Held**
SIC: 8721 Certified public accountant

(P-26214)
HAGEN STREIFF NEWTON OSHIRO
1990 N Calif Blvd Ste 320, Walnut Creek
(94596-3781)
PHONE..................925 941-1050
Mark Newton, *Partner*
EMP: 50
SALES (est): 1.3MM **Privately Held**
SIC: 8721 Certified public accountant

(P-26215)
HANSEN ICC LLC
2111 Palomar Airport Rd, Carlsbad
(92011-1418)
PHONE..........................760 268-7299
Guy Tennant, *General Mgr*
Ali Valinasab, *Software Engr*
EMP: 100
SQ FT: 8,016
SALES (est): 8.5MM **Privately Held**
SIC: 8721 Billing & bookkeeping service
HQ: Hansen Technologies North America,
    Inc.
    350 5th Ave Ste 6510
    New York NY 10118
    -

(P-26216)
HEALTHCARE COST SOLUTIONS INC
Also Called: H C S
1200 Newprt Cntr Dr 190, Newport Beach
(92660)
PHONE..........................949 721-2795
Bridget T Gallagher, *CEO*
EMP: 60 EST: 1994
SALES (est): 3.3MM **Privately Held**
WEB: www.hcsstat.com
SIC: 8721 8742 Auditing services; hospital
& health services consultant

(P-26217)
HEMMING MORSE LLP (PA)
1390 Willow Pass Rd # 410, Concord
(94520-7943)
PHONE..........................415 836-4000
Greg McKinnon, *Managing Prtnr*
Jim Andersen, *Partner*
David Callaghan, *Partner*
Colin Johns, *Managing Prtnr*
Joan Ledbetter, *Admin Mgr*
EMP: 95
SALES (est): 9.9MM **Privately Held**
SIC: 8721 Certified public accountant

(P-26218)
HMWC CPAS & BUSINESS ADVISORS
Also Called: Yosemite Capital Management
17501 17th St Ste 100, Tustin
(92780-7924)
PHONE..........................714 505-9000
Steven Williams, *President*
Gerald Herter, *Partner*
Phr A Ferran, *COO*
Michaele Garcia, *Executive Asst*
Debra Leon, *Executive Asst*
EMP: 57 EST: 1972
SALES (est): 6.2MM **Privately Held**
SIC: 8721 Certified public accountant

(P-26219)
HOLTHOUSE CARLIN VAN TRIGT LLP
350 W Colo Blvd Fl 5 Flr 5, Pasadena
(91105)
PHONE..........................626 243-5100
Kevin Cordano, *Principal*
EMP: 70 **Privately Held**
SIC: 8721 Certified public accountant
PA: Holthouse Carlin Van Trigt Llp
    11444 W Olympic Blvd # 11
    Los Angeles CA 90064
    -

(P-26220)
HOLTHOUSE CARLIN VAN TRIGT LLP
400 W Ventura Blvd # 250, Camarillo
(93010-9137)
PHONE..........................805 374-8555
Kathleen H Jones, *Principal*
Beth Salverson, *Principal*
EMP: 70 **Privately Held**
SIC: 8721 Certified public accountant
PA: Holthouse Carlin Van Trigt Llp
    11444 W Olympic Blvd # 11
    Los Angeles CA 90064
    -

(P-26221)
HOLTHOUSE CARLIN VAN TRIGT LLP
15760 Ventura Blvd # 1700, Encino
(91436-3028)
PHONE..........................818 849-3140
Norman Tamkin, *President*
EMP: 70 **Privately Held**
SIC: 8721 Certified public accountant
PA: Holthouse Carlin Van Trigt Llp
    11444 W Olympic Blvd # 11
    Los Angeles CA 90064
    -

(P-26222)
HOLTHOUSE CARLIN VAN TRIGT LLP
18565 Jamboree Rd Ste 400, Irvine
(92612-2562)
PHONE..........................714 361-7600
Donna Hansen, *Owner*
EMP: 70 **Privately Held**
SIC: 8721 Certified public accountant
PA: Holthouse Carlin Van Trigt Llp
    11444 W Olympic Blvd # 11
    Los Angeles CA 90064
    -

(P-26223)
HOLTHOUSE CARLIN VAN TRIGT LLP (PA)
11444 W Olympic Blvd # 11, Los Angeles
(90064-1500)
PHONE..........................310 477-5551
Philip Holthouse, *Managing Prtnr*
David Bierhorst, *Partner*
James Carlin, *Partner*
Blake Christian, *Partner*
Greg Hutchins, *Partner*
EMP: 110
SALES (est): 44.4MM **Privately Held**
WEB: www.hcvt.com
SIC: 8721 Certified public accountant

(P-26224)
HOOD & STRONG LLP (PA)
275 Battery St Ste 900, San Francisco
(94111-3332)
PHONE..........................415 781-0793
Robert Raffo, *Managing Prtnr*
Raul Hernandez, *Partner*
Steve Piuma, *Partner*
Alexandra Hernandez, *Managing Dir*
EMP: 75
SQ FT: 13,000
SALES (est): 14.7MM **Privately Held**
WEB: www.hoodstrong.com
SIC: 8721 Certified public accountant

(P-26225)
HUTCHINSON & BLOODGOOD LLP (PA)
550 N Brand Blvd Fl 14, Glendale
(91203-1952)
P.O. Box 1917 (91209-1917)
PHONE..........................818 637-5000
Richard Preciado, *Managing Prtnr*
Michael Benneian, *Partner*
Gary Carruthers, *Partner*
Jenny Chen, *Partner*
Juan Daukowski, *Partner*
EMP: 125
SALES (est): 21MM **Privately Held**
WEB: www.hbllp.com
SIC: 8721 Certified public accountant

(P-26226)
I L S WEST INC
17501 17th St Ste 100, Tustin
(92780-7924)
PHONE..........................714 505-7530
EMP: 50
SALES (est): 1.5MM **Privately Held**
SIC: 8721

(P-26227)
INDEVIA ACCOUNTING INC
2667 Camino Del Rio S # 101, San Diego
(92108-3707)
PHONE..........................858 450-2981
Dev Purkayastha, *President*
Wendy A McGuire, *COO*
EMP: 60
SQ FT: 200

SALES: 1MM **Privately Held**
SIC: 8721 Accounting, auditing & bookkeeping

(P-26228)
INFINEON TECH AMERICAS CORP
Interntnal Rctfr/Ccunting Dept
222 Kansas St, El Segundo (90245-4315)
PHONE..........................310 726-8000
Michael McGee, *Manager*
Mike Seidl, *President*
Michael Barrow, *Exec VP*
Marc Rougee, *Exec VP*
David Poon, *Vice Pres*
EMP: 699
SALES (corp-wide): 8.3B **Privately Held**
WEB: www.irf.com
SIC: 8721 3674 Accounting, auditing &
bookkeeping; semiconductors & related
devices
HQ: Infineon Technologies Americas Corp.
    101 N Pacific Coast Hwy
    El Segundo CA 90245
    310 726-8000

(P-26229)
INNOVTIVE EMPLYEE SLUTIONS INC
9665 Gran Rdge Dr Ste 420, San Diego
(92123)
PHONE..........................858 715-5100
Karla Hertzog, *CEO*
Peter Limone, *CFO*
Darlene Bruder, *Vice Pres*
Tania Fiero, *Vice Pres*
Trevor Foster, *Vice Pres*
EMP: 1500
SQ FT: 6,641
SALES (est): 85.1MM **Privately Held**
WEB: www.innovative-solution.com
SIC: 8721 Payroll accounting service

(P-26230)
INTERPACIFIC GROUP INC
576 Beale St, San Francisco (94105-2019)
PHONE..........................415 442-0711
Dave Smith, *President*
David Smith, *Admin Sec*
EMP: 1306
SALES (est): 41.8MM **Privately Held**
WEB: www.interpacific-group.com
SIC: 8721 Accounting, auditing & book-
keeping

(P-26231)
JMT CHARITABLE FOUNDATION
1 Market Ste 620, San Francisco
(94105-5105)
PHONE..........................415 974-6000
John Williamson, *Managing Prtnr*
Carlotta L Henneman, *Administration*
Jesse Kaplan, *Finance Mgr*
Corina Evans, *Manager*
Yvonne Yang, *Manager*
EMP: 70
SALES (corp-wide): 276.3MM **Privately Held**
SIC: 8721 Certified public accountant
PA: Eisneramper Llp
    750 3rd Ave Fl 16
    New York NY 10017
    212 949-8700

(P-26232)
JOSHUA J BODENSTADT CPA A PROF
4225 Executive Sq Ste 900, La Jolla
(92037-1485)
PHONE..........................858 642-5050
Joshua J Bodenstadt, *Partner*
EMP: 50
SALES (est): 159.2K **Privately Held**
SIC: 8721 Certified public accountant

(P-26233)
JPMORGAN XIGN CORPORATION
7077 Koll Center Pkwy, Pleasanton
(94566-3142)
PHONE..........................925 469-9446
Thomas M Glassanos, *President*
Jerry Ulrich, *Treasurer*
Bill Williamson, *Vice Pres*
EMP: 85

SQ FT: 26,000
SALES (est): 35.8K
SALES (corp-wide): 99.6B **Publicly Held**
WEB: www.xign.com
SIC: 8721 Billing & bookkeeping service
HQ: Jpmorgan Chase Bank, National Asso-
    ciation
    1111 Polaris Pkwy
    Columbus OH 43240
    614 436-3055

(P-26234)
KELLOGG ANDLSON ACCNTANCY CORP (PA)
21700 Oxnard St Ste 800, Woodland Hills
(91367-7500)
PHONE..........................818 971-5100
Christian Payne, *CEO*
James F Walters, *President*
William Wall, *Vice Pres*
EMP: 85
SALES (est): 5MM **Privately Held**
WEB: www.k-a.com
SIC: 8721 Certified public accountant

(P-26235)
KIECKHAFER SCHIFFER & CO LLP (PA)
6201 Oak Cyn Ste 200, Irvine
(92618-5231)
PHONE..........................949 250-3900
Jim Kieckhafer, *Partner*
Scott Schiffer, *Partner*
Emily Anderson, *Tax Mgr*
Zach Walter, *Tax Mgr*
Romeo Santos, *Accountant*
EMP: 50
SALES (est): 9.7MM **Privately Held**
WEB: www.ksandco.com
SIC: 8721 Certified public accountant

(P-26236)
KPMG LLP
9171 Wilshire Blvd # 500, Beverly Hills
(90210-5530)
PHONE..........................310 273-2770
Melvin Ozur, *Branch Mgr*
Rhonika Hodge, *Admin Asst*
Gaby Passarelli, *Human Resources*
EMP: 50
SALES (corp-wide): 5.1B **Privately Held**
WEB: www.rkco.com
SIC: 8721 Certified public accountant
PA: Kpmg Llp
    1676 Intl Dr Ste 1200
    Mclean VA 22102
    703 286-8000

(P-26237)
KPMG LLP
4655 Executive Dr # 1100, San Diego
(92121-3132)
PHONE..........................858 750-7100
Elizabeth Altman, *Branch Mgr*
Conrad Kreutzer, *Partner*
Elton E Winston, *Principal*
Tanya Nesta, *Admin Asst*
Stephanie Isaacson, *Auditing Mgr*
EMP: 150
SALES (corp-wide): 5.1B **Privately Held**
SIC: 8721 Certified public accountant
PA: Kpmg Llp
    1676 Intl Dr Ste 1200
    Mclean VA 22102
    703 286-8000

(P-26238)
KPMG LLP
55 2nd St Ste 1400, San Francisco
(94105-4557)
PHONE..........................415 963-5100
Louis P Miramontes, *Managing Prtnr*
Barbara Carbone, *Partner*
Alan Chinn, *Partner*
Glenn M Farrell, *Partner*
Brad Fisher, *Partner*
EMP: 50
SQ FT: 4,325
SALES (corp-wide): 5.1B **Privately Held**
SIC: 8721 Certified public accountant
PA: Kpmg Llp
    1676 Intl Dr Ste 1200
    Mclean VA 22102
    703 286-8000

(P-26239)
KPMG LLP
550 S Hope St Ste 1500, Los Angeles
(90071-2629)
PHONE............................703 286-8175
Daniel Smith, *Manager*
Julie Hansen, *Broker*
Geeta Anand, *Sr Associate*
Mike Levine, *Sr Associate*
Liwei Shi, *Sr Associate*
EMP: 99
SALES (corp-wide): 5.1B **Privately Held**
SIC: 8721　Certified public accountant
PA: Kpmg Llp
　　1676 Intl Dr Ste 1200
　　Mclean VA 22102
　　703 286-8000

(P-26240)
KPMG LLP
550 S Hope St Ste 1500, Los Angeles
(90071-2629)
PHONE............................212 758-9700
Joseph T Boyle, *Manager*
Bob Siegal, *Director*
EMP: 3000
SALES (corp-wide): 5.1B **Privately Held**
SIC: 8721　Certified public accountant
PA: Kpmg Llp
　　1676 Intl Dr Ste 1200
　　Mclean VA 22102
　　703 286-8000

(P-26241)
KPMG LLP
2175 N Calif Blvd # 1000, Walnut Creek
(94596-3579)
PHONE............................925 946-1300
Todd Goldman, *Manager*
EMP: 50
SALES (corp-wide): 5.1B **Privately Held**
WEB: www.rkco.com
SIC: 8721　Certified public accountant
PA: Kpmg Llp
　　1676 Intl Dr Ste 1200
　　Mclean VA 22102
　　703 286-8000

(P-26242)
KPMG LLP
500 Capitol Mall Ste 2100, Sacramento
(95814-4754)
PHONE............................916 448-4700
Rich Wise, *Partner*
Tiffany Ellis, *Manager*
Sikender Mohammad, *Contractor*
Eric Castillo, *Associate*
Laura Gutierrez, *Associate*
EMP: 110
SALES (corp-wide): 5.1B **Privately Held**
SIC: 8721　Certified public accountant
PA: Kpmg Llp
　　1676 Intl Dr Ste 1200
　　Mclean VA 22102
　　703 286-8000

(P-26243)
KPMG LLP
21700 Oxnard St Ste 1800, Woodland Hills
(91367-3659)
PHONE............................818 227-6900
Mort Erlich, *Manager*
Keith Catlow, *Managing Dir*
Joseph Quinn, *Sr Associate*
Rachel Fonseca, *Manager*
Ryan Hall, *Manager*
EMP: 50
SALES (corp-wide): 5.1B **Privately Held**
SIC: 8721　Certified public accountant
PA: Kpmg Llp
　　1676 Intl Dr Ste 1200
　　Mclean VA 22102
　　703 286-8000

(P-26244)
**KRANZ & ASSOC HOLDINGS
LLC**
830 Menlo Ave Ste 100, Menlo Park
(94025-4734)
PHONE............................650 854-4400
Deborah Kranz,
EMP: 90
SQ FT: 750
SALES (est): 1.3MM **Privately Held**
SIC: 8721　Accounting services, except au-
diting

(P-26245)
**LAVINE LOFGREN MORRIS
ENGELB**
4180 La Jolla Village Dr # 300, La Jolla
(92037-1402)
PHONE............................858 455-1200
Von Morris, *Mng Member*
Andy Goodman, *COO*
Shawn Goll, *Admin Asst*
Donna Luniewski, *Administration*
Julie Vadnais, *Webmaster*
EMP: 50
SQ FT: 5,000
SALES (est): 6.3MM **Privately Held**
SIC: 8721　Certified public accountant

(P-26246)
LINDQUIST LLP (PA)
5000 Executive Pkwy # 400, San Ramon
(94583-4210)
PHONE............................925 277-9100
Barry Omahen, *Partner*
Alan C Lindquist, *Partner*
Kimberly Ray, *Partner*
Robert Bellerose, *Administration*
Deborah R Dimery, *CPA*
EMP: 51
SALES (est): 9.4MM **Privately Held**
SIC: 8721　Certified public accountant

(P-26247)
LLP MOSS ADAMS
2882 Prospect Park Dr # 300, Rancho Cor-
dova (95670-6059)
PHONE............................916 503-8100
Robert Ahern, *Branch Mgr*
Mary Michela, *Admin Asst*
Heather Cole, *CPA*
Shane Hunt, *Senior Mgr*
Matthew Montez, *Senior Mgr*
EMP: 78
SALES (corp-wide): 350.4MM **Privately
Held**
SIC: 8721　Certified public accountant
PA: Moss Adams Llp
　　999 3rd Ave Ste 2800
　　Seattle WA 98104
　　206 302-6800

(P-26248)
LLP MOSS ADAMS
21700 Oxnard St Ste 300, Woodland Hills
(91367-7561)
PHONE............................818 577-1822
Gidget Furness, *COO*
Bob Terada, *Office Mgr*
Chris Lheureux, *Technology*
Norma Higbee, *Purch Agent*
EMP: 78
SALES (corp-wide): 350.4MM **Privately
Held**
SIC: 8721　Certified public accountant
PA: Moss Adams Llp
　　999 3rd Ave Ste 2800
　　Seattle WA 98104
　　206 302-6800

(P-26249)
LLP MOSS ADAMS
3121 W March Ln Ste 100, Stockton
(95219-2367)
PHONE............................209 955-6100
David Gellerman, *Principal*
Heidi Berenbrok, *CPA*
Heather Schlenger, *Manager*
EMP: 50
SALES (corp-wide): 350.4MM **Privately
Held**
SIC: 8721　Certified public accountant
PA: Moss Adams Llp
　　999 3rd Ave Ste 2800
　　Seattle WA 98104
　　206 302-6800

(P-26250)
LLP MOSS ADAMS
101 2nd St Ste 900, San Francisco
(94105-3650)
PHONE............................415 956-1500
Joy Robinson, *Branch Mgr*
Dan Cheyney, *Partner*
Steven Schechter, *Partner*
Caryl Thorp, *Partner*
Eric Tostenrud, *Partner*
EMP: 140

SALES (corp-wide): 318.6MM **Privately
Held**
WEB: www.mossadams.com
SIC: 8721　Certified public accountant
PA: Moss Adams Llp
　　999 3rd Ave Ste 2800
　　Seattle WA 98104
　　206 302-6800

(P-26251)
LLP MOSS ADAMS
635 Campbell Tech Pkwy # 100, Campbell
(95008-5071)
PHONE............................408 369-2400
Vid Lock, *Partner*
Liana Felix, *Partner*
Clare Piech, *Partner*
Kevin Maddock, *Auditor*
Al Domingo, *Assistant*
EMP: 200
SALES (corp-wide): 350.4MM **Privately
Held**
SIC: 8721　Certified public accountant
PA: Moss Adams Llp
　　999 3rd Ave Ste 2800
　　Seattle WA 98104
　　206 302-6800

(P-26252)
LLP MOSS ADAMS
2040 Main St Ste 900, Irvine (92614-8213)
PHONE............................949 221-4000
Roger Weninger, *Branch Mgr*
Simon Dufour, *Auditing Mgr*
Roger Burggrabe, *Senior Mgr*
Doug Buurma, *Senior Mgr*
Wendy Todd, *Senior Mgr*
EMP: 50
SALES (corp-wide): 318.6MM **Privately
Held**
WEB: www.mossadams.com
SIC: 8721　Certified public accountant
PA: Moss Adams Llp
　　999 3rd Ave Ste 2800
　　Seattle WA 98104
　　206 302-6800

(P-26253)
LLP MOSS ADAMS
4747 Executive Dr # 1300, San Diego
(92121-3114)
PHONE............................858 627-1400
Laura Roos, *Partner*
Carisa Wisniewski, *Managing Prtnr*
Beth Gayvert, *Executive Asst*
Simone Edwards, *Admin Asst*
Kim Bryant, *Sales Mgr*
EMP: 65
SALES (corp-wide): 318.6MM **Privately
Held**
WEB: www.mossadams.com
SIC: 8721　Certified public accountant
PA: Moss Adams Llp
　　999 3rd Ave Ste 2800
　　Seattle WA 98104
　　206 302-6800

(P-26254)
**LODGEN LACHER GOLDITCH
SARD**
16530 Ventura Blvd # 305, Encino
(91436-4554)
PHONE............................818 783-0570
Ben Frankel, *Partner*
Patricia Bates, *Partner*
Bernard S Golditch, *Partner*
Dan Howard, *Partner*
Stephen P Lacher, *Partner*
EMP: 50
SQ FT: 12,000
SALES (est): 4.2MM **Privately Held**
WEB: www.fllgsh.com
SIC: 8721　Certified public accountant

(P-26255)
**MACIAS GINI & OCONNELL LLP
(PA)**
3000 S St Ste 300, Sacramento
(95816-7014)
PHONE............................916 928-4600
Kenneth A Macias, *Partner*
Ernest Gini, *Partner*
Jim Godsey, *Partner*
Rick Green, *Partner*
Scott Hammon, *Partner*
EMP: 75

SQ FT: 12,000
SALES: 33.4MM **Privately Held**
WEB: www.mgocpa.com
SIC: 8721　Certified public accountant

(P-26256)
MARCUM LLP
303 2nd St Ste 950, San Francisco
(94107-1366)
PHONE............................415 543-6900
Jeffrey M Weiner, *Branch Mgr*
EMP: 55
SALES (corp-wide): 341MM **Privately
Held**
SIC: 8721　Certified public accountant
PA: Marcum Llp
　　750 3rd Ave Fl 11
　　New York NY 10017
　　212 485-5500

(P-26257)
MARCUM LLP
2049 Century Park E # 300, Los Angeles
(90067-3105)
PHONE............................310 432-7400
Ron Friedman, *Branch Mgr*
Claudia Herrera, *Office Admin*
Ken Gryske, *Director*
Lori Rock, *Manager*
EMP: 75
SALES (corp-wide): 341MM **Privately
Held**
SIC: 8721　Accounting services, except au-
diting; certified public accountant
PA: Marcum Llp
　　750 3rd Ave Fl 11
　　New York NY 10017
　　212 485-5500

(P-26258)
MED-DATA INCORPORATED
3741 Douglas Blvd Ste 170, Roseville
(95661-4271)
PHONE............................916 771-1362
Bruce Stewart, *Branch Mgr*
EMP: 100
SALES (corp-wide): 16.5MM **Privately
Held**
SIC: 8721　Accounting services, except au-
diting
PA: Med-Data, Incorporated
　　3326 160th Ave Se Ste 440
　　Bellevue WA 98008
　　800 261-0048

(P-26259)
**MEDAMERICA BILLING SVCS
INC (HQ)**
Also Called: California Emergency Physician
1601 Cummins Dr Ste D, Modesto
(95358-6411)
PHONE............................209 491-7710
Michael F Harrington, *CEO*
Erik Davenport, *Partner*
Jaime Rivas, *Partner*
James V Proffitt, *Officer*
Melissa Foreman, *Division Mgr*
EMP: 67
SQ FT: 75,000
SALES (est): 29.7MM
SALES (corp-wide): 500MM **Privately
Held**
WEB: www.cep.com
SIC: 8721　Billing & bookkeeping service
PA: California Emergency Physicians Foun-
dation
　　2100 Powell St Ste 900
　　Emeryville CA 94608
　　510 350-2700

(P-26260)
**MEDEX PRATICE SOLUTIONS
INC**
4725 Enterprise Way Ste 1, Modesto
(95356-8967)
P.O. Box 188, Oakdale (95361-0188)
PHONE............................209 845-1346
Bryan Williamson, *President*
Michael Mc Gann, *Vice Pres*
EMP: 60
SALES (est): 3.2MM **Privately Held**
SIC: 8721　Billing & bookkeeping service

(P-26261)
MSC SERVICE CO
Also Called: Morley Construction
3330 Ocean Park Blvd # 101, Santa Monica
(90405-3202)
PHONE..................................310 399-1600
Mark Benjamin, *CEO*
Burt Lewitt, *President*
Todd Paris, *CFO*
Jon Sansom, *Marketing Mgr*
EMP: 85
SQ FT: 20,000
SALES (est): 2.8MM
SALES (corp-wide): 168.7MM **Privately Held**
WEB: www.mscservice.com
SIC: 8721 1542 1522 1521 Auditing services; nonresidential construction; residential construction; single-family housing construction
PA: Morley Builders, Inc.
3330 Ocean Park Blvd # 101
Santa Monica CA 90405
310 399-1600

(P-26262)
NOVOGRADAC AND CO LLP
246 1st St Ste 500, San Francisco
(94105-4699)
PHONE..................................415 356-8000
M J Novogradac, *Partner*
EMP: 50
SALES (est): 1MM **Privately Held**
SIC: 8721 Certified public accountant

(P-26263)
OUM & CO LLP (PA)
601 California St # 1800, San Francisco
(94108-2823)
PHONE..................................415 434-3744
James E Ullakko, *Partner*
Paul Ainslie, *Partner*
Chris S Millias, *Partner*
John Muranishi, *Partner*
Craig Tatlonghari, *Partner*
EMP: 68 **EST:** 1976
SQ FT: 7,700
SALES (est): 16.2MM **Privately Held**
WEB: www.oumcpa.com
SIC: 8721 Certified public accountant

(P-26264)
PASADENA BILLING ASSOCIATES
225 S Lake Ave Ste 535, Pasadena
(91101-3010)
PHONE..................................626 795-6596
Dale W Zeh Jr, *President*
Lauri G Zeh, *Vice Pres*
Kerith Kelly, *Manager*
EMP: 70
SQ FT: 5,000
SALES (est): 3.3MM **Privately Held**
WEB: www.dobilling.com
SIC: 8721 Billing & bookkeeping service

(P-26265)
PAYCHEX INC
9 E River Park Pl E # 210, Fresno
(93720-1530)
PHONE..................................559 432-1100
Kevin Hardwick, *Branch Mgr*
Michael Carner, *Sales Staff*
Erin Nestor, *Consultant*
EMP: 60
SALES (corp-wide): 3.3B **Publicly Held**
WEB: www.paychex.com
PA: Paychex, Inc.
911 Panorama Trl S
Rochester NY 14625
585 385-6666

(P-26266)
PAYCHEX INC
10150 Meanley Dr Ste 200, San Diego
(92131-3008)
PHONE..................................858 547-2920
Ed Nunn, *Manager*
Christina Marino, *Administration*
EMP: 100
SALES (corp-wide): 3.3B **Publicly Held**
WEB: www.paychex.com
SIC: 8721 8742 7374 Payroll accounting service; management consulting services; data processing & preparation

PA: Paychex, Inc.
911 Panorama Trl S
Rochester NY 14625
585 385-6666

(P-26267)
PAYCHEX INC
1420 Iowa Ave Ste 100, Riverside
(92507-0510)
PHONE..................................951 682-6100
Karry Zolz, *Manager*
EMP: 50
SALES (corp-wide): 3.3B **Publicly Held**
WEB: www.paychex.com
SIC: 8721 Payroll accounting service
PA: Paychex, Inc.
911 Panorama Trl S
Rochester NY 14625
585 385-6666

(P-26268)
PAYCHEX INC
300 Crprate Pinte Ste 150, Culver City
(90230)
PHONE..................................310 338-7900
Debbie Woods, *Manager*
Caroline Carmona, *Purch Dir*
Debi Wood, *Mktg Dir*
David Beach, *Sales Mgr*
Bob Gilbow, *Manager*
EMP: 100
SALES (corp-wide): 3.3B **Publicly Held**
WEB: www.paychex.com
SIC: 8721 Payroll accounting service
PA: Paychex, Inc.
911 Panorama Trl S
Rochester NY 14625
585 385-6666

(P-26269)
PAYROLLINGCOM CORP
Also Called: Kaizen Staffing
4626 Albuquerque St Uppr, San Diego
(92109-3858)
PHONE..................................858 866-2626
Laverne Kato, *CEO*
Samer Khouli, *CEO*
Susan Kelly, *Principal*
EMP: 50
SQ FT: 10,000
SALES (est): 4.6MM **Privately Held**
WEB: www.payrolling.com
SIC: 8721 Payroll accounting service

(P-26270)
PERRY-SMITH LLP
400 Capitol Mall Ste 1400, Sacramento
(95814-4498)
PHONE..................................916 441-1000
Gary A Fox, *Managing Prtnr*
David T Becker, *Partner*
Jeffrey A Bertleson, *Partner*
Jeffrey Claire, *Partner*
Sue Cordonnier, *Partner*
EMP: 100
SALES (est): 6.4MM **Privately Held**
WEB: www.perry-smith.com
SIC: 8721 Accounting, auditing & bookkeeping

(P-26271)
PHYSICIANS CHOICE LLC
21860 Burbank Blvd # 120, Woodland Hills
(91367-6477)
P.O. Box 4419 (91365-4419)
PHONE..................................818 340-9988
John D Uphold,
Clare Nicholson, *Vice Pres*
Michelle Reckleff,
Jonathan Sturm,
EMP: 80
SQ FT: 10,000
SALES (est): 6.2MM **Privately Held**
WEB: www.physchoice.com
SIC: 8721 Billing & bookkeeping service

(P-26272)
PKF CERTIF PUB ACCTS A PROF (PA)
550 N Brand Blvd Ste 950, Glendale
(91203-1973)
PHONE..................................818 630-7630
Rex H Poulsen, *President*
Mark Hennelly, *Treasurer*
John Engelbrecht, *Vice Pres*
EMP: 60

SALES: 3.1MM **Privately Held**
WEB: www.pkfla.com
SIC: 8721 Auditing services

(P-26273)
PREMIER MANAGEMENT COMPANY (PA)
1141 S Beverly Dr Fl 3, Los Angeles
(90035-1119)
PHONE..................................310 286-3074
Jacob Graff, *President*
Pnina Graff, *Admin Sec*
EMP: 58
SQ FT: 1,000
SALES (est): 4.8MM **Privately Held**
SIC: 8721 8741 Billing & bookkeeping service; nursing & personal care facility management

(P-26274)
PRICEWATERHOUSECOOPERS LLP
2020 Main St Ste 400, Irvine (92614-8243)
PHONE..................................949 437-5200
Diana Franklin, *Manager*
Patrick Fitzgerald, *Partner*
Mike Reid, *Managing Dir*
Michael Wellington, *Mktg Dir*
Rony Mansour, *Senior Mgr*
EMP: 260
SALES (corp-wide): 6.8B **Privately Held**
WEB: www.pwcglobal.com
SIC: 8721 Certified public accountant
PA: Pricewaterhousecoopers Llp
300 Madison Ave Fl 24
New York NY 10017
646 471-4000

(P-26275)
PRICEWATERHOUSECOOPERS LLP
488 Almaden Blvd Ste 1800, San Jose
(95110-2768)
PHONE..................................408 817-3700
Don McGovern, *Branch Mgr*
Timothy Scott, *Partner*
Rich Zook, *Partner*
Christine Galloni, *Executive*
Joe Tort, *Executive*
EMP: 700
SALES (corp-wide): 6.8B **Privately Held**
WEB: www.pwcglobal.com
SIC: 8721 Certified public accountant
PA: Pricewaterhousecoopers Llp
300 Madison Ave Fl 24
New York NY 10017
646 471-4000

(P-26276)
PRICEWATERHOUSECOOPERS LLP
5375 Mira Sorrento Pl, San Diego
(92121-3809)
PHONE..................................858 677-2400
Christina Nordvall, *Manager*
Mansoor Nazzal, *Auditor*
George Wood, *Senior Mgr*
Emily Cook, *Manager*
Garret McBride, *Manager*
EMP: 275
SALES (corp-wide): 6.8B **Privately Held**
SIC: 8721 Certified public accountant
PA: Pricewaterhousecoopers Llp
300 Madison Ave Fl 24
New York NY 10017
646 471-4000

(P-26277)
PRICEWATERHOUSECOOPERS LLP
400 Capitol Mall Ste 600, Sacramento
(95814-4423)
PHONE..................................916 930-8100
Robert Kittredge, *Branch Mgr*
Susan Coleman, *Admin Sec*
Jon Sperring, *Client Mgr*
EMP: 84
SQ FT: 1,000
SALES (corp-wide): 6.8B **Privately Held**
WEB: www.pwcglobal.com
SIC: 8721 Certified public accountant
PA: Pricewaterhousecoopers Llp
300 Madison Ave Fl 24
New York NY 10017
646 471-4000

(P-26278)
PRICEWATERHOUSECOOPERS LLP
3 Embarcadero Ctr Fl 20, San Francisco
(94111-4004)
PHONE..................................415 498-5000
John McCaffery, *Partner*
Jason S Miller, *Senior Mgr*
EMP: 275
SALES (corp-wide): 6.8B **Privately Held**
WEB: www.pwcglobal.com
SIC: 8721 Accounting, auditing & bookkeeping
PA: Pricewaterhousecoopers Llp
300 Madison Ave Fl 24
New York NY 10017
646 471-4000

(P-26279)
QBI LLC (PA)
Also Called: Qualified Benefits
21031 Ventura Blvd # 1200, Woodland Hills
(91364-2229)
PHONE..................................818 594-4900
Nicholas H Stonnington, *Mng Member*
Victor Pantin, *CFO*
Sandy Duncan, *Admin Asst*
Mike Parker, *CIO*
Janice Hammett, *Opers Mgr*
EMP: 90
SALES (est): 10MM **Privately Held**
SIC: 8721 6411 Payroll accounting service; pension & retirement plan consultants

(P-26280)
RAND MEDICAL BILLING INC
Also Called: Orion - Rand
1633 Erringer Rd Fl 1, Simi Valley
(93065-3557)
PHONE..................................805 578-8300
Marvin Retsky, *President*
Patty Artist, *Office Mgr*
EMP: 100
SQ FT: 10,000
SALES (est): 5.5MM
SALES (corp-wide): 76.7MM **Publicly Held**
SIC: 8721 Billing & bookkeeping service
HQ: Orion Healthcorp, Inc.
3200 Wilcrest Dr Ste 550
Houston TX 77042
713 432-1100

(P-26281)
ROSERYAN INC
35473 Dumbarton Ct, Newark
(94560-1100)
PHONE..................................510 456-3056
Kathleen M Ryan, *President*
Maureen Ryan, *President*
Pat Voll, *Vice Pres*
Jason Barker, *Executive*
Stan Fels, *Business Dir*
EMP: 60
SALES (est): 4.3MM **Privately Held**
WEB: www.roseryan.com
SIC: 8721 Accounting, auditing & bookkeeping

(P-26282)
RSM US LLP
44 Montgomery St Ste 3900, San Francisco
(94104-4602)
PHONE..................................415 848-5300
Tim Tiefenthaler, *Managing Prtnr*
Janis Parthun, *Manager*
EMP: 99
SALES (corp-wide): 1.8B **Privately Held**
SIC: 8721 Certified public accountant
PA: Rsm Us Llp
1 S Wacker Dr Ste 800
Chicago IL 60606
312 384-6000

(P-26283)
RSM US LLP
18401 Von Karman Ave # 500, Irvine
(92612-1542)
PHONE..................................949 255-6500
Gretchen Valentine, *Managing Prtnr*
Ryan Lemond, *Auditing Mgr*
Todd Sigler, *Director*
Atul Sapra, *Manager*
EMP: 71
SALES (corp-wide): 1.8B **Privately Held**
SIC: 8721 Certified public accountant

PA: Rsm Us Llp
1 S Wacker Dr Ste 800
Chicago IL 60606
312 384-6000

(P-26284)
RSM US LLP
100 W San Fernando St, San Jose
(95113-2219)
PHONE....................408 572-4440
Dennis Young, *Branch Mgr*
EMP: 84
SALES (corp-wide): 1.8B **Privately Held**
SIC: 8721 Certified public accountant
PA: Rsm Us Llp
1 S Wacker Dr Ste 800
Chicago IL 60606
312 384-6000

(P-26285)
S L G G CONSULTING GROUP LLC (PA)
10960 Wilshire Blvd # 1100, Los Angeles
(90024-3714)
PHONE....................310 477-3924
Harvey Goldstein,
Norman Greebaum,
Donald Leve,
Eric Ouellette,
Simon William,
EMP: 250
SALES (est): 7.5MM **Privately Held**
SIC: 8721 Accounting, auditing & book-keeping

(P-26286)
SANTA CLARA COUNTY OF
Also Called: Valley Med Ctr Billing Dept
2325 Enborg Ln Fl 4, San Jose
(95128-2649)
PHONE....................408 885-7200
Mary Wells, *Director*
EMP: 150 **Privately Held**
WEB: www.countyairports.org
SIC: 8721 9311 Billing & bookkeeping service; finance, taxation & monetary policy;
PA: County Of Santa Clara
3180 Newberry Dr Ste 150
San Jose CA 95118
408 299-5105

(P-26287)
SANTA CLARA COUNTY OF
Also Called: Santa Clara Vlly Health/Hosptl
751 S Bascom Ave Fl 4, San Jose
(95128-2604)
PHONE....................408 885-7354
Art Gamez, *Branch Mgr*
EMP: 160 **Privately Held**
WEB: www.countyairports.org
SIC: 8721 9431 Billing & bookkeeping service; administration of public health programs;
PA: County Of Santa Clara
3180 Newberry Dr Ste 150
San Jose CA 95118
408 299-5105

(P-26288)
SEILER LLP (PA)
3 Lagoon Dr Ste 400, Redwood City
(94065-5157)
P.O. Box 8043 (94063-0943)
PHONE....................650 365-4646
James G B Demartini III, *Partner*
Mark Berryman, *Partner*
James G B Demartini III, *Partner*
Brian J Dinsmore, *Partner*
Kenneth Everett, *Partner*
EMP: 140
SQ FT: 31,142
SALES (est): 24.6MM **Privately Held**
SIC: 8721 Certified public accountant

(P-26289)
SEILER LLP
220 Montgomery St Ste 300, San Francisco
(94104-3436)
PHONE....................415 392-2123
Brian Jeffs, *Manager*
Arlan Kertz, *Partner*
Linda Johnson, *Office Mgr*
Maggie Chan, *Admin Asst*
Kiana Evans, *Admin Asst*
EMP: 57

SQ FT: 10,230
SALES (corp-wide): 24.6MM **Privately Held**
SIC: 8721 Accounting services, except auditing
PA: Seiler Llp
3 Lagoon Dr Ste 400
Redwood City CA 94065
650 365-4646

(P-26290)
SHEA LABAGH DOBBERSTEIN CPA (PA)
44 Montgomery St Ste 3200, San Francisco
(94104-4805)
PHONE....................415 731-0100
James Dobberstein, *President*
Ron Simonian, *Treasurer*
Gregory T Labagh, *Vice Pres*
Tom Jackson, *Admin Sec*
Karen Salinas, *Admin Asst*
EMP: 50
SQ FT: 15,000
SALES (est): 11.1MM **Privately Held**
SIC: 8721 Certified public accountant

(P-26291)
SIERRA BOOKKEEPING & TAX SVC
5777 Madison Ave Ste 615, Sacramento
(95841-3312)
PHONE....................916 349-7610
Joannie D Utley, *Principal*
EMP: 60
SALES (est): 1.8MM **Privately Held**
SIC: 8721 Billing & bookkeeping service

(P-26292)
SIERRA HEALTH SERVICES LLC
2423 W March Ln Ste 100, Stockton
(95207-8250)
P.O. Box 7096 (95267-0096)
PHONE....................209 956-7725
Earl Ohgman, *Mng Member*
Paul Tausendfreund, *Info Tech Mgr*
Cindy Birmingham,
Candice Almonte, *Director*
Gianelli Buensuceso CPC, *Director*
EMP: 50
SALES (est): 4.6MM **Privately Held**
SIC: 8721 8011 Billing & bookkeeping service; specialized medical practitioners, except internal; physicians' office, including specialists

(P-26293)
SINGERLEWAK LLP (PA)
10960 Wilshire Blvd, Los Angeles
(90024-3702)
PHONE....................310 477-3924
Jim Pitrat, *Managing Prtnr*
Marc Abrams, *Partner*
David Free, *Partner*
Norman Greenbaum, *Partner*
Janice McKenna, *Partner*
EMP: 120
SQ FT: 24,000
SALES (est): 47.7MM **Privately Held**
WEB: www.singerlewak.com
SIC: 8721 8742 Certified public accountant; business consultant

(P-26294)
SINGERLEWAK LLP
2050 Main St Ste 700, Irvine (92614-8259)
PHONE....................949 261-8600
David Krajanowski, *Branch Mgr*
EMP: 52
SALES (corp-wide): 47.7MM **Privately Held**
SIC: 8721 8742 Certified public accountant; business consultant
PA: Singerlewak Llp
10960 Wilshire Blvd
Los Angeles CA 90024
310 477-3924

(P-26295)
SINGERLEWAK LLP
21550 Oxnard St Ste 1000, Woodland Hills
(91367-7148)
PHONE....................818 999-3924
Elizabeth Vanderroest, *Branch Mgr*
EMP: 52

SALES (corp-wide): 47.7MM **Privately Held**
SIC: 8721 8742 Certified public accountant; business consultant
PA: Singerlewak Llp
10960 Wilshire Blvd
Los Angeles CA 90024
310 477-3924

(P-26296)
SOREN MCADAM CHRISTIANSON LLP
2068 Orange Tree Ln # 100, Redlands
(92374-4555)
P.O. Box 8010 (92375-1210)
PHONE....................909 798-2222
James L Soren, *Partner*
Gary Christianson, *Partner*
Ken Goddard, *Partner*
Jason Lewis, *Partner*
Doug McAdam, *Partner*
EMP: 59
SQ FT: 14,000
SALES (est): 5MM **Privately Held**
WEB: www.smc-cpas.com
SIC: 8721 Certified public accountant

(P-26297)
SQUAR MILNER PETERSON (PA)
4100 Nwport Pl Dr Ste 300, Newport Beach
(92660)
PHONE....................949 222-2999
Steve Milner, *Managing Prtnr*
Scott Burack, *Partner*
Ray Hermanson, *Partner*
Stan Luker, *Partner*
Steve Speier, *Partner*
EMP: 122
SQ FT: 11,500
SALES (est): 45.4MM **Privately Held**
WEB: www.squarmilner.com
SIC: 8721 Accounting services, except auditing

(P-26298)
SSAE 16 PROFESSIONALS LLP
3419 E Chapman Ave # 334, Orange
(92869-3812)
PHONE....................866 480-9485
Jim Jimenez, *Partner*
John Mason, *Principal*
Gary Pennington, *Principal*
Tim Roncevich, *Principal*
Joe Jimenez, *Director*
EMP: 55
SALES (est): 767K **Privately Held**
SIC: 8721 Certified public accountant

(P-26299)
SURGICAL CARE AFFILIATE
Also Called: TAC Rbo
2450 Venture Oaks Way # 120, Sacramento (95833-3292)
PHONE....................916 529-4590
EMP: 50 EST: 2011
SALES (est): 2.7MM **Privately Held**
SIC: 8721

(P-26300)
TANNER MAINSTAIN BLATT & GLY
10866 Wilshire Blvd Fl 10, Los Angeles
(90024-4350)
PHONE....................310 446-2700
William Tanner, *President*
Steve Blatt, *Vice Pres*
Michael Glynn, *Vice Pres*
Brad Johnson, *Vice Pres*
Elena Chapovsky, *Executive Asst*
EMP: 70
SQ FT: 13,000
SALES: 7MM **Privately Held**
WEB: www.tmbgcpa.com
SIC: 8721 Accounting services, except auditing

(P-26301)
TAXRESOURCES INC (PA)
Also Called: Taxaudit.com
600 Coolidge Dr Ste 300, Folsom
(95630-4211)
PHONE....................877 369-7827
Mark D Olander, *CEO*
Dave E Du Val, *Vice Pres*

Nancy K Farwell, *Vice Pres*
Jane T Smith, *Vice Pres*
EMP: 120
SQ FT: 3,000
SALES (est): 40MM **Privately Held**
WEB: www.taxaudit.com
SIC: 8721 Certified public accountant

(P-26302)
THE TEAM COMPANIES LLC (PA)
Also Called: Team Services
901 W Alameda Ave Ste 100, Burbank
(91506-2849)
PHONE....................818 558-3261
Justin Kramer, *CEO*
Geoffrey Matus, *Ch of Bd*
An De Vooght, *CFO*
Carl Zucker, *Vice Pres*
Carol Davies, *Comms Mgr*
EMP: 90
SQ FT: 20,000
SALES: 1.3B **Privately Held**
WEB: www.teamservices.net
SIC: 8721 Payroll accounting service

(P-26303)
THOMAS WIRIG DOLL & CO CPAS
Also Called: Thomas Doll & Company
165 Lennon Ln Ste 200, Walnut Creek
(94598-2447)
P.O. Box 30307 (94598-9307)
PHONE....................925 939-2500
Brent P Thomas, *President*
Sherman Doll, *Admin Sec*
Glenda Craine, *Supervisor*
EMP: 66
SQ FT: 9,000
SALES (est): 5.6MM **Privately Held**
SIC: 8721 Certified public accountant

(P-26304)
TRI CITY EMERGENCY MED GROUP
5050 Avenida Encinas # 200, Carlsbad
(92008-4383)
P.O. Box 5567, Oceanside (92052-5567)
PHONE....................760 439-1963
Richard P Buruss, *Partner*
Sue Kruger, *CPA*
EMP: 50
SALES (est): 5.3MM **Privately Held**
SIC: 8721 8011 Billing & bookkeeping service; physicians' office, including specialists

(P-26305)
US LOAN AUDITORS LLC
7485 Rush Rver Dr Ste 710, Sacramento
(95831)
PHONE....................916 248-8625
Shane Barker, *Mng Member*
EMP: 100 EST: 2009
SALES (est): 3.7MM **Privately Held**
SIC: 8721 Accounting, auditing & book-keeping

(P-26306)
VAVRINEK TRINE DAY & CO LLP (PA)
10681 Fthill Blvd Ste 300, Rancho Cucamonga (91730)
PHONE....................909 466-4410
Ron White, *Partner*
Joe Aguilar, *Partner*
Roger E Alfaro, *Partner*
Rick Alonzo, *Partner*
Heidi L Aschenbrenner, *Partner*
EMP: 140 EST: 1948
SQ FT: 10,000
SALES (est): 42.7MM **Privately Held**
WEB: www.vtdcpa.com
SIC: 8721 Certified public accountant

(P-26307)
WINDES INC (PA)
111 W Ocean Blvd Ste 22, Long Beach
(90802-4653)
P.O. Box 87 (90801-0087)
PHONE....................562 435-1191
John L Dicarlo, *CEO*
Jim Jimenez, *Partner*
Rebecca Christiansen, *Opers Staff*
Scott J Dionne, *Director*
EMP: 100

SQ FT: 26,560
SALES (est): 21MM **Privately Held**
WEB: www.windes.com
SIC: 8721 Certified public accountant

8731 Commercial Physical & Biological Research

(P-26308)
A3 LABS LLC
130 Webster St, Oakland (94607-3756)
PHONE..................................925 274-8503
Sheila Gibson, *Principal*
Kamili Moreland, *Admin Sec*
EMP: 50
SALES (est): 1.1MM **Privately Held**
SIC: 8731 Commercial physical research

(P-26309)
ACEA BIOSCIENCES INC
6779 Mesa Ridge Rd # 100, San Diego (92121-2996)
PHONE..................................858 724-0928
Xiao Xu, *President*
Long Mao, *Associate Dir*
Nicholle Winn-Peraccchino, *Office Mgr*
Angela Scigliano, *Admin Asst*
Xiaobo Wang, *CTO*
▲ EMP: 85
SALES: 300K **Privately Held**
WEB: www.aceabio.com
SIC: 8731 Medical research, commercial

(P-26310)
ACHATES POWER INC
4060 Sorrento Valley Blvd A, San Diego (92121-1428)
PHONE..................................858 535-9920
David Johnson, *CEO*
John Koszewnik, *Principal*
Carol Mottershead, *Finance Dir*
Jerome Paye, *Opers Staff*
EMP: 95
SALES (est): 17.1MM **Privately Held**
WEB: www.achatespower.com
SIC: 8731 Commercial physical research

(P-26311)
ACTIVE MOTIF INC (PA)
Also Called: Timelogic
1914 Palomar Oaks Way # 150, Carlsbad (92008-6509)
PHONE..................................760 431-1263
Joseph Fernandez, *CEO*
Joel Harris, *Managing Prtnr*
Theodore Defrank, *President*
Laura Carpenter, *Vice Pres*
Madeleine Craske, *Research*
EMP: 53
SQ FT: 16,000
SALES (est): 13.2MM **Privately Held**
WEB: www.activemotif.com
SIC: 8731 Biotechnical research, commercial

(P-26312)
ADVANCED CELL DIAGNOSTICS INC
Also Called: A C D
7707 Gateway Blvd, Newark (94560-1160)
PHONE..................................510 576-8800
Yuling Luo, *President*
Steve Chen, *COO*
Jessie Qian Wang, *CFO*
Tom Olenic, *Ch Credit Ofcr*
Rob Monroe, *Chief Mktg Ofcr*
EMP: 66
SQ FT: 2,500
SALES (est): 8.5MM
SALES (corp-wide): 563MM **Publicly Held**
WEB: www.genospectra.com
SIC: 8731 2835 Biotechnical research, commercial; microbiology & virology diagnostic products
PA: Bio-Techne Corporation
614 Mckinley Pl Ne
Minneapolis MN 55413
612 379-8854

(P-26313)
AEMETIS INC (PA)
20400 Stevens, Cupertino (95014)
PHONE..................................408 213-0940

Eric A McAfee, *Ch of Bd*
Andrew B Foster, *COO*
Todd A Waltz, *CFO*
Francis Barton, *Bd of Directors*
Andy Foster, *Exec VP*
EMP: 135
SQ FT: 9,238
SALES: 150.1MM **Publicly Held**
SIC: 8731 2911 Energy research; diesel fuels

(P-26314)
AFFYMETRIX INC
5893 Oberlin Dr, San Diego (92121-3773)
PHONE..................................858 642-2058
EMP: 200
SALES (corp-wide): 20.9B **Publicly Held**
SIC: 8731 Biotechnical research, commercial
HQ: Affymetrix, Inc.
3380 Central Expy
Santa Clara CA 95051

(P-26315)
ALLCELLS LLC
1301 Harbor Bay Pkwy # 200, Alameda (94502)
PHONE..................................510 521-2600
Jie Tong,
Robert Wong, *General Mgr*
John Ng, *Info Tech Mgr*
Keith Cervantes, *Technician*
Johnny Chau, *Accounting Mgr*
EMP: 52
SALES: 12.8MM **Privately Held**
WEB: www.allcells.com
SIC: 8731 Biotechnical research, commercial

(P-26316)
ALLIANT TCHSYSTEMS OPRTONS LLC
9401 Corbin Ave, Northridge (91324-2400)
PHONE..................................818 887-8195
Ronald Hill, *Principal*
EMP: 400
SALES (est): 126.5MM **Publicly Held**
WEB: www.mrcwdc.com
SIC: 8731 Commercial physical research
HQ: Northrop Grumman Innovation Systems, Inc.
45101 Warp Dr
Dulles VA 20166
703 406-5000

(P-26317)
ALLOGENE THERAPEUTICS INC
210 E Grand Ave, South San Francisco (94080-4811)
PHONE..................................650 457-2700
David Chang, *President*
Arie Belldegrun, *Ch of Bd*
Eric Schmidt, *CFO*
Alison Moore, *CTO*
EMP: 78
SQ FT: 68,000
SALES (est): 1.7MM **Privately Held**
SIC: 8731 2836 Biological research; biological products, except diagnostic

(P-26318)
ALPHA TEKNOVA INC
2290 Bert Dr, Hollister (95023-2567)
PHONE..................................831 637-1100
Thomas Davis, *CEO*
Richard Alan Goozh, *CFO*
Amy Wildey, *QA Dir*
Luis Alvarez, *Info Tech Mgr*
Kimberly Gibson, *QC Mgr*
EMP: 75
SQ FT: 34,000
SALES: 9.7MM **Privately Held**
WEB: www.teknova.com
SIC: 8731 Biotechnical research, commercial

(P-26319)
AMSEC LLC
9444 Balboa Ave Ste 400, San Diego (92123-4378)
PHONE..................................858 522-6319
Michelle Wurl, *Director*
EMP: 289 **Publicly Held**

SIC: 8731 8711 Commercial physical research; engineering services
HQ: Amsec Llc
5701 Cleveland St
Virginia Beach VA 23462
757 463-6666

(P-26320)
ANASPEC INC (HQ)
Also Called: Anaspec Egt Group
34801 Campus Dr, Fremont (94555-3606)
PHONE..................................800 452-5530
Philippe Cronet, *President*
Masanobu Sugawara, *President*
Susan Garcia, *Vice Pres*
Anita Hong, *General Mgr*
Lamarr Kelly, *Info Tech Dir*
EMP: 50
SALES (est): 14.9MM
SALES (corp-wide): 5.6B **Privately Held**
WEB: www.anaspec.com
SIC: 8731 Chemical laboratory, except testing; biotechnical research, commercial
PA: Kaneka Corporation
2-3-18, Nakanoshima, Kita-Ku
Osaka OSK 530-0
662 265-050

(P-26321)
APPLIED MOLECULAR EVOLUTION (HQ)
10300 Campus Point Dr # 200, San Diego (92121-1504)
PHONE..................................858 597-4990
Thomas Bumol, *President*
Melissa Baker, *Officer*
EMP: 50
SQ FT: 43,000
SALES (est): 9.1MM
SALES (corp-wide): 22.8B **Publicly Held**
WEB: www.amevolution.com
SIC: 8731 Commercial physical research
PA: Eli Lilly And Company
Lilly Corporate Ctr
Indianapolis IN 46285
317 276-2000

(P-26322)
APPLIED P & CH LABORATORY SOUT
Also Called: APC Lab
13760 Magnolia Ave, Chino (91710-7018)
PHONE..................................909 590-1828
Jack Zhang, *President*
Mary Luo, *Corp Secy*
EMP: 60
SQ FT: 30,000
SALES (est): 3.6MM **Privately Held**
WEB: www.apclab.com
SIC: 8731 Environmental research

(P-26323)
APPLIED RESEARCH ASSOC INC
5425 Hollister Ave # 220, Santa Barbara (93111-3370)
PHONE..................................805 962-4810
Joan Rothenberg, *Branch Mgr*
Rob Sues, *President*
EMP: 61
SALES (corp-wide): 229.9MM **Privately Held**
SIC: 8731 8711 Commercial physical research; consulting engineer
PA: Applied Research Associates, Inc.
4300 San Mateo Blvd Ne A220
Albuquerque NM 87110
505 883-3636

(P-26324)
AQUATIC SCIENCE CENTER
4911 Central Ave, Richmond (94804-5803)
PHONE..................................510 746-7334
Warner Chabot, *Exec Dir*
Jim Kelly, *Exec Dir*
Lawrence Sim, *Software Dev*
EMP: 50
SALES (est): 1.7MM **Privately Held**
SIC: 8731 Environmental research

(P-26325)
ARAGEN BIOSCIENCE INC
380 Woodview Ave, Morgan Hill (95037-2823)
PHONE..................................408 779-1700

JB Gupta, *CEO*
Manmahesh Kantipudi, *Ch of Bd*
Manni Kantipudi, *CEO*
EMP: 50
SALES: 9MM **Privately Held**
WEB: www.aragenbio.com
SIC: 8731 Biotechnical research, commercial; medical research, commercial
HQ: Gvk Biosciences Private Limited
1st Floor, Nrm-Iv, Plot No.28a, Ida
Hyderabad TS 50007

(P-26326)
ARCUS BIOSCIENCES INC
3928 Point Eden Way, Hayward (94545-3719)
PHONE..................................510 694-6200
Terry Rosen, *CEO*
Juan Carlos Jaen, *President*
Jennifer Jarrett, *COO*
Joyson Joseph Karakunnel, *Vice Pres*
Steven Chan,
EMP: 83
SALES: 1.4MM **Privately Held**
SIC: 8731 Biotechnical research, commercial

(P-26327)
ARETE ASSOCIATES
103 Johnson St, Windsor (95492-7435)
PHONE..................................818 885-2200
Dave Kier, *CEO*
Terry Frazier, *Senior Engr*
EMP: 57
SALES (corp-wide): 49.2MM **Privately Held**
SIC: 8731 Commercial physical research
PA: Arete Associates
9301 Corbin Ave Ste 2000
Northridge CA 91324
818 885-2200

(P-26328)
ARETE ASSOCIATES (PA)
9301 Corbin Ave Ste 2000, Northridge (91324-2508)
PHONE..................................818 885-2200
David Campion, *President*
Christopher Choi, *CFO*
Charles Agnew, *Officer*
Sallie Di Vincenzo, *Vice Pres*
Doug Deprospo, *Security Dir*
EMP: 125
SQ FT: 170,000
SALES (est): 49.2MM **Privately Held**
WEB: www.arete-dc.com
SIC: 8731 Commercial physical research

(P-26329)
ARIOSA DIAGNOSTICS INC
5945 Optical Ct, San Jose (95138-1400)
PHONE..................................408 229-7500
Kenneth Song MD, *CEO*
Dave Mullarkey, *COO*
Thomas Musci MD, *Chief Mktg Ofcr*
Natalie A Cummins, *Vice Pres*
Thomas J Musci, *Vice Pres*
EMP: 140
SALES (est): 28.5MM
SALES (corp-wide): 53.9B **Publicly Held**
SIC: 8731 Biotechnical research, commercial
HQ: Roche Holdings, Inc.
1 Dna Way
South San Francisco CA 94080

(P-26330)
ASTERIAS BIOTHERAPEUTICS INC
6300 Dumbarton Cir, Fremont (94555-3644)
PHONE..................................510 456-3800
Michael H Mulroy, *President*
Don M Bailey, *Ch of Bd*
Jane S Lebkowski, *President*
Katharine E Spink, *COO*
Ryan D Chavez, *CFO*
EMP: 55
SQ FT: 44,000
SALES: 4MM **Privately Held**
SIC: 8731 2836 Biological research; biological products, except diagnostic

(P-26331)
ATK SPACE SYSTEMS INC
370 N Halstead St, Pasadena
(91107-3122)
PHONE..................626 351-0205
Joe Tellegrino, *Manager*
EMP: 70 **Publicly Held**
SIC: 8731 3826 8711 Commercial physical research; engineering laboratory, except testing; instruments measuring thermal properties; engineering services
HQ: Atk Space Systems Inc.
11310 Frederick Ave
Beltsville MD 20705
301 595-5500

(P-26332)
ATYR PHARMA INC
3545 John Hopkins Ct, San Diego
(92121-1108)
PHONE..................858 731-8389
Sanjay S Shukla, *President*
John K Clarke, *Ch of Bd*
Jill Broadfoot, *CFO*
James Blair, *Bd of Directors*
John Mendlein, *Bd of Directors*
EMP: 65
SQ FT: 24,494
SALES (est): 13.4MM **Privately Held**
SIC: 8731 Biotechnical research, commercial

(P-26333)
AURORA ALGAE INC
3325 Investment Blvd, Hayward
(94545-3808)
PHONE..................510 266-5000
Paul Angelico, *President*
Bill Roeschlein, *CFO*
Lee Covert, *Senior VP*
Matthew Caspari, *Vice Pres*
Guido Radaelli, *Vice Pres*
EMP: 100
SALES (est): 13.6MM **Privately Held**
WEB: www.aurorabiofuels.com
SIC: 8731 Commercial physical research

(P-26334)
AUTOGENOMICS INC
1600 Faraday Ave, Carlsbad (92008-7313)
PHONE..................760 477-2248
Fareed Kureshy, *CEO*
Thomas V Hennessey, *COO*
Robert B Cole, *CFO*
Jim Canfield, *Vice Pres*
Sherman Chang, *Vice Pres*
EMP: 80
SQ FT: 120,000
SALES (est): 16.4MM **Privately Held**
WEB: www.autogenomics.com
SIC: 8731 Biotechnical research, commercial

(P-26335)
AVERY CORP
207 N Goode Ave Fl 6, Glendale
(91203-1364)
PHONE..................626 304-2000
Dean Scarborough, *President*
David Maxson, *Director*
EMP: 200
SALES (est): 9.6MM
SALES (corp-wide): 6.6B **Publicly Held**
WEB: www.avery.com
SIC: 8731 Biological research
PA: Avery Dennison Corporation
207 N Goode Ave Ste 500
Glendale CA 91203
626 304-2000

(P-26336)
AVIVA SYSTEMS BIOLOGY CORP (PA)
7700 Ronson Rd Ste 100, San Diego
(92111-1553)
PHONE..................858 552-6979
Lingxun Duan, *President*
Yi-Chun Wang, *COO*
Huajie Wen, *Exec VP*
Stephen Hill, *Controller*
EMP: 55 EST: 2001
SQ FT: 2,600
SALES: 3MM **Privately Held**
WEB: www.avivasysbio.com
SIC: 8731 Biotechnical research, commercial

(P-26337)
AXONICS MODULATION TECH INC
26 Technology Dr, Irvine (92618-2380)
PHONE..................949 396-6322
Raymond W Cohen, *CEO*
Raphael Wisniewski, *Ch of Bd*
Danny L Dearen, *President*
Rinda Sama, *COO*
Karen Noblett, *Chief Mktg Ofcr*
EMP: 72
SALES: 128.1K **Privately Held**
SIC: 8731 Biotechnical research, commercial; commercial physical research; commercial research laboratory

(P-26338)
BIOCEPT INC
5810 Nancy Ridge Dr # 150, San Diego
(92121-2840)
PHONE..................858 320-8200
Michael W Nall, *President*
David F Hale, *Ch of Bd*
Timothy C Kennedy, *CFO*
Lyle J Arnold, *Senior VP*
Michael Terry, *Senior VP*
EMP: 95
SQ FT: 48,000
SALES: 5MM **Privately Held**
WEB: www.biocept.com
SIC: 8731 Biotechnical research, commercial

(P-26339)
BIOCLINCA
Also Called: Synarc Reiscdronate
7707 Gateway Blvd Ste 300, Newark
(94560-1160)
PHONE..................503 284-3334
Elfa Griffith, *Director*
EMP: 50
SALES (corp-wide): 44MM **Privately Held**
WEB: www.synarc.com
SIC: 8731 Commercial physical research
PA: Bioclinca
7707 Gateway Blvd Fl 3
Newark CA 94560
415 817-8900

(P-26340)
BIOMEDICURE LLC
7940 Silverton Ave # 107, San Diego
(92126-6340)
PHONE..................858 586-1888
Yong Qian,
EMP: 55
SALES: 100K **Privately Held**
SIC: 8731 Biotechnical research, commercial

(P-26341)
BIONETICS CORPORATION
Mercury Consolidated Div
P.O. Box 115, Moffett Field (94035-0115)
PHONE..................650 604-5327
Charles Spectre, *Branch Mgr*
EMP: 50
SALES (corp-wide): 47.1MM **Privately Held**
WEB: www.bionetics.com
SIC: 8731 Commercial research laboratory
PA: The Bionetics Corporation
101 Production Dr Ste 100
Yorktown VA 23693
757 873-0900

(P-26342)
BOEING COMPANY
5753 W Las Positas Blvd, Pleasanton
(94588-4084)
PHONE..................925 398-7664
W James McNerney Jr, *Manager*
EMP: 70
SALES (corp-wide): 93.3B **Publicly Held**
SIC: 8731 8711 3674 3672 Computer (hardware) development; engineering services; semiconductors & related devices; printed circuit boards
PA: The Boeing Company
100 N Riverside Plz
Chicago IL 60606
312 544-2000

(P-26343)
BPS BIOSCIENCE INC
6042 Cornerstone Ct W B, San Diego
(92121-4746)
PHONE..................858 202-1401
Henry Zhu, *President*
Pavel Shashkin, *Associate Dir*
Jill Ruesch, *Administration*
Jie Zhu, *Research*
Andrew C Newman, *Marketing Staff*
EMP: 50
SALES (est): 399.2K **Privately Held**
SIC: 8731 Biotechnical research, commercial; biological research

(P-26344)
BYTON NORTH AMERICA CORP
4201 Burton Dr, Santa Clara (95054-1512)
PHONE..................408 966-5078
EMP: 120 EST: 2016
SALES (est): 10.1MM **Privately Held**
SIC: 8731

(P-26345)
CALIFORNIA INSTITUTE TECH
360 S Wilson Ave, Pasadena (91106-3268)
PHONE..................626 395-8700
Bill Nunez, *Manager*
EMP: 200
SQ FT: 3,536
SALES (corp-wide): 2.8B **Privately Held**
WEB: www.caltech.edu
SIC: 8731 Biological research
PA: California Institute Of Technology
1200 E California Blvd
Pasadena CA 91125
626 395-6811

(P-26346)
CCINTEGRATION INC (PA)
2060 Corporate Ct, San Jose
(95131-1753)
PHONE..................408 228-1314
Hank C Ta, *President*
Wes Hook, *Business Dir*
Philisia Vuong, *Admin Asst*
Jared Beckman, *Business Mgr*
Hoai Ta, *Opers Staff*
EMP: 50
SQ FT: 235,000
SALES (est): 16.2MM **Privately Held**
WEB: www.ccintegration.com
SIC: 8731 7371 Computer (hardware) development; computer software development

(P-26347)
CGI TECHNOLOGIES SOLUTIONS INC
860 Stillwater Rd Ste 210, West Sacramento (95605-1684)
PHONE..................916 281-3200
Janet Loveall, *QC Mgr*
Aniket Goundaje, *Sr Consultant*
EMP: 50
SALES (corp-wide): 8.6B **Privately Held**
SIC: 8731 Commercial physical research
HQ: Cgi Technologies And Solutions Inc.
11325 Random Hills Rd
Fairfax VA 22030
703 267-8000

(P-26348)
CIR
1745 Celeste Dr, San Mateo (94402-2603)
PHONE..................650 574-6900
Dan Collins, *Owner*
EMP: 105
SQ FT: 13,500
SALES (est): 4.2MM **Privately Held**
WEB: www.cirlabs.com
SIC: 8731 5169 5191 2899 Industrial laboratory, except testing; chemicals & allied products; chemicals, industrial & heavy; pesticides; fertilizer & fertilizer materials; chemical preparations; insecticides & pesticides; phosphatic fertilizers

(P-26349)
COLSA CORPORATION
41240 12th St W, Palmdale (93551-1449)
PHONE..................661 273-3859
Tom Berard, *Director*
EMP: 238

SALES (corp-wide): 190.1MM **Privately Held**
SIC: 8731 Computer (hardware) development
PA: Colsa Corporation
6728 Odyssey Dr Nw
Huntsville AL 35806
256 964-5361

(P-26350)
COMPARENETWORKS INC (PA)
Also Called: Biocompare
395 Oyster Point Blvd # 321, South San Francisco (94080-1931)
PHONE..................650 873-9031
Brian Cowley, *CEO*
Paul Gatti, *President*
Matthew McLean, *COO*
Bo Purtic, *Officer*
Joan Boyce, *Vice Pres*
EMP: 74
SQ FT: 16,152
SALES (est): 9.8MM **Privately Held**
WEB: www.biocompare.com
SIC: 8731 Commercial physical research

(P-26351)
COVANCE INC
10300 Campus Point Dr # 225, San Diego
(92121-1515)
PHONE..................858 352-2300
MO Chaudry, *Manager*
EMP: 85 **Publicly Held**
SIC: 8731 Biological research
HQ: Covance Inc.
206 Carnegie Ctr
Princeton NJ 08540

(P-26352)
DART NEUROSCIENCE LLC
12278 Scripps Summit Dr, San Diego
(92131-3697)
PHONE..................858 736-3060
Kenneth E Johns Jr, *CEO*
Ted Stmartin, *CFO*
Ted St Martin, *CFO*
Tim Tully, *Officer*
Phil Perera, *Vice Pres*
EMP: 220
SALES (est): 43.3MM **Privately Held**
SIC: 8731 8733 Biotechnical research, commercial; medical research

(P-26353)
DEPOSITION SCIENCES INC
Also Called: D S I
3300 Coffey Ln, Santa Rosa (95403-1917)
PHONE..................707 573-6700
Lee Bartolomei, *President*
Thomas Chambers, *Director*
EMP: 96
SQ FT: 8,400
SALES (est): 13.2MM **Publicly Held**
WEB: www.depsci.com
SIC: 8731 3827 Industrial laboratory, except testing; lens coating equipment
PA: Lockheed Martin Corporation
6801 Rockledge Dr
Bethesda MD 20817

(P-26354)
DISNEY RESEARCH PITTSBURGH
532 Paula Ave, Glendale (91201-2328)
PHONE..................412 623-1800
Jessica K Hodgins, *Lab Dir*
EMP: 137
SALES (est): 21.5MM **Publicly Held**
SIC: 8731 Commercial research laboratory
HQ: Walt Disney Imagineering Research & Development, Inc.
1401 Flower St
Glendale CA 91201
818 544-6500

(P-26355)
DSM BIOMEDICAL INC
Also Called: Polymer Technology Group, The
2810 7th St, Berkeley (94710-2703)
PHONE..................510 841-8800
Christophe Dardel, *CEO*
Patrick Gray, *Manager*
Yuan Tian, *Manager*
EMP: 120

▲ = Import ▼=Export
◆ =Import/Export

SQ FT: 55,000
SALES (est): 23.3MM
SALES (corp-wide): 10.1B Privately Held
WEB: www.polymertech.com
SIC: 8731 2836 Commercial physical research; biological products, except diagnostic
PA: Koninklijke Dsm N.V.
Het Overloon 1
Heerlen 6411
455 788-111

(P-26356)
DT RESEARCH INC (PA)
2000 Concourse Dr, San Jose
(95131-1701)
PHONE.....................408 934-6220
Yuan D Tsai, President
Yuan-Daw Tsai, President
David Hale, Vice Pres
Soon Poh, Vice Pres
Sam Hall, Info Tech Mgr
EMP: 51
SQ FT: 20,000
SALES (est): 21.7MM Privately Held
WEB: www.dtresearch.com
SIC: 8731 Computer (hardware) development

(P-26357)
E-SCEPTRE INC
16800 Gale Ave, City of Industry
(91745-1804)
PHONE.....................888 350-8989
Stephen Liu, President
Steven Liu, CEO
Richard Gallegos, Exec VP
EMP: 60
SQ FT: 80,000
SALES (est): 4.2MM Privately Held
SIC: 8731 Computer (hardware) development
PA: Sceptre Industries Inc
16800 Gale Ave
City Of Industry CA 91745
-

(P-26358)
ELAN DRUG DELIVERY INC
Also Called: Elan Drug Technologies
180 Oyster Point Blvd, South San Francisco (94080-1909)
PHONE.....................770 531-8100
David Czekai, President
James L Botkin, Senior VP
Gary Liversidge, CTO
EMP: 52
SALES (est): 2.5MM Privately Held
SIC: 8731 4215 Medical research, commercial; courier services, except by air
PA: Alkermes Public Limited Company
Connacht House
Dublin
-

(P-26359)
ELECTRIC POWER RES INST INC (PA)
3420 Hillview Ave, Palo Alto (94304-1382)
P.O. Box 10412 (94303-0813)
PHONE.....................650 855-2000
Michael Howard, CEO
Gil C Quiniones, Ch of Bd
Terry Boston, President
Patricia Vincent-Collawn, Vice Ch Bd
Mark F McGranaghan, Vice Pres
EMP: 600
SQ FT: 300,000
SALES (est): 408.7MM Privately Held
WEB: www.epri.com
SIC: 8731 Energy research

(P-26360)
EMERALD CLOUD LAB INC
844 Dubuque Ave, South San Francisco
(94080-1804)
PHONE.....................650 257-7554
Daniel Jerome Kleinbaum, Co-CEO
Brian Frezza, Co-CEO
Micah Merrick, Vice Pres
EMP: 60 EST: 2009
SALES (est): 3.7MM Privately Held
SIC: 8731 Biotechnical research, commercial

(P-26361)
ENERGY INNOVATIONS INC
130 W Union St, Pasadena (91103-3628)
PHONE.....................626 585-6900
Joseph Budano, CEO
Bill Gross, President
Marcia Goodstein, COO
Greg Chrisney, CFO
Doug McPherson, Executive
EMP: 200
SALES (est): 14.4MM Privately Held
WEB: www.energyinnovations.com
SIC: 8731 Commercial physical research

(P-26362)
ENVIRONMENTAL SCIENCE ASSOC (PA)
Also Called: ESA
550 Kearny St Ste 800, San Francisco
(94108-2512)
PHONE.....................415 896-5900
Leslie Moulton, President
Gary Oates, Senior VP
EMP: 65
SQ FT: 20,000
SALES: 80K Privately Held
WEB: www.esassoc.com
SIC: 8731 8748 Environmental research; environmental consultant

(P-26363)
EPITOMICS INC (HQ)
863 Mitten Rd Ste 103, Burlingame
(94010-1311)
PHONE.....................650 583-6688
Guo-Liang Yu, Ch of Bd
Zhiqiang An, Officer
Brad S Lee, Exec VP
Taiying Chen, Vice Pres
Robert Pytela, Security Dir
EMP: 56
SALES (est): 13.6MM
SALES (corp-wide): 281.1MM Privately Held
WEB: www.epitomics.com
SIC: 8731 Biotechnical research, commercial
PA: Abcam Plc
330 Cambridge Science Park
Cambridge CAMBS CB4 0
122 369-6000

(P-26364)
EUROFINS FOOD
Covance Food Solutions
2441 Constitution Dr, Livermore
(94551-7573)
PHONE.....................609 452-4440
EMP: 4167
SALES (corp-wide): 64.1MM Privately Held
SIC: 8731 Commercial physical research
PA: Eurofins Food Chemistry Testing Us, Inc.
3301 Kinsman Blvd
Madison WI 53704
717 656-2300

(P-26365)
FERRING RESEARCH INSTITUTE INC
4245 Sorrento Valley Blvd, San Diego
(92121-1408)
PHONE.....................858 657-1400
Pierre Riviere, President
EMP: 65
SQ FT: 30,000
SALES (est): 10.1MM Privately Held
SIC: 8731 Biotechnical research, commercial
HQ: Ferring Pharmaceuticals Sa
Chemin De La Vergognausaz 50
Saint-Prex VD
583 010-000

(P-26366)
FIT ELECTRONICS INC (HQ)
Also Called: Foxconn Electronics
500 S Kraemer Blvd # 100, Brea
(92821-6728)
PHONE.....................714 988-9388
Mike Unger, President
Ralph Gillespie, CEO
EMP: 133 EST: 1997

SALES (est): 35.6MM
SALES (corp-wide): 60.3B Privately Held
SIC: 8731 5065 Electronic research; electronic parts
PA: Hon Hai Precision Industry Co., Ltd.
66, Zhongshan Rd.,
New Taipei City 23680
222 683-477

(P-26367)
FLUIDIGM CORPORATION (PA)
7000 Shoreline Ct Ste 100, South San
Francisco (94080-7603)
PHONE.....................650 266-6000
S Christopher Linthwaite, President
Samuel D Colella, Ch of Bd
Stephen Christopher Linthwaite, President
Vikram Jog, CFO
Joanna Lowe, Treasurer
EMP: 148
SQ FT: 94,000
SALES: 101.9MM Publicly Held
WEB: www.fluidigm.com
SIC: 8731 Biotechnical research, commercial

(P-26368)
FUJITSU LABORATORIES AMER INC (DH)
1240 E Arques Ave 345, Sunnyvale
(94085-5401)
PHONE.....................408 530-4500
Hiromu Hayashi, President
Nobuaki Kawato, Exec VP
Masami Yamamoto, Principal
Naomi Hadatsuki, Manager
EMP: 80
SALES (est): 650MM
SALES (corp-wide): 38.4B Privately Held
WEB: www.fujitsulabs.com
SIC: 8731 Commercial physical research
HQ: Fujitsu Laboratories Ltd.
4-1-1, Kamikodanaka, Nakahara-Ku
Kawasaki KNG 211-0
447 542-613

(P-26369)
GENEOHM SCIENCES INC
11085 N Torrey Pines Rd # 210, La Jolla
(92037-1015)
PHONE.....................201 847-5824
Peter Klemm, President
Jamie Condy, President
EMP: 150
SQ FT: 22,000
SALES (est): 6.1MM
SALES (corp-wide): 12B Publicly Held
WEB: www.geneohm.com
SIC: 8731 Commercial physical research
PA: Becton, Dickinson And Company
1 Becton Dr
Franklin Lakes NJ 07417
201 847-6800

(P-26370)
GENERAL ATOMICS (HQ)
3550 General Atomics Ct, San Diego
(92121-1194)
P.O. Box 85608 (92186-5608)
PHONE.....................858 455-2810
J Neal Blue, President
Liam Kelly, CFO
Anthony Navarra, Treasurer
Frank Pace, Exec VP
Linden Blue, Senior VP
▲ EMP: 2015 EST: 1955
SQ FT: 1,000,000
SALES (est): 1.3B Privately Held
WEB: www.generalatomics.com
SIC: 8731 Energy research

(P-26371)
GENERAL ATOMICS
16969 Mesamint St, San Diego
(92127-2407)
PHONE.....................858 676-7100
Anthony Navarra, Vice Pres
Robert Laird, Vice Pres
Lloyd Wood, Program Mgr
Luis Cardenas, Engineer
Steve Pidcoe, Engineer
EMP: 99 Privately Held
WEB: www.generalatomics.com
SIC: 8731 Commercial physical research

HQ: General Atomics
3550 General Atomics Ct
San Diego CA 92121
858 455-2810

(P-26372)
GENERAL ATOMICS
Also Called: General Atomics Energy Pdts
4949 Greencraig Ln, San Diego
(92123-1675)
PHONE.....................858 455-4000
Joel Ennis, General Mgr
Claudio Pereida, President
Kristin Spivey, Program Mgr
Emelie Galace, Admin Asst
Dwayne Williams, Planning
EMP: 170 Privately Held
WEB: www.generalatomics.com
SIC: 8731 7371 3823 Commercial physical research; custom computer programming services; industrial instrmnts msrmnt display/control process variable
HQ: General Atomics
3550 General Atomics Ct
San Diego CA 92121
858 455-2810

(P-26373)
GENTEX CORPORATION
Also Called: Western Operations
9859 7th St, Rancho Cucamonga
(91730-5244)
PHONE.....................909 481-7667
Robert McCay, Branch Mgr
Michael Tran, IT/INT Sup
John Lopata, Engineer
Lorenzo Petty, Engineer
EMP: 90
SALES (corp-wide): 139.6MM Privately Held
WEB: www.gentex.net
SIC: 8731 3845 3841 Commercial research laboratory; biological research; electromedical equipment; surgical & medical instruments
PA: Gentex Corporation
324 Main St
Simpson PA 18407
570 282-3550

(P-26374)
GEOLOGICAL SURVEY US DEPT
345 Middlefield Rd, Menlo Park
(94025-3561)
PHONE.....................650 329-5229
Maria McNutt, Director
EMP: 70 Publicly Held
SIC: 8731 9511 Commercial physical research; air, water & solid waste management;
HQ: United States Dept Of Geological Survey
12201 Sunrise Valley Dr # 100
Reston VA 20192

(P-26375)
HELIX HOLDINGS I LLC
1 Circle Star Way Fl 2, San Carlos
(94070-6234)
PHONE.....................415 805-3360
Robin Thurston, CEO
EMP: 100
SALES (est): 1.3MM Privately Held
SIC: 8731 Biological research

(P-26376)
HELIX OPCO LLC
1 Circle Star Way Fl 2, San Carlos
(94070-6234)
PHONE.....................415 805-3360
Robin Thurston, CEO
EMP: 169
SQ FT: 103,948
SALES: 2MM Privately Held
SIC: 8731 Biological research

(P-26377)
HMCLAUSE INC
Also Called: Harris Moran
9241 Mace Blvd, Davis (95618-9614)
PHONE.....................530 747-3235
Lincoln Moehle, Manager
EMP: 80

SALES (corp-wide): 185.5MM **Privately Held**
WEB: www.harrismoran.com
SIC: 8731 Agricultural research
HQ: Hm.Clause, Inc.
   260 Cousteau Pl Ste 210
   Davis CA 95618
   800 320-4672

(P-26378)
HOWARD HUGHES MEDICAL INST
Also Called: H H M I
279 Campus Dr Rm B202, Stanford (94305-5101)
PHONE....................650 725-8252
John Kennedy, *Manager*
EMP: 100
SALES (corp-wide): 2.3B **Privately Held**
SIC: 8731 6732
PA: Howard Hughes Medical Institute Inc
   4000 Jones Bridge Rd
   Chevy Chase MD 20815
   301 215-8500

(P-26379)
HOWARD HUGHES MEDICAL INST
1550 4th St Rm 190, San Francisco (94143-2324)
PHONE....................415 476-9668
John Flickinger, *Branch Mgr*
Teresa Tucker, *Admin Asst*
EMP: 120
SALES (corp-wide): 2.3B **Privately Held**
SIC: 8731 Biological research
PA: Howard Hughes Medical Institute Inc
   4000 Jones Bridge Rd
   Chevy Chase MD 20815
   301 215-8500

(P-26380)
IBIS BIOSCIENCES INC
2251 Faraday Ave Ste 150, Carlsbad (92008-7209)
PHONE....................760 476-3200
Andrea Wainer, *CEO*
Jayme Laforte, *Administration*
Lee Ann Paaton, *Administration*
EMP: 120
SALES (est): 15.3MM
SALES (corp-wide): 27.3B **Publicly Held**
SIC: 8731 Biological research
PA: Abbott Laboratories
   100 Abbott Park Rd
   Abbott Park IL 60064
   224 667-6100

(P-26381)
IMPACT ASSESSMENT INC
2166 Avenida De La Playa F, La Jolla (92037-3214)
PHONE....................858 459-0142
John S Petterson, *President*
Mario Amanzio, *Business Anlyst*
Jeff Sanchez, *Director*
EMP: 60 **EST:** 1981
SQ FT: 1,700
SALES (est): 5.6MM **Privately Held**
WEB: www.impactassessment.net
SIC: 8731 Environmental research; commercial research laboratory

(P-26382)
INCLIN INC
2655 Campus Dr Ste 100, San Mateo (94403-2520)
PHONE....................650 961-3422
Taylor Kilfoil, *CEO*
Dirk Thye, *CEO*
Tony Pantuso, *COO*
Arnold Wong, *CFO*
Anita Das, *Vice Pres*
EMP: 75
SQ FT: 9,800
SALES (est): 8.3MM **Privately Held**
SIC: 8731 Biotechnical research, commercial

(P-26383)
INOVA DIAGNOSTICS INC (HQ)
9900 Old Grove Rd, San Diego (92131-1638)
PHONE....................858 586-9900
Roger Ingles, *CEO*
Pere Solagagles, *CFO*

Michael Mahler, *Vice Pres*
Patricia Swartwood, *Vice Pres*
Gary Norman, *Admin Asst*
▲ **EMP:** 285
SQ FT: 81,000
SALES (est): 75.5MM
SALES (corp-wide): 157.1MM **Privately Held**
WEB: www.inovadx.com
SIC: 8731 2835 Medical research, commercial; in vitro diagnostics
PA: Werfenlife Sa.
   Plaza Europa, 21 - 23
   L'hospitalet De Llobregat 08908
   934 010-101

(P-26384)
INTARCIA THERAPEUTICS INC
Also Called: Hayward Manufacturing
24650 Industrial Blvd, Hayward (94545-2234)
PHONE....................510 782-7800
Kurt Graves, *CEO*
Owen Hughes, *Officer*
Michelle Baron, *Vice Pres*
David Franklin, *Vice Pres*
Kristina Yu-Isenberg, *Vice Pres*
EMP: 68
SALES (corp-wide): 19.4MM **Privately Held**
SIC: 8731 Biotechnical research, commercial
PA: Intarcia Therapeutics, Inc.
   1 Marina Park Dr Ste 13
   Boston MA 02210
   617 936-2500

(P-26385)
INTEGRIUM LLC (PA)
Also Called: Integrex Innovations
14351 Myford Rd Ste A, Tustin (92780-7038)
PHONE....................714 541-5591
David Smith MD,
EMP: 54
SQ FT: 40,000
SALES (est): 11MM **Privately Held**
WEB: www.integrium.com
SIC: 8731 8742 Medical research, commercial; industry specialist consultants

(P-26386)
INTERNATIONAL BUS MCHS CORP
Also Called: IBM
650 Harry Rd, San Jose (95120-6001)
PHONE....................408 927-1080
Mark Dean, *Vice Pres*
Jim Modak, *Info Tech Dir*
Eileen Wang, *Software Dev*
John Palmer, *Research*
Lily Boterenbrood, *Technology*
EMP: 500
SALES (corp-wide): 79.1B **Publicly Held**
WEB: www.ibm.com
SIC: 8731 Commercial research laboratory
PA: International Business Machines Corporation
   1 New Orchard Rd Ste 1 # 1
   Armonk NY 10504
   914 499-1900

(P-26387)
ISOTIS ORTHOBIOLOGICS INC
2 Goodyear Ste A, Irvine (92618-2052)
PHONE....................949 595-8710
Keith Valentine, *CEO*
Peter J Arduini, *President*
Christian S Schade, *Exec VP*
Trudy Jackson, *Executive*
Nancy Toledo, *Principal*
EMP: 150
SALES (est): 17.8MM **Privately Held**
SIC: 8731 5047 Biological research; surgical equipment & supplies
HQ: Isotis International Sarl
   C/O Fidulem Sa
   Lausanne VD 1005
   216 132-525

(P-26388)
JANSSEN ALZHEIMER IMMUNOTHERA
700 Gateway Blvd, South San Francisco (94080-7020)
PHONE....................650 794-2500

Dr Stefaan Heylen, *President*
Nadine De Leeuw, *Manager*
Marc Nicholson, *Manager*
EMP: 100
SALES (est): 5.6MM
SALES (corp-wide): 76.4B **Publicly Held**
SIC: 8731 Commercial physical research
HQ: Janssen Research & Development, Llc
   920 Us Highway 202
   Raritan NJ 08869
   908 704-4000

(P-26389)
KAPL INC
1126 N Brookhurst St, Anaheim (92801-1702)
PHONE....................714 991-9543
EMP: 254 **Privately Held**
SIC: 8731 Energy research
PA: Kapl, Inc.
   2401 River Rd
   Schenectady NY 12309

(P-26390)
KINEMED INC
40 Lincoln Ave, Piedmont (94611-3845)
PHONE....................510 655-6525
Robert Stein, *CEO*
David Fineman, *President*
Hank Settle, *CFO*
Patrick James Doyle, *Officer*
Irwin Heyman, *Exec VP*
EMP: 54 **EST:** 2001
SQ FT: 10,000
SALES (est): 7.7MM **Privately Held**
WEB: www.kinemed.com
SIC: 8731 Biotechnical research, commercial

(P-26391)
KITE PHARMA INC (HQ)
2400 Broadway Ste 100, Santa Monica (90404-3058)
PHONE....................310 824-9999
Robin L Washington, *President*
Richard L Wang, *CEO*
Anthony J Polverino, *Vice Pres*
Rizwana F Sproule, *Vice Pres*
Mario De Vera, *Engineer*
EMP: 129
SQ FT: 20,000
SALES: 22.1MM
SALES (corp-wide): 26.1B **Publicly Held**
SIC: 8731 2836 Commercial physical research; biological products, except diagnostic
PA: Gilead Sciences, Inc.
   333 Lakeside Dr
   Foster City CA 94404
   650 574-3000

(P-26392)
L3 APPLIED TECHNOLOGIES INC
2700 Merced St, San Leandro (94577-5602)
PHONE....................510 577-7100
Janet Luna, *Director*
EMP: 109
SALES (corp-wide): 9.5B **Publicly Held**
SIC: 8731 Commercial physical research
HQ: L3 Applied Technologies, Inc.
   10180 Barnes Canyon Rd
   San Diego CA 92121
   858 404-7824

(P-26393)
LA JOLLA PHARMACEUTICAL CO (PA)
4550 Towne Centre Ct, San Diego (92121-1900)
PHONE....................858 207-4264
George F Tidmarsh, *President*
Kevin C Tang, *Ch of Bd*
Jennifer A Carver, *COO*
Dennis M Mulroy, *CFO*
Lakhmir S Chawla, *Chief Mktg Ofcr*
EMP: 123
SQ FT: 83,008
SALES: 616K **Publicly Held**
WEB: www.ljpc.com
SIC: 8731 2834 Biotechnical research, commercial; pharmaceutical preparations

(P-26394)
LAB-GISTICS LLC
885 Pacific Ave, San Jose (95126-4821)
PHONE....................650 309-2627
Minh Phan,
EMP: 200
SQ FT: 60,000
SALES: 25MM **Privately Held**
SIC: 8731 Computer (hardware) development

(P-26395)
LABCYTE INC (PA)
Also Called: Echo
170 Rose Orchard Way # 200, San Jose (95134-1374)
PHONE....................408 747-2000
Mark F Colbrie, *CEO*
Tammy Cameron, *CFO*
Stephen Bates, *Exec VP*
Mathew Bramwell, *Vice Pres*
Michae Miller, *Vice Pres*
EMP: 74
SQ FT: 19,200
SALES (est): 18.1MM **Privately Held**
WEB: www.labcyte.com
SIC: 8731 Commercial physical research

(P-26396)
LEIDOS INC
Also Called: Reveal Imaging
2985 Scott St, Vista (92081-8339)
PHONE....................858 826-9090
John Jumper, *CEO*
Marcus Edwards, *Engineer*
EMP: 130
SALES (corp-wide): 10.1B **Publicly Held**
WEB: www.saic.com
SIC: 8731 3829 3826 Commercial physical research; measuring & controlling devices; analytical instruments
HQ: Leidos, Inc.
   11951 Freedom Dr Ste 500
   Reston VA 20190
   571 526-6000

(P-26397)
LEIDOS INC
4035 Hancock St, San Diego (92110-5105)
PHONE....................858 826-5552
Diane Malito, *Branch Mgr*
EMP: 377
SALES (corp-wide): 10.1B **Publicly Held**
WEB: www.saic.com
SIC: 8731 Commercial physical research
HQ: Leidos, Inc.
   11951 Freedom Dr Ste 500
   Reston VA 20190
   571 526-6000

(P-26398)
LEIDOS INC
1874 S Pacific Coast Hwy, Redondo Beach (90277-6117)
PHONE....................310 791-9671
Alexander Preston, *Branch Mgr*
EMP: 82
SALES (corp-wide): 10.1B **Publicly Held**
WEB: www.saic.com
SIC: 8731 Commercial physical research
HQ: Leidos, Inc.
   11951 Freedom Dr Ste 500
   Reston VA 20190
   571 526-6000

(P-26399)
LEIDOS INC
9455 Towne Centre Dr # 200, San Diego (92121-3079)
PHONE....................858 535-4499
Jim Taylor, *Manager*
John Jumper, *CEO*
EMP: 112
SALES (corp-wide): 10.1B **Publicly Held**
WEB: www.saic.com
SIC: 8731 Commercial physical research
HQ: Leidos, Inc.
   11951 Freedom Dr Ste 500
   Reston VA 20190
   571 526-6000

(P-26400)
LEIDOS INC
Also Called: Saic
10260 Campus Point Dr C, San Diego
(92121-1522)
PHONE.......................703 676-4300
Jere Drummond, *Director*
Brian Dealy, *President*
John Hensley, *President*
Suzan Yeager, *President*
Barry Wallis, *Officer*
EMP: 148
SALES (corp-wide): 10.1B **Publicly Held**
SIC: 8731 Commercial physical research
HQ: Leidos, Inc.
    11951 Freedom Dr Ste 500
    Reston VA 20190
    571 526-6000

(P-26401)
LEIDOS INC
4161 Campus Point Ct, San Diego
(92121-1513)
PHONE.......................858 826-9416
Paul Chang, *Manager*
Roger Krone, *CEO*
EMP: 208
SALES (corp-wide): 10.1B **Publicly Held**
WEB: www.saic.com
SIC: 8731 Commercial physical research
HQ: Leidos, Inc.
    11951 Freedom Dr Ste 500
    Reston VA 20190
    571 526-6000

(P-26402)
LEIDOS INC
Saic
590 W Central Ave Ste I, Brea
(92821-3019)
PHONE.......................714 257-6400
Fax: 714 257-9886
EMP: 93
SALES (corp-wide): 7B **Publicly Held**
SIC: 8731
HQ: Leidos, Inc.
    11951 Freedom Dr Ste 500
    Reston VA 20190
    571 526-6000

(P-26403)
LEIDOS INC
300 N Sepulveda Blvd, El Segundo
(90245-4472)
PHONE.......................310 524-3134
Ronald Graves, *Manager*
Tom Bosmans, *Vice Pres*
EMP: 182
SALES (corp-wide): 10.1B **Publicly Held**
WEB: www.saic.com
SIC: 8731 Commercial physical research
HQ: Leidos, Inc.
    11951 Freedom Dr Ste 500
    Reston VA 20190
    571 526-6000

(P-26404)
LEIDOS INC
10740 Thornmint Rd, San Diego
(92127-2700)
PHONE.......................858 826-6616
Sarita Ambris, *Branch Mgr*
EMP: 93
SALES (corp-wide): 10.1B **Publicly Held**
WEB: www.saic.com
SIC: 8731 Commercial physical research
HQ: Leidos, Inc.
    11951 Freedom Dr Ste 500
    Reston VA 20190
    571 526-6000

(P-26405)
LEIDOS INC
2000 Powell St Ste 1090, Emeryville
(94608-1780)
PHONE.......................510 428-2550
EMP: 93
SALES (corp-wide): 10.1B **Publicly Held**
WEB: www.saic.com
SIC: 8731 Commercial physical research;
energy research; environmental research;
medical research, commercial
HQ: Leidos, Inc.
    11951 Freedom Dr Ste 500
    Reston VA 20190
    571 526-6000

(P-26406)
LEIDOS INC
1299 Prospect St, La Jolla (92037-3623)
PHONE.......................858 826-6000
EMP: 350
SALES (corp-wide): 10.1B **Publicly Held**
WEB: www.saic.com
SIC: 8731 Commercial physical research
HQ: Leidos, Inc.
    11951 Freedom Dr Ste 500
    Reston VA 20190
    571 526-6000

(P-26407)
LEIDOS INC
Also Called: National Security
4065 Hancock St, San Diego (92110-5151)
PHONE.......................858 826-6000
Gordon Saakamodo, *Manager*
EMP: 93
SALES (corp-wide): 10.1B **Publicly Held**
WEB: www.saic.com
SIC: 8731 Commercial physical research;
energy research; environmental research;
medical research, commercial
HQ: Leidos, Inc.
    11951 Freedom Dr Ste 500
    Reston VA 20190
    571 526-6000

(P-26408)
LEIDOS INC
10010 Campus Point Dr, San Diego
(92121-1518)
PHONE.......................858 826-7129
Joel Colbourn, *Branch Mgr*
EMP: 241
SQ FT: 64,800
SALES (corp-wide): 10.1B **Publicly Held**
WEB: www.saic.com
SIC: 8731 Energy research; environmental
research; medical research, commercial
HQ: Leidos, Inc.
    11951 Freedom Dr Ste 500
    Reston VA 20190
    571 526-6000

(P-26409)
LEIDOS INC
Also Called: Saic
505 14th St Ste 900, Oakland
(94612-1468)
PHONE.......................510 466-7138
April Pierson, *Manager*
EMP: 93
SALES (corp-wide): 10.1B **Publicly Held**
SIC: 8731 Commercial physical research
HQ: Leidos, Inc.
    11951 Freedom Dr Ste 500
    Reston VA 20190
    571 526-6000

(P-26410)
LEIDOS INC
N Depo Rd Bldg 4530, Fort Irwin (92310)
PHONE.......................910 574-4597
Cassidy Smith, *Manager*
EMP: 93
SALES (corp-wide): 10.1B **Publicly Held**
SIC: 8731 Commercial physical research
HQ: Leidos, Inc.
    11951 Freedom Dr Ste 500
    Reston VA 20190
    571 526-6000

(P-26411)
LEIDOS ENGRG & SCIENCES LLC
1330 30th St Ste A, San Diego
(92154-3471)
PHONE.......................619 542-3130
Karen Parizeau, *Manager*
James Sleeth, *Principal*
EMP: 95
SALES (corp-wide): 10.1B **Publicly Held**
SIC: 8731 Natural resource research
HQ: Leidos Engineering & Sciences, Llc
    700 N Frederick Ave
    Gaithersburg MD 20879
    301 240-7000

(P-26412)
LIGHTWAVES 2020 INC
1323 Great Mall Dr, Milpitas (95035-8013)
PHONE.......................408 503-8888
J J Pan, *Ch of Bd*

Jewel Chang, *Principal*
EMP: 50
SALES (est): 6.2MM **Privately Held**
WEB: www.lightwaves2020.com
SIC: 8731 Electronic research

(P-26413)
MA LABORATORIES INC
Also Called: MA Labs
18725 San Jose Ave, City of Industry
(91748-1324)
PHONE.......................626 820-8988
Christine Pan, *Manager*
EMP: 53
SALES (corp-wide): 427.6MM **Privately Held**
SIC: 8731 Commercial physical research
PA: Ma Laboratories, Inc.
    2075 N Capitol Ave
    San Jose CA 95132
    408 941-0808

(P-26414)
MANNKIND CORPORATION (PA)
30930 Russell Ranch Rd # 300, Westlake Village (91362-7379)
PHONE.......................818 661-5000
Matthew J Pfeffer, *CEO*
Kent Kresa, *Ch of Bd*
Michael E Castagna, *CEO*
Steven Binder, *CFO*
Ronald Consiglio, *Bd of Directors*
▲ EMP: 148
SQ FT: 142,000
SALES: 11.7MM **Publicly Held**
WEB: www.mannkindcorp.com
SIC: 8731 2834 Biotechnical research,
commercial; pharmaceutical preparations

(P-26415)
MEMBRANE TECHNOLOGY & RES INC (PA)
Also Called: M T R
39630 Eureka Dr, Newark (94560-4805)
PHONE.......................650 328-2228
Colin Bailey, *Chairman*
Hans Wijmans, *President*
Nicolas Wynn, *COO*
Meryl Rains, *CFO*
Janet Farrant, *Exec VP*
EMP: 70
SQ FT: 60,000
SALES (est): 16.6MM **Privately Held**
WEB: www.mtrinc.com
SIC: 8731 3823 Commercial research lab-
oratory; on-stream gas/liquid analysis in-
struments, industrial

(P-26416)
MEMORIAL HEALTHTEC LABRATORIES
9920 Talbert Ave, Fountain Valley
(92708-5153)
PHONE.......................714 962-4677
Marcia Manker, *Manager*
Jeff Desrocher, *Info Tech Dir*
Lori Debold, *Med Doctor*
Kevin Tauris, *Director*
Debbie Marino, *Manager*
EMP: 875
SALES (corp-wide): 2.2B **Privately Held**
SIC: 8731 Commercial physical research
HQ: Memorial Healthtec Labratories Inc
    2865 Atlantic Ave Ste 203
    Long Beach CA 90806

(P-26417)
MICROCONSTANTS INC
9050 Camino Santa Fe, San Diego
(92121-3203)
PHONE.......................858 652-4600
Gilbert Lam, *Officer*
Jose Buenviaje, *Vice Pres*
Moira Brown, *Info Tech Mgr*
Karen Trout, *Project Dir*
Cynthia Gomez, *Project Mgr*
EMP: 50
SQ FT: 34,000
SALES (est): 8.3MM **Privately Held**
SIC: 8731 Biotechnical research, commer-
cial

(P-26418)
MIDWEST ENVIROMENTAL CONTROL
22430 13th St, Santa Clarita (91321-1104)
PHONE.......................661 255-0722
Dale Brouhl, *Owner*
EMP: 50
SALES (est): 1.8MM **Privately Held**
SIC: 8731 Environmental research

(P-26419)
MONTEREY BAY AQUARIUM RES INST
Also Called: Mbari
7700 Sandholdt Rd, Moss Landing
(95039-9644)
PHONE.......................831 775-1700
Christopher A Scholin, *President*
Marcia McNutt, *President*
Basilio Martinez, *CFO*
Frank Flores, *Chief Mktg Ofcr*
Julie Packard, *Vice Pres*
▲ EMP: 220
SQ FT: 17,000
SALES: 58.9MM **Privately Held**
WEB: www.mbari.org
SIC: 8731 Commercial physical research

(P-26420)
MOTECH AMERICAS LLC
Also Called: GE Energy
1300 Valley Vista Dr # 207, Diamond Bar
(91765-3940)
PHONE.......................302 451-7500
Peng Heng Chang, *CEO*
Eric Kuo, *President*
Dr Alan Wu, *President*
EMP: 320
SALES (est): 23.8MM
SALES (corp-wide): 770.4MM **Privately Held**
SIC: 8731 3674 Energy research; solar
cells
PA: Motech Industries Inc.
    6f, 248, Pei Shen Rd., Sec. 3,
    New Taipei City 22204
    226 625-093

(P-26421)
NATIONAL MARINE FISHERIES SVC
Also Called: Southwest Fsheries Science Ctr
8604 La Jolla Shores Dr, La Jolla
(92037-1508)
PHONE.......................858 546-7081
William W Fox Jr, *Director*
Anne Allen, *Admin Asst*
EMP: 150 **Publicly Held**
SIC: 8731 9512 Biological research; land,
mineral & wildlife conservation;
HQ: Western Pacific Regional Fishery Man-
agement Council
    1315 E West Hwy
    Silver Spring MD 20910

(P-26422)
NEBULA INC
Also Called: Nebula Systems
1100 La Avenida St, Mountain View
(94043-1452)
PHONE.......................650 539-9900
Gordon Stitt, *CEO*
Chris C Kemp, *CEO*
Kim Broadbeck, *Vice Pres*
Tina Nolte, *Vice Pres*
Steve O'Hara, *Vice Pres*
EMP: 67
SALES (est): 8.2MM **Privately Held**
WEB: www.nebula.com
SIC: 8731 7373 Computer (hardware) de-
velopment; computer integrated systems
design

(P-26423)
NEUROPACE INC
455 Bernardo Ave, Mountain View
(94043-5237)
PHONE.......................650 237-2700
Frank Fischer, *President*
Rebecca Kuhn, *Officer*
Isabella Abati, *Vice Pres*
Debra Smolley, *Vice Pres*
Pamela Maher, *Director*
EMP: 90

SQ FT: 37,500
SALES (est): 18.8MM Privately Held
WEB: www.neuropace.com
SIC: 8731 Medical research, commercial

(P-26424)
NORTHROP GRUMMAN SYSTEMS CORP
1 Rancho Carmel Dr, San Diego (92128)
PHONE..............................858 592-3000
Rudy Lozano, *Manager*
Jerry Wheeler, *Admin Asst*
Covey Darin, *Planning*
Majid Azimi, *Design Engr*
James Worley, *Design Engr*
EMP: 1300
SQ FT: 211,000 Publicly Held
WEB: www.trw.com
SIC: 8731 8711 7373 3812 Commercial physical research; engineering services; computer integrated systems design; search & navigation equipment
HQ: Northrop Grumman Systems Corporation
2980 Fairview Park Dr
Falls Church VA 22042
703 280-2900

(P-26425)
ORBITAL SCIENCES CORPORATION
Also Called: Advanced Programs Group
2401 E El Segundo Blvd # 200, El Segundo (90245-4631)
PHONE..............................703 406-5000
Antonio Elias, *Exec VP*
EMP: 500 Publicly Held
SIC: 8731 Commercial physical research
HQ: Orbital Sciences Corporation
45101 Warp Dr
Dulles VA 20166
703 406-5000

(P-26426)
ORGANOVO HOLDINGS INC (PA)
6275 Nncy Rdge Dr Ste 110, San Diego (92121)
PHONE..............................858 224-1000
Taylor Crouch, *President*
Kirk Malloy, *Ch of Bd*
Craig Kussman, *CFO*
Eric David, *Officer*
Jennifer Kinsbruner Bush, *Senior VP*
EMP: 75
SQ FT: 45,580
SALES: 4.6MM Publicly Held
SIC: 8731 Biological research

(P-26427)
OSTENDO TECHNOLOGIES INC (PA)
6185 Paseo Del Norte # 200, Carlsbad (92011-1152)
PHONE..............................760 710-3003
Hussein S El-Ghoroury, *CEO*
Benjamin Haskell, *President*
Joaquin Silva, *President*
Wayne Lutje, *Vice Pres*
Jason McDowall, *Vice Pres*
EMP: 52
SQ FT: 10,000
SALES (est): 24.3MM Privately Held
WEB: www.ostendotech.com
SIC: 8731 Electronic research

(P-26428)
PALL FORTEBIO LLC
47661 Fremont Blvd, Fremont (94538-6577)
PHONE..............................650 322-1360
Joseph D Keegan, *CEO*
Jack H Fuchs, *CFO*
Robert Wicke, *Vice Pres*
EMP: 94
SALES (est): 17.9MM
SALES (corp-wide): 18.3B Publicly Held
WEB: www.fortebio.com
SIC: 8731 Biotechnical research, commercial; biological research
HQ: Pall Corporation
25 Harbor Park Dr
Port Washington NY 11050
516 484-5400

(P-26429)
PALO ALTO MEDICAL FOUNDATION
Research Institute
795 El Camino Real, Palo Alto (94301-2302)
PHONE..............................650 326-8120
EMP: 50
SALES (corp-wide): 12.4B Privately Held
SIC: 8731 Medical research, commercial
HQ: Palo Alto Medical Foundation For Health Care, Research And Education (Inc)
795 El Camino Real
Palo Alto CA 94301
650 321-4121

(P-26430)
PALO ALTO RESEARCH CENTER INC
Also Called: Parc
3333 Coyote Hill Rd, Palo Alto (94304-1314)
PHONE..............................650 812-4000
Tolga Kurtoglu, *CEO*
Mark Bernstein, *President*
John Knights, *President*
John Pauksta, *CFO*
Jonathan R Wolter, *CFO*
EMP: 250
SQ FT: 200,000
SALES (est): 51.9MM
SALES (corp-wide): 10.2B Publicly Held
WEB: www.parc.com
SIC: 8731 Medical research, commercial
PA: Xerox Corporation
201 Merritt 7
Norwalk CT 06851
203 968-3000

(P-26431)
PANASONIC CORP NORTH AMERICA
Panasonic Research & Dev
10900 N Tantau Ave 200, Cupertino (95014-0713)
PHONE..............................408 861-3900
Thomas Eccleston, *Branch Mgr*
Peter Fung, *Technology*
EMP: 140
SALES (corp-wide): 74.9B Privately Held
SIC: 8731 Electronic research
HQ: Panasonic Corporation Of North America
2 Riverfront Plz Ste 200
Newark NJ 07102
201 348-7000

(P-26432)
PAREXEL INTERNATIONAL CORP
1560 E Chevy Chase Dr # 140, Glendale (91206-4197)
PHONE..............................818 254-7076
Mollie Barrett, *Director*
Simon Soden, *Info Tech Mgr*
Kimberly Dao, *Research*
Joan Ignosci, *Research*
Doreen Dawson, *Human Res Dir*
EMP: 200
SALES (corp-wide): 2.4B Privately Held
SIC: 8731 Medical research, commercial
HQ: Parexel International Corporation
195 West St
Waltham MA 02451
781 487-9900

(P-26433)
PARSONS GOVERNMENT SVCS INC (HQ)
25531 Commercentre Dr, Lake Forest (92630-8873)
PHONE..............................949 768-8161
Charles L Harrington, *CEO*
Sean Collins, *Officer*
Garth Bloxham, *Vice Pres*
Michael Byers, *Vice Pres*
Michael Cox, *Vice Pres*
EMP: 53
SALES (est): 126.1MM
SALES (corp-wide): 3.1B Privately Held
WEB: www.sparta.com
SIC: 8731 Commercial physical research

PA: The Parsons Corporation
100 W Walnut St
Pasadena CA 91124
626 440-2000

(P-26434)
PAXVAX INC
3985 Sorrento Valley Blvd A, San Diego (92121-1421)
PHONE..............................858 450-9595
Ali Pina, *Branch Mgr*
EMP: 50
SALES (corp-wide): 560.8MM Publicly Held
SIC: 8731 Biotechnical research, commercial
HQ: Paxvax, Inc.
555 Twin Dolphin Dr # 360
Redwood City CA 94065

(P-26435)
PERLEGEN SCIENCES INC
35473 Dumbarton Ct, Newark (94560-1100)
PHONE..............................650 625-4500
Bradley Margus, *President*
Stephen Fodor, *Ch of Bd*
William W Sims, *CFO*
David R Cox MD, *Officer*
Mark McCamish MD, *Officer*
EMP: 102
SQ FT: 58,000
SALES (est): 5.5MM Privately Held
WEB: www.perlegen.com
SIC: 8731 8071 Biotechnical research, commercial; medical laboratories

(P-26436)
PERSONALIS INC
1330 Obrien Dr, Menlo Park (94025-1436)
PHONE..............................650 752-1300
John West, *CEO*
Richard Chen, *Officer*
Lloyd Hsu, *Vice Pres*
Fitzpatrick Michael, *Vice Pres*
Carol Tillis, *Vice Pres*
EMP: 70
SQ FT: 30,000
SALES (est): 12.6MM Privately Held
SIC: 8731 Commercial research laboratory; biotechnical research, commercial

(P-26437)
PETER H MATTSON & CO INC
343 Hatch Dr, Foster City (94404-1162)
PHONE..............................650 356-2500
Steve Gundrum, *President*
Peter H Mattson, *Chairman*
Patricia Mattson, *Corp Secy*
Barbara Stuckey, *Officer*
Doug Berg, *Vice Pres*
EMP: 70
SQ FT: 20,000
SALES (est): 11.2MM Privately Held
WEB: www.protothink.com
SIC: 8731 Food research

(P-26438)
PHYSICAL OPTICS CORPORATION (PA)
1845 W 205th St, Torrance (90501-1510)
PHONE..............................310 320-3088
Joanna Jannson, *CEO*
Min-Yi Shih, *President*
Gajendra Savant, *COO*
Gordon Drew, *CFO*
Tomasz Jannson, *Senior VP*
EMP: 244
SQ FT: 45,000
SALES: 82.4MM Privately Held
WEB: www.poc.com
SIC: 8731 7299 Commercial research laboratory; information services, consumer

(P-26439)
POLYPEPTIDE LABS SAN DIEGO LLC
9395 Cabot Dr, San Diego (92126-4310)
PHONE..............................858 408-0808
Timothy Culberth, *CEO*
Trishul Shah, *Associate Dir*
Terry Wyant, *Info Tech Mgr*
Phil Morrgavo, *Buyer*
Felix Smith, *Buyer*
EMP: 72

SQ FT: 43,000
SALES: 14MM Privately Held
WEB: www.neomps.com
SIC: 8731 2834 2833 Biotechnical research, commercial; pharmaceutical preparations; medicinals & botanicals
HQ: Polypeptide Laboratories Inc.
365 Maple Ave
Torrance CA 90503

(P-26440)
PROMAB BIOTECHNOLOGIES INC
2600 Hilltop Dr, San Pablo (94806-1971)
PHONE..............................510 860-4615
Lijun Wu, *President*
Vita Golubovskaya, *Business Dir*
EMP: 80 EST: 2001
SALES (est): 2MM Privately Held
SIC: 8731 Biotechnical research, commercial

(P-26441)
PROSCIENTO INC
855 Third Ave Ste 3340, Chula Vista (91911-1350)
PHONE..............................619 427-1300
Marcus Hompesch, *CEO*
Brian Mooney, *COO*
Linda Morrow, *COO*
Markus Hofmann, *CFO*
Christian Weyer, *Officer*
EMP: 170
SQ FT: 20,000
SALES (est): 32.2MM Privately Held
WEB: www.profilinstitute.com
SIC: 8731 Biotechnical research, commercial

(P-26442)
PULSE-LINK INC
2730 Loker Ave W, Carlsbad (92010-6603)
PHONE..............................760 448-4690
John Santhoff, *CEO*
Paul Dillon, *President*
Bruce Watkins, *President*
Rusty Cashman, *Engineer*
Dan Grantz, *Senior Engr*
EMP: 75
SQ FT: 33,000
SALES (est): 5.7MM Privately Held
WEB: www.pulselink.net
SIC: 8731 Electronic research

(P-26443)
QUANTUM CORPORATION (PA)
224 Airport Pkwy Ste 550, San Jose (95110-1097)
PHONE..............................408 944-4000
James J Lerner, *CEO*
Raghavendra Rau, *Ch of Bd*
J Michael Dodson, *CFO*
William C Britts, *Senior VP*
Robert S Clark, *Senior VP*
▲ EMP: 314
SALES (est): 505.3MM Publicly Held
WEB: www.quantum.com
SIC: 8731 3572 Computer (hardware) development; tape storage units, computer

(P-26444)
RAVEN BIOTECHNOLOGIES INC
1 Corporate Dr, South San Francisco (94080-7043)
PHONE..............................650 624-2600
George Schreiner, *CEO*
Michael Kranda, *Ch of Bd*
John B Whelan, *COO*
William R Rohn, *Vice Ch Bd*
Lucille W S Chang, *Vice Pres*
EMP: 66
SQ FT: 68,000
SALES (est): 5.7MM
SALES (corp-wide): 157.7MM Publicly Held
WEB: www.ravenbio.com
SIC: 8731 Biotechnical research, commercial; commercial research laboratory
PA: Macrogenics, Inc.
9704 Medical Center Dr
Rockville MD 20850
301 251-5172

(P-26445)
ROCHE MOLECULAR SYSTEMS INC
1145 Atlantic Ave Ste 100, Alameda (94501-1145)
PHONE....................510 814-2800
Terrance Taford, *Branch Mgr*
EMP: 135
SALES (corp-wide): 53.9B **Privately Held**
SIC: 8731 Biotechnical research, commercial
HQ: Roche Molecular Systems, Inc.
4300 Hacienda Dr
Pleasanton CA 94588

(P-26446)
ROCHE MOLECULAR SYSTEMS INC (DH)
4300 Hacienda Dr, Pleasanton (94588-2722)
P.O. Box 9002 (94566-9002)
PHONE....................925 730-8000
Paul Brown, *President*
Maria Horga, *Vice Pres*
Kathleen Lake, *Associate Dir*
Ricardo Guerrero, *Principal*
Toni Pergola, *Asst Admin*
EMP: 400
SALES (est): 163.2MM
SALES (corp-wide): 53.9B **Privately Held**
SIC: 8731 Biotechnical research, commercial

(P-26447)
SAMSUNG RESEARCH AMERICA INC (DH)
Also Called: Sisa
665 Clyde Ave, Mountain View (94043-2235)
PHONE....................408 544-5700
Young Joon Gil, *President*
Doochan Daniel Eum, *CEO*
Oh-Hyun Kwon, *CEO*
K E Jang, *CFO*
Ju-Hwa Yoon, *CFO*
EMP: 50
SQ FT: 32,000
SALES (est): 65.1MM
SALES (corp-wide): 148.1B **Privately Held**
WEB: www.cnl-samsung.com
SIC: 8731 7371 Computer (hardware) development; computer software development & applications
HQ: Samsung Electronics America, Inc.
85 Challenger Rd Fl 7
Ridgefield Park NJ 07660
201 229-4000

(P-26448)
SANGAMO THERAPEUTICS INC (PA)
501 Canal Blvd, Richmond (94804-3559)
PHONE....................510 970-6000
Alexander D Macrae, *President*
Kathy Y Yi, *CFO*
Stephen Dilly, *Bd of Directors*
Roger Jeffs, *Bd of Directors*
John Larson, *Bd of Directors*
EMP: 117
SQ FT: 45,600
SALES: 36.5MM **Publicly Held**
WEB: www.sangamo.com
SIC: 8731 Biotechnical research, commercial

(P-26449)
SANSA TECHNOLOGY LLC
6990 Village Pkwy, Dublin (94568-2438)
PHONE....................866 204-3710
EMP: 50
SALES (est): 2.6MM **Privately Held**
SIC: 8731

(P-26450)
SCIENTIFIC APPLICATIONS & RES (PA)
Also Called: SARA
6300 Gateway Dr, Cypress (90630-4844)
PHONE....................714 828-1465
Parviz Parhami, *CEO*
James Wes, *President*
Amy Dockendorf, *COO*
Michael Zintl, *Program Mgr*

Bill Bickford, *Administration*
EMP: 58
SQ FT: 43,000
SALES: 26MM **Privately Held**
WEB: www.sarainc.com
SIC: 8731 Commercial physical research

(P-26451)
SCRIPPS HEALTH
Scripps Health Research
10550 N Torrey Pines Rd, La Jolla (92037-1000)
PHONE....................858 652-5504
Robert Sarnoff, *Branch Mgr*
EMP: 165
SALES (corp-wide): 2.9B **Privately Held**
SIC: 8731 Medical research, commercial
PA: Scripps Health
10140 Campus Point Dr Ax415
San Diego CA 92121
800 727-4777

(P-26452)
SEMINIS INC
500 Lucy Brown Rd, San Juan Bautista (95045-9713)
PHONE....................831 623-4554
Nancy Bergamini, *Manager*
EMP: 60
SALES (corp-wide): 41.2B **Privately Held**
WEB: www.seminis.com
SIC: 8731 Agricultural research
HQ: Seminis, Inc.
2700 Camino Del Sol
Oxnard CA 93030
-

(P-26453)
SEMINIS INC (DH)
2700 Camino Del Sol, Oxnard (93030-7967)
PHONE....................805 485-7317
Bruno Ferrari, *President*
Eugenio N Solorzano, *President*
Charles E Green, *Senior VP*
Oscar J Velasco, *Senior VP*
Enrique Lopez, *Vice Pres*
EMP: 300
SALES (est): 87.4MM
SALES (corp-wide): 41.2B **Privately Held**
WEB: www.seminis.com
SIC: 8731 8742 2099 Agricultural research; food research; productivity improvement consultant; marketing consulting services; food preparations
HQ: Monsanto Company
800 N Lindbergh Blvd
Saint Louis MO 63167
314 694-1000

(P-26454)
SENOMYX INC
4767 Nexus Center Dr, San Diego (92121-3051)
PHONE....................858 646-8300
John Poyhonen, *President*
Kent Snyder, *Ch of Bd*
David Humphrey, *CFO*
Sharon Wicker, *Senior VP*
Catherine C Lee, *Vice Pres*
EMP: 59
SQ FT: 65,000
SALES: 29.3MM
SALES (corp-wide): 3.3B **Privately Held**
WEB: www.senomyx.com
SIC: 8731 6794 Food research; franchises, selling or licensing
HQ: Firmenich Incorporated
250 Plainsboro Rd
Plainsboro NJ 08536
609 452-1000

(P-26455)
SEQUENOM INC (HQ)
3595 John Hopkins Ct, San Diego (92121-1121)
PHONE....................858 202-9000
Dirk Van Den Boom, *President*
Carolyn D Beaver, *CFO*
Daniel S Grosu, *Chief Mktg Ofcr*
Mathias Ehrich, *Officer*
Jeffrey D Linton, *Senior VP*
EMP: 80
SALES (est): 128.2MM **Publicly Held**
WEB: www.sequenom.com
SIC: 8731 Biological research

(P-26456)
SIMBOL INC (PA)
Also Called: Simbol Materials
6920 Koll Center Pkwy # 216, Pleasanton (94566-3156)
PHONE....................925 226-7400
Luka Erceg, *President*
EMP: 75
SALES (est): 16.4MM **Privately Held**
SIC: 8731 Natural resource research

(P-26457)
SORRENTO THERAPEUTICS INC (PA)
4955 Directors Pl, San Diego (92121-3836)
PHONE....................858 203-4100
Henry Ji, *Ch of Bd*
Jiong Shao, *CFO*
Jerome Zeldis, *Chief Mktg Ofcr*
George K Ng, *Officer*
EMP: 107 EST: 2006
SQ FT: 43,000
SALES: 151.8MM **Publicly Held**
SIC: 8731 Biotechnical research, commercial; biological research

(P-26458)
SPREADTRUM CMMNCATIONS USA INC
10180 Telesis Ct Ste 500, San Diego (92121-2787)
PHONE....................858 546-0895
Daniel LI, *CFO*
Shawn Pollard, *Office Mgr*
Charlie Hanes, *Info Tech Dir*
Robert Mix, *Technology*
Meng Chung, *Engineer*
EMP: 70
SALES (est): 11.6MM **Privately Held**
WEB: www.spreadtrum.com
SIC: 8731 Electronic research
HQ: Spreadtrum Communications (Shanghai) Co., Ltd.
Building 1, Exhibition Center, 2288, Zuchongzhi Road, China (Sha
Shanghai 20120
212 036-0600

(P-26459)
STELLARTECH RESEARCH CORP (PA)
560 Cottonwood Dr, Milpitas (95035-7403)
PHONE....................408 331-3134
Roger A Stern, *President*
Jerome Jackson, *Vice Pres*
Edison Manuel, *Vice Pres*
Jerry Smith, *Vice Pres*
Vincent Sullivan, *Vice Pres*
EMP: 100
SQ FT: 20,000
SALES (est): 30.3MM **Privately Held**
SIC: 8731 3842 Medical research, commercial; surgical appliances & supplies

(P-26460)
STRATEGY FOR WATER & LAND RESO
49 Donovan, Irvine (92620-3882)
PHONE....................949 572-3034
Douglas Hamilton,
EMP: 50
SALES (est): 1.2MM **Privately Held**
SIC: 8731 Natural resource research

(P-26461)
SUN INNOVATIONS INC
43241 Osgood Rd, Fremont (94539-5657)
PHONE....................510 573-3913
Ted Sun, *President*
Donna George, *Sales Dir*
EMP: 50
SQ FT: 2,200
SALES (est): 2.8MM **Privately Held**
WEB: www.superimaging.com
SIC: 8731 Commercial physical research

(P-26462)
SUN PHARMACEUTICALS INC
Also Called: Research
13718 Sorbonne Ct, San Diego (92128-4760)
PHONE....................858 380-8865
Meng Sun, *President*
Zuolin Zhu, *CTO*
EMP: 102

SALES (est): 2.7MM **Privately Held**
SIC: 8731 Biotechnical research, commercial

(P-26463)
SUNSYSTEM TECHNOLOGY LLC (PA)
2731 Citrus Rd Ste D, Rancho Cordova (95742-6303)
PHONE....................916 671-3351
Kurtis Bank, *President*
Nick Snow, *Director*
EMP: 375 EST: 2014
SALES (est): 52.2MM **Privately Held**
SIC: 8731 Commercial physical research

(P-26464)
SYNTERACTHCR INC (DH)
5909 Sea Otter Pl Ste 100, Carlsbad (92010-6674)
PHONE....................760 268-8200
Ellen Morgan, *President*
Karl Deonanan, *CFO*
Keith Kelson, *CFO*
Richard Paul, *Chief Mktg Ofcr*
Russ Holmes, *Exec VP*
EMP: 330
SQ FT: 30,000
SALES: 65.4MM
SALES (corp-wide): 66.7MM **Privately Held**
WEB: www.synteract.com
SIC: 8731 Medical research, commercial
HQ: Synteracthcr Corporation
5909 Sea Otter Pl Ste 100
Carlsbad CA 92010
760 268-8200

(P-26465)
SYNTERACTHCR CORPORATION (HQ)
5909 Sea Otter Pl Ste 100, Carlsbad (92010-6674)
PHONE....................760 268-8200
Steve Powell, *CEO*
Keith Kelson, *CFO*
Cheryl Murphy, *Senior VP*
Ren Daren, *Vice Pres*
Martine Dehlinger-Kremer, *Vice Pres*
EMP: 330 EST: 2008
SALES (est): 66.7MM **Privately Held**
SIC: 8731 Commercial physical research
PA: Synteracthcr Holdings Corporation
5909 Sea Otter Pl Ste 100
Carlsbad CA 92010
760 268-8200

(P-26466)
SYNTERACTHCR HOLDINGS CORP (PA)
5909 Sea Otter Pl Ste 100, Carlsbad (92010-6674)
PHONE....................760 268-8200
Steve Powell, *CEO*
Keith Kelson, *CFO*
Frank Santoro, *Chief Mktg Ofcr*
Stewart Bieler, *Officer*
Dieter Seitz-Tutter, *Opers Staff*
EMP: 350 EST: 2008
SALES (est): 66.7MM **Privately Held**
SIC: 8731 Commercial physical research

(P-26467)
SYNTHETIC GENOMICS INC (DH)
11149 N Torrey Pines Rd, La Jolla (92037-1009)
PHONE....................858 754-2900
Oliver Fetzer, *CEO*
Aristides Patrinos, *President*
Joseph Mahler, *CFO*
Hamilton O Smith, *Security Dir*
James Flatt, *CTO*
EMP: 123
SQ FT: 45,000
SALES (est): 48MM **Privately Held**
WEB: www.syntheticgenomics.com
SIC: 8731 Biotechnical research, commercial
HQ: Genting Plantations Berhad
10th Floor Wisma Genting
Kuala Lumpur KLP
323 336-408

P R O D U C T S & S V C S

(P-26468)
TAE TECHNOLOGIES INC (PA)
19631 Pauling, Foothill Ranch
(92610-2607)
P.O. Box 7010, Rcho STA Marg (92688-7010)
PHONE..............................949 830-2117
Michl Binderbauer, *CEO*
Mark J Lewis, *President*
Brandon Cholodenko, *Sr Ntwrk Engine*
David Ewing, *CIO*
Don Bui, *Design Engr*
EMP: 155
SALES (est): 50.3MM **Privately Held**
SIC: 8731 Energy research

(P-26469)
TAKARA BIO USA INC
Also Called: Clontech
1290 Terra Bella Ave, Mountain View
(94043-1837)
PHONE..............................650 919-7300
Carol Lou, *President*
Kazuki Yamamoto, *COO*
Leslee McLennan Bonino, *Vice Pres*
Michelle Moreno, *Executive Asst*
Joe Antona, *Administration*
EMP: 175
SQ FT: 100,000
SALES: 95.6MM
SALES (corp-wide): 2.5B **Privately Held**
WEB: www.clontech.com
SIC: 8731 2836 Biotechnical research,
commercial; biological products, except
diagnostic
HQ: Takara Bio Inc.
7-4-38, Nojihigashi
Kusatsu SGA 525-0
775 656-920

(P-26470)
TANVEX BIOPHARMA USA INC (PA)
Also Called: L J B
2030 Main St Ste 600, Irvine (92614-7235)
PHONE..............................858 210-4100
Allen Chao, *CEO*
CHI-Chuan Chen, *President*
Dilip Joshi, *Vice Pres*
Hugh Murray, *Research*
Kevin TSE, *Research*
EMP: 71
SALES (est): 26MM **Privately Held**
SIC: 8731 Biological research

(P-26471)
TEGILE SYSTEMS INC
7999 Gateway Blvd Ste 120, Newark
(94560-1144)
PHONE..............................510 791-7900
Rohit Kshetrapal, *CEO*
Renato Maranon, *President*
James Yu, *President*
Ian Edmundson, *CFO*
Michael Morgan, *CFO*
EMP: 130
SQ FT: 6,500
SALES (est): 27.2MM **Privately Held**
SIC: 8731 3572 Computer (hardware) de-
velopment; computer storage devices

(P-26472)
TELEDYNE SCENTIFIC IMAGING LLC
5212 Verdugo Way, Camarillo
(93012-8662)
PHONE..............................805 373-4979
James Beletic, *President*
EMP: 150
SQ FT: 54,295
SALES (corp-wide): 2.6B **Publicly Held**
SIC: 8731 Commercial physical research
HQ: Teledyne Scientific & Imaging, Llc
1049 Camino Dos Rios
Thousand Oaks CA 91360

(P-26473)
TELEDYNE SCENTIFIC IMAGING LLC (HQ)
Also Called: Teledyne Scientific Company
1049 Camino Dos Rios, Thousand Oaks
(91360-2362)
PHONE..............................805 373-4545
Robert Mehrabian,

James Beletic, *President*
Berinder Brar, *President*
Aldo Pichelli, *President*
Roxanne Austin, *Bd of Directors*
EMP: 125
SQ FT: 161,000
SALES (est): 78MM
SALES (corp-wide): 2.6B **Publicly Held**
WEB: www.teledyne-si.com
SIC: 8731 8732 8733 Commercial physi-
cal research; commercial nonphysical re-
search; noncommercial research
organizations
PA: Teledyne Technologies Inc
1049 Camino Dos Rios
Thousand Oaks CA 91360
805 373-4545

(P-26474)
THE EXECUTIVE OFFICE OF
Also Called: Governors Office Plg & RES
1400 10th St Rm 100, Sacramento
(95814-5502)
PHONE..............................916 322-2318
Sean Walsh, *Director*
EMP: 80 **Privately Held**
SIC: 8731 9111 Environmental research;
governors' offices;
HQ: Executive Office Of The State Of Cali-
fornia
Governors Ofc
Sacramento CA 95814

(P-26475)
TOSHIBA MEMORY AMERICA INC
35 Iron Point Cir Ste 100, Folsom
(95630-8588)
PHONE..............................916 986-4707
Robert Reed, *Branch Mgr*
EMP: 50
SALES (corp-wide): 37B **Privately Held**
SIC: 8731 Electronic research
HQ: Toshiba Memory America, Inc.
2610 Orchard Pkwy
San Jose CA 95134
408 526-2400

(P-26476)
TRANSPHORM INC (PA)
115 Castilian Dr, Goleta (93117-3025)
PHONE..............................805 456-1300
Umesh Mishra, *CEO*
Yifeng Wu, *President*
Primit Parikh, *COO*
Cameron McAulay, *CFO*
Ronald Barr, *Vice Pres*
EMP: 53
SQ FT: 3,000
SALES (est): 9MM **Privately Held**
SIC: 8731 3674 Commercial physical re-
search; semiconductors & related devices

(P-26477)
TRILINK BIOTECHNOLOGIES LLC
9955 Mesa Rim Rd, San Diego
(92121-2911)
PHONE..............................858 546-0004
Richard Hogrefe, *President*
Terry Beck, *Senior VP*
Jennifer Bartels, *Prdtn Mgr*
Kaitlin Matthys, *Production*
Craig Dobbs, *VP Mktg*
EMP: 72
SQ FT: 40,000
SALES (est): 13MM **Privately Held**
WEB: www.trilinkbiotech.com
SIC: 8731 8748 Biotechnical research,
commercial; biological research; test de-
velopment & evaluation service

(P-26478)
TRUESDAIL LABORATORIES INC
3337 Michelson Dr, Irvine (92612-1699)
PHONE..............................714 730-6239
Ed Wilson, *CEO*
John Hill, *President*
Brian K Service, *Chairman*
Wogderess Berhe, *Project Mgr*
Randy Gates, *Manager*
EMP: 50 **EST:** 1931
SQ FT: 40,000

SALES: 4.8MM **Privately Held**
WEB: www.truesdail.com
SIC: 8731 8734 1711 Commercial physical research; water testing laboratory;
plumbing contractors

(P-26479)
UNITED STATES DEPT OF ENERGY
1 Cyclotron Rd, Berkeley (94720-8099)
PHONE..............................510 486-4936
Fax: 510 486-7192
EMP: 2351 **Publicly Held**
SIC: 8731
HQ: United States Dept Of Energy
1000 Independence Ave Sw
Washington DC 20585
202 586-5000

(P-26480)
UNITED STATES DEPT OF ENERGY
Also Called: Lawrence Livermore Nat Lab
7000 East Ave, Livermore (94550-9698)
P.O. Box 808 (94551-0808)
PHONE..............................925 422-1100
Fax: 925 423-3597
EMP: 7000 **Publicly Held**
SIC: 8731 9611
HQ: United States Dept Of Energy
1000 Independence Ave Sw
Washington DC 20585
202 586-5000

(P-26481)
UNITED STATES DEPT OF NAVY
Also Called: Naval Research
937 N Harbor Dr, San Diego (92132-5001)
PHONE..............................619 532-1897
Erickson Gary, *Branch Mgr*
EMP: 50 **Publicly Held**
SIC: 8731 9711 Commercial physical re-
search; Navy;
HQ: United States Department Of The Navy
1200 Navy Pentagon
Washington DC 20350

(P-26482)
UNITED STATES DEPT OF NAVY
Also Called: Naval Research Lab
7 Grace Hopper Ave Stop 2, Monterey
(93943-5598)
PHONE..............................831 656-4613
Phillip Merilees, *Branch Mgr*
EMP: 64 **Publicly Held**
SIC: 8731 9711 Commercial physical re-
search; Navy;
HQ: United States Department Of The Navy
1200 Navy Pentagon
Washington DC 20350

(P-26483)
UNITY BIOTECHNOLOGY INC
3280 Byshore Blvd Ste 100, Brisbane
(94005)
PHONE..............................650 416-1192
Keith R Leonard Jr, *Ch of Bd*
Nathaniel E David, *President*
Bob Goeltz, *CFO*
Robert C Goeltz II, *CFO*
Jamie Dananberg, *Chief Mktg Ofcr*
EMP: 70
SQ FT: 39,000
SALES: 1.3MM **Privately Held**
SIC: 8731 Medical research, commercial

(P-26484)
UNIVERSITY CALIFORNIA IRVINE
Also Called: Henry Samueli School Engrg
2220 Engineering Gateway, Irvine
(92697-0001)
PHONE..............................949 824-2819
Dr GP LI, *Director*
Tammy Phan, *Programmer Anys*
Kathleen Glynn, *Financial Analy*
Andrew Cassidy, *Internal Med*
EMP: 55 **Privately Held**
SIC: 8731 8221 9411 Electronic research;
university; administration of educational
programs;

HQ: University Of California, Irvine
510 Aldrich Hall
Irvine CA 92697
949 824-8343

(P-26485)
UNIVERSITY SOUTHERN CALIFORNIA
1000 S Fremont Ave Unit 7, Alhambra
(91803-8897)
PHONE..............................626 457-4240
Mary Ann Pentz, *Director*
Douglas Spencer, *Manager*
EMP: 100
SALES (corp-wide): 2.6B **Privately Held**
WEB: www.usc.edu
SIC: 8731 8221 Medical research, com-
mercial; university
PA: University Of Southern California
3720 S Flower St Fl 3
Los Angeles CA 90089
213 740-7762

(P-26486)
US DEPT OF THE AIR FORCE
Also Called: Chem Lab Rkfe
10 E Saturn Dr, Edwards (93524-7201)
PHONE..............................661 275-5410
Joan Larue, *Manager*
EMP: 85 **Publicly Held**
WEB: www.af.mil
SIC: 8731 9711 Chemical laboratory, ex-
cept testing; Air Force;
HQ: United States Department Of The Air
Force
1000 Air Force Pentagon
Washington DC 20330

(P-26487)
USDA FOREST SERVICE
4955 Canyon Crest Dr, Riverside
(92507-6071)
PHONE..............................951 680-1560
Irene Powell, *Administration*
EMP: 75 **Publicly Held**
WEB: www.defendtheforests.org
SIC: 8731 9512 Environmental research;
land conservation agencies;
HQ: Us Dept Of Agriculture Forest Service
201 14th St Sw
Washington DC 20024

(P-26488)
VENTURE DESIGN SERVICES INC (PA)
1051 S East St, Anaheim (92805-5749)
PHONE..............................714 765-3740
Wong Ngit Liong, *Chairman*
Tan Kian Seng, *President*
E H SOO, *CEO*
Soin Sign, *Treasurer*
Lee Ghai Keen, *Exec VP*
EMP: 170
SQ FT: 60,000
SALES (est): 13MM **Privately Held**
SIC: 8731 Commercial physical research

(P-26489)
VERINATA HEALTH INC
Also Called: Illumina-Redwood City
200 Lincoln Centre Dr, Foster City
(94404-1122)
PHONE..............................650 632-1680
Jeff Bird, *CEO*
Vance Vanier, *President*
Lisa Robison, *Research*
Jeff Skredenske, *Research*
James Blake, *Engineer*
EMP: 55
SALES (est): 8.7MM
SALES (corp-wide): 2.7B **Publicly Held**
WEB: www.livingmicrosystems.com
SIC: 8731 2835 Biotechnical research,
commercial; in vitro & in vivo diagnostic
substances
PA: Illumina, Inc.
5200 Illumina Way
San Diego CA 92122
858 202-4500

(P-26490)
VERTEX PHRMCTCALS SAN DEGO LLC (HQ)
3215 Merryfield Row, San Diego (92121-1126)
PHONE..............................858 404-6600
Joshua S Boger, *Bd of Directors*
Suzanne Pryor-Tillotson, *Vice Pres*
Damian Wilmot, *Vice Pres*
Anita Hintsala, *Executive Asst*
Huy Nguyen, *Software Dev*
EMP: 235
SQ FT: 81,000
SALES (est): 18.5MM
SALES (corp-wide): 2.4B **Publicly Held**
SIC: 8731 Biotechnical research, commercial
PA: Vertex Pharmaceuticals Incorporated
50 Northern Ave
Boston MA 02210
617 341-6100

(P-26491)
VIA COMMUNICATIONS INC
940 Mission Ct, Fremont (94539-8202)
PHONE..............................510 687-4650
Wen-CHI Chen, *CEO*
Jonathan Chang, *CFO*
EMP: 250
SQ FT: 3,300
SALES (est): 9.1MM **Privately Held**
SIC: 8731 Computer (hardware) development

(P-26492)
VIRIDENT SYSTEMS INC
1745 Tech Dr Ste 700, San Jose (95110)
PHONE..............................408 573-5000
Mike Gustafson, *Senior VP*
Bruce Horn, *CFO*
Mark Delsman, *Vice Pres*
Kumar Ganapathy, *Vice Pres*
Ken Grohe, *Vice Pres*
EMP: 110
SALES (est): 12.2MM
SALES (corp-wide): 20.6B **Publicly Held**
SIC: 8731 Computer (hardware) development
HQ: Hgst, Inc.
5601 Great Oaks Pkwy
San Jose CA 95119
408 717-6000

(P-26493)
WESTON SOLUTIONS INC
5817 Dryden Pl Ste 101, Carlsbad (92008-5576)
PHONE..............................760 795-6900
Lisa Marie Kay, *Branch Mgr*
Andrea Crumpacker, *Opers Mgr*
Michelle Patzius, *Manager*
EMP: 65
SALES (corp-wide): 637.8MM **Privately Held**
WEB: www.rfweston.com
SIC: 8731 Environmental research
HQ: Weston Solutions, Inc.
1400 Weston Way
West Chester PA 19380
610 701-3000

(P-26494)
WILLOW GARAGE INC
921 E Charleston Rd, Palo Alto (94303-4903)
PHONE..............................650 322-2584
Scott Wendell Hassan, *CEO*
Steve Cousins, *President*
Udit Jain, *CTO*
Vilas Mahajan, *Software Dev*
Varsha Narkhede, *Software Dev*
EMP: 59
SQ FT: 10,000
SALES (est): 6.4MM **Privately Held**
SIC: 8731 Electronic research

(P-26495)
ZYMO RESEARCH CORP (PA)
17062 Murphy Ave, Irvine (92614-5914)
PHONE..............................949 679-1190
Xiyu Jia MD, *President*
LI Zhang, *Shareholder*
Angela Kim, *Admin Sec*
Danice Cabaya, *Research*
Brandon Pollack, *Engineer*
EMP: 57

SQ FT: 10,000
SALES (est): 17.6MM **Privately Held**
WEB: www.zymoresearch.com
SIC: 8731 Biotechnical research, commercial; medical research, commercial

---

8732 Commercial Economic, Sociological & Educational Research

---

(P-26496)
ACTIVE MEASURE INC
Also Called: Survey Junkie
550 N Brand Blvd Ste 1850, Glendale (91203-1943)
PHONE..............................818 237-8417
Armen Adjemian, *CEO*
Drew Kutcharian, *CTO*
EMP: 60
SALES (est): 2.2MM **Privately Held**
SIC: 8732 7375 Market analysis or research; on-line data base information retrieval

(P-26497)
ADDED VALUE LLC (DH)
3400 Cahuenga Blvd W B, Los Angeles (90068-1376)
PHONE..............................323 254-4326
Meggy Taylor, *President*
EMP: 190
SQ FT: 9,800
SALES (est): 19.5MM
SALES (corp-wide): 20.1B **Privately Held**
WEB: www.us.millwardbrown.com
SIC: 8732 Market analysis or research
HQ: Kantar Llc
11 Madison Ave Ste 1201
New York NY 10010
212 548-7200

(P-26498)
ADEPT CONSUMER TESTING INC
16130 Ventura Blvd # 200, Encino (91436-2580)
PHONE..............................310 279-4600
Mark Tobias, *President*
EMP: 50
SQ FT: 12,000
SALES (est): 6.4MM **Privately Held**
WEB: www.adeptconsumer.com
SIC: 8732 Market analysis or research

(P-26499)
ADVANTAGE SALES & MKTG LLC (HQ)
Also Called: Advantage Solutions
18100 Von Karman Ave # 900, Irvine (92612-7195)
PHONE..............................949 797-2900
Sonny King, *Chairman*
Susie Orendain, *Partner*
Brian Stevens, *COO*
Robert Murray, *Treasurer*
Tanya Domier, *Chief Mktg Ofcr*
EMP: 250
SALES (est): 2B
SALES (corp-wide): 8.4B **Privately Held**
SIC: 8732 8742 8743 Marketing consulting services; sales (including sales management) consultant; sales promotion; market analysis or research
PA: Advantage Sales & Marketing Inc.
18100 Von Karman Ave # 900
Irvine CA 92612
949 797-2900

(P-26500)
AMER ZOETROPE RESEARCH LLC
1991 Saint Helana Hwy, Rutherford (94573)
PHONE..............................707 963-9230
Jay Shoemaker, *President*
EMP: 150
SALES (est): 3.4MM **Privately Held**
SIC: 8732 Market analysis or research

(P-26501)
BANK AMERICA NATIONAL ASSN
555 California St Ste 4, San Francisco (94104-1532)
PHONE..............................415 913-3438
John Walter, *Senior VP*
EMP: 100
SALES (corp-wide): 100.2B **Publicly Held**
WEB: www.bofa.com
SIC: 8732 Business analysis
HQ: Bank Of America, National Association
100 S Tryon St
Charlotte NC 28202
704 386-5681

(P-26502)
BAY ALARM COMPANY
9836 Kitty Ln, Oakland (94603-1070)
PHONE..............................510 452-3211
Delores Nielsen, *Manager*
Mark Terry, *Human Resources*
Bryan Lubbers, *Opers Staff*
Shawn Maccallister, *Manager*
EMP: 81
SALES (corp-wide): 163.5MM **Privately Held**
WEB: www.bayalarm.com
SIC: 8732 1731 7382 5063 Commercial nonphysical research; electrical work; security systems services; electrical apparatus & equipment
PA: Bay Alarm Company
5130 Commercial Cir
Concord CA 94520
925 935-1100

(P-26503)
CAPITOL CORPORATE SERVICES
455 Capitol Mall Ste 217, Sacramento (95814-4405)
PHONE..............................916 444-6787
John H Robinson, *Vice Pres*
Cheryl Roberts, *President*
EMP: 50
SALES (est): 4.7MM **Privately Held**
WEB: www.capitolcorporateservices.com
SIC: 8732 Research services, except laboratory

(P-26504)
CIC RESEARCH INC
8361 Vickers St Ste 308, San Diego (92111-2112)
PHONE..............................858 637-4000
Gordon H Kubota PHD, *President*
Skip Hull, *Vice Pres*
Warren L Hull, *Vice Pres*
Joyce G Revlett, *Vice Pres*
Julie Spinazzola, *Office Mgr*
EMP: 65 **EST:** 1965
SQ FT: 15,000
SALES: 3.1MM **Privately Held**
WEB: www.cicresearch.com
SIC: 8732 Economic research; market analysis or research

(P-26505)
COHERENT INC
1100 La Avenida St, Mountain View (94043-1452)
PHONE..............................408 764-4000
Richard Pierce, *CEO*
John H N Fisher, *Principal*
Mike Mielke, *Security Dir*
EMP: 82
SQ FT: 42,000
SALES (est): 15.9MM **Privately Held**
WEB: www.raydiance-inc.com
SIC: 8732 3826 3821 Research services, except laboratory; laser scientific & engineering instruments; laser beam alignment devices

(P-26506)
COMPETITIVE EDGE RES COMM INC
1620 5th Ave Ste 825, San Diego (92101-2750)
PHONE..............................619 702-2372
John E Nienstedt, *President*
EMP: 60
SQ FT: 4,000

SALES: 1.5MM **Privately Held**
WEB: www.cerc.net
SIC: 8732 Opinion research

(P-26507)
CORNERSTONE RESEARCH INC
633 W 5th St Fl 31, Los Angeles (90071-2005)
PHONE..............................213 553-2500
Richard Dalbeck, *Vice Pres*
Maria Rivas, *Admin Asst*
Jordan Finley, *Administration*
Donald Hsueh, *Analyst*
Shane Oka, *Analyst*
EMP: 73
SALES (corp-wide): 88.4MM **Privately Held**
SIC: 8732 Market analysis, business & economic research
PA: Cornerstone Research, Inc.
1000 El Camino Real # 250
Menlo Park CA 94025
650 853-1660

(P-26508)
DAS GLOBAL CAPITAL CORP
42 Peninsula Ctr Ste 317, Rllng HLS Est (90274-3506)
PHONE..............................702 967-1688
Cleooarta Y Natt, *CEO*
EMP: 59 **Privately Held**
SIC: 8732 Merger, acquisition & reorganization research
PA: Das Global Capital Corp
1785 E Sahara Ave Ste 490
Las Vegas NV 89104

(P-26509)
DAVIS RESEARCH LLC
23801 Calabasas Rd # 1036, Calabasas (91302-3319)
PHONE..............................818 591-2408
William A Davis III, *Mng Member*
Robert Davis,
EMP: 150
SQ FT: 16,000
SALES (est): 10.6MM **Privately Held**
WEB: www.davisresearch.com
SIC: 8732 Market analysis or research

(P-26510)
DECIPHER INC (HQ)
7 E River Park Pl E # 110, Fresno (93720-1669)
PHONE..............................559 436-6940
Jamin Brazil, *President*
Kristin Luck, *President*
Ian Duffield, *COO*
Jayme Plunkett, *Co-CEO*
Ji Yeong Kim, *Senior VP*
EMP: 60
SQ FT: 13,000
SALES (est): 11MM
SALES (corp-wide): 50.3MM **Privately Held**
WEB: www.decipherinc.com
SIC: 8732 Economic research
PA: Focusvision Worldwide, Inc.
1266 E Main St Ste 3
Stamford CT 06902
203 355-9020

(P-26511)
DIRECTIONS IN RESEARCH INC (PA)
9665 Gran Rdge Dr Ste 550, San Diego (92123)
PHONE..............................619 299-5883
David Phife, *President*
Susan Phife, *Vice Pres*
EMP: 290
SQ FT: 3,500
SALES (est): 23.5MM **Privately Held**
WEB: www.diresearch.com
SIC: 8732 Market analysis or research

(P-26512)
DIRECTLINE TECHNOLOGIES INC
1600 N Carpenter Rd, Modesto (95351-1185)
PHONE..............................209 491-2020
Martha Connor, *CEO*

Gary Connor, *Admin Sec*
Marian De Ramos-Maverro, *Accountant*
EMP: 75
SQ FT: 9,000
SALES (est): 2.8MM **Privately Held**
WEB: www.directline-tech.com
SIC: 8732 Market analysis or research

(P-26513)
ECKER CONSUMER
RECRUITING INC (PA)
Also Called: Ecker & Associates
1303 Melbourne St, Foster City
(94404-3739)
PHONE...................................650 871-6800
Leon Ecker, *President*
Bette Rosenthal, *Vice Pres*
EMP: 50
SQ FT: 5,300
SALES: 2.5MM **Privately Held**
WEB: www.eckersf.com
SIC: 8732 Opinion research

(P-26514)
ELECTRONIC ENTRMT DESIGN
& RES
Also Called: Eedar
2075 Corte Del Nogal B, Carlsbad
(92011-1413)
PHONE...................................760 579-7100
Gregory Short, *CEO*
Geoffrey Zatkiin, *President*
Shelli Francoise, *Office Admin*
Ryan Stelzner, *Analyst*
Robert Felix, *Director*
EMP: 53
SQ FT: 11,000
SALES (est): 5.3MM **Privately Held**
WEB: www.eedar.com
SIC: 8732 Market analysis or research

(P-26515)
ELLIOTT BENSON MARKET
RESEARCH
1226 H St, Sacramento (95814-1911)
PHONE...................................916 325-1670
Jaclyn Benson, *Owner*
EMP: 50
SALES (est): 956.3K **Privately Held**
WEB: www.elliottbenson.com
SIC: 8732 Market analysis or research

(P-26516)
ERNEST GALLO CLINIC & RES
CTR
5980 Horton St Ste 370, Emeryville
(94608-2058)
PHONE...................................510 985-3856
Raymond L White PHD, *President*
John De Luca, *Chairman*
William Sawyers, *Vice Pres*
EMP: 115
SQ FT: 87,200
SALES: 1.4MM **Privately Held**
WEB: www.gallo.ucsf.edu
SIC: 8732 8731 Commercial nonphysical
　research; commercial physical research

(P-26517)
FLEISCHMAN FIELD RESEARCH
INC
250 Sutter St Fl 2, San Francisco
(94108-4462)
P.O. Box 641620 (94164-1620)
PHONE...................................415 398-4140
Molly Fleischman, *President*
Andrew Fleischman, *CEO*
Andy Fleischman, *Research*
Lauren Fleischman, *Human Res Dir*
EMP: 130
SALES (est): 9.1MM **Privately Held**
WEB: www.ffrsf.com
SIC: 8732 Market analysis or research

(P-26518)
FRANCE TELECOM RES & DEV
LLC
Also Called: Orange Labs
60 Spear St Ste 1100, San Francisco
(94105-1599)
PHONE...................................415 284-9765
Elie Girard,
Thierry Souche, *Senior VP*
Christian Luginbuhl, *Vice Pres*
Jean-Jacques Pany, *Vice Pres*

Mark Plakias, *Vice Pres*
EMP: 65
SALES (est): 12MM
SALES (corp-wide): 27.3B **Privately Held**
WEB: www.francetelecom.com
SIC: 8732 Market analysis or research
PA: Orange
　78 84
　Paris 75015
　153 867-790

(P-26519)
FRANK N MAGID ASSOCIATES
INC
15260 Ventura Blvd # 1840, Sherman Oaks
(91403-5379)
PHONE...................................818 263-3300
Brent Magid, *Owner*
EMP: 70 **EST:** 2001
SALES (est): 3.2MM **Privately Held**
SIC: 8732 Market analysis or research

(P-26520)
FRANK N MAGID ASSOCIATES
INC
15260 Vntr Blvd Ste 1840, Sherman Oaks
(91403)
PHONE...................................818 263-3300
Frank N Magid, *Branch Mgr*
EMP: 105
SALES (corp-wide): 21.4MM **Privately**
Held
SIC: 8732 Market analysis or research
PA: Frank N. Magid Associates, Inc.
　1 Research Ctr
　Marion IA 52302
　319 377-7349

(P-26521)
GARTNER INC
11845 W Olympic Blvd 505w, Los Angeles
(90064-5057)
PHONE...................................310 479-2108
Bill Kumagai, *Manager*
James Park, *Sr Consultant*
Ernst Rampen, *Director*
EMP: 55
SALES (corp-wide): 3.3B **Publicly Held**
WEB: www.gartner.com
SIC: 8732 Market analysis or research
PA: Gartner, Inc.
　56 Top Gallant Rd
　Stamford CT 06902
　203 316-1111

(P-26522)
GFK CUSTOM RESEARCH LLC
360 Pine St Fl 6, San Francisco
(94104-3226)
PHONE...................................415 398-2812
Xiaoyan Zhao, *Branch Mgr*
Rob Hernandez, *Vice Pres*
Daniel Rosen, *Vice Pres*
Eric Wagatha, *Vice Pres*
Diane Forgione, *Admin Asst*
EMP: 54
SALES (corp-wide): 2.4MM **Privately**
Held
WEB: www.gfknop.com
SIC: 8732 8713 Market analysis or re-
　search; surveying services
HQ: Gfk Custom Research, Llc
　200 Liberty St Fl 4
　New York NY 10281
　212 240-5300

(P-26523)
GFK CUSTOM RESEARCH LLC
879 W 190th St Ste 390, Gardena
(90248-4229)
PHONE...................................310 527-2100
Donna Miller, *Senior VP*
Jaroslaw Muszynski, *Technical Staff*
Tyler Amos, *Marketing Staff*
Maikel Verhaaren, *Director*
EMP: 112
SALES (corp-wide): 2.4MM **Privately**
Held
SIC: 8732 Market analysis or research
HQ: Gfk Custom Research, Llc
　200 Liberty St Fl 4
　New York NY 10281
　212 240-5300

(P-26524)
GLASS LEWIS & CO LLC (HQ)
255 California St # 1100, San Francisco
(94111-4927)
PHONE...................................415 678-4110
Katherine Rabin, *CEO*
John Wieck, *COO*
Robert McCormick,
David Eaton, *Vice Pres*
Nichol Garzon-Mitchell, *Vice Pres*
EMP: 60
SALES (est): 18.9MM
SALES (corp-wide): 140B **Privately Held**
WEB: www.glasslewis.com
SIC: 8732 Business analysis
PA: Ontario Teachers' Pension Plan Board
　5650 Yonge St Suite 300
　North York ON M2M 4
　416 228-5900

(P-26525)
GLOBAL INDUSTRY ANALYSTS
INC
6150 Hellyer Ave Ste 100, San Jose
(95138-1072)
PHONE...................................408 528-9966
Kalakoti S Reddy, *CEO*
EMP: 700
SALES (est): 29.5MM **Privately Held**
WEB: www.sisinfotech.com
SIC: 8732 Market analysis or research

(P-26526)
HANLEY WOOD MKT
INTELLIGENCE (HQ)
Also Called: Meyers Group
555 Anton Blvd Ste 950, Costa Mesa
(92626-7811)
PHONE...................................714 540-8500
Jeff Meyers, *CEO*
Karen Meyers, *Managing Prtnr*
Tom Flynn, *President*
EMP: 55
SALES (est): 6.8MM
SALES (corp-wide): 164.8MM **Privately**
Held
SIC: 8732 Market analysis, business &
　economic research
PA: Hw Holdco, Llc
　1 Thomas Cir Nw Ste 600
　Washington DC 20005
　202 452-0800

(P-26527)
HIGH DESERT PARTNERSHIP
Also Called: NORTON SCIENCE AND LAN-
GUAGE AC
17500 Mana Rd, Apple Valley
(92307-2181)
PHONE...................................760 946-5414
Lisa Lamb, *CEO*
Gordon Soholt, *General Mgr*
Teresa Dowd, *Executive Asst*
David Kenneally, *Info Tech Dir*
Jim Quinn, *Info Tech Mgr*
EMP: 350
SQ FT: 35,000
SALES: 22.4MM **Privately Held**
WEB: www.lcer.org
SIC: 8732 Commercial nonphysical re-
　search

(P-26528)
HONDA R&D AMERICAS INC
7514 Reseda Blvd, Reseda (91335-2820)
PHONE...................................818 345-7922
David Colby, *Branch Mgr*
EMP: 50
SALES (corp-wide): 144.1B **Privately**
Held
WEB: www.hra.com
SIC: 8732 Market analysis or research
HQ: Honda R&D Americas, Inc.
　1900 Harpers Way
　Torrance CA 90501
　310 781-5500

(P-26529)
IBISWORLD INC (DH)
11755 Wilshire Blvd # 1100, Los Angeles
(90025-1506)
PHONE...................................800 330-3772
Phil Ruthven, *Principal*
Quinn Callaway, *President*
Karen Parker-Masarone, *President*

Justin Ruthven, *President*
Jason Baker, *COO*
EMP: 67
SALES (est): 17.3MM **Privately Held**
SIC: 8732 Market analysis or research
HQ: Ibisworld Pty Ltd
　L3 1 Collins St
　Melbourne VIC 3000
　396 553-881

(P-26530)
INTERVIEWING SERVICE AMER
INC
200 S Grfield Ave Ste 302, Alhambra
(91801)
PHONE...................................626 979-4140
Kelly Simmoms, *Manager*
EMP: 100
SALES (corp-wide): 25MM **Privately**
Held
SIC: 8732 Market analysis or research
PA: Interviewing Service Of America, Llc
　15400 Sherman Way Ste 400
　Van Nuys CA 91406
　818 989-1044

(P-26531)
INTERVIEWING SERVICE AMER
LLC (PA)
Also Called: ISA
15400 Sherman Way Ste 400, Van Nuys
(91406-4211)
PHONE...................................818 989-1044
Michael Halberstam, *Chairman*
Tony Kretzmer, *President*
Vicky Agalsoff, *Vice Pres*
John Fitzpatrick, *Vice Pres*
Gabriel Oshen, *Vice Pres*
EMP: 250
SQ FT: 20,000
SALES: 25MM **Privately Held**
SIC: 8732 Market analysis or research

(P-26532)
IPSOS OTX CORPORATION (HQ)
300 Crprate Pinte Ste 500, Culver City
(90230)
PHONE...................................310 736-3400
Shelley Zalis, *CEO*
Jeff Dean, *CFO*
Catherine Martell, *Director*
EMP: 210
SALES (est): 18MM
SALES (corp-wide): 475.9K **Privately**
Held
SIC: 8732 Market analysis or research
PA: Ipsos
　35 Rue Du Val De Marne
　Paris 75013
　141 989-000

(P-26533)
IPSOS PUBLIC AFFAIRS INC
3402 N Blackstone Ave, Fresno
(93726-5395)
PHONE...................................559 451-2820
Jorge Zelada, *Branch Mgr*
EMP: 111
SALES (corp-wide): 475.9K **Privately**
Held
SIC: 8732 Market analysis or research
HQ: Ipsos Public Affairs, Inc.
　222 S Rverside Plz Fl 4 Flr 4
　Chicago IL 60606
　312 526-4000

(P-26534)
J PAUL GETTY TRUST
Also Called: Getty Conservation Institute
1200 Getty Center Dr # 400, Los Angeles
(90049-1657)
PHONE...................................310 440-7325
Tim Wayland, *Branch Mgr*
EMP: 70
SALES (corp-wide): 200.9MM **Privately**
Held
SIC: 8732 Commercial nonphysical re-
　search
PA: The J Paul Getty Trust
　1200 Getty Center Dr # 500
　Los Angeles CA 90049
　310 440-7300

(P-26535)
JD POWER (HQ)
3200 Park Center Dr Fl 13, Costa Mesa
(92626-7154)
PHONE...............................714 621-6200
Dave Habiger, *President*
Joseph Damour, *CFO*
Deirdre Borrego, *Vice Pres*
John Humphrey, *Vice Pres*
Finbarr O'Neill, *Principal*
EMP: 250
SQ FT: 45,000
SALES (est): 125.4MM
SALES (corp-wide): 5.9MM **Privately Held**
WEB: www.jdpower.com
SIC: 8732 8742 Survey service: marketing, location, etc.; management consulting services
PA: Xio (Uk) Llp
    Suite 1502
    London SE1 9
    203 608-1331

(P-26536)
JD POWER
30870 Russell Ranch Rd, Westlake Village
(91362-7366)
PHONE...............................805 418-8000
Keith Webster, *Vice Pres*
Deidre Borrego, *President*
Monica Favorite, *President*
Dave Letson, *Senior VP*
Geoffrey Broderick, *Vice Pres*
EMP: 280
SALES (corp-wide): 5.9MM **Privately Held**
WEB: www.jdpower.com
SIC: 8732 Market analysis or research
HQ: J.D. Power
    3200 Park Center Dr Fl 13
    Costa Mesa CA 92626
    714 621-6200

(P-26537)
LELAND STANFORD JUNIOR UNIV
Stanf CNT Rsch & Ds Prntn
1070 Arastradero Rd # 100, Palo Alto
(94304-1336)
PHONE...............................650 723-6254
Steven Fortmann, *Director*
EMP: 163
SALES (corp-wide): 5.6B **Privately Held**
SIC: 8732 8221 Educational research; university
PA: Leland Stanford Junior University
    450 Serra Mall
    Stanford CA 94305
    650 723-2300

(P-26538)
LELAND STANFORD JUNIOR UNIV
476 Lomita Mall, Palo Alto (94305-4008)
PHONE...............................650 723-7546
Larry Candido, *Manager*
Paul McIntyre, *Manager*
EMP: 300
SALES (corp-wide): 5.6B **Privately Held**
SIC: 8732 8221 Educational research; university
PA: Leland Stanford Junior University
    450 Serra Mall
    Stanford CA 94305
    650 723-2300

(P-26539)
LIEBERMAN RES WORLDWIDE LLC (PA)
1900 Ave Of The Sts 160, Los Angeles
(90067)
PHONE...............................310 553-0550
David Sackman, *President*
Arnold Fishman, *Ch of Bd*
Peter Von Oy, *Project Mgr*
EMP: 140 **EST:** 1973
SQ FT: 24,560
SALES (est): 43.9MM **Privately Held**
WEB: www.lrwonline.com
SIC: 8732 Market analysis or research

(P-26540)
LOS ANGELES BIO MED RES INST
1124 W Carson St Rm 5l2, Torrance
(90502-2006)
PHONE...............................310 222-3604
Eli Ipp, *Principal*
EMP: 50
SALES: 75.4MM **Privately Held**
SIC: 8732 Research services, except laboratory

(P-26541)
LUTH RESEARCH INC (PA)
Also Called: Surveysavvy.com
1365 4th Ave, San Diego (92101-4208)
PHONE...............................619 234-5884
Roseanne Luth, *President*
Charles Rosen, *Exec VP*
Marcos Gill, *Vice Pres*
Candice Rab, *Vice Pres*
Ellen Romer, *Vice Pres*
EMP: 305
SQ FT: 15,000
SALES (est): 51.7MM **Privately Held**
WEB: www.luthresearch.com
SIC: 8732 Market analysis or research

(P-26542)
MARITZCX RESEARCH LLC
3901 Via Oro Ave Ste 200, Long Beach
(90810-1800)
PHONE...............................310 525-1300
Christopher Gerth, *Branch Mgr*
EMP: 526
SALES (corp-wide): 1.2B **Privately Held**
SIC: 8732 Market analysis or research
HQ: Maritzcx Research Llc
    1355 N Highway Dr
    Fenton MO 63026
    636 827-4000

(P-26543)
MCCANN-ERICKSON USA INC
Also Called: McKann World Group
600 Battery St Fl 1, San Francisco
(94111-1834)
PHONE...............................415 262-5600
Mike Parsons, *Branch Mgr*
Deborah Leighton, *Vice Pres*
Scott Duchon, *Creative Dir*
Darrin Mackie, *Info Tech Mgr*
Ken Krausgill, *Business Mgr*
EMP: 200
SALES (corp-wide): 7.8B **Publicly Held**
SIC: 8732 7311 Market analysis or research; advertising agencies
HQ: Mccann-Erickson Usa, Inc.
    622 3rd Ave Fl 3
    New York NY 10017
    646 865-2000

(P-26544)
MEYERS RESEARCH LLC
3200 Bristol St Ste 640, Costa Mesa
(92626-1863)
PHONE...............................714 619-7800
Kevin Gillen, *Officer*
Michelle Weedon, *Senior VP*
Jon Cruse, *Vice Pres*
John Weeden, *Sales Dir*
Keishawn Spells, *Sales Staff*
EMP: 79
SALES (corp-wide): 9.6MM **Privately Held**
SIC: 8732 Business research service
PA: Meyers Research, Llc
    151 El Camino Dr
    Beverly Hills CA 90212
    858 381-4390

(P-26545)
MICHAEL A MECZKA
5757 W Century Blvd # 120, Los Angeles
(90045-6401)
PHONE...............................310 670-4824
Michael A Meczka, *President*
Dona Browne, *Vice Pres*
EMP: 50
SALES (est): 2MM **Privately Held**
WEB: www.mmrcinc.com
SIC: 8732 Commercial nonphysical research

(P-26546)
MILLWARD BROWN LLC
2425 Olympic Blvd 240e, Santa Monica
(90404-4076)
PHONE...............................310 309-3352
Nile Rowan, *Branch Mgr*
EMP: 50
SALES (corp-wide): 20.1B **Privately Held**
SIC: 8732 Market analysis or research
HQ: Millward Brown, Llc
    11 Madison Ave Ste 1200
    New York NY 10010
    212 548-7200

(P-26547)
MONTEREY COUNTY OFFICE EDUCATN
Technology Information Svcs
901 Blanco Cir, Salinas (93901-4401)
PHONE...............................831 755-0324
Dave Paulson, *CTO*
EMP: 85 **Privately Held**
SIC: 8732 7374 Educational research; computer processing services
PA: Monterey County Office Of Education
    901 Blanco Cir
    Salinas CA 93901

(P-26548)
NATIONAL ECNOMIC RES ASSOC INC
777 S Figueroa St # 1950, Los Angeles
(90017-5800)
PHONE...............................213 346-3000
Gary Dorman, *VP Mktg*
Hethie Parmesano, *Vice Pres*
Katie Orlandi, *Analyst*
Andrew Hund, *Human Res Mgr*
Joan Wolff, *Sr Associate*
EMP: 62
SALES (corp-wide): 14B **Publicly Held**
SIC: 8732 Business economic service
HQ: National Economic Research Associates, Inc.
    1166 Ave Of The Americas
    New York NY 10036
    212 345-3000

(P-26549)
NATIONAL RESEARCH GROUP INC
6255 W Sunset Blvd Fl 19, Los Angeles
(90028-7420)
PHONE...............................323 817-2000
Jon Penn, *CEO*
Jeff Hall, *Exec VP*
James McNamara, *Exec VP*
Ray Ydoyaga, *Exec VP*
Andrew Fielder, *Vice Pres*
EMP: 400
SALES (est): 41.7MM
SALES (corp-wide): 125.6MM **Privately Held**
WEB: www.nrg.com
SIC: 8732 Market analysis or research; business research service
PA: The Stagwell Group Llc
    1808 I St Nw Ste 600
    Washington DC 20006
    202 524-4364

(P-26550)
NIELSEN COMPANY (US) LLC
Also Called: Nielsen Media Research
6255 W Sunset Blvd Fl 20, Los Angeles
(90028-7405)
PHONE...............................323 817-2000
Tom Borys, *Manager*
Yesenia Nunez, *Client Mgr*
Pedro Albizures, *Manager*
Doug Whittenburg, *Manager*
EMP: 400
SALES (corp-wide): 6.5B **Privately Held**
WEB: www.nielsenmedia.com
SIC: 8732 Market analysis or research
HQ: The Nielsen Company Us Llc
    85 Broad St
    New York NY 10004

(P-26551)
NIELSEN COMPANY (US) LLC
5375 Mira Sorrento Pl # 400, San Diego
(92121-3809)
PHONE...............................858 677-9542
Teri Jacobson, *Branch Mgr*
Keith Peterson, *COO*
Hugo Borda, *Vice Pres*
Doug Diem, *Vice Pres*
Mark Nelson, *Vice Pres*
EMP: 127
SALES (corp-wide): 6.5B **Privately Held**
SIC: 8732 Market analysis or research
HQ: The Nielsen Company Us Llc
    85 Broad St
    New York NY 10004

(P-26552)
NIELSEN COMPANY (US) LLC
6255 W Sunset Blvd Fl 19, Los Angeles
(90028-7420)
PHONE...............................323 462-0050
Adam Levy, *Vice Pres*
EMP: 80
SALES (corp-wide): 6.5B **Privately Held**
SIC: 8732 Market analysis or research
HQ: The Nielsen Company Us Llc
    85 Broad St
    New York NY 10004

(P-26553)
NITTO DENKO TECHNICAL CORP
501 Via Del Monte, Oceanside
(92058-1251)
PHONE...............................760 435-7011
Kenji Matsumoto, *President*
EMP: 100
SALES (est): 19.3MM
SALES (corp-wide): 8B **Privately Held**
WEB: www.nitto.co.jp
SIC: 8732 3089 3462 Research services, except laboratory; automotive parts, plastic; automotive & internal combustion engine forgings
PA: Nitto Denko Corporation
    4-20, Ofukacho, Kita-Ku
    Osaka OSK 530-0
    676 322-101

(P-26554)
NOVOZYMES INC (DH)
Also Called: Novo Nordisk Biotech
1445 Drew Ave, Davis (95618-4880)
PHONE...............................530 757-8100
Peder Holk Nielsen, *CEO*
Ejner B Jensen, *President*
Prashant V Iyer, *Associate*
EMP: 70
SQ FT: 64,000
SALES (est): 20.4MM
SALES (corp-wide): 20.7B **Privately Held**
WEB: www.novozymesbiotech.com
SIC: 8732 Commercial nonphysical research
HQ: Novozymes North America, Inc.
    77 Perry Chapel Church Rd
    Franklinton NC 27525
    919 494-2014

(P-26555)
OTR GLOBAL LLC
155 Montgomery St Ste 501, San Francisco
(94104-4110)
PHONE...............................415 675-7660
Otr Global, *Branch Mgr*
EMP: 50 **Privately Held**
SIC: 8732 Market analysis or research
PA: Otr Global Llc
    4 Manhattanville Rd # 205
    Purchase NY 10577

(P-26556)
PACIFICA KATIE AVENUE LLC
1775 Hancock St Ste 100, San Diego
(92110-2035)
PHONE...............................619 296-9000
Deepak Israni,
EMP: 80
SALES (est): 5.7MM **Privately Held**
SIC: 8732 Merger, acquisition & reorganization research

(P-26557)
PROXIM WIRELESS CORPORATION
2114 Ringwood Ave, San Jose
(95131-1715)
PHONE...................408 383-7600
David Renauld, *Vice Pres*
EMP: 240
SALES (corp-wide): 31MM **Publicly Held**
SIC: 8732 Research services, except laboratory
PA: Proxim Wireless Corporation
2114 Ringwood Ave
San Jose CA 95131
408 383-7600

(P-26558)
QUINTILES PACIFIC INCORPORATED (HQ)
448 E Middlefield Rd, Mountain View
(94043-4006)
PHONE...................650 567-2000
Joe Colintino, *President*
John Sneed, *Director*
EMP: 50
SQ FT: 13,500
SALES (est): 13.8MM **Publicly Held**
SIC: 8732 Research services, except laboratory

(P-26559)
QURI INC
655 Montgomery St Lbby 1, San Francisco
(94111-2638)
PHONE...................415 413-0100
Justin Behar, *CEO*
John Mecklenburg, *COO*
EMP: 50
SALES (est): 5MM **Privately Held**
SIC: 8732 Market analysis or research

(P-26560)
RDP ACQUISITION COMPANY
Also Called: Dreyers Grnd Ice Cream Hldings
5929 College Ave, Oakland (94618-1325)
PHONE...................510 652-8187
Gary T Rogers, *Principal*
EMP: 350
SALES (est): 6.3MM
SALES (corp-wide): 90.8B **Privately Held**
SIC: 8732 Merger, acquisition & reorganization research
HQ: Dreyer's Grand Ice Cream Holdings, Inc.
5929 College Ave
Oakland CA 94618
510 652-8187

(P-26561)
REDHILL GROUP INC
Also Called: SCR
18010 Sky Park Cir # 275, Irvine
(92614-6439)
PHONE...................949 752-5900
Mark McCourt, *President*
Judith McCourt, *Vice Pres*
Ryan Mak, *Research Analys*
EMP: 61
SQ FT: 4,000
SALES (est): 5.8MM **Privately Held**
WEB: www.redhillgroup.com
SIC: 8732 Market analysis or research

(P-26562)
RETAILNEXT INC
845 Market St Ste 450, San Francisco
(94103-1938)
PHONE...................408 298-2585
EMP: 150
SALES (corp-wide): 56.3MM **Privately Held**
SIC: 8732 Market analysis or research
PA: Retailnext, Inc.
60 S Market St Ste 1000
San Jose CA 95113
408 884-2162

(P-26563)
S K & A INFORMATION SVCS INC (DH)
Also Called: SK&a
2601 Main St Ste 650, Irvine (92614-4228)
PHONE...................949 476-2051
David Escalante Jr, *President*
Al M Cosentino, *CFO*

Jaqueline Aguilera, *Director*
EMP: 87
SQ FT: 12,000
SALES (est): 7.8MM
SALES (corp-wide): 6.8MM **Privately Held**
WEB: www.skainfo.com
SIC: 8732 Market analysis or research

(P-26564)
SMARTREVENUECOM INC
101 Cooper St Ste 205, Santa Cruz
(95060-4526)
PHONE...................203 733-9156
John Dranow, *CEO*
EMP: 492
SALES (corp-wide): 46.7MM **Privately Held**
SIC: 8732 Market analysis or research
PA: Smartrevenue.Com, Inc.
60 Twin Ridge Rd
Ridgefield CT 06877
203 733-9156

(P-26565)
SOCRATIC TECHNOLOGIES INC (PA)
208 Utah St Ste 350, San Francisco
(94103-4881)
P.O. Box 411587 (94141-1587)
PHONE...................415 430-2200
Bill Macelroy, *President*
Michael Gray, *Vice Pres*
EMP: 65
SQ FT: 14,000
SALES (est): 8.4MM **Privately Held**
WEB: www.sotech.com
SIC: 8732 Market analysis or research

(P-26566)
SOLEIL COMMUNICATIONS LLC
Also Called: Prodata Research
2655 Camino DI Rio N 11, San Diego
(92108)
PHONE...................619 624-2888
Michael Gehrig, *Mng Member*
John Lewis,
EMP: 70
SALES (est): 4.9MM
SALES (corp-wide): 100.2MM **Privately Held**
SIC: 8732 Market analysis or research
PA: The Welk Group Inc
8860 Lawrence Welk Dr
Escondido CA 92026
760 749-3000

(P-26567)
SUNING CMMERCE R D CTR USA INC
Also Called: Suning USA
845 Page Mill Rd, Palo Alto (94304-1011)
PHONE...................650 834-9800
Enlong Hou, *CEO*
Jin Ming, *President*
EMP: 60
SQ FT: 9,800
SALES (est): 4.5MM
SALES (corp-wide): 28.3B **Privately Held**
SIC: 8732 Commercial nonphysical research
PA: Suning.Com Co., Ltd.
No.1, Suning Avenue, Xuanwu Dist.
Nanjing 21004
258 441-8888

(P-26568)
SURVEY SAMPLING INTL LLC
Also Called: Instantly
16501 Ventura Blvd # 300, Encino
(91436-2007)
PHONE...................866 872-4006
EMP: 200
SALES (corp-wide): 96.6MM **Privately Held**
SIC: 8732 Market analysis or research; market analysis, business & economic research; survey service: marketing, location, etc.
HQ: Survey Sampling International, Llc
6 Research Dr Ste 200
Shelton CT 06484
203 567-7200

(P-26569)
TECHAISLE LLC
5053 Doyle Rd Ste 105, San Jose
(95129-4228)
PHONE...................408 253-4416
Anurag Agrawal,
Arun Mishra, *Managing Dir*
EMP: 50
SALES: 172K **Privately Held**
WEB: www.techaisle.com
SIC: 8732 Market analysis or research

(P-26570)
TIGER ANALYTICS LLC
4701 Patrick Henry Dr, Santa Clara
(95054-1819)
PHONE...................408 508-4430
Mahesh Kumar,
Aseem Sharma, *Analyst*
EMP: 60 EST: 2011
SALES (est): 2.5MM **Privately Held**
SIC: 8732 Business analysis

(P-26571)
TOSHIBA EDUCATION CENTER
9740 Irvine Blvd, Irvine (92618-1651)
PHONE...................949 583-3000
Ted Flati, *Principal*
EMP: 55
SALES (est): 5.6MM
SALES (corp-wide): 36.4B **Privately Held**
WEB: www.tams.com
SIC: 8732 Educational research
HQ: Canon Medical Systems Usa, Inc.
2441 Michelle Dr
Tustin CA 92780
714 730-5000

(P-26572)
TREDENCE INC (PA)
1900 Camden Ave Ste 66, San Jose
(95124-2948)
PHONE...................408 819-2336
Subhankar Bhowmick, *CEO*
Sumit Mehra, *President*
Shashank Kumar Dubey, *Vice Pres*
EMP: 250 EST: 2014
SQ FT: 500
SALES (est): 15.5MM **Privately Held**
SIC: 8732 Market analysis, business & economic research

(P-26573)
TRENDSOURCE INC
Also Called: Examine Your Practice
4891 Pacific Hwy Ste 200, San Diego
(92110-4026)
PHONE...................619 718-7467
Rodney Moll, *Chairman*
Bob Post, *COO*
Neil A Wykes, *CFO*
EMP: 57
SQ FT: 7,500
SALES (est): 7.6MM **Privately Held**
WEB: www.trendsource.com
SIC: 8732 Market analysis, business & economic research

(P-26574)
TROTTA ASSOCIATES
13160 Mindanao Way # 100, Marina Del Rey (90292-7900)
PHONE...................310 306-6866
Diane Trotta, *CEO*
EMP: 80
SALES (est): 7.7MM **Privately Held**
SIC: 8732 Market analysis or research

(P-26575)
UNIVERSITY CAL RIVERSIDE
Also Called: Uc Riverside RES Economic Dev
900 University Ave, Riverside
(92521-0001)
PHONE...................951 827-4801
Stan Fletcher, *Director*
Laurie Gustafson, *CFO*
Iqbal Pittalwala, *Officer*
Stacy Sweeney, *Officer*
Charles Brinkley, *Vice Pres*
EMP: 72 **Privately Held**
SIC: 8732 8221 9411 Economic research; university; administration of educational programs;

HQ: University Cal Riverside
900 University Ave
Riverside CA 92521
951 827-1012

(P-26576)
VERANCE CORPORATION
10089 Willow Creek Rd, San Diego
(92131-1697)
PHONE...................858 202-2800
Linesh Shah, *CEO*
Clifford Friedman, *Ch of Bd*
F Mario Petrocco, *CFO*
Dr Joe Winograd, *Exec VP*
EMP: 65
SALES (est): 8.6MM **Privately Held**
WEB: www.verance.com
SIC: 8732 Research services, except laboratory

(P-26577)
XDBS CORPORATION
Also Called: Xdbsb2b
3501 Jack Northrop Ave, Hawthorne
(90250-4433)
PHONE...................302 566-3006
Julie Strong, *CEO*
Kartik Anand, *Chairman*
Nuzhat Ansari, *Executive*
Gorav Mohan, *Associate Dir*
Prakash Nair, *Sales Staff*
EMP: 100
SQ FT: 4,000
SALES (est): 3MM **Privately Held**
SIC: 8732 7389 5963 8742 Survey service: marketing, location, etc.; telemarketing services; direct sales, telemarketing; sales (including sales management) consultant

---

8733 Noncommercial Research Organizations

(P-26578)
AEROSPACE CORPORATION (PA)
2310 E El Segundo Blvd, El Segundo
(90245-4609)
P.O. Box 92957, Los Angeles (90009-2957)
PHONE...................310 336-5000
Steven Isakowitz, *President*
Hung Nguyen, *Vice Chairman*
Ellen M Beatty, *CFO*
Thomas Oconnor, *Treasurer*
Rufus A Fulton, *Trustee*
EMP: 2313 EST: 1960
SQ FT: 1,167,251
SALES: 900MM **Privately Held**
SIC: 8733 8711 8731 Scientific research agency; engineering services; commercial physical research

(P-26579)
AEROSPACE CORPORATION
2745 E Sherman Ave, Orange
(92869-3216)
PHONE...................714 248-1194
EMP: 345
SALES (corp-wide): 900MM **Privately Held**
SIC: 8733 Scientific research agency
PA: The Aerospace Corporation
2310 E El Segundo Blvd
El Segundo CA 90245
310 336-5000

(P-26580)
AEROSPACE CORPORATION
P.O. Box 5068 (93437-0068)
PHONE...................805 320-9599
William Sandberg, *Branch Mgr*
Matthew Ogan, *Project Engr*
EMP: 99
SALES (corp-wide): 900MM **Privately Held**
SIC: 8733 Noncommercial research organizations
PA: The Aerospace Corporation
2310 E El Segundo Blvd
El Segundo CA 90245
310 336-5000

(P-26581)
AEROSPACE CORPORATION
2009 Harkness St, Manhattan Beach
(90266-4112)
PHONE.................................310 336-1025
Joe Barger, *Branch Mgr*
EMP: 345
SALES (corp-wide): 900MM **Privately Held**
SIC: 8733 Noncommercial research organizations
PA: The Aerospace Corporation
2310 E El Segundo Blvd
El Segundo CA 90245
310 336-5000

(P-26582)
AEROSPACE CORPORATION
3171 Grangemount Rd, Glendale (91206)
PHONE.................................818 952-6075
Milton F Pope, *Branch Mgr*
EMP: 345
SALES (corp-wide): 900MM **Privately Held**
SIC: 8733 Scientific research agency
PA: The Aerospace Corporation
2310 E El Segundo Blvd
El Segundo CA 90245
310 336-5000

(P-26583)
AEROSPACE CORPORATION
624 N Guadalupe Ave, Redondo Beach
(90277-2953)
PHONE.................................310 374-8866
Robert W Hosken, *Branch Mgr*
EMP: 99
SALES (corp-wide): 900MM **Privately Held**
SIC: 8733 Scientific research agency
PA: The Aerospace Corporation
2310 E El Segundo Blvd
El Segundo CA 90245
310 336-5000

(P-26584)
AFFYMAX RESEARCH INSTITUTE
4001 Miranda Ave, Palo Alto (94304-1218)
PHONE.................................650 812-8700
Gordon Ringold PHD, *CEO*
Lauren Stevens, *President*
Mark Thompson, *CFO*
Helen S Kim, *Officer*
Emily Lee Kelly, *Vice Pres*
EMP: 50
SQ FT: 103,000
SALES (est): 4.1MM **Privately Held**
SIC: 8733 8732 8731 Medical research; commercial nonphysical research; commercial physical research

(P-26585)
AIR FORCE US DEPT OF
Also Called: Aerospace Federally Funded RES
2310 E El Segundo Blvd, El Segundo
(90245-4609)
PHONE.................................310 336-5000
EMP: 391 **Publicly Held**
SIC: 8733 9711 Noncommercial research organizations; Air Force
HQ: United States Department Of The Air Force
1000 Air Force Pentagon
Washington DC 20330

(P-26586)
AIR FORCE US DEPT OF
Also Called: Project Air Force
1776 Main St, Santa Monica (90401-3208)
PHONE.................................310 393-0411
EMP: 391 **Publicly Held**
SIC: 8733 9711 Noncommercial research organizations; Air Force
HQ: United States Department Of The Air Force
1000 Air Force Pentagon
Washington DC 20330

(P-26587)
AKELA PHARMA INC
11011 Torreyana Rd 100, San Diego
(92121-1104)
PHONE.................................512 391-3525
Rudy Emmelot, *President*
Seth E Lemler, *Ch of Bd*
Fr D Ric Dumais, *Vice Pres*
EMP: 50 EST: 2008
SALES (est): 5.5MM **Privately Held**
SIC: 8733 Noncommercial research organizations

(P-26588)
ALFRED E MANN FOUNDATION (PA)
Also Called: Aemf
25134 Rye Canyon Loop # 200, Valencia
(91355-5028)
PHONE.................................661 702-6700
John Petrovich, *CEO*
Robert Greenberg, *Ch of Bd*
Mark Chamberlain, *COO*
Farah Boroomand, *CFO*
Sarah Lundy, *HR Admin*
EMP: 67
SQ FT: 67,000
SALES: 454.8K **Privately Held**
SIC: 8733 8641 Medical research; civic social & fraternal associations

(P-26589)
AMERICAN CANCER SOC CAL DIV (PA)
1001 Marina Village Pkwy, Alameda
(94501-1091)
PHONE.................................510 893-7900
Carolyn F Katzin, *CEO*
Marilyn Broussard, *CFO*
Carolyn P Williams-Goldma, *Vice Pres*
Marlene Yip, *Regional Mgr*
James Kelly, *Manager*
EMP: 100
SQ FT: 47,000
SALES (est): 38.2MM **Privately Held**
SIC: 8733 Noncommercial research organizations

(P-26590)
AMERICAN INSTITUTE OF AERONAUT
3198 E Fox Run Way, San Diego
(92111-7721)
PHONE.................................619 545-3736
Keith Glassman, *Principal*
EMP: 99
SALES (est): 3.3MM **Privately Held**
SIC: 8733 Noncommercial research organizations

(P-26591)
AMERICAN INSTITUTE RESEARCH
2151 River Plaza Dr # 320, Sacramento
(95833-3881)
PHONE.................................916 286-8800
EMP: 329
SALES (corp-wide): 474MM **Privately Held**
SIC: 8733 Noncommercial social research organization
PA: American Institutes For Research In The Behavioral Sciences
1000 Thmas Jfferson St Nw
Washington DC 20007
202 403-5000

(P-26592)
AMGEN PHARMACEUTICALS INC
1 Amgen Center Dr, Thousand Oaks
(91320-1799)
PHONE.................................805 447-1000
Gordon Binder, *President*
EMP: 4200
SALES (est): 69.9MM
SALES (corp-wide): 22.8B **Publicly Held**
SIC: 8733 Biotechnical research, noncommercial
PA: Amgen Inc.
1 Amgen Center Dr
Thousand Oaks CA 91320
805 447-1000

(P-26593)
ASIA FOUNDATION (PA)
465 California St Fl 9, San Francisco
(94104-1892)
P.O. Box 193223 (94119-3223)
PHONE.................................415 982-4640
David D Arnold, *President*
Suzanne Siskel, *COO*
Ken Krug, *CFO*
Amory Sharpe, *Officer*
Richard H Fuller, *Vice Pres*
EMP: 90
SQ FT: 17,207
SALES: 108.1MM **Privately Held**
SIC: 8733 Noncommercial research organizations

(P-26594)
ATK SPACE SYSTEMS INC
Also Called: Space Components Division
7130 Miramar Rd Ste 100b, San Diego
(92121-2340)
PHONE.................................858 621-5700
Doan La, *Branch Mgr*
EMP: 300 **Publicly Held**
SIC: 8733 Scientific research agency
HQ: Atk Space Systems Inc.
6033 Bandini Blvd
Commerce CA 90040
323 722-0222

(P-26595)
BAY AREA ENVMTL RES INST
Also Called: Baer Institute
Nasa Resrch Park 101, Moffett Field
(94035)
PHONE.................................707 938-9387
Robert W Bergstrom, *President*
Mark Sittloh, *Exec Dir*
Helene Hendriks, *Analyst*
EMP: 87
SQ FT: 750
SALES: 18.2MM **Privately Held**
WEB: www.baeri.org
SIC: 8733 Noncommercial research organizations

(P-26596)
BECKMAN RESEARCH INST HOPE
1500 Duarte Rd, Duarte (91010-3012)
PHONE.................................626 359-8111
Michael A Friedman, *CEO*
Robert Stone, *President*
Harlan Levine, *CEO*
William Sargeant, *COO*
Terry Blackwood, *CFO*
EMP: 250
SALES: 298.9MM
SALES (corp-wide): 1.4B **Privately Held**
SIC: 8733 Medical research
PA: City Of Hope
1500 Duarte Rd
Duarte CA 91010
626 256-4673

(P-26597)
BERKELEY LIGHTS INC (PA)
5858 Horton St Ste 320, Emeryville
(94608-2183)
PHONE.................................510 898-1433
Eric Hobbs, *CEO*
Kevin Chapman, *Officer*
Jonathan Lazarus, *Vice Pres*
Igor Khandros, *Principal*
Pete Hallesy, *Sr Software Eng*
EMP: 63
SALES (est): 33.4MM **Privately Held**
SIC: 8733 Research institute

(P-26598)
BRENTWOOD BMDICAL RES INST INC
11301 Wilshire Blvd B114, Los Angeles
(90073-1003)
P.O. Box 25027 (90025-0027)
PHONE.................................310 312-1554
Kenneth Hickman, *CEO*
Thoyd Ellis, *CFO*
EMP: 130
SQ FT: 1,500
SALES: 7.2MM **Privately Held**
SIC: 8733 Medical research

(P-26599)
BUCK INST FOR RES ON AGING (PA)
8001 Redwood Blvd, Novato (94945-1400)
PHONE.................................415 209-2000
Eric M Verdin, *President*
Dale Bredesen MD, *President*
Raja Kamal, *Senior VP*
Nancy Derr, *Vice Pres*
Remy Gross III, *Vice Pres*
EMP: 175
SQ FT: 185,000
SALES: 38.7MM **Privately Held**
SIC: 8733 Medical research

(P-26600)
CALIFORNIA CMPLTE CNT CNSUS
400 R St Ste 350, Sacramento
(95811-6213)
PHONE.................................916 852-2020
Ditas Katague, *Principal*
EMP: 60
SALES (est): 908.1K **Privately Held**
SIC: 8733 Noncommercial research organizations

(P-26601)
CALIFRNIA INST FOR BMDICAL RES
11119 N Torrey Pines Rd, La Jolla
(92037-1046)
PHONE.................................858 242-1000
Peter G Schultz, *Director*
EMP: 110
SQ FT: 6,320
SALES (est): 18.3MM **Privately Held**
SIC: 8733 Medical research

(P-26602)
CALIFRNIA PCF MED CTR FNDATION (PA)
2015 Steiner St, San Francisco
(94115-2627)
P.O. Box 7999 (94120-7999)
PHONE.................................415 600-4400
Sloan Barnett, *Ch of Bd*
Doug Nelson, *President*
Karen Jeu, *Vice Pres*
EMP: 58
SALES (est): 7.6MM **Privately Held**
SIC: 8733 Noncommercial research organizations

(P-26603)
CANCER PREVENTION INST CAL (PA)
Also Called: CPIC
2201 Walnut Ave Ste 300, Fremont
(94538-2334)
PHONE.................................510 608-5000
Donna M Randall, *CEO*
Don Neilsen, *Exec Dir*
Anil Narayan, *Finance Dir*
Amber Shomo, *Controller*
David Rost, *Manager*
EMP: 150 EST: 1974
SQ FT: 33,598
SALES: 13MM **Privately Held**
SIC: 8733 Medical research

(P-26604)
CANJI INC
3525 John Hopkins Ct, San Diego
(92121-1121)
PHONE.................................858 597-0177
Steven Chang, *Vice Pres*
Donald R Conklin, *Ch of Bd*
Raul E Cesan, *President*
Joseph C Conners, *Exec VP*
Thomas H Kelly, *Exec VP*
EMP: 78
SQ FT: 48,000
SALES (est): 1.9MM
SALES (corp-wide): 40.1B **Publicly Held**
WEB: www.canji.com
SIC: 8733 Biotechnical research, noncommercial
PA: Merck & Co., Inc.
2000 Galloping Hill Rd
Kenilworth NJ 07033
908 740-4000

(P-26605)
CAPRION PROTEOMICS USA LLC
1455 Adams Dr Ste 2124, Menlo Park (94025-1438)
P.O. Box 16044, San Francisco (94116-0044)
PHONE................650 470-2300
Martin Leblanc, *CEO*
Dr Daniel Chelsky, *Principal*
Suman Gupta, *Director*
Tom Mahony, *Director*
EMP: 50
SALES (est): 4.8MM **Privately Held**
SIC: 8733
PA: Caprion Proteomique Inc
201 Av Du President-Kennedy Bureau 3900
Montreal QC H2X 3
514 360-3600

(P-26606)
CARNEGIE INSTITUTION WASH
Also Called: Observatories of The Carnegie
813 Santa Barbara St, Pasadena (91101-1232)
PHONE................626 577-1122
Wendy L Freedman, *Director*
Jovan Tadic, *Research*
Andrew McWilliam, *Human Res Mgr*
Sharon Kelly, *Buyer*
Yue Meng, *Manager*
EMP: 100
SQ FT: 24,075
SALES (est): 13.1MM
SALES (corp-wide): 161.4MM **Privately Held**
WEB: www.gl.ciw.edu
SIC: 8733 7999 Scientific research agency; observation tower operation
PA: Carnegie Institution Of Washington
1530 P St Nw
Washington DC 20005
202 387-6400

(P-26607)
CATHOLIC CHARITIES OF LA INC (PA)
1531 James M Wood Blvd, Los Angeles (90015-1112)
P.O. Box 15095 (90015-0095)
PHONE................213 251-3400
Monsignor G Cox, *Exec Dir*
James E Bathker, *CFO*
Ronald Lopez, *Officer*
Sarah Elder, *Vice Pres*
John Vavoudis, *Info Tech Dir*
EMP: 55
SQ FT: 18,000
SALES: 34.2MM **Privately Held**
SIC: 8733 8322 Noncommercial research organizations; individual & family services

(P-26608)
CELERA CORPORATION (HQ)
33608 Ortega Hwy, San Juan Capistrano (92675-2042)
PHONE................510 749-4200
Kathy Ordoez, *CEO*
Mathew J Budoff, *Co-Owner*
H R Superko MD, *Officer*
Tom White, *Officer*
Paul Arata, *Senior VP*
EMP: 77
SQ FT: 48,000
SALES (est): 44.1MM
SALES (corp-wide): 7.7B **Publicly Held**
SIC: 8733 8731 Scientific research agency; commercial physical research
PA: Quest Diagnostics Incorporated
500 Plaza Dr Ste G
Secaucus NJ 07094
973 520-2700

(P-26609)
CENTER FOR CIVIC EDUCATION (PA)
5115 Douglas Fir Rd Ste J, Calabasas (91302-2590)
PHONE................818 591-9321
Charles N Quigley, *Exec Dir*
Jim Heredia, *Officer*
Sharon Moran, *Vice Pres*
Michael Fischer, *Executive*
John Hale, *Associate Dir*

EMP: 60
SQ FT: 16,000
SALES: 6MM **Privately Held**
WEB: www.civiced.org
SIC: 8733 8748 Educational research agency; educational consultant

(P-26610)
CENTRAL CALIFORNIA TR
22847 Road 140, Tulare (93274-9367)
PHONE................559 686-4973
Marylou Polek, *Prgrmr*
Vic Corkins, *Chairman*
Dean Gillette, *Admin Sec*
EMP: 55
SQ FT: 12,500
SALES: 1.6MM **Privately Held**
WEB: www.cctea.org
SIC: 8733 Bacteriological research

(P-26611)
CG2 INC
Also Called: Quantum3d Government Systems
1759 Mccarthy Blvd, Milpitas (95035-7416)
PHONE................407 737-8800
EMP: 69
SALES (est): 3.2MM **Privately Held**
SIC: 8733

(P-26612)
CHILDRENS HOSP OKLAND RES INST
5700 Martin Luther, Oakland (94609)
PHONE................510 450-7600
Antonie H Paap, *President*
Jenison Soriano, *Receiver*
David Lynch, *Vice Pres*
Betsy Lathrop, *Administration*
Jennifer Beckstead, *Research*
EMP: 100
SALES (est): 10.3MM
SALES (corp-wide): 178.6MM **Privately Held**
SIC: 8733 Scientific research agency
PA: Children's Hospital & Research Center At Oakland
747 52nd St
Oakland CA 94609
510 428-3000

(P-26613)
CHILDRENS HOSPITAL LOS ANGELES
Also Called: Saban Research Institute, The
4661 W Sunset Blvd, Los Angeles (90027-6042)
PHONE................323 361-2751
Cheryl Saban, *Branch Mgr*
EMP: 450
SALES (corp-wide): 1B **Privately Held**
SIC: 8733 Medical research
PA: The Childrens Hospital Los Angeles
4650 W Sunset Blvd
Los Angeles CA 90027
323 660-2450

(P-26614)
CHILDRENS INST LOS ANGELES (PA)
2121 W Temple St, Los Angeles (90026-4915)
PHONE................213 385-5100
Bradley Myslinski, *President*
Eugene Straub, *Treasurer*
Martine Singer, *Vice Pres*
Dena M Scott, *Psychologist*
EMP: 1000 EST: 2011
SALES: 696.7K **Privately Held**
SIC: 8733 Noncommercial research organizations

(P-26615)
COMPLETE GENOMICS INC
2904 Orchard Pkwy, San Jose (95134-2009)
PHONE................650 943-2800
Clifford A Reid PHD, *Ch of Bd*
Ajay Bansal, *CFO*
Keith Raffel, *Ch Credit Ofcr*
Arthur W Homan, *Senior VP*
Ethan Knowlden, *Senior VP*
EMP: 255
SQ FT: 66,000

SALES (est): 66.1MM
SALES (corp-wide): 34.2MM **Privately Held**
SIC: 8733 Biotechnical research, noncommercial
HQ: Beijing Genomics Institute At Shenzhen
Zonghe Building, Beishan Industrial Zone, Yantian Street, Yantia Shenzhen
755 223-2454

(P-26616)
DOHENY EYE INSTITUTE
3158 Kings Ct, Los Angeles (90077-1900)
P.O. Box 86228 (90086-0228)
PHONE................323 442-6682
EMP: 106
SALES (corp-wide): 27.3MM **Privately Held**
SIC: 8733 Medical research
PA: Doheny Eye Institute
1355 San Pablo St
Los Angeles CA 90033
323 342-7120

(P-26617)
ENERGY LIVERMORE OFF US DEPT
Also Called: Lawrence Livermore Nat Lab
539 Peralta Ave, San Francisco (94110-5338)
PHONE................415 648-3878
Thomas McVey, *Research*
EMP: 398 **Privately Held**
SIC: 8733 9611 Noncommercial research organizations; energy development & conservation agency, government;
PA: United States Department Of Energy Livermore Office
7000 East Ave
Livermore CA 94550
925 422-1100

(P-26618)
ENERGY LIVERMORE OFF US DEPT
Also Called: Lawrence Livermore Nat Lab
1413 Willowtree Ct, San Jose (95118-1155)
PHONE................408 267-1413
David Zalk, *Branch Mgr*
EMP: 398 **Privately Held**
SIC: 8733 9611 Noncommercial research organizations; energy development & conservation agency, government;
PA: United States Department Of Energy Livermore Office
7000 East Ave
Livermore CA 94550
925 422-1100

(P-26619)
FAIR TRADE USA
1500 Broadway Ste 400, Oakland (94612-2079)
PHONE................510 663-5260
Paul Rice, *President*
Dave Rochlin, *COO*
Joan Catherine Braun, *CFO*
EMP: 80
SQ FT: 23,600
SALES: 14.5MM **Privately Held**
SIC: 8733 Noncommercial social research organization

(P-26620)
GARY MARY W WIRELESS HLTH INST
10350 N Torrey Pines Rd, La Jolla (92037-1018)
PHONE................858 412-8600
Donald M Casey Jr, *CEO*
Michael Caponetto, *CFO*
Gary West, *Chairman*
Dr Joseph Smith, *Chief Mktg Ofcr*
Dr Eric Topol, *Chief Mktg Ofcr*
EMP: 50
SALES: 184.6K **Privately Held**
SIC: 8733 Medical research

(P-26621)
HORIZON PHARMACEUTICAL LLC (HQ)
7 Hamilton Landing # 100, Novato (94949-8209)
PHONE................415 408-6200
Timothy P Walbert, *President*
Barry J Moze, *COO*
Paul W Hoelscher, *CFO*
Robert F Carey, *Officer*
David A Happel, *Exec VP*
EMP: 74
SQ FT: 52,319
SALES: 94.2MM **Privately Held**
WEB: www.torreypinestherapeutics.com
SIC: 8733 2834 Medical research; pharmaceutical preparations

(P-26622)
HRL LABORATORIES LLC
Also Called: Hughes Research Laboratories
3011 Malibu Canyon Rd, Malibu (90265-4797)
PHONE................310 317-5000
Penrose Albright, *President*
Roger Gronwald, *CFO*
Conilee Kirkpatrick, *Vice Pres*
Carole Johnson, *Executive*
Albert Cosand, *Principal*
EMP: 500
SQ FT: 250,000
SALES (est): 8.7MM **Privately Held**
WEB: www.hrl.com
SIC: 8733 8731 Research institute; commercial physical research

(P-26623)
HUNTINGTON MED RES INSTITUTES
734 Fairmount Ave, Pasadena (91105-3104)
PHONE................626 397-5804
William Opel, *Manager*
EMP: 60
SALES (est): 3.5MM
SALES (corp-wide): 15.5MM **Privately Held**
WEB: www.hmri.org
SIC: 8733
PA: Huntington Medical Research Institutes
686 S Fair Oaks Ave
Pasadena CA 91105
626 795-4343

(P-26624)
IDUN PHARMACEUTICALS INC
9380 Judicial Dr, San Diego (92121-3830)
PHONE................858 622-3000
Martin Mackay, *CEO*
David Shapiro, *Exec VP*
EMP: 50
SQ FT: 43,000
SALES (est): 1.4MM
SALES (corp-wide): 35.3MM **Publicly Held**
SIC: 8733 Medical research
PA: Conatus Pharmaceuticals Inc.
16745 W Bernardo Dr # 200
San Diego CA 92127
858 376-2600

(P-26625)
INSTITUTE FOR LA JOLLA
Also Called: La Jolla Inst For Allergy & Im
9420 Athena Cir, La Jolla (92037-1387)
PHONE................858 752-6500
Mitchell Kronenberg, *President*
Skip Carpowich, *CFO*
Gina Kirchweger, *Officer*
Chris Lee, *Officer*
Charles A Carpowich Jr, *Exec VP*
EMP: 240
SQ FT: 87,000
SALES: 61.5MM **Privately Held**
SIC: 8733 Medical research

(P-26626)
INTERNTIONAL CMPT SCIENCE INST
Also Called: I C S I
1947 Center St Ste 600, Berkeley (94704-1159)
PHONE................510 643-9153
Rebecca Pieraccini, *President*
Orpheus Crutchfield, *Managing Dir*

Maria Quintana, *General Mgr*
Cindy Ngu, *Admin Asst*
Albert Park, *Admin Asst*
EMP: 50
SQ FT: 26,000
SALES: 7.8MM **Privately Held**
SIC: 8733 Research institute

(P-26627)
J CRAIG VENTER INSTITUTE INC (PA)
4120 Capricorn Ln, La Jolla (92037-3498)
PHONE..................301 795-7000
J Craig Venter, *CEO*
Karen Nelson, *President*
Robert Friedman, *COO*
Harold Davies, *CFO*
Kathleen L Mattis, *Admin Sec*
EMP: 325
SQ FT: 125,000
SALES (est): 39.9MM **Privately Held**
WEB: www.jcvi.org
SIC: 8733 8731 Research institute; biological research

(P-26628)
JBS INTERNATIONAL INC
555 Airport Blvd Ste 400, Burlingame (94010-2036)
PHONE..................650 373-4900
Cynthia Currin, *Principal*
Claudia Birmingham, *Comp Spec*
Julio Campero, *Research*
Craig Mathson, *Technology*
EMP: 55
SALES (corp-wide): 61.2MM **Privately Held**
SIC: 8733 Medical research
PA: Jbs International, Inc.
5515 Security Ln Ste 800
North Bethesda MD 20852
301 495-1080

(P-26629)
JOHN WAYNE INSTITUTE FOR CTR
2200 Santa Monica Blvd, Santa Monica (90404-2312)
PHONE..................310 449-5253
Patrick Wayne, *Ch of Bd*
Gary Grubbs, *COO*
EMP: 160
SQ FT: 57,000
SALES: 13.9MM **Privately Held**
SIC: 8733 Research institute

(P-26630)
JWCH INSTITUTE INC
6912 Ajax Ave, Bell (90201-4057)
PHONE..................323 562-5813
Annabel Munoz, *Manager*
Teresa I Bertao, *Nurse Practr*
EMP: 62
SALES (corp-wide): 33.9MM **Privately Held**
SIC: 8733 Noncommercial research organizations
PA: Jwch Institute, Inc.
5650 Jillson St
Commerce CA 90040
323 477-1171

(P-26631)
JWCH INSTITUTE INC
12360 Firestone Blvd, Norwalk (90650-4324)
PHONE..................562 281-0306
Oyamendan Itohan, *COO*
EMP: 78
SALES (corp-wide): 33.9MM **Privately Held**
SIC: 8733 Noncommercial research organizations
PA: Jwch Institute, Inc.
5650 Jillson St
Commerce CA 90040
323 477-1171

(P-26632)
LAS CUMBRES OBSERVATORY GLOBAL
6740 Cortona Dr Ste 102, Goleta (93117-5575)
PHONE..................805 880-1600
Wayne Rosing, *President*

Dorothy Largay, *Treasurer*
Michael Falarsky, *Exec VP*
EMP: 50
SQ FT: 37,795
SALES: 7MM **Privately Held**
WEB: www.lcogt.net
SIC: 8733 Scientific research agency

(P-26633)
LELAND STANFORD JUNIOR UNIV
Blum, John Erthquake Engrg Ctr
Melcode 4020 Bldg 540, Stanford (94305)
PHONE..................650 723-4150
Greg Dierlein, *Director*
EMP: 70
SALES (corp-wide): 5.6B **Privately Held**
SIC: 8733 8221 Research institute; university
PA: Leland Stanford Junior University
450 Serra Mall
Stanford CA 94305
650 723-2300

(P-26634)
LELAND STANFORD JUNIOR UNIV
Also Called: Ginzton Laboratory
450 Via Palou Mall, Stanford (94305-4014)
PHONE..................650 723-0107
Marilynn Elverson, *Director*
Haim Mendelson, *Professor*
EMP: 150
SALES (corp-wide): 5.6B **Privately Held**
SIC: 8733 8221 Physical research, noncommercial; university
PA: Leland Stanford Junior University
450 Serra Mall
Stanford CA 94305
650 723-2300

(P-26635)
LELAND STANFORD JUNIOR UNIV
Also Called: Stanford Univ Earth Secinces
397 Panama Mall Ste 360, Stanford (94305-2237)
PHONE..................650 724-8899
Pamila Matson, *Principal*
Pamela Matson, *Manager*
EMP: 150
SALES (corp-wide): 5.6B **Privately Held**
SIC: 8733 8731 Scientific research agency; commercial physical research
PA: Leland Stanford Junior University
450 Serra Mall
Stanford CA 94305
650 723-2300

(P-26636)
LELAND STANFORD JUNIOR UNIV
Diagnostic Radiology
1201 Welch Rd, Palo Alto (94305-5102)
PHONE..................650 723-4733
Robert Herfkens, *Principal*
EMP: 67
SALES (corp-wide): 5.6B **Privately Held**
SIC: 8733 8221 Medical research; university
PA: Leland Stanford Junior University
450 Serra Mall
Stanford CA 94305
650 723-2300

(P-26637)
LUMINAR TECHNOLOGIES INC
1891 Page Mill Rd 200, Palo Alto (94304-1211)
PHONE..................626 629-8686
Austin Russell, *CEO*
EMP: 87
SALES (corp-wide): 3MM **Privately Held**
SIC: 8733 Noncommercial research organizations
PA: Luminar Technologies, Inc.
12601 Research Pkwy
Orlando FL 32826
800 532-2417

(P-26638)
MEDIDATA SOLUTIONS INC
343 Sansome St Ste 1400, San Francisco (94104-5607)
PHONE..................415 295-4300

Joe Rincon, *Office Mgr*
EMP: 207 **Publicly Held**
SIC: 8733 Medical research
PA: Medidata Solutions, Inc.
350 Hudson St Fl 9
New York NY 10014

(P-26639)
MICROBIOLOGY & QULTY ASSOC INC
2341 Stanwell Dr, Concord (94520-4808)
PHONE..................925 288-1400
Juan Munoz, *President*
Renee Johnston, *Lab Dir*
Jeneill Knight, *QA Dir*
Mimi Leong, *Sales Staff*
Ramon Mendoza, *Director*
EMP: 50
SQ FT: 50,000
SALES: 5MM **Privately Held**
SIC: 8733 Physical research, noncommercial
PA: Analytical Lab Group, Llc
1285 Corp Ctr Dr Ste 110
Saint Paul MN 55121
612 845-3618

(P-26640)
MILKEN INSTITUTE
1250 4th St Fl 2, Santa Monica (90401-1418)
PHONE..................310 570-4600
Michael L Klowden, *CEO*
Michael Milken, *Ch of Bd*
Richard Ditizio, *President*
John Hunter, *CFO*
Carole Biau, *Associate Dir*
EMP: 50
SALES (est): 61.8MM **Privately Held**
WEB: www.milkeninstitute.com
SIC: 8733 Economic research, noncommercial

(P-26641)
MIND RESEARCH INSTITUTE
Also Called: Music Intllgnce Neuro Dev Inst
111 Academy Ste 100, Irvine (92617-3046)
PHONE..................949 345-8700
Brett Woudenberg, *CEO*
Laura Hanson, *Partner*
Andrew R Coulson, *President*
Gregory Blevins, *CFO*
Josephine Garrett, *CFO*
EMP: 160
SALES: 29MM **Privately Held**
WEB: www.mindinst.org
SIC: 8733 Medical research

(P-26642)
NAVIGATE BIOPHARMA SVCS INC
1890 Rutherford Rd, Carlsbad (92008-7344)
PHONE..................866 992-4939
Kevin Zou, *CEO*
EMP: 180
SALES (est): 588.9K
SALES (corp-wide): 49.1B **Privately Held**
SIC: 8733
HQ: Novartis Finance Corporation
230 Park Ave Fl 21
New York NY 10169

(P-26643)
NOVARTIS INSTITUT
Also Called: Genomics Inst. O
10675 John J Hopkins Dr, San Diego (92121-1127)
PHONE..................858 812-1976
Genevieve Welch, *Principal*
Andrey Santrosyan, *Associate Dir*
Kelly Milliken, *Info Tech Mgr*
Aleksey Galipchak, *IT/INT Sup*
Jason Matzen, *Research*
EMP: 51
SALES (est): 8.6MM **Privately Held**
SIC: 8733 Research institute

(P-26644)
NT SUNSET INC
2220 Livingston St # 201, Oakland (94606-5216)
PHONE..................510 420-3772
Wilbur Ross, *Ch of Bd*

James Curley, *President*
Mark Brutten, *Senior VP*
Dirk Keunen, *Senior VP*
Kelvin Chen, *Vice Pres*
EMP: 50 **EST:** 1998
SALES (est): 5.7MM **Privately Held**
WEB: www.nano-tex.com
SIC: 8733 Noncommercial research organizations

(P-26645)
OLIVE VIEW/UCLA EDUCATION &
14445 Olive View Dr, Sylmar (91342-1437)
PHONE..................818 364-3434
Denise Tritt, *General Mgr*
Lisa Gipti, *Accountant*
EMP: 75
SQ FT: 1,326
SALES: 3MM **Privately Held**
SIC: 8733 Medical research

(P-26646)
PALO ALTO VTERANS INST FOR RES
Also Called: Pavir
3801 Miran Ave Bldg 101a, Palo Alto (94304)
PHONE..................650 858-3970
Kerstin Lynam, *CEO*
Mary Thornton, *COO*
Bonnie Liang, *CFO*
Orr Sharpe, *Lab Dir*
Karamjeet Kaur, *Administration*
EMP: 218
SQ FT: 5,500
SALES: 28.2MM **Privately Held**
WEB: www.paire.org
SIC: 8733 Medical research; noncommercial biological research organization; scientific research agency

(P-26647)
PARKINSONS INSTITUTE
675 Almanor Ave Ste 101, Sunnyvale (94085-2930)
PHONE..................800 786-2958
Carrolee Barlow, *CEO*
Irwin Helford, *Ch of Bd*
EMP: 85
SQ FT: 40,000
SALES: 8.8MM **Privately Held**
WEB: www.parkinsonsinstitute.org
SIC: 8733 8011 Medical research; clinic, operated by physicians

(P-26648)
POINT REYES BIRD OBSERVATORY
Also Called: PRBO
3820 Cypress Dr Ste 11, Petaluma (94954-6964)
PHONE..................707 781-2555
Ellie M Cohen, *President*
Luke Petersen, *Partner*
Corey Shake, *Partner*
Edward Sarti, *Ch of Bd*
Laurie Tahcott, *CFO*
EMP: 85
SQ FT: 2,000
SALES: 12.3MM **Privately Held**
SIC: 8733 8748 Noncommercial biological research organization; business consulting

(P-26649)
PREMIER SOURCE LLC
999 Bayhill Dr Fl 3, San Bruno (94066-3070)
PHONE..................415 349-2010
Kenneth Wicks,
Sinead Foley,
EMP: 65
SQ FT: 13,000
SALES (est): 3.4MM
SALES (corp-wide): 153.1B **Publicly Held**
SIC: 8733
PA: Amerisourcebergen Corporation
1300 Morris Dr Ste 100
Chesterbrook PA 19087
610 727-7000

(P-26650)
PROTHENA BIOSCIENCES INC
331 Oyster Point Blvd, South San Francisco (94080-1913)
PHONE...................650 837-8550
Dale Schenk, *CEO*
Tran Nguyen, *CFO*
A W Homan, *Principal*
Martin Koller MD, *Principal*
Sarah Huntley, *Information Mgr*
EMP: 50
SALES (est): 9.9MM **Privately Held**
SIC: 8733 Medical research

(P-26651)
PUBLIC HEALTH INSTITUTE (PA)
555 12th St Ste 1050, Oakland (94607-3630)
PHONE...................510 285-5500
Mary Pittman, *President*
Melange Matthews, *COO*
Bob Wolfson, *COO*
Tamar Dorfman, *CFO*
Matthew Marsom, *Vice Pres*
EMP: 630
SQ FT: 50,000
SALES: 96MM **Privately Held**
WEB: www.bmsg.org
SIC: 8733 Scientific research agency; medical research

(P-26652)
RADIABEAM TECHNOLOGIES LLC
1717 Stuart St, Santa Clara (95054)
PHONE...................310 822-5845
Salime Boubher,
EMP: 50
SALES: 5MM **Privately Held**
SIC: 8733 3826 Physical research, noncommercial; laser scientific & engineering instruments

(P-26653)
RANCHO RESEARCH INSTITUTE
Also Called: RRI
7601 Imperial Hwy, Downey (90242-3456)
P.O. Box 3500 (90242-3500)
PHONE...................562 401-8111
Julia Laplount, *CEO*
Yaga Szlachcic, *President*
EMP: 175
SQ FT: 15,000
SALES: 6.8MM **Privately Held**
WEB: www.larei.org
SIC: 8733 Educational research agency; scientific research agency

(P-26654)
REGULUS THERAPEUTICS INC
10614 Science Center Dr, San Diego (92121-1150)
PHONE...................858 202-6300
Stelios Papadopoulos, *Ch of Bd*
Joseph P Hagan, *President*
Daniel Chevallard, *CFO*
Hugh Rosen, *Bd of Directors*
Dan Chevallard, *Vice Pres*
EMP: 63 EST: 2008
SQ FT: 59,000
SALES: 72K **Privately Held**
SIC: 8733 Biotechnical research, noncommercial

(P-26655)
RIVERSIDE RESEARCH INSTITUTE
3333 W Coast Hwy Ste 101, Newport Beach (92663-4039)
PHONE...................949 631-0107
Rosemary Ellis, *Director*
EMP: 50
SALES (corp-wide): 88.1MM **Privately Held**
SIC: 8733 8092 Research institute; kidney dialysis centers
PA: Riverside Research Institute
156 William St Fl 9
New York NY 10038
212 563-4545

(P-26656)
SAFC CARLSBAD INC
6219 El Camino Real, Carlsbad (92009-1604)
PHONE...................760 710-6100
Jefferey Strobel, *Director*
Don Linehan, *General Mgr*
Mark A Logomasini, *Finance Dir*
Wolf Klump, *Senior Mgr*
Jefferey L Strobel, *Director*
EMP: 65
SQ FT: 24,000
SALES (est): 3.5MM
SALES (corp-wide): 18B **Privately Held**
WEB: www.molecularmed.com
SIC: 8733 Medical research
HQ: Bioreliance Corporation
14920 Broschart Rd
Rockville MD 20850
301 738-1000

(P-26657)
SANFORD BURNHAM PREBYS MEDICAL (PA)
Also Called: SBP
10901 N Torrey Pines Rd, La Jolla (92037-1005)
PHONE...................858 795-5000
Perry Nisen, *CEO*
Kristiina Vuori, *President*
Gary Chessum, *CFO*
Robin Ryan, *Vice Pres*
Sylvie E Blondelle, *Associate Dir*
EMP: 966
SQ FT: 397,000
SALES: 132.5MM **Privately Held**
SIC: 8733 Research institute

(P-26658)
SANTEN INCORPORATED
6401 Hollis St Ste 125, Emeryville (94608-1462)
PHONE...................415 268-9100
Akihiro Aki Tsujimura, *Principal*
Xavier Avat, *President*
Reza M Haque, *Senior VP*
Peter Sallstig, *Senior VP*
EMP: 100
SQ FT: 46,000
SALES (est): 25.7MM
SALES (corp-wide): 2.1B **Privately Held**
WEB: www.santeninc.com
SIC: 8733 8011 8731 Noncommercial biological research organization; offices & clinics of medical doctors; commercial physical research
PA: Santen Pharmaceutical Co., Ltd.
4-20, Ofukacho, Kita-Ku
Osaka OSK 530-0
663 217-000

(P-26659)
SCRIPPS RESEARCH INSTITUTE (PA)
10550 N Torrey Pines Rd, La Jolla (92037-1000)
PHONE...................858 784-1000
Peter G Schultz, *CEO*
Ronald L Davis, *Ch of Bd*
John D Diekman, *Ch of Bd*
Steve A Kay, *President*
Cary E Thomas, *CFO*
EMP: 99
SALES: 348.5MM **Privately Held**
SIC: 8733 Research institute

(P-26660)
SETI INSTITUTE
Also Called: Seti Institute, The
189 Bernardo Ave 100, Mountain View (94043-5203)
PHONE...................650 961-6633
Matthew Doan, *President*
Dr John Billingham, *Vice Chairman*
Edna Devor, *CEO*
Shannon Atkinson, *CFO*
Dr Greg Papadopolous, *Chairman*
EMP: 115
SQ FT: 19,737
SALES (est): 18.9MM **Privately Held**
WEB: www.voyagesthroughtime.org
SIC: 8733 Research institute

(P-26661)
SRI INTERNATIONAL (PA)
333 Ravenswood Ave, Menlo Park (94025-3493)
P.O. Box 2203 (94026-2203)
PHONE...................650 859-2000
William Jeffrey, *CEO*
Richard Brewer, *Managing Prtnr*
Denise Glyn Borders, *President*
Stephen Ciesinski, *President*
Manish Kothari, *President*
▲ EMP: 1430
SQ FT: 1,300,000
SALES: 503.9MM **Privately Held**
WEB: www.sri.com
SIC: 8733 8748 Scientific research agency; noncommercial social research organization; business consulting

(P-26662)
SRI INTERNATIONAL
4111 Broad St Ste 220, San Luis Obispo (93401-8743)
PHONE...................805 542-9330
EMP: 142
SALES (corp-wide): 550MM **Privately Held**
SIC: 8733
PA: Sri International
333 Ravenswood Ave
Menlo Park CA 94025
650 859-2000

(P-26663)
STANFORD UNIV FRMAN SPGLI INST
616 Serra St, Stanford (94305-6008)
PHONE...................650 723-8681
Michael McFaul, *Director*
EMP: 250
SALES (est): 3.3MM **Privately Held**
SIC: 8733 Research institute

(P-26664)
STUDY US RESEARCH INST INC
1335 N La Brea Ave 2-205, Los Angeles (90028-3905)
PHONE...................213 840-9575
Tiffany S Bennett, *President*
EMP: 99
SALES: 250K **Privately Held**
SIC: 8733 Noncommercial research organizations

(P-26665)
TAKEDA CALIFORNIA INC
Also Called: Tcal
10410 Science Center Dr, San Diego (92121-1119)
PHONE...................858 622-8528
Keith Wilson, *President*
David Weitz, *Vice Pres*
Paul Eiler, *General Mgr*
Joel Hunter, *General Mgr*
Gary Lavaliere, *General Mgr*
EMP: 220
SALES (est): 41.9MM
SALES (corp-wide): 16.6B **Privately Held**
WEB: www.takedasd.com
SIC: 8733 Biotechnical research, noncommercial
PA: Takeda Pharmaceutical Company Limited
2-1-1, Nihombashihoncho
Chuo-Ku TKY 103-0
332 782-111

(P-26666)
THE NATIONAL FOOD LAB LLC
365 N Canyons Pkwy # 201, Livermore (94551-7703)
PHONE...................925 828-1440
Austin Sharp, *President*
Julie Hill, *Vice Pres*
Debbie Lohmeyer, *Vice Pres*
Wilfredo Ocasio, *Vice Pres*
Jena Roberts, *Vice Pres*
EMP: 150 EST: 1991
SQ FT: 21,000
SALES (est): 23.5MM **Privately Held**
WEB: www.thenfl.com
SIC: 8733 Scientific research agency

(P-26667)
TOYOTA RESEARCH INSTITUTE INC
4440 El Camino Real, Los Altos (94022-1003)
PHONE...................703 231-6680
Krshan Toursohi, *General Mgr*
EMP: 94
SALES (corp-wide): 275.7B **Privately Held**
SIC: 8733 Research institute
HQ: Toyota Research Institute, Inc.
1 Kendall Sq Ste B200
Cambridge MA 02139
857 285-6160

(P-26668)
UNITED STATES DEPT OF ENERGY
Also Called: Lawrence Berkeley National Lab
1 Cyclotron Rd, Berkeley (94720-8099)
PHONE...................510 486-4000
EMP: 5000 **Publicly Held**
SIC: 8733 9611
HQ: United States Dept Of Energy
1000 Independence Ave Sw
Washington DC 20585
202 586-5000

(P-26669)
UNIVERSITY CAL SAN FRANCISCO
Also Called: Uscf Caps Department Medicine
500 Parnassus Ave, San Francisco (94143-2203)
PHONE...................415 476-9000
EMP: 87
SALES (corp-wide): 9.5B **Privately Held**
SIC: 8733 8221 9411
HQ: University Of California, San Francisco
505 Parnassus Ave
San Francisco CA 94143
415 476-9000

(P-26670)
UNIVERSITY CALIFORNIA BERKELEY
Also Called: Lawrence Berkeley National Lab
5885 Hollis St, Emeryville (94608-2404)
PHONE...................510 495-2490
Michael Witherell, *Director*
EMP: 3304 **Privately Held**
SIC: 8733 8221 9411 Noncommercial research organizations; university; administration of educational programs;
HQ: The University California Berkeley
200 Clfrnia Hall Spc 1500
Berkeley CA 94720
510 642-6000

(P-26671)
VIACYTE INC
3550 General Atomics Ct B2-503, San Diego (92121-1122)
PHONE...................858 455-3708
Paul K Laikind, *President*
Kevin D'Amour, *Officer*
Anthony Gringeri, *Officer*
Allan Robins, *Senior VP*
Liz Bui, *Vice Pres*
EMP: 55
SQ FT: 12,000
SALES (est): 10.3MM **Privately Held**
WEB: www.novocell.com
SIC: 8733 2836 Medical research; biological products, except diagnostic

(P-26672)
WCCT GLOBAL INC (PA)
5630 Cerritos Ave, Cypress (90630-4738)
PHONE...................714 668-1500
Bill Taaffe, *CEO*
Bill Van Nostrand, *Exec VP*
Lee Barsky, *Vice Pres*
Yves Grenon, *Vice Pres*
Joanne Hollenbach, *Vice Pres*
EMP: 74
SALES (est): 32.2MM **Privately Held**
SIC: 8733 Research institute

(P-26673)
WESTED
300 Lakeside Dr Fl 25th, Oakland (94612-3534)
PHONE...................510 302-4200

Teresa Johnson, *Branch Mgr*
Richard Whitmore, *Administration*
Joaquin Petersen, *Technology*
Brian Williams, *Human Res Mgr*
Robert Montgomery, *Sr Project Mgr*
EMP: 62
SALES (corp-wide): 102.8MM **Privately Held**
WEB: www.edgateway.net
SIC: 8733 8732 Educational research agency; commercial nonphysical research
PA: Wested
730 Harrison St Ste 500
San Francisco CA 94107
415 565-3000

(P-26674)
WESTED
180 Harbor Dr Ste 112, Sausalito
(94965-2845)
PHONE.................................415 289-2300
Peter Mangione, *Branch Mgr*
Kyle Walsh, *Analyst*
EMP: 51
SALES (corp-wide): 102.8MM **Privately Held**
WEB: www.edgateway.net
SIC: 8733 8732 Educational research agency; commercial nonphysical research
PA: Wested
730 Harrison St Ste 500
San Francisco CA 94107
415 565-3000

(P-26675)
WESTED (PA)
730 Harrison St Ste 500, San Francisco
(94107-1242)
PHONE.................................415 565-3000
Glen H Harvey, *CEO*
Beverly Hurley, *Bd of Directors*
David Sperry, *Bd of Directors*
Juan Bojorquez, *Vice Pres*
John Flaherty, *Associate Dir*
EMP: 115
SQ FT: 85,000
SALES (est): 102.8MM **Privately Held**
WEB: www.edgateway.net
SIC: 8733 Educational research agency

(P-26676)
WESTED
730 Harrison St Ste 500, San Francisco
(94107-1242)
PHONE.................................415 565-3000
Judy Gilbert, *Manager*
EMP: 172
SALES (corp-wide): 102.8MM **Privately Held**
WEB: www.edgateway.net
SIC: 8733 8732 Educational research agency; commercial nonphysical research
PA: Wested
730 Harrison St Ste 500
San Francisco CA 94107
415 565-3000

(P-26677)
WESTERN STATES INFO NETWRK INC
1825 Bell St Ste 205, Sacramento
(95825-1020)
PHONE.................................916 263-1180
Karen Aumond, *Exec Dir*
EMP: 78
SALES: 5.3MM **Privately Held**
SIC: 8733 Noncommercial research organizations

(P-26678)
WHITTIER INST FOR DIABETES
10140 Campus Point Dr, San Diego
(92121-1520)
PHONE.................................877 944-8843
Athena Tsimikas, *Exec Dir*
EMP: 80 **EST:** 1980
SALES (est): 3.9MM
SALES (corp-wide): 2.9B **Privately Held**
WEB: www.scripps.org
SIC: 8733 Medical research
PA: Scripps Health
10140 Campus Point Dr Ax415
San Diego CA 92121
800 727-4777

(P-26679)
ZONARE MEDICAL SYSTEMS INC
420 Bernardo Ave, Mountain View
(94043-5209)
P.O. Box 760, Alviso (95002-0760)
PHONE.................................650 230-2800
Donald Southard, *CEO*
Timothy A Marcotte, *President*
Steve Edwards, *Vice Pres*
Michael Gabler, *Vice Pres*
Jon Livak, *Vice Pres*
EMP: 65
SALES (est): 19.1MM **Privately Held**
WEB: www.zonare.com
SIC: 8733 5047 Research institute; hospital equipment & supplies
PA: Mindray Medical International Limited
C/O: Conyers Trust Company (Cayman) Limited
George Town GR CAYMAN

8734 Testing Laboratories

(P-26680)
ACCION LABS US INC
4633 Old Ironsides Dr # 304, Santa Clara
(95054-1807)
PHONE.................................408 970-9809
William Flavin, *General Mgr*
EMP: 1465
SALES (corp-wide): 7.3MM **Privately Held**
SIC: 8734 Testing laboratories
PA: Accion Labs Us, Inc.
1225 Wash Pike Ste 401
Bridgeville PA 15017
724 260-5139

(P-26681)
AGRICULTURE AND PRIORITY POLLU (PA)
Also Called: Appl
908 N Temperance Ave, Clovis
(93611-8606)
PHONE.................................559 275-2175
Diane Anderson, *President*
Bradford Anderson, *Corp Secy*
Sharon Dehmlow, *General Mgr*
Cynthia Clark, *Project Mgr*
Rene Patterson, *Safety Mgr*
EMP: 50
SQ FT: 8,000
SALES (est): 9.1MM **Privately Held**
SIC: 8734 Pollution testing

(P-26682)
AIRCRAFT XRAY LABORATORIES INC
5216 Pacific Blvd, Huntington Park
(90255-2595)
PHONE.................................323 587-0164
EMP: 67
SQ FT: 60,000
SALES (est): 11.6MM **Privately Held**
WEB: www.aircraftxray.com
SIC: 8734 7384 3471 Testing laboratories; photograph developing & retouching; plating & polishing

(P-26683)
ALS SERVICES USA CORP
1875 Coronado Ave, Long Beach
(90755-1245)
PHONE.................................562 597-3932
Pete Guebara, *Branch Mgr*
EMP: 100 **Privately Held**
SIC: 8734 Testing laboratories
HQ: Als Services Usa, Corp.
10450 Stncliff Rd Ste 210
Houston TX 77099
281 530-5656

(P-26684)
BABCOCK LABORATORIES INC
Also Called: E. S. Babcock & Sons
6100 Quail Valley Ct, Riverside
(92507-0704)
P.O. Box 432 (92502-0432)
PHONE.................................951 653-3351
Allison Mackenzie, *CEO*
Carol Kase, *COO*

Brad Meadows, *Vice Pres*
Tami Kearns, *Admin Asst*
Nicole Greenwood, *Technician*
EMP: 70
SQ FT: 20,000
SALES (est): 14MM **Privately Held**
WEB: www.babcocklabs.com
SIC: 8734 Water testing laboratory; food testing service

(P-26685)
BC LABORATORIES INC
4100 Atlas Ct, Bakersfield (93308-4510)
PHONE.................................661 327-4911
Carolyn I Jackson, *President*
Richard Eglin, *Shareholder*
Stuart Buttram, *Lab Dir*
Robert Cortez, *Department Mgr*
Miranda Sonia, *QA Dir*
EMP: 93
SQ FT: 18,000
SALES (est): 10.4MM **Privately Held**
WEB: www.bclabs.com
SIC: 8734 Water testing laboratory

(P-26686)
BIOSCREEN TESTING SERVICES INC (PA)
3904 Del Amo Blvd Ste 801, Torrance
(90503-2183)
PHONE.................................602 277-1154
Bradford L Rope, *President*
Ranil M Fernando, *Vice Pres*
David Heuer, *Director*
EMP: 85
SQ FT: 20,000
SALES (est): 21.2MM **Privately Held**
WEB: www.bioscreen.com
SIC: 8734 8731 Testing laboratories; commercial physical research

(P-26687)
CALIFORNIA LAB SCIENCES LLC
Also Called: West Pacific Medical Lab
10200 Pioneer Blvd # 500, Santa Fe Springs (90670-6000)
PHONE.................................562 758-6900
William McDonald,
EMP: 300
SALES (est): 32.6MM **Privately Held**
SIC: 8734 Testing laboratories

(P-26688)
CATALENT SAN DIEGO INC
7330 Carroll Rd Ste 200, San Diego
(92121-2364)
PHONE.................................858 805-6383
Timothy Scott, *President*
Jordan Lin, *Engineer*
Allison Hernandez, *Human Resources*
Jason Everett, *Mfg Dir*
Kimberly Scholz, *Marketing Staff*
EMP: 120
SQ FT: 6,600
SALES (est): 18MM **Publicly Held**
WEB: www.pharmatek.com
SIC: 8734 8731 Testing laboratories; commercial research laboratory
HQ: Catalent Pharma Solutions, Inc.
14 Schoolhouse Rd
Somerset NJ 08873

(P-26689)
CENTRAL COUNTIES
241 Business Park Way, Atwater
(95301-9487)
PHONE.................................209 356-0355
Christine Hackler, *Principal*
EMP: 70
SALES (est): 5.5MM **Privately Held**
SIC: 8734 Testing laboratories

(P-26690)
COOPER & JACKSON INC
310 Shaw Rd Ste D, South San Francisco
(94080-6615)
PHONE.................................408 437-2750
Kevin Waldron, *President*
Jeanine Waldron, *Vice Pres*
EMP: 200
SQ FT: 52,000

SALES (est): 11.1MM **Privately Held**
SIC: 8734 1521 Testing laboratories; repairing fire damage, single-family houses; single-family home remodeling, additions & repairs

(P-26691)
DACOR HOLDINGS INC
14425 Clark Ave, City of Industry
(91745-1235)
P.O. Box 90070 (91715-0070)
PHONE.................................626 626-4461
Michael Joseph, *President*
EMP: 150
SALES (est): 11.4MM **Privately Held**
SIC: 8734 Testing laboratories

(P-26692)
DE PAR INC
Also Called: Associated Laboratories
931 W Barkley Ave, Orange (92868-1208)
PHONE.................................714 771-6900
Tito L Parola, *President*
Robert Webber, *Treasurer*
Edward Behare, *Admin Sec*
Kristen Walker, *Project Mgr*
EMP: 85 **EST:** 1924
SQ FT: 17,000
SALES (est): 10.5MM **Privately Held**
WEB: www.associatedlabs.com
SIC: 8734 Testing laboratories

(P-26693)
DICKSON TESTING CO INC (DH)
11126 Palmer Ave, South Gate
(90280-7492)
PHONE.................................562 862-8378
Robert Lyddon, *President*
Jim Scanell, *Vice Pres*
EMP: 80
SQ FT: 40,000
SALES (est): 15.2MM
SALES (corp-wide): 242.1B **Publicly Held**
WEB: www.dicksontesting.com
SIC: 8734 Metallurgical testing laboratory
HQ: Precision Castparts Corp.
4650 Sw Mcdam Ave Ste 300
Portland OR 97239
503 946-4800

(P-26694)
EAG INC (HQ)
Also Called: Eag Laboratories
2710 Walsh Ave, Santa Clara
(95051-0963)
PHONE.................................408 454-4600
Siddhartha Kadia, *CEO*
Lance Jones, *President*
Stefan Karnavas, *CFO*
Amanda Halford, *Exec VP*
Patricia M Lindley, *Exec VP*
EMP: 148
SQ FT: 70,000
SALES (est): 221.8MM **Privately Held**
WEB: www.eaglabs.com
SIC: 8734 Product testing laboratories
PA: Eurofins Pharma Us Holdings Ii, Inc
2425 New Holland Pike
Lancaster PA 17601
717 656-2300

(P-26695)
ELEMENT MTRLS TECH HB INC
18100 S Wilmington Ave, Compton
(90220-5909)
PHONE.................................310 632-8500
Chuck Gee, *General Mgr*
Cindy Castellanos, *Purchasing*
EMP: 86
SALES (corp-wide): 533MM **Privately Held**
WEB: www.stork.com
SIC: 8734 Metallurgical testing laboratory
HQ: Element Materials Technology Huntington Beach Inc.
15062 Bolsa Chica St
Huntington Beach CA 92649
714 892-1961

(P-26696)
ELEMENT MTRLS TECH HB INC (DH)
15062 Bolsa Chica St, Huntington Beach
(92649-1023)
PHONE.................................714 892-1961

Charles Noall, *President*
Eelco Niermeijer, *CFO*
Pete Regan, *Chairman*
Jeff Joyce, *Exec VP*
Jo Wetz, *Exec VP*
EMP: 80
SQ FT: 4,500
SALES (est): 41.6MM
SALES (corp-wide): 533MM **Privately
Held**
WEB: www.stork.com
SIC: 8734 Metallurgical testing laboratory
HQ: Element Materials Technology Group
Us Holdings Inc.
15062 Bolsa Chica St
Huntington Beach CA 92649
714 892-1961

(P-26697)
ELLIOTT LABORATORIES INC
41039 Boyce Rd, Fremont (94538-2434)
PHONE...............................510 440-9500
Conrad Chu, *Principal*
Gaylon Morris, *Manager*
EMP: 50
SALES (est): 2.3MM **Privately Held**
SIC: 8734 Testing laboratories

(P-26698)
EMAX LABORATORIES INC
1835 W 205th St, Torrance (90501-1510)
PHONE...............................310 618-8889
Caspar J Pang, *CEO*
Kam P Yee, *President*
Richard Beauvil, *Officer*
Regina Chamberlain, *Executive*
Sing C Pang, *Admin Sec*
EMP: 50
SQ FT: 14,000
SALES (est): 11.2MM **Privately Held**
WEB: www.emaxlabs.com
SIC: 8734 8748 8731 Pollution testing;
environmental consultant; environmental
research

(P-26699)
**EMERY SMITH LABORATORIES
INC**
781 E Washington Blvd, Los Angeles
(90021-3043)
PHONE...............................213 745-5333
James E Partridge, *CEO*
EMP: 135
SALES (est): 14.7MM **Privately Held**
SIC: 8734 Testing laboratories

(P-26700)
**ENVIRONMENTAL HEALTH
HAZARD**
1515 Clay St Ste 1600, Oakland
(94612-1499)
PHONE...............................510 622-3200
EMP: 70 **Privately Held**
WEB: www.oehha.ca.gov
SIC: 8734 9511 Hazardous waste testing;
air, water & solid waste management;
HQ: California Office Of Environmental
Health Hazard Assessment
1001 I St
Sacramento CA 95814
916 324-7572

(P-26701)
EUROFINS AIR TOXICS LLC
180 Blue Ravine Rd Ste B, Folsom
(95630-4703)
PHONE...............................916 985-1000
J Wilson Hershey, *Ch of Bd*
Robert Mitzel, *President*
Thomas E Wolgemuth, *Corp Secy*
Stephany Mason, *Vice Pres*
Bob Mitzel, *VP Bus Dvlpt*
EMP: 55
SQ FT: 24,000
SALES (est): 8.9MM
SALES (corp-wide): 11.5MM **Privately
Held**
WEB: www.airtoxics.com
SIC: 8734 Water testing laboratory
PA: Eurofins Environment Testing Us Hold-
ings, Inc.
2200 Rittenhouse St # 175
Des Moines IA 50321
515 698-5039

(P-26702)
**FORENSIC ANALYTICAL SPC
INC (PA)**
3777 Depot Rd Ste 409, Hayward
(94545-2761)
PHONE...............................510 887-8828
David Kuhane, *President*
Richard Bernius, *COO*
John Martinelli, *Branch Mgr*
Dan Coltrin, *CTO*
Tiffany Rivera, *Accountant*
EMP: 120
SQ FT: 40,000
SALES (est): 12.3MM **Privately Held**
WEB: www.forensica.com
SIC: 8734 8748 Forensic laboratory; envi-
ronmental consultant

(P-26703)
GENZYME CORPORATION
2440 S Sepulveda Blvd # 100, Los Angeles
(90064-1784)
PHONE...............................310 482-5000
Richard Adleson, *Branch Mgr*
Robert V Pierre, *Pathologist*
Ronald Paler, *Med Doctor*
EMP: 200
SALES (corp-wide): 609.6MM **Privately
Held**
WEB: www.genzyme.com
SIC: 8734 8731 Testing laboratories; com-
mercial physical research
HQ: Genzyme Corporation
50 Binney St
Cambridge MA 02142
617 252-7500

(P-26704)
HORIZON WEST INC
Also Called: Oakwood Village
3388 Bell Rd, Auburn (95603-9242)
PHONE...............................530 889-8122
Roubah Moredhesal, *President*
EMP: 55
SALES (corp-wide): 103.7MM **Privately
Held**
SIC: 8734 8361 Food testing service; resi-
dential care
PA: Horizon West, Inc.
4020 Sierra College Blvd
Rocklin CA 95677
916 624-6230

(P-26705)
**IMAGING HLTHCARE
SPCALISTS LLC**
6386 Alvarado Ct, San Diego (92120-4905)
PHONE...............................619 229-2299
EMP: 61 **Privately Held**
SIC: 8734 Testing laboratories
PA: Imaging Healthcare Specialists, Llc
150 W Washington St
San Diego CA 92103

(P-26706)
INTERTEK GROUP INC
25800 Commercentre Dr, Lake Forest
(92630-8804)
PHONE...............................949 448-4100
Anuj Kumar, *President*
John Magelnicki, *Project Engr*
Christina Martinez, *Supervisor*
EMP: 63
SALES (corp-wide): 660.6MM **Privately
Held**
SIC: 8734 Testing laboratories
PA: Intertek Group Inc.
545 E Algonquin Rd Ste F
Arlington Heights IL 60005
847 871-1020

(P-26707)
**INTERTEK TESTING SVCS NA
INC**
25800 Commercentre Dr, Lake Forest
(92630-8804)
PHONE...............................949 448-4100
EMP: 65
SALES (corp-wide): 3.6B **Privately Held**
SIC: 8734 Testing laboratories
HQ: Intertek Testing Services Na, Inc.
3933 Us Route 11
Cortland NY 13045
607 753-6711

(P-26708)
INTERTEK USA INC
Also Called: Intertek Pharmaceutical Svcs
10420 Wateridge Cir, San Diego
(92121-5773)
PHONE...............................858 558-2599
Arron Xu, *Manager*
EMP: 100
SALES (corp-wide): 3.6B **Privately Held**
SIC: 8734 Testing laboratories
HQ: Intertek Usa Inc.
200 Westlke Prk Blvd 40
Houston TX 77079
713 543-3600

(P-26709)
INVITAE CORPORATION (PA)
1400 16th St, San Francisco (94103-5110)
PHONE...............................415 374-7782
Randal W Scott, *Ch of Bd*
Sean George, *CEO*
Lee Bendekgey, *CFO*
Shelly Guyer, *CFO*
Robert L Nussbaum, *Chief Mktg Ofcr*
EMP: 100
SQ FT: 7,795
SALES (est): 68.2MM **Publicly Held**
SIC: 8734 Testing laboratories

(P-26710)
ISE LABS INC
46800 Bayside Pkwy, Fremont
(94538-6592)
PHONE...............................510 687-2500
Cezar Simoniak, *Manager*
EMP: 50 **Privately Held**
WEB: www.iselabs.com
SIC: 8734 8731 Testing laboratories; com-
mercial physical research
HQ: Ise Labs, Inc.
46800 Bayside Pkwy
Fremont CA 94538
510 687-2500

(P-26711)
ISE LABS INC (DH)
46800 Bayside Pkwy, Fremont
(94538-6592)
PHONE...............................510 687-2500
Tien Wu, *CEO*
Jeff Thompson, *Vice Pres*
EMP: 200
SQ FT: 69,000
SALES (est): 52.5MM **Privately Held**
WEB: www.iselabs.com
SIC: 8734 3672 Calibration & certification;
printed circuit boards

(P-26712)
MCCAMPBELL ANALYTICAL INC
1534 Willow Pass Rd, Pittsburg
(94565-1701)
PHONE...............................925 252-9262
Edward Hamilton, *CEO*
Jill Miller, *Officer*
Ed Hamilton, *Lab Dir*
Rosa Venegas, *Business Dir*
Yen Cao, *Admin Asst*
EMP: 63
SQ FT: 12,896
SALES (est): 10.5MM **Privately Held**
WEB: www.mccampbell.com
SIC: 8734 Testing laboratories

(P-26713)
**MICHELSON LABORATORIES
INC (PA)**
6280 Chalet Dr, Commerce (90040-3761)
PHONE...............................562 928-0553
Grant Michelson, *President*
Jack E Michelson, *CEO*
Eva Vasco, *Administration*
Benjamin Garcia, *Info Tech Mgr*
Aaron Kaisber, *Marketing Staff*
EMP: 65
SQ FT: 20,000
SALES (est): 12.9MM **Privately Held**
WEB: www.michelsonlab.com
SIC: 8734 Food testing service

(P-26714)
MILLENNIUM HEALTH LLC (PA)
16981 Via Tazon Ste F, San Diego
(92127-1645)
PHONE...............................877 451-3534
Jennifer Strickland, *CEO*

Eugene I Davis, *Ch of Bd*
Howard Appel, *President*
David Cohen, *COO*
Mark A Winham, *COO*
EMP: 258
SALES (est): 66.1MM **Privately Held**
SIC: 8734 Testing laboratories

(P-26715)
**MIRION TECHNOLOGIES GDS
INC (HQ)**
Also Called: Global Dosimetry Solutions
2652 Mcgaw Ave, Irvine (92614-5840)
PHONE...............................949 419-1000
Thomas Logan, *CEO*
Sander Perle, *President*
James Hippel, *CFO*
Jack Pacheco, *CFO*
Tony Rabb, *CFO*
EMP: 125
SALES (est): 35.6MM **Privately Held**
WEB: www.mirion.com
SIC: 8734 Radiation dosimetry laboratory

(P-26716)
MISTRAS GROUP INC
2230 E Artesia Blvd, Long Beach
(90805-1739)
PHONE...............................562 597-3932
EMP: 58 **Publicly Held**
SIC: 8734 Testing laboratories
PA: Mistras Group, Inc.
195 Clarksville Rd Ste 2
Princeton Junction NJ 08550

(P-26717)
MISTRAS GROUP INC
6170 Egret Ct, Benicia (94510-1269)
PHONE...............................707 746-5870
Chuck Penley, *General Mgr*
EMP: 50 **Publicly Held**
SIC: 8734 Testing laboratories
PA: Mistras Group, Inc.
195 Clarksville Rd Ste 2
Princeton Junction NJ 08550

(P-26718)
**MONTROSE ENVMTL GROUP
INC**
2825 Verne Roberts Cir, Antioch
(94509-7902)
PHONE...............................925 680-4300
WEI Marcus Tan, *Principal*
EMP: 322 **Privately Held**
SIC: 8734 Pollution testing
PA: Montrose Environmental Corporation
1 Park Plz Ste 1000
Irvine CA 92614

(P-26719)
**MOORE TWINING ASSOCIATES
INC (PA)**
2527 Fresno St, Fresno (93721-1804)
PHONE...............................559 268-7021
Harry D Moore, *President*
Ruth E Moore, *Corp Secy*
Brian Boudreau, *Vice Pres*
EMP: 85 **EST:** 1898
SQ FT: 22,500
SALES (est): 18.8MM **Privately Held**
WEB: www.mooretwining.com
SIC: 8734 8711 Testing laboratories; engi-
neering services

(P-26720)
**NANOLAB TECHNOLOGIES INC
(PA)**
Also Called: Fib Lab
1708 Mccarthy Blvd, Milpitas (95035-7454)
PHONE...............................408 433-3320
John P Traub, *President*
Carol Traub, *Treasurer*
Xiu Han, *Vice Pres*
John Olson, *Vice Pres*
Jein Shyue, *Vice Pres*
EMP: 65
SQ FT: 15,000
SALES (est): 11.9MM **Privately Held**
WEB: www.nanolab1.com
SIC: 8734 Water testing laboratory

1132   2019 Directory of California
Wholesalers and Services Companies   ▲ = Import ▼=Export
◆ =Import/Export

(P-26721)
NATIONAL EVERCLEAN SVCS INC
28632 Roadside Dr Ste 275, Agoura Hills (91301-6052)
PHONE.............................877 532-5326
John McShane, *President*
EMP: 100
SQ FT: 2,500
SALES (est): 6.6MM
SALES (corp-wide): 728MM **Privately Held**
WEB: www.evercleanservices.com
SIC: 8734 8711 Food testing service; engineering services
PA: Underwriters Laboratories Inc.
333 Pfingsten Rd
Northbrook IL 60062
847 272-8800

(P-26722)
NITTO AVECIA PHARMA SERVICES (PA)
10 Vanderbilt, Irvine (92618-2010)
PHONE.............................949 951-4425
Assad Kazeminy, *President*
Raymond Kaczmarek, *President*
William Stowell, *CFO*
Adam Fox, *Exec VP*
Jack Wright, *Vice Pres*
EMP: 73
SQ FT: 62,000
SALES (est): 37.8MM **Privately Held**
WEB: www.irvinepharma.com
SIC: 8734 Product testing laboratories

(P-26723)
NORTH AMERCN SCIENCE ASSOC INC
N A M S A
9 Morgan, Irvine (92618-2005)
PHONE.............................949 951-3110
Dennis Nivens, *Vice Pres*
EMP: 60
SQ FT: 40,000
SALES (corp-wide): 126.5MM **Privately Held**
WEB: www.namsa.com
SIC: 8734 8071 8999 Testing laboratories; medical laboratories; chemical consultant
PA: North American Science Associates, Inc.
6750 Wales Rd
Northwood OH 43619
419 666-9455

(P-26724)
NTS TECHNICAL SYSTEMS
3505 E 3rd St, San Bernardino (92408-0201)
P.O. Box 160, Norco (92860-0160)
PHONE.............................909 382-2360
Doug Anderson, *Branch Mgr*
William McGinnis, *CEO*
EMP: 86
SALES (corp-wide): 273.9MM **Privately Held**
WEB: www.wylelabs.com
SIC: 8734 Testing laboratories
HQ: Nts Technical Systems
24007 Ventura Blvd # 200
Calabasas CA 91302
818 591-0776

(P-26725)
NTS TECHNICAL SYSTEMS
1536 E Valencia Dr, Fullerton (92831-4734)
PHONE.............................714 998-4351
Hector Paez, *General Mgr*
Rachel Joshi, *Business Dir*
Marty McCormick, *Department Mgr*
George Fogg, *Engineer*
Timothy Sturkie, *Facilities Mgr*
EMP: 121
SALES (corp-wide): 273.9MM **Privately Held**
WEB: www.ntscorp.com
SIC: 8734 8711 Radiation laboratories; sanitary engineers
HQ: Nts Technical Systems
24007 Ventura Blvd # 200
Calabasas CA 91302
818 591-0776

(P-26726)
PACIFIC TOXICOLOGY LABS
Also Called: Forensic Toxicology Associates
9348 De Soto Ave, Chatsworth (91311-4926)
PHONE.............................818 598-3110
Jeff Lanzolatta, *CEO*
Sue Barbosa, *COO*
Ken Kodama, *COO*
Greg Carroll, *CFO*
Neil Patel Carroll, *CFO*
EMP: 75
SQ FT: 19,000
SALES (est): 13MM **Privately Held**
WEB: www.pactox.com
SIC: 8734 Testing laboratories

(P-26727)
PHAMATECH INCORPORATED
15175 Innovation Dr, San Diego (92128-3401)
PHONE.............................858 643-5555
Tuan Pham, *CEO*
Tuan H Pham, *CEO*
EMP: 200
SQ FT: 50,000
SALES (est): 31.2MM **Privately Held**
WEB: www.phamatech.com
SIC: 8734 5047 Forensic laboratory; medical laboratory equipment

(P-26728)
PSYCHEMEDICS CORPORATION
5832 Uplander Way, Culver City (90230-6608)
PHONE.............................310 216-7776
Michael Schaffer, *Manager*
EMP: 75
SALES (est): 8MM
SALES (corp-wide): 39.7MM **Publicly Held**
WEB: www.psychemedics.com
SIC: 8734 Testing laboratories
PA: Psychemedics Corporation
289 Great Rd Ste 200
Acton MA 01720
978 206-8220

(P-26729)
SCST INC (PA)
6280 Riverdale St, San Diego (92120-3308)
PHONE.............................619 280-4321
Neal Clements, *CEO*
John Kirschbaum, *COO*
EMP: 74
SQ FT: 15,482
SALES: 12.2MM **Privately Held**
WEB: www.scst.com
SIC: 8734 8711 Testing laboratories; engineering services

(P-26730)
SGS NORTH AMERICA INC
1759 S Main St Ste 116, Milpitas (95035-6765)
PHONE.............................408 588-0200
James A Gordon, *Director*
EMP: 95
SALES (corp-wide): 6.4B **Privately Held**
SIC: 8734 Water testing laboratory
HQ: Sgs North America Inc.
201 Route 17
Rutherford NJ 07070
201 508-3000

(P-26731)
SIGNET TESTING LABS INC (HQ)
3526 Breakwater Ct, Hayward (94545-3611)
PHONE.............................510 887-8484
Robert V Tadlock, *President*
EMP: 250
SALES (est): 19.2MM
SALES (corp-wide): 16.4MM **Privately Held**
SIC: 8734 Testing laboratories
PA: United Engineering Resources, Inc.
498 N 3rd St
Sacramento CA 95811
916 375-6700

(P-26732)
SILLIKER LABS GROUP INC
6360 Gateway Dr, Cypress (90630-4844)
PHONE.............................714 226-0000

Vidyha Ganger, *Managing Dir*
Hanna Lee, *Opers Spvr*
Helen Andrews, *Opers Mgr*
EMP: 50
SALES (est): 5.1MM **Privately Held**
SIC: 8734 Product testing laboratories
HQ: Silliker, Inc.
111 E Wacker Dr Ste 2300
Chicago IL 60601
312 938-5151

(P-26733)
TESTAMERICA LABORATORIES INC
17461 Derian Ave Ste 100, Irvine (92614-5845)
PHONE.............................949 261-1022
Fred Haley, *Branch Mgr*
EMP: 177
SALES (corp-wide): 983.9MM **Privately Held**
WEB: www.stl-inc.com
SIC: 8734 Water testing laboratory
HQ: Testamerica Laboratories, Inc.
4101 Shuffel St Nw # 100
North Canton OH 44720
800 456-9396

(P-26734)
TESTAMERICA LABORATORIES INC
880 Riverside Pkwy, West Sacramento (95605-1500)
PHONE.............................916 373-5600
Roger Freize, *Manager*
EMP: 100
SALES (corp-wide): 983.9MM **Privately Held**
WEB: www.stl-inc.com
SIC: 8734 8731 2899 Testing laboratories; commercial physical research; chemical preparations
HQ: Testamerica Laboratories, Inc.
4101 Shuffel St Nw # 100
North Canton OH 44720
800 456-9396

(P-26735)
TUV SUD AMERICA INC
10040 Mesa Rim Rd, San Diego (92121-2912)
PHONE.............................858 546-3999
Gerhard Abel, *Branch Mgr*
EMP: 58 **Privately Held**
WEB: www.tuvamerica.com
SIC: 8734 Product testing laboratories
HQ: Tuv Sud America Inc.
10 Centennial Dr Ste 207
Peabody MA 01960
978 573-2500

(P-26736)
TWINING INC (PA)
Also Called: Twining Laboratories
2883 E Spring St Ste 300, Long Beach (90806-6847)
PHONE.............................562 426-3355
Edward Butch M Twining Jr, *CEO*
Brian Kramer, *President*
Talin Astourian, *Vice Pres*
Richard S Hazen, *Vice Pres*
Steve Schiffer, *Vice Pres*
EMP: 94
SQ FT: 13,600
SALES (est): 41.1MM **Privately Held**
WEB: www.twininglabs.com
SIC: 8734 Testing laboratories

(P-26737)
UNDERWRITERS LABORATORIES INC
455 E Trimble Rd, San Jose (95131-1230)
PHONE.............................248 427-5300
Eric Swerrie, *Branch Mgr*
EMP: 300
SALES (corp-wide): 728MM **Privately Held**
WEB: www.ul.com
SIC: 8734 Testing laboratories
PA: Underwriters Laboratories Inc.
333 Pfingsten Rd
Northbrook IL 60062
847 272-8800

(P-26738)
UNDERWRITERS LABORATORIES INC
47173 Benicia St, Fremont (94538-7366)
PHONE.............................510 771-1000
Robert W Miller, *Branch Mgr*
EMP: 487
SALES (corp-wide): 728MM **Privately Held**
WEB: www.ul.com
SIC: 8734 Testing laboratories
PA: Underwriters Laboratories Inc.
333 Pfingsten Rd
Northbrook IL 60062
847 272-8800

(P-26739)
UNDERWRITERS LABORATORIES INC
4510 Riding Club Ct, Hayward (94542-2238)
PHONE.............................408 754-6500
EMP: 180
SALES (corp-wide): 22.6MM **Privately Held**
SIC: 8734
PA: Underwriters Laboratories Inc.
333 Pfingsten Rd
Northbrook IL 60062
847 272-8800

(P-26740)
UNDERWRITERS LABORATORIES INC
2191 Zanker Rd, San Jose (95131-2109)
PHONE.............................408 493-9910
EMP: 102
SALES (corp-wide): 728MM **Privately Held**
SIC: 8734 Product testing laboratory, safety or performance
PA: Underwriters Laboratories Inc.
333 Pfingsten Rd
Northbrook IL 60062
847 272-8800

(P-26741)
UNITED MFG ASSEMBLY INC
44169 Fremont Blvd, Fremont (94538-6044)
PHONE.............................510 490-1065
Yonwen Chou, *President*
Lisian Pan, *Project Mgr*
May Mah, *Finance*
May Wah, *Controller*
Margie Vo, *Human Res Mgr*
EMP: 95
SALES (est): 13.2MM **Privately Held**
WEB: www.umai.com
SIC: 8734 3672 Testing laboratories; printed circuit boards

(P-26742)
VALLEY INDUSTRIAL X-RA
3700 Pegasus Dr 100, Bakersfield (93308-6825)
PHONE.............................661 399-8497
Larry Williams, *President*
Terry Campbell, *Vice Pres*
Don Carlon, *Executive*
Hector Lopez, *Manager*
EMP: 200
SQ FT: 18,000
SALES (est): 19.5MM
SALES (corp-wide): 82.3MM **Privately Held**
WEB: www.vxray.com
SIC: 8734 X-ray inspection service, industrial
HQ: Rontgen Technische Dienst B.V.
Delftweg 144
Rotterdam 3046
107 166-000

8741 Management Services

(P-26743)
800 DEGREES LLC
10889 Lindbrook Dr, Los Angeles (90024-3027)
PHONE.............................310 443-1911
Adam Fleischman,
Anthony Carron,

P
R
O
D
U
C
T
S

&

S
V
C
S

Allen Ravert,
EMP: 50
SQ FT: 2,900
SALES (est): 4.3MM **Privately Held**
SIC: 8741 Restaurant management

(P-26744)
ACCESS INFO MGT SHRED SVCS LLC
13950 Cerritos Corprt Dr C, Cerritos (90703-2468)
PHONE..................805 529-6866
Elaine Pahulu, *Branch Mgr*
EMP: 51 **Privately Held**
SIC: 8741 Business management
PA: Access Information Management Shared Services, Llc
500 Unicorn Park Dr # 503
Woburn MA 01801

(P-26745)
ACEPEX MANAGEMENT CORPORATION
13401 Yorba Ave, Chino (91710-5055)
PHONE..................909 591-1999
EMP: 306
SALES (corp-wide): 37.5MM **Privately Held**
SIC: 8741
PA: Acepex Management Corporation
10643 Mills Ave
Montclair CA 91763
909 625-6900

(P-26746)
ACTIVCARE LIVING INC (PA)
9619 Chesapeake Dr # 103, San Diego (92123-1368)
PHONE..................858 565-4424
William Major Chance, *CEO*
Todd A Shetter, *COO*
Todd Shetter, *COO*
B Renee Barnard, *CFO*
Dkevin Moriarty, *Vice Pres*
EMP: 180
SQ FT: 9,000
SALES (est): 36.5MM **Privately Held**
WEB: www.healthcaregrp.com
SIC: 8741 Nursing & personal care facility management

(P-26747)
ACTIVE WELLNESS LLC
600 California St Fl 11, San Francisco (94108-2727)
P.O. Box 2358 (94126-2358)
PHONE..................415 741-3300
Jill Stevens Kinney, *Chairman*
William Joseph McBride III, *President*
Carey White, *CFO*
Elizabeth Studebaker, *Senior Mgr*
EMP: 1100
SQ FT: 1,000
SALES: 40MM **Privately Held**
SIC: 8741 7991 Hospital management; nursing & personal care facility management; health club

(P-26748)
ADVANCED BIOSERVICES LLC (PA)
19255 Vanowen St, Reseda (91335-5021)
PHONE..................818 342-0100
Anna Kane,
EMP: 65
SALES (est): 13.9MM **Privately Held**
SIC: 8741 Administrative management

(P-26749)
ADVANCED MEDICAL MGT INC
5000 Arprt Plz Dr Ste 150, Long Beach (90815)
PHONE..................562 766-2000
Stephen Hegstrom, *CEO*
Kathy Hegstrom, *President*
Paul Pew, *Exec VP*
Courtney Plank, *Human Res Mgr*
EMP: 60
SALES (est): 8.7MM **Privately Held**
WEB: www.duongnet.com
SIC: 8741 8721 Hospital management; nursing & personal care facility management; accounting, auditing & bookkeeping

(P-26750)
AEG MANAGEMENT LACC LLC
Also Called: Los Angeles Convention Center
1201 S Figueroa St, Los Angeles (90015-1308)
PHONE..................213 741-1151
Brad Gessner, *Senior VP*
Estella M Flores, *Bd of Directors*
Kathleen Clariett, *Vice Pres*
Keith Hilsgen, *Vice Pres*
Carisa Malanum, *Vice Pres*
EMP: 220
SALES (est): 20MM
SALES (corp-wide): 20.2MM **Privately Held**
SIC: 8741 Business management
PA: Aeg Facilities, Llc
800 W Olympic Blvd # 305
Los Angeles CA 90015
213 763-7700

(P-26751)
AIR FORCE US DEPT OF
Also Called: 30th Cpts-Financial Management
1031 California Blvd # 11777, Lompoc (93437-6248)
PHONE..................805 606-5355
Steve Kam, *Branch Mgr*
EMP: 65 **Publicly Held**
WEB: www.af.mil
SIC: 8741 9711 Management services; Air Force
HQ: United States Department Of The Air Force
1000 Air Force Pentagon
Washington DC 20330

(P-26752)
AJIT HEALTHCARE INC
316 S Westlake Ave, Los Angeles (90057-4500)
PHONE..................213 484-0510
Jasvant N Modi, *President*
Ramon Perez, *Administration*
EMP: 80
SALES (est): 5.9MM **Privately Held**
SIC: 8741 Nursing & personal care facility management

(P-26753)
ALL IN ONE INC
Also Called: Act 1 Personnel Services
1999 W 190th St, Torrance (90504-6202)
P.O. Box 29048, Glendale (91209-9048)
PHONE..................310 538-3374
Janice B Howroyd, *President*
Michael A Hoyal, *CFO*
Tina Bryant, *Admin Sec*
Michael Hoyal, *Assistant VP*
EMP: 120
SALES (est): 13.1MM **Privately Held**
SIC: 8741 Administrative management

(P-26754)
ALL SYSTEM PERSONNEL MGMT
16885 W Bernardo Dr # 150, San Diego (92127-1618)
PHONE..................858 674-4090
Laurie Gerrard, *Executive*
EMP: 50
SALES (est): 1.1MM **Privately Held**
SIC: 8741 Management services

(P-26755)
ALLEGIS RESIDENTIAL SVCS INC
Also Called: Aspm-Sandiego
9340 Hazard Way Ste B2, San Diego (92123-1228)
PHONE..................858 430-5700
Karen Martinez, *CEO*
Steve Howe, *COO*
Jorge Martinez, *CFO*
Hanna Kruz, *Treasurer*
Nina Lynes, *Opers Staff*
EMP: 80
SQ FT: 4,000
SALES (est): 1.6MM **Privately Held**
SIC: 8741 Business management
PA: S.H.E. Manages Properties, Inc.
9340 Hazard Way Ste B2
San Diego CA 92123

(P-26756)
AMERICAN INTGRTED RSOURCES INC
2341 N Pacific St, Orange (92865-2601)
PHONE..................714 921-4100
Thomas C Stevens, *CEO*
Megan Duffy, *Office Mgr*
Manish Patel, *Controller*
Gerald Adkerson, *Assistant*
EMP: 80
SALES (est): 2MM **Privately Held**
SIC: 8741 Construction management

(P-26757)
AMERICAN MZHOU DNGPO GROUP INC
4520 Maine Ave, Baldwin Park (91706-2671)
PHONE..................626 820-9239
Gang Wang, *CEO*
EMP: 100
SALES (est): 636.5K **Privately Held**
SIC: 8741 Restaurant management

(P-26758)
AMERISOURCEBERGEN CORPORATION
1368 Metropolitan Dr, Orange (92868)
P.O. Box 247, Thorofare NJ (08086-0247)
PHONE..................610 727-7000
Daniel Ramirez, *Manager*
Liz Carbon, *Vice Pres*
Lisa Keeley, *Analyst*
Wesley Behar, *Sales Staff*
Steve Gabourie, *Manager*
EMP: 180
SALES (corp-wide): 153.1B **Publicly Held**
WEB: www.amerisourcebergen.net
SIC: 8741 Administrative management
PA: Amerisourcebergen Corporation
1300 Morris Dr Ste 100
Chesterbrook PA 19087
610 727-7000

(P-26759)
AMERISOURCEBERGEN CORPORATION
505 City Pkwy W, Orange (92868-2924)
PHONE..................714 704-4407
EMP: 180
SALES (corp-wide): 153.1B **Publicly Held**
SIC: 8741 Administrative management
PA: Amerisourcebergen Corporation
1300 Morris Dr Ste 100
Chesterbrook PA 19087
610 727-7000

(P-26760)
ANAHEIM FIRST FMLY DNTL GROUP
Also Called: Affd
1161 N Euclid St, Anaheim (92801-1938)
PHONE..................714 999-5050
Mary Ann De Santiago, *President*
John Delaney DDS, *Vice Pres*
EMP: 54
SALES (est): 4MM **Privately Held**
SIC: 8741 Office management

(P-26761)
APEX GROUP
17101 Superior St, Northridge (91325-1961)
PHONE..................818 885-0513
Damon Zumwalt, *President*
EMP: 200
SALES (est): 9MM **Privately Held**
SIC: 8741 8721 Administrative management; accounting, auditing & bookkeeping

(P-26762)
APPLECARE MEDICAL MGT LLC
18 Centerpointe Dr # 100, La Palma (90623-1028)
P.O. Box 6014, Artesia (90702-6014)
PHONE..................714 443-4507
Vinod Jivrajka, *Principal*
EMP: 108

SALES (est): 13.1MM
SALES (corp-wide): 201.1B **Publicly Held**
SIC: 8741 Nursing & personal care facility management
PA: Unitedhealth Group Incorporated
9900 Bren Rd E Ste 300w
Minnetonka MN 55343
952 936-1300

(P-26763)
ARCHIVES MANAGEMENT CORP (PA)
Also Called: Bay Management
2301 S El Camino Real, San Mateo (94403-2213)
PHONE..................650 544-2200
Harlan Shapers, *President*
EMP: 180
SQ FT: 12,000
SALES (est): 18.1MM **Privately Held**
WEB: www.adultsupersource.com
SIC: 8741 8742 Business management; management consulting services

(P-26764)
ARNEL INTERIOR CORP
Also Called: Arnel and Afflate
949 S Coast Dr Ste 600, Costa Mesa (92626-7734)
PHONE..................714 481-5100
George Argyrox, *Ch of Bd*
Dan Russo, *CEO*
Tony Roxtrom, *Vice Pres*
EMP: 300
SQ FT: 4,000
SALES (est): 6.6MM **Privately Held**
SIC: 8741 Construction management

(P-26765)
ARNOLD PALMER GOLF MGT LLC
300 Finley Rd, San Francisco (94129-1196)
P.O. Box 29063 (94129-0063)
PHONE..................415 561-4670
EMP: 70
SALES (corp-wide): 48.4MM **Privately Held**
SIC: 8741 7992
HQ: Arnold Palmer Golf Management, Llc
5430 Lbj Fwy Ste 1400
Dallas TX 75240
972 419-1400

(P-26766)
ARTIST SILVA MANAGEMENT LLC (PA)
Also Called: Silva Artist Management,
722 Seward St, Los Angeles (90038-3504)
PHONE..................323 856-8222
John Silva,
John Cutcliffe, *Vice Pres*
Gary Gersh,
Kristen Welsh, *Director*
Michael Meisel, *Manager*
EMP: 120
SALES (est): 9.1MM **Privately Held**
WEB: www.sammusicbiz.com
SIC: 8741 Business management

(P-26767)
ASHFORD TRS NICKEL LLC
Also Called: Sheraton Sn Diego Htl Msn Vly
1433 Camino Del Rio S, San Diego (92108-3521)
PHONE..................619 260-0111
Mike Rice, *Manager*
EMP: 60 **Privately Held**
SIC: 8741 5813 5812 Hotel or motel management; drinking places; eating places
PA: Ashford Trs Nickel, Llc
1345 Treat Blvd
Walnut Creek CA 94597

(P-26768)
ASSET ATHENE MANAGEMENT L P (HQ)
2121 Rosecrans Ave # 5300, El Segundo (90245-4750)
PHONE..................310 698-4444
James R Belardi, *CEO*
Mark Suter, *Officer*
Jeff Boland, *Exec VP*

James Hassett, *Exec VP*
Angelo Lombardo, *Senior VP*
EMP: 69
SALES (est): 13.2MM **Publicly Held**
SIC: 8741 Financial management for business

(P-26769)
ATRIA SENIOR LIVING GROUP INC
Also Called: Golden
33 Creek Rd Side, Irvine (92604-4792)
PHONE...................................949 786-5665
Sandra McDaniel, *Manager*
Maureen Salonga, *Nursing Dir*
Bruce Miller, *Director*
EMP: 60 **Privately Held**
WEB: www.atriacom.com
SIC: 8741 6531 Hotel or motel management; real estate brokers & agents
PA: Atria Senior Living Group Inc
　　300 E Market St Ste 100
　　Louisville KY 40202
　　-

(P-26770)
AUDIO VISUAL MGT SOLUTIONS
Also Called: AV Management
12812 Garden Grove Blvd M, Garden Grove (92843-2009)
PHONE...................................714 590-8755
Just Cameron, *Branch Mgr*
EMP: 198 **Privately Held**
SIC: 8741 Business management
PA: Audio Visual Management Solutions, Inc
　　814 6th Ave S
　　Seattle WA 98134
　　-

(P-26771)
AVIATION CONSULTANTS INC (PA)
Also Called: Epic Jet Centre
945 Airport Dr, San Luis Obispo (93401-8354)
PHONE...................................805 548-1300
William Borgsmiller, *President*
Nathan Ross, *CFO*
Crystal Heavers, *Mktg Dir*
Ryan Andrews, *Manager*
Stephanie Austin, *Manager*
EMP: 62
SQ FT: 6,100
SALES (est): 9.5MM **Privately Held**
WEB: www.aviationconsultants.net
SIC: 8741 7363 Management services; pilot service, aviation

(P-26772)
BACCHUS VINEYARD MGT LLC
1720 River Rd, Fulton (95439-8843)
PHONE...................................707 837-8304
James G Alexander, *Mng Member*
EMP: 60
SALES (est): 7.8MM **Privately Held**
SIC: 8741 Business management

(P-26773)
BANK AMERICA NATIONAL ASSN
73525 El Paseo, Palm Desert (92260-4341)
PHONE...................................760 636-7500
EMP: 138
SALES (corp-wide): 100.2B **Publicly Held**
SIC: 8741 6282 6029 6021 Business management; investment advice; commercial banks; national commercial banks
HQ: Bank Of America, National Association
　　100 S Tryon St
　　Charlotte NC 28202
　　704 386-5681

(P-26774)
BANK AMERICA NATIONAL ASSN
555 Capitol Mall, Sacramento (95814-4504)
PHONE...................................916 326-3161
Maria Barry, *Branch Mgr*
EMP: 138

SALES (corp-wide): 100.2B **Publicly Held**
SIC: 8741 6282 6029 6021 Business management; investment advice; commercial banks; national commercial banks
HQ: Bank Of America, National Association
　　100 S Tryon St
　　Charlotte NC 28202
　　704 386-5681

(P-26775)
BARRETT BUSINESS SERVICES INC
1840 Gateway Dr, San Mateo (94404-4027)
PHONE...................................650 653-7588
EMP: 5003
SALES (corp-wide): 920.4MM **Publicly Held**
SIC: 8741 Business management
PA: Barrett Business Services Inc
　　8100 Ne Parkway Dr # 200
　　Vancouver WA 98662
　　360 828-0700

(P-26776)
BAY VISTA SENIOR HOUSING
6120 Stoneridge, Pleasanton (94588)
PHONE...................................925 924-7100
Grace Chrisostomo, *Governor*
Linda Coleman, *Governor*
Andrew McDonald, *Governor*
Susan Tolentino, *Governor*
EMP: 104
SALES (est): 1.2MM
SALES (corp-wide): 178.8MM **Privately Held**
SIC: 8741 Management services
HQ: Humangood Affordable Housing
　　6120 Stoneridge Mall Rd # 100
　　Pleasanton CA 94588
　　925 924-7163

(P-26777)
BAYSCAPE MANAGEMENT INC
Also Called: Coast Landscape Management
1350 Pacific Ave, Alviso (95002)
P.O. Box 880 (95002-0880)
PHONE...................................408 288-2940
Thomas Ellington, *President*
EMP: 70
SALES (est): 9.5MM **Privately Held**
SIC: 8741 Management services

(P-26778)
BECHTEL CAPITAL MGT CORP
50 Beale St, San Francisco (94105-1813)
PHONE...................................415 768-1234
Riley Bechtel, *Chairman*
Brendan Bechtel, *President*
Bill Dudley, *CEO*
Peter Dawson, *CFO*
Anshul Maheshwari, *Treasurer*
EMP: 2000
SQ FT: 600,000
SALES (est): 49.2MM
SALES (corp-wide): 10.4B **Privately Held**
WEB: www.bechtelgroup.com
SIC: 8741 Financial management for business
PA: Bechtel Group, Inc.
　　50 Beale St Bsmt 1
　　San Francisco CA 94105
　　415 768-1234

(P-26779)
BEECH STREET CORPORATION (DH)
25550 Commercentre Dr # 200, Lake Forest (92630-8893)
PHONE...................................949 672-1000
William Fickling Jr, *Chairman*
William Hale, *President*
Jon Bird, *CFO*
Rick Markus, *Exec VP*
Norm Werthwein, *Senior VP*
EMP: 350
SQ FT: 60,000
SALES (est): 18.9MM
SALES (corp-wide): 3.7B **Publicly Held**
WEB: www.beechstreet.com
SIC: 8741 Administrative management
HQ: Concentra Operating Corporation
　　5080 Spectrum Dr Ste 400w
　　Addison TX 75001
　　972 364-8000

(P-26780)
BEVERLY HEALTH CARE CORP (PA)
5445 Everglades St, Ventura (93003-6523)
PHONE...................................805 642-1736
Carol Tradeway, *Director*
Rose Taylor-Calhoun, *CEO*
Philip Drescher, *Principal*
Harry Maynard, *Principal*
Gary Wolfe, *Principal*
EMP: 50
SQ FT: 85,000
SALES (est): 16.9MM **Privately Held**
SIC: 8741 Management services

(P-26781)
BLACK CANYON CAPITAL LLC
2000 Avenue Of The, Los Angeles (90067)
PHONE...................................310 272-1800
Michael Hooks, *Mng Member*
Bradley Spencer, *CFO*
Paras Mehta,
Cameron Reilly,
Tom Barber, *Mng Member*
EMP: 172
SALES: 21MM **Privately Held**
WEB: www.blackcanyoncapital.com
SIC: 8741 Personnel management

(P-26782)
BML WORKS NA LLC
228 Hamilton Ave Fl 3, Palo Alto (94301-2583)
PHONE...................................650 268-8305
George Ferrier,
EMP: 52
SALES (est): 2.5MM **Privately Held**
SIC: 8741 Management services

(P-26783)
BOARDVANTAGE INC (HQ)
4300 Bohannon Dr Ste 110, Menlo Park (94025-1042)
PHONE...................................212 401-8700
Joe Ruck, *President*
Anirban Datta, *Chief Mktg Ofcr*
Mary De Frnchi, *Exec VP*
Jianya Zhou, *Admin Asst*
Tom Bartos, *Administration*
EMP: 64
SQ FT: 7,000
SALES (est): 19.6MM
SALES (corp-wide): 3.9B **Publicly Held**
WEB: www.boardvantage.com
SIC: 8741 8742 Management services; personnel management consultant
PA: Nasdaq, Inc.
　　1 Liberty Plz Ste 4900
　　New York NY 10006
　　212 401-8700

(P-26784)
BPG STORAGE SOLUTIONS INC
2033 N Main St Ste 340, Walnut Creek (94596-3727)
PHONE...................................562 467-2000
Michael Barker, *President*
EMP: 60
SALES (est): 3.1MM
SALES (corp-wide): 13.5MM **Privately Held**
WEB: www.barkerpacific.com
SIC: 8741 Management services
PA: Barker Pacific Group, Inc.
　　101 Ygnacio Valley Rd # 210
　　Walnut Creek CA 94596
　　415 884-9977

(P-26785)
BRET BOYLAN PROPERTY MGT
Also Called: Bret Boylan
35 N Alboni Pl Apt 409, Long Beach (90802-5438)
P.O. Box 14690 (90853-4690)
PHONE...................................562 437-7886
Bret Boylan, *Owner*
EMP: 50
SQ FT: 300
SALES (est): 2MM **Privately Held**
SIC: 8741

(P-26786)
BROUGHTON HOSPITALITY GROUP (PA)
2400 E Katella Ave # 300, Anaheim (92806-5957)
PHONE...................................714 908-4237
Larry Broughton, *President*
Robert Rycroft, *CFO*
Robert Srycrodt, *CFO*
Teri Serrano, *Vice Pres*
Shawna Shope, *Vice Pres*
EMP: 240
SALES (est): 19.5MM **Privately Held**
WEB: www.broughtonhospitality.com
SIC: 8741 Hotel or motel management

(P-26787)
BUCKINGHAM AFFRDBL APRTMNTS LP
Also Called: Buckingham Apartments
11911 San Vicente Blvd, Los Angeles (90049-5086)
PHONE...................................424 273-6162
Adam Cutler, *Vice Pres*
EMP: 60
SALES (est): 1.7MM **Privately Held**
SIC: 8741 Business management

(P-26788)
BUCKLAND VINEYARD MANAGEMENT (PA)
4560 Slodusty Rd, Garden Valley (95633-9244)
PHONE...................................530 333-1534
Alfred Buckland, *President*
EMP: 60
SALES (est): 3.5MM **Privately Held**
SIC: 8741 Management services

(P-26789)
BUONA TERRA FARMING CO INC
2380 A St, Santa Maria (93455-1009)
PHONE...................................805 614-9229
John Belfy, *President*
EMP: 100
SALES (est): 11.6MM **Privately Held**
SIC: 8741 0762 Management services; farm management services

(P-26790)
BUTTE BASIN MANAGEMENT CO
1624 Poole Blvd, Yuba City (95993-2610)
P.O. Box 3775 (95992-3775)
PHONE...................................530 674-2060
Samuel Neves, *President*
Dominic Neves, *Vice Pres*
EMP: 50
SALES (est): 2.5MM **Privately Held**
SIC: 8741 Management services

(P-26791)
C/O UC SAN FRANCISCO (PA)
Also Called: University of CA Office
1111 Franklin St Fl 12, Oakland (94607-5201)
PHONE...................................858 534-7323
John Fox, *Principal*
Arthur A Castillo, *Officer*
Marina Arseniev, *Associate Dir*
Ronald James, *Associate Dir*
Robert M Neuhard, *Associate Dir*
EMP: 148
SALES (est): 49.8MM **Privately Held**
SIC: 8741 Restaurant management

(P-26792)
CAL CARE INC
Also Called: Atherton Healthcare
1275 Crane St, Menlo Park (94025-4212)
PHONE...................................650 325-8600
Chris Green, *Administration*
Nana Cocachvili, *Administration*
EMP: 115
SALES (est): 11.2MM **Privately Held**
SIC: 8741 Nursing & personal care facility management

(P-26793)
CAL PINNACLE MLTARY CMMUNITIES
3200 4th Ave Ste 201, San Diego (92103-5716)
P.O. Box 10034, Fort Irwin (92310-0034)
PHONE...............................619 764-5087
Shawn Sommerville, *Director*
EMP: 55 EST: 2010
SALES (est): 1.4MM **Privately Held**
SIC: 8741 Management services

(P-26794)
CAL POLY CORPORATION
Also Called: Cal Poly Foundation
Bldg 15, San Luis Obispo (93407)
PHONE...............................805 756-1131
Hank A Mumford, *Exec Dir*
EMP: 210
SALES (corp-wide): 46.7MM **Privately Held**
WEB: www.calpolyarts.org
SIC: 8741 Business management
PA: Cal Poly Corporation
1 Grand Ave Bldg 15
San Luis Obispo CA 93407
805 756-1131

(P-26795)
CALIFORNIA STATE UNIV AUX SVCS
Also Called: UNIVERSITY BOOKSTORE
5151 State University Dr Ge314, Los Angeles (90032-4226)
PHONE...............................323 343-2531
R Dean Calvo, *Exec Dir*
EMP: 600
SQ FT: 108,000
SALES: 30.8MM **Privately Held**
SIC: 8741 5942 5651 5812 Business management; financial management for business; college book stores; unisex clothing stores; cafeteria

(P-26796)
CAMARILLO HEALTHCARE CENTER
205 Granada St, Camarillo (93010-7715)
PHONE...............................805 482-9805
Erica Olsen, *Administration*
Angie Chavz, *Administration*
Brett Watson, *Administration*
EMP: 1127
SALES (est): 3MM
SALES (corp-wide): 1.8B **Publicly Held**
SIC: 8741 Nursing & personal care facility management
PA: The Ensign Group Inc
27101 Puerta Real Ste 450
Mission Viejo CA 92691
949 487-9500

(P-26797)
CARRINGTON MRTG HOLDINGS LLC
1600 S Douglass Rd # 110, Anaheim (92806-5948)
PHONE...............................888 267-0584
Phil Grassbaugh, *Vice Pres*
Lori Grigg, *Exec VP*
Steve Patton, *Exec VP*
Rick Sharga, *Exec VP*
Rob Petruska, *Senior VP*
EMP: 123
SQ FT: 192,000
SALES (est): 21.5MM
SALES (corp-wide): 32.8MM **Privately Held**
SIC: 8741 Management services
PA: Carrington Capital Management Llc
7 Greenwich Office Park
Greenwich CT 06831
203 661-6186

(P-26798)
CASTLEBLACK OWNER HOLDINGS LLC
601 James Way, Pismo Beach (93449-3502)
PHONE...............................805 773-6020
Gordon Jackson, *Manager*
EMP: 50
SALES (corp-wide): 19.7MM **Privately Held**
SIC: 8741 Hotel or motel management

PA: Castleblack Owner Holdings, Llc
399 Park Ave Fl 18
New York NY 10022
212 547-2609

(P-26799)
CATHAY BANK
977 N Broadway Ste 306, Los Angeles (90012-1786)
PHONE...............................213 687-1300
Dunson K Cheng, *Ch of Bd*
EMP: 354
SALES (corp-wide): 612.4MM **Publicly Held**
SIC: 8741 6021 Management services; national commercial banks
HQ: Cathay Bank
9650 Flair Dr
El Monte CA 91731
626 279-3698

(P-26800)
CBS TELEVISION DISTRIBUTION (PA)
Also Called: CBS Enterprises
2450 Colo Ave Ste 500e, Santa Monica (90404)
PHONE...............................310 264-3300
Paul Franklin, *President*
Bruce Pottash, *Exec VP*
Lisa Lasarenko, *Vice Pres*
Maria Galan, *Manager*
EMP: 20000 EST: 2010
SQ FT: 20,000
SALES: 13.6B **Privately Held**
SIC: 8741 Management services

(P-26801)
CHEVRON INVESTOR INC
100 Chevron Way, Richmond (94801-2016)
PHONE...............................510 242-3000
Mark Logan, *Branch Mgr*
EMP: 100
SALES (corp-wide): 141.7B **Publicly Held**
SIC: 8741 8731 Management services; commercial physical research
HQ: Chevron Investor Inc
6001 Bollinger Canyon Rd
San Ramon CA 94583
925 842-1000

(P-26802)
CHILIS 898 CORONA
3579 Grand Oaks, Corona (92881-4634)
PHONE...............................951 734-7275
Deann Demarso, *President*
Deann De Marso, *President*
Perry Schoulten, *Office Mgr*
EMP: 90
SALES (est): 3.1MM **Privately Held**
SIC: 8741 Restaurant management

(P-26803)
CHOOSING INDEPENDENCE INC
7615 Louise Ave, Northridge (91325-4523)
PHONE...............................818 257-0323
Christian Richards Jr, *CEO*
EMP: 53
SQ FT: 3,500
SALES: 1.7MM **Privately Held**
SIC: 8741 Nursing & personal care facility management

(P-26804)
CIK POWER DISTRIBUTORS LLC
240 W Grove Ave, Orange (92865-3204)
PHONE...............................714 938-0297
Chris A Christopher, *Mng Member*
Marc Oslund, *Project Mgr*
Stephen G Carter,
Robert M Tulley,
EMP: 53
SALES (est): 11.9MM **Privately Held**
SIC: 8741 Construction management

(P-26805)
CIRCLE WOOD SERVICES INC
3670 W Temple Ave, Pomona (91768-2588)
PHONE...............................909 784-0733
Don Watson, *President*
EMP: 70 EST: 2007
SQ FT: 1,400

SALES (est): 5.9MM **Privately Held**
SIC: 8741 Business management

(P-26806)
CITIZENHAWK INC
Also Called: Wolters Kluwer Corp Legal Svcs
135 Columbia, Aliso Viejo (92656-4108)
PHONE...............................949 427-3002
Richard Flynn, *CEO*
Thomas Nestor, *VP Finance*
EMP: 94 EST: 2009
SALES (est): 17MM
SALES (corp-wide): 5.2B **Privately Held**
SIC: 8741 Management services
HQ: C T Corporation System
111 8th Ave Fl 13
New York NY 10011
212 894-8940

(P-26807)
CITRUS VLY HLTH PARTNERS INC (PA)
Also Called: Inter Community Hospital
210 W San Bernardino Rd, Covina (91723-1515)
P.O. Box 6108 (91722-5108)
PHONE...............................626 331-7331
Robert Curry, *CEO*
James Yoshioka, *President*
Alvia Polk, *COO*
Lois Conyers, *CFO*
Paveljit Bindra, *Chief Mktg Ofcr*
EMP: 2800
SQ FT: 237,000
SALES: 64.4MM **Privately Held**
WEB: www.cvhp.com
SIC: 8741 Administrative management

(P-26808)
CITY & COUNTY OF SAN FRANCISCO
Also Called: Administrative Services
1 Carlton B Goodlett Pl # 234, San Francisco (94102-4604)
PHONE...............................415 554-4799
Corrine Mehgan, *Mng Officer*
Alvin C Moses, *Manager*
EMP: 100 **Privately Held**
SIC: 8741 9199 Management services; general government administration; ;
PA: City & County Of San Francisco
1 Dr Carlton B Goodlett P
San Francisco CA 94102
415 554-7500

(P-26809)
CITY ALAMEDA HEALTH CARE CORP
2070 Clinton Ave, Alameda (94501-4399)
PHONE...............................510 814-4000
Deborah E Stebbins, *Branch Mgr*
EMP: 436
SALES (corp-wide): 85.9MM **Privately Held**
SIC: 8741 Hospital management
PA: City Of Alameda Health Care Corporation
2070 Clinton Ave
Alameda CA 94501
510 522-3700

(P-26810)
CLARIZEN INC
2755 Campus Dr Ste 300, San Mateo (94403-2538)
PHONE...............................866 502-9813
Boaz Chalamish, *CEO*
Shiri Kerman, *Vice Pres*
EMP: 55
SALES (est): 10.1MM **Privately Held**
SIC: 8741 Management services
PA: Clarizen Ltd
4 Hacharash, Floor 10
Hod Hasharon
979 443-00

(P-26811)
CLOROX SERVICES COMPANY
5060 Johnson Dr, Pleasanton (94588-3333)
PHONE...............................925 425-6748
Tinoco Adelita, *Manager*
EMP: 64
SALES (corp-wide): 6.1B **Publicly Held**
SIC: 8741 Management services

HQ: Clorox Services Company
1221 Broadway Fl 13
Oakland CA 94612

(P-26812)
CLOROX SERVICES COMPANY (HQ)
1221 Broadway Fl 13, Oakland (94612-1837)
PHONE...............................510 271-7000
R A Llenado, *Ch of Bd*
C E Williams, *President*
Ausfahl Cutter, *Vice Pres*
Oscar Lopez, *Manager*
Michael McGowan, *Manager*
EMP: 100
SALES (est): 81.9MM
SALES (corp-wide): 6.1B **Publicly Held**
WEB: www.clorox.com
SIC: 8741 Management services
PA: The Clorox Company
1221 Broadway Ste 1300
Oakland CA 94612
510 271-7000

(P-26813)
CMTS LLC
5777 W Century Blvd # 1105, Los Angeles (90045-5637)
PHONE...............................310 215-0237
K Hezekiah Harris II, *CEO*
Ejaz Ahmad, *President*
Bill Blalock, *President*
Winifred Harris, *Vice Pres*
Rick Zabel, *Manager*
EMP: 120
SQ FT: 1,500
SALES (est): 12.2MM **Privately Held**
SIC: 8741 Construction management

(P-26814)
COLLECTIVE MGT GROUP LLC
8383 Wilshire Blvd # 1050, Beverly Hills (90211-2425)
PHONE...............................323 655-8585
Michael Green, *CEO*
Jordan Toplitzky, *CFO*
Kendall Durkee, *Office Admin*
Jordan Berliant,
Gary Binkow,
EMP: 110
SQ FT: 15,000
SALES: 50MM **Privately Held**
SIC: 8741 Management services

(P-26815)
COLUSA REGIONAL MEDICAL CENTER
Also Called: Women's Health Center
199 E Webster St Ste 1, Colusa (95932-2954)
PHONE...............................530 458-5821
David Zwald, *Principal*
EMP: 180
SQ FT: 48,000
SALES: 21.1MM **Privately Held**
WEB: www.colusamedicalcenter.org
SIC: 8741 8062 Hospital management; general medical & surgical hospitals

(P-26816)
COMMUNITY HOUSING OPPORT
Also Called: Sterling Asset Management
5030 Bus Center Dr # 260, Fairfield (94534-6884)
PHONE...............................707 759-6043
Nancy Conk, *Exec Dir*
EMP: 50
SALES (corp-wide): 7.8MM **Privately Held**
WEB: www.chochousing.org
SIC: 8741 Management services
PA: Community Housing Opportunities Corporation
5030 Business Center Dr # 260
Fairfield CA 94534
530 757-4444

(P-26817)
COMPUTERIZED MGT SVCS INC
Also Called: CMS
4100 Guardian St Ste 205, Simi Valley (93063-6721)
P.O. Box 190 (93062-0190)
PHONE...............................805 522-5940

J Daryl Favale, *President*
EMP: 100
SQ FT: 7,500
SALES (est): 9.3MM **Privately Held**
SIC: 8741 Business management

(P-26818)
CONSTRUCTION TESTING SERVICES (PA)
2118 Rheem Dr, Pleasanton (94588-2775)
PHONE..............................925 462-5151
Patrick Greenan, *President*
Aaren Solis, *Vice Pres*
Amanda Frey, *Admin Asst*
Cathy Rangel, *Admin Asst*
Yate Chhoun-Le, *Project Mgr*
EMP: 50 **EST:** 1994
SQ FT: 5,000
SALES (est): 11.5MM **Privately Held**
WEB: www.cts-1.com
SIC: 8741 Construction management

(P-26819)
COOPER PUGEDA MANAGEMENT INC
Also Called: CPM Services
65 Mccoppin St, San Francisco (94103-1235)
PHONE..............................415 543-6251
Ismael Pugeda, *President*
Jeff Cooper, *Vice Pres*
Laurane Delfin, *Office Mgr*
Stephanie Clarke-Finch, *Administration*
Jeff J Cooper, *Info Tech Mgr*
EMP: 50
SQ FT: 2,500
SALES (est): 6.2MM **Privately Held**
WEB: www.schedulers.com
SIC: 8741 1542 Construction management; nonresidential construction

(P-26820)
CORNERSTONE HOTEL MANAGEMENT (DH)
222 Kearny St Ste 200, San Francisco (94108-4537)
PHONE..............................415 397-5572
Tom La Tour, *President*
J Kirke Wrench, *CFO*
Nir Margalit, *Admin Sec*
EMP: 75
SALES (est): 7.5MM
SALES (corp-wide): 1.7B **Privately Held**
SIC: 8741 Management services
HQ: Alexis Hotel Management Inc
222 Kearny St Ste 200
San Francisco CA
415 397-5572

(P-26821)
CORVEL CORPORATION (PA)
2010 Main St Ste 600, Irvine (92614-7272)
PHONE..............................949 851-1473
V Gordon Clemons, *Ch of Bd*
Michael G Combs, *President*
Kenneth S Cragun, *CFO*
Diane J Blaha, *Chief Mktg Ofcr*
Diane Blaha, *Chief Mktg Ofcr*
EMP: 148
SQ FT: 13,000
SALES: 558.3MM **Publicly Held**
WEB: www.corvel.com
SIC: 8741 8011 Nursing & personal care facility management; internal medicine practitioners; medical insurance associations

(P-26822)
COUNTRY VILLA SERVICE CORP
3002 Rowena Ave, Los Angeles (90039-2005)
PHONE..............................323 666-1544
Stephen Rissman, *President*
EMP: 120
SALES (corp-wide): 125.3MM **Privately Held**
WEB: www.countryvillahealth.com
SIC: 8741 8051 Nursing & personal care facility management; skilled nursing care facilities
PA: Country Villa Service Corp.
2400 E Katella Ave # 800
Anaheim CA 92806
310 574-3733

(P-26823)
COUNTRY VILLA SERVICE CORP (PA)
Also Called: Country Villa Health Services
2400 E Katella Ave # 800, Anaheim (92806-5955)
PHONE..............................310 574-3733
Stephen Reissman, *CEO*
Diane Reissman, *Exec VP*
Cheryl Petterson, *Vice Pres*
Mauricio Vejar, *Director*
Katherine Wisnoski, *Manager*
EMP: 80 **EST:** 1972
SQ FT: 24,000
SALES (est): 125.3MM **Privately Held**
WEB: www.countryvillahealth.com
SIC: 8741 Nursing & personal care facility management; hospital management

(P-26824)
COUNTRY VILLA SERVICE CORP
1730 Grand Ave, Long Beach (90804-2011)
PHONE..............................562 597-8817
Nenita Bartolome, *Financial Exec*
EMP: 110
SALES (corp-wide): 125.3MM **Privately Held**
SIC: 8741 Nursing & personal care facility management
PA: Country Villa Service Corp.
2400 E Katella Ave # 800
Anaheim CA 92806
310 574-3733

(P-26825)
COUNTRY VILLA SERVICE CORP
615 W Duarte Rd, Monrovia (91016-4436)
PHONE..............................626 358-4547
Sam Chia, *Branch Mgr*
EMP: 110
SALES (corp-wide): 125.3MM **Privately Held**
SIC: 8741 Management services
PA: Country Villa Service Corp.
2400 E Katella Ave # 800
Anaheim CA 92806
310 574-3733

(P-26826)
COUNTRY VILLA SERVICE CORP
Also Called: Country Villa E Convalescent
2415 S Western Ave, Los Angeles (90018-2608)
PHONE..............................323 734-1101
Phadra Johnson, *Manager*
Imad E Asmar, *Director*
Gigi Garcia, *Director*
EMP: 120
SALES (corp-wide): 125.3MM **Privately Held**
WEB: www.countryvillahealth.com
SIC: 8741 8051 8011 8059 Nursing & personal care facility management; skilled nursing care facilities; clinic, operated by physicians; convalescent home
PA: Country Villa Service Corp.
2400 E Katella Ave # 800
Anaheim CA 92806
310 574-3733

(P-26827)
COUNTRY VILLA SERVICE CORP
3533 Motor Ave, Los Angeles (90034-4806)
PHONE..............................310 574-3733
EMP: 110
SALES (corp-wide): 125.3MM **Privately Held**
SIC: 8741
PA: Country Villa Service Corp.
2400 E Katella Ave # 800
Anaheim CA 92806
310 574-3733

(P-26828)
COUNTRY VILLA SERVICE CORP
3233 W Pico Blvd, Los Angeles (90019-3640)
PHONE..............................323 734-9122
Mike Demchuck, *Manager*
Norma Rojas, *Vice Pres*
EMP: 100

SALES (corp-wide): 125.3MM **Privately Held**
WEB: www.countryvillahealth.com
SIC: 8741 8051 Nursing & personal care facility management; skilled nursing care facilities
PA: Country Villa Service Corp.
2400 E Katella Ave # 800
Anaheim CA 92806
310 574-3733

(P-26829)
COUNTRYSIDE INN-CORONA LP
1015 W Colton Ave, Redlands (92374-2933)
PHONE..............................909 335-9024
Donald B Ayres Jr, *Branch Mgr*
EMP: 50
SALES (corp-wide): 34.4MM **Privately Held**
SIC: 8741 Management services
PA: Countryside Inn-Corona, L.P.
1900 Bollero Pl
Corona CA 92882
714 540-6060

(P-26830)
COUNTRYSIDE INN-CORONA LP
12850 Seal Beach Blvd, Seal Beach (90740-2714)
PHONE..............................562 596-8330
Bill Tolen, *Manager*
EMP: 50
SALES (corp-wide): 34.4MM **Privately Held**
WEB: www.ayreshotelsealbeach.com
SIC: 8741 1531 Management services; operative builders
PA: Countryside Inn-Corona, L.P.
1900 Bollero Pl
Corona CA 92882
714 540-6060

(P-26831)
COUNTY OF LOS ANGELES
Also Called: Social Service Dept- Admin
12900 Crssrds Pkwy S 20, City of Industry (91746)
PHONE..............................562 908-8400
Phillip Browning, *Director*
EMP: 400 **Privately Held**
WEB: www.co.la.ca.us
SIC: 8741 9441 Management services;
PA: County Of Los Angeles
500 W Temple St Ste 437
Los Angeles CA 90012
213 974-1101

(P-26832)
COUNTY OF SAN MATEO
Also Called: Human Resources Department
400 County Ctr, Redwood City (94063-1662)
PHONE..............................650 363-4915
Greg Munks, *Sheriff*
Michelle Makino, *Program Mgr*
Nancy Lapolla, *Director*
Tony Harwood, *Manager*
EMP: 145 **Privately Held**
WEB: www.ci.sanmateo.ca.us
SIC: 8741 9441 Personnel management;
PA: County Of San Mateo
400 County Ctr
Redwood City CA 94063
650 363-4123

(P-26833)
COUNTY OF SAN MATEO
Also Called: Human Resources Department
455 County Ctr, Redwood City (94063-9700)
PHONE..............................650 363-4343
Donna Vaillancourt, *Director*
EMP: 50 **Privately Held**
WEB: www.ci.sanmateo.ca.us
SIC: 8741 9441 Personnel management;
PA: County Of San Mateo
400 County Ctr
Redwood City CA 94063
650 363-4123

(P-26834)
CRESTLINE HOTELS & RESORTS LLC
535 S Grand Ave, Los Angeles (90071-2601)
PHONE..............................213 624-0000
Eddie Andre, *Manager*
Ruth Newman, *Executive*
Iddie Andre, *General Mgr*
EMP: 88
SALES (corp-wide): 45.4MM **Privately Held**
SIC: 8741 Hotel or motel management
PA: Crestline Hotels & Resorts, Llc
3950 University Dr # 301
Fairfax VA 22030
571 529-6100

(P-26835)
CRESTLINE HOTELS & RESORTS LLC
1250 Columbus Ave, San Francisco (94133-1327)
PHONE..............................415 775-7555
Amy Arbuckle, *Manager*
EMP: 175
SALES (corp-wide): 48.6MM **Privately Held**
SIC: 8741 Hotel or motel management
PA: Crestline Hotels & Resorts, Llc
3950 University Dr # 301
Fairfax VA 22030
571 529-6100

(P-26836)
CSI FINANCIAL SERVICES LLC
3636 Nobel Dr Ste 250, San Diego (92122-1042)
PHONE..............................858 200-9200
Janet Shanks, *CFO*
Bruce J Haupt, *Vice Pres*
Laurie Heavey, *Vice Pres*
Vince Koch, *Vice Pres*
Linne Buffington, *Executive Asst*
EMP: 50
SQ FT: 4,050
SALES (est): 6.2MM **Privately Held**
WEB: www.csifinancial.com
SIC: 8741 8742 Management services; hospital & health services consultant

(P-26837)
DERJJAN ASSOCIATES INC (PA)
2025 Soquel Ave, Santa Cruz (95062-1323)
PHONE..............................831 423-4111
Larry Deghetaldi, *President*
Gary Loveridge, *Ch of Bd*
Wayne Boss, *President*
Lowell M Sprague, *VP Finance*
EMP: 185
SQ FT: 60,000
SALES (est): 11.2MM **Privately Held**
WEB: www.williamrichards.com
SIC: 8741 6512 Administrative management; bank building operation

(P-26838)
DEWOLF REALTY CO INC
4330 California St, San Francisco (94118-1316)
P.O. Box 591540 (94159-1540)
PHONE..............................415 221-2032
William A Talmage, *President*
Marie Wayne, *Corp Secy*
Aaron Sinel, *Vice Pres*
EMP: 60 **EST:** 1879
SALES (est): 6.5MM **Privately Held**
WEB: www.dewolfsf.com
SIC: 8741 6531 Management services; appraiser, real estate; real estate brokers & agents

(P-26839)
DHS CONSULTING INC
1820 E 1st St Ste 410, Santa Ana (92705-8311)
PHONE..............................714 276-1135
Sudhir Damle, *President*
Eric Slaasted, *Senior VP*
Hemalata Damle, *Vice Pres*
Melanie Estes, *Vice Pres*
Craig Reiter, *Vice Pres*
EMP: 56
SQ FT: 6,000

P R O D U C T S & S V C S

SALES: 12MM **Privately Held**
SIC: 8741 Construction management

(P-26840)
DIGITAL MEDIA MANAGEMENT LLC
5670 Wilshire Blvd Fl 11, Los Angeles
(90036-5627)
PHONE.................................323 378-6505
Luigi Picarazzi, *Mng Member*
Adam Reynolds, *Vice Pres*
Kolleen Figiel, *Office Mgr*
David Blaise, *Graphic Designe*
Dave Giglio, *Opers Staff*
EMP: 65
SALES (est): 2.4MM **Privately Held**
SIC: 8741 Management services

(P-26841)
DIRECTORATE OF MWR FMD USAG
420 Montgomery St, San Francisco
(94104-1207)
PHONE.................................210 466-1376
Christine Brunner, *Manager*
EMP: 99
SALES (est): 1.9MM **Privately Held**
SIC: 8741 Management services

(P-26842)
DOCTORS OF AFFILIATED
600 City Pkwy W Ste 400, Orange
(92868-2900)
PHONE.................................714 539-3100
Frank Rubino, *President*
John Ernsberger, *CEO*
Prakesh Bondade, *Chairman*
EMP: 59
SQ FT: 10,000
SALES (est): 6.4MM **Privately Held**
WEB: www.adoc.us
SIC: 8741 Management services

(P-26843)
DONALD LUCKY LLC
Also Called: Babe's Bbq Grill
4029 Westerly Pl Ste 111, Newport Beach
(92660-2329)
PHONE.................................949 752-0647
Donald Callender,
EMP: 120 EST: 2001
SALES (est): 5.1MM **Privately Held**
SIC: 8741 Restaurant management

(P-26844)
DOSSE ENTERTAINMENT MGMT
8942 Wilshire Blvd, Beverly Hills
(90211-1908)
PHONE.................................323 366-9173
Ricardo Hardin, *CEO*
Yulissa Henderson, *Executive Asst*
EMP: 100
SQ FT: 3,500
SALES: 2.7MM **Privately Held**
SIC: 8741 8743 Management services;
public relations services

(P-26845)
E3 HEALTHCARE MANAGEMENT LLC
375 Forest Ave, Palo Alto (94301-2521)
PHONE.................................650 324-0600
Carole Wilson, *Mng Member*
EMP: 100
SALES (est): 3.9MM **Privately Held**
SIC: 8741 Hospital management

(P-26846)
ECONNECTIONS INC
75 N Fair Oaks Ave, Pasadena
(91103-3651)
PHONE.................................626 307-6200
Robert Rodin, *President*
Henry W Chin, *Exec VP*
EMP: 150
SALES (est): 5.3MM **Privately Held**
WEB: www.econnections.com
SIC: 8741 5065 8742 Management services; electronic parts & equipment; management consulting services

(P-26847)
EMULEX CORPORATE SERVICES CORP
3333 Susan St, Costa Mesa (92626-1632)
PHONE.................................714 662-5600
Paul Folino, *President*
Brian Reed, *President*
Matt McSweeney, *Vice Pres*
Michael J Rockenbach, *Vice Pres*
Mary Scott, *Admin Asst*
EMP: 79
SQ FT: 30,000
SALES (est): 8.1MM **Privately Held**
SIC: 8741 Business management

(P-26848)
ENERGY SALVAGE INC
8231 Alpine Ave Ste 3, Sacramento
(95826-4746)
P.O. Box 255009 (95865-5009)
PHONE.................................916 737-8640
Michael P Lien, *President*
Norman Lien, *CFO*
Timothy S Lien, *Vice Pres*
EMP: 50
SALES (est): 2.1MM **Privately Held**
SIC: 8741 6512 Business management; financial management for business; non-residential building operators

(P-26849)
EPIC MANAGEMENT LP (PA)
1615 Orange Tree Ln, Redlands
(92374-4501)
P.O. Box 19020, San Bernardino (92423-9020)
PHONE.................................909 799-1818
John D Goodman, *CEO*
David Hutchinson, *CFO*
Jean Meeks, *Treasurer*
Brian R Fraser, *Vice Pres*
Fred Hollaus, *Vice Pres*
EMP: 148
SALES (est): 50.3MM **Privately Held**
SIC: 8741 Nursing & personal care facility management

(P-26850)
ET CAPITAL SOLAR PARTNERS USA
4900 Hopyard Rd Ste 2, Pleasanton
(94588-3344)
PHONE.................................925 460-9898
Boris Schubert, *CEO*
Elaine Jones, *President*
EMP: 50
SALES (est): 980.6K **Privately Held**
SIC: 8741 3674 Financial management for business; solar cells
PA: Et Solar Group

(P-26851)
ETHOS MANAGEMENT INC (PA)
560 W Main St, Alhambra (91801-3374)
PHONE.................................626 456-3669
Nhac Vy Ngo, *CEO*
EMP: 50
SALES (est): 2.8MM **Privately Held**
SIC: 8741 Management services

(P-26852)
EUGENE BURGER MANAGEMENT CORP
555 Capitol Mall Ste 725, Sacramento
(95814-4515)
PHONE.................................916 443-6637
Eugene Burger, *Principal*
James Evenson, *Accounting Mgr*
Carol Melendez, *Supervisor*
EMP: 122
SALES (corp-wide): 19.4MM **Privately Held**
SIC: 8741 Business management
PA: Eugene Burger Management Corp
6600 Hunter Dr
Rohnert Park CA 94928
707 584-5123

(P-26853)
EVEREST SILICON VALLEY MGT LP
8200 Gateway Blvd, Newark (94560-8000)
PHONE.................................510 494-8800
Marshall Young, *CEO*
Li Hui Lo, *COO*
EMP: 54
SQ FT: 7,500
SALES: 450K
SALES (corp-wide): 1.2MM **Privately Held**
SIC: 8741 Hotel or motel management
PA: Everest Hotel Group, Llc
2140 S Dupont Hwy
Camden DE 19934
213 272-0088

(P-26854)
EVOLUTION HOSPITALITY LLC (PA)
1211 Puerta Del Sol # 170, San Clemente
(92673-6353)
PHONE.................................949 325-1350
John Murphy, *President*
Bhavesh Patel, *Senior VP*
Christopher Conrad, *Vice Pres*
Lynn Kozlowski, *Vice Pres*
David Kreizinger, *Vice Pres*
EMP: 91 EST: 2010
SALES (est): 194.5MM **Privately Held**
SIC: 8741 7011 Hotel or motel management; hotels & motels

(P-26855)
FACILITY OPERATIONS PLUS
118 W Olive Ave, Monrovia (91016-3410)
PHONE.................................800 789-9608
James Demonaco, *President*
Walt Van Eyk, *Exec VP*
EMP: 80
SQ FT: 10,000
SALES (est): 3.9MM **Privately Held**
WEB: www.foplus.com
SIC: 8741 6531 1542 Management services; real estate managers; commercial & office building, new construction

(P-26856)
FACILITY SERVICES PARTNERS
1 University Dr, Aliso Viejo (92656-8081)
PHONE.................................949 480-4090
Malcolm Thomas, *President*
Scott Collins, *Managing Prtnr*
EMP: 62 EST: 2008
SALES (est): 4MM **Privately Held**
SIC: 8741 7349 Industrial management; building maintenance services

(P-26857)
FALCON AEROSPACE HOLDINGS LLC
Also Called: Wesco Aircraft
27727 Avenue Scott, Valencia
(91355-1219)
PHONE.................................661 775-7200
Randy J Snyder, *Ch of Bd*
Gregory A Hann, *Exec VP*
Tommy Lee, *Exec VP*
EMP: 1250
SALES (est): 37.6MM **Privately Held**
SIC: 8741 Management services

(P-26858)
FBD VANGUARD CONSTRUCTION INC
550 Greenville Rd, Livermore
(94550-9297)
PHONE.................................925 245-1300
Billie Sposeto, *President*
Madison Adkins, *Administration*
Troy Ravazza, *Manager*
EMP: 120
SALES (est): 21MM **Privately Held**
SIC: 8741 Construction management

(P-26859)
FIVE STAR QUALITY CARE INC
Also Called: Palm Springs Health Care Ctr
277 S Sunrise Way, Palm Springs
(92262-6738)
PHONE.................................760 327-8541
Darrin Tharp, *Administration*
EMP: 100 **Publicly Held**
WEB: www.fivestarqualitycare.com
SIC: 8741 8322 Nursing & personal care facility management; rehabilitation services
PA: Five Star Senior Living Inc.
400 Centre St
Newton MA 02458

(P-26860)
FOR HOSPITAL COMMITTEE
Also Called: Valleycare Health System
1111 E Stanley Blvd, Livermore
(94550-4115)
PHONE.................................925 447-7000
Marcelina L Feit, *CEO*
Isabel Chen, *Exec Dir*
Virgil De Leon, *Network Analyst*
John Gozun, *Nurse*
EMP: 1000
SALES: 273.3MM **Privately Held**
SIC: 8741 Administrative management; hospital management

(P-26861)
FORT JAMES CORPORATION
Also Called: Fort James Communications
Pprs
2000 Powell St, Emeryville (94608-1804)
PHONE.................................510 594-4900
Miles Marsh, *Branch Mgr*
EMP: 100
SALES (corp-wide): 42.9B **Privately Held**
WEB: www.fortjames.com
SIC: 8741 Administrative management
HQ: Fort James Corporation
133 Peachtree St Ne
Atlanta GA 30303
404 652-4000

(P-26862)
FORTE ENTERPRISES INC (PA)
Also Called: St Francis Pavillion
99 Escuela Dr, Daly City (94015-4003)
PHONE.................................650 994-3200
Thomas J Nico, *President*
EMP: 240
SQ FT: 14,000
SALES (est): 9.8MM **Privately Held**
SIC: 8741 8721 Nursing & personal care facility management; accounting, auditing & bookkeeping

(P-26863)
FPI MANAGEMENT INC
1107 Luchessi Dr, San Jose (95118-3739)
PHONE.................................408 267-3952
EMP: 248
SALES (corp-wide): 89.5MM **Privately Held**
SIC: 8741 6513 Business management; apartment building operators
PA: Fpi Management, Inc.
800 Iron Point Rd
Folsom CA 95630
916 357-5300

(P-26864)
FRITO-LAY NORTH AMERICA INC
1500 Francisco St, Torrance (90501-1329)
PHONE.................................310 224-5600
Dexter Matt, *General Mgr*
EMP: 200
SQ FT: 75,861
SALES (corp-wide): 63.5B **Publicly Held**
WEB: www.fritolay.com
SIC: 8741 2099 2096 Management services; food preparations; potato chips & similar snacks
HQ: Frito-Lay North America, Inc.
7701 Legacy Dr
Plano TX 75024

(P-26865)
FRONT LINE MGT GROUP INC
1100 Glendon Ave Ste 2000, Los Angeles
(90024-3524)
PHONE.................................310 209-3100
Irving Azoff, *President*
EMP: 90
SALES (est): 3.9MM
SALES (corp-wide): 10.3B **Publicly Held**
SIC: 8741 Management services

HQ: Flmg Holdings Corp.
9348 Civic Center Dr
Beverly Hills CA 90210
310 867-7000

(P-26866)
GAFCON INC (PA)
5960 Cornerstone Ct W # 100, San Diego
(92121-3780)
PHONE..............................858 875-0010
Yehudi Gaffen, *CEO*
Pam Gaffen, *President*
Robin Duveen, *COO*
Casey Sanfilippo, *COO*
Jon Rodriguez, *CFO*
EMP: 60
SQ FT: 14,000
SALES (est): 18.8MM **Privately Held**
SIC: 8741 8111 Construction management; legal services

(P-26867)
GARDNER NEUROLOGIC ORTHOPEDIC
Also Called: Internal Associates Med Group
6167 Bristol Pkwy Ste 200, Culver City
(90230-6649)
PHONE..............................310 649-5824
Elias Munoz, *Principal*
EMP: 70
SALES (est): 1.9MM **Privately Held**
SIC: 8741 Management services

(P-26868)
GEO GROUP INC
10400 Rancho Rd, Adelanto (92301-2237)
P.O. Box 6005 (92301-1190)
PHONE..............................760 246-1171
Jerardo Acevedo, *Warden*
EMP: 100
SALES (corp-wide): 2.2B **Privately Held**
WEB: www.thegeogroupinc.com
SIC: 8741 Management services
PA: The Geo Group Inc
621 Nw 53rd St Ste 700
Boca Raton FL 33487
561 893-0101

(P-26869)
GEO GROUP INC
Also Called: Golden State Crrctional Fcilty
611 Frontage Rd, Mc Farland
(93250-1075)
P.O. Box 1518 (93250-0118)
PHONE..............................661 792-2731
Wanda Wilson, *Warden*
EMP: 120
SALES (corp-wide): 2.2B **Privately Held**
WEB: www.thegeogroupinc.com
SIC: 8741 Management services
PA: The Geo Group Inc
621 Nw 53rd St Ste 700
Boca Raton FL 33487
561 893-0101

(P-26870)
GILARDI & CO LLC
3301 Kerner Blvd Ste 100, San Rafael
(94901-4896)
PHONE..............................415 461-0410
Bryan Butvick, *CEO*
Daniel Burke, *Exec VP*
Lara McDermott, *Exec VP*
Kim Wagner, *Exec VP*
Rich Pentimonti, *Managing Dir*
EMP: 80
SQ FT: 16,000
SALES (est): 10.5MM **Privately Held**
WEB: www.gilardi.com
SIC: 8741 8111 Management services; legal services
HQ: Kurtzman Carson Consultants, Inc
2335 Alaska Ave
El Segundo CA 90245
310 823-9000

(P-26871)
GILBANE BUILDING COMPANY
Also Called: Gilbane Construction
1798 Tech Dr Ste 120, San Jose (95110)
PHONE..............................408 660-4400
Bob Crowder, *Director*
EMP: 64

SALES (corp-wide): 4.9B **Privately Held**
WEB: www.gilbaneco.com
SIC: 8741 1542 Construction management; commercial & office building, new construction
HQ: Gilbane Building Company
7 Jackson Walkway Ste 2
Providence RI 02903
401 456-5800

(P-26872)
GLOBAL 360 INC
1080 Marina Village Pkwy # 300, Alameda
(94501-6427)
PHONE..............................510 263-4800
Nina Abbott, *Branch Mgr*
EMP: 65
SALES (corp-wide): 2.2B **Privately Held**
WEB: www.global360.com
SIC: 8741 Management services
PA: Open Text Corporation
275 Frank Tompa Dr
Waterloo ON N2L 0
519 888-7111

(P-26873)
GLOBAL-DINING INC CALIFORNIA
1212 3rd Street Promenade, Santa Monica
(90401-1308)
PHONE..............................310 576-9922
Kozo Hasegawa, *CEO*
EMP: 140
SALES: 6.2MM
SALES (corp-wide): 87.6MM **Privately Held**
SIC: 8741 Restaurant management
PA: Global-Dining, Inc.
7-1-5, Minamiaoyama
Minato-Ku TKY 107-0
354 693-223

(P-26874)
GOLDMAN AVRAM
Also Called: Nrt
1855 Gateway Blvd Ste 750, Concord
(94520-3290)
PHONE..............................925 275-3000
Avram Goldman, *President*
Jamie A Schlicher, *Vice Pres*
EMP: 75
SALES (est): 3.3MM **Privately Held**
SIC: 8741 6531 Management services; real estate brokers & agents

(P-26875)
GONZALEZ MANAGEMENT CO INC
10147 San Fernando Rd, Pacoima
(91331-2617)
PHONE..............................818 485-0596
Luis Gonzalez, *President*
EMP: 65 EST: 2004
SQ FT: 20,000
SALES (est): 6.8MM **Privately Held**
SIC: 8741 Management services

(P-26876)
GRANVILLE GLENDALE INC
Also Called: Granville Cafe
807 Americana Way, Glendale
(91210-1509)
PHONE..............................818 550-0472
Jonathan Weiss, *CEO*
EMP: 75 EST: 2008
SALES (est): 4.5MM **Privately Held**
SIC: 8741 Restaurant management

(P-26877)
GREYSTAR MANAGEMENT SVCS LP
17885 Von Karman Ave, Irvine
(92614-5223)
PHONE..............................949 705-0010
Jennifer Jackson, *Regional Mgr*
Eileen Nelson, *Regional Mgr*
EMP: 334 **Privately Held**
SIC: 8741 Business management
PA: Greystar Management Services, L.P.
750 Bering Dr Ste 300
Houston TX 77057

(P-26878)
GRIFFIN GROUP LLC (PA)
4 Rebelo Ln Ste D, Novato (94947-3629)
PHONE..............................415 892-4569
Keith Greggor, *CEO*
Crystal Marty, *CFO*
Tony Foglio, *Chairman*
Lynn Lackey, *Vice Pres*
Chad Farmer, *CTO*
EMP: 110
SALES (est): 5MM **Privately Held**
SIC: 8741 Business management

(P-26879)
GRIFFIN SLR MANAGEMENT INC
9454 Wilshire Blvd # 700, Beverly Hills
(90212-2931)
PHONE..............................310 270-4031
Sol L Rabin, *President*
Coleen Rabin, *Principal*
EMP: 66
SALES (est): 3.6MM **Privately Held**
SIC: 8741 Management services

(P-26880)
GRM INFORMATION MGT SERVICES
8500 Mercury Ln, Pico Rivera
(90660-3796)
PHONE..............................562 373-9000
Lev Spivak, *Vice Pres*
John Buglino, *Marketing Staff*
EMP: 50
SALES (est): 1.8MM **Privately Held**
SIC: 8741 Management services

(P-26881)
GRM INFORMATION MGT SVCS INC
8500 Mercury Ln, Pico Rivera
(90660-3796)
PHONE..............................562 373-9000
Jack Grimdjean, *Manager*
EMP: 54 **Privately Held**
SIC: 8741 Business management
PA: Grm Information Management Services, Inc.
215 Coles St
Jersey City NJ 07310

(P-26882)
GSG ASSOCIATES INC
1010 E Union St Ste 203, Pasadena
(91106-1756)
PHONE..............................626 585-1808
Glenda S Garrard, *CEO*
Jay Garrard, *President*
Maureen Stratton, *President*
EMP: 100
SQ FT: 3,800
SALES (est): 9MM **Privately Held**
WEB: www.gsga.net
SIC: 8741 Nursing & personal care facility management

(P-26883)
HALL MANAGEMENT CORP
Also Called: Land & Personnel Management
759 S Madera Ave, Kerman (93630-1744)
PHONE..............................559 846-7382
Stacy Hampton, *President*
James Randles, *Vice Pres*
EMP: 2000
SQ FT: 5,000
SALES (est): 98.4MM **Privately Held**
SIC: 8741 Personnel management

(P-26884)
HARBOR-UCLA MED FOUNDATION INC (PA)
Also Called: Harbor Ucla Med Foundation
21840 S Norm Ave, Torrance (90502)
PHONE..............................310 222-5015
Chester Choi, *CEO*
EMP: 100
SQ FT: 45,000
SALES: 11.2MM **Privately Held**
WEB: www.harborucla.org
SIC: 8741 Hospital management

(P-26885)
HEALTHCARE MGT PARTNERS LLC
20 Executive Park Ste 155, Irvine
(92614-4733)
PHONE..............................949 263-8620
Claudia Dwyer,
Douglas Cassel,
Chris Kellogg,
Brigette Labar,
Jay Lichman,
EMP: 260
SALES (est): 11.6MM **Privately Held**
WEB: www.hmpllc.com
SIC: 8741 8721 Hospital management; nursing & personal care facility management; accounting, auditing & bookkeeping

(P-26886)
HOSTMARK INVESTORS LTD PARTNR
Also Called: Santa Clara Hilton, The
4949 Great America Pkwy, Santa Clara
(95054-1216)
PHONE..............................408 330-0001
Roy Truitt, *General Mgr*
EMP: 180 **Privately Held**
SIC: 8741 7991 5813 5812 Hotel or motel management; physical fitness facilities; drinking places; eating places; hotel, franchised
PA: Hostmark Investors Limited Partnership
1300 E Wdfield Rd Ste 400
Schaumburg IL 60173

(P-26887)
HOTEL MANAGERS GROUP LLC
11590 W Bernardo Ct # 211, San Diego
(92127-1622)
PHONE..............................858 673-1534
Joel Biggs, *Mng Member*
Michele Demayo, *Exec VP*
Michelle Demayo, *Exec VP*
Emad Alwer, *Vice Pres*
Alan Bowles, *Vice Pres*
EMP: 400
SALES (est): 33.4MM **Privately Held**
WEB: www.hotelmanagersgroup.com
SIC: 8741 7011 7041 Hotel or motel management; hotels & motels; membership-basis organization hotels

(P-26888)
HRONOPOULOS
110 W A St Ste 900, San Diego
(92101-3705)
PHONE..............................619 237-6161
Andreas Hronopoulos, *CEO*
George Hronopoulos, *CFO*
Shannon McCampbell, *Admin Asst*
Jordan Yerkes, *Info Tech Dir*
Kevin Kachman,
EMP: 50 EST: 2010
SQ FT: 10,000
SALES: 4MM **Privately Held**
SIC: 8741 Business management

(P-26889)
HRP CAPITAL INC
Also Called: PhyCor
27699 Jefferson Ave # 201, Temecula
(92590-2661)
PHONE..............................951 676-0171
Rolando Atigoa, *Branch Mgr*
EMP: 53
SALES (corp-wide): 12.4MM **Privately Held**
SIC: 8741 8011 Nursing & personal care facility management; primary care medical clinic
PA: Hrp Capital, Inc.
173 Bridge Plz N
Fort Lee NJ 07024
201 242-4938

(P-26890)
HUNT CONVENIENCE STORES LLC
5750 S Watt Ave, Sacramento
(95829-9349)
P.O. Box 277670 (95827-7670)
PHONE..............................916 383-4868
Joshua M Hunt, *Mng Member*

Daniel Maue, *CFO*
EMP: 50 **EST:** 2014
SQ FT: 3,200
SALES: 5MM **Privately Held**
SIC: 8741 Administrative management

(P-26891)
IKEA PURCHASING SVCS US INC
600 N San Fernando Blvd, Burbank
(91502-1021)
PHONE..............................818 841-3500
Chris Maynard, *Manager*
EMP: 300 **Privately Held**
SIC: 8741 8721 5712 Administrative management; accounting, auditing & bookkeeping; furniture stores
HQ: Ikea Purchasing Services (Us) Inc.
7810 Katy Fwy
Houston TX 77024
888 888-4532

(P-26892)
INLAND CNTIES REGIONAL CTR INC (PA)
Also Called: INLAND REGIONAL CENTER
1365 S Waterman Ave, San Bernardino
(92408-2804)
P.O. Box 19037 (92423-9037)
PHONE..............................909 890-3000
Carol A Fitzgibbons, *CEO*
Carol Fitzgibbons, *Exec Dir*
Kaye Quintero, *Controller*
Carmela Aquino, *Psychologist*
Reina Campos, *Psychologist*
EMP: 83
SQ FT: 82,000
SALES: 463.3MM **Privately Held**
SIC: 8741 Management services

(P-26893)
INNOVATIVE EDUCATION MGT INC
1166 Broadway Ste Q, Placerville
(95667-5745)
PHONE..............................530 295-3566
Randy Gaschler, *President*
Denise Williams, *Admin Asst*
Katy Mann, *Administration*
Eugene Linger, *Info Tech Dir*
Susan Jenkins, *Research*
EMP: 154
SQ FT: 2,000
SALES: 20MM **Privately Held**
SIC: 8741 Management services

(P-26894)
INTELLECTUAL VENTURES LLC
200 California Ave # 200, Palo Alto
(94306-1635)
PHONE..............................650 941-1330
EMP: 287
SALES (corp-wide): 118.8MM **Privately Held**
SIC: 8741 Management services
PA: Intellectual Ventures, Llc
3150 139th Ave Se Ste 500
Bellevue WA 98005
425 467-2300

(P-26895)
INTERSTATE HOTELS RESORTS INC
4685 Macarthur Ct Ste 480, Newport Beach
(92660-8850)
PHONE..............................949 783-2500
Mark Burden, *Branch Mgr*
Chris Vaughn, *General Mgr*
EMP: 61 **Privately Held**
SIC: 8741 Hotel or motel management
HQ: Interstate Hotels & Resorts, Inc.
4501 Fairfax Dr Ste 500
Arlington VA 22203
703 387-3100

(P-26896)
INTERSTATE HOTELS RESORTS INC
Also Called: Hilton Garden Inn Carlsbad Bch
6450 Carlsbad Blvd, Carlsbad
(92011-1058)
PHONE..............................760 476-0800
Bob Moore, *Manager*
EMP: 70 **Privately Held**
WEB: www.sheratonokc.com

SIC: 8741 Hotel or motel management
HQ: Interstate Hotels & Resorts, Inc.
4501 Fairfax Dr Ste 500
Arlington VA 22203
703 387-3100

(P-26897)
INTERSTATE HOTELS RESORTS INC
Also Called: Doral Palm Sprngs Rsrt & Golf
67 967 Vst Chno At Lndau, Palm Springs
(92263)
P.O. Box 1644 (92263-1644)
PHONE..............................760 322-7000
Elie Zod, *Manager*
EMP: 200 **Privately Held**
WEB: www.sheratonokc.com
SIC: 8741 Hotel or motel management
HQ: Interstate Hotels & Resorts, Inc.
4501 Fairfax Dr Ste 500
Arlington VA 22203
703 387-3100

(P-26898)
INTERSTATE HOTELS RESORTS INC
Also Called: Embassy Suites Walnut Creek
1345 Treat Blvd, Walnut Creek
(94597-2173)
PHONE..............................925 934-2500
David Cano, *Manager*
EMP: 130 **Privately Held**
WEB: www.sheratonokc.com
SIC: 8741 Hotel or motel management
HQ: Interstate Hotels & Resorts, Inc.
4501 Fairfax Dr Ste 500
Arlington VA 22203
703 387-3100

(P-26899)
INTERSTATE HOTELS RESORTS INC
Also Called: Claremont Resort
41 Tunnel Rd, Berkeley (94705-2429)
PHONE..............................510 843-3000
Mike Czarcinski, *General Mgr*
EMP: 99 **Privately Held**
WEB: www.sheratonokc.com
SIC: 8741 Hotel or motel management
HQ: Interstate Hotels & Resorts, Inc.
4501 Fairfax Dr Ste 500
Arlington VA 22203
703 387-3100

(P-26900)
INTERSTATE HOTELS RESORTS INC
Also Called: Hilton
18800 Macarthur Blvd, Irvine (92612-1410)
PHONE..............................949 833-9999
Ted Holmquist, *General Mgr*
Dori Familiant, *General Mgr*
Tina Vu, *Manager*
EMP: 185 **Privately Held**
WEB: www.sheratonokc.com
SIC: 8741 Hotel or motel management
HQ: Interstate Hotels & Resorts, Inc.
4501 Fairfax Dr Ste 500
Arlington VA 22203
703 387-3100

(P-26901)
INTERSTELLAR INC
292 Ivy St Ste E, San Francisco
(94102-4480)
PHONE..............................415 598-0346
Adam Ludwin, *CEO*
Jed McCaleb, *CTO*
EMP: 60
SALES (est): 798.5K **Privately Held**
SIC: 8741 Management services

(P-26902)
INVESTORS CAPITAL MGT GROUP
Also Called: Cuisine Partners USA
10390 Santa Monica Blvd, Los Angeles
(90025-5058)
PHONE..............................310 553-5175
EMP: 277
SQ FT: 7,800
SALES (est): 11MM **Privately Held**
SIC: 8741

(P-26903)
JC RESORTS LLC
Also Called: Surf Sand Hotel
1555 S Coast Hwy, Laguna Beach
(92651-3226)
PHONE..............................949 376-2779
Blaise Bartell, *Branch Mgr*
EMP: 300 **Privately Held**
WEB: www.surfandsandresort.com
SIC: 8741 5813 5812 7011 Hotel or motel management; drinking places; eating places; hotels
PA: Jc Resorts Llc
533 Coast Blvd S
La Jolla CA 92037

(P-26904)
JC RESORTS LLC
Also Called: Encinitas Ranch Golf Course
1275 Quail Gardens Dr, Encinitas
(92024-2368)
PHONE..............................760 944-1936
Rod Landville, *Manager*
EMP: 100
SALES (est): 5.2MM **Privately Held**
WEB: www.surfandsandresort.com
SIC: 8741 7992 Hotel or motel management; public golf courses
PA: Jc Resorts Llc
533 Coast Blvd S
La Jolla CA 92037

(P-26905)
JENKINS GALES & MARTINEZ INC
6033 W Century Blvd # 601, Los Angeles
(90045-6414)
PHONE..............................310 645-0561
Earl Gales Jr, *Ch of Bd*
Ray David, *Corp Secy*
Starla Gale, *Vice Pres*
Ryan Gales, *Marketing Staff*
Michael Neilson, *Sr Project Mgr*
EMP: 70
SQ FT: 5,000
SALES: 3.9MM **Privately Held**
WEB: www.jgminc.com
SIC: 8741 8712 7389 8711 Construction management; architectural engineering; mapmaking or drafting, including aerial; construction & civil engineering

(P-26906)
JESSE LEE GROUP INC
Also Called: Castro Valley Care Centers
300 Crprate Pinte Ste 550, Culver City
(90230)
PHONE..............................510 351-3700
George Davis, *Manager*
EMP: 91
SALES (corp-wide): 7.6MM **Privately Held**
SIC: 8741 8051 8059 Hospital management; skilled nursing care facilities; convalescent home
PA: Jesse Lee Group, Inc
5212 Village Creek Dr
Plano TX 75093
972 931-3800

(P-26907)
JESSE LEE GROUP INC
Also Called: New Hope Care Center
2586 Buthmann Ave, Tracy (95376-2165)
PHONE..............................209 832-2273
Ruby Rakow, *President*
EMP: 120
SALES (corp-wide): 7.6MM **Privately Held**
SIC: 8741 8051 Hospital management; convalescent home with continuous nursing care
PA: Jesse Lee Group, Inc
5212 Village Creek Dr
Plano TX 75093
972 931-3800

(P-26908)
JIPC MANAGEMENT INC
Also Called: John's Incredible Pizza Co
22342 Avenida Empresa # 220, Rcho STA
Marg (92688-2161)
PHONE..............................949 916-2000
John M Parlet, *President*

Natalie Cervantes, *Admin Asst*
Alice Louie, *Admin Asst*
Kenneth Perkins, *Software Engr*
Julie Peterson, *Accountant*
EMP: 1000
SALES (est): 77.2MM **Privately Held**
SIC: 8741 Restaurant management

(P-26909)
JOIE DE VIVRE HOSPITALITY LLC (PA)
1750 Geary Blvd, San Francisco
(94115-3715)
PHONE..............................415 835-0300
Stephen T Conley Jr, *CEO*
Greg Smith, *Exec VP*
Jorge Trevino, *Exec VP*
Brett Blass, *Vice Pres*
Karlene Holloman, *Vice Pres*
EMP: 50
SALES: 231.8MM **Privately Held**
WEB: www.hotelbijou.com
SIC: 8741 Hotel or motel management

(P-26910)
JOIE DE VIVRE HOSPITALITY LLC
Also Called: Maxwell Hotel, The
386 Geary St, San Francisco (94102-1802)
PHONE..............................415 986-2000
Steven Conley, *Manager*
EMP: 60
SALES (corp-wide): 231.8MM **Privately Held**
WEB: www.hotelbijou.com
SIC: 8741 7011 Hotel or motel management; motels
PA: Joie De Vivre Hospitality, Llc
1750 Geary Blvd
San Francisco CA 94115
415 835-0300

(P-26911)
JOIE DE VIVRE HOSPITALITY LLC
Also Called: Costanoa
2001 Rossi Rd, Pescadero (94060-9732)
PHONE..............................650 879-1100
Daniel Medellin, *Branch Mgr*
Teri Giordani, *Sales Staff*
EMP: 65
SALES (corp-wide): 231.8MM **Privately Held**
WEB: www.hotelbijou.com
SIC: 8741 Hotel or motel management
PA: Joie De Vivre Hospitality, Llc
1750 Geary Blvd
San Francisco CA 94115
415 835-0300

(P-26912)
JUVENILE JUSTICE DIVISION CAL
Also Called: Ventura Yuth Crrctional Fcilty
3100 Wright Rd, Camarillo (93010-8307)
PHONE..............................805 485-7951
Vivian Craford, *Superintendent*
Gary Collins, *Principal*
EMP: 350 **Privately Held**
WEB: www.cya.ca.gov
SIC: 8741 9223 Office management; house of correction, government
HQ: Juvenile Justice Division, California
1515 S St Ste 502s
Sacramento CA 95811

(P-26913)
KA MANAGEMENT INC
5820 Oberlin Dr Ste 201, San Diego
(92121-3743)
PHONE..............................858 404-6080
Kayvon Agahnia, *CEO*
Jill Muller, *Manager*
EMP: 90
SALES: 12MM **Privately Held**
SIC: 8741 Management services

(P-26914)
KAISER HLTH PLAN ASSET MGT INC
Also Called: KAISER PERMANENTE
1 Kaiser Plz Ste 1333, Oakland
(94612-3604)
PHONE..............................510 271-5910

Thomas R Meier, *President*
Tony Nottonson, *Manager*
EMP: 50
SALES: 31.6MM
SALES (corp-wide): 94.1B **Privately Held**
WEB: www.kaiser.com
SIC: 8741 Hospital management
PA: Kaiser Foundation Health Plan, Inc.
1 Kaiser Plz
Oakland CA 94612
510 271-5800

(P-26915)
KAL KRISHNAN CONSULTING SVCS (PA)
800 S Figueroa St # 1210, Los Angeles
(90017-2521)
PHONE..................................510 893-3500
Kalliana R Krishnan, *President*
Dev Krishnan, *President*
Ron Anderson, *Vice Pres*
Stan Tomlinson, *Vice Pres*
Rajesh Iyer, *Principal*
EMP: 94
SQ FT: 1,000
SALES (est): 11.5MM **Privately Held**
WEB: www.kalkrishnan.com
SIC: 8741 Construction management

(P-26916)
KEIRO SERVICES
Also Called: Keiro Senior Health Care
420 E 3rd St Ste 1000, Los Angeles
(90013-1648)
PHONE..................................213 873-5700
Shawn Miyake, *CEO*
Kanako Fukuyama, *Analyst*
EMP: 500
SQ FT: 26,000
SALES: 3.4MM **Privately Held**
SIC: 8741 Nursing & personal care facility management

(P-26917)
KERN AROUND CLOCK FOUNDATION
Also Called: Around The Clock Linkage
5251 Office Park Dr # 400, Bakersfield
(93309-0667)
PHONE..................................661 324-3221
Mary Vasinda, *President*
Stacie Dollar, *VP Mktg*
Mark Berg, *Manager*
EMP: 50
SALES (est): 269.9K **Privately Held**
WEB: www.bakersfieldcare.com
SIC: 8741 8322 Business management;
individual & family services

(P-26918)
KFI
1 Sansome St Fl 32, San Francisco
(94104-4436)
PHONE..................................415 956-9812
Gary Burison, *CEO*
Alla Olshansky, *Accountant*
EMP: 50
SALES (est): 1.5MM **Privately Held**
SIC: 8741 Management services

(P-26919)
KIMPTON HOTEL & REST GROUP LLC
Also Called: Hotel Moneco
501 Geary St, San Francisco (94102-1640)
PHONE..................................415 292-0100
Jimmy Hord, *Manager*
EMP: 88
SALES (corp-wide): 1.7B **Privately Held**
WEB: www.kuletos.com
SIC: 8741 7011 5812 Hotel or motel man-
agement; hotels & motels; eating places
HQ: Kimpton Hotel & Restaurant Group Llc
222 Kearny St Ste 200
San Francisco CA 94108
415 397-5572

(P-26920)
KINTETSU ENTERPRISES
328 E 1st St, Los Angeles (90012-3902)
PHONE..................................213 687-2000
EMP: 90

SALES: 5MM
SALES (corp-wide): 11.4B **Privately Held**
WEB: www.miyakoinn.com
SIC: 8741 6531
PA: Kintetsu Group Holdings Co., Ltd.
6-1-55, Uehonmachi, Tennoji-Ku
Osaka OSK 543-0
667 753-355

(P-26921)
KISCO SENIOR LIVING LLC
Also Called: Bridgepoint At San Francisco
1601 19th Ave Ofc, San Francisco
(94122-3478)
PHONE..................................415 664-6264
Susan Edwards, *Branch Mgr*
EMP: 66
SALES (corp-wide): 138.2MM **Privately Held**
WEB: www.kiscosl.com
SIC: 8741 Nursing & personal care facility management
PA: Senior Kisco Living Llc
5790 Fleet St Ste 300
Carlsbad CA 92008
760 804-5900

(P-26922)
KOR HOTEL GROUPS INC
530 Pico Blvd, Santa Monica (90405-1223)
PHONE..................................310 309-8066
Micheal D'Amodio, *President*
EMP: 99
SALES (est): 3.3MM **Privately Held**
SIC: 8741 Hotel or motel management

(P-26923)
KRM RISK MANAGEMENT SVCS INC
4270 W Richert Ave # 101, Fresno
(93722-6334)
P.O. Box 9549 (93793-9549)
PHONE..................................559 277-4800
Steve Wigh, *Vice Pres*
EMP: 51 **Privately Held**
WEB: www.krmrisk.com
SIC: 8741 Management services
PA: Krm Risk Management Services, Inc.
4270 W Richert Ave 101
Fresno CA 93722

(P-26924)
KSL II MNGEMENT OPERATIONS LLC
50905 Avenida Bermudas, La Quinta
(92253-8910)
PHONE..................................760 564-8000
Scott Dalecio, *President*
EMP: 60
SALES (est): 5MM **Privately Held**
SIC: 8741 Management services

(P-26925)
LA JOIE JERRY
Also Called: La Joie Construction
418 Sonora Dr, San Mateo (94402-2342)
PHONE..................................650 375-1808
Jerry La Joie, *Owner*
EMP: 50
SALES (est): 2.9MM **Privately Held**
SIC: 8741 1542 1521 Construction man-
agement; commercial & office building,
new construction; new construction, sin-
gle-family houses

(P-26926)
LA VOIE & SONS CONSTRUCTION
1061 Nichols Ct, Rocklin (95765-1325)
PHONE..................................916 408-6900
EMP: 50
SALES (est): 2.6MM **Privately Held**
SIC: 8741

(P-26927)
LAKESIDE SYSTEMS INC
Also Called: Lakeside Medical Systems
8510 Balboa Blvd Ste 150, Northridge
(91325-5810)
PHONE..................................866 654-3471
Richard Merkin, *CEO*
EMP: 700
SQ FT: 20,000

SALES (est): 31.2MM
SALES (corp-wide): 46.4MM **Privately Held**
SIC: 8741 8742 6411 Management services; management consulting services; insurance agents, brokers & service
PA: Heritage Provider Network Inc
8510 Balboa Blvd Ste 285
Northridge CA 91325
818 654-3461

(P-26928)
LEDCOR MANAGEMENT SERVICES INC
6405 Mira Mesa Blvd Ste 1, San Diego
(92121-4147)
PHONE..................................858 527-6400
Dave Lede, *CEO*
EMP: 50
SALES (est): 4.6MM **Privately Held**
SIC: 8741 Business management

(P-26929)
LEDESMA & MEYER DEV INC
9441 Haven Ave, Rancho Cucamonga
(91730-5844)
PHONE..................................909 476-0590
Joseph Ledesma, *CEO*
Kris Meyer, *Vice Pres*
EMP: 55
SQ FT: 16,480
SALES (est): 3.3MM **Privately Held**
SIC: 8741 Construction management

(P-26930)
LEGACY PRTNERS RESIDENTIAL INC
5141 California Ave # 100, Irvine
(92617-3060)
PHONE..................................949 930-6600
Deborah Dodd, *Branch Mgr*
Erik Hansen, *Manager*
EMP: 319
SALES (corp-wide): 83.6MM **Privately Held**
SIC: 8741 Management services
PA: Legacy Partners Residential, Inc.
4000 E 3rd Ave Ste 600
Foster City CA 94404
650 571-2250

(P-26931)
LEGACY PRTNERS RESIDENTIAL INC (PA)
4000 E 3rd Ave Ste 600, Foster City
(94404-4828)
PHONE..................................650 571-2250
C Preston Butcher, *Ch of Bd*
Gary J Rossi, *CFO*
Kathy Drossel, *Office Admin*
Amelia Johnson, *VP Human Res*
Timothy Labrier, *Senior Mgr*
EMP: 180
SALES (est): 83.6MM **Privately Held**
SIC: 8741 Management services

(P-26932)
LENDLEASE US CONSTRUCTION INC
800 W 6th St Ste 1600, Los Angeles
(90017-2719)
PHONE..................................213 430-4660
Mike Concannon, *Branch Mgr*
EMP: 100
SALES (corp-wide): 12.4B **Privately Held**
SIC: 8741 8742 1541 1542 Construction
management; construction project management consultant; industrial buildings,
new construction; nonresidential construction
HQ: Lendlease (Us) Construction Inc.
200 Park Ave Fl 9
New York NY 10166
212 592-6700

(P-26933)
LEXXIOM INC
7945 Cartilla Ave A, Rancho Cucamonga
(91730-3069)
PHONE..................................909 481-2536
Robert Lemelin, *President*
Brian Lemelin, *COO*
Leo Lemelin, *CFO*
Ron Fakhoury, *VP Opers*
EMP: 360

SALES (est): 24MM **Privately Held**
WEB: www.thedebtmediator.com
SIC: 8741 Administrative management

(P-26934)
LIBSOURCE LLC
10390 Santa Monica Blvd, Los Angeles
(90025-5058)
PHONE..................................323 852-1083
Deborah Schwarz, *CEO*
Robert Corrao, *COO*
EMP: 140
SQ FT: 2,500
SALES: 20MM **Privately Held**
SIC: 8741 Financial management for busi-
ness

(P-26935)
LION-VALLEN LTD PARTNERSHIP
22 Area Aven A Bldg 2234, Camp Pendle-
ton (92055)
P.O. Box 555045 (92055-5045)
PHONE..................................760 385-4885
EMP: 50 **Privately Held**
SIC: 8741 Management services
PA: Lion-Vallen Limited Partnership
7200 Poe Ave Ste 400
Dayton OH 45414

(P-26936)
LIVINGSTON MEM VNA HLTH CORP
Also Called: Livingston Mem Vst Nrs Associa
1996 Eastman Ave Ste 101, Ventura
(93003-5768)
PHONE..................................805 642-0239
Lanyard K Dial MD, *President*
Charles Hair MD, *Ch of Bd*
Judy Hecox, *President*
Jeffrey Paul, *Treasurer*
Stephanie Montenegro, *Social Dir*
EMP: 200
SQ FT: 12,600
SALES: 17MM **Privately Held**
WEB: www.lmvna.org
SIC: 8741 8082 Hospital management;
nursing & personal care facility manage-
ment; home health care services

(P-26937)
MANUFACTURING SOLUTIONS INC (PA)
1738 N Neville St, Orange (92865-4214)
PHONE..................................714 453-0100
Anthony Puccio, *President*
Joe Puccio, *COO*
Gilles Madelmont, *CFO*
EMP: 370
SQ FT: 15,000
SALES (est): 14.7MM **Privately Held**
SIC: 8741 Management services

(P-26938)
MAVERICK HOTEL PARTNERS LLC
Also Called: Filament Hospitality
2 Embarcadero Ctr Fl 8, San Francisco
(94111-3833)
PHONE..................................415 655-9526
Ingrid Summerfield, *Mng Member*
EMP: 300
SQ FT: 2,000
SALES: 75K **Privately Held**
SIC: 8741 Hotel or motel management

(P-26939)
MAX SPORTSTERS INC
Also Called: Wheeler and Company
10050 N Foothill Blvd # 200, Cupertino
(95014-5661)
PHONE..................................408 446-8330
David Wheeler, *President*
EMP: 50
SALES (est): 1.1MM **Privately Held**
SIC: 8741 Restaurant management

(P-26940)
MCKINLEY PLAZA LLC
2401 E Division St, National City
(91950-1901)
PHONE..................................619 405-6307
Roshan Gupta,
EMP: 99

SALES: 950K **Privately Held**
SIC: **8741** Hotel or motel management

(P-26941)
MCMILLAN FARM MANAGEMENT
29379 Rancho California R, Temecula (92591-5208)
PHONE...................................951 676-2045
Gary McMillan, *Owner*
EMP: 150
SALES (est): 14MM Privately Held
SIC: **8741** 0174 Management services; citrus fruits

(P-26942)
MEDICAL NETWORK INC
Also Called: MBC Systems
1809 E Dyer Rd Ste 311, Santa Ana (92705-5740)
PHONE...................................949 863-0022
David Conrad, *President*
Erica Weinstein, *Executive*
Kimmie Le, *Director*
EMP: 80
SQ FT: 3,500
SALES (est): 9.4MM Privately Held
WEB: www.mbcsystems.org
SIC: **8741** Hospital management; nursing & personal care facility management

(P-26943)
MENTOR MEDIA (USA) SUP
3768 Milliken Ave Ste A, Eastvale (91752-1037)
PHONE...................................909 930-0800
Kok Khoon Lim, *CEO*
Kok Choy, *President*
EMP: 80
SALES (est): 15MM
SALES (corp-wide): 5.8B Privately Held
SIC: **8741** 8742 Business management; business planning & organizing services
HQ: Mentor Media Ltd
　　47 Jalan Buroh
　　Singapore 61949
　　663 133-33

(P-26944)
MGT INDUSTRIES INC
19034 S Vermont Ave, Gardena (90248-4412)
PHONE...................................310 324-3152
EMP: 69
SALES (corp-wide): 63.5MM Privately Held
SIC: **8741** Management services
PA: Mgt Industries, Inc.
　　13889 S Figueroa St
　　Los Angeles CA 90061
　　310 516-5900

(P-26945)
MIDNIGHT SNACK LP
Also Called: Ford's Filling Station
4182 Irving Pl, Culver City (90232-2812)
PHONE...................................310 202-1470
Benjamin Ford, *Partner*
Wild Hog, *Partner*
EMP: 50
SALES (est): 4.8MM Privately Held
SIC: **8741** 8742 Restaurant management; restaurant & food services consultants

(P-26946)
MIG MANAGEMENT SERVICES LLC
660 Newport Center Dr, Newport Beach (92660-6401)
PHONE...................................949 474-5800
Paul Merage, *CEO*
EMP: 80
SALES (est): 3.3MM
SALES (corp-wide): 133.7K Privately Held
SIC: **8741** Management services
PA: Mig Capital, Llc
　　660 Newport Center Dr # 450
　　Newport Beach CA 92660
　　949 474-5800

(P-26947)
MIKE ROVNER CONSTRUCTION INC
22600 Lambert St, Lake Forest (92630-6201)
PHONE...................................949 458-1562
Mike Rovner, *Branch Mgr*
EMP: 171 **Privately Held**
SIC: **8741** 1522 1521 Construction management; residential construction; single-family housing construction
PA: Mike Rovner Construction, Inc.
　　5400 Tech Cir
　　Moorpark CA 93021

(P-26948)
MIMG MEDICAL MANAGEMENT LLC
26522 La Alameda Ste 120, Mission Viejo (92691-6330)
PHONE...................................949 282-1600
EMP: 60
SQ FT: 1,800
SALES (est): 2.6MM Privately Held
SIC: **8741**

(P-26949)
MONTAGE HEALTH (PA)
23625 Holman Hwy, Monterey (93940-5902)
P.O. Box Hh (93942-6032)
PHONE...................................831 625-4830
Steven Packer MD, *President*
Laura Zehm, *CFO*
Terril Lowe, *Vice Pres*
Tim Nylen, *Vice Pres*
Cynthia Peck, *Vice Pres*
EMP: 1650
SQ FT: 350,000
SALES: 200MM Privately Held
SIC: **8741** Hospital management

(P-26950)
MORRISON MGT SPECIALISTS INC
Also Called: Morrison Health Care
1150 N Indian Canyon Dr, Palm Springs (92262-4872)
PHONE...................................760 323-6296
Rick Tinsley, *Director*
EMP: 97
SALES (corp-wide): 28.9B Privately Held
SIC: **8741** 5812 8742 5813 Management services; eating places; food & beverage consultant; drinking places
HQ: Morrison Management Specialists, Inc.
　　400 Northridge Rd Ste 600
　　Sandy Springs GA 30350

(P-26951)
MORRISON MGT SPECIALISTS INC
1531 Esplanade, Chico (95926-3310)
PHONE...................................530 332-7557
EMP: 97
SALES (corp-wide): 28.9B Privately Held
WEB: www.iammorrison.com
SIC: **8741** Management services
HQ: Morrison Management Specialists, Inc.
　　400 Northridge Rd Ste 600
　　Sandy Springs GA 30350

(P-26952)
MORRISON MGT SPECIALISTS INC
14445 Olive View Dr, Sylmar (91342-1437)
PHONE...................................818 364-4219
Kathy Dagg, *Manager*
EMP: 78
SALES (corp-wide): 28.9B Privately Held
WEB: www.iammorrison.com
SIC: **8741** 5812 Restaurant management; eating places
HQ: Morrison Management Specialists, Inc.
　　400 Northridge Rd Ste 600
　　Sandy Springs GA 30350

(P-26953)
MOSAIC
Also Called: Mosaic Quest
10991 Via Banco, San Diego (92126-7423)
PHONE...................................858 397-2261
EMP: 79
SALES (corp-wide): 236.4MM Privately Held
SIC: **8741** Management services
PA: Mosaic
　　4980 S 118th St
　　Omaha NE 68137
　　402 896-3884

(P-26954)
NASDAQ INC
4300 Bohannon Dr Ste 110, Menlo Park (94025-1042)
PHONE...................................510 705-8951
EMP: 150
SALES (corp-wide): 3.9B Publicly Held
SIC: **8741** 8742 Management services; personnel management consultant
PA: Nasdaq, Inc.
　　1 Liberty Plz Ste 4900
　　New York NY 10006
　　212 401-8700

(P-26955)
NAVIGANT CYMETRIX CORPORATION
1515 W 190th St Ste 350, Gardena (90248-4910)
PHONE...................................424 201-6300
Jeff Macdonald, *Branch Mgr*
Karen Ladika, *Principal*
EMP: 125
SALES (corp-wide): 1B Publicly Held
WEB: www.hmsintl.com
SIC: **8741** Management services
HQ: Navigant Cymetrix Corporation
　　1 Park Plz Ste 1050
　　Irvine CA 92614
　　714 361-6800

(P-26956)
NB ENTERPRISES & DIST INC
603 Wilshire Blvd, Los Angeles (90017-3207)
PHONE...................................866 216-1515
Neal B Platt, *President*
William Saller, *Vice Pres*
EMP: 85
SQ FT: 1,500
SALES: 15.3MM Privately Held
SIC: **8741** Management services

(P-26957)
NETWORK MANAGEMENT GROUP INC (PA)
1100 S Flower St Ste 3110, Los Angeles (90015-2287)
PHONE...................................323 263-2632
John Park, *President*
EMP: 160
SQ FT: 2,039
SALES (est): 9.8MM Privately Held
WEB: www.networkm.com
SIC: **8741** 8742 Business management; management consulting services

(P-26958)
NETWORK MEDICAL MANAGEMENT INC
1668 S Grfeld Ave Ste 100, Alhambra (91801)
PHONE...................................626 282-0288
Thomas Lam MD, *Co-CEO*
Gary Augusta, *President*
Hing Ang, *COO*
Mihir Shah, *CFO*
Warren Hosseinion MD, *Co-CEO*
EMP: 130
SQ FT: 14,000
SALES (est): 9.3MM Publicly Held
WEB: www.nmm.cc
SIC: **8741** Hospital management; nursing & personal care facility management
PA: Apollo Medical Holdings, Inc.
　　700 N Brand Blvd Ste 1400
　　Glendale CA 91203

(P-26959)
NEW SOLAR INCORPORATED
1525 Mccarthy Blvd, Milpitas (95035-7451)
PHONE...................................888 886-0103
Charles Ng, *President*
Porter Wong, *Corp Secy*
Ralph Chern, *Sales Executive*
EMP: 50
SALES (est): 1.8MM Privately Held
WEB: www.newsolarinc.com
SIC: **8741** 5063 1731 4931 Financial management for business; electrical apparatus & equipment; electrical work; electric & other services combined; solar energy contractor

(P-26960)
NEWPORT GROUP INC (PA)
1350 Treat Blvd Ste 300, Walnut Creek (94597-7959)
PHONE...................................925 328-4540
Greg W Tschider, *CEO*
Nancy Worth, *COO*
Jackie Ward, *Officer*
Martha Sadler, *Exec VP*
Tom Hinsch, *Vice Pres*
EMP: 115
SALES (est): 68.4MM Privately Held
SIC: **8741** Administrative management

(P-26961)
NO SHNACKS INC
7480 Harvard Ct, Fontana (92336-3432)
PHONE...................................909 293-8747
Gary Clark, *Owner*
EMP: 50
SALES (est): 1.3MM Privately Held
SIC: **8741** Business management

(P-26962)
NORTH AMERICAN HEALTH CARE
Also Called: Cottonwood Post-Acute Rehab
625 Cottonwood St, Woodland (95695-3614)
PHONE...................................530 662-9193
Jason Bliss, *Manager*
Donald Laws, *Principal*
James Ellissherinian, *Info Tech Mgr*
EMP: 80
SALES (corp-wide): 69.3MM Privately Held
WEB: www.nahci.com
SIC: **8741** 8051 Nursing & personal care facility management; skilled nursing care facilities
PA: North American Health Care, Inc.
　　5150 E A Palma Ave 206
　　Anaheim CA 92807
　　949 240-2423

(P-26963)
NORTH AMERICAN HEALTH CARE INC (PA)
5150 E A Palma Ave 206, Anaheim (92807)
PHONE...................................949 240-2423
John L Sorensen, *Ch of Bd*
Timothy J Paulsen, *CEO*
Tim Paulson, *CFO*
Donald G Laws, *Chairman*
Darian Dahl, *Vice Pres*
EMP: 175
SALES (est): 69.3MM Privately Held
WEB: www.nahci.com
SIC: **8741** Nursing & personal care facility management

(P-26964)
NORTH AMERICAN MED MGT CAL INC (DH)
3281 E Guasti Rd Fl 7, Ontario (91761-7622)
PHONE...................................909 605-8000
Richard A Shinto MD, *CEO*
Glen Marconcini, *Exec VP*
Mollie Van Hofwegen, *Executive Asst*
Rick De Avila, *Project Mgr*
Karen Donan, *Financial Analy*
EMP: 75
SALES (est): 7.6MM
SALES (corp-wide): 1B Privately Held
SIC: **8741** Nursing & personal care facility management

(P-26965)
NORTHSTAR SENIOR LIVING INC
Also Called: Mountain Lakes Senior Living
2334 Washington Ave Ste A, Redding
(96001-2159)
PHONE..................................530 242-8300
Rick Jensen, *CEO*
Brian Uhlir, *CFO*
EMP: 586
SALES (est): 42MM **Privately Held**
SIC: 8741 Nursing & personal care facility management

(P-26966)
NTREPID CORPORATION
10201 Wtridge Cir Ste 300, San Diego
(92121)
PHONE..................................800 921-2414
Mike Simpson, *Program Mgr*
Timothy Ritenour, *Network Tech*
Chris Bertolero, *Opers Staff*
Carl Agbayani, *Manager*
EMP: 77 **Privately Held**
SIC: 8741 7371 Management services; software programming applications
HQ: Ntrepid Llc
12801 Worldgate Dr # 800
Herndon VA 20170
-

(P-26967)
ONRAD INC
Also Called: Onrad Medical Group
1770 Iowa Ave Ste 280, Riverside
(92507-7401)
PHONE..................................800 848-5876
David Engert, *President*
Samuel Salen, *Ch of Bd*
Scott Castle, *CFO*
Lisa Maulit, *Executive*
EMP: 79
SQ FT: 1,500
SALES: 9MM **Privately Held**
SIC: 8741 Business management

(P-26968)
ORANGE COUNTY DEPT EDUCATION
Tustin Unified School District
300 S C St, Tustin (92780-3633)
PHONE..................................714 730-7301
Peter Gorman, *Superintendent*
EMP: 1600
SALES (corp-wide): 284.9MM **Privately Held**
WEB: www.ocprob.com
SIC: 8741 Administrative management
PA: Orange County Superintendent Of Schools
200 Kalmus Dr
Costa Mesa CA 92626
714 966-4000

(P-26969)
OREQ CORPORATION
Also Called: Pool Pals Division
42306 Remington Ave, Temecula
(92590-2512)
PHONE..................................951 296-5076
Jess L Hetzner, *CEO*
Ron Hetzner, *Exec VP*
EMP: 50
SALES (est): 10.9MM **Privately Held**
WEB: www.oreqcorp.com
SIC: 8741 5091 5941 Business management; spa equipment & supplies; water sport equipment

(P-26970)
OVATIONS FANFARE
Also Called: Fanfare Enterprises
88 Fair Dr, Costa Mesa (92626-6521)
PHONE..................................714 708-1880
Juan Quintero, *Manager*
EMP: 75
SALES (corp-wide): 5.6MM **Privately Held**
SIC: 8741 5812 Management services; caterers
PA: Ovations Fanfare
61 Haas Pavilion
Berkeley CA 94720
510 704-8361

(P-26971)
PACIFIC PARK MANAGEMENT
1300 Fillmore St, San Francisco
(94115-4113)
PHONE..................................415 440-4840
EMP: 56 **Privately Held**
SIC: 8741 7521 Business management; indoor parking services
PA: Pacific Park Management Inc
465 California St Ste 473
San Francisco CA 94104

(P-26972)
PACIFIC PARTNERS MGT SVCS INC
Also Called: Pacific Partners MSI
1051 E Hillsdale Blvd, Foster City
(94404-1640)
P.O. Box 5860, San Mateo (94402-5860)
PHONE..................................650 358-5804
Lori Vatcher, *CEO*
M L Bonham MD, *President*
EMP: 100
SALES (est): 12.7MM **Publicly Held**
WEB: www.ppmsi.com
SIC: 8741 8748 Business management; business consulting
PA: Hca Healthcare, Inc.
1 Park Plz
Nashville TN 37203
-

(P-26973)
PACIFIC PROGRAM/DESIGN MANAGEM
100 W Walnut St, Pasadena (91124-0001)
PHONE..................................626 440-2000
Mary Ann Hopkins, *Manager*
Ozzie Gallo, *Controller*
EMP: 99
SALES (est): 49.9K **Privately Held**
SIC: 8741 8711 Business management; engineering services

(P-26974)
PACIFIC VENTURES LTD
Also Called: Jacmar Companies, The
2200 W Valley Blvd, Alhambra
(91803-1928)
PHONE..................................626 576-0737
William H Tilley, *CEO*
Jim Dalpozzo, *President*
Randy Hill, *Exec VP*
EMP: 250 EST: 1976
SQ FT: 20,000
SALES (est): 11.4MM **Privately Held**
SIC: 8741 6722 Restaurant management; management investment, open-end

(P-26975)
PACKARD HOSPITALITY GROUP LLC
9555 Chesapeake Dr # 202, San Diego
(92123-6301)
PHONE..................................858 277-4305
Michael Goldstein,
Steve Carr,
Michael Hercbergs, *Manager*
EMP: 120
SQ FT: 4,000
SALES: 75MM **Privately Held**
SIC: 8741 Hotel or motel management

(P-26976)
PACWEND INC
Also Called: Wendy's
1308 Kansas Ave Ste 6, Modesto
(95351-1530)
PHONE..................................209 577-6690
Joe Johal, *CEO*
EMP: 65
SALES (est): 2.1MM **Privately Held**
SIC: 8741 Restaurant management

(P-26977)
PACWEND III INC
Also Called: Wendy's
1308 Kansas Ave Ste 6, Modesto
(95351-1530)
PHONE..................................209 577-6690
Joe Johal, *CEO*
EMP: 100
SALES (est): 3.9MM **Privately Held**
SIC: 8741 Restaurant management

(P-26978)
PAMA MANAGEMENT CO
123 N Inez St Ste 16, Hemet (92543-4169)
PHONE..................................951 929-0340
EMP: 50
SALES (est): 2.4MM **Privately Held**
SIC: 8741

(P-26979)
PARAMUNT MADOWS NURSING CTR LP
Also Called: Affinity Health Care
7039 Alondra Blvd, Paramount
(90723-3925)
PHONE..................................562 531-0990
Carlos Aragon, *Administration*
EMP: 99 EST: 2015
SQ FT: 10,000
SALES (est): 2.8MM **Privately Held**
SIC: 8741 Nursing & personal care facility management

(P-26980)
PARSONS CONSTRUCTORS INC
Also Called: Operations/Risk Group
100 W Walnut St, Pasadena (91124-0001)
PHONE..................................626 440-2000
Chuck Harrington, *CEO*
Robert Camp, *Admin Sec*
EMP: 5905
SALES (est): 98.4MM
SALES (corp-wide): 3.1B **Privately Held**
SIC: 8741 8711 Management services; engineering services
PA: The Parsons Corporation
100 W Walnut St
Pasadena CA 91124
626 440-2000

(P-26981)
PARTHENON DCS HOLDINGS LLC
4 Embarcadero Ctr, San Francisco
(94111-4106)
PHONE..................................925 960-4800
EMP: 1400
SALES (est): 25.2MM **Privately Held**
SIC: 8741 Financial management for business

(P-26982)
PATEL BROTHERS INC
Also Called: Burger King
693 Hillcrest Ter, Fremont (94539-6224)
PHONE..................................510 590-6914
Jayant F Patel, *CEO*
Pyaneta Patel, *President*
Anju Chugh, *Manager*
EMP: 150
SALES (est): 85.4K **Privately Held**
SIC: 8741 5812 Restaurant management; fast-food restaurant, independent

(P-26983)
PATHWAY CAPITAL MANAGEMENT LP (PA)
18575 Jamboree Rd Ste 700, Irvine
(92612-2546)
PHONE..................................949 622-1000
Milt M Best,
Gerard Branka, *President*
Linda Chaffin, *Senior VP*
John Brescia, *Vice Pres*
Paul De Groot, *Vice Pres*
EMP: 100
SQ FT: 13,302
SALES (est): 15.1MM **Privately Held**
WEB: www.pathwaycapital.com
SIC: 8741 6282 Financial management for business; investment advice

(P-26984)
PEN-CAL ADMINISTRATORS INC
Also Called: P C A
7633 Suthfront Rd Ste 120, Livermore
(94551)
PHONE..................................925 251-3400
Kirk Penland, *CEO*
Sergio Amiri, *Vice Pres*
Steve Schwaderer, *Vice Pres*
Christian Penland, *Executive*
Dan Golesh, *Managing Dir*
EMP: 75
SQ FT: 15,000

SALES (est): 10.3MM
SALES (corp-wide): 8.6B **Publicly Held**
WEB: www.pencal.com
SIC: 8741 Financial management for business
PA: Voya Financial, Inc.
230 Park Ave Fl 14
New York NY 10169
212 309-8200

(P-26985)
PHYSICIAN MANAGEMENT GROUP INC
Also Called: Childrens Specialist San Diego
3860 Calle Fortunada # 210, San Diego
(92123-4800)
PHONE..................................858 309-6300
Fax: 858 309-6298
EMP: 105
SALES (est): 6.5MM **Privately Held**
WEB: www.pmgservices.org
SIC: 8741

(P-26986)
PHYSICIAN WEBLINK OF CAL (HQ)
7 Technology Dr, Irvine (92618-2302)
PHONE..................................949 923-3201
Jay Cohen, *President*
Bartley Asner, *CEO*
Jacob Furgacth, *COO*
Richard Greene, *CFO*
EMP: 165
SQ FT: 25,000
SALES (est): 4.9MM **Privately Held**
SIC: 8741 Business management

(P-26987)
PIERCEY MANAGEMENT SVCS INC (PA)
Also Called: Piercey Automotive Group
16901 Millikan Ave, Irvine (92606-5011)
PHONE..................................949 379-3701
William R Piercey, *President*
Tom A Chadwell, *CFO*
Tom Chadwell, *CFO*
Bill Clements, *Info Tech Dir*
Rich Dusablon, *Prgrmr*
EMP: 54 EST: 1994
SALES (est): 62.1MM **Privately Held**
WEB: www.pierceyautomotivegroup.com
SIC: 8741 Management services

(P-26988)
PIONEER HEALTH CARE SERVICES
1640 School St Ste 100, Moraga
(94556-1119)
PHONE..................................925 631-9100
Charles Patterson, *President*
EMP: 200
SQ FT: 2,300
SALES (est): 6.7MM **Privately Held**
WEB: www.pioneerhealthcareservices.com
SIC: 8741 Hospital management; nursing & personal care facility management

(P-26989)
PK MANAGEMENT LLC
15301 Ventura Blvd # 570, Sherman Oaks
(91403-3102)
PHONE..................................818 808-0600
Robert Krensky, *Mng Member*
Gregory Perlman,
EMP: 500
SALES (est): 21.9MM **Privately Held**
SIC: 8741 Business management

(P-26990)
PRE CON INDUSTRIES INC
Also Called: Premier Drywall
514 Work St, Salinas (93901-4350)
P.O. Box 5728, Santa Maria (93456-5728)
PHONE..................................805 345-3147
John Amburgey, *CEO*
Jose Rosas, *Vice Pres*
EMP: 50
SALES (est): 931.4K **Privately Held**
SIC: 8741 Management services

P
R
O
D
U
C
T
S

&

S
V
C
S

(P-26991)
PREMIER HLTHCARE SOLUTIONS INC
Also Called: Premier IMS Insurance Services
12225 El Camino Real, San Diego
(92130-2084)
PHONE..................................858 569-8629
Susan Devore, *Branch Mgr*
EMP: 305
SALES (corp-wide): 1.4B **Publicly Held**
SIC: 8741 Management services
HQ: Premier Healthcare Solutions, Inc.
13034 Balntyn Corp Pl
Charlotte NC 28277
704 357-0022

(P-26992)
PRIMARY CARE ASSOD MED GROUP (PA)
1635 Lake Marcos Dr # 201, San Marcos (92078-4661)
PHONE..................................760 471-7505
Robert Mongeon, *President*
EMP: 70
SALES (est): 6.6MM **Privately Held**
SIC: 8741 Administrative management

(P-26993)
PRIMARY PROVIDER MGT CO INC (PA)
Also Called: Ppmc
2115 Compton Ave Ste 301, Corona
(92881-7272)
PHONE..................................951 280-7700
Robert Dukes, *CEO*
Maureen B Tyson, *President*
Renee Szafirowski, *Manager*
EMP: 195
SQ FT: 23,500
SALES (est): 23MM **Privately Held**
WEB: www.missionmedicalgroup.net
SIC: 8741 Business management

(P-26994)
PRIMED MGT CONSULTING SVCS INC
2409 Camino Ramon, San Ramon
(94583-4285)
P.O. Box 5080 (94583-0980)
PHONE..................................925 327-6710
Cardoza Darryl, *CEO*
Steve McDermott, *President*
Tim Richards, *CFO*
Robert Ramsey, *Vice Pres*
Vrajeta Joshi, *Program Mgr*
EMP: 500
SQ FT: 30,000
SALES (est): 53.9MM **Privately Held**
SIC: 8741 8742 Management services;
management consulting services

(P-26995)
PRO UNLIMITED INC
1350 Bayshore Hwy Ste 350, Burlingame
(94010-1831)
PHONE..................................650 344-1099
Allie Shlomo, *COO*
EMP: 50 **Privately Held**
SIC: 8741 Financial management for business
PA: Pro Unlimited, Inc.
7777 Glades Rd Ste 208
Boca Raton FL 33434

(P-26996)
PRO-MED HLTH CARE ADMNISTRATOR
4150 Concours Ste 100, Ontario
(91764-5914)
PHONE..................................909 932-1045
Kit Thapar, *CEO*
Jeereddi A Prasad, *President*
EMP: 75
SQ FT: 20,000
SALES (est): 1.7MM **Privately Held**
WEB: www.promedhealth.com
SIC: 8741 Administrative management
PA: Pamona Valley Medical Group Inc
9302 Pttsbrgh Ave Ste 220
Rancho Cucamonga CA 91730

(P-26997)
PROACTIVE BUS SOLUTIONS INC
428 13th St Fl 5, Oakland (94612-2617)
PHONE..................................510 302-0120
Deidrie Towery, *CEO*
Jay A Copeland, *CFO*
Don Gholston, *Office Mgr*
Proactive Dennawi, *Admin Asst*
Gina Salazar, *Admin Asst*
EMP: 250 EST: 1998
SQ FT: 3,000
SALES: 10MM **Privately Held**
WEB: www.proactiveok.com
SIC: 8741 8742 Management services;
business consultant

(P-26998)
PROACTIVE RISK MANAGEMENT INC
1111 S Grand Ave Apt 611, Los Angeles
(90015-2763)
PHONE..................................213 840-8856
Benoit Grenier, *CEO*
Simon Talbot, *IT/INT Sup*
EMP: 100
SALES: 15MM **Privately Held**
SIC: 8741 Business management

(P-26999)
PROFESSIONAL GOLF MGT LLC
49155 Vista Estrella, La Quinta
(92253-6343)
P.O. Box 5566 (92248-5565)
PHONE..................................760 564-0804
Raymond Holohan, *Mng Member*
Carol Holohan,
EMP: 70
SALES (est): 5.8MM **Privately Held**
WEB:
www.professionalgolfmanagement.com
SIC: 8741 Management services

(P-27000)
PROJECT MANAGEMENT INSTITUTE
8895 Towne Centre Dr, San Diego
(92122-5542)
PHONE..................................760 458-6198
Tieman Chang, *Vice Pres*
EMP: 99
SALES: 249.5K **Privately Held**
SIC: 8741 Office management

(P-27001)
PROSPECT MEDICAL GROUP INC (HQ)
1920 E 17th St Ste 200, Santa Ana
(92705-8626)
PHONE..................................714 796-5900
Jacob Y Terner MD, *President*
Mitchell Lew, *CEO*
Mike Heather, *CFO*
Lourdes Alberto, *Vice Pres*
Rick Jacob, *Vice Pres*
EMP: 350
SQ FT: 2,420
SALES (est): 31.6MM
SALES (corp-wide): 815.3MM **Privately Held**
WEB: www.prospectcorona.com
SIC: 8741 Hospital management; nursing & personal care facility management
PA: Prospect Medical Holdings, Inc.
3415 S Sepulveda Blvd # 9
Los Angeles CA 90034
310 943-4500

(P-27002)
PROSPECT MEDICAL SYSTEMS INC (HQ)
Also Called: Genesis Health Care
600 City Pkwy W Ste 800, Orange
(92868-2948)
PHONE..................................714 667-8156
Mitchell Lew MD, *CEO*
Eric Samuels, *President*
Fitsum Tesfay, *Senior VP*
Ryan Bayne, *Vice Pres*
Rosa Catalano, *Vice Pres*
EMP: 121

SALES (est): 23.5MM
SALES (corp-wide): 815.3MM **Privately Held**
SIC: 8741 Hospital management; nursing & personal care facility management
PA: Prospect Medical Holdings, Inc.
3415 S Sepulveda Blvd # 9
Los Angeles CA 90034
310 943-4500

(P-27003)
PROVIDENCE HEALTH SYSTEM
Little Company Mary Pathology
4101 Torrance Blvd, Torrance
(90503-4607)
PHONE..................................310 303-6970
Angie Bugg, *Branch Mgr*
Kim Giles, *Executive Asst*
Toni Spencer, *Analyst*
EMP: 102
SALES (corp-wide): 17.6B **Privately Held**
SIC: 8741 8071 Hospital management;
pathological laboratory
HQ: Providence Health System-Southern California
1801 Lind Ave Sw
Renton WA 98057
425 525-3355

(P-27004)
PROVIDENT FINANCIAL MANAGEMENT
3130 Wilshire Blvd # 600, Santa Monica
(90403-2349)
P.O. Box 4084 (90411-4084)
PHONE..................................310 282-0477
Ivan Axelrod, *Managing Prtnr*
Barry Siegel, *Partner*
EMP: 95
SQ FT: 34,000
SALES (est): 2.7MM **Privately Held**
WEB: www.providentfm.com
SIC: 8741 Financial management for business

(P-27005)
PS24 INC
Also Called: Grove - Design District, The
65 Division St, San Francisco
(94103-5215)
PHONE..................................415 834-5105
Kenneth Zankel, *Principal*
Charles Baldwin, *General Mgr*
EMP: 100 EST: 2017
SALES: 500K **Privately Held**
SIC: 8741 Restaurant management

(P-27006)
PTR GROUP INC
Also Called: Glad I'M Not Driving.com
652 S Joyce Ave, Rialto (92376-7178)
PHONE..................................951 965-1822
Paul Rodriguez, *President*
EMP: 50
SALES (est): 1.3MM **Privately Held**
SIC: 8741 7389 Business management;

(P-27007)
R & V MANAGEMENT CORPORATION
768 Hollister St, San Diego (92154-1333)
PHONE..................................619 429-3305
EMP: 61
SALES (corp-wide): 34.3MM **Privately Held**
SIC: 8741 Management services
PA: R & V Management Corporation
3444 Camno Dl Rio N 202
San Diego CA 92108
619 285-5500

(P-27008)
RADNET MANAGEMENT INC
Also Called: Modesto Imaging Center
157 E Coolidge Ave, Modesto
(95350-4504)
PHONE..................................209 524-6800
Kim Davis, *Branch Mgr*
EMP: 60 **Publicly Held**
WEB: www.radnetmgt.com
SIC: 8741 Management services
HQ: Radnet Management, Inc.
1510 Cotner Ave
Los Angeles CA 90025
310 445-2800

(P-27009)
RADNET MANAGEMENT INC
8750 Wilshire Blvd # 100, Beverly Hills
(90211-2708)
PHONE..................................323 549-3000
Taryn D Dartz, *Branch Mgr*
EMP: 100 **Publicly Held**
WEB: www.radnetmgt.com
SIC: 8741 Management services
HQ: Radnet Management, Inc.
1510 Cotner Ave
Los Angeles CA 90025
310 445-2800

(P-27010)
RADY CHLD HOSPITAL-SAN DIEGO
Also Called: Bernardy Ctr For Medcly Frgled
8022 Birmingham Dr # 22, San Diego
(92123-2707)
PHONE..................................858 966-5833
Kathleen Sellick, *Manager*
Kim Looney, *Software Dev*
Xenia Hom, *Med Doctor*
Amanda Abbott, *Counsel*
Pamela Dixon, *Director*
EMP: 60 **Privately Held**
SIC: 8741 8051 Nursing & personal care facility management; skilled nursing care facilities
HQ: Rady Children's Hospital-San Diego
3020 Childrens Way
San Diego CA 92123
858 576-1700

(P-27011)
RAINMAKER SYSTEMS INC
Also Called: Rmkr
1821 S Bascom Ave Ste 385, Campbell
(95008-2309)
PHONE..................................408 659-1800
Terry Lydon, *CEO*
Bryant Tolles, *CFO*
EMP: 150
SALES: 17.6MM **Privately Held**
WEB: www.rmkr.com
SIC: 8741 8742 Management services;
marketing consulting services; sales (including sales management) consultant

(P-27012)
RAYMOND GROUP (PA)
Also Called: Orange Cnty George M Raymond N
520 W Walnut Ave, Orange (92868-5008)
P.O. Box 1727 (92856-0727)
PHONE..................................714 771-7670
Travis Winsor, *CEO*
James Watson, *President*
Mary Raymond, *Treasurer*
Buster Peterson, *Exec VP*
Kendra Eilers, *Senior VP*
EMP: 95
SQ FT: 20,000
SALES (est): 35.5MM **Privately Held**
SIC: 8741 Construction management

(P-27013)
REIGN ACCESSORIES INC
4000 Redondo Beach Ave, Redondo Beach
(90278-1109)
PHONE..................................310 297-6400
Jon Hirschberg, *President*
EMP: 50
SALES (est): 2MM **Privately Held**
WEB: www.rainforestventures.com
SIC: 8741 Business management

(P-27014)
RELIABLE INTERIORS INC
104 S Maple St, Corona (92880-1704)
P.O. Box 2618 (92878-2618)
PHONE..................................951 371-3390
Gerald C Crowther, *President*
William J Klotz, *President*
Glenn L Crowther, *Vice Pres*
Ralph G Prentiss, *Vice Pres*
Lee Scott, *Vice Pres*
EMP: 200
SALES (est): 7.6MM **Privately Held**
SIC: 8741 1742 Construction management; drywall

1144   2019 Directory of California
Wholesalers and Services Companies   ▲ = Import ▼=Export
◆ =Import/Export

(P-27015)
RENOVO SOLUTIONS LLC
4 Executive Cir Ste 185, Irvine
(92614-6791)
PHONE.............................714 599-7969
Sandy Morford, *CEO*
Haresh Saitiani, *COO*
Haresh Satiani, *COO*
Don Carson, *Exec VP*
Donald K Carson, *Vice Pres*
EMP: 300
SQ FT: 5,400
SALES: 70MM **Privately Held**
SIC: 8741 Hospital management

(P-27016)
RESIDNTIAL ALZHEIMERS CARE INC
9619 Chesapeake Dr # 103, San Diego
(92123-1368)
PHONE.............................858 565-4424
William M Chance, *President*
EMP: 180
SQ FT: 9,000
SALES (est): 4.5MM **Privately Held**
SIC: 8741 Nursing & personal care facility
management

(P-27017)
RESPONSELOGIX INC
2001 Gateway Pl Ste 750w, San Jose
(95110-1080)
PHONE.............................408 220-6505
Lionel Thomas Mohr, *CEO*
EMP: 150
SALES (corp-wide): 19.9MM **Privately Held**
SIC: 8741 Management services
PA: Responselogix, Inc.
6991 E Camelback Rd B300
Scottsdale AZ 85251
408 220-6545

(P-27018)
RHS CORP
Also Called: Redlands Community Hospital
350 Terracina Blvd, Redlands
(92373-4850)
PHONE.............................909 335-5500
James R Holmes, *President*
Gary Marais, *Research*
Mohsen Mabudian, *Allrgy & Immnlg*
John Zdrojewski, *Dermatology*
James Agee, *Urology*
EMP: 1450
SQ FT: 265,000
SALES: 256.8K **Privately Held**
SIC: 8741 Hospital management

(P-27019)
RROMEO CORPORATION
535 Anton Blvd Ste 200, Costa Mesa
(92626-7680)
PHONE.............................714 640-3800
Richard Putnam, *Branch Mgr*
John Casasante, *Vice Pres*
EMP: 80
SALES (corp-wide): 11.5B **Privately Held**
WEB: www.rref.com
SIC: 8741 6531 Management services;
real estate managers
HQ: The Rromeo Corporation
101 California St Fl 24
San Francisco CA 94111
415 781-3300

(P-27020)
S W K PROPERTIES LLC (PA)
Also Called: Sheraton Ontario Airport Hotel
3807 Wilshire Blvd # 1226, Los Angeles
(90010-3101)
PHONE.............................213 383-9204
Eric Cha,
EMP: 70
SQ FT: 3,000
SALES (est): 10MM **Privately Held**
SIC: 8741 7011 Hotel or motel manage-
ment; hotels

(P-27021)
SAN JOSE ARENA MANAGEMENT LLC
44388 Old Warm Sprng Blvd, Fremont
(94538-6148)
PHONE.............................510 623-7200

Greg Jamison, *Branch Mgr*
EMP: 128
SALES (corp-wide): 16.8MM **Privately Held**
SIC: 8741 Management services
PA: San Jose Arena Management, Llc
525 W Santa Clara St
San Jose CA 95113
408 287-7070

(P-27022)
SANTA CLARITA HEALTH CARE ASSN (PA)
23845 Mcbean Pkwy, Santa Clarita
(91355-2001)
PHONE.............................661 253-8000
Roger Seaver, *President*
Paul Salomon, *COO*
C R Hudson, *CFO*
James D Hicken, *Treasurer*
John Barstis, *Admin Sec*
EMP: 65
SQ FT: 130,000
SALES (est): 18.9MM **Privately Held**
SIC: 8741 Hospital management; nursing
& personal care facility management

(P-27023)
SCCH INC
Also Called: Courtyard Care Center
1880 Dawson Ave, Signal Hill
(90755-5913)
PHONE.............................562 494-5188
Julie Javier, *Administration*
Spencer Olsen, *Treasurer*
EMP: 99
SALES (est): 6.9MM **Privately Held**
WEB: www.nahci.com
SIC: 8741 8052 8051 Management serv-
ices; intermediate care facilities; skilled
nursing care facilities

(P-27024)
SCRIPPS CLINIC FOUNDATION
12395 El Camino Real, San Diego
(92130-3082)
PHONE.............................858 554-9000
Dr Hugh Greenway, *CEO*
Sheldon Kleiman, *Diag Radio*
EMP: 1600
SALES (est): 78.2MM
SALES (corp-wide): 2.9B **Privately Held**
WEB: www.scripps.org
SIC: 8741 Management services
PA: Scripps Health
10140 Campus Point Dr Ax415
San Diego CA 92121
800 727-4777

(P-27025)
SEABREEZE MANAGEMENT COMPANY (PA)
26840 Aliso Viejo Pkwy # 100, Aliso Viejo
(92656-2624)
PHONE.............................949 855-1800
Isaiah S Henry, *CEO*
Susan Larson, *President*
Brandon Tryon, *Exec VP*
Eron Kaylor, *Vice Pres*
Sarah Atha, *General Mgr*
EMP: 69
SQ FT: 22,000
SALES (est): 17.3MM **Privately Held**
WEB: www.seabreezemgmt.com
SIC: 8741 Management services

(P-27026)
SETHI MANAGEMENT INC
6100 Innovation Way, Carlsbad
(92009-1728)
P.O. Box 235927, Encinitas (92023-5927)
PHONE.............................760 692-5288
Jeetander Sethi, *CEO*
Gaurav Sethi, *Vice Pres*
EMP: 154
SALES (est): 40MM **Privately Held**
SIC: 8741 Business management

(P-27027)
SEVILLE GROUP (PA)
Also Called: S G I
199 S Hudson Ave Ste 101, Pasadena
(91101-2917)
PHONE.............................626 395-7474
Connie Flores, *CEO*
Rene J Flores Sr, *President*

Lawrence R Varone, *CFO*
Lawrence Varone, *CFO*
Lance Jackson, *Senior VP*
EMP: 83
SQ FT: 5,000
SALES (est): 9.4MM **Privately Held**
WEB: www.sgicm.com
SIC: 8741 8742 8711 Construction man-
agement; construction project manage-
ment consultant; engineering services

(P-27028)
SHELL VACATIONS LLC
Also Called: Donatello
501 Post St, San Francisco (94102-1228)
PHONE.............................415 441-7100
Alan Hompkins, *Principal*
EMP: 60 **Publicly Held**
SIC: 8741 7011 7389 Hotel or motel man-
agement; hotels & motels; office facilities
& secretarial service rental
HQ: Shell Vacations L.L.C.
40 Skokie Blvd Ste 350
Northbrook IL 60062

(P-27029)
SILVER CREEK HOME OWNERS
Also Called: Silver Crk Vlly Ctry CLB HM Ow
1935 Dry Creek Rd Ste 203, Campbell
(95008-3631)
PHONE.............................408 559-1977
Tim Johnson, *CEO*
Marianne Hudkins, *Principal*
EMP: 50
SALES (est): 3.5MM **Privately Held**
SIC: 8741 Management services

(P-27030)
SIMPSON & SIMPSON
633 W 5th St Ste 3320, Los Angeles
(90071-3542)
PHONE.............................213 736-6664
Brainard Simpson, *Principal*
Carl P Simpson, *Principal*
Harverth Cameron, *Auditor*
Gunther Liedl, *Sr Project Mgr*
Etta Hur, *Manager*
EMP: 61
SQ FT: 5,500
SALES (est): 7.4MM **Privately Held**
WEB: www.simpsonandsimpsoncpas.com
SIC: 8741 8721 Financial management for
business; accounting, auditing & book-
keeping; certified public accountant

(P-27031)
SMART MANAGEMENT & COMPANIES
Also Called: G Moroni Comp
1501 Corp Way Ste 200, Sacramento
(95831)
PHONE.............................916 392-3000
Tony Lutsi, *Owner*
Greg Moroni, *Co-Owner*
EMP: 400
SQ FT: 2,000
SALES (est): 15.1MM **Privately Held**
WEB: www.smartmanagement.us
SIC: 8741 8742 Management services;
management consulting services

(P-27032)
SMILE BRANDS GROUP INC (PA)
Also Called: Bright Now Dental
100 Spectrum Center Dr # 1500, Irvine
(92618-4962)
PHONE.............................714 668-1300
Steven C Bilt, *CEO*
Stan Andrakowicz, *President*
Bradley Schmidt, *CFO*
Victoria Harvey,
Yolanda Joblin, *Executive Asst*
EMP: 90
SQ FT: 15,000
SALES (est): 540.5MM **Privately Held**
WEB: www.brightnow.com
SIC: 8741 8021 Management services;
dental clinics & offices

(P-27033)
SMITH BROADCASTING GROUP INC (PA)
2315 Red Rose Way, Santa Barbara
(93109-1259)
PHONE.............................805 965-0400

Debrah Egar, *Exec Sec*
David A Fitz, *Vice Pres*
EMP: 165 EST: 1985
SALES (est): 15.2MM **Privately Held**
SIC: 8741 8742 Business management;
management consulting services

(P-27034)
SMITH BROTHERS RESTAURANT INC
100 Corson St Lbby, Pasadena
(91103-3854)
PHONE.............................626 577-2400
Robert Smith, *President*
Jason Tirona, *CFO*
Toni Taylor, *Executive*
Greg Smith, *Admin Sec*
EMP: 55
SALES (est): 5.5MM **Privately Held**
SIC: 8741 8742 8721 Restaurant man-
agement; management consulting serv-
ices; accounting, auditing & bookkeeping

(P-27035)
SNF MANAGEMENT
9200 W Sunset Blvd # 700, West Holly-
wood (90069-3502)
PHONE.............................310 385-1090
Lee Samson, *President*
Ken Cess, *Shareholder*
Lawrence Feigen, *COO*
Christine Houser, *CFO*
Heidi Capela, *Vice Pres*
EMP: 64
SALES (est): 13MM **Privately Held**
SIC: 8741 Management services

(P-27036)
SOC/GENERAL SERVICES/BPM
455 Golden Gate Ave # 2600, San Fran-
cisco (94102-3670)
PHONE.............................415 703-5341
Sam Flores, *General Mgr*
Paul Gates, *Technician*
Anthony Lewis, *Technician*
Angela Noble, *Technician*
Sylvia Smith, *Technician*
EMP: 60
SALES (est): 3.4MM **Privately Held**
SIC: 8741 Construction management

(P-27037)
SODEXO MANAGEMENT INC
Also Called: Cific Energy Center
851 Howard St, San Francisco
(94103-3009)
PHONE.............................925 325-9657
Jim Wasley, *Branch Mgr*
EMP: 82
SALES (corp-wide): 139.1MM **Privately Held**
SIC: 8741 Management services
HQ: Sodexo Management Inc.
9801 Washingtonian Blvd
Gaithersburg MD 20878

(P-27038)
SODEXO MANAGEMENT INC
1 University Cir, Turlock (95382-3200)
PHONE.............................209 667-3634
Tom Welton, *Manager*
EMP: 75
SALES (corp-wide): 139.1MM **Privately Held**
WEB: www.compass-mgmt.com
SIC: 8741 Management services
HQ: Sodexo Management Inc.
9801 Washingtonian Blvd
Gaithersburg MD 20878

(P-27039)
SODEXO OPERATIONS LLC
100 Campus Ctr Bldg 16, Seaside
(93955-8000)
PHONE.............................831 582-3838
Charles Wesley, *General Mgr*
EMP: 100
SALES (corp-wide): 139.1MM **Privately Held**
SIC: 8741 5812 Restaurant management;
eating places

PRODUCTS & SVCS

HQ: Sodexo Operations, Llc
9801 Washingtonian Blvd
Gaithersburg MD 20878
301 987-4000

(P-27040)
SOLPAC CONSTRUCTION INC
Also Called: SOLTEK PACIFIC CONSTRUC-
TION CO
2424 Congress St, San Diego
(92110-2819)
PHONE..............................619 296-6247
Stephen Thompson, *CEO*
Brandon Richie, *President*
Dave Carlin, *COO*
Kevin Cammall, *Vice Pres*
John Myers, *Vice Pres*
EMP: 235
SQ FT: 12,291
SALES: 154.7MM **Privately Held**
SIC: 8741 1542 1611 Construction man-
agement; commercial & office building
contractors; design & erection, combined:
non-residential; general contractor, high-
way & street construction

(P-27041)
**SOUTHERN CALIFORNIA
PHYSICIA**
6760 Top Gun St Ste 100, San Diego
(92121-4152)
PHONE..............................858 824-7000
Joyce Cook, *CEO*
Marcia Aeschaleman, *CFO*
Marcia Aeschleman, *CFO*
Patrick Rousseau, *Controller*
Arlys Bartholomew, *Director*
EMP: 65 EST: 1996
SQ FT: 17,000
SALES: 8.2MM **Privately Held**
WEB: www.scpmcs.org
SIC: 8741 Administrative management

(P-27042)
SOUTHERN IMPLANTS INC
5 Holland Ste 209, Irvine (92618-2576)
PHONE..............................949 273-8505
Michael Kehoe, *President*
Michael Nealon, *CFO*
EMP: 125
SALES (est): 249.9K **Privately Held**
SIC: 8741 Management services

(P-27043)
SRG MANAGEMENT LLC
500 Stevens Ave Ste 100, Solana Beach
(92075-2055)
PHONE..............................858 792-9300
Michael S Grust, *CEO*
EMP: 204
SALES (est): 41.9K
SALES (corp-wide): 94.1MM **Privately
Held**
SIC: 8741 Business management
HQ: Srg Holdings, Llc
500 Stevens Ave Ste 100
Solana Beach CA 92075
858 792-9300

(P-27044)
SRHT PROPERTY MGMT CO
1317 E 7th St, Los Angeles (90021-1101)
PHONE..............................213 683-0522
Michael Alvidrez, *Director*
Joanne Cohen, *Admin Asst*
EMP: 100 EST: 1994
SALES: 4.3MM **Privately Held**
SIC: 8741 Management services

(P-27045)
**STAN TASHMAN & ASSOCIATES
INC**
8675 Wash Blvd Ste 203, Culver City
(90232-7486)
PHONE..............................310 460-7600
Richard Tashman, *CEO*
Stan Tashman, *CFO*
Ty Olson, *Vice Pres*
EMP: 650
SQ FT: 14,000
SALES (est): 38.1MM **Privately Held**
WEB: www.tashman.com
SIC: 8741 Management services

(P-27046)
**STANFORD MANAGEMENT
COMPANY**
635 Knight Way, Stanford (94305-7297)
PHONE..............................650 721-2200
Rob Wallace, *CEO*
EMP: 60
SALES (est): 342.4K **Privately Held**
SIC: 8741 Management services

(P-27047)
**STARZZ MANAGEMENT
SERVICES (PA)**
528 Stonehaven Ct, Hayward
(94544-6696)
PHONE..............................510 632-5533
Monica Walton, *President*
Monica Thompkins, *CFO*
Joe Thompkins, *Vice Pres*
EMP: 92
SQ FT: 2,100
SALES (est): 6.1MM **Privately Held**
SIC: 8741 Management services

(P-27048)
STEWARDSHIP COMPANY LLC
1 Rancho San Carlos Rd, Carmel
(93923-7999)
PHONE..............................831 620-6700
Thomas A Gray,
Don W Wilcoxon,
EMP: 200
SQ FT: 2,000
SALES (est): 13MM **Privately Held**
SIC: 8741 Management services

(P-27049)
STRAIGHT LANDER INC
8335 W Sunset Blvd # 320, Los Angeles
(90069-1500)
PHONE..............................323 337-9075
David Yashar, *President*
EMP: 58 EST: 1998
SALES (est): 2MM **Privately Held**
SIC: 8741 Business management

(P-27050)
**SUN MAR MANAGEMENT
SERVICES**
Also Called: Laurel Convelescent Center
7509 Laurel Ave, Fontana (92336-2315)
PHONE..............................909 822-8066
Blaine Hendrickson, *President*
EMP: 86
SALES (corp-wide): 50.5MM **Privately
Held**
WEB: www.extendedcarehospital.com
SIC: 8741 8051 Management services;
skilled nursing care facilities
PA: Sun Mar Management Services
3050 Saturn St Ste 201
Brea CA 92821
714 577-3880

(P-27051)
**SUN MAR MANAGEMENT
SERVICES**
Also Called: Sun Mar Health Care
3136 Del Mar Ave, Rosemead
(91770-2326)
PHONE..............................626 288-8353
Steve Montelli, *Administration*
EMP: 60
SALES (corp-wide): 50.5MM **Privately
Held**
WEB: www.extendedcarehospital.com
SIC: 8741 8051 Management services;
skilled nursing care facilities
PA: Sun Mar Management Services
3050 Saturn St Ste 201
Brea CA 92821
714 577-3880

(P-27052)
**SUN MAR MANAGEMENT
SERVICES**
Also Called: North Valley Nursing Center
7660 Wyngate St, Tujunga (91042-1736)
PHONE..............................818 352-1454
Katherine Rodriguez, *Manager*
EMP: 100

SALES (corp-wide): 50.5MM **Privately
Held**
WEB: www.extendedcarehospital.com
SIC: 8741 8059 Management services;
convalescent home
PA: Sun Mar Management Services
3050 Saturn St Ste 201
Brea CA 92821
714 577-3880

(P-27053)
**SUNAMERICA INVESTMENTS
INC (DH)**
1 Sun America Ctr Fl 37, Los Angeles
(90067-6103)
PHONE..............................310 772-6000
Eli Broad, *President*
EMP: 80
SQ FT: 76,000
SALES: 2B
SALES (corp-wide): 49.5B **Publicly Held**
WEB: www.opfa.com
SIC: 8741 6211 6282 7311 Administrative
management; financial management for
business; security brokers & dealers; in-
vestment advisory service; advertising
agencies
HQ: Sunamerica Inc.
1 Sun America Ctr Fl 38
Los Angeles CA 90067
310 772-6000

(P-27054)
**SUPERIOR SUPPORT SERVICES
INC**
Also Called: Superior Services
702 Civic Center Dr, Oceanside
(92054-2504)
PHONE..............................559 458-0507
Sheila Guarderas, *President*
EMP: 500
SQ FT: 6,000
SALES: 17MM **Privately Held**
WEB: www.superiorservices.com
SIC: 8741 7349 Restaurant management;
janitorial service, contract basis

(P-27055)
SYLMARK INC (PA)
Also Called: Sylmark Group
7821 Orion Ave Ste 200, Van Nuys
(91406-2032)
PHONE..............................818 217-2000
Peter Spiegel, *President*
Mark Funk, *CFO*
Steven Ober, *Vice Pres*
EMP: 90
SALES (est): 20MM **Privately Held**
SIC: 8741 Management services

(P-27056)
SYNERMED
711 W College St Fl 4, Los Angeles
(90012-3177)
P.O. Box 2002, Monterey Park (91754-
0952)
PHONE..............................213 626-4556
John Edwards, *President*
Jonathan Kan, *Project Mgr*
Roberto Castellanos, *Technology*
Kate Good, *Human Resources*
EMP: 65
SALES (est): 5.8MM **Privately Held**
SIC: 8741 Hospital management

(P-27057)
**T3W BUSINESS SOLUTIONS
INC**
3921 Ampudia St, San Diego (92110-2813)
PHONE..............................619 298-0888
Lisa Carman, *President*
Holly Andrews, *CFO*
Deb West, *Contract Mgr*
EMP: 65
SQ FT: 2,523
SALES: 4.6MM **Privately Held**
SIC: 8741 8713 8711 7371 Business
management; surveying services; engi-
neering services; custom computer pro-
gramming services; data processing &
preparation; facilities support services

(P-27058)
TCM GROUP LLC
3130 Inland Empire Blvd, Ontario
(91764-6569)
PHONE..............................909 527-8580
Rima Tahan, *President*
S Michael Tahan, *Vice Pres*
Carol Larsen, *Administration*
Bryce Nielsen, *Controller*
Ivan Benavidez, *Sr Project Mgr*
EMP: 50
SALES (est): 2.2MM
SALES (corp-wide): 483.7MM **Publicly
Held**
SIC: 8741 8742 Construction manage-
ment; construction project management
consultant
PA: Hill International, Inc.
2005 Market St Fl 17
Philadelphia PA 19103
215 309-7700

(P-27059)
TCV MANAGEMENT 2004 LLC
528 Ramona St, Palo Alto (94301-1709)
PHONE..............................650 614-8200
Jay C Hoag, *Manager*
EMP: 50
SALES: 2.5MM **Privately Held**
SIC: 8741 Management services

(P-27060)
**TEXTAINER GROUP HOLDINGS
LTD (HQ)**
650 California St Fl 16, San Francisco
(94108-2720)
PHONE..............................415 434-0551
John A Maccarone, *President*
Jim Hoelter, *Bd of Directors*
Alvin Chong, *Vice Pres*
Lionel Vargas, *Admin Asst*
Lynda Kwong, *Controller*
EMP: 55 EST: 1994
SALES (est): 10.3MM **Privately Held**
SIC: 8741 Business management

(P-27061)
**THE FOR HOSPITAL
COMMITTEE (DH)**
Also Called: Valley Care Health System, The
5555 W Las Positas Blvd, Pleasanton
(94588-4000)
PHONE..............................925 847-3000
Scott Gregerson, *CEO*
Gina Teeples, *Officer*
Doreen Montemayer, *QC Dir*
Eileen Shaw,
Christopher Cooley,
EMP: 500
SALES (est): 101MM
SALES (corp-wide): 5.6B **Privately Held**
WEB: www.valleycare.com
SIC: 8741 8062 Hospital management;
general medical & surgical hospitals
HQ: Stanford Health Care
300 Pasteur Dr
Stanford CA 94305
650 723-4000

(P-27062)
**TISHMAN CONSTRUCTION
CORP CAL**
444 S Flower St Ste 2500, Los Angeles
(90071-2926)
PHONE..............................213 542-6400
John L Tishman, *Ch of Bd*
Larry Schwarzwalder, *Treasurer*
Thomas McCaslin, *Exec VP*
EMP: 70
SQ FT: 14,000
SALES (est): 6.1MM
SALES (corp-wide): 20.1B **Publicly Held**
SIC: 8741 Construction management
HQ: Tishman Realty & Construction Co,
Inc.
100 Park Ave Fl 5
New York NY 10017
212 708-6800

(P-27063)
**TOFASCO OF AMERICA INC
(PA)**
1661 Fairplex Dr, La Verne (91750-5871)
PHONE..............................909 392-8282
Edward Zheng, *President*

Xiu Jun Liang, *Vice Pres*
Albert Sheih, *Vice Pres*
Babby Chao, *Administration*
Vanessa Chan, *MIS Dir*
EMP: 60
SQ FT: 160,554
SALES: 9MM **Privately Held**
SIC: 8741 Financial management for business

(P-27064)
TOP OF MARKET
Also Called: San Diego Fish Market
750 N Harbor Dr, San Diego (92101-5806)
PHONE...................................619 234-4867
Jim Wentler, *Owner*
Alfonso Deanda, *Owner*
Bob Wilson, *Owner*
Fred Ducket, *Partner*
Dan Houte, *Manager*
EMP: 280
SALES (est): 10.1MM **Privately Held**
SIC: 8741 5813 Restaurant management; cocktail lounge

(P-27065)
TRADESMEN INTERNATIONAL LLC
15500 Rockfield Blvd, Irvine (92618-2725)
PHONE...................................949 588-3280
Jason Hammer, *Branch Mgr*
EMP: 60 **Privately Held**
SIC: 8741 7361 Construction management; employment agencies
PA: Tradesmen International, Llc
9760 Shepard Rd
Macedonia OH 44056

(P-27066)
TRI-MARINE FISHING MGT LLC
Also Called: Trimarine Fish Group
220 Cannery St, San Pedro (90731-7308)
PHONE...................................310 547-1144
Vince Torre, *Manager*
Phil Roberts, *Principal*
Kevin Stark, *Technology*
Renato Curto,
Renato C Member,
EMP: 50
SQ FT: 8,000
SALES (est): 1.8MM **Privately Held**
SIC: 8741 Management services

(P-27067)
TRICOM MANAGEMENT INC
Also Called: United Owners Services
4025 E La Palma Ave # 101, Anaheim (92807-1734)
PHONE...................................714 630-2029
Woody Cary, *President*
Fernando Celis, *Vice Pres*
Tom Jay, *Manager*
EMP: 200
SQ FT: 9,000
SALES (est): 19.3MM **Privately Held**
SIC: 8741 7389 Management services; time-share condominium exchange

(P-27068)
TRILAR MANAGEMENT GROUP
1025 S Gilbert St, Hemet (92543-7090)
PHONE...................................951 925-2021
Susan A York, *Branch Mgr*
EMP: 124
SALES (corp-wide): 9.1MM **Privately Held**
SIC: 8741 Business management
PA: Trilar Management Group
2101 Camino Vida Roble A
Carlsbad CA 92011
760 603-3205

(P-27069)
TRITON MANAGEMENT SERVICES LLC
1000 Aviara Dr Ste 300, Carlsbad (92011-4218)
PHONE...................................760 431-9911
Bob Lloyd, *Principal*
Dave Schaefer, *CFO*
Peter Botz, *General Counsel*
EMP: 53
SALES (est): 9.6MM **Privately Held**
SIC: 8741 Management services

(P-27070)
TROON GOLF LLC
Also Called: Indian Wells Golf Resort
44500 Indian Wells Ln, Indian Wells (92210-8746)
PHONE...................................760 346-4653
Rich Carter, *General Mgr*
Brian Hampson, *Director*
Beth Widdowson, *Associate*
EMP: 130 **Privately Held**
WEB: www.americangolf.com
SIC: 8741 7997 Management services; country club, membership
PA: Troon Golf, L.L.C.
15044 N Scottsdale Rd # 300
Scottsdale AZ 85254

(P-27071)
TWENTY4SEVEN HOTELS CORP
520 Newport Center Dr # 520, Newport Beach (92660-7020)
PHONE...................................949 734-6400
David Wani, *CEO*
Drew Hardy, *President*
Leesa Gibbons, *Vice Pres*
Brett Myers, *General Mgr*
MBA Grant, *Finance*
EMP: 500
SQ FT: 15,000
SALES (est): 20.9MM **Privately Held**
SIC: 8741 Hotel or motel management

(P-27072)
UCD MC HOME CARE SERVICES
Also Called: Uc David Home Care Services
3630 Business Dr, Sacramento (95820-2163)
PHONE...................................916 734-2458
Glenda Wegner, *Manager*
John McMillan, *Director*
EMP: 200
SALES (est): 8MM **Privately Held**
SIC: 8741 Nursing & personal care facility management

(P-27073)
UNITED BEHAVIORAL HEALTH
3111 Cmino Del Rio N 50, San Diego (92108)
P.O. Box 601370 (92160-1370)
PHONE...................................619 641-6800
Chris Janick, *Manager*
EMP: 100
SALES (corp-wide): 201.1B **Publicly Held**
WEB: www.unitedbehavioralhealth.com
SIC: 8741 8322 Nursing & personal care facility management; individual & family services
HQ: United Behavioral Health
425 Market St Fl 18
San Francisco CA 94105
415 547-1403

(P-27074)
UNITED BEHAVIORAL HEALTH (HQ)
425 Market St Fl 18, San Francisco (94105-2493)
PHONE...................................415 547-1403
Saul Feldman, *Ch of Bd*
Keith Dickson, *President*
Ann Mc Clanathan, *COO*
Karen Schievelbein, *CFO*
William Goldman Sr, *Exec VP*
EMP: 250
SQ FT: 20,000
SALES (est): 32.7MM
SALES (corp-wide): 201.1B **Publicly Held**
WEB: www.unitedbehavioralhealth.com
SIC: 8741 8742 Management services; management consulting services
PA: Unitedhealth Group Incorporated
9900 Bren Rd E Ste 300w
Minnetonka MN 55343
952 936-1300

(P-27075)
UNITED PARADYNE CORPORATION
P.O. Box 5368 (93150-5368)
PHONE...................................805 734-2359
Randy Cobb, *Manager*

EMP: 52 **Privately Held**
SIC: 8741 Management services
PA: United Paradyne Corporation
2370 Skyway Dr Ste 203
Santa Maria CA

(P-27076)
US SKILLSERVE INC (PA)
4115 E Broadway Ste A, Long Beach (90803-1532)
PHONE...................................562 930-0777
Simcha Mandeldaum, *CEO*
EMP: 1000
SQ FT: 1,000
SALES (est): 74.8MM **Privately Held**
SIC: 8741 Hospital management; nursing & personal care facility management

(P-27077)
USAG ANSBACH FINANCIAL MGT DIV
420 Montgomery St, San Francisco (94104-1207)
PHONE...................................210 466-1376
Karen McGrail, *Manager*
EMP: 99
SALES (est): 2.1MM **Privately Held**
SIC: 8741 Management services

(P-27078)
USAG RHEINLAND PFALZ FINCL MGT
420 Montgomery St, San Francisco (94104-1207)
PHONE...................................210 466-1376
Tanja Lee, *Manager*
EMP: 99
SALES (est): 5.4MM **Privately Held**
WEB: www.usajobs.org
SIC: 8741 Management services

(P-27079)
USAG VICENZA ITALY DMWR F M D
420 Montgomery St, San Francisco (94104-1207)
PHONE...................................210 466-1376
David Floyd, *Manager*
EMP: 99
SALES (est): 1.6MM **Privately Held**
SIC: 8741 Financial management for business

(P-27080)
USAG WIESBADEN FINCL MGT DIV
420 Montgomery St, San Francisco (94104-1207)
PHONE...................................210 466-1376
Sabine Norton, *Manager*
EMP: 99
SALES (est): 5.5MM **Privately Held**
SIC: 8741 Management services

(P-27081)
VALLEY MANAGEMENT SERVICES
Also Called: Valley Power System
425 S Hacienda Blvd, City of Industry (91745-1123)
PHONE...................................626 333-1243
H Clark Lee, *Chairman*
EMP: 425
SALES (est): 22.2MM **Privately Held**
SIC: 8741 Business management; administrative management

(P-27082)
VALLEY PHYSICIANS ALLIANCE
255 E Rver Pk Cir Ste 240, Fresno (93720)
P.O. Box 27500 (93729-7500)
PHONE...................................559 538-3000
Michelle Brown, *Opers Staff*
Duane Oswald, *President*
EMP: 81
SALES (est): 1.1MM **Privately Held**
SIC: 8741 Management services

(P-27083)
VANIR CONSTRUCTION MGT INC (PA)
4540 Duckhorn Dr Ste 300, Sacramento (95834-2597)
PHONE...................................916 444-3700
Dorene C Dominguez, *Ch of Bd*
John Kuprenas, *CEO*
Alex Leon, *CFO*
Ray Nez, *CFO*
Bruce Russo, *Executive*
EMP: 70
SQ FT: 16,000
SALES (est): 69.8MM **Privately Held**
WEB: www.vanir.com
SIC: 8741 Construction management

(P-27084)
VENDOR DIRECT SOLUTIONS LLC
515 S Figueroa St # 1900, Los Angeles (90071-3336)
PHONE...................................213 362-5622
Jules Buenabenta, *Principal*
Jim Young, *Exec VP*
Stephanie Simmons, *Human Resources*
Elysha Puga, *Marketing Staff*
Angel E Nevarez, *General Counsel*
EMP: 250
SQ FT: 1,200
SALES (est): 41.3MM **Privately Held**
SIC: 8741 Business management

(P-27085)
VENTURA MEDICAL MANAGEMENT LLC
2601 E Main St, Ventura (93003-2801)
PHONE...................................805 477-6220
Jim Malone,
Deborah Carlson MD,
Kent Coleman PHD,
John Pritchard MD,
EMP: 325
SALES (est): 11.3MM **Privately Held**
SIC: 8741 Hospital management

(P-27086)
VICTUS GROUP INC
2350 W Shaw Ave, Fresno (93711-3401)
PHONE...................................559 429-8080
Bob Young Yoon, *CEO*
EMP: 176
SALES: 2.8MM **Privately Held**
SIC: 8741 Hotel or motel management

(P-27087)
VIVA SOMA LESSEE INC
Also Called: Park Central Ht San Francisco
50 3rd St, San Francisco (94103-3106)
PHONE...................................415 974-6400
John Anderson, *Branch Mgr*
Christina Tang, *Human Res Mgr*
Jay Heidenreich, *Sales Dir*
Heather Knight, *Manager*
Henree Weiner, *Manager*
EMP: 511
SALES (corp-wide): 1.1B **Privately Held**
SIC: 8741 Hotel or motel management; restaurant management
HQ: Viva Soma Lessee, Inc.
7550 Wisconsin Ave Fl 10
Bethesda MD

(P-27088)
VPM MANAGEMENT INC
2400 Main St Ste 201, Irvine (92614-6271)
PHONE...................................949 863-1500
Philip H McNamee, *CEO*
Mark Ellis,
Steve Tomlin,
Scott J Barker, *Mng Member*
EMP: 150
SALES (est): 18.7MM **Privately Held**
SIC: 8741 Management services

(P-27089)
WARNER BROS DISTRIBUTING INC
Warner Bros. Pictures Domestic
4000 Warner Blvd Bldg 154, Burbank (91522-0002)
PHONE...................................818 954-6000
Dan Fellman, *Branch Mgr*
Jorge Ferran, *Manager*

**P
R
O
D
U
C
T
S

&

S
V
C
S**

EMP: 122
SALES (corp-wide): 160.5B **Publicly Held**
SIC: 8741 7822 Management services; distribution, exclusive of production: motion picture
HQ: Warner Bros. Distributing Inc.
　　4000 Warner Blvd
　　Burbank CA 91522

(P-27090)
WASTEXPERTS INCORPORATED
440 Boulder Ct Ste 200, Pleasanton (94566-8313)
P.O. Box 2099, Martinez (94553-0209)
PHONE.....................925 484-1057
David Lentz, *President*
Justin Costa, *Admin Mgr*
Mindy Santillan, *Admin Asst*
Alexandra White, *Portfolio Mgr*
Matt Liberatore, *Director*
EMP: 80
SALES (est): 11.2MM **Privately Held**
SIC: 8741 Management services

(P-27091)
WEALTH EDUCATORS INC
5209 Wilshire Blvd, Los Angeles (90036-4311)
PHONE.....................310 623-9145
Veronica Sesma, *CEO*
EMP: 112
SQ FT: 1,800
SALES (est): 3.8MM **Privately Held**
SIC: 8741 Financial management for business

(P-27092)
WESCO AIRCRAFT HOLDINGS INC (PA)
24911 Avenue Stanford, Valencia (91355-1281)
PHONE.....................661 775-7200
Todd S Renehan, *CEO*
Randy J Snyder, *Ch of Bd*
Alex Murray, *President*
Kerry A Shiba, *CFO*
Thomas Bancroft, *Bd of Directors*
EMP: 62
SALES: 1.4B **Publicly Held**
SIC: 8741 5072 Management services; hardware

(P-27093)
WESTERN MEDICAL MANAGEMENT LLC
3333 Michelson Dr Ste 735, Irvine (92612-7679)
PHONE.....................949 260-6575
Baruch Fogel, *Partner*
Rachel Fogel, *Partner*
EMP: 50
SALES (est): 3.9MM **Privately Held**
WEB: www.1wmm.com
SIC: 8741

(P-27094)
WESTERN NATIONAL CONTRACTORS
8 Executive Cir, Irvine (92614-6746)
PHONE.....................949 862-6200
Michael Hayde, *CEO*
Randy Avery, *Vice Pres*
John Townsend, *Vice Pres*
Jeffrey R Scott, *Admin Sec*
Larry Johnson, *Director*
EMP: 88
SALES (est): 16.4MM **Privately Held**
SIC: 8741 Construction management

(P-27095)
WESTLAKE DEVELOPMENT GROUP LLC
520 El Camino Real Fl 9, Belmont (94002)
PHONE.....................650 579-1010
T M Chang, *Branch Mgr*
EMP: 100
SQ FT: 600
SALES (corp-wide): 12.4MM **Privately Held**
WEB: www.westlake-global.com
SIC: 8741 Administrative management

PA: Westlake Development Group, Llc
　　520 S El Camino Real # 900
　　San Mateo CA 94402
　　650 579-1010

(P-27096)
WHISKEY GIRL
702 5th Ave, San Diego (92101-6918)
PHONE.....................619 236-1616
Jerry Lopez, *General Mgr*
David Schissman, *Co-Owner*
EMP: 83
SALES (est): 5.5MM
SALES (corp-wide): 6.1MM **Privately Held**
SIC: 8741 5813 Restaurant management; night clubs
PA: Buffalo Joe's Lp
　　1620 5th Ave Ste 770
　　San Diego CA 92101
　　619 235-6796

(P-27097)
WHITE CARNIVAL LLC
11812 San Vicente Blvd # 4, Los Angeles (90049-5022)
PHONE.....................310 914-1600
Matt Lichtenberg,
EMP: 50
SALES (est): 1.1MM **Privately Held**
SIC: 8741 Management services

(P-27098)
WORD & BROWN INSURANCE
Also Called: Conexis
721 S Parker St Ste 200, Orange (92868-4772)
PHONE.....................714 567-4398
John Word, *President*
Ivonne Roca, *Executive*
John Ball, *Managing Dir*
Andrew Russell, *Broker*
EMP: 215
SALES (corp-wide): 383.5MM **Privately Held**
SIC: 8741 Administrative management
PA: Word & Brown, Insurance Administrators, Inc.
　　721 S Parker St Ste 300
　　Orange CA 92868
　　714 835-5006

(P-27099)
WORLDSTAGE INC (PA)
1111 Bell Ave Ste A, Tustin (92780-6463)
PHONE.....................714 508-1858
Gary Standard, *CEO*
Josh Weisberg, *President*
Stan Jacobs, *CFO*
Rodney Miller, *CFO*
Gregg Whitaker, *CFO*
EMP: 53
SALES (est): 27.6MM **Privately Held**
SIC: 8741 Business management

(P-27100)
WYNDHAM IRVN-ORANGE CNTY ARPRT
17941 Von Karman Ave, Irvine (92614-6253)
PHONE.....................949 863-1999
Paul Gibbs, *Principal*
Justin Gammon, *General Mgr*
Bill Acuna, *Director*
EMP: 90
SQ FT: 1,000
SALES: 15MM **Privately Held**
SIC: 8741 7011 7389 Management services; hotels & motels; hotel & motel reservation service

(P-27101)
XTRA DEPARTMENT INC
12631 Imperial Hwy F106, Santa Fe Springs (90670-4710)
PHONE.....................562 462-3800
Richard Anzalone, *President*
EMP: 60
SALES (est): 3.7MM **Privately Held**
WEB: www.xtradepartment.com
SIC: 8741 Business management

(P-27102)
ZAHARONI HOLDINGS
5400 W Rosecrans Ave Lowr, Hawthorne (90250-6686)
PHONE.....................310 297-9722
Isaac Zaharoni, *Principal*
Dan Zaharoni, *Treasurer*
Patty Steiman, *Vice Pres*
Gil Zaharoni, *Admin Sec*
EMP: 50
SQ FT: 75,000
SALES: 80MM **Privately Held**
WEB: www.zaharoni.com
SIC: 8741 Financial management for business

8742 Management Consulting Services

(P-27103)
A T KEARNEY INC
555 Mission St Ste 1800, San Francisco (94105-0924)
PHONE.....................415 490-4000
Charity Reyes, *Office Mgr*
Pat McCarty, *Associate*
Steffen Oder, *Associate*
EMP: 98
SALES (corp-wide): 1.1B **Privately Held**
SIC: 8742 Business consultant
HQ: A. T. Kearney, Inc.
　　227 W Monroe St
　　Chicago IL 60606
　　312 648-0111

(P-27104)
A WORLD FIT FOR KIDS
678 S La Fayette Park Pl, Los Angeles (90057-3206)
PHONE.....................213 387-7712
Normandie Nigh, *Exec Dir*
Samantha Sorbo, *Vice Pres*
Martha Cordero, *Program Mgr*
Ian Keiller, *Director*
EMP: 110
SQ FT: 4,800
SALES: 2MM **Privately Held**
WEB: www.worldfitforkids.org
SIC: 8742 8641 8322 Management consulting services; civic social & fraternal associations; youth center

(P-27105)
ACCENTURE FEDERAL SERVICES LLC
Also Called: Accenture National SEC Svcs
1615 Murray Canyon Rd # 400, San Diego (92108-4314)
PHONE.....................619 574-2400
Jim Wangler, *Branch Mgr*
EMP: 145 **Privately Held**
SIC: 8742 7361 8711 7373 Business consultant; employment agencies; engineering services; computer integrated systems design; computer software development
HQ: Accenture Federal Services Llc
　　800 N Glebe Rd Ste 300
　　Arlington VA 22203
　　703 947-2000

(P-27106)
ACCENTURE LLP
2141 Rosecrans Ave # 3100, El Segundo (90245-7518)
PHONE.....................310 726-2700
Joyce Nitz, *Branch Mgr*
Rebecca Hernandez, *Partner*
Robert Wollan, *Managing Prtnr*
Andrea Lucchesi, *Executive*
Prashant Lad, *Project Mgr*
EMP: 350 **Privately Held**
WEB: www.wavesecurities.com
SIC: 8742 Business consultant
HQ: Accenture Llp
　　161 N Clark St Ste 1100
　　Chicago IL 60601
　　312 693-0161

(P-27107)
ACCENTURE LLP
2 Santa Ana Ct, Belvedere Tiburon (94920-1620)
PHONE.....................415 537-5860

Bill Moon, *Vice Pres*
Dave Alverado, *Software Dev*
EMP: 208 **Privately Held**
WEB: www.wavesecurities.com
SIC: 8742 Business consultant
HQ: Accenture Llp
　　161 N Clark St Ste 1100
　　Chicago IL 60601
　　312 693-0161

(P-27108)
ACCENTURE LLP
560 Mission St Fl 12, San Francisco (94105-2927)
PHONE.....................415 537-5000
Christopher S Digiorgio, *Principal*
Arunkumar Natarajan, *Vice Pres*
Reynold Bryan, *Executive*
Kirk Kirkpatrick, *Principal*
Courtney Rosen, *Principal*
EMP: 310 **Privately Held**
WEB: www.wavesecurities.com
SIC: 8742 Business consultant
HQ: Accenture Llp
　　161 N Clark St Ste 1100
　　Chicago IL 60601
　　312 693-0161

(P-27109)
ACCENTURE LLP
50 W San Fernando St # 1208, San Jose (95113-2429)
PHONE.....................408 817-2100
Jackson Wilson, *Manager*
John Gingrich, *Managing Dir*
Ramadurai Ramalingam, *Managing Dir*
Michael Redding, *Managing Dir*
Richard Desmond, *Technology*
EMP: 218 **Privately Held**
WEB: www.wavesecurities.com
SIC: 8742 Business consultant
HQ: Accenture Llp
　　161 N Clark St Ste 1100
　　Chicago IL 60601
　　312 693-0161

(P-27110)
ACCENTURE LLP
50 W San Fernando St # 1200, San Jose (95113-2429)
PHONE.....................650 213-2000
Christopher S Digiorgio, *Manager*
Paul Hasenwinkel, *Principal*
Vincent Hui, *Principal*
Clifford Jury, *Principal*
Carlisle Kirkpatrick, *Principal*
EMP: 175 **Privately Held**
SIC: 8742 8748 Business consultant; business consulting
HQ: Accenture Llp
　　161 N Clark St Ste 1100
　　Chicago IL 60601
　　312 693-0161

(P-27111)
ACCENTURE LLP
1415 L St Ste 700, Sacramento (95814-3964)
PHONE.....................916 557-2200
Christopher S Digiorgio, *Branch Mgr*
Mark Noriega, *Managing Dir*
John Nichols, *Manager*
EMP: 175 **Privately Held**
WEB: www.wavesecurities.com
SIC: 8742 Business consultant; management information systems consultant
HQ: Accenture Llp
　　161 N Clark St Ste 1100
　　Chicago IL 60601
　　312 693-0161

(P-27112)
ACCOUNTNOW INC
2603 Camino Ramon Ste 485, San Ramon (94583-9131)
P.O. Box 1966 (94583-6966)
PHONE.....................925 498-1800
James G Jones, *CEO*
David J Petrini, *CFO*
Paul Rosenfeld, *Chief Mktg Ofcr*
Preethi Janardhanan, *Info Tech Dir*
Jenn Cordeiro, *Technology*
EMP: 618

SALES (est): 13.6MM
SALES (corp-wide): 890.1MM **Publicly Held**
SIC: 8742 Financial consultant
PA: Green Dot Corporation
　　3465 E Foothill Blvd # 100
　　Pasadena CA 91107
　　626 765-2000

(P-27113)
ADIVO ASSOCIATES LLC
1 Post St Ste 2750, San Francisco
(94104-5246)
PHONE..............................415 992-1449
Maik Klasen, *Managing Dir*
Anna Santos, *Executive*
Ryan Goulding, *Managing Dir*
Lilia Carmen, *Administration*
Brandi Baughman, *Consultant*
EMP: 90
SQ FT: 2,000
SALES (est): 4.3MM **Privately Held**
SIC: 8742 Business consultant

(P-27114)
ADMINISTRATIVE SVCS COOP INC
2129 W Rosecrans Ave, Gardena
(90249-2933)
PHONE..............................310 715-1968
Martiros Manukyan, *CEO*
Raymond McGreevy, *President*
William J Rouse, *General Mgr*
EMP: 200
SALES (est): 19.8MM **Privately Held**
SIC: 8742 Administrative services consultant

(P-27115)
AECOM C&E INC
Also Called: Aecom Consulting
1999 Avenue Of The Stars, Los Angeles
(90067-6022)
PHONE..............................213 593-8100
Bill Mehol, *Branch Mgr*
George Sholy, *Assoc VP*
Carla Christofferson, *Exec VP*
Christopher Choa, *Vice Pres*
Mark Duda, *Vice Pres*
EMP: 200
SALES (corp-wide): 20.1B **Publicly Held**
SIC: 8742 9441 Human resource consulting services; administration of social & human resources
HQ: Aecom C&E, Inc
　　250 Apollo Dr
　　Chelmsford MA 01824
　　978 905-2100

(P-27116)
AEG GLOBAL PARTNERSHIPS LLC
1100 S Flower St Ste 3200, Los Angeles
(90015-2125)
PHONE..............................213 763-7700
Todd Goldstein, *President*
EMP: 50
SALES (est): 1.8MM **Privately Held**
SIC: 8742 Management consulting services
HQ: Anschutz Entertainment Group, Inc.
　　1100 S Flower St
　　Los Angeles CA 90015
　　213 337-5052

(P-27117)
AEROMEDEVAC INC
1860 Joe Crosson Dr, El Cajon
(92020-1227)
PHONE..............................619 284-7910
Adam Williams, *President*
John Olson, *CEO*
Raul Mendoza, *Vice Pres*
Michael Weiland, *Business Dir*
Sheila Navarro, *Info Tech Mgr*
EMP: 54
SALES (est): 6.3MM **Privately Held**
WEB: www.aeromedevac.com
SIC: 8742 Management consulting services

(P-27118)
AGAMA SOLUTIONS INC
39159 Paseo Padre Pkwy # 216, Fremont
(94538-1689)
PHONE..............................510 796-9300

Shivani G Sanan, *CEO*
Tanu Kalra, *President*
Pankaj Kalra, *Vice Pres*
Ashish Sanan, *Vice Pres*
EMP: 175
SQ FT: 9,000
SALES (est): 22.9MM **Privately Held**
SIC: 8742 7371 Management consulting services; computer software development

(P-27119)
AGR GROUP INC
13902 Harbor Blvd Ste 2c, Garden Grove
(92843-4013)
PHONE..............................714 245-7151
EMP: 750
SQ FT: 15,500
SALES: 16MM **Privately Held**
WEB: www.agrgroupinc.com
SIC: 8742

(P-27120)
AGREEYA SOLUTIONS INC (PA)
605 Coolidge Dr Ste 200, Folsom
(95630-4210)
PHONE..............................916 294-0075
Neerja Khosla, *President*
Sangeeta Khazanchi, *CFO*
Sanjay Khosla, *Vice Pres*
Ajay Kaul, *Admin Sec*
EMP: 55
SQ FT: 14,000
SALES (est): 40MM **Privately Held**
WEB: www.agreeya.com
SIC: 8742 7371 Management consulting services; computer software systems analysis & design, custom

(P-27121)
AKQA INC (HQ)
360 3rd St Ste 500, San Francisco
(94107-2165)
PHONE..............................415 645-9400
Tom Bedecarre, *CEO*
Miranda Molen, *Partner*
Romain Lartigue, *Managing Dir*
Nicole Rathbun, *Administration*
Chris Marsh, *Sr Software Eng*
EMP: 400
SQ FT: 28,000
SALES (est): 69.5MM
SALES (corp-wide): 20.1B **Privately Held**
WEB: www.akqa.com
SIC: 8742 Marketing consulting services
PA: Wpp Plc
　　Queensway House Hilgrove Street St Helier
　　Jersey JE1 1
　　207 408-2204

(P-27122)
ALAN B WHITSON COMPANY INC
1507 W Alton Ave, Santa Ana
(92704-7219)
P.O. Box 9229, Newport Beach (92658-9229)
PHONE..............................949 955-1200
Alan B Whitson, *President*
EMP: 750
SQ FT: 18,000
SALES: 41.4MM **Privately Held**
SIC: 8742 1389 5411 Corporation organizing; servicing oil & gas wells; convenience stores, chain

(P-27123)
ALIGHT (US) LLC
100 Bayview Cir Ste 100 # 100, Newport Beach (92660-2963)
P.O. Box 6300 (92658-6300)
PHONE..............................949 725-4500
Eric Watkins, *Manager*
Dale Macrae, *Vice Pres*
Gabriella Ludwig, *Admin Asst*
Mark Vincenti, *Administration*
Melissa Wallace, *Director*
EMP: 200
SALES (corp-wide): 5.6B **Privately Held**
WEB: www.hewitt.com
SIC: 8742 8748 Compensation & benefits planning consultant; business consulting
HQ: Alight (Us), Llc
　　200 E Randolph St Ll3
　　Chicago IL 60601
　　312 381-1000

(P-27124)
ALTEGRA HEALTH
3415 S Sepulveda Blvd # 900, Los Angeles
(90034-6981)
PHONE..............................310 776-4001
EMP: 99
SALES (est): 6.6MM **Privately Held**
SIC: 8742

(P-27125)
ALVAREZ & MARSAL HOLDINGS LLC
100 Pine St Fl 9, San Francisco
(94111-5111)
PHONE..............................415 490-2300
Bill Kosturos, *Manager*
Mark Stott, *Managing Dir*
EMP: 180
SALES (corp-wide): 229.3MM **Privately Held**
SIC: 8742 3523 3448 Financial consultant; farm machinery & equipment; prefabricated metal buildings
HQ: Alvarez & Marsal, Inc.
　　600 Madison Ave Fl 8
　　New York NY 10022
　　212 759-4433

(P-27126)
AMCO FOODS INC
601 E Glenoaks Blvd # 108, Glendale
(91207-1760)
PHONE..............................818 247-4716
Bobken Amirian, *President*
Brian Polthow, *CFO*
Nick Amirian, *Corp Secy*
Nareg Amirian, *Principal*
EMP: 475 EST: 1999
SALES: 5.8MM **Privately Held**
SIC: 8742 Business consultant

(P-27127)
AMERICA CONSULTING GROUP LLC
23 Corporate Plaza Dr # 150, Newport Beach (92660-7911)
PHONE..............................714 390-3105
Alan Ford, *CEO*
EMP: 200 EST: 2017
SALES: 5MM **Privately Held**
SIC: 8742 Business consultant

(P-27128)
AMERICAN ALL RISK LOSS ADM
4270 W Richert Ave # 101, Fresno
(93722-6334)
P.O. Box 9783 (93794-9783)
PHONE..............................559 277-4960
Steve Wigh, *President*
Luis Feliz, *Admin Sec*
EMP: 125
SALES (est): 12.6MM **Privately Held**
SIC: 8742 Administrative services consultant

(P-27129)
AMERICAN FINANCIAL NETWORK INC
14241 Firestone Blvd, La Mirada
(90638-5530)
PHONE..............................562 926-2401
Dan Piumpunyalerd, *Branch Mgr*
EMP: 74
SALES (corp-wide): 177.5MM **Privately Held**
SIC: 8742 7389 6162 Financial consultant; financial services; mortgage bankers & correspondents
PA: American Financial Network, Inc.
　　10 Pointe Dr Ste 330
　　Brea CA 92821
　　909 606-3905

(P-27130)
AMERICAN FINANCIAL NETWORK INC
3400 Inland Empire Blvd # 101, Ontario
(91764-5577)
PHONE..............................951 582-2655
EMP: 111
SALES (corp-wide): 177.5MM **Privately Held**
SIC: 8742 7389 6162 Financial consultant; financial services; mortgage bankers & correspondents

PA: American Financial Network, Inc.
　　10 Pointe Dr Ste 330
　　Brea CA 92821
　　909 606-3905

(P-27131)
AMGREEN SOLUTIONS INC
1367 Venice Blvd Fl 2, Los Angeles
(90006-5519)
PHONE..............................213 388-5647
Changhwan Ko, *President*
Michael Kim, *Sales Dir*
Nick Guillen, *Director*
EMP: 50
SALES: 8MM **Privately Held**
SIC: 8742 7389 Management engineering; water softener service

(P-27132)
AMMUNITION LLC
1500 Sansome St Ste 110, San Francisco
(94111-1015)
PHONE..............................415 632-1170
Peter Rack, *Managing Dir*
Darcy Dinucci, *Vice Pres*
Victoria Slaker, *Vice Pres*
Robert Kanes, *Program Mgr*
Meghan Durney, *Office Mgr*
EMP: 51
SQ FT: 5,200
SALES (est): 14.6MM **Privately Held**
SIC: 8742 Industrial consultant

(P-27133)
AMS VENTURES INC
39141 Civic Center Dr, Fremont
(94538-5818)
PHONE..............................301 980-5087
Stephen Zuppas, *CFO*
EMP: 70
SALES (est): 995.7K **Privately Held**
SIC: 8742 Marketing consulting services

(P-27134)
AMTROW GROUP INC
8306 Wilshire Blvd 1042, Beverly Hills
(90211-2304)
PHONE..............................310 557-0857
Samuel Neiderberg, *President*
Mikhail Aptor, *Vice Pres*
EMP: 86
SQ FT: 1,400
SALES (est): 3.6MM **Privately Held**
SIC: 8742 8741 1542 1522 Industry specialist consultants; construction management; nonresidential construction; residential construction

(P-27135)
ANDERSON KAYNE INV MGT INC (PA)
1800 Avenue Of The Stars # 200, Los Angeles (90067-4204)
PHONE..............................310 556-2721
Richard Kayne, *Ch of Bd*
John Anderson, *CEO*
Paul Stapleton, *Treasurer*
David J Shladovsky, *Admin Sec*
Thuc Tran, *Administration*
EMP: 55
SQ FT: 20,000
SALES (est): 22.2MM **Privately Held**
SIC: 8742 6211 6726 6282 Financial consultant; investment firm, general brokerage; investment offices; investment advice

(P-27136)
ANDERSONPENNA PARTNERS INC
3737 Birch St Ste 250, Newport Beach
(92660-2682)
PHONE..............................949 428-1500
Lisa Penna, *President*
Steve Badum, *President*
Angelique M Lucero, *CFO*
David R Anderson, *Exec VP*
Dino D'Emilia, *Vice Pres*
EMP: 75
SALES (est): 7.9MM **Privately Held**
SIC: 8742 8711 Transportation consultant; engineering services
PA: Ardurra Group Llc
　　3012 26th St
　　Metairie LA 70002
　　504 454-3866

(P-27137)
ANJANEYAP INC
830 Hillview Ct Ste 140, Milpitas
(95035-4552)
PHONE..............................408 922-9690
Sundeep Bhandal, *President*
Swapnil Anand, *Vice Pres*
Taresh Anand, *Vice Pres*
Akshatha Sreenivas, *Recruiter*
EMP: 53
SQ FT: 4,300
SALES: 37.7MM **Privately Held**
SIC: 8742 Business consultant

(P-27138)
AON CONSULTING INC
2570 N 1st St Ste 500, San Jose
(95131-1018)
PHONE..............................408 321-2500
Steve Radford, *Manager*
Daniel Coleman, *Associate*
EMP: 65
SALES (corp-wide): 10B **Privately Held**
WEB: www.radford.com
SIC: 8742 Compensation & benefits plan-
ning consultant
HQ: Aon Consulting, Inc.
200 E Randolph St Ll3
Chicago IL 60601
312 381-1000

(P-27139)
APA INCORPORATED
405 S Beverly Dr Ste 500, Beverly Hills
(90212-4425)
P.O. Box 45 (90213-0045)
PHONE..............................310 888-4200
Kat Cafeler, *President*
Brian Dow, *Bd of Directors*
Marc Kamler, *Vice Pres*
Larry Sheffield, *Vice Pres*
James Gosnell, *Info Tech Mgr*
EMP: 150
SALES (est): 11.4MM **Privately Held**
SIC: 8742 Business consultant

(P-27140)
APERIAN GLOBAL INC (PA)
1 Kaiser Plz Ste 785, Oakland
(94612-3611)
PHONE..............................628 222-3773
Ernest Gundling, *President*
Dave Eaton, *President*
Theodore Dale, *COO*
David Reilly, *CFO*
Ted Dale, *Officer*
EMP: 62
SQ FT: 4,000
SALES (est): 9MM **Privately Held**
WEB: www.meridianglobal.com
SIC: 8742 Business consultant

(P-27141)
**APN BUSINESS RESOURCES
INC**
21418 Osborne St, Canoga Park
(91304-1520)
PHONE..............................818 717-9980
Michael Noori, *CEO*
EMP: 85
SALES: 15MM **Privately Held**
SIC: 8742 8748 Business planning & or-
ganizing services; business consulting

(P-27142)
**ARCO ENVMTL REMEDIATION
LLC**
Also Called: Am/PM Food Mart
5472 Orangethorpe Ave, La Palma
(90623-1005)
PHONE..............................714 523-5674
Bruce Niemeyer, *President*
Yolanda Ramos, *Site Mgr*
EMP: 68 EST: 1996
SALES (est): 1.7MM
SALES (corp-wide): 240.2B **Privately
Held**
WEB: www.bpamoco.com
SIC: 8742 8748 6794 Management con-
sulting services; environmental consult-
ant; franchises, selling or licensing
HQ: Bp Corporation North America Inc.
501 Westlake Park Blvd
Houston TX 77079
281 366-2000

(P-27143)
ASHLEY MANAGEMENT GROUP
300 Spectrum Center Dr # 400, Irvine
(92618-4925)
PHONE..............................949 754-3120
Lance Ashley, *President*
EMP: 50
SALES: 5MM **Privately Held**
SIC: 8742 Business consultant

(P-27144)
**ASSET MARKETING SYSTEMS
INSU**
Also Called: AMS
15050 Ave Of Science # 100, San Diego
(92128-3418)
PHONE..............................888 303-8755
Mike Botkin, *CEO*
Dee Costa, *President*
Louise Kinard Erdman, *CFO*
Jeff Stemler, *Exec VP*
Todd Greider, *Train & Dev Mgr*
EMP: 70
SQ FT: 19,000
SALES (est): 8.6MM **Privately Held**
WEB: www.assetmarketingsystems.net
SIC: 8742 Marketing consulting services

(P-27145)
AUTISM PARTNERSHIP INC
200 Marina Dr C, Seal Beach
(90740-6023)
PHONE..............................562 431-9293
Ronald Leaf, *President*
John McEachin, *Admin Sec*
Julie McEachin, *Administration*
Andrea Waks, *Client Mgr*
EMP: 95
SALES (est): 6MM **Privately Held**
WEB: www.autismpartnership.com
SIC: 8742 Hospital & health services con-
sultant

(P-27146)
AVANTI HEALTH SYSTEM LLC
222 N Pacific Coast Hwy # 950, El Se-
gundo (90245-5627)
PHONE..............................310 356-0550
Steve Dixon,
Maria Guerrero, *Administration*
Mark Bell, *Mng Member*
Poe Corn, *Mng Member*
James Macpherson, *Mng Member*
EMP: 446 EST: 2008
SALES (est): 49.5MM **Privately Held**
SIC: 8742 Hospital & health services con-
sultant

(P-27147)
AXA ADVISORS LLC
88 Kearny St Fl 20, San Francisco
(94108-5548)
PHONE..............................415 276-2100
Daniel W Worthington, *Manager*
EMP: 70 **Publicly Held**
WEB: www.axacs.com
SIC: 8742 Financial consultant
HQ: Axa Advisors, Llc
1290 Ave Of Amrcs Fl Cnc1
New York NY 10104
212 554-1234

(P-27148)
**B A TECHNOLINKS
CORPORATION**
4677 Old Ironsides Dr # 440, Santa Clara
(95054-1826)
PHONE..............................408 940-5921
Kiran Maruvada, *CEO*
Krishna Vemuri, *President*
EMP: 70 EST: 2010
SALES (est): 5.8MM **Privately Held**
SIC: 8742 Business consultant

(P-27149)
**BABCOCK & BROWN ELEC MGT
LLC**
4350 La Jolla Village Dr, San Diego
(92122-1243)
PHONE..............................858 587-5820
Sean McLaughlin, *Branch Mgr*
EMP: 151

SALES (corp-wide): 18.1MM **Privately
Held**
SIC: 8742 Management consulting services
PA: Babcock & Brown Electronics Management Llc
4 Embarcadero Ctr Ste 700
San Francisco CA 94111
415 512-1515

(P-27150)
BAIN & COMPANY INC
1901 Ave Of The Sts 200, Los Angeles
(90067)
PHONE..............................310 229-3000
Kevin Badkoubehi, *Branch Mgr*
Peter Ratajczak, *Mktg Coord*
Hubert Shen, *Sr Associate*
Joon Choi, *Manager*
Sarah Pura, *Manager*
EMP: 80
SALES (corp-wide): 422.3MM **Privately
Held**
WEB: www.bain.com
SIC: 8742 Business consultant
PA: Bain & Company, Inc.
131 Dartmouth St Ste 901
Boston MA 02116
617 572-2000

(P-27151)
BAIN & COMPANY INC
1 Embarcadero Ctr # 3500, San Francisco
(94111-3628)
PHONE..............................415 627-1000
Vernon Altman, *Manager*
Stephen Bertrand, *Partner*
Julie Lin, *Executive Asst*
Yesenia Pulido, *Executive Asst*
Katie Schenkkan, *Hum Res Coord*
EMP: 109
SALES (corp-wide): 422.3MM **Privately
Held**
WEB: www.bain.com
SIC: 8742 Business consultant
PA: Bain & Company, Inc.
131 Dartmouth St Ste 901
Boston MA 02116
617 572-2000

(P-27152)
BAINBRIDGE INC (PA)
4435 Estgate Mall Ste 130, San Diego
(92121)
PHONE..............................858 638-1800
Steven Stucker, *President*
Gregory Bribiesca, *Vice Pres*
Nick Chini, *Manager*
EMP: 61
SALES (est): 6.3MM **Privately Held**
WEB: www.bbridge.com
SIC: 8742 8732 Management consulting
services; market analysis or research

(P-27153)
**BASELINE CONSULTING GROUP
INC**
15300 Ventura Blvd # 200, Sherman Oaks
(91403-3138)
PHONE..............................818 906-7638
Evan Levy, *President*
Jill Dyche, *Vice Pres*
EMP: 50
SQ FT: 5,000
SALES: 3.4MM
SALES (corp-wide): 3B **Privately Held**
WEB: www.baseline-consulting.com
SIC: 8742 Management consulting serv-
ices
HQ: Dataflux Corporation Llc
100 Sas Campus Dr
Cary NC 27513
919 447-3000

(P-27154)
**BASKETBALL MARKETING CO
INC**
Also Called: and 1
101 Enterprise Ste 100, Aliso Viejo
(92656-2604)
PHONE..............................866 866-1232
EMP: 78
SALES (est): 4MM
SALES (corp-wide): 2.7B **Publicly Held**
SIC: 8742

HQ: American Sporting Goods Corp
101 Enterprise Ste 200
Aliso Viejo CA 92656
949 267-2800

(P-27155)
BBCERT
510 S Highway 1, Bodega Bay (94923)
PHONE..............................480 220-3799
Linda Stout, *President*
EMP: 50
SALES (est): 924.5K **Privately Held**
SIC: 8742 Training & development consult-
ant

(P-27156)
**BEACON ACCUNTING
RESOURCES LLC**
1818 Glenwood Ln, Newport Beach
(92660-4317)
PHONE..............................949 981-5946
EMP: 50
SALES (est): 1.8MM **Privately Held**
SIC: 8742 Business planning & organizing
services

(P-27157)
BEACON RESOURCES LLC
4 Corporate Plaza Dr # 101, Newport
Beach (92660-7906)
PHONE..............................949 955-1773
Colleen Freeman,
Mike Kelly,
EMP: 50
SALES (est): 3.4MM **Privately Held**
SIC: 8742 Business planning & organizing
services
HQ: David M. Lewis Company, Llc
21800 Oxnard St Ste 980
Woodland Hills CA 91367

(P-27158)
**BEATING WALL STREET INC
(PA)**
14934 Dickens St Apt 16, Sherman Oaks
(91403-3419)
PHONE..............................818 332-9696
Hamed Khorsand, *President*
EMP: 230
SQ FT: 8,000
SALES (est): 7.6MM **Privately Held**
WEB: www.beatingwallstreet.com
SIC: 8742 Financial consultant

(P-27159)
BECKETT ENTERPRISE
Also Called: Selu College
900 Kincaid Ave K8, Inglewood
(90302-2021)
PHONE..............................310 686-3817
Tyesha Beckett, *CEO*
EMP: 50 EST: 2017
SALES (est): 924.5K **Privately Held**
SIC: 8742 Corporation organizing

(P-27160)
BENTLEY HEALTH CARE INC
9777 Wilshire Blvd Fl 4, Beverly Hills
(90212-1904)
PHONE..............................310 967-3300
Bernard Salick MD, *President*
Barbara Bromley-Williams, *Vice Pres*
EMP: 70
SQ FT: 32,000
SALES (est): 3.4MM **Privately Held**
SIC: 8742 Hospital & health services con-
sultant

(P-27161)
**BITE COMMUNICATIONS LLC
(HQ)**
100 Montgomery St # 1103, San Francisco
(94104-4388)
PHONE..............................415 365-0222
Tim Dyson, *Mng Member*
Andrea Cunningham, *President*
Alisa Macdonnell, *Senior VP*
Will Willis, *Senior VP*
Jeanine Bran, *Vice Pres*
EMP: 75
SQ FT: 10,000

SALES (est): 12.6MM
SALES (corp-wide): 262.9MM **Privately Held**
WEB: www.bitepr.com
SIC: 8742 8743 Marketing consulting services; public relations services
PA: Next Fifteen Communications Group Plc
75 Bermondsey Street
London SE1 3
207 908-6444

(P-27162)
BLACKSTONE CONSULTING INC (PA)
11726 San Vicente Blvd # 550, Los Angeles (90049-5089)
PHONE....................................310 826-4389
Ronald Joseph Blackstone, *President*
Gary Meek, *CFO*
Joe Blackstone, *General Mgr*
Alejandra Ordaz, *Administration*
Laura Ritenour, *Project Mgr*
EMP: 148
SQ FT: 1,500
SALES (est): 108.2MM **Privately Held**
WEB: www.blackstone-consulting.com
SIC: 8742 Management consulting services

(P-27163)
BLANCHARD TRAINING AND DEV INC (PA)
Also Called: Ken Blanchard Companies, The
125 State Pl, Escondido (92029-1323)
PHONE....................................760 489-5005
Thomas J McKee, *CEO*
Maritza Dominguez, *Partner*
John Hester, *Partner*
Joanne Hum, *Partner*
Howard Farfel, *President*
▼ EMP: 200
SALES: 61.2MM **Privately Held**
SIC: 8742 Training & development consultant

(P-27164)
BLB RESOURCES INC (PA)
16845 Von Karman Ave # 100, Irvine (92606-4961)
PHONE....................................949 261-9155
Rod Gaston, *CEO*
Susan Gaston, *President*
Denise Johnson, *CFO*
Khiem Nguyen, *Info Tech Dir*
Christine Cooper, *Project Mgr*
EMP: 105
SQ FT: 20,000
SALES (est): 14.5MM **Privately Held**
SIC: 8742 Management consulting services

(P-27165)
BON APPETIT MANAGEMENT CO
1259 E Colton Ave, Redlands (92374-3755)
PHONE....................................909 748-8970
Bret Martin, *General Mgr*
EMP: 120
SALES (corp-wide): 28.9B **Privately Held**
WEB: www.cafebonappetit.com
SIC: 8742 Administrative services consultant
HQ: Bon Appetit Management Co.
100 Hamilton Ave Ste 400
Palo Alto CA 94301
650 798-8000

(P-27166)
BOOZ ALLEN HAMILTON INC
5220 Pacific Concourse Dr # 390, Los Angeles (90045-6244)
PHONE....................................310 297-2100
Ralph Shrader, *CEO*
Jake Montes, *Engineer*
Sanjana Venkatraman, *Analyst*
Elizabeth McNally, *Sr Associate*
Amanda Cohen, *Associate*
EMP: 52 **Publicly Held**
SIC: 8742 Management consulting services
HQ: Booz Allen Hamilton Inc.
8283 Greensboro Dr # 700
Mc Lean VA 22102
703 902-5000

(P-27167)
BOOZ ALLEN HAMILTON INC
1615 Murray Canyon Rd # 900, San Diego (92108-4314)
PHONE....................................619 725-6500
Foster Rich, *Vice Pres*
Philip Summerly, *Social Dir*
Kristy Brierton, *Admin Asst*
Amabel Bautista, *Administration*
Shane Doyle, *Network Enginr*
EMP: 52 **Publicly Held**
WEB: www.bah.com
SIC: 8742 Management consulting services
HQ: Booz Allen Hamilton Inc.
8283 Greensboro Dr # 700
Mc Lean VA 22102
703 902-5000

(P-27168)
BOOZ ALLEN HAMILTON INC
555 S Flower St Fl 36, Los Angeles (90071-2300)
PHONE....................................213 620-1900
Wayne Gilles, *Branch Mgr*
EMP: 52 **Publicly Held**
WEB: www.bah.com
SIC: 8742 Management consulting services
HQ: Booz Allen Hamilton Inc.
8283 Greensboro Dr # 700
Mc Lean VA 22102
703 902-5000

(P-27169)
BOSTON CONSULTING GROUP INC
355 S Grand Ave Ste 3300, Los Angeles (90071-1592)
PHONE....................................213 621-2772
Angela Johnson, *Director*
EMP: 70
SALES (corp-wide): 5B **Privately Held**
WEB: www.bcg.com
SIC: 8742 Business consultant
PA: The Boston Consulting Group Inc
200 Pier 4 Blvd Fl 11
Boston MA 02210
617 973-1200

(P-27170)
BRAD MILLER
Also Called: Infotech Consulting
340 Pine St Ste 504, San Francisco (94104-3211)
PHONE....................................415 986-5400
Brad Miller, *Owner*
EMP: 200
SALES: 8MM **Privately Held**
SIC: 8742 Management information systems consultant

(P-27171)
BRANDREP INC
16812 Armstrong Ave, Irvine (92606-4916)
PHONE....................................800 405-7119
Banir Ganatra, *Owner*
Drew Gockel, *Vice Pres*
Vasile Popovici, *Controller*
Dylan Ramsey, *Sales Staff*
Jen Sandoval, *Sales Staff*
EMP: 50 EST: 2013
SALES (est): 7.2MM **Privately Held**
SIC: 8742 Marketing consulting services

(P-27172)
BRIDGWTER CONSULTING GROUP INC
18881 Von Karman Ave, Irvine (92612-1500)
PHONE....................................949 535-1755
Mark Montgomery, *President*
EMP: 90
SQ FT: 1,600
SALES: 13.5MM **Privately Held**
SIC: 8742 7379 Management consulting services;

(P-27173)
BROKER SOLUTIONS INC (PA)
Also Called: New American Funding
14511 Myford Rd Ste 100, Tustin (92780-7057)
PHONE....................................800 450-2010
Rick Arvielo, *CEO*

Patricia Arvielo, *President*
Christy Bunce, *COO*
Frank Fuentes, *Vice Pres*
EMP: 650
SALES (est): 161.9MM **Privately Held**
SIC: 8742 6162 Financial consultant; bond & mortgage companies

(P-27174)
BROWN AND STREZA LLP
40 Pacifica Ste 1500, Irvine (92618-7496)
PHONE....................................949 453-2900
Richard Streza, *President*
David Brown, *Vice Pres*
Ashley Razee, *Admin Sec*
Dawn Alewine, *Admin Asst*
Daniel Beck, *Admin Asst*
EMP: 60
SQ FT: 1,000
SALES (est): 8.6MM **Privately Held**
WEB: www.brownandstreza.com
SIC: 8742 8111 Business planning & organizing services; general practice attorney, lawyer

(P-27175)
BUSINESS FOR SCIAL RSPNSBILITY (PA)
Also Called: B S R
88 Kearny St Fl 12, San Francisco (94108-5539)
PHONE....................................415 984-3200
Aron Cramer, *CEO*
MEI Cheung, *Opers Staff*
Eric Stryson, *Director*
EMP: 130
SQ FT: 20,000
SALES: 21.2MM **Privately Held**
WEB: www.bsr.org
SIC: 8742 General management consultant

(P-27176)
BUSINESS INTELLIGENCE
2131 Palomar Airport Rd # 328, Carlsbad (92011-1466)
P.O. Box 99973, San Diego (92169-1973)
PHONE....................................858 452-8200
Sean Lesher, *Mng Member*
John Vasek,
Chris Stoffel, *Consultant*
EMP: 50
SQ FT: 700
SALES (est): 12MM **Privately Held**
SIC: 8742 Management information systems consultant

(P-27177)
BUSINESSCOM INC
2120 Colorado Ave Fl 3, Santa Monica (90404-5510)
PHONE....................................310 586-4000
Ryan Peddycord, *CEO*
Brian Barnum, *President*
Jeffrey Grow, *Director*
EMP: 52
SQ FT: 22,000
SALES (est): 4.7MM
SALES (corp-wide): 41.9MM **Privately Held**
WEB: www.business.com
SIC: 8742 7375 Management consulting services; information retrieval services
HQ: Business.Com Media, Inc.
1900 Wright Pl Ste 250
Carlsbad CA 92008
888 441-4466

(P-27178)
CALIF INSTITUTE HUMAN SER
1801 E Cotati Ave, Rohnert Park (94928-3613)
PHONE....................................707 664-2416
Tony Apolloni, *Director*
EMP: 70 EST: 1980
SALES (est): 2.6MM **Privately Held**
SIC: 8742 Human resource consulting services

(P-27179)
CALIFORNIA MFG TECH CONSULTING
Also Called: Cmtc
690 Knox St Ste 200, Torrance (90502-1323)
PHONE....................................310 263-3060

James Watson, *President*
Bill Doxakis, *Partner*
John J Vanburen, *CFO*
Jack Van Buren, *Executive*
Edith Leyden, *Admin Asst*
EMP: 73
SQ FT: 10,000
SALES: 29.9MM **Privately Held**
SIC: 8742 8711 Consulting engineer; marketing consulting services

(P-27180)
CALIFRNIA IND SYS OPRATOR CORP
110 Blue Ravine Rd, Folsom (95630-4711)
PHONE....................................916 608-7000
Terry Winter, *President*
Terri Moreland, *Director*
Heather Kelley, *Manager*
EMP: 150 **Privately Held**
WEB: www.caiso.com
SIC: 8742 Human resource consulting services
PA: California Independent System Operator Corporation
250 Outcropping Way
Folsom CA 95630
-

(P-27181)
CAPTAIN MARKETING INC
3577 N Figueroa St, Los Angeles (90065-2445)
PHONE....................................310 402-9709
EMP: 77
SALES (corp-wide): 10MM **Privately Held**
SIC: 8742 Marketing consulting services
PA: Captain Marketing, Inc.
4505 Las Virgenes Rd # 210
Calabasas CA 91302
888 297-9977

(P-27182)
CARANYTHINGCOM INC
Also Called: Customerlink Systems
22 4th St Fl 12, San Francisco (94103-3176)
PHONE....................................916 781-4344
Mark Hockridge, *CEO*
EMP: 59
SQ FT: 11,366
SALES (est): 5.7MM **Privately Held**
WEB: www.customerlink.com
SIC: 8742 Marketing consulting services

(P-27183)
CARLETON BOOKER MARKETING INC
5042 Wilshire Blvd # 31584, Los Angeles (90036-4305)
PHONE....................................510 999-1682
Carleton C Booker, *CEO*
EMP: 52
SALES (est): 1.6MM **Privately Held**
SIC: 8742 Marketing consulting services

(P-27184)
CASA ALLEGRA COMMUNITY SVCS
35 Mitchell Blvd Ste 8, San Rafael (94903-2012)
PHONE....................................415 499-1116
Jeanne Santangelo, *Director*
Mia Brown, *Bd of Directors*
EMP: 70
SALES: 4.7MM **Privately Held**
SIC: 8742 Human resource consulting services

(P-27185)
CBRE GLOBAL INVESTORS LLC (DH)
Also Called: Global Innovation Partner
515 S Flower St Ste 3100, Los Angeles (90071-2233)
PHONE....................................213 683-4200
Ritson Ferguson, *CEO*
Maurice Voskuilen, *CFO*
Kathy Matson, *Vice Pres*
Matthew Yao, *Vice Pres*
Maura Bilafer, *Managing Dir*
EMP: 150
SQ FT: 60,000

SALES (est): 142.5MM
SALES (corp-wide): 14.2B **Publicly Held**
WEB: www.cbreglobalindestors.com
SIC: 8742 Real estate consultant
HQ: Cbre, Inc.
    400 S Hope St Ste 25
    Los Angeles CA 90071
    213 613-3333

(P-27186)
CBRE GLOBAL INVESTORS LLC
3501 Jamboree Rd Ste 100, Newport
Beach (92660-2940)
PHONE..........................949 725-8500
Steven Swerdlow, *Principal*
EMP: 350
SALES (corp-wide): 14.2B **Publicly Held**
SIC: 8742 6531 Management consulting
  services; real estate agent, commercial
HQ: Cbre Global Investors, Llc
    515 S Flower St Ste 3100
    Los Angeles CA 90071
    213 683-4200

(P-27187)
CBRE SERVICES INC
400 S Hope St Ste 25, Los Angeles
(90071-2800)
PHONE..........................213 613-3333
Robert Sulentic, *CEO*
Robert Stillman, *Vice Chairman*
Randall Brown, *President*
Lou Nutter, *Senior VP*
James Bach, *Vice Pres*
EMP: 70
SALES (est): 7.4MM
SALES (corp-wide): 14.2B **Publicly Held**
WEB: www.cbrichardellis.com
SIC: 8742 6531 Real estate consultant;
  real estate agent, commercial
PA: Cbre Group, Inc.
    400 S Hope St Ste 25
    Los Angeles CA 90071
    213 613-3333

(P-27188)
CELERITY CONSULTING GROUP INC (PA)
2 Gough St Ste 300, San Francisco
(94103-5420)
PHONE..........................415 986-8850
Rachelle Yowell, *CEO*
Christopher Yowell, *President*
Norman Yee, *COO*
Steffani Aranas, *Vice Pres*
Kevin Liu, *Vice Pres*
EMP: 61
SQ FT: 28,000
SALES (est): 15.8MM **Privately Held**
WEB: www.celerityconsulting.net
SIC: 8742 7371 7379 7375 Management
  consulting services; management infor-
  mation systems consultant; computer
  software development & applications;
  data processing consultant; on-line data
  base information retrieval; data process-
  ing service

(P-27189)
CHASE GROUP LLC
Also Called: Center At Parkwest, The
6740 Wilbur Ave, Reseda (91335-5179)
PHONE..........................818 708-3533
Phil Chase, *Branch Mgr*
EMP: 100 **Privately Held**
SIC: 8742 8049 Management consulting
  services; nurses & other medical assis-
  tants
PA: The Chase Group Llc
    3075 E Thousand Oaks Blvd
    Thousand Oaks CA 91362

(P-27190)
CHASE GROUP LLC
Also Called: Simi Vly Care & Rehabilitation
5270 E Los Angeles Ave, Simi Valley
(93063-4137)
PHONE..........................805 522-9155
Phil Chase, *Manager*
Maria Curiel, *Office Mgr*
Floyd Rhoades, *Administration*
EMP: 100 **Privately Held**
SIC: 8742 8732 Management consulting
  services; research services, except labo-
  ratory

PA: The Chase Group Llc
    3075 E Thousand Oaks Blvd
    Thousand Oaks CA 91362
    -

(P-27191)
CHECK DISC LABS
4121 W Vanowen Pl, Burbank
(91505-1131)
PHONE..........................818 847-2255
Jonathan Burk, *General Mgr*
Jeremiah Magan, *Technician*
EMP: 70
SQ FT: 8,000
SALES (est): 3.5MM **Privately Held**
SIC: 8742 Quality assurance consultant

(P-27192)
CIPHERMAX INC (PA)
1975 Concourse Dr, San Jose
(95131-1708)
PHONE..........................408 382-6500
Nelson Bye, *President*
Ray KAO, *Ch of Bd*
EMP: 55
SQ FT: 23,000
SALES (est): 5.3MM **Privately Held**
WEB: www.maxxan.com
SIC: 8742 Management consulting serv-
  ices

(P-27193)
CITY OF FULLERTON
Maintenance Dept
1580 W Commonwealth Ave, Fullerton
(92833-2728)
PHONE..........................714 738-6897
Robert Savage, *Director*
Charles Kovac, *Project Mgr*
Kevin Coe, *Supervisor*
Bill Roseberry, *Supervisor*
EMP: 150 **Privately Held**
SIC: 8742 Maintenance management con-
  sultant
PA: City Of Fullerton
    303 W Commonwealth Ave
    Fullerton CA 92832
    714 738-6300

(P-27194)
CITY OF IRVINE
Also Called: Dept of Public Works
6427 Oak Cyn, Irvine (92618-5202)
P.O. Box 19575 (92623-9575)
PHONE..........................949 724-7600
Allison Hart, *Manager*
EMP: 70 **Privately Held**
SIC: 8742 9111 8748 7349 Public utilities
  consultant; mayors' offices; business con-
  sulting; building maintenance services;
  lawn & garden services
PA: City Of Irvine
    1 Civic Center Plz
    Irvine CA 92606
    949 724-6000

(P-27195)
CLOUDTRIGGER INC
760 Garden View Ct # 120, Encinitas
(92024-2473)
PHONE..........................858 367-5272
Doug McLean, *Vice Pres*
EMP: 70
SALES (est): 5.3MM **Privately Held**
SIC: 8742 Management consulting serv-
  ices

(P-27196)
CODE FOR AMERICA LABS INC
155 9th St, San Francisco (94103-2620)
PHONE..........................415 625-9633
Jennifer Pahlka, *President*
Meghan Reilly, *Vice Pres*
Abhi Nemani, *Software Engr*
Rebecca Rangel, *Project Mgr*
Manya Scheps, *Senior Mgr*
EMP: 80
SALES (est): 12.8MM **Privately Held**
SIC: 8742 Marketing consulting services

(P-27197)
COHEN BROWN MGT GROUP INC (PA)
11835 W Olympic Blvd 920e, Los Angeles
(90064-5001)
PHONE..........................310 966-1001

Martin L Cohen, *CEO*
Edward G Brown, *President*
Ruben Rubinstein, *COO*
Christopher Phillips, *Vice Pres*
Jorge Maldonado, *Info Tech Mgr*
EMP: 64
SQ FT: 5,500
SALES (est): 10.1MM **Privately Held**
WEB: www.cbmg.com
SIC: 8742 Training & development consult-
  ant

(P-27198)
COMPSPEC INC
425 E Colorado St Ste 410, Glendale
(91205-1675)
PHONE..........................818 551-4200
Nabil Haddad, *President*
Terri Pina, *Executive*
Monica Peinado, *Info Tech Mgr*
Shelly Murph, *Marketing Staff*
Shelle Mitchell, *Director*
EMP: 100
SALES (est): 10.9MM **Privately Held**
WEB: www.compspecinc.com
SIC: 8742 7299 Hospital & health services
  consultant; debt counseling or adjustment
  service, individuals

(P-27199)
CONSUMER RESOURCE NETWORK LLC
Also Called: Launchpad Communications
4420 E Miraloma Ave Ste J, Anaheim
(92807-1839)
PHONE..........................800 291-4794
Mark Osborne,
Alex Kim, *CFO*
Brian Pick, *Vice Pres*
Greg Hall,
Benjamin Kim,
EMP: 340
SQ FT: 27,519
SALES (est): 19.5MM **Privately Held**
WEB: www.consumerresourcenetwork.net
SIC: 8742 Marketing consulting services

(P-27200)
COOPERATIVE PERSONNEL SERVICES (PA)
Also Called: CPS Hr Consulting
2450 Del Paso Rd Ste 220, Sacramento
(95834-9664)
PHONE..........................916 263-3600
Jerry Greenwell, *CEO*
Tim Howald, *CFO*
Sarah Williams, *Admin Asst*
Teresa Webster, *Recruiter*
Jill Engelmann, *Sr Consultant*
EMP: 139
SQ FT: 34,000
SALES (est): 31.2MM **Privately Held**
SIC: 8742 Personnel management consult-
  ant

(P-27201)
CORPORATE VISIONS INC (PA)
3875 Hopyard Rd Ste 275, Pleasanton
(94588-8527)
PHONE..........................415 464-4400
Erik Peterson, *CEO*
Joseph Terry, *President*
Gloria Fan, *CFO*
Mike Finley, *Ch Credit Ofcr*
EMP: 53 **EST:** 2011
SALES (est): 31.4MM **Privately Held**
SIC: 8742 Management consulting serv-
  ices

(P-27202)
CORPORATE VISIONS INC
2705 Avenida De Anita # 29, Carlsbad
(92010-8355)
PHONE..........................760 458-0914
Mark Valle, *Principal*
Lexin Chen, *Accountant*
EMP: 91
SALES (corp-wide): 31.4MM **Privately Held**
SIC: 8742 Management consulting serv-
  ices
PA: Corporate Visions Inc
    3875 Hopyard Rd Ste 275
    Pleasanton CA 94588
    415 464-4400

(P-27203)
CPE HR INC
9000 W Sunset Blvd # 900, West Holly-
wood (90069-5801)
PHONE..........................310 270-9800
Harold Walt, *CEO*
Faith Branvold, *President*
Grace Drulias, *CFO*
Walt Robinson, *Vice Pres*
Victor Sacks,
EMP: 90
SALES (est): 15.8MM **Privately Held**
SIC: 8742 Human resource consulting
  services

(P-27204)
CREATIVE EVENTS ENTERPRISES
4872 Topanga Canyon Blvd # 406, Wood-
land Hills (91364-4229)
PHONE..........................818 610-7000
Frank Biedka, *President*
Irving Shanske, *Vice Pres*
Arthur Webb, *Vice Pres*
EMP: 170
SALES (est): 7.2MM **Privately Held**
SIC: 8742 7389 7999 Business consult-
  ant; convention & show services; picnic
  ground operation

(P-27205)
CROWN GOLF PROPERTIES LP
Also Called: Tustin Ranch Golf Club
12442 Tustin Ranch Rd, Tustin
(92782-1000)
PHONE..........................714 730-1611
Steve Plummer, *Manager*
Jessica Tjan, *Manager*
EMP: 200
SALES (corp-wide): 85.5MM **Privately Held**
WEB: www.rvrgolf.com
SIC: 8742 7997 7992 Business consult-
  ant; membership sports & recreation
  clubs; public golf courses
PA: Crown Golf Properties, Lp
    222 N La Salle St # 2000
    Chicago IL 60601
    312 395-7701

(P-27206)
CROWN GOLF PROPERTIES LP
Also Called: Empire Lake Golf Course
791 Camarillo Springs Rd, Camarillo
(93012-8111)
PHONE..........................909 481-6663
Eugene Park, *Manager*
EMP: 60
SALES (corp-wide): 85.5MM **Privately Held**
WEB: www.rvrgolf.com
SIC: 8742 Business consultant
PA: Crown Golf Properties, Lp
    222 N La Salle St # 2000
    Chicago IL 60601
    312 395-7701

(P-27207)
CT LIEN SOLUTION
330 N Brand Blvd Ste 700, Glendale
(91203-2336)
PHONE..........................818 662-4100
CT Cor System, *Branch Mgr*
EMP: 148
SALES (corp-wide): 5.2B **Privately Held**
SIC: 8742 Management consulting serv-
  ices
HQ: Ct Lien Solution
    2929 Allen Pkwy Ste 3300
    Houston TX 77019
    713 533-4600

(P-27208)
CUNNINGHAM GROUP INC
5616 Circle View Dr, Bonsall (92003-5301)
PHONE..........................303 295-1982
Paul Cunningham, *CEO*
Troy Cunningham, *President*
EMP: 57
SALES (est): 2.8MM **Privately Held**
SIC: 8742 Financial consultant

(P-27209)
CUSTOMER LOYALTY BUILDERS INC
Also Called: Service Quality
1063 Todos Santos, Concord (94522)
PHONE....................................888 478-7787
Jeff Kasper, *President*
Michael Mendona, *Principal*
EMP: 100
SALES (est): 4.5MM **Privately Held**
SIC: 8742 8211 Marketing consulting services; seminary

(P-27211)
CUSTOMIZED DIST SVCS INC
3355 E Cedar St, Ontario (91761-7632)
PHONE....................................909 947-0084
Mark Tuttle, *Branch Mgr*
Melinda Ramirez, *Executive*
Corina Perryman, *Human Resources*
EMP: 100
SALES (corp-wide): 91.1MM **Privately Held**
WEB: www.cds3pl.com
SIC: 8742 7319 8741 Transportation consultant; distribution of advertising material or sample services; management services
PA: Customized Distribution Services, Inc.
20 Harry Shupe Blvd
Wharton NJ 07885
973 366-5090

(P-27211)
DEEP FOCUS INC
6922 Hollywood Blvd Fl 10, Hollywood (90028-6130)
PHONE....................................323 790-5340
EMP: 600
SALES (corp-wide): 50.7MM **Privately Held**
SIC: 8742 8743 Marketing consulting services; promotion service
HQ: Deep Focus, Inc.
229 W 43rd St Fl 8
New York NY 10036
212 792-6800

(P-27212)
DELOITTE CONSULTING LLP
Also Called: Bersin By Deloitte
555 Mission St, San Francisco (94105-0920)
PHONE....................................510 251-4400
Joshua Bersin, *Principal*
Sebnem Tokcan, *Information Mgr*
EMP: 63
SALES (corp-wide): 6.6B **Privately Held**
SIC: 8742 Financial consultant
HQ: Deloitte Consulting Llp
30 Rockefeller Plz
New York NY 10112
212 492-4000

(P-27213)
DELOITTE CONSULTING LLP
695 Town Center Dr # 1200, Costa Mesa (92626-1924)
PHONE....................................714 436-7100
Robert Lupcenpi, *Branch Mgr*
James Yu, *Partner*
Kim Peterson, *Business Dir*
John Fitzgerald, *Managing Dir*
Scott Plutko, *Managing Dir*
EMP: 63
SALES (corp-wide): 6.6B **Privately Held**
WEB: www.dctoolset.com
SIC: 8742 Management consulting services
HQ: Deloitte Consulting Llp
30 Rockefeller Plz
New York NY 10112
212 492-4000

(P-27214)
DENTISTAT INC
Also Called: Insurance Dentists Amer Idoa
1688 Dell Ave Ste 210, Campbell (95008-6926)
PHONE....................................408 376-0336
Richard H Guenther, *Ch of Bd*
Richard H Guenther DMD, *Ch of Bd*
Bret W Guenther, *President*
Richard L Garwood DDS, *CEO*
Harry J Kaplan, *Corp Secy*
EMP: 65

SQ FT: 7,661
SALES (est): 6.9MM **Privately Held**
WEB: www.dentistat.com
SIC: 8742 8748 Hospital & health services consultant; business consulting

(P-27215)
DEVELPMENT DIMENSIONS INTL INC
4160 Dublin Blvd Ste 450, Dublin (94568-7723)
PHONE....................................925 361-4246
Daniel Prachar, *Director*
EMP: 288
SALES (corp-wide): 188.4MM **Privately Held**
SIC: 8742 Training & development consultant
PA: Development Dimensions International, Inc.
1225 Washington Pike
Bridgeville PA 15017
412 257-0600

(P-27216)
DIGITALTHINK INC (DH)
601 Brannan St, San Francisco (94107-1511)
PHONE....................................415 625-4000
Michael W Pope, *President*
Jon Madonna, *Ch of Bd*
Robert J Krolik, *CFO*
Adam D Levy, *Vice Pres*
EMP: 250
SQ FT: 51,000
SALES (est): 15.6MM
SALES (corp-wide): 17B **Publicly Held**
WEB: www.digitalthink.com
SIC: 8742 Marketing consulting services
HQ: Convergys Customer Management Group Inc.
201 E 4th St Bsmt
Cincinnati OH 45202
513 723-6104

(P-27217)
DOWLING ADVISORY GROUP
3579 E Foothill Blvd # 651, Pasadena (91107-3119)
PHONE....................................626 319-1369
James Dowling, *Owner*
EMP: 100
SALES: 1MM **Privately Held**
SIC: 8742 Business consultant

(P-27218)
DPK CONSULTING
Also Called: Tetra Tech Dpk
605 Market St Ste 800, San Francisco (94105-3210)
PHONE....................................415 495-7772
Robert W Page, *President*
EMP: 100
SALES (est): 6.5MM
SALES (corp-wide): 2.7B **Publicly Held**
WEB: www.dpkconsulting.com
SIC: 8742 Business consultant
HQ: Ard, Inc.
159 Bank St Ste 300
Burlington VT 05401
802 658-3890

(P-27219)
DRAWBRIDGE INC
2121 S El Camino Real 7th, San Mateo (94403-1855)
PHONE....................................650 513-2323
Kamakshi Sivaramakrishnan, *CEO*
Jon Degennaro, *President*
Matt Gallatin, *CFO*
Christina Park, *Vice Pres*
Ryan Tokar, *Executive*
EMP: 85
SALES (est): 1.2MM **Privately Held**
SIC: 8742 Marketing consulting services

(P-27220)
DUFF & PHELPS LLC
1950 University Ave # 400, East Palo Alto (94303-2250)
PHONE....................................650 798-5500
Greg Franceschi, *Director*
EMP: 65
SALES (corp-wide): 558.1MM **Privately Held**
SIC: 8742 Financial consultant

HQ: Duff & Phelps, Llc
55 E 52nd St Fl 31
New York NY 10055
212 871-2000

(P-27221)
DUFF & PHELPS LLC
350 S Grand Ave Ste 3100, Los Angeles (90071-3420)
PHONE....................................213 270-2300
EMP: 67
SALES (corp-wide): 97.4MM **Privately Held**
SIC: 8742
HQ: Duff & Phelps, Llc
55 E 52nd St Fl 31
New York NY 10055
212 871-6777

(P-27222)
EASTERN GOLDFIELDS INC
1660 Hotel Cir N Ste 207, San Diego (92108-2803)
PHONE....................................619 497-2555
Michael McChesney, *CEO*
Derrick Short, *Credit Mgr*
Mike Tonkins, *Manager*
EMP: 218
SALES (est): 4.7MM **Privately Held**
SIC: 8742 Management consulting services

(P-27223)
ECORP CONSULTING INC (PA)
2525 Warren Dr, Rocklin (95677-2167)
PHONE....................................916 782-9100
James Stewart, *President*
James D Stewart, *CEO*
Bjorn Gregersen, *CFO*
Peter Balfour, *Vice Pres*
Harold Freeman, *Vice Pres*
EMP: 55
SQ FT: 6,950
SALES (est): 17.2MM **Privately Held**
WEB: www.ecorpconsulting.com
SIC: 8742 8748 Industry specialist consultants; business consulting

(P-27224)
EK HEALTH SERVICES INC (PA)
992 S De Anza Blvd Ste 10, San Jose (95129-2777)
PHONE....................................408 973-0888
Eunhee Kim, *President*
Kerri Wilson, *President*
Sang Kim, *CFO*
Douglas Benner, *Chief Mktg Ofcr*
Joseph N Desantis, *Vice Pres*
EMP: 53
SQ FT: 6,500
SALES (est): 12MM **Privately Held**
WEB: www.ekhealth.com
SIC: 8742 Hospital & health services consultant; human resource consulting services; personnel management consultant

(P-27225)
ENBIO CORP
150 E Olive Ave Ste 212, Burbank (91502-1850)
PHONE....................................818 953-9976
Arthur Zenian, *CEO*
Irving Flores, *Admin Asst*
Stefan Boghossian, *Technician*
Jay Trujillo, *Technician*
Matthew Euen, *Engineer*
EMP: 142
SQ FT: 1,500
SALES: 7.8MM **Privately Held**
SIC: 8742 Hospital & health services consultant

(P-27226)
ENSIGHTEN INC (HQ)
226 Airport Pkwy Ste 390, San Jose (95110-1026)
PHONE....................................650 249-4712
Josh Manion, *CEO*
Olivier Silvestre, *Vice Pres*
John Chambers, *Executive*
Jerome Cail, *Business Dir*
Kaitlyn Huffman, *Admin Asst*
EMP: 59 **EST:** 2012

SALES (est): 31.1MM
SALES (corp-wide): 3.2MM **Privately Held**
SIC: 8742 8741 Management consulting services; management services
PA: Tagman Limited
Henry Wood House 7th Floor
London W1W 7
203 770-7641

(P-27227)
ENTERPRISE EVENTS GROUP INC
950 Northgate Dr Ste 100, San Rafael (94903-3430)
PHONE....................................415 499-4444
Matt Gillam, *CEO*
Rich A Calcaterra, *Vice Pres*
Maggie Gillespie, *Executive*
Christopher Shavor, *Executive*
Jennifer Haskins, *Admin Asst*
EMP: 150
SQ FT: 18,000
SALES (est): 32.2MM **Privately Held**
WEB: www.eegweb.com
SIC: 8742 8743 Incentive or award program consultant; promotion service

(P-27228)
EVERWISE CORPORATION
2 Embarcadero Ctr Fl 8, San Francisco (94111-3833)
PHONE....................................888 250-6219
EMP: 77
SALES (corp-wide): 8.2MM **Privately Held**
SIC: 8742 Training & development consultant
PA: Everwise Corporation
18 W 21st St Fl 7
New York NY

(P-27229)
EXCEL MANAGED CARE DISA
3840 Watt Ave Bldg C, Sacramento (95821-2640)
PHONE....................................916 944-7185
Stephen Smetana, *Vice Pres*
Steve Smetana, *Vice Pres*
Brenda Smith, *Vice Pres*
William V Spaller, *Principal*
Paula Weissel, *Manager*
EMP: 92
SQ FT: 3,600
SALES (est): 9.7MM **Privately Held**
WEB: www.excelmanagedcare.com
SIC: 8742 Hospital & health services consultant

(P-27230)
EXPERIAN INFO SOLUTIONS INC
Also Called: Experian Marketing
841 Apollo St Ste 200, El Segundo (90245-4722)
PHONE....................................310 343-6700
Dana Shupe, *Branch Mgr*
Harry Tsoi, *Manager*
EMP: 110
SALES (corp-wide): 4.6B **Privately Held**
SIC: 8742 Marketing consulting services
HQ: Experian Information Solutions, Inc.
475 Anton Blvd
Costa Mesa CA 92626
714 830-7000

(P-27231)
EXPRESSWORKS INTERNATIONAL LLC (PA)
2410 Camino Ramon Ste 167, San Ramon (94583-4328)
PHONE....................................925 244-0900
John Quereto, *President*
Deborah Bernardi, *Info Tech Mgr*
Tony Harter, *Senior Mgr*
Stephen Zaruba, *Mng Member*
Cynthia Morrow, *Director*
EMP: 130
SQ FT: 12,000
SALES (est): 9.4MM **Privately Held**
WEB: www.expressworks.com
SIC: 8742 Marketing consulting services

P R O D U C T S & S V C S

(P-27232)
EXULT INC
121 Innovation Dr Ste 200, Irvine
(92617-3094)
P.O. Box 6300, Newport Beach (92658-6300)
PHONE..........................949 856-8800
James C Madden, *Ch of Bd*
Jim Aselta, *Partner*
Kevin Campbell, *President*
John Adams, *CFO*
Robert E Ball,
EMP: 2424
SQ FT: 22,000
SALES (est): 78.3MM
SALES (corp-wide): 5.6B **Privately Held**
SIC: 8742 Human resource consulting
 services
HQ: Alight (Us), Llc
 200 E Randolph St Ll3
 Chicago IL 60601
 312 381-1000

(P-27233)
FDSI LOGISTICS LLC
5703 Corsa Ave, Westlake Village
(91362-4001)
PHONE..........................818 971-3300
David Kolchins, *Vice Pres*
Dee Weller, *Marketing Staff*
John Hudson, *Director*
EMP: 75
SQ FT: 8,000
SALES: 13MM
SALES (corp-wide): 136.8B **Publicly
 Held**
WEB: www.fdsi.com
SIC: 8742 4731 Transportation consultant;
 freight transportation arrangement
PA: Cardinal Health, Inc.
 7000 Cardinal Pl
 Dublin OH 43017
 614 757-5000

(P-27234)
FINANCIAL ENGINES LLC (HQ)
1050 Enterprise Way Fl 3, Sunnyvale
(94089-1414)
PHONE..........................408 498-6000
Lawrence M Raffone, *President*
John B Bunch, *COO*
Craig L Foster, *CFO*
Robert Huret, *Bd of Directors*
Lewis E Antone Jr, *Exec VP*
EMP: 170 EST: 1996
SQ FT: 80,995
SALES: 480.5MM **Privately Held**
WEB: www.financialadvice.com
SIC: 8742 6282 6411 Financial consult-
 ant; investment advice; pension & retire-
 ment plan consultants
PA: Financial Engines Edelman, L.P.
 4000 Legato Rd Fl 9
 Fairfax VA 22033
 800 706-3916

(P-27235)
**FINANCIAL HEALTHCARE
SERVICES**
690 E Green St Ste 300, Pasadena
(91101-2121)
PHONE..........................626 356-7950
Esther Yatman, *President*
Lon Yatman, *Treasurer*
Weng Tang, *Controller*
EMP: 50
SQ FT: 10,000
SALES (est): 3.5MM **Privately Held**
WEB: www.uai-unifi.com
SIC: 8742 Administrative services consult-
 ant

(P-27236)
**FIRST CAPITOL CONSULTING
INC**
3530 Wilshire Blvd # 1460, Los Angeles
(90010-2334)
PHONE..........................213 382-1115
Robert Sheen, *President*
David Song, *Opers Staff*
Joanna H Kim, *General Counsel*
EMP: 73
SALES (est): 2.8MM **Privately Held**
WEB: www.fccila.net
SIC: 8742 Management consulting serv-
 ices

(P-27237)
FIRST PAGE SAGE LLC
2250 Union St, San Francisco
(94123-3900)
PHONE..........................415 624-3526
Evan Bailyn, *Mng Member*
Bradley Bailyn,
Katie Morris, *Accounts Exec*
EMP: 51
SALES (est): 83.2K **Privately Held**
SIC: 8742 Marketing consulting services

(P-27238)
**FISHERIES RESOURCE VLNTR
CORPS**
109 Stanford Ln, Seal Beach (90740-2533)
PHONE..........................562 596-9261
Thomas J Walsh, *President*
EMP: 113
SALES (est): 133.2K **Privately Held**
SIC: 8742 Business planning & organizing
 services

(P-27239)
**FOOD MANAGEMENT
ASSOCIATES INC**
22349 La Palma Ave # 115, Yorba Linda
(92887-3810)
PHONE..........................714 694-2828
Richard Warmolts, *President*
Laura Warmolts, *Vice Pres*
Rich Warlmots, *Marketing Mgr*
EMP: 50
SQ FT: 1,800
SALES (est): 7.2MM **Privately Held**
SIC: 8742 Business consultant

(P-27240)
**FOSTERING EXECUTIVE
LEADERSHIP**
4790 Irvine Blvd 105-432, Irvine
(92620-1973)
PHONE..........................949 651-6250
Tammy Wong, *President*
Sid Benes, *Opers Mgr*
Chris Martell, *Opers Staff*
EMP: 99
SALES (est): 4MM **Privately Held**
SIC: 8742 Training & development consult-
 ant

(P-27241)
**FRANK GATES SERVICE
COMPANY**
1107 Investment Blvd, El Dorado Hills
(95762-5736)
PHONE..........................916 934-0812
Chanteo Kvigne, *Manager*
EMP: 70
SALES (corp-wide): 2.3B **Privately Held**
WEB: www.fgsc.com
SIC: 8742 Management consulting serv-
 ices
HQ: The Frank Gates Service Company
 5000 Bradenton Ave # 100
 Dublin OH 43017
 614 793-8000

(P-27242)
FREIGHT MANAGEMENT INC
Also Called: F M I
2900 E La Palma Ave, Anaheim
(92806-2616)
PHONE..........................714 632-1440
Robert J Walters, *President*
Heidi Calamusa, *Vice Pres*
Tim Ponder, *Vice Pres*
Angela Shackford, *Vice Pres*
EMP: 53
SQ FT: 9,000
SALES: 60.6MM **Privately Held**
SIC: 8742 Transportation consultant

(P-27243)
FUTUREDONTICS INC (PA)
Also Called: 1-800 Dentist
6060 Center Dr Fl 7, Los Angeles
(90045-1596)
PHONE..........................310 215-6400
Michael Turner, *CEO*
Ronald Joyal, *COO*
Gary St Denis, *Chairman*
Jonathan Kass, *Vice Pres*
Bret McAllister, *CIO*
EMP: 102

SQ FT: 35,000
SALES (est): 37.4MM **Privately Held**
WEB: www.futuredontics.com
SIC: 8742 Marketing consulting services

(P-27244)
GALLUP INC
Also Called: Gallup Organization, The
18300 Von Karman Ave, Irvine
(92612-1057)
PHONE..........................949 474-2700
Kelly Aylward, *Partner*
Angel Hernandez, *Sales Staff*
Craig Kamins, *Associate*
EMP: 50
SALES (corp-wide): 175.4MM **Privately
 Held**
SIC: 8742 Marketing consulting services
PA: Gallup, Inc.
 901 F St Nw Ste 400
 Washington DC 20004
 202 715-3030

(P-27245)
**GAVIN DE BECKER &
ASSOCIATES**
11684 Ventura Blvd # 440, Studio City
(91604-2699)
PHONE..........................818 760-4213
Gavin De Becker, *President*
Michael La Fever, *Exec VP*
Ryan Davis, *Vice Pres*
Alan Peng, *Vice Pres*
Val Xharra, *Vice Pres*
EMP: 180
SQ FT: 1,600
SALES (est): 32.1MM **Privately Held**
SIC: 8742 Business consultant

(P-27246)
**GLOBAL MANAGEMENT
COMPANY LLC**
3150 E Pico Blvd, Los Angeles
(90023-3632)
PHONE..........................323 261-8114
Sandra Berg,
EMP: 100
SALES (est): 2.5MM **Privately Held**
SIC: 8742 Management consulting serv-
 ices

(P-27247)
GLOBAL WORK GROUP LLC
Also Called: Global Realty Group
17224 San Fernando, Granada Hills
(91344)
PHONE..........................424 220-9994
Geoff Mills, *Mng Member*
Jill Henson, *Treasurer*
EMP: 75
SALES: 30MM **Privately Held**
SIC: 8742 7389 Materials mgmt. (purchas-
 ing, handling, inventory) consultant;

(P-27248)
GOETZMAN GROUP INC (PA)
21700 Oxnard St Ste 1540, Woodland Hills
(91367-3644)
PHONE..........................818 595-1112
Greg Goetzman, *President*
EMP: 75
SQ FT: 4,500
SALES (est): 8.9MM **Privately Held**
WEB: www.goetzmangroup.com
SIC: 8742 8721 Management consulting
 services; accounting, auditing & book-
 keeping

(P-27249)
GOLD TREE INC
Also Called: New Wave Transport
11643 E Telg Rd St 204, Santa Fe Springs
(90670)
PHONE..........................562 801-0218
Jose S Funes, *CEO*
EMP: 60
SALES (est): 2.8MM **Privately Held**
SIC: 8742 Transportation consultant

(P-27250)
GORILLA TECH AMERICAS INC
2678 Bishop Dr Ste 290, San Ramon
(94583)
PHONE..........................925 365-1161
Carlo Tortora, *President*
EMP: 99

SALES (est): 6MM **Privately Held**
SIC: 8742 Marketing consulting services

(P-27251)
GPS FLYERS
527 Prospect Ave, Hermosa Beach
(90254-4940)
PHONE..........................951 588-7777
Patrick Antrim, *Owner*
EMP: 51
SQ FT: 3,000
SALES: 1.1MM **Privately Held**
SIC: 8742 Marketing consulting services

(P-27252)
GRAND VIEW RESEARCH INC
201 Spear St Ste 1100, San Francisco
(94105-6164)
PHONE..........................415 349-0058
Brian Haven, *CEO*
Shomali Naranje, *Executive*
Thomas Philip, *Executive*
Sakshi Bedi, *Research*
Poorva Chaudhari, *Research*
EMP: 50
SQ FT: 1,000
SALES (est): 4MM **Privately Held**
SIC: 8742 Marketing consulting services

(P-27253)
GRAPHIC ORB INC
8687 Melrose Ave Ste 8, West Hollywood
(90069-5746)
PHONE..........................310 967-2350
John Thompson, *President*
Denis Adair, *Vice Pres*
EMP: 64 EST: 1970
SQ FT: 35,000
SALES (est): 4.3MM **Privately Held**
WEB: www.graphicorb.com
SIC: 8742 Marketing consulting services

(P-27254)
GREAT DESTINATIONS INC
25510 Commercentre Dr, Lake Forest
(92630-8855)
PHONE..........................949 667-9401
Andrew Gennuso, *President*
Nishant Machado, *Vice Pres*
Sarahi Maldonado, *Office Mgr*
EMP: 95
SQ FT: 3,000
SALES: 9MM **Privately Held**
SIC: 8742 Marketing consulting services

(P-27255)
GREENSPIRE LLC
11620 Wilshire Blvd # 410, Los Angeles
(90025-6805)
PHONE..........................310 477-7686
David Murray, *CEO*
Mitchel Young, *Controller*
Lindsie Garrison, *Human Res Dir*
EMP: 80
SQ FT: 4,000
SALES (est): 1.6MM **Privately Held**
SIC: 8742 7389 Marketing consulting
 services;

(P-27256)
HAMILTON PARTNERS
1301 Shoreway Rd Ste 250, Burlingame
(94010)
PHONE..........................650 347-8800
John Hamilton, *President*
EMP: 55
SALES (est): 293.1K **Privately Held**
SIC: 8742 Training & development consult-
 ant

(P-27257)
HARRIS MYCFO INC
2200 Geng Rd Ste 100, Palo Alto
(94303-3358)
PHONE..........................480 348-7725
Michael Montogomery, *President*
John Benevides, *President*
Craig Rawlins, *President*
Ross Kari, *CFO*
Harvey Armstrong, *Managing Dir*
EMP: 90
SALES (est): 16.2MM **Privately Held**
SIC: 8742 Financial consultant

(P-27258)
HDR ENGINEERING INC
8690 Balboa Ave Ste 200, San Diego
(92123-6507)
PHONE..................................858 712-8400
Bill Bennett, *Branch Mgr*
EMP: 50
SALES (corp-wide): 2.3B **Privately Held**
SIC: 8742 8711 Management consulting
services; engineering services
HQ: Hdr Engineering, Inc.
1917 S 67th St
Omaha NE 68106
402 399-1000

(P-27259)
HDR ENGINEERING INC
350 S Grand Ave Ste 2900, Los Angeles
(90071-3406)
PHONE..................................626 584-1700
Al Korth, *Manager*
EMP: 130
SALES (corp-wide): 2.3B **Privately Held**
SIC: 8742 8711 Management consulting
services; engineering services
HQ: Hdr Engineering, Inc.
1917 S 67th St
Omaha NE 68106
402 399-1000

(P-27260)
HDR ENGINEERING INC
201 California St # 1500, San Francisco
(94111-5002)
PHONE..................................415 546-4200
Michael Orr, *Manager*
EMP: 99
SALES (corp-wide): 2.3B **Privately Held**
SIC: 8742 8711 Management consulting
services; engineering services
HQ: Hdr Engineering, Inc.
1917 S 67th St
Omaha NE 68106
402 399-1000

(P-27261)
HDR ENGINEERING INC
2365 Iron Point Rd # 300, Folsom
(95630-8711)
PHONE..................................916 817-4700
Brent Felker, *Branch Mgr*
EMP: 86
SALES (corp-wide): 2.3B **Privately Held**
SIC: 8742 Construction project manage-
ment consultant
HQ: Hdr Engineering, Inc.
1917 S 67th St
Omaha NE 68106
402 399-1000

(P-27262)
**HEALTH EDUC ECONOMIC
DEVLPMNT**
304 Coral Reef Rd, Alameda (94501-5929)
PHONE..................................510 604-6143
Leeda Rashid, *President*
EMP: 99
SALES (est): 2.7MM **Privately Held**
SIC: 8742 Hospital & health services con-
sultant

(P-27263)
HIS MANNA INC
Also Called: Workforce
150 Felker St Ste B, Santa Cruz
(95060-2849)
P.O. Box 1527 (95061-1527)
PHONE..................................831 423-5515
Gordon Agrella, *President*
Carolyn Agrella, *Vice Pres*
Baisy Alvarez, *Admin Asst*
EMP: 200 **EST:** 1972
SQ FT: 4,200
SALES (est): 12.2MM **Privately Held**
WEB: www.hismanna.com
SIC: 8742 7549 7349 Management con-
sulting services; automotive maintenance
services; building maintenance, except
repairs

(P-27264)
**HORIZON ACTUARIAL
SERVICES LLC**
5200 Lankershim Blvd, North Hollywood
(91601-3155)
PHONE..................................818 691-2000
Larry H Weitzner,
Ron Stonehill, *Associate*
EMP: 92
SALES (corp-wide): 16.3MM **Privately
Held**
SIC: 8742 Compensation & benefits plan-
ning consultant
PA: Horizon Actuarial Services Llc
8601 Georgia Ave Ste 700
Silver Spring MD 20910
240 247-4600

(P-27265)
HORNBLOWER YACHTS INC
2825 5th Ave, San Diego (92103-6326)
PHONE..................................619 234-8687
Jim Unger, *Branch Mgr*
EMP: 160
SALES (corp-wide): 126.6MM **Privately
Held**
WEB: www.hornbloweryachts.com
SIC: 8742 7999 7389 7299 Restaurant &
food services consultants; pleasure boat
rental; convention & show services; wed-
ding chapel, privately operated
PA: Hornblower Yachts, Llc
On The Embarcadero Pier 3 St Pier
San Francisco CA 94111
415 788-8866

(P-27266)
HP CAPITAL LLC
3111 Camino Del Rio N, San Diego
(92108-5720)
PHONE..................................858 753-8486
Samuel A Price,
EMP: 65
SQ FT: 600
SALES: 500K **Privately Held**
SIC: 8742 Management consulting serv-
ices

(P-27267)
HUMETRIX INC
1155 Camino Del Mar Ste 5, Del Mar
(92014-2605)
PHONE..................................858 259-8987
Bettina Experton, *President*
Claudia M Ellison, *Vice Pres*
EMP: 50
SALES (est): 4.3MM **Privately Held**
WEB: www.humetrix.com
SIC: 8742 5047 3841 Hospital & health
services consultant; medical & hospital
equipment; surgical & medical instru-
ments

(P-27268)
ICF CONSULTING GROUP INC
101 Lucas Valley Rd # 249, San Rafael
(94903-1700)
PHONE..................................703 934-3000
Berlin Brett, *Branch Mgr*
EMP: 509
SALES (corp-wide): 1.2B **Publicly Held**
SIC: 8742 Business consultant
HQ: Icf Consulting Group, Inc.
9300 Lee Hwy Ste G130
Fairfax VA 22031
703 934-3000

(P-27269)
ICF JONES & STOKES INC
1 Ada Ste 100, Irvine (92618-5339)
PHONE..................................949 333-6600
David Freytag, *Manager*
EMP: 99
SALES (corp-wide): 1.2B **Publicly Held**
SIC: 8742 8748 Business consultant; busi-
ness consulting
HQ: Icf Jones & Stokes, Inc
9300 Lee Hwy
Fairfax VA 22031
703 934-3000

(P-27270)
**INDIGO HOSPITALITY
MANAGEMENT**
Also Called: Indigo Hotels
1817 N Sepulveda Blvd, Manhattan Beach
(90266-2901)
PHONE..................................310 787-7795
B C Patel, *President*
Barrett Patel, *Director*
EMP: 50 **EST:** 1992
SALES (est): 2.3MM **Privately Held**
WEB: www.indigohotels.com
SIC: 8742 Real estate consultant

(P-27271)
INDUCTIVE AUTOMATION LLC
90 Blue Ravine Rd, Folsom (95630-4715)
PHONE..................................800 266-7798
Steve Hechtman, *President*
Wendi-Lynn Hechtman, *Vice Pres*
Katharina Jeschke,
Jason Waits, *Principal*
Don Pearson, *Security Dir*
EMP: 100
SALES (est): 259.1K **Privately Held**
SIC: 8742 5734 Automation & robotics
consultant; computer software & acces-
sories

(P-27272)
INDVLS
9 Macarthur Pl Unit 2306, Santa Ana
(92707-6755)
PHONE..................................818 703-3855
Ze'shawn Campbell,
EMP: 50
SQ FT: 3,000
SALES: 5MM **Privately Held**
SIC: 8742 7311 Marketing consulting serv-
ices; advertising agencies

(P-27273)
**INFORMA RESEARCH SERVICES
INC (DH)**
26565 Agoura Rd Ste 300, Calabasas
(91302-1942)
PHONE..................................818 880-8877
Michael E Adler, *President*
Charles A Miwa, *COO*
Lori Jomsky, *Senior VP*
Brian Richards, *Vice Pres*
Steven Fordham, *Engineer*
EMP: 193
SQ FT: 16,000
SALES (est): 37MM **Privately Held**
WEB: www.informars.com
SIC: 8742 Banking & finance consultant
HQ: Informa Plc
Mortimer House
London W1T 3
207 017-5000

(P-27274)
INKLING SYSTEMS INC
343 Sansome St Fl 8, San Francisco
(94104-1303)
PHONE..................................415 975-4420
Matt Macinnis, *CEO*
Rob Cromwell, *President*
Charles Macinnis, *President*
Harper Casimiro, *Admin Asst*
Jessica Jenkins, *Software Engr*
EMP: 66
SALES (est): 10.9MM **Privately Held**
SIC: 8742 Management consulting serv-
ices
PA: Marlin Equity Partners, Llc
338 Pier Ave
Hermosa Beach CA 90254

(P-27275)
INSPERITY INC
1440 Bridgegate Dr # 200, Diamond Bar
(91765-3935)
PHONE..................................909 569-1000
Richard Cleek, *General Mgr*
EMP: 100
SALES (corp-wide): 3.3B **Publicly Held**
WEB: www.administaff.com
SIC: 8742 Human resource consulting
services

PA: Insperity, Inc.
19001 Crescent Springs Dr
Kingwood TX 77339
281 358-8986

(P-27276)
INTELISYS INC
1318 Redwood Way Ste 120, Petaluma
(94954-6542)
PHONE..................................800 615-8330
Jay Bradley, *President*
EMP: 80 **Publicly Held**
SIC: 8742 Marketing consulting services
HQ: Intelisys, Inc.
6 Logue Ct
Greenville SC 29615
800 944-2432

(P-27277)
INTER CON SECURITY INC
2801 Camino Del Rio S 300h, San Diego
(92108-3800)
PHONE..................................619 523-0291
Rick Hernadez, *President*
Collette Sobray, *Personnel*
Andrew Wright, *Director*
EMP: 50
SALES (est): 2.7MM **Privately Held**
WEB: www.interconsecurity.com
SIC: 8742 7381 Industry specialist con-
sultants; security guard service

(P-27278)
**INTERNATIONAL BUS MCHS
CORP**
Also Called: IBM
4000 Executive Pkwy # 300, San Ramon
(94583-4257)
PHONE..................................925 277-5000
Lynn Dail, *Branch Mgr*
Dana Grove, *Program Mgr*
Richard Sweda, *Analyst*
Jamie Mendez, *Marketing Mgr*
Karin Ball, *Marketing Staff*
EMP: 186
SALES (corp-wide): 79.1B **Publicly Held**
WEB: www.ibm.com
SIC: 8742 Sales (including sales manage-
ment) consultant
PA: International Business Machines Cor-
poration
1 New Orchard Rd Ste 1 # 1
Armonk NY 10504
914 499-1900

(P-27279)
**INTERNET MARKETING ASSN
INC**
10 Mar Del Rey, San Clemente
(92673-2761)
PHONE..................................949 443-9300
Sinan Kanatsiz, *Principal*
Rachel Reenders, *Exec Dir*
Chanelle Dayrit, *Accounts Exec*
EMP: 65
SALES (est): 4.1MM **Privately Held**
SIC: 8742 Marketing consulting services

(P-27280)
**INTERSTATE ELECTRONICS
CORP**
Also Called: Human Resources
708 E Vermont Ave, Anaheim (92805-5611)
PHONE..................................714 758-0500
EMP: 600
SALES (corp-wide): 9.5B **Publicly Held**
SIC: 8742 Human resource consulting
services
HQ: Interstate Electronics Corporation
602 E Vermont Ave
Anaheim CA 92805
714 758-0500

(P-27281)
INTRAVAS INC
Also Called: Review Boost
6300 Yarrow Dr, Carlsbad (92011-1542)
PHONE..................................760 650-4040
Guillermo Rivas, *CEO*
EMP: 65
SALES (est): 3.9MM **Privately Held**
SIC: 8742 Marketing consulting services

(P-27282)
ISYS SOLUTIONS INC
2601 Saturn St Ste 302, Brea
(92821-6702)
PHONE..............................714 521-7656
Chris Loumakis, *CEO*
EMP: 69
SALES (est): 9.3MM **Privately Held**
WEB: www.isyscal.com
SIC: 8742 Hospital & health services consultant

(P-27283)
ITA GROUP INC
455 Market St Ste 1450, San Francisco
(94105-2442)
PHONE..............................415 277-3200
Deborah Ebsen, *General Mgr*
EMP: 119
SALES (corp-wide): 145.9MM **Privately Held**
SIC: 8742 Incentive or award program consultant
PA: Ita Group, Inc
4600 Westown Pkwy Ste 100
West Des Moines IA 50266
515 326-3400

(P-27284)
J P CONSULTING
4690 E 2nd St Ste 3, Benicia (94510-1008)
PHONE..............................707 747-4800
Jody Hoberson, *Co-Owner*
Robert Perkey, *Co-Owner*
EMP: 50
SALES (est): 3.6MM **Privately Held**
SIC: 8742 Management consulting services

(P-27285)
JACK NADEL INC (PA)
Also Called: Jack Nadel International
8701 Bellanca Ave, Los Angeles
(90045-4411)
P.O. Box 8342, Pasadena (91109-8342)
PHONE..............................310 815-2600
Craig Nadel, *CEO*
Sarah Kliewer, *Partner*
Robert Kritzler, *CFO*
Jack Nadel, *Chairman*
Debbie Abergel, *Senior VP*
EMP: 70 **EST:** 1953
SQ FT: 30,000
SALES (est): 106MM **Privately Held**
WEB: www.nadel.com
SIC: 8742 5199 Incentive or award program consultant; gifts & novelties

(P-27286)
JACOBS PROJECT MANAGEMENT CO
300 Frank H Ogawa Plz, Oakland
(94612-2037)
PHONE..............................510 457-2436
Steve Paquette, *Manager*
Frank Joyce, *Contract Mgr*
EMP: 95
SALES (est): 2.5MM
SALES (corp-wide): 10B **Publicly Held**
SIC: 8742 Management consulting services
PA: Jacobs Engineering Group Inc.
1999 Bryan St Ste 1200
Dallas TX 75201
214 583-8500

(P-27287)
JACOBUS CONSULTING INC
15375 Barranca Pkwy B202, Irvine
(92618-2213)
PHONE..............................949 727-0720
Sandra Jacobs, *President*
Alan Hall, *Vice Pres*
Nelson Matt, *Vice Pres*
Lynette Johnson, *Executive Asst*
Arizdelsy Vega, *Executive Asst*
EMP: 50
SQ FT: 1,800
SALES (est): 5.8MM **Privately Held**
SIC: 8742 Hospital & health services consultant

(P-27288)
JB UPLAND LTD LIABILITY CO
9087 Arrow Rte Ste 140, Rancho Cucamonga (91730-4431)
PHONE..............................909 944-5456
Mary R McDonagh,
EMP: 50
SALES (est): 2.4MM **Privately Held**
SIC: 8742 Marketing consulting services

(P-27289)
JNR INC
19900 Macarthur Blvd # 700, Irvine
(92612-8416)
PHONE..............................949 476-2788
James Jalet III, *CEO*
Luann Jalet, *COO*
Greg Moody, *CFO*
Thomas Chiang, *Exec VP*
Simca Le, *Administration*
EMP: 60
SQ FT: 15,000
SALES (est): 12MM **Privately Held**
WEB: www.jnrinc.com
SIC: 8742 7389 4724 Incentive or award program consultant; convention & show services; tourist agency arranging transport, lodging & car rental

(P-27290)
JOBVITE INC
1300 S El Camino Real # 400, San Mateo
(94402-2970)
PHONE..............................650 376-7200
Dan Finnigan, *CEO*
Charles Stryker, *President*
Peter Maloney, *CFO*
John Winkenbach, *CFO*
Kimberley Kasper, *Chief Mktg Ofcr*
EMP: 100
SALES (est): 15.9MM **Privately Held**
SIC: 8742 Human resource consulting services

(P-27291)
K & S TOWING & TRANSPORT
Also Called: K & S Auto, Truck & Tractor
2780 Willow Pass Rd, Bay Point
(94565-6603)
PHONE..............................925 709-0759
Khurram Shah, *Owner*
EMP: 55
SQ FT: 10,000
SALES: 5.6MM **Privately Held**
WEB: www.kandstowing.com
SIC: 8742 7299 Transportation consultant; personal item care & storage services

(P-27292)
KABLER CONSTRUCTION SVCS INC
467 Miller Ave, Mill Valley (94941-2941)
PHONE..............................415 888-8812
Sophia Kabler Cowley, *President*
John Kabler, *Vice Pres*
EMP: 50
SALES: 536K **Privately Held**
SIC: 8742 1771 8741 Construction project management consultant; concrete work; construction management

(P-27293)
KASPICK & CO LLC (DH)
Also Called: Teachers Insurance and Annuity
203 Redwood Shores Pkwy # 300, Redwood City (94065-6121)
PHONE..............................650 585-4100
Lindy Sherwood, *Managing Dir*
Thomas Grenville, *Officer*
Michael Kahn, *Managing Dir*
Dave Libengood, *General Mgr*
Andrew King, *Admin Asst*
EMP: 60
SALES (est): 6.4MM
SALES (corp-wide): 30.3B **Privately Held**
WEB: www.kaspick.com
SIC: 8742 Financial consultant
HQ: Teachers Insurance And Annuity Association-College Retirement Equities Fund
730 3rd Ave Ste 2a
New York NY 10017
212 490-9000

(P-27294)
KENSHOO INC (HQ)
22 4th St Fl 7, San Francisco (94103-3141)
PHONE..............................877 536-7462
Yoav Izhar-Prato, *CEO*
Timothy Doherty, *Partner*
Shirley Grill-Rachman, *COO*
Sarit Firon, *CFO*
Igal Shany, *CFO*
EMP: 110
SALES (est): 18.6MM **Privately Held**
SIC: 8742 Marketing consulting services
PA: Kenshoo Ltd
30 Habarzel
Tel Aviv-Jaffa
732 862-507

(P-27295)
KORN/FERRY INTERNATIONAL (PA)
Also Called: KORN FERRY
1900 Avenue Stars, Los Angeles (90067)
PHONE..............................310 552-1834
Gary D Burnison, *President*
Michael Rottblatt, *Senior Partner*
Craig Dunlevie, *Partner*
Matthew Page, *Partner*
Rafael A Sierra, *Partner*
EMP: 136 **EST:** 1969
SALES: 1.8B **Publicly Held**
WEB: www.kornferry.com
SIC: 8742 7361 Management consulting services; executive placement

(P-27296)
KPC GROUP LLC (PA)
6800 Indiana Ave Ste 130, Riverside
(92506-4266)
PHONE..............................951 782-8812
Kali Chaudhuri, *Mng Member*
Mike Mortru,
Kali P Chaudhuri, *Mng Member*
Michael O'Brien, *Mng Member*
EMP: 167
SALES (est): 12.4MM **Privately Held**
SIC: 8742 Financial consultant

(P-27297)
LABMED PARTNERS
5000 Birch St, Newport Beach
(92660-2127)
PHONE..............................949 242-9925
EMP: 50
SALES (est): 1.3MM **Privately Held**
SIC: 8742

(P-27298)
LANCASHIRE GROUP INCORPORATED
Also Called: Tlg
37053 Cherry St Ste 210, Newark
(94560-3782)
P.O. Box 1138 (94560-6138)
PHONE..............................510 792-9384
Ian McDonnell, *President*
Johnny Lambert, *COO*
John Cerelli, *CFO*
John Lambert, *Senior VP*
EMP: 279
SQ FT: 2,400
SALES (est): 25.5MM **Privately Held**
WEB: www.tlg-inc.com
SIC: 8742 Industry specialist consultants

(P-27299)
LBA INC (PA)
Also Called: Layton-Belling & Associates
3347 Michelson Dr Ste 200, Irvine
(92612-0687)
PHONE..............................949 833-0400
Philip Belling, *CEO*
Steve Layton, *President*
Tom Rutherford, *CFO*
Kim Cart, *Property Mgr*
EMP: 120
SALES (est): 13.5MM **Privately Held**
SIC: 8742 Real estate consultant

(P-27300)
LEAF COMMERCIAL CAPITAL INC
1100 Town & Country Rd, Orange
(92868-4600)
PHONE..............................866 219-7924
Rich Vohra, *Vice Pres*

EMP: 50 **Publicly Held**
SIC: 8742 Financial consultant
HQ: Leaf Commercial Capital, Inc.
2005 Market St Fl 14
Philadelphia PA 19103
800 819-5556

(P-27301)
LEEKILPATRICK MANAGEMENT INC
Also Called: Management Success
324 S Myrtle Ave, Monrovia (91016-2849)
PHONE..............................818 500-9631
Bill Kilpatrick, *President*
EMP: 60
SQ FT: 18,200
SALES (est): 6.8MM **Privately Held**
SIC: 8742 7538 Business consultant; general automotive repair shops

(P-27302)
LEGACY MARKETING GROUP (PA)
2090 Marina Ave, Petaluma (94954-6714)
PHONE..............................707 778-8638
Lynda R Pitts, *CEO*
Preston Pitts, *President*
Chris Eaken, *Vice Pres*
Dayna Wells, *Vice Pres*
EMP: 215
SALES (est): 13.9MM **Privately Held**
WEB: www.legacynet.com
SIC: 8742 Marketing consulting services

(P-27303)
LEK CONSULTING LLC
1100 Glendon Ave Ste 2100, Los Angeles
(90024-3592)
PHONE..............................310 209-9800
Sherice Lenons, *Manager*
William Frack, *Exec Dir*
Chelsey Kobuch, *Admin Asst*
Matthias Kleinz, *Manager*
Nicholas Fritz-Zavacki, *Associate*
EMP: 60 **Privately Held**
WEB: www.lek.com
SIC: 8742 8748 Business consultant; business consulting
PA: L.E.K. Consulting, Llc
75 State St Ste 1901
Boston MA 02109

(P-27304)
LINARDOS ENTERPRISES INC
75 Broadway, San Francisco (94111-1422)
PHONE..............................415 644-0827
Peter Lionardo, *President*
Ashley Pease, *Office Mgr*
EMP: 58
SQ FT: 800
SALES: 5.7MM **Privately Held**
SIC: 8742 General management consultant

(P-27305)
LLP MOSS ADAMS
1000 Main St, NAPA (94559-2645)
PHONE..............................707 224-4001
Jennifer Rabanal, *Branch Mgr*
EMP: 69
SALES (corp-wide): 350.4MM **Privately Held**
SIC: 8742 Financial consultant
PA: Moss Adams Llp
999 3rd Ave Ste 2800
Seattle WA 98104
206 302-6800

(P-27306)
LOS ANGELES GUILD LLC
Also Called: Guild, The
3437 W El Segundo Blvd, Hawthorne
(90250-4816)
PHONE..............................323 733-5033
Jeffrey C Hatfield,
Peter Brown,
Sam Ewan,
Jeffrey Hatfield,
EMP: 201 **EST:** 2007
SALES (est): 22.7MM **Privately Held**
SIC: 8742 7319 Marketing consulting services; display advertising service

1156 2019 Directory of California
Wholesalers and Services Companies ▲ = Import ▼=Export
◆ =Import/Export

(P-27307)
LOS ANGELES CLIPPERS FOUNDATION
Also Called: Lac Club
1111 S Figueroa St # 1100, Los Angeles (90015-1300)
PHONE..................213 742-7555
Donald Sterling, *President*
EMP: 55
SALES: 1.3MM **Privately Held**
SIC: 8742 Sales (including sales management) consultant

(P-27308)
LOTUS INTERWORKS INC
10801 National Blvd # 500, Los Angeles (90064-4152)
PHONE..................310 442-3330
Bhaskarpilai Gopinath, *Ch of Bd*
EMP: 200
SQ FT: 10,000
SALES (est): 13.3MM **Privately Held**
WEB: www.lotusinterworks.com
SIC: 8742 Management consulting services

(P-27309)
LYNUP CORPORATION
16875 W Bernardo Dr # 110, San Diego (92127-1670)
PHONE..................858 207-4610
Parvin Garbo-Inkumsah, *President*
Drew Brickweg, *Exec VP*
Aaron J Gaeir, *Vice Pres*
EMP: 60 EST: 2010
SALES (est): 5.7MM **Privately Held**
SIC: 8742 Marketing consulting services

(P-27310)
M E NOLLKAMPER INC (PA)
940 Manor Way, Corona (92882-7979)
PHONE..................951 737-9300
Milton Nollkamper, *President*
EMP: 50
SALES (est): 3MM **Privately Held**
SIC: 8742 8711 Public utilities consultant; consulting engineer

(P-27311)
M F SALTA CO INC (PA)
Also Called: Atlas Advertising
20 Executive Park Ste 150, Irvine (92614-4732)
PHONE..................562 421-2512
Mike Salta, *President*
James Smith, *Treasurer*
EMP: 70
SALES (est): 3.6MM **Privately Held**
SIC: 8742 Management consulting services

(P-27312)
M SQUARED CONSULTING INC (HQ)
111 Sutter St Ste 900, San Francisco (94104-4523)
PHONE..................415 391-1038
John Kunzweiler, *CEO*
Dirk Sodestrom, *CFO*
David Graves, *Vice Pres*
Anita Kratka, *Vice Pres*
John Pennock, *Vice Pres*
EMP: 240
SQ FT: 9,600
SALES (est): 24.5MM
SALES (corp-wide): 43.3MM **Privately Held**
WEB: www.msquared.com
SIC: 8742 Business consultant
PA: Edwards Solomon Group Llc
1255 Drummers Ln Ste 200
Wayne PA 19087
610 902-0440

(P-27313)
MALCO SERVICES INC
3703 E Melville Way, Anaheim (92806-2122)
PHONE..................714 630-0194
Duane Malone, *President*
Joe Malone, *COO*
EMP: 100
SQ FT: 15,831

SALES: 4MM **Privately Held**
SIC: 8742 Maintenance management consultant

(P-27314)
MANAGEMENT TRUST ASSN INC
12607 Hiddencreek Way R, Cerritos (90703-2146)
PHONE..................562 926-3372
Christie Alviso, *Administration*
EMP: 109 **Privately Held**
SIC: 8742 8741 Management consulting services; business management
PA: The Management Trust Association Inc
15661 Red Hill Ave # 201
Tustin CA 92780

(P-27315)
MANSION HOSPITALITY SERVICES
3410 Westover St, McClellan (95652-1005)
PHONE..................916 643-6222
Russell A Dazzio, *Chairman*
Roland Moritz, *Corp Secy*
EMP: 60
SALES (est): 2.2MM **Privately Held**
SIC: 8742 Management consulting services

(P-27316)
MAPP DIGITAL US LLC
9276 Scranton Rd Ste 500, San Diego (92121-7707)
PHONE..................619 295-1856
Steve Warren, *CEO*
Jonah Sulak, *President*
Claire Long, *CFO*
Eric Hinkle, *Chairman*
Matthew Langie, *Chief Mktg Ofcr*
EMP: 125 EST: 2000
SQ FT: 14,000
SALES (est): 9.2MM **Privately Held**
WEB: www.bluehornet.com
SIC: 8742 Marketing consulting services
PA: Marlin Equity Partners, Llc
338 Pier Ave
Hermosa Beach CA 90254

(P-27317)
MARCUS BUCKINGHAM COMPANY
8350 Wilshire Blvd # 200, Beverly Hills (90211-2327)
PHONE..................323 302-9810
Marcus Buckingham, *CEO*
Christian Gomez, *President*
EMP: 60
SALES (est): 8.7MM
SALES (corp-wide): 13.3B **Publicly Held**
SIC: 8742 Human resource consulting services
PA: Automatic Data Processing, Inc.
1 Adp Blvd Ste 1 # 1
Roseland NJ 07068
973 974-5000

(P-27318)
MARGINPOINT (PA)
23046 Avnida De La Crlota Carlota, Laguna Hills (92653)
PHONE..................949 766-9933
Vince Sheeran, *CEO*
Michael J Hammons, *President*
Stephen Desantis, *CFO*
Scott Poteracki, *CFO*
Anton Visser, *Chief Mktg Ofcr*
EMP: 70
SALES (est): 10MM **Privately Held**
WEB: www.nexiant.com
SIC: 8742 Management consulting services

(P-27319)
MARKETBRIDGE CORP
601 Montgomery St Ste 650, San Francisco (94111-2608)
PHONE..................240 752-1800
Ashok Nayyar, *Branch Mgr*
EMP: 62 **Privately Held**
SIC: 8742 Marketing consulting services

PA: Marketbridge Corp.
4800 Montgomery Ln # 500
Bethesda MD 20814

(P-27320)
MARKETING PROFESSIONALS INC
5100 E La Palma Ave # 116, Anaheim (92807-2081)
PHONE..................714 578-0500
Joseph L Smith, *President*
Cynthia A Simms, *CFO*
George M Schnitzer, *Chairman*
EMP: 350
SQ FT: 900
SALES (est): 18.5MM **Privately Held**
WEB: www.marketingprofessionals.org
SIC: 8742 7319 Marketing consulting services; retail trade consultant; display advertising service

(P-27321)
MARKSYS LLC
3725 Cincinnati Ave # 200, Rocklin (95765-1220)
PHONE..................916 745-4883
Jerod Meents, *Principal*
Kyle Schubert, *Mktg Dir*
Melissa Barrett, *Marketing Staff*
Ryan Gutshall,
EMP: 60
SQ FT: 45,000
SALES: 34MM **Privately Held**
SIC: 8742

(P-27322)
MATERIALS MARKETING
250 Baker St Ste 100, Costa Mesa (92626-4574)
PHONE..................949 729-9881
John Cina, *Manager*
EMP: 100
SALES (est): 4.9MM **Privately Held**
SIC: 8742 Marketing consulting services

(P-27323)
MATT CONSTRUCTION CORPORATION (PA)
9814 Norwalk Blvd Ste 100, Santa Fe Springs (90670-2997)
PHONE..................562 903-2277
Steve F Matt, *President*
Paul J Matt, *CEO*
Marvin Wheat, *COO*
Kenneth Blakeley, *CFO*
Alan B Matt, *Corp Secy*
EMP: 131
SQ FT: 21,000
SALES (est): 32MM **Privately Held**
WEB: www.mattconstruction.com
SIC: 8742 Construction project management consultant

(P-27324)
MAXIMUS INC
Also Called: Maximus CA Healthy Family
625 Coolidge Dr Ste 100, Folsom (95630-3197)
PHONE..................916 673-2175
John Antifino, *Principal*
Jeff Dew, *Project Dir*
EMP: 70
SALES (corp-wide): 2.4B **Publicly Held**
WEB: www.maxinc.com
SIC: 8742 Business consultant
PA: Maximus, Inc.
1891 Metro Center Dr
Reston VA 20190
703 251-8500

(P-27325)
MAXIMUS INC
625 Coolidge Dr Ste 100, Folsom (95630-3197)
PHONE..................916 673-4162
Michael Lemburg, *Manager*
EMP: 50
SALES (corp-wide): 2.4B **Publicly Held**
WEB: www.maxinc.com
SIC: 8742 Management consulting services
PA: Maximus, Inc.
1891 Metro Center Dr
Reston VA 20190
703 251-8500

(P-27326)
MAXWELL PETERSEN ASSOCIATES
Also Called: Dynamic Chiropractic
13950 Milton Ave Ste 200, Westminster (92683-2939)
PHONE..................714 230-3150
Donald M Petersen, *President*
Peter Crownfield, *COO*
Gabrielle Lindsley, *Business Mgr*
Evelyn Petersen, *Payroll Mgr*
Carla Rubie, *Production*
EMP: 50
SQ FT: 2,000
SALES (est): 5.4MM **Privately Held**
WEB: www.mpamedia.com
SIC: 8742 Business consultant

(P-27327)
MCB-CJS LLC
5312 Bolsa Ave, Huntington Beach (92649-1051)
PHONE..................714 230-3600
Joan Heid, *Partner*
Chet Seto, *Partner*
David Dowell, *Finance*
EMP: 99
SQ FT: 70,000
SALES (est): 2.3MM **Privately Held**
SIC: 8742 Management consulting services

(P-27328)
MCCLELLAN BUSINESS PARK LLC
Also Called: Mp Holdings
3140 Peacekeeper Way, McClellan (95652-2508)
PHONE..................916 965-7100
Larry Kelley, *President*
Jay Hecklively, *Exec VP*
Debra Compton, *Senior VP*
Tiffany Garcia, *Senior VP*
Ken Giannotti, *Senior VP*
EMP: 99 EST: 1999
SQ FT: 22,000
SALES (est): 21MM **Privately Held**
WEB: www.mcclellanpark.com
SIC: 8742 Real estate consultant

(P-27329)
MCKINSEY & COMPANY INC
2000 Avenue Of The Stars # 800, Los Angeles (90067-4714)
PHONE..................424 249-1000
John Durat, *General Mgr*
Bruce Simpson, *Chief Mktg Ofcr*
David Court, *Managing Dir*
Joseph Percoco, *Business Anlyst*
Eduardo Hernandez, *Data Proc Staff*
EMP: 50
SALES (corp-wide): 2.3B **Privately Held**
WEB: www.mckinsey.com
SIC: 8742 Marketing consulting services
PA: Mckinsey & Company, Inc.
55 E 52nd St Fl 16
New York NY 10055
212 446-7000

(P-27330)
MCKINSEY & COMPANY INC
555 California St #4800, San Francisco (94104-1779)
PHONE..................415 981-0250
Gary Pinkus, *Manager*
Lenny Mendonca, *Exec Dir*
Bernadette Uniacke, *Opers Mgr*
Roberta Casey, *Manager*
Nicholas Donoghoe, *Manager*
EMP: 300
SALES (corp-wide): 2.3B **Privately Held**
WEB: www.mckinsey.com
SIC: 8742 Marketing consulting services
PA: Mckinsey & Company, Inc.
55 E 52nd St Fl 16
New York NY 10055
212 446-7000

(P-27331)
MCKINSEY & COMPANY INC
3075 Hansen Way Bldg A, Palo Alto (94304-1025)
PHONE..................650 494-6262
Jon Duane, *Manager*
Joan Isaksen, *Executive Asst*

Kelly Kramer, *Info Tech Mgr*
Yuan Jialei, *Project Mgr*
Tony Hansen, *Director*
EMP: 75
SALES (corp-wide): 2.3B **Privately Held**
WEB: www.mckinsey.com
SIC: 8742 Marketing consulting services
PA: Mckinsey & Company, Inc.
　　55 E 52nd St Fl 16
　　New York NY 10055
　　212 446-7000

(P-27332)
MEDICAL MANAGEMENT CONS INC
Also Called: MMC
6046 Cornerstone Ct W, San Diego
(92121-4758)
PHONE......................858 587-0609
Rahmani, *Manager*
EMP: 4950
SALES (corp-wide): 71.4MM **Privately Held**
WEB: www.mmchr.com
SIC: 8742 Hospital & health services consultant
PA: Medical Management Consultants, Inc.
　　8150 Beverly Blvd
　　Los Angeles CA 90048
　　310 659-3835

(P-27333)
MEDICAL RECEIVABLES SOLUTIONS
Also Called: M R S
101 W American Canyon Rd, American Canyon (94503-1162)
PHONE......................707 980-6733
Aleshia L Hunter, *President*
EMP: 50
SALES (est): 7.2MM **Privately Held**
SIC: 8742 Business consultant

(P-27334)
MEDICAL SPECIALTIES MANAGERS
Also Called: Medical Specialty Billing
1 City Blvd W Ste 1100, Orange
(92868-3647)
PHONE......................714 571-5000
Barry Haberman, *President*
Charles Caporale, *CFO*
Uri Klugman, *CFO*
Monica Bahr, *Vice Pres*
Randy Brooks, *Vice Pres*
EMP: 115
SQ FT: 29,000
SALES (est): 17.5MM **Privately Held**
WEB: www.msmnet.com
SIC: 8742 8721 Hospital & health services consultant; billing & bookkeeping service

(P-27335)
MEDSPHERE SYSTEMS CORPORATION (PA)
1903 Wright Pl Ste 120, Carlsbad
(92008-6584)
PHONE......................760 692-3700
Kenneth W Kizer MD MPH, *Ch of Bd*
Ronald L Gue PH D, *President*
Zubin Emsley, *President*
Irv H Lichtenwald, *CEO*
Irv Lichtenwald, *CEO*
EMP: 71
SALES (est): 20.4MM **Privately Held**
WEB: www.medsphere.com
SIC: 8742 Hospital & health services consultant

(P-27336)
MERCER (US) INC
777 S Figueroa St # 2400, Los Angeles
(90017-5800)
PHONE......................213 346-2200
Nancy McLean, *Manager*
Elizabeth Dill, *Investment Ofcr*
Joseph Ziomek, *Sr Associate*
EMP: 200
SALES (corp-wide): 14B **Publicly Held**
SIC: 8742 Compensation & benefits planning consultant
HQ: Mercer (Us) Inc.
　　1166 Ave Of The Americ
　　New York NY 10036
　　212 345-7000

(P-27337)
MERCER (US) INC
4 Embarcadero Ctr Lbby 4 # 4, San Francisco (94111-4112)
PHONE......................415 743-8700
Jerry Murphy, *Manager*
Gary W Blank, *Principal*
Kenia Casarreal, *Principal*
Beverly Croydon, *Principal*
Cheryl V Doege, *Principal*
EMP: 250
SALES (corp-wide): 14B **Publicly Held**
SIC: 8742 Compensation & benefits planning consultant
HQ: Mercer (Us) Inc.
　　1166 Ave Of The Americ
　　New York NY 10036
　　212 345-7000

(P-27338)
MERCER (US) INC
17901 Von Karman Ave # 1100, Irvine
(92614-6297)
PHONE......................949 222-1300
Kathy Spear, *Manager*
Heather Cushnie, *Executive Asst*
Kari Zoolakis, *Human Res Dir*
Anca De Maio, *Director*
EMP: 100
SALES (corp-wide): 14B **Publicly Held**
SIC: 8742 Compensation & benefits planning consultant; personnel management consultant
HQ: Mercer (Us) Inc.
　　1166 Ave Of The Americ
　　New York NY 10036
　　212 345-7000

(P-27339)
MERCER HEALTH & BENEFITS LLC
3 Embarcadero Ctr, San Francisco
(94111-4003)
PHONE......................415 743-8751
Susan Snow, *Principal*
EMP: 99
SALES (corp-wide): 14B **Publicly Held**
SIC: 8742 Hospital & health services consultant
HQ: Mercer Health & Benefits Llc
　　1166 Ave Of Americas Flr 30
　　New York NY 10036
　　212 345-7000

(P-27340)
MERIDIAN KNWLDGE SOLUTIONS LLC
80 Iron Pont Cir Ste 100, Folsom (95630)
PHONE......................913 985-9625
Jonna Ward, *CEO*
Ruben Mercado, *Info Tech Mgr*
Emily Marcovich, *Marketing Staff*
Tom Harisis, *Manager*
EMP: 90
SQ FT: 32,481
SALES (est): 11.5MM **Privately Held**
WEB: www.meridianksi.com
SIC: 8742 Training & development consultant
HQ: Visionary Integration Professionals, Llc
　　80 Iron Point Cir Ste 100
　　Folsom CA 95630
　　916 985-9625

(P-27341)
MERIT TECHNOLOGIES LLC
Also Called: MTI
10509 Vista Sorrento Pkwy # 420, San Diego (92121-2743)
PHONE......................858 623-9800
Donald Wang PHD, *Mng Member*
Don Wang, *Managing Dir*
Steeve Higgins, *Controller*
EMP: 60
SQ FT: 2,000
SALES (est): 4MM **Privately Held**
SIC: 8742 Construction project management consultant

(P-27342)
MESA COUNSELLING
850 E Foothill Blvd, Rialto (92376-5230)
PHONE......................909 421-9301
Sherwin Farr, *General Mgr*
EMP: 50

SALES (est): 1.8MM **Privately Held**
SIC: 8742 Management consulting services

(P-27343)
METRON INCORPORATED
12250 El Camino Real # 260, San Diego
(92130-2226)
PHONE......................858 792-8904
EMP: 50
SALES (corp-wide): 39.9MM **Privately Held**
SIC: 8742 8731 8733 8711
PA: Metron, Incorporated
　　1818 Library St Ste 600
　　Reston VA 20190
　　703 467-5641

(P-27344)
METROPOLITAN MARKETING INC (PA)
Also Called: Valley Indoor Swap Meet
6320 Canoga Ave Ste 1630, Woodland Hills
(91367-2564)
PHONE......................909 620-5083
Glenn A Malkin, *President*
Ronald C Wolfe, *CFO*
Stuart E Siegel, *Vice Pres*
EMP: 70
SQ FT: 2,500
SALES (est): 7.3MM **Privately Held**
WEB: www.indoorswap.com
SIC: 8742 Marketing consulting services

(P-27345)
MF SERVICES COMPANY LLC (HQ)
4350 Von Karman Ave # 400, Newport Beach (92660-2007)
PHONE......................949 474-5800
Paul Merage, *Mng Member*
Richard Merage,
EMP: 60
SALES (est): 2.4MM
SALES (corp-wide): 133.7K **Privately Held**
SIC: 8742 Financial consultant
PA: Mig Capital, Llc
　　660 Newport Center Dr # 450
　　Newport Beach CA 92660
　　949 474-5800

(P-27346)
MICHAELSON CONNOR & BOUL (PA)
5312 Bolsa Ave, Huntington Beach
(92649-1051)
PHONE......................714 230-3600
Joan Heid, *President*
Firmin Boul, *Corp Secy*
Michael Ryan, *Vice Pres*
David Dowell, *Director*
EMP: 100
SQ FT: 12,500
SALES (est): 12.9MM **Privately Held**
WEB: www.mcbreo.com
SIC: 8742 Real estate consultant

(P-27347)
MIDLAND EXPRESS CREDIT LLC
2037 W Bullard Ave # 316, Fresno
(93711-1200)
PHONE......................800 961-3904
Walter Daniels, *President*
EMP: 52
SALES (est): 1.4MM **Privately Held**
SIC: 8742 Marketing consulting services

(P-27348)
MILLENNIA HOLDINGS INC
Also Called: Mellennia Holdings
3731 Wilshire Blvd # 618, Los Angeles
(90010-2876)
PHONE......................213 252-1230
Hiroki Tarui, *CEO*
Chugo Rionie, *CFO*
Yumiko Pardi, *Human Resources*
Mitsuteru Morimoto, *Consultant*
EMP: 60
SALES (est): 8.4MM **Privately Held**
WEB: www.mhiholdings.com
SIC: 8742 Hospital & health services consultant

(P-27349)
MLSLISTINGS INC
Also Called: RE Infolink
740 Kifer Rd, Sunnyvale (94086-5121)
PHONE......................408 874-0200
Gerald J Harrison, *President*
EMP: 58 **EST:** 2007
SALES: 14MM **Privately Held**
SIC: 8742 Real estate consultant

(P-27350)
MODERN HR INC
9000 W Sunset Blvd # 900, West Hollywood (90069-5801)
PHONE......................310 270-9800
Harold Walt, *CEO*
Faith Branvold, *President*
Grace Drulias, *CFO*
EMP: 400
SALES: 1MM **Privately Held**
SIC: 8742 Human resource consulting services

(P-27351)
MOLECULE LABS INC
524 Stone Rd # 107, Benicia (94510-1120)
PHONE......................714 892-3133
EMP: 50 **EST:** 2016
SALES (est): 78.8K **Privately Held**
SIC: 8742 Business consultant

(P-27352)
MUNISERVICES LLC (DH)
Also Called: Avenu Muniservices
7625 N Palm Ave Ste 108, Fresno
(93711-5785)
PHONE......................800 800-8181
Steve Roberts, *President*
Brenda Narayan, *Chief Mktg Ofcr*
Doug Jensen, *Vice Pres*
Peter Haggard, *Software Dev*
Kelli Parker, *Business Anlyst*
EMP: 113
SQ FT: 16,000
SALES (est): 15.1MM
SALES (corp-wide): 75.4MM **Privately Held**
WEB: www.muniservices.com
SIC: 8742 Industry specialist consultants
HQ: Avenu Insights & Analytics, Llc
　　555 Madison Ave Fl 16
　　New York NY 10022
　　757 519-9300

(P-27353)
MV MEDICAL MANAGEMENT
1860 Colo Blvd Ste 200, Los Angeles
(90041)
PHONE......................323 257-7637
Eva Vargas, *President*
Daniel E Vargas Jr, *COO*
Alma Moreno, *Treasurer*
Evy Vargas, *Admin Sec*
Margaret Shao, *Administration*
EMP: 60
SQ FT: 7,400
SALES (est): 8.9MM **Privately Held**
WEB: www.mvmedical.com
SIC: 8742 Management consulting services

(P-27354)
MW PARTNERS
201 Sandpointe Ave # 200, Santa Ana
(92707-5778)
PHONE......................949 705-0682
Rich Low, *Principal*
Michael Willner, *Managing Prtnr*
Richard Low, *General Mgr*
SOO Lim, *Technology*
Prateek Gangula, *Opers Mgr*
EMP: 100
SALES (est): 763K **Privately Held**
SIC: 8742 Management consulting services

(P-27355)
MW2 CONSULTING LLC
981 Manor Way, Los Altos (94024-5622)
PHONE......................408 573-6310
Michael Morris,
Alice Harmon,
Uwe Wienkauf,
EMP: 85
SQ FT: 5,700

SALES (est): 4.7MM **Privately Held**
WEB: www.mw2consulting.com
SIC: **8742** Management consulting services

(P-27356)
N COMPASS INTERNATIONAL INC
Also Called: Ncompass International
8223 Santa Monica Blvd, West Hollywood (90046-5912)
PHONE....................................323 785-1700
Donna Direnzo Graves, *CEO*
Kae Erickson, *COO*
EMP: 138
SQ FT: 20,000
SALES (est): 28.2MM **Privately Held**
WEB: www.ncompassinternational.com
SIC: **8742** Marketing consulting services

(P-27357)
NAN MCKAY AND ASSOCIATES INC
1810 Gillespie Way # 202, El Cajon (92020-0920)
PHONE....................................619 258-1855
Nan McKay, *President*
John McKay, *CEO*
Raymond Adair, *Vice Pres*
Dorian Jenkins, *Vice Pres*
James McKay, *Vice Pres*
EMP: 58
SQ FT: 14,000
SALES: 30MM **Privately Held**
WEB: www.nanmckay.com
SIC: **8742** 7371 2731 Training & development consultant; computer software development; textbooks: publishing & printing

(P-27358)
NATIONAL EMPLOYEE BENEFITS LLC
3200 E Guasti Rd Ste 100, Ontario (91761-8661)
PHONE....................................877 778-8330
Cheryl Gollnick, *Mng Member*
EMP: 208
SALES (est): 7.8MM **Privately Held**
WEB: www.manageyouremployees.com
SIC: **8742** Compensation & benefits planning consultant

(P-27359)
NATIONAL FNCL SRVCS CNSRTM LLC
3161 Los Prados St, San Mateo (94403-2013)
PHONE....................................650 572-2872
Tony Quintero,
EMP: 99
SALES (est): 2.6MM **Privately Held**
SIC: **8742**

(P-27360)
NAVIGANT CONSULTING INC
300 S Grand Ave Ste 3850, Los Angeles (90071-3174)
PHONE....................................213 452-4516
Mike Wallace, *Vice Pres*
Angela Sabbe, *Associate Dir*
EMP: 100
SALES (corp-wide): 1B **Publicly Held**
WEB: www.navigantconsulting.com
SIC: **8742** Business consultant
PA: Navigant Consulting, Inc.
150 N Riverside Plz # 2100
Chicago IL 60606
312 573-5600

(P-27361)
NBC CONSULTING INC
Also Called: Pacific Health and Welness
2110 Artesia Blvd Ste 323, Redondo Beach (90278-3073)
PHONE....................................310 798-5000
Neal M Bychek, *President*
Robin Bychek, *CFO*
EMP: 100
SALES: 1MM **Privately Held**
WEB: www.nbcconsulting.com
SIC: **8742** Hospital & health services consultant

(P-27362)
NEARDATA INC
Also Called: Neardata Systems
4502 Dyer St Ste 103, La Crescenta (91214-2854)
PHONE....................................818 249-2469
Samuel S Chilingurian, *President*
EMP: 76
SQ FT: 5,600
SALES (est): 6.5MM **Privately Held**
SIC: **8742** 7371 Management consulting services; computer software development

(P-27363)
NET4SITE LLC
3350 Scott Blvd Bldg 34b, Santa Clara (95054-3105)
PHONE....................................408 427-3004
C K Singla,
Gautam Gauba, *Officer*
Roger Diaz, *Business Dir*
EMP: 78
SQ FT: 3,000
SALES: 10MM **Privately Held**
SIC: **8742** Management information systems consultant

(P-27364)
NETBASE SOLUTIONS INC (PA)
3960 Freedom Cir 201, Santa Clara (95054-1204)
PHONE....................................650 810-2100
Peter M Caswell, *CEO*
Bob Pape, *CFO*
Bob Ciccone, *Vice Pres*
Steve Winters, *Vice Pres*
David Yehle, *Vice Pres*
EMP: 56
SALES (est): 13.5MM **Privately Held**
WEB: www.accelovation.com
SIC: **8742** Business planning & organizing services

(P-27365)
NETLINE CORPORATION (PA)
750 University Ave # 200, Los Gatos (95032-7697)
PHONE....................................408 374-4200
Robert S Alvin, *CEO*
Werner Mansfeld, *President*
Mark Bowman, *Vice Pres*
David Fortino, *Vice Pres*
Jayaram Kalpathy, *Vice Pres*
EMP: 53
SALES (est): 8.8MM **Privately Held**
WEB: www.netline.com
SIC: **8742** Marketing consulting services

(P-27366)
NEWMARK & COMPANY RE INC
Also Called: Newmark Grubb Knight Frank
1551 N Tustin Ave Ste 300, Santa Ana (92705-8638)
PHONE....................................714 667-8252
Ryan Bohls, *Managing Dir*
Matt Davidson, *Managing Dir*
Paul Fischetti, *Managing Dir*
Debra Gould, *Director*
Frank Nelson, *Director*
EMP: 60
SALES (corp-wide): 3.3B **Publicly Held**
SIC: **8742** 6531 Real estate consultant; real estate agent, commercial; housing authority operator
HQ: Newmark & Company Real Estate, Inc.
125 Park Ave
New York NY 10017
212 372-2000

(P-27367)
NEXT IMAGE MEDICAL INC (PA)
3390 Carmel Mountain Rd # 150, San Diego (92121-1055)
PHONE....................................858 847-9185
Elizabeth Griggs, *CEO*
EMP: 60
SALES (est): 8.4MM **Privately Held**
SIC: **8742** Business consultant

(P-27368)
NEXT MANAGEMENT LLC
Also Called: Next Management Co
8447 Wilshire Blvd # 301, Beverly Hills (90211-3226)
PHONE....................................323 782-0038
Faith Kates, *President*

EMP: 50
SALES (corp-wide): 12.5MM **Privately Held**
SIC: **8742** 8021 Management consulting services; offices & clinics of dentists
PA: Next Management, Llc
15 Watts St Fl 6
New York NY 10013
212 925-5100

(P-27369)
NFP PROPERTY & CASUALTY SVCS
Also Called: Nfp Advisors
2450 Tapo St, Simi Valley (93063-2454)
PHONE....................................805 579-1900
Mary Lue, *CEO*
EMP: 50
SALES (est): 115K **Privately Held**
SIC: **8742** Financial consultant

(P-27370)
NI KI CRUZ LLC
5255 Stevens Creek Blvd, Santa Clara (95051-6664)
PHONE....................................408 332-7616
Carlos R Cruz Jr, *Partner*
EMP: 99
SALES (est): 58.9K **Privately Held**
SIC: **8742** Marketing consulting services

(P-27371)
NINES RESTAURANT
Also Called: Bunkers Grille
100 Summerset Dr, Brentwood (94513-6426)
PHONE....................................925 516-3413
James A Shoemaker, *President*
Sally Shoemaker, *Vice Pres*
EMP: 60
SQ FT: 14,000
SALES (est): 4.2MM **Privately Held**
WEB: www.bunkersgrille.com
SIC: **8742** Management consulting services

(P-27372)
NPS MARKETING
3381 Sage Rose Ln, Placerville (95667-5452)
P.O. Box 2392 (95667-2392)
PHONE....................................916 941-5510
Scott Becker, *Owner*
EMP: 300
SALES: 2.5MM **Privately Held**
SIC: **8742** 7389 Marketing consulting services;

(P-27373)
OMEGA 2 ALPHA SERVICES LLC
Also Called: O2a
935 Riverside Ave Ste 23, Paso Robles (93446-2605)
PHONE....................................805 610-2249
Daniel McGee,
Robert Cidemiller, *Mng Member*
EMP: 53 EST: 2014
SALES (est): 1.1MM **Privately Held**
SIC: **8742** Construction project management consultant

(P-27374)
OMEGA WASTE MANAGEMENT INC
Also Called: Omega Management Services
957 Colusa St, Corning (96021-2224)
P.O. Box 495 (96021-0495)
PHONE....................................530 824-1890
Robert O'Conner, *President*
Karen O'Conner, *Vice Pres*
Dan O'Connor, *Vice Pres*
Laurie Spindler, *Human Res Mgr*
Laura Bachelor, *Accounts Mgr*
EMP: 68
SQ FT: 6,000
SALES (est): 12.6MM **Privately Held**
WEB: www.omegawastemanagement.com
SIC: **8742** Management consulting services

(P-27375)
OMNI CONSULTING GROUP LLP
Also Called: Omni Research Group
3531 Mono Pl Ste 100, Davis (95618-6049)
P.O. Box 4128 (95617-4128)
PHONE....................................530 750-5199
Frank J Bernard, *Partner*
Michael G Ashworth, *Partner*
Lawrence C Barrington, *Partner*
Frank J Bernhard, *Partner*
John P Evans, *Partner*
EMP: 78 EST: 1989
SQ FT: 8,500
SALES (est): 3.4MM **Privately Held**
WEB: www.omniconsultinggroup.com
SIC: **8742** Marketing consulting services

(P-27376)
ONE CALL MEDICAL INC
8501 Fllbrook Ave Ste 100, Canoga Park (91304)
PHONE....................................818 346-8700
Julie Moss, *Manager*
Barbara Hess, *Executive Asst*
Donna Knight, *Human Res Dir*
EMP: 68 **Privately Held**
SIC: **8742** Compensation & benefits planning consultant
PA: One Call Medical, Inc.
841 Prudential Dr Ste 900
Jacksonville FL 32207

(P-27377)
ONE MAIN FINANCIAL SERVICES
1121 E Alosta Ave, Azusa (91702-2740)
PHONE....................................626 335-0617
Cristo Gomez, *Manager*
EMP: 126
SALES (corp-wide): 3.2B **Privately Held**
SIC: **8742** 7389 Financial consultant; financial services
PA: Springleaf Financial Holdings, Llc
601 Nw 2nd St
Evansville IN 47708
800 961-5577

(P-27378)
ONE MAIN FINANCIAL SERVICES
711 Stony Point Rd, Santa Rosa (95407-6802)
PHONE....................................707 546-5162
EMP: 126
SALES (corp-wide): 2.5B **Privately Held**
SIC: **8742** 7389 6162 6141 Financial consultant; financial services; mortgage bankers & correspondents; personal credit institutions
PA: Springleaf Financial Holdings, Llc
601 Nw 2nd St
Evansville IN 47708
800 961-5577

(P-27379)
ONE10 LLC
180 Montgomery St, San Francisco (94104-4205)
PHONE....................................415 398-3534
EMP: 100
SALES (corp-wide): 1.8B **Privately Held**
SIC: **8742**
HQ: One10 Llc
100 N 6th St Ste 700b
Minneapolis MN 55403
763 445-3000

(P-27380)
ONE10 LLC
735 Battery St Fl 1, San Francisco (94111-1535)
PHONE....................................415 844-2200
Fax: 415 844-2248
EMP: 70
SALES (corp-wide): 1.8B **Privately Held**
SIC: **8742**
HQ: One10 Llc
100 N 6th St Ste 700b
Minneapolis MN 55403
763 445-3000

(P-27381)
OPEN HARBOR INC
1123 Industrial Rd, San Francisco (94111)
PHONE.................................650 413-4200
Bill Walsh, *President*
EMP: 83
SALES (est): 3.2MM **Privately Held**
SIC: 8742 Management consulting services

(P-27382)
OPERATIX INC
111 N Market St Ste 300, San Jose
(95113-1116)
PHONE.................................408 332-5796
Graham Curme, *CEO*
Aurelien Mottier, *Vice Pres*
EMP: 65 EST: 2013
SALES (est): 3.2MM **Privately Held**
SIC: 8742 Marketing consulting services

(P-27383)
OPINION DYNAMICS CORP FLA INC
1999 Harrison St Ste 1250, Oakland
(94612-4709)
PHONE.................................510 444-5050
Randy Lampkin, *Principal*
EMP: 90
SALES (corp-wide): 14.6MM **Privately Held**
SIC: 8742 Marketing consulting services
PA: Opinion Dynamics Corporation Of
    Florida, Inc.
    1000 Winter St
    Waltham MA 02451
    617 492-1400

(P-27384)
P H S MANAGEMENT GROUP (PA)
721 N Eckhoff St, Orange (92868-1005)
PHONE.................................714 547-7551
Kevin O Lewand, *President*
EMP: 50
SALES (est): 5.3MM **Privately Held**
SIC: 8742 Hospital & health services consultant

(P-27385)
P K B INVESTMENTS INC
Also Called: Home Instead Senior Care
745 E Locust Ave Ste 105, Fresno
(93720-3000)
PHONE.................................559 243-1224
David Phillips, *President*
April Cavanaugh, *CFO*
Patrick Cavanaugh, *Admin Sec*
EMP: 140
SALES (est): 1.9MM **Privately Held**
SIC: 8742 8322 Management consulting
services; individual & family services

(P-27386)
PACIFIC SECURED EQUITIES INC
Also Called: Intercare Holdings Insur Svcs
6020 West Oaks Blvd # 100, Rocklin
(95765-5472)
P.O. Box 579, Roseville (95661-0579)
PHONE.................................916 677-2500
George W McCleary Jr, *CEO*
Agnes Hoeberling, *COO*
Richard Rothman, *Exec VP*
Kathleen Cooper, *Senior VP*
Alan Avriett, *Vice Pres*
EMP: 300
SQ FT: 21,000
SALES (est): 499K **Privately Held**
WEB: www.intercareins.com
SIC: 8742 Administrative services consultant

(P-27387)
PALORAS CORPORATION
228 Hamilton Ave Fl 3, Palo Alto
(94301-2583)
PHONE.................................650 440-7663
Ramki Pitchuiyer, *CEO*
EMP: 55
SALES (est): 8MM **Privately Held**
SIC: 8742 Business consultant

(P-27388)
PARSONS BRNCKRHOFF HLDINGS INC
2329 Oakes Dr Ste 200, Sacramento
(95833)
PHONE.................................916 567-2500
Michelle Poe, *Technology*
Doris Piper, *Manager*
EMP: 70
SALES (corp-wide): 230.6MM **Privately Held**
SIC: 8742 Management consulting services
PA: Parsons Brinckerhoff Holdings Inc.
    1 Penn Plz
    New York NY 10119
    212 465-5000

(P-27389)
PARTNERS IN LEADERSHIP LLC (HQ)
27555 Ynez Rd Ste 300, Temecula
(92591-4678)
PHONE.................................951 694-5596
Gordon Treadway, *CEO*
Marcus Nicolls, *Senior Partner*
Brad Burton, *President*
Maury Hiers, *President*
Jared Jones, *President*
EMP: 95
SQ FT: 12,000
SALES: 31MM
SALES (corp-wide): 4.3MM **Privately Held**
WEB: www.ozprinciple.com
SIC: 8742 Business consultant
PA: Partners In Leadership Intermediate
    Holdings Llc
    27555 Ynez Rd
    Temecula CA 92591
    951 506-6878

(P-27390)
PARTNERS IN LEADERSHIP INTERME (PA)
27555 Ynez Rd, Temecula (92591-4687)
PHONE.................................951 506-6878
Yvon Wagner, *Director*
EMP: 95
SALES (est): 4.3MM **Privately Held**
SIC: 8742 Business consultant

(P-27391)
PENNYMAC FINANCIAL SVCS INC
36 Discovery, Irvine (92618-3751)
PHONE.................................949 341-0020
Stanford L Kurland, *Ch of Bd*
EMP: 1070
SALES (corp-wide): 1.1B **Publicly Held**
SIC: 8742 Financial consultant
PA: Pennymac Financial Services, Inc.
    3043 Townsgate Rd
    Westlake Village CA 91361
    818 224-7442

(P-27392)
PERKSTREET FINANCIAL INC
1100 La Avenida St Ste A, Mountain View
(94043-1453)
PHONE.................................978 801-1177
Laurence Stock, *CFO*
EMP: 50 EST: 2008
SALES (est): 4.4MM **Privately Held**
SIC: 8742 Banking & finance consultant

(P-27393)
PERMANENTE FEDERATION LLC
1 Kaiser Plz Fl 27, Oakland (94612-3610)
PHONE.................................510 625-6920
Cal James, *CEO*
Claire Tamo, *CFO*
EMP: 80 EST: 1997
SQ FT: 18,663
SALES (est): 8.9MM **Privately Held**
SIC: 8742 Management consulting services

(P-27394)
PG&E CAPITAL LLC
1 Market, San Francisco (94105-1596)
PHONE.................................415 321-4600
Anthony Earley Hr, *Chairman*

EMP: 354
SALES (est): 74.4K **Publicly Held**
SIC: 8742 Marketing consulting services
PA: Pg&E Corporation
    77 Beale St
    San Francisco CA 94105
    -

(P-27395)
PHENOMENON MKTG & ENTRMT LLC (PA)
5900 Wilshire Blvd Fl 28, Los Angeles
(90036-5013)
PHONE.................................323 648-4000
Krishnan Menon, *CEO*
Chris Adams, *Creative Dir*
Tim Bateman, *Creative Dir*
Keara Sexton, *Executive Asst*
Kayla Stormont, *Executive Asst*
EMP: 60
SQ FT: 15,289
SALES (est): 20MM **Privately Held**
SIC: 8742 Marketing consulting services

(P-27396)
PNC BANK NATIONAL ASSOCIATION
26901 Agoura Rd Ste 200, Calabasas
(91301-5109)
PHONE.................................818 880-3300
Tim White, *Branch Mgr*
Joe G Basurto, *Senior VP*
Gary Baratta, *Vice Pres*
Patricia Rhodes, *Loan Officer*
EMP: 80
SALES (corp-wide): 18B **Publicly Held**
SIC: 8742 Financial consultant
HQ: Pnc Bank, National Association
    222 Delaware Ave
    Wilmington DE 19801
    877 762-2000

(P-27397)
PRECISE ENTERPRISES LLC
Also Called: Precise Auto Protection
751 W 9th St, Azusa (91702-2340)
P.O. Box 305 (91702-0305)
PHONE.................................818 599-6450
Harry Pambuckchyan, *Mng Member*
Gina Pambuckchyan,
Sitta Saghoejian,
EMP: 50
SQ FT: 6,500
SALES (est): 3.8MM **Privately Held**
SIC: 8742 Marketing consulting services

(P-27398)
PRESCRIPTION SOLUTIONS
2858 Loker Ave E Ste 100, Carlsbad
(92010-6673)
PHONE.................................760 804-2370
Bobby Robert Bliatout, *President*
Richard Swartz, *Vice Pres*
Phil Haworth, *Info Tech Mgr*
Jessica Flores, *Graphic Designe*
Shaun Davis, *Senior Mgr*
EMP: 1000
SALES (est): 73.4MM **Privately Held**
SIC: 8742 Hospital & health services consultant

(P-27399)
PREVENTION INSTITUTE
221 Oak St Ste A, Oakland (94607-4595)
PHONE.................................510 444-4133
Larry Cohen, *Exec Dir*
Emily Kemp, *Officer*
Veonna Washington, *Officer*
Jessica Berthold, *Comms Mgr*
Linda Benson, *Bookkeeper*
EMP: 56 EST: 2001
SQ FT: 2,612
SALES (est): 4.4MM **Privately Held**
SIC: 8742 Training & development consultant

(P-27400)
PRIME HEALTHCARE SERVICES - SH
4929 Van Nuys Blvd, Sherman Oaks
(91403-1702)
PHONE.................................818 981-7111
Prem Reddy, *CEO*
EMP: 900

SALES (est): 38.1K
SALES (corp-wide): 3.4B **Privately Held**
SIC: 8742 Hospital & health services consultant
PA: Prime Healthcare Foundation, Inc.
    3300 E Guasti Rd Fl 3
    Ontario CA 91761
    909 235-4400

(P-27401)
PRIMUS GROUP INC (PA)
Also Called: Primus Labs
2810 Industrial Pkwy, Santa Maria
(93455-1812)
PHONE.................................805 922-0055
Robert F Stovicek, *Principal*
Brian Mansfield, *Business Dir*
Clint Sanvictores, *CIO*
Curtis Wilson, *Technology*
Kara Christopher, *Accountant*
EMP: 50
SQ FT: 12,000
SALES (est): 22.1MM **Privately Held**
WEB: www.primuslabs.com
SIC: 8742 8734 8731 Food & beverage
consultant; food testing service; commercial physical research

(P-27402)
PRIZE PROZ
1500 S Hellman Ave, Ontario (91761-7634)
PHONE.................................909 509-8600
Dennis Foland, *Owner*
EMP: 50 EST: 2011
SALES (est): 214.3K **Privately Held**
SIC: 8742 Incentive or award program consultant

(P-27403)
PRODUCT SLINGSHOT INC
Also Called: Forecast 3d
2221 Rutherford Rd, Carlsbad
(92008-8815)
PHONE.................................760 929-9380
Corey Douglas Weber, *President*
Corey Weber, *CFO*
Donovan Weber, *Vice Pres*
Norma Martinez, *Executive*
Greg Lee, *Administration*
EMP: 96
SQ FT: 28,000
SALES (est): 15.3MM **Privately Held**
WEB: www.forecast3d.com
SIC: 8742 3544 3082 3089 Productivity
improvement consultant; industrial molds;
unsupported plastics profile shapes; casting of plastic; coloring & finishing of plastic products; injection molded finished
plastic products

(P-27404)
PROMO SHOP INC (PA)
5420 Mcconnell Ave, Los Angeles
(90066-7037)
PHONE.................................310 821-1780
Guillermo Kahan, *President*
Bob Golden, *CFO*
Matthew Mason, *Vice Pres*
Frank Nordyke, *Vice Pres*
Dawn Rogers, *Vice Pres*
EMP: 55
SALES: 39.6MM **Privately Held**
WEB: www.promoshopinc.com
SIC: 8742 Marketing consulting services

(P-27405)
PROMOTE MEDIA LP
8484 Wilshire Blvd # 630, Beverly Hills
(90211-3227)
PHONE.................................323 433-7950
Jeffrey Essebag,
EMP: 60
SALES (est): 881.9K **Privately Held**
SIC: 8742 Marketing consulting services

(P-27406)
PROPHET BRAND STRATEGY (PA)
1 Bush St Fl 7, San Francisco
(94104-4413)
PHONE.................................415 677-0909
Michael Dunn, *President*
Rune Gustafson, *President*
Simon Marlow, *COO*
Jeani Vance, *CIO*
Tosson El Noshokaty, *Director*

EMP: 50
SQ FT: 1,744
SALES: 100MM **Privately Held**
SIC: 8742 Marketing consulting services

(P-27407)
PROTIVITI INC
2613 Camino Ramon, San Ramon
(94583-4289)
PHONE.....................415 402-3663
Keith Waddell, *Manager*
EMP: 58
SALES (corp-wide): 5.2B **Publicly Held**
SIC: 8742 8721 Management consulting services; accounting, auditing & book-keeping
HQ: Protiviti Inc.
   2884 Sand Hill Rd Ste 200
   Menlo Park CA 94025
   650 234-6000

(P-27408)
PROTIVITI INC (HQ)
2884 Sand Hill Rd Ste 200, Menlo Park
(94025-7072)
PHONE.....................650 234-6000
Joseph A Tarantino, *Principal*
Brian Christensen, *Exec VP*
Bradley Nelson, *Technology*
Timothy R Maloney, *Auditing Mgr*
Jason Allen, *Assistant*
EMP: 100
SALES (est): 261MM
SALES (corp-wide): 5.2B **Publicly Held**
SIC: 8742 8721 Industry specialist consultants; auditing services
PA: Robert Half International Inc.
   2884 Sand Hill Rd Ste 200
   Menlo Park CA 94025
   650 234-6000

(P-27409)
PROTIVITI INC
400 S Hope St Ste 900, Los Angeles
(90071-2808)
PHONE.....................213 327-1400
Paul Sacks, *Branch Mgr*
EMP: 100
SALES (corp-wide): 5.2B **Publicly Held**
SIC: 8742 Food & beverage consultant
HQ: Protiviti Inc.
   2884 Sand Hill Rd Ste 200
   Menlo Park CA 94025
   650 234-6000

(P-27410)
PROVIDENCE SEMINARS INC
6349 Palomar Oaks Ct, Carlsbad
(92011-1428)
PHONE.....................760 827-2100
Russell Carroll, *President*
EMP: 75
SQ FT: 15,000
SALES (est): 2.5MM **Privately Held**
SIC: 8742 Real estate consultant

(P-27411)
PUBLIC CONSULTING GROUP INC
Also Called: Pcg Technology Consulting
2150 River Plaza Dr # 380, Sacramento
(95833-4138)
PHONE.....................916 565-8090
Lori Duff, *Manager*
EMP: 60
SALES (corp-wide): 379.7MM **Privately Held**
SIC: 8742 Business consultant
PA: Public Consulting Group, Inc.
   148 State St Fl 10
   Boston MA 02109
   617 426-2026

(P-27412)
PWC STRATEGY& (US) LLC
3 Embarcadero Ctr Fl 20, San Francisco
(94111-4004)
PHONE.....................415 498-5000
Ralph W Shrader, *Branch Mgr*
William T Reed, *Principal*
EMP: 200
SALES (corp-wide): 6.8B **Privately Held**
SIC: 8742 Management consulting services

HQ: Pwc Strategy& (Us) Llc
   101 Park Ave Fl 18
   New York NY 10178
   -

(P-27413)
Q ANALYSTS LLC (PA)
4320 Stevens Creek Blvd # 130, San Jose
(95129-1280)
PHONE.....................408 907-8500
Ross Fernandes,
Joe Lawlor, *President*
Thuy To, *Executive*
Jason Knight, *Business Dir*
Raul Deleon, *QA Dir*
EMP: 70
SALES (est): 10.4MM **Privately Held**
WEB: www.qanalysts.com
SIC: 8742 7379 Quality assurance consultant; computer related consulting services

(P-27414)
QLM CONSULTING INC
2400 Bridgeway Ste 290, Sausalito
(94965-2851)
P.O. Box 982 (94966-0982)
PHONE.....................415 331-9292
Michael McCartney, *CEO*
EMP: 50
SALES (est): 2.1MM **Privately Held**
WEB: www.qlmconsulting.com
SIC: 8742 Construction project management consultant

(P-27415)
QUALITY PLANNING CORPORATION
388 Market St Ste 750, San Francisco
(94111-5352)
PHONE.....................415 369-0707
Raj Bhat, *President*
EMP: 54
SALES (est): 5.2MM **Publicly Held**
WEB: www.qualityplanning.com
SIC: 8742 Financial consultant
HQ: Insurance Services Office, Inc.
   545 Washington Blvd Fl 12
   Jersey City NJ 07310
   201 469-2000

(P-27416)
QY RESEARCH INC
17890 Castleton St, City of Industry
(91748-1756)
PHONE.....................626 295-2442
Song Chunming, *President*
Diao Hongwei, *Vice Pres*
Zhang Dong, *Director*
EMP: 61
SALES (est): 1.5MM **Privately Held**
SIC: 8742 Management consulting services

(P-27417)
R3 STRATEGIC SUPPORT GROUP INC
1050 B Ave Ste A, Coronado (92118-3430)
PHONE.....................800 418-2040
Randall Packard, *President*
Clark Nichols, *Principal*
Mark Sanders, *Principal*
Bart Davis, *Technology*
Linda Runyeon, *VP Finance*
EMP: 67
SALES (est): 1.2MM **Privately Held**
SIC: 8742 Business consultant

(P-27418)
RAINIER FINANCIAL GROUP LLC
2321 Rosecrans Ave # 4270, El Segundo
(90245-4964)
PHONE.....................310 335-9200
Kevin Neustadt, *Managing Prtnr*
EMP: 50
SALES (est): 3.4MM **Privately Held**
SIC: 8742 Financial consultant

(P-27419)
RAY W CHOI
Also Called: Ictp
731 E Ball Rd Ste 100, Anaheim
(92805-5951)
PHONE.....................714 783-1000

Ray W Choi, *Owner*
EMP: 92
SQ FT: 10,000
SALES (est): 4.2MM **Privately Held**
SIC: 8742 7379 Training & development consultant; computer related consulting services

(P-27420)
RED PEAK GROUP LLC
23975 Park Sorrento # 410, Calabasas
(91302-4031)
PHONE.....................818 222-7762
Michael Birkin, *CEO*
EMP: 90
SALES (est): 4.8MM **Privately Held**
SIC: 8742 Marketing consulting services

(P-27421)
REDSTONE PRINT & MAIL INC
910 Riverside Pkwy Ste 40, West Sacramento (95605-1510)
PHONE.....................916 318-6450
Ledi Cody, *President*
EMP: 60 EST: 2015
SALES: 20MM **Privately Held**
SIC: 8742 Marketing consulting services

(P-27422)
REPUTATION IMPRESSION LLC
9245 Activity Rd Ste 106, San Diego
(92126-4442)
PHONE.....................858 633-4500
Scott Spencer, *CEO*
EMP: 85
SALES (est): 7.6MM **Privately Held**
SIC: 8742 Industry specialist consultants

(P-27423)
REPUTATION MANAGEMENT CONS INC
1720 E Garry Ave Ste 103, Santa Ana
(92705-5831)
P.O. Box 92, Irvine (92650-0092)
PHONE.....................949 682-7906
Gary P Hagins, *President*
Anthony Asuncion, *Project Mgr*
Adam Reifman, *Opers Staff*
EMP: 65
SQ FT: 4,000
SALES: 9MM **Privately Held**
SIC: 8742 Business consultant

(P-27424)
RESEARCH TRIANGLE INSTITUTE
2150 Shattuck Ave Ste 800, Berkeley
(94704-1352)
PHONE.....................510 849-4942
E Wayne Holden, *Branch Mgr*
Jan Van Bruaene, *President*
Jiantong Wang, *Director*
Wally Campbell, *Manager*
EMP: 72
SALES (corp-wide): 972.2MM **Privately Held**
SIC: 8742 8732 Management consulting services; educational research
PA: Research Triangle Institute Inc
   3040 Cornwallis Rd
   Durham NC 27709
   919 541-6000

(P-27425)
RESORT PROCOMM INC
9550 Waples St Ste 105, San Diego
(92121-2984)
PHONE.....................858 866-6280
Will Dougherty, *President*
EMP: 61
SALES (est): 2.1MM **Privately Held**
SIC: 8742 Marketing consulting services

(P-27426)
RESOURCES CONNECTION INC
Also Called: Resources Global Professionals
695 Town Center Dr # 600, Costa Mesa
(92626-1924)
PHONE.....................714 430-6550
Donald Murray, *Principal*
Lorelei Heisler, *Managing Dir*
Chris Paik-Phong, *Opers Mgr*
Joan Lieberman, *Director*
Doris Owens, *Director*
EMP: 86 **Publicly Held**

SIC: 8742 Management consulting services
PA: Resources Connection, Inc.
   17101 Armstrong Ave # 100
   Irvine CA 92614

(P-27427)
RESOURCES CONNECTION INC (PA)
17101 Armstrong Ave # 100, Irvine
(92614-5742)
PHONE.....................714 430-6400
Kate W Duchene, *President*
Donald B Murray, *Ch of Bd*
Herbert M Mueller, *CFO*
Omar Ligot, *Vice Pres*
John D Bower,
EMP: 732
SQ FT: 56,200
SALES: 654.1MM **Publicly Held**
SIC: 8742 7389 8721 Business consultant; business planning & organizing services; financial services; legal & tax services; accounting, auditing & bookkeeping; auditing services

(P-27428)
RHODES RETAIL SERVICES INC
8603 Excelsior Rd, Elk Grove
(95624-9661)
PHONE.....................916 714-9233
Chris Rhodes, *President*
Valerie Rhodes, *CFO*
EMP: 90
SQ FT: 1,200
SALES (est): 8.4MM **Privately Held**
WEB: www.rhodesretail.com
SIC: 8742 Merchandising consultant

(P-27429)
RIVIERA PARTNERS LLC (PA)
141 10th St, San Francisco (94103-2604)
PHONE.....................877 748-4372
Will Hunsinger, *CEO*
Kevin Buckby, *Partner*
Andy Grosso, *Partner*
Tyna Huynh, *Accountant*
Ali Behnam, *Mng Member*
EMP: 53
SALES (est): 7.7MM **Privately Held**
SIC: 8742 Business consultant

(P-27430)
RMD GROUP INC
2311 E South St, Long Beach
(90805-4424)
PHONE.....................562 866-9288
Ralph Holguin, *President*
Laura Milanes, *Officer*
Caitlin Stafford, *Executive*
Eli Saiz, *General Mgr*
Samantha Lopez, *Executive Asst*
EMP: 300
SALES (est): 35.8MM **Privately Held**
SIC: 8742 Marketing consulting services

(P-27431)
ROBERT HALF MGT RESOURCES
1999 Harrison St Ste 1100, Oakland
(94612-4708)
PHONE.....................510 271-0910
Robert Gardener, *Manager*
EMP: 50
SALES (est): 2.2MM **Privately Held**
SIC: 8742 Management consulting services

(P-27432)
ROBERTSON PIPER MANAGEMENT LLC
963 Fremont Ave, Los Altos (94024-6098)
PHONE.....................650 625-8333
Robertson Piper, *Principal*
EMP: 185
SALES (est): 4.8MM **Privately Held**
SIC: 8742 Management consulting services

(P-27433)
ROCKPORT ADM SVCS LLC (PA)
Also Called: Rockport Healthcare Services
5900 Wilshire Blvd # 1600, Los Angeles
(90036-5016)
PHONE.....................323 330-6500
Vincent S Hambright, *CEO*
Brad Gibson, *CFO*
Michael Wasserman, *Chief Mktg Ofcr*
Steven Stroll, *Mng Member*
Yehuda Kaplan, *Director*
EMP: 75
SQ FT: 4,800
SALES (est): 33MM **Privately Held**
SIC: 8742 Hospital & health services consultant

(P-27434)
RUBY CREEK RESOURCES
1835 W Olympic Blvd, Los Angeles
(90006-3701)
PHONE.....................212 671-0404
Robert Slavik, *CEO*
EMP: 50
SALES: 10MM **Privately Held**
SIC: 8742 Business planning & organizing services

(P-27435)
RUSSON FINANCIAL SERVICES INC
Also Called: New England Financial
19935 Ventura Blvd # 100, Woodland Hills
(91364-9605)
PHONE.....................818 999-2800
Tony Russon, *CEO*
EMP: 60
SQ FT: 10,000
SALES (est): 3.6MM **Privately Held**
SIC: 8742 Financial consultant

(P-27436)
S E O P INC
1621 Alton Pkwy Ste 150, Irvine
(92606-4875)
PHONE.....................949 682-7906
Gary Hagins, *CEO*
Rhonda Spears, *President*
Abram Serrano, *Manager*
EMP: 150
SALES (est): 15.3MM **Privately Held**
WEB: www.seop.com
SIC: 8742 Marketing consulting services

(P-27437)
SABAN BRANDS LLC (HQ)
10100 Santa Monica Blvd # 500, Los Angeles (90067-4121)
PHONE.....................310 557-5230
Elie Dekel, *President*
Jack Sorensen, *President*
Janet Scardino, *COO*
William Kehoe, *CFO*
Frederic Soulie, *Senior VP*
EMP: 88
SQ FT: 605,000
SALES (est): 16.5MM
SALES (corp-wide): 50.4MM **Privately Held**
SIC: 8742 General management consultant
PA: Global Reach 18, Inc.
10100 Santa Monica Blvd # 900
Los Angeles CA 90067
310 203-5850

(P-27438)
SACKETT NATIONAL HOLDINGS INC
2605 Camino Del Rio S # 400, San Diego
(92108-3706)
PHONE.....................866 834-6242
EMP: 63
SALES (corp-wide): 44.2MM **Privately Held**
SIC: 8742 7389 Management consulting services; financial services
PA: Sackett National Holdings, Inc.
7373 Peak Dr
Las Vegas NV 89128
702 900-1791

(P-27439)
SANDISK LLC
951 Sandisk Dr, Milpitas (95035-7933)
PHONE.....................408 801-1000
Dennis Segers, *Branch Mgr*
Carol Kurimsky, *Vice Pres*
Erez Schwartz, *Vice Pres*
Vishal Sharma, *Program Mgr*
Mia Lane, *Executive Asst*
EMP: 104
SALES (corp-wide): 20.6B **Publicly Held**
WEB: www.sdcard.com
SIC: 8742 Management consulting services
HQ: Sandisk Llc
951 Sandisk Dr
Milpitas CA 95035
408 801-1000

(P-27440)
SAVIYNT INC (PA)
1301 E El Segundo Blvd, El Segundo
(90245-4303)
PHONE.....................310 641-1664
Amit Saha, *CEO*
Jerod Curley, *Vice Pres*
Bob Maynard, *Vice Pres*
Matt Schmidt, *Vice Pres*
Jim Vouloumanos, *Vice Pres*
EMP: 122
SQ FT: 10,000
SALES (est): 21.6MM **Privately Held**
SIC: 8742 Management consulting services

(P-27441)
SEARCH OPTICS LLC (PA)
5770 Oberlin Dr, San Diego (92121-1723)
PHONE.....................858 678-0707
David Ponn, *CEO*
Eduardo Cortez, *President*
David Cox, *President*
Troy Smith, *President*
Jason Stesney, *Treasurer*
EMP: 60
SQ FT: 16,500
SALES (est): 26.3MM **Privately Held**
WEB: www.searchoptics.com
SIC: 8742 Marketing consulting services

(P-27442)
SECOVA INC
3090 Bristol St Ste 200, Costa Mesa
(92626-3061)
PHONE.....................714 384-0530
Venkat Tadanki, *President*
V Chandrasekaran, *COO*
Joel Carter, *Senior VP*
Robert G Parke, *Senior VP*
Karen Kerns, *Vice Pres*
EMP: 186
SQ FT: 7,662
SALES (est): 8.1MM **Privately Held**
WEB: www.secova.com
SIC: 8742 Human resource consulting services
HQ: Secova Eservices, Inc.
3090 Bristol St Ste 200
Costa Mesa CA 92626
714 384-0655

(P-27443)
SECOVA ESERVICES INC (HQ)
3090 Bristol St Ste 200, Costa Mesa
(92626-3061)
PHONE.....................714 384-0655
Venkat R Tadanki, *CEO*
Robert G Parke, *Admin Sec*
V Chandrasekaran, *CTO*
Suresh Murugesan, *Network Mgr*
Zahid Chaudhry, *Finance*
EMP: 84
SQ FT: 6,713
SALES (est): 30.6MM **Privately Held**
WEB: www.ultralink.com
SIC: 8742 Human resource consulting services

(P-27444)
SEQUOIA BNEFITS INSUR SVCS LLC
1850 Gateway Dr Ste 600, San Mateo
(94404-4064)
PHONE.....................650 369-0200
Greg Golub,
Sean Martin, *President*

Michele Floriani, *Chief Mktg Ofcr*
Hall Kesmodel, *Officer*
Cris Barrett, *Vice Pres*
EMP: 70 **EST:** 2001
SQ FT: 2,000
SALES (est): 11.7MM **Privately Held**
WEB: www.sequoiabenefits.com
SIC: 8742 Compensation & benefits planning consultant

(P-27445)
SET FREE SERVICES INC
3300 Veda St, Redding (96001-3511)
P.O. Box 993544 (96099-3544)
PHONE.....................530 243-3373
Robert Lincoln Hancock, *President*
Jim Dahl,
Lisa Freres,
Tammy Lucarelli,
Dan Mullens,
EMP: 53
SQ FT: 10,000
SALES (est): 1.8MM **Privately Held**
SIC: 8742 8748 Management consulting services; business consulting

(P-27446)
SEVILLE CONSTRUCTION SVCS INC
199 S Hudson Ave, Pasadena
(91101-2917)
PHONE.....................626 204-0800
Jeffrey S Flores, *President*
Michelle Acero, *Manager*
EMP: 75
SQ FT: 3,300
SALES (est): 8.7MM **Privately Held**
WEB: www.sevillecs.com
SIC: 8742 Construction project management consultant

(P-27447)
SHANNON RANCHES INC
12601 E Highway 20, Clearlake Oaks
(95423-8312)
P.O. Box 2037 (95423-2037)
PHONE.....................707 998-9656
Clay Shannon, *President*
Margarita Shannon, *Treasurer*
Craig Shannon, *Vice Pres*
EMP: 250 **EST:** 1993
SQ FT: 2,100
SALES (est): 36.4MM **Privately Held**
WEB: www.shannonridge.com
SIC: 8742 Administrative services consultant

(P-27448)
SIERRA SYSTEMS INC (PA)
222 N Pacific Coast Hwy, El Segundo
(90245-5648)
PHONE.....................310 536-6288
Calvin Yonker, *President*
Patricia Kaiser, *COO*
Brian Fees, *CFO*
Tim Vanderhoof, *Software Dev*
Sheila Schuetz, *Manager*
EMP: 200
SALES (est): 13.1MM **Privately Held**
WEB: www.sierrasys.com
SIC: 8742 Management consulting services

(P-27449)
SIGMAWAYS INC
39737 Paseo Padre Pkwy, Fremont
(94538-2996)
PHONE.....................510 573-4208
Prakash Sadasivam, *CEO*
Sudha Kadirvelu, *Human Res Mgr*
Geetha Kannan, *Recruiter*
Priya Raj, *Recruiter*
Bhuvana Ravi, *Recruiter*
EMP: 60
SQ FT: 5,000
SALES (est): 6MM **Privately Held**
SIC: 8742 7379 7373 Management consulting services; computer related consulting services; systems software development services

(P-27450)
SIMI RADIOLOGY & IMAGING
Also Called: Computerized Management/Event Svcs
4100 Guardian St Ste 205, Simi Valley
(93063-6721)
P.O. Box 190 (93062-0190)
PHONE.....................805 522-5978
Daryl Favale, *Owner*
EMP: 100
SALES (est): 5.2MM **Privately Held**
SIC: 8742 Hospital & health services consultant

(P-27451)
SITESTUFF YARDI SYSTEMS I (PA)
430 S Fairview Ave, Goleta (93117-3637)
PHONE.....................805 966-3666
Steven Sewell, *Principal*
Phil Privette, *Technical Staff*
Martin Gedny, *Marketing Staff*
Cheri Quattlebaum, *Manager*
Aaron Wells, *Accounts Mgr*
EMP: 68
SALES (est): 13.6MM **Privately Held**
SIC: 8742 Real estate consultant

(P-27452)
SITRICK BRINCKO GROUP LLC
1840 Century Park E # 800, Los Angeles
(90067-2101)
PHONE.....................310 788-2850
Michael Sitrick, *Mng Member*
John Brincko,
EMP: 60
SALES (est): 3.6MM **Publicly Held**
SIC: 8742 8743 Management consulting services; public relations services
PA: Resources Connection, Inc.
17101 Armstrong Ave # 100
Irvine CA 92614

(P-27453)
SKYLIGHT HALTHCARE SYSTEMS INC
10935 Vista Sorrento Pkwy # 350, San Diego (92130-2651)
PHONE.....................858 523-3700
David J Schofield, *CEO*
Fitz Patrick, *CFO*
Lisa Romano, *Ch Credit Ofcr*
Rich Holbrook, *CTO*
Angelo Spagnolo, *Network Tech*
EMP: 56
SQ FT: 11,000
SALES (est): 10.5MM
SALES (corp-wide): 57.3MM **Privately Held**
WEB: www.skylight.com
SIC: 8742 Hospital & health services consultant
PA: Getwellnetwork, Inc.
7700 Old Georgtwn Rd Fl 4
Bethesda MD 20814
240 482-3200

(P-27454)
SKYLINE CONSULTING GROUP
13186 Skyline Blvd, Woodside
(94062-4542)
PHONE.....................650 529-3455
Gustavo Rabin, *Owner*
Stacy Shamberger, *Exec VP*
Annie Abrams, *Vice Pres*
Melissa Lind, *Vice Pres*
Stacy McCarthy, *Principal*
EMP: 119
SALES (est): 6.3MM **Privately Held**
WEB: www.skylineconsulting.com
SIC: 8742 Training & development consultant

(P-27455)
SMARTZIP ANALYTICS INC (PA)
4450 Rosewood Dr Ste 300, Pleasanton
(94588-3063)
PHONE.....................925 218-1900
Tom Glassanos, *President*
Scott Baumgartner, *CFO*
Frank Richards, *Chairman*
Rajeev Kalavar, *Vice Pres*
Michael Ametrano, *Executive*
EMP: 77

▲ = Import ▼=Export
◆ =Import/Export

SALES (est): 11.7MM **Privately Held**
SIC: 8742 Marketing consulting services;
real estate consultant

(P-27456)
SMG HOLDINGS INC
Also Called: Palm Springs Convention Center
277 N Avenida Caballeros, Palm Springs
(92262-6440)
PHONE...................................760 325-6611
Jim Dunn, *Branch Mgr*
Gabe Rios, *Opers Mgr*
Kristie Dore, *Manager*
Ashley Yanez, *Manager*
EMP: 60
SALES (corp-wide): 24.5B **Privately Held**
WEB: www.smgworld.com
SIC: 8742 7389 Business consultant; con-
vention & show services
HQ: Smg Holdings, Llc
300 Cnshohckn State Rd # 450
Conshohocken PA 19428

(P-27457)
SMITH-EMERY COMPANY (PA)
781 E Washington Blvd, Los Angeles
(90021-3091)
PHONE...................................213 745-5312
James Partridge, *Ch of Bd*
James E Partridge, *Ch of Bd*
EMP: 70 EST: 1904
SQ FT: 35,000
SALES (est): 28.1MM **Privately Held**
WEB: www.smithemery.com
SIC: 8742 Construction project manage-
ment consultant

(P-27458)
SNAP TECHNOLOGIES INC
130 W Union St, Pasadena (91103-3628)
PHONE...................................626 585-6900
Tom McGovern, *President*
Anmol Malhotra, *Partner*
Rachel Racusen, *Comms Dir*
Michael Wandell, *Technical Staff*
Florus Beuting, *Asst Controller*
EMP: 50 EST: 2004
SALES: 10MM **Privately Held**
SIC: 8742 4813 Financial consultant;

(P-27459)
SOAPROJECTS INC (PA)
495 N Whisman Rd Ste 100, Mountain View
(94043-5725)
PHONE...................................650 960-9900
Manpreet Grover, *President*
Mark Gonzalez, *Business Dir*
Rick Gutierrez, *Business Dir*
Lisa Loder, *Admin Asst*
Evangeline Sotelo, *Admin Asst*
EMP: 51
SALES (est): 17.2MM **Privately Held**
SIC: 8742 7379 8721 Financial consult-
ant; computer related consulting services;
accounting, auditing & bookkeeping

(P-27460)
SODEXO INC
1812 Verdugo Blvd Fl 1, Glendale
(91208-1407)
PHONE...................................818 952-2201
Ron Reed, *Manager*
Dominic Bull, *Manager*
EMP: 90
SALES (corp-wide): 139.1MM **Privately
Held**
SIC: 8742 Hospital & health services con-
sultant
HQ: Sodexo, Inc.
9801 Washingtonian Blvd # 1
Gaithersburg MD 20878
301 987-4000

(P-27461)
SOLO W-2 INC
Also Called: Solo Workforce
3478 Buskirk Ave Ste 1000, Pleasant Hill
(94523-4378)
PHONE...................................925 680-0200
James R Ziegler, *President*
Sara M Wilkison, *CFO*
Elizabeth Murphy, *Vice Pres*
Sandi Buchanan, *Human Res Dir*
EMP: 110 EST: 1997
SQ FT: 800

SALES: 10MM **Privately Held**
WEB: www.pacepros.com
SIC: 8742 8721 Compensation & benefits
planning consultant; billing & bookkeeping
service

(P-27462)
SPRINGLEAF FINCL HOLDINGS LLC
905 E Hospitality Ln B, San Bernardino
(92408-2865)
PHONE...................................909 796-1603
EMP: 126
SALES (corp-wide): 3.2B **Privately Held**
SIC: 8742 7389 Financial consultant; fi-
nancial services
PA: Springleaf Financial Holdings, Llc
601 Nw 2nd St
Evansville IN 47708
800 961-5577

(P-27463)
SPRINGLEAF FINCL HOLDINGS LLC
26451 Ynez Rd, Temecula (92591-4628)
PHONE...................................951 296-0135
EMP: 126
SALES (corp-wide): 2.5B **Privately Held**
SIC: 8742 7389 6162 6141 Financial
consultant; financial services; mortgage
bankers & correspondents; personal
credit institutions
PA: Springleaf Financial Holdings, Llc
601 Nw 2nd St
Evansville IN 47708
800 961-5577

(P-27464)
SPRINGLEAF FINCL HOLDINGS LLC
17140 Bear Valley Rd, Victorville
(92395-8312)
PHONE...................................760 241-1451
EMP: 126
SALES (corp-wide): 2.5B **Privately Held**
SIC: 8742 7389 6141 Financial consultant; financial services; personal credit institutions
PA: Springleaf Financial Holdings, Llc
601 Nw 2nd St
Evansville IN 47708
800 961-5577

(P-27465)
SQA SERVICES INC
550 Silver Spur Rd # 300, Rllng HLS Est
(90275-3605)
PHONE...................................310 544-6888
James C McKay, *CEO*
J Michael McKay, *President*
Gerard Pearce, *Vice Pres*
Vamika Jackson, *Administration*
Ray Silverio, *Info Tech Dir*
EMP: 267
SQ FT: 8,000
SALES (est): 32.4MM **Privately Held**
WEB: www.sqaservices.com
SIC: 8742 Quality assurance consultant

(P-27466)
ST JUDE HOSPITAL YORBA LINDA (PA)
251 Imperial Hwy Ste 481, Fullerton
(92835-1058)
PHONE...................................714 449-4800
Lee Penrose, *Principal*
EMP: 60
SALES (est): 10.3MM **Privately Held**
SIC: 8742 Management consulting serv-
ices

(P-27467)
STAGE 4 SOLUTIONS INCORPORATED
19200 Portos Dr, Saratoga (95070-5123)
PHONE...................................408 868-9739
Niti Agrawal, *CEO*
EMP: 50
SALES (est): 596.7K **Privately Held**
WEB: www.stage4solutions.com
SIC: 8742 New products & services con-
sultants

(P-27468)
STATE GROUP LLC
Also Called: Seven Hospitality
36 Umbria, Irvine (92618-8877)
PHONE...................................949 612-2879
Matt Pannek,
Michelle Pannek,
EMP: 280
SQ FT: 8,800
SALES (est): 17.6MM **Privately Held**
SIC: 8742 Restaurant & food services con-
sultants

(P-27469)
STERLING CONSULTING GROUP LLC
Also Called: Sterling Brand
55 Union St Fl 3, San Francisco
(94111-1244)
PHONE...................................415 248-7900
Austin McGhie, *Manager*
Corey Allen, *Accountant*
Lisa Grant, *Receptionist*
EMP: 84 **Privately Held**
SIC: 8742 Marketing consulting services
PA: Sterling Consulting Group Llc
75 Varick St Fl 8
New York NY 10013

(P-27470)
STERLING MKTG & FINCL CORP
Also Called: T3 Direct
4660 Spyres Way Ste 1, Modesto
(95356-9801)
PHONE...................................209 593-1140
Albert W Dadesho, *President*
Susie Dadesho, *Vice Pres*
EMP: 50
SQ FT: 8,000
SALES (est): 5.5MM **Privately Held**
SIC: 8742 Marketing consulting services

(P-27471)
STRATEGIC BUS INSIGHTS INC (PA)
333 Ravenswood Ave, Menlo Park
(94025-3453)
PHONE...................................650 859-4600
William Guns, *CEO*
William Ralston, *CFO*
Eilif Trondsen, *Senior VP*
Larry Cohen, *Vice Pres*
Chulho Park, *Principal*
EMP: 63 EST: 2000
SQ FT: 10,000
SALES (est): 10.6MM **Privately Held**
WEB: www.sricbi.com
SIC: 8742 Marketing consulting services

(P-27472)
STRATEGIC ENLACE INC
281 N Puente St, Brea (92821-3825)
PHONE...................................714 256-8648
Alberto Fernandez, *President*
Marina Arreola, *Office Mgr*
Julia Pacheco, *Marketing Staff*
Brian Kannisto, *Director*
Hector Velazquez, *Accounts Mgr*
EMP: 55
SQ FT: 6,000
SALES (est): 4.8MM **Privately Held**
WEB: www.strategicenlace.com
SIC: 8742 Marketing consulting services;
sales (including sales management) con-
sultant

(P-27473)
STRATEGIC STAFFING SVCS INC
Also Called: Total Hr Management
35 N Lake Ave Ste 140, Pasadena
(91101-1898)
PHONE...................................818 248-0049
James E Harwood, *President*
EMP: 735
SALES (est): 1.8MM
SALES (corp-wide): 390.3MM **Privately
Held**
SIC: 8742 Human resource consulting
services
PA: Coadvantage Corporation
6407 Parkland Dr
Sarasota FL 34243
941 925-2990

(P-27474)
SULLIVANCURTISMONROE INSURANCE (PA)
1920 Main St Ste 600, Irvine (92614-7226)
P.O. Box 19763 (92623-9763)
PHONE...................................800 427-3253
John Monroe, *CEO*
David Kummer, *President*
Mark Eckenweiler, *CFO*
Frances Leiva, *CFO*
Amanda C Griffin, *Assoc VP*
EMP: 103
SQ FT: 22,000
SALES (est): 38.7MM **Privately Held**
WEB: www.sullicurt.com
SIC: 8742 6411 Management consulting
services; insurance brokers

(P-27475)
SUMMIT HR WORLDWIDE INC
Also Called: Echo Staffing
220 Main St Ste 208a, San Jose (95112)
PHONE...................................408 884-7100
Priyaranjan Sinha, *Ch of Bd*
Vidhya Singaradel, *Info Tech Mgr*
Rex Fernando, *Manager*
EMP: 100
SALES (est): 4.1MM **Privately Held**
SIC: 8742 Human resource consulting
services

(P-27476)
SUN PACIFIC MARKETING COOP INC
33502 Lerdo Hwy, Bakersfield
(93308-9438)
PHONE...................................213 612-9957
Berne H Evans III, *Branch Mgr*
EMP: 843
SALES (corp-wide): 221.8MM **Privately
Held**
SIC: 8742 Marketing consulting services
PA: Sun Pacific Marketing Cooperative, Inc.
1095 E Green St
Pasadena CA 91106
213 612-9957

(P-27477)
SUTTER HEALTH
633 Folsom St Fl 5, San Francisco
(94107-3623)
PHONE...................................415 600-3311
Victor Wong, *Technology*
Nina Fong, *Recruiter*
Edward Holt, *Director*
Bob Sypher, *Director*
EMP: 345
SALES (corp-wide): 12.4B **Privately Held**
SIC: 8742 Business planning & organizing
services
PA: Sutter Health
2200 River Plaza Dr
Sacramento CA 95833
916 733-8800

(P-27478)
SUTTER PHYSICIAN SERVICES (HQ)
10470 Old Placrvl Rd # 100, Sacramento
(95827-2539)
P.O. Box 254707 (95865-4707)
PHONE...................................916 854-6600
Jeremy Eaves, *CEO*
Damon Lang, *Associate Dir*
Balbir Singh, *Database Admin*
Kevin Yamamoto, *Financial Analy*
Amber McCauslin, *Human Resources*
EMP: 800
SQ FT: 87,000
SALES (est): 52.6MM
SALES (corp-wide): 12.4B **Privately Held**
WEB: www.sutterconnect.com
SIC: 8742 8741 8721 Hospital & health
services consultant; management infor-
mation systems consultant; management
services; accounting, auditing & book-
keeping
PA: Sutter Health
2200 River Plaza Dr
Sacramento CA 95833
916 733-8800

(P-27479)
SWANDER PACE CAPITAL LLC (PA)
101 Mission St Ste 1900, San Francisco (94105-1726)
PHONE...................................415 477-8500
Andrew Richards, *Principal*
Heather Fraser, *CFO*
Ann Kim, *Vice Pres*
Nathan Ngai, *Vice Pres*
Heather Smith Thorne, *Vice Pres*
EMP: 567
SQ FT: 5,000
SALES (est): 35.3MM **Privately Held**
WEB: www.spcap.com
SIC: 8742 Restaurant & food services consultants

(P-27480)
SYNERGY HEALTH AST LLC (DH)
Also Called: Americas Regional Division
9020 Activity Rd Ste D, San Diego (92126-4454)
PHONE...................................858 586-1166
Rebecca Aldhizer,
Jeff Maybruck, *Vice Pres*
Dottie Lucas, *QC Mgr*
Kevin Smith, *Maintence Staff*
Meridith Erickson, *Cust Mgr*
▲ EMP: 54
SALES (est): 10.6MM
SALES (corp-wide): 2.6B **Privately Held**
WEB: www.beam-one.com
SIC: 8742 Hospital & health services consultant
HQ: Steris Corporation
5960 Heisley Rd
Mentor OH 44060
440 354-2600

(P-27481)
TECHNOLOGY ASSOCIATES EC INC
3115 Melrose Dr Ste 110, Carlsbad (92010-6531)
PHONE...................................760 765-5275
Walter Oleski, *CEO*
EMP: 74
SALES: 13.7MM **Privately Held**
SIC: 8742 General management consultant

(P-27482)
TECOLOTE RESEARCH INC
2120 E Grand Ave Ste 200, El Segundo (90245-5024)
PHONE...................................310 640-4700
James Takayesu, *President*
EMP: 114
SALES (corp-wide): 89.8MM **Privately Held**
WEB: www.tecolote.com
SIC: 8742 8731 Management consulting services; commercial physical research
PA: Tecolote Research, Inc.
420 S Fairview Ave # 201
Goleta CA 93117
805 571-6366

(P-27483)
TELEGRAPH HILL PARTNERS INVEST (PA)
360 Post St Ste 601, San Francisco (94108-4909)
PHONE...................................415 765-6980
J Matthew Mackowski, *Chairman*
Rob C Hart Cfa, *Vice Pres*
M Celeste Salvatto, *Administration*
Deval A Lashkari PHD,
Jeanette M Welsh JD,
EMP: 50
SALES (est): 35MM **Privately Held**
SIC: 8742 6799 Management consulting services; investors

(P-27484)
TELENAV INC
4655 Great America Pkwy # 300, Santa Clara (95054-1236)
PHONE...................................360 765-0058
Ravi Acharya, *Branch Mgr*
EMP: 450

SALES (corp-wide): 169.5MM **Publicly Held**
SIC: 8742 Marketing consulting services
PA: Telenav, Inc.
4655 Great America Pkwy # 300
Santa Clara CA 95054
408 245-3800

(P-27485)
TELESTAR CONSULTING INC
519 N Alta Dr, Beverly Hills (90210-3501)
PHONE...................................310 748-0008
Karl Angel, *President*
EMP: 50
SALES (est): 2.4MM **Privately Held**
SIC: 8742 Hospital & health services consultant

(P-27486)
TERRACARE ASSOCIATES LLC
921 Arnold Dr, Martinez (94553-4102)
PHONE...................................925 374-0060
Todd Williams, *Principal*
EMP: 87 **Privately Held**
SIC: 8742 Management consulting services
PA: Terracare Associates, Llc
8201 Southpark Ln Ste 110
Littleton CO 80120
-

(P-27487)
TETRA TECH INC
1230 Columbia St Ste 1000, San Diego (92101-8588)
PHONE...................................619 525-7188
Roger Argus, *Branch Mgr*
Lawrence D Romine Jr, *Engineer*
EMP: 68
SALES (corp-wide): 2.7B **Publicly Held**
SIC: 8742 8744 8711 Management consulting services; facilities support services; engineering services
PA: Tetra Tech, Inc.
3475 E Foothill Blvd
Pasadena CA 91107
626 351-4664

(P-27488)
THIEL CAPITAL LLC (PA)
1 Letterman Dr Ste 400, San Francisco (94129-1496)
PHONE...................................415 567-7360
Peter Thiel,
Jory Shoell, *CFO*
Timothy Van Voris, *Officer*
Timothy Voris, *Officer*
Kellie Ammerman, *Vice Pres*
EMP: 65
SALES (est): 9.7MM **Privately Held**
SIC: 8742 Financial consultant

(P-27489)
THRESHOLD DIGITAL RESEARCH LAB
1649 11th St, Santa Monica (90404-3707)
PHONE...................................310 452-8885
Larry Kasanoff, *President*
EMP: 50 EST: 1996
SALES (est): 2.9MM **Privately Held**
WEB: www.threshold-digital.com
SIC: 8742 Management consulting services

(P-27490)
TOP TIER CONSULTING
21550 Oxnard St Fl 3, Woodland Hills (91367-7105)
PHONE...................................818 338-2121
Brad Armstrong, *Principal*
Gregory Anderson, *Principal*
Christopher Downey, *Principal*
EMP: 70
SQ FT: 2,000
SALES: 19MM **Privately Held**
SIC: 8742 7379 Management consulting services; computer related consulting services

(P-27491)
TOPDOWN CONSULTING INC
530 Divisadero St Ste 310, San Francisco (94117-2213)
PHONE...................................888 644-8445
Juan Porter, *President*
Mike Davies, *COO*

EMP: 80 EST: 2000
SALES (est): 8.6MM **Privately Held**
WEB: www.topdownconsulting.com
SIC: 8742

(P-27492)
TRACE3 INC
2120 E Grand Ave Ste 145, El Segundo (90245-5024)
PHONE...................................310 220-0164
Teresa Chavez, *Office Mgr*
EMP: 65
SALES (corp-wide): 104.8MM **Privately Held**
SIC: 8742 Sales (including sales management) consultant
PA: Trace3, Llc
7565 Irvine Center Dr
Irvine CA 92618
949 333-2300

(P-27493)
TRACE3 LLC (PA)
7565 Irvine Center Dr, Irvine (92618-4918)
PHONE...................................949 333-2300
Hayes Drumwright, *CEO*
Tyler Beecher, *CEO*
Terri Cooper, *Vice Pres*
Danielle Rodriguez, *Vice Pres*
James Franklin, *Project Mgr*
EMP: 100
SQ FT: 10,000
SALES (est): 104.8MM **Privately Held**
WEB: www.trace3.com
SIC: 8742 Sales (including sales management) consultant

(P-27494)
TRANSIRIS CORPORATION
555 Airport Blvd Ste 325, Burlingame (94010-2062)
PHONE...................................650 303-3495
Silvian Centiu, *CEO*
Simona Nan, *Director*
EMP: 75
SALES (est): 6.3MM **Privately Held**
SIC: 8742 Marketing consulting services

(P-27495)
TRANZEAL INC
2107 N 1st St Ste 500, San Jose (95131-2028)
PHONE...................................408 834-8711
Akhil Khera, *Partner*
Murali Kolli, *COO*
Karan Singh, *Senior Mgr*
Santhosh Lakshmipathy, *Manager*
Andrew Mukherjee, *Manager*
EMP: 50
SQ FT: 2,200
SALES (est): 281.6K **Privately Held**
SIC: 8742 Management consulting services

(P-27496)
TREELINE AND ASSOCIATES
9330 Baseline Rd Ste 106, Rancho Cucamonga (91701-5827)
PHONE...................................909 476-2757
John Metters, *Owner*
EMP: 99
SALES (est): 2.6MM **Privately Held**
SIC: 8742 Marketing consulting services

(P-27497)
TRIAGE CONSULTING GROUP (PA)
221 Main St Ste 1100, San Francisco (94105-1927)
PHONE...................................415 512-9400
Brian Neece, *President*
Damon Lewis, *Treasurer*
Shauna Stewart, *Vice Pres*
Melissa Sorenson, *Program Mgr*
Kim Mc Lemore, *Office Mgr*
EMP: 280
SQ FT: 21,665
SALES: 98MM **Privately Held**
WEB: www.triageconsulting.com
SIC: 8742 8748 Hospital & health services consultant; business consulting

(P-27498)
TRIPLE RING TECHNOLOGIES INC
39655 Eureka Dr, Newark (94560-4806)
PHONE...................................510 592-3000
Joseph A Heanue, *CEO*
Marc Whyte, *Ch of Bd*
Barclay Dorman, *Vice Pres*
Ryan Gaunt, *Vice Pres*
Peter Holst, *Vice Pres*
EMP: 50
SALES (est): 11.7MM **Privately Held**
WEB: www.tripleringtech.com
SIC: 8742 Business consultant

(P-27499)
TRIPLECURVE LLC
5716 Corsa Ave Ste 110, Westlake Village (91362-7354)
PHONE...................................855 874-2878
Joseph Demike,
Brianna Demike, *Partner*
EMP: 100 EST: 2012
SALES (est): 3.6MM **Privately Held**
SIC: 8742 2741 7371 Management consulting services; ; custom computer programming services

(P-27500)
TSMC NORTH AMERICA (HQ)
2851 Junction Ave, San Jose (95134-1910)
PHONE...................................408 382-8000
Richard B Cassidy II, *CEO*
Rick Cassidy, *President*
Pan-WEI Lai, *President*
Peter Bonfield, *Bd of Directors*
Thomas Engibous, *Bd of Directors*
EMP: 108
SALES (est): 33.1MM
SALES (corp-wide): 32.4B **Privately Held**
SIC: 8742 8711 5065 3674 Marketing consulting services; consulting engineer; electronic parts & equipment; semiconductor circuit networks
PA: Taiwan Semiconductor Manufacturing Company Limited
8, Li Hsing 6th Rd., Hsinchu Science Park,
Hsinchu City 30077
356 366-88

(P-27501)
UNITED TALENT AGENCY LLC
1880 Century Park E # 711, Los Angeles (90067-1618)
PHONE...................................310 385-2800
Grant Ledger, *Owner*
Bruce Solar, *Technology*
EMP: 284
SALES (corp-wide): 29.6MM **Privately Held**
SIC: 8742 Management consulting services
PA: United Talent Agency, Llc
9336 Civic Center Dr
Beverly Hills CA 90210
310 273-6700

(P-27502)
UPLIFT INC
801 El Camino Real, Menlo Park (94025-4807)
PHONE...................................844 257-5400
Brian Edward Barth, *CEO*
Rob Soderbery, *President*
Tom Botts, *Officer*
Noha Carrington, *Officer*
Chris Vukelich, *Senior VP*
EMP: 70
SALES (est): 708.3K **Privately Held**
SIC: 8742 7371 Marketing consulting services; computer software development & applications

(P-27503)
US TOURNAMENT GOLF LTD LBLTY
5464 Topaz St, Rancho Cucamonga (91701-1317)
P.O. Box 3373 (91729-3373)
PHONE...................................909 987-6695
Robert E Harrington, *Mng Member*
Bob Harrington, *Admin Sec*
EMP: 50
SQ FT: 1,000

SALES: 5MM **Privately Held**
SIC: 8742 Business planning & organizing services

(P-27504)
USA FACT INC (PA)
6200 Box Springs Blvd B, Riverside (92507-0790)
PHONE..............................951 656-7800
Matt Davidson, *CEO*
Laurie Beem, *Vice Pres*
Daniel Doherty, *Vice Pres*
Cheryl Franklin, *Vice Pres*
Marina Ashshahid, *QA Dir*
EMP: 54
SALES (est): 10.9MM **Privately Held**
WEB: www.usafact.com
SIC: 8742 Human resource consulting services

(P-27505)
VALUE-CENTERED SOLUTIONS INC
2300 Stanwell Dr Ste A, Concord (94520-4841)
PHONE..............................510 662-3333
Michael E Parker, *President*
Darral Brown, *CFO*
Bella Survine, *Executive Asst*
Sharmayne Thompson, *Accounting Mgr*
Rita Johnson, *Business Mgr*
EMP: 50
SQ FT: 7,000
SALES (est): 1.6MM **Privately Held**
SIC: 8742 Management consulting services

(P-27506)
VAN ETTEN SUZUMOTO BECKET LLP
1620 26th St Ste 6000n, Santa Monica (90404-4074)
PHONE..............................310 315-8284
David Van Etten,
EMP: 65
SALES (est): 3.3MM **Privately Held**
SIC: 8742 Management consulting services

(P-27507)
VARIS LLC
3915 Security Park Dr B, Rancho Cordova (95742-6903)
PHONE..............................916 294-0860
Dean B Wilkie, *Manager*
EMP: 70
SALES (est): 3MM
SALES (corp-wide): 10.3MM **Privately Held**
SIC: 8742 Hospital & health services consultant
PA: Varis Llc
9245 Sierra College Blvd
Roseville CA 95661
916 294-0860

(P-27508)
VARIS LLC (PA)
9245 Sierra College Blvd, Roseville (95661-5919)
PHONE..............................916 294-0860
Joy A Wilkie, *Mng Member*
Dean Wilkie, *General Mgr*
Kaye Perryman, *Administration*
Amaniese Roberts, *Administration*
Edward Wadsworth, *Software Engr*
EMP: 110
SQ FT: 5,600
SALES (est): 10.3MM **Privately Held**
WEB: www.varis1.com
SIC: 8742 Hospital & health services consultant

(P-27509)
VAYAN MARKETING GROUP LLC
10877 Wilshire Blvd Fl 12, Los Angeles (90024-4332)
PHONE..............................310 943-4990
Jesse Lo RE,
Laura Kall,
Michael Medema,
Brad Morrison,
EMP: 50
SQ FT: 7,000

SALES (est): 3.3MM **Privately Held**
WEB: www.vayan.com
SIC: 8742 Marketing consulting services

(P-27510)
VERIFI INC
8391 Beverly Blvd Ste 310, Los Angeles (90048-2633)
P.O. Box 310 (90078-0310)
PHONE..............................323 655-5789
Matthew G Katz, *CEO*
Jennifer Schulz, *CEO*
Ronald B Cushey, *CFO*
Jeff Sawitke,
Tony Wootton, *Risk Mgmt Dir*
EMP: 65
SALES (est): 13MM **Privately Held**
SIC: 8742 Quality assurance consultant

(P-27511)
VERTICALRESPONSE INC
550 Kearny St Ste 710, San Francisco (94108-2589)
PHONE..............................866 683-7842
Janine Popick, *President*
Dave Shiba, *COO*
David Shiba, *COO*
Mindy Rosso, *Senior VP*
Richard Tan, *Administration*
EMP: 110
SALES (est): 19.3MM
SALES (corp-wide): 1.9B **Publicly Held**
WEB: www.verticalresponse.com
SIC: 8742 Marketing consulting services
PA: Deluxe Corporation
3680 Victoria St N
Shoreview MN 55126
651 483-7111

(P-27512)
VIDHWAN INC (PA)
Also Called: E-Solutions
2 N Market St Ste 400, San Jose (95113-1213)
PHONE..............................408 289-8200
Priyanka Gupta, *CEO*
Ashish Pandey, *Executive*
Anish Kumar, *Tech Recruiter*
Harender Singh, *Tech Recruiter*
Tanvi Sood, *Tech Recruiter*
EMP: 150
SQ FT: 2,000
SALES (est): 24.7MM **Privately Held**
SIC: 8742 Human resource consulting services; training & development consultant

(P-27513)
VINCE SOLUTIONS (PA)
3910 Riverbend Ter, Fremont (94555-1505)
PHONE..............................510 432-0852
Ashok Yalamati, *President*
Sridhar Vadlapudi, *Admin Sec*
Srini Sirigina, *CTO*
Venkata Kodali, *Manager*
EMP: 55
SQ FT: 1,600
SALES (est): 2.6MM **Privately Held**
WEB: www.janvisoft.com
SIC: 8742 Administrative services consultant

(P-27514)
VISIO INTEG PROFE LLC (HQ)
Also Called: Visionary Intgrtion Prfssonals
80 Iron Point Cir Ste 100, Folsom (95630-8592)
PHONE..............................916 985-9625
Jonna A Ward, *CEO*
Patti Bennion, *CFO*
Steve Carpenter, *Vice Pres*
EMP: 95
SQ FT: 9,000
SALES: 100MM **Privately Held**
SIC: 8742 7379 Management consulting services; computer related maintenance services

(P-27515)
VISIONSTAR INC
3435 Wilsh Blvd Ste 2120, Los Angeles (90010)
PHONE..............................213 387-3700
Mark Anav, *CEO*
EMP: 90

SALES (est): 7.4MM **Privately Held**
SIC: 8742 Marketing consulting services

(P-27516)
VISTAGE INTERNATIONAL INC (PA)
Also Called: Executive Committee, The
4840 Eastgate Mall, San Diego (92121-1977)
PHONE..............................858 523-6800
Rafael Pastor, *Ch of Bd*
Peter J Campbell, *Managing Prtnr*
Richard Carr, *Vice Chairman*
Gaye Van Den Hombergh, *President*
Ken Jacobson, *CEO*
EMP: 115
SALES (est): 25.4MM **Privately Held**
WEB: www.teconline.com
SIC: 8742 Business planning & organizing services

(P-27517)
VISTANCIA MARKETING LLC
Also Called: Shea Homes Ltd Prtnershp
655 Brea Canyon Rd, Walnut (91789-3078)
PHONE..............................909 594-9500
John Francisshea, *Principal*
EMP: 51
SALES (est): 3.1MM
SALES (corp-wide): 2.2B **Privately Held**
SIC: 8742 Marketing consulting services
HQ: Shea Homes Limited Partnership, A California Limited Partnership
655 Brea Canyon Rd
Walnut CA 91789
-

(P-27518)
WAGEWORKS INC (PA)
1100 Park Pl Fl 4, San Mateo (94403-1599)
PHONE..............................650 577-5200
Joseph L Jackson, *CEO*
Stuart C Harvey, *Ch of Bd*
Edgar O Montes, *President*
Ismail Dawood, *CFO*
Kimberly L Wilford, *Senior VP*
EMP: 113
SQ FT: 37,937
SALES: 364.7MM **Publicly Held**
SIC: 8742 Compensation & benefits planning consultant

(P-27519)
WASSERMAN MEDIA GROUP LLC (PA)
10900 Wilshire Blvd, Los Angeles (90024-6501)
PHONE..............................310 407-0200
Casey Wasserman, *Mng Member*
Marc Murphy, *President*
Tim Chadwick, *COO*
Dean Christopher, *CFO*
Christopher Dean, *CFO*
EMP: 115
SQ FT: 40,000
SALES (est): 65MM **Privately Held**
SIC: 8742 Marketing consulting services

(P-27520)
WEST COAST AVIATION SVCS LLC (PA)
Also Called: West Coast Charters
19711 Campus Dr Ste 200, Santa Ana (92707-5203)
PHONE..............................949 852-8340
Gary Standell, *President*
Chris Kramer, *Finance Mgr*
Barbara Hunt, *Marketing Staff*
Chris Little, *Director*
Laura Trenerry, *Manager*
EMP: 50
SQ FT: 2,000
SALES (est): 9MM **Privately Held**
WEB: www.westcoastcharters.com
SIC: 8742 5088 Industry specialist consultants; aircraft & parts

(P-27521)
WESTERN HEALTH RESOURCES
440 Greenfield Ave Ste B, Hanford (93230-3568)
PHONE..............................559 537-2860

Sandy Delarosa, *Director*
EMP: 50
SALES (corp-wide): 59.7MM **Privately Held**
SIC: 8742 Hospital & health services consultant
PA: Western Health Resources
2100 Douglas Blvd
Roseville CA
916 781-2000

(P-27522)
WILSHIRE ASSOCIATES INC (PA)
1299 Ocean Ave Ste 700, Santa Monica (90401-1085)
PHONE..............................310 451-3051
Dennis A Tito, *CEO*
John Hindman, *President*
Andrew Junkin, *President*
Suehyun Kim, *Vice Pres*
EMP: 210
SQ FT: 57,530
SALES (est): 56.2MM **Privately Held**
WEB: www.wilshire.com
SIC: 8742 Financial consultant

(P-27523)
WIPFLI LLP
Also Called: Wipli HFS Consultants
505 14th St Ste 1220, Oakland (94612-1419)
PHONE..............................510 768-0066
EMP: 100
SALES (corp-wide): 432.2MM **Privately Held**
SIC: 8742 Hospital & health services consultant
PA: Wipfli Llp
10000 W Innovation Dr 250-260
Milwaukee WI 53226
414 431-9300

(P-27524)
WPROMOTE LLC (PA)
2100 E Grand Ave Fl 1, El Segundo (90245-5150)
PHONE..............................310 421-4844
Michael Mothner, *President*
Michael Block, *COO*
Brian Rubin, *Officer*
Kelly Mulvey, *Administration*
Brock Honma, *Graphic Designe*
EMP: 76
SALES: 12.2MM **Privately Held**
WEB: www.wpromote.com
SIC: 8742 Marketing consulting services

(P-27525)
WSP USA INC
16689 Foothill Blvd, Fontana (92335-8414)
PHONE..............................909 427-9166
EMP: 61
SALES (corp-wide): 5.4B **Privately Held**
SIC: 8742 Management consulting services
HQ: Wsp Usa Inc.
1 Penn Plz Ste 200
New York NY 10119
212 465-5000

(P-27526)
WTW DELAWARE HOLDINGS LLC
Also Called: Willis Towers Watson
345 California St Fl 15, San Francisco (94104-2629)
PHONE..............................415 733-4100
Jacque Leger, *Principal*
EMP: 125 **Privately Held**
WEB: www.watsonwyatt.com
SIC: 8742 8999 7371 6411 Compensation & benefits planning consultant; human resource consulting services; actuarial consultant; computer software systems analysis & design, custom; computer software development; pension & retirement plan consultants
HQ: Wtw Delaware Holdings Llc
800 N Glebe Rd
Arlington VA 22203
-

PRODUCTS & SVCS

(P-27527)
WTW DELAWARE HOLDINGS LLC
Also Called: Willis Towers Watson
10955 Vista Sorrento Pkwy # 300, San Diego (92130-8699)
PHONE..................................858 523-5500
EMP: 80 **Privately Held**
WEB: www.watsonwyatt.com
SIC: 8742 Management consulting services
HQ: Wtw Delaware Holdings Llc
800 N Glebe Rd
Arlington VA 22203

(P-27528)
XAD INC
189 Bernardo Ave 100, Mountain View (94043-5203)
PHONE..................................650 386-6867
EMP: 189
SALES (corp-wide): 46.8MM **Privately Held**
SIC: 8742 Marketing consulting services
PA: Xad, Inc.
1 World Trade Ctr Fl 60
New York NY

(P-27529)
YMARKETING LLC
4000 Macarthur Blvd # 350, Newport Beach (92660-2517)
PHONE..................................714 545-2550
Ryan Lash, CEO
Brian Yun, COO
Jennifer Jee, Officer
EMP: 70
SALES (est): 454K
SALES (corp-wide): 31.3MM **Privately Held**
SIC: 8742 Marketing consulting services
PA: The Sandbox Group Llc
1 E Wacker Dr Ste 3200
Chicago IL 60601
312 803-1900

(P-27530)
YODLEE INC (HQ)
3600 Bridge Pkwy Ste 200, Redwood City (94065-6139)
PHONE..................................650 980-3600
Anil Arora, President
Mike Armsby, CFO
Bill Parsons, Ch Credit Ofcr
David Lee, Chief Mktg Ofcr
Richard Fitzgerald, Vice Pres
▲ EMP: 146 EST: 1999
SQ FT: 35,000
SALES (est): 80.1MM
SALES (corp-wide): 683.6MM **Publicly Held**
SIC: 8742 Banking & finance consultant
PA: Envestnet, Inc.
35 E Wacker Dr Ste 2400
Chicago IL 60601
312 827-2800

(P-27531)
YOUAPPI INC
2 Embarcadero Ctr # 2310, San Francisco (94111-3823)
PHONE..................................646 854-3390
EMP: 70 EST: 2011
SALES (est): 176.4K **Privately Held**
SIC: 8742 7313

(P-27532)
ZIPLINE INTERNATIONAL INC
529 Railroad Ave, South San Francisco (94080-3450)
PHONE..................................415 993-0604
Keller Rinaudo, CEO
Keenan Wyrobek, CTO
Marina Yang, Director
EMP: 150
SALES (est): 25.1MM **Privately Held**
SIC: 8742 Automation & robotics consultant

(P-27533)
ZIPRECRUITER INC
604 Arizona Ave, Santa Monica (90401-1610)
PHONE..................................800 557-9015

Ian Howard Siegel, CEO
Evan Lasiewicz, Executive
Craig Glendenning, Administration
Killian Jackson, Engineer
Suzanne B Harrison, Human Resources
EMP: 600
SQ FT: 1,800
SALES (est): 7.3MM **Privately Held**
SIC: 8742 Human resource consulting services

(P-27534)
ZS ASSOCIATES INC
2535 W Hillcrest Dr # 100, Thousand Oaks (91320-2457)
PHONE..................................805 413-5900
EMP: 62
SALES (corp-wide): 291.2MM **Privately Held**
SIC: 8742 Marketing consulting services
PA: Zs Associates, Inc.
1560 Sherman Ave Ste 800
Evanston IL 60201
847 492-3600

(P-27535)
ZS ASSOCIATES INC
4365 Executive Dr # 1530, San Diego (92121-2129)
PHONE..................................858 677-2200
EMP: 62
SALES (corp-wide): 291.2MM **Privately Held**
SIC: 8742 7378 Marketing consulting services; computer maintenance & repair
PA: Zs Associates, Inc.
1560 Sherman Ave Ste 800
Evanston IL 60201
847 492-3600

8743 Public Relations Svcs

(P-27536)
ACCESS PUBLIC RELATIONS LLC
Also Called: Access Communications
720 California St Fl 5, San Francisco (94108-2453)
PHONE..................................415 904-7070
Susan Butenhoff,
Danielle Caff, Senior VP
Nancy Blair, Vice Pres
Ken Bruno, Accounting Mgr
Matt Afflixio,
EMP: 64
SQ FT: 17,000
SALES (est): 8.1MM
SALES (corp-wide): 15.2B **Publicly Held**
WEB: www.accesspr.com
SIC: 8743 Public relations & publicity
HQ: Ketchum Incorporated
1285 Avenue Of The Americ
New York NY 10019
646 935-3900

(P-27537)
ARYAKA NETWORKS INC (PA)
1800 Gateway Dr Ste 200, San Mateo (94404-4072)
PHONE..................................408 273-8420
Matt Carter, CEO
Shawn Farshchi, President
Ram Gupta, Chairman
Mike Hoffman, Officer
EMP: 73
SALES (est): 43.8MM **Privately Held**
SIC: 8743 Sales promotion

(P-27538)
AT&T CORP
50 Fremont St, San Francisco (94105-2276)
PHONE..................................415 442-5900
Dennis Williams, Branch Mgr
EMP: 150
SALES (corp-wide): 160.5B **Publicly Held**
WEB: www.att.com
SIC: 8743 Sales promotion
HQ: At&T Corp.
1 At&T Way
Bedminster NJ 07921
800 403-3302

(P-27539)
B T B EVENTS INC
Also Called: California Special Events
10950 Virginia Cir, Fountain Valley (92708-7010)
PHONE..................................714 415-3313
Christopher P Chapin, CEO
Robert G Traxel, President
Roger Janke, Vice Pres
John P Regas, VP Opers
EMP: 75
SALES (est): 12.9MM **Privately Held**
SIC: 8743 8742 7359 6512 Sales promotion; public relations & publicity; sales (including sales management) consultant; equipment rental & leasing; nonresidential building operators

(P-27540)
BAKER WINOKUR
Also Called: Bwrpr
9100 Wilshire Blvd 500w, Beverly Hills (90212-3426)
PHONE..................................310 248-6169
M Sorel, President
Cindy Guagenti, Managing Dir
Courtney Sybesma, Accounts Exec
EMP: 70 EST: 1979
SALES: 10MM **Privately Held**
WEB: www.bwrpr.com
SIC: 8743 Public relations & publicity

(P-27541)
BEHR PROCESS SALES COMPANY
3000 S Main St Apt 84e, Santa Ana (92707-4225)
P.O. Box 1287 (92702-1287)
PHONE..................................714 545-7101
Kevin Jaffe, Partner
John V Croul, Partner
EMP: 150
SQ FT: 54,000
SALES (est): 9.8MM **Privately Held**
SIC: 8743 2851 5198 Sales promotion; varnishes; paints & paint additives; stains; varnish, oil or wax; lacquer: bases, dopes, thinner; paints, varnishes & supplies

(P-27542)
BENDER/HELPER IMPACT INC (PA)
11500 W Olympic Blvd # 655, Los Angeles (90064-1530)
PHONE..................................310 473-4147
Lee Helper, President
Dean Bender, Vice Pres
Adam Krell, Executive
Jonah Keel, Business Dir
Jerry Griffin, General Mgr
EMP: 55
SQ FT: 9,314
SALES (est): 6.5MM **Privately Held**
WEB: www.bhimpact.com
SIC: 8743 Public relations & publicity

(P-27543)
BNI ENTERPRISES INC
Also Called: B N I
545 College Commerce Way, Upland (91786-4377)
PHONE..................................909 305-1818
Ivan Misner, Chairman
Mike Fitton, Marketing Staff
EMP: 600
SQ FT: 33,000
SALES (est): 81.7MM **Privately Held**
WEB: www.bni.com
SIC: 8743 Promotion service

(P-27544)
BWR PUBLIC RELATIONS
Also Called: Baker Winokur Ryder
9100 Wilshire Blvd 500w, Beverly Hills (90212-3415)
PHONE..................................310 248-6100
Larry Winokur, President
Neal Cohen, Officer
Jeffrey Chassen, Executive
Lauren Peteroy, Executive
Paulette V Kam, Managing Dir
EMP: 67
SALES (est): 2.2MM **Privately Held**
SIC: 8743 Public relations & publicity

(P-27545)
CALIBRE INTERNATIONAL LLC (PA)
Also Called: High Caliber Line
6250 N Irwindale Ave, Irwindale (91702-3208)
PHONE..................................626 969-4660
Daniel Oas,
Kenan Ozcan, CFO
Les Dorfman, VP Sales
Catherine Oas,
Patty Gomez, Accounts Exec
◆ EMP: 165
SQ FT: 100,000
SALES: 28MM **Privately Held**
WEB: www.calibr.com
SIC: 8743 2759 Promotion service; promotional printing

(P-27546)
CAROLINE PROMOTIONS INC
809 S Adams St Apt 7, Glendale (91205-4424)
PHONE..................................818 507-7666
Caroline Jovenich, President
EMP: 55
SQ FT: 600
SALES (est): 3.4MM **Privately Held**
WEB: www.carolinepromotions.com
SIC: 8743 Sales promotion

(P-27547)
CATALINA EVENTS INC
2605 184th St, Redondo Beach (90278-4508)
PHONE..................................310 925-6986
John Ellis, CEO
EMP: 50
SALES (est): 843.2K **Privately Held**
SIC: 8743 Promotion service

(P-27548)
CITY OF CORONA
400 S Vicentia Ave, Corona (92882-2187)
PHONE..................................951 279-3647
Kit Field, Branch Mgr
EMP: 250 **Privately Held**
SIC: 8743 Public relations services
PA: City Of Corona
400 S Vicentia Ave
Corona CA 92882
951 736-2372

(P-27549)
CMP FILM & DESIGN BURBANK LLC
Also Called: Mocean
2717 W Olive Ave, Burbank (91505-4532)
PHONE..................................818 729-0800
Craig Murray, Mng Member
Matthew Hurst, Production
EMP: 65
SQ FT: 12,000
SALES (est): 4.1MM **Privately Held**
SIC: 8743 7812 Promotion service; video tape production

(P-27550)
COMPETITOR GROUP EVENTS INC
5452 Oberlin Dr, San Diego (92121-1715)
PHONE..................................858 450-6510
Tim Murphy, President
EMP: 50
SQ FT: 12,500
SALES (est): 3.6MM
SALES (corp-wide): 127MM **Privately Held**
WEB: www.eliteracing.com
SIC: 8743 Promotion service
HQ: Competitor Group, Inc.
6420 Sequence Dr
San Diego CA 92121

(P-27551)
DANIEL J EDELMAN INC
Also Called: Edelman Public Relations
525 Market St, San Francisco (94105-2708)
PHONE..................................415 222-9944
Jay Porter, General Mgr
Tom Parker, Creative Dir
EMP: 99

▲ = Import ▼=Export
◆ =Import/Export

SALES (corp-wide): 580.4MM **Privately Held**
SIC: **8743** Public relations & publicity
HQ: Daniel J. Edelman, Inc.
200 E Randolph St Fl 63
Chicago IL 60601
312 240-3000

(P-27552)
DANIEL J EDELMAN INC
Also Called: Edelman Public Relations
5670 Wilshire Blvd # 2500, Los Angeles
(90036-5679)
PHONE...................................323 857-9100
Gail Becker, *Principal*
Ben White, *Vice Pres*
Katie Nafius, *Supervisor*
EMP: 65
SALES (corp-wide): 580.4MM **Privately Held**
SIC: **8743** 7313 Public relations & publicity; electronic media advertising representatives; printed media advertising representatives
HQ: Daniel J. Edelman, Inc.
200 E Randolph St Fl 63
Chicago IL 60601
312 240-3000

(P-27553)
FENTON COMMUNICATIONS INC
182 2nd St Ste 400, San Francisco
(94105-3801)
PHONE...................................415 255-1946
Parker Blackman, *Manager*
Michael Huttner, *Director*
EMP: 50
SALES (corp-wide): 13.8MM **Privately Held**
WEB: www.dhs.gov
SIC: **8743** Public relations & publicity
PA: Fenton Communications, Inc.
1010 Vermont Ave Nw # 1100
Washington DC 20005
202 822-5200

(P-27554)
FLEISHMAN-HILLARD INC
720 California St Fl 6, San Francisco
(94108-2478)
PHONE...................................415 318-4000
Tim O'Keeffe, *General Mgr*
EMP: 50
SALES (corp-wide): 15.2B **Publicly Held**
WEB: www.fleishmanhillard.com
SIC: **8743** Public relations & publicity
HQ: Fleishman-Hillard Inc.
200 N Broadway
Saint Louis MO 63102
314 982-1700

(P-27555)
HAVAS FORMULA LLC
1215 Cushman Ave, San Diego
(92110-3904)
PHONE...................................619 234-0345
Michael A Olguin, *President*
David Heimlich, *President*
Tara Reid, *Assoc VP*
Alexis McCance, *Senior VP*
Ditas Mauricio, *Vice Pres*
EMP: 100
SQ FT: 2,700
SALES (est): 16MM
SALES (corp-wide): 78.4MM **Privately Held**
WEB: www.formulapr.com
SIC: **8743** 7319 Public relations & publicity; transit advertising services
HQ: Havas
29 30
Puteaux 92800
158 478-000

(P-27556)
HILL & KNOWLTON STRATEGIES LLC
Blanc & Otus
60 Green St, San Francisco (94111-1435)
PHONE...................................415 281-7120
Quinn Daly, *General Mgr*
EMP: 55
SALES (corp-wide): 20.1B **Privately Held**
SIC: **8743** Public relations & publicity

HQ: Hill And Knowlton Strategies, Llc
466 Lexington Ave Frnt 4
New York NY 10017
212 885-0300

(P-27557)
HOFFMAN AGENCY (PA)
325 S 1st St Ste 300, San Jose
(95113-2830)
PHONE...................................408 286-2611
Lou Hoffman, *CEO*
Laurie Jones, *Info Tech Dir*
Bonnie Lamb, *Director*
Steve Burkhart, *Manager*
EMP: 53
SQ FT: 23,000
SALES (est): 4.9MM **Privately Held**
WEB: www.hoffman.com
SIC: **8743** Public relations & publicity

(P-27558)
KETCHUM INCORPORATED
12777 W Jefferson Blvd # 120, Los Angeles
(90066-7038)
PHONE...................................310 437-2600
Melissa Kinch, *Director*
Maxine Enciso, *Vice Pres*
Matthew Dernoga, *Research*
Joanne Zhu, *Research*
Stacy Kika, *Accounts Exec*
EMP: 60
SALES (corp-wide): 15.2B **Publicly Held**
SIC: **8743** 7311 Public relations & publicity; advertising agencies
HQ: Ketchum Incorporated
1285 Avenue Of The Americ
New York NY 10019
646 935-3900

(P-27559)
KETCHUM INCORPORATED
1050 Battery St, San Francisco
(94111-1286)
PHONE...................................415 984-6100
Melissa Kinch, *Director*
David Allan, *Vice Pres*
Bob Conrad, *Vice Pres*
Rebekah Earp, *Vice Pres*
Sarah Gates, *Vice Pres*
EMP: 75
SALES (corp-wide): 15.2B **Publicly Held**
WEB: www.imsfastpak.com
SIC: **8743** Public relations & publicity
HQ: Ketchum Incorporated
1285 Avenue Of The Americ
New York NY 10019
646 935-3900

(P-27560)
LEAGUE OF CALIFORNIA CITIES (PA)
Also Called: WESTERN CITY MAGAZINE
1400 K St Fl 4, Sacramento (95814-3916)
PHONE...................................916 658-8200
Carolyn Coleman, *Exec Dir*
Norman Coppinger, *CFO*
Kayla Boutros, *Admin Asst*
Kimberly Brady, *Admin Asst*
Kristy Jensen, *Admin Asst*
EMP: 80
SQ FT: 32,000
SALES: 300.6K **Privately Held**
WEB: www.cacities.org
SIC: **8743** 2721 Lobbyist; magazines: publishing only, not printed on site

(P-27561)
LEWIS PR INC (DH)
111 Sutter St Ste 850, San Francisco
(94104-4506)
PHONE...................................415 432-2400
Chris Lewis, *CEO*
James Oehlcke, *CFO*
Fernando Batista, *Top Exec*
Andres Wittermann, *Exec VP*
Heather Bliss, *Senior VP*
EMP: 53
SALES (est): 15.2MM
SALES (corp-wide): 65.5MM **Privately Held**
SIC: **8743** Public relations & publicity
HQ: Lewis Communications Limited
22 Floor, Millbank Tower
London SW1P
207 802-2626

(P-27562)
LIPPIN GROUP INC (PA)
6100 Wilshire Blvd # 400, Los Angeles
(90048-5109)
PHONE...................................323 965-1990
Richard B Lippin, *President*
Don Ciaramella, *President*
Shelly Saarella, *CFO*
Matt Biscuiti, *Vice Pres*
David Gardner, *Vice Pres*
EMP: 50
SQ FT: 8,000
SALES (est): 6.6MM **Privately Held**
SIC: **8743** Public relations & publicity

(P-27563)
MAGIC WORKFORCE SOLUTIONS LLC
9100 Wilsh Blvd Ste 700e, Beverly Hills
(90212)
PHONE...................................310 246-6153
Earvin Johnson, *CEO*
Eric Holoman, *President*
Kawanna Brown, *COO*
EMP: 4539 EST: 2007
SALES (est): 3.1MM
SALES (corp-wide): 506.3MM **Privately Held**
SIC: **8743** Promotion service
PA: Magic Johnson Enterprises, Inc.
9100 Wilshire Blvd 700e
Beverly Hills CA 90212
310 247-2033

(P-27564)
MURPHY OBRIEN INC
11444 W Olympic Blvd # 600, Los Angeles
(90064-1549)
PHONE...................................310 453-2539
Karen Murphy O'Brien, *CEO*
Brett O'Brien, *Managing Prtnr*
EMP: 55
SQ FT: 7,159
SALES (est): 4.6MM **Privately Held**
WEB: www.murphyobrien.com
SIC: **8743** Public relations & publicity

(P-27565)
NATIONAL PRODUCT SERVICES LLC
1005 Marvista Ave, Seal Beach
(90740-5841)
PHONE...................................562 594-8206
Nancy Sawyer,
EMP: 50 EST: 2001
SQ FT: 600
SALES (est): 2.6MM **Privately Held**
SIC: **8743** Sales promotion

(P-27566)
OGILVY PUB RLTONS WRLDWIDE INC
1530 J St, Sacramento (95814-2052)
PHONE...................................916 231-7700
EMP: 74
SALES (corp-wide): 20.1B **Privately Held**
SIC: **8743** Public relations & publicity
HQ: Ogilvy Public Relations Worldwide Inc.
636 11th Ave
New York NY 10036
212 880-5200

(P-27567)
OUTCAST AGENCY LLC
100 Montgomery St # 1200, San Francisco
(94104-4331)
PHONE...................................415 392-8282
Tim Dyson,
Lara Cohen, *Vice Pres*
Devon Corvasce, *Vice Pres*
Meg D'Incecco, *Vice Pres*
Sophie Fischman, *Vice Pres*
EMP: 120
SALES (est): 12.1MM **Privately Held**
SIC: **8743** Public relations services

(P-27568)
PMK-BNC INC (PA)
1840 Century Park E # 1400, Los Angeles
(90067-2115)
PHONE...................................310 854-0455
Michael Nyman, *CEO*
Chris Robichaud, *President*
John Lundy, *CFO*
Doug Piwinski, *Exec VP*

Deknatel Alison, *Vice Pres*
EMP: 130
SQ FT: 4,000
SALES (est): 29.1MM **Privately Held**
SIC: **8743** Public relations & publicity

(P-27569)
PMK-BNC INC
8687 Melrose Ave Fl 8th, Los Angeles
(90069-5746)
PHONE...................................310 854-4800
Eunice Ko, *Branch Mgr*
Dana Berkowitz, *Director*
EMP: 50
SALES (corp-wide): 29.1MM **Privately Held**
SIC: **8743** Public relations & publicity
PA: Pmk-Bnc, Inc.
1840 Century Park E # 1400
Los Angeles CA 90067
310 854-0455

(P-27570)
POSITEA INV & PUB RELATIONS
Also Called: Mathews & Clark Communications
710 Lakeway Dr, Sunnyvale (94085-4006)
PHONE...................................408 736-1120
Stuart Chalmers, *President*
Stephen Howse, *Manager*
EMP: 50
SALES (est): 1.4MM **Privately Held**
SIC: **8743** Public relations services

(P-27571)
RPMC INC (PA)
Also Called: R P M C Travel
23975 Park Sorrento # 410, Calabasas
(91302-4031)
PHONE...................................818 222-7762
Robert Olshever, *President*
Kelly Weinberg, *Exec VP*
Murray Schwartz, *Vice Pres*
Angelica Diaz, *Senior Mgr*
Jacqueline Bao, *Director*
EMP: 95
SQ FT: 10,000
SALES (est): 11.3MM **Privately Held**
SIC: **8743** 8742 Promotion service; marketing consulting services

(P-27572)
WEBER SHANDWICK
600 Battery St Fl 1, San Francisco
(94111-1820)
PHONE...................................415 262-5600
Luca Penati, *General Mgr*
EMP: 60
SALES (est): 593.2K **Privately Held**
SIC: **8743** Public relations services

8744 Facilities Support Mgmt Svcs

(P-27573)
ACEPEX MANAGEMENT CORPORATION
10643 Mills Ave, Montclair (91763-4612)
PHONE...................................909 625-6900
Henry C Rhee, *CEO*
Nancy Escobar, *Executive Asst*
Helen Ward, *Project Mgr*
Drew Feldmann, *Controller*
Tracey Daniels, *Clerk*
EMP: 150
SQ FT: 7,000
SALES: 22.8MM **Privately Held**
WEB: www.acepex.com
SIC: **8744** Base maintenance (providing personnel on continuing basis)

(P-27574)
ADVANCED CLEANUP TECH INC (PA)
20928 S Lamberton Ave, Carson
(90810-1024)
P.O. Box 5270, Compton (90224-5270)
PHONE...................................310 763-1423
Ruben Garcia, *CEO*
Andy Chavez, *Manager*
EMP: 120
SALES (est): 28.5MM **Privately Held**
WEB: www.actird.com
SIC: **8744**

(P-27575)
AGUATIERRA ASSOCIATES INC (PA)
Also Called: Weiss Associates
2000 Powell St Ste 555, Emeryville (94608-1838)
PHONE..................................510 450-6000
Michael D Dresen, *President*
Richard B Weiss, *CFO*
Scott Bourne, *Vice Pres*
Robert Devany, *Vice Pres*
Roshy Mozafar, *Engineer*
EMP: 55
SQ FT: 13,000
SALES (est): 6.2MM **Privately Held**
SIC: 8744 4959 8748 Facilities support services; environmental cleanup services; environmental consultant

(P-27576)
AMERICAN INTEGRATED SVCS INC (PA)
1502 E Opp St, Wilmington (90744-3927)
P.O. Box 92316, Long Beach (90809-2316)
PHONE..................................310 522-1168
Paul David Herrera, *President*
John Georgagi, *Vice Pres*
Gary Runnells, *Vice Pres*
Sandi Schafer, *Vice Pres*
Kelly Stater, *Vice Pres*
EMP: 50
SQ FT: 77,000
SALES (est): 33.1MM **Privately Held**
WEB: www.americanintegrated.com
SIC: 8744

(P-27577)
AMERITAC INC (PA)
640 Logan Ln, Danville (94526-1512)
P.O. Box 279 (94526-0279)
PHONE..................................925 743-8398
Isiah Harris, *President*
Lawrence Stevens, *Vice Pres*
Larry Stevens, *Marketing Mgr*
EMP: 80
SQ FT: 2,024
SALES: 3.5MM **Privately Held**
WEB: www.ameritac.net
SIC: 8744 Base maintenance (providing personnel on continuing basis)

(P-27578)
ARGUS MANAGEMENT COMPANY LLC
Also Called: Argus Medical Management
5150 E Pacific Coast Hwy # 500, Long Beach (90804-3328)
PHONE..................................562 299-5200
Robert C Boullon,
Irene Valenzuela, *Regional Mgr*
Geegee Reynoso, *Admin Sec*
Misun Kim, *Analyst*
Karen Hale, *Opers Mgr*
EMP: 300
SQ FT: 2,500
SALES (est): 19.1MM **Privately Held**
WEB: www.argusmso.com
SIC: 8744 Facilities support services

(P-27579)
CAPE ENVIRONMENTAL MGT INC
18012 Cowan Ste 150, Irvine (92614-6817)
PHONE..................................949 236-3000
Amir Matin, *Manager*
EMP: 265
SALES (corp-wide): 243.8MM **Privately Held**
SIC: 8744
PA: Cape Environmental Management Inc.
500 Pinnacle Ct Ste 100
Norcross GA 30071
770 908-7200

(P-27580)
CASA DSCANSO CONVALESCENT HOSP
Also Called: Huntington Child Care Center
4515 Huntington Dr S, Los Angeles (90032-1940)
PHONE..................................323 225-5991
Jack Gindi, *President*
EMP: 107
SALES (est): 5.6MM **Privately Held**
SIC: 8744 Facilities support services

(P-27581)
CITY OF BREA
Also Called: Maintenance Dept
1 Civic Center Cir Fl 3, Brea (92821-5758)
PHONE..................................714 990-7650
Bill Higgins, *Director*
EMP: 57 **Privately Held**
WEB: www.cityofbrea.net
SIC: 8744 Base maintenance (providing personnel on continuing basis)
PA: City Of Brea
1 Civic Center Cir Fl 3
Brea CA 92821
714 990-7600

(P-27582)
CITY OF WOODLAND
Also Called: Public Works Department
655 N Pioneer Ave, Woodland (95776-6112)
PHONE..................................530 661-5962
Greg Mayer, *Director*
EMP: 200 **Privately Held**
WEB: www.ci.woodland.ca.us
SIC: 8744 Base maintenance (providing personnel on continuing basis)
PA: City Of Woodland
300 1st St
Woodland CA 95695
530 661-5830

(P-27583)
CORECIVIC INC
Also Called: San Diego Correctional Fcilty
446 Alta Rd, San Diego (92158-0001)
P.O. Box 439049, San Ysidro (92143-9049)
PHONE..................................619 661-9119
EMP: 243
SALES (corp-wide): 1.7B **Publicly Held**
WEB: www.correctionscorp.com
SIC: 8744 Correctional facility
PA: Corecivic, Inc.
10 Burton Hills Blvd
Nashville TN 37215
615 263-3000

(P-27584)
CORECIVIC INC
Also Called: California Cy Correctional Ctr
22844 Virginia Blvd, California City (93505)
P.O. Box 2590 (93504-0590)
PHONE..................................760 373-1764
Charles Gilkey, *Warden*
EMP: 150
SALES (corp-wide): 1.7B **Publicly Held**
WEB: www.correctionscorp.com
SIC: 8744 Correctional facility
PA: Corecivic, Inc.
10 Burton Hills Blvd
Nashville TN 37215
615 263-3000

(P-27585)
CORNELL COMPANIES INC
759 Lakeview Ave, San Francisco (94112-2203)
PHONE..................................415 346-9769
EMP: 92
SALES (corp-wide): 2.2B **Privately Held**
SIC: 8744 Correctional facility
HQ: Cornell Companies, Inc.
621 Nw 53rd St Ste 700
Boca Raton FL 33487
-

(P-27586)
CORRECTIONAL SERVICES CORP LLC
7805 Arjons Dr, San Diego (92126-4368)
PHONE..................................858 566-9816
EMP: 51
SALES (corp-wide): 2.2B **Privately Held**
SIC: 8744 Correctional facility
HQ: Correctional Services Corporation, Llc
621 Nw 53rd St Ste 700
Boca Raton FL 33487
-

(P-27587)
COUNTY OF MONTEREY
Also Called: County Jail
1410 Natividad Rd, Salinas (93906-3102)
PHONE..................................831 755-3782
John Davidson, *Principal*
EMP: 179 **Privately Held**
WEB: www.montereycountyfarmbureau.org

SIC: 8744 Jails, privately operated
PA: County Of Monterey
168 W Alisal St Fl 2
Salinas CA 93901
831 755-5040

(P-27588)
COUNTY OF SACRAMENTO
Also Called: Sheriff's Dept
12500 Bruceville Rd, Elk Grove (95757-9784)
PHONE..................................916 874-1927
James Babcock, *Branch Mgr*
EMP: 250 **Privately Held**
WEB: www.sna.com
SIC: 8744 9223 Correctional facility; correctional institutions;
PA: County Of Sacramento
700 H St Ste 7650
Sacramento CA 95814
916 874-5544

(P-27589)
CVE NB CONTRACTING GROUP INC
Also Called: Central Valley Environmental
135 Utility Ct A, Rohnert Park (94928-1616)
PHONE..................................707 584-1900
Tim Williamson, *CEO*
Glenn Accornero, *COO*
EMP: 50 EST: 2015
SQ FT: 4,700
SALES: 12.5MM **Privately Held**
SIC: 8744

(P-27590)
GEO GROUP INC
Also Called: Taft Correctional Institution
1500 Cadet Rd, Taft (93268-4800)
P.O. Box 7000 (93268-7000)
PHONE..................................661 763-2510
Michael Denop, *Warden*
EMP: 387
SALES (corp-wide): 2.2B **Privately Held**
WEB: www.thegeogroupinc.com
SIC: 8744 Correctional facility
PA: The Geo Group Inc
621 Nw 53rd St Ste 700
Boca Raton FL 33487
561 893-0101

(P-27591)
GERWEND ENTERPRISES INC
Also Called: Integrity Management Entps
2952 Market St, San Diego (92102-3241)
PHONE..................................619 254-5018
Carlos Buzon, *President*
Tony Pizarro, *Vice Pres*
EMP: 150
SQ FT: 4,000
SALES (est): 6.9MM **Privately Held**
SIC: 8744 Facilities support services

(P-27592)
GILBANE AECOM JV
1655 Grant St Fl 12, Concord (94520-2600)
PHONE..................................925 946-3100
Eric Banks, *Manager*
Harvey Coppage, *Manager*
Natalia Rahkman, *Manager*
Matt Tierney, *Manager*
EMP: 54 EST: 2016
SALES (est): 1.2MM
SALES (corp-wide): 4.9B **Privately Held**
SIC: 8744 Facilities support services
HQ: Gilbane Federal
1655 Grant St Fl 12
Concord CA 94520
-

(P-27593)
HUMAN POTENTIAL CONS LLC
500 E Carson Plaza Dr # 127, Carson (90746-7370)
PHONE..................................310 756-1560
Garnett Newcombe, *CEO*
Tiffani Clegg, *General Mgr*
Camille Chapman, *Administration*
Leonora Vides, *Info Tech Mgr*
Marty Hill, *Case Mgr*
EMP: 63 EST: 1997
SQ FT: 3,500

SALES: 3.5MM **Privately Held**
SIC: 8744 7349 8741 Facilities support services; janitorial service, contract basis; personnel management

(P-27594)
IAP WORLD SERVICES INC
567 Dugan South Akron Rd, Mountain View (94035)
PHONE..................................650 604-0451
Travis Durano, *Project Mgr*
EMP: 68
SALES (corp-wide): 661.5MM **Privately Held**
WEB: www.jcwsi.com
SIC: 8744 Facilities support services
HQ: Iap World Services, Inc.
7315 N Atlantic Ave
Cape Canaveral FL 32920
321 784-7100

(P-27595)
IAP WORLD SERVICES INC
510 S Loop 1st St Bldg T, Fort Irwin (92310)
PHONE..................................760 380-6772
Jeffrey D Williamson, *Manager*
EMP: 290
SALES (corp-wide): 661.5MM **Privately Held**
WEB: www.jcwsi.com
SIC: 8744 Facilities support services
HQ: Iap World Services, Inc.
7315 N Atlantic Ave
Cape Canaveral FL 32920
321 784-7100

(P-27596)
INDYNE INC
1036 California Blvd # 11013, Vandenberg Afb (93437)
PHONE..................................805 606-7225
Kenneth A Cinal, *Branch Mgr*
David Miller, *Principal*
EMP: 700
SALES (corp-wide): 268.7MM **Privately Held**
WEB: www.indyneinc.com
SIC: 8744 Base maintenance (providing personnel on continuing basis)
PA: Indyne, Inc.
21351 Gentry Dr Ste 205
Sterling VA 20166
703 903-6900

(P-27597)
INNOVATIVE CNSTR SOLUTIONS
4011 W Chandler Ave, Santa Ana (92704-5201)
PHONE..................................714 893-6366
Hirad Emadi, *President*
Greg Sherman, *Vice Pres*
John R White, *Vice Pres*
Monique Stefanovic, *Office Mgr*
Chad Castro, *Project Mgr*
EMP: 105
SQ FT: 2,000
SALES (est): 20.8MM **Privately Held**
SIC: 8744 1795 ; demolition, buildings & other structures

(P-27598)
JLS ENVIRONMENTAL SERVICES INC
3460 Swetzer Rd, Loomis (95650-7624)
PHONE..................................916 660-1525
Larry Walker, *President*
John G Sheehan, *CEO*
David Locke, *CFO*
Shane Lesher, *General Mgr*
Cigi Ramesbottom, *Office Mgr*
EMP: 70
SALES (est): 7.7MM **Privately Held**
WEB: www.jls-inc.com
SIC: 8744 8999 ; earth science services

(P-27599)
LEIGHTON GROUP INC (PA)
17781 Cowan, Irvine (92614-6009)
PHONE..................................949 477-4040
Terry Brennan, *Ch of Bd*
Vincent Ip, *Vice Pres*
Carl Kim, *Vice Pres*
Gareth Mills, *Vice Pres*
Tom Mills, *Vice Pres*
EMP: 270

SALES (est): 30.7MM **Privately Held**
WEB: www.leightongroup.com
SIC: 8744

(P-27600)
M & E TECHNICAL SERVICES L L C (PA)
Also Called: Mets//
3601 Bayview Dr, Manhattan Beach (90266-3225)
PHONE..............................256 964-6486
Gary Olney, *CEO*
David Smith, *President*
Garry Olney, *CEO*
Harry Seggelke, *CFO*
Jack Bailey, *Vice Pres*
EMP: 90
SALES (est): 5.5MM **Privately Held**
SIC: 8744 4225 4731 7539 Facilities support services; general warehousing & storage; freight transportation arrangement; automotive repair shops

(P-27601)
OLYMPUS BUILDING SERVICES INC
441 La Moree Rd, San Marcos (92078-5017)
PHONE..............................760 750-4629
Anthony Hipple, *Branch Mgr*
EMP: 1090
SALES (corp-wide): 23MM **Privately Held**
SIC: 8744 Facilities support services
PA: Olympus Building Services Inc
1430 E Missouri Ave B205
Phoenix AZ 85014
480 284-8018

(P-27602)
ONE SILVER SERVE INC
Also Called: SERVPRO Encino/Sherman Oaks
17835 Ventura Blvd # 108, Encino (91316-3634)
PHONE..............................818 995-6444
Alan Reed, *CEO*
Elia Morales, *Receptionist*
EMP: 50
SALES (est): 1.5MM **Privately Held**
SIC: 8744

(P-27603)
ONE WORKPLACE L FERRARI LLC
Also Called: One Work Place
475 Brannan St Ste 210, San Francisco (94107-5498)
PHONE..............................415 357-2200
Mark Smith, *VP Sales*
EMP: 82
SALES (corp-wide): 225.6MM **Privately Held**
WEB: www.oneworkplace.com
SIC: 8744 Facilities support services
PA: One Workplace L. Ferrari, Llc
2500 De La Cruz Blvd
Santa Clara CA 95050
669 800-2500

(P-27604)
SERVICON SYSTEMS INC (PA)
Also Called: Pacifica Consulting Services
3965 Landmark St, Culver City (90232-2399)
PHONE..............................310 204-5040
Michael Mahdesian, *Chairman*
Laurie Sewell, *President*
Maritza Aguilar, *CFO*
Robert Harrelson, *Officer*
Enio Martinez, *Vice Pres*
EMP: 1500
SQ FT: 11,500
SALES (est): 98.4MM **Privately Held**
WEB: www.janitorial.com
SIC: 8744 7349 1771 Facilities support services; building maintenance services; flooring contractor

(P-27605)
SMG
Also Called: Smg Stockton
3445 S El Dorado St, Stockton (95206)
PHONE..............................209 937-7433
Kandra Clark, *General Mgr*

EMP: 400
SQ FT: 25,000
SALES (est): 4.9MM
SALES (corp-wide): 24.5B **Privately Held**
SIC: 8744 Facilities support services
HQ: Smg Holdings, Llc
300 Cnshohckn State Rd # 450
Conshohocken PA 19428
-

(P-27606)
SUPPORT ASSOCIATES INC
22901 Mill Creek Dr, Laguna Hills (92653-1215)
PHONE..............................949 595-4379
John Shadwick, *President*
Larry Cory, *Shareholder*
Peggy Norman, *Shareholder*
Susan Shadwick, *Administration*
Mitchell Glavas, *Marketing Staff*
EMP: 170
SALES (est): 10MM **Privately Held**
WEB: www.supportassociates.com
SIC: 8744 Facilities support services

(P-27607)
SWISS PORT CORP
Also Called: Swissport
11001 Aviation Blvd, Los Angeles (90045-6123)
PHONE..............................310 417-0258
Armin Unternaehrer, *Vice Pres*
Steve Gomez, *Vice Pres*
EMP: 500
SALES (est): 33.6MM **Privately Held**
SIC: 8744 4581 Facilities support services; airports, flying fields & services

(P-27608)
TECHFLOW INC (PA)
9889 Willow Creek Rd, San Diego (92131-1119)
PHONE..............................858 412-8000
Robert Baum, *CEO*
Mark Carter, *COO*
Lorie Atoe, *CFO*
Jon Baker, *Admin Asst*
Darren Taplin, *Administration*
EMP: 104
SQ FT: 19,000
SALES (est): 47.3MM **Privately Held**
WEB: www.techflow.com
SIC: 8744 8711 8748 Facilities support services; engineering services; systems analysis & engineering consulting services

(P-27609)
VANGUARD RESOURCES CORP
13816 Fontanelle Pl, San Diego (92128-4755)
P.O. Box 420355 (92142-0355)
PHONE..............................858 336-7147
Nicole Murray, *President*
EMP: 60
SALES (est): 2MM **Privately Held**
WEB: www.vanguardresourcescorp.com
SIC: 8744 Facilities support services

(P-27610)
WEST COAST STORM INC (PA)
9701 Wilshire Blvd # 1000, Beverly Hills (90212-2020)
PHONE..............................909 890-5700
Michelle Padilla, *President*
Renata Salo, *CFO*
Rafael Padilla, *Vice Pres*
EMP: 50
SQ FT: 48,000
SALES (est): 6.7MM **Privately Held**
WEB: www.wcstorm.net
SIC: 8744

(P-27611)
WORKCARE INC
300 S Harbor Blvd Ste 600, Anaheim (92805-3718)
PHONE..............................714 978-7488
Dr Peter P Greaney, *CEO*
Bill Nixon, *CFO*
William E Nixon, *CFO*
Paula Sandrock, *Vice Pres*
Dennis Stephens, *Vice Pres*
EMP: 181
SQ FT: 11,000

SALES (est): 26.7MM **Privately Held**
WEB: www.workcare.com
SIC: 8744 8011 Facilities support services; offices & clinics of medical doctors

(P-27612)
ZERO WASTE SOLUTIONS INC
1850 Gateway Blvd # 1030, Concord (94520-3279)
P.O. Box 5097 (94524-0097)
PHONE..............................925 270-3339
Shavila Singh, *CEO*
EMP: 200
SQ FT: 3,000
SALES (est): 23.3MM **Privately Held**
WEB: www.zerowastesolutions.com
SIC: 8744 Facilities support services

8748 Business Consulting Svcs, NEC

(P-27613)
500 STARTUPS INCUBATOR LLC
814 Mission St Ste 600, San Francisco (94103-3025)
PHONE..............................415 974-6343
Melissa Grody, *Executive Asst*
EMP: 118
SALES (corp-wide): 15MM **Privately Held**
SIC: 8748 Educational consultant
PA: 500 Startups Incubator, L.L.C.
444 Castro St Ste 1200
Mountain View CA 94041
650 743-4738

(P-27614)
500 STARTUPS INCUBATOR LLC (PA)
444 Castro St Ste 1200, Mountain View (94041-2064)
PHONE..............................650 743-4738
Dave McClure, *Principal*
Christine Tsai, *Principal*
EMP: 120 EST: 2010
SALES (est): 15MM **Privately Held**
SIC: 8748 Educational consultant

(P-27615)
8020 CONSULTING LLC
6303 Owensmouth Ave Fl 10, Woodland Hills (91367-2262)
PHONE..............................818 523-3201
David Lewis, *Mng Member*
Kelly Swartzel, *COO*
Michael Laborde, *Director*
Ellen Vayner, *Manager*
Radha Abboy, *Consultant*
EMP: 50
SALES (est): 15MM **Privately Held**
SIC: 8748 Business consulting

(P-27616)
ABSG CONSULTING INC
505 14th St Ste 900, Oakland (94612-1468)
PHONE..............................510 508-6289
William Keogh, *Branch Mgr*
EMP: 50
SALES (corp-wide): 980.6MM **Privately Held**
WEB: www.absconsulting.com
SIC: 8748 Safety training service; systems analysis & engineering consulting services; testing services
HQ: Absg Consulting Inc.
16855 Northchase Dr
Houston TX 77060
281 673-2800

(P-27617)
ABSG CONSULTING INC
300 Commerce Ste 200, Irvine (92602-1305)
PHONE..............................714 734-4242
Melinda Arjonilla, *Branch Mgr*
EMP: 68
SALES (corp-wide): 980.6MM **Privately Held**
WEB: www.absconsulting.com
SIC: 8748 Safety training service; testing services; systems analysis & engineering consulting services

HQ: Absg Consulting Inc.
16855 Northchase Dr
Houston TX 77060
281 673-2800

(P-27618)
AC SQUARE INC
4590 Qantas Ln, Stockton (95206-3903)
PHONE..............................650 293-2730
EMP: 239
SALES (corp-wide): 43.7MM **Privately Held**
SIC: 8748
PA: Ac Square, Inc.
371 Foster City Blvd
Foster City CA 94404
650 293-2730

(P-27619)
ACC-GWG LLC
Also Called: American Commodity Co.
6133 Abel Rd, Williams (95987-5816)
P.O. Box 236 (95987-0236)
PHONE..............................530 473-2827
Chris Crutchfield, *President*
Bob Watts, *President*
Nicole Montna Van Vleck, *Admin Sec*
Paul Crutchfield,
Al Montna,
EMP: 60
SALES (est): 5.6MM **Privately Held**
SIC: 8748 Agricultural consultant

(P-27620)
ACRT PACIFIC LLC
3443 Deer Park Dr Ste B, Stockton (95219-2306)
PHONE..............................330 945-7500
Brad S Schroeder,
Alan Rothenbuecher,
EMP: 450
SALES (est): 50MM **Privately Held**
SIC: 8748 Business consulting

(P-27621)
AE & ASSOCIATES LLC
506 Queensland Cir, Corona (92879-1381)
PHONE..............................951 278-3477
Arnold Ardevela,
Ester Ardevela,
EMP: 60 EST: 1999
SQ FT: 3,755
SALES (est): 750K **Privately Held**
SIC: 8748 Business consulting

(P-27622)
AECOM GLOBAL II LLC
2870 Gateway Oaks Dr # 300, Sacramento (95833-3577)
PHONE..............................916 679-8700
Victor Auvinen, *Branch Mgr*
EMP: 185
SQ FT: 12,000
SALES (corp-wide): 20.1B **Publicly Held**
SIC: 8748 Environmental consultant
HQ: Aecom Global Ii, Llc
1999 Avenue Of The Stars
Los Angeles CA 90067
213 593-8100

(P-27623)
AECOM GLOBAL II LLC
915 Wilshire Blvd Ste 800, Los Angeles (90017-3488)
PHONE..............................213 996-2200
Dave Wu, *Branch Mgr*
Jennifer Jauch, *Safety Dir*
EMP: 200
SALES (corp-wide): 20.1B **Publicly Held**
SIC: 8748 Systems analysis & engineering consulting services
HQ: Aecom Global Ii, Llc
1999 Avenue Of The Stars
Los Angeles CA 90067
213 593-8100

(P-27624)
AECOM GLOBAL II LLC
310 Golden Shore Ste 100, Long Beach (90802-4240)
PHONE..............................310 343-6977
Edward Andrechak, *Branch Mgr*
EMP: 65
SALES (corp-wide): 20.1B **Publicly Held**
SIC: 8748 Environmental consultant

P R O D U C T S & S V C S

HQ: Aecom Global Ii, Llc
1999 Avenue Of The Stars
Los Angeles CA 90067
213 593-8100

(P-27625)
AECOM TECHNICAL SERVICES INC (HQ)
300 S Grand Ave Ste 1100, Los Angeles (90071-3173)
PHONE...................213 593-8000
Timothy H Keener, *CEO*
EMP: 100 EST: 1970
SQ FT: 43,000
SALES (est): 1.2B
SALES (corp-wide): 20.1B **Publicly Held**
WEB: www.earthtech.com
SIC: 8748 4953 8742 8711 Environmental consultant; refuse systems; industry specialist consultants; engineering services
PA: Aecom
1999 Avenue Of The Stars # 2600
Los Angeles CA 90067
213 593-8000

(P-27626)
AECOM USA INC
515 S Figueroa St Ste 400, Los Angeles (90071-3323)
PHONE...................213 330-7200
EMP: 104
SALES (corp-wide): 20.1B **Publicly Held**
SIC: 8748 Business consulting
HQ: Aecom Usa, Inc.
605 3rd Ave
New York NY 10158
212 973-2900

(P-27627)
AECOM USA INC
100 W San Fernando St, San Jose (95113-2219)
PHONE...................408 392-0670
EMP: 104
SALES (corp-wide): 17.4B **Publicly Held**
SIC: 8748
HQ: Aecom Usa, Inc.
605 3rd Ave
New York NY 10158
212 973-2900

(P-27628)
AECOM USA INC
300 S Grand Ave Ste 1100, Los Angeles (90071-3173)
PHONE...................213 593-8000
Tom Joldersma, *CFO*
EMP: 500
SALES (corp-wide): 20.1B **Publicly Held**
SIC: 8748 Business consulting
HQ: Aecom Usa, Inc.
605 3rd Ave
New York NY 10158
212 973-2900

(P-27629)
AECOM USA INC
999 W Town And Country Rd, Orange (92868-4713)
PHONE...................714 567-2501
Bruce Toro, *Manager*
EMP: 60
SALES (corp-wide): 20.1B **Publicly Held**
SIC: 8748 Business consulting
HQ: Aecom Usa, Inc.
605 3rd Ave
New York NY 10158
212 973-2900

(P-27630)
AHTNA-CDM SMITH JV
3200 El Camino Real, Irvine (92602-1378)
PHONE...................714 824-3471
Craig O'Rourke, *Partner*
John Czapor, *Partner*
Matt Tisher, *CFO*
EMP: 89
SALES (est): 2.7MM **Privately Held**
SIC: 8748 1794 8711 1611 Environmental consultant; excavation & grading, building construction; building construction consultant; highway & street construction

(P-27631)
ALIANTEL INC
1940 W Corporate Way, Anaheim (92801-5373)
PHONE...................714 829-1650
Suresh Sachdeva, *CEO*
John Kelly, *Principal*
EMP: 90
SALES (est): 12.9MM **Privately Held**
SIC: 8748 7389 Telecommunications consultant; telephone services

(P-27632)
ALL ENVIRONMENTAL INC
Also Called: Aei Consultants
1200 Main St Ste D, Irvine (92614-6749)
PHONE...................949 752-9300
Craig Hertz, *Owner*
EMP: 76 **Privately Held**
SIC: 8748 Environmental consultant
PA: All Environmental, Inc.
2500 Camino Diablo
Walnut Creek CA 94597

(P-27633)
ALL ENVIRONMENTAL INC
Also Called: Aei Consultants
2447 Pcf Cast Hwy Ste 101, Hermosa Beach (90254)
PHONE...................310 798-4255
Adam Bennett, *Manager*
EMP: 150 **Privately Held**
WEB: www.allenvironmental.com
SIC: 8748 Environmental consultant
PA: All Environmental, Inc.
2500 Camino Diablo
Walnut Creek CA 94597

(P-27634)
ALL-CITY MANAGEMENT SVCS INC
10440 Pioneer Blvd Ste 5, Santa Fe Springs (90670-8238)
PHONE...................310 202-8284
Baron Farwell, *CEO*
Ronald Farwell, *CFO*
Koree Yancy, *Executive Asst*
Ron Farwell, *Admin Sec*
Carmen Sjelin, *Manager*
EMP: 1800
SQ FT: 3,500
SALES (est): 96.9MM **Privately Held**
SIC: 8748 Traffic consultant

(P-27635)
ALLIED INDUSTRIES INC (PA)
Also Called: Allied Environmental Services
21650 Oxnard St Ste 500, Woodland Hills (91367-4911)
PHONE...................818 781-2490
Ernesto Gutierrez, *President*
Fernando Gutierrez, *COO*
EMP: 150
SQ FT: 11,000
SALES (est): 24.5MM **Privately Held**
SIC: 8748 Environmental consultant

(P-27636)
AMATEL INC (PA)
1017 S Mountain Ave, Monrovia (91016-3642)
PHONE...................323 801-0199
Joe Nwankwo, *President*
EMP: 50
SQ FT: 5,500
SALES (est): 14.9MM **Privately Held**
WEB: www.amatel.com
SIC: 8748 8711 Telecommunications consultant; engineering services

(P-27637)
AMBREEN ENTERPRISES INC
20370 Via Badalona, Yorba Linda (92887-3136)
PHONE...................909 620-1339
EMP: 80 EST: 2011
SALES (est): 157.4K **Privately Held**
SIC: 8748

(P-27638)
AMERICAN INFRASTRUCTURE MLP FU
950 Tower Ln Ste 800, Foster City (94404-2191)
PHONE...................650 854-6000
George McCown, *Partner*
Nandit Gandhi, *Partner*
Nancy Katz, *Vice Pres*
Paul Ho, *Managing Dir*
Mia Gonzalez, *Executive Asst*
EMP: 51
SALES (est): 7.5MM **Privately Held**
SIC: 8748 Business consulting

(P-27639)
AMERICAN NURSING HOME MGT INC
Also Called: Briercrest Inglewoodhealthcare
301 Centinela Ave, Inglewood (90302-3231)
PHONE...................310 672-1012
Bill Belamger, *Administration*
EMP: 100
SALES (corp-wide): 7.5MM **Privately Held**
SIC: 8748 8051 Business consulting; skilled nursing care facilities
PA: American Nursing Home Management, Inc.
17000 Ventura Blvd # 212
Encino CA

(P-27640)
AMERICAN TECHNOLOGIES INC
8444 Miralani Dr Ste 200, San Diego (92126-4389)
PHONE...................858 530-2400
Eric Gotsom, *Branch Mgr*
Eric Gotham, *Project Mgr*
Nicholas Sekol, *Project Mgr*
Stan Schritt, *Sr Project Mgr*
Mike Carroll, *Superintendent*
EMP: 55
SALES (corp-wide): 236.5MM **Privately Held**
WEB: www.amer-tech.com
SIC: 8748 Business consulting
PA: American Technologies Inc.
210 W Baywood Ave
Orange CA 92865
714 283-9990

(P-27641)
AMTEL INC
950 S Bascom Ave Ste 2002, San Jose (95128-3538)
PHONE...................408 615-0522
Pankaj Gupta, *CEO*
Chet Jackson, *President*
Sidney Hill, *Manager*
EMP: 50
SALES (est): 8.6MM **Privately Held**
WEB: www.amtelnet.com
SIC: 8748 7371 Telecommunications consultant; computer software development
HQ: Netplus Buyer, Inc.
9707 Key West Ave Ste 202
Rockville MD 20850
800 989-5566

(P-27642)
ANELLO SEC & CONSULTING LLC
17348 Tiara St, Encino (91316-1355)
PHONE...................818 632-3277
Michael Anello, *Principal*
EMP: 65 EST: 2008
SALES (est): 2.5MM **Privately Held**
SIC: 8748 Business consulting

(P-27643)
APX INC (PA)
2001 Gateway Pl Ste 315w, San Jose (95110-1045)
PHONE...................408 517-2100
Joseph Varnas, *CEO*
EMP: 50
SALES: 18.5MM **Privately Held**
WEB: www.apx.com
SIC: 8748 Energy conservation consultant

(P-27644)
ASHOK THUMMALACHETTY
44721 Aguila Ter, Fremont (94539-6293)
PHONE...................510 687-9797
Ashok Thummalachetty, *President*
William Lynch, *Vice Pres*
EMP: 115
SQ FT: 3,000
SALES (est): 5.5MM **Privately Held**
WEB: www.fortuna.com
SIC: 8748 7379 1731 Business consulting; computer related consulting services; electrical work

(P-27645)
ASSOCTED LRNG LNGAGE SPCIALIST (PA)
1060 Twin Dolphin Dr # 100, Redwood City (94065-1133)
P.O. Box 1389, San Carlos (94070-7389)
PHONE...................650 631-9999
Pamela Joy, *Director*
Karen Gilbert, *Finance*
Sanimata Kautai, *Human Res Mgr*
Kelli Ferreira, *Program Dir*
Liz Field, *Director*
EMP: 58
SQ FT: 9,400
SALES: 2MM **Privately Held**
WEB: www.allsinc.com
SIC: 8748 8049 Educational consultant; speech pathologist

(P-27646)
ASSURE CONSULTING INC
257 Castro St Ste 205, Mountain View (94041-1287)
PHONE...................650 966-1967
Murugesh Ramiah, *Chairman*
Vina Vivek, *President*
EMP: 90
SALES (est): 3.4MM **Privately Held**
WEB: www.assure-usa.com
SIC: 8748 Business consulting

(P-27647)
AT&T CORP
16201 Raymer St, Van Nuys (91406-1210)
PHONE...................818 997-5998
Laurie Tossie, *Manager*
EMP: 100
SALES (corp-wide): 160.5B **Publicly Held**
WEB: www.swbell.com
SIC: 8748 Telecommunications consultant
HQ: At&T Corp.
1 At&T Way
Bedminster NJ 07921
800 403-3302

(P-27648)
AT&T SERVICES INC
Also Called: SBC
5650 Aldrin Ct, Bakersfield (93313-2110)
PHONE...................661 324-2046
Tim Frazure, *Manager*
EMP: 108
SALES (corp-wide): 160.5B **Publicly Held**
WEB: www.dsdllc.com
SIC: 8748 Telecommunications consultant
HQ: At&T Services, Inc.
208 S Akard St Ste 110
Dallas TX 75202
210 821-4105

(P-27649)
ATKINS NORTH AMERICA INC
332 Pine St Ste 500, San Francisco (94104-3225)
PHONE...................916 325-4800
Rod Jeung, *Manager*
EMP: 50
SALES (corp-wide): 7.3B **Privately Held**
WEB: www.cargillemt.com
SIC: 8748 8742 8711 Environmental consultant; planning consultant; consulting engineer
HQ: Snc-Lavalin Inc
455 Boul Rene-Levesque O
Montreal QC H2Z 1
514 393-1000

(P-27650)
ATRILOGY SOLUTIONS GROUP INC (PA)
23422 Mill Creek Dr # 105, Laguna Hills (92653-7920)
PHONE.....................................949 777-4700
David Charest, *President*
Douglas Lins, *CFO*
Rodney Rihela, *Vice Pres*
CJ Dickinson, *Info Tech Mgr*
Kyle Eve, *Tech Recruiter*
EMP: 50
SQ FT: 5,528
SALES: 22MM **Privately Held**
WEB: www.atrilogy.com
SIC: 8748 Business consulting

(P-27651)
AUCTIVA CORPORATION
360 E 6th St, Chico (95928-5631)
PHONE.....................................530 894-7400
Mark A Schwartz, *CEO*
Jeff Schlicht, *President*
Shawn Horswill, *Info Tech Mgr*
Crystal Estes CPA, *Finance*
Jeff Mengoli, *General Counsel*
EMP: 80
SALES (est): 6.3MM **Privately Held**
WEB: www.theonlineseller.com
SIC: 8748 Business consulting

(P-27652)
AVA THE RABBIT HAVEN INC
Also Called: RABBIT HAVEN THE
1261 S Mary St, Scotts Valley (95067)
P.O. Box 66594 (95067-6594)
PHONE.....................................831 600-7479
Heather Bechtel, *Director*
Richard Jacobel, *President*
EMP: 80
SALES: 111.1K **Privately Held**
SIC: 8748 Testing service, educational or personnel

(P-27653)
AXIOM GLOBAL TECHNOLOGIES INC
220 N Wiget Ln, Walnut Creek (94598-2404)
PHONE.....................................925 393-5800
Mohit Sishu Arora, *CEO*
Priya Arora, *Ch of Bd*
Sumit Singh, *Technology*
Janice Mills, *Manager*
EMP: 125 **EST:** 2001
SALES (est): 1.8MM **Privately Held**
WEB: www.acg-usa.com
SIC: 8748 Business consulting

(P-27654)
B & L CONSULTING LLC
164 N 2nd Ave 9, Upland (91786-6001)
PHONE.....................................682 238-6994
Bayandre Lewis, *Mng Member*
EMP: 63
SQ FT: 5,000
SALES: 5.2MM **Privately Held**
SIC: 8748 Business consulting

(P-27655)
BARSTOW REDEVELOPMENT AGENCY
220 E Mountain View St B, Barstow (92311-7304)
PHONE.....................................760 256-3531
Paul Warmer, *President*
Chris Heldreth, *General Mgr*
Tommy Alva, *Director*
Mike Brown, *Director*
EMP: 126
SQ FT: 1,039
SALES (est): 87.9K **Privately Held**
SIC: 8748 Economic consultant

(P-27656)
BAY AREA AIR QUALITY (PA)
375 Beale St Ste 600, San Francisco (94105-2097)
P.O. Box 420434 (94142-0434)
PHONE.....................................415 749-4900
Jack Broadbent, *CEO*
Ricardo Cardenas, *Principal*
EMP: 350
SQ FT: 101,000

SALES (est): 50.2MM **Privately Held**
WEB: www.baaqmd.gov
SIC: 8748 Environmental consultant

(P-27657)
BERKELEY RESEARCH GROUP LLC (PA)
2200 Powell St Ste 1200, Emeryville (94608-1833)
PHONE.....................................510 285-3300
David Teece, *Chairman*
Marvin Tenenbaum, *President*
Sebastien Belanger, *COO*
David M Johnson, *CFO*
Eric Miller, *Senior VP*
EMP: 138
SALES (est): 152.8MM **Privately Held**
SIC: 8748 Business consulting

(P-27658)
BLACKSTONE TECHNOLOGY GROUP (PA)
455 Market St Ste 620, San Francisco (94105-2449)
PHONE.....................................415 837-1400
David Mysona, *CEO*
Casey Courneen, *President*
Giles Kesteloot, *President*
Patrick James, *COO*
Rakesh Agrawal, *Exec VP*
EMP: 100
SQ FT: 10,000
SALES (est): 42.9MM **Privately Held**
WEB: www.bstonetech.com
SIC: 8748 Business consulting

(P-27659)
BLAINE TECH SERVICES INC (PA)
1680 Rogers Ave, San Jose (95112-1105)
PHONE.....................................408 573-0555
Sigrid J Blaine, *President*
Richard C Blaine, *Vice Pres*
Francis P Thie, *Vice Pres*
Deilavonce Frazier, *Info Tech Mgr*
Michael Ninokata, *Sr Project Mgr*
EMP: 66
SQ FT: 16,000
SALES (est): 10MM **Privately Held**
WEB: www.blainetech.com
SIC: 8748 Environmental consultant

(P-27660)
BMV DIRECT II LP
17190 Bernardo Center Dr, San Diego (92128-7030)
PHONE.....................................858 485-9840
EMP: 59
SALES (est): 1.7MM
SALES (corp-wide): 674.6MM **Privately Held**
SIC: 8748 Business consulting
HQ: Biomed Realty, L.P.
17190 Bernardo Center Dr
San Diego CA 92128
858 485-9840

(P-27661)
BOCA MESA INCORPORATED
3130 Skyway Dr Ste 701, Santa Maria (93455-1800)
PHONE.....................................805 934-9470
EMP: 69
SALES (est): 4.7MM **Privately Held**
SIC: 8748 7349

(P-27662)
BRANDNET INC
724 Battery St 3, San Francisco (94111-1559)
PHONE.....................................415 216-4152
John Farrar, *President*
Andy Atherton, *COO*
EMP: 60
SALES (est): 5.9MM **Privately Held**
SIC: 8748 Business consulting
HQ: Valassis Communications, Inc.
19975 Victor Pkwy
Livonia MI 48152
734 591-3000

(P-27663)
BROCADE CMMNCTIONS SYSTEMS INC
110 Holger Way, San Jose (95134-1376)
PHONE.....................................408 333-4300
EMP: 71
SALES (corp-wide): 13.2B **Privately Held**
SIC: 8748
HQ: Brocade Communications Systems Llc
130 Holger Way
San Jose CA 95134

(P-27664)
BURBANK PLG & ZONING DIV OF
150 N 3rd St Fl 2, Burbank (91502-1264)
PHONE.....................................818 238-5250
Joy Forbes, *Director*
EMP: 50
SALES (est): 110.4K **Privately Held**
SIC: 8748 Urban planning & consulting services

(P-27665)
BUREAU VERITAS NORTH AMER INC
Also Called: Clayton Group Services
1940 E Deere Ave Ste 210, Santa Ana (92705-5718)
PHONE.....................................714 431-4100
Sandi Schafer, *Vice Pres*
Lisa Townsend, *Social Dir*
Yuliana Sanchez, *Manager*
EMP: 70
SALES (corp-wide): 316.4MM **Privately Held**
SIC: 8748 Business consulting
HQ: Bureau Veritas North America, Inc.
1601 Sawgrs Corp Pkwy
Sunrise FL 33323
954 236-8100

(P-27666)
BUXTON CONSULTING
5976 W Las Positas Blvd # 208, Pleasanton (94588-8506)
PHONE.....................................925 467-0700
James T Buxton, *President*
Chandra Reddy, *Vice Pres*
EMP: 90
SQ FT: 6,500
SALES (est): 11.4MM **Privately Held**
WEB: www.us-buxton.com
SIC: 8748 Systems analysis & engineering consulting services

(P-27667)
BY REFERRAL ONLY INC
2035 Corte Del Nogal # 200, Carlsbad (92011-1445)
PHONE.....................................760 707-1300
Joseph F Stumpf, *President*
Daniel Paris, *Technology*
Toby Seward, *Technology*
Lori Westbay, *Marketing Mgr*
Sarah Warren,
EMP: 100
SALES (est): 10.1MM **Privately Held**
SIC: 8748 Educational consultant

(P-27668)
CAL SOUTHERN ASSN GOVERNMENTS (PA)
Also Called: S C A G
900 Wilshire Blvd # 1700, Los Angeles (90017-4701)
PHONE.....................................213 236-1800
Hasan Ikhrata, *Exec Dir*
Basil Panas, *CFO*
EMP: 130
SQ FT: 50,000
SALES: 40MM **Privately Held**
SIC: 8748 Urban planning & consulting services

(P-27669)
CALI HSG FINANCE AGCY
500 Capitol Mall Ste 1400, Sacramento (95814-4740)
PHONE.....................................916 326-8627
Janet Louie, *Manager*
EMP: 99 **EST:** 2011

SALES (est): 4MM **Privately Held**
SIC: 8748 Urban planning & consulting services

(P-27670)
CALIFORNIA COML INV GROUP INC
Also Called: Ccig
4530 E Thousand Oaks Blvd # 100, West-lake Village (91362-3897)
PHONE.....................................805 495-8400
Gary Collett, *President*
Louis Mellman, *Vice Pres*
EMP: 50
SALES (est): 5.3MM **Privately Held**
SIC: 8748 Urban planning & consulting services

(P-27671)
CALIFORNIA DEPT TRANSPORTATION
Also Called: Caltrans District 1
1656 Union St, Eureka (95501-2229)
P.O. Box 3700 (95502-3700)
PHONE.....................................707 445-6600
Charlie Fielder, *Director*
EMP: 500 **Privately Held**
WEB: www.caltip.org
SIC: 8748 4789 9621 Business consulting; railroad maintenance & repair services;
HQ: California Dept Of Transportation
1120 N St
Sacramento CA 95814

(P-27672)
CALIFORNIA ENVMTL HLTH ASSN
Also Called: C E H A
2000 A De Las Pulgas 10, San Mateo (94403)
PHONE.....................................650 363-4726
Liberty Cerezo, *Treasurer*
Todd A Frantz, *President*
EMP: 70
SQ FT: 500
SALES (est): 6.1MM **Privately Held**
SIC: 8748 Environmental consultant

(P-27673)
CALIFORNIA TRAFFIC SAFETY INST
Also Called: CTSI
209 E Avenue K8 Ste 210, Lancaster (93535-4535)
PHONE.....................................661 940-1907
Wanda Paulson, *President*
Michael Atmore, *CFO*
Carrie Pierce, *Vice Pres*
Tiffany Coronado, *Exec Dir*
EMP: 160
SQ FT: 42,000
SALES: 4.7MM **Privately Held**
WEB: www.ctsi-courtnetwork.org
SIC: 8748 Educational consultant

(P-27674)
CAMPESINOS UNIDOS INC (PA)
1005 C St, Brawley (92227-2020)
P.O. Box 39 (92227-0039)
PHONE.....................................760 370-5100
Jose Lopez, *Exec Dir*
Jose Delgado, *Treasurer*
Socorro Juarez, *Vice Pres*
Maria Acuna, *Admin Sec*
Vianey Durazo, *Admin Sec*
EMP: 162
SQ FT: 65,000
SALES: 4.7MM **Privately Held**
SIC: 8748 Employee programs administration

(P-27675)
CAPITAL OVERSIGHT INC (PA)
2118 Wilshire Blvd, Santa Monica (90403-5704)
PHONE.....................................310 453-8000
Dayne Williams, *CEO*
Matthew Denti, *Vice Pres*
Kenneth Mays, *Vice Pres*
Tamara Stewart, *Vice Pres*
Patricia Sewell, *Admin Sec*
EMP: 328 **EST:** 2002
SQ FT: 11,000

SALES: 7.7MM **Privately Held**
SIC: 8748 7323 7389 7299 Business consulting; credit clearinghouse; ; personal financial services

(P-27676)
CATALINA ENTERPRISE INC
206 Catalina Rd, Fullerton (92835-2506)
PHONE...................949 637-3091
Stanley Johnson, *CEO*
Easter Johnson, *Vice Pres*
EMP: 52 **EST:** 2015
SALES (est): 929.7K **Privately Held**
SIC: 8748 Systems engineering consultant, ex. computer or professional

(P-27677)
CAVISSON SYSTEMS INC
5201 Great America Pkwy, Santa Clara (95054-1122)
PHONE...................800 701-6125
Anil Kumar, *President*
Raj Sajankila, *Vice Pres*
Arun Goel, *Technical Mgr*
Anupam Chaudhary, *Software Engr*
Shakti Jha, *Software Engr*
EMP: 500
SQ FT: 10,000
SALES: 20MM **Privately Held**
SIC: 8748 Systems analysis & engineering consulting services

(P-27678)
CDSNET LLC
Also Called: Fmsinfoserv
6053 W Century Blvd, Los Angeles (90045-6430)
PHONE...................310 981-9500
Michael Griffus, *President*
Francis G Homan, *CFO*
EMP: 65
SALES (est): 3.3MM **Privately Held**
WEB: www.tectransinc.com
SIC: 8748 Business consulting
HQ: Keolis Transit America, Inc.
　　6053 W Century Blvd # 900
　　Los Angeles CA 90045

(P-27679)
CEMTEK ENVIRONMENTAL INC
3041 Orange Ave, Santa Ana (92707-4247)
PHONE...................714 437-7100
Tyron Smith, *CEO*
Johnny Vu, *Project Engr*
Jeremy Vana, *Engineer*
Quang Nguyen, *Sales Mgr*
Dee Bester, *Sales Associate*
EMP: 50
SQ FT: 15,500
SALES: 17.8MM **Privately Held**
WEB: www.cemteks.com
SIC: 8748 Environmental consultant

(P-27680)
CENTER FOR AUTISM RELATED SVCS
5949 Lankershim Blvd, North Hollywood (91601-1006)
PHONE...................323 850-7177
Susan Kumaer, *Administration*
Susan Kumar, *Administration*
Luz Uribe, *Manager*
EMP: 50
SALES (est): 173K **Privately Held**
WEB: www.center4autism.com
SIC: 8748 7361 Educational consultant; employment agencies

(P-27681)
CENTER FOR SUSTAINABLE ENERGY
3980 Sherman St Ste 170, San Diego (92110-4314)
PHONE...................858 244-1177
Michael Akavan, *Chairman*
Fred Baranowski, *Treasurer*
Mary McGroarty, *Admin Sec*
Heather Shepard, *Director*
Michael Arvizu, *Associate*
EMP: 87
SALES: 90MM **Privately Held**
WEB: www.sdenergy.org
SIC: 8748 Environmental consultant

(P-27682)
CETECOM INC (DH)
411 Dixon Landing Rd, Milpitas (95035-2579)
PHONE...................408 586-6200
Maan Ghanma, *CEO*
Willfried Klassmann, *President*
Heiko Strehlow, *COO*
Clorinda Sammis, *Corp Secy*
Jens Passe, *Managing Dir*
EMP: 85
SQ FT: 48,000
SALES (est): 24.9MM
SALES (corp-wide): 300.2MM **Privately Held**
WEB: www.cetecomusa.com
SIC: 8748 8734 Communications consulting; testing laboratories
HQ: Cetecom Gmbh
　　Im Teelbruch 116
　　Essen 45219
　　205 495-190

(P-27683)
CHALLENGER INDUSTRIES INC
Also Called: Challenger Ent
2971 E White Star Ave, Anaheim (92806-2630)
PHONE...................714 630-4344
Gregory Joseph Martin, *President*
Ron Flicker, *Exec VP*
EMP: 60
SQ FT: 4,000
SALES (est): 7.3MM **Privately Held**
WEB: www.challengerenterprises.com
SIC: 8748 Systems analysis & engineering consulting services

(P-27684)
CHAMBERS GROUP INC
17671 Cowan Ste 100, Irvine (92614-6074)
P.O. Box N Centre D, Santa Ana (92707)
PHONE...................949 261-5414
Sherman Smith, *President*
EMP: 50
SALES (corp-wide): 18.9MM **Privately Held**
WEB: www.chambersgroupinc.com
SIC: 8748 Environmental consultant
PA: Chambers Group, Inc.
　　5 Hutton Cntre Dr Ste 750
　　Santa Ana CA 92707
　　949 261-5414

(P-27685)
CHIKPEA INC
1 Market St Spear Spear Tower, San Francisco (94127)
PHONE...................888 342-3828
Adam Kleinberg, *CEO*
Bhaskar Roy, *Principal*
Asit Mahato, *Software Engr*
Christina Low, *Mktg Dir*
Jordan Connor, *Marketing Mgr*
EMP: 50
SALES (est): 2.5MM **Privately Held**
SIC: 8748 Telecommunications consultant

(P-27686)
CITY OF MORGAN HILL
Also Called: Public Works Department
100 Edes St, Morgan Hill (95037-5301)
PHONE...................408 776-7333
Jim Ashcraft, *Director*
EMP: 52 **Privately Held**
WEB: www.mhcommunitycenter.com
SIC: 8748 9111 City planning; mayors' offices
PA: City Of Morgan Hill
　　17575 Peak Ave
　　Morgan Hill CA 95037
　　408 778-6480

(P-27687)
CITY OF NORCO
Also Called: Successor Agency To The Norco
2870 Clark Ave, Norco (92860-1903)
PHONE...................951 270-5617
Greg Newton, *Mayor*
EMP: 100 **Privately Held**
SIC: 8748 Urban planning & consulting services
PA: City Of Norco
　　2870 Clark Ave
　　Norco CA 92860
　　951 270-5617

(P-27688)
CITY OF SAN DIEGO
Also Called: Enginring Capitl Projects Dept
1010 2nd Ave Ste 800, San Diego (92101-4907)
PHONE...................619 533-3012
Patti Boekamp, *Deputy Dir*
Brian P Fennessy, *Chief*
EMP: 50 **Privately Held**
WEB: www.eayo.com
SIC: 8748 9621 Traffic consultant; regulation, administration of transportation;
PA: City Of San Diego
　　202 C St
　　San Diego CA 92101
　　619 236-6330

(P-27689)
CLEARESULT CONSULTING INC
Also Called: Peci
1 Sansome St Fl 35, San Francisco (94104-4436)
PHONE...................415 848-1250
Karen Healey, *Branch Mgr*
EMP: 77
SALES (corp-wide): 585.3MM **Privately Held**
SIC: 8748 Energy conservation consultant
PA: Clearesult Consulting Inc.
　　4301 Westbank Dr Ste A250
　　Austin TX 78746
　　512 327-9200

(P-27690)
COASSURE INC
4100 Moorpark Ave Ste 122, San Jose (95117-1707)
P.O. Box 234, Los Altos (94023-0234)
PHONE...................408 244-0400
Zaydoon Jawadi, *President*
EMP: 100
SALES (est): 2.9MM **Privately Held**
WEB: www.coassure.com
SIC: 8748 Testing services

(P-27691)
COHEN VENTURES INC (PA)
Also Called: Energy Solutions
449 15th St Ste 402, Oakland (94612-2828)
PHONE...................510 482-4420
Samuel D Cohen, *President*
Chris Burmester, *Vice Pres*
Jamillah Spears, *Executive*
Simone Young-Tem, *Executive Asst*
Daniel Young, *Web Proj Mgr*
EMP: 74
SQ FT: 11,000
SALES (est): 16.7MM **Privately Held**
WEB: www.energy-solution.com
SIC: 8748 Energy conservation consultant

(P-27692)
COMMODITY DISTRIBUTION SERVICE
10035 Painter Ave, Santa Fe Springs (90670-3015)
PHONE...................562 777-9969
Dan Nagel, *President*
Mitchell Patton, *CFO*
EMP: 50
SQ FT: 40,000
SALES (est): 2.3MM **Privately Held**
WEB: www.cdscold.com
SIC: 8748 Business consulting

(P-27693)
COMMUNICATION CONSULTANTS (PA)
3001 Coffee Rd Ste 5, Modesto (95355-1764)
P.O. Box 578353 (95357-8353)
PHONE...................209 869-5206
Richard Costa, *Owner*
EMP: 60
SALES (est): 2.6MM **Privately Held**
SIC: 8748 Telecommunications consultant

(P-27694)
COMMUNITY HOUSING OPPORT (PA)
Also Called: C H O C
5030 Business Center Dr # 260, Fairfield (94534-6884)
PHONE...................530 757-4444
Manuela Silva, *Exec Dir*
Peter Lundberg, *Vice Pres*
EMP: 50
SQ FT: 3,000
SALES: 7.8MM **Privately Held**
WEB: www.chochousing.org
SIC: 8748 Urban planning & consulting services

(P-27695)
COMMUNITY REDEVELOPMENT AGENCY (PA)
Also Called: C R A
448 S Hill St Ste 1200, Los Angeles (90013-1153)
PHONE...................213 977-1600
Cecilia V Estolano, *Administration*
Christine Essel, *CEO*
Craig Bullock, *Officer*
Cesar Delacruz, *Officer*
Estevan Valenzuela, *Principal*
EMP: 165 **EST:** 1948
SQ FT: 80,000
SALES: 7.2MM **Privately Held**
SIC: 8748 Urban planning & consulting services

(P-27696)
CONDOR EARTH TECHNOLOGIES INC (PA)
21663 Brian Ln, Sonora (95370-9065)
P.O. Box 3905 (95370-3905)
PHONE...................209 532-0361
Robert John Job, *CEO*
Barry Hillman, *President*
Bob Job, *Vice Pres*
Glenn Nunelley, *Vice Pres*
Tiffany Harrell, *Admin Asst*
EMP: 110
SQ FT: 9,000
SALES (est): 12.2MM **Privately Held**
WEB: www.condordataserver.com
SIC: 8748 7349 Environmental consultant; cleaning service, industrial or commercial

(P-27697)
CONSORTM ON REACHNG EXCELLNCE
Also Called: Core
3112 Cedar Ravine Rd, Placerville (95667-6506)
PHONE...................510 540-4200
Linda Diamond, *CEO*
Bill Honig, *President*
Mark Simmons, *Officer*
EMP: 50
SALES (est): 4MM **Privately Held**
WEB: www.corelearn.com
SIC: 8748 Educational consultant

(P-27698)
CORNERSTONE CNSULTING TECH INC
241 5th St, San Francisco (94103-4102)
PHONE...................415 705-7800
Wayne Perry, *CEO*
Charles Jones, *Officer*
EMP: 50
SQ FT: 1,400
SALES (est): 4.4MM **Privately Held**
WEB: www.cornerstoneconcilium.com
SIC: 8748 8742 7379 Educational consultant; management consulting services; computer related consulting services

(P-27699)
CORNERSTONE RESEARCH INC (PA)
1000 El Camino Real # 250, Menlo Park (94025-4315)
PHONE...................650 853-1660
Cynthia Zollinger, *Chairman*
Michael E Burton, *President*
Lee Reamy, *CFO*
Catherine Galley, *Senior VP*
Michael Keeley, *Senior VP*
EMP: 100
SQ FT: 40,000
SALES (est): 88.4MM **Privately Held**
WEB: www.cornerstone.com
SIC: 8748 7389 Economic consultant; financial services

(P-27700)
CORNERSTONE RESEARCH INC
2 Embarcadero Ctr Fl 20, San Francisco (94111-3922)
PHONE.................................415 229-8100
Cynthia Zollinger, *CEO*
Nora Sawyer, *Technology*
Kathleen Easterbrook, *Associate*
EMP: 52
SALES (corp-wide): 88.4MM **Privately Held**
SIC: 8748 Economic consultant
PA: Cornerstone Research, Inc.
1000 El Camino Real # 250
Menlo Park CA 94025
650 853-1660

(P-27701)
COUNTY OF SAN DIEGO
Human Resources Dept
1600 Pacific Hwy Ste 207, San Diego (92101-2422)
PHONE.................................619 236-2191
Janice Horning, *Branch Mgr*
EMP: 150 **Privately Held**
WEB: www.sdlcc.org
SIC: 8748 9441 Employee programs administration; administration of social & human resources
PA: County Of San Diego
1600 Pacific Hwy Ste 209
San Diego CA 92101
619 531-5880

(P-27702)
DAIRY COUNCIL OF CALIFORNIA (PA)
1418 N Market Blvd # 500, Sacramento (95834-1945)
PHONE.................................949 756-7892
Peggy Biltz, *CEO*
EMP: 50 **EST:** 1919
SQ FT: 10,000
SALES (est): 5.8MM **Privately Held**
WEB: www.dairycouncilofca.org
SIC: 8748 Agricultural consultant; systems engineering consultant, ex. computer or professional

(P-27703)
DATA RECOGNITION CORPORATION
Also Called: C T B
20 Ryan Ranch Rd, Monterey (93940-6439)
PHONE.................................831 393-0700
Mike Limbach, *Vice Pres*
Christy Montejo, *Project Mgr*
EMP: 50
SALES (corp-wide): 260.3MM **Privately Held**
SIC: 8748 Business consulting
PA: Data Recognition Corporation
13490 Bass Lake Rd
Maple Grove MN 55311
763 268-2000

(P-27704)
DECISION TOOLBOX INC
5319 University Dr 521, Irvine (92612-2965)
PHONE.................................562 377-5600
Kim Shepherd, *President*
Anice Alexander, *Partner*
Rina Altaras, *Partner*
Kris Cable, *Partner*
Melissa Curtis, *Partner*
EMP: 85
SQ FT: 300
SALES (est): 7.4MM **Privately Held**
SIC: 8748 Business consulting

(P-27705)
DESTINATION SCIENCE LLC
953 N Elm St, Orange (92867-5454)
PHONE.................................714 289-9100
Heena Desai,
Sharon Fogg,
Kathy Heraghty,
Nina Conway, *Director*
▲ **EMP:** 150
SQ FT: 5,000

SALES (est): 1MM **Privately Held**
WEB: www.destinationscience.org
SIC: 8748 Educational consultant

(P-27706)
DIVERSIFIED RE PACKAGING CORP
1118 S La Cienega Blvd, Los Angeles (90035-2519)
PHONE.................................310 855-1946
Jeffrie Green, *President*
EMP: 700
SALES (est): 13.5MM **Privately Held**
SIC: 8748 Business consulting

(P-27707)
DNV GL ENERGY INSIGHTS USA INC
Also Called: K E M A
155 Grand Ave Ste 500, Oakland (94612-3747)
PHONE.................................510 891-0446
Rich Barnes, *Branch Mgr*
David Cesio, *Business Dir*
William Vail, *Administration*
Michael Rufo, *Director*
Cynthia Hester, *Manager*
EMP: 50
SALES (corp-wide): 2.3B **Privately Held**
SIC: 8748 Energy conservation consultant
HQ: Dnv Gl Energy Insights Usa, Inc.
1400 Ravello Rd
Katy TX 77449
281 396-1000

(P-27708)
E & J GALLO WINERY
Also Called: Ranch Winery, The
105a Zinfandel Ln, Saint Helena (94574-1631)
PHONE.................................707 967-9284
EMP: 50
SALES (corp-wide): 2.6B **Privately Held**
SIC: 8748 5182 Business consulting; wine
PA: E. & J. Gallo Winery
600 Yosemite Blvd
Modesto CA 95354
209 341-3111

(P-27709)
EAG HOLDINGS LLC
2710 Walsh Ave, Santa Clara (95051-0963)
PHONE.................................408 530-3500
Siddhartha Kadia, *CEO*
EMP: 700
SQ FT: 70,000
SALES (est): 18.8MM **Privately Held**
SIC: 8748 Business consulting

(P-27710)
EALLIANT LLC
1202 Morena Blvd Ste 100, San Diego (92110-3842)
PHONE.................................619 255-9344
Allen F Maxwell, *Mng Member*
Clarence Carter,
EMP: 50 **EST:** 2012
SALES (est): 1.5MM **Privately Held**
SIC: 8748 Business consulting

(P-27711)
ECHELON SECURITY INC
1604 Kerley Dr, San Jose (95112-4815)
PHONE.................................408 436-8844
Steve Brown, *President*
EMP: 67
SQ FT: 2,000
SALES (est): 5.1MM **Privately Held**
SIC: 8748 7381 Business consulting; guard services; security guard service

(P-27712)
ECO BAY SERVICES INC
1501 Minnesota St, San Francisco (94107-3521)
PHONE.................................415 643-7777
Trent Scott Michels, *CEO*
EMP: 65 **EST:** 2007
SQ FT: 80,000
SALES (est): 32.5MM **Privately Held**
SIC: 8748 Environmental consultant

(P-27713)
ECONOMIC DEV CORP OF LA COUNTY
Also Called: Los Angeles Cnty Economic Dev
444 S Flower St Ste 3700, Los Angeles (90071-2972)
PHONE.................................213 622-4300
William C Allen, *President*
Scott Somers, *Managing Prtnr*
Jill Yoshimi, *President*
David A Flaks, *COO*
Susan D Stel, *CFO*
EMP: 50 **EST:** 1981
SQ FT: 18,000
SALES (est): 5.5MM **Privately Held**
WEB: www.laedc.org
SIC: 8748 Business consulting

(P-27714)
EDGE MORTGAGE ADVISORY CO LLC
2125 E Katella Ave # 350, Anaheim (92806-6072)
PHONE.................................714 564-5800
Robin Auerbach, *President*
Doug Speaker, *Senior VP*
EMP: 88
SALES (est): 9.7MM **Privately Held**
SIC: 8748 Business consulting

(P-27715)
ELEVATE SERVICES INC (PA)
201 S Santa Fe Ave # 100, Los Angeles (90012-4338)
PHONE.................................310 853-8448
Liam Brown, *Chairman*
John Croft, *President*
Mark Redmayne, *President*
Lokendra Tomar, *CEO*
Anurag Grover, *COO*
EMP: 300
SALES: 25MM **Privately Held**
SIC: 8748 Business consulting

(P-27716)
ELS
Also Called: Els Architecture
2040 Addison St, Berkeley (94704-1104)
PHONE.................................510 549-2929
Barry Elbasani, *President*
Janette Gross, *Treasurer*
Carol Shen, *Admin Sec*
Cheri Lafontaine, *Admin Asst*
Lina Toledo, *Accounting Mgr*
EMP: 65 **EST:** 1967
SQ FT: 12,000
SALES (est): 7.4MM **Privately Held**
WEB: www.elsarch.com
SIC: 8748 8712 Urban planning & consulting services; architectural services

(P-27717)
EMERGENT VENTURES INTL INC
1156 Clement St, San Francisco (94118-2115)
PHONE.................................415 655-6617
Ashutosh Pandey, *President*
Thomas Rosenberg, *Vice Pres*
EMP: 99
SALES (est): 2.9MM **Privately Held**
SIC: 8748 Energy conservation consultant

(P-27718)
ENERGY EXPERTS INTERNATIONAL
7111 N Fresno St Ste 260, Fresno (93720-2959)
PHONE.................................559 449-1124
Dennis Martinez, *Associate*
EMP: 117
SALES (corp-wide): 1MM **Privately Held**
SIC: 8748 8742 Energy conservation consultant; management consulting services
PA: Energy Experts International
555 Twin Dolphin Dr # 150
Redwood City CA 94065
650 593-4261

(P-27719)
ENTERPRISE SOLUTIONS INC
2855 Kifer Rd, Santa Clara (95051-0814)
PHONE.................................408 727-3627
Lucy Phang, *CFO*
EMP: 185 **Privately Held**

SIC: 8748 Systems engineering consultant, ex. computer or professional
PA: Enterprise Solutions, Inc.
500 E Diehl Rd Ste 130
Naperville IL 60563

(P-27720)
ENVENT CORPORATION (PA)
3220 E 29th St, Long Beach (90806-2321)
PHONE.................................562 997-9465
Steve Sellinger, *President*
Thomas Kerscher, *Vice Pres*
JD Jaeger, *General Mgr*
Nancy Savady, *Office Admin*
Laikyn Hilborn, *Admin Asst*
EMP: 131
SQ FT: 6,400
SALES: 33.3MM **Privately Held**
WEB: www.enventcorporation.com
SIC: 8748 Environmental consultant

(P-27721)
ENVIRONMENTAL RESOLUTIONS INC
Also Called: Cardno Eri
25371 Commercentre Dr # 250, Lake Forest (92630-8867)
PHONE.................................949 457-8950
Steve M Zigan, *CEO*
Robert L Kroeger, *Vice Pres*
James Chappell, *Program Mgr*
Sean Guiltinan, *Sr Project Mgr*
Gary Decarlo, *Manager*
EMP: 300
SQ FT: 14,100
SALES (est): 411.2K
SALES (corp-wide): 882.1MM **Privately Held**
WEB: www.eri-us.com
SIC: 8748 8744 Environmental consultant;
HQ: Cardno Usa, Inc.
10004 Park Meadows Dr # 300
Lone Tree CO 80124

(P-27722)
EPCM PROF SVC PARTNERS LLC
2017 Palo Verde Ave, Long Beach (90815-3300)
PHONE.................................562 936-1000
F P Kallina, *Mng Member*
Frederick Paul Kallina, *Mng Member*
EMP: 52
SQ FT: 5,000
SALES (est): 1.1MM **Privately Held**
SIC: 8748 Systems analysis & engineering consulting services

(P-27723)
ES ENGINEERING INC
1 Park Plz Ste 1000, Irvine (92614-8507)
PHONE.................................714 919-6500
Niu Jinghui, *President*
EMP: 60
SQ FT: 2,300
SALES: 25MM **Privately Held**
SIC: 8748 Environmental consultant

(P-27724)
EUROGENTEC NORTH AMERICA INC
34801 Campus Dr, Fremont (94555-3606)
PHONE.................................510 791-9560
Jean-Pierre Delwart, *President*
Lamarr Kelley, *Technology*
EMP: 115
SQ FT: 11,000
SALES (est): 2.5MM
SALES (corp-wide): 5.6B **Privately Held**
WEB: www.eurogentec.com
SIC: 8748 Business consulting
HQ: Kaneka Eurogentec Sa
Rue Du Bois Saint-Jean 5
Seraing 4102
437 274-00

(P-27725)
EXPERIAN MKTG SOLUTIONS LLC
475 Anton Blvd, Costa Mesa (92626-7037)
PHONE.................................714 830-7000
Kevin Dean, *President*
Marlene Rossi, *Director*

EMP: 501
SQ FT: 4,000
SALES (est): 5.5MM **Privately Held**
SIC: 8748 Business consulting

(P-27726)
FAIR ISAAC CORPORATION (PA)
181 Metro Dr Ste 700, San Jose
(95110-1346)
PHONE..............................408 535-1500
William J Lansing, *CEO*
Leslie Charney, *Partner*
Chris Smith, *Partner*
Alexandre Soares, *Partner*
Braden R Kelly, *Ch of Bd*
▲ EMP: 366
SQ FT: 55,000
SALES: 932.1MM **Publicly Held**
WEB: www.fairisaac.com
SIC: 8748 7389 7372 Business consult-
ing; financial services; business oriented
computer software

(P-27727)
FAITH COM INC (PA)
Also Called: Fci Management
3850 E Gilman St, Long Beach
(90815-1752)
PHONE..............................562 719-9300
Patricia Watts, *President*
Donald Gregg, *COO*
EMP: 58
SQ FT: 7,000
SALES (est): 12.7MM **Privately Held**
WEB: www.fcimgt.com
SIC: 8748 Energy conservation consultant

(P-27728)
FAME ASSISTANCE CORPORATION
2270 S Harvard Blvd, Los Angeles
(90018-2142)
PHONE..............................323 373-7720
Denise Hunter, *President*
EMP: 75
SQ FT: 33,748
SALES: 1.7MM **Privately Held**
SIC: 8748 Business consulting

(P-27729)
FAMILY AND CHILDREN SERVICES
950 W Julian St, San Jose (95126-2719)
PHONE..............................408 292-9353
Diana Nemen, *CEO*
Cory Brier, *Office Mgr*
Lisa Weisenreder, *Office Mgr*
Cristina Trujillo, *Admin Asst*
Anita Inagandla, *Human Resources*
EMP: 70
SQ FT: 9,500
SALES (est): 4.6MM **Privately Held**
SIC: 8748 Business consulting

(P-27730)
FORENSIC ANALYTICAL
Also Called: Facs
3111 Camino DI Rio N 43, San Diego
(92108)
PHONE..............................858 859-3322
EMP: 75 **Privately Held**
SIC: 8748 Business consulting
PA: Forensic Analytical Consulting Serv-
ices, Inc.
21228 Cabot Blvd
Hayward CA 94545

(P-27731)
FOX TRANSPORTATION INC (PA)
8610 Helms Ave, Rancho Cucamonga
(91730-4520)
P.O. Box 3119 (91729-3119)
PHONE..............................909 291-4646
Michael K Fox, *CEO*
Mary Anne Fox, *Shareholder*
Chad Shearer, *President*
David Langrehr, *Senior VP*
David Burns, *Vice Pres*
EMP: 60
SALES (est): 21.8MM **Privately Held**
SIC: 8748 4213 Business consulting;
trucking, except local

(P-27732)
FRYS ELECTRONICS INC
4100 Northgate Blvd, Sacramento
(95834-1240)
PHONE..............................916 286-5800
Mark Ashby, *Branch Mgr*
EMP: 300
SALES (corp-wide): 21.8MM **Privately Held**
WEB: www.frys.com
SIC: 8748 5731 Business consulting;
radio, television & electronic stores
PA: Fry's Electronics, Inc.
600 E Brokaw Rd
San Jose CA 95112
408 487-4500

(P-27733)
FTI CONSULTING INC
50 California St Ste 1900, San Francisco
(94111-4620)
PHONE..............................415 283-4200
Jerry Keeler, *Manager*
Michelle Solis, *Executive Asst*
EMP: 80
SALES (corp-wide): 1.8B **Publicly Held**
SIC: 8748 Business consulting
PA: Fti Consulting, Inc.
555 12th St Nw Ste 3
Washington DC 20004
202 312-9100

(P-27734)
FUSE PROJECT LLC
1401 16th St, San Francisco (94103-5109)
PHONE..............................415 908-1492
Yves Behar, *President*
Helen Fu Thomas, *Ch of Bd*
Mitch Pergola, *COO*
Christina Park, *Program Mgr*
Hillary Hayden, *Executive Asst*
EMP: 60
SQ FT: 22,000
SALES (est): 3.8MM **Privately Held**
WEB: www.fuseproject.com
SIC: 8748 Business consulting

(P-27735)
FUSIONSTORM
2 Bryant St Ste 150, San Francisco
(94105-1641)
PHONE..............................415 623-2626
Daniel Serpico, *President*
Brian Siu, *Accountant*
Adam Forsblom, *Counsel*
Mike Costabile, *Manager*
Steve Campagnone, *Accounts Exec*
EMP: 119
SALES (corp-wide): 5B **Privately Held**
SIC: 8748 Systems engineering consult-
ant, ex. computer or professional
HQ: Fusionstorm
124 Grove St Ste 311
Franklin MA 02038
508 520-5000

(P-27736)
GENPACT LLC
3300 Hillview Ave, Palo Alto (94304-1203)
PHONE..............................203 690-9308
Sanjay Srivastava, *Principal*
EMP: 50 **Privately Held**
SIC: 8748 Business consulting
HQ: Genpact Llc
1155 Avenue Of The Americ
New York NY 10036
212 896-6600

(P-27737)
GEOCON CONSULTANTS INC (PA)
6960 Flanders Dr, San Diego (92121-3992)
PHONE..............................858 558-6900
Michael Chapin, *CEO*
Joe Vettel, *President*
John Hoobs, *Vice Pres*
Neal Berliner, *Principal*
John Juhrend, *Principal*
EMP: 85
SQ FT: 10,000
SALES (est): 25.7MM **Privately Held**
WEB: www.geoconinc.com
SIC: 8748 8711 Environmental consultant;
engineering services

(P-27738)
GLASSFAB TEMPERING SVCS INC (PA)
Also Called: Glass Fab Tempering Sv
1448 Mariani Ct, Tracy (95376-2825)
PHONE..............................209 229-1060
Jagmohan Singh, *CEO*
Surinderpal Bains, *President*
Usha Mhay, *CFO*
EMP: 56
SQ FT: 60,000
SALES (est): 16MM **Privately Held**
SIC: 8748 Business consulting

(P-27739)
GLOBAL INFOTECH CORPORATION
2890 Zanker Rd Ste 202, San Jose
(95134-2118)
PHONE..............................408 567-0600
Atul Sharma, *President*
Nitin Prasad, *Vice Pres*
Roshni Chopra, *Technology*
EMP: 550 EST: 1995
SQ FT: 3,000
SALES (est): 46.1MM **Privately Held**
WEB: www.global-infotech.com
SIC: 8748 Systems analysis & engineering
consulting services

(P-27740)
GOLDEN GATE CAPITOL
1 Embarcadero Ctr # 3900, San Francisco
(94111-3628)
PHONE..............................415 983-2700
Jacob Mizrahi, *Principal*
EMP: 500
SALES (est): 10.9MM **Privately Held**
SIC: 8748 Business consulting

(P-27741)
GORDON E BTTY I MORE FUNDATION
1661 Page Mill Rd, Palo Alto (94304-1209)
PHONE..............................650 213-3000
Lewis W Coleman, *President*
Denise Strack, *Ch Invest Ofcr*
Chris McCrum,
EMP: 75
SALES (est): 284.4MM **Privately Held**
WEB: www.moorefoundation.org
SIC: 8748 Economic consultant

(P-27742)
GTT COMMUNICATIONS (MP) INC
555 Anton Blvd Ste 200, Costa Mesa
(92626-7811)
PHONE..............................714 327-2000
Steve Schilling, *President*
Steve Chisholm, *Vice Pres*
Tadashi Egami, *Vice Pres*
Arnaud Gautier, *Vice Pres*
Brenda Viloria, *Vice Pres*
EMP: 64 **Publicly Held**
SIC: 8748 Telecommunications consultant
HQ: Gtt Communications (Mp), Inc.
6700 Koll Center Pkwy
Pleasanton CA 94566
925 201-2500

(P-27743)
H & F GRAIN FARMS LLC
1181 S Wolff Rd, Oxnard (93033-2105)
PHONE..............................805 754-4449
Robert Boelts,
EMP: 70
SALES (est): 4.5MM **Privately Held**
SIC: 8748 0191 Agricultural consultant;
general farms, primarily crop

(P-27744)
HANLEY WOOD MKT INTELLIGENCE (PA)
555 Anton Blvd Ste 950, Costa Mesa
(92626-7811)
PHONE..............................714 540-8500
Thomas Flynn, *President*
Shawn Edwards, *Vice Pres*
EMP: 175
SQ FT: 15,000
SALES (est): 20MM **Privately Held**
SIC: 8748 8742 Publishing consultant;
real estate consultant

(P-27745)
HARRIS & SLOAN CONSULTING
2295 Gateway Oaks Dr # 165, Sacramento
(95833-4211)
PHONE..............................916 921-2800
Timothy Sloan, *President*
Alyssa Gutierrez, *Design Engr*
Danielle Jurado, *Project Mgr*
EMP: 50
SALES (est): 1.9MM **Privately Held**
WEB: www.hscgi.com
SIC: 8748 Business consulting

(P-27746)
HERE FILMS
10990 Wilshire Blvd, Los Angeles
(90024-3913)
PHONE..............................310 806-4288
EMP: 50
SALES (est): 1.2MM **Privately Held**
SIC: 8748

(P-27747)
HETROSYS LLC
3858 Carrera Ct, San Jose (95148-3716)
PHONE..............................408 270-0240
Harpreet Soni, *CEO*
EMP: 56
SQ FT: 2,800
SALES: 3.1MM **Privately Held**
SIC: 8748 7389 Telecommunications con-
sultant;

(P-27748)
HINTTECH INC
505 Montgomery St Fl 11, San Francisco
(94111-2585)
PHONE..............................415 874-3200
Egbert Hendricks, *President*
Terry Francis, *Technical Staff*
EMP: 120
SALES: 17MM **Privately Held**
SIC: 8748 Business consulting

(P-27749)
HUMBOLDT STATE UNIVERSITY SPON
Also Called: Hsu Foundation
1 Harpst St, Arcata (95521-8299)
P.O. Box 1185 (95518-1185)
PHONE..............................707 826-4189
Steven Karp, *Exec Dir*
Erika Wright, *General Mgr*
EMP: 100
SALES: 25.7MM **Privately Held**
WEB: www.hsujacks.com
SIC: 8748 Educational consultant

(P-27750)
HUNTER-LA PURISIMA CORP
5060 California Ave # 640, Bakersfield
(93309-0728)
PHONE..............................661 616-0600
Kenneth J Hunter III, *President*
EMP: 52 EST: 1984
SALES (est): 1.9MM **Privately Held**
SIC: 8748 Urban planning & consulting
services

(P-27751)
IBASET INC
27442 Portola Pkwy # 300, Foothill Ranch
(92610-2822)
PHONE..............................949 598-5200
Ladeira Poonian, *CEO*
Vikram Sial, *President*
Diana CHI, *Accountant*
EMP: 99
SQ FT: 28,000
SALES (est): 2.6MM **Privately Held**
SIC: 8748 7371 7372 Business consult-
ing; custom computer programming serv-
ices; application computer software

(P-27752)
INFOSOFT INC
7891 Westwood Dr Ste 113, Gilroy
(95020-4786)
PHONE..............................408 659-4326
Ashish Chopra, *President*
Raj Chopra, *Vice Pres*
Vick Pandey, *Tech Recruiter*
Manoranjan Das, *Recruiter*
Gary Giri, *Recruiter*
EMP: 80

SALES (est): 272.3K **Privately Held**
SIC: **8748** 7361 Systems engineering consultant, ex. computer or professional; placement agencies

(P-27753)
INSTITUTE FOR MULTICULTURAL
121 W Lexington Dr, Glendale (91203-2203)
PHONE....................................818 240-4311
Tara Pir, *Manager*
Nima Nouri, *Psychologist*
EMP: 70 **Privately Held**
SIC: **8748** Educational consultant
PA: Institute For Multicultural Counseling And Educational Services Inc.
3580 Wilshire Blvd # 2000
Los Angeles CA 90010
-

(P-27754)
INTERNATIONAL ADVISORS LLC
31248 Oak Crest Dr, Westlake Village (91361-4692)
PHONE....................................497 961-7988
Steven Bronson, *President*
EMP: 100
SALES (est): 8MM **Privately Held**
SIC: **8748** Business consulting

(P-27755)
INTERNATIONAL MGT SYSTEMS
Also Called: IMS
4640 Admiralty Way # 500, Marina Del Rey (90292-6621)
PHONE....................................310 822-2022
Harry M Thorpe Jr, *President*
Becky Valdez, *Administration*
Kristi Newman, *Human Res Mgr*
EMP: 90
SQ FT: 6,000
SALES (est): 3.9MM **Privately Held**
WEB: www.imssvs.com
SIC: **8748** 7374 Systems engineering consultant, ex. computer or professional; data processing & preparation

(P-27756)
INTRINSIK ENVMTL SCIENCES INC
1608 Pacific Ave Ste 201, Venice (90291-5112)
PHONE....................................310 392-6462
EMP: 67
SALES (corp-wide): 3.5MM **Privately Held**
SIC: **8748**
PA: Intrinsik Environmental Sciences Inc
6605 Hurontario St Suite 605
Mississauga ON L5T 0
905 364-7800

(P-27757)
ITC SRVICE GROUP ACQSITION LLC (PA)
Also Called: I T C
7777 Greenback Ln Ste 201, Citrus Heights (95610-5800)
PHONE....................................877 370-4482
Timothy S Sauer, *President*
Jim Rush, *COO*
Jeremy Elmas, *CFO*
Robert Bradley, *Vice Pres*
Boe Cunningham, *Vice Pres*
EMP: 50 EST: 1999
SQ FT: 11,843
SALES (est): 80.7MM **Privately Held**
WEB: www.callitc.com
SIC: **8748** Telecommunications consultant

(P-27758)
JACOBS CONSULTANCY INC
555 Airport Blvd Ste 300, Burlingame (94010-2036)
PHONE....................................650 579-7722
Nick Davidson, *Branch Mgr*
EMP: 85
SALES (corp-wide): 10B **Publicly Held**
WEB: www.jacobsconsultancy.com
SIC: **8748** 8742 Business consulting; management consulting services

HQ: Jacobs Consultancy Inc.
5995 Rogerdale Rd
Houston TX 77072
832 351-6000

(P-27759)
JAG PROFESSIONAL SERVICES INC
2008 Walnut Ave, Manhattan Beach (90266-2841)
P.O. Box 3007, El Segundo (90245-8107)
PHONE....................................310 945-5648
Judith Hinkley, *CEO*
Bob Warnke, *Director*
EMP: 126
SQ FT: 1,000
SALES (est): 10MM **Privately Held**
WEB: www.jagprof.com
SIC: **8748** Business consulting

(P-27760)
JK CONSULTANTS
160 Station Way Unit 102, Arroyo Grande (93421-5008)
PHONE....................................209 532-7772
Fred Khachi, *President*
Elaine Khachi, *Exec VP*
Lorraine Pinto, *Administration*
EMP: 50
SQ FT: 3,000
SALES (est): 25MM **Privately Held**
WEB: www.jksuccess.com
SIC: **8748** 8742 Business consulting; management consulting services

(P-27761)
JULIO GONZALEZ
1417 S Fairfax Ave Apt 4, Los Angeles (90019-3736)
PHONE....................................310 310-4055
Julio Gonzalez, *Owner*
EMP: 99
SALES: 950K **Privately Held**
SIC: **8748** Business consulting

(P-27762)
JUSTICE CALIFORNIA DEPARTMENT
Also Called: Testing and Selection
1300 I St Ste 720, Sacramento (95814-2958)
PHONE....................................916 324-5039
Richard Busman, *Branch Mgr*
Jeanne Wolfe,
EMP: 1000 **Privately Held**
WEB: www.doj.state.wi.us
SIC: **8748** 9222 Testing services; systems engineering consultant, ex. computer or professional; legal counsel & prosecution;
HQ: California Department Of Justice
1300 I St Ste 1142
Sacramento CA 95814
-

(P-27763)
KATZ MEDIA GROUP INC
5700 Wilshire Blvd # 100, Los Angeles (90036-3659)
PHONE....................................323 966-5000
K Thornton, *Manager*
Michael Canter, *Executive*
David Hall, *Executive*
Elizabeth Batista, *Research*
Christina Lind, *Sales Staff*
EMP: 85 **Publicly Held**
WEB: www.ctvsales.com
SIC: **8748** Business consulting
HQ: Katz Media Group Inc
125 W 55th St Fl 11
New York NY 10019
-

(P-27764)
KLEINFELDER INC
3880 Lemon St Ste 300, Riverside (92501-3301)
PHONE....................................951 801-3681
John Lohman, *Manager*
Aaron Kidd, *Lab Dir*
Kim Harlow, *Purch Agent*
EMP: 55

SALES (corp-wide): 249.4MM **Privately Held**
WEB: www.kleinfelder.com
SIC: **8748** 7389 Environmental consultant; systems engineering consultant, ex. computer or professional; air pollution measuring service
HQ: Kleinfelder, Inc.
550 W C St Ste 1200
San Diego CA 92101
619 831-4600

(P-27765)
KLEINFELDER ASSOCIATES
550 W C St Ste 1200, San Diego (92101-3532)
PHONE....................................619 831-4600
George J Pierson, *President*
Bart Patton, *COO*
John Pilkington, *CFO*
Larry Peterson, *Senior VP*
Russ Carey, *Vice Pres*
EMP: 1500
SALES (est): 61.6MM
SALES (corp-wide): 249.4MM **Privately Held**
SIC: **8748** Environmental consultant
PA: The Kleinfelder Group Inc
550 W C St Ste 1200
San Diego CA 92101
619 831-4600

(P-27766)
KLH CONSULTING INC
2324 Bethards Dr, Santa Rosa (95405-8537)
PHONE....................................707 575-9986
Soni Lampert, *CEO*
Hub Lampert, *CFO*
EMP: 55 EST: 1978
SALES (est): 9.1MM **Privately Held**
WEB: www.klhconsulting.com
SIC: **8748** 7371 7372 Systems engineering consultant, ex. computer or professional; custom computer programming services; business oriented computer software

(P-27767)
KRAZAN & ASSOCIATES (PA)
215 W Dakota Ave, Clovis (93612-5608)
PHONE....................................559 348-2200
Dean L Alexander, *President*
Jodi Ragsdale, *CFO*
Emilo Vargas, *CFO*
Thomas P Krazan, *Chairman*
Mike Thomas, *Lab Dir*
EMP: 68
SQ FT: 21,000
SALES: 19MM **Privately Held**
WEB: www.krazan.com
SIC: **8748** 8734 8742 Environmental consultant; product testing laboratory, safety or performance; management engineering

(P-27768)
KROS-WISE
3111 Camino Del Rio N, San Diego (92108-5720)
PHONE....................................619 223-1980
Lily Aragon, *President*
EMP: 85
SALES (est): 5.8MM **Privately Held**
WEB: www.kroswise.com
SIC: **8748** Business consulting

(P-27769)
L S A ASSOCIATES INC (PA)
20 Executive Park Ste 200, Irvine (92614-4739)
PHONE....................................949 553-0666
Les Card, *CEO*
Rob McCann, *President*
James Baum, *CFO*
Marco Perez, *Regional Mgr*
Natalie Frey, *General Mgr*
EMP: 110
SQ FT: 22,000
SALES (est): 52.6MM **Privately Held**
WEB: www.lsa-assoc.com
SIC: **8748** Environmental consultant

(P-27770)
LAND DESIGN CONSULTANTS INC
2700 E Foothill Blvd # 200, Pasadena (91107-3443)
PHONE....................................626 578-7000
Robert Sims, *President*
Larry Mar, *CFO*
Steve Hunter, *Vice Pres*
Jimmy Lee, *Planning*
EMP: 70
SALES: 9.6MM **Privately Held**
WEB: www.ldcla.com
SIC: **8748** 8711 8713 Urban planning & consulting services; environmental consultant; civil engineering; surveying services

(P-27771)
LAYNE CHRISTENSEN COMPANY
Colog Div
1717 W Park Ave, Redlands (92373-8049)
PHONE....................................909 390-2833
David Singleton, *General Mgr*
EMP: 140
SALES (corp-wide): 2.9B **Publicly Held**
WEB: www.laynechristensen.com
SIC: **8748** 7699 5084 Environmental consultant; pumps & pumping equipment repair; pumps & pumping equipment
HQ: Layne Christensen Company
1800 Hughes Landing Blvd
The Woodlands TX 77380
281 475-2600

(P-27772)
LEED INTERNATIONAL LLC
1583 Shanghai Cir, San Jose (95131-2411)
PHONE....................................650 861-7883
Hong Zhang, *Chairman*
EMP: 50
SALES (est): 594.2K **Privately Held**
SIC: **8748** 5961 Business consulting; catalog & mail-order houses

(P-27773)
LEIGHTON AND ASSOCIATES INC (PA)
17781 Cowan, Irvine (92614-6009)
PHONE....................................949 250-1421
Terry Brennan, *President*
Robert Riha, *COO*
Gareth Mills, *Vice Pres*
Iraj Poormand, *Vice Pres*
Kris Lutton, *Office Mgr*
EMP: 70
SQ FT: 30,000
SALES (est): 14.7MM **Privately Held**
SIC: **8748** 8711 Environmental consultant; engineering services

(P-27774)
LESLEY FOUNDATION
701 Arnold Way Bldg A, Half Moon Bay (94019-2199)
PHONE....................................650 726-4888
Sarah Lambert, *Exec Dir*
EMP: 65
SALES: 11.4MM **Privately Held**
SIC: **8748** Urban planning & consulting services

(P-27775)
LEVEL FOUR BUSINESS MGT LLC
11812 San Vicente Blvd # 400, Los Angeles (90049-6625)
PHONE....................................310 914-1600
Mark Friedman, *Mng Member*
Linda Collison, *Executive Asst*
Jeremy Marcusc, *Business Mgr*
Melina Schroeder, *Business Mgr*
Shiela Soles, *Persnl Mgr*
EMP: 50
SALES (est): 1.5MM **Privately Held**
SIC: **8748** Business consulting

(P-27776)
LIVEVOX INC (PA)
655 Montgomery St # 1190, San Francisco (94111-2647)
PHONE....................................415 671-6000
Louis Summe, *CEO*
Larry Siegel, *COO*

Michael Leraris, *CFO*
Ashley Maciel, *Admin Asst*
Taylor Stephens, *Project Mgr*
EMP: 85
SALES (est): 34MM **Privately Held**
WEB: www.tfhinc.net
SIC: 8748 Telecommunications consultant

(P-27777)
LUMETRA HEALTHCARE SOLUTIONS
550 Kearny St Ste 300, San Francisco
(94108-2597)
PHONE........................415 677-2000
Patricia Daniel, *CEO*
Lewy Roth, *Office Mgr*
Consuela Bejan, *Executive Asst*
Merry Tantaros, *Project Mgr*
Annie Auyeung, *Accountant*
EMP: 50
SQ FT: 5,000
SALES (est): 4.5MM **Privately Held**
WEB: www.lumetra.com
SIC: 8748 Business consulting

(P-27778)
LUSIVE DECOR
Also Called: Luxe Light and Home
3400 Medford St, Los Angeles
(90063-2530)
PHONE........................323 227-9207
Jason Kai Cooper, *CEO*
Terra Clark, *General Mgr*
Wesley Colmenares, *Office Mgr*
Carlos Gutierrez, *Project Mgr*
Paula Machado, *Project Mgr*
EMP: 50 **EST:** 2006
SALES (est): 8.6MM **Privately Held**
SIC: 8748 3646 Lighting consultant; ceiling systems, luminous

(P-27779)
LYLE COMPANY
3140 Gold Camp Dr Ste 30, Rancho Cordova (95670-6192)
P.O. Box 2255 (95741-2255)
PHONE........................916 266-7000
Lanny G Lyle, *Ch of Bd*
Randy Cobb, *Vice Pres*
Steve Zito, *Info Tech Mgr*
Nancy Griggs, *Project Mgr*
Lisa M Connolly, *Accountant*
EMP: 60
SALES (est): 5.7MM **Privately Held**
WEB: www.lyleco.com
SIC: 8748 Business consulting

(P-27780)
MANAGEMENT TECH CONSULTING LLC
7738 Skyhill Dr, Los Angeles (90068-1232)
PHONE........................323 851-5008
Darryl Henderson, *CEO*
Rebecca Waldera, *Admin Asst*
Nitesh Agarwal, *Manager*
EMP: 65
SQ FT: 2,800
SALES (est): 3.7MM **Privately Held**
SIC: 8748 Business consulting

(P-27781)
MANTECH SYSTEMS ENGRG CORP
8328 Clairemont Mesa Blvd # 100, San Diego (92111-1328)
PHONE........................858 292-9000
Brad Geiger, *Systems Mgr*
EMP: 70
SALES (corp-wide): 1.7B **Publicly Held**
SIC: 8748 Business consulting
HQ: Mantech Systems Engineering Corporation
12015 Lee Jackson Hwy # 110
Fairfax VA 22033
703 218-6000

(P-27782)
MASSDROP INC
710 Sansome St, San Francisco
(94111-1704)
PHONE........................415 340-2999
Steve El-Hage, *CEO*
Anne Morrissey, *Vice Pres*
Eric Stender, *Sr Software Eng*
Jasper Chan, *CTO*

Jonathan Liu, *Software Engr*
EMP: 70
SQ FT: 11,839
SALES (est): 15.5MM **Privately Held**
SIC: 8748 Systems engineering consultant, ex. computer or professional

(P-27783)
MAXIM PLANNING GROUP
1214 E Colorado Blvd, Pasadena
(91106-1899)
PHONE........................818 425-4343
Steve Vivanco, *Owner*
EMP: 60
SALES (est): 3MM **Privately Held**
SIC: 8748 Business consulting

(P-27784)
MCWONG ENVMTL & ENRGY GROUP
1921 Arena Blvd, Sacramento
(95834-3770)
PHONE........................916 371-8080
Margaret Wong, *President*
EMP: 50 **EST:** 2001
SQ FT: 7,800
SALES (est): 16MM **Privately Held**
WEB: www.mcwonginc.com
SIC: 8748 Energy conservation consultant; environmental consultant

(P-27785)
MENKE & ASSOCIATES INC (PA)
1 Kaiser Plz Ste 505, Oakland
(94612-3611)
PHONE........................415 362-5200
John Menke, *President*
W Kyle Coltman, *CEO*
Nancy Menke, *Admin Sec*
EMP: 55
SQ FT: 12,500
SALES (est): 9MM **Privately Held**
WEB: www.menke.com
SIC: 8748 Employee programs administration

(P-27786)
MICHAEL BAKER INTL INC
2729 Prospect Park Dr # 220, Rancho Cordova (95670-6291)
PHONE........................916 361-8384
Phil Carter, *Manager*
Kurt Bergman, *CEO*
EMP: 99
SALES (corp-wide): 592.9MM **Privately Held**
SIC: 8748 Business consulting
HQ: Baker Michael International Inc
500 Grant St Ste 5400
Pittsburgh PA 15219
412 269-6300

(P-27787)
MICHAEL BAKER INTL INC
9755 Clairemont Mesa Blvd, San Diego
(92124-1333)
PHONE........................858 453-3602
Phil Carter, *Manager*
EMP: 75
SALES (corp-wide): 592.9MM **Privately Held**
WEB: www.rbf.com
SIC: 8748 Business consulting
HQ: Baker Michael International Inc
500 Grant St Ste 5400
Pittsburgh PA 15219
412 269-6300

(P-27788)
MICHAEL BAKER INTL INC
3300 E Guasti Rd Ste 100, Ontario
(91761-8656)
PHONE........................909 974-4900
Ron Craig, *Manager*
EMP: 50
SALES (corp-wide): 592.9MM **Privately Held**
SIC: 8748 Business consulting
HQ: Baker Michael International Inc
14725 Alton Pkwy
Irvine CA 92618
949 472-3505

(P-27789)
MIND DRAGON INC
36002 Pansy St, Winchester (92596-8735)
PHONE........................877 367-6060
Jefferson Nunn, *President*
Fern Rudin, *CFO*
Jim Alexander, *Vice Pres*
Alan Gerson, *Vice Pres*
EMP: 50
SQ FT: 1,700
SALES: 600K **Privately Held**
WEB: www.mindragon.com
SIC: 8748 Business consulting

(P-27790)
MIRAMED GLOBAL SERVICES INC
Also Called: On Call Consulting
199 E Thsand Oaks Blvd, Thousand Oaks
(91360)
PHONE........................805 277-1017
Ron Manzani, *Branch Mgr*
EMP: 579 **Privately Held**
SIC: 8748 Business consulting
PA: Miramed Global Services, Inc.
255 W Michigan Ave
Jackson MI 49201

(P-27791)
MONTE VSTA MEM SCHLRSHP ASSOC
2 School Way, Watsonville (95076-9716)
PHONE........................831 722-8178
Stephen Sharp, *Administration*
EMP: 50
SALES (est): 3MM **Privately Held**
SIC: 8748 Business consulting

(P-27792)
MONTROSE ENVMTL GROUP INC (PA)
1 Park Plz Ste 1000, Irvine (92614-8507)
PHONE........................949 988-3500
Vijay Manthripragada, *CEO*
Allan Dicks, *CFO*
Jose Revuelta, *Officer*
Yvonne Senouci, *Vice Pres*
Tanya Jackson, *Project Mgr*
EMP: 52
SALES (est): 179.4MM **Privately Held**
SIC: 8748 Environmental consultant

(P-27793)
MONTROSE ENVMTL GROUP INC
1631 E Saint Andrew Pl, Santa Ana
(92705-4932)
PHONE........................714 332-8646
EMP: 714
SALES (corp-wide): 179.4MM **Privately Held**
SIC: 8748 Environmental consultant
PA: Montrose Environmental Group, Inc.
1 Park Plz Ste 1000
Irvine CA 92614
949 988-3500

(P-27794)
MOORE IACOFANO GOLTSMAN INC (PA)
Also Called: M I G
800 Hearst Ave, Berkeley (94710-2018)
PHONE........................510 845-7549
Susan M Goltsman, *President*
Daniel Iacofano, *CEO*
Carolyn Verheyen, *COO*
Donna Sonoda, *Business Dir*
Rachael Husted, *Office Mgr*
EMP: 63
SQ FT: 6,000
SALES (est): 19.5MM **Privately Held**
WEB: www.migcom.com
SIC: 8748 Environmental consultant; communications consulting

(P-27795)
MOUNTAIN TOP COMM SVCS LLC
1902 Orange Tree Ln, Redlands
(92374-2888)
PHONE........................909 798-4400
Diodore Pesquera,
Joseph Jacobson,

Justin Mata,
EMP: 50 **EST:** 2011
SQ FT: 4,025
SALES (est): 368.5K **Privately Held**
SIC: 8748 Telecommunications consultant

(P-27796)
MSLA MANAGEMENT LLC
1294 E Colorado Blvd, Pasadena
(91106-1901)
PHONE........................626 824-6020
Michael Lambert, *CEO*
Sahniah Siciarz-Lambert, *President*
Robert Worth Oberrender, *Treasurer*
Thomas Shaun McGlinch, *Asst Treas*
Paul Timothy Runice, *Asst Treas*
EMP: 173
SALES (est): 1.9MM
SALES (corp-wide): 201.1B **Publicly Held**
SIC: 8748 Business consulting
HQ: Logistics Health, Inc.
328 Front St S
La Crosse WI 54601
866 284-8788

(P-27797)
MYOSCIENCE INC
46400 Fremont Blvd, Fremont
(94538-6469)
PHONE........................510 933-1500
Timothy I Still, *President*
Brian Farley, *Ch of Bd*
Matt Franklin, *CFO*
Peter Osborne, *CFO*
James Berger, *Info Tech Mgr*
EMP: 50
SALES (est): 8.9MM **Privately Held**
SIC: 8748 Business consulting

(P-27798)
NATIONAL INSURANCE HOUSING
Also Called: National Insurance Associates
265 Santa Helena Ste 210, Solana Beach
(92075-1546)
PHONE........................800 550-1911
Susan Swan, *Executive*
EMP: 99
SALES (est): 3.2MM **Privately Held**
SIC: 8748 Urban planning & consulting services

(P-27799)
NATIONAL SAFETY SERVICES
3400 Avenue Of The Arts, Costa Mesa
(92626-1927)
PHONE........................714 679-9118
EMP: 50
SALES (est): 2.7MM **Privately Held**
SIC: 8748 8999

(P-27800)
NEWTON SOFTED INC
Also Called: Pm2net
2807 Mcgaw Ave, Irvine (92614-5835)
PHONE........................949 396-6192
Carson Synh, *CEO*
Joel Morrison, *Project Mgr*
Michael Wynn, *Sales Staff*
EMP: 50
SALES (est): 2MM **Privately Held**
SIC: 8748 7379 Systems analysis & engineering consulting services; computer related consulting services

(P-27801)
NEXANT INC (PA)
101 2nd St Ste 1000, San Francisco
(94105-3651)
PHONE........................415 369-1000
John Gustafson, *CEO*
Arjun Gupta, *Chairman*
Terry Fry, *Senior VP*
Michael Sullivan, *Senior VP*
Eric Bober, *Vice Pres*
EMP: 80
SQ FT: 17,462
SALES (est): 150.5MM **Privately Held**
WEB: www.nexant.com
SIC: 8748 Energy conservation consultant

(P-27802)
NINYO & MOORE
GEOTECHNICAL (PA)
5710 Ruffin Rd, San Diego (92123-1013)
PHONE..................................858 576-1000
Avram Ninyo, *CEO*
Madan Chirumalla, *Admin Sec*
Angelique Frederick, *Admin Asst*
Tiffany Hooper, *Admin Asst*
Tim Timmerman, *CTO*
EMP: 80
SQ FT: 24,000
SALES: 50.9MM **Privately Held**
SIC: 8748 Environmental consultant

(P-27803)
NINYO & MOORE
GEOTECHNICAL
475 Goddard Ste 200, Irvine (92618-4622)
PHONE..................................949 753-7070
Carol Price, *Manager*
Avram Ninyo, *President*
EMP: 65
SALES (corp-wide): 50.9MM **Privately**
Held
SIC: 8748 8711 8734 Environmental consultant; pollution control engineering; soil analysis
PA: Ninyo & Moore Geotechnical & Environmental Sciences Consultants
5710 Ruffin Rd
San Diego CA 92123
858 576-1000

(P-27804)
NMS DATA INC
Also Called: Neilson Marketing Services
23172 Plaza Pointe Dr # 205, Laguna Hills (92653-1477)
PHONE..................................949 472-2700
Lawrence Neilson, *CEO*
Jeffrey Neilson, *President*
Neilson Paul, *Vice Pres*
Jolie Eritano, *Accountant*
Mike Neilson, *VP Opers*
EMP: 50
SQ FT: 9,500
SALES: 5MM **Privately Held**
SIC: 8748 Business consulting

(P-27805)
NORTH LA COUNTY REGIONAL
CTR (PA)
15400 Sherman Way Ste 170, Van Nuys (91406-4272)
PHONE..................................818 778-1900
George Stevens, *Director*
Kim Rolfes, *CFO*
EMP: 350
SQ FT: 57,000
SALES: 433.3MM **Privately Held**
SIC: 8748 Test development & evaluation service

(P-27806)
NORTH LA COUNTY REGIONAL
CTR
Also Called: Regional Center For Devlpmtnly
43210 Gingham Ave Ste 6, Lancaster (93535-4512)
PHONE..................................661 945-6761
Joan Daniels, *Manager*
EMP: 70
SALES (corp-wide): 433.3MM **Privately**
Held
SIC: 8748 Test development & evaluation service
PA: North La County Regional Center Inc
15400 Sherman Way Ste 170
Van Nuys CA 91406
818 778-1900

(P-27807)
NTS TECHNICAL SYSTEMS
Also Called: Saugus Division
20970 Centre Pointe Pkwy, Santa Clarita (91350-2975)
PHONE..................................661 259-8184
Rick Reyes, *General Mgr*
Bob Carpenter, *Program Mgr*
Jori Czajkowski, *Department Mgr*
Mark Kawai, *Technician*
Pat Leblanc, *Manager*
EMP: 56

SALES (corp-wide): 273.9MM **Privately**
Held
WEB: www.ntscorp.com
SIC: 8748 8734 Environmental consultant; product testing laboratories
HQ: Nts Technical Systems
24007 Ventura Blvd # 200
Calabasas CA 91302
818 591-0776

(P-27808)
O C JONES & SONS INC
155 Filbert St Ste 209, Oakland (94607-2524)
PHONE..................................510 663-6911
Carla Radosta, *Branch Mgr*
EMP: 100
SALES (corp-wide): 114.3MM **Privately**
Held
SIC: 8748 Business consulting
PA: O. C. Jones & Sons, Inc.
1520 4th St
Berkeley CA 94710
510 526-3424

(P-27809)
OCEAN PARK COMMUNITY
CENTER
Turning Point
1447 16th St, Santa Monica (90404-2715)
PHONE..................................310 828-6717
Patricia Bauman, *Director*
EMP: 51
SALES (corp-wide): 13.5MM **Privately**
Held
SIC: 8748 Urban planning & consulting services
PA: Ocean Park Community Center
1453 16th St
Santa Monica CA 90404
310 264-6646

(P-27810)
OFFICE OF THE LEGISLATIVE
COUN
Also Called: Legislative Counsel Tstg Off
925 L St Ste 900, Sacramento (95814-3702)
PHONE..................................916 445-3796
Alison Raymer, *Manager*
EMP: 1000 **Privately Held**
WEB: www.lc.ca.gov
SIC: 8748 9121 Testing services; legislative bodies;
HQ: Office Of The Legislative Counsel
State Cpitol Bldg Rm 3021
Sacramento CA 95814

(P-27811)
ONE DIVERSIFIED LLC
3275 Edward Ave, Santa Clara (95054-2340)
PHONE..................................408 969-1972
EMP: 91
SALES (corp-wide): 459MM **Privately**
Held
SIC: 8748 7373 Systems analysis & engineering consulting services; systems integration services
PA: One Diversified, Llc
2975 Northwoods Pkwy
Peachtree Corners GA 30071
770 447-1001

(P-27812)
ONSITE CONSULTING LLC
5042 Wilshire Blvd # 135, Los Angeles (90036-4305)
PHONE..................................323 401-3190
James D Sinclair, *Mng Member*
EMP: 65
SALES: 9.5MM **Privately Held**
SIC: 8748 Business consulting

(P-27813)
OPALLIOS INC
4633 Old Ironsides Dr # 315, Santa Clara (95054-1846)
PHONE..................................408 769-4594
Omcar Paradkar, *Principal*
Pulkit Mathur, *Sales Staff*
EMP: 50
SALES (est): 2MM **Privately Held**
SIC: 8748 Business consulting

(P-27814)
OPENPOPCOM INC (PA)
5422 Beach Blvd, Buena Park (90621-1234)
PHONE..................................714 249-7044
Sun Jong Baek, *President*
EMP: 75
SALES (est): 4.5MM **Privately Held**
SIC: 8748 Telecommunications consultant

(P-27815)
ORANGE SILICON VALLEY
60 Spear St Ste 1100, San Francisco (94105-1599)
PHONE..................................415 243-1500
EMP: 60 EST: 2012
SALES (est): 3.6MM **Privately Held**
SIC: 8748

(P-27816)
OUTSOURCE TESTING INC
Also Called: Ostcs
1278 Center Court Dr, Covina (91724-3601)
PHONE..................................909 592-8898
Brian Steven Pinkus, *President*
Rafael Garcia, *Technician*
Melanie Pinkus, *Director*
EMP: 75
SQ FT: 8,000
SALES (est): 5.6MM **Privately Held**
WEB: www.outsourcetesting.com
SIC: 8748 Testing services

(P-27817)
P8GE CONSULTING INC
Also Called: Fame Hardwood Floors
8406 Beverly Blvd, Los Angeles (90048-3402)
PHONE..................................310 666-2301
Pedram Youav Nazarian, *CEO*
EMP: 50
SQ FT: 1,500
SALES: 10MM **Privately Held**
SIC: 8748 Business consulting

(P-27818)
PACIFIC COMMUNICATIONS
ASSOC
761 2nd St, Brentwood (94513-1352)
P.O. Box 1147 (94513-3147)
PHONE..................................925 634-1203
Peter Petrovich, *President*
Fred Valverde, *CFO*
Rhonda Petrovich, *Vice Pres*
Mark Isidoro, *VP Opers*
EMP: 50
SQ FT: 600
SALES (est): 2.7MM **Privately Held**
WEB: www.pacific-communications.com
SIC: 8748 Communications consulting

(P-27819)
PARAGON PARTNERS LTD (PA)
5660 Katella Ave Ste 100, Cypress (90630-5058)
PHONE..................................714 379-3376
Neilia A La Valle, *President*
Norm Henenberg, *Vice Pres*
Joel Sewell, *Vice Pres*
Kathy Viodes, *Asst Controller*
Susan Spaulding, *Human Resources*
EMP: 65
SQ FT: 10,000
SALES (est): 18.6MM **Privately Held**
WEB: www.paragon-partners.com
SIC: 8748 Business consulting

(P-27820)
PCS LINK INC
Also Called: Greenwood & Hall
12424 Wilshire Blvd # 1030, Los Angeles (90025-1031)
PHONE..................................949 655-5000
John R Hall, *CEO*
Jonathan Newcomb, *Ch of Bd*
Zantine Greenwood, *CFO*
Brad Johnson, *Exec VP*
Harvey Ross, *Exec VP*
EMP: 310
SQ FT: 25,000
SALES (est): 35.3MM **Privately Held**
WEB: www.pcslink.com
SIC: 8748 Communications consulting

(P-27821)
PEOPLES SELF-HELP HOUSING
CORP
Also Called: Los Adobes De Maria
1026 W Boone St, Santa Maria (93458-5499)
PHONE..................................805 349-9341
John Fowler, *Director*
EMP: 65
SALES (corp-wide): 10MM **Privately**
Held
SIC: 8748 Urban planning & consulting services
PA: Peoples' Self-Help Housing Corporation
3533 Empleo St
San Luis Obispo CA 93401
805 781-3088

(P-27822)
PINNACLE ELECTRICAL SVCS
INC
Also Called: Pinnacle Networking Services
730 Fairmont Ave Ste 100, Glendale (91203-1079)
PHONE..................................818 241-6009
Avo Amirian, *CEO*
Joe Lucurst, *President*
EMP: 56 EST: 1991
SQ FT: 2,500
SALES (est): 3.1MM **Privately Held**
SIC: 8748 Telecommunications consultant

(P-27823)
POLARIS RESEARCH &
DEVELOPMENT
390 4th St Fl 1, San Francisco (94107-1289)
PHONE..................................415 777-3229
Mike Jang, *Vice Pres*
Ernie Fazio, *President*
Rosa Osman, *CFO*
Carol McGruder, *Director*
EMP: 70
SQ FT: 10,000
SALES (est): 3.9MM **Privately Held**
SIC: 8748 Environmental consultant

(P-27824)
PONDER ENVIRONMENTAL
SVCS INC (PA)
4563 E 2nd St, Benicia (94510-1032)
P.O. Box 1427 (94510-4427)
PHONE..................................707 748-7775
Jim Ponder, *President*
Curtis Fox, *Area Mgr*
Joe Anderson, *General Mgr*
Sharon Taylor, *Safety Dir*
Justin Ponder, *Opers Mgr*
EMP: 60
SQ FT: 15,000
SALES: 17.9MM **Privately Held**
WEB:
www.ponderenvironmentalservices.com
SIC: 8748 Environmental consultant

(P-27825)
PREMIER EXEC SOLUTIONS INC
269 S Beverly Dr Ste 981, Beverly Hills (90212-3851)
PHONE..................................310 989-9925
Manny Salazar, *President*
EMP: 50
SALES (est): 1.9MM **Privately Held**
SIC: 8748 Business consulting

(P-27826)
PROFIT RECOVERY PARTNERS
LLC
Also Called: P R P
2995 Red Hill Ave Ste 200, Costa Mesa (92626-5984)
PHONE..................................949 851-2777
Donald Steiner, *President*
Jeremy Linehan, *President*
Marty Bozarth, *COO*
Paul J Bottiaux, *CFO*
Paul Bottiaux, *CFO*
EMP: 75
SQ FT: 260,000
SALES (est): 12.9MM **Privately Held**
WEB: www.prpllc.com
SIC: 8748 Business consulting

(P-27827)
PROJECT CONSULTING SPECIALISTS
425 N Whisman Rd Ste 600, Mountain View (94043-5733)
PHONE..................650 265-2400
Brendan McIntyre, *President*
EMP: 50
SQ FT: 2,200
SALES (est): 5.7MM **Privately Held**
SIC: 8748 Systems engineering consultant, ex. computer or professional

(P-27828)
PROJECT DESIGN CONSULTANTS
701 B St Ste 800, San Diego (92101-8162)
PHONE..................619 235-6471
Gregory M Shields, *CEO*
William R Dick, *President*
Mark Kestel, *President*
Chris Morrow, *Vice Pres*
Debby Reece, *Vice Pres*
EMP: 100
SQ FT: 22,000
SALES (est): 9.8MM **Privately Held**
WEB: www.projectdesign.com
SIC: 8748 8711 8713 Urban planning & consulting services; civil engineering; surveying services

(P-27829)
PS ARTS
Also Called: CROSSROADS COMMUNITY FOUNDATIO
6701 Center Dr W Ste 550, Los Angeles (90045-1556)
PHONE..................310 586-1017
Kristin Paglia, *Exec Dir*
Amy Shario, *Exec Dir*
Lora Cawelti, *Program Mgr*
Kristen Paglia, *General Mgr*
Jen Garratt, *Director*
EMP: 50
SALES: 3.7MM **Privately Held**
WEB: www.psarts.org
SIC: 8748 Educational consultant

(P-27830)
QUADRIX INFORMATION TECH INC
Also Called: Quadrixit
10736 Jefferson Blvd # 132, Culver City (90230-4933)
PHONE..................424 603-2140
Joseph Gutwirth, *CEO*
Naida Gutwirth, *COO*
Dennis Rojas, *Exec VP*
EMP: 50 EST: 2010
SALES (est): 2.1MM **Privately Held**
SIC: 8748 7379 Systems engineering consultant, ex. computer or professional; computer related consulting services

(P-27831)
QUALITYLOGIC INC (PA)
2245 1st St Ste 103, Simi Valley (93065-0904)
PHONE..................805 531-9030
Dave Jollota, *CEO*
Gary James, *CEO*
Steve Butterfield, *Principal*
Bill Campbell, *Principal*
James Mater, *Principal*
EMP: 120
SALES: 10MM **Privately Held**
WEB: www.qualitylogic.com
SIC: 8748 7372 Testing services; application computer software

(P-27832)
QUOVA INC
401 Castro St Fl 3, Mountain View (94041-2089)
PHONE..................650 965-2898
Marie Alexander, *President*
Gary P Jackson, *COO*
Jean-Louis Casabonne, *CFO*
EMP: 60
SQ FT: 10,000
SALES: 4.2MM
SALES (corp-wide): 119MM **Privately Held**
WEB: www.quova.com
SIC: 8748 Business consulting

HQ: Neustar, Inc.
21575 Ridgetop Cir
Sterling VA 20166
571 434-5400

(P-27833)
QUOVERA INC (PA)
788 Stone Ln, Palo Alto (94303-4413)
PHONE..................650 691-0114
Austin R Erlich, *CEO*
Metin Gokcen, *Vice Pres*
Guy Wilnai, *Vice Pres*
EMP: 150
SQ FT: 8,000
SALES (est): 10.6MM **Privately Held**
WEB: www.quovera.com
SIC: 8748 Systems analysis & engineering consulting services

(P-27834)
QUOVERA INC
19800 Macarthur Blvd, Irvine (92612-2421)
PHONE..................949 224-3825
Hector Rodriguez, *Branch Mgr*
EMP: 50 **Privately Held**
WEB: www.quovera.com
SIC: 8748 Business consulting
PA: Quovera, Inc
788 Stone Ln
Palo Alto CA 94303

(P-27835)
RAMBOLL ENVIRON US CORPORATION
2200 Powell St Ste 700, Emeryville (94608-1877)
PHONE..................510 655-7400
Douglas Daugherty, *Manager*
EMP: 70
SALES (corp-wide): 314.9MM **Privately Held**
WEB: www.environcorp.com
SIC: 8748 Environmental consultant
HQ: Ramboll Us Corporation
4350 Fairfax Dr Ste 300
Arlington VA 22203
703 516-2300

(P-27836)
RAMBOLL ENVIRON US CORPORATION
Also Called: Ramboll Environment & Health
5 Park Plz Ste 500, Irvine (92614-8525)
PHONE..................949 261-5151
George Linkletter, *Manager*
EMP: 65
SALES (corp-wide): 314.9MM **Privately Held**
WEB: www.environcorp.com
SIC: 8748 8711 Environmental consultant; pollution control engineering
HQ: Ramboll Us Corporation
4350 Fairfax Dr Ste 300
Arlington VA 22203
703 516-2300

(P-27837)
RANGE GENERATION NEXT LLC
Also Called: Rgnext
Pillar Point Air Sta, El Granada (94018)
PHONE..................310 647-9438
Tom Kennedy, *CEO*
Donna Mc Cullough, *Manager*
EMP: 50
SQ FT: 100
SALES (est): 2.5MM **Privately Held**
SIC: 8748 Systems analysis or design

(P-27838)
RAPID PRODUCT DEV GROUP INC
300 W Grand Ave, Escondido (92025-2659)
PHONE..................760 703-5770
Tony Moran, *CEO*
EMP: 110
SALES (est): 5.4MM **Privately Held**
WEB: www.rpdg.com
SIC: 8748 Business consulting

(P-27839)
RECON ENVIRONMENTAL INC (PA)
1927 5th Ave Ste 200, San Diego (92101-2357)
PHONE..................619 308-9333
Charles Bull, *Ch of Bd*
Robert Macaller, *President*
Diane Pearson Bull, *CFO*
Paul Fromer, *Vice Pres*
Roberta Herdes, *Vice Pres*
EMP: 100
SQ FT: 18,500
SALES (est): 21.9MM **Privately Held**
WEB: www.recon-us.com
SIC: 8748 Environmental consultant

(P-27840)
REDEVELOPMENT AGENCY OF THE CI
Also Called: SUISUN REDEVELOPMENT AGENCY
701 Civic Center Blvd, Suisun City (94585-2617)
PHONE..................707 421-7309
Suzanne Bragdon, *Manager*
Pete Sanchez, *Mayor*
Jason Garben, *Director*
EMP: 68
SALES: 12.6MM **Privately Held**
SIC: 8748 Urban planning & consulting services

(P-27841)
REGENESIS BIOREMEDIATION PDTS (PA)
1011 Calle Sombra, San Clemente (92673-4204)
PHONE..................949 366-8000
Scott B Wilson, *President*
Christopher Graham, *CFO*
Gavin Herbert Jr, *Chairman*
Rick Gillespie, *Vice Pres*
Craig Sandefur, *Vice Pres*
EMP: 50
SQ FT: 15,000
SALES: 24.3MM **Privately Held**
SIC: 8748 Environmental consultant

(P-27842)
RESOLUTION ECONOMICS GROUP LLC (PA)
1925 Century Park E Fl 15, Los Angeles (90067-2701)
PHONE..................310 275-9137
Trevor Sturges, *CFO*
Ali Leeman, *Managing Prtnr*
EMP: 54 EST: 2011
SALES (est): 2.8MM **Privately Held**
SIC: 8748 Economic consultant

(P-27843)
RETAIL SERVICES & SYSTEMS INC
2765 E Bidwell St, Folsom (95630-6405)
PHONE..................916 984-6923
EMP: 78
SALES (corp-wide): 794MM **Privately Held**
SIC: 8748 5921 Business consulting; wine
PA: Retail Services & Systems, Inc.
6600 Rockledge Dr Ste 150
Bethesda MD 20817
301 795-1000

(P-27844)
RETAIL SERVICES & SYSTEMS INC
394 N Moorpark Rd, Thousand Oaks (91360-4303)
PHONE..................805 494-0108
Bill Mazal, *Branch Mgr*
EMP: 78
SALES (corp-wide): 794MM **Privately Held**
SIC: 8748 5921 Business consulting; wine
PA: Retail Services & Systems, Inc.
6600 Rockledge Dr Ste 150
Bethesda MD 20817
301 795-1000

(P-27845)
ROI COMMUNICATIONS INC (PA)
5274 Scotts Valley Dr # 107, Scotts Valley (95066-3538)
PHONE..................831 430-0170
Barbara Fagan Smith, *President*
Charlie Wrench, *President*
Sheryl Lewis, *COO*
Joann Webster, *Officer*
Janice Collins, *Vice Pres*
EMP: 56
SALES (est): 9MM **Privately Held**
WEB: www.roico.com
SIC: 8748 Communications consulting

(P-27846)
ROSE INTERNATIONAL INC
4000 Executive Pkwy # 150, San Ramon (94583-4314)
PHONE..................636 812-4000
Mary Coats, *Branch Mgr*
Simon Ghimire, *Tech Recruiter*
Samar Singh, *Tech Recruiter*
EMP: 200 **Privately Held**
SIC: 8748 7371 7363 7361 Systems engineering consultant, ex. computer or professional; computer software development; help supply services; employment agencies
PA: Rose International, Inc.
16401 Swingley Ridge Rd
Chesterfield MO 63017

(P-27847)
ROSE INTERNATIONAL INC
18952 Macarthur Blvd # 440, Irvine (92612-1402)
PHONE..................636 812-4000
Jonnie Gray, *Branch Mgr*
EMP: 50 **Privately Held**
SIC: 8748 7371 7363 7361 Systems engineering consultant, ex. computer or professional; computer software development; help supply services; employment agencies
PA: Rose International, Inc.
16401 Swingley Ridge Rd
Chesterfield MO 63017

(P-27848)
ROUX ASSOCIATES INC
5150 E Pacific Coast Hwy # 450, Long Beach (90804-3328)
PHONE..................562 446-8600
Wai Kwan, *President*
EMP: 51
SALES (corp-wide): 85MM **Privately Held**
SIC: 8748 Environmental consultant
PA: Roux Associates, Inc.
209 Shafter St
Islandia NY 11749
631 232-2600

(P-27849)
S R I C B I
333 Ravenswood Ave, Menlo Park (94025-3453)
PHONE..................650 859-4865
William Guns, *President*
William Rolston, *CFO*
EMP: 70
SALES: 9MM **Privately Held**
SIC: 8748 Business consulting

(P-27850)
SA PHOTONICS INC
120 Knowles Dr, Los Gatos (95032-1828)
PHONE..................408 560-3500
James Coward, *President*
Dave Pechner, *Officer*
Andrea Singewald, *Officer*
Rick Streeter, *Program Mgr*
Toan Nguyen, *Admin Mgr*
EMP: 51
SQ FT: 30,000
SALES (est): 7.5MM **Privately Held**
WEB: www.saphotonics.com
SIC: 8748 Business consulting

▲ = Import ▼=Export
◆ =Import/Export

(P-27851)
SACRAMNTO MTRO A QULTY MGT DST
777 12th St Ste 300, Sacramento (95814-1928)
PHONE..................................916 874-4800
Larry Greene, *Exec Dir*
Dave Grose, *Division Mgr*
Tim Taylor, *Division Mgr*
Brigette Tollstrup, *Division Mgr*
Donald Dumaine, *Technical Staff*
EMP: 82
SALES (est): 12MM **Privately Held**
SIC: 8748 Environmental consultant

(P-27852)
SAN DIEGO COMMUNITY HSING CORP
230 Catania St, San Diego (92113-1864)
PHONE..................................619 527-4633
Garl Vaughn, *CEO*
John Piper, *CFO*
EMP: 250
SQ FT: 2,200
SALES (est): 1.2MM **Privately Held**
SIC: 8748 Urban planning & consulting services

(P-27853)
SAN JOAQUIN VAL UNI AIR POL (PA)
Also Called: Valley Air District
1990 E Gettysburg Ave, Fresno (93726-0244)
PHONE..................................559 230-6000
Seyed Sadredin, *Exec Dir*
Theresa Haywood, *Office Admin*
David Lee, *Programmer Anys*
Seng Lee, *Programmer Anys*
Carlos Garcia, *Technology*
EMP: 200
SQ FT: 60,000
SALES (est): 24.7MM **Privately Held**
SIC: 8748 Environmental consultant

(P-27854)
SAN JOAQUIN VAL UNI AIR POL
Also Called: Southern Regional Office
2700 M St Ste 275, Bakersfield (93301-2373)
PHONE..................................209 497-1000
Linda Phillips, *Manager*
EMP: 56 **Privately Held**
SIC: 8748 Environmental consultant
PA: San Joaquin Valley Unified Air Pollution Control District
1990 E Gettysburg Ave
Fresno CA 93726

(P-27855)
SAN JOAQUIN VALLEY A P C D
Also Called: Air Polution Control District
1990 E Gettysburg Ave, Fresno (93726-0244)
PHONE..................................559 230-6000
David L Crow, *Director*
Steve Shaw, *Executive*
Alex Krivobok, *Administration*
Bryan Wong, *Administration*
Adriana Myovich, *Teacher*
EMP: 100
SALES (est): 6.7MM **Privately Held**
SIC: 8748 Environmental consultant

(P-27856)
SAN JOSE REDEVELOPMENT AGENCY
200 E Santa Clara St 14th, San Jose (95113-1903)
PHONE..................................408 535-8500
Harry Mavrogenes, *Exec Dir*
Julie Amato, *Officer*
John Wise, *Deputy Dir*
EMP: 140
SQ FT: 10,045
SALES (est): 7.8MM **Privately Held**
WEB: www.sjredevelopment.org
SIC: 8748 Urban planning & consulting services
PA: City Of San Jose
200 E Santa Clara St
San Jose CA 95113
408 535-3500

(P-27857)
SEALASKA ENVMTL SVCS LLC
3838 Camino Del Rio N # 240, San Diego (92108-1741)
PHONE..................................619 564-8329
Derik Frederiksen,
EMP: 65
SALES (est): 2.5MM
SALES (corp-wide): 293.3MM **Privately Held**
SIC: 8748 4959 Environmental consultant; environmental cleanup services
PA: Sealaska Corporation
1 Sealaska Plz Ste 400
Juneau AK 99801
907 586-1512

(P-27858)
SENSITY SYSTEMS INC (HQ)
1237 E Arques Ave, Sunnyvale (94085-4701)
PHONE..................................408 841-4200
Hugh Martin, *CEO*
Sean Harrington, *COO*
Phil Rehkemper, *CFO*
Scott Shipman,
Geoff Arnold, *CTO*
EMP: 58
SALES (est): 19MM
SALES (corp-wide): 126B **Publicly Held**
SIC: 8748 Lighting consultant
PA: Verizon Communications Inc.
1095 Ave Of The Americas
New York NY 10036
212 395-1000

(P-27859)
SIGNATURE CONSULTANTS LLC
8560 W Sunset Blvd, Los Angeles (90069-2311)
PHONE..................................310 229-5731
EMP: 90 **Privately Held**
SIC: 8748 Business consulting
PA: Signature Consultants Llc
200 W Cypress Creek Rd # 400
Fort Lauderdale FL 33309

(P-27860)
SILICON VALLEY EXEC NETWRK
1336 Nelson Way, Sunnyvale (94087-3135)
PHONE..................................408 746-5803
Brian Reynard, *CEO*
EMP: 901
SALES (est): 16.4MM **Privately Held**
SIC: 8748 Business consulting

(P-27861)
SILV COMMUNICATION INC
3460 Wilshire Blvd # 1100, Los Angeles (90010-2206)
PHONE..................................213 381-7999
John Shaikh, *President*
Sk Golam Ahia, *Vice Pres*
EMP: 56
SQ FT: 7,500
SALES: 8MM **Privately Held**
SIC: 8748 Telecommunications consultant

(P-27862)
SMART SOFTWARE TSTG SOLUTIONS
2450 Peralta Blvd Ste 202, Fremont (94536-3826)
PHONE..................................833 778-7872
Pankaj Goel, *CEO*
EMP: 60 **EST:** 2016
SALES (est): 895.4K **Privately Held**
SIC: 8748 7371 Testing services; computer software development & applications

(P-27863)
SOLUGENIX CORPORATION (PA)
601 Valencia Ave, Brea (92823-6358)
PHONE..................................866 749-7658
Shashi Jasthi, *CEO*
Suneetha Menon, *COO*
Damola Akinola, *Vice Pres*
Michael Bradish, *Business Dir*
Crystal A Kolosick, *Executive Asst*
EMP: 56
SQ FT: 1,600

SALES (est): 42.8MM **Privately Held**
WEB: www.solugenix.com
SIC: 8748 Telecommunications consultant

(P-27864)
SOLVE HEALTHCARE CORPORATION (PA)
1300 Bristol St N Ste 285, Newport Beach (92660-8902)
PHONE..................................949 891-0300
Sheel Mehta, *President*
Sajjad Khan, *Officer*
Mary Elliott, *Consultant*
EMP: 75
SALES (est): 4.2MM **Privately Held**
SIC: 8748 Business consulting

(P-27865)
SONOMA TECHNOLOGY INC
1450 N Mcdowell Blvd, Petaluma (94954-6515)
PHONE..................................707 665-9900
Lyle R Chinkin, *President*
Fred Lurmann, *Chairman*
Barbara A Austin, *Exec VP*
Paul T Roberts, *Exec VP*
Timothy S Dye, *Senior VP*
EMP: 65
SQ FT: 29,011
SALES: 9.9MM **Privately Held**
WEB: www.sonomatech.com
SIC: 8748 Environmental consultant

(P-27866)
SOURCE 44 LLC
Also Called: Source Intelligence
1921 Palomar Oaks Way # 205, Carlsbad (92008-6523)
PHONE..................................877 916-6337
Jess F Kraus, *CEO*
Matt Thorn, *COO*
Dan Dague, *Officer*
Alex Eng, *Officer*
Jennifer Kraus, *Officer*
EMP: 111
SALES (est): 10.1MM **Privately Held**
SIC: 8748 7371 Business consulting; computer software development

(P-27867)
SOUTH CAPITOL COTTAGE
15054 Daisy Rd, Adelanto (92301-4824)
PHONE..................................951 662-3026
Carol James, *Exec Dir*
Felica Taylor, *President*
Dorothy Shorter, *CFO*
Emma Nash, *Exec VP*
Theodore Nash, *Vice Pres*
EMP: 80
SALES: 450K **Privately Held**
SIC: 8748 Urban planning & consulting services

(P-27868)
SOUTH COAST AIR QULTY MGT DST (PA)
Also Called: A Q M D
21865 Copley Dr, Diamond Bar (91765-4178)
P.O. Box 4940 (91765-0940)
PHONE..................................909 396-2000
Raymond E Robinson, *CEO*
Marcia Crane, *President*
Rebecca Garcia, *President*
Jo Ghosh, *Officer*
Michael O'Kelly, *Officer*
EMP: 780 **EST:** 1955
SQ FT: 350
SALES (est): 98.4MM **Privately Held**
SIC: 8748 Environmental consultant

(P-27869)
SPECTRUM SERVICES GROUP INC
4600 Northgate Blvd # 120, Sacramento (95834-1159)
PHONE..................................916 760-7913
Tasawwar Ali, *CEO*
Shane Ali, *President*
Shannon Dawson, *Info Tech Mgr*
Hasnain Ali, *Project Mgr*
Janet Berry, *Sls & Mktg Exec*
EMP: 85
SQ FT: 2,000

SALES (est): 12.3MM **Privately Held**
SIC: 8748 8744 8741 Business consulting; facilities support services; construction management

(P-27870)
SPRINGBOARD SOLUTIONS LLC
Also Called: CREDIT.ORG
4351 Latham St, Riverside (92501-1749)
PHONE..................................951 779-7739
Todd Emerson, *Principal*
Al Nemerofsky, *Administration*
EMP: 150
SALES: 15.9MM
SALES (corp-wide): 24.5MM **Privately Held**
SIC: 8748 Business consulting
PA: Springboard Nonprofit Consumer Credit Management, Inc.
4351 Latham St
Riverside CA 92501
951 781-0114

(P-27871)
SUCCESSOR TO SAN FRANCISCO
Also Called: Office Cmnty Inv Infrstructure
1 S Van Ness Ave Fl 5, San Francisco (94103-5416)
PHONE..................................415 749-2400
Marcia Rosen, *Principal*
Tiffany Bohee, *Exec Dir*
Annie Wong, *Manager*
Don Rice, *Accounts Mgr*
EMP: 99
SALES (est): 5.5MM **Privately Held**
SIC: 8748 Economic consultant

(P-27872)
SWCA INCORPORATED
Also Called: Swca Environmental Consultants
51 W Dayton St Ste 100, Pasadena (91105-2025)
PHONE..................................626 240-0587
Cara Corsetti, *Branch Mgr*
EMP: 89
SALES (corp-wide): 162.7MM **Privately Held**
WEB: www.swca.com
SIC: 8748 8733 Environmental consultant; archeological expeditions
PA: Swca, Incorporated
20 E Thomas Rd Ste 1700
Phoenix AZ 85012
602 274-3831

(P-27873)
SYNAGRO WEST LLC
1499 Bayshore Hwy Ste 111, Burlingame (94010-1723)
PHONE..................................650 652-6531
EMP: 99
SALES: 950K
SALES (corp-wide): 43.6K **Privately Held**
SIC: 8748
HQ: Synagro Technologies, Inc.
435 Williams Ct Ste 100
Baltimore MD 21220

(P-27874)
SYPARTNERS LLC (HQ)
475 Brannan St Ste 100, San Francisco (94107-5419)
PHONE..................................415 536-6600
Susan Schuman, *CEO*
Nancy Hawley, *Vice Pres*
Mickey Stretton, *Creative Dir*
Jarin Tabata, *Creative Dir*
Jessica Tillyer, *Creative Dir*
EMP: 73
SALES (est): 21.6MM
SALES (corp-wide): 12.5B **Privately Held**
WEB: www.sypartners.com
SIC: 8748 Business consulting
PA: Hakuhodo Dy Holdings Incorporated
5-3-1, Akasaka
Minato-Ku TKY 107-0
364 419-033

(P-27875)
T-FORCE INC (PA)
4695 Macarthur Ct, Newport Beach (92660-1882)
PHONE..................................949 208-1527
Raid Al-Khawaldeh, *President*

Peter Nguyen, *Vice Pres*
Ala Alhajali, *Branch Mgr*
EMP: 98
SALES (est): 8.1MM **Privately Held**
WEB: www.t-force.com
SIC: 8748 7379 Telecommunications consultant;

(P-27876)
TAHOE TRCKE UNFD SCH DIS FINCN
Also Called: Truckee High School
11725 Donner Past Rd, Truckee (96160)
PHONE...................530 582-7630
John Carlson, *Principal*
Trent Kirschner, *Teacher*
EMP: 73
SALES (est): 3.6MM
SALES (corp-wide): 63.1MM **Privately Held**
WEB: www.ttusd.k12.ca.us
SIC: 8748 8211 Business consulting; public senior high school
PA: Tahoe Truckee Unified School District Financing Corporation
11603 Donner Pass Rd
Truckee CA 96161
530 582-2500

(P-27877)
TEAM RISK MGT STRATEGIES LLC
Also Called: Trust Employee ADM & MGT
3131 Camino Del Rio N # 650, San Diego (92108-5751)
PHONE...................877 767-8728
Terence J Keating, *President*
Arthur D Candland, *CFO*
Cheryl Doss, *Vice Pres*
Susanne Schellpeper, *Payroll Mgr*
Sharon Novak, *Human Resources*
EMP: 2500
SALES (est): 98.4MM **Privately Held**
SIC: 8748 Employee programs administration

(P-27878)
TELECOM TECHNOLOGY SVCS INC
Also Called: Tts
7901 Stoneridge Dr # 500, Pleasanton (94588-3969)
PHONE...................925 224-7812
Lin Weng, *CEO*
EMP: 130
SQ FT: 7,102
SALES (est): 18.3MM **Privately Held**
WEB: www.ttswireless.com
SIC: 8748 Telecommunications consultant

(P-27879)
TEMPEST TELECOM SOLUTIONS LLC (PA)
136 W Canon Perdido St # 100, Santa Barbara (93101-3242)
PHONE...................805 879-4800
Jessica Firestone, *CEO*
Dan Firestone, *COO*
Julie Lubin, *CFO*
Richard Smith, *Vice Pres*
Ellen Cole, *Admin Asst*
EMP: 60
SQ FT: 9,000
SALES (est): 42.4MM **Privately Held**
WEB: www.tempesttelecom.com
SIC: 8748 Systems analysis & engineering consulting services; telecommunications consultant

(P-27880)
TETRA TECH INC
3201 Airpark Dr Ste 108, Santa Maria (93455-1834)
PHONE...................805 739-2600
Jeff Matthew, *Branch Mgr*
EMP: 63
SALES (corp-wide): 2.7B **Publicly Held**
WEB: www.tetratech.com
SIC: 8748 Environmental consultant
PA: Tetra Tech, Inc.
3475 E Foothill Blvd
Pasadena CA 91107
626 351-4664

(P-27881)
TETRA TECH EC INC
1230 Columbia St Ste 750, San Diego (92101-8536)
PHONE...................619 234-8690
Andy Bolt, *Branch Mgr*
EMP: 67
SALES (corp-wide): 2.7B **Publicly Held**
SIC: 8748 Testing services
HQ: Tetra Tech Ec, Inc.
6 Century Dr Ste 3
Parsippany NJ 07054
973 630-8000

(P-27882)
TETRA TECH EC INC
2969 Prospect Park Dr # 100, Rancho Cordova (95670-6187)
PHONE...................916 852-8300
Anh Nghiem, *Manager*
EMP: 1000
SALES (corp-wide): 2.7B **Publicly Held**
SIC: 8748 Environmental consultant
HQ: Tetra Tech Ec, Inc.
6 Century Dr Ste 3
Parsippany NJ 07054
973 630-8000

(P-27883)
TETRA TECH NUS INC
3475 E Foothill Blvd, Pasadena (91107-6024)
PHONE...................412 921-7090
Dan L Batrack, *CEO*
Steven M Burdick, *Exec VP*
John Trepanowski, *Vice Pres*
Ronald Chu, *Principal*
Janet Mandel, *Director*
EMP: 100
SALES (est): 5.4MM
SALES (corp-wide): 2.7B **Publicly Held**
WEB: www.ttnus.com
SIC: 8748 Environmental consultant
PA: Tetra Tech, Inc.
3475 E Foothill Blvd
Pasadena CA 91107
626 351-4664

(P-27884)
THOMSON REUTERS (LEGAL) INC
2440 W El Camino Real, Mountain View (94040-1497)
PHONE...................650 210-1900
Steve Robinson, *Manager*
EMP: 100 **Privately Held**
SIC: 8748 Business consulting
HQ: Thomson Reuters (Legal) Inc.
610 Opperman Dr
Eagan MN 55123
651 687-7000

(P-27885)
THOMSON REUTERS (LEGAL) INC
50 California St Ste 200, San Francisco (94111-4605)
PHONE...................415 344-6000
Heather Cameron, *Manager*
EMP: 100 **Privately Held**
SIC: 8748 Business consulting
HQ: Thomson Reuters (Legal) Inc.
610 Opperman Dr
Eagan MN 55123
651 687-7000

(P-27886)
TM FINANCIAL FORENSICS LLC (PA)
2 Embarcadero Ctr # 2510, San Francisco (94111-3924)
PHONE...................415 692-6350
Paul Meyer, *President*
Jeff Colditz, *Vice Pres*
Brian Hammer, *Vice Pres*
John Hansen, *Vice Pres*
Angela Izuel, *Vice Pres*
EMP: 50 **EST:** 2009
SALES (est): 10.4MM **Privately Held**
SIC: 8748 Communications consulting

(P-27887)
TOTAL EDUCATION SOLUTIONS INC (PA)
625 Fair Oaks Ave Ste 300, South Pasadena (91030-5805)
PHONE...................323 341-5580
Nancy Lavelle, *President*
Piero Stillitano, *CFO*
Meaghan Donahue, *Vice Pres*
Dana Rivera, *Program Mgr*
Lynne Porter, *Regional Mgr*
EMP: 593
SALES (est): 56MM **Privately Held**
SIC: 8748 Educational consultant

(P-27888)
TRC SOLUTIONS INC (DH)
Also Called: Alton Geoscience
9685 Research Dr Ste 100, Irvine (92618-4657)
PHONE...................949 753-0101
Christopher P Vincze, *Ch of Bd*
Thomas W Bennet Jr, *CFO*
EMP: 125
SQ FT: 47,000
SALES (est): 31MM
SALES (corp-wide): 165.4MM **Privately Held**
WEB: www.trcsolutions.com
SIC: 8748 8711 Environmental consultant; engineering services
HQ: Trc Companies, Inc.
650 Suffolk St
Lowell MA 01854
978 970-5600

(P-27889)
TRILLIANT INCORPORATED
1100 Island Dr Ste 201, Redwood City (94065-5187)
PHONE...................650 204-5050
Andy White, *President*
Salim Khan, *COO*
Bob Habig, *CFO*
Juan Otero, *Admin Sec*
Mimish Mehta, *VP Finance*
EMP: 93
SALES (est): 17.6MM **Privately Held**
SIC: 8748 Environmental consultant

(P-27890)
TRIMARK OPERATIONS CENTER
2365 Iron Point Rd # 100, Folsom (95630-8711)
PHONE...................916 357-5970
Mark J Morosky, *President*
Dean Schoeder, *COO*
Bob Wood, *CTO*
Robert Hinchman, *Director*
EMP: 53 **EST:** 2000
SQ FT: 108,000
SALES (est): 10.5MM **Privately Held**
WEB: www.trimarkmdma.com
SIC: 8748 Energy conservation consultant

(P-27891)
TRIPLE HS INC (PA)
Also Called: H. T. Harvey & Associates
983 University Ave Bldg D, Los Gatos (95032-7637)
PHONE...................408 458-3200
Karin Hunsicker, *CEO*
Ronald R Duke, *President*
Cynthia Pollard Bell, *Controller*
David Ainley, *Chief*
Patrick Reynolds, *Associate*
EMP: 98 **EST:** 1971
SQ FT: 15,000
SALES (est): 9.2MM **Privately Held**
WEB: www.harveyecology.com
SIC: 8748 8731 Environmental consultant; environmental research

(P-27892)
UNIVERSAL NETWORK DEV CORP (PA)
Also Called: Undc
2555 3rd St Ste 112, Sacramento (95818-1100)
PHONE...................916 475-1200
Cinthia Larkin Kazee, *President*
EMP: 97
SQ FT: 1,600

SALES (est): 11.4MM **Privately Held**
WEB: www.undc.com
SIC: 8748 8711 Communications consulting; telecommunications consultant; professional engineer

(P-27893)
VALLE SANIT AND FLOOD CONTR DI
450 Ryder St, Vallejo (94590-7217)
PHONE...................707 644-8949
Melissa Morton, *CEO*
Mary A Morris, *CFO*
Ron Matheson, *District Mgr*
Holly M Charlety, *Admin Sec*
Jason Kaduk, *Info Tech Mgr*
EMP: 86 **EST:** 1952
SQ FT: 10,000
SALES: 27.9MM **Privately Held**
WEB: www.vsfcd.com
SIC: 8748 Environmental consultant; traffic consultant; economic consultant

(P-27894)
VENCORE INC
2750 Womble Rd Ste 202, San Diego (92106-6114)
PHONE...................571 313-6000
John Curtis, *CEO*
Stephen Costalas, *Senior VP*
Jennifer Felix, *Senior VP*
David Papas, *Senior VP*
Frank Anstett, *Vice Pres*
EMP: 50
SQ FT: 10,000
SALES (est): 1.1MM **Privately Held**
SIC: 8748 7373 Systems analysis & engineering consulting services; systems engineering, computer related

(P-27895)
VENUE MANAGEMENT SERVICES INC
500 N 1st Ave Ste 4, Arcadia (91006-2898)
PHONE...................626 445-6000
Charles E McIntyre, *President*
EMP: 280
SALES (est): 6.8MM **Privately Held**
WEB: www.venueservices.com
SIC: 8748 Business consulting

(P-27896)
VERIDIAM ALLIED SWISS
4645 North Ave, Oceanside (92056-3593)
PHONE...................760 941-1702
Thomas Cresante, *Owner*
EMP: 53
SALES (est): 3.4MM
SALES (corp-wide): 143.6MM **Privately Held**
WEB: www.veridiam.com
SIC: 8748 Business consulting
HQ: Veridiam, Inc.
1717 N Cuyamaca St
El Cajon CA 92020
619 448-1000

(P-27897)
VERIZON COMMUNICATIONS INC
180 N Mirage Ave, Lindsay (93247-2538)
PHONE...................559 562-0000
Seiden Berg, *Manager*
EMP: 53
SALES (corp-wide): 126B **Publicly Held**
WEB: www.gte.com
SIC: 8748 Telecommunications consultant
PA: Verizon Communications Inc.
1095 Ave Of The Americas
New York NY 10036
212 395-1000

(P-27898)
VETERANS AFFAIRS CAL DEPT
Also Called: Veterans Affairs Testing Off
1227 O St Ste 105, Sacramento (95814-5891)
PHONE...................916 653-2535
Karen Escobar, *Director*
EMP: 347 **Privately Held**
WEB: www.californiachronicle.com
SIC: 8748 9451 Testing services; administration of veterans' affairs;

HQ: California Department Of Veterans Affairs
1227 O St Ste 105
Sacramento CA 95814
800 952-5626

(P-27899)
VETERANS EZ INFO INC
1901 1st Ave Ste 192, San Diego (92101-2356)
PHONE.............................866 839-1329
James Miner, *Ch of Bd*
Phonprapha Miner, *Senior VP*
EMP: 138
SQ FT: 1,200
SALES: 24MM **Privately Held**
SIC: 8748 Business consulting

(P-27900)
VILLA REAL INC
421 S El Dorado St Ste D1, Stockton (95203-3459)
P.O. Box 447 (95201-0447)
PHONE.............................209 460-5069
Greg Arnaudo, *Ch of Bd*
EMP: 100
SALES: 41.9K **Privately Held**
SIC: 8748 Urban planning & consulting services

(P-27901)
VIMO INC (PA)
Also Called: Getinsured.com
1305 Terra Bella Ave, Mountain View (94043-1851)
PHONE.............................650 618-4600
Srinivasan Krishnan, *CEO*
Paul Neutz, *President*
Shankar Srinivasan, *COO*
Krzysztof Kujawa, *Vice Pres*
Scott Osler, *Vice Pres*
EMP: 84
SQ FT: 20,000
SALES (est): 27.3MM **Privately Held**
WEB: www.vimo.com
SIC: 8748 6411 7371 7373 Business consulting; insurance brokers; computer software development & applications; systems software development services

(P-27902)
VINCULUMS SERVICES INC
10 Pasteur Ste 100, Irvine (92618-3823)
PHONE.............................949 783-3552
Paul Foster, *CEO*
Brian Woodward, *COO*
Norm Alexander, *CFO*
Bart Van Aardenne, *Chairman*
Cindy Holbrook, *Program Mgr*
EMP: 220 **EST:** 2005
SQ FT: 8,000
SALES (est): 39.1MM **Privately Held**
SIC: 8748 Telecommunications consultant

(P-27903)
VOLT TELECOM GROUP INC
Also Called: Volt Telecom Group
218 Helicopter Cir, Corona (92880-2531)
PHONE.............................800 548-6602
Frank Dalessio, *CEO*
EMP: 50
SALES (corp-wide): 24.3MM **Privately Held**
SIC: 8748 Telecommunications consultant
PA: Volt Telecommunications Group, Inc.
560 Lexington Ave Fl 14
New York NY 10022
212 704-2400

(P-27904)
VOLT TELECOM GROUP INC
Also Called: Volt Telecom Group
218 Helicopter Cir, Corona (92880-2531)
PHONE.............................951 493-8900
Frank D'Alessio, *CEO*
Kingsley H Nelson, *Principal*
EMP: 250
SALES (corp-wide): 24.3MM **Privately Held**
SIC: 8748 Telecommunications consultant
PA: Volt Telecommunications Group, Inc.
560 Lexington Ave Fl 14
New York NY 10022
212 704-2400

(P-27905)
VOX NETWORK SOLUTIONS INC
8000 Marina Blvd Ste 130, Brisbane (94005-1882)
PHONE.............................650 989-1000
Scott Landis, *Ch of Bd*
Nick Kolintzas, *Vice Pres*
Aileen Meraz, *Vice Pres*
Elaine Flores, *Sr Software Eng*
David Waybright, *Project Mgr*
EMP: 150
SQ FT: 3,904
SALES: 44.9MM **Privately Held**
WEB: www.voxnetworksolutions.com
SIC: 8748 3661 Telecommunications consultant; switching equipment, telephone; telephone central office equipment, dial or manual; telephone sets, all types except cellular radio

(P-27906)
VSC SPORTS INC
Also Called: Yorba Bena Ice Skting Bowl Ctr
750 Folsom St, San Francisco (94107-1276)
PHONE.............................415 820-3525
Michael Paikin, *Owner*
EMP: 60
SALES (corp-wide): 4.8MM **Privately Held**
WEB: www.vscsports.com
SIC: 8748 Business consulting
PA: Vsc Sports Inc
14909 Magnolia Blvd # 202
Sherman Oaks CA 91403
818 994-3229

(P-27907)
W CORPORATION
Also Called: Vantage Company
1643 W Orange Grove Ave, Orange (92868-1116)
PHONE.............................714 532-8800
Kenneth Watkins, *President*
Marvin Anderson, *CFO*
Tony Watterson, *General Mgr*
Chris Hernandez, *Manager*
EMP: 120 **EST:** 2001
SALES: 24.5MM **Privately Held**
SIC: 8748 1542 1522 Telecommunications consultant; commercial & office building, new construction; residential construction

(P-27908)
WARNER BROS CONSUMER PDTS INC (DH)
4001 W Olive Ave, Burbank (91505-4272)
PHONE.............................818 954-7980
Brad Globe, *President*
Dan Romanelli, *President*
Randy Blotky, *Senior VP*
Ana De Castro, *Senior VP*
John Schulman, *Admin Sec*
▲ **EMP:** 112
SALES (est): 17.5MM
SALES (corp-wide): 160.5B **Publicly Held**
SIC: 8748 5961 Business consulting; novelty merchandise, mail order
HQ: Warner Bros. Entertainment Inc.
4000 Warner Blvd
Burbank CA 91522
818 954-6000

(P-27909)
WEISSCOMM GROUP LTD (PA)
Also Called: Wcg World
50 Francisco St Ste 400, San Francisco (94133-2114)
PHONE.............................415 362-5018
James Weiss, *CEO*
Paulo Simas, *Managing Prtnr*
Mary Corcoran, *President*
Chris Deri, *President*
Angela Gillespie, *President*
EMP: 75
SQ FT: 16,000
SALES (est): 116.1MM **Privately Held**
WEB: www.wcgworld.com
SIC: 8748 Communications consulting

(P-27910)
WILLIAM S HART PONY & SOFTBALL
Also Called: Wm S Hart Pony & Softball
23437 Valencia Blvd, Valencia (91355-1702)
PHONE.............................661 254-9780
Dave Scripture, *President*
Mike Clare, *Treasurer*
Ken Underwood, *Exec VP*
Paul Silveri, *Admin Sec*
Randy Sreden, *Commissioner*
EMP: 55
SALES (est): 2.3MM **Privately Held**
SIC: 8748 Environmental consultant

(P-27911)
WRIGHT BROADBAND GROUP INC
4413 La Jolla Village Dr, San Diego (92122-1264)
PHONE.............................858 362-0380
Leroy Wright, *President*
EMP: 75
SQ FT: 3,000
SALES: 7MM **Privately Held**
SIC: 8748 Telecommunications consultant

(P-27912)
X3 MANAGEMENT SERVICES INC
2128 Auto Park Way, Escondido (92029-1344)
PHONE.............................760 597-9336
David G Cranford, *CEO*
Arlette Zuniga, *CFO*
Bonnie Pierce, *Controller*
John Dykes, *Opers Staff*
Anthony Kachinsky, *Manager*
EMP: 72
SALES: 6.3MM **Privately Held**
SIC: 8748 1731 1531 1541 Telecommunications consultant; electrical work; fiber optic cable installation; operative builders; industrial buildings & warehouses; solar energy contractor

(P-27913)
YCG LLC
Also Called: You Consulting Group
566 Shanas Ln, Encinitas (92024-2435)
P.O. Box 231423 (92023-1423)
PHONE.............................760 230-8016
David Hackett, *Mng Member*
Dr Zannah Hackett,
EMP: 52
SALES: 250K **Privately Held**
SIC: 8748 Business consulting

(P-27914)
YUCAIPA COMPANIES LLC (PA)
9130 W Sunset Blvd, Los Angeles (90069-3110)
PHONE.............................310 789-7200
Ronald W Burkle, *Mng Member*
Scott Stedman,
EMP: 150
SALES (est): 1.4B **Privately Held**
SIC: 8748 6719 6726 Business consulting; investment holding companies, except banks; investment offices

(P-27915)
ZELOS CONSULTING LLC
2400 Wyandotte St B103, Mountain View (94043-2373)
PHONE.............................650 968-2881
Stephen Chiu,
Poline Chiu,
Tony Quintong,
EMP: 50
SQ FT: 5,000
SALES (est): 3.5MM **Privately Held**
WEB: www.zelos.com
SIC: 8748 Systems analysis & engineering consulting services

8999 Services Not Elsewhere Classified

(P-27916)
ACTIVE LAWYERS REFERRAL SVC
9301 Wilshire Blvd # 508, Beverly Hills (90210-5424)
PHONE.............................310 247-0425
Paul Mehdizadeh, *President*
Vincent Mehdizadeh, *Manager*
EMP: 60
SALES (est): 1.1MM **Privately Held**
SIC: 8999 7299 Information bureau; information services, consumer

(P-27917)
AEROSPACE & MARINE INTL
6910 Santa Teresa Blvd, San Jose (95119-1339)
PHONE.............................408 360-0440
George Carlsgaard, *President*
Paul Xander, *Sr Software Eng*
Victor Kremer, *Technology*
Colin King, *Opers-Prdtn-Mfg*
Frank Bowman, *Sales Executive*
EMP: 50
SALES (est): 1.7MM **Privately Held**
WEB: www.amiwx.com
SIC: 8999 Weather related services

(P-27918)
ANKA BEHAVIORAL HEALTH INC
2507 Evelyn Ave, Rosemead (91770-3070)
PHONE.............................626 573-5902
EMP: 69
SALES (corp-wide): 40.4MM **Privately Held**
SIC: 8999 Actuarial consultant
PA: Anka Behavioral Health, Incorporated
1850 Gateway Blvd Ste 900
Concord CA 94520
925 825-4700

(P-27919)
ASSISTED HOME RECOVERY INC
1900 W Garvey Ave S # 210, West Covina (91790-2656)
PHONE.............................626 915-5595
EMP: 66
SALES (corp-wide): 11.5MM **Privately Held**
SIC: 8999 Artists & artists' studios
PA: Assisted Home Recovery Inc
8550 Balboa Blvd Lbby
Northridge CA 91325
818 894-8117

(P-27920)
ASSOCIATED STUDENTS INC
Also Called: Associated Students, Inc.
1 Grand Ave, San Luis Obispo (93407-9000)
PHONE.............................805 756-1281
Richard Johnson, *Exec Dir*
Dwayne Brummett, *Exec Dir*
EMP: 68
SALES (corp-wide): 12.7MM **Privately Held**
SIC: 8999 Artists & artists' studios
PA: Associated Students Inc Of California Polytechnic State University At San Luis Obispo
University Un Bldg 65
San Luis Obispo CA 93407
805 756-1281

(P-27921)
AT&T CORP
1188 W Evelyn Ave, Sunnyvale (94086-5742)
PHONE.............................650 960-2313
EMP: 68
SALES (corp-wide): 160.5B **Publicly Held**
SIC: 8999 Communication services
HQ: At&T Corp.
1 At&T Way
Bedminster NJ 07921
800 403-3302

(P-27922)
BUCK GLOBAL LLC
1801 Century Park E # 500, Los Angeles
(90067-2302)
PHONE..................................310 282-8232
Harold Love, *Branch Mgr*
EMP: 55
SALES (corp-wide): 600MM **Privately Held**
SIC: 8999 8742 6282 2741 Actuarial consultant; compensation & benefits planning consultant; investment advice; technical papers: publishing only, not printed on site
PA: Buck Global, Llc
420 Lexington Ave Rm 2220
New York NY 10170
212 330-1000

(P-27923)
CALIFORNIA TAHOE CONSERVANCY
1061 3rd St, South Lake Tahoe
(96150-3475)
PHONE..................................530 542-5580
Patrick Wright, *Exec Dir*
Russell Maloney, *Principal*
David Gregorich, *Administration*
EMP: 50
SALES (est): 1.9MM **Privately Held**
SIC: 8999 Natural resource preservation service
HQ: California Natural Resources Agency
1416 9th St Ste 1311
Sacramento CA 95814

(P-27924)
CARDINAL CARTRIDGE INC
20450 Plummer St, Chatsworth
(91311-5372)
PHONE..................................818 727-9740
Dan Ghammachi, *Principal*
EMP: 69
SALES (corp-wide): 45.1MM **Privately Held**
SIC: 8999 Artists & artists' studios
HQ: Cardinal Cartridge, Inc.
20450 Plummer St
Chatsworth CA 91311
775 624-8135

(P-27925)
CONSERVATION LIQUIDATION
100 Pine St Fl 12, San Francisco
(94111-5114)
PHONE..................................415 676-5000
David Wilson, *CEO*
EMP: 75
SALES (est): 2.7MM **Privately Held**
SIC: 8999 Natural resource preservation service

(P-27926)
COUNTY OF SAN MATEO
Also Called: Information Services Dept
455 County Ctr Fl 3, Redwood City
(94063-9728)
PHONE..................................650 363-4548
Jon Walton, *CIO*
EMP: 150 **Privately Held**
WEB: www.ci.sanmateo.ca.us
SIC: 8999 9199 Information bureau;
PA: County Of San Mateo
400 County Ctr
Redwood City CA 94063
650 363-4123

(P-27927)
DATA TRACE INFO SVCS LLC (HQ)
4 First American Way, Santa Ana
(92707-5913)
PHONE..................................714 250-6700
Mike Henney Sr,
Amanda Price, *Vice Pres*
Felix Uy, *Technical Mgr*
Andrea Henney, *Project Mgr*
Donna Schopper, *Client Mgr*
EMP: 100
SALES (est): 8.3MM
SALES (corp-wide): 1.8B **Publicly Held**
SIC: 8999 Information bureau

PA: Corelogic, Inc.
40 Pacifica Ste 900
Irvine CA 92618
949 214-1000

(P-27928)
FORT MASON CENTER
2 Marina Blvd Bldg A, San Francisco
(94123-1284)
PHONE..................................415 345-7500
Caroline Werth, *President*
Jovanne Reilly, *Executive*
Rich Hillis, *Exec Dir*
Matt White, *Technician*
Leanna Louie, *Accountant*
EMP: 56
SQ FT: 300,000
SALES: 8.6MM **Privately Held**
WEB: www.fortmason.org
SIC: 8999 Art related services

(P-27929)
GLOBAL BUILDING SERVICES INC
17618 Murphy Pkwy, Lathrop (95330-8629)
PHONE..................................209 858-9501
EMP: 298
SALES (corp-wide): 37.3MM **Privately Held**
SIC: 8999 Actuarial consultant
PA: Global Building Services, Inc.
25129 The Old Rd Ste 102
Stevenson Ranch CA 91381
661 288-5733

(P-27930)
GOLDEN GATE NAT PRKS CNSRVANCY
Also Called: Golden Gate Nat Prks Cnsrvancy
1600 Los Gamos Dr, San Rafael
(94903-1806)
PHONE..................................415 785-4787
EMP: 86
SALES (corp-wide): 61.5MM **Privately Held**
SIC: 8999 Natural resource preservation service
PA: Golden Gate National Parks Conservancy
Fort Mason Bldg 201
San Francisco CA 94123
415 561-3000

(P-27931)
GOLDEN GATE NAT PRKS CNSRVANCY (PA)
Fort Mason Bldg 201, San Francisco
(94123)
PHONE..................................415 561-3000
Greg Moore, *CEO*
Alison Campbell, *Partner*
Laurie Wetzel, *CFO*
Gordon Ritter, *Treasurer*
Nicolas Elsishans, *Exec VP*
▲ EMP: 70
SQ FT: 5,000
SALES: 61.5MM **Privately Held**
WEB: www.parksconservancy.org
SIC: 8999 Natural resource preservation service

(P-27932)
HEALTHCARE SERVICES GROUP INC
5199 E Pacific Coast Hwy # 402, Long Beach (90804-3309)
PHONE..................................562 494-7939
Mike Hammond, *Principal*
EMP: 5008
SALES (corp-wide): 1.8B **Publicly Held**
SIC: 8999 Artists & artists' studios
PA: Healthcare Services Group Inc
3220 Tillman Dr Ste 300
Bensalem PA 19020
215 639-4274

(P-27933)
INDYME SOLUTIONS LLC
8295 Aero Pl Ste 260, San Diego
(92123-2029)
PHONE..................................858 268-0717
Joe Joseph Eudano, *CEO*
Jack Hetzel, *CFO*
Larry Cleary, *Vice Pres*

Bill Kepner, *Vice Pres*
Jay Standiford, *Vice Pres*
EMP: 50
SQ FT: 18,000
SALES (est): 3.2MM **Privately Held**
SIC: 8999 Communication services

(P-27934)
INTERIM INC
Also Called: Interim Services
339 Pajaro St Ste B, Salinas (93901-3400)
PHONE..................................831 754-3838
Fred Harris, *Branch Mgr*
EMP: 122
SALES (corp-wide): 12.5MM **Privately Held**
SIC: 8999 Personal services
PA: Interim, Inc.
604 Pearl St Frnt
Monterey CA 93940
831 649-4399

(P-27935)
J RIVERA ASSOCIATES INC
Also Called: 4 Su Salud Medical Contact Ctr
139 S Guild Ave, Lodi (95240-0867)
PHONE..................................415 617-5660
Jose R Rivera MPH, *CEO*
EMP: 92
SQ FT: 5,000
SALES: 2MM **Privately Held**
SIC: 8999 Communication services

(P-27936)
JAQUI FOUNDATION INC
675 Hegenberger Rd # 209, Oakland
(94621-1919)
P.O. Box 4938 (94605-6938)
PHONE..................................510 562-4721
Robert L Porter Jr, *CEO*
Dorothy M Jones, *Treasurer*
Dawson Andrews, *Admin Sec*
EMP: 50
SQ FT: 600
SALES: 1.5MM **Privately Held**
WEB: www.jaquifoundation.org
SIC: 8999 Personal services

(P-27937)
KCI ENVIRONMENTAL INC
207 Suburban Rd Ste 6, San Luis Obispo
(93401-7559)
P.O. Box 3307 (93403-3307)
PHONE..................................805 543-3311
Curt Boutwell, *President*
Jim Gorter, *General Mgr*
Ernie Peterson, *Project Mgr*
Kim Nunez, *Controller*
EMP: 50
SALES (est): 2.8MM **Privately Held**
WEB: www.kcienv.com
SIC: 8999 Earth science services

(P-27938)
KINGS RIVER CONSERVATION DST
4886 E Jensen Ave, Fresno (93725-1899)
PHONE..................................559 237-5567
Mark McKean, *President*
Brent Graham, *Vice Pres*
David Orth, *General Mgr*
EMP: 64
SQ FT: 8,500
SALES (est): 6.7MM **Privately Held**
WEB: www.krcd.org
SIC: 8999 Natural resource preservation service

(P-27939)
LUCILE SALTER PACKARD CHIL
725 Welch Rd, Palo Alto (94304-1601)
PHONE..................................650 736-4030
Simone Esson, *Branch Mgr*
EMP: 286
SALES (corp-wide): 1.4B **Privately Held**
SIC: 8999 Artists & artists' studios
PA: Lucile Salter Packard Children's Hospital At Stanford
725 Welch Rd
Palo Alto CA 94304
650 497-8000

(P-27940)
M4 WIND SERVICES INC
4020 Long Beach Blvd Fl 2, Long Beach
(90807-2683)
PHONE..................................562 981-7797
Myles Baker, *President*
Steve Doyle, *Analyst*
Scott Young, *Manager*
EMP: 99
SALES (est): 1.4MM **Privately Held**
SIC: 8999 Artists & artists' studios

(P-27941)
MALKA COMMUNICATIONS GROUP INC
15260 Ventura Blvd, Sherman Oaks
(91403-5307)
PHONE..................................818 239-4431
Nataly Malka, *CEO*
Robert Malka, *COO*
EMP: 50
SQ FT: 1,900
SALES (est): 1.2MM **Privately Held**
SIC: 8999 Communication services

(P-27942)
MAXUS USA
6300 Wilshire Blvd # 720, Los Angeles
(90048-5204)
PHONE..................................323 202-4650
AMA Korankyi, *Supervisor*
Juli Suk, *Supervisor*
EMP: 560
SALES (est): 76K
SALES (corp-wide): 20.1B **Privately Held**
SIC: 8999 Communication services
HQ: Maxus Communications Llc
498 Fashion Ave
New York NY 10018
212 297-8300

(P-27943)
MCCLATCHY COMPANY
2100 Q St, Sacramento (95816-6816)
PHONE..................................916 321-1941
EMP: 10000
SALES (est): 72.8K **Privately Held**
SIC: 8999

(P-27944)
MGM AND UA SERVICES COMPANY
245 N Beverly Dr, Beverly Hills
(90210-5319)
PHONE..................................310 449-3000
Gary Barber, *President*
EMP: 560
SALES (est): 76.3K
SALES (corp-wide): 1.1B **Privately Held**
SIC: 8999 Artists & artists' studios
HQ: Metro-Goldwyn-Mayer, Inc.
245 N Beverly Dr
Beverly Hills CA 90210

(P-27945)
MIDPENINSUL RGNL OPN SP
330 Distel Cir, Los Altos (94022-1404)
PHONE..................................650 691-1200
Craig Britton, *President*
Bill Korbholz, *COO*
EMP: 65
SQ FT: 12,000
SALES: 47MM **Privately Held**
SIC: 8999 Natural resource preservation service

(P-27946)
MILLIMAN INC
650 California St Fl 21, San Francisco
(94108-2602)
PHONE..................................415 403-1333
Steve White, *Manager*
Bob Helliesen, *Principal*
Jim Walbridge, *Principal*
Rich Wright, *General Mgr*
Gale I Yarymowicz, *Office Mgr*
EMP: 50
SALES (corp-wide): 937.6MM **Privately Held**
WEB: www.millimanglobal.com
SIC: 8999 6411 Actuarial consultant; ratemaking organizations, insurance

PA: Milliman, Inc.
1301 5th Ave Ste 3800
Seattle WA 98101
206 624-7940

(P-27947)
OPTIMA NETWORK SERVICES INC (DH)
15345 Fairfield Ranch Rd # 225, Chino Hills (91709-8859)
PHONE..................................305 599-1800
Robert E Apple, *CEO*
Michael Mosel, *President*
William Appel, *Opers Mgr*
Kyle Meyer, *Opers Staff*
Eric Bengtson, *Manager*
EMP: 75
SQ FT: 6,475
SALES (est): 7.9MM
SALES (corp-wide): 6.6B **Publicly Held**
WEB: www.optimanet.net
SIC: 8999 Communication services
HQ: Mastec North America, Inc.
800 S Douglas Rd Ste 1200
Coral Gables FL 33134
305 599-1800

(P-27948)
ORACLE CORP
17901 Von Karman Ave # 800, Irvine (92614-5241)
PHONE..................................650 506-7000
EMP: 567
SALES (est): 27.1MM **Privately Held**
SIC: 8999

(P-27949)
ORANGEPEOPLE LLC
300 Spectrum Center Dr, Irvine (92618-4925)
PHONE..................................949 535-1308
Raghav Putrevu, *President*
Jessica Balaji, *Technology*
Mary George, *Technical Staff*
Jenny Alex, *Manager*
EMP: 76
SQ FT: 8,000
SALES (est): 12MM **Privately Held**
SIC: 8999 7374 7371 8742 Cloud seeding; data processing service; computer software development; construction project management consultant

(P-27950)
OVERSEAS SERVICE CORPORATION
Also Called: Ocean Service
8221 Arjons Dr Ste B2, San Diego (92126-6319)
PHONE..................................858 408-0751
Paul Hogan, *President*
Tomoko Phillips, *Buyer*
EMP: 232
SALES (corp-wide): 46.6MM **Privately Held**
SIC: 8999 Actuarial consultant
PA: Overseas Service Corporation
1100 Northpoint Pkwy # 200
West Palm Beach FL 33407
561 683-4090

(P-27951)
PANGEA CORPORATION
34145 Pacific Coast Hwy, Dana Point (92629-2808)
PHONE..................................949 443-0666
John Schulte, *CEO*
John Besmehn, *CEO*
Cheryl Ann Wong, *Director*
Cheryl Wong, *Director*
EMP: 50
SALES (est): 1.2MM **Privately Held**
WEB: www.pangeacorp.com
SIC: 8999 8742 7336 8743 Advertising copy writing; writing for publication; new products & services consultants; creative services to advertisers, except writers; graphic arts & related design; public relations services; video tape production; audio-visual program production

(P-27952)
PARADIGM INFORMATION SERVICES
10755 F Scrps Pwy Pkwy424, San Diego (92131)
PHONE..................................858 693-6115
Elizabeth Bentz, *CEO*
Richard Scheiner, *President*
Gwen Scheiner, *Corp Secy*
Mark Barrett, *Technical Staff*
Kristi Jennings, *Assistant*
EMP: 75
SALES (est): 2.3MM **Privately Held**
WEB: www.paradigmplacements.com
SIC: 8999 8711 7336 7371 Technical writing; consulting engineer; electrical or electronic engineering; graphic arts & related design; computer software development & applications; educational services

(P-27953)
PARTNERS RISK SPECIALISTS
6136 Mission Gorge Rd # 125, San Diego (92120-3494)
PHONE..................................619 326-0840
Jona Barnes, *Principal*
EMP: 50
SALES (est): 281.4K **Privately Held**
SIC: 8999 Services

(P-27954)
PLACER COUNTY ADM SVCS
2962 Richardson Dr, Auburn (95603-2640)
PHONE..................................530 886-5401
Jerry Gamaz, *Director*
EMP: 126
SALES (est): 5.1MM **Privately Held**
SIC: 8999 9199 Information bureau; general government administration

(P-27955)
PRIDE INDUSTRIES
1281 National Dr, Sacramento (95834-1902)
PHONE..................................916 649-9499
Allan Ruzick, *Branch Mgr*
Randy Beck, *Senior Engr*
Karelle Hatcher, *Manager*
Mark Polek, *Supervisor*
EMP: 220
SALES (corp-wide): 290.6MM **Privately Held**
SIC: 8999 Personal services
PA: Pride Industries
10030 Foothills Blvd
Roseville CA 95747
916 788-2100

(P-27956)
RADAR MEDICAL SYSTEMS INC
1510 Cotner Ave, Los Angeles (90025-3303)
PHONE..................................440 337-9521
Florence Present, *Principal*
EMP: 79 **EST:** 2015
SALES (est): 65.3K **Publicly Held**
SIC: 8999 Communication services
HQ: Radnet Managed Imaging Services, Inc.
1510 Cotner Ave
Los Angeles CA 90025
310 445-2800

(P-27957)
RAMBOLL US CORPORATION
Also Called: Ramboll Environ
18100 Von Karman Ave # 600, Irvine (92612-7198)
PHONE..................................949 798-3604
Anne Pena, *Manager*
EMP: 50
SALES (corp-wide): 314.9MM **Privately Held**
SIC: 8999 8748 Earth science services; environmental consultant
HQ: Ramboll Us Corporation
4350 Fairfax Dr Ste 300
Arlington VA 22203
703 516-2300

(P-27958)
RIVERSIDE COUNTY FLOOD CONTROL
1995 Market St, Riverside (92501-1719)
PHONE..................................951 955-1200

Jason Uhley, *Principal*
Aldous Tsang, *Admin Sec*
Joe Barcenas, *Engineer*
Kevin Cunningham, *Engineer*
Mekbib Degaga, *Engineer*
EMP: 210
SALES (est): 8.2MM **Privately Held**
SIC: 8999 Natural resource preservation service

(P-27959)
STORMGEO (DH)
Also Called: Applied Weather Technology Inc
140 Kifer Ct, Sunnyvale (94086-5120)
PHONE..................................408 731-8600
Robert Haydn Jones, *CEO*
Haydn Jones, *President*
William Lapworth, *CFO*
Cynthia Lin, *CFO*
Joe Stacey, *Vice Pres*
EMP: 166
SQ FT: 19,000
SALES (est): 21.4MM **Privately Held**
SIC: 8999 Weather forecasting
HQ: Stormgeo As
Nordre Nostekaien 1
Bergen 5011
557 061-70

(P-27960)
UNIVERSAL CYLINDER EXCH INC
692 N Cypress St Ste B, Orange (92867-6665)
P.O. Box 6147 (92863-6147)
PHONE..................................714 744-1036
Pamela A Ogier, *President*
Blaine Ogier, *Manager*
EMP: 85
SALES (est): 1.6MM **Privately Held**
SIC: 8999 Natural resource preservation service

(P-27961)
VICTOR CMNTY SUPPORT SVCS INC
900 E Main St Ste 201, Grass Valley (95945-5853)
PHONE..................................530 273-2244
Rachel Pena, *Exec Dir*
EMP: 205
SALES (corp-wide): 37.7MM **Privately Held**
SIC: 8999 Artists & artists' studios
PA: Victor Community Support Services, Inc.
1360 E Lassen Ave
Chico CA 95973
530 893-0758

(P-27962)
WESTVIEW SERVICES INC
11728 Magnolia Ave Ste D, Riverside (92503-4970)
PHONE..................................951 343-2356
Greg Drann, *Branch Mgr*
EMP: 88
SALES (corp-wide): 16.6MM **Privately Held**
SIC: 8999 Artists & artists' studios
PA: Westview Services, Inc
10522 Katella Ave
Anaheim CA 92804
714 517-6606

(P-27963)
WOODMONT REAL ESTATE SVCS LP
3883 Airway Dr, Santa Rosa (95403-1670)
PHONE..................................707 569-0582
Ron Granville, *Branch Mgr*
EMP: 279 **Privately Held**
SIC: 8999 Artists & artists' studios
PA: Woodmont Real Estate Services, L.P.
1050 Ralston Ave
Belmont CA 94002

(P-27964)
WU YEE CHILDRENS SERVICES
Also Called: Wu Yee Child Care Center
831 Broadway, San Francisco (94133-4218)
PHONE..................................415 677-0100
Alyson Suzeuki, *Program Dir*

David Ziegler, *Admin Sec*
EMP: 68
SALES (corp-wide): 20.4MM **Privately Held**
SIC: 8999 Artists & artists' studios
PA: Wu Yee Children's Services
827 Broadway
San Francisco CA 94133
415 230-7504

(P-27965)
ZOE HOLDING COMPANY INC
44 Montgomery St, San Francisco (94104-4602)
PHONE..................................415 421-4900
John Unick, *Branch Mgr*
EMP: 131
SALES (corp-wide): 60.6MM **Privately Held**
SIC: 8999 Artists & artists' studios
PA: Zoe Holding Company, Inc.
3131 E Camelback Rd # 200
Phoenix AZ 85016
602 508-1883

P
R
O
D
U
C
T
S

&

S
V
C
S

ALPHABETIC SECTION

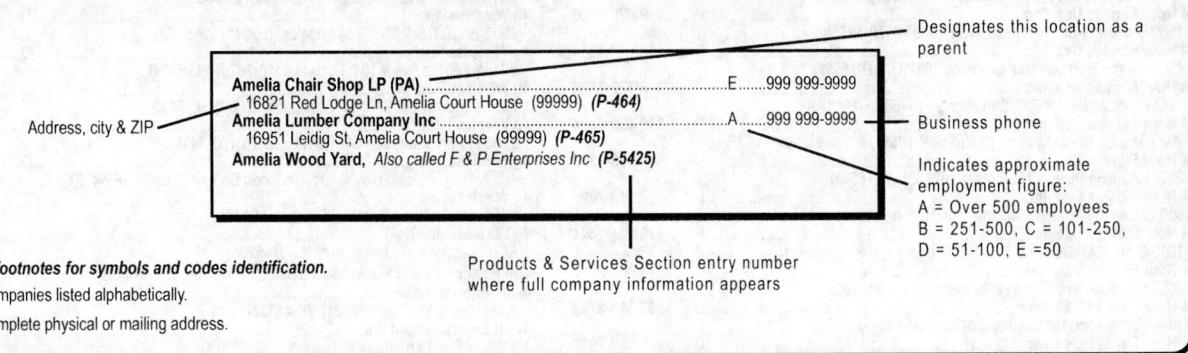

Designates this location as a parent

Amelia Chair Shop LP (PA) .... E....999 999-9999
16821 Red Lodge Ln, Amelia Court House (99999) *(P-464)*
Amelia Lumber Company Inc .... A....999 999-9999
16951 Leidig St, Amelia Court House (99999) *(P-465)*
Amelia Wood Yard, *Also called F & P Enterprises Inc* *(P-5425)*

Address, city & ZIP

Business phone

Indicates approximate employment figure:
A = Over 500 employees
B = 251-500, C = 101-250,
D = 51-100, E =50

See footnotes for symbols and codes identification.
* Companies listed alphabetically.
* Complete physical or mailing address.

Products & Services Section entry number where full company information appears

---

(a) Tool Shed Inc (PA) ....D......831 477-7133
3700 Soquel Ave Santa Cruz (95062) *(P-14463)*
0epi, Carmichael *Also called Eskaton Properties Inc* *(P-20411)*
1-800 Dentist, Los Angeles *Also called Futuredontics Inc* *(P-27243)*
1-800 Radiator & A/C (PA) ....D......707 747-7400
4401 Park Rd Benicia (94510) *(P-6616)*
1-800-4-insure Insurance Svcs ....C......818 701-3733
9310 Reseda Blvd Northridge (91324) *(P-10506)*
1-800-Radiator, Benicia *Also called 1-800 Radiator & A/C* *(P-6616)*
1-Carasight Surveillance, San Diego *Also called Inseego North America LLC* *(P-15978)*
1000 Aguajito Op Co LLC ....D......831 373-6141
1000 Aguajito Rd Monterey (93940) *(P-12286)*
1000 Executive Parkway LLC ....C......530 533-7335
1000 Executive Pkwy Oroville (95966) *(P-20213)*
101communications Holdings LLC (HQ) ....D......818 734-1520
9201 Oakdale Ave Ste 101 Chatsworth (91311) *(P-13932)*
106 Sacramento Mhrc, Sacramento *Also called Crestwood Behavioral Hlth Inc* *(P-21946)*
10632 Bolsa Avenue LP ....D......949 673-1221
500 Nwport Ctr Dr Ste 200 Newport Beach (92660) *(P-10967)*
107 San Jose Mhrc, San Jose *Also called Crestwood Behavioral Hlth Inc* *(P-24493)*
10up Inc ....D......888 571-7130
2765 Carradale Dr Roseville (95661) *(P-15905)*
11 Main Inc ....C......530 892-9191
527 Flume St Chico (95928) *(P-5428)*
1105 Government Group, Chatsworth *Also called 101communications Holdings LLC* *(P-13932)*
1105 Media Inc ....C......949 265-1520
4 Venture Ste 150 Irvine (92618) *(P-5968)*
111 Vallejo IMD, Vallejo *Also called Crestwood Behavioral Hlth Inc* *(P-21949)*
112 Modesto Snf, Modesto *Also called Crestwood Behavioral Hlth Inc* *(P-21945)*
1125 Sir Francis Drake Bouleva ....C......415 456-9680
1125 Sir Francis Drake Bl Kentfield (94904) *(P-21994)*
1130 W La Palma Ave Inc ....D......562 930-0777
4115 E Broadway Long Beach (90803) *(P-20214)*
1135 N Leisure Ct Inc ....C......714 772-1353
1135 N Leisure Ct Anaheim (92801) *(P-20215)*
115 Bakersfield Mhrc, Bakersfield *Also called Crestwood Behavioral Hlth Inc* *(P-23762)*
120 Fremont Snf, Redding *Also called Crestwood Behavioral Hlth Inc* *(P-24494)*
120 Fremont Snf, Fremont *Also called Crestwood Behavioral Hlth Inc* *(P-24497)*
120 South Los Angeles Street H ....D......213 629-1200
120 S Los Angeles St Los Angeles (90012) *(P-12287)*
123ewireless, Rcho STA Marg *Also called Sarco Inc* *(P-7539)*
1260 Bb Property LLC ....B......805 969-2261
1260 Channel Dr Santa Barbara (93108) *(P-12288)*
1334 Partners LP ....D......310 546-5656
1330 Park View Ave Manhattan Beach (90266) *(P-18814)*
134 Alameda Snf, Fremont *Also called Crestwood Behavioral Hlth Inc* *(P-24495)*
137 Bakersfield Bridge, Bakersfield *Also called Crestwood Behavioral Hlth Inc* *(P-22015)*
1370 Realty Corp ....C......818 817-0092
14545 Friar St Ste 101 Van Nuys (91411) *(P-11182)*
144 Pleasant Hill The Pathway, Pleasant Hill *Also called Crestwood Behavioral Hlth Inc* *(P-21951)*
145 Fresno Bridge, Fresno *Also called Crestwood Behavioral Hlth Inc* *(P-21947)*
14545 Friar LLC ....D......818 817-0082
14545 Friar St Ste 105 Van Nuys (91411) *(P-10843)*
14766 Wash Ave Operations LLC ....A......510 352-2211
14766 Washington Ave San Leandro (94578) *(P-20973)*
152 Vallejo Rcfe, Vallejo *Also called Crestwood Behavioral Hlth Inc* *(P-24496)*
1524 Abbot Kinney LLC ....D......310 907-6517
1746 Abbot Kinney Blvd Venice (90291) *(P-11183)*
153 American River PHF, Carmichael *Also called Crestwood Behavioral Hlth Inc* *(P-21950)*
15th & L Investors LLC ....D......916 267-6805
1121 15th St Sacramento (95814) *(P-12289)*
1658 Camden LLC ....E......818 769-1944
12147 Riverside Dr North Hollywood (91607) *(P-10968)*
16700 Roscoe Associates LLC ....D......818 989-2300
16700 Roscoe Blvd Van Nuys (91406) *(P-18815)*
1755 Efm 1 LLC ....D......323 231-4174
1755 Kings Way Los Angeles (90069) *(P-11184)*
1800-R-Ado, Los Angeles *Also called Wilshire Consumer Credit* *(P-9729)*
180Ia LLC ....C......310 382-1400
12555 W Jefferson Blvd # 200 Los Angeles (90066) *(P-13783)*

1835 Columbia Street LP ....D......619 564-3993
1835 Columbia St San Diego (92101) *(P-12290)*
19 Entertainment Worldwide LLC ....D......310 777-1940
401 Wilshire Blvd Lbby Santa Monica (90401) *(P-18416)*
19 Management, Santa Monica *Also called 19 Entertainment Worldwide LLC* *(P-18416)*
1906 Lodge, Coronado *Also called Four Sisters Inns* *(P-12589)*
1928 Jewelry Company, Burbank *Also called Mel Bernie and Company Inc* *(P-8010)*
1k Studios, Burbank *Also called One K Studios LLC* *(P-14124)*
1life Healthcare Inc ....D......415 644-5265
130 Sutter St Fl 2 San Francisco (94104) *(P-22720)*
1nteger LLC ....E......424 320-2977
1437 7th St Ste 400 Santa Monica (90401) *(P-13712)*
1on1 LLC ....E......310 448-5376
12015 Waterfront Dr # 261 Playa Vista (90094) *(P-15563)*
1st Class Laundry Services, Union City *Also called Specialized Laundry Svcs Inc* *(P-13621)*
1st Interstate Bank Building, Oakland *Also called San Francisco Bay Area Rapid* *(P-3706)*
1st Light Energy Inc (PA) ....E......209 824-5500
1869 Moffat Blvd Manteca (95336) *(P-3478)*
1st Team Real Estate, Tustin *Also called First Team RE - Orange Cnty* *(P-11464)*
1st United Services Credit Un (PA) ....D......800 649-0193
5901 Gibraltar Dr Pleasanton (94588) *(P-9537)*
2 G Fitness LLC ....D......925 838-9200
730 Camino Ramon Ste 200 Danville (94526) *(P-18546)*
20/20 Plumbing & Heating Inc ....C......951 396-2020
7343 Orangewood Dr Ste B Riverside (92504) *(P-2076)*
20/20 Recycle Centers, Redlands *Also called Contain-A-Way Inc* *(P-6382)*
2100 Trust LLC (PA) ....C......877 469-7344
625 N Grand Ave Santa Ana (92701) *(P-12087)*
211 La County, San Gabriel *Also called Information & Referral Fed Los* *(P-13751)*
21st Century Health Club (PA) ....D......707 795-0400
680a E Cotati Ave Cotati (94931) *(P-22495)*
21st Century Insurance Company (HQ) ....A......877 310-5687
6301 Owensmouth Ave Woodland Hills (91367) *(P-10507)*
21st Century Lf & Hlth Co Inc (PA) ....C......818 887-4436
21600 Oxnard St Ste 1500 Woodland Hills (91367) *(P-10154)*
21st Century Super Stars., Rcho STA Marg *Also called C-21 Super Stars* *(P-11258)*
2253 Apparel Inc (PA) ....D......323 837-9800
1708 Aeros Way Montebello (90640) *(P-8284)*
22nd Century Technologies Inc ....D......866 537-9191
6203 San Ignacio Ave San Jose (95119) *(P-14948)*
2300 West El Secundo LP ....D......310 769-6669
11916 Eucalyptus Ave Hawthorne (90250) *(P-11185)*
23andme Inc ....B......510 381-7237
349 Oyster Point Blvd # 100 South San Francisco (94080) *(P-16204)*
23andme Inc (PA) ....B......650 961-7152
899 W Evelyn Ave Mountain View (94041) *(P-16205)*
24 7ai Inc (PA) ....C......650 385-2247
2001 All Programable San Jose (95124) *(P-16299)*
24 Hour Fitness Usa Inc ....E......916 984-1924
1006 Riley St Folsom (95630) *(P-18547)*
24 Hour Fitness Usa Inc ....E......707 536-0048
6345 Commerce Blvd Rohnert Park (94928) *(P-22721)*
24 Hour Fitness Usa Inc ....E......510 795-6666
39300 Paseo Padre Pkwy Fremont (94538) *(P-18548)*
24 Hour Fitness Usa Inc ....E......818 531-0257
1903 W Empire Ave Burbank (91504) *(P-22722)*
24 Hour Fitness Usa Inc ....E......949 610-0651
1870 Harbor Blvd Ste 124 Costa Mesa (92627) *(P-22723)*
24 Hour Fitness Usa Inc ....D......760 918-4790
5964 La Place Ct Carlsbad (92008) *(P-18549)*
24 Hour Fitness Usa Inc ....D......760 602-5001
1265 Laurel Tree Ln # 100 Carlsbad (92011) *(P-18550)*
24 Hour Fitness Usa Inc ....D......310 553-7600
9911 W Pico Blvd Ste A Los Angeles (90035) *(P-18551)*
24 Hour Fitness Usa Inc ....D......626 795-7121
525 E Colorado Blvd Bsmt Pasadena (91101) *(P-18552)*
24 Hour Fitness Usa Inc ....D......909 944-1000
11787 Foothill Blvd Rancho Cucamonga (91730) *(P-18553)*
24 Hour Fitness Usa Inc ....E......310 652-7440
8612 Santa Monica Blvd West Hollywood (90069) *(P-18554)*
24 Hour Fitness Usa Inc ....D......949 650-3600
555 W 19th St Costa Mesa (92627) *(P-18555)*
24 Hour Fitness Usa Inc (HQ) ....C......925 543-3100
12647 Alcosta Blvd # 500 San Ramon (94583) *(P-18556)*

A L P H A B E T I C

Employee Codes: A=Over 500 employees, B=251-500
C=101-250, D=51-100, E=50

2019 Directory of California
Wholesalers and Services Companies

© Mergent Inc. 1-800-342-5647

1185

24 Hour Fitness Usa Inc ...... E 714 525-9924
1430 N Lemon St Anaheim (92801) *(P-18557)*
24 Hour Fitness Usa Inc ...... D 619 425-6600
1660 Broadway Ste 19 Chula Vista (91911) *(P-18558)*
24 Hour Fitness Usa Inc ...... D 818 247-4334
450 N Brand Blvd Ste 100 Glendale (91203) *(P-18559)*
24 Hour Fitness Usa Inc ...... D 916 722-7588
12647 Alcosta Blvd # 500 San Ramon (94583) *(P-18560)*
24 Hour Fitness Usa Inc ...... D 310 450-4464
2929 31st St Santa Monica (90405) *(P-18561)*
24 Hour Fitness Usa Inc ...... D 949 830-4213
26781 Rancho Pkwy Lake Forest (92630) *(P-18562)*
24 Hour Fitness Usa Inc ...... E 650 343-7922
500 El Camino Real Burlingame (94010) *(P-18563)*
24 Hour Fitness Usa Inc ...... E 619 294-2424
1640 Camino Del Rio N # 315 San Diego (92108) *(P-18564)*
24 Hour Fitness Usa Inc ...... D 818 887-2582
6653 Fallbrook Ave Canoga Park (91307) *(P-18565)*
24 Hour Fitness Usa Inc ...... D 562 943-3771
10125 Whittwood Dr Whittier (90603) *(P-18566)*
24 Hour Fitness Usa Inc ...... D 925 930-7900
2033 N Main St Ste 110 Walnut Creek (94596) *(P-18567)*
24 Hour Fitness Usa Inc ...... E 650 941-2268
550 Showers Dr Ste 1 Mountain View (94040) *(P-18568)*
24 Hour Fitness Usa Inc ...... E 858 538-4400
10025 Carmel Mountain Rd San Diego (92129) *(P-18569)*
24 Hour Fitness Usa Inc ...... D 510 264-3275
24727 Amador St Hayward (94544) *(P-18570)*
24 Hour Fitness Worldwide Inc (PA) ...... D 925 543-3100
12647 Alcosta Blvd # 500 San Ramon (94583) *(P-18571)*
24 Hour Fitness Worldwide Inc ...... E 310 374-4524
1601 Pcf Cast Hwy Ste 100 Hermosa Beach (90254) *(P-18572)*
24 Hour In Motion Fitness, Chico *Also called B A M I Inc (P-18575)*
24-Hour Med Staffing Svcs LLC ...... C 909 895-8960
21700 Copley Dr Ste 270 Diamond Bar (91765) *(P-14805)*
24hr Homecare LLC (PA) ...... D 310 906-3683
300 N Pacific Coast Hwy # 1065 El Segundo (90245) *(P-22175)*
29 Palms Enterprises Corp ...... A 760 775-5566
46200 Harrison Pl Coachella (92236) *(P-19089)*
2h Construction Inc ...... D 562 424-5567
2653 Walnut Ave Signal Hill (90755) *(P-1451)*
2nd Floor Main Street Concepts ...... E 714 969-9000
126 Main St Ste 201 Huntington Beach (92648) *(P-10969)*
2ndgear LLC (HQ) ...... C 714 702-1023
611 Anton Blvd Ste 700 Costa Mesa (92626) *(P-16274)*
2wire Inc (HQ) ...... C 408 235-5500
2450 Walsh Ave Santa Clara (95051) *(P-5429)*
3-Way Farms (PA) ...... E 831 722-0748
428 Browns Valley Rd Watsonville (95076) *(P-241)*
3067 Orange Avenue LLC ...... C 714 827-2440
3067 W Orange Ave Anaheim (92804) *(P-20216)*
30th Cpts-Financial Management, Lompoc *Also called Air Force US Dept of (P-26751)*
314e Corporation ...... D 510 371-6736
47102 Mission Falls Ct # 219 Fremont (94539) *(P-14949)*
32nd District-Orange Cnty Fair, Costa Mesa *Also called Food & Agriculture Cal Dept (P-19176)*
3900 West Lane Bowl Inc ...... E 209 466-6100
3900 West Ln Stockton (95204) *(P-18476)*
3dna Corp (PA) ...... D 213 394-4623
520 S Grand Ave Fl 2 Los Angeles (90071) *(P-14950)*
3k Technologies LLC ...... C 408 716-5900
1114 Cadillac Ct Milpitas (95035) *(P-14951)*
3M Company ...... C 909 974-3004
5151 E Philadelphia St Ontario (91761) *(P-4520)*
3m/Pharmaceuticals ...... D 818 341-1300
19901 Nordhoff St Northridge (91324) *(P-2795)*
3scale Inc ...... E 415 349-5187
995 Market St San Francisco (94103) *(P-16864)*
3vr Security Inc ...... D 415 513-4577
814 Mission St Fl 4 San Francisco (94103) *(P-16865)*
4 Cs, Santa Rosa *Also called Community Chld Cre Cncl Sonoma (P-24301)*
4 CS Council ...... C 408 487-0747
2515 N 1st St San Jose (95131) *(P-24255)*
4 Earth Farms Inc (PA) ...... D 323 201-5800
5555 E Olympic Blvd Commerce (90022) *(P-8636)*
4 Su Salud Medical Contact Ctr, Lodi *Also called J Rivera Associates Inc (P-27935)*
4 Wheel Parts Performance Ctrs, Compton *Also called Tap Worldwide LLC (P-6679)*
40 Hours Staffing, San Jose *Also called 40 Hrs Inc (P-14559)*
40 Hrs Inc ...... A 408 414-0158
1669 Flanigan Dr San Jose (95121) *(P-14559)*
417 Stockton St LLC ...... D 323 327-9656
1180 S Beverly Dr Ste 508 Los Angeles (90035) *(P-12291)*
425 North Point Street LLC ...... D 800 648-4626
101 California St Ste 950 San Francisco (94111) *(P-12292)*
4290 El Camino Properties LP ...... C 650 857-0787
4290 El Camino Real Palo Alto (94306) *(P-12293)*
42nd Street Moon ...... E 415 255-8207
601 Van Ness Ave San Francisco (94102) *(P-18335)*
48123 CA Investors LLC ...... C 831 667-2331
48123 Highway 1 Big Sur (93920) *(P-12294)*
495 Geary LLC ...... C 415 775-4700
495 Geary St San Francisco (94102) *(P-12295)*
4d Inc ...... C 408 557-4600
95 S Market St Ste 240 San Jose (95113) *(P-14952)*
4g Wireless Inc ...... D 562 928-2972
7220 Eastern Ave Bell (90201) *(P-5430)*
4g Wireless Inc ...... D 925 307-8990
4620 Tassajara Rd Dublin (94568) *(P-5431)*

4g Wireless Inc ...... D 310 429-9048
8342 Lincoln Blvd Los Angeles (90045) *(P-5432)*
4g Wireless Inc ...... D 323 679-9991
4925 Eagle Rock Blvd Los Angeles (90041) *(P-5433)*
4g Wireless Inc ...... D 760 705-7133
501 W Felicita Ave # 104 Escondido (92025) *(P-5434)*
4g Wireless Inc ...... D 760 828-2543
2635 Gateway Rd Ste 103 Carlsbad (92009) *(P-5435)*
4g Wireless Inc ...... D 951 210-7980
2560 N Perris Blvd Ste G8 Perris (92571) *(P-5436)*
4g Wireless Inc ...... D 310 376-2299
407 N Pacific Coast Hwy # 101 Redondo Beach (90277) *(P-5437)*
4g Wireless Inc ...... D 562 432-7744
285 E 5th St Long Beach (90802) *(P-5438)*
4g Wireless Inc (PA) ...... C 949 748-6100
8871 Research Dr Irvine (92618) *(P-5255)*
4inkjets.com, Long Beach *Also called Ld Products Inc (P-7070)*
4wall Entertainment Inc ...... C 702 263-3858
400 N Berry St Brea (92821) *(P-18336)*
4wall Entertainment Inc ...... D 818 252-7481
5435 W San Fernando Rd Los Angeles (90039) *(P-18337)*
5 Day Business Forms Mfg Inc (PA) ...... D 213 623-3577
2910 E La Cresta Ave Anaheim (92806) *(P-8072)*
5 Day Business Forms Mfg Inc ...... D 714 632-8674
2921 E La Cresta Ave Anaheim (92806) *(P-8073)*
5 Design Inc ...... D 323 308-3558
1024 N Orange Dr Ste 215 Los Angeles (90038) *(P-26016)*
5 Diamond Protection Inc ...... D 949 466-1367
2901 W Macarthur Blvd Santa Ana (92704) *(P-10844)*
5 Nine Group Inc ...... C 805 880-2948
1125 Lindero Canyon Rd Westlake Village (91362) *(P-14953)*
5 Star Pool Plaster Inc ...... D 209 599-3111
7275 National Dr Ste A Livermore (94550) *(P-1369)*
500 Startups Incubator LLC ...... C 415 974-6343
814 Mission St Ste 600 San Francisco (94103) *(P-27613)*
500 Startups Incubator LLC ...... C 650 743-4738
444 Castro St Ste 1200 Mountain View (94041) *(P-27614)*
500 Startups Management Co LLC ...... C 650 743-4738
444 Castro St Ste 1200 Mountain View (94041) *(P-12195)*
51 Minds Entertainment LLC ...... D 323 466-9200
5200 Lankershim Blvd # 200 North Hollywood (91601) *(P-18417)*
51st St & 8th Ave Corp ...... A 619 424-4000
4000 Coronado Bay Rd Coronado (92118) *(P-12296)*
525 Studios Inc ...... D 310 525-1234
1632 5th St Santa Monica (90401) *(P-18174)*
550 Flower St Operations LLC ...... C 213 892-8080
550 S Flower St Los Angeles (90071) *(P-12297)*
5design, Los Angeles *Also called 5 Design Inc (P-26016)*
5th & Sunset Productions, Los Angeles *Also called Fifth & Sunset Enterprises LLC (P-14505)*
5th Avenue Partners LLC ...... B 619 515-3000
1047 5th Ave San Diego (92101) *(P-12298)*
6417 Selma Hotel LLC ...... C 323 844-6417
6417 Selma Ave Los Angeles (90028) *(P-12299)*
6500 Hllister Ave Partners LLC ...... D 805 722-1362
6500 Hollister Ave Goleta (93117) *(P-10845)*
6wind Usa Inc ...... A 408 816-1366
2975 Scott Blvd Ste 115 Santa Clara (95054) *(P-14954)*
7 Diamonds Clothing, Tustin *Also called M & S Trading Inc (P-8269)*
7 Layers Inc ...... D 949 716-6512
15 Musick Irvine (92618) *(P-25490)*
711 Hope LP ...... C 213 365-5000
3470 Wilshire Blvd # 700 Los Angeles (90010) *(P-11162)*
72andsunny LLC ...... C 310 215-9009
12101 Bluff Creek Dr Playa Vista (90094) *(P-13784)*
741 Studios LLC ...... C 925 407-2063
2950 Buskirk Ave Ste 300 Walnut Creek (94597) *(P-16300)*
7410 Woodman Avenue LLC ...... D 805 496-4336
22837 Ventura Blvd # 201 Woodland Hills (91364) *(P-10970)*
76, San Diego *Also called Cosco Fire Protection Inc (P-2172)*
7days Inc ...... C 424 255-5872
3503 Jack Northrop Ave Hawthorne (90250) *(P-7432)*
7th Avenue Center LLC ...... D 831 476-1700
1171 7th Ave Santa Cruz (95062) *(P-21921)*
7th Standard Ranch Company ...... B 661 399-0416
33374 Lerdo Hwy Bakersfield (93308) *(P-127)*
800 Degrees LLC ...... E 310 443-1911
10889 Lindbrook Dr Los Angeles (90024) *(P-26743)*
8020 Consulting LLC ...... E 818 523-3201
6303 Owensmouth Ave Fl 10 Woodland Hills (91367) *(P-27615)*
8110 Aero Holding LLC ...... C 858 277-8888
8110 Aero Dr San Diego (92123) *(P-12300)*
834 W Arrow Highway LP ...... D 213 355-1024
4032 Wilshire Blvd # 600 Los Angeles (90010) *(P-20914)*
8520 Western Ave Inc ...... C 714 828-8222
10811 Kiowa Rd Apt 2a Apple Valley (92308) *(P-20974)*
8x8 Inc (PA) ...... C 408 727-1885
2125 Onel Dr San Jose (95131) *(P-5439)*
901 West Olympic Blvd LP ...... C 347 992-5707
901 W Olympic Blvd Los Angeles (90015) *(P-12301)*
95cs/Scxc Comp, Edwards *Also called US Dept of the Air Force (P-6004)*
9th Medical Group, Marysville *Also called US Dept of the Air Force (P-21889)*
A & A Home Care Services ...... D 760 416-6769
7756 Cntry Clb Dr Bldg A Palm Springs (92263) *(P-22176)*
A & A Mechanical Contractors ...... D 408 225-1321
2943 Daylight Way San Jose (95111) *(P-2077)*
A & B Construction, Berkeley *Also called Andrew M Jordan Inc (P-3414)*
A & C Convatescent Hospital, Millbrae *Also called A & C Health Care Services Inc (P-19266)*

Mergent e-mail: customerrelations@mergent.com
1186

2019 Directory of California
Wholesalers and Services Companies

(P-0000) Products & Services Section entry number
(PA)=Parent Co (HQ)=Headquarters (DH)=Div Headquarters

A & C Health Care Services Inc ....C 650 689-5784
33 Mateo Ave Millbrae (94030) (P-19266)
A & D Fire Protection Inc ....D 619 258-7697
11465 Woodside Ave Fl 1 Santee (92071) (P-2078)
A & D General Contracting, Santee Also called A & D Fire Protection Inc (P-2078)
A & D Hauling Services Inc ....D 310 514-8969
13337 South St Cerritos (90703) (P-3957)
A & G Grove Service ....D 760 728-5447
32731 Mesa Lilac Rd Escondido (92026) (P-471)
A & H Communications Inc ....C 949 250-4555
1791 Reynolds Ave Irvine (92614) (P-1889)
A & I Color Laboratory, Burbank Also called Jake Hey Incorporated (P-16962)
A & I Transportation, Watsonville Also called A & I Trucking Inc (P-3958)
A & I Trucking Inc (PA) ....E 831 763-7805
123 Lee Rd Ste E Watsonville (95076) (P-3958)
A & P Towing-Metropro Rd Svcs, Santa Ana Also called Metropro Road Services Inc (P-17866)
A & R Electric, Fullerton Also called Swinford Electric Inc (P-2757)
A & R Wholesale Distrs Inc ....D 714 777-7742
1765 W Penhall Way Anaheim (92801) (P-8542)
A & S Technologies, Northridge Also called Ikano Communications Inc (P-16144)
A & W Maintenance ....D 310 619-8694
7573 Cibola Trl Yucca Valley (92284) (P-1106)
A A A Automobile Club So Cal, Los Angeles Also called Automobile Club Southern Cal (P-10554)
A A A Automobile Club So Cal, Laguna Hills Also called Automobile Club Southern Cal (P-25391)
A A A Couriers, Los Angeles Also called Classic Couriers Inc (P-4395)
A A A Five Star Adventures ....E 760 320-1500
611 S Palm Canyon Dr Palm Springs (92264) (P-18816)
A A A Furnace AC Co ....D 408 293-4717
1712 Stone Ave Ste 1 San Jose (95125) (P-2079)
A A A Furnace Company, San Jose Also called Rando AAA Hvac Inc (P-2328)
A A A Packing and Shipping Inc ....E 626 310-7787
2000 E 49th St Vernon (90058) (P-3959)
A A Gonzalez Inc ....D 818 367-2242
13264 Ralston Ave Sylmar (91342) (P-2833)
A A U C, Los Angeles Also called African American Unity Center (P-23461)
A B C D Associates ....C 916 363-4843
10410 Coloma Rd Rancho Cordova (95670) (P-20217)
A B S, City of Industry Also called Magnell Associate Inc (P-7073)
A B S Auto Auctions, Corona Also called Auto Buyline Systems Inc (P-6579)
A Better Life Together Inc ....D 619 741-1548
3322 Sweetwater Springs B Spring Valley (91977) (P-22177)
A Better Solution In Home Care ....C 619 447-1528
1409 N 2nd St El Cajon (92021) (P-22178)
A Better Way Inc (PA) ....C 510 601-0203
3200 Adeline St Berkeley (94703) (P-24727)
A Buchalter Professional Corp (PA) ....C 213 891-0700
1000 Wilshire Blvd # 1500 Los Angeles (90017) (P-22903)
A C D, Newark Also called Advanced Cell Diagnostics Inc (P-26312)
A C F, Covina Also called Acf Components & Fasteners Inc (P-7571)
A C Freight Systems Inc (PA) ....C 408 392-8900
850 Service St San Jose (95112) (P-4088)
A C G, Laguna Hills Also called American Capital Group Inc (P-9752)
A C I Communications, Calabasas Also called Able Cable Inc (P-17901)
A C M, Santa Ana Also called Advanced Clnroom McRclean Corp (P-14182)
A C N, City of Industry Also called America Chung Nam LLC (P-7967)
A C Rentals LLC ....E 858 271-8571
8540 Production Ave Ste A San Diego (92121) (P-2080)
A C S Security, Los Angeles Also called ACS Security Industries Inc (P-16867)
A C T Box Office, San Francisco Also called American Conservatory (P-18343)
A C T S, Bloomington Also called Acts For Children (P-24406)
A Caos Medical Corporation ....D 800 362-2731
2655 Camino Del R San Diego (92108) (P-22179)
A Caregiver LLC ....E 951 676-4190
31520 Rr Cyn Rd Ste A Canyon Lake (92587) (P-22180)
A Coach USA Company, Sacramento Also called All West Coachlines Inc (P-3893)
A Colmenero Plastering Inc ....D 559 435-3606
1710 W San Madele Ave Fresno (93711) (P-2834)
A Comcast, Modesto Also called Comcast Corporation (P-5874)
A Community For Peace ....D 916 728-5613
6060 Sunrise Vista Dr # 2340 Citrus Heights (95610) (P-24728)
A Community of Friends ....D 213 480-0809
3701 Wilshire Blvd # 700 Los Angeles (90010) (P-10971)
A Complete Drywall Co, San Rafael Also called Michael B Mayock Inc (P-2918)
A Cori Partnership ....D 818 368-2802
10626 Balboa Blvd Granada Hills (91344) (P-20975)
A Csg-Nova Joint Venture ....D 916 371-7303
3960 Industrial Blvd # 500 West Sacramento (95691) (P-1710)
A D Bilich Inc ....E 925 820-5557
11 Crow Canyon Ct Ste 100 San Ramon (94583) (P-9767)
A D G, San Diego Also called Affinity Development Group Inc (P-25374)
A D S, Los Angeles Also called Advanced Digital Services Inc (P-18011)
A Development Stage Company, San Francisco Also called Brience Inc (P-15035)
A E W/Careage Ops, Bakersfield Also called Glenwood Gardens (P-20458)
A F C, Rancho Dominguez Also called Advanced Fresh Concepts Corp (P-12133)
A F Evans Company Inc ....D 925 937-1700
1700 Tice Valley Blvd Ofc Walnut Creek (94595) (P-16969)
A F Gilmore Company ....D 323 939-1191
6301 W 3rd St Los Angeles (90036) (P-11186)
A F V W Health Center ....B 951 697-2025
17050 Arnold Dr Ofc Riverside (92518) (P-20218)
A Filml Inc ....D 213 977-8600
6255 W Sunset Blvd Fl 12 Los Angeles (90028) (P-18175)
A G A, Fremont Also called Homelegance Inc (P-6725)
A G Hacienda Incorporated ....B 661 792-2418
32794 Sherwood Ave Mc Farland (93250) (P-3960)
A G Paceman Inc ....D 650 592-7282
1100 Industrial Rd Ste 11 San Carlos (94070) (P-11163)
A G Spanos Management Inc ....E 209 478-7954
10100 Trinity Pkwy Fl 5 Stockton (95219) (P-11187)
A Growing Concern Landscapes ....D 714 843-5137
17382 Gothard St Huntington Beach (92647) (P-724)
A I H, Glendale Also called Access Integrated Healthcare (P-20979)
A I S-Auto Insur Specialists, Long Beach Also called Auto Insur Spcialists-Long Bch (P-10552)
A I T Development Corp ....D 818 407-5533
21021 Devonshire St # 205 Chatsworth (91311) (P-1107)
A Is For Apple Inc ....C 877 991-0009
1485 Saratoga Ave Ste 200 San Jose (95129) (P-20160)
A Its Laugh Productions Inc ....D 818 848-8787
914 N Victory Blvd Burbank (91502) (P-18008)
A J Esprit ....E 619 223-8171
5102 N Harbor Dr San Diego (92106) (P-12302)
A J Excavation Inc ....C 559 408-5908
514 N Brawley Ave Fresno (93706) (P-1711)
A J Parent Company Inc (PA) ....D 714 521-1100
6910 Aragon Cir Ste 6 Buena Park (90620) (P-16970)
A J R Trucking Inc ....D 562 989-9555
915 Monterey Rd Glendale (91206) (P-3961)
A L Gilbert Company ....D 209 537-0766
4431 Jessup Rd Keyes (95328) (P-8903)
A L S Industries Inc (PA) ....E 310 532-9262
1942 Artesia Blvd Torrance (90504) (P-7943)
A Lighting By Design, Anaheim Also called Albd Electric and Cable (P-2503)
A M I Encn-Trzana Rgnal Med Ce, Tarzana Also called AMI-Hti Tarzana Encino Joint V (P-21284)
A M Ortega Construction Inc ....D 951 360-1352
58 Kellogg St Ventura (93001) (P-1108)
A M Ortega Construction Inc (PA) ....C 619 390-1988
10125 Channel Rd Lakeside (92040) (P-2495)
A M R, Irwindale Also called American Med (P-3746)
A M S Partnership (PA) ....D 310 312-6698
1517 S Sepulveda Blvd Los Angeles (90025) (P-11851)
A Meissners Hhld & Indus Svc ....D 916 920-2121
2417 Cormorant Way Sacramento (95815) (P-7718)
A O Reed & Co ....B 858 565-4131
4777 Ruffner St San Diego (92111) (P-2081)
A P Express Worldwide, Pico Rivera Also called AP Express LLC (P-5009)
A P H Technological Consulting ....E 626 796-0331
2500 E Colo Blvd Ste 300 Pasadena (91107) (P-25491)
A P I Property Management, Newport Beach Also called Amarik Properties Inc (P-11210)
A P R Consulting Inc ....A 714 544-3696
17852 17th St Ste 206 Tustin (92780) (P-16301)
A P R Inc ....C 805 379-3400
100 E Thsnd Oaks Blvd Thousand Oaks (91360) (P-14806)
A Plus In Home Care ....D 559 224-9442
5150 N 6th St Ste 111 Fresno (93710) (P-22181)
A Plus Mini Market, Fresno Also called A Plus In Home Care (P-22181)
A Plus Senior Care Inc ....E 909 989-2563
4701 Arrow Hwy Montclair (91763) (P-23453)
A Q M D, Diamond Bar Also called South Coast Air Qulty MGT Dst (P-27868)
A R C Fastener Supply, Corona Also called ARC Fastener Supply & Mfg (P-7828)
A R Wilson Quarry & Asp Plant, Aromas Also called Granite Rock Co (P-6896)
A Ruiz Cnstr Co & Assoc Inc ....E 415 647-4010
1601 Cortland Ave San Francisco (94110) (P-1452)
A S A P Professional Services ....D 800 303-2727
2440 Camino Ramon Ste 313 San Ramon (94583) (P-14560)
A S E C International Inc ....A 803 939-4809
11400 W Olympic Blvd Los Angeles (90064) (P-16082)
A S I, Long Beach Also called Associated Students California (P-25094)
A S I, Fremont Also called Asi Computer Technologies Inc (P-7009)
A S I Corporation ....C 714 526-5533
1308 N Patt St Anaheim (92801) (P-13785)
A S S U, Stanford Also called Associated Students Stanford (P-25095)
A Smwm California Corporation ....D 415 546-0400
185 Berry St Ste 5100 San Francisco (94107) (P-26017)
A T Associates Inc ....E 510 649-6670
2223 Ashby Ave Berkeley (94705) (P-20976)
A T Associates Inc ....D 510 261-8564
2919 Fruitvale Ave Oakland (94602) (P-20977)
A T Associates Inc (PA) ....D 925 808-6540
535 School St Pittsburg (94565) (P-20978)
A T Kearney Inc ....D 415 490-4000
555 Mission St Ste 1800 San Francisco (94105) (P-27103)
A T S, Los Angeles Also called Authorized Taxi Cab (P-16877)
A Taxi Cab, Newport Beach Also called A White and Yellow Cab Inc (P-3863)
A Teichert & Son Inc (HQ) ....C 916 484-3011
3500 American River Dr Sacramento (95864) (P-6874)
A Tool Shed Equipment Rentals, Santa Cruz Also called (a) Tool Shed Inc (P-14463)
A Touch of Kindness ....D 323 997-6500
353 1/2 N La Brea Ave Los Angeles (90036) (P-23454)
A Transportation, Tarzana Also called Airey Enterprises LLC (P-7905)
A Ursgi-Bmdc Joint Venture ....D 858 812-9292
4225 Executive Sq # 1600 La Jolla (92037) (P-25492)
A V Nursing Care Center, Lancaster Also called Antelope Vly Retirement HM Inc (P-20994)
A W Properties West LLC ....D 858 832-1462
16236 San Dieguito Rd # 310 Rancho Santa Fe (92091) (P-1109)
A White and Yellow Cab Inc ....C 714 258-1000
2082 Se Bristol St # 212 Newport Beach (92660) (P-3863)

Employee Codes: A=Over 500 employees, B=251-500
C=101-250, D=51-100, E=50
2019 Directory of California
Wholesalers and Services Companies
© Mergent Inc. 1-800-342-5647
1187

A World Fit For Kids.....C.....213 387-7712
678 S La Fayette Park Pl Los Angeles (90057) ***(P-27104)***
A Yafa Pen Company.....E.....818 704-8888
21306 Gault St Canoga Park (91303) ***(P-8074)***
A&E Television Networks LLC.....C.....310 201-6015
2049 Century Park E # 800 Los Angeles (90067) ***(P-5855)***
A&S Floors, Benicia *Also called Anthony Trevino* ***(P-3094)***
A-1 Delivery Co.....D.....909 444-1220
1777 S Vintage Ave Ontario (91761) ***(P-3962)***
A-1 Electric Service Co Inc.....E.....310 204-1077
4204 Sepulveda Blvd Culver City (90230) ***(P-2496)***
A-1 Elite Painting Inc.....E.....760 365-6702
56409 Yuma Trl Yucca Valley (92284) ***(P-2417)***
A-1 Event & Party Rentals.....D.....626 967-0500
251 E Front St Covina (91723) ***(P-13713)***
A-1 Express Delivery Service (PA).....E.....323 585-4440
4520 S Maywood Ave Vernon (90058) ***(P-3963)***
A-1 Hospice Care Inc.....D.....818 237-2700
217 E Alameda Ave Ste 306 Burbank (91502) ***(P-22182)***
A-1 Party Rentals, Covina *Also called Cwf Inc* ***(P-14498)***
A-1 Pomona Linen, Paramount *Also called Braun Linen Service Inc* ***(P-13519)***
A-Able Inc (PA).....D.....323 658-5779
17801 Ventura Blvd Encino (91316) ***(P-14135)***
A-C Electric Company (PA).....B.....661 410-0000
2921 Hanger Way Bakersfield (93308) ***(P-2497)***
A-C Electric Company.....D.....661 633-5368
315 30th St Bakersfield (93301) ***(P-25493)***
A-Check America Inc (PA).....C.....951 750-1501
1501 Research Park Dr Riverside (92507) ***(P-14028)***
A-Check America Inc.....C.....800 872-2677
1501 Research Park Dr Riverside (92507) ***(P-14029)***
A-Check America, Member Act 1, Riverside *Also called A-Check America Inc* ***(P-14028)***
A-Mark Precious Metals Inc (PA).....E.....310 587-1477
2121 Rosecrans Ave # 6300 El Segundo (90245) ***(P-8000)***
A-Para Transit Corp.....C.....510 562-5500
1400 Doolittle Dr San Leandro (94577) ***(P-3739)***
A-Star Staffing Inc.....C.....619 574-7600
3636 Camino Del Rio N # 102 San Diego (92108) ***(P-14561)***
A-Throne Co Inc.....D.....562 981-1197
1850 E 33rd St Long Beach (90807) ***(P-14464)***
A-Z Bus Sales Inc (PA).....D.....951 781-7188
1900 S Riverside Ave Colton (92324) ***(P-6570)***
A.M. Services, Fremont *Also called Ardenbrook Inc* ***(P-11216)***
A1 Building Management Inc.....C.....714 447-3800
2461 E Orangethorpe Ave # 200 Fullerton (92831) ***(P-14166)***
A1 Event & Party Rentals, Covina *Also called A-1 Event & Party Rentals* ***(P-13713)***
A1 Protective Services Inc.....D.....415 467-7200
5 Thomas Mellon Cir San Francisco (94134) ***(P-16540)***
A1 Protective Services LLC.....E.....916 421-3000
7000 Franklin Blvd Sacramento (95823) ***(P-16541)***
A10 Networks Inc (PA).....A.....408 325-8668
3 W Plumeria Dr San Jose (95134) ***(P-15906)***
A3 Labs LLC.....E.....925 274-8503
130 Webster St Oakland (94607) ***(P-26308)***
A3M CO, Los Angeles *Also called Little Tokyo Service Center* ***(P-23901)***
AA Autmtive Personnel Svcs Inc.....C.....310 914-3012
2251 Federal Ave Los Angeles (90064) ***(P-17844)***
Aa/Acme Locksmiths Inc.....D.....510 483-6584
1660 Factor Ave San Leandro (94577) ***(P-2498)***
AAA, Oakland *Also called American Automobile Assctn* ***(P-25379)***
AAA, Encino *Also called Automobile Club Southern Cal* ***(P-25383)***
AAA, Torrance *Also called Automobile Club Southern Cal* ***(P-25384)***
AAA, Ventura *Also called Automobile Club Southern Cal* ***(P-25385)***
AAA, Glendora *Also called Automobile Club Southern Cal* ***(P-25386)***
AAA, Bakersfield *Also called Automobile Club Southern Cal* ***(P-25387)***
AAA, Northridge *Also called Automobile Club Southern Cal* ***(P-25388)***
AAA, Woodland Hills *Also called Automobile Club Southern Cal* ***(P-25389)***
AAA, Capitola *Also called CA Ste Atom Assoc Intr-Ins Bur* ***(P-17855)***
AAA, San Mateo *Also called CA Ste Atom Assoc Intr-Ins Bur* ***(P-10341)***
AAA, Mountain View *Also called CA Ste Atom Assoc Intr-Ins Bur* ***(P-10568)***
AAA, La Mesa *Also called Automobile Club Southern Cal* ***(P-25394)***
AAA Accounting Services.....D.....949 791-7368
2 Enterprise Apt 1211 Aliso Viejo (92656) ***(P-26138)***
AAA Auto Club, Costa Mesa *Also called Automobile Club Southern Cal* ***(P-10555)***
AAA Drain Patrol.....E.....916 348-3098
3437 Myrtle Ave Ste 440 North Highlands (95660) ***(P-2082)***
AAA Elctrcal Cmmunications Inc (PA).....C.....800 892-4784
25007 Anza Dr Valencia (91355) ***(P-2499)***
AAA Fire Protection Service, Union City *Also called AAA Restaurant Fire Ctrl Inc* ***(P-16971)***
AAA Property Services, Valencia *Also called AAA Elctrcal Cmmunications Inc* ***(P-2499)***
AAA Restaurant Fire Ctrl Inc.....D.....510 786-9555
30113 Union City Blvd Union City (94587) ***(P-16971)***
AAA Restoration Inc.....E.....951 471-5828
29850 2nd St Lake Elsinore (92532) ***(P-3479)***
AAA Signs Inc.....D.....916 568-3456
2020 Railroad Dr Sacramento (95815) ***(P-17748)***
AAA Travel.....E.....650 572-5600
1650 S Delaware St San Mateo (94402) ***(P-10329)***
Aaaaa Rent-A-Space, Castro Valley *Also called Ras Management Inc* ***(P-4624)***
Aaaza Inc.....D.....213 380-8333
3250 Wilshire Blvd # 1901 Los Angeles (90010) ***(P-13786)***
Aab Water Company Inc.....D.....559 497-2700
226 S Avenue 54 Los Angeles (90042) ***(P-6205)***
Aadlen Brothers Auto Wrecking (PA).....D.....323 875-1400
11590 Tuxford St Sun Valley (91352) ***(P-7964)***
Aah Hudson LP.....A.....626 794-9179
1255 N Hudson Ave Pasadena (91104) ***(P-10972)***
Aai Termite Pest Control, Salida *Also called Royce Corporation* ***(P-14156)***
Aall Care In Home Services, San Diego *Also called Faith Jones & Associates Inc* ***(P-22296)***
AAM, Anaheim *Also called Anaheim Arena Management LLC* ***(P-18503)***
Aamcom LLC.....E.....310 318-8100
800 N Pacific Coast Hwy Redondo Beach (90277) ***(P-5440)***
AAR Manufacturing Inc.....D.....916 830-7011
5307 Luce Ave Bldg 243e McClellan (95652) ***(P-17899)***
AAR Manufacturing Inc.....D.....800 422-2213
5239 Luce Ave Bldg 243d McClellan (95652) ***(P-17900)***
Aardex Inc.....D.....805 928-7600
1550 E Main St Santa Maria (93454) ***(P-1453)***
Aardvark Staffing Inc.....E.....916 774-7115
3017 Douglas Blvd Fl 3 Roseville (95661) ***(P-14807)***
Aaron Dowling Incorporated.....D.....559 432-4500
8080 N Palm Ave Ste 300 Fresno (93711) ***(P-22904)***
Aaron Thomas Company Inc (PA).....C.....714 894-4468
7421 Chapman Ave Garden Grove (92841) ***(P-16972)***
Aat Kings Tours USA Inc.....D.....714 456-0505
801 E Katella Ave Fl 3 Anaheim (92805) ***(P-4959)***
Aat Torrey Reserve 6 LLC.....D.....858 350-2600
11455 El Cmino Real Ste 2 San Diego (92130) ***(P-10846)***
Aatcaa Headstart, Sonora *Also called Amador Tlmne Cmnty Action Agcy* ***(P-24733)***
Aauw Action Fund Inc.....D.....650 574-9160
P.O. Box 1239 San Mateo (94401) ***(P-25373)***
Aaxis Pacific, Lomita *Also called Aaxis Pharmaceuticals Inc* ***(P-7147)***
Aaxis Pharmaceuticals Inc.....C.....424 263-5294
1835 262nd St Lomita (90717) ***(P-7147)***
AB Cellular Holding LLC.....A.....562 468-6846
1452 Edinger Ave Tustin (92780) ***(P-5441)***
AB Closing Corporation.....D.....707 766-1777
1304 Southpoint Blvd Petaluma (94954) ***(P-14562)***
Ab/SW 70 S Lake Owner LLC.....E.....650 571-2200
70 S Lake Ave Pasadena (91101) ***(P-11164)***
Aba Holdings LLC.....C.....858 565-4131
4777 Ruffner St San Diego (92111) ***(P-11959)***
Abacus Business Capital Inc.....E.....909 594-8080
738 Epperson Dr City of Industry (91748) ***(P-8369)***
Abacus Data Systems Inc (HQ).....D.....858 452-4280
9171 Towne Centre Dr # 200 San Diego (92122) ***(P-14955)***
Abacus Service Corporation.....B.....916 288-8948
1725 23rd St Sacramento (95816) ***(P-14956)***
Abacusnext, San Diego *Also called Abacus Data Systems Inc* ***(P-14955)***
Abad Foam Inc.....E.....714 994-2223
6560 Caballero Blvd Buena Park (90620) ***(P-9191)***
ABB Enterprise Software Inc.....C.....415 527-2850
60 Spear St San Francisco (94105) ***(P-15564)***
ABB Optical Group, Alameda *Also called Abb/Con-Cise Optical Group LLC* ***(P-7232)***
Abb/Con-Cise Optical Group LLC.....D.....800 852-8089
1750 N Loop Rd Ste 150 Alameda (94502) ***(P-7231)***
Abb/Con-Cise Optical Group LLC.....D.....510 483-9400
1750 N Loop Rd Ste 150 Alameda (94502) ***(P-7232)***
Abba Bail Bonds (PA).....E.....213 680-1400
900 Avila St Ste 2 Los Angeles (90012) ***(P-16973)***
Abbey Management Company LLC.....D.....562 243-2100
330 Golden Shore Ste 300 Long Beach (90802) ***(P-11960)***
Abbey Partner VI.....E.....951 785-8800
7207 Arlington Ave Ste D Riverside (92503) ***(P-11188)***
Abbey-Properties LLC (PA).....D.....562 435-2100
12447 Lewis St Ste 203 Garden Grove (92840) ***(P-10847)***
Abbood Zeyad.....E.....619 212-2820
7914 La Mesa Blvd Apt 6 La Mesa (91942) ***(P-25494)***
Abbott Stringham An.....D.....408 377-8700
1530 Meridian Ave 2 San Jose (95125) ***(P-26139)***
Abbyson Living Corp.....B.....805 465-5500
26500 W Agrra Rd 102-87 Calabasas (91302) ***(P-6705)***
Abbyy USA Software House Inc (HQ).....C.....408 457-9777
890 Hillview Ct Ste 300 Milpitas (95035) ***(P-14957)***
Abc Inc.....B.....818 863-7801
500 Circle Seven Dr Glendale (91201) ***(P-5763)***
ABC 30, Fresno *Also called Kfsn Television LLC* ***(P-5806)***
ABC Bus Inc.....D.....714 444-5888
1485 Dale Way Costa Mesa (92626) ***(P-6571)***
ABC Bus Inc.....D.....650 368-3364
3508 Haven Ave Redwood City (94063) ***(P-6572)***
ABC Cable Networks Group.....C.....415 954-7911
900 Front St San Francisco (94111) ***(P-5764)***
ABC Cable Networks Group.....C.....818 560-4365
698 S Buena Vista St Burbank (91521) ***(P-18234)***
ABC Cable Networks Group (HQ).....C.....818 460-7477
500 S Buena Vista St Burbank (91521) ***(P-5688)***
ABC Cable Networks Group.....C.....323 860-5900
6834 Hollywood Blvd Los Angeles (90028) ***(P-5689)***
ABC Corona, Corona *Also called Amerisourcebergen Drug Corp* ***(P-8143)***
ABC Family Worldwide Inc (HQ).....B.....818 560-1000
500 S Buena Vista St Burbank (91521) ***(P-18009)***
ABC Home Health Care Llc.....C.....858 455-5000
5090 Shoreham Pl Ste 209 San Diego (92122) ***(P-22183)***
ABC Phones North Carolina Inc.....D.....510 314-0981
3935 E Castro Valley Blvd Castro Valley (94552) ***(P-5256)***
ABC Phones North Carolina Inc.....D.....530 541-9500
2230 Lake Tahoe Blvd # 130 South Lake Tahoe (96150) ***(P-5257)***
ABC Sacramento Striker, Sacramento *Also called Amerisourcebergen Drug Corp* ***(P-8142)***
ABC School Equipment Inc.....D.....951 817-2200
1451 E 6th St Corona (92879) ***(P-7239)***
ABC Security Service Inc (PA).....C.....510 436-0666
1840 Embarcadero Oakland (94606) ***(P-16542)***
ABC Valencia, Valencia *Also called Amerisourcebergen Drug Corp* ***(P-8141)***
Abc7 Broadcast Center, San Francisco *Also called Kgo Television Inc* ***(P-5808)***
Abco Insulation, Azusa *Also called Oj Insulation LP* ***(P-2927)***

Mergent e-mail: customerrelations@mergent.com
1188
2019 Directory of California
Wholesalers and Services Companies
(P-0000) Products & Services Section entry number
(PA)=Parent Co (HQ)=Headquarters (DH)=Div Headquarters

Abd Insurance & Fincl Svcs Inc (PA).....D.....650 488-8565
3 Waters Park Dr Ste 100 San Mateo (94403) ***(P-10508)***
Abe Entercom Holdings LLC.....D.....619 291-9797
1615 Murray Canyon Rd # 710 San Diego (92108) ***(P-5690)***
Abe-El Produce.....B.....559 528-3030
42143 Road 120 Orosi (93647) ***(P-32)***
ABF Freight System Inc.....E.....408 435-8550
2135 Otoole Ave San Jose (95131) ***(P-4089)***
ABF Freight System Inc.....E.....323 773-2580
8001 Telegraph Rd Pico Rivera (90660) ***(P-4090)***
ABF Freight System Inc.....D.....510 533-8575
4575 Tidewater Ave Oakland (94601) ***(P-4091)***
ABF Freight System Inc.....E.....714 974-2485
1601 N Batavia St Orange (92867) ***(P-4092)***
ABF Freight System Inc.....D.....916 428-3531
3250 47th Ave Sacramento (95824) ***(P-4093)***
ABF Freight System Inc.....C.....909 355-9805
10744 Almond Ave Fontana (92337) ***(P-4094)***
Abhe & Svoboda Inc.....D.....619 659-1320
880 Tavern Rd Alpine (91901) ***(P-1454)***
ABI Attorneys Service Inc (PA).....D.....909 793-0613
2015 W Park Ave Redlands (92373) ***(P-14069)***
ABI Document Support Svcs LLC.....E.....909 793-0613
11010 White Rock Rd # 160 Rancho Cordova (95670) ***(P-16974)***
ABI Document Support Svcs LLC.....D.....909 793-0613
10459 Mountain View Ave E Loma Linda (92354) ***(P-16975)***
ABI VIP Attorney Service, Redlands *Also called ABI Attorneys Service Inc* ***(P-14069)***
Abilities United (PA).....C.....650 494-0550
525 E Charleston Rd Palo Alto (94306) ***(P-23455)***
Ability Counts Inc (PA).....D.....951 734-6595
775 Trademark Cir Ste 101 Corona (92879) ***(P-24144)***
Abilityfirst.....D.....213 748-7309
3812 S Grand Ave Los Angeles (90037) ***(P-23456)***
Abilty First.....D.....562 426-6161
3770 E Willow St Long Beach (90815) ***(P-24405)***
ABLE, Azusa *Also called California Pediatric Fmly Svcs* ***(P-23524)***
Able Building Maintenance, Santa Ana *Also called Crown Building Maintenance Co* ***(P-14238)***
Able Building Maintenance, Los Angeles *Also called Crown Building Maintenance Co* ***(P-14241)***
Able Cable Inc (PA).....C.....818 223-3600
5115 Douglas Fir Rd Ste A Calabasas (91302) ***(P-17901)***
Able Engineering Services, Los Angeles *Also called Crown Energy Services Inc* ***(P-14242)***
Able Exterminators Inc.....D.....408 251-6500
68 N Sunset Ave San Jose (95116) ***(P-14136)***
Able Hands Inc.....D.....626 965-2233
18780 Amar Rd Ste 207 Walnut (91789) ***(P-22184)***
ABLE INDUSTRIES, Visalia *Also called Tulare Cty Trng Ctr Hndcpd* ***(P-24239)***
Able Patrol & Guard, San Diego *Also called Locator Services Inc* ***(P-16720)***
Able Services, South San Francisco *Also called Crown Energy Services Inc* ***(P-25631)***
Able Services Inc.....D.....800 461-9577
868 Folsom St San Francisco (94107) ***(P-25495)***
Ablitt's Fine Cleaners, Santa Barbara *Also called Santa Barbara Fabricare Inc* ***(P-13568)***
ABM Aviation Inc.....B.....650 872-5400
601 Gateway Blvd Ste 1145 South San Francisco (94080) ***(P-4867)***
ABM Distributors Inc.....D.....310 401-0434
811 W 7th St Ste 1040 Los Angeles (90017) ***(P-18010)***
ABM Elctrcal Ltg Solutions Inc.....D.....408 399-3030
6940 Koll Center Pkwy # 100 Pleasanton (94566) ***(P-14167)***
ABM Elctrcal Ltg Solutions Inc.....D.....866 226-2838
14201 Franklin Ave Tustin (92780) ***(P-14168)***
ABM Engineering, Oakland *Also called ABM Facility Services Inc* ***(P-14169)***
ABM Facility Services Inc (HQ).....D.....510 251-0381
1266 14th St Ste 103 Oakland (94607) ***(P-14169)***
ABM Industries Incorporated.....E.....323 720-4020
5300 S Eastrn Ave Ste 110 Los Angeles (90040) ***(P-14170)***
ABM Janitorial Services Inc.....A.....213 384-0600
3580 Wilshire Blvd # 1130 Los Angeles (90010) ***(P-9911)***
ABM Janitorial Services Inc.....D.....559 651-1612
1335 N Plaza Dr Ste C Visalia (93291) ***(P-14171)***
ABM Janitorial Services Inc.....B.....559 276-9096
4747 N Bendel Ave Ste 104 Fresno (93722) ***(P-14172)***
ABM Janitorial Services Inc.....B.....925 924-0270
6671 Owens Dr Pleasanton (94588) ***(P-14173)***
ABM Janitorial Services Inc.....B.....916 374-1739
830 Riverside Pkwy Ste 40 West Sacramento (95605) ***(P-14174)***
ABM Janitorial Services Inc.....C.....909 987-3700
11955 Jack Benny Dr # 104 Rancho Cucamonga (91739) ***(P-14175)***
ABM Janitorial Services Inc.....C.....209 983-3923
2385 Arch Airport Rd # 100 Stockton (95206) ***(P-14176)***
ABM Parking Services.....D.....213 955-7945
945 W 8th St Los Angeles (90017) ***(P-17661)***
ABM Parking Services (PA).....C.....619 235-4500
3585 Corporate Ct San Diego (92123) ***(P-17662)***
ABM Securities, Los Angeles *Also called ABM Janitorial Services Inc* ***(P-9911)***
Abode Communities.....C.....213 629-2702
1149 S Hill St Fl 7 Los Angeles (90015) ***(P-11189)***
Abode Services (PA).....D.....510 657-7409
40849 Fremont Blvd Fremont (94538) ***(P-23457)***
Above Hlth HM Care Sltions LLC.....D.....714 585-2185
960 S Peregrine Pl Anaheim (92806) ***(P-22185)***
Abp Liquidating Corp.....E.....650 871-7689
299 Lawrence Ave South San Francisco (94080) ***(P-8637)***
Abraham Jsha Hschl Dy Schl Wst.....D.....818 707-2365
27400 Canwood St Agoura (91301) ***(P-24256)***
Abrazar Inc.....D.....714 893-3581
7101 Wyoming St Westminster (92683) ***(P-23458)***
ABRAZAR ELDERLY ASSISTANCE, Westminster *Also called Abrazar Inc* ***(P-23458)***

ABS Capital Partners III LP.....D.....415 617-2800
101 California St Fl 24 San Francisco (94111) ***(P-12196)***
ABS Computer Technologies, Whittier *Also called Magnell Associate Inc* ***(P-4590)***
ABS Computer Technologies, City of Industry *Also called Magnell Associate Inc* ***(P-7074)***
ABS Consulting Inc.....D.....714 734-4242
300 Commerce Ste 200 Irvine (92602) ***(P-25496)***
ABS Group, Irvine *Also called ABS Consulting Inc* ***(P-25496)***
Abs-American Building Supply, Sacramento *Also called American Building Supply Inc* ***(P-6806)***
ABS-Cbn International (HQ).....C.....800 527-2820
2001 Junipero Serra Blvd # 200 Daly City (94014) ***(P-5856)***
Absg Consulting Inc.....E.....510 508-6289
505 14th St Ste 900 Oakland (94612) ***(P-27616)***
Absg Consulting Inc.....D.....714 734-4242
300 Commerce Ste 200 Irvine (92602) ***(P-27617)***
Abshear Landscape Development.....E.....916 660-1617
3171b Rippey Rd Loomis (95650) ***(P-725)***
Abso.....C.....800 943-2589
101 Creekside Ridge Ct # 2 Roseville (95678) ***(P-14563)***
Absolutdata Technologies Inc.....D.....510 748-9922
1320 Harbor Bay Pkwy # 170 Alameda (94502) ***(P-16976)***
Absolute Exhibits Inc (PA).....D.....714 685-2800
1382 Valencia Ave Ste H Tustin (92780) ***(P-16977)***
Absolute Return Portfolio.....A.....800 800-7646
700 Newport Center Dr Newport Beach (92660) ***(P-12019)***
Absolute Towing-Hollenbeck Div.....E.....323 225-9294
4760 Valley Blvd Los Angeles (90032) ***(P-17845)***
Abtech Support, Carlsbad *Also called Abtech Technologies Inc* ***(P-16302)***
Abtech Technologies Inc.....D.....760 827-5100
2042 Corte Del Nogal D Carlsbad (92011) ***(P-16302)***
Abx Engineering Inc.....D.....650 552-2300
875 Stanton Rd Burlingame (94010) ***(P-7433)***
Abzooba Inc.....C.....650 453-8760
1551 Mccarthy Blvd # 204 Milpitas (95035) ***(P-14958)***
AC Enterprises, Hayward *Also called Andrew Chekene Enterprises Inc* ***(P-1118)***
AC Hotel San Jose Downtown, San Jose *Also called Sj Hotel Manager LLC* ***(P-13241)***
AC Square Inc.....C.....650 293-2730
4590 Qantas Ln Stockton (95206) ***(P-27618)***
AC TRANSIT, Oakland *Also called Alameda-Contra Costa Trnst Dst* ***(P-3638)***
Aca Financial Guaranty Corp.....D.....323 255-3583
7189 N Figueroa St Los Angeles (90042) ***(P-9867)***
Academy Foundation (HQ).....D.....310 247-3000
8949 Wilshire Blvd Beverly Hills (90211) ***(P-18176)***
Academy Mpic Arts & Sciences (PA).....D.....310 247-3000
8949 Wilshire Blvd Beverly Hills (90211) ***(P-24992)***
Academy Swim Club.....D.....661 702-8585
28079 Smyth Dr Valencia (91355) ***(P-18817)***
Academy TV Arts & Sciences.....D.....818 754-2800
5220 Lankershim Blvd North Hollywood (91601) ***(P-24993)***
Acalvio Technologies Inc.....D.....408 931-6160
2520 Mission College Blvd # 110 Santa Clara (95054) ***(P-16866)***
ACC Senior Services, Sacramento *Also called Asian Community Center of Sac* ***(P-23493)***
ACC West Coast, Benicia *Also called American Civil Const* ***(P-1718)***
ACC-Gwg LLC.....D.....530 473-2827
6133 Abel Rd Williams (95987) ***(P-27619)***
Accel Biotech LLC.....D.....408 354-1700
103 Cooper Ct Los Gatos (95032) ***(P-25497)***
Accel North America Inc.....C.....408 514-5199
4633 Old Ironsides Dr # 400 Santa Clara (95054) ***(P-6995)***
Accela Inc (PA).....C.....925 659-3200
2633 Camino Ramon Ste 500 San Ramon (94583) ***(P-15565)***
Accelerated Envmtl Svcs Inc.....D.....661 765-4003
23601 Taft Hwy Bakersfield (93311) ***(P-14177)***
Accelerize Inc (PA).....D.....949 515-2141
20411 Sw Birch St Ste 250 Newport Beach (92660) ***(P-14959)***
Accelon Inc.....E.....925 216-5735
2410 Camino Ramon Ste 194 San Ramon (94583) ***(P-14564)***
Accent Service Company Inc.....D.....877 611-0131
2001 Lemnos Dr Costa Mesa (92626) ***(P-14178)***
Accentcare Inc.....A.....858 576-7410
5050 Mrphy Knyan Rd St200 San Diego (92123) ***(P-22186)***
Accentcare HM Hlth Scrmnto Inc.....D.....916 852-5888
2880 Sunrise Blvd Ste 218 Rancho Cordova (95742) ***(P-22187)***
Accentcare Home Health.....E.....760 352-4022
2344 S 2nd St Ste A El Centro (92243) ***(P-22188)***
Accentcare Home Health Cal Inc.....D.....925 356-6066
2300 Contra Costa Blvd # 125 Pleasant Hill (94523) ***(P-22189)***
Accentcare Home Health Cal Inc.....E.....818 528-8855
15455 San Fernando Ste Mission Hills (91345) ***(P-22190)***
Accentcare Home Health Cal Inc.....D.....909 605-7000
1455 Auto Center Dr # 200 Ontario (91761) ***(P-22191)***
Accentcare Home Health Cal Inc.....C.....858 576-7410
5050 Murphy Canyon Rd # 200 San Diego (92123) ***(P-22192)***
Accentcare Home Health Cal Inc.....D.....949 250-0133
3636 Birch St Ste 195 Newport Beach (92660) ***(P-22193)***
Accenture Federal Services LLC.....C.....619 574-2400
1615 Murray Canyon Rd # 400 San Diego (92108) ***(P-27105)***
Accenture LLP.....B.....310 726-2700
2141 Rosecrans Ave # 3100 El Segundo (90245) ***(P-27106)***
Accenture LLP.....C.....415 537-5860
2 Santa Ana Ct Belvedere Tiburon (94920) ***(P-27107)***
Accenture LLP.....B.....415 537-5000
560 Mission St Fl 12 San Francisco (94105) ***(P-27108)***
Accenture LLP.....C.....408 817-2100
50 W San Fernando St # 1208 San Jose (95113) ***(P-27109)***
Accenture LLP.....C.....650 213-2000
50 W San Fernando St # 1200 San Jose (95113) ***(P-27110)***
Accenture LLP.....C.....916 557-2200
1415 L St Ste 700 Sacramento (95814) ***(P-27111)***

ALPHABETIC

Employee Codes: A=Over 500 employees, B=251-500
C=101-250, D=51-100, E=50
2019 Directory of California
Wholesalers and Services Companies
© Mergent Inc. 1-800-342-5647
1189

Accenture National SEC Svcs, San Diego *Also called Accenture Federal Services LLC* ***(P-27105)***
Access Biologicals LLC....D....760 597-9749
995 Park Center Dr Vista (92081) ***(P-8137)***
Access Business Group Intl LLC....C....800 879-2732
6500 Beach Blvd Buena Park (90621) ***(P-16978)***
Access Capital Services Inc (PA)....D....559 627-5221
1625 E Shaw Ave Ste 137 Fresno (93710) ***(P-13988)***
Access Communications, San Francisco *Also called Access Public Relations LLC* ***(P-27536)***
Access Dental Centers, Sacramento *Also called Access Dental Plan* ***(P-20106)***
Access Dental Plan (PA)....D....916 922-5000
8890 Cal Center Dr Sacramento (95826) ***(P-20106)***
Access Finance Inc....E....310 826-4000
3415 S Sepulveda Blvd # 400 Los Angeles (90034) ***(P-16979)***
Access Hollywood....C....818 840-4444
3000 W Alameda Ave Burbank (91523) ***(P-5765)***
Access Info MGT Shred Svcs LLC....D....805 529-6866
13950 Cerritos Corprt Dr C Cerritos (90703) ***(P-26744)***
Access Info MGT Shred Svcs LLC....D....925 461-5352
4501 Pell Dr Sacramento (95838) ***(P-4664)***
Access Integrated Healthcare....D....866 460-7465
550 N Brand Blvd Fl 20 Glendale (91203) ***(P-20979)***
Access Nurses Inc....D....858 458-4400
5935 Cornerstone Ct W San Diego (92121) ***(P-14565)***
Access Pacific Inc....E....626 792-0616
755 E Washington Blvd Pasadena (91104) ***(P-1455)***
Access Paratransit, El Monte *Also called Access Services* ***(P-3635)***
Access Public Relations LLC....D....415 904-7070
720 California St Fl 5 San Francisco (94108) ***(P-27536)***
Access Services....D....213 270-6000
3449 Santa Anita Ave El Monte (91731) ***(P-3635)***
Access Spclty Animal Hospitals....D....310 558-6100
9599 Jefferson Blvd Culver City (90232) ***(P-592)***
Access Systems Americas Inc....A....408 400-3000
3965 Freedom Cir Ste 200 Santa Clara (95054) ***(P-14960)***
Access To Loans For Learning....E....310 979-4700
1230 Rosecrans Ave # 560 Manhattan Beach (90266) ***(P-9868)***
Accessory Power, Westlake Village *Also called AP Global Inc* ***(P-7438)***
Accidental Fire & Casualty, Lancaster *Also called Wilshire Insurance Company* ***(P-10831)***
Accion Labs Us Inc....A....408 970-9809
4633 Old Ironsides Dr # 304 Santa Clara (95054) ***(P-26680)***
Acco Engineered Systems Inc....D....323 727-7765
3421 S Malt Ave Commerce (90040) ***(P-17889)***
Acco Engineered Systems Inc....C....510 346-4300
1133 Aladdin Ave San Leandro (94577) ***(P-2083)***
Acco Engineered Systems Inc....E....323 201-0931
6446 E Washington Blvd Commerce (90040) ***(P-16980)***
Accor Bus & Leisure N Amer LLC....C....650 598-9000
223 Twin Dolphin Dr Redwood City (94065) ***(P-12303)***
Accor Corp....C....310 278-5444
8555 Beverly Blvd Los Angeles (90048) ***(P-12304)***
Accor Services US LLC....B....310 319-3122
101 Wilshire Blvd Santa Monica (90401) ***(P-12305)***
Accor Services US LLC (HQ)....A....415 772-5000
950 Mason St San Francisco (94108) ***(P-12306)***
Account Control Technology Inc....E....661 395-5702
5531 Bus Park S Ste 100 Bakersfield (93309) ***(P-13989)***
Accountable Health Staff Inc....B....916 286-7667
7777 Greenback Ln Ste 205 Citrus Heights (95610) ***(P-14566)***
Accountants 4 Contract....D....415 781-8644
235 Montgomery St Ste 630 San Francisco (94104) ***(P-26140)***
Accountemps, San Francisco *Also called Robert Half International Inc* ***(P-14736)***
Accountemps, Menlo Park *Also called Robert Half International Inc* ***(P-14738)***
Accounting Department, Orland *Also called City of Orland* ***(P-6227)***
Accountnow Inc....A....925 498-1800
2603 Camino Ramon Ste 485 San Ramon (94583) ***(P-27112)***
Accounts Payable Department, Ontario *Also called Technicolor HM Entrmt Svcs Inc* ***(P-18226)***
Accredited Nursing Care, Pasadena *Also called Accredited Nursing Services* ***(P-20219)***
Accredited Nursing Care, Woodland Hills *Also called Dunn & Berger Inc* ***(P-22287)***
Accredited Nursing Care, Costa Mesa *Also called Accredited Nursing Services* ***(P-22194)***
Accredited Nursing Services....D....626 573-1234
80 S Lake Ave Ste 630 Pasadena (91101) ***(P-20219)***
Accredited Nursing Services....D....714 973-1234
950 S Coast Dr Ste 215 Costa Mesa (92626) ***(P-22194)***
Accretive Solutions Inc (HQ)....A....312 994-4600
17101 Armstrong Ave # 100 Irvine (92614) ***(P-26141)***
Accs, San Clemente *Also called American Corrective Counseling* ***(P-23473)***
Acct Holdings LLC....A....916 971-1981
5949 Fair Oaks Blvd Carmichael (95608) ***(P-16981)***
ACCU, Glendora *Also called Americas Christian Credit Un* ***(P-9621)***
Accu-Bore Directional Drilling, Benicia *Also called Mdr Inc* ***(P-25815)***
Accu-Count Inventory Svcs Inc....D....805 231-6310
1024 N Citrus Ave Covina (91722) ***(P-16982)***
Accumen Inc (PA)....D....858 777-8160
5414 Oberlin Dr Ste 200 San Diego (92121) ***(P-22195)***
Accunex Inc....E....818 882-5858
20700 Lassen St Chatsworth (91311) ***(P-2500)***
Accurate Background LLC (PA)....B....800 784-3911
7515 Irvine Center Dr Irvine (92618) ***(P-16206)***
Accurate Courier Services Inc....D....310 481-3937
11022 Santa Monica Blvd # 360 Los Angeles (90025) ***(P-3964)***
Accurate Delivery Systems Inc....D....951 823-8870
173 Resource Dr Bloomington (92316) ***(P-3965)***
Accurate Electronics, Chatsworth *Also called Accunex Inc* ***(P-2500)***
Accurate Express, Los Angeles *Also called Accurate Services Inc* ***(P-9667)***
Accurate Services Inc....C....323 906-1000
3429 Glendale Blvd Los Angeles (90039) ***(P-9667)***
Accutherm Air Heating & Coolg, Garden Grove *Also called Accutherm Refrigeraton Inc* ***(P-2084)***
Accutherm Refrigeraton Inc....D....714 766-7800
11264 Monarch St Ste A Garden Grove (92841) ***(P-2084)***
Ace Beverage Co....D....323 266-6238
550 S Mission Rd Los Angeles (90033) ***(P-8975)***
Ace Cash Express Inc....C....951 509-3506
6302 Van Buren Blvd Riverside (92503) ***(P-9668)***
Ace Duraflo Pipe Restoration, Santa Ana *Also called Pipe Restoration Inc* ***(P-2310)***
Ace Fence Company, La Puente *Also called Apw Construction Inc* ***(P-1874)***
Ace Financial Services Inc....D....510 790-4600
39300 Civic Center Dr # 290 Fremont (94538) ***(P-10509)***
Ace Floor Co Inc....D....805 955-9000
5155 Goldman Ave Moorpark (93021) ***(P-3093)***
Ace Hardware, Fresno *Also called Fresno Plumbing & Heating Inc* ***(P-2215)***
Ace Hardware, Bishop *Also called High Country Lumber Inc* ***(P-6831)***
Ace High Entertainnment LLC....E....916 243-5515
125 Sconce Way Sacramento (95838) ***(P-18502)***
Ace Industrial Supply Inc (PA)....E....818 252-1981
7535 N San Fernando Rd Burbank (91505) ***(P-1110)***
Ace Parking Management Inc....C....510 589-2313
1901 Harrison St Ste 102 Oakland (94612) ***(P-17663)***
Ace Parking Management Inc....C....858 552-0237
4352 La Jolla Village Dr San Diego (92122) ***(P-17664)***
Ace Parking Management Inc....D....415 345-8354
711 Van Ness Ave San Francisco (94102) ***(P-17665)***
Ace Parking Management Inc....C....510 272-9788
2101 Webster St Oakland (94612) ***(P-17666)***
Ace Parking Management Inc....C....510 251-0509
1330 Broadway Ste 915 Oakland (94612) ***(P-17667)***
Ace Parking Management Inc....C....949 727-1470
71 Fortune Dr Ste 916 Irvine (92618) ***(P-17668)***
Ace Parking Management Inc....C....619 238-4765
110 W A St Ste 105 San Diego (92101) ***(P-17669)***
Ace Parking Management Inc....D....415 749-1949
415 Taylor St San Francisco (94102) ***(P-17670)***
Ace Parking Management Inc (PA)....E....619 233-6624
645 Ash St San Diego (92101) ***(P-17671)***
Ace Parking Management Inc....D....408 437-2185
2050 Gateway Pl San Jose (95110) ***(P-17672)***
Ace Parking Management Inc....C....714 845-8000
21500 Pacific Coast Hwy Huntington Beach (92648) ***(P-17673)***
Ace Parking Management Inc....D....619 230-0003
440 11th Ave San Diego (92101) ***(P-17674)***
Ace Parking Management Inc....C....619 232-1234
1 Market Pl San Diego (92101) ***(P-17675)***
Ace Property & Casualty, Fremont *Also called Ace Financial Services Inc* ***(P-10509)***
Ace Relocation Systems Inc (PA)....D....858 677-5500
5608 Eastgate Dr San Diego (92121) ***(P-3966)***
Ace Relocation Systems Inc....E....310 632-2800
189 W Victoria St Long Beach (90805) ***(P-3967)***
Ace Tomato Company Inc....D....209 982-0734
777 N Pershing Ave Ste 1a Stockton (95203) ***(P-33)***
Ace USA....D....510 790-4695
39300 Civic Center Dr # 290 Fremont (94538) ***(P-10510)***
Acea Biosciences Inc....D....858 724-0928
6779 Mesa Ridge Rd # 100 San Diego (92121) ***(P-26309)***
Acemi Nursery Inc....D....559 842-7766
3626 N Howard Ave Kerman (93630) ***(P-199)***
Acepex Management Corporation....B....909 591-1999
13401 Yorba Ave Chino (91710) ***(P-26745)***
Acepex Management Corporation....C....909 625-6900
10643 Mills Ave Montclair (91763) ***(P-27573)***
Acer America Corporation (HQ)....D....408 533-7700
333 W San Carlos St San Jose (95110) ***(P-16303)***
Acera, Oakland *Also called Alameda County Employees Retir* ***(P-10475)***
Acetech Construction Inc....E....213 637-4702
3699 Wilshire Blvd # 655 Los Angeles (90010) ***(P-25498)***
Aceteck Roofing Co Inc....E....323 231-6060
5830 Woodlawn Ave Los Angeles (90003) ***(P-3121)***
Aceva Technologies Inc....C....650 227-5500
1810 Gateway Dr Ste 360 San Mateo (94404) ***(P-14030)***
Acf Components & Fasteners Inc....D....949 833-0506
742 Arrow Grand Cir Covina (91722) ***(P-7571)***
Achates Power Inc....D....858 535-9920
4060 Sorrento Valley Blvd A San Diego (92121) ***(P-26310)***
Achates Security Agency, Salinas *Also called J Waters Inc* ***(P-16707)***
Achem Industry America Inc (PA)....E....562 802-0998
13226 Alondra Blvd Cerritos (90703) ***(P-7824)***
Achiever Christian Pre-Schl &....E....408 264-2345
540 Sands Dr San Jose (95125) ***(P-24257)***
Achievo Corporation (PA)....D....925 498-8864
1400 Terra Bella Ave E Mountain View (94043) ***(P-14961)***
Aci International (PA)....D....310 889-3400
844 Moraga Dr Los Angeles (90049) ***(P-8342)***
ACI Construction Company Inc....E....909 391-4477
207 W State St Ontario (91762) ***(P-25499)***
Acm Technologies Inc (PA)....D....951 738-9898
2535 Research Dr Corona (92882) ***(P-6948)***
Acme Building Maintenance Co (HQ)....D....408 263-5911
941 Catherine St Alviso (95002) ***(P-14179)***
Acme Construction Company Inc....D....209 523-2674
1565 Cummins Dr Modesto (95358) ***(P-1370)***
Acme Furniture Industry Inc (PA)....D....626 964-3456
18895 Arenth Ave City of Industry (91748) ***(P-6706)***
Acme Metals & Steel Supply Inc, Gardena *Also called Acme Metals LLC* ***(P-7251)***

Mergent e-mail: customerrelations@mergent.com
1190
2019 Directory of California Wholesalers and Services Companies
(P-0000) Products & Services Section entry number
(PA)=Parent Co (HQ)=Headquarters (DH)=Div Headquarters

Acme Metals LLC...D...310 329-2263
14930 S San Pedro St Gardena (90248) *(P-7251)*
Acme Staffing, El Centro *Also called I N C Builders Inc (P-14860)*
Acme Television Holdings LLC...B...714 245-9499
4790 Irvine Blvd Ste 105 Irvine (92620) *(P-5766)*
Acme Trading, City of Industry *Also called Acme Furniture Industry Inc (P-6706)*
Acme-Hardesty Co., Santa Barbara *Also called Jacob Stern & Sons Inc (P-8929)*
Acmpc California 3 LLC...C...559 591-6140
38773 Rd 48 Lindsay (93247) *(P-200)*
Acom Solutions Inc (PA)...E...562 424-7899
2850 E 29th St Long Beach (90806) *(P-15907)*
Acon Laboratories Inc (PA)...D...858 875-8000
10125 Mesa Rim Rd San Diego (92121) *(P-7148)*
Acosta Inc...C...714 988-1500
915 W Imperial Hwy # 200 Brea (92821) *(P-8370)*
Acosta Inc...D...925 600-3500
5735 W Las Positas Blvd # 300 Pleasanton (94588) *(P-8371)*
Acosta Sales & Marketing, Brea *Also called Acosta Inc (P-8370)*
Acoustical Contractor, Thousand Oaks *Also called S A Cali-U Acoustics Inc (P-2954)*
Acrobat Staffing, San Diego *Also called SE Scher Corporation (P-14755)*
Acrobat Staffing, Rocklin *Also called SE Scher Corporation (P-14756)*
Acronics Systems Inc...C...408 432-0888
2102 Commerce Dr San Jose (95131) *(P-25500)*
Across Systems Inc...D...877 922-7677
100 N Brand Blvd Ste 100 Glendale (91203) *(P-6996)*
Acrt Pacific LLC...B...330 945-7500
3443 Deer Park Dr Ste B Stockton (95219) *(P-27620)*
ACS, Huntington Beach *Also called Applied Computer Solutions (P-14990)*
ACS Communications Inc...E...310 767-2145
680 Knox St Ste 150 Torrance (90502) *(P-2501)*
ACS Security Industries Inc...D...310 475-9016
1964 Westwood Blvd # 235 Los Angeles (90025) *(P-16867)*
Acss, Beaumont *Also called Anderson Chrnesky Strl Stl Inc (P-3359)*
Act 1 Group Inc (PA)...D...310 532-1529
1999 W 190th St Torrance (90504) *(P-14567)*
Act 1 Personnel Services, Torrance *Also called All In One Inc (P-26753)*
Act Associates, Folsom *Also called Matthew Burns (P-1589)*
Act Fulfillment Inc...C...909 930-9083
3155 Universe Dr Mira Loma (91752) *(P-4521)*
Act Home Health Inc...D...714 560-0800
12431 Lewis St Ste 101 Garden Grove (92840) *(P-22196)*
ACT Lighting Inc...A...818 707-0884
2313 N Valley St Burbank (91505) *(P-7324)*
Actian Corporation (PA)...D...650 587-5500
2300 Geng Rd Ste 150 Palo Alto (94303) *(P-15908)*
Action Day Nrseries Prmry Plus...D...408 370-0350
18720 Bucknall Rd Saratoga (95070) *(P-24258)*
Action Day Nrseries Prmry Plus...E...408 266-8952
2148 Lincoln Ave San Jose (95125) *(P-24259)*
Action Force Security...E...310 715-6053
1212 W Gardena Blvd Ste C Gardena (90247) *(P-16543)*
Action Home Nursing Services...D...530 756-2600
561 Torero Way El Dorado Hills (95762) *(P-22197)*
Action Messenger Service, Los Angeles *Also called Peach Inc (P-4426)*
Action Property Management Inc...C...800 400-2284
530 S Hewitt St Los Angeles (90013) *(P-25090)*
Action Property Management Inc (PA)...D...949 450-0202
2603 Main St Ste 500 Irvine (92614) *(P-11146)*
Action Roofing, Santa Barbara *Also called JM Roofing Company Inc (P-3169)*
Action Sales, Monterey Park *Also called JC Foodservice Inc (P-7138)*
Action Sports Retailer...D...949 226-5744
31910 Del Obispo St # 200 San Juan Capistrano (92675) *(P-16983)*
Activcare Living Inc (PA)...C...858 565-4424
9619 Chesapeake Dr # 103 San Diego (92123) *(P-26746)*
Active Lawyers Referral Svc...D...310 247-0425
9301 Wilshire Blvd # 508 Beverly Hills (90210) *(P-27916)*
Active Measure Inc...D...818 237-8417
550 N Brand Blvd Ste 1850 Glendale (91203) *(P-26496)*
Active Motif Inc (PA)...D...760 431-1263
1914 Palomar Oaks Way # 150 Carlsbad (92008) *(P-26311)*
Active Storage Inc...E...818 709-1133
2295 Jefferson St Torrance (90501) *(P-16984)*
Active Wellness LLC...A...415 741-3300
600 California St Fl 11 San Francisco (94108) *(P-26747)*
Actividentity Corporation...C...510 574-0100
6623 Dumbarton Cir Fremont (94555) *(P-16083)*
Activision Blizzard Inc...C...415 881-9100
4 Hamilton Landing Novato (94949) *(P-15566)*
Activision Blizzard Inc...C...310 581-4700
3420 Ocean Park Blvd # 2000 Santa Monica (90405) *(P-14962)*
Activision Blizzard Inc (PA)...B...310 255-2000
3100 Ocean Park Blvd Santa Monica (90405) *(P-15567)*
Activision Blizzard Inc...D...949 955-1380
3 Blizzard Irvine (92618) *(P-15568)*
Activision Blizzard Inc...C...310 431-4000
653 W Fallbrook Ave # 104 Fresno (93711) *(P-4522)*
Activision Publishing Inc (HQ)...A...310 255-2000
3100 Ocean Park Blvd Santa Monica (90405) *(P-15569)*
Acts For Children (PA)...D...909 877-5499
18136 Jurupa Ave Bloomington (92316) *(P-24406)*
Actual Reality Pictures Inc...E...818 325-8800
16030 Ventura Blvd # 380 Encino (91436) *(P-11190)*
Acumen LLC...C...650 558-8882
500 Airport Blvd Ste 100 Burlingame (94010) *(P-15909)*
ACWD, Fremont *Also called Alameda County Water District (P-6206)*
Acxiom Corporation...E...714 636-3093
8801 Elmer Ln Garden Grove (92841) *(P-16207)*
Acxiom Corporation...D...650 356-3400
100 Redwood Shores Pkwy Redwood City (94065) *(P-16208)*
Ad Force Private Security, Stockton *Also called California Guard Inc (P-16596)*
Ad Land Venture LP...D...916 853-9015
3217 Fitzgerald Rd Rancho Cordova (95742) *(P-794)*
Ad Results Media LLC...D...858 480-5223
111 C St Encinitas (92024) *(P-13933)*
Adair Enterprises...D...714 998-5551
2390 N American Way Orange (92865) *(P-18338)*
Adams & Barnes Inc...E...626 358-1858
433 W Foothill Blvd Monrovia (91016) *(P-11191)*
Adams Early Childhood Lrng Ctr, La Quinta *Also called Adams Learning Center (P-24260)*
Adams Learning Center...E...760 777-4260
50800 Desert Club Dr La Quinta (92253) *(P-24260)*
Adams Pool Specialties, Sacramento *Also called Dave Gross Enterprises Inc (P-3509)*
Adams Steel, Anaheim *Also called Self Serve Auto Dismantlers (P-6475)*
Adams Streeter Civil Engineers...D...949 474-2330
15 Corporate Park Irvine (92606) *(P-25501)*
Adaptamed LLC...C...877 478-7773
6699 Alvarado Rd Ste 2301 San Diego (92120) *(P-14963)*
Adaptive Insights Inc (HQ)...C...650 528-7500
3350 W Byshore Rd Ste 200 Palo Alto (94303) *(P-15570)*
Adaptive Spectrum and Signal A...D...650 264-2667
333 Twin Dolphin Dr # 300 Redwood City (94065) *(P-5442)*
Adassured, Oceanside *Also called Pepperjam LLC (P-15350)*
Adco Container Company...E...818 998-2565
9959 Canoga Ave Chatsworth (91311) *(P-7825)*
Adcolony Inc...D...650 625-1262
11400 W Olympic Blvd # 1200 Los Angeles (90064) *(P-14964)*
Adcom Interactive Media Inc...D...800 296-7104
901 W Alameda Ave Ste 102 Burbank (91506) *(P-16304)*
Add Media, Los Angeles *Also called Admarketing Inc (P-13788)*
Add2net Inc (PA)...E...714 521-8150
931 E La Habra Blvd La Habra (90631) *(P-16305)*
Added Value LLC (HQ)...C...323 254-4326
3400 Cahuenga Blvd W B Los Angeles (90068) *(P-26497)*
Addepar Inc (PA)...D...855 464-6268
303 Bryant St Mountain View (94041) *(P-14965)*
Addiction RES & Trtmnt Inc...D...415 928-7800
433 Turk St San Francisco (94102) *(P-22496)*
Addison-Penzak Jewish Communit...C...408 358-3636
14855 Oka Rd Ste 201 Los Gatos (95032) *(P-18573)*
Addus Healthcare Inc...D...209 526-8451
817 Coffee Rd Ste B1 Modesto (95355) *(P-22198)*
Addus Healthcare Inc...E...530 566-0405
936 Mangrove Ave Chico (95926) *(P-22199)*
Addus Healthcare Inc...B...650 638-7943
1730 S Amphlett Blvd San Mateo (94402) *(P-22200)*
Addus Healthcare Inc...D...530 247-0858
2851 Park Marina Dr # 150 Redding (96001) *(P-20161)*
Adee Plumbing and Heating Inc (PA)...D...323 296-8787
5457 Crenshaw Blvd Los Angeles (90043) *(P-2085)*
Adelphia, Fullerton *Also called Spectrum MGT Holdg Co LLC (P-5938)*
Adelson Testan Brundo Novel (PA)...E...805 604-1816
31330 Oak Crest Dr Westlake Village (91361) *(P-22905)*
Adept Consumer Testing Inc...E...310 279-4600
16130 Ventura Blvd # 200 Encino (91436) *(P-26498)*
Aderholt Specialty Company Inc...D...209 526-2000
1557 Cummins Dr Modesto (95358) *(P-2835)*
Adesa Auction, Sacramento *Also called Adesa Corporation LLC (P-6573)*
Adesa Corporation LLC...C...916 388-8899
8649 Kiefer Blvd Sacramento (95826) *(P-6573)*
Adesa Corporation LLC...E...951 361-9400
11625 Nino Way Mira Loma (91752) *(P-6574)*
Adesa Corporation LLC...C...619 661-5565
2175 Cactus Rd San Diego (92154) *(P-6575)*
Adesso Inc...C...909 839-2929
160 Commerce Way Walnut (91789) *(P-6997)*
Adeste Program Company...B...213 251-3551
1531 James M Wood Blvd Los Angeles (90015) *(P-24261)*
Adexa Inc (PA)...E...310 642-2100
5777 W Century Blvd # 1100 Los Angeles (90045) *(P-15571)*
Adg Corporation...E...415 864-4090
1871 Market St San Francisco (94103) *(P-12197)*
Adhei Enterprises Inc...E...818 788-7680
4627 Lemona Ave Sherman Oaks (91403) *(P-14180)*
ADI, San Bernardino *Also called Aviation & Defense Inc (P-4874)*
Adia LLC...D...310 370-0555
3625 Del Amo Blvd Ste 225 Torrance (90503) *(P-22201)*
Adicio Inc...D...760 602-9502
5993 Avenida Encinas # 100 Carlsbad (92008) *(P-5443)*
Adir International LLC...C...213 639-7716
4444 Ayers Ave Vernon (90058) *(P-1371)*
Adir International LLC...D...213 386-4412
4444-46 Ayers Ave Los Angeles (90023) *(P-4523)*
Adivo Associates LLC...D...415 992-1449
1 Post St Ste 2750 San Francisco (94104) *(P-27113)*
Adj Products LLC (PA)...C...323 582-2650
6122 S Eastern Ave Commerce (90040) *(P-7325)*
Adkan Engineers, Riverside *Also called Adkison Engineers Inc (P-25502)*
Adkison Engineers Inc...D...951 688-0241
6879 Airport Dr Riverside (92504) *(P-25502)*
Adlink Cable Advertising LLC...C...310 477-3994
11150 Santa Monica Blvd # 100 Los Angeles (90025) *(P-13787)*
ADM Furniture Inc...D...310 762-2800
11680 Wright Rd Lynwood (90262) *(P-6707)*
Admarketing Inc...D...310 203-8400
1801 Century Park E # 2100 Los Angeles (90067) *(P-13788)*
Admedia, Burbank *Also called Adcom Interactive Media Inc (P-16304)*

ALPHABETIC

Employee Codes: A=Over 500 employees, B=251-500
C=101-250, D=51-100, E=50
2019 Directory of California
Wholesalers and Services Companies
© Mergent Inc. 1-800-342-5647
1191

Admhs, Santa Barbara *Also called County of Santa Barbara Alcoho* ***(P-22557)***
Admin, Bakersfield *Also called County of Kern* ***(P-19408)***
Administration, Los Angeles *Also called County of Los Angeles* ***(P-24879)***
Administration of Public Works, Martinez *Also called County of Contra Costa* ***(P-1747)***
Administrative Office, Redding *Also called Mercy HM Svcs A Cal Ltd Partnr* ***(P-19686)***
ADMINISTRATIVE OFFICES, Upland *Also called Inland Valley Drug & Alcohol* ***(P-23856)***
Administrative Services, San Francisco *Also called City & County of San Francisco* ***(P-26808)***
Administrative Services SD......E......619 398-2314
3473 Kurtz St San Diego (92110) ***(P-3864)***
Administrative Svcs Coop Inc......C......310 715-1968
2129 W Rosecrans Ave Gardena (90249) ***(P-27114)***
Administrative Systems Inc......D......916 563-1121
1651 Response Rd Ste 350 Sacramento (95815) ***(P-16985)***
Adminstrtive Office of US Crts......D......408 535-5200
280 S 1st St San Jose (95113) ***(P-23459)***
Adminstrtive Office of US Crts......C......619 557-6650
101 W Broadway Ste 700 San Diego (92101) ***(P-23460)***
Admiral Home Health Inc......D......562 421-0777
4010 Watson Plaza Dr # 140 Lakewood (90712) ***(P-22202)***
Admiral Security Services Inc......B......888 471-1128
2151 Salvio St Ste 260 Concord (94520) ***(P-16868)***
Admiralty Partners Inc......D......310 471-3772
1170 Somera Rd Los Angeles (90077) ***(P-12198)***
Adobe Animal Hospital Inc......D......650 948-9661
4470 El Camino Real Los Altos (94022) ***(P-593)***
Adobe Inc (PA)......A......408 536-6000
345 Park Ave San Jose (95110) ***(P-15572)***
Adobe Packing Company (PA)......C......831 753-6195
367 W Market St Salinas (93901) ***(P-488)***
Adobe Systems Incorporated......A......415 832-2000
601 And 625 Townsend St San Francisco (94103) ***(P-15573)***
Adolph Gasser Inc......C......415 495-3852
4340 Redwood Hwy Ste 227 San Rafael (94903) ***(P-6939)***
Adolph Gasser Photography, San Rafael *Also called Adolph Gasser Inc* ***(P-6939)***
Adopt-A-Beach, Costa Mesa *Also called Adopt-A-Highway Maintenance* ***(P-1712)***
Adopt-A-Highway Maintenance......C......800 200-0003
3158 Red Hill Ave Ste 200 Costa Mesa (92626) ***(P-1712)***
Adorno Construction Inc......D......408 369-8675
520 Westchester Dr Ste A Campbell (95008) ***(P-3212)***
ADP, Buena Park *Also called Automatic Data Processing Inc* ***(P-16085)***
ADP, Rancho Cucamonga *Also called Automatic Data Processing Inc* ***(P-16086)***
ADP, Camarillo *Also called Automatic Data Processing Inc* ***(P-16087)***
ADP, San Francisco *Also called Automatic Data Processing Inc* ***(P-16088)***
ADP, San Dimas *Also called Automatic Data Processing Inc* ***(P-16089)***
ADP, Redwood City *Also called Automatic Data Processing Inc* ***(P-16090)***
ADP, Novato *Also called Automatic Data Processing Inc* ***(P-16091)***
ADP, Irvine *Also called Automatic Data Processing Inc* ***(P-16092)***
ADP, Milpitas *Also called Automatic Data Processing Inc* ***(P-16093)***
ADP, La Palma *Also called Automatic Data Processing Inc* ***(P-16094)***
ADP, San Dimas *Also called Automatic Data Processing Inc* ***(P-16096)***
ADP, Los Angeles *Also called Automatic Data Processing Inc* ***(P-16097)***
ADP, San Diego *Also called Automatic Data Processing Inc* ***(P-16098)***
Adrianas Insurance Svcs Inc (PA)......D......909 291-4040
9445 Charles Smith Ave Rancho Cucamonga (91730) ***(P-10511)***
Adroll Inc (PA)......D......877 723-7655
2300 Harrison St Fl 2 San Francisco (94110) ***(P-13789)***
ADS, Bloomington *Also called Accurate Delivery Systems Inc* ***(P-3965)***
ADS Techonlogy, Walnut *Also called Adesso Inc* ***(P-6997)***
ADT Security Corporation......E......925 251-9088
2150 John Glenn Dr # 100 Concord (94520) ***(P-16869)***
Adtek Engineering Service......D......800 451-0782
2090 N Tustin Ave Ste 160 Santa Ana (92705) ***(P-25503)***
Adult & Childrens Dental Group, South Gate *Also called Scott Jacks DDS Inc* ***(P-20137)***
ADULT DAY CARE CENTER, San Francisco *Also called Institute On Aging* ***(P-23859)***
Adult Mddlhlth Otptient Clinic, Fairfield *Also called County of Solano* ***(P-20926)***
Adult Probation Department, San Francisco *Also called City & County of San Francisco* ***(P-23573)***
Adult Probation Department, San Jose *Also called Santa Clara County of* ***(P-24030)***
Advance Beverage Co Inc......D......661 833-3783
5200 District Blvd Bakersfield (93313) ***(P-8976)***
Advance Building Maintenance......B......310 247-0077
9601 Wilshire Blvd Gl25 Beverly Hills (90210) ***(P-14181)***
Advance Disposal Company, Hesperia *Also called Best Way Disposal Co Inc* ***(P-6353)***
Advance Health Solutions LLC......D......858 876-0136
7825 Fay Ave Ste 200 La Jolla (92037) ***(P-22203)***
Advance Services Inc......A......408 767-2797
8021 Kern Ave Gilroy (95020) ***(P-17919)***
Advance Staffing Inc......B......408 205-6154
2060 Walsh Ave Ste 101 Santa Clara (95050) ***(P-14808)***
Advanced Acoustics......E......925 299-0515
3430 Golden Gate Way Lafayette (94549) ***(P-2836)***
Advanced Air LLC......D......310 676-4673
12101 Crenshaw Blvd Ste 1 Hawthorne (90250) ***(P-4855)***
Advanced Bioservices LLC (PA)......D......818 342-0100
19255 Vanowen St Reseda (91335) ***(P-26748)***
Advanced Cable Technologies......E......818 262-6484
13400 Saticoy St Ste 30 North Hollywood (91605) ***(P-1890)***
Advanced Cell Diagnostics Inc......D......510 576-8800
7707 Gateway Blvd Newark (94560) ***(P-26312)***
Advanced Cleanup Tech Inc (PA)......C......310 763-1423
20928 S Lamberton Ave Carson (90810) ***(P-27574)***
Advanced Clnroom McRclean Corp......C......714 751-1152
3250 S Susan St Ste A Santa Ana (92704) ***(P-14182)***
Advanced Commercial Corporatio......C......760 431-8500
5900 Pasteur Ct Ste 200 Carlsbad (92008) ***(P-12020)***
Advanced Communication Service......C......909 210-9328
2650 Flora Spiegel Way Corona (92881) ***(P-16986)***
Advanced Critical Care Emerge......D......818 887-2262
20051 Ventura Blvd Ste I Woodland Hills (91364) ***(P-594)***
Advanced Dcument Solutions Inc (PA)......E......661 251-0337
24307 Magic Mountain Pkwy Valencia (91355) ***(P-26126)***
Advanced Dental Imaging LLC......E......805 687-5571
4028 Via Laguna Santa Barbara (93110) ***(P-22161)***
Advanced Digital Services Inc (PA)......D......323 962-8585
948 N Cahuenga Blvd Los Angeles (90038) ***(P-18011)***
Advanced Electronic Solutions, Irvine *Also called Patric Communications Inc* ***(P-2676)***
Advanced Environmental Inc......E......909 356-9025
13579 Whittram Ave Fontana (92335) ***(P-3968)***
Advanced Fabrication Tech, Hayward *Also called R2g Enterprises Inc* ***(P-3193)***
Advanced Fresh Concepts Corp (PA)......D......310 604-3630
19205 S Laurel Park Rd Rancho Dominguez (90220) ***(P-12133)***
Advanced HM Hlth & Hospice Inc......D......916 978-0744
4354 Auburn Blvd Sacramento (95841) ***(P-20107)***
Advanced Home Health Inc......D......916 978-0744
4354 Auburn Blvd Sacramento (95841) ***(P-22204)***
Advanced Home House, Sacramento *Also called Advanced HM Hlth & Hospice Inc* ***(P-20107)***
Advanced Image Direct, Fullerton *Also called Real Estate Image Inc* ***(P-14061)***
Advanced Industrial Cmpt Inc (PA)......D......909 895-8989
21808 Garcia Ln City of Industry (91789) ***(P-6998)***
Advanced Industrial Services, Bakersfield *Also called CL Knox Inc* ***(P-1054)***
Advanced Industrial Svcs Cal, Paramount *Also called Advanced Industrial Svcs Inc* ***(P-2418)***
Advanced Industrial Svcs Inc......D......562 940-8305
7831 Alondra Blvd Paramount (90723) ***(P-2418)***
Advanced Lighting Concepts Inc......E......858 521-0233
11235 W Bernardo Ct # 102 San Diego (92127) ***(P-7326)***
Advanced Logistics MGT Inc......E......310 638-0715
19067 S Reyes Ave Compton (90221) ***(P-4095)***
Advanced Medical Imaging, Fresno *Also called Community Medical Centers* ***(P-21339)***
Advanced Medical MGT Inc......D......562 766-2000
5000 Arprt Plz Dr Ste 150 Long Beach (90815) ***(P-26749)***
Advanced Medical Placement......C......818 996-9812
18425 Burbank Blvd # 508 Tarzana (91356) ***(P-24729)***
Advanced Medical Reviews Inc......D......310 575-0900
600 Crprate Pinte Ste 300 Culver City (90230) ***(P-14809)***
Advanced Mp Technology Inc (PA)......C......949 492-6589
1010 Calle Sombra San Clemente (92673) ***(P-7434)***
Advanced Office, Santa Ana *Also called Integrus LLC* ***(P-6962)***
Advanced Programs Group, El Segundo *Also called Orbital Sciences Corporation* ***(P-26425)***
Advanced Protection Inds Inc......E......800 662-1711
25341 Commercentre Dr # 100 Lake Forest (92630) ***(P-16870)***
Advanced Rehabilitation Tech......D......858 621-5959
7950 Dunbrook Rd San Diego (92126) ***(P-7149)***
Advanced Resources, Fontana *Also called Advanced Environmental Inc* ***(P-3968)***
Advanced Rsrvation Systems Inc......D......858 300-8600
2445 Truxtun Rd Ste 205 San Diego (92106) ***(P-16306)***
Advanced Software Design Inc......D......925 975-0691
1371 Oakland Blvd Ste 100 Walnut Creek (94596) ***(P-14966)***
Advanced Software Dynamics, Walnut Creek *Also called Advanced Software Design Inc* ***(P-14966)***
Advanced Sterlization......D......909 350-6987
13135 Napa St Fontana (92335) ***(P-4524)***
Advanced Surgery Institute LLC......C......707 528-6331
1739 4th St Santa Rosa (95404) ***(P-19267)***
Advanced Test Eqp Rentals, San Diego *Also called Advanced Test Equipment Corp* ***(P-14465)***
Advanced Test Equipment Corp......D......858 558-6500
10401 Roselle St San Diego (92121) ***(P-14465)***
Advanced Trans Grp, Compton *Also called Advanced Logistics MGT Inc* ***(P-4095)***
Advanced Veterinary Care Ctr......D......310 542-8018
15926 Hawthorne Blvd Lawndale (90260) ***(P-595)***
Advantage Framing Solutions......E......530 742-7660
1965 N Beale Rd Marysville (95901) ***(P-1456)***
Advantage Ground Trnsp, Costa Mesa *Also called Advantage Ground Trnsp Corp* ***(P-3740)***
Advantage Ground Trnsp Corp......D......714 557-2465
2960 Airway Ave Ste B102 Costa Mesa (92626) ***(P-3740)***
Advantage Logistics Inc......C......408 943-6300
2071 Ringwood Ave Ste D San Jose (95131) ***(P-4995)***
Advantage Mailing LLC (PA)......C......714 538-3881
1600 N Kraemer Blvd Anaheim (92806) ***(P-14040)***
Advantage Mailing Service, Anaheim *Also called Advantage Mailing LLC* ***(P-14040)***
Advantage Media Services Inc......D......661 705-7588
28220 Industry Dr Valencia (91355) ***(P-4525)***
Advantage Plumbing Group Inc......D......714 898-6020
3331 Orangewood Ave Los Alamitos (90720) ***(P-2086)***
Advantage Pntg Solutions Inc......D......951 739-9204
14734 Yorba Ct Chino (91710) ***(P-2419)***
Advantage Produce Inc......E......213 627-2777
1511 Bay St Los Angeles (90021) ***(P-8638)***
Advantage Sales & Marketing......C......925 463-5600
5064 Franklin Dr Pleasanton (94588) ***(P-8372)***
Advantage Sales & Mktg Inc......C......310 321-6869
200 N Pacific Coast Hwy # 1000 El Segundo (90245) ***(P-8373)***
Advantage Sales & Mktg Inc (PA)......C......949 797-2900
18100 Von Karman Ave # 900 Irvine (92612) ***(P-8374)***
Advantage Sales & Mktg LLC......D......925 463-5600
6700 Koll Center Pkwy # 300 Pleasanton (94566) ***(P-8375)***
Advantage Sales & Mktg LLC (HQ)......C......949 797-2900
18100 Von Karman Ave # 900 Irvine (92612) ***(P-26499)***
Advantage Solutions, Irvine *Also called Advantage Sales & Mktg Inc* ***(P-8374)***
Advantage Solutions, Irvine *Also called Advantage Sales & Mktg LLC* ***(P-26499)***

Mergent e-mail: customerrelations@mergent.com
1192
2019 Directory of California
Wholesalers and Services Companies
(P-0000) Products & Services Section entry number
(PA)=Parent Co (HQ)=Headquarters (DH)=Div Headquarters

Advantage Waypoint LLC ....D....717 424-4973
2642 Michelle Dr Tustin (92780) *(P-8376)*
Advantage-Crown Sls & Mktg LLC (HQ) ....A....714 780-3000
1400 S Douglass Rd # 200 Anaheim (92806) *(P-8377)*
Advantech Corporation (HQ) ....D....408 519-3800
380 Fairview Way Milpitas (95035) *(P-6999)*
Advantedge Technology Inc ....D....805 488-0405
271 Market St Ste 15 Port Hueneme (93041) *(P-25504)*
Advantis Global Inc (PA) ....C....415 850-1500
301 Howard St Ste 1400 San Francisco (94105) *(P-16307)*
Advent Group Ministries Inc ....D....408 281-0708
90 Great Oaks Blvd # 108 San Jose (95119) *(P-24407)*
Advent Resources Inc ....D....310 241-1500
235 W 7th St San Pedro (90731) *(P-15574)*
Advent Securities Investments (PA) ....E....562 920-5467
9631 Alondra Blvd Ste 202 Bellflower (90706) *(P-9912)*
Advent Software Inc (HQ) ....C....415 543-7696
600 Townsend St Fl 5 San Francisco (94103) *(P-14967)*
ADVENTIST HEALTH, Hanford *Also called Hanford Community Hospital (P-21438)*
Adventist Health Clearlake (HQ) ....B....707 994-6486
15630 18th Ave Clearlake (95422) *(P-21263)*
Adventist Health Cmnty. Care, Dinuba *Also called Adventist Health System (P-19268)*
Adventist Health Homecare Svcs, Glendale *Also called Glendale Adventist Medical Ctr (P-22301)*
Adventist Health Sonora (HQ) ....A....209 532-5000
1000 Greenley Rd Sonora (95370) *(P-21264)*
Adventist Health System ....A....559 595-9890
250 W El Monte Way Dinuba (93618) *(P-19268)*
Adventist Health System/West ....C....707 995-4888
14880 Olympic Dr Clearlake (95422) *(P-19269)*
Adventist Health System/West (PA) ....B....916 781-2000
2100 Douglas Blvd Roseville (95661) *(P-21265)*
Adventist Health System/West ....E....818 409-8540
381 Merrill Ave Glendale (91206) *(P-21266)*
Adventist Health System/West ....E....707 995-4500
15230 Lakeshore Dr Clearlake (95422) *(P-21267)*
Adventist Health System/West ....B....707 994-6486
18th Ave Hwy 53 Clearlake (95422) *(P-19270)*
Adventist Hlth Med Foundation, Glendale *Also called Adventist Health System/West (P-21266)*
Adventist Media Center Inc (PA) ....D....805 955-7777
11291 Pierce St Riverside (92505) *(P-18339)*
Adventist Medical Center-Selma ....B....559 891-1000
1141 Rose Ave Selma (93662) *(P-21268)*
Adventres Rlling Cross-Country ....C....415 332-5075
242 Redwd Hwy Frntge 1 Mill Valley (94941) *(P-13442)*
Adventure City Inc ....D....714 821-3311
1238 S Beach Blvd Anaheim (92804) *(P-19090)*
Adventure Connection Inc ....D....530 626-7385
986 Lotus Rd Lotus (95651) *(P-19091)*
Adventureplex ....E....310 546-7708
1701 Marine Ave Manhattan Beach (90266) *(P-18574)*
Adventures Cross-Country, Mill Valley *Also called Adventres Rlling Cross-Country (P-13442)*
Adventures In Hospitality Inc ....D....760 356-2806
633 W Canal St Calexico (92231) *(P-18818)*
Advertising, Santa Ana *Also called Dgwb Ventures LLC (P-13819)*
Advertising Consultants Inc (PA) ....C....310 233-2750
330 Golden Shore Ste 410 Long Beach (90802) *(P-13963)*
Advertising Department, Long Beach *Also called Comcast Corporation (P-5882)*
Advintist Hlth Clearlake Hosp ....B....707 994-6486
18th Ave & Hwy 53 Clearlake (95422) *(P-21269)*
Advisorsquare, Culver City *Also called Liveoffice LLC (P-15743)*
Ae & Associates LLC ....D....951 278-3477
506 Queensland Cir Corona (92879) *(P-27621)*
Aecom ....C....661 266-0802
1023 E Avenue J10 Lancaster (93535) *(P-26018)*
Aecom (PA) ....C....213 593-8000
1999 Avenue Of The Stars # 2600 Los Angeles (90067) *(P-25505)*
Aecom C&E Inc ....D....805 388-3775
1220 Avenida Acaso Camarillo (93012) *(P-25506)*
Aecom C&E Inc ....C....213 593-8100
1999 Avenue Of The Stars Los Angeles (90067) *(P-27115)*
Aecom Consulting, Los Angeles *Also called Aecom C&E Inc (P-27115)*
Aecom Design, Los Angeles *Also called Aecom Services Inc (P-26019)*
Aecom E&C Holdings Inc (HQ) ....C....213 593-8000
1999 Avenue Of The Stars Los Angeles (90067) *(P-25507)*
Aecom Energy & Cnstr Inc (HQ) ....C....213 593-8100
1999 Avenue Of The Stars Los Angeles (90067) *(P-1872)*
Aecom Energy & Cnstr Inc ....B....858 481-9502
2850 Carmel Valley Rd Del Mar (92014) *(P-1713)*
Aecom Energy & Cnstr Inc ....C....714 228-4300
16711 Knott Ave La Mirada (90638) *(P-25508)*
Aecom Environment, Camarillo *Also called Aecom C&E Inc (P-25506)*
Aecom Global II LLC ....D....415 774-2700
1320 S Simpson Cir Anaheim (92806) *(P-25509)*
Aecom Global II LLC ....D....805 692-0600
130 Robin Hill Rd Ste 100 Goleta (93117) *(P-25510)*
Aecom Global II LLC (HQ) ....D....213 593-8100
1999 Avenue Of The Stars Los Angeles (90067) *(P-25511)*
Aecom Global II LLC ....B....916 679-2000
2870 Gateway Oaks Dr # 150 Sacramento (95833) *(P-25512)*
Aecom Global II LLC ....C....916 679-8700
2870 Gateway Oaks Dr # 300 Sacramento (95833) *(P-27622)*
Aecom Global II LLC ....D....415 774-2700
600 Montgomery St San Francisco (94111) *(P-25513)*
Aecom Global II LLC ....D....530 827-2406
74 C St Herlong (96113) *(P-25514)*
Aecom Global II LLC ....C....559 347-5669
5168 E Dakota Ave Fresno (93727) *(P-25515)*
Aecom Global II LLC ....C....213 996-2200
915 Wilshire Blvd Ste 800 Los Angeles (90017) *(P-27623)*
Aecom Global II LLC ....D....310 343-6977
310 Golden Shore Ste 100 Long Beach (90802) *(P-27624)*
Aecom Services Inc (HQ) ....C....213 593-8000
300 S Grand Ave Fl 2 Los Angeles (90071) *(P-26019)*
Aecom Technical Services Inc (HQ) ....D....213 593-8000
300 S Grand Ave Ste 1100 Los Angeles (90071) *(P-27625)*
Aecom Technical Services Inc ....C....510 834-4304
1333 Broadway Ste 800 Oakland (94612) *(P-25516)*
Aecom Technical Services Inc ....D....909 554-5000
901 Via Piemonte Ste 400 Ontario (91764) *(P-25517)*
Aecom Technical Services Inc ....D....619 610-7600
401 W A St Ste 1200 San Diego (92101) *(P-25518)*
Aecom Technology Corporation ....D....916 414-5800
2020 L St Ste 400 Sacramento (95811) *(P-25519)*
Aecom Usa Inc ....C....213 330-7200
515 S Figueroa St Ste 400 Los Angeles (90071) *(P-27626)*
Aecom Usa Inc ....C....408 392-0670
100 W San Fernando St San Jose (95113) *(P-27627)*
Aecom Usa Inc ....B....213 593-8000
300 S Grand Ave Ste 1100 Los Angeles (90071) *(P-27628)*
Aecom Usa Inc ....D....714 567-2501
999 W Town And Country Rd Orange (92868) *(P-27629)*
Aecom-TSE Joint Venture ....D....510 285-6639
300 Lakeside Dr Ste 400 Oakland (94612) *(P-25520)*
Aedis Architech and Planning, San Jose *Also called Aedis Architects (P-26020)*
Aedis Architects (PA) ....E....949 496-6191
387 S 1st St Ste 300 San Jose (95113) *(P-26020)*
AEG Global Partnerships LLC ....E....213 763-7700
1100 S Flower St Ste 3200 Los Angeles (90015) *(P-27116)*
AEG Management Lacc LLC ....C....213 741-1151
1201 S Figueroa St Los Angeles (90015) *(P-26750)*
AEG Presents LLC (HQ) ....C....323 930-5700
425 W 11th St Los Angeles (90015) *(P-18340)*
AEG Worldwide, Los Angeles *Also called Anschutz Entrmt Group Inc (P-18418)*
Aegis Ambulance Service Inc (PA) ....D....626 685-9410
1059 E Bedmar St Carson (90746) *(P-3741)*
Aegis Assisted Living, Aptos *Also called Aegis Senior Communities LLC (P-22207)*
Aegis Assisted Living, Carmichael *Also called Aegis Senior Communities LLC (P-20220)*
Aegis Asssted Living Prpts LLC ....E....510 739-1515
3850 Walnut Ave 228 Fremont (94538) *(P-24408)*
Aegis Asssted Living Prpts LLC ....D....760 806-3600
1440 S Melrose Dr Oceanside (92056) *(P-24409)*
Aegis At Shadowridge, Oceanside *Also called Aegis Asssted Living Prpts LLC (P-24409)*
Aegis Enterprises Inc ....D....925 417-5550
500 Boulder Ct Ste A Pleasanton (94566) *(P-2087)*
Aegis Fire Systems, Pleasanton *Also called Aegis Enterprises Inc (P-2087)*
Aegis Gardens, Fremont *Also called Aegis Senior Communities LLC (P-22205)*
Aegis Living, Pleasant Hill *Also called Aegis Senior Communities LLC (P-22206)*
AEgis of Carmichael ....D....916 972-1313
4050 Walnut Ave Carmichael (95608) *(P-24410)*
Aegis of Fremont, Fremont *Also called Aegis Asssted Living Prpts LLC (P-24408)*
Aegis of Granada Hills, Granada Hills *Also called Aegis Senior Communities LLC (P-22208)*
Aegis of Laguna Niguel, Laguna Niguel *Also called Aegis Senior Communities LLC (P-24411)*
Aegis of San Francisco, South San Francisco *Also called Ageis Living (P-24412)*
Aegis Senior Communities LLC ....E....510 739-0909
36281 Fremont Blvd Fremont (94536) *(P-22205)*
Aegis Senior Communities LLC ....D....925 588-7030
1660 Oak Park Blvd Pleasant Hill (94523) *(P-22206)*
Aegis Senior Communities LLC ....E....831 684-2700
125 Heather Ter Aptos (95003) *(P-22207)*
Aegis Senior Communities LLC ....E....949 496-8080
32170 Niguel Rd Laguna Niguel (92677) *(P-24411)*
Aegis Senior Communities LLC ....B....916 972-1313
4050 Walnut Ave Carmichael (95608) *(P-20220)*
Aegis Senior Communities LLC ....D....818 363-3373
10801 Lindley Ave Granada Hills (91344) *(P-22208)*
Aegis Software Inc ....E....858 551-1652
5580 La Jolla Blvd # 436 La Jolla (92037) *(P-13964)*
Aegis Treatment Centers LLC (PA) ....E....818 206-0360
7246 Remmet Ave Canoga Park (91303) *(P-22497)*
Aei Consultants, Irvine *Also called All Environmental Inc (P-27632)*
Aei Consultants, Hermosa Beach *Also called All Environmental Inc (P-27633)*
Aem Corporation, Camarillo *Also called Applied Engineering MGT Corp (P-14991)*
Aemetis Inc (PA) ....C....408 213-0940
20400 Stevens Cupertino (95014) *(P-26313)*
Aemf, Valencia *Also called Alfred E Mann Foundation (P-26588)*
AEP Span Inc ....D....916 372-0933
2110 Enterprise Blvd West Sacramento (95691) *(P-3122)*
Aer Electronics Inc (PA) ....D....510 300-0500
42744 Boscell Rd Fremont (94538) *(P-6335)*
Aer Technologies Inc ....B....714 871-7357
650 Columbia St Brea (92821) *(P-17927)*
Aera Energy LLC (HQ) ....A....661 665-5000
10000 Ming Ave Bakersfield (93311) *(P-1032)*
Aera Energy LLC ....D....661 665-3200
29235 Highway 33 Maricopa (93252) *(P-1033)*
Aera Energy South Midway, Maricopa *Also called Aera Energy LLC (P-1033)*
Aera Technology Inc ....C....408 524-2222
707 California St Mountain View (94041) *(P-14968)*
Aerelectronics, Fremont *Also called Aer Electronics Inc (P-6335)*
Aerial Applicators, Biggs *Also called Chuck Jones Flying Service (P-461)*
Aeris Communications Inc (PA) ....D....408 557-1900
1745 Tech Dr Ste 700 San Jose (95110) *(P-5444)*

ALPHABETIC

Employee Codes: A=Over 500 employees, B=251-500
C=101-250, D=51-100, E=50
2019 Directory of California
Wholesalers and Services Companies
© Mergent Inc. 1-800-342-5647
1193

Aero Port Services Inc (PA)	D	310 623-8230
216 W Florence Ave Inglewood (90301) *(P-16871)*		
Aero-Engines Inc		323 663-3961
2641 Roseview Ave Los Angeles (90065) *(P-17928)*		
Aeroflot Rssina Internatl Arln, Beverly Hills *Also called Aeroflot Russian Airlines (P-4756)*		
Aeroflot Russian Airlines	D	323 272-4861
8383 Wilshire Blvd # 648 Beverly Hills (90211) *(P-4756)*		
Aeroground Inc (HQ)	A	650 266-6965
270 Lawrence Ave South San Francisco (94080) *(P-4868)*		
Aerohive Networks Inc (PA)	A	408 510-6100
1011 Mccarthy Blvd Milpitas (95035) *(P-15910)*		
Aeromedevac Inc	D	619 284-7910
1860 Joe Crosson Dr El Cajon (92020) *(P-27117)*		
Aeronautical Radio Inc	D	925 294-8400
6011 Industrial Way Livermore (94551) *(P-5258)*		
Aerospace & Marine Intl	E	408 360-0440
6910 Santa Teresa Blvd San Jose (95119) *(P-27917)*		
Aerospace Corporation (PA)	A	310 336-5000
2310 E El Segundo Blvd El Segundo (90245) *(P-26578)*		
Aerospace Corporation	B	714 248-1194
2745 E Sherman Ave Orange (92869) *(P-26579)*		
Aerospace Corporation	D	805 320-9599
P.O. Box 5068 Lompoc (93437) *(P-26580)*		
Aerospace Corporation	A	310 336-1025
2009 Harkness St Manhattan Beach (90266) *(P-26581)*		
Aerospace Corporation	B	818 952-6075
3171 Grangemount Rd Glendale (91206) *(P-26582)*		
Aerospace Corporation	D	310 374-8866
624 N Guadalupe Ave Redondo Beach (90277) *(P-26583)*		
Aerospace Federally Funded RES, El Segundo *Also called Air Force US Dept of (P-26585)*		
Aerospace Material Division, Bay Point *Also called Henkel Corporation (P-25732)*		
Aerotransporte De Carge Union	B	310 649-0069
5625 W Imperial Hwy Los Angeles (90045) *(P-4757)*		
Aerounion, Los Angeles *Also called Aerotransporte De Carge Union (P-4757)*		
Aerovironment Inc	D	626 357-9983
900 Enchanted Way Simi Valley (93065) *(P-25521)*		
Aerovironment Inc	C	805 581-2187
900 Innovators Way Simi Valley (93065) *(P-24940)*		
AES Alamitos LLC	D	562 493-7891
690 N Studebaker Rd Long Beach (90803) *(P-6008)*		
AES Huntington Beach LLC	E	714 374-1476
21730 Newland St Huntington Beach (92646) *(P-6009)*		
AES Networks, San Jose *Also called Vormetric Inc (P-16529)*		
AES Southland LLC	D	562 430-8685
690 N Studebaker Rd Long Beach (90803) *(P-6010)*		
Aesthetic Maintenance Corp	E	213 353-1525
1625 Palo Alto St Ste 301 Los Angeles (90026) *(P-14183)*		
Aestiva Software Inc	E	310 697-0338
3551 Voyager St Ste 201 Torrance (90503) *(P-14969)*		
Aetna Health California Inc	D	415 645-8200
1 Embarcadero Ctr Ste 300 San Francisco (94111) *(P-10175)*		
Aetna Health California Inc	D	619 656-3104
727 Pueblo Pl Chula Vista (91914) *(P-10176)*		
Aetna Health California Inc (HQ)	C	925 543-9223
2409 Camino Ramon San Ramon (94583) *(P-10177)*		
Aewestjv	E	619 233-1023
363 5th Ave Ste 202 San Diego (92101) *(P-26021)*		
AF Software Holdings Inc	B	888 317-3395
1825 S Grant St Ste 900 San Mateo (94402) *(P-11961)*		
AF Software Parent Inc	B	888 317-3395
1825 S Grant St Ste 900 San Mateo (94402) *(P-11962)*		
AFA Constrctn Grp/Cal Inc JV	D	707 446-7996
2040 Peabody Rd Ste 400 Vacaville (95687) *(P-1457)*		
Afc Distribution Corp	E	310 604-3630
19205 S Laurel Park Rd Rancho Dominguez (90220) *(P-8378)*		
Afex, Woodland Hills *Also called Associated Foreign Exch Inc (P-9670)*		
Affd, Anaheim *Also called Anaheim First Fmly Dntl Group (P-26760)*		
Affiliated Communications Inc	E	805 650-4949
3601 Calle Tecate Ste 200 Camarillo (93012) *(P-16987)*		
Affiliated Funding Corporation	D	714 619-3100
5 Hutton Centre Dr # 1100 Santa Ana (92707) *(P-9869)*		
Affiliated Temporary Help	B	323 771-1383
4359 Florence Ave Bell (90201) *(P-14810)*		
Affinity Auto Programs Inc	D	858 643-9324
10251 Vista Cerento Pkwy San Diego (92121) *(P-16988)*		
Affinity Development Group Inc	C	858 643-9324
10251 Vista Sorrento Pkwy # 300 San Diego (92121) *(P-25374)*		
Affinity Group, Ventura *Also called Agi Holding Corp (P-18819)*		
Affinity Health Care, Paramount *Also called Paramunt Madows Nursing Ctr LP (P-26979)*		
Affirm Inc	C	415 984-0490
650 California St Fl 12 San Francisco (94108) *(P-9730)*		
Affirm Identity, San Francisco *Also called Affirm Inc (P-9730)*		
Affordable Engrg Svcs Inc	D	973 890-8915
1455 Frazee Rd Ste 860 San Diego (92108) *(P-25522)*		
Affordable Installations, Nevada City *Also called Patrick Dean Bryan (P-3565)*		
Affymax Research Institute	E	650 812-8700
4001 Miranda Ave Palo Alto (94304) *(P-26584)*		
Affymetrix Inc	C	858 642-2058
5893 Oberlin Dr San Diego (92121) *(P-26314)*		
AFL, Rancho Cucamonga *Also called Ccna Vons Athletes For Life (P-25408)*		
AFL-CIO #1245, Vacaville *Also called International Brthrhd of Elctr (P-25063)*		
Afm & Sag-Aftra Intellectual	D	818 255-7980
4705 Laurel Canyon Blvd # 400 Valley Village (91607) *(P-16989)*		
African American Unity Center	D	323 789-7300
944 W 53rd St Los Angeles (90037) *(P-23461)*		
After Market Group Inc (HQ)	D	916 361-1687
10173 Croydon Way Ste 1 Sacramento (95827) *(P-7150)*		

After-Party2 Inc (HQ)	C	310 202-0011
901 W Hillcrest Blvd Inglewood (90301) *(P-14466)*		
After-Party2 Inc	D	310 535-3660
2310 E Imperial Hwy El Segundo (90245) *(P-14467)*		
Aftershock La Studios Inc		650 450-9660
3633 Lenawee Ave Ste 100 Los Angeles (90016) *(P-14970)*		
AG Air Conditioning & Htg Inc	E	818 988-5388
14620 Keswick St Van Nuys (91405) *(P-2088)*		
AG Facilities Operations LLC	A	323 651-1808
6380 Wilshire Blvd # 800 Los Angeles (90048) *(P-20980)*		
AG Heating and AC, Van Nuys *Also called AG Air Conditioning & Htg Inc (P-2088)*		
AG Redlands LLC	C	909 793-2678
700 E Highland Ave Redlands (92374) *(P-20981)*		
AG Rx (PA)	D	805 487-0696
751 S Rose Ave Oxnard (93030) *(P-9071)*		
Ag-Wise Enterprises Inc (PA)	C	661 325-1567
5100 California Ave # 209 Bakersfield (93309) *(P-679)*		
Agama Solutions Inc	C	510 796-9300
39159 Paseo Padre Pkwy # 216 Fremont (94538) *(P-27118)*		
Agamerica Fcb (PA)	D	651 282-8800
3636 American River Dr # 100 Sacramento (95864) *(P-9692)*		
Agape In Home Care Inc	E	661 835-0364
4800 District Blvd Ste A Bakersfield (93313) *(P-22209)*		
Age Advantage HM Care Svcs	D	619 449-5900
5480 Baltimore Dr Ste 214 La Mesa (91942) *(P-20982)*		
Age Concerns Inc	B	619 544-1622
2650 Camino Del Rio N # 203 San Diego (92108) *(P-23462)*		
Age Well Senior Services Inc (PA)	D	949 855-8033
24461 Ridge Route Dr # 220 Laguna Hills (92653) *(P-23463)*		
Ageis Living		650 952-6100
2280 Gellert Blvd South San Francisco (94080) *(P-24412)*		
Agemark Corporation (PA)	C	925 257-4671
25 Avenida De Orinda Orinda (94563) *(P-20221)*		
Agency For Performing Arts Inc (PA)	C	310 557-9049
405 S Beverly Dr Ste 500 Beverly Hills (90212) *(P-18341)*		
Agencycom LLC	B	415 817-3800
5353 Grosvenor Blvd Los Angeles (90066) *(P-15575)*		
Agendia Inc	C	949 540-6300
22 Morgan Irvine (92618) *(P-22498)*		
Agent Franchise LLC	C	949 930-5025
9518 9th St Ste C2 Rancho Cucamonga (91730) *(P-10155)*		
Aggregate West Coast, Thermal *Also called West Coast Aggregate Supply (P-1096)*		
Agi Holding Corp (PA)	D	805 667-4100
2575 Vista Del Mar Dr Ventura (93001) *(P-18819)*		
Agile 1, Torrance *Also called Act 1 Group Inc (P-14567)*		
Agile Sourcing Partners Inc	C	951 279-4154
2385 Railroad St Corona (92880) *(P-6194)*		
Agilent Technologies Inc		805 566-6655
6392 Via Real Carpinteria (93013) *(P-8138)*		
Agility Holdings Inc (HQ)	D	714 617-6300
310 Commerce Ste 250 Irvine (92602) *(P-4996)*		
Agility Logistics, Irvine *Also called Agility Holdings Inc (P-4996)*		
Agility Logistics Corp	D	310 507-6700
21906 Arnold Center Rd Carson (90810) *(P-4997)*		
Agilon Health Inc		562 256-3800
1 World Trade Ctr Long Beach (90831) *(P-10178)*		
Agilysys Inc		805 692-6339
5383 Hollister Ave # 120 Santa Barbara (93111) *(P-7000)*		
Agilysys Inc	E	702 759-4879
1900 Powell St Ste 230 Emeryville (94608) *(P-7001)*		
Aging & Adult Services, Bakersfield *Also called County of Kern (P-23647)*		
Aging & Adult Services, Taft *Also called County of Kern (P-23649)*		
Aging & Adult Services, Bakersfield *Also called County of Kern (P-23651)*		
Aging & Adult Services, Victorville *Also called County of San Bernardino (P-23719)*		
Agire Mortgage Corporation	E	714 564-5821
2125 E Katella Ave # 350 Anaheim (92806) *(P-9768)*		
Agnews Developmental Center, San Jose *Also called Developmental Svcs Cal Dept (P-20928)*		
Agostini and Associates Inc	E	925 691-7300
1470 Civic Ct Ste 1760 Concord (94520) *(P-14811)*		
Agostini Health Care Staffing, Concord *Also called Agostini and Associates Inc (P-14811)*		
Agoura Hills Renaissance Hotel, Agoura Hills *Also called Davidson Hotel Partners Lp (P-12513)*		
AGR Group Inc	A	714 245-7151
13902 Harbor Blvd Ste 2c Garden Grove (92843) *(P-27119)*		
Agreeya Solutions Inc (PA)	D	916 294-0075
605 Coolidge Dr Ste 200 Folsom (95630) *(P-27120)*		
Agreserves Inc	D	530 343-5365
6100 Wilson Landing Rd Chico (95973) *(P-184)*		
Agri Valley Services	D	559 253-0104
1532 N West Ave Fresno (93728) *(P-26142)*		
Agri-Feed Industries, Imperial *Also called Western Meat Processors Inc (P-402)*		
Agri-Mix Transport Inc	C	661 833-6280
1400 S Union Ave Ste 110 Bakersfield (93307) *(P-3969)*		
Agri-World Cooperative	E	559 673-1306
31545 Donald Ave Madera (93636) *(P-680)*		
Agrian Inc (PA)	D	559 437-5700
352 W Spruce Ave Clovis (93611) *(P-16308)*		
Agrichem, Fowler *Also called Kandarian Agri Enterprises (P-151)*		
Agriculture and Priority Pollu	E	559 275-2175
908 N Temperance Ave Clovis (93611) *(P-26681)*		
Agriholding Inc	D	559 738-5880
3330 S Fairway St Visalia (93277) *(P-4998)*		
Agriland Holding Inc	D	559 665-2100
23400 Road 24 Chowchilla (93610) *(P-232)*		
Agritec International Ltd	E	626 812-7200
5820 Martin Rd Irwindale (91706) *(P-8016)*		

Mergent e-mail: customerrelations@mergent.com
1194

2019 Directory of California
Wholesalers and Services Companies

(P-0000) Products & Services Section entry number
(PA)=Parent Co (HQ)=Headquarters (DH)=Div Headquarters

Agro-Jal Farms Inc.....D.....805 928-2682
257 Kathleen Ct Santa Maria (93458) *(P-489)*
Agsource Services LLC.....E.....559 735-9700
222 N Garden St Ste 400 Visalia (93291) *(P-636)*
Agua Caliente Casino & Resort, Rancho Mirage *Also called Agua Clnte Band Chilla Indians (P-12307)*
Agua Caliente Development Auth.....D.....760 699-6800
5401 Dinah Shore Dr Palm Springs (92264) *(P-11192)*
Agua Clnte Band Chilla Indians.....A.....760 321-2000
32250 Bob Hope Dr Rancho Mirage (92270) *(P-12307)*
Agua Clnte Band Chilla Indians (PA).....C.....760 699-6800
5401 Dinah Shore Dr Palm Springs (92264) *(P-25375)*
Agua Clnte Band Chilla Indians.....A.....800 854-1279
401 E Amado Rd Palm Springs (92262) *(P-12308)*
Aguatierra Associates Inc (PA).....D.....510 450-6000
2000 Powell St Ste 555 Emeryville (94608) *(P-27575)*
Ahm Gemch Inc.....C.....626 579-7777
1701 Santa Anita Ave El Monte (91733) *(P-21270)*
Ahmc, Anaheim *Also called Anaheim Regional Medical Ctr (P-19292)*
Ahmc Garfield Medical Ctr LP.....C.....626 573-2222
525 N Garfield Ave Monterey Park (91754) *(P-20222)*
Ahmc Healthcare.....C.....626 570-0612
55 S Raymond Ave Ste 105 Alhambra (91801) *(P-21271)*
Ahmc Healthcare Inc.....A.....626 248-3452
500 E Main St Alhambra (91801) *(P-22724)*
Ahmc Healthcare Inc (PA).....C.....626 943-7526
1000 S Fremont Ave Unit 6 Alhambra (91803) *(P-21272)*
Ahmc Healthcare Inc.....A.....626 579-7777
1701 Santa Anita Ave South El Monte (91733) *(P-21273)*
Ahmc Whittier Hosp Med Ctr LP.....A.....562 945-3561
9080 Colima Rd Whittier (90605) *(P-21274)*
Ahr Professionals, Lake Forest *Also called Validus Group Inc (P-14792)*
Ahrens Landscape & Maintenance, Sacramento *Also called Jma Investments Ltd (P-870)*
Ahtna Government Services Corp.....D.....916 372-2000
3100 Beacon Blvd West Sacramento (95691) *(P-1458)*
Ahtna-CDM JV.....E.....714 824-3470
3200 El Camino Real Irvine (92602) *(P-1372)*
Ahtna-CDM Smith JV.....D.....714 824-3471
3200 El Camino Real Irvine (92602) *(P-27630)*
Ai Inc/CSC Grou.....D.....661 775-8400
28001 Smyth Dr Ste 107 Valencia (91355) *(P-16544)*
AIA Holdings Inc (PA).....D.....818 222-4999
26560 Agoura Rd Ste 100 Calabasas (91302) *(P-10420)*
Aic Inc USA, City of Industry *Also called Advanced Industrial Cmpt Inc (P-6998)*
Aicent Inc.....C.....408 324-1316
900 E Hamilton Ave # 600 Campbell (95008) *(P-16309)*
Aichinger International Inc.....D.....310 375-1533
5423 Littlebow Rd Pls Vrds Pnsl (90275) *(P-6576)*
Aico, Pico Rivera *Also called Amini Innovation Corp (P-6709)*
AID FOR AIDS, Los Angeles *Also called Alliance For Housing & Healing (P-20915)*
AIDS PROJECT LA, Los Angeles *Also called Apla Health & Wellness (P-19301)*
AIDS PROJECT LA, Los Angeles *Also called Aids Project Los Angeles (P-23464)*
Aids Project Los Angeles (PA).....D.....213 201-1600
611 S Kingsley Dr Los Angeles (90005) *(P-23464)*
Aids Svcs Fndation Orange Cnty.....D.....949 809-5700
17982 Sky Park Cir Ste J Irvine (92614) *(P-23465)*
AIDS WALK ORANGE COUNTY, Irvine *Also called Aids Svcs Fndation Orange Cnty (P-23465)*
AIG, San Francisco *Also called American Gen Lf Insur Co Del (P-10127)*
AIG Direct Insurance Svcs Inc.....B.....858 309-3000
9640 Gran Rdge Dr Ste 200 San Diego (92123) *(P-10512)*
AIG Private Client Group, San Diego *Also called American Intl Group Inc (P-10521)*
Aii Group, Santa Ana *Also called Atlas International Inc (P-7610)*
Aimloan.com, A Direct Lender, San Diego *Also called American Internet Mortgage Inc (P-9773)*
Air Cargo Handling Service, South San Francisco *Also called Aeroground Inc (P-4868)*
Air Control Systems Inc.....E.....909 786-4230
1940 S Grove Ave Ontario (91761) *(P-2089)*
Air Force US Dept of.....D.....805 606-5355
1031 California Blvd # 11777 Lompoc (93437) *(P-26751)*
Air Force US Dept of.....B.....310 336-5000
2310 E El Segundo Blvd El Segundo (90245) *(P-26585)*
Air Force US Dept of.....B.....310 393-0411
1776 Main St Santa Monica (90401) *(P-26586)*
Air Force Village West Inc.....B.....951 697-2000
17050 Arnold Dr Riverside (92518) *(P-20223)*
Air France (air Nationale).....D.....415 877-0179
San Francisco Intl A San Francisco (94125) *(P-4758)*
Air Lease Corporation (PA).....D.....310 553-0555
2000 Avenue Of The Stars 1000n Los Angeles (90067) *(P-14468)*
Air Mechanical Inc.....D.....714 995-3947
608 S Vicki Ln Anaheim (92804) *(P-2090)*
Air New Zealand Limited.....D.....310 648-7000
222 N Pacific Coast Hwy # 900 El Segundo (90245) *(P-4759)*
Air Polution Control District, Fresno *Also called San Joaquin Valley A P C D (P-27855)*
Air Systems Service & Cnstr.....C.....916 368-0336
10381 Old Placerville Rd # 100 Sacramento (95827) *(P-2091)*
Air Tiger Express (usa) Inc.....E.....626 965-8647
17000 Gale Ave City of Industry (91745) *(P-4999)*
Air Treatment Corporation (PA).....D.....909 869-7975
640 N Puente St Brea (92821) *(P-7642)*
Air-Sea Forwarders Inc (PA).....D.....310 216-1616
9009 S La Cienega Blvd Inglewood (90301) *(P-5000)*
Air-TEC, Carson *Also called Clay Dunn Enterprises Inc (P-2162)*
Airbnb Inc (PA).....A.....415 800-5959
888 Brannan St Ste 300 San Francisco (94103) *(P-13471)*
Airco Mechanical Inc (PA).....C.....916 381-4523
8210 Demetre Ave Sacramento (95828) *(P-2092)*
Airco Mechanical Inc.....C.....415 982-4726
401 13th St San Francisco (94130) *(P-2093)*
Aircraft Xray Laboratories Inc.....D.....323 587-0164
5216 Pacific Blvd Huntington Park (90255) *(P-26682)*
Airdrome Orchards Inc (PA).....E.....408 297-6461
111 E Alma Ave San Jose (95112) *(P-201)*
Aire-Rite AC & Rfrgn Inc.....D.....714 895-2338
15122 Bolsa Chica St Huntington Beach (92649) *(P-2094)*
Airemasters Air Conditioning, Santa Fe Springs *Also called Scorpio Enterprises (P-2350)*
Airespring Inc.....D.....818 786-8990
7800 Woodley Ave Van Nuys (91406) *(P-5445)*
Airey Enterprises LLC.....E.....818 530-3362
5530 Corbin Ave Ste 325 Tarzana (91356) *(P-7905)*
Airfield Maintenance, Sacramento *Also called County of Sacramento (P-14234)*
Airframer R, Torrance *Also called Sonic Industries Inc (P-25919)*
Airgas Inc.....B.....530 241-1544
653 N Market St Redding (96003) *(P-7719)*
Airgas Inc.....C.....858 279-8200
9010 Clairemont Mesa Blvd San Diego (92123) *(P-7720)*
Airgas Safety Inc.....D.....562 699-5239
2355 Workman Mill Rd City of Industry (90601) *(P-7721)*
Airgas Usa LLC.....C.....858 279-8200
9010 Clairemont Mesa Blvd San Diego (92123) *(P-8916)*
Airgas Usa LLC.....D.....323 568-2244
11711 S Alameda St Los Angeles (90059) *(P-7722)*
Airgas Usa LLC.....D.....408 998-6380
441 Hobson St San Jose (95110) *(P-7723)*
Airline Coach Service, Burlingame *Also called Jeremiah Phillips LLC (P-4028)*
Airline Coach Service Inc (PA).....D.....650 697-7733
863 Malcolm Rd Burlingame (94010) *(P-3636)*
Airmotive Carburetor Co, Burbank *Also called William F Kellogg Corporation (P-7920)*
Airpark Partners, Riverside *Also called Abbey Partner VI (P-11188)*
Airport Century Inn.....D.....310 649-4000
5547 W Century Blvd Los Angeles (90045) *(P-12309)*
Airport Cinemas 12, Santa Rosa *Also called North American Cinemas Inc (P-18307)*
Airport Club.....C.....707 528-2582
432 Aviation Blvd Santa Rosa (95403) *(P-18820)*
Airport Commisions.....A.....650 821-5000
San Francisco Intl Arprt San Francisco (94128) *(P-4869)*
Airport Connection Inc.....C.....805 389-8196
95 Dawson Dr Camarillo (93012) *(P-3637)*
Airport Health Club, Santa Rosa *Also called Airport Club (P-18820)*
Airport Parking Services, San Bruno *Also called Skypark Inc (P-13774)*
Airpush Inc.....C.....877 944-2490
11400 W Olympic Blvd Los Angeles (90064) *(P-13790)*
Ais Construction Company.....D.....805 928-9467
713 Rincon Hill Rd Santa Maria (93455) *(P-1459)*
Ais, Associated Insurance Svc, Tustin *Also called Apollo Agencies Inc (P-10539)*
Alsha Academy.....D.....310 908-1962
706 S Pershing Ave Stockton (95203) *(P-13437)*
Ait Worldwide Logistics Inc.....D.....310 538-4383
19901 Hamilton Ave Ste D Torrance (90502) *(P-5001)*
AJ Kirkwood & Associates Inc.....B.....714 505-1977
2752 Walnut Ave Tustin (92780) *(P-2502)*
AJ Oster West LLC.....D.....714 692-1000
22833 La Palma Ave Yorba Linda (92887) *(P-7252)*
Ajax Portable Services.....E.....831 384-5000
11240 Commercial Pkwy Castroville (95012) *(P-14469)*
Ajc Sandblasting Inc.....D.....562 436-3606
932 Schley Ave Wilmington (90744) *(P-3480)*
Ajit Healthcare Inc.....D.....213 484-0510
316 S Westlake Ave Los Angeles (90057) *(P-26752)*
AJM Packaging Corporation.....D.....619 448-4007
1160 Vernon Way El Cajon (92020) *(P-9192)*
Ajo, Yorba Linda *Also called AJ Oster West LLC (P-7252)*
Ajr Trucking Inc.....C.....562 989-9555
2700 Rose Ave Ste A Signal Hill (90755) *(P-3970)*
AJW Restoration Services LLC.....E.....858 429-5641
7445 Raytheon Rd San Diego (92111) *(P-1460)*
AK Constructors Inc.....D.....951 280-0269
1751 Jenks Dr Corona (92880) *(P-1461)*
AK Electrical Services, Corona *Also called AK Constructors Inc (P-1461)*
Akela Pharma Inc.....E.....512 391-3525
11011 Torreyana Rd 100 San Diego (92121) *(P-26587)*
Akin Gump Strauss.....D.....310 229-1000
2029 Century Park E # 2400 Los Angeles (90067) *(P-22906)*
Akin Gump Strauss Hauer & Fel.....C.....415 765-9500
580 California St # 1500 San Francisco (94104) *(P-22907)*
Akland Healthcare Wellness Ctr, Oakland *Also called Oakland Healthcare & Wellness (P-20672)*
Akqa Inc (HQ).....B.....415 645-9400
360 3rd St Ste 500 San Francisco (94107) *(P-27121)*
Al Anwa USA Incorporated.....C.....310 301-2000
4200 Admiralty Way Marina Del Rey (90292) *(P-12310)*
Al Barcellos Et.....E.....209 826-2636
17599 Ward Rd Los Banos (93635) *(P-10)*
Al-Tar Services Inc.....D.....866 522-3499
823 Kifer Rd Sunnyvale (94086) *(P-17929)*
Ala Costa Center Program For (PA).....D.....510 527-2550
1300 Rose St Berkeley (94702) *(P-24262)*
Alabbasi, Perris *Also called Mamco Inc (P-1810)*
Aladdin Bail Bonds, Carlsbad *Also called Two Jinn Inc (P-17526)*
Aladdin Sonora Motor Inn.....E.....209 533-4971
14260 Mono Way Sonora (95370) *(P-12311)*
Alaidandrew Corporation.....D.....661 334-2200
1205 8th St Bakersfield (93304) *(P-20983)*
Alain Pinel Realtors.....D.....831 622-1040
Junipero Between 5 & 6 # 56 Carmel (93921) *(P-11193)*

ALPHABETIC

Employee Codes: A=Over 500 employees, B=251-500
C=101-250, D=51-100, E=50
2019 Directory of California
Wholesalers and Services Companies
© Mergent Inc. 1-800-342-5647
1195

Alain Pinel Realtors Inc........D.......415 814-6690
2001 Union St Ste 200 San Francisco (94123) ***(P-11194)***
Alain Pinel Realtors Inc........D.......415 755-1111
101 Nellen Ave Corte Madera (94925) ***(P-11195)***
Alain Pinel Realtors Inc........D.......650 548-1111
520 S El Camino Real # 100 San Mateo (94402) ***(P-11196)***
Alain Pinel Realtors Inc........D.......408 358-1111
750 University Ave # 150 Los Gatos (95032) ***(P-11197)***
Alain Pinel Realtors Inc........D.......707 636-3800
2911 Cleveland Ave Santa Rosa (95403) ***(P-11198)***
Alain Pinel Realtors Inc........D.......925 251-1111
900 Main St Ste 101 Pleasanton (94566) ***(P-11199)***
Alain Pinel Realtors Inc........D.......650 375-1111
1440 Chapin Ave Ste 200 Burlingame (94010) ***(P-11200)***
Alain Pinel Realtors Inc........C.......650 323-1111
578 University Ave Palo Alto (94301) ***(P-11201)***
Alain Pinel Realtors Inc........D.......650 941-1111
167 S San Antonio Rd # 1 Los Altos (94022) ***(P-11202)***
Alain Pinel Realtors Inc........D.......650 462-1111
1550 El Camino Real # 100 Menlo Park (94025) ***(P-11203)***
Alakor Healthcare LLC........C.......626 408-9800
323 S Heliotrope Ave Monrovia (91016) ***(P-21275)***
Alameda Alliance For Health........C.......510 747-4555
1240 S Loop Rd Alameda (94502) ***(P-10179)***
Alameda Bureau Elec Imprv Corp (HQ)........D.......510 748-3902
2000 Grand St Alameda (94501) ***(P-6011)***
Alameda Care Center, Burbank *Also called Artesia Healthcare Inc* ***(P-20235)***
Alameda Care Center, Alameda *Also called Shoreline S Intermediate Care* ***(P-20957)***
Alameda Chapel of The Chimes, Hayward *Also called Chapel of Chimes* ***(P-11939)***
Alameda Cnty Cmnty Fd Bnk Inc........D.......510 635-3663
7900 Edgewater Dr Oakland (94621) ***(P-23466)***
Alameda Corridor Engrg Team........D.......310 816-0460
1 Civic Plaza Dr Ste 600 Carson (90745) ***(P-25523)***
Alameda County AG Fair Assn........D.......925 426-7600
4501 Pleasanton Ave Pleasanton (94566) ***(P-19092)***
Alameda County Employees Retir........D.......510 628-3000
475 14th St Ste 1000 Oakland (94612) ***(P-10475)***
Alameda County Fair, Pleasanton *Also called Alameda County AG Fair Assn* ***(P-19092)***
Alameda County Industries Inc........E.......510 357-7282
610 Aladdin Ave San Leandro (94577) ***(P-6336)***
Alameda County Water District (PA)........C.......510 668-4200
43885 S Grimmer Blvd Fremont (94538) ***(P-6206)***
Alameda Family Services........D.......510 629-6300
2325 Clement Ave Alameda (94501) ***(P-24263)***
Alameda Halthcare Wellness Ctr, Alameda *Also called Alameda Hlthcare & Wellnss Ctr* ***(P-20224)***
Alameda Health System (PA)........D.......510 437-4800
1411 E 31st St Oakland (94602) ***(P-21276)***
Alameda Hlthcare & Wellnss Ctr........D.......510 523-8857
430 Willow St Alameda (94501) ***(P-20224)***
ALAMEDA HOSPITAL, Alameda *Also called City Alameda Health Care Corp* ***(P-21327)***
Alameda Municipal Power, Alameda *Also called Alameda Bureau Elec Imprv Corp* ***(P-6011)***
Alameda Produce Market LLC........D.......213 221-3400
761 Terminal St Ste 2 Los Angeles (90021) ***(P-11204)***
Alameda, County Medical Center, San Leandro *Also called County of Alameda* ***(P-19407)***
Alameda-Contra Costa Trnst Dst (PA)........C.......510 891-4777
1600 Franklin St Oakland (94612) ***(P-3638)***
Alameda-Contra Costa Trnst Dst........C.......510 577-8816
10626 International Blvd Oakland (94603) ***(P-3949)***
Alamitos Blmont Rhblttion Hosp, Long Beach *Also called Alamitos-Belmont Rehab Inc* ***(P-20225)***
Alamitos Convalescent Hospital, Los Alamitos *Also called Goodman Group Inc* ***(P-20490)***
Alamitos Enterprises LLC (PA)........D.......562 596-1827
3311 Katella Ave Los Alamitos (90720) ***(P-17846)***
Alamitos W Convalescent Hosp, Los Alamitos *Also called Katella Properties* ***(P-20552)***
Alamitos-Belmont Rehab Inc........C.......562 434-8421
3901 E 4th St Long Beach (90814) ***(P-20225)***
Alamo Medical Group, Alamo *Also called John Muir Physician Network* ***(P-19521)***
Alamo Rent A Car, Inglewood *Also called Alamo Rental (us) Inc* ***(P-17621)***
Alamo Rent A Car, Newport Beach *Also called Alamo Rental (us) Inc* ***(P-17622)***
Alamo Rental (us) Inc........D.......310 649-2242
9020 Aviation Blvd Inglewood (90301) ***(P-17621)***
Alamo Rental (us) Inc........E.......949 852-0403
4500 Campus Dr Ste 300 Newport Beach (92660) ***(P-17622)***
Alan B Whitson Company Inc........A.......949 955-1200
1507 W Alton Ave Santa Ana (92704) ***(P-27122)***
Alan Smith Pool Plastering Inc........D.......714 628-9494
227 W Carleton Ave Orange (92867) ***(P-2837)***
Alaska Airlines Inc........D.......800 426-0333
1800 W Airport Dr Han Hangar Ontario (91761) ***(P-4760)***
Alaska Airlines Inc........C.......310 925-2409
600 World Way Los Angeles (90045) ***(P-4761)***
Alaska Airlines Inc........E.......619 238-2042
2357 Airlane Rd Ste D San Diego (92101) ***(P-4762)***
Alaska Airlines Inc........D.......510 577-5813
1 Alan Shepard Way Oakland (94621) ***(P-4763)***
Alaska Diesel Electric........C.......626 934-6211
425 S Hacienda Blvd City of Industry (91745) ***(P-17791)***
Albd Electric and Cable........D.......949 440-1216
995 E Discovery Ln Anaheim (92801) ***(P-2503)***
Albert A Webb Associates (PA)........C.......951 686-1070
3788 Mccray St Riverside (92506) ***(P-25524)***
Albert D Seeno Cnstr Co Inc........D.......925 671-7711
4021 Port Chicago Hwy Concord (94520) ***(P-1329)***
Albertsons Brea Dist Ctr, Brea *Also called Albertsons LLC* ***(P-4528)***
Albertsons Dist Ctr 8760, La Habra *Also called Albertsons LLC* ***(P-4527)***
Albertsons Dist Ctr 8795, Vacaville *Also called Albertsons LLC* ***(P-4526)***
Albertsons LLC........B.......707 446-5922
700 Crocker Dr Vacaville (95688) ***(P-4526)***
Albertsons LLC........D.......714 578-4670
777 S Harbor Blvd La Habra (90631) ***(P-4527)***
Albertsons LLC........A.......714 990-8200
200 N Puente St Brea (92821) ***(P-4528)***
Albion River Inn Incorporated........D.......707 937-1919
3790 N Highway 1 Albion (95410) ***(P-12312)***
Albireo Energy, Poway *Also called Electronic Control Systems LLC* ***(P-2576)***
Alca Trax Sea Foods, Santa Rosa *Also called North Coast Fisheries LLC* ***(P-8584)***
Alcal Specialty Contg Inc (HQ)........D.......916 929-3100
946 N Market Blvd Sacramento (95834) ***(P-3123)***
Alcatraz Cruises LLC........C.......415 981-7625
Hornb Alcat Landi Pier 33 St Pier San Francisco (94111) ***(P-4960)***
Alco Iron & Metal Co (PA)........D.......510 562-1107
2140 Davis St San Leandro (94577) ***(P-7965)***
Alcohol DRG Program Yolo Cnty........E.......530 666-8650
137 N Cottonwood St Ste 1 Woodland (95695) ***(P-22499)***
Alcone Marketing Group Inc (HQ)........D.......949 595-5322
4 Studebaker Irvine (92618) ***(P-13791)***
Alcorn Fence Company (PA)........C.......818 983-0650
9901 Glenoaks Blvd Sun Valley (91352) ***(P-3481)***
Aldersly Retirement Center........D.......415 453-9271
326 Mission Ave San Rafael (94901) ***(P-10973)***
ALDERSLY RETIREMENT COMMUNITY, San Rafael *Also called Aldersly Retirement Center* ***(P-10973)***
Alderson Convalescent Hospital, Woodland *Also called United Health Systems Inc* ***(P-20846)***
Alderwood Inc........D.......626 289-4439
115 Bridge St San Gabriel (91775) ***(P-20984)***
Alderwood Child Development, Irvine *Also called Child Development Incorporated* ***(P-24285)***
Alderwoods (delaware) Inc........E.......209 883-0411
900 Santa Fe Ave Hughson (95326) ***(P-11938)***
Aldoc Inc........D.......714 836-8477
304 N Townsend St Ste D Santa Ana (92703) ***(P-2095)***
Aldon Ter Convalsent Hosptial, Los Angeles *Also called Longwood Management Corp* ***(P-21142)***
Aldridge Pite LLP........C.......858 750-7700
4375 Jutland Dr Ste 200 San Diego (92117) ***(P-22908)***
Alecto Healthcare Services LLC (PA)........A.......323 938-3161
16310 Bake Pkwy Ste 200 Irvine (92618) ***(P-21277)***
Alegrecare Inc........B.......415 974-3530
1375 Sutter St Ste 110 San Francisco (94109) ***(P-22210)***
Aleks Corporation........C.......714 245-7191
15640 Laguna Canyon Rd Irvine (92618) ***(P-15576)***
Aleks Educational Systems, Irvine *Also called Aleks Corporation* ***(P-15576)***
Alemeda County Industries LLC........D.......510 357-7282
610 Aladdin Ave San Leandro (94577) ***(P-6337)***
Alert Communications, Camarillo *Also called Affiliated Communications Inc* ***(P-16987)***
Alert Insulation Company Inc........D.......626 961-9113
15913 Old Valley Blvd A La Puente (91744) ***(P-2838)***
Alex Moving & Storage, Camarillo *Also called Uribe Trucking Inc* ***(P-4383)***
Alexander Delu........D.......209 334-6660
15175 N Devries Rd Lodi (95242) ***(P-128)***
Alexander Properties Company........E.......925 866-0100
2600 Camino Ramon Ste 201 San Ramon (94583) ***(P-10848)***
Alexander's Grand Salon & Spa, Anaheim *Also called Alexanders Grand Salon* ***(P-13644)***
Alexanders Grand Salon........D.......714 282-6438
5579 E Santa Ana Cyn Rd Anaheim (92807) ***(P-13644)***
Alexandria Care Center LLC........C.......323 660-1800
1515 N Alexandria Ave Los Angeles (90027) ***(P-20985)***
Alexandria Clayton........E.......530 262-5961
2051 Hilltop Dr Ste A16c Redding (96002) ***(P-15911)***
Alfa Tech Cnslting Engners Inc (PA)........D.......408 487-1200
1321 Ridder Park Dr 50 San Jose (95131) ***(P-25525)***
Alfa Tech Consulting Entps, San Jose *Also called Alfa Tech Cnslting Engners Inc* ***(P-25525)***
Alfred E Mann Foundation (PA)........D.......661 702-6700
25134 Rye Canyon Loop # 200 Valencia (91355) ***(P-26588)***
Alfreds Pictures Frames Inc........E.......714 434-4838
1580 Sunflower Ave Costa Mesa (92626) ***(P-16990)***
Alfresco Software Inc (PA)........D.......888 317-3395
1825 S Grant St Ste 900 San Mateo (94402) ***(P-15577)***
Algonquin Power and Utilities........B.......530 543-5288
933 Eloise Ave South Lake Tahoe (96150) ***(P-2504)***
Algos Inc A Medical Corp (PA)........D.......626 696-1400
224 N Fair Oaks Ave Pasadena (91103) ***(P-22500)***
Alhambra Convalescent Hosp LLC........D.......925 228-2020
331 Ilene St Martinez (94553) ***(P-20226)***
Alhambra Healthcare & Wellness........D.......626 282-3151
415 S Garfield Ave Alhambra (91801) ***(P-20227)***
Alhambra Hospital Med Ctr LP........C.......626 570-1606
100 S Raymond Ave Alhambra (91801) ***(P-21278)***
Alhambra/Sierra Springs........D.......408 727-0677
485 Vista Way Milpitas (95035) ***(P-8750)***
Aliantel Inc........D.......714 829-1650
1940 W Corporate Way Anaheim (92801) ***(P-27631)***
Alicia Arroyo Inc........C.......831 675-2850
800 Johnson Cyn Rd 4 Gonzales (93926) ***(P-637)***
Alienvault LLC (HQ)........D.......650 713-3333
1100 Park Pl Ste 300 San Mateo (94403) ***(P-15578)***
Alight (us) LLC........C.......949 725-4500
100 Bayview Cir Ste 100 # 100 Newport Beach (92660) ***(P-27123)***
Alignment Health Plan........D.......323 728-7232
1100 W Town & Country Orange (92868) ***(P-10180)***
Alignment Healthcare USA LLC (PA)........D.......844 310-2247
1100 W Town And Country R Orange (92868) ***(P-22725)***
Alion Science and Tech Corp........D.......805 488-8761
266 E Scott St Port Hueneme (93041) ***(P-25526)***

Mergent e-mail: customerrelations@mergent.com
1196
2019 Directory of California
Wholesalers and Services Companies
(P-0000) Products & Services Section entry number
(PA)=Parent Co (HQ)=Headquarters (DH)=Div Headquarters

Alisal Guest Ranch, Solvang *Also called Alisal Properties* ***(P-13443)***
Alisal Health Center, Salinas *Also called County of Monterey* ***(P-19417)***
Alisal Properties (PA).....C.....805 688-6411
1054 Alisal Rd Solvang (93463) ***(P-13443)***
Alisam Oxnard Operating.....C.....310 877-7179
212 26th St Ste 246 Santa Monica (90402) ***(P-10849)***
Aliso Air Conditioning & Htg, Rancho Santa Margari *Also called Jct Company LLC* ***(P-2242)***
Aliso Creek Inn and Golf Crse, Laguna Beach *Also called Laguna Bch Golf Bnglow Vlg LLC* ***(P-18725)***
Aliso Mechanical Incorporated.....C.....949 544-1601
29736 A De Las Bandera Rancho Santa Margari (92688) ***(P-2096)***
Aliso Viejo Country Club, Aliso Viejo *Also called Aliso Viejo Golf Club Inc* ***(P-18679)***
Aliso Viejo Golf Club Inc.....C.....949 598-9200
33 Santa Barbara Dr Aliso Viejo (92656) ***(P-18679)***
Aliso Viejo Medical Offices, Aliso Viejo *Also called Kaiser Foundation Hospitals* ***(P-19524)***
All Action Security Inc.....D.....800 482-7371
20501 Ventura Blvd # 275 Woodland Hills (91364) ***(P-16545)***
All American Agrigate, Corona *Also called All American Asphalt* ***(P-1714)***
All American Asphalt (PA).....D.....951 736-7600
400 E 6th St Corona (92879) ***(P-1714)***
All American Asphalt.....C.....951 736-7617
1776 All American Way Corona (92879) ***(P-1715)***
All American Asphalt.....C.....951 736-7617
1776 All American Way Corona (92879) ***(P-1716)***
All American Decorative Con, Irvine *Also called Home Franchise Concepts LLC* ***(P-3266)***
All American Maintenance, Chatsworth *Also called Marotto Corporation* ***(P-14313)***
All American Plastic & Packg, National City *Also called Ghazal & Sons Inc* ***(P-8106)***
All American Service & Sups.....D.....951 736-3880
1776 All American Way Corona (92879) ***(P-17930)***
All Area Plumbing Inc.....C.....323 939-9990
5742 Venice Blvd Los Angeles (90019) ***(P-2097)***
All California Mortgage Inc (PA).....D.....415 925-5225
17 E Sr Frncis Drke Bl200 Larkspur (94939) ***(P-9769)***
All Care Industries Inc.....D.....562 623-4009
16747 1/2 Parkside Ave Cerritos (90703) ***(P-14184)***
All Care Medical Group Inc.....D.....408 278-3550
31 Crescent St Huntington Park (90255) ***(P-19271)***
All Care Services Inc.....D.....714 669-1148
17671 Irvine Blvd Ste 110 Tustin (92780) ***(P-23467)***
All Commercial Landscape Svc.....E.....559 453-1670
5213 E Pine Ave Fresno (93727) ***(P-795)***
All Control Cleaning Inc.....D.....805 987-4210
124 N Aviador St Ste 1 Camarillo (93010) ***(P-14185)***
All Counties Courier Inc.....C.....949 224-0900
14811 Myford Rd Tustin (92780) ***(P-4392)***
All Direct Mail Services Inc.....C.....818 833-7773
5091 4th St Baldwin Park (91706) ***(P-14041)***
All Environmental Inc.....D.....949 752-9300
1200 Main St Ste D Irvine (92614) ***(P-27632)***
All Environmental Inc.....C.....310 798-4255
2447 Pcf Cast Hwy Ste 101 Hermosa Beach (90254) ***(P-27633)***
All Fab Prcsion Sheetmetal Inc.....D.....408 279-1099
1015 Timothy Dr San Jose (95133) ***(P-3124)***
All For You Home Care, Sacramento *Also called Careability Health Svcs Corp* ***(P-22253)***
All Hallows Garden Apartments, San Francisco *Also called All Hallows Preservation LP* ***(P-10974)***
All Hallows Preservation LP.....A.....415 285-3909
54 Navy Rd San Francisco (94124) ***(P-10974)***
All Health Services Corp (PA).....D.....559 583-9101
206 W 8th St Hanford (93230) ***(P-14568)***
All Hnds Crwash Dtail Ctr Lube.....D.....949 716-3600
22952 Pacific Park Dr Aliso Viejo (92656) ***(P-17800)***
All In One Inc.....C.....310 538-3374
1999 W 190th St Torrance (90504) ***(P-26753)***
All In One Complete Bldg Svcs, Vacaville *Also called Mark Garcia* ***(P-14312)***
All Motorists Insurance Agency.....C.....818 880-9070
5230 Las Virgenes Rd # 100 Calabasas (91302) ***(P-10513)***
All Nation Security Svcs Inc (PA).....C.....213 769-4510
3701 Wilshire Blvd # 530 Los Angeles (90010) ***(P-16546)***
All Phase Business Supplies.....E.....310 631-1900
1920 E Gladwick St Compton (90220) ***(P-8075)***
All Pro Drywall.....E.....530 722-5182
22148 Buckeye Pl Cottonwood (96022) ***(P-2839)***
All Seasons Framing Corp.....E.....714 634-2324
644 N Eckhoff St Orange (92868) ***(P-3015)***
All Seasons Homecare.....D.....408 378-0900
262 E Hamilton Ave Ste C Campbell (95008) ***(P-22211)***
All South Bay Central Office.....D.....310 618-1180
1411 Marcelina Ave Torrance (90501) ***(P-25376)***
All Star Automotive Products.....D.....626 960-5164
4257 Auction Ave Ste N Baldwin Park (91706) ***(P-6617)***
All Star Glass Inc (PA).....E.....619 275-3343
1845 Morena Blvd San Diego (92110) ***(P-17751)***
All Star Maintenance Inc.....D.....858 259-0900
12250 El Camino Real # 300 San Diego (92130) ***(P-3482)***
All Star Seed (PA).....D.....760 482-9400
2015 Silsbee Rd El Centro (92243) ***(P-490)***
All Stars.....B.....858 259-0900
12250 El Camino Real # 300 San Diego (92130) ***(P-3483)***
All State Association Inc.....C.....877 425-2558
11487 San Fernando Rd San Fernando (91340) ***(P-24941)***
All System Personnel Mgmt.....E.....858 674-4090
16885 W Bernardo Dr # 150 San Diego (92127) ***(P-26754)***
All Taxi Electronics, San Francisco *Also called Yellow Cab Cooperative Inc* ***(P-3875)***
All Tmperatures Controlled Inc.....D.....818 882-1478
9720 Topanga Canyon Pl Chatsworth (91311) ***(P-2098)***
All Types of Baseboard, San Diego *Also called Juan Lopez* ***(P-1186)***
All Valley Home Care, San Diego *Also called All Valley Home Hlth Care Inc* ***(P-22212)***
All Valley Home Hlth Care Inc.....D.....619 276-8001
3665 Ruffin Rd Ste 103 San Diego (92123) ***(P-22212)***
All Valley Washer Service Inc.....D.....818 787-1100
15008 Delano St Van Nuys (91411) ***(P-13556)***
All West Coachlines, Sacramento *Also called Cusa AWC LLC* ***(P-3644)***
All West Coachlines Inc.....D.....916 423-4000
7701 Wilbur Way Sacramento (95828) ***(P-3893)***
All-City Management Svcs Inc.....A.....310 202-8284
10440 Pioneer Blvd Ste 5 Santa Fe Springs (90670) ***(P-27634)***
All-Guard Alarm Systems Inc (PA).....D.....800 255-4273
1306 Stealth St Livermore (94551) ***(P-2505)***
All-Phase Electric Supply, Burbank *Also called Consolidated Elec Distrs Inc* ***(P-7350)***
All-Points Petroleum LLC.....D.....707 745-1116
640 Noyes Ct Benicia (94510) ***(P-8948)***
All-Pro Bail Bonds Inc (PA).....D.....858 481-1200
512 Via De La Valle # 303 Solana Beach (92075) ***(P-16991)***
All-Pro Bail Bonds Inc.....D.....760 941-4100
530 Hacienda Dr Ste 104d Vista (92081) ***(P-16992)***
All-Pro Remodeling.....D.....714 288-1314
706 N Tustin St Orange (92867) ***(P-1111)***
All-Rite Leasing Company Inc.....B.....714 530-7074
950 S Coast Dr Ste 110 Costa Mesa (92626) ***(P-14186)***
Allan Automatic Sprinkler Corp.....D.....714 993-9500
3233 Enterprise St Brea (92821) ***(P-2099)***
Allan Company, Baldwin Park *Also called Cedarwood-Young Company* ***(P-6371)***
Allan Company, Baldwin Park *Also called Cedarwood-Young Company* ***(P-7973)***
Allana Buick & Bers Inc (PA).....D.....650 543-5600
990 Commercial St Ste 200 Palo Alto (94303) ***(P-25527)***
Allaquaria LLC.....D.....310 645-1107
5420 W 104th St Los Angeles (90045) ***(P-9193)***
Allcells LLC.....D.....510 521-2600
1301 Harbor Bay Pkwy # 200 Alameda (94502) ***(P-26315)***
Alldata LLC.....D.....916 684-5200
9650 W Taron Dr Ste 100 Elk Grove (95757) ***(P-15579)***
Alldayeveryday Productions LLC.....E.....323 556-6200
2028 E 7th St Los Angeles (90021) ***(P-18012)***
Alldragon International Inc.....E.....408 410-6248
4285 Payne Ave 10028 San Jose (95117) ***(P-14971)***
Alldrin Brothers Inc.....E.....855 667-4231
584 Hi Tech Pkwy Oakdale (95361) ***(P-491)***
Alldrin Brothers Almonds, Oakdale *Also called Alldrin Brothers Inc* ***(P-491)***
Allegis Group Inc.....C.....650 425-6950
1 Waters Park Dr San Mateo (94403) ***(P-14812)***
Allegis Residential Svcs Inc.....D.....858 430-5700
9340 Hazard Way Ste B2 San Diego (92123) ***(P-26755)***
Allen Spees Family Homes.....E.....559 432-3664
524 W Roberts Ave Fresno (93704) ***(P-24413)***
Allen Construction Inc.....E.....818 879-5334
31356 Via Colinas Ste 107 Westlake Village (91362) ***(P-3016)***
Allen Development Partners LLC (PA).....D.....559 732-5425
125 Sbridge 100 Visalia (93291) ***(P-11852)***
Allen Drywall & Associates.....D.....650 579-0664
380 Lang Rd Burlingame (94010) ***(P-2840)***
Allen Edwards Beauty Salon (PA).....D.....818 981-7711
16101 Ventura Blvd # 155 Encino (91436) ***(P-13645)***
Allen Edwards Salons, Woodland Hills *Also called Canter/Edwards Enterprises* ***(P-13649)***
Allen L Bender Inc.....C.....916 372-2190
6625 Quail Crossing Ln Granite Bay (95746) ***(P-1462)***
Allen Lund Company LLC (HQ).....D.....818 790-1110
4529 Angeles Crest Hwy # 300 La Canada Flintridge (91011) ***(P-5002)***
Allen Lund Company LLC.....D.....650 358-9454
1825 S Grant St Ste 320 San Mateo (94402) ***(P-5003)***
Allen Lund Corporation (PA).....E.....818 790-8412
4529 Angeles Crest Hwy La Canada Flintridge (91011) ***(P-5004)***
Allen Matkins, San Francisco *Also called Eileen Nottoli* ***(P-23059)***
Allen Matkins Leck Gmble.....D.....415 837-1515
3 Embarcadero Ctr # 1200 San Francisco (94111) ***(P-22909)***
Allen Matkins Leck Gmble (PA).....B.....213 622-5555
865 S Figueroa St # 2800 Los Angeles (90017) ***(P-22910)***
Allen Matkins Leck Gmble.....D.....949 553-1313
1900 Main St Fl 5 Irvine (92614) ***(P-22911)***
Allen Medical Group Inc.....E.....818 698-8444
14416 Victory Blvd # 211 Van Nuys (91401) ***(P-19272)***
Allen Transportation Co, Sacramento *Also called Amador Stage Lines Inc* ***(P-3887)***
Allergan Sales LLC (HQ).....A.....862 261-7000
2525 Dupont Dr 14th Irvine (92612) ***(P-8139)***
Alliance Bay Funding Inc.....D.....510 742-6600
37600 Central Ct Ste 264 Newark (94560) ***(P-11205)***
Alliance Capital Markets, Orange *Also called Alliance Funding Group* ***(P-18177)***
Alliance Construction, Costa Mesa *Also called Empire Leasing Inc* ***(P-3032)***
Alliance Credit Union (PA).....D.....408 445-3386
3315 Almaden Expy Ste 55 San Jose (95118) ***(P-9619)***
Alliance Fc.....E.....909 784-0005
3496 Little League Dr San Bernardino (92407) ***(P-25377)***
Alliance For Housing & Healing (PA).....D.....323 344-4885
825 Colorado Blvd Ste 100 Los Angeles (90041) ***(P-20915)***
Alliance Funding Group.....D.....800 978-8817
3745 W Chapman Ave # 200 Orange (92868) ***(P-18177)***
Alliance Ground Intl LLC.....D.....310 646-2446
6181 W Imperial Hwy Los Angeles (90045) ***(P-4870)***
Alliance Ground Intl LLC.....D.....650 821-0855
648 Rest Field Rd San Francisco (94128) ***(P-4871)***
Alliance Healthcare Svcs Inc (HQ).....C.....949 242-5300
18201 Von Karman Ave Irvine (92612) ***(P-22058)***
Alliance Hospital Services.....E.....650 697-6900
100 S San Mateo Dr San Mateo (94401) ***(P-22213)***
Alliance Information Technolog (PA).....D.....925 462-9787
7041 Koll Center Pkwy # 140 Pleasanton (94566) ***(P-14972)***

ALPHABETIC

Employee Codes: A=Over 500 employees, B=251-500
C=101-250, D=51-100, E=50
2019 Directory of California
Wholesalers and Services Companies
© Mergent Inc. 1-800-342-5647
1197

Alliance Medical Center Inc D 707 431-8234
1381 University St Healdsburg (95448) ***(P-19273)***
Alliance Member Services Inc D 831 459-0980
333 Front St Ste 200 Santa Cruz (95060) ***(P-25378)***
Alliance Nrsing Rhbltation Ctr, El Monte *Also called Georgia Atkison Snf LLC* ***(P-20453)***
Alliance Rdwods Cnfrnce Grunds D 707 874-3507
6250 Bohemian Hwy Occidental (95465) ***(P-13444)***
Alliance Roofing Company Inc (PA) E 800 579-2595
630 Martin Ave Santa Clara (95050) ***(P-3125)***
Alliance Rvrside Hsptality LLC E 949 229-3168
21520 Yorba Linda Blvd Yorba Linda (92887) ***(P-12313)***
Alliance Title, Glendale *Also called Wfg National Title Insur Co* ***(P-10474)***
Alliance Wall Systems Inc E 530 740-7800
4638 Skyway Dr Marysville (95901) ***(P-2841)***
Alliance Work Net, Modesto *Also called County of Stanislaus* ***(P-24177)***
Alliancebernstein LP D 310 286-6000
1999 Ave Of The Sts 215 Los Angeles (90067) ***(P-12021)***
Allianceit, Pleasanton *Also called Alliance Information Technolog* ***(P-14972)***
Alliant Asset MGT Co LLC (PA) D 818 668-2805
21600 Oxnard St Ste 1200 Woodland Hills (91367) ***(P-11206)***
Alliant Educational Foundation C 559 456-2777
5130 E Clinton Way Fresno (93727) ***(P-22501)***
Alliant Insurance Services Inc (PA) C 949 756-0271
1301 Dove St Ste 200 Newport Beach (92660) ***(P-10514)***
Alliant Insurance Services Inc D 619 238-1828
701 B St Ste 600 San Diego (92101) ***(P-10515)***
Alliant Tchsystems Oprtons LLC B 818 887-8195
9401 Corbin Ave Northridge (91324) ***(P-26316)***
Allianz Globl Corp & Specialty, Burbank *Also called Allianz Underwriters Insur Co* ***(P-10332)***
Allianz Globl Invstors Amer LP (HQ) D 949 219-2200
680 Nwport Ctr Dr Ste 250 Newport Beach (92660) ***(P-10050)***
Allianz Globl Risks US Insur (HQ) C 818 260-7500
2350 W Empire Ave Burbank (91504) ***(P-10330)***
Allianz Globl Risks US Insur B 415 899-3758
1465 N Mcdowell Blvd Petaluma (94954) ***(P-10331)***
Allianz Insurance Company, Petaluma *Also called Allianz Globl Risks US Insur* ***(P-10331)***
Allianz Technology America Inc C 415 899-2713
1465 N Mcdowell Blvd Petaluma (94954) ***(P-16310)***
Allianz Underwriters Insur Co D 818 260-7500
2350 W Empire Ave Burbank (91504) ***(P-10332)***
Allied Anesthesia Med Group D 951 830-9816
400 N Tustin Ave Santa Ana (92705) ***(P-19274)***
Allied Artists International, City of Industry *Also called Allied Entertainment Group Inc* ***(P-18013)***
Allied Auto Store, Fremont *Also called Serrato-Mcdermott Inc* ***(P-6673)***
Allied Beverage LLC B 818 493-6400
13235 Golden State Rd Sylmar (91342) ***(P-7661)***
Allied Building Products Corp E 714 647-9792
1201 E Mcfadden Ave Santa Ana (92705) ***(P-6916)***
Allied Building Products Corp E 909 796-6926
456 Industrial Rd San Bernardino (92408) ***(P-6805)***
Allied Building Products Corp E 707 584-7599
4159 Santa Rosa Ave Santa Rosa (95407) ***(P-6917)***
Allied Building Products Corp D 323 721-9011
1620 S Maple Ave Montebello (90640) ***(P-6918)***
Allied Company Holdings Inc (PA) B 818 493-6400
13235 Golden State Rd Sylmar (91342) ***(P-8977)***
Allied Digital Services LLC (HQ) C 310 431-2375
680 Knox St Ste 200 Torrance (90502) ***(P-16264)***
Allied Electric Motor Svc Inc (PA) D 559 486-4222
4690 E Jensen Ave Fresno (93725) ***(P-7327)***
Allied Entertainment Group Inc (PA) B 626 330-0600
273 W Allen Ave City of Industry (91746) ***(P-18013)***
Allied Environmental Services, Woodland Hills *Also called Allied Industries Inc* ***(P-27635)***
Allied Farming Company, Exeter *Also called Sun Pacific Farming Coop Inc* ***(P-713)***
Allied Fire Protection C 510 533-5516
555 High St Oakland (94601) ***(P-2100)***
Allied Food Distributors Inc D 925 432-1625
1225 California Ave Pittsburg (94565) ***(P-8751)***
Allied Framers Inc C 707 452-7050
4990 Allison Pkwy Vacaville (95688) ***(P-3017)***
Allied Gardens Towing Inc (HQ) D 619 563-4060
9150 Chesapeake Dr # 240 San Diego (92123) ***(P-17847)***
Allied High Tech Products Inc D 310 635-2466
2376 E Pacifica Pl Rancho Dominguez (90220) ***(P-7826)***
Allied Industries Inc (PA) C 818 781-2490
21650 Oxnard St Ste 500 Woodland Hills (91367) ***(P-27635)***
Allied Interstate Inc (HQ) D 818 575-5400
30699 Russell Ranch Rd # 250 Westlake Village (91362) ***(P-13990)***
Allied Intl San Franisco, Hayward *Also called Nor-Cal Moving Services* ***(P-4361)***
Allied Landscape Svcs S Inc D 408 310-8476
5542 Monterey Hwy Ste 277 San Jose (95138) ***(P-726)***
Allied Lube Texas LP (PA) D 949 486-4008
4440 Von Karman Ave # 100 Newport Beach (92660) ***(P-17848)***
Allied Medical Service of Cal E 415 931-1400
2570 Bush St San Francisco (94115) ***(P-3742)***
Allied Prof Nursing Care D 909 949-1066
2345 W Fthlls Blvd Ste 14 Upland (91786) ***(P-22214)***
Allied Protection Services Inc D 310 330-8314
19164 Van Ness Ave Torrance (90501) ***(P-16547)***
Allied Refrigeration Inc D 310 202-2220
3650 Holdrege Ave Los Angeles (90016) ***(P-7643)***
Allied Risk Management Inc D 661 305-0455
2010 W Avenue K 395 Lancaster (93536) ***(P-16548)***
Allied Steel Co Inc D 951 241-7000
1027 Palmyrita Ave Riverside (92507) ***(P-3358)***
Allied Swift, Oceanside *Also called Allied Swiss Limited* ***(P-10850)***
Allied Swiss Limited C 760 941-1702
2636 Vista Pacific Dr Oceanside (92056) ***(P-10850)***
Allied Universal, Santa Ana *Also called Universal Services America LP* ***(P-16850)***
Allied Universal Security Svcs, Santa Ana *Also called Universal Protection Svc LP* ***(P-16848)***
Alliedbarton Security Svcs LLC C 626 213-3100
765 The City Dr S Ste 150 Orange (92868) ***(P-16549)***
Alliedbarton Security Svcs LLC C 951 801-7300
3120 Chicago Ave Ste 190 Riverside (92507) ***(P-16550)***
Alliedbarton Security Svcs LLC C 310 324-1219
637 E Albertoni St # 202 Carson (90746) ***(P-16551)***
Alliedbarton Security Svcs LLC C 916 489-8280
8950 Cal Center Dr # 150 Sacramento (95826) ***(P-16552)***
Alliedbarton Security Svcs LLC D 805 983-1204
300 E Esplanade Dr # 1510 Oxnard (93036) ***(P-16553)***
Alliedbarton Security Svcs LLC B 562 906-4800
10330 Pioneer Blvd # 235 Santa Fe Springs (90670) ***(P-16554)***
Alliedbarton Security Svcs LLC B 510 839-4041
1600 Riviera Ave Ste 375 Walnut Creek (94596) ***(P-16555)***
Alliedbarton Security Svcs LLC B 408 954-8274
2540 N 1st St Ste 101 San Jose (95131) ***(P-16556)***
Alliedbarton Security Svcs LLC B 858 874-8200
7670 Opportunity Rd # 210 San Diego (92111) ***(P-16557)***
Alliedbarton Security Svcs LLC B 800 418-6423
3701 Wilshire Blvd # 600 Los Angeles (90010) ***(P-16558)***
Alliedbarton Security Svcs LLC C 714 260-0805
765 The City Dr S Ste 105 Orange (92868) ***(P-16559)***
Allison Dowdy D 707 303-3472
1045 College Ave Santa Rosa (95404) ***(P-11207)***
Allison, Amanda Dvm, Elk Grove *Also called Bradshaw Veterinary Clinic* ***(P-598)***
Allmark Inc (PA) D 909 989-7556
10070 Arrow Rte Rancho Cucamonga (91730) ***(P-11208)***
Allogene Therapeutics Inc D 650 457-2700
210 E Grand Ave South San Francisco (94080) ***(P-26317)***
Alloy Construction Inc D 661 203-2592
701 Gardner Field Rd Taft (93268) ***(P-2005)***
Allpro Industry Solutions LLC E 661 854-3613
7850 White Ln Bakersfield (93309) ***(P-5005)***
Allred Child Developement Ctr, San Bernardino *Also called San Bernardino City Unf School* ***(P-24376)***
Allsafe Selfstorage, Danville *Also called Cubix Construction Company* ***(P-1389)***
Allstar Commercial Cleaning E 858 715-0500
4805 Mercury St Ste H San Diego (92111) ***(P-17931)***
Allstar Home Services, Rancho Cucamonga *Also called Infinity Service Group Inc* ***(P-2234)***
Allstate, Corona *Also called Acm Technologies Inc* ***(P-6948)***
Allstate, Torrance *Also called Janet Hilton* ***(P-10660)***
Allstate Building Maintenance D 714 739-8080
4890 Saint Andrews Ave Buena Park (90621) ***(P-14187)***
Allstate Communications ASC, Chatsworth *Also called US Interstate Distrg Inc* ***(P-5658)***
Allstate Construction Co E 310 652-6942
1364 Londonderry Pl Los Angeles (90069) ***(P-1112)***
Allstate Imaging Inc (PA) D 818 678-4550
21621 Nordhoff St Chatsworth (91311) ***(P-6949)***
Allstate Insurance Company A 909 612-5504
21950 Copley Dr Ste 130 Diamond Bar (91765) ***(P-10333)***
Allstate Research and Plg Ctr D 650 833-6200
4200 Bohannon Dr Ste 200 Menlo Park (94025) ***(P-10516)***
Alltech Services, Los Alamitos *Also called Mggb Inc* ***(P-25818)***
Alltek Company U S A Inc E 714 375-9785
18281 Gothard St Ste 102 Huntington Beach (92648) ***(P-7724)***
Alltoss, Glendale *Also called Durini Luis Carlos Estrada* ***(P-17142)***
Alltrade Tools LLC E 310 522-9008
6122 Katella Ave Cypress (90630) ***(P-7572)***
ALMA VIA OF CAMARILLO, Alameda *Also called Elder Care Alliance Camarillo* ***(P-24516)***
Almaden Golf & Country Club D 408 323-4812
6663 Hampton Dr San Jose (95120) ***(P-18821)***
Almaden Health & Rehab Ctr, San Jose *Also called Mariner Health Care Inc* ***(P-20625)***
Almaden Valley Athletic Club D 408 445-4900
5400 Camden Ave San Jose (95124) ***(P-18822)***
Almavia of San Francisco D 415 337-1339
1 Thomas More Way San Francisco (94132) ***(P-20228)***
Almond Board of California E 209 549-8262
1150 9th St Ste 1500 Modesto (95354) ***(P-24942)***
Aloft El Sgnd-Los Angles Arprt, El Segundo *Also called Rubicon B Hacienda LLC* ***(P-13152)***
Aloft Ontario-Rancho Cucamonga D 909 484-2018
10480 4th St Rancho Cucamonga (91730) ***(P-12314)***
Aloft Sfo, Millbrae *Also called Millbrae Wcp Hotel II LLC* ***(P-12929)***
Alogent Holdings Inc D 760 410-9000
5868 Owens Ave Ste 200 Carlsbad (92008) ***(P-14973)***
Alois LLC D 215 297-4492
548 Market St Ste 47970 San Francisco (94104) ***(P-14569)***
Alois Staffing, San Francisco *Also called Alois LLC* ***(P-14569)***
Alom Technologies Corporation (PA) D 510 360-3600
48105 Warm Springs Blvd Fremont (94539) ***(P-16993)***
Alondra Golf Course Inc D 310 217-9915
16400 Prairie Ave Lawndale (90260) ***(P-18680)***
Alonso Construction, Spring Valley *Also called Hugo Alonso Inc* ***(P-1408)***
Alorica Customer Care Inc A 619 298-7103
8885 Rio San Diego Dr San Diego (92108) ***(P-16994)***
Alorica Inc (PA) D 949 527-4600
5 Park Plz Ste 1100 Irvine (92614) ***(P-16084)***
Alpert & Alpert Iron & Met Inc E 562 624-8833
2350 W 16th St Long Beach (90813) ***(P-7253)***
ALPERT JEWISH COMMUNITY CENTRE, Long Beach *Also called Jewish Community Ctr Long Bch* ***(P-23872)***
Alpha Connection Group Home D 760 247-6370
22675 Anoka Rd Apple Valley (92308) ***(P-25053)***

Mergent e-mail: customerrelations@mergent.com
1198
2019 Directory of California
Wholesalers and Services Companies
(P-0000) Products & Services Section entry number
(PA)=Parent Co (HQ)=Headquarters (DH)=Div Headquarters

ALPHA CONNECTION YOUTH FAMILY, Apple Valley *Also called Alpha Connection Group Home* ***(P-25053)***
Alpha Mechanical Inc ....D....858 278-3500
4990 Greencraig Ln Ste A San Diego (92123) ***(P-2101)***
Alpha Mechanical Inc (PA) ....D....858 278-3500
4885 Greencraig Ln San Diego (92123) ***(P-2102)***
Alpha Net Consulting LLC ....D....408 330-0896
3080 Olcott St Ste C235 Santa Clara (95054) ***(P-14974)***
Alpha Professional Resources, Thousand Oaks *Also called A P R Inc* ***(P-14806)***
Alpha Project For Homeless (PA) ....D....619 542-1877
3737 5th Ave Ste 203 San Diego (92103) ***(P-23468)***
Alpha Swimming Pool & Spa ....D....714 879-4667
2600 Athena Pl Fullerton (92833) ***(P-16995)***
Alpha Systems Fire Protection ....E....323 227-0700
7356 Fulton Ave North Hollywood (91605) ***(P-8017)***
Alpha Teknova Inc ....D....831 637-1100
2290 Bert Dr Hollister (95023) ***(P-26318)***
Alpha-Winfield Contractors Inc ....D....510 652-4712
1096 Yerba Buena Ave Emeryville (94608) ***(P-1113)***
Alphabet Inc (PA) ....D....650 253-0000
1600 Amphitheatre Pkwy Mountain View (94043) ***(P-14975)***
Alpine Camp Conference Ctr Inc ....D....909 337-6287
415 Clubhouse Dr Blue Jay (92317) ***(P-19093)***
Alpine Carpets, Culver City *Also called Alpine Interiors Corporation* ***(P-6746)***
Alpine Convalescent Center Inc ....D....619 659-3120
2120 Alpine Blvd Alpine (91901) ***(P-22502)***
Alpine Electronics America Inc ....C....310 783-7391
2012 Abalone Ave Ste D Torrance (90501) ***(P-7407)***
Alpine Electronics America Inc (HQ) ....C....310 326-8000
19145 Gramercy Pl Torrance (90501) ***(P-7408)***
Alpine Inn Restaurant, Torrance *Also called Alpine Village* ***(P-10851)***
Alpine Interiors Corporation (PA) ....D....310 390-7639
3961 Sepulveda Blvd # 205 Culver City (90230) ***(P-6746)***
Alpine Meadows Ski Area ....E....530 583-4232
2600 Alpine Meadows Rd Alpine Meadows (96146) ***(P-12315)***
Alpine Meadows Ski Resort, Alpine Meadows *Also called Alpine Meadows Ski Area* ***(P-12315)***
Alpine Special Treatment Ctr, Alpine *Also called Alpine Convalescent Center Inc* ***(P-22502)***
Alpine Village ....C....310 327-4384
833 Torrance Blvd Ste 1a Torrance (90502) ***(P-10851)***
Als Services Usa Corp ....D....562 597-3932
1875 Coronado Ave Long Beach (90755) ***(P-26683)***
Alsco - Geyer Irrigation Inc ....D....530 476-2253
700 5th St Arbuckle (95912) ***(P-7699)***
Alsco Inc ....D....510 237-9634
1009 Factory St Richmond (94801) ***(P-13493)***
Alsco Inc ....C....323 465-5111
900 N Highland Ave Los Angeles (90038) ***(P-13494)***
Alsco Inc ....D....805 650-6578
2215 Palma Dr Ventura (93003) ***(P-13495)***
Alsco Inc ....C....619 234-7291
705 W Grape St San Diego (92101) ***(P-13496)***
Alsco Inc ....D....415 648-9266
1575 Indiana St San Francisco (94107) ***(P-13497)***
Alsco Inc ....D....714 774-4165
1750 S Zeyn St Anaheim (92802) ***(P-13498)***
Alsco Inc ....D....707 523-3311
3311 Industrial Dr Santa Rosa (95403) ***(P-13499)***
Alsco Inc ....C....408 279-2345
2275 Junction Ave San Jose (95131) ***(P-13500)***
Alsco Inc ....C....707 751-0652
5159 Commercial Cir Concord (94520) ***(P-13501)***
Alsco Inc ....D....916 454-5545
3391 Lanatt St Sacramento (95819) ***(P-13502)***
Alston & Bird LLP ....C....213 626-8830
333 S Hope St Ste 1600 Los Angeles (90071) ***(P-22912)***
Alston & Bird LLP ....B....202 239-3673
2815 Townsgate Rd Ste 200 Westlake Village (91361) ***(P-22913)***
Alston Construction Co Inc (PA) ....D....916 340-2400
8775 Folsom Blvd Ste 201 Sacramento (95826) ***(P-1463)***
Alta Bates Summit Medical Ctr, Berkeley *Also called Surgery Center of Alta Bates* ***(P-21796)***
Alta Btes Cmprhnsive Cncer Ctr, Berkeley *Also called Surgery Center of Alta Bates* ***(P-19956)***
Alta Cal Regional Ctr Inc ....B....530 674-3070
950 Tharp Rd Ste 202 Yuba City (95993) ***(P-23469)***
Alta Care Center LLC ....C....714 530-6322
13075 Blackbird St Garden Grove (92843) ***(P-20986)***
Alta Drywall, Escondido *Also called Innovative Drywall Systems Inc* ***(P-2895)***
Alta Equipment Leasing Company ....D....415 875-1000
50 California St Fl 24 San Francisco (94111) ***(P-14470)***
Alta Healthcare System LLC ....C....818 787-1511
14433 Emelita St Van Nuys (91401) ***(P-24730)***
Alta Healthcare System LLC (HQ) ....C....323 267-0477
4081 E Olympic Blvd Los Angeles (90023) ***(P-24731)***
Alta Hollywood Community Hsptl ....C....818 787-1511
14433 Emelita St Van Nuys (91401) ***(P-21922)***
Alta Hospitals System LLC ....C....323 267-0477
4081 E Olympic Blvd Los Angeles (90023) ***(P-21279)***
Alta Hospitals System LLC ....A....714 619-7700
14662 Newport Ave Tustin (92780) ***(P-21280)***
Alta Hospitals System LLC (HQ) ....C....310 943-4500
10780 Santa Monica Blvd # 400 Los Angeles (90025) ***(P-21281)***
Alta Interiors Inc ....D....951 784-1400
847 Palmyrita Ave Riverside (92507) ***(P-2842)***
Alta Loma Assisted Living LLC ....D....909 481-2600
9428 19th St Murrieta (92562) ***(P-23470)***
ALTA ONE FCU, Ridgecrest *Also called Altaone Federal Credit Union* ***(P-9538)***
Alta Sierra Country Club Inc ....E....530 273-2041
11897 Tammy Way Grass Valley (95949) ***(P-18823)***
Alta Vista Country Club LLC ....D....714 524-1591
777 Alta Vista St Placentia (92870) ***(P-18824)***
Alta Vista Healthcare and Well ....C....951 688-8200
9020 Garfield St Riverside (92503) ***(P-19275)***
Alta Vista Healthcare Center, Riverside *Also called Kindred Healthcare Operating* ***(P-21129)***
Alta Vista Solutions ....C....510 594-0510
3260 Blume Dr Ste 500 Richmond (94806) ***(P-25528)***
Alta-Dena Certified Dairy LLC ....D....858 292-6930
4656 Cardin St San Diego (92111) ***(P-8511)***
Altaba Inc ....C....408 349-5080
3420 Central Expy Santa Clara (95051) ***(P-5446)***
Altadena Town and Country Club ....D....626 345-9088
2290 Country Club Dr Altadena (91001) ***(P-18825)***
Altaf Zahid Engineering Svcs ....E....760 481-9072
42051 Orange Blossom Dr Temecula (92591) ***(P-16996)***
Altamed Health Services Corp ....D....323 980-4466
5427 Whittier Blvd Los Angeles (90022) ***(P-19276)***
Altamed Health Services Corp ....C....714 635-0593
1820 W Lincoln Ave Anaheim (92801) ***(P-19277)***
Altamed Health Services Corp ....D....626 214-1480
535 S 2nd Ave Covina (91723) ***(P-10156)***
Altamed Health Services Corp ....D....562 949-6069
9436 Slauson Ave Pico Rivera (90660) ***(P-19278)***
Altamed Health Services Corp ....C....323 889-7847
10454 Valley Blvd El Monte (91731) ***(P-22726)***
Altamed Health Services Corp (PA) ....C....323 725-8751
2040 Camfield Ave Commerce (90040) ***(P-19279)***
Altamed Health Services Corp ....D....562 949-8717
9436 Slauson Ave Pico Rivera (90660) ***(P-22727)***
Altamed Health Services Corp ....A....877 462-2582
10418 Valley Blvd Ste B El Monte (91731) ***(P-19280)***
Altamed Health Services Corp ....E....323 980-4000
5425 Pomona Blvd Los Angeles (90022) ***(P-19281)***
Altamed Health Services Corp ....C....714 780-5690
1814 W Lincoln Ave Anaheim (92801) ***(P-19282)***
Altametrics LLC ....C....800 676-1281
3191 Red Hill Ave Ste 100 Costa Mesa (92626) ***(P-7002)***
Altamont Infrastructure Co ....D....925 245-5500
6185 Industrial Way Livermore (94551) ***(P-6012)***
Altaone Federal Credit Union (PA) ....C....760 371-7000
701 S China Lake Blvd Ridgecrest (93555) ***(P-9538)***
Altcare Cedar Creek LLC ....D....510 527-7282
868 Ensenada Ave Berkeley (94707) ***(P-24414)***
Altec Products Inc (PA) ....D....949 727-1248
23422 Mill Creek Dr # 225 Laguna Hills (92653) ***(P-16997)***
Altech Services Inc ....B....888 725-8324
400 Continental Blvd Fl 6 El Segundo (90245) ***(P-14813)***
Altegra Health ....D....310 776-4001
3415 S Sepulveda Blvd # 900 Los Angeles (90034) ***(P-27124)***
Alten Construction Inc ....D....510 234-4200
1141 Marina Way S Richmond (94804) ***(P-1464)***
Altenheim Inc ....D....510 530-4013
1720 Macarthur Blvd Oakland (94602) ***(P-10975)***
Altera Real Estate ....B....949 547-7351
33522 Niguel Rd Ste 200 Dana Point (92629) ***(P-11209)***
Altium Inc (HQ) ....D....858 864-1661
4225 Executive Sq Ste 700 La Jolla (92037) ***(P-14976)***
Altium LLC ....D....800 544-4186
4275 Executive Sq Ste 825 La Jolla (92037) ***(P-15580)***
Altman Plants, Vista *Also called Altman Specialty Plants Inc* ***(P-9123)***
Altman Specialty Plants Inc (PA) ....A....800 348-4881
3742 Blue Bird Canyon Rd Vista (92084) ***(P-9123)***
Alton Geoscience, Irvine *Also called TRC Solutions Inc* ***(P-27888)***
Alton Irvine Inc ....D....949 428-4141
2052 Alton Pkwy Irvine (92606) ***(P-6708)***
Altoon Partners LLP (PA) ....D....213 225-1900
617 W 7th St Ste 400 Los Angeles (90017) ***(P-26022)***
Altoon Porter, Los Angeles *Also called Altoon Partners LLP* ***(P-26022)***
Altour International Inc ....C....310 571-6000
12100 W Olympic Blvd # 300 Los Angeles (90064) ***(P-4928)***
Altour International Inc (PA) ....D....310 571-6000
12100 W Olympic Blvd # 300 Los Angeles (90064) ***(P-4929)***
Altour Travel Master, Los Angeles *Also called Altour International Inc* ***(P-4928)***
Altria Group Distribution Co ....C....804 274-2000
3500 W Olive Ave Ste 1490 Burbank (91505) ***(P-8909)***
Altria Group Distribution Co ....D....626 792-2900
3500 W Olive Ave Ste 1490 Burbank (91505) ***(P-9181)***
Altura Centers For Health ....D....559 686-9097
1201 N Cherry St Tulare (93274) ***(P-19283)***
Altura Comm Solutions LLC (HQ) ....D....714 948-8400
1335 S Acacia Ave Fullerton (92831) ***(P-7435)***
Altura Communication Systems, Fullerton *Also called Altura Comm Solutions LLC* ***(P-7435)***
Altura Credit Union (PA) ....D....888 883-7228
2847 Campus Pkwy Riverside (92507) ***(P-9620)***
Alumatec Inc ....D....818 609-7460
18411 Sherman Way Reseda (91335) ***(P-1034)***
Aluminum Precision Pdts Inc (PA) ....A....714 546-8125
3333 W Warner Ave Santa Ana (92704) ***(P-7254)***
Alvarado Hospital LLC (HQ) ....D....619 287-3270
6655 Alvarado Rd San Diego (92120) ***(P-21282)***
Alvarado Parkway Institute, La Mesa *Also called Helix Healthcare Inc* ***(P-21957)***
Alvaradosmith A Prof Corp (PA) ....C....714 852-6800
1 Macarthur Pl Ste 200 Santa Ana (92707) ***(P-22914)***
Alvarez & Marsal Holdings LLC ....C....415 490-2300
100 Pine St Fl 9 San Francisco (94111) ***(P-27125)***
Alvarion Inc (HQ) ....E....650 314-2500
555 N Mathilda Ave # 210 Sunnyvale (94085) ***(P-7436)***
Alventive Inc (PA) ....D....408 969-8000
2790 Walsh Ave Santa Clara (95051) ***(P-15581)***

ALPHABETIC

Employee Codes: A=Over 500 employees, B=251-500
C=101-250, D=51-100, E=50
2019 Directory of California
Wholesalers and Services Companies
© Mergent Inc. 1-800-342-5647
1199

Alves, Robert L, Selma *Also called Robert Alves Farms Inc* ***(P-170)***
Alvizia Landscape Co LLC..........C.......619 661-6557
2520 Cactus Rd San Diego (92154) ***(P-796)***
Always Best, City of Industry *Also called Rongcheng Trading LLC* ***(P-8629)***
Always Home Nursing Svc Inc..........C.......916 989-6420
7777 Greenback Ln Ste 208 Citrus Heights (95610) ***(P-22215)***
Always There Live In Care LLC..........D.......888 606-8880
7121 Magnolia Ave Riverside (92504) ***(P-22216)***
Alzheimer's Living Center, Fresno *Also called Community Medical Centers* ***(P-21338)***
Alzheimers Care Since 1983..........E.......714 641-0959
3730 S Greenville St Santa Ana (92704) ***(P-22217)***
Alzheimers Greater Los Angeles..........D.......323 938-3379
4221 Wilshire Blvd # 400 Los Angeles (90010) ***(P-23471)***
AM Products Inc..........E.......714 662-4454
1661 Palm St Santa Ana (92701) ***(P-7255)***
Am-PM Sewer & Drain Cleaning, San Diego *Also called Bill Howe Plumbing Inc* ***(P-2144)***
Am-TEC Security, Chino *Also called Am-TEC Total Security Inc* ***(P-16872)***
Am-TEC Total Security Inc (PA)..........D.......909 573-4678
4075 Schaefer Ave Chino (91710) ***(P-16872)***
Am/PM Food Mart, La Palma *Also called Arco Envmtl Remediation LLC* ***(P-27142)***
Amada America Inc (HQ)..........D.......714 739-2111
7025 Firestone Blvd Buena Park (90621) ***(P-7725)***
Amada Capital Corporation..........D.......714 739-2111
7025 Firestone Blvd Buena Park (90621) ***(P-14471)***
Amada Enterprises Inc..........C.......323 757-1881
12619 Avalon Blvd Los Angeles (90061) ***(P-20229)***
Amadeus Salon Inc (PA)..........D.......626 795-0969
2817 E Foothill Blvd Pasadena (91107) ***(P-13646)***
Amador Development, Azusa *Also called David L Amador Inc* ***(P-3245)***
Amador Stage Lines Inc..........D.......916 444-7880
1331 C St Sacramento (95814) ***(P-3887)***
Amador Tlmne Cmnty Action Agcy (PA)..........C.......209 296-2785
10590 State Highway 88 Jackson (95642) ***(P-24732)***
Amador Tlmne Cmnty Action Agcy..........E.......209 533-1397
427 Highway 49 Sonora (95370) ***(P-24733)***
Amador Water Agency..........D.......209 223-3018
12800 Ridge Rd Sutter Creek (95685) ***(P-6207)***
Amador-Tolumne Cmnty Resources..........D.......209 223-1485
10590 State Highway 88 Jackson (95642) ***(P-24734)***
Amanecer Cmnty Counseling Svc..........D.......213 481-7464
1200 Wilshire Blvd # 200 Los Angeles (90017) ***(P-22503)***
Amar Transportation Inc (PA)..........C.......831 728-8209
144 W Lake Ave Ste C Watsonville (95076) ***(P-4096)***
AMARAL RANCHES, Chualar *Also called C & G Farms Inc* ***(P-40)***
Amarik Properties Inc (PA)..........D.......714 505-5200
1400 Bristol St N Ste 220 Newport Beach (92660) ***(P-11210)***
Amatel Inc (PA)..........E.......323 801-0199
1017 S Mountain Ave Monrovia (91016) ***(P-27636)***
Amato Industries Incorporated..........D.......650 697-5548
1550 Gilbreth Rd Burlingame (94010) ***(P-3743)***
Amaturo Sonoma Media Group LLC..........D.......707 543-0126
1410 Neotomas Ave Ste 200 Santa Rosa (95405) ***(P-5691)***
Amawaterways LLC (PA)..........C.......800 626-0126
26010 Mureau Rd Calabasas (91302) ***(P-5205)***
Amax Computer, Fremont *Also called Amax Engineering Corporation* ***(P-7003)***
Amax Engineering Corporation (PA)..........C.......510 651-8886
1565 Reliance Way Fremont (94539) ***(P-7003)***
Ambassador Gaming Inc..........C.......714 969-8730
660 Newport Center Dr # 1050 Newport Beach (92660) ***(P-19094)***
Amber Financial Group LLC (PA)..........C.......858 487-7209
11415 W Bernardo Ct San Diego (92127) ***(P-9770)***
Amber Holdings Inc..........A.......415 765-6500
150 California St San Francisco (94111) ***(P-14977)***
Amber Mortgage, San Diego *Also called Amber Financial Group LLC* ***(P-9770)***
Amberfin Limited..........E.......818 768-8948
7590 N Glenoaks Blvd # 101 Burbank (91504) ***(P-7004)***
Ambiente Enterprises Inc..........C.......760 674-1905
73726 Alessandro Dr # 203 Palm Desert (92260) ***(P-22218)***
Amblin/Reliance Holding Co LLC..........D.......818 733-6272
100 Universal City Plz Universal City (91608) ***(P-18014)***
Ambreen Enterprises Inc..........D.......909 620-1339
20370 Via Badalona Yorba Linda (92887) ***(P-27637)***
Ambrose Recreation & Park Dst..........D.......925 458-1601
3105 Willow Pass Rd Bay Point (94565) ***(P-19095)***
Ambry Genetics Corporation (HQ)..........D.......949 900-5500
15 Argonaut Aliso Viejo (92656) ***(P-22059)***
Ambulnz Health LLC..........B.......877 311-5555
12531 Vanowen St North Hollywood (91605) ***(P-3744)***
AMC, Burbank *Also called American Multi-Cinema Inc* ***(P-18257)***
AMC, San Diego *Also called American Multi-Cinema Inc* ***(P-18258)***
AMC, Monterey Park *Also called American Multi-Cinema Inc* ***(P-18259)***
AMC, Fair Oaks *Also called Sunset Pet Hospital Inc* ***(P-609)***
AMC, Covina *Also called American Multi-Cinema Inc* ***(P-18260)***
AMC, San Francisco *Also called American Multi-Cinema Inc* ***(P-18261)***
AMC, Torrance *Also called American Multi-Cinema Inc* ***(P-18262)***
AMC, Orange *Also called American Multi-Cinema Inc* ***(P-18263)***
AMC, Fullerton *Also called American Multi-Cinema Inc* ***(P-18264)***
AMC, Pasadena *Also called American Multi-Cinema Inc* ***(P-18265)***
AMC, Norwalk *Also called American Multi-Cinema Inc* ***(P-18266)***
AMC, Los Angeles *Also called Aesthetic Maintenance Corp* ***(P-14183)***
AMC, Los Angeles *Also called American Multi-Cinema Inc* ***(P-18267)***
AMC, San Diego *Also called American Multi-Cinema Inc* ***(P-18268)***
AMC, City of Industry *Also called American Multi-Cinema Inc* ***(P-18269)***
AMC, Montebello *Also called American Multi-Cinema Inc* ***(P-18270)***
AMC Entertainment Inc..........E.......909 476-1288
4549 Mills Cir Ontario (91764) ***(P-18256)***
AMC&, Los Angeles *Also called Anderson McPharlin Conners LLP* ***(P-22916)***
Amcal Communities Inc..........E.......818 706-0694
30141 Agoura Rd Ste 100 Agoura Hills (91301) ***(P-11853)***
Amcap Fund Inc..........B.......213 486-9200
333 S Hope St Ste Levb Los Angeles (90071) ***(P-12022)***
Amco Foods Inc..........B.......818 247-4716
601 E Glenoaks Blvd # 108 Glendale (91207) ***(P-27126)***
Amcom Food Service, City of Industry *Also called Klm Management Company* ***(P-8523)***
AMD Trading Company Inc..........C.......415 391-0601
1021 Stockton St San Francisco (94108) ***(P-9194)***
Amdal In-Home Care Inc (PA)..........E.......559 686-6611
147 N K St Tulare (93274) ***(P-20987)***
Amdal In-Home Care Inc..........D.......559 227-1701
4848 N 1st St Ste 104 Fresno (93726) ***(P-20988)***
Amdocs Inc..........B.......916 934-7000
1104 Investment Blvd El Dorado Hills (95762) ***(P-14978)***
Amdocs Bcs Inc..........B.......916 934-7000
1104 Investment Blvd El Dorado Hills (95762) ***(P-14979)***
Amdx Laboratory Sciences, San Diego *Also called Progenity Inc* ***(P-22126)***
Amec Fster Wheler E C Svcs Inc..........C.......951 273-7400
250 E Rincon St Ste 204 Corona (92879) ***(P-25529)***
Amen Clinics Inc A Med Corp (PA)..........E.......888 564-2700
3150 Bristol St Ste 400 Costa Mesa (92626) ***(P-22060)***
Amen Clinics Inc A Med Corp..........E.......650 416-7830
350 N Wiget Ln Ste 105 Walnut Creek (94598) ***(P-19284)***
Amer Zoetrope Research LLC..........C.......707 963-9230
1991 Saint Helana Hwy Rutherford (94573) ***(P-26500)***
Ameri-Kleen..........B.......831 722-8888
313 W Beach St Watsonville (95076) ***(P-14188)***
Ameri-Kleen..........C.......805 546-0706
1023 E Grand Ave Arroyo Grande (93420) ***(P-14189)***
Ameri-Kleen Building Services, Watsonville *Also called Ameri-Kleen* ***(P-14188)***
Ameri-Kleen Building Services, Arroyo Grande *Also called Ameri-Kleen* ***(P-14189)***
Ameri-West Medical Associates, La Habra *Also called Jayasinghe Medical Group Inc* ***(P-19518)***
America Chung Nam (group) (PA)..........C.......909 839-8383
1163 Fairway Dr City of Industry (91789) ***(P-7966)***
America Chung Nam LLC (HQ)..........C.......909 839-8383
1163 Fairway Dr Fl 3 City of Industry (91789) ***(P-7967)***
America Consulting Group LLC..........C.......714 390-3105
23 Corporate Plaza Dr # 150 Newport Beach (92660) ***(P-27127)***
America Drean Realty, Santa Cruz *Also called David Lyng & Associates Inc* ***(P-11393)***
America Shredding..........D.......702 262-3607
6565 Smith Ave Newark (94560) ***(P-16998)***
America West Airlines Inc..........C.......619 231-7340
3835 N Harbor Dr Ste 128 San Diego (92101) ***(P-4764)***
America West Airlines Inc..........D.......949 852-5471
18601 Airport Way Ste 238 Santa Ana (92707) ***(P-4765)***
American AC Distrs LLC..........D.......407 850-0147
16900 Chestnut St City of Industry (91748) ***(P-2103)***
American Academy of Opthalmlgy (PA)..........C.......415 561-8500
655 Beach St Fl 1 San Francisco (94109) ***(P-24994)***
American Ace International Co..........D.......626 937-6116
313 Newquist Pl Ste A City of Industry (91745) ***(P-8379)***
American Ace Intl Trdg Co, City of Industry *Also called American Ace International Co* ***(P-8379)***
American Advisors Group (PA)..........E.......866 948-0003
3800 W Chapman Ave Fl 3 Orange (92868) ***(P-10051)***
American Agcredit Flca (PA)..........D.......707 545-1200
400 Aviation Blvd Ste 100 Santa Rosa (95403) ***(P-9751)***
American Air, Visalia *Also called American Incorporated* ***(P-2105)***
American Airlines Inc..........D.......408 291-3800
2077 Airport Blvd Ste 103 San Jose (95110) ***(P-4766)***
American Airlines Inc..........B.......650 877-6000
International Airport San Francisco (94128) ***(P-4767)***
American Airlines Inc..........C.......310 215-7054
5950 Avion Dr Los Angeles (90045) ***(P-4768)***
American Airlines Inc..........C.......949 852-5470
18601 Airport Way Ste 213 Santa Ana (92707) ***(P-4769)***
American Airlines Inc..........C.......213 935-6045
7000 World Way W Los Angeles (90045) ***(P-4770)***
American Airlines Inc..........B.......310 646-0093
100 World Way Ste D Los Angeles (90045) ***(P-4771)***
American Airlines Inc..........E.......619 574-0615
3707 N Harbor Dr Ste 103 San Diego (92101) ***(P-4772)***
American Airlines Inc..........C.......310 646-3013
7183 World Way W Los Angeles (90045) ***(P-4773)***
American Airlines Inc..........D.......805 988-0407
3100 Wright Rd Camarillo (93010) ***(P-4774)***
American Airlines Group Inc..........A.......310 251-9184
3543 Carlisle St Perris (92571) ***(P-4775)***
American All Risk Loss Adm..........C.......559 277-4960
4270 W Richert Ave # 101 Fresno (93722) ***(P-27128)***
American Ambulance, Fresno *Also called K W P H Enterprises* ***(P-3812)***
American Asp Repr Rsrfcing Inc (PA)..........D.......510 723-0280
24200 Clawiter Rd Hayward (94545) ***(P-3213)***
American Asphalt South Inc..........D.......909 427-8276
14436 Santa Ana Ave Fontana (92337) ***(P-1717)***
American Automobile..........D.......925 279-2300
3055 Oak Rd Walnut Creek (94597) ***(P-10517)***
American Automobile Asscth..........C.......510 350-2042
1982 Pleasant Valley Ave A Oakland (94611) ***(P-25379)***
American Automobile Asscth..........B.......510 596-3669
1277 Treat Blvd Ste 1000 Walnut Creek (94597) ***(P-25380)***
American Automobile Asscth..........C.......707 566-4000
1501 Farmers Ln Santa Rosa (95405) ***(P-10334)***
American Automobile Asscth..........E.......209 952-4100
3116 W March Ln Ste 100 Stockton (95219) ***(P-25381)***

Mergent e-mail: customerrelations@mergent.com
1200
2019 Directory of California
Wholesalers and Services Companies
(P-0000) Products & Services Section entry number
(PA)=Parent Co (HQ)=Headquarters (DH)=Div Headquarters

American Automobile Associatio.....B.....510 596-3669
1277 Treat Blvd Ste 1000 Walnut Creek (94597) ***(P-10335)***
American Baptist Homes of West, Redlands *Also called American Baptist Homes of West* ***(P-10976)***
American Baptist Homes of West.....C.....909 335-3077
460 E Fern Ave Redlands (92373) ***(P-10976)***
American Baptist Homes of West.....C.....559 439-4770
5555 N Fresno St Fresno (93710) ***(P-24415)***
American Baptist Homes of West.....C.....510 654-7172
110 41st St Ofc Oakland (94611) ***(P-24416)***
American Baptist Homes of West.....C.....661 834-0620
1401 New Stine Rd Bakersfield (93309) ***(P-20989)***
American Baptist Homes of West.....C.....909 793-1233
900 Salem Dr Redlands (92373) ***(P-20990)***
American Baptist Homes of West (HQ).....D.....925 924-7100
6120 Stoneridge Mall Rd # 300 Pleasanton (94588) ***(P-10977)***
American Baptist Homes of West.....C.....650 948-8291
373 Pine Ln Los Altos (94022) ***(P-20991)***
American Baptist Homes of West.....C.....805 687-1571
900 Calle De Los Amigos Santa Barbara (93105) ***(P-10978)***
American Baptist Homes of West.....C.....408 357-1100
800 Blossom Hill Rd Ofc Los Gatos (95032) ***(P-20992)***
American Beef Packers Inc.....C.....909 628-4888
13677 Yorba Ave Chino (91710) ***(P-623)***
American Bldg Maint Co of Ill.....E.....510 573-1618
44870 Osgood Rd Fremont (94539) ***(P-14190)***
American Bldg Maint Co-West (HQ).....C.....415 733-4000
75 Broadway Ste 111 San Francisco (94111) ***(P-14191)***
American Bolt & Screw Mfg Corp (PA).....D.....909 390-0522
14650 Miller Ave Ste 200 Fontana (92336) ***(P-7573)***
American Brdge/Fluor Entps Inc.....D.....510 808-4623
1390 Willow Pass Rd Concord (94520) ***(P-1873)***
American Building Maint Co NY.....A.....415 733-4000
101 California St San Francisco (94111) ***(P-14192)***
American Building Maintenance, Los Angeles *Also called Century Plaza Garage* ***(P-17681)***
American Building Service Inc.....D.....510 483-5120
4578 Crow Canyon Pl Castro Valley (94552) ***(P-14193)***
American Building Supply Inc (HQ).....C.....916 503-4100
8360 Elder Creek Rd Sacramento (95828) ***(P-6806)***
American Building Supply Inc.....D.....209 941-8852
1488 Tillie Lewis Dr Stockton (95206) ***(P-6807)***
American Cancer Soc Cal Div (PA).....D.....510 893-7900
1001 Marina Village Pkwy Alameda (94501) ***(P-26589)***
American Cancer Soc Cal Div.....E.....408 265-5535
1103 Branham Ln San Jose (95118) ***(P-24735)***
American Capital Group Inc.....D.....949 271-5800
23382 Mill Creek Dr # 115 Laguna Hills (92653) ***(P-9752)***
American Care Givers Westwood.....D.....310 208-8005
947 Tiverton Ave Ste 533 Los Angeles (90024) ***(P-23472)***
American Carequest Inc (PA).....D.....415 885-3324
819 Cowan Rd Ste C Burlingame (94010) ***(P-22219)***
American Century Inv MGT Inc.....C.....650 965-8300
1665 Charleston Rd Mountain View (94043) ***(P-10052)***
American Century Investments, Mountain View *Also called American Century Inv MGT Inc* ***(P-10052)***
American Chemical & Sanitary, Brea *Also called American Sanitary Supply Inc* ***(P-7879)***
American Civil Const.....D.....707 746-8028
2990 Bay Vista Ct Ste D Benicia (94510) ***(P-1718)***
American Civil Constrs LLC.....C.....707 746-8028
3701 Mallard Dr Benicia (94510) ***(P-2006)***
American Commodity Co., Williams *Also called ACC-Gwg LLC* ***(P-27619)***
American Companies, Pico Rivera *Also called Three Sons Inc* ***(P-8631)***
American Concrete.....D.....760 471-9907
1125 Linda Vista Dr Ste 1 San Marcos (92078) ***(P-3214)***
American Concrete Cutting Inc.....D.....714 547-7181
620 N Poinsettia St Santa Ana (92701) ***(P-3445)***
American Conservatory.....D.....415 749-2228
415 Geary St San Francisco (94102) ***(P-18342)***
American Conservatory.....D.....415 749-2228
405 Geary St San Francisco (94102) ***(P-18343)***
American Conservatory Theater.....C.....415 439-2379
1117 Market St San Francisco (94103) ***(P-13714)***
American Contractors Inc.....D.....714 282-5700
404 W Blueridge Ave Orange (92865) ***(P-2104)***
American Contrs Indemnity Co (HQ).....C.....213 330-1309
801 S Figueroa St Ste 700 Los Angeles (90017) ***(P-10421)***
American Corporate SEC Inc (PA).....D.....562 216-7440
1 World Trade Ctr # 1240 Long Beach (90831) ***(P-16560)***
American Corporation.....D.....310 274-1800
315 N Doheny Dr Beverly Hills (90211) ***(P-6701)***
American Corrective Counseling.....B.....949 369-6210
180 Avenida La Pata # 200 San Clemente (92673) ***(P-23473)***
American Crclation Innovations, Long Beach *Also called Advertising Consultants Inc* ***(P-13963)***
American Cstm Private SEC Inc.....D.....209 369-1200
446 E Vine St Ste A Stockton (95202) ***(P-16561)***
American De Rosa Lamparts LLC (PA).....D.....800 777-4440
1945 S Tubeway Ave Commerce (90040) ***(P-7328)***
American Deck Systems, San Diego *Also called Magnesite Specialties Inc* ***(P-3113)***
American Dj Group of Companies, Commerce *Also called D J American Supply Inc* ***(P-8024)***
American Dmlton/Concrete Cutng, Santa Ana *Also called American Concrete Cutting Inc* ***(P-3445)***
American Dntl Partners of Cal.....C.....951 689-5031
7251 Magnolia Ave Riverside (92504) ***(P-20108)***
American Dream.....D.....916 613-4917
300 Portinao Cir Sacramento (95831) ***(P-1114)***
American Eagle Pro.....D.....310 412-0019
425 W Kelso St Inglewood (90301) ***(P-16562)***
American Eagle Protective Svcs, Inglewood *Also called American Eagle Pro* ***(P-16562)***
American Eagle Services Inc.....D.....574 859-2055
1320 Arrow Hwy La Verne (91750) ***(P-14814)***
American Electric Supply Inc (PA).....D.....951 734-7910
361 S Maple St Corona (92880) ***(P-7329)***
American Electrical Svcs Inc.....C.....831 638-1737
501 San Benito St Fl 3 Hollister (95023) ***(P-2506)***
American Electronic Warfare As.....C.....858 524-6119
16766 Bernardo Center Dr San Diego (92128) ***(P-25530)***
American Engrg Contrs Inc.....C.....209 229-1591
25445 S Schulte Rd Tracy (95377) ***(P-2507)***
American Etc Inc.....B.....650 873-5353
1140 San Mateo Ave South San Francisco (94080) ***(P-13482)***
American Express Travel.....D.....949 453-7123
15353 Barranca Pkwy Irvine (92618) ***(P-4930)***
American Farms LLC.....D.....831 424-1815
1107 Harkins Rd Salinas (93901) ***(P-20)***
American Faucet Coatings Corp.....E.....760 598-5895
3280 Corporate Vw Vista (92081) ***(P-6747)***
American Fencing, Fresno *Also called A J Excavation Inc* ***(P-1711)***
American Fidelity Assurance Co.....D.....909 941-1175
3200 Inland Empire Blvd # 260 Ontario (91764) ***(P-10518)***
American Fidelity Assurance Co.....D.....559 230-2107
3649 W Beechwood Ave # 103 Fresno (93711) ***(P-10519)***
American Financial Network Inc.....D.....562 926-2401
14241 Firestone Blvd La Mirada (90638) ***(P-27129)***
American Financial Network Inc.....D.....562 861-1414
8505 Florence Ave Downey (90240) ***(P-10053)***
American Financial Network Inc.....C.....951 582-2655
3400 Inland Empire Blvd # 101 Ontario (91764) ***(P-27130)***
American Financial Network Inc.....D.....909 287-7585
14748 Pipeline Ave Ste A Chino Hills (91709) ***(P-10054)***
American Financial Network Inc (PA).....C.....909 606-3905
10 Pointe Dr Ste 330 Brea (92821) ***(P-9771)***
American Financial Network Inc.....D.....925 705-7710
2125 Oak Grove Rd Walnut Creek (94598) ***(P-10055)***
American First Credit Union (PA).....D.....562 691-1112
700 N Harbor Blvd La Habra (90631) ***(P-9539)***
American Fish and Seafood, Los Angeles *Also called Prospect Enterprises Inc* ***(P-8596)***
American Force Private SEC Inc.....D.....909 384-9820
1585 S D St Ste 208 San Bernardino (92408) ***(P-16563)***
American Freightways LP.....D.....866 326-5902
10845 Rancho Bernardo Rd # 100 San Diego (92127) ***(P-4097)***
American Funding.....D.....408 269-4238
5369 Camden Ave Ste 240 San Jose (95124) ***(P-9870)***
American Funds Distrs Inc (HQ).....C.....213 486-9200
333 S Hope St Ste Levb Los Angeles (90071) ***(P-12023)***
American Funds Service Company.....E.....949 975-5000
6455 Irvine Center Dr Irvine (92618) ***(P-10124)***
American Future Tech Corp.....C.....888 462-3899
529 Baldwin Park Blvd City of Industry (91746) ***(P-7005)***
American Gen Lf Insur Co Del.....B.....415 836-2700
1 Montgomery St Fl 25 San Francisco (94104) ***(P-10127)***
American General Life Insur.....D.....650 994-6679
455 Hickey Blvd Ste 500 Daly City (94015) ***(P-10520)***
American GNC Corporation.....E.....805 582-0582
888 E Easy St Simi Valley (93065) ***(P-25531)***
American Golf Construction, Canoga Park *Also called American Landscape Inc* ***(P-727)***
American Golf Corporation.....C.....858 755-6768
1505 Lomas Santa Fe Dr Solana Beach (92075) ***(P-18826)***
American Golf Corporation.....D.....805 495-5407
4155 Erbes Rd Thousand Oaks (91360) ***(P-18827)***
American Golf Corporation.....C.....949 786-1224
1 Ethel Coplen Way Irvine (92612) ***(P-18828)***
American Golf Corporation (PA).....C.....310 664-4000
909 N Pacific Coast Hwy El Segundo (90245) ***(P-18829)***
American Golf Corporation.....E.....562 421-0550
3101 Carson St Lakewood (90712) ***(P-18681)***
American Golf Corporation.....C.....310 476-2411
12445 Mountain Gate Dr Los Angeles (90049) ***(P-18830)***
American Golf Corporation.....E.....209 477-4653
6301 W Eight Mile Rd Stockton (95219) ***(P-18831)***
American Golf Corporation.....D.....714 779-2461
19400 Mountain View Ave Yorba Linda (92886) ***(P-18832)***
American Golf Corporation.....E.....562 494-4424
5001 Deukmejian Dr Long Beach (90804) ***(P-18682)***
American Golf Corporation.....D.....702 431-2191
68311 Paseo Real Cathedral City (92234) ***(P-18833)***
American Golf Corporation.....D.....805 343-1214
1490 Golf Course Ln Nipomo (93444) ***(P-18834)***
American Golf Corporation.....D.....714 536-8866
6501 Palm Ave Huntington Beach (92648) ***(P-18835)***
American Golf Corporation.....D.....909 861-5757
22751 Golden Springs Dr Diamond Bar (91765) ***(P-18836)***
American Golf Corporation.....D.....925 672-9737
1001 Peacock Creek Dr Clayton (94517) ***(P-18837)***
American Golf Corporation.....E.....408 262-8813
1500 Country Club Dr Milpitas (95035) ***(P-18838)***
American Golf Corporation.....D.....760 757-2100
3202 Vista Way Oceanside (92056) ***(P-18839)***
American Golf Corporation.....D.....310 377-7370
7000 Los Verdes Dr Ste 1 Rancho Palos Verdes (90275) ***(P-18840)***
American Golf Corporation.....D.....714 846-1364
16782 Graham St Huntington Beach (92649) ***(P-18841)***
American Golf Corporation.....D.....831 688-3213
610 Clubhouse Dr Rear Aptos (95003) ***(P-18842)***
American Golf Corporation.....E.....760 568-9311
41500 Monterey Ave Palm Desert (92260) ***(P-18843)***
American Golf Corporation.....D.....562 943-7123
15501 Alicante Rd La Mirada (90638) ***(P-18683)***

Employee Codes: A=Over 500 employees, B=251-500
C=101-250, D=51-100, E=50
2019 Directory of California
Wholesalers and Services Companies
© Mergent Inc. 1-800-342-5647
1201

American Golf Corporation.....E.....805 522-0803
5031 Alamo St Simi Valley (93063) ***(P-18844)***
American Golf Corporation.....D.....805 527-9663
301 Wood Ranch Pkwy Simi Valley (93065) ***(P-18684)***
American Golf Corporation.....D.....714 672-6800
1440 E Bastanchury Rd Fullerton (92835) ***(P-18685)***
American Guard Services Inc (PA).....B.....310 645-6200
1125 W 190th St Gardena (90248) ***(P-16564)***
American Health Care, Rocklin *Also called American Hlthcare ADM Svcs Inc* ***(P-22728)***
American Health Connection.....B.....424 226-0420
8484 Wilshire Blvd # 501 Beverly Hills (90211) ***(P-16999)***
American Health Services LLC.....C.....661 254-6630
26460 Summit Cir Santa Clarita (91350) ***(P-19285)***
American Heart Association Inc.....E.....213 291-7000
816 S Figueroa St Los Angeles (90017) ***(P-24995)***
American Hlthcare ADM Svcs Inc.....B.....916 773-7227
3850 Atherton Rd Rocklin (95765) ***(P-22728)***
American Home Alarms Inc.....C.....888 531-5065
1012 S Baldwin Ave Ste A Arcadia (91007) ***(P-2508)***
American Home Assurance Co.....B.....213 689-3500
777 S Figueroa St Ste 300 Los Angeles (90017) ***(P-10336)***
American Homes Trust.....D.....619 694-7821
450 Camino Hermoso San Marcos (92078) ***(P-12149)***
American Honda, Eastvale *Also called Meiko America Inc* ***(P-4593)***
American Honda Finance Corp (HQ).....C.....310 972-2239
20800 Madrona Ave Torrance (90503) ***(P-9701)***
American Honda Finance Corp.....D.....714 816-8110
10801 Walker St Ste 140 Cypress (90630) ***(P-9702)***
American Honda Motor Co Inc (HQ).....A.....310 783-2000
1919 Torrance Blvd Torrance (90501) ***(P-6577)***
American Hospital Mgt Corp (PA).....B.....707 822-3621
3800 Janes Rd Arcata (95521) ***(P-21283)***
American Hritg Protection Svcs, Winnetka *Also called Memon Aamir* ***(P-16730)***
American Incorporated.....B.....559 651-1776
1345 N American St Visalia (93291) ***(P-2105)***
American Indian Health & Svcs.....E.....805 681-7356
4141 State St Ste B11 Santa Barbara (93110) ***(P-22729)***
American Industrial Supply.....D.....818 841-7788
9817 Variel Ave Chatsworth (91311) ***(P-7827)***
American Infrastructure Mlp Fu.....D.....650 854-6000
950 Tower Ln Ste 800 Foster City (94404) ***(P-27638)***
American Institute of Aeronaut.....D.....619 545-3736
3198 E Fox Run Way San Diego (92111) ***(P-26590)***
American Institute Research.....B.....916 286-8800
2151 River Plaza Dr # 320 Sacramento (95833) ***(P-26591)***
American Insurance Company Inc.....A.....415 899-2000
1465 N Mcdowell Blvd Petaluma (94954) ***(P-10337)***
American Integrated Svcs Inc (PA).....E.....310 522-1168
1502 E Opp St Wilmington (90744) ***(P-27576)***
American Interbanc Mrtg LLC.....E.....714 957-9430
4 Park Plz Ste 650 Irvine (92614) ***(P-9772)***
American International Inds, Commerce *Also called Glamour Industries Co* ***(P-8170)***
American International Inds, Camarillo *Also called Bml Industries Inc* ***(P-7339)***
American Internet Mortgage Inc.....C.....888 411-4246
4121 Camino Del Rio S San Diego (92108) ***(P-9773)***
American Intgrted Rsources Inc.....D.....714 921-4100
2341 N Pacific St Orange (92865) ***(P-26756)***
American Intl Group Inc.....B.....213 689-3500
777 S Figueroa St # 1800 Los Angeles (90017) ***(P-10496)***
American Intl Group Inc.....C.....619 682-4058
9350 Waxie Way Ste 300 San Diego (92123) ***(P-10521)***
American Janitor Services, Thousand Oaks *Also called American Services and Products* ***(P-14194)***
American Kal Enterprises Inc (PA).....D.....626 338-7308
4265 Puente Ave Baldwin Park (91706) ***(P-7574)***
American Landscape Inc.....C.....818 999-2041
7013 Owensmouth Ave Canoga Park (91303) ***(P-727)***
American Landscape Management.....E.....805 647-5077
1607 Los Angeles Ave I Ventura (93004) ***(P-797)***
American Landscape Management (PA).....B.....818 999-2041
7013 Owensmouth Ave Canoga Park (91303) ***(P-728)***
American Leak Detection Inc.....E.....714 836-8477
304 N Townsend St Ste D Santa Ana (92703) ***(P-2106)***
American Legal Copy-Or LLC.....D.....415 777-4449
98 Battery St Ste 220 San Francisco (94111) ***(P-14070)***
American Legion Ambulance Svc.....D.....209 223-2963
11350 American Legion Dr Sutter Creek (95685) ***(P-25091)***
AMERICAN LEGION HALL, Sutter Creek *Also called American Legion Ambulance Svc* ***(P-25091)***
American Liberty Capital Corp.....C.....949 623-0288
19000 Macarthur Blvd # 400 Irvine (92612) ***(P-9871)***
American Liberty Funding, Irvine *Also called American Liberty Capital Corp* ***(P-9871)***
American Marketing Systems Inc.....D.....800 747-7784
2800 Van Ness Ave San Francisco (94109) ***(P-11211)***
American Mdsg Specialists Inc.....B.....925 516-3220
958 Dainty Ave Brentwood (94513) ***(P-13965)***
American Med.....C.....909 793-7676
600 Iowa St Redlands (92373) ***(P-3745)***
American Med.....B.....626 633-4600
5257 Vincent Ave Irwindale (91706) ***(P-3746)***
American Med.....C.....650 235-1333
1510 Rollins Rd Burlingame (94010) ***(P-3747)***
American Med.....C.....510 895-7600
7575 Southfront Rd Livermore (94551) ***(P-3748)***
American Med.....C.....909 948-1714
7925 Center Ave Rancho Cucamonga (91730) ***(P-3749)***
American Med Resp Amblnc Svc.....D.....707 536-0400
930 S A St Santa Rosa (95404) ***(P-3750)***
American Med Rspnse Sthern Cal.....A.....661 945-9310
1055 W Avenue J Lancaster (93534) ***(P-3751)***
American Medical Response, Palm Springs *Also called Springs Ambulance Service Inc* ***(P-3850)***
American Medical Response.....C.....925 454-6000
2400 Bisso Ln Concord (94520) ***(P-3752)***
American Medical Response.....B.....916 563-0600
1041 Fee Dr Sacramento (95815) ***(P-3753)***
American Medical Response.....D.....415 922-9400
1300 Illinois St San Francisco (94107) ***(P-3754)***
American Medical Response.....D.....831 423-7030
116 Hubbard St Santa Cruz (95060) ***(P-3755)***
American Medical Response (HQ).....D.....951 782-5200
879 Marlborough Ave Riverside (92507) ***(P-3756)***
American Medical Response.....D.....650 235-1333
1510 Rollins Rd Burlingame (94010) ***(P-3757)***
American Medical Response Inc.....C.....925 602-1300
2400 Bisso Ln Concord (94520) ***(P-3758)***
American Medical Response Inc.....C.....209 567-4030
1420 Lander Ave Turlock (95380) ***(P-3759)***
American Medical Response Inc.....C.....951 658-2826
208 E Devonshire Ave A Hemet (92543) ***(P-3760)***
American Medical Response Inc.....C.....858 492-3500
3465 Camino Del Rio S # 410 San Diego (92108) ***(P-3761)***
American Medical Response Inc.....A.....858 492-8111
3465 Camino Del Rio S # 410 San Diego (92108) ***(P-3762)***
American Medical Response Inc.....C.....805 688-6550
240 E Highway 246 Ste 300 Buellton (93427) ***(P-3763)***
American Medical Response Inc.....C.....760 883-5000
1111 Montalvo Way Palm Springs (92262) ***(P-3764)***
American Medical Response Inc.....C.....831 718-9555
4548 A St Marina (93933) ***(P-3765)***
American Medical Response Inc.....C.....951 765-3900
208 E Devonshire Ave A Hemet (92543) ***(P-3766)***
American Medical Response Inc.....C.....831 636-9391
1870 Hillcrest Rd Hollister (95023) ***(P-3767)***
American Medical Response Inc.....E.....530 887-9440
13146 Lincoln Way Auburn (95603) ***(P-3768)***
American Medical Response Inc.....C.....415 794-9204
13992 Catalina St San Leandro (94577) ***(P-3769)***
American Medical Response West.....B.....209 948-5136
3755 West Ln Stockton (95204) ***(P-3770)***
American Medical Tech Inc.....D.....949 553-0359
17595 Cartwright Rd Irvine (92614) ***(P-7151)***
American Medical Technologies, Irvine *Also called Gordian Medical Inc* ***(P-7182)***
American Merchant Center Inc.....D.....818 947-1700
6819 Sepulveda Blvd # 311 Van Nuys (91405) ***(P-9731)***
American Messaging Svcs LLC.....D.....510 889-2300
2181 W Winton Ave Hayward (94545) ***(P-5447)***
American Metal & Iron Inc.....D.....408 452-0777
2377 Tulip Rd San Jose (95128) ***(P-7968)***
American Metals Corporation (HQ).....C.....916 371-7700
1499 Parkway Blvd West Sacramento (95691) ***(P-7256)***
American Mobile Healthcare, San Diego *Also called Amn Healthcare Services Inc* ***(P-20162)***
American Multi-Cinema Inc.....D.....818 953-4020
125 E Palm Ave Burbank (91502) ***(P-18257)***
American Multi-Cinema Inc.....E.....619 296-0370
7037 Friars Rd San Diego (92108) ***(P-18258)***
American Multi-Cinema Inc.....D.....626 407-0240
450 N Atlantic Blvd Monterey Park (91754) ***(P-18259)***
American Multi-Cinema Inc.....D.....626 974-8624
1414 N Azusa Ave Covina (91722) ***(P-18260)***
American Multi-Cinema Inc.....E.....415 674-4630
1000 Van Neca Ave Ste A San Francisco (94109) ***(P-18261)***
American Multi-Cinema Inc.....C.....310 326-5011
2591 Airport Dr Torrance (90505) ***(P-18262)***
American Multi-Cinema Inc.....D.....714 769-4288
20 City Blvd W Ste E1 Orange (92868) ***(P-18263)***
American Multi-Cinema Inc.....E.....714 992-6961
1001 S Lemon St Ste A Fullerton (92832) ***(P-18264)***
American Multi-Cinema Inc.....E.....626 585-8900
42 Miller Aly Pasadena (91103) ***(P-18265)***
American Multi-Cinema Inc.....E.....562 864-6206
12300 Civic Center Dr Norwalk (90650) ***(P-18266)***
American Multi-Cinema Inc.....E.....310 228-5500
10250 Snta Mnca Bld Ste 196 Los Angeles (90067) ***(P-18267)***
American Multi-Cinema Inc.....D.....619 296-2737
1640 Cmino Del Rio N 20 San Diego (92108) ***(P-18268)***
American Multi-Cinema Inc.....D.....626 810-7949
1560 S Azusa Ave City of Industry (91748) ***(P-18269)***
American Multi-Cinema Inc.....E.....323 722-4583
1475 N Montebello Blvd Montebello (90640) ***(P-18270)***
American Multimedia TV USA.....D.....626 466-1038
530 S Lake Ave Unit 368 Pasadena (91101) ***(P-5767)***
American Mutual Fund Inc.....C.....213 486-9200
333 S Hope St Fl 51 Los Angeles (90071) ***(P-12024)***
American Mzhou Dngpo Group Inc.....D.....626 820-9239
4520 Maine Ave Baldwin Park (91706) ***(P-26757)***
American National Red Cross.....C.....510 594-5100
6230 Claremont Ave Oakland (94618) ***(P-22730)***
American National Red Cross.....E.....714 481-5300
601 N Golden Circle Dr Santa Ana (92705) ***(P-23474)***
American National Red Cross.....C.....415 427-8134
1663 Market St San Francisco (94103) ***(P-23475)***
American National Red Cross.....E.....925 603-7400
1300 Alberta Way Concord (94521) ***(P-23476)***
American National Red Cross.....A.....909 859-7006
100 Red Cross Cir Pomona (91768) ***(P-22731)***
American National Red Cross.....D.....858 309-1200
3950 Calle Fortunada San Diego (92123) ***(P-23477)***

Mergent e-mail: customerrelations@mergent.com
1202
2019 Directory of California Wholesalers and Services Companies
(P-0000) Products & Services Section entry number
(PA)=Parent Co (HQ)=Headquarters (DH)=Div Headquarters

American Nursing Home MGT Inc ....D....310 672-1012
301 Centinela Ave Inglewood (90302) ***(P-27639)***

American Nwland Communities LP (PA) ....E....858 455-7503
9820 Towne Centre Dr # 100 San Diego (92121) ***(P-11854)***

American Pacific Mortgage Corp ....E....415 891-8706
300 Tamal Plz Ste 250 Corte Madera (94925) ***(P-9872)***

American Pacific Mortgage Corp (PA) ....C....916 960-1325
3000 Lava Ridge Ct # 200 Roseville (95661) ***(P-9774)***

American Paper & Plastics Inc ....C....626 444-0000
550 S 7th Ave City of Industry (91746) ***(P-8093)***

American Paper & Provisions, City of Industry *Also called American Paper & Plastics Inc* ***(P-8093)***

American Patriot Security ....D....916 706-2449
10293 Rockingham Dr # 104 Sacramento (95827) ***(P-16565)***

American Paving Co ....E....559 268-9886
315 N Thorne Ave Fresno (93706) ***(P-1719)***

American Plus Bank (PA) ....E....626 821-9188
630 W Duarte Rd Arcadia (91007) ***(P-9275)***

American Portwell Tech Inc (PA) ....D....510 403-3399
44200 Christy St Fremont (94538) ***(P-7006)***

American President Lines LLC ....D....510 272-3990
1579 Middle Harbor Rd Oakland (94607) ***(P-5006)***

American Pride Gen Engrg Inc ....E....760 736-4056
529 W 4th Ave Ste B Escondido (92025) ***(P-25532)***

American Private Duty Inc ....D....818 386-6358
13111 Ventura Blvd # 100 Studio City (91604) ***(P-22220)***

American Prof Ambulance Corp ....C....818 996-2200
16945 Sherman Way Van Nuys (91406) ***(P-3771)***

American Property Management ....C....925 463-8000
7050 Johnson Dr Pleasanton (94588) ***(P-12316)***

American Protection Group Inc (PA) ....C....818 279-2433
8551 Vesper Ave Panorama City (91402) ***(P-16566)***

American Prprty-Mnagement Corp ....C....619 232-3121
326 Broadway San Diego (92101) ***(P-12317)***

American Realty, San Jose *Also called American Funding* ***(P-9870)***

American Realty Advisors ....D....818 545-1152
515 S Flower St Ste 4900 Los Angeles (90071) ***(P-12150)***

American Realty Centre Inc ....D....323 666-6111
120 S Glendale Ave Glendale (91205) ***(P-11212)***

American Recovery Center, Pomona *Also called Behavioral Health Services Inc* ***(P-23507)***

American Recovery Service, El Dorado Hills *Also called Patrick K Willis Company Inc* ***(P-17393)***

American Red Cross, Concord *Also called American National Red Cross* ***(P-23476)***

American Red Cross ....D....310 445-9900
11355 Ohio Ave Los Angeles (90025) ***(P-23478)***

American Red Cross La Chapter (PA) ....B....310 445-9900
11355 Ohio Ave Los Angeles (90025) ***(P-23479)***

American Red Cross San Diego (PA) ....D....858 309-1200
3950 Calle Fortunada San Diego (92123) ***(P-24736)***

American Reprographics Co LLC ....D....213 745-3145
934 Venice Blvd Los Angeles (90015) ***(P-14071)***

American Reprographics Co LLC ....D....916 443-1322
1322 V St Sacramento (95818) ***(P-14072)***

American Reprographics Co LLC ....D....626 289-5021
616 Monterey Pass Rd Monterey Park (91754) ***(P-14073)***

American Reprographics Co LLC ....D....408 295-5770
821 Martin Ave Santa Clara (95050) ***(P-14074)***

American Reprographics Co LLC ....C....714 751-2680
345 Clinton St Costa Mesa (92626) ***(P-14075)***

American Reprographics Co LLC ....D....951 686-0530
4295 Main St Riverside (92501) ***(P-14076)***

American Residential Svcs LLC ....D....858 457-5547
9895 Olson Dr Ste A San Diego (92121) ***(P-2107)***

American Residential Svcs LLC ....E....310 808-0279
15707 S Main St Gardena (90248) ***(P-2108)***

American Residential Svcs LLC ....D....858 677-5445
6162 Nncy Rdge Dr Ste 100 San Diego (92121) ***(P-2109)***

American Residential Svcs LLC ....D....858 292-4452
P.O. Box 1592 El Cajon (92022) ***(P-2110)***

American Residential Svcs LLC ....D....650 856-1612
1965 Kyle Park Ct San Jose (95125) ***(P-2111)***

American Residential Svcs LLC ....D....951 341-9371
1520 W Linden St Riverside (92507) ***(P-2112)***

American Residential Svcs LLC ....D....510 729-6227
1618 Doolittle Dr San Leandro (94577) ***(P-2113)***

American Residential Svcs LLC ....D....510 657-7601
29196 Simms Ct Hayward (94544) ***(P-2114)***

American Residential Svcs LLC ....D....408 435-3810
2305 Paragon Dr San Jose (95131) ***(P-17932)***

American Residential Svcs LLC ....D....714 634-1826
740 N Hariton St Orange (92868) ***(P-2115)***

American Residential Svcs LLC ....D....818 833-6677
12507 San Fernando Rd Sylmar (91342) ***(P-2116)***

American Restoration Services, Hayward *Also called American Technologies Inc* ***(P-3485)***

American Restoration Services, Simi Valley *Also called American Technologies Inc* ***(P-1117)***

American Retirement Corp ....C....310 399-3227
2107 Ocean Ave Santa Monica (90405) ***(P-20230)***

American River Care, Carmichael *Also called Sunbridge Brittany Rehab Centr* ***(P-20787)***

American Rlction Logistics Inc ....D....562 229-3600
13565 Larwin Cir Santa Fe Springs (90670) ***(P-4328)***

American Sanitary Supply Inc ....E....714 632-3010
592 Explorer St Brea (92821) ***(P-7879)***

American Security Force Inc ....C....323 722-8585
5400 E Olympic Blvd # 225 Commerce (90022) ***(P-16567)***

American Service Industries ....D....323 779-4000
2930 W Imperial Hwy # 332 Inglewood (90303) ***(P-16873)***

American Services and Products ....D....805 375-2858
949 Camino Dos Rios Thousand Oaks (91360) ***(P-14194)***

American Sign, Van Nuys *Also called Dee Sign Co* ***(P-17128)***

American Solar Solution Inc ....D....877 946-8855
6400 Laurel Canyon Blvd # 550 North Hollywood (91606) ***(P-1115)***

American Spclty Hlth Group Inc (HQ) ....B....858 754-2000
10221 Wateridge Cir # 201 San Diego (92121) ***(P-22221)***

American Specialty Health Inc (PA) ....C....858 754-2000
10221 Wateridge Cir # 201 San Diego (92121) ***(P-10522)***

American State Water Company, San Dimas *Also called Golden State Water Company* ***(P-6259)***

American Sunrise Inc ....D....858 610-4766
7404 Santa Fe Canyon Pl San Diego (92129) ***(P-14980)***

American Synergy Asbestos Remo ....D....510 444-2333
28436 Satellite St Hayward (94545) ***(P-3484)***

American Tech Service ....D....951 372-9664
1761 3rd St Ste 105 Norco (92860) ***(P-25533)***

American Technical Svcs Inc ....D....818 590-7784
9520 Topanga Canyon Blvd Chatsworth (91311) ***(P-25534)***

American Technologies Inc ....D....510 429-5000
25000 Industrial Blvd Hayward (94545) ***(P-3485)***

American Technologies Inc (PA) ....C....714 283-9990
210 W Baywood Ave Orange (92865) ***(P-1116)***

American Technologies Inc ....E....818 700-5060
2688 Westhills Ct Simi Valley (93065) ***(P-1117)***

American Technologies Inc ....D....858 530-2400
8444 Miralani Dr Ste 200 San Diego (92126) ***(P-27640)***

American Textile Maint Co ....E....213 749-4433
1705 Hooper Ave Los Angeles (90021) ***(P-13503)***

American Textile Maint Co ....D....562 438-7656
3001 E Anaheim St Long Beach (90804) ***(P-13504)***

American Textile Maint Co ....D....562 438-1126
3001 E Anaheim St Long Beach (90804) ***(P-13505)***

American Textile Maint Co ....C....323 735-1661
1664 W Washington Blvd Los Angeles (90007) ***(P-13506)***

American Textile Maint Co ....C....562 424-1607
2201 E Carson St Long Beach (90807) ***(P-13581)***

American Tile Brick Veneer Inc ....E....562 595-9293
1389 E 28th St Signal Hill (90755) ***(P-2986)***

American Tire Distributors ....E....408 435-3340
645 Dado St San Jose (95131) ***(P-6689)***

American Transport Inc ....D....714 567-8000
3910 Prospect Ave Ste A Yorba Linda (92886) ***(P-9775)***

American Travel Solutions LLC ....D....818 359-6514
26707 Agoura Rd Ste 204 Calabasas (91302) ***(P-4931)***

American Two-Way, North Hollywood *Also called Emergency Technologies Inc* ***(P-7359)***

American Union Fincl Svcs Inc ....C....714 619-2520
210 S Orange Grove Blvd # 1 Pasadena (91105) ***(P-9703)***

American Untd HM Care Crp-Priv, Studio City *Also called American Private Duty Inc* ***(P-22220)***

American Vision Windows Inc ....C....805 582-1833
2125 N Madera Rd Ste A Simi Valley (93065) ***(P-17933)***

American Voice Mail Inc (PA) ....E....310 478-4949
11150 W Olympic Blvd # 975 Los Angeles (90064) ***(P-5259)***

American Water Works Co Inc ....D....916 568-4236
4701 Beloit Dr Sacramento (95838) ***(P-6208)***

American Way Cultural Center, Orange *Also called Adair Enterprises* ***(P-18338)***

American West ....E....805 926-2800
511 Zaca Ln Ste 120 San Luis Obispo (93401) ***(P-4098)***

American West Worldwide Ex Inc (PA) ....D....800 788-4534
51 Zaca Ln Ste 120 San Luis Obispo (93401) ***(P-4329)***

American Wht Mssn In Sthrn ....D....714 522-4599
7212 Orangethorpe Ave 7a Buena Park (90621) ***(P-23480)***

American Wrecking Inc ....D....626 350-8303
2459 Lee Ave South El Monte (91733) ***(P-3446)***

American Zettler Inc (HQ) ....D....949 360-5830
75 Columbia Aliso Viejo (92656) ***(P-7437)***

American-1 Airtight SEC Co ....E....714 997-0605
2510 N Grand Ave Ste 207 Santa Ana (92705) ***(P-16568)***

Americantours Intl LLC (HQ) ....C....310 641-9953
6053 W Century Blvd Los Angeles (90045) ***(P-4961)***

Americare Ambulance Service, Huntington Beach *Also called Americare Medservices Inc* ***(P-3772)***

Americare Hlth Retirement Inc ....D....760 744-4484
1550 Security Pl Ofc San Marcos (92078) ***(P-10852)***

Americare Medservices Inc (PA) ....C....310 632-1141
6524 Fremont Cir Huntington Beach (92648) ***(P-3772)***

Americas Christian Credit Un (PA) ....D....626 208-5400
2100 E Route 66 Ste 100 Glendora (91740) ***(P-9621)***

Americas Finest Carpet Co, Chula Vista *Also called Home Carpet Investment Inc* ***(P-3106)***

Americas Flood Services Inc ....D....916 636-9460
3350 Country Club Dr # 201 Cameron Park (95682) ***(P-10523)***

Americas Lemonade Stand Inc ....C....707 745-1274
5100 Park Rd Benicia (94510) ***(P-17000)***

Americas Printer.com, Buena Park *Also called A J Parent Company Inc* ***(P-16970)***

Americas Regional Division, San Diego *Also called Synergy Health Ast LLC* ***(P-27480)***

Americash ....E....714 994-7554
3080 Bristol St Ste 300 Costa Mesa (92626) ***(P-9776)***

Americold Logistics LLC ....A....714 993-3533
2750 Orbiter St Brea (92821) ***(P-4492)***

Americold Logistics LLC ....D....678 441-1468
1415 N Raymond Ave Anaheim (92801) ***(P-4493)***

Americold Logistics LLC ....E....831 424-1537
950 S Sanborn Rd Salinas (93901) ***(P-4494)***

Americold Logistics LLC ....E....909 390-4950
700 Malaga St Ontario (91761) ***(P-4495)***

Americold Logistics LLC ....D....323 581-0025
3420 E Vernon Ave Vernon (90058) ***(P-4496)***

Americold Realty, Ontario *Also called Americold Logistics LLC* ***(P-4495)***

Americor Funding Inc ....C....866 333-8686
18200 Von Karman Ave # 600 Irvine (92612) ***(P-13715)***

ALPHABETIC

Employee Codes: A=Over 500 employees, B=251-500
C=101-250, D=51-100, E=50
2019 Directory of California
Wholesalers and Services Companies
© Mergent Inc. 1-800-342-5647
1203

Ameriflight LLC.....D.....510 569-6000
21889 Skywest Dr Hayward (94541) ***(P-4776)***
Amerifreight Inc.....A.....909 839-2600
218 Machlin Ct Walnut (91789) ***(P-4529)***
AmeriGas Propane LP.....D.....916 852-7400
11030 White Rock Rd # 100 Rancho Cordova (95670) ***(P-8949)***
Amerine Systems Incorporated.....E.....209 847-5968
10866 Cleveland Ave Oakdale (95361) ***(P-729)***
Ameripath Mortgage Corporation.....C.....949 753-9211
6410 Oak Cyn Ste 200 Irvine (92618) ***(P-9777)***
Ameripride Services Inc.....D.....805 239-9449
109 Calle Propano Ste C Paso Robles (93446) ***(P-13507)***
Ameripride Services Inc.....E.....530 242-0564
3750 Eastside Rd Redding (96001) ***(P-13508)***
Ameripride Services Inc.....C.....661 324-7941
335 Washington St Bakersfield (93307) ***(P-13509)***
Ameripride Services Inc.....D.....559 266-0627
1050 W Whites Bridge Ave Fresno (93706) ***(P-13582)***
Ameripride Services Inc.....E.....209 982-0020
4206 S B St Stockton (95206) ***(P-13510)***
Ameripride Services Inc.....E.....714 385-8991
2230 W Chapman Ave Orange (92868) ***(P-13511)***
Ameripride Services Inc.....E.....800 748-6178
3701 Collins Ave Ste 5b Richmond (94806) ***(P-13512)***
Ameripride Services Inc.....E.....800 882-5326
1356 Dayton St Ste R Salinas (93901) ***(P-13513)***
Ameripride Unifom Svcs, Bakersfield *Also called Ameripride Services Inc* ***(P-13509)***
Ameripride Uniform Services, Fresno *Also called Ameripride Services Inc* ***(P-13582)***
Ameriquest Capital Corporation (PA).....B.....714 564-0600
1100 W Twn Cntry Rd R Orange (92868) ***(P-9873)***
Amerisourcebergen Corporation.....C.....610 727-7000
1368 Metropolitan Dr Orange (92868) ***(P-26758)***
Amerisourcebergen Corporation.....C.....951 493-2339
215 Deininger Cir Corona (92880) ***(P-8140)***
Amerisourcebergen Corporation.....C.....714 704-4407
505 City Pkwy W Orange (92868) ***(P-26759)***
Amerisourcebergen Drug Corp.....C.....661 257-6400
24903 Avenue Kearny Valencia (91355) ***(P-8141)***
Amerisourcebergen Drug Corp.....C.....916 830-4500
1325 Striker Ave Sacramento (95834) ***(P-8142)***
Amerisourcebergen Drug Corp.....C.....951 371-2000
1851 California Ave Corona (92881) ***(P-8143)***
Amerisuites, Ontario *Also called Todays Vi LLC* ***(P-13331)***
Amerit Fleet Solutions Inc (HQ).....D.....877 512-6374
1331 N Calif Blvd Ste 150 Walnut Creek (94596) ***(P-17849)***
Ameritac Inc (PA).....D.....925 743-8398
640 Logan Ln Danville (94526) ***(P-27577)***
Ameritech Mortgage, Walnut Creek *Also called Izt Mortgage Inc* ***(P-9888)***
Ameriwest Industries Inc.....E.....909 930-1898
2910 S Archibald Ave A Ontario (91761) ***(P-7575)***
AMF Bowling Centers Inc.....E.....323 728-9161
1201 W Beverly Blvd Montebello (90640) ***(P-18477)***
AMF Bowling Centers Inc.....E.....661 324-4966
1819 30th St Bakersfield (93301) ***(P-18478)***
AMF Bowling Centers Inc.....E.....949 770-0055
22771 Centre Dr Lake Forest (92630) ***(P-18479)***
AMG Construction Group.....D.....800 310-2609
1103 W Gardena Blvd # 201 Gardena (90248) ***(P-1720)***
AMG Huntington Beach LLC.....E.....714 894-9802
5416 Argosy Ave Huntington Beach (92649) ***(P-25535)***
Amgen Distribution Inc.....D.....760 989-4424
1244 Valley View Rd # 119 Glendale (91202) ***(P-4099)***
Amgen Pharmaceuticals Inc.....A.....805 447-1000
1 Amgen Center Dr Thousand Oaks (91320) ***(P-26592)***
Amgreen Solar and Electrics.....E.....213 388-5647
1367 Venice Blvd Los Angeles (90006) ***(P-2117)***
Amgreen Solutions Inc.....E.....213 388-5647
1367 Venice Blvd Fl 2 Los Angeles (90006) ***(P-27131)***
Amgreen-Karena Ht Partnr Ltd (PA).....D.....818 707-9494
5743 Corsa Ave Ste 200 Westlake Village (91362) ***(P-12318)***
Amh Portfolio One LLC.....C.....480 921-4600
30601 Agoura Rd Ste 200 Agoura Hills (91301) ***(P-12151)***
AMI Manufacturing, Sacramento *Also called Airco Mechanical Inc* ***(P-2092)***
AMI-Hti Tarzana Encino Joint V.....A.....818 881-0800
18321 Clark St Tarzana (91356) ***(P-21284)***
Amica Mutual Insurance Company.....D.....877 972-6422
3200 Park Center Dr # 650 Costa Mesa (92626) ***(P-10338)***
Amini Innovation Corp.....C.....562 222-2500
8725 Rex Rd Pico Rivera (90660) ***(P-6709)***
Amir Ahmad MD.....D.....805 545-8100
628 California Blvd Ste D San Luis Obispo (93401) ***(P-19286)***
Amisub (irvine Regional Hospi).....A.....949 916-7556
1400 S Douglass Rd # 250 Anaheim (92806) ***(P-21285)***
Amisub of California Inc (HQ).....A.....818 881-0800
18321 Clark St Tarzana (91356) ***(P-21286)***
Amk Foodservices Inc.....C.....805 544-7600
830 Capitolio Way San Luis Obispo (93401) ***(P-8380)***
Amkotron Inc.....D.....562 921-3330
12620 Hiddencreek Way Cerritos (90703) ***(P-16276)***
Ammunition LLC.....D.....415 632-1170
1500 Sansome St Ste 110 San Francisco (94111) ***(P-27132)***
Amn Healthcare Inc (HQ).....C.....858 792-0711
12400 High Bluff Dr San Diego (92130) ***(P-19287)***
Amn Healthcare Services Inc.....A.....858 792-0711
12400 High Bluff Dr # 100 San Diego (92130) ***(P-20162)***
Amn Healthcare Services Inc (PA).....C.....866 871-8519
12400 High Bluff Dr San Diego (92130) ***(P-14815)***
Amobee Inc (HQ).....C.....650 353-4399
901 Marshall St 200 Redwood City (94063) ***(P-13792)***
Amoeba Music Inc.....D.....415 831-1200
1855 Haight St San Francisco (94117) ***(P-17001)***
AMP Technologies LLC (PA).....C.....877 442-2824
445 Melrose Ct San Ramon (94582) ***(P-14981)***
Ampam Parks Mechanical Inc.....A.....310 835-1532
17036 Avalon Blvd Carson (90746) ***(P-2118)***
Ampco Contracting Inc.....C.....949 955-2255
1420 S Allec St Anaheim (92805) ***(P-6529)***
Ampla Health (PA).....C.....530 674-4261
935 Market St Yuba City (95991) ***(P-20109)***
Ampla Health.....D.....530 342-4395
680 Cohasset Rd Chico (95926) ***(P-19288)***
Ampla Health.....D.....530 743-4614
4941 Olivehurst Ave Olivehurst (95961) ***(P-19289)***
Amplify Education Inc.....D.....562 209-7875
1032 Irving St Ste 445 San Francisco (94122) ***(P-14982)***
Ampronix Inc.....D.....949 273-8000
15 Whatney Irvine (92618) ***(P-7152)***
AMR, Los Angeles *Also called American Airlines Inc* ***(P-4768)***
AMR Appraisals Inc.....D.....925 400-6066
5000 Executive Pkwy # 270 San Ramon (94583) ***(P-11213)***
AMR Eagle, San Diego *Also called Envoy Air Inc* ***(P-4888)***
AMS, San Diego *Also called Asset Marketing Systems Insu* ***(P-27144)***
AMS, San Bernardino *Also called Allied Building Products Corp* ***(P-6805)***
AMS, Montebello *Also called Allied Building Products Corp* ***(P-6918)***
AMS - Exotic LLC.....D.....213 612-5888
720 S Alameda St Los Angeles (90021) ***(P-8639)***
AMS American Mech Svcs MD Inc.....D.....714 888-6820
2116 E Walnut Ave Fullerton (92831) ***(P-2119)***
AMS Bekins Van Lines, Burlingame *Also called AMS Relocation Incorporated* ***(P-4330)***
AMS Electric Inc.....D.....925 961-1600
6905 Sierra Ct Ste A Dublin (94568) ***(P-2509)***
AMS Fulfillment, Valencia *Also called Advantage Media Services Inc* ***(P-4525)***
AMS Paving Inc (PA).....E.....909 357-0711
11060 Rose Ave Fontana (92337) ***(P-1721)***
AMS Relocation Incorporated.....D.....650 697-3530
1873 Rollins Rd Burlingame (94010) ***(P-4330)***
AMS Ventures Inc.....D.....301 980-5087
39141 Civic Center Dr Fremont (94538) ***(P-27133)***
Amsec LLC.....B.....858 522-6319
9444 Balboa Ave Ste 400 San Diego (92123) ***(P-26319)***
Amsi Real Estate Services, San Francisco *Also called American Marketing Systems Inc* ***(P-11211)***
Amsnet Inc (PA).....E.....925 245-6100
502 Commerce Way Livermore (94551) ***(P-15912)***
Amstar/Davidson Robles LLC.....D.....626 577-1000
168 S Los Robles Ave Pasadena (91101) ***(P-12319)***
Amsurg, Torrance *Also called Torrance Surgery Center LP* ***(P-20008)***
Amsurg, San Diego *Also called Mission Valley Hts Surgery Ctr* ***(P-19695)***
Amsurg, Glendale *Also called Glendale Eye Medical Group* ***(P-19484)***
Amtel Inc.....E.....408 615-0522
950 S Bascom Ave Ste 2002 San Jose (95128) ***(P-27641)***
Amtrak, San Diego *Also called National Railroad Pass Corp* ***(P-3621)***
Amtrav, Calabasas *Also called American Travel Solutions LLC* ***(P-4931)***
Amtrow Group Inc.....D.....310 557-0857
8306 Wilshire Blvd 1042 Beverly Hills (90211) ***(P-27134)***
Amtv USA, Pasadena *Also called American Multimedia TV USA* ***(P-5767)***
Amwins Insurance Brkg Cal LLC (HQ).....D.....818 772-1774
21550 Oxnard St Ste 1100 Woodland Hills (91367) ***(P-10524)***
Amzn Mobile LLC.....B.....925 348-4580
525 Market St Fl 19 San Francisco (94105) ***(P-14983)***
An Open Check, Costa Mesa *Also called North American Acceptance Corp* ***(P-9725)***
Ana Nacapa Surgical Associates, Ventura *Also called Ventura County Medical Center* ***(P-20054)***
Ana Trading Corp USA (HQ).....D.....310 542-2500
3625 Del Amo Blvd Ste 300 Torrance (90503) ***(P-7726)***
Anabella Hotel The, Anaheim *Also called Fjs Inc* ***(P-12577)***
Anaheim Arena, Anaheim *Also called City of Anaheim* ***(P-10864)***
Anaheim Arena Management LLC.....A.....714 704-2400
2695 E Katella Ave Anaheim (92806) ***(P-18503)***
Anaheim Arts Council.....C.....714 868-6094
P.O. Box 1364 Anaheim (92815) ***(P-24863)***
Anaheim Ca LLC.....D.....714 634-4500
100 The City Dr S Orange (92868) ***(P-12320)***
Anaheim Crest Nursing Center, Anaheim *Also called 3067 Orange Avenue LLC* ***(P-20216)***
Anaheim Ducks Hockey Club LLC (PA).....D.....714 940-2900
2695 E Katella Ave Anaheim (92806) ***(P-18504)***
Anaheim First Fmly Dntl Group.....D.....714 999-5050
1161 N Euclid St Anaheim (92801) ***(P-26760)***
Anaheim Gateway Sport Club, Anaheim *Also called 24 Hour Fitness Usa Inc* ***(P-18557)***
Anaheim General Hospital, Los Angeles *Also called Pacific Health Corporation* ***(P-21621)***
Anaheim Global Medical Center.....B.....714 533-6220
1025 S Anaheim Blvd Anaheim (92805) ***(P-21287)***
Anaheim Harbor Medical Group (PA).....C.....714 533-4511
710 N Euclid St Anaheim (92801) ***(P-19290)***
Anaheim Hills Auto Body Inc.....D.....714 632-8266
3500 E La Palma Ave Anaheim (92806) ***(P-17711)***
Anaheim Hills Medical Offices, Anaheim *Also called Kaiser Foundation Hospitals* ***(P-19541)***
Anaheim Hotel LLC.....C.....714 750-1811
1855 S Harbor Blvd Anaheim (92802) ***(P-12321)***
Anaheim Ice.....D.....714 535-7465
300 W Lincoln Ave Anaheim (92805) ***(P-19096)***
Anaheim Kraemer Medical Offs, Anaheim *Also called Kaiser Foundation Hospitals* ***(P-19543)***
Anaheim Majestic Garden Hotel, Anaheim *Also called Ken Real Estate Lease Ltd* ***(P-12802)***
Anaheim Medical Center.....D.....714 774-1450
1111 W La Palma Ave Anaheim (92801) ***(P-19291)***

Mergent e-mail: customerrelations@mergent.com
1204
2019 Directory of California
Wholesalers and Services Companies
(P-0000) Products & Services Section entry number
(PA)=Parent Co (HQ)=Headquarters (DH)=Div Headquarters

Anaheim Park Hotel C 714 992-1700
222 W Houston Ave Fullerton (92832) ***(P-12322)***
Anaheim Park Inn and Camelot D 714 635-7275
1520 S Harbor Blvd Anaheim (92802) ***(P-12323)***
Anaheim Plaza Hotel & Suites, Anaheim *Also called Anaheim Plaza Hotel Inc* ***(P-12324)***
Anaheim Plaza Hotel Inc C 714 772-5900
1700 S Harbor Blvd Anaheim (92802) ***(P-12324)***
Anaheim Regional Medical Ctr A 714 774-1450
1111 W La Palma Ave Anaheim (92801) ***(P-21288)***
Anaheim Regional Medical Ctr B 714 999-3847
1111 W La Palma Ave Anaheim (92801) ***(P-19292)***
Anaheim Regional Medical Ctr (PA) E 714 774-1450
1111 W La Palma Ave Anaheim (92801) ***(P-21995)***
Anaheim V A Clinic, Anaheim *Also called Veterans Health Administration* ***(P-20081)***
Anaheim/Orange Cnty Visitor Bu (PA) D 714 765-8888
2099 S State College Blvd Anaheim (92806) ***(P-17002)***
Anaheim/Orange Hilton Suites, Orange *Also called Hit Portfolio II Trs LLC* ***(P-12687)***
Analytic US Market Neutral Off D 213 688-3015
555 W 5th St Fl 50 Los Angeles (90013) ***(P-9913)***
Anand Software Inc D 209 287-1708
4719 Quail Lakes Dr Stockton (95207) ***(P-14984)***
Anaplan Inc (PA) C 415 742-8199
50 Hawthorne St San Francisco (94105) ***(P-16311)***
Anaspec Inc (HQ) E 800 452-5530
34801 Campus Dr Fremont (94555) ***(P-26320)***
Anaspec Egt Group, Fremont *Also called Anaspec Inc* ***(P-26320)***
Anatec International Inc (HQ) D 949 498-3350
2950 E Birch St Brea (92821) ***(P-25536)***
Anberry Rehabilitation Hosp, Atwater *Also called Tjd LLC* ***(P-21229)***
Ancca Corporation D 949 553-0084
7 Goddard Irvine (92618) ***(P-2843)***
Anchor General Insurance Agcy C 858 527-3600
10256 Meanley Dr San Diego (92131) ***(P-10525)***
Anchor J Dairy, Stevinson *Also called James J Stevinson A Corp* ***(P-418)***
Anchor Loans LP C 310 395-0010
5230 Las Virgenes Rd # 105 Calabasas (91302) ***(P-12152)***
Anchor Nationwide Loans, Calabasas *Also called Anchor Loans LP* ***(P-12152)***
Ancon Marine D 310 952-8160
2209 Zeus Ct Bakersfield (93308) ***(P-17934)***
and 1, Aliso Viejo *Also called Basketball Marketing Co Inc* ***(P-27154)***
and Syndicated Productions Inc D 818 308-5200
3500 W Olive Ave Ste 1000 Burbank (91505) ***(P-18015)***
Andatha International Inc (PA) D 415 398-8600
611 Mission St Fl 4 San Francisco (94105) ***(P-22915)***
Andaz Sandiego, San Diego *Also called Hit Portfolio I Misc Trs LLC* ***(P-12684)***
Andersen & Sons Shelling Inc D 530 839-2236
4530 Rowles Rd Vina (96092) ***(P-492)***
Andersen Hotels Inc D 949 494-1151
92 Argonaut Ste 150 Aliso Viejo (92656) ***(P-12325)***
Andersen Nut Company E 209 854-6820
3050 S Hunt Rd Gustine (95322) ***(P-493)***
Andersen Tax LLC C 213 593-2300
400 Suth Hope St Ste 2000 Los Angeles (90071) ***(P-13701)***
Andersncttonwood Disposal Svcs D 530 824-4700
3281 State Highway 99w S Corning (96021) ***(P-3971)***
Anderson Rowe & Buckley Inc C 415 282-1625
2833 3rd St San Francisco (94107) ***(P-2120)***
Anderson & Howard Electric Inc C 949 250-4555
1791 Reynolds Ave Irvine (92614) ***(P-2510)***
Anderson & Martella Inc E 925 934-3831
1200 Mt Diablo Blvd # 400 Walnut Creek (94596) ***(P-3468)***
Anderson Air Conditioning LP D 714 998-6850
2100 E Walnut Ave Fullerton (92831) ***(P-2121)***
Anderson Associates Staffing (PA) C 323 930-3170
8200 Wilshire Blvd # 200 Beverly Hills (90211) ***(P-14816)***
Anderson Burton Construction D 626 441-2464
1510 Oxley St Ste G South Pasadena (91030) ***(P-1465)***
Anderson Chrnesky Strl Stl Inc D 951 769-5700
353 Risco Cir Beaumont (92223) ***(P-3359)***
Anderson Direct Marketing, Poway *Also called T G T Enterprises Inc* ***(P-14064)***
Anderson Hay & Grain Co Inc C 310 518-2935
915 E Colon St Wilmington (90744) ***(P-8904)***
Anderson Homes, Lodi *Also called Lodi Development Inc* ***(P-11885)***
Anderson House, Concord *Also called Youth Homes Incorporated* ***(P-24726)***
Anderson Howard, Irvine *Also called Anderson & Howard Electric Inc* ***(P-2510)***
Anderson Kayne Capital B 800 231-7414
1800 Avenue Of The Los Angeles (90067) ***(P-10056)***
Anderson Kayne Inv MGT Inc (PA) D 310 556-2721
1800 Avenue Of The Stars # 200 Los Angeles (90067) ***(P-27135)***
Anderson Lumber, North Highlands *Also called Pacific Coast Supply LLC* ***(P-6847)***
Anderson McPharlin Conners LLP (PA) D 213 688-0080
707 Wilshire Blvd # 4000 Los Angeles (90017) ***(P-22916)***
Anderson News LLC D 714 892-7766
15172 Goldenwest Cir Westminster (92683) ***(P-9108)***
Anderson PCF Engrg Cnstr Inc D 408 970-9900
1390 Norman Ave Santa Clara (95054) ***(P-2007)***
Anderson Plbg Htg A Condition, El Cajon *Also called Walter Anderson Plumbing Inc* ***(P-2403)***
Anderson Pump Company D 559 665-4477
24719 Robertson Blvd Chowchilla (93610) ***(P-6209)***
Andersonpenna Partners Inc D 949 428-1500
3737 Birch St Ste 250 Newport Beach (92660) ***(P-27136)***
Andover Maintenance Inc D 626 254-1651
45 La Porte St Arcadia (91006) ***(P-14195)***
Andregg Geomatics D 530 885-7072
11661 Blocker Dr Ste 200 Auburn (95603) ***(P-26127)***
Andreini & Company (PA) D 650 573-1111
220 W 20th Ave San Mateo (94403) ***(P-10526)***
Andrew and Williamson Sales Co (PA) D 619 661-6000
9940 Marconi Dr San Diego (92154) ***(P-8640)***
Andrew Chekene Enterprises Inc C 650 588-1001
21965 Meekland Ave Hayward (94541) ***(P-1118)***
Andrew L Youngquist Cnstr Inc D 949 862-5611
3187 Red Hill Ave Ste 200 Costa Mesa (92626) ***(P-1466)***
Andrew Lauren Company Inc C 949 861-4222
15225 Alton Pkwy Unit 300 Irvine (92618) ***(P-17003)***
Andrew M Golden MD D 619 528-5342
4647 Zion Ave San Diego (92120) ***(P-19293)***
Andrew M Jordan Inc D 510 999-6000
1350 4th St Berkeley (94710) ***(P-3414)***
Andrew Williamson Fresh Prod, San Diego *Also called Andrew and Williamson Sales Co* ***(P-8640)***
Andrews Air Corporation C 650 871-4747
50 Tanforan Ave South San Francisco (94080) ***(P-5007)***
Andrews Electronics, Santa Clarita *Also called Partsearch Technologies Inc* ***(P-7523)***
Andrews Group Inc (PA) D 707 422-4844
1801 Walters Ct Fairfield (94533) ***(P-2122)***
Andrews International Inc C 818 260-9586
455 N Moss St Burbank (91502) ***(P-16569)***
Andrews International Inc C 805 409-4160
455 N Moss St Burbank (91502) ***(P-16570)***
Andrews International Inc (PA) A 818 487-4060
455 N Moss St Burbank (91502) ***(P-16571)***
Andrews International Inc C 626 407-2290
455 N Moss St Burbank (91502) ***(P-16572)***
Andrian Inc E 408 434-0730
1935 Lundy Ave San Jose (95131) ***(P-3486)***
Andrighetto Produce Inc D 650 588-0930
155 Terminal Ct Stalls 15 Stalls South San Francisco (94083) ***(P-3487)***
Andwin Corporation (PA) C 818 999-2828
6636 Variel Ave Woodland Hills (91303) ***(P-8094)***
Andwin Scientific, Woodland Hills *Also called Andwin Corporation* ***(P-8094)***
Andy Boy, Salinas *Also called DArrigo Broscoof California* ***(P-47)***
Andy Gump Inc D 818 255-0650
11551 Hart St North Hollywood (91605) ***(P-14472)***
Ane Productions Inc D 818 972-0777
3500 W Olive Ave Ste 1000 Burbank (91505) ***(P-18016)***
Anello SEC & Consulting LLC D 818 632-3277
17348 Tiara St Encino (91316) ***(P-27642)***
Anesthesia Business Cons Inc D 925 951-1366
1600 Riviera Ave Ste 420 Walnut Creek (94596) ***(P-19294)***
Anesthesia Consultants of Cont, Walnut Creek *Also called Anesthesia Business Cons Inc* ***(P-19294)***
Anesthesia Service Med Group E 858 277-4767
3626 Ruffin Rd San Diego (92123) ***(P-19295)***
Anfinson Lumber Sales Inc (PA) D 951 681-4707
13041 Union Ave Fontana (92337) ***(P-6808)***
Angel Care Home Health Inc E 818 248-8811
850 Colorado Blvd Ste 103 Los Angeles (90041) ***(P-22222)***
Angel Island Co, Red Bluff *Also called Concessionaires Urban Park* ***(P-19147)***
Angel View Inc E 760 322-2440
454 N Indian Canyon Dr Palm Springs (92262) ***(P-24417)***
Angel View Resale Store, Palm Springs *Also called Angel View Inc* ***(P-24417)***
Angeles Contractor Inc (PA) D 714 523-1021
783 Phillips Rowland Heights (91748) ***(P-1373)***
Angeles Home Health Care Inc C 213 487-5131
3701 Wilshire Blvd # 900 Los Angeles (90010) ***(P-22223)***
Angeles Los Equestrian Center C 818 840-9063
480 W Riverside Dr Burbank (91506) ***(P-19097)***
Angelika Film Center and Cafe, San Diego *Also called Reading International Inc* ***(P-18314)***
Angels Baseball LP (PA) A 714 940-2000
2000 E Gene Autry Way Anaheim (92806) ***(P-18505)***
Angels In Motion LLC D 909 590-9102
4091 Riverside Dr Ste 111 Chino (91710) ***(P-22224)***
Angels Nursing Center, Los Angeles *Also called Gva Enterprises Inc* ***(P-21103)***
Angels Nursing Center, Los Angeles *Also called Gva Enterprises Inc* ***(P-20500)***
Angelus Western Ppr Fibers Inc D 213 623-9221
2474 Porter St Los Angeles (90021) ***(P-7969)***
Angioscore Inc C 510 933-7900
5055 Brandin Ct Fremont (94538) ***(P-7153)***
Anheuser-Busch LLC B 707 429-7595
3101 Busch Dr Fairfield (94534) ***(P-7727)***
Anheuser-Busch LLC C 951 782-3935
1400 Marlborough Ave Riverside (92507) ***(P-8978)***
Anheuser-Busch LLC C 310 761-4600
20499 S Reeves Ave Carson (90810) ***(P-8979)***
Anheuser-Busch LLC C 949 263-9270
18952 Macarthur Blvd Irvine (92612) ***(P-8980)***
Animal Care Center D 707 584-4343
6470 Redwood Dr Rohnert Park (94928) ***(P-596)***
Animoto LLC D 415 987-3139
333 Kearny St Fl 6 San Francisco (94108) ***(P-14985)***
Anitsa Inc C 213 237-0533
6032 Shull St Bell Gardens (90201) ***(P-13483)***
Anixter Inc D 916 563-7560
855 National Dr Ste 103 Sacramento (95834) ***(P-7330)***
Anixter Inc E 858 571-6571
7140 Opportunity Rd San Diego (92111) ***(P-7331)***
Anixter Inc D 800 854-2088
7140 Opportunity Rd San Diego (92111) ***(P-7880)***
Anixter Inc D 510 477-2400
30061 Ahern Ave Union City (94587) ***(P-7332)***
Anixter Inc E 925 469-8500
5000 Franklin Dr 200 Pleasanton (94588) ***(P-7333)***
Anjana Software Solutions Inc D 805 583-0121
1445 E Los Angeles Ave # 305 Simi Valley (93065) ***(P-14986)***

ALPHABETIC

Employee Codes: A=Over 500 employees, B=251-500
C=101-250, D=51-100, E=50
2019 Directory of California
Wholesalers and Services Companies
© Mergent Inc. 1-800-342-5647
1205

Anjaneyap Inc ....D 408 922-9690
830 Hillview Ct Ste 140 Milpitas (95035) ***(P-27137)***
Anka Behavioral Health Inc ....D 626 573-5902
2507 Evelyn Ave Rosemead (91770) ***(P-27918)***
Anka Behavioral Health Inc ....D 209 982-4697
458 Almond Dr Lodi (95240) ***(P-22732)***
Anka Behavioral Health Inc ....D 916 722-3700
7515 Willow Way Citrus Heights (95610) ***(P-22733)***
Anka Behavioral Health Inc ....C 951 929-2744
2100 State St Hemet (92543) ***(P-10527)***
Anka Behavioral Health Inc ....D 510 494-1567
5149 Winston Ct Fremont (94536) ***(P-22734)***
Anka Behavioral Health Inc (PA) ....C 925 825-4700
1850 Gateway Blvd Ste 900 Concord (94520) ***(P-22504)***
Anka Behavioral Health Inc ....D 909 622-8217
942 Barbara Ln Pomona (91767) ***(P-19296)***
Anna Corporation ....E 951 736-6037
2078 2nd St Norco (92860) ***(P-2420)***
Annabel Investment Company ....D 925 866-0100
2600 Camino Ramon Ste 201 San Ramon (94583) ***(P-11855)***
Annandale Golf Club ....C 626 796-6125
1 N San Rafael Ave Pasadena (91105) ***(P-18845)***
Anne M Kent MD ....D 949 650-7100
500 Superior Ave Ste 310 Newport Beach (92663) ***(P-19297)***
Anne Sppi Clnic Riverside Rnch, Bakersfield *Also called Sippi Anne Riverside Ranch LLP* ***(P-24675)***
Annenberg Foundation Trust (PA) ....D 760 202-2222
37977 Bob Hope Dr Rancho Mirage (92270) ***(P-12088)***
Annie App Inc (HQ) ....D 844 277-2664
23 Geary St Ste 400800 San Francisco (94108) ***(P-14987)***
Annies Homegrown Inc ....D 510 558-7500
1610 5th St Berkeley (94710) ***(P-8752)***
Anning-Johnson Company ....C 510 670-0100
22955 Kidder St Hayward (94545) ***(P-2844)***
Anning-Johnson Company ....E 626 369-7131
13250 Temple Ave City of Industry (91746) ***(P-2845)***
Annuzzi Concrete Service Inc ....E 415 468-2795
85 Elmira St San Francisco (94124) ***(P-1722)***
Anomali Incorporated ....D 408 800-4050
808 Winslow St Redwood City (94063) ***(P-14988)***
Anonymous Content LLC (PA) ....D 310 558-6000
3532 Hayden Ave Culver City (90232) ***(P-18017)***
Anova Food LLC ....D 858 715-4000
280 10th Ave San Diego (92101) ***(P-8568)***
Ans World Service Inc ....D 714 441-2400
2751 E Chapman Ave # 204 Fullerton (92831) ***(P-5219)***
Ansafone Contact Centers, Santa Ana *Also called Ephonamationcom Inc* ***(P-17153)***
Ansar Gallery ....C 949 220-0000
2505 El Camino Rd Tustin (92782) ***(P-8381)***
Anschutz Entrmt Group Inc (HQ) ....C 213 337-5052
1100 S Flower St Los Angeles (90015) ***(P-18418)***
Anschutz Film Group ....A 310 887-1000
1888 Century Park E # 1400 Los Angeles (90067) ***(P-2846)***
Anschutz So Calif Sports Compl ....C 310 630-2000
18400 Avalon Blvd Ste 100 Carson (90746) ***(P-18506)***
Ansira Partners Inc ....D 818 461-6100
5000 Van Nuys Blvd Sherman Oaks (91403) ***(P-17004)***
Answer Financial Inc (HQ) ....C 818 644-4000
15910 Ventura Blvd Fl 6 Encino (91436) ***(P-17005)***
Ant Farm LLC ....C 323 850-0700
1027 W Edgeware Rd Los Angeles (90026) ***(P-18178)***
Antelope Valley Country Club ....C 661 947-3142
39800 Country Club Dr Palmdale (93551) ***(P-18846)***
Antelope Valley Foundation ....E 661 945-7290
646 W Lancaster Blvd # 109 Lancaster (93534) ***(P-23481)***
Antelope Valley Health Center, Lancaster *Also called County of Los Angeles* ***(P-22549)***
Antelope Valley Hlth Care Dst, Lancaster *Also called Antelope Valley Hospital Inc* ***(P-21289)***
Antelope Valley Hospital, Lancaster *Also called Kaiser Foundation Hospitals* ***(P-21492)***
Antelope Valley Hospital Inc ....D 661 949-1550
1601 W Avenue J Ste 201 Lancaster (93534) ***(P-19298)***
Antelope Valley Hospital Inc ....C 661 726-6180
1600 W Avenue J Lancaster (93534) ***(P-19299)***
Antelope Valley Hospital Inc (PA) ....A 661 949-5000
1600 W Avenue J Lancaster (93534) ***(P-21289)***
Antelope Valley Mall ....D 661 266-9150
1233 W Rancho Vista Blvd # 405 Palmdale (93551) ***(P-10853)***
Antelope Valley Medical Group ....E 661 945-2783
44469 10th St W Lancaster (93534) ***(P-19300)***
Antelope Vly Convalecent Hosp, Lancaster *Also called Antelope Vly Retirement HM Inc* ***(P-20993)***
Antelope Vly Dom Vlnce Council (PA) ....D 661 723-7772
43434 Sahuayo St Lancaster (93535) ***(P-23482)***
Antelope Vly Retirement HM Inc ....B 661 948-7501
44445 15th St W Lancaster (93534) ***(P-20993)***
Antelope Vly Retirement HM Inc ....C 661 949-5524
44567 15th St W Lancaster (93534) ***(P-20994)***
Antelope Vly Schl Trnsp Agcy ....C 661 945-3621
670 W Avenue L8 Lancaster (93534) ***(P-3907)***
Anthony Botelho ....D 831 623-4228
382 Olympia Ave San Juan Bautista (95045) ***(P-213)***
Anthony Harvesting Inc ....C 831 385-6460
401 S Vanderhurst Ave King City (93930) ***(P-472)***
Anthony Lambe ....D 559 268-0709
1521 W Nielsen Ave Ste 69 Fresno (93706) ***(P-6618)***
Anthony P Garofalo A Dental ....D 619 440-0071
742 Broadway El Cajon (92021) ***(P-20110)***
Anthony Soto Emplyment Trining, Santa Rosa *Also called California Human Dev Corp* ***(P-24161)***
Anthony Trevino ....D 707 747-4776
938 Adams St Ste A Benicia (94510) ***(P-3094)***
Anthony Vineyards Inc (PA) ....C 661 858-6211
5512 Valpredo Ave Bakersfield (93307) ***(P-129)***
Anthonys Fish Grotto ....D 619 713-1853
9530 Murray Dr La Mesa (91942) ***(P-8569)***
Antimite Associates Inc ....D 619 231-2900
5458 Complex St 401 San Diego (92123) ***(P-14137)***
Antioch Convalescent Hospital, Antioch *Also called Norcal Care Centers Inc* ***(P-21166)***
Antioch Public Golf Corp ....D 925 706-4220
4800 Golf Course Rd Antioch (94531) ***(P-18686)***
Antioch Rotary Club ....E 925 757-1800
324 G St Antioch (94509) ***(P-18847)***
Antonini Freight Express Inc (PA) ....C 209 466-4900
287 N Cardinal Ave Stockton (95215) ***(P-3972)***
Anvil Builders Inc ....C 415 285-5000
1475 Donner Ave San Francisco (94124) ***(P-1723)***
Ao Freight Corporation (PA) ....E 310 419-8833
419 N Oak St Inglewood (90302) ***(P-5008)***
AOC Technologies Inc ....B 925 875-0808
5960 Inglewood Dr Pleasanton (94588) ***(P-7257)***
AON, Los Angeles *Also called Schirmer Fire Protection Eng* ***(P-10765)***
AON Benfield Fac Inc ....C 415 486-6900
199 Fremont St Fl 15 San Francisco (94105) ***(P-10157)***
AON Consulting Inc ....D 408 321-2500
2570 N 1st St Ste 500 San Jose (95131) ***(P-27138)***
AON Consulting Inc ....D 818 506-4300
707 Wilshire Blvd # 2500 Los Angeles (90017) ***(P-10528)***
AON Consulting Inc ....D 800 558-0655
3461 Fair Oaks Blvd Sacramento (95864) ***(P-10529)***
AON Consulting Inc ....D 562 345-4700
21900 Burbank Blvd # 101 Woodland Hills (91367) ***(P-10530)***
AON Consulting Inc ....D 800 283-1667
851 Van Ness Ave Fl 2 San Francisco (94109) ***(P-10531)***
AON Consulting Inc ....D 800 815-1823
160 Via Verde Ste 200 San Dimas (91773) ***(P-10532)***
AON Consulting Inc ....C 415 486-6226
199 Fremont St Fl 11 San Francisco (94105) ***(P-10533)***
AON Consulting Inc ....D 562 496-2888
5000 E Spring St Ste 100 Long Beach (90815) ***(P-10534)***
AON Consulting Inc ....D 626 683-5200
255 S Lake Ave Ste 900 Pasadena (91101) ***(P-10535)***
AON Consulting & Insur Svcs ....D 415 486-7500
199 Fremont St Fl 14 San Francisco (94105) ***(P-10536)***
AON Risk Svcs Companies Inc ....D 213 630-3200
707 Wilshire Blvd # 2600 Los Angeles (90017) ***(P-10537)***
Aopen America Incorporated ....D 408 586-1200
2150 N 1st St Ste 300 San Jose (95131) ***(P-7007)***
AP Express LLC ....D 562 236-2250
8500 Rex Rd Pico Rivera (90660) ***(P-5009)***
AP Express International LLC ....D 562 236-2250
8500 Rex Rd Pico Rivera (90660) ***(P-5220)***
AP Global Inc ....D 818 707-3167
31352 Via Colinas Ste 101 Westlake Village (91362) ***(P-7438)***
AP Tech, Fremont *Also called American Portwell Tech Inc* ***(P-7006)***
APA Incorporated ....C 310 888-4200
405 S Beverly Dr Ste 500 Beverly Hills (90212) ***(P-27139)***
APC Lab, Chino *Also called Applied P & Ch Laboratory Sout* ***(P-26322)***
Apeiro, Oceanside *Also called Shieldx Networks Inc* ***(P-15442)***
Aperian Global Inc (PA) ....D 628 222-3773
1 Kaiser Plz Ste 785 Oakland (94612) ***(P-27140)***
Aperio Group LLC ....D 415 339-4300
3 Harbor Dr Ste 204 Sausalito (94965) ***(P-17006)***
Apex Bulk Commodities Inc ....D 909 854-9991
14080 Slover Ave Fontana (92337) ***(P-10044)***
Apex Communications, Fremont *Also called Netversant - Silicon Vly Inc* ***(P-2660)***
Apex Computer Systems Inc ....D 562 926-6820
13875 Cerritos Corprt Dr A Cerritos (90703) ***(P-16277)***
Apex Development Inc ....C 818 887-0400
23679 Calabasas Rd # 764 Calabasas (91302) ***(P-1263)***
Apex Group ....C 818 885-0513
17101 Superior St Northridge (91325) ***(P-26761)***
Apex Healthcare Med Ctr Inc (PA) ....D 951 765-0700
2390 E Florida Ave # 201 Hemet (92544) ***(P-20163)***
Apex Logistics Intl Inc (PA) ....D 310 665-0288
17511 S Susana Rd Compton (90221) ***(P-5010)***
Apex Machine Works Inc ....D 310 393-5987
2118 Wilshire Blvd # 258 Santa Monica (90403) ***(P-25537)***
Apex Mechanical Systems Inc ....D 858 536-8700
7440 Trade St Ste A San Diego (92121) ***(P-2123)***
Apex Medical Group Lab, Hemet *Also called Apex Healthcare Med Ctr Inc* ***(P-20163)***
Apex Parks Group LLC (PA) ....C 949 349-8461
27061 Aliso Creek Rd # 100 Aliso Viejo (92656) ***(P-18790)***
Apex Parks Group LLC ....D 909 981-5251
1500 W 7th St Upland (91786) ***(P-19098)***
Apex Parks Group LLC ....D 210 341-6663
27061 Aliso Creek Rd # 100 Aliso Viejo (92656) ***(P-19099)***
Apex Staffing Service ....E 909 941-0267
10134 6th St Ste A Rancho Cucamonga (91730) ***(P-14817)***
Apexcare Inc (PA) ....A 916 924-9111
1418 Howe Ave Ste B Sacramento (95825) ***(P-22225)***
Apfeld & Neal Insurance Svcs ....E 714 821-7041
11022 Winners Cir Ste 100 Los Alamitos (90720) ***(P-10538)***
Apic Hotels Group LLC (HQ) ....C 415 692-1502
5 Thomas Mellon Cir # 305 San Francisco (94134) ***(P-12326)***
Apical Industries Inc ....D 760 724-5300
3030 Enterprise Ct Ste A Vista (92081) ***(P-7906)***
Apigee Corporation ....C 408 343-7300
1600 Amphitheatre Pkwy Mountain View (94043) ***(P-14989)***

Mergent e-mail: customerrelations@mergent.com
1206
2019 Directory of California
Wholesalers and Services Companies
(P-0000) Products & Services Section entry number
(PA)=Parent Co (HQ)=Headquarters (DH)=Div Headquarters

APL Logistics Ltd..........C......310 548-8700
180 E Ocean Blvd Ste 800 Long Beach (90802) ***(P-4695)***
Apla Health & Wellness..........D......213 201-1546
611 S Kingsley Dr Los Angeles (90005) ***(P-19301)***
APM Terminals Pacific LLC..........E......310 221-4000
2500 Navy Way Pier 400 San Pedro (90731) ***(P-5011)***
APM Terminals Pacific LLC (HQ)..........C......704 571-2768
2500 Navy Way San Pedro (90731) ***(P-4723)***
APM Terminals Pacific Ltd..........B......510 992-6430
5801 Christie Ave Emeryville (94608) ***(P-5012)***
Apn Business Resources Inc..........D......818 717-9980
21418 Osborne St Canoga Park (91304) ***(P-27141)***
Apn Software Services Inc (PA)..........D......510 623-5050
39899 Balentine Dr # 385 Newark (94560) ***(P-16312)***
Apolis, El Segundo *Also called Rjt Compuquest Inc* ***(P-16473)***
Apollo Agencies Inc (PA)..........D......714 832-2100
700 W 1st St Ste 2 Tustin (92780) ***(P-10539)***
Apollo Couriers Inc (PA)..........D......310 337-0377
1039 W Hillcrest Blvd Inglewood (90301) ***(P-4393)***
Apollo Cpr, Pico Rivera *Also called Ionics Altrpure Wtr Crparation* ***(P-8807)***
Apollo Div Ionics Ultrapure, San Jose *Also called Suez Wts Systems Usa Inc* ***(P-7638)***
Apollo Electric..........D......714 256-8414
330 N Basse Ln Brea (92821) ***(P-2511)***
App Wholesale LLC..........B......323 980-3746
3686 E Olympic Blvd Los Angeles (90023) ***(P-8753)***
Appdirect Inc (PA)..........D......415 852-3924
650 California St Fl 25 San Francisco (94108) ***(P-15582)***
Appdynamics LLC (HQ)..........C......415 442-8400
303 2nd St Fl 8 San Francisco (94107) ***(P-15583)***
Appdynamics, Inc., San Francisco *Also called Appdynamics LLC* ***(P-15583)***
Appellation Tours Inc..........E......707 938-9390
21707 8th St E Sonoma (95476) ***(P-4962)***
Appery LLC..........D......925 602-5504
1340 Treat Blvd Ste 375 Walnut Creek (94597) ***(P-15584)***
Appetize Technologies Inc..........C......877 559-4225
6601 Center Dr W Ste 700 Los Angeles (90045) ***(P-15585)***
Appfolio Inc (PA)..........C......805 364-6093
50 Castilian Dr Ste 101 Santa Barbara (93117) ***(P-15586)***
Appfolio Inc..........A......866 648-1536
9201 Spectrum San Diego (92123) ***(P-15587)***
Appl, Clovis *Also called Agriculture and Priority Pollu* ***(P-26681)***
Apple Eght Hospitality MGT Inc..........D......714 827-1010
5865 Katella Ave Cypress (90630) ***(P-12327)***
Apple Hospitality Reit Inc..........D......916 568-5400
2540 Venture Oaks Way Sacramento (95833) ***(P-12328)***
Apple Inns Inc..........E......510 895-1311
68 Monarch Bay Dr San Leandro (94577) ***(P-12329)***
Apple Nine Hospitality MGT..........D......858 573-0700
8651 Spectrum Center Blvd San Diego (92123) ***(P-12330)***
Apple One Employment, Glendale *Also called Howroyd-Wright Emplymnt Agcy* ***(P-14639)***
Apple Store Glendale Galleria, Glendale *Also called Glendale Associates Ltd* ***(P-10884)***
Apple Valley Care & Rehab, Sebastopol *Also called Apple Vly Cnvalescent Hosp Inc* ***(P-20231)***
Apple Valley Care Center, Apple Valley *Also called Front Porch Communities & Svcs* ***(P-20442)***
Apple Valley Golf Club..........C......760 242-3653
15200 Rancherias Rd Apple Valley (92307) ***(P-18848)***
Apple Valley Golf Course, Apple Valley *Also called Apple Valley Golf Club* ***(P-18848)***
Apple Vlley/ Vctrvlle Cnsrtium..........D......760 240-7000
14955 Dale Evans Pkwy Apple Valley (92307) ***(P-13716)***
Apple Vly Cnvalescent Hosp Inc..........C......707 823-7675
1035 Gravenstein Hwy N Sebastopol (95472) ***(P-20231)***
Applebee Leasing Inc..........D......818 612-6218
4 Maidstone Dr Newport Beach (92660) ***(P-17007)***
Applecare Medical MGT LLC..........C......714 443-4507
18 Centerpointe Dr # 100 La Palma (90623) ***(P-26762)***
Appleone Employment Services, Glendale *Also called Howroyd-Wright Emplymnt Agcy* ***(P-14640)***
Applewood Care Center..........E......916 446-2506
1090 Rio Ln Sacramento (95822) ***(P-20232)***
APPLEWOOD OPERATING, Redding *Also called Copper Ridge Care Center* ***(P-20323)***
Appliance Recycling Ctrs Amer..........D......310 223-2800
1920 S Acacia Ave Compton (90220) ***(P-6338)***
Applied Biosystems LLC (HQ)..........C......650 638-5000
5791 Van Allen Way Carlsbad (92008) ***(P-15588)***
Applied Companies..........E......661 257-0090
28020 Avenue Stanford Santa Clarita (91355) ***(P-25538)***
Applied Companies RE LLC..........E......661 257-0090
28020 Avenue Stanford Valencia (91355) ***(P-10854)***
Applied Computer Solutions (HQ)..........D......714 861-2200
15461 Springdale St Huntington Beach (92649) ***(P-14990)***
Applied Engineering MGT Corp..........C......805 484-1909
760 Paseo Camarillo # 101 Camarillo (93010) ***(P-14991)***
Applied Geokinetics..........D......949 502-5353
77 Bunsen Irvine (92618) ***(P-25539)***
Applied Language Solutions LLC..........C......800 579-5010
1250 W Sunflower La Habra (90631) ***(P-17008)***
Applied Materials, Roseville *Also called Cokeva Inc* ***(P-16280)***
Applied Molecular Evolution (HQ)..........E......858 597-4990
10300 Campus Point Dr # 200 San Diego (92121) ***(P-26321)***
Applied P & Ch Laboratory Sout..........D......909 590-1828
13760 Magnolia Ave Chino (91710) ***(P-26322)***
Applied Research Assoc Inc..........D......805 962-4810
5425 Hollister Ave # 220 Santa Barbara (93111) ***(P-26323)***
Applied Underwriters Inc..........E......415 656-5000
950 Tower Ln Ste 1400 Foster City (94404) ***(P-10540)***
Applied Weather Technology Inc, Sunnyvale *Also called Stormgeo* ***(P-27959)***
Appraisal Trend, Encino *Also called Valuation Concepts LLC* ***(P-11811)***
Appraiser Loft LLC..........E......858 832-8334
3027 Townsgate Rd Ste 140 Westlake Village (91361) ***(P-11214)***
Apprendre Technologies Inc..........D......561 244-9917
1781 S Campton Ave # 217 Anaheim (92805) ***(P-14992)***
Apprentice & Journeymen Traini..........D......818 464-4579
7850 Haskell Ave Van Nuys (91406) ***(P-2124)***
Apprentice & Journeymen Trn Tr..........D......323 636-9871
7850 Haskell Ave Van Nuys (91406) ***(P-24145)***
Appsflyer Ltd..........D......415 636-9430
111 New Montgomery St San Francisco (94105) ***(P-13934)***
Appster Inc..........D......415 926-2741
180 Sansome St Fl 4 San Francisco (94104) ***(P-14993)***
Apptivo Inc..........C......650 906-1034
34364 Eucalyptus Ter Fremont (94555) ***(P-14994)***
Apria Healthcare Group Inc (HQ)..........D......949 639-2000
26220 Enterprise Ct Lake Forest (92630) ***(P-22226)***
Apria Healthcare LLC..........D......530 669-6441
1680 Tide Ct Ste B Woodland (95776) ***(P-22735)***
Apria Healthcare LLC..........C......209 223-7727
220 Scttsvlle Blvd Bldg A Jackson (95642) ***(P-22736)***
Apria Healthcare LLC..........D......650 588-9744
480 Carlton Ct South San Francisco (94080) ***(P-7154)***
Apria Healthcare LLC..........C......805 278-6700
2150 Trabajo Dr Ste B Oxnard (93030) ***(P-14431)***
Apria Healthcare LLC..........D......858 653-6800
10090 Willow Creek Rd San Diego (92131) ***(P-14432)***
Apria Healthcare LLC..........C......949 639-2000
26220 Enterprise Ct Lake Forest (92630) ***(P-22737)***
Apria Healthcare LLC..........C......530 677-2713
1450 Expo Pkwy Sacramento (95815) ***(P-7155)***
Apria Healthcare LLC (HQ)..........B......949 639-2163
26220 Enterprise Ct Lake Forest (92630) ***(P-7156)***
Apria Healthcare LLC..........D......925 827-8800
2510 Dean Lesher Dr Ste D Concord (94520) ***(P-7157)***
Apria Healthcare LLC..........D......949 639-2163
1931 Lundy Ave San Jose (95131) ***(P-14433)***
Apria Healthcare LLC..........D......707 543-0979
3636 N Laughlin Rd # 190 Santa Rosa (95403) ***(P-14434)***
Apria Healthcare LLC..........D......951 320-1100
815 Marlborough Ave # 200 Riverside (92507) ***(P-22227)***
Apria Healthcare LLC..........D......510 346-4000
2476 Verna Ct San Leandro (94577) ***(P-22228)***
Apriso Corporation..........C......562 951-8000
301 E Ocean Blvd Ste 1200 Long Beach (90802) ***(P-15913)***
Apteligent Inc..........D......415 371-1402
1100 La Avenida St Ste A Mountain View (94043) ***(P-15589)***
Aptim Corp..........A......925 288-2011
4005 Port Chicago Hwy Concord (94520) ***(P-25540)***
Aptim Corp..........D......949 261-6441
18100 Von Karman Ave Irvine (92612) ***(P-25541)***
Aptiv Digital Inc..........D......818 295-6789
2210 W Olive Ave Fl 2 Burbank (91506) ***(P-15590)***
Aptos Berry Farms Inc..........D......831 724-3256
730 S A St Oxnard (93030) ***(P-90)***
Apttus Corporation (PA)..........C......650 445-7700
1400 Fashion Island Blvd # 100 San Mateo (94404) ***(P-15914)***
Apu Inc (PA)..........D......661 948-2880
14939 Oxnard St Van Nuys (91411) ***(P-6619)***
Apumac LLC..........C......888 248-7775
6404 Wilshire Blvd # 106 Los Angeles (90048) ***(P-7439)***
Apumac.com, Los Angeles *Also called Apumac LLC* ***(P-7439)***
Apw Construction Inc (PA)..........D......626 820-0812
727 Glendora Ave La Puente (91744) ***(P-1874)***
Apw Construction Inc..........D......626 855-1720
15135 Salt Lake Ave City of Industry (91746) ***(P-3488)***
Apw International Inc..........C......310 884-5003
1073 E Artesia Blvd Carson (90746) ***(P-6620)***
Apw Knox-Seeman Warehouse Inc (HQ)..........D......310 604-4373
1073 E Artesia Blvd Carson (90746) ***(P-6621)***
Apx Inc (PA)..........E......408 517-2100
2001 Gateway Pl Ste 315w San Jose (95110) ***(P-27643)***
Aqua Gunite Inc..........E......408 271-2782
5830 S Naylor Rd Livermore (94551) ***(P-3489)***
Aqua-Serv Engineers Inc (HQ)..........D......951 681-9696
13560 Colombard Ct Fontana (92337) ***(P-8917)***
Aquaclean Janitorial..........D......858 537-9090
9403 Compass Point Dr S San Diego (92126) ***(P-14196)***
Aqualine Piping Inc..........D......408 745-7100
2108 Bering Dr Ste C San Jose (95131) ***(P-2125)***
Aquarium of Pacific..........D......562 590-3100
310 Golden Shore Ste 300 Long Beach (90802) ***(P-24922)***
Aquarium of Pacific (PA)..........B......562 590-3100
100 Aquarium Way Long Beach (90802) ***(P-24923)***
AQUARIUM OF THE BAY, THE, San Francisco *Also called Bayorg* ***(P-24924)***
Aquatic Designing Inc..........E......707 822-4629
4801 West End Rd Arcata (95521) ***(P-25542)***
Aquatic Science Center..........E......510 746-7334
4911 Central Ave Richmond (94804) ***(P-26324)***
Aquinas Corporation..........C......408 248-7100
3580 Payne Ave San Jose (95117) ***(P-20233)***
Aquirecorps Norwalk Auto Auctn..........C......562 864-7464
12405 Rosecrans Ave Norwalk (90650) ***(P-6578)***
AR Preservation LP..........D......415 776-2151
201 Eddy St San Francisco (94102) ***(P-10979)***
AR Wilson Quarry, Aromas *Also called Granite Rock Co* ***(P-1092)***
Araco Enterprises LLC..........B......818 767-0675
9189 De Garmo Ave Sun Valley (91352) ***(P-6339)***
Aragen Bioscience Inc..........E......408 779-1700
380 Woodview Ave Morgan Hill (95037) ***(P-26325)***

ALPHABETIC

Employee Codes: A=Over 500 employees, B=251-500
C=101-250, D=51-100, E=50
2019 Directory of California
Wholesalers and Services Companies
© Mergent Inc. 1-800-342-5647
1207

Aragon Commercial Ldscpg Inc.....C.....408 998-0600
2305 S Vasco Rd Livermore (94550) ***(P-798)***
Aragon Construction Inc.....D.....909 621-2200
5440 Arrow Hwy Montclair (91763) ***(P-1467)***
Arakelian Enterprises Inc.....C.....818 768-0689
11121 Pendleton St Sun Valley (91352) ***(P-6340)***
Arakelian Enterprises Inc.....B.....626 336-3636
15045 Salt Lake Ave City of Industry (91746) ***(P-6341)***
Arakelian Enterprises Inc.....C.....951 342-3300
687 Iowa Ave Riverside (92507) ***(P-6342)***
Arakelian Enterprises Inc.....D.....818 768-1477
14048 Valley Blvd La Puente (91746) ***(P-6343)***
Arakelian Enterprises Inc (PA).....C.....626 336-3636
14048 Valley Blvd City of Industry (91746) ***(P-6344)***
Arakelian Enterprises Inc.....C.....818 768-1492
11121 Pendleton St Sun Valley (91352) ***(P-3973)***
Aramark Facility Services LLC.....C.....213 740-8968
941 W 35th St Los Angeles (90007) ***(P-14197)***
Aramark Facility Services LLC.....E.....714 372-0683
5301 Bolsa Ave Bldg 10 Huntington Beach (92647) ***(P-14198)***
Aramark Services Inc.....C.....831 372-8016
800 Asilomar Blvd Pacific Grove (93950) ***(P-12331)***
Aramark Services Inc.....D.....323 587-7661
1405 E 58th Pl Los Angeles (90001) ***(P-13629)***
Aramark Services Inc.....D.....310 635-5000
17044 Montanero Ave Ste 4 Carson (90746) ***(P-17009)***
Aramark Spt & Entrmt Group LLC.....C.....408 999-5735
525 W Santa Clara St San Jose (95113) ***(P-18419)***
Aramark Spt & Entrmt Group LLC.....C.....213 740-1224
3400 S Figueroa St Los Angeles (90007) ***(P-18420)***
Aramark Spt & Entrmt Group LLC.....C.....831 648-9809
886 Cannery Row Monterey (93940) ***(P-18421)***
Aramark Spt & Entrmt Group LLC.....D.....408 748-7030
5001 Great America Pkwy Santa Clara (95054) ***(P-18422)***
Aramark Unf & Career AP LLC.....D.....209 368-9785
1617 Jim Way Modesto (95358) ***(P-13583)***
Aramark Unf & Career AP LLC.....D.....818 973-3700
115 N First St Burbank (91502) ***(P-13584)***
Aramark Unf & Career AP LLC.....B.....916 286-4100
1419 National Dr Sacramento (95834) ***(P-13585)***
Aramark Unf & Career AP LLC (HQ).....C.....818 973-3700
115 N First St Ste 203 Burbank (91502) ***(P-13586)***
Aramark Unf & Career AP LLC.....D.....408 243-9824
855 Mckendrie St San Jose (95126) ***(P-13514)***
Aramark Unf & Career AP LLC.....D.....530 241-6433
755 Butte St Redding (96001) ***(P-13587)***
Aramark Unf & Career AP LLC.....D.....323 774-4216
15525 Garfield Ave Paramount (90723) ***(P-13515)***
Aramark Unf & Career AP LLC.....C.....510 835-9285
330 Chestnut St Oakland (94607) ***(P-13588)***
Aramark Unf & Career AP LLC.....C.....323 266-0555
4422 Dunham St Los Angeles (90023) ***(P-13589)***
Aramark Unf & Career AP LLC.....E.....858 550-1131
5665 Eastgate Dr San Diego (92121) ***(P-13516)***
Aramark Unf & Career AP LLC.....D.....714 545-4877
3101 W Adams St Santa Ana (92704) ***(P-13590)***
Aramark Unf & Career AP LLC.....C.....559 291-6631
3333 N Sabre Dr Fresno (93727) ***(P-13517)***
Aramark Unf & Career AP LLC.....D.....510 487-1855
31148 San Antonio St Hayward (94544) ***(P-13591)***
Aramark Unf & Career AP LLC.....D.....925 827-3782
5000 Forni Dr Concord (94520) ***(P-13592)***
Aramark Unf & Career AP LLC.....C.....858 550-5200
5665 Eastgage Dr San Diego (92121) ***(P-13593)***
Aramark Unf & Career AP LLC.....D.....818 364-8272
15372 Cobalt St Sylmar (91342) ***(P-13594)***
Aramark Unf & Career AP LLC.....D.....650 244-9332
440 N Canal St South San Francisco (94080) ***(P-13595)***
Aramark Unf & Career AP LLC.....C.....415 244-8332
440 Carolina St San Francisco (94107) ***(P-13518)***
Aramark Uniform Services.....D.....916 286-4100
1419 National Dr Sacramento (95834) ***(P-13596)***
Ararat Home of Los Angeles.....C.....818 837-1800
15099 Mission Hills Rd Mission Hills (91345) ***(P-20995)***
Ararat Home of Los Angeles (PA).....B.....818 365-3000
15105 Mission Hills Rd Mission Hills (91345) ***(P-20996)***
Ararat Nursing Facility, Mission Hills *Also called Ararat Home of Los Angeles* ***(P-20995)***
ARARAT RESIDENTAIL CARE FACILI, Mission Hills *Also called Ararat Home of Los Angeles* ***(P-20996)***
ARB, Lake Forest *Also called Juniper Rock Corporation* ***(P-1089)***
Arb Inc (HQ).....C.....949 598-9242
26000 Commercentre Dr Lake Forest (92630) ***(P-2008)***
Arb Inc.....E.....925 432-3649
1875 Loveridge Rd Pittsburg (94565) ***(P-4530)***
Arb Inc.....E.....805 643-4188
2235 N Ventura Ave Ventura (93001) ***(P-1891)***
Arb Inc.....E.....415 206-1015
50 Quint St San Francisco (94124) ***(P-1468)***
Arbitech LLC.....D.....949 376-6650
64 Fairbanks Irvine (92618) ***(P-7008)***
Arbor Employment & Training, Canoga Park *Also called Canoga Park Worksource Center* ***(P-14583)***
Arbor Medical Group Inc (PA).....D.....805 614-7591
1502 Marilyn Way Santa Maria (93454) ***(P-19302)***
Arbor Vly Nrsing Rhbltion Ctr, Modesto *Also called Kissito Health Case Inc* ***(P-20567)***
Arbormed Inc (PA).....C.....714 689-1500
725 W Town And Country Rd Orange (92868) ***(P-22738)***
Arbors, The, San Diego *Also called G & L Penasquitos Inc* ***(P-23820)***
Arborwell Inc (PA).....D.....510 881-4260
2337 American Ave Hayward (94545) ***(P-965)***
ARC, Torrance *Also called Good Sports Plus Ltd* ***(P-15184)***
ARC - Imperial Valley (PA).....C.....760 352-0180
298 E Ross Ave El Centro (92243) ***(P-23483)***
ARC - Imperial Valley.....D.....760 768-1944
340 E 1st St Calexico (92231) ***(P-22505)***
ARC - SD E Cnty Training Ctrs, El Cajon *Also called ARC of San Diego* ***(P-24738)***
ARC Community Enrichment, Ojai *Also called ARC of Ventura County Inc* ***(P-22506)***
ARC Document Solutions Inc.....C.....818 242-6555
655 N Central Ave Glendale (91203) ***(P-14077)***
ARC Document Solutions Inc.....D.....626 333-7005
1207 John Reed Ct Ste A City of Industry (91745) ***(P-14078)***
ARC Document Solutions Inc.....D.....949 660-1150
345 Clinton St Costa Mesa (92626) ***(P-14079)***
ARC Document Solutions Inc.....E.....415 495-8700
945 Bryant St Ste 1000 San Francisco (94103) ***(P-14080)***
ARC Document Solutions Inc.....C.....818 908-0222
15019 Califa St Van Nuys (91411) ***(P-14081)***
ARC ENTERPRISES, San Diego *Also called ARC of San Diego* ***(P-24737)***
ARC Fastener Supply & Mfg.....D.....909 481-8171
2104 Wembley Ln Corona (92881) ***(P-7828)***
ARC Fresno/Madera Counties (PA).....D.....559 226-6268
4490 E Ashlan Ave Fresno (93726) ***(P-24146)***
ARC Imaging Resources, Monterey Park *Also called American Reprographics Co LLC* ***(P-14073)***
ARC Industries.....D.....805 520-0399
5143 Cochran St Ste 93063 Simi Valley (93063) ***(P-24418)***
ARC Los Angles Orange Counties (PA).....D.....562 803-1556
12049 Woodruff Ave Downey (90241) ***(P-24147)***
ARC Mid-Cities Inc.....C.....310 329-9272
14208 Towne Ave Los Angeles (90061) ***(P-24148)***
ARC of Alameda County (PA).....C.....510 357-3569
14700 Doolittle Dr San Leandro (94577) ***(P-23484)***
ARC of Alameda County.....C.....510 582-8151
1101 Walpert St Hayward (94541) ***(P-24149)***
ARC of Butte County (PA).....C.....530 891-5865
2030 Park Ave Chico (95928) ***(P-23485)***
ARC of San Diego, Chula Vista *Also called ARC Starlight Center* ***(P-23486)***
ARC of San Diego (PA).....A.....619 685-1175
3030 Market St San Diego (92102) ***(P-24737)***
ARC of San Diego.....C.....619 448-2415
1855 John Towers Ave El Cajon (92020) ***(P-24738)***
ARC of Ventura County Inc.....D.....805 650-8611
210 Canada St Ojai (93023) ***(P-22506)***
ARC of Ventura County Inc.....C.....805 644-0880
4277 Transport St Ste F Ventura (93003) ***(P-22507)***
ARC San Francisco (PA).....C.....415 255-7200
1500 Howard St San Francisco (94103) ***(P-24150)***
ARC Starlight Center.....D.....619 427-7524
1280 Nolan Ave Chula Vista (91911) ***(P-23486)***
Arca Los Angeles, Compton *Also called Appliance Recycling Ctrs Amer* ***(P-6338)***
Arcadia Convalescent Hosp Inc (PA).....C.....323 681-1504
1601 S Baldwin Ave Arcadia (91007) ***(P-20997)***
Arcadia Gardens MGT Corp.....D.....626 574-8571
720 W Camino Real Ave Arcadia (91007) ***(P-20916)***
Arcadia Health Care Center, Arcadia *Also called Arcadia Convalescent Hosp Inc* ***(P-20997)***
Arcadia Health Services Inc.....D.....209 572-7650
1400 Florida Ave Ste 206 Modesto (95350) ***(P-22229)***
Arcadia Healthcare, Redding *Also called Northern California Hlth Care* ***(P-22374)***
Arcadia Management Service Co.....E.....408 286-4440
5185 Cherry Ave Ste 10 San Jose (95118) ***(P-11215)***
Arcadia Services Inc.....D.....248 352-7530
4340 Redwood Hwy Ste 123 San Rafael (94903) ***(P-14818)***
Arcadia Transit Inc.....E.....818 252-0630
7955 San Fernando Rd Sun Valley (91352) ***(P-3639)***
Arcana Corporation.....E.....805 882-1305
118 Nopalitos Way Santa Barbara (93103) ***(P-17010)***
Arch Bay Holdings LLC.....D.....949 679-2400
327 W Maple Ave Monrovia (91016) ***(P-11963)***
Arch Health Partners Inc (HQ).....D.....858 675-3100
15611 Pomerado Rd Ste 575 Poway (92064) ***(P-21290)***
Archer Norris A Prof Law Corp (PA).....C.....925 930-6000
2033 N Main St Ste 800 Walnut Creek (94596) ***(P-22917)***
Archer Western Contractors LLC.....D.....858 715-7200
9915 Mira Mesa Blvd # 230 San Diego (92131) ***(P-1724)***
Archer-Daniels-Midland Company.....D.....559 233-6262
3390 S Chestnut Ave Fresno (93725) ***(P-8754)***
Architects Orange.....C.....714 639-9860
144 N Orange St Orange (92866) ***(P-26023)***
Architectural Coatings Inc.....E.....714 701-1360
1565 E Edinger Ave Santa Ana (92705) ***(P-2421)***
Architectural GL & Alum Co Inc (PA).....C.....925 583-2460
6400 Brisa St Livermore (94550) ***(P-7258)***
Architecture Division, Los Angeles *Also called City of Los Angeles* ***(P-26037)***
Architrends Inc.....D.....925 648-8800
3860 Blackhawk Rd Ste 160 Danville (94506) ***(P-25543)***
Archives Management Corp (PA).....C.....650 544-2200
2301 S El Camino Real San Mateo (94403) ***(P-26763)***
Arciero Brothers Inc.....C.....714 238-6600
5614 E La Palma Ave Anaheim (92807) ***(P-3215)***
Arclight Cinema Company.....D.....818 501-0753
15301 Ventura Blvd Bldg A Sherman Oaks (91403) ***(P-18271)***
Arclight Cinema Company.....C.....323 464-1465
120 N Robertson Blvd Fl 3 Los Angeles (90048) ***(P-18272)***
Arco Envmtl Remediation LLC.....D.....714 523-5674
5472 Orangethorpe Ave La Palma (90623) ***(P-27142)***

Mergent e-mail: customerrelations@mergent.com
1208
2019 Directory of California
Wholesalers and Services Companies
(P-0000) Products & Services Section entry number
(PA)=Parent Co (HQ)=Headquarters (DH)=Div Headquarters

Arco Olympic Training Center, Chula Vista *Also called United Sttes Olympic Committee* ***(P-18536)***

Arconic Fastening Systems, Simi Valley *Also called Arconic Global Fas & Rings Inc* ***(P-7832)***

Arconic Fstening Systems Rings, City of Industry *Also called Arconic Global Fas & Rings Inc* ***(P-7829)***

Arconic Fstening Systems Rings, Torrance *Also called Arconic Global Fas & Rings Inc* ***(P-7830)***

Arconic Fstening Systems Rings, Torrance *Also called Arconic Global Fas & Rings Inc* ***(P-7831)***

Arconic Fstening Systems Rings, Fullerton *Also called Arconic Global Fas & Rings Inc* ***(P-7833)***

Arconic Fstening Systems Rings, Torrance *Also called Arconic Global Fas & Rings Inc* ***(P-7834)***

Arconic Fstening Systems Rings, Tracy *Also called Arconic Global Fas & Rings Inc* ***(P-7576)***

Arconic Fstening Systems Rings, Torrance *Also called Arconic Global Fas & Rings Inc* ***(P-7835)***

Arconic Global Fas & Rings Inc ....B.......626 968-3831
135 N Unruh Ave City of Industry (91744) ***(P-7829)***

Arconic Global Fas & Rings Inc ....D.......310 784-0700
3000 Lomita Blvd Torrance (90505) ***(P-7830)***

Arconic Global Fas & Rings Inc ....B.......310 530-2220
3014 Lomita Blvd Torrance (90505) ***(P-7831)***

Arconic Global Fas & Rings Inc (HQ) ....C.......805 527-3600
3990a Heritage Oak Ct Simi Valley (93063) ***(P-7832)***

Arconic Global Fas & Rings Inc ....D.......714 871-1550
800 S State College Blvd Fullerton (92831) ***(P-7833)***

Arconic Global Fas & Rings Inc ....E.......310 530-2220
3000 Lomita Blvd Torrance (90505) ***(P-7834)***

Arconic Global Fas & Rings Inc ....D.......209 839-3005
1925 N Macarthur Dr # 200 Tracy (95376) ***(P-7576)***

Arconic Global Fas & Rings Inc ....A.......310 530-2220
3018 Lomita Blvd Torrance (90505) ***(P-7835)***

Arconix USA, Camarillo *Also called Arconix/Usa Inc* ***(P-7440)***

Arconix/Usa Inc ....D.......805 388-2525
880 Avenida Acaso Ste 100 Camarillo (93012) ***(P-7440)***

Arcs Commercial Mortgage Co LP (HQ) ....C.......818 676-3274
26901 Agoura Rd Ste 200 Calabasas (91301) ***(P-9778)***

Arcsoft Inc (PA) ....D.......510 440-9901
46605 Fremont Blvd Fremont (94538) ***(P-14995)***

Arctouch LLC ....C.......415 944-2000
303 2nd St Ste 800s San Francisco (94107) ***(P-14996)***

Arcules Inc ....D.......949 439-0053
17875 Von Karman Ave # 450 Irvine (92614) ***(P-14997)***

Arcus Biosciences Inc ....D.......510 694-6200
3928 Point Eden Way Hayward (94545) ***(P-26326)***

Ardcore Senior Living ....D.......714 974-2226
525 S Anaheim Hills Rd Anaheim (92807) ***(P-24419)***

Arden Health & Rehab Ctr, Sacramento *Also called Mariner Health Care Inc* ***(P-20630)***

Arden Hills Country Club Inc ....D.......916 482-6111
1220 Arden Hills Ln Sacramento (95864) ***(P-18849)***

Arden-Mayfair Inc ....E.......310 638-2842
6191 Peachtree St Commerce (90040) ***(P-4531)***

Ardenbrook Inc (PA) ....D.......510 797-7980
4725 Thornton Ave Fremont (94536) ***(P-11216)***

Ardenwood Farm, Fremont *Also called City of Fremont* ***(P-24872)***

Ardwin Freight, Burbank *Also called Ardwin Inc* ***(P-4100)***

Ardwin Inc ....C.......818 767-7777
2940 N Hollywood Way Burbank (91505) ***(P-4100)***

Are- Maryland No 31 LLC ....E.......626 578-0777
385 E Colo Blvd Ste 299 Pasadena (91101) ***(P-10855)***

Area Distributing Co, San Jose *Also called J T R Company Inc* ***(P-8180)***

Area Distributing Company, San Jose *Also called J T R Company Inc* ***(P-4579)***

Area Housing Authority (PA) ....E.......805 480-9991
1400 W Hillcrest Dr Newbury Park (91320) ***(P-11217)***

Arena Painting Contractors Inc ....D.......310 316-2446
525 E Alondra Blvd Gardena (90248) ***(P-2422)***

Arena Solutions Inc (PA) ....D.......650 513-3500
989 E Hillsdale Blvd # 250 Foster City (94404) ***(P-14998)***

Arena Stuart Rentals Inc ....C.......408 856-3232
454 S Abbott Ave Milpitas (95035) ***(P-14473)***

Arent Fox LLP ....C.......213 629-7400
555 W 5th St Ste 4800 Los Angeles (90013) ***(P-22918)***

Ares Management LP (PA) ....D.......310 201-4100
2000 Avenue Of The Stars # 12 Los Angeles (90067) ***(P-12025)***

Ares Management LLC (HQ) ....D.......310 201-4100
2000 Avenue Of The Stars # 12 Los Angeles (90067) ***(P-12199)***

Ares Management LLC ....C.......310 201-4100
1999 Ave Of Stars Fl 37 Los Angeles (90067) ***(P-12026)***

Arete Associates ....D.......818 885-2200
103 Johnson St Windsor (95492) ***(P-26327)***

Arete Associates (PA) ....C.......818 885-2200
9301 Corbin Ave Ste 2000 Northridge (91324) ***(P-26328)***

Arete Hotels LLC ....D.......209 602-7952
2229 Den Helder Dr Modesto (95356) ***(P-12332)***

AREY JONES EDUCATIONAL SOLUTIO, San Diego *Also called Broadway Typewriter Co Inc* ***(P-7020)***

Argent Hotel, The, San Francisco *Also called L-O Soma Hotel Inc* ***(P-12826)***

Argent Management Co LLC ....D.......949 777-4070
2392 Morse Ave Irvine (92614) ***(P-11218)***

Argent Management LLC (PA) ....B.......949 777-4000
2392 Morse Ave Irvine (92614) ***(P-11219)***

Argo Ai LLC (HQ) ....D.......412 709-6992
100 W Evelyn Ave Ste 1 Mountain View (94041) ***(P-14999)***

Argon Enterprises Inc ....D.......310 349-8777
13658 Hawthorne Blvd Hawthorne (90250) ***(P-11220)***

Argonaut Constructors ....C.......707 542-4862
360 Sutton Pl Santa Rosa (95407) ***(P-1725)***

Argonaut Hotel ....C.......415 563-0800
495 Jefferson St San Francisco (94109) ***(P-12333)***

Argonaut Kensington Associates ....D.......925 943-1121
1580 Geary Rd Ofc Walnut Creek (94597) ***(P-23487)***

Argonne YMCA After School, San Francisco *Also called Young Mens Christian Assoc SF* ***(P-25321)***

Argus Management Company LLC ....B.......562 299-5200
5150 E Pacific Coast Hwy # 500 Long Beach (90804) ***(P-27578)***

Argus Medical Management, Long Beach *Also called Argus Management Company LLC* ***(P-27578)***

Aria Group Incorporated ....D.......949 475-2915
17395 Daimler St Irvine (92614) ***(P-25544)***

Aria Systems Inc (PA) ....D.......415 852-7250
100 Pine St Ste 2450 San Francisco (94111) ***(P-15591)***

Ariba Inc (HQ) ....C.......650 849-4000
3420 Hillview Ave Bldg 3 Palo Alto (94304) ***(P-15592)***

Aricent Technologies, Santa Clara *Also called Aricent US Inc* ***(P-15000)***

Aricent US Inc (HQ) ....E.......408 329-7400
3979 Freedom Cir Ste 950 Santa Clara (95054) ***(P-15000)***

Aries Filterworks ....E.......323 262-1600
13850 Van Ness Ave Gardena (90249) ***(P-7836)***

ARINC Incorporated ....D.......310 301-9040
4553 Glencoe Ave Ste 100 Marina Del Rey (90292) ***(P-25545)***

Arinwine Arcft Maint Svcs LLC ....D.......310 338-0063
1720 E Holly Ave El Segundo (90245) ***(P-4872)***

Ariosa Diagnostics Inc ....C.......408 229-7500
5945 Optical Ct San Jose (95138) ***(P-26329)***

Arise LLC ....D.......559 485-0881
1033 Van Ness Ave Fresno (93721) ***(P-19100)***

Arise Construction Inc ....D.......559 449-8989
5390 E Pine Ave Fresno (93727) ***(P-2126)***

Arise Solar, Fresno *Also called Arise Construction Inc* ***(P-2126)***

Arizona and 21st Corp ....D.......310 829-5377
2021 Arizona Ave Santa Monica (90404) ***(P-20998)***

Arizona Channel Isla ....D.......480 788-0755
300 W 9th St Oxnard (93030) ***(P-19101)***

Arizona Pipeline Company (PA) ....B.......760 244-8212
17372 Lilac St Hesperia (92345) ***(P-1892)***

Arizona Pipeline Company ....C.......951 270-3100
1745 Sampson Ave Corona (92879) ***(P-1893)***

Arizona Tile LLC ....D.......714 978-6403
1620 S Lewis St Anaheim (92805) ***(P-6875)***

Arkebauer Properties, Irvine *Also called Western National Properties* ***(P-1326)***

Arko Foods International Inc (PA) ....D.......323 257-1888
3410 N San Fernando Rd # 1 Los Angeles (90065) ***(P-8382)***

Arlene Keller MD ....E.......415 923-3598
2100 Webster St Ste 423 San Francisco (94115) ***(P-19303)***

ARLINGTON GARDENS CARE CENTER, Riverside *Also called Honey Flower Holdings LLC* ***(P-20532)***

Arlo Technologies Inc (HQ) ....B.......408 890-3900
2200 Faraday Ave Ste 150 Carlsbad (92008) ***(P-16874)***

Armada Trucking Group Inc ....D.......800 620-8592
225 Hermosa Ave Unit 202 Long Beach (90802) ***(P-3974)***

Armand Hammer Museum ....C.......310 443-7000
10899 Wilshire Blvd Los Angeles (90024) ***(P-24864)***

Armando C Ibarra CPA ....D.......619 422-1348
371 E St Chula Vista (91910) ***(P-26143)***

Armando Gonzalez Contracting ....B.......661 792-3785
32380 Elmo Hwy Mc Farland (93250) ***(P-638)***

Armanino LLP ....C.......310 478-4148
11766 Wilshire Blvd Fl 9 Los Angeles (90025) ***(P-26144)***

Armanino LLP (PA) ....C.......925 790-2600
12657 Alcosta Blvd # 500 San Ramon (94583) ***(P-26145)***

Armc, Colton *Also called Arrowhead Regional Medical Ctr* ***(P-21291)***

Armed Courier Service, Santa Clara *Also called Dan Connolly Inc* ***(P-16625)***

Armed Forces Officials Assn ....E.......858 672-1438
14532 Penasquitos Dr San Diego (92129) ***(P-24996)***

Armenian Amrcn Cuncil On Aging ....E.......818 241-8690
407 E Colorado St Glendale (91205) ***(P-23488)***

ARMENIAN-AMERICAN COUNCIL ON A, Glendale *Also called Armenian Amrcn Cuncil On Aging* ***(P-23488)***

Arminak & Associates LLC ....D.......626 358-4804
4832 Azusa Canyon Rd A Irwindale (91706) ***(P-9195)***

Armstrong Construction Co, Emeryville *Also called Armstrong Installation Service* ***(P-2423)***

Armstrong Installation Service ....D.......408 777-1234
4575 San Pablo Ave Emeryville (94608) ***(P-2423)***

Arnaudo Bros Transport Inc (PA) ....D.......209 835-0406
16505 S Tracy Blvd Tracy (95304) ***(P-323)***

Arnaudo Bros Trucking, Tracy *Also called Arnaudo Bros Transport Inc* ***(P-323)***

Arnel and Affliate, Costa Mesa *Also called Arnel Interior Corp* ***(P-26764)***

Arnel Development Company ....D.......760 599-6111
3146 Tiger Run Ct Ste 108 Carlsbad (92010) ***(P-1264)***

Arnel Interior Corp ....B.......714 481-5100
949 S Coast Dr Ste 600 Costa Mesa (92626) ***(P-26764)***

Arnies Supplies Service Ltd ....D.......323 263-1696
1501 N Ditman Ave Los Angeles (90063) ***(P-17935)***

Arnold & Porter LLP ....B.......818 788-8081
3 Embarcadero Ctr Fl 7 San Francisco (94111) ***(P-22919)***

Arnold & Porter PC ....B.......415 434-1600
3 Embarcadero Ctr Fl 7 San Francisco (94111) ***(P-22920)***

Arnold Palmer Golf MGT LLC ....D.......415 561-4670
300 Finley Rd San Francisco (94129) ***(P-26765)***

Arnold Porter Kaye Scholer LLP ....D.......650 319-4500
3000 El Camino Real 2-500 Palo Alto (94306) ***(P-22921)***

Arnold Porter Kaye Scholer LLP ....C.......310 788-1000
1999 Avenue Of The Stars # 1600 Los Angeles (90067) ***(P-22922)***

ALPHABETIC

Arntz Builders Inc..........E.......415 382-1188
431 Payran St Ste A Petaluma (94952) *(P-1374)*
Aroma Spa & Sports LLC..........D.......213 387-2111
3680 Wilshire Blvd # 301 Los Angeles (90010) *(P-19102)*
Aroma Wilshire Center, Los Angeles *Also called Hanil Development Inc (P-11944)*
Aroma Wilshire Center, Los Angeles *Also called Aroma Spa & Sports LLC (P-19102)*
Around The Clock Home Care, Bakersfield *Also called Vasindas Around The Clock Care (P-24709)*
Around The Clock Linkage, Bakersfield *Also called Kem Around Clock Foundation (P-26917)*
Arq LLC..........D.......888 384-0971
3002 Dow Ave Ste 416 Tustin (92780) *(P-25546)*
Arrand Properties LLC..........E.......925 289-1032
5032 Westside Dr San Ramon (94583) *(P-1119)*
Arraycon LLC (PA)..........E.......916 925-0201
1143 Blumenfeld Dr # 200 Sacramento (95815) *(P-2127)*
Arreolas Complete Ldscp Svc, Sacramento *Also called Arreolas Complete Ldscp Svc (P-799)*
Arreolas Complete Ldscp Svc..........E.......916 387-6777
8671 Morrison Creek Dr # 100 Sacramento (95828) *(P-799)*
Arriaga Usa Inc..........D.......818 982-9559
11831 Vose St North Hollywood (91605) *(P-2987)*
Arriaga Usa Inc (PA)..........C.......818 982-9559
12000 Sherman Way North Hollywood (91605) *(P-6876)*
Arriba Juntos (PA)..........D.......415 487-3240
1850 Mission St San Francisco (94103) *(P-24151)*
Arrival Communications Inc (HQ)..........D.......661 322-7375
1800 19th St Bakersfield (93301) *(P-17011)*
Arrow Alliance Group, Santa Clara *Also called Arrow Electronics Inc (P-7441)*
Arrow Bell, Woodland Hills *Also called Arrow Electronics Inc (P-7442)*
Arrow Disposal Services Inc..........E.......626 336-2255
14332 Valley Blvd La Puente (91746) *(P-6345)*
Arrow Electronics Inc..........C.......631 847-2918
3000 Bowers Ave Santa Clara (95051) *(P-7441)*
Arrow Electronics Inc..........D.......818 932-1022
20935 Warner Center Ln A Woodland Hills (91367) *(P-7442)*
Arrow Tools Fas & Saw Inc..........E.......818 780-1464
7635 Burnet Ave Van Nuys (91405) *(P-7577)*
Arrow USA..........D.......951 845-6144
1105 Highland Ct Beaumont (92223) *(P-7881)*
Arrow Wire & Cable Inc (PA)..........E.......909 282-1940
13911 Yorba Ave Chino (91710) *(P-7334)*
Arrowhead Central Credit Union (PA)..........B.......866 212-4333
8686 Haven Ave Rancho Cucamonga (91730) *(P-9540)*
Arrowhead Convalescent Home..........D.......909 886-4731
4343 N Sierra Way San Bernardino (92407) *(P-20234)*
Arrowhead Gen Insur Agcy Inc (HQ)..........C.......619 881-8600
701 B St Ste 2100 San Diego (92101) *(P-10339)*
Arrowhead Home, San Bernardino *Also called Arrowhead Convalescent Home (P-20234)*
Arrowhead Management Company (HQ)..........D.......800 669-1889
701 B St Ste 2100 San Diego (92101) *(P-10541)*
Arrowhead Mountain Spring Wtr, Cabazon *Also called Nestle Waters North Amer Inc (P-8834)*
Arrowhead Regional Medical Ctr..........A.......909 580-1000
400 N Pepper Ave Colton (92324) *(P-21291)*
Arrowhead Water, Orange *Also called Nestle Waters North Amer Inc (P-8833)*
Arroyo & Coates Inc..........D.......415 445-7800
425 California St # 2000 San Francisco (94104) *(P-11221)*
Arroyo Developmental Services..........D.......626 307-2240
1839 Potrero Grande Dr Monterey Park (91755) *(P-23489)*
Arroyo Grande Care Center, Arroyo Grande *Also called Compass Health Inc (P-21043)*
Arroyo Grande Community Hosp, Arroyo Grande *Also called Dignity Health (P-21374)*
Arroyo Insurance Services Inc (PA)..........D.......626 799-9532
440 E Huntington Dr # 100 Arcadia (91006) *(P-10542)*
Arroyo Labor Contracting Svc, Gonzales *Also called Alicia Arroyo Inc (P-637)*
Arroyo Seco Medical Group (PA)..........D.......626 795-7556
301 S Fair Oaks Ave # 300 Pasadena (91105) *(P-19304)*
ARROYO VISTA FAMILY HEALTH CEN, Los Angeles *Also called Arroyo Vsta Fmly Hlth Fndation (P-19305)*
Arroyo Vsta Fmly Hlth Fndation (PA)..........C.......323 254-5221
6000 N Figueroa St Los Angeles (90042) *(P-19305)*
ARS, Whittier *Also called Assocted Reproduction Svcs Inc (P-14082)*
ARS American Residential (HQ)..........D.......760 941-7000
2373 La Mirada Dr Vista (92081) *(P-2128)*
ARS National Services Inc (PA)..........C.......800 456-5053
201 W Grand Ave Escondido (92025) *(P-13991)*
ARS of San Diego-8112, San Diego *Also called American Residential Svcs LLC (P-2109)*
ARS West LLC..........D.......760 480-6631
780 W El Norte Pkwy Escondido (92026) *(P-17850)*
Art & Logic Inc..........D.......818 500-1933
87 N Raymond Ave Pasadena (91103) *(P-15915)*
Art Piccadilly Shaw LLC (PA)..........B.......559 348-5520
2305 W Shaw Ave Fresno (93711) *(P-12334)*
Art Piccadilly Shaw LLC..........D.......559 375-7760
5115 E Mckinley Ave Fresno (93727) *(P-12335)*
Art Piccadilly Shaw LLC..........C.......559 224-4200
4961 N Cedar Ave Fresno (93726) *(P-12336)*
Art Supply Enterprises Inc (PA)..........C.......510 428-9011
1375 Ocean Ave Emeryville (94608) *(P-9196)*
Arta Western Medical Group..........C.......949 260-6575
1665 Scenic Ave Ste 100 Costa Mesa (92626) *(P-10158)*
Artesia Christian Home Inc..........C.......562 865-5218
11614 183rd St Artesia (90701) *(P-20999)*
Artesia Healthcare Inc..........D.......818 843-1771
925 W Alameda Ave Burbank (91506) *(P-20235)*
Arthrtis Fundation PCF Reg Inc..........E.......323 954-5760
800 W 6th St Ste 1250 Los Angeles (90017) *(P-25092)*
Arthur J Gallagher & Co..........E.......949 349-9800
18201 Von Karman Ave # 200 Irvine (92612) *(P-10543)*
Arthur J Gallagher & Co..........C.......818 539-2300
505 N Brand Blvd Ste 600 Glendale (91203) *(P-10544)*
Arthur J Gallagher & Co..........C.......415 546-9300
1 Market Spear Tower San Francisco (94105) *(P-10545)*
Arthur J Gallagher & Co..........D.......559 436-0833
7910 N Ingram Ave Ste 201 Fresno (93711) *(P-10546)*
Arthur J Gallagher & Co..........E.......925 299-1112
3697 Mt Diablo Blvd # 300 Lafayette (94549) *(P-10547)*
Arthur Kunde & Sons Inc..........E.......707 833-5501
9825 Sonoma Hwy Kenwood (95452) *(P-681)*
Arthur Loussararian MD, Mission Viejo *Also called Mission Internal Med Group Inc (P-19690)*
Arthur Schawlow Center, Paradise *Also called California Vocations Inc (P-21029)*
Artiano Shinoff Abed (PA)..........D.......619 232-3122
16935 W Bernardo Dr # 114 San Diego (92127) *(P-22923)*
Artic Mechanical Inc (PA)..........D.......909 980-2539
10440 Trademark St Rancho Cucamonga (91730) *(P-2129)*
Artichoke Joe's Casino, San Bruno *Also called Artichoke Joes Inc (P-19103)*
Artichoke Joes Inc..........B.......650 589-8812
659 Huntington Ave San Bruno (94066) *(P-19103)*
Artificial Solutions Inc..........D.......650 943-2325
800 W El Camino Real Mountain View (94040) *(P-15001)*
Artimex Iron Company Inc..........C.......619 444-3155
315 Cypress Ln El Cajon (92020) *(P-3360)*
Artimisa & Co..........D.......530 283-3700
220 Forest Knoll Ln Quincy (95971) *(P-25547)*
Artisan Bakers..........D.......707 939-1765
21684 8th St E Ste 400 Sonoma (95476) *(P-8755)*
Artisan Entertainment Inc..........A.......310 449-9200
2700 Colorado Ave Ste 200 Santa Monica (90404) *(P-18018)*
Artisan Pictures Inc..........C.......310 449-9200
2700 Colorado Ave Fl 2 Santa Monica (90404) *(P-8018)*
Artisan Sotheby's Intl. Realty, Santa Rosa *Also called Realogy Holdings Corp (P-11717)*
Artist Silva Management LLC (PA)..........C.......323 856-8222
722 Seward St Los Angeles (90038) *(P-26766)*
Artistic Entrmt Svcs LLC..........D.......626 334-9388
120 N Aspan Ave Azusa (91702) *(P-18423)*
Artistic Maintenance Inc..........D.......909 390-5156
603 S Milliken Ave Ste A Ontario (91761) *(P-800)*
Artistic Maintenance Inc..........C.......949 733-8690
16092 Construction Cir E Irvine (92606) *(P-801)*
Artists of River Town..........D.......530 534-7690
56 Highlands Blvd Oroville (95966) *(P-24997)*
Artists Studio Gallery..........D.......424 206-9902
5504 Crestridge Rd Rancho Palos Verdes (90275) *(P-19104)*
Artizen Incorporated..........C.......650 261-9400
101 Golf Course Dr # 300 Rohnert Park (94928) *(P-15002)*
Artlogic, Pasadena *Also called Art & Logic Inc (P-15915)*
Arts and Services For Disabled..........E.......562 377-0302
3626 E Pacific Coast Hwy Long Beach (90804) *(P-23490)*
Arts Elegance Inc (PA)..........D.......626 405-1522
739 E Walnut St Ste 200 Pasadena (91101) *(P-8001)*
Artwear Inc..........E.......310 217-1393
13621 S Main St Los Angeles (90061) *(P-8249)*
Arup North America Limited..........C.......310 578-4182
12777 W Jefferson Blvd Los Angeles (90066) *(P-25548)*
Arup North America Limited (HQ)..........C.......415 957-9445
560 Mission St Fl 7 San Francisco (94105) *(P-25549)*
Arvin-Edison Water Storage Dst (PA)..........E.......661 854-5573
20401 E Bear Mtn Blvd Arvin (93203) *(P-6553)*
Arxan Technologies Inc (PA)..........D.......415 247-0900
650 California St Fl 2750 San Francisco (94108) *(P-16313)*
Arya Design Group, Los Angeles *Also called Arya Group Inc (P-1120)*
Arya Group Inc..........E.......310 446-7000
10490 Santa Monica Blvd Los Angeles (90025) *(P-1120)*
Arya Ice Cream Distrg Co Inc..........D.......323 234-2994
914 E 31st St Los Angeles (90011) *(P-8512)*
Aryaka Networks Inc (PA)..........D.......408 273-8420
1800 Gateway Dr Ste 200 San Mateo (94404) *(P-27537)*
Aryzta LLC..........E.......209 469-4920
920 Shaw Rd Stockton (95215) *(P-8756)*
Asai, Glendale *Also called Automated Systems America Inc (P-17936)*
Asana Integrated Medical Group..........D.......888 212-7545
26135 Mureau Rd Ste 101 Calabasas (91302) *(P-23491)*
ASAP Professional Services, San Ramon *Also called A S A P Professional Services (P-14560)*
Asbestos Instant Response Inc..........D.......323 733-0508
3517 W Washington Blvd Los Angeles (90018) *(P-3490)*
Asbury Environmental Services (PA)..........D.......310 886-3400
1300 S Santa Fe Ave Compton (90221) *(P-3975)*
Asbury Pk Nrsing Rhblttion Ctr..........C.......916 649-2000
2257 Fair Oaks Blvd Sacramento (95825) *(P-21000)*
Asbury Transportation Co..........D.......661 327-2271
2144 Mohawk St Bakersfield (93308) *(P-4101)*
ASC Building Products, West Sacramento *Also called ASC Profiles LLC (P-7259)*
ASC Profiles LLC (HQ)..........D.......916 372-6851
2110 Enterprise Blvd West Sacramento (95691) *(P-7259)*
Ascar Inc..........D.......805 966-3331
110 E De La Guerra St Santa Barbara (93101) *(P-16314)*
Ascend Clinical LLC (PA)..........D.......650 780-5500
1400 Industrial Way Redwood City (94063) *(P-22061)*
Ascend Distribution, City of Industry *Also called Eforcity Corp - Nfm (P-7470)*
Ascendantfx Capital USA Inc..........D.......201 633-4667
3478 Buskirk Ave Ste 1000 Pleasant Hill (94523) *(P-9669)*
Ascendify Corporation..........E.......415 528-5503
580 California St Bsmt San Francisco (94104) *(P-15003)*
Ascent Services Group Inc..........B.......925 627-4900
1001 Galaxy Way Ste 408 Concord (94520) *(P-14819)*

Asco, Fontana *Also called Automotive Sup Co Southern Cal* ***(P-6624)***
Ascon Recycle Company..........E.......661 533-0154
6500 E Avenue T Littlerock (93543) ***(P-6346)***
Ascon Recycling Co..........C.......760 948-1538
17671 Bear Valley Rd Hesperia (92345) ***(P-6347)***
Ascot Hotel LP..........C.......310 476-6411
170 N Church Ln Los Angeles (90049) ***(P-12337)***
Asec Group, Los Angeles *Also called A S E C International Inc* ***(P-16082)***
Asgn Incorporated (PA)..........C.......818 878-7900
26745 Malibu Hills Rd Calabasas (91301) ***(P-14570)***
Ash Holdings LLC..........D.......909 793-2609
1620 W Fern Ave Redlands (92373) ***(P-20236)***
Ashbury Market Inc..........D.......650 952-8889
179 Starlite St South San Francisco (94080) ***(P-8757)***
Ashford Trs Nickel LLC (PA)..........D.......925 934-2500
1345 Treat Blvd Walnut Creek (94597) ***(P-12338)***
Ashford Trs Nickel LLC..........D.......619 260-0111
1433 Camino Del Rio S San Diego (92108) ***(P-26767)***
Ashland Distribution, Commerce *Also called Ashland LLC* ***(P-8919)***
Ashland LLC..........D.......310 223-3505
20915 S Wilmington Ave Carson (90810) ***(P-8918)***
Ashland LLC..........D.......323 767-1300
6608 E 26th St Commerce (90040) ***(P-8919)***
Ashland Performance Materials, Carson *Also called Ashland LLC* ***(P-8918)***
Ashley Home Care Services LLC..........E.......323 286-2831
200 Spectrum Center Dr # 300 Irvine (92618) ***(P-22230)***
Ashley Lane Cherry Orchards LP..........E.......209 546-0426
500 N Jack Tone Rd Stockton (95215) ***(P-214)***
Ashley Ltc Inc..........D.......707 528-2100
446 Arrowood Dr Santa Rosa (95407) ***(P-20237)***
Ashley Management Group..........E.......949 754-3120
300 Spectrum Center Dr # 400 Irvine (92618) ***(P-27143)***
Ashok Thummalachetty..........C.......510 687-9797
44721 Aguila Ter Fremont (94539) ***(P-27644)***
Ashunya Inc..........D.......714 385-1900
642 N Eckhoff St Orange (92868) ***(P-15004)***
Ashwood Construction Inc..........E.......559 253-7240
5755 E Kings Canyon Rd # 110 Fresno (93727) ***(P-1265)***
Asi Computer Technologies Inc (PA)..........C.......510 226-8000
48289 Fremont Blvd Fremont (94538) ***(P-7009)***
ASI Hastings Inc..........C.......619 590-9300
4870 Vewridge Ave Ste 200 San Diego (92123) ***(P-2130)***
Asi Heating, Air and Solar, San Diego *Also called ASI Hastings Inc* ***(P-2130)***
Asia Foundation (PA)..........D.......415 982-4640
465 California St Fl 9 San Francisco (94104) ***(P-26593)***
Asia Pacific Capital..........D.......213 628-8800
345 Suth Fgroa St Ste 100 Los Angeles (90071) ***(P-12057)***
Asiainfo-Linkage Inc..........A.......408 970-9788
5201 Great America Pkwy # 356 Santa Clara (95054) ***(P-5448)***
Asian Amercn Recovery Svcs Inc (PA)..........C.......650 243-4888
1115 Mission Rd 2 South San Francisco (94080) ***(P-23492)***
Asian Amercn Recovery Svcs Inc..........C.......408 271-3900
1340 Tully Rd Ste 304 San Jose (95122) ***(P-21996)***
ASIAN ART MEUSUEM OF SF, San Francisco *Also called Asian Art Museum Found San Fra* ***(P-24865)***
Asian Art Museum, San Francisco *Also called City & County of San Francisco* ***(P-24871)***
Asian Art Museum Found San Fra..........C.......415 581-3500
200 Larkin St San Francisco (94102) ***(P-24865)***
Asian Cmnty Mental Hlth Svcs, Oakland *Also called Asian Community Mental Hlth Bd* ***(P-22508)***
Asian Commodities Company, Los Angeles *Also called Arko Foods International Inc* ***(P-8382)***
Asian Community Center of Sac (PA)..........C.......916 394-6399
7334 Park City Dr Sacramento (95831) ***(P-23493)***
Asian Community Mental Hlth Bd..........D.......510 869-6000
310 8th St Ste 201 Oakland (94607) ***(P-22508)***
Asian Health Services..........D.......510 986-0601
270 13th St Oakland (94612) ***(P-19306)***
Asian Health Services (PA)..........C.......510 986-6800
101 8th St Oakland (94607) ***(P-19307)***
Asian PCF Hlth Care Ventr Inc (PA)..........C.......323 644-3880
4216 Fountain Ave Los Angeles (90029) ***(P-24739)***
Asian Rehabilitation Svc Inc (PA)..........D.......562 632-1141
7009 Washington Ave Whittier (90602) ***(P-24152)***
Asics America Corporation (HQ)..........C.......949 453-8888
80 Technology Dr Irvine (92618) ***(P-8343)***
Asics Tiger, Irvine *Also called Asics America Corporation* ***(P-8343)***
Asig, Ontario *Also called Menzies Aviation (texas) Inc* ***(P-4901)***
Asilomar Conference Center, Pacific Grove *Also called Pacific Grove Aslmar Oper Corp* ***(P-12997)***
Asist Inc..........D.......559 251-7701
1974 N Gateway Blvd # 102 Fresno (93727) ***(P-22231)***
Asistencia Villa, Redlands *Also called Redlands Cmnty Hosp Foundation* ***(P-21193)***
Asistencia Villa Rehab & Care, Redlands *Also called Silverscreen Healthcare Inc* ***(P-21217)***
Ask.com, Oakland *Also called IAC Search & Media Inc* ***(P-16231)***
Asmg, San Diego *Also called Anesthesia Service Med Group* ***(P-19295)***
Asociacon De Bomberos Del Esta..........D.......949 355-4249
1100 Calle Del Cerro 52d San Clemente (92672) ***(P-24943)***
Aspect Software Inc..........E.......408 595-5002
101 Academy Ste 130 Irvine (92617) ***(P-15593)***
Aspects Furniture Mfg Inc..........C.......909 606-5806
15830 El Prado Rd Ste A Chino (91708) ***(P-6710)***
Aspen Apts I..........D.......415 673-5879
165 Eddy St San Francisco (94102) ***(P-10980)***
Aspen Grove Apartments LLC..........D.......408 848-6400
450 E 8th St Gilroy (95020) ***(P-10981)***
Aspen Youth Inc..........D.......562 567-5507
17777 Center Court Dr N # 300 Cerritos (90703) ***(P-23494)***
Asphalt Management Inc..........E.......562 630-6811
7243 Somerset Blvd Paramount (90723) ***(P-3216)***
Aspiranet..........D.......415 759-3690
3925 Noriega St San Francisco (94122) ***(P-24420)***
Aspiranet..........D.......209 669-2582
151 E Canal Dr Turlock (95380) ***(P-24421)***
Aspiranet..........D.......209 667-0327
2513 Youngstown Rd Turlock (95380) ***(P-23495)***
Aspiriant LLC..........E.......415 371-7800
50 California St Ste 2600 San Francisco (94111) ***(P-17012)***
Asplundh Tree Expert Co..........D.......805 964-9216
6100 Francis Botello Rd C Goleta (93117) ***(P-966)***
Asplundh Tree Expert LLC..........D.......805 641-0528
2055 N Ventura Ave Ventura (93001) ***(P-967)***
Asplundh Tree Expert LLC..........C.......714 893-2405
6101 Gateway Dr Cypress (90630) ***(P-968)***
Aspm-Sandiego, San Diego *Also called Allegis Residential Svcs Inc* ***(P-26755)***
Asr, San Juan Capistrano *Also called Action Sports Retailer* ***(P-16983)***
Asr Constructors Inc..........B.......951 779-6580
33891 Mission Trl Wildomar (92595) ***(P-1469)***
Asrc Industrial Services LLC (HQ)..........C.......707 644-7455
2300 Clayton Rd Ste 1050 Concord (94520) ***(P-14820)***
Assa Abloy Rsdential Group Inc..........B.......626 369-4718
600 Balwin Park Blvd City of Industry (91746) ***(P-7578)***
Assertive Security Services &..........A.......818 888-2405
20501 Ventura Blvd # 150 Woodland Hills (91364) ***(P-16875)***
Assessor-Recorder's Office, Fresno *Also called County of Fresno* ***(P-25014)***
Asset Athene Management L P (HQ)..........D.......310 698-4444
2121 Rosecrans Ave # 5300 El Segundo (90245) ***(P-26768)***
Asset Marketing Systems Insu..........D.......888 303-8755
15050 Ave Of Science # 100 San Diego (92128) ***(P-27144)***
ASset Private Security Inc..........D.......831 809-9779
36 Quail Run Cir Ste O Salinas (93907) ***(P-16573)***
Assetmark Inc (HQ)..........E.......925 521-1040
1655 Grant St Ste 1000 Concord (94520) ***(P-10057)***
Assi Security (PA)..........D.......949 955-0244
1370 Reynolds Ave Ste 201 Irvine (92614) ***(P-2512)***
ASSICIATED STUDENTS, San Luis Obispo *Also called Associated Students Inc* ***(P-23497)***
Assign Corporation..........C.......818 247-7100
200 N Maryland Ave # 204 Glendale (91206) ***(P-16315)***
Assist 65 Plus..........E.......323 557-4426
111 W 7th St Ste 211 Los Angeles (90014) ***(P-17013)***
Assista Hlthcare Prfssnals LLC..........C.......650 393-4293
2006 Pioneer Ct San Mateo (94403) ***(P-23496)***
Assistance In Home Care, Garden Grove *Also called Our Watch* ***(P-22385)***
Assistance League Foothill Com..........C.......909 987-2813
8555 Archibald Ave 8593 Rancho Cucamonga (91730) ***(P-24740)***
Assistance League of Redlands..........C.......909 792-2675
506 W Colton Ave Redlands (92374) ***(P-24741)***
ASSISTANCE LEAGUE THRIFT SHOP, Redlands *Also called Assistance League of Redlands* ***(P-24741)***
Assisted Home Care, Northridge *Also called Assisted Home Recovery Inc* ***(P-14571)***
Assisted Home Care, Thousand Oaks *Also called Staff Assistance Inc* ***(P-14768)***
Assisted Home Recovery Inc..........D.......626 915-5595
1900 W Garvey Ave S # 210 West Covina (91790) ***(P-27919)***
Assisted Home Recovery Inc (PA)..........C.......818 894-8117
8550 Balboa Blvd Lbby Northridge (91325) ***(P-14571)***
Assita In-Home Care, San Mateo *Also called Assista Hlthcare Prfssnals LLC* ***(P-23496)***
Assoc For Retarded Citizens..........D.......909 884-6484
796 E 6th St San Bernardino (92410) ***(P-24153)***
Associate Mechanical Contrs..........D.......760 294-3517
622 S Vinewood St Escondido (92029) ***(P-2131)***
Associated Bond, Calabasas *Also called AIA Holdings Inc* ***(P-10420)***
Associated Entrtmt Releasing (PA)..........E.......323 934-7044
4401 Wilshire Blvd Los Angeles (90010) ***(P-18019)***
Associated Feed & Supply Co (PA)..........C.......209 667-2708
5213 W Main St Turlock (95380) ***(P-9072)***
Associated Foreign Exch Inc (HQ)..........D.......888 307-2339
21045 Califa St Woodland Hills (91367) ***(P-9670)***
Associated Group, Commerce *Also called Associated Landscape* ***(P-17014)***
Associated Indemnity Corp..........A.......415 899-2000
1465 N Mcdowell Blvd # 100 Petaluma (94954) ***(P-10128)***
Associated Internal Medicine (PA)..........D.......510 465-6700
350 30th St Ste 320 Oakland (94609) ***(P-19308)***
Associated Intl Insur Co, Woodland Hills *Also called Markel Corp* ***(P-10676)***
Associated Koi Clubs America..........D.......949 650-5225
P.O. Box 10879 Costa Mesa (92627) ***(P-18850)***
Associated Laboratories, Orange *Also called De Par Inc* ***(P-26692)***
Associated Landscape..........D.......714 558-6100
2420 S Eastern Ave Commerce (90040) ***(P-17014)***
Associated Pathology Med Group..........D.......831 462-7625
1555 Soquel Dr Santa Cruz (95065) ***(P-19309)***
Associated Pension Cons Inc (PA)..........D.......530 343-4233
2035 Forest Ave Chico (95928) ***(P-10548)***
Associated Press..........D.......213 626-1200
221 S Figueroa St Ste 300 Los Angeles (90012) ***(P-16952)***
Associated Realtors..........D.......949 813-1888
27411 Viana Mission Viejo (92692) ***(P-11222)***
Associated Students Californi..........D.......657 278-2468
800 N State College Blvd Fullerton (92831) ***(P-25093)***
Associated Students California..........B.......562 985-4994
1212 N Bellflower Blvd # 220 Long Beach (90815) ***(P-25094)***
Associated Students Cdc..........D.......408 924-6988
460 S 8th St San Jose (95112) ***(P-24264)***
Associated Students Inc..........E.......760 750-4990
333 S Twin Oaks Valley Rd San Marcos (92096) ***(P-13472)***

ALPHABETIC

Associated Students Inc (PA).....D.....805 756-1281
University Un Bldg 65 San Luis Obispo (93407) ***(P-23497)***
Associated Students Inc.....D.....805 756-1281
1 Grand Ave San Luis Obispo (93407) ***(P-27920)***
Associated Students San Diego (PA).....A.....619 594-0234
5500 Campanile Dr San Diego (92182) ***(P-25382)***
Associated Students Stanford (PA).....D.....650 723-4331
201 Tresidder Un Stanford (94305) ***(P-25095)***
Associated Students Uc Irvine, Irvine *Also called Student Government Associat* ***(P-4952)***
Associated Students UCLA (PA).....B.....310 825-4321
308 Westwood Plz Los Angeles (90095) ***(P-24742)***
Associated Students UCLA.....C.....310 794-0242
924 Westwood Blvd Los Angeles (90024) ***(P-24743)***
Associated Students UCLA.....A.....310 825-9451
650 Chrls Yng S Rm 23 120 Los Angeles (90095) ***(P-19310)***
Associated Students, Inc., San Luis Obispo *Also called Associated Students Inc* ***(P-27920)***
Associated Television Intl, Los Angeles *Also called Associated Entrmt Releasing* ***(P-18019)***
Association For Retarded (PA).....D.....562 597-7716
4519 E Stearns St Long Beach (90815) ***(P-24154)***
Association of CA Schl Admnstr, La Mirada *Also called Norwalk La Mirada Unif* ***(P-25031)***
Associations of United Nurses (PA).....D.....909 599-8622
955 Overland Ct Ste 150 San Dimas (91773) ***(P-25054)***
Assocted Fgn Exch Holdings Inc (PA).....D.....818 386-2702
21045 Califa St Woodland Hills (91367) ***(P-9671)***
Assocted Gstrntrlogy Med Group (PA).....D.....714 778-1300
1211 W La Palma Ave Anaheim (92801) ***(P-19311)***
Assocted Lrng Lngage Spcialist (PA).....D.....650 631-9999
1060 Twin Dolphin Dr # 100 Redwood City (94065) ***(P-27645)***
Assocted Reproduction Svcs Inc.....C.....562 696-1181
13925 Whittier Blvd Whittier (90605) ***(P-14082)***
Assocted Third Pty Admnstrtors.....C.....619 358-8140
2831 Camino Del Rio S San Diego (92108) ***(P-10476)***
Assurant Inc.....B.....714 571-3900
2677 N Main St Ste 600 Santa Ana (92705) ***(P-10129)***
Assure Consulting Inc.....D.....650 966-1967
257 Castro St Ste 205 Mountain View (94041) ***(P-27646)***
Assure Detective Agency, Corona *Also called Chief Protective Services Inc* ***(P-16602)***
Assuredpartners Inc.....D.....916 443-0200
1455 Response Rd Ste 260 Sacramento (95815) ***(P-10549)***
Asterias Biotherapeutics Inc.....D.....510 456-3800
6300 Dumbarton Cir Fremont (94555) ***(P-26330)***
Astoria Convalescent Hospital.....C.....818 367-5881
14040 Astoria St Sylmar (91342) ***(P-20238)***
Astoria Nursing & Rehab Center, Sylmar *Also called Astoria Convalescent Hospital* ***(P-20238)***
Astoria Nursing and Rehab Ctr, Sylmar *Also called G and E Healthcare Svcs LLC* ***(P-20444)***
Astoria Software.....E.....415 956-3917
160 Spear St Ste 1100 San Francisco (94105) ***(P-15594)***
Astro Realty Inc.....D.....562 924-3381
11305 183rd St Cerritos (90703) ***(P-11223)***
Asus Computer International.....C.....510 739-3777
48720 Kato Rd Fremont (94538) ***(P-7010)***
Asylum, The, Glendale *Also called Global Asylum Incorporated* ***(P-18056)***
At & T Wireless Service, Tustin *Also called AB Cellular Holding LLC* ***(P-5441)***
At Home Caregivers, Novato *Also called Bear Flag Marketing Corp* ***(P-22235)***
At Road Inc (HQ).....B.....510 668-1638
888 Tasman Dr Milpitas (95035) ***(P-15916)***
At Your Home Familycare.....C.....858 625-0406
6540 Lusk Blvd Ste C266 San Diego (92121) ***(P-13717)***
At Your Svc Htg & Coolg LLC.....D.....602 550-6946
333 H St Ste 5000 Chula Vista (91910) ***(P-1470)***
AT&T, Artesia *Also called New Cingular Wireless Svcs Inc* ***(P-5611)***
AT&T Corp.....D.....714 965-4685
10035 Adams Ave Huntington Beach (92646) ***(P-5260)***
AT&T Corp.....D.....925 603-9476
2390 Monument Blvd Pleasant Hill (94523) ***(P-5261)***
AT&T Corp.....D.....415 970-8520
2410 Mission St San Francisco (94110) ***(P-5262)***
AT&T Corp.....D.....619 448-1798
50 Town Center Pkwy Santee (92071) ***(P-5263)***
AT&T Corp.....A.....415 442-2600
795 Folsom St San Francisco (94107) ***(P-5449)***
AT&T Corp.....D.....714 258-8290
2219 Park Ave Ste 8a Tustin (92782) ***(P-5264)***
AT&T Corp.....D.....909 646-9644
12379 S Mainstreet Rancho Cucamonga (91739) ***(P-5265)***
AT&T Corp.....D.....909 930-6508
2508 S Grove Ave Ontario (91761) ***(P-5266)***
AT&T Corp.....D.....626 912-0600
830 W Arrow Hwy San Dimas (91773) ***(P-5267)***
AT&T Corp.....D.....310 225-3028
20810 Avalon Blvd Carson (90746) ***(P-5268)***
AT&T Corp.....D.....949 364-4052
27762 Antonio Pkwy Ste L3 Ladera Ranch (92694) ***(P-5269)***
AT&T Corp.....D.....310 303-3888
1100 Pacific Coast Hwy # 5 Hermosa Beach (90254) ***(P-5270)***
AT&T Corp.....D.....323 589-7045
6833 Pacific Blvd Huntington Park (90255) ***(P-5271)***
AT&T Corp.....D.....949 559-1457
6328 Irvine Blvd Irvine (92620) ***(P-5272)***
AT&T Corp.....D.....310 473-3649
2333 S Sepulveda Blvd Los Angeles (90064) ***(P-5273)***
AT&T Corp.....D.....626 396-0100
83 E Colorado Blvd Pasadena (91105) ***(P-5274)***
AT&T Corp.....D.....805 562-0121
7060 Market Place Dr Goleta (93117) ***(P-5275)***
AT&T Corp.....D.....310 547-0400
980 N Western Ave Ste H San Pedro (90732) ***(P-5276)***
AT&T Corp.....D.....661 297-1720
26453 Bouquet Canyon Rd Santa Clarita (91350) ***(P-5277)***
AT&T Corp.....D.....714 284-3818
217 N Lemon St Rm 205 Anaheim (92805) ***(P-5278)***
AT&T Corp.....D.....661 799-0800
24935 Pico Canyon Rd Stevenson Ranch (91381) ***(P-5279)***
AT&T Corp.....D.....951 275-8801
3977 Chicago Ave Riverside (92507) ***(P-5280)***
AT&T Corp.....D.....323 568-2006
4332 Tweedy Blvd South Gate (90280) ***(P-5450)***
AT&T Corp.....D.....925 356-6204
2745 Cloverdale Ave Concord (94518) ***(P-5451)***
AT&T Corp.....D.....530 891-2025
3750 Morrow Ln Chico (95928) ***(P-5281)***
AT&T Corp.....D.....805 445-6562
1955 E Daily Dr Camarillo (93010) ***(P-5282)***
AT&T Corp.....D.....530 822-2700
1054 Harter Pkwy Ste 9 Yuba City (95993) ***(P-5283)***
AT&T Corp.....D.....760 752-3273
133 S Las Posas Rd # 141 San Marcos (92078) ***(P-5284)***
AT&T Corp.....D.....213 787-0055
624 S Grand Ave Ste 2940 Los Angeles (90017) ***(P-5452)***
AT&T Corp.....D.....415 721-1470
835 4th St San Rafael (94901) ***(P-5285)***
AT&T Corp.....D.....831 465-6771
1855 41st Ave Capitola (95010) ***(P-5286)***
AT&T Corp.....D.....805 583-9483
1263 Simi Town Center Way Simi Valley (93065) ***(P-5287)***
AT&T Corp.....D.....209 956-8324
1610 W Yosemite Ave Ste 2 Manteca (95337) ***(P-5453)***
AT&T Corp.....D.....858 693-0815
8225 Mira Mesa Blvd San Diego (92126) ***(P-5288)***
AT&T Corp.....D.....530 661-7724
1810 E Main St Woodland (95776) ***(P-5289)***
AT&T Corp.....D.....818 374-6458
6920 Van Nuys Blvd Rm 100 Van Nuys (91405) ***(P-5454)***
AT&T Corp.....D.....818 373-6896
14709 Vanoan St Van Nuys (91405) ***(P-5455)***
AT&T Corp.....D.....650 960-2313
1188 W Evelyn Ave Sunnyvale (94086) ***(P-27921)***
AT&T Corp.....D.....650 780-1005
1121 Jefferson Ave Rm 222 Redwood City (94063) ***(P-5456)***
AT&T Corp.....C.....415 394-3000
2600 Camino Ramon San Ramon (94583) ***(P-5457)***
AT&T Corp.....D.....323 874-7000
7100 Santa Monica Blvd # 125 West Hollywood (90046) ***(P-5290)***
AT&T Corp.....D.....925 327-7100
134 Sunset Dr San Ramon (94583) ***(P-5291)***
AT&T Corp.....D.....408 729-8400
1705 Story Rd San Jose (95122) ***(P-5292)***
AT&T Corp.....D.....408 871-3870
1546 Saratoga Ave San Jose (95129) ***(P-5293)***
AT&T Corp.....D.....949 622-8240
17675 Harvard Ave Ste B Irvine (92614) ***(P-5294)***
AT&T Corp.....D.....818 506-9118
6000 Lankershim Blvd North Hollywood (91606) ***(P-5295)***
AT&T Corp.....D.....925 275-8048
2600 Camino Ramon San Ramon (94583) ***(P-5458)***
AT&T Corp.....B.....925 560-5011
5130 Hacienda Dr Fl 1 Dublin (94568) ***(P-17015)***
AT&T Corp.....D.....310 659-7600
998 S Robertson Blvd # 103 Los Angeles (90035) ***(P-5296)***
AT&T Corp.....D.....818 997-5998
16201 Raymer St Van Nuys (91406) ***(P-27647)***
AT&T Corp.....A.....925 823-5388
2600 Camino Ramon 2w856 San Ramon (94583) ***(P-5459)***
AT&T Corp.....D.....714 666-5504
3925 E Coronado St Anaheim (92807) ***(P-5460)***
AT&T Corp.....C.....415 442-5900
50 Fremont St San Francisco (94105) ***(P-27538)***
AT&T Corp.....B.....916 830-5000
4130 S Market Ct Sacramento (95834) ***(P-5461)***
AT&T Corp.....D.....559 294-5431
3375 Peach Ave Clovis (93612) ***(P-5462)***
AT&T Corp.....D.....909 381-7729
455 W 2nd St San Bernardino (92401) ***(P-5463)***
AT&T Corp.....D.....408 980-2004
3025 Raymond St Santa Clara (95054) ***(P-5464)***
AT&T Corp.....D.....510 965-9714
2105 Macdonald Ave Richmond (94801) ***(P-5465)***
AT&T Corp.....D.....831 642-0100
400 Del Monte Ctr Monterey (93940) ***(P-5297)***
AT&T Corp.....D.....562 923-3032
8420 Firestone Blvd Downey (90241) ***(P-5298)***
AT&T Corp.....D.....415 276-0039
625 Ellis St Ste 205 Mountain View (94043) ***(P-5466)***
AT&T Corp.....D.....213 787-0055
700 S Flower St Ste 810 Los Angeles (90017) ***(P-5467)***
AT&T Corp.....D.....925 776-1200
2701 Verne Roberts Cir Antioch (94509) ***(P-5468)***
AT&T Datacomm LLC.....E.....714 675-9752
16755 Von Karman Ave # 120 Irvine (92606) ***(P-5469)***
AT&T Services.....D.....925 901-9318
2 Circle E Ranch Pl San Ramon (94583) ***(P-5470)***
AT&T Services Inc.....C.....619 515-5100
101 Broadway San Diego (92101) ***(P-5471)***
AT&T Services Inc.....C.....661 398-2000
4300 Ming Ave Bakersfield (93309) ***(P-5472)***
AT&T Services Inc.....D.....831 394-2690
161 Calle Del Oaks Monterey (93940) ***(P-5473)***

Mergent e-mail: customerrelations@mergent.com
1212
2019 Directory of California
Wholesalers and Services Companies
(P-0000) Products & Services Section entry number
(PA)=Parent Co (HQ)=Headquarters (DH)=Div Headquarters

AT&T Services Inc ... C ... 415 545-9051
610 Brannan St San Francisco (94107) ***(P-5474)***
AT&T Services Inc ... C ... 209 223-0012
303 Church St Jackson (95642) ***(P-5475)***
AT&T Services Inc ... B ... 559 454-3579
5555 E Olive Ave Ste A315 Fresno (93727) ***(P-5476)***
AT&T Services Inc ... B ... 661 327-6030
50101 Office Park Dr Bakersfield (93304) ***(P-5477)***
AT&T Services Inc ... C ... 210 886-4922
200 W Center Street Prome Anaheim (92805) ***(P-5478)***
AT&T Services Inc ... C ... 858 886-2762
7337 Trade St Rm 3600 San Diego (92121) ***(P-5479)***
AT&T Services Inc ... C ... 714 259-4441
1834 W Victoria Ave Anaheim (92804) ***(P-5480)***
AT&T Services Inc ... C ... 805 237-9503
908 28th St Paso Robles (93446) ***(P-5481)***
AT&T Services Inc ... C ... 951 369-2282
3580 Warm St Riverside (92501) ***(P-5482)***
AT&T Services Inc ... D ... 831 649-2029
787 Munras Ave Monterey (93940) ***(P-5483)***
AT&T Services Inc ... C ... 650 960-2255
360 Pioneer Way Mountain View (94041) ***(P-5484)***
AT&T Services Inc ... C ... 916 972-2248
3464 El Camino Ave Sacramento (95821) ***(P-5485)***
AT&T Services Inc ... D ... 626 578-4168
3280 E Foothill Blvd Pasadena (91107) ***(P-5486)***
AT&T Services Inc ... C ... 661 324-2046
5650 Aldrin Ct Bakersfield (93313) ***(P-27648)***
AT&T Services Inc ... A ... 213 975-4089
1010 Wilshire Blvd Los Angeles (90017) ***(P-5487)***
AT&T Services Inc ... A ... 925 823-1443
2600 Camino Ramon 2e750ll San Ramon (94583) ***(P-5488)***
AT&T Services Inc ... D ... 415 545-9058
666 Folsom St Rm 1132 San Francisco (94107) ***(P-5489)***
AT&T Services Inc ... B ... 510 836-6889
1270 Arroyo Way Walnut Creek (94596) ***(P-5490)***
AT&T Services Inc ... C ... 916 638-6096
2615 Mercantile Dr Rancho Cordova (95742) ***(P-5491)***
AT&T Services Inc ... C ... 707 545-5000
2125 Occidental Rd Santa Rosa (95401) ***(P-5492)***
AT&T Services Inc ... C ... 650 579-5266
1480 Burlingame Ave Burlingame (94010) ***(P-5493)***
AT&T Services Inc ... B ... 707 428-2512
1122 Western St Fairfield (94533) ***(P-5494)***
AT&T Services Inc ... E ... 213 741-3111
1900 S Grand Ave Rm 100 Los Angeles (90007) ***(P-5495)***
AT&T Services Inc ... C ... 408 554-3335
485 S Monroe St 13a San Jose (95128) ***(P-5496)***
AT&T Services Inc ... B ... 415 394-3000
140 New Montgomery St San Francisco (94105) ***(P-5497)***
AT&T Services Inc ... D ... 510 791-6605
44900 Industrial Dr Fremont (94538) ***(P-5498)***
AT&T Services Inc ... C ... 760 489-3519
146 S Broadway Escondido (92025) ***(P-5499)***
AT&T Services Inc ... D ... 714 992-3359
8925 Orangethorpe Ave Buena Park (90621) ***(P-5500)***
AT&T Services Inc ... D ... 925 671-1902
1714 Colfax St Ste 300 Concord (94520) ***(P-5501)***
AT&T Services Inc ... C ... 415 774-1957
2345 Pine St San Francisco (94115) ***(P-5502)***
AT&T Services Inc ... C ... 510 732-0830
7701 Artesia Blvd Buena Park (90621) ***(P-5503)***
AT&T Services Inc ... D ... 916 453-6267
1821 24th St Rm 122 Sacramento (95816) ***(P-5504)***
AT&T Services Inc ... C ... 760 722-7261
2727 Oceanside Blvd Oceanside (92054) ***(P-5505)***
AT&T Services Inc ... C ... 916 972-2423
3707 Kings Way Sacramento (95821) ***(P-5506)***
AT&T Services Inc ... B ... 925 671-1059
1033 Shary Cir Ste A Concord (94518) ***(P-5507)***
AT&T Services Inc ... B ... 858 495-3907
7650 Convoy Ct Ste 106 San Diego (92111) ***(P-5508)***
AT&T Services Inc ... B ... 760 489-3187
950 W Washington Ave Escondido (92025) ***(P-5509)***
AT&T Services Inc ... B ... 925 943-4383
1755 Locust St Fl 2 Walnut Creek (94596) ***(P-5510)***
AT&T Services Inc ... B ... 323 468-6813
1429 N Gower St Los Angeles (90028) ***(P-5511)***
AT&T Services Inc ... B ... 626 308-8582
501 S Marengo Ave Alhambra (91803) ***(P-5512)***
AT&T Services Inc ... C ... 415 823-0993
2600 Camino Ramon Rm 1-E San Ramon (94583) ***(P-5513)***
AT&T Services Inc ... C ... 510 645-7684
504 C 1550 Oakland (94612) ***(P-5514)***
AT&T Services Inc ... D ... 408 973-7504
5285 Doyle Rd Rm 3 San Jose (95129) ***(P-5515)***
AT&T Services Inc ... C ... 510 645-4507
1587 Franklin St Rm 1353 Oakland (94612) ***(P-5516)***
AT&T Services Inc ... C ... 916 376-2006
3900 Channel Dr West Sacramento (95691) ***(P-5517)***
AT&T Wireless, Santa Fe Springs *Also called New Cingular Wireless Svcs Inc* ***(P-5411)***
Ata Engineering Inc (PA) ... D ... 858 480-2000
13290 Evening Creek Dr S # 250 San Diego (92128) ***(P-25550)***
Atac (PA) ... D ... 408 736-2822
2770 De La Cruz Blvd Santa Clara (95050) ***(P-15917)***
Atascadero Hotel Partners LLC ... D ... 805 462-3500
900 El Camino Real Atascadero (93422) ***(P-12339)***
Atascadero State Hospital, Atascadero *Also called Califrnia Dept State Hospitals* ***(P-21935)***
Atc Services Inc ... B ... 213 593-8100
999 W Town And Country Rd Orange (92868) ***(P-26024)***
Atcaa, Jackson *Also called Amador Tlmne Cmnty Action Agcy* ***(P-24732)***
Atchesons Express Inc ... E ... 714 808-9199
1590 S Archibald Ave Ontario (91761) ***(P-3976)***
Atcr, Jackson *Also called Amador-Tolumne Cmnty Resources* ***(P-24734)***
Atech Logistics Inc ... C ... 707 526-1910
7 College Ave Santa Rosa (95401) ***(P-5013)***
Atech Warehousing & Dist Inc (PA) ... D ... 707 526-1910
7 College Ave Santa Rosa (95401) ***(P-4102)***
Atel Capital Group (PA) ... D ... 800 543-2835
600 Montgomery St Fl 9 San Francisco (94111) ***(P-9753)***
Atel Corporation ... D ... 415 989-8800
600 Montgomery St Ste 900 San Francisco (94111) ***(P-17016)***
Atelier Ace LLC ... E ... 503 546-6836
3191 Casitas Ave Ste 116 Los Angeles (90039) ***(P-14100)***
Aten Technology Inc ... D ... 949 428-1111
15365 Barranca Pkwy Irvine (92618) ***(P-7011)***
Athens Administrators, Concord *Also called Athens Insurance Service Inc* ***(P-10550)***
Athens Disposal Company Inc (PA) ... B ... 626 336-3636
14048 Valley Blvd La Puente (91746) ***(P-6348)***
Athens Environmental Services, Sun Valley *Also called Araco Enterprises LLC* ***(P-6339)***
Athens Insurance, Concord *Also called James C Jenkins Insur Svc Inc* ***(P-10658)***
Athens Insurance Service Inc ... C ... 925 826-1000
2552 Stanwell Dr Ste 100 Concord (94520) ***(P-10550)***
Athens Services, City of Industry *Also called Arakelian Enterprises Inc* ***(P-6341)***
Athens Services, City of Industry *Also called Arakelian Enterprises Inc* ***(P-6344)***
Athens Services, Sun Valley *Also called Arakelian Enterprises Inc* ***(P-3973)***
Atherton Baptist Homes ... C ... 626 863-1710
214 S Atlantic Blvd Alhambra (91801) ***(P-20239)***
Atherton Healthcare, Menlo Park *Also called Cal Care Inc* ***(P-26792)***
Athicon ... E ... 213 454-0662
6310 San Vicente Blvd Los Angeles (90048) ***(P-25551)***
Athletic Department, Stockton *Also called University of Pacific* ***(P-19254)***
Athletics Investment Group LLC (PA) ... C ... 510 638-4900
7000 Coliseum Way Ste 3 Oakland (94621) ***(P-18507)***
Athoc Inc (HQ) ... D ... 925 242-5660
3001 Bishop Dr Ste 400 San Ramon (94583) ***(P-15005)***
ATI, Danville *Also called Architrends Inc* ***(P-25543)***
ATI, Orange *Also called American Technologies Inc* ***(P-1116)***
ATI Architects & Engineers, Pleasanton *Also called Martin ATI-AC Inc* ***(P-26094)***
ATI Machinery Inc ... E ... 559 884-2471
21436 S Lassen Ave Five Points (93624) ***(P-7700)***
Atk Audiotek ... D ... 661 705-3700
28238 Avenue Crocker Valencia (91355) ***(P-2513)***
Atk Services, Valencia *Also called Atk Audiotek* ***(P-2513)***
Atk Space Systems Inc ... D ... 626 351-0205
370 N Halstead St Pasadena (91107) ***(P-26331)***
Atk Space Systems Inc ... B ... 858 621-5700
7130 Miramar Rd Ste 100b San Diego (92121) ***(P-26594)***
Atkins North America Inc ... D ... 858 874-1810
9275 Sky Park Ct Ste 200 San Diego (92123) ***(P-25552)***
Atkins North America Inc ... E ... 916 325-4800
332 Pine St Ste 500 San Francisco (94104) ***(P-27649)***
Atkinson And Ly Rd & Rm Lw (PA) ... C ... 562 653-3200
12800 Center Court Dr S # 300 Cerritos (90703) ***(P-22924)***
Atkinson Andelson Loya, Cerritos *Also called Atkinson And Ly Rd & Rm Lw* ***(P-22924)***
Atkinson Construction Inc ... B ... 303 410-2540
18201 Von Karman Ave # 800 Irvine (92612) ***(P-1726)***
Atkinson Youth Services Inc ... D ... 916 927-1863
4253 Balsam St Sacramento (95838) ***(P-23498)***
Atkinson Youth Services Inc (PA) ... D ... 916 257-0637
1906 El Camino Ave Sacramento (95815) ***(P-24422)***
Atkinson-Baker Inc (PA) ... C ... 818 551-7300
500 N Brand Blvd Fl 3 Glendale (91203) ***(P-14132)***
Atlanta Seafoods LLC ... D ... 626 626-4900
10501 Valley Blvd # 1820 El Monte (91731) ***(P-8570)***
Atlantic Aviation Svc ... E ... 408 297-7552
1250 Aviation Ave Hngr E2 San Jose (95110) ***(P-4873)***
Atlantic Express of California, Long Beach *Also called Atlantic Express Trnsp* ***(P-3773)***
Atlantic Express Trnsp ... C ... 562 997-6868
2450 Long Beach Blvd Long Beach (90806) ***(P-3773)***
Atlantic Mem Healthcare Assoc (PA) ... C ... 562 424-8101
2750 Atlantic Ave Long Beach (90806) ***(P-20240)***
ATLANTIC MEMORIAL HEALTHCARE C, Long Beach *Also called Atlantic Mem Healthcare Assoc* ***(P-20240)***
Atlantic Optical Co Inc ... D ... 818 407-1890
20801 Nordhoff St Chatsworth (91311) ***(P-7233)***
Atlantic Recording Corp ... B ... 818 238-6800
3400 W Olive Ave Burbank (91505) ***(P-17017)***
Atlas Advertising, Irvine *Also called M F Salta Co Inc* ***(P-27311)***
Atlas Construction Supply Inc (PA) ... D ... 858 277-2100
4640 Brinnell St San Diego (92111) ***(P-6877)***
Atlas Database Software Corp (PA) ... D ... 818 340-7080
26679 Agoura Rd Ste 200 Calabasas (91302) ***(P-15006)***
Atlas Development, Calabasas *Also called Atlas Database Software Corp* ***(P-15006)***
Atlas Digital LLC (PA) ... D ... 323 762-2626
170 S Flower St Burbank (91502) ***(P-18020)***
Atlas Disposal Industries LLC ... D ... 916 455-2800
3000 Power Inn Rd Sacramento (95826) ***(P-6349)***
Atlas Entertainment Inc ... E ... 310 786-4900
9200 W Sunset Blvd Ste 10 West Hollywood (90069) ***(P-18021)***
Atlas General Insur Svcs LLC ... C ... 858 529-6700
4365 Executive Dr Ste 400 San Diego (92121) ***(P-10551)***
Atlas Heating, San Jose *Also called American Residential Svcs LLC* ***(P-2111)***
Atlas Hospitality Group ... D ... 949 622-3400
1901 Main St Ste 175 Irvine (92614) ***(P-11224)***
Atlas International Inc ... E ... 714 622-1550
500 W Warner Ave Ste A Santa Ana (92707) ***(P-7610)***

Employee Codes: A=Over 500 employees, B=251-500
C=101-250, D=51-100, E=50

2019 Directory of California
Wholesalers and Services Companies

1213

Atlas Lift Tech Inc....C....415 283-1804
210 Porter Dr Ste 300 San Ramon (94583) ***(P-22739)***
ATLAS MOVER SERVICES, Rancho Dominguez *Also called Mover Services Inc* ***(P-3552)***
Atlas Security & Patrol Inc....E....510 791-7380
39465 Paseo Padre Pkwy # 2800 Fremont (94538) ***(P-16574)***
Atlas Security Inc....E....323 876-1401
11862 Balboa Blvd Ste 395 Granada Hills (91344) ***(P-16876)***
Atlas/Eastern Van Lines, Pomona *Also called W Why W Enterprises Inc* ***(P-4388)***
Atlassian Inc (HQ)....C....415 701-1110
1098 Harrison St San Francisco (94103) ***(P-15595)***
Atlaz Inc....D....415 671-6142
10721 Fair Oaks Blvd Fair Oaks (95628) ***(P-15007)***
Atrenta Inc (HQ)....D....408 453-3333
690 E Middlefield Rd Mountain View (94043) ***(P-15008)***
Atria Grand Oaks, Lake Forest *Also called Atria Senior Living Inc* ***(P-24424)***
Atria Park Pacific Palisades, Pacific Palisades *Also called Atria Senior Living Inc* ***(P-24423)***
Atria Senior Living Inc....D....310 573-9545
15441 W Sunset Blvd Pacific Palisades (90272) ***(P-24423)***
Atria Senior Living Inc....D....805 370-5400
22032 Arrowhead Ln Lake Forest (92630) ***(P-24424)***
Atria Senior Living Group Inc....D....805 482-9771
24 Las Posas Rd Camarillo (93010) ***(P-24425)***
Atria Senior Living Group Inc....C....949 661-1220
32353 San Juan Creek Rd San Juan Capistrano (92675) ***(P-24426)***
Atria Senior Living Group Inc....D....925 938-6611
1400 Montego Walnut Creek (94598) ***(P-24427)***
Atria Senior Living Group Inc....D....408 266-1660
1660 Gaton Dr Ofc San Jose (95125) ***(P-24428)***
Atria Senior Living Group Inc....E....415 892-0944
853 Tamalpais Ave Ofc Novato (94947) ***(P-24429)***
Atria Senior Living Group Inc....D....949 786-5665
33 Creek Rd Side Irvine (92604) ***(P-26769)***
Atria Senior Living Group Inc....D....916 488-5722
2426 Garfield Ave Ofc Carmichael (95608) ***(P-24430)***
Atria Senior Living Group Inc....D....760 341-0890
44600 Monterey Ave Ofc Palm Desert (92260) ***(P-24431)***
Atrilogy Solutions Group Inc (PA)....E....949 777-4700
23422 Mill Creek Dr # 105 Laguna Hills (92653) ***(P-27650)***
Atrium Capital Corp....A....650 233-7878
3000 Sand Hill Rd 2-130 Menlo Park (94025) ***(P-9914)***
Atrium Hotel, Irvine *Also called Golden Hotels Ltd Partnership* ***(P-12608)***
Atrium of San Jose, San Jose *Also called Brookdale Lving Cmmunities Inc* ***(P-24441)***
Atrium Plaza LLC....C....650 653-6000
1770 S Amphlett Blvd San Mateo (94402) ***(P-12340)***
Atsugi Kokusai Kanko USA Inc....D....951 924-4444
28095 John F Kennedy Dr Moreno Valley (92555) ***(P-18851)***
Attendant Care Referrals Inc....D....310 399-2904
2801 Ocean Park Blvd # 192 Santa Monica (90405) ***(P-22232)***
Attn Inc....C....323 413-2878
729 Seward St Los Angeles (90038) ***(P-13935)***
Attorney Recovery Systems Inc (PA)....D....818 774-1420
18757 Burbank Blvd # 300 Tarzana (91356) ***(P-13992)***
Attorneys At Law, Fresno *Also called Lang Richert & Patch* ***(P-23183)***
Atypon Systems LLC (PA)....D....408 988-1240
5201 Great America Pkwy # 510 Santa Clara (95054) ***(P-15596)***
Atyr Pharma Inc....D....858 731-8389
3545 John Hopkins Ct San Diego (92121) ***(P-26332)***
Auberge Du Soleil, Rutherford *Also called Terre Du Soleil Ltd* ***(P-13323)***
Auburn Constructors Inc....D....916 924-0344
730 W Stadium Ln Sacramento (95834) ***(P-2009)***
Auburn Gardens Care Center, Auburn *Also called Madera Convalescent Hospital* ***(P-21148)***
Auburn Oaks Care Center....D....650 949-7777
3400 Bell Rd Auburn (95603) ***(P-20241)***
Auburn Old Town Gallery....D....530 887-9150
218 Washington St Ste A Auburn (95603) ***(P-19105)***
Auburn Placer Disposal Service....D....530 885-3735
12305 Shale Ridge Ln Auburn (95602) ***(P-6350)***
Auburn Pride, Auburn *Also called Pride Industries* ***(P-24220)***
Auburn Ravine Terrace, Auburn *Also called Retirement Housing Foundation* ***(P-24651)***
Auburn Ravine Terrace, Auburn *Also called Congrgtnal Ch Retirement Cmnty* ***(P-11004)***
Auburn-Placer Recycling Center, Auburn *Also called Auburn Placer Disposal Service* ***(P-6350)***
Auchante Inc....D....562 231-1880
6730 Florence Ave Bell Gardens (90201) ***(P-11225)***
Auction.com, San Mateo *Also called Ten-X LLC* ***(P-11788)***
Auctioncom Inc....C....800 499-6199
1 Mauchly Ste 27 Irvine (92618) ***(P-11226)***
Auctioncom LLC (PA)....D....949 859-2777
1 Mauchly Irvine (92618) ***(P-11227)***
Auctiva Corporation....D....530 894-7400
360 E 6th St Chico (95928) ***(P-27651)***
Audaexplore, San Diego *Also called Audatex North America Inc* ***(P-15597)***
Audatex North America Inc (HQ)....C....858 946-1900
15030 Ave Of San Diego (92128) ***(P-15597)***
Audio Visual Headquarters (HQ)....E....310 603-0652
16320 Arthur St Cerritos (90703) ***(P-14474)***
Audio Visual MGT Solutions....C....714 590-8755
12812 Garden Grove Blvd M Garden Grove (92843) ***(P-26770)***
Audiobahn Inc....D....714 988-0400
114 S Berry St Brea (92821) ***(P-7443)***
Audioquest, Irvine *Also called Quest Group* ***(P-8051)***
Audiovisions, Lake Forest *Also called Inspiria Inc* ***(P-25748)***
Auditboard Inc (PA)....E....877 769-5444
12800 Center Court Dr S # 100 Cerritos (90703) ***(P-15009)***
Auditor Controller Department, San Bernardino *Also called County of San Bernardino* ***(P-26174)***
Audrey Adams MD....E....408 354-2114
718 University Ave # 211 Los Gatos (95032) ***(P-19312)***
Augmedix Inc....D....855 720-2929
1161 Mission St Ste 210 San Francisco (94103) ***(P-17018)***
Augustine Consulting Inc (PA)....D....831 920-1754
24560 Silver Cloud Ct # 102 Monterey (93940) ***(P-25553)***
Augustine Ideas, Roseville *Also called D Augustine & Associates* ***(P-13807)***
Aurora Algae Inc....D....510 266-5000
3325 Investment Blvd Hayward (94545) ***(P-26333)***
Aurora Behavioral Health....D....707 800-7700
1287 Fulton Rd Santa Rosa (95401) ***(P-21923)***
Aurora Behavioral Health Care....C....858 487-3200
11878 Avenue Of Industry San Diego (92128) ***(P-21924)***
Aurora Behavioral Hlth Care, San Diego *Also called Aurora Healthcare Inc* ***(P-21292)***
Aurora Healthcare Inc....E....858 487-3200
11878 Avenue Of Industry San Diego (92128) ***(P-21292)***
Aurora Las Encinas LLC....C....626 795-9901
2900 E Del Mar Blvd Pasadena (91107) ***(P-21925)***
Aurora Las Encinas Hospital, Pasadena *Also called Aurora Las Encinas LLC* ***(P-21925)***
Aurora Resurgence Fund LP....A....310 551-0101
10877 Wilshire Blvd # 2100 Los Angeles (90024) ***(P-12027)***
Aurora World Inc....C....562 205-1222
8820 Mercury Ln Pico Rivera (90660) ***(P-7944)***
Aus Decking Inc....D....916 373-5320
2999 Promenade St Ste 100 West Sacramento (95691) ***(P-3217)***
Ausenco PSI LLC (HQ)....D....925 939-4420
1320 Willow Pass Rd # 300 Concord (94520) ***(P-25554)***
Ausenco USA Inc (PA)....D....925 939-4420
1320 Willow Pass Rd Concord (94520) ***(P-25555)***
Ausgar Technologies Inc....C....855 428-7427
10721 Treena St San Diego (92131) ***(P-25556)***
Austin Veum Rbbins Prtners Inc (PA)....D....619 231-1960
501 W Broadway Ste A San Diego (92101) ***(P-26025)***
Authority Tax Services LLC....D....213 486-5135
777 S Figueroa St # 1900 Los Angeles (90017) ***(P-17019)***
Authorized Taxi Cab....D....323 776-5324
6150 W 96th St Los Angeles (90045) ***(P-16877)***
Autism Otrach Southern Cal LLC....D....619 795-9925
3110 Cmino Del Rio S 30 San Diego (92108) ***(P-23499)***
Autism Partnership Inc....D....562 431-9293
200 Marina Dr C Seal Beach (90740) ***(P-27145)***
Auto Body Management Inc....E....818 888-7654
7654 Tampa Ave Reseda (91335) ***(P-17712)***
Auto Buyline Systems Inc (PA)....E....909 881-7828
341 Corporate Terrace Cir Corona (92879) ***(P-6579)***
Auto Club Enterprises (PA)....A....714 850-5111
3333 Fairview Rd Msa451 Costa Mesa (92626) ***(P-10159)***
Auto Club Enterprises....B....310 914-8500
8761 Santa Monica Blvd West Hollywood (90069) ***(P-10160)***
Auto Club Speedway, Fontana *Also called California Speedway Corp* ***(P-18537)***
Auto Collection, Escondido *Also called Lincoln Witt Mercury* ***(P-17770)***
Auto Expressions LLC....D....310 639-0666
505 E Euclid Ave Compton (90222) ***(P-6622)***
Auto Insur Spcialists-Long Bch....D....562 496-2888
5000 E Spring St Ste 100 Long Beach (90815) ***(P-10552)***
Auto Insurance Specialists LLC (HQ)....C....562 345-6247
17785 Center Court Dr N # 110 Cerritos (90703) ***(P-10553)***
Auto Parts Group, Rancho Cordova *Also called Pick Pull Auto Dismantling Inc* ***(P-6703)***
Auto Parts Warehouse Inc (PA)....E....800 913-6119
16941 Keegan Ave Carson (90746) ***(P-6623)***
Auto Pride, Anaheim *Also called Cal-State Auto Parts Inc* ***(P-6629)***
Auto Repair Specialist, La Mesa *Also called C & D Towing Specialists Inc* ***(P-17854)***
Auto Strap Transport LLC (PA)....C....909 795-4088
15252 Slover Ave Fontana (92337) ***(P-5014)***
Auto Town Inc....D....209 473-2513
2150 E Hammer Ln Stockton (95210) ***(P-17754)***
Auto World Car Wash LLC....A....408 345-6532
15951 Los Gatos Blvd Los Gatos (95032) ***(P-17801)***
Autobody Depot, San Diego *Also called Tcp Global Corporation* ***(P-9190)***
Autocrib Inc....C....714 274-0400
2882 Dow Ave Tustin (92780) ***(P-17020)***
Autodesk Inc....D....415 356-0700
1 Market St San Francisco (94105) ***(P-15598)***
Autodesk Inc (PA)....B....415 507-5000
111 Mcinnis Pkwy San Rafael (94903) ***(P-15599)***
Autodesk Inc....C....415 507-5000
3950 Civic Center Dr San Rafael (94903) ***(P-15600)***
Autofarm, Fremont *Also called Novariant Inc* ***(P-25847)***
Autogenomics Inc....D....760 477-2248
1600 Faraday Ave Carlsbad (92008) ***(P-26334)***
Automate Parking Inc....D....310 674-3396
8405 Pershing Dr Ste 301 Playa Del Rey (90293) ***(P-17676)***
AUTOMATED CONTROLS AND TECHNIC, Bakersfield *Also called A-C Electric Company* ***(P-2497)***
Automated Ctrl Technical Svcs, Bakersfield *Also called A-C Electric Company* ***(P-25493)***
Automated Systems America Inc....D....877 500-0002
101 N Brand Blvd Ste 1230 Glendale (91203) ***(P-17936)***
Automatic Data Processing Inc....C....714 690-7000
7000 Village Dr Ste 200 Buena Park (90621) ***(P-16085)***
Automatic Data Processing Inc....C....800 225-5237
9445 Fairway View Pl # 200 Rancho Cucamonga (91730) ***(P-16086)***
Automatic Data Processing Inc....C....805 383-8630
5153 Camino Ruiz Ste 100 Camarillo (93012) ***(P-16087)***
Automatic Data Processing Inc....E....800 225-5237
600 California St Fl 11 San Francisco (94108) ***(P-16088)***
Automatic Data Processing Inc....C....909 592-6411
620 W Covina Blvd San Dimas (91773) ***(P-16089)***

Mergent e-mail: customerrelations@mergent.com
1214
2019 Directory of California Wholesalers and Services Companies
(P-0000) Products & Services Section entry number
(PA)=Parent Co (HQ)=Headquarters (DH)=Div Headquarters

Automatic Data Processing Inc...................C......800 225-5237
720 Bay Rd Redwood City (94063) (P-16090)
Automatic Data Processing Inc...................C......415 899-7300
505 San Marin Dr Ste A110 Novato (94945) (P-16091)
Automatic Data Processing Inc...................C......949 751-0360
3972 Barranca Pkwy J610 Irvine (92606) (P-16092)
Automatic Data Processing Inc...................B......408 876-6600
820 N Mccarthy Blvd # 120 Milpitas (95035) (P-16093)
Automatic Data Processing Inc...................D......714 994-2000
5355 Orangethorpe Ave La Palma (90623) (P-16094)
Automatic Data Processing Inc...................D......925 251-5300
4125 Hopyard Rd Pleasanton (94588) (P-16095)
Automatic Data Processing Inc...................C......800 225-5237
400 W Covina Blvd San Dimas (91773) (P-16096)
Automatic Data Processing Inc...................D......800 225-5237
600 Crprate Pinte Ste 450 Los Angeles (90230) (P-16097)
Automatic Data Processing Inc...................D......619 293-4800
1450 Frazee Rd Ste 601 San Diego (92108) (P-16098)
Automation Anywhere Inc (PA)....................D......888 484-3535
633 River Oaks Pkwy San Jose (95134) (P-7012)
Automation Engrg Systems Inc....................D......858 967-8650
10815 Rancho Bernardo Rd San Diego (92127) (P-15918)
Automattic Inc.................................D......877 273-3049
60 29th St Ste 343 San Francisco (94110) (P-5518)
Automobile Club Southern Cal (PA)...............C......213 741-3686
2601 S Figueroa St Los Angeles (90007) (P-10554)
Automobile Club Southern Cal....................E......818 997-6230
15503 Ventura Blvd # 150 Encino (91436) (P-25383)
Automobile Club Southern Cal....................D......310 325-3111
23001 Hawthorne Blvd Torrance (90505) (P-25384)
Automobile Club Southern Cal....................D......805 644-7171
1501 S Victoria Ave Ventura (93003) (P-25385)
Automobile Club Southern Cal....................E......626 963-8531
1301s S Grand Ave Glendora (91740) (P-25386)
Automobile Club Southern Cal....................E......661 327-4661
1500 Commercial Way Bakersfield (93309) (P-25387)
Automobile Club Southern Cal....................D......818 993-1616
9440 Reseda Blvd Northridge (91324) (P-25388)
Automobile Club Southern Cal....................E......818 883-2660
22708 Victory Blvd Woodland Hills (91367) (P-25389)
Automobile Club Southern Cal....................D......951 684-4250
3700 Central Ave Riverside (92506) (P-25390)
Automobile Club Southern Cal....................E......949 951-1400
25181 Paseo De Alicia Laguna Hills (92653) (P-25391)
Automobile Club Southern Cal....................C......714 885-1343
3333 Fairview Rd Costa Mesa (92626) (P-10555)
Automobile Club Southern Cal....................C......909 392-1444
2488 Foothill Blvd Ste A La Verne (91750) (P-25392)
Automobile Club Southern Cal....................C......760 247-4110
19201 Bear Valley Rd C Apple Valley (92308) (P-25393)
Automobile Club Southern Cal....................C......909 980-0233
10540 Fthill Blvd Ste 100 Rancho Cucamonga (91730) (P-10556)
Automobile Club Southern Cal....................C......858 481-7181
2666 Del Mar Heights Rd Del Mar (92014) (P-10557)
Automobile Club Southern Cal....................D......619 464-7001
8765 Fletcher Pkwy La Mesa (91942) (P-25394)
Automotive Expediters, Van Nuys Also called K Automotive Distributors (P-6650)
Automotive Service Council......................D......800 810-4272
10813 Airport Dr El Cajon (92020) (P-25395)
Automotive Services Division, Ontario Also called Securitas SEC Svcs USA Inc (P-16793)
Automotive Services Division, Northridge Also called Securitas SEC Svcs USA Inc (P-16813)
Automotive Sup Co Southern Cal (PA).............C......909 428-9072
10580 Mulberry Ave Fontana (92337) (P-6624)
Automotive Tstg & Dev Svcs Inc (PA).............C......909 390-1100
400 Etiwanda Ave Ontario (91761) (P-17851)
Autonomy Interwoven, Sunnyvale Also called Entco LLC (P-15668)
Autoreturn, San Francisco Also called Tegsco LLC (P-17875)
Autoweb Inc (PA)................................C......949 225-4500
18872 Macarthur Blvd Irvine (92612) (P-16209)
Autry Museum of American West...................C......323 667-2000
4700 Western Heritage Way Los Angeles (90027) (P-24866)
Autumn Hills Convalescent Home, Glendale Also called Mariner Health Care Inc (P-20619)
Auxiliary of Mission............................D......949 364-1400
27700 Medical Center Rd Mission Viejo (92691) (P-21293)
Auxilio Solutions, Inc., Mission Viejo Also called Ctek Solutions Inc (P-14084)
AV Brands Inc...................................E......410 884-9463
635 Broadway Ste 2 Sonoma (95476) (P-9031)
AV Builder Corp (PA)............................D......858 622-9200
6373 Nancy Ridge Dr San Diego (92121) (P-1266)
AV Management, Garden Grove Also called Audio Visual MGT Solutions (P-26770)
AV Occupational Medicine, Lancaster Also called Daniel O Mongiano MD A PR (P-19426)
Ava Enterprises Inc.............................E......805 988-0192
3451 Lunar Ct Oxnard (93030) (P-7409)
Ava The Rabbit Haven Inc........................D......831 600-7479
1261 S Mary St Scotts Valley (95067) (P-27652)
Avac, San Jose Also called Almaden Valley Athletic Club (P-18822)
Avadyne Health, San Diego Also called H & R Accounts Inc (P-15195)
Avalon A Cerritos...............................E......562 865-9500
11000 New Falcon Way Ofc # 177 Cerritos (90703) (P-23500)
Avalon At Newport, Newport Beach Also called Ventage Senior Housing (P-11131)
Avalon At Newport LLC...........................D......949 631-3555
393 Hospital Rd Newport Beach (92663) (P-24432)
Avalon At Newport Beach, Newport Beach Also called Avalon At Newport LLC (P-24432)
Avalon At Penasquitos Hills, Irvine Also called Avalonbay Communities Inc (P-11228)
Avalon Building Maintenance (PA)................C......714 693-2407
3148 E La Palma Ave Ste A Anaheim (92806) (P-14199)

Avalon Care Cen.................................D......209 723-1056
3170 M St Merced (95348) (P-20242)
Avalon Care Center..............................C......209 754-3823
900 Mountain Ranch Rd San Andreas (95249) (P-20243)
Avalon Care Center - Merced.....................D......209 722-6231
3169 M St Merced (95348) (P-20244)
Avalon Care Center - Modesto....................D......209 526-1775
1900 Coffee Rd Modesto (95355) (P-20245)
Avalon Care Ctr - Chwchlla LLC..................D......559 665-4826
1010 Ventura Ave Chowchilla (93610) (P-20246)
Avalon Care Ctr - Madera LLC....................D......559 673-9278
1700 Howard Rd Madera (93637) (P-20247)
Avalon Care Ctr - Modesto LLC...................D......209 529-0516
515 E Orangeburg Ave Modesto (95350) (P-20248)
Avalon Care Ctr - Newman LLC....................D......209 862-2862
709 N St Newman (95360) (P-20249)
Avalon Care Ctr - Sonora LLC....................D......209 533-2500
19929 Greenley Rd Sonora (95370) (P-20250)
Avalon Golden Gate LLC..........................D......415 664-6264
1601 19th Ave Apt 122 San Francisco (94122) (P-24433)
Avalon Health Care - Madera, Madera Also called Avalon Care Ctr - Madera LLC (P-20247)
AVALON HEALTH CARE GROUP, Sonora Also called Avalon Care Ctr - Sonora LLC (P-20250)
Avalon Hotel, Beverly Hills Also called Honeymoon Real Estate LP (P-12698)
Avalon Malibu, Malibu Also called Snb Corporation (P-24051)
Avalon Staffing, Westlake Village Also called Jackie Hoofring (P-14654)
Avalon Staffing LLC.............................D......925 626-7138
550 Harvest Park Dr Ste B Brentwood (94513) (P-14572)
Avalon Transportation Co, Culver City Also called Virgin Fish Inc (P-3857)
Avalonbay Communities Inc.......................E......949 955-6200
2050 Main St Ste 1200 Irvine (92614) (P-11228)
Avanquest North America Inc., Calabasas Also called Avanquest North America LLC (P-15010)
Avanquest North America LLC (HQ)................D......818 591-9600
23801 Calabasas Rd # 2005 Calabasas (91302) (P-15010)
Avanti Agency Corporation.......................B......714 935-0900
282 S Anita Dr Orange (92868) (P-17021)
Avanti Health System LLC........................B......310 356-0550
222 N Pacific Coast Hwy # 950 El Segundo (90245) (P-27146)
Avantica Technologies, Mountain View Also called Group Avantica Inc (P-15192)
Avantra Financial, Arcadia Also called Avantra Real Estate Services (P-11229)
Avantra Real Estate Services....................E......626 357-7028
148 E Fthill Blvd Ste 100 Arcadia (91006) (P-11229)
Avar Construction Inc...........................D......510 354-2000
47375 Fremont Blvd Fremont (94538) (P-1727)
Avar Construction Systems Inc (PA)..............E......510 354-2000
47375 Fremont Blvd Fremont (94538) (P-1875)
Avaya Inc (HQ)..................................C......908 953-6000
4655 Great America Pkwy Santa Clara (95054) (P-17022)
Avaya Inc.......................................C......949 225-5678
18201 Von Karman Ave # 600 Irvine (92612) (P-5519)
Ave Maria Convalescent Hosp.....................D......831 373-1216
1249 Josselyn Canyon Rd Monterey (93940) (P-20251)
Ave Maria Senior Living, Monterey Also called Ave Maria Convalescent Hosp (P-20251)
Avenidas (PA)...................................D......650 289-5400
4000 Middlefield Rd Ste I Palo Alto (94303) (P-23501)
Avenidas Senior Hlth Day Hlth, Palo Alto Also called Avenidas (P-23501)
Aveniu Brands, Sonoma Also called AV Brands Inc (P-9031)
Avenu Muniservices, Fresno Also called Muniservices LLC (P-27352)
Avenue H LLC....................................D......909 795-2476
35253 Avenue H Yucaipa (92399) (P-20252)
Avenue of Arts Wyndham Hotel, Costa Mesa Also called Rosanna Inc (P-13138)
Avenuesocial Inc................................C......510 275-4485
440 N Wolfe Rd Sunnyvale (94085) (P-15011)
Aver Information Inc............................E......408 263-3828
668 Mission Ct Fremont (94539) (P-7013)
Avery Corp......................................C......626 304-2000
207 N Goode Ave Fl 6 Glendale (91203) (P-26335)
Aveva Software LLC (HQ).........................B......949 727-3200
26561 Rancho Pkwy S Lake Forest (92630) (P-15919)
AVI Systems Inc.................................C......415 915-2070
44150 S Grimmer Blvd Fremont (94538) (P-7444)
Avia Tech LLC...................................D......858 777-5000
7220 Trade St Ste 300 San Diego (92121) (P-13793)
Aviar Golf Club, Carlsbad Also called Four Seasons Resort Aviara (P-18714)
Aviara Fsrc Associates Limited..................A......760 603-6800
7100 Aviara Resort Dr Carlsbad (92011) (P-12341)
Aviara Resort Associates (PA)...................A......760 448-1234
7100 Aviara Resort Dr Carlsbad (92011) (P-12342)
Aviation & Defense Inc..........................C......909 382-3487
255 S Leland Norton Way San Bernardino (92408) (P-4874)
Aviation Consultants Inc (PA)...................D......805 548-1300
945 Airport Dr San Luis Obispo (93401) (P-26771)
Aviation Port Services LLC, San Leandro Also called Aviation Port Services LLc (P-4724)
Aviation Port Services LLc......................D......510 636-8790
2081 Adams Ave San Leandro (94577) (P-4724)
Aviation Safeguards, Los Angeles Also called Command Security Corporation (P-16610)
Aviation Safeguards, San Jose Also called Command Security Corporation (P-16611)
Avida Caregivers Inc............................A......323 498-1500
11500 W Olympic Blvd # 400 Los Angeles (90064) (P-22233)
Avionics & Electronics, Valencia Also called Curtiss-Wright Controls (P-25634)
Avis Budget Car Rentals, San Leandro Also called Avis Rent A Car System Inc (P-17624)
Avis Rent A Car System Inc......................D......909 974-2192
3450 E Airport Dr Ste 500 Ontario (91761) (P-17623)
Avis Rent A Car System Inc......................C......510 562-8828
390 Doolittle Dr San Leandro (94577) (P-17624)

Employee Codes: A=Over 500 employees, B=251-500
C=101-250, D=51-100, E=50

2019 Directory of California
Wholesalers and Services Companies

© Mergent Inc. 1-800-342-5647

1215

Avis Rent A Car System Inc...D....510 577-6360
1 Airport Dr Oakland (94621) *(P-17625)*
Avis Rent A Car System Inc...C....916 922-5601
6520 Mcnair Cir Sacramento (95837) *(P-17626)*
Avis Rent A Car System Inc...D....650 616-0150
513 Eccles Ave Ste A South San Francisco (94080) *(P-17627)*
Avis Rent A Car System Inc...D....818 566-3001
4209 W Vanowen Pl Burbank (91505) *(P-17628)*
Avis Rent A Car Systems, Sacramento *Also called Avis Rent A Car System Inc (P-17626)*
Avita Medical Americas LLC...D....661 367-9170
28159 Ave Stnford Ste 220 Valencia (91355) *(P-7158)*
Avitas Systems Inc...D....650 233-3900
2882 Sand Hill Rd Ste 240 Menlo Park (94025) *(P-17023)*
Aviva Center, Los Angeles *Also called Hamburger Home (P-24546)*
Aviva Systems Biology Corp (PA)...D....858 552-6979
7700 Ronson Rd Ste 100 San Diego (92111) *(P-26336)*
Avnet Inc...D....949 789-4100
220 Commerce Ste 100 Irvine (92602) *(P-7445)*
Avnet Inc...D....818 594-8310
20951 Burbank Blvd Ste A Woodland Hills (91367) *(P-7446)*
Avnet Inc...D....408 501-3925
2110 Zanker Rd San Jose (95131) *(P-7447)*
Avnet Inc...B....760 946-5030
1400 Montefino Ave # 100 Diamond Bar (91765) *(P-7448)*
Avnet Inc...B....858 385-7500
15231 Avenue Of Science # 150 San Diego (92128) *(P-7449)*
Avnet Computers, Irvine *Also called Avnet Inc (P-7445)*
Avnet Computers, Woodland Hills *Also called Avnet Inc (P-7446)*
Avnet Computers, San Jose *Also called Avnet Inc (P-7447)*
Avnet Computers, San Diego *Also called Avnet Inc (P-7449)*
Avoca Productions Inc...D....310 244-4000
10202 Washington Blvd Culver City (90232) *(P-18022)*
Avocado Post Acute, El Cajon *Also called Eldorado Care Center LP (P-20388)*
Avolent Inc...D....415 553-6400
444 De Haro St Ste 100 San Francisco (94107) *(P-15601)*
Avongard Products USa Ltd...E....310 319-2300
12777 W Jefferson Blvd # 100 Los Angeles (90066) *(P-18179)*
Aware Point, San Diego *Also called Awarepoint Corporation (P-15012)*
Awarepoint Corporation (PA)...D....858 345-5000
600 W Broadway Ste 250 San Diego (92101) *(P-15012)*
Awe, San Diego *Also called Herring Networks Inc (P-5799)*
AWH Burbank Hotel LLC...C....813 843-6000
2500 N Hollywood Way Burbank (91505) *(P-12343)*
AWR, San Dimas *Also called Golden State Water Company (P-6258)*
Awt Construction Group Inc...D....707 746-7500
4740 E 2nd St Ste 22 Benicia (94510) *(P-1121)*
Axa Advisors LLC...D....213 251-1600
3435 Wilshire Blvd # 2500 Los Angeles (90010) *(P-10058)*
Axa Advisors LLC...D....415 276-2100
88 Kearny St Fl 20 San Francisco (94108) *(P-27147)*
Axa Advisors LLC...D....619 239-0018
701 B St Ste 1500 San Diego (92101) *(P-10130)*
Axa Equitable Life Insur Co...D....858 552-1234
3777 La Jolla Village Dr San Diego (92122) *(P-10558)*
Axaio Industries LLC...E....323 504-1074
538 S Oxford Ave Apt 302 Los Angeles (90020) *(P-5520)*
Axcient Inc (HQ)...D....650 314-7300
1161 San Antonio Rd Mountain View (94043) *(P-15013)*
Axiom Global Technologies Inc...C....925 393-5800
220 N Wiget Ln Walnut Creek (94598) *(P-27653)*
Axiom Home Warranty LLC...C....844 562-9466
2015 Manhattan B Redondo Beach (90278) *(P-10422)*
Axiom Memory Solutions Inc...D....949 581-1450
15 Chrysler Irvine (92618) *(P-7014)*
Axis, Culver City *Also called Rick Solomon Enterprises Inc (P-8276)*
Axis Community Health Inc...D....925 462-1755
4361 Railroad Ave Pleasanton (94566) *(P-22509)*
Axis Construction, Hayward *Also called Axis Services Inc (P-1267)*
Axis Services Inc...C....510 732-6111
2566 Barrington Ct Hayward (94545) *(P-1267)*
Axminster Medical Group Inc (PA)...D....310 670-3255
11539 Hawthorne Blvd Fl 6 Hawthorne (90250) *(P-19313)*
Axonics Modulation Tech Inc...D....949 396-6322
26 Technology Dr Irvine (92618) *(P-26337)*
Aya Healthcare Inc (PA)...D....858 458-4410
5930 Cornerstone Ct W # 300 San Diego (92121) *(P-14821)*
Ayala Corporation...C....559 867-5700
21510 S Chteau Fresno Ave Riverdale (93656) *(P-14573)*
Ayala Drywall...E....805 487-3392
2600 Alexander St Oxnard (93033) *(P-2847)*
Ayala Farms, Riverdale *Also called Ayala Corporation (P-14573)*
Ayco Company LP...C....949 955-1544
17885 Von Karman Ave # 300 Irvine (92614) *(P-10059)*
Aylesva Inc...C....562 688-0592
14537 Garfield Ave Paramount (90723) *(P-8344)*
Ayoob & Peery Plumbing Co Inc...D....415 550-0975
975 Indiana St San Francisco (94107) *(P-2132)*
Ayres - Chino Hills, Chino Hills *Also called Ayres Group (P-12345)*
Ayres Group...D....310 220-6447
14400 Hindry Ave Hawthorne (90250) *(P-12344)*
Ayres Group...D....909 631-2922
4785 Chino Hills Pkwy Chino Hills (91709) *(P-12345)*
Ayres Group (PA)...D....714 540-6060
355 Bristol St Costa Mesa (92626) *(P-12346)*
Ayres Hotel Laguna Woods, Laguna Woods *Also called Countryside Inn-Corona LP (P-12486)*
Ayres Hotel Manhattan Beach, Hawthorne *Also called Ayres Group (P-12344)*
Ayzenberg Group Inc...D....626 584-4070
49 E Walnut St Pasadena (91103) *(P-13794)*
AZ West, Compton *Also called Az/CFS West Inc (P-4665)*
Az/CFS West Inc...D....310 898-2090
250 W Manville St Compton (90220) *(P-4665)*
Azalea & Rose Co...E....909 949-2442
1420 N Campus Ave Upland (91786) *(P-242)*
Azcona Harvesting LLC...C....831 674-2526
44 El Camino Real Unit A Greenfield (93927) *(P-473)*
Azimc Investments Inc (HQ)...C....818 678-6571
8901 Canoga Ave Canoga Park (91304) *(P-6625)*
Aztec Engineering Group Inc...D....951 471-6190
2151 Michelson Dr Ste 100 Irvine (92612) *(P-25557)*
Aztec Harvesting...A....760 922-7348
1075 N Broadway Blythe (92225) *(P-639)*
Aztec Landscaping Inc (PA)...C....619 464-3303
7980 Lemon Grove Way Lemon Grove (91945) *(P-802)*
Aztec Sheet Metal Inc...D....619 937-0005
11222 Woodside Ave N Santee (92071) *(P-3126)*
Aztlan Graphics, Chico *Also called Gonzales Enterprises Inc (P-8262)*
Azubu North America Inc...E....310 759-9529
15303 Ventura Blvd # 900 Sherman Oaks (91403) *(P-7945)*
Azumio Inc (PA)...C....719 310-3774
230 California Ave # 212 Palo Alto (94306) *(P-15014)*
Azure Acres, Sebastopol *Also called Camp Recovery Centers LP (P-22001)*
B & B Concrete, Santa Clara *Also called Robert A Bothman Inc (P-3317)*
B & B Nurseries Inc...C....951 352-8383
9505 Cleveland Ave Riverside (92503) *(P-9124)*
B & B Plastics Recyclers Inc (PA)...D....909 829-3606
3040 N Locust Ave Rialto (92377) *(P-7970)*
B & B Specialties Inc...D....714 985-3075
4321 E La Palma Ave Anaheim (92807) *(P-7579)*
B & B Specialty Metals, Bakersfield *Also called B & B Surplus Inc (P-7260)*
B & B Surplus Inc (PA)...D....661 589-0381
7020 Rosedale Hwy Bakersfield (93308) *(P-7260)*
B & C, Oakland *Also called B&C Transit Inc (P-25558)*
B & E Convalescent Center Inc (PA)...D....562 923-9449
11627 Telg Rd Ste 200 Santa Fe Springs (90670) *(P-21001)*
B & E Farms Inc...E....714 893-8166
9112 Mcfadden Ave Westminster (92683) *(P-91)*
B & G Delivery System Inc...C....916 921-4401
2549 Harris Ave Sacramento (95838) *(P-3977)*
B & K Electric Wholesale (PA)...D....626 965-5040
1225 S Johnson Dr City of Industry (91745) *(P-7335)*
B & L Consulting LLC...D....682 238-6994
164 N 2nd Ave 9 Upland (91786) *(P-27654)*
B & M Contractors Inc...D....805 581-5480
4473 Cochran St Simi Valley (93063) *(P-3218)*
B & M Racing, Santa Rosa *Also called Driven Performance Brands Inc (P-6636)*
B & R Farm Labor Contractor...C....805 524-1346
422 Mockingbird Ln Fillmore (93015) *(P-14574)*
B & R Tevelde...D....559 583-1277
2911 Hanford Armona Rd Hanford (93230) *(P-406)*
B A M I Inc...E....530 343-5678
1293 E 1st Ave Chico (95926) *(P-18575)*
B A S, Diamond Bar *Also called Tetra Tech Bas Inc (P-25948)*
B A Technolinks Corporation...D....408 940-5921
4677 Old Ironsides Dr # 440 Santa Clara (95054) *(P-27148)*
B B & K Fund Services Inc...E....650 571-5800
950 Tower Ln Ste 1900 Foster City (94404) *(P-9915)*
B B & K Holdings (PA)...E....650 571-5800
950 Tower Ln Ste 1900 Foster City (94404) *(P-10060)*
B B & T Management Corp...C....916 428-8060
1453 Blair Ave Sacramento (95822) *(P-6809)*
B B G Management Group (PA)...D....909 797-9581
12164 California St Yucaipa (92399) *(P-8543)*
B B S I, San Diego *Also called Barrett Business Services Inc (P-22935)*
B Boston & Associates Inc (PA)...C....323 264-3915
4871 S Santa Fe Ave Vernon (90058) *(P-8285)*
B C C S Inc (PA)...D....408 379-5500
1711 Dell Ave Campbell (95008) *(P-1471)*
B C Life & Health Insurance Co...D....818 703-2345
21555 Oxnard St Woodland Hills (91367) *(P-10161)*
B C Rentals Inc...D....714 974-1190
638 W Southern Ave Orange (92865) *(P-7728)*
B C S, Canoga Park *Also called Buyers Consultation Svc Inc (P-7453)*
B E Giovannetti & Sons (PA)...E....530 662-1729
403 Court St Woodland (95695) *(P-1)*
B F C Inc...C....415 495-3085
675 Davis St San Francisco (94111) *(P-2514)*
B F Management...D....323 931-7776
117 N Fuller Ave Los Angeles (90036) *(P-11230)*
B H C Alhambra Hospital, Rosemead *Also called Psychiatric Solutions Inc (P-22657)*
B H R Operations LLC...D....408 321-9500
777 Bellew Dr Milpitas (95035) *(P-12347)*
B I A, Emeryville *Also called Behavioral Intervention Assn (P-14824)*
B Jacqueline and Assoc Inc...B....626 844-1400
1192 N Lake Ave Pasadena (91104) *(P-15015)*
B L S Limousine Service, Los Angeles *Also called Bls Lmsine Svc Los Angeles Inc (P-3779)*
B M D, Galt *Also called Building Material Distrs Inc (P-6813)*
B M S, Irvine *Also called Bankruptcy MGT Solutions Inc (P-22932)*
B N E U S A, City of Industry *Also called Ettv America Corp (P-5912)*
B N I, Upland *Also called Bni Enterprises Inc (P-27543)*
B O S S, Berkeley *Also called Building Opportunities (P-23521)*
B R Funsten & Co...D....209 825-5375
105 Lndustrial Park Manteca (95337) *(P-6748)*
B R Funsten & Co...D....707 863-8300
5200 Watt Ct Ste B Fairfield (94534) *(P-6749)*

B Riley Financial Inc (PA)......C......818 884-3737
21255 Burbank Blvd # 400 Woodland Hills (91367) ***(P-17024)***
B S A Partners......D......714 523-2800
14419 Firestone Blvd La Mirada (90638) ***(P-12348)***
B S Hand & Sons Inc......E......818 983-1155
4450 Shopping Ln Simi Valley (93063) ***(P-3219)***
B S I Holdings Inc......A......831 622-1840
100 Clock Tower Pl # 200 Carmel (93923) ***(P-2848)***
B S K Analytical Laboratories, Fresno *Also called BSK Associates* ***(P-25583)***
B S R, San Francisco *Also called Business For Scial Rspnsbility* ***(P-27175)***
B T & T Travel Inc......D......559 237-9410
2609 E Mckinley Ave Ste N Fresno (93703) ***(P-4932)***
B T B Events Inc......D......714 415-3313
10950 Virginia Cir Fountain Valley (92708) ***(P-27539)***
B T Mancini Co Inc (PA)......B......408 942-7900
876 S Milpitas Blvd Milpitas (95035) ***(P-3095)***
B T W, West Sacramento *Also called Bytheways Manufacturing Inc* ***(P-6754)***
B Z Plumbing Company Inc......C......916 645-1600
1901 Aviation Blvd Lincoln (95648) ***(P-2133)***
B&B Industrial Services Inc (PA)......D......909 428-3167
14549 Manzanita Dr Fontana (92335) ***(P-2796)***
B&C Transit Inc (PA)......D......510 483-3560
1924 Franklin St Ste 200 Oakland (94612) ***(P-25558)***
B-Per Electronic Inc......D......626 912-0600
1600 N Brwy Santa Ana (92706) ***(P-5299)***
B-Spring Valley LLC......D......619 797-3991
9009 Campo Rd Spring Valley (91977) ***(P-20253)***
B.T. Mancini Company, Milpitas *Also called B T Mancini Co Inc* ***(P-3095)***
B2b Payroll Services, Cypress *Also called B2b Staffing Services Inc* ***(P-14822)***
B2b Staffing Services Inc......B......714 243-4104
4501 Cerritos Ave Ste 201 Cypress (90630) ***(P-14822)***
Ba Leasing & Capital Corp (HQ)......C......415 765-1804
555 California St Fl 4 San Francisco (94104) ***(P-14475)***
Baart Behavioral Hlth Svcs Inc......D......415 928-7800
433 Turk St San Francisco (94102) ***(P-22510)***
Baart Community Healthcare......D......415 928-7800
433 Turk St San Francisco (94102) ***(P-22511)***
Baaz Global, San Francisco *Also called Baaz Inc* ***(P-15016)***
Baaz Inc......D......408 621-6912
1 Hallidie Plz Ste 200 San Francisco (94102) ***(P-15016)***
Babcock & Brown Elec MGT LLC......C......858 587-5820
4350 La Jolla Village Dr San Diego (92122) ***(P-27149)***
Babcock & Brown Holdings Inc (HQ)......C......415 512-1515
1 Pier Ste 3 San Francisco (94111) ***(P-9916)***
Babcock & Brown Latin America......D......415 512-1515
2 Harrison St Fl 6 San Francisco (94105) ***(P-9754)***
Babcock Laboratories Inc......D......951 653-3351
6100 Quail Valley Ct Riverside (92507) ***(P-26684)***
Babe's Bbq Grill, Newport Beach *Also called Donald Lucky LLC* ***(P-26843)***
Babycenter LLC (HQ)......E......415 537-0900
163 Freelon St San Francisco (94107) ***(P-13718)***
Babyfirst Americas LLC......D......310 442-9853
10390 Santa Monica Blvd Los Angeles (90025) ***(P-15017)***
Bacchus Vineyard MGT LLC......D......707 837-8304
1720 River Rd Fulton (95439) ***(P-26772)***
Bacci Glinn Physcl Therapy Inc......E......559 733-2478
5533 W Hillsdale Ave A Visalia (93291) ***(P-20164)***
Bachelor Productions Inc......D......310 567-9249
2121 Avenue Of The Stars Los Angeles (90067) ***(P-18023)***
Bachem Americas Inc......D......760 597-8820
1271 Avenida Chelsea Vista (92081) ***(P-8920)***
Back Street Fitness Inc......E......707 254-7200
3175 California Blvd NAPA (94558) ***(P-18576)***
Backproject Corporation......D......408 730-1111
170 N Wolfe Rd Sunnyvale (94086) ***(P-7159)***
Backroads (PA)......B......510 527-1555
801 Cedar St Berkeley (94710) ***(P-4963)***
Backweb Technologies Inc......E......408 933-1700
2727 Walsh Ave Ste 102 Santa Clara (95051) ***(P-7015)***
Baco Realty Corporation......D......916 974-9898
6310 Stockton Blvd Sacramento (95824) ***(P-16575)***
Baco Realty Corporation......D......925 275-0100
2071 Camino Ramon San Ramon (94583) ***(P-4532)***
Bacome Insurance Agency, Fresno *Also called James G Parker Insurance Assoc* ***(P-10659)***
Bacon's Multivision, Oakland *Also called Multivision Inc* ***(P-17339)***
Bacr, San Francisco *Also called Ruth Barajas* ***(P-24000)***
Bad Boys Bail Bonds Inc (PA)......D......408 298-3333
595 Park Ave Ste 200 San Jose (95110) ***(P-17025)***
Badalian Enterprises Inc......D......714 635-4082
1540 S Harbor Blvd Anaheim (92802) ***(P-12349)***
Badger Farming Company Inc......D......559 592-5520
150 W Pine St Exeter (93221) ***(P-202)***
Badgeville Inc......E......650 323-6668
805 Veterans Blvd Ste 307 Redwood City (94063) ***(P-15602)***
Bae Sys Sierra Detroit Allison (HQ)......D......510 635-8991
1755 Adams Ave San Leandro (94577) ***(P-17755)***
Baechler Investigative Svcs......D......619 464-5600
1935 N Marshall Ave Ste C El Cajon (92020) ***(P-16576)***
Baer Institute, Moffett Field *Also called Bay Area Envmtl Res Inst* ***(P-26595)***
Bagatelos Glass Systems Inc (PA)......D......916 364-3600
2750 Redding Ave Sacramento (95820) ***(P-3402)***
Bagatlos Archtctral GL Systems, Sacramento *Also called Bagatelos Glass Systems Inc* ***(P-3402)***
Bagley, William T, San Francisco *Also called Nossaman LLP* ***(P-23293)***
Bahia Resort Hotels, San Diego *Also called Bh Partn A Calif Limit Partne* ***(P-12383)***
Bahia Sternwheelers Inc......E......858 539-7720
998 W Mission Bay Dr San Diego (92109) ***(P-4709)***
Baid Vivek......D......888 550-8553
2335 Irvine Ave Newport Beach (92660) ***(P-5521)***
Bail Hotline Bail Bonds, Riverside *Also called Dmcg Inc* ***(P-17133)***
Bailard, Foster City *Also called B B & K Holdings* ***(P-10060)***
Bailard Inc (HQ)......E......650 571-5800
950 Tower Ln Ste 1900 Foster City (94404) ***(P-10061)***
Bailey, Rollin C MD, Lompoc *Also called Valley Medical Group of Lompoc* ***(P-20044)***
Bain & Company Inc......D......310 229-3000
1901 Ave Of The Sts 200 Los Angeles (90067) ***(P-27150)***
Bain & Company Inc......C......415 627-1000
1 Embarcadero Ctr # 3500 San Francisco (94111) ***(P-27151)***
Bainbridge Inc (PA)......D......858 638-1800
4435 Estgate Mall Ste 130 San Diego (92121) ***(P-27152)***
Baird-Neece Packing Corp......C......559 784-3393
60 S E St Porterville (93257) ***(P-494)***
Baja Construction Co Inc (PA)......D......925 229-0732
223 Foster St Martinez (94553) ***(P-3361)***
Baja Freight Forwarders Inc (PA)......D......619 671-3100
8662 Siempre Viva Rd San Diego (92154) ***(P-5015)***
Baja Life Online Partners......E......949 376-4619
P.O. Box 4917 Laguna Beach (92652) ***(P-15018)***
Bakbone Software Inc (HQ)......D......858 450-9009
9540 Towne Centre Dr # 100 San Diego (92121) ***(P-15019)***
Baker Keener & Nahra......E......213 241-0900
633 W 5th St Ste 5500 Los Angeles (90071) ***(P-22925)***
Baker & Hostetler LLP......D......310 820-8800
11601 Wilshire Blvd Fl 14 Los Angeles (90025) ***(P-22926)***
Baker & McKenzie LLP......C......415 576-3000
2 Embarcadero Ctr # 1100 San Francisco (94111) ***(P-22927)***
Baker & McKenzie LLP......D......650 856-2400
660 Hansen Way Ste 1 Palo Alto (94304) ***(P-22928)***
Baker & Taylor LLC......C......858 457-2500
10350 Barnes Canyon Rd # 100 San Diego (92121) ***(P-9109)***
Baker Distributing Company LLC......D......760 708-4201
241 Market Pl Escondido (92029) ***(P-7644)***
Baker Hghes Olfld Oprtions LLC......E......661 834-9654
5700 Doolittle Ave Shafter (93263) ***(P-1048)***
Baker Hughes A GE Company LLC......D......661 387-1010
1127 Carrier Parkway Ave Bakersfield (93308) ***(P-1049)***
Baker Hughes A GE Company LLC......D......661 831-7686
3901 Fanucchi Way Shafter (93263) ***(P-1050)***
Baker Hughes A GE Company LLC......D......800 229-7447
5145 Boylan St Bakersfield (93308) ***(P-1051)***
Baker Keener & Nahra, Los Angeles *Also called Baker Keener & Nahra* ***(P-22925)***
Baker Mnock Jensen A Prof Corp......C......559 432-5400
5260 N Palm Ave Ste 421 Fresno (93704) ***(P-22929)***
Baker Mnock Jnsen Attys At Law, Fresno *Also called Baker Mnock Jensen A Prof Corp* ***(P-22929)***
Baker Petrolite LLC......D......661 325-4138
5125 Boylan St Bakersfield (93308) ***(P-1052)***
Baker Places Inc......C......415 503-3137
101 Gough St San Francisco (94102) ***(P-22512)***
Baker Places Inc (PA)......C......415 864-4655
1000 Brannan St Ste 401 San Francisco (94103) ***(P-24434)***
Baker Winokur......D......310 248-6169
9100 Wilshire Blvd 500w Beverly Hills (90212) ***(P-27540)***
Baker Winokur Ryder, Beverly Hills *Also called Bwr Public Relations* ***(P-27544)***
Bakercorp (HQ)......C......562 430-6262
3020 Old Ranch Pkwy # 220 Seal Beach (90740) ***(P-14476)***
Bakersfield Assc Rtrd Ctzns......C......661 834-2272
2240 S Union Ave Bakersfield (93307) ***(P-24155)***
Bakersfield Community Based, Bakersfield *Also called Veterans Health Administration* ***(P-20082)***
Bakersfield Country Club......D......661 871-4000
4200 Country Club Dr Bakersfield (93306) ***(P-18852)***
Bakersfield District Office, Bakersfield *Also called State Compensation Insur Fund* ***(P-10396)***
Bakersfield Family Med Group......D......661 846-3605
5601 Auburn St Unit A Bakersfield (93306) ***(P-22740)***
Bakersfield Family Medical Ctr, Bakersfield *Also called Heritage Medical Group* ***(P-19499)***
Bakersfield Healthcare......D......661 872-2121
2211 Mount Vernon Ave Bakersfield (93306) ***(P-20254)***
Bakersfield Kitchen & Bath......D......661 836-2284
3529 Pegasus Dr Bakersfield (93308) ***(P-2134)***
Bakersfield Memorial Hospital......A......661 327-1792
420 34th St Bakersfield (93301) ***(P-21294)***
Bakersfield Moving & Storage......E......661 397-4521
3820 Herring Rd Arvin (93203) ***(P-4331)***
Bakersfield Symphony Orch......D......661 323-7928
1328 34th St Ste A Bakersfield (93301) ***(P-18424)***
Bakersfield Vet Center, Bakersfield *Also called Veterans Health Administration* ***(P-20084)***
Bakery Ex Southern Cal LLC......D......714 446-9470
1910 W Malvern Ave Fullerton (92833) ***(P-8758)***
Bakkavor Foods Usa Inc (HQ)......B......704 522-1977
18201 Central Ave Carson (90746) ***(P-8759)***
Balance Staffing, San Jose *Also called Staffing Solutions Inc* ***(P-14770)***
Balance4kids......D......831 464-8669
4500 Soquel Dr Soquel (95073) ***(P-25096)***
Balboa Bay Club Inc (HQ)......B......949 645-5000
1221 W Coast Hwy Ste 145 Newport Beach (92663) ***(P-18853)***
Balboa Bay Club and Resort, Newport Beach *Also called International Bay Clubs LLC* ***(P-18938)***
Balboa Capital Corporation (PA)......C......949 756-0800
575 Anton Blvd Fl 12 Costa Mesa (92626) ***(P-9704)***
Balboa Enterprises Inc......C......650 961-6161
2530 Solace Pl Mountain View (94040) ***(P-20255)***
Balboa Plaza Admin Offices, Granada Hills *Also called Kaiser Foundation Hospitals* ***(P-19561)***

Employee Codes: A=Over 500 employees, B=251-500
C=101-250, D=51-100, E=50
2019 Directory of California
Wholesalers and Services Companies
© Mergent Inc. 1-800-342-5647
1217

Balboa Yacht Club ....E....949 673-3515
1801 Bayside Dr Corona Del Mar (92625) ***(P-18854)***
Bald Eagle Security Svcs Inc ....D....619 230-0022
3626 Main St San Diego (92113) ***(P-16577)***
Baldwin Hospitality LLC ....D....626 962-6000
14635 Baldwin Ave Baldwin Park (91706) ***(P-12350)***
Balfour Beatty Cnstr LLC ....C....510 903-2060
2335 Broadway Ste 300 Oakland (94612) ***(P-1472)***
Bali Construction Inc ....D....626 442-8003
9852 Joe Vargas Way South El Monte (91733) ***(P-1894)***
Ball Horticultural Company ....C....805 343-2723
400 Obispo St Guadalupe (93434) ***(P-243)***
Ball Tagawa Growers ....E....805 481-7526
819 Zenon Way Arroyo Grande (93420) ***(P-244)***
Ballard Clothing Design, Los Angeles *Also called W Scott Bllard Dsign Arch Inc* ***(P-17577)***
Ballard Rehabilitation Hosp, San Bernardino *Also called Vibra Hosp San Bernardino LLC* ***(P-21908)***
Ballard Rosenberg Golper Sav (PA) ....D....818 508-3700
15760 Ventura Blvd # 1800 Encino (91436) ***(P-22930)***
Ballard Spahr LLP ....D....424 204-4400
2029 Century Park E # 800 Los Angeles (90067) ***(P-22931)***
Balletto Ranch Inc (PA) ....D....707 568-2455
5700 Occidental Rd Santa Rosa (95401) ***(P-34)***
Balliet Bros Construction Corp ....E....650 871-9000
390 Swift Ave Ste 14 South San Francisco (94080) ***(P-1473)***
Baloian Farm, Fresno *Also called Baloian Packing Co Inc* ***(P-35)***
Baloian Farms, Fresno *Also called Baloian Packing Co Inc* ***(P-36)***
Baloian Packing Co Inc (PA) ....D....559 485-9200
446 N Blythe Ave Fresno (93706) ***(P-35)***
Baloian Packing Co Inc ....D....559 441-7043
3138 W Whites Bridge Ave Fresno (93706) ***(P-36)***
Baltazar Construction Inc ....E....626 339-8620
236 E Arrow Hwy Covina (91722) ***(P-3220)***
Bamko Inc ....C....310 470-5859
11620 Wilshire Blvd # 610 Los Angeles (90025) ***(P-13926)***
Bana Home Loan Servicing ....A....213 345-7975
31303 Agoura Rd Westlake Village (91361) ***(P-9276)***
Banamex USA, Los Angeles *Also called Busa Servicing Inc* ***(P-9422)***
Banamex USA Bancorp (HQ) ....C....310 203-3440
2029 Century Park E Fl 42 Los Angeles (90067) ***(P-11952)***
Banc America Lsg & Capitl LLC (HQ) ....C....415 765-7349
555 California St Fl 4 San Francisco (94104) ***(P-9755)***
Banc California National Assn (HQ) ....D....877 770-2262
3 Macarthur Pl Santa Ana (92707) ***(P-9277)***
Banc California National Assn ....E....310 286-0710
10100 Santa Monica Blvd Los Angeles (90067) ***(P-9278)***
Banc of California Inc (PA) ....C....855 361-2262
3 Macarthur Pl Ste 100 Santa Ana (92707) ***(P-9279)***
Bandai Namco Entrmt Amer Inc ....C....408 235-2000
2051 Mission College Blvd Santa Clara (95054) ***(P-7946)***
Baney Corporation ....D....530 899-9090
2035 Business Ln Chico (95928) ***(P-12351)***
Bangkit (usa) Inc ....D....626 672-0888
10511 Valley Blvd El Monte (91731) ***(P-8076)***
Bangs Avenue Medical Offices, Modesto *Also called Kaiser Foundation Hospitals* ***(P-19571)***
Banister Electrical Inc ....D....925 778-7801
2532 Verne Roberts Cir Antioch (94509) ***(P-2515)***
Bank America National Assn ....D....559 445-7731
5292 N Palm Ave Fresno (93704) ***(P-9280)***
Bank America National Assn ....E....800 432-1000
1525 Market St San Francisco (94103) ***(P-9281)***
Bank America National Assn ....D....805 520-5100
450 American St Simi Valley (93065) ***(P-9732)***
Bank America National Assn ....C....415 913-5891
345 Montgomery St San Francisco (94104) ***(P-9282)***
Bank America National Assn ....D....530 891-7019
400 Broadway St Chico (95928) ***(P-9283)***
Bank America National Assn ....D....800 432-1000
345 N Brand Blvd Glendale (91203) ***(P-9284)***
Bank America National Assn ....E....562 624-4330
6351 E Spring St Long Beach (90808) ***(P-9285)***
Bank America National Assn ....D....818 898-3033
120 S Brand Blvd San Fernando (91340) ***(P-9286)***
Bank America National Assn ....E....800 432-1000
212 E Main St Visalia (93291) ***(P-9287)***
Bank America National Assn ....C....760 636-7500
73525 El Paseo Palm Desert (92260) ***(P-26773)***
Bank America National Assn ....D....310 384-4562
550 S Hill St Ste 101 Los Angeles (90013) ***(P-9288)***
Bank America National Assn ....C....916 326-3161
555 Capitol Mall Sacramento (95814) ***(P-26774)***
Bank America National Assn ....E....714 973-8495
13220 Harbor Blvd Garden Grove (92843) ***(P-9289)***
Bank America National Assn ....D....949 474-8801
275 Valencia Ave Brea (92823) ***(P-9779)***
Bank America National Assn ....E....951 929-8614
1687 E Florida Ave Hemet (92544) ***(P-9290)***
Bank America National Assn ....D....800 432-1000
1450 W Redondo Beach Blvd Gardena (90247) ***(P-9291)***
Bank America National Assn ....D....818 577-2000
5901 Canoga Ave Woodland Hills (91367) ***(P-9292)***
Bank America National Assn ....D....909 393-3002
4100 Chino Hills Pkwy Chino Hills (91709) ***(P-9293)***
Bank America National Assn ....D....951 676-4114
27489 Ynez Rd Temecula (92591) ***(P-9294)***
Bank America National Assn ....D....415 913-3438
555 California St Ste 4 San Francisco (94104) ***(P-26501)***
Bank Leumi Le, Los Angeles *Also called Bank Leumi USA* ***(P-9295)***
Bank Leumi USA ....D....323 966-4700
555 W 5th St Fl 33 Los Angeles (90013) ***(P-9295)***
Bank of America, San Francisco *Also called Bankamerica Financial Inc* ***(P-9733)***
Bank of Commerce Mortgage, San Ramon *Also called Commerce Home Mortgage Inc* ***(P-9878)***
Bank of Hope (HQ) ....C....213 639-1700
3731 Wilshire Blvd # 400 Los Angeles (90010) ***(P-9296)***
Bank of Marin ....D....415 472-2265
4460 Redwood Hwy Ste 1 San Rafael (94903) ***(P-9413)***
Bank of Marin Bancorp (PA) ....C....415 763-4520
504 Redwood Blvd Ste 100 Novato (94947) ***(P-9414)***
Bank of Orient (HQ) ....C....415 338-0668
100 Pine St Ste 600 San Francisco (94111) ***(P-9415)***
Bank of Sierra, San Luis Obispo *Also called Bank of Sierra* ***(P-9297)***
Bank of Sierra ....D....805 541-0400
500 Marsh St San Luis Obispo (93401) ***(P-9297)***
Bank of Sierra (HQ) ....C....559 782-4300
90 N Main St Porterville (93257) ***(P-9416)***
Bank of Stockton (HQ) ....C....209 929-1600
301 E Miner Ave Stockton (95202) ***(P-9417)***
BANK OF THE WEST (HQ) ....A....415 765-4800
180 Montgomery St # 1400 San Francisco (94104) ***(P-9418)***
Bank of Tokyo, Los Angeles *Also called Mufg Bank Ltd* ***(P-9513)***
Bank of Tokyo Ltd ....A....213 488-3700
445 S Figueroa St # 2700 Los Angeles (90071) ***(P-9495)***
Bankamerica Financial Inc ....A....415 622-3521
315 Montgomery St San Francisco (94104) ***(P-9733)***
Bankcard Services, Torrance *Also called Credit Card Services Inc* ***(P-17112)***
Bankcard Services (PA) ....C....213 365-1122
21281 S Western Ave Torrance (90501) ***(P-17026)***
Bankcard USA Merchant Srvc ....D....818 597-7000
5701 Lindero Canyon Rd Westlake Village (91362) ***(P-6950)***
Bankers Diversified Mortgage, Yorba Linda *Also called American Transport Inc* ***(P-9775)***
Bankruptcy Management Cons, El Segundo *Also called BMC Group Inc* ***(P-22951)***
Bankruptcy MGT Solutions Inc (PA) ....D....949 222-1212
5 Peters Canyon Rd # 200 Irvine (92606) ***(P-22932)***
Banner Bank ....D....916 648-2100
1750 Howe Ave Ste 100 Sacramento (95825) ***(P-9419)***
Banner Bank ....D....916 685-6546
9340 E Stockton Blvd Elk Grove (95624) ***(P-9298)***
Banner Bank ....E....619 243-7900
1350 Rosecrans St San Diego (92106) ***(P-9420)***
Banner Health ....C....530 251-3147
1800 Spring Ridge Dr Susanville (96130) ***(P-21295)***
Banner Lassen Medical Center ....C....530 252-2000
1800 Spring Ridge Dr Susanville (96130) ***(P-21296)***
Banquet Facilities ....E....951 360-2081
6000 Camino Real Riverside (92509) ***(P-13719)***
Banyan Solutions Inc ....D....650 766-9338
2809 Blue Oak Ct Brentwood (94513) ***(P-14823)***
Banyon Transcription, Brentwood *Also called Banyan Solutions Inc* ***(P-14823)***
Bapko Metal Inc ....D....714 639-9380
180 S Anita Dr Orange (92868) ***(P-3362)***
Bar Architects ....D....415 293-5700
901 Battery St Ste 300 San Francisco (94111) ***(P-26026)***
Bar Asscation of San Francisco (PA) ....D....415 982-1600
301 Battery St Fl 3 San Francisco (94111) ***(P-24998)***
Bara Construction, Danville *Also called Bara Infoware Inc* ***(P-25559)***
Bara Construction Services ....E....925 790-0130
2678 Bishop Dr Ste 116 San Ramon (94583) ***(P-1330)***
Bara Infoware Inc (PA) ....D....925 790-0130
4115 Blackhawk Plaza Cir Danville (94506) ***(P-25559)***
Barazani Outdoors Inc ....D....818 701-6977
14101 Valleyheart Dr # 104 Sherman Oaks (91423) ***(P-730)***
Barazani Pave Stone Inc ....C....818 701-6977
14546 Hamlin St Ste 201 Van Nuys (91411) ***(P-2797)***
Barbaccia Properties ....D....408 225-1010
165 Blossom Hill Rd San Jose (95123) ***(P-11157)***
Barbara Worth Resort, Calexico *Also called Adventures In Hospitality Inc* ***(P-18818)***
Barbour & Floyd Medical Assoc, Lynwood *Also called South Cntl Heatlh & Rehab Prog* ***(P-22682)***
Barcelo Enterprises Inc ....D....760 728-3444
4400 Macarthur Blvd # 980 Newport Beach (92660) ***(P-245)***
Barcelon Associates MGT Corp ....C....925 627-7000
590 Lennon Ln Ste 110 Walnut Creek (94598) ***(P-11231)***
Barclays Capital Inc ....D....650 289-6000
155 Linfield Dr Menlo Park (94025) ***(P-12200)***
Barclays Capital Inc ....D....310 481-4100
10250 Santa Monica Blvd # 24 Los Angeles (90067) ***(P-9917)***
Barcott Frank A SEC Invstgtons ....C....714 891-8556
6446 San Andres Ave Cypress (90630) ***(P-16578)***
Barcott SEC & Investigations, Cypress *Also called Barcott Frank A SEC Invstgtons* ***(P-16578)***
Bare Elegance, Monrovia *Also called Imperial Project Inc* ***(P-18441)***
Barger & Wolen LLP ....E....415 434-2800
275 Battery St Ste 480 San Francisco (94111) ***(P-22933)***
Barkers Food Machinery, Irwindale *Also called Service Solutions Group LLC* ***(P-17912)***
Barlow Group (PA) ....C....213 250-4200
2000 Stadium Way Los Angeles (90026) ***(P-21997)***
Barlow Respiratory Hospital (PA) ....C....213 250-4200
2000 Stadium Way Los Angeles (90026) ***(P-21998)***
Barlow Respitory Hospital, Los Angeles *Also called Barlow Group* ***(P-21997)***
Barnes & Thornburg LLP ....C....310 284-3880
2029 Century Park E # 300 Los Angeles (90067) ***(P-22934)***
Barnes and Berger ....E....760 922-6136
1091 S Intake Blvd Blythe (92225) ***(P-474)***
Barnum & Celillo Electric Inc (PA) ....D....916 646-4661
135 Main Ave Ste A Sacramento (95838) ***(P-2516)***

Mergent e-mail: customerrelations@mergent.com
1218
2019 Directory of California
Wholesalers and Services Companies
(P-0000) Products & Services Section entry number
(PA)=Parent Co (HQ)=Headquarters (DH)=Div Headquarters

Baron Pool Plst Sthern Cal Inc.....D.....909 792-8891
495 Industrial Rd San Bernardino (92408) *(P-3491)*
Barona Creek Golf Club.....D.....619 387-7018
1932 Wildcat Canyon Rd Lakeside (92040) *(P-18687)*
Barona Resort & Casino.....A.....619 443-2300
1932 Wildcat Canyon Rd Lakeside (92040) *(P-12352)*
Baronhr LLC.....C.....909 517-3800
13085 Central Ave Ste 4 Chino (91710) *(P-14575)*
Barr Engineering Inc.....D.....562 944-1722
12612 Clark St Santa Fe Springs (90670) *(P-2135)*
Barra LLC (HQ).....B.....510 548-5442
2100 Milvia St Berkeley (94704) *(P-15603)*
Barra, Inc., Berkeley *Also called Barra LLC (P-15603)*
Barracuda Networks Inc (HQ).....C.....408 342-5400
3175 Winchester Blvd Campbell (95008) *(P-15604)*
Barranca Medical Offices, Irvine *Also called Kaiser Foundation Hospitals (P-21475)*
Barraza Farm Labor Contractor, Calipatria *Also called Frank Barraza (P-649)*
Barrel Ten Quarter Circle Inc.....B.....707 265-4000
33 Harlow Ct NAPA (94558) *(P-9032)*
Barrett Business Services Inc.....A.....858 314-1100
8880 Rio San Diego Dr # 800 San Diego (92108) *(P-22935)*
Barrett Business Services Inc.....A.....909 890-3633
862 E Hospitality Ln San Bernardino (92408) *(P-14576)*
Barrett Business Services Inc.....A.....650 653-7588
1840 Gateway Dr San Mateo (94404) *(P-26775)*
Barrick Gold Corporation.....D.....707 995-6070
26775 Morgan Valley Rd Lower Lake (95457) *(P-1004)*
Barry Bishop.....D.....510 596-0888
6001 Shellmound St # 875 Emeryville (94608) *(P-22936)*
Barry McPherson Inc.....C.....425 343-5000
1932 E Deere Ave Ste 240 Santa Ana (92705) *(P-10559)*
Barrys Bootcamp Holdings LLC (PA).....B.....270 535-5005
7373 Beverly Blvd Los Angeles (90036) *(P-7922)*
Barrys Security Services Inc (PA).....C.....951 789-7575
16739 Van Buren Blvd Riverside (92504) *(P-16579)*
Barrys Security Services Inc.....C.....562 493-7007
5480 Katella Ave Ste 203 Los Alamitos (90720) *(P-16580)*
Barstow Community Hospital, Barstow *Also called Hospital of Barstow Inc (P-21455)*
Barstow Redevelopment Agency.....C.....760 256-3531
220 E Mountain View St B Barstow (92311) *(P-27655)*
Bart, Oakland *Also called San Francisco Bay Area Rapid (P-3710)*
Bartco Lighting Inc.....D.....714 230-3200
5761 Research Dr Huntington Beach (92649) *(P-7336)*
Bartell Hotels.....C.....619 224-3411
2303 Shelter Island Dr San Diego (92106) *(P-12353)*
Bartell Hotels.....C.....619 222-6440
1710 W Mission Bay Dr San Diego (92109) *(P-12354)*
Bartell Hotels.....E.....858 581-3500
610 Diamond St San Diego (92109) *(P-12355)*
Bartell Hotels.....D.....619 222-0561
2051 Shelter Island Dr San Diego (92106) *(P-12356)*
Bartell Hotels.....D.....858 453-5500
3299 Holiday Ct La Jolla (92037) *(P-12357)*
Bartholomew Barry & Associates.....D.....818 543-4000
701 N Brand Blvd Ste 800 Glendale (91203) *(P-22937)*
Bartko Zankel Tarrant & Mil.....D.....415 956-1900
1 Embarcadero Ctr Ste 800 San Francisco (94111) *(P-22938)*
Bartlett Pringle & Wolf LLP.....E.....805 564-2103
1123 Chapala St Ste 300 Santa Barbara (93101) *(P-26146)*
Bartley Optical, Irwindale *Also called Essilor Laboratories Amer Inc (P-7234)*
Barton Hospital.....A.....530 543-5685
2170 South Ave South Lake Tahoe (96150) *(P-21297)*
Baseline Consulting Group Inc.....E.....818 906-7638
15300 Ventura Blvd # 200 Sherman Oaks (91403) *(P-27153)*
Basic Occpational Training Ctr, Perris *Also called Basic Occpational Training Ctr (P-24744)*
Basic Occpational Training Ctr.....C.....951 657-8028
1323 Jet Way Perris (92571) *(P-24744)*
Basic Resources Inc (PA).....E.....209 521-9771
928 12th St Ste 700 Modesto (95354) *(P-1728)*
Basile Construction Inc.....E.....858 278-2739
7952 Armour St San Diego (92111) *(P-1895)*
Basis Worldwide.....E.....424 261-2354
1557 7th St Santa Monica (90401) *(P-13795)*
Bask Jewelry Inc.....D.....831 479-8849
2607 S Main St Soquel (95073) *(P-8002)*
Basket Basics, Carson *Also called Kole Imports (P-9228)*
Basketball Marketing Co Inc.....D.....866 866-1232
101 Enterprise Ste 100 Aliso Viejo (92656) *(P-27154)*
Basquez Tiburcio Health Center.....C.....510 471-5907
33255 9th St Union City (94587) *(P-22513)*
Bass Tickets, Concord *Also called Bay Area Seating Service Inc (P-19106)*
Bassard Convalescent & Med Hm (PA).....D.....510 537-6700
3269 D St Hayward (94541) *(P-21002)*
Bassard Convalscent Home, Hayward *Also called Bassard Convalescent & Med Hm (P-21002)*
Bassenian/Lagoni Architects.....D.....949 553-9100
2031 Orchard Dr Ste 100 Newport Beach (92660) *(P-26027)*
Basslake LLC.....D.....559 642-3121
39255 Marina Dr Bass Lake (93604) *(P-12358)*
Bassmnt, Newport Beach *Also called Downtown SD Ventures LLC (P-19160)*
Bastille Networks Inc.....E.....800 530-3341
499 Lake Ave Santa Cruz (95062) *(P-15020)*
Batchmaster Software, Irvine *Also called Eworkplace Solutions Inc (P-7047)*
Bates Display & Packaging, Chino Hills *Also called Bates Sample Case Company Inc (P-17027)*
Bates Sample Case Company Inc.....D.....951 371-4922
5995 W Park Dr Chino Hills (91709) *(P-17027)*
Battery Agency, Hollywood *Also called Battery Marketing Inc (P-13796)*
Battery Assist, Los Angeles *Also called Club Assist US LLC (P-6631)*
Battery Marketing Inc.....D.....323 467-7267
6515 W Sunset Blvd # 200 Hollywood (90028) *(P-13796)*
Battery The, San Francisco *Also called Mxb Battery Operations LP (P-25204)*
Batth Farms, Caruthers *Also called Charanjit Singh Batth (P-185)*
Bauer Hockey Inc.....B.....818 782-6445
3500 Willow Ln Thousand Oaks (91361) *(P-7923)*
Bauers Intelligent Trnsp Inc (PA).....C.....415 522-1212
50 Pier San Francisco (94158) *(P-3774)*
Bautista, Jennifer L, San Jose *Also called Robinson and Wood Inc (P-23357)*
Bavaria Holdings Inc.....A.....415 418-2900
1 Letterman Dr Bldg C San Francisco (94129) *(P-11964)*
Bavarian Lion Company Cal (PA).....C.....707 545-8530
2777 4th St Santa Rosa (95405) *(P-12359)*
Bavc, San Francisco *Also called Bay Area Video Coalition Inc (P-18180)*
Baxco Pharmaceutical Inc.....C.....909 595-0826
2393 Bateman Ave Duarte (91010) *(P-8144)*
Baxter Healthcare Corporation.....A.....805 372-3000
1 Baxter Way Ste 100 Westlake Village (91362) *(P-8145)*
Bay Advanced Tech 0045, Newark *Also called Bay Advanced Technologies LLC (P-7729)*
Bay Advanced Technologies LLC.....D.....510 857-0900
8100 Central Ave Newark (94560) *(P-7729)*
Bay Alarm Company (PA).....D.....925 935-1100
5130 Commercial Cir Concord (94520) *(P-2517)*
Bay Alarm Company.....D.....510 452-3211
9836 Kitty Ln Oakland (94603) *(P-26502)*
Bay Area Air Quality (PA).....B.....415 749-4900
375 Beale St Ste 600 San Francisco (94105) *(P-27656)*
Bay Area At Home, Belmont *Also called Silverado Senior Living Inc (P-21208)*
Bay Area Beverage, Richmond *Also called T F Louderback Inc (P-9028)*
Bay Area Beverage Co.....C.....510 965-6120
700 National Ct Richmond (94804) *(P-9033)*
Bay Area Cnstr Framers Inc.....C.....925 454-8514
1150 W Center St Ste 105 Manteca (95337) *(P-3018)*
Bay Area Community Med Group, Los Angeles *Also called Santa Monica Bay Physicians He (P-19859)*
Bay Area Community Svcs Inc (PA).....E.....510 613-0330
390 40th St Oakland (94609) *(P-23502)*
Bay Area Credit Service LLC.....A.....858 653-3824
10562 Caminito Flores San Diego (92126) *(P-9622)*
Bay Area Distributing Coinc.....E.....510 232-8554
1061 Factory St Richmond (94801) *(P-8981)*
Bay Area Envmtl Res Inst.....D.....707 938-9387
Nasa Resrch Park 101 Moffett Field (94035) *(P-26595)*
Bay Area Garment, Hayward *Also called Early Transportation Services (P-4134)*
Bay Area Installations Inc (PA).....D.....510 895-8196
2481 Verna Ct San Leandro (94577) *(P-3492)*
Bay Area Kenworth, San Leandro *Also called Ssmb Pacific Holding Co Inc (P-6609)*
Bay Area News Group E Bay LLC (HQ).....D.....925 302-1683
6270 Houston Pl Ste A Dublin (94568) *(P-13966)*
Bay Area Pdatric Med Group Inc (PA).....D.....650 992-4200
901 Campus Dr Ste 111 Daly City (94015) *(P-19314)*
BAY AREA RESCUE MISSION, Richmond *Also called Richmond Rescue Mission (P-23997)*
Bay Area Seating Service Inc.....B.....925 671-4000
1855 Gateway Blvd Ste 630 Concord (94520) *(P-19106)*
Bay Area Senior Services Inc.....C.....650 579-5500
1 Baldwin Ave Ofc San Mateo (94401) *(P-23503)*
Bay Area Surgical MGT LLC.....E.....408 297-3432
2110 Forest Ave Fl 2 San Jose (95128) *(P-19315)*
Bay Area Techworkers (PA).....D.....925 359-2200
2000 Crow Canyon Pl # 150 San Ramon (94583) *(P-14577)*
Bay Area Video Coalition Inc.....D.....415 861-3282
2727 Mariposa St Fl 2 San Francisco (94110) *(P-18180)*
Bay Area/Diablo Petroleum Co (HQ).....C.....925 228-2222
1340 Arnold Dr Ste 231 Martinez (94553) *(P-8950)*
Bay Area/Diablo Petroleum Co.....C.....925 228-2222
1800 Sutter St Concord (94520) *(P-8951)*
Bay Bread LLC.....D.....415 440-0356
2325 Pine St San Francisco (94115) *(P-8760)*
Bay Brokerage Inc.....E.....650 413-1721
17 Woodleaf Ave Redwood City (94061) *(P-8383)*
Bay Cities Crane & Rigging Inc (PA).....E.....510 232-7222
457 Parr Blvd Richmond (94801) *(P-14477)*
Bay Cities Pav & Grading Inc.....C.....925 687-6666
1450 Civic Ct Bldg B Concord (94520) *(P-3415)*
Bay City Equipment Inds Inc.....D.....619 938-8200
13625 Danielson St Poway (92064) *(P-7337)*
Bay City Flower Co (PA).....B.....650 726-5535
2265 Cabrillo Hwy S Half Moon Bay (94019) *(P-9125)*
Bay City Flower Co.....C.....650 712-8147
1450 Cabrillo Hwy S Half Moon Bay (94019) *(P-246)*
Bay City Mechanical Inc.....C.....510 233-7000
4124 Lakeside Dr Richmond (94806) *(P-2136)*
Bay City Television Inc (PA).....D.....858 279-6666
8253 Ronson Rd San Diego (92111) *(P-5768)*
Bay Club Golden Gateway LLC.....E.....415 616-8800
370 Drumm St San Francisco (94111) *(P-18855)*
Bay Club Golden Gateway Inc, San Francisco *Also called Bay Club Golden Gateway LLC (P-18855)*
Bay Club Holdings III LLC.....D.....415 433-2936
370 Drumm St San Francisco (94111) *(P-19107)*
Bay Club Hotel and Marina A C.....D.....619 224-8888
2131 Shelter Island Dr San Diego (92106) *(P-12360)*
Bay Club Marin, Corte Madera *Also called Bay Clubs Inc (P-18856)*
Bay Clubs Inc.....D.....415 945-3000
220 Corte Madera Town Ctr Corte Madera (94925) *(P-18856)*
Bay Clubs Inc.....D.....408 738-2582
3250 Central Expy Santa Clara (95051) *(P-18577)*

ALPHABETIC

Employee Codes: A=Over 500 employees, B=251-500 C=101-250, D=51-100, E=50
2019 Directory of California Wholesalers and Services Companies
© Mergent Inc. 1-800-342-5647
1219

Bay Clubs Inc D 818 884-5034
22235 Sherman Way Canoga Park (91303) ***(P-18857)***
Bay Clubs Inc D 650 593-1112
200 Redwood Shr Pkwy Redwood City (94065) ***(P-18578)***
Bay Counties Waste Svcs Inc D 408 565-9900
3355 Thomas Rd Santa Clara (95054) ***(P-6351)***
Bay Federal Credit Union (PA) C 831 479-6000
3333 Clares St Capitola (95010) ***(P-9541)***
Bay Grove Capital Group LLC (PA) E 415 229-7953
801 Montgomery St Fl 5 San Francisco (94133) ***(P-12028)***
Bay Imaging Cons Med Group Inc (PA) D 925 296-7150
175 Lennon Ln Ste 100 Walnut Creek (94598) ***(P-19316)***
Bay Management, San Mateo *Also called Archives Management Corp* ***(P-26763)***
Bay Marine & Indus Sup LLC E 510 337-9122
2900 Main St Alameda (94501) ***(P-8019)***
Bay Meadows Racing Association C 650 573-4500
2600 S Delaware St San Mateo (94403) ***(P-24944)***
Bay Medic Transportation Inc D 800 689-9511
959 Detroit Ave Concord (94518) ***(P-3775)***
Bay Medical Management LLC C 925 296-7150
2125 Oak Grove Rd Ste 200 Walnut Creek (94598) ***(P-19317)***
Bay Photo Inc C 831 475-6090
2959 Park Ave Ste A Soquel (95073) ***(P-13639)***
Bay Point Healthcare Center, Hayward *Also called Kissito Health Care Inc* ***(P-22354)***
Bay Standard Inc D 925 634-1181
24485 Marsh Creek Rd Brentwood (94513) ***(P-7837)***
Bay Standard Manufacturing Inc (PA) E 925 634-1181
24485 Marsh Creek Rd Brentwood (94513) ***(P-7580)***
Bay Valley Medical Group Inc (PA) D 510 785-5000
27212 Calaroga Ave Hayward (94545) ***(P-19318)***
Bay Valley Mortgage, La Palma *Also called Pacific Bay Lending Group* ***(P-9900)***
Bay View Rhbilitation Hosp LLC D 510 521-5600
516 Willow St Alameda (94501) ***(P-20256)***
Bay Vista Senior Housing C 925 924-7100
6120 Stoneridge Pleasanton (94588) ***(P-26776)***
Bay West Shwplace Invstors LLC (PA) D 415 490-5800
2 Henry Adams St Ste 450 San Francisco (94103) ***(P-10856)***
Baybridge Employment Services, Eureka *Also called Humboldt Commnty Accss Resrc* ***(P-23848)***
Bayco Financial Corporation (PA) D 310 378-8181
24050 Madison St Ste 101 Torrance (90505) ***(P-11232)***
Bayer Protective Services Inc C 916 486-5800
3436 Amrcn Rver Dr Ste 10 Sacramento (95864) ***(P-16878)***
Baymarr Constructors Inc (PA) D 661 395-1676
6950 Mcdivitt Dr Bakersfield (93313) ***(P-3221)***
Baynote Inc D 866 921-0919
75 E Santa Clara St # 600 San Jose (95113) ***(P-7016)***
Bayonet/Blackhorse Golf Course, Seaside *Also called Bsl Golf Corp* ***(P-18690)***
Bayorg D 415 623-5300
Embarcadero At Beach St San Francisco (94133) ***(P-24924)***
Baypoint Trading, San Francisco *Also called Btig LLC* ***(P-9920)***
Bayscape Management Inc D 408 288-2940
1350 Pacific Ave Alviso (95002) ***(P-26777)***
Bayshore Ambulance Inc (PA) D 650 525-9700
370 Hatch Dr Foster City (94404) ***(P-3776)***
Bayshore Healthcare Inc C 805 544-5100
3033 Augusta St San Luis Obispo (93401) ***(P-20257)***
Bayside Care Center, Morro Bay *Also called Compass Health Inc* ***(P-21042)***
Bayside Insulation & Cnstr D 925 288-8960
1635 Challenge Dr Concord (94520) ***(P-1474)***
Bayside Interiors Inc (PA) C 510 438-9171
3220 Darby Cmn Fremont (94539) ***(P-2849)***
Bayside Medical Group, San Ramon *Also called Lucile Salter Packard Chil* ***(P-19664)***
Bayspring Medical Group A Pro E 415 674-2600
1199 Bush St Ste 500 San Francisco (94109) ***(P-19319)***
Bayview Engrg & Cnstr Co Inc D 916 939-8986
5040 Rbert J Mathews Pkwy El Dorado Hills (95762) ***(P-2137)***
Bayview Hospital and Mental C 619 426-6311
330 Moss St Chula Vista (91911) ***(P-21926)***
Bayview Hunters Point Foundati (PA) D 415 468-5100
150 Executive Park Blvd San Francisco (94134) ***(P-25396)***
Bayview Hunters Point Y M C A D 415 822-7728
1601 Lane St San Francisco (94124) ***(P-25097)***
Bayview Preservation LP A 415 285-7344
5 Commer Ct San Francisco (94124) ***(P-10982)***
Bayview Properties Inc D 831 655-7650
2600 Sand Dunes Dr Monterey (93940) ***(P-12361)***
Bayview Properties Inc D 831 624-1841
3665 Rio Rd Carmel (93923) ***(P-12362)***
Bayview Properties Inc (PA) D 831 394-3321
2600 Sand Dunes Dr Monterey (93940) ***(P-12363)***
Baywood Court (PA) D 510 733-2102
21966 Dolores St Apt 279 Castro Valley (94546) ***(P-22234)***
Baywood Court Retirement Ctr, Castro Valley *Also called Baywood Court* ***(P-22234)***
Bazan Mario AG Services & Vine D 707 945-0718
1984 Yountville Cross Rd Yountville (94599) ***(P-130)***
Bazan Mrio Vinyrd Mgmt AG Svcs, Yountville *Also called Bazan Mario AG Services & Vine* ***(P-130)***
Bazic Product, El Monte *Also called Bangkit (usa) Inc* ***(P-8076)***
BB&k, Riverside *Also called Best Best & Krieger LLP* ***(P-22944)***
Bbam Arcft Holdings 137 Labuan D 415 267-1600
50 California St Fl 14 San Francisco (94111) ***(P-14478)***
Bbam Arcft Holdings 139 Labuan, San Francisco *Also called Bbam US LP* ***(P-9918)***
Bbam US LP B 415 267-1600
50 California St Fl 14 San Francisco (94111) ***(P-9918)***
Bbccsd, Big Bear City *Also called Big Bear City Cmnty Svcs Dst* ***(P-6320)***
Bbcert E 480 220-3799
510 S Highway 1 Bodega Bay (94923) ***(P-27155)***
Bbcn Bank E 213 389-5550
550 S Western Ave Los Angeles (90020) ***(P-9421)***
BBDO Worldwide Inc D 415 808-6200
600 California St Fl 8 San Francisco (94108) ***(P-13797)***
Bbg, Irvine *Also called Burleigh Point Ltd* ***(P-11254)***
Bbk Performance Inc D 951 296-1771
27440 Bostik Ct Temecula (92590) ***(P-6626)***
Bc Contractors, Gonzales *Also called Bulmaro Castro Contractors* ***(P-14579)***
Bc Laboratories Inc D 661 327-4911
4100 Atlas Ct Bakersfield (93308) ***(P-26685)***
Bc Traffic Specialists, Orange *Also called B C Rentals Inc* ***(P-7728)***
Bc2 Environmental, Orange *Also called Beks Acquisition Inc* ***(P-3348)***
Bcbg Max Azria Group LLC D 323 589-2224
2761 Fruitland Ave Vernon (90058) ***(P-8286)***
Bcbg Max Azria Group LLC (HQ) B 323 589-2224
2761 Fruitland Ave Vernon (90058) ***(P-8287)***
Bcci Builders, San Francisco *Also called Bcci Construction Company* ***(P-1475)***
Bcci Construction Company (PA) C 415 817-5100
1160 Battery St Ste 250 San Francisco (94111) ***(P-1475)***
BCII, North Hills *Also called Brentwood Cmmncations Intl Inc* ***(P-18025)***
BCM Construction Company Inc E 530 342-1722
2990 State Highway 32 # 100 Chico (95973) ***(P-1375)***
Bcp Systems Inc D 714 202-3900
1560 S Sinclair St Anaheim (92806) ***(P-16278)***
Bctc Corporation D 323 888-9388
5500 E Olympic Blvd Ste B Commerce (90022) ***(P-8288)***
Bdc Distribution Center, Redlands *Also called Becton Dickinson and Company* ***(P-7160)***
Bdl Prosthetics, Irvine *Also called James R Glidewell Dental* ***(P-22169)***
Bdna Corporation (PA) D 650 625-9530
339 Bernardo Ave Ste 206 Mountain View (94043) ***(P-15605)***
Bdo Usa LLP C 415 397-7900
1 Bush St Fl 18 San Francisco (94104) ***(P-26147)***
Bdo Usa LLP D 858 404-9200
3570 Carmel Mountain Rd # 400 San Diego (92130) ***(P-26148)***
Bdo Usa LLP D 408 278-0220
300 Park Ave Ste 900 San Jose (95110) ***(P-26149)***
Bdo Usa LLP D 714 957-3200
600 Anton Blvd Ste 500 Costa Mesa (92626) ***(P-26150)***
Bdp Bowl Inc E 650 878-0300
900 King Plz Daly City (94015) ***(P-18480)***
BDR Industries Inc (PA) D 661 940-8554
820 E Avenue L12 Lancaster (93535) ***(P-5857)***
BDS Marketing LLC (HQ) C 800 234-4237
10 Holland Irvine (92618) ***(P-13798)***
BDS Plumbing Inc D 925 939-1004
2125 Youngs Ct Walnut Creek (94596) ***(P-2138)***
BDS Solutions Group LLC (HQ) A 949 472-6700
10 Holland Irvine (92618) ***(P-13799)***
Be Wise Ranch, Escondido *Also called William Brammer* ***(P-8748)***
Bea Systems Inc (HQ) A 650 506-7000
2315 N 1st St San Jose (95131) ***(P-15021)***
Beach & Tennis Club, Pebble Beach *Also called Lone Cypress Company LLC* ***(P-18958)***
Beach and La Mirada Car Wash E 714 994-1099
5231 Beach Blvd Buena Park (90621) ***(P-17802)***
Beach Cities 16 Cinemas, El Segundo *Also called Pacific Theaters Inc* ***(P-18309)***
Beach Cities Health District C 310 318-7939
514 N Prospect Ave Fl 3 Redondo Beach (90277) ***(P-24745)***
Beach Cities Invest & Protctn B 310 322-4724
2500 Via Cabrillo Marina San Pedro (90731) ***(P-16581)***
Beach Cities Memory Care Cmnty, Redondo Beach *Also called Silverado Senior Living Inc* ***(P-20765)***
Beach Club D 310 395-3254
201 Palisades Beach Rd Santa Monica (90402) ***(P-18858)***
Beach House Ht - Half Moon Bay, Half Moon Bay *Also called Pacific Beach House LLC* ***(P-12994)***
Beach Motel Partners Ltd D 800 755-0222
28 W Cabrillo Blvd Santa Barbara (93101) ***(P-12364)***
Beachbody LLC (PA) B 310 883-9000
3301 Exposition Blvd Fl 3 Santa Monica (90404) ***(P-13936)***
Beachside Nursing Center, Huntington Beach *Also called Sea Breeze Health Care Inc* ***(P-20750)***
Beachside Realtors (PA) B 714 969-6100
19671 Beach Blvd Ste 101 Huntington Beach (92648) ***(P-11233)***
Beachside Realtors D 909 606-1299
4197 Chino Hills Pkwy Chino Hills (91709) ***(P-3493)***
Beachside Realtors D 562 947-7834
15820 Whittier Blvd Ste B Whittier (90603) ***(P-11234)***
Beachsports Inc E 310 372-2202
600 N Catalina Ave Redondo Beach (90277) ***(P-13445)***
Beacon Accunting Resources LLC E 949 981-5946
1818 Glenwood Ln Newport Beach (92660) ***(P-27156)***
Beacon Health Options Inc C 714 763-2405
10805 Holder St Ste 300 Cypress (90630) ***(P-23504)***
Beacon Healthcare Services D 949 650-9750
1501 E 16th St Newport Beach (92663) ***(P-21927)***
Beacon Resources LLC E 949 955-1773
4 Corporate Plaza Dr # 101 Newport Beach (92660) ***(P-27157)***
Beacon Roofing Supply Inc D 408 293-5947
200 San Jose Ave San Jose (95125) ***(P-6919)***
Beacon Roofing Supply Inc D 818 768-4661
8501 Telfair Ave Sun Valley (91352) ***(P-7838)***
Beacon Sales Acquisition Inc C 714 288-1974
1201 E Mcfadden Ave Santa Ana (92705) ***(P-6920)***
Beacon West Energy Group LLC D 805 816-2790
1145 Eugenia Pl Ste 101 Carpinteria (93013) ***(P-25560)***
Bead Society C 805 495-2550
1454 Valley High Ave Thousand Oaks (91362) ***(P-25397)***
Bead Society , The, Thousand Oaks *Also called Bead Society* ***(P-25397)***

Beador Construction Co Inc.....D.....951 674-7352
26320 Lester Cir Corona (92883) ***(P-1729)***
Beale Air Force Base Outreach, Marysville *Also called Yuba Community College Dst* ***(P-24141)***
Beam "easy Living" Center, Grass Valley *Also called Beam Vacuums California Inc* ***(P-2518)***
Beam Vacuums California Inc.....E.....916 564-3279
422 Henderson St Grass Valley (95945) ***(P-2518)***
Bear Creek Golf & Country Club, Murrieta *Also called Bear Creek Golf Club Inc* ***(P-18859)***
Bear Creek Golf Club Inc.....D.....951 677-8621
22640 Bear Creek Dr N Murrieta (92562) ***(P-18859)***
Bear Creek Manor.....E.....209 723-4674
2929 M St Merced (95348) ***(P-10983)***
Bear Creek Partners LLC.....D.....951 677-8621
22640 Bear Creek Dr N Murrieta (92562) ***(P-18860)***
Bear Flag Marketing Corp.....C.....415 899-8466
7599 Redwood Blvd Ste 200 Novato (94945) ***(P-22235)***
Bear River Casino.....B.....707 733-9644
11 Bear Paws Way Loleta (95551) ***(P-12365)***
Bear River Casino Hotel, Loleta *Also called Bear River Casino* ***(P-12365)***
Bear Stearns, Del Mar *Also called JP Morgan Securities LLC* ***(P-9967)***
Bear Stearns Companies LLC.....A.....949 856-8300
1833 Alton Pkwy Irvine (92606) ***(P-9780)***
Bear Stern Residential Mrtg, Irvine *Also called Bear Stearns Companies LLC* ***(P-9780)***
Bear Trucking Inc.....D.....909 799-1616
19768 Kendall Dr San Bernardino (92407) ***(P-4332)***
Bear Valley Mountain Resort, Bear Valley *Also called Bear Valley Ski Co* ***(P-19108)***
Bear Valley Ski Co.....B.....209 753-2301
2280 State Rte 207 Bear Valley (95223) ***(P-19108)***
Bear Valley Springs Assn.....C.....661 821-5537
29541 Rollingoak Dr Tehachapi (93561) ***(P-25098)***
Bear Vly Cmnty Healthcare Dst (PA).....C.....909 866-6501
41870 Garstin Dr Big Bear Lake (92315) ***(P-21298)***
Bear Vly Fbrcators Stl Sup Inc.....D.....760 247-5381
10700 Civic Center Dr 100c Rancho Cucamonga (91730) ***(P-1376)***
Bearing Engineers Inc (PA).....D.....949 586-7442
27 Argonaut Aliso Viejo (92656) ***(P-7839)***
Beating Wall Street Inc (PA).....C.....818 332-9696
14934 Dickens St Apt 16 Sherman Oaks (91403) ***(P-27158)***
Beats Music LLC.....D.....415 590-5104
235 2nd St San Francisco (94105) ***(P-15606)***
Beau Wine Tours, Sonoma *Also called Appellation Tours Inc* ***(P-4962)***
Beauchamp Distributing Company.....D.....310 639-5320
1911 S Santa Fe Ave Compton (90221) ***(P-8982)***
Beaudry R V San Marcos Inc.....C.....760 736-8800
251 Travelers Way San Marcos (92069) ***(P-17852)***
Beaudry Rv, San Marcos *Also called Beaudry R V San Marcos Inc* ***(P-17852)***
Beaumont Care Center, Cherry Valley *Also called David-Kleis Inc* ***(P-20368)***
Beaumont Unified School Dst.....A.....951 845-3010
1001 Cougar Way Beaumont (92223) ***(P-3908)***
Beauties of Life Inc.....C.....415 297-6765
960 Jackson St San Francisco (94133) ***(P-15022)***
Beautitudes Beauty Supply LLC.....D.....800 830-6076
7850 White Ln Ste E Bakersfield (93309) ***(P-7882)***
Beauty 21 Cosmetics Inc.....C.....909 945-2220
2021 S Archibald Ave Ontario (91761) ***(P-8146)***
Beauty Bazar Inc.....D.....650 326-8522
36 Stanford Shopping Ctr Palo Alto (94304) ***(P-13647)***
Beauty Recognized LP.....D.....310 278-7646
224 Via Rodeo Dr Beverly Hills (90210) ***(P-13648)***
Beautycounter, Santa Monica *Also called Counter Brands LLC* ***(P-8164)***
Beaver Medical Clinic, Highland *Also called Beaver Medical Group LP* ***(P-19321)***
Beaver Medical Clinic Inc (PA).....C.....909 793-3311
1615 Orange Tree Ln Redlands (92374) ***(P-19320)***
Beaver Medical Group LP (HQ).....C.....909 425-3321
7000 Boulder Ave Highland (92346) ***(P-19321)***
Beazer Pre-Owned Rental Homes, Agoura Hills *Also called Amh Portfolio One LLC* ***(P-12151)***
Becho Inc.....D.....818 362-8391
15901 Olden St Sylmar (91342) ***(P-1730)***
Bechtel, Livermore *Also called National Security Tech LLC* ***(P-25841)***
Bechtel Capital MGT Corp.....A.....415 768-1234
50 Beale St San Francisco (94105) ***(P-26778)***
Bechtel Energy Corporation.....A.....415 768-1234
50 Beale St Bsmt 1 San Francisco (94105) ***(P-25561)***
Bechtel Enterprises Holdings (HQ).....D.....415 768-1234
50 Beale St Ste 2200 San Francisco (94105) ***(P-25562)***
Bechtel Entps Holdings Inc.....B.....415 768-6745
50 Beale St Bsmt 1 San Francisco (94105) ***(P-1476)***
Bechtel Global Energy Inc.....A.....415 768-1234
50 Beale St Bsmt 1 San Francisco (94105) ***(P-25563)***
Bechtel Group Inc (PA).....A.....415 768-1234
50 Beale St Bsmt 1 San Francisco (94105) ***(P-2010)***
Bechtel Intl Systems Inc (HQ).....D.....415 768-1234
50 Beale St San Francisco (94105) ***(P-25564)***
Beck Group, The, Beverly Hills *Also called Beck International Inc* ***(P-1377)***
Beck International Inc.....B.....310 281-2980
9641 Sunset Blvd Beverly Hills (90210) ***(P-1377)***
Beckett Enterprise.....E.....310 686-3817
900 Kincaid Ave K8 Inglewood (90302) ***(P-27159)***
Beckman Research Inst Hope.....C.....626 359-8111
1500 Duarte Rd Duarte (91010) ***(P-26596)***
Becton Dickinson and Company.....D.....909 748-7300
2200 W San Bernardino Ave Redlands (92374) ***(P-7160)***
Bedon Construction Inc.....D.....951 246-9005
27989 Holland Rd Menifee (92584) ***(P-25565)***
Bedrock Company.....D.....951 273-1931
2970 Myers St Riverside (92503) ***(P-3222)***
Bedrosian Farms Inc.....E.....559 834-5981
8333 S Sunnyside Ave Fowler (93625) ***(P-131)***
Bedrosian's Tile & Marble, Anaheim *Also called Paragon Industries Inc* ***(P-6903)***
Beech Street Corporation (HQ).....B.....949 672-1000
25550 Commercentre Dr # 200 Lake Forest (92630) ***(P-26779)***
Beethoven Holdings Inc.....C.....559 733-4100
400 E Main St Ste 110 Visalia (93291) ***(P-11235)***
Begroup (PA).....D.....818 638-4563
516 Burchett St Glendale (91203) ***(P-21003)***
Begroup.....D.....626 359-9371
1763 Royal Oaks Dr Ofc Duarte (91010) ***(P-20258)***
Behavioral H Bakersfield.....C.....661 398-1800
5201 White Ln Bakersfield (93309) ***(P-21928)***
Behavioral Health, Lancaster *Also called Kaiser Foundation Hospitals* ***(P-19566)***
Behavioral Health Center, Palm Springs *Also called San Gorgonio Memorial Hospital* ***(P-22674)***
Behavioral Health Resources.....C.....951 275-8400
5900 Brockton Ave Riverside (92506) ***(P-21929)***
Behavioral Health Services, Mount Shasta *Also called County of Siskiyou* ***(P-22558)***
Behavioral Health Services Inc (PA).....E.....310 679-9031
15519 Crenshaw Blvd Gardena (90249) ***(P-23505)***
Behavioral Health Services Inc.....D.....562 599-4194
1775 Chestnut Ave Long Beach (90813) ***(P-23506)***
Behavioral Health Services Inc.....D.....909 865-2336
2180 Valley Blvd Pomona (91768) ***(P-23507)***
Behavioral Health Svcs Dept, Long Beach *Also called Childnet Youth & Fmly Svcs Inc* ***(P-24464)***
Behavioral Health Works Inc.....D.....800 249-1266
1301 E Orangewood Ave Anaheim (92805) ***(P-22741)***
Behavioral Hlth Recovery Svcs, Modesto *Also called County of Stanislaus* ***(P-24773)***
Behavioral Intervention Assn.....E.....510 652-7445
2354 Powell St A Emeryville (94608) ***(P-14824)***
Behavioral Learning Center Inc.....D.....661 254-7086
28245 Avenue Crocker # 220 Valencia (91355) ***(P-23508)***
Behavioral Medicine Center, Redlands *Also called Loma Linda University Med Ctr* ***(P-21563)***
Behavoral Autism Therapies LLC (PA).....C.....909 483-5000
2930 Inland Empire Blvd Ontario (91764) ***(P-23509)***
Behr Process Sales Company.....C.....714 545-7101
3000 S Main St Apt 84e Santa Ana (92707) ***(P-27541)***
Behringer Harvard Wilshire Blv.....D.....310 475-8711
10740 Wilshire Blvd Los Angeles (90024) ***(P-12366)***
Being Fit Fitness Centers, San Diego *Also called Being Fit Inc* ***(P-18579)***
Being Fit Inc (PA).....D.....858 549-3456
8292 Mira Mesa Blvd San Diego (92126) ***(P-18579)***
Being Fit Inc.....D.....858 483-9294
4971 Clairemont Dr Ste A San Diego (92117) ***(P-18580)***
Beitler & Associates Inc (PA).....C.....310 820-2955
825 S Barrington Ave Los Angeles (90049) ***(P-11236)***
Beitler Commercial Realty Svcs, Los Angeles *Also called Beitler & Associates Inc* ***(P-11236)***
Bejac Corporation (PA).....D.....714 528-6224
569 S Van Buren St Placentia (92870) ***(P-7730)***
Bekins Moving & Storage, Santa Fe Springs *Also called Bekins Moving Solutions Inc* ***(P-4333)***
Bekins Moving Solutions Inc (PA).....D.....562 356-9460
12610 Shoemaker Ave Santa Fe Springs (90670) ***(P-4333)***
Beks Acquisition Inc.....E.....714 744-2990
1150 W Trenton Ave Orange (92867) ***(P-3348)***
Bel Air Lighting Inc (PA).....C.....818 768-5511
28104 Witherspoon Pkwy Valencia (91355) ***(P-7338)***
Bel Esprit Builders Inc.....E.....949 709-3500
23112 Alcalde Dr Ste A Laguna Hills (92653) ***(P-1477)***
Bel Vista Convalescent Hosp, Long Beach *Also called Villa De La Mar Inc* ***(P-21247)***
Bel Vista Convalescent Hosp, Pasadena *Also called Robert C Hamilton* ***(P-24655)***
Bel-Air Bay Club Ltd.....C.....310 230-4700
16801 Pacific Coast Hwy Pacific Palisades (90272) ***(P-25099)***
Bel-Air Country Club.....C.....310 472-9563
10768 Bellagio Rd Los Angeles (90077) ***(P-18861)***
Belcampo Group Inc.....D.....530 842-5200
329 N Phillipe Ln Yreka (96097) ***(P-13720)***
Belcampo Group Inc (PA).....D.....510 250-7810
65 Webster St Oakland (94607) ***(P-445)***
Belcampo Meat, Yreka *Also called Belcampo Group Inc* ***(P-13720)***
Belectric Inc (HQ).....D.....510 896-3940
951 Mariners Island Blvd San Mateo (94404) ***(P-2011)***
Belkin Components, Playa Vista *Also called Belkin International Inc* ***(P-7450)***
Belkin International Inc (HQ).....B.....310 751-5100
12045 Waterfront Dr Playa Vista (90094) ***(P-7450)***
Bell Gardens Bicycle Club Inc.....A.....562 806-4646
888 Bicycle Casino Dr Bell Gardens (90201) ***(P-19109)***
Bell Integrator Inc (PA).....A.....650 943-2415
1735 N 1st St Ste 102 San Jose (95112) ***(P-15920)***
Bell Pipe & Supply Co.....E.....714 772-3200
215 E Ball Rd Anaheim (92805) ***(P-7840)***
Bell Private Security Inc.....D.....714 964-9381
18030 Brookhurst St Fountain Valley (92708) ***(P-16582)***
Bell Products Inc.....D.....707 255-1811
722 Soscol Ave NAPA (94559) ***(P-2139)***
Bella Terra Carwash, Huntington Beach *Also called Russell Fisher Partnership* ***(P-17837)***
Bella Terra Technologies Inc.....D.....650 316-6660
1600 Amphitheatre Pkwy Mountain View (94043) ***(P-5969)***
Bella Vista Healthcare Center.....D.....909 985-2731
933 E Deodar St Ontario (91764) ***(P-20259)***
Bella Vsta Trnstional Care Ctr, San Luis Obispo *Also called Bayshore Healthcare Inc* ***(P-20257)***
Bellavista Landscape Svcs Inc.....D.....831 461-1761
340 Twin Pines Dr Scotts Valley (95066) ***(P-731)***

Employee Codes: A=Over 500 employees, B=251-500
C=101-250, D=51-100, E=50
2019 Directory of California
Wholesalers and Services Companies
© Mergent Inc. 1-800-342-5647
1221

Bellis Steel Company Inc (PA)..........D.......818 886-5601
8740 Vanalden Ave Northridge (91324) ***(P-3363)***
Belmont Athletic Club..........D.......562 438-3816
4918 E 2nd St Long Beach (90803) ***(P-18862)***
Belmont Bruns Construction Inc..........D.......408 977-1708
1125 Mabury Rd San Jose (95133) ***(P-1478)***
BELMONT CONVALESCENT HOSPITAL, Long Beach *Also called Country Villa Blmnt Hght Hlth* ***(P-21045)***
Belmont Corporation..........D.......530 542-1101
901 Park Ave South Lake Tahoe (96150) ***(P-12367)***
Belmont Oaks Academy..........D.......650 593-6175
2200 Carlmont Dr Belmont (94002) ***(P-24265)***
Belmont Shores Kindercare, Long Beach *Also called Kindercare Learning Ctrs LLC* ***(P-24336)***
Belmont Village LP..........D.......408 720-8498
1039 E El Camino Real Sunnyvale (94087) ***(P-10984)***
Belmont Village LP..........D.......858 486-5020
13075 Evening Creek Dr S San Diego (92128) ***(P-21004)***
Belmont Village LP..........D.......818 972-2405
455 E Angeleno Ave Burbank (91501) ***(P-10985)***
Belmont Village LP..........D.......310 377-9977
5701 Crestridge Rd Rancho Palos Verdes (90275) ***(P-10986)***
Belmont Village LP..........E.......323 874-7711
2051 N Highland Ave Los Angeles (90068) ***(P-10987)***
Belmont Village At Sabre Sprng, San Diego *Also called Belmont Village LP* ***(P-21004)***
Belmont Village of Hollywood, Los Angeles *Also called Belmont Village LP* ***(P-10987)***
Belmont Village of Sunnyvale, Sunnyvale *Also called Belmont Village LP* ***(P-10984)***
Belvedere Hotel Partnership..........B.......310 551-2888
9882 Santa Monica Blvd Beverly Hills (90212) ***(P-12368)***
Belvedere Partnership..........B.......310 551-2888
9882 Santa Monica Blvd Beverly Hills (90212) ***(P-12369)***
Belville Enterprises Inc..........D.......858 652-6960
6225 Nancy Ridge Dr San Diego (92121) ***(P-19322)***
Bemus Landscape Inc..........B.......714 557-7910
1225 Puerta Del Sol # 500 San Clemente (92673) ***(P-2012)***
Ben Bennett Inc (PA)..........C.......949 209-9712
3419 Via Lido 646 Newport Beach (92663) ***(P-21005)***
Ben Bollinger Productions Inc..........D.......909 626-3296
455 W Foothill Blvd Claremont (91711) ***(P-18344)***
Ben F Smith Inc..........C.......858 271-4320
8655 Miramar Pl Ste B San Diego (92121) ***(P-3223)***
Ben Myerson Candy Co Inc (PA)..........B.......800 331-2829
6550 E Washington Blvd Commerce (90040) ***(P-9034)***
Ben Myerson Candy Co Inc..........D.......510 236-2233
3463 Collins Ave Richmond (94806) ***(P-9035)***
Benchmark Internet Group LLC..........D.......562 286-6820
10621 Calle Lee Ste 141 Los Alamitos (90720) ***(P-16316)***
Benchmark Landscape Inc..........C.......858 513-7190
12575 Stowe Dr Poway (92064) ***(P-803)***
Benchmark-Tech Corporation..........C.......831 475-5600
1 Chaminade Ln Santa Cruz (95065) ***(P-17028)***
Benco Dental Supply Co..........D.......714 424-0977
3590 Harbor Gtwy N Costa Mesa (92626) ***(P-7161)***
Bender Miles Construction, San Bernardino *Also called Michael Reyes* ***(P-1594)***
Bender/Helper Impact Inc (PA)..........D.......310 473-4147
11500 W Olympic Blvd # 655 Los Angeles (90064) ***(P-27542)***
Beneficent Technology Inc..........E.......650 644-3400
480 California Ave # 201 Palo Alto (94306) ***(P-17029)***
Beneficial Administration, Irvine *Also called Pension Administrators Inc* ***(P-14057)***
Beneficial Administration Co..........D.......949 756-1000
17701 Mitchell N Irvine (92614) ***(P-10560)***
Beneficial State Bank (HQ)..........D.......510 550-8420
1438 Webster St Ste 100 Oakland (94612) ***(P-9496)***
Benefit & Risk Management Svcs..........C.......916 467-1200
80 Iron Point Cir Ste 200 Folsom (95630) ***(P-10561)***
Benefit Planning, Marina Del Rey *Also called Veba Administrators Inc* ***(P-10823)***
Benefitvision Inc..........D.......818 348-3100
5550 Topanga Canyon Blvd # 180 Woodland Hills (91367) ***(P-24156)***
Benetech, Palo Alto *Also called Beneficent Technology Inc* ***(P-17029)***
Benetech Inc (PA)..........D.......916 484-6811
3947 Lennane Dr Ste 250 Sacramento (95834) ***(P-10562)***
Benetech Inc..........E.......916 484-6811
4420 Auburn Blvd Fl 2 Sacramento (95841) ***(P-10563)***
Benetrac, San Diego *Also called Paychex Benefit Tech Inc* ***(P-5622)***
Benettis Italia Inc..........D.......310 537-8036
3037 E Maria St Compton (90221) ***(P-6711)***
Benex LLC..........D.......310 675-6200
169 Saxony Rd Ste 111 Encinitas (92024) ***(P-7883)***
Benicia Plumbing Inc..........D.......707 745-2930
265 W Channel Rd Benicia (94510) ***(P-2140)***
Benjamin Kurzban Son Ctrl Inc..........E.......347 227-3425
24533 Stagg St Canoga Park (91304) ***(P-1331)***
Bennathon Corp (PA)..........D.......916 405-2100
10278 Iron Rock Way Elk Grove (95624) ***(P-1479)***
Bennett & Bennett Inc (PA)..........E.......559 582-9336
955 S Commerce Way Lemoore (93245) ***(P-2141)***
Bennett & Bennett Irrigation, Lemoore *Also called Bennett & Bennett Inc* ***(P-2141)***
Bennett Enterprises A CA..........D.......310 534-3543
25889 Belle Porte Ave Harbor City (90710) ***(P-804)***
Bennett Landscape, Harbor City *Also called Bennett Enterprises A CA* ***(P-804)***
Benq America Corp (HQ)..........D.......714 559-4900
3200 Park Center Dr # 150 Costa Mesa (92626) ***(P-7017)***
Bens Asphalt & Maint Co Inc..........E.......951 248-1103
2537 Rubidoux Blvd Riverside (92509) ***(P-1731)***
Bent Tree Nursing Center Inc..........C.......760 945-3033
247 E Bobier Dr Vista (92084) ***(P-20260)***
Bentley Health Care Inc..........D.......310 967-3300
9777 Wilshire Blvd Fl 4 Beverly Hills (90212) ***(P-27160)***
Bentley Systems Incorporated..........D.......925 933-2525
1600 Riviera Ave Ste 300 Walnut Creek (94596) ***(P-15023)***
Bentley-Simonson Inc..........D.......805 650-2794
1746 S Victoria Ave Ste F Ventura (93003) ***(P-1012)***
Bento Box Entertainment LLC..........B.......818 333-7700
5161 Lankershim Blvd # 1 North Hollywood (91601) ***(P-18425)***
Benz - One Complete Operation, Tehachapi *Also called Pjbs Holdings Inc* ***(P-6428)***
Benzara Inc..........D.......562 633-7612
8600 Mercury Ln Pico Rivera (90660) ***(P-6750)***
Berding & Weil LLP (PA)..........D.......925 838-2090
2175 N Calif Blvd Ste 500 Walnut Creek (94596) ***(P-22939)***
Beres Consulting..........D.......310 476-9941
470 S Bentley Ave Los Angeles (90049) ***(P-24945)***
Beresford Arms, The, San Francisco *Also called Beresford Corporation* ***(P-12370)***
Beresford Corp..........C.......415 981-7386
582 Market St Ste 912 San Francisco (94104) ***(P-203)***
Beresford Corporation..........D.......415 673-9900
635 Sutter St San Francisco (94102) ***(P-12370)***
Berg Injury Lawyers, Alameda *Also called Berg Wlliam L Attorney At Law* ***(P-22940)***
Berg Lacquer Co (PA)..........D.......323 261-8114
3150 E Pico Blvd Los Angeles (90023) ***(P-9188)***
Berg Wlliam L Attorney At Law (PA)..........D.......510 523-3200
2440 Santa Clara Ave Alameda (94501) ***(P-22940)***
Bergelectric Corp (PA)..........C.......310 337-1377
5650 W Centinela Ave Los Angeles (90045) ***(P-2519)***
Bergelectric Corp..........A.......760 746-1003
650 Opper St Escondido (92029) ***(P-2520)***
Bergelectric Corp..........D.......916 636-1880
11333 Sunrise Park Dr Rancho Cordova (95742) ***(P-2521)***
Bergelectric Corp..........D.......949 250-7005
1935 Deere Ave Irvine (92606) ***(P-2522)***
Bergen Brunswig Drug Company..........A.......714 385-4000
4000 W Metropolitan Dr # 200 Orange (92868) ***(P-8147)***
Bergensons Property Svcs Inc..........A.......760 631-5111
3605 Ocean Ranch Blvd # 200 Oceanside (92056) ***(P-14200)***
Berger Kahn (PA)..........D.......310 578-6800
4551 Glencoe Ave Ste 245 Marina Del Rey (90292) ***(P-22941)***
Berger Kahn..........E.......310 821-9000
2 Park Plz Ste 650 Irvine (92614) ***(P-22942)***
Berglund & Johnson Law Office, Woodland Hills *Also called Law Offices Berglund & Johnson* ***(P-23194)***
Bergman Kprs LLC (PA)..........C.......714 924-7000
2850 Saturn St Ste 100 Brea (92821) ***(P-1480)***
Berkadia Commercial Mrtg LLC..........D.......951 506-2787
1 Better World Cir # 210 Temecula (92590) ***(P-11237)***
Berkeley 75 Hsing Partners LP..........E.......510 705-1488
1936 University Ave # 130 Berkeley (94704) ***(P-11238)***
Berkeley Albany YMCA, Concord *Also called Young MNS Chrstn Assn of E Bay* ***(P-25355)***
Berkeley Cement Inc..........C.......510 525-8175
1200 6th St Berkeley (94710) ***(P-3224)***
Berkeley Clinic Auxuillary..........D.......510 525-7844
10052 San Pablo Ave El Cerrito (94530) ***(P-25398)***
Berkeley Country Club..........D.......510 233-7550
7901 Cutting Blvd El Cerrito (94530) ***(P-18863)***
Berkeley E Convalescent Hosp, Santa Monica *Also called Berkeley E Convalescent Hosp* ***(P-21006)***
Berkeley E Convalescent Hosp..........C.......310 829-5377
2021 Arizona Ave Santa Monica (90404) ***(P-21006)***
Berkeley Electronic Press, Berkeley *Also called Internet-Journals LLC* ***(P-16406)***
Berkeley Farms LLC (HQ)..........B.......510 265-8600
25500 Clawiter Rd Hayward (94545) ***(P-8513)***
Berkeley Lights Inc (PA)..........D.......510 898-1433
5858 Horton St Ste 320 Emeryville (94608) ***(P-26597)***
Berkeley Pines Care Center, Berkeley *Also called A T Associates Inc* ***(P-20976)***
Berkeley Repertory Theatre (PA)..........D.......510 204-8901
2025 Addison St Berkeley (94704) ***(P-18345)***
Berkeley Research Group LLC (PA)..........C.......510 285-3300
2200 Powell St Ste 1200 Emeryville (94608) ***(P-27657)***
Berkeley Student Coop Inc..........D.......510 848-1936
2424 Ridge Rd Berkeley (94709) ***(P-13473)***
Berkeley Symphony Orchestra..........E.......510 841-2800
1942 University Ave # 207 Berkeley (94704) ***(P-18426)***
Berkeley Unified School Dst..........E.......510 644-6182
1314 7th St Berkeley (94710) ***(P-3909)***
Berkley East Convalescent Hosp, Santa Monica *Also called Arizona and 21st Corp* ***(P-20998)***
Berkley Vly Cnvlscent Hosp Inc..........C.......818 786-0020
6600 Sepulveda Blvd Van Nuys (91411) ***(P-20261)***
Berkshire Hathaway, Lancaster *Also called V Troth Inc* ***(P-11810)***
Berkshire Hathaway Homestates..........D.......619 686-8424
2020 Camino Del Rio N San Diego (92108) ***(P-10564)***
Berkshire Hattaway Home Servcs..........D.......626 913-2808
16404 Colima Rd Hacienda Heights (91745) ***(P-11239)***
Berkshire Mortgage Fin Corp..........D.......949 754-6300
7575 Irvine Center Dr # 200 Irvine (92618) ***(P-9781)***
Bermuda Dunes Country Club..........E.......760 360-2481
42765 Adams St Bermuda Dunes (92203) ***(P-18864)***
Bermuda Dunes Learning Ctr Inc..........E.......760 772-7127
42115 Yucca Ln Bermuda Dunes (92203) ***(P-24266)***
Bernard Osher Marin Jewish Com..........C.......415 444-8000
200 N San Pedro Rd San Rafael (94903) ***(P-23510)***
Bernard Perrin Supowitz Inc..........E.......323 981-2800
5496 Lindbergh Ln Bell (90201) ***(P-8384)***
Bernardo Hts Healthcare Inc..........D.......858 673-0101
11895 Avenue Of Industry San Diego (92128) ***(P-21007)***
Bernards Builders Inc..........B.......818 898-1521
555 1st St San Fernando (91340) ***(P-1268)***

Mergent e-mail: customerrelations@mergent.com
1222
2019 Directory of California
Wholesalers and Services Companies
(P-0000) Products & Services Section entry number
(PA)=Parent Co (HQ)=Headquarters (DH)=Div Headquarters

Bernardy Ctr For Medcly Frgled, San Diego *Also called Rady Chld Hospital-San Diego* ***(P-27010)***
Bernel Inc ....C....714 778-6070
501 W Southern Ave Orange (92865) ***(P-2142)***
Berro Management ....D....562 432-3444
3950 Parmnt Blvd Ste 115 Lakewood (90712) ***(P-11240)***
Berry & Berry Inc (PA) ....D....559 674-2491
413 W Yosemite Ave # 106 Madera (93637) ***(P-1122)***
Berry & Berry Law Firm ....D....510 250-0200
475 14th St Ste 550 Oakland (94612) ***(P-22943)***
Berry Construction, Madera *Also called Berry & Berry Inc* ***(P-1122)***
Berry Petroleum Company LLC (HQ) ....D....661 616-3900
5201 Truxtun Ave Ste 100 Bakersfield (93309) ***(P-1013)***
Berry Seed & Feed, Keyes *Also called A L Gilbert Company* ***(P-8903)***
Berry-Hinckley, Auburn *Also called Western Energetix LLC* ***(P-8947)***
Berryman Health Inc ....D....707 462-8864
1349 S Dora St Ukiah (95482) ***(P-21008)***
Bershtel Enterprises LLC (PA) ....C....626 301-9214
2745 Huntington Dr Duarte (91010) ***(P-17030)***
Bersin By Deloitte, San Francisco *Also called Deloitte Consulting LLP* ***(P-27212)***
Bert E Jessup Transportation ....D....408 848-3390
641 Old Gilroy St Gilroy (95020) ***(P-4103)***
Bertolottis Ceres Disposal ....D....209 537-8000
231 Flamingo Rd Ceres (95307) ***(P-6352)***
Bertram Capital Management LLC ....B....650 358-5000
800 Concar Dr Ste 100 San Mateo (94402) ***(P-12201)***
Bess Testlab Inc ....E....408 988-0101
2461 Tripaldi Way Hayward (94545) ***(P-1896)***
Best Best & Krieger LLP (PA) ....C....951 686-1450
3390 University Ave # 500 Riverside (92501) ***(P-22944)***
Best Best & Krieger LLP ....E....949 263-2600
18101 Von Karman Ave # 1000 Irvine (92612) ***(P-22945)***
BEST Consulting Inc ....E....916 448-2050
8795 Folsom Blvd Ste 103 Sacramento (95826) ***(P-20917)***
Best Contracting Services Inc ....D....510 886-7240
4301 Bettencourt Way Union City (94587) ***(P-3127)***
Best Contracting Services Inc (PA) ....B....310 328-9176
19027 S Hamilton Ave Gardena (90248) ***(P-3128)***
Best Financial, The, Signal Hill *Also called First American Team Realty Inc* ***(P-11450)***
Best Friends Animal Society ....B....818 643-3989
15321 Brand Blvd Mission Hills (91345) ***(P-25399)***
Best Interiors Inc (PA) ....C....714 490-7999
2100 E Via Burton Anaheim (92806) ***(P-2850)***
Best Life and Health Insur Co ....D....949 253-4080
17701 Mitchell N Irvine (92614) ***(P-10131)***
Best Overnight Express, Irwindale *Also called Best Overnite Express Inc* ***(P-3978)***
Best Overnite Express Inc (PA) ....C....626 256-6340
406 Live Oak Ave Irwindale (91706) ***(P-3978)***
Best Plans, Irvine *Also called Beneficial Administration Co* ***(P-10560)***
Best Tours & Travel, Fresno *Also called B T & T Travel Inc* ***(P-4932)***
Best Valet Parking Corporation ....D....800 708-2538
12792 Valley View St # 201 Garden Grove (92845) ***(P-13721)***
Best Way Disposal Co Inc ....D....760 244-9773
17105 Mesa St Hesperia (92345) ***(P-6353)***
Best Western, San Simeon *Also called Cavalier Inn Incorporated* ***(P-12441)***
Best Western, Monterey *Also called Bayview Properties Inc* ***(P-12361)***
Best Western, South Lake Tahoe *Also called Belmont Corporation* ***(P-12367)***
Best Western, Santa Barbara *Also called Encina Pepper Tree Joint Ventr* ***(P-12559)***
Best Western, Aptos *Also called Seacliff Inn Inc* ***(P-13199)***
Best Western, San Diego *Also called Tic World-Wide Corp* ***(P-13328)***
Best Western, Victorville *Also called L & S Investment Co Inc* ***(P-12824)***
Best Western, South San Francisco *Also called Grosvenor Properties Ltd* ***(P-12631)***
Best Western, Carpinteria *Also called Carpinteria Motor Inn Inc* ***(P-12433)***
Best Western Amador Inn, Jackson *Also called Sita Ram LLC* ***(P-13232)***
Best Western Bayshore Inn ....E....707 268-8005
3500 Broadway Eureka (95503) ***(P-12371)***
Best Western Bayside Inn, San Diego *Also called T I C Hotels Inc* ***(P-13315)***
Best Western Canterbury Hotel, San Francisco *Also called Canterbury Hotel Corp* ***(P-12425)***
Best Western Golden Sails Ht, Torrance *Also called Long Beach Golden Sails Inc* ***(P-12862)***
Best Western Half Moon Bay, Half Moon Bay *Also called Pacifica Hotel Company* ***(P-13009)***
Best Western Hilltop Inn ....E....530 221-6100
2300 Hilltop Dr Redding (96002) ***(P-12372)***
Best Western Hotel Tomo ....E....415 921-4000
1800 Sutter St San Francisco (94115) ***(P-12373)***
Best Western International Inc ....D....559 592-8118
805 S Kaweah Ave Exeter (93221) ***(P-12374)***
Best Western Island Palms, San Diego *Also called Bartell Hotels* ***(P-12356)***
Best Western Oxnard Inn ....E....805 483-9581
1156 S Oxnard Blvd Oxnard (93030) ***(P-12375)***
Best Western Park Place, Anaheim *Also called Best Western Stovalls Inn* ***(P-12377)***
Best Western Pasada At Harbor, San Diego *Also called Tesi Investment Company LLC* ***(P-13324)***
Best Western Plus-Heritage Inn ....E....209 474-3301
111 E March Ln Stockton (95207) ***(P-12376)***
Best Western Stockton Inn, Stockton *Also called Westland Hotel Corporation* ***(P-13394)***
Best Western Stovalls Inn ....E....714 776-4800
1544 S Harbor Blvd Anaheim (92802) ***(P-12377)***
Best Western Stovalls Inn (PA) ....D....714 956-4430
1110 W Katella Ave Anaheim (92802) ***(P-12378)***
Best Western, The Beach Resort, Monterey *Also called Bayview Properties Inc* ***(P-12363)***
Best Wstn Carmel Mission Inn, Carmel *Also called Trevi Partners A Calif LP* ***(P-13343)***
Best Wstn El Rancho Inn Suites, Millbrae *Also called El Rancho Motel Inc* ***(P-12553)***
Best Wstn Half Moon Bay Lodge, Half Moon Bay *Also called Half Moon Bay Lodge* ***(P-12636)***
Best-Way Distributing Co, Sylmar *Also called Allied Company Holdings Inc* ***(P-8977)***
Bestitcom Inc (PA) ....D....602 667-5613
1464 Madera Rd Simi Valley (93065) ***(P-16317)***
Beston Development ....D....619 232-6315
1055 1st Ave San Diego (92101) ***(P-12379)***
Bestway Delivery, Van Nuys *Also called Mercury Messenger Service Inc* ***(P-17322)***
Bestway Recycling Company Inc (PA) ....D....323 588-8157
2268 Firestone Blvd Los Angeles (90002) ***(P-7971)***
Bet Tzedek ....D....323 939-0506
3250 Wilshire Blvd Fl 13 Los Angeles (90010) ***(P-22946)***
Beta Healthcare Group (PA) ....D....925 838-6070
1443 Danville Blvd Alamo (94507) ***(P-10423)***
Bethel Lutheran Home Inc ....D....559 896-4900
2280 Dockery Ave Selma (93662) ***(P-21009)***
Bethel Retirement Community ....D....209 577-1901
2345 Scenic Dr Modesto (95355) ***(P-21010)***
Bethesda Lthran Cmmunities Inc ....D....559 636-6300
5440 W Wren Ave Visalia (93291) ***(P-24435)***
Bethesda University California ....D....714 517-1945
730 N Euclid St Anaheim (92801) ***(P-12073)***
Bettendorf Enterprises Inc ....D....530 365-1937
20943 Bettendorf Way Anderson (96007) ***(P-4104)***
Bettendorf Trucking, Anderson *Also called Bettendorf Enterprises Inc* ***(P-4104)***
Better Homes and Gardens Mason ....D....925 776-2740
5887 Lone Tree Way Ste A Antioch (94531) ***(P-11241)***
Better Life Organic Produce, Los Angeles *Also called Better Life Produce Inc* ***(P-8641)***
Better Life Produce Inc ....E....213 623-0640
2020 E 7th Pl Los Angeles (90021) ***(P-8641)***
Better Living Brands LLC ....C....888 723-3929
11555 Dublin Canyon Rd Pleasanton (94588) ***(P-17031)***
Better Mens Clothes, Los Angeles *Also called Hirsh Inc* ***(P-1064)***
Better Way Services ....D....661 326-6444
5329 Office Center Ct # 100 Bakersfield (93309) ***(P-23511)***
Betterworks Systems Inc ....D....650 656-9013
999 Main St Redwood City (94063) ***(P-15607)***
Betty Ford Center (HQ) ....C....760 773-4100
39000 Bob Hope Dr Rancho Mirage (92270) ***(P-21999)***
Betty Jimenez, Brawley *Also called Clinicas De Slud Del Peblo Inc* ***(P-19391)***
Beutler Heating & AC, Fairfield *Also called Villara Corporation* ***(P-3209)***
Beutler Heating & AC, Manteca *Also called Villara Corporation* ***(P-2400)***
Beutler Heating & Air, McClellan *Also called Villara Corporation* ***(P-2401)***
Beven-Herron Inc ....C....714 523-5870
14511 Industry Cir La Mirada (90638) ***(P-3129)***
Beverly, Fresno *Also called Golden Living LLC* ***(P-20461)***
Beverly, Fowler *Also called Golden Living LLC* ***(P-20462)***
Beverly, Beverly Hills *Also called Bhrac LLC* ***(P-17629)***
Beverly, Ridgecrest *Also called Golden Living LLC* ***(P-22305)***
Beverly Blvd Leaseco LLC ....D....310 278-5444
8555 Beverly Blvd Los Angeles (90048) ***(P-12380)***
Beverly Center, Los Angeles *Also called La Cienega Associates* ***(P-11555)***
Beverly Community Hosp Assn ....B....323 889-2452
101 E Beverly Blvd # 104 Montebello (90640) ***(P-21299)***
Beverly Community Hosp Assn (PA) ....C....323 726-1222
309 W Beverly Blvd Montebello (90640) ***(P-21300)***
Beverly Community Hosp Assn ....A....323 725-1519
1920 W Whittier Blvd Montebello (90640) ***(P-21301)***
Beverly Health Care Corp (PA) ....E....805 642-1736
5445 Everglades St Ventura (93003) ***(P-26780)***
Beverly Healthcare, Panorama City *Also called Golden Living LLC* ***(P-21084)***
Beverly Healthcare, Costa Mesa *Also called Golden Living LLC* ***(P-20463)***
Beverly Healthcare, Montrose *Also called Golden Living LLC* ***(P-21085)***
Beverly Healthcare, San Francisco *Also called Golden Living LLC* ***(P-20466)***
Beverly Healthcare, Sonora *Also called Golden Living LLC* ***(P-21087)***
Beverly Healthcare, Modesto *Also called Golden Living LLC* ***(P-21088)***
Beverly Healthcare, Los Gatos *Also called Golden Living LLC* ***(P-21089)***
Beverly Healthcare, Seal Beach *Also called Golden Living LLC* ***(P-21090)***
Beverly Healthcare, Oxnard *Also called Golden Living LLC* ***(P-20468)***
Beverly Healthcare, Ventura *Also called Golden Living LLC* ***(P-20469)***
Beverly Healthcare, Lodi *Also called Golden Living LLC* ***(P-20470)***
Beverly Healthcare, West Covina *Also called Golden Living LLC* ***(P-20472)***
Beverly Healthcare, Madera *Also called Golden Living LLC* ***(P-21091)***
Beverly Healthcare, Capistrano Beach *Also called Golden Living LLC* ***(P-20475)***
Beverly Healthcare, Murrieta *Also called Golden Living LLC* ***(P-23824)***
Beverly Healthcare, Fresno *Also called Golden Living LLC* ***(P-20478)***
Beverly Healthcare, San Jose *Also called Golden Living LLC* ***(P-24540)***
Beverly Healthcare, Modesto *Also called Golden Living LLC* ***(P-20480)***
Beverly Healthcare, Los Gatos *Also called Golden Living LLC* ***(P-20481)***
Beverly Healthcare, Chico *Also called Golden Living LLC* ***(P-20484)***
Beverly Healthcare, Merced *Also called Golden Living LLC* ***(P-21095)***
Beverly Healthcare, Newman *Also called Golden Living LLC* ***(P-20485)***
Beverly Hills Active Club, Los Angeles *Also called 24 Hour Fitness Usa Inc* ***(P-18551)***
Beverly Hills Country Club ....C....310 836-4400
3084 Motor Ave Los Angeles (90064) ***(P-11856)***
Beverly Hills Hotel, Beverly Hills *Also called Sajahtera Inc* ***(P-13163)***
Beverly Hills Lingual Inst ....E....323 651-5000
8383 Wilshire Blvd # 250 Beverly Hills (90211) ***(P-17032)***
Beverly Hills Luxury Hotel LLC ....B....310 274-9999
1801 Century Park E # 1200 Los Angeles (90067) ***(P-12381)***
Beverly Hills Luxury Interiors, Los Angeles *Also called Kenneth Brdwick Intr Dsgns Inc* ***(P-17272)***
Beverly Hills Plaza Hotel, Los Angeles *Also called Donald T Sterling Corporation* ***(P-12538)***
Beverly Hills Polc Ofcrs Assoc ....D....310 288-1755
464 N Rexford Dr Beverly Hills (90210) ***(P-24999)***
Beverly Hospital, Montebello *Also called Beverly Community Hosp Assn* ***(P-21300)***

ALPHABETIC

Employee Codes: A=Over 500 employees, B=251-500
C=101-250, D=51-100, E=50
2019 Directory of California
Wholesalers and Services Companies
© Mergent Inc. 1-800-342-5647
1223

Beverly Pl Memory Care Cmnty, Los Angeles *Also called Silverado Senior Living Inc (P-21216)*
Beverly Radiology Med Group (PA)....C....310 975-1500
465 N Roxbury Dr Ste 101 Beverly Hills (90210) ***(P-19323)***
Beverly Sunstone Hills LLC....D....310 228-4100
1177 S Beverly Dr Los Angeles (90035) ***(P-12382)***
Beverly West Health Care Inc....D....323 938-2451
1020 S Fairfax Ave Los Angeles (90019) ***(P-20262)***
Beverlywood Realty Inc....E....310 836-8322
2800 S Robertson Blvd Los Angeles (90034) ***(P-11242)***
Bex Portfolio LLC....D....650 494-3700
925 E Meadow Dr Palo Alto (94303) ***(P-17033)***
Beyer Park Villas LLC....D....209 236-1900
3529 Forest Glenn Dr Modesto (95355) ***(P-24436)***
BFI Waste Services LLC....D....559 275-1551
5501 N Golden State Blvd Fresno (93722) ***(P-6354)***
BFI Waste Systems N Amer Inc....D....805 965-5248
800 Cacique St Santa Barbara (93103) ***(P-6355)***
BFI Waste Systems N Amer Inc....D....831 775-3850
271 Rianda St Salinas (93901) ***(P-6356)***
BFI Waste Systems N Amer Inc....D....510 657-1350
42600 Boyce Rd Fremont (94538) ***(P-6357)***
Bfp Fire Protection Inc....D....831 461-1100
17 Janis Way Scotts Valley (95066) ***(P-2143)***
Bgm, San Jose *Also called Brilliant General Maintinc (P-14203)*
Bh Partn A Calif Limit Partne (PA)....B....858 539-7635
998 W Mission Bay Dr San Diego (92109) ***(P-12383)***
Bh Partn A Calif Limit Partne....D....858 453-4420
11480 N Torrey Pines Rd A La Jolla (92037) ***(P-12384)***
Bh-SD Opco LLC....D....619 465-4411
7050 Parkway Dr La Mesa (91942) ***(P-21930)***
Bhandal Bros Inc....E....831 728-2691
2490 San Juan Rd Hollister (95023) ***(P-4105)***
Bhandal Bros Trucking Inc....D....831 728-2691
2490 San Juan Rd Hollister (95023) ***(P-4106)***
Bho LLC....E....951 845-2220
5801 Sun Lakes Blvd Banning (92220) ***(P-24437)***
Bhrac LLC....D....310 862-1933
9777 Wilshire Blvd # 517 Beverly Hills (90212) ***(P-17629)***
Bi-County Ambulance Service....E....530 674-2780
1700 Poole Blvd Yuba City (95993) ***(P-3777)***
Bi-Rite Foodservice Distrs, Brisbane *Also called Bi-Rite Restaurant Sup Co Inc (P-8385)*
Bi-Rite Restaurant Sup Co Inc....B....415 656-0187
123 S Hill Dr Brisbane (94005) ***(P-8385)***
Biagi Bros Inc....D....707 642-4412
1200 Green Island Rd American Canyon (94503) ***(P-4533)***
Biagi Bros Inc....C....909 390-6910
3655 E Airport Dr Ontario (91761) ***(P-4107)***
Biagi Bros Inc....D....707 745-8115
650 Stone Rd Benicia (94510) ***(P-4108)***
Biagi Brothers Bezzerides Co, Benicia *Also called Biagi Bros Inc (P-4108)*
Bianchi Ag Services Inc (PA)....C....530 882-4575
1210 Richvale Hwy Richvale (95974) ***(P-7701)***
Bianchi Ag Services Inc....D....530 923-7675
3056 Colusa Hwy Yuba City (95993) ***(P-682)***
Biarca Inc (PA)....D....408 564-4465
1060 Hyde Ave San Jose (95129) ***(P-16318)***
Bicara Ltd....B....310 316-6222
318 Avenue I Ste 65 Redondo Beach (90277) ***(P-8611)***
Bickmore and Associates Inc (HQ)....D....916 244-1100
1750 Creekside Oaks Dr # 200 Sacramento (95833) ***(P-10565)***
Bickmore Risk Svcs Consulting, Sacramento *Also called Bickmore and Associates Inc (P-10565)*
Bicycle Casino LP....A....562 806-4646
888 Bicycle Casino Dr Bell Gardens (90201) ***(P-12385)***
Bicycle Club Casino, Bell Gardens *Also called Bell Gardens Bicycle Club Inc (P-19109)*
Bicycle Hotel and Casino, Bell Gardens *Also called Bicycle Casino LP (P-12385)*
Bidmail, Tustin *Also called Internet Blueprint Inc (P-15231)*
Bienvenidos Childrens Center (PA)....C....213 785-5906
501 S Atlantic Blvd Los Angeles (90022) ***(P-23512)***
Bienvenidos Community Hlth Ctr, Los Angeles *Also called Via Care Cmnty Hlth Ctr Inc (P-20086)*
BIENVENIDOS FAMILY SERVICES, Los Angeles *Also called Bienvenidos Childrens Center (P-23512)*
Big 5 Sporting Goods Corp....B....323 755-2663
11310 Crenshaw Blvd Inglewood (90303) ***(P-19110)***
Big Bear City Cmnty Svcs Dst (PA)....D....909 585-2565
139 E Big Bear Blvd Big Bear City (92314) ***(P-6320)***
Big Bulb Ideas Inc....E....408 888-2346
5655 Silver Creek Vlley R San Jose (95138) ***(P-15024)***
Big Canyon Country Club....C....949 644-5404
1 Big Canyon Dr Newport Beach (92660) ***(P-18865)***
Big City Access Inc (PA)....D....916 428-4090
3131 52nd Ave West Sacramento (95691) ***(P-7668)***
Big F Company Inc....D....805 928-2333
1445 Jason Way Santa Maria (93455) ***(P-9073)***
Big Four Restaurant, San Francisco *Also called Nob Hill Properties Inc (P-12958)*
Big Joe California North Inc (PA)....C....510 785-6900
25932 Eden Landing Rd Hayward (94545) ***(P-7731)***
Big Joe Handling Systems, Hayward *Also called Big Joe California North Inc (P-7731)*
Big League Dreams Jurupa LLC....D....951 685-6900
10550 Cntu Gllano Rnch Rd Mira Loma (91752) ***(P-18508)***
Big Lgue Drams Chino Hills LLC....D....909 287-6900
16333 Fairfield Ranch Rd Chino Hills (91709) ***(P-18509)***
Big Lgue Dreams Consulting LLC....C....619 846-8855
2155 Trumble Rd Perris (92571) ***(P-18510)***
Big Lgue Dreams Consulting LLC....C....760 324-5600
33700 Date Palm Dr Cathedral City (92234) ***(P-13446)***
Big Lgue Dreams Consulting LLC....C....530 223-1177
20155 Viking Way Redding (96003) ***(P-18866)***
Big Lgue Dreams Consulting LLC....C....626 839-1100
2100 S Azusa Ave West Covina (91792) ***(P-18511)***
Big Oak Hardwood Floor Co Inc....D....650 591-8651
1731 Leslie St San Mateo (94402) ***(P-3096)***
Big River Lodge, Mendocino *Also called Big River Ltd-Design (P-12386)*
Big River Ltd-Design....D....707 937-5615
44850 Comptche Ukiah Rd Mendocino (95460) ***(P-12386)***
Big Sandy Rancheria, Auberry *Also called Mono Wind Casino (P-12936)*
Big Sky Country Club LLC....D....805 522-4653
3301 Lost Canyons Dr Simi Valley (93063) ***(P-18688)***
Big Star, South Gate *Also called Koos Manufacturing Inc (P-17278)*
Big Switch Networks Inc (PA)....D....650 322-6510
3111 Coronado Dr Bldg A Santa Clara (95054) ***(P-15608)***
Big Valley Mortgage, Roseville *Also called American Pacific Mortgage Corp (P-9774)*
Big3 Basketball LLC....D....213 417-2013
644 S Figueroa St Los Angeles (90017) ***(P-18512)***
Bigbyte Corporation....D....510 249-1100
47430 Seabridge Dr Fremont (94538) ***(P-16279)***
Biggest Lser Ftnes Rdge Malibu, Malibu *Also called Fitness Ridge Malibu LLC (P-12576)*
Biggie Crane and Ritting, San Leandro *Also called Galena Equipment Rental LLC (P-14440)*
Biggs Cardosa Associates Inc (PA)....D....408 296-5515
865 The Alameda San Jose (95126) ***(P-25566)***
Bigham Taylor Roofing Corp....D....510 886-0197
22721 Alice St Hayward (94541) ***(P-3130)***
Bighorn Golf Club....C....760 773-2468
255 Palowet Dr Palm Desert (92260) ***(P-18867)***
Bigrentz Inc....D....855 999-5438
1063 Mcgaw Ave Ste 200 Irvine (92614) ***(P-14437)***
Bigrentz.com, Irvine *Also called Bigrentz Inc (P-14437)*
Bill Brown Construction Co....D....408 297-3738
242 Phelan Ave San Jose (95112) ***(P-1269)***
Bill Brown Construction Co....D....408 297-3738
242 Phelan Ave San Jose (95112) ***(P-1123)***
Bill Howe Plumbing Inc....D....800 245-5469
9085 Aero Dr Ste B San Diego (92123) ***(P-2144)***
Bill Nelson GEC, Fresno *Also called Bill Nlson Gen Engrg Cnstr Inc (P-1897)*
Bill Nlson Gen Engrg Cnstr Inc....D....559 439-1756
7600 N Ingram Ave Ste 126 Fresno (93711) ***(P-1897)***
Bill Papich Construction Inc....E....805 489-9420
398 Sunrise Ter Arroyo Grande (93420) ***(P-2013)***
Bill Wilson Center (PA)....D....408 243-0222
3490 The Alameda Santa Clara (95050) ***(P-23513)***
Billcom Inc....C....650 353-3301
1810 Embarcadero Rd Palo Alto (94303) ***(P-15609)***
Billing Services Plus DBA Apex....D....415 604-3515
70 Dorman Ave San Francisco (94124) ***(P-14201)***
Bilt-Well Roofing & Mtl Co, Los Angeles *Also called Sbb Roofing Inc (P-3199)*
Biltmore Hotel....C....408 988-8411
2151 Laurelwood Rd Santa Clara (95054) ***(P-12387)***
Biltwell Roofing, Los Angeles *Also called R F R Corporation (P-11909)*
Binding Site Inc (PA)....D....858 453-9177
6730 Mesa Ridge Rd Ste B San Diego (92121) ***(P-7162)***
Binex Line Corp (PA)....D....310 416-8600
19515 S Vermont Ave Torrance (90502) ***(P-5016)***
Bio Industries Inc....E....530 529-3290
2060 Montgomery Rd Red Bluff (96080) ***(P-458)***
Bio-Mdcal Applications Cal Inc....D....562 920-2070
10116 Rosecrans Ave Bellflower (90706) ***(P-22466)***
Bio-Mdcal Applications Cal Inc....E....626 457-9002
1801 W Valley Blvd # 102 Alhambra (91803) ***(P-22467)***
Bio-Mdcal Applications Cal Inc....D....951 343-7700
3470 La Sierra Ave Ste E Riverside (92503) ***(P-22468)***
Bio-Mdical Applications Rl Inc....D....559 221-6311
3636 N 1st St Ste 144 Fresno (93726) ***(P-22469)***
Bio-Med Services Inc....D....909 235-4400
3300 E Guasti Rd Ontario (91761) ***(P-22742)***
Bio-Reference Laboratories Inc....C....408 341-8600
2605 Winchester Blvd Campbell (95008) ***(P-22062)***
Biocept Inc....D....858 320-8200
5810 Nancy Ridge Dr # 150 San Diego (92121) ***(P-26338)***
Bioclinca (PA)....C....415 817-8900
7707 Gateway Blvd Fl 3 Newark (94560) ***(P-15025)***
Bioclinca....E....503 284-3334
7707 Gateway Blvd Ste 300 Newark (94560) ***(P-26339)***
Biocompare, South San Francisco *Also called Comparenetworks Inc (P-26350)*
Biomarin Inc....C....415 761-8600
7250 Redwood Blvd Ste 300 Novato (94945) ***(P-7163)***
Biomat Usa Inc....A....310 772-7777
2410 Lillyvale Ave Los Angeles (90032) ***(P-22743)***
Biomat Usa Inc (HQ)....E....323 225-2221
2410 Lillyvale Ave Los Angeles (90032) ***(P-22744)***
Biomat Usa Inc....D....661 863-0621
246 Bernard St Bakersfield (93305) ***(P-22745)***
Biomed Realty LP (HQ)....E....858 485-9840
17190 Bernardo Center Dr San Diego (92128) ***(P-12153)***
Biomedical Engineering Center, Sacramento *Also called Sutter Health (P-21828)*
Biomedical Life Systems Inc....D....760 727-5600
2448 Cades Way Vista (92081) ***(P-7164)***
Biomedicure LLC....D....858 586-1888
7940 Silverton Ave # 107 San Diego (92126) ***(P-26340)***
Bionetics Corporation....E....650 604-5327
P.O. Box 115 Moffett Field (94035) ***(P-26341)***
Bioscreen Testing Services Inc (PA)....D....602 277-1154
3904 Del Amo Blvd Ste 801 Torrance (90503) ***(P-26686)***
Biosite Inc....D....510 683-9063
9975 Summers Ridge Rd San Diego (92121) ***(P-7165)***

Mergent e-mail: customerrelations@mergent.com
1224
2019 Directory of California Wholesalers and Services Companies
(P-0000) Products & Services Section entry number
(PA)=Parent Co (HQ)=Headquarters (DH)=Div Headquarters

Biotheranostics Inc (PA) ....D....877 886-6739
9640 Towne Centre Dr # 200 San Diego (92121) ***(P-22063)***
Birch Aquarium At Scripps ....E....858 534-4109
2300 Expedition Way La Jolla (92037) ***(P-24925)***
Birch Ptrick Convalescent Cntr, Chula Vista *Also called Sharp Healthcare* ***(P-20757)***
Bird Mrlla Bxer Wlpert A Prof ....D....310 201-2100
1875 Century Park E Fl 23 Los Angeles (90067) ***(P-22947)***
Birkenstock Usa Lp (HQ) ....D....415 884-3200
8171 Redwood Blvd Novato (94945) ***(P-8345)***
Birnam Wood Golf Club ....C....805 969-2223
1941 E Valley Rd Santa Barbara (93108) ***(P-18868)***
Birst Inc ....B....415 766-4800
45 Fremont St Ste 1800 San Francisco (94105) ***(P-15026)***
Birtcher Andrson Investors LLC ....E....949 545-0526
31910 Del Obispo St # 100 San Juan Capistrano (92675) ***(P-12202)***
Birtcher Andrson Property Svcs (PA) ....D....949 831-0707
27611 La Paz Rd Ste D Laguna Niguel (92677) ***(P-11243)***
Birtcher/Aetna Laguna Hills ....D....949 458-2311
24903 Moulton Pkwy Ofc Laguna Hills (92653) ***(P-10988)***
Birth Choice of San Marco ....D....760 744-1313
277 S Rancho Santa Fe Rd San Marcos (92078) ***(P-23514)***
Bishop Paiute Gaming Corp ....C....760 872-6005
2742 N Sierra Hwy Bishop (93514) ***(P-19111)***
Bishop Ranch Veterinary Center (PA) ....D....925 743-9300
2000 Bishop Dr San Ramon (94583) ***(P-597)***
Bishop Waste Disposal Inc ....E....760 872-6561
100 Snland Reservation Rd Bishop (93514) ***(P-6358)***
Bissell Bros Bldg Maint Servic, Rancho Cordova *Also called Bissell Brothers Janitorial* ***(P-14202)***
Bissell Brothers Janitorial ....D....916 635-1852
3207 Luyung Dr Rancho Cordova (95742) ***(P-14202)***
Bite Communications LLC (HQ) ....D....415 365-0222
100 Montgomery St # 1103 San Francisco (94104) ***(P-27161)***
Bitech-Ace A Joint Venture ....D....714 521-1477
7371 Walnut Ave Buena Park (90620) ***(P-3225)***
Bitfone Corporation (PA) ....E....949 234-7000
32451 Golden Lantern # 301 Laguna Niguel (92677) ***(P-15027)***
Bitgravity, Burlingame *Also called Tata Communications Amer Inc* ***(P-17496)***
Bittorrent Inc ....E....408 641-4219
612 Howard St Ste 400 San Francisco (94105) ***(P-15028)***
Bizcom Electronics Inc (HQ) ....C....408 262-7877
1171 Montague Expy Milpitas (95035) ***(P-7018)***
Bizmatics Inc (PA) ....C....408 873-3030
4010 Moorpark Ave Ste 222 San Jose (95117) ***(P-15610)***
Bizringer.com, Newport Beach *Also called Baid Vivek* ***(P-5521)***
Bjj Company LLC (PA) ....D....209 941-8361
1040 W Kettleman Ln Lodi (95240) ***(P-4109)***
BJs Restaurants Inc ....C....209 526-8850
3401 Dale Rd Ste 840 Modesto (95356) ***(P-8003)***
Bkf Engineers (PA) ....C....650 482-6300
255 Shoreline Dr Ste 200 Redwood City (94065) ***(P-25567)***
BKK Corporation (PA) ....D....626 965-0911
2210 S Azusa Ave West Covina (91792) ***(P-6359)***
BKM Officeworks, San Diego *Also called Wmk Office San Diego LLC* ***(P-6745)***
Bl Daily, San Francisco *Also called Beauties of Life Inc* ***(P-15022)***
Blach Construction Company (PA) ....D....408 244-7100
2244 Blach Pl Ste 100 San Jose (95131) ***(P-1378)***
Black & Veatch Corporation ....E....913 458-2000
5 Peters Canyon Rd # 300 Irvine (92606) ***(P-25568)***
Black & White TV Inc ....E....310 855-1040
8756 Dorrington Ave West Hollywood (90048) ***(P-17882)***
Black Bear Security Services ....C....415 559-5159
2016 Oakdale Ave Ste B San Francisco (94124) ***(P-16583)***
Black Box Network Services, Los Angeles *Also called Scottel Voice & Data Inc* ***(P-17910)***
Black Canyon Capital LLC ....C....310 272-1800
2000 Avenue Of The Los Angeles (90067) ***(P-26781)***
Black Diamond Electric Inc ....D....925 777-3440
2595 W 10th St Antioch (94509) ***(P-2523)***
Black Dog Farms of California ....C....760 356-2951
530 W 6th St Holtville (92250) ***(P-37)***
Black Dot Wireless LLC ....D....949 502-3800
27271 Las Ramblas Ste 300 Mission Viejo (92691) ***(P-5300)***
Black Gold Golf Club ....D....714 961-0060
1 Black Gold Dr Yorba Linda (92886) ***(P-18689)***
Black Jack Farms, Santa Maria *Also called Blackjack Farms De La Costa CN* ***(P-324)***
Black Knght RE Data Sltons LLC ....C....626 808-9000
3100 New York Dr Pasadena (91107) ***(P-11244)***
Black Knight Data & Analytics, Pasadena *Also called Black Knght RE Data Sltons LLC* ***(P-11244)***
Black Lake Golf Course, Nipomo *Also called American Golf Corporation* ***(P-18834)***
Black Meadow Landing ....D....760 663-4901
156100 Black Meadow Rd Parker Dam (92267) ***(P-12388)***
Black Oak Casino ....D....209 928-9300
19400 Tuolumne Rd N Tuolumne (95379) ***(P-19112)***
Black Tie Transportation LLC ....C....925 847-0747
7080 Commerce Dr Pleasanton (94588) ***(P-3778)***
Blackarrow Inc (HQ) ....D....408 642-6400
4 N 2nd St Ste 1100 San Jose (95113) ***(P-15029)***
Blackbaud Internet Solutions, San Diego *Also called Kintera Inc* ***(P-15730)***
Blackbeard's Family Fun Center, Fresno *Also called GLad Entertainment Inc* ***(P-19178)***
Blackhawk Country Club ....C....925 736-6500
599 Blackhawk Club Dr Danville (94506) ***(P-18869)***
Blackhawk Network Inc (HQ) ....A....925 226-9990
6220 Stoneridge Mall Rd Pleasanton (94588) ***(P-9672)***
Blackhawk Network Holdings Inc (HQ) ....B....925 226-9990
6220 Stoneridge Mall Rd Pleasanton (94588) ***(P-9673)***
Blackjack Farms De La Costa CN ....C....805 347-1333
2385 A St Santa Maria (93455) ***(P-324)***
Blackline Systems Inc (HQ) ....C....818 746-4700
21300 Victory Blvd Fl 12 Woodland Hills (91367) ***(P-15611)***
Blackrock Funds III ....D....415 597-2000
400 Howard St San Francisco (94105) ***(P-12029)***
Blackrock Global Investors ....A....415 670-2000
400 Howard St San Francisco (94105) ***(P-10062)***
Blackrock Holdco 2 Inc ....D....415 678-2000
50 California St Ste 200 San Francisco (94111) ***(P-11245)***
Blackrock Instnl Tr Nat Assn (HQ) ....A....415 597-2000
400 Howard St San Francisco (94105) ***(P-12030)***
Blackrock Logistics Inc ....C....925 523-3878
7031 Koll Center Pkwy # 250 Pleasanton (94566) ***(P-5017)***
Blackstone Consulting Inc (PA) ....C....310 826-4389
11726 San Vicente Blvd # 550 Los Angeles (90049) ***(P-27162)***
Blackstone Technology Group (PA) ....D....415 837-1400
455 Market St Ste 620 San Francisco (94105) ***(P-27658)***
Bladium Inc (PA) ....C....510 814-4999
800 W Tower Ave Bldg 40 Alameda (94501) ***(P-18581)***
Bladium Sports Clubs, Alameda *Also called Bladium Inc* ***(P-18581)***
Blaine Convention Services Inc ....A....714 522-8270
114 S Berry St Brea (92821) ***(P-17034)***
Blaine Tech Services Inc (PA) ....D....408 573-0555
1680 Rogers Ave San Jose (95112) ***(P-27659)***
Blair Engineering Inc (PA) ....D....559 326-1400
451 Clovis Ave Ste 200 Clovis (93612) ***(P-25569)***
Blair Television Inc ....D....714 537-5923
11111 Santa Monica Blvd # 1900 Los Angeles (90025) ***(P-18024)***
Blair TV Communication, Los Angeles *Also called Blair Television Inc* ***(P-18024)***
Blair, Church & Flynn, Clovis *Also called Blair Engineering Inc* ***(P-25569)***
Blake H Brown Inc (HQ) ....D....310 764-0110
1300 W Artesia Blvd Compton (90220) ***(P-7732)***
Blanchard Training and Dev Inc (PA) ....C....760 489-5005
125 State Pl Escondido (92029) ***(P-27163)***
Blanchardcoachingcom Inc ....B....760 489-5005
125 State Pl Escondido (92029) ***(P-24157)***
Blank Rome LLP ....D....424 239-3400
2029 Century Park E Fl 6 Los Angeles (90067) ***(P-22948)***
Blare's Air & Ground Services, Lemoore *Also called R & D Leasing Inc* ***(P-14539)***
Blayne Pacelli ....D....310 383-6281
12345 Ventura Blvd Ste A Studio City (91604) ***(P-11246)***
Blazer Wilkinson LP ....B....831 455-3700
19040 Portola Dr Salinas (93908) ***(P-8642)***
Blazing Industrial Steel Inc ....C....951 360-8340
9040 Jurupa Rd Riverside (92509) ***(P-3364)***
Blazona Concrete Cnstr Inc ....D....916 375-8337
525 Harbor Blvd Ste 10 West Sacramento (95691) ***(P-1481)***
Blb Resources Inc (PA) ....C....949 261-9155
16845 Von Karman Ave # 100 Irvine (92606) ***(P-27164)***
Bleacher Report Inc ....D....415 777-5505
609 Mission St San Francisco (94105) ***(P-16099)***
Bleacher Report Inc ....C....415 777-5505
153 Kearny St Fl 2 San Francisco (94108) ***(P-18235)***
Bledsoe Masonry Inc ....D....951 360-6140
4680 Felspar St Ste A Riverside (92509) ***(P-2798)***
Bleu Chateau Assisted Living, Burbank *Also called Le Bleu Chateau Inc* ***(P-24576)***
Blh Construction Company ....C....818 905-3837
21031 Ventura Blvd # 200 Woodland Hills (91364) ***(P-1270)***
Blind Childrens Lrng Ctr Inc ....E....714 573-8888
18542 Vanderlip Ave Ste B Santa Ana (92705) ***(P-24267)***
Blize Healthcare Cal Inc ....D....800 343-2549
750 Alfred Nobel Dr # 202 Hercules (94547) ***(P-22236)***
Blizzard Entertainment Inc (HQ) ....D....949 955-1380
1 Blizzard Irvine (92618) ***(P-15612)***
Blocka Construction Inc ....D....510 657-3686
4455 Enterprise St Fremont (94538) ***(P-2145)***
Blockr.io, San Francisco *Also called Coinbase Inc* ***(P-9674)***
Blois Construction Inc ....C....805 485-0011
3201 Sturgis Rd Oxnard (93030) ***(P-1898)***
Blomberg Window, Sacramento *Also called B B & T Management Corp* ***(P-6809)***
Blood Bank of Redwoods (PA) ....C....707 545-1222
3505 Industrial Dr Santa Rosa (95403) ***(P-22746)***
Blood Bank of San Bernardino A (PA) ....B....909 885-6503
384 W Orange Show Rd San Bernardino (92408) ***(P-22747)***
Blood Center of The Pacific, Santa Rosa *Also called Blood Bank of Redwoods* ***(P-22746)***
Blood Centers of Pacific (PA) ....C....415 567-6400
270 Masonic Ave San Francisco (94118) ***(P-22748)***
Blood Centers of Pacific ....E....707 428-6001
1325 Gateway Blvd Ste C1 Fairfield (94533) ***(P-22749)***
Blood Systems, Hayward *Also called Vitalant* ***(P-22900)***
Bloodsource Inc (PA) ....B....916 456-1500
10536 Peter A Mccuen Blvd Mather (95655) ***(P-22750)***
Bloodsource Inc ....D....209 724-0428
382 E Yosemite Ave Merced (95340) ***(P-22751)***
Bloodsource Inc ....E....916 488-1701
3099 Fair Oaks Blvd Sacramento (95864) ***(P-22752)***
Bloom David Law Offices of ....E....323 938-5248
3530 Wilshire Blvd # 1300 Los Angeles (90010) ***(P-22949)***
Bloom Hergott Diemer Cook LLC ....D....310 859-6800
150 S Rodeo Dr Fl 3 Beverly Hills (90212) ***(P-22950)***
Bloom, Jacob A, Beverly Hills *Also called Bloom Hergott Diemer Cook LLC* ***(P-22950)***
Bloomberg LP ....D....415 912-2960
345 California St Fl 35 San Francisco (94104) ***(P-16953)***
Blossom Valley Cnstr Inc ....D....408 993-0766
1125 Mabury Rd San Jose (95133) ***(P-805)***
Blower-Dempsay Corporation (PA) ....C....714 481-3800
4042 W Garry Ave Santa Ana (92704) ***(P-9197)***
Bls Lmsine Svc Los Angeles Inc (PA) ....B....323 644-7166
2860 Fletcher Dr Los Angeles (90039) ***(P-3779)***

ALPHABETIC

Employee Codes: A=Over 500 employees, B=251-500
C=101-250, D=51-100, E=50
2019 Directory of California
Wholesalers and Services Companies
© Mergent Inc. 1-800-342-5647
1225

BLT & Associates Inc ....C....323 860-4000
6430 W Sunset Blvd # 800 Los Angeles (90028) *(P-14101)*
Blu Homes Inc ....C....415 625-0809
1015 Walnut Ave Vallejo (94592) *(P-1124)*
Blue and Gold Fleet ....D....415 705-8200
Marine Terminal Pier 41 St Pier San Francisco (94133) *(P-4710)*
Blue Banner Company Inc (PA) ....D....951 682-6183
2601 3rd St Riverside (92507) *(P-495)*
Blue Box Opco LLC (PA) ....D....800 840-4916
10025 Mesa Rim Rd San Diego (92121) *(P-7947)*
Blue Bus Tours LLC ....C....415 353-5310
50 Quint St San Francisco (94124) *(P-19113)*
Blue Casa Communications Inc ....E....805 966-1669
114 E Haley St Ste A Santa Barbara (93101) *(P-5522)*
Blue Chip Inventory Service ....D....818 461-1765
14852 Ventura Blvd # 112 Sherman Oaks (91403) *(P-17035)*
Blue Chip Mayflower, Hawthorne *Also called Blue Chip Moving and Stor Inc (P-4110)*
Blue Chip Moving and Stor Inc ....D....323 463-6888
13525 Crenshaw Blvd Hawthorne (90250) *(P-4110)*
Blue Chip Stamps ....A....626 585-6700
301 E Colo Blvd Ste 300 Pasadena (91101) *(P-7261)*
Blue Coat LLC ....A....408 220-2200
350 Ellis St Mountain View (94043) *(P-15613)*
Blue Coat Systems LLC (HQ) ....D....650 527-8000
350 Ellis St Mountain View (94043) *(P-15921)*
Blue Cross & Blue Shield Mich ....C....323 782-3046
6300 Wilshire Blvd # 970 Los Angeles (90048) *(P-10181)*
Blue Cross of California (HQ) ....C....805 557-6050
4553 La Tienda Rd Westlake Village (91362) *(P-10182)*
Blue Devils Lessee LLC ....C....310 399-9344
530 Pico Blvd Santa Monica (90405) *(P-12389)*
Blue Diamond Growers ....C....209 545-6221
4800 Sisk Rd Modesto (95356) *(P-496)*
Blue Diamond Materials, Brea *Also called Sully-Miller Contracting Co (P-1856)*
Blue Eagle Contracting Inc ....D....530 272-0287
2059 Nev Cy Hwy Ste 204 Grass Valley (95945) *(P-3979)*
Blue Earth Inc (PA) ....C....702 608-5476
235 Pine St Ste 1100 San Francisco (94104) *(P-11965)*
Blue Freight, Tarzana *Also called Blue Sky Services Inc (P-5018)*
Blue Harbor, Aliso Viejo *Also called By Wind Inc (P-15042)*
Blue Haven Pools, San Diego *Also called P & A Holdings Inc (P-11957)*
Blue Jeans Network Inc (PA) ....D....408 550-2828
516 Clyde Ave Mountain View (94043) *(P-5970)*
Blue Lake Casino ....E....707 668-5101
777 Casino Way Blue Lk Blue Lake Blue Lake (95525) *(P-12390)*
Blue Mountain Air, Vacaville *Also called Blue Mountain Cnstr Svcs Inc (P-2146)*
Blue Mountain Cnstr Svcs Inc ....C....800 889-2085
707 Aldridge Rd Ste B Vacaville (95688) *(P-2146)*
Blue Planet International Inc ....E....323 526-9999
2945 E 12th St Los Angeles (90023) *(P-8289)*
Blue River Seafood Inc ....E....510 300-6800
25447 Industrial Blvd Hayward (94545) *(P-8571)*
Blue Rose Concrete Contrs Inc ....C....909 823-6190
14636 Ceres Ave Fontana (92335) *(P-3226)*
Blue Sheild of California, Walnut Creek *Also called California Physicians Service (P-10184)*
Blue Shield of California, San Francisco *Also called California Physicians Service (P-10185)*
Blue Shield of California, El Dorado Hills *Also called California Physicians Service (P-10187)*
Blue Shield of California, El Segundo *Also called California Physicians Service (P-10188)*
Blue Shield of California, Woodland Hills *Also called California Physicians Service (P-10189)*
Blue Skies Landscape Maint, Encinitas *Also called Cielo Azul Inc (P-812)*
Blue Sky Services Inc ....D....818 609-8779
5530 Corbin Ave Ste 220 Tarzana (91356) *(P-5018)*
Blue-Grace Logistics LLC ....D....858 427-5093
8765 Aero Dr Ste 133 San Diego (92123) *(P-5019)*
Bluebeam Inc (PA) ....C....626 788-4100
55 S Lake Ave Ste 900 Pasadena (91101) *(P-15030)*
Bluebridge Professional Svcs ....D....909 625-6151
420 W Baseline Rd Ste D Claremont (91711) *(P-22237)*
Bluegill Solar, Moreno Valley *Also called Bluegill Technologies LLC (P-16879)*
Bluegill Technologies LLC ....D....877 765-2770
11884 Welby Pl Ste 101 Moreno Valley (92557) *(P-16879)*
Blueline Construction, Rancho Cordova *Also called Ron Nurss Inc (P-3318)*
Bluevine Capital Inc ....D....888 216-9619
401 Warren St Ste 300 Redwood City (94063) *(P-9734)*
Bluewater Envmtl Svcs Inc ....D....510 346-8800
2075 Williams St San Leandro (94577) *(P-3494)*
Blufocus Inc ....D....818 294-7695
2233 N Ontario St 130 Burbank (91504) *(P-15031)*
Blumenthal Distributing Inc (PA) ....C....909 930-2000
1901 S Archibald Ave Ontario (91761) *(P-6712)*
Blx Group Inc ....D....760 776-6622
71534 Sahara Rd Rancho Mirage (92270) *(P-247)*
Blx Group LLC ....D....213 612-2400
777 S Figueroa St # 3200 Los Angeles (90017) *(P-10063)*
Blythe Nursing Care Center ....D....760 922-8176
285 W Chanslor Way Blythe (92225) *(P-20263)*
BMA Long Beach, Long Beach *Also called Fresenius Med Care Long Beach (P-22476)*
BMA San Gabriel, Alhambra *Also called Bio-Mdcal Applications Cal Inc (P-22467)*
BMC Group Inc ....D....310 321-5555
300 N Cntntl Blvd Ste 570 El Segundo (90245) *(P-22951)*
Bmi Imaging Systems Inc (PA) ....D....916 924-6666
1115 E Arques Ave Sunnyvale (94085) *(P-16100)*
Bml Industries Inc ....D....805 388-6800
1040 Avenida Acaso Camarillo (93012) *(P-7339)*
Bml Works Na LLC ....D....650 268-8305
228 Hamilton Ave Fl 3 Palo Alto (94301) *(P-26782)*
Bmp, Glendale *Also called Bunim-Murray Productions (P-18027)*
Bmr 21 Erie St LLC ....D....858 485-9840
17190 Bernardo Center Dr San Diego (92128) *(P-11247)*
Bmr Apps Inc ....D....954 651-1412
548 Market St San Francisco (94104) *(P-16319)*
Bms Parent Inc (PA) ....D....909 981-2341
1220 Dewey Way Ste F Upland (91786) *(P-26151)*
Bmt International SEC Svcs, Oakland *Also called Rory V Parker (P-16777)*
Bmt Scientific Marine Svcs Inc (HQ) ....D....760 737-3505
955 Borra Pl Ste 100 Escondido (92029) *(P-25570)*
Bmv Direct II LP ....D....858 485-9840
17190 Bernardo Center Dr San Diego (92128) *(P-27660)*
BMW Designworks ....C....503 614-3403
2201 Corporate Center Dr Newbury Park (91320) *(P-6627)*
BNC Real Estate (PA) ....B....858 481-3000
990 Highland Dr Ste 203 Solana Beach (92075) *(P-11248)*
Bni Enterprises Inc ....A....909 305-1818
545 College Commerce Way Upland (91786) *(P-27543)*
Bnn, Los Angeles *Also called Breitbart News Network LLC (P-13937)*
Bnsf Railway Company ....C....909 386-4002
740 Carnegie Dr San Bernardino (92408) *(P-3614)*
Bnsf Railway Company ....C....760 255-7803
200 N Avenue H Barstow (92311) *(P-3615)*
Bnsf Railway Company ....C....323 869-3002
6300 Sheila St Commerce (90040) *(P-3616)*
Bnsf Railway Company ....C....323 267-4133
3770 E Washington Blvd Vernon (90058) *(P-3617)*
Boardvantage Inc (HQ) ....D....212 401-8700
4300 Bohannon Dr Ste 110 Menlo Park (94025) *(P-26783)*
Boatworks, San Leandro *Also called Stepping Stn Grwth Ctr Fr Chld (P-24234)*
Bob Dillon Construction Inc ....C....805 495-2607
856 Calle Margarita Thousand Oaks (91360) *(P-3019)*
Bob Hope Health Center, Woodland Hills *Also called Motion Picture and TV Fund (P-21598)*
Bob Hubbard Horse Trnsp Inc (PA) ....E....951 369-3770
3730 S Riverside Ave Colton (92324) *(P-3980)*
Boca Mesa Incorporated ....D....805 934-9470
3130 Skyway Dr Ste 701 Santa Maria (93455) *(P-27661)*
Bockmon & Woody Elc Co Inc ....C....209 464-4878
1528 El Pinal Dr Stockton (95205) *(P-2524)*
Bodega Bay Associates ....D....650 330-8888
1100 Alma St Ste 106 Menlo Park (94025) *(P-12391)*
Bodega Bay Lodge, Bodega Bay *Also called NAPA Valley Lodge LP (P-12949)*
Bodega Bay Lodge, Menlo Park *Also called Bodega Bay Associates (P-12391)*
Bodega Harbour Golf Links, Bodega Bay *Also called Bodega Harbour Homeowners Assn (P-25100)*
Bodega Harbour Homeowners Assn ....D....707 875-3519
21301 Heron Dr Bodega Bay (94923) *(P-25100)*
Body Transformations, Lodi *Also called R DS For Healthcare (P-20198)*
Boeing Company ....D....805 606-6340
Slc 2 Bldg 1628 San Luis Obispo (93401) *(P-4875)*
Boeing Company ....B....650 316-3732
329 Bernardo Ave Mountain View (94043) *(P-25571)*
Boeing Company ....D....925 398-7664
5753 W Las Positas Blvd Pleasanton (94588) *(P-26342)*
Boeing Company ....E....818 466-8800
5800 Woolsey Canyon Rd Canoga Park (91304) *(P-25572)*
Boething Treeland Farms Inc ....A....650 851-4770
2923 Alpine Rd Portola Valley (94028) *(P-984)*
Boething Treeland Farms Inc (PA) ....D....818 883-1222
23475 Long Valley Rd Woodland Hills (91367) *(P-985)*
Boething Treeland Farms Inc ....C....209 727-3741
20601 E Kettleman Ln Lodi (95240) *(P-986)*
Boething Treeland Nursery, Lodi *Also called Boething Treeland Farms Inc (P-986)*
Bogart Construction Inc ....D....949 453-1400
9980 Irvine Center Dr # 200 Irvine (92618) *(P-1482)*
Bogh Engineering Inc ....D....951 845-5130
401 W Fourth St Beaumont (92223) *(P-3227)*
Bohemian Club (PA) ....C....415 885-2440
624 Taylor St San Francisco (94102) *(P-25101)*
BOHEMIAN GROVE, San Francisco *Also called Bohemian Club (P-25101)*
Bohm Law Group Inc (PA) ....E....916 927-5574
4600 Northgate Blvd # 210 Sacramento (95834) *(P-22952)*
Boiling Point Rest Sca Inc ....B....626 551-5181
13668 Valley Blvd Unit C2 City of Industry (91746) *(P-14578)*
Bolin Builders Inc ....E....209 772-9721
3848 Berkesey Ln Valley Springs (95252) *(P-1125)*
Bollingers Candelight Pavilion, Claremont *Also called Ben Bollinger Productions Inc (P-18344)*
Bolsa Medical Group, Westminster *Also called Co D L Pham MD (P-19392)*
Bolthouse Farms ....A....661 366-7205
3200 E Brundage Ln Bakersfield (93304) *(P-38)*
Bombard Mar & Resort MGT Svcs (PA) ....B....310 519-7971
95 Berth San Pedro (90731) *(P-4711)*
Bomel Construction Co Inc ....C....760 431-6360
701 Palomar Airport Rd # 270 Carlsbad (92011) *(P-1379)*
Bomel Construction Co Inc (PA) ....D....714 921-1660
96 Corporate Park Ste 100 Irvine (92606) *(P-1380)*
Bon Appetit Management Co ....C....909 748-8970
1259 E Colton Ave Redlands (92374) *(P-27165)*
Bonanza Plumbing Inc (PA) ....D....951 360-8262
2259 Hamner Ave Norco (92860) *(P-2147)*
Bonanza Productions Inc ....A....818 954-4212
4000 Warner Blvd Burbank (91522) *(P-18427)*
Bonded Carpet, San Diego *Also called Bonded Inc (P-13572)*
Bonded Inc (PA) ....D....858 576-8400
7831 Ostrow St San Diego (92111) *(P-13572)*
Bondi-Nderson Assoc Insur Brks, Santa Rosa *Also called Northwest Insurance Agency (P-10719)*

Mergent e-mail: customerrelations@mergent.com
1226
2019 Directory of California Wholesalers and Services Companies
(P-0000) Products & Services Section entry number
(PA)=Parent Co (HQ)=Headquarters (DH)=Div Headquarters

Bongmi Inc ....E....415 823-8595
68 Harriet St Unit 3 San Francisco (94103) *(P-7166)*
Bonhams Bttrflds Actneers Corp (HQ) ....C....415 861-7500
220 San Bruno Ave San Francisco (94103) *(P-17036)*
Bonhams Corporation ....C....415 861-7500
220 San Bruno Ave San Francisco (94103) *(P-17037)*
Bonita Golf Club, Bonita *Also called Crockett & Coinc (P-18702)*
Bonita House Inc ....D....510 923-0180
6333 Telg Ave Ste 102 Oakland (94609) *(P-23515)*
Bonita Medical Offices, Bonita *Also called Kaiser Foundation Hospitals (P-21514)*
Bonne Bridge Muell Okeef & (PA) ....D....213 480-1900
3699 Wilsh Boule Fl 10 Flr 10 Los Angeles (90010) *(P-22953)*
Bonneville International Corp ....E....323 634-1800
5900 Wilshire Blvd # 1900 Los Angeles (90036) *(P-5692)*
Bonneville International Corp ....D....415 764-1021
2013rd St Ste 1200 San Francisco (94103) *(P-5693)*
Bonneville International Corp ....E....415 777-0965
201 3rd St Fl 12 San Francisco (94103) *(P-5694)*
Bonneville Steel Inc ....D....866 956-8323
13654 Live Oak Ln Irwindale (91706) *(P-3365)*
Bonnie Brae Cnvlscent Hosp Inc (PA) ....D....213 483-8144
420 S Bonnie Brae St Los Angeles (90057) *(P-21011)*
Bontadelli Inc ....D....831 423-8572
2611 Mission St Santa Cruz (95060) *(P-8643)*
Bonterra Psomas, Santa Ana *Also called Psomas (P-26132)*
Boom-Boom Jeans, Los Angeles *Also called Blue Planet International Inc (P-8289)*
Boomers, Newport Beach *Also called Festival Fun Parks LLC (P-19170)*
Boomers, Vista *Also called Festival Fun Parks LLC (P-19172)*
Boornazian Jensen & Garthe A ....D....510 834-4350
555 12th St Oakland (94607) *(P-22954)*
Booth Ranches LLC ....D....559 626-4472
440 Anchor Ave Orange Cove (93646) *(P-447)*
Booz Allen Hamilton Inc ....D....310 297-2100
5220 Pacific Concourse Dr # 390 Los Angeles (90045) *(P-27166)*
Booz Allen Hamilton Inc ....D....619 725-6500
1615 Murray Canyon Rd # 900 San Diego (92108) *(P-27167)*
Booz Allen Hamilton Inc ....D....310 524-1557
2250 E Imperial Hwy # 540 El Segundo (90245) *(P-25573)*
Booz Allen Hamilton Inc ....D....213 620-1900
555 S Flower St Fl 36 Los Angeles (90071) *(P-27168)*
Borbon Incorporated ....C....714 994-0170
7312 Walnut Ave Buena Park (90620) *(P-2424)*
Border Valley Trading Ltd ....D....760 344-6700
604 Mead Rd Brawley (92227) *(P-9074)*
Border Valley Trading Ltd (PA) ....D....209 669-6000
14503 W Harding Rd Turlock (95380) *(P-9075)*
Boreal Ridge Corporation ....C....530 426-1012
19749 Boreal Ridge Rd Soda Springs (95728) *(P-12392)*
Boreal Ski Area, Soda Springs *Also called Boreal Ridge Corporation (P-12392)*
Boretech Resrce Recovry Engine ....E....209 373-2588
1820 Industrial Dr Stockton (95206) *(P-7733)*
Boretech Rsurce Recovery Engrg, Stockton *Also called Boretech Resrce Recovry Engine (P-7733)*
Borg Redwood Fences, Livermore *Also called Selex Inc (P-3582)*
Borgens & Borgens Inc ....D....209 547-2980
141 E Acacia St Ste D Stockton (95202) *(P-16584)*
Borjon Iscander ....C....209 245-6289
18586 Highway 49 Plymouth (95669) *(P-640)*
Borland Software Corporation ....D....650 286-1900
951 Mariners Isl Blvd # 460 San Mateo (94404) *(P-15614)*
Borrego Cmnty Hlth Foundation ....B....760 765-1223
2721 Washington Julian (92036) *(P-19324)*
Borrego Cmnty Hlth Foundation (PA) ....C....760 767-5051
4343 Yaqui Pass Rd Borrego Springs (92004) *(P-19325)*
Borrego Medical Center, Borrego Springs *Also called Borrego Cmnty Hlth Foundation (P-19325)*
Borrmann Metal Center (PA) ....D....818 846-7171
110 W Olive Ave Burbank (91502) *(P-7262)*
Borunda Private SEC Patrol Inc ....E....559 299-2662
1070 Brookhaven Dr Clovis (93612) *(P-16585)*
Boshart Automotive Tstg Svcs ....D....909 466-1602
1840 S Carlos Ave 15 Ontario (91761) *(P-17038)*
Boskovich Farms Inc (PA) ....C....805 487-2299
711 Diaz Ave Oxnard (93030) *(P-497)*
Boskovich Farms Inc ....B....805 987-1443
4224 Pleasant Valley Rd Camarillo (93012) *(P-39)*
Bosman Dairy LLC ....C....559 752-7018
6802 Avenue 120 A Tipton (93272) *(P-407)*
Boss Audio Systems, Oxnard *Also called Ava Enterprises Inc (P-7409)*
Bossard North America Inc ....D....562 906-2003
2000 Chabot Ct Tracy (95304) *(P-7841)*
Boston Brick & Stone Inc ....E....626 269-2622
2005 Lincoln Ave Pasadena (91103) *(P-2799)*
Boston Consulting Group Inc ....D....213 621-2772
355 S Grand Ave Ste 3300 Los Angeles (90071) *(P-27169)*
Bostonia Medical Offices, El Cajon *Also called Kaiser Foundation Hospitals (P-21499)*
Botanica Landscapes, Yuba City *Also called United Landscape Resource Inc (P-955)*
Bottomley Distributing Co Inc ....D....408 945-0660
755 Yosemite Dr Milpitas (95035) *(P-8983)*
Boulder Active Club, Carlsbad *Also called 24 Hour Fitness Usa Inc (P-18550)*
Boulder Creek Post Acute, Poway *Also called Pomerado Operations LLC (P-20711)*
Boulevard Entertainment Inc ....C....818 840-6969
903 S Lake St Ste 202 Burbank (91502) *(P-17039)*
Boutique Air Inc ....B....415 449-0505
5 3rd St Ste 925 San Francisco (94103) *(P-4856)*
Bowers Ambulance Service, Baldwin Park *Also called Bowers Companies Inc (P-3780)*
Bowers Companies Inc (HQ) ....D....562 988-6460
5257 Vincent Ave Baldwin Park (91706) *(P-3780)*
Bowie Enterprises ....D....559 732-2988
1920 S Mooney Blvd Visalia (93277) *(P-17803)*
Bowie Enterprises (PA) ....D....559 227-6221
4411 N Blackstone Ave Fresno (93726) *(P-17804)*
Bowie Enterprises ....D....559 292-6565
801 W Shaw Ave Clovis (93612) *(P-17805)*
Bowie Enterprises ....D....559 227-3400
4411 N Blackstone Ave Fresno (93726) *(P-17853)*
Bowie Limited ....D....716 610-2480
18351 Colima Rd Ste 255 Rowland Heights (91748) *(P-15032)*
Bowlero Corp ....D....626 339-1286
1060 W San Bernardino Rd Covina (91722) *(P-18481)*
Bowlero Corp ....D....626 960-3636
675 S Glendora Ave West Covina (91790) *(P-18482)*
Bowlero Corp ....E....909 945-9392
7930 Haven Ave Ste 101 Rancho Cucamonga (91730) *(P-18483)*
Bowlero Corp ....E....951 698-2202
40440 California Oaks Rd Murrieta (92562) *(P-18484)*
Bowles & Verna ....E....925 935-3300
2121 N Calif Blvd Ste 875 Walnut Creek (94596) *(P-22955)*
Bowles Farming Co Inc ....E....209 827-3000
11609 Hereford Rd Los Banos (93635) *(P-325)*
Bowman & Brooke-Attys, Torrance *Also called Bowman and Brooke LLP (P-22956)*
Bowman and Brooke LLP ....D....310 768-3068
970 W 190th St Ste 700 Torrance (90502) *(P-22956)*
Bowman Pipeline Contractors, Bakersfield *Also called Southwest Contractors (P-1982)*
Bowsmith Inc (PA) ....D....559 592-9485
131 2nd St Exeter (93221) *(P-13597)*
Box Inc (PA) ....C....877 729-4269
900 Jefferson Ave Redwood City (94063) *(P-15615)*
Box Bros Corp ....E....310 394-8660
825 Wilshire Blvd Santa Monica (90401) *(P-17040)*
BOY SCOUTS OF AMERICA, Piedmont *Also called Boyscout of America (P-25118)*
Boy Scouts of America (PA) ....D....213 353-9879
2333 Scout Way Los Angeles (90026) *(P-25102)*
Boy's & Girls Club Bakersfield, Bakersfield *Also called Boys Girls Clubs of Kern Cnty (P-25113)*
Boyd & Associates ....D....805 988-8298
445 E Esplanade Dr # 210 Oxnard (93036) *(P-16586)*
Boyd & Associates (PA) ....C....818 752-1888
2191 E Thompson Blvd Ventura (93001) *(P-16587)*
Boyd & Associates ....C....714 835-5423
3151 Airway Ave Ste K105 Costa Mesa (92626) *(P-16588)*
Boyd Corporation ....C....714 777-5995
4990 E Hunter Ave Anaheim (92807) *(P-7842)*
Boyd Flotation Inc ....D....909 357-6400
7551 Cherry Ave Fontana (92336) *(P-6713)*
Boyett Construction Inc (PA) ....D....510 264-9100
2404 Tripaldi Way Hayward (94545) *(P-2851)*
Boykin Mgt Co Ltd Lblty Co ....E....619 299-6633
3888 Greenwood St San Diego (92110) *(P-12393)*
Boykin Mgt Co Ltd Lblty Co ....B....510 548-7920
200 Marina Blvd Berkeley (94710) *(P-12394)*
Boyle Engineering Corporation (HQ) ....D....949 476-3300
999 W Town And Country Rd Orange (92868) *(P-25574)*
Boyle Engineering Corporation ....D....714 543-5274
999 W Town And Country Rd Orange (92868) *(P-25575)*
Boys & Girls CLB of Peninsula ....D....650 322-6255
401 Pierce Rd Menlo Park (94025) *(P-18870)*
BOYS & GIRLS CLUB OF SAN PEDRO, San Pedro *Also called Boys and Girls Clubs of The La (P-25108)*
Boys & Girls Club of Tracy (PA) ....E....209 832-2582
753 W Lowell Ave Tracy (95376) *(P-25103)*
Boys & Girls Club Silicon Vly ....D....408 957-9685
518 Valley Way Milpitas (95035) *(P-23516)*
Boys & Girls Club Simi Vly Inc ....E....805 527-4437
2850 Lemon Dr Simi Valley (93063) *(P-25104)*
Boys & Girls Clubs Cent Sonoma ....C....707 528-7977
1400 N Dutton Ave Ste 14 Santa Rosa (95401) *(P-25105)*
Boys & Girls Clubs of Marin A ....D....707 769-5322
1400 N Dutton Ave Ste 23 Santa Rosa (95401) *(P-25106)*
Boys & Girls Clubs of N Vly ....D....530 899-0335
601 Wall St Chico (95928) *(P-25107)*
BOYS & GIRLS CLUBS OF SAN DIEG, Solana Beach *Also called Boys Grls Clubs of San Deguito (P-25116)*
Boys and Girls Club ....E....818 225-8406
22450 Mulholland Hwy Calabasas (91302) *(P-18871)*
Boys and Girls Clubs of The La (PA) ....D....310 833-1322
1200 S Cabrillo Ave San Pedro (90731) *(P-25108)*
Boys and Girls Clubs of The La ....D....310 833-1322
1501 S Cabrillo Ave San Pedro (90731) *(P-25109)*
Boys and Girls Clubs of The La ....D....310 833-1322
1700 Gulf Ave Wilmington (90744) *(P-25110)*
Boys Girls CLB Huntington Vly (PA) ....D....714 531-2582
16582 Brookhurst St Fountain Valley (92708) *(P-25111)*
Boys Girls CLB Imperial Beach ....D....619 424-2266
847 Encina Ave Imperial Beach (91932) *(P-25112)*
Boys Girls Clubs of Kern Cnty ....D....661 325-3730
801 Niles St Bakersfield (93305) *(P-25113)*
Boys Girls Clubs Santa Monica, Santa Monica *Also called Boys Grls CLB Snta Monica Inc (P-25114)*
Boys Grls CLB Snta Monica Inc ....D....310 361-8500
1220 Lincoln Blvd Santa Monica (90401) *(P-25114)*
Boys Grls Clubs Grdn Grove Inc ....C....714 537-8833
13645 Clinton St Garden Grove (92843) *(P-25115)*
Boys Grls Clubs of San Deguito (PA) ....D....858 755-9371
533 Lomas Santa Fe Dr Solana Beach (92075) *(P-25116)*
Boys Grls Clubs of Squoias Inc ....D....559 592-4074
1003 San Juan Ave Exeter (93221) *(P-25117)*

ALPHABETIC

Employee Codes: A=Over 500 employees, B=251-500
C=101-250, D=51-100, E=50
2019 Directory of California
Wholesalers and Services Companies
© Mergent Inc. 1-800-342-5647
1227

Boys Republic (PA).......C.......909 902-6690
1907 Boys Republic Dr Chino Hills (91709) ***(P-24438)***
Boyscout of America.......D.......510 547-4493
10 Highland Way Piedmont (94611) ***(P-25118)***
BP Industries Incorporated.......D.......909 481-0227
5300 E Concours St Ontario (91764) ***(P-6751)***
BP Products W Coast Refinery, Carson *Also called BP West Coast Products LLC* ***(P-8941)***
BP West Coast Products LLC.......B.......310 816-8787
22600 Wilmington Ave Carson (90745) ***(P-1014)***
BP West Coast Products LLC.......B.......510 231-4724
1306 Canal Blvd Richmond (94804) ***(P-1015)***
BP West Coast Products LLC.......C.......310 549-6204
1801 E Sepulveda Blvd Carson (90745) ***(P-8941)***
Bpaz Holdings 6 LLC.......D.......415 295-8080
1 Sansome St Ste 1500 San Francisco (94104) ***(P-11966)***
Bpg Storage Solutions Inc.......D.......562 467-2000
2033 N Main St Ste 340 Walnut Creek (94596) ***(P-26784)***
Bpo Management Services Inc (PA).......D.......714 972-2670
8175 E Kaiser Blvd 100 Anaheim (92808) ***(P-15033)***
Bpr Properties Berkeley LLC.......C.......650 424-1400
953 Industrial Ave # 100 Palo Alto (94303) ***(P-10857)***
Bps Bioscience Inc.......E.......858 202-1401
6042 Cornerstone Ct W B San Diego (92121) ***(P-26343)***
Bps Supply Group (PA).......D.......661 589-9141
3301 Zachary Ave Shafter (93263) ***(P-7263)***
BQE Software Inc.......D.......310 602-4020
3825 Del Amo Blvd Trrance Torrance Torrance (90503) ***(P-15616)***
BR Funsten, Manteca *Also called B R Funsten & Co* ***(P-6748)***
Bracket Global LLC.......D.......415 293-1340
303 2nd St Ste 700 San Francisco (94107) ***(P-15034)***
Brad Miller.......C.......415 986-5400
340 Pine St Ste 504 San Francisco (94104) ***(P-27170)***
Brad Rambo & Associates Inc (PA).......D.......949 366-9911
1341 Calle Avanzado San Clemente (92673) ***(P-8250)***
Brad Watkins Masonry Inc.......D.......818 360-3796
10315 Woodley Ave Ste 130 Granada Hills (91344) ***(P-2800)***
Braddock & Logan Group II LP.......C.......925 736-4000
4155 Blackhawk Plaza Cir # 201 Danville (94506) ***(P-11857)***
Braddock & Logan Inc.......D.......925 229-1747
3600 Pine St Apt 3600 # 3600 Martinez (94553) ***(P-10989)***
Braddock & Logan Services Inc.......C.......925 736-4000
4155 Blackhawk Plaza Cir # 201 Danville (94506) ***(P-1483)***
Braden Partners LP A Calif.......D.......661 632-1979
7500 District Blvd Bakersfield (93313) ***(P-7167)***
Braden Partners LP A Calif (HQ).......D.......415 893-1518
1304 Sthpint Blvd Ste 130 Petaluma (94954) ***(P-22238)***
Bradford & Barthel LLP (PA).......C.......916 569-0790
2518 River Plaza Dr Sacramento (95833) ***(P-22957)***
Bradford Messenger Service.......D.......559 252-0775
4955 E Andersen Ave # 118 Fresno (93727) ***(P-17041)***
BRADLEY COURT, Chula Vista *Also called Healthcare MGT Systems Inc* ***(P-20519)***
Bradley Grdns Convalescent Ctr, San Jacinto *Also called Healthcare MGT Systems Inc* ***(P-20520)***
Bradley Melissa Real Estate.......D.......415 459-1010
851 Irwin St Ste 104 San Rafael (94901) ***(P-11249)***
Bradshaw Home, Rancho Cucamonga *Also called Bradshaw International Inc* ***(P-6752)***
Bradshaw International Inc (HQ).......B.......909 476-3884
9409 Buffalo Ave Rancho Cucamonga (91730) ***(P-6752)***
Bradshaw Veterinary Clinic.......D.......916 685-2494
9609 Bradshaw Rd Elk Grove (95624) ***(P-598)***
Brady Vorwerck Rydr & Cspno (PA).......D.......480 456-9888
19200 Von Karman Ave Irvine (92612) ***(P-22958)***
Brady Company.......D.......415 644-0836
795 Folsom St San Francisco (94107) ***(P-16320)***
Brady Company/Central Cal.......C.......831 633-3315
13540 Blackie Rd Castroville (95012) ***(P-2852)***
Brady Company/Los Angeles Inc.......D.......714 533-9850
1010 N Olive St Anaheim (92801) ***(P-2853)***
Brady Company/San Diego Inc.......B.......619 462-2600
8100 Center St La Mesa (91942) ***(P-2854)***
Brady Gce II.......D.......858 496-0500
2655 Camino San Diego (92108) ***(P-25576)***
Brady Socal Incorporated.......D.......619 462-2600
8100 Center St La Mesa (91942) ***(P-2855)***
Braemar Country Club Inc.......C.......323 873-6880
4001 Reseda Blvd Tarzana (91356) ***(P-18872)***
Braemar Partnership.......B.......858 488-1081
3999 Mission Blvd San Diego (92109) ***(P-12395)***
Bragg Crane & Rigging, Richmond *Also called Bay Cities Crane & Rigging Inc* ***(P-14477)***
Bragg Crane & Rigging, Long Beach *Also called Bragg Investment Company Inc* ***(P-17042)***
Bragg Investment Company Inc (PA).......A.......562 984-2400
6251 N Paramount Blvd Long Beach (90805) ***(P-17042)***
Braille Institute America Inc (PA).......C.......323 663-1111
741 N Vermont Ave Los Angeles (90029) ***(P-23517)***
Bramasol Inc.......D.......408 831-0046
3979 Freedom Cir Ste 620 Santa Clara (95054) ***(P-7019)***
Branch, Walnut Creek *Also called Moffatt & Nichol* ***(P-25830)***
Brand Flower Farms Inc (PA).......C.......805 684-5531
5300 Foothill Rd Carpinteria (93013) ***(P-9126)***
Brand Precision, Benicia *Also called Clean Hrbors Es Indus Svcs Inc* ***(P-17938)***
Brand Scaffold Service, Richmond *Also called Brand Services LLC* ***(P-3495)***
Brand Services Inc.......E.......707 603-3400
535 Watt Dr Fairfield (94534) ***(P-7669)***
Brand Services LLC.......D.......510 231-9640
940 Hensley St Richmond (94801) ***(P-3495)***
Brand Services of California, Fairfield *Also called Brand Services Inc* ***(P-7669)***
Branded Entrmt Netwrk Inc (PA).......C.......310 342-1500
15250 Ventura Blvd # 300 Sherman Oaks (91403) ***(P-14096)***
Brandel Manor, Turlock *Also called Emanuel Medical Center Inc* ***(P-21405)***
Branderscom Inc (PA).......D.......650 292-2752
2551 Casey Ave Mountain View (94043) ***(P-9198)***
Brandes Inv Partners Inc (PA).......C.......858 755-0239
11988 Charmaine Way Ste 6 San Diego (92131) ***(P-12031)***
Brandnet Inc.......D.......415 216-4152
724 Battery St 3 San Francisco (94111) ***(P-27662)***
Brandrep Inc.......E.......800 405-7119
16812 Armstrong Ave Irvine (92606) ***(P-27171)***
Brandt Cattle, Calipatria *Also called Brandt Co Inc* ***(P-396)***
Brandt Co Inc.......D.......760 348-2295
7015 Brandt Rd Calipatria (92233) ***(P-396)***
Brandvia Alliance Inc.......D.......408 955-0500
2159 Bering Dr San Jose (95131) ***(P-9199)***
Branlyn Prominence Inc.......C.......760 843-5655
13334 Amargosa Rd Victorville (92392) ***(P-22239)***
Branlyn Prominence Inc (PA).......D.......909 476-9030
9213 Archibald Ave Rancho Cucamonga (91730) ***(P-22240)***
Brannon Inc.......C.......805 621-5000
1340 W Betteravia Rd Santa Maria (93455) ***(P-1381)***
Braswell Col Care Redlands CA.......C.......909 792-6050
1618 Laurel Ave Redlands (92373) ***(P-21012)***
Braswells Villa Monte Vista.......C.......858 487-6242
12696 Monte Vista Rd Poway (92064) ***(P-21013)***
Braswells Yucaipa Valley C.......D.......909 795-2476
35253 Avenue H Yucaipa (92399) ***(P-20264)***
Braun Electric Company Inc (HQ).......B.......661 633-1451
3000 E Belle Ter Bakersfield (93307) ***(P-2525)***
Braun Electric Company Inc.......C.......661 763-1531
111 Main St Taft (93268) ***(P-2526)***
Braun Linen Service Inc (PA).......C.......909 623-2678
16514 Garfield Ave Paramount (90723) ***(P-13519)***
Braun Linen Service Inc.......D.......909 623-2678
396 La Mesa St Pomona (91766) ***(P-13484)***
Bravante Produce, Reedley *Also called Cal Packing & Storage LP* ***(P-4497)***
Bravo Tech Inc.......E.......714 230-8333
14600 Industry Cir La Mirada (90638) ***(P-5301)***
Brayton Purcell APC (PA).......C.......415 898-1555
222 Rush Landing Rd Novato (94945) ***(P-22959)***
Bre Diamond Hotel LLC.......C.......650 712-7000
1 Miramontes Point Rd Half Moon Bay (94019) ***(P-12396)***
Bre El Segundo Property Owner, El Segundo *Also called Bshh II LLC* ***(P-12408)***
Bre El Sgundo Property Owner B, El Segundo *Also called Bshh II LLC* ***(P-12409)***
Bre Select Hotels Oper LLC.......D.......408 719-1313
30 Ranch Dr Milpitas (95035) ***(P-12397)***
Bre/Japantown Owner LLC.......D.......415 922-3200
1625 Post St San Francisco (94115) ***(P-12398)***
Brea Dialysis Center, Brea *Also called Renal Treatment Ctrs - Cal Inc* ***(P-22485)***
Break Floor Productions LLC (PA).......E.......818 432-1234
5446 Satsuma Ave North Hollywood (91601) ***(P-18346)***
Break Media, Beverly Hills *Also called Nextpoint Inc* ***(P-5614)***
Breakout Prison Outreach.......D.......408 702-2405
1560 Berger Dr San Jose (95112) ***(P-23518)***
Breast Diagnostic Center.......E.......310 517-4709
3275 Skypark Dr Ste A Torrance (90505) ***(P-19326)***
Breast Imaging Center, Sacramento *Also called Sutter Health* ***(P-19979)***
Breeders Choice Pet Foods, Irwindale *Also called Central Garden & Pet Company* ***(P-9205)***
Brehm Communities (PA).......D.......760 448-2420
1935 Camino Vida Roble # 200 Carlsbad (92008) ***(P-1126)***
Brehm Communities LLC (PA).......D.......760 448-2420
1825 Aston Ave Ste B Carlsbad (92008) ***(P-1127)***
Breitbart News Network LLC.......D.......424 371-0585
149 S Barrington Ste 735 Los Angeles (90049) ***(P-13937)***
Breitburn Energy Co, Santa Fe Springs *Also called Strand Energy Company* ***(P-1029)***
Breitburn GP LLC.......A.......213 225-5900
707 Wilshire Blvd # 4600 Los Angeles (90017) ***(P-1016)***
Bremer Whyte Brown Omeara, Newport Beach *Also called Bremer Whyte Brown Omeara LLP* ***(P-22960)***
Bremer Whyte Brown Omeara LLP (PA).......E.......949 221-1000
20320 Sw Birch St Ste 200 Newport Beach (92660) ***(P-22960)***
Brendan Tours (PA).......C.......818 428-6000
801 E Katella Ave Anaheim (92805) ***(P-4964)***
Brendan Worldwide Vacations, Anaheim *Also called Brendan Tours* ***(P-4964)***
Brenden Theatre Corporation.......D.......707 469-0180
531 Davis St Vacaville (95688) ***(P-18273)***
Brenden Theatre Corporation.......D.......209 491-7770
1021 10th St Frnt Modesto (95354) ***(P-18274)***
Brenden Theatre Corporation (PA).......C.......925 677-0462
1985 Willow Pass Rd Ste C Concord (94520) ***(P-18275)***
Brennan Electric Inc.......C.......909 772-2263
460 S Stoddard Ave Ste 3 San Bernardino (92401) ***(P-2527)***
Brenntag Pacific Inc (HQ).......C.......562 903-9626
10747 Patterson Pl Santa Fe Springs (90670) ***(P-8921)***
Brentwood Bmdical RES Inst Inc.......C.......310 312-1554
11301 Wilshire Blvd B114 Los Angeles (90073) ***(P-26598)***
Brentwood Cmmncations Intl Inc.......E.......818 333-3680
16135 Roscoe Blvd North Hills (91343) ***(P-18025)***
Brentwood Country Club.......C.......310 451-8011
590 S Burlingame Ave Los Angeles (90049) ***(P-18873)***
Brentwood Health Care Center, Santa Monica *Also called Coastal Health Care Inc* ***(P-20318)***
Brentwood Medical Tech Corp.......D.......800 624-8950
1125 W 190th St Gardena (90248) ***(P-7168)***
Brentwood Skill Nursng & Rehab.......D.......530 527-2046
1795 Walnut St Red Bluff (96080) ***(P-21014)***
Brentwood Sklled Nursng Rhbltn, Red Bluff *Also called Brentwood Skill Nursng & Rehab* ***(P-21014)***

Mergent e-mail: customerrelations@mergent.com
1228
2019 Directory of California
Wholesalers and Services Companies
(P-0000) Products & Services Section entry number
(PA)=Parent Co (HQ)=Headquarters (DH)=Div Headquarters

Brer Affiliates LLC (HQ) ....C....949 794-7900
18500 Von Karman Ave # 400 Irvine (92612) ***(P-12134)***
Bret Boylan, Long Beach *Also called Bret Boylan Property Mgt* ***(P-26785)***
Bret Boylan Property Mgt ....E....562 437-7886
35 N Alboni Pl Apt 409 Long Beach (90802) ***(P-26785)***
Brethren Inc ....E....714 836-4800
1170 E Fruit St Santa Ana (92701) ***(P-8020)***
Brethren Hillcrest Homes ....C....909 593-4917
2705 Mountain View Dr Ofc La Verne (91750) ***(P-24439)***
Breville Usa Inc ....E....310 755-3000
19400 S Western Ave Torrance (90501) ***(P-6753)***
Brewer Crane & Rigging, Lakeside *Also called LLC Brewer Crane* ***(P-14445)***
Brewster Marble Co Inc ....E....818 834-2195
20801 Dearborn St Chatsworth (91311) ***(P-2988)***
Brewsters Automotive Inc ....D....714 528-4683
17357 Los Angeles St Yorba Linda (92886) ***(P-17756)***
Briar Golf LP ....D....760 328-6571
68311 Paseo Real Cathedral City (92234) ***(P-19114)***
Briarcrest Nursing Center Inc ....C....562 927-2641
5648 Gotham St Bell (90201) ***(P-20265)***
Briarpatch Coop Nev Cnty Inc ....C....530 272-5333
290 Sierra College Dr A Grass Valley (95945) ***(P-25400)***
Briarpatch Coop-Community Mkt, Grass Valley *Also called Briarpatch Coop Nev Cnty Inc* ***(P-25400)***
Briarwood Health Care Inc ....E....916 383-2741
5901 Lemon Hill Ave Sacramento (95824) ***(P-21015)***
Brickley Construction Co Inc ....E....909 888-2010
957 Reece St San Bernardino (92411) ***(P-3496)***
Brickley Environmental, San Bernardino *Also called Brickley Construction Co Inc* ***(P-3496)***
Bricsnet FM America Inc ....D....202 756-1840
1820 Harvest Rd Pleasanton (94566) ***(P-16321)***
Bridge Bank, San Jose *Also called Western Alliance Bank* ***(P-9494)***
Bridge Bay Resort & Marina ....D....530 275-3021
10300 Bridge Bay Rd Redding (96003) ***(P-12399)***
Bridge Group Hh Inc ....C....858 455-5000
5090 Shoreham Pl Ste 209 San Diego (92122) ***(P-11967)***
Bridge Housing Acquisition ....D....415 989-1111
1 Hawthorne St Ste 400 San Francisco (94105) ***(P-10858)***
Bridge Housing Corporation (PA) ....D....415 989-1111
600 California St Fl 9 San Francisco (94108) ***(P-11858)***
Bridge Partners Inc (PA) ....D....925 256-9448
1850 Mt Diablo Blvd # 410 Walnut Creek (94596) ***(P-12203)***
Bridgepoint At San Francisco, San Francisco *Also called Kisco Senior Living LLC* ***(P-26921)***
Bridges At Gale Ranch LLC ....D....925 735-4253
9000 S Gale Ridge Rd San Ramon (94582) ***(P-18874)***
Bridges At Sn Pdro Pnnsla Hspt ....D....310 514-5359
1300 W 7th St Fl 4 San Pedro (90732) ***(P-22514)***
Bridges Club At Rancho SA ....C....858 759-7200
18550 Seven Bridges Rd Rancho Santa Fe (92091) ***(P-25119)***
Bridges From School To Work, Oakland *Also called Marriott Foundation For People* ***(P-24203)***
Bridges Golf Club, The, San Ramon *Also called Bridges At Gale Ranch LLC* ***(P-18874)***
Bridgford Foods, Anaheim *Also called A S I Corporation* ***(P-13785)***
Bridgford Marketing Company (HQ) ....D....714 526-5533
1308 N Patt St Anaheim (92801) ***(P-8612)***
Bridgwter Consulting Group Inc ....D....949 535-1755
18881 Von Karman Ave Irvine (92612) ***(P-27172)***
Brieck Restoration Inc ....E....858 679-9928
13750 Danielson St Poway (92064) ***(P-1128)***
Brience Inc (HQ) ....D....415 974-5300
128 Spear St Fl 3 San Francisco (94105) ***(P-15035)***
Brier Oak On Sunset LLC ....C....323 663-3951
8318 S Main St Apt 1 Los Angeles (90003) ***(P-21016)***
Brier Oak On Sunset Rehab, Los Angeles *Also called Skilled Healthcare LLC* ***(P-20768)***
Brier Oak On Sunset Rehab Ctr, Los Angeles *Also called Brier Oak On Sunset LLC* ***(P-21016)***
Briercrest Inglewoodhealthcare, Inglewood *Also called American Nursing Home MGT Inc* ***(P-27639)***
Briggs Electric Inc (PA) ....D....714 544-2500
14381 Franklin Ave Tustin (92780) ***(P-2528)***
Bright Bristol Street LLC ....D....714 557-3000
3131 Bristol St Costa Mesa (92626) ***(P-12400)***
Bright Caregivers, Huntington Beach *Also called Medical Diagnostic* ***(P-21156)***
Bright Event Rentals LLC (PA) ....C....310 202-0011
1640 W 190th St Torrance (90501) ***(P-14479)***
Bright Event Rentals LLC ....A....858 496-9700
7069 Consolidated Way San Diego (92121) ***(P-14480)***
Bright Event Rentals LLC ....C....310 202-0011
22674 Broadway Ste A Sonoma (95476) ***(P-14481)***
Bright Expectations Inc ....E....951 360-2070
8175 Limonite Ave Ste C Riverside (92509) ***(P-22241)***
Bright Health Physicians (PA) ....C....562 947-8478
15725 Whittier Blvd # 500 Whittier (90603) ***(P-19327)***
Bright Horizons Chld Ctrs LLC ....C....805 447-6793
1 Amgen Center Dr Thousand Oaks (91320) ***(P-24268)***
Bright Horizons Chld Ctrs LLC ....C....408 853-2196
800 Barber Ln Milpitas (95035) ***(P-24269)***
Bright House Networks LLC ....D....661 634-2200
4450 California Ave Ste A Bakersfield (93309) ***(P-5858)***
Bright Now Dental, Irvine *Also called Smile Brands Group Inc* ***(P-27032)***
Bright Pharmaceutical Services ....D....818 981-9100
4570 Van Nuys Blvd Sherman Oaks (91403) ***(P-8148)***
Brightcloud Inc ....C....858 652-4803
4370 La Jolla Village Dr # 820 San Diego (92122) ***(P-16880)***
Brightcurrent Inc ....D....877 896-3306
426 17th St Ste 700 Oakland (94612) ***(P-17043)***
Brightedge Technologies Inc (PA) ....C....800 578-8023
989 E Hillsdale Blvd Foster City (94404) ***(P-15036)***
Brighter Inc ....D....888 230-4413
501 Santa Monica Blvd # 403 Santa Monica (90401) ***(P-20111)***
Brighter Beginnings (PA) ....D....510 903-7503
3478 Buskirk Ave Ste 105 Pleasant Hill (94523) ***(P-23519)***
Brightercom, Santa Monica *Also called Brighter Inc* ***(P-20111)***
Brighterion Inc ....D....415 986-5600
150 Spear St Ste 1000 San Francisco (94105) ***(P-15037)***
Brightertech Incorporated ....E....310 909-4940
510 Strtford Ct Unit 204a Del Mar (92014) ***(P-5523)***
Brighton Convalescent Center ....D....626 798-9124
1836 N Fair Oaks Ave Pasadena (91103) ***(P-21017)***
Brighton Gardens Inc ....D....858 259-2222
13101 Hartfield Ave San Diego (92130) ***(P-20266)***
Brighton Gardens of Camarillo, Camarillo *Also called Sunrise Senior Living LLC* ***(P-20830)***
Brighton Gardens of Sunrise, Palm Desert *Also called Sunrise Senior Living Inc* ***(P-20796)***
Brighton Health Alliance (PA) ....D....619 461-0376
8322 Clairemont Mesa Blvd San Diego (92111) ***(P-20267)***
Brighton Place East Inc ....D....619 461-3222
8625 Lamar St Spring Valley (91977) ***(P-20268)***
Brighton Place of San Diego, San Diego *Also called Brighton Health Alliance* ***(P-20267)***
Brighton Place San Diego ....C....619 263-2166
1350 Euclid Ave San Diego (92105) ***(P-20269)***
Brighton Place Spring Valley, Spring Valley *Also called B-Spring Valley LLC* ***(P-20253)***
Brightscope, San Diego *Also called Strategic Insights Inc* ***(P-15866)***
Brightstar Health, Torrance *Also called Smart Choice Investments Inc* ***(P-14761)***
Brightview Companies LLC ....C....209 993-9277
2447 Stagecoach Rd Stockton (95215) ***(P-732)***
Brightview Companies LLC ....C....626 574-3940
201 Longden Ave Irwindale (91706) ***(P-733)***
Brightview Companies LLC (HQ) ....C....818 223-8500
24151 Ventura Blvd Calabasas (91302) ***(P-2014)***
Brightview Golf Maint Inc ....E....805 968-6400
405 Glen Annie Rd Santa Barbara (93117) ***(P-2015)***
Brightview Golf Maint Inc (HQ) ....D....818 223-8500
24151 Ventura Blvd Calabasas (91302) ***(P-2016)***
Brightview Landscape Dev Inc (HQ) ....E....818 223-8500
24151 Ventura Blvd Calabasas (91302) ***(P-734)***
Brightview Landscape Dev Inc ....B....858 458-9900
8450 Miramar Pl San Diego (92121) ***(P-2017)***
Brightview Landscape Dev Inc ....D....818 838-4700
13691 Vaughn St San Fernando (91340) ***(P-2148)***
Brightview Landscape Dev Inc ....B....714 546-7975
11555 Cley Rver Cir Ste A Fountain Valley (92708) ***(P-2149)***
Brightview Landscape Dev Inc ....D....714 546-7843
1960 S Yale St Santa Ana (92704) ***(P-735)***
Brightview Landscape Svcs Inc ....E....510 487-4826
20551b Corsair Blvd Hayward (94545) ***(P-736)***
Brightview Landscape Svcs Inc ....C....858 458-1900
8500 Miramar Pl San Diego (92121) ***(P-737)***
Brightview Landscape Svcs Inc ....D....925 957-8831
4677 Pacheco Blvd Martinez (94553) ***(P-738)***
Brightview Landscape Svcs Inc ....D....714 546-7843
1960 S Yale St Santa Ana (92704) ***(P-739)***
Brightview Landscape Svcs Inc ....D....916 381-2800
5745 Alder Ave Sacramento (95828) ***(P-740)***
Brightview Landscape Svcs Inc ....D....925 924-8900
7039 Commerce Cir Ste B Pleasanton (94588) ***(P-741)***
Brightview Landscape Svcs Inc ....C....310 327-8700
17813 S Main St Ste 105 Gardena (90248) ***(P-742)***
Brightview Landscapes LLC ....D....760 438-3551
2420 Cougar Dr Carlsbad (92010) ***(P-743)***
Brightview Landscapes LLC ....D....619 644-8584
9090 Birch St Spring Valley (91977) ***(P-744)***
Brightview Tree Company ....C....818 951-5500
9500 Foothill Blvd Sunland (91040) ***(P-987)***
Brightview Tree Company ....C....714 546-7975
3200 W Telegraph Rd Fillmore (93015) ***(P-988)***
Brightview Tree Company ....D....925 862-2485
8501 Calaveras Rd Sunol (94586) ***(P-989)***
Brightview Tree Company ....D....209 886-5511
28915 E Funck Rd Farmington (95230) ***(P-990)***
Brilliance Investment LLC ....D....510 568-1880
8350 Edes Ave Oakland (94621) ***(P-12401)***
Brilliant General Maintinc ....C....408 287-6708
954 Chestnut St San Jose (95110) ***(P-14203)***
Brilliant Sftwr Solutions Inc ....D....510 742-5120
2400 Camino Ramon Ste 170 San Ramon (94583) ***(P-15922)***
Brillstein Entrmt Partners LLC (PA) ....B....310 205-5100
9150 Wilshire Blvd # 350 Beverly Hills (90212) ***(P-18026)***
Brillstein Grey Entertainment, Beverly Hills *Also called Brillstein Entrmt Partners LLC* ***(P-18026)***
Brinderson LP (HQ) ....C....714 466-7100
19000 Macarthur Blvd # 800 Irvine (92612) ***(P-25577)***
Brinderson LP ....D....714 466-7100
19000 Macarthur Blvd # 800 Irvine (92612) ***(P-25578)***
Brinks Incorporated ....C....818 503-8630
1120 Venice Blvd Los Angeles (90015) ***(P-16589)***
Brinks Incorporated ....C....916 452-5279
8178 Alpine Ave Unit A Sacramento (95826) ***(P-16590)***
Brinks Incorporated ....C....619 263-6615
4520 Federal Blvd Ste A San Diego (92102) ***(P-16591)***
Brinks Incorporated ....D....408 436-7717
1630 Old Bayshore Hwy San Jose (95112) ***(P-16592)***
Brinks Incorporated ....E....323 262-2646
1821 S Soto St Los Angeles (90023) ***(P-16593)***
Brisam Lax (de) LLC ....D....310 649-5151
9901 S La Cienega Blvd Los Angeles (90045) ***(P-12402)***
Brisbane Mechanical, Brisbane *Also called FW Spencer & Son Inc* ***(P-2217)***

ALPHABETIC

Employee Codes: A=Over 500 employees, B=251-500
C=101-250, D=51-100, E=50
2019 Directory of California
Wholesalers and Services Companies
© Mergent Inc. 1-800-342-5647
1229

Bristlecone Incorporated....A....650 386-4000
10 Almaden Blvd Ste 600 San Jose (95113) *(P-15038)*
Bristol Hotel....D....619 232-6141
1055 1st Ave San Diego (92101) *(P-12403)*
Bristol Park Medical Group, Fountain Valley *Also called St Jude Hospital Yorba Linda (P-19942)*
Bristol, The, San Diego *Also called Beston Development (P-12379)*
Brita Products Company....D....510 271-7000
1221 Broadway Ste 290 Oakland (94612) *(P-7611)*
Brite Media LLC....C....818 826-5790
16027 Ventura Blvd # 210 Encino (91436) *(P-13938)*
Brite Promotions, Encino *Also called Brite Media LLC (P-13938)*
Briteworks Inc....D....626 337-0099
620 N Commercial Ave Covina (91723) *(P-14204)*
Brithinee Electric....D....909 825-7971
620 S Rancho Ave Colton (92324) *(P-7340)*
Brittany House LLC....D....562 421-4717
5401 E Centralia St Long Beach (90808) *(P-24440)*
Brittney House....D....562 421-4717
5401 E Centralia St Long Beach (90808) *(P-22242)*
Britz Fertilizers Inc....D....559 884-2421
21817 S Frsno Coalinga Rd Five Points (93624) *(P-9076)*
Brix Group Inc (PA)....D....559 457-4700
838 N Laverne Ave Fresno (93727) *(P-7451)*
Broadcast Co of Americas LLC (PA)....D....858 453-0658
6160 Cornerstone Ct E San Diego (92121) *(P-5695)*
Broadmoor Hotel (PA)....C....415 776-7034
1499 Sutter St San Francisco (94109) *(P-10990)*
Broadmoor Hotel....D....415 673-8445
1465 65th St Apt 274 Emeryville (94608) *(P-12404)*
Broadmoor Hotel....D....415 673-2511
1000 Sutter St San Francisco (94109) *(P-12405)*
Broadrach Cpitl Prtners Fund I....A....650 331-2500
248 Homer Ave Palo Alto (94301) *(P-12032)*
Broadreach Capitl Partners LLC....A....310 691-5760
6430 W Sunset Blvd # 504 Los Angeles (90028) *(P-12204)*
Broadreach Capitl Partners LLC (PA)....A....650 331-2500
855 El Camino Real Palo Alto (94301) *(P-9919)*
Broadreach Capitl Partners LLC....A....415 354-4640
235 Montgomery St # 1018 San Francisco (94104) *(P-12205)*
Broadsoft Contact Center Inc....E....408 338-0900
930 Hamlin Ct Sunnyvale (94089) *(P-15039)*
Broadspire Inc....D....213 785-8043
19425 Soled Canyo Rd Ste Santa Clarita (91351) *(P-5524)*
Broadstone Raquet Club, Folsom *Also called Spare-Time Inc (P-19054)*
Broadstreet Power, Van Nuys *Also called Broadstreet Solar Inc (P-2150)*
Broadstreet Solar Inc....E....818 206-1464
16112 Hart St Van Nuys (91406) *(P-2150)*
Broadview Inc....E....323 221-9174
4570 Griffin Ave Los Angeles (90031) *(P-20270)*
Broadvision Inc (PA)....D....650 331-1000
460 Seaport Ct Ste 102 Redwood City (94063) *(P-15617)*
Broadway By Bay....C....650 579-5565
853 Industrial Rd Ste H San Carlos (94070) *(P-18347)*
Broadway Manor Care Center, Glendale *Also called Longwood Management Corp (P-21140)*
Broadway Mech - Contrs Inc....C....510 746-4000
873 81st Ave Oakland (94621) *(P-2151)*
Broadway Sacramento (PA)....C....916 446-5880
1510 J St Ste 200 Sacramento (95814) *(P-18348)*
Broadway Typewriter Co Inc....D....800 998-9199
1055 6th Ave Ste 101 San Diego (92101) *(P-7020)*
Brocade Cmmnctions Systems Inc....D....408 333-4300
110 Holger Way San Jose (95134) *(P-27663)*
Brocchini Farms Inc....E....209 599-4229
27011 S Austin Rd Ripon (95366) *(P-132)*
Brock LLC (PA)....D....925 371-2184
333 N Canyons Pkwy # 221 Livermore (94551) *(P-5020)*
Brock Transportation, Livermore *Also called Brock LLC (P-5020)*
Broder Bros Co....D....559 233-9900
3443 E Central Ave Fresno (93725) *(P-8251)*
Broderick Gen Enginneering Inc....E....707 996-7809
21750 8th St E Ste B Sonoma (95476) *(P-1732)*
Brokaw Nursery LLC....D....805 647-2262
5501 Elizabeth Rd Ventura (93004) *(P-248)*
Broker Solutions Inc....D....800 450-2010
233 Milford Dr Corona Del Mar (92625) *(P-9782)*
Broker Solutions Inc (PA)....A....800 450-2010
14511 Myford Rd Ste 100 Tustin (92780) *(P-27173)*
Brokerage Lgstics Slutions Inc....D....619 671-0276
1659 Gailes Blvd Ste 101 San Diego (92154) *(P-5021)*
Brook Furniture Clearance Ctr, Hayward *Also called Brook Furniture Rental Inc (P-14482)*
Brook Furniture Rental Inc....E....510 487-4440
30985 Santana St Hayward (94544) *(P-14482)*
Brook Side Development, Stockton *Also called Groupe Development Associates (P-11879)*
Brookdale Clairemont, San Diego *Also called Emeritus Corporation (P-20391)*
Brookdale Elk Grove, Elk Grove *Also called Brookdale Senior Living Inc (P-20272)*
Brookdale Folsom, Folsom *Also called Brookdale Senior Living Inc (P-21020)*
Brookdale Lving Cmmunities Inc....C....408 445-7770
1009 Blossom River Way San Jose (95123) *(P-24441)*
Brookdale Lving Cmmunities Inc....D....650 366-3900
485 Woodside Rd Ofc Redwood City (94061) *(P-20271)*
Brookdale Redwood City, Redwood City *Also called Brookdale Lving Cmmunities Inc (P-20271)*
Brookdale Senior Living Inc....D....714 671-7898
285 W Central Ave Brea (92821) *(P-24442)*
Brookdale Senior Living Inc....D....209 835-1000
355 W Grant Line Rd Ofc Tracy (95376) *(P-24443)*
Brookdale Senior Living Inc....D....760 340-5999
72201 Country Club Dr Rancho Mirage (92270) *(P-21018)*
Brookdale Senior Living Inc....D....916 683-1881
6727 Laguna Park Dr Elk Grove (95758) *(P-20272)*
Brookdale Senior Living Inc....D....760 346-7772
72750 Country Club Dr Rancho Mirage (92270) *(P-21019)*
Brookdale Senior Living Inc....D....916 983-9300
780 Harrington Way Folsom (95630) *(P-21020)*
Brookdale Senior Living Inc....D....951 744-9861
1001 N Lyon Ave Hemet (92545) *(P-21021)*
Brookdale Senior Living Inc....D....951 808-9387
2005 Kellogg Ave Corona (92879) *(P-21022)*
Brookdale Snior Lving Cmmnties....D....909 796-5421
25585 Van Leuven St Loma Linda (92354) *(P-21023)*
Brookdale Sunwest, Hemet *Also called Brookdale Senior Living Inc (P-21021)*
Brooker Associates....D....949 559-4877
16372 Cnstr Cir E 5 Irvine (92618) *(P-969)*
Brookfeld Bay Area Hldings LLC....D....925 743-8000
500 La Gonda Way Ste 100 Danville (94526) *(P-11859)*
Brookfeld Sthland Holdings LLC....C....714 427-6868
3200 Park Center Dr # 1000 Costa Mesa (92626) *(P-1129)*
Brookfield 1996 California, Del Mar *Also called Brookfield Homes of California (P-1130)*
Brookfield Dtla Fund Office....D....626 792-2727
191 N Los Robles Ave Pasadena (91101) *(P-12406)*
Brookfield Dtla Fund Office....D....213 626-3300
355 S Grand Ave Ste 3300 Los Angeles (90071) *(P-12154)*
Brookfield Homes, Danville *Also called Brookfeld Bay Area Hldings LLC (P-11859)*
Brookfield Homes of California....E....858 481-8500
12865 Pointe Del Mar Way # 200 Del Mar (92014) *(P-1130)*
Brookfield Homes Pacific Inc (HQ)....D....858 481-8500
12865 Pointe Del 200 Del Mar (92014) *(P-1131)*
Brookfield Properties, Los Angeles *Also called Trz Holdings II Inc (P-11805)*
Brookfield Residential, Costa Mesa *Also called Brookfeld Sthland Holdings LLC (P-1129)*
Brookside Community Health Ctr....E....510 215-5001
1030 Nevin Ave Richmond (94801) *(P-19328)*
Brookside Country Club....D....209 956-6200
3603 Saint Andrews Dr Stockton (95219) *(P-18875)*
Brookside Golf Course, Pasadena *Also called City of Pasadena (P-18697)*
Brooktrails Lodge LLC....D....707 459-1596
24675 Birch St Willits (95490) *(P-12407)*
Brosamer & Wall Inc....C....925 932-7900
1777 Oakland Blvd Ste 300 Walnut Creek (94596) *(P-25579)*
Brosamer & Wall LLC....E....925 932-7900
1777 Oakland Blvd Ste 300 Walnut Creek (94596) *(P-11250)*
Brother Benno Foundation Inc (PA)....D....760 439-1244
970 Vine St Apt 209 Oceanside (92054) *(P-24444)*
BROTHER BENNO'S FOUNDATION, Oceanside *Also called Brother Benno Foundation Inc (P-24444)*
Broughton Hospitality Group (PA)....C....714 908-4237
2400 E Katella Ave # 300 Anaheim (92806) *(P-26786)*
Broward Builders Inc....D....530 666-5635
1200 E Kentucky Ave Woodland (95776) *(P-1484)*
Brower Mechanical Inc....D....530 749-0808
4060 Alvis Ct Rocklin (95677) *(P-17890)*
Brown & Toland Medical Group (PA)....C....415 972-4162
1221 Broadway Ste 700 Oakland (94612) *(P-19329)*
Brown & Toland Medical Group....C....415 752-8038
3905 Sacramento St # 301 San Francisco (94118) *(P-19330)*
Brown and Caldwell (PA)....C....925 937-9010
201 N Civic Dr Ste 115 Walnut Creek (94596) *(P-25580)*
Brown and Caldwell....D....530 747-0650
1590 Drew Ave Ste 210 Davis (95618) *(P-25581)*
Brown and Caldwell....D....858 514-8822
9665 Chesapeake Dr # 201 San Diego (92123) *(P-25582)*
Brown and Streza LLP....D....949 453-2900
40 Pacifica Ste 1500 Irvine (92618) *(P-27174)*
Brown Armstrong Accntancy Corp....D....661 324-4971
4200 Truxtun Ave Ste 300 Bakersfield (93309) *(P-26152)*
Brown Armstrong Cpas, Bakersfield *Also called Brown Armstrong Accntancy Corp (P-26152)*
Brown Construction Inc....D....916 374-8616
1465 Entp Blvd Ste 100 West Sacramento (95691) *(P-1485)*
Brownco Construction Co Inc....D....714 935-9600
1000 E Katella Ave Anaheim (92805) *(P-1486)*
Browne Child Development Ctr, Oceanside *Also called Business and Support Services (P-24270)*
Brownie's Digital Imaging, Sacramento *Also called American Reprographics Co LLC (P-14072)*
Browning Apartments....E....213 252-8847
1104 Browning Blvd Los Angeles (90037) *(P-10991)*
Browning-Ferris Industries Inc....C....818 790-5410
9200 Glenoaks Blvd Sun Valley (91352) *(P-6360)*
Browning-Ferris Industries LLC....D....408 262-1401
1601 Dixon Landing Rd Milpitas (95035) *(P-6361)*
Bruce Olson Construction Inc....D....530 581-1087
7320 River Rd Tahoe City (96145) *(P-1271)*
Bruce Olson Construction Inc....C....530 581-1087
7320 River Rd Olympic Valley (96146) *(P-1132)*
Bruck Lighting Systems, Tustin *Also called Ledra Brands Inc (P-6773)*
Brudvik Inc (PA)....D....760 320-4429
600 S Eugene Rd Palm Springs (92264) *(P-2529)*
BRUDVIK RENTAL DIVISION, Palm Springs *Also called Brudvik Inc (P-2529)*
Bruml Management LLC....E....800 733-3629
2051 Alpine Way Hayward (94545) *(P-8290)*
Brunswick Cal Oaks Bowl, Murrieta *Also called Bowlero Corp (P-18484)*
Brunswick Corner Partnership....E....916 649-7500
550 Howe Ave Ste 200 Sacramento (95825) *(P-11251)*
Brunswick Covino Lanes, Covina *Also called Bowlero Corp (P-18481)*
Brunswick Deer Creks Lnes 213, Rancho Cucamonga *Also called Bowlero Corp (P-18483)*

Mergent e-mail: customerrelations@mergent.com
1230
2019 Directory of California
Wholesalers and Services Companies
(P-0000) Products & Services Section entry number
(PA)=Parent Co (HQ)=Headquarters (DH)=Div Headquarters

Brutoco Engrg & Cnstr Inc ....C....909 350-3535
1272 Center Court Dr # 101 Covina (91724) ***(P-1733)***
Bryan Cave Lighton Paisner LLP ....E....415 675-3400
333 Market St Fl 25 San Francisco (94105) ***(P-22961)***
Bryan Cave Lighton Paisner LLP ....D....949 223-7000
3161 Michelson Dr # 1500 Irvine (92612) ***(P-22962)***
Bryan Cave Lighton Paisner LLP ....C....310 576-2100
120 Broadway Ste 300 Santa Monica (90401) ***(P-22963)***
Bryant Ranch Prepack ....E....818 764-7225
1919 N Victory Pl Burbank (91504) ***(P-8149)***
Bryce Canyon Resorts, El Portal *Also called Yosemite Management Group LLC* ***(P-13435)***
Bsgs Five Points, Five Points *Also called Britz Fertilizers Inc* ***(P-9076)***
Bshh II LLC ....E....310 356-4587
475 N Sepulveda Blvd El Segundo (90245) ***(P-12408)***
Bshh II LLC ....D....310 356-4577
525 N Pacific Coast Hwy El Segundo (90245) ***(P-12409)***
BSK Associates ....D....559 497-2888
1414 Stanislaus St Fresno (93706) ***(P-25583)***
Bsl Golf Corp ....C....831 899-7271
1 Mcclure Way Seaside (93955) ***(P-18690)***
Bsm UNI ....E....213 626-2557
712 Ceres Ave Los Angeles (90021) ***(P-8572)***
Bsmi, Brentwood *Also called Bay Standard Manufacturing Inc* ***(P-7580)***
Bsnap LLC ....D....657 269-4410
4 Hutton Centre Dr Fl 10 Santa Ana (92707) ***(P-9783)***
Bssp, Sausalito *Also called Butler Shine Stern Prtners LLC* ***(P-13800)***
Bst Enterprises Inc ....D....310 638-1222
17801 S Susana Rd Compton (90221) ***(P-6628)***
BT Americas Inc ....D....646 487-7400
2160 E Grand Ave El Segundo (90245) ***(P-7452)***
BT Holdings Inc ....E....707 279-4317
4150 Soda Bay Rd Kelseyville (95451) ***(P-215)***
BT Infonet, El Segundo *Also called Infonet Services Corporation* ***(P-5585)***
Bti Wireless, La Mirada *Also called Bravo Tech Inc* ***(P-5301)***
Btig LLC (PA) ....D....415 248-2200
600 Montgomery St Fl 6 San Francisco (94111) ***(P-9920)***
Bubbla Inc ....E....818 884-2000
7931 Deering Ave Canoga Park (91304) ***(P-9200)***
Bubbles Devine Bakeries Inc ....D....818 786-1700
15215 Keswick St Van Nuys (91405) ***(P-8761)***
Buchalter Nemer A Prof Corp ....D....714 549-5150
18400 Von Karman Ave # 800 Irvine (92612) ***(P-22964)***
BUCHALTER NEMER, A PROFESSIONAL CORPORATION, Irvine *Also called Buchalter Nemer A Prof Corp* ***(P-22964)***
Buchanan Dental Center, San Francisco *Also called U C S F School of Dentistry* ***(P-20141)***
Buchanan Fund I LLC ....D....949 721-1414
620 Newport Ctr Dr Ste 850 Newport Beach (92660) ***(P-12206)***
Buchanan Street Partners LP ....D....949 721-1414
3501 Jamboree Rd Ste 4200 Newport Beach (92660) ***(P-11252)***
Buck Global LLC ....D....310 282-8232
1801 Century Park E # 500 Los Angeles (90067) ***(P-27922)***
Buck Inst For RES On Aging (PA) ....C....415 209-2000
8001 Redwood Blvd Novato (94945) ***(P-26599)***
Buckelew Programs (PA) ....C....415 457-6964
555 Northgate Dr Ste 100 San Rafael (94903) ***(P-23520)***
Buckeye Fire Equipment Company ....B....510 483-1815
2416 Teagarden St San Leandro (94577) ***(P-7734)***
Buckingham Affrdbl Aprtmnts LP ....D....424 273-6162
11911 San Vicente Blvd Los Angeles (90049) ***(P-26787)***
Buckingham Apartments, Los Angeles *Also called Buckingham Affrdbl Aprtmnts LP* ***(P-26787)***
Buckingham Property Management ....D....559 322-1105
12609 Moffatt Ln Fresno (93730) ***(P-13722)***
Buckland Vineyard Management (PA) ....D....530 333-1534
4560 Slodusty Rd Garden Valley (95633) ***(P-26788)***
Buckles-Smith Electric Company (PA) ....D....408 280-7777
540 Martin Ave Santa Clara (95050) ***(P-7735)***
Budget Electric, Tracy *Also called American Engrg Contrs Inc* ***(P-2507)***
Budget Electrical Contrs Inc ....C....909 381-2646
25051 5th St San Bernardino (92410) ***(P-2530)***
Budget Rent-A-Car, Beverly Hills *Also called Star Lax LLC* ***(P-17648)***
Budget Rent-A-Car, Valley Village *Also called Eam Inc* ***(P-17631)***
Buds & Son Trucking Inc ....D....619 443-4200
12570 Highway 67 Lakeside (92040) ***(P-3981)***
Budway Enterprises Inc (PA) ....D....909 463-0500
13600 Napa St Fontana (92335) ***(P-4111)***
Budway Trucking & Warehousing, Fontana *Also called Budway Enterprises Inc* ***(P-4111)***
Buena Park Medical Group Inc (PA) ....D....714 994-5290
6301 Beach Blvd Ste 101 Buena Park (90621) ***(P-19331)***
Buena Park Nursing Center, Apple Valley *Also called 8520 Western Ave Inc* ***(P-20974)***
Buena Park Police Association ....D....714 562-3901
6650 Beach Blvd Buena Park (90621) ***(P-25055)***
Buena Ventura Care Center Inc (PA) ....D....323 268-0106
1016 S Record Ave Los Angeles (90023) ***(P-20273)***
Buena Ventura Care Center Inc ....D....818 247-4476
1505 Colby Dr Glendale (91205) ***(P-21024)***
Buena Vista Care Center, Santa Barbara *Also called Covenant Care California LLC* ***(P-20347)***
Buena Vista Care Center Inc ....D....714 535-7264
1440 S Euclid St Anaheim (92802) ***(P-20274)***
Buena Vista Food Products Inc (HQ) ....C....626 815-8859
823 W 8th St Azusa (91702) ***(P-8762)***
Buena Vista International Inc (HQ) ....E....818 560-1000
500 S Buena Vista St Burbank (91521) ***(P-18236)***
Buena Vista Manor, Duarte *Also called Cal Southern Presbt Homes* ***(P-20278)***
Buena Vista Pictures Dist, Burbank *Also called ABC Cable Networks Group* ***(P-18234)***
Buena Vista Television (HQ) ....C....818 560-1878
500 S Buena Vista St Burbank (91521) ***(P-16954)***
Buena Vista TV Advg Sls, Burbank *Also called Buena Vista Television* ***(P-16954)***
Buenaventura Medical Group (PA) ....B....805 477-6000
888 S Hill Rd Ventura (93003) ***(P-19332)***
Buenaventura Medical Group ....D....805 477-6220
2601 E Main St Ste 104 Ventura (93003) ***(P-19333)***
Buffalo Distribution ....E....510 475-9810
1624 Pacific St Union City (94587) ***(P-8346)***
Buffini & Company (PA) ....C....760 827-2100
6349 Palomar Oaks Ct Carlsbad (92011) ***(P-24158)***
Build Group Inc (PA) ....C....415 367-9399
457 Minna St Ste 100 San Francisco (94103) ***(P-1487)***
Build Group Inc ....D....408 986-8711
1210 Coleman Ave Santa Clara (95050) ***(P-1488)***
Build Rehabilitation Inds (PA) ....D....818 485-8560
12432 Foothill Blvd Sylmar (91342) ***(P-24159)***
Build Sjc, Santa Clara *Also called Build Group Inc* ***(P-1488)***
Buildcom Inc ....B....800 375-3403
402 Otterson Dr Ste 100 Chico (95928) ***(P-7612)***
Builders & Tradesmens ....D....916 772-9200
6610 Sierra College Blvd Rocklin (95677) ***(P-10566)***
Builders & Tradesmens Insur ....D....916 772-9200
6610 Sierra College Blvd Rocklin (95677) ***(P-10132)***
Builders Firstsource Inc ....E....619 440-7711
1262 E Main St El Cajon (92021) ***(P-6810)***
Builders Firstsource Inc ....E....619 425-6660
3450 Highland Ave National City (91950) ***(P-6811)***
Builders Firstsource Inc ....D....858 755-0246
663 Lomas Santa Fe Dr Solana Beach (92075) ***(P-6812)***
Building & Safety Department, Fremont *Also called City of Fremont* ***(P-26036)***
Building and Property MGT BR, Los Angeles *Also called General Services Cal Dept* ***(P-14275)***
Building Cleaning Systems, Santa Ana *Also called Carrasco Heleo* ***(P-14208)***
Building Elctronic Contrls Inc (PA) ....E....909 305-1600
2246 Lindsay Way Glendora (91740) ***(P-2531)***
Building Inspection, Long Beach *Also called City of Long Beach* ***(P-17078)***
Building Material Distrs Inc (PA) ....C....209 745-3001
225 Elm Ave Galt (95632) ***(P-6813)***
Building Opportunities (PA) ....C....510 649-1930
1918 University Ave 2a Berkeley (94704) ***(P-23521)***
Building Services, San Bernardino *Also called San Bernardino City Unf School* ***(P-14374)***
Building Services/System Inc ....D....925 688-1234
2575 Stanwell Dr Concord (94520) ***(P-10859)***
Buildingminds Inc ....E....973 397-6510
1200 Seaport Blvd Redwood City (94063) ***(P-15040)***
Buildrite, Chico *Also called Cleanrite Inc* ***(P-3505)***
Bulk Transportation (PA) ....D....909 594-2855
415 S Lemon Ave Walnut (91789) ***(P-4112)***
Bullup Inc ....E....566 997-2543
4365 Via Scorpresa San Diego (92124) ***(P-15041)***
Bully Pictures Inc (PA) ....C....310 395-6500
1220 Cabrillo Ave Venice (90291) ***(P-18349)***
Bulmaro Castro Contractors ....C....831 675-2927
349 Belden St Gonzales (93926) ***(P-14579)***
Bungalow 16 Entertainment LLC ....E....310 226-7870
8113 Melrose Ave Los Angeles (90046) ***(P-8004)***
Bunim-Murray Productions ....C....818 756-5100
1015 Grandview Ave Glendale (91201) ***(P-18027)***
Bunker Hill Club Inc ....D....213 620-9662
555 S Flower St Ste 5100 Los Angeles (90071) ***(P-25120)***
Bunkers Grille, Brentwood *Also called Nines Restaurant* ***(P-27371)***
Bunzl Distribution Cal LLC (HQ) ....D....714 688-1900
3310 E Miraloma Ave Anaheim (92806) ***(P-8095)***
Bunzl Retail Services LLC ....D....909 476-2457
8449 Milliken Ave Ste 102 Rancho Cucamonga (91730) ***(P-8096)***
Bunzl Usa Inc ....D....314 997-5959
15959 Piuma Ave Cerritos (90703) ***(P-8097)***
Buona Terra Farming Co Inc ....D....805 614-9229
2380 A St Santa Maria (93455) ***(P-26789)***
Burbank Airport Mariott Hotel, Burbank *Also called PHF II Burbank LLC* ***(P-13059)***
Burbank Bob Hope Airport, Burbank *Also called Jetblue Airways Corporation* ***(P-4786)***
Burbank Dental Laboratory Inc ....C....818 841-2256
2101 Floyd St Burbank (91504) ***(P-7169)***
Burbank Housing Dev Corp ....C....707 526-9782
790 Sonoma Ave Santa Rosa (95404) ***(P-11860)***
Burbank Plg & Zoning Div of ....E....818 238-5250
150 N 3rd St Fl 2 Burbank (91502) ***(P-27664)***
Burbank Television Entps LLC ....C....818 954-6000
4000 Warner Blvd Burbank (91522) ***(P-5769)***
Burbank Water & Power, Burbank *Also called City of Burbank* ***(P-6181)***
Burch Construction Company Inc ....E....760 788-9370
405 Maple St Ste C-101 Ramona (92065) ***(P-1489)***
Burdette De Cock Inc ....C....310 542-0563
3625 Del Amo Blvd Ste 105 Torrance (90503) ***(P-22243)***
Burdick Painting ....D....408 567-1330
705 Nuttman St Santa Clara (95054) ***(P-3497)***
Bureau Veritas North Amer Inc ....D....714 431-4100
1940 E Deere Ave Ste 210 Santa Ana (92705) ***(P-27665)***
Burford Family Farming Co LP (PA) ....C....559 431-0902
1443 W Sample Ave Fresno (93711) ***(P-326)***
Burford Ranch, Fresno *Also called Burford Family Farming Co LP* ***(P-326)***
Burger King, Fremont *Also called Patel Brothers Inc* ***(P-26982)***
Burger Physcl Therapy Svcs Inc (HQ) ....C....916 983-5900
1301 E Bidwell St Ste 201 Folsom (95630) ***(P-20165)***
Burger Physcl Thrapy Rhblttion, Folsom *Also called Burger Physcl Therapy Svcs Inc* ***(P-20165)***

A L P H A B E T I C

Employee Codes: A=Over 500 employees, B=251-500
C=101-250, D=51-100, E=50
2019 Directory of California
Wholesalers and Services Companies
© Mergent Inc. 1-800-342-5647
1231

Burger Physical Therapy....E....916 983-5900
1301 E Bidwell St Ste 101 Folsom (95630) ***(P-20166)***
Burger Rhblitation Systems Inc....D....916 617-2400
2101 Stone Blvd Ste 175 West Sacramento (95691) ***(P-20167)***
Burger Rhblitation Systems Inc....D....916 863-5785
6614 Mercy Ct Ste C Fair Oaks (95628) ***(P-20168)***
Burger Rhblitation Systems Inc (PA)....C....800 900-8491
1301 E Bidwell St Ste 201 Folsom (95630) ***(P-20169)***
Burgett Incorporated....D....916 567-9999
4111a N Freeway Blvd Sacramento (95834) ***(P-8021)***
Burke Williams & Sorensen LLP (PA)....D....213 236-0600
444 S Flower St Ste 2400 Los Angeles (90071) ***(P-22965)***
Burkshire Has A Way Home Servc....D....818 501-4800
16810 Ventura Blvd Fl 1 Encino (91436) ***(P-11253)***
Burleigh Point Ltd (HQ)....C....949 428-3200
117 Waterworks Way Irvine (92618) ***(P-11254)***
Burlingame Country Club....D....650 696-8100
80 New Place Rd Hillsborough (94010) ***(P-18876)***
Burlingame Healtcare Center, Burlingame *Also called Burlingame Senior Care LLC* ***(P-21025)***
Burlingame Industries Inc (PA)....D....909 355-7000
3546 N Riverside Ave Rialto (92377) ***(P-13459)***
Burlingame Industries Inc....C....909 887-7038
277 Lytle Creek Rd Lytle Creek (92358) ***(P-13460)***
Burlingame Industries Inc....D....209 464-9001
4555 Mckinley Ave Stockton (95206) ***(P-6921)***
Burlingame Long Term Care, Burlingame *Also called San Mateo Healthcare & Wellnes* ***(P-20742)***
Burlingame Senior Care LLC....B....650 692-3758
1100 Trousdale Dr Burlingame (94010) ***(P-21025)***
Burlington Convalescent Hosp (PA)....D....213 381-5585
845 S Burlington Ave Los Angeles (90057) ***(P-20275)***
Burlington Convalescent Hosp....D....323 295-7737
3737 Don Felipe Dr Los Angeles (90008) ***(P-20276)***
Burlington Northern, San Bernardino *Also called Bnsf Railway Company* ***(P-3614)***
Burlington Northern, Barstow *Also called Bnsf Railway Company* ***(P-3615)***
Burlington Northern, Commerce *Also called Bnsf Railway Company* ***(P-3616)***
Burlington Northern, Vernon *Also called Bnsf Railway Company* ***(P-3617)***
Burn 60 LLC....E....310 476-5656
159 S Barrington Pl Los Angeles (90049) ***(P-18582)***
Burnham & Brown, Oakland *Also called Burnham Brown A Prof Corp* ***(P-22966)***
Burnham Brown A Prof Corp....C....510 444-6800
1901 Harrison St Ste 1100 Oakland (94612) ***(P-22966)***
Burnham Real Estate, San Diego *Also called Christian and Wakefield* ***(P-11316)***
Burns & McDonnell Inc....D....714 256-1595
140 S State College Blvd Brea (92821) ***(P-25584)***
Burns and Sons Trucking Inc....D....619 460-5394
9210 Olive Dr Spring Valley (91977) ***(P-3982)***
Burr Pilger Mayer....D....707 544-4078
110 Stony Point Rd # 210 Santa Rosa (95401) ***(P-26153)***
Burr Pilger Mayer (PA)....C....415 421-5757
600 California St Fl 6 San Francisco (94108) ***(P-26154)***
Burr Pilger Mayer Inc....E....408 961-6355
60 S Market St Ste 800 San Jose (95113) ***(P-26155)***
Burr Pilger Mayer Inc....E....650 855-6800
2000 University Ave East Palo Alto (94303) ***(P-26156)***
Burrtec Waste Group Inc....D....760 256-2730
2340 W Main St Barstow (92311) ***(P-3983)***
Burrtec Waste Industries Inc (HQ)....C....909 429-4200
9890 Cherry Ave Fontana (92335) ***(P-6362)***
Burtch Construction, Bakersfield *Also called Burtch Trucking Inc* ***(P-1734)***
Burtch Trucking Inc....D....661 399-1736
18815 Highway 65 Bakersfield (93308) ***(P-1734)***
Burtech Pipeline Incorporated....D....760 634-2822
102 2nd St Encinitas (92024) ***(P-1899)***
Burton P Scott, Los Angeles *Also called Morgan Lewis & Bockius LLP* ***(P-23265)***
Burton-Way House Ltd A CA....C....805 214-8075
2 Dole Dr Westlake Village (91362) ***(P-12410)***
Burton-Way House Ltd A CA....C....310 273-2222
300 S Doheny Dr Los Angeles (90048) ***(P-12411)***
Burton-Way House Ltd A CA (PA)....E....310 552-6623
2029 Century Park E # 2200 Los Angeles (90067) ***(P-12412)***
Bus Company, Santa Clarita *Also called Santa Clarita City of* ***(P-3883)***
Busa Servicing Inc (HQ)....C....310 203-3400
2029 Century Park E # 4200 Los Angeles (90067) ***(P-9422)***
Busa Servicing Inc....C....800 222-1234
2029 Century Park E # 4200 Los Angeles (90067) ***(P-9423)***
Bushnell Gardens....D....916 791-4199
5255 Douglas Blvd Granite Bay (95746) ***(P-9127)***
Bushnell's Landscape Creations, Granite Bay *Also called Bushnell Gardens* ***(P-9127)***
Business and Support Services....D....760 830-6873
P.O. Box 6001 Twentynine Palms (92278) ***(P-18877)***
Business and Support Services....B....760 725-5187
Camp Pendleton Mc Base Oceanside (92055) ***(P-20112)***
Business and Support Services....E....760 725-2817
Santa Jancinto Rd 20286 Oceanside (92054) ***(P-24270)***
Business and Support Services....A....858 577-1061
Mccs Bldg 2273 Elrod Ave San Diego (92145) ***(P-19115)***
Business Connections....D....530 527-6229
332 Pine St Red Bluff (96080) ***(P-14580)***
Business Department, Murrieta *Also called Southwest Healthcare Sys Aux* ***(P-21771)***
Business For Scial Rspnsbility (PA)....C....415 984-3200
88 Kearny St Fl 12 San Francisco (94108) ***(P-27175)***
Business Furn Solutions Inc (PA)....D....408 325-3100
2150 N 1st St Ste 100 San Jose (95131) ***(P-6714)***
Business Intelligence....E....858 452-8200
2131 Palomar Airport Rd # 328 Carlsbad (92011) ***(P-27176)***
Business of Finance, San Francisco *Also called Airport Commisions* ***(P-4869)***
Business Services Network....D....415 282-8161
1275 Fairfax Ave Ste 103 San Francisco (94124) ***(P-14042)***
Businesscom Inc....D....310 586-4000
2120 Colorado Ave Fl 3 Santa Monica (90404) ***(P-27177)***
Butcher's Brand, San Leandro *Also called Webers Quality Meats Inc* ***(P-8634)***
Butler America LLC (HQ)....A....805 880-1965
3820 State St Ste B Santa Barbara (93105) ***(P-25585)***
Butler International Inc (PA)....C....805 882-2200
3820 State St Ste A Santa Barbara (93105) ***(P-14825)***
Butler Service Group Inc (HQ)....D....201 891-5312
3820 State St Ste A Santa Barbara (93105) ***(P-14826)***
Butler Shine Stern Prtners LLC....C....415 331-6049
20 Liberty Ship Way Sausalito (94965) ***(P-13800)***
Butte Basin Management Co....E....530 674-2060
1624 Poole Blvd Yuba City (95993) ***(P-26790)***
Butte County Employment Center, Oroville *Also called County of Butte* ***(P-23631)***
Butte County Mental Hlth Svcs, Chico *Also called County of Butte* ***(P-22540)***
Butte County Office Education....B....530 532-5786
1859 Bird St Oroville (95965) ***(P-25401)***
Butte County Probation, Oroville *Also called County of Butte* ***(P-23626)***
BUTTE HOME HEALTH & HOSPICE, Chico *Also called Butte Home Health Inc* ***(P-22244)***
Butte Home Health Inc....C....530 895-0462
10 Constitution Dr Chico (95973) ***(P-22244)***
Butte Primary Care Med Group....D....530 877-0762
6585 Clark Rd Ste 200 Paradise (95969) ***(P-19334)***
Butte-Yb-Stter Wtr Qlty Cltion....D....530 673-5131
625 Cooper Ave Yuba City (95991) ***(P-4488)***
Butter Paddle....D....408 395-1678
33 N Santa Cruz Ave Los Gatos (95030) ***(P-17044)***
Butter Paddle, The, Los Gatos *Also called Butter Paddle* ***(P-17044)***
Butterfield Electric Inc (PA)....C....530 666-2116
2101 Freeway Dr Ste A Woodland (95776) ***(P-2532)***
Butterwick Dr Kimberly Jane MD....D....858 657-1002
9339 Genesee Ave Ste 300 San Diego (92121) ***(P-19335)***
Button & Turkovich....D....530 795-2090
24604 Buckeye Rd Winters (95694) ***(P-327)***
Button Transportation Inc....C....707 678-1983
7000 Button Ln Dixon (95620) ***(P-4113)***
Buttonwillow Warehouse Co Inc (HQ)....D....661 695-6500
3430 Unicorn Rd Bakersfield (93308) ***(P-9077)***
Buxton Consulting....D....925 467-0700
5976 W Las Positas Blvd # 208 Pleasanton (94588) ***(P-27666)***
Buy Fresh Produce Inc....D....323 796-0127
6636 E 26th St Commerce (90040) ***(P-8644)***
Buyefficient LLC....D....949 382-3129
903 Calle Amanecer # 200 San Clemente (92673) ***(P-7132)***
Buyerlink, Walnut Creek *Also called One Planet Ops Inc* ***(P-13873)***
Buyers Consultation Svc Inc (PA)....D....818 341-4820
8735 Remmet Ave Canoga Park (91304) ***(P-7453)***
Buzz Oates Management Services....E....916 381-3843
555 Capitol Mall Ste 900 Sacramento (95814) ***(P-11255)***
Buzztime Inc....C....760 476-1976
2231 Rutherford Rd # 210 Carlsbad (92008) ***(P-5770)***
BV General Inc....D....323 651-0043
619 N Fairfax Ave Los Angeles (90036) ***(P-21026)***
BVHP, San Francisco *Also called Bayview Hunters Point Foundati* ***(P-25396)***
Bvk Gaming Inc....D....707 644-8853
3466 Broadway St American Canyon (94503) ***(P-19116)***
Bvls, Plymouth *Also called Borjon Iscander* ***(P-640)***
Bvs Entertainment Inc (HQ)....E....818 460-6917
500 S Buena Vista St Burbank (91521) ***(P-18028)***
Bwr Public Relations....D....310 248-6100
9100 Wilshire Blvd 500w Beverly Hills (90212) ***(P-27544)***
Bwrpr, Beverly Hills *Also called Baker Winokur* ***(P-27540)***
Bws Group Co., Santa Fe Springs *Also called Ob Usa Inc* ***(P-9018)***
Bx Construction LLC....D....951 509-9412
11671 Sterling Ave Ste K Riverside (92503) ***(P-1133)***
By Referral Only Inc....D....760 707-1300
2035 Corte Del Nogal # 200 Carlsbad (92011) ***(P-27667)***
By The Blue Sea LLC....B....310 458-0030
1 Pico Blvd Santa Monica (90405) ***(P-12413)***
By Wind Inc....D....949 385-6219
15 Enterprise Ste 520 Aliso Viejo (92656) ***(P-15042)***
By-The-Bay Investments Inc....B....510 793-2581
37000 Fremont Blvd Fremont (94536) ***(P-12207)***
Bycor General Contractors Inc....D....858 587-1901
6490 Marindustry Dr Ste A San Diego (92121) ***(P-1490)***
Byers Enterprises Inc....D....530 272-7777
11773 Slow Poke Ln Grass Valley (95945) ***(P-3131)***
Byers Leafguard Gutter Systems, Grass Valley *Also called Byers Enterprises Inc* ***(P-3131)***
Bynd LLC....D....415 944-2293
100 Montgomery St # 1102 San Francisco (94104) ***(P-15043)***
Byrd Harvest Inc....B....805 343-1608
192 Guadalupe St Guadalupe (93434) ***(P-475)***
Byrd Produce, Guadalupe *Also called Byrd Harvest Inc* ***(P-475)***
Byrom-Davey Inc....E....858 513-7199
13220 Evnng Crk Dr S # 103 San Diego (92128) ***(P-2018)***
Byron Park, Walnut Creek *Also called A F Evans Company Inc* ***(P-16969)***
Byte Mobile, Santa Clara *Also called Bytemobile Inc* ***(P-5971)***
Bytemobile Inc....B....408 327-7700
2860 De La Cruz Blvd # 200 Santa Clara (95050) ***(P-5971)***
Bytheways Manufacturing Inc....B....916 453-1212
2080 Enterprise Blvd West Sacramento (95691) ***(P-6754)***
Byton North America Corp....C....408 966-5078
4201 Burton Dr Santa Clara (95054) ***(P-26344)***
C & B Delivery Services....D....909 623-4708
230 Diamond St Laguna Beach (92651) ***(P-4534)***

Mergent e-mail: customerrelations@mergent.com
1232
2019 Directory of California
Wholesalers and Services Companies
(P-0000) Products & Services Section entry number
(PA)=Parent Co (HQ)=Headquarters (DH)=Div Headquarters

C & C Boats Inc........E.......805 445-9456
1861 Baja Vista Way Camarillo (93010) *(P-4753)*
C & C Construction Inc........E.......916 434-5280
7941 E Hidden Lakes Dr Granite Bay (95746) *(P-1491)*
C & C Security Patrol Inc (PA)........C.......510 713-1260
4615 Enterprise Cmn Fremont (94538) *(P-16594)*
C & D Towing Specialists Inc (PA)........D.......619 463-8697
8332 Case St La Mesa (91942) *(P-17854)*
C & G Farms Inc........C.......831 679-2978
25453 Iverson Rd Chualar (93925) *(P-40)*
C & I, Spring Valley *Also called Commercial Indus Roofg Co Inc (P-3140)*
C & L Refrigeration Corp........C.......800 901-4822
4111 N Palm St Fullerton (92835) *(P-2152)*
C & M Transfer San Diego Inc........D.......619 562-6111
8787 Olive Ln Santee (92071) *(P-4334)*
C & O Painting Inc........E.......408 279-8011
1500 N 4th St San Jose (95112) *(P-2425)*
C & R Systems Inc (PA)........E.......951 270-0255
1835 Capital St Corona (92880) *(P-2533)*
C & S Draperies Inc........C.......209 466-5371
4210 Kiernan Ave Modesto (95356) *(P-13573)*
C & S Wholesale Grocers Inc........B.......916 383-5275
8301 Fruitridge Rd Sacramento (95826) *(P-4535)*
C A A, Los Angeles *Also called Creative Artists Agency LLC (P-18361)*
C A C, Goleta *Also called Community Action Commsn Santa (P-24757)*
C A H H S........D.......916 552-7507
1215 K St Ste 800 Sacramento (95814) *(P-24946)*
C A Hofmann Construction Inc........E.......909 484-5888
8923 Laramie Dr Rancho Cucamonga (91737) *(P-2856)*
C A L M, Santa Barbara *Also called Child Abuse Lstening Mediation (P-23556)*
C A Rasmussen Inc (PA)........E.......661 367-9040
28548 Livingston Ave Valencia (91355) *(P-2019)*
C B B Z S Inc........D.......818 908-1900
7015 Valjean Ave Van Nuys (91406) *(P-2426)*
C B Coast Newport Properties........D.......949 644-1600
840 Nwport Ctr Dr Ste 100 Newport Beach (92660) *(P-11256)*
C B Richard Ellis Investors, Los Angeles *Also called T C W Realty Fund VI (P-12189)*
C B S Marketwatch, San Francisco *Also called Marketwatch Inc (P-16956)*
C C Connection Inc........D.......925 937-0100
2950 Buskirk Ave Ste 140 Walnut Creek (94597) *(P-11257)*
C C S, Los Angeles *Also called Creative Channel Services LLC (P-13805)*
C D C, Costa Mesa *Also called Creative Design Cons Inc (P-17110)*
C D I, Sacramento *Also called Creative Design Interiors Inc (P-3098)*
C D Lyon Construction Inc (PA)........D.......805 653-0173
380 W Stanley Ave Ventura (93001) *(P-25586)*
C D Payroll Inc........D.......818 848-1562
2300 W Empire Ave Burbank (91504) *(P-26157)*
C D R, Oxnard *Also called Child Development Resources of (P-23562)*
C D R Enterprises Inc........D.......661 940-0344
42302 8th St E Lancaster (93535) *(P-2857)*
C E B M Inc........E.......909 975-4440
3100 E Cedar St Ste 17 Ontario (91761) *(P-14205)*
C E D, Orange *Also called County Whl Elc Co Los Angeles (P-7352)*
C E H A, San Mateo *Also called California Envmtl Hlth Assn (P-27672)*
C E I, Oakland *Also called Center For Elders Independence (P-10192)*
C E P........D.......909 580-1456
400 N Pepper Ave Ste 107 Colton (92324) *(P-19336)*
C E T, San Jose *Also called Center For Employment Training (P-24164)*
C E Toland & Son........C.......707 747-1000
5300 Industrial Way Benicia (94510) *(P-3498)*
C F I, Los Angeles *Also called Commodity Forwarders Inc (P-5035)*
C F X, Carson *Also called City Fashion Express Inc (P-5033)*
C H I, Modesto *Also called Community Hospice Inc (P-20922)*
C H O C, Fairfield *Also called Community Housing Opport (P-27694)*
C H Reynolds Electric Inc........B.......408 436-9280
1281 Wayne Ave San Jose (95131) *(P-2534)*
C H Robinson Intl Inc........D.......310 763-6080
680 Knox St Ste 210 Torrance (90502) *(P-5022)*
C I C C, Covelo *Also called Covelo Indian Community Center (P-11387)*
C I Container Line, Los Angeles *Also called Carmichael International Svc (P-5025)*
C I Design, Lake Forest *Also called Commercial Indus Design Co Inc (P-7024)*
C I G A, Glendale *Also called Califrnia Insur Guarantee Assn (P-10497)*
C I W, Pittsburg *Also called Concord Iron Works Inc (P-3374)*
C J Foods, Los Angeles *Also called CJ America Inc (P-8768)*
C J Health Services Inc........D.......510 793-3000
38650 Mission Blvd Fremont (94536) *(P-20277)*
C J Vandergeest Ldscp Care Inc........D.......805 650-0726
2476 Palma Dr Ste G Ventura (93003) *(P-806)*
C L A, Van Nuys *Also called Clay Lacy Aviation Inc (P-4881)*
C L Bryant Inc........C.......209 566-5000
7401 Del Cielo Way Modesto (95356) *(P-8942)*
C M A, Sacramento *Also called California Medical Association (P-25003)*
C M A Alliance........E.......818 981-0800
16542 Ventura Blvd # 210 Encino (91436) *(P-10567)*
C M C Steel Fabricators Inc........C.......909 899-9993
12451 Arrow Rte Etiwanda (91739) *(P-3366)*
C M C Steel Fabricators Inc........D.......909 873-3060
2755 S Willow Ave Bloomington (92316) *(P-3367)*
C M S Hospitality, Los Angeles *Also called Concession Management Svcs Inc (P-19146)*
C M Service, San Carlos *Also called Commercial Mechanical Svc Inc (P-17893)*
C N B Commercial Banking Ctr, Riverside *Also called City National Bank (P-9338)*
C N L Hotel Del Partners LP........A.......619 522-8299
1500 Orange Ave San Diego (92118) *(P-12414)*
C O T S Inc (PA)........D.......714 751-5466
6242 Cherry Ave Long Beach (90805) *(P-3781)*
C Overaa & Co (PA)........C.......510 234-0926
200 Parr Blvd Richmond (94801) *(P-1382)*
C Overaa & Co........C.......510 235-0540
2555 El Portal Dr San Pablo (94806) *(P-1383)*
C P Construction Co Inc........E.......909 981-1091
105 N Loma Pl Upland (91786) *(P-1900)*
C P Document Technologies LLC (PA)........D.......213 617-4040
800 W 6th St Ste 1400 Los Angeles (90017) *(P-7454)*
C P S Express (HQ)........D.......951 685-1041
3401 Etiwanda Ave B Mira Loma (91752) *(P-3984)*
C P T C, Anaheim *Also called California Private Trnsp Co LP (P-5214)*
C R A, Los Angeles *Also called Community Redevelopment Agency (P-27695)*
C R I, Torrance *Also called Contract Recruiting Inc (P-14592)*
C R S Drywall Inc........D.......408 998-4360
135 San Jose Ave San Jose (95125) *(P-2858)*
C S C, Northridge *Also called Contemporary Services Corp (P-14590)*
C S D P, Irvine *Also called Customer Srvc Dlvry Pltfrm Crp (P-16339)*
C S I, Simi Valley *Also called Cardservice International Inc (P-17056)*
C S I, Santa Fe Springs *Also called Csi Electrical Contractors Inc (P-2555)*
C S I Patrol Services........D.......562 981-8988
3605 Long Beach Blvd # 205 Long Beach (90807) *(P-16595)*
C S S, Bakersfield *Also called Construction Specialty Svc Inc (P-1911)*
C S Transport Inc........D.......760 666-5661
425 E Heber Rd Ste 200 Heber (92249) *(P-3985)*
C T and F Inc........D.......562 927-2339
7228 Scout Ave Bell Gardens (90201) *(P-2535)*
C T B, Monterey *Also called Data Recognition Corporation (P-27703)*
C T Corporation System........D.......925 287-9801
2875 Michelle Ste 100 Irvine (92606) *(P-22967)*
C T I, Rancho Cucamonga *Also called Collection Technology Inc (P-13999)*
C Team Construction Inc........D.......619 579-6572
1272 Greenfield Dr El Cajon (92021) *(P-3228)*
C V S Optical Lab Div, Rancho Cordova *Also called Vision Service Plan (P-10327)*
C V Water District, Coachella *Also called Coachella Valley Water Dst (P-6229)*
C W 5, San Diego *Also called Kswb Inc (P-5815)*
C W Driver Incorporated (PA)........D.......626 351-8800
468 N Rosemead Blvd Pasadena (91107) *(P-1492)*
C W Hotels Ltd........C.......310 395-9700
1740 Ocean Ave Santa Monica (90401) *(P-12415)*
C W S, San Diego *Also called Communction Wirg Spcalists Inc (P-2548)*
C Y S, Fresno *Also called Comprehensive Youth Ser (P-23614)*
C&C Jewelry Mfg Inc........D.......213 623-6800
323 W 8th St Fl 4 Los Angeles (90014) *(P-8005)*
C&M Relocation Systems, Santee *Also called C & M Transfer San Diego Inc (P-4334)*
C&R Maintance, Oxnard *Also called HE Julien & Associates Inc (P-857)*
C&S Wholesale Grocers Inc........B.......559 442-4700
2797 S Orange Ave Fresno (93725) *(P-8386)*
C-21 Super Stars........D.......949 389-1600
22342 Avenida Empresa Rcho STA Marg (92688) *(P-11258)*
C-Air International Inc........D.......310 695-3400
9841 Arprt Blvd Ste 1400 Los Angeles (90045) *(P-5023)*
C.E.G. Construction, Pico Rivera *Also called Chalmers Corporation (P-1385)*
C.H.M.B., Escondido *Also called California Healthcare (P-10573)*
C.O.M.P.A.S.S., Redding *Also called Care Options Management Plans (P-22248)*
C.R. B Cnsulting Engineers Inc, Carlsbad *Also called Clark Richardson and Biskup (P-25617)*
C/O Longwood Management, Los Angeles *Also called Magnolia Ventures Ltd (P-17309)*
C/O Uc San Francisco........D.......310 794-1841
1245 16th St Ste 225 Santa Monica (90404) *(P-19337)*
C/O Uc San Francisco (PA)........C.......858 534-7323
1111 Franklin St Fl 12 Oakland (94607) *(P-26791)*
C2 Financial Corporation........C.......925 938-1300
3000 Citrus Cir Ste 118 Walnut Creek (94598) *(P-10064)*
C2 Financial Corporation........C.......559 824-2300
978 Burlingame Ave Clovis (93612) *(P-10065)*
C2 Financial Corporation........C.......858 220-2112
703 Sunset Ct San Diego (92109) *(P-10066)*
C2 Imaging, Costa Mesa *Also called Crisp Enterprises Inc (P-14083)*
C21 Peak........C.......818 363-1717
11011 Balboa Blvd Granada Hills (91344) *(P-11259)*
C3 Iot Inc........C.......650 503-2200
1300 Seaport Blvd Ste 500 Redwood City (94063) *(P-15618)*
C9 Edge Inc........D.......650 561-7855
177 Bovet Rd Ste 520 San Mateo (94402) *(P-7021)*
C9 Inc........D.......650 561-7855
177 Bovet Rd Ste 520 San Mateo (94402) *(P-15044)*
Ca Inc........C.......800 225-5224
3965 Freedom Cir Fl 6 Santa Clara (95054) *(P-15619)*
Ca Inc........D.......631 342-6000
10180 Telesis Ct Ste 500 San Diego (92121) *(P-15620)*
CA Landscape and Design, Upland *Also called California Ldscp & Design Inc (P-809)*
CA Station Management Inc........C.......909 245-6251
3200 E Guasti Rd Ste 100 Ontario (91761) *(P-1901)*
CA Ste Atom Assoc Intr-Ins Bur........A.......415 565-2012
150 Van Ness Ave San Francisco (94102) *(P-10340)*
CA Ste Atom Assoc Intr-Ins Bur........D.......831 824-9128
4400 Capitola Rd Ste 100 Capitola (95010) *(P-17855)*
CA Ste Atom Assoc Intr-Ins Bur........D.......650 572-5600
1650 S Delaware St San Mateo (94402) *(P-10341)*
CA Ste Atom Assoc Intr-Ins Bur........D.......650 623-3200
900 Miramonte Ave Mountain View (94040) *(P-10568)*
Caa Sports LLC (HQ)........D.......424 288-2000
2000 Avenue Of The Stars # 100 Los Angeles (90067) *(P-18513)*
Cabana Hotel, Palo Alto *Also called 4290 El Camino Properties LP (P-12293)*
Cabazon Band Mission Indians........A.......760 342-5000
84245 Indio Springs Dr Indio (92203) *(P-12416)*

ALPHABETIC

Employee Codes: A=Over 500 employees, B=251-500
C=101-250, D=51-100, E=50
2019 Directory of California
Wholesalers and Services Companies
© Mergent Inc. 1-800-342-5647
1233

Cableconn Industries Inc..........D.......858 571-7111
7198 Convoy Ct San Diego (92111) ***(P-7341)***
Cabrillo College Children Ctr..........D.......831 479-6352
6500 Soquel Dr Aptos (95003) ***(P-24271)***
Cabrillo Economic Dev Corp (PA)..........D.......805 659-3791
702 County Square Dr # 100 Ventura (93003) ***(P-1272)***
Cabrillo Gen Insur Agcy Inc..........D.......858 244-0550
7071 Convoy Ct Ste 201 San Diego (92111) ***(P-10569)***
Cac Studios, Malibu *Also called Creating Arts Company **(P-18360)***
Cache Creek Casino Resort..........A.......530 796-3118
14455 State Highway 16 Brooks (95606) ***(P-12417)***
Cacho Landscape Maintenance Co..........E.......818 365-0773
711 Truman St San Fernando (91340) ***(P-807)***
Caci Inc - Federal..........E.......619 881-6000
1455 Frazee Rd Ste 700 San Diego (92108) ***(P-15923)***
Caci Nss Inc..........C.......703 841-7800
3201 Airpark Dr Ste 109 Santa Maria (93455) ***(P-7022)***
Cacique Inc..........C.......626 961-3399
14923 Proctor Ave La Puente (91746) ***(P-8514)***
Cactus Recycling Inc (PA)..........C.......619 661-1283
8710 Avenida Fuente San Diego (92154) ***(P-6363)***
Cadence Design Systems Inc (PA)..........A.......408 943-1234
2655 Seely Ave Bldg 5 San Jose (95134) ***(P-15621)***
Cadent Inc..........C.......408 470-1000
2560 Orchard Pkwy San Jose (95131) ***(P-15924)***
Cadforce Inc..........A.......310 876-1800
10811 Wash Blvd Ste 302 Culver City (90232) ***(P-17045)***
Cadnchev Inc..........D.......562 944-6422
13603 Foster Rd Santa Fe Springs (90670) ***(P-6702)***
Cadreon LLC..........C.......415 262-5900
600 Battery St San Francisco (94111) ***(P-13801)***
Cadreon LLC..........D.......415 262-5900
653 Front St San Francisco (94111) ***(P-13802)***
Caesar and Seider Insur Svcs (PA)..........D.......805 682-2571
40 E Alamar Ave Ste 4 Santa Barbara (93105) ***(P-10570)***
Caesars Entrtnment Oprting Inc..........A.......760 751-3100
777 Harrahs Rincon Way Valley Center (92082) ***(P-19117)***
Caffeine Productions..........D.......323 860-8111
1040 N Las Palmas Ave Los Angeles (90038) ***(P-18029)***
Cahill Contractors Inc (PA)..........D.......415 986-0600
425 California St # 2200 San Francisco (94104) ***(P-1493)***
Cahill Contractors LLC..........D.......415 986-0600
425 California St # 2200 San Francisco (94104) ***(P-1494)***
Cahuilla Creek Casino, Anza *Also called Cahuilla Creek Rest & Casino **(P-19118)***
Cahuilla Creek Rest & Casino..........C.......951 763-1200
52702 Us Highway 371 Anza (92539) ***(P-19118)***
Cai, Corona *Also called Combustion Associates Inc **(P-6021)***
Cai Company, Brea *Also called California Automobile Insur Co **(P-10342)***
Cai International Inc (PA)..........D.......415 788-0100
1 Market Plz Ste 900 San Francisco (94105) ***(P-14483)***
Caine & Weiner Company Inc (PA)..........D.......818 226-6000
5805 Sepulvda Blvd # 400 Van Nuys (91411) ***(P-13993)***
Caito Fisheries Inc (PA)..........D.......707 964-6368
19400 Harbor Ave Fort Bragg (95437) ***(P-8573)***
Cake Corporation..........D.......650 215-7777
101 Redwood Ave Redwood City (94061) ***(P-15045)***
Cal Americas Wholesale Florist, Vista *Also called United Floral Exchange Inc **(P-9171)***
Cal Bowl Enterprises LLC..........E.......562 421-8448
2500 Carson St Lakewood (90712) ***(P-18485)***
Cal Care Inc..........C.......650 325-8600
1275 Crane St Menlo Park (94025) ***(P-26792)***
Cal Chamber, Sacramento *Also called California Chamber Commerce **(P-24949)***
Cal Citrus Packing Co..........D.......559 562-2536
111 N Mount Vernon Ave Lindsay (93247) ***(P-498)***
Cal Coast Financial Inc..........D.......510 683-9850
39355 California St # 101 Fremont (94538) ***(P-9874)***
Cal Coast Financial Corp (PA)..........D.......510 683-9850
43801 Mssion Blvd Ste 201 Fremont (94539) ***(P-11260)***
Cal Coast Telecom, San Jose *Also called Radonich Corp **(P-2691)***
Cal Coffee Shop, Lakewood *Also called Nationwide Theatres Corp **(P-18496)***
Cal Color Growers LLC..........D.......408 778-0835
330 Peebles Ave Morgan Hill (95037) ***(P-9128)***
Cal Consolidated Communications..........D.......916 786-6141
211 Lincoln St Roseville (95678) ***(P-5525)***
Cal Courts, Eureka *Also called Nor-Wall Inc **(P-18988)***
Cal Custom Tile..........D.......559 875-1460
1300 Commerce Way Sanger (93657) ***(P-2989)***
Cal Empire Engineering Inc..........E.......626 915-8030
628 E Edna Pl Covina (91723) ***(P-3447)***
Cal Facilities Management Co, San Jose *Also called Yang C Park **(P-14801)***
Cal Fresco LLC..........C.......714 690-7700
6850 Artesia Blvd Buena Park (90620) ***(P-8645)***
Cal Gran Theatres LLC..........E.......805 934-1582
3170 Santa Maria Way Santa Maria (93455) ***(P-18276)***
Cal Micro, Ontario *Also called Ruuhwa Dann and Associates Inc **(P-6454)***
Cal Mutual Inc..........D.......888 700-4650
2040 S Santa Cruz St # 115 Anaheim (92805) ***(P-9784)***
Cal Packing & Storage LP..........D.......559 638-2929
1356 S Buttonwillow Ave Reedley (93654) ***(P-4497)***
Cal Pinnacle Mltary Cmmunities..........D.......619 764-5087
3200 4th Ave Ste 201 San Diego (92103) ***(P-26793)***
Cal Poly Corporation..........D.......805 756-1587
Cal Poly Bldg 31 San Luis Obispo (93407) ***(P-13438)***
Cal Poly Corporation..........C.......805 756-1131
Bldg 15 San Luis Obispo (93407) ***(P-26794)***
Cal Poly Foundation, San Luis Obispo *Also called Cal Poly Corporation **(P-26794)***
Cal Poly Pomona Foundation Inc (PA)..........A.......909 869-2950
3801 W Temple Ave Bldg 55 Pomona (91768) ***(P-25402)***
Cal Shakes, Berkeley *Also called California Shakespeare Theater **(P-18351)***
Cal Sierra Construction Inc..........D.......916 416-7901
5904 Van Alstine Ave 1 Carmichael (95608) ***(P-1902)***
Cal Southern Assn Governments (PA)..........C.......213 236-1800
900 Wilshire Blvd # 1700 Los Angeles (90017) ***(P-27668)***
Cal Southern Illumination..........E.......949 622-3000
240 Commerce Irvine (92602) ***(P-7342)***
Cal Southern Presbt Homes..........C.......949 854-9500
19191 Harvard Ave Ofc Irvine (92612) ***(P-10992)***
Cal Southern Presbt Homes..........C.......858 454-4201
7450 Olivetas Ave Ofc La Jolla (92037) ***(P-24445)***
Cal Southern Presbt Homes (PA)..........D.......818 247-0420
516 Burchett St Glendale (91203) ***(P-10993)***
Cal Southern Presbt Homes..........C.......818 244-7219
1230 E Windsor Rd Ofc Glendale (91205) ***(P-10994)***
Cal Southern Presbt Homes..........D.......626 359-8141
802 Buena Vista St Duarte (91010) ***(P-20278)***
Cal Southern Presbt Homes..........D.......818 247-0420
516 Burchett St Glendale (91203) ***(P-10995)***
Cal Southern Presbt Homes..........C.......626 357-1632
1763 Royal Oaks Dr Ofc Duarte (91010) ***(P-10996)***
Cal Southern Presbt Homes..........C.......760 747-4306
710 W 13th Ave Escondido (92025) ***(P-24446)***
Cal Southern Presbt Homes..........D.......760 737-5110
500 E Valley Pkwy Ofc Escondido (92025) ***(P-24447)***
Cal Southern Services..........D.......626 281-5942
419 Mcgroarty St San Gabriel (91776) ***(P-13520)***
Cal Southern Sound Image Inc (PA)..........D.......760 737-3900
2425 Auto Park Way Escondido (92029) ***(P-7455)***
Cal Southern United Food..........C.......714 220-2297
6425 Katella Ave Cypress (90630) ***(P-10477)***
Cal Strs, West Sacramento *Also called Califor State Teach Retire Sys **(P-10478)***
Cal Tech Emplyees Fderal Cr Un (PA)..........D.......818 952-4444
528 Foothill Blvd La Canada Flintridge (91011) ***(P-9542)***
Cal West Enterprises, San Diego *Also called Wamc Company Inc **(P-11139)***
Cal West General Engrg Inc..........E.......619 469-5811
5480 Baltimore Dr Ste 215 La Mesa (91942) ***(P-14484)***
Cal West Underground Inc..........D.......951 371-6775
951 6th St Norco (92860) ***(P-2020)***
Cal-A-Vie, Vista *Also called Spa Havens LP **(P-18657)***
Cal-Coast Healthcare Inc..........D.......415 479-5149
81 Professional Ctr Pkwy San Rafael (94903) ***(P-20279)***
Cal-Lift Inc..........D.......562 566-1400
13027 Crossroads Pkwy S La Puente (91746) ***(P-7736)***
Cal-Med Ambulance, South El Monte *Also called California Med Response Inc **(P-3783)***
Cal-Organic Farms, Lamont *Also called Grimmway Enterprises Inc **(P-8694)***
Cal-Pacific Construction Inc..........E.......650 557-1238
1009 Terra Nova Blvd Pacifica (94044) ***(P-1495)***
Cal-State Auto Parts Inc (PA)..........C.......714 630-5954
1361 N Red Gum St Anaheim (92806) ***(P-6629)***
Cal-State Steel Corporation..........C.......310 632-2772
1801 W Compton Blvd Compton (90220) ***(P-3368)***
Cal-Steam, San Francisco *Also called Ferguson Enterprises Inc **(P-7617)***
Cal-West Concrete Cutting Inc (PA)..........D.......510 656-0253
3000 Tara Ct Union City (94587) ***(P-3229)***
Cal-West Nurseries Inc..........C.......951 270-0667
138 North Dr Norco (92860) ***(P-808)***
Cal/Pac Paintings & Coatings..........D.......714 628-1514
608 N Eckhoff St Orange (92868) ***(P-2427)***
Calabasas Country Club, Calabasas *Also called Knight-Calabasas LLC **(P-18942)***
Calabasas Country Club..........D.......818 222-8111
4515 Park Entrada Calabasas (91302) ***(P-18878)***
Calance, Buena Park *Also called Partners Information Tech Inc **(P-16451)***
Calatlantic Group Inc..........C.......760 602-6824
5750 Fleet St Ste 200 Carlsbad (92008) ***(P-1134)***
Calatlantic Group Inc..........D.......951 898-5500
355 E Rincon St Ste 300 Corona (92879) ***(P-1135)***
Calatlantic Group Inc..........D.......805 379-6600
757 Nile River Dr Oxnard (93036) ***(P-1136)***
Calatlantic Group Inc..........E.......925 847-8700
3825 Hopyard Rd Ste 195 Pleasanton (94588) ***(P-1332)***
Calatlantic Group Inc..........D.......949 789-1600
15360 Barranca Pkwy Irvine (92618) ***(P-1137)***
Calatlantic Group Inc..........D.......310 821-9843
13200 Fiji Way Marina Del Rey (90292) ***(P-1138)***
Calatlantic Group Inc..........D.......949 789-1600
26 Technology Dr Irvine (92618) ***(P-1139)***
Calatlantic Group Inc..........D.......760 931-4414
5740 Fleet St Ste 200 Carlsbad (92008) ***(P-1333)***
Calatlantic Homes, Irvine *Also called Calatlantic Group Inc **(P-1137)***
Calaveras County Water Dst..........D.......209 754-3543
120 Toma Ct San Andreas (95249) ***(P-6210)***
Calavo Foods, Santa Paula *Also called Calavo Growers Inc **(P-5206)***
Calavo Growers Inc (PA)..........C.......805 525-1245
1141 Cummings Rd Ste A Santa Paula (93060) ***(P-8646)***
Calavo Growers Inc..........D.......805 525-5511
15765 W Telegraph Rd Santa Paula (93060) ***(P-5206)***
Calavo Growers Inc..........E.......951 676-7331
28410 Vincent Moraga Dr Temecula (92590) ***(P-8647)***
Calbee North America LLC..........E.......707 427-2500
2600 Maxwell Way Fairfield (94534) ***(P-8489)***
Calbond, Rancho Dominguez *Also called Calpipe Industries LLC **(P-7264)***
Calcom Solar, Visalia *Also called California Coml Solar Inc **(P-2154)***
Calculi Corporation..........E.......408 970-0007
3945 Freedom Cir Santa Clara (95054) ***(P-15925)***
Calderon Building Maintenance..........D.......619 269-5940
3822 Sherman St San Diego (92110) ***(P-14206)***
Caldwell Banker Inc..........D.......760 941-6888
40 Main St Ste E100 Vista (92083) ***(P-11261)***

Caldwell Realty ...D.......562 907-5655
14831 Whittier Blvd # 102 Whittier (90605) ***(P-11262)***
Caldwell Ventures LLC ...E.......530 899-0814
1351 E Lassen Ave Ofc Chico (95973) ***(P-20280)***
Calenergy LLC ...B.......402 231-1527
7030 Gentry Rd Calipatria (92233) ***(P-2536)***
CALEX, Northridge *Also called Valley Hospital Medical Center* ***(P-21895)***
Calex Engineering Inc ...D.......661 254-1866
23651 Pine St Newhall (91321) ***(P-3416)***
California Fruit Exchange LLC (PA) ...C.......209 365-2340
6011 E Pine St Lodi (95240) ***(P-8648)***
Calhot Illinios LLC ...C.......310 536-9800
5250 W El Segundo Blvd Hawthorne (90250) ***(P-12418)***
Calhoun Construction Inc ...C.......916 434-8356
110 Gateway Dr Ste 260 Lincoln (95648) ***(P-1140)***
Cali Calmecac Language Academy ...D.......707 837-7747
9491 Starr Rd Windsor (95492) ***(P-25121)***
Cali Hsg Finance Agcy ...D.......916 326-8627
500 Capitol Mall Ste 1400 Sacramento (95814) ***(P-27669)***
Caliber Bodyworks Texas Inc ...D.......310 392-7662
1100 Colorado Ave Santa Monica (90401) ***(P-17713)***
Caliber Bodyworks Texas Inc ...C.......714 436-5010
1399 Logan Ave Costa Mesa (92626) ***(P-17714)***
Caliber Bodyworks Texas Inc ...D.......714 665-3905
5 Auto Center Dr Tustin (92782) ***(P-17715)***
Caliber Bodyworks Texas Inc ...D.......408 972-0300
3517 Hillcap Ave San Jose (95136) ***(P-17716)***
Caliber Bodyworks Texas Inc ...E.......909 598-1113
20601 Valley Blvd Walnut (91789) ***(P-17717)***
Caliber Capital Group LLC ...A.......714 507-1998
5900 Katella Ave Ste A101 Cypress (90630) ***(P-10067)***
Caliber Collision Centers, Tustin *Also called Caliber Bodyworks Texas Inc* ***(P-17715)***
Caliber Collision Centers, San Jose *Also called Caliber Bodyworks Texas Inc* ***(P-17716)***
Caliber Holdings Corporation ...D.......323 913-4000
3020 Riverside Dr Los Angeles (90039) ***(P-17718)***
Caliber Home Loans Inc ...D.......925 417-3491
6600 Koll Center Pkwy Pleasanton (94566) ***(P-9785)***
Caliber Home Loans Inc ...B.......707 432-1000
3700 Hilborn Rd Ste 700 Fairfield (94534) ***(P-9786)***
Caliber Home Loans Inc ...D.......805 883-6800
1111 Chapala St Santa Barbara (93101) ***(P-9787)***
Calibre International LLC (PA) ...C.......626 969-4660
6250 N Irwindale Ave Irwindale (91702) ***(P-27545)***
Calico Brands Inc ...E.......909 930-5000
2055 S Haven Ave Ontario (91761) ***(P-9201)***
Calico Building Services Inc ...C.......949 380-8707
15550 Rockfield Blvd C Irvine (92618) ***(P-14207)***
Calidad Industries Inc ...D.......510 534-6666
1301 30th Ave Oakland (94601) ***(P-24160)***
Caliente Farms, Delano *Also called M Caratan Inc* ***(P-159)***
Calif Institute Human Ser ...D.......707 664-2416
1801 E Cotati Ave Rohnert Park (94928) ***(P-27178)***
Calif Land Management, South Lake Tahoe *Also called California Land Mgt Svcs Corp* ***(P-13461)***
Calif Stat Univ Fres Foun ...C.......559 278-0850
5370 N Chestnut Ave Fresno (93725) ***(P-25403)***
Califia Farms LLC ...D.......661 679-1000
33502 Lerdo Hwy Bakersfield (93308) ***(P-328)***
Califor State Teach Retire Sys (HQ) ...C.......800 228-5453
100 Waterfront Pl West Sacramento (95605) ***(P-10478)***
California Academy Sciences (PA) ...A.......415 379-8000
55 Music Concourse Dr San Francisco (94118) ***(P-24926)***
California Access Scaffold LLC ...D.......310 324-3388
331 Vineland Ave City of Industry (91746) ***(P-3499)***
California Air Cartage Inc (PA) ...D.......619 291-8544
2357 Airlane Rd Ste B San Diego (92101) ***(P-4777)***
California American Water Co (HQ) ...D.......619 409-7703
655 W Broadway Ste 1410 San Diego (92101) ***(P-6211)***
California American Water Co ...D.......619 656-2400
880 Kuhn Dr Chula Vista (91914) ***(P-6212)***
California American Water Co ...E.......707 542-1717
4787 Old Redwood Hwy Santa Rosa (95403) ***(P-6213)***
California American Water Co ...E.......916 568-4216
4701 Beloit Dr Sacramento (95838) ***(P-6214)***
California and Nevada IBEW/Nec ...D.......925 828-6322
5934 Gibraltar Dr Ste 205 Pleasanton (94588) ***(P-2537)***
California Anesthesia Asso Med ...D.......800 888-2186
400 N Tustin Ave Ste 400 # 400 Santa Ana (92705) ***(P-19338)***
CALIFORNIA ARMENIAN HOME, Fresno *Also called California HM For The Aged Inc* ***(P-21028)***
California Artichoke & Vegetab ...D.......831 633-2144
10855 Ocean Mist Pkwy Castroville (95012) ***(P-499)***
California Assn Realtors Inc (PA) ...C.......213 739-8200
525 S Virgil Ave Los Angeles (90020) ***(P-24947)***
California Association O (PA) ...D.......916 443-7401
1215 K St Ste 800 Sacramento (95814) ***(P-25000)***
California Automobile Insur Co ...A.......714 232-8669
555 W Imperial Hwy Brea (92821) ***(P-10342)***
California Baking Company ...B.......619 591-8289
681 Anita St Chula Vista (91911) ***(P-8763)***
California Bank & Trust, Culver City *Also called Zb National Association* ***(P-9412)***
California Basic, Santa Fe Springs *Also called Mias Fashion Mfg Co Inc* ***(P-8321)***
California Bistro At Fo ...D.......760 603-3700
7100 Aviara Resort Dr Carlsbad (92011) ***(P-12419)***
California Bread Co., Chula Vista *Also called California Baking Company* ***(P-8763)***
California Broadcast Ctr LLC ...C.......310 233-2425
3800 Via Oro Ave Long Beach (90810) ***(P-5859)***
California Business Bureau Inc (PA) ...C.......626 303-1515
1711 S Mountain Ave Monrovia (91016) ***(P-13994)***
California Cancer Asssctes ...D.......559 447-4949
7130 N Millbrook Ave Fresno (93720) ***(P-19339)***
California Cancer Center, Fresno *Also called Community Medical Center* ***(P-21337)***
California Capital Insur Co (PA) ...C.......831 233-5500
2300 Garden Rd Monterey (93940) ***(P-10343)***
California Casuality, San Mateo *Also called California Casualty Mgt Co* ***(P-10344)***
California Casualty Mgt Co (HQ) ...C.......650 574-4000
1875 S Grant St Ste 800 San Mateo (94402) ***(P-10344)***
California Cereal Products Inc (PA) ...D.......510 452-4500
1267 14th St Oakland (94607) ***(P-8905)***
California Certified Organic ...D.......831 423-2263
2155 Delaware Ave Ste 150 Santa Cruz (95060) ***(P-24948)***
California Chamber Commerce (PA) ...D.......916 444-6670
1215 K St Ste 1400 Sacramento (95814) ***(P-24949)***
California Child Care Resourc ...E.......510 658-0381
5232 Claremont Ave Oakland (94618) ***(P-23522)***
California Child Care Resource (PA) ...D.......415 882-0234
1182 Market St Ste 300 San Francisco (94102) ***(P-23523)***
California Choice, Orange *Also called Choic Admini Insur Servi* ***(P-10582)***
California Citrus Cooperative ...D.......951 683-4045
859 Center St Riverside (92507) ***(P-204)***
California Clinical Trials ...C.......310 945-1780
3828 Delmas Ter 2 Culver City (90232) ***(P-10571)***
California Closet Co, San Diego *Also called Dehart Inc* ***(P-3510)***
California Closet Co O ...D.......760 773-4784
42210 Cook St Ste E Palm Desert (92211) ***(P-3500)***
California Club ...C.......213 622-1391
538 S Flower St Los Angeles (90071) ***(P-25122)***
California Club Lucky Lady ...E.......619 287-6690
5526 El Cajon Blvd San Diego (92115) ***(P-12420)***
California Club of CA ...D.......415 474-3516
1750 Clay St San Francisco (94109) ***(P-25123)***
California Cmnty Foundation (PA) ...D.......213 413-4130
221 S Figueroa St Ste 400 Los Angeles (90012) ***(P-12074)***
California Cmplte CNT Cnsus ...D.......916 852-2020
400 R St Ste 350 Sacramento (95811) ***(P-26600)***
California Coast Credit Union (PA) ...C.......858 495-1600
9201 Spectrum Center Blvd # 300 San Diego (92123) ***(P-9623)***
California Coast Credit Union ...C.......858 495-1600
5890 Pcf Ctr Blvd Frnt San Diego (92121) ***(P-9543)***
California Coast Credit Union ...D.......858 495-1600
8131 Allison Ave La Mesa (91942) ***(P-9624)***
California Comfort Systems USA ...B.......858 564-1100
7740 Kenamar Ct San Diego (92121) ***(P-2153)***
California Coml Inv Group Inc ...E.......805 495-8400
4530 E Thousand Oaks Blvd # 100 Westlake Village (91362) ***(P-27670)***
California Coml Solar Inc ...D.......559 667-9200
635 S Atwood St Visalia (93277) ***(P-2154)***
California Commerce Club Inc ...A.......323 721-2100
6131 Telegraph Rd Commerce (90040) ***(P-12421)***
California Contrs Sups Inc ...D.......818 785-8823
7729 Burnet Ave Van Nuys (91405) ***(P-7670)***
California Convalescent Center, Los Angeles *Also called Bonnie Brae Cnvlscent Hosp Inc* ***(P-21011)***
California Convalescent Hosp ...D.......805 682-1355
2225 De La Vina St Santa Barbara (93105) ***(P-21027)***
California Convalescent Hosptl ...D.......626 793-5114
120 Bellefontaine St Pasadena (91105) ***(P-20281)***
California Correctnl Peace Ofc (PA) ...D.......916 372-6060
755 Riverpoint Dr West Sacramento (95605) ***(P-25056)***
California Country Club ...D.......626 333-4571
1509 Workman Mill Rd City of Industry (90601) ***(P-18879)***
California Creations Inc ...E.......323 722-9832
1100 S Vail Ave Montebello (90640) ***(P-6715)***
California Credit Union ...D.......818 291-5434
11331 Camarillo St North Hollywood (91602) ***(P-9544)***
California Credit Union ...D.......213 975-1254
333 S Beaudry Ave Ste 215 Los Angeles (90017) ***(P-9545)***
California Credit Union (PA) ...C.......818 291-6700
701 N Brand Blvd Ste 100 Glendale (91203) ***(P-9625)***
California Credit Union ...D.......310 671-1080
3550 W Century Blvd # 103 Inglewood (90303) ***(P-9626)***
California Credits Group LLC ...E.......626 584-9800
251 S Lake Ave Ste 400 Pasadena (91101) ***(P-17046)***
California Cryobank Inc ...B.......650 635-1420
611 Gateway Blvd Ste 820 South San Francisco (94080) ***(P-22753)***
California Cryobank Inc (PA) ...D.......310 443-5244
11915 La Grange Ave Los Angeles (90025) ***(P-22754)***
California Cy Correctional Ctr, California City *Also called Corecivic Inc* ***(P-27584)***
California Dental Arts LLC ...D.......408 255-1020
20421 Pacifica Dr Cupertino (95014) ***(P-22162)***
California Dental Association (PA) ...C.......916 443-0505
1201 K St Fl 14 Sacramento (95814) ***(P-25001)***
California Dept Fish Wildlife ...C.......916 358-2900
1701 Nimbus Rd Ste A Gold River (95670) ***(P-13447)***
California Dept Rehabilitation ...D.......415 904-7100
301 Howard St Ste 900 San Francisco (94105) ***(P-14581)***
California Dept Tax & Fee ADM ...D.......800 400-7115
450 N St Sacramento (95814) ***(P-13702)***
California Dept Transportation ...B.......707 445-6600
1656 Union St Eureka (95501) ***(P-27671)***
California Drywall Co (PA) ...C.......408 292-7500
2290 S 10th St San Jose (95112) ***(P-2859)***
California Eastern Labs Inc (PA) ...D.......408 919-2500
4590 Patrick Henry Dr Santa Clara (95054) ***(P-7456)***
California Emergency Physician, Modesto *Also called Medamerica Billing Svcs Inc* ***(P-26259)***
California Empire Bancorp Inc ...E.......909 484-7988
10681 Fthill Blvd Ste 200 Rancho Cucamonga (91730) ***(P-9788)***

ALPHABETIC

Employee Codes: A=Over 500 employees, B=251-500
C=101-250, D=51-100, E=50
2019 Directory of California
Wholesalers and Services Companies
© Mergent Inc. 1-800-342-5647
1235

California Endive Farm, Rio Vista *Also called California Vegetable Spc Inc (P-8650)*
California Endowment (PA)....D....800 449-4149
1000 N Alameda St Los Angeles (90012) **(P-24746)**
California Envmtl Hlth Assn....D....650 363-4726
2000 A De Las Pulgas 10 San Mateo (94403) **(P-27672)**
California Envmtl Systems Inc....D....530 820-3693
12265 Locksley Ln Auburn (95602) **(P-25587)**
California Eye Institute....C....559 449-5000
Low Vision Dept St Agnes Fresno (93720) **(P-19340)**
California Fair Plan Assn....D....213 487-0111
3435 Wilshire Blvd # 1200 Los Angeles (90010) **(P-10572)**
California Family Fitness, Elk Grove *Also called California Family Health LLC (P-18583)*
California Family Health LLC....E....916 685-3355
8569 Bond Rd Ste 130 Elk Grove (95624) **(P-18583)**
California Farms Meat Co Inc....D....323 581-3663
4401 S Downey Rd Vernon (90058) **(P-8613)**
California Field Ironwrkrs, San Bernardino *Also called Iron Workers Local 433 (P-12099)*
California First Nat Bancorp (PA)....D....949 255-0500
28 Executive Park Ste 200 Irvine (92614) **(P-9299)**
California First National Bank....D....949 255-0500
28 Executive Park Ste 200 Irvine (92614) **(P-9497)**
California Forensic Med Group....D....858 694-4690
2801 Meadow Lark Dr San Diego (92123) **(P-22755)**
California Forensic Med Group....D....805 654-3343
800 S Victoria Ave Ventura (93009) **(P-22756)**
California Forensic Med Group....D....209 525-5670
200 E Hackett Rd Modesto (95358) **(P-19341)**
CALIFORNIA FORENSIC MEDICAL GROUP INC, Modesto *Also called California Forensic Med Group (P-19341)*
California Friends Homes....B....714 530-9100
12151 Dale Ave Stanton (90680) **(P-24448)**
California Fuji International....E....818 889-6680
901 Encinal Canyon Rd Malibu (90265) **(P-18691)**
California Golden Realty....A....408 822-6000
26752 Calaroga Ave Hayward (94545) **(P-11263)**
California Golf Association....D....831 625-4653
3200 Lopez Rd Pebble Beach (93953) **(P-24950)**
California Govrnmnt Opr Agncy....A....800 228-5453
7667 Folsom Blvd Fl 3 Sacramento (95826) **(P-10479)**
California Guard Inc....D....209 465-8420
3108 N Cherryland Ave Stockton (95215) **(P-16596)**
California Health Benefit Exch....D....916 228-8210
1601 Exposition Blvd Sacramento (95815) **(P-25002)**
California Health Insur Exch, Sacramento *Also called California Health Benefit Exch (P-25002)*
California Healthcare, Van Nuys *Also called Golden Living LLC (P-22304)*
California Healthcare....C....760 520-1333
700 La Terraza Blvd # 200 Escondido (92025) **(P-10573)**
CALIFORNIA HEALTHCARE AND REHA, Van Nuys *Also called Normand/Wlshire Rtrment Ht Inc (P-11084)*
California Hispanic Com....C....562 942-9625
9033 Washington Blvd Pico Rivera (90660) **(P-22000)**
California Hlth Collaborative (PA)....D....559 221-6315
1680 W Shaw Ave Fresno (93711) **(P-17047)**
California HM For The Aged Inc....C....559 251-8414
6720 E Kings Canyon Rd Fresno (93727) **(P-21028)**
California Home Care Inc....B....619 521-5858
3078 El Cajon Blvd San Diego (92104) **(P-22245)**
California Hospital Assn Cha, Sacramento *Also called California Association O (P-25000)*
California Hospital Med Ctr, Los Angeles *Also called Dignity Health (P-21378)*
California Human Dev Corp (PA)....C....707 523-1155
3315 Airway Dr Santa Rosa (95403) **(P-24161)**
California Hydronics Corp (PA)....D....510 293-1993
2293 Tripaldi Way Hayward (94545) **(P-7645)**
California Imaging Nework, Los Angeles *Also called Oaks Diagnostics Inc (P-19727)*
California Institute Tech....C....626 395-8700
360 S Wilson Ave Pasadena (91106) **(P-26345)**
CALIFORNIA ISO, Folsom *Also called Califrnia Ind Sys Oprator Corp (P-6013)*
California Kidney Med Group....C....805 497-7775
375 Rolling Oaks Dr # 100 Thousand Oaks (91361) **(P-19342)**
California Lab Sciences LLC....B....562 758-6900
10200 Pioneer Blvd # 500 Santa Fe Springs (90670) **(P-26687)**
California Land Mgt Svcs Corp....E....530 544-5994
2165 Fallen Leaf Rd South Lake Tahoe (96150) **(P-13461)**
California Ldscp & Design Inc....C....909 949-1601
273 N Benson Ave Upland (91786) **(P-809)**
California Lighting Sales Inc (PA)....D....626 775-6000
4900 Rivergrade Rd D110 Baldwin Park (91706) **(P-7343)**
California Limousines....D....949 581-7531
23016 Lake Forest Dr A Laguna Hills (92653) **(P-3782)**
California Linen, Pasadena *Also called Dydee Service of Pasedena (P-13632)*
California Linen Service, Pasadena *Also called Dy-Dee Service Pasadena Inc (P-13631)*
California Linen Services Inc....D....626 564-4576
40 E California Blvd Pasadena (91105) **(P-13521)**
California Lmcc/Ibew-Neca, Pleasanton *Also called California and Nevada IBEW/Nec (P-2537)*
California Marine Cleaning Inc (PA)....C....619 231-8788
2049 Main St San Diego (92113) **(P-6364)**
California Marketing, San Diego *Also called Mabie Marketing Group Inc (P-17306)*
California Materials Inc....E....209 472-7422
3736 S Highway 99 Stockton (95215) **(P-3986)**
California Mayoreo-Y-Menudeo, Calexico *Also called California Super Market (P-4536)*
California Med Response Inc....D....562 968-1818
1557 Santa Anita Ave South El Monte (91733) **(P-3783)**
California Medical Association (PA)....D....916 444-5532
1201 J St Ste 200 Sacramento (95814) **(P-25003)**
California Mentor, Bakersfield *Also called National Mentor Inc (P-24811)*
California Mfg Tech Consulting....D....310 263-3060
690 Knox St Ste 200 Torrance (90502) **(P-27179)**
California Mission Inn, Rosemead *Also called Ensign Group Inc (P-20401)*
California Motorcycle Club....D....510 534-6222
742 45th Ave Oakland (94601) **(P-18880)**
California Nurses Association (PA)....D....510 273-2200
155 Grand Ave Ste 115 Oakland (94612) **(P-25004)**
CALIFORNIA NURSING & REHABILIT, Palm Springs *Also called California Nursing and Rehab (P-20282)*
California Nursing and Rehab....C....760 325-2937
2299 N Indian Ave Palm Springs (92262) **(P-20282)**
California Oak Valley Golf....E....951 769-9771
1888 Golf Club Dr Beaumont (92223) **(P-18692)**
California Odd Fellows (PA)....D....707 257-7885
1800 Atrium Pkwy NAPA (94559) **(P-10997)**
California Odd Fellows....D....707 257-7885
1800 Atrium Pkwy NAPA (94559) **(P-10998)**
California Oregon Broadcasting (HQ)....D....530 243-7777
755 Auditorium Dr Redding (96001) **(P-5771)**
California Overnight, Stockton *Also called Express Messenger Systems Inc (P-4402)*
California Overnight, Anaheim *Also called Express Messenger Systems Inc (P-4403)*
California Overnight, Sacramento *Also called Express Messenger Systems Inc (P-4408)*
California Overnight, San Francisco *Also called Express Messenger Systems Inc (P-4410)*
California Pacific CA....E....415 345-0940
2100 Webster St Ste 516 San Francisco (94115) **(P-21302)**
California Pacific Homes Inc (PA)....D....949 833-6000
16530 Bake Pkwy Ste 200 Irvine (92618) **(P-1334)**
California Pacific Medical Ctr, San Francisco *Also called Sutter Bay Hospitals (P-21799)*
California Pacific Medical Ctr....D....415 600-1378
2100 Webster St Ste 115 San Francisco (94115) **(P-21303)**
California Pajarosa....D....831 722-6374
133 Hughes Rd Watsonville (95076) **(P-249)**
California Pajarosa Floral....E....831 722-6374
133 Hughes Rd Watsonville (95076) **(P-9129)**
California Parking Company (PA)....D....415 781-4896
768 Sansome St San Francisco (94111) **(P-11165)**
California Pav Grading Co Inc....D....323 372-5920
3253 Verdugo Rd Los Angeles (90065) **(P-1735)**
California Pavement Maint Inc....D....916 381-8033
9390 Elder Creek Rd Sacramento (95829) **(P-1736)**
California Pediatric Fmly Svcs....D....626 812-0055
326 E Foothill Blvd Azusa (91702) **(P-23524)**
California Peo Home....D....626 300-0400
849 Foothill Blvd Ste 8 La Canada Flintridge (91011) **(P-24449)**
California Physicians Service....C....661 631-2277
2020 17th St Bakersfield (93301) **(P-10183)**
California Physicians Service....C....925 927-7419
2066 Camel Ln Apt 24 Walnut Creek (94596) **(P-10184)**
California Physicians Service....D....818 228-2010
6300 Canoga Ave Ste A Woodland Hills (91367) **(P-10424)**
California Physicians Service (PA)....A....415 229-5000
50 Beale St Bsmt 2 San Francisco (94105) **(P-10185)**
California Physicians Service....C....530 351-6115
4700 Bechelli Ln Redding (96002) **(P-10186)**
California Physicians Service....B....916 350-7800
4203 Town Center Blvd El Dorado Hills (95762) **(P-10187)**
California Physicians Service....C....310 744-2668
100 N Pacific Coast Hwy # 2000 El Segundo (90245) **(P-10188)**
California Physicians Service....B....818 598-8000
6300 Canoga Ave Ste A Woodland Hills (91367) **(P-10189)**
California Pools, Coachella *Also called Teserra (P-3592)*
California Preferred Bldrs Inc....E....818 402-3345
20335 Ventura Blvd # 422 Woodland Hills (91364) **(P-1141)**
California Private Trnsp Co LP....D....714 637-9191
180 N Rverview Dr Ste 200 Anaheim (92808) **(P-5214)**
California Produce, San Juan Bautista *Also called Christopher Ranch LLC (P-8655)*
California Produce Wholsalers....E....562 776-5770
6818 Watcher St Commerce (90040) **(P-8649)**
California Public Emplyees Ret....C....916 795-3000
400 P St Ste 1204 Sacramento (95814) **(P-10480)**
California Public Emplyees Ret (HQ)....A....916 795-3000
400 Q St Sacramento (95811) **(P-10481)**
California Rain Company Inc....D....213 623-6061
1213 E 14th St Los Angeles (90021) **(P-8291)**
California Repertory Company....E....562 985-7891
1250 N Bellflower Blvd # 124 Long Beach (90840) **(P-18350)**
California Resources Corp (PA)....D....888 848-4754
9200 Oakdale Ave Ste 900 Chatsworth (91311) **(P-1040)**
California Resources Corp....C....562 624-3400
111 W Ocean Blvd Ste 800 Long Beach (90802) **(P-1017)**
California Resources Prod Corp....D....805 483-8017
3450 E 5th St Oxnard (93033) **(P-1018)**
California Resources Prod Corp (HQ)....C....661 869-8000
11109 River Run Blvd Bakersfield (93311) **(P-1019)**
California Rural Indian Health....D....916 437-0104
1020 Sun Down Way Roseville (95661) **(P-24747)**
California Safety Agency....E....866 996-6990
8932 Katella Ave Ste 108 Anaheim (92804) **(P-16597)**
California Schl Employees Assn (PA)....C....408 473-1000
2045 Lundy Ave San Jose (95131) **(P-25057)**
California Schl Employees Assn....B....626 258-3300
4600 Santa Anita Ave El Monte (91731) **(P-14827)**
California School Boards Assn....D....800 266-3382
3251 Beacon Blvd West Sacramento (95691) **(P-24951)**
California Search Services, Red Bluff *Also called Business Connections (P-14580)*
California Security Cons....C....209 465-8420
3108 N Cherryland Ave Stockton (95215) **(P-16598)**
California Shakespeare Theater....C....510 548-3422
701 Heinz Ave Berkeley (94710) **(P-18351)**

Mergent e-mail: customerrelations@mergent.com
1236
2019 Directory of California Wholesalers and Services Companies
(P-0000) Products & Services Section entry number
(PA)=Parent Co (HQ)=Headquarters (DH)=Div Headquarters

California Shellfish Co Inc..........B.......707 542-9490
1280 Columbus Ave 300r San Francisco (94133) ***(P-8574)***
California Shtmtl Works Inc..........D.......619 562-7010
1020 N Marshall Ave El Cajon (92020) ***(P-1384)***
California Sierra Express Inc..........C.......916 375-7070
2975 Oates St Ste 30 West Sacramento (95691) ***(P-5024)***
California Silver-Agriculture..........E.......559 562-3795
831 Ash Ave Lindsay (93247) ***(P-997)***
California Skateparks..........C.......909 949-1601
285 N Benson Ave Upland (91786) ***(P-17048)***
California Special Events, Fountain Valley *Also called B T B Events Inc* ***(P-27539)***
California Speedway Corp..........E.......909 429-5000
9300 Cherry Ave Fontana (92335) ***(P-18537)***
California State Automobile (HQ)..........A.......925 287-7600
1276 S California Blvd Walnut Creek (94596) ***(P-10345)***
California State Univ Aux Svcs..........A.......323 343-2531
5151 State University Dr Ge314 Los Angeles (90032) ***(P-26795)***
California Strl Concepts Inc..........D.......661 257-6903
28358 Constellation Rd # 660 Valencia (91355) ***(P-1496)***
California Subshine Inc..........D.......310 374-4900
561 N Pacific Coast Hwy Redondo Beach (90277) ***(P-17049)***
California Sun Centers Inc..........D.......916 789-9767
8265 Sierra College Blvd Roseville (95661) ***(P-13723)***
California Suncare Inc..........D.......310 578-4400
12777 W Jefferson Blvd Los Angeles (90066) ***(P-8150)***
California Super Market..........D.......760 357-3065
363 W 2nd St Calexico (92231) ***(P-4536)***
California Supply Inc (PA)..........D.......310 532-2500
491 E Compton Blvd Gardena (90248) ***(P-8098)***
California Survey Res Svcs..........C.......818 780-2777
15350 Sherman Way Ste 480 Van Nuys (91406) ***(P-16101)***
California Tahoe Conservancy..........E.......530 542-5580
1061 3rd St South Lake Tahoe (96150) ***(P-27923)***
California Tan, Los Angeles *Also called California Suncare Inc* ***(P-8150)***
California Teachers Assn..........D.......530 622-8013
222 Judy Dr Kelsey (95667) ***(P-25005)***
California Teachers Assn (PA)..........C.......650 697-1400
1705 Murchison Dr Burlingame (94010) ***(P-25006)***
California Ticketscom Inc..........C.......925 671-4000
1855 Gateway Blvd Ste 630 Concord (94520) ***(P-18352)***
California Ticketscom Inc (HQ)..........D.......714 327-5400
555 Anton Blvd Fl 11 Costa Mesa (92626) ***(P-18353)***
California Tile Installers, San Jose *Also called U S Perma Inc* ***(P-3014)***
California Title Co Nthrn Cal..........C.......909 825-8800
1955 Hunts Ln Ste 102 San Bernardino (92408) ***(P-10434)***
California Title Company..........D.......619 516-5227
2365 Northside Dr Ste 250 San Diego (92108) ***(P-10435)***
California Title Company (PA)..........D.......949 582-8709
28202 Cabot Rd Ste 625 Laguna Niguel (92677) ***(P-10436)***
California Traffic Control..........D.......562 595-7575
3333 Cherry Ave Long Beach (90807) ***(P-17050)***
California Traffic Ctrl Svcs, Long Beach *Also called California Traffic Control* ***(P-17050)***
California Traffic Safety Inst..........C.......661 940-1907
209 E Avenue K8 Ste 210 Lancaster (93535) ***(P-27673)***
California Transit Inc..........D.......323 234-8750
3201 Hooper Ave Los Angeles (90011) ***(P-3640)***
California United Mech Inc (PA)..........B.......408 232-9000
2185 Oakland Rd San Jose (95131) ***(P-2155)***
California University Long Bch, Long Beach *Also called California Repertory Company* ***(P-18350)***
California Valley Land Co Inc (PA)..........D.......559 945-9292
18036 Gale Huron (93234) ***(P-460)***
California Vegetable Spc Inc..........D.......707 374-2111
15 Poppy House Rd Rio Vista (94571) ***(P-8650)***
California Villa, Van Nuys *Also called Longwood Management Corp* ***(P-11057)***
California Vocations Inc..........C.......530 877-0937
1620 Cypress Ln Paradise (95969) ***(P-21029)***
California Waste Services LLC..........C.......310 538-5998
621 W 152nd St Gardena (90247) ***(P-6365)***
California Waste Solutions Inc..........D.......408 292-0830
1820 10th St Oakland (94607) ***(P-6366)***
California Waste Solutions Inc (PA)..........D.......510 832-8111
1005 Timothy Dr San Jose (95133) ***(P-6367)***
California Water Service Co (HQ)..........C.......408 367-8200
1720 N 1st St San Jose (95112) ***(P-6215)***
California Water Service Co..........D.......661 396-2400
3725 S H St Bakersfield (93304) ***(P-6216)***
California Water Service Co..........D.......209 547-7900
1505 E Sonora St Stockton (95205) ***(P-6217)***
California Watercress Inc (PA)..........D.......805 524-4808
550 E Telegraph Rd Fillmore (93015) ***(P-41)***
California Wireless Solutions..........D.......408 771-1249
4095 Evergrn Vlg S 200 Milpitas (95035) ***(P-5302)***
California Yacht Club, Marina Del Rey *Also called Laaco Ltd* ***(P-18950)***
California Yacht Marina Inc (PA)..........E.......310 534-8436
22905 Lockness Ave Torrance (90501) ***(P-4748)***
California Youth Outreach, San Jose *Also called Breakout Prison Outreach* ***(P-23518)***
Californian-Pasadena, Pasadena *Also called California Convalescent Hosptl* ***(P-20281)***
Califrn/Nvada Developments LLC..........C.......714 677-5721
3010 Old Ranch Pkwy # 330 Seal Beach (90740) ***(P-11166)***
Califrnia Atism Foundation Inc (PA)..........C.......510 758-0433
4075 Lakeside Dr Richmond (94806) ***(P-24748)***
Califrnia Auto Dalers Exch LLC..........B.......714 996-2400
1320 N Tustin Ave Anaheim (92807) ***(P-6580)***
Califrnia CPA Edcatn Fundation..........D.......800 922-5272
1800 Gateway Dr Ste 200 San Mateo (94404) ***(P-25007)***
Califrnia Cryobank Lf Sciences, South San Francisco *Also called California Cryobank Inc* ***(P-22753)***
Califrnia Cslty Indemnity Exch (PA)..........C.......650 574-4000
1900 Almeda De Las Pulgas San Mateo (94403) ***(P-10346)***
Califrnia Dept State Hospitals..........B.......559 935-4300
24511 W Jayne Ave Coalinga (93210) ***(P-21931)***
Califrnia Dept State Hospitals..........A.......714 957-5000
2501 Harbor Blvd Costa Mesa (92626) ***(P-21932)***
Califrnia Dept State Hospitals..........A.......707 253-5000
2100 Napa Vallejo Hwy NAPA (94558) ***(P-21933)***
Califrnia Dept State Hospitals..........A.......909 425-7000
3102 E Highland Ave Patton (92369) ***(P-21934)***
Califrnia Dept State Hospitals..........A.......805 468-2000
10333 El Camino Real Atascadero (93422) ***(P-21935)***
Califrnia Erctors Bay Area Inc..........C.......707 746-1990
4500 California Ct Benicia (94510) ***(P-3369)***
Califrnia Frnsic Med Group Inc..........C.......831 755-3886
1410 Natividad Rd Salinas (93906) ***(P-19343)***
Califrnia Golf CLB San Frncsco..........D.......650 588-9021
844 W Orange Ave South San Francisco (94080) ***(P-18881)***
Califrnia High Speed Rail Auth..........D.......916 324-1541
770 L St Ste 620 Sacramento (95814) ***(P-3618)***
Califrnia Hlth Care Foundation (PA)..........D.......510 891-3963
1438 Webster St Ste 400 Oakland (94612) ***(P-25124)***
Califrnia Hlth Humn Srvcs Agcy..........B.......916 739-7640
3301 S St Sacramento (95816) ***(P-16102)***
Califrnia Hosp Med Ctr Fndtion..........A.......213 748-2411
1401 S Grand Ave Los Angeles (90015) ***(P-21304)***
Califrnia Ind Sys Oprator Corp..........C.......916 608-7000
110 Blue Ravine Rd Folsom (95630) ***(P-27180)***
Califrnia Ind Sys Oprator Corp (PA)..........A.......916 351-4400
250 Outcropping Way Folsom (95630) ***(P-6013)***
Califrnia Inst For Bmdical RES..........C.......858 242-1000
11119 N Torrey Pines Rd La Jolla (92037) ***(P-26601)***
Califrnia Insur Guarantee Assn..........C.......818 844-4300
101 N Brand Blvd Ste 600 Glendale (91203) ***(P-10497)***
Califrnia Intermodal Assoc Inc (PA)..........D.......323 562-7788
6666 E Washington Blvd Commerce (90040) ***(P-4114)***
Califrnia Leag Cnsrvtion Vters (PA)..........D.......510 271-0900
350 Frank H Ogawa Plz # 1100 Oakland (94612) ***(P-25369)***
Califrnia Nrsing Rhbltion Ctr, Palm Springs *Also called Cnrc LLC* ***(P-20316)***
Califrnia PCF Med Ctr Fndation (PA)..........D.......415 600-4400
2015 Steiner St San Francisco (94115) ***(P-26602)***
Califrnia Physcn Reimbursement..........D.......530 241-0473
1321 Butte St Apt 202 Redding (96001) ***(P-10574)***
Califrnia Psychtric Trnsitions..........D.......209 667-9304
9234n Hinton Ave Delhi (95315) ***(P-19344)***
Califrnia Rgional Intranet Inc..........D.......858 974-5080
8929 Complex Dr Ste A San Diego (92123) ***(P-5526)***
Califrnia Rsurces Long Bch Inc..........C.......562 624-3204
111 W Ocean Blvd Ste 800 Long Beach (90802) ***(P-1053)***
Califrnia Schl For Deaf Frmont, Fremont *Also called Education California Dept* ***(P-24317)***
Califrnia Scnce Ctr Foundation..........B.......213 744-2545
700 Exposition Park Dr Los Angeles (90037) ***(P-24867)***
Califrnia Shock Truma A Rescue (PA)..........D.......916 921-4000
4933 Bailey Loop McClellan (95652) ***(P-4857)***
Califrnia State Employees Assn (PA)..........B.......916 444-8134
1108 O St Ste 405 Sacramento (95814) ***(P-25058)***
Califrnia Tchers Rtirement Sys, Sacramento *Also called California Govrnmnt Opr Agncy* ***(P-10479)***
Califrnia Yuth Soccer Assn Inc..........D.......925 426-5437
1040 Serpentine Ln # 206 Pleasanton (94566) ***(P-25404)***
Califrnia-Nevada Methdst Homes (PA)..........C.......510 893-8989
201 19th St Ste 100 Oakland (94612) ***(P-24450)***
Califrnia-Nevada Methdst Homes..........D.......510 835-5511
1850 Alice St Ofc Oakland (94612) ***(P-21030)***
Califrnias Gnite Pool Plst Inc..........D.......925 960-9500
510 Greenville Rd Livermore (94550) ***(P-3501)***
Califronia Department of State..........A.......805 468-2501
10333 El Camino Real Atascadero (93422) ***(P-21936)***
Calimesa Operations LLC..........C.......909 795-2421
13542 2nd St Yucaipa (92399) ***(P-20283)***
Calimesa Post Acute, Yucaipa *Also called Calimesa Operations LLC* ***(P-20283)***
Calistoga Spa Hot Springs, Calistoga *Also called Calistoga Spa Inc* ***(P-18584)***
Calistoga Spa Inc..........D.......707 942-6269
1006 Washington St Calistoga (94515) ***(P-18584)***
Calko Transport Company Inc..........D.......310 816-0602
720 E Watson Center Rd Carson (90745) ***(P-4335)***
Call & Jensen APC..........E.......949 717-3000
610 Nwport Ctr Dr Ste 700 Newport Beach (92660) ***(P-22968)***
Call Center Services Intl LLC..........D.......858 427-8500
809 Bowsprit Rd Ste 204 Chula Vista (91914) ***(P-17051)***
Call To Action LLC (PA)..........D.......310 996-7200
11601 Wilshire Blvd Fl 23 Los Angeles (90025) ***(P-12208)***
Callan LLC (PA)..........C.......415 974-5060
600 Montgomery St Ste 800 San Francisco (94111) ***(P-10068)***
Callan Management Corporation..........B.......818 846-2215
2919 W Burbank Blvd Ste C Burbank (91505) ***(P-16881)***
Callaway Golf Ball Oprtons Inc..........A.......760 931-1771
2180 Rutherford Rd Carlsbad (92008) ***(P-7924)***
Calleguas Municipal Water Dict..........D.......805 526-9323
2100 E Olsen Rd Thousand Oaks (91360) ***(P-6218)***
Callfire Inc..........D.......213 221-2289
1410 2nd St Ste 200 Santa Monica (90401) ***(P-15046)***
Callidus Software Inc (HQ)..........C.......925 251-2200
4140 Dublin Blvd Ste 400 Dublin (94568) ***(P-15047)***
Calliduscloud, Dublin *Also called Callidus Software Inc* ***(P-15047)***
Callison LLC..........C.......310 394-8460
1453 3rd Street Promenade # 400 Santa Monica (90401) ***(P-26028)***
Callisonrtkl Inc..........C.......213 627-7373
818 W 7th St Ste 300 Los Angeles (90017) ***(P-26029)***

ALPHABETIC

Callisonrtkl Inc....C....213 633-6000
333 S Hope St Ste C200 Los Angeles (90071) ***(P-26030)***
Calmet Inc (PA)....C....323 721-8120
7202 Petterson Ln Paramount (90723) ***(P-6368)***
Calmex Engineering Inc....D....909 546-1311
2764 S Vista Ave Bloomington (92316) ***(P-3230)***
Calnev Pipe Line LLC....C....714 560-4400
1100 W Town And Cntry Rd Orange (92868) ***(P-25588)***
Calpella Distribution Center, Calpella *Also called Mendocino Forest Pdts Co LLC* ***(P-6841)***
Calpers, Sacramento *Also called Public Employees Retirement* ***(P-10492)***
Calpers Investment Office, Sacramento *Also called California Public Emplyees Ret* ***(P-10480)***
Calpine Containers Inc....D....559 591-6555
42779 Road 80 Dinuba (93618) ***(P-8099)***
Calpine Corporation....E....530 821-2075
5029 S Township Rd Yuba City (95993) ***(P-6014)***
Calpine Energy Solutions LLC (HQ)....D....877 273-6772
401 W A St Ste 500 San Diego (92101) ***(P-6180)***
Calpipe Industries LLC (HQ)....C....562 803-4388
19440 S Dminguez Hills Dr Rancho Dominguez (90220) ***(P-7264)***
Calply, San Diego *Also called L & W Supply Corporation* ***(P-6898)***
Calply, Hayward *Also called L & W Supply Corporation* ***(P-6899)***
Calstar, McClellan *Also called Califrnia Shock Truma A Rescue* ***(P-4857)***
Calstars....E....916 445-0211
915 L St Fl 7 Sacramento (95814) ***(P-26158)***
Caltech Efcu, La Canada Flintridge *Also called Cal Tech Emplyees Fderal Cr Un* ***(P-9542)***
Calteck USA Inc....E....949 786-4854
33 Goldenrod Irvine (92614) ***(P-17792)***
CALTRAIN, San Carlos *Also called Peninsula Crrdor Jint Pwers Bd* ***(P-3697)***
Caltrans, Fairfield *Also called Transportation California Dept* ***(P-1864)***
Caltrans District 1, Eureka *Also called California Dept Transportation* ***(P-27671)***
Caltrans Eastern Reg Rd Maint, Whittier *Also called Transportation California Dept* ***(P-1865)***
Caltronics Business Systems, Sacramento *Also called JJR Enterprises Inc* ***(P-17905)***
Calvary Baptist Ch Los Gatos....D....408 356-5126
16330 Los Gatos Blvd Los Gatos (95032) ***(P-24272)***
Calvary Cemetery, Santa Barbara *Also called Roman Cath Arch of Los Angels* ***(P-13695)***
Calvary Church Santa Ana Inc....C....714 973-4800
1010 N Tustin Ave Santa Ana (92705) ***(P-24273)***
Calvary Infant Care Center, Los Gatos *Also called Calvary Baptist Ch Los Gatos* ***(P-24272)***
Calvey Incorporated....D....916 681-4800
8670 Fruitridge Rd # 300 Sacramento (95826) ***(P-8100)***
Calworks Partnr Conference....E....858 292-2900
5151 Murphy Canyon Rd # 220 San Diego (92123) ***(P-12075)***
CAM Services, Culver City *Also called Common Area Maint Svcs Inc* ***(P-14223)***
Camanche Lake, Ione *Also called Parks and Recreation Cal Dept* ***(P-19215)***
Camanche Northshore Store, Ione *Also called Concessionaires Urban Park* ***(P-19149)***
Camanche Recreation-North, Ione *Also called Concessionaires Urban Park* ***(P-19148)***
Camarena Health....D....559 664-4000
505 E Almond Ave Madera (93637) ***(P-19345)***
Camarena Health....D....559 642-6724
49169 Road 426 Oakhurst (93644) ***(P-19346)***
Camarillo Family YMCA, Camarillo *Also called Channel Islands Young Mens Ch* ***(P-25131)***
Camarillo Healthcare Center....A....805 482-9805
205 Granada St Camarillo (93010) ***(P-26796)***
Camarillo Ranch Foundation....D....805 389-8182
201 Camarillo Ranch Rd Camarillo (93012) ***(P-17052)***
Camaro Cleaners Corp (PA)....D....650 343-4296
1515 Wedgewood Dr Hillsborough (94010) ***(P-13563)***
Cambium Business Group Inc (PA)....C....714 670-1171
6950 Noritsu Ave Buena Park (90620) ***(P-6716)***
Cambium Networks Inc....C....847 640-3809
2010 N 1st St San Jose (95131) ***(P-5972)***
Camble Center....D....818 242-2434
6512 San Fernando Rd Glendale (91201) ***(P-24162)***
Cambria El Segundo Lax, El Segundo *Also called Fc El Segundo LLC* ***(P-12571)***
Cambria Pines Lodge, Cambria *Also called Pacific Cambria Inc* ***(P-12995)***
Cambrian Homecare Inc....D....760 955-2250
15401 Anacapa Rd Ste 2 Victorville (92392) ***(P-22246)***
Cambridge Design Partnr Inc....D....650 387-7812
228 Hamilton Ave Fl 3 Palo Alto (94301) ***(P-25589)***
CAMELLIA GARDENS CARE CENTER, Pasadena *Also called Camellia Gardens Care Ctr* ***(P-20284)***
Camellia Gardens Care Ctr....D....626 798-6777
1920 N Fair Oaks Ave Pasadena (91103) ***(P-20284)***
Camelot Park Santa Maria, Santa Maria *Also called Festival Fun Parks LLC* ***(P-19171)***
Cameron Family YMCA, Santee *Also called YMCA of San Diego County* ***(P-25304)***
Cameron Intrstate Pipeline LLC....C....619 696-3110
488 8th Ave San Diego (92101) ***(P-1903)***
Cameron Park Country Club Inc....D....530 672-9840
3201 Royal Dr Cameron Park (95682) ***(P-18882)***
Cameron Surface Systems, Bakersfield *Also called Cameron West Coast Inc* ***(P-7671)***
Cameron West Coast Inc....D....661 837-4980
4316 Yeager Way Bakersfield (93313) ***(P-7671)***
Camflor Inc....C....831 726-1330
2364 Riverside Rd Watsonville (95076) ***(P-250)***
Camico Mutual Insurance Co (PA)....D....650 378-6874
1800 Gateway Dr Ste 300 San Mateo (94404) ***(P-10575)***
Caminar....D....530 343-4421
376 Rio Lindo Ave Chico (95926) ***(P-22515)***
Camino Dialysis Svcs Oak 110, Mountain View *Also called El Camino Hospital* ***(P-22475)***
Camino Real Group LLC....E....650 964-1700
840 E El Camino Real Mountain View (94040) ***(P-12422)***
Camino Ruiz Suite 235, San Diego *Also called Operation Samahan Inc* ***(P-19737)***
Camp Amgen, Thousand Oaks *Also called Bright Horizons Chld Ctrs LLC* ***(P-24268)***
Camp Bow Wow Franchising Inc....D....310 571-6500
12401 W Olympic Blvd Los Angeles (90064) ***(P-599)***
Camp Dresser & McKee, Carlsbad *Also called CDM SMITH INC* ***(P-25599)***
Camp Fire USA Long Beach Cncl....E....562 421-2725
7070 E Carson St Long Beach (90808) ***(P-25125)***
Camp Harmon Easter Seal Soc, Boulder Creek *Also called Easter Seals Inc* ***(P-13449)***
Camp Pendleton Billeting Fund, Camp Pendleton *Also called Marine Corps United States* ***(P-12876)***
Camp Pendleton Hospital, Oceanside *Also called Marine Corps United States* ***(P-22034)***
Camp Recovery Centers LP....A....707 823-3385
2264 Green Hill Rd Sebastopol (95472) ***(P-22001)***
Camp Recovery Centers LLP....D....831 438-1868
3192 Glen Canyon Rd Santa Cruz (95066) ***(P-22516)***
Camp Royaneh Boy Scout....D....707 632-5291
P.O. Box 39 Cazadero (95421) ***(P-25126)***
CAMP WINNARAINBOW, Berkeley *Also called Winnarainbow Inc* ***(P-13458)***
Campaign Monitor USA Inc....D....888 533-8098
123 Mission St Fl 26 San Francisco (94105) ***(P-15048)***
Campanile II LP....B....323 939-6813
13721 Ventura Blvd Sherman Oaks (91423) ***(P-8764)***
Campanile Restaurant, Sherman Oaks *Also called Campanile II LP* ***(P-8764)***
Campbell Hhg Hotel Dev LP....E....408 626-9590
655 Creekside Way Campbell (95008) ***(P-12423)***
Campesinos Unidos Inc (PA)....C....760 370-5100
1005 C St Brawley (92227) ***(P-27674)***
Campion, Catherine A MD, Newport Beach *Also called Newport Fmly Mdcne/A Med Group* ***(P-19712)***
Campo Band Missions Indians....B....619 938-6000
1800 Golden Acorn Way Campo (91906) ***(P-18781)***
Campos Dmetrio Frm Labor Contr, Woodland *Also called Campos Dmetrio Frm Labor Contr* ***(P-14582)***
Campos Dmetrio Frm Labor Contr....D....530 662-4143
117 W Main St Ste 19 Woodland (95695) ***(P-14582)***
Campos Family Farms LLC....D....559 275-3000
4726 W Jacquelyn Ave Fresno (93722) ***(P-329)***
Campton Place Hotel, San Francisco *Also called Southbourne Inc* ***(P-13250)***
Campton Place, A Taj Hotel, San Francisco *Also called Ihms (sf) LLC* ***(P-12761)***
Campus Explorer Inc....D....310 574-2243
2850 Ocean Park Blvd # 310 Santa Monica (90405) ***(P-5527)***
Campus Laundry, Watsonville *Also called Monterey Bay Acadamy Laundry* ***(P-13488)***
Campus Laundry, Watsonville *Also called Oceanside Laundry LLC* ***(P-13560)***
Camstar International Inc....D....909 931-2540
939 W 9th St Upland (91786) ***(P-7581)***
Can-AM Plumbing Inc....C....925 846-1833
151 Wyoming St Pleasanton (94566) ***(P-2156)***
Can-Do....D....646 228-7049
578 Washington Blvd 39o Marina Del Rey (90292) ***(P-23525)***
Can-West Directory Distrs, Monterey *Also called Clum Morford Distributing* ***(P-17088)***
Canadian Imperial Bank....D....949 759-4718
620 Newport Center Dr Newport Beach (92660) ***(P-9300)***
Cancer Federation Inc (PA)....C....951 849-4325
711 W Ramsey St Banning (92220) ***(P-24749)***
Cancer Prevention Inst Cal (PA)....C....510 608-5000
2201 Walnut Ave Ste 300 Fremont (94538) ***(P-26603)***
Candle Center The, Sacramento *Also called Therapeutic Pathways Inc* ***(P-20208)***
CANDLE LIGHTERS THE, Fremont *Also called Fremont Candle Lighters* ***(P-25423)***
Candlewood Suites, Santa Clara *Also called Hpt Trs Ihg-2 Inc* ***(P-12734)***
Canedy Court Reporting, San Diego *Also called Rett Inc* ***(P-14133)***
Canepas Car Wash (PA)....D....209 948-1636
642 N Hunter St Stockton (95202) ***(P-17806)***
Canessa Investments N V....E....310 273-8543
9434 Cherokee Ln Beverly Hills (90210) ***(P-12209)***
Canew Inc....C....818 703-5100
22135 Roscoe Blvd Canoga Park (91304) ***(P-22163)***
Canfab, Corona *Also called Cannon Fabrication Inc* ***(P-3132)***
Canine Cmpnons For Indpendence (PA)....D....707 577-1700
2965 Dutton Ave Santa Rosa (95407) ***(P-626)***
Canji Inc....D....858 597-0177
3525 John Hopkins Ct San Diego (92121) ***(P-26604)***
Cannon Cochran MGT Svcs Inc....D....949 474-6500
18881 Von Karman Ave # 380 Irvine (92612) ***(P-10576)***
Cannon Corporation (PA)....D....805 544-7407
1050 Southwood Dr San Luis Obispo (93401) ***(P-26128)***
Cannon Fabrication Inc....D....951 278-1830
182 Granite St Ste 101 Corona (92879) ***(P-3132)***
Canoga Hotel Corporation....C....818 595-1000
6360 Canoga Ave Woodland Hills (91367) ***(P-12424)***
Canoga Park Worksource Center....E....818 596-4448
21010 Vanowen St Canoga Park (91303) ***(P-14583)***
Canoga Park/West Hills Club, Canoga Park *Also called 24 Hour Fitness Usa Inc* ***(P-18565)***
Canon Bus Solutions-West Inc....B....310 217-3000
110 W Walnut St Gardena (90248) ***(P-6951)***
Canon Medical Systems USA Inc (HQ)....B....714 730-5000
2441 Michelle Dr Tustin (92780) ***(P-7170)***
Canon Recruiting Group LLC....B....661 252-7400
26531 Summit Cir Santa Clarita (91350) ***(P-14828)***
Canon Solutions America Inc....D....800 323-4827
203 S Waterman Ave El Centro (92243) ***(P-6952)***
Canon Solutions America Inc....D....800 333-6395
15975 Alton Pkwy Irvine (92618) ***(P-7737)***
Canon Solutions America Inc....D....760 438-6990
2382 Faraday Ave Ste 250 Carlsbad (92008) ***(P-17053)***
Canon Solutions America Inc....D....909 390-7400
3237 E Guasti Rd Ste 200 Ontario (91761) ***(P-6953)***
Canon Solutions America Inc....D....415 743-7300
201 California St Ste 100 San Francisco (94111) ***(P-6954)***

Canon Solutions America Inc....D....949 753-4200
123 Paularino Ave Costa Mesa (92626) ***(P-6955)***
Canon USA Inc....B....949 753-4000
15955 Alton Pkwy Irvine (92618) ***(P-6940)***
Canopy Energy, Van Nuys *Also called Energy Enterprises USA Inc* ***(P-2200)***
Cantamar Property MGT Inc....E....562 862-4470
9550 Firestone Blvd # 105 Downey (90241) ***(P-11264)***
Canteen Vending, Garden Grove *Also called Compass Group Usa Inc* ***(P-14488)***
Canteen Vending - San Diego....D....619 527-1900
5515 Market St San Diego (92114) ***(P-8544)***
Canter/Edwards Enterprises (PA)....E....818 887-7330
23251 Collins St Woodland Hills (91367) ***(P-13649)***
Canterbury Hotel Corp....C....415 345-3200
750 Sutter St San Francisco (94109) ***(P-12425)***
Canterbury Woods, Pacific Grove *Also called Covia Communities* ***(P-24488)***
Canterbury, The, Pls Vrds Pnsl *Also called Episcopal Communities & Servic* ***(P-20405)***
Canton Food Co Inc....C....213 688-7707
750 S Alameda St Los Angeles (90021) ***(P-8387)***
Cantor Art Ctr Stanford Univ, Palo Alto *Also called Leland Stanford Junior Univ* ***(P-21547)***
Cantor Fitzgerald L P....D....310 282-6500
1925 Century Park E # 700 Los Angeles (90067) ***(P-9921)***
Canvas Worldwide LLC....C....424 303-4300
12015 Bluff Creek Dr Los Angeles (90094) ***(P-13939)***
Canyon Country Medical Offices, Santa Clarita *Also called Kaiser Foundation Hospitals* ***(P-19587)***
Canyon Crest Country Club Inc....D....951 274-7900
975 Country Club Dr Riverside (92506) ***(P-18883)***
Canyon Crest Mental Hlth Offs, Riverside *Also called Kaiser Foundation Hospitals* ***(P-19579)***
Canyon Hills Club, Anaheim *Also called Ardcore Senior Living* ***(P-24419)***
Canyon Insulation Inc....D....951 278-9200
645 E Harrison St Ste 100 Corona (92879) ***(P-2860)***
Canyon Lk Property Owners Assn....D....951 244-6841
31512 Railroad Canyon Rd Canyon Lake (92587) ***(P-25127)***
Canyon Manor Residential Treat, Novato *Also called Marin County Sart Program* ***(P-21965)***
Canyon Partners Incorporated (HQ)....D....310 272-1000
2000 Ave Of The Sts Fl 11 Los Angeles (90067) ***(P-9922)***
Canyon Properties III LLC....D....818 890-0430
11723 Fenton Ave Sylmar (91342) ***(P-21031)***
Canyon Ridge Hospital Inc....C....909 590-3700
5353 G St Chino (91710) ***(P-21937)***
Canyon View Capital Inc....D....831 480-6335
331 Soquel Ave Ste 100 Santa Cruz (95062) ***(P-12155)***
Canyon Way Nursery, Studio City *Also called Wurzel Landscape Maintenance* ***(P-963)***
Cap Diagnostics LLC....D....714 966-1221
17661 Cowan Irvine (92614) ***(P-22064)***
Cap-Mpt, Los Angeles *Also called Coopertive Amrcn Physcians Inc* ***(P-25012)***
Cap-Mpt (PA)....C....213 473-8600
333 S Hope St Fl 8 Los Angeles (90071) ***(P-10425)***
Capacity LLC....C....732 745-7770
19852 Business Pkwy Walnut (91789) ***(P-4666)***
Capay Fruits and Vegetables, West Sacramento *Also called Capay Incorporated* ***(P-8765)***
Capay Incorporated (PA)....D....530 796-0730
3880 Seaport Blvd West Sacramento (95691) ***(P-8765)***
Capay Organic, West Sacramento *Also called Farm Fresh To You* ***(P-343)***
Capc Inc....C....562 693-8826
7200 Greenleaf Ave # 170 Whittier (90602) ***(P-24750)***
Capcom Entertainment Inc....D....650 350-6500
185 Berry St Ste 1200 San Francisco (94107) ***(P-7948)***
Capcom U S A Inc (HQ)....C....650 350-6500
185 Berry St Ste 1200 San Francisco (94107) ***(P-7949)***
Capcom U.S.a, San Francisco *Also called Capcom Entertainment Inc* ***(P-7948)***
Cape Clear Software Inc....D....408 879-7365
900 E Hamilton Ave # 100 Campbell (95008) ***(P-15049)***
Cape Environmental MGT Inc....B....949 236-3000
18012 Cowan Ste 150 Irvine (92614) ***(P-27579)***
Capeconnect, Campbell *Also called Cape Clear Software Inc* ***(P-15049)***
Capgemini America Inc....D....415 796-6777
1160 Battery St Ste 275 San Francisco (94111) ***(P-16322)***
Capiot Software Inc....C....650 766-2469
3000 El Cam Palo Alto (94306) ***(P-16323)***
Capistrano Beach Extended....D....949 496-5786
35410 Del Rey Capistrano Beach (92624) ***(P-20285)***
Capital Athletic Club Inc....D....916 442-3927
1515 8th St Sacramento (95814) ***(P-18585)***
Capital Beverage Company (PA)....C....916 371-8164
2500 Del Monte St West Sacramento (95691) ***(P-8984)***
Capital Brands LLC (HQ)....D....310 996-7200
11601 Wilshire Blvd Fl 23 Los Angeles (90025) ***(P-8766)***
Capital Builders, Brentwood *Also called V Development Inc* ***(P-1324)***
Capital City Drywall Inc....D....916 331-9200
6525 32nd St Ste B1 North Highlands (95660) ***(P-2861)***
Capital Commercial Flrg Inc....E....916 569-1960
3709 Bradview Dr Ste 100 Sacramento (95827) ***(P-3097)***
Capital Commercial Property, Culver City *Also called Property Management Assoc Inc* ***(P-11688)***
Capital Drywall LP....C....909 599-6818
333 S Grand Ave Ste 4070 Los Angeles (90071) ***(P-2862)***
Capital Engineering Cons Inc (PA)....D....916 851-3500
11020 Sun Center Dr # 100 Rancho Cordova (95670) ***(P-25590)***
Capital Group Companies Inc....B....310 996-6238
11100 Santa Monica Blvd # 1500 Los Angeles (90025) ***(P-10069)***
Capital Group Companies Inc (PA)....A....213 486-9200
333 S Hope St Fl 55 Los Angeles (90071) ***(P-10070)***
Capital Group Companies Inc....B....213 486-1698
1 Market Plz Ste 1800 San Francisco (94105) ***(P-10071)***
Capital Group Companies Inc....B....949 975-5000
6455 Irvine Center Dr Irvine (92618) ***(P-10072)***
Capital Group Private Markets, Irvine *Also called Capital Group Companies Inc* ***(P-10072)***
Capital Group, The, Los Angeles *Also called Capital Group Companies Inc* ***(P-10070)***
Capital Guardian Trust Company (HQ)....D....213 486-9200
333 S Hope St Fl 52 Los Angeles (90071) ***(P-12089)***
Capital Insurance Group, Monterey *Also called California Capital Insur Co* ***(P-10343)***
Capital Invstmnts Vntures Corp (PA)....C....949 858-0647
30151 Tomas Rcho STA Marg (92688) ***(P-25008)***
Capital Mortgage Services, Ventura *Also called E&S Financial Group Inc* ***(P-9879)***
Capital Oversight Inc (PA)....B....310 453-8000
2118 Wilshire Blvd Santa Monica (90403) ***(P-27675)***
Capital Plus Financial Corp....E....619 744-1900
909 W Laurel St Ste 250 San Diego (92101) ***(P-9789)***
Capital Public Radio Inc....E....916 278-8900
7055 Folsom Blvd Sacramento (95826) ***(P-5696)***
Capital Research and MGT Co (HQ)....B....213 486-9200
333 S Hope St Fl 55 Los Angeles (90071) ***(P-10073)***
Capital Research and MGT Co....D....949 975-5000
6455 Irvine Center Dr Irvine (92618) ***(P-10074)***
Capital Transitional Care, Sacramento *Also called Covenant Care California LLC* ***(P-20346)***
Capitol Casino....C....916 446-0700
411 N 16th St Sacramento (95811) ***(P-19119)***
Capitol Corporate Services....E....916 444-6787
455 Capitol Mall Ste 217 Sacramento (95814) ***(P-26503)***
Capitol Records LLC....A....213 462-6252
1750 Vine St Los Angeles (90028) ***(P-17054)***
Capitol Regency LLC....B....916 443-1234
1209 L St Sacramento (95814) ***(P-12426)***
Capitola Care Center Inc....D....831 477-0329
1098 38th Ave Santa Cruz (95062) ***(P-21032)***
Capitola Manor, Santa Cruz *Also called Capitola Care Center Inc* ***(P-21032)***
Caprion Proteomics USA LLC....E....650 470-2300
1455 Adams Dr Ste 2124 Menlo Park (94025) ***(P-26605)***
Capsbc, San Bernardino *Also called Community Action Prtnship Sb C* ***(P-24764)***
Captain Marketing Inc....D....310 402-9709
3577 N Figueroa St Los Angeles (90065) ***(P-27181)***
Captiva Software Corporation (HQ)....D....858 320-1000
10145 Pacific Hts Blvd San Diego (92121) ***(P-15926)***
Captured Sea Inc....D....714 856-3358
5901 Warner Ave Huntington Beach (92649) ***(P-1497)***
Capurro Farms, Moss Landing *Also called Capurro Marketing LLC* ***(P-8651)***
Capurro Marketing LLC....D....831 728-1767
2250 Highway 1 Moss Landing (95039) ***(P-8651)***
Car Park Inc....C....323 462-6060
6541 Hollywood Blvd Hollywood (90028) ***(P-17677)***
Car Spa Inc....E....951 279-1422
996 Mountain Ave Norco (92860) ***(P-17856)***
Car Wash Partners Inc....C....661 837-9485
3201 Panama Ln Bakersfield (93313) ***(P-17807)***
Cara Communications Corp....E....310 442-5600
12233 W Olympic Blvd # 170 Los Angeles (90064) ***(P-18030)***
Caranythingcom Inc....D....916 781-4344
22 4th St Fl 12 San Francisco (94103) ***(P-27182)***
Carat....D....415 541-2700
85 2nd St Fl 6 San Francisco (94105) ***(P-13967)***
Carat N Amer Dntsu Ageis Ntwrk....C....310 255-1000
5800 Bristol Pkwy Fl 5 Culver City (90230) ***(P-13968)***
Caraustar Industries Inc....C....209 476-7710
2800 W March Ln Ste 480 Stockton (95219) ***(P-6369)***
Carbon California Company LLC....D....805 933-1901
270 Quail Ct Ste B Santa Paula (93060) ***(P-1020)***
Carbon Five, San Francisco *Also called Carbonfive Incorporated* ***(P-15050)***
Carbonfive Incorporated....D....415 546-0500
585 Howard St Fl 2 San Francisco (94105) ***(P-15050)***
Cardenas Bros Farming Company....D....805 928-1559
1141 Tama Ln Santa Maria (93455) ***(P-92)***
Cardflex Inc....D....714 361-1900
2900 Bristol St Bldg F Costa Mesa (92626) ***(P-17055)***
Cardiac Noninvasive Laboratory, Los Angeles *Also called Cedars-Sinai Medical Center* ***(P-19360)***
Cardiac Unit, Anaheim *Also called Anaheim Regional Medical Ctr* ***(P-21288)***
Cardic Arithmias....E....650 617-8100
770 Welch Rd Ste 100 Palo Alto (94304) ***(P-19347)***
Cardiff Transportation, Palm Desert *Also called Gary Cardiff Enterprises Inc* ***(P-3799)***
Cardinal Cartridge Inc....D....818 727-9740
20450 Plummer St Chatsworth (91311) ***(P-27924)***
Cardinal Health Inc....D....909 824-1820
793 Via Lata Colton (92324) ***(P-8151)***
Cardinal Health Inc....D....951 360-2199
1100 Bird Center Dr Palm Springs (92262) ***(P-7171)***
Cardinal Health Inc....C....916 372-9880
3238 Dwight Rd Elk Grove (95758) ***(P-8152)***
Cardinal Health Inc....C....530 406-3600
700 Vaughn Rd Dixon (95620) ***(P-8153)***
Cardinal Health Inc....D....510 232-2030
1007 Canal Blvd Richmond (94804) ***(P-8154)***
Cardinal Health Inc....D....559 448-0788
7330 N Palm Ave Ste 104 Fresno (93711) ***(P-8155)***
Cardinal Health Inc....D....530 225-8735
1935 Pine St Redding (96001) ***(P-8156)***
Cardinal Health Inc....D....909 605-0900
4551 E Philadelphia St Ontario (91761) ***(P-8157)***
Cardinal Health Inc....C....661 295-6100
27680 Avenue Mentry Valencia (91355) ***(P-8158)***
Cardinal Health 200 LLC....C....951 686-8900
3750 Torrey View Ct San Diego (92130) ***(P-7172)***
Cardinal Point Captains Inc....D....760 438-7361
5005 Texas St Ste 104 San Diego (92108) ***(P-14829)***
Cardinal Transportation, Gardena *Also called First Student Inc* ***(P-3936)***

ALPHABETIC

Employee Codes: A=Over 500 employees, B=251-500
C=101-250, D=51-100, E=50
2019 Directory of California
Wholesalers and Services Companies
© Mergent Inc. 1-800-342-5647
1239

Cardio Pulmonary Services, La Jolla *Also called Professional Health Tech* ***(P-19797)***
Cardiodx Inc....C....650 475-2788
600 Saginaw Dr Redwood City (94063) ***(P-22065)***
Cardiology Department, Los Angeles *Also called Usc Care Medical Group Inc* ***(P-21890)***
Cardiovascular Consultants Hea....D....559 432-4303
1207 E Herndon Ave Fresno (93720) ***(P-19348)***
Cardivsclr Mdcl Grp of Sthrn....E....310 278-3400
414 N Camden Dr Ste 1100 Beverly Hills (90210) ***(P-19349)***
Cardno Eri, Lake Forest *Also called Environmental Resolutions Inc* ***(P-27721)***
Cardservice International Inc....A....800 217-4622
4565 Industrial St Ste 7k Simi Valley (93063) ***(P-17056)***
Cardservice International Inc....D....714 773-1778
1538 W Commonwealth Ave Fullerton (92833) ***(P-17057)***
Cardservice International Inc (HQ)....B....805 648-1425
5898 Condor Dr 220 Moorpark (93021) ***(P-17058)***
Care Inc....E....818 232-7940
15315 Magnolia Blvd # 306 Sherman Oaks (91403) ***(P-20918)***
Care 1st Health Plan (PA)....C....323 889-6638
601 Potrero Grande Dr # 2 Monterey Park (91755) ***(P-22757)***
Care 2....D....650 622-0860
203 Redwood Shores Pkwy # 230 Redwood City (94065) ***(P-25405)***
Care 4 U LLC....D....818 593-7911
22726 Eccles St West Hills (91304) ***(P-23526)***
Care A Van Transport, Carlsbad *Also called CAV Inc* ***(P-3784)***
Care Ambulance, San Diego *Also called Care Medical Trnsp Inc* ***(P-14830)***
Care Associates Inc....D....626 330-4048
15125 Gale Ave Hacienda Heights (91745) ***(P-24451)***
Care Choice Health Systems Inc....D....760 798-4508
338 Via Vera Cruz Ste 120 San Marcos (92078) ***(P-21033)***
Care Choice Home Care, San Marcos *Also called Care Choice Health Systems Inc* ***(P-21033)***
Care Medical Trnsp Inc....C....858 653-4520
9770 Candida St San Diego (92126) ***(P-14830)***
Care Options Management Plans....D....925 551-3227
7000 Village Pkwy Ste A Dublin (94568) ***(P-22247)***
Care Options Management Plans (PA)....D....530 242-8580
1020 Market St Redding (96001) ***(P-22248)***
Care Plus Home Care Inc....C....949 716-2273
22931 Triton Way Ste 133 Laguna Hills (92653) ***(P-22249)***
Care Plus Home Health, Laguna Hills *Also called Care Plus Nursing Services Inc* ***(P-22250)***
Care Plus North of San Diego....D....619 421-0807
2337 Eastridge Loop Chula Vista (91915) ***(P-14584)***
Care Plus Nursing Services Inc....C....949 600-7194
22931 Triton Way Ste 236 Laguna Hills (92653) ***(P-22250)***
Care Solution Associates LLC....D....925 443-1000
179 Contractors Ave Livermore (94551) ***(P-22251)***
Care Tech Inc....D....909 882-2965
4280 Cypress Dr San Bernardino (92407) ***(P-20286)***
Care Unlimited Health Systems....D....626 332-3767
1025 W Arrow Hwy Ste 105 Glendora (91740) ***(P-22252)***
Care With Dignity Convalescent, San Diego *Also called Care With Dignity Healthcare* ***(P-20288)***
Care With Dignity Healthcare....D....619 447-1020
1340 E Madison Ave El Cajon (92021) ***(P-20287)***
Care With Dignity Healthcare (PA)....C....858 278-4750
8060 Frost St San Diego (92123) ***(P-20288)***
Care Wst-Wrner Mtn Nursing Ctr, Alturas *Also called County of Modoc* ***(P-20332)***
Careability Health Svcs Corp....D....916 479-8554
1329 Howe Ave Ste 100 Sacramento (95825) ***(P-22253)***
Careage Inc....E....408 238-9751
2501 Alvin Ave San Jose (95121) ***(P-20289)***
Carecredit LLC....C....800 300-3046
2995 Red Hill Ave Ste 100 Costa Mesa (92626) ***(P-17059)***
Caredx Inc (PA)....C....415 287-2300
3260 Bayshore Blvd Brisbane (94005) ***(P-22066)***
Career Dev Inst For Excptnl....E....951 337-3678
1470 Marsh Way Riverside (92501) ***(P-11861)***
Career Group Inc (PA)....A....310 277-8188
10100 Santa Monica Blvd # 900 Los Angeles (90067) ***(P-14585)***
Career Transition Center....C....562 570-9675
3447 Atlantic Ave Ste 100 Long Beach (90807) ***(P-24163)***
Carefusion Corporation....D....760 778-7200
1100 Bird Center Dr Palm Springs (92262) ***(P-22758)***
Carefusion Solutions LLC (HQ)....A....858 617-2100
3750 Torrey View Ct San Diego (92130) ***(P-7173)***
Caremark Rx Inc....D....909 822-1164
1851 N Riverside Ave Rialto (92376) ***(P-19350)***
Caremark Rx LLC....E....760 948-6606
15576 Main St Hesperia (92345) ***(P-19351)***
Caremark Rx LLC....E....209 957-7050
800 Douglas Rd Stockton (95207) ***(P-19352)***
Caremore Health Plan (HQ)....D....562 622-2950
12900 Park Plaza Dr # 150 Cerritos (90703) ***(P-19353)***
Caremore Insurance Services, Cerritos *Also called Caremore Health Plan* ***(P-19353)***
Caremore Medical Group, Downey *Also called Conrad A Cox* ***(P-19404)***
Caremore Medical Group Inc....B....562 622-2900
12900 Park Plz Ste 150 Lakewood (90805) ***(P-10162)***
Careonsite Inc....D....562 437-0381
1805 Arnold Dr Martinez (94553) ***(P-19354)***
Careonsite Inc (PA)....E....562 437-0831
1250 Pacific Ave Long Beach (90813) ***(P-19355)***
Cares, San Diego *Also called Center For Autsm Rsrch Evltn* ***(P-22522)***
Cares Community Health....C....916 443-3299
1500 21st St Sacramento (95811) ***(P-19356)***
Carescope LLC....D....916 780-1384
1455 Response Rd Ste 120 Sacramento (95815) ***(P-23527)***
Caresouth Home Health Svcs LLC....E....408 378-6131
815 Pollard Rd Los Gatos (95032) ***(P-22254)***
Carfax Studios....D....562 377-0223
3937 Carfax Ave Long Beach (90808) ***(P-13724)***
Carfinance Capital LLC....A....800 900-5150
7525 Irvine Center Dr # 250 Irvine (92618) ***(P-12210)***
Cargill Incorporated....C....510 797-1820
7220 Central Ave Newark (94560) ***(P-8922)***
Cargo Service Center, Los Angeles *Also called Swissport Cargo Services LP* ***(P-4914)***
Caribbean South Amercn Council....E....925 709-3433
12 Ambrose Ave Bay Point (94565) ***(P-4933)***
Carinet, San Diego *Also called Califrnia Rgional Intranet Inc* ***(P-5526)***
Caring Cmpanions Referral Agcy, Hemet *Also called Caring Companions Home* ***(P-22255)***
Caring Companions Home....D....951 765-1441
116 Las Lunas St Hemet (92543) ***(P-22255)***
Caritas Management Corporation....D....415 647-7191
1358 Valencia St San Francisco (94110) ***(P-11265)***
Carl's Jr., San Ramon *Also called T W M Industries* ***(P-12071)***
Carleton Booker Marketing Inc....D....510 999-1682
5042 Wilshire Blvd # 31584 Los Angeles (90036) ***(P-27183)***
Carlilemacy Inc....E....707 542-6451
15 3rd St Santa Rosa (95401) ***(P-25591)***
Carlisle Construction Mtls Inc....D....909 591-7425
5635 Schaefer Ave Chino (91710) ***(P-6922)***
Carlisle Construction Mtls Inc....D....707 678-6900
1155 Business Park Dr Dixon (95620) ***(P-6923)***
Carlisle Research Corporation....D....818 785-8677
7100 Hayvenhurst Ave Ph F Van Nuys (91406) ***(P-15927)***
Carlsbad By The Sea, Carlsbad *Also called Front Porch Communities* ***(P-21071)***
Carlsbad Inn Vactn Condo Ownrs....D....760 434-7542
3001 Carlsbad Blvd Carlsbad (92008) ***(P-25128)***
Carlsbad Medical Offices, Carlsbad *Also called Kaiser Foundation Hospitals* ***(P-19621)***
Carlsbad Municipal Water Dst....E....760 438-2722
5950 El Camino Real Carlsbad (92008) ***(P-6219)***
Carlsbad Surgery Center LLC....E....760 448-2488
6121 Paseo Del Norte # 100 Carlsbad (92011) ***(P-22517)***
Carlson, Tustin *Also called Corland Companies* ***(P-11384)***
Carlson Barbee & Gibson Inc....D....925 866-0322
2633 Camino Ramon Ste 350 San Ramon (94583) ***(P-25592)***
Carlton Hotel Properties LP....D....415 673-0242
1075 Sutter St San Francisco (94109) ***(P-12427)***
Carlton Plaza of Fremont, Fremont *Also called Retirement Lf Care Communities* ***(P-24652)***
Carlton Plaza of San Leandro, San Leandro *Also called Carlton Senior Living* ***(P-11266)***
Carlton Senior Living....D....925 935-1001
175 Cleaveland Rd Pleasant Hill (94523) ***(P-22256)***
Carlton Senior Living....D....510 636-0660
1000 E 14th St San Leandro (94577) ***(P-11266)***
Carlton Senior Living Inc....D....408 972-1400
380 Branham Ln Ofc Ofc San Jose (95136) ***(P-10577)***
Carlton Senior Living Inc....E....916 714-2404
6915 Elk Grove Blvd Elk Grove (95758) ***(P-11267)***
Carlton Senior Living Inc....C....916 971-4800
1075 Fulton Ave Sacramento (95825) ***(P-24452)***
Carlton Senior Living Inc....D....925 935-1660
2770 Pleasant Hill Rd Ofc Concord (94523) ***(P-11862)***
Carmel Architectural Sales....D....714 630-7221
2300 E Katella Ave # 370 Anaheim (92806) ***(P-3133)***
Carmel Hills Care Center, Monterey *Also called Pater Digintas Inc* ***(P-20698)***
Carmel Marina, Castroville *Also called USA Waste of California Inc* ***(P-4078)***
Carmel Mission Inn, Carmel *Also called Bayview Properties Inc* ***(P-12362)***
Carmel Mission Inn....D....831 624-1841
3665 Rio Rd Carmel (93923) ***(P-12428)***
Carmel Mtn Rhab Healthcare Ctr, San Diego *Also called Bernardo Hts Healthcare Inc* ***(P-21007)***
Carmel Partners Inc (PA)....C....415 273-2900
1000 Sansome St Fl 1 San Francisco (94111) ***(P-11268)***
Carmel Valley Manor, Carmel *Also called Northern CA Cngrgtnl Rtmt* ***(P-21167)***
Carmel Valley Medical Offices, San Diego *Also called Kaiser Foundation Hospitals* ***(P-19581)***
Carmel Valley Packing Inc....C....831 771-8860
26965 Encinal Rd Salinas (93908) ***(P-500)***
Carmel Valley Ranch....C....831 625-9500
1 Old Ranch Rd Carmel (93923) ***(P-12429)***
Carmel Valley Ranch Hotel, Carmel *Also called Carmel Valley Ranch* ***(P-12429)***
Carmel Valley Resort, Carmel *Also called Carmel Vly Mrtg Borrower LLC* ***(P-12430)***
Carmel Vlg Rtirement Residence....D....714 962-6667
17077 San Mateo St # 3113 Fountain Valley (92708) ***(P-10999)***
Carmel Vly Mrtg Borrower LLC....D....831 625-9500
1 Old Ranch Rd Carmel (93923) ***(P-12430)***
Carmichael Care Inc....C....916 483-8103
6041 Fair Oaks Blvd Carmichael (95608) ***(P-20290)***
Carmichael International Svc (HQ)....D....213 353-0800
533 Glendale Blvd Ste 102 Los Angeles (90026) ***(P-5025)***
Carmichael Recreation & Pk Dst....C....916 485-5322
5750 Grant Ave Carmichael (95608) ***(P-23528)***
Carnahan Occupational Therapy....E....805 737-1604
116 E College Ave Ste G Lompoc (93436) ***(P-22518)***
Carnegie Agency Inc....E....805 445-1470
2101 Corp Cntr Dr Ste 150 Newbury Park (91320) ***(P-10578)***
Carnegie Institution Wash....D....626 577-1122
813 Santa Barbara St Pasadena (91101) ***(P-26606)***
Carneros Inn LLC....B....707 299-4880
4048 Sonoma Hwy NAPA (94559) ***(P-12431)***
Carneros Resort and Spa, NAPA *Also called GF Carneros Tenant LLC* ***(P-13660)***
Carnival Corporation....A....562 843-5569
231 Windsor Way Long Beach (90802) ***(P-4934)***
Carnival Corporation....A....562 901-3232
231 Windsor Way Long Beach (90802) ***(P-4935)***
Carol Electric Company Inc....D....562 431-1870
3822 Cerritos Ave Los Alamitos (90720) ***(P-2538)***
Caroline Promotions Inc....D....818 507-7666
809 S Adams St Apt 7 Glendale (91205) ***(P-27546)***

Mergent e-mail: customerrelations@mergent.com
1240
2019 Directory of California
Wholesalers and Services Companies
(P-0000) Products & Services Section entry number
(PA)=Parent Co (HQ)=Headquarters (DH)=Div Headquarters

Carollo Engineers Inc (PA)....D....925 932-1710
2700 Ygnacio Valley Rd # 300 Walnut Creek (94598) *(P-25593)*
Carollo Engineers Inc....D....714 540-4300
3100 S Harbor Blvd # 200 Santa Ana (92704) *(P-25594)*
Carollo Engineers Inc....C....858 505-1020
701 Palomar Airport Rd Carlsbad (92011) *(P-25595)*
Carolyn E Wylie Center....D....951 683-5193
4164 Brockton Ave Ste A Riverside (92501) *(P-24274)*
Carone & Company Inc....D....925 602-8800
5009 Forni Dr Ste A Concord (94520) *(P-3417)*
Carparts Technologies....C....949 488-8860
32122 Camn Capistrano # 100 San Juan Capistrano (92675) *(P-15622)*
Carpenter Fund Manager Gp LLC....C....949 261-8888
5 Park Plz Ste 950 Irvine (92614) *(P-9301)*
Carpenter Funds....D....510 633-0333
265 Hegenberger Rd # 100 Oakland (94621) *(P-12090)*
Carpenters Southwest ADM Corp (PA)....D....213 386-8590
533 S Fremont Ave Los Angeles (90071) *(P-12432)*
Carpet Care By Tri-Star, Northridge *Also called Tri - Star Win Coverings Inc (P-6795)*
Carpet Solutions....E....310 886-3800
28126 Peacock Ridge Dr # 115 Rancho Palos Verdes (90275) *(P-13574)*
Carpinteria Motor Inn Inc....E....805 684-0473
4558 Carpinteria Ave Carpinteria (93013) *(P-12433)*
Carquinez Dialysis, Vallejo *Also called Total Renal Care Inc (P-22493)*
Carr & Ferrell....D....650 812-3400
120 Constitution Dr Menlo Park (94025) *(P-22969)*
Carr & Ferrell LLP (PA)....D....650 812-3400
120 Constitution Dr Menlo Park (94025) *(P-22970)*
Carr Mc Clellan Ingersoll Thom (PA)....D....650 342-9600
216 Park Rd Burlingame (94010) *(P-22971)*
Carr, McClellan, Burlingame *Also called Carr Mc Clellan Ingersoll Thom (P-22971)*
Carrara Marble Co Amer Inc (PA)....D....626 961-6010
15939 Phoenix Dr City of Industry (91745) *(P-6878)*
Carrasco Heleo....C....714 639-1759
2510 N Grand Ave Ste 102 Santa Ana (92705) *(P-14208)*
Carriage Inn, Daly City *Also called Reneson Hotels Inc (P-13115)*
Carrier Commercial Service, Sacramento *Also called Carrier Corporation (P-17891)*
Carrier Corporation....E....916 928-9500
1168 National Dr Ste 60 Sacramento (95834) *(P-17891)*
Carrier Johnson (PA)....D....619 236-9462
1301 3rd Ave San Diego (92101) *(P-26031)*
Carrier Totaline (PA)....D....714 578-5200
205 S Puente St Brea (92821) *(P-7738)*
Carrington Mrtg Holdings LLC....C....888 267-0584
1600 S Douglass Rd # 110 Anaheim (92806) *(P-26797)*
Carroll Burdick Mc Donough LLP (PA)....C....415 989-5900
275 Battery St Ste 2600 San Francisco (94111) *(P-22972)*
Carrollco Inc....E....559 396-3939
3104 N Miami Ave Fresno (93727) *(P-1142)*
Carson Capital Corp (PA)....D....951 684-9585
42882 Ivy St Murrieta (92562) *(P-6581)*
Carson Community Center, Carson *Also called City of Carson (P-23578)*
Carson Gang Diversion Team, Carson *Also called County of Los Angeles (P-25059)*
Carson Kurtzman Consultants (HQ)....C....310 823-9000
2335 Alaska Ave El Segundo (90245) *(P-22973)*
CARSON LANDSCAPE INDUSTRIES, Sacramento *Also called Frank Carson Ldscp & Maint Inc (P-842)*
Carson Medical Offices, Gardena *Also called Kaiser Foundation Hospitals (P-19560)*
Carson Operating Company LLC....D....310 830-9200
2 Civic Plaza Dr Carson (90745) *(P-12434)*
Carson Senior Assisted Living, Carson *Also called Secrom Inc (P-21205)*
Carson Senior Assisted Living....D....310 830-4010
345 E Carson St Carson (90745) *(P-24453)*
Cartel Marketing Inc....C....818 483-1130
5230 Las Virgenes Rd # 250 Calabasas (91302) *(P-10579)*
Carters Details Plus, Burbank *Also called Jim & Doug Carters Automotive (P-17689)*
Cartridge Family Inc....C....510 658-0400
1940 Union St Ste 29 Oakland (94607) *(P-8077)*
Cartridge Family Ink, Oakland *Also called Cartridge Family Inc (P-8077)*
Cartwright Termite & Pest Ctrl....E....760 771-6091
51360 Calle Guatemala La Quinta (92253) *(P-14138)*
Caruso MGT Ltd A Cal Ltd Prtnr....D....323 900-8100
101 The Grove Dr Los Angeles (90036) *(P-11269)*
Carver Preschool, Garden Grove *Also called Garden Grove Unified Schl Dst (P-24324)*
Casa Allegra Community Svcs....D....415 499-1116
35 Mitchell Blvd Ste 8 San Rafael (94903) *(P-27184)*
Casa Colin Comprehensive....C....909 596-7733
255 E Bonita Ave Pomona (91767) *(P-22519)*
Casa Colina Inc (PA)....A....909 596-7733
255 E Bonita Ave Pomona (91767) *(P-23529)*
CASA COLINA CENTERS FOR REHABILITATION, Pomona *Also called Casa Colina Hospital and Cente (P-21305)*
Casa Colina Hospital & Ctr, Pomona *Also called Casa Colina Inc (P-23529)*
Casa Colina Hospital and Cente (HQ)....B....909 596-7733
255 E Bonita Ave Pomona (91767) *(P-21305)*
Casa Coloma Health Care Center, Rancho Cordova *Also called A B C D Associates (P-20217)*
Casa De Amparo (PA)....D....760 754-5500
325 Buena Creek Rd San Marcos (92069) *(P-24454)*
Casa De Las Campanas Inc (PA)....C....858 451-9152
18655 W Bernardo Dr # 489 San Diego (92127) *(P-24455)*
Casa De Santa Fe of Rocklin....D....916 435-8800
3201 Santa Fe Way Apt 1 Rocklin (95765) *(P-21034)*
Casa Dorinda, Santa Barbara *Also called Montecito Retirement Assn (P-20650)*
Casa Dscanso Convalescent Hosp....C....323 225-5991
4515 Huntington Dr S Los Angeles (90032) *(P-27580)*
Casa Fremont, Fremont *Also called Anka Behavioral Health Inc (P-22734)*
Casa Madrona Hotel and Spa LLC....D....415 332-0502
801 Bridgeway Sausalito (94965) *(P-12435)*
Casa Munras Garden Hotel, Monterey *Also called Portfolio Hotels & Resorts LLC (P-13074)*
Casa Munras Hotel LLC....D....831 375-2411
700 Munras Ave Monterey (93940) *(P-12436)*
Casa Pacifica Adult Day H, San Diego *Also called J Gelt Corporation (P-23868)*
Casa Pacifica Centers (PA)....C....805 482-3260
1722 S Lewis Rd Camarillo (93012) *(P-23530)*
Casa Palmera Care Center, Del Mar *Also called Lee Johnson (P-21133)*
Casa Real Estate Ltd Partnr....D....760 320-4117
415 S Belardo Rd Palm Springs (92262) *(P-12437)*
Casa Sandoval LLC....D....510 727-1700
1200 Russell Way Hayward (94541) *(P-11000)*
Casa-Pacifica Inc....B....951 658-3369
2200 W Acacia Ave Ofc Hemet (92545) *(P-24456)*
Casa-Pacifica Inc....D....951 766-5116
2400 W Acacia Ave Hemet (92545) *(P-24457)*
Casablanca Alzheimer's Care, Oak View *Also called Casablanca Alzheimers Resid (P-24458)*
Casablanca Alzheimers Resid....D....805 649-5143
158 Rockaway Rd Oak View (93022) *(P-24458)*
Casanova Pndrill Pblicidad Inc (PA)....D....949 474-5001
275 Mccormick Ave Ste 1a Costa Mesa (92626) *(P-13803)*
Casas - Comprehensive....D....858 292-2900
5151 Murphy Canyon Rd # 220 San Diego (92123) *(P-25406)*
Casas International Brkg Inc (PA)....D....619 661-6162
9355 Airway Rd Ste 4 San Diego (92154) *(P-4537)*
Casavina Foundation Corp....C....408 238-9751
2501 Alvin Ave San Jose (95121) *(P-20291)*
Casbn Investment Inc....D....650 991-2800
345 Gellert Blvd Ste A Daly City (94015) *(P-11270)*
Cascade Drilling LP....E....909 946-1605
1333 W 9th St Upland (91786) *(P-3349)*
Cascade Logistics, Tracy *Also called Es3 LLC (P-4554)*
Cascade Logistics LLC....D....209 832-4205
857 Stonebridge Dr Tracy (95376) *(P-4538)*
Casden Builders LLC....E....310 274-5553
9090 Wilshire Blvd Fl 3 Beverly Hills (90211) *(P-10860)*
Casden Company LLC....D....310 274-5553
9606 Santa Monica Blvd # 3 Beverly Hills (90210) *(P-11863)*
Case Dealer Holding Co LLC....C....916 649-0096
1751 Bell Ave Sacramento (95838) *(P-7672)*
Case Medical Group, Sacramento *Also called Central Anesthesia Service (P-19363)*
Case Vlott Cattle....E....559 665-7399
20330 Road 4 Chowchilla (93610) *(P-408)*
Casecentral Inc (HQ)....D....415 989-2300
1055 E Colo Blvd Ste 400 Pasadena (91106) *(P-17060)*
Casecentral.com, Pasadena *Also called Casecentral Inc (P-17060)*
Casestack Inc (PA)....D....310 473-8885
3000 Ocean Park Blvd Santa Monica (90405) *(P-5026)*
Casewise Systems Inc (HQ)....D....424 284-4101
9465 Wilshire Blvd # 300 Beverly Hills (90212) *(P-7023)*
Casey Company (PA)....C....562 436-9685
180 E Ocean Blvd Ste 1010 Long Beach (90802) *(P-8952)*
Casey Securities Inc (PA)....D....415 544-5030
301 Pine St San Francisco (94104) *(P-9923)*
Casey-Fogli Con Contrs Inc....D....510 887-0837
1970 National Ave Hayward (94545) *(P-3231)*
Cash It Here, Santa Ana *Also called Continental Currency Svcs Inc (P-9676)*
Cashcall Inc....A....949 752-4600
1 City Blvd W Ste 102 Orange (92868) *(P-9705)*
Cashedge Inc....D....408 541-3900
525 Almanor Ave Ste 150 Sunnyvale (94085) *(P-17061)*
Casino, Hopland *Also called Hopland Band Pomo Indians Inc (P-19182)*
Casino Morongo....D....951 849-3080
49500 Seminole Dr Cabazon (92230) *(P-18791)*
Casino San Pablo, San Pablo *Also called Lytton Rancheria (P-19201)*
Casitas Care Center, Granada Hills *Also called A Cori Partnership (P-20975)*
Cask Technologies LLC (PA)....C....858 458-9951
9350 Waxie Way Ste 210 San Diego (92123) *(P-15051)*
Caspar Community....E....707 964-4997
15051 Caspar Rd Caspar (95420) *(P-23531)*
Casper Company....C....619 589-6001
3825 Bancroft Dr Spring Valley (91977) *(P-3448)*
Caspian Commercial Plbg Inc....D....818 649-2500
711 Ivy St Glendale (91204) *(P-2157)*
Cass Inc (PA)....C....510 893-6476
2730 Peralta St Oakland (94607) *(P-7972)*
Cass Construction Inc (PA)....C....619 590-0929
1100 Wagner Dr El Cajon (92020) *(P-1904)*
Cassidy Medical Group Inc (PA)....D....760 630-5487
145 Thunder Dr Vista (92083) *(P-19357)*
Cassidy Trly Prop MGT Sn Frncs....D....415 781-8100
201 California St Ste 800 San Francisco (94111) *(P-11271)*
Cast & Crew Payroll LLC (PA)....C....818 848-6022
2300 W Empire Ave # 500 Burbank (91504) *(P-26159)*
Cast and Crew Entrmt Svcs, Burbank *Also called Cast & Crew Payroll LLC (P-26159)*
Castaic Lk Wtr Agcy Fing Corp (PA)....C....661 259-2737
27234 Bouquet Canyon Rd Santa Clarita (91350) *(P-6220)*
Caster Family Enterprises Inc....C....619 287-8893
4607 Mission Gorge Pl San Diego (92120) *(P-12211)*
Castlblack Pismo Bch Owner LLC....E....805 773-6020
601 James Way Pismo Beach (93449) *(P-12438)*
Castle & Cooke Inc....A....714 385-9641
2099 S State College Blvd Anaheim (92806) *(P-9924)*
Castle & Cooke Inc....A....951 245-0476
17600 Collier Ave C120 Lake Elsinore (92530) *(P-1273)*
Castle & Cooke Calaveras Inc....A....310 208-3636
1 Dole Dr Westlake Village (91362) *(P-1498)*

ALPHABETIC

Employee Codes: A=Over 500 employees, B=251-500
C=101-250, D=51-100, E=50
2019 Directory of California
Wholesalers and Services Companies
© Mergent Inc. 1-800-342-5647
1241

Castle & Cooke California Inc.....E.....661 664-6500
10000 Stockdale Hwy # 300 Bakersfield (93311) ***(P-6370)***
Castle & Cooke Commercial CA.....D.....661 665-1540
10000 Stockdale Hwy # 300 Bakersfield (93311) ***(P-11864)***
Castle & Cooke Mortgage, Anaheim *Also called Castle & Cooke Inc* ***(P-9924)***
Castle Dental.....E.....323 567-1227
4433 Tweedy Blvd South Gate (90280) ***(P-20113)***
Castle Family Health Ctrs Inc (PA).....D.....209 381-2000
3605 Hospital Rd Ste H Atwater (95301) ***(P-22520)***
Castle Manor Convalescent Ctr, National City *Also called Castle Manor Inc* ***(P-20292)***
Castle Manor Inc.....D.....619 791-7900
541 S V Ave National City (91950) ***(P-20292)***
Castleblack Owner Holdings LLC.....E.....805 773-6020
601 James Way Pismo Beach (93449) ***(P-26798)***
Castlehill Properties Inc (PA).....D.....209 472-9800
3240 W March Ln Stockton (95219) ***(P-12439)***
Castlewood Country Club.....C.....925 846-2871
707 Country Club Cir Pleasanton (94566) ***(P-18884)***
Castlight Health Inc (PA).....D.....415 829-1400
150 Spear St Ste 400 San Francisco (94105) ***(P-16103)***
Caston Inc.....D.....909 381-1619
354 S Allen St San Bernardino (92408) ***(P-2863)***
Castro Valley Care Centers, Culver City *Also called Jesse Lee Group Inc* ***(P-26906)***
Castro Valley Health Inc.....C.....510 690-1930
2410 Camino Ramon Ste 331 San Ramon (94583) ***(P-22257)***
Caswell Bay Inc.....D.....925 933-8181
1777 N Calif Blvd Ste 210 Walnut Creek (94596) ***(P-22258)***
CAT Logistics Inc.....D.....909 390-1920
5491 E Francis St Ontario (91761) ***(P-4539)***
Catalent San Diego Inc.....C.....858 805-6383
7330 Carroll Rd Ste 200 San Diego (92121) ***(P-26688)***
Catalina Business Entps Inc.....E.....310 510-1600
635 Crescent Ave Avalon (90704) ***(P-19120)***
Catalina Channel Express Inc (HQ).....B.....310 519-7971
385 E Swinford St San Pedro (90731) ***(P-4712)***
Catalina Channel Express Inc.....C.....562 435-8686
320 Golden Shore Lbby Long Beach (90802) ***(P-4725)***
Catalina Channel Express Inc.....C.....562 495-3565
1046 Queens Hwy Long Beach (90802) ***(P-4713)***
Catalina Enterprise Inc.....D.....949 637-3091
206 Catalina Rd Fullerton (92835) ***(P-27676)***
Catalina Events Inc.....E.....310 925-6986
2605 184th St Redondo Beach (90278) ***(P-27547)***
Catalina Express, Long Beach *Also called Catalina Channel Express Inc* ***(P-4725)***
Catalina Express, Long Beach *Also called Catalina Channel Express Inc* ***(P-4713)***
Catalina Express Cruises, San Pedro *Also called Catalina Channel Express Inc* ***(P-4712)***
Catalina Glassbottom Boat Inc.....D.....310 510-2888
1 Cabrillo Mole Avalon (90704) ***(P-4714)***
Catalina Solar 2 LLC.....A.....888 903-6926
15445 Innovation Dr San Diego (92128) ***(P-6015)***
Catalina Solar Lessee LLC.....A.....888 903-6926
11585 Willow Springs Rd Rosamond (93560) ***(P-6016)***
Catalyst Development Corp.....E.....760 228-9653
56925 Yucca Trl Yucca Valley (92284) ***(P-15623)***
Catamaran Resort Hotel, San Diego *Also called Braemar Partnership* ***(P-12395)***
Catamount Broadcasting of Chic (PA).....C.....530 893-2424
3460 Silverbell Rd Chico (95973) ***(P-5772)***
Catania Hijar Corporation.....C.....800 400-3401
11487 Woodside Ave Santee (92071) ***(P-1905)***
Cataphora Inc (PA).....D.....650 622-9840
3425 Edison Way Menlo Park (94025) ***(P-15052)***
Catasys Inc (PA).....D.....310 444-4300
11601 Wilshire Blvd # 1100 Los Angeles (90025) ***(P-21938)***
Catati Rohnert Park Inc.....E.....707 792-4531
1400 Magnolia Ave Rohnert Park (94928) ***(P-17062)***
Catered Manor, Long Beach *Also called Covenant Care California LLC* ***(P-20339)***
Caterpillar, San Diego *Also called Hawthorne Machinery Co* ***(P-17767)***
Caterpillar, Ontario *Also called CAT Logistics Inc* ***(P-4539)***
Caterpillar Authorized Dealer, Riverside *Also called Johnson Machinery Co* ***(P-7684)***
Caterpillar Authorized Dealer, West Sacramento *Also called Holt of California* ***(P-7680)***
Caterpillar Authorized Dealer, City of Industry *Also called Quinn Shepherd Machinery* ***(P-7691)***
Caterpillar Authorized Dealer, Salinas *Also called Quinn Lift Inc* ***(P-7789)***
Caterpillar Authorized Dealer, San Diego *Also called Hawthorne Machinery Co* ***(P-14443)***
Caterpillar Authorized Dealer, Oxnard *Also called Quinn Group Inc* ***(P-7708)***
Caterpillar Authorized Dealer, Imperial *Also called Empire Southwest LLC* ***(P-7674)***
Caterpillar Authorized Dealer, Bakersfield *Also called Quinn Company* ***(P-7687)***
Caterpillar Authorized Dealer, Oxnard *Also called Quinn Company* ***(P-7688)***
Caterpillar Authorized Dealer, Santa Maria *Also called Quinn Company* ***(P-7689)***
Caterpillar Authorized Dealer, Salinas *Also called Quinn Group Inc* ***(P-7690)***
Caterpillar Authorized Dealer, San Diego *Also called Hawthorne Machinery Co* ***(P-7677)***
Cathay Bank (HQ).....C.....626 279-3698
9650 Flair Dr El Monte (91731) ***(P-9424)***
Cathay Bank.....D.....626 588-1911
250 S Atlantic Blvd Monterey Park (91754) ***(P-9425)***
Cathay Bank.....B.....213 687-1300
977 N Broadway Ste 306 Los Angeles (90012) ***(P-26799)***
Cathay Bank.....D.....213 896-0098
800 W 6th St Ste 200 Los Angeles (90017) ***(P-9426)***
Cathay Bank.....C.....626 452-1582
4128 Temple City Blvd Rosemead (91770) ***(P-9427)***
Cathay Pacific Airways Limited.....D.....310 615-1113
1960 E Grand Ave Ste 540 El Segundo (90245) ***(P-4986)***
Cathedral Bookstore, Los Angeles *Also called Cathedral Center of St Paul* ***(P-25407)***
Cathedral Center of St Paul.....D.....213 482-2040
840 Echo Park Ave Los Angeles (90026) ***(P-25407)***
Cathedral Cyn Golf Tennis CLB, Cathedral City *Also called Briar Golf LP* ***(P-19114)***
Cathedral Oaks Athletic Club, Goleta *Also called Cathedral Oaks Tennis Swim Ath* ***(P-18885)***
Cathedral Oaks Tennis Swim Ath.....D.....805 964-7762
5800 Cathedral Oaks Rd Goleta (93117) ***(P-18885)***
Cathedral Pioneer Church Homes (PA).....D.....916 442-4906
415 P St Ofc Sacramento (95814) ***(P-20293)***
Catholic Charities.....E.....408 468-0100
2625 Zanker Rd Ste 200 San Jose (95134) ***(P-19358)***
Catholic Charities Diocese (PA).....D.....209 444-5900
1106 N El Dorado St Stockton (95202) ***(P-23532)***
Catholic Charities Diocese San.....E.....619 287-9454
4575 Mission Gorge Pl A San Diego (92120) ***(P-23533)***
CATHOLIC CHARITIES OF EAST BAY, Oakland *Also called Catholic Charities of The Dioc* ***(P-23538)***
Catholic Charities of La Inc (PA).....D.....213 251-3400
1531 James M Wood Blvd Los Angeles (90015) ***(P-26607)***
Catholic Charities of La Inc.....E.....818 883-6015
21600 Hart St Canoga Park (91303) ***(P-23534)***
Catholic Charities of La Inc.....D.....213 251-3400
1400 James M Wood Blvd Los Angeles (90015) ***(P-23535)***
Catholic Charities of Santa CL (PA).....C.....408 468-0100
2625 Zanker Rd Ste 200 San Jose (95134) ***(P-23536)***
Catholic Charities of Santa CL.....D.....805 643-4694
303 N Ventura Ave Ste A Ventura (93001) ***(P-23537)***
Catholic Charities of The Dioc (PA).....D.....510 768-3100
433 Jefferson St Oakland (94607) ***(P-23538)***
Catholic Chrts Cyo Archdiocs.....D.....415 743-0017
810 Avenue D San Francisco (94130) ***(P-23539)***
Catholic Chrts Cyo Archdiocs.....D.....415 405-2000
141 Leland Ave San Francisco (94134) ***(P-23540)***
Catholic Chrts Cyo Archdiocs.....E.....650 757-2110
699 Serramonte Blvd 210 Daly City (94015) ***(P-3910)***
Catholic Chrts Cyo Archdiocs.....D.....415 334-5550
1111 Junipero Serra Blvd San Francisco (94132) ***(P-23541)***
Catholic Chrts Cyo Archdiocs.....D.....415 553-8700
20 Franklin St San Francisco (94102) ***(P-23542)***
Catholic Chrts Cyo Archdiocs (PA).....D.....415 972-1200
990 Eddy St San Francisco (94109) ***(P-23543)***
Catholic Chrts Cyo Archdiocs.....B.....415 507-2000
1 Saint Vincents Dr San Rafael (94903) ***(P-23544)***
CATHOLIC YOUTH ORGANIZATION, Daly City *Also called Catholic Chrts Cyo Archdiocs* ***(P-3910)***
Caton Moving & Storage, Alameda *Also called Chipman Corporation* ***(P-4336)***
Cats U S A Pest Control, North Hollywood *Also called Cats USA Inc* ***(P-14139)***
Cats USA Inc.....D.....818 506-1000
5683 Whitnall Hwy North Hollywood (91601) ***(P-14139)***
Catta Verdera Country Club.....D.....916 645-7200
1111 Catta Verdera Lincoln (95648) ***(P-18886)***
Cattail Farms Inc.....D.....916 207-6580
3970 Cr95b Knights Landing (95645) ***(P-4)***
Cattlemens.....D.....925 447-1224
2882 Kitty Hawk Rd Livermore (94551) ***(P-13725)***
Cattlemens Restaurant, Livermore *Also called Cattlemens* ***(P-13725)***
Cattrac Construction Inc.....D.....909 355-1146
15030 Slover Ave Fontana (92337) ***(P-2021)***
CAV Inc.....D.....760 729-5199
5411 Avenida Encinas # 210 Carlsbad (92008) ***(P-3784)***
Cavalier Inn Inc.....D.....805 927-4688
9415 Hearst Dr San Simeon (93452) ***(P-12440)***
Cavalier Inn Incorporated.....D.....805 927-6444
250 San Simeon Ave Ste 4c San Simeon (93452) ***(P-12441)***
Cavalier Oceanfront Resort, San Simeon *Also called Cavalier Inn Inc* ***(P-12440)***
Cavallo Point LLC (PA).....D.....415 339-4700
601 Murray Cir Sausalito (94965) ***(P-12442)***
Cavendish Kinetics Inc.....E.....408 627-4504
2960 N 1st St San Jose (95134) ***(P-7457)***
Caviar Inc (HQ).....D.....888 978-5619
220 Montgomery St Ste 370 San Francisco (94104) ***(P-23545)***
Cavisson Systems Inc.....B.....800 701-6125
5201 Great America Pkwy Santa Clara (95054) ***(P-27677)***
CB Associates Inc.....E.....424 777-8214
11659 Haynes St North Hollywood (91606) ***(P-13995)***
CB C&C Properties/Comm Di Inc.....D.....530 221-7551
2120 Churn Creek Rd Redding (96002) ***(P-11272)***
CB North LLC.....A.....831 786-1642
480 W Beach St Watsonville (95076) ***(P-330)***
CB Richard Ellis RE Svcs LLC.....D.....213 613-3333
355 S Grand Ave Ste 2700 Los Angeles (90071) ***(P-11273)***
CB Richard Ellis Strategic Par.....D.....213 614-6862
515 S Flower St Ste 3100 Los Angeles (90071) ***(P-12212)***
CB Richard Ellis Strtgc Prtnrs.....D.....213 683-4200
515 S Flower St Los Angeles (90071) ***(P-10861)***
Cb-1 Hotel.....D.....415 633-3838
757 Market St San Francisco (94103) ***(P-12443)***
Cbabr Inc (PA).....D.....951 640-7056
31620 Rr Cyn Rd Ste A Canyon Lake (92587) ***(P-11274)***
Cbest Inc.....D.....310 445-2378
11620 Wilshire Blvd # 450 Los Angeles (90025) ***(P-22002)***
Cbiz Mayor Hoffman Mechan (PA).....D.....858 795-2000
10616 Scripps Summit Ct San Diego (92131) ***(P-26160)***
Cbizmhm LLC.....E.....661 325-7500
5060 California Ave # 800 Bakersfield (93309) ***(P-26161)***
Cbol Corporation.....C.....818 704-8200
19850 Plummer St Chatsworth (91311) ***(P-7458)***
Cbre Inc.....D.....916 446-6800
500 Capitol Mall Ste 2400 Sacramento (95814) ***(P-11275)***
Cbre Inc (HQ).....C.....213 613-3333
400 S Hope St Ste 25 Los Angeles (90071) ***(P-12058)***

Mergent e-mail: customerrelations@mergent.com
1242
2019 Directory of California
Wholesalers and Services Companies
(P-0000) Products & Services Section entry number
(PA)=Parent Co (HQ)=Headquarters (DH)=Div Headquarters

Cbre Inc ....C....714 939-2100
2125 E Katella Ave # 100 Anaheim (92806) ***(P-11276)***
Cbre Inc ....B....626 814-7900
4900 Rivergrade Rd A110 Baldwin Park (91706) ***(P-11277)***
Cbre Inc ....D....818 907-4600
15303 Ventura Blvd # 200 Van Nuys (91403) ***(P-11278)***
Cbre Inc ....D....408 453-7400
225 W Santa Clara St # 1050 San Jose (95113) ***(P-11279)***
Cbre Inc ....C....310 363-4900
2221 Rosecrans Ave # 100 El Segundo (90245) ***(P-11280)***
Cbre Inc ....D....818 502-6700
234 S Brand Blvd Ste 800 Glendale (91204) ***(P-11281)***
Cbre Inc ....D....310 550-2500
1840 Century Park E # 900 Los Angeles (90067) ***(P-11282)***
Cbre Inc ....C....858 546-4600
4365 Executive Dr # 1600 San Diego (92121) ***(P-11283)***
Cbre Inc ....D....909 418-2000
4141 Inland Empire Blvd # 100 Ontario (91764) ***(P-11284)***
Cbre Capstone, Los Angeles *Also called Cbre Inc* ***(P-11282)***
Cbre Global Investors LLC (HQ) ....C....213 683-4200
515 S Flower St Ste 3100 Los Angeles (90071) ***(P-27185)***
Cbre Global Investors LLC ....B....949 725-8500
3501 Jamboree Rd Ste 100 Newport Beach (92660) ***(P-27186)***
Cbre Group Inc (PA) ....C....213 613-3333
400 S Hope St Ste 25 Los Angeles (90071) ***(P-11285)***
Cbre Services Inc ....D....213 613-3333
400 S Hope St Ste 25 Los Angeles (90071) ***(P-27187)***
Cbre Valuation and Advisory, Los Angeles *Also called CB Richard Ellis RE Svcs LLC* ***(P-11273)***
CBS Broadcasting Inc ....B....415 765-0928
855 Battery St San Francisco (94111) ***(P-5773)***
CBS Broadcasting Inc ....D....415 765-4097
A65 Battery St San Francisco (94111) ***(P-5697)***
CBS Broadcasting Inc ....B....818 655-2000
4200 Radford Ave Studio City (91604) ***(P-5774)***
CBS Broadcasting Inc ....D....323 575-2345
7800 Beverly Blvd Los Angeles (90036) ***(P-25596)***
CBS Corporation ....D....323 575-2345
7800 Beverly Blvd Los Angeles (90036) ***(P-5775)***
CBS Corporation ....D....415 765-4000
865 Battery St Fl 2/3 San Francisco (94111) ***(P-5698)***
CBS Corporation ....D....760 343-5700
31276 Dunham Way Thousand Palms (92276) ***(P-5776)***
CBS Enterprises, Santa Monica *Also called CBS Television Distribution* ***(P-26800)***
CBS Farms LLC ....E....831 724-0700
80 Sakata Ln Watsonville (95076) ***(P-93)***
CBS Interactive Inc ....C....415 344-1813
2900 W Alameda Ave Burbank (91505) ***(P-13969)***
CBS Interactive Inc (HQ) ....A....415 344-2000
235 2nd St San Francisco (94105) ***(P-13970)***
CBS Maxpreps Inc ....E....530 676-6440
4364 Town Center Blvd # 320 El Dorado Hills (95762) ***(P-5528)***
CBS Network News, Los Angeles *Also called Merlot Film Productions Inc* ***(P-18078)***
CBS Radio Inc ....C....559 490-0106
1071 W Shaw Ave Fresno (93711) ***(P-5699)***
CBS Radio Inc ....D....415 765-4097
865 Battery St Fl 3 San Francisco (94111) ***(P-5700)***
CBS Radio Inc ....C....323 525-0980
5670 Wilshire Blvd # 200 Los Angeles (90036) ***(P-5701)***
CBS Radio Inc ....D....909 825-9525
900 E Washington St # 315 Colton (92324) ***(P-5702)***
CBS Radio Inc ....D....323 930-1067
5901 Venice Blvd Los Angeles (90034) ***(P-5703)***
CBS Radio Inc ....C....323 930-7580
5901 Venice Blvd Los Angeles (90034) ***(P-5704)***
CBS Radio Inc ....D....916 923-6800
280 Commerce Cir Sacramento (95815) ***(P-5705)***
CBS Studio Center, Studio City *Also called Radford Studio Center Inc* ***(P-18398)***
CBS Television Distribution (PA) ....A....310 264-3300
2450 Colo Ave Ste 500e Santa Monica (90404) ***(P-26800)***
Cbsi, San Francisco *Also called CBS Interactive Inc* ***(P-13970)***
Cbsj Financial Corporation ....D....408 792-4600
1735 N 1st St Ste 250 San Jose (95112) ***(P-13996)***
Cbsrr Inc ....D....909 336-2131
27206 Hwy 189 Blue Jay (92317) ***(P-11286)***
CC Wellness LLC (HQ) ....D....661 295-1700
29000 Hancock Pkwy Valencia (91355) ***(P-8159)***
Cc-Palo Alto Inc ....C....650 853-5000
620 Sand Hill Rd Palo Alto (94304) ***(P-20919)***
Ccare West, Fresno *Also called California Cancer Assctes* ***(P-19339)***
Ccbc Reference Lab, Fresno *Also called Central California Blood Ctr* ***(P-22761)***
CCC Property Holdings LLC ....C....310 609-1957
500 S Alameda St Compton (90221) ***(P-11968)***
Ccc2931 LLC ....D....562 590-8591
2401 E Pacific Coast Hwy Wilmington (90744) ***(P-4667)***
Cccc Growth Fund LLC ....D....626 441-8770
899 El Centro St South Pasadena (91030) ***(P-12213)***
Cch Computax, Torrance *Also called CCH Incorporated* ***(P-16104)***
CCH Incorporated ....B....310 800-9800
20101 Hamilton Ave # 200 Torrance (90502) ***(P-16104)***
Ccig, Westlake Village *Also called California Coml Inv Group Inc* ***(P-27670)***
Ccintegration Inc (PA) ....E....408 228-1314
2060 Corporate Ct San Jose (95131) ***(P-26346)***
Ccmsi, Irvine *Also called Cannon Cochran MGT Svcs Inc* ***(P-10576)***
Ccna Vons Athletes For Life ....D....805 453-2499
10670 6th St Ste 113 Rancho Cucamonga (91730) ***(P-25408)***
CCOF CERTIFICATION SERVICES, Santa Cruz *Also called California Certified Organic* ***(P-24948)***
CCPOA, West Sacramento *Also called California Correctnl Peace Ofc* ***(P-25056)***
CCS, Hayward *Also called Controlled Contamination Svcs* ***(P-14227)***
Ccts, Santa Ana *Also called Satellite Management Co* ***(P-11754)***
Cdc San Francisco LLC ....D....415 616-6512
888 Howard St San Francisco (94103) ***(P-12444)***
Cdcr - California Men's Colony, San Luis Obispo *Also called Correctons Rhbltation Cal Dept* ***(P-22539)***
Cdcr Cal Instn For Men Hosp, Chino *Also called Correctons Rhbltation Cal Dept* ***(P-21344)***
CDI, Woodland Hills *Also called Child Development Institute* ***(P-23561)***
CDI Marine Company LLC ....E....619 407-4010
694 Moss St Chula Vista (91911) ***(P-25597)***
CDM Constructors Inc ....D....909 579-3500
9220 Cleveland Ave # 100 Rancho Cucamonga (91730) ***(P-1906)***
CDM SMITH INC ....D....949 752-5452
46 Discovery Ste 250 Irvine (92618) ***(P-25598)***
CDM SMITH INC ....D....760 438-7755
703 Palomar Airport Rd # 300 Carlsbad (92011) ***(P-25599)***
CDM SMITH INC ....D....617 452-6000
2300 Clayton Rd Ste 950 Concord (94520) ***(P-25600)***
Cdnetworks Inc (HQ) ....D....408 228-3379
1919 S Bascom Ave Ste 600 Campbell (95008) ***(P-5529)***
Cds Moving Equipment Inc (PA) ....D....310 631-1100
375 W Manville St Rancho Dominguez (90220) ***(P-7739)***
Cdsnet LLC ....D....310 981-9500
6053 W Century Blvd Los Angeles (90045) ***(P-27678)***
Cdw, Anaheim *Also called Consolidated Design West Inc* ***(P-14106)***
CE Allencompany Inc ....E....562 989-6100
2109 Gundry Ave Long Beach (90755) ***(P-2022)***
Ce2 Kleinfelder JV ....D....925 463-7301
7901 Stoneridge Dr # 315 Pleasanton (94588) ***(P-25601)***
Cea-Pack Logistics, Cerritos *Also called Cea-Pack Services Inc* ***(P-4394)***
Cea-Pack Services Inc ....C....562 407-0660
12607 Hiddencreek Way Cerritos (90703) ***(P-4394)***
CEC, La Canada *Also called Child Educational Center* ***(P-24287)***
Cecchini & Cecchini, Brentwood *Also called Robert Cecchini Inc* ***(P-77)***
Cecelia Packing Corporation ....C....559 626-5000
24780 E South Ave Orange Cove (93646) ***(P-501)***
Cecico Inc ....D....323 269-7000
1016 Towne Ave Unit 110 Los Angeles (90021) ***(P-8292)***
Cecico Town, Los Angeles *Also called Cecico Inc* ***(P-8292)***
Cecilla Gonzalez De Al Hoya CA, Los Angeles *Also called White Memorial Medical Center* ***(P-21916)***
Cecos ....E....805 982-5400
3502 Goodspeed St Ste 1 Port Hueneme (93043) ***(P-25602)***
Cedar Creek Alzhimers Dementia, Berkeley *Also called Altcare Cedar Creek LLC* ***(P-24414)***
CEDAR CREST NURSING & REHABILITATION CENTER, Sunnyvale *Also called Ghc of Sunnyvale LLC* ***(P-21081)***
Cedar Fair LP ....C....408 988-1776
4701 Great America Pkwy Santa Clara (95054) ***(P-18792)***
Cedar Holdings LLC ....D....909 862-0611
7534 Palm Ave Highland (92346) ***(P-20294)***
Cedar House Rehabilitation Ctr, Bloomington *Also called Social Science Service Center* ***(P-22050)***
Cedar Management LLC ....D....310 396-3100
3233 Dnald Douglas Loop S Santa Monica (90405) ***(P-11287)***
Cedar Mountain Post Acute, Yucaipa *Also called Cedar Operations LLC* ***(P-20295)***
Cedar Operations LLC ....C....909 790-2273
11970 4th St Yucaipa (92399) ***(P-20295)***
Cedar Signature, Santa Monica *Also called Cedar Management LLC* ***(P-11287)***
Cedar Sinai Medical Group, Beverly Hills *Also called Medical Group Bverly Hills Inc* ***(P-19676)***
CEDARS SINAI MEDICAL GROUP, Beverly Hills *Also called Medical Group Bverly Hills Inc* ***(P-19675)***
Cedars-Sinai Medical Center ....C....310 824-3664
8635 W 3rd St Ste 1195 Los Angeles (90048) ***(P-19359)***
Cedars-Sinai Medical Center ....B....310 423-3849
127 S San Vicente Blvd # 3417 Los Angeles (90048) ***(P-19360)***
Cedars-Sinai Medical Center ....A....323 866-8483
8631 W 3rd St Ste 730 Los Angeles (90048) ***(P-19361)***
Cedars-Sinai Medical Center ....C....310 385-3400
250 N Robertson Blvd # 101 Beverly Hills (90211) ***(P-21306)***
Cedarwood-Young Company (PA) ....C....626 962-4047
14620 Joanbridge St Baldwin Park (91706) ***(P-6371)***
Cedarwood-Young Company ....D....626 962-4047
14618 Arrow Hwy Baldwin Park (91706) ***(P-7973)***
Cederlind Farms LP ....D....209 606-8586
2514 Kenney Ave Winton (95388) ***(P-133)***
Cei, San Jose *Also called Cupertino Electric Inc* ***(P-2557)***
Celebrity Casinos Inc ....B....310 631-3838
123 E Artesia Blvd Compton (90220) ***(P-12445)***
Celebrity Pink USA, Montebello *Also called 2253 Apparel Inc* ***(P-8284)***
Celera Corporation (HQ) ....D....510 749-4200
33608 Ortega Hwy San Juan Capistrano (92675) ***(P-26608)***
Celerity Consulting Group Inc (PA) ....D....415 986-8850
2 Gough St Ste 300 San Francisco (94103) ***(P-27188)***
Celestica LLC ....B....909 418-6986
895 S Rockefeller Ave # 102 Ontario (91761) ***(P-7459)***
Celestix Networks Inc ....D....510 668-0700
215 Fourier Ave Ste 140 Fremont (94539) ***(P-15928)***
Celex Solutions, Brea *Also called Contract Services Group Inc* ***(P-14225)***
Celgene Corporation ....C....858 677-0034
10300 Campus Point Dr # 100 San Diego (92121) ***(P-8160)***
Celgene Signal Research, San Diego *Also called Celgene Corporation* ***(P-8160)***
Cell Design Labs Inc ....E....510 398-0501
5858 Horton St Ste 240 Emeryville (94608) ***(P-8161)***

ALPHABETIC

Employee Codes: A=Over 500 employees, B=251-500
C=101-250, D=51-100, E=50
2019 Directory of California
Wholesalers and Services Companies
© Mergent Inc. 1-800-342-5647
1243

Cell Site Management Group LLC..............E.......800 906-9778
25109 Jefferson Ave Murrieta (92562) *(P-5303)*
Cell-Crete Corporation..............D.......510 471-7257
995 Zephyr Ave Hayward (94544) *(P-3232)*
Cellarstone Inc (PA)..............D.......650 242-0008
1650 Borel Pl Ste 100 San Mateo (94402) *(P-16324)*
Cellco Partnership..............D.......951 769-0985
1484 E Second St Beaumont (92223) *(P-5304)*
Cellco Partnership..............D.......951 296-3499
26480 Ynez Rd Temecula (92591) *(P-5305)*
Cellco Partnership..............D.......310 891-6991
24329 Crenshaw Blvd Ste D Torrance (90505) *(P-5306)*
Cellco Partnership..............D.......925 245-0494
2428 Las Positas Rd Livermore (94551) *(P-5307)*
Cellco Partnership..............D.......831 644-0858
1680 Del Monte Ctr Monterey (93940) *(P-5308)*
Cellco Partnership..............D.......714 921-5130
1500 E Village Way # 2205 Orange (92865) *(P-5309)*
Cellco Partnership..............D.......925 626-3480
6471 Lone Tree Way Brentwood (94513) *(P-5310)*
Cellco Partnership..............D.......951 697-3035
2851 Canyon Springs Pkwy Riverside (92507) *(P-5311)*
Cellco Partnership..............D.......805 376-8917
2535 W Hillcrest Dr Thousand Oaks (91320) *(P-5312)*
Cellco Partnership..............D.......212 395-1000
255 Parkshore Dr Folsom (95630) *(P-5313)*
Cellco Partnership..............D.......805 596-2300
1101 Los Olivos Ave Los Osos (93402) *(P-5314)*
Cellco Partnership..............D.......559 454-0803
550 S Clovis Ave Ste 105 Fresno (93727) *(P-5315)*
Cellco Partnership..............D.......714 427-0733
901 S Coast Dr Ste K120 Costa Mesa (92626) *(P-5316)*
Cellco Partnership..............D.......951 361-1850
12459 Limonite Ave C-2 Eastvale (91752) *(P-5317)*
Cellco Partnership..............D.......916 786-6151
1900 Douglas Blvd Ste D Roseville (95661) *(P-5318)*
Cellco Partnership..............A.......949 286-7000
15505 Sand Canyon Ave Irvine (92618) *(P-5319)*
Cellco Partnership..............D.......831 786-0267
1051 S Green Valley Rd Watsonville (95076) *(P-5320)*
Cellco Partnership..............D.......562 694-8630
1401 W Imperial Hwy Ste C La Habra (90631) *(P-5321)*
Cellco Partnership..............D.......714 564-0050
691 S Main St Ste 80 Orange (92868) *(P-5322)*
Cellco Partnership..............D.......760 738-0088
711 Center Dr Ste 6a San Marcos (92069) *(P-5323)*
Cellco Partnership..............D.......831 475-3100
1440 41st Ave Ste B Capitola (95010) *(P-5324)*
Cellco Partnership..............D.......661 827-8728
2701 Ming Ave Spc 100a Bakersfield (93304) *(P-5325)*
Cellco Partnership..............D.......760 720-8400
1846 Marron Rd Carlsbad (92008) *(P-5326)*
Cellco Partnership..............D.......415 924-9084
125 Corte Madera Town Ctr Corte Madera (94925) *(P-5327)*
Cellco Partnership..............D.......619 596-7201
1571 N Magnolia Ave # 212 El Cajon (92020) *(P-5328)*
Cellco Partnership..............D.......559 451-0556
7723 N Blackstone Ave # 102 Fresno (93720) *(P-5329)*
Cellco Partnership..............D.......562 809-5650
12607 Artesia Blvd Cerritos (90703) *(P-5330)*
Cellco Partnership..............D.......530 892-6900
1950 E 20th St Ste 803 Chico (95928) *(P-5331)*
Cellco Partnership..............D.......951 549-6400
2210 Griffin Way Ste 101 Corona (92879) *(P-5332)*
Cellco Partnership..............D.......510 490-3800
39050 Argonaut Way Fremont (94538) *(P-5333)*
Cellco Partnership..............D.......714 256-6015
2500 E Imperial Hwy # 178 Brea (92821) *(P-5334)*
Cellco Partnership..............D.......818 500-7779
1023 E Colorado St Glendale (91205) *(P-5335)*
Cellco Partnership..............D.......858 625-7751
10525 Vista Sorrento Pkwy # 150 San Diego (92121) *(P-5336)*
Cellco Partnership..............D.......818 920-4848
8300 Van Nuys Blvd Panorama City (91402) *(P-5337)*
Cellco Partnership..............D.......805 650-0410
488 S Mills Rd Ventura (93003) *(P-5338)*
Cellco Partnership..............D.......805 237-8200
205 Oak Hill Rd Paso Robles (93446) *(P-5339)*
Cellco Partnership..............D.......760 642-0430
258 N El Cmino Real Ste A Encinitas (92024) *(P-5340)*
Cellco Partnership..............D.......951 898-0980
2540 Tuscany St Corona (92881) *(P-5341)*
Cellco Partnership..............D.......916 408-7958
125 Cyber Ct Rocklin (95765) *(P-5342)*
Cellco Partnership..............D.......818 842-2722
1729 N Victory Pl Burbank (91502) *(P-5343)*
Cellco Partnership..............D.......626 472-6196
14510 Baldwn Prk Town Ctr Baldwin Park (91706) *(P-5344)*
Cellco Partnership..............D.......408 846-5170
6965 Camino Arroyo Ste 60 Gilroy (95020) *(P-5345)*
Cellco Partnership..............D.......626 395-0956
368 S Lake Ave Pasadena (91101) *(P-5346)*
Cellco Partnership..............D.......916 331-6833
5051 Auburn Blvd Sacramento (95841) *(P-5347)*
Cellco Partnership..............D.......760 568-5542
71800 Highway 111 A110 Rancho Mirage (92270) *(P-5348)*
Cellco Partnership..............D.......408 263-1960
172 Ranch Dr Milpitas (95035) *(P-5349)*
Cellco Partnership..............D.......949 472-0700
23718 El Toro Rd Ste A Lake Forest (92630) *(P-5350)*
Cellco Partnership..............D.......415 402-0640
768 Market St San Francisco (94102) *(P-5351)*
Cellco Partnership..............D.......209 668-9579
3202 W Monte Vista Ave Turlock (95380) *(P-5352)*
Cellco Partnership..............D.......925 743-9327
18012 Bollinger Canyon Rd San Ramon (94583) *(P-5353)*
Cellco Partnership..............D.......661 663-9451
5508 Young St Bakersfield (93311) *(P-5973)*
Cellco Partnership..............D.......818 990-4610
17237 Ventura Blvd Encino (91316) *(P-5354)*
Cellco Partnership..............D.......619 216-5840
2015 Birch Rd Ste 1805 Chula Vista (91915) *(P-5355)*
Cellco Partnership..............D.......510 267-0731
3264 Lakeshore Ave Oakland (94610) *(P-5356)*
Cellco Partnership..............D.......415 258-8404
333 Biscayne Dr San Rafael (94901) *(P-5357)*
Cellco Partnership..............D.......916 419-6200
3635 N Freeway Blvd Sacramento (95834) *(P-5358)*
Cellco Partnership..............D.......818 980-4200
11265 Ventura Blvd Studio City (91604) *(P-5359)*
Cellco Partnership..............D.......925 472-0487
1199 Dunsyre Dr Lafayette (94549) *(P-5360)*
Cellco Partnership..............D.......562 401-1045
12006 Lakewood Blvd Downey (90242) *(P-5361)*
Cellco Partnership..............D.......760 662-5914
12821 Main St Hesperia (92345) *(P-5362)*
Cellco Partnership..............D.......559 325-1420
1398 Shaw Ave Clovis (93612) *(P-5363)*
Cellco Partnership..............D.......661 274-2112
39575 Trade Center Dr Palmdale (93551) *(P-5364)*
Cellco Partnership..............D.......714 847-8799
16120 Beach Blvd Huntington Beach (92647) *(P-5365)*
Cellco Partnership..............D.......310 659-0775
100 N La Cienega Blvd # 233 Los Angeles (90048) *(P-5366)*
Cellco Partnership..............B.......916 357-1000
255 Parkshore Dr Bldg B Folsom (95630) *(P-5367)*
Cellco Partnership..............D.......209 543-6500
3801 Pelandale Ave Ste B3 Modesto (95356) *(P-5368)*
Cellco Partnership..............D.......213 738-9771
3785 Wilshire Blvd Los Angeles (90010) *(P-5369)*
Cellco Partnership..............D.......310 329-9325
20820 Avalon Blvd Carson (90746) *(P-5370)*
Cellco Partnership..............D.......323 465-0640
1503 Vine St Hollywood (90028) *(P-5371)*
Cellco Partnership..............D.......323 603-0369
7100 Santa Monica Blvd West Hollywood (90046) *(P-5372)*
Cellco Partnership..............D.......415 695-8400
2654 Mission St San Francisco (94110) *(P-5373)*
Cellco Partnership..............D.......510 324-5740
30935 Courthouse Dr Spc 1 Union City (94587) *(P-5374)*
Cellco Partnership..............D.......661 286-2399
24201 Valencia Blvd Valencia (91355) *(P-5375)*
Cellco Partnership..............D.......714 899-4690
6856 Katella Ave Cypress (90630) *(P-5376)*
Cellco Partnership..............D.......760 337-5508
880 N Imperial Ave El Centro (92243) *(P-5377)*
Cellco Partnership..............D.......805 955-9035
1555 Simi Town Center Way Simi Valley (93065) *(P-5378)*
Cellco Partnership..............D.......818 715-9143
6600 Topanga Canyon Blvd Canoga Park (91303) *(P-5379)*
Cellco Partnership..............D.......831 421-0753
110 Cooper St Ste A Santa Cruz (95060) *(P-5380)*
Cellco Partnership..............D.......909 381-0576
500 Inland Center Dr # 459 San Bernardino (92408) *(P-5381)*
Cellco Partnership..............D.......916 536-0440
6065 Sunrise Blvd Citrus Heights (95610) *(P-5382)*
Cellco Partnership..............D.......415 351-1700
1 Daniel Burnham Ct Bsmt San Francisco (94109) *(P-5383)*
Cellco Partnership..............D.......562 789-0911
12376 Washington Blvd A Whittier (90606) *(P-5384)*
Cellco Partnership..............D.......858 614-0011
7061 Clairemont Mesa Blvd San Diego (92111) *(P-5385)*
Cellco Partnership..............D.......909 591-9740
3825 Grand Ave Chino (91710) *(P-5386)*
Cellco Partnership..............D.......530 674-8007
1145 Colusa Ave Ste A Yuba City (95991) *(P-5387)*
Cellco Partnership..............D.......949 831-3955
27040 Alicia Pkwy Ste E Laguna Niguel (92677) *(P-5388)*
Cellco Partnership..............D.......805 569-2525
2980 State St Santa Barbara (93105) *(P-5389)*
Cellco Partnership..............D.......707 525-5010
844 4th St Santa Rosa (95404) *(P-5390)*
Cellco Partnership..............D.......714 449-0715
503 N State College Blvd Fullerton (92831) *(P-5391)*
Cellco Partnership..............D.......650 323-6127
219 University Ave Palo Alto (94301) *(P-5392)*
Cellco Partnership..............D.......805 549-6260
994 Mill St Ste 100 San Luis Obispo (93401) *(P-5393)*
Cellco Partnership..............D.......714 775-0600
3770 W Mcfadden Ave Ste H Santa Ana (92704) *(P-5394)*
Cellco Partnership..............D.......323 826-9880
6400 Pacific Blvd Huntington Park (90255) *(P-5974)*
Cellco Partnership..............C.......858 618-2100
11134 Rancho Carmel Dr # 101 San Diego (92128) *(P-5395)*
Cellco Partnership..............D.......661 726-4762
43458 10th St W Ste C Lancaster (93534) *(P-5396)*
Cellco Partnership..............D.......949 488-9990
638 Camino De Ls Mrs H140 San Clemente (92673) *(P-5397)*
Cellco Partnership..............D.......323 725-9750
5438 Whittier Blvd Commerce (90022) *(P-5398)*

Cellco Partnership...D...562 942-8527
8724 Washington Blvd Pico Rivera (90660) ***(P-5399)***
Cellmark Inc (HQ)...D...415 927-1700
88 Rowland Way Ste 300 Novato (94945) ***(P-8022)***
Cellmatics...E...760 692-2424
2309 Masters Rd Carlsbad (92008) ***(P-15929)***
Cello & Maudru Cnstr Co Inc...E...707 257-0454
2505 Oak St NAPA (94559) ***(P-1499)***
Cellular Palace Inc...D...310 278-2007
10435 Santa Monica Blvd F Los Angeles (90025) ***(P-7460)***
Celluphone LLC...C...323 727-9131
6119 E Washington Blvd Commerce (90040) ***(P-7461)***
Celmol Inc...D...714 259-1000
1611 E Saint Andrew Pl Santa Ana (92705) ***(P-9202)***
Cels Enterprises Inc (PA)...D...310 838-0280
3485 S La Cienega Blvd A Los Angeles (90016) ***(P-8347)***
Cem - Victorville River Plant, Victorville *Also called Cemex Cnstr Mtls PCF LLC* ***(P-6880)***
Cem Builders Inc...E...408 395-1490
37 S 4th St Campbell (95008) ***(P-25603)***
Cemak Trucking Inc (PA)...D...949 253-2800
4621 Teller Ave Ste 130 Newport Beach (92660) ***(P-3987)***
Cement Cutting Inc...D...619 296-9592
3610 Hancock St Frnt Frnt San Diego (92110) ***(P-3233)***
Cement Mason Health & Welfare...D...707 864-3300
220 Campus Ln Suisun City (94534) ***(P-24751)***
Cemex Cement Inc...C...626 969-1747
1201 W Gladstone St Azusa (91702) ***(P-6879)***
Cemex Cnstr Mtls PCF LLC...C...760 381-7600
16888 E St Victorville (92394) ***(P-6880)***
Cemtek Environmental Inc...E...714 437-7100
3041 Orange Ave Santa Ana (92707) ***(P-27679)***
Cen Cal Plastering Inc...B...209 858-1045
1256 W Lathrop Rd Manteca (95336) ***(P-2864)***
Cencal Health, Santa Barbara *Also called Santa Barbara San Luis Obispo* ***(P-10171)***
Centene Corporation...D...530 626-5773
550 Main St Placerville (95667) ***(P-10190)***
Centene Corporation...D...314 505-6689
12033 Foundation Pl Gold River (95670) ***(P-10191)***
Center At Parkwest, The, Reseda *Also called Chase Group Llc* ***(P-27189)***
Center Cnslng Edctn & Crisis...D...925 462-1755
4361 Railroad Ave Pleasanton (94566) ***(P-23546)***
Center Coast Home Help Care, Monterey *Also called Visiting Nurse Association* ***(P-22447)***
Center For Achievement Center, Bakersfield *Also called New Advances For People Disabi* ***(P-24812)***
Center For Atism Rlted Dsrders...E...949 203-8872
106 Discovery Irvine (92618) ***(P-22521)***
Center For Autism & (PA)...C...818 345-2345
21600 Oxnard St Ste 1800 Woodland Hills (91367) ***(P-20170)***
Center For Autism Related Svcs...E...323 850-7177
5949 Lankershim Blvd North Hollywood (91601) ***(P-27680)***
Center For Autsm Rsrch Evltn...C...858 444-8823
10174 Old Grove Rd San Diego (92131) ***(P-22522)***
Center For Better Health and...D...714 751-8110
1520 Nutmeg Pl Ste 220 Costa Mesa (92626) ***(P-22759)***
Center For Civic Education (PA)...D...818 591-9321
5115 Douglas Fir Rd Ste J Calabasas (91302) ***(P-26609)***
Center For Discovery, Lakewood *Also called Discovery Practice Management* ***(P-19446)***
Center For Dscovery Adoloscent...E...562 425-6404
4136 Ann Arbor Rd Lakewood (90712) ***(P-22003)***
Center For Elders Independence...C...510 433-1150
510 17th St Ste 400 Oakland (94612) ***(P-10192)***
Center For Employment Training (PA)...D...408 287-7924
701 Vine St San Jose (95110) ***(P-24164)***
Center For Ind Living Inc (PA)...D...510 841-4776
2490 Mariner Square Loop # 210 Alameda (94501) ***(P-23547)***
Center For Indvdual and Fam Th...D...714 558-9266
840 W Town And Country Rd Orange (92868) ***(P-23548)***
CENTER FOR INJURY PREVENTION, Chula Vista *Also called Racelegal Com* ***(P-25453)***
Center For Learning and...B...800 538-8365
424 Peninsula Ave San Mateo (94401) ***(P-23549)***
Center For Sustainable Energy...D...858 244-1177
3980 Sherman St Ste 170 San Diego (92110) ***(P-27681)***
Center For Ventr Philanthropy, San Mateo *Also called Peninsula Community Foundation* ***(P-12082)***
Center Glass Co No 3...D...619 469-6181
7853 El Cajon Blvd La Mesa (91942) ***(P-3403)***
Center Medical Company...E...626 575-7500
12100 Valley Blvd 109a El Monte (91732) ***(P-19362)***
Center of Rehabilitation...C...714 826-2330
9021 Knott Ave Buena Park (90620) ***(P-20296)***
Center Point Inc (PA)...D...415 492-4444
135 Paul Dr San Rafael (94903) ***(P-23550)***
Center Thtre Group Los Angeles (PA)...C...213 972-7344
601 W Temple St Los Angeles (90012) ***(P-18354)***
Center To Promote Healthcare A (PA)...D...510 834-1300
1951 Webster St Fl 2 Oakland (94612) ***(P-22760)***
CENTER, THE, San Diego *Also called San Diego Lesbian Gay Bisexu* ***(P-24011)***
Centerline Wood Products...D...760 246-4530
10007 Yucca Rd Adelanto (92301) ***(P-8023)***
Centerplate, San Francisco *Also called Volume Services Inc* ***(P-19257)***
Centerplate, Lake Elsinore *Also called Volume Services Inc* ***(P-19260)***
Centex Homes Inc...C...949 453-0113
27401 Los Altos Ste 400 Mission Viejo (92691) ***(P-1143)***
Centex Homes Inc...C...949 453-0113
250 Commerce Ste 100 Irvine (92602) ***(P-1144)***
Centimark Corporation...E...909 652-9280
1420 S Archibald Ave Ontario (91761) ***(P-3134)***
Centimark Corporation...C...510 921-5500
2380 W Winton Ave Hayward (94545) ***(P-3135)***
Centimark Roofing Systems, Hayward *Also called Centimark Corporation* ***(P-3135)***
Centinela Frman Rgonal Med Ctr, Marina Del Rey *Also called Cfhs Holdings Inc* ***(P-21308)***
Centinela Frman Rgonal Med Ctr, Marina Del Rey *Also called Cfhs Holdings Inc* ***(P-21309)***
Centinela Frman Rgonal Med Ctr, Inglewood *Also called Cfhs Holdings Inc* ***(P-21310)***
Centinela Hospital Medical Ctr, Inglewood *Also called Prime Healthcare Centinela LLC* ***(P-21657)***
Centinela Skilled Nursing and...D...310 674-3216
950 S Flower St Inglewood (90301) ***(P-20297)***
Centinela Skld Nrng Wlns Cntr, Inglewood *Also called West Cntinela Vly Care Ctr Inc* ***(P-20882)***
Centinela Skld Nrsng & Wllnss...D...310 674-3216
1001 S Osage Ave Inglewood (90301) ***(P-20298)***
Centinela Valley Care Center...C...310 674-3216
950 S Flower St Inglewood (90301) ***(P-24459)***
Centra Freight Services Inc (PA)...D...650 873-8147
279 Lawrence Ave South San Francisco (94080) ***(P-5207)***
Central Anesthesia Service...D...916 481-6800
3315 Watt Ave Sacramento (95821) ***(P-19363)***
Central Branch YMCA, San Jose *Also called YMCA of Silicon Valley* ***(P-25311)***
Central Business Solutions Inc (PA)...D...510 573-5500
37600 Central Ct Ste 214 Newark (94560) ***(P-16325)***
Central Cal Healthcare Sys, Fresno *Also called Veterans Health Administration* ***(P-20062)***
Central Cal Nikkei Foundation...D...559 237-4006
540 S Peach Ave Fresno (93727) ***(P-24460)***
Central California Blood Ctr...D...559 389-5433
4343 W Herndon Ave Fresno (93722) ***(P-22761)***
Central California Blood Ctr...D...559 324-1211
8094 N Cedar Ave Fresno (93720) ***(P-22762)***
Central California Blood Ctr (PA)...C...559 389-5433
4343 W Herndon Ave Fresno (93722) ***(P-22763)***
Central California Ear Nose...E...559 432-3724
1351 E Spruce Ave Fresno (93720) ***(P-19364)***
Central California Faculty Med...B...209 620-6937
1085 W Minnesota Ave Turlock (95382) ***(P-22764)***
Central California Faculty Med (PA)...D...559 453-5200
2625 E Divisadero St Fresno (93721) ***(P-19365)***
Central California Tr...D...559 686-4973
22847 Road 140 Tulare (93274) ***(P-26610)***
Central Cardiology Med Clinic...C...661 395-0000
2901 Sillect Ave Ste 100 Bakersfield (93308) ***(P-19366)***
Central Cast Vsting Nurse Assn, Monterey *Also called Central Coast Cmnty Hlth Care* ***(P-22259)***
Central Cleaning Co, Pleasanton *Also called Dan Lofgren* ***(P-14248)***
Central Coast Cmnty Hlth Care...C...831 372-6668
5 Lower Ragsdale Dr # 102 Monterey (93940) ***(P-21035)***
Central Coast Cmnty Hlth Care...B...831 648-4200
40 Ragsdale Dr Ste 150 Monterey (93940) ***(P-22259)***
Central Coast Cooling LLC...D...831 422-7265
1107 Merrill St Salinas (93901) ***(P-4498)***
Central Coast Distributing LLC...D...805 922-2108
815 S Blosser Rd Santa Maria (93458) ***(P-8985)***
Central Coast Management, Ventura *Also called Pierpont Inn Inc* ***(P-13063)***
Central Coast Packing, Soledad *Also called Vasquez Brothers Inc* ***(P-583)***
Central Coast Pathology Lab, Bakersfield *Also called Physicians Automated Lab Inc* ***(P-22122)***
Central Coast Pub Safety Inc...D...805 556-4450
222 Carmen Ln Ste 202 Santa Maria (93458) ***(P-16599)***
Central Coast Vna & Hospice (PA)...C...831 372-6668
5 Lower Ragsdle Dr 102 Monterey (93940) ***(P-22260)***
Central Coast Vna & Hospice...D...831 758-8243
45 Plaza Cir Salinas (93901) ***(P-22261)***
Central Cold Storage, Castroville *Also called Vps Companies Inc* ***(P-8508)***
Central Contra Costa Sanit...D...925 228-9500
5019 Imhoff Pl Martinez (94553) ***(P-6321)***
Central Counties...D...209 356-0355
241 Business Park Way Atwater (95301) ***(P-26689)***
Central Courier LLC...D...805 654-1145
1957 Eastman Ave Ste C Ventura (93003) ***(P-3988)***
Central Freight Lines Inc...D...800 782-5036
1621 Main Ave Sacramento (95838) ***(P-4115)***
Central Freight Lines Inc...D...559 233-5559
4575 S Chestnut Ave Fresno (93725) ***(P-3989)***
Central Garden & Pet Company...D...858 695-0743
9235 Activity Rd San Diego (92126) ***(P-9203)***
Central Garden & Pet Company...C...562 926-5252
13227 Orden Dr Santa Fe Springs (90670) ***(P-9204)***
Central Garden & Pet Company...D...626 334-9301
16321 Arrow Hwy Irwindale (91706) ***(P-9205)***
CENTRAL GARDENS CONVALESCENT H, San Francisco *Also called Central Gardens Inc* ***(P-20299)***
Central Gardens Inc...C...415 567-2967
1355 Ellis St San Francisco (94115) ***(P-20299)***
Central Health Plan Cal Inc...A...626 938-7120
1055 Park View Dr Ste 355 Covina (91724) ***(P-22262)***
Central Indiana Hdwr Co Inc (PA)...C...317 558-5700
3512 Seagate Way Ste 190 Oceanside (92056) ***(P-7582)***
Central Medical Offices, Bakersfield *Also called Kaiser Foundation Hospitals* ***(P-19542)***
Central Orange County Svc Ctr, Santa Ana *Also called Southern California Edison Co* ***(P-6125)***
Central Parking Corporation...D...510 832-7227
1624 Franklin St Ste 722 Oakland (94612) ***(P-17678)***
Central Parking System Inc...D...714 751-2855
3420 Bristol St Ste 225 Costa Mesa (92626) ***(P-17679)***
Central Parking System Inc...D...916 441-1074
716 10th St Ste 101 Sacramento (95814) ***(P-17680)***

ALPHABETIC

Employee Codes: A=Over 500 employees, B=251-500
C=101-250, D=51-100, E=50
2019 Directory of California
Wholesalers and Services Companies
© Mergent Inc. 1-800-342-5647
1245

Central Payment Co LLC....D....415 462-8335
2350 Kerner Blvd Ste 300 San Rafael (94901) ***(P-17063)***
Central Purchasing LLC (PA)....B....805 388-1000
26541 Agoura Rd Calabasas (91302) ***(P-7843)***
Central Reference Lab Inc (PA)....C....909 861-6966
1470 Valley Vista Dr # 100 Pomona (91765) ***(P-22067)***
Central Refill Pharmaceuticals....D....562 401-4214
9521 Dalen St Downey (90242) ***(P-8162)***
Central Reinforcing Corp....D....909 773-0840
14166 Slover Ave Fontana (92337) ***(P-3370)***
Central Retail Pharmaceuticals, Downey *Also called Central Refill Pharmaceuticals* ***(P-8162)***
Central Roofing Company, Gardena *Also called Claud Townsley Inc* ***(P-3138)***
Central State Pre-School....E....760 432-2499
2310 Aldergrove Ave Escondido (92029) ***(P-24275)***
Central Svc Ctr & Exec Offs....E....909 307-6555
1751 Plum Ln Redlands (92374) ***(P-17064)***
Central Technologies, Irvine *Also called Inductors Inc* ***(P-7493)***
Central Valley AG Transload, Oakdale *Also called Central Valley AG Trnspt Inc* ***(P-502)***
Central Valley AG Trnspt Inc....D....209 544-9246
5509 Langworth Rd Oakdale (95361) ***(P-502)***
Central Valley Autism Project....D....209 521-4791
3425 Coffee Rd Ste C2 Modesto (95355) ***(P-23551)***
Central Valley Cheese Inc....D....209 664-1080
115 S Kilroy Rd Turlock (95380) ***(P-8515)***
Central Valley Clinic Inc....E....408 885-5400
2425 Enborg Ln San Jose (95128) ***(P-22523)***
Central Valley Cmnty Bancorp (PA)....C....559 298-1775
7100 N Fincl Dr Ste 101 Fresno (93720) ***(P-9428)***
Central Valley Community Bank....D....559 625-8733
120 N Floral St Visalia (93291) ***(P-9429)***
Central Valley Community Bank....E....916 985-8700
905 Sutter St Ste 100 Folsom (95630) ***(P-9430)***
Central Valley Community Bank (HQ)....C....559 323-3384
600 Pollasky Ave Clovis (93612) ***(P-9431)***
Central Valley Community Bank....C....559 298-1775
7100 N Fincl Dr Ste 101 Fresno (93720) ***(P-9498)***
Central Valley Concrete Inc (PA)....C....209 723-8846
3823 N State Highway 59 Merced (95348) ***(P-3990)***
Central Valley Environmental, Rohnert Park *Also called Cve Nb Contracting Group Inc* ***(P-27589)***
Central Valley Fund, The, Davis *Also called Cvf Capital Partners Inc* ***(P-12219)***
Central Valley General Hosp (HQ)....B....559 583-2100
1025 N Douty St Hanford (93230) ***(P-21307)***
Central Valley Indian Hlth Inc (PA)....D....559 299-2578
2740 Herndon Ave Clovis (93611) ***(P-19367)***
Central Valley Oprtnty Ctr Inc (PA)....C....209 357-0062
6838 Bridget Ct Winton (95388) ***(P-24165)***
Central Valley Party Supply....E....209 569-0399
3250 Dale Rd Ste I Modesto (95356) ***(P-14485)***
Central Valley Trucking, Merced *Also called Central Valley Concrete Inc* ***(P-3990)***
Central Valley YMCA, Fresno *Also called Central Vly Yng MNS Chrn Assoc* ***(P-25129)***
Central Vly Chld Svcs Netwrk....D....559 456-1100
1911 N Helm Ave Fresno (93727) ***(P-23552)***
Central Vly Regional Ctr Inc....C....559 738-2200
5441 W Cypress Ave Visalia (93277) ***(P-22524)***
Central Vly Specialty Hosp Inc....D....209 248-7700
730 17th St Modesto (95354) ***(P-20300)***
Central Vly Yng MNS Chrn Assoc....E....559 225-9191
4045 N Fresno St Ste 101 Fresno (93726) ***(P-25129)***
Centre Care Management Co LLC....C....858 613-6255
15611 Pomerado Rd Ste 400 Poway (92064) ***(P-19368)***
Centre For Health Care, Poway *Also called Centre Care Management Co LLC* ***(P-19368)***
Centre For Neuro Skills (PA)....C....661 872-3408
5215 Ashe Rd Bakersfield (93313) ***(P-22525)***
Centrelink Ins & Fincl Svcs, Woodland Hills *Also called Centrelink Insur & Fincl Svcs* ***(P-17065)***
Centrelink Insur & Fincl Svcs....D....818 587-2001
20750 Ventura Blvd # 300 Woodland Hills (91364) ***(P-17065)***
Centrescapes Inc....D....909 392-3303
165 Gentry St Pomona (91767) ***(P-810)***
Centrify Corporation (PA)....C....669 444-5200
3300 Tannery Way Santa Clara (95054) ***(P-15053)***
Centrl Territrl Salvation Army....D....714 832-7100
10200 Pioneer Rd Tustin (92782) ***(P-23553)***
Centro Inc....C....415 788-6190
115 Sansome St Ste 1200 San Francisco (94104) ***(P-15930)***
Centro De Salud De La (PA)....D....619 428-4463
4004 Beyer Blvd San Ysidro (92173) ***(P-22526)***
Centro De Salud De La....D....619 477-0165
1420 E Plaza Blvd Ste E4 National City (91950) ***(P-23554)***
Centurion Group, The, Los Angeles *Also called Mulholland SEC & Patrol Inc* ***(P-16736)***
Centurion Group, The, Los Angeles *Also called Centurion Security Inc* ***(P-16600)***
Centurion Security Inc....C....818 755-0202
11454 San Vicente Blvd Los Angeles (90049) ***(P-16600)***
Centurion Security Svcs Inc (PA)....D....949 474-0444
20102 Sw Cypress St Newport Beach (92660) ***(P-16601)***
Century 14, Roseville *Also called Century Theatres Inc* ***(P-18325)***
Century 21, Downey *Also called First Family Homes* ***(P-11453)***
Century 21, Inglewood *Also called Smith Coleman Inc* ***(P-11767)***
Century 21, Huntington Beach *Also called Beachside Realtors* ***(P-11233)***
Century 21, Downey *Also called Steve Roberson* ***(P-11779)***
Century 21, Monrovia *Also called Adams & Bames Inc* ***(P-11191)***
Century 21, Laguna Woods *Also called Rainbow Realty Corporation* ***(P-11700)***
Century 21, Redlands *Also called Lois Lauer Realty* ***(P-11566)***
Century 21, Porter Ranch *Also called Coast To Coast Realty* ***(P-11324)***
Century 21, Oakdale *Also called Premier Valley Inc* ***(P-11678)***
Century 21, Walnut Creek *Also called Kropa Realty* ***(P-11554)***
Century 21, Lakewood *Also called Rainbow Properties Inc* ***(P-11699)***
Century 21, Fresno *Also called Century Adanalian & Vasquez* ***(P-11309)***
Century 21, Rancho Cucamonga *Also called Excellnce of Inland Empire Inc* ***(P-11425)***
Century 21, Fullerton *Also called John G Shipley* ***(P-11533)***
Century 21, San Dimas *Also called National Credit Industries Inc* ***(P-9898)***
Century 21, Bellflower *Also called Leroy Durbin* ***(P-11564)***
Century 21, Cerritos *Also called Astro Realty Inc* ***(P-11223)***
Century 21, Whittier *Also called Beachside Realtors* ***(P-11234)***
Century 21....E....707 429-2121
301 Dickson Hill Rd Ste A Fairfield (94533) ***(P-11288)***
Century 21 A Better Svc Rlty....D....562 287-0230
8077 2nd St Fl Fl Downey (90241) ***(P-11289)***
Century 21 A Better Svc Rlty....D....562 806-1000
5831 Firestone Blvd Ste J South Gate (90280) ***(P-10580)***
Century 21 Able Inc....D....858 450-2100
3202 Governor Dr Ste 100 San Diego (92122) ***(P-11290)***
Century 21 Alpha LLC....D....408 369-2000
1630 W Campbell Ave Ste 1 Campbell (95008) ***(P-11291)***
Century 21 Amber Realty Inc....D....310 625-4363
21024 Wood Ave Apt A Torrance (90503) ***(P-11292)***
Century 21 Beachside....D....562 430-2121
6265 E 2nd St Ste 103 Long Beach (90803) ***(P-11293)***
Century 21 Beverlywood Realty....D....310 836-8321
2800 S Robertson Blvd Los Angeles (90034) ***(P-11294)***
Century 21 Crest....D....818 248-9100
4005 Foothill Blvd La Crescenta (91214) ***(P-11295)***
Century 21 Dstnctive Prpts Inc....D....707 678-9211
1450 Ary Ln Ste A Dixon (95620) ***(P-11296)***
Century 21 E, Diamond Bar *Also called E-N Realty II* ***(P-11413)***
Century 21 Excellence....E....562 948-4553
5207 Rosemead Blvd Ste 1 Pico Rivera (90660) ***(P-11297)***
Century 21 Exclusive Realtors....C....310 373-5252
22831 Hawthorne Blvd Torrance (90505) ***(P-11298)***
Century 21 Experience, Alta Loma *Also called Expreal Inc* ***(P-11426)***
Century 21 Golden Hills, San Jose *Also called Qal Affiliate Inc* ***(P-11697)***
Century 21 Golden Realty (PA)....D....626 797-6680
482 N Rosemead Blvd Pasadena (91107) ***(P-11299)***
Century 21 Green Gable RE, Dixon *Also called Century 21 Dstnctive Prpts Inc* ***(P-11296)***
Century 21 Haley & Associates....D....916 782-1500
699 Wshington Blvd Ste B5 Roseville (95678) ***(P-11300)***
Century 21 Hill Top Realtors, Simi Valley *Also called First & La Realty Corp* ***(P-11448)***
Century 21 Home Realtors (PA)....D....909 591-0158
4110 Edison Ave Ste 210 Chino (91710) ***(P-11301)***
Century 21 Home Realtors....D....909 980-8000
8338 Day Creek Blvd # 101 Rancho Cucamonga (91739) ***(P-11302)***
Century 21 King Realtors, Rancho Cucamonga *Also called Century 21 Home Realtors* ***(P-11302)***
Century 21 Landmark Properties....E....562 422-0911
1650 Ximeno Ave Ste 120 Long Beach (90804) ***(P-11303)***
Century 21 Les Ryan Realty (PA)....D....707 468-0423
495 E Perkins St Ste A Ukiah (95482) ***(P-11304)***
Century 21 Les Ryan Realty....D....707 577-7777
1057 College Ave Ofc Ste Santa Rosa (95404) ***(P-11305)***
Century 21 Ludecke Inc (PA)....D....626 445-0123
34 E Foothill Blvd Arcadia (91006) ***(P-11306)***
Century 21 Masters....D....626 732-6184
480 W Rowland St Ste B Covina (91723) ***(P-11307)***
Century 21 Powerhouse Realty, Huntington Park *Also called Powerhouse Realty Inc* ***(P-11675)***
Century 21 Showcase Inc....D....909 936-9334
7835 Church St Highland (92346) ***(P-11308)***
Century 8, North Hollywood *Also called Century Theatres Inc* ***(P-18327)***
Century Adanalian & Vasquez....D....559 244-6000
1415 W Shaw Ave Fresno (93711) ***(P-11309)***
Century Bankcard Services....D....818 700-3100
25129 The Old Rd Ste 222 Stevenson Ranch (91381) ***(P-17066)***
Century City Primary Care....E....310 553-3189
2080 Century Park E # 1605 Los Angeles (90067) ***(P-19369)***
Century Commercial Service....E....530 823-1004
12820 Earhart Ave Auburn (95602) ***(P-7344)***
Century Contract Services Inc....C....858 672-4118
15815 Camino Codorniz San Diego (92127) ***(P-14209)***
Century Electronics, Newbury Park *Also called Perillo Industries Inc* ***(P-7524)***
Century Finance Incorporated....D....310 281-3081
2461 Santa Monica Blvd Santa Monica (90404) ***(P-9790)***
Century Huntington Beach & Xd, Huntington Beach *Also called Cinemark Usa Inc* ***(P-18280)***
Century National, Encino *Also called Kramer-Wilson Company Inc* ***(P-10365)***
Century National Properties (PA)....D....818 760-0880
12200 Sylvan St Ste 250 North Hollywood (91606) ***(P-10862)***
Century Pk Capitl Partners LLC (PA)....C....310 867-2210
2101 Rosecrans Ave # 4275 El Segundo (90245) ***(P-12059)***
Century Plaza Garage....C....310 226-7495
2049 Century Park E Ste D Los Angeles (90067) ***(P-17681)***
Century Properties Owners Assn....E....310 272-8580
1 W Century Dr Los Angeles (90067) ***(P-11310)***
Century Skill Care....D....310 672-1012
301 Centinela Ave Inglewood (90302) ***(P-20301)***
Century Skilled Nursing Care, Inglewood *Also called Century Skill Care* ***(P-20301)***
Century Stadium....D....916 922-4241
1590 Ethan Way Sacramento (95825) ***(P-18277)***
Century Stadium 21, Sacramento *Also called Century Stadium* ***(P-18277)***
Century Theatres Inc....D....916 797-3466
1555 Eureka Rd Roseville (95661) ***(P-18325)***

Century Theatres Inc......D......510 758-9626
3200 Klose Way Richmond (94806) *(P-18326)*
Century Theatres Inc......D......818 508-1943
12827 Victory Blvd North Hollywood (91606) *(P-18327)*
Century Vision Developers Inc......E......925 588-7390
3000 Oak Rd Ste 360 Walnut Creek (94597) *(P-1500)*
Century West Plumbing, Westlake Village *Also called Sdg Enterprises (P-2351)*
Century Wilshire Hotel, Culver City *Also called Century Wilshire Inc (P-12446)*
Century Wilshire Inc......D......310 558-9400
9400 Culver Blvd Culver City (90232) *(P-12446)*
Century, The, Los Angeles *Also called Century Properties Owners Assn (P-11310)*
Century-National Insurance Co (HQ)......B......818 760-0880
16650 Sherman Way Ste 200 Van Nuys (91406) *(P-10133)*
Cep America LLC......D......510 350-2691
2100 Powell St Ste 900 Emeryville (94608) *(P-19370)*
Ceps, Sacramento *Also called Consultnts In Edctl Per Skills (P-23616)*
Ceramic Decorating Company Inc......E......323 268-5135
4651 Sheila St Commerce (90040) *(P-17067)*
Ceramic Tile Art Inc......D......818 767-9088
11601 Pendleton St Sun Valley (91352) *(P-2990)*
Cerebral Palsy Assn San Joaqui, Stockton *Also called United Cerebral Palsy Assoc (P-25048)*
Cerenzia Foods Inc......D......909 989-4000
8585 White Oak Ave Rancho Cucamonga (91730) *(P-8388)*
Ceridian LLC......D......310 719-7400
1515 W 190th St Ste 100 Gardena (90248) *(P-26162)*
Ceridian Tax Service Inc......B......714 963-1311
17390 Brookhurst St # 100 Fountain Valley (92708) *(P-26163)*
Cerritos Cinemas 10, Artesia *Also called Edwards Theatres Circuit Inc (P-18296)*
Cerritos Medical Office Bldg, Cerritos *Also called Kaiser Foundation Hospitals (P-19547)*
Certainteed Gypsum Inc......E......949 282-5300
27442 Portola Pkwy # 100 El Toro (92610) *(P-6814)*
Certapro Painters, San Francisco *Also called Norcal Painters Inc (P-2461)*
Certent Inc (PA)......C......925 730-4300
1548 Eureka Rd Ste 100 Roseville (95661) *(P-15054)*
Certified Air Conditioning Inc......C......858 292-5740
12520 High Bluff Dr # 312 San Diego (92130) *(P-2158)*
Certified Aviation Svcs LLC......D......310 338-1224
5720 Avion Dr Los Angeles (90045) *(P-4876)*
Certified Coatings Company......D......707 639-4414
2320 Cordelia Rd Fairfield (94534) *(P-2428)*
Certified Frt Logistics Inc (PA)......C......805 925-9900
1344 White Ct Santa Maria (93458) *(P-4116)*
Certified Nursing Registry Inc......C......626 912-1877
2707 E Valley Blvd # 309 West Covina (91792) *(P-14586)*
Certified Trnsp Svcs Inc......D......714 835-8676
1038 N Custer St Santa Ana (92701) *(P-3911)*
Cerutti Bros Inc......D......209 862-2249
26118 Mcclintock Rd Newman (95360) *(P-42)*
Cesar Chavez Student Center......C......415 338-7362
1650 Holloway Ave Rm C134 San Francisco (94132) *(P-10863)*
Cesars Productions......E......415 821-1156
91 Miguel St San Francisco (94131) *(P-17068)*
Cessna Scrmnto Ctation Svc Ctr, Sacramento *Also called Textron Aviation Inc (P-4919)*
CETEC SOLUTIONS, Gardena *Also called Charles E Thomas Company Inc (P-1501)*
Cetecom Inc (HQ)......D......408 586-6200
411 Dixon Landing Rd Milpitas (95035) *(P-27682)*
Cetera Financial Group Inc (PA)......C......866 489-3100
200 N Pacific Coast Hwy # 11 El Segundo (90245) *(P-17069)*
Ceva Inc......B......650 417-7900
1174 Castro St Ste 210 Mountain View (94040) *(P-12135)*
Ceva Freight LLC......D......310 972-5500
19600 S Western Ave Torrance (90501) *(P-5027)*
Ceva Freight LLC......C......916 379-6000
8670 Younger Creek Dr Sacramento (95828) *(P-5028)*
Ceva Logistics LLC......B......310 223-6500
19600 S Western Ave Torrance (90501) *(P-5029)*
Ceva Logistics US Inc......E......951 332-3202
11290 Cntu Gllano Rnch Rd Mira Loma (91752) *(P-4668)*
Ceva Ocean Line, Torrance *Also called Ceva Freight LLC (P-5027)*
Ceva Ocean Line, Sacramento *Also called Ceva Freight LLC (P-5028)*
CF Merced La Sierra LLC......D......209 723-4224
2424 M St Merced (95340) *(P-20302)*
CF San Rafael LLC......D......415 479-5161
81 Professional Ctr Pkwy San Rafael (94903) *(P-20303)*
CF Watsonville LLC......D......831 724-7505
525 Auto Center Dr Watsonville (95076) *(P-20304)*
CF Watsonville East LLC......D......310 574-3733
535 Auto Center Dr Watsonville (95076) *(P-20305)*
CF Watsonville West LLC......D......831 724-7505
525 Auto Center Dr Watsonville (95076) *(P-20306)*
Cfgi LLC......C......415 670-9041
600 California St Fl 14 San Francisco (94108) *(P-26164)*
Cfhc, Los Angeles *Also called Essential Access Health (P-24780)*
Cfhs Holdings Inc......A......310 823-8911
4650 Lincoln Blvd Marina Del Rey (90292) *(P-21308)*
Cfhs Holdings Inc......A......310 448-7800
4640 Admiralty Way # 650 Marina Del Rey (90292) *(P-21309)*
Cfhs Holdings Inc......A......310 673-4660
555 E Hardy St Inglewood (90301) *(P-21310)*
Cfp Fire Protection Inc......D......949 338-4280
17461 Derian Ave Ste 114 Irvine (92614) *(P-2159)*
Cfr Rinkens LLC (PA)......D......310 639-7725
15501 Texaco Ave Paramount (90723) *(P-5030)*
CFS Income Tax, Simi Valley *Also called CFS Tax Software (P-15624)*
CFS Tax Software......D......805 522-1157
1445 E Los Angeles Ave # 214 Simi Valley (93065) *(P-15624)*
Cg2 Inc......D......407 737-8800
1759 Mccarthy Blvd Milpitas (95035) *(P-26611)*
CGB, Gardena *Also called Pulp Studio Incorporated (P-14127)*
Cgi Technologies Solutions Inc......E......916 281-3200
860 Stillwater Rd Ste 210 West Sacramento (95605) *(P-26347)*
Cgi Technologies Solutions Inc......D......510 238-5300
505 14th St Fl 9 Oakland (94612) *(P-16326)*
Cgl Companies LLC......D......916 678-7890
2485 Natomas Park Dr # 300 Sacramento (95833) *(P-26032)*
Cgp Holdings LLC......D......760 764-1300
2 Gill Station Coastal Rd Little Lake (93542) *(P-6551)*
Cgtech (PA)......E......949 753-1050
9000 Research Dr Irvine (92618) *(P-15931)*
Cgtech Vericut, Irvine *Also called Cgtech (P-15931)*
Ch Cupertino Owner LLC......C......408 253-8900
10050 S De Anza Blvd Cupertino (95014) *(P-12447)*
Ch Market Center Inc......D......909 628-9100
4200 Chino Health Ste 325 Chino Hills (91709) *(P-11311)*
Ch Reynolds, San Jose *Also called C H Reynolds Electric Inc (P-2534)*
CH Robinson Freight Svcs Ltd......E......310 515-7755
680 Knox St Ste 210 Torrance (90502) *(P-5031)*
Ch2m Hill Inc......E......916 920-0300
2485 Natomas Park Dr # 600 Sacramento (95833) *(P-26033)*
Ch2m Hill Inc......C......530 243-5832
2525 Airpark Dr Redding (96001) *(P-25604)*
Ch2m Hill Inc......A......916 920-0300
2485 Natomas Park Dr # 600 Sacramento (95833) *(P-25605)*
Ch2m Hill Inc......C......510 604-4144
155 Grand Ave Ste 800 Oakland (94612) *(P-25606)*
Ch2m Hill Inc......E......408 436-4936
1737 N 1st St Ste 300 San Jose (95112) *(P-26034)*
Ch2m Hill Constructors Inc......B......916 920-0212
2485 Natomas Park Dr # 600 Sacramento (95833) *(P-1907)*
Cha Hollywood Medical Ctr LP (PA)......A......213 413-3000
1300 N Vermont Ave Los Angeles (90027) *(P-21311)*
Cha-Dor Realty......D......916 624-0627
4243 Dominguez Rd Rocklin (95677) *(P-6815)*
Chabad House, San Diego *Also called Friends Chbad Lbvtch San Diego (P-23815)*
Chad Garrett Investigations, North Hollywood *Also called Protection Specialists (P-16768)*
Chaduxtt JV......D......619 525-7188
1230 Columbia St Ste 1000 San Diego (92101) *(P-25607)*
Chadwick Center For Children &......E......858 966-5814
3020 Childrens Way San Diego (92123) *(P-19371)*
Challenge Dairy Products Inc......E......323 724-3130
5741 Smithway St Commerce (90040) *(P-8516)*
Challenge Dairy Products Inc (HQ)......D......925 828-6160
6701 Donlon Way Dublin (94568) *(P-8517)*
Challenger Ent, Anaheim *Also called Challenger Industries Inc (P-27683)*
Challenger Industries Inc......D......714 630-4344
2971 E White Star Ave Anaheim (92806) *(P-27683)*
Challenger Schools......D......408 723-0111
4949 Harwood Rd San Jose (95124) *(P-24276)*
Challenger Schools......E......408 266-7073
4949 Harwood Rd San Jose (95124) *(P-24277)*
Challenger Sheet Metal Inc......D......619 596-8040
9353 Abraham Way Ste A Santee (92071) *(P-3136)*
Chalmers Corporation......D......562 948-4850
7901 Crossway Dr Pico Rivera (90660) *(P-1385)*
Chamberlains Children Ctr Inc......D......831 636-2121
1850 Cienega Rd Hollister (95023) *(P-24461)*
Chamberpac, San Jose *Also called San Jose Silicon Valley Cham (P-24979)*
Chambers Belt Company......D......760 602-9688
5840 El Camino Real Ste 1 Carlsbad (92008) *(P-8348)*
Chambers Group Inc......D......949 261-5414
17671 Cowan Ste 100 Irvine (92614) *(P-27684)*
Chaminade At Santa Cruz, Santa Cruz *Also called Chaminade Ltd (P-12448)*
Chaminade Ltd......C......831 475-5600
1 Chaminade Ln Santa Cruz (95065) *(P-12448)*
Chaminade of Santa Cruz, Santa Cruz *Also called Lho Santa Cruz One Lesse Inc (P-12851)*
Chaminade of Santa Cruz, Santa Cruz *Also called Benchmark-Tech Corporation (P-17028)*
Champagne Landscape Nurs Inc......D......559 277-8188
3233 N Cornelia Ave Fresno (93722) *(P-811)*
Champion Electric Inc......D......951 276-9619
3950 Garner Rd Riverside (92501) *(P-2539)*
Champion Signs Incorporated......E......858 751-2900
7835 Wilkerson Ct San Diego (92111) *(P-14102)*
Champion Transportation Svcs, Pico Rivera *Also called AP Express International LLC (P-5220)*
Championship Golf Services Inc......C......951 272-4340
2340 Silver Oak Cir Corona (92882) *(P-18693)*
Chamson Management Inc......D......714 751-2400
7 Hutton Centre Dr Santa Ana (92707) *(P-12449)*
Chance Group LLC......E......310 343-3766
911 E 106th St Los Angeles (90002) *(P-8293)*
Chancellor Hlth Care Cal I Inc (PA)......D......909 796-0235
25383 Cole St Loma Linda (92354) *(P-21036)*
Chandler Convalescent Hospital......D......818 240-1610
525 S Central Ave Glendale (91204) *(P-20307)*
Change Healthcare Tech LLC......C......559 455-4000
5110 E Clinton Way # 101 Fresno (93727) *(P-17070)*
Change Hlthcare Operations LLC......D......805 777-7773
241 Lombard St Thousand Oaks (91360) *(P-16105)*
Changeorg Inc......C......415 817-1840
383 Rhode Island St # 300 San Francisco (94103) *(P-16210)*
Changing Tides Family Services (PA)......C......707 444-8293
2259 Myrtle Ave Eureka (95501) *(P-24278)*
Channel 4-NBC 4 Television, Burbank *Also called Access Hollywood (P-5765)*

ALPHABETIC

Employee Codes: A=Over 500 employees, B=251-500
C=101-250, D=51-100, E=50
2019 Directory of California
Wholesalers and Services Companies
© Mergent Inc. 1-800-342-5647
1247

Channel 40 Inc ....C....916 454-4422
4655 Fruitridge Rd Sacramento (95820) ***(P-5777)***
Channel Intelligence Inc (HQ) ....D....321 939-5600
1600 Amphitheatre Pkwy Mountain View (94043) ***(P-5530)***
Channel Islands Young Mens Ch ....D....805 736-3483
201 W College Ave Lompoc (93436) ***(P-25130)***
Channel Islands Young Mens Ch ....D....805 484-0423
3111 Village Park Dr Camarillo (93012) ***(P-25131)***
Channel Islands Young Mens Ch ....C....805 687-7727
36 Hitchcock Way Santa Barbara (93105) ***(P-25132)***
Channel Islands Young Mens Ch ....D....805 969-3288
591 Santa Rosa Ln Santa Barbara (93108) ***(P-25133)***
Channel Islands Young Mens Ch ....C....805 484-0423
3760 Telegraph Rd Ventura (93003) ***(P-25134)***
Channel Islands Young Mens Ch ....D....805 686-2037
900 N Refugio Rd Santa Ynez (93460) ***(P-25135)***
Channel Islnds Vgtble Frms Inc (PA) ....D....805 984-1910
595 Victoria Ave Oxnard (93030) ***(P-309)***
Channel Medical Center, Stockton *Also called Community Medical Centers Inc* ***(P-19400)***
Channing House ....D....650 327-0950
850 Webster St Ofc Palo Alto (94301) ***(P-21037)***
Chap, Pasadena *Also called Community Hlth Alance Pasadena* ***(P-21331)***
Chapa-De Indian Health (PA) ....D....530 887-2800
11670 Atwood Rd Auburn (95603) ***(P-19372)***
Chaparral Foundation ....D....510 848-8774
1309 Allston Way Berkeley (94702) ***(P-20308)***
Chaparral House, Berkeley *Also called Chaparral Foundation* ***(P-20308)***
Chapel Funding Corporation ....C....949 580-1800
26521 Rancho Pkwy S Lake Forest (92630) ***(P-9791)***
Chapel of Chimes (HQ) ....D....510 471-3363
32992 Mission Blvd Hayward (94544) ***(P-11939)***
Chapel of Chimes ....E....510 654-1288
4499 Piedmont Ave Oakland (94611) ***(P-13687)***
Chapel of Chimes ....D....650 349-4411
100 Lifemark Rd Redwood City (94062) ***(P-11940)***
Chapman Family Health, Orange *Also called Chapman Global Medical Center* ***(P-21312)***
Chapman Global Medical Center ....B....714 633-0011
2601 E Chapman Ave Orange (92869) ***(P-21312)***
Chapman Golf Development LLC ....D....760 564-8723
78505 Avenue 52 La Quinta (92253) ***(P-18887)***
Chapman Hbr Sklled Nrsing Care ....D....714 971-5517
12232 Chapman Ave Garden Grove (92840) ***(P-20309)***
Chapman University ....C....714 997-6821
625 N Glassell St Orange (92867) ***(P-17071)***
Chapman/Leonard Studio Eqp Inc (PA) ....C....323 877-5309
12950 Raymer St North Hollywood (91605) ***(P-18181)***
Chapmn-Hrbor Sklled Nrsing Ctr, Garden Grove *Also called Chapman Hbr Sklled Nrsing Care* ***(P-20309)***
Chappellet Vineyard ....E....707 286-4219
1581 Sage Canyon Rd Saint Helena (94574) ***(P-134)***
Charanjit Singh Batth ....D....559 864-9421
5434 W Kamm Ave Caruthers (93609) ***(P-185)***
Chardonnay, NAPA *Also called NAPA Golf Associates LLC* ***(P-18983)***
Chardonnay Golf Club, NAPA *Also called Chardonnay/ Club Shakespeare* ***(P-18888)***
Chardonnay/ Club Shakespeare ....D....707 257-1900
2555 Jamieson Canyon Rd NAPA (94558) ***(P-18888)***
Chargers Football Company LLC (PA) ....D....619 280-2121
3333 Susan St Costa Mesa (92626) ***(P-18514)***
Chariot Travelware, Ontario *Also called Damao Luggage Intl Inc* ***(P-8025)***
Charlee Family Care ....D....951 845-3588
136 E Sixth St Beaumont (92223) ***(P-24462)***
Charles & Cynthia Eberly Inc ....D....323 937-6468
8383 Wilshire Blvd # 906 Beverly Hills (90211) ***(P-11001)***
Charles Brooks Cmnty Swim Ctr, Woodland *Also called City of Woodland* ***(P-19145)***
Charles Culberson Inc ....C....650 335-4730
1084 Allen Way Campbell (95008) ***(P-2865)***
Charles Drew Univ Mdcine Scnce ....C....310 605-0164
135 W Victoria St Long Beach (90805) ***(P-24279)***
Charles Dunn Co Inc ....C....213 481-1800
800 W 6th St Ste 800 # 800 Los Angeles (90017) ***(P-11312)***
Charles Dunn Raltor State Svcs, Los Angeles *Also called Charles Dunn Co Inc* ***(P-11312)***
Charles Dunn RE Svcs Inc (PA) ....D....213 270-6200
800 W 6th St Ste 600 Los Angeles (90017) ***(P-11313)***
Charles E Thomas Company Inc (PA) ....D....310 323-6730
13701 Alma Ave Gardena (90249) ***(P-1501)***
Charles Fenley Enterprises ....E....209 523-2832
1109 Oakdale Rd Modesto (95355) ***(P-17808)***
Charles M Kamiya and Sons Inc ....D....310 781-2066
373 Van Ness Ave Ste 200 Torrance (90501) ***(P-10581)***
Charles McMurray Co (PA) ....D....559 292-5751
2520 N Argyle Ave Fresno (93727) ***(P-7583)***
Charles Pankow Bldrs Ltd A Cal (PA) ....E....626 304-1190
199 S Los Robles Ave # 300 Pasadena (91101) ***(P-1502)***
Charles Pankow Bldrs Ltd A Cal ....B....510 893-5170
1111 Broadway Ste 200 Oakland (94607) ***(P-1503)***
Charles Schwab & Co Inc, Brea *Also called Charles Schwab Corporation* ***(P-9927)***
Charles Schwab Corporation (PA) ....C....415 667-7000
211 Main St Fl 17 San Francisco (94105) ***(P-9925)***
Charles Schwab Corporation ....D....951 587-2840
27580 Ynez Rd Ste A Temecula (92591) ***(P-17072)***
Charles Schwab Corporation ....D....530 448-8038
10770 Donner Pass Rd # 103 Truckee (96161) ***(P-9926)***
Charles Schwab Corporation ....D....714 385-6000
3421 E Imperial Hwy Brea (92823) ***(P-9927)***
Charles Schwab Corporation ....D....415 294-3503
1400 Grant Ave Ste 101 Novato (94945) ***(P-9928)***
Charles Schwab Corporation ....E....858 523-2454
12481 High Bluff Dr # 100 San Diego (92130) ***(P-9929)***
Charles W Bowers Museum Corp ....D....714 567-3600
2002 N Main St Santa Ana (92706) ***(P-24868)***
Charleston Company, Los Angeles *Also called Walter J Conn & Associates* ***(P-26118)***
Charlie Mitchell Chld Clinic, Madera *Also called Valley Childrens Hospital* ***(P-21893)***
Charlie W Shaeffer Jr MD ....D....760 346-0642
39000 Bob Hope Dr Rancho Mirage (92270) ***(P-19373)***
Charlies Enterprises ....C....559 445-8600
1888 S East Ave Fresno (93721) ***(P-8652)***
Charming Trim & Packaging ....A....415 302-7021
28 Brookside Ct Novato (94947) ***(P-8223)***
Charolais Care V Inc ....D....415 921-5038
1426 Fillmore St Ste 207 San Francisco (94115) ***(P-22263)***
Charter Behavioral Health Syst ....D....626 966-1632
1161 E Covina Blvd Covina (91724) ***(P-21939)***
Charter Cmmnctons Oprating LLC ....D....760 452-8609
12180 Ridgecrest Rd # 102 Victorville (92395) ***(P-5860)***
Charter Cmmnctons Oprating LLC ....B....310 971-4001
4031 Via Oro Ave Long Beach (90810) ***(P-5861)***
Charter Cmmnctons Oprating LLC ....E....530 241-7352
5797 Eastside Rd Redding (96001) ***(P-5862)***
Charter Hospice Inc ....C....909 825-2969
1007 E Cooley Dr Ste 100 Colton (92324) ***(P-20920)***
Charter Oak Hospital, Covina *Also called Charter Behavioral Health Syst* ***(P-21939)***
Charter Realty Group Inc (PA) ....D....310 826-3174
12400 Wilshire Blvd Los Angeles (90025) ***(P-11314)***
Chase Bros Dairy, Ventura *Also called Hailwood Inc* ***(P-10890)***
Chase Care Center Inc ....C....323 935-8490
1101 Crenshaw Blvd Los Angeles (90019) ***(P-21038)***
Chase Credit Systems Inc ....D....818 762-6262
300 E Magnolia Blvd # 502 Burbank (91502) ***(P-15055)***
Chase Group Llc ....D....818 708-3533
6740 Wilbur Ave Reseda (91335) ***(P-27189)***
Chase Group Llc ....D....805 522-9155
5270 E Los Angeles Ave Simi Valley (93063) ***(P-27190)***
Chase Receivables, Sonoma *Also called Credit Bureau NAPA County Inc* ***(P-14001)***
Chase Suite and Woodfin Hotels, San Diego *Also called Woodfin Suite Hotels LLC* ***(P-13416)***
Chaser, Gardena *Also called Houston Salem Inc* ***(P-8307)***
Chateau At River's Edge, Sacramento *Also called Hank Fisher Properties Inc* ***(P-21104)***
Chateau La Jolla Inn ....E....858 459-4451
233 Prospect St La Jolla (92037) ***(P-12450)***
Chateau Lake San Marcos Homeow ....D....760 471-0083
1502 Circa Del Lago San Marcos (92078) ***(P-25136)***
Chateau On Capitol Avenue, The, Sacramento *Also called Hank Fisher Properties Inc* ***(P-24548)***
Chateau Pleasant Hill 2, Concord *Also called Carlton Senior Living Inc* ***(P-11862)***
Chateau San Juan, San Juan Capistrano *Also called Atria Senior Living Group Inc* ***(P-24426)***
Chateaux Framing Inc ....C....209 537-6799
3701 Georgeann Pl Ceres (95307) ***(P-3020)***
Chatham Inc ....E....800 222-2002
300 Rancheros Dr Ste 360 San Marcos (92069) ***(P-8006)***
Chatsworth Health & Rehab, Chatsworth *Also called Golden State Health Ctrs Inc* ***(P-21098)***
Chatsworth Park Hlth Care Ctr, Chatsworth *Also called Cpcc Inc* ***(P-21052)***
CHC, Los Angeles *Also called Covenant House California* ***(P-24485)***
Chcg Architects, Pasadena *Also called Gonzalez/Goodale Architects* ***(P-26051)***
Check Disc Labs ....D....818 847-2255
4121 W Vanowen Pl Burbank (91505) ***(P-27191)***
Check Point Software Tech Inc (HQ) ....C....650 628-2000
959 Skyway Rd Ste 300 San Carlos (94070) ***(P-15625)***
Checker Cab Co ....D....818 488-5088
14943 Califa St Van Nuys (91411) ***(P-3865)***
Cheema Freightlines LLC ....D....209 599-0777
223 W 5th St Ripon (95366) ***(P-5032)***
Cheema Logistics, Ripon *Also called Cheema Freightlines LLC* ***(P-5032)***
Cheese Plant, Hanford *Also called Marquez Brothers Intl Inc* ***(P-8426)***
Chef Works Inc (PA) ....C....858 643-5600
12325 Kerran St Poway (92064) ***(P-8252)***
Chefs Warehouse Westcoast LLC (HQ) ....D....626 465-4200
16633 Gale Ave City of Industry (91745) ***(P-8389)***
Chelbay Schuler & Chelbay (PA) ....D....408 288-4400
6800 Santa Teresa Blvd # 100 San Jose (95119) ***(P-10482)***
Chelsio Communications Inc ....C....408 962-3600
209 N Fair Oaks Ave Sunnyvale (94085) ***(P-15056)***
Chem Lab Rkfe, Edwards *Also called US Dept of the Air Force* ***(P-26486)***
Chem Quip Inc ....D....800 821-1678
2551 Land Ave Sacramento (95815) ***(P-7925)***
Chemical Dependency Recovery ....E....916 482-1132
2829 Watt Ave Ste 150 Sacramento (95821) ***(P-8923)***
Chemical Waste Management Inc ....D....559 386-9711
35251 Old Skyline Rd Kettleman City (93239) ***(P-6372)***
Chemtrans, Gardena *Also called Radford Alexander Corporation* ***(P-4053)***
Chen Dvid MD Dgnstc Med Group ....C....626 566-3900
25 N Santa Anita Ave Arcadia (91006) ***(P-7174)***
Cheque Guard Inc ....D....818 563-9335
512 S Verdugo Dr Burbank (91502) ***(P-15057)***
Cher Ae Heights Casino, Trinidad *Also called Cher-Ae Heights Indian Cmnty* ***(P-19121)***
Cher-Ae Heights Indian Cmnty ....C....707 677-3611
27 Scenic Dr Trinidad (95570) ***(P-19121)***
Cherokee Freight Lines, Stockton *Also called Scan-Vino LLC* ***(P-4259)***
Cherry Avenue Auction Inc ....E....559 266-9856
4640 S Cherry Ave Fresno (93706) ***(P-17073)***
Cherry City Electric, City of Industry *Also called Morrow-Meadows Corporation* ***(P-2652)***
Chesapeake Lodging Trust ....D....415 296-2900
333 Battery St Lbby San Francisco (94111) ***(P-12451)***
Chester Avenue Medical Offices, Bakersfield *Also called Kaiser Foundation Hospitals* ***(P-19544)***

Mergent e-mail: customerrelations@mergent.com
1248
2019 Directory of California Wholesalers and Services Companies
(P-0000) Products & Services Section entry number
(PA)=Parent Co (HQ)=Headquarters (DH)=Div Headquarters

Chester Avenue Medical Offs II, Bakersfield *Also called Kaiser Foundation Hospitals (P-19545)*
Chester C Lehmann Co Inc (PA)............D.......408 293-5818
1135 Auzerais Ave San Jose (95126) *(P-7345)*
Chester Public Utility Dst............D.......530 258-2171
251 Chester Airport Rd Chester (96020) *(P-6195)*
Chevron, Modesto *Also called Charles Fenley Enterprises (P-17808)*
Chevron, Campbell *Also called Lark Avenue Car Wash (P-17824)*
Chevron, Davis *Also called Tera Investments Inc (P-12274)*
Chevron Energy Technology Co (HQ)............D.......510 242-5059
100 Chevron Way Richmond (94801) *(P-25608)*
Chevron Investor Inc (HQ)............B.......925 842-1000
6001 Bollinger Canyon Rd San Ramon (94583) *(P-12214)*
Chevron Investor Inc............D.......510 242-3000
100 Chevron Way Richmond (94801) *(P-26801)*
Chevron Mining Inc............B.......760 856-7625
67750 Bailey Rd Mountain Pass (92366) *(P-1008)*
Chevron USA Inc............D.......925 842-0855
6001 Bollinger Canyon Rd San Ramon (94583) *(P-1021)*
Chhp Management LLC............D.......323 583-1931
2623 E Slauson Ave Huntington Park (90255) *(P-21313)*
Chiala, George Packing, Morgan Hill *Also called George Chiala Farms Inc (P-57)*
CHIBI CHAN PRESCHOOL, San Francisco *Also called Japanese Cmnty Youth Council (P-24792)*
Chicago Title & Escrow............E.......760 746-3882
316 W Mission Ave Ste 110 Escondido (92025) *(P-10437)*
Chicago Title and Trust Co............E.......818 548-0222
535 N Brnd Blvrd Fl 3 Flr 3 Glendale (91203) *(P-10438)*
Chicago Title Company............C.......619 230-6340
701 B St Ste 1120 San Diego (92101) *(P-10439)*
Chicago Title Company............D.......213 488-4375
725 S Figueroa St Ste 200 Los Angeles (90017) *(P-10440)*
Chicago Title Company............D.......559 451-3700
7330 N Palm Ave Ste 101 Fresno (93711) *(P-10441)*
Chicago Title Insurance Co............D.......209 952-5500
3127 Transworld Dr # 103 Stockton (95206) *(P-11847)*
Chicago Title Insurance Co............E.......916 985-0300
105 Lake Forest Way Folsom (95630) *(P-10442)*
Chicago Title Insurance Co............D.......805 656-1300
500 E Esplanade Dr # 102 Oxnard (93036) *(P-10443)*
Chicago Title Insurance Co............D.......760 546-1000
316 W Mission Ave Ste 110 Escondido (92025) *(P-10444)*
Chicago Title Insurance Co............B.......916 783-7195
925 Highland Pointe Dr # 340 Roseville (95678) *(P-10445)*
Chicago Title Insurance Co (HQ)............C.......805 565-6900
4050 Calle Real Santa Barbara (93110) *(P-10446)*
Chicago Title Insurance Co............D.......559 733-3814
120 N Floral St Visalia (93291) *(P-10447)*
Chicken of Sea International, El Segundo *Also called Tri-Union Seafoods LLC (P-8608)*
Chicken Ranch Bingo & Casino............C.......209 984-3000
16929 Chicken Ranch Rd Jamestown (95327) *(P-19122)*
Chico Area Recreation & Pk Dst (PA)............C.......530 895-4711
545 Vallombrosa Ave Chico (95926) *(P-19123)*
Chico Creek Care Rhabilitation, Chico *Also called Helios Healthcare LLC (P-21107)*
Chico Csu............D.......530 898-3917
400 W 1st St Chico (95929) *(P-22765)*
Chico Csu Research Foundation............A.......530 898-6811
25 Main St Unit 203 Chico (95928) *(P-25137)*
Chico Electric Inc............D.......530 891-1933
36 W Eaton Rd Chico (95973) *(P-2540)*
Chico Family Health Center, Chico *Also called Ampla Health (P-19288)*
Chico Immdate Care Med Ctr Inc (PA)............E.......530 891-1676
376 Vallombrosa Ave Chico (95926) *(P-19374)*
Chico Paramedic Rescue, Chico *Also called First Rsponder Emrgncy Med Svc (P-3797)*
Chico Produce Inc (PA)............C.......530 893-0596
70 Pepsi Way Durham (95938) *(P-8653)*
Chico Sports Club, Chico *Also called Jeff Stover Inc (P-18616)*
Chico V A Outpatient Clinic, Chico *Also called Veterans Health Administration (P-20067)*
Chidren's Hospital Center, Los Angeles *Also called Childrens Hospital Los Angeles (P-22007)*
Chief Engineering Co, Lake Elsinore *Also called Chief Trnsp & Engrg Contrs Inc (P-1737)*
Chief Protective Services Inc............D.......951 738-0881
1344 W 6th St Ste 300 Corona (92882) *(P-16602)*
Chief San Diego Hotel LLC............D.......619 239-2400
601 Pacific Hwy San Diego (92101) *(P-12452)*
Chief Trnsp & Engrg Contrs Inc............D.......951 258-6607
4056 Tamarind Rdg Lake Elsinore (92530) *(P-1737)*
Chikpea Inc............E.......888 342-3828
1 Market St Spear Spear Tower San Francisco (94127) *(P-27685)*
Child & Family Center............C.......661 259-9439
21545 Centre Pointe Pkwy Santa Clarita (91350) *(P-23555)*
Child & Family Services, Orland *Also called Glenn County Office Education (P-24325)*
Child Abuse Lstening Mediation............E.......805 965-2376
1236 Chapala St Santa Barbara (93101) *(P-23556)*
CHILD ABUSE PREVENTION, Oakland *Also called Family Paths Inc (P-22578)*
Child Action Inc (PA)............B.......916 369-4460
9800 Old Winery Pl Sacramento (95827) *(P-24280)*
Child and Family Guidance Ctr............D.......661 265-8627
310 E Plmdle Blvd G Palmdale (93550) *(P-22527)*
Child and Family Guidance Ctr (PA)............C.......818 739-5140
9650 Zelzah Ave Northridge (91325) *(P-22528)*
Child and Family Guidance Ctr............E.......818 830-0200
8550 Balboa Blvd Ste 150 Northridge (91325) *(P-22529)*
Child Care, Fresno *Also called Kid Iq 24 Hr Childcare (P-24331)*
Child Care Coordinating Counsi............E.......650 517-1400
330 Twin Dolphin Dr # 119 Redwood City (94065) *(P-23557)*
Child Care Resource Center Inc (PA)............C.......818 717-1000
20001 Prairie St Chatsworth (91311) *(P-23558)*
Child Care Resource Center Inc............B.......661 255-2474
20001 Prairie St Chatsworth (91311) *(P-23559)*
Child Care Resource Center Inc............E.......661 723-3246
250 Grand Cypress Ave # 601 Palmdale (93551) *(P-23560)*
Child Day School (PA)............D.......925 284-7092
1049 Stuart St Lafayette (94549) *(P-24281)*
Child Development Assoc Inc (PA)............C.......619 427-4411
180 Otay Lakes Rd Ste 310 Bonita (91902) *(P-24282)*
Child Development Center............E.......858 794-7160
309 N Rios Ave Solana Beach (92075) *(P-24283)*
Child Development Centers, Morgan Hill *Also called Child Development Incorporated (P-24284)*
Child Development Incorporated (PA)............E.......408 556-7300
350 Woodview Ave Morgan Hill (95037) *(P-24284)*
Child Development Incorporated............B.......714 842-4064
17341 Jacquelyn Ln Huntington Beach (92647) *(P-11315)*
Child Development Incorporated............A.......949 725-0961
2005 Knollcrest Irvine (92603) *(P-24285)*
Child Development Incorporated............A.......949 854-5060
5151 Amalfi Dr Irvine (92603) *(P-24286)*
Child Development Institute............E.......818 888-4559
6340 Variel Ave Ste A Woodland Hills (91367) *(P-23561)*
Child Development Office, The, Santa Monica *Also called Santa Monica City of (P-24379)*
Child Development Resources of (PA)............C.......805 485-7878
221 Ventura Blvd Oxnard (93036) *(P-23562)*
Child Educational Center............D.......818 354-3418
140 Foothill Blvd La Canada (91011) *(P-24287)*
Child Family & Cmnty Svcs Inc............C.......510 796-9512
32980 Alvarado Niles Rd # 856 Union City (94587) *(P-24288)*
Child Help Head Start Center, Beaumont *Also called Childhelp Inc (P-24463)*
Child Start Inc (PA)............C.......707 252-8931
439 Devlin Rd NAPA (94558) *(P-24289)*
Child Support Services, Commerce *Also called County of Los Angeles (P-23657)*
Child Support Services, San Francisco *Also called San Francisco City & County (P-24018)*
Child Support Svcs, Martinez *Also called County of Contra Costa (P-23634)*
Child Support Svcs Cal Dept (HQ)............D.......916 464-5000
11120 International Dr Rancho Cordova (95670) *(P-23563)*
Child360, Los Angeles *Also called Los Angles Universal Preschool (P-24343)*
Childcare Careers LLC............A.......650 372-0211
2000 Sierra Point Pkwy # 702 Brisbane (94005) *(P-14831)*
Childerns Spec of San Deigo, San Diego *Also called Stanley M Kirkpatrick MD (P-19944)*
Childhelp Inc............C.......951 845-6737
14700 Manzanita Rd Beaumont (92223) *(P-24463)*
Childnet Youth & Fmly Svcs Inc (PA)............C.......562 498-5500
4155 Outer Traffic Cir Long Beach (90804) *(P-23564)*
Childnet Youth & Fmly Svcs Inc............D.......562 492-9983
5150 E Pacific Cst Hwy # 100 Long Beach (90804) *(P-24464)*
Children & Family Serivces, Orange *Also called County of Orange (P-23700)*
Children & Family Svcs Dept, Santa Fe Springs *Also called County of Los Angeles (P-23659)*
Children & Family Svcs Dept, Los Angeles *Also called County of Los Angeles (P-23668)*
Children of Rainbow Inc (PA)............C.......619 615-0652
4890 Logan Ave San Diego (92113) *(P-24290)*
Children of The Rainbow Head............C.......619 266-7311
4890 Logan Ave San Diego (92113) *(P-24291)*
Children Services, San Bernardino *Also called County of San Bernardino (P-24483)*
CHILDREN'S DISCOVERY MUSEUM, Rancho Mirage *Also called Childrens Museum of Desert (P-24870)*
Children's Health Center, Chico *Also called Enloe Medical Center (P-19462)*
Children's Protective Services, Redding *Also called County of Shasta (P-23742)*
Childrens Angelcare Aid Intl............C.......619 795-6234
4535 58th St San Diego (92115) *(P-23565)*
Childrens Associated Med Group, San Diego *Also called Childrens Specialist of San D (P-19380)*
Childrens Botique, The, Rancho Cucamonga *Also called Childrens Btq At Stevens Hope (P-8294)*
Childrens Btq At Stevens Hope............E.......909 256-0100
10730 Fthill Blvd Ste 170 Rancho Cucamonga (91730) *(P-8294)*
Childrens Bureau Southern Cal (PA)............C.......213 342-0100
1910 Magnolia Ave Los Angeles (90007) *(P-24465)*
Childrens Clinic serving Chl............B.......562 264-4638
701 E 28th St Ste 200 Long Beach (90806) *(P-19375)*
Childrens Creativity Museum............D.......415 820-3320
221 4th St San Francisco (94103) *(P-24869)*
Childrens Crisis Cntr Stanisls............D.......209 577-4413
1244 Fiori Ave Modesto (95350) *(P-23566)*
Childrens Cuncil San Francisco (PA)............C.......415 343-3378
445 Church St San Francisco (94114) *(P-23567)*
Childrens Day School............E.......415 861-5432
333 Dolores St San Francisco (94110) *(P-24292)*
Childrens Healthcare Cal............A.......714 997-3000
455 S Main St Orange (92868) *(P-19376)*
Childrens Healthcare Cal (PA)............A.......714 997-3000
1201 W La Veta Ave Orange (92868) *(P-22004)*
Childrens Home of Stockton............D.......209 466-0853
430 N Pilgrim St Stockton (95205) *(P-24466)*
Childrens Home Southern Cal (PA)............E.......818 592-2960
22455 Victory Blvd West Hills (91307) *(P-24467)*
Childrens Hosp La Med Group, Los Angeles *Also called Childrens Hospital Los (P-19377)*
Childrens Hosp Okland Res Inst............D.......510 450-7600
5700 Martin Luther Oakland (94609) *(P-26612)*
Childrens Hospital Los (PA)............D.......323 361-2336
6430 W Sunset Blvd # 600 Los Angeles (90028) *(P-19377)*
Childrens Hospital Los Angeles............C.......818 728-4930
5359 Balboa Blvd Encino (91316) *(P-21314)*

ALPHABETIC

Employee Codes: A=Over 500 employees, B=251-500
C=101-250, D=51-100, E=50
2019 Directory of California
Wholesalers and Services Companies
© Mergent Inc. 1-800-342-5647
1249

Childrens Hospital Los Angeles....C....323 361-2153
5000 W Sunset Blvd # 400 Los Angeles (90027) ***(P-21315)***
Childrens Hospital Los Angeles (PA)....D....323 660-2450
4650 W Sunset Blvd Los Angeles (90027) ***(P-22005)***
Childrens Hospital Los Angeles....C....626 795-7177
468 E Santa Clara St Arcadia (91006) ***(P-21316)***
Childrens Hospital Los Angeles....C....310 820-8608
1301 20th St Ste 460 Santa Monica (90404) ***(P-19378)***
Childrens Hospital Los Angeles....B....323 361-2119
4650 W Sunset Blvd Los Angeles (90027) ***(P-19379)***
Childrens Hospital Los Angeles....C....323 361-2215
800 N Brand Blvd Glendale (91203) ***(P-22006)***
Childrens Hospital Los Angeles....B....323 361-2751
4661 W Sunset Blvd Los Angeles (90027) ***(P-26613)***
Childrens Hospital Los Angeles....B....714 841-4990
7891 Talbert Ave Ste 103 Huntington Beach (92648) ***(P-20114)***
Childrens Hospital Los Angeles....D....323 660-2450
4650 W Sunset Blvd Los Angeles (90027) ***(P-21317)***
Childrens Hospital Los Angeles....C....323 361-5702
4661 W Sunset Blvd Los Angeles (90027) ***(P-22007)***
Childrens Hospital Orange Cnty (PA)....D....714 997-3000
1201 W La Veta Ave Orange (92868) ***(P-22008)***
Childrens Hospital Orange Cnty....B....949 365-2416
455 S Main St Orange (92868) ***(P-22009)***
Childrens Hospital Orange Cnty....A....949 631-2062
500 Superior Ave Newport Beach (92663) ***(P-24293)***
Childrens Hospital Orange Cnty....A....949 387-2586
980 Roosevelt Irvine (92620) ***(P-21318)***
Childrens Hospotal & Research (PA)....A....510 428-3000
747 52nd St Oakland (94609) ***(P-21319)***
Childrens Inst Los Angeles....A....213 383-2765
679 S New Hampshire Ave Los Angeles (90005) ***(P-23568)***
Childrens Inst Los Angeles (PA)....A....213 385-5100
2121 W Temple St Los Angeles (90026) ***(P-26614)***
Childrens Institute Inc (PA)....B....213 385-5100
2121 W Temple St Los Angeles (90026) ***(P-23569)***
Childrens Laboratory, Encino *Also called Childrens Hospital Los Angeles* ***(P-21314)***
Childrens Law Center Cal (PA)....C....323 980-8700
101 Centre Plaza Dr Monterey Park (91754) ***(P-22974)***
Childrens Museum of Desert....E....760 321-0602
71701 Gerald Ford Dr Rancho Mirage (92270) ***(P-24870)***
Childrens Protective Services....D....530 749-6311
5730 Packard Ave Marysville (95901) ***(P-23570)***
Childrens Rcvery Ctr Nthrn Cal, Campbell *Also called Subacute Chld Hosp Cal Inc* ***(P-22052)***
Childrens Recvg Hm Sacramento....C....916 482-2370
3555 Auburn Blvd Sacramento (95821) ***(P-24468)***
Childrens Services....D....530 458-0300
345 5th St Ste A Colusa (95932) ***(P-23571)***
Childrens Specialist of San D (PA)....B....858 576-1700
3020 Childrens Way San Diego (92123) ***(P-19380)***
Childrens Specialist San Diego, San Diego *Also called Physician Management Group Inc* ***(P-26985)***
Childrens Vlg of Sonoma Cnty....E....707 566-7044
1321 Lia Ln Santa Rosa (95404) ***(P-24469)***
Chilis 898 Corona....D....951 734-7275
3579 Grand Oaks Corona (92881) ***(P-26802)***
China Airlines Ltd (HQ)....C....310 646-4233
11201 Aviation Blvd Los Angeles (90045) ***(P-4778)***
China Brma India Veterans Assn, San Jose *Also called General George W Sliney Basha* ***(P-25159)***
China Peak Mountain Resort LLC....D....559 233-2500
59265 Hwy 168 Lakeshore (93634) ***(P-12453)***
China Pearl, Pacoima *Also called CPI Luxury Group* ***(P-8007)***
China Yngxin Phrmceuticals Inc....A....626 581-9098
927 Canada Ct City of Industry (91748) ***(P-7175)***
Chinaamerica Film Distributors, San Marino *Also called Tricor Entertainment Inc* ***(P-18136)***
Chinatown Service Center (PA)....C....213 808-1700
767 N Hill St Ste 200b Los Angeles (90012) ***(P-24166)***
Chinese Cnsld Benevolent Assn....D....415 982-6000
843 Stockton St San Francisco (94108) ***(P-25138)***
Chinese Hospital Association (PA)....B....415 982-2400
845 Jackson St San Francisco (94133) ***(P-21320)***
Chinese Laundry Inc....E....310 945-3299
3485 S La Cienega Blvd Los Angeles (90016) ***(P-8349)***
Chinese Laundry Shoes, Los Angeles *Also called Cels Enterprises Inc* ***(P-8347)***
Chinese Laundry Shoes, Los Angeles *Also called Chinese Laundry Inc* ***(P-8349)***
Chino Grading Inc....D....909 364-8667
3613 Philadelphia St Chino (91710) ***(P-3418)***
Chino Medical Group Inc....D....909 591-6446
5475 Walnut Ave Chino (91710) ***(P-19381)***
Chino Rdological Registry Corp....D....909 591-6688
6719 Eagle Dr Chino (91710) ***(P-21321)***
Chino Valley Healthcare Center....D....909 628-1245
2351 S Towne Ave Pomona (91766) ***(P-20310)***
CHINO VALLEY MEDICAL CENTER, Chino *Also called Veritas Health Services Inc* ***(P-21897)***
Chino Valley Rock, Ontario *Also called Chino Valley Sawdust Inc* ***(P-6373)***
Chino Valley Sawdust Inc....D....909 947-5983
13434 S Ontario Ave Ontario (91761) ***(P-6373)***
Chino-Pacific Warehouse Corp (PA)....D....909 545-8100
3601 Jurupa St Ontario (91761) ***(P-4540)***
Chipman Corporation (PA)....E....510 748-8700
1040 Marina Village Pkwy # 100 Alameda (94501) ***(P-4336)***
Chipman Corporation....D....510 748-8787
1555 Zephyr Ave Hayward (94544) ***(P-4117)***
Chiquita Brands Intl Inc....D....213 488-0925
746 Market Ct Los Angeles (90021) ***(P-8654)***
Chiquita Fresh North Amer LLC....B....954 924-5642
1440 E 3rd St Oxnard (93030) ***(P-233)***
Chirag Hospitality Inc....D....415 922-0244
2440 Lombard St San Francisco (94123) ***(P-12454)***
Chiro Inc (PA)....D....909 879-1160
2260 S Vista Ave Bloomington (92316) ***(P-7884)***
Chiron Corporation....D....510 655-8730
4560 Horton St Emeryville (94608) ***(P-22766)***
Chlb LLC....D....562 997-2000
2776 Pacific Ave Long Beach (90806) ***(P-21940)***
Choa Hope LLC....E....712 277-4101
515 W Washington Ave Escondido (92025) ***(P-12455)***
Choc, Orange *Also called Childrens Hospital Orange Cnty* ***(P-22008)***
Choc Health Alliance....D....714 565-5100
1120 W La Veta Ave # 450 Orange (92868) ***(P-10193)***
Choc Mission, Orange *Also called Childrens Hospital Orange Cnty* ***(P-22009)***
Chodorow De Castro West....D....310 478-2541
10960 Wilshire Blvd # 1400 Los Angeles (90024) ***(P-22975)***
Choic Admini Insur Servi....B....714 542-4200
721 S Parker St Ste 200 Orange (92868) ***(P-10582)***
Choice Hotels Intl Inc....D....661 764-5207
20688 Tracy Ave Buttonwillow (93206) ***(P-12456)***
Choice In Aging (PA)....D....925 682-6330
490 Golf Club Rd Pleasant Hill (94523) ***(P-22530)***
Choice Internet, Irvine *Also called Cie Digital Labs LLC* ***(P-13971)***
Choice Medical Group Inc....D....916 483-2885
2322 Butano Dr Ste 205 Sacramento (95825) ***(P-22531)***
Choice Pak Products, Maywood *Also called Jack H Caldwell & Sons Inc* ***(P-8697)***
Choices For Children (PA)....D....408 297-3295
111 N Market St Ste 700 San Jose (95113) ***(P-24294)***
CHOICESS, Arcadia *Also called Community Housing Options* ***(P-23605)***
Chong Partners Architecher Inc....C....613 995-8210
901 Market St Ste 600 San Francisco (94103) ***(P-26035)***
Chooljian & Sons Inc (PA)....D....559 888-2031
5287 S Del Rey Ave Del Rey (93616) ***(P-503)***
Chooljian Bros Packing Co Inc....E....559 875-5501
3192 S Indianola Ave Sanger (93657) ***(P-8767)***
Choosing Independence Inc....D....818 257-0323
7615 Louise Ave Northridge (91325) ***(P-26803)***
Chopra Center For Wellbeing, Carlsbad *Also called Chopra Cntre For Wll-Being LLC* ***(P-19124)***
Chopra Cntre For Wll-Being LLC....D....760 494-1600
2013 Costa Del Mar Rd Carlsbad (92009) ***(P-19124)***
Choura Events....D....310 320-6200
540 Hawaii Ave Torrance (90503) ***(P-14486)***
Choura Venue Services....D....562 426-0555
4101 E Willow St Long Beach (90815) ***(P-13726)***
Choura Vnue Svcs At Carson Ctr, Long Beach *Also called Choura Venue Services* ***(P-13726)***
Chowchilla Conv. Center, Chowchilla *Also called Avalon Care Ctr - Chwchlla LLC* ***(P-20246)***
Chowchilla Medical Center, Chowchilla *Also called Madera Community Hospital* ***(P-21573)***
Chowchilla Mem Hlth Care Dst (PA)....D....559 665-3781
1104 Ventura Ave Chowchilla (93610) ***(P-20311)***
Chownow Inc....D....888 707-2469
12181 Bluff Creek Dr # 200 Playa Vista (90094) ***(P-15626)***
Chrisp Company (PA)....C....510 656-2840
43650 Osgood Rd Fremont (94539) ***(P-1738)***
Christensen & Giannini LLC....D....831 449-2494
1588 Moffett St Ste B Salinas (93905) ***(P-43)***
Christian and Wakefield (PA)....D....619 236-1555
110 W A St Ste 900 San Diego (92101) ***(P-11316)***
Christian Church Homes....C....510 893-2998
251 28th St Oakland (94611) ***(P-11317)***
Christian Community Credit Un (PA)....D....626 915-7551
255 N Lone Hill Ave San Dimas (91773) ***(P-9627)***
Christian Conference Grounds, Mount Hermon *Also called Mount Hermon Association Inc* ***(P-13453)***
Christian Counseling Centers....D....408 559-1115
3880 S Bascom Ave Ste 202 San Jose (95124) ***(P-23572)***
Christian Kirkwood Schools (PA)....D....562 862-4251
10822 Brookshire Ave Downey (90241) ***(P-24295)***
Christiansen Amusements Corp....D....760 735-8542
1725 S Escondido Blvd E Escondido (92025) ***(P-19125)***
Christie Dgtal Systems USA Inc (HQ)....D....714 527-7056
10550 Camden Dr Cypress (90630) ***(P-6941)***
Christmas Bonus Fund of The Pl....D....213 385-6161
501 Shatto Pl Ste 5 Los Angeles (90020) ***(P-12091)***
Christopher Ranch LLC (PA)....C....408 847-1100
305 Bloomfield Ave Gilroy (95020) ***(P-21)***
Christopher Ranch LLC....D....831 636-8722
1690 Freitas Rd San Juan Bautista (95045) ***(P-8655)***
Christopher Ransom Corporation (PA)....C....510 345-9144
1300 Clay St Ste 600 Oakland (94612) ***(P-12060)***
Chroma Systems....D....714 557-8480
3201 S Susan St Santa Ana (92704) ***(P-13575)***
Chromalloy San Diego Corp....C....858 877-2800
7007 Consolidated Way San Diego (92121) ***(P-17937)***
Chrome River Technologies Inc (PA)....D....323 857-5800
5757 Wilshire Blvd # 270 Los Angeles (90036) ***(P-15058)***
Chronicle Broadcasting Co....B....415 561-8000
900 Front St San Francisco (94111) ***(P-5778)***
Chronicle LLC....D....650 214-5199
250 Mayfield Ave Mountain View (94043) ***(P-16882)***
Chrysler Plymouth Dodge Jeep, Watsonville *Also called Marty Franich Leasing Co* ***(P-17656)***
Chsp Trs Fisherman Wharf LLC....C....415 563-1234
555 N Point St San Francisco (94133) ***(P-12457)***
Chsp Trs Los Angeles LLC....D....213 624-0000
535 S Grand Ave Los Angeles (90071) ***(P-12458)***

Mergent e-mail: customerrelations@mergent.com
1250
2019 Directory of California
Wholesalers and Services Companies
(P-0000) Products & Services Section entry number
(PA)=Parent Co (HQ)=Headquarters (DH)=Div Headquarters

Chubb, Los Angeles *Also called Pacific Indemnity Company* ***(P-10725)***
Chubb, San Francisco *Also called Federal Insurance Company* ***(P-10627)***
Chubb US Holding Inc.......D.......415 547-4400
455 Market St Ste 500 San Francisco (94105) ***(P-10583)***
Chubb US Holding Inc.......C.......619 563-2400
3131 Camino Del Rio N San Diego (92108) ***(P-10584)***
Chubb US Holding Inc.......C.......818 428-3600
9200 Oakdale Ave Chatsworth (91311) ***(P-10585)***
Chuck Jones Flying Service (PA).......E.......530 868-5798
216 W Hamilton Rd Biggs (95917) ***(P-461)***
Chukchansi Gold Resort Casino.......A.......866 794-6946
711 Lucky Ln Coarsegold (93614) ***(P-12459)***
Chula Vista Active Club, Chula Vista *Also called 24 Hour Fitness Usa Inc* ***(P-18558)***
Chula Vista Veterans Center, Chula Vista *Also called Veterans Health Administration* ***(P-20070)***
Chumash Casino Resort (HQ).......C.......805 686-0855
3400 E Highway 246 Santa Ynez (93460) ***(P-19126)***
Church & Larsen Inc.......C.......626 303-8741
16103 Avenida Padilla Irwindale (91702) ***(P-2866)***
Church Brothers LLC (PA).......D.......831 796-1000
19065 Portola Dr Ste C Salinas (93908) ***(P-8656)***
Church of Vly Rtrment Hmes Inc.......D.......408 241-7750
390 N Winchester Blvd Santa Clara (95050) ***(P-24470)***
Churchill Downs Incorporated.......A.......502 638-3879
800 W El Camino Real # 400 Mountain View (94040) ***(P-18538)***
Churchill MGT Group Corp.......E.......877 937-7110
5900 Wilshire Blvd # 400 Los Angeles (90036) ***(P-10075)***
CIC Research Inc.......D.......858 637-4000
8361 Vickers St Ste 308 San Diego (92111) ***(P-26504)***
Cicileo Landscapes.......E.......805 967-3939
4565 Hollister Ave Santa Barbara (93110) ***(P-745)***
Cie Digital Labs LLC (PA).......D.......949 381-6200
19900 Macarthur Blvd # 1000 Irvine (92612) ***(P-13971)***
Cie Games LLC.......E.......415 800-6100
500 Howard St Ste 300 San Francisco (94105) ***(P-15059)***
Cielo Azul Inc.......D.......855 863-8503
1545 Lake Dr Encinitas (92024) ***(P-812)***
Cierra Wireless.......C.......760 476-8700
2738 Loker Ave W Ste A Carlsbad (92010) ***(P-25609)***
Cific Energy Center, San Francisco *Also called Sodexo Management Inc* ***(P-27037)***
Cigna Healthcare Cal Inc.......C.......415 374-2500
1 Front St Ste 1700 San Francisco (94111) ***(P-10194)***
Cigna Healthcare Cal Inc (HQ).......B.......818 500-6262
400 N Brand Blvd Ste 400 # 400 Glendale (91203) ***(P-10195)***
Cigna Healthcare Cal Inc.......C.......805 230-8300
2801 Townsgate Rd Ste 121 Thousand Oaks (91361) ***(P-10196)***
Cigna Healthcare Cal Inc.......B.......559 738-2000
5300 W Tulare Ave Ste 100 Visalia (93277) ***(P-10197)***
Cik Power Distributors LLC.......D.......714 938-0297
240 W Grove Ave Orange (92865) ***(P-26804)***
Cim Group LP (PA).......D.......323 860-4900
4700 Wilshire Blvd Ste 1 Los Angeles (90010) ***(P-11318)***
Cim/Oakland City Center LLC.......D.......510 451-4000
1001 Broadway Oakland (94607) ***(P-12460)***
Cimatron Gibbs LLC.......D.......805 523-0004
323 Science Dr Moorpark (93021) ***(P-15060)***
Cinelease Inc (HQ).......E.......855 441-5500
5375 W San Fernando Rd Los Angeles (90039) ***(P-18182)***
Cinema City Theaters.......E.......714 970-0865
5635 E La Palma Ave Anaheim (92807) ***(P-18278)***
Cinemark 16 Bayfair.......D.......510 276-9684
15555 E 14th St Ste 600 San Leandro (94578) ***(P-18279)***
Cinemark Usa Inc.......D.......714 373-4573
7777 Edinger Ave Ste 170 Huntington Beach (92647) ***(P-18280)***
Cinemastar Luxury Theaters.......B.......760 945-2500
1949 Avenida Del Oro # 100 Oceanside (92056) ***(P-18281)***
Cinepolis Luxury Cinemas.......D.......323 556-6340
6420 Wilshire Blvd # 900 Los Angeles (90048) ***(P-18282)***
Cinnabar.......C.......818 842-8190
4571 Electronics Pl Los Angeles (90039) ***(P-14103)***
Cinnabar California Inc.......D.......818 842-8190
4571 Electronics Pl Los Angeles (90039) ***(P-14104)***
Cinnabar Hills Golf Club, San Jose *Also called Traditions Golf LLC* ***(P-18773)***
Cinovation Inc.......D.......818 246-3160
6527 San Fernando Rd Glendale (91201) ***(P-18031)***
Cintas Corporation.......D.......925 743-1745
3201 Dnville Blvd Ste 285 Alamo (94507) ***(P-13522)***
Cintas Corporation No 2.......D.......310 635-8713
18050 Central Ave Carson (90746) ***(P-13727)***
Cintas Corporation No 2.......D.......408 292-6700
2188 Del Franco St Ste 70 San Jose (95131) ***(P-13598)***
Cintas Corporation No 2.......D.......714 288-8400
4320 E Miraloma Ave Anaheim (92807) ***(P-9206)***
Cintas Corporation No 3.......D.......661 282-4300
5500 Young St Bakersfield (93311) ***(P-13599)***
Cintas Corporation No 3.......C.......619 239-1001
675 32nd St San Diego (92102) ***(P-13600)***
Cintas Corporation No 3.......D.......562 692-8741
2829 Workman Mill Rd Whittier (90601) ***(P-13523)***
Cintas Corporation No 3.......E.......510 352-6330
777 139th Ave San Leandro (94578) ***(P-13728)***
Cintas Corporation No 3.......C.......562 368-3200
7735 Paramount Blvd Pico Rivera (90660) ***(P-13524)***
Cintas Corporation No 3.......C.......909 930-9096
2150 Proforma Ave Ontario (91761) ***(P-13525)***
Cintas Corporation No 3.......D.......661 310-7400
28334 Industry Dr Valencia (91355) ***(P-13526)***
Cintas Corporation No 3.......D.......510 352-6330
20929 Cabot Blvd Hayward (94545) ***(P-13601)***
Cintas Corporation No 3.......D.......310 725-2850
20100 S Susana Rd Compton (90221) ***(P-13602)***
Cintas Corporation No 3.......C.......916 419-8519
1231 National Dr Sacramento (95834) ***(P-13603)***
Cintas Corporation No 3.......D.......909 390-4912
1851 S Wineville Ave Ontario (91761) ***(P-13604)***
Cintas Corporation No 3.......D.......650 589-4300
220 Demeter St East Palo Alto (94303) ***(P-13605)***
Cintiva Financial Corporation.......D.......877 246-8482
10145 Pacific Hts 800 San Diego (92121) ***(P-9875)***
Ciphercloud Inc (PA).......D.......408 519-6930
2581 Junction Ave Ste 200 San Jose (95134) ***(P-15627)***
Ciphermax Inc (PA).......D.......408 382-6500
1975 Concourse Dr San Jose (95131) ***(P-27192)***
Cir.......C.......650 574-6900
1745 Celeste Dr San Mateo (94402) ***(P-26348)***
Circle K Ranch.......D.......559 834-1571
8640 E Manning Ave Selma (93662) ***(P-135)***
Circle Marina Car Wash Inc.......E.......562 494-4698
4800 E Pacific Coast Hwy Long Beach (90804) ***(P-17809)***
Circle Marina Hand Car Wash, Long Beach *Also called Circle Marina Car Wash Inc* ***(P-17809)***
Circle W Enterprises Inc.......E.......661 257-2400
27737 Avenue Hopkins Valencia (91355) ***(P-7346)***
Circle Wood Services Inc.......D.......909 784-0733
3670 W Temple Ave Pomona (91768) ***(P-26805)***
Circulating Air Inc (PA).......D.......818 764-0530
7337 Varna Ave North Hollywood (91605) ***(P-2160)***
Cirks Construction Inc.......D.......916 362-5460
3300 Industrial Blvd West Sacramento (95691) ***(P-1504)***
Cirrus Enterprises LLC.......D.......310 204-6159
18027 Bishop Ave Carson (90746) ***(P-8912)***
Cirrus Health II LP.......C.......949 855-0562
24331 El Toro Rd Ste 150 Laguna Hills (92637) ***(P-19382)***
Cirtech Inc.......E.......714 921-0860
250 E Emerson Ave Orange (92865) ***(P-17074)***
CIS Security, Fresno *Also called Geil Enterprises Inc* ***(P-16664)***
Cisco Ironport Systems LLC (HQ).......B.......650 989-6500
170 W Tasman Dr San Jose (95134) ***(P-15628)***
Cisco Systems Capital Corp (HQ).......C.......610 386-5870
170 W Tasman Dr San Jose (95134) ***(P-17075)***
Cisco Webex LLC (HQ).......A.......408 435-7000
170 W Tasman Dr San Jose (95134) ***(P-17076)***
CIT Bank NA.......D.......760 771-3498
78010 Main St La Quinta (92253) ***(P-9302)***
CIT Bank NA.......D.......310 727-5660
1570 Rosecrans Ave Manhattan Beach (90266) ***(P-9303)***
CIT Bank NA.......D.......909 631-2560
3410 Grand Ave Ste A Chino Hills (91709) ***(P-9304)***
CIT Bank NA.......D.......310 475-4594
2920 N Beverly Glen Cir Los Angeles (90077) ***(P-9305)***
CIT Bank NA.......D.......310 372-8473
1100 Pacific Coast Hwy Hermosa Beach (90254) ***(P-9306)***
CIT Bank NA.......D.......818 502-8400
1111 N Brand Blvd Ste A Glendale (91202) ***(P-9307)***
CIT Bank NA.......D.......310 452-3802
1750 Ocean Park Blvd Santa Monica (90405) ***(P-9308)***
CIT Bank NA.......D.......562 433-0972
3500 E 7th St Long Beach (90804) ***(P-9309)***
CIT Bank NA.......D.......818 817-5320
17050 Ventura Blvd # 100 Encino (91316) ***(P-9310)***
CIT Bank NA.......D.......805 465-1053
1727 E Daily Dr Camarillo (93010) ***(P-9311)***
CIT Bank NA.......D.......310 390-7745
5573 Sepulveda Blvd Culver City (90230) ***(P-9312)***
CIT Bank NA.......D.......310 559-7222
10784 Jefferson Blvd Culver City (90230) ***(P-9313)***
CIT Bank NA.......D.......310 477-0546
11310 National Blvd Los Angeles (90064) ***(P-9314)***
CIT Bank NA.......D.......818 525-3760
1001 N San Fernando Blvd Burbank (91504) ***(P-9315)***
CIT Bank NA.......D.......949 347-7014
27620 Marguerite Pkwy B Mission Viejo (92692) ***(P-9316)***
CIT Bank NA.......D.......949 598-9621
23072 Alicia Pkwy Mission Viejo (92692) ***(P-9317)***
CIT Bank NA.......D.......949 675-2890
3700 E Coast Hwy Corona Del Mar (92625) ***(P-9318)***
CIT Bank NA (HQ).......D.......626 859-5400
75 N Fair Oaks Ave Fl 1 Pasadena (91103) ***(P-9319)***
CIT Bank NA.......D.......805 379-5520
199 E Thousand Oaks Blvd Thousand Oaks (91360) ***(P-9320)***
CIT Bank National Association.......D.......818 885-9065
20505 Devonshire St Chatsworth (91311) ***(P-9321)***
CIT Bank National Association.......D.......626 435-2260
220 N Hacienda Blvd City of Industry (91744) ***(P-9322)***
CIT Bank National Association.......D.......310 394-1640
401 Wilshire Blvd Santa Monica (90401) ***(P-9323)***
CIT Bank National Association.......D.......310 820-9650
12401 Wilshire Blvd Los Angeles (90025) ***(P-9324)***
CIT Bank National Association.......D.......310 577-6142
13405 Washington Blvd Marina Del Rey (90292) ***(P-9325)***
CIT Bank National Association.......D.......310 829-4477
1630 Montana Ave Santa Monica (90403) ***(P-9326)***
CIT Bank National Association.......D.......323 838-6881
5701 S Eastrn Ave Ste 108 Commerce (90040) ***(P-9327)***
CIT Bank National Association.......D.......310 265-1656
30019 Hawthorne Blvd Rancho Palos Verdes (90275) ***(P-9328)***
Citadel Group Solutions Inc.......D.......310 649-7500
1999 Avenue Of The Stars Los Angeles (90067) ***(P-15932)***

Citadel Roofing & Solar.......C.......707 446-5500
4980 Allison Pkwy Vacaville (95688) *(P-3137)*
Citadel Security Inc.......C.......562 248-2300
5199 E Pacific Cst Hwy # 200 Long Beach (90804) *(P-16603)*
Citibank FSB (HQ).......B.......415 627-6000
1 Sansome St San Francisco (94104) *(P-9522)*
Citibank National Association.......C.......805 497-7361
3967 E Thousand Oaks Blvd Westlake Village (91362) *(P-9329)*
Citibank National Association.......C.......800 627-3999
3580 Tyler St Riverside (92503) *(P-9330)*
Citibank National Association.......C.......619 870-0609
2240 Otay Lakes Rd 304-3 Chula Vista (91915) *(P-9331)*
Citibank National Association.......C.......415 431-6940
150 Pennsylvania Ave San Francisco (94107) *(P-9332)*
Citigroup Global Markets Inc.......C.......213 486-8811
444 S Flower St Fl 35 Los Angeles (90071) *(P-9930)*
Citigroup Global Markets Inc.......D.......310 727-9533
2381 Rosecrans Ave # 115 El Segundo (90245) *(P-9931)*
Citigroup Global Markets Inc.......E.......916 567-2056
155 Cadillac Dr Fl 1 Sacramento (95825) *(P-9932)*
Citigroup Global Markets Inc.......D.......858 597-7777
4350 La Jolla Village Dr San Diego (92122) *(P-9933)*
Citigroup Global Markets Inc.......E.......310 540-9511
21250 Hawthorne Blvd # 650 Torrance (90503) *(P-9934)*
Citigroup Global Markets Inc.......D.......949 955-7500
1901 Main St Ste 800 Irvine (92614) *(P-9935)*
Citigroup Global Markets Inc.......D.......858 456-4900
1225 Prospect St La Jolla (92037) *(P-9936)*
Citigroup Global Markets Inc.......E.......559 438-2542
5250 N Palm Ave Ste 321 Fresno (93704) *(P-9937)*
Citigroup Global Markets Inc.......D.......310 544-3600
609 Deep Valley Dr # 400 Rllng HLS Est (90274) *(P-9938)*
Citigroup Global Markets Inc.......D.......909 625-0781
456 W Foothill Blvd Claremont (91711) *(P-9939)*
Citigroup Global Markets Inc.......C.......650 926-7600
2775 Sand Hill Rd Ste 120 Menlo Park (94025) *(P-9940)*
Citigroup Inc.......D.......805 557-0930
325 E Hillcrest Dr Thousand Oaks (91360) *(P-9333)*
Citigroup Inc.......D.......909 335-0547
300 E State St Redlands (92373) *(P-9334)*
Citigroup Inc.......D.......949 726-5124
3996 Barranca Pkwy # 130 Irvine (92606) *(P-9335)*
Citigroup Inc.......D.......619 498-3158
352 H St Chula Vista (91910) *(P-9336)*
Citigroup Inc.......D.......415 617-8524
1 Sansome St Fl 27 San Francisco (94104) *(P-9941)*
Citigroup Inc.......D.......714 938-0748
840 N Eckhoff St Ste 140 Orange (92868) *(P-9792)*
Citimortgage Inc.......E.......925 730-3800
6160 Stoneridge Mall Rd # 150 Pleasanton (94588) *(P-9942)*
Citiscape Prprty MGT Group LLC.......D.......415 674-1440
3450 3rd St Ste 1a San Francisco (94124) *(P-11319)*
Citivest Inc.......D.......949 474-0440
4340 Von Karman Ave # 110 Newport Beach (92660) *(P-11320)*
Citizenhawk Inc.......D.......949 427-3002
135 Columbia Aliso Viejo (92656) *(P-26806)*
Citizens Business Bank (HQ).......C.......909 980-4030
701 N Haven Ave Ste 350 Ontario (91764) *(P-9432)*
Citizens Business Bank.......E.......951 808-8940
255 E Rincon St Ste 312 Corona (92879) *(P-9499)*
Citizens Business Bank.......D.......949 440-5200
1401 Dove St Ste 100 Newport Beach (92660) *(P-9433)*
Citizens Business Bank.......E.......626 577-1700
460 Serra Madre Villa Ave Pasadena (91107) *(P-9434)*
Citizens Business Bank.......D.......818 843-0707
4100 W Alameda Ave # 101 Burbank (91505) *(P-9435)*
Citizens Business Bank.......D.......661 281-0300
1230 17th St Bakersfield (93301) *(P-9436)*
Citizens Choice Health Plan, Orange *Also called Alignment Health Plan (P-10180)*
Citizens Development Corp (PA).......D.......760 744-0120
1105 La Bonita Dr San Marcos (92078) *(P-18889)*
Citizens Financial Svc., Costa Mesa *Also called Citizens Financial Svcs Inc (P-14487)*
Citizens Financial Svcs Inc.......D.......714 751-6100
3130 Harbor Blvd Costa Mesa (92626) *(P-14487)*
Citrix Systems Inc.......D.......408 790-8000
4988 Great America Pkwy Santa Clara (95054) *(P-15061)*
Citrus Heights Sport Club, San Ramon *Also called 24 Hour Fitness Usa Inc (P-18560)*
Citrus North Venture.......D.......256 428-2000
6591 Collins Dr Ste E11 Moorpark (93021) *(P-12461)*
CITRUS VALLEY HOME HEALTH, West Covina *Also called Citrus Valley Hospice (P-20312)*
Citrus Valley Hospice.......D.......626 859-2263
820 N Phillips Ave West Covina (91791) *(P-20312)*
Citrus Valley Medical Ctr Inc (PA).......A.......626 962-4011
1115 S Sunset Ave West Covina (91790) *(P-21322)*
Citrus Valley Medical Ctr Inc.......A.......626 858-8515
140 W College St Covina (91723) *(P-21323)*
Citrus Valley Medical Ctr Inc.......A.......626 963-8411
1115 S Sunset Ave West Covina (91790) *(P-21324)*
Citrus Valley Medical Ctr Inc.......A.......626 331-7331
210 W San Bernardino Rd Covina (91723) *(P-21325)*
Citrus Vly Hlth Partners Inc.......B.......626 962-4011
1115 S Sunset Ave West Covina (91790) *(P-19383)*
Citrus Vly Hlth Partners Inc (PA).......A.......626 331-7331
210 W San Bernardino Rd Covina (91723) *(P-26807)*
Citrus Vly Hlth Partners Inc.......A.......626 732-3100
1325 N Grand Ave Ste 300 Covina (91724) *(P-22767)*
Citrusbits Inc.......E.......925 452-6012
5776 Stoneridge Mall Rd # 298 Pleasanton (94588) *(P-15062)*
City & County of San Francisco.......C.......415 553-1706
850 Bryant St Ste 200 San Francisco (94103) *(P-23573)*
City & County of San Francisco.......D.......415 621-6600
401 Van Ness Ave Ste 110 San Francisco (94102) *(P-18355)*
City & County of San Francisco.......A.......415 551-3000
525 Golden Gate Ave San Francisco (94102) *(P-6221)*
City & County of San Francisco.......D.......415 621-6600
401 Van Ness Ave Ste 110 San Francisco (94102) *(P-18356)*
City & County of San Francisco.......D.......415 581-3500
200 Larkin St San Francisco (94102) *(P-24871)*
City & County of San Francisco.......A.......415 206-8000
1001 Potrero Ave San Francisco (94110) *(P-21326)*
City & County of San Francisco.......D.......415 557-4713
30 Van Ness Ave Ste 4100 San Francisco (94102) *(P-25009)*
City & County of San Francisco.......C.......415 554-4700
1 Carlton B Goodlett Pl # 234 San Francisco (94102) *(P-22976)*
City & County of San Francisco.......C.......415 553-1752
850 Bryant St Ste 600 San Francisco (94103) *(P-22977)*
City & County of San Francisco.......D.......415 753-7561
375 Woodside Ave 1 San Francisco (94127) *(P-23574)*
City & County of San Francisco.......D.......415 554-4799
1 Carlton B Goodlett Pl # 234 San Francisco (94102) *(P-26808)*
City Alameda Health Care Corp (PA).......D.......510 522-3700
2070 Clinton Ave Alameda (94501) *(P-21327)*
City Alameda Health Care Corp.......B.......510 814-4000
2070 Clinton Ave Alameda (94501) *(P-26809)*
CITY ARTS ACADEMY, San Diego *Also called Harmonium Inc (P-24326)*
City Attorney, Los Angeles *Also called City of Los Angeles (P-22981)*
City Attorney, San Francisco *Also called City & County of San Francisco (P-22976)*
City Attorneys Office, Long Beach *Also called City of Long Beach (P-22979)*
City Club LLC.......D.......415 362-2480
155 Sansome St Fl 9 San Francisco (94104) *(P-18890)*
City Club of San Francisco, San Francisco *Also called City Club LLC (P-18890)*
City Club On Bunker Hill, Los Angeles *Also called Bunker Hill Club Inc (P-25120)*
City Corporation Yard, Delano *Also called City of Delano (P-18695)*
City Distribution Services, Carson *Also called Tri-Modal Dist Svcs Inc (P-4381)*
City Fashion Express Inc.......D.......310 223-1010
2888 E El Presidio St Carson (90810) *(P-5033)*
City Fibers Inc (PA).......D.......323 583-1013
2500 S Santa Fe Ave Vernon (90058) *(P-7974)*
City Fibers Inc.......D.......323 583-1013
2525 E 25th St Vernon (90058) *(P-4541)*
City Hall, Ventura *Also called Ventura Streets Dept (P-1256)*
City Hall Pblc Wrks Eng Dpt, San Bernardino *Also called San Bernardino California City (P-24977)*
City Hanford Public Imprv Corp.......D.......559 585-2550
900 S 10th Ave Hanford (93230) *(P-1908)*
City Hope National Medical Ctr.......A.......626 256-4673
1500 Duarte Rd Duarte (91010) *(P-21328)*
City II Enterprises Inc.......E.......408 275-1200
845 Earle Ave San Jose (95126) *(P-813)*
City Impact.......E.......415 292-1770
230 Jones St Fl 1 San Francisco (94102) *(P-25409)*
City Impact Inc.......D.......805 983-3636
555 S A St Ste 175 Oxnard (93030) *(P-23575)*
City Leasing & Rentals.......C.......619 276-6171
2111 Morena Blvd San Diego (92110) *(P-17652)*
City Long Bch Prkg Enforcement, Long Beach *Also called City of Long Beach (P-6532)*
City Los Angeles General Svcs, Los Angeles *Also called City of Los Angeles (P-22980)*
City Mnterey Pk Recreation Ctr, Monterey Park *Also called City of Monterey Park (P-19137)*
City National Bank (HQ).......B.......310 888-6000
555 S Flower St Fl 21 Los Angeles (90071) *(P-9337)*
City National Bank.......E.......951 276-8800
3484 Central Ave Riverside (92506) *(P-9338)*
City National Bank.......D.......619 645-6100
225 Broadway Ste 500 San Diego (92101) *(P-9339)*
City National Bank.......C.......310 297-6606
2100 Park Pl Ste 150 El Segundo (90245) *(P-9340)*
City National Investments, San Diego *Also called City National Bank (P-9339)*
City National SEC Svcs Inc.......D.......310 641-6666
5901 W Century Blvd # 806 Los Angeles (90045) *(P-16604)*
City of Anaheim.......B.......714 704-2400
2695 E Katella Ave Anaheim (92806) *(P-10864)*
City of Antioch.......D.......925 779-6950
1201 W 4th St Antioch (94509) *(P-6530)*
City of Arcadia.......B.......626 574-5435
240 W Huntington Dr Arcadia (91007) *(P-3641)*
City of Bakersfield.......C.......661 852-7300
1001 Truxtun Ave Bakersfield (93301) *(P-23576)*
City of Baldwin Park.......D.......626 960-1955
14403 Pacific Ave Baldwin Park (91706) *(P-25410)*
City of Bell.......D.......323 773-1596
6330 Pine Ave Bell (90201) *(P-23577)*
City of Berkeley.......A.......510 981-6750
2180 Milvia St Berkeley (94704) *(P-26165)*
City of Beverly Hills.......B.......310 285-2552
342 Foothill Rd Beverly Hills (90210) *(P-17682)*
City of Brea.......D.......714 990-7650
1 Civic Center Cir Fl 3 Brea (92821) *(P-27581)*
City of Burbank.......B.......818 238-3550
164 W Magnolia Blvd Burbank (91502) *(P-6181)*
City of Burlingame.......E.......650 558-7670
1361 N Carolan Ave Burlingame (94010) *(P-1739)*
City of Carson.......D.......310 835-0212
3 Civic Plaza Dr Carson (90745) *(P-23578)*
City of Chino.......D.......909 591-9843
5050 Schaefer Ave Chino (91710) *(P-6531)*
City of Commerce.......B.......323 722-4805
2535 Commerce Way Commerce (90040) *(P-19127)*

Mergent e-mail: customerrelations@mergent.com
1252
2019 Directory of California
Wholesalers and Services Companies
(P-0000) Products & Services Section entry number
(PA)=Parent Co (HQ)=Headquarters (DH)=Div Headquarters

City of Compton	D	310 635-3484
1108 N Oleander Ave Compton (90222) *(P-19128)*		
City of Concord	B	925 692-2400
2000 Kirker Pass Rd Concord (94521) *(P-18357)*		
City of Concord	D	925 686-6262
4050 Port Chicago Hwy Concord (94520) *(P-18694)*		
City of Corona	C	951 279-3647
400 S Vicentia Ave Corona (92882) *(P-27548)*		
City of Corona	D	951 736-2266
400 S Vicentia Ave # 210 Corona (92882) *(P-6196)*		
City of Coronado	D	619 522-7342
1845 Strand Way Coronado (92118) *(P-19129)*		
City of Coronado	D	619 522-7380
101 B Ave Coronado (92118) *(P-6182)*		
City of Daly City	D	650 991-8064
333 90th St Fl 1 Daly City (94015) *(P-25610)*		
City of Delano	E	661 721-3350
725 S Lexington St Delano (93215) *(P-18695)*		
City of Downey	D	562 861-8211
8435 Firestone Blvd Downey (90241) *(P-18358)*		
City of El Centro	C	760 337-4505
307 W Brighton Ave El Centro (92243) *(P-1740)*		
City of Encinitas	E	760 633-2850
160 Calle Magdalena Encinitas (92024) *(P-1741)*		
City of Fairfield	C	707 428-7435
1000 Webster St Fairfield (94533) *(P-10865)*		
City of Folsom	D	916 355-7285
48 Natoma St Folsom (95630) *(P-19130)*		
City of Foster City	E	650 286-3380
650 Shell Blvd Foster City (94404) *(P-19131)*		
City of Fremont	C	510 791-4196
34600 Ardenwood Blvd Fremont (94555) *(P-24872)*		
City of Fremont	C	510 494-4460
39550 Liberty St Fremont (94538) *(P-26036)*		
City of Fresno	B	559 621-7433
2223 G St Fresno (93706) *(P-3642)*		
City of Fresno	C	559 621-5300
1910 E University Ave Fresno (93703) *(P-6222)*		
City of Fresno	D	559 445-8200
700 M St Fresno (93721) *(P-17077)*		
City of Fullerton	C	714 738-6897
1580 W Commonwealth Ave Fullerton (92833) *(P-27193)*		
City of Galt	D	209 366-7180
660 Chabolla Ave Galt (95632) *(P-19132)*		
City of Gardena	D	310 324-1475
13999 S Western Ave Gardena (90249) *(P-3643)*		
City of Glendale	D	818 548-3945
633 E Broadway Ste 205 Glendale (91206) *(P-25611)*		
City of Glendale	D	818 548-3950
541 W Chevy Chase Dr Glendale (91204) *(P-18515)*		
City of Glendale	B	818 548-3300
141 N Glendale Ave Fl 2 Glendale (91206) *(P-6017)*		
City of Glendale	E	818 548-3980
634 Bekins Way Glendale (91201) *(P-6018)*		
City of Glendale	C	818 548-2011
800 Air Way Glendale (91201) *(P-6223)*		
City of Industry Disposal Co	E	626 336-5439
17445 Railroad St City of Industry (91748) *(P-6374)*		
City of Inglewood	D	310 412-5370
700 Warren Ln Inglewood (90302) *(P-19133)*		
City of Irvine	D	949 724-7600
6427 Oak Cyn Irvine (92618) *(P-27194)*		
City of Irvine	D	949 724-7740
6443 Oak Cyn Irvine (92618) *(P-19134)*		
City of Irvine	D	949 724-7101
1 Civic Center Plz Irvine (92606) *(P-25010)*		
City of Irvine	D	949 724-6728
4531 Bryan Ave Irvine (92620) *(P-19135)*		
City of Irvine	D	949 724-6900
20 Lake Rd Irvine (92604) *(P-23579)*		
City of La Habra	E	562 905-9708
101 W La Habra Blvd La Habra (90631) *(P-23580)*		
City of La Mesa	E	619 667-1450
8152 Commercial St La Mesa (91942) *(P-1742)*		
City of Lemoore	E	559 924-6744
711 W Cinnamon Dr Lemoore (93245) *(P-6375)*		
City of Livermore	E	925 960-8100
101 W Jack London Blvd Livermore (94551) *(P-2023)*		
City of Lomita	E	310 325-9830
24373 Walnut St Lomita (90717) *(P-6224)*		
City of Long Beach	B	562 570-7298
333 W Ocean Blvd Fl 4 Long Beach (90802) *(P-17078)*		
City of Long Beach	C	562 570-2828
2600 Temple Ave Long Beach (90806) *(P-17757)*		
City of Long Beach	D	562 570-5423
2600 Temple Ave Long Beach (90806) *(P-22978)*		
City of Long Beach	C	562 570-2890
2929 E Willow St Long Beach (90806) *(P-6532)*		
City of Long Beach	C	562 570-2000
2400 E Spring St Long Beach (90806) *(P-6189)*		
City of Long Beach	D	562 570-2600
4100 E Don Douglas Dr Fl Flr 2 Long Beach (90808) *(P-4877)*		
City of Long Beach	B	562 436-3636
300 E Ocean Blvd Long Beach (90802) *(P-17079)*		
City of Long Beach	D	562 570-6919
333 W Ocean Blvd Lbby Long Beach (90802) *(P-22979)*		
City of Long Beach	B	562 570-6383
333 W Ocean Blvd Ste 9 Long Beach (90802) *(P-1743)*		
City of Long Beach	D	562 570-2390
1800 E Wardlow Rd Long Beach (90807) *(P-6225)*		

City of Los Angeles	A	213 978-0259
600 S Spring St Unit 200 Los Angeles (90014) *(P-25612)*		
City of Los Angeles	C	213 978-4049
111 E 1st St Ste 401 Los Angeles (90012) *(P-22980)*		
City of Los Angeles	B	310 732-3550
500 Pier A Pl Wilmington (90744) *(P-3950)*		
City of Los Angeles	C	213 473-0800
2800 E Observatory Ave Los Angeles (90027) *(P-24873)*		
City of Los Angeles	D	213 485-4282
1149 S Broadway Ste 800 Los Angeles (90015) *(P-26037)*		
City of Los Angeles	A	818 756-8022
6262 Van Nuys Blvd # 451 Van Nuys (91401) *(P-25613)*		
City of Los Angeles	D	213 202-5500
201 N Figueroa St # 1400 Los Angeles (90012) *(P-25411)*		
City of Los Angeles	D	213 847-2799
3330 W 36th St Los Angeles (90018) *(P-14210)*		
City of Los Angeles	C	310 732-7681
425 S Palos Verdes St San Pedro (90731) *(P-4726)*		
City of Los Angeles	A	213 978-8100
200 N Main St Ste 800 Los Angeles (90012) *(P-22981)*		
City of Los Angeles	E	323 467-7193
3200 Canyon Dr Los Angeles (90068) *(P-13448)*		
City of Los Angeles	D	213 485-4981
2513 E 24th St Vernon (90058) *(P-3951)*		
City of Los Angeles	D	818 908-5950
16461 Sherman Way Ste 210 Van Nuys (91406) *(P-4878)*		
City of Mill Valley	E	415 383-1370
180 Camino Alto Mill Valley (94941) *(P-19136)*		
City of Mill Valley	E	415 388-4033
26 Corte Madera Ave Mill Valley (94941) *(P-1744)*		
City of Monterey Park	D	626 307-1388
320 W Newmark Ave Fl 1 Monterey Park (91754) *(P-19137)*		
City of Moorpark	D	805 517-6261
799 Moorpark Ave Moorpark (93021) *(P-23581)*		
City of Morgan Hill	D	408 776-7333
100 Edes St Morgan Hill (95037) *(P-27686)*		
City of Morro Bay, Morro Bay *Also called Morro Bay Public Works* *(P-1821)*		
City of NAPA	E	707 255-7631
1151 Pearl St NAPA (94559) *(P-3876)*		
City of Norco	D	951 270-5632
2870 Clark Ave Norco (92860) *(P-6226)*		
City of Norco	D	951 270-5617
2870 Clark Ave Norco (92860) *(P-27687)*		
City of Norwalk, Norwalk *Also called Norwalk Transit System* *(P-3691)*		
City of Oakland	B	510 238-6796
150 Frank H Ogawa Plz # 3332 Oakland (94612) *(P-23582)*		
City of Oakland	E	510 238-3494
250 Frank H Ogawa Plz # 6300 Oakland (94612) *(P-19138)*		
City of Oakland	E	510 268-9000
519 18th St Oakland (94612) *(P-19139)*		
City of Orange	D	714 744-7264
230 E Chapman Ave Orange (92866) *(P-23583)*		
City of Orange	E	714 744-7272
230 E Chapman Ave Orange (92866) *(P-19140)*		
City of Orland (PA)	E	530 865-1610
815 4th St Orland (95963) *(P-6227)*		
City of Oxnard	D	805 385-8019
350 N C St Oxnard (93030) *(P-23584)*		
City of Oxnard	D	805 385-8136
251 S Hayes Ave Oxnard (93030) *(P-6228)*		
City of Oxnard	D	805 385-7950
1060 Pacific Ave Oxnard (93030) *(P-18793)*		
City of Oxnard	A	805 983-4653
2401 W Vineyard Ave Oxnard (93036) *(P-18696)*		
CITY OF OXNARD PERFORMING ARTS, Oxnard *Also called Oxnard Perfrmn Arts & Convtn (P-17381)*		
City of Pacifica-Vallemar	E	650 738-7466
170 Santa Maria Ave Pacifica (94044) *(P-24296)*		
City of Palm Springs	D	760 318-3800
3400 E Tahquitz Canyon Wa Palm Springs (92262) *(P-4879)*		
City of Palmdale	C	661 267-5338
39101 3rd St E Palmdale (93550) *(P-14211)*		
City of Palo Alto	D	650 329-2598
2501 Embarcadero Way Palo Alto (94303) *(P-17080)*		
City of Pasadena	D	626 744-4311
117 E Colorado Blvd Pasadena (91105) *(P-14212)*		
City of Pasadena	D	626 543-4708
1133 Rosemont Ave Pasadena (91103) *(P-18697)*		
City of Pomona	B	909 397-5506
2040 W Holt Ave Fl 2 Pomona (91768) *(P-24752)*		
City of Pomona	C	909 620-2361
636 W Monterey Ave Pomona (91768) *(P-6376)*		
City of Redlands	E	909 798-7525
35 Cajon St Redlands (92373) *(P-6377)*		
City of Richmond	D	510 620-6788
3230 Macdonald Ave Fl 2 Richmond (94804) *(P-19141)*		
City of Riverside	D	951 346-4700
3485 Mission Inn Ave Riverside (92501) *(P-17081)*		
City of Salinas	D	831 758-7233
426 Work St Salinas (93901) *(P-14213)*		
City of San Diego	E	619 533-3012
1010 2nd Ave Ste 800 San Diego (92101) *(P-27688)*		
City of San Diego	D	619 533-6518
202 C St Ms37c San Diego (92101) *(P-22010)*		
City of San Diego	C	858 627-3210
9573 Chesapeake Dr San Diego (92123) *(P-25614)*		
City of San Jose	B	408 277-5277
408 Almaden Blvd San Jose (95110) *(P-17082)*		
City of San Jose	D	408 794-6400
1300 Senter Rd San Jose (95112) *(P-24927)*		

Employee Codes: A=Over 500 employees, B=251-500
C=101-250, D=51-100, E=50

2019 Directory of California
Wholesalers and Services Companies

© Mergent Inc. 1-800-342-5647
1253

A L P H A B E T I C

City of San Jose......B......408 392-3600
1701 Arprt Blvd Ste B1130 San Jose (95110) ***(P-4880)***
City of San Jose......C......408 226-6765
200 Edenvale Ave San Jose (95136) ***(P-12462)***
City of San Mateo......D......650 522-7300
1949 Pacific Blvd San Mateo (94403) ***(P-14214)***
City of Santa Clara......D......408 615-3770
2600 Benton St Santa Clara (95051) ***(P-3502)***
City of Santa Clara......E......408 615-2300
1500 Warburton Ave Santa Clara (95050) ***(P-6019)***
City of Santa Clara......C......408 615-2046
1705 Martin Ave Santa Clara (95050) ***(P-6020)***
City of Santa Clra Parks Svc, Santa Clara *Also called City of Santa Clara* ***(P-3502)***
City of South Lake Tahoe......D......530 542-6056
1180 Rufus Allen Blvd South Lake Tahoe (96150) ***(P-19142)***
City of Sunnyvale......D......408 730-7451
456 W Olive Ave Sunnyvale (94086) ***(P-13474)***
City of Sunnyvale......C......408 730-7510
221 Commercial St Sunnyvale (94085) ***(P-17083)***
City of Torrance......D......310 781-6901
20500 Madrona Ave Torrance (90503) ***(P-19143)***
City of Tulare......D......559 684-4200
3981 S K St Tulare (93274) ***(P-6378)***
City of Vacaville......D......707 449-6122
1100 Alamo Dr Vacaville (95687) ***(P-23585)***
City of Vacaville......B......707 449-5170
650 Merchant St Vacaville (95688) ***(P-25615)***
City of Vallejo......B......707 644-4000
1001 Fairgrounds Dr Vallejo (94589) ***(P-18794)***
City of Visalia......D......559 713-4000
303 E Acequia Ave Visalia (93291) ***(P-17084)***
City of Vista......C......760 940-9283
101 Wave Dr Vista (92083) ***(P-19144)***
City of Whittier......D......562 567-9446
7630 Washington Ave Whittier (90602) ***(P-23586)***
City of Woodland......C......530 661-5878
2001 East St Woodland (95776) ***(P-19145)***
City of Woodland......C......530 661-5962
655 N Pioneer Ave Woodland (95776) ***(P-27582)***
City of Woodland......D......530 661-5961
42929 County Road 24 Woodland (95776) ***(P-25616)***
City Park, San Francisco *Also called Imperial Parking (us) LLC* ***(P-17684)***
City Rescue Mission, San Diego *Also called San Diego Rescue Mission Inc* ***(P-24837)***
City Rise Inc (PA)......C......209 333-0807
1225 S Sacramento St Lodi (95240) ***(P-17085)***
City Rise Services, Lodi *Also called City Rise Inc* ***(P-17085)***
City Security Co Inc......D......626 458-2325
430 S Grfield Ave Ste 401 Alhambra (91801) ***(P-16605)***
City Service Contracting Inc (PA)......D......714 632-6610
920 Lawrence St Placentia (92870) ***(P-3503)***
City Service Paving, Placentia *Also called City Service Contracting Inc* ***(P-3503)***
City Towel & Dust Service Inc......E......707 542-0391
3016 Dutton Ave Santa Rosa (95407) ***(P-13527)***
City Wire Cloth, Fontana *Also called Daniel Gerard Worldwide Inc* ***(P-7268)***
Citywide Plumbing Heating......E......619 231-2022
9825 Carroll Centre Rd San Diego (92126) ***(P-2161)***
Civco, Rcho STA Marg *Also called Capital Invstmnts Vntures Corp* ***(P-25008)***
Civic Auditorium, Santa Monica *Also called Santa Monica City of* ***(P-10933)***
CIVIC THEATRE, San Diego *Also called San Diego Theatres Inc* ***(P-10932)***
Civicorps......C......510 992-7800
6315 San Leandro St Oakland (94621) ***(P-6379)***
CJ America Inc (HQ)......C......213 427-5566
5700 Wilshire Blvd # 550 Los Angeles (90036) ***(P-8768)***
CJ Construction & Dev Inc......D......760 247-6868
78206 Varner Rd Ste D Palm Desert (92211) ***(P-1274)***
CJ Model Home Maintenance Inc......D......925 485-3280
240 Spring St Pleasanton (94566) ***(P-14215)***
CJJ Farming Inc......E......805 739-1723
125 W Mill St Santa Maria (93458) ***(P-94)***
CK Enterprises Inc......D......760 967-8863
102 Copperwood Way Ste H Oceanside (92058) ***(P-17086)***
CK Franchising Inc (HQ)......D......800 498-8144
1 Park Plz Ste 300 Irvine (92614) ***(P-22264)***
Ckl Construction Inc......B......408 244-7042
967 W Hedding St San Jose (95126) ***(P-1275)***
Cks Business Services, Bakersfield *Also called Cbizmhm LLC* ***(P-26161)***
CL Knox Inc......D......661 837-0477
34933 Imperial St Bakersfield (93308) ***(P-1054)***
Claim Jumper Restaurant......C......949 461-7170
27845 Snta Margarita Pkwy Mission Viejo (92691) ***(P-1505)***
Claimremedi Inc......D......707 827-1274
2235 Mercury Way Ste 107 Santa Rosa (95407) ***(P-14031)***
Claims Management Inc......C......916 631-1250
1101 Crksde Rdge Dr 100 Roseville (95678) ***(P-10586)***
Clairemont Healthcare......D......858 278-4750
8060 Frost St San Diego (92123) ***(P-20313)***
Clairemont Medical Offices, San Diego *Also called Kaiser Foundation Hospitals* ***(P-19604)***
Clara Baldwin Stocker Home......E......626 962-7151
527 S Valinda Ave West Covina (91790) ***(P-20314)***
Clarbec Inc......E......707 996-4012
19368 Orange Ave Sonoma (95476) ***(P-136)***
Clare Foundation Inc (PA)......D......310 314-6200
909 Pico Blvd Santa Monica (90405) ***(P-23587)***
Clare Foundation Inc......D......310 314-6200
1871 9th St Santa Monica (90404) ***(P-23588)***
Claremont Club, The, Claremont *Also called Claremont Tennis Club* ***(P-18892)***
Claremont Country Club......D......510 653-6789
5295 Broadway Ter Oakland (94618) ***(P-18891)***
Claremont Hotel Club & Spa, Berkeley *Also called Claremont Ht Prpts Ltd Partnr* ***(P-12463)***
Claremont House Incorporated......D......510 658-9266
4500 Gilbert St Oakland (94611) ***(P-24471)***
Claremont Ht Prpts Ltd Partnr......A......510 843-3000
41 Tunnel Rd Berkeley (94705) ***(P-12463)***
Claremont Manor, Claremont *Also called Front Porch Communities* ***(P-21072)***
Claremont Outpatient Clinic, Claremont *Also called Pomona Valley Hospital Med Ctr* ***(P-21653)***
Claremont Resort, Berkeley *Also called Interstate Hotels Resorts Inc* ***(P-26899)***
Claremont Retirement MGT, Oakland *Also called Claremont House Incorporated* ***(P-24471)***
Claremont Star LP......E......909 482-0124
555 W Foothill Blvd Claremont (91711) ***(P-12464)***
Claremont Tennis Club......C......909 625-9515
1777 Monte Vista Ave Claremont (91711) ***(P-18892)***
Clarient Diagnostic Svcs Inc......B......888 443-3310
31 Columbia Aliso Viejo (92656) ***(P-22068)***
Clarion Construction Inc......E......909 598-4060
21067 Commerce Point Dr Walnut (91789) ***(P-1386)***
Clarion Corporation America (HQ)......D......310 327-9100
6200 Gateway Dr Cypress (90630) ***(P-7410)***
Clarion Hotel, Anaheim *Also called Comfort California Inc* ***(P-12480)***
Clarion Hotel, Ridgecrest *Also called Peekay Investments Prpts LLC* ***(P-13055)***
Clarion Hotel San Jose Airport......D......408 453-5340
1355 N 4th St San Jose (95112) ***(P-12465)***
Clarizen Inc......D......866 502-9813
2755 Campus Dr Ste 300 San Mateo (94403) ***(P-26810)***
Clark Booker T (PA)......E......510 482-8900
1569 Solano Ave Berkeley (94707) ***(P-14216)***
Clark Richardson and Biskup......D......760 496-3714
3207 Grey Hawk Ct Ste 150 Carlsbad (92010) ***(P-25617)***
Clark & Sullivan Builders Inc......C......916 338-7707
2024 Opportunity Dr # 150 Roseville (95678) ***(P-1506)***
Clark Bros Farming Inc......E......209 392-6144
19772 State Highway 33 Dos Palos (93620) ***(P-11)***
Clark Cnstr Group-California......B......714 754-0764
18201 Von Karman Ave # 800 Irvine (92612) ***(P-1387)***
Clark Cnstr Grup-California LP......B......714 429-9779
18201 Von Karman Ave Irvine (92612) ***(P-1507)***
Clark Pest Ctrl Stockton Inc (PA)......D......209 368-7152
555 N Guild Ave Lodi (95240) ***(P-14140)***
Clark Pest Ctrl Stockton Inc......D......209 524-6384
480 E Service Rd Modesto (95358) ***(P-14141)***
Clark Pest Ctrl Stockton Inc......D......916 925-7000
5822 Roseville Rd Sacramento (95842) ***(P-14142)***
Clark Pest Ctrl Stockton Inc......E......707 446-9748
811 U Banks Vacaville (95688) ***(P-14143)***
Clark Pest Ctrl Stockton Inc......E......209 474-3204
4816 Clowes St Stockton (95210) ***(P-14144)***
Clark Pest Ctrl Stockton Inc......D......408 945-3600
199 Topaz St Milpitas (95035) ***(P-14145)***
Clark Pest Ctrl Stockton Inc......D......925 449-6203
2313 Research Dr Livermore (94550) ***(P-14146)***
Clark Pest Ctrl Stockton Inc......E......916 635-7770
11285 White Rock Rd Rancho Cordova (95742) ***(P-14147)***
Clark Plumbing Co, Van Nuys *Also called Valley Clark Plbg & Htg Co Inc* ***(P-2394)***
Clarklift Los Angeles Inc......C......562 949-1006
8314 Slauson Ave Pico Rivera (90660) ***(P-7740)***
Clarklift-West Inc......C......916 381-5674
4750 Illinois Ave Fair Oaks (95628) ***(P-7741)***
Claro Pool Services Inc......D......760 341-3377
42161 Beacon Hl Palm Desert (92211) ***(P-3504)***
Class, San Mateo *Also called Center For Learning and* ***(P-23549)***
Class Act Hair & Nail Salon......D......530 223-3442
2795 Bechelli Ln Redding (96002) ***(P-13650)***
Classic, Torrance *Also called I C Class Components Corp* ***(P-7491)***
Classic Bowling Center, Daly City *Also called Bdp Bowl Inc* ***(P-18480)***
Classic Car Wash Inc (PA)......C......408 371-2414
871 E Hamilton Ave Ste C Campbell (95008) ***(P-17810)***
Classic Car Washes, San Jose *Also called Lark Avenue Car Wash* ***(P-17823)***
Classic Collision Center 2, Los Angeles *Also called Caliber Holdings Corporation* ***(P-17718)***
Classic Couriers Inc (PA)......D......323 461-3741
1601 N El Centro Ave Los Angeles (90028) ***(P-4395)***
Classic Custom Vacations, San Jose *Also called Classic Vacations LLC* ***(P-4966)***
Classic Custom Vacations Inc......C......800 221-3949
5893 Rue Ferrari San Jose (95138) ***(P-4965)***
Classic Distrg & Bev Group Inc......B......626 934-3700
120 Puente Ave City of Industry (91746) ***(P-8986)***
Classic Hardwood Floors, San Diego *Also called Davenport Development Corp* ***(P-3099)***
Classic Installs Inc......D......951 678-9906
22475 Baxter Rd Wildomar (92595) ***(P-3469)***
Classic Park Lane Partnership......D......831 373-0101
200 Glenwood Cir Ofc Monterey (93940) ***(P-11002)***
Classic Parking Inc......B......408 278-1444
34 S Autumn St San Jose (95110) ***(P-17683)***
Classic Party Rentals, Sonoma *Also called CP Opco LLC* ***(P-14491)***
Classic Party Rentals, San Diego *Also called CP Opco LLC* ***(P-14492)***
Classic Party Rentals, Los Angeles *Also called CP Opco LLC* ***(P-14493)***
Classic Party Rentals, Inglewood *Also called CP Opco LLC* ***(P-13735)***
Classic Party Rentals, Inglewood *Also called After-Party2 Inc* ***(P-14466)***
Classic Party Rentals, Los Angeles *Also called CP Opco LLC* ***(P-14494)***
Classic Party Rentals, Sonoma *Also called CP Opco LLC* ***(P-14495)***
Classic Party Rentals, Carpinteria *Also called CP Opco LLC* ***(P-14496)***
Classic Party Rentals, Santa Ana *Also called CP Opco LLC* ***(P-14497)***
Classic Protection Inc......E......213 742-1238
3208 Royal St Los Angeles (90007) ***(P-16606)***

Mergent e-mail: customerrelations@mergent.com
1254
2019 Directory of California
Wholesalers and Services Companies
(P-0000) Products & Services Section entry number
(PA)=Parent Co (HQ)=Headquarters (DH)=Div Headquarters

Classic Riverdale Inc ....D....831 373-0101
200 Glenwood Cir Monterey (93940) **(P-12466)**
Classic Rsdence Mgt Ltd Partnr ....D....831 373-0101
200 Glenwood Cir Ofc Monterey (93940) **(P-12467)**
Classic Soft Trim Inc ....D....510 782-4911
3201 Diablo Ave Hayward (94545) **(P-9207)**
Classic Tile & Mosaic Inc (PA) ....D....310 538-9605
14463 S Broadway Gardena (90248) **(P-6881)**
Classic Vacations LLC ....C....800 221-3949
5893 Rue Ferrari San Jose (95138) **(P-4966)**
Classified Advertising ....D....805 564-5200
715 Anacapa St Santa Barbara (93101) **(P-9110)**
Classmates Media Corporation ....B....818 287-3600
21301 Burbank Blvd Woodland Hills (91367) **(P-13729)**
Claud Townsley Inc ....D....310 527-6770
555 W 182nd St Gardena (90248) **(P-3138)**
Claude Laval Corporation ....D....559 255-1601
1365 N Clovis Ave Fresno (93727) **(P-7742)**
Claudia Richard Inc ....D....323 264-3915
4871 S Santa Fe Ave Vernon (90058) **(P-8295)**
Clauss Construction ....D....619 390-4940
9911 Maine Ave Lakeside (92040) **(P-3449)**
Clay Dunn Enterprises Inc ....C....310 549-1698
1606 E Carson St Carson (90745) **(P-2162)**
Clay Lacy Aviation Inc (PA) ....B....818 989-2900
7435 Valjean Ave Van Nuys (91406) **(P-4881)**
Clay Miranda Trucking Inc ....D....559 275-6250
3220 W Belmont Ave Fresno (93722) **(P-3991)**
Clayton Group Services, Santa Ana *Also called Bureau Veritas North Amer Inc* **(P-27665)**
CLC Incorporated (PA) ....E....916 789-7600
3001 Lava Ridge Ct # 250 Roseville (95661) **(P-14587)**
Clean Energy ....A....949 437-1000
4675 Macarthur Ct Ste 800 Newport Beach (92660) **(P-6157)**
Clean Energy Fuels Corp (PA) ....C....949 437-1000
4675 Macarthur Ct Ste 800 Newport Beach (92660) **(P-6190)**
Clean Enviroment ....D....619 521-0543
4570 Alvarado Canyon Rd C San Diego (92120) **(P-14217)**
Clean Harbors Envmtl Svcs Inc ....D....707 747-6699
4101 Industrial Way Benicia (94510) **(P-6380)**
Clean Hrbors Es Indus Svcs Inc ....D....707 745-1581
4501 California Ct Benicia (94510) **(P-17938)**
Clean King Laundry Systems Inc ....E....818 363-5500
15431 Chatsworth St Mission Hills (91345) **(P-13557)**
Clean Power Finance Inc ....C....899 525-2123
50 Osgood Pl Ste 400 San Francisco (94133) **(P-17939)**
Clean Up, San Bernardino *Also called Universal* **(P-14417)**
Clean-A-Rama Maint Svc LLC ....D....415 495-5298
526 Columbus Ave Fl 2 San Francisco (94133) **(P-14218)**
CLEANERIFIC, San Francisco *Also called Jewish Family and Chld Svcs* **(P-23873)**
Cleaning Services ....E....408 778-9251
7828 Monterey St Gilroy (95020) **(P-17940)**
Cleanrite Inc (PA) ....D....530 891-0333
1200 W East Ave Chico (95926) **(P-3505)**
Cleanstreet ....C....310 329-3078
1937 W 169th St Gardena (90247) **(P-6533)**
Cleantech Environmental, Irwindale *Also called Agritec International Ltd* **(P-8016)**
Clear Channel Riverside, Riverside *Also called Iheartcommunications Inc* **(P-5722)**
Clear Credit Capital, Agoura Hills *Also called Quality Home Loans* **(P-9852)**
Clear World Communications ....B....714 445-3900
3100 S Harbor Blvd # 300 Santa Ana (92704) **(P-5531)**
Clearbalance Holdings LLC ....E....858 535-0870
3636 Nobel Dr Ste 250 San Diego (92122) **(P-11969)**
Clearcapitalcom Inc ....C....530 550-2500
10266 Truckee Airport Rd Truckee (96161) **(P-11321)**
Clearcapitalcom Inc ....D....530 582-5011
1410 Rocky Ridge Dr # 250 Roseville (95661) **(P-11322)**
Clearcaptions LLC ....E....866 868-8695
3001 Lava Ridge Ct # 100 Roseville (95661) **(P-5532)**
Clearesult Consulting Inc ....D....415 848-1250
1 Sansome St Fl 35 San Francisco (94104) **(P-27689)**
Clearlake Family Health Center, Clearlake *Also called Adventist Health System/West* **(P-21267)**
Clearpath Lending ....C....949 502-3577
15635 Alton Pkwy Ste 300 Irvine (92618) **(P-9876)**
Clearpath Management Group Inc (PA) ....B....209 239-8700
1215 W Center St Ste 102 Manteca (95337) **(P-14832)**
Clearpath Workforce MGT Inc ....B....209 239-8700
1215 W Center St Ste 102 Manteca (95337) **(P-14833)**
Clearslide Inc (HQ) ....D....877 360-3366
45 Fremont St Fl 32 San Francisco (94105) **(P-15629)**
Clearview Capital LLC ....A....310 806-9555
12100 Wilshire Blvd # 800 Los Angeles (90025) **(P-12215)**
Clearwell Systems Inc ....C....877 253-2793
350 Ellis St Mountain View (94043) **(P-15630)**
Clem-Trans Inc ....E....909 877-4450
213 W Valley Blvd Rialto (92376) **(P-3992)**
Clement Preschool, Saratoga *Also called Precious Enterprises Inc* **(P-24372)**
Clement Support Services Inc ....D....408 227-1171
1001 Yosemite Dr Milpitas (95035) **(P-7265)**
Clendenen Vineyard MGT LLC ....D....707 473-0881
9235 W Dry Creek Rd Healdsburg (95448) **(P-137)**
Cleveland Marble LP ....E....714 998-3280
219 E Bristol Ln Orange (92865) **(P-2801)**
Cleveland Wrecking Company (HQ) ....D....626 967-4287
999 W Town And Country Rd Orange (92868) **(P-3450)**
Cli, Indio *Also called Commercial Lighting Inds Inc* **(P-7348)**
Click Labs Inc ....A....415 658-5227
315 Montgomery St Fl 8 San Francisco (94104) **(P-15063)**
Clif Bar & Company (PA) ....C....510 596-6300
1451 66th St Emeryville (94608) **(P-8769)**
Cliff House Restaurant, Fort Bragg *Also called Tradewinds Lodge* **(P-13338)**
Cliff View Terrace Inc ....D....805 682-7443
623 W Junipero St Santa Barbara (93105) **(P-24472)**
Clifford & Brown A Prof Corp ....D....661 322-6023
1430 Truxtun Ave Ste 900 Bakersfield (93301) **(P-22982)**
Clift Hotel Four Season, San Francisco *Also called Morgans Hotel Group MGT LLC* **(P-12944)**
Clift Hotels, San Francisco *Also called 495 Geary LLC* **(P-12295)**
Cliftonlarsonallen LLP ....B....916 784-7800
925 Highland Pointe Dr # 450 Roseville (95678) **(P-26166)**
Cliftonlarsonallen LLP ....D....626 857-7300
2210 E Route 66 Ste 100 Glendora (91740) **(P-26167)**
Cliftonlarsonallen LLP ....D....310 273-2501
1925 Century Park E Fl 16 Los Angeles (90067) **(P-26168)**
Clima-Tech Inc ....D....909 613-5513
187 W Orangethorpe Ave G Placentia (92870) **(P-17892)**
Climate Corporation (HQ) ....D....415 363-0500
201 3rd St Ste 1100 San Francisco (94103) **(P-683)**
Climatec LLC ....E....858 391-7000
13715 Stowe Dr Poway (92064) **(P-2541)**
Clinapps Inc ....D....858 866-0228
9530 Towne Centre Dr # 120 San Diego (92121) **(P-15064)**
Clinic Business, San Diego *Also called Scripps Health* **(P-19874)**
Clinic Inc (PA) ....D....323 730-1920
3834 S Western Ave Los Angeles (90062) **(P-22532)**
Clinica Medica Familiar ....D....714 541-0870
517 N Main St Ste 100 Santa Ana (92701) **(P-19384)**
Clinica Msr Oscar A Romero (PA) ....D....213 989-7700
123 S Alvarado St Los Angeles (90057) **(P-19385)**
Clinica Popular Medical Group ....E....213 381-7175
101 S Rossmore Ave Los Angeles (90004) **(P-19386)**
Clinica Sagrado Corazon ....E....714 491-7777
831 S Harbor Blvd Anaheim (92805) **(P-19387)**
Clinica Sierra Vista ....D....559 457-6900
3727 N 1st St Ste 106 Fresno (93726) **(P-23589)**
Clinica Sierra Vista ....E....661 326-6490
1430 Truxtun Ave Ste 300 Bakersfield (93301) **(P-22768)**
Clinica Sierra Vista (PA) ....D....661 635-3050
1430 Truxtun Ave Ste 400 Bakersfield (93301) **(P-19388)**
Clinica Sierra Vista ....D....559 457-5292
7202 N Millbrook Ave Fresno (93720) **(P-19389)**
Clinicas De Slud Del Peblo Inc (PA) ....D....760 344-9951
1166 K St Brawley (92227) **(P-19390)**
Clinicas De Slud Del Peblo Inc ....D....760 344-6471
900 Main St Brawley (92227) **(P-19391)**
Clinicas Del Camino Real Inc ....D....805 487-5351
650 Meta St Oxnard (93030) **(P-22533)**
Clinicas Del Camino Real Inc (PA) ....C....805 647-6322
200 S Wells Rd Ste 200 # 200 Ventura (93004) **(P-22534)**
Clinicomp International Inc (PA) ....D....858 546-8202
9655 Towne Centre Dr San Diego (92121) **(P-15933)**
Clipper Corporation (PA) ....E....310 533-8585
21124 Figueroa St Carson (90745) **(P-7133)**
Clocktower Inn ....D....805 652-0141
181 E Santa Clara St Ventura (93001) **(P-12468)**
Cloisters Mssion Hills Hosp HM, San Diego *Also called Mission Hills Post Acute Care* **(P-24601)**
Cloisters of La Jolla Inc ....D....858 459-4361
7160 Fay Ave La Jolla (92037) **(P-20315)**
Clontech, Mountain View *Also called Takara Bio Usa Inc* **(P-26469)**
Clorox Services Company ....D....925 425-6748
5060 Johnson Dr Pleasanton (94588) **(P-26811)**
Clorox Services Company (HQ) ....D....510 271-7000
1221 Broadway Fl 13 Oakland (94612) **(P-26812)**
Closet World Inc ....B....626 855-0846
14438 Don Julian Rd City of Industry (91746) **(P-3021)**
Closet World, The, City of Industry *Also called Home Organizers Inc* **(P-3043)**
Closingcorp Inc ....D....858 551-1500
3111 Camino Del Rio N # 200 San Diego (92108) **(P-16327)**
Cloud Automation Division, Aliso Viejo *Also called Quest Software Inc* **(P-15838)**
Cloudera Inc (PA) ....C....650 362-0488
395 Page Mill Rd Ste 300 Palo Alto (94306) **(P-15065)**
Cloudflare Inc (PA) ....D....650 319-8930
101 Townsend St San Francisco (94107) **(P-16883)**
Cloudpeople Global ....E....530 591-7028
2485 Notre Dame Blvd Chico (95928) **(P-15066)**
Cloudtrigger Inc ....D....858 367-5272
760 Garden View Ct # 120 Encinitas (92024) **(P-27195)**
Clover Network Inc ....D....650 210-7888
415 N Mathilda Ave Sunnyvale (94085) **(P-5533)**
Clover Sonoma, Petaluma *Also called Clover-Stornetta Farms Inc* **(P-8770)**
Clover-Stornetta Farms Inc (PA) ....C....707 769-3282
1800 S Mcdowell Blvd Petaluma (94954) **(P-8770)**
Cloverdale Healthcare Center, Cloverdale *Also called Ensign Cloverdale LLC* **(P-20394)**
Cloverleaf Bowl, Fremont *Also called Fremont Sports Inc* **(P-18490)**
Clovis Community Living, Fresno *Also called Community Medical Center* **(P-21336)**
Clovis Community Medical Ctr, Clovis *Also called Fresno Cmnty Hosp & Med Ctr* **(P-21421)**
Clovis Custom Drywall Inc ....E....559 297-7073
141 Sunnyside Ave Ste 108 Clovis (93611) **(P-2867)**
Clovis Unified School District ....B....559 327-3900
885 Gettysburg Ave Clovis (93612) **(P-18332)**
Clp Resources Inc ....E....415 508-0910
1485 Bay Shore Blvd # 138 San Francisco (94124) **(P-14834)**
Clp Resources Inc ....E....707 569-0200
1260 N Dutton Ave Santa Rosa (95401) **(P-14835)**

ALPHABETIC

Employee Codes: A=Over 500 employees, B=251-500
C=101-250, D=51-100, E=50
2019 Directory of California
Wholesalers and Services Companies
© Mergent Inc. 1-800-342-5647
1255

Clp Resources Inc ....D.......916 788-0300
1000 Sunrise Ave Ste 8a Roseville (95661) *(P-14836)*
Clp Resources Inc ....C.......650 261-2100
570 El Cmino Real Ste 170 Redwood City (94063) *(P-14837)*
Clp Resources Inc ....E.......415 446-7000
4460 Redwood Hwy Ste 14 San Rafael (94903) *(P-14838)*
Clp Resources Inc ....D.......714 300-0510
741 E Ball Rd Ste 100 Anaheim (92805) *(P-14839)*
Clp Resources Inc ....D.......818 260-9190
111 N First St Ste 100 Burbank (91502) *(P-14840)*
Clpf - Sycamore ....D.......212 883-2500
6721 Sycamore Canyon Blvd Riverside (92507) *(P-11323)*
Cls Landscape Management Inc ....B.......909 628-3005
4711 Schaefer Ave Unit A Chino (91710) *(P-970)*
Cls Trnsprttion Los Angles LLC (HQ) ....C.......310 414-8189
600 S Allied Way El Segundo (90245) *(P-3785)*
Club Assist North America Inc (PA) ....D.......213 388-4333
888 W 6th St Ste 300 Los Angeles (90017) *(P-6630)*
Club Assist US LLC ....C.......213 388-4333
888 W 6th St Ste 300 Los Angeles (90017) *(P-6631)*
Club At Los Gatos Inc ....D.......408 867-5110
14428 Big Basin Way Ste A Saratoga (95070) *(P-18586)*
Club At Shnndoah Sprng Vlg Inc ....E.......760 343-3497
32700 Desert Moon Dr Thousand Palms (92276) *(P-18893)*
Club Nautique (PA) ....D.......510 521-5544
1150 Ballena Blvd Ste 161 Alameda (94501) *(P-18894)*
Club of Sunrise Country ....D.......760 328-6549
71601 Country Club Dr Rancho Mirage (92270) *(P-18895)*
Club One At Petaluma ....D.......707 766-8080
1201 Redwood Way Petaluma (94954) *(P-18896)*
Club One Casino Inc ....B.......559 497-3000
1033 Van Ness Ave Fresno (93721) *(P-12469)*
Club Quarters San Francisco ....D.......415 268-3606
424 Clay St San Francisco (94111) *(P-12470)*
Club Sport of Fremont ....C.......510 226-8500
46650 Landing Pkwy Fremont (94538) *(P-17087)*
Club Tan, Bakersfield *Also called Europro Inc (P-13743)*
Clubcorp Usa Inc ....C.......858 756-2471
5690 Cancha De Golf Rancho Santa Fe (92091) *(P-18897)*
Clubcorp Usa Inc ....E.......916 434-9100
1525 Highway 193 Lincoln (95648) *(P-18698)*
Clubsport of Fremont, Fremont *Also called Leisure Sports Inc (P-18625)*
Clubsport San Ramon LLC ....C.......925 283-4000
4000 Mt Diablo Blvd Lafayette (94549) *(P-18587)*
Clubsport San Ramon LLC (PA) ....B.......925 735-1182
350 Bollinger Canyon Ln San Ramon (94582) *(P-18588)*
Clum Morford Distributing (PA) ....D.......831 333-1100
20 Ragsdale Dr Ste 100 Monterey (93940) *(P-17088)*
Clutter Inc (PA) ....C.......800 805-4023
3526 Hayden Ave Culver City (90232) *(P-13730)*
Clyde & Co US LLP ....D.......415 365-9800
101 2nd St Fl 24 San Francisco (94105) *(P-22983)*
Clyde Miles Cnstr Co Inc ....D.......925 427-4473
1110 Burnett Ave Ste C Concord (94520) *(P-1145)*
CM Concrete Inc ....C.......805 520-8100
650 E Easy St Simi Valley (93065) *(P-3234)*
CM Laundry LLC ....D.......310 436-6170
14919 S Figueroa St Gardena (90248) *(P-13630)*
CM Wind Down Topco Inc ....D.......415 995-6800
750 Battery St Ste 300 San Francisco (94111) *(P-5706)*
CMA Fire Protection (PA) ....D.......661 322-9344
4300 Stine Rd Ste 800 Bakersfield (93313) *(P-2163)*
Cmac Cnstr Refinery & Pipeline, Long Beach *Also called Cmac Construction Company (P-1909)*
Cmac Construction Company ....D.......562 435-5611
1450 Santa Fe Ave Long Beach (90813) *(P-1909)*
Cmat, Stockton *Also called California Materials Inc (P-3986)*
Cmb Laboratory, Cypress *Also called Consoldted Med Bo-Analysis Inc (P-22069)*
CMC Fontana Steel ....B.......909 899-9993
12451 Arrow Rte Rancho Cucamonga (91739) *(P-3371)*
CMC Rebar ....D.......909 899-9993
12451 Arrow Rte Rancho Cucamonga (91739) *(P-3372)*
CMC Rebar Fabricators, Bloomington *Also called C M C Steel Fabricators Inc (P-3367)*
Cmf Inc ....D.......714 637-2409
1317 W Grove Ave Orange (92865) *(P-3139)*
Cmg Financial Services ....D.......925 983-3073
3160 Crow Canyon Rd # 400 San Ramon (94583) *(P-17089)*
Cmg Mortgage Inc (PA) ....B.......619 554-1327
3160 Crow Canyon Rd # 400 San Ramon (94583) *(P-9877)*
Cmp Film & Design Burbank LLC ....D.......818 729-0800
2717 W Olive Ave Burbank (91505) *(P-27549)*
Cmre Financial Services Inc ....B.......714 528-3200
3075 E Imperial Hwy # 200 Brea (92821) *(P-13997)*
CMS, Simi Valley *Also called Computerized Mgt Svcs Inc (P-26817)*
CMS Llnl ....D.......925 422-5584
7000 East Ave Msl090 Livermore (94550) *(P-18183)*
Cmsc, San Francisco *Also called Costless Maintenance Svcs Co (P-14230)*
Cmtc, Torrance *Also called California Mfg Tech Consulting (P-27179)*
Cmts LLC ....C.......310 215-0237
5777 W Century Blvd # 1105 Los Angeles (90045) *(P-26813)*
CNA Financial Corporation ....C.......714 255-2200
1800 E Imperial Hwy # 200 Brea (92821) *(P-10587)*
CNA Insurance, Brea *Also called CNA Financial Corporation (P-10587)*
CNA Surety Corporation ....D.......619 682-3550
1455 Frazee Rd Ste 801 San Diego (92108) *(P-10588)*
Cncml A California Ltd Partnr ....D.......530 583-1578
1920 Squaw Valley Rd Olympic Valley (96146) *(P-12471)*
Cnet Networks Inc ....A.......415 344-2000
235 2nd St San Francisco (94105) *(P-15934)*
Cnet Technology Corporation (HQ) ....C.......408 392-9966
26291 Prod Ave Ste 205 Hayward (94545) *(P-7462)*
Cnh Industrial America LLC ....E.......510 351-2015
1919 Williams St San Leandro (94577) *(P-7673)*
Cni Thl Ops LLC ....D.......408 943-0600
1801 Barber Ln Milpitas (95035) *(P-12472)*
Cni Thl Propco Fe LLC ....D.......661 325-9700
5101 California Ave Bakersfield (93309) *(P-12473)*
Cnn America Inc ....D.......323 993-5000
6430 W Sunset Blvd # 300 Los Angeles (90028) *(P-5863)*
Cnrc LLC ....D.......760 325-2937
2299 N Indian Ave Palm Springs (92262) *(P-20316)*
Cns Logistics Inc ....D.......562 229-1133
108 W Walnut St Ste 270 Gardena (90248) *(P-5034)*
Cntry Vlla Merced Hlthcre Cntr, Merced *Also called Country Villa Service Corp (P-23624)*
CNX Media Inc ....D.......415 229-8300
1 Beach St Ste 300 San Francisco (94133) *(P-18032)*
Co D L Pham MD ....E.......714 531-2091
10362 Bolsa Ave Ste 110 Westminster (92683) *(P-19392)*
Co Team Staffing ....D.......209 578-4286
1608 Sunrise Ave Ste D Modesto (95350) *(P-14841)*
CO-OP NETWORK, Rancho Cucamonga *Also called CU Cooperative Systems Inc (P-9678)*
Co-Optimum, Sherman Oaks *Also called Ansira Partners Inc (P-17004)*
Co-Sales, Pleasanton *Also called Impact Group LLC (P-8416)*
Coa Inc (PA) ....C.......562 944-7899
12928 Sandoval St Santa Fe Springs (90670) *(P-6717)*
Coach Bus Lines, San Francisco *Also called Cusa Fl LLC (P-3894)*
Coach Usa Inc ....C.......714 978-8855
2001 S Manchester Ave Anaheim (92802) *(P-4967)*
Coachella Valley Water Dst (PA) ....C.......760 398-2651
85995 Avenue 52 Coachella (92236) *(P-6229)*
Coachella Valley Water Dst ....C.......760 398-2651
75515 Hovley Ln E Palm Desert (92211) *(P-6230)*
Coachella Valley Water Dst ....C.......760 398-2651
75 525 Hovley Ln Palm Desert (92260) *(P-6231)*
Coachella Vly Rescue Mission ....E.......760 347-3512
82873 Via Venecia Indio (92201) *(P-23590)*
Coact Designworks ....E.......916 930-5900
801 T St Sacramento (95811) *(P-26038)*
Coadna Holdings Inc (HQ) ....D.......408 736-1100
1020 Stewart Dr Sunnyvale (94085) *(P-11970)*
Coalinga Dstngished Cmnty Care ....D.......559 935-5939
834 Maple Rd Coalinga (93210) *(P-20317)*
Coalinga Regional Medical Cent ....C.......559 935-6400
1191 Phelps Ave Coalinga (93210) *(P-21329)*
Coalinga State Hospital, Coalinga *Also called Califrnia Dept State Hospitals (P-21931)*
Coalition For Family Harmony ....D.......805 983-6014
1030 N Ventura Rd Oxnard (93030) *(P-23591)*
Coan Construction Co Inc ....D.......909 868-6812
1481 E Grand Ave Pomona (91766) *(P-3235)*
Coassure Inc ....D.......408 244-0400
4100 Moorpark Ave Ste 122 San Jose (95117) *(P-27690)*
Coast Alum & Architectural Inc (PA) ....C.......562 946-6061
10628 Fulton Wells Ave Santa Fe Springs (90670) *(P-7266)*
Coast Building Products, San Jose *Also called Coast Insulation Contrs Inc (P-2868)*
Coast Building Products, Salinas *Also called Superior Contracting Corp (P-2965)*
Coast Capital, San Jose *Also called ECi Corporation A Corp Nev (P-9801)*
Coast Carwash LP ....E.......562 961-5555
5677 E 7th St Long Beach (90804) *(P-17811)*
Coast Central Credit Union (PA) ....C.......707 445-8801
2650 Harrison Ave Eureka (95501) *(P-9546)*
Coast Citrus Distributors (PA) ....D.......619 661-7950
7597 Bristow Ct San Diego (92154) *(P-8657)*
Coast Citrus Distributors ....C.......213 955-3444
1601 E Olympic Blvd Los Angeles (90021) *(P-8658)*
Coast Citrus Distributors ....E.......650 588-0707
131 Terminal Ct 13 South San Francisco (94080) *(P-8659)*
Coast Counties Peterbilt, San Leandro *Also called Coast Counties Truck & Eqp Co (P-6582)*
Coast Counties Truck & Eqp Co ....D.......510 568-6933
260 Doolittle Dr San Leandro (94577) *(P-6582)*
Coast Environmental Inc ....D.......760 929-9570
2221 Las Palmas Dr Ste J Carlsbad (92011) *(P-17090)*
Coast Farms Inc ....D.......805 383-0455
645 Laguna Rd Camarillo (93012) *(P-44)*
Coast Hand Car Wash, Long Beach *Also called Coast Carwash LP (P-17811)*
Coast Insulation Contrs Inc (HQ) ....D.......386 304-2222
1341 Old Oakland Rd San Jose (95112) *(P-2868)*
Coast Iron & Steel Co ....E.......562 946-4421
12300 Lakeland Rd Santa Fe Springs (90670) *(P-3373)*
Coast Landscape Management, Alviso *Also called Bayscape Management Inc (P-26777)*
Coast Nurseries Inc (PA) ....C.......805 386-4253
5870 E Los Angeles Ave Somis (93066) *(P-251)*
Coast Personnel Services Inc (PA) ....A.......408 653-2100
2295 De La Cruz Blvd Santa Clara (95050) *(P-14588)*
Coast Plaza Doctors Hospital (PA) ....D.......562 868-3751
13100 Studebaker Rd Norwalk (90650) *(P-21330)*
Coast Plaza Hospital, Norwalk *Also called Cph Hospital Management LLC (P-22280)*
Coast Produce Company (PA) ....C.......213 955-4900
1791 Bay St Los Angeles (90021) *(P-8660)*
Coast To Coast Bus Eqp Inc (PA) ....D.......949 457-7300
8 Vanderbilt Ste 200 Irvine (92618) *(P-6956)*
Coast To Coast Realty ....D.......818 360-2609
18879 Brasilia Dr Porter Ranch (91326) *(P-11324)*
Coast To Coast Restoration, Sun Valley *Also called Coast To Coast Water Damage (P-14219)*
Coast To Coast Water Damage ....E.......818 255-3323
10881 La Tuna Canyon Rd Sun Valley (91352) *(P-14219)*
Coast Tropical, San Diego *Also called Coast Citrus Distributors (P-8657)*

Mergent e-mail: customerrelations@mergent.com
1256
2019 Directory of California
Wholesalers and Services Companies
(P-0000) Products & Services Section entry number
(PA)=Parent Co (HQ)=Headquarters (DH)=Div Headquarters

Coast Tropical, South San Francisco *Also called Coast Citrus Distributors* ***(P-8659)***
Coast Waste Management .... C 760 753-9412
5960 El Camino Real Carlsbad (92008) ***(P-6381)***
Coastal Alliance Holdings Inc .... C 562 370-1000
1650 Ximeno Ave Ste 120 Long Beach (90804) ***(P-11325)***
Coastal Building Services Inc .... B 714 775-2855
718 N Hariton St Orange (92868) ***(P-14220)***
Coastal Closeouts Inc .... D 323 589-7900
100 Oceangate Ste 1200 Long Beach (90802) ***(P-17091)***
Coastal Cmnty Senior Care LLC .... C 562 596-4884
5500 E Atherton St # 216 Long Beach (90815) ***(P-22265)***
Coastal Community College, Westminster *Also called Orange County One Stop Center* ***(P-14682)***
Coastal Community Hospital, Santa Ana *Also called Health Resources Corp* ***(P-21444)***
Coastal Grading and Excavating .... E 805 445-6433
756 Calle Plano Camarillo (93012) ***(P-3419)***
Coastal Harvesting Inc .... B 805 525-6250
503 S Palm Ave Santa Paula (93060) ***(P-641)***
Coastal Health Care Inc .... D 310 828-5596
1321 Franklin St Santa Monica (90404) ***(P-20318)***
Coastal International Inc (PA) .... A 415 339-1700
3 Harbor Dr Ste 211 Sausalito (94965) ***(P-17092)***
Coastal Intl Cnstr Svcs, Sausalito *Also called Coastal International Inc* ***(P-17092)***
Coastal Marine Services Inc (PA) .... E 619 291-8176
2255 National Ave San Diego (92113) ***(P-3506)***
Coastal Mirage Landscapes .... D 949 496-7070
26362 Via De Anza San Juan Capistrano (92675) ***(P-746)***
Coastal Pacific Fd Distrs Inc (PA) .... C 909 947-2066
1015 Performance Dr Stockton (95206) ***(P-8390)***
Coastal Pacific Fd Distrs Inc .... C 909 947-2066
1520 E Mission Blvd Ste B Ontario (91761) ***(P-8391)***
Coastal Pacific Foods, Ontario *Also called Coastal Pacific Fd Distrs Inc* ***(P-8391)***
Coastal Paving Incorporated .... D 408 988-5559
1295 Norman Ave Santa Clara (95054) ***(P-3236)***
Coastal Radiation Oncology Med .... D 805 494-4483
1240 S Westlake Blvd Westlake Village (91361) ***(P-19393)***
Coastal Rubbish, Sun Valley *Also called Crown Disposal Company Inc* ***(P-6387)***
Coastal Select Insurance Co .... E 707 863-3700
4820 Busineca Ctr Dr 20 Fairfield (94534) ***(P-10589)***
Coastal The, North Hollywood *Also called Coastal Tile Inc* ***(P-2991)***
Coastal Tile Inc .... D 818 988-6134
7403 Greenbush Ave North Hollywood (91605) ***(P-2991)***
Coastal Traffic Systems Inc .... D 714 641-3744
9391 Power Dr Huntington Beach (92646) ***(P-7347)***
Coastal Transport Co Inc .... D 619 584-1055
9950 San Diego Mission Rd F San Diego (92108) ***(P-3993)***
Coastal View Halthcare Ctr LLC .... D 805 642-4101
4904 Telegraph Rd Ventura (93003) ***(P-21039)***
Coaster Company of America, Santa Fe Springs *Also called Coa Inc* ***(P-6717)***
Coasthills Credit Union (PA) .... D 805 733-7600
3880 Constellation Rd Lompoc (93436) ***(P-9628)***
Coastline Cnstr & Awng Co Inc .... D 714 891-9798
5742 Research Dr Huntington Beach (92649) ***(P-1146)***
Coastside Senior Housing Limit .... E 415 355-7100
925 Main St Half Moon Bay (94019) ***(P-11326)***
Cobalt Construction Company .... D 805 577-6222
2259 Ward Ave Ste 200 Simi Valley (93065) ***(P-1276)***
Cobb Property Services, Orange *Also called Cobb Waterblasting Inc* ***(P-14221)***
Cobb Waterblasting Inc .... D 714 769-2622
1145 W Shelley Ct Orange (92868) ***(P-14221)***
Coblentz Patch Duffy Bass LLP .... D 510 655-4598
1 Montgomery St Ste 3000 San Francisco (94104) ***(P-22984)***
Cockrell Electric Inc .... D 760 864-6233
79553 Country Club Dr B Bermuda Dunes (92203) ***(P-2542)***
Codding Construction Co .... E 707 795-3550
1400 Valley House Dr # 100 Rohnert Park (94928) ***(P-1508)***
Code America Inc .... D 562 502-7365
235 E Broadway Ste 960 Long Beach (90802) ***(P-14589)***
Code and Theory LLC .... D 415 839-6455
250 Montgomery St Ste 800 San Francisco (94104) ***(P-9208)***
Code For America Labs Inc .... D 415 625-9633
155 9th St San Francisco (94103) ***(P-27196)***
Coelho West Custom Farming .... D 559 884-2566
26979 S Butte Ave Five Points (93624) ***(P-331)***
Cofa Media Group LLC .... D 877 293-2007
5650 El Camino Real Carlsbad (92008) ***(P-5534)***
Coffman Specialties Inc (PA) .... C 858 536-3100
9685 Via Excelencia # 200 San Diego (92126) ***(P-3237)***
Cofiroute Usa LLC .... C 949 754-0198
200 Spectrum Center Dr # 1650 Irvine (92618) ***(P-5215)***
Cogar International Enrgy Corp (PA) .... E 626 494-8157
5286 Industrial Dr Huntington Beach (92649) ***(P-2543)***
Cogent Financial Group .... D 562 985-1388
5199 E Pacific Coast Hwy Long Beach (90804) ***(P-9735)***
Cognitive Medical Systems Inc .... D 858 509-4949
9444 Waples St Ste 300 San Diego (92121) ***(P-15067)***
Cognitiveclouds Software Inc .... D 415 234-3611
5433 Ontario Cmn Fremont (94555) ***(P-15068)***
Cognix Automation Inc .... E 925 464-8822
3423 Torlano Pl Pleasanton (94566) ***(P-15935)***
Cohen Brown MGT Group Inc (PA) .... D 310 966-1001
11835 W Olympic Blvd 920e Los Angeles (90064) ***(P-27197)***
Cohen Richard Ldscp & Cnstr .... E 949 768-0599
20795 Canada Rd El Toro (92630) ***(P-814)***
Cohen Ventures Inc (PA) .... D 510 482-4420
449 15th St Ste 402 Oakland (94612) ***(P-27691)***
Coherent Inc .... D 408 764-4000
1100 La Avenida St Mountain View (94043) ***(P-26505)***
Cohesity Inc (PA) .... D 408 645-0041
300 Park Ave Ste 800 San Jose (95110) ***(P-17093)***
Cohn Wholesale Fruit & Grocery (PA) .... C 619 528-1113
3511 Camino Del Rio S # 306 San Diego (92108) ***(P-8661)***
Cohnreznick LLP .... D 818 205-2600
21600 Oxnard St Ste 700 Woodland Hills (91367) ***(P-26169)***
Cohnreznick LLP .... E 310 477-3722
11755 Wilshire Blvd # 1700 Los Angeles (90025) ***(P-26170)***
Coinbase Inc (PA) .... D 415 275-2890
548 Market St Ste 23008 San Francisco (94104) ***(P-9674)***
Coinmach Corporation (PA) .... D 818 637-4300
3628 San Fernando Rd Glendale (91204) ***(P-13558)***
Coit Restoration Services, Modesto *Also called C & S Draperies Inc* ***(P-13573)***
Coit Services Inc .... E 949 760-0760
1297 Logan Ave Costa Mesa (92626) ***(P-13564)***
Cokeva Inc .... C 916 462-6001
9000 Foothills Blvd Roseville (95747) ***(P-16280)***
Coldwater Care Center LLC .... D 818 766-6105
12750 Riverside Dr North Hollywood (91607) ***(P-20319)***
Coldwell Banker, West Hollywood *Also called Coldwer Banker Previews* ***(P-11366)***
Coldwell Banker, Davis *Also called Doug Arnold Real Estate Inc* ***(P-11406)***
Coldwell Banker, Pasadena *Also called Nrt Commercial Utah LLC* ***(P-11637)***
Coldwell Banker, Canyon Lake *Also called Cbabr Inc* ***(P-11274)***
Coldwell Banker, Bakersfield *Also called Preferred Brokers Inc* ***(P-11677)***
Coldwell Banker, Valencia *Also called Vista Valencia Group Inc* ***(P-11815)***
Coldwell Banker, Vista *Also called Caldwell Banker Inc* ***(P-11261)***
Coldwell Banker .... D 916 447-5900
730 Alhambra Blvd Ste 150 Sacramento (95816) ***(P-11327)***
Coldwell Banker .... D 650 596-5400
580 El Camino Real San Carlos (94070) ***(P-10590)***
Coldwell Banker .... D 619 460-6600
9332 Fuerte Dr La Mesa (91941) ***(P-11328)***
Coldwell Banker .... D 760 753-5616
740 Garden View Ct # 100 Encinitas (92024) ***(P-11329)***
Coldwell Banker .... D 650 324-4456
1377 El Camino Real Menlo Park (94025) ***(P-11330)***
Coldwell Banker .... E 650 726-1100
248 Main St Ste 200 Half Moon Bay (94019) ***(P-11331)***
Coldwell Banker Affiliates .... D 650 941-7040
161 S San Antonio Rd # 1 Los Altos (94022) ***(P-11332)***
Coldwell Banker Amaral & Assoc .... D 925 439-7400
3775 Main St Ste E Oakley (94561) ***(P-11333)***
Coldwell Banker and Associates (PA) .... D 951 304-2900
23823 Clinton Keith Rd # 102 Wildomar (92595) ***(P-9943)***
Coldwell Banker Coastl Aliance, Long Beach *Also called Coastal Alliance Holdings Inc* ***(P-11325)***
Coldwell Banker Hartwig Co, Lancaster *Also called Hartwig Realty Inc* ***(P-11500)***
Coldwell Banker Home Source .... D 760 684-8100
15500 W Sand St Ste 2 Victorville (92392) ***(P-11334)***
Coldwell Banker Inland Brokers, Wildomar *Also called Coldwell Banker and Associates* ***(P-9943)***
Coldwell Banker Premier Prpts .... D 805 565-2200
1498 E Valley Rd Santa Barbara (93108) ***(P-11335)***
Coldwell Banker Prof Group .... D 408 383-1044
2860 Zanker Rd Ste 204 San Jose (95134) ***(P-11336)***
Coldwell Banker Property Shop .... D 805 646-7288
727 W Ojai Ave Ojai (93023) ***(P-11337)***
Coldwell Banker RE Corp .... D 818 995-2424
15490 Ventura Blvd # 100 Sherman Oaks (91403) ***(P-11338)***
Coldwell Banker RE Corp .... E 408 981-7200
1000 Sunset Dr Ste 190 Roseville (95678) ***(P-11339)***
Coldwell Banker RE Corp .... E 909 792-4147
501 W Redlands Blvd Ste A Redlands (92373) ***(P-11340)***
Coldwell Banker RE LLC .... D 408 491-1600
1045 Willow St San Jose (95125) ***(P-11341)***
Coldwell Banker Residential RE, San Jose *Also called Terry Meyer* ***(P-11792)***
Coldwell Banker Residential RE (HQ) .... B 949 367-1800
27271 Las Ramblas Mission Viejo (92691) ***(P-11342)***
Coldwell Banker Residential RE .... D 626 445-5500
15 E Foothill Blvd Arcadia (91006) ***(P-11343)***
Coldwell Banker Sky Ridge Rlty, Blue Jay *Also called Cbsrr Inc* ***(P-11286)***
Coldwell Banker Solano Pacific, Benicia *Also called Solano Pacific Corporation* ***(P-11770)***
Coldwell Banker Town & Country .... D 626 966-3688
345 E Rowland St Covina (91723) ***(P-11344)***
Coldwell Bankers Residential .... D 510 583-5400
21060 Redwood Rd Ste 100 Castro Valley (94546) ***(P-11345)***
Coldwell Bankers Residential (PA) .... C 818 575-2660
604 Lindero Canyon Rd Agoura Hills (91377) ***(P-11346)***
Coldwell Bnkr First Class Rlty .... D 323 721-7430
7825 Florence Ave A Downey (90240) ***(P-11347)***
Coldwell Bnkr Residential Brkg .... D 650 558-6800
181 2nd Ave Ste 100 San Mateo (94401) ***(P-11348)***
Coldwell Bnkr Residential Brkg .... D 530 823-7653
500 Auburn Folsom Rd # 300 Auburn (95603) ***(P-11349)***
Coldwell Bnkr Residential Brkg (HQ) .... D 925 275-3000
1855 Gateway Blvd Ste 750 Concord (94520) ***(P-11350)***
Coldwell Bnkr Residential Brkg .... D 650 558-4200
1427 Chapin Ave Burlingame (94010) ***(P-11351)***
Coldwell Bnkr Residential Brkg .... D 831 462-9000
2140 41st Ave Ste 100 Capitola (95010) ***(P-11352)***
Coldwell Bnkr Residential Brkg .... D 310 273-3113
166 N Canon Dr Ste 200 Beverly Hills (90210) ***(P-11353)***
Coldwell Bnkr Residential Brkg .... D 415 447-8800
1801 Lombard St San Francisco (94123) ***(P-11354)***
Coldwell Bnkr Residential Brkg .... D 760 325-4500
1081 N Palm Canyon Dr Palm Springs (92262) ***(P-11355)***
Coldwell Bnkr Residential Brkg .... D 916 966-8200
5034 Sunrise Blvd Fair Oaks (95628) ***(P-11356)***

ALPHABETIC

Coldwell Bnkr Residential Brkg...E...714 832-0020
21580 Yorba Linda Blvd Yorba Linda (92887) ***(P-11357)***
Coldwell Bnkr Residential Brkg...D...818 222-0023
23647 Calabasas Rd Calabasas (91302) ***(P-11358)***
Coldwell Bnkr Residential Brkg...D...760 776-9898
72605 Highway 111 Ste B2 Palm Desert (92260) ***(P-11359)***
Coldwell Bnkr Residential Brkg...D...760 771-5454
45000 Club Dr Indian Wells (92210) ***(P-11360)***
Coldwell Bnkr Residential Brkg...D...831 420-2628
410 Sims Rd Santa Cruz (95060) ***(P-11361)***
Coldwell Bnkr Residential Brkg...D...510 608-7600
3340 Walnut Ave Ste 110 Fremont (94538) ***(P-11362)***
Coldwell Bnkr Rsdential RE LLC...D...408 355-1500
410 N Santa Cruz Ave Los Gatos (95030) ***(P-11363)***
Coldwell Bnkr Rsdntial, Newport Beach *Also called C B Coast Newport Properties* ***(P-11256)***
Coldwell Bnkr Rsdntial RE Svcs...D...916 933-1155
4370 Town Center Blvd # 270 El Dorado Hills (95762) ***(P-11364)***
Coldwell Bnkr Rsdntial Re Svcs (PA)...D...949 367-1800
27271 Las Ramblas Mission Viejo (92691) ***(P-11365)***
Coldwer Banker Previews...C...310 278-9470
9069 W Sunset Blvd # 100 West Hollywood (90069) ***(P-11366)***
Cole-Schaefer Ambulance Svc, Pomona *Also called Schaefer Ambulance Service Inc* ***(P-3845)***
Colfin Esh Funding LLC...B...310 282-8820
2450 Broadway Fl 6 Santa Monica (90404) ***(P-12033)***
Colich & Sons, Gardena *Also called Colich Sons* ***(P-1910)***
Colich Sons...C...323 770-2920
547 W 140th St Gardena (90248) ***(P-1910)***
Collabria Care...D...707 258-9080
414 S Jefferson St NAPA (94559) ***(P-22266)***
Collabrus Inc...C...415 288-1826
111 Sutter St Ste 900 San Francisco (94104) ***(P-26171)***
Collectech Systems Inc (HQ)...C...818 597-7500
2290 Agate Ct 1a Simi Valley (93065) ***(P-13998)***
Collected Group Company LLC...E...323 277-3900
5300 S Santa Fe Ave Vernon (90058) ***(P-8296)***
Collection Technology Inc...D...800 743-4284
10801 6th St Ste 200 Rancho Cucamonga (91730) ***(P-13999)***
Collective Digital Studio, LLC, Beverly Hills *Also called Studio 71 LP* ***(P-13956)***
Collective Health, San Francisco *Also called Collectivehealth Inc* ***(P-10591)***
Collective MGT Group LLC...C...323 655-8585
8383 Wilshire Blvd # 1050 Beverly Hills (90211) ***(P-26814)***
Collectivehealth Inc...B...650 376-3804
85 Bluxome St San Francisco (94107) ***(P-10591)***
Collectors Universe Inc (PA)...D...949 567-1234
1610 E Saint Andrew Pl Santa Ana (92705) ***(P-17941)***
College Hospital Inc (PA)...A...562 924-9581
10802 College Pl Cerritos (90703) ***(P-21941)***
College Hospital Cerritos, Cerritos *Also called College Hospital Inc* ***(P-21941)***
College Medical Center, Long Beach *Also called Chlb LLC* ***(P-21940)***
College Movers, San Diego *Also called Student Movers Inc* ***(P-4377)***
College Operations LLC...E...559 353-0576
1730 S College Ave Dinuba (93618) ***(P-24297)***
College Park Realty Inc (PA)...C...562 594-6753
10791 Los Alamitos Blvd Los Alamitos (90720) ***(P-11367)***
College Park Realty Inc...E...562 982-0300
2610 Los Coyotes Diagonal Long Beach (90815) ***(P-11368)***
College Vsta Convalescent Hosp, Los Angeles *Also called Notellage Corporation* ***(P-21170)***
Collier Warehouse Inc...E...415 920-9720
90 Dorman Ave San Francisco (94124) ***(P-6816)***
Colliers International...D...415 788-3100
101 2nd St Ste 1100 San Francisco (94105) ***(P-11369)***
Colliers Intl Prperty Cons Inc...E...858 455-1515
4660 La Jolla Village Dr # 100 San Diego (92122) ***(P-11370)***
Colliers Intl Prperty Cons Inc...D...916 929-5999
301 University Ave # 100 Sacramento (95825) ***(P-11371)***
Colliers Investment Services, San Jose *Also called Colliers Parrish Intl Inc* ***(P-11372)***
Colliers Parrish Intl Inc...D...408 282-3800
450 W Santa Clara St San Jose (95113) ***(P-11372)***
Colliers Parrish Intl Inc...D...925 279-1050
1850 Mt Diablo Blvd # 200 Walnut Creek (94596) ***(P-11373)***
Collins Avenue LLC...E...323 930-6633
5410 Wilshire Blvd # 800 Los Angeles (90036) ***(P-5779)***
Collins Cllins Muir Stwart LLP...E...626 243-1100
1100 El Centro St Frnt South Pasadena (91030) ***(P-22985)***
Collins Electrical Company Inc (PA)...B...209 466-3691
3412 Metro Dr Stockton (95215) ***(P-2544)***
Collins Electrical Company Inc...C...209 466-3691
1902 Channel Dr West Sacramento (95691) ***(P-2545)***
Collins Electrical Company Inc...D...831 384-0114
385 Reservation Rd Marina (93933) ***(P-2546)***
Collwood Ter Stellar Care Inc...D...619 287-2920
4518 54th St San Diego (92115) ***(P-21040)***
Colonial Care Center, Long Beach *Also called Longwood Management Corp* ***(P-21145)***
Colonial Gardens Nursing Home, Pico Rivera *Also called Rivera Sanitarium Inc* ***(P-20724)***
Colonial Home Care Svcs Inc...C...714 289-7220
326 W Katella Ave Ste F Orange (92867) ***(P-22267)***
COLONIAL MANOR CONVALESCENT HOSPITAL, West Covina *Also called Wicoro Inc* ***(P-21255)***
Colony Advisors, Los Angeles *Also called Colony Management Inc* ***(P-11374)***
Colony Capitl Inv Advisors LLC...D...310 282-8820
515 S Flower St Fl 44 Los Angeles (90071) ***(P-12216)***
Colony Management Inc...D...310 282-8820
1999 Ave Of The Los Angeles (90067) ***(P-11374)***
Colony Northstar Inc...D...310 882-7230
11601 Wilshire Blvd # 1600 Los Angeles (90025) ***(P-11375)***
Colony Palms Hotel LLC...D...760 969-1800
572 N Indian Canyon Dr Palm Springs (92262) ***(P-12474)***

Color Ad Inc...E...310 632-5500
18601 S Santa Fe Ave Compton (90221) ***(P-13804)***
Color By Deluxe, Burbank *Also called Deluxe Laboratories Inc* ***(P-18187)***
Color Concepts, Canoga Park *Also called Rte Enterprises Inc* ***(P-2477)***
Color Spot Lodi, Lodi *Also called Sg Personnel LLC* ***(P-300)***
Color Spot Nurseries Inc...D...310 549-7470
321 W Sepulveda Blvd Carson (90745) ***(P-9130)***
Colorado River Adventures Inc (PA)...C...760 663-3737
2715 Parker Dam Rd Earp (92242) ***(P-13462)***
Colorado River Medical Center, Needles *Also called Lifepoint Health Inc* ***(P-21554)***
Colorado River Medical Center...D...760 326-4531
1401 Bailey Ave Needles (92363) ***(P-19394)***
Colorama Wholesale Nursery, Azusa *Also called Richard Wilson Wellington* ***(P-294)***
Colorescience Inc...C...866 426-5673
2141 Palomar Airport Rd R Carlsbad (92011) ***(P-8163)***
Colorexa, Van Nuys *Also called Exandal Corporation* ***(P-8404)***
Colortokens Inc...E...408 341-6030
2101 Tasman Dr Ste 201 Santa Clara (95054) ***(P-15631)***
Colosseum Athletics Corp...D...310 667-8341
2400 S Wilmington Ave Compton (90220) ***(P-8253)***
Colrich Communities Inc...D...858 350-7672
444 W Beech St Ste 300 San Diego (92101) ***(P-11865)***
Cols Inc...C...714 720-6100
1611 S Melrose Dr 253&278 Vista (92081) ***(P-3786)***
Colsa Corporation...C...661 273-3859
41240 12th St W Palmdale (93551) ***(P-26349)***
Colt Security Services, Palm Desert *Also called Dlo Enterprises Inc* ***(P-16631)***
Colt Services Inc...D...858 271-9910
9655 Via Excelencia San Diego (92126) ***(P-13576)***
Colton Joint Unified Schl Dst...D...909 876-4240
471 Agua Mansa Rd Colton (92324) ***(P-24298)***
Colton Real Estate Group (PA)...D...949 475-4200
515 Cabrillo Park Dr # 305 Santa Ana (92701) ***(P-11167)***
Columbia Hospitality Inc...C...831 646-8900
652 Cannery Row Monterey (93940) ***(P-12475)***
Columbia Hospitality Inc...D...831 373-5700
300 Pacific St Monterey (93940) ***(P-12476)***
Columbia Hospitality Inc...E...831 373-8000
487 Foam St Monterey (93940) ***(P-12477)***
Columbia Hydronics Co., Hayward *Also called California Hydronics Corp* ***(P-7645)***
Columbia Pictures Inds Inc (HQ)...C...310 244-4000
10202 Washington Blvd Culver City (90232) ***(P-18033)***
Columbia San Clemente Hospital, San Clemente *Also called HCA Inc* ***(P-21443)***
Columbia Specialty Company Inc (PA)...D...562 634-6425
5875 Obispo Ave Long Beach (90805) ***(P-2164)***
Columbia Woodlake LLC...D...206 728-9063
500 Leisure Ln Sacramento (95815) ***(P-12478)***
Columbus Tech & Svcs Inc (PA)...B...310 356-5600
1960 E Grand Ave El Segundo (90245) ***(P-25618)***
Column Five Media Inc (PA)...E...949 614-0759
5151 California Ave # 230 Irvine (92617) ***(P-14105)***
Colusa Casino, Colusa *Also called Colusa Indian Cmnty Council* ***(P-24753)***
Colusa Casino Resort, Colusa *Also called New Colusa Indian Bingo* ***(P-19208)***
Colusa City Office Education, Colusa *Also called Childrens Services* ***(P-23571)***
Colusa Cnty Sbstnce Abuse Svcs...D...530 458-0520
162 E Carson St Ste A Colusa (95932) ***(P-23592)***
Colusa County Behavioral Hlth, Colusa *Also called Colusa Cnty Sbstnce Abuse Svcs* ***(P-23592)***
Colusa Indian Cmnty Council...A...530 458-6572
3740 Highway 45 Colusa (95932) ***(P-24753)***
Colusa Produce Corporation...D...530 696-0121
1954 Progress Rd Meridian (95957) ***(P-8771)***
Colusa Regional Medical Center...C...530 458-5821
199 E Webster St Ste 1 Colusa (95932) ***(P-26815)***
Colusa, Glenn, Trinity Commut, Willows *Also called Glenn Cnty Humn Resource Agcy* ***(P-24185)***
Comak Trading Inc A Cal Corp...D...323 261-3404
2550 S Soto St Vernon (90058) ***(P-8297)***
Comav Technical Services LLC...C...760 530-2400
18438 Readiness St Victorville (92394) ***(P-4882)***
Combustion Associates Inc...E...951 272-6999
555 Monica Cir Corona (92880) ***(P-6021)***
Comca Sport Net Bay Area...C...415 896-2557
360 3rd St Fl 2 San Francisco (94107) ***(P-5864)***
Comcast Cable, San Jose *Also called Comcast Corporation* ***(P-5878)***
Comcast Cable, Madera *Also called Comcast Corporation* ***(P-5879)***
Comcast Cable, Fresno *Also called Comcast Corporation* ***(P-5880)***
Comcast Cable, NAPA *Also called Comcast Corporation* ***(P-5881)***
Comcast California Ix Inc...D...215 286-3345
1111 Andersen Dr San Rafael (94901) ***(P-5865)***
Comcast Cble Cmmunications LLC...E...310 216-3500
6320 Arizona Cir Los Angeles (90045) ***(P-5866)***
Comcast Cble Cmmunications LLC...C...415 715-0524
1485 Bay Shore Blvd # 125 San Francisco (94124) ***(P-5867)***
Comcast Cble Cmmunications LLC...C...559 253-4050
1031 N Plaza Dr Visalia (93291) ***(P-5868)***
Comcast Cble Cmmunications LLC...C...310 216-3686
6357 Arizona Cir Los Angeles (90045) ***(P-5869)***
Comcast Corporation...D...916 459-2964
2860 Gateway Oaks Dr Sacramento (95833) ***(P-5870)***
Comcast Corporation...D...650 689-5392
860 Stanton Rd Burlingame (94010) ***(P-5871)***
Comcast Corporation...D...415 665-5507
1 La Avanzada St Rm 111 San Francisco (94131) ***(P-5872)***
Comcast Corporation...D...707 266-7584
166 Watson Ln American Canyon (94503) ***(P-5873)***

Mergent e-mail: customerrelations@mergent.com
1258
2019 Directory of California
Wholesalers and Services Companies
(P-0000) Products & Services Section entry number
(PA)=Parent Co (HQ)=Headquarters (DH)=Div Headquarters

Comcast Corporation......D......209 222-3656
3801 Pelandale Ave A11 Modesto (95356) ***(P-5874)***
Comcast Corporation......D......415 367-4153
221 2nd St Sausalito (94965) ***(P-5875)***
Comcast Corporation......D......510 266-3200
23525 Clawiter Rd Hayward (94545) ***(P-5876)***
Comcast Corporation......D......951 268-9378
425 Corona Mall Corona (92879) ***(P-5877)***
Comcast Corporation......D......408 216-2878
203 N 27th St San Jose (95116) ***(P-5878)***
Comcast Corporation......D......559 474-4194
1300 W Yosemite Ave Madera (93637) ***(P-5879)***
Comcast Corporation......D......559 718-9917
2414 E Acacia Ave Fresno (93726) ***(P-5880)***
Comcast Corporation......D......707 266-7012
810 Randolph St NAPA (94559) ***(P-5881)***
Comcast Corporation......D......800 240-3640
5462 E Del Amo Blvd 239 Long Beach (90808) ***(P-5882)***
Comcast Corporation......D......925 432-0500
550 Garcia Ave Pittsburg (94565) ***(P-5883)***
Comcast Corporation......B......916 830-6790
1750 Creekside Oaks Dr # 100 Sacramento (95833) ***(P-5884)***
Comcast Corporation......D......415 835-5700
50 Francisco St Fl 3 San Francisco (94133) ***(P-5885)***
Comcast Corporation......D......209 955-6521
6505 Tam O Shanter Dr Stockton (95210) ***(P-5886)***
Comcast Corporation......D......323 993-8000
900 N Cahuenga Blvd Los Angeles (90038) ***(P-5887)***
Comcast Corporation......B......925 271-9794
2001 Diamond Blvd 150 Concord (94520) ***(P-5888)***
Comcast Corporation......D......831 657-6095
2455 Henderson Way Monterey (93940) ***(P-5889)***
Comcast of California/Colo......D......925 424-0273
3055 Comcast Pl Livermore (94551) ***(P-5400)***
Comcast West Bay Area, San Francisco *Also called Comcast Cble Cmmunications LLC* ***(P-5867)***
Come Land Maint Svc Co Inc......A......818 567-2455
1419 N San Fernando Blvd # 250 Burbank (91504) ***(P-14222)***
Comerica Bank......D......925 941-1900
1442 N Main St Walnut Creek (94596) ***(P-9341)***
Comerit Inc......C......888 556-5990
2201 Francisco Dr # 140283 El Dorado Hills (95762) ***(P-16328)***
Comet Building Maintenance Inc......D......415 383-1035
21 Commercial Blvd Ste 12 Novato (94949) ***(P-747)***
Comet Electric Inc......C......818 340-0965
21625 Prairie St Chatsworth (91311) ***(P-2547)***
Comfort Air Inc......D......209 466-4601
1607 French Camp Tpke Stockton (95206) ***(P-2165)***
Comfort California Inc......E......415 928-5000
2775 Van Ness Ave San Francisco (94109) ***(P-12479)***
Comfort California Inc......D......714 750-3131
616 W Convention Way Anaheim (92802) ***(P-12480)***
Comfort Inn, San Francisco *Also called Comfort California Inc* ***(P-12479)***
Comfort Inn, Monterey *Also called V I P Associates Inc* ***(P-13361)***
Comfort Inn, South San Francisco *Also called Comfort Suites* ***(P-12481)***
Comfort Inn, San Diego *Also called A J Esprit* ***(P-12302)***
Comfort Keepers, El Cajon *Also called Way Cool Homecare Inc* ***(P-22462)***
Comfort Keepers, Irvine *Also called CK Franchising Inc* ***(P-22264)***
Comfort Keepers, Claremont *Also called Bluebridge Professional Svcs* ***(P-22237)***
Comfort Keepers - 509, Orange *Also called Cornerstone Family Svcs LLC* ***(P-22277)***
Comfort Suites, Healdsburg *Also called H2 Hotel LLC* ***(P-12635)***
Comfort Suites......D......650 589-7100
121 E Grand Ave South San Francisco (94080) ***(P-12481)***
Comfort Systems Usa Inc......D......909 390-6677
4189 Santa Ana St Ste D Ontario (91761) ***(P-2166)***
Comfort Zone, Sacramento *Also called Villara Corporation* ***(P-2399)***
Comglobal Systems Inc (HQ)......D......619 321-6000
1315 Dell Ave Campbell (95008) ***(P-15936)***
Command & Control Systems, San Diego *Also called Engility LLC* ***(P-25665)***
Command Delivery Systems Inc (PA)......D......909 444-1475
20935 Currier Rd Walnut (91789) ***(P-3994)***
Command Guard Services, Torrance *Also called Resource Collection Inc* ***(P-14365)***
Command International SEC Svcs......D......818 997-1666
6819 Sepulveda Blvd Van Nuys (91405) ***(P-16607)***
Command Security Corporation......C......714 557-9355
8840 Warner Ave Ste 301 Fountain Valley (92708) ***(P-16608)***
Command Security Corporation......C......510 623-2355
890 Hillview Ct Ste 100 Milpitas (95035) ***(P-16609)***
Command Security Corporation......A......310 981-4530
8929 S Sepulveda Blvd # 300 Los Angeles (90045) ***(P-16610)***
Command Security Corporation......D......650 574-0911
1701 Airport Blvd Ste 205 San Jose (95110) ***(P-16611)***
Commerce Casino, Commerce *Also called California Commerce Club Inc* ***(P-12421)***
Commerce Center Theatres......D......323 722-5577
950 Goodrich Blvd Commerce (90022) ***(P-18283)***
Commerce Home Mortgage Inc (HQ)......D......925 830-1500
3130 Crow Canyon Pl # 300 San Ramon (94583) ***(P-9878)***
Commerce Velocity LLC......E......949 756-8950
1 Technology Dr Ste J725 Irvine (92618) ***(P-15632)***
Commerce West Insurance Co......D......925 730-6400
6130 Stoneridge Mall Rd # 400 Pleasanton (94588) ***(P-9706)***
Commercial Carriers Insur Agcy......C......562 404-4900
4 Centerpointe Dr Ste 300 La Palma (90623) ***(P-10347)***
Commercial Casting Co, Fontana *Also called Hartman Industries* ***(P-7279)***
Commercial Coating Company Inc......D......323 256-1331
2809 W Avenue 37 Los Angeles (90065) ***(P-1745)***
Commercial Door Company Inc......D......714 529-2179
1374 E 9th St Pomona (91766) ***(P-3022)***
Commercial Finance & L......D......858 866-8525
12626 High Bluff Dr # 370 San Diego (92130) ***(P-9500)***
Commercial Indus Design Co Inc......D......949 273-6199
20372 N Sea Cir Lake Forest (92630) ***(P-7024)***
Commercial Indus Roofg Co Inc......D......619 465-3737
9239 Olive Dr Spring Valley (91977) ***(P-3140)***
Commercial Inv MGT Group, Los Angeles *Also called Cim Group LP* ***(P-11318)***
Commercial Landscape Svc......D......949 660-8655
1821 Reynolds Ave Irvine (92614) ***(P-748)***
Commercial Lbr & Pallet Co Inc......C......626 968-0631
135 Long Ln City of Industry (91746) ***(P-6817)***
Commercial Lighting Inds Inc......D......800 755-0155
81161 Indio Blvd Indio (92201) ***(P-7348)***
Commercial Mechanical Svc Inc (PA)......E......650 610-8440
981 Bing St San Carlos (94070) ***(P-17893)***
Commercial Paving, Los Angeles *Also called Commercial Coating Company Inc* ***(P-1745)***
Commercial Prgrm Systems Inc (PA)......C......818 308-8560
4400 Coldwater Canyon Ave # 200 Studio City (91604) ***(P-16329)***
Commercial Property Management (PA)......D......213 739-2000
3251 W 6th St Ste 109 Los Angeles (90020) ***(P-11003)***
Commercial Protective Svcs Inc......A......310 515-5290
3400 E Airport Way Long Beach (90806) ***(P-16612)***
Commercial Rfrgn Spcalists LLC (HQ)......C......510 784-8990
3480 Arden Rd Hayward (94545) ***(P-2167)***
Commercial Roofing Systems Inc......D......626 359-5354
11735 Goldring Rd Arcadia (91006) ***(P-3141)***
Commercial Site Imprvs Inc......E......209 785-1920
192 Poker Flat Rd Copperopolis (95228) ***(P-3420)***
Commercial Spport Svcs Antioch, Antioch *Also called Contra Costa ARC* ***(P-24171)***
Commercial Support Services, Richmond *Also called Contra Costa ARC* ***(P-24475)***
Commodity Distribution Service......E......562 777-9969
10035 Painter Ave Santa Fe Springs (90670) ***(P-27692)***
Commodity Forwarders Inc (HQ)......D......310 348-8855
11101 S La Cienega Blvd Los Angeles (90045) ***(P-5035)***
Commodity Resource Envmtl Inc (PA)......D......818 843-2811
116 E Prospect Ave Burbank (91502) ***(P-7975)***
Common Area Maint Svcs Inc (PA)......D......310 390-3552
5664 Selmaraine Dr Culver City (90230) ***(P-14223)***
Commons At Calabasas, The, Los Angeles *Also called Caruso MGT Ltd A Cal Ltd Prtnr* ***(P-11269)***
Commonweal......D......415 868-0970
451 Mesa Rd Bolinas (94924) ***(P-23593)***
Commonwealth Central Credit Un (PA)......D......408 531-3100
5890 Silver Creek Vly Rd San Jose (95138) ***(P-9547)***
Commonwealth Equity Svcs LLP......D......949 336-6440
20 Corporate Park Ste 150 Irvine (92606) ***(P-13703)***
Commonwealth Financial Network, Irvine *Also called Commonwealth Equity Svcs LLP* ***(P-13703)***
Commonwealth International......E......626 279-9201
968 Durfee Ave South El Monte (91733) ***(P-16613)***
Commonwealth Land Title Co......D......949 460-4500
6 Executive Cir Ste 100 Irvine (92614) ***(P-10448)***
Communction Wirg Spcalists Inc......D......858 278-4545
8909 Complex Dr Ste F San Diego (92123) ***(P-2548)***
Communicare Health Centers......C......530 758-2060
2051 John Jones Rd Davis (95616) ***(P-19395)***
Communication & Info Tech, Sacramento *Also called County of Sacramento* ***(P-16266)***
Communication Consultants (PA)......D......209 869-5206
3001 Coffee Rd Ste 5 Modesto (95355) ***(P-27693)***
Communication Svc For Deaf Inc......E......209 475-5000
81 W March Ln Stockton (95207) ***(P-24754)***
Communications Supply Corp......D......714 670-7711
6251 Knott Ave Buena Park (90620) ***(P-5975)***
Communigate Systems, Richmond *Also called Stalker Software Inc* ***(P-15864)***
Community & Senior Svcs, Lancaster *Also called County of Los Angeles* ***(P-23662)***
Community Access Network......D......951 279-1333
2275 S Main St Ste 201 Corona (92882) ***(P-23594)***
Community Action Brd of Snt Cr......E......831 724-0206
406 Main St Ste 202 Watsonville (95076) ***(P-25139)***
Community Action Commsn Santa......C......805 343-0615
4545 10th St Guadalupe (93434) ***(P-24755)***
Community Action Commsn Santa......B......805 614-0786
1890 Sandalwood Dr Santa Maria (93455) ***(P-24756)***
Community Action Commsn Santa (PA)......E......805 964-8857
5638 Hollister Ave # 230 Goleta (93117) ***(P-24757)***
Community Action Commsn Santa......D......805 922-2243
201 W Chapel St Santa Maria (93458) ***(P-24758)***
Community Action Marin......C......415 459-6330
1108 Tamalpais Ave San Rafael (94901) ***(P-22535)***
Community Action Marine, San Rafael *Also called Community Action Marin* ***(P-22535)***
Community Action Partnershi (PA)......D......714 897-6670
11870 Monarch St Garden Grove (92841) ***(P-23595)***
Community Action Partnership......B......805 541-4122
3970 Short St San Luis Obispo (93401) ***(P-23596)***
Community Action Partnership......C......805 489-4026
1152 E Grand Ave Arroyo Grande (93420) ***(P-22986)***
Community Action Partnership (PA)......D......805 544-4355
1030 Southwood Dr San Luis Obispo (93401) ***(P-23597)***
Community Action Partnership O......C......707 544-0120
141 Stony Cir Ste 210 Santa Rosa (95401) ***(P-24759)***
Community Action Partnr Kern......D......661 845-3901
7998 Alicante Ave Lamont (93241) ***(P-24760)***
Community Action Partnr Kern......D......661 758-0129
1600 Poplar Ave Wasco (93280) ***(P-24299)***
Community Action Partnr Kern......D......661 336-0317
2400 Truxtun Ave Bakersfield (93301) ***(P-24761)***
Community Action Partnr Kern......C......760 371-1469
814 N Norma St Ridgecrest (93555) ***(P-24762)***

ALPHABETIC

Employee Codes: A=Over 500 employees, B=251-500
C=101-250, D=51-100, E=50
2019 Directory of California
Wholesalers and Services Companies
© Mergent Inc. 1-800-342-5647
1259

Community Action Partnr Kern.......D.......661 792-1066
217 W Kern Ave Mc Farland (93250) *(P-23598)*
Community Action Partnr Kern.......D.......661 366-5953
4404 Pioneer Dr Bakersfield (93306) *(P-24763)*
Community Action Partnr Kern (PA).......E.......661 336-5236
5005 Business Park N Bakersfield (93309) *(P-23599)*
Community Action Prtnrshp (PA).......C.......559 673-9173
1225 Gill Ave Madera (93637) *(P-24300)*
Community Action Prtnship Sb C.......D.......909 723-1500
696 S Tippecanoe Ave San Bernardino (92408) *(P-24764)*
Community Actv Rhbltn & Emplym, Crescent City *Also called Full Spectrum Services Inc (P-23818)*
COMMUNITY ADVOCATE FOR PEOPLE', Whittier *Also called Capc Inc (P-24750)*
Community Blood Bank Inc.......D.......760 773-4190
70025 Highway 111 Ste 101 Rancho Mirage (92270) *(P-22769)*
Community Bridges.......C.......831 724-2024
114 E 5th St Watsonville (95076) *(P-23600)*
Community Build Inc (PA).......D.......323 290-6560
4305 Degnan Blvd Ste 102 Los Angeles (90008) *(P-25140)*
COMMUNITY CARE & REHABILITATIO, Riverside *Also called Community Care Rehab Ctr LLC (P-20320)*
Community Care Adhc Inc.......D.......626 614-8999
9917 Las Tunas Dr Temple City (91780) *(P-23601)*
Community Care Center, Duarte *Also called Kf Community Care LLC (P-21124)*
Community Care Management Corp (PA).......E.......707 468-9347
301 S State St Ukiah (95482) *(P-23602)*
Community Care On Palm, Riverside *Also called South Coast Health Wellness (P-20772)*
Community Care Rehab Ctr LLC.......C.......951 680-6500
4070 Jurupa Ave Riverside (92506) *(P-20320)*
Community Care Rhblitation Ctr, Newport Beach *Also called Ben Bennett Inc (P-21005)*
Community Caregivers Inc.......D.......831 645-1434
80 Garden Ct Ste 105 Monterey (93940) *(P-22268)*
Community Catalysts California.......E.......760 471-3700
935 W San Marcos Blvd # 103 San Marcos (92078) *(P-24167)*
Community Chld Cre Cncl Sonoma (PA).......D.......707 522-1413
131a Stony Cir Ste 300 Santa Rosa (95401) *(P-24301)*
Community Clinics Hlth Netwrk.......E.......619 542-4300
3710 Ruffin Rd San Diego (92123) *(P-25011)*
Community Convalescent Center.......D.......909 621-4751
9620 Fremont Ave Montclair (91763) *(P-20321)*
Community Convalescent Hospita.......D.......626 963-6091
638 E Colorado Ave Glendora (91740) *(P-20322)*
Community Dev Inst Head Start.......D.......858 668-2985
12988 Bowron Rd Poway (92064) *(P-24302)*
Community Facilities Dst No 6, Los Angeles *Also called County of Los Angeles (P-6235)*
Community Family Guidance Ctr (PA).......D.......562 865-6444
10929 South St Ste 208b Cerritos (90703) *(P-22536)*
Community Gatepath.......C.......650 259-8500
350 Twin Dolphin Dr # 123 Redwood City (94065) *(P-23603)*
Community Health Agency, Riverside *Also called County of Riverside (P-24771)*
Community Health Agency, Riverside *Also called County of Riverside (P-19420)*
Community Health Agency, Moreno Valley *Also called County of Riverside (P-19421)*
COMMUNITY HEALTH CENTER, Bakersfield *Also called Omni Family Health (P-19732)*
Community Health Centers (PA).......C.......805 929-3211
150 Tejas Pl Nipomo (93444) *(P-19396)*
Community Health Ctrs Cntrl (PA).......D.......805 346-3900
2050 S Blosser Rd Santa Maria (93458) *(P-23604)*
Community Health Group.......C.......800 224-7766
2420 Fenton St Ste 100 Chula Vista (91914) *(P-19397)*
Community Health Network LLC.......D.......951 265-8281
25102 Jefferson Ave Ste B Murrieta (92562) *(P-22269)*
Community Health Netwrk of San, San Francisco *Also called Ocean Park Health Center (P-19728)*
Community Health Plan, Alhambra *Also called County of Los Angeles (P-10198)*
Community Health System, Fresno *Also called Community Hospitals Centl Cal (P-21334)*
Community Health Systems Inc.......C.......951 571-2300
22675 Alessandro Blvd # 1 Moreno Valley (92553) *(P-19398)*
Community Hlth Alance Pasadena (PA).......D.......626 398-6300
1855 N Fair Oaks Ave # 200 Pasadena (91103) *(P-21331)*
Community Home Health Agency, Santa Barbara *Also called Sansum Clinic (P-22411)*
Community Home Partners LLC.......D.......408 985-5252
2384 Pacific Dr Santa Clara (95051) *(P-20921)*
Community Hosp Recovery Ctr, Monterey *Also called Monterey Peninsula Hospital (P-21597)*
Community Hosp San Bernardino (HQ).......B.......909 887-6333
1805 Medical Center Dr San Bernardino (92411) *(P-21332)*
Community Hospice Inc (PA).......C.......209 578-6300
4368 Spyres Way Modesto (95356) *(P-20922)*
Community Hospice Inc.......E.......209 578-6380
2201 Euclid Ave Hughson (95326) *(P-20923)*
Community Hospital Long Beach.......A.......562 494-0600
1760 Termino Ave Ste 105 Long Beach (90804) *(P-21333)*
COMMUNITY HOSPITAL OF HUNTINGTON PARK, Huntington Park *Also called Chhp Management LLC (P-21313)*
Community Hospitals Centl Cal.......C.......559 459-2916
1140 T St Fresno (93721) *(P-16106)*
Community Hospitals Centl Cal (PA).......A.......559 459-6000
2823 Fresno St Fresno (93721) *(P-21334)*
Community Hospitals Centl Cal.......A.......559 459-6000
2823 Fresno St Fresno (93721) *(P-21335)*
Community Housing Inc.......E.......650 328-3300
437 Webster St Palo Alto (94301) *(P-24473)*
Community Housing Opport (PA).......E.......530 757-4444
5030 Business Center Dr # 260 Fairfield (94534) *(P-27694)*
Community Housing Opport.......E.......707 759-6043
5030 Bus Center Dr # 260 Fairfield (94534) *(P-26816)*
Community Housing Options.......D.......626 359-3300
348 E Foothill Blvd Arcadia (91006) *(P-23605)*
Community Human Services (PA).......C.......831 658-3811
2560 Garden Rd Ste 201b Monterey (93940) *(P-23606)*
Community Integrated Work Prog.......E.......559 276-8564
4623 W Jacquelyn Ave Fresno (93722) *(P-24168)*
Community Integrated Work Prog.......E.......510 487-9768
1875 Whipple Rd Hayward (94544) *(P-23607)*
Community Integration Program, Sacramento *Also called Develop Disabilities Svc Org (P-23769)*
Community Interface Services.......D.......760 729-3866
2621 Roosevelt St Ste 100 Carlsbad (92008) *(P-23608)*
Community Intgrted Work Prgram, Hayward *Also called Community Integrated Work Prog (P-23607)*
Community Med Group of Rvrside.......C.......951 274-3414
4444 Magnolia Ave Riverside (92501) *(P-19399)*
Community Medical Center.......C.......559 222-7416
3003 N Mariposa St Fresno (93703) *(P-21336)*
Community Medical Center.......D.......559 447-4050
7257 N Fresno St Fresno (93720) *(P-21337)*
Community Medical Centers.......C.......559 320-2200
668 E Bullard Ave Fresno (93710) *(P-21338)*
Community Medical Centers.......D.......559 447-4000
6297 N Fresno St Fresno (93710) *(P-21339)*
Community Medical Centers Inc.......D.......209 944-4700
701 E Channel St Stockton (95202) *(P-19400)*
Community Medical Centers Inc (PA).......D.......209 373-2800
7210 Murray Dr Stockton (95210) *(P-22537)*
Community Mem HSP/Sn Benua.......D.......805 652-5072
147 N Brent St Ventura (93003) *(P-21340)*
Community Memorial Health Sys (PA).......A.......805 652-5011
147 N Brent St Ventura (93003) *(P-21341)*
Community Memorial Health Sys.......C.......805 646-1401
1306 Maricopa Hwy Ojai (93023) *(P-21342)*
COMMUNITY MEMORIAL HOSPITAL, Ventura *Also called Community Memorial Health Sys (P-21341)*
Community Mental Health Clinic, Greenbrae *Also called County of Marin (P-22550)*
Community Mental Health Svcs, San Luis Obispo *Also called County of San Luis Obispo (P-22555)*
Community Orthopedic Medical.......D.......949 348-4000
26401 Crown Valley Pkwy # 101 Mission Viejo (92691) *(P-19401)*
Community Partners (PA).......D.......213 346-3200
1000 N Alameda St Ste 240 Los Angeles (90012) *(P-24765)*
Community Partners Intl.......C.......510 225-9676
2560 9th St Ste 315b Berkeley (94710) *(P-12076)*
Community Redevelopment Agency (PA).......C.......213 977-1600
448 S Hill St Ste 1200 Los Angeles (90013) *(P-27695)*
Community Regional Medical Ctr, Fresno *Also called Community Hospitals Centl Cal (P-21335)*
Community Services, Modesto *Also called County of Stanislaus (P-23747)*
Community Services Department, La Habra *Also called City of La Habra (P-23580)*
Community Services For Deaf, Stockton *Also called Communication Svc For Deaf Inc (P-24754)*
Community Support Options Inc.......C.......661 758-5331
1401 Poso Dr Wasco (93280) *(P-23609)*
Community Therapies.......E.......661 945-7878
19040 Soledad Canyon Rd Santa Clarita (91351) *(P-20171)*
Community Therapies Baby Steps, Santa Clarita *Also called Community Therapies (P-20171)*
Community Transit Services, El Monte *Also called First Student Inc (P-3650)*
Community TV Southern Cal, Burbank *Also called Kcetlink (P-5805)*
Community West Bank.......D.......805 692-5821
445 Pine Ave Goleta (93117) *(P-9342)*
Communty Convlscnt Hosp Mntclr, Montclair *Also called US Skillserve Inc (P-20847)*
Communty Slns For Chldrn Fmls (PA).......C.......408 779-2113
9015 Murray Ave Ste 100 Gilroy (95020) *(P-23610)*
Companion Home Hlth & Hospice.......D.......714 560-8177
2041 W Orangewood Ave B Orange (92868) *(P-22270)*
Companion Hospice, Orange *Also called Companion Home Hlth & Hospice (P-22270)*
Companion Hospice and.......D.......310 338-1257
6133 Bristol Parkday 11 # 110 Culver City (90230) *(P-22271)*
Companion Hospice Care LLC.......C.......562 944-2711
8130 Florence Ave Ste 200 Downey (90240) *(P-22272)*
Companion Hospice LLC.......D.......562 944-2711
8130 Florence Ave Ste 200 Downey (90240) *(P-22273)*
Company 3 Inc.......D.......310 255-6600
1661 Lincoln Blvd Ste 400 Santa Monica (90404) *(P-18184)*
Comparenetworks Inc (PA).......D.......650 873-9031
395 Oyster Point Blvd # 321 South San Francisco (94080) *(P-26350)*
Compass Actn Netwk Dirct Outcm, Marina Del Rey *Also called Can-Do (P-23525)*
Compass Bank.......B.......951 279-7071
195 W Ontario Ave Corona (92882) *(P-9501)*
Compass Bank.......B.......951 672-4829
27851 Bradley Rd Ste 125 Sun City (92586) *(P-9343)*
Compass Bank.......B.......209 239-1381
201 N Main St Manteca (95336) *(P-9437)*
Compass Bank.......B.......209 473-6925
2427 W Hammer Ln Stockton (95209) *(P-9438)*
Compass Bank.......B.......209 939-3288
2562 Pacific Ave Stockton (95204) *(P-9439)*
Compass Children's Center, San Francisco *Also called Compass Family Services (P-24304)*
COMPASS CLARA HOUSE, San Francisco *Also called Compass Family Services (P-23613)*
Compass Connecting Point, San Francisco *Also called Compass Family Services (P-23611)*
Compass Family Services.......D.......415 644-0504
37 Grove St San Francisco (94102) *(P-24303)*

Mergent e-mail: customerrelations@mergent.com
1260
2019 Directory of California
Wholesalers and Services Companies
(P-0000) Products & Services Section entry number
(PA)=Parent Co (HQ)=Headquarters (DH)=Div Headquarters

Compass Family Services ....D....415 644-0504
144 Leavenworth St San Francisco (94102) ***(P-24304)***
Compass Family Services ....C....415 644-0504
37 Grove St San Francisco (94102) ***(P-23611)***
Compass Family Services ....D....415 644-0504
626 Polk St San Francisco (94102) ***(P-23612)***
Compass Family Services ....D....415 644-0504
111 Page St San Francisco (94102) ***(P-23613)***
Compass Group Usa Inc ....C....714 899-2520
12640 Knott St Garden Grove (92841) ***(P-14488)***
Compass Health Inc ....D....805 543-0210
1425 Woodside Dr San Luis Obispo (93401) ***(P-21041)***
Compass Health Inc ....C....805 772-7372
1405 Teresa Dr Morro Bay (93442) ***(P-21042)***
Compass Health Inc ....C....805 489-8137
1212 Farroll Ave Arroyo Grande (93420) ***(P-21043)***
Compass Health Inc ....D....805 466-9254
10805 El Camino Real Atascadero (93422) ***(P-21044)***
Compass Transportation Charter, South San Francisco *Also called Sfo Airporter Inc* ***(P-3724)***
Competent Care HM Hlth Nursing, Costa Mesa *Also called Competent Care Inc* ***(P-22274)***
Competent Care Inc ....D....714 545-4818
2900 Bristol St Ste D107 Costa Mesa (92626) ***(P-22274)***
Competitive Edge RES Comm Inc ....D....619 702-2372
1620 5th Ave Ste 825 San Diego (92101) ***(P-26506)***
Competitor Group Events Inc ....E....858 450-6510
5452 Oberlin Dr San Diego (92121) ***(P-27550)***
Compex Legal Services Inc (PA) ....C....310 782-1801
325 Maple Ave Torrance (90503) ***(P-22987)***
Complete Coach Works (HQ) ....B....951 682-2557
1863 Service Ct Riverside (92507) ***(P-17857)***
Complete Food Service Inc ....D....951 685-8490
3815 Wabash Dr Mira Loma (91752) ***(P-8772)***
Complete Genomics Inc ....B....650 943-2800
2904 Orchard Pkwy San Jose (95134) ***(P-26615)***
Complete Landscape Care Inc ....D....562 946-4441
13316 Leffingwell Rd Whittier (90605) ***(P-815)***
Complete Linen Services, South San Francisco *Also called Complete Linen Svc* ***(P-13528)***
Complete Linen Svc ....D....650 873-1221
290 S Maple Ave South San Francisco (94080) ***(P-13528)***
Complete Logistics Company ....C....909 427-9800
13831 Slover Ave Fontana (92337) ***(P-3995)***
Complete Millwork Services Inc ....D....408 567-9664
405 Aldo Ave Santa Clara (95054) ***(P-6818)***
Complete Office California Inc ....D....714 880-1222
12724 Moore St Cerritos (90703) ***(P-6718)***
Complete Relocation Svcs Inc ....D....714 901-7411
7361 Doig Dr Garden Grove (92841) ***(P-4337)***
Completely Fresh Foods Inc ....C....323 722-9136
4401 S Downey Rd Vernon (90058) ***(P-8773)***
Complex Studios ....E....310 477-1938
2323 Corinth Ave Los Angeles (90064) ***(P-17094)***
Complex The, Los Angeles *Also called Complex Studios* ***(P-17094)***
Complianceonline, Palo Alto *Also called Metricstream Inc* ***(P-15758)***
Composite Software LLC (HQ) ....D....800 553-6387
755 Sycamore Dr Milpitas (95035) ***(P-15633)***
Comppartners Inc ....D....949 253-3111
333 City Blvd W Ste 1500 Orange (92868) ***(P-22275)***
Comprehensive Autism Ctr Inc ....D....951 813-4035
7839 University Ave # 105 La Mesa (91942) ***(P-20172)***
Comprehensive Child Dev Ctr, San Pedro *Also called Comprehensive Child Dev Inc* ***(P-24305)***
Comprehensive Child Dev Inc ....D....310 514-4998
769 W 3rd St San Pedro (90731) ***(P-24305)***
Comprehensive Cmnty Hlth Ctr ....E....323 344-4144
5059 York Blvd Los Angeles (90042) ***(P-19402)***
Comprehensive Community Health ....E....818 265-2264
801 S Chevy Chase Dr Glendale (91205) ***(P-22276)***
Comprehensive Dist Svcs Inc ....C....310 523-1546
18726 S Wstn Ave Ste 300 Gardena (90248) ***(P-5221)***
Comprehensive Enviro ....E....619 294-9400
1615 Murray Canyon Rd San Diego (92108) ***(P-25619)***
Comprehensive SEC Svcs Inc (PA) ....D....916 683-3605
10535 E Stockton Blvd G Elk Grove (95624) ***(P-16614)***
Comprehensive Youth Ser ....D....559 229-3561
4545 N West Ave Ste 101 Fresno (93705) ***(P-23614)***
Compremex LLC ....C....714 739-1348
14849 Firestone Blvd La Mirada (90638) ***(P-4396)***
Comprhnsive Trning Systems Inc ....E....619 424-6650
497 11th St Ste 4 Imperial Beach (91932) ***(P-24169)***
Comps Inc ....C....858 658-0576
4535 Towne Centre Ct San Diego (92121) ***(P-16211)***
Compspec Inc ....D....818 551-4200
425 E Colorado St Ste 410 Glendale (91205) ***(P-27198)***
Compton Adult Day Care, Compton *Also called Lynwood Developmental Care* ***(P-21146)***
Compton Family Mhc Fsp, Compton *Also called County of Los Angeles* ***(P-22773)***
Compton Hauling, Compton *Also called USA Waste of California Inc* ***(P-6498)***
Compton Service Center, Compton *Also called Southern California Edison Co* ***(P-6130)***
Compton Training Center, Van Nuys *Also called Apprentice & Journeymen Tm Tr* ***(P-24145)***
Compulaw LLC ....E....310 553-3355
200 Crprate Pinte Ste 400 Culver City (90230) ***(P-15069)***
Compulink Business Systems Inc ....C....805 446-2050
1100 Business Center Cir Newbury Park (91320) ***(P-15634)***
Compulink Management Ctr Inc ....C....562 988-1688
3545 Long Beach Blvd Long Beach (90807) ***(P-15635)***
Compumail Information Svcs Inc ....D....925 689-7100
4057 Port Chicago Hwy # 300 Concord (94520) ***(P-17095)***

Computer Consulting (PA) ....A....310 568-5000
600 Corporate Pointe # 1010 Culver City (90230) ***(P-5535)***
Computer History Museum ....D....650 810-1010
1401 N Shoreline Blvd Mountain View (94043) ***(P-24874)***
Computer Proc Unlimited Inc ....D....858 530-0875
9235 Activity Rd Ste 104 San Diego (92126) ***(P-15070)***
Computer Programming Dept, Novato *Also called County of Marin* ***(P-16109)***
Computer Resources Group Inc ....C....415 398-3535
275 Battery St Ste 800 San Francisco (94111) ***(P-15071)***
Computer Sciences Corporation ....D....510 645-3000
1111 Broadway Fl 13 Oakland (94607) ***(P-16330)***
Computer Task Group Inc ....C....408 573-6070
2033 Gateway Pl Fl 5 San Jose (95110) ***(P-15072)***
Computer Task Group Inc ....B....800 992-5350
101 Metro Dr Ste 530 San Jose (95110) ***(P-15073)***
Computerized Management ....D....805 522-5999
40 W Cochran St Simi Valley (93065) ***(P-14842)***
Computerized Management Svcs, Simi Valley *Also called Simi Radiology & Imaging* ***(P-27450)***
Computerized Mgt Svcs Inc ....D....805 522-5940
4100 Guardian St Ste 205 Simi Valley (93063) ***(P-26817)***
Computrition Inc (HQ) ....D....818 961-3999
8521 Fllbrook Ave Ste 100 Canoga Park (91304) ***(P-15074)***
Compvue Inc ....D....408 892-9909
440 N Wolfe Rd Sunnyvale (94085) ***(P-15075)***
Compwest Insurance Company ....D....714 641-9500
3 Hutton Cntre Dr Ste 550 Santa Ana (92707) ***(P-10348)***
Comrade Inc ....E....510 277-3400
484 9th St Oakland (94607) ***(P-17096)***
Comstock Crosser Assoc Dev Inc ....E....310 546-5781
321 12th St Ste 200 Manhattan Beach (90266) ***(P-11866)***
Comstock Homes, Manhattan Beach *Also called Comstock Crosser Assoc Dev Inc* ***(P-11866)***
Comtel Pro Media, Burbank *Also called Edgewise Media Services Inc* ***(P-7469)***
Comtel Systems Technology ....D....408 543-5600
1292 Hammerwood Ave Sunnyvale (94089) ***(P-2549)***
Con-Way, Blythe *Also called Xpo Logistics Freight Inc* ***(P-4319)***
Con-Way, Lakeport *Also called Xpo Enterprise Services Inc* ***(P-4308)***
Con-Way, Santa Rosa *Also called Xpo Logistics Freight Inc* ***(P-4320)***
Conam Management Corporation (PA) ....C....858 614-7200
3990 Ruffin Rd Ste 100 San Diego (92123) ***(P-11376)***
Concentrix Corporation ....D....510 668-3717
44201 Nobel Dr Fremont (94538) ***(P-16331)***
Concept Enterprises Inc ....D....626 968-8827
152 S Brent Cir Walnut (91789) ***(P-7411)***
Concept Green Enrgy Sltons Inc ....A....855 459-6535
13824 Yorba Ave Chino (91710) ***(P-17097)***
Concerro Inc (HQ) ....E....858 882-8500
9276 Scranton Rd Ste 400 San Diego (92121) ***(P-15076)***
Concerto Healthcare Inc (PA) ....C....949 537-3400
85 Enterprise Ste 200 Aliso Viejo (92656) ***(P-23615)***
Concession Management Svcs Inc ....C....310 846-5830
6033 W Century Blvd # 890 Los Angeles (90045) ***(P-19146)***
Concessionaires Urban Park (PA) ....B....530 529-1512
2150 Main St Ste 5 Red Bluff (96080) ***(P-19147)***
Concessionaires Urban Park ....E....209 763-5121
2000 Camanche Rd Ofc Ofc Ione (95640) ***(P-19148)***
Concessionaires Urban Park ....D....209 763-5166
2000 Camanche Rd Ofc Ofc Ione (95640) ***(P-19149)***
Concessionaires Urban Park ....D....530 529-1596
34600 Ardenwood Blvd Fremont (94555) ***(P-19150)***
Concessionaires Urban Park ....D....530 529-1513
18013 Bollinger Canyon Rd San Ramon (94583) ***(P-19151)***
Conco Cement Company, Concord *Also called Gonsalves & Santucci Inc* ***(P-3259)***
Conco Cement Company, Concord *Also called Gonsalves & Santucci Inc* ***(P-3375)***
Conco Pumping ....D....909 350-0503
13052 Dahlia St Fontana (92337) ***(P-3238)***
Concord Foods Inc (PA) ....D....909 975-2000
4601 E Guasti Rd Ontario (91761) ***(P-8392)***
Concord Hotel LLC ....D....925 521-3751
45 John Glenn Dr Concord (94520) ***(P-12482)***
Concord Iron Works Inc ....E....925 432-0136
1501 Loveridge Rd Ste 15 Pittsburg (94565) ***(P-3374)***
Concord Jet Service Inc (PA) ....E....925 682-4830
1380 Galaxy Way Ste B Concord (94520) ***(P-14489)***
Concord Pavillion, Concord *Also called City of Concord* ***(P-18357)***
Concorde Battery Corporation ....C....626 962-4006
1125 N Azusa Canyon Rd West Covina (91790) ***(P-4542)***
Concourse Hotel At, Los Angeles *Also called Humnit Hotel At Lax LLC* ***(P-12741)***
Concrete Concepts Inc ....D....760 737-5470
2317 Auto Park Way Escondido (92029) ***(P-3239)***
Concrete Construction, San Diego *Also called Ben F Smith Inc* ***(P-3223)***
Concrete Contractor, Mission Viejo *Also called Cs Concrete Solutions Inc* ***(P-3243)***
Concrete Holding Co Cal Inc ....B....818 788-4228
15821 Ventura Blvd # 475 Encino (91436) ***(P-11971)***
Concrete Images International ....D....858 676-1253
17237 Saint Andrews Dr Poway (92064) ***(P-3240)***
Concrete North Inc ....D....209 745-7400
10274 Iron Rock Way Elk Grove (95624) ***(P-3241)***
Concrete Tie Industries Inc (PA) ....D....310 886-1000
130 E Oris St Compton (90222) ***(P-6882)***
Condon-Johnson & Assoc Inc (PA) ....E....510 636-2100
480 Roland Way Ste 200 Oakland (94621) ***(P-3242)***
Condor Earth Technologies Inc (PA) ....C....209 532-0361
21663 Brian Ln Sonora (95370) ***(P-27696)***
Condor Productions LLC ....D....310 449-3000
245 N Beverly Dr Beverly Hills (90210) ***(P-18185)***
Conduit Inc ....C....650 340-1550
180 Sansome St 18 San Francisco (94104) ***(P-5536)***

ALPHABETIC

Employee Codes: A=Over 500 employees, B=251-500 C=101-250, D=51-100, E=50
2019 Directory of California Wholesalers and Services Companies
© Mergent Inc. 1-800-342-5647
1261

Conduit Lngage Specialists Inc .... D 859 299-3178
  22720 Ventura Blvd # 100 Woodland Hills (91364) *(P-13731)*
Cone Collision Center, Downey *Also called Mullahey Chevrolet Inc (P-17731)*
Conejo Pacific Technologies 805 498-5315
  1560 Newbury Rd Ste 1 Newbury Park (91320) *(P-1388)*
Conejo Valley Unified Schl Dst .... D 805 496-9035
  100 S Conejo School Rd Thousand Oaks (91362) *(P-24306)*
Conejo Valley Unified Schl Dst .... C 805 492-3531
  620 Velarde Dr Thousand Oaks (91360) *(P-25141)*
Conejo Vly Nghborhood For Lrng, Thousand Oaks *Also called Conejo Valley Unified Schl Dst (P-24306)*
Conestoga Hotel .... D 714 535-0300
  1240 S Walnut St Anaheim (92802) *(P-12483)*
Conexis, Orange *Also called Word & Brown Insurance (P-27098)*
Conexis Bneft Admnistrators LP (HQ) .... C 714 835-5006
  721 S Parker St Ste 300 Orange (92868) *(P-10592)*
Confi-Chek Inc (PA) .... D 800 718-8997
  1915 21st St Sacramento (95811) *(P-16212)*
Confie Seguros Inc (HQ) .... D 714 252-2500
  7711 Center Ave Ste 200 Huntington Beach (92647) *(P-10593)*
Confire J P A .... D 909 356-2375
  1743 Miro Way Rialto (92376) *(P-17098)*
Conforti Plumbing Inc .... A 530 622-0202
  6080 Pleasant Valley Rd C El Dorado (95623) *(P-2168)*
Conglobal Industries LLC .... D 310 518-2850
  1711 Alameda St Wilmington (90744) *(P-4669)*
Congregation of Poor Sisters .... D 559 237-3444
  2121 N 1st St Fresno (93703) *(P-24474)*
Congress Med Surgery Ctr LLC .... D 626 396-8100
  800 S Raymond Ave Pasadena (91105) *(P-19403)*
Congrgtnal Ch Retirement Cmnty .... D 530 823-6131
  750 Auburn Ravine Rd Auburn (95603) *(P-11004)*
Connect Computers, Tustin *Also called General Procurement Inc (P-7054)*
Connect Your Home LLC 949 777-0100
  1 Park Plz Ste 600 Irvine (92614) *(P-1509)*
Connectx Inc .... E 310 702-8686
  909 N Avi Blvd Unit 6 Manhattan Beach (90266) *(P-16332)*
Connexity Inc (HQ) .... C 310 571-1235
  2120 Colorado Ave Ste 400 Santa Monica (90404) *(P-5537)*
Connexsys Engineering Inc 510 243-2050
  1320 Willow Pass Rd # 500 Concord (94520) *(P-25620)*
Connotate Technologies Inc .... E 949 270-1916
  2601 Main St Ste 830 Irvine (92614) *(P-15077)*
Conrad A Cox .... E 562 927-0033
  9040 Telegraph Rd Downey (90240) *(P-19404)*
Conrad Acceptance Corporation .... E 760 735-5000
  476 W Vermont Ave Escondido (92025) *(P-9736)*
Conrad Credit, Escondido *Also called Conrad Acceptance Corporation (P-9736)*
Conrad Credit Corporation .... E 760 735-5000
  476 W Vermont Ave Escondido (92025) *(P-14000)*
Conrad Imports Inc .... D 415 626-3303
  540 Barneveld Ave Ste H San Francisco (94124) *(P-6755)*
Conrad Lab, The, Lodi *Also called Lodi Memorial Hosp Assn Inc (P-21558)*
Conroy Farms Inc .... B 805 981-0537
  520 Maulhardt Ave Oxnard (93030) *(P-95)*
Consensus Health, Emeryville *Also called Onebody Inc (P-22380)*
Consensus Orthopedics Inc .... D 916 355-7110
  1115 Windfield Way # 100 El Dorado Hills (95762) *(P-7176)*
Conservation Corps Long Beach .... C 562 986-1249
  340 Nieto Ave Long Beach (90814) *(P-24170)*
Conservation Liquidation .... D 415 676-5000
  100 Pine St Fl 12 San Francisco (94111) *(P-27925)*
Considine & Considine An Acco .... D 619 231-1977
  8989 Rio San Diego Dr # 250 San Diego (92108) *(P-26172)*
Consoldted Fire Protection LLC (HQ) .... A 949 727-3277
  153 Technology Dr Ste 200 Irvine (92618) *(P-17099)*
Consoldted Med Bo-Analysis Inc (PA) .... D 714 657-7369
  10700 Walker St Cypress (90630) *(P-22069)*
Consoldted Med Bo-Analysis Inc .... D 714 657-7389
  7631 Wyoming St Ste 105a Westminster (92683) *(P-22070)*
Consoldted Med Bo-Analysis Inc .... D 714 467-0240
  12665 Garden Grove Blvd Garden Grove (92843) *(P-22071)*
Consolidated Cleaning Services .... D 510 663-2585
  6353 Westover Dr Oakland (94611) *(P-14224)*
Consolidated Design West Inc .... D 714 999-1476
  1345 S Lewis St Anaheim (92805) *(P-14106)*
Consolidated Elec Distrs Inc .... D 858 268-1020
  5457 Ruffin Rd San Diego (92123) *(P-7349)*
Consolidated Elec Distrs Inc .... D 626 345-0000
  3020 W Empire Ave Burbank (91504) *(P-7350)*
Consolidated Plastics Corp (PA) .... D 909 393-8222
  14954 La Palma Dr Chino (91710) *(P-8913)*
Consolidated Reprographics, Costa Mesa *Also called American Reprographics Co LLC (P-14075)*
Consolidated Tribal Health Prj .... D 707 485-5115
  6991 N State St Redwood Valley (95470) *(P-22538)*
Consortium For Community Svcs, Sacramento *Also called Quality Group Homes Inc (P-1220)*
Consortm On Reachng Excellnce 510 540-4200
  3112 Cedar Ravine Rd Placerville (95667) *(P-27697)*
Consorzio, Berkeley *Also called Homegrown Natural Foods Inc (P-8413)*
Constance Dehaan Dvm, Rohnert Park *Also called Animal Care Center (P-596)*
Constellation Newenergy Inc .... D 213 576-6001
  350 S Grand Ave Ste 3800 Los Angeles (90071) *(P-6022)*
Construction, Fresno *Also called Quiring General LLC (P-1622)*
Construction Customer Service .... E 714 701-1858
  1320 N Hancock St Ste A Anaheim (92807) *(P-1147)*

Construction Specialty Svc Inc .... D 661 864-7573
  4550 Buck Owens Blvd Bakersfield (93308) *(P-1911)*
Construction Temps, Signal Hill *Also called Wannajob Inc (P-14942)*
Construction Testing Services (PA) .... E 925 462-5151
  2118 Rheem Dr Pleasanton (94588) *(P-26818)*
Construction Tstg & Engrg Inc (PA) .... D 760 746-4955
  1441 Montiel Rd Ste 115 Escondido (92026) *(P-25621)*
Consultants For Adhc, Temple City *Also called Community Care Adhc Inc (P-23601)*
Consultnts In Edctl Per Skills (PA) .... D 916 348-1890
  5825 Auburn Blvd Ste 1 Sacramento (95841) *(P-23616)*
Consumer Credit Counseling Svc (PA) .... D 415 788-0288
  595 Market St Ste 1500 San Francisco (94105) *(P-13732)*
Consumer Portfolio Svcs Inc .... C 949 788-5695
  19500 Jamboree Rd Irvine (92612) *(P-9707)*
Consumer Portfolio Svcs Inc .... D 949 753-6800
  16355 Laguna Canyon Rd Irvine (92618) *(P-9708)*
Consumer Resource Network LLC .... B 800 291-4794
  4420 E Miraloma Ave Ste J Anaheim (92807) *(P-27199)*
Contact Security Inc .... C 714 572-6760
  3000 E Birch St Ste 111 Brea (92821) *(P-16615)*
Contactual Inc .... E 650 292-4408
  810 W Maude Ave Sunnyvale (94085) *(P-15636)*
Contain-A-Way Inc .... B 909 796-2860
  25837 Bus Ctr Dr Ste F Redlands (92374) *(P-6382)*
Contec Microelectronics USA .... D 949 250-4025
  17811 Gillette Ave Fl 1 Irvine (92614) *(P-7025)*
Contec USA, Irvine *Also called Contec Microelectronics USA (P-7025)*
Contemporary Services Corp .... C 310 320-8418
  369 Van Ness Way Ste 702 Torrance (90501) *(P-16884)*
Contemporary Services Corp (PA) .... C 818 885-5150
  17101 Superior St Northridge (91325) *(P-14590)*
Contemporary Services Corp .... D 909 740-3834
  4365 E Lowell St Ste A Ontario (91761) *(P-16265)*
Contemporary Services Corp .... C 559 225-9325
  2650 E Shaw Ave Fresno (93710) *(P-16616)*
Contemprary Hstrical Vhcl Assn .... D 707 448-7266
  430 Oak View Dr Vacaville (95688) *(P-25142)*
Content Guru Inc .... D 408 559-3988
  1901 S Bascom Ave # 1100 Campbell (95008) *(P-5538)*
Conti Life Comm Plea LLC .... D 925 227-6800
  3300 Stoneridge Creek Way Pleasanton (94588) *(P-17100)*
Contiki Holidays, Anaheim *Also called Contiki US Holdings Inc (P-4968)*
Contiki US Holdings Inc .... D 714 935-0808
  801 E Katella Ave Frnt Anaheim (92805) *(P-4968)*
Continental 155 5th Corp .... E 310 640-1520
  2041 Rosecrans Ave # 200 El Segundo (90245) *(P-11377)*
Continental Agency Inc (PA) .... D 909 595-8884
  1768 W 2nd St Pomona (91766) *(P-5036)*
Continental Airlines, Los Angeles *Also called United Airlines Inc (P-4809)*
Continental Commercial Group, Glendale *Also called L A Commercial Group Inc (P-14012)*
Continental Currency Svcs Inc (HQ) .... E 714 569-0300
  1108 E 17th St Santa Ana (92701) *(P-9675)*
Continental Currency Svcs Inc (PA) .... D 714 569-0300
  1108 E 17th St Santa Ana (92701) *(P-9676)*
Continental Data Graphics, Long Beach *Also called Continental Graphics Corp (P-14107)*
Continental Data Graphics, Long Beach *Also called Continental Graphics Corp (P-25622)*
Continental Dntl Ceramics Inc .... E 310 618-8821
  1873 Western Way Torrance (90501) *(P-22164)*
Continental Ex Money Order Co, Santa Ana *Also called Continental Currency Svcs Inc (P-9675)*
Continental Exch Solutions Inc (HQ) 714 522-7044
  6565 Knott Ave Buena Park (90620) *(P-9677)*
Continental Graphics Corp (PA) .... C 714 503-4200
  4060 N Lakewood Blvd Long Beach (90808) *(P-14107)*
Continental Graphics Corp .... A 714 503-4200
  2401 E Wardlow Rd Long Beach (90807) *(P-25622)*
Continental Sales Co., Los Angeles *Also called Val-Pro Inc (P-8741)*
Continental Trnsp Svcs, Long Beach *Also called C O T S Inc (P-3781)*
Continuing Lf Communities LLC (PA) .... D 760 704-6400
  1940 Levante St Carlsbad (92009) *(P-14591)*
Contra Costa ARC .... D 925 755-4925
  2505 W 10th St Antioch (94509) *(P-24171)*
Contra Costa ARC .... D 510 233-7303
  1420 Regatta Blvd Richmond (94804) *(P-24475)*
Contra Costa Country Club .... D 925 798-7135
  801 Golf Club Rd Pleasant Hill (94523) *(P-18898)*
Contra Costa Electric Inc (HQ) .... B 925 229-4250
  825 Howe Rd Martinez (94553) *(P-2550)*
Contra Costa Electric Inc .... C 661 322-4036
  3208 Landco Dr Bakersfield (93308) *(P-2551)*
Contra Costa Metal Fabricators, Oakland *Also called Monterey Mechanical Co (P-2047)*
Contra Costa Newspapers Inc .... E 925 757-2525
  1650 Cavallo Rd Antioch (94509) *(P-9111)*
Contra Costa Vet Med Emrgcy CL .... E 925 798-5830
  1145 Turtle Rock Ln Concord (94521) *(P-600)*
Contra Costa Water District (PA) .... C 925 688-8000
  1331 Concord Ave Concord (94520) *(P-6232)*
Contract, San Juan Capistrano *Also called Emerald Expositions LLC (P-17151)*
Contract Recruiting Inc (PA) .... D 310 792-7100
  3625 Del Amo Blvd Ste 300 Torrance (90503) *(P-14592)*
Contract Services Group Inc .... C 714 582-1800
  480 Capricorn St Brea (92821) *(P-14225)*
Contractor Warehouse .... D 562 633-1428
  5950 N Paramount Blvd Lakewood (90805) *(P-1510)*
Contractors Cargo Company, Compton *Also called CCC Property Holdings LLC (P-11968)*
Contractors Cargo Company .... C 310 609-1957
  500 S Alameda St Compton (90221) *(P-4118)*
Contractors Complete Surety, Wildomar *Also called Asr Constructors Inc (P-1469)*

Mergent e-mail: customerrelations@mergent.com
1262

2019 Directory of California
Wholesalers and Services Companies

(P-0000) Products & Services Section entry number
(PA)=Parent Co (HQ)=Headquarters (DH)=Div Headquarters

Contractors Flrg Svc Cal Inc ....C....714 556-6100
300 E Dyer Rd Santa Ana (92707) ***(P-6756)***
Contractors Labor Pool of La, Burbank *Also called Clp Resources Inc* ***(P-14840)***
Contractors Rigging & Erectors, Compton *Also called Contractors Cargo Company* ***(P-4118)***
Contrlled Cntmination Svcs LLC ....C....888 263-9886
6150 Lusk Blvd Ste B205 San Diego (92121) ***(P-14226)***
Control AC Svc Corp ....D....714 777-8600
5200 E La Palma Ave Anaheim (92807) ***(P-2169)***
Control Air Conditioning Corp ....C....760 744-2727
1390 Armorlite Dr San Marcos (92069) ***(P-17894)***
Control Air Conditioning Corp (PA) ....C....714 777-8600
5200 E La Palma Ave Anaheim (92807) ***(P-2170)***
Controlco (PA) ....D....800 800-7126
3451 Vincent Rd Ste C Pleasant Hill (94523) ***(P-7743)***
Controlled Contamination Svcs, San Diego *Also called Contrlled Cntmination Svcs LLC* ***(P-14226)***
Controlled Contamination Svcs ....D....510 728-1106
23595 Cabot Blvd Ste 115 Hayward (94545) ***(P-14227)***
Convention Center Booking Off, Richmond *Also called City of Richmond* ***(P-19141)***
Conventions Arts & Entrmt, San Jose *Also called City of San Jose* ***(P-17082)***
Convergint Technologies LLC ....E....510 300-2800
5860 W Las Positas Blvd # 7 Pleasanton (94588) ***(P-16885)***
Conversant LLC (HQ) ....C....818 575-4500
30699 Russell Ranch Rd # 250 Westlake Village (91362) ***(P-16213)***
Converse Inc ....D....415 433-1174
838 Market St San Francisco (94102) ***(P-8350)***
Converse Inc ....D....909 625-6655
2150 E Montclair Plaza Ln Montclair (91763) ***(P-8351)***
Converse Inc ....D....310 451-0314
1437-39 3rd St Promenade Santa Monica (90401) ***(P-8352)***
Converse Inc ....D....909 974-5695
4450 E Lowell St Ontario (91761) ***(P-8353)***
Converseai Inc (HQ) ....C....415 919-7891
548 Market St San Francisco (94104) ***(P-15078)***
Convo Communications LLC ....C....925 227-5500
6601 Owens Dr Ste 155 Pleasanton (94588) ***(P-5976)***
Convoy Inc ....E....415 403-2770
1020 Kearny St San Francisco (94133) ***(P-16281)***
Cook Cabinets Inc ....D....530 621-0851
6428 Capitol Ave Diamond Springs (95619) ***(P-3023)***
Cook King, La Mirada *Also called Stainless Stl Fabricators Inc* ***(P-7805)***
Cook Realty Inc ....C....916 451-6702
4305 Freeport Blvd Sacramento (95822) ***(P-11378)***
Cook Realty Sales, Sacramento *Also called Cook Realty Inc* ***(P-11378)***
Cookie Jar Entrmt USA Inc ....C....818 955-5400
4100 W Alameda Ave # 101 Burbank (91505) ***(P-18034)***
Cooksey Toolen Gage Duffy (PA) ....D....714 431-1100
535 Anton Blvd Fl 10 Costa Mesa (92626) ***(P-22988)***
Cool Roofing Systems Inc (PA) ....D....209 825-0818
1286 Dupont Ct Manteca (95336) ***(P-3142)***
Cool Transport, Colton *Also called Van Dyk Tank Lines Inc* ***(P-4084)***
Cooley Godward Kronish, San Francisco *Also called Cooley LLP* ***(P-22989)***
Cooley LLP ....D....415 693-2000
101 California St Fl 5 San Francisco (94111) ***(P-22989)***
Cooley LLP (PA) ....B....650 843-5000
3175 Hanover St Palo Alto (94304) ***(P-22990)***
Cooley LLP ....C....650 843-5124
4 Palo Alto Sq Palo Alto (94306) ***(P-22991)***
Cooley LLP ....C....858 550-6000
4401 Eastgate Mall San Diego (92121) ***(P-22992)***
Cooper & Jackson Inc ....C....408 437-2750
310 Shaw Rd Ste D South San Francisco (94080) ***(P-26690)***
Cooper Crane & Rigging Inc (PA) ....D....707 765-4646
1175 Nimitz Ave Ste 104 Vallejo (94592) ***(P-2024)***
Cooper Pugeda Management Inc ....E....415 543-6251
65 Mccoppin St San Francisco (94103) ***(P-26819)***
Cooper Vali & Associates Inc (HQ) ....D....510 446-8301
1850 Gateway Blvd Ste 100 Concord (94520) ***(P-25623)***
Cooper White & Cooper LLP (PA) ....C....415 433-1900
201 California St Fl 17 San Francisco (94111) ***(P-22993)***
Cooperative Personnel Services (PA) ....C....916 263-3600
2450 Del Paso Rd Ste 220 Sacramento (95834) ***(P-27200)***
Coopertive Amrcn Physcians Inc (PA) ....D....213 473-8600
333 S Hope St Fl 8 Los Angeles (90071) ***(P-25012)***
Coordnted Dlvry Instllion Inc ....D....714 501-4040
905 E Katella Ave Anaheim (92805) ***(P-3996)***
Copart ....E....707 863-0297
5251 Business Center Dr Fairfield (94534) ***(P-6583)***
Copier Source Inc (PA) ....D....909 890-4040
650 E Hospitality Ln # 500 San Bernardino (92408) ***(P-6957)***
Copley Press Inc ....C....760 767-0100
3845 Yaqui Pass Borrego Springs (92004) ***(P-12484)***
Copley Press Inc ....D....619 718-5200
2375 Northside Dr Ste 300 San Diego (92108) ***(P-15637)***
Coppel Corporation ....D....760 357-3707
503 Scaroni Ave Calexico (92231) ***(P-6719)***
Copper Eagle Patrol & Security, Santa Clarita *Also called S C Security Inc* ***(P-16779)***
Copper Ridge Care Center ....C....530 222-2273
201 Hartnell Ave Redding (96002) ***(P-20323)***
Copper River Country Club LP (PA) ....D....559 434-5200
2140 E Clubhouse Dr Fresno (93730) ***(P-18899)***
Coppersmith Global Logistics, El Segundo *Also called L E Coppersmith Inc* ***(P-5100)***
Coptic Clinics ....D....562 900-2692
3803 W Mission Blvd Pomona (91766) ***(P-19405)***
Copypage, Los Angeles *Also called C P Document Technologies LLC* ***(P-7454)***
Cora Constructors Inc ....E....760 674-3201
75140 Saint Charles Pl A Palm Desert (92211) ***(P-25624)***
Corcoran District Hospital ....D....559 992-3300
1310 Hanna Ave Corcoran (93212) ***(P-21343)***
Cordelia Lighting Inc ....C....310 886-3490
20101 S Santa Fe Ave Compton (90221) ***(P-7351)***
Cordevalle Golf Club LLC ....C....408 695-4500
1 Cordevalle Club Dr San Martin (95046) ***(P-18900)***
Cordilleras Mental Health Ctr, Redwood City *Also called Telecare Corporation* ***(P-21987)***
Cordoba Corporation ....D....213 895-0224
1401 N Broadway Los Angeles (90012) ***(P-15937)***
Core, Placerville *Also called Consortm On Reachng Excellnce* ***(P-27697)***
Core Communications Group LLC ....D....714 729-8404
2749 Saturn St Brea (92821) ***(P-11379)***
Core Group Inc (PA) ....C....909 438-2626
14544 Central Ave Ste 42 Chino (91710) ***(P-17101)***
Core Group, The, Milpitas *Also called Tcg Builders Inc* ***(P-1670)***
Core Medstaff, Los Angeles *Also called Total Professional Network* ***(P-14783)***
Core Nutrition LLC ....D....310 640-0500
100 N Pacific Coast Hwy # 325 El Segundo (90245) ***(P-8774)***
Core Nutrition LLC ....E....310 640-0500
1222 E Grand Ave Ste 102 El Segundo (90245) ***(P-8775)***
Core Realty Holdings LLC (PA) ....D....949 863-1031
1600 Dove St Ste 450 Newport Beach (92660) ***(P-12156)***
Core Realty Holdings MGT Inc ....D....949 863-1031
1600 Dove St Ste 450 Newport Beach (92660) ***(P-11380)***
Core-Mark Corona 2 ....E....800 622-1206
1550 Magnolia Ave Corona (92879) ***(P-8393)***
Core-Mark Holding Company Inc (PA) ....D....650 589-9445
395 Oyster Point Blvd # 415 South San Francisco (94080) ***(P-8394)***
Core-Mark International, South San Francisco *Also called Core-Mark Midcontinent Inc* ***(P-9183)***
Core-Mark International Inc ....C....661 366-2673
200 Coremark Ct Bakersfield (93307) ***(P-8776)***
Core-Mark International Inc ....C....661 366-2673
8333 Edison Hwy Bakersfield (93307) ***(P-9182)***
Core-Mark International Inc ....C....323 583-6531
2311 E 48th St Vernon (90058) ***(P-8777)***
Core-Mark International Inc ....C....509 535-9768
3030 Mulvany Pl West Sacramento (95691) ***(P-8778)***
Core-Mark International Inc ....C....510 487-3000
31300 Medallion Dr Hayward (94544) ***(P-8779)***
Core-Mark International Inc (HQ) ....D....650 589-9445
395 Oyster Point Blvd # 415 South San Francisco (94080) ***(P-8395)***
Core-Mark Midcontinent Inc (HQ) ....C....650 589-9445
395 Oyster Point Blvd # 415 South San Francisco (94080) ***(P-9183)***
Core-Mark Sacramento 2 ....E....866 791-4210
2959 Thomas Pl Ste 150 West Sacramento (95691) ***(P-8396)***
Corecare I I I ....C....714 256-8000
800 Morningside Dr Fullerton (92835) ***(P-24476)***
Corecare V A Cal Ltd Partnr ....C....714 256-1000
2525 Brea Blvd Fullerton (92835) ***(P-20324)***
Corecivic Inc ....C....619 661-9119
446 Alta Rd San Diego (92158) ***(P-27583)***
Corecivic Inc ....C....760 373-1764
22844 Virginia Blvd California City (93505) ***(P-27584)***
Corelogic Inc ....E....714 250-6400
201 Spear St Fl 4 San Francisco (94105) ***(P-11381)***
Corelogic Inc ....D....916 431-2146
11010 White Rock Rd Rancho Cordova (95670) ***(P-14032)***
Corelogic Inc ....E....714 250-6400
40 Pacifica Ste 900 Irvine (92618) ***(P-11382)***
Corelogic Credco LLC (HQ) ....C....949 214-1000
40 Pacifica Ste 900 Irvine (92618) ***(P-14033)***
Corelogic Dorado, Oakland *Also called Dorado Network Systems Corp* ***(P-15652)***
Corelogic Info Solutions, Rancho Cordova *Also called Corelogic Inc* ***(P-14032)***
Corelynx Inc ....C....877 267-3599
11501 Dublin Blvd Ste 200 Dublin (94568) ***(P-15079)***
Coretechs Staffing Inc ....D....650 363-7960
50 Woodside Plz Ste 604 Redwood City (94061) ***(P-15080)***
Corey Delta Constructors Inc ....D....925 370-9808
261 Arthur Rd Fairfield (94533) ***(P-2171)***
Corey Nursery Co Inc (PA) ....D....909 621-6886
1650 Monte Vista Ave Claremont (91711) ***(P-9131)***
Corinthian Intl Prkg Svcs Inc ....B....408 867-7275
19925 Stevens Creek Blvd B Cupertino (95014) ***(P-13733)***
Corinthian Parking Services, Cupertino *Also called Corinthian Intl Prkg Svcs Inc* ***(P-13733)***
Corinthian Realty LLC ....D....510 487-8653
3902 Smith St Union City (94587) ***(P-11383)***
Corinthian Title Company Inc ....D....619 299-4800
5030 Camino De La Siesta San Diego (92108) ***(P-10449)***
Corizon Health Inc ....C....925 551-6500
5325 Broder Blvd Dublin (94568) ***(P-19406)***
Corkys Pest Control Inc ....D....760 432-8801
909 Rancheros Dr San Marcos (92069) ***(P-14148)***
Corland Companies (PA) ....D....714 573-7780
17542 17th St Ste 420 Tustin (92780) ***(P-11384)***
Cornell Companies Inc ....D....415 346-9769
759 Lakeview Ave San Francisco (94112) ***(P-27585)***
Cornell Corrections Cal Inc (HQ) ....B....805 644-8700
1811 Knoll Dr Ventura (93003) ***(P-23617)***
Corner Bakery Store ....E....714 459-1420
1040 W Imperial Hwy Ste A La Habra (90631) ***(P-8780)***
Corner Products Company ....D....800 876-8889
17110 Armstrong Ave Irvine (92614) ***(P-7463)***
Cornerstone Cnsulting Tech Inc ....E....415 705-7800
241 5th St San Francisco (94103) ***(P-27698)***
Cornerstone Family Svcs LLC ....D....714 744-3800
1748 W Katella Ave # 207 Orange (92867) ***(P-22277)***
Cornerstone Healthcare Inc ....C....805 777-1133
143 Triunfo Canyon Rd # 103 Westlake Village (91361) ***(P-20924)***

ALPHABETIC

Employee Codes: A=Over 500 employees, B=251-500
C=101-250, D=51-100, E=50
2019 Directory of California
Wholesalers and Services Companies
© Mergent Inc. 1-800-342-5647
1263

Cornerstone Hospice Cal LLC...D.......909 872-8100
1461 E Cooley Dr Ste 220 Colton (92324) ***(P-22278)***
Cornerstone Hotel Management (HQ)...D.......415 397-5572
222 Kearny St Ste 200 San Francisco (94108) ***(P-26820)***
Cornerstone Marketing Alliance, Encino *Also called C M A Alliance* ***(P-10567)***
Cornerstone Medical Group...E.......909 890-4353
1881 Commercenter E # 112 San Bernardino (92408) ***(P-20153)***
Cornerstone Ondemand Inc (PA)...C.......310 752-0200
1601 Cloverfield Blvd 620s Santa Monica (90404) ***(P-15638)***
Cornerstone Research Inc...D.......213 553-2500
633 W 5th St Fl 31 Los Angeles (90071) ***(P-26507)***
Cornerstone Research Inc (PA)...D.......650 853-1660
1000 El Camino Real # 250 Menlo Park (94025) ***(P-27699)***
Cornerstone Research Inc...D.......415 229-8100
2 Embarcadero Ctr Fl 20 San Francisco (94111) ***(P-27700)***
Coroc, Bakersfield *Also called Weatherford International LLC* ***(P-1086)***
Corodata Corporation (PA)...D.......858 748-1100
12375 Kerran St Poway (92064) ***(P-4670)***
Corona - College Heights Ora...B.......951 359-6451
8000 Lincoln Ave Riverside (92504) ***(P-504)***
Corona Clipper Inc...D.......951 737-6515
22440 Temescal Canyon Rd # 102 Corona (92883) ***(P-7584)***
Corona Medical Offices, Corona *Also called Kaiser Foundation Hospitals* ***(P-12109)***
Corona Regional Med Ctr Hosp, Corona *Also called Uhs-Corona Inc* ***(P-21865)***
Corona Regional Medical Center, Corona *Also called Uhs-Corona Inc* ***(P-22704)***
Corona Rgional Med Ctr Bus Off, Corona *Also called Quadramed Corporation* ***(P-14019)***
Coronado Financial Corp...E.......619 946-1900
940 Eastlake Pkwy Chula Vista (91914) ***(P-11385)***
Coronado Royale, Coronado *Also called GK Management Co Inc* ***(P-11483)***
Coronado YMCA, Richmond *Also called Young MNS Chrstn Assn of E Bay* ***(P-25362)***
Coronel Construction Inc...D.......661 725-4400
2328 Venice Dr Delano (93215) ***(P-1148)***
Corovan Corporation (PA)...C.......858 762-8100
12302 Kerran St Poway (92064) ***(P-4338)***
Corovan Moving & Storage Co (HQ)...D.......858 748-1100
12302 Kerran St Poway (92064) ***(P-4339)***
Corp of Church of Christ Ld St...C.......323 268-7281
2720 E 11th St Los Angeles (90023) ***(P-17921)***
Corpinfo Services, Santa Monica *Also called K-Micro Inc* ***(P-7068)***
Corporate Building Svcs Inc...C.......213 252-0999
3325 Wilshire Blvd # 1240 Los Angeles (90010) ***(P-14228)***
Corporate Image Maintenance, Santa Ana *Also called Gamboa Service Inc* ***(P-14272)***
Corporate Production Designs...E.......310 937-9663
1427 Goodman Ave Redondo Beach (90278) ***(P-18035)***
Corporate Risk Hldings III Inc...A.......949 428-5839
3349 Michelson Dr Ste 150 Irvine (92612) ***(P-17102)***
Corporate Soul LLC...B.......707 431-7781
433 Hudson St Healdsburg (95448) ***(P-13734)***
Corporate Visions Inc (PA)...D.......415 464-4400
3875 Hopyard Rd Ste 275 Pleasanton (94588) ***(P-27201)***
Corporate Visions Inc...D.......760 458-0914
2705 Avenida De Anita # 29 Carlsbad (92010) ***(P-27202)***
Corporate Yard, San Mateo *Also called City of San Mateo* ***(P-14214)***
Corporate Yard, Hayward *Also called Hayward Area Recreation Pkdist* ***(P-4573)***
Corporation of The President...D.......916 482-1480
3000 Auburn Blvd Ste B Sacramento (95821) ***(P-24172)***
Corporation Service Company...D.......302 636-5400
2710 Gateway Oaks Dr Sacramento (95833) ***(P-14229)***
Corportion of Fine Arts Mseums...D.......415 750-3600
75 Tea Garden Dr San Francisco (94118) ***(P-24875)***
Corportion of Fine Arts Mseums...C.......415 750-3600
50 Hagiwara Tea Garden Dr San Francisco (94118) ***(P-24876)***
Corportion of Fine Arts Mseums...C.......415 750-3600
50 Golden Gate Pk Hgiwara San Francisco (94118) ***(P-24877)***
Corportion of Fine Arts Mseums (PA)...C.......415 750-3600
50 Hagiwara Tea Garden Dr San Francisco (94118) ***(P-24878)***
CORPRATE OFFICE, Blythe *Also called Blythe Nursing Care Center* ***(P-20263)***
Corptax LLC...D.......818 316-2400
21550 Oxnard St Ste 700 Woodland Hills (91367) ***(P-15081)***
Corral De Tierra Country Club...D.......831 484-1325
81 Corral De Tierra Rd Salinas (93908) ***(P-18901)***
Corral Del Tierra...D.......831 372-6244
81 Corral De Tierra Rd Salinas (93908) ***(P-18902)***
Correctional Medical Grp, Monterey *Also called Southwest Correctional Medical* ***(P-22685)***
Correctional Services Corp LLC...D.......858 566-9816
7805 Arjons Dr San Diego (92126) ***(P-27586)***
Correctons Rhbltation Cal Dept...D.......707 445-6520
930 3rd St Ste 100 Eureka (95501) ***(P-23618)***
Correctons Rhbltation Cal Dept...D.......909 806-3516
303 W 5th St San Bernardino (92401) ***(P-23619)***
Correctons Rhbltation Cal Dept...C.......909 597-1821
14901 Central Ave Chino (91710) ***(P-21344)***
Correctons Rhbltation Cal Dept...A.......805 547-7900
Hwy 1 N San Luis Obispo (93409) ***(P-22539)***
Correctons Rhbltation Cal Dept...C.......916 358-2319
1920 Alabama Ave Sacramento (95825) ***(P-16107)***
Corridor Capital LLC (PA)...C.......310 442-7000
12400 Walsh Ave Ste 645 Los Angeles (90066) ***(P-12217)***
Corridor Recycling Inc...D.......310 835-3849
22500 S Alameda St Long Beach (90810) ***(P-6383)***
Corru Kraft Buena Pk Div 5058, Buena Park *Also called Orora North America* ***(P-8117)***
Corru Kraft Fullerton Div 5068, Fullerton *Also called Orora Packaging Solutions* ***(P-8123)***
Cort Business Services Corp...D.......562 582-1515
14350 Grfield Ave Ste 500 Paramount (90723) ***(P-14490)***
Cortel Inc...D.......650 703-7217
14621 Arroyo Hondo San Diego (92127) ***(P-5401)***
Corvel Corporation...C.......909 257-3700
10750 4th St Ste 100 Rancho Cucamonga (91730) ***(P-10594)***
Corvel Corporation (PA)...C.......949 851-1473
2010 Main St Ste 600 Irvine (92614) ***(P-26821)***
Corvel Enterprise Comp Inc...D.......949 851-1473
2010 Main St Ste 600 Irvine (92614) ***(P-10595)***
Corventis Inc (PA)...D.......408 790-9300
2033 Gateway Pl Ste 100 San Jose (95110) ***(P-16214)***
Cosco Agencies (los Angeles) (HQ)...D.......213 689-6700
588 Harbor Scenic Way Long Beach (90802) ***(P-5037)***
Cosco Fire Protection Inc...D.......925 455-2751
7455 Longard Rd Livermore (94551) ***(P-2552)***
Cosco Fire Protection Inc...D.......858 444-2000
4990 Greencraig Ln San Diego (92123) ***(P-2172)***
Cosco Fire Protection Inc...C.......714 989-1800
1075 W Lambert Rd Ste D Brea (92821) ***(P-2173)***
Cosmopro West Inc...E.......714 258-8301
15773 Gateway Cir Tustin (92780) ***(P-22279)***
Coso Operating Company LLC...D.......760 764-1300
2 Gill Station Coso Rd Little Lake (93542) ***(P-6023)***
Costa Mesa Country Club, Costa Mesa *Also called Mesa Verde Partners* ***(P-18733)***
Costa Mesa Marriott Suites, Costa Mesa *Also called Host Hotels & Resorts LP* ***(P-12711)***
Costa Mesa Sport Club, Costa Mesa *Also called 24 Hour Fitness Usa Inc* ***(P-18555)***
Costa Sons...E.......831 678-0799
36817 Foothill Rd Soledad (93960) ***(P-45)***
Costa View Farms...E.......559 675-3131
16800 Road 15 Madera (93637) ***(P-409)***
Costa View Farms Shop, Madera *Also called Costa View Farms* ***(P-409)***
Costanoa, Pescadero *Also called Joie De Vivre Hospitality LLC* ***(P-26911)***
Costanoa, Pescadero *Also called King-Reynolds Ventures LLC* ***(P-17275)***
Costar Group Inc...C.......858 458-4900
8910 University Center Ln # 300 San Diego (92122) ***(P-11386)***
Costco Auto Program, San Diego *Also called Affinity Auto Programs Inc* ***(P-16988)***
Costco Wholesale Corporation...C.......909 823-8270
16505 Sierra Lakes Pkwy Fontana (92336) ***(P-9209)***
Costless Maintenance Svcs Co...D.......415 550-8819
3254 19th St San Francisco (94110) ***(P-14230)***
Cosumnes Community Svcs Dst...B.......916 405-7150
9355 E Stockton Blvd Elk Grove (95624) ***(P-19152)***
Coto De Caza Golf Club Inc...C.......949 766-7886
25291 Vista Del Verde Trabuco Canyon (92679) ***(P-18516)***
Coto De Caza Golf Racquet CLB, Trabuco Canyon *Also called Coto De Caza Golf Racquet CLB* ***(P-18903)***
Coto De Caza Golf Racquet CLB...C.......949 858-4100
25291 Vista Del Verde Trabuco Canyon (92679) ***(P-18903)***
Cottage Care Center...C.......805 682-7111
2415 De La Vina St Santa Barbara (93105) ***(P-21345)***
Cottage Health (PA)...A.......805 682-7111
400 W Pueblo St Santa Barbara (93105) ***(P-21346)***
Cottage Health...C.......805 688-6432
2050 Viborg Rd Solvang (93463) ***(P-21347)***
COTTAGE HEALTH SYSTEM, Santa Barbara *Also called Goleta Valley Cottage Hospital* ***(P-21430)***
Cottage Health System...A.......805 967-3411
351 S Patterson Ave Goleta (93111) ***(P-21348)***
Cottage Hospital Childrens Ctr, Santa Barbara *Also called Santa Barbara Cottage Hospital* ***(P-21715)***
Cottonwood Cyn Healthcare Ctr, El Cajon *Also called Plum Healthcare Group LLC* ***(P-20708)***
Cottonwood Golf Club, El Cajon *Also called Premier Golf Properties LP* ***(P-18745)***
Cottonwood Post-Acute Rehab, Woodland *Also called North American Health Care* ***(P-26962)***
Couch Distributing Company Inc...C.......831 724-0649
104 Lee Rd Watsonville (95076) ***(P-8987)***
Council On Aging - S Cali Inc...D.......714 479-0107
2 Executive Cir Ste 175 Irvine (92614) ***(P-23620)***
Council On Aging Svcs For SRS (PA)...C.......707 525-0143
30 Kawana Springs Rd Santa Rosa (95404) ***(P-23621)***
Counseling and Research Assoc (PA)...C.......310 715-2020
108 W Victoria St Gardena (90248) ***(P-24477)***
Counseling and Research Assoc...D.......661 726-5500
314 E Avenue K4 Lancaster (93535) ***(P-24478)***
Counsyl Inc...B.......888 268-6795
180 Kimball Way South San Francisco (94080) ***(P-22072)***
Counter Brands LLC (PA)...D.......310 828-0111
2803 Colorado Ave Santa Monica (90404) ***(P-8164)***
Country Archer Jerky, San Bernardino *Also called S&E Gourmet Cuts Inc* ***(P-8567)***
Country Builders Inc...C.......925 373-1020
5915 Graham Ct Livermore (94550) ***(P-1277)***
Country Builders Construction, Livermore *Also called Country Builders Inc* ***(P-1277)***
Country Club Lanes, Sacramento *Also called Pinsetters Inc* ***(P-18497)***
Country Floors America LLC (PA)...D.......310 657-0510
8735 Melrose Ave Vernon (90058) ***(P-6883)***
Country Floral Supply Inc (PA)...D.......805 520-8026
3802 Weatherly Cir Westlake Village (91361) ***(P-9132)***
Country Furnishings, Westlake Village *Also called Country Floral Supply Inc* ***(P-9132)***
Country Hills Health Care Inc...C.......619 441-8745
1580 Broadway El Cajon (92021) ***(P-20325)***
Country Inn &SUite By Carlson...E.......909 937-6000
231 N Vineyard Ave Ontario (91764) ***(P-12485)***
Country Manor Health Care, Sylmar *Also called Canyon Properties III LLC* ***(P-21031)***
Country Oaks Care Center, Pomona *Also called Country Oaks Partners LLC* ***(P-20327)***
Country Oaks Care Center Inc...D.......805 922-6657
830 E Chapel St Santa Maria (93454) ***(P-20326)***
Country Oaks Partners LLC...D.......909 622-1067
215 W Pearl St Pomona (91768) ***(P-20327)***
Country Suites By Carlson, Fremont *Also called Merrill Gardens* ***(P-11150)***

Country Villa Blmnt Hght Hlth	D	562 597-8817
1730 Grand Ave Long Beach (90804) *(P-21045)*		
Country Villa E Convalescent, Los Angeles *Also called Country Villa Service Corp (P-26826)*		
Country Villa East LP	C	323 939-3184
5916 W Pico Blvd Los Angeles (90035) *(P-21046)*		
Country Villa Glendale, Glendale *Also called Glendale Healthcare Center (P-20456)*		
Country Villa Health Services, Anaheim *Also called Country Villa Service Corp (P-26823)*		
Country Villa Imperial LLC	C	323 666-1544
3002 Rowena Ave Los Angeles (90039) *(P-20328)*		
Country Villa Los Feliz, Los Angeles *Also called Country Villa Imperial LLC (P-20328)*		
Country Villa Rancho	C	760 340-0053
39950 Vista Del Sol Rancho Mirage (92270) *(P-23622)*		
Country Villa Service Corp	C	323 666-1544
3002 Rowena Ave Los Angeles (90039) *(P-26822)*		
Country Villa Service Corp	D	562 598-2477
3000 N Gate Rd Seal Beach (90740) *(P-23623)*		
Country Villa Service Corp	D	209 723-2911
510 W 26th St Merced (95340) *(P-23624)*		
Country Villa Service Corp (PA)	D	310 574-3733
2400 E Katella Ave # 800 Anaheim (92806) *(P-26823)*		
Country Villa Service Corp	C	562 597-8817
1730 Grand Ave Long Beach (90804) *(P-26824)*		
Country Villa Service Corp	D	818 246-5516
1208 S Central Ave Glendale (91204) *(P-20329)*		
Country Villa Service Corp	C	626 358-4547
615 W Duarte Rd Monrovia (91016) *(P-26825)*		
Country Villa Service Corp	C	626 285-2165
112 E Broadway San Gabriel (91776) *(P-21047)*		
Country Villa Service Corp	D	626 445-2421
400 W Huntington Dr Arcadia (91007) *(P-20330)*		
Country Villa Service Corp	C	323 734-1101
2415 S Western Ave Los Angeles (90018) *(P-26826)*		
Country Villa Service Corp	D	760 340-0053
39950 Vista Del Sol Rancho Mirage (92270) *(P-17103)*		
Country Villa Service Corp	D	310 574-3733
3533 Motor Ave Los Angeles (90034) *(P-26827)*		
Country Villa Service Corp	D	323 734-9122
3233 W Pico Blvd Los Angeles (90019) *(P-26828)*		
Country Villa Service Corp	D	310 537-2500
3611 E Imperial Hwy Lynwood (90262) *(P-20331)*		
Country Villa Terrace (PA)	D	323 653-3980
6050 W Pico Blvd Los Angeles (90035) *(P-21048)*		
Country Villa Terrace	E	323 939-3184
5916 W Pico Blvd Los Angeles (90035) *(P-21049)*		
COUNTRY VILLA WESTWOOD NURSING, Los Angeles *Also called Westwood Healthcare Center LP (P-20890)*		
Country Vlla Convalescent Hosp, Los Angeles *Also called Country Villa Terrace (P-21048)*		
Country Vlla Nrsing Rhbltation, Los Angeles *Also called Country Villa East LP (P-21046)*		
Countryside Inn-Corona LP	E	909 335-9024
1015 W Colton Ave Redlands (92374) *(P-26829)*		
Countryside Inn-Corona LP	D	949 588-0131
24341 El Toro Rd Laguna Woods (92637) *(P-12486)*		
Countryside Inn-Corona LP	E	562 596-8330
12850 Seal Beach Blvd Seal Beach (90740) *(P-26830)*		
Countryside Inn-Corona LP	D	714 549-0300
325 Bristol St Costa Mesa (92626) *(P-12487)*		
Countryside Mushrooms Inc	D	408 683-2748
11300 Center Ave Gilroy (95020) *(P-310)*		
Countryside Suites By Ayres, Costa Mesa *Also called Countryside Inn-Corona LP (P-12487)*		
Countrywide Capital Mkts LLC (HQ)	C	818 225-3000
4500 Park Granada Calabasas (91302) *(P-9793)*		
Countrywide Financial Corp (HQ)	A	818 225-3000
4500 Park Granada Calabasas (91302) *(P-9794)*		
Countrywide Home Loans Inc (HQ)	A	818 225-3000
225 W Hillcrest Dr Thousand Oaks (91360) *(P-9795)*		
Countrywide Home Loans Inc	C	818 550-8700
801 N Brand Blvd Ste 750 Glendale (91203) *(P-9796)*		
Countrywide Securities Corp	B	818 225-3000
4500 Park Granada Calabasas (91302) *(P-9944)*		
County Building Materials Inc	D	408 274-4920
2927 S King Rd San Jose (95122) *(P-6819)*		
COUNTY CLUB OF RANCHO BERNARDO, San Diego *Also called Rancho Bernardo Golf Club (P-19007)*		
County Engineers Assn Cal	D	707 762-3492
120 Round Ct Petaluma (94952) *(P-25625)*		
County General Hospital, San Luis Obispo *Also called County of San Luis Obispo (P-21358)*		
County Government, San Luis Obispo *Also called County of San Luis Obispo (P-25630)*		
County Jail, Salinas *Also called County of Monterey (P-27587)*		
County Lake Health Services	D	707 263-1090
922 Bevins Ct Lakeport (95453) *(P-25013)*		
County Los Angles Prbtion Dept, Pomona *Also called County of Los Angeles (P-23674)*		
County Monterey Social Svcs	D	831 899-8001
1281 Broadway Ave Seaside (93955) *(P-23625)*		
County of Alameda	B	510 670-5455
399 Elmhurst St Hayward (94544) *(P-1746)*		
County of Alameda	E	510 670-5700
24100 Amador St Ste 130 Hayward (94544) *(P-24173)*		
County of Alameda	C	510 481-4141
2060 Fairmont Dr San Leandro (94578) *(P-19407)*		
County of Butte	C	530 538-7661
42 County Center Dr Oroville (95965) *(P-23626)*		
County of Butte	B	530 538-7721
25 County Center Dr # 110 Oroville (95965) *(P-23627)*		
County of Butte	B	530 872-6328
5910 Clark Rd Ste W Paradise (95969) *(P-23628)*		
County of Butte	A	530 538-7572
202 Mira Loma Dr Oroville (95965) *(P-23629)*		

County of Butte	B	530 538-6802
205 Mira Loma Dr Oroville (95965) *(P-23630)*		
County of Butte	A	530 538-7711
78 Table Mountain Blvd Oroville (95965) *(P-23631)*		
County of Butte	B	530 891-2850
107 Parmac Rd Ste 4 Chico (95926) *(P-22540)*		
County of Calaveras	D	209 754-6402
891 Mountain Ranch Rd San Andreas (95249) *(P-23632)*		
County of Contra Costa	C	925 313-4000
50 Douglas Dr Ste 200 Martinez (94553) *(P-23633)*		
County of Contra Costa	C	925 313-2000
255 Glacier Dr Martinez (94553) *(P-1747)*		
County of Contra Costa	D	925 646-5877
2099 Arnold Industrial Wa Concord (94520) *(P-14231)*		
County of Contra Costa	D	925 313-7052
2467 Waterbird Way Martinez (94553) *(P-14232)*		
County of Contra Costa	C	866 901-3212
50 Douglas Dr Ste 100 Martinez (94553) *(P-23634)*		
County of Contra Costa	C	925 313-1500
40 Douglas Dr Martinez (94553) *(P-23635)*		
County of Contra Costa	C	925 370-5000
2500 Alhambra Ave Martinez (94553) *(P-21349)*		
County of Contra Costa	E	925 646-5480
1420 Willow Pass Rd # 140 Concord (94520) *(P-22541)*		
County of Del Norte	C	707 464-3191
880 Northcrest Dr Crescent City (95531) *(P-24766)*		
County of El Dorado, Placerville *Also called El Dorado County Health Dept (P-19456)*		
County of El Dorado	D	530 626-4141
3940 Hwy 49 Diamond Springs (95619) *(P-6384)*		
County of El Dorado	D	530 621-6210
935b Spring St Placerville (95667) *(P-21942)*		
County of El Dorado	D	530 621-5845
3000 Fairlane Ct Ste 2 Placerville (95667) *(P-14233)*		
County of El Dorado	C	530 621-5625
3974 Durock Rd Ste 205 Shingle Springs (95682) *(P-23636)*		
County of El Dorado	D	530 642-7130
3057 Briw Rd Ste A Placerville (95667) *(P-23637)*		
County of Fresno	D	559 600-3420
1130 O St Fresno (93724) *(P-22994)*		
County of Fresno	D	559 600-3800
2212 N Winery Ave Ste 122 Fresno (93703) *(P-23638)*		
County of Fresno	D	559 600-5127
333 W Pontiac Way Clovis (93612) *(P-23639)*		
County of Fresno	D	559 600-3546
2220 Tulare St Ste 300 Fresno (93721) *(P-22995)*		
County of Fresno	D	559 600-4600
4417 E Inyo St Bldg 333 Fresno (93702) *(P-22542)*		
County of Fresno	D	559 600-3534
2281 Tulare St Ste 201 Fresno (93721) *(P-25014)*		
County of Fresno	C	559 600-3996
3333 E American Ave Ste B Fresno (93725) *(P-23640)*		
County of Fresno	C	559 488-3275
P.O. Box 352 Fresno (93708) *(P-23641)*		
County of Glenn	D	530 934-6582
247 N Villa Ave Willows (95988) *(P-22770)*		
County of Glenn	C	530 934-6530
777 N Colusa St Willows (95988) *(P-1748)*		
County of Glenn	D	530 934-6453
525 W Sycamore St Ste A1 Willows (95988) *(P-23642)*		
County of Glenn	C	530 934-6514
420 E Laurel St Willows (95988) *(P-23643)*		
County of Glenn	D	530 934-6582
242 N Villa Ave Willows (95988) *(P-22543)*		
County of Humboldt	B	707 445-6180
929 Koster St Eureka (95501) *(P-23644)*		
County of Humboldt	C	707 476-4054
720 Wood St Eureka (95501) *(P-22544)*		
County of Imperial	C	760 482-4441
935 Broadway Ave El Centro (92243) *(P-22771)*		
County of Imperial	D	760 355-1748
304 E 4th St Imperial (92251) *(P-1749)*		
County of Imperial	C	760 336-3581
324 Applestille Rd El Centro (92243) *(P-23645)*		
County of Imperial	C	760 482-4120
202 N 8th St El Centro (92243) *(P-22545)*		
County of Inyo	D	760 878-0292
224 N Edwards St Independence (93526) *(P-17605)*		
County of Kern	A	661 868-4100
2005 Ridge Rd Bakersfield (93305) *(P-23646)*		
County of Kern	D	661 392-2010
2014 Calloway Dr Bakersfield (93312) *(P-23647)*		
County of Kern	D	661 336-6800
2001 28th St Ste C Bakersfield (93301) *(P-23648)*		
County of Kern	E	661 868-8360
1721 Westwind Dr Bakersfield (93301) *(P-19408)*		
County of Kern	A	661 326-2054
1700 Mount Vernon Ave Bakersfield (93306) *(P-21350)*		
County of Kern	D	661 763-1535
5357 Truxtun Ave Taft (93268) *(P-23649)*		
County of Kern	E	661 763-4246
500 Cascade Pl Taft (93268) *(P-19153)*		
County of Kern	D	661 721-5134
1816 Cecil Ave Delano (93215) *(P-23650)*		
County of Kern	A	661 631-6346
100 E California Ave Bakersfield (93307) *(P-24767)*		
County of Kern	D	661 363-8910
6601 Niles Senior St Bakersfield (93306) *(P-23651)*		
County of Kern	D	661 868-2000
1215 Truxtun Ave Fl 4 Bakersfield (93301) *(P-22996)*		
County of Kings	C	559 584-1411
330 Campus Dr Hanford (93230) *(P-10163)*		

Employee Codes: A=Over 500 employees, B=251-500
C=101-250, D=51-100, E=50

2019 Directory of California
Wholesalers and Services Companies

© Mergent Inc. 1-800-342-5647

1265

A
L
P
H
A
B
E
T
I
C

County of Kings .... C 559 852-4316
1424 Forum Dr Hanford (93230) *(P-23652)*

County of Los Angeles .... C 818 364-1555
14445 Olive View Dr 2b Sylmar (91342) *(P-21351)*

County of Los Angeles .... C 818 837-6969
1212 Pico St San Fernando (91340) *(P-19409)*

County of Los Angeles .... C 626 356-5281
300 E Walnut St Dept 200 Pasadena (91101) *(P-23653)*

County of Los Angeles .... D 661 223-8700
30500 Arrastre Canyon Rd Acton (93510) *(P-22011)*

County of Los Angeles .... D 323 869-7063
5555 Ferguson Dr Commerce (90022) *(P-24768)*

County of Los Angeles .... C 626 299-5300
1000 S Fremont Ave Unit 4 Alhambra (91803) *(P-10198)*

County of Los Angeles .... C 626 575-4059
11234 Valley Blvd Ste 103 El Monte (91731) *(P-23654)*

County of Los Angeles .... D 213 739-2360
600 S Commwl Ave Fl 2 Flr 2 Los Angeles (90005) *(P-22772)*

County of Los Angeles .... C 213 974-0515
320 W Temple St Fl 9 Los Angeles (90012) *(P-16215)*

County of Los Angeles .... D 310 885-2100
546 W Compton Blvd Compton (90220) *(P-22773)*

County of Los Angeles .... B 661 940-4181
5300 W Avenue I Lancaster (93536) *(P-23655)*

County of Los Angeles .... C 562 401-9413
7601 Imperial Hwy Downey (90242) *(P-23656)*

County of Los Angeles .... B 310 222-2401
1000 W Carson St Fl 8 Flr 8 Palos Verdes Peninsu (90274) *(P-21352)*

County of Los Angeles .... B 323 889-3405
5770 S Eastern Ave Fl 4th Commerce (90040) *(P-23657)*

County of Los Angeles .... C 661 723-4051
349 E Avenue K6 Ste B Lancaster (93535) *(P-23658)*

County of Los Angeles .... A 562 401-7088
7601 Imperial Hwy Downey (90242) *(P-22546)*

County of Los Angeles .... A 213 974-7284
515 E 6th St Los Angeles (90021) *(P-22012)*

County of Los Angeles .... C 310 668-4545
12025 Wilmington Ave Los Angeles (90059) *(P-21353)*

County of Los Angeles .... B 562 903-5000
10355 Slusher Dr Santa Fe Springs (90670) *(P-23659)*

County of Los Angeles .... B 562 908-8400
12900 Crssrds Pkwy S 20 City of Industry (91746) *(P-26831)*

County of Los Angeles .... C 310 222-4220
1000 W Carson St Torrance (90502) *(P-19410)*

County of Los Angeles .... B 562 497-3500
4060 Watson Plaza Dr Lakewood (90712) *(P-23660)*

County of Los Angeles .... D 323 226-8611
1605 Eastlake Ave Los Angeles (90033) *(P-24479)*

County of Los Angeles .... B 323 226-6221
1200 N State St Los Angeles (90033) *(P-19411)*

County of Los Angeles .... C 323 265-1804
1000 Corp Ctr Dr Ste 200b Monterey Park (91754) *(P-23661)*

County of Los Angeles .... C 661 948-2320
777 W Jackman St Lancaster (93534) *(P-23662)*

County of Los Angeles .... B 213 744-3677
2829 S Grand Ave Los Angeles (90007) *(P-19412)*

County of Los Angeles .... C 818 374-2161
210 W Temple St Fl 18 Los Angeles (90012) *(P-23663)*

County of Los Angeles .... C 323 226-8998
1601 Eastlake Ave Ste 4 Los Angeles (90033) *(P-22997)*

County of Los Angeles .... D 818 364-2011
16350 Filbert St Sylmar (91342) *(P-24480)*

County of Los Angeles .... D 310 668-6845
921 E Compton Blvd Compton (90221) *(P-22774)*

County of Los Angeles .... D 626 229-3825
532 E Colorado Blvd Fl 8 Pasadena (91101) *(P-22775)*

County of Los Angeles .... A 213 922-6210
1 Gateway Plz Los Angeles (90012) *(P-14108)*

County of Los Angeles .... C 909 620-3330
300 S Park Ave Ste 770 Pomona (91766) *(P-22998)*

County of Los Angeles .... A 323 267-2136
1100 N Eastern Ave Los Angeles (90063) *(P-26173)*

County of Los Angeles .... C 213 974-9331
320 W Temple St Ste 1101 Los Angeles (90012) *(P-23664)*

County of Los Angeles .... A 213 240-8412
313 N Figueroa St Fl 9 Los Angeles (90012) *(P-25015)*

County of Los Angeles .... D 909 629-1166
1875 Fairplex Dr Pomona (91768) *(P-18699)*

County of Los Angeles .... C 562 908-3119
8240 Broadway Ave Whittier (90606) *(P-23665)*

County of Los Angeles .... B 323 586-7263
1740 E Gage Ave Los Angeles (90001) *(P-23666)*

County of Los Angeles .... D 323 769-7800
5205 Melrose Ave Los Angeles (90038) *(P-22547)*

County of Los Angeles .... C 323 226-8511
1601 Eastlake Ave Los Angeles (90033) *(P-23667)*

County of Los Angeles .... A 323 226-3468
1240 N Mission Rd Los Angeles (90033) *(P-22013)*

County of Los Angeles .... A 562 462-2094
12400 Imperial Hwy Norwalk (90650) *(P-16108)*

County of Los Angeles .... D 213 351-5600
425 Shatto Pl Los Angeles (90020) *(P-23668)*

County of Los Angeles .... C 323 727-1639
5445 Whittier Blvd Fl 400 Los Angeles (90022) *(P-23669)*

County of Los Angeles .... C 323 560-5001
8130 Atlantic Ave Cudahy (90201) *(P-24769)*

County of Los Angeles .... C 805 237-3110
530 12th St Fl 1 Paso Robles (93446) *(P-23670)*

County of Los Angeles .... C 661 723-6088
44933 Fern Ave Lancaster (93534) *(P-25626)*

County of Los Angeles .... B 213 744-5601
2707 S Grand Ave Los Angeles (90007) *(P-23671)*

County of Los Angeles .... D 213 351-7800
3530 Wilshire Blvd Fl 9 Los Angeles (90010) *(P-22776)*

County of Los Angeles .... A 661 948-8581
335 E Avenue I Lancaster (93535) *(P-19413)*

County of Los Angeles .... C 323 226-6021
1100 N Mission Rd Rm 236 Los Angeles (90033) *(P-21354)*

County of Los Angeles .... D 661 298-3406
27233 Camp Plenty Rd Canyon Country (91351) *(P-10483)*

County of Los Angeles .... C 562 945-2581
9402 Greenleaf Ave Whittier (90605) *(P-3912)*

County of Los Angeles .... D 310 222-2357
1000 W Crson St Bsmnt 404 Basement Torrance (90502) *(P-8165)*

County of Los Angeles .... D 562 861-0316
5525 Imperial Hwy South Gate (90280) *(P-22777)*

County of Los Angeles .... D 323 857-6000
5905 Wilshire Blvd Los Angeles (90036) *(P-24879)*

County of Los Angeles .... C 818 362-6437
14555 Osborne St Ofc Van Nuys (91402) *(P-23672)*

County of Los Angeles .... C 213 367-3176
6801 E 2nd St Long Beach (90803) *(P-6233)*

County of Los Angeles .... C 626 854-4987
17171 Gale Ave City of Industry (91745) *(P-23673)*

County of Los Angeles .... D 213 240-7780
313 N Figueroa St Los Angeles (90012) *(P-22778)*

County of Los Angeles .... C 626 337-1277
14747 Ramona Blvd Baldwin Park (91706) *(P-25627)*

County of Los Angeles .... D 909 469-4500
1660 W Mission Blvd Pomona (91766) *(P-23674)*

County of Los Angeles .... D 310 266-3711
1725 Main St Rm 125 Santa Monica (90401) *(P-23675)*

County of Los Angeles .... D 818 374-2000
14414 Delano St Van Nuys (91401) *(P-23676)*

County of Los Angeles .... E 626 821-5858
330 E Live Oak Ave Arcadia (91006) *(P-23677)*

County of Los Angeles .... E 562 402-0688
17707 Studebaker Rd Artesia (90703) *(P-22548)*

County of Los Angeles .... D 310 518-8800
1325 Broad Ave Wilmington (90744) *(P-19414)*

County of Los Angeles .... C 818 896-1903
13300 Van Nuys Blvd Pacoima (91331) *(P-19415)*

County of Los Angeles .... C 661 947-7173
38126 Sierra Hwy Palmdale (93550) *(P-1750)*

County of Los Angeles .... B 626 458-4000
900 S Fremont Ave Alhambra (91803) *(P-6234)*

County of Los Angeles .... C 310 603-7483
200 W Compton Blvd # 700 Compton (90220) *(P-22999)*

County of Los Angeles .... D 626 455-4700
4024 Durfee Ave Rm 225 El Monte (91732) *(P-24481)*

County of Los Angeles .... C 213 974-2811
210 W Temple St Fl 19 Los Angeles (90012) *(P-23000)*

County of Los Angeles .... C 310 603-7271
200 W Compton Blvd Fl 8 Compton (90220) *(P-23001)*

County of Los Angeles .... D 323 780-2185
4849 Civic Center Way Los Angeles (90022) *(P-23678)*

County of Los Angeles .... C 562 807-7860
12727 Norwalk Blvd Norwalk (90650) *(P-23679)*

County of Los Angeles .... C 310 222-3552
20221 Hamilton Ave Torrance (90502) *(P-23002)*

County of Los Angeles .... A 213 351-7257
501 Shatto Pl Ste 301 Los Angeles (90020) *(P-23680)*

County of Los Angeles .... D 323 586-6469
8526 Grape St Los Angeles (90001) *(P-23681)*

County of Los Angeles .... C 310 603-7311
200 W Compton Blvd # 300 Compton (90220) *(P-23682)*

County of Los Angeles .... C 626 458-1700
1525 Alcazar St Bldg 1 Los Angeles (90033) *(P-1751)*

County of Los Angeles .... D 626 356-5281
199 N Euclid Ave Pasadena (91101) *(P-23683)*

County of Los Angeles .... D 818 374-2406
6230 Sylmar Ave Ste 201 Van Nuys (91401) *(P-23003)*

County of Los Angeles .... D 661 524-2005
335 E Avenue K6 Ste B Lancaster (93535) *(P-22549)*

County of Los Angeles .... B 562 940-2476
9150 Imperial Hwy Downey (90242) *(P-23684)*

County of Los Angeles .... C 323 267-2771
1100 N Eastern Ave Los Angeles (90063) *(P-17104)*

County of Los Angeles .... C 562 599-9200
2600 Redondo Ave 3 Long Beach (90806) *(P-19416)*

County of Los Angeles .... C 818 557-4164
3307 N Glenoaks Blvd Burbank (91504) *(P-23685)*

County of Los Angeles .... B 213 473-6100
450 Bauchet St Los Angeles (90012) *(P-21355)*

County of Los Angeles .... C 626 308-5542
200 W Woodward Ave Alhambra (91801) *(P-23686)*

County of Los Angeles .... C 818 889-1353
427 Encinal Canyon Rd Malibu (90265) *(P-23687)*

County of Los Angeles .... C 213 974-4561
441 Bauchet St Los Angeles (90012) *(P-5222)*

County of Los Angeles .... C 559 675-7739
209 W Yosemite Ave Madera (93637) *(P-23688)*

County of Los Angeles .... C 213 974-8301
500 W Temple St Ste 525 Los Angeles (90012) *(P-6235)*

County of Los Angeles .... C 310 847-4018
21356 Avalon Blvd Carson (90745) *(P-25059)*

County of Madera .... D 559 675-7811
200 W 4th St Madera (93637) *(P-17858)*

County of Marin .... B 415 332-6158
164 Donahue St Sausalito (94965) *(P-23689)*

Mergent e-mail: customerrelations@mergent.com
1266

2019 Directory of California
Wholesalers and Services Companies

(P-0000) Products & Services Section entry number
(PA)=Parent Co (HQ)=Headquarters (DH)=Div Headquarters

County of Marin....B....415 499-6970
120 N Redwood Dr San Rafael (94903) ***(P-23690)***
County of Marin....D....415 499-7060
371 Bel Marin Keys Blvd # 100 Novato (94949) ***(P-16109)***
County of Marin....D....415 448-1500
250 Bon Air Rd Greenbrae (94904) ***(P-22550)***
County of Marin....C....415 499-7877
1600 Los Gamos Dr Ste 200 San Rafael (94903) ***(P-25628)***
County of Medocina Dept of Mnt, Ukiah *Also called County of Mendocino* ***(P-22551)***
County of Mendocino....D....707 463-4363
340 Lake Mendocino Dr Ukiah (95482) ***(P-4883)***
County of Mendocino....B....707 463-2437
737 S State St Ukiah (95482) ***(P-23691)***
County of Mendocino....C....707 463-4363
340 Lake Mendocino Dr Ukiah (95482) ***(P-1752)***
County of Mendocino....C....707 463-4396
860a N Bush St Ukiah (95482) ***(P-22551)***
County of Merced....C....209 724-2000
1205 W 18th St Merced (95340) ***(P-24174)***
County of Modoc....C....530 233-6223
204 S Court St Ste 6 Alturas (96101) ***(P-17105)***
County of Modoc....D....530 233-6501
120 N Main St Alturas (96101) ***(P-23692)***
County of Modoc....C....530 233-3416
228 W Mcdowell Ave Alturas (96101) ***(P-20332)***
County of Modoc....D....530 233-6400
204 S Court St Ste 6 Alturas (96101) ***(P-23693)***
County of Monterey....D....831 755-4944
855 E Laurel Dr Ste D Salinas (93905) ***(P-17106)***
County of Monterey....D....831 755-5027
240 Church St Ste 116 Salinas (93901) ***(P-17107)***
County of Monterey....E....831 755-4500
1270 Natividad Rd Salinas (93906) ***(P-24770)***
County of Monterey....A....831 755-4201
1441 Constitution Blvd # 100 Salinas (93906) ***(P-21356)***
County of Monterey....E....831 769-8800
559 E Alisal St Ste 201 Salinas (93905) ***(P-19417)***
County of Monterey....B....831 755-3700
1414 Natividad Rd Salinas (93906) ***(P-25412)***
County of Monterey....A....831 755-8500
1000 S Main St Ste 216 Salinas (93901) ***(P-23694)***
County of Monterey....C....831 755-3782
1410 Natividad Rd Salinas (93906) ***(P-27587)***
County of Monterey....B....831 755-4800
168 W Alisal St Fl 3 Salinas (93901) ***(P-1753)***
County of Monterey Social Svcs, Seaside *Also called County Monterey Social Svcs* ***(P-23625)***
County of NAPA....B....707 253-4625
650 Imperial Way Ste 101 NAPA (94559) ***(P-23695)***
County of NAPA....E....707 253-4361
212 Walnut St NAPA (94559) ***(P-23696)***
County of NAPA....B....707 253-4461
2261 Elm St NAPA (94559) ***(P-22552)***
County of Orange....D....714 896-7188
8141 13th St Westminster (92683) ***(P-23697)***
County of Orange....D....714 937-4500
1535 E Orangewood Ave Anaheim (92805) ***(P-23698)***
County of Orange....D....714 896-7500
14180 Beach Blvd Ste 120 Westminster (92683) ***(P-23699)***
County of Orange....E....714 834-8385
1729 W 17th St Santa Ana (92706) ***(P-22073)***
County of Orange....C....949 252-5006
3160 Airway Ave Costa Mesa (92626) ***(P-4884)***
County of Orange....E....714 626-3700
1440 N Harbor Blvd # 400 Fullerton (92835) ***(P-23004)***
County of Orange....B....714 834-4000
300 N Sunflower Ste 400 Santa Ana (92703) ***(P-6385)***
County of Orange....C....714 704-8000
800 N Eckhoff St Bldg 121 Orange (92868) ***(P-23700)***
County of Orange....E....714 567-7500
1300 S Grand Ave Ste C Santa Ana (92705) ***(P-25370)***
County of Orange....D....714 834-8899
2020 W Walnut St Santa Ana (92703) ***(P-23701)***
County of Orange....A....714 834-6021
405 W 5th St Ofc Santa Ana (92701) ***(P-20925)***
County of Orange....D....714 935-6435
341 The City Dr S Orange (92868) ***(P-23702)***
County of Placer....D....530 886-1870
379 Nevada St Auburn (95603) ***(P-23703)***
County of Placer....D....530 889-7215
11584 B Ave Auburn (95603) ***(P-22553)***
County of Placer....C....530 889-7500
3091 County Center Dr # 220 Auburn (95603) ***(P-25629)***
County of Placer....C....530 823-4300
11512 B Ave Auburn (95603) ***(P-23704)***
County of Placer....C....530 889-7900
2929 Richardson Dr Ste B Auburn (95603) ***(P-23705)***
County of Riverside....C....951 955-6000
4075 Main St Riverside (92501) ***(P-23005)***
County of Riverside....E....951 272-5400
3178 Hamner Ave Norco (92860) ***(P-23706)***
County of Riverside....D....951 955-0840
5256 Mission Blvd Riverside (92509) ***(P-19418)***
County of Riverside....D....951 443-2262
2560 N Perris Blvd Ste N1 Perris (92571) ***(P-23707)***
County of Riverside....B....951 358-5306
4065 County Circle Dr Riverside (92503) ***(P-24771)***
County of Riverside....D....951 486-4000
26520 Cactus Ave Moreno Valley (92555) ***(P-19419)***
County of Riverside....D....951 358-6000
7140 Indiana Ave Riverside (92504) ***(P-19420)***
County of Riverside....B....951 486-4000
26520 Cactus Ave Moreno Valley (92555) ***(P-19421)***
County of Riverside....D....951 245-3060
1400 W Minthorn St Lake Elsinore (92530) ***(P-23708)***
County of Riverside....D....951 600-6500
43264 Business Park Dr # 102 Temecula (92590) ***(P-23709)***
County of Riverside....C....951 955-3100
1325 Spruce St Ste 100 Riverside (92507) ***(P-23710)***
County of Riverside....D....760 863-8283
47923 Oasis St Ste A Indio (92201) ***(P-19422)***
County of Riverside....D....951 245-3100
1400 W Minthorn St Lake Elsinore (92530) ***(P-23711)***
County of Riverside....D....760 863-7600
47 665 Oasis St Indio (92201) ***(P-24482)***
County of Riverside....D....951 275-8783
4168 12th St Riverside (92501) ***(P-23712)***
County of Riverside....D....760 863-8247
82503 Us Highway 111 Indio (92201) ***(P-19154)***
County of Riverside....D....951 697-4699
6296 River Crest Dr Ste K Riverside (92507) ***(P-23713)***
County of Riverside....E....951 486-7700
4080 Lemon St Fl 3 Riverside (92501) ***(P-16333)***
County of Riverside....A....951 955-0905
3960 Orange St Ste 500 Riverside (92501) ***(P-23714)***
County of Riverside....D....951 358-4415
10000 County Farm Rd Riverside (92503) ***(P-23715)***
County of Riverside....B....951 955-4800
3133 Mission Inn Ave Riverside (92507) ***(P-1149)***
County of Riverside....D....951 955-3100
3403 10th St Ste 500 Riverside (92501) ***(P-24175)***
County of Riverside Department (PA)....D....951 358-5000
4065 County Circle Dr Riverside (92503) ***(P-25413)***
County of Riverside Department....D....760 320-1048
554 S Paseo Dorotea Palm Springs (92264) ***(P-22779)***
County of Sacramento....B....916 874-7752
799 G St Sacramento (95814) ***(P-16266)***
County of Sacramento....D....916 875-2711
9700 Goethe Rd Ste D Sacramento (95827) ***(P-1876)***
County of Sacramento....D....916 875-0900
9616 Micron Ave Ste 750 Sacramento (95827) ***(P-20333)***
County of Sacramento....C....916 874-5411
700 H St Ste 270 Sacramento (95814) ***(P-23006)***
County of Sacramento....D....916 874-0746
7207 Earhart Dr Sacramento (95837) ***(P-14234)***
County of Sacramento....D....916 363-8383
10361 Rockingham Dr # 100 Sacramento (95827) ***(P-18795)***
County of Sacramento....C....916 874-1927
12500 Bruceville Rd Elk Grove (95757) ***(P-27588)***
County of Sacramento....C....916 875-4467
9750 Bus Park Dr Ste 104 Sacramento (95827) ***(P-23716)***
County of San Bernardino....D....909 891-3300
412 W Hospitality Ln Fl 2 San Bernardino (92415) ***(P-23717)***
County of San Bernardino....C....909 580-1000
400 N Pepper Ave Colton (92324) ***(P-22074)***
County of San Bernardino....D....909 387-5455
385 N Arrowhead Ave San Bernardino (92415) ***(P-24307)***
County of San Bernardino....D....909 387-2363
250 S Lena Rd San Bernardino (92415) ***(P-24308)***
County of San Bernardino....D....909 945-4000
8303 Haven Ave Rancho Cucamonga (91730) ***(P-23718)***
County of San Bernardino....D....909 387-0535
860 E Gilbert St San Bernardino (92415) ***(P-24483)***
County of San Bernardino....C....909 386-8818
222 W Hospitality Ln San Bernardino (92415) ***(P-26174)***
County of San Bernardino....D....760 843-5100
17270 Bear Valley Rd # 108 Victorville (92395) ***(P-23719)***
County of San Bernardino....D....760 228-5234
56357 Pima Trl Yucca Valley (92284) ***(P-23720)***
County of San Bernardino....E....909 425-0785
26887 5th St Highland (92346) ***(P-24309)***
County of San Diego....D....858 694-5141
6950 Levant St San Diego (92111) ***(P-23721)***
County of San Diego....D....866 262-9881
130 E Alvarado St Fallbrook (92028) ***(P-23722)***
County of San Diego....D....858 495-5537
5560 Overland Ave Ste 310 San Diego (92123) ***(P-23723)***
County of San Diego....D....619 515-8202
330 W Broadway Ste 1100 San Diego (92101) ***(P-23724)***
County of San Diego....D....619 531-4040
330 W Broadway Ste 1020 San Diego (92101) ***(P-23007)***
County of San Diego....C....760 754-3456
1320 Union Plaza Ct Oceanside (92054) ***(P-23725)***
County of San Diego....D....619 479-1832
8735 Jamacha Blvd Spring Valley (91977) ***(P-23726)***
County of San Diego....C....619 236-2191
1600 Pacific Hwy Ste 207 San Diego (92101) ***(P-27701)***
County of San Diego....E....858 694-2895
9320 Farnham St San Diego (92123) ***(P-21357)***
County of San Diego....B....619 692-8200
3853 Rosecrans St San Diego (92110) ***(P-21943)***
County of San Diego....D....619 563-2765
3255 Camino Del Rio S San Diego (92108) ***(P-23727)***
County of San Diego....D....619 531-4521
5570 Overland Ave Ste 101 San Diego (92123) ***(P-22780)***
County of San Diego....C....619 236-8725
4588 Market St San Diego (92102) ***(P-23728)***
County of San Joaquin....B....209 468-2601
826 N California St Stockton (95202) ***(P-23729)***

ALPHABETIC

County of San Joaquin...D...209 468-4100
24 S Hunter St Ste 201 Stockton (95202) ***(P-23730)***
County of San Joaquin...B...209 468-8750
1212 N California St Stockton (95202) ***(P-22554)***
County of San Joaquin...D...209 468-3021
1810 E Hazelton Ave Stockton (95205) ***(P-24772)***
County of San Joaquin...C...209 468-3500
56 S Lincoln St Stockton (95203) ***(P-24176)***
County of San Joaquin...D...209 468-6966
500 W Hospital Rd French Camp (95231) ***(P-23731)***
County of San Luis Obispo...B...805 781-4800
2180 Johnson Ave San Luis Obispo (93401) ***(P-21358)***
County of San Luis Obispo...C...805 781-5437
3433 S Higuera St San Luis Obispo (93401) ***(P-23732)***
County of San Luis Obispo...C...805 781-4700
2178 Johnson Ave San Luis Obispo (93401) ***(P-22555)***
County of San Luis Obispo...B...805 781-1864
3433 S Higuera St San Luis Obispo (93401) ***(P-23733)***
County of San Luis Obispo...C...805 781-5258
Government Center Rm 207 San Luis Obispo (93408) ***(P-25630)***
County of San Mateo...C...650 599-7336
680 Warren St Redwood City (94063) ***(P-23734)***
County of San Mateo...C...650 312-5327
222 Paul Scannell Dr San Mateo (94402) ***(P-23735)***
County of San Mateo...B...650 312-8887
222 Paul Scannell Dr Fl 2 San Mateo (94402) ***(P-23736)***
County of San Mateo...C...650 363-4915
400 County Ctr Redwood City (94063) ***(P-26832)***
County of San Mateo...E...650 363-4343
455 County Ctr Redwood City (94063) ***(P-26833)***
County of San Mateo...D...650 853-3139
2277 University Ave East Palo Alto (94303) ***(P-23737)***
County of San Mateo...C...650 363-4548
455 County Ctr Fl 3 Redwood City (94063) ***(P-27926)***
County of San Mateo...D...650 363-1910
555 County Ctr Fl 2 Redwood City (94063) ***(P-23738)***
County of San Mateo...C...650 802-6470
400 Harbor Blvd Bldg B Belmont (94002) ***(P-23739)***
County of San Mateo...D...650 372-8540
150 W 20th Ave San Mateo (94403) ***(P-22556)***
County of San Mateo...C...650 312-8803
222 Paul Scannell Dr San Mateo (94402) ***(P-23740)***
County of San Mateo...D...650 363-4020
455 County Ctr Fl 4 Redwood City (94063) ***(P-13463)***
County of San Mateo...C...650 363-4244
400 County Ctr Fl 5 Redwood City (94063) ***(P-23741)***
County of Santa Barbara Alcoho...D...805 681-4093
300 N San Antonio Rd Santa Barbara (93110) ***(P-22557)***
County of Shasta...D...530 225-5000
1400 California St Redding (96001) ***(P-10484)***
County of Shasta...D...530 225-5554
1313 Yuba St Redding (96001) ***(P-23742)***
County of Shasta...D...530 347-6276
19897 Gas Point Rd Cottonwood (96022) ***(P-25143)***
County of Shasta...D...530 245-6300
1355 West St Redding (96001) ***(P-23008)***
County of Shasta...E...530 225-2999
43 Hilltop Dr Redding (96003) ***(P-24310)***
County of Siskiyou...D...530 918-7200
1107 Ream Ave Mount Shasta (96067) ***(P-22558)***
County of Siskiyou...D...530 841-2700
818 S Main St Yreka (96097) ***(P-23743)***
County of Solano...D...707 784-8400
275 Beck Ave Fairfield (94533) ***(P-23744)***
County of Solano...D...707 451-6090
810 Vaca Valley Pkwy # 203 Vacaville (95688) ***(P-6236)***
County of Solano...C...707 784-7600
475 Union Ave Fairfield (94533) ***(P-23745)***
County of Solano...D...707 784-2080
2101 Courage Dr Fairfield (94533) ***(P-20926)***
County of Sonoma...C...707 823-8511
501 Petaluma Ave Sebastopol (95472) ***(P-21359)***
County of Sonoma...D...707 565-4850
3322 Chanate Rd Santa Rosa (95404) ***(P-21944)***
County of Sonoma...C...707 527-2911
2615 Paulin Dr Santa Rosa (95403) ***(P-16110)***
County of Sonoma...C...707 565-2209
600 Administration Dr 212j Santa Rosa (95403) ***(P-23009)***
County of Sonoma...D...707 527-2641
2300 County Center Dr B100 Santa Rosa (95403) ***(P-23746)***
County of Sonoma...D...707 527-2911
2300 Prof Dr Rear Door B Santa Rosa (95403) ***(P-16111)***
County of Stanislaus...C...209 525-4130
1716 Morgan Rd Modesto (95358) ***(P-6534)***
County of Stanislaus...A...209 525-7000
830 Scenic Dr Modesto (95350) ***(P-21360)***
County of Stanislaus...D...209 558-8828
830 Scenic Dr Modesto (95350) ***(P-23747)***
County of Stanislaus...C...209 567-4120
801 11th St Modesto (95354) ***(P-23748)***
County of Stanislaus...C...209 558-7377
108 Campus Way Modesto (95350) ***(P-23749)***
County of Stanislaus...C...209 558-9675
251 E Hackett Rd Modesto (95358) ***(P-23750)***
County of Stanislaus...D...209 525-6225
800 Scenic Dr Modesto (95350) ***(P-24773)***
County of Stanislaus...C...209 525-7423
800 Scenic Dr Bldg B Modesto (95350) ***(P-22559)***
County of Stanislaus...D...209 558-2500
108 Campus Way Modesto (95350) ***(P-23751)***
County of Stanislaus...C...209 558-2100
251 E Hackett Rd Ste 2 Modesto (95358) ***(P-24177)***
County of Sutter...C...530 822-7250
1965 Live Oak Blvd Yuba City (95991) ***(P-22560)***
County of Tehama...C...530 527-5631
1860 Walnut St Red Bluff (96080) ***(P-23752)***
County of Tehama...D...530 527-4052
1840 Walnut St Red Bluff (96080) ***(P-23753)***
County of Tuolumne...B...209 533-5561
2 S Green St Sonora (95370) ***(P-16112)***
County of Tuolumne...C...209 533-5711
20075 Cedar Rd N Sonora (95370) ***(P-23754)***
County of Ventura...C...805 654-2561
800 S Victoria Ave Ventura (93009) ***(P-23755)***
County of Ventura...D...805 654-3456
4651 Telephone Rd Ste 300 Ventura (93003) ***(P-23756)***
County of Ventura...C...805 385-8654
1400 Vanguard Dr Fl 2nd Oxnard (93033) ***(P-23757)***
County of Ventura...E...805 240-2701
300 W 9th St Oxnard (93030) ***(P-24311)***
County of Ventura...D...805 654-3152
800 S Victoria Ave 1540 Ventura (93009) ***(P-26175)***
County of Ventura...A...805 652-6000
3291 Loma Vista Rd Ventura (93003) ***(P-23758)***
County of Ventura...B...805 654-5529
5171 Verdugo Way Camarillo (93012) ***(P-23759)***
County of Yolo...D...530 666-8630
292 W Beamer St Woodland (95695) ***(P-22561)***
County of Yuba...D...530 749-5470
915 8th St Ste 123 Marysville (95901) ***(P-11867)***
County of Yuba...C...530 749-7550
215 5th St Ste 154 Marysville (95901) ***(P-23760)***
County Probation, El Monte *Also called County of Los Angeles* ***(P-23654)***
County Sandiego Dept Chldspprt...B...619 578-6660
3666 Krny Vlla Rd Ste 100 San Diego (92123) ***(P-23761)***
County Santtn Dist 2 of La Co (PA)...A...562 699-7411
1955 Workman Mill Rd Whittier (90601) ***(P-6535)***
County Santtn Dist 2 of La Co...B...310 830-2400
24501 Figueroa St Carson (90745) ***(P-6536)***
County Santtn Dist 2 of La Co...D...562 699-5204
2800 Workman Mill Rd Whittier (90601) ***(P-6386)***
County Santtn Dist 2 of La Co...D...310 638-1161
920 S Alameda St Compton (90221) ***(P-6537)***
County Ventura Human Resources, Ventura *Also called County of Ventura* ***(P-23755)***
County Whl Elc Co Los Angeles...D...714 633-3801
560 N Main St Orange (92868) ***(P-7352)***
Countywide Childrens Case MGT, Los Angeles *Also called County of Los Angeles* ***(P-22772)***
Countywide Mech Systems Inc...C...619 449-9900
1400 N Johnson Ave # 114 El Cajon (92020) ***(P-2174)***
Coupa Software Incorporated (PA)...C...650 931-3200
1855 S Grant St San Mateo (94402) ***(P-15639)***
Courseco Inc (PA)...A...707 763-0335
1039 N Mcdowell Blvd B Petaluma (94954) ***(P-18700)***
Coursera Inc (PA)...D...650 963-9884
381 E Evelyn Ave Mountain View (94041) ***(P-15082)***
Court House, Torrance *Also called County of Los Angeles* ***(P-23002)***
Courtesy Security Inc...D...888 572-5545
37420 Cedar Blvd Ste D Newark (94560) ***(P-16617)***
Courthuse Tours-Docent Council, Santa Barbara *Also called Santa Barbara City of* ***(P-4978)***
Courtland Farming, Courtland *Also called Delta Breeze Farming Inc* ***(P-334)***
Courtney Inc (PA)...D...949 222-2050
16781 Millikan Ave Irvine (92606) ***(P-3507)***
Courtside Club, Los Gatos *Also called Courtside Tennis Club* ***(P-18904)***
Courtside Tennis Club...D...408 395-7111
14675 Winchester Blvd Los Gatos (95032) ***(P-18904)***
Courtyard & Residence Inn La, Los Angeles *Also called 901 West Olympic Blvd LP* ***(P-12301)***
Courtyard By Marr San Diego Ai, San Diego *Also called Liberty Station Hhg Hotel LP* ***(P-12853)***
Courtyard By Marriott, San Francisco *Also called Marriot Courtyard* ***(P-12877)***
Courtyard By Marriott, Pleasant Hill *Also called Courtyard Management Corp* ***(P-12493)***
Courtyard By Marriott, Monrovia *Also called Sage Hospitality Resources LLC* ***(P-13161)***
Courtyard By Marriott, Pasadena *Also called Rt Pasad Hotel Partners LP* ***(P-13149)***
Courtyard By Marriott, Baldwin Park *Also called Baldwin Hospitality LLC* ***(P-12350)***
Courtyard By Marriott, Rancho Cordova *Also called Courtyard Management Corp* ***(P-12494)***
Courtyard By Marriott, San Diego *Also called San Diego Hotel Lease LLC* ***(P-13170)***
Courtyard By Marriott, El Segundo *Also called Marriott International Inc* ***(P-12898)***
Courtyard By Marriott, Richmond *Also called Pacific Hotel Management LLC* ***(P-13000)***
Courtyard By Marriott, Culver City *Also called Force-Oakleaf LP* ***(P-12580)***
Courtyard By Marriott...D...619 291-5720
595 Hotel Cir S San Diego (92108) ***(P-12488)***
Courtyard By Marriott...D...805 786-4200
1605 Calle Joaquin San Luis Obispo (93405) ***(P-12489)***
Courtyard By Marriott...D...415 925-1800
2500 Larkspur Landing Cir Larkspur (94939) ***(P-12490)***
Courtyard By Marriott...D...626 965-1700
1905 S Azusa Ave Hacienda Heights (91745) ***(P-12491)***
Courtyard By Marriott S, Sacramento *Also called Gccfc 2005-Gg5 Y St Ltd Partnr* ***(P-12599)***
Courtyard By Marriott San Dieg, San Diego *Also called Courtyard-Central* ***(P-12496)***
Courtyard By Marriott San Jose, Campbell *Also called Campbell Hhg Hotel Dev LP* ***(P-12423)***
Courtyard By Marroitt Oxnard, Oxnard *Also called Recp Cy Oxnard LLC* ***(P-13102)***
Courtyard By Mrriott Riverside, Yorba Linda *Also called Alliance Rvrside Hsptality LLC* ***(P-12313)***
Courtyard Care Center, Signal Hill *Also called SCCH Inc* ***(P-27023)***

Mergent e-mail: customerrelations@mergent.com
1268
2019 Directory of California
Wholesalers and Services Companies
(P-0000) Products & Services Section entry number
(PA)=Parent Co (HQ)=Headquarters (DH)=Div Headquarters

Courtyard Care Center, San Jose *Also called SSC San Jose Operating Co LP* ***(P-20778)***

Courtyard Cypress, Cypress *Also called Apple Eght Hospitality MGT Inc* ***(P-12327)***

Courtyard Management Corp ....D....818 999-2200
21101 Ventura Blvd Woodland Hills (91364) ***(P-12492)***

Courtyard Management Corp ....E....925 691-1444
2250 Contra Costa Blvd Pleasant Hill (94523) ***(P-12493)***

Courtyard Management Corp ....E....916 638-3800
10683 White Rock Rd Rancho Cordova (95670) ***(P-12494)***

Courtyard Marriott Mission Vly, San Diego *Also called Mbp Land LLC* ***(P-12917)***

Courtyard Oxnard ....D....805 988-3600
600 E Esplanade Dr Oxnard (93036) ***(P-12495)***

Courtyard Oxnard Ventura, Oxnard *Also called Js Hospitality Group LLC* ***(P-12795)***

Courtyard Plaza ....E....818 780-5005
6951 Lennox Ave Van Nuys (91405) ***(P-20334)***

Courtyard Sacramento-Midtown, Sacramento *Also called Cy Sac Operator LLC* ***(P-12510)***

Courtyard San Diego Carlsbad, Carlsbad *Also called Hit Portfolio II NTC Trs LP* ***(P-12686)***

Courtyard San Diego Central, San Diego *Also called Apple Nine Hospitality MGT* ***(P-12330)***

Courtyard San Diego Gaslamp, San Diego *Also called Cy Gaslamp LLC* ***(P-12509)***

Courtyard-Central ....D....858 573-0700
8651 Spectrum Center Blvd San Diego (92123) ***(P-12496)***

Courtyards At Pine Creek Inc ....E....925 798-3900
1081 Mohr Ln Concord (94518) ***(P-24484)***

Couts Heating & Cooling Inc ....D....951 278-5560
1693 Rimpau Ave Corona (92881) ***(P-2175)***

Covad Communications, San Jose *Also called Megapath Group Inc* ***(P-5599)***

Covance Inc ....D....858 352-2300
10300 Campus Point Dr # 225 San Diego (92121) ***(P-26351)***

Covanta Delano Inc ....E....661 792-3067
31500 Pond Rd Delano (93215) ***(P-6024)***

Cove Builders Inc ....C....714 436-2973
2264 Arroyo Dr Riverside (92506) ***(P-1278)***

Cove Electric Inc ....D....760 568-9924
77971 Wildcat Dr Ste F Palm Desert (92211) ***(P-2553)***

Covelo Indian Community Center ....D....707 983-8478
Hwy 162 Covelo (95428) ***(P-11387)***

Covenant Aviation Security LLC ....A....650 219-3473
1000 Marina Blvd Ste 100 Brisbane (94005) ***(P-16618)***

Covenant Care LLC ....D....831 476-0770
1935 Wharf Rd Capitola (95010) ***(P-20335)***

Covenant Care California LLC ....D....562 923-9301
13007 Paramount Blvd Downey (90242) ***(P-20336)***

Covenant Care California LLC ....C....209 477-5252
9289 Branstetter Pl Stockton (95209) ***(P-20337)***

Covenant Care California LLC ....D....415 327-0511
911 Bryant St Palo Alto (94301) ***(P-20338)***

Covenant Care California LLC ....D....562 426-0394
4010 N Virginia Rd Long Beach (90807) ***(P-20339)***

Covenant Care California LLC ....D....408 248-3736
410 N Winchester Blvd Santa Clara (95050) ***(P-20340)***

Covenant Care California LLC ....D....510 261-2628
2124 57th Ave Oakland (94621) ***(P-20341)***

Covenant Care California LLC ....D....562 427-7493
2725 Pacific Ave Long Beach (90806) ***(P-20342)***

Covenant Care California LLC ....C....805 488-3696
5225 S J St Oxnard (93033) ***(P-20343)***

Covenant Care California LLC ....C....323 589-5941
6425 Miles Ave Huntington Park (90255) ***(P-20344)***

Covenant Care California LLC ....C....559 251-8463
577 S Peach Ave Fresno (93727) ***(P-20345)***

Covenant Care California LLC ....D....916 391-6011
6821 24th St Sacramento (95822) ***(P-20346)***

Covenant Care California LLC ....C....805 964-4871
160 S Patterson Ave Santa Barbara (93111) ***(P-20347)***

Covenant Care California LLC ....C....209 632-3821
1111 E Tuolumne Rd Turlock (95382) ***(P-20348)***

Covenant Care California LLC ....C....408 842-9311
8170 Murray Ave Gilroy (95020) ***(P-20349)***

Covenant Care California LLC (HQ) ....E....949 349-1200
27071 Aliso Creek Rd # 100 Aliso Viejo (92656) ***(P-20350)***

Covenant Care California LLC ....E....760 745-1288
1025 W 2nd Ave Escondido (92025) ***(P-20351)***

Covenant Care California LLC ....C....209 521-2094
3620 Dale Rd Ste B Modesto (95356) ***(P-21050)***

Covenant Care California LLC ....C....714 554-9700
1929 N Fairview St Santa Ana (92706) ***(P-20352)***

Covenant Care California LLC ....D....650 964-0543
1949 Grant Rd Mountain View (94040) ***(P-21361)***

Covenant Care California LLC ....C....650 941-5255
809 Fremont Ave Los Altos (94024) ***(P-20353)***

Covenant Care Indiana Inc (HQ) ....D....949 349-1200
27071 Aliso Creek Rd # 100 Aliso Viejo (92656) ***(P-20354)***

Covenant Care La Jolla LLC ....C....858 453-5810
2552 Torrey Pines Rd # 1 La Jolla (92037) ***(P-20355)***

Covenant House California ....C....323 461-3131
1325 N Western Ave Los Angeles (90027) ***(P-24485)***

Covenant Industries Inc ....D....951 808-3708
110 Pine Ave Ste 910 Long Beach (90802) ***(P-14593)***

Covenant Players (PA) ....C....805 486-7155
1741 Fiske Pl Oxnard (93033) ***(P-18359)***

Covenant Rtirement Communities ....C....619 479-4790
325 Kempton St Spring Valley (91977) ***(P-21051)***

Covenant Rtirement Communities ....C....209 632-9976
2125 N Olive Ave Ofc Turlock (95382) ***(P-24486)***

Covenant Village of Turlock, Turlock *Also called Covenant Rtirement Communities* ***(P-24486)***

Coventry Court Health Center ....C....714 636-2800
2040 S Euclid St Anaheim (92802) ***(P-20356)***

Coventry Cove Apartments, Fresno *Also called Buckingham Property Management* ***(P-13722)***

Coverity LLC (HQ) ....D....415 321-5200
185 Berry St Ste 6500 San Francisco (94107) ***(P-15083)***

Covey Auto Express Inc (PA) ....C....253 826-0461
1444 El Pinal Dr Stockton (95205) ***(P-17859)***

Covey, The, Carmel *Also called Quail Lodge Inc* ***(P-13087)***

Covia Affordable Communities ....C....925 956-7400
2185 N Calif Blvd Ste 215 Walnut Creek (94596) ***(P-20357)***

Covia Communities ....C....510 835-4700
100 Bay Pl Ofc Oakland (94610) ***(P-24487)***

Covia Communities ....D....831 373-3111
651 Sinex Ave Pacific Grove (93950) ***(P-24488)***

Covia Communities ....B....707 538-8400
5555 Montgomery Dr Santa Rosa (95409) ***(P-24489)***

Covia Communities ....C....415 776-0500
1661 Pine St Apt 911 San Francisco (94109) ***(P-24490)***

Covina Bowl Inc ....D....626 339-1286
675 S Glendora Ave West Covina (91790) ***(P-18486)***

Covina Rehabilitation Center ....C....626 967-3874
261 W Badillo St Covina (91723) ***(P-20358)***

Covina Service Center, San Dimas *Also called Southern California Edison Co* ***(P-6137)***

Covington & Burling LLP ....C....650 632-4700
333 Twin Dolphin Dr # 700 Redwood City (94065) ***(P-23010)***

Covington & Burling LLP ....E....415 591-6000
1 Front St Fl 35 San Francisco (94111) ***(P-23011)***

Covington & Burling LLP ....B....424 332-4800
1999 Avenue Of The Stars # 3500 Los Angeles (90067) ***(P-23012)***

Cowboy Poetry, Santa Clarita *Also called Santa Clarita City of* ***(P-19234)***

Cowell Homeowners Association (PA) ....D....925 825-0250
4498 Lawson Ct Concord (94521) ***(P-25144)***

Cowell Student Health Center, Davis *Also called University California Davis* ***(P-20031)***

Cowell Student Health Service, Stanford *Also called Leland Stanford Junior Univ* ***(P-19648)***

Cowles California Media Co ....D....831 422-3500
1550 Moffett St Salinas (93905) ***(P-5780)***

Cox Castle & Nicholson LLP (PA) ....C....310 284-2200
2029 Cntury Nicholson Llp Los Angeles (90067) ***(P-23013)***

Cox Automotive Inc ....C....626 573-8001
8001 Garvey Ave Rosemead (91770) ***(P-6584)***

Cox Automotive Inc ....A....404 843-5000
10700 Beech Ave Fontana (92337) ***(P-6585)***

Cox Automotive Inc ....B....510 786-4500
29900 Auction Ct Hayward (94544) ***(P-6586)***

Cox Automotive Inc ....B....951 689-6000
6446 Fremont St Riverside (92504) ***(P-6587)***

Cox Automotive Inc ....B....760 754-3600
691 Calle Joven Oceanside (92057) ***(P-6588)***

Cox California Telcom LLC ....D....310 377-1800
43 Peninsula Ctr Rllng HLS Est (90274) ***(P-5539)***

Cox California Telcom LLC ....C....760 966-0447
1922 Avenida Del Oro Oceanside (92056) ***(P-5977)***

Cox Castle, Los Angeles *Also called Cox Castle & Nicholson LLP* ***(P-23013)***

Cox Communications Inc ....D....949 716-2020
140 Columbia Aliso Viejo (92656) ***(P-5890)***

Cox Communications Inc ....D....858 715-4500
1535 Euclid Ave San Diego (92105) ***(P-5891)***

Cox Communications Inc ....C....949 240-1212
26181 Avenida Aeropuerto San Juan Capistrano (92675) ***(P-5540)***

Cox Communications Inc ....D....805 681-6600
3303 State St Santa Barbara (93105) ***(P-5892)***

Cox Communications Inc ....D....949 546-1000
6771 Quail Hill Pkwy Irvine (92603) ***(P-5893)***

Cox Communications Cal LLC ....B....619 562-9820
1175 N Cuyamaca St El Cajon (92020) ***(P-5894)***

Cox Communications Cal LLC ....B....619 262-1122
5159 Federal Blvd San Diego (92105) ***(P-5895)***

Cox Communications Cal LLC ....B....619 263-9251
581 Telegraph Canyon Rd Chula Vista (91910) ***(P-5896)***

Cox Petroleum Transport, Bakersfield *Also called H F Cox Inc* ***(P-4189)***

Coyote Creek Consulting Inc ....D....408 383-9200
1551 Mccarthy Blvd # 115 Milpitas (95035) ***(P-16334)***

Coyote Creek Golf Club ....D....408 463-1400
1 Coyote Creek Golf Dr Morgan Hill (95037) ***(P-18701)***

Coyote Hills Golf Course, Fullerton *Also called American Golf Corporation* ***(P-18685)***

CP Development Co LLC ....D....415 995-1770
1 Sansome St Ste 3200 San Francisco (94104) ***(P-11868)***

CP Opco LLC ....D....707 253-2332
22674 Broadway A Sonoma (95476) ***(P-14491)***

CP Opco LLC ....D....858 496-9700
7069 Cnsld Way Ste 300 San Diego (92121) ***(P-14492)***

CP Opco LLC ....D....209 524-1966
333 S Grand Ave Ste 4070 Los Angeles (90071) ***(P-14493)***

CP Opco LLC (HQ) ....A....310 966-4900
901 W Hillcrest Blvd A Inglewood (90301) ***(P-13735)***

CP Opco LLC ....D....310 966-4900
11766 Wilshire Blvd # 380 Los Angeles (90025) ***(P-14494)***

CP Opco LLC ....D....650 652-0300
22674 Broadway A Sonoma (95476) ***(P-14495)***

CP Opco LLC ....D....805 566-3566
1120 Mark Ave Carpinteria (93013) ***(P-14496)***

CP Opco LLC ....D....714 540-6111
3101 S Harbor Blvd Santa Ana (92704) ***(P-14497)***

CP Technologies, Irvine *Also called Corner Products Company* ***(P-7463)***

CPC Services Inc ....D....626 852-6200
2025 E Fincl Way Ste 200 Glendora (91741) ***(P-6884)***

Cpcc Inc ....D....818 882-3200
10610 Owensmouth Ave Chatsworth (91311) ***(P-21052)***

Cpe Hr Inc ....D....310 270-9800
9000 W Sunset Blvd # 900 West Hollywood (90069) ***(P-27203)***

Cpe Peo Inc ....D....310 385-1000
9200 W Sunset Blvd West Hollywood (90069) ***(P-14843)***

Employee Codes: A=Over 500 employees, B=251-500
C=101-250, D=51-100, E=50
2019 Directory of California
Wholesalers and Services Companies
© Mergent Inc. 1-800-342-5647
1269

Cph Hospital Management LLC.....A.....562 838-3751
13100 Studebaker Rd Norwalk (90650) ***(P-22280)***
Cph Monarch Hotel LLC.....A.....949 234-3200
1 Monarch Beach Resort Dana Point (92629) ***(P-12497)***
CPI Econco Division (HQ).....D.....530 662-7553
1318 Commerce Ave Woodland (95776) ***(P-17902)***
CPI International.....D.....707 521-6327
5580 Skylane Blvd Santa Rosa (95403) ***(P-7240)***
CPI Luxury Group.....D.....818 249-9888
10220 Norris Ave Pacoima (91331) ***(P-8007)***
CPIC, Fremont *Also called Cancer Prevention Inst Cal* ***(P-26603)***
CPM Ltd Inc (PA).....A.....619 237-9900
1855 1st Ave Ste 300 San Diego (92101) ***(P-14844)***
CPM Services, San Francisco *Also called Cooper Pugeda Management Inc* ***(P-26819)***
Cpmc, San Francisco *Also called Sutter Health* ***(P-21804)***
Cpn Wild Horse Geothermal LLC.....B.....707 431-6229
10350 Socrates Mine Rd Middletown (95461) ***(P-6025)***
Cpo Commerce LLC.....D.....626 585-3600
120 W Bellevue Dr Ste 300 Pasadena (91105) ***(P-7585)***
CPS, Studio City *Also called Commercial Prgrm Systems Inc* ***(P-16329)***
CPS, Burlingame *Also called Kotobuki-Ya Inc* ***(P-3663)***
CPS Hr Consulting, Sacramento *Also called Cooperative Personnel Services* ***(P-27200)***
CPS Security, Long Beach *Also called Commercial Protective Svcs Inc* ***(P-16612)***
CPS Security Solutions Inc (PA).....D.....310 818-1030
3400 E Airport Way Long Beach (90806) ***(P-16619)***
Cpu Medical Management Systems, San Diego *Also called Computer Proc Unlimited Inc* ***(P-15070)***
Cr Drywall, San Jose *Also called C R S Drywall Inc* ***(P-2858)***
Craft Resources Inc.....C.....310 937-3744
220 S Pcifc Cst Hwy 112 Redondo Beach (90277) ***(P-14845)***
Craftman Concrete.....D.....559 298-8864
755 N Peach Ave Ste F11 Clovis (93611) ***(P-1150)***
Craftsman Lath and Plaster Inc.....B.....951 685-9922
8325 63rd St Riverside (92509) ***(P-3024)***
Craftworks Rest Breweries Inc.....E.....415 292-5800
600 Polk St San Francisco (94102) ***(P-17108)***
Craig Realty Group, Newport Beach *Also called Eureka Realty Partners Inc* ***(P-11874)***
Cramer Painting Inc.....E.....909 397-5770
4080 Mission Blvd Montclair (91763) ***(P-2429)***
Crane Acquisition Inc.....D.....415 922-1666
2700 Geary Blvd San Francisco (94118) ***(P-14149)***
Crane Co.....C.....562 426-2531
3201 Walnut Ave Long Beach (90755) ***(P-7844)***
Crane Pest Control, San Francisco *Also called Crane Acquisition Inc* ***(P-14149)***
Craniofacial Department, Loma Linda *Also called Loma Linda University Med Ctr* ***(P-21560)***
Crash Inc Short Term I.....E.....619 282-7274
4161 Marlborough Ave San Diego (92105) ***(P-22562)***
CRAYCROFT YOUTH CENTER, Fresno *Also called Rescue Children Inc* ***(P-23991)***
Crazy Gideons, Los Angeles *Also called F O C Electronics Corporation* ***(P-7415)***
CRC Health Corporate.....D.....714 542-3581
2101 E 1st St Santa Ana (92705) ***(P-22563)***
CRC Health Corporate (HQ).....D.....408 367-0044
20400 Stevens Cupertino (95014) ***(P-22564)***
CRC Health Corporation (HQ).....D.....877 272-8668
20400 Stevens Creek Blvd # 600 Cupertino (95014) ***(P-22014)***
CRC Health Group Inc (HQ).....D.....877 272-8668
20400 Stev Creek Blvd 6 Flr 6 Cupertino (95014) ***(P-22781)***
Crdn of Southern La County, Long Beach *Also called Foasberg Laundry & Clrs Inc* ***(P-13530)***
Cre, Burbank *Also called Commodity Resource Envmtl Inc* ***(P-7975)***
Create Music Group Inc.....D.....310 623-0696
1320 N Wilton Pl Los Angeles (90028) ***(P-17109)***
Creating Arts Company.....E.....310 804-0223
4380 Hillview Dr Malibu (90265) ***(P-18360)***
Creative Alternatives.....C.....209 668-9361
2855 Geer Rd Ste A Turlock (95382) ***(P-24491)***
Creative Artists Agency LLC (PA).....A.....424 288-2000
2000 Avenue Of The Stars # 100 Los Angeles (90067) ***(P-18361)***
Creative Channel Services LLC (HQ).....D.....310 482-6500
12777 W Jefferson Blvd # 120 Los Angeles (90066) ***(P-13805)***
Creative Child Care Inc (PA).....B.....209 941-9100
4719 Quail Lakes Dr G-237 Stockton (95207) ***(P-24312)***
Creative Circle LLC (HQ).....D.....323 930-2333
5900 Wilshire Blvd # 1100 Los Angeles (90036) ***(P-14594)***
Creative Design Cons Inc (PA).....D.....714 641-4868
2915 Red Hill Ave G201 Costa Mesa (92626) ***(P-17110)***
Creative Design Interiors Inc (PA).....D.....916 641-1121
737 Del Paso Rd Sacramento (95834) ***(P-3098)***
Creative Energy Foods Inc.....D.....510 638-8668
9957 Medford Ave Ste 4 Oakland (94603) ***(P-8781)***
Creative Events Enterprises.....C.....818 610-7000
4872 Topanga Canyon Blvd # 406 Woodland Hills (91364) ***(P-27204)***
Creative Group, The, Menlo Park *Also called Robert Half International Inc* ***(P-14739)***
Creative Housing & Services.....C.....626 403-5454
605 E Huntington Dr # 207 Monrovia (91016) ***(P-11005)***
Creative Labs Inc (HQ).....C.....408 428-6600
1901 Mccarthy Blvd Milpitas (95035) ***(P-7026)***
Creative Living Options Inc.....C.....916 372-2102
2945 Ramco St Ste 120 West Sacramento (95691) ***(P-24492)***
Creative Maintenance Systems.....D.....949 852-2871
1340 Reynolds Ave Ste 111 Irvine (92614) ***(P-14235)***
Creative Nail Design Inc.....C.....760 599-2900
9560 Towne Centre Dr # 200 San Diego (92121) ***(P-13651)***
Creative Recreation, Los Angeles *Also called Kommonwealth Inc* ***(P-8360)***
Creative Security Company Inc.....B.....408 295-2600
150 S Autumn St Ste B San Jose (95110) ***(P-16620)***
Creative Technology Group Inc (HQ).....D.....818 779-2400
14000 Arminta St Panorama City (91402) ***(P-17111)***

Creativebug LLC.....C.....415 325-5926
835 Market St Ste 700 San Francisco (94103) ***(P-15084)***
Credit Bureau NAPA County Inc.....C.....707 940-3000
1247 Broadway Sonoma (95476) ***(P-14001)***
Credit Card Services Inc (PA).....D.....213 365-1122
21281 S Western Ave Torrance (90501) ***(P-17112)***
Credit Counselor of California, San Francisco *Also called Consumer Credit Counseling Svc* ***(P-13732)***
Credit Karma Inc (PA).....C.....415 510-5059
760 Market St Ste 500 San Francisco (94102) ***(P-17113)***
Credit Solutions Corp.....C.....858 650-0812
13520 Evening Creek Dr N # 500 San Diego (92128) ***(P-9709)***
Credit Ssse Securities USA LLC.....D.....213 253-2600
10880 Wilshire Blvd Los Angeles (90024) ***(P-9945)***
Credit Suisse (usa) Inc.....D.....415 249-2100
650 California St Fl 31 San Francisco (94108) ***(P-9946)***
Credit Suisse (usa) Inc.....E.....415 678-3940
650 California St Fl 28 San Francisco (94108) ***(P-9947)***
Credit Union Southern Cal (PA).....E.....562 698-8326
8028 Greenleaf Ave Whittier (90602) ***(P-9548)***
CREDIT.ORG, Riverside *Also called Springboard Solutions LLC* ***(P-27870)***
Credo Mobile Inc.....D.....415 369-2000
101 Market St Ste 700 San Francisco (94105) ***(P-5541)***
Creedence Lessee LLC.....D.....415 561-1100
425 N Point St San Francisco (94133) ***(P-12498)***
Creekside Cnvalescent Hosp Inc.....C.....707 544-7750
850 Sonoma Ave Santa Rosa (95404) ***(P-20359)***
Creekside Comet Education Fund.....D.....925 314-2000
6011 Massara St Danville (94506) ***(P-12077)***
Creekside Healthcare Ctr.....E.....510 235-5514
1900 Church Ln San Pablo (94806) ***(P-20360)***
Creekside Rehab and Behavioral.....C.....707 524-7030
850 Sonoma Ave Santa Rosa (95404) ***(P-20361)***
Crenshaw Bowling.....E.....310 326-5120
24600 Crenshaw Blvd Torrance (90505) ***(P-18487)***
Crenshaw Nursing, Los Angeles *Also called Longwood Management Corp* ***(P-20601)***
Crenshaw YMCA.....D.....323 290-9113
3820 Santa Rosalia Dr Los Angeles (90008) ***(P-25145)***
Crescent Court Nursing Home.....E.....209 367-7400
1334 S Ham Ln Lodi (95242) ***(P-21053)***
Crescent Cy Convalescent Hosp, Crescent City *Also called North Shore Investment Inc* ***(P-20663)***
Crescent Healthcare Inc (HQ).....C.....714 520-6300
11980 Telg Rd Ste 100 Santa Fe Springs (90670) ***(P-22281)***
Crescent Solutions, Irvine *Also called Crescent Staffing Inc* ***(P-15085)***
Crescent Staffing Inc (PA).....C.....949 724-0304
17871 Mitchell N Ste 100 Irvine (92614) ***(P-15085)***
Crescenta-Canada YMCA (PA).....B.....818 790-0123
1930 Foothill Blvd La Canada (91011) ***(P-25146)***
Crescenta-Canada YMCA.....E.....818 352-3255
6840 Foothill Blvd Tujunga (91042) ***(P-25147)***
Cresse Mark School of Baseball.....D.....714 892-6145
58 Fulmar Ln Aliso Viejo (92656) ***(P-19155)***
Crest Beverage, San Diego *Also called Reyes Holdings LLC* ***(P-10011)***
Crest Beverage Company Inc.....C.....858 452-2300
3840 Via De La Valle Del Mar (92014) ***(P-8988)***
Crest Digital, Laguna Beach *Also called National Film Laboratories* ***(P-18204)***
Crest Financial Corporation (HQ).....D.....562 733-6500
12641 166th St Cerritos (90703) ***(P-10596)***
Crest R E O & Relocation, La Crescenta *Also called EAM Enterprises Inc* ***(P-11414)***
Crest Steel Corporation.....D.....310 830-2651
6580 General Rd Riverside (92509) ***(P-7267)***
Cresta Loma, Alameda *Also called Telecare Corporation* ***(P-21988)***
Crestline Funding Corporation.....E.....949 863-8600
18851 Pardeen Ave San Diego (92108) ***(P-9797)***
Crestline Hotels & Resorts Inc.....C.....213 629-1200
120 S Los Angeles St 11 Los Angeles (90012) ***(P-12499)***
Crestline Hotels & Resorts LLC.....D.....213 624-0000
535 S Grand Ave Los Angeles (90071) ***(P-26834)***
Crestline Hotels & Resorts LLC.....C.....415 775-7555
1250 Columbus Ave San Francisco (94133) ***(P-26835)***
Crestline Hotels & Resorts LLC.....C.....760 322-6000
888 E Tahquitz Canyon Way Palm Springs (92262) ***(P-12500)***
Crestmont Capital LLC.....C.....800 949-0401
2030 Main St Irvine (92614) ***(P-12218)***
Creston Village, Paso Robles *Also called Emeritus Corporation* ***(P-11013)***
Crestview Cnvalescent Hosp Inc.....C.....909 877-1361
1471 S Riverside Ave Rialto (92376) ***(P-20362)***
CRESTWOOD BEHAVIORAL HEALTH, Stockton *Also called Dreamctchers Empwerment Netwrk* ***(P-24508)***
Crestwood Behavioral Hlth Inc.....C.....209 526-8050
1400 Celeste Dr Modesto (95355) ***(P-21945)***
Crestwood Behavioral Hlth Inc.....D.....408 275-1067
1425 Fruitdale Ave San Jose (95128) ***(P-24493)***
Crestwood Behavioral Hlth Inc.....D.....530 221-0976
3062 Churn Creek Rd Redding (96002) ***(P-24494)***
Crestwood Behavioral Hlth Inc.....C.....510 651-1244
4303 Stevenson Blvd Fremont (94538) ***(P-24495)***
Crestwood Behavioral Hlth Inc.....C.....916 452-1431
2600 Stockton Blvd Sacramento (95817) ***(P-21946)***
Crestwood Behavioral Hlth Inc.....C.....707 552-0215
115 Oddstad Dr Vallejo (94589) ***(P-24496)***
Crestwood Behavioral Hlth Inc.....D.....510 793-8383
2171 Mowry Ave Fremont (94538) ***(P-24497)***
Crestwood Behavioral Hlth Inc.....D.....661 363-8127
6700 Eucalyptus Dr Ste A Bakersfield (93306) ***(P-23762)***
Crestwood Behavioral Hlth Inc.....D.....559 445-9094
153 N U St Fresno (93701) ***(P-21947)***

Crestwood Behavioral Hlth Inc..........D.......707 558-1777
2201 Tuolumne St Vallejo (94589) ***(P-21948)***
Crestwood Behavioral Hlth Inc..........D.......707 552-0215
115 Oddstad Dr Vallejo (94589) ***(P-21949)***
Crestwood Behavioral Hlth Inc..........C.......661 363-6711
6744 Eucalyptus Dr Bakersfield (93306) ***(P-22015)***
Crestwood Behavioral Hlth Inc..........D.......916 977-0949
4741 Engle Rd Carmichael (95608) ***(P-21950)***
Crestwood Behavioral Hlth Inc..........D.......925 938-8050
550 Patterson Blvd Pleasant Hill (94523) ***(P-21951)***
Crew Creative Advertising LLC..........C.......310 451-3225
7966 Beverly Blvd Los Angeles (90048) ***(P-13806)***
Crew Inc..........D.......310 608-6860
19618 S Susana Rd Compton (90221) ***(P-3421)***
Crh Management, Newport Beach *Also called Core Realty Holdings MGT Inc* ***(P-11380)***
CRI HELP DRUG REHABILITATION, North Hollywood *Also called Cri-Help Inc* ***(P-24498)***
Cri-Help Inc (PA)..........C.......818 985-8323
11027 Burbank Blvd North Hollywood (91601) ***(P-24498)***
Cricket Communications LLC (HQ)..........D.......858 882-6000
7337 Trade St San Diego (92121) ***(P-5402)***
Cricket Indiana Property Co..........D.......858 587-2648
10307 Pacific Center Ct San Diego (92121) ***(P-5403)***
Cricket Stx, San Diego *Also called Stx Wireless Operations LLC* ***(P-5417)***
Cricket Wireless, San Diego *Also called Cricket Communications LLC* ***(P-5402)***
Crime Impact Security & Patrol, Los Angeles *Also called Crime Impact Security Patrol* ***(P-16621)***
Crime Impact Security Patrol..........D.......323 296-6406
3860 Crenshaw Blvd # 223 Los Angeles (90008) ***(P-16621)***
Crimetek Security..........B.......209 668-6208
3448 N Golden State Blvd Turlock (95382) ***(P-16622)***
Cripts Health Care..........E.......858 554-8646
10666 N Torrey Pines Rd La Jolla (92037) ***(P-19423)***
Crisp California Walnuts, Stratford *Also called Crisp Warehouse Inc* ***(P-505)***
Crisp Enterprises Inc (PA)..........D.......714 668-5955
3180 Pullman St Costa Mesa (92626) ***(P-14083)***
Crisp Warehouse Inc..........D.......559 947-9221
20500 Main St Stratford (93266) ***(P-505)***
Cristophe Salon, Beverly Hills *Also called Hair Fashion Inc* ***(P-13661)***
Critchfeld Mech Inc Sthern Cal..........D.......949 390-2900
1821 Mcgaw Ave Irvine (92614) ***(P-2176)***
Critchfield Mechanical Inc..........B.......650 321-7801
4085 Campbell Ave Menlo Park (94025) ***(P-2177)***
CRITTENTON SERVICES FOR CHILDR, Fullerton *Also called Florence Crittenton Services* ***(P-24530)***
Crmc, Coalinga *Also called Coalinga Regional Medical Cent* ***(P-21329)***
Crocker Art Museum, Sacramento *Also called Crocker Art Museum Association* ***(P-25414)***
Crocker Art Museum Association..........D.......916 808-7000
216 O St Sacramento (95814) ***(P-25414)***
Crocker Group LLC..........D.......714 221-5621
1101 E Orangewood Ave Anaheim (92805) ***(P-11388)***
Crockett & Coinc..........D.......619 267-1103
5540 Sweetwater Rd Bonita (91902) ***(P-18702)***
Crockett Garbage Service, Richmond *Also called Richmond Sanitary Service Inc* ***(P-6547)***
Crocodile Bay Lodge..........C.......707 559-7990
731 Southpoint Blvd Petaluma (94954) ***(P-13439)***
Crocus Holdings LLC..........D.......916 782-1238
1161 Cirby Way Roseville (95661) ***(P-20363)***
Crooks, Jerry C MD, Stockton *Also called Stockton Orthpd Med Group Inc* ***(P-19952)***
Crosby National Golf Club LLC..........D.......858 756-6310
17102 Bing Crosby Blvd Rancho Santa Fe (92067) ***(P-18905)***
Cross Country Healthcare Inc..........B.......951 786-7683
1700 Iowa Ave Ste 210 Riverside (92507) ***(P-14595)***
Cross Link Inc..........D.......415 495-3191
Bldg C Pier 50 San Francisco (94158) ***(P-4745)***
Cross Rock, Paso Robles *Also called Pearce Services LLC* ***(P-1968)***
Crosscap Media Services Inc (PA)..........D.......415 217-8860
311 California St Ste 320 San Francisco (94104) ***(P-15086)***
Crosscheck Inc (PA)..........C.......707 665-2100
1440 N Mcdowell Blvd Petaluma (94954) ***(P-17114)***
Crosslink Prof Tax Sltions LLC (PA)..........D.......209 835-1360
7575 W Linne Rd Tracy (95304) ***(P-15087)***
Crossmark Inc..........D.......714 464-6318
2401 E Katella Ave # 625 Anaheim (92806) ***(P-8397)***
Crossmark Inc..........B.......925 463-3555
3875 Hopyard Rd Ste 250 Pleasanton (94588) ***(P-8398)***
Crossmark Sales & Marketing, Pleasanton *Also called Crossmark Inc* ***(P-8398)***
Crossroad Services Inc..........B.......510 895-5055
2360 Alvarado St San Leandro (94577) ***(P-17115)***
CROSSROADS COMMUNITY FOUNDATIO, Los Angeles *Also called PS Arts* ***(P-27829)***
Crossroads Diversfd Svcs Inc..........D.......916 676-2540
7011 Sylvan Rd Ste A Citrus Heights (95610) ***(P-14596)***
Crossroads Facility Svcs Inc..........D.......916 568-5230
9300 Tech Center Dr # 100 Sacramento (95826) ***(P-14236)***
Crossroads Medical Offices, City of Industry *Also called Kaiser Foundation Hospitals* ***(P-19550)***
Crowd Management, Fresno *Also called Contemporary Services Corp* ***(P-16616)***
Crowdstrike Inc (HQ)..........C.......888 512-8906
150 Mathilda Pl Ste 300 Sunnyvale (94086) ***(P-16335)***
Crowdstrike Holdings Inc (PA)..........C.......888 512-8906
15440 Laguna Canyon Rd Irvine (92618) ***(P-16336)***
Crowe LLP..........C.......818 501-5200
15233 Ventura Blvd Fl 9 Sherman Oaks (91403) ***(P-26176)***
Crowell & Moring LLP..........D.......415 986-2800
275 Battery St Ste 2200 San Francisco (94111) ***(P-23014)***
Crowell & Moring LLP..........E.......949 263-8400
3 Park Plz Ste 2000 Irvine (92614) ***(P-23015)***
Crowell, Weedon & Co., Los Angeles *Also called DA Davidson & Co* ***(P-9948)***
Crown Building Maintenance Co..........A.......916 920-9556
1832 Tribute Rd Ste H Sacramento (95815) ***(P-14237)***
Crown Building Maintenance Co..........E.......714 434-9494
3300 W Macarthur Blvd Santa Ana (92704) ***(P-14238)***
Crown Building Maintenance Co..........B.......303 680-3713
235 Pine St Ste 600 San Francisco (94104) ***(P-14239)***
Crown Building Maintenance Co..........C.......858 560-5785
5482 Complex St Ste 108 San Diego (92123) ***(P-14240)***
Crown Building Maintenance Co..........E.......213 765-7800
2601 S Figueroa St # 299 Los Angeles (90007) ***(P-14241)***
Crown Cove Senior Care Cmnty..........D.......949 760-2800
3901 E Coast Hwy Ofc Corona Del Mar (92625) ***(P-24499)***
Crown Disposal Company Inc..........C.......818 767-0675
9189 De Garmo Ave Sun Valley (91352) ***(P-6387)***
Crown Energy Services Inc..........A.......415 546-6534
611 Gateway Blvd South San Francisco (94080) ***(P-25631)***
Crown Energy Services Inc..........A.......213 765-7800
2601 S Figueroa St Fl 1 Los Angeles (90007) ***(P-14242)***
Crown Facility Solutions..........E.......657 266-0821
3617 W Macarthur Blvd Santa Ana (92704) ***(P-14243)***
Crown Fence Co..........D.......562 864-5177
12118 Bloomfield Ave Santa Fe Springs (90670) ***(P-3508)***
Crown Golf Properties LP..........C.......714 730-1611
12442 Tustin Ranch Rd Tustin (92782) ***(P-27205)***
Crown Golf Properties LP..........D.......909 481-6663
791 Camarillo Springs Rd Camarillo (93012) ***(P-27206)***
Crown Hardware Inc..........C.......760 334-0300
745 S Coast Highway 101 # 104 Encinitas (92024) ***(P-7586)***
Crown Limousine L.A., Los Angeles *Also called Crown Transportation Inc* ***(P-3787)***
Crown Media United States LLC (HQ)..........D.......818 755-2400
12700 Ventura Blvd # 100 Studio City (91604) ***(P-5897)***
Crown Plaza, Pleasanton *Also called Six Continents Hotels Inc* ***(P-13238)***
Crown Plaza, Milpitas *Also called B H R Operations LLC* ***(P-12347)***
Crown Plaza La Harbor Hotel, San Pedro *Also called Spf Capital Real Estate LLC* ***(P-13254)***
Crown Plaza Los Angeles, Los Angeles *Also called Ihg Management (maryland) LLC* ***(P-12760)***
Crown Plaza SD..........D.......619 297-1101
2270 Hotel Cir N San Diego (92108) ***(P-12501)***
Crown Pointe Retirement, Corona *Also called Provident Group Crown Pnte LLC* ***(P-11100)***
Crown Transportation Inc..........D.......310 737-0888
12300 W Washington Blvd Los Angeles (90066) ***(P-3787)***
Crown Vly Precision Machining, Irwindale *Also called Sinecera Inc* ***(P-17471)***
Crowne Plaza, Irvine *Also called Intercontinental Hotels Group* ***(P-12766)***
Crowne Plaza, Los Angeles *Also called Hpt Trs Ihg-2 Inc* ***(P-12736)***
Crowne Plaza, Redondo Beach *Also called Hpt Trs Ihg-2 Inc* ***(P-12737)***
Crowne Plaza, Fullerton *Also called Huoyen International Inc* ***(P-12743)***
Crowne Plaza Concord, Concord *Also called Concord Hotel LLC* ***(P-12482)***
Crowne Plaza Costa Mesa, Costa Mesa *Also called Bright Bristol Street LLC* ***(P-12400)***
Crowne Plaza Hotel, Foster City *Also called Founders Management II Corp* ***(P-12583)***
Crowne Plaza Irvine-Orange Cou, Irvine *Also called Intercontinental Hotels Group* ***(P-12773)***
Crowne Plaza Lax LLC..........C.......310 258-1321
5985 W Century Blvd Los Angeles (90045) ***(P-12502)***
Crowne Plaza Ventura Beach, Ventura *Also called Ventura Hsptality Partners LLC* ***(P-13366)***
Crowne Plz Los Angeles Hbr Ht, San Pedro *Also called Proficient LLC* ***(P-13081)***
Crowne Plz Los Angeles Hbr Ht, Long Beach *Also called Nhca Inc* ***(P-12956)***
Crowne Plz Scramento Northeast, Sacramento *Also called Khanna Entps - II Ltd Partnr* ***(P-12805)***
Crowner Sheet Metal Pdts Inc..........E.......626 960-4971
14346 Arrow Hwy Baldwin Park (91706) ***(P-3143)***
Crp Centinela LP..........C.......901 821-4117
6161 W Centinela Ave Culver City (90230) ***(P-12503)***
CRS, Hayward *Also called Commercial Rfrgn Spcalists LLC* ***(P-2167)***
CRST International Inc..........C.......909 829-1313
10641 Calabash Ave Fontana (92337) ***(P-4119)***
Crstb Partners LLC..........C.......916 645-7200
3075 Twelve Bridges Dr Lincoln (95648) ***(P-18703)***
Crucible..........D.......510 444-0919
1260 7th St Oakland (94607) ***(P-23763)***
Cruisers Carwash & Diner, Northridge *Also called M K H Inc* ***(P-17831)***
Crum & Forster, Los Angeles *Also called United States Fire Insur Co* ***(P-10811)***
Crunch LLC..........D.......323 654-4550
8000 W Sunset Blvd # 220 West Hollywood (90046) ***(P-18589)***
Crunch LLC..........C.......415 495-1939
345 Spear St Ste 104 San Francisco (94105) ***(P-18590)***
Crunch Fitness, West Hollywood *Also called Crunch LLC* ***(P-18589)***
Crunch Fitness..........D.......805 522-5454
19867 Prairie St Ste 200 Chatsworth (91311) ***(P-18591)***
Crunchyroll, San Francisco *Also called Ellation Inc* ***(P-15133)***
Cruz Hoffstetter LLC..........D.......626 915-5621
519 W Badillo St Covina (91722) ***(P-17116)***
Cruz Modular Inc (PA)..........D.......714 283-2890
249 W Baywood Ave Ste B Orange (92865) ***(P-4340)***
Cruz Veterinary Hospital..........D.......831 475-5400
2585 Soquel Dr Santa Cruz (95065) ***(P-601)***
Crystal Aire Country Club Golf..........E.......661 944-2112
15701 Boca Raton Ave Llano (93544) ***(P-18906)***
Crystal Art of Florida, Vernon *Also called Rggd Inc* ***(P-8053)***
Crystal Casino & Hotel, Compton *Also called Celebrity Casinos Inc* ***(P-12445)***
Crystal Chrysler Plymuth Dodge..........D.......760 324-9375
36444 Auto Park Dr Cathedral City (92234) ***(P-17758)***
Crystal Creamery, Modesto *Also called Foster Dairy Farms* ***(P-412)***
Crystal Cruises LLC (HQ)..........C.......310 785-9300
11755 Wilshire Blvd # 900 Los Angeles (90025) ***(P-4707)***
Crystal Dynamics Inc..........D.......650 421-7600
1400a Saport Blvd Ste 300 Redwood City (94063) ***(P-15640)***

ALPHABETIC

Employee Codes: A=Over 500 employees, B=251-500
C=101-250, D=51-100, E=50
2019 Directory of California
Wholesalers and Services Companies
© Mergent Inc. 1-800-342-5647
1271

Crystal Organic Farms LLC ....B.......661 845-5200
6900 Mountain View Rd Bakersfield (93307) ***(P-332)***

Crystal Springs Golf Course, Burlingame *Also called Crystal Springs Golf Partners* ***(P-18907)***

Crystal Springs Golf Partners ....E.......650 342-4188
6650 Golf Course Dr Burlingame (94010) ***(P-18907)***

Crystal Stairs Inc (PA) ....B.......323 299-8998
5110 W Goldleaf Cir # 150 Los Angeles (90056) ***(P-23764)***

Crystal Valet Parking Inc ....D.......323 663-7275
4477 Hollywood Blvd 209 Los Angeles (90027) ***(P-13736)***

Crystalaire Country Club, Llano *Also called Crystal Aire Country Club Golf* ***(P-18906)***

Cs Concrete Solutions Inc ....D.......949 285-3122
47 Goldbriar Way Mission Viejo (92692) ***(P-3243)***

Csaa Insur Group Walnut Creek, Irvine *Also called Western United Insurance Co* ***(P-10829)***

Csaa Insurance AAA, Santa Rosa *Also called American Automobile Assctn* ***(P-10334)***

Csaa Insurance Exchange (PA) ....C.......800 922-8228
3055 Oak Rd Walnut Creek (94597) ***(P-10597)***

Csaa Travel Agency, Walnut Creek *Also called American Automobile Assctn* ***(P-25380)***

Csaa Travel Agency, Walnut Creek *Also called American Automobile Associatio* ***(P-10335)***

Csaa Travel Agency, Stockton *Also called American Automobile Assctn* ***(P-25381)***

Csaa Travel Agency, Walnut Creek *Also called American Automobile* ***(P-10517)***

Csac Excess Insurance Auth ....D.......916 850-7300
75 Iron Point Cir Ste 200 Folsom (95630) ***(P-10598)***

Csba, West Sacramento *Also called California School Boards Assn* ***(P-24951)***

CSC Auto Salv Dismantling Inc ....D.......818 532-4624
12207 Branford St Sun Valley (91352) ***(P-5038)***

CSC Consulting Inc ....D.......310 563-2062
2100 E Grand Ave B360 El Segundo (90245) ***(P-16337)***

CSC Covansys Corporation ....C.......510 304-3430
34740 Tuxedo Cmn Fremont (94555) ***(P-15088)***

CSC Serviceworks Holdings Inc ....C.......510 429-0900
32910 Alvarado Niles Rd # 150 Union City (94587) ***(P-13559)***

CSCU, Lompoc *Also called Coasthills Credit Union* ***(P-9628)***

Csdvrs LLC (PA) ....C.......727 443-1218
595 Menlo Dr Rocklin (95765) ***(P-17117)***

Cse Holdings Inc (HQ) ....D.......408 436-1907
650 Brennan St San Jose (95131) ***(P-7885)***

CSEA, Sacramento *Also called Califrnia State Employees Assn* ***(P-25058)***

Csea, San Jose *Also called California Schl Employees Assn* ***(P-25057)***

Csfe, Port Hueneme *Also called Cecos* ***(P-25602)***

Csg Consultants Inc (PA) ....E.......650 522-2500
550 Pilgrim Dr Foster City (94404) ***(P-25632)***

Csi, Fullerton *Also called Cardservice International Inc* ***(P-17057)***

Csi Cold Storage 4150, Anaheim *Also called US Foods Inc* ***(P-8896)***

Csi Electrical Contractors Inc ....D.......661 723-0869
41769 11th St W Ste B Palmdale (93551) ***(P-2554)***

Csi Electrical Contractors Inc (PA) ....C.......562 946-0700
10623 Fulton Wells Ave Santa Fe Springs (90670) ***(P-2555)***

Csi Financial Services LLC ....E.......858 200-9200
3636 Nobel Dr Ste 250 San Diego (92122) ***(P-26836)***

Csl Solutions, Fair Oaks *Also called Wightman Enterprises Inc* ***(P-14945)***

CSRA LLC ....A.......619 225-2600
4045 Hancock St San Diego (92110) ***(P-16267)***

CSRA LLC ....D.......951 898-3015
2727 Hamner Ave Norco (92860) ***(P-15089)***

CSRA LLC ....C.......703 876-1026
1520 Rr Ave Marie Is Marie Island Vallejo (94592) ***(P-16268)***

CSRA Systems & Solutions LLC ....E.......951 735-3300
2727 Hamner Ave Norco (92860) ***(P-16338)***

CSS Holdings Inc ....D.......888 884-9224
7486 La Jolla Blvd La Jolla (92037) ***(P-15090)***

Csu Holding Company ....E.......707 746-0353
531 Stone Rd Benicia (94510) ***(P-11972)***

Csub Nursing Class of 2006 ....D.......408 219-5914
9001 Stockdale Hwy Bakersfield (93311) ***(P-17118)***

Csus Children's Center, Sacramento *Also called Students of Associated* ***(P-24389)***

CSX Corporation ....C.......626 336-1377
14863 Clark Ave Hacienda Heights (91745) ***(P-3619)***

CT Lien Solution ....C.......818 662-4100
330 N Brand Blvd Ste 700 Glendale (91203) ***(P-27207)***

Ctc Food International Inc (PA) ....E.......650 873-7600
50 W Ohio Ave Richmond (94804) ***(P-8782)***

Ctc Group Inc (HQ) ....C.......310 540-0500
21333 Hawthorne Blvd Torrance (90503) ***(P-12504)***

Ctdn - Redding, Redding *Also called Donor Network West* ***(P-22792)***

Ctek Solutions Inc ....C.......949 614-0700
27271 Las Ramblas Ste 200 Mission Viejo (92691) ***(P-14084)***

Ctg, San Jose *Also called Computer Task Group Inc* ***(P-15073)***

Ctm, Gardena *Also called Classic Tile & Mosaic Inc* ***(P-6881)***

Ctour Holiday LLC ....B.......323 261-8811
222 E Huntington Dr # 105 Monrovia (91016) ***(P-19156)***

CTS Advantage Logistics, San Jose *Also called Advantage Logistics Inc* ***(P-4995)***

CTSI, Lancaster *Also called California Traffic Safety Inst* ***(P-27673)***

CU Cooperative Systems Inc (PA) ....B.......909 948-2500
9692 Haven Ave Rancho Cucamonga (91730) ***(P-9678)***

CU Direct Corporation (PA) ....C.......909 481-2300
2855 E Guasti Rd Ste 500 Ontario (91761) ***(P-15091)***

Cubic Corporation ....A.......858 277-6780
9233 Balboa Ave San Diego (92123) ***(P-15938)***

Cubic Defense Systems, San Diego *Also called Cubic Corporation* ***(P-15938)***

Cubic Global Defense Inc ....D.......858 277-8760
2280 Historic Decatur Rd # 200 San Diego (92106) ***(P-25633)***

Cubix Construction Company (PA) ....C.......925 314-0770
5 Meadowbrook Ln Danville (94526) ***(P-1389)***

Cucamonga Valley Water Dst ....D.......909 987-2591
10440 Ashford St Rancho Cucamonga (91730) ***(P-6237)***

Cudahy Medical Offices, Cudahy *Also called Kaiser Foundation Hospitals* ***(P-21500)***

Cudc, Ontario *Also called CU Direct Corporation* ***(P-15091)***

Cuisine Partners USA, Los Angeles *Also called Investors Capital MGT Group* ***(P-26902)***

Culberson Drywall, Campbell *Also called Charles Culberson Inc* ***(P-2865)***

Culinary Hispanic Foods Inc ....A.......619 955-6101
805 Bow St Chula Vista (91914) ***(P-8783)***

Culinary Services America Inc ....E.......323 965-7582
6363 Wilshire Blvd # 305 Los Angeles (90048) ***(P-14846)***

Culinary Staffing Service, Los Angeles *Also called Culinary Services America Inc* ***(P-14846)***

Culture, San Diego *Also called Carrier Johnson* ***(P-26031)***

Culver City Roofing Company ....D.......323 930-1311
5741 W Adams Blvd Los Angeles (90016) ***(P-3144)***

Culver West Health Center LLC ....D.......310 390-9506
4035 Grand View Blvd Los Angeles (90066) ***(P-21054)***

Culver-Melin Enterprises ....D.......209 726-9182
2150 Wardrobe Ave Merced (95341) ***(P-14244)***

Cummings Transportation, Shafter *Also called Cummings Vacuum Service Inc* ***(P-1055)***

Cummings Vacuum Service Inc ....D.......661 746-1786
19605 Broken Ct Shafter (93263) ***(P-1055)***

Cummings-Violich Inc ....D.......530 894-5494
1750 Dayton Rd Chico (95928) ***(P-684)***

Cummings-Vlich Inc-Orchard MGT, Chico *Also called Cummings-Violich Inc* ***(P-684)***

Cummins Pacific LLC ....B.......510 351-6101
14775 Wicks Blvd San Leandro (94577) ***(P-7744)***

Cumulus Intrmdate Holdings Inc ....D.......310 840-4900
3321 S La Cienega Blvd Los Angeles (90016) ***(P-5707)***

Cumulus Intrmdate Holdings Inc ....C.......209 766-5103
3136 Boeing Way 125 Stockton (95206) ***(P-5708)***

Cumulus Media, San Francisco *Also called CM Wind Down Topco Inc* ***(P-5706)***

Cumulus Networks Inc (PA) ....C.......650 383-6700
185 E Dana St Mountain View (94041) ***(P-15641)***

Cuneo Black Ward Missler A Law ....E.......916 363-8822
700 University Ave # 110 Sacramento (95825) ***(P-23016)***

Cuneo, Black, Ward & Missler, Sacramento *Also called Cuneo Black Ward Missler A Law* ***(P-23016)***

Cunha Draying Inc ....D.......209 858-1400
1500 Madruga Rd Lathrop (95330) ***(P-4120)***

Cuningham Group Arch Inc ....E.......310 895-2200
8665 Hayden Pl Culver City (90232) ***(P-26039)***

Cuningham Group, The, Culver City *Also called Cuningham Group Arch Inc* ***(P-26039)***

Cunningham Group Inc ....D.......303 295-1982
5616 Circle View Dr Bonsall (92003) ***(P-27208)***

Cupertino Electric Inc ....A.......408 808-8260
350 Lenore Way Felton (95018) ***(P-2556)***

Cupertino Electric Inc (PA) ....B.......408 808-8000
1132 N 7th St San Jose (95112) ***(P-2557)***

Cupertino Electric Inc ....D.......415 970-3400
1740 Cesar Chavez Fl 2 San Francisco (94124) ***(P-2558)***

Cupertino Healthcare ....D.......408 253-9034
22590 Voss Ave Cupertino (95014) ***(P-20364)***

Cupertino Hlthcare Wllness Ctr, Cupertino *Also called Cupertino Healthcare* ***(P-20364)***

Cupertino Inn, Cupertino *Also called Forge-Vidovich Motel Limited* ***(P-12581)***

Cupertino Lessee LLC ....C.......908 253-8900
10050 S De Anza Blvd Cupertino (95014) ***(P-12505)***

Curatel LLC ....B.......213 427-7411
1605 W Olympic Blvd # 600 Los Angeles (90015) ***(P-5542)***

Curran's Disposal, San Bernardino *Also called Empire Disposal LLC* ***(P-6398)***

Current Tv LLC ....C.......415 995-8328
118 King St San Francisco (94107) ***(P-17119)***

Curtco Publishing LLC (PA) ....D.......310 589-7700
29160 Heathercliff Rd # 1 Malibu (90265) ***(P-13940)***

Curti Family Inc ....D.......559 688-8323
3235 Avenue 199 Tulare (93274) ***(P-410)***

Curtis Legal Group A Professi ....E.......209 521-1800
1300 K St Fl 2 Modesto (95354) ***(P-23017)***

Curtiss-Wright Controls (HQ) ....D.......626 851-3100
28965 Avenue Penn Valencia (91355) ***(P-25634)***

Curtiss-Wright Controls ....C.......661 257-4430
28965 Avenue Penn Santa Clarita (91355) ***(P-25635)***

Curtiss-Wright Controls (HQ) ....C.......661 702-1494
28965 Avenue Penn Santa Clarita (91355) ***(P-25636)***

Curvature LLC (HQ) ....B.......800 230-6638
6500 Hollister Ave # 210 Santa Barbara (93117) ***(P-7027)***

Cusa AWC LLC ....E.......916 423-4000
7701 Wilbur Way Sacramento (95828) ***(P-3644)***

Cusa Fl LLC ....C.......415 642-9400
41 Pier San Francisco (94133) ***(P-3894)***

Cusa Gcbs LLC ....D.......619 266-7365
3888 Beech St San Diego (92105) ***(P-4969)***

Cushman & Wakefield Inc ....C.......408 664-5403
800 W El Camino Real Mountain View (94040) ***(P-14245)***

Cushman & Wakefield Inc ....E.......650 347-3700
1350 Bayshore Hwy Ste 900 Burlingame (94010) ***(P-11389)***

Cushman & Wakefield Cal Inc (HQ) ....C.......408 275-6730
1 Maritime Plz Ste 900 San Francisco (94111) ***(P-11390)***

Cushman & Wakefield Cal Inc ....E.......949 474-4004
18111 Von Karman Ave # 1000 Irvine (92612) ***(P-11391)***

Custom Alloy Scrap Sales Inc (HQ) ....E.......510 893-6476
2730 Peralta St Oakland (94607) ***(P-7976)***

Custom Bilt Holdings LLC ....D.......909 664-1587
15133 Sierra Bonita Ln Chino (91710) ***(P-7745)***

Custom Building Products Inc ....E.......562 598-8808
7711 Center Ave Ste 500 Huntington Beach (92647) ***(P-1151)***

Custom Business Solutions Inc (PA) ....D.......949 380-7674
12 Morgan Irvine (92618) ***(P-6958)***

Custom Commercial Dry Clrs Inc (PA) ....E.......510 723-1000
3201 Investment Blvd Hayward (94545) ***(P-13565)***

Mergent e-mail: customerrelations@mergent.com
1272
2019 Directory of California
Wholesalers and Services Companies
(P-0000) Products & Services Section entry number
(PA)=Parent Co (HQ)=Headquarters (DH)=Div Headquarters

Custom Companies Inc...D...310 672-8800
13012 Molette St Santa Fe Springs (90670) ***(P-5039)***
Custom Cooler Inc...D...909 592-1111
420 E Arrow Hwy San Dimas (91773) ***(P-7662)***
Custom Craft Company, Santa Fe Springs *Also called Interntonal Win Treatments Inc* ***(P-6768)***
Custom Crome, Visalia *Also called Dae-IL Usa Inc* ***(P-6632)***
Custom Design Co Inc...E...818 507-5959
20969 Ventura Blvd # 217 Woodland Hills (91364) ***(P-1511)***
Custom Drywall Inc...D...408 263-1616
1570 Gladding Ct Milpitas (95035) ***(P-2869)***
Custom Drywall Service, Clovis *Also called Clovis Custom Drywall Inc* ***(P-2867)***
Custom Goods LLC (PA)...E...310 241-6700
1035 E Watson Center Rd Carson (90745) ***(P-4543)***
Custom Hotel LLC...D...310 645-0400
8639 Lincoln Blvd Los Angeles (90045) ***(P-12506)***
Custom House Hotel LP...D...831 649-4511
2 Portola Plz Monterey (93940) ***(P-12507)***
Custom Lawn Services, Ventura *Also called American Landscape Management* ***(P-797)***
Custom Lawn Services, Canoga Park *Also called American Landscape Management* ***(P-728)***
Custom Medical Products Inc...C...619 461-2068
9680 Alto Dr La Mesa (91941) ***(P-7177)***
Custom Metal Fabricators, Orange *Also called Cmf Inc* ***(P-3139)***
Custom Product Dev Corp...D...925 960-0577
4603 Las Positas Rd Ste A Livermore (94551) ***(P-3145)***
Custom Service Systems, Riverside *Also called Ghossain & Truelock Entps Inc* ***(P-14276)***
Custom Tours Inc...D...310 274-8819
24003 Ventura Blvd 100a Calabasas (91302) ***(P-4987)***
Custom Vinyls, Fontana *Also called Patrick Industries Inc* ***(P-6904)***
Customcare Home Hlth Svcs Inc...D...916 714-1155
9826 Bond Rd Ste A Elk Grove (95624) ***(P-22282)***
Customer Loan Depot, Foothill Ranch *Also called Loandepotcom LLC* ***(P-9829)***
Customer Loyalty Builders Inc...D...888 478-7787
1063 Todos Santos Concord (94522) ***(P-27209)***
Customer Srvc Dlvry Pltfrm Crp...E...717 896-8489
15615 Alton Pkwy Ste 310 Irvine (92618) ***(P-16339)***
Customerlink Systems, San Francisco *Also called Caranythingcom Inc* ***(P-27182)***
Customfab Inc...C...714 891-9119
7345 Orangewood Ave Garden Grove (92841) ***(P-17120)***
Customized Dist Svcs Inc...D...909 947-0084
3355 E Cedar St Ontario (91761) ***(P-27210)***
Customized Performance Inc...C...408 437-1720
780 Montague Expy Ste 201 San Jose (95131) ***(P-14246)***
Customline Professional...B...714 996-1333
567 S Melrose St Placentia (92870) ***(P-14109)***
Customzed Svcs Admnstrtors Inc...C...858 810-2000
4181 Ruffin Rd Ste 150 San Diego (92123) ***(P-10599)***
Cut N Clean Greens, Oxnard *Also called San Miguel Produce Inc* ***(P-79)***
Cutler Group LP...E...415 645-6745
101 Montgomery St Ste 700 San Francisco (94104) ***(P-17121)***
Cutting Edge Drywall Inc...E...858 408-0870
7046 Convoy Ct San Diego (92111) ***(P-2870)***
Cutting Edge Protection I...E...949 307-1596
381 Crosby St Altadena (91001) ***(P-13684)***
Cutting Edge Staffing Inc...D...951 587-0550
27715 Jefferson Ave Temecula (92590) ***(P-14597)***
Cve Nb Contracting Group Inc...E...707 584-1900
135 Utility Ct A Rohnert Park (94928) ***(P-27589)***
Cvf Capital Partners Inc...C...530 757-7004
1590 Drew Ave Ste 110 Davis (95618) ***(P-12219)***
Cvh Home Health Services, San Ramon *Also called Castro Valley Health Inc* ***(P-22257)***
Cvoc, Winton *Also called Central Valley Oprtnty Ctr Inc* ***(P-24165)***
Cvpartners Inc (HQ)...C...415 543-8600
505 Sansome St Ste 1100 San Francisco (94111) ***(P-14598)***
CVRM, Indio *Also called Coachella Vly Rescue Mission* ***(P-23590)***
CVS, Camarillo *Also called Kaiser Foundation Hospitals* ***(P-10267)***
Cw Healthcare Inc...E...510 636-9000
2884 Wakefield Dr Belmont (94002) ***(P-14847)***
Cw Network LLC (PA)...C...818 977-2500
3300 W Olive Ave Fl 3 Burbank (91505) ***(P-5781)***
CW Welding Service Inc...D...661 399-5422
761 Majors Ct Bakersfield (93308) ***(P-8008)***
CWC Acquisition, Orange *Also called Cleveland Wrecking Company* ***(P-3450)***
Cwf Inc...D...626 967-0500
251 E Front St Covina (91723) ***(P-14498)***
Cwgp Limited Partnership...D...310 395-9700
1740 Ocean Ave Santa Monica (90401) ***(P-12508)***
Cwi, San Francisco *Also called Collier Warehouse Inc* ***(P-6816)***
Cwip, Fresno *Also called Community Integrated Work Prog* ***(P-24168)***
Cwn Management, Mission Viejo *Also called Claim Jumper Restaurant* ***(P-1505)***
Cwp Cabinets Inc...C...760 246-4530
10007 Yucca Rd Adelanto (92301) ***(P-3025)***
Cwpfl Inc...E...714 564-7900
1682 Langley Ave Irvine (92614) ***(P-17122)***
Cws Apartment Homes LLC (PA)...B...949 640-4200
14 Corporate Plaza Dr # 210 Newport Beach (92660) ***(P-11392)***
Cws Capital Partners, Newport Beach *Also called Cws Apartment Homes LLC* ***(P-11392)***
Cws Utility Services Corp...B...408 367-8200
1720 N 1st St San Jose (95112) ***(P-24952)***
Cwtv, Burbank *Also called Cw Network LLC* ***(P-5781)***
Cy Gaslamp LLC...D...619 544-1004
453 6th Ave San Diego (92101) ***(P-12509)***
Cy Sac Operator LLC...D...916 455-6800
4422 Y St Sacramento (95817) ***(P-12510)***
Cyara Solutions Corp...C...650 549-8522
999 Main St Ste 101 Redwood City (94063) ***(P-7028)***
Cyber Policy...C...877 626-9991
1 California St Ste 1100 San Francisco (94111) ***(P-10600)***
Cyber Technology LLC (PA)...E...614 207-2955
1901 Newport Blvd Ste 300 Costa Mesa (92627) ***(P-10601)***
Cybercoders Inc...C...949 885-5151
6591 Irvine Center Dr # 200 Irvine (92618) ***(P-14599)***
Cybercsi Inc...D...408 727-2900
3511 Thomas Rd Ste 5 Santa Clara (95054) ***(P-7029)***
Cyberdefender Corporation...B...323 449-0774
617 W 7th St Fl 10 Los Angeles (90017) ***(P-15092)***
Cybernet Entertainment LLC (PA)...D...415 865-0230
1800 Mission St San Francisco (94103) ***(P-18036)***
Cyberpower Inc...D...626 813-7730
730 Baldwin Park Blvd City of Industry (91746) ***(P-7030)***
Cyberscientific, Irvine *Also called Cybercoders Inc* ***(P-14599)***
Cybersource Corporation (HQ)...C...650 432-7350
900 Metro Center Blvd Foster City (94404) ***(P-16113)***
Cybrex Consulting Inc...D...513 999-2109
4470 W Sunset Blvd Los Angeles (90027) ***(P-15642)***
Cylance Inc (PA)...C...949 375-3380
400 Spectrum Center Dr Irvine (92618) ***(P-15643)***
Cynergistek Inc (PA)...D...949 614-0700
27271 Las Ramblas Ste 200 Mission Viejo (92691) ***(P-14085)***
Cyphort Inc...E...408 841-4665
1133 Innovation Way Sunnyvale (94089) ***(P-7031)***
Cypress College Foundation...D...714 484-7128
9200 Valley View Ave Whittier (90603) ***(P-25148)***
Cypress Creek Holdings LLC...D...310 581-6299
3250 Ocean Park Blvd # 355 Santa Monica (90405) ***(P-6026)***
Cypress Ctr For Fmly Medicine...D...562 799-4801
10601 Walker St Ste 250 Cypress (90630) ***(P-19424)***
Cypress Education Foundation...D...714 220-6900
9470 Moody St Cypress (90630) ***(P-25149)***
Cypress Funeral Services Inc...C...650 550-8808
1370 El Camino Real Colma (94014) ***(P-13688)***
Cypress Garden At Citrus Hts...E...916 729-2722
7375 Stock Ranch Rd Citrus Heights (95621) ***(P-20927)***
Cypress Garden Villas...D...562 860-9260
21600 Bloomfield Ave Hawaiian Gardens (90716) ***(P-11006)***
Cypress Gardens Convalescent H...C...951 688-3643
9025 Colorado Ave Riverside (92503) ***(P-21055)***
Cypress Halthcare Partners LLC (PA)...C...831 649-1000
100 Wilson Rd Ste 100 # 100 Monterey (93940) ***(P-19425)***
Cypress Hotel, Cupertino *Also called Ch Cupertino Owner LLC* ***(P-12447)***
Cypress Lawn Funeral Home, Colma *Also called Cypress Funeral Services Inc* ***(P-13688)***
Cypress Ridge Golf Course...E...805 474-7979
780 Cypress Ridge Pkwy Arroyo Grande (93420) ***(P-18704)***
Cypress Security LLC (PA)...D...866 345-1277
478 Tehama St San Francisco (94103) ***(P-16623)***
Cypress Security LLC...D...562 222-4197
9926 Pioneer Blvd Ste 106 Santa Fe Springs (90670) ***(P-16624)***
Cytosport Holdings Inc...C...707 751-3942
1340 Treat Blvd Ste 350 Walnut Creek (94597) ***(P-11973)***
Czech Commerce Ltd...D...831 649-4633
3063 Larkin Rd Pebble Beach (93953) ***(P-8924)***
Cznd Inc...D...323 378-6505
8444 Wilshire Blvd Fl 5 Beverly Hills (90211) ***(P-18428)***
D & C Care Center Inc...D...626 798-1175
1640 N Fair Oaks Ave Pasadena (91103) ***(P-21056)***
D & D Wholesale Distrs Inc...D...626 333-2111
777 Baldwin Park Blvd City of Industry (91746) ***(P-8662)***
D & H Landscaping Inc...D...510 223-6597
4221 Appian Way El Sobrante (94803) ***(P-816)***
D & J Plumbing Inc...D...916 922-4888
4341 Winters St Sacramento (95838) ***(P-2178)***
D & J Tile Company Inc...D...650 632-4000
1045 Terminal Way San Carlos (94070) ***(P-2992)***
D & K Engineering (PA)...C...858 451-8999
15890 Bernardo Center Dr San Diego (92127) ***(P-25637)***
D & L Produce, Selma *Also called Serimian M S D L Ranch* ***(P-380)***
D & W LLC...D...310 345-0075
3501 Rindge Ln Redondo Beach (90278) ***(P-12511)***
D - Link, Fountain Valley *Also called D-Link Systems Incorporated* ***(P-7032)***
D A McCosker Construction Co...E...925 686-1780
3911 Laura Alice Way Concord (94520) ***(P-1754)***
D A V Industries...D...619 337-9244
1049 Elkelton Blvd Spring Valley (91977) ***(P-25150)***
D A Wood Construction Inc...D...209 491-4970
601 Albers Rd Modesto (95357) ***(P-25638)***
D and D Concrete Cnstr Inc...D...619 518-9737
13795 Blaisdell Pl # 201 Poway (92064) ***(P-3244)***
D and S Landscaping Inc...C...925 455-4630
26901 Hansen Rd Tracy (95377) ***(P-817)***
D Augustine & Associates...D...916 774-9600
532 Gibson Dr Ste 250 Roseville (95678) ***(P-13807)***
D B Specialty Farms, Santa Maria *Also called Darensberries LLC* ***(P-96)***
D C Golf A CA Partnership...E...626 797-3821
1456 E Mendocino St Altadena (91001) ***(P-18705)***
D C M Data Systems, Fremont *Also called Dcm Technologies Inc* ***(P-15097)***
D C N Wireless, Woodland Hills *Also called Digital Communications Network* ***(P-5404)***
D C S, Brea *Also called Diversfied Cmmnctions Svcs Inc* ***(P-5549)***
D C Taylor Co...E...925 603-1100
5060 Forni Dr Ste B Concord (94520) ***(P-3146)***
D C Vient Inc (PA)...B...209 578-1224
1556 Cummins Dr Modesto (95358) ***(P-2430)***
D E F Express Corporation...D...559 264-0500
2626 S Railroad Ave Fresno (93725) ***(P-4121)***
D E L T A Rescue, Acton *Also called Dedication & Everlasting Love* ***(P-627)***
D E X, Camarillo *Also called Data Exchange Corporation* ***(P-7033)***

ALPHABETIC

Employee Codes: A=Over 500 employees, B=251-500
C=101-250, D=51-100, E=50
2019 Directory of California
Wholesalers and Services Companies
© Mergent Inc. 1-800-342-5647
1273

D F Rios Construction Inc....D....510 226-7467
45847 Warm Springs Blvd Fremont (94539) *(P-3026)*
D G A, Los Angeles *Also called Directors Guild America Inc (P-18188)*
D J American Supply Inc....C....323 582-2650
6122 S Eastern Ave Commerce (90040) *(P-8024)*
D J Farm Management....E....661 792-6222
11298 Magnolia Ave Wasco (93280) *(P-685)*
D K Fortune & Associates Inc....C....310 391-7266
5240 Sepulveda Blvd Culver City (90230) *(P-21057)*
D M Electric Inc....D....909 888-8639
336 S Waterman Ave Ste K San Bernardino (92408) *(P-2559)*
D M S, Fremont *Also called DMS Facility Services Inc (P-14253)*
D P S Inc....D....714 564-7900
1682 Langley Ave Irvine (92614) *(P-2431)*
D R C, Sacramento *Also called Disability Rights California (P-23042)*
D S I, Santa Rosa *Also called Deposition Sciences Inc (P-26353)*
D S P Janitorial Service, Hayward *Also called D S P Service Inc (P-14247)*
D S P Service Inc....E....510 782-2200
23762 Foley St Ste 3 Hayward (94545) *(P-14247)*
D S R Inc....D....805 275-0039
3503 Arundell Cir Ste A Ventura (93003) *(P-17942)*
D S S Company....E....209 948-0302
655 W Clay St Stockton (95206) *(P-1912)*
D W Nicholson Corporation (PA)....C....510 887-0900
24747 Clawiter Rd Hayward (94545) *(P-2179)*
D W Powell Construction Inc....E....909 356-8880
8555 Banana Ave Fontana (92335) *(P-1755)*
D&A Enterprises Inc....B....510 445-1600
34943 Newark Blvd Newark (94560) *(P-8399)*
D&B, San Francisco *Also called Dun & Bradstreet Inc (P-14034)*
D&D Equipment Rental LLC....E....562 595-4555
2596 Mission St Ste 201 San Marino (91108) *(P-14438)*
D'Andrea Graphics, Cypress *Also called DAndrea Graphic Corportion (P-14110)*
D'Angelo, Michael L, Irvine *Also called Sean P OConnor (P-23369)*
D'Best Produce, Fresno *Also called De Benedetto Farms Inc (P-186)*
D-Link Systems Incorporated....C....714 885-6000
17595 Mount Herrmann St Fountain Valley (92708) *(P-7032)*
D/K Mechanical Contractors Inc....C....714 970-0180
3870 E Eagle Dr Anaheim (92807) *(P-2180)*
D2j Inc....D....323 589-1374
6351 Regent St Ste 100 Huntington Park (90255) *(P-17123)*
D3 Go, Encino *Also called D3publisher of America Inc (P-15644)*
D3publisher of America Inc....D....310 268-0820
15910 Ventura Blvd # 800 Encino (91436) *(P-15644)*
D7 Roofing Services Inc....D....916 447-2175
2851 Gold Tailings Ct Rancho Cordova (95670) *(P-3147)*
DA Davidson & Co....B....213 620-1850
624 S Grand Ave Ste 2600 Los Angeles (90017) *(P-9948)*
Daart Engineering Company Inc....D....909 888-8696
1598 N H St San Bernardino (92405) *(P-2181)*
DAB, Santa Fe Springs *Also called Disabled Amrcn Vtrans Dept Cal (P-25152)*
DAC, Palm Springs *Also called Desert Arts Center (P-24880)*
Dacare Inc (PA)....D....760 344-4654
643 Main St Brawley (92227) *(P-23765)*
Dacor Holdings Inc....C....626 626-4461
14425 Clark Ave City of Industry (91745) *(P-26691)*
Dae-IL Usa Inc....D....559 651-5170
7227 W Sunnyview Ave Visalia (93291) *(P-6632)*
Dager Corporation (PA)....D....916 989-4229
8004 Flsom Hydre Aburn Rd Folsom (95630) *(P-13652)*
Dahl-Beck Electric Co....D....510 237-2325
2775 Goodrick Ave Richmond (94801) *(P-7353)*
Dahlin Group Inc (PA)....D....925 251-7200
5865 Owens Dr Pleasanton (94588) *(P-26040)*
Dailey & Associates....D....310 360-3100
8687 Melrose Ave G300 Los Angeles (90069) *(P-13808)*
Daily Journal Corporation....E....213 229-5500
915 E 1st St Los Angeles (90012) *(P-13941)*
Daily Saw Service Inc....E....323 564-1791
4481 Firestone Blvd South Gate (90280) *(P-7845)*
Dailylook Inc....D....888 888-6645
2445 E 12th St Ste B Los Angeles (90021) *(P-17124)*
Dairy Council of California (PA)....E....949 756-7892
1418 N Market Blvd # 500 Sacramento (95834) *(P-27702)*
Dairyamerica Inc (PA)....D....559 251-0992
7815 N Palm Ave Ste 250 Fresno (93711) *(P-8518)*
Daiwa Corporation....D....562 375-6800
11137 Warland Dr Cypress (90630) *(P-7926)*
Daiwa Golf Company Division, Cypress *Also called Daiwa Corporation (P-7926)*
Daiwa House California Inc....B....310 228-5675
1901 Avenue Of The Stars # 264 Los Angeles (90067) *(P-1152)*
Dal Cais Inc....D....916 381-8080
5101 Florin Perkins Rd Sacramento (95826) *(P-1512)*
Dal-Tile Corporation....D....949 260-0488
1132 Duryea Ave Irvine (92614) *(P-6885)*
Dal-Tile Corporation....D....858 571-0283
7484 Raytheon Rd Ste A San Diego (92111) *(P-6886)*
Dal-Tile Corporation....D....510 357-6197
2303 Merced St San Leandro (94577) *(P-6887)*
Dal-Tile Corporation....D....909 390-7000
3625 Jurupa St Ontario (91761) *(P-6888)*
Dal-Tile Corporation....D....209 543-0924
4201 Technology Dr Modesto (95356) *(P-6889)*
Dalaklis McKeown Entertainment....D....310 545-0120
2517 Crest Dr Manhattan Beach (90266) *(P-18037)*
Daleo Inc....D....408 846-9621
550 E Luchessa Ave Gilroy (95020) *(P-1913)*
Daley, Lakeside *Also called Nicholas Grant Corporation (P-1826)*
Daley & Heft Attorneys....E....858 755-5666
462 Stevens Ave Ste 201 Solana Beach (92075) *(P-23018)*
Daleys Drywall and Taping Inc....A....408 378-9500
960 Camden Ave Campbell (95008) *(P-2871)*
Dallas Union Hotel Inc....C....626 356-1000
150 Corson St Pasadena (91103) *(P-12157)*
Dalton Trucking Inc (PA)....C....909 823-0663
13560 Whittram Ave Fontana (92335) *(P-3997)*
Damao Luggage Intl Inc....A....909 923-6531
1909 S Vineyard Ave Ontario (91761) *(P-8025)*
Dameron Hospital Association (PA)....A....209 944-5550
525 W Acacia St Stockton (95203) *(P-21362)*
Damon Electrical....D....818 426-3450
7800 Bobbyboyar Ave West Hills (91304) *(P-2560)*
Damrell Nelson Schrimp Pall....E....209 848-3500
703 W F St Oakdale (95361) *(P-23019)*
Dan Avila and Sons....D....209 495-3899
2718 Roberts Rd Ceres (95307) *(P-46)*
Dan Connolly Inc....D....408 241-0910
855 Civic Center Dr Ste 5 Santa Clara (95050) *(P-16625)*
Dan Freitas Electric....D....559 686-9572
983 E Levin Ave Tulare (93274) *(P-2561)*
Dan Lofgren....D....925 846-6632
7707 Forsythia Ct Pleasanton (94588) *(P-14248)*
Dan R Costa Inc....C....209 234-2004
17239 Louise Ave Escalon (95320) *(P-333)*
Dana Middle Schl Bys Girls CLB, San Pedro *Also called Boys and Girls Clubs of The La (P-25109)*
Danco Builders Inc....D....707 822-9000
5251 Ericson Way Ste A Arcata (95521) *(P-1279)*
Danco Communities....D....707 822-9000
5251 Ericson Way Ste A Arcata (95521) *(P-11869)*
DAndrea Graphic Corportion....D....310 642-0260
6100 Gateway Dr Cypress (90630) *(P-14110)*
Danell Custom Harvesting LLC....C....559 582-1251
8265 Hanford Armona Rd Hanford (93230) *(P-476)*
Danerica Enterprises Inc....D....818 774-1813
23901 Calabasas Rd # 1068 Calabasas (91302) *(P-13737)*
Dang Quinten....D....626 429-6332
11272 Frankmont Ct El Monte (91732) *(P-5978)*
Danger Inc....C....650 323-9700
3101 Park Blvd Palo Alto (94306) *(P-5543)*
Daniel Gerard Worldwide Inc....D....951 361-1111
13055 Jurupa Ave Fontana (92337) *(P-7268)*
Daniel J Edelman Inc....D....415 222-9944
525 Market St San Francisco (94105) *(P-27551)*
Daniel J Edelman Inc....D....323 857-9100
5670 Wilshire Blvd # 2500 Los Angeles (90036) *(P-27552)*
Daniel J Edelman Inc....D....650 762-2800
201 Baldwin Ave San Mateo (94401) *(P-13942)*
Daniel J Edelman Inc....D....323 857-9100
5900 Wilshire Blvd # 2400 Los Angeles (90036) *(P-13943)*
Daniel Loria Novartis....C....510 655-8729
4560 Horton St Emeryville (94608) *(P-22016)*
Daniel O Mongiano MD A PR....E....661 951-9195
42220 10th St W Ste 109 Lancaster (93534) *(P-19426)*
Daniel Robert Knowlton....D....760 265-5293
68368 Madrid Rd Cathedral City (92234) *(P-23020)*
Daniels Kent Personnel Agency, Walnut *Also called Kent Daniels & Associates Inc (P-14656)*
Daniels Western Mt Packers Inc....D....562 948-2254
5217 Industry Ave Pico Rivera (90660) *(P-8614)*
Danish Care Center, Atascadero *Also called Compass Health Inc (P-21044)*
Danish Environment Inc....D....818 992-6722
9424 Eton Ave Ste G Chatsworth (91311) *(P-14249)*
Danlil Enterprise Inc....D....714 776-7705
1440 S State College Blvd Anaheim (92806) *(P-14250)*
Danning Gill Damnd Kollitz LLP....D....310 277-0077
1900 Avenue Of The Stars # 11 Los Angeles (90067) *(P-23021)*
Dannis Wlver Klley A Prof Corp (PA)....D....415 543-4111
275 Battery St Ste 1150 San Francisco (94111) *(P-23022)*
Danny Mahagna Shapprie....E....760 341-5070
73280 Highway 111 Palm Desert (92260) *(P-18429)*
Danny Ryan Precision Contg Inc....D....949 642-6664
1818 N Orangethorpe Park Anaheim (92801) *(P-3451)*
Dans Landscape Service Inc....D....714 241-9591
718 Aleppo St Newport Beach (92660) *(P-818)*
Dansk Enterprises Inc....D....714 751-0347
3419 Via Lido 345 Newport Beach (92663) *(P-16626)*
Danville Long-Term Care Inc....D....925 837-4566
336 Diablo Rd Danville (94526) *(P-20365)*
Danville Post Acute Rehab, Danville *Also called Danville Long-Term Care Inc (P-20365)*
Danville Rehsbilitation, Danville *Also called Danville Village Skilled Nursn (P-20366)*
Danville Village Skilled Nursn....D....925 837-4566
336 Diablo Rd Danville (94526) *(P-20366)*
Dapcon Inc....D....408 573-7200
877 Commercial St San Jose (95112) *(P-2432)*
Daps Naval Hosp, Lemoore *Also called United States Dept of Navy (P-21872)*
Daqri LLC (PA)....D....213 375-8830
1201 W 5th St Ste T800 Los Angeles (90017) *(P-15093)*
Darco Construction, Stanton *Also called Denver D Darling Inc (P-1390)*
Darden Architects Inc....D....559 448-8051
6790 N West Ave Ste 104 Fresno (93711) *(P-26041)*
Darensberries LLC....C....805 937-8000
714 S Blosser Rd Santa Maria (93458) *(P-96)*
Darensburg Roghair & Renier....E....760 256-6891
1520 E Main St Barstow (92311) *(P-12512)*
Darr & Pitcairn AG Inc....E....661 758-5156
16674 Wasco Ave Wasco (93280) *(P-477)*

Mergent e-mail: customerrelations@mergent.com
1274
2019 Directory of California
Wholesalers and Services Companies
(P-0000) Products & Services Section entry number
(PA)=Parent Co (HQ)=Headquarters (DH)=Div Headquarters

Darrell L Green Inc D 559 688-0686
12652 Avenue 240 Tulare (93274) ***(P-4341)***
DArrigo Broscoof California (PA) E 831 455-4500
21777 Harris Rd Salinas (93908) ***(P-47)***
Dart Aerospace, Vista *Also called Apical Industries Inc* ***(P-7906)***
Dart Entities, Commerce *Also called Dart International A Corp* ***(P-4342)***
Dart International A Corp (HQ) C 323 264-8746
1430 S Eastman Ave Commerce (90023) ***(P-4342)***
Dart Neuroscience LLC C 858 736-3060
12278 Scripps Summit Dr San Diego (92131) ***(P-26352)***
Das Global Capital Corp D 702 967-1688
42 Peninsula Ctr Ste 317 Rllng HLS Est (90274) ***(P-26508)***
Dassault Systemes Americas C 818 999-2500
6320 Canoga Ave Fl 3 Woodland Hills (91367) ***(P-15094)***
Dassels Petroleum Inc E 831 636-5100
340 El Camino Real S Salinas (93901) ***(P-8953)***
Data 911, Poway *Also called Hubb Systems LLC* ***(P-15973)***
Data Center, Sacramento *Also called Correctons Rhbltation Cal Dept* ***(P-16107)***
Data Control Corporation D 916 774-4000
P.O. Box 2069 Granite Bay (95746) ***(P-15939)***
Data Domain LLC A 408 980-4800
2421 Mission College Blvd Santa Clara (95054) ***(P-15940)***
Data Exchange, Camarillo *Also called Dex Corporation* ***(P-25643)***
Data Exchange Corporation (PA) B 805 388-1711
3600 Via Pescador Camarillo (93012) ***(P-7033)***
Data Recognition Corporation E 831 393-0700
20 Ryan Ranch Rd Monterey (93940) ***(P-27703)***
Data Specialties Inc (PA) D 714 523-8489
8400 Kass Dr Buena Park (90621) ***(P-2562)***
Data Trace Info Svcs LLC (HQ) D 714 250-6700
4 First American Way Santa Ana (92707) ***(P-27927)***
Data-Image Systems, Rancho Cordova *Also called Ricoh Usa Inc* ***(P-6974)***
Database Marketing Group Inc B 714 727-0800
5 Peters Canyon Rd # 150 Irvine (92606) ***(P-14043)***
Datallegro Inc D 949 680-3000
85 Enterprise Ste 200 Aliso Viejo (92656) ***(P-7034)***
Datapark Inc D 510 483-7275
1631 Neptune Dr San Leandro (94577) ***(P-15941)***
Dataprose Inc D 805 278-7430
1451 N Rice Ave Ste A Oxnard (93030) ***(P-16114)***
Datasafe Inc (PA) E 650 875-3800
574 Eccles Ave South San Francisco (94080) ***(P-4671)***
Datasafe Inc E 650 875-3800
3160 W Bayshore Rd Palo Alto (94303) ***(P-4672)***
Datastax Inc (PA) D 650 389-6000
3975 Freedom Cir Ste 400 Santa Clara (95054) ***(P-16115)***
Davalan Fresh, Los Angeles *Also called Davalan Sales Inc* ***(P-8663)***
Davalan Sales Inc C 213 623-2500
1601 E Olympic Blvd # 325 Los Angeles (90021) ***(P-8663)***
Dave Calhoun and Assoc LLC (PA) C 925 688-1234
2575 Stanwell Dr Ste 100 Concord (94520) ***(P-14251)***
Dave Gross Enterprises Inc D 916 388-2000
7 Wayne Ct Sacramento (95829) ***(P-3509)***
Dave Spurr Excavating Inc E 805 238-0834
935 Riverside Ave Ste 18 Paso Robles (93446) ***(P-3422)***
Dave Williams Plbg & Elec Inc C 760 296-1397
75140 Saint Charles Pl C Palm Desert (92211) ***(P-2182)***
Dave Wilson Nursery Inc (PA) E 209 874-1821
19701 Lake Rd Hickman (95323) ***(P-252)***
Davenport Development Corp E 858 300-3333
8360 Clairemont Mesa Blvd # 111 San Diego (92111) ***(P-3099)***
Davey Tree Surgery Company D 530 378-2674
6915 Eastside Rd Ste 94 Anderson (96007) ***(P-971)***
Davey Tree Surgery Company (HQ) A 925 443-1723
2617 S Vasco Rd Livermore (94550) ***(P-972)***
Davey Tree Surgery Company D 760 975-0225
1914 Mission Rd Ste N Escondido (92029) ***(P-973)***
David & Goliath LLC C 310 445-5200
909 N Pacific Coast Hwy # 700 El Segundo (90245) ***(P-13809)***
DAVID & MARGARET YOUTH AND FAM, La Verne *Also called David and Margaret Home Inc* ***(P-24500)***
David and Margaret Home Inc C 909 596-5921
1350 3rd St La Verne (91750) ***(P-24500)***
David Civalier MD Inc E 530 244-4034
2510 Airpark Dr Ste 104 Redding (96001) ***(P-19427)***
David D Bohannon Organization (PA) D 650 345-8222
60 31st Ave San Mateo (94403) ***(P-10866)***
David Darroch D 510 835-9100
300 Lakeside Dr Fl 24 Oakland (94612) ***(P-23023)***
David Evans and Associates Inc E 909 481-5750
4141 Inland Empire Blvd # 250 Ontario (91764) ***(P-25639)***
David Evans Enterprises Inc A 213 337-3680
201 S Figueroa St Ste 240 Los Angeles (90012) ***(P-25640)***
David King Convalescent Hosp D 310 451-9706
1340 15th St Santa Monica (90404) ***(P-21058)***
David L Amador Inc D 626 334-2011
762 N Loren Ave Azusa (91702) ***(P-3245)***
David Levy Co Inc E 562 404-9998
12753 Moore St Cerritos (90703) ***(P-7464)***
David Lyng & Associates Inc D 831 429-5700
1041 41st Ave Ste A Santa Cruz (95062) ***(P-11393)***
David Morse & Assoc., Glendale *Also called Dma Claims Inc* ***(P-10608)***
David N Schultz Inc (PA) C 818 240-1070
715 N Central Ave Ste 300 Glendale (91203) ***(P-11394)***
David Ollis Landscape Dev Inc E 909 307-1911
450 Kansas St Ste 104 Redlands (92373) ***(P-819)***
David Ross Inc D 323 684-7673
1899 N Raymond Ave Pasadena (91103) ***(P-20367)***
David Santos Farming D 209 826-1065
720 Jefferson Ave Los Banos (93635) ***(P-17125)***
David W Golen D 213 716-0706
20253 Gifford St Winnetka (91306) ***(P-3998)***
David-Kleis Inc C 951 845-1166
9246 Avenida Miravilla Cherry Valley (92223) ***(P-20368)***
Davidon Five Star Corp D 925 945-8000
1600 S Main St Ste 150 Walnut Creek (94596) ***(P-12220)***
Davidon Homes, Walnut Creek *Also called Davidon Five Star Corp* ***(P-12220)***
Davidson Builders, Del Mar *Also called Davidson Communities LLC* ***(P-11870)***
Davidson Communities LLC (PA) E 858 259-8500
1302 Camino Del Mar Del Mar (92014) ***(P-11870)***
Davidson Hotel Partners Lp C 818 707-1220
30100 Agoura Rd Agoura Hills (91301) ***(P-12513)***
Davie Brown Entertainment Inc D 310 979-1980
12777 W Jefferson Blvd # 120 Los Angeles (90066) ***(P-18362)***
Davis Brothers Framing Inc C 909 944-4899
8780 Prestige Ct Rancho Cucamonga (91730) ***(P-3027)***
Davis Cmnty Clnic Dntl Program, Davis *Also called Davis Community Clinic* ***(P-19428)***
Davis Community Clinic (PA) D 530 758-2060
2040 Sutter Pl Davis (95616) ***(P-19428)***
Davis Framing Inc E 619 463-2394
8103 Commercial St La Mesa (91942) ***(P-3028)***
Davis Hallmark Partnership E 530 753-3320
110 F St Davis (95616) ***(P-12514)***
Davis Medical Offices, Davis *Also called Kaiser Foundation Hospitals* ***(P-19606)***
Davis Research LLC C 818 591-2408
23801 Calabasas Rd # 1036 Calabasas (91302) ***(P-26509)***
Davis Trucking LLC (PA) E 619 229-9997
7345 Mission Gorge Rd H San Diego (92120) ***(P-3999)***
Davis Wright Tremaine LLP D 415 276-6500
505 Montgomery St Ste 800 San Francisco (94111) ***(P-23024)***
Davis Wright Tremaine LLP D 213 633-6800
865 S Figueroa St # 2400 Los Angeles (90017) ***(P-23025)***
Davis Ziff Publishing Inc C 415 551-4800
235 2nd St San Francisco (94105) ***(P-5544)***
Daviselen Advertising Inc (PA) C 213 688-7000
865 S Figueroa St # 1200 Los Angeles (90017) ***(P-13810)***
Daviselen Advertising Inc D 858 847-0789
420 Stevens Ave Ste 240 Solana Beach (92075) ***(P-13811)***
Davita Dialysis, Irvine *Also called Renal Treatment Ctrs - Cal Inc* ***(P-22486)***
Davita Hesperia Dialysis Ctr, Hesperia *Also called Total Renal Care Inc* ***(P-22494)***
Davita Inc B 949 930-4400
15271 Laguna Canyon Rd Irvine (92618) ***(P-22470)***
Davita Inc D 310 536-2400
601 Hawaii St El Segundo (90245) ***(P-22471)***
Davita Magan Management Inc (HQ) C 626 331-6411
420 W Rowland St Covina (91723) ***(P-19429)***
Davita Magan Management Inc D 909 592-9712
330 W Covina Blvd San Dimas (91773) ***(P-19430)***
Davita Medical Management LLC D 323 720-1144
2601 Via Campo Montebello (90640) ***(P-19431)***
Davita Medical Management LLC D 626 444-0333
3144 Santa Anita Ave # 201 El Monte (91733) ***(P-19432)***
Davita Medical Management LLC (HQ) A 310 354-4200
2175 Park Pl El Segundo (90245) ***(P-19433)***
Davlor Company D 949 244-9748
12 Oakbrook Trabuco Canyon (92679) ***(P-1513)***
Davlor Constructio Corp, Trabuco Canyon *Also called Davlor Company* ***(P-1513)***
Daw Industries Inc E 858 622-4955
6610 Nncy Rdge Dr Ste 100 San Diego (92121) ***(P-8026)***
Dawn Ranch Lodge & Rd Hse Rest D 707 869-0656
16467 Hwy 116 Guerneville (95446) ***(P-12515)***
Day Star Educational Center, Fullerton *Also called Westview Services Inc* ***(P-24132)***
Day Star Fixtures E 714 838-4613
1802 Riverford Rd Tustin (92780) ***(P-3029)***
Day Wireless Systems, San Diego *Also called U S Mbile Wrless Cmmunications* ***(P-5424)***
Daybreak Care Center (PA) E 818 504-6154
9040 Sunland Blvd Sun Valley (91352) ***(P-24501)***
Daybreak Game Company LLC B 858 239-0500
15051 Avenue Of Science San Diego (92128) ***(P-15095)***
Daylight Foods Inc C 408 284-7300
660 Vista Way Milpitas (95035) ***(P-8664)***
Daylight Transport LLC (PA) D 310 507-8200
1501 Hughes Way Ste 200 Long Beach (90810) ***(P-4122)***
Daymark Properties Realty, San Diego *Also called Daymark Realty Advisors Inc* ***(P-11395)***
Daymark Realty Advisors Inc B 714 975-2999
750 B St Ste 2620 San Diego (92101) ***(P-11395)***
Dayout Brawley, Brawley *Also called Dacare Inc* ***(P-23765)***
Days Inn, Glendale *Also called JP Allen Extended Stay* ***(P-12794)***
Days Inn, Oakland *Also called Brilliance Investment LLC* ***(P-12401)***
Days Inn Bakersfield C 661 324-6666
818 Real Rd Bakersfield (93309) ***(P-12516)***
DAYSTAR FOUNDATION, Lancaster *Also called Antelope Valley Foundation* ***(P-23481)***
Daytona Surfise, North Hollywood *Also called Century National Properties* ***(P-10862)***
Daz Systems LLC (HQ) D 310 640-1300
880 Apollo St Ste 201 El Segundo (90245) ***(P-15096)***
Dazian LLC D 818 287-3800
10671 Lorne St Sun Valley (91352) ***(P-8224)***
Dazian's, Sun Valley *Also called Dazian LLC* ***(P-8224)***
Db Custom Farming, Bakersfield *Also called Donald Valpredo Farming Inc* ***(P-50)***
DB Roberts Inc D 805 988-4882
880 Avenida Acaso Ste 100 Camarillo (93012) ***(P-7846)***
Dbi Beverage Inc D 209 524-2477
4140 Brew Master Dr Ceres (95307) ***(P-8989)***
Dbi Beverage Sacramento (HQ) D 916 373-5700
3500 Carlin Dr West Sacramento (95691) ***(P-9036)***

ALPHABETIC

Employee Codes: A=Over 500 employees, B=251-500
C=101-250, D=51-100, E=50
2019 Directory of California
Wholesalers and Services Companies

1275

Dbi Beverage San Francisco........C.......415 643-9900
245 S Spruce Ave Ste 100 South San Francisco (94080) ***(P-8990)***
Dbi Beverage San Joaquin........D.......209 948-9400
4547 Frontier Way Stockton (95215) ***(P-8991)***
Dbi Services Inc........D.......805 523-7114
2775 Hollister St Simi Valley (93065) ***(P-1914)***
DC Solar Solutions Inc........E.......925 203-1088
4901 Park Rd Benicia (94510) ***(P-2183)***
DC Transport Inc........D.......916 438-0888
5411 Raley Blvd Sacramento (95838) ***(P-4123)***
Dcm Data Systems, Fremont *Also called Dcm Limited* ***(P-16340)***
Dcm Limited........D.......510 494-2321
39159 Paseo Padre Pkwy # 303 Fremont (94538) ***(P-16340)***
Dcm Technologies Inc........D.......510 791-2182
39159 Paseo Padre Pkwy # 303 Fremont (94538) ***(P-15097)***
Dcor LLC (PA)........D.......805 535-2000
290 Maple Ct Ste 290 # 290 Ventura (93003) ***(P-1041)***
Dcor LLC........D.......805 576-1200
290 Maple Ct Ste 290 Ventura (93003) ***(P-1042)***
Dcp Jl Triton Sf LLC........E.......844 808-0290
342 Grant Ave San Francisco (94108) ***(P-12517)***
Dcp Rights LLC........E.......310 255-4600
2900 Olympic Blvd Santa Monica (90404) ***(P-18038)***
DCS, Lathrop *Also called Performant Recovery Inc* ***(P-14016)***
Dcss, Modesto *Also called County of Stanislaus* ***(P-23750)***
Dct, Fontana *Also called Desert Coastal Transport Inc* ***(P-4128)***
DDB Worldwide........C.......310 907-1500
340 Main St Venice (90291) ***(P-13812)***
DDB Worldwide........C.......415 732-3600
600 California St Fl 7 San Francisco (94108) ***(P-13813)***
Ddso Inc (PA)........D.......916 456-5166
5051 47th Ave Sacramento (95824) ***(P-23766)***
De Anza Campland LLC (PA)........D.......858 581-4200
2211 Pacific Beach Dr San Diego (92109) ***(P-13464)***
De Anza Land & Leisure Corp........E.......619 423-2727
2170 Coronado Ave San Diego (92154) ***(P-18284)***
De Anza Square Shopping Center........D.......408 738-4444
1306 S Mary Ave 1370 Sunnyvale (94087) ***(P-1335)***
De Benedetto AG, Chowchilla *Also called J & R Debenedetto Orchards Inc* ***(P-695)***
De Benedetto Farms Inc........D.......559 276-2400
1547 N Marks Ave Fresno (93722) ***(P-186)***
De Hart Plumbing Htg & A Inc........E.......209 523-4578
311 Bitritto Way Modesto (95356) ***(P-2184)***
De La Torre Landscape & Maint........C.......951 549-3525
656 Paseo Grande Corona (92882) ***(P-820)***
De Lasalle Institute, NAPA *Also called Retreat & Conference Center* ***(P-13771)***
De Mattei Construction Inc........D.......408 295-7516
1794 The Alameda San Jose (95126) ***(P-1153)***
De Mello Roofing Inc........D.......415 456-0741
45 Jordan St San Rafael (94901) ***(P-3148)***
De Oliviera Concrete Inc........E.......661 252-7522
14111 Soledad Canyon Rd Santa Clarita (91387) ***(P-3246)***
De Par Inc........D.......714 771-6900
931 W Barkley Ave Orange (92868) ***(P-26692)***
Deacon Construction - Cal........D.......916 969-0900
7745 Greenback Ln Ste 250 Citrus Heights (95610) ***(P-1514)***
Deacon Corp........D.......949 222-9060
17880 Fitch Irvine (92614) ***(P-1515)***
Deacon Holdings Inc (PA)........D.......916 969-0900
7745 Greenback Ln Ste 250 Citrus Heights (95610) ***(P-1516)***
Dealersocket Inc (PA)........D.......949 900-0300
100 Avenida La Pata San Clemente (92673) ***(P-15098)***
Dealertrack Collte Manag Servi........C.......916 368-5300
9750 Goethe Rd Sacramento (95827) ***(P-16341)***
Dealey Renton and Associates........D.......510 465-3090
530 Water St Fl 7th Oakland (94607) ***(P-10602)***
Dealix Corporation........C.......650 599-5500
720 Bay Rd Ste 200 Redwood City (94063) ***(P-6589)***
Dean Goodman Inc........D.......714 229-8999
10833 Valley View St # 240 Cypress (90630) ***(P-11396)***
Dean Socal LLC........C.......951 734-3950
17637 E Valley Blvd City of Industry (91744) ***(P-8519)***
Deanco Healthcare LLC........A.......818 787-2222
14850 Roscoe Blvd Panorama City (91402) ***(P-21952)***
Deardorff Family Farm, Oxnard *Also called Deardorff-Jackson Co* ***(P-8665)***
Deardorff-Jackson Co........E.......805 487-7801
400 Lombard St Oxnard (93030) ***(P-8665)***
Death Valley 49ers Inc........D.......559 297-5691
1442 Carson Ave Clovis (93611) ***(P-25415)***
Debisys Inc (PA)........D.......949 699-1401
27442 Portola Pkwy # 150 Foothill Ranch (92610) ***(P-9679)***
Debtmerica LLC........D.......714 389-4200
3100 S Harbor Blvd # 250 Santa Ana (92704) ***(P-13738)***
Debtmerica Relief, Santa Ana *Also called Debtmerica LLC* ***(P-13738)***
Decarta Inc........D.......408 294-8400
1455 Market St Fl 4 San Francisco (94103) ***(P-15099)***
Decathalon Club, San Francisco *Also called Executives Outlet Inc* ***(P-18598)***
Decathlon Club, Santa Clara *Also called Bay Clubs Inc* ***(P-18577)***
Decathlon Club Inc........C.......408 738-2582
3250 Central Expy Santa Clara (95051) ***(P-18592)***
Dechert LLP........C.......949 442-6000
650 Town Center Dr # 700 Costa Mesa (92626) ***(P-23026)***
Dechert LLP........C.......213 489-1357
633 W 5th St Ste 3700 Los Angeles (90071) ***(P-23027)***
Dechert LLP........E.......415 262-4500
1 Bush St Ste 1600 San Francisco (94104) ***(P-23028)***
Decimal Inc........D.......855 980-6612
1160 Battery St Ste 350 San Francisco (94111) ***(P-17126)***
Decipher Inc (HQ)........D.......559 436-6940
7 E River Park Pl E # 110 Fresno (93720) ***(P-26510)***
Decision Minds........C.......408 309-8051
1525 Mccarthy Blvd # 224 Milpitas (95035) ***(P-16116)***
Decision Ready Solutions Inc........E.......949 400-1126
2855 Michelle Ste 350 Irvine (92606) ***(P-9798)***
Decision Sciences Intl Corp........D.......858 571-1900
12345 First American Way # 100 Poway (92064) ***(P-7465)***
Decision Toolbox Inc........D.......562 377-5600
5319 University Dr 521 Irvine (92612) ***(P-27704)***
Decisionlogic LLC........E.......858 586-0202
9820 Willow Creek Rd # 310 San Diego (92131) ***(P-15645)***
Decker Elc Co Inc Elec Contrs........D.......650 635-1390
147 Beacon St South San Francisco (94080) ***(P-2563)***
Decker Landscaping Inc........D.......916 652-1780
13265 Bill Francis Dr Auburn (95603) ***(P-821)***
Decky Co Inc (PA)........D.......310 608-2726
2121 S Wilmington Ave Compton (90220) ***(P-8254)***
Declara Inc........D.......650 800-7695
977 Commercial St Palo Alto (94303) ***(P-16342)***
Decton Inc........C.......949 851-0111
19800 Macarthur Blvd # 600 Irvine (92612) ***(P-14600)***
Decurion Corporation (PA)........D.......310 659-9432
120 N Robertson Blvd Fl 3 Los Angeles (90048) ***(P-18285)***
Dedicated Fleet Systems Inc (PA)........D.......909 590-8209
1350 Philadelphia St Pomona (91766) ***(P-4000)***
Dedicated Management Group LLC........C.......209 385-0694
3876 E Childs Ave Merced (95341) ***(P-17127)***
Dedicated Media Inc (PA)........D.......310 524-9400
909 N Pacific Coast Hwy # 320 El Segundo (90245) ***(P-13814)***
Dedication & Everlasting Love........D.......661 269-4010
6021 Shannon Valley Rd Acton (93510) ***(P-627)***
Dee Sign Co........D.......818 904-3400
7950 Woodley Ave Van Nuys (91406) ***(P-17128)***
Deep Focus Inc........A.......323 790-5340
6922 Hollywood Blvd Fl 10 Hollywood (90028) ***(P-27211)***
Deepak Chopra LLC........E.......760 494-1600
2013 Costa Del Mar Rd Carlsbad (92009) ***(P-18593)***
Deer Park Pharmacy, Saint Helena *Also called St Helena Hospital* ***(P-21775)***
Defenders Trnsp Svcs Inc........C.......909 854-7000
14562 Slover Ave Fontana (92337) ***(P-5040)***
Defenseweb Technologies Inc........D.......858 272-8505
10188 Telesis Ct Ste 300 San Diego (92121) ***(P-16343)***
Defined Contribution Trust Fun........D.......213 385-6161
501 Shatto Pl Ste 500 Los Angeles (90020) ***(P-12092)***
Defy Media LLC........D.......310 360-4141
8750 Wilshire Blvd # 200 Beverly Hills (90211) ***(P-13815)***
Degenkolb Engineers (PA)........C.......415 392-6952
375 Beale St Ste 500 San Francisco (94105) ***(P-25641)***
Dehart Inc........D.......858 695-0882
7550 Miramar Rd Ste 300 San Diego (92126) ***(P-3510)***
Dejuno Corporation........D.......909 230-6744
6275 Providence Way Eastvale (92880) ***(P-9210)***
Dekra-Lite Industries Inc........D.......714 436-0705
3102 W Alton Ave Santa Ana (92704) ***(P-17129)***
Del AMO Construction........D.......310 378-6203
23840 Madison St Torrance (90505) ***(P-1517)***
Del AMO Diagnostic Center........E.......310 316-2424
3531 Fashion Way Torrance (90503) ***(P-22565)***
Del AMO Grdns Cnvlscnt Hosp &........D.......310 378-4233
22419 Kent Ave Torrance (90505) ***(P-20369)***
Del AMO Hospital Inc........B.......310 530-1151
23700 Camino Del Sol Torrance (90505) ***(P-21953)***
Del AMO Insurance Services........D.......310 534-3444
910 Lomita Blvd Ste E Harbor City (90710) ***(P-10603)***
Del Contes Landscaping Inc........D.......510 353-6030
41900 Boscell Rd Fremont (94538) ***(P-822)***
Del Mar Convalescent Hospital........D.......626 288-8353
3136 Del Mar Ave Rosemead (91770) ***(P-21363)***
Del Mar Country Club Inc........D.......858 759-5500
6001 Clubhouse Dr Rancho Santa Fe (92067) ***(P-18908)***
Del Mar French Laundry........E.......831 375-9597
508 Del Monte Ave Monterey (93940) ***(P-13485)***
Del Mar Holding LLC........A.......313 659-7300
1022 Bay Marina Dr 10 National City (91950) ***(P-8615)***
Del Mar Plastering Inc........D.......951 343-5955
7085 Jurupa Ave Ste 2 Riverside (92504) ***(P-2872)***
Del Mar Seafoods Inc........C.......805 850-0421
1449 Spinnaker Dr Ventura (93001) ***(P-8575)***
Del Mar Thoroughbred Club........B.......858 755-1141
2260 Jimmy Durante Blvd Del Mar (92014) ***(P-18539)***
Del Monaco Specialty Foods Inc........D.......408 500-4100
18675 Madrone Pkwy # 150 Morgan Hill (95037) ***(P-8400)***
Del Norte Distribution, Oxnard *Also called Seaboard Produce Distrs Inc* ***(P-7712)***
Del Norte Workforce Center........E.......707 464-8347
875 5th St Ste 12 Crescent City (95531) ***(P-24178)***
Del Paso Country Club........C.......916 489-3681
3333 Marconi Ave Sacramento (95821) ***(P-18909)***
Del Puerto Health Care Dst........D.......209 892-9100
875 E St Patterson (95363) ***(P-19434)***
Del Puerto Health Center, Patterson *Also called Del Puerto Health Care Dst* ***(P-19434)***
Del Rey Packing Co, Del Rey *Also called Chooljian & Sons Inc* ***(P-503)***
Del Rey Systems and Tech Inc (PA)........D.......858 874-8992
7844 Convoy Ct San Diego (92111) ***(P-16344)***
Del Rio Convalescent, Bell Gardens *Also called Del Rio Sanitarium Inc* ***(P-20371)***
Del Rio Convalescent Center, Whittier *Also called Del Rio Health Care Inc* ***(P-20370)***
Del Rio Golf & Country Club........C.......209 341-2414
801 Stewart Rd Modesto (95356) ***(P-18910)***
Del Rio Health Care Inc........C.......562 947-5221
16016 Rio Florida Dr Whittier (90603) ***(P-20370)***

Del Rio Sanitarium Inc........C......562 927-6586
7002 Gage Ave Bell Gardens (90201) *(P-20371)*
Del Rosa Villa Inc........D......909 885-3261
2018 Del Rosa Ave San Bernardino (92404) *(P-20372)*
Delancey Street Coach Service, San Francisco *Also called Delancey Street Foundation (P-24502)*
Delancey Street Foundation (PA)........B......415 957-9800
600 The Embarcadero San Francisco (94107) *(P-24502)*
Delano Dst Sklled Nrsing Fclty........C......661 720-2100
1509 Tokay St Delano (93215) *(P-20373)*
Delano Energy, Delano *Also called Covanta Delano Inc (P-6024)*
Delegata Corporation........D......916 609-5400
2450 Venture Oaks Way # 400 Sacramento (95833) *(P-15942)*
Delicate Productions Inc (PA)........D......415 484-1174
874 Verdulera St Camarillo (93010) *(P-18363)*
Delimex Holdings Inc........A......619 210-2700
7878 Airway Rd San Diego (92154) *(P-11974)*
Dell, San Jose *Also called Force10 Networks Inc (P-15957)*
Della Maggiore Tile Inc........D......408 286-3991
87 N 30th St San Jose (95116) *(P-2993)*
Delmart Cold Storage Co Inc........D......661 849-8608
1401 19th St Bakersfield (93301) *(P-4499)*
Delmart Farms Inc........D......661 746-2148
30988 Riverside Cntrl Vly Shafter (93263) *(P-138)*
Deloitte & Touche LLP........A......213 688-0800
555 W 5th St Ste 2700 Los Angeles (90013) *(P-26177)*
Deloitte & Touche LLP........C......619 232-6500
655 W Broadway Ste 700 San Diego (92101) *(P-26178)*
Deloitte & Touche LLP........A......714 436-7419
695 Town Center Dr # 1200 Costa Mesa (92626) *(P-26179)*
Deloitte & Touche LLP........B......415 783-4000
555 Mission St Ste 1400 San Francisco (94105) *(P-26180)*
Deloitte & Touche LLP........B......408 704-4000
225 W Santa Clara St # 600 San Jose (95113) *(P-26181)*
Deloitte & Touche LLP........D......559 449-6300
5250 N Palm Ave Ste 300 Fresno (93704) *(P-26182)*
Deloitte & Touche LLP........C......415 782-4020
6210 Stoneridge Mall Rd Pleasanton (94588) *(P-26183)*
Deloitte & Touche LLP........C......213 688-0800
555 W 5th St Ste 2700 Los Angeles (90013) *(P-26184)*
Deloitte Consulting LLP........D......510 251-4400
555 Mission St San Francisco (94105) *(P-27212)*
Deloitte Consulting LLP........D......714 436-7100
695 Town Center Dr # 1200 Costa Mesa (92626) *(P-27213)*
Deloitte Tax LLP........B......415 783-4000
555 Mission St Ste 1400 San Francisco (94105) *(P-26185)*
Deloitte Tax LLP........B......408 704-4000
225 W Santa Clara St # 600 San Jose (95113) *(P-26186)*
Delphi Productions Inc (PA)........C......510 748-7494
950 W Tower Ave Alameda (94501) *(P-13816)*
Delphix Corp (PA)........E......650 494-1645
1400 Saport Blvd Ste 200a Redwood City (94063) *(P-15646)*
Delta Air Lines Inc........D......310 646-9614
5625 W Imperial Hwy Los Angeles (90045) *(P-5041)*
Delta Air Lines Inc........D......323 417-7374
500 World Way Los Angeles (90045) *(P-4779)*
Delta Airlines, Los Angeles *Also called Delta Air Lines Inc (P-5041)*
Delta Airlines, Los Angeles *Also called Delta Air Lines Inc (P-4779)*
Delta America Ltd (HQ)........C......510 668-5100
46101 Fremont Blvd Fremont (94538) *(P-7466)*
Delta Blood Bank........D......209 943-3830
1900 W Orangeburg Ave Modesto (95350) *(P-22782)*
Delta Blood Bank (HQ)........D......800 244-6794
65 N Commerce St Stockton (95202) *(P-22783)*
Delta Brands Inc........D......209 522-9044
3700 Finch Rd Modesto (95357) *(P-8992)*
Delta Breeze Farming Inc........C......916 775-2055
11566 State Highway 160 Courtland (95615) *(P-334)*
Delta Computer Consulting........C......310 541-9440
25550 Hawthorne Blvd # 106 Torrance (90505) *(P-16345)*
Delta Creative Inc........C......800 423-4135
2690 Pellissier Pl City of Industry (90601) *(P-7950)*
Delta Dental of California........B......619 683-2549
1450 Frazee Rd Ste 200 San Diego (92108) *(P-10199)*
Delta Dental of California (PA)........B......415 972-8300
560 Mission St Fl 13 San Francisco (94105) *(P-10200)*
Delta Dental of California........A......916 853-7373
11155 International Dr Sacramento (95826) *(P-10201)*
Delta Dental Plan, Sacramento *Also called Delta Dental of California (P-10201)*
Delta Disposal Service Co, Tracy *Also called Tracy Dlta Solid Waste Mgt Inc (P-6483)*
Delta Electronics Americas Ltd (HQ)........D......510 668-5100
46101 Fremont Blvd Fremont (94538) *(P-7467)*
Delta Floral Distributors Inc........C......323 751-8116
6810 West Blvd Los Angeles (90043) *(P-9133)*
Delta Galil USA Inc........D......949 296-0380
16912 Von Karman Ave Irvine (92606) *(P-8298)*
Delta Growers, Stockton *Also called Heritage Land Company Inc (P-266)*
Delta Hawkeye Security Inc........D......209 957-3333
7400 Shoreline Dr Ste 2 Stockton (95219) *(P-16627)*
Delta Health Systems, Stockton *Also called Wm Michael Stemler Inc (P-10834)*
Delta Hlth Care MGT Svcs Corp (PA)........D......209 444-8300
4662 Precissi Ln Ste 200 Stockton (95207) *(P-22566)*
Delta Max........E......949 759-8529
23 Curl Dr Corona Del Mar (92625) *(P-16346)*
Delta Nrsing Rhabilitation Ctr, Visalia *Also called Delta Nrsing Rhbilitation Hosp (P-20374)*
Delta Nrsing Rhbilitation Hosp........D......559 625-4003
514 N Bridge St Visalia (93291) *(P-20374)*
Delta One Security Inc........D......707 425-9346
342 Acacia St Fairfield (94533) *(P-16628)*
Delta Personnel Services Inc........D......925 356-3034
1820 Galindo St Ste 3 Concord (94520) *(P-16629)*
Delta PHI Chapter, Goleta *Also called Gamma PHI Beta Sorority Inc (P-13475)*
Delta Products, Fremont *Also called Delta America Ltd (P-7466)*
Delta Protective Services, Stockton *Also called Borgens & Borgens Inc (P-16584)*
Delta Rescue Inc........D......661 269-4010
P.O. Box 9 Glendale (91209) *(P-25416)*
Delta Scientific Corporation (PA)........C......661 575-1100
40355 Delta Ln Palmdale (93551) *(P-16886)*
Delta Tech Service Inc (PA)........D......707 745-2080
397 W Channel Rd Benicia (94510) *(P-14252)*
Delta Truck Center, French Camp *Also called Fresno Truck Center (P-6594)*
Delta-T Group Inc........A......619 543-0556
4420 Hotel Circle Ct # 205 San Diego (92108) *(P-22283)*
Deluxe Auto Carriers Inc........D......909 746-0900
4788 Brookhollow Cir Jurupa Valley (92509) *(P-4001)*
Deluxe Digital Dist Inc........E......818 260-6202
2400 W Empire Ave Ste 200 Los Angeles (90027) *(P-18186)*
Deluxe Entrmt Svcs Group Inc (PA)........D......818 565-3600
2400 W Empire Ave Ste 200 Burbank (91504) *(P-18430)*
Deluxe Laboratories Inc (HQ)........A......323 462-6171
2400 W Empire Ave Ste 200 Burbank (91504) *(P-18187)*
Deluxe Media Services........B......818 526-3700
2130 N Hollywood Way Burbank (91505) *(P-16117)*
Deluxe Media Services LLC........A......323 462-6171
1377 N Serrano Ave Los Angeles (90027) *(P-18039)*
Demand Chain Inc........C......800 466-3786
301 Howard St Fl 20 San Francisco (94105) *(P-7035)*
Demand Media, Santa Monica *Also called Leaf Group Ltd (P-13948)*
Demandbase Inc (PA)........D......415 683-2660
680 Folsom St Ste 400 San Francisco (94107) *(P-15647)*
Demandtec LLC........B......914 499-1900
1 Franklin Pkwy Bldg 910 San Mateo (94403) *(P-15100)*
Demaria Landtech........E......858 481-5500
5631 Palmer Way Ste C Carlsbad (92010) *(P-823)*
Demaria Landtech Inc........E......858 481-5500
2789 High Mead Cir Vista (92084) *(P-824)*
Demenno Kerdoon........C......310 537-7100
2000 N Alameda St Compton (90222) *(P-1043)*
Demenno-Kerdoon........B......310 898-3848
1300 S Santa Fe Ave Compton (90221) *(P-4002)*
Demko Drywall & Demolition Co........E......619 590-0025
419 S Marshall Ave El Cajon (92020) *(P-2873)*
Demler Armstrong & Rowland LLP........E......562 597-0029
4500 E Pacific Cst Hwy # 400 Long Beach (90804) *(P-23029)*
Demler Egg Ranch........E......661 758-4577
28198 Gromer Ave Wasco (93280) *(P-430)*
Demo Deluxe, Yorba Linda *Also called IMG (P-17232)*
Dena Corp........D......415 375-3170
185 Berry St Ste 3000 San Francisco (94107) *(P-15101)*
Denios Roseville Farmers........C......916 782-2704
2013 Opportunity Dr Roseville (95678) *(P-17130)*
Denken Solutions Inc........C......949 630-5263
220 Technology Dr Ste 220 # 220 Irvine (92618) *(P-15102)*
Dennett Tile & Stone Inc........E......707 541-3700
4536 Bennett View Dr Santa Rosa (95404) *(P-2994)*
Dennis & Leen, Los Angeles *Also called EC Group Inc (P-6720)*
Dennis Allen Associates (PA)........D......805 884-8777
201 N Milpas St Santa Barbara (93103) *(P-1154)*
Dennis Blazona Construction........D......916 375-8337
525 Harbor Blvd Ste 10 West Sacramento (95691) *(P-3247)*
Dennis Foland Inc........D......909 930-9900
1500 S Hellman Ave Ontario (91761) *(P-8027)*
Dennis Hyde Construction Inc........D......661 393-1077
7112 Darrin Ave Bakersfield (93308) *(P-1155)*
Dennis M McCoy & Sons Inc (PA)........D......818 874-3872
32107 Lindero Canyon Rd # 212 Westlake Village (91361) *(P-1756)*
Denova Home Sales Inc........D......925 852-0545
1500 Willow Pass Ct Concord (94520) *(P-11397)*
Denova Homes, Concord *Also called Denova Home Sales Inc (P-11397)*
Denso Pdts & Svcs Americas Inc (HQ)........C......310 834-6352
3900 Via Oro Ave Long Beach (90810) *(P-6633)*
Dental, San Diego *Also called Veterans Health Administration (P-20143)*
Dental Office, Oxnard *Also called Clinicas Del Camino Real Inc (P-22533)*
Dentalville, Panorama City *Also called Leonid M Glosman DDS A D (P-20125)*
Dentistat Inc........D......408 376-0336
1688 Dell Ave Ste 210 Campbell (95008) *(P-27214)*
Dentists Insurance Company (HQ)........C......916 443-4567
1201 K St Ste 1600 Sacramento (95814) *(P-10604)*
Dentons US LLP........D......650 798-0300
1530 Page Mill Rd Ste 200 Palo Alto (94304) *(P-23030)*
Dentons US LLP........C......949 732-3700
4675 Macarthur Ct # 1250 Newport Beach (92660) *(P-23031)*
Dentons US LLP........D......619 595-5400
750 B St Ste 3300 San Diego (92101) *(P-23032)*
Dentons US LLP........B......619 236-1414
4655 Executive Dr Ste 700 San Diego (92121) *(P-23033)*
Dentons US LLP........C......415 882-5000
1 Market Plz Fl 24 San Francisco (94105) *(P-23034)*
Dentons US LLP........C......213 623-9300
601 S Figueroa St # 2500 Los Angeles (90017) *(P-23035)*
Dentons US LLP........C......213 688-1000
300 S Grand Ave Fl 14 Los Angeles (90071) *(P-23036)*
Denver D Darling Inc........D......714 761-8299
8402 Katella Ave Stanton (90680) *(P-1390)*
Department Behavioral Health, Fresno *Also called County of Fresno (P-22542)*
Department Child Support Svcs, Camarillo *Also called County of Ventura (P-23759)*
Department Children Fmly Svcs, Los Angeles *Also called County of Los Angeles (P-23680)*

ALPHABETIC

Employee Codes: A=Over 500 employees, B=251-500
C=101-250, D=51-100, E=50
2019 Directory of California
Wholesalers and Services Companies
© Mergent Inc. 1-800-342-5647
1277

Department Health Care Svcs ....D......510 412-3700
  850 Marina Bay Pkwy Richmond (94804) *(P-22075)*
Department of Ane, Sacramento *Also called University California Davis* *(P-21885)*
Department of Cultural Affairs, Los Angeles *Also called City of Los Angeles* *(P-25411)*
Department of Health, Los Angeles *Also called County of Los Angeles* *(P-22776)*
Department of Health Services, Los Angeles *Also called County of Los Angeles* *(P-22013)*
Department of Health Services, Martinez *Also called County of Contra Costa* *(P-21349)*
Department of Health Services, Concord *Also called County of Contra Costa* *(P-22541)*
Department of Mental Health, Los Angeles *Also called County of Los Angeles* *(P-16215)*
Department of Mental Health, Willows *Also called County of Glenn* *(P-22543)*
Department of Public Safety, Stanford *Also called Leland Stanford Junior Univ* *(P-2631)*
Department of Public Works, Alhambra *Also called County of Los Angeles* *(P-6234)*
Department of Public Works, Mill Valley *Also called City of Mill Valley* *(P-1744)*
Department of Public Works, San Rafael *Also called County of Marin* *(P-25628)*
Department of Regional Parks, Sacramento *Also called County of Sacramento* *(P-18795)*
Department of Social Services, Alturas *Also called County of Modoc* *(P-23692)*
Department of Social Services, San Luis Obispo *Also called County of San Luis Obispo* *(P-23732)*
Department of Social Services, Paso Robles *Also called County of Los Angeles* *(P-23670)*
Department of Social Services, Placerville *Also called County of El Dorado* *(P-23637)*
Department of Transportation, Ukiah *Also called County of Mendocino* *(P-4883)*
Department of Urology, San Francisco *Also called University Cal San Francisco* *(P-21881)*
Department Public Social Svcs, Cudahy *Also called County of Los Angeles* *(P-24769)*
Dependable Aircargo Ex Inc ....C......310 537-2000
  19201 S Susana Rd Compton (90221) *(P-5042)*
Dependable Disposal and Recycl, Spring Valley *Also called Burns and Sons Trucking Inc* *(P-3982)*
Dependable Furniture Mfrs, San Francisco *Also called Van Sark Inc* *(P-6739)*
Dependable Highway Express Inc ....D......909 923-0065
  1351 S Campus Ave Ontario (91761) *(P-4124)*
Dependable Highway Express Inc ....C......209 342-0184
  1343 Lone Palm Ave Modesto (95351) *(P-4125)*
Dependable Highway Express Inc ....E......510 357-2223
  3012 Alvarado St San Leandro (94577) *(P-4544)*
Dependable Highway Express Inc (PA) ....B......323 526-2200
  2555 E Olympic Blvd Los Angeles (90023) *(P-4126)*
Dependable Highway Express Inc ....D......510 357-2223
  3199 Alvarado St San Leandro (94577) *(P-4127)*
Dependable Highway Express Inc ....E......916 374-0782
  830 E St West Sacramento (95605) *(P-4003)*
Deployment Solutions LLC ....E......317 281-9682
  332 Bandini Pl Vista (92083) *(P-2564)*
Depo Auto Parts, Fontana *Also called Maxzone Vehicle Lighting Corp* *(P-6656)*
Deposition Sciences Inc ....D......707 573-6700
  3300 Coffey Ln Santa Rosa (95403) *(P-26353)*
Depot, Porterville *Also called Tharp Truck Rental Inc* *(P-17996)*
Dept Children and Family Svcs, Lakewood *Also called County of Los Angeles* *(P-23660)*
Dept of Building Inspection, Salinas *Also called County of Monterey* *(P-17107)*
Dept of Child Support, Stockton *Also called County of San Joaquin* *(P-23729)*
Dept of Community Services, Bell *Also called City of Bell* *(P-23577)*
Dept of Maintenance, Antioch *Also called City of Antioch* *(P-6530)*
Dept of Mental Health, Woodland *Also called County of Yolo* *(P-22561)*
Dept of Public Works, Irvine *Also called City of Irvine* *(P-27194)*
Dept of Social Services, Eureka *Also called County of Humboldt* *(P-23644)*
Dept of Social Services Dss, San Luis Obispo *Also called County of San Luis Obispo* *(P-23733)*
Der Manouel Insurance Group, Fresno *Also called Hub Intrntional Insur Svcs Inc* *(P-10648)*
Derek Silva Community, San Francisco *Also called Catholic Chrts Cyo Archdiocs* *(P-23542)*
Derjjan Associates Inc (PA) ....C......831 423-4111
  2025 Soquel Ave Santa Cruz (95062) *(P-26837)*
Des Architects + Engineers Inc ....C......650 364-6453
  399 Bradford St Ste 300 Redwood City (94063) *(P-26042)*
Deser Sands Unifi Schoo Distr ....D......760 777-4200
  47950 Dune Palms Rd La Quinta (92253) *(P-24313)*
Deseret Farms of California, Chico *Also called Agreserves Inc* *(P-184)*
Deseret Industries, Sacramento *Also called Corporation of The President* *(P-24172)*
Desert Aids Project (PA) ....D......760 323-2118
  1695 N Sunrise Way Bldg 1 Palm Springs (92262) *(P-23767)*
Desert Air Conditioning Inc ....E......760 323-3383
  590 S Williams Rd Palm Springs (92264) *(P-3149)*
Desert Area Resources Training ....D......760 375-8494
  201 E Ridgecrest Blvd Ridgecrest (93555) *(P-24774)*
Desert Arts Center ....D......760 323-7973
  550 N Palm Canyon Dr Palm Springs (92262) *(P-24880)*
Desert Cardiology Cons Med G, Rancho Mirage *Also called Desert Cardiology Consultants* *(P-19435)*
Desert Cardiology Consultants ....D......760 346-0642
  39000 Bob Hope Dr Rancho Mirage (92270) *(P-19435)*
Desert Cities Dialysis, Victorville *Also called Jamboor Medical Corporation* *(P-22480)*
Desert Cncpts Ldscpg Maint Inc ....C......760 200-9007
  79469 Country Club Dr I Bermuda Dunes (92203) *(P-749)*
Desert Coastal Transport Inc (PA) ....D......909 357-3395
  10686 Banana Ave Fontana (92337) *(P-4128)*
Desert Dental Group, Victorville *Also called Joseph A Foroosh Dental Corp* *(P-20120)*
Desert Falls Country Club Inc ....D......760 340-5646
  1111 Desert Falls Pkwy Palm Desert (92211) *(P-18911)*
Desert Haven Enterprises Inc (PA) ....A......661 948-8402
  43437 Copeland Cir Lancaster (93535) *(P-825)*
Desert Haven Enterprises Inc ....B......661 948-8402
  43437 Copeland Cir Lancaster (93535) *(P-826)*
DESERT HORIZONS COUNTRY CLUB, Indian Wells *Also called Dhccnp* *(P-18913)*
Desert Hot Springs Real Proper ....D......760 329-6000
  10805 Palm Dr Desert Hot Springs (92240) *(P-10867)*

Desert Hot Springs Spa Hotel, Desert Hot Springs *Also called Whatever It Takes Inc* *(P-13397)*
Desert Hot Springs Spa Hotel, Desert Hot Springs *Also called Desert Hot Springs Real Proper* *(P-10867)*
Desert Knlls Convalescent Hosp, Victorville *Also called Knolls Convalescent Hospital* *(P-20568)*
Desert Knolls Convalescent, Victorville *Also called Knolls Convalescent Hospital* *(P-20569)*
Desert Manor Care Center LP ....D......760 365-0717
  8515 Cholla Ave Yucca Valley (92284) *(P-24503)*
Desert Mechanical Inc ....A......702 873-7333
  15870 Olden St Sylmar (91342) *(P-2185)*
Desert Medical Group Inc (PA) ....C......760 320-8814
  275 N El Cielo Rd D-402 Palm Springs (92262) *(P-19436)*
Desert Medical Group Inc ....C......760 323-8657
  275 N El Cielo Rd Ste C Palm Springs (92262) *(P-19437)*
Desert Oaks Apartments, Visalia *Also called Kern 2008 Cmnty Partners LP* *(P-1299)*
Desert Oasis Healthcare, Palm Springs *Also called Desert Medical Group Inc* *(P-19436)*
Desert Orthopdc Center A Mdcl (PA) ....D......760 568-2684
  39000 Bob Hope Dr W301 Rancho Mirage (92270) *(P-19438)*
Desert Princess Hoa, Cathedral City *Also called Desert Prncess Homeowners Assn* *(P-25151)*
Desert Princess Home ....E......760 322-1655
  28555 Landau Blvd Cathedral City (92234) *(P-18912)*
Desert Prncess Homeowners Assn ....D......760 322-1907
  28555 Landau Blvd Cathedral City (92234) *(P-25151)*
Desert Recreation District (PA) ....D......760 347-3484
  45305 Oasis St Indio (92201) *(P-19157)*
Desert Recycling Inc ....E......760 948-3122
  17105 Mesa St Hesperia (92345) *(P-6388)*
Desert Regional Med Ctr Inc (HQ) ....A......760 323-6511
  1150 N Indian Canyon Dr Palm Springs (92262) *(P-21364)*
Desert Regional Med Ctr Inc ....C......760 323-6640
  1695 N Sunrise Way Palm Springs (92262) *(P-22017)*
Desert Resort Management ....D......760 831-0172
  42635 Melanie Pl Ste 103 Palm Desert (92211) *(P-11398)*
Desert Rose Golf Course, Cathedral City *Also called American Golf Corporation* *(P-18833)*
Desert Springs Healthcare, Indio *Also called Indio Hlthcare Wllness Ctr LLC* *(P-20542)*
Desert Springs Hotel ....E......760 251-3399
  10805 Palm Dr Desert Hot Springs (92240) *(P-10868)*
Desert Star Co ....E......661 259-5848
  23119 Drayton St Saugus (91350) *(P-8925)*
Desert Sun Science Center, The, Idyllwild *Also called Guided Discoveries Inc* *(P-13450)*
Desert Television LLC ....D......760 343-5700
  73185 Highway 111 Ste D Palm Desert (92260) *(P-5782)*
Desert Valley Date Inc ....E......760 398-0999
  86740 Industrial Way Coachella (92236) *(P-506)*
Desert Valley Hospital Inc (HQ) ....C......760 241-8000
  16850 Bear Valley Rd Victorville (92395) *(P-21365)*
DESERT VALLEY INDUSTRIES, Palm Desert *Also called Desertarc* *(P-23768)*
Desert Valley Med Group Inc ....D......760 245-2474
  12401 Hesperia Rd Ste 9 Victorville (92395) *(P-19439)*
Desert Valley Med Group Inc (PA) ....B......760 241-8000
  16850 Bear Valley Rd Victorville (92395) *(P-19440)*
Desert View Auto Auctions Inc (PA) ....C......760 788-6955
  14280 Danielson St A Poway (92064) *(P-6590)*
Desert View Funeral Home ....E......760 244-0007
  11478 Amargosa Rd Victorville (92392) *(P-13689)*
Desert Water Agency Fing Corp ....D......760 323-4971
  1200 S Gene Autry Trl Palm Springs (92264) *(P-6238)*
Desert Willow Golf Course, Palm Desert *Also called Desert Willow Golf Resort Inc* *(P-18706)*
Desert Willow Golf Resort Inc ....C......760 346-0015
  38995 Desert Willow Dr Palm Desert (92260) *(P-18706)*
Desertarc ....B......760 346-1611
  73255 Country Club Dr Palm Desert (92260) *(P-23768)*
Design Collection Inc ....D......323 277-9200
  2209 S Santa Fe Ave Los Angeles (90058) *(P-8225)*
Design Machine and Mfg ....E......559 897-7374
  2491 Simpson St Kingsburg (93631) *(P-17943)*
Design Masonry Inc ....D......661 252-2784
  20703 Santa Clara St Canyon Country (91351) *(P-2802)*
Designed MBL Systems Inds Inc ....C......209 892-6298
  800 S State Highway 33 Patterson (95363) *(P-1518)*
Designers LLC (PA) ....D......209 982-0600
  235 Frank West Cir Stockton (95206) *(P-13577)*
Desilva Gates Construction LP ....C......916 386-9708
  7700 College Town Dr # 230 Sacramento (95826) *(P-1757)*
Desilva Gates Construction LP (PA) ....D......925 361-1380
  11555 Dublin Blvd Dublin (94568) *(P-1758)*
Desmond Mail Delivery Service ....D......323 262-1085
  4600 Worth St Los Angeles (90063) *(P-4004)*
Destination Moon LP ....D......415 675-7777
  615 Battery St Fl 6 San Francisco (94111) *(P-14111)*
Destination Residences LLC ....E......760 346-4647
  45750 San Luis Rey Ave Palm Desert (92260) *(P-12518)*
Destination Residences LLC ....B......858 550-1000
  9700 N Torrey Pines Rd La Jolla (92037) *(P-13739)*
Destination Science LLC ....C......714 289-9100
  953 N Elm St Orange (92867) *(P-27705)*
Destination Shuttle Svcs LLC ....C......310 338-9466
  6150 W 96th St Los Angeles (90045) *(P-3645)*
Destination Webcam, La Jolla *Also called Aegis Software Inc* *(P-13964)*
Destiny Arts Center ....E......510 597-1619
  970 Grace Ave Oakland (94608) *(P-19158)*
Deutsch La Inc ....D......310 862-3000
  5454 Beethoven St Los Angeles (90066) *(P-13817)*
Deutsche Bank National Tr Co (HQ) ....D......213 620-8200
  2000 Avenue Of The Stars Los Angeles (90067) *(P-9693)*

Deutsche Bank National Tr Co ....D....714 247-6000
1761 E Saint Andrew Pl Santa Ana (92705) ***(P-12093)***
Deutsche Bank National Tr Co ....D....714 247-6054
1761 E Saint Andrew Pl Santa Ana (92705) ***(P-9665)***
Deutsche Bank Tr Co Americas ....C....415 617-4200
101 California St # 4500 San Francisco (94111) ***(P-9949)***
Deutsche Inv MGT Americas Inc ....E....415 648-9408
101 California St # 2400 San Francisco (94111) ***(P-10076)***
Devcon Construction Inc (PA) ....B....408 942-8200
690 Gibraltar Dr Milpitas (95035) ***(P-1391)***
Develop Disabilities Svc Org ....D....916 973-1951
2331 Saint Marks Way G1 Sacramento (95864) ***(P-23769)***
Develop Point Education ....E....805 624-6171
9909 Topanga Canyon Blvd # 346 Chatsworth (91311) ***(P-13740)***
Developers Surety Indemnity Co, Irvine *Also called Insco Insurance Services Inc* ***(P-10650)***
Developers Surety Indemnity Co (HQ) ....D....949 263-3300
17771 Cowan Ste 100 Irvine (92614) ***(P-10426)***
Development Exchange, Mountain View *Also called Devxcom Inc* ***(P-5545)***
Development Resource Cons Inc (PA) ....D....714 685-6860
160 S Old Springs Rd # 210 Anaheim (92808) ***(P-25642)***
Developmental Svcs Cal Dept ....A....559 782-2222
26501 Avenue 140 Porterville (93257) ***(P-20375)***
Developmental Svcs Cal Dept ....A....408 451-6000
3500 Zanker Rd San Jose (95134) ***(P-20928)***
Developmental Svcs Cal Dept ....A....714 957-5151
2501 Harbor Blvd Costa Mesa (92626) ***(P-24179)***
Developmental Svcs Continuum ....D....619 460-7333
7944 Golden Ave Lemon Grove (91945) ***(P-24504)***
Developmentally Research Ctr, San Marcos *Also called San Diego-Imperial Counties De* ***(P-24015)***
Develpment Dimensions Intl Inc ....B....925 361-4246
4160 Dublin Blvd Ste 450 Dublin (94568) ***(P-27215)***
Devereux California Center, Goleta *Also called Devereux Foundation* ***(P-22567)***
Devereux Center In California, Goleta *Also called Devereux Foundation* ***(P-12094)***
Devereux Foundation ....B....805 968-2525
7055 Seaway Dr Goleta (93117) ***(P-22567)***
Devereux Foundation ....B....805 968-2525
El Colegio Rd Goleta (93117) ***(P-12094)***
Device Anywhere ....D....650 655-6400
777 Mariners Isl Blvd # 250 San Mateo (94404) ***(P-15103)***
Devincenzi Concrete Cnstr ....E....707 568-4370
3276 Dutton Ave Santa Rosa (95407) ***(P-3248)***
Devine & Son Trucking Co Inc (PA) ....C....559 486-7440
3870 Channel Dr West Sacramento (95691) ***(P-4704)***
Devine Intermodal, West Sacramento *Also called Devine & Son Trucking Co Inc* ***(P-4704)***
Devonshire Care Center LLC ....D....951 925-2571
1350 E Devonshire Ave Hemet (92544) ***(P-20376)***
Devxcom Inc ....E....650 390-6553
310 Villa St Mountain View (94041) ***(P-5545)***
Dewhurst & Associates ....D....858 456-5345
7533 Girard Ave La Jolla (92037) ***(P-1156)***
Dewmobile USA Inc ....E....408 550-2818
2901 Tasman Dr Ste 107 Santa Clara (95054) ***(P-15104)***
Dewolf Realty Co Inc ....D....415 221-2032
4330 California St San Francisco (94118) ***(P-26838)***
Dex Corporation ....C....805 388-1711
3600 Via Pescador Camarillo (93012) ***(P-25643)***
Dexyp, Glendale *Also called Yellowpagescom LLC* ***(P-17603)***
Deyoung Museum, San Francisco *Also called Corportion of Fine Arts Mseums* ***(P-24878)***
Dfa of California ....C....530 345-5077
6100 Wilson Landing Rd Chico (95973) ***(P-25417)***
Dfa of California ....D....209 465-2289
1050 Diamond St Stockton (95205) ***(P-17131)***
Dfds International Corporation ....D....310 414-1516
898 N Pacific Coast Hwy # 6 El Segundo (90245) ***(P-5043)***
Dfds Transport US, El Segundo *Also called Dfds International Corporation* ***(P-5043)***
DFI Technologies LLC ....D....916 568-1234
1065 National Dr Ste 1 Sacramento (95834) ***(P-7036)***
Dfs Flooring Inc (PA) ....C....818 374-5200
15651 Saticoy St Van Nuys (91406) ***(P-3100)***
Dfusion Software Inc ....E....323 617-5577
5900 Wilshire Blvd # 2550 Los Angeles (90036) ***(P-15105)***
Dg Architects Inc (PA) ....D....650 943-1660
550 Ellis St Mountain View (94043) ***(P-26043)***
Dga Plnning L Arch L Interiors, Mountain View *Also called Dg Architects Inc* ***(P-26043)***
Dga Services Inc (PA) ....D....408 232-4800
1075 Montague Expy Milpitas (95035) ***(P-4343)***
Dgwb Inc ....D....714 881-2300
217 N Main St Ste 200 Santa Ana (92701) ***(P-13818)***
Dgwb Advg & Communications, Santa Ana *Also called Dgwb Inc* ***(P-13818)***
Dgwb Ventures LLC ....D....714 881-2308
217 N Main St Ste 200 Santa Ana (92701) ***(P-13819)***
DH Smith Company Inc ....D....408 532-7617
6000 Hellyer Ave Ste 150 San Jose (95138) ***(P-2874)***
Dhap Digital Inc ....E....415 962-4900
235 Montgomery St # 1320 San Francisco (94104) ***(P-15106)***
Dharne & Company ....D....949 293-5675
19200 Von Karman Ave # 400 Irvine (92612) ***(P-16347)***
Dhccnp ....D....760 340-4646
44900 Desert Horizons Dr Indian Wells (92210) ***(P-18913)***
Dhe, Ontario *Also called Dependable Highway Express Inc* ***(P-4124)***
Dhe, San Leandro *Also called Dependable Highway Express Inc* ***(P-4127)***
Dhl Express (usa) Inc ....D....415 826-7338
401 23rd St San Francisco (94107) ***(P-4816)***
Dhl Supply Chain (usa) ....C....415 531-0596
485 Valley Dr Brisbane (94005) ***(P-5044)***
Dhl Supply Chain (usa) ....E....909 350-6976
9211 Kaiser Way Fontana (92335) ***(P-4545)***
Dhl Supply Chain (usa) ....D....510 784-7360
2391 W Winton Ave Hayward (94545) ***(P-4546)***
Dhl Supply Chain (usa) ....D....623 907-2338
5576 Ontario Mills Pkwy Ontario (91764) ***(P-4547)***
Dhs Consulting Inc ....D....714 276-1135
1820 E 1st St Ste 410 Santa Ana (92705) ***(P-26839)***
Dhs Member Services ....E....562 595-5151
3833 Atlantic Ave Long Beach (90807) ***(P-20115)***
Dhv Industries Inc ....D....661 392-8948
3451 Pegasus Dr Bakersfield (93308) ***(P-7847)***
Dhx-Dependable Hawaiian Ex Inc ....C....510 686-2600
2375 Davis St San Leandro (94577) ***(P-5045)***
Dhx-Dependable Hawaiian Ex Inc (PA) ....C....310 537-2000
19201 S Susana Rd Compton (90221) ***(P-5046)***
Diablo Country Club ....D....925 837-4221
1700 Club House Rd Diablo (94528) ***(P-18914)***
Diablo Country Club ....E....925 837-4221
1700 Clubhouse Rd Diablo (94528) ***(P-18915)***
Diablo Grande Ltd Partnership ....D....209 892-7421
9521 Morton Davis Dr Patterson (95363) ***(P-11871)***
Diablo Landscape Inc ....D....408 487-9620
1655 Berryessa Rd San Jose (95133) ***(P-827)***
Diablo Realty Inc ....E....925 933-9300
975 Ygnacio Valley Rd Walnut Creek (94596) ***(P-11399)***
Diablo Valley Rock, Concord *Also called Carone & Company Inc* ***(P-3417)***
Diablo Vly College Foundation (PA) ....C....925 685-1230
321 Golf Club Rd Pleasant Hill (94523) ***(P-17132)***
Diageo North America Inc ....D....707 939-6200
21468 8th St E Sonoma (95476) ***(P-9037)***
Diageo North America Inc ....D....949 421-3974
30 Journey Aliso Viejo (92656) ***(P-9038)***
Diagnostic and Interventio ....D....310 574-0400
13160 Mindanao Way # 150 Marina Del Rey (90292) ***(P-19441)***
Diagnostic Labs & Rdlgy, Burbank *Also called Kan-Di-Ki LLC* ***(P-22101)***
Diagnstic Med Group Sthern Cal, Arcadia *Also called Chen Dvid MD Dgnstc Med Group* ***(P-7174)***
Dial Communications, Camarillo *Also called Dial Security* ***(P-16887)***
Dial Global Digital, Culver City *Also called Triton Media Group LLC* ***(P-5757)***
Dial Security (PA) ....C....805 389-6700
760 W Ventura Blvd Camarillo (93010) ***(P-16887)***
Dialog Semiconductor Inc ....C....408 327-8800
1515 Wyatt Dr Santa Clara (95054) ***(P-7468)***
Dialysis Centers Ventura Cnty ....D....805 658-9211
4567 Telephone Rd Ste 101 Ventura (93003) ***(P-22472)***
Dialysis Clinic Inc ....E....916 453-0803
1771 Stockton Blvd # 200 Sacramento (95816) ***(P-22473)***
Diamond Bar Golf Course, Diamond Bar *Also called American Golf Corporation* ***(P-18836)***
Diamond Bar Medical Offices, Diamond Bar *Also called Kaiser Foundation Hospitals* ***(P-19553)***
Diamond Environmental Svcs LP ....D....760 744-7191
807 E Mission Rd San Marcos (92069) ***(P-14499)***
Diamond Intl Investment LLC ....D....559 226-2200
3737 N Blackstone Ave Fresno (93726) ***(P-12519)***
Diamond Learning Center Inc ....D....559 241-0580
1620 W Fairmont Ave Fresno (93705) ***(P-23770)***
Diamond Mike Plbg Htg AC Elec, Culver City *Also called Mike Diamond Plumbing Inc* ***(P-2281)***
Diamond Mountain Casino ....C....530 252-1100
900 Skyline Dr Susanville (96130) ***(P-12520)***
Diamond Products LLC (PA) ....C....818 772-0100
21350 Lassen St Chatsworth (91311) ***(P-9211)***
Diamond Reference Laboratory, Pomona *Also called Central Reference Lab Inc* ***(P-22067)***
Diamond Resorts LLC ....D....760 866-1800
2800 S Palm Canyon Dr Palm Springs (92264) ***(P-12521)***
Diamond Ridge Corporation ....C....909 949-0605
121 S Mountain Ave Upland (91786) ***(P-9799)***
Diamond Ridge Healthcare Ctr, Pittsburg *Also called SSC Pittsburg Operating Co LP* ***(P-21220)***
Diamond W Floorcovering, City of Industry *Also called W Diamond Supply Co* ***(P-6803)***
Diamondpeo LLC ....C....714 728-5186
27442 Calle Arroyo Ste A San Juan Capistrano (92675) ***(P-14601)***
Diamondrock San Dego Tnant LLC ....B....619 239-4500
400 W Broadway San Diego (92101) ***(P-12522)***
Diani Building Corp (PA) ....D....805 925-9533
351 N Blosser Rd Santa Maria (93458) ***(P-1519)***
Dianne Adair Day Care Centers (PA) ....D....925 429-3232
1862 Bailey Rd Concord (94521) ***(P-24314)***
Diaz Plastering Inc ....D....661 244-8228
4900 California Ave 210b Bakersfield (93309) ***(P-2875)***
Diazyme Laboratories Inc ....D....858 455-4754
12889 Gregg Ct Poway (92064) ***(P-22076)***
Dibuduo Dfendis Insur Brks LLC (PA) ....D....559 432-0222
6873 N West Ave Fresno (93711) ***(P-10605)***
Dicalite Minerals Corp ....D....530 335-5451
36994 Summit Lake Rd Burney (96013) ***(P-17944)***
Dicaperl Corporation (HQ) ....D....610 667-6640
23705 Crenshaw Blvd Torrance (90505) ***(P-1102)***
Dick Anderson & Sons Farming ....C....559 945-2511
15900 W Dorris Ave Huron (93234) ***(P-335)***
Dickenson Peatman & Fogarty A (PA) ....E....707 252-7122
1455 1st St Ste 301 NAPA (94559) ***(P-23037)***
Dickinson, Diane MD, Arcata *Also called Northcountry Clinic* ***(P-19718)***
Dickson Testing Co Inc (HQ) ....D....562 862-8378
11126 Palmer Ave South Gate (90280) ***(P-26693)***
Didi Hirsch Community Mental, Culver City *Also called Didi Hirsch Psychiatric Svc* ***(P-23771)***
Didi Hirsch Psychiatric Svc (PA) ....C....310 390-6612
4760 Sepulveda Blvd Culver City (90230) ***(P-23771)***

ALPHABETIC

Diede Construction Inc ....D.......209 369-8255
12393 N Hwy 99 Lodi (95240) ***(P-1520)***
Diehard Security Solutions Inc ....C.......510 995-8450
1151 Harbor Bay Pkwy # 140 Alameda (94502) ***(P-16630)***
Diepenbrock Elkin LLP ....D.......916 492-5000
500 Capitol Mall Ste 650 Sacramento (95814) ***(P-23038)***
Diesel Parts and Service, Long Beach *Also called Harbor Diesel and Eqp Inc* ***(P-7755)***
Diestel Turkey Ranch ....C.......209 984-0826
14111 High Tech Dr C Jamestown (95327) ***(P-437)***
Diestel Turkey Ranch (PA) ....C.......209 532-4950
22200 Lyons Bald Mtn Rd Sonora (95370) ***(P-438)***
Dietrich Post Co Inc ....E.......510 596-0080
945 Bryant St San Francisco (94103) ***(P-8078)***
Dietz Glmor Chazen A Prof Corp (PA) ....E.......858 565-0269
7071 Convoy Ct Ste 300 San Diego (92111) ***(P-23039)***
Diez & Leis RE Group Inc ....D.......916 487-4287
5120 Manzanita Ave # 120 Carmichael (95608) ***(P-11400)***
Digex Inc ....E.......408 468-5000
2950 Zanker Rd San Jose (95134) ***(P-5546)***
Digicentury Corporation ....D.......408 213-0146
2303 Camino Ramon Ste 202 San Ramon (94583) ***(P-15107)***
Digiquest Corp ....E.......951 776-4344
989 Talcey Ter Riverside (92506) ***(P-7037)***
Digital Chocolate Inc ....D.......650 372-1600
1855 S Grant St Ste 200 San Mateo (94402) ***(P-15108)***
Digital Communications Network (PA) ....D.......818 227-3333
6300 Canoga Ave Ste 1625 Woodland Hills (91367) ***(P-5404)***
Digital Domain 30 Inc (PA) ....B.......310 314-2800
12641 Beatrice St Los Angeles (90066) ***(P-18040)***
Digital Film Labs, Los Angeles *Also called Point360* ***(P-18210)***
Digital Foundry Inc ....E.......415 789-1600
1707 Tiburon Blvd Belvedere Tiburon (94920) ***(P-16348)***
Digital Guardian Inc ....B.......408 716-4200
2101 Tasman Dr Ste 210 Santa Clara (95054) ***(P-15109)***
Digital Insight Corporation ....C.......818 879-1010
5601 Lindero Canyon Rd # 100 Westlake Village (91362) ***(P-16216)***
Digital Insight Corporation (HQ) ....C.......818 879-1010
1300 Seaport Blvd Ste 300 Redwood City (94063) ***(P-16217)***
Digital Keystone Inc ....E.......650 938-7301
21631 Stevns Crk Blvd A Cupertino (95014) ***(P-15943)***
Digital Kitchen LLC ....E.......310 499-9255
3585 Hayden Ave Culver City (90232) ***(P-18041)***
Digital Map Products Inc ....D.......949 333-5111
5201 California Ave # 200 Irvine (92617) ***(P-5979)***
Digital Media Management LLC ....D.......323 378-6505
5670 Wilshire Blvd Fl 11 Los Angeles (90036) ***(P-26840)***
Digital Networks Group Inc ....D.......949 428-6333
20382 Hermana Cir Lake Forest (92630) ***(P-15944)***
Digital Path Inc ....E.......800 676-7284
1065 Marauder St Chico (95973) ***(P-5547)***
Digital Realty Trust Inc (PA) ....C.......415 738-6500
4 Embarcadero Ctr # 3200 San Francisco (94111) ***(P-16349)***
Digital Realty Trust LP ....A.......415 738-6500
4 Embarcadero Ctr # 3200 San Francisco (94111) ***(P-12158)***
Digitalist USA Ltd ....A.......949 278-1354
128 Spear St Lbby San Francisco (94105) ***(P-15945)***
Digitalmojo Inc (PA) ....D.......800 413-5916
3111 Camino Del Rio N # 400 San Diego (92108) ***(P-5548)***
Digitalthink Inc (HQ) ....C.......415 625-4000
601 Brannan St San Francisco (94107) ***(P-27216)***
Digitaria, San Diego *Also called Mirum Inc* ***(P-14121)***
Digite Inc ....D.......408 418-3834
21060 Homestead Rd # 220 Cupertino (95014) ***(P-15110)***
Dignity Health ....C.......916 861-1100
3215 Prospect Park Dr Rancho Cordova (95670) ***(P-21366)***
Dignity Health ....B.......213 484-7111
2131 W 3rd St Los Angeles (90057) ***(P-21367)***
Dignity Health ....C.......916 983-7400
1650 Creekside Dr Folsom (95630) ***(P-21368)***
Dignity Health ....B.......805 739-3000
1400 E Church St Santa Maria (93454) ***(P-21369)***
Dignity Health ....E.......916 681-1600
7601 Hospital Dr Ste 103 Sacramento (95823) ***(P-21370)***
Dignity Health ....A.......916 537-5151
6501 Coyle Ave Fl 6 Carmichael (95608) ***(P-21371)***
Dignity Health ....B.......805 384-8071
5051 Verdugo Way Ste 100 Camarillo (93012) ***(P-21372)***
Dignity Health ....D.......805 489-4261
1054 E Grand Ave Ste A Arroyo Grande (93420) ***(P-22284)***
Dignity Health ....C.......916 851-2153
3400 Data Dr Rancho Cordova (95670) ***(P-21373)***
Dignity Health ....B.......805 473-7626
345 S Halcyon Rd Arroyo Grande (93420) ***(P-21374)***
Dignity Health ....B.......415 438-5500
1700 Montgomery St # 300 San Francisco (94111) ***(P-21375)***
Dignity Health ....A.......562 491-9000
1050 Linden Ave Long Beach (90813) ***(P-21376)***
Dignity Health (PA) ....C.......415 438-5500
185 Berry St Ste 300 San Francisco (94107) ***(P-21377)***
Dignity Health ....C.......916 667-0000
8120 Timberlake Way # 201 Sacramento (95823) ***(P-19442)***
Dignity Health ....A.......213 748-2411
1401 S Grand Ave Los Angeles (90015) ***(P-21378)***
Dignity Health ....A.......916 537-5000
6501 Coyle Ave Carmichael (95608) ***(P-21379)***
Dignity Health ....C.......209 467-6430
2102 N California St Stockton (95204) ***(P-22077)***
Dignity Health ....D.......661 832-8300
2301 Ashe Rd Bakersfield (93309) ***(P-24315)***

Dignity Health ....B.......916 983-7400
1650 Creekside Dr Folsom (95630) ***(P-21380)***
Dignity Health ....C.......530 225-6345
2175 Rosaline Ave Ste A Redding (96001) ***(P-21381)***
Dignity Health ....C.......530 666-8828
20 N Cottonwood St Woodland (95695) ***(P-21382)***
Dignity Health ....A.......831 462-7700
1555 Soquel Dr Santa Cruz (95065) ***(P-21383)***
Dignity Health ....C.......209 754-3521
768 Mountain Ranch Rd San Andreas (95249) ***(P-21384)***
Dignity Health ....C.......916 423-5940
7500 Hospital Dr Sacramento (95823) ***(P-21385)***
Dignity Health ....A.......916 453-4545
4001 J St Sacramento (95819) ***(P-21386)***
Dignity Health ....E.......916 851-3800
3400 Data Dr Rancho Cordova (95670) ***(P-4548)***
Dignity Health ....C.......805 739-3830
124 S College Dr Santa Maria (93454) ***(P-22285)***
Dignity Health ....C.......805 739-3650
1530 Cypress Way Santa Maria (93454) ***(P-20377)***
Dignity Health ....E.......661 663-6767
551 Shanley Ct Bakersfield (93311) ***(P-21387)***
Dignity Health ....D.......916 983-7988
1600 Creekside Dr # 3700 Folsom (95630) ***(P-19443)***
Dignity Health ....C.......805 389-5800
2309 Antonio Ave Camarillo (93010) ***(P-21388)***
Dignity Health ....A.......916 423-3000
7500 Hospital Dr Sacramento (95823) ***(P-21389)***
Dignity Health ....A.......805 739-3100
505 Plaza Dr Santa Maria (93454) ***(P-21390)***
Dignity Health ....A.......805 988-2500
1600 N Rose Ave Oxnard (93030) ***(P-21391)***
Dignity Health ....A.......415 668-1000
450 Stanyan St San Francisco (94117) ***(P-21392)***
Dignity Health ....E.......209 943-4663
2333 W March Ln Ste B Stockton (95207) ***(P-22286)***
Dignity Health ....C.......661 632-5279
400 Old River Rd Bakersfield (93311) ***(P-21393)***
Dignity Health ....A.......916 453-4453
4001 J St Sacramento (95819) ***(P-22078)***
Dignity Health ....D.......916 536-2420
8350 Auburn Blvd Ste 200 Citrus Heights (95610) ***(P-19444)***
Dignity Health ....B.......661 632-5000
2215 Truxtun Ave Bakersfield (93301) ***(P-21394)***
Dignity Health Med Foundation ....D.......916 681-6300
6615 Valley Hi Dr Sacramento (95823) ***(P-22784)***
Dignity Health Med Foundation ....D.......831 475-8834
1667 Dominican Way # 134 Santa Cruz (95065) ***(P-22785)***
Dignity Health Med Foundation ....D.......831 535-1560
9515 Soquel Dr Ste 100 Aptos (95003) ***(P-22786)***
Dignity Health Med Foundation ....A.......916 379-2840
3400 Data Dr Rancho Cordova (95670) ***(P-22787)***
Dignity Health Med Foundation ....D.......916 787-0404
2110 Prfcional Dr Ste 120 Roseville (95661) ***(P-22788)***
Dignity Health Med Foundation (HQ) ....C.......916 379-2840
3400 Data Dr Rancho Cordova (95670) ***(P-21395)***
Dignity Health Medical Grp, Santa Cruz *Also called Dignity Health Med Foundation* ***(P-22785)***
Dignity Hlth Med Grp-Dominican, Aptos *Also called Dignity Health Med Foundation* ***(P-22786)***
Dignity Hlth Med Grp-Dominican, Rancho Cordova *Also called Dignity Health Med Foundation* ***(P-22787)***
Dignity Hlth Med Grp-Dominican, Rancho Cordova *Also called Dignity Health Med Foundation* ***(P-21395)***
Dilbeck Inc (PA) ....D.......818 790-6774
1030 Foothill Blvd La Canada (91011) ***(P-11401)***
Dilbeck Inc ....D.......818 248-2248
2943 Foothill Blvd La Crescenta (91214) ***(P-11402)***
Dilbeck Inc ....E.......805 379-1880
850 Hampshire Rd Ste A Westlake Village (91361) ***(P-11403)***
Dilbeck Inc ....D.......626 584-0101
225 E Colorado Blvd Pasadena (91101) ***(P-11404)***
Dilbeck Realtors, La Canada *Also called Dilbeck Inc* ***(P-11401)***
Dilbeck Realtors, Westlake Village *Also called Dilbeck Inc* ***(P-11403)***
Dilbeck Realtors, Pasadena *Also called Dilbeck Inc* ***(P-11404)***
Dimare Company, Newman *Also called Dimare Enterprises Inc* ***(P-48)***
Dimare Enterprises Inc (PA) ....C.......209 827-2900
1406 N St Newman (95360) ***(P-48)***
Dimare Fresh ....B.......916 921-6302
4050 Pell Cir Sacramento (95838) ***(P-8666)***
Dimension Data Cloud Solutions (HQ) ....D.......408 567-2000
5201 Great America Pkwy # 122 Santa Clara (95054) ***(P-15111)***
Dimension Data North Amer Inc ....D.......925 226-8378
5000 Hopyard Rd Pleasanton (94588) ***(P-15946)***
Dimension Development Two LLC ....D.......619 233-8408
1531 Pacific Hwy San Diego (92101) ***(P-12523)***
Dimension Development Two LLC ....D.......858 485-9250
11611 Bernardo Plaza Ct San Diego (92128) ***(P-12524)***
Dincloud Inc ....D.......310 929-1101
27520 Hawthorne Blvd # 185 Rllng HLS Est (90274) ***(P-15648)***
Dinuba Medical Center, Dinuba *Also called Dinuba Medical Clinic* ***(P-19445)***
Dinuba Medical Clinic (PA) ....D.......559 591-1820
271 N L St Dinuba (93618) ***(P-19445)***
Dinyari Construction Inc ....E.......408 289-5400
500 Phelan Ave San Jose (95112) ***(P-1280)***
Diplomat Packaging, Sylmar *Also called Winning Performance Pdts Inc* ***(P-17598)***
Direct Access Insurance Svcs, Grass Valley *Also called Networked Insurance Agents LLC* ***(P-10699)***
Direct Delivery Center, Ontario *Also called Sears Roebuck and Co* ***(P-17987)***

Mergent e-mail: customerrelations@mergent.com
1280
2019 Directory of California
Wholesalers and Services Companies
(P-0000) Products & Services Section entry number
(PA)=Parent Co (HQ)=Headquarters (DH)=Div Headquarters

Direct Flow Medical Inc (PA)....D....707 576-0420
3945 Freedom Cir Ste 560 Santa Clara (95054) ***(P-22789)***
Direct Partners Inc (HQ)....D....310 482-4200
12777 W Jefferson Blvd # 120 Los Angeles (90066) ***(P-13820)***
Direct Technology, Roseville *Also called Directapps Inc* ***(P-16350)***
Directapps Inc (PA)....C....916 787-2200
3009 Douglas Blvd Ste 300 Roseville (95661) ***(P-16350)***
Directions In Research Inc (PA)....B....619 299-5883
9665 Gran Rdge Dr Ste 550 San Diego (92123) ***(P-26511)***
Directline Technologies Inc....D....209 491-2020
1600 N Carpenter Rd Modesto (95351) ***(P-26512)***
Directorate of Mwr Fmd Usag....D....210 466-1376
420 Montgomery St San Francisco (94104) ***(P-26841)***
Directors Guild America Inc (PA)....C....310 289-2000
7920 W Sunset Blvd # 600 Los Angeles (90046) ***(P-18188)***
Directv Inc....A....888 388-4249
2230 E Imperial Hwy El Segundo (90245) ***(P-5898)***
Directv LLC....D....909 509-4790
1055 E Francis St Ontario (91761) ***(P-5899)***
Directv Enterprises LLC....A....310 535-5000
2230 E Imperial Hwy El Segundo (90245) ***(P-5900)***
Directv Group Inc....C....707 452-7409
340 Commerce Ave Fairfield (94533) ***(P-5901)***
Directv Group Inc....C....510 481-1324
1129 B St San Lorenzo (94580) ***(P-5902)***
Directv Group Holdings LLC (HQ)....C....310 964-5000
2260 E Imperial Hwy El Segundo (90245) ***(P-5903)***
Directv Group Inc (HQ)....C....310 964-5000
2260 E Imperial Hwy El Segundo (90245) ***(P-5904)***
Directv International Inc (HQ)....C....310 964-6460
2230 E Imperial Hwy Fl 10 El Segundo (90245) ***(P-5905)***
Dirt Cheap Demolition Inc....E....619 426-9598
171 Mace St Ste A4 Chula Vista (91911) ***(P-3452)***
Dirt Farmer & Co Inc....D....707 833-2054
9725 Los Guilicos Ave Kenwood (95452) ***(P-139)***
Dirtmarket , The, Campbell *Also called Cem Builders Inc* ***(P-25603)***
Disability Group Inc....B....310 829-5100
1014 23rd St Santa Monica (90403) ***(P-23040)***
Disability Insurance, Stockton *Also called E D D 2100* ***(P-10164)***
Disability Rights California....D....213 213-8000
350 S Bixel St Los Angeles (90017) ***(P-23041)***
Disability Rights California (PA)....D....916 488-9950
1831 K St Sacramento (95811) ***(P-23042)***
Disabled Amrcn Vtrans Dept Cal (PA)....D....562 404-1266
13733 Rosecrans Ave Santa Fe Springs (90670) ***(P-25152)***
Discharge Resource Group....C....650 877-8111
400 Oyster Point Blvd # 440 South San Francisco (94080) ***(P-14848)***
Discount Builders Supply....D....415 285-2800
1695 Mission St San Francisco (94103) ***(P-6820)***
Discount Tire Center, Northridge *Also called Discount Tire Ctr* ***(P-17793)***
Discount Tire Ctr....D....818 993-4758
19545 Parthenia St Ste 3 Northridge (91324) ***(P-17793)***
Discoverready LLC....D....661 284-6401
27200 Tourney Rd Ste 450 Valencia (91355) ***(P-23043)***
Discovery Bay Ctry Club, Byron *Also called New Discovery Inc* ***(P-18986)***
Discovery Bay Golf & Cntry CLB, Byron *Also called New Discovery Inc* ***(P-18740)***
Discovery Communications Inc (PA)....B....310 975-5906
10100 Santa Monica Blvd Los Angeles (90067) ***(P-5980)***
Discovery Plz Med & Admin Offs, Bakersfield *Also called Kaiser Foundation Hospitals* ***(P-19546)***
Discovery Practice Management....E....562 425-6404
4136 Ann Arbor Rd Lakewood (90712) ***(P-19446)***
Discovery Scnce Ctr Ornge Cnty....C....866 552-2823
2500 N Main St Santa Ana (92705) ***(P-18796)***
Discovery Shop, San Jose *Also called American Cancer Soc Cal Div* ***(P-24735)***
Dish Network Corporation....D....909 381-4767
396 Orange Show Ln San Bernardino (92408) ***(P-5906)***
Dish Network Corporation....E....818 334-8740
1297 N Verdugo Rd Glendale (91206) ***(P-5907)***
Dish Network Corporation....E....714 424-0503
2602 Halladay St Santa Ana (92705) ***(P-5908)***
Dish Network Corporation....E....916 381-5084
5671 Warehouse Way Sacramento (95826) ***(P-5909)***
Dish Systems, Irvine *Also called Connect Your Home LLC* ***(P-1509)***
Disney Construction Inc....D....650 689-5149
533 Airport Blvd Ste 120 Burlingame (94010) ***(P-1759)***
Disney Enterprises Inc (HQ)....A....818 560-1000
500 S Buena Vista St Burbank (91521) ***(P-18042)***
Disney Enterprises Inc....A....714 778-6600
1150 W Magic Way Anaheim (92802) ***(P-12525)***
Disney Enterprises Inc....B....818 560-3692
3235 S Buena Vista St Burbank (91521) ***(P-18043)***
Disney Enterprises Inc....B....714 999-0990
1717 S Disneyland Dr Anaheim (92802) ***(P-12526)***
Disney Incorporated (HQ)....C....818 560-1000
500 S Buena Vista St Burbank (91521) ***(P-18044)***
Disney Interactive Studios Inc....C....818 560-1000
601 Circle Seven Dr Glendale (91201) ***(P-15112)***
Disney Interactive Studios Inc....C....818 553-5000
681 W Buena Vista St Burbank (91521) ***(P-15113)***
Disney Interfinance Corp....B....818 560-1000
500 S Buena Vista St Burbank (91521) ***(P-18237)***
Disney Regional Entrmt Inc (HQ)....C....818 560-1000
500 S Buena Vista St Burbank (91521) ***(P-19159)***
Disney Research Pittsburgh....C....412 623-1800
532 Paula Ave Glendale (91201) ***(P-26354)***
Disneyland, Anaheim *Also called Walt Disney Company* ***(P-13377)***
Disneyland Hotel, Anaheim *Also called WCO Hotels Inc* ***(P-13384)***
Disneyland International....C....714 781-4000
105 S Harbor Blvd Anaheim (92805) ***(P-18797)***
Disneyland International....B....714 956-6746
1580 S Disneyland Dr Anaheim (92802) ***(P-12527)***
Disneyland International (HQ)....C....818 560-1000
500 S Buena Vista St Burbank (91521) ***(P-18798)***
Dispatch Commodity Trucking, Fontana *Also called Dispatch Transportation LLC* ***(P-14500)***
Dispatch Office, Oakland *Also called First Transit Inc* ***(P-3655)***
Dispatch Transportation LLC....C....909 355-5531
14032 Santa Ana Ave Fontana (92337) ***(P-14500)***
Dispatch Trucking LLC (PA)....D....909 355-5531
14032 Santa Ana Ave Fontana (92337) ***(P-5047)***
Dist Attorney's Office, Redding *Also called County of Shasta* ***(P-23008)***
Distil Networks Inc....D....415 423-0831
115 Sansome St Ste 600 San Francisco (94104) ***(P-16888)***
Distillery Inc....D....415 505-5446
90 Heron Ct San Quentin (94964) ***(P-15649)***
Distinctive Concrete Inc....E....858 277-9707
9320 Chesapeake Dr # 214 San Diego (92123) ***(P-3249)***
Distribution Alternatives Inc....C....909 673-1000
17820 Slover Ave Bloomington (92316) ***(P-4549)***
Distribution Warehouse, Woodland *Also called Apria Healthcare LLC* ***(P-22735)***
District Attorney, Westminster *Also called County of Orange* ***(P-23697)***
District Attorney, Santa Maria *Also called Santa Barbara County of* ***(P-23366)***
District Attorney, Compton *Also called County of Los Angeles* ***(P-22999)***
District Attorney, Santa Rosa *Also called County of Sonoma* ***(P-23009)***
District Attorney, Van Nuys *Also called County of Los Angeles* ***(P-23003)***
District Attorney's Office, San Francisco *Also called City & County of San Francisco* ***(P-22977)***
District Attroney's Office, San Jose *Also called Santa Clara County of* ***(P-23367)***
District Council DC (PA)....D....510 638-7600
9235 San Leandro St Oakland (94603) ***(P-23772)***
District Office East, Bakersfield *Also called Panama-Buena Vista Un Schl Dst* ***(P-14340)***
District Warehouse, Placentia *Also called Linda Placentia-Yorba* ***(P-4585)***
Distritution Center, Ontario *Also called Converse Inc* ***(P-8353)***
Diva Systems Corporation....C....650 779-3000
800 Saginaw Dr Redwood City (94063) ***(P-5910)***
Divergent Technologies Inc....D....310 339-1186
19601 Hamilton Ave Torrance (90502) ***(P-25644)***
Diverscape Inc....D....951 245-1686
21730 Bundy Canyon Rd Wildomar (92595) ***(P-828)***
Diverse Journeys Inc (PA)....D....310 643-7403
525 S Douglas St Ste 210 El Segundo (90245) ***(P-23773)***
Diversfied Cmmnctions Svcs Inc....D....562 696-9660
1260 Pioneer St Brea (92821) ***(P-5549)***
Diversfied Envmtl Ctalysts Inc (PA)....B....818 994-1908
14645 Keswick St Van Nuys (91405) ***(P-6634)***
Diversified Clinical Services....D....714 579-8400
4225 E La Palma Ave Anaheim (92807) ***(P-22790)***
Diversified Health Svcs Del....E....626 798-6753
2585 E Washington Blvd Pasadena (91107) ***(P-24505)***
Diversified Health Svcs Del (PA)....C....510 231-6200
136 Washington Ave Richmond (94801) ***(P-21059)***
DIVERSIFIED INDUSTRIES, Montclair *Also called Oparc* ***(P-24213)***
Diversified Landscape Co, Wildomar *Also called Diverscape Inc* ***(P-828)***
Diversified Metal Works, Orange *Also called Rika Corporation* ***(P-3395)***
Diversified RE Packaging Corp....A....310 855-1946
1118 S La Cienega Blvd Los Angeles (90035) ***(P-27706)***
Diversified Transport Systems....E....559 268-2760
3150 S Willow Ave Fresno (93725) ***(P-4550)***
Diversified Transportation LLC....D....310 981-9500
6053 W Century Blvd # 900 Los Angeles (90045) ***(P-3646)***
Diversified Trnsp Svcs, Torrance *Also called DTM Services Inc* ***(P-5049)***
Diversified Utility Svcs Inc....B....661 325-3212
3105 Unicorn Rd Bakersfield (93308) ***(P-1915)***
Diversity Bus Solutions Inc....C....909 395-0243
2515 S Euclid Ave Ontario (91762) ***(P-14602)***
Divine Home Care, San Leandro *Also called Wild Karma Inc* ***(P-20891)***
Division 1, Los Angeles *Also called Los Angeles County MTA* ***(P-3669)***
Division 7, Venice *Also called Los Angeles County MTA* ***(P-3677)***
Division 8 Inc....E....619 741-7552
1920 Cordell Ct Ste 105 El Cajon (92020) ***(P-3404)***
Division Infectious Diseases, La Jolla *Also called Scripps Clinic Carmel Valley* ***(P-19861)***
Division of Rheumatology, Los Angeles *Also called Childrens Hospital Los Angeles* ***(P-19379)***
Division of State Architect, Oakland *Also called General Services Cal Dept* ***(P-26047)***
Division of State Architect, Los Angeles *Also called General Services Cal Dept* ***(P-26048)***
Division Three Cnstr Svcs....D....951 609-3043
30620 Plumas St Lake Elsinore (92530) ***(P-1521)***
Dix Metals Inc....D....714 677-0777
14801 Able Ln Ste 101 Huntington Beach (92647) ***(P-7269)***
DJ Scheffler Inc (PA)....E....909 595-2924
2500 Pomona Blvd Pomona (91768) ***(P-2803)***
Djont/Cmb Ssf Leasing LLC....D....650 589-3400
250 Gateway Blvd South San Francisco (94080) ***(P-12528)***
Dkd Property Management, San Jose *Also called Property Maintenance Company* ***(P-14359)***
Dkn Hotel LLC (PA)....B....714 427-4320
42 Corporate Park Ste 200 Irvine (92606) ***(P-12529)***
Dkn Hotel LLC....D....714 535-0300
1240 S Walnut St Anaheim (92802) ***(P-12530)***
Dl Imaging, Santa Ana *Also called Dekra-Lite Industries Inc* ***(P-17129)***
DL Long Landscaping Inc....D....909 628-5531
5475 G St Chino (91710) ***(P-750)***
Dla Piper LLP (us)....B....213 330-7700
550 S Hope St Ste 2400 Los Angeles (90071) ***(P-23044)***

ALPHABETIC

Employee Codes: A=Over 500 employees, B=251-500
C=101-250, D=51-100, E=50
2019 Directory of California
Wholesalers and Services Companies
© Mergent Inc. 1-800-342-5647
1281

Dla Piper LLP (us) B 650 833-2000
2000 University Ave # 100 East Palo Alto (94303) ***(P-23045)***

Dla Piper LLP (us) D 310 595-3000
2000 Avenue Of The Stars 400n Los Angeles (90067) ***(P-23046)***

Dla Piper LLP (us) B 650 833-2000
2000 University Ave # 100 East Palo Alto (94303) ***(P-23047)***

Dla Piper LLP (us) C 619 699-2700
401 B St Ste 1700 San Diego (92101) ***(P-23048)***

Dla Piper LLP (us) D 858 677-1400
4365 Executive Dr # 1100 San Diego (92121) ***(P-23049)***

Dlc, Cerritos *Also called David Levy Co Inc* ***(P-7464)***

Dlh Davinci LLC D 818 703-5100
22135 Roscoe Blvd Ste 101 West Hills (91304) ***(P-22165)***

Dlo Enterprises Inc D 760 346-8033
41865 Boardwalk Ste 216 Palm Desert (92211) ***(P-16631)***

Dlr Group Inc C 626 796-8230
700 S Flower St Fl 22 Los Angeles (90017) ***(P-26044)***

Dlr Group Inc (HQ) C 213 800-9400
700 Suth Flwr St Fl 22 Flr 22 Los Angeles (90017) ***(P-26045)***

Dlt Growers Inc E 909 947-8198
13131 S Bon View Ave Ontario (91761) ***(P-253)***

Dma Claims Inc (PA) D 323 342-6800
330 N Brand Blvd Ste 230 Glendale (91203) ***(P-10606)***

Dma Claims Inc D 800 649-7602
7188 Via Carmela San Jose (95139) ***(P-10607)***

Dma Claims Inc D 323 342-6800
330 N Brand Blvd Ste 230 Glendale (91203) ***(P-10608)***

Dma Claims Services, Glendale *Also called Dma Claims Inc* ***(P-10606)***

Dma Greencare Contracting Inc E 714 630-9470
3000 E Coronado St Anaheim (92806) ***(P-829)***

DMC Construction Incorporated D 831 656-1600
2110 Del Monte Ave Monterey (93940) ***(P-1522)***

Dmcg Inc (PA) E 951 683-9685
3605 10th St Riverside (92501) ***(P-17133)***

Dmf Inc D 323 934-7779
1118 E 223rd St Carson (90745) ***(P-7354)***

Dmf Lighting, Carson *Also called Dmf Inc* ***(P-7354)***

Dmi, Sylmar *Also called Desert Mechanical Inc* ***(P-2185)***

DMS Facility Services Inc A 510 656-9400
3137 Skyway Ct Fremont (94539) ***(P-14253)***

DMS Facility Services LLC C 858 560-4191
5735 Krny Vlla Rd Ste 108 San Diego (92123) ***(P-25645)***

Dna Specialty Inc D 310 767-4070
200 W Artesia Blvd Compton (90220) ***(P-6635)***

DNC Prks Resorts At Tenaya Inc (HQ) D 877 247-9241
1122 Highway 41 Fish Camp (93623) ***(P-12531)***

DNC Prks Rsrts At Yosemite Inc A 209 372-1001
9001 Village Dr Yosemite Ntpk (95389) ***(P-12532)***

Dnj Parking, San Francisco *Also called California Parking Company* ***(P-11165)***

Dnow LP D 310 900-3900
1111 W Artesia Blvd Compton (90220) ***(P-4673)***

Dns Electronics, Sunnyvale *Also called Screen Spe Usa LLC* ***(P-7540)***

Dnv GL Energy Insights USA Inc E 510 891-0446
155 Grand Ave Ste 500 Oakland (94612) ***(P-27707)***

Dobler & Sons LLC B 831 724-6727
174 Struve Rd Moss Landing (95039) ***(P-49)***

Docircle Inc E 415 484-4221
2544 W Woodland Dr Anaheim (92801) ***(P-5550)***

Docker Inc (PA) D 800 764-4847
144 Townsend St Ste 100 San Francisco (94107) ***(P-15114)***

Dockside Machine & Ship Repair, Wilmington *Also called Marine Technical Services Inc* ***(P-17310)***

Docler Media LLC (HQ) D 424 777-3999
8000 Beverly Blvd Los Angeles (90048) ***(P-16118)***

Docmagic Inc D 800 649-1362
1800 W 213th St Torrance (90501) ***(P-17134)***

Doctor On Demand Inc D 415 935-4447
275 Battery St Ste 650 San Francisco (94111) ***(P-15650)***

Doctors Ambulance Services, Laguna Hills *Also called Herren Enterprises Inc* ***(P-3808)***

Doctors Company D 707 226-0289
185 Greenwood Rd NAPA (94558) ***(P-19447)***

Doctors Company Insurance Svcs B 707 226-0100
185 Greenwood Rd NAPA (94558) ***(P-10427)***

Doctors Hospital Manteca Inc B 209 823-3111
1205 E North St Manteca (95336) ***(P-22018)***

Doctors Hospital W Covina Inc C 626 338-8481
725 S Orange Ave West Covina (91790) ***(P-21396)***

Doctors Management Company (HQ) C 707 226-0100
185 Greenwood Rd NAPA (94558) ***(P-10609)***

Doctors Med Ctr Modesto Inc (HQ) D 209 578-1211
1441 Florida Ave Modesto (95350) ***(P-21397)***

Doctors of Affiliated D 714 539-3100
600 City Pkwy W Ste 400 Orange (92868) ***(P-26842)***

Document Proc Solutions Inc (PA) D 714 482-2060
590 W Lambert Rd Brea (92821) ***(P-16119)***

Document Systems, Torrance *Also called Docmagic Inc* ***(P-17134)***

Document Technologies LLC D 415 495-4100
275 Battery St Ste 250 San Francisco (94111) ***(P-17135)***

Document Technologies LLC D 213 892-9000
350 S Figueroa St Ste 750 Los Angeles (90071) ***(P-17136)***

Document Technologies LLC D 650 485-2705
3600 W Bayshore Rd Palo Alto (94303) ***(P-17137)***

Docusign Inc (PA) B 415 489-4940
221 Main St Ste 1000 San Francisco (94105) ***(P-15651)***

DOD Constructors A JV D 707 265-1100
185 Devlin Rd NAPA (94558) ***(P-2025)***

DOD Fueling Constructors A JV D 707 265-1100
185 Devlin Rd NAPA (94558) ***(P-2026)***

DOD Marine Constructors A JV D 707 265-1100
185 Devlin Rd NAPA (94558) ***(P-2027)***

Dodge & Cox C 415 981-1710
555 California St # 4000 San Francisco (94104) ***(P-12034)***

Dodge Ridge Corporation B 209 536-5300
1 Dodge Ridge Rd Pinecrest (95364) ***(P-12533)***

Dodge Ridge Winter Sports Area, Pinecrest *Also called Dodge Ridge Corporation* ***(P-12533)***

Dodger Stadium, Los Angeles *Also called Fox BSB Holdco Inc* ***(P-18518)***

Doheny Eye Institute C 323 442-6682
3158 Kings Ct Los Angeles (90077) ***(P-26616)***

Dokken Engineering (PA) D 916 858-0642
110 Blue Ravine Rd # 200 Folsom (95630) ***(P-25646)***

Dolan Concrete Construction D 408 869-3250
3045 Alfred St Santa Clara (95054) ***(P-3250)***

Dolby Labs Licensing Corp C 415 558-0200
100 Potrero Ave San Francisco (94103) ***(P-12136)***

Dolce Hayes Mansion, San Jose *Also called City of San Jose* ***(P-12462)***

Dolce International / NAPA LLC B 707 257-0200
1600 Atlas Peak Rd NAPA (94558) ***(P-12534)***

Dole Food Company Inc (HQ) C 818 874-4000
1 Dole Dr Westlake Village (91362) ***(P-234)***

Dole Fresh Fruit Company (HQ) B 818 874-4000
1 Dole Dr Westlake Village (91362) ***(P-8667)***

Dole Fresh Vegetables Inc C 559 945-2591
16199 9th St Huron (93234) ***(P-507)***

Dole Fresh Vegetables Inc C 831 678-5030
32655 Camphora Rd Soledad (93960) ***(P-8668)***

Dole Holding Company LLC A 818 879-6600
1 Dole Dr Westlake Village (91362) ***(P-235)***

Dole Holdings Inc (PA) D 818 879-6600
1 Dole Dr Westlake Village (91362) ***(P-8669)***

Doll Fresh Vegestable, Huron *Also called Royal Packing Dcf* ***(P-78)***

Doll House Footwear, City of Industry *Also called J P Original Corp* ***(P-8359)***

Dollar Smart, Oxnard *Also called G P M M Money Centers Inc* ***(P-9684)***

Dollar Thrifty Auto Group Inc A 619 298-7635
4420 Pacific Hwy San Diego (92110) ***(P-17630)***

Dolphin Bay Hotel & Residences, Shell Beach *Also called Dolphin Bay Ht & Residence Inc* ***(P-12535)***

Dolphin Bay Ht & Residence Inc D 805 773-4300
2727 Shell Beach Rd Shell Beach (93449) ***(P-12535)***

Dolphin Hkg Ltd (PA) D 310 215-3356
1125 W Hillcrest Blvd Inglewood (90301) ***(P-9212)***

Dolphin Imaging MGT Solutions, Chatsworth *Also called Patterson Dental Supply Inc* ***(P-15347)***

Dolphin Imaging Systems LLC E 818 435-1368
9200 Oakdale Ave Ste 500 Chatsworth (91311) ***(P-15115)***

Dolphin International, Inglewood *Also called Dolphin Hkg Ltd* ***(P-9212)***

Dolphins Cove Resort Ltd D 714 980-0830
465 W Orangewood Ave Anaheim (92802) ***(P-12536)***

Domaine Carneros Ltd D 707 257-0101
1240 Duhig Rd NAPA (94559) ***(P-140)***

Domestic Horizons, Beverly Hills *Also called Global Horizons Inc* ***(P-14627)***

Domestic Linen Supply Co Inc (HQ) E 213 749-6300
1600 Compton Ave Los Angeles (90021) ***(P-13529)***

Dominator Radiology Systems, San Diego *Also called DR Systems Inc* ***(P-22079)***

Dominguez Firm Inc D 213 388-7788
3250 Wilshire Blvd # 1200 Los Angeles (90010) ***(P-23050)***

Dominguez Landscape Svcs Inc D 916 381-8855
8376 Rovana Cir Sacramento (95828) ***(P-830)***

Dominican Hospital Foundation C 831 457-7057
610 Frederick St Santa Cruz (95062) ***(P-24506)***

Dominican Hospital Foundation (HQ) C 831 462-7700
1555 Soquel Dr Santa Cruz (95065) ***(P-21398)***

Dominican Oaks Corporation D 831 462-6257
3400 Paul Sweet Rd Ofc Santa Cruz (95065) ***(P-11007)***

Dominican Rehab Services, Santa Cruz *Also called Dominican Hospital Foundation* ***(P-24506)***

Dominion International Inc D 916 683-9545
2305 Longport Ct Elk Grove (95758) ***(P-12537)***

Dominos Pizza LLC C 909 390-1990
301 S Rockefeller Ave Ontario (91761) ***(P-4674)***

Domus Construction & Design E 916 381-7500
8864 Fruitridge Rd Sacramento (95826) ***(P-1157)***

Don Brandel Plumbing Inc E 562 408-0400
15100 Texaco Ave Paramount (90723) ***(P-2186)***

Don Gragnani Farms D 559 693-4352
12910 S Napa Ave Tranquillity (93668) ***(P-336)***

Don Kinzel Construction Inc D 661 322-9105
4300 Easton Dr Ste 2 Bakersfield (93309) ***(P-3030)***

Don Lee Farms, Inglewood *Also called Goodman Food Products Inc* ***(P-8408)***

Don Sebastiani & Sons Internat (PA) D 707 933-1704
19150 Sonoma Hwy 12 Sonoma (95476) ***(P-9039)***

Don Turner and Associates, Fresno *Also called Turner Security Systems Inc* ***(P-16840)***

Donaghy Sales Inc C 559 486-0901
2363 S Cedar Ave Fresno (93725) ***(P-8993)***

Donahue Gallager Woods LLP (PA) D 415 381-4161
1999 Harrison St Ste 2500 Oakland (94612) ***(P-23051)***

Donahue Schrber Rlty Group Inc (PA) D 714 545-1400
200 Baker St Ste 100 Costa Mesa (92626) ***(P-11405)***

Donahue Schriber Rlty Group LP (PA) D 714 545-1400
200 Baker St Ste 100 Costa Mesa (92626) ***(P-10869)***

Donahue Schriber Rlty Group LP D 714 545-1400
5082 N Palm Ave Fresno (93704) ***(P-10870)***

Donahue Schriber Rlty Group LP D 714 283-3535
8020 E Santa Ana Cyn Rd Anaheim (92808) ***(P-10871)***

Donahue Schriber Rlty Group LP D 858 793-5757
12925 El Camino Real J22 San Diego (92130) ***(P-10872)***

Donald J Scheffler Cnstr, Azusa *Also called Heidi Corporation* ***(P-1288)***

Mergent e-mail: customerrelations@mergent.com
1282
2019 Directory of California Wholesalers and Services Companies
(P-0000) Products & Services Section entry number
(PA)=Parent Co (HQ)=Headquarters (DH)=Div Headquarters

Donald Lawrence Company, Visalia *Also called Donald Lawrence Fulbright Co* ***(P-1336)***
Donald Lawrence Fulbright Co.....D.....559 625-0762
32557 Road 138 Visalia (93292) ***(P-1336)***
Donald Lucky LLC.....C.....949 752-0647
4029 Westerly Pl Ste 111 Newport Beach (92660) ***(P-26843)***
Donald P Dick AC Inc (PA).....D.....559 255-1644
1444 N Whitney Ave Fresno (93703) ***(P-2187)***
Donald T Sterling Corporation.....D.....310 275-5575
10300 Wilshire Blvd Los Angeles (90024) ***(P-12538)***
Donald Valpredo Farming Inc.....D.....661 858-2245
2101 Mttler Frontage Rd E Bakersfield (93307) ***(P-50)***
Donatello, San Francisco *Also called Shell Vacations LLC* ***(P-27028)***
Dongalen Enterprises Inc (PA).....C.....916 422-3110
330 Commerce Cir Sacramento (95815) ***(P-8914)***
Donor Network West (PA).....C.....925 480-3100
12667 Alcosta Blvd # 500 San Ramon (94583) ***(P-22791)***
Donor Network West.....D.....510 418-0336
5800 Airport Rd Ste B Redding (96002) ***(P-22792)***
Donovan Bros Golf LLC.....D.....805 531-9300
15187 Tierra Rejada Rd Moorpark (93021) ***(P-18707)***
Donovan Golf Courses MGT (PA).....C.....714 554-0672
3017 W 5th St Santa Ana (92703) ***(P-18708)***
Donovan Golf Courses MGT.....E.....714 528-6400
1800 Carbon Canyon Rd Chino (91708) ***(P-18709)***
Doose Landscape Incorporated.....D.....760 591-4500
785 E Mission Rd San Marcos (92069) ***(P-831)***
Dorado Network Systems Corp.....C.....650 227-7300
555 12th St Ste 1100 Oakland (94607) ***(P-15652)***
Dorado Software Inc.....D.....916 673-1100
4805 Golden Foothill Pkwy El Dorado Hills (95762) ***(P-15116)***
Doral Palm Sprngs Rsrt & Golf, Palm Springs *Also called Interstate Hotels Resorts Inc* ***(P-26897)***
Dorani Limited.....D.....213 355-7230
777 S Alameda St Los Angeles (90021) ***(P-15117)***
Doremus & Company.....E.....415 273-7800
550 3rd St San Francisco (94107) ***(P-13821)***
Dorfman Pacific, Stockton *Also called Dorfman-Pacific Co* ***(P-8255)***
Dorfman-Pacific Co (HQ).....C.....209 982-1400
2615 Boeing Way Stockton (95206) ***(P-8255)***
Dorothy Johnson Center, Chico *Also called Chico Area Recreation & Pk Dst* ***(P-19123)***
Dos Palos Mem Rur Hlth Clinic, Dos Palos *Also called Dos Palos Memorial Hosp Inc* ***(P-19448)***
Dos Palos Memorial Hosp Inc.....D.....209 392-6121
2118 Marguerite St Dos Palos (93620) ***(P-19448)***
Dos Pueblos Ranch, Goleta *Also called Schulte Ranches* ***(P-379)***
Dosse Entertainment Mgmt.....D.....323 366-9173
8942 Wilshire Blvd Beverly Hills (90211) ***(P-26844)***
DOT Foods Inc.....C.....209 581-9090
2200 Nickerson Dr Modesto (95358) ***(P-8401)***
DOT Leasing Company.....C.....949 474-1100
2424 Mcgaw Ave Irvine (92614) ***(P-8069)***
DOT Printer Inc.....E.....949 752-7730
1801 S Standard Ave Santa Ana (92707) ***(P-4551)***
DOT Printer Warehouse, Santa Ana *Also called DOT Printer Inc* ***(P-4551)***
DOT-Line Transportation Inc.....D.....877 900-7768
4366 E 26th St Vernon (90058) ***(P-4129)***
Double D Transportation Co.....D.....510 783-2335
22991 Clawiter Rd Hayward (94545) ***(P-4005)***
Double Day Office Services Inc.....E.....650 872-6600
340 Shaw Rd South San Francisco (94080) ***(P-4344)***
Double Eagle Trnsp Corp.....C.....760 956-3770
12135 Scarbrough Ct Oak Hills (92344) ***(P-4130)***
Double G Productions Ltd.....D.....310 479-0978
11301 W Olympic Blvd # 115 Los Angeles (90064) ***(P-18431)***
Double Three Htlirvinespectrum, Irvine *Also called Spectrum Hotel Group LLC* ***(P-13252)***
Double Tree Club Ht San Diego, San Diego *Also called Pbp Hotel LLC* ***(P-11906)***
Double Tree Past Acute, Sacramento *Also called Sacramento Operating Co LP* ***(P-20736)***
Doubledutch Inc (PA).....D.....800 748-9024
350 Rhode Island St # 375 San Francisco (94103) ***(P-15653)***
Doubleline Capital LP.....C.....213 633-8200
333 S Grand Ave Fl 18 Los Angeles (90071) ***(P-17138)***
DoubleTree by Hilton, San Diego *Also called Swvp Del Mar Hotel LLC* ***(P-13311)***
Doubletree By Hilton, San Diego *Also called San Diego Lessee LLC* ***(P-13171)***
Doubletree By Hilton, San Diego *Also called Gringteam Inc* ***(P-12628)***
Doubletree By Hilton Brky Mrna, Berkeley *Also called Westpost Berkeley LLC* ***(P-13395)***
Doubletree By Hilton Carson, Carson *Also called Carson Operating Company LLC* ***(P-12434)***
Doubletree By Hilton Fresno, Fresno *Also called Uniwell Fresno Hotel LLC* ***(P-13356)***
Doubletree By Hilton Hotel.....C.....310 322-0999
1985 E Grand Ave El Segundo (90245) ***(P-12539)***
Doubletree By Hilton Hotel.....D.....619 881-6900
1515 Hotel Cir S San Diego (92108) ***(P-12540)***
Doubletree By Hilton La - Com, Commerce *Also called Tpg La Commerce LLC* ***(P-13335)***
Doubletree By Hilton San Jose, San Jose *Also called San Jose Lessee LLC* ***(P-13178)***
Doubletree Hotel, Commerce *Also called W2005 Wyn Hotels LP* ***(P-13376)***
Doubletree Hotel, San Diego *Also called Gringteam Inc* ***(P-12621)***
Doubletree Hotel, Santa Ana *Also called Chamson Management Inc* ***(P-12449)***
Doubletree Hotel, Ontario *Also called Gringteam Inc* ***(P-12622)***
Doubletree Hotel, Anaheim *Also called Doubltree Suites By Hilton LLC* ***(P-12542)***
Doubletree Hotel, San Jose *Also called Gringteam Inc* ***(P-12623)***
Doubletree Hotel, Irvine *Also called Spectrum Hotel Group LLC* ***(P-13253)***
Doubletree Hotel, Santa Ana *Also called Gringteam Inc* ***(P-12625)***
Doubletree Hotel, Sacramento *Also called Gringteam Inc* ***(P-12626)***
Doubletree Hotel, Santa Barbara *Also called Fess Prker-Red Lion Gen Partnr* ***(P-12574)***
Doubletree Hotel, El Segundo *Also called European Hotl Invstrs of CA* ***(P-12566)***
Doubletree Hotel, Torrance *Also called Ctc Group Inc* ***(P-12504)***
Doubletree Hotel, Modesto *Also called Gringteam Inc* ***(P-12627)***
Doubletree Hotel, Claremont *Also called Claremont Star LP* ***(P-12464)***
Doubletree Hotel, Burlingame *Also called Gringteam Inc* ***(P-12629)***
Doubletree Hotel, Santa Monica *Also called Santa Monica Hsr Ltd Partnr* ***(P-13190)***
Doubletree Hotel, Dana Point *Also called Gringteam Inc* ***(P-12630)***
Doubletree Hotel.....D.....323 722-8800
888 Montebello Blvd Rosemead (91770) ***(P-12541)***
Doubletree Hotel Modesto, Modesto *Also called Modesto Hospitality Lessee LLC* ***(P-12935)***
Doubletree Hotel-Lax, El Segundo *Also called Tri-Star Ccw Management L P* ***(P-13345)***
Doubletree Ht San Diego Dwntwn, San Diego *Also called Harbor View Hotel Ventures LLC* ***(P-12643)***
Doubletree Suites, Santa Monica *Also called Santa Monica Hotel Owner LLC* ***(P-13189)***
Doubletree Suites Doheny, Dana Point *Also called Ergs Aim Hotel Realty LLC* ***(P-12562)***
Doubltree By Hilton Ht Modesto, Modesto *Also called Modesto Hospitality LLC* ***(P-12934)***
Doubltree By Hlton Ht Bkrsfeld, Bakersfield *Also called Gringteam Inc* ***(P-12624)***
Doubltree By Hlton Scrmento Ht, Sacramento *Also called Wmk Sacramento LLC* ***(P-13415)***
Doubltree Ht Anhim-Orange Cnty, Orange *Also called Anaheim Ca LLC* ***(P-12320)***
Doubltree Los Angeles Westside, Culver City *Also called Crp Centinela LP* ***(P-12503)***
Doubltree Suites By Hilton LLC.....C.....714 750-3000
2085 S Harbor Blvd Anaheim (92802) ***(P-12542)***
Doudell Trucking Company (PA).....C.....408 263-7300
1505 N 4th St San Jose (95112) ***(P-4131)***
Doug Arnold Real Estate Inc (PA).....E.....530 758-3080
505 2nd St Davis (95616) ***(P-11406)***
Douglas Elliman Real Estate.....E.....310 595-3888
150 El Camino Dr Beverly Hills (90212) ***(P-11407)***
Douglas Emmett Realty Fund 199.....D.....310 255-7700
808 Wilshire Blvd Ste 200 Santa Monica (90401) ***(P-11408)***
Douglas Fir Holdings LLC.....C.....714 842-5551
8382 Newman Ave Huntington Beach (92647) ***(P-20378)***
Douglas L Myovich Trucking Inc.....D.....559 233-8242
1895 W Jefferson Ave Fresno (93706) ***(P-4006)***
Douglas Ranch LLC.....E.....949 500-7009
33200 E Carmel Valley Rd Carmel Valley (93924) ***(P-448)***
Douglas Ross Construction Inc.....D.....408 429-7700
900 E Hamilton Ave # 140 Campbell (95008) ***(P-1281)***
Douglas Steel Supply Inc (PA).....D.....323 587-7676
4804 Laurel Canyon Blvd Valley Village (91607) ***(P-7270)***
Douglas Steel Supply Co., Valley Village *Also called Douglas Steel Supply Inc* ***(P-7270)***
Douglas W Jackson MD.....D.....562 424-6666
2760 Atlantic Ave Long Beach (90806) ***(P-19449)***
Doumit Communication Inc.....D.....916 362-3519
25 Cadillac Dr Ste 134 Sacramento (95825) ***(P-1760)***
Dove Ceilings Inc (PA).....E.....949 597-1794
22991 Belquest Dr Lake Forest (92630) ***(P-2876)***
Dowling Advisory Group.....D.....626 319-1369
3579 E Foothill Blvd # 651 Pasadena (91107) ***(P-27217)***
Down River, Stockton *Also called Signode Industrial Group LLC* ***(P-7798)***
Downey Brand LLP (PA).....C.....916 444-1000
621 Capitol Mall Fl 18 Sacramento (95814) ***(P-23052)***
Downey Care Center, Downey *Also called Covenant Care California LLC* ***(P-20336)***
Downey Civic Theatre, Downey *Also called City of Downey* ***(P-18358)***
Downey Community Health Center.....C.....562 862-6506
8425 Iowa St Downey (90241) ***(P-20379)***
Downey Family Y M C A, Downey *Also called Young Mens Chrstn Assn of La* ***(P-25346)***
Downey Orthopedic Med Group, Lawndale *Also called Southwestern Orthpd Med Corp* ***(P-19929)***
Downey Regional Medical Center, Downey *Also called Pih Health Hospital - Whitti* ***(P-21648)***
Downey YMCA, Downey *Also called Young Mens Chrstn Assn of La* ***(P-24137)***
Downs Fuel Transport Inc.....E.....951 256-8286
1296 Magnolia Ave Corona (92879) ***(P-8954)***
Downtown Berkeley YMCA, Berkeley *Also called Young MNS Chrstn Assn of E Bay* ***(P-25360)***
Downtown Business Fincl Ctr, Bakersfield *Also called Citizens Business Bank* ***(P-9436)***
Downtown Community Dev YMCA, Long Beach *Also called Young Mens Christian Associat* ***(P-25331)***
Downtown Los Angeles Branch, Los Angeles *Also called Israel Discount Bank New York* ***(P-9464)***
Downtown Metro.....E.....760 398-3310
1030 6th St Ste 16 Coachella (92236) ***(P-5405)***
Downtown San Diego Partnr Inc (PA).....D.....619 234-0201
401 B St Ste 100 San Diego (92101) ***(P-24953)***
Downtown San Diego Partnr Inc.....D.....619 234-8900
1111 6th Ave Ste 101 San Diego (92101) ***(P-24954)***
Downtown SD Ventures LLC.....D.....619 231-9200
20162 Sw Birch St Ste 350 Newport Beach (92660) ***(P-19160)***
DP Technology Corp (PA).....D.....805 388-6000
1150 Avenida Acaso Camarillo (93012) ***(P-15118)***
Dpi Specialty Foods West Inc (HQ).....C.....909 975-1019
601 S Rockefeller Ave Ontario (91761) ***(P-8402)***
Dpk Consulting.....D.....415 495-7772
605 Market St Ste 800 San Francisco (94105) ***(P-27218)***
Dppm Inc.....D.....415 695-7707
4040 24th St San Francisco (94114) ***(P-11409)***
Dpr Construction Inc.....E.....408 370-2322
1510 S Winchester Blvd San Jose (95128) ***(P-1392)***
Dpr Construction Inc (PA).....A.....650 474-1450
1450 Veterans Blvd Redwood City (94063) ***(P-1393)***
Dpr Construction Inc.....B.....916 568-3434
2480 Natomas Park Dr # 100 Sacramento (95833) ***(P-1523)***
Dpr Construction Inc.....B.....858 646-0757
5010 Shoreham Pl Ste 100 San Diego (92122) ***(P-1394)***
Dpr Construction Inc.....E.....949 955-3771
4665 Macarthur Ct Ste 100 Newport Beach (92660) ***(P-1524)***

Employee Codes: A=Over 500 employees, B=251-500
C=101-250, D=51-100, E=50
2019 Directory of California
Wholesalers and Services Companies
© Mergent Inc. 1-800-342-5647
1283

Dpr Construction A Gen Partnr .... E......916 568-3434
  2480 Natomas Park Dr # 100 Sacramento (95833) *(P-1395)*
Dpr Construction A Gen Partnr (HQ) .... A......650 474-1450
  1450 Veterans Blvd Redwood City (94063) *(P-1396)*
Dpr Holdings LLC .... E......323 761-9829
  4804 Laurel Canyon Blvd Studio City (91607) *(P-11975)*
Dpss, Burbank *Also called County of Los Angeles (P-23685)*
Dr Fresh LLC .... D......714 690-1573
  6 Centerpointe Dr Ste 640 La Palma (90623) *(P-8166)*
DR Horton Inc .... E......951 272-9000
  2280 Wardlow Cir Ste 100 Corona (92880) *(P-1337)*
DR Systems Inc .... C......858 625-3344
  10140 Mesa Rim Rd San Diego (92121) *(P-22079)*
Draftfcb, San Francisco *Also called Fcb Worldwide Inc (P-13829)*
Dragados/Flatiron Joint Ventr .... D......559 847-5388
  14555 S Peach Ave Selma (93662) *(P-1525)*
Dragon Engineering, Chowchilla *Also called Anderson Pump Company (P-6209)*
Drain Doctor .... E......408 970-3800
  480 Aldo Ave Santa Clara (95054) *(P-2188)*
Drain Patrol .... D......858 560-1137
  7764 Arjons Dr San Diego (92126) *(P-2189)*
Draios Inc .... D......916 521-3802
  1949 5th St Ste 104 Davis (95616) *(P-15119)*
Drake Larson Ranchs .... C......760 399-5494
  89780 Ave 60 Thermal (92274) *(P-141)*
Drake Terrace, San Rafael *Also called Kisco Senior Living LLC (P-11043)*
Drawbridge Inc .... D......650 513-2323
  2121 S El Camino Real 7th San Mateo (94403) *(P-27219)*
Drchrono Inc .... E......650 600-2079
  328 Gibraltar Dr Sunnyvale (94089) *(P-15120)*
DREAM HOLLYWOOD, Los Angeles *Also called 6417 Selma Hotel LLC (P-12299)*
Dream Home & Investments Rlty, Lomita *Also called Long Beach Investment Group (P-9830)*
Dream Home Care Inc .... D......562 595-9021
  3939 Atlantic Ave Ste 213 Long Beach (90807) *(P-24507)*
Dream Home Estates Inc .... E......949 415-4646
  2901 W Coast Hwy Ste 200 Newport Beach (92663) *(P-11410)*
Dream Lounge Inc .... A......213 688-7888
  11271 Ventura Blvd 456 Studio City (91604) *(P-8256)*
Dream River, Commerce *Also called Shason Inc (P-8243)*
Dreamctchers Empwerment Netwrk (PA) .... A......209 478-5291
  7590 Shoreline Dr Ste B Stockton (95219) *(P-24508)*
Dreamctchers Empwerment Netwrk .... C......925 935-6630
  1911 Oak Park Blvd Pleasant Hill (94523) *(P-24509)*
Dreamctchers Empwerment Netwrk .... D......209 477-4817
  6940 Pacific Ave Stockton (95207) *(P-24510)*
Dreamhost.com, Brea *Also called New Dream Network LLC (P-5612)*
Dreamhost.com, Los Angeles *Also called New Dream Network LLC (P-5613)*
Dreamscape Ldscp & Maint Inc .... E......619 583-4439
  7192 Mission Gorge Rd San Diego (92120) *(P-751)*
Dreamworks Animation LLC .... D......818 695-5000
  1000 Flwr St Cmpnile Bldg Glendale (91201) *(P-18045)*
Dreamworks Animation Pubg LLC .... B......818 695-5000
  1000 Flower St Glendale (91201) *(P-18046)*
Dreamworks Animation TV, Glendale *Also called Dreamworks Animation LLC (P-18045)*
DREIER'S NURSING CARE CENTER, Glendale *Also called Ksm Healthcare Inc (P-20570)*
Dreisbach Enterprises Inc (PA) .... C......510 533-6600
  575 Maritime St Oakland (94607) *(P-11168)*
Dreisbach Freight Services, Oakland *Also called Dreisbach Enterprises Inc (P-11168)*
Dresick Farms Inc (PA) .... D......559 945-2513
  19536 Jayne Ave Huron (93234) *(P-51)*
Drew Chain Security Corp .... D......626 457-8626
  55 S Raymond Ave Ste 303 Alhambra (91801) *(P-16632)*
Drew Child Dev Corp Inc (PA) .... C......323 249-2950
  1770 E 118th St Los Angeles (90059) *(P-23774)*
Drew Health Foundation .... E......650 328-1619
  1191 Runnymede St East Palo Alto (94303) *(P-24775)*
Dreyer Bbich Bccola Cllham LLP .... D......916 379-3500
  20 Bicentennial Cir Sacramento (95826) *(P-23053)*
Dreyer's Grand Ice Cream, Walnut *Also called Nestle Dreyers Ice Cream Co (P-8525)*
Dreyers Grand Ice Cream Hold (HQ) .... C......510 652-8187
  5929 College Ave Oakland (94618) *(P-8520)*
Dreyers Grnd Ice Cream Hldings, Oakland *Also called Rdp Acquisition Company (P-26560)*
DRG Health Care Staffing, South San Francisco *Also called Discharge Resource Group (P-14848)*
Driftwood Convalescent Hosp, Davis *Also called Mariner Health Care Inc (P-20618)*
Driftwood Health Care Ctr, Torrance *Also called Mariner Health Care Inc (P-20610)*
Driftwood Healthcare Center, Hayward *Also called Mariner Health Care Inc (P-20622)*
Drinker Biddle & Reath LLP .... C......310 229-1282
  1800 Century Park E # 1400 Los Angeles (90067) *(P-23054)*
Drinker Biddle & Reath LLP .... C......415 591-7500
  4 Embarcadero Ctr Lbby San Francisco (94111) *(P-23055)*
Drinks Holdings Inc .... C......310 441-8400
  1125 E Broadway 173 Glendale (91205) *(P-9040)*
Driscolls Inc (PA) .... D......831 424-0506
  345 Westridge Dr Watsonville (95076) *(P-8670)*
Driscolls Inc .... D......800 871-3333
  150 Westridge Dr Watsonville (95076) *(P-8671)*
Driscolls Inc .... E......831 763-5100
  1750 San Juan Rd Aromas (95004) *(P-8672)*
Drive Thru Technology Inc .... C......323 576-1400
  1755 N Main St Los Angeles (90031) *(P-16889)*
Driveai Inc .... C......650 729-0499
  365 Ravendale Dr Mountain View (94043) *(P-15654)*
Driven Performance Brands Inc (PA) .... D......707 544-4761
  100 Stony Point Rd # 125 Santa Rosa (95401) *(P-6636)*
Driver Inc .... D......415 999-4960
  438 Shotwell St San Francisco (94110) *(P-15655)*

Driver Spg .... E......855 300-4774
  1501 S Harris Ct Anaheim (92806) *(P-17139)*
Drivesavers Inc .... D......415 382-2000
  400 Bel Marin Keys Blvd Novato (94949) *(P-16218)*
Drivesavers Data Recovery, Novato *Also called Drivesavers Inc (P-16218)*
Drohan Trade Center, Rancho Cordova *Also called McKesson Corporation (P-8194)*
Droisys Inc (PA) .... B......408 874-8333
  4800 Patrick Henry Dr Santa Clara (95054) *(P-15947)*
Drop Lot Services, San Juan Capistrano *Also called Merit Logistics LLC (P-5109)*
Dropbox Inc (PA) .... C......415 857-6800
  333 Brannan St San Francisco (94107) *(P-15656)*
Dropcar Inc .... D......707 421-1300
  521 Railroad Ave Suisun City (94585) *(P-5551)*
Dropzone Waterpark .... C......951 210-1600
  2165 Trumble Rd Perris (92571) *(P-19161)*
Drug & Alcohol Services of .... D......805 781-4275
  2180 Johnson Ave Ste A San Luis Obispo (93401) *(P-22568)*
Drug Abuse Alternatives Center (PA) .... C......707 544-3295
  2403 Prof Dr Ste 102 Santa Rosa (95403) *(P-23775)*
Drug Abuse Alternatives Center .... E......707 571-2233
  2403 Prof Dr Ste 103 Santa Rosa (95403) *(P-22569)*
Drum Security Service Inc .... D......818 708-7914
  4509 Callada Pl Tarzana (91356) *(P-16633)*
Drummond Medical Group Inc .... C......760 446-4571
  900 N Heritage Dr Ste A Ridgecrest (93555) *(P-19450)*
Druva Inc (HQ) .... D......650 241-3501
  150 Mathilda Pl Ste 450 Sunnyvale (94086) *(P-15657)*
Dry Creek Lath & Plaster Inc .... D......209 367-8607
  27940 Kennefick Rd Galt (95632) *(P-2877)*
Dryco Construction (PA) .... C......510 438-6500
  42745 Boscell Rd Fremont (94538) *(P-1761)*
Drywall Works Inc .... D......916 383-6667
  5451 Whse Way Ste 105 Sacramento (95826) *(P-2878)*
Ds Services of America Inc .... D......818 787-9397
  7817 Haskell Ave Van Nuys (91406) *(P-8784)*
Ds Services of America Inc .... C......626 472-7201
  4548 Azusa Canyon Rd Irwindale (91706) *(P-8785)*
DSC Logistics Inc .... D......909 363-4354
  1895 Marigold Ave Redlands (92374) *(P-4132)*
DSC Logistics Inc .... B......540 377-2302
  5690 Industrial Pkwy San Bernardino (92407) *(P-5048)*
DSC Logistics Inc .... D......209 362-2232
  1565 N Macarthur Dr Tracy (95376) *(P-4552)*
DSC Logistics Inc .... D......909 605-7233
  12350 Philadelphia Ave Eastvale (91752) *(P-4007)*
Dsca, Long Beach *Also called Denso Pdts & Svcs Americas Inc (P-6633)*
Dsd Trucking Inc (PA) .... D......310 338-3395
  2411 Santa Fe Ave Redondo Beach (90278) *(P-4885)*
Dsh Graphics, Yorba Linda *Also called Dsh West Inc (P-14112)*
Dsh West Inc .... D......714 692-8777
  5455 Camino De Bryant Yorba Linda (92887) *(P-14112)*
DSM Biomedical Inc .... C......510 841-8800
  2810 7th St Berkeley (94710) *(P-26355)*
Dsp Group Inc (PA) .... D......408 986-4300
  691 S Milpitas Blvd # 212 Milpitas (95035) *(P-15121)*
Dst Output California Inc .... C......916 939-4617
  5220 Rbert J Mathews Pkwy El Dorado Hills (95762) *(P-16282)*
DSV Solutions LLC .... D......714 630-0110
  3454 E Miraloma Ave Anaheim (92806) *(P-5223)*
Dt Club Hotel Santa Ana, Santa Ana *Also called Jhc Investment Inc (P-12790)*
Dt Floormasters Inc .... D......510 476-1000
  31164 Huntwood Ave Hayward (94544) *(P-3101)*
Dt Research Inc (PA) .... D......408 934-6220
  2000 Concourse Dr San Jose (95131) *(P-26356)*
Dtex Systems Inc .... E......408 418-3786
  3055 Olin Ave Ste 2000 San Jose (95128) *(P-15122)*
Dti Inc .... D......310 635-9002
  1628 S Sportsman Dr Compton (90221) *(P-4008)*
Dti Services Inc (PA) .... D......213 670-1100
  601 S Figueroa St # 4300 Los Angeles (90017) *(P-16351)*
DTM Services Inc (PA) .... D......310 521-1200
  19829 Hamilton Ave Torrance (90502) *(P-5049)*
Dtrs Santa Monica LLC .... B......310 458-6700
  1700 Ocean Ave Santa Monica (90401) *(P-12543)*
Dts, Sacramento *Also called Technology Services Cal Dept (P-16509)*
Dts Inc (HQ) .... C......818 436-1000
  5220 Las Virgenes Rd Calabasas (91302) *(P-18189)*
Dtt, Los Angeles *Also called Drive Thru Technology Inc (P-16889)*
Dual Diagnosis Trtmnt Ctr Inc .... C......424 289-9031
  12832 Short Ave Los Angeles (90066) *(P-22080)*
Dual Diagnosis Trtmnt Ctr Inc .... C......949 324-4531
  69640 Highway 111 Rancho Mirage (92270) *(P-22793)*
Dual Diagnosis Trtmnt Ctr Inc (PA) .... C......949 276-5553
  1211 Puerta Del Sol # 200 San Clemente (92673) *(P-22570)*
Dual Diagnosis Trtmnt Ctr Inc .... C......424 207-2220
  6167 Bristol Pkwy Culver City (90230) *(P-22571)*
Duane Morris LLP .... C......415 957-3000
  1 Market Plz Ste 2200 San Francisco (94105) *(P-23056)*
Duarte Manor, Los Angeles *Also called Emp III Inc (P-12223)*
Duarte Nursery Inc .... B......209 887-3409
  23456 E Flood Rd Linden (95236) *(P-254)*
Duarte Nursery (PA) .... B......209 531-0351
  1555 Baldwin Rd Hughson (95326) *(P-255)*
Duarte Properties, Hughson *Also called Duarte Nursery Inc (P-255)*
Dublin Hstrcal Prsrvation Assn .... D......925 785-2898
  7172 Regional St Pmb 316 Dublin (94568) *(P-24881)*
Dublin San Ramon Services Dst (PA) .... C......925 875-2276
  7051 Dublin Blvd Dublin (94568) *(P-6239)*

Dublin San Ramon Services Dst ....D 925 846-4565
7399 Johnson Dr Pleasanton (94588) *(P-6240)*
Duckor Spradling Metzger ....D 619 209-3000
101 W Broadway Ste 1700 San Diego (92101) *(P-23057)*
Duckpunk Productions Inc ....D 310 836-3818
10728 Westminster Ave Los Angeles (90034) *(P-18047)*
Ducks Unlimited Inc ....E 916 852-2000
3074 Gold Canal Dr Rancho Cordova (95670) *(P-1003)*
Ducky's Car Wash, San Carlos *Also called Duckys of San Carlos Inc (P-17812)*
Duckys of San Carlos Inc ....E 650 637-1301
1301 Old County Rd San Carlos (94070) *(P-17812)*
Dudek (PA) ....D 760 942-5147
605 3rd St Encinitas (92024) *(P-25647)*
Dudek ....B 760 942-5147
605 3rd St Encinitas (92024) *(P-25648)*
Duff & Phelps LLC ....D 650 798-5500
1950 University Ave # 400 East Palo Alto (94303) *(P-27220)*
Duff & Phelps LLC ....D 213 270-2300
350 S Grand Ave Ste 3100 Los Angeles (90071) *(P-27221)*
Duff & Phelps LLC ....D 415 693-5300
345 California St # 2100 San Francisco (94104) *(P-17140)*
Duggan & Associates Inc ....D 323 965-1502
1442 W 135th St Gardena (90249) *(P-2433)*
Dui Program, Santa Monica *Also called Clare Foundation Inc (P-23588)*
Duke Energy Corporation ....C 949 727-7434
8001 Irvine Center Dr Irvine (92618) *(P-6027)*
Duke Financial Co Inc ....C 858 694-1215
100 N Rancho Santa Fe Rd # 117 San Marcos (92069) *(P-13653)*
Duke Pacific Inc ....D 909 591-0191
13950 Monte Vista Ave Chino (91710) *(P-3150)*
DULCINEA FARMS, Los Angeles *Also called Pacific Trellis Fruit LLC (P-8714)*
Duleys Landscape Inc ....E 559 855-5090
28876 Topaz Rd Tollhouse (93667) *(P-832)*
Dun & Bradstreet Inc ....D 415 343-6540
1 Embarcadero Ctr # 2060 San Francisco (94111) *(P-14034)*
Dun & Bradstreet Emerging (HQ) ....C 310 456-8271
22761 Pacific Coast Hwy # 226 Malibu (90265) *(P-17141)*
Dunbar Armored Inc ....D 510 569-7400
629 Whitney St San Leandro (94577) *(P-16634)*
Dunlap Property Group Inc ....D 714 879-0111
801 E Chapman Ave Ste 233 Fullerton (92831) *(P-11411)*
Dunn & Berger Inc ....B 818 986-1234
5955 De Soto Ave Ste 160 Woodland Hills (91367) *(P-22287)*
Duplo USA Corporation (PA) ....D 949 752-8222
3050 Daimler St Santa Ana (92705) *(P-6959)*
Dura Freight Lines, Walnut *Also called Patina Freight Inc (P-4606)*
Dura Metrics Inc (PA) ....D 707 546-5138
816 Piner Rd Santa Rosa (95403) *(P-22166)*
Duran Human Capital Partners ....E 408 540-0070
300 Orchard Cy Dr Ste 142 Campbell (95008) *(P-14603)*
Durham School Services ....D 408 448-0740
3001 Ross Ave Ste 11 San Jose (95124) *(P-3913)*
Durham School Services L P ....C 310 767-5820
16627 Avalon Blvd Ste B Carson (90746) *(P-3914)*
Durham School Services L P ....C 408 377-6655
1506 White Oaks Rd Campbell (95008) *(P-3915)*
Durham School Services L P ....D 805 495-8338
365 E Avnda De Los Alvare Thousand Oaks (91360) *(P-3916)*
Durham School Services L P ....C 714 542-8989
2818 W 5th St Santa Ana (92703) *(P-3952)*
Durham School Services L P ....C 510 887-6005
27577 Industrial Blvd A Hayward (94545) *(P-3917)*
Durham School Services L P ....D 530 273-7282
10701 E Bennett Rd Grass Valley (95945) *(P-3918)*
Durham School Services L P ....C 925 686-3391
2121 Piedmont Way Pittsburg (94565) *(P-3919)*
Durham School Services L P ....C 626 573-3769
2713 River Ave Rosemead (91770) *(P-3920)*
Durini Luis Carlos Estrada ....E 502 474-3112
100 W Broadway Ste 100 # 100 Glendale (91210) *(P-17142)*
Durkee Drayage Company ....D 510 970-7550
539 Stone Rd Benicia (94510) *(P-4345)*
Dust Networks Inc ....D 510 400-2900
32990 Alvrdo Niles Rd # 910 Union City (94587) *(P-5406)*
Dutch LLC (HQ) ....C 323 277-3900
5301 S Santa Fe Ave Vernon (90058) *(P-8299)*
Duthie Electric Service Corp ....E 562 790-1772
2335 E Cherry Indus Cir Long Beach (90805) *(P-17903)*
Duthie Power Services, Long Beach *Also called Duthie Electric Service Corp (P-17903)*
Dutra Dredging, San Rafael *Also called Dutra Group (P-2029)*
Dutra Dredging Company (HQ) ....D 415 721-2131
2350 Kerner Blvd Ste 200 San Rafael (94901) *(P-2028)*
Dutra Group (PA) ....D 415 258-6876
2350 Kerner Blvd Ste 200 San Rafael (94901) *(P-2029)*
Dutra Manson JV ....D 415 258-6876
1000 Point San Pedro Rd San Rafael (94901) *(P-2030)*
Dutra Materials, San Rafael *Also called San Rafael Rock Quarry Inc (P-1090)*
Dutra Realty, Pleasanton *Also called Mason-Mcduffie Real Estate Inc (P-11593)*
Duxford Financial Inc ....E 949 471-2010
4490 Von Karman Ave Newport Beach (92660) *(P-9800)*
Dv Custom Farming LLC ....D 661 858-2888
2101 Mettler Frontage E Bakersfield (93307) *(P-337)*
Dva Renal Healthcare Inc ....D 949 588-9211
23141 Plaza Pointe Dr Laguna Hills (92653) *(P-22474)*
Dw Berry Farms LLC ....B 805 795-8403
3960 N Rose Ave Oxnard (93036) *(P-338)*
Dw Logistix, Winnetka *Also called David W Golen (P-3998)*
DW Morgan LLC ....D 925 460-2700
4185 Blackhawk Danville (94506) *(P-5050)*
DWA, Palm Springs *Also called Desert Water Agency Fing Corp (P-6238)*
Dwa Holdings LLC (HQ) ....D 818 695-5000
1000 Flower St Glendale (91201) *(P-18048)*
Dwa Nova LLC ....D 818 695-5000
1000 Flower St Glendale (91201) *(P-15658)*
Dwayne Nash Industries Inc ....C 916 253-1900
8825 Washington Blvd # 100 Roseville (95678) *(P-3151)*
Dwaynes Engineering & Cnstr ....D 661 762-7261
3655 Addie Ave Mc Kittrick (93251) *(P-1056)*
Dwiw Inc ....E 949 574-7147
700 W 16th St Costa Mesa (92627) *(P-833)*
Dwn, Hickman *Also called Dave Wilson Nursery Inc (P-252)*
Dy-Dee Service Pasadena Inc ....D 626 792-6183
40 E California Blvd Pasadena (91105) *(P-13631)*
Dya Assoc ....D 323 364-4270
8335 W Sunset Blvd # 320 Los Angeles (90069) *(P-11872)*
Dydee Service of Pasedena ....D 626 240-0115
40 E California Blvd Pasadena (91105) *(P-13632)*
Dykema Gossett PLLC ....D 213 457-1800
333 S Grand Ave Ste 2100 Los Angeles (90071) *(P-23058)*
Dynalectric Company ....C 805 517-1253
668 Flinn Ave Moorpark (93021) *(P-2565)*
Dynalectric Company ....B 858 712-4700
9505 Chesapeake Dr San Diego (92123) *(P-2566)*
Dynalectric Company ....C 714 236-2242
4462 Corporate Center Dr Los Alamitos (90720) *(P-2567)*
Dynalectric Company ....C 415 487-4700
825 Howe Rd Martinez (94553) *(P-2568)*
Dynamex Inc ....D 209 464-7008
4790 Frontier Way Ste A Stockton (95215) *(P-4397)*
Dynamex Operations West Inc ....E 714 994-1615
16900 Valley View Ave La Mirada (90638) *(P-4398)*
Dynamic Auto Images Inc ....B 714 981-4367
1407 N Batavia St Ste 102 Orange (92867) *(P-17813)*
Dynamic Chiropractic, Westminster *Also called Maxwell Petersen Associates (P-27326)*
Dynamic Detail, Orange *Also called Dynamic Auto Images Inc (P-17813)*
Dynamic Home Care Service Inc (PA) ....C 818 981-4446
14260 Ventura Blvd # 301 Sherman Oaks (91423) *(P-22288)*
Dynamic Maintenance Svcs Inc ....D 925 228-7434
837 Arnold Dr Ste 220 Martinez (94553) *(P-14254)*
Dynamic Plumbing Commercial ....D 951 343-1200
7343 Orangewood Dr Ste B Riverside (92504) *(P-2190)*
Dynamic Plumbing Systems Inc ....B 951 343-1200
5920 Winterhaven Ave Riverside (92504) *(P-2191)*
Dynamic Realty Corp ....D 626 931-3200
800 S Barranca Ave # 260 Covina (91723) *(P-11412)*
Dynamic Staffing Inc (PA) ....C 916 773-3900
920 Reserve Dr Ste 150 Roseville (95678) *(P-14604)*
Dynamo Aviation Inc ....D 818 785-9561
16760 Schoenborn St North Hills (91343) *(P-4886)*
Dyncorp ....C 619 522-2222
Nas Nrth Is Bldg 1479 San Diego (92135) *(P-15948)*
Dyncorp International LLC ....D 817 224-8200
896 Langford Lake Rd Fort Irwin (92310) *(P-4887)*
Dynegy Moss Landing LLC ....D 831 633-6618
7301 Highway 1 Moss Landing (95039) *(P-6028)*
Dyntek Inc (PA) ....C 949 271-6700
5241 California Ave # 150 Irvine (92617) *(P-16352)*
Dz Trading Ltd ....C 951 479-5700
12492 Feather Dr Eastvale (91752) *(P-8028)*
Dzyne Technologies Inc ....E 703 454-0704
11 Vanderbilt Irvine (92618) *(P-25649)*
E & B Ntral Resources Mgt Corp (PA) ....D 661 679-1714
1600 Norris Rd Bakersfield (93308) *(P-1022)*
E & C Fashion Inc ....B 323 262-0099
3600 E Olympic Blvd Los Angeles (90023) *(P-17143)*
E & E Co Ltd ....B 530 669-5991
2222 E Beamer St Woodland (95776) *(P-1158)*
E & E Co Ltd ....C 530 669-5991
2222 E Beamer St Woodland (95776) *(P-6757)*
E & E Co Ltd (PA) ....C 510 490-9788
45875 Northport Loop E Fremont (94538) *(P-6758)*
E & J Gallo Inc ....D 209 287-1716
3430 Tully Rd Ste 20 Modesto (95350) *(P-15949)*
E & J Gallo Winery ....D 707 431-5400
11447 Old Redwood Hwy Healdsburg (95448) *(P-142)*
E & J Gallo Winery ....E 707 967-9284
105a Zinfandel Ln Saint Helena (94574) *(P-27708)*
E & J Gallo Winery ....D 209 394-6271
5953 Weir Ave Livingston (95334) *(P-686)*
E & M AG Svc Inc A Cal Corp ....E 559 627-2724
2446 W Border Links Dr Visalia (93291) *(P-687)*
E & M Concrete Construction ....D 805 658-2888
2842 Sherwin Ave Ste A Ventura (93003) *(P-3251)*
E & M Electric and McHy Inc (PA) ....E 707 433-5578
126 Mill St Healdsburg (95448) *(P-7746)*
E & S International Entps Inc (PA) ....C 818 887-0700
7801 Hayvenhurst Ave Van Nuys (91406) *(P-7412)*
E & S Rsidential Care Svcs LLC ....D 559 275-3555
6083 N Marks Ave Fresno (93711) *(P-24511)*
E & T Foods Inc ....B 760 843-7730
14827 Seventh St Victorville (92395) *(P-449)*
E A Com Inc ....C 650 628-1500
209 Redwood Shores Pkwy Redwood City (94065) *(P-15123)*
E and B Natural Resources ....D 661 679-1700
1600 Norris Rd Bakersfield (93308) *(P-1044)*
E B C F, Oakland *Also called East Bay Community Foundation (P-24776)*
E B Stone & Son Inc ....D 707 426-2500
6111 Lambie Rd Suisun City (94585) *(P-9078)*

ALPHABETIC

E Business Solutions Inc E 800 660-2669
1271 Dodson Way Riverside (92507) ***(P-13822)***

E C R M C, El Centro *Also called El Centro Regional Medical Ctr* ***(P-21403)***

E C Wise Inc (PA) D 415 355-9473
1299 4th St Ste 505 San Rafael (94901) ***(P-16120)***

E Center C 530 634-1200
1506 Starr Dr Yuba City (95993) ***(P-24316)***

E D C, Torrance *Also called Electronic Data Care Inc* ***(P-15951)***

E D D 2100 D 209 941-6501
3127 Transworld Dr # 150 Stockton (95206) ***(P-10164)***

E E G and E P, Chico *Also called Enloe Medical Center* ***(P-21412)***

E Film Digital Labratories, Los Angeles *Also called Efilm LLC* ***(P-18050)***

E G Ayers Distributing Inc E 707 445-2077
5819 S Broadway St Eureka (95503) ***(P-8403)***

E H Summit Inc (PA) C 310 476-6571
11461 W Sunset Blvd Los Angeles (90049) ***(P-12544)***

E H Summit Inc D 310 273-0300
360 N Rodeo Dr Beverly Hills (90210) ***(P-12545)***

E I I, Bakersfield *Also called Electrcal Instrumentation Intl* ***(P-2572)***

E J Harrison & Sons Inc C 805 647-1414
1589 Lirio Ave Ventura (93004) ***(P-6389)***

E J Williams Property MGT D 209 473-4022
5637 N Pershing Ave Ste D Stockton (95207) ***(P-11008)***

E Jordan Brookes Co Inc (PA) D 562 968-2100
10634 Shoemaker Ave Santa Fe Springs (90670) ***(P-7241)***

E Jordan Brookes Co., Santa Fe Springs *Also called E Jordan Brookes Co Inc* ***(P-7241)***

E K T Farms, Watsonville *Also called Edward J Kelly* ***(P-340)***

E L Payne Heating Company E 310 275-5331
226 S Lucerne Blvd Los Angeles (90004) ***(P-2192)***

E L S, Los Angeles *Also called J C Entertainment Ltg Svcs Inc* ***(P-18375)***

E M S Trading Inc E 909 581-7800
5161 Richton St Montclair (91763) ***(P-8354)***

E M Tharp Inc (PA) D 559 782-5800
15243 Road 192 Porterville (93257) ***(P-6591)***

E O S International, Carlsbad *Also called Electronic Online Systems Intl* ***(P-15952)***

E P A, Sacramento *Also called Environmental Protection Agcy* ***(P-6540)***

E P U, Fresno *Also called Exceptnal Prents Unlimited Inc* ***(P-23791)***

E R G Home Health Provider D 562 403-1070
11700 South St Ste 200 Artesia (90701) ***(P-22289)***

E R I T Inc (PA) D 760 433-6024
251 Airport Rd Oceanside (92058) ***(P-24512)***

E R I T Inc C 760 721-1706
251 Airport Rd Oceanside (92058) ***(P-24513)***

E S 3, San Diego *Also called Enginring Sftwr Sys Sltons Inc* ***(P-25667)***

E S Q, Cupertino *Also called Esq Business Services Inc* ***(P-15672)***

E Street Cold Logistics LLC (PA) E 310 233-7300
901 E E St Wilmington (90744) ***(P-4500)***

E T Horn Company (PA) D 714 523-8050
16050 Canary Ave La Mirada (90638) ***(P-8926)***

E Tradeshowgirlscom D 949 661-4177
1 Ocean Rdg Laguna Niguel (92677) ***(P-17144)***

E W C H Inc D 510 783-4811
1805 West St Hayward (94545) ***(P-20380)***

E W Merritt Farms (PA) D 559 784-8916
11188 Road 192 Porterville (93257) ***(P-339)***

E Z Data Inc (HQ) D 626 585-3505
251 S Lake Ave Ste 200 Pasadena (91101) ***(P-15124)***

E Z Staffing Inc (PA) B 818 845-2500
801 N Brand Blvd Ste 1120 Glendale (91203) ***(P-14605)***

E&M, Healdsburg *Also called E & M Electric and McHy Inc* ***(P-7746)***

E&S Financial Group Inc D 805 644-1621
4253 Transport St Ventura (93003) ***(P-9879)***

E-Loan Inc (HQ) A 925 847-6200
6230 Stoneridge Mall Rd Pleasanton (94588) ***(P-9880)***

E-N Realty II E 909 597-1736
1081 Grand Ave Diamond Bar (91765) ***(P-11413)***

E-Sceptre Inc D 888 350-8989
16800 Gale Ave City of Industry (91745) ***(P-26357)***

E-Solutions, San Jose *Also called Vidhwan Inc* ***(P-27512)***

E-Times Corporation Ltd B 213 452-6720
601 S Figueroa St # 5000 Los Angeles (90017) ***(P-16219)***

E. S. Babcock & Sons, Riverside *Also called Babcock Laboratories Inc* ***(P-26684)***

E.V. Roberts, Carson *Also called Cirrus Enterprises LLC* ***(P-8912)***

E2 Consulting Engineers Inc B 510 652-1164
1900 Powell St Ste 250 Emeryville (94608) ***(P-25650)***

E2 Corp D 818 904-5660
8121 Van Nuys Blvd # 308 Panorama City (91402) ***(P-15950)***

E2 Solutions, Panorama City *Also called E2 Corp* ***(P-15950)***

E3 Healthcare Management LLC D 650 324-0600
375 Forest Ave Palo Alto (94301) ***(P-26845)***

Ea, Redwood City *Also called Electronic Arts Inc* ***(P-15664)***

Ea Consulting Inc E 916 357-6767
1024 Iron Point Rd Folsom (95630) ***(P-16353)***

Ea Mobile Inc B 310 754-7125
5510 Lincoln Blvd Los Angeles (90094) ***(P-5407)***

Eag Inc (HQ) C 408 454-4600
2710 Walsh Ave Santa Clara (95051) ***(P-26694)***

Eag Holdings LLC A 408 530-3500
2710 Walsh Ave Santa Clara (95051) ***(P-27709)***

Eag Laboratories, Santa Clara *Also called Eag Inc* ***(P-26694)***

Eagle Community Credit Union (PA) D 949 588-9400
23021 Lake Center Dr Lake Forest (92630) ***(P-9629)***

Eagle Glen Country Club LLC D 951 272-4653
1800 Eagle Glen Pkwy Corona (92883) ***(P-18710)***

Eagle Glen Golf Club, Corona *Also called Eagle Glen Country Club LLC* ***(P-18710)***

Eagle High Reach Equipment LLC D 619 265-2637
14241 Alondra Blvd La Mirada (90638) ***(P-14501)***

Eagle Intermodel Services, San Bernardino *Also called Eagle Systems Inc* ***(P-4133)***

Eagle Lath & Plaster Inc D 916 925-1435
4350 Warehouse Ct North Highlands (95660) ***(P-1526)***

Eagle Rafting C 760 376-3648
13226 Sierra Way Kernville (93238) ***(P-4715)***

Eagle Resources Inc D 805 922-0000
516 W Boone St Santa Maria (93458) ***(P-14606)***

Eagle Ridge Golf Club, Gilroy *Also called Eagle Ridge Golf Cntry CLB LLC* ***(P-18916)***

Eagle Ridge Golf Cntry CLB LLC C 408 846-4531
2951 Club Dr Gilroy (95020) ***(P-18916)***

Eagle Roofing Products, Rialto *Also called Burlingame Industries Inc* ***(P-13459)***

Eagle Roofing Products, Stockton *Also called Burlingame Industries Inc* ***(P-6921)***

Eagle Security Service Inc C 310 532-1626
12903 S Normandie Ave Gardena (90249) ***(P-16635)***

Eagle Systems Inc C 909 386-4343
395 N Mount Vernon Ave San Bernardino (92411) ***(P-4133)***

Eagle Systems Intl Inc B 510 259-1700
28436 Satellite St Hayward (94545) ***(P-2193)***

Eagle Vnes Vnyrds Golf CLB LLC D 707 257-4470
580 S Kelly Rd American Canyon (94503) ***(P-18917)***

EAGLES HALL, Roseville *Also called Fraternal Order Eagles 1582* ***(P-10878)***

Eah Elena Gardens LP B 415 295-8840
1902 Lakewood Dr San Jose (95132) ***(P-11009)***

Eah Housing, San Rafael *Also called Eah Inc* ***(P-11147)***

Eah Inc (PA) D 415 258-1800
22 Pelican Way San Rafael (94901) ***(P-11147)***

Elliant LLC E 619 255-9344
1202 Morena Blvd Ste 100 San Diego (92110) ***(P-27710)***

Eam Inc (PA) D 213 342-1760
5404 Whitsett Ave Ste 50 Valley Village (91607) ***(P-17631)***

EAM Enterprises Inc (PA) B 818 248-9100
4005 Foothill Blvd La Crescenta (91214) ***(P-11414)***

Eappraiseit LLC (PA) D 800 281-6200
12395 First American Way Poway (92064) ***(P-11415)***

Earl's Organic Produce, San Francisco *Also called Earls Organic* ***(P-8673)***

Earle M Jorgensen Company D 510 487-2700
31100 Wiegman Rd Hayward (94544) ***(P-7271)***

Earle M Jorgensen Company D 323 567-1122
350 S Grand Ave Ste 5100 Los Angeles (90071) ***(P-7272)***

Earls Organic D 415 824-7419
2101 Jerrold Ave Ste 100 San Francisco (94124) ***(P-8673)***

Earlwood LLC D 310 371-1228
20820 Earl St Torrance (90503) ***(P-20381)***

Earlwood Convalescent Hospital, Torrance *Also called Earlwood LLC* ***(P-20381)***

Early Childhood Education, La Quinta *Also called Deser Sands Unifi Schoo Distr* ***(P-24313)***

Early Childhood Services, Ridgecrest *Also called Desert Area Resources Training* ***(P-24774)***

Early Morning LLC D 503 912-5261
30135 Mc Combs Rd Wasco (93280) ***(P-256)***

Early Transportation Services D 510 324-1119
30796 San Clemente St Hayward (94544) ***(P-4134)***

Earth Island Institute Inc D 510 859-9100
2150 Allston Way Ste 460 Berkeley (94704) ***(P-25418)***

Earth Systems Southwest (HQ) D 760 345-1588
79811 Country Club Dr B Bermuda Dunes (92203) ***(P-25651)***

Earth Technology Corp USA A 213 593-8000
1999 Avenue Of Los Angeles (90067) ***(P-6390)***

Earthbound Farm LLC (HQ) A 831 623-7880
1721 San Juan Hwy San Juan Bautista (95045) ***(P-508)***

Earthbound Productions LLC D 504 734-3337
849 N Occidental Blvd Los Angeles (90026) ***(P-18049)***

Earthco, Santa Ana *Also called Morrison Landscaping Inc* ***(P-7323)***

Earthtech, Oakland *Also called Kaiser Group Holdings Inc* ***(P-25775)***

Easia Golf Investment LLC D 760 775-2000
84000 Terra Lago Pkwy Indio (92203) ***(P-12221)***

East Area Office, Walnut Creek *Also called East Bay Municipl Utilty Distr* ***(P-6244)***

East Bay Airport Shuttle, San Jose *Also called South Bay Airport Shuttle* ***(P-3729)***

East Bay Airport Shuttle, Pleasant Hill *Also called East Bay Connection Inc* ***(P-3647)***

East Bay Asian Local Dev Corp C 510 267-1917
1825 San Pablo Ave # 200 Oakland (94612) ***(P-11010)***

East Bay Asian Youth Center E 510 533-1092
2025 E 12th St Oakland (94606) ***(P-23776)***

East Bay Btncal Zoological Soc D 510 632-9525
9777 Golf Links Rd Oakland (94605) ***(P-19162)***

East Bay Clarklift Inc D 559 268-6621
4646 E Jensen Ave Fresno (93725) ***(P-7747)***

East Bay Community Foundation D 510 836-3223
200 Frank H Ogawa Plz Oakland (94612) ***(P-24776)***

East Bay Connection Inc E 925 609-1920
140 Mayhew Way Ste 1002 Pleasant Hill (94523) ***(P-3647)***

East Bay Foundation Grad Med D 510 437-4197
1411 E 31st St Oakland (94602) ***(P-22794)***

East Bay Innovations D 510 618-1580
2450 Washington Ave # 240 San Leandro (94577) ***(P-17145)***

East Bay Municipal Utility Dst D 866 403-2683
2149 Union St Oakland (94607) ***(P-6241)***

East Bay Municipl Utilty Distr D 866 403-2683
1100 21st St Oakland (94607) ***(P-6242)***

East Bay Municipl Utilty Distr C 866 403-2683
3999 Lakeside Dr Richmond (94806) ***(P-6243)***

East Bay Municipl Utilty Distr D 866 403-2683
2551 N Main St Walnut Creek (94597) ***(P-6244)***

East Bay Municipl Utilty Distr D 866 403-2683
2020 Wake Ave Oakland (94607) ***(P-6391)***

East Bay Municipl Utilty Distr (PA) A 866 403-2683
375 11th St Oakland (94607) ***(P-6245)***

East Bay Municipl Utilty Distr D 510 287-0760
375 11th St Oakland (94607) ***(P-6246)***

Mergent e-mail: customerrelations@mergent.com
1286
2019 Directory of California Wholesalers and Services Companies
(P-0000) Products & Services Section entry number
(PA)=Parent Co (HQ)=Headquarters (DH)=Div Headquarters

East Bay Nephrology.....E.....510 235-1057
2089 Vale Rd Ste 32 San Pablo (94806) **(P-19451)**

East Bay Regional Park Dst.....D.....510 881-1833
17930 Lake Chabot Rd Castro Valley (94546) **(P-19163)**

East Bay Regional Park Public, Castro Valley *Also called East Bay Regional Park Dst* **(P-19163)**

East Bay Transitional Homes, Oakland *Also called Bay Area Community Svcs Inc* **(P-23502)**

East Crson II Hsing Prtners LP.....D.....310 522-9606
401 W Carson St Carson (90745) **(P-11416)**

East Hall Investors Inc.....D.....530 328-1900
11601 Blocker Dr Ste 200 Auburn (95603) **(P-12222)**

East L A Remarkable Citizens (PA).....D.....323 223-3079
3839 Selig Pl Los Angeles (90031) **(P-23777)**

East Lion Corporation.....E.....626 912-1818
318 Brea Canyon Rd Walnut (91789) **(P-8355)**

East Los Angeles Community Un (PA).....E.....323 721-1655
5400 E Olympic Blvd Fl 3 Commerce (90022) **(P-9737)**

East Los Angeles Doctors Hosp, Los Angeles *Also called Eladh LP* **(P-21404)**

East Los Angeles Mental Hlth.....D.....323 725-1337
1436 Goodrich Blvd Commerce (90022) **(P-22572)**

East Palo Alto Hotel Dev Inc.....C.....650 566-1200
2050 University Ave East Palo Alto (94303) **(P-12546)**

East Palo Alto Y M C A.....E.....650 328-9622
550 Bell St East Palo Alto (94303) **(P-25153)**

East San Gbriel Vly Consortium.....D.....626 960-3964
5200 Irwindale Ave # 210 Irwindale (91706) **(P-3788)**

East Valley Cmnty Hlth Ctr Inc (PA).....D.....626 919-3402
420 S Glendora Ave West Covina (91790) **(P-22573)**

East Valley Family YMCA Dcc, North Hollywood *Also called Young Mens Chrstn Assn of La* **(P-24402)**

East Valley Glendora Hosp LLC.....B.....626 852-5000
150 W Route 66 Glendora (91740) **(P-21399)**

East Valley Hospital Med Ctr, Glendora *Also called East Valley Glendora Hosp LLC* **(P-21399)**

East Valley Tourist Dev Auth.....A.....760 342-5000
84245 Indio Springs Dr Indio (92203) **(P-19164)**

East Valley Water District.....D.....909 889-9501
31111 Greenspot Rd Highland (92346) **(P-6247)**

East West, Cerritos *Also called Global Med Services Inc* **(P-22302)**

East West Bank (HQ).....B.....626 768-6000
135 N Ls Rbls Ave 100 Pasadena (91101) **(P-9440)**

East West Bank.....C.....415 391-8912
555 Montgomery St Bsmt San Francisco (94111) **(P-9441)**

East West Bank.....D.....626 280-1688
228 W Garvey Ave Monterey Park (91754) **(P-9533)**

Eastbiz Corporation (PA).....D.....310 212-7134
3501 Jack Northrop Ave Hawthorne (90250) **(P-19165)**

Easter Seal Soc Superior Cal (PA).....C.....916 485-6711
3205 Hurley Way Sacramento (95864) **(P-22795)**

Easter Seal Society, Lancaster *Also called Easter Seals Southern Cal Inc* **(P-24778)**

Easter Seals Inc.....D.....831 338-3383
16403 Highway 9 Boulder Creek (95006) **(P-13449)**

Easter Seals Central Cal.....B.....831 684-2166
9010 Soquel Dr Aptos (95003) **(P-23778)**

Easter Seals Main Office, Sacramento *Also called Easter Seal Soc Superior Cal* **(P-22795)**

Easter Seals Southern Cal Inc.....D.....818 551-0128
710 W Broadway Glendale (91204) **(P-24777)**

Easter Seals Southern Cal Inc.....E.....661 723-3414
340 E Avenue I Ste 101 Lancaster (93535) **(P-24778)**

Eastern California Museum (PA).....B.....760 878-0292
155 N Grant St Independence (93526) **(P-24882)**

Eastern Goldfields Inc.....C.....619 497-2555
1660 Hotel Cir N Ste 207 San Diego (92108) **(P-27222)**

Eastern Los Angeles RE (PA).....B.....626 299-4700
1000 S Fremont Ave # 40 Alhambra (91803) **(P-23779)**

Eastern Municipal Water Dst (PA).....B.....951 928-3777
2270 Trumble Rd Perris (92572) **(P-6248)**

Eastern Plumas Health Care.....D.....530 993-1225
700 3rd St Loyalton (96118) **(P-20382)**

Eastern Plumas Health Care (PA).....C.....530 832-4277
500 1st Ave Portola (96122) **(P-22796)**

Eastern Plumas Hospital, Portola *Also called Eastern Plumas Health Care* **(P-22796)**

Eastern Sierra Transit Auth.....E.....760 872-1901
703 Airport Rd Bishop (93514) **(P-3877)**

Eastern Star Homes California (PA).....D.....714 986-2380
16850 Bastanchury Rd Yorba Linda (92886) **(P-23780)**

EASTERN STAR PROFESSIONAL BUIL, Yorba Linda *Also called Eastern Star Homes California* **(P-23780)**

Eastland Executive Office, West Covina *Also called Eastland Tower Partnership* **(P-11169)**

Eastland Tower Partnership.....E.....626 858-2000
1932 E Garvey Ave S West Covina (91791) **(P-11169)**

Eastman Music Company (PA).....D.....909 868-1777
2158 Pomona Blvd Pomona (91768) **(P-8029)**

Eastmans Guitars, Pomona *Also called Eastman Music Company* **(P-8029)**

Easton Hockey, Thousand Oaks *Also called Bauer Hockey Inc* **(P-7923)**

Eastrdge Prsonnel of Las Vegas.....D.....415 248-2567
530 Davis St San Francisco (94111) **(P-14607)**

Eastrdge Prsonnel of Las Vegas (PA).....E.....619 260-2000
2355 Northside Dr Ste 120 San Diego (92108) **(P-14608)**

Eastridge ADM Staffing, San Diego *Also called Eplica Inc* **(P-14850)**

Eastridge Infotech, San Diego *Also called Eastrdge Prsonnel of Las Vegas* **(P-14608)**

Eastridge Workforce Solutions, San Diego *Also called Teg Staffing Inc* **(P-14778)**

Eastside Group Corporation.....C.....213 368-9777
1830 W Olympic Blvd # 202 Los Angeles (90006) **(P-16636)**

Eastside Management Co Inc.....C.....209 578-9852
1131 12th St Ste C Modesto (95354) **(P-688)**

Eastwestproto Inc.....C.....888 535-5728
1120 S Maple Ave Ste 200 Montebello (90640) **(P-3789)**

Easun Inc.....C.....916 929-8855
2001 Point West Way Sacramento (95815) **(P-12547)**

Easy Care Mso LLC.....B.....562 676-9600
3900 Kilroy Airport Way # 110 Long Beach (90806) **(P-22797)**

Easy Fuel, Aliso Viejo *Also called Efuel LLC* **(P-8956)**

Easy Ride Transportation.....D.....424 999-8830
1820 W Carson St Ste 202 Torrance (90501) **(P-5224)**

Easypost, San Francisco *Also called Simpler Postage Inc* **(P-5169)**

Easyturf Inc (HQ).....D.....760 745-7026
2750 La Mirada Dr Vista (92081) **(P-3511)**

Eaton Canyon Golf Course, Altadena *Also called D C Golf A CA Partnership* **(P-18705)**

Eaton Corporation.....B.....818 409-0200
4690 Colorado Blvd Los Angeles (90039) **(P-7355)**

Eb, Santa Rosa *Also called Exchange Bank* **(P-9534)**

EBA & M Corporation (PA).....D.....714 668-8920
3505 Cadillac Ave O201 Costa Mesa (92626) **(P-10202)**

Ebc Inc (PA).....D.....310 753-6407
219 Manhattan Beach Blvd Manhattan Beach (90266) **(P-1159)**

EBM Janitorial Services Inc.....D.....805 523-3700
5260 Bonsai Ave Ste E Moorpark (93021) **(P-14255)**

Ebmud, Oakland *Also called East Bay Municipl Utilty Distr* **(P-6242)**

Ebmud, Richmond *Also called East Bay Municipl Utilty Distr* **(P-6243)**

Ebmud, Oakland *Also called East Bay Municipl Utilty Distr* **(P-6391)**

EBMUD, Oakland *Also called East Bay Municipl Utilty Distr* **(P-6245)**

Ebmud, Oakland *Also called East Bay Municipl Utilty Distr* **(P-6246)**

Ebmud - Construction and Maint, Oakland *Also called East Bay Municipal Utility Dst* **(P-6241)**

Ebs Concrete Inc.....E.....951 279-6869
1320 E 6th St Ste 100 Corona (92879) **(P-3252)**

Ebs General Engineering Inc.....D.....951 279-6869
1320 E 6th St Ste 100 Corona (92879) **(P-1762)**

EBSC LP.....D.....510 547-2244
3875 Telegraph Ave Oakland (94609) **(P-19452)**

EC Davis Health Services, Sacramento *Also called Internal Mdcine Rsdncy Affairs* **(P-25021)**

EC Group Inc (PA).....D.....310 815-2700
5960 Bowcroft St Los Angeles (90016) **(P-6720)**

Ecamsecure.....D.....888 246-0556
3400 E Airport Way Long Beach (90806) **(P-16890)**

ECB Corp (PA).....D.....714 385-8900
6400 Artesia Blvd Buena Park (90620) **(P-2194)**

Ecc, Burlingame *Also called Environmental Chemical Corp* **(P-25670)**

ECCU, Brea *Also called Evangelical Christian Cr Un* **(P-9634)**

Echelon Security Inc.....D.....408 436-8844
1604 Kerley Dr San Jose (95112) **(P-27711)**

Echo, San Jose *Also called Labcyte Inc* **(P-26395)**

Echo Landscape.....D.....510 481-8614
2401 Grant Ave San Lorenzo (94580) **(P-834)**

Echo Staffing, San Jose *Also called Summit Hr Worldwide Inc* **(P-27475)**

Echo, A Heatlhstream Company, San Diego *Also called Healthstream Inc* **(P-15702)**

ECi Corporation A Corp Nev (PA).....D.....408 941-9268
4300 Stevens Creek Blvd # 275 San Jose (95129) **(P-9801)**

Ecker & Associates, Foster City *Also called Ecker Consumer Recruiting Inc* **(P-26513)**

Ecker Consumer Recruiting Inc (PA).....E.....650 871-6800
1303 Melbourne St Foster City (94404) **(P-26513)**

Eclipse Berry Farms LLC.....D.....310 207-7879
11812 San Vicente Blvd # 250 Los Angeles (90049) **(P-97)**

Eclipse Solutions Inc.....D.....916 565-8090
2150 River Plaza Dr # 380 Sacramento (95833) **(P-16354)**

Ecmc-CA, Rancho Cordova *Also called Educational Credit MGT Corp* **(P-9694)**

Eco Bay Services Inc.....D.....415 643-7777
1501 Minnesota St San Francisco (94107) **(P-27712)**

Eco Farm Field Inc.....D.....951 676-4047
28790 Las Haciendas St Temecula (92590) **(P-689)**

Eco Farms Avocados Inc (PA).....D.....951 694-3013
28790 Las Haciendas St Temecula (92590) **(P-509)**

Eco Farms Sales Inc (PA).....D.....951 694-3013
28790 Las Haciendas St Temecula (92590) **(P-8674)**

Eco Flow Transportation LLC.....D.....310 816-0260
18735 S Ferris Pl Rancho Dominguez (90220) **(P-5051)**

Ecola Services Inc.....D.....818 920-7301
15314 Devonshire St Ste F Mission Hills (91345) **(P-14150)**

Ecologic Brands Inc.....E.....209 239-3600
550 Carnegie St Manteca (95337) **(P-9213)**

Ecology Control Industries.....D.....510 235-1393
255 Parr Blvd Richmond (94801) **(P-6538)**

Ecompanies LLC.....E.....310 586-4000
2120 Colorado Ave Fl 3 Santa Monica (90404) **(P-5552)**

Econa Corp.....E.....619 722-6555
1344 Paizay Pl Unit 732 Chula Vista (91913) **(P-26187)**

Econco Broadcast Service, Woodland *Also called CPI Econco Division* **(P-17902)**

Econnections Inc.....C.....626 307-6200
75 N Fair Oaks Ave Pasadena (91103) **(P-26846)**

Econo Air, Brea *Also called Mddr Inc* **(P-2276)**

Econo Air Conditioning Inc.....E.....714 630-3090
3366 E La Palma Ave Anaheim (92806) **(P-2195)**

Econo Lodge Inn & Suites, Buttonwillow *Also called Choice Hotels Intl Inc* **(P-12456)**

Economic Dev Corp of La County.....E.....213 622-4300
444 S Flower St Ste 3700 Los Angeles (90071) **(P-27713)**

Economic Development, Riverside *Also called County of Riverside* **(P-24175)**

Economic Development Dept, Riverside *Also called County of Riverside* **(P-23710)**

Economy Inn.....E.....760 256-5601
1243 E Main St Barstow (92311) **(P-12548)**

Econosoft Inc.....D.....408 442-3663
2375 Zanker Rd Ste 250 San Jose (95131) **(P-15125)**

Employee Codes: A=Over 500 employees, B=251-500
C=101-250, D=51-100, E=50
2019 Directory of California
Wholesalers and Services Companies
© Mergent Inc. 1-800-342-5647
1287

Econtactlive Inc ....D....209 548-4300
6436 Oakdale Rd Riverbank (95367) ***(P-17146)***
Ecorp Consulting Inc (PA) ....D....916 782-9100
2525 Warren Dr Rocklin (95677) ***(P-27223)***
Ecotech Rfrgn & Hvac Inc ....D....888 833-8100
630 S Sunkist St Ste R Anaheim (92806) ***(P-2196)***
Ecrio Inc ....D....408 973-7290
19925 Stevens Creek Blvd # 100 Cupertino (95014) ***(P-15659)***
Ecs, San Francisco *Also called Episcopal Comm Svc San Fran* ***(P-23788)***
Ecs South Bay Head Start, Chula Vista *Also called Episcopal Community* ***(P-23789)***
Ecullet Inc ....D....650 493-7300
1 Vintage Ct Woodside (94062) ***(P-6392)***
Ed Rocha Livestock Trnsp Inc ....D....209 538-1302
2400 Nickerson Dr Modesto (95358) ***(P-4135)***
ED Safety Services Inc ....C....209 333-0807
1040 W Kettleman Ln # 388 Lodi (95240) ***(P-1763)***
Ed Staub & Sons Petroleum Inc ....D....530 233-2610
406 W 8th St Alturas (96101) ***(P-8955)***
Ed Thoming & Sons Inc ....D....209 835-2792
33600 S Koster Rd Tracy (95304) ***(P-187)***
Edata Solutions Inc ....A....510 574-5380
39180 Liberty St Ste 125 Fremont (94538) ***(P-16121)***
Edaw Inc ....D....619 233-1454
401 W A St Ste 1200 San Diego (92101) ***(P-752)***
Edaw Inc ....D....916 414-5800
2020 L St Ste 400 Sacramento (95811) ***(P-753)***
Edaw Inc (HQ) ....C....415 955-2800
300 California St Fl 5 San Francisco (94104) ***(P-11873)***
Edc Probation, Shingle Springs *Also called County of El Dorado* ***(P-23636)***
Edc Service Corporation (del) ....D....909 390-4747
415 N Vineyard Ave # 205 Ontario (91764) ***(P-9680)***
Edco Disposal Corporation Inc (PA) ....C....619 287-7555
2755 California Ave Signal Hill (90755) ***(P-6393)***
Edco Disposal Corporation Inc ....D....714 522-3577
6762 Stanton Ave Buena Park (90621) ***(P-6394)***
Edco Drywall Company, Westminster *Also called Edco Drywall Inc* ***(P-2879)***
Edco Drywall Inc ....E....714 799-9886
7200 Hazard Ave Westminster (92683) ***(P-2879)***
Edco Waste & Recycl Svcs Inc (HQ) ....D....760 744-2700
224 S Las Posas Rd San Marcos (92078) ***(P-6395)***
EDCTA, Diamond Springs *Also called El Dorado County Transit Auth* ***(P-3648)***
Edd Payroll Services, Sacramento *Also called Employment Dev Cal Dept* ***(P-14613)***
Edelman Productions, San Francisco *Also called New Paradigm Productions Inc* ***(P-18084)***
Edelman Public Relations, San Francisco *Also called Daniel J Edelman Inc* ***(P-27551)***
Edelman Public Relations, Los Angeles *Also called Daniel J Edelman Inc* ***(P-27552)***
Edelman Public Relations, San Mateo *Also called Daniel J Edelman Inc* ***(P-13942)***
Edelman Public Relations, Los Angeles *Also called Daniel J Edelman Inc* ***(P-13943)***
Eden Area Regnl Occupational P ....D....510 293-2900
26316 Hesperian Blvd Hayward (94545) ***(P-24180)***
Eden Area Rop School, Hayward *Also called Eden Area Regnl Occupational P* ***(P-24180)***
Eden Housing Inc (PA) ....D....510 582-1460
22645 Grand St Hayward (94541) ***(P-1282)***
Eden Housing Inc ....D....925 297-4297
3428 Mt Diablo Blvd Lafayette (94549) ***(P-1283)***
Eden Housing Management Inc (PA) ....E....510 582-1460
22645 Grand St Hayward (94541) ***(P-11417)***
Eden Labs Med Group Inc ....E....510 537-1234
20103 Lake Chabot Rd Castro Valley (94546) ***(P-19453)***
Eden Medical Center, Castro Valley *Also called Eden Township Hospital Dst* ***(P-21400)***
Eden Medical Center, Sacramento *Also called Sutter Health* ***(P-21831)***
Eden Township Hospital Dst ....A....510 538-2031
20400 Lake Chabot Rd # 303 Castro Valley (94546) ***(P-21400)***
Eden Villa, Castro Valley *Also called Ku Kyoung* ***(P-20571)***
Eden West Rehabilitation ....D....510 783-4811
1805 West St Hayward (94545) ***(P-20383)***
Edf Msschstts Spnsor Mmber LLC ....A....888 903-6926
15445 Innovation Dr San Diego (92128) ***(P-6029)***
Edf Renewable Energy, San Diego *Also called Milo Wind Project LLC* ***(P-6053)***
Edf Renewables Inc (PA) ....C....858 521-3300
15445 Innovation Dr San Diego (92128) ***(P-2197)***
Edf Renewables Services Inc (HQ) ....D....858 521-3575
15445 Innovation Dr San Diego (92128) ***(P-17794)***
Edf Rnwbles Asset Holdings Inc ....A....888 903-6926
15445 Innovation Dr San Diego (92128) ***(P-6030)***
Edge Financial Inc ....E....323 857-5809
10100 Santa Monica Blvd Los Angeles (90067) ***(P-13704)***
Edge Mortgage Advisory Co LLC ....D....714 564-5800
2125 E Katella Ave # 350 Anaheim (92806) ***(P-27714)***
Edge Systems LLC (PA) ....C....800 603-4996
2165 E Spring St Long Beach (90806) ***(P-7178)***
Edgemine Inc ....C....323 267-8222
1801 E 50th St Los Angeles (90058) ***(P-8300)***
Edges Electrical Group LLC (HQ) ....D....408 293-5818
1135 Auzerais Ave San Jose (95126) ***(P-7356)***
Edgewater Convalescent Hosp ....D....562 434-0974
2625 E 4th St Long Beach (90814) ***(P-20384)***
Edgewater Networks Inc ....D....408 351-7200
5225 Hellyer Ave Ste 100 San Jose (95138) ***(P-5553)***
Edgewater Plumbing of Benicia ....E....707 747-9204
5143 Port Chicago Hwy Concord (94520) ***(P-2198)***
Edgewater Skilled Nursing Ctr, Long Beach *Also called Edgewater Convalescent Hosp* ***(P-20384)***
Edgewave Inc ....D....800 782-3762
4225 Executive Sq # 1600 La Jolla (92037) ***(P-15660)***
Edgewise Media Services Inc (PA) ....D....714 919-2020
4518 W Vanowen St Burbank (91505) ***(P-7469)***
Edgewood Center, Azusa *Also called RES-Care California Inc* ***(P-20951)***
Edgewood Ctr For Childrens (PA) ....B....415 681-3211
1801 Vicente St San Francisco (94116) ***(P-24514)***
Edgewood Partners Insur Ctr ....C....415 356-3900
1390 Willow Pass Rd # 800 Concord (94520) ***(P-10610)***
Edgewood Partners Insur Ctr ....D....415 456-4323
1010 B St Ste 423 San Rafael (94901) ***(P-10611)***
Edgewood Properties (PA) ....D....925 838-2847
3096 Sandstone Rd Alamo (94507) ***(P-11011)***
Edgewood Prtners Insur Ctr Inc (PA) ....D....415 356-3900
1390 Willow Pass Rd # 800 Concord (94520) ***(P-10612)***
Edinger Medical Group Inc (PA) ....C....714 965-2500
9900 Talbert Ave 302 Fountain Valley (92708) ***(P-19454)***
Edison Capital (HQ) ....D....909 594-3789
18101 Von Karman Ave Irvine (92612) ***(P-6031)***
Edison International (PA) ....D....626 302-2222
2244 Walnut Grove Ave Rosemead (91770) ***(P-6032)***
Edison Mission Energy (HQ) ....E....626 302-5778
2244 Walnut Grove Ave Rosemead (91770) ***(P-6033)***
Edison Mssion Midwest Holdings ....A....626 302-2222
2244 Walnut Grove Ave Rosemead (91770) ***(P-6034)***
Edith Witt Senior Community, San Francisco *Also called Mercy Hsing California Xxxiv* ***(P-11066)***
Edmin Open Systems Inc (PA) ....D....858 712-9341
5471 Krny Vlla Rd Ste 310 San Diego (92123) ***(P-16355)***
Edmunds Holding Company (PA) ....A....310 309-6300
2401 Colorado Ave Santa Monica (90404) ***(P-16220)***
Edmunds.com, Santa Monica *Also called Edmunds Holding Company* ***(P-16220)***
Edmundscom Inc (HQ) ....A....310 309-6300
2401 Colorado Ave Santa Monica (90404) ***(P-13944)***
Edo LLC ....C....914 641-2000
3500 Willow Ln Thousand Oaks (91361) ***(P-25652)***
EDS West LLC ....D....323 887-7367
6666 E Washington Blvd Commerce (90040) ***(P-4009)***
Education California Dept ....B....510 794-3666
39350 Gallaudet Dr Fremont (94538) ***(P-24317)***
Educational Credit MGT Corp ....B....800 367-1590
P.O. Box 419045 Rancho Cordova (95741) ***(P-9694)***
Educational Employees Cr Un (PA) ....C....559 437-7700
2222 W Shaw Ave Fresno (93711) ***(P-9549)***
Educational Employees Cr Un ....E....559 587-4460
1460 W 7th St Hanford (93230) ***(P-9630)***
Educational Employees Cr Un ....D....559 896-0222
3488 W Shaw Ave Fresno (93711) ***(P-9631)***
Educational Media Foundation (PA) ....B....916 251-1600
5700 West Oaks Blvd Rocklin (95765) ***(P-5709)***
Educational Services Division, Ontario *Also called American Fidelity Assurance Co* ***(P-10518)***
Edward B Ward & Company Inc (HQ) ....E....415 330-6600
99 S Hill Dr Ste B Brisbane (94005) ***(P-7646)***
Edward E Straine CPA ....D....916 646-6464
1760 Creekside Oaks Dr Sacramento (95833) ***(P-26188)***
Edward J Kelly ....C....831 724-0832
959 Riverside Rd Watsonville (95076) ***(P-340)***
Edward Straling ....E....760 887-3673
2940 Grace Ln Ste C Costa Mesa (92626) ***(P-2569)***
Edward Thomas Companies ....D....714 782-7500
640 W Katella Ave Anaheim (92802) ***(P-12549)***
Edward Thomas Hospitality Corp ....B....310 458-0030
1 Pico Blvd Santa Monica (90405) ***(P-12550)***
Edward Vincent Park, Inglewood *Also called City of Inglewood* ***(P-19133)***
Edwardo Z Garcia ....C....661 854-5414
380 Tucker St Arvin (93203) ***(P-642)***
Edwards Brea 10 West ....E....714 672-4136
255 W Birch St Brea (92821) ***(P-18286)***
Edwards Cinemas University, Irvine *Also called Edwards Theatres Circuit Inc* ***(P-18299)***
Edwards Lifesciences LLC (HQ) ....A....949 250-2500
1 Edwards Way Irvine (92614) ***(P-19455)***
Edwards Technologies Inc ....D....310 536-7070
139 Maryland St El Segundo (90245) ***(P-2570)***
Edwards Theaters, Camarillo *Also called Edwards Theatres Circuit Inc* ***(P-18298)***
Edwards Theatres Circuit Inc ....D....951 361-1917
8032 Limonite Ave Riverside (92509) ***(P-18287)***
Edwards Theatres Circuit Inc ....D....714 428-0962
901 S Coast Dr Costa Mesa (92626) ***(P-18288)***
Edwards Theatres Circuit Inc ....D....619 660-3460
2951 Jamacha Rd El Cajon (92019) ***(P-18289)***
Edwards Theatres Circuit Inc ....D....949 582-4078
27741 Crown Valley Pkwy # 323 Mission Viejo (92691) ***(P-18290)***
Edwards Theatres Circuit Inc ....D....858 635-7716
10733 Westview Pkwy San Diego (92126) ***(P-18291)***
Edwards Theatres Circuit Inc ....D....714 557-5701
1561 W Sunflower Ave Santa Ana (92704) ***(P-18292)***
Edwards Theatres Circuit Inc (HQ) ....C....949 640-4600
300 Newport Center Dr Newport Beach (92660) ***(P-18293)***
Edwards Theatres Circuit Inc ....D....562 429-3321
7501 Carson Blvd Long Beach (90808) ***(P-18294)***
Edwards Theatres Circuit Inc ....D....760 471-3734
1180 W San Marcos Blvd San Marcos (92078) ***(P-18295)***
Edwards Theatres Circuit Inc ....D....562 403-1133
12761 Towne Center Dr Artesia (90703) ***(P-18296)***
Edwards Theatres Circuit Inc ....D....951 296-0144
40750 Winchester Rd Temecula (92591) ***(P-18297)***
Edwards Theatres Circuit Inc ....D....805 383-8866
680 Ventura Blvd Camarillo (93010) ***(P-18298)***
Edwards Theatres Circuit Inc ....D....949 854-8811
4245 Campus Dr Irvine (92612) ***(P-18299)***
Edwards Theatres Circuit Inc ....D....805 526-4329
1457 E Los Angeles Ave Simi Valley (93065) ***(P-18300)***

Mergent e-mail: customerrelations@mergent.com
1288
2019 Directory of California
Wholesalers and Services Companies
(P-0000) Products & Services Section entry number
(PA)=Parent Co (HQ)=Headquarters (DH)=Div Headquarters

Edwards Theatres Circuit Inc ....D....805 347-1164
1521 S Bradley Rd Santa Maria (93454) ***(P-18301)***

Edwards, Allen Beauty Salon, Encino *Also called Allen Edwards Beauty Salon* ***(P-13645)***

Eedar, Carlsbad *Also called Electronic Entrmt Design & RES* ***(P-26514)***

Ees Residential Group Homes ....D....408 265-8780
5369 Camden Ave Ste 280 San Jose (95124) ***(P-24515)***

Effort, The, Sacramento *Also called Wellspace Health* ***(P-22714)***

Efi, Fremont *Also called Electronics For Imaging Inc* ***(P-15132)***

Efilm LLC ....C....323 463-7041
1144 N Las Palmas Ave Los Angeles (90038) ***(P-18050)***

Eforcity Corp - Nfm ....D....626 442-3168
18525 Railroad St City of Industry (91748) ***(P-7470)***

Efront Financial Solutions Inc ....D....415 653-3239
135 Main St Ste 1330 San Francisco (94105) ***(P-15126)***

Efs West ....E....661 705-8200
28472 Constellation Rd Valencia (91355) ***(P-25653)***

Efuel LLC ....D....949 330-7145
65 Enterprise Fl 3 Aliso Viejo (92656) ***(P-8956)***

Egain Corporation (PA) ....C....408 636-4500
1252 Borregas Ave Sunnyvale (94089) ***(P-15661)***

Eggleston Youth Centers Inc (PA) ....D....626 480-8107
13001 Ramona Blvd Ste E Irwindale (91706) ***(P-23781)***

Egnyte Inc (PA) ....D....650 968-4018
1350 W Middlefield Rd Mountain View (94043) ***(P-15127)***

Ego Inc ....C....626 447-0296
444 E Huntington Dr # 300 Arcadia (91006) ***(P-26189)***

Egomotion Inc ....E....415 849-4662
729 Minna St San Francisco (94103) ***(P-15662)***

Eharmony Inc (PA) ....C....424 258-1199
10900 Wilshire Blvd Los Angeles (90024) ***(P-13741)***

Eharmony.com, Los Angeles *Also called Eharmony Inc* ***(P-13741)***

EHC LIFEBUILDERS, Milpitas *Also called Homefrst Svcs Santa Clara Cnty* ***(P-23842)***

Ehealth Inc (PA) ....D....650 584-2700
440 E Middlefield Rd Mountain View (94043) ***(P-10613)***

Ehealth Insurance.com, Gold River *Also called Ehealthinsurance Services Inc* ***(P-15128)***

Ehealthinsurance Services Inc (HQ) ....D....650 584-2700
440 E Middlefield Rd Mountain View (94043) ***(P-10614)***

Ehealthinsurance Services Inc ....C....916 608-6101
11919 Foundation Pl # 100 Gold River (95670) ***(P-15128)***

Ehealthwirecom Inc ....C....916 924-8092
2450 Venture Oaks Way # 100 Sacramento (95833) ***(P-22798)***

Ehmcke Sheet Metal Corp ....D....619 477-6484
840 W 19th St National City (91950) ***(P-3152)***

Ehs Medical Group, Monterey Park *Also called Synermed* ***(P-19997)***

Eichleay Engineers Inc ....B....925 689-7000
1390 Willow Pass Rd # 360 Concord (94520) ***(P-25654)***

Eichleay Inc ....C....562 256-8600
3780 Kilroy Airport Way # 440 Long Beach (90806) ***(P-25655)***

Eichleay Inc (PA) ....C....925 689-7000
1390 Willow Pass Rd # 600 Concord (94520) ***(P-25656)***

Eie Electric, Costa Mesa *Also called Pmd Industries Inc* ***(P-2682)***

Eight Star Commodities, El Centro *Also called All Star Seed* ***(P-490)***

Eight Star Equipment, El Centro *Also called Noblesse Oblige Inc* ***(P-482)***

Eighty Eight, Los Angeles *Also called Ms Bubbles Inc* ***(P-8324)***

Eighty One Enterprise Inc ....E....626 371-1980
9401 Whitmore St El Monte (91731) ***(P-8301)***

Eileen Nottoli ....D....415 837-1515
3 Embarcadero Ctr # 1200 San Francisco (94111) ***(P-23059)***

Eineridge Care Center, Sylmar *Also called Quality Long Term Care Nev Inc* ***(P-20713)***

Einfochips Inc (HQ) ....C....408 496-1882
2025 Gateway Pl Ste 270 San Jose (95110) ***(P-15129)***

Einstein Dental, San Diego *Also called Einstein Industries Inc* ***(P-15130)***

Einstein Industries Inc ....C....858 459-1182
6825 Flanders Dr San Diego (92121) ***(P-15130)***

Eis Group Inc ....C....415 402-2622
731 Sansome St Fl 4 San Francisco (94111) ***(P-15663)***

Eisenberg International Corp (PA) ....D....818 365-8161
9128 Jordan Ave Chatsworth (91311) ***(P-8257)***

Eisenberg Village, Reseda *Also called Los Angles Jewish HM For Aging* ***(P-20604)***

Eisenhower Desert Crdiolgy Ctr, Rancho Mirage *Also called Charlie W Shaeffer Jr MD* ***(P-19373)***

Eisenhower Medical Center (PA) ....A....760 340-3911
39000 Bob Hope Dr Rancho Mirage (92270) ***(P-21401)***

Eisner Pediatric Fmly Med Ctr, Los Angeles *Also called Pediatric & Family Medical Ctr* ***(P-22639)***

Eiu of California, Bakersfield *Also called Electrical & Instrumentation* ***(P-2575)***

Ejm Kyrene LLC (PA) ....E....310 278-1830
9061 Santa Monica Blvd Los Angeles (90069) ***(P-1338)***

Ejm Property Management, Los Angeles *Also called Ejm Kyrene LLC* ***(P-1338)***

Ek Health Services Inc (PA) ....D....408 973-0888
992 S De Anza Blvd Ste 10 San Jose (95129) ***(P-27224)***

Ekedal Concrete Inc ....D....949 720-8011
19600 Fairchild Ste 123 Irvine (92612) ***(P-2804)***

El & El Wood Products Corp (PA) ....C....909 591-0339
6011 Schaefer Ave Chino (91710) ***(P-6821)***

El Al Israel Airlines Ltd ....C....323 852-1252
6404 Wilshire Blvd # 1250 Los Angeles (90048) ***(P-4988)***

EL ARCA, Los Angeles *Also called East L A Remarkable Citizens* ***(P-23777)***

El Aviso Magazine ....B....323 586-9199
4850 Gage Ave Bell (90201) ***(P-9112)***

El Caballero Country Club ....C....818 654-3000
18300 Tarzana Dr Tarzana (91356) ***(P-18918)***

El Cajon Ford, El Cajon *Also called El Cajon Motors* ***(P-17653)***

El Cajon Medical Offices, El Cajon *Also called Kaiser Foundation Hospitals* ***(P-21501)***

El Cajon Motors (PA) ....D....619 579-8888
1595 E Main St El Cajon (92021) ***(P-17653)***

El Cajon Plumbing & Htg Sup Co ....E....619 449-7300
1655 N Magnolia Ave El Cajon (92020) ***(P-7647)***

El Cajon Vly Convalescent Ctr ....C....619 440-1211
510 E Washington Ave El Cajon (92020) ***(P-20385)***

El Camino Care Center, Carmichael *Also called Helios Healthcare LLC* ***(P-20522)***

El Camino Children & Fmly Svcs ....E....562 364-1258
9900 Lakewood Blvd # 104 Downey (90240) ***(P-23782)***

El Camino Country Club, Oceanside *Also called American Golf Corporation* ***(P-18839)***

El Camino Gardens, Carmichael *Also called Atria Senior Living Group Inc* ***(P-24430)***

El Camino Hospital ....C....650 988-7444
1503 Grant Rd Ste 120 Mountain View (94040) ***(P-23783)***

El Camino Hospital ....C....650 940-7000
2240 Tully Rd San Jose (95122) ***(P-22081)***

El Camino Hospital ....D....650 940-7310
2505 Hospital Dr Ste 1 Mountain View (94040) ***(P-22475)***

El Camino Hospital ....C....650 988-4825
625 Ellis St Ste 100 Mountain View (94043) ***(P-22019)***

El Camino Hospital Auxiliary ....A....650 940-7214
2500 Grant Rd Mountain View (94040) ***(P-22290)***

El Camino Labor LLC ....D....831 809-9537
815 Broadway St King City (93930) ***(P-643)***

El Camino Mem Pk & Mortuary, San Diego *Also called Stewart Enterprises Inc* ***(P-13699)***

El Camino Mem Pk & Mortuary, San Diego *Also called San Diego Cemetery Assn* ***(P-13697)***

El Camino Rental ....E....760 722-7368
1833 Oceanside Blvd Ste D Oceanside (92054) ***(P-14502)***

El Camino Surgery Center LLC ....D....650 961-1200
2480 Grant Rd Fl 1 Mountain View (94040) ***(P-21402)***

El Camino YMCA, Mountain View *Also called YMCA of Silicon Valley* ***(P-25312)***

El Capitan Canyon LLC ....D....805 685-3887
11560 Calle Real Santa Barbara (93117) ***(P-13465)***

El Centro Regional Medical Ctr (PA) ....A....760 339-7100
1415 Ross Ave El Centro (92243) ***(P-21403)***

El Clasificado (PA) ....D....323 837-4095
11205 Imperial Hwy Norwalk (90650) ***(P-13945)***

El Concilio San Mateo Cnty Inc ....E....650 373-1080
3180 Middlefield Rd Redwood City (94063) ***(P-23784)***

El Cordova Hotel ....D....619 435-4131
1351 Orange Ave Coronado (92118) ***(P-12551)***

El Dorado Country Club ....C....760 346-8081
46000 Fairway Dr Indian Wells (92210) ***(P-18919)***

El Dorado County Health Dept ....D....530 621-6100
931 Spring St Placerville (95667) ***(P-19456)***

El Dorado County Transit Auth ....D....530 642-5383
6565 Commerce Way Ste A Diamond Springs (95619) ***(P-3648)***

El Dorado Enterprises Inc ....A....310 719-9800
1000 W Redondo Beach Blvd Gardena (90247) ***(P-12552)***

El Dorado Hills County Wtr Dst ....D....916 933-6623
1050 Wilson Blvd El Dorado Hills (95762) ***(P-6249)***

El Dorado Hills Fire Dept, El Dorado Hills *Also called El Dorado Hills County Wtr Dst* ***(P-6249)***

El Dorado Irrigation District ....B....530 622-4513
2890 Mosquito Rd Placerville (95667) ***(P-6250)***

El Dorado Savings Bank (PA) ....D....530 622-1492
4040 El Dorado Rd Placerville (95667) ***(P-9523)***

El Dorado Water & Shower Svc ....E....530 622-8995
5821 Mother Lode Dr Placerville (95667) ***(P-6251)***

El Encanto Healthcare & Rehab ....C....626 336-1274
555 El Encanto Rd City of Industry (91745) ***(P-20386)***

EL ENCANTO HOME HEALTH CARE, City of Industry *Also called El Encanto Healthcare & Rehab* ***(P-20386)***

El Guapo Spices and Herbs Pkg, Commerce *Also called El Guapo Spices Inc* ***(P-8786)***

El Guapo Spices Inc (PA) ....D....213 312-1300
6200 E Slauson Ave Commerce (90040) ***(P-8786)***

El Macero Country Club Inc ....D....530 753-3363
44571 Clubhouse Dr El Macero (95618) ***(P-18920)***

El Mexicano, Montebello *Also called Marquez Brothers Intl Inc* ***(P-8425)***

El Monte Community Credit Un ....D....626 444-0501
11718 Ramona Blvd El Monte (91732) ***(P-9632)***

El Monte Convalescent Hospital ....D....626 442-1500
4096 Easy St El Monte (91731) ***(P-21060)***

El Monte Rents Inc (HQ) ....C....562 404-9300
12818 Firestone Blvd Santa Fe Springs (90670) ***(P-17659)***

El Monte Rv, Santa Fe Springs *Also called El Monte Rents Inc* ***(P-17659)***

El Nido Family Centers (PA) ....C....818 830-3646
10200 Sepulveda Blvd # 350 Mission Hills (91345) ***(P-23785)***

El Pas-Los Angles Lmsne Ex Inc ....E....213 623-2323
260 E 6th St Los Angeles (90014) ***(P-3895)***

El Paseo Limousine, Santa Clara *Also called Worldwide Ground Transportatio* ***(P-3862)***

El Pollo Loco Holdings Inc (PA) ....C....714 599-5000
3535 Harbor Blvd Ste 100 Costa Mesa (92626) ***(P-12137)***

El Prado Golf Course LP ....D....909 597-1751
6555 Pine Ave Chino (91708) ***(P-18711)***

El Rancho Motel Inc ....C....650 588-8500
1100 El Camino Real Millbrae (94030) ***(P-12553)***

El Rancho Vista Hlth Care Ctr, Pico Rivera *Also called Mariner Health Care Inc* ***(P-20623)***

El Segundo Eductl Foundation ....B....310 615-2650
641 Sheldon St El Segundo (90245) ***(P-24779)***

El Toro Water Distr Public Fac (PA) ....D....949 837-1662
24251 Los Alisos Blvd Lake Forest (92630) ***(P-6252)***

El-Com Cabletek, Garden Grove *Also called Elrob Inc* ***(P-7472)***

Eladh LP ....D....323 268-5514
4060 Whittier Blvd Los Angeles (90023) ***(P-21404)***

Elaine Null ....C....415 345-4428
1388 Sutter St Fl 11 San Francisco (94109) ***(P-17147)***

Elan Drug Delivery Inc ....D....770 531-8100
180 Oyster Point Blvd South San Francisco (94080) ***(P-26358)***

Elan Drug Technologies, South San Francisco *Also called Elan Drug Delivery Inc* ***(P-26358)***

ALPHABETIC

Elance Inc (HQ)..........C.......650 316-7500
441 Logue Ave Ste 150 Mountain View (94043) ***(P-13823)***
Elasticsearch Inc (PA)..........D.......650 458-2620
800 W El Camino Real # 350 Mountain View (94040) ***(P-15131)***
Elavon Inc..........A.......954 776-7990
1281 9th Ave Unit 706 San Diego (92101) ***(P-16221)***
Elavon Inc..........B.......925 734-8939
4234 Hacienda Dr Ste 250 Pleasanton (94588) ***(P-16222)***
Elcor Electric Inc..........C.......408 986-1320
3310 Bassett St Santa Clara (95054) ***(P-2571)***
Elder Care Alliance Camarillo..........D.......510 769-2700
1301 Marina Village Pkwy # 210 Alameda (94501) ***(P-24516)***
Elder Care Alliance San Rafael..........D.......510 769-2700
1301 Marina Village Pkwy # 210 Alameda (94501) ***(P-20387)***
Elder Options (PA)..........E.......530 626-6939
82 Main St Placerville (95667) ***(P-23786)***
Eldorado Care Center LP..........B.......619 440-1211
510 E Washington Ave El Cajon (92020) ***(P-20388)***
Eldorado Community Service Ctr..........D.......424 227-7971
335 E Manchester Blvd Inglewood (90301) ***(P-19457)***
Electra Owners Assoc..........C.......619 236-3310
700 W E St San Diego (92101) ***(P-24955)***
Electrcal Instrumentation Intl..........B.......661 836-9466
6950 District Blvd Bakersfield (93313) ***(P-2572)***
Electric Cloud Inc (PA)..........D.......408 419-4300
125 S Market St Ste 400 San Jose (95113) ***(P-7038)***
Electric Department, Santa Clara *Also called City of Santa Clara* ***(P-6020)***
Electric Lightwa..........D.......707 284-4000
3700 Old Redwood Hwy Santa Rosa (95403) ***(P-17148)***
Electric Motor & Supply Co., Fresno *Also called Electric Motor Shop* ***(P-7357)***
Electric Motor Shop..........D.......559 233-1153
250 Broadway St Fresno (93721) ***(P-7357)***
Electric Power RES Inst Inc (PA)..........A.......650 855-2000
3420 Hillview Ave Palo Alto (94304) ***(P-26359)***
Electric Sales Unlimited..........E.......562 463-8300
9023 Norwalk Blvd Santa Fe Springs (90670) ***(P-7358)***
Electric Svc & Sup Co Pasadena..........D.......626 795-8641
2668 E Foothill Blvd Pasadena (91107) ***(P-2573)***
Electric Tech Construction Inc..........D.......925 849-5324
1910 Mark Ct Ste 130 Concord (94520) ***(P-1916)***
Electric USA..........E.......800 921-1151
480 Aldo Ave Santa Clara (95054) ***(P-2574)***
Electrical & Instrumentation..........C.......661 836-9466
6950 District Blvd Bakersfield (93313) ***(P-2575)***
Electrical Distributors Co, San Jose *Also called Chester C Lehmann Co Inc* ***(P-7345)***
Electro Rent Corporation (PA)..........C.......818 786-2525
8511 Fllbrook Ave Ste 200 West Hills (91304) ***(P-14503)***
Electrolux Home Products Inc..........D.......909 605-9448
701 Malaga St Ontario (91761) ***(P-7413)***
Electronic Arts Inc (PA)..........B.......650 628-1500
209 Redwood Shores Pkwy Redwood City (94065) ***(P-15664)***
Electronic Clearing House Inc (HQ)..........D.......805 419-8700
730 Paseo Camarillo Camarillo (93010) ***(P-15665)***
Electronic Commerce LLC..........D.......800 770-5520
1 City Blvd W Ste 1850 Orange (92868) ***(P-9756)***
Electronic Control Systems LLC..........C.......858 513-1911
12575 Kirkham Ct Ste 1 Poway (92064) ***(P-2576)***
Electronic Data Care Inc..........D.......310 791-2600
23670 Hawthorne Blvd # 208 Torrance (90505) ***(P-15951)***
Electronic Entrmt Design & RES..........D.......760 579-7100
2075 Corte Del Nogal B Carlsbad (92011) ***(P-26514)***
Electronic Online Systems Intl..........D.......760 431-8400
2292 Faraday Ave Frnt Carlsbad (92008) ***(P-15952)***
Electronic Recyclers..........D.......253 736-2627
7815 N Palm Ave Ste 140 Fresno (93711) ***(P-6396)***
Electronic Recyclers America, Fresno *Also called Electronic Recyclers Intl Inc* ***(P-6397)***
Electronic Recyclers Intl Inc (PA)..........C.......800 374-3473
7815 N Palm Ave Ste 140 Fresno (93711) ***(P-6397)***
Electronics For Imaging Inc (PA)..........E.......650 357-3500
6750 Dumbarton Cir Fremont (94555) ***(P-15132)***
Electrosonic Inc (HQ)..........C.......818 333-3600
3320 N San Fernando Blvd Burbank (91504) ***(P-25657)***
Elegance Exotic Wood Flooring, Fontana *Also called Elegance Wood Products Inc* ***(P-6759)***
Elegance Wood Products Inc..........D.......909 484-7676
7351 Mcguire Ave Fontana (92336) ***(P-6759)***
Elegant Surfaces..........D.......209 823-9388
3640 Amrcn Rver Dr 150 Sacramento (95864) ***(P-6890)***
Eleganza Tiles Inc (PA)..........D.......714 224-1700
3125 E Coronado St Anaheim (92806) ***(P-2995)***
Element Mtrls Tech HB Inc..........D.......310 632-8500
18100 S Wilmington Ave Compton (90220) ***(P-26695)***
Element Mtrls Tech HB Inc (HQ)..........D.......714 892-1961
15062 Bolsa Chica St Huntington Beach (92649) ***(P-26696)***
Elements Behavioral Health Inc (PA)..........C.......562 741-6470
5000 Arprt Plz Dr Ste 100 Long Beach (90815) ***(P-22574)***
Elena Gardens Apartments, San Jose *Also called Eah Elena Gardens LP* ***(P-11009)***
Elena Villa Healthcare Center..........D.......562 868-0591
13226 Studebaker Rd Norwalk (90650) ***(P-21061)***
Elevate Credit Inc..........C.......817 928-1500
11710 El Camino Real San Diego (92130) ***(P-9710)***
Elevate Property Services LP..........E.......562 219-2101
19700 Fairchild Ste 150 Irvine (92612) ***(P-11170)***
Elevate Services Inc (PA)..........B.......310 853-8448
201 S Santa Fe Ave # 100 Los Angeles (90012) ***(P-27715)***
Eleven Inc..........C.......415 707-1111
500 Sansome St Ste 100 San Francisco (94111) ***(P-13824)***
Eleven Communications, San Francisco *Also called Eleven Inc* ***(P-13824)***
Eleven Western Builders Inc (PA)..........C.......760 796-6346
2862 Executive Pl Escondido (92029) ***(P-1527)***

Elias Elliott Lampasi Fehn (PA)..........D.......951 689-5031
7251 Magnolia Ave Riverside (92504) ***(P-20116)***
Elica Health Centers..........D.......916 454-2345
3701 J St Ste 201 Sacramento (95816) ***(P-19458)***
Elim Alzheimers & Rehab..........D.......559 320-2200
668 E Bullard Ave Fresno (93710) ***(P-20389)***
Elioco Produce Inc..........C.......831 424-5450
367 W Market St Ste A Salinas (93901) ***(P-644)***
Eliseo Esparza Delgadillo..........E.......209 745-3937
88 Wildflower Dr Galt (95632) ***(P-645)***
Elite, Culver City *Also called West Publishing Corporation* ***(P-16077)***
Elite & Associates..........D.......805 582-0353
18605 Parthenia St Northridge (91324) ***(P-3153)***
Elite Airways LLC..........C.......805 496-3334
4607 Lakeview Canyon Rd Westlake Village (91361) ***(P-4989)***
Elite Anywhere Corp..........D.......917 860-9247
82585 Showcase Pkwy Indio (92203) ***(P-5052)***
Elite Aviation LLC..........D.......818 988-5387
7501 Hayvenhurst Pl Van Nuys (91406) ***(P-4858)***
Elite Craftsman (PA)..........C.......562 989-3511
2763 Saint Louis Ave Long Beach (90755) ***(P-14256)***
Elite Electric..........D.......951 681-5811
9415 Bellegrave Ave Riverside (92509) ***(P-2577)***
Elite Enfrcment SEC Sltons Inc..........E.......866 354-8308
29970 Technology Dr Murrieta (92563) ***(P-16637)***
Elite Information Group Inc (HQ)..........B.......323 642-5200
5100 W Goldleaf Cir # 100 Los Angeles (90056) ***(P-15953)***
Elite Landscaping Inc..........C.......559 292-7760
2972 Larkin Ave Clovis (93612) ***(P-835)***
Elite Maintenance Services Inc..........D.......619 516-7000
7770 Regents Rd Ste 113 San Diego (92122) ***(P-14257)***
Elite Nursing Services Inc..........E.......714 919-7898
1915 W Orangewood Ave # 110 Orange (92868) ***(P-14609)***
Elite Power Inc..........D.......916 739-1580
6530 Asher Ln Sacramento (95828) ***(P-2578)***
Elite Roofing Company, Northridge *Also called Elite & Associates* ***(P-3153)***
Elite Security Services Inc..........B.......949 222-2203
18006 Sky Park Cir # 205 Irvine (92614) ***(P-16638)***
Elite Show Services Inc..........A.......619 574-1589
2878 Camino Del Rio S # 260 San Diego (92108) ***(P-16639)***
Elite Tek Services Inc..........D.......714 881-5301
131 Mercer Way Costa Mesa (92627) ***(P-16356)***
Elite Tile, Livermore *Also called Mthuron Inc* ***(P-3005)***
Elitecare Medical Staffing LLC..........D.......559 438-7700
761 E Locust Ave Ste 103 Fresno (93720) ***(P-14610)***
Elitegroup Cmpt Systems Inc..........C.......510 226-7333
6851 Mowry Ave Newark (94560) ***(P-7039)***
Elizabeth Glaser Pedia..........A.......310 231-0400
16130 Ventura Blvd # 250 Encino (91436) ***(P-22799)***
Elizabeth Hospice Inc (PA)..........C.......760 737-2050
500 La Terraza Blvd # 130 Escondido (92025) ***(P-22291)***
Elizabeth Larson..........D.......415 409-7300
3736 Jackson St San Francisco (94118) ***(P-11418)***
Elizabethan Inn Associates LP..........D.......916 448-1300
1935 Wright St Apt 231 Sacramento (95825) ***(P-12554)***
Elk Grove Adult Cmnty Training..........D.......916 431-3162
8810 Elk Grove Blvd Elk Grove (95624) ***(P-24956)***
Elk Grove Montessori School, Sacramento *Also called Montessori Learning Commons* ***(P-24350)***
Elk Grove Park District..........B.......916 685-9502
8820 Elk Grove Blvd Ste 2 Elk Grove (95624) ***(P-19166)***
Elk Grove Unified School Dst..........C.......916 686-7733
8421 Gerber Rd Sacramento (95828) ***(P-3921)***
Elk Hills Power LLC..........C.......661 763-2730
101 Ash St San Diego (92101) ***(P-6035)***
Elk Valley Casino Inc..........C.......707 464-1020
2500 Howland Hill Rd Crescent City (95531) ***(P-12555)***
Elkay Plastics Co Inc (PA)..........D.......323 722-7073
6000 Sheila St Commerce (90040) ***(P-8101)***
Elkhorn Berry Farms LLC..........D.......831 722-2472
262 E Lake Ave Watsonville (95076) ***(P-341)***
Elkor Properties, Santa Monica *Also called Roscoe Real Estate Ltd Partnr* ***(P-13139)***
Ellation Inc (PA)..........C.......415 796-3560
835 Market St Ste 700 San Francisco (94103) ***(P-15133)***
Ellen Degeneres Show, The, Burbank *Also called Wad Productions Inc* ***(P-18152)***
Ellie Fashion Group Inc..........D.......818 355-3812
1735 Stewart St Fl 2 Santa Monica (90404) ***(P-17149)***
Ellie Mae Inc (PA)..........C.......925 227-7000
4420 Rosewood Dr Ste 500 Pleasanton (94588) ***(P-15666)***
Ellie Mae Inc..........B.......818 223-2000
24025 Park Sorrento # 210 Calabasas (91302) ***(P-15134)***
Elliott Auto Supply Co Inc..........E.......800 278-6394
448 W Katella Ave Orange (92867) ***(P-6637)***
Elliott Auto Supply Co Inc..........D.......310 527-2500
1600 E Orangethorpe Ave Fullerton (92831) ***(P-6638)***
Elliott Benson Market Research..........E.......916 325-1670
1226 H St Sacramento (95814) ***(P-26515)***
Elliott Homes Inc (PA)..........C.......916 984-1300
340 Palladio Pkwy Ste 521 Folsom (95630) ***(P-1160)***
Elliott Laboratories Inc..........E.......510 440-9500
41039 Boyce Rd Fremont (94538) ***(P-26697)***
Ellis Building Contractors, Manhattan Beach *Also called Ebc Inc* ***(P-1159)***
Ellison Construction-Framing, Brentwood *Also called Ellison Framing Inc* ***(P-3031)***
Ellison Framing Inc..........C.......925 516-9269
160 Guthrie Ln Ste 13 Brentwood (94513) ***(P-3031)***
Ellison Machinery Co (HQ)..........D.......562 949-8311
9912 Pioneer Blvd Santa Fe Springs (90670) ***(P-7748)***
Ellison Technologies, Santa Fe Springs *Also called Ellison Machinery Co* ***(P-7748)***

Mergent e-mail: customerrelations@mergent.com
1290
2019 Directory of California
Wholesalers and Services Companies
(P-0000) Products & Services Section entry number
(PA)=Parent Co (HQ)=Headquarters (DH)=Div Headquarters

Ellison Technologies Inc D 562 949-8311
9912 Pioneer Blvd Santa Fe Springs (90670) ***(P-7749)***
Elljay Acoustics Inc D 714 961-1173
511 Cameron St Placentia (92870) ***(P-2880)***
Elma Electronic Inc E 209 858-2411
17700 Shideler Pkwy Lathrop (95330) ***(P-7471)***
Elmco Sales Inc (PA) D 626 855-4831
15070 Proctor Ave City of Industry (91746) ***(P-7613)***
Elmco/Duddy Inc (HQ) E 626 333-9942
15070 Proctor Ave City of Industry (91746) ***(P-7614)***
Elms Convalescent Hospital, Thousand Oaks *Also called Elms Sanitarium Inc* ***(P-20390)***
Elms Sanitarium Inc D 818 240-6720
3247 Windmist Ave Thousand Oaks (91362) ***(P-20390)***
Elmwood Care Center, Berkeley *Also called Shattuck Health Care Inc* ***(P-20758)***
Elo Touch Solutions Inc (HQ) C 408 597-8000
670 N Mccarthy Blvd # 100 Milpitas (95035) ***(P-7040)***
Elrob Inc D 714 230-6100
12691 Monarch St Garden Grove (92841) ***(P-7472)***
Els D 510 549-2929
2040 Addison St Berkeley (94704) ***(P-27716)***
Els Architecture, Berkeley *Also called Els* ***(P-27716)***
Els Investments C 916 388-0308
9980 Horn Rd Sacramento (95827) ***(P-754)***
Elsinore Vly Municpl Wtr Dst (PA) D 951 674-3146
31315 Chaney St Lake Elsinore (92530) ***(P-6253)***
Elston Masonry Inc D 760 728-3593
1422 Santa Margarita Dr Fallbrook (92028) ***(P-2805)***
Elvira Sandoval C 530 473-5718
2154 Hill Rd Williams (95987) ***(P-14611)***
Elvis Schoenberg Production E 323 344-1745
549 Marie Ave Los Angeles (90042) ***(P-18364)***
Elysium Jennings LLC C 661 679-1700
1600 Norris Rd Bakersfield (93308) ***(P-1035)***
Elyxir Distributing LLC C 831 761-6400
270 W Riverside Dr Watsonville (95076) ***(P-8994)***
Emagia Corporation E 408 654-6575
4701 P Henry Dr Bldg 20 Santa Clara (95054) ***(P-17150)***
Emagined Security Inc E 415 944-2977
2816 San Simeon Way San Carlos (94070) ***(P-16891)***
Emanuel Medical Center Inc C 209 667-5600
1801 N Olive Ave Turlock (95382) ***(P-21405)***
Emanuel Medical Center Inc (HQ) A 209 667-4200
825 Delbon Ave Turlock (95382) ***(P-21406)***
Emanuel Medical Center Inc C 209 664-2520
2121 Colorado Ave Ste A Turlock (95382) ***(P-21407)***
Emax Laboratories Inc E 310 618-8889
1835 W 205th St Torrance (90501) ***(P-26698)***
Embarcadero Homes Assn Inc D 954 776-2611
Lincoln Sq Condos Stockton (95207) ***(P-25154)***
Embarcadero Inn Associates C 415 495-2100
155 Steuart St San Francisco (94105) ***(P-12556)***
Embarcadero Systems Corp C 510 749-7400
1601 Harbor Bay Pkwy # 120 Alameda (94502) ***(P-15135)***
Embarcadero, The, San Francisco *Also called Crunch LLC* ***(P-18590)***
Embassador Private Securities D 415 822-8811
1341 Evans Ave San Francisco (94124) ***(P-9950)***
Embassy Sites-So San Francisco, South San Francisco *Also called Djont/Cmb Ssf Leasing LLC* ***(P-12528)***
Embassy Stes Monterey Bay Htl, Seaside *Also called Tucson Hotels LP* ***(P-13350)***
Embassy Stes San Dego-La Jolla, San Diego *Also called Sunstone Top Gun LLC* ***(P-13307)***
Embassy Suites, Milpitas *Also called Park Hotels & Resorts Inc* ***(P-13019)***
Embassy Suites, Palmdale *Also called Sunstone Hotel Investors LLC* ***(P-13295)***
Embassy Suites, NAPA *Also called Park Hotels & Resorts Inc* ***(P-13025)***
Embassy Suites, NAPA *Also called NAPA Es Leasing LLC* ***(P-12948)***
Embassy Suites, Covina *Also called Park Hotels & Resorts Inc* ***(P-13029)***
Embassy Suites, Burlingame *Also called Park Hotels & Resorts Inc* ***(P-13032)***
Embassy Suites, Arcadia *Also called Park Hotels & Resorts Inc* ***(P-13033)***
Embassy Suites, Downey *Also called Park Hotels & Resorts Inc* ***(P-13034)***
Embassy Suites, Buena Park *Also called Park Hotels & Resorts Inc* ***(P-13035)***
Embassy Suites, Irvine *Also called Park Hotels & Resorts Inc* ***(P-13038)***
Embassy Suites, Los Angeles *Also called Sunstone Hotel Investors Inc* ***(P-13293)***
Embassy Suites, San Rafael *Also called Hospitality Ventures MGT LLC* ***(P-12700)***
Embassy Suites, Brea *Also called Windsor Capital Group Inc* ***(P-13407)***
Embassy Suites, Temecula *Also called Windsor Capital Group Inc* ***(P-13408)***
Embassy Suites, Anaheim *Also called Park Hotels & Resorts Inc* ***(P-13041)***
Embassy Suites, Santa Ana *Also called Windsor Capital Group Inc* ***(P-13411)***
Embassy Suites, South San Francisco *Also called Park Hotels & Resorts Inc* ***(P-13042)***
Embassy Suites, South Lake Tahoe *Also called Park Hotels & Resorts Inc* ***(P-13043)***
Embassy Suites Anaheim Orange, Orange *Also called Ergs Aim Hotel Realty LLC* ***(P-12561)***
Embassy Suites Arcadia, Santa Monica *Also called Windsor Capital Group Inc* ***(P-13404)***
Embassy Suites Brea, Brea *Also called Park Hotels & Resorts Inc* ***(P-13020)***
Embassy Suites By Hilton San, San Diego *Also called Sunstone Top Gun Lessee Inc* ***(P-13308)***
Embassy Suites El Paso, Santa Monica *Also called Windsor Capital Group Inc* ***(P-13410)***
Embassy Suites Lompoc, Santa Monica *Also called Windsor Capital Group Inc* ***(P-13405)***
Embassy Suites Management LLC C 858 453-0400
4550 La Jolla Village Dr San Diego (92122) ***(P-12557)***
Embassy Suites Walnut Creek, Walnut Creek *Also called Interstate Hotels Resorts Inc* ***(P-26898)***
Embassy Suites- Santa Clara, Santa Clara *Also called Msr Hotels & Resorts Inc* ***(P-12947)***
Embassy Suites- Santa Clara, Santa Clara *Also called Santa Clara Tenant Corp* ***(P-13186)***
Embee Processing LLC B 714 546-9842
2136 S Hathaway St Santa Ana (92705) ***(P-25658)***
Embee Processing, Inc., Santa Ana *Also called Embee Processing LLC* ***(P-25658)***

Embrane Inc E 408 550-2700
2350 Mission College Blvd # 703 Santa Clara (95054) ***(P-15136)***
Emco High Voltage, Jackson *Also called Xp Power LLC* ***(P-7567)***
Emcor Fclities Svcs N Amer Inc C 858 712-4700
9505 Chesapeake Dr San Diego (92123) ***(P-2199)***
Emcor Services, Irvine *Also called Mesa Energy Systems Inc* ***(P-2278)***
Emerald Brook LLC E 760 345-4770
76000 Frank Sinatra Dr Palm Desert (92211) ***(P-13466)***
Emerald Cloud Lab Inc D 650 257-7554
844 Dubuque Ave South San Francisco (94080) ***(P-26360)***
Emerald Connect LLC (HQ) D 800 233-2834
15050 Avenue Of Sci 200 San Diego (92128) ***(P-16122)***
Emerald Desert Rv Resort, Palm Desert *Also called Emerald Brook LLC* ***(P-13466)***
Emerald Expositions LLC (HQ) B 949 226-5700
31910 Del Obispo St # 200 San Juan Capistrano (92675) ***(P-17151)***
Emerald Landscape Services D 714 844-2200
1041 N Kemp St Anaheim (92801) ***(P-836)***
Emerald Site Services Inc D 916 685-7211
9883 Kent St Elk Grove (95624) ***(P-3423)***
Emerald Ter Convalescent Hosp, Los Angeles *Also called Equicare Medical Supply Inc* ***(P-20406)***
Emerald Textiles LLC B 619 330-7077
1725 Dornoch Ct San Diego San Diego (92154) ***(P-13486)***
Emerald Trans Los Angeles LLC E 323 277-2500
5756 Alba St Los Angeles (90058) ***(P-4010)***
Emercon Construction Inc (PA) D 714 630-9615
2906 E Coronado St Anaheim (92806) ***(P-1161)***
Emerge Digital Inc D 415 839-5055
543 Howard St Lbby San Francisco (94105) ***(P-16357)***
Emerge Digital Group, San Francisco *Also called Emerge Digital Inc* ***(P-16357)***
Emergency Ambulance Service D 714 990-1331
3200 E Birch St Ste A Brea (92821) ***(P-3790)***
Emergency Groups Office, Arcadia *Also called Ego Inc* ***(P-26189)***
Emergency Med Group of Folsom D 916 983-7470
1650 Creekside Dr Folsom (95630) ***(P-19459)***
Emergency Medicine Specialist D 714 543-8911
1010 W La Veta Ave # 755 Orange (92868) ***(P-21408)***
Emergency Physicians Med Group, Citrus Heights *Also called Dignity Health* ***(P-19444)***
Emergency Reporting Systems, El Monte *Also called ERs SEC Alarm Systems Inc* ***(P-7360)***
Emergency Technologies Inc D 818 765-4421
7345 Varna Ave North Hollywood (91605) ***(P-7359)***
Emergent Medical Associates (PA) D 310 379-2134
111 N Sepulveda Blvd # 210 Manhattan Beach (90266) ***(P-19460)***
Emergent Ventures Intl Inc D 415 655-6617
1156 Clement St San Francisco (94118) ***(P-27717)***
Emerging Markets Growth Fund, Irvine *Also called American Funds Service Company* ***(P-10124)***
Emerik Hotel Corp D 213 748-1291
1020 S Figueroa St Los Angeles (90015) ***(P-12558)***
Emeritus At Casa Glendale, Glendale *Also called Emeritus Corporation* ***(P-20931)***
Emeritus At Villa Colima, Walnut *Also called Emeritus Corporation* ***(P-20932)***
Emeritus Corporation E 858 292-8044
5219 Clairemont Mesa Blvd San Diego (92117) ***(P-20391)***
Emeritus Corporation E 707 552-3336
2261 Tuolumne St Vallejo (94589) ***(P-20929)***
Emeritus Corporation E 707 996-7101
800 Oregon St Sonoma (95476) ***(P-20930)***
Emeritus Corporation E 760 741-3055
1351 E Washington Ave Escondido (92027) ***(P-11012)***
Emeritus Corporation E 818 246-7457
426 Piedmont Ave Glendale (91206) ***(P-20931)***
Emeritus Corporation E 909 595-5030
19850 Colima Rd Walnut (91789) ***(P-20932)***
Emeritus Corporation E 805 239-1313
1919 Creston Rd Ofc Paso Robles (93446) ***(P-11013)***
Emerson Elementary D 818 558-5419
720 E Cypress Ave Burbank (91501) ***(P-25155)***
Emery Financial Inc (PA) D 949 219-0640
620 Nwport Ctr Dr Ste 800 Newport Beach (92660) ***(P-9881)***
Emery Marina, Emeryville *Also called Young MNS Chrstn Assn of E Bay* ***(P-25357)***
Emery Smith Laboratories Inc C 213 745-5333
781 E Washington Blvd Los Angeles (90021) ***(P-26699)***
Emery Smith Laboratories Inc D 714 238-6133
1195 N Tustin Ave Anaheim (92807) ***(P-25659)***
Emeter Corporation C 650 227-7770
4000 E 3rd Ave Ste 400 Foster City (94404) ***(P-15137)***
EMI Music Distribution, Los Angeles *Also called Capitol Records LLC* ***(P-17054)***
EMI Publishing, Santa Monica *Also called Screen Gems-EMI Music Inc* ***(P-17461)***
Emida Technologies, Foothill Ranch *Also called Debisys Inc* ***(P-9679)***
Eminence Home Health Care Inc E 818 830-7113
16921 Parthenia St # 301 Northridge (91343) ***(P-22292)***
EMJ Hayward, Hayward *Also called Earle M Jorgensen Company* ***(P-7271)***
Emmanuel Cnvlscent Hosp Almeda D 510 521-5765
508 Westline Dr Alameda (94501) ***(P-21062)***
Emmi Inc D 213 622-7234
631 S Olive St Ste 302 Los Angeles (90014) ***(P-8009)***
Emmi Universal Fine Jeweller, Los Angeles *Also called Emmi Inc* ***(P-8009)***
Emmis Communications Corp C 818 238-6705
2600 W Olive Ave Fl 8 Burbank (91505) ***(P-5710)***
Emmis Communications Corp C 626 484-4440
790 E Colorado Blvd Fl 9 Pasadena (91101) ***(P-5711)***
Emmis Publishing Corporation D 323 801-0100
5900 Wilshire Blvd Fl 10 Los Angeles (90036) ***(P-9113)***
Emn8, San Diego *Also called Tillster Inc* ***(P-16513)***
Emotiv Systems Inc E 415 503-3601
1770 Post St Ste 350 San Francisco (94115) ***(P-18782)***

Employee Codes: A=Over 500 employees, B=251-500
C=101-250, D=51-100, E=50
2019 Directory of California
Wholesalers and Services Companies
© Mergent Inc. 1-800-342-5647
1291

Emove Express Company.....D.......650 377-0913
688 Matsonia Dr Foster City (94404) ***(P-16123)***
Emovexpress.com, Foster City *Also called Emove Express Company* ***(P-16123)***
Emp III Inc.....D.......323 231-4174
1755 Mrtn Lthr Kng Jr Blv Los Angeles (90058) ***(P-12223)***
Empcc Inc.....D.......714 564-7900
1682 Langley Ave Fl 2 Irvine (92614) ***(P-2434)***
Emperor's Clge & Clnc Tradtn, Santa Monica *Also called Emperors Clg Trdtnl Orntl Mdc* ***(P-20173)***
Emperors Clg Trdtnl Orntl Mdc.....D.......310 453-8383
1807 Wilshire Blvd Ste B Santa Monica (90403) ***(P-20173)***
Empire Building Services Inc.....D.......714 836-7700
1570 E Edinger Ave Ste D Santa Ana (92705) ***(P-14258)***
Empire Chauffeur Service Ltd.....D.......310 414-8189
600 S Allied Way El Segundo (90245) ***(P-4011)***
Empire Cls Worldwide, El Segundo *Also called Cls Trnsprttion Los Angles LLC* ***(P-3785)***
Empire Community Painting, Irvine *Also called Empcc Inc* ***(P-2434)***
Empire Community Painting, Irvine *Also called D P S Inc* ***(P-2431)***
Empire Company LLC.....D.......951 742-5273
31 Heron Ln Riverside (92507) ***(P-6822)***
Empire Demolition Inc.....D.......909 393-8300
1623 Leeson Ln Corona (92879) ***(P-3253)***
Empire Disposal LLC.....E.......909 797-9125
5455 Industrial Pkwy San Bernardino (92407) ***(P-6398)***
Empire Enterprises Inc.....C.......562 529-2676
8800 Park St Bellflower (90706) ***(P-3791)***
Empire Estates Inc.....D.......909 980-3100
10750 Civic Center Dr # 100 Rancho Cucamonga (91730) ***(P-11419)***
Empire Golf Inc (PA).....D.......916 314-3150
14670 Cantova Way Ste 228 Rancho Murieta (95683) ***(P-18712)***
Empire Internation, El Segundo *Also called Empire Chauffeur Service Ltd* ***(P-4011)***
Empire Lake Golf Course, Camarillo *Also called Crown Golf Properties LP* ***(P-27206)***
Empire Leasing Inc.....D.......949 646-7400
2045 Placentia Ave Ste A Costa Mesa (92627) ***(P-3032)***
Empire Oil Co.....D.......909 877-0226
2756 S Riverside Ave Bloomington (92316) ***(P-8957)***
Empire Parking, Bellflower *Also called Empire Enterprises Inc* ***(P-3791)***
Empire Realty Associates Inc.....D.......925 217-5000
380 Diablo Rd Danville (94526) ***(P-11420)***
Empire Southwest LLC.....B.......760 545-6200
3393 Us Highway 86 Imperial (92251) ***(P-7674)***
Empire Transportation.....B.......562 529-2676
8800 Park St Bellflower (90706) ***(P-3888)***
Employbridge LLC (HQ).....C.......805 882-2200
301 Mentor Dr 210 Santa Barbara (93111) ***(P-14849)***
Employee Benefits Security ADM.....D.......626 229-1000
1055 E Colo Blvd Ste 200 Pasadena (91106) ***(P-10485)***
Employee Solutions, Van Nuys *Also called ME and ME Inc* ***(P-14878)***
Employees Benefit ADM & MGT, Costa Mesa *Also called EBA & M Corporation* ***(P-10202)***
Employment & Community Options.....C.......858 565-9870
5050 Murphy Canyon Rd # 220 San Diego (92123) ***(P-24181)***
Employment & Human Services, Martinez *Also called County of Contra Costa* ***(P-23635)***
Employment Dev Cal Dept.....D.......805 614-1550
1410 S Broadway Ste E Santa Maria (93454) ***(P-14612)***
Employment Dev Cal Dept.....A.......916 654-7867
751 N St Fl 6 Sacramento (95814) ***(P-14613)***
Employment Intake Training Ctr, Los Angeles *Also called Swissport Usa Inc* ***(P-4916)***
Employment Training Academy.....E.......209 475-1529
4045 Coronado Ave Stockton (95204) ***(P-25419)***
Employnet Inc.....A.......831 316-1814
445 Tyler St Monterey (93940) ***(P-14614)***
Employnet Inc.....A.......831 233-9999
838 S Main St Ste B Salinas (93901) ***(P-14615)***
Empres Financial Services LLC.....D.......707 643-2793
1527 Springs Rd Vallejo (94591) ***(P-20392)***
Empres Post Acute Rhbilitation, Petaluma *Also called Evergreen At Petaluma LLC* ***(P-20418)***
Empresas Del Bosque Inc.....B.......209 364-6428
51481 W Shields Ave Firebaugh (93622) ***(P-342)***
Empress Care Center.....D.......408 287-0616
1299 S Bascom Ave San Jose (95128) ***(P-21063)***
Empyr Incorporated.....D.......888 664-5669
11010 Roselle St Ste 150 San Diego (92121) ***(P-13742)***
Emq Familiesfirst, Campbell *Also called Uplift Family Services* ***(P-24704)***
Emq Familiesfirst, Los Gatos *Also called Uplift Family Services* ***(P-22708)***
EMR Cpr LLC.....B.......408 471-6804
48511 Warm Springs Blvd # 206 Fremont (94539) ***(P-15954)***
Ems Construction Inc.....D.......858 679-8292
12185 Dearborn Pl Poway (92064) ***(P-1528)***
Emser International LLC (PA).....D.......323 650-2000
8431 Santa Monica Blvd Los Angeles (90069) ***(P-6891)***
Emser Tile LLC.....D.......909 974-1600
5300 Shea Center Dr Ontario (91761) ***(P-2996)***
Emsoc, Orange *Also called Emergency Medicine Specialist* ***(P-21408)***
Emt LLC (PA).....D.......707 584-5123
6600 Hunter Dr Rohnert Park (94928) ***(P-12159)***
Emulex Corporate Services Corp.....D.......714 662-5600
3333 Susan St Costa Mesa (92626) ***(P-26847)***
En Pointe Technologies Sls LLC.....C.......310 337-6151
1940 E Mariposa Ave El Segundo (90245) ***(P-7041)***
Enbio Corp.....C.......818 953-9976
150 E Olive Ave Ste 212 Burbank (91502) ***(P-27225)***
Encina Pepper Tree Joint Ventr (PA).....D.......805 687-5511
3850 State St Santa Barbara (93105) ***(P-12559)***
Encina Wastewater Authority.....D.......760 438-3941
6200 Avenida Encinas Carlsbad (92011) ***(P-6322)***
Encina Water Pollution Control, Carlsbad *Also called Encina Wastewater Authority* ***(P-6322)***
Encinitas Memory Care Cmnty, Encinitas *Also called Silverado Senior Living Inc* ***(P-21214)***
Encinitas Ranch Golf Course, Encinitas *Also called JC Resorts LLC* ***(P-26904)***
Encino Branch, Encino *Also called Umpqua Bank* ***(P-9374)***
Encino Center Car Wash Inc.....E.......818 788-6300
16300 Ventura Blvd Encino (91436) ***(P-17814)***
Encino Hospital Medical Center.....B.......818 995-5000
16237 Ventura Blvd Encino (91436) ***(P-21409)***
Encino Trzana Regional Med Ctr.....B.......818 995-5000
16237 Ventura Blvd Encino (91436) ***(P-21410)***
Enclarity Inc.....D.......949 614-8110
16815 Von Karman Ave # 125 Irvine (92606) ***(P-16124)***
Encompass Community Services.....B.......831 724-3885
225 Westridge Dr Watsonville (95076) ***(P-23787)***
Encompass Fmly Phy Med Grp Inc (PA).....D.......619 660-6212
10225 Austin Dr Ste 103 Spring Valley (91978) ***(P-20146)***
Encompass Health Corporation.....C.......714 832-9200
14851 Yorba St Tustin (92780) ***(P-22575)***
Encompass Health Corporation.....C.......661 323-5500
5001 Commerce Dr Bakersfield (93309) ***(P-24517)***
Encompass Health Corporation.....D.......510 547-2244
3875 Telegraph Ave Oakland (94609) ***(P-22020)***
Encore Aerospace LLC.....D.......562 344-1700
1729 Apollo Ct Seal Beach (90740) ***(P-3512)***
Encore Capital Group Inc (PA).....D.......877 445-4581
3111 Camino Del Rio N # 103 San Diego (92108) ***(P-9738)***
Encore Cnsmr Capitl Fund II LP (PA).....D.......415 296-9850
111 Pine St Ste 1825 San Francisco (94111) ***(P-12224)***
Encore Fund LP.....D.......415 676-4000
555 California St # 2975 San Francisco (94104) ***(P-12035)***
Encore Gymnstics Dnce Climbing, Concord *Also called Encore Inc* ***(P-19167)***
Encore Inc.....E.......925 932-1033
999 Bancroft Rd Concord (94518) ***(P-19167)***
Encore Media Services Inc.....D.......661 705-1323
24853 Avenue Rockefeller Valencia (91355) ***(P-18190)***
Encore Semi Inc.....D.......858 225-4993
9444 Waples St Ste 150 San Diego (92121) ***(P-25660)***
Encore Senior Living III LLC.....E.......951 360-1616
6280 Clay St Riverside (92509) ***(P-11014)***
Encore Senior Vlg At Riverside, Riverside *Also called Encore Senior Living III LLC* ***(P-11014)***
End-Time Message & Support.....E.......323 756-6252
855 W 125th St Los Angeles (90044) ***(P-12225)***
Endemol.....D.......310 860-9914
9255 W Sunset Blvd # 1100 West Hollywood (90069) ***(P-18365)***
Endocrine Sciences Inc.....C.......818 880-8040
4301 Lost Hills Rd Calabasas (91301) ***(P-22082)***
Endorse Corp.....A.......617 470-8332
60 E 3rd Ave San Mateo (94401) ***(P-7042)***
Endsight.....D.......510 655-6500
1440 4th St Ste B Berkeley (94710) ***(P-16358)***
Endurance Lending Network, San Francisco *Also called Funding Circle Usa Inc* ***(P-9713)***
Enercon Services Inc.....D.......805 242-0600
364 Pacific St San Luis Obispo (93401) ***(P-25661)***
Energetic Lath & Plaster, North Highlands *Also called Energetic Pntg & Drywall Inc* ***(P-2881)***
Energetic Pntg & Drywall Inc (PA).....C.......916 488-8455
2929 Orange Grove Ave North Highlands (95660) ***(P-2881)***
Energy Enterprises USA Inc (PA).....D.......424 339-0005
6842 Van Nuys Blvd # 800 Van Nuys (91405) ***(P-2200)***
Energy Experts International.....C.......559 449-1124
7111 N Fresno St Ste 260 Fresno (93720) ***(P-27718)***
Energy Innovations Inc.....C.......626 585-6900
130 W Union St Pasadena (91103) ***(P-26361)***
Energy Livermore Off US Dept.....B.......415 648-3878
539 Peralta Ave San Francisco (94110) ***(P-26617)***
Energy Livermore Off US Dept.....B.......408 267-1413
1413 Willowtree Ct San Jose (95118) ***(P-26618)***
Energy Resource Center, Downey *Also called Southern California Gas Co* ***(P-6175)***
Energy Salvage Inc.....E.......916 737-8640
8231 Alpine Ave Ste 3 Sacramento (95826) ***(P-26848)***
Energy Solutions, Oakland *Also called Cohen Ventures Inc* ***(P-27691)***
Energy Store of California Inc.....D.......916 825-8751
14958 Venado Dr Rancho Murieta (95683) ***(P-2201)***
Enerpath Services Inc.....D.......909 335-1699
1758 Orange Tree Ln Redlands (92374) ***(P-2579)***
Enertis Solar Inc.....E.......415 400-5271
1750 Montgomery St # 127 San Francisco (94111) ***(P-25662)***
Engage Technologies Inc.....B.......415 829-1400
150 Spear St Ste 400 San Francisco (94105) ***(P-15138)***
Engagio Inc.....E.......650 265-2264
101 S San Mateo Dr Fl 4 San Mateo (94401) ***(P-15667)***
Enganering and Technical Svcs, Santa Maria *Also called Caci Nss Inc* ***(P-7022)***
Engie Services US Inc (HQ).....D.......844 678-3772
500 12th St Ste 300 Oakland (94607) ***(P-25663)***
Engility LLC.....C.......510 357-4610
2700 Merced St San Leandro (94577) ***(P-25664)***
Engility LLC.....C.......858 552-9500
7580 Metro Dr Ste 207 San Diego (92108) ***(P-25665)***
Engility LLC.....A.......703 633-8300
200 W Los Angeles Ave Simi Valley (93065) ***(P-25666)***
Engineered Forest Products LLC.....D.......925 376-0881
1340 Bollinger Cyn Moraga (94556) ***(P-12226)***
Engineered Soil Repairs Inc.....D.......408 297-2150
1267 Springbrook Rd Walnut Creek (94597) ***(P-2806)***
Engineered Well Svc Intl Inc.....C.......866 913-6283
3120 Standard St Bakersfield (93308) ***(P-1057)***
Engineering Division, Lancaster *Also called County of Los Angeles* ***(P-25626)***
Engineering Public Works, Glendale *Also called City of Glendale* ***(P-25611)***
Engineering/Remdtn Rsrcs Grp (PA).....D.......925 839-2200
4585 Pacheco Blvd Ste 200 Martinez (94553) ***(P-6539)***

Mergent e-mail: customerrelations@mergent.com
1292
2019 Directory of California
Wholesalers and Services Companies
(P-0000) Products & Services Section entry number
(PA)=Parent Co (HQ)=Headquarters (DH)=Div Headquarters

Enginring Capitl Projects Dept, San Diego *Also called City of San Diego* ***(P-27688)***
Enginring Sftwr Sys Sltons Inc (PA)..........D.......619 338-0380
550 W C St Ste 1630 San Diego (92101) ***(P-25667)***
Englekirk Institutional Inc (PA)..........E.......323 733-2640
888 S Figueroa St Ste 180 Los Angeles (90017) ***(P-25668)***
Englekirk Structural Engineers (PA)..........E.......323 733-6673
888 S Figueroa St # 1800 Los Angeles (90017) ***(P-25669)***
English Oaks Convalescent..........C.......209 577-1001
2633 W Rumble Rd Modesto (95350) ***(P-20393)***
ENGLISH OAKS CONVALESCENT & RE, Modesto *Also called English Oaks Convalescent* ***(P-20393)***
Engstrom Lipscomb and Lack A (PA)..........D.......310 552-3800
10100 Santa Monica Blvd # 1200 Los Angeles (90067) ***(P-23060)***
Enhanced Landscape MGT Inc..........D.......805 557-2737
1938 E Thousand Oaks Blvd Thousand Oaks (91362) ***(P-837)***
Enloe Homecare Services, Chico *Also called Enloe Medical Center* ***(P-22293)***
Enloe Hospt-Phys Thrpy..........C.......530 891-7300
1444 Magnolia Ave Chico (95926) ***(P-21411)***
Enloe Medical Center..........D.......530 332-4111
560 Cohasset Rd Chico (95926) ***(P-21412)***
Enloe Medical Center..........B.......530 332-7522
175 W 5th Ave Chico (95926) ***(P-19461)***
Enloe Medical Center..........B.......530 332-6050
1390 E Lassen Ave Chico (95973) ***(P-22293)***
Enloe Medical Center..........D.......530 332-6138
340 W East Ave Chico (95926) ***(P-20174)***
Enloe Medical Center..........C.......530 332-6400
888 Lakeside Vlg Cmns Chico (95928) ***(P-21413)***
Enloe Medical Center..........B.......530 332-6000
277 Cohasset Rd Chico (95926) ***(P-19462)***
Enloe Outpatient Center, Chico *Also called Enloe Medical Center* ***(P-21413)***
Enloe Rehabilitation Center, Chico *Also called Enloe Medical Center* ***(P-20174)***
Enns Farms, Kingsburg *Also called Enns Packing Company Inc* ***(P-216)***
Enns Packing Company Inc..........E.......559 897-7700
1911 Bergren Ct Kingsburg (93631) ***(P-216)***
Enpower Management Corp..........E.......925 244-1100
2420 Camino Ramon Ste 101 San Ramon (94583) ***(P-6036)***
Enquero Inc..........D.......408 406-3203
1551 Mccarthy Blvd # 207 Milpitas (95035) ***(P-15955)***
Enrichment Eductl Experiences..........D.......818 989-7509
4400 Coldwater Canyon Ave # 300 Studio City (91604) ***(P-24318)***
Enrichment Program, Rocklin *Also called Star Inc* ***(P-24073)***
Ensighten Inc (HQ)..........D.......650 249-4712
226 Airport Pkwy Ste 390 San Jose (95110) ***(P-27226)***
Ensign Cloverdale LLC..........D.......707 894-5201
300 Cherry Creek Rd Cloverdale (95425) ***(P-20394)***
Ensign Group Inc..........C.......805 925-8713
1405 E Main St Santa Maria (93454) ***(P-24518)***
Ensign Group Inc..........D.......949 642-0387
340 Victoria St Costa Mesa (92627) ***(P-20395)***
Ensign Group Inc..........C.......818 893-6385
9541 Van Nuys Blvd Panorama City (91402) ***(P-20396)***
Ensign Group Inc..........C.......562 947-7817
10426 Bogardus Ave Whittier (90603) ***(P-20397)***
Ensign Group Inc..........C.......707 525-1250
3751 Montgomery Dr Santa Rosa (95405) ***(P-20398)***
Ensign Group Inc..........D.......760 746-0303
201 N Fig St Escondido (92025) ***(P-20399)***
Ensign Group Inc..........D.......626 607-2400
4800 Delta Ave Rosemead (91770) ***(P-20400)***
Ensign Group Inc..........C.......626 287-0438
8417 Mission Dr Rosemead (91770) ***(P-20401)***
Ensign Palm I LLC..........D.......760 323-2638
2990 E Ramon Rd Palm Springs (92264) ***(P-20402)***
Ensign Services Inc..........D.......949 487-9500
27101 Puerta Real Ste 450 Mission Viejo (92691) ***(P-20403)***
Ensign Southland LLC..........C.......949 487-9500
27101 Puerta Real Ste 450 Mission Viejo (92691) ***(P-20404)***
Ensign Willits LLC..........D.......707 459-5592
64 Northbrook Way Willits (95490) ***(P-21064)***
Ent Facial Surgery Center, Fresno *Also called Central California Ear Nose* ***(P-19364)***
Entco LLC (HQ)..........B.......312 580-9100
1140 Enterprise Way Sunnyvale (94089) ***(P-15668)***
Entercom Communications Corp..........C.......916 766-5000
5345 Madison Ave Sacramento (95841) ***(P-5712)***
Entercom Communications Corp..........C.......610 660-5610
201 3rd St Fl 12 San Francisco (94103) ***(P-5713)***
Entercom Communications Corp..........C.......916 334-7777
5345 Madison Ave Ste 100 Sacramento (95841) ***(P-5714)***
Enterprise Events Group Inc..........C.......415 499-4444
950 Northgate Dr Ste 100 San Rafael (94903) ***(P-27227)***
Enterprise Holdings Inc..........D.......559 261-9221
780 W Pinedale Ave Fresno (93711) ***(P-17632)***
Enterprise Rent-A-Car..........D.......760 772-0281
78385 Varner Rd Ste D Palm Desert (92211) ***(P-17633)***
Enterprise Rent-A-Car..........D.......619 297-0311
2942 Kettner Blvd San Diego (92101) ***(P-17634)***
Enterprise Rent-A-Car (HQ)..........D.......657 221-4400
333 City Blvd W Ste 1000 Orange (92868) ***(P-17654)***
Enterprise Rent-A-Car..........D.......949 373-9350
28112 Camino Capistrano Laguna Niguel (92677) ***(P-17635)***
Enterprise Rent-A-Car Compan..........D.......916 576-3164
6320 Mcnair Cir Sacramento (95837) ***(P-17636)***
Enterprise Rent-A-Car Compan (HQ)..........E.......916 787-4500
150 N Sunrise Ave Roseville (95661) ***(P-17655)***
Enterprise Roofing Service Inc..........D.......925 689-8100
2400 Bates Ave Concord (94520) ***(P-3154)***
Enterprise Services LLC..........A.......916 636-1000
3215 Prospect Park Dr Rancho Cordova (95670) ***(P-16125)***
Enterprise Services LLC..........B.......619 817-3851
3990 Sherman St San Diego (92110) ***(P-16126)***
Enterprise Services LLC..........C.......310 331-1074
1 Hornet Way El Segundo (90245) ***(P-16127)***
Enterprise Signal Inc..........D.......877 256-8303
440 N Wolfe Rd Sunnyvale (94085) ***(P-15669)***
Enterprise Solutions Inc..........C.......408 727-3627
2855 Kifer Rd Santa Clara (95051) ***(P-27719)***
Enterprise Vineyards..........E.......707 996-6513
16600 Norrbom Rd Sonoma (95476) ***(P-143)***
Entertainment & Sports Today..........D.......213 388-9050
2966 Wilshire Blvd Ste C Los Angeles (90010) ***(P-5783)***
Entertainment Partners (PA)..........B.......818 955-6000
2835 N Naomi St Burbank (91504) ***(P-26190)***
Entertinment Studios Media Inc (PA)..........D.......310 277-3500
1925 Century Park E # 1025 Los Angeles (90067) ***(P-18432)***
Enthusiast Network Inc (PA)..........B.......310 531-9900
2221 Rosecrans Ave # 195 El Segundo (90245) ***(P-5053)***
Entitlement LLC..........E.......224 336-2669
1236 Euclid St Santa Monica (90404) ***(P-18433)***
Entravision Radio, Sacramento *Also called Entravsion Communications Corp* ***(P-5787)***
Entravsion Communications Corp..........E.......831 333-9736
67 Garden Ct Monterey (93940) ***(P-5784)***
Entravsion Communications Corp..........D.......323 900-6100
5700 Wilshire Blvd # 250 Los Angeles (90036) ***(P-5785)***
Entravsion Communications Corp..........D.......760 568-3636
72920 Parkview Dr Palm Desert (92260) ***(P-5786)***
Entravsion Communications Corp..........E.......916 646-4000
1436 Auburn Blvd Sacramento (95815) ***(P-5715)***
Entravsion Communications Corp..........E.......916 648-6029
1436 Auburn Blvd Sacramento (95815) ***(P-5787)***
Entravsion Communications Corp (PA)..........C.......310 447-3870
2425 Olympic Blvd Ste 600 Santa Monica (90404) ***(P-5788)***
Entrepreneur Preferred, Murrieta *Also called Inzunza Real Estate Inc* ***(P-11523)***
Entrepreneurial Capital Corp..........C.......949 809-3900
4100 Nwport Pl Dr Ste 400 Newport Beach (92660) ***(P-10873)***
Entrepreneurial Hospitality..........C.......951 346-4700
3485 Mission Inn Ave Riverside (92501) ***(P-17152)***
Event Corporation (PA)..........C.......562 997-9465
3220 E 29th St Long Beach (90806) ***(P-27720)***
Enviance Inc (HQ)..........D.......760 496-0200
5780 Fleet St Ste 200 Carlsbad (92008) ***(P-15139)***
Enviro Tech Chemical Svcs Inc (PA)..........C.......209 581-9576
500 Winmoore Way Modesto (95358) ***(P-8927)***
Environment Control, Visalia *Also called Tim Hofer Inc* ***(P-14407)***
Environment Control..........E.......559 456-9791
1849 N Helm Ave Ste 105 Fresno (93727) ***(P-14259)***
Environmental Chemical Corp (PA)..........D.......650 347-1555
1240 Bayshore Hwy Burlingame (94010) ***(P-25670)***
Environmental Construction Inc..........D.......818 449-8920
21550 Oxnard St Ste 1060 Woodland Hills (91367) ***(P-1529)***
Environmental Health Hazard..........D.......510 622-3200
1515 Clay St Ste 1600 Oakland (94612) ***(P-26700)***
Environmental Industries, Fillmore *Also called Brightview Tree Company* ***(P-988)***
Environmental Ldscp Solutions, Sacramento *Also called Els Investments* ***(P-754)***
Environmental Lights, San Diego *Also called Advanced Lighting Concepts Inc* ***(P-7326)***
Environmental Protection Agcy..........D.......916 324-7572
1001 I St Ste 19b Sacramento (95814) ***(P-6540)***
Environmental Resolutions Inc..........B.......949 457-8950
25371 Commercentre Dr # 250 Lake Forest (92630) ***(P-27721)***
Environmental Resources MGT, Walnut Creek *Also called Erm-West Inc* ***(P-25675)***
Environmental Science Assoc (PA)..........D.......415 896-5900
550 Kearny St Ste 800 San Francisco (94108) ***(P-26362)***
Environmental Systems Inc (PA)..........D.......408 980-1711
3353 De La Cruz Blvd Santa Clara (95054) ***(P-2202)***
Environmental Systems Research..........D.......916 448-2412
1600 K St Ste 4c Sacramento (95814) ***(P-7043)***
Environments For Learning Inc (PA)..........D.......949 855-5630
24291 Muirlands Blvd Lake Forest (92630) ***(P-24319)***
Environments Plus (PA)..........D.......805 375-5727
1700 1st St San Fernando (91340) ***(P-3513)***
Envise..........D.......714 901-5800
12131 Western Ave Garden Grove (92841) ***(P-2203)***
Envivio Inc..........C.......650 243-2700
535 Mission St Fl 27 San Francisco (94105) ***(P-5554)***
Envoy Inc..........D.......415 787-7871
410 Townsend St Ste 410 # 410 San Francisco (94107) ***(P-15140)***
Envoy Air Inc..........E.......619 260-9069
3707 N Harbor Dr Ste 124 San Diego (92101) ***(P-4888)***
Enxco, San Diego *Also called Edf Renewables Services Inc* ***(P-17794)***
Enzennauer Vineyard Managment..........D.......707 433-0532
18501 Ida Clayton Rd Calistoga (94515) ***(P-690)***
Eoc Resource Development, Fresno *Also called Fresno Cnty Economic Opportunt* ***(P-17176)***
Eon Reality Inc (PA)..........E.......949 460-2000
39 Parker Ste 100 Irvine (92618) ***(P-7044)***
Epak9, El Cajon *Also called Executive Protection Agency K-* ***(P-16643)***
Epcm Prof Svc Partners LLC..........D.......562 936-1000
2017 Palo Verde Ave Long Beach (90815) ***(P-27722)***
Ephesoft Inc (PA)..........D.......949 335-5335
8707 Research Dr Irvine (92618) ***(P-7045)***
Ephonamationcom Inc..........C.......714 560-1000
145 E Columbine Ave Santa Ana (92707) ***(P-17153)***
Epic, Concord *Also called Edgewood Prtners Insur Ctr Inc* ***(P-10612)***
Epic Jet Centre, San Luis Obispo *Also called Aviation Consultants Inc* ***(P-26771)***
Epic Management LP (PA)..........C.......909 799-1818
1615 Orange Tree Ln Redlands (92374) ***(P-26849)***
Epic Sciences Inc..........D.......858 356-6610
9381 Judicial Dr Ste 200 San Diego (92121) ***(P-22083)***

ALPHABETIC

Employee Codes: A=Over 500 employees, B=251-500
C=101-250, D=51-100, E=50
2019 Directory of California
Wholesalers and Services Companies
© Mergent Inc. 1-800-342-5647
1293

Epic Ventures Inc (PA).......E.......831 219-9100
200 Concourse Blvd Santa Rosa (95403) **(P-9041)**
Epic War, Palo Alto *Also called Machine Zone Inc* **(P-15267)**
Epic Wines, Santa Rosa *Also called Epic Ventures Inc* **(P-9041)**
Epicenter Live Inc.......C.......424 235-4835
4040 Mahaila Ave Unit A San Diego (92122) **(P-18366)**
Epicentro Advertising Mktg Svc.......E.......408 453-0353
2370 Qume Dr Ste B San Jose (95131) **(P-13825)**
Epicor Software Corporation.......C.......925 361-9900
4120 Dublin Blvd Ste 300 Dublin (94568) **(P-15670)**
Epidendio Construction Inc.......E.......707 994-5100
11325 Highway 29 Lower Lake (95457) **(P-3254)**
Episcopal Comm Svc San Fran (PA).......C.......415 487-3300
165 8th St Fl 3 San Francisco (94103) **(P-23788)**
Episcopal Communities & Servic.......D.......310 544-2204
5801 Crestridge Rd Pls Vrds Pnsl (90275) **(P-20405)**
Episcopal Community.......D.......619 228-2800
1261 Third Ave Ste B Chula Vista (91911) **(P-23789)**
Episcopal Senior Communities.......C.......408 354-0211
110 Wood Rd Ofc Los Gatos (95030) **(P-24519)**
Epitec Inc.......A.......760 650-2515
515 Olive Ave Vista (92083) **(P-15141)**
Epitome Enterprises LLC.......D.......909 625-4728
821 Mary Pl Claremont (91711) **(P-15142)**
Epitomics Inc (HQ).......D.......650 583-6688
863 Mitten Rd Ste 103 Burlingame (94010) **(P-26363)**
Eplica Inc (PA).......C.......619 260-2000
2355 Northside Dr Ste 120 San Diego (92108) **(P-14850)**
Epochcom LLC.......C.......310 664-5700
2644 30th St Fl 2 Santa Monica (90405) **(P-16128)**
Epocrates Inc (HQ).......E.......650 227-1700
50 Hawthorne St San Francisco (94105) **(P-22800)**
Eppink of California Inc.......E.......562 633-1275
11900 Center St South Gate (90280) **(P-3033)**
Epri Csg, Palo Alto *Also called Eprisolutions Inc* **(P-25671)**
Eprisolutions Inc.......D.......650 855-8900
3412 Hillview Ave Palo Alto (94304) **(P-25671)**
Eps Corporate Holdings Inc.......D.......714 635-3131
1235 S Lewis St Anaheim (92805) **(P-7615)**
Epsilon Mission Solutions Inc.......D.......619 702-1700
9242 Lightwave Ave # 100 San Diego (92123) **(P-25672)**
Epsilon Systems Solutions Inc.......C.......619 702-1700
5482 Complex St Ste 109 San Diego (92123) **(P-25673)**
Epsilon Systems Solutions Inc (PA).......D.......619 702-1700
9242 Lightwave Ave # 100 San Diego (92123) **(P-25674)**
Epson America Inc.......C.......562 290-5855
1650 Glenn Curtiss St Carson (90746) **(P-4553)**
Epson West, Carson *Also called Epson America Inc* **(P-4553)**
Epstein Becker & Green PC.......D.......310 556-8861
1875 Century Park E # 500 Los Angeles (90067) **(P-23061)**
Eqal Inc.......C.......818 276-6300
5250 Lankershim Blvd # 720 North Hollywood (91601) **(P-13826)**
Equal Access International.......D.......415 561-4884
1212 Market St Ste 200 San Francisco (94102) **(P-2580)**
Equator LLC (HQ).......C.......310 469-9500
6060 Center Dr Ste 500 Los Angeles (90045) **(P-15143)**
Equator Business Solutions, Los Angeles *Also called Equator LLC* **(P-15143)**
Equator Coffees LLC.......D.......415 485-2213
115 Jordan St San Rafael (94901) **(P-7134)**
Equicare Medical Supply Inc.......D.......213 385-1715
1154 S Alvarado St Los Angeles (90006) **(P-20406)**
Equilar Inc.......C.......877 441-6090
1100 Marshall St Redwood City (94063) **(P-17154)**
Equinix Inc (PA).......C.......650 598-6000
1 Lagoon Dr Ste 400 Redwood City (94065) **(P-12160)**
Equinix (us) Enterprises Inc (HQ).......D.......650 598-6363
1 Lagoon Dr Redwood City (94065) **(P-5981)**
Equinox Fitness Club, San Francisco *Also called Equinox Holdings Inc* **(P-18594)**
Equinox Fitness Club, Irvine *Also called Equinox-76th Street Inc* **(P-18596)**
Equinox Holdings Inc.......B.......415 243-0492
747 Market St San Francisco (94103) **(P-18594)**
Equinox-76th Street Inc.......D.......415 398-0747
301 Pine St San Francisco (94104) **(P-18595)**
Equinox-76th Street Inc.......D.......949 296-1700
19540 Jamboree Rd Irvine (92612) **(P-18596)**
Equinox-76th Street Inc.......B.......949 975-8400
1980 Main St Fl 4 Irvine (92614) **(P-20175)**
Equistar Irvine Company LLC.......D.......949 833-3331
18800 Macarthur Blvd Irvine (92612) **(P-12560)**
Equitable Life Assurance, San Diego *Also called Axa Equitable Life Insur Co* **(P-10558)**
Equitable Variable Lf Insur Co.......D.......619 239-0018
701 B St Ste 1500 San Diego (92101) **(P-10134)**
Equity Title Company (HQ).......D.......818 291-4400
801 N Brand Blvd Ste 400 Glendale (91203) **(P-10450)**
ERA Realty Center.......D.......530 295-2900
49 Placerville Dr Placerville (95667) **(P-11421)**
Erepublic Inc (PA).......C.......916 932-1300
100 Blue Ravine Rd Folsom (95630) **(P-17155)**
Erewhon Natural Foods Market, Calabasas *Also called Nowher Partners LLC* **(P-8841)**
Ergomotion Inc.......D.......805 979-9400
6790 Navigator Way Goleta (93117) **(P-6721)**
Ergs Aim Hotel Realty LLC.......D.......714 938-1111
400 N State College Blvd Orange (92868) **(P-12561)**
Ergs Aim Hotel Realty LLC.......D.......949 661-1100
34402 Pacific Coast Hwy Dana Point (92624) **(P-12562)**
Eri Economic Research Inst Inc.......D.......800 627-3697
111 Academy Ste 270 Irvine (92617) **(P-15671)**
Eric D Feldman MD Inc.......E.......562 424-6666
2760 Atlantic Ave Long Beach (90806) **(P-19463)**
Eric Jones Customs Brokerage.......E.......310 348-3777
9841 Arprt Blvd Ste 1400 Los Angeles (90045) **(P-5054)**
Eric Stark Interiors Inc.......D.......408 441-6136
2284 Paragon Dr San Jose (95131) **(P-2882)**
Ericksen Arbuthnot Kilduff (PA).......D.......925 947-1702
570 Lennon Ln Walnut Creek (94598) **(P-23062)**
Erickson Construction LP.......C.......916 774-1100
8350 Industrial Ave Roseville (95678) **(P-3034)**
Erickson-Hall Construction Co (PA).......D.......760 796-7700
500 Corporate Dr Escondido (92029) **(P-1530)**
Ericsson Inc.......A.......408 750-5000
2755 Augustine Dr Santa Clara (95054) **(P-5555)**
Ericsson Inc.......A.......408 597-3600
100 Headquarters Dr San Jose (95134) **(P-15956)**
Erlanger Distribution Ctr Inc.......E.......951 784-5147
797 Palmyrita Ave Riverside (92507) **(P-9214)**
Erlanger Sales, Riverside *Also called Erlanger Distribution Ctr Inc* **(P-9214)**
Erm-West Inc (HQ).......D.......925 946-0455
1277 Treat Blvd Ste 500 Walnut Creek (94597) **(P-25675)**
Ernest Gallo Clinic & RES Ctr.......C.......510 985-3856
5980 Horton St Ste 370 Emeryville (94608) **(P-26516)**
Ernest Packaging (PA).......C.......800 233-7788
5777 Smithway St Commerce (90040) **(P-9215)**
Ernest Packaging Solutions, Sacramento *Also called Calvey Incorporated* **(P-8100)**
Ernest Paper, Commerce *Also called Ernest Packaging* **(P-9215)**
Ernie & Sons Scaffolding.......C.......925 446-4442
1960 Olivera Rd Concord (94520) **(P-3514)**
Ernst & Young LLP.......A.......213 977-3200
725 S Figueroa St Ste 200 Los Angeles (90017) **(P-26191)**
Ernst & Young LLP.......C.......310 725-1764
200 N Pacific Coast Hwy # 2 El Segundo (90245) **(P-26192)**
Ernst & Young LLP.......D.......415 894-8000
560 Mission St Ste 1600 San Francisco (94105) **(P-26193)**
Ernst & Young LLP.......C.......650 496-1600
1451 California Ave Palo Alto (94304) **(P-26194)**
Ernst & Young LLP.......A.......408 947-5500
303 Almaden Blvd Ste 1000 San Jose (95110) **(P-26195)**
Ernst & Young LLP.......C.......858 535-7200
4370 La Jolla Village Dr # 500 San Diego (92122) **(P-26196)**
Ernst & Young LLP.......B.......949 794-2300
18101 Von Karman Ave # 1700 Irvine (92612) **(P-26197)**
Ernst & Young LLP.......C.......949 838-3300
18006 Sky Park Cir # 106 Irvine (92614) **(P-26198)**
Ernst & Young LLP.......D.......805 778-7000
2931 Townsgate Rd Ste 100 Westlake Village (91361) **(P-26199)**
Ernst & Young LLP.......C.......650 802-4500
275 Shoreline Dr Ste 600 Redwood City (94065) **(P-26200)**
Ernst & Young LLP.......C.......916 218-1900
2901 Douglas Blvd Ste 300 Roseville (95661) **(P-26201)**
Ernst & Young LLP.......C.......925 734-6388
4301 Hacienda Dr Ste 450 Pleasanton (94588) **(P-26202)**
Ernst & Young LLP.......A.......415 894-8000
560 Mission St Ste 1600 San Francisco (94105) **(P-26203)**
Ero-Tech Corp.......D.......415 468-5600
2301 S El Camino Real San Mateo (94403) **(P-18238)**
Errama Trucking Company Inc.......E.......818 381-3341
11336 Montgomery Ave Granada Hills (91344) **(P-4136)**
Errecas Inc.......D.......619 390-6400
12570 Slaughter House Lakeside (92040) **(P-3424)**
Errg, Martinez *Also called Engineering/Remdtn Rsrcs Grp* **(P-6539)**
ERs SEC Alarm Systems Inc.......D.......626 579-2525
4538 Santa Anita Ave El Monte (91731) **(P-7360)**
Erwin Street Medical Offices, Woodland Hills *Also called Kaiser Foundation Hospitals* **(P-21504)**
Es Engineering Inc.......D.......714 919-6500
1 Park Plz Ste 1000 Irvine (92614) **(P-27723)**
Es Engineering Services LLC.......D.......949 988-3500
1 Park Plz Ste 1000 Irvine (92614) **(P-25676)**
Es3 LLC.......E.......209 832-4205
857 Stonebridge Dr Tracy (95376) **(P-4554)**
ESA, San Francisco *Also called Environmental Science Assoc* **(P-26362)**
ESA P Prtfolio Oper Lessee LLC.......E.......949 851-2711
4881 Birch St Newport Beach (92660) **(P-12563)**
ESA P Prtfolio Oper Lessee LLC.......D.......714 639-8608
1635 W Katella Ave Orange (92867) **(P-12564)**
ESA Risk Management, San Jose *Also called SCC ESA Dept of Risk Mgmt* **(P-10764)**
Esc Entertainment Inc.......C.......818 954-1018
4000 Warner Blvd Burbank (91522) **(P-18191)**
Escalate Inc (HQ).......B.......858 457-3888
10680 Treena St Ste 170 San Diego (92131) **(P-15144)**
Escalate Retail, San Diego *Also called Escalate Inc* **(P-15144)**
Escondido Medical Offices, Escondido *Also called Kaiser Foundation Hospitals* **(P-19605)**
Escondido Memory Care Cmnty, Escondido *Also called Silverado Senior Living Inc* **(P-21213)**
Escondido Post Acute Rehab, Escondido *Also called Mek Escondido LLC* **(P-20639)**
Escondido Veterans Center, Escondido *Also called Veterans Health Administration* **(P-20071)**
Eset LLC (HQ).......D.......619 876-5400
610 W Ash St Ste 1700 San Diego (92101) **(P-7046)**
Eset North America, San Diego *Also called Eset LLC* **(P-7046)**
Eskaton (PA).......A.......916 334-0296
5105 Manzanita Ave Ste D Carmichael (95608) **(P-10874)**
Eskaton.......D.......916 852-7900
11390 Coloma Rd Ofc Gold River (95670) **(P-24520)**
Eskaton Center of Greenhaven, Sacramento *Also called Eskaton Properties Inc* **(P-20410)**
Eskaton Lodge.......E.......916 789-0326
22 Cadillac Dr Apt 301 Sacramento (95825) **(P-24521)**
Eskaton Properties Inc.......A.......916 974-2060
3847 Walnut Ave Carmichael (95608) **(P-20407)**

Eskaton Properties Inc.....D.....916 331-8513
5318 Manzanita Ave Carmichael (95608) *(P-20408)*
Eskaton Properties Inc.....D.....916 334-0810
1650 Eskaton Loop Roseville (95747) *(P-24522)*
Eskaton Properties Inc.....C.....916 965-4663
11300 Fair Oaks Blvd Fair Oaks (95628) *(P-20409)*
Eskaton Properties Inc.....C.....916 393-2550
455 Florin Rd Sacramento (95831) *(P-20410)*
Eskaton Properties Inc (PA).....D.....916 334-0810
5105 Manzanita Ave Ste A Carmichael (95608) *(P-20411)*
Eskaton Properties Inc.....C.....916 974-2000
3939 Walnut Ave Unit 399 Carmichael (95608) *(P-24523)*
Eskaton Village Care Center, Carmichael *Also called Eskaton Properties Inc (P-20407)*
Eskaton Village Charmichael, Carmichael *Also called Eskaton Properties Inc (P-24523)*
Eskaton Village Roseville, Roseville *Also called Eskaton Properties Inc (P-24522)*
Esl, Burbank *Also called Turtle Entertainment America (P-18469)*
Esl Technologies Inc.....B.....916 677-4500
8875 Washington Blvd B Roseville (95678) *(P-16283)*
Esna Corporation.....E.....661 206-6010
44300 Lowtree Ave Ste 100 Lancaster (93534) *(P-9882)*
Esolar Inc (HQ).....D.....818 303-9500
900 Glenneyre St Laguna Beach (92651) *(P-2031)*
Esoterix Ctr For Clncal Trails, Calabasas *Also called Endocrine Sciences Inc (P-22082)*
ESP Group Ltd.....D.....626 301-0280
2397 Bateman Ave Duarte (91010) *(P-8302)*
Esparza Enterprises Inc.....B.....760 344-2031
251 W Main St Ste G&F Brawley (92227) *(P-691)*
Esparza Enterprises Inc (PA).....A.....661 831-0002
3851 Fruitvale Ave Bakersfield (93308) *(P-14851)*
Esparza Enterprises Inc.....D.....661 831-0002
3851 Fruitvale Ave A Bakersfield (93308) *(P-14616)*
Esparza Enterprises Inc.....A.....760 398-0349
51335 Harrison St Ste 112 Coachella (92236) *(P-14617)*
Esparza Enterprises Inc.....A.....661 631-0347
500 Workman St Bakersfield (93307) *(P-4137)*
Espn Inc.....B.....212 456-7439
800 W Olympic Blvd Los Angeles (90015) *(P-5911)*
Esprit, Camarillo *Also called DP Technology Corp (P-15118)*
Esq Business Services Inc (PA).....D.....925 734-9800
20660 Stevens Cupertino (95014) *(P-15672)*
Esquire Landscape Inc.....E.....858 530-2949
8380 Miralani Dr Ste B San Diego (92126) *(P-838)*
Ess.....D.....888 303-6424
5227 Dantes View Dr Agoura Hills (91301) *(P-2204)*
Essco, Pasadena *Also called Electric Svc & Sup Co Pasadena (P-2573)*
Essendant Co.....C.....626 961-0011
918 S Stimson Ave City of Industry (91745) *(P-8079)*
Essendant Co.....C.....916 344-6707
5440 Stationers Way Sacramento (95842) *(P-8080)*
Essential Access Health (PA).....D.....213 386-5614
3600 Wilshire Blvd # 600 Los Angeles (90010) *(P-24780)*
Essential Products Inc.....D.....650 300-0000
380 Portage Ave Palo Alto (94306) *(P-15145)*
Essex Management Corporation (HQ).....D.....650 494-3700
925 E Meadow Dr Palo Alto (94303) *(P-12161)*
Essex Properties LLC.....D.....949 798-8100
18012 Sky Park Cir # 200 Irvine (92614) *(P-11422)*
Essex Property, San Mateo *Also called Essex Queen Anne LLC (P-11171)*
Essex Property Trust Inc.....D.....916 381-0345
8795 Folsom Blvd Ste 101 Sacramento (95826) *(P-12162)*
Essex Property Trust Inc (PA).....D.....650 655-7800
1100 Park Pl Ste 200 San Mateo (94403) *(P-11015)*
Essex Queen Anne LLC.....D.....650 849-1600
1100 Park Pl Ste 200 San Mateo (94403) *(P-11171)*
Essilor Laboratories Amer Inc.....D.....626 969-6181
1300 W Optical Dr Irwindale (91702) *(P-7234)*
Essrig Taylor Constructions, San Diego *Also called Etc Building & Design Inc (P-17156)*
Estate Investment Group, Dublin *Also called New Home Professionals (P-11626)*
Estes Express Lines Inc.....C.....714 994-3770
14727 Alondra Blvd La Mirada (90638) *(P-4138)*
Estes Express Lines Inc.....D.....909 427-9850
10736 Cherry Ave Fontana (92337) *(P-4139)*
Estes Express Lines Inc.....D.....626 333-9090
13327 Temple Ave City of Industry (91746) *(P-4140)*
Estes Express Lines Inc.....E.....408 286-3894
1634 S 7th St San Jose (95112) *(P-4141)*
Estes Express Lines Inc.....D.....510 635-0165
1750 Adams Ave San Leandro (94577) *(P-4142)*
Estes Express Lines Inc.....D.....818 504-4155
9120 San Fernando Rd Sun Valley (91352) *(P-4143)*
Estes Express Lines Inc.....D.....209 982-1841
7611 S Airport Way Stockton (95206) *(P-4144)*
Estes Express Lines Inc.....D.....310 549-7306
1531 Blinn Ave Wilmington (90744) *(P-4145)*
Estes Express Lines Inc.....D.....714 523-1122
14727 Alondra Blvd La Mirada (90638) *(P-4146)*
Estralla Inn & Spa, Palm Springs *Also called Casa Real Estate Ltd Partnr (P-12437)*
Estrella Inc.....C.....562 925-6418
17836 Woodruff Ave Bellflower (90706) *(P-20412)*
Estrella Communications Inc.....D.....818 260-5700
3000 W Alameda Ave Burbank (91523) *(P-5789)*
Estuate Inc.....D.....408 946-0002
830 Hillview Ct Ste 280 Milpitas (95035) *(P-15146)*
Esurance Insurance Svcs Inc (HQ).....C.....415 875-4500
650 Davis St San Francisco (94111) *(P-10615)*
Esys Energy Control Company.....D.....661 833-1902
4520 Stine Rd Ste 7 Bakersfield (93313) *(P-7750)*
Et Capital Solar Partners USA.....E.....925 460-9898
4900 Hopyard Rd Ste 2 Pleasanton (94588) *(P-26850)*
Et Whitehall Seascape LLC.....C.....310 581-5533
1910 Ocean Way Santa Monica (90405) *(P-12565)*
Etairos Consulting.....E.....844 219-7027
6711 Studio Pl Riverside (92509) *(P-16359)*
Etap, Irvine *Also called Operation Technology Inc (P-15332)*
Etc Building & Design Inc (PA).....C.....858 554-1150
6805 Nancy Ridge Dr San Diego (92121) *(P-17156)*
Etchandy Farms LLC.....D.....805 983-4700
4324 E Vineyard Ave Oxnard (93036) *(P-98)*
Etchegaray Farms LLC.....E.....661 393-0920
32324 Famoso Rd Mc Farland (93250) *(P-405)*
Ethan Conrad Properties Inc.....D.....916 779-1000
1300 National Dr Ste 100 Sacramento (95834) *(P-10875)*
Etherwan Systems Inc.....D.....714 779-3800
2301 E Winston Rd Anaheim (92806) *(P-16360)*
Ethiopian World Federation.....E.....323 844-1826
422 E 41st St Los Angeles (90011) *(P-24781)*
Ethos Management Inc (PA).....E.....626 456-3669
560 W Main St Alhambra (91801) *(P-26851)*
Ethosenergy Field Services LLC (HQ).....D.....310 639-3523
10455 Slusher Dr Bldg 12 Santa Fe Springs (90670) *(P-1058)*
Etiwanda Historical Society.....D.....909 899-8432
7150 Etiwanda Ave Rancho Cucamonga (91739) *(P-24883)*
Etiwanda Power Plant, Rancho Cucamonga *Also called NRG California South LP (P-6059)*
Etna Police Activities League.....C.....530 467-3400
448 Main St Etna (96027) *(P-23790)*
Etouch Systems Corp.....A.....510 795-4800
6627 Dumbarton Cir Fremont (94555) *(P-16361)*
Etrigue Corporation.....E.....408 490-2900
6399 San Ignacio Ave # 200 San Jose (95119) *(P-15147)*
Ettv America Corp.....D.....626 581-8899
18430 San Jose Ave Ste A City of Industry (91748) *(P-5912)*
Euclid Parking, Porterville *Also called Exeter Packers Inc (P-512)*
Eugene Burger Management Corp.....C.....916 443-6637
555 Capitol Mall Ste 725 Sacramento (95814) *(P-26852)*
Eugene N Townsend.....D.....619 442-8807
609 S Marshall Ave El Cajon (92020) *(P-17719)*
Eurasia Power LLC.....E.....805 383-1234
4022 Cmino Ranchero Ste D Camarillo (93012) *(P-7473)*
Eureka District Office, Eureka *Also called State Compensation Insur Fund (P-10407)*
Eureka Realty Partners Inc (PA).....B.....949 224-4100
4100 Macarthur Blvd # 200 Newport Beach (92660) *(P-11874)*
Eureka Rehab & Wellness Center.....D.....707 445-3261
2353 23rd St Eureka (95501) *(P-20413)*
Eureka Rhbltation Wellness Ctr, Eureka *Also called Eureka Rehab & Wellness Center (P-20413)*
Eureka Veterans Clinic, Eureka *Also called Veterans Health Administration (P-20068)*
Eurodent Inc.....D.....818 832-1325
9310 Topanga Canyon Blvd # 200 Chatsworth (91311) *(P-22167)*
Eurodrip USA Inc.....D.....559 674-2670
1850 W Almond Ave Madera (93637) *(P-7702)*
Eurofins Air Toxics LLC.....D.....916 985-1000
180 Blue Ravine Rd Ste B Folsom (95630) *(P-26701)*
Eurofins Food.....A.....609 452-4440
2441 Constitution Dr Livermore (94551) *(P-26364)*
Eurogentec North America Inc.....C.....510 791-9560
34801 Campus Dr Fremont (94555) *(P-27724)*
European Hotl Invstrs of CA.....E.....310 322-0999
1985 E Grandave El Segundo (90245) *(P-12566)*
European Hotl Invstrs of CA (PA).....D.....949 474-7368
2532 Dupont Dr Irvine (92612) *(P-12567)*
European Paving Designs Inc.....D.....408 283-5230
1474 Berger Dr San Jose (95112) *(P-2435)*
Europro Inc (PA).....D.....661 615-6610
9539 Langley Rd Bakersfield (93312) *(P-13743)*
Ev Ray Inc.....E.....818 346-5381
6400 Variel Ave Woodland Hills (91367) *(P-6760)*
Evangelical Christian Cr Un.....C.....714 671-5700
955 W Imperial Hwy # 100 Brea (92821) *(P-9633)*
Evangelical Christian Cr Un (PA).....D.....714 671-5700
955 W Imperial Hwy # 100 Brea (92821) *(P-9634)*
Evangelical Covenant Church.....D.....619 931-1114
325 Kempton St Spring Valley (91977) *(P-24524)*
Evangelical Covenant Church.....C.....805 687-0701
2550 Treasure Dr Santa Barbara (93105) *(P-24525)*
Evans Hardy & Young Inc.....E.....805 963-5841
829 De La Vina St Ste 100 Santa Barbara (93101) *(P-13827)*
Evans Dedicated Systems Inc (PA).....C.....323 725-2928
6001 E Wash Blvd Ste 200 Commerce (90040) *(P-4147)*
Evans/Sipes Inc (PA).....C.....805 644-1242
5720 Ralston St Ste 100 Ventura (93003) *(P-11423)*
Eveg Inc.....E.....844 221-3359
16540 Aston Irvine (92606) *(P-15148)*
Event Guard Services Inc.....D.....626 531-6772
1823 Business Center Dr Duarte (91010) *(P-16640)*
Event Rentals San Diego, San Diego *Also called Bright Event Rentals LLC (P-14480)*
Eventbrite Inc (PA).....C.....415 692-7779
155 5th St Fl 7 San Francisco (94103) *(P-16362)*
Ever Win International Corp.....E.....626 810-8218
17579 Railroad St City of Industry (91748) *(P-7474)*
Everest Consulting Group Inc.....D.....510 494-8440
39650 Mission Blvd Fremont (94539) *(P-15149)*
Everest Silicon Valley MGT LP.....D.....510 494-8800
8200 Gateway Blvd Newark (94560) *(P-26853)*
Everest Wtrprfing Rstrtion Inc.....D.....415 282-9800
1270 Missouri St San Francisco (94107) *(P-13744)*
Everett Basham.....D.....408 261-3000
3567 Benton St Ste 300 Santa Clara (95051) *(P-5556)*

ALPHABETIC

Employee Codes: A=Over 500 employees, B=251-500
C=101-250, D=51-100, E=50
2019 Directory of California
Wholesalers and Services Companies
© Mergent Inc. 1-800-342-5647
1295

Everett Mall 01 LLC....E....818 505-6777
12411 Ventura Blvd Studio City (91604) ***(P-11172)***
Evergent Technologies Inc....D....408 718-5453
1250 Borregas Ave Sunnyvale (94089) ***(P-15150)***
Evergreen At Chico LLC....C....530 342-4885
1200 Springfield Dr Chico (95928) ***(P-20414)***
Evergreen At Lakeport LLC (PA)....D....707 263-6382
1291 Craig Ave Lakeport (95453) ***(P-20415)***
Evergreen At Lakeport LLC....C....661 871-3133
6212 Tudor Way Bakersfield (93306) ***(P-20416)***
Evergreen At Oroville LLC....D....530 533-7335
1000 Executive Pkwy Oroville (95966) ***(P-20417)***
Evergreen At Petaluma LLC....C....707 763-6887
300 Douglas St Petaluma (94952) ***(P-20418)***
Evergreen Cleaning Systems Inc....E....213 386-3260
3325 Wilshire Blvd # 622 Los Angeles (90010) ***(P-14260)***
Evergreen Company Inc....D....916 257-5994
847 E Turner Rd Lodi (95240) ***(P-17157)***
Evergreen Distributors Inc (PA)....E....858 481-0622
13650 Carmel Valley Rd San Diego (92130) ***(P-257)***
Evergreen Dstntion Hldings LLC....D....209 379-2606
33160 Evergreen Rd Groveland (95321) ***(P-12568)***
Evergreen Fullerton Healthcare, Fullerton *Also called Pavilion At Sunny Hills* ***(P-20699)***
Evergreen Health Care LLC....D....661 854-4475
323 Campus Dr Arvin (93203) ***(P-20419)***
Evergreen Healthcare Center, Bakersfield *Also called Evergreen At Lakeport LLC* ***(P-20416)***
Evergreen Lkport Halthcare Ctr, Lakeport *Also called Evergreen At Lakeport LLC* ***(P-20415)***
Evergreen Lodge, Groveland *Also called Evergreen Dstntion Hldings LLC* ***(P-12568)***
Evergreen Nursery, San Diego *Also called Evergreen Distributors Inc* ***(P-257)***
Evergreen Solar Services, Agoura Hills *Also called Ess* ***(P-2204)***
Evernote Corporation (PA)....D....650 216-7700
305 Walnut St Redwood City (94063) ***(P-5557)***
Eversoft Inc (PA)....D....562 495-7766
707 W 16th St Long Beach (90813) ***(P-7616)***
Eversoft Products, Long Beach *Also called Eversoft Inc* ***(P-7616)***
Everwise Corporation....D....888 250-6219
2 Embarcadero Ctr Fl 8 San Francisco (94111) ***(P-27228)***
Everyone Counts Inc....D....858 427-4673
4250 Executive Sq Ste 600 La Jolla (92037) ***(P-15151)***
Evgo Services LLC....D....310 954-2900
11390 W Olympic Blvd Fl 2 Los Angeles (90064) ***(P-17860)***
Evidentio Inc (HQ)....C....855 933-1337
7901 Stoneridge Dr # 150 Pleasanton (94588) ***(P-15152)***
Evidera Archimedes Inc....D....415 490-0400
450 Sansome St Ste 650 San Francisco (94111) ***(P-10616)***
Evikecom Inc....D....626 286-0360
2801 W Mission Rd Alhambra (91803) ***(P-7927)***
Evisions Inc (PA)....D....949 833-1384
440 Exchange Ste 200 Irvine (92602) ***(P-15153)***
Evolent Health Inc....B....571 389-6000
1 Kearny St Ste 300 San Francisco (94108) ***(P-22801)***
Evolution Fresh Inc (HQ)....D....800 794-9986
11655 Jersey Blvd Rancho Cucamonga (91730) ***(P-8675)***
Evolution Hospitality LLC (PA)....D....949 325-1350
1211 Puerta Del Sol # 170 San Clemente (92673) ***(P-26854)***
Evolution Juice, Rancho Cucamonga *Also called Evolution Fresh Inc* ***(P-8675)***
Evolve Discovery, San Francisco *Also called Andatha International Inc* ***(P-22915)***
Evolve Growth Initiatives LLC....E....424 281-5000
820 Moraga Dr Los Angeles (90049) ***(P-24526)***
Evolve Treatment Centers, Los Angeles *Also called Evolve Growth Initiatives LLC* ***(P-24526)***
Evoq Properties Inc....D....213 988-8890
1318 E 7th St Ste 200 Los Angeles (90021) ***(P-11424)***
Evotek Inc (PA)....D....858 362-5083
6150 Lusk Blvd Ste 204 San Diego (92121) ***(P-16363)***
Evotek Solutions, San Diego *Also called Evotek Inc* ***(P-16363)***
Evox Productions LLC (PA)....D....310 605-1400
2363 E Pacifica Pl 305 Compton (90220) ***(P-15154)***
Evriholder Products LLC (HQ)....E....714 490-7878
1500 S Lewis St Anaheim (92805) ***(P-6761)***
EW Scripps Company....C....619 237-1010
4600 Air Way San Diego (92102) ***(P-5790)***
Ewing-Foley Inc (PA)....E....408 342-1201
10061 Bubb Rd Ste 100 Cupertino (95014) ***(P-7475)***
Eworkplace Solutions Inc....C....949 583-1646
9861 Irvine Center Dr Irvine (92618) ***(P-7047)***
Exablox Corporation....D....408 773-8477
1156 Sonora Ct Sunnyvale (94086) ***(P-16223)***
Exactax Inc (PA)....D....714 284-4802
1100 E Orangethorpe Ave # 100 Anaheim (92801) ***(P-13705)***
Exadel Inc (PA)....D....925 363-9510
1340 Treat Blvd Walnut Creek (94597) ***(P-15673)***
Exagen Diagnostics Inc....D....505 272-7966
1221 Liberty Way Ste A Vista (92081) ***(P-22084)***
Examine Your Practice, San Diego *Also called Trendsource Inc* ***(P-26573)***
Examone World Wide Inc....D....619 299-3926
7480 Mission Valley Rd # 101 San Diego (92108) ***(P-22802)***
Exandal Corporation....C....818 705-9497
17620 Sherman Way Ste 207 Van Nuys (91406) ***(P-8404)***
Excalibur Well Services Corp (PA)....D....661 589-5338
22034 Rosedale Hwy Bakersfield (93314) ***(P-1036)***
Exceed, Hemet *Also called Valley Rsrce Ctr For Retarded* ***(P-24856)***
Excel Academy....D....949 387-7822
1200 Quail St Ste 175 Newport Beach (92660) ***(P-25420)***
Excel Auto Transporting Towing, Jurupa Valley *Also called Deluxe Auto Carriers Inc* ***(P-4001)***
Excel Building Services LLC....A....925 474-1080
1061 Serpentine Ln Ste H Pleasanton (94566) ***(P-14261)***
Excel Construction Svcs Inc (PA)....D....714 680-9200
1950 Raymer Ave Fullerton (92833) ***(P-1397)***
Excel Contractors Inc....D....661 942-6944
348 E Avenue K8 Ste B Lancaster (93535) ***(P-1162)***
Excel Home Health Inc....E....619 460-6622
5575 Lake Park Way # 220 La Mesa (91942) ***(P-22294)***
Excel Landscape Inc....C....951 735-9650
710 Rimpau Ave Ste 108 Corona (92879) ***(P-839)***
Excel Managed Care Disa....D....916 944-7185
3840 Watt Ave Bldg C Sacramento (95821) ***(P-27229)***
Excel Mdular Scaffold Lsg Corp....A....760 598-0050
2555 Birch St Vista (92081) ***(P-3515)***
Excel Moving Services....D....800 392-3596
30047 Ahern Ave Union City (94587) ***(P-4346)***
Excel Paving Co, Long Beach *Also called Palp Inc* ***(P-1832)***
Excell Care Ctr, Oakland *Also called Mariner Health Care Inc* ***(P-20626)***
Excell Center, The, Turlock *Also called Aspiranet* ***(P-23495)***
Excell Health Care Center, Oakland *Also called SSC Oakland Excell Oper Co LP* ***(P-20777)***
Excell Staffing & SEC Svcs, El Cajon *Also called Xl Staffing Inc* ***(P-14800)***
Excellence Ventures Inc....D....323 262-6800
149 S Mednik Ave Los Angeles (90022) ***(P-17158)***
Excellent Building Maintenance, Moorpark *Also called EBM Janitorial Services Inc* ***(P-14255)***
Excellnce of Inland Empire Inc....C....909 758-4311
9568 Archibald Ave 110 Rancho Cucamonga (91730) ***(P-11425)***
Excelta Corporation (PA)....D....805 686-4686
60 Easy St Ste F Buellton (93427) ***(P-7587)***
Exceptional Chld Foundation (PA)....C....310 204-3300
5350 Machado Ln Culver City (90230) ***(P-24182)***
Exceptional Chld Foundation....C....310 204-3300
5350 Machado Ln Culver City (90230) ***(P-24183)***
Exceptnal Prents Unlimited Inc....D....559 229-2000
4440 N 1st St Fresno (93726) ***(P-23791)***
Exchange Bank (HQ)....C....707 524-3000
440 Aviation Blvd Santa Rosa (95403) ***(P-9534)***
Exchange Bank....C....707 524-3399
440 Aviation Blvd Santa Rosa (95403) ***(P-9344)***
Exchange Bank....D....707 762-5555
2 E Washington St Petaluma (94952) ***(P-9442)***
Exchange Bank....B....707 584-7300
6290 Commerce Blvd Rohnert Park (94928) ***(P-9443)***
Exchange Bank/Loan Service Ctr, Santa Rosa *Also called Exchange Bank* ***(P-9344)***
Exchange La, Sherman Oaks *Also called WERM Investments LLC* ***(P-18475)***
Execusheld Prtection Group LLC....D....707 439-6351
301 Georgia St Ste 307 Vallejo (94590) ***(P-16641)***
Execushield Inc....D....415 508-0825
4104 24th St Ste 501 San Francisco (94114) ***(P-16642)***
Executive Briefing Center, Sunnyvale *Also called Juniper Networks Inc* ***(P-15990)***
Executive Committee, The, San Diego *Also called Vistage International Inc* ***(P-27516)***
Executive Ex Mssngr-Air Curier, Newport Beach *Also called Executive Express Inc* ***(P-4399)***
Executive Express Inc (PA)....D....949 852-0450
2007 Quail St Newport Beach (92660) ***(P-4399)***
Executive Financial HM Ln Corp....E....818 285-5626
12501 Chandler Blvd Valley Village (91607) ***(P-9802)***
Executive Fitness Management....E....818 259-6753
226 E Palm Ave Burbank (91502) ***(P-18597)***
Executive Home Loan, Valley Village *Also called Executive Financial HM Ln Corp* ***(P-9802)***
Executive Inn Inc....D....408 245-5330
1217 Wildwood Ave Sunnyvale (94089) ***(P-12569)***
Executive Landscape Inc....C....760 731-9036
2131 Huffstatler St Fallbrook (92028) ***(P-840)***
Executive Living Apartments, Stockton *Also called Grupe Properties Co* ***(P-4569)***
Executive Network Entps Inc....D....310 457-8822
1224 21st St Apt E Santa Monica (90404) ***(P-3792)***
Executive Network Entps Inc (PA)....D....310 447-2759
13440 Beach Ave Marina Del Rey (90292) ***(P-3793)***
Executive Personnel Services....B....714 310-9506
17842 Irvine Blvd Ste 236 Tustin (92780) ***(P-14618)***
Executive Protection Agency K-....E....619 442-5771
1175 N 2nd St Ste 102 El Cajon (92021) ***(P-16643)***
Executives Outlet Inc....C....415 433-6044
1 Lombard St Lbby San Francisco (94111) ***(P-18598)***
Exel N Amercn Logistics Inc....D....209 942-0102
3735 Imperial Way Stockton (95215) ***(P-4501)***
Exel N Amercn Logistics Inc....D....209 932-2400
4512 Frontier Way Stockton (95215) ***(P-4502)***
Exeter Engineering Inc....D....559 592-3161
109 W Pine St Exeter (93221) ***(P-510)***
Exeter Packers Inc (PA)....A....559 592-5168
1250 E Myer Ave Exeter (93221) ***(P-511)***
Exeter Packers Inc....C....661 399-0416
33374 Lerdo Hwy Bakersfield (93308) ***(P-4503)***
Exeter Packers Inc....C....559 784-8820
23744 Avenue 181 Porterville (93257) ***(P-512)***
Exeter-Ivanhoe Citrus Assn....D....559 592-3141
901 Rocky Hill Dr Exeter (93221) ***(P-513)***
Exigen (usa) Inc (PA)....A....415 402-2600
345 California St Fl 22 San Francisco (94104) ***(P-15155)***
Exigen Group, San Francisco *Also called Exigen (usa) Inc* ***(P-15155)***
Exis Inc....E....408 944-4600
1570 The Alameda Ste 150 San Jose (95126) ***(P-7476)***
Exodus Recovery, Culver City *Also called Solano County Mental Health* ***(P-24054)***
Exodus Recovery Inc (PA)....D....310 945-3350
9808 Venice Blvd Ste 700 Culver City (90232) ***(P-22576)***
Exodus Recovery Ctr At Brotman (PA)....D....310 253-9494
3828 Delmas Ter Culver City (90232) ***(P-22021)***
Exp US Services Inc....D....858 597-0555
5670 Oberlin Dr San Diego (92121) ***(P-25677)***

Mergent e-mail: customerrelations@mergent.com
1296
2019 Directory of California
Wholesalers and Services Companies
(P-0000) Products & Services Section entry number
(PA)=Parent Co (HQ)=Headquarters (DH)=Div Headquarters

Expeditors Intl Wash Inc ....E....415 657-3600
425 Valley Dr Brisbane (94005) ***(P-5055)***
Expeditors Intl Wash Inc ....C....919 489-7431
578 Eccles Ave South San Francisco (94080) ***(P-5056)***
Expeditors Intl Wash Inc ....D....310 343-6200
5757 W Century Blvd Los Angeles (90045) ***(P-5057)***
Expeditors Intl Wash Inc ....C....310 343-6200
5757 W Century Blvd Los Angeles (90045) ***(P-5058)***
Expeditors Intl Wash Inc ....D....619 710-1900
1470 Expo Way Ste 110 San Diego (92154) ***(P-5059)***
Experian Corporation ....A....714 830-7000
475 Anton Blvd Santa Ana (92704) ***(P-14035)***
Experian Info Solutions Inc (HQ) ....A....714 830-7000
475 Anton Blvd Costa Mesa (92626) ***(P-14036)***
Experian Info Solutions Inc ....C....310 343-6700
841 Apollo St Ste 200 El Segundo (90245) ***(P-27230)***
Experian Info Solutions Inc ....C....949 567-3731
18500 Von Karman Ave # 400 Irvine (92612) ***(P-14037)***
Experian Marketing, El Segundo *Also called Experian Info Solutions Inc* ***(P-27230)***
Experian Mktg Solutions LLC ....A....714 830-7000
475 Anton Blvd Costa Mesa (92626) ***(P-27725)***
Experience Unlimited, Capitola *Also called Profile of Santa Cruz* ***(P-14704)***
Experienced Home Care Registry ....D....760 724-0880
110 Civic Center Dr # 206 Vista (92084) ***(P-22295)***
Experts Exch Exprts-Xchangecom, San Luis Obispo *Also called Experts Exchange LLC* ***(P-16364)***
Experts Exchange LLC ....D....805 787-0603
2701 Mcmillan Ave Ste 160 San Luis Obispo (93401) ***(P-16364)***
Exploratorium (PA) ....B....415 528-4462
17 Pier Ste 100 San Francisco (94111) ***(P-24884)***
Exponent Inc (PA) ....C....650 326-9400
149 Commonwealth Dr Menlo Park (94025) ***(P-25678)***
Exponential Interactive Inc (HQ) ....D....510 250-5500
5858 Horton St Ste 300 Emeryville (94608) ***(P-13828)***
Expreal Inc ....D....909 373-4400
7168 Archibald Ave # 100 Alta Loma (91701) ***(P-11426)***
Exprescom LLC ....D....619 271-0531
10145 Via De La Amistad San Diego (92154) ***(P-7414)***
Exprescom S.A. De C.V., San Diego *Also called Exprescom LLC* ***(P-7414)***
Express Cable Communication ....D....951 272-2029
350 S Maple St Ste L Corona (92880) ***(P-5913)***
Express Contractors Inc ....D....951 360-6500
11625 Industry Ave Fontana (92337) ***(P-13578)***
Express Financial, San Ysidro *Also called Nigal Inc* ***(P-5686)***
Express Imaging Services Inc ....D....888 846-8804
1805 W 208th St Ste 202 Torrance (90501) ***(P-4675)***
Express Messenger Systems Inc ....D....323 725-2100
5829 Smithway St Commerce (90040) ***(P-4400)***
Express Messenger Systems Inc ....D....209 234-8255
1627 Industrial Dr Stockton (95206) ***(P-4401)***
Express Messenger Systems Inc ....D....209 234-8255
555 Zephyr St Stockton (95206) ***(P-4402)***
Express Messenger Systems Inc ....D....949 235-1400
1240 S Allec St Anaheim (92805) ***(P-4403)***
Express Messenger Systems Inc ....D....800 488-2829
914 W Boone St Santa Maria (93458) ***(P-4404)***
Express Messenger Systems Inc ....C....818 504-9043
11085 Olinda St Sun Valley (91352) ***(P-4405)***
Express Messenger Systems Inc ....D....800 359-2959
375 W Apra St Compton (90220) ***(P-4406)***
Express Messenger Systems Inc ....D....650 553-4001
250 Utah Ave South San Francisco (94080) ***(P-4407)***
Express Messenger Systems Inc ....D....916 921-6016
1635 Main Ave Ste 3 Sacramento (95838) ***(P-4408)***
Express Messenger Systems Inc ....D....559 277-4910
4603 N Brawley Ave # 103 Fresno (93722) ***(P-4409)***
Express Messenger Systems Inc ....D....415 495-7300
101 Spear St Ste A1 San Francisco (94105) ***(P-4410)***
Express Personnel Services ....D....530 671-9202
870 W Onstott Frontage Rd E Yuba City (95991) ***(P-14619)***
Express System Intermodal Inc ....C....801 302-6625
2633 Camino Ramon Ste 400 San Ramon (94583) ***(P-5060)***
Expressworks International LLC (PA) ....C....925 244-0900
2410 Camino Ramon Ste 167 San Ramon (94583) ***(P-27231)***
Extended Care Hosp Westminster ....C....714 891-2769
206 Hospital Cir Westminster (92683) ***(P-20420)***
Extended Stay America, Newport Beach *Also called ESA P Prtfolio Oper Lessee LLC* ***(P-12563)***
Extended Stay America, Orange *Also called ESA P Prtfolio Oper Lessee LLC* ***(P-12564)***
Exterior Solutions Inc ....D....310 400-3510
25752 Simpson Pl Calabasas (91302) ***(P-6924)***
Exterran Inc ....D....626 455-0739
3449 Santa Anita Ave El Monte (91731) ***(P-14439)***
Extra Express (cerritos) Inc ....E....714 985-6000
20405 Business Pkwy Walnut (91789) ***(P-5061)***
Extreme Telecom Inc ....C....818 902-4821
9221 Corbin Ave Ste 260 Northridge (91324) ***(P-5558)***
Exult Inc ....A....949 856-8800
121 Innovation Dr Ste 200 Irvine (92617) ***(P-27232)***
Exyte US Inc ....E....415 621-1199
1453 Mission St Fl 2 San Francisco (94103) ***(P-25679)***
Ey, Los Angeles *Also called Ernst & Young LLP* ***(P-26191)***
Ey, El Segundo *Also called Ernst & Young LLP* ***(P-26192)***
Ey, San Francisco *Also called Ernst & Young LLP* ***(P-26193)***
Ey, Palo Alto *Also called Ernst & Young LLP* ***(P-26194)***
Ey, San Jose *Also called Ernst & Young LLP* ***(P-26195)***
Ey, San Diego *Also called Ernst & Young LLP* ***(P-26196)***
Ey, Irvine *Also called Ernst & Young LLP* ***(P-26197)***
Ey, Irvine *Also called Ernst & Young LLP* ***(P-26198)***
Ey, Westlake Village *Also called Ernst & Young LLP* ***(P-26199)***
Ey, Redwood City *Also called Ernst & Young LLP* ***(P-26200)***
Ey, Roseville *Also called Ernst & Young LLP* ***(P-26201)***
Eye Medical Center of Fresno, Fresno *Also called Eye Medical Clinic Fresno Inc* ***(P-19464)***
Eye Medical Clinic Fresno Inc ....D....559 486-5000
1360 E Herndon Ave # 301 Fresno (93720) ***(P-19464)***
Eye Physican Medical Group, El Cajon *Also called Sharp Healthcare* ***(P-19882)***
Eye Q Vision Care (PA) ....C....559 486-2000
7075 N Sharon Ave Fresno (93720) ***(P-19465)***
EZ Acceptance Inc ....C....858 278-8351
7651 Ronson Rd San Diego (92111) ***(P-14504)***
EZ Electric, Roseville *Also called Vexillum Inc* ***(P-6147)***
EZ Lube LLC (PA) ....D....714 556-1312
3540 Howard Way Ste 200 Costa Mesa (92626) ***(P-17861)***
F & A Federal Credit Union ....D....323 268-1226
2625 Corporate Pl Monterey Park (91754) ***(P-9550)***
F & F Contracting Inc ....C....559 276-2418
4145 W Alamos Ave Fresno (93722) ***(P-646)***
F & G Biagi Transportation, Ontario *Also called Biagi Bros Inc* ***(P-4107)***
F & H Construction (PA) ....D....209 931-3738
1115 E Lockeford St Lodi (95240) ***(P-1531)***
F and A Farms, Stevinson *Also called Frank J Gomes Dairy A Califo* ***(P-413)***
F C I, Anaheim *Also called Fci Lender Services Inc* ***(P-14002)***
F D I C, Roseville *Also called Federal Deposit Insurance Corp* ***(P-10501)***
F E A, Sunnyvale *Also called Fujitsu Electronics Amer Inc* ***(P-25695)***
F E E, Rcho STA Marg *Also called Fakouri Electrical Engrg Inc* ***(P-16284)***
F F M L R, Moss Beach *Also called Friends Fitzgerald Mar Reserve* ***(P-24782)***
F I N, Van Nuys *Also called Financial Information Network* ***(P-15160)***
F J Hoover Plumbing Inc ....D....951 360-8262
2259 Hamner Ave Norco (92860) ***(P-2205)***
F Korbel & Bros ....C....707 525-1875
4384 Becker Blvd Santa Rosa (95403) ***(P-4889)***
F M I, Anaheim *Also called Freight Management Inc* ***(P-27242)***
F M T, Carlsbad *Also called Fmt Consultants LLC* ***(P-16366)***
F M Tarbell Co ....D....951 471-5333
18295 Collier Ave Lake Elsinore (92530) ***(P-11427)***
F M Tarbell Co ....D....951 677-3565
39028 Winchester Rd # 101 Murrieta (92563) ***(P-11428)***
F M Tarbell Co ....D....714 772-8990
321 S State College Blvd Anaheim (92806) ***(P-11429)***
F M Tarbell Co ....E....714 637-7240
6396 E Santa Ana Cyn Rd Anaheim (92807) ***(P-11430)***
F M Tarbell Co (HQ) ....C....714 972-0988
1403 N Tustin Ave Ste 380 Santa Ana (92705) ***(P-11431)***
F M Tarbell Co ....C....951 280-6040
315 Magnolia Ave Corona (92879) ***(P-11432)***
F M Tarbell Co ....D....949 830-6030
25201 La Paz Rd Laguna Hills (92653) ***(P-11433)***
F M Tarbell Co ....D....951 301-5932
27701 Scott Rd Ste 103 Menifee (92584) ***(P-11434)***
F M Tarbell Co ....C....951 303-0307
31990 Temecula Pkwy # 101 Temecula (92592) ***(P-11435)***
F M Tarbell Co ....D....909 861-3100
22632 Golden Springs Dr # 290 Diamond Bar (91765) ***(P-11436)***
F M Tarbell Co ....E....714 639-0677
4040 Barranca Pkwy # 100 Irvine (92604) ***(P-11437)***
F M Tarbell Co ....D....949 559-8451
4000 Barranca Pkwy # 160 Irvine (92604) ***(P-11438)***
F M Tarbell Co ....D....951 471-5333
18295 Collier Ave Lake Elsinore (92530) ***(P-11439)***
F M Tarbell Co ....D....951 270-1022
2409 S Vineyard Ave Ste A Ontario (91761) ***(P-11440)***
F M Tarbell Co ....E....760 346-7405
74245 Highway 111 Ste 100 Palm Desert (92260) ***(P-11441)***
F M Tarbell Co ....C....909 982-8881
1365 E 19th St Ste A Upland (91784) ***(P-11442)***
F O C Electronics Corporation ....E....213 625-5775
830 Traction Ave Los Angeles (90013) ***(P-7415)***
F P I, Shafter *Also called Farm Pump & Irrigation Co Inc* ***(P-7751)***
F R A LP ....D....714 633-1442
1702 Fairhaven Ave Santa Ana (92705) ***(P-13690)***
F R Ghianni Drywall Cnstr Co, El Cajon *Also called F R Ghianni Enterprises Inc* ***(P-1163)***
F R Ghianni Enterprises Inc ....D....619 279-1073
1937 Friendship Dr Ste A El Cajon (92020) ***(P-1163)***
F R H I, San Jose *Also called Fertility & Reproductive* ***(P-19473)***
F R T International Inc ....C....909 390-4892
2825 Jurupa St Ontario (91761) ***(P-5062)***
F R T International Inc (PA) ....C....310 604-8208
1700 N Alameda St Compton (90222) ***(P-4555)***
F&E Aircraft Maintenance, El Segundo *Also called Arinwine Arcft Maint Svcs LLC* ***(P-4872)***
F&E Aircraft Maintenance (PA) ....B....310 338-0063
531 Main St El Segundo (90245) ***(P-4890)***
F&M Bank, Long Beach *Also called Farmers Merchants Bnk Long Bch* ***(P-9444)***
F-Secure Inc ....E....888 432-8233
470 Ramona St Palo Alto (94301) ***(P-7048)***
F3 and Associates Inc (PA) ....D....707 748-4300
701 E H St Benicia (94510) ***(P-26129)***
Faberware Div, Fairfield *Also called Meyer Corporation US* ***(P-6776)***
Fabric Barn ....C....562 494-3450
3123 E Anaheim St Long Beach (90804) ***(P-8226)***
Fabulous & Company LLC ....E....818 261-7242
19553 Enadia Way Reseda (91335) ***(P-13654)***
Facebook Inc (PA) ....A....650 543-4800
1 Hacker Way Bldg 10 Menlo Park (94025) ***(P-16224)***
Facey Medical Foundation ....C....805 206-2000
2655 1st St Simi Valley (93065) ***(P-20147)***

ALPHABETIC

Facey Medical Foundation C 818 861-7831
191 S Buena Vista St Burbank (91505) ***(P-20148)***
Facey Medical Foundation (PA) C 818 365-9531
15451 San Fernando Msn Mission Hills (91345) ***(P-22803)***
Facey Medical Foundation C 818 837-5677
11211 Sepulveda Blvd Mission Hills (91345) ***(P-22804)***
Facey Medical Foundation D 661 250-5225
17909 Soledad Canyon Rd Santa Clarita (91387) ***(P-22805)***
Facey Medical Foundation D 661 513-2100
27924 Seco Canyon Rd Santa Clarita (91350) ***(P-19466)***
Facey Medical Foundation C 818 365-9531
11165 Sepulveda Blvd Mission Hills (91345) ***(P-19467)***
Facey Medical Foundation D 626 576-0800
1237 E Main St San Gabriel (91776) ***(P-22806)***
Facey Medical Group, Santa Clarita *Also called Facey Medical Foundation* ***(P-22805)***
Facial Reconstructive Surg &, East Palo Alto *Also called Facial Reconstructive Surgery* ***(P-19468)***
Facial Reconstructive Surgery E 650 328-0511
1900 University Ave 101e East Palo Alto (94303) ***(P-19468)***
Facilities Management, Oakland *Also called Oakland Unified School Dst* ***(P-14335)***
Facilities Operation and Trnsp D 209 826-1936
2657 E Pacheco Blvd Los Banos (93635) ***(P-3922)***
Facility Masters Inc (PA) B 408 436-9090
1604 Kerley Dr San Jose (95112) ***(P-14262)***
Facility Operations Plus D 800 789-9608
118 W Olive Ave Monrovia (91016) ***(P-26855)***
Facility Services Partners D 949 480-4090
1 University Dr Aliso Viejo (92656) ***(P-26856)***
Facility Solutions Group Inc D 714 993-3966
801 Richfield Rd Placentia (92870) ***(P-7361)***
Facs, San Diego *Also called Forensic Analytical* ***(P-27730)***
Fact Foundation D 818 729-8105
303 N Glenoaks Blvd Burbank (91502) ***(P-17159)***
Facter Direct Ltd C 323 634-1999
4751 Wilshire Blvd # 140 Los Angeles (90010) ***(P-17160)***
Factory 2-U Import Export Inc D 323 587-9900
13034 Delano St Van Nuys (91401) ***(P-8303)***
Factory Motor Parts, Orange *Also called Elliott Auto Supply Co Inc* ***(P-6637)***
Factory Mutual Insurance Co C 925 934-2200
1333 N Calif Blvd Ste 200 Walnut Creek (94596) ***(P-10349)***
Factory Mutual Insurance Co D 818 227-2200
6320 Canoga Ave Ste 1100 Woodland Hills (91367) ***(P-10350)***
Factory R D D 949 900-3460
23192 Verdugo Dr Laguna Hills (92653) ***(P-7242)***
Faculty Physcans Srgeons Llusm D 909 558-4000
11370 Anderson St Loma Linda (92354) ***(P-19469)***
Fair Isaac Corporation (PA) B 408 535-1500
181 Metro Dr Ste 700 San Jose (95110) ***(P-27726)***
Fair Isaac International Corp (HQ) A 415 446-6000
200 Smith Ranch Rd San Rafael (94903) ***(P-15674)***
Fair Trade Corner Inc E 530 566-1405
11591 Meridian Rd Chico (95973) ***(P-514)***
Fair Trade USA D 510 663-5260
1500 Broadway Ste 400 Oakland (94612) ***(P-26619)***
Fairbanks Ranch Cntry CLB Inc C 858 259-8811
15150 San Dieguito Rd Rancho Santa Fe (92067) ***(P-18921)***
Fairchild Medical Center, Yreka *Also called Siskiyou Hospital Inc* ***(P-21757)***
Fairfield Community Center, Fairfield *Also called City of Fairfield* ***(P-10865)***
Fairfield Development Inc (PA) C 858 457-2123
5510 Morehouse Dr Ste 200 San Diego (92121) ***(P-1284)***
Fairfield Family YMCA, Long Beach *Also called Young Mens Chrstn Assc Gr L B* ***(P-25337)***
Fairfield Healthcare Center, Fairfield *Also called Fairfield Nursing & Rehab Ctr* ***(P-20421)***
Fairfield Inn, San Diego *Also called RPC Old Town Avenue Owner LLC* ***(P-13146)***
Fairfield Inn, El Segundo *Also called Rubicon B Hacienda LLC* ***(P-13151)***
Fairfield Inn, Rancho Cordova *Also called Presidio Hotel Group LLC* ***(P-13080)***
Fairfield Medical Offices, Fairfield *Also called Kaiser Foundation Hospitals* ***(P-19556)***
Fairfield Nursing & Rehab Ctr D 707 425-0623
1255 Travis Blvd Fairfield (94533) ***(P-20421)***
Fairfield-Suisun Sewer Dst D 707 429-8930
1010 Chadbourne Rd Fairfield (94534) ***(P-6399)***
Fairfight, Pasadena *Also called Myinternetservicescom LLC* ***(P-5607)***
Fairgrounds Golf Center, Rancho Murieta *Also called Empire Golf Inc* ***(P-18712)***
Fairmont Designs, Buena Park *Also called Cambium Business Group Inc* ***(P-6716)***
Fairmont Hotel, San Francisco *Also called Accor Services US LLC* ***(P-12306)***
Fairmont Miramar Hotel, Santa Monica *Also called Ocean Avenue LLC* ***(P-12968)***
Fairmont San Francisco, San Francisco *Also called Mason Street Opco LLC* ***(P-12914)***
Fairmont Snoma Mission Inn Spa, Sonoma *Also called Sonoma Hotel Operator Inc* ***(P-13246)***
Fairplex Enterprises Inc D 909 623-3111
1101 W Mckinley Ave Pomona (91768) ***(P-19168)***
Fairplex Rv Park, Pomona *Also called Los Angeles County Fair Assn* ***(P-19199)***
Fairsite Preschool, Galt *Also called Galt Joint Union School Dst* ***(P-24323)***
Fairview Developmental Center, Costa Mesa *Also called Califrnia Dept State Hospitals* ***(P-21932)***
Fairview Developmental Center, Costa Mesa *Also called Developmental Svcs Cal Dept* ***(P-24179)***
Fairway Technologies Inc D 858 454-4471
7825 Fay Ave Ste 100 La Jolla (92037) ***(P-16365)***
Fairwinds Woodward Park, Fresno *Also called Leisure Care LLC* ***(P-24578)***
Fairwinds-West Hills, Canoga Park *Also called Leisure Care LLC* ***(P-20938)***
Fairwood Apartments, Carmichael *Also called Fairwood Associates Apts* ***(P-11016)***
Fairwood Associates Apts D 916 944-0152
8893 Fair Oaks Blvd Ofc Carmichael (95608) ***(P-11016)***
Faith Bumper Service, Gilroy *Also called Faith T & B Plating Inc* ***(P-17161)***
Faith Com Inc (PA) D 562 719-9300
3850 E Gilman St Long Beach (90815) ***(P-27727)***
Faith Electric LLC (PA) C 909 767-2682
12350 Hesperia Rd Ste 215 Victorville (92395) ***(P-2581)***
Faith Enterprises Inc E 209 835-6034
545 W Beverly Pl Tracy (95376) ***(P-20422)***
Faith Jones & Associates Inc (PA) D 619 297-9601
7801 Mission Center Ct # 106 San Diego (92108) ***(P-22296)***
Faith Quality Auto Body Inc D 951 698-8215
41130 Nick Ln Murrieta (92562) ***(P-17720)***
Faith T & B Plating Inc D 408 986-1226
8475 Forest St Gilroy (95020) ***(P-17161)***
Fakouri Electrical Engrg Inc D 949 888-2400
30001 Comercio Rcho STA Marg (92688) ***(P-16284)***
Falcon Aerospace Holdings LLC A 661 775-7200
27727 Avenue Scott Valencia (91355) ***(P-26857)***
Falcon Auto Repair, Gardena *Also called Raymak Automotive Inc* ***(P-17780)***
Falcon Trading Company (PA) C 831 786-7000
423 Salinas Rd Royal Oaks (95076) ***(P-8787)***
Falconwood Inc D 619 297-9080
1011 Camino Del Rio S San Diego (92108) ***(P-16285)***
Falken Tire, Rancho Cucamonga *Also called Sumitomo Rubber North Amer Inc* ***(P-6695)***
Falken Tire Holdings Inc D 800 723-2553
8656 Haven Ave Rancho Cucamonga (91730) ***(P-6690)***
Falken Tires, Rancho Cucamonga *Also called Falken Tire Holdings Inc* ***(P-6690)***
Fallbrook Fire Protection Dst D 760 723-2010
315 E Ivy St Fallbrook (92028) ***(P-17162)***
Fallbrook Public Utility Dst D 760 728-1125
990 E Mission Rd Fallbrook (92028) ***(P-6254)***
Fallbrook Sklled Nrsing Fcilty D 760 728-2330
325 Potter St Fallbrook (92028) ***(P-20423)***
Fallon Land Company Inc E 213 880-1279
4 Corporate Plaza Dr # 210 Newport Beach (92660) ***(P-7273)***
Fam LLC D 323 888-7755
5553 Bandini Blvd Ste B Bell (90201) ***(P-8258)***
Fam Brands, Bell *Also called Fam LLC* ***(P-8258)***
Famand Inc D 707 255-9295
1604 Airport Blvd Santa Rosa (95403) ***(P-2206)***
Fame Assistance Corporation D 323 373-7720
2270 S Harvard Blvd Los Angeles (90018) ***(P-27728)***
Fame Hardwood Floors, Los Angeles *Also called P8ge Consulting Inc* ***(P-27817)***
Fame Systems Inc E 805 485-0808
301 Hearst Dr Oxnard (93030) ***(P-14263)***
Family & Children Services D 650 326-6576
375 Cambridge Ave Palo Alto (94306) ***(P-23792)***
Family and Children Services D 408 292-9353
950 W Julian St San Jose (95126) ***(P-27729)***
Family Assessment Cnslng Edctn E 714 447-9024
1651 E 4th St Ste 128 Santa Ana (92701) ***(P-23793)***
Family Bridges Inc C 510 839-2270
168 11th St Oakland (94607) ***(P-23794)***
Family Care Network Inc (PA) D 805 503-6240
1255 Kendall Rd San Luis Obispo (93401) ***(P-24320)***
Family Circle Inc D 805 385-4180
2100 Outlet Center Dr # 380 Oxnard (93036) ***(P-23795)***
Family Health Center, Pomona *Also called Keith T Kusunis MD* ***(P-22605)***
Family Health Program, Long Beach *Also called Healthcare Partners LLC* ***(P-22813)***
Family Health Services Clinic, Madera *Also called Madera Community Hospital* ***(P-21572)***
Family Healthcare Network C 559 734-1939
501 N Bridge St Visalia (93291) ***(P-20176)***
Family Healthcare Network B 559 781-7242
1137 W Poplar Ave Porterville (93257) ***(P-19470)***
Family Healthcare Network C 559 798-1877
33025 159th Rd Ivanhoe (93235) ***(P-19471)***
Family Hlth Ctrs San Diego Inc (PA) D 619 515-2303
823 Gateway Center Way San Diego (92102) ***(P-22577)***
Family Mdcine Rsidency Program D 559 499-6450
155 N Fresno St Ste 326 Fresno (93701) ***(P-21414)***
Family Mrale Wlfare Recreation D 760 380-3493
1317 Normandy Dr Fort Irwin (92310) ***(P-18922)***
Family Paths Inc (PA) D 510 893-9230
1727 M L King Jr Way Oakland (94612) ***(P-22578)***
Family Plg Assoc Med Group D 562 595-5653
2777 Long Beach Blvd # 150 Long Beach (90806) ***(P-17163)***
Family Plg Assoc Med Group (PA) D 213 738-7283
3050 E Airport Way Long Beach (90806) ***(P-19472)***
Family Radio, Alameda *Also called Family Stations Inc* ***(P-5716)***
Family Resource & Referral Ctr D 209 948-1553
509 W Weber Ave Ste 101 Stockton (95203) ***(P-23796)***
Family Savings Bank, Los Angeles *Also called Oneunited Bank* ***(P-9468)***
Family Service Agency, San Rafael *Also called Family Svcs Agcy Marin Cnty* ***(P-23801)***
Family Service Agency E 805 735-4376
101 S B St Ste A Lompoc (93436) ***(P-23797)***
Family Services E 559 741-7310
807 W Oak Ave Visalia (93291) ***(P-25421)***
Family Services Tulare County D 559 732-1970
815 W Oak Ave Visalia (93291) ***(P-23798)***
Family Stations Inc (PA) C 510 568-6200
1350 S Loop Rd Alameda (94502) ***(P-5716)***
Family Stress Center, Northridge *Also called Child and Family Guidance Ctr* ***(P-22529)***
Family Support Bureau, San Francisco *Also called San Francisco City & County* ***(P-24019)***
Family Support Division, Modesto *Also called County of Stanislaus* ***(P-23751)***
Family Support Services (PA) D 510 834-2443
401 Grand Ave Ste 500 Oakland (94610) ***(P-23799)***
Family Svc Agcy San Francisco (PA) D 415 474-7310
1500 Franklin St San Francisco (94109) ***(P-14852)***
Family Svc Agcy Santa Barbara D 805 965-1001
123 W Gutierrez St Santa Barbara (93101) ***(P-23800)***

Mergent e-mail: customerrelations@mergent.com
1298
2019 Directory of California
Wholesalers and Services Companies
(P-0000) Products & Services Section entry number
(PA)=Parent Co (HQ)=Headquarters (DH)=Div Headquarters

Family Svcs Agcy Marin Cnty (PA).....D.....415 491-5700
555 Northgate Dr San Rafael (94903) ***(P-23801)***
Family Tree Produce Inc.....C.....714 693-5688
5510 E La Palma Ave Anaheim (92807) ***(P-8676)***
Family Urgent Care Center, Anaheim *Also called Anaheim Harbor Medical Group* ***(P-19290)***
Family YMCA of Desert.....D.....760 423-5860
42575 Valley Dr Palm Desert (92210) ***(P-23802)***
Famma Group Inc (PA).....D.....323 826-9600
4510 Loma Vista Ave Vernon (90058) ***(P-8259)***
Famous Ramona Water Inc.....E.....760 789-0174
250 Aqua Ln Ramona (92065) ***(P-8788)***
Famous Software LLC (PA).....D.....559 438-3600
8080 N Palm Ave Ste 210 Fresno (93711) ***(P-15156)***
Fanfare Enterprises, Costa Mesa *Also called Ovations Fanfare* ***(P-26970)***
Fantasea Yacht Charters, Marina Del Rey *Also called USG Enterprises Inc* ***(P-4722)***
Fantasy Springs Resort Casino, Indio *Also called East Valley Tourist Dev Auth* ***(P-19164)***
Fao ROC Holdings LLC.....C.....949 900-6501
15 Cushing Irvine (92618) ***(P-7951)***
Fao Schwarz, Irvine *Also called Fao ROC Holdings LLC* ***(P-7951)***
Far East Broadcasting Co Inc.....D.....562 947-4651
15700 Imperial Hwy La Mirada (90638) ***(P-5717)***
Far East Home Care Inc.....C.....949 673-3100
3407 W 6th St Ste 710 Los Angeles (90020) ***(P-22297)***
Far Northern Coordinating Coun.....D.....530 895-8633
1377 E Lassen Ave Chico (95973) ***(P-23803)***
Far Northern Coordinating Coun (PA).....D.....530 222-4791
1900 Churn Creek Rd # 114 Redding (96002) ***(P-23804)***
Far Northern Regional Center, Redding *Also called Far Northern Coordinating Coun* ***(P-23804)***
Far West Electric Inc.....D.....909 684-8661
6094 Keswick Ave Riverside (92506) ***(P-2582)***
Far West Inc.....D.....559 627-1241
4444 W Meadow Ave Visalia (93277) ***(P-20424)***
Far West Inc.....D.....323 564-7761
8455 State St South Gate (90280) ***(P-20425)***
Far West Inc.....C.....559 733-0901
4525 W Tulare Ave Visalia (93277) ***(P-21065)***
Far West Inc.....D.....909 884-4781
467 E Gilbert St San Bernardino (92404) ***(P-20426)***
Far West Management Corp (PA).....D.....949 863-1757
17941 Mitchell S Ste A Irvine (92614) ***(P-11443)***
Faraday & Future, Gardena *Also called FARaday&future Inc* ***(P-25680)***
FARaday&future Inc.....A.....424 276-7616
18455 S Figueroa St Gardena (90248) ***(P-25680)***
Farallon Capital Partners LP (PA).....D.....415 421-2132
1 Maritime Plz Ste 2100 San Francisco (94111) ***(P-12036)***
Fargo Colonial LLC.....D.....858 454-2181
910 Prospect St La Jolla (92037) ***(P-12570)***
Farm Fresh To You (PA).....C.....916 303-7145
3880 Seaport Blvd West Sacramento (95691) ***(P-343)***
Farm Pump & Irrigation Co Inc (PA).....D.....661 589-6901
535 N Shafter Ave Shafter (93263) ***(P-7751)***
FARM SUPPLY COMPANY, San Luis Obispo *Also called San Luis Obispo Cnty Frm Inc* ***(P-9096)***
Farmers Group Inc (HQ).....A.....323 932-3200
6301 Owensmouth Ave Woodland Hills (91367) ***(P-10351)***
Farmers Group Inc.....D.....213 615-2500
700 S Flower St Ste 2800 Los Angeles (90017) ***(P-10135)***
Farmers Group Inc.....D.....909 839-2020
13950 Ramona Ave Chino (91710) ***(P-10617)***
Farmers Group Inc.....E.....408 557-1100
429 Llewellyn Ave Campbell (95008) ***(P-10618)***
Farmers Group Inc.....B.....925 847-3100
11555 Dublin Canyon Rd Pleasanton (94588) ***(P-10619)***
Farmers Group Inc.....D.....818 249-3000
550 S Hill St Ste 1309 Los Angeles (90013) ***(P-10620)***
Farmers Group Inc.....D.....916 727-4600
6518 Antelope Rd Citrus Heights (95621) ***(P-10621)***
Farmers Group Inc.....A.....805 583-7400
6303 Owensmouth Ave Fl 1 Woodland Hills (91367) ***(P-10622)***
Farmers Insurance, Woodland Hills *Also called Farmers Group Inc* ***(P-10351)***
Farmers Insurance, Los Angeles *Also called Farmers Group Inc* ***(P-10135)***
Farmers Insurance, Chino *Also called Farmers Group Inc* ***(P-10617)***
Farmers Insurance, Campbell *Also called Farmers Group Inc* ***(P-10618)***
Farmers Insurance, Pleasanton *Also called Farmers Group Inc* ***(P-10619)***
Farmers Insurance, Los Angeles *Also called Farmers Group Inc* ***(P-10620)***
Farmers Insurance, Citrus Heights *Also called Farmers Group Inc* ***(P-10621)***
Farmers Insurance, Woodland Hills *Also called Farmers Group Inc* ***(P-10622)***
Farmers Insurance Exchange (HQ).....A.....323 932-3200
6301 Owensmouth Ave # 300 Woodland Hills (91367) ***(P-10623)***
Farmers Insurance Exchange.....B.....559 594-4149
411 E Pine St Ste A Exeter (93221) ***(P-10624)***
Farmers Insurance Fed Cred UNI (PA).....C.....323 209-6000
4601 Wilshire Blvd # 110 Los Angeles (90010) ***(P-9551)***
Farmers International Inc.....E.....530 566-1405
1260 Muir Ave Chico (95973) ***(P-188)***
Farmers Merchants Bnk Long Bch (HQ).....C.....562 437-0011
302 Pine Ave Long Beach (90802) ***(P-9444)***
Farmers Merchants Bnk Long Bch.....C.....562 430-4724
1695 Adolfo Lopez Dr Seal Beach (90740) ***(P-9445)***
Farmers Mrchants Bnk Centl Cal.....C.....916 394-3200
8799 Elk Grove Blvd Elk Grove (95624) ***(P-9446)***
Farmers W Flowers & Bouquets, Carpinteria *Also called Brand Flower Farms Inc* ***(P-9126)***
Farmex Land Management Inc.....C.....559 875-7181
11156 E Annadale Ave Sanger (93657) ***(P-17164)***
Farmington Fresh Sales LLC (PA).....C.....209 983-9700
7735 S Highway 99 Stockton (95215) ***(P-217)***
Farms Golf Club Inc.....D.....858 756-5585
8500 San Andrews Rd Rancho Santa Fe (92067) ***(P-18923)***
Farms of Amador.....D.....209 257-0112
12200b Airport Rd Jackson (95642) ***(P-25422)***
Faro Logistics, Norwalk *Also called Faro Services Inc* ***(P-4556)***
Faro Services Inc.....C.....562 483-7799
15625 Shoemaker Ave Norwalk (90650) ***(P-4556)***
Farwest Corrosion Control Co (PA).....C.....310 532-9524
12029 Regentview Ave Downey (90241) ***(P-3516)***
Farwest Insulation Contracting.....E.....310 634-2800
2741 Yates Ave Commerce (90040) ***(P-2883)***
Farwest Trading, Turlock *Also called Associated Feed & Supply Co* ***(P-9072)***
Faschings Car Wash, Arcadia *Also called George Fasching* ***(P-17815)***
Fashion Resources, Los Angeles *Also called Tarrant Apparel Group* ***(P-8338)***
Fashion Wheel, Fresno *Also called Anthony Lambe* ***(P-6618)***
Fashioncraft Floors Inc (PA).....E.....714 255-8400
1630 Faraday Ave Carlsbad (92008) ***(P-3102)***
Fast Deer Bus Chrtr Incrprtion.....D.....323 201-8988
8105 Slauson Ave Montebello (90640) ***(P-3896)***
Fast Lane Container Services, Wilmington *Also called Fast Lane Transportation Inc* ***(P-4148)***
Fast Lane Transportation Inc (PA).....D.....562 435-3000
2400 E Pacific Coast Hwy Wilmington (90744) ***(P-4148)***
Fast Pro Inc.....D.....408 566-0200
2555 Lafayette St Ste 103 Santa Clara (95050) ***(P-6639)***
Fast Undercar, Santa Clara *Also called Fast Pro Inc* ***(P-6639)***
Fast Undercar Stockton, Antioch *Also called Jamm Management LLC* ***(P-6649)***
Fastclick Inc.....D.....805 689-9839
530 E Montecito St Santa Barbara (93103) ***(P-13972)***
Fastclick.com, Santa Barbara *Also called Fastclick Inc* ***(P-13972)***
Fastech, Buena Park *Also called Fueling and Service Tech Inc* ***(P-7752)***
Fastly Inc (PA).....D.....415 488-6329
475 Brannan St Ste 300 San Francisco (94107) ***(P-15157)***
Fathers of St Charles.....C.....818 768-6500
10631 Vinedale St Sun Valley (91352) ***(P-11017)***
Faucetdirect.com, Chico *Also called Buildcom Inc* ***(P-7612)***
Faulkner Trucking Inc.....D.....559 684-9298
3645 S K St Tulare (93274) ***(P-4149)***
Fault Line Plumbing.....E.....925 443-6450
7640 National Dr Livermore (94550) ***(P-2207)***
Fayaka Airways LLC.....C.....800 771-5489
659 Macarthur Blvd San Leandro (94577) ***(P-4859)***
Fba Inc (PA).....E.....510 265-1888
1675 Sabre St Hayward (94545) ***(P-25681)***
Fbd Vanguard Construction Inc.....C.....925 245-1300
550 Greenville Rd Livermore (94550) ***(P-26858)***
Fc El Segundo LLC.....D.....702 439-7945
199 Continental Blvd El Segundo (90245) ***(P-12571)***
Fc Landscape Inc.....D.....760 347-6600
43216 Madison St Indio (92201) ***(P-755)***
Fc Metropolitan Lofts Inc.....D.....213 488-0010
949 S Hope St Ste 100 Los Angeles (90015) ***(P-11875)***
Fcb Worldwide Inc.....A.....415 820-8545
1160 Battery St Ste 250 San Francisco (94111) ***(P-13829)***
Fcb Worldwide Inc.....C.....415 820-8000
1160 Battery St Ste 250 San Francisco (94111) ***(P-13830)***
Fce Benefit Administrators Inc (PA).....C.....650 341-0306
1528 S El Camino Real # 307 San Mateo (94402) ***(P-10625)***
Fci Lender Services Inc.....C.....714 974-1945
8180 E Kaiser Blvd Anaheim (92808) ***(P-14002)***
Fci Management, Long Beach *Also called Faith Com Inc* ***(P-27727)***
Fcrta, Fresno *Also called Fresno County Rural Trnst Agcy* ***(P-3657)***
Fcs Medical Corporation.....D.....323 317-9200
1701 E Cesar E Chavez Ave # 230 Los Angeles (90033) ***(P-20149)***
Fcs Software Solutions Limited.....D.....408 324-1203
2375 Zanker Rd Ste 250 San Jose (95131) ***(P-15158)***
Fcti Inc (PA).....D.....310 405-0022
11766 Wilshire Blvd # 1100 Los Angeles (90025) ***(P-9681)***
Fdi Collateral Management, Sacramento *Also called Dealertrack Collte Manag Servi* ***(P-16341)***
FDIC, Los Angeles *Also called Federal Deposit Insurance Corp* ***(P-10500)***
FDIC-San Frncisco Regional Off, San Francisco *Also called Federal Deposit Insurance Corp* ***(P-10499)***
Fdsi Logistics LLC.....D.....818 971-3300
5703 Corsa Ave Westlake Village (91362) ***(P-27233)***
Feather Falls Casino, Oroville *Also called Mooretown Rancheria* ***(P-18785)***
Feather Falls Casino, Oroville *Also called Mooretown Rancheria* ***(P-19204)***
Feather River Home Health, Paradise *Also called Feather River Hospital* ***(P-21416)***
Feather River Hospital (PA).....A.....530 877-9361
5974 Pentz Rd Paradise (95969) ***(P-21415)***
Feather River Hospital.....D.....530 872-3378
6626 Clark Rd Ste P Paradise (95969) ***(P-21416)***
Feather River Hospital.....C.....530 876-7216
1295 Bille Rd Paradise (95969) ***(P-7179)***
Feather River Hospital HM Oxgn, Paradise *Also called Feather River Hospital* ***(P-7179)***
Feather Rver Recreation Pk Dst.....D.....530 533-2011
1875 Feather River Blvd Oroville (95965) ***(P-19169)***
Fed Air Security Corporation.....D.....626 535-2200
210 S De Lacey Ave Pasadena (91105) ***(P-16892)***
Fedelity National Title Co Org.....D.....818 758-6849
5000 Van Nuys Blvd 500 Sherman Oaks (91403) ***(P-10451)***
Federal Deposit Insurance Corp.....C.....626 359-7152
1333 S Mayflower Ave # 450 Monrovia (91016) ***(P-10498)***
Federal Deposit Insurance Corp.....C.....415 546-0160
25 Jessie St Ste 2300 San Francisco (94105) ***(P-10499)***
Federal Deposit Insurance Corp.....C.....323 545-9260
5150 W Goldleaf Cir # 405 Los Angeles (90056) ***(P-10500)***

Employee Codes: A=Over 500 employees, B=251-500
C=101-250, D=51-100, E=50
2019 Directory of California
Wholesalers and Services Companies
© Mergent Inc. 1-800-342-5647
1299

Federal Deposit Insurance Corp ....C......916 789-8580
   1532 Eureka Rd Ste 102 Roseville (95661) *(P-10501)*
Federal Dfenders San Diego Inc (PA) ....D......619 234-8467
   225 Broadway Ste 900 San Diego (92101) *(P-23063)*
Federal Express Corporation ....D......800 463-3339
   3541 Regional Pkwy Petaluma (94954) *(P-4817)*
Federal Express Corporation ....C......800 463-3339
   1650 47th St San Diego (92102) *(P-4818)*
Federal Express Corporation ....C......800 463-3339
   1330 Fortress St Chico (95973) *(P-4819)*
Federal Express Corporation ....D......800 463-3339
   1286 Lawrence Station Rd Sunnyvale (94089) *(P-4820)*
Federal Express Corporation ....C......800 463-3339
   12600 Prairie Ave Hawthorne (90250) *(P-4821)*
Federal Express Corporation ....C......800 463-3339
   11340 Sherman Way Sun Valley (91352) *(P-4780)*
Federal Express Corporation ....C......800 463-3339
   1500 Nichols Dr Rocklin (95765) *(P-4781)*
Federal Express Corporation ....D......800 463-3339
   2660 Research Park Dr Soquel (95073) *(P-4411)*
Federal Express Corporation ....C......800 463-3339
   2495 Faraday Ave Carlsbad (92010) *(P-17165)*
Federal Express Corporation ....C......800 463-3339
   1081 Fullerton Rd City of Industry (91748) *(P-4412)*
Federal Express Corporation ....B......800 463-3339
   200 N Pacific Coast Hwy # 800 El Segundo (90245) *(P-17166)*
Federal Express Corporation ....C......800 463-3339
   1111 Bird Center Dr Palm Springs (92262) *(P-4782)*
Federal Express Corporation ....C......510 347-2430
   1601 Aurora Dr San Leandro (94577) *(P-4822)*
Federal Express Corporation ....D......800 463-3339
   1650 Sunflower Ave Costa Mesa (92626) *(P-4823)*
Federal Express Corporation ....D......800 463-3339
   3333 S Grand Ave Los Angeles (90007) *(P-4150)*
Federal Express Corporation ....D......800 463-3339
   7275 Johnson Dr Pleasanton (94588) *(P-17167)*
Federal Express Corporation ....D......800 463-3339
   1 Lower Ragsdale Dr # 4 Monterey (93940) *(P-4824)*
Federal Express Corporation ....C......800 463-3339
   710 Dado St San Jose (95131) *(P-4413)*
Federal Express Corporation ....B......510 382-2344
   9190 Edes Ave Oakland (94603) *(P-4414)*
Federal Express Corporation ....C......510 465-5209
   500 12th St Ste 139 Oakland (94607) *(P-4825)*
Federal Express Corporation ....D......800 463-3339
   8455 Pardee Dr Oakland (94621) *(P-4826)*
Federal Express Corporation ....C......800 463-3339
   6775 Woodrum Cir Redding (96002) *(P-4827)*
Federal Express Corporation ....E......800 463-3339
   935 Performance Dr Stockton (95206) *(P-4828)*
Federal Express Corporation ....D......800 463-3339
   9339 Ann St Santa Fe Springs (90670) *(P-4829)*
Federal Express Corporation ....C......800 463-3339
   9510 W Airport Dr Visalia (93277) *(P-4830)*
Federal Express Corporation ....B......800 463-3339
   7000 Barranca Pkwy Irvine (92618) *(P-17168)*
Federal Express Corporation ....B......800 463-3339
   3371 E Francis St Ontario (91761) *(P-17169)*
Federal Express Corporation ....D......909 390-3237
   2060 S Wineville Ave B Ontario (91761) *(P-4831)*
Federal Express Corporation ....C......800 463-3339
   1600 63rd St Emeryville (94608) *(P-4012)*
Federal Express Corporation ....C......800 463-3339
   2500 Kimberly Ave Fullerton (92831) *(P-4832)*
Federal Express Corporation ....D......800 463-3339
   3150 Paseo Mercado Oxnard (93036) *(P-4833)*
Federal Express Corporation ....D......916 361-5500
   8950 Cal Center Dr # 370 Sacramento (95826) *(P-4834)*
Federal Express Corporation ....C......800 463-3339
   2221 W Washington St San Diego (92110) *(P-5063)*
Federal Express Corporation ....C......800 463-3339
   1875 Marin St San Francisco (94124) *(P-4835)*
Federal Express Corporation ....C......800 463-3339
   2451 N Palm Dr Long Beach (90755) *(P-4836)*
Federal Express Corporation ....C......949 862-4500
   2601 Main St Ste 1000 Irvine (92614) *(P-4783)*
Federal Express Corporation ....C......562 522-4014
   1 World Trade Ctr Ste 191 Long Beach (90831) *(P-4837)*
Federal Hm Ln Bnk San Frncisco (PA) ....B......415 616-1000
   600 California St San Francisco (94108) *(P-9695)*
Federal Insurance Company ....D......818 596-6100
   21820 Burbank Blvd # 330 Woodland Hills (91367) *(P-10626)*
Federal Insurance Company ....D......415 273-6300
   275 Battery St Fl 12 San Francisco (94111) *(P-10627)*
Federal Rsrve Bnk San Frncisco (HQ) ....A......415 974-2000
   101 Market St San Francisco (94105) *(P-9273)*
Federal Rsrve Bnk San Frncisco ....A......213 683-2300
   950 S Grand Ave Los Angeles (90015) *(P-9274)*
Federico Beauty Institute ....E......916 929-4242
   1515 Sports Dr Ste 100 Sacramento (95834) *(P-13655)*
Federted Indans Grton Rncheria ....B......707 588-7100
   630 Park Ct Rohnert Park (94928) *(P-12572)*
Fedex, Petaluma *Also called Federal Express Corporation* *(P-4817)*
Fedex, San Diego *Also called Federal Express Corporation* *(P-4818)*
Fedex, Chico *Also called Federal Express Corporation* *(P-4819)*
Fedex, Sunnyvale *Also called Federal Express Corporation* *(P-4820)*
Fedex, Hawthorne *Also called Federal Express Corporation* *(P-4821)*
Fedex, Sun Valley *Also called Federal Express Corporation* *(P-4780)*
Fedex, Rocklin *Also called Federal Express Corporation* *(P-4781)*

Fedex, Soquel *Also called Federal Express Corporation* *(P-4411)*
Fedex, Carlsbad *Also called Federal Express Corporation* *(P-17165)*
Fedex, City of Industry *Also called Federal Express Corporation* *(P-4412)*
Fedex, El Segundo *Also called Federal Express Corporation* *(P-17166)*
Fedex, Palm Springs *Also called Federal Express Corporation* *(P-4782)*
Fedex, San Leandro *Also called Federal Express Corporation* *(P-4822)*
Fedex, Costa Mesa *Also called Federal Express Corporation* *(P-4823)*
Fedex, Los Angeles *Also called Federal Express Corporation* *(P-4150)*
Fedex, Pleasanton *Also called Federal Express Corporation* *(P-17167)*
Fedex, Monterey *Also called Federal Express Corporation* *(P-4824)*
Fedex, San Jose *Also called Federal Express Corporation* *(P-4413)*
Fedex, Oakland *Also called Federal Express Corporation* *(P-4414)*
Fedex, Oakland *Also called Federal Express Corporation* *(P-4825)*
Fedex, Oakland *Also called Federal Express Corporation* *(P-4826)*
Fedex, Redding *Also called Federal Express Corporation* *(P-4827)*
Fedex, Stockton *Also called Federal Express Corporation* *(P-4828)*
Fedex, Santa Fe Springs *Also called Federal Express Corporation* *(P-4829)*
Fedex, Visalia *Also called Federal Express Corporation* *(P-4830)*
Fedex, Irvine *Also called Federal Express Corporation* *(P-17168)*
Fedex, Ontario *Also called Federal Express Corporation* *(P-17169)*
Fedex, Ontario *Also called Federal Express Corporation* *(P-4831)*
Fedex, Emeryville *Also called Federal Express Corporation* *(P-4012)*
Fedex, Fullerton *Also called Federal Express Corporation* *(P-4832)*
Fedex, Oxnard *Also called Federal Express Corporation* *(P-4833)*
Fedex, Sacramento *Also called Federal Express Corporation* *(P-4834)*
Fedex, San Diego *Also called Federal Express Corporation* *(P-5063)*
Fedex, San Francisco *Also called Federal Express Corporation* *(P-4835)*
Fedex, Long Beach *Also called Federal Express Corporation* *(P-4836)*
Fedex, Irvine *Also called Federal Express Corporation* *(P-4783)*
Fedex, Long Beach *Also called Federal Express Corporation* *(P-4837)*
Fedex Corporation ....E......415 657-0403
   50 Cypress Ln Brisbane (94005) *(P-17170)*
Fedex Freight Corporation ....E......714 637-9346
   310 W Grove Ave Orange (92865) *(P-4691)*
Fedex Freight Corporation ....C......323 269-9800
   4500 Bandini Blvd Vernon (90058) *(P-4151)*
Fedex Freight Corporation ....C......714 996-8720
   1379 N Miller St Anaheim (92806) *(P-4152)*
Fedex Freight Corporation ....C......909 887-3970
   7250 Cajon Blvd San Bernardino (92407) *(P-4153)*
Fedex Freight Corporation ....D......760 873-8655
   193 Willow St Bishop (93514) *(P-4154)*
Fedex Freight Corporation ....D......619 710-0268
   2250 Airway Ln San Diego (92154) *(P-4155)*
Fedex Freight Corporation ....B......310 323-5230
   15200 S Main St Gardena (90248) *(P-4156)*
Fedex Freight Corporation ....B......800 288-0743
   3200 Workman Mill Rd Whittier (90601) *(P-4692)*
Fedex Freight Corporation ....E......408 988-2111
   3255 Victor St Santa Clara (95054) *(P-4013)*
Fedex Freight Corporation ....B......510 895-0440
   29001 Hopkins St Hayward (94545) *(P-4157)*
Fedex Freight Corporation ....D......818 899-1141
   11911 Branford St Sun Valley (91352) *(P-4158)*
Fedex Freight Corporation ....C......209 466-7726
   4520 S Highway 99 Stockton (95215) *(P-4159)*
Fedex Freight Corporation ....D......800 706-1687
   56 Fairbanks Irvine (92618) *(P-4160)*
Fedex Freight West Inc ....D......650 244-9522
   3050 Teagarden St San Leandro (94577) *(P-4161)*
Fedex Freight West Inc ....C......559 266-0732
   4570 S Maple Ave Fresno (93725) *(P-4162)*
Fedex Freight West Inc ....B......909 357-3555
   11153 Mulberry Ave Fontana (92337) *(P-4163)*
Fedex Freight West Inc. ....E......707 778-3191
   1230 N Mcdowell Blvd Petaluma (94954) *(P-4164)*
Fedex Ground Package Sys Inc ....E......800 463-3339
   1497 George Dr Ste G Redding (96003) *(P-4165)*
Fedex Ground Package Sys Inc ....C......800 463-3339
   590 E Orangethorpe Ave Anaheim (92801) *(P-4166)*
Fedex Ground Package Sys Inc ....C......800 463-3339
   10132 Airway Rd San Diego (92154) *(P-4415)*
Fedex Ground Package Sys Inc ....D......800 463-3339
   1844 S Haster St Anaheim (92802) *(P-4167)*
Fedex Ground Package Sys Inc ....C......800 463-3339
   9999 Olson Dr Ste 100 San Diego (92121) *(P-4838)*
Fedex Ground Package Sys Inc ....D......800 463-3339
   1 Carousel Ln Unit B Ukiah (95482) *(P-4168)*
Fedex Ground Package Sys Inc ....C......800 463-3339
   101 Book Farm Rd Durham (95938) *(P-4169)*
Fedex Ground Package Sys Inc ....C......800 463-3339
   1725 Charles Willard St Carson (90746) *(P-4170)*
Fedex Ground Package Sys Inc ....C......800 463-3339
   311 Otterson Dr Chico (95928) *(P-4171)*
Fedex Ground Package Sys Inc ....C......800 463-3339
   375 Airport Rd Bishop (93514) *(P-4172)*
Fedex Ground Package Sys Inc ....C......800 463-3339
   500 Caletti Ave Windsor (95492) *(P-4173)*
Fedex Ground Package Sys Inc ....E......800 463-3339
   1070 San Mateo Ave South San Francisco (94080) *(P-4416)*
Fedex Ground Package Sys Inc ....D......800 463-3339
   601 Stone Rd Benicia (94510) *(P-4417)*
Fedex Ground Package Sys Inc ....D......800 463-3339
   1500 E Wooley Rd Ste B Oxnard (93030) *(P-4174)*

Fedex Ground Package Sys Inc ....B....800 463-3339
696 E Trimble Rd Ste 10 San Jose (95131) *(P-4175)*
Fedex Ground Package Sys Inc ....A....800 463-3339
330 Resource Dr Bloomington (92316) *(P-4839)*
Fedex Ground Package Sys Inc ....D....800 463-3339
300 Manabe Ow Rd Watsonville (95076) *(P-4176)*
Fedex Ground Package Sys Inc ....D....800 463-3339
9175 San Fernando Rd Sun Valley (91352) *(P-4177)*
Fedex Home Delivery, Oxnard *Also called Fedex Ground Package Sys Inc (P-4174)*
Fedex Office & Print Svcs Inc ....E....805 379-1552
2799 E Thousand Oaks Blvd Thousand Oaks (91362) *(P-14086)*
Fedex Office & Print Svcs Inc ....D....562 942-1953
8642 Whittier Blvd Pico Rivera (90660) *(P-4418)*
Fedex Office & Print Svcs Inc ....E....310 827-2297
13488 Maxella Ave Marina Del Rey (90292) *(P-14087)*
Fedex Office & Print Svcs Inc ....D....805 339-2000
4360 E Main St Ste A Ventura (93003) *(P-14088)*
Fedex Office & Print Svcs Inc ....E....213 892-1700
800 Wilshire Blvd Los Angeles (90017) *(P-14089)*
Fedex Smartpost Inc ....D....323 888-8879
5560 Ferguson Dr Commerce (90022) *(P-4419)*
Fedex Supply Chain ....E....909 605-9210
1670 Champagne Ave Ontario (91761) *(P-4557)*
Fehr & Peers (PA) ....D....925 977-3200
100 Pringle Ave Ste 600 Walnut Creek (94596) *(P-25682)*
Fei Enterprises Inc ....E....323 937-0856
5242 W Adams Blvd Los Angeles (90016) *(P-2583)*
Feiwell, Lawrence MD, Los Alamitos *Also called Marinow Harry MD Facs Inc (P-19668)*
Felina Lingerie, Chatsworth *Also called Piege Co (P-8273)*
Felson Companies Inc ....D....510 538-1150
1290 B St Ste 210 Hayward (94541) *(P-11444)*
Felson Management Corp (PA) ....E....510 538-1150
1290 B St Ste 210 Hayward (94541) *(P-11445)*
Felton Institute, San Francisco *Also called Family Svc Agcy San Francisco (P-14852)*
Fenagh Engineering & Tstg LLC ....E....925 462-5151
9070 Center Ave Rancho Cucamonga (91730) *(P-17171)*
Fencecorp Inc (HQ) ....B....951 686-3170
18440 Van Buren Blvd Riverside (92508) *(P-3517)*
Fenceworks Inc ....D....714 238-0091
2861 E La Cresta Ave Anaheim (92806) *(P-3518)*
Fenceworks Inc (PA) ....C....951 788-5620
870 Main St Riverside (92501) *(P-3519)*
Fenceworks Inc ....D....661 265-0082
891 Corporation St Santa Paula (93060) *(P-3520)*
Fender Digital LLC (HQ) ....D....323 462-2198
1575 N Gower St Ste 170 Los Angeles (90028) *(P-15159)*
Fenderscape Inc ....C....562 988-2228
1446 E Hill St Signal Hill (90755) *(P-841)*
Fennel Inc ....D....951 284-2020
1169 Sherborn St Corona (92879) *(P-3035)*
Fenton Communications Inc ....E....415 255-1946
182 2nd St Ste 400 San Francisco (94105) *(P-27553)*
Fenton Scripps Landing LLC ....D....858 586-0206
9970 Erma Rd San Diego (92131) *(P-11018)*
Fenty Beauty LLC ....C....818 973-2709
425 Market St Fl 19 San Francisco (94105) *(P-8167)*
Fenwick & West LLP (PA) ....B....650 988-8500
801 California St Mountain View (94041) *(P-23064)*
Fenwick & West LLP ....C....415 875-2300
555 California St # 1200 San Francisco (94104) *(P-23065)*
Feralloy PDM Steel Service, Stockton *Also called PDM Steel Service Centers (P-7300)*
Fergadis Enterprises, Bell *Also called Bernard Perrin Supowitz Inc (P-8384)*
Ferguson 601, Van Nuys *Also called Ferguson Enterprises Inc (P-7623)*
Ferguson 667, San Diego *Also called Ferguson Enterprises Inc (P-7620)*
Ferguson 677, Westminster *Also called Ferguson Enterprises Inc (P-7622)*
Ferguson Enterprises Inc ....D....408 441-7276
777 Mariposa St San Francisco (94107) *(P-7617)*
Ferguson Enterprises Inc ....D....626 965-0724
18825 San Jose Ave City of Industry (91748) *(P-7618)*
Ferguson Enterprises Inc ....E....559 253-2900
704 N Laverne Ave Fresno (93727) *(P-7619)*
Ferguson Enterprises Inc ....D....619 515-0300
3280 Market St San Diego (92102) *(P-7620)*
Ferguson Enterprises Inc ....C....909 364-8700
9750 S Town Ave Pomona (91766) *(P-7621)*
Ferguson Enterprises Inc ....C....714 893-1936
6421 Industry Way Westminster (92683) *(P-7622)*
Ferguson Enterprises Inc ....E....818 786-9720
7651 Woodman Ave Van Nuys (91402) *(P-7623)*
Ferguson Fire Fabrication Inc (HQ) ....D....909 517-3085
2750 S Towne Ave Pomona (91766) *(P-7624)*
Ferguson Salon Management ....E....760 434-4141
2946 State St Ste F Carlsbad (92008) *(P-13656)*
Ferguson Salon Management Inc ....E....760 434-5008
1104 Knowles Ave Carlsbad (92008) *(P-13657)*
Fern Oaks Frms A Cal Gen Prtnr ....E....559 684-8220
17001 Avenue 160 Porterville (93257) *(P-411)*
Fernandes & Sons Gen Contrs ....D....408 626-9090
2110 S Bascom Ave Ste 201 Campbell (95008) *(P-14853)*
Fernview Convalescent Hospital ....D....626 285-3131
126 N San Gabriel Blvd San Gabriel (91775) *(P-20427)*
Ferrado Garden Court LLC ....D....650 543-2224
520 Cowper St Ste 100 Palo Alto (94301) *(P-12573)*
Ferrees Group Home Inc ....D....951 849-1927
878 Highland Home Rd Banning (92220) *(P-24527)*
Ferreira Service Inc (PA) ....D....925 831-9330
2600 Old Crow Canyon Rd # 100 San Ramon (94583) *(P-2208)*
Ferring Research Institute Inc ....D....858 657-1400
4245 Sorrento Valley Blvd San Diego (92121) *(P-26365)*

Fertility & Reproductive ....D....408 358-2500
2581 Samaritan Dr Ste 302 San Jose (95124) *(P-19473)*
Fess Prker-Red Lion Gen Partnr ....B....805 564-4333
633 E Cabrillo Blvd Santa Barbara (93103) *(P-12574)*
Festival Companies, The, Los Angeles *Also called Festival Management Corp (P-11446)*
Festival Fun Parks LLC ....D....951 785-3000
3500 Polk St Riverside (92505) *(P-18799)*
Festival Fun Parks LLC ....C....954 921-1411
4590 Macarthur Blvd # 400 Newport Beach (92660) *(P-19170)*
Festival Fun Parks LLC ....C....805 922-1574
2250 Preisker Ln Santa Maria (93458) *(P-19171)*
Festival Fun Parks LLC ....A....909 802-2200
111 Raging Waters Dr San Dimas (91773) *(P-7928)*
Festival Fun Parks LLC ....D....760 945-9474
1525 W Vista Way Vista (92083) *(P-19172)*
Festival Fun Parks LLC ....E....949 261-0404
4590 Macarthur Blvd # 400 Newport Beach (92660) *(P-18800)*
Festival Fun Parks LLC ....D....949 559-8336
3405 Michelson Dr Irvine (92612) *(P-19173)*
Festival Management Corp (PA) ....D....310 665-9610
5901 W Century Blvd # 700 Los Angeles (90045) *(P-11446)*
Festival of Arts Laguna Beach ....D....949 494-1145
650 Laguna Canyon Rd Laguna Beach (92651) *(P-19174)*
Ffd II, San Diego *Also called Fairfield Development Inc (P-1284)*
Fff Enterprises Inc (PA) ....B....951 296-2500
44000 Winchester Rd Temecula (92590) *(P-8168)*
Ffna, Foothill Ranch *Also called Frontech N Fujitsu Amer Inc (P-15960)*
Fhar Fmly Hsing Adult Rsources ....D....650 573-3341
205 W 20th Ave San Mateo (94403) *(P-23805)*
Fhpa, Gold River *Also called Health Net Inc (P-10206)*
Fib Lab, Milpitas *Also called Nanolab Technologies Inc (P-26720)*
Fiber Optic Technologies, Torrance *Also called ACS Communications Inc (P-2501)*
Fibertron Corporation ....D....714 670-7711
6400 Artesia Blvd Buena Park (90620) *(P-7477)*
Ficcadenti & Waggoner Consul (PA) ....D....949 474-0502
16969 Von Karman Ave # 240 Irvine (92606) *(P-25683)*
Fidelity Home Energy Inc (PA) ....D....858 220-7784
2235 Polvorosa Ave # 230 San Leandro (94577) *(P-2209)*
Fidelity Nat HM Warranty Co ....C....925 356-0194
1850 Gateway Blvd Ste 400 Concord (94520) *(P-10428)*
Fidelity National Fincl Inc ....D....949 622-5000
1300 Dove St Ste 310 Newport Beach (92660) *(P-10628)*
Fidelity National Title Co ....E....818 881-7800
42544 10th St W Lancaster (93534) *(P-10452)*
Fidelity Roof Company (PA) ....D....510 547-6330
1075 40th St Oakland (94608) *(P-3155)*
Fidelity Security Services Inc ....C....661 295-5007
25133 Avenue Tibbitts H Valencia (91355) *(P-16644)*
Field Foundation ....E....562 921-3567
15306 Carmenita Rd Santa Fe Springs (90670) *(P-1059)*
Field Fresh Farms LLC ....D....831 722-1422
320 Industrial Rd Watsonville (95076) *(P-8677)*
Fields Construction Services ....D....925 294-8183
5715 Southfront Rd Ste B1 Livermore (94551) *(P-14264)*
Fields Win Clg Win Protection, Livermore *Also called Fields Construction Services (P-14264)*
Fieldserver Technologies ....E....408 262-2299
1991 Tarob Ct Milpitas (95035) *(P-6191)*
Fieldstone Communities Inc ....E....949 790-5400
16 Technology Dr Ste 125 Irvine (92618) *(P-1164)*
Fieldstone Communities Inc (PA) ....C....949 790-5400
16 Technology Dr Ste 125 Irvine (92618) *(P-1339)*
Fieno Inc ....D....760 352-2996
11583 Big Canyon Ln San Diego (92131) *(P-515)*
Fierce Wombat Games Inc ....E....650 996-2910
910 E Hamilton Ave Fl 6 Campbell (95008) *(P-16129)*
Fiesta De Reyes, San Diego *Also called Old Town Fmly Hospitality Corp (P-12977)*
Fifth & Sunset Enterprises LLC ....D....310 979-0212
12322 Exposition Blvd Los Angeles (90064) *(P-14505)*
Fifty Peninsula Partners ....D....650 344-8200
850 N El Camino Real Ofc San Mateo (94401) *(P-11019)*
Fig Garden Golf Course Inc ....D....559 439-2928
7700 N Van Ness Blvd Fresno (93711) *(P-18924)*
Fig Holdings LLC ....D....209 524-4817
1310 W Granger Ave Modesto (95350) *(P-20428)*
Figi Acquisition Company LLC ....C....800 678-3444
3636 Gateway Center Ave San Diego (92102) *(P-9216)*
Figure Eight Technologies Inc ....D....415 471-1920
940 Howard St San Francisco (94103) *(P-16130)*
Fiji Water Company LLC (HQ) ....E....310 966-5700
11444 W Olympic Blvd # 250 Los Angeles (90064) *(P-8789)*
Filament Hospitality, San Francisco *Also called Maverick Hotel Partners LLC (P-26938)*
Filemaker Inc (HQ) ....C....408 987-7000
5201 Patrick Henry Dr Santa Clara (95054) *(P-15675)*
Filice Insurance Agency, San Jose *Also called Ron Filice Enterprises Inc (P-10759)*
Fillmore Convalescent Ctr LLC ....D....805 524-0083
118 B St Fillmore (93015) *(P-21066)*
Fillmore Farm Management, Fillmore *Also called Wonderful Citrus Packing LLC (P-210)*
Fillmore Marketplace I, San Francisco *Also called Fillmore Marketplace LP (P-11447)*
Fillmore Marketplace LP ....E....415 921-6514
1223 Webster St San Francisco (94115) *(P-11447)*
Film Payroll Services Inc (PA) ....D....310 440-9600
500 S Sepulveda Blvd Fl 4 Los Angeles (90049) *(P-26204)*
Film Roman Llc ....C....818 748-4000
6320 Canoga Ave Ste 450 Woodland Hills (91367) *(P-18051)*
Film Roman LLC ....C....818 748-4000
6320 Canoga Ave Ste 450 Woodland Hills (91367) *(P-18052)*
FILML.A, Los Angeles *Also called A Filml Inc (P-18175)*

ALPHABETIC

Filmquest Pictures Corporation..........C.......818 905-1006
15331 Stonewood Ter Sherman Oaks (91403) ***(P-18053)***
Filoli Center..........D.......650 364-8300
86 Canada Rd Woodside (94062) ***(P-24928)***
FILOLI GARDEN SHOP, Woodside *Also called Filoli Center* ***(P-24928)***
Filter Recycling Services Inc (PA)..........D.......909 873-4141
180 W Monte Ave Rialto (92376) ***(P-6400)***
Filyn Corporation..........C.......714 632-0225
2950 E La Jolla St Anaheim (92806) ***(P-3794)***
Final Film..........D.......323 467-0700
3620 W Valhalla Dr Burbank (91505) ***(P-14113)***
Finance America LLC (HQ)..........C.......949 440-1000
1901 Main St Ste 150 Irvine (92614) ***(P-9803)***
Finance America Mortgage LLC..........B.......562 478-4664
13200 Crossroads Pkwy N City of Industry (91746) ***(P-9804)***
Financial Credit Network Inc (PA)..........E.......559 733-7550
1300 W Main St Visalia (93291) ***(P-14003)***
Financial Division, Imperial Beach *Also called Jpmorgan Chase Bank Nat Assn* ***(P-9509)***
Financial Engines LLC (HQ)..........C.......408 498-6000
1050 Enterprise Way Fl 3 Sunnyvale (94089) ***(P-27234)***
Financial Healthcare Services..........E.......626 356-7950
690 E Green St Ste 300 Pasadena (91101) ***(P-27235)***
Financial Information Network..........D.......818 782-0331
6656 Valjean Ave Van Nuys (91406) ***(P-15160)***
Financial Pacific Insurance Co..........D.......916 630-5000
3850 Atherton Rd Rocklin (95765) ***(P-10629)***
Financial Partners Credit Un (PA)..........D.......562 904-3000
7800 Imperial Hwy Downey (90242) ***(P-9552)***
Financial Statement Svcs Inc (PA)..........C.......714 436-3326
3300 S Fairview St Santa Ana (92704) ***(P-14044)***
Financial Transaction, Roseville *Also called Safe Credit Union* ***(P-9584)***
Financialforcecom Inc (HQ)..........D.......866 743-2220
595 Market St Ste 2700 San Francisco (94105) ***(P-15161)***
Finastra Merchant Services Inc (PA)..........D.......415 277-9900
333 Bush St Fl 26 San Francisco (94104) ***(P-9682)***
Fine Arts Mseums San Francisco, San Francisco *Also called Corportion of Fine Arts Mseums* ***(P-24875)***
Fine Arts Museum, Santa Barbara *Also called Santa Barbara Museum of Art* ***(P-24912)***
Fine Chemicals Holdings Corp..........B.......916 357-6880
Highway 50 And Hazel Ave Rancho Cordova (95741) ***(P-11976)***
Fine Line Group Inc..........E.......415 777-4070
457 Minna St San Francisco (94103) ***(P-1532)***
Fine Northern Oak, NAPA *Also called Seguin Mreau NAPA Coperage Inc* ***(P-7870)***
Finest Produce, Bellflower *Also called Produce Company* ***(P-8720)***
Finezi Inc..........D.......510 790-4768
31080 Blvd Ste 212 Union City (94587) ***(P-14620)***
Finley Swim Center..........E.......707 543-3760
2060 W College Ave Santa Rosa (95401) ***(P-19175)***
Finn Holding Corporation (PA)..........A.......310 712-1850
360 N Crescent Dr Beverly Hills (90210) ***(P-4705)***
Fiorano Software Inc..........D.......650 326-1136
230 California Ave # 103 Palo Alto (94306) ***(P-15676)***
Fire and Police..........E.......562 961-0066
4645 E Anaheim St Long Beach (90804) ***(P-24957)***
Fire Insurance Exchange (PA)..........A.......323 932-3200
4680 Wilshire Blvd Los Angeles (90010) ***(P-10630)***
Fire Safe Systems Inc..........D.......310 542-0585
1312 Kingsdale Ave Redondo Beach (90278) ***(P-2210)***
Fire Safety First, Santa Ana *Also called Brethren Inc* ***(P-8020)***
Fire Sprinkler Systems Inc (PA)..........D.......800 915-3473
705 E Harrison St Ste 200 Corona (92879) ***(P-2211)***
Firearms Academy, Santa Ana *Also called OC Special Events SEC Inc* ***(P-16745)***
Fireeye Inc (PA)..........C.......408 321-6300
601 Mccarthy Blvd Milpitas (95035) ***(P-15677)***
Firefighter Cancer Support Ntw..........E.......866 994-3276
3460 Fletcher Ave El Monte (91731) ***(P-23806)***
Firefighters First Credit Un (PA)..........C.......323 254-1700
815 Colorado Blvd Los Angeles (90041) ***(P-9553)***
Firemans Fund Insurance Co (HQ)..........A.......415 899-2000
1465 N Mcdowell Blvd # 100 Petaluma (94954) ***(P-10352)***
Firemans Fund Insurance Co..........C.......858 492-3019
9275 Sky Park Ct San Diego (92123) ***(P-10353)***
Firemans Fund Insurance Co..........C.......818 953-6533
2350 W Empire Ave Ste 200 Burbank (91504) ***(P-10354)***
Firm A Chugh Professional Corp..........D.......562 229-1220
15925 Carmenita Rd Cerritos (90703) ***(P-23066)***
Firm A Chugh Professional Corp..........E.......408 970-0100
4800 Great America Pkwy # 310 Santa Clara (95054) ***(P-23067)***
First & La Realty Corp (PA)..........D.......805 581-0021
1301 E Los Angeles Ave Simi Valley (93065) ***(P-11448)***
First Alarm..........A.......831 649-1111
1 Lower Ragsdale Dr # 3700 Monterey (93940) ***(P-2584)***
First Alarm (PA)..........C.......831 476-1111
1111 Estates Dr Aptos (95003) ***(P-2585)***
First Alarm SEC & Patrol Inc..........B.......209 473-1110
5250 Claremont Ave Stockton (95207) ***(P-16893)***
First Alarm SEC & Patrol Inc..........B.......925 295-1260
1801 Oakland Blvd Ste 315 Walnut Creek (94596) ***(P-16894)***
First Alarm SEC & Patrol Inc..........B.......707 584-1110
1240 Briggs Ave Santa Rosa (95401) ***(P-16895)***
First Alarm SEC & Patrol Inc (PA)..........C.......408 866-1111
1731 Tech Dr Ste 800 San Jose (95110) ***(P-16645)***
First Allied Securities Inc (PA)..........D.......619 702-9600
655 W Broadway Fl 11 San Diego (92101) ***(P-9951)***
First Amercn Lenders Advantage, Concord *Also called First American Title Insur Co* ***(P-10461)***
First Amercn Prof RE Svcs Inc (PA)..........C.......714 250-1400
200 Commerce Irvine (92602) ***(P-11449)***
First Amercn Title of Stockton (PA)..........D.......209 929-4800
2800 W March Ln Ste 210 Stockton (95219) ***(P-11848)***
First American Card Service..........E.......951 677-8720
25060 Hancock Ave Ste 103 Murrieta (92562) ***(P-17172)***
First American Casualty Insur, Santa Ana *Also called First American Title Insur Co* ***(P-10460)***
First American Financial Corp (PA)..........C.......714 250-3000
1 First American Way Santa Ana (92707) ***(P-10453)***
First American Mortgage Svcs..........B.......714 250-4210
3 First American Way Santa Ana (92707) ***(P-10454)***
First American Team Realty Inc (PA)..........C.......562 427-7765
2501 Cherry Ave Ste 100 Signal Hill (90755) ***(P-11450)***
First American Title Insur Co..........D.......925 356-7000
1001 Galaxy Way Ste 101 Concord (94520) ***(P-11451)***
First American Title Insur Co (HQ)..........C.......800 854-3643
1 First American Way Santa Ana (92707) ***(P-10455)***
First American Title Insur Co..........C.......619 238-1776
411 Ivy St San Diego (92101) ***(P-10456)***
First American Title Insur Co..........C.......909 889-0311
1855 W Rdlands Blvd 100 Redlands (92373) ***(P-10457)***
First American Title Insur Co (HQ)..........C.......831 426-5000
330 Soquel Ave Santa Cruz (95062) ***(P-10458)***
First American Title Insur Co..........E.......805 543-8900
899 Pacific St San Luis Obispo (93401) ***(P-10459)***
First American Title Insur Co..........C.......714 800-3000
9 First American Way Santa Ana (92707) ***(P-10460)***
First American Title Insur Co..........D.......925 798-2800
1855 Gateway Blvd Ste 700 Concord (94520) ***(P-10461)***
First American Title Insur Co..........A.......714 250-4000
3 First American Way Santa Ana (92707) ***(P-10462)***
First American Trust Company (HQ)..........D.......714 560-7856
5 First American Way Santa Ana (92707) ***(P-10077)***
First Avenue Inc..........D.......626 856-2076
5105 Heintz St Baldwin Park (91706) ***(P-3156)***
First Baptist Head Start..........D.......925 473-2000
3890 Railroad Ave Pittsburg (94565) ***(P-24321)***
First Building Maintenance, Berkeley *Also called Clark Booker T* ***(P-14216)***
First California Mrtg Co II..........D.......415 209-0910
1400 N Mcdowell Blvd # 300 Petaluma (94954) ***(P-9805)***
First Call Nursing Svcs Inc..........C.......408 262-1533
1313 N Milpitas Blvd # 210 Milpitas (95035) ***(P-14621)***
First Capitol Consulting Inc..........D.......213 382-1115
3530 Wilshire Blvd # 1460 Los Angeles (90010) ***(P-27236)***
First Choice Bank..........D.......213 617-0082
420 E 3rd St Ste 100 Los Angeles (90013) ***(P-9447)***
First Choice Bank (HQ)..........D.......562 345-9092
17785 Center Court Dr N # 750 Cerritos (90703) ***(P-9448)***
First City Credit Union (PA)..........C.......213 482-3477
717 W Temple St Ste 400 Los Angeles (90012) ***(P-9554)***
First Community Bancorp..........D.......858 756-3023
5900 La Place Ct Ste 200 Carlsbad (92008) ***(P-9345)***
First Community Investments..........D.......951 238-8322
3636 E Florence Ave Huntington Park (90255) ***(P-11452)***
First Databank Inc..........D.......650 588-5454
701 Gateway Blvd Ste 600 San Francisco (94188) ***(P-16131)***
First Entertainment Credit Un (PA)..........D.......323 851-3673
6735 Forest Lawn Dr # 100 Los Angeles (90068) ***(P-9555)***
First Evang Lutheran Ch & Schl..........D.......310 320-9920
2900 W Carson St Torrance (90503) ***(P-24322)***
First Family Homes..........E.......562 862-7373
12027 Paramount Blvd Downey (90242) ***(P-11453)***
First Fire Systems Inc (PA)..........D.......310 559-0900
5947 Burchard Ave Los Angeles (90034) ***(P-16896)***
First Group of America, Santa Maria *Also called First Transit* ***(P-3652)***
First Hotels International Inc..........C.......909 884-9364
295 N E St San Bernardino (92401) ***(P-12575)***
First Interstate Security Inc..........C.......818 995-6664
20548 Ventura Blvd # 118 Woodland Hills (91364) ***(P-16646)***
First Legal Support Svcs LLC (PA)..........D.......213 250-1111
1517 Beverly Blvd Los Angeles (90026) ***(P-23068)***
First Marin Realty Inc..........D.......415 383-9393
145 Lomita Dr Mill Valley (94941) ***(P-11454)***
First National Bank..........B.......858 756-3023
6110 El Tordo Rancho Santa Fe (92067) ***(P-9346)***
First National Bank (PA)..........D.......619 233-5588
401 W A St Ste 200 San Diego (92101) ***(P-12095)***
First Nationwide Mortgage Corp..........C.......818 209-3134
18440 Bermuda St Northridge (91326) ***(P-9883)***
First Northern Bank of Dixon (HQ)..........D.......707 678-4422
195 N 1st St Dixon (95620) ***(P-9449)***
First Northern Community, Dixon *Also called First Northern Bank of Dixon* ***(P-9449)***
First Page Sage LLC..........D.......415 624-3526
2250 Union St San Francisco (94123) ***(P-27237)***
First Place For Youth (PA)..........E.......510 272-0979
426 17th St Ste 100 Oakland (94612) ***(P-23807)***
First Priority Financial Inc..........B.......707 432-1000
3700 Hilborn Rd Ste 700 Fairfield (94534) ***(P-9806)***
First Regional Bancorp..........B.......310 552-1776
1801 Century Park E # 800 Los Angeles (90067) ***(P-9450)***
First Republic Bank..........C.......415 389-0880
750 Redwood Hwy Frontage # 1218 Mill Valley (94941) ***(P-9451)***
First Republic Bank..........D.......415 392-1400
101 Pine St San Francisco (94111) ***(P-9502)***
First Republic Bank..........C.......415 392-3888
44 Montgomery St Ste 110 San Francisco (94104) ***(P-9452)***
First Republic Bank..........C.......650 233-8880
2550 Sand Hill Rd Ste 100 Menlo Park (94025) ***(P-9453)***
First Republic Bank..........C.......213 239-8883
888 S Figueroa St Ste 100 Los Angeles (90017) ***(P-9454)***
First Republic Bank..........C.......925 254-8993
224 Brookwood Rd Orinda (94563) ***(P-9455)***

Mergent e-mail: customerrelations@mergent.com
1302
2019 Directory of California
Wholesalers and Services Companies
(P-0000) Products & Services Section entry number
(PA)=Parent Co (HQ)=Headquarters (DH)=Div Headquarters

First Republic Bank ...C...619 238-9088
1280 4th Ave San Diego (92101) ***(P-9456)***
First Republic Bank ...C...415 564-8881
653 Irving St San Francisco (94122) ***(P-9457)***
First Republic Bank ...C...415 487-0888
1355 Market St Ste 140 San Francisco (94103) ***(P-9458)***
First Republic Bank ...C...415 975-3877
405 Howard St Ste 110 San Francisco (94105) ***(P-9459)***
First Republic Bank ...D...310 712-1888
1888 Century Park E # 200 Los Angeles (90067) ***(P-9503)***
First Republic Bank (PA) ...B...415 392-1400
111 Pine St Fl 2 San Francisco (94111) ***(P-9504)***
First Republic Bank ...C...650 470-8888
1215 El Camino Real Menlo Park (94025) ***(P-9505)***
First Responder Ems Inc ...C...916 381-3780
10161 Croydon Way Ste 1 Sacramento (95827) ***(P-3795)***
First Responder Ems Inc ...D...530 897-6345
333 Huss Dr Ste 100 Chico (95928) ***(P-3796)***
First Rsponder Emrgncy Med Svc ...C...530 891-4357
333 Huss Dr Ste 300 Chico (95928) ***(P-3797)***
First Security Services, San Jose *Also called First Alarm SEC & Patrol Inc* ***(P-16645)***
First State, Huntington Beach *Also called First Team RE - Orange Cnty* ***(P-11461)***
First Step Ind Living Program, Rancho Cucamonga *Also called National Mentor Inc* ***(P-24209)***
First Student Inc ...D...510 237-6677
436 Parr Blvd Richmond (94801) ***(P-3923)***
First Student Inc ...D...707 678-8679
550 E C St Dixon (95620) ***(P-3649)***
First Student Inc ...D...925 676-1976
2477 Arnold Indus Way Concord (94520) ***(P-3897)***
First Student Inc ...D...650 685-8245
991 E Poplar Ave San Mateo (94401) ***(P-3924)***
First Student Inc ...C...951 736-3234
300 S Buena Vista Ave Corona (92882) ***(P-3953)***
First Student Inc ...D...909 383-1640
234 S I St San Bernardino (92410) ***(P-3925)***
First Student Inc ...D...760 320-4659
5006 E Calle San Raphael Palm Springs (92264) ***(P-3926)***
First Student Inc ...C...209 466-7737
2005 Navy Dr Stockton (95206) ***(P-3927)***
First Student Inc ...D...909 383-7104
844 E 9th St San Bernardino (92410) ***(P-3928)***
First Student Inc ...D...626 448-9446
4337 Rowland Ave El Monte (91731) ***(P-3650)***
First Student Inc ...C...310 715-6122
14800 S Avalon Blvd Gardena (90248) ***(P-3929)***
First Student Inc ...B...415 647-9012
2270 Jerrold Ave San Francisco (94124) ***(P-3930)***
First Student Inc ...D...510 237-6365
436 Parr Blvd Richmond (94801) ***(P-3931)***
First Student Inc ...D...818 707-2082
5320 Derry Ave Ste O Agoura Hills (91301) ***(P-3932)***
First Student Inc ...D...714 850-7578
3401 W Castor St Santa Ana (92704) ***(P-3933)***
First Student Inc ...C...925 754-4878
801 Wilbur Ave Antioch (94509) ***(P-3651)***
First Student Inc ...C...818 896-0333
11233 San Fernando Rd San Fernando (91340) ***(P-3934)***
First Student Inc ...C...559 661-7433
123 N E St Ste 102 Madera (93638) ***(P-3935)***
First Student Inc ...C...310 769-2400
14800 S Avalon Blvd Gardena (90248) ***(P-3936)***
First Team RE - Orange Cnty ...D...760 340-9911
74855 Country Club Dr Palm Desert (92260) ***(P-11455)***
First Team RE - Orange Cnty ...D...909 861-1380
1950 S Brea Canyon Rd # 1 Diamond Bar (91765) ***(P-11456)***
First Team RE - Orange Cnty ...D...714 223-2143
18180 Yorba Linda Blvd # 501 Yorba Linda (92886) ***(P-11457)***
First Team RE - Orange Cnty ...C...562 596-9911
12501 Seal Beach Blvd # 100 Seal Beach (90740) ***(P-11458)***
First Team RE - Orange Cnty ...D...949 759-5747
4 Corporate Plaza Dr # 100 Newport Beach (92660) ***(P-11459)***
First Team RE - Orange Cnty (PA) ...C...888 236-1943
108 Pacifica Ste 300 Irvine (92618) ***(P-11460)***
First Team RE - Orange Cnty ...D...714 965-2244
20100 Brookhurst St Huntington Beach (92646) ***(P-11461)***
First Team RE - Orange Cnty ...D...562 346-5088
42 64th Pl Long Beach (90803) ***(P-11462)***
First Team RE - Orange Cnty ...C...949 240-7979
32451 Golden Lantern # 210 Laguna Niguel (92677) ***(P-11463)***
First Team RE - Orange Cnty ...C...714 544-5456
17240 17th St Tustin (92780) ***(P-11464)***
First Team RE - Orange Cnty ...D...714 974-9191
8028 E Santa Ana Cyn Rd Anaheim (92808) ***(P-11465)***
First Team RE - Orange Cnty ...C...949 389-0004
26711 Aliso Creek Rd # 200 Aliso Viejo (92656) ***(P-11466)***
First Team S S Estate, Diamond Bar *Also called First Team RE - Orange Cnty* ***(P-11456)***
First Team Walk-In Realty, Irvine *Also called First Team RE - Orange Cnty* ***(P-11460)***
First Technology Federal Cr Un (PA) ...D...855 855-8805
1335 Terra Bella Ave Mountain View (94043) ***(P-9556)***
First Technology Federal Cr Un ...C...855 855-8805
1011 Sunset Blvd Ste 210 Rocklin (95765) ***(P-9557)***
First Transit ...D...805 925-5254
1303 Fairway Dr Santa Maria (93455) ***(P-3652)***
First Transit Inc ...D...310 515-8270
2400 E Dominguez St Long Beach (90810) ***(P-3653)***
First Transit Inc ...D...510 535-9192
411 High St Oakland (94601) ***(P-3654)***
First Transit Inc ...D...510 437-8990
407 High St Oakland (94601) ***(P-3655)***
First US Community Credit Un (PA) ...D...916 576-5700
580 University Ave # 100 Sacramento (95825) ***(P-9558)***
Firstat Nursing Services Inc ...C...619 220-7600
411 Camino Del Rio S # 100 San Diego (92108) ***(P-22298)***
Firstcall (PA) ...C...415 781-4300
1 Sansome St Ste 3500 San Francisco (94104) ***(P-16647)***
Firstfed Financial Corp ...A...562 618-0573
6320 Canoga Ave Woodland Hills (91367) ***(P-9347)***
Firstline Security Systems Inc (PA) ...D...714 937-1440
2211 E Howell Ave Anaheim (92806) ***(P-16897)***
Firstservice Residential (HQ) ...C...949 448-6000
15241 Laguna Canyon Rd Irvine (92618) ***(P-11467)***
Firstsight Vision Services Inc (HQ) ...D...909 920-5008
1202 Monte Vista Ave # 17 Upland (91786) ***(P-20157)***
Firstsrvice Rsidential Cal Inc (HQ) ...D...909 981-4131
195 N Euclid Ave Upland (91786) ***(P-11468)***
Fischer Inc ...D...909 881-2910
1372 W 26th St San Bernardino (92405) ***(P-2212)***
Fischer Tile and Marble Inc ...C...916 452-1426
1800 23rd St Sacramento (95816) ***(P-2997)***
Fiserv Inc ...D...909 595-9074
19935 E Walnut Dr N City of Industry (91789) ***(P-16132)***
Fiserv Inc ...D...909 598-8700
19935 E Walnut Dr N Walnut (91789) ***(P-16133)***
Fiserv Inc ...D...408 242-3011
525 Almanor Ave Sunnyvale (94085) ***(P-16134)***
Fiserv Inc ...D...805 532-9100
405 Science Dr Moorpark (93021) ***(P-16135)***
Fiserv Inc ...D...909 595-9074
19935 E Walnut Dr N Walnut (91789) ***(P-16136)***
Fish & Richardson PC ...D...650 839-5070
500 Arguello St Ste 500 # 500 Redwood City (94063) ***(P-23069)***
Fish & Richardson PC ...C...858 678-5070
12390 El Camino Real San Diego (92130) ***(P-23070)***
Fishel Company ...D...714 668-9268
647 Young St Santa Ana (92705) ***(P-1917)***
Fisher & Paykel Healthcare Inc ...C...949 453-4000
173 Technology Dr Ste 100 Irvine (92618) ***(P-7180)***
Fisher & Phillips LLP ...D...949 851-2424
2050 Main St Ste 1000 Irvine (92614) ***(P-23071)***
Fisher Communications Inc ...D...661 327-7955
1901 Westwind Dr Bakersfield (93301) ***(P-5791)***
Fisher Ranch LLC ...D...760 922-4151
10610 Ice Plant Rd Blythe (92225) ***(P-516)***
Fisher Scientific Company LLC ...D...909 393-2100
6722 Bickmore Ave Chino (91708) ***(P-7243)***
Fisheries Resource Vlntr Corps ...C...562 596-9261
109 Stanford Ln Seal Beach (90740) ***(P-27238)***
Fishers Nursery ...D...209 599-3412
24081 S Austin Rd Ripon (95366) ***(P-9134)***
Fishman Supply Company ...D...707 763-8161
1345 Industrial Ave Petaluma (94952) ***(P-7886)***
Fisk Electric Company ...C...818 884-1166
15870 Olden St Sylmar (91342) ***(P-2586)***
Fit Electronics Inc (HQ) ...C...714 988-9388
500 S Kraemer Blvd # 100 Brea (92821) ***(P-26366)***
Fitness 2000 Inc ...E...510 791-2481
35145 Newark Blvd Newark (94560) ***(P-18599)***
Fitness Evolution ...D...209 545-9055
4120 Dale Rd Ste G Modesto (95356) ***(P-18600)***
Fitness International LLC ...E...949 421-6082
24491 Alicia Pkwy Mission Viejo (92691) ***(P-18601)***
Fitness International LLC ...E...858 550-5912
10535 Heater Ct San Diego (92121) ***(P-18602)***
Fitness Ridge Malibu LLC ...D...818 874-1300
277 Latigo Canyon Rd Malibu (90265) ***(P-12576)***
Fitness SF, Corte Madera *Also called Jackovics Enterprises Inc* ***(P-18614)***
Fitz Fresh Inc ...E...831 763-4440
211 Lee Rd Watsonville (95076) ***(P-311)***
Fitzgrald Abbott Beardsley LLP ...D...510 451-3300
1221 Broadway Fl 21 Oakland (94612) ***(P-23072)***
Five Acres-The Boys & Girls & ...B...626 798-6793
760 Mountain View St Altadena (91001) ***(P-24528)***
Five Star Auto Repair and Wash, Rocklin *Also called Jkf Auto Service Inc* ***(P-17821)***
Five Star Auto Repr & Car Wash, Rocklin *Also called Jemtown Inc* ***(P-17820)***
Five Star Packing LLC ...A...760 356-4103
437 W 5th St Holtville (92250) ***(P-647)***
Five Star Quality Care Inc ...E...760 479-1818
1350 S El Camino Real Encinitas (92024) ***(P-24529)***
Five Star Quality Care Inc ...D...760 327-8541
277 S Sunrise Way Palm Springs (92262) ***(P-26859)***
Five Star Quality Care Inc ...E...209 951-6500
3530 Deer Park Dr Stockton (95219) ***(P-22299)***
Five Star Quality Care Inc ...C...949 642-8044
466 Flagship Rd Newport Beach (92663) ***(P-20429)***
Five Star Quality Care Inc ...C...209 466-2066
537 E Fulton St Stockton (95204) ***(P-20430)***
Five Star Quality Care Inc ...D...818 997-1841
6835 Hazeltine Ave Van Nuys (91405) ***(P-20431)***
Five Star Quality Care Inc ...C...805 492-2444
93 W Avnida De Los Arbles Thousand Oaks (91360) ***(P-20432)***
Five Star Quality Care Inc ...B...858 673-6300
16925 Hierba Dr San Diego (92128) ***(P-20433)***
Five Star Quality Care Inc ...C...559 446-6226
6075 N Marks Ave Fresno (93711) ***(P-20434)***
Five Star Transportation Inc ...E...310 348-0820
8703 La Tijera Blvd # 102 Los Angeles (90045) ***(P-4990)***
Five9 Inc (PA) ...C...925 201-2000
4000 Executive Pkwy # 400 San Ramon (94583) ***(P-15678)***
Fix Shore, Downey *Also called Westar Manufacturing Inc* ***(P-3610)***

ALPHABETIC

Employee Codes: A=Over 500 employees, B=251-500
C=101-250, D=51-100, E=50
2019 Directory of California
Wholesalers and Services Companies
© Mergent Inc. 1-800-342-5647
1303

FJ Willert Contracting Co.....C.....619 421-1980
1869 Nirvana Ave Chula Vista (91911) ***(P-3425)***
Fjs Inc.....C.....714 905-1050
888 S Disneyland Dr # 400 Anaheim (92802) ***(P-12577)***
Fkc Partners A Cal Ltd Partnr.....E.....714 528-9864
180 N Rverview Dr Ste 100 Anaheim (92808) ***(P-11469)***
Fkc Properties, Anaheim *Also called Fkc Partners A Cal Ltd Partnr* ***(P-11469)***
Flagship Credit Acceptance LLC.....C.....949 748-7172
7525 Irvine Center Dr Irvine (92618) ***(P-17173)***
Flagship Health Care Center, Newport Beach *Also called Five Star Quality Care Inc* ***(P-20429)***
Flagship Healthcare Center, Newport Beach *Also called SSC Newport Beach Oper Co LP* ***(P-20776)***
Flagstar Bancorp Inc.....C.....714 549-9100
949 S Coast Dr Ste 100 Costa Mesa (92626) ***(P-9683)***
Flair Building Maintanance, Santa Clara *Also called Flair Building Services Inc* ***(P-14265)***
Flair Building Services Inc.....D.....408 987-4040
3470 Edward Ave Santa Clara (95054) ***(P-14265)***
Flamingo Resort Hotel, Santa Rosa *Also called Bavarian Lion Company Cal* ***(P-12359)***
Flanders Pointe Apts, Tustin *Also called Steadfast Management Co Inc* ***(P-11117)***
Flash Point Graphix, Burbank *Also called Final Film* ***(P-14113)***
Flash Transport Inc.....D.....909 829-1369
14796 Washington Dr Fontana (92335) ***(P-4178)***
Flatiron Electric Group Inc.....E.....714 228-9631
15335 Fairfield Ranch Rd # 200 Chino Hills (91709) ***(P-2587)***
Flatiron West Inc.....C.....707 742-6000
2100 Goodyear Rd Benicia (94510) ***(P-1877)***
Flatiron West Inc.....D.....909 597-8413
16341 Chino Corona Rd Chino (91708) ***(P-1878)***
Fleet Maintenance Dept, Santa Cruz *Also called Santa Cruz Metro Trnst Dst* ***(P-3884)***
Fleet Mangement Solutions, Garden Grove *Also called Teletrac Inc* ***(P-5999)***
Fleischman Field Research Inc.....C.....415 398-4140
250 Sutter St Fl 2 San Francisco (94108) ***(P-26517)***
Fleishman-Hillard Inc.....E.....415 318-4000
720 California St Fl 6 San Francisco (94108) ***(P-27554)***
Flexcare LLC.....A.....866 564-3589
990 Reserve Dr Ste 200 Roseville (95678) ***(P-14854)***
Flexcare Medical Staffing, Roseville *Also called Flexcare LLC* ***(P-14854)***
Flexport Inc (PA).....D.....415 231-5252
760 Market St Fl 8 San Francisco (94102) ***(P-5225)***
Flextronics Global Services, Milpitas *Also called Flextronics Intl USA Inc* ***(P-5559)***
Flextronics Intl USA Inc.....C.....408 576-6769
890 Yosemite Dr Bldg 14 Milpitas (95035) ***(P-5559)***
Flintco Pacific Inc.....D.....916 757-1000
401 Derek Pl Roseville (95678) ***(P-25684)***
Flir Commercial Systems Inc (HQ).....B.....805 964-9797
6769 Hollister Ave # 100 Goleta (93117) ***(P-7478)***
Flo Health Inc.....D.....510 303-9307
541 Jefferson Ave Ste 100 Redwood City (94063) ***(P-15162)***
Floorgate Inc.....D.....323 478-2000
3350 N San Fernando Rd Los Angeles (90065) ***(P-3103)***
Floormasters, The, Hayward *Also called Dt Floormasters Inc* ***(P-3101)***
Flor Do Oakley Club, Oakley *Also called Flordo Oakley Hall* ***(P-10876)***
Flora Ter Convalescent Hosp, Los Angeles *Also called Country Villa Terrace* ***(P-21049)***
Flora Terra Landscape MGT, San Jose *Also called City II Enterprises Inc* ***(P-813)***
Flordo Oakley Hall.....C.....925 625-4076
520 2nd St Oakley (94561) ***(P-10876)***
Florence Crittenton Services.....B.....714 680-9000
801 E Chapman Ave Ste 203 Fullerton (92831) ***(P-24530)***
Florence Filter Corporation.....D.....310 637-1137
530 W Manville St Compton (90220) ***(P-7648)***
Florence Office, Los Angeles *Also called County of Los Angeles* ***(P-23666)***
Florence Villa Hotel.....C.....415 397-7700
225 Powell St San Francisco (94102) ***(P-12578)***
Florence Villa Hotel LLC.....D.....415 397-7700
225 Powell St San Francisco (94102) ***(P-12579)***
Flores Labor Contracting.....B.....661 792-3061
501 6th St Mc Farland (93250) ***(P-648)***
Florida Beauty Flora Inc.....B.....805 642-1633
6205 Ventura Blvd Ventura (93003) ***(P-13658)***
Florida Conditioning, City of Industry *Also called American AC Distrs LLC* ***(P-2103)***
Floyd Johnston Cnstr Co Inc.....D.....559 299-7373
2301 Herndon Ave Clovis (93611) ***(P-1918)***
Floyd Skeren & Kelly LLP (PA).....D.....818 206-9222
101 Moody Ct Ste 200 Thousand Oaks (91360) ***(P-23073)***
Flt Inc.....C.....916 355-1500
12747 Folsom Blvd Folsom (95630) ***(P-17759)***
Fluid Inc (HQ).....D.....877 343-3240
1611 Telegraph Ave Fl 4 Oakland (94612) ***(P-15163)***
Fluidigm Corporation (PA).....C.....650 266-6000
7000 Shoreline Ct Ste 100 South San Francisco (94080) ***(P-26367)***
Fluor Corporation.....D.....949 349-2000
3 Polaris Way Aliso Viejo (92656) ***(P-25685)***
Fluor Daniel, Aliso Viejo *Also called Fluor Plant Services Intl Inc* ***(P-25688)***
Fluor Daniel Construction Co (HQ).....B.....949 349-2000
3 Polaris Way Aliso Viejo (92656) ***(P-1879)***
Fluor Enterprises Inc.....D.....408 256-0853
5600 Cottle Rd San Jose (95123) ***(P-25686)***
Fluor Enterprises Inc.....D.....949 349-2000
9701 Jeronimo Rd Irvine (92618) ***(P-25687)***
Fluor Enterprises Inc.....D.....469 398-7000
1 Fluor Daniel Dr Aliso Viejo (92698) ***(P-3521)***
Fluor Enterprises Inc.....C.....949 349-2000
3 Polaris Way Aliso Viejo (92656) ***(P-7675)***
Fluor Facility & Plant Svcs.....C.....408 256-1333
124 Blossom Hill Rd Ste H San Jose (95123) ***(P-14266)***
Fluor Industrial Services Inc.....A.....949 439-2000
1 Enterprise Aliso Viejo (92656) ***(P-14267)***
Fluor Plant Services Intl Inc.....D.....949 349-2000
1 Enterprise Aliso Viejo (92656) ***(P-25688)***
Fluoramec LLC (HQ).....E.....949 349-2000
1 Enterprise Aliso Viejo (92656) ***(P-25689)***
Flurish Inc.....D.....855 253-6387
225 Bush St Ste 1100 San Francisco (94104) ***(P-9711)***
Flw Inc.....D.....714 751-7512
5672 Bolsa Ave Huntington Beach (92649) ***(P-7416)***
Flyers Energy LLC.....B.....661 321-9961
4200 Buck Owens Blvd Bakersfield (93308) ***(P-8958)***
Flyers Energy LLC.....C.....909 877-2441
571 W Slover Ave Bloomington (92316) ***(P-8959)***
Flyers Energy LLC.....D.....707 546-0766
444 Yolanda Ave Ste A Santa Rosa (95404) ***(P-8960)***
Flyers Energy LLC.....D.....760 949-3356
11211 G Ave Hesperia (92345) ***(P-8943)***
Flynn Industries Inc (PA).....D.....415 776-7337
825 Van Ness Ave Ste 501 San Francisco (94109) ***(P-258)***
Flynn Properties Inc.....E.....415 835-0225
225 Bush St Ste 1470 San Francisco (94104) ***(P-11470)***
FM Global, Walnut Creek *Also called Factory Mutual Insurance Co* ***(P-10349)***
FM Global, Woodland Hills *Also called Factory Mutual Insurance Co* ***(P-10350)***
FM Seoul Bang Song Inc.....E.....323 525-1650
4525 Wilshire Blvd Fl 3 Los Angeles (90010) ***(P-5718)***
FMC Dialysis Svcs Bellflower, Bellflower *Also called Bio-Mdcal Applications Cal Inc* ***(P-22466)***
FMC Dialysis Svcs Riverside, Riverside *Also called Bio-Mdcal Applications Cal Inc* ***(P-22468)***
Fmr LLC.....C.....800 225-6447
1995 University Ave Berkeley (94704) ***(P-10078)***
Fmr LLC.....C.....916 784-3649
1220 Rsville Pkwy Ste 100 Roseville (95678) ***(P-10079)***
Fmsinfoserv, Los Angeles *Also called Cdsnet LLC* ***(P-27678)***
Fmt Consultants LLC (PA).....D.....844 369-4593
2310 Camino Vida Roble # 101 Carlsbad (92011) ***(P-16366)***
Fmwr, Fort Irwin *Also called Family Mrale Wlfare Recreation* ***(P-18922)***
Fnc Inc.....D.....714 866-1099
40 Pacifica Ste 900 Irvine (92618) ***(P-15164)***
Fns Inc (PA).....D.....661 615-2300
1545 Francisco St Torrance (90501) ***(P-5064)***
FNS Customs Brokers Inc.....E.....310 667-4880
18301 S Broadwick St Compton (90220) ***(P-5065)***
Fnti Fidelity Nat Tech Imagin.....E.....408 942-1780
2123 Ringwood Ave San Jose (95131) ***(P-16367)***
Foam Co, The, Van Nuys *Also called Grht Inc* ***(P-9222)***
Foam Distributors Incorporated.....D.....510 441-8377
31009 San Antonio St Hayward (94544) ***(P-9217)***
Foam Fabrication For Packaging, Hayward *Also called Foam Distributors Incorporated* ***(P-9217)***
Foasberg Laundry & Clrs Inc (PA).....D.....562 426-7345
640 E Wardlow Rd Long Beach (90807) ***(P-13530)***
Focus 360 Inc.....D.....949 234-0008
27721 La Paz Rd Ste B Laguna Niguel (92677) ***(P-15165)***
Focus Diagnostics Inc.....B.....714 220-1900
11331 Valley View St # 150 Cypress (90630) ***(P-22085)***
Focus Technologies Holding Co.....B.....800 838-4548
10703 Progress Way Cypress (90630) ***(P-22086)***
Foley & Lardner LLP.....C.....650 856-3700
975 Page Mill Rd Palo Alto (94304) ***(P-23074)***
Foley & Lardner LLP.....D.....415 434-4484
555 California St # 1700 San Francisco (94104) ***(P-23075)***
Foley & Lardner LLP.....C.....213 972-4500
555 S Flower St Ste 3300 Los Angeles (90071) ***(P-23076)***
Foley & Lardner LLP.....D.....858 847-6700
3579 Vly Cntre Dr Ste 300 San Diego (92130) ***(P-23077)***
Folio Wine Company LLC (PA).....C.....707 254-9885
550 Gateway Dr Ste 220 NAPA (94558) ***(P-9042)***
Folio Wine Company LLC.....D.....707 256-2757
1285 Dealy Ln NAPA (94559) ***(P-9043)***
Folio Wine Company Imports, NAPA *Also called Folio Wine Company LLC* ***(P-9042)***
Folsom Ambulatory Surgery Ctr, Folsom *Also called Kaiser Foundation Hospitals* ***(P-19559)***
Folsom Lake Bank, Folsom *Also called Central Valley Community Bank* ***(P-9430)***
Folsom Lake Toyota, Folsom *Also called Flt Inc* ***(P-17759)***
Folsom Manlove Venture, Sacramento *Also called Oates Buzz Enterprises* ***(P-10921)***
Folsom Recreation Corp.....D.....916 983-4411
511 E Bidwell St Folsom (95630) ***(P-18488)***
Folsom Sport Club, Folsom *Also called 24 Hour Fitness Usa Inc* ***(P-18547)***
Fonda & Frazer LLP (PA).....D.....310 553-3320
1925 Century Park E # 1360 Los Angeles (90067) ***(P-23078)***
Fontana Mental Health Offices, Fontana *Also called Kaiser Foundation Hospitals* ***(P-19558)***
Fontana Resources At Work.....C.....909 428-3833
8608 Live Oak Ave Fontana (92335) ***(P-24184)***
Fontana Steel, Etiwanda *Also called C M C Steel Fabricators Inc* ***(P-3366)***
Fontana Water Company, El Monte *Also called San Gabriel Valley Water Co* ***(P-6304)***
Food & Agriculture Cal Dept.....D.....714 751-3247
88 Fair Dr Costa Mesa (92626) ***(P-19176)***
Food 4 Less, Downey *Also called Ralphs Grocery Company* ***(P-4620)***
Food Express Inc.....E.....323 589-1417
5127 Maywood Ave Maywood (90270) ***(P-4014)***
Food Management Associates Inc.....E.....714 694-2828
22349 La Palma Ave # 115 Yorba Linda (92887) ***(P-27239)***
Food Sales West Inc (PA).....D.....714 966-2900
235 Baker St Costa Mesa (92626) ***(P-8405)***
Foodcraft Cof Refreshment Svcs, Long Beach *Also called Steuber Corporation* ***(P-7146)***
Foods and Produce, Buena Park *Also called Walong Marketing Inc* ***(P-8901)***

Footh The / Easte Trans Corri.....D.....949 754-3400
125 Pacifica Ste 100 Irvine (92618) ***(P-1764)***
Footh-De Anza Commun Colleg Di.....D.....650 949-7260
12345 S El Monte Rd # 6202 Los Altos Hills (94022) ***(P-5719)***
Foothill Distributing Co Inc.....C.....530 243-3932
1530 Beltline Rd Redding (96003) ***(P-8995)***
Foothill Estates Inc.....D.....831 422-7819
400 Griffin St Salinas (93901) ***(P-11876)***
Foothill Federal Credit Union (PA).....E.....626 445-0950
30 S 1st Ave Arcadia (91006) ***(P-9559)***
Foothill Health Center Inc.....C.....408 729-4290
2670 S White Rd Ste 200 San Jose (95148) ***(P-19474)***
Foothill Hospital-Morris L Jo (PA).....B.....626 857-3145
250 S Grand Ave Glendora (91741) ***(P-21417)***
Foothill Oaks Care Center Inc.....D.....530 888-6257
3400 Bell Rd Auburn (95603) ***(P-20435)***
Foothill Packing Inc.....B.....805 925-7900
2255 S Broadway Santa Maria (93454) ***(P-8406)***
FOOTHILL PRESBYTERIAN HOSPITAL, Glendora *Also called Foothill Hospital-Morris L Jo* ***(P-21417)***
Foothill Ranch Medical Offices, Foothill Ranch *Also called Kaiser Foundation Hospitals* ***(P-19557)***
Foothill Ranch Sport Club, Lake Forest *Also called 24 Hour Fitness Usa Inc* ***(P-18562)***
Foothill Regional Medical Ctr, Tustin *Also called Alta Hospitals System LLC* ***(P-21280)***
Foothill Transit Service Corp (PA).....D.....626 967-3147
100 S Vincent Ave Ste 200 West Covina (91790) ***(P-3656)***
Foothill Waste Reclamation Inc.....D.....818 897-5099
12221 Lopez Canyon Rd Sylmar (91342) ***(P-6401)***
For Hospital Committee.....A.....925 447-7000
1111 E Stanley Blvd Livermore (94550) ***(P-26860)***
Force Electronics, Visalia *Also called Heilind Electronics Inc* ***(P-7486)***
Force Framing Inc.....E.....714 970-3888
21520 Yorba Linda Blvd G Yorba Linda (92887) ***(P-3036)***
Force Measurement Systems, Anaheim *Also called Wasser Filtration Inc* ***(P-7819)***
Force-Oakleaf LP.....D.....310 484-7000
6333 Bristol Pkwy Culver City (90230) ***(P-12580)***
Force10 Networks Inc.....A.....707 665-4400
350 Holger Way San Jose (95134) ***(P-15957)***
Ford Construction Company Inc.....D.....209 333-1116
300 W Pine St Lodi (95240) ***(P-2032)***
Ford Graphics, Los Angeles *Also called American Reprographics Co LLC* ***(P-14071)***
Ford Motor Company.....C.....323 267-6121
812 Union St Montebello (90640) ***(P-4558)***
Ford Motor Company.....C.....209 824-6600
1269 Phoenix Dr Manteca (95336) ***(P-6640)***
Ford Motor Company.....D.....925 351-6205
4900 Hopyard Rd Ste 220 Pleasanton (94588) ***(P-9712)***
Ford Motor Company.....B.....949 341-5800
3 Glen Bell Way Ste 200 Irvine (92618) ***(P-23079)***
Ford Motor Land Dev Corp.....B.....949 242-6606
3 Glen Bell Way Ste 100 Irvine (92618) ***(P-25690)***
Ford Plastering Inc.....B.....714 921-0624
732 W Grove Ave Orange (92865) ***(P-3255)***
Ford Street Project Inc.....E.....707 462-1934
139 Ford St Ukiah (95482) ***(P-24531)***
Ford's Filling Station, Culver City *Also called Midnight Snack LP* ***(P-26945)***
Forecast 3d, Carlsbad *Also called Product Slingshot Inc* ***(P-27403)***
Foreign Prnt Is Alanz AG Mnchn, Newport Beach *Also called Allianz Globl Invstors Amer LP* ***(P-10050)***
Foremost Healthcare Centers.....D.....760 244-5579
17581 Sultana St Hesperia (92345) ***(P-11020)***
Foremost Operations LLC.....E.....760 244-5579
17581 Sultana St Hesperia (92345) ***(P-24532)***
Foremost Terrace Room, Hesperia *Also called Foremost Operations LLC* ***(P-24532)***
Forensic Analytical.....D.....858 859-3322
3111 Camino Dl Rio N 43 San Diego (92108) ***(P-27730)***
Forensic Analytical Spc Inc (PA).....C.....510 887-8828
3777 Depot Rd Ste 409 Hayward (94545) ***(P-26702)***
Forensic Toxicology Associates, Chatsworth *Also called Pacific Toxicology Labs* ***(P-26726)***
Forescout Technologies Inc (PA).....C.....408 213-3191
190 W Tasman Dr San Jose (95134) ***(P-15166)***
Forest City Rental Prpts Corp.....D.....661 266-9150
1233 W Avenue P Ste 900 Palmdale (93551) ***(P-10877)***
FOREST HILL MANOR, Oakland *Also called Califrnia-Nevada Methdst Homes* ***(P-24450)***
Forest Lawn Memorial & Mortuar, Cypress *Also called Forest Lawn Memorial-Park Assn* ***(P-11941)***
Forest Lawn Memorial-Park Assn.....D.....714 828-3131
4471 Lincoln Ave Cypress (90630) ***(P-11941)***
Forest Lawn Memorial-Park Assn.....D.....323 254-7251
6300 Forest Lawn Dr Los Angeles (90068) ***(P-11942)***
Forest Lawn Memorial-Park Assn.....D.....562 424-1631
1500 E San Antonio Dr Long Beach (90807) ***(P-11943)***
Forest Park Cabana Club.....E.....408 244-1884
2911 Pruneridge Ave Santa Clara (95051) ***(P-18925)***
Forest Products Distrs Inc.....D.....707 443-7024
1090 W Waterfront Dr Eureka (95501) ***(P-6823)***
Forestry and Fire Protection.....C.....530 225-2418
875 Cypress Ave Redding (96001) ***(P-998)***
Forever Firewood Inc (PA).....E.....831 461-0634
46 El Pueblo Rd Ste A Santa Cruz (95066) ***(P-3157)***
Forever Link International Inc.....E.....877 839-9899
455 Brea Canyon Rd Walnut (91789) ***(P-8356)***
Forex Capital Markets LLC.....D.....415 343-4874
201 Mission St Ste 290 San Francisco (94105) ***(P-9952)***
Forge-Vidovich Motel Limited.....D.....408 996-7700
10889 N De Anza Blvd Cupertino (95014) ***(P-12581)***
Forgerock Inc (PA).....D.....415 599-1100
201 Mission St Ste 2900 San Francisco (94105) ***(P-15679)***
Forgerock US Inc (HQ).....D.....415 599-1100
201 Mission St San Francisco (94105) ***(P-15680)***
Foria International Inc (PA).....C.....626 912-8836
18689 Arenth Ave City of Industry (91748) ***(P-8260)***
Formation Inc.....D.....650 257-2277
35 Stillman St San Francisco (94107) ***(P-15681)***
Formation Systems, San Francisco *Also called Formation Inc* ***(P-15681)***
Formula One Systems Inc (HQ).....D.....562 424-7899
2850 E 29th St Long Beach (90806) ***(P-15167)***
Fornaca Inc (PA).....C.....866 308-9461
2400 National City Blvd National City (91950) ***(P-17721)***
Forrest City Development, Los Angeles *Also called Fc Metropolitan Lofts Inc* ***(P-11875)***
Forsys Inc.....D.....408 409-2567
6036 Stevenson Blvd Fremont (94538) ***(P-16368)***
Forsythe Technology LLC.....D.....424 217-6500
222 N Pacific Coast Hwy # 1426 El Segundo (90245) ***(P-16369)***
Fort Hill Construction (PA).....D.....323 656-7425
12711 Ventura Blvd # 390 Studio City (91604) ***(P-1165)***
Fort James Communications Pprs, Emeryville *Also called Fort James Corporation* ***(P-26861)***
Fort James Corporation.....D.....510 594-4900
2000 Powell St Emeryville (94608) ***(P-26861)***
Fort Mason Center.....D.....415 345-7500
2 Marina Blvd Bldg A San Francisco (94123) ***(P-27928)***
Fort Wash Golf & Cntry CLB.....D.....559 434-1702
10272 N Millbrook Ave Fresno (93730) ***(P-18926)***
Fort Washington Parent Assoc.....D.....559 327-6600
960 E Teague Ave Fresno (93720) ***(P-25156)***
FORT, THE, Fresno *Also called Fort Wash Golf & Cntry CLB* ***(P-18926)***
Forta (PA).....D.....626 446-7027
671 W Naomi Ave Arcadia (91007) ***(P-20177)***
Fortanasce & Associates, Arcadia *Also called Forta* ***(P-20177)***
Forte Enterprises Inc (PA).....C.....650 994-3200
99 Escuela Dr Daly City (94015) ***(P-26862)***
Fortinet Inc (PA).....C.....408 235-7700
899 Kifer Rd Sunnyvale (94086) ***(P-15682)***
Fortress Holding Group LLC.....D.....714 202-8710
5500 E Santa Ana Canyon R Anaheim (92807) ***(P-11977)***
Fortress Investment Group LLC.....D.....310 228-3030
10250 Constellation Blvd # 2300 Los Angeles (90067) ***(P-12037)***
Fortress Investment Group LLC.....D.....415 284-7400
42 Florida St Flr San Francisco (94103) ***(P-12038)***
Fortress Resources LLC (PA).....C.....562 633-9951
24200 Main St Carson (90745) ***(P-17760)***
Fortuna Enterprises LP.....B.....310 410-4000
5711 W Century Blvd Los Angeles (90045) ***(P-12582)***
Fortune Avenue Foods Inc.....D.....909 930-5989
2117 Pointe Ave Ontario (91761) ***(P-8407)***
Fortune Dynamic Inc.....D.....909 979-8318
21923 Ferrero City of Industry (91789) ***(P-8357)***
Forty Four Group LLC.....D.....949 407-6360
11397 Slater Ave Fountain Valley (92708) ***(P-13831)***
Forty Niners Football Co LLC.....D.....408 562-4949
4949 Mrie P Debartolo Way Santa Clara (95054) ***(P-18517)***
Forum At Rancho San Antonio, Cupertino *Also called Rancho San Antonio Retirement* ***(P-24643)***
Forum Enterprises Inc.....E.....310 330-7300
333 W Florence Ave Inglewood (90301) ***(P-18434)***
Forum Healthcare Center.....C.....650 944-0200
23600 Via Esplendor Cupertino (95014) ***(P-20436)***
Forward Air Inc.....E.....415 570-6040
30108 Eigenbrodt Way # 100 Union City (94587) ***(P-5066)***
Forward Management LLC.....D.....415 869-6300
101 California St # 1600 San Francisco (94111) ***(P-10080)***
Forward Slope Incorporated.....D.....619 299-4400
2020 Camino Del Rio N San Diego (92108) ***(P-25691)***
Forward Slope., San Diego *Also called Forward Slope Incorporated* ***(P-25691)***
Foshay Electric Coinc.....D.....858 277-7676
1555 Laurel Bay Ln San Diego (92154) ***(P-2588)***
Foss Maritime Co Inc.....D.....562 435-0171
Berth 35 Pier D Long Beach (90802) ***(P-4746)***
Foss Maritime Company.....D.....510 307-4271
1316 Canal Blvd Richmond (94804) ***(P-4696)***
Foss Maritime Company.....C.....562 435-0171
Berth 35 Pier D Long Beach (90801) ***(P-4697)***
Foster Care Licensing & Svc, Ventura *Also called County of Ventura* ***(P-23756)***
Foster Dairy Farms (PA).....A.....209 576-3400
529 Kansas Ave Modesto (95351) ***(P-412)***
Foster Dairy Farms.....E.....510 783-1270
3440 Enterprise Ave Hayward (94545) ***(P-8521)***
Foster Dairy Farms.....C.....209 874-9605
1472 Hall Rd Hickman (95323) ***(P-17945)***
Foster Dairy Products Distrg (PA).....A.....209 576-3400
529 Kansas Ave Modesto (95351) ***(P-8522)***
Foster Farms, Fresno *Also called Foster Poultry Farms* ***(P-443)***
Foster Farms LLC.....B.....559 793-5501
770 N Plano St Porterville (93257) ***(P-431)***
Foster Poultry Farms.....A.....559 457-6509
4107 Ave 360 Traver (93673) ***(P-9079)***
Foster Poultry Farms.....A.....209 394-7901
843 Davis St Livingston (95334) ***(P-440)***
Foster Poultry Farms.....D.....209 668-5922
1033 S Center St Turlock (95380) ***(P-441)***
Foster Poultry Farms.....A.....559 265-2000
900 W Belgravia Ave Fresno (93706) ***(P-442)***
Foster Poultry Farms.....A.....559 442-3771
2960 S Cherry Ave Fresno (93706) ***(P-443)***
Foster Turkey Live Haul, Turlock *Also called Foster Poultry Farms* ***(P-441)***
Foster Wheeler Energy Svcs Inc.....E.....800 500-1993
9645 Scranton Rd Ste 230 San Diego (92121) ***(P-3470)***

ALPHABETIC

Employee Codes: A=Over 500 employees, B=251-500
C=101-250, D=51-100, E=50
2019 Directory of California
Wholesalers and Services Companies
© Mergent Inc. 1-800-342-5647
1305

Fostering Executive Leadership ....D....949 651-6250
4790 Irvine Blvd 105-432 Irvine (92620) ***(P-27240)***
Foto Kem Film & Video, Burbank *Also called Foto-Kem Industries Inc* ***(P-18192)***
Foto-Kem Industries Inc (PA) ....B....818 846-3102
2801 W Alameda Ave Burbank (91505) ***(P-18192)***
Foto-Kem Industries Inc ....B....818 846-3102
2801 W Olive Ave Burbank (91505) ***(P-18193)***
Fotokem, Burbank *Also called Foto-Kem Industries Inc* ***(P-18193)***
Foundation 9 Entertainment Inc (PA) ....C....949 698-1500
30211 A De Las Bandera200 Rancho Santa Margari (92688) ***(P-15683)***
Foundation Building Material, San Jose *Also called Railway Distributing Inc* ***(P-6906)***
Foundation Building Mtls LLC (HQ) ....D....714 380-3127
2741 Walnut Ave Ste 200 Tustin (92780) ***(P-2884)***
Foundation Constructors Inc (PA) ....D....925 754-6633
81 Big Break Rd Oakley (94561) ***(P-2033)***
Foundation For Dance Education ....D....909 482-1590
9061 Central Ave Montclair (91763) ***(P-18333)***
Foundation For Early Childhood (PA) ....D....626 572-5107
3360 Flair Dr Ste 100 El Monte (91731) ***(P-23808)***
Foundation Laboratory, Pomona *Also called Latara Enterprise Inc* ***(P-22104)***
Foundation Repair of CA, Livermore *Also called Smp Construction & Maint Inc* ***(P-1653)***
Foundation Super Skateboard, San Diego *Also called Tum Yeto Inc* ***(P-7941)***
Founders Healthcare LLC ....D....626 683-5401
170 N Daisy Ave Pasadena (91107) ***(P-22300)***
Founders Management II Corp ....B....650 570-5700
1221 Chess Dr Foster City (94404) ***(P-12583)***
Foundstone Inc ....D....949 297-5600
27201 Puerta Real Ste 400 Mission Viejo (92691) ***(P-15684)***
Foundtion For Cal Cmnty Cllges (PA) ....C....916 325-4300
1102 Q St Ste 4800 Sacramento (95811) ***(P-24958)***
Foundtion For Hispanic Educatn (PA) ....D....408 585-5022
14271 Story Rd San Jose (95127) ***(P-25157)***
Fountain, San Francisco *Also called Onboardiq Inc* ***(P-16239)***
Fountain Court Essex ....E....818 227-2100
22102 Clarendon St # 200 Woodland Hills (91367) ***(P-11471)***
Fountain Grove Golf & Athc CLB ....D....707 521-3207
1525 Fountaingrove Pkwy Santa Rosa (95403) ***(P-18713)***
Fountain Valley Body Works M2 ....E....714 751-8812
17481 Newhope St Fountain Valley (92708) ***(P-17722)***
Fountain Valley Regl Hospl ....A....714 966-7200
17100 Euclid St Fountain Valley (92708) ***(P-21418)***
Fountain Valley School Dst ....D....714 668-5882
17330 Mount Herrmann St Fountain Valley (92708) ***(P-14268)***
Fountaingrove Inn LLC ....D....707 578-6101
101 Fountaingrove Pkwy Santa Rosa (95403) ***(P-12584)***
Fountains At Sea Bluffs, Dana Point *Also called Sunrise Senior Living Inc* ***(P-20804)***
Fountains At The Carlotta, Palm Desert *Also called Sunrise Senior Living LLC* ***(P-20833)***
Fountains At The Carlotta, The, Palm Desert *Also called Watermark Rtrment Cmmnties Inc* ***(P-20877)***
FOUNTAINS, THE, Yuba City *Also called United Com Serve* ***(P-20845)***
Fountainwood Residential Care ....D....916 988-2200
8773 Oak Ave Orangevale (95662) ***(P-24533)***
Fountngrove Inn Conference Ctr, Santa Rosa *Also called Fountaingrove Inn LLC* ***(P-12584)***
Four CS Service Inc ....D....559 237-3990
1560 H St Fresno (93721) ***(P-3158)***
Four Medica Inc ....D....310 348-4100
13160 Mindanao Way # 280 Marina Del Rey (90292) ***(P-5982)***
Four Points Bakersfield, Bakersfield *Also called Cni Thl Propco Fe LLC* ***(P-12473)***
Four Points By Sheraton, San Diego *Also called Pinnacle 1617 LLC* ***(P-13065)***
Four Points By Sheraton ....D....310 645-4600
9750 Airport Blvd Los Angeles (90045) ***(P-12585)***
Four Points by Sheraton LAX, Los Angeles *Also called Irp Lax Hotel LLC* ***(P-12780)***
Four Points San Diego-Seaworld, San Diego *Also called Greenwood Holdings LLC* ***(P-12620)***
Four Points San Jose Downtown ....E....408 282-8800
211 S 1st St San Jose (95113) ***(P-12586)***
Four Points San Rafael, San Rafael *Also called San Rafael Hillcrest LLC* ***(P-13182)***
Four Points Sheraton Lax, Los Angeles *Also called Lax Hotel Ventures LLC* ***(P-12841)***
Four Points Sheraton Ventura, Ventura *Also called Harbor Island Hotel Group LP* ***(P-12642)***
Four Seasons Healthcare ....D....818 985-1814
5335 Laurel Canyon Blvd North Hollywood (91607) ***(P-20437)***
Four Seasons Hotel, Westlake Village *Also called Burton-Way House Ltd A CA* ***(P-12410)***
Four Seasons Hotel, Los Angeles *Also called Burton-Way House Ltd A CA* ***(P-12411)***
Four Seasons Hotel, Los Angeles *Also called Burton-Way House Ltd A CA* ***(P-12412)***
Four Seasons Hotel, San Francisco *Also called Cb-1 Hotel* ***(P-12443)***
Four Seasons Hotel Inc ....A....415 633-3441
735 Market St Fl 6 San Francisco (94103) ***(P-12587)***
Four Seasons Hotel Inc ....A....650 566-1200
2050 University Ave East Palo Alto (94303) ***(P-12588)***
Four Seasons Hotel Silicon Vly, East Palo Alto *Also called East Palo Alto Hotel Dev Inc* ***(P-12546)***
Four Seasons Landscaping, Van Nuys *Also called S G D Enterprises* ***(P-933)***
Four Seasons Landscaping, Van Nuys *Also called S D Property Management Inc* ***(P-11749)***
Four Seasons Resort Aviara, Carlsbad *Also called California Bistro At Fo* ***(P-12419)***
Four Seasons Resort Aviara ....D....760 603-6900
7447 Batiquitos Dr Carlsbad (92011) ***(P-18714)***
Four Sisters Inns ....C....619 437-1900
1060 Adella Ave Coronado (92118) ***(P-12589)***
Four Ssons Hotel-San Francisco, San Francisco *Also called Four Seasons Hotel Inc* ***(P-12587)***
Four Ssons Rsort Santa Barbara, Santa Barbara *Also called 1260 Bb Property LLC* ***(P-12288)***
Fourth Phase Los Angeles, San Fernando *Also called Prg (california) Inc* ***(P-18099)***
Fourth Street Bowl ....E....408 453-5555
1441 N 4th St San Jose (95112) ***(P-18489)***
Fourthfloor Fashion Talent, Los Angeles *Also called Career Group Inc* ***(P-14585)***
Fowler Convalescent Hospital ....E....559 834-2542
1306 E Sumner Ave Fowler (93625) ***(P-21067)***
Fowler Labor Service Inc ....B....559 834-3723
633 W Fresno St Fowler (93625) ***(P-14622)***
Fowler Packing Company Inc ....C....559 834-5911
8570 S Cedar Ave Fresno (93725) ***(P-517)***
Fox Inc (HQ) ....A....310 369-1000
2121 Ave Of The Los Angeles (90067) ***(P-5792)***
Fox Animation Studios Inc ....B....323 857-8800
5700 Wilshire Blvd # 325 Los Angeles (90036) ***(P-18054)***
Fox Broadcasting Company (HQ) ....C....310 369-1000
10201 W Pico Blvd Los Angeles (90064) ***(P-5793)***
Fox BSB Holdco Inc ....A....323 224-1500
1000 Vin Scully Ave Los Angeles (90090) ***(P-18518)***
Fox Factory Holding Corp ....A....619 768-1800
750 Vernon Way Ste 101 El Cajon (92020) ***(P-6641)***
Fox Family Channel, Burbank *Also called International Fmly Entrtmt Inc* ***(P-5922)***
Fox Films Entertainment, Los Angeles *Also called Twentieth Cntury Fox Film Corp* ***(P-18140)***
Fox Head Inc (PA) ....C....888 369-7223
16752 Armstrong Ave Irvine (92606) ***(P-8261)***
Fox Luggage Inc ....D....323 588-1688
5353 E Slauson Ave Commerce (90040) ***(P-8030)***
Fox Network Center, Los Angeles *Also called Fox Networks Group Inc* ***(P-5915)***
Fox Networks Group Inc ....C....310 369-5104
10201 W Pico Blvd Los Angeles (90064) ***(P-5914)***
Fox Networks Group Inc (HQ) ....D....310 369-9369
10201 W Pico Blvd 101 Los Angeles (90064) ***(P-5915)***
Fox Racing, Irvine *Also called Fox Head Inc* ***(P-8261)***
Fox Rent A Car Inc (PA) ....E....310 342-5155
5500 W Century Blvd Los Angeles (90045) ***(P-17637)***
Fox Television Stations Inc (HQ) ....B....310 584-2000
1999 S Bundy Dr Los Angeles (90025) ***(P-5794)***
Fox Transportation Inc (PA) ....D....909 291-4646
8610 Helms Ave Rancho Cucamonga (91730) ***(P-27731)***
Foxconn Electronics, Brea *Also called Fit Electronics Inc* ***(P-26366)***
Foxy, Salinas *Also called Nunes Company Inc* ***(P-8710)***
FP, San Francisco *Also called Francisco Partners LP* ***(P-15958)***
Fphs2, Corona *Also called Advanced Communication Service* ***(P-16986)***
FPI Management Inc ....C....408 267-3952
1107 Luchessi Dr San Jose (95118) ***(P-26863)***
FPI Management Inc (PA) ....E....916 357-5300
800 Iron Point Rd Folsom (95630) ***(P-11472)***
Fpk Investigaions, Valencia *Also called Fpk Security Inc* ***(P-16648)***
Fpk Security Inc ....B....661 702-9091
28348 Constellation Rd # 880 Valencia (91355) ***(P-16648)***
Fpl LLC ....D....805 643-6144
550 San Jon Rd Ventura (93001) ***(P-12590)***
Fragomen Del Rey Bernse ....D....858 793-1600
11238 El Camino Real # 100 San Diego (92130) ***(P-23080)***
Fragomen Del Rey Bernse ....E....310 820-3322
11150 W Olympic Blvd # 1000 Los Angeles (90064) ***(P-23081)***
Fragomen Del Rey Bernse ....D....949 660-3504
18401 Von Karman Ave # 255 Irvine (92612) ***(P-23082)***
Fragomen Del Rey Bernse ....D....408 919-0600
2121 Tasman Dr Santa Clara (95054) ***(P-23083)***
Framing Associates Inc ....C....619 336-9991
1320 Coolidge Ave National City (91950) ***(P-1285)***
Framing Fabrics, Los Angeles *Also called Neuberg Nuberg Importers Group* ***(P-6777)***
Fran-Jom Inc ....D....626 443-3028
5101 Tyler Ave Temple City (91780) ***(P-21068)***
France Telecom RES & Dev LLC ....D....415 284-9765
60 Spear St Ste 1100 San Francisco (94105) ***(P-26518)***
Franciscan Conv. Hospital, Merced *Also called Avalon Care Center - Merced* ***(P-20244)***
Franciscan Lines Inc ....C....415 642-9400
41 Pier San Francisco (94133) ***(P-3798)***
Francisco Emilio Assoc Law Off ....D....949 474-2222
17532 Von Karman Ave Irvine (92614) ***(P-23084)***
Francisco Partners LP (HQ) ....D....415 418-2900
1 Letterman Dr Bldg C San Francisco (94129) ***(P-15958)***
Francisco Partners MGT LP (PA) ....E....415 418-2900
1 Letterman Dr Ste 410 San Francisco (94129) ***(P-12227)***
Franconnect LLC ....C....760 720-5354
300 Carlsbad Village Dr 302a Carlsbad (92008) ***(P-15959)***
Frandzel Share Robins Bloom Lc ....D....323 852-1000
1000 Wilshire Blvd # 1900 Los Angeles (90017) ***(P-23085)***
Frank Rimerman & Co LLP ....D....415 439-1144
1 Embarcadero Ctr # 2410 San Francisco (94111) ***(P-26205)***
Frank Barraza ....D....760 348-7363
147 E Alamo Calipatria (92233) ***(P-649)***
Frank C Alegre Trucking Inc (PA) ....C....209 334-2112
5100 W Highway 12 Lodi (95242) ***(P-4179)***
Frank Carson Ldscp & Maint Inc ....C....916 856-5400
9530 Elder Creek Rd Sacramento (95829) ***(P-842)***
Frank D Lanterman Regional Ctr, Los Angeles *Also called Los Angeles Cnty Dev Svc Fndtn* ***(P-22836)***
Frank D Yelian MD PC ....E....949 788-1133
3500 Barranca Pkwy # 300 Irvine (92606) ***(P-19475)***
Frank Gates Service Company ....D....916 934-0812
1107 Investment Blvd El Dorado Hills (95762) ***(P-27241)***
Frank Gates Service Company ....D....800 994-4611
2400 E Katella Ave # 650 Anaheim (92806) ***(P-10355)***
Frank Ghiglione Inc (PA) ....C....510 483-7000
14327 Washington Ave San Leandro (94578) ***(P-4015)***
Frank Ghiglione Inc ....D....510 483-2063
2972 Alvarado St Ste H San Leandro (94577) ***(P-4016)***

Mergent e-mail: customerrelations@mergent.com
1306
2019 Directory of California
Wholesalers and Services Companies
(P-0000) Products & Services Section entry number
(PA)=Parent Co (HQ)=Headquarters (DH)=Div Headquarters

Frank Howard Allen Fincl Corp....D....415 456-3000
1016 Irwin St San Rafael (94901) *(P-11473)*
Frank Howard Allen Fincl Corp....D....707 523-3000
460 Mission Blvd Santa Rosa (95409) *(P-11474)*
Frank Howard Allen Real Estate, San Rafael *Also called Frank Howard Allen Fincl Corp (P-11473)*
Frank J Gomes Dairy A Califo....D....209 669-7978
5301 Deangelis Rd Stevinson (95374) *(P-413)*
Frank M Booth Inc (PA)....C....530 742-7134
222 3rd St Marysville (95901) *(P-25692)*
Frank N Magid Associates Inc....D....818 263-3300
15260 Ventura Blvd # 1840 Sherman Oaks (91403) *(P-26519)*
Frank N Magid Associates Inc....C....818 263-3300
15260 Vntr Blvd Ste 1840 Sherman Oaks (91403) *(P-26520)*
Frank S Smith Masonry Inc....D....909 468-0525
2830 Pomona Blvd Pomona (91768) *(P-2807)*
Frank Schipper Construction Co....E....805 963-4359
610 E Cota St Santa Barbara (93103) *(P-1533)*
Frank Sciarrino Marble G....D....858 695-8030
7505 Trade St San Diego (92121) *(P-6892)*
Frank Toyata & Scion, National City *Also called Fornaca Inc (P-17721)*
Frank-Lin Distillers Pdts Ltd (PA)....C....408 259-8900
2455 Huntington Dr Fairfield (94533) *(P-9044)*
Franke Con J Electric Inc....D....209 462-0717
317 N Grant St Stockton (95202) *(P-2589)*
Franklin Advisers Inc (HQ)....A....650 312-2000
1 Franklin Pkwy San Mateo (94403) *(P-10081)*
Franklin Data, Westlake Village *Also called 5 Nine Group Inc (P-14953)*
Franklin Resources Inc (PA)....D....650 312-2000
1 Franklin Pkwy San Mateo (94403) *(P-12039)*
Franklin Templeton Investment, Rancho Cordova *Also called Franklin Tmpleton Inv Svcs LLC (P-9953)*
Franklin Templeton Svcs LLC....A....650 312-3000
1 Franklin Pkwy San Mateo (94403) *(P-10082)*
Franklin Tmpleton Inv Svcs LLC....C....650 312-2000
3366 Quality Dr Rancho Cordova (95670) *(P-10083)*
Franklin Tmpleton Inv Svcs LLC....C....925 875-2619
5130 Hacienda Dr Fl 4 Dublin (94568) *(P-10084)*
Franklin Tmpleton Inv Svcs LLC (HQ)....A....916 463-1500
3344 Quality Dr Rancho Cordova (95670) *(P-9953)*
Frantz Wholesale Nursery LLC....C....209 874-1459
12161 Delaware Rd Hickman (95323) *(P-259)*
Franza Sanger Winery, Sanger *Also called Wine Group Inc (P-9061)*
Frasco Inc (PA)....D....818 848-3888
215 W Alameda Ave Burbank (91502) *(P-16649)*
Frasco Investigative Services, Burbank *Also called Frasco Inc (P-16649)*
Fraternal Order Eagles 1582....C....916 782-2694
124 Vernon St Roseville (95678) *(P-10878)*
Frazier Nut Farms Inc....E....209 522-1406
10830 Yosemite Blvd Waterford (95386) *(P-189)*
Freckle Education Inc....E....215 896-9896
100 Bush St Ste 700 San Francisco (94104) *(P-15168)*
Fred H Lundblade Jr....D....707 442-8049
939 Koster St Ste B Eureka (95501) *(P-10879)*
Fred Leeds Properties....E....310 826-2466
3860 Crenshaw Blvd # 201 Los Angeles (90008) *(P-11021)*
Fredericka Manor....D....619 422-9271
183 Third Ave Chula Vista (91910) *(P-24534)*
FREDERICKA MANOR CARE CENTER, Burbank *Also called Fact Foundation (P-17159)*
Fredericka Manor Care Center, Glendale *Also called Front Porch Communities (P-21070)*
Fredericka Manor Care Center, Chula Vista *Also called Front Porch Communities (P-21073)*
Fredericksen Tank Lines Inc (PA)....D....916 371-4960
840 Delta Ln West Sacramento (95691) *(P-4180)*
Free Conferencing Corporation....C....562 437-1411
4300 E Pacific Coast Hwy Long Beach (90804) *(P-5560)*
Free Stream Media Corp (PA)....D....415 889-6404
123 Townsend St 5 San Francisco (94107) *(P-9218)*
Freeconferencecall.com, Long Beach *Also called Free Conferencing Corporation (P-5560)*
Freedom Debt Relief, San Mateo *Also called Freedom Financial Network LLC (P-13745)*
Freedom Financial Network LLC (PA)....D....650 393-6619
1875 S Grant St Ste 400 San Mateo (94402) *(P-13745)*
Freedom Painting Inc....E....562 696-0785
8822 Calmada Ave Whittier (90605) *(P-2436)*
Freedom Properties, Hemet *Also called Casa-Pacifica Inc (P-24456)*
Freedom Properties Village, Hemet *Also called Casa-Pacifica Inc (P-24457)*
Freedom Solar Services....C....951 696-9506
43445 Bus Pk Dr Ste 110 Temecula (92590) *(P-2213)*
Freedom Staff Leasing Inc....B....310 834-6621
3142 Pacific Coast Hwy Torrance (90505) *(P-14855)*
Freedom Village Healthcare Ctr....D....949 472-4733
23442 El Toro Rd Bldg 2 Lake Forest (92630) *(P-20438)*
Freeman Freeman & Smiley (PA)....D....310 398-6100
1888 Century Park E Fl 19 Los Angeles (90067) *(P-23086)*
Freeman Audio Visual LLC....C....714 254-3400
901 E South St Anaheim (92805) *(P-14506)*
Freeman Expositions LLC....C....714 254-3400
901 E South St Anaheim (92805) *(P-17174)*
Freeman Expositions LLC....D....650 878-6023
245 S Spruce Ave South San Francisco (94080) *(P-17175)*
Freeman Freeman & Smiley LLP, Los Angeles *Also called Freeman Freeman & Smiley (P-23086)*
Freemont Health Care Center, Fremont *Also called Mariner Health Care Inc (P-20611)*
Freemont Rideout Health Group....D....530 751-4000
989 Plumas St Yuba City (95991) *(P-19476)*
Freeport-Mcmoran Oil & Gas LLC....D....661 322-7600
1200 Discovery Dr Ste 500 Bakersfield (93309) *(P-1023)*
Freeway Insurance, Huntington Beach *Also called Confie Seguros Inc (P-10593)*
Freeway Insurance (PA)....C....714 252-2500
7711 Center Ave Ste 200 Huntington Beach (92647) *(P-10631)*
Freight Management Inc....D....714 632-1440
2900 E La Palma Ave Anaheim (92806) *(P-27242)*
Freight Solution Providers, Rancho Cordova *Also called Kls Air Express Inc (P-5094)*
Freitas Brothers....E....805 343-3134
Hwy 1 Guadalupe (93434) *(P-52)*
Freixenet Usa Inc....D....707 996-7256
23555 Arnold Dr Sonoma (95476) *(P-9045)*
Fremantle Media, Burbank *Also called Prdctions N Fremantle Amer Inc (P-18395)*
Fremont Ambltory Srgery Ctr LP....D....510 456-4600
39350 Civic Center Dr Fremont (94538) *(P-19477)*
Fremont Bank (HQ)....C....510 505-5226
39150 Fremont Blvd Fremont (94538) *(P-9460)*
Fremont Candle Lighters....C....510 796-0595
39261 Fremont Hub Fremont (94538) *(P-25423)*
Fremont Dental Group, Fremont *Also called John J Maguire DDS (P-20119)*
FREMONT HOSPITAL, Mariposa *Also called John C Fremont Healthcare Dst (P-21461)*
Fremont Hospital....A....530 751-4000
620 J St Marysville (95901) *(P-21419)*
Fremont Marriott....C....510 413-3700
46100 Landing Pkwy Fremont (94538) *(P-12591)*
Fremont Medical Center, Marysville *Also called Fremont Hospital (P-21419)*
Fremont Mutual Funds Inc....D....800 548-4539
333 Market St Ste 2600 San Francisco (94105) *(P-9954)*
Fremont Properties Inc....E....415 284-8500
199 Fremont St Ste 1900 San Francisco (94105) *(P-10880)*
Fremont Realty Capital LP....D....415 284-8665
199 Fremont St Fl 19 San Francisco (94105) *(P-11173)*
Fremont Sports Inc....E....510 656-4411
40645 Fremont Blvd Ste 3 Fremont (94538) *(P-18490)*
Fremont Surgery Center, Fremont *Also called Fremont Ambltory Srgery Ctr LP (P-19477)*
Fremont Unified School Dst....D....510 657-0761
43772 S Grimmer Blvd Fremont (94538) *(P-14269)*
French Hosp Med Ctr Foundation (HQ)....B....805 543-5353
1911 Johnson Ave San Luis Obispo (93401) *(P-21420)*
French Laundry Restaurant Corp (PA)....D....707 944-0167
6540 Washington St Yountville (94599) *(P-13633)*
French Park Care Center....C....714 973-1656
600 E Washington Ave Santa Ana (92701) *(P-20439)*
French Redwood Inc....C....650 598-9000
223 Twin Dolphin Dr Redwood City (94065) *(P-12592)*
Freschi Air Systems Inc....D....925 827-9761
715 Fulton Shipyard Rd Antioch (94509) *(P-2214)*
Freschi Service Experts, Antioch *Also called Freschi Air Systems Inc (P-2214)*
Fresenius Med Care Long Beach....E....562 432-4444
440 W Ocean Blvd Long Beach (90802) *(P-22476)*
Fresenius Medical Care, Fresno *Also called Bio-Mdical Applications Rl Inc (P-22469)*
Fresh Air Environmental Svcs....D....323 913-1965
10675 Rush St South El Monte (91733) *(P-3522)*
Fresh Farms Inc....E....831 385-3285
700 Airport Rd King City (93930) *(P-53)*
Fresh Grill LLC....C....714 444-2126
111 E Garry Ave Santa Ana (92707) *(P-8790)*
Fresh Leaf Farms LLC (HQ)....E....831 422-7405
1250 Hansen St Salinas (93901) *(P-54)*
Fresh Lifelines For Youth Inc....D....408 263-2630
568 Valley Way Milpitas (95035) *(P-23809)*
Fresh Origins LLC....B....760 736-4072
570 Quarry Rd San Marcos (92069) *(P-22)*
Fresh Pick Produce....E....408 315-4612
195 San Pedro Ave Ste D Morgan Hill (95037) *(P-8031)*
Fresh Start Bakeries, Stockton *Also called Aryzta LLC (P-8756)*
Fresh Venture Farms LLC....D....805 754-4449
1181 S Wolff Rd Oxnard (93033) *(P-55)*
Freshko Produce Services Inc....C....559 497-7000
2155 E Muscat Ave Fresno (93725) *(P-8678)*
Fresholgy Inc....D....818 847-1888
12400 Wilshire Blvd # 1180 Los Angeles (90025) *(P-8791)*
Freshpoint Inc....C....510 476-5900
30336 Whipple Rd Union City (94587) *(P-8679)*
Freshpoint Inc....C....626 855-1400
155 N Orange Ave City of Industry (91744) *(P-8680)*
Freshpoint Central California....C....209 216-0200
5900 N Golden State Blvd Turlock (95382) *(P-8681)*
Freshpoint Las Vegas, City of Industry *Also called Freshpoint Inc (P-8680)*
Freshpoint Southern Cal Inc....C....626 855-1400
155 N Orange Ave City of Industry (91744) *(P-8682)*
Freshpoint Southern California, City of Industry *Also called Freshpoint Southern Cal Inc (P-8682)*
Freshway Farms LLC....C....805 349-7170
2165 W Main St Santa Maria (93458) *(P-99)*
Fresno Airport Hotels LLC....D....559 252-3611
5090 E Clinton Way Fresno (93727) *(P-12593)*
Fresno Auto Dealers Auction....C....559 268-8051
278 N Marks Ave Fresno (93706) *(P-6592)*
Fresno Beverage Company Inc....C....559 650-1500
3525 S East Ave Fresno (93725) *(P-8996)*
Fresno Cmnty Hosp & Med Ctr....D....559 324-4000
2755 Herndon Ave Clovis (93611) *(P-21421)*
Fresno Cmnty Hosp & Med Ctr (HQ)....A....559 459-6000
2823 Fresno St Fresno (93721) *(P-21422)*
Fresno Cnty Economic Opportunt....A....559 263-1000
1900 Mariposa Mall # 300 Fresno (93721) *(P-23810)*
Fresno Cnty Economic Opportunt (PA)....A....559 263-1010
1920 Mariposa Mall # 300 Fresno (93721) *(P-23811)*
Fresno Cnty Economic Opportunt....B....559 263-1013
1920 Mariposa Mall Fresno (93721) *(P-17176)*

ALPHABETIC

Employee Codes: A=Over 500 employees, B=251-500
C=101-250, D=51-100, E=50
2019 Directory of California
Wholesalers and Services Companies
© Mergent Inc. 1-800-342-5647
1307

Fresno Cnty Economic Opportunt...D....559 485-3733
3120 W Nielsen Ave # 102 Fresno (93706) ***(P-23812)***
Fresno Cnty Sprntndent Schools...D....559 644-1000
16644 S Elm Ave Caruthers (93609) ***(P-3937)***
Fresno Convention Center, Fresno *Also called City of Fresno* ***(P-17077)***
Fresno County Private Security...D....559 233-9800
2150 Tulare St Fresno (93721) ***(P-16650)***
Fresno County Rural Trnst Agcy (PA)...D....559 233-6789
2035 Tulare St Fresno (93721) ***(P-3657)***
Fresno District Office, Fresno *Also called State Compensation Insur Fund* ***(P-10401)***
Fresno Eoc, Fresno *Also called Fresno Cnty Economic Opportunt* ***(P-23810)***
FRESNO EOC, Fresno *Also called Fresno Cnty Economic Opportunt* ***(P-23811)***
Fresno Hauling, Fresno *Also called USA Waste of California Inc* ***(P-6496)***
Fresno Hauling, Visalia *Also called USA Waste of California Inc* ***(P-6501)***
Fresno Heart Hospital LLC...B....559 433-8000
15 E Audubon Dr Fresno (93720) ***(P-21423)***
Fresno Heritage Partners...E....559 446-6226
6075 N Marks Ave Fresno (93711) ***(P-24535)***
Fresno Hotel Partners LP...D....559 224-4040
324 E Shaw Ave Fresno (93710) ***(P-12594)***
Fresno Irrigation District...D....559 233-7161
2907 S Maple Ave Fresno (93725) ***(P-6554)***
Fresno Metro Flood Ctrl Dst...D....559 456-3292
5469 E Olive Ave Fresno (93727) ***(P-17177)***
Fresno Plumbing & Heating Inc (PA)...C....559 294-0200
2585 N Larkin Ave Fresno (93727) ***(P-2215)***
Fresno Rescue Mission Inc (PA)...E....559 268-0839
263 G St Fresno (93706) ***(P-23813)***
Fresno Roofing Co Inc...D....559 255-8377
5950 E Olive Ave Fresno (93727) ***(P-3159)***
Fresno Skilled Nursing...D....559 268-5361
1665 M St Fresno (93721) ***(P-20440)***
Fresno Surgery Center LP (PA)...C....559 431-8000
6125 N Fresno St Fresno (93710) ***(P-21424)***
Fresno Surgical Hospital, Fresno *Also called Fresno Surgery Center LP* ***(P-21424)***
Fresno Truck Center...D....559 486-4310
2727 E Central Ave Fresno (93725) ***(P-6593)***
Fresno Truck Center...C....209 983-2400
10182 S Harlan Rd French Camp (95231) ***(P-6594)***
Fresno Unified School District...C....559 457-3074
4600 N Brawley Ave Fresno (93722) ***(P-14270)***
Fresno-Madera Federal Land...D....559 674-2437
305 N I St Madera (93637) ***(P-9696)***
Fresnos Chaffee Zoo Corp...C....559 498-5910
894 W Belmont Ave Fresno (93728) ***(P-24929)***
Freund Baking Co, Hayward *Also called Oakhurst Industries Inc* ***(P-8437)***
Frey Farming & Tpsry Vineyards...D....805 937-1542
2203 Fallen Leaf Dr Santa Maria (93455) ***(P-692)***
Friant Water Authority (PA)...E....559 562-6305
854 N Harvard Ave Lindsay (93247) ***(P-6255)***
Friant Water Users Association...D....559 562-6305
854 N Harvard Ave Lindsay (93247) ***(P-6256)***
Friant Water Users Authority, Lindsay *Also called Friant Water Users Association* ***(P-6256)***
Frick Paper Company...C....323 726-8200
2164 N Batavia St Orange (92865) ***(P-8102)***
Friedas Inc...D....714 733-7655
4465 Corporate Center Dr Los Alamitos (90720) ***(P-8683)***
Friedas Specialty Produce, Los Alamitos *Also called Friedas Inc* ***(P-8683)***
Friedman Professional Mgt Co...D....714 842-1426
17752 Beach Blvd Side Huntington Beach (92647) ***(P-19478)***
Friendly Hills Country Club...C....562 698-0331
8500 Villaverde Dr Whittier (90605) ***(P-18927)***
Friendly Valley Recrtl Assn...E....661 252-3223
19345 Avenue Of The Oaks Santa Clarita (91321) ***(P-23814)***
FRIENDLY VILLAGE COMMUNITY ASS, Santa Clarita *Also called Friendly Valley Recrtl Assn* ***(P-23814)***
Friends Chbad Lbvtch San Diego (PA)...E....619 265-7700
6115 Montezuma Rd San Diego (92115) ***(P-23815)***
Friends Fitzgerald Mar Reserve...D....650 728-3584
200 Nevada Ave Moss Beach (94038) ***(P-24782)***
Friends Group Express Inc...D....909 346-6814
14520 Village Dr Apt 1013 Fontana (92337) ***(P-4181)***
Friends of Cultural Center Inc...D....760 346-6505
73000 Fred Waring Dr Palm Desert (92260) ***(P-18367)***
Friends of Family...E....818 988-4430
16861 Parthenia St Northridge (91343) ***(P-23816)***
Friends of Max Rose LLC...D....424 901-1260
1639 11th St Ste 260 Santa Monica (90404) ***(P-18055)***
Friends of The Los Angeles...C....323 653-0440
8405 Beverly Blvd Los Angeles (90048) ***(P-24783)***
Friends Outside...C....209 955-0701
7272 Murray Dr Stockton (95210) ***(P-23817)***
Friends Santa Cruz State Parks...D....831 429-1840
1543 Pacific Ave Ste 206 Santa Cruz (95060) ***(P-25158)***
Fritch Eye Care Medical Center...D....661 665-2020
9000 Ming Ave Ste L2 Bakersfield (93311) ***(P-19479)***
Frito-Lay North America Inc...C....530 671-7854
401 Burns Dr Yuba City (95991) ***(P-8545)***
Frito-Lay North America Inc...C....925 734-3100
26672 Towne Centre Dr Foothill Ranch (92610) ***(P-8546)***
Frito-Lay North America Inc...B....626 855-1300
14600 Proctor Ave City of Industry (91746) ***(P-8547)***
Frito-Lay North America Inc...C....310 224-5600
1500 Francisco St Torrance (90501) ***(P-26864)***
Frito-Lay North America Inc...B....909 941-6214
9535 Archibald Ave Rancho Cucamonga (91730) ***(P-8548)***
Frito-Lay North America Inc...C....661 328-6034
28801 Highway 58 Bakersfield (93314) ***(P-8549)***
Frito-Lay North America Inc...C....559 226-8153
3630 N Hazel Ave Fresno (93722) ***(P-8550)***
Frito-Lay North America Inc...D....661 951-1399
751 W Avenue L8 Lancaster (93534) ***(P-8551)***
Frito-Lay North America Inc...D....559 312-8553
1774 Automation Pkwy San Jose (95131) ***(P-8552)***
Frito-Lay North America Inc...D....415 467-1860
151 W Hill Pl Brisbane (94005) ***(P-8553)***
Frito-Lay North America Inc...C....916 372-5400
3810 Seaport Blvd West Sacramento (95691) ***(P-8554)***
Frito-Lay North America Inc...E....661 835-0347
6320 District Blvd Bakersfield (93313) ***(P-8555)***
Frito-Lay North America Inc...D....510 769-5000
1450 S Loop Rd Alameda (94502) ***(P-8556)***
Frito-Lay North America Inc...D....760 727-6022
1390 Vantage Ct Vista (92081) ***(P-8557)***
Frito-Lay North America Inc...D....949 586-4644
26962 Vista Ter El Toro (92630) ***(P-8558)***
Frito-Lay North America Inc...D....559 651-1334
8316 W Elowin Ct Visalia (93291) ***(P-8559)***
Frito-Lay North America Inc...C....209 544-5424
4029 Leckron Rd Modesto (95357) ***(P-8560)***
Frito-Lay North America Inc...E....310 322-5001
1924 E Maple Ave El Segundo (90245) ***(P-8561)***
Frize Corporation...D....800 834-2127
16605 Gale Ave City of Industry (91745) ***(P-1398)***
Frog Design Inc (HQ)...C....415 442-4804
1130 Howard St San Francisco (94103) ***(P-14114)***
Fromer Inc...D....818 341-3896
22225 Acorn St Chatsworth (91311) ***(P-1166)***
Front Line MGT Group Inc...D....310 209-3100
1100 Glendon Ave Ste 2000 Los Angeles (90024) ***(P-26865)***
Front Porch Inc (PA)...D....209 288-5500
905 Mono Way Sonora (95370) ***(P-15169)***
Front Porch Communities...C....323 661-1128
1055 N Kingsley Dr Los Angeles (90029) ***(P-20441)***
Front Porch Communities...C....714 776-7150
1401 W Ball Rd Anaheim (92802) ***(P-21069)***
Front Porch Communities...D....858 454-2151
849 Coast Blvd La Jolla (92037) ***(P-11022)***
Front Porch Communities (PA)...D....818 729-8100
800 N Brand Blvd Fl 19 Glendale (91203) ***(P-21070)***
Front Porch Communities...B....858 274-4110
2567 2nd Ave Unit 312 San Diego (92103) ***(P-11023)***
Front Porch Communities...C....760 729-4983
2855 Carlsbad Blvd Carlsbad (92008) ***(P-21071)***
Front Porch Communities...C....909 626-1227
650 Harrison Ave Claremont (91711) ***(P-21072)***
Front Porch Communities...C....619 427-2777
111 Third Ave Chula Vista (91910) ***(P-21073)***
Front Porch Communities & Svcs...C....626 796-8162
842 E Villa St Pasadena (91101) ***(P-24536)***
Front Porch Communities & Svcs...D....818 729-8100
303 N Glenoaks Blvd # 1000 Burbank (91502) ***(P-21074)***
Front Porch Communities & Svcs...C....562 868-9761
11701 Studebaker Rd Norwalk (90650) ***(P-21075)***
Front Porch Communities & Svcs...D....760 240-5051
11959 Apple Valley Rd Apple Valley (92308) ***(P-20442)***
Front Prch Cmmunities/Services...C....805 687-0793
3775 Modoc Rd Santa Barbara (93105) ***(P-21076)***
Front St Inc...C....831 420-0120
2115 7th Ave Santa Cruz (95062) ***(P-21077)***
Front St Residential Care, Santa Cruz *Also called Front St Inc* ***(P-21077)***
Frontapp Inc...D....415 680-3048
525 Brannan St Ste 300 San Francisco (94107) ***(P-15685)***
Frontech N Fujitsu Amer Inc...D....408 982-3697
2933 Bunker Hill Ln # 101 Santa Clara (95054) ***(P-15170)***
Frontech N Fujitsu Amer Inc (HQ)...C....949 855-5500
27121 Towne Centre Dr # 100 Foothill Ranch (92610) ***(P-15960)***
Frontier California Inc...D....760 342-0500
83793 Dr Carreon Blvd Indio (92201) ***(P-5561)***
Frontier California Inc...D....805 925-0000
200 W Church St Santa Maria (93458) ***(P-5562)***
Frontier California Inc...D....760 256-3511
135 Cozy Ln Barstow (92311) ***(P-5563)***
Frontier California Inc...D....909 941-4068
9000 Hellman Ave Rancho Cucamonga (91730) ***(P-4017)***
Frontier California Inc...C....818 365-0542
510 Park Ave San Fernando (91340) ***(P-5564)***
Frontier California Inc...C....209 239-4128
525 E Yosemite Ave Manteca (95336) ***(P-5565)***
Frontier California Inc...A....805 372-6000
112 S Lakeview Canyon Rd Westlake Village (91362) ***(P-7479)***
Frontier California Inc...D....805 372-6000
1 Wellpoint Way Westlake Village (91362) ***(P-5566)***
Frontier California Inc...D....559 592-2100
200 W Firebaugh Ave Exeter (93221) ***(P-5567)***
Frontier California Inc...D....559 224-9222
5195 N Blackstone Ave Fresno (93710) ***(P-5408)***
Frontier Communities, Ontario *Also called Shii LLC* ***(P-11764)***
Frontier Land Companies...E....209 957-8112
10100 Trinity Pkwy # 420 Stockton (95219) ***(P-1167)***
Frontier Logistics Services, Ontario *Also called F R T International Inc* ***(P-5062)***
Frontier Logistics Services, Compton *Also called F R T International Inc* ***(P-4555)***
Frontier Mechanical Inc...D....661 589-6203
6309 Seven Seas Ave Bakersfield (93308) ***(P-2216)***
Frontier Plumbing, Bakersfield *Also called Frontier Mechanical Inc* ***(P-2216)***
Frontier Title Co (PA)...E....707 427-5400
1499 Oliver Rd Fairfield (94534) ***(P-10463)***

Mergent e-mail: customerrelations@mergent.com
1308
2019 Directory of California Wholesalers and Services Companies
(P-0000) Products & Services Section entry number
(PA)=Parent Co (HQ)=Headquarters (DH)=Div Headquarters

Frontiir Corporation...C...510 996-2071
1586 Parkview Ave Apt 3 San Jose (95130) *(P-5568)*
Frontrange Holding Inc...B...408 601-2800
490 N Mccarthy Blvd Milpitas (95035) *(P-15686)*
Frontrs-Frnters Land Companies, Stockton *Also called Frontier Land Companies (P-1167)*
Frsteam By Custom Commercial, Hayward *Also called Custom Commercial Dry Clrs Inc (P-13565)*
Fruit Guys...D...714 826-2993
4465 Corporate Center Dr Los Alamitos (90720) *(P-8684)*
Fruit Patch Sales LLC...B...559 591-1170
38773 Road 48 Dinuba (93618) *(P-8685)*
Fruitvale Long Term Care LLC...D...510 261-5613
3020 E 15th St Oakland (94601) *(P-20443)*
Fry, Opal W & Son Farming, Bakersfield *Also called Opal Fry and Son (P-74)*
Frys Electronics Inc...B...916 286-5800
4100 Northgate Blvd Sacramento (95834) *(P-27732)*
Frys Electronics Inc...C...310 364-3797
3600 N Sepulveda Blvd Manhattan Beach (90266) *(P-7049)*
FS Commercial Landscape Inc (PA)...D...951 360-7070
5151 Pedley Rd Riverside (92509) *(P-843)*
FS&k, Thousand Oaks *Also called Floyd Skeren & Kelly LLP (P-23073)*
FSA, Lompoc *Also called Family Service Agency (P-23797)*
Fscc, Santa Barbara *Also called Frank Schipper Construction Co (P-1533)*
Fsq Rio Las Palmas Business Tr...D...209 957-4711
877 E March Ln Apt 378 Stockton (95207) *(P-11024)*
Fssi, Santa Ana *Also called Financial Statement Svcs Inc (P-14044)*
Fst Sand & Gravel Inc...E...951 277-8440
21780 Temescal Canyon Rd Corona (92883) *(P-6893)*
Ft USA, Ontario *Also called Inqbrands Inc (P-16397)*
FT. WASHINGTON ELEM., Fresno *Also called Fort Washington Parent Assoc (P-25156)*
Ftdi West Inc...D...909 473-1111
3375 Enterprise Dr Bloomington (92316) *(P-4559)*
Fti Consulting Inc...D...213 689-1200
350 S Grand Ave Ste 3000 Los Angeles (90071) *(P-25693)*
Fti Consulting Inc...D...415 283-4200
50 California St Ste 1900 San Francisco (94111) *(P-27733)*
Fts Global, Visalia *Also called Agriholding Inc (P-4998)*
Fuel Delivery Services Inc...D...209 751-2185
4895 S Airport Way Stockton (95206) *(P-4182)*
Fuel TV...D...310 444-8564
1440 S Sepulveda Blvd Los Angeles (90025) *(P-5795)*
Fueling and Service Tech Inc...D...714 523-0194
7050 Village Dr Ste D Buena Park (90621) *(P-7752)*
Fuentes Farms Ag Inc...B...209 722-7201
2346 Glen Ave Merced (95340) *(P-14623)*
Fugro USA Land Inc...E...925 256-6070
1777 Botelho Dr Ste 262 Walnut Creek (94596) *(P-25694)*
Fuji Food Products Inc (PA)...D...562 404-2590
14420 Bloomfield Ave Santa Fe Springs (90670) *(P-8792)*
Fuji Food Products Inc...C...619 268-3118
8660 Miramar Rd Ste N San Diego (92126) *(P-8793)*
Fuji Natural Foods Inc (HQ)...D...909 947-1008
13500 S Hamner Ave Ontario (91761) *(P-312)*
Fuji Photo Film, Cypress *Also called Fujifilm North America Corp (P-6942)*
Fujifilm North America Corp...C...714 372-4200
6200 Phyllis Dr Cypress (90630) *(P-6942)*
Fujitsu America Inc (HQ)...B...408 746-6000
1250 E Arques Ave Sunnyvale (94085) *(P-15961)*
Fujitsu America Inc...D...408 746-8419
3113 Knights Bridge Rd San Jose (95132) *(P-15962)*
Fujitsu America Inc...C...408 992-3561
317 Eureka St San Francisco (94114) *(P-15963)*
Fujitsu America Inc...C...310 563-7000
2250 E Imperial Hwy # 200 El Segundo (90245) *(P-15964)*
Fujitsu Computer Pdts Amer Inc (HQ)...B...408 746-7000
1250 E Arques Ave Sunnyvale (94085) *(P-7050)*
Fujitsu Electronics Amer Inc (HQ)...D...408 737-5600
1250 E Arques Ave Sunnyvale (94085) *(P-25695)*
Fujitsu Glovia Inc (HQ)...C...310 563-7000
200 Continental Blvd Fl 3 El Segundo (90245) *(P-15171)*
Fujitsu Laboratories Amer Inc (HQ)...D...408 530-4500
1240 E Arques Ave 345 Sunnyvale (94085) *(P-26368)*
Fujitsu Ten Corp of America...C...310 327-2151
19600 S Vermont Ave Torrance (90502) *(P-7417)*
Full Circle Wireless Inc...E...949 783-7979
8900 Research Dr Irvine (92618) *(P-7480)*
Full Spectrum Services Inc...E...707 465-1460
1570 S Railroad Ave Crescent City (95531) *(P-23818)*
Full Throttle...C...323 474-8417
125 E 56th St Los Angeles (90011) *(P-17178)*
Fullclip USA, Garden Grove *Also called Customfab Inc (P-17120)*
Fullmer Cattle Nthrn Cal LLC...C...909 597-3274
16600 Hellman Ave Corona (92880) *(P-399)*
Fullmer Construction...C...909 947-9467
1725 S Grove Ave Ontario (91761) *(P-1399)*
Fullscreen Inc (HQ)...D...310 202-3333
12180 Millennium Ste 100 Playa Vista (90094) *(P-13832)*
Fulwider and Patton LLP...D...310 824-5555
6100 Center Dr Ste 1200 Los Angeles (90045) *(P-23087)*
Fumai Industrial Inc...D...626 272-1788
735 W Duarte Rd Arcadia (91007) *(P-7481)*
Fume-A-Pest & Termite Control, Encino *Also called A-Able Inc (P-14135)*
Fund Services Advisors Inc...E...213 612-2196
777 S Figueroa St # 3200 Los Angeles (90017) *(P-10085)*
Fundbox Inc...C...415 509-1343
300 Montgomery St Ste 900 San Francisco (94104) *(P-9757)*
Funding Circle Usa Inc...D...855 385-5356
747 Front St Fl 4 San Francisco (94111) *(P-9713)*
Funny or Die Inc...E...650 461-3929
1041 N Formosa Ave West Hollywood (90046) *(P-16370)*
Furnace Creek Ranch & Inn, Death Valley *Also called Xanterra Parks & Resorts Inc (P-13431)*
Furniture America Cal Inc (PA)...D...909 718-7276
19605 E Walnut Dr N City of Industry (91789) *(P-6722)*
Furniture America California, City of Industry *Also called Furniture America Cal Inc (P-6722)*
Furniture Trnsp Systems...D...909 869-1200
3100 Pomona Blvd Pomona (91768) *(P-5067)*
Fuscoe Engineering Inc (PA)...D...949 474-1960
16795 Von Karman Ave # 100 Irvine (92606) *(P-25696)*
Fuse Project LLC...D...415 908-1492
1401 16th St San Francisco (94103) *(P-27734)*
Fusefx LLC...B...818 237-5052
14823 Califa St Van Nuys (91411) *(P-18194)*
Fusion Mphc Holding Corp...C...925 201-2500
6800 Koll Center Pkwy Pleasanton (94566) *(P-15687)*
Fusion Real Estate Network Inc...D...916 448-3174
1300 National Dr Ste 170 Sacramento (95834) *(P-11475)*
Fusionone Inc...D...408 282-1200
55 Almaden Blvd Ste 500 San Jose (95113) *(P-15172)*
Fusionstorm...C...415 623-2626
2 Bryant St Ste 150 San Francisco (94105) *(P-27735)*
Fusionzone Automotive Inc...E...888 576-1136
1011 Swarthmore Ave Pacific Palisades (90272) *(P-16371)*
Future Dial Incorporated...D...408 245-8880
392 Potrero Ave Sunnyvale (94085) *(P-16372)*
Future Energy Corporation...D...760 477-9700
4120 Avenida De La Plata Oceanside (92056) *(P-2885)*
Future Energy Corporation (PA)...C...800 985-0733
8980 Grant Line Rd Upland (91786) *(P-2886)*
Future Energy Savers, Upland *Also called Future Energy Corporation (P-2886)*
Future Homes International, Moraga *Also called Engineered Forest Products LLC (P-12226)*
Future State...D...925 956-4200
2101 Webster St Ste 520 Oakland (94612) *(P-16373)*
Futuredontics Inc (PA)...C...310 215-6400
6060 Center Dr Fl 7 Los Angeles (90045) *(P-27243)*
Futurenet Technologies Corp...C...909 396-4000
1320 Valley Vista Dr # 202 Diamond Bar (91765) *(P-15173)*
Futures Explored...D...925 332-7183
2380 Salvio St Ste 302 Concord (94520) *(P-23819)*
Futuro Infantil Hispano Ffa...E...626 339-1824
2227 E Garvey Ave N West Covina (91791) *(P-24537)*
Fvbw, Fountain Valley *Also called Fountain Valley Body Works M2 (P-17722)*
FW Spencer & Son Inc...C...415 468-5000
99 S Hill Dr Brisbane (94005) *(P-2217)*
Fx Networks LLC...C...310 369-1000
10201 W Pico Blvd Los Angeles (90064) *(P-5916)*
G & G Construction Co, Atwater *Also called Gino/Giuseppe Inc (P-3256)*
G & H Dental Arts Inc (PA)...D...310 214-8007
4212 Artesia Blvd Torrance (90504) *(P-22168)*
G & L Penasquitos Inc...D...858 538-0802
10584 Rancho Carmel Dr San Diego (92128) *(P-23820)*
G A T X Rail, Colton *Also called GATX Corporation (P-5226)*
G and E Healthcare Svcs LLC...C...818 367-5881
14040 Astoria St Sylmar (91342) *(P-20444)*
G and L Brock Cnstr Co Inc...E...209 931-3626
4145 Calloway Ct Stockton (95215) *(P-3426)*
G B & P Citrus Co Inc (PA)...D...213 312-1380
1601 E Olympic Blvd # 111 Los Angeles (90021) *(P-10881)*
G B Group Inc (PA)...D...408 848-8118
8921 Murray Ave Gilroy (95020) *(P-1286)*
G Brothers Construction Inc...E...714 590-3070
7070 Patterson Dr Garden Grove (92841) *(P-2887)*
G D B, San Rafael *Also called Guide Dogs For Blind Inc (P-628)*
G I L C Inc...E...831 724-1011
585 W Beach St Watsonville (95076) *(P-1168)*
G J Sullivan Co Inc...D...213 626-1000
800 W 6th St Ste 1800 Los Angeles (90017) *(P-10632)*
G K Tool Corp...D...626 338-7300
4265 Puente Ave Baldwin Park (91706) *(P-7588)*
G Katen Partners Ltd Lblty Co...A...424 354-3241
9903 Santa Monica Blvd Beverly Hills (90212) *(P-5068)*
G M A C-One Source Realty...D...619 405-6231
898 Jackman St El Cajon (92020) *(P-11476)*
G M Floral Company...E...213 489-7055
740 Maple Ave Los Angeles (90014) *(P-9135)*
G M Floral Supply, Los Angeles *Also called G M Floral Company (P-9135)*
G M I, San Diego *Also called Guard Management Inc (P-16667)*
G Moroni Comp, Sacramento *Also called Smart Management & Companies (P-27031)*
G P M M Money Centers Inc...E...619 288-7607
1460 Doris Ave Oxnard (93030) *(P-9684)*
G P Resources, Compton *Also called General Petroleum Corporation (P-8961)*
G P S, Taft *Also called General Production Svc Cal Inc (P-1920)*
G R Helm Inc...D...916 933-9697
5050 Rbert J Mathews Pkwy El Dorado Hills (95762) *(P-14856)*
G S C Ball, Commerce *Also called Grocers Specialty Company (P-8412)*
G S N, Santa Monica *Also called Game Show Network LLC (P-5917)*
G S R, Pleasanton *Also called Global Software Resources Inc (P-16386)*
G T Global Staffing, Los Angeles *Also called Global Staffing Inc (P-14629)*
G W Maintenance Inc (PA)...D...714 541-2211
1101 E 6th St Santa Ana (92701) *(P-7848)*
G W Surfaces (PA)...C...805 642-5004
2432 Palma Dr Ventura (93003) *(P-3523)*
G&H Dental Arts Cushman Dental, Torrance *Also called G & H Dental Arts Inc (P-22168)*
G&K Services Inc...D...916 381-5500
5900 Alder Ave Sacramento (95828) *(P-13606)*

ALPHABETIC

G&K Services LLC ... E ... 925 427-4401
1229 California Ave Pittsburg (94565) ***(P-13607)***
G/M Business Interiors, San Diego *Also called Goforth & Marti* ***(P-6723)***
G2 Direct and Digital ... E ... 415 421-1000
612 Howard St Ste 400 San Francisco (94105) ***(P-15174)***
G2 Software Systems Inc ... C ... 619 222-8025
4025 Hancock St Ste 105 San Diego (92110) ***(P-25697)***
G3 Enterprises, Modesto *Also called United Sttes Intrmdal Svcs LLC* ***(P-5191)***
G3 Enterprises Inc (PA) ... C ... 209 341-7515
502 E Whitmore Ave Modesto (95358) ***(P-5069)***
G3 Enterprises Inc ... C ... 209 341-3441
1300 Camino Diablo Rd Byron (94514) ***(P-5070)***
G3 Enterprises Inc ... D ... 209 341-4045
500 S Santa Rosa Ave Modesto (95354) ***(P-5071)***
G4s Government Services, Irvine *Also called G4s Justice Services LLC* ***(P-16898)***
G4s Justice Services LLC ... C ... 800 589-6003
201 Technology Dr Irvine (92618) ***(P-16898)***
G4s Secure Solutions (usa) ... C ... 661 834-3454
4400 Ashe Rd Ste 206 Bakersfield (93313) ***(P-16651)***
G4s Secure Solutions (usa) ... B ... 323 938-9100
4929 Wilshire Blvd # 601 Los Angeles (90010) ***(P-16652)***
G4s Secure Solutions (usa) ... B ... 951 341-3000
1450 Iowa Ave Riverside (92507) ***(P-16653)***
G4s Secure Solutions (usa) ... C ... 925 543-0008
1 Annabel Ln Ste 208 San Ramon (94583) ***(P-16654)***
G4s Secure Solutions USA Inc ... C ... 619 295-2394
5030 Camino De La Siesta # 404 San Diego (92108) ***(P-16655)***
G4s Secure Solutions USA Inc ... C ... 415 591-0780
200 Pine St Fl 7 San Francisco (94104) ***(P-16656)***
G4s Secure Solutions USA Inc ... C ... 714 939-4900
2300 E Katella Ave # 150 Anaheim (92806) ***(P-16657)***
G4s Secure Solutions USA Inc ... C ... 818 889-1113
5655 Lindero Canyon Rd # 504 Westlake Village (91362) ***(P-16658)***
G5 Global Partners Ix LLC ... D ... 619 291-6500
2151 Hotel Cir S San Diego (92108) ***(P-12595)***
G7 Productivity Systems ... D ... 858 675-1095
16885 W Bernardo Dr # 290 San Diego (92127) ***(P-15688)***
GA Services LLC ... E ... 949 752-6515
1681 Kettering Irvine (92614) ***(P-16374)***
Gable House Inc ... D ... 310 378-2265
22501 Hawthorne Blvd Torrance (90505) ***(P-18491)***
Gable House Bowl, Torrance *Also called Gable House Inc* ***(P-18491)***
Gables of Ojai LLC ... D ... 805 646-1446
701 N Montgomery St Ojai (93023) ***(P-11025)***
Gabriella Foundation ... D ... 213 365-2491
639 S Commwl Ave Ste B Los Angeles (90005) ***(P-18334)***
Gachina Landscape MGT Inc ... B ... 650 853-0400
1130 Obrien Dr Menlo Park (94025) ***(P-844)***
GAF Holdings Inc ... B ... 559 734-3333
1300 E Mineral King Ave Visalia (93292) ***(P-11978)***
GAF Materials, Stockton *Also called Standard Industries Inc* ***(P-6930)***
GAF Materials, Shafter *Also called Standard Industries Inc* ***(P-6931)***
Gafcon Inc (PA) ... D ... 858 875-0010
5960 Cornerstone Ct W # 100 San Diego (92121) ***(P-26866)***
Gahvejian Enterprises Inc ... E ... 559 834-5956
2004 S Temperance Ave Fowler (93625) ***(P-8103)***
Gaia Interactive Inc ... C ... 408 573-8800
2540 N 1st St Ste 101 San Jose (95131) ***(P-5569)***
Gaia Online, San Jose *Also called Gaia Interactive Inc* ***(P-5569)***
Gaithers Family Home ... E ... 559 781-0301
1408 S Newcomb St Porterville (93257) ***(P-21078)***
Gaju Market Corporation ... C ... 213 382-9444
450 S Western Ave Los Angeles (90020) ***(P-9219)***
Galassos Bakery (PA) ... C ... 951 360-1211
10820 San Sevaine Way Mira Loma (91752) ***(P-8794)***
Galaxy Building Systems Inc ... C ... 818 340-6557
23978 Craftsman Rd Calabasas (91302) ***(P-14271)***
Gale Lina Inc ... D ... 909 595-8898
230 S 9th Ave City of Industry (91746) ***(P-8169)***
Gale/Triangle, San Pedro *Also called Performance Team Frt Sys Inc* ***(P-4610)***
Galena Equipment Rental LLC ... E ... 510 638-8100
10700 Bigge St San Leandro (94577) ***(P-14440)***
Galice Inc ... D ... 323 731-8200
30140 Tuttle Ct Tehachapi (93561) ***(P-17179)***
Galkos Construction Inc (PA) ... D ... 714 373-8545
15262 Pipeline Ln Huntington Beach (92649) ***(P-13746)***
Gallagher Bassett, Irvine *Also called Arthur J Gallagher & Co* ***(P-10543)***
Gallagher Construction Svcs, San Francisco *Also called Arthur J Gallagher & Co* ***(P-10545)***
Gallagher Pediatric Therapy, Fullerton *Also called Therapy For Kids Inc* ***(P-20209)***
Gallaher Construction Inc ... E ... 707 535-3200
220 Concourse Blvd Santa Rosa (95403) ***(P-1169)***
Galleano Enterprises Inc ... D ... 951 685-5376
4231 Wineville Ave Mira Loma (91752) ***(P-144)***
Galleher LLC (PA) ... C ... 562 944-8885
9303 Greenleaf Ave Santa Fe Springs (90670) ***(P-6762)***
Galleria Park Associates LLC ... D ... 415 781-3060
191 Sutter St San Francisco (94104) ***(P-12596)***
Galleria Park Hotel, San Francisco *Also called Galleria Park Associates LLC* ***(P-12596)***
Galli Produce Company ... D ... 408 436-6100
1650 Old Bayshore Hwy San Jose (95112) ***(P-8686)***
Gallo Cattle Co A Ltd Partnr ... B ... 209 394-7984
10561 State Highway 140 Atwater (95301) ***(P-414)***
Gallo Sales Company Inc (HQ) ... C ... 510 476-5000
30825 Wiegman Rd Hayward (94544) ***(P-9046)***
Galloway Lucchese Everson ... E ... 925 930-9090
2300 Contra Costa Blvd Walnut Creek (94596) ***(P-23088)***
Gallup Inc ... E ... 949 474-2700
18300 Von Karman Ave Irvine (92612) ***(P-27244)***
Gallup & Stribling Orchids LLC ... E ... 805 684-1998
3450 Via Real Carpinteria (93013) ***(P-260)***
Gallup and Stribling Holdings, Carpinteria *Also called Gallup & Stribling Orchids LLC* ***(P-260)***
Gallup Organization, The, Irvine *Also called Gallup Inc* ***(P-27244)***
Galt Joint Union School Dst ... E ... 209 745-1546
902 Caroline Ave Galt (95632) ***(P-24323)***
Galt Park Recreation, Galt *Also called City of Galt* ***(P-19132)***
Gama Berry Farms LLC ... D ... 805 483-1000
730 S A St Oxnard (93030) ***(P-100)***
Gama Contracting Services Inc ... C ... 626 442-7200
1835 Floradale Ave South El Monte (91733) ***(P-7676)***
Gamboa Service Inc ... D ... 714 966-5325
2116 S Wright St Santa Ana (92705) ***(P-14272)***
Game Show Network LLC (HQ) ... D ... 310 255-6800
2150 Colorado Ave Ste 100 Santa Monica (90404) ***(P-5917)***
Gamefly Inc (PA) ... C ... 310 568-8224
6080 Center Dr Fl 8 Los Angeles (90045) ***(P-16375)***
Gameworks, Los Angeles *Also called Sega Entertainment USA Inc* ***(P-18789)***
Gamma PHI Beta Sorority Inc ... D ... 805 968-4221
890 Camino Pescadero Goleta (93117) ***(P-13475)***
Gamut Construction Company Inc ... D ... 909 948-0500
9340 Santa Anita Ave # 105 Rancho Cucamonga (91730) ***(P-12228)***
Gano Excel (usa) Inc ... D ... 626 338-8081
15439 Dupont Ave Chino (91710) ***(P-8795)***
Gar Enterprises (PA) ... D ... 626 574-1175
418 E Live Oak Ave Arcadia (91006) ***(P-7051)***
Garage Door Specialists, Sacramento *Also called Singley Enterprises* ***(P-6865)***
Garcia Juarez Construction Inc (PA) ... D ... 951 657-3535
6801 Atlantic Ave Long Beach (90805) ***(P-25698)***
Garcia Roofing Inc ... E ... 661 325-5736
201 Mount Vernon Ave Bakersfield (93307) ***(P-3160)***
Garda CL Technical Svcs Inc ... D ... 818 362-7011
15640 Roxford St Sylmar (91342) ***(P-16659)***
Garda CL West Inc ... E ... 909 574-2676
372 S Arrowhead Ave San Bernardino (92408) ***(P-16660)***
Garda CL West Inc (HQ) ... B ... 213 383-3611
1612 W Pico Blvd Los Angeles (90015) ***(P-16661)***
Garda CL West Inc ... D ... 800 883-8305
301 N Lake Ave Ste 600 Pasadena (91101) ***(P-16662)***
Garden City Inc ... A ... 408 244-3333
1887 Matrix Blvd San Jose (95110) ***(P-19177)***
Garden City Casino & Rest, San Jose *Also called Garden City Inc* ***(P-19177)***
GARDEN CITY HEALTHCARE CENTER, Modesto *Also called Fig Holdings LLC* ***(P-20428)***
Garden Court Hotel ... D ... 650 322-9000
520 Cowper St Ste 100 Palo Alto (94301) ***(P-12597)***
Garden Crest Convalesce ... D ... 323 663-8281
909 Lucile Ave Los Angeles (90026) ***(P-20445)***
Garden Crest Rtrment Residence, Los Angeles *Also called Garden Crest Convalesce* ***(P-20445)***
Garden Grove Advanced Imaging ... C ... 310 445-2800
1510 Cotner Ave Los Angeles (90025) ***(P-22087)***
Garden Grove Convales ... C ... 714 638-9470
12882 Shackelford Ln Garden Grove (92841) ***(P-21079)***
GARDEN GROVE HOSPITAL, Garden Grove *Also called Kenneth Corp* ***(P-21531)***
Garden Grove Hospital Med Ctr, Garden Grove *Also called Prime Health Care Svcs Grdn Gr* ***(P-21655)***
Garden Grove Unified Schl Dst ... D ... 714 663-6437
8371 Orangewood Ave Garden Grove (92841) ***(P-24324)***
Garden Medical Offices, Downey *Also called Kaiser Foundation Hospitals* ***(P-19555)***
Garden Terrace Health Care Ctr, Vista *Also called Bent Tree Nursing Center Inc* ***(P-20260)***
Garden View Inc ... E ... 626 303-4043
417 E Huntington Dr Monrovia (91016) ***(P-756)***
Garden View Care Center Inc ... D ... 626 962-7095
14475 Garden View Ln Baldwin Park (91706) ***(P-20446)***
Garden, The, Santa Ana *Also called Alzheimers Care Since 1983* ***(P-22217)***
Gardena Convalescent Center, Santa Fe Springs *Also called B & E Convalescent Center Inc* ***(P-21001)***
Gardena Flores Inc ... D ... 310 323-4570
14165 Purche Ave Gardena (90249) ***(P-20447)***
Gardena Hospital LP ... A ... 310 532-4200
1145 W Redondo Beach Blvd Gardena (90247) ***(P-21425)***
Gardena Medical Offices, Gardena *Also called Kaiser Foundation Hospitals* ***(P-21503)***
Gardena Municipal Bus Lines, Gardena *Also called City of Gardena* ***(P-3643)***
Gardeners Guild Inc ... C ... 415 457-0400
2780 Goodrick Ave Richmond (94801) ***(P-845)***
Gardner Family Care Corp ... C ... 408 935-3906
160 E Virginia St Ste 280 San Jose (95112) ***(P-22579)***
Gardner Family Hlth Netwrk Inc (PA) ... E ... 408 200-2291
1621 Gold St Alviso (95002) ***(P-22580)***
Gardner Logistics, Chino *Also called Gardner Trucking Inc* ***(P-4183)***
Gardner Neurologic Orthopedic ... D ... 310 649-5824
6167 Bristol Pkwy Ste 200 Culver City (90230) ***(P-26867)***
Gardner Pool Company Inc (PA) ... D ... 619 593-8880
801 Gable Way El Cajon (92020) ***(P-3524)***
Gardner Pool Plastering, El Cajon *Also called Gardner Pool Company Inc* ***(P-3524)***
Gardner Trucking Inc ... D ... 909 563-5606
9032 Merrill Ave Chino (91708) ***(P-4183)***
Gardner Trucking Inc (HQ) ... B ... 909 563-5606
1219 E Elm St Ontario (91761) ***(P-4184)***
Garfield Nuerobehavioral Ctr, Oakland *Also called Telecare Corporation* ***(P-21982)***
Garfield Nursing Home Inc ... C ... 510 582-7676
1100 Marina Village Pkwy # 100 Alameda (94501) ***(P-20448)***
Garibaldi Company, Stockton *Also called Mgd Inc* ***(P-11077)***
Garich Inc (PA) ... B ... 858 453-1331
6336 Greenwich Dr Ste A San Diego (92122) ***(P-14624)***

Mergent e-mail: customerrelations@mergent.com
1310
2019 Directory of California
Wholesalers and Services Companies
(P-0000) Products & Services Section entry number
(PA)=Parent Co (HQ)=Headquarters (DH)=Div Headquarters

Garich Inc ....A....951 302-4750
504 E Alvarado St Ste 201 Fallbrook (92028) *(P-14625)*
Garlic Company ....C....661 393-4212
18602 S Zerker Rd Shafter (93263) *(P-23)*
Garment Industry Laundry ....C....323 752-8335
710 W 58th St Los Angeles (90037) *(P-13608)*
Garovibridge, Novato *Also called Johann B Garovi* *(P-1882)*
Garrad Hassan America Inc (HQ) ....D....858 836-3370
9665 Chesapeake Dr # 435 San Diego (92123) *(P-25699)*
Garrett J Gentry Gen Engrg Inc ....D....909 693-3391
1297 W 9th St Upland (91786) *(P-25700)*
Garrick Motors Inc ....C....760 489-2656
559 S Pine St Escondido (92025) *(P-17761)*
Garris Plastering, Orange *Also called Padilla Construction Company* *(P-2936)*
Gartner Inc ....D....310 479-2108
11845 W Olympic Blvd 505w Los Angeles (90064) *(P-26521)*
Gary Cardiff Enterprises Inc ....D....760 568-1403
75255 Sheryl Ave Palm Desert (92211) *(P-3799)*
Gary Lask ....D....310 825-0631
200 Ucla Medical Plz 4 Los Angeles (90095) *(P-19480)*
Gary Mary W Wireless Hlth Inst ....E....858 412-8600
10350 N Torrey Pines Rd La Jolla (92037) *(P-26620)*
Gary R Edwards Inc ....D....619 299-8700
3930 Utah St Ste C San Diego (92104) *(P-17180)*
Gary Steel Division, Santa Fe Springs *Also called Kloeckner Metals Corporation* *(P-7286)*
Garys Construction Inc ....C....760 639-4456
2517 Dos Lomas Fallbrook (92028) *(P-6541)*
GAS COMPANY, THE, Los Angeles *Also called Southern California Gas Co* *(P-6163)*
Gas Transmission Systems Inc ....C....530 893-6711
130 Amber Grove Dr # 134 Chico (95973) *(P-25701)*
Gaslamp Hotel Management Inc ....C....619 234-0977
202 Island Ave San Diego (92101) *(P-12598)*
Gastroenterology Division ....E....415 206-8823
1001 Potrero Ave Ste 1e21 San Francisco (94110) *(P-19481)*
Gat - Arln Ground Support Inc ....C....818 847-9127
2627 N Hollywood Way Burbank (91505) *(P-4991)*
Gat - Arln Ground Support Inc ....B....916 923-2349
6701 Lindbergh Dr Sacramento (95837) *(P-4891)*
Gatan Inc (HQ) ....D....925 463-0200
5794 W Las Positas Blvd Pleasanton (94588) *(P-25702)*
Gate City Beverage Bear Trckg, San Bernardino *Also called Bear Trucking Inc* *(P-4332)*
Gate City Beverage Distrs (PA) ....B....909 799-0281
2505 Steele Rd San Bernardino (92408) *(P-8997)*
Gate City Beverage Distrs ....B....760 775-5483
31315 Plantation Dr Thousand Palms (92276) *(P-8998)*
Gate Five Group LLC ....E....415 339-9500
200 Gate 5 Rd Ste 116 Sausalito (94965) *(P-6763)*
Gate of Heaven Cemetery, Los Altos *Also called Roman Cthlic Bishp of San Jose* *(P-11948)*
Gate Three Healthcare LLC ....C....949 770-3348
24962 Calle Aragon Laguna Hills (92637) *(P-24538)*
Gatehouse Msi LLC ....E....562 623-3000
15511 Carmenita Rd Santa Fe Springs (90670) *(P-3037)*
Gates of Spain Wibel ....E....626 441-3078
2545 Mission St Pasadena (91108) *(P-13659)*
Gateway, Los Angeles *Also called County of Los Angeles* *(P-14108)*
Gateway Auto Auction Group, Fresno *Also called Gateway Auto Sales & Lsg Inc* *(P-6595)*
Gateway Auto Sales & Lsg Inc ....D....800 921-4336
3260 E Annadale Ave Fresno (93725) *(P-6595)*
Gateway Ctr of Monterey Cnty (PA) ....D....831 372-8002
850 Congress Ave Pacific Grove (93950) *(P-24539)*
Gateway Home Realty, Brea *Also called American Financial Network Inc* *(P-9771)*
Gateway Landscape Cnstr Inc ....D....925 875-0000
6735 Sierra Ct Ste A Dublin (94568) *(P-846)*
Gateway Limousine, Burlingame *Also called Amato Industries Incorporated* *(P-3743)*
Gateway Post Acute, Porterville *Also called Valley Careidence Opco LLC* *(P-20849)*
Gateway Security Inc ....A....310 410-0790
5757 W Century Blvd Los Angeles (90045) *(P-16663)*
Gateways Hosp Mental Hlth Ctr ....D....323 644-2026
340 N Madison Ave Los Angeles (90004) *(P-21954)*
Gateways Hosp Mental Hlth Ctr (PA) ....C....323 644-2000
1891 Effie St Los Angeles (90026) *(P-21955)*
GATX Corporation ....D....909 825-3043
20878 Slover St Colton (92324) *(P-5226)*
Gavin De Becker & Associates ....C....818 760-4213
11684 Ventura Blvd # 440 Studio City (91604) *(P-27245)*
Gaw Van Male Smith Myers ....D....707 425-1250
1411 Oliver Rd Ste 300 Fairfield (94534) *(P-23089)*
Gb3, Clovis *Also called George Browns Sports Club* *(P-18603)*
Gbc Concrete Masnry Cnstr Inc ....C....951 245-2355
561 Birch St Lake Elsinore (92530) *(P-2808)*
GBI Tile & Stone Inc (PA) ....E....949 567-1880
5900 Skylab Rd Ste 150 Huntington Beach (92647) *(P-6894)*
Gbp Intermediate Corp (HQ) ....A....424 254-9774
2321 Rosecrans Ave # 3255 El Segundo (90245) *(P-11979)*
Gbp Parent Corp (HQ) ....A....424 254-9774
2321 Rosecrans Ave # 3255 El Segundo (90245) *(P-11980)*
GBS Financial Corp ....D....310 937-0073
904 Manhattan Ave Ste 3 Manhattan Beach (90266) *(P-17181)*
GBS Linens Inc (PA) ....D....714 778-6448
305 N Muller St Anaheim (92801) *(P-13531)*
GBS Party Linens, Anaheim *Also called GBS Linens Inc* *(P-13531)*
GBT Inc ....D....626 854-9338
17358 Railroad St City of Industry (91748) *(P-7052)*
Gc Services Ltd Partnership ....C....626 851-8227
4900 Rivergrade Rd # 210 Irwindale (91706) *(P-14004)*
Gcc, Santa Rosa *Also called Ghilotti Construction Co Inc* *(P-2034)*
Gcccd Auxiliary, El Cajon *Also called Grossmont-Cuyamaca Community* *(P-25170)*

Gccfc 2005-Gg5 Y St Ltd Partnr ....D....916 455-6800
4422 Y St Sacramento (95817) *(P-12599)*
GCI Construction Inc ....E....714 957-0233
1031 Calle Recodo Ste D San Clemente (92673) *(P-1765)*
Gcl Solar Energy Inc ....D....415 362-2601
1 Market Er 00 Steuart Tow San Francisco (94105) *(P-2218)*
Gcl W, Los Angeles *Also called Garda CL West Inc* *(P-16661)*
Gco Inc (PA) ....E....510 786-3333
27750 Industrial Blvd Hayward (94545) *(P-7625)*
Gct Semiconductor Inc (PA) ....C....408 434-6040
2121 Ringwood Ave Ste A San Jose (95131) *(P-7482)*
Gcti, Los Angeles *Also called Gentlecare Transport Inc* *(P-3800)*
Gcu Trucking Inc ....D....209 845-2117
7819 Crane Rd Oakdale (95361) *(P-4185)*
GD Heil Inc ....C....714 687-9100
1031 Segovia Cir Placentia (92870) *(P-3453)*
GD Nielson Construction Inc ....D....707 253-8774
147 Camino Oruga NAPA (94558) *(P-1919)*
Gda Technologies Inc (HQ) ....D....408 753-1191
25 Metro Dr Fl 3 San Jose (95110) *(P-25703)*
Gdf Parent LLC ....D....714 743-7209
1510 1/2 W 228th St Torrance (90501) *(P-17182)*
Gdr Group Inc ....D....949 453-8818
3 Park Plz Ste 1700 Irvine (92614) *(P-16376)*
Gdsa-Lincoln Inc (PA) ....D....916 645-8961
1501 Aviation Blvd Lincoln (95648) *(P-17904)*
GE, Mission Viejo *Also called Swiss RE America Holding Corp* *(P-10146)*
GE Aviation Systems LLC ....C....661 277-7308
295 N Wolfe Ave Bldg 3810 Edwards Afb (93524) *(P-4892)*
GE Digital LLC (HQ) ....B....925 242-6200
2623 Camino Ramon San Ramon (94583) *(P-15689)*
GE Energy, Diamond Bar *Also called Motech Americas LLC* *(P-26420)*
Geary Darling Lessee Inc ....C....415 292-0100
501 Geary St San Francisco (94102) *(P-12600)*
Gebbs Software Intl Inc ....D....201 227-0088
4640 Admiralty Way Fl 9 Marina Del Rey (90292) *(P-16377)*
Geek Squad Inc ....D....805 278-9555
2300 N Rose Ave Oxnard (93036) *(P-16378)*
Geek Squad Inc ....D....800 433-5778
120 Imperial Hwy Fullerton (92835) *(P-16379)*
Geek Squad Inc ....D....800 433-5778
1490 Fitzgerald Dr Pinole (94564) *(P-16380)*
Geek Squad Inc ....D....714 434-0132
901 S Coast Dr Ste F Costa Mesa (92626) *(P-16381)*
Geek Squad Inc ....D....714 938-0380
3741 W Chapman Ave Orange (92868) *(P-16382)*
Gehr Development Corporation (HQ) ....D....323 728-5558
7400 E Slauson Ave Commerce (90040) *(P-10882)*
Gehry Partners LLP ....C....310 482-3000
12541 Beatrice St Los Angeles (90066) *(P-26046)*
Gei Consultants Inc ....D....916 631-4500
2868 Prospect Park Dr # 400 Rancho Cordova (95670) *(P-25704)*
Geico Corporation ....C....707 448-7172
2033 Arden Way Ste C Sacramento (95825) *(P-10633)*
Geico General Insurance Co ....B....858 848-8200
14111 Danielson St Poway (92064) *(P-10634)*
Geil Enterprises Inc (PA) ....C....559 495-3000
1945 N Helm Ave Ste 102 Fresno (93727) *(P-16664)*
Gel Pak LLC ....D....510 576-2220
31398 Huntwood Ave Hayward (94544) *(P-14115)*
Gelfand Rennert & Feldman LLP (PA) ....C....310 553-1707
1880 Century Park E # 1600 Los Angeles (90067) *(P-17183)*
Gels Logistics Inc ....D....909 610-2277
20275 Business Pkwy City of Industry (91789) *(P-5072)*
Gelshmal Enterprises LLC ....E....310 672-9090
945 W Hyde Park Blvd Inglewood (90302) *(P-6943)*
Gem Mortgage, Barstow *Also called Golden Empire Mortgage Inc* *(P-9809)*
Gem Trans Care, Pasadena *Also called Gem Transitional Care Center* *(P-20449)*
Gem Transitional Care Center ....D....626 737-0560
716 S Fair Oaks Ave Pasadena (91105) *(P-20449)*
Gemalto Cogent Inc (HQ) ....D....626 325-9600
639 N Rosemead Blvd Pasadena (91107) *(P-15965)*
Gemini Moving Specialists, Toluca Lake *Also called James B Branch Inc* *(P-4352)*
Gemmm Corp ....D....805 267-2700
587 W Los Angeles Ave Moorpark (93021) *(P-11477)*
Gemmm Corp ....D....818 522-0740
2211 Memory Ln Westlake Village (91361) *(P-11478)*
Gemmm Corp (PA) ....D....805 496-0555
2860 E Thousand Oaks Blvd Thousand Oaks (91362) *(P-11479)*
Gemperle Enterprises ....D....209 667-2651
10218 Lander Ave Turlock (95380) *(P-432)*
Gemperle Farms, Turlock *Also called Gemperle Enterprises* *(P-432)*
Genco, Ontario *Also called Fedex Supply Chain* *(P-4557)*
Gene A Garcia Construction ....E....559 352-6173
1663 E Poppy Hills Dr Fresno (93730) *(P-1170)*
Gene M Accito ....D....530 674-3179
331 Pelican Pl Yuba City (95993) *(P-24)*
Gene Townsend's Auto Body, El Cajon *Also called Eugene N Townsend* *(P-17719)*
Gene Watson Construction A CA ....A....661 763-5254
801 Kern St Taft (93268) *(P-1060)*
Gene Wheeler Farms Inc ....C....661 951-2100
444 W Avenue H6 Lancaster (93534) *(P-344)*
Gene's Cooperage, El Monte *Also called Pacific Coast Drum Company* *(P-7862)*
Genea Energy Partners Inc ....D....714 694-0536
19100 Von Karman Ave # 550 Irvine (92612) *(P-15966)*
Geneohm Sciences Inc ....C....201 847-5824
11085 N Torrey Pines Rd # 210 La Jolla (92037) *(P-26369)*
General Atomics (HQ) ....A....858 455-2810
3550 General Atomics Ct San Diego (92121) *(P-26370)*

ALPHABETIC

Employee Codes: A=Over 500 employees, B=251-500
C=101-250, D=51-100, E=50
2019 Directory of California
Wholesalers and Services Companies
© Mergent Inc. 1-800-342-5647
1311

General Atomics..........D.......858 676-7100
16969 Mesamint St San Diego (92127) ***(P-26371)***
General Atomics..........C.......858 455-4000
4949 Greencraig Ln San Diego (92123) ***(P-26372)***
General Atomics Energy Pdts, San Diego *Also called General Atomics* ***(P-26372)***
General Brands Packing, Sun Valley *Also called Sugar Foods Corporation* ***(P-17491)***
General Coatings Corporation..........C.......909 204-4150
9349 Feron Blvd Rancho Cucamonga (91730) ***(P-2437)***
General Coatings Corporation..........C.......858 587-1277
600 W Freedom Ave Orange (92865) ***(P-2438)***
General Coatings Corporation (PA)..........C.......858 587-1277
6711 Nancy Ridge Dr San Diego (92121) ***(P-2439)***
General Coatings Corporation..........C.......559 495-4004
1220 E North Ave Fresno (93725) ***(P-2440)***
General Contractor, Palm Desert *Also called Cora Constructors Inc* ***(P-25624)***
General Dynamics Advanced Info..........A.......650 966-2000
100 Ferguson Dr Mountain View (94043) ***(P-25705)***
General Dynamics Info Tech Inc..........E.......619 881-8989
1615 Murray Canyon Rd # 600 San Diego (92108) ***(P-16383)***
General Dynmics Mssion Systems..........C.......954 846-3400
250 S Milpitas Blvd Milpitas (95035) ***(P-7053)***
General Electric Company..........B.......909 605-7603
2264 E Avion Ave Ontario (91761) ***(P-17946)***
General Electric Company..........C.......650 725-0516
288 Campus Dr Bldg 14105 Stanford (94305) ***(P-6037)***
General Electric Company..........D.......707 469-8346
428 Ballindine Dr Vacaville (95688) ***(P-2590)***
General Electric Company..........C.......916 286-8020
3100 Zinfandel Dr Ste 255 Rancho Cordova (95670) ***(P-9739)***
General Electric Company..........D.......925 242-6200
2623 Camino Ramon San Ramon (94583) ***(P-15690)***
General Electric Company..........C.......626 359-7988
1303 Bloomdale St Duarte (91010) ***(P-16286)***
General Electric Company..........C.......714 434-4111
2995 Red Hill Ave Ste 100 Costa Mesa (92626) ***(P-9758)***
General Electric Company..........D.......925 602-5950
2120 Diamond Blvd Ste 100 Concord (94520) ***(P-25706)***
General Electric Company..........C.......949 838-3043
17901 Von Karman Ave # 600 Irvine (92614) ***(P-9759)***
General Engineering Wstn Inc (PA)..........D.......714 630-3200
1140 N Red Gum St Anaheim (92806) ***(P-2219)***
General Environmental..........D.......916 351-0980
11855 White Rock Rd Rancho Cordova (95742) ***(P-17184)***
General George W Sliney Basha..........D.......408 296-3423
4839 Rio Vista Ave San Jose (95129) ***(P-25159)***
General Home Medical Sup Inc..........D.......805 449-1559
4607 Lakeview Canyon Rd # 584 Westlake Village (91361) ***(P-7181)***
General Motors LLC..........C.......800 521-7300
9150 Hermosa Ave Rancho Cucamonga (91730) ***(P-4560)***
General Motors LLC..........D.......951 361-6302
11900 Cabernet Dr Dr1 Fontana (92337) ***(P-4561)***
General Networks Corporation..........D.......818 249-1962
3524 Ocean View Blvd Glendale (91208) ***(P-16384)***
General Petroleum Corporation (HQ)..........C.......562 983-7300
19501 S Santa Fe Ave Compton (90221) ***(P-8961)***
General Petroleum Corporation..........D.......209 537-1056
237 E Whitmore Ave Modesto (95358) ***(P-8944)***
General Pool & Spa Supply Inc (PA)..........D.......916 853-2401
11285 Sunco Dr Rancho Cordova (95742) ***(P-7929)***
General Procurement Inc (PA)..........E.......949 679-7960
2601 Walnut Ave Tustin (92780) ***(P-7054)***
General Prod A Cal Ltd Partnr (PA)..........C.......916 441-6431
1330 N B St Sacramento (95811) ***(P-8687)***
General Produce, Vernon *Also called V & L Produce Inc* ***(P-8740)***
General Production Svc Cal Inc..........C.......661 765-5330
1333 Kern St Taft (93268) ***(P-1920)***
General Restaurant Equipment, Los Angeles *Also called South China Sheet Metal Inc* ***(P-2367)***
General Services, Los Angeles *Also called City of Los Angeles* ***(P-14210)***
General Services, Concord *Also called County of Contra Costa* ***(P-14231)***
General Services, Martinez *Also called County of Contra Costa* ***(P-14232)***
General Services, Vernon *Also called City of Los Angeles* ***(P-3951)***
General Services Cal Dept..........C.......916 845-4942
9645 Butterfield Way # 1503 Sacramento (95827) ***(P-14273)***
General Services Cal Dept..........D.......510 622-3101
1515 Clay St Ste 1201 Oakland (94612) ***(P-26047)***
General Services Cal Dept..........D.......213 897-3995
700 N Alameda St Ste 500 Los Angeles (90012) ***(P-26048)***
General Services Cal Dept..........B.......916 657-9960
601 Sequoia Pacific Blvd Sacramento (95811) ***(P-25707)***
General Services Cal Dept..........D.......562 342-7212
4665 Lampson Ave Los Alamitos (90720) ***(P-16137)***
General Services Cal Dept..........B.......916 657-9903
601 Sequoia Pacific Blvd Sacramento (95811) ***(P-25708)***
General Services Cal Dept..........A.......916 445-4566
1304 O St Ste 301 Sacramento (95814) ***(P-14274)***
General Services Cal Dept..........D.......213 897-2241
300 S Spring St Ste 1726 Los Angeles (90013) ***(P-14275)***
General Tool Inc..........D.......949 261-2322
2025 Alton Pkwy Irvine (92606) ***(P-7849)***
General Underground..........C.......714 632-8646
701 W Grove Ave Orange (92865) ***(P-2220)***
Generation Construction Inc..........C.......909 923-2077
15650 El Prado Rd Chino (91710) ***(P-1534)***
Generation Contracting & Emerg..........E.......858 679-9928
13685 Stowe Dr Ste B Poway (92064) ***(P-1171)***
Genesis Health Care, Orange *Also called Prospect Medical Systems Inc* ***(P-27002)***
Genesis Healthcare Corporation..........D.......310 391-8266
3951 East Blvd Los Angeles (90066) ***(P-20450)***
Genesis Healthcare Corporation..........E.......909 622-1069
1425 Laurel Ave Pomona (91768) ***(P-20451)***
Genesis Healthcare Corporation..........C.......909 628-6024
2335 S Towne Ave Pomona (91766) ***(P-20452)***
Genesis Healthcare Partners PC..........C.......619 230-0400
2466 1st Ave Ste B San Diego (92101) ***(P-22581)***
Genesis Healthcare Partners PC (PA)..........C.......858 810-7200
3444 Kearny Villa Rd San Diego (92123) ***(P-22582)***
Genesis Home Health Inc..........E.......805 520-7100
1687 Erringer Rd Ste 202 Simi Valley (93065) ***(P-14857)***
Genesis Logistics Inc..........D.......510 476-0790
4013 Whipple Rd Union City (94587) ***(P-4562)***
Genesis Tech Partners LLC..........C.......800 950-2647
21540 Plummer St Ste A Chatsworth (91311) ***(P-17947)***
Genesys Telecom Labs, Daly City *Also called Genesys Telecom Labs Inc* ***(P-15691)***
Genesys Telecom Labs Inc (HQ)..........B.......650 466-1100
2001 Junipero Serra Blvd Daly City (94014) ***(P-15691)***
Genetic Dsase Screning Program, Richmond *Also called Public Health California Dept* ***(P-19808)***
Genex (HQ)..........C.......424 672-9500
800 Corporate Pointe # 100 Culver City (90230) ***(P-15175)***
Gengo Inc..........E.......650 585-4390
307 2nd Ave San Mateo (94401) ***(P-17185)***
Genium Inc..........C.......415 240-0442
585 Broadway St Redwood City (94063) ***(P-15176)***
Genius Products Inc..........C.......310 453-1222
3301 Expo Blvd Ste 100 Santa Monica (90404) ***(P-8032)***
Genmark Automation (HQ)..........D.......510 897-3400
46723 Lakeview Blvd Fremont (94538) ***(P-7753)***
Genmark Diagnostics Inc (PA)..........C.......760 448-4300
5964 La Place Ct Ste 100 Carlsbad (92008) ***(P-22088)***
Genomedx Biosciences Corp..........D.......888 975-4540
10355 Science Center Dr # 240 San Diego (92121) ***(P-22089)***
Genomic Health Inc (PA)..........C.......650 556-9300
301 Penobscot Dr Redwood City (94063) ***(P-22090)***
Genomic Health Inc..........B.......650 269-0545
101 University Ave Palo Alto (94301) ***(P-22091)***
Genomic Health Inc..........B.......650 556-9300
101 Galveston Dr Redwood City (94063) ***(P-22092)***
Genomics Inst. O, San Diego *Also called Novartis Institut* ***(P-26643)***
Genoptix Inc (PA)..........C.......760 268-6200
2131 Faraday Ave Carlsbad (92008) ***(P-22093)***
Genoptix Inc..........B.......760 268-6200
2110 Rutherford Rd Carlsbad (92008) ***(P-22094)***
Genoptix Mdcial Lab A Novartis, Carlsbad *Also called Genoptix Inc* ***(P-22094)***
Genoptix Medical Laboratory, Carlsbad *Also called Genoptix Inc* ***(P-22093)***
Genpact LLC..........E.......203 690-9308
3300 Hillview Ave Palo Alto (94304) ***(P-27736)***
Genpact Mortgage Services Inc (HQ)..........D.......949 417-5131
15420 Laguna Canyon Rd Irvine (92618) ***(P-9807)***
Gensler and Associates, Los Angeles *Also called M Arthur Gensler Jr Assoc Inc* ***(P-26090)***
Genstar Capital LP..........A.......415 834-2350
4 Embarcadero Ctr # 1500 San Francisco (94111) ***(P-9955)***
Gentek Media Inc..........E.......909 476-3818
13900 Sycamore Way Chino (91710) ***(P-7055)***
Gentex Corporation..........D.......909 481-7667
9859 7th St Rancho Cucamonga (91730) ***(P-26373)***
Gentle Giant Studios Inc..........D.......818 504-3555
7511 N San Fernando Rd Burbank (91505) ***(P-17186)***
Gentlecare Transport Inc..........D.......323 662-8777
3539 Casitas Ave Los Angeles (90039) ***(P-3800)***
Gentry Associates LLC..........D.......619 296-0057
525 Spruce St San Diego (92103) ***(P-12601)***
Gentry Group LLC..........E.......310 968-5399
555 N Rockingham Ave Los Angeles (90049) ***(P-18435)***
Genuent Usa LLC..........D.......916 772-3700
2240 Douglas Blvd Ste 100 Roseville (95661) ***(P-15177)***
Genuine Parts Distributors..........D.......562 692-9034
3200 E Guasti Rd Ste 100 Ontario (91761) ***(P-6642)***
Genzyme Corporation..........C.......310 482-5000
2440 S Sepulveda Blvd # 100 Los Angeles (90064) ***(P-26703)***
Geo Group Inc..........D.......760 246-1171
10400 Rancho Rd Adelanto (92301) ***(P-26868)***
Geo Group Inc..........B.......661 763-2510
1500 Cadet Rd Taft (93268) ***(P-27590)***
Geo Group Inc..........C.......661 792-2731
611 Frontage Rd Mc Farland (93250) ***(P-26869)***
Geo Mmi Engineering, Oakland *Also called Geosyntec Consultants Inc* ***(P-25711)***
Geo Telecom..........E.......949 362-0921
252 Woodcrest Ln Aliso Viejo (92656) ***(P-1921)***
Geocities, Santa Clara *Also called Altaba Inc* ***(P-5446)***
Geocon Consultants Inc (PA)..........D.......858 558-6900
6960 Flanders Dr San Diego (92121) ***(P-27737)***
Geocon Incorporated..........D.......858 558-6900
6960 Flanders Dr San Diego (92121) ***(P-25709)***
Geodis Logistics LLC..........D.......310 604-8185
301 W Walnut St Compton (90220) ***(P-4563)***
Geodis Logistics LLC..........D.......909 801-3145
2301 W San Bernardino Ave Redlands (92374) ***(P-4564)***
Geodis Logistics LLC..........D.......909 240-6298
1710 W Base Line Rd Rialto (92376) ***(P-4565)***
Geodis Logistics LLC..........D.......951 571-2481
3285 De Forest Cir Mira Loma (91752) ***(P-4566)***
Geodis Wilson Usa Inc..........C.......650 692-9850
229 Littlefield Ave Ste 1 South San Francisco (94080) ***(P-5073)***
Geographic Expeditions Inc..........D.......415 922-0448
1008 General Kennedy Ave # 3 San Francisco (94129) ***(P-4936)***
Geological Survey US Dept..........D.......650 329-5229
345 Middlefield Rd Menlo Park (94025) ***(P-26374)***

Georg Fischer LLC (HQ)....D....714 731-8800
9271 Jeronimo Rd Irvine (92618) *(P-7274)*
Georg Fischer Piping, Irvine *Also called Georg Fischer LLC (P-7274)*
George Amaral Ranches Inc....D....831 679-2977
25453 Iverson Rd Gonzales (93926) *(P-56)*
George Brazil Plbg Htg & AC, Culver City *Also called L A Services Inc (P-2253)*
George Brazil Plbg Htg & AC, Santa Ana *Also called Orange County Services Inc (P-2299)*
George Browns Sports Club (PA)....D....559 297-8656
1155 N Fowler Ave Ste 500 Clovis (93611) *(P-18603)*
George Chiala Farms Inc....C....408 778-0562
15500 Hill Rd Morgan Hill (95037) *(P-57)*
George E Masker Inc....D....510 568-1206
7699 Edgewater Dr Oakland (94621) *(P-2441)*
George Fasching....E....626 446-0654
425 N Santa Anita Ave Arcadia (91006) *(P-17815)*
George G Sharp Inc....D....619 425-4211
1065 Bay Blvd Ste D Chula Vista (91911) *(P-25710)*
George L Mee Memorial Hospital, King City *Also called Southern Mnterey Cnty Mem Hosp (P-21768)*
George M Rajacich MD PC....E....818 787-2020
14914 Sherman Way Van Nuys (91405) *(P-19482)*
George M Robinson & Co (PA)....D....510 632-7017
1461 Atteberry Ln San Jose (95131) *(P-2221)*
George P Johnson Company....C....650 226-0600
999 Skyway Rd Ste 300 San Carlos (94070) *(P-9220)*
George Richard....D....619 805-6751
P.O. Box 712002 Santee (92072) *(P-1400)*
Georges Yellow Taxi Cab Co, Santa Rosa *Also called Neese Inc (P-3867)*
Georgia Atkison Snf LLC....C....626 444-2535
3825 Durfee Ave El Monte (91732) *(P-20453)*
Georgia-Pacific LLC....C....559 651-5500
9525 W Nicholas Ct Visalia (93291) *(P-8104)*
Georgia-Pacific LLC....B....562 861-6226
9206 Santa Fe Springs Rd Santa Fe Springs (90670) *(P-8105)*
Georgia-Pacific LLC....D....562 926-8888
15500 Valley View Ave La Mirada (90638) *(P-7977)*
Georgian Hotel....D....310 395-9945
1415 Ocean Ave Santa Monica (90401) *(P-12602)*
Geosyntec Consultants Inc....D....714 969-0800
2100 Main St Ste 150 Huntington Beach (92648) *(P-25160)*
Geosyntec Consultants Inc....E....510 836-3034
1111 Broadway Fl 6th Oakland (94607) *(P-25711)*
Geovera Specialty Insurance Co....D....707 863-3700
1455 Oliver Rd Fairfield (94534) *(P-10635)*
Gerawan Farming Partners Inc....B....559 787-8780
15749 E Ventura Ave Sanger (93657) *(P-462)*
Gerber Ambulance Company Inc....C....310 542-6464
19801 Mariner Ave Torrance (90503) *(P-3801)*
Gerber Ambulance Service, Torrance *Also called Gerber Ambulance Company Inc (P-3801)*
Gerdau Reinforcing Steel (HQ)....E....858 737-7700
3880 Murphy Canyon Rd # 100 San Diego (92123) *(P-1401)*
Gerdau Reinforcing Steel....D....909 713-1130
5425 Industrial Pkwy San Bernardino (92407) *(P-7275)*
Geri Care Inc....D....310 320-0961
21521 S Vermont Ave Torrance (90502) *(P-20454)*
Geri-Care II Inc....C....310 328-0812
22035 S Vermont Ave Torrance (90502) *(P-21080)*
Gersh Agency Inc (PA)....D....310 274-6611
9465 Wilshire Blvd Fl 6 Beverly Hills (90212) *(P-18368)*
Gerson Bakar & Associates, Palo Alto *Also called Oak Creek Apartments (P-11086)*
Gerson Baker & Associates....D....650 756-0959
333 Park Plaza Dr Ofc Daly City (94015) *(P-11026)*
Gerwend Enterprises Inc....C....619 254-5018
2952 Market St San Diego (92102) *(P-27591)*
Ges, Chula Vista *Also called Global Exprnce Specialists Inc (P-17193)*
Get Heal Inc....D....310 528-4957
528 Palisades Dr Ste 176 Pacific Palisades (90272) *(P-14858)*
Get Tested Coachella Valley, Palm Springs *Also called Desert Aids Project (P-23767)*
Get-A-Lift Handicap Bus Trnsp, Bakersfield *Also called Golden Empire Transit District (P-3658)*
Getaround Inc (PA)....D....866 438-2768
1177 Harrison St San Francisco (94103) *(P-17638)*
Getinsured.com, Mountain View *Also called Vimo Inc (P-27901)*
Getmedlegal, San Dimas *Also called Legal Solutions Holdings Inc (P-23199)*
Getright Ventures Inc....D....510 402-4816
3675 Rocky Shore Ct Vallejo (94591) *(P-9884)*
Gettler-Ryan Inc (PA)....D....925 551-7555
6805 Sierra Ct Ste G Dublin (94568) *(P-3525)*
Getty Conservation Institute, Los Angeles *Also called J Paul Getty Trust (P-26534)*
Getty Images Inc....D....323 202-4200
6300 Wilshire Blvd # 1600 Los Angeles (90048) *(P-17187)*
Gettyone Image Bank, Los Angeles *Also called Getty Images Inc (P-17187)*
GF Carneros Tenant LLC....E....707 299-4900
4048 Sonoma Hwy NAPA (94559) *(P-13660)*
Gfk Custom Research LLC....D....415 398-2812
360 Pine St Fl 6 San Francisco (94104) *(P-26522)*
Gfk Custom Research LLC....C....310 527-2100
879 W 190th St Ste 390 Gardena (90248) *(P-26523)*
Gfp Oceanside Block 21 LLC....D....760 722-1003
110 N Myers St Oceanside (92054) *(P-12603)*
Ggec America Inc....D....714 750-2280
20450 Stevens Creek Blvd # 220 Cupertino (95014) *(P-7483)*
Ggis Insurance Services Inc....C....818 553-2110
600 N Brand Blvd Ste 300 Glendale (91203) *(P-10636)*
Ggwh LLC....E....310 786-1700
9440 Santa Monica Blvd # 610 Beverly Hills (90210) *(P-12604)*
Ghazal & Sons Inc (PA)....D....619 474-6677
3020 Hoover Ave National City (91950) *(P-8106)*
Ghc of Lompoc LLC....C....805 735-4010
1428 W North Ave Lompoc (93436) *(P-22583)*
Ghc of Sunnyvale LLC....C....408 738-4880
797 E Fremont Ave Sunnyvale (94087) *(P-21081)*
Ghd Inc....E....707 443-8326
718 3rd St Eureka (95501) *(P-25712)*
Ghd Inc....D....707 523-1010
2235 Mercury Way Ste 150 Santa Rosa (95407) *(P-25713)*
Ghg Properties LLC....D....562 945-8511
7320 Greenleaf Ave Whittier (90602) *(P-12605)*
Ghilotti Bros Inc....B....415 454-7011
525 Jacoby St San Rafael (94901) *(P-1766)*
Ghilotti Construction Co Inc....C....707 556-9145
600 S Napa Junction Rd American Canyon (94503) *(P-1767)*
Ghilotti Construction Co Inc (PA)....C....707 585-1221
246 Ghillotti Ave Santa Rosa (95407) *(P-2034)*
Ghio Seafood Products, La Mesa *Also called Anthonys Fish Grotto (P-8569)*
Ghossain & Truelock Entps Inc....D....951 781-9345
783 Palmyrita Ave Ste A Riverside (92507) *(P-14276)*
Ghost Management Group LLC....C....949 870-1400
41 Discovery Irvine (92618) *(P-13946)*
GI GP IV LLC (PA)....E....415 688-4800
188 The Embarcadero # 700 San Francisco (94105) *(P-9956)*
GI Industries....D....805 522-2150
195 W Los Angeles Ave Simi Valley (93065) *(P-6402)*
GI Partners, San Francisco *Also called Global Innovation Partners LLC (P-17194)*
GI Partners, San Francisco *Also called GI GP IV LLC (P-9956)*
Giampolini & Co....C....415 673-1236
1482 67th St Emeryville (94608) *(P-2442)*
Giampolini/Courtney, Emeryville *Also called Giampolini & Co (P-2442)*
Giannas Baking Company....D....831 633-3700
11165 Commercial Pkwy Castroville (95012) *(P-8796)*
Giant Bicycle Inc (HQ)....D....805 267-4600
3587 Old Conejo Rd Newbury Park (91320) *(P-7930)*
Giant Creative Strategy Llc....C....415 655-5200
1700 Montgomery St # 485 San Francisco (94111) *(P-13833)*
Giant Sport Paintball Park, Bellflower *Also called Hollywood Sports Park LLC (P-17224)*
Giarretto Institute....E....408 453-7616
232 E Gish Rd San Jose (95112) *(P-23821)*
Gibbs Giden Locher....D....310 552-3400
1880 Century Park E # 1200 Los Angeles (90067) *(P-23090)*
Gibbs & Associates, Moorpark *Also called Cimatron Gibbs LLC (P-15060)*
Gibbs International Inc (PA)....C....805 485-0551
2201 Ventura Blvd Oxnard (93036) *(P-17762)*
Gibbs International Truck Ctrs, Oxnard *Also called Gibbs International Inc (P-17762)*
Gibralter Convalescent Hosp....D....626 443-9425
2720 Nevada Ave El Monte (91733) *(P-21082)*
Gibson Dunn & Crutcher LLP....D....650 849-5300
1881 Page Mill Rd Palo Alto (94304) *(P-23091)*
Gibson Dunn & Crutcher LLP....C....949 451-3800
3161 Michelson Dr # 1200 Irvine (92612) *(P-23092)*
Gibson Dunn & Crutcher LLP (PA)....B....213 229-7000
333 S Grand Ave Ste 4600 Los Angeles (90071) *(P-23093)*
Gibson Dunn & Crutcher LLP....D....310 552-8500
2029 Century Park E # 4000 Los Angeles (90067) *(P-23094)*
Gibson Dunn & Crutcher LLP....C....415 393-8200
555 Mission St Ste 3000 San Francisco (94105) *(P-23095)*
Gibson Outlet, Commerce *Also called Gibson Overseas Inc (P-6764)*
Gibson Overseas Inc....A....323 832-8900
2410 Yates Ave Commerce (90040) *(P-6764)*
Gic Real Estate Inc (HQ)....D....415 229-1800
1 Bush St Ste 1100 San Francisco (94104) *(P-11480)*
Gico Management....D....209 599-7131
23073 S Frederick Rd Ripon (95366) *(P-8562)*
Gieg Chevron LLC....D....831 755-8000
905 Abbott St 945 Salinas (93901) *(P-17816)*
Gierahn Dry Wall Inc....E....661 257-7900
28490 Westinghouse Pl # 150 Santa Clarita (91355) *(P-2888)*
Giga Omni Media Inc....D....415 974-6355
1613a Lyon St San Francisco (94115) *(P-16955)*
Gigabyte Technology, City of Industry *Also called GBT Inc (P-7052)*
Gigamon Inc (HQ)....C....408 831-4000
3300 Olcott St Santa Clara (95054) *(P-15692)*
Gigsurf Inc....B....415 894-2445
217 Dore St San Francisco (94103) *(P-14626)*
Gigya Inc (HQ)....D....650 353-7230
2513 E Char Rd Ste 200 Mountain View (94043) *(P-15178)*
Gilardi & Co LLC....D....415 461-0410
3301 Kerner Blvd Ste 100 San Rafael (94901) *(P-26870)*
Gilbane Aecom JV....D....925 946-3100
1655 Grant St Fl 12 Concord (94520) *(P-27592)*
Gilbane Building Company....D....408 660-4400
1798 Tech Dr Ste 120 San Jose (95110) *(P-26871)*
Gilbane Construction, San Jose *Also called Gilbane Building Company (P-26871)*
Gilbane Federal (HQ)....C....925 946-3100
1655 Grant St Fl 12 Concord (94520) *(P-25714)*
Gilbane Smcc LLC....D....925 946-3100
1655 Grant St 12f Concord (94520) *(P-1535)*
Gilbert Klly Crwley Jnnett LLP (PA)....D....213 615-7000
550 S Hope St Ste 2200 Los Angeles (90071) *(P-23096)*
Gilbert Service Corp....C....909 393-7575
6725 Kimball Ave Chino (91708) *(P-4347)*
Gilbert West, Chino *Also called Gilbert Service Corp (P-4347)*
Gilkey Farms Inc....D....559 992-2136
2411 Whitley Ave Corcoran (93212) *(P-12)*
Gill Transport LLC....B....805 240-1979
1051 Pacific Ave Oxnard (93030) *(P-4186)*
Gillette Citrus Company....D....559 626-4236
10175 S Anchor Ave Dinuba (93618) *(P-518)*

ALPHABETIC

Employee Codes: A=Over 500 employees, B=251-500
C=101-250, D=51-100, E=50
2019 Directory of California
Wholesalers and Services Companies
© Mergent Inc. 1-800-342-5647
1313

Gilliam & Sons Inc..........E.......661 589-0913
9831 Rosedale Hwy Bakersfield (93312) ***(P-3427)***

Gills Onions LLC..........D.......805 240-1983
1051 Pacific Ave Oxnard (93030) ***(P-8688)***

Gilroy Fitness Inc (PA)..........E.......408 848-1234
8540 Church St Gilroy (95020) ***(P-18604)***

Gilroy Gardens Family Theme Pk..........C.......408 840-7100
3050 Hecker Pass Rd Gilroy (95020) ***(P-18801)***

Gilroy Health & Rehab Ctr, Gilroy *Also called Mariner Health Care Inc* ***(P-20612)***

Gilroy Health and Fitness, Gilroy *Also called Gilroy Fitness Inc* ***(P-18604)***

Gilroy Health Care, Gilroy *Also called Covenant Care California LLC* ***(P-20349)***

Gils Distributing Service (PA)..........C.......213 627-0539
718 E 8th St Los Angeles (90021) ***(P-13973)***

Gilton Resource Recovery..........D.......209 527-3781
755 S Yosemite Ave Oakdale (95361) ***(P-6403)***

Gilton Solid Waste MGT Inc..........C.......209 527-3781
755 S Yosemite Ave Oakdale (95361) ***(P-6404)***

Gina B Ltd Inc..........D.......310 366-7926
1601 W 134th St Gardena (90249) ***(P-6765)***

Gina B Showroom, Gardena *Also called Gina B Ltd Inc* ***(P-6765)***

Gino Rinaldi Inc..........D.......831 761-0195
51 Fremont St Royal Oaks (95076) ***(P-2998)***

Gino/Giuseppe Inc..........C.......209 358-0556
700 Enterprise Ct Ste A Atwater (95301) ***(P-3256)***

Ginzton Laboratory, Stanford *Also called Leland Stanford Junior Univ* ***(P-26634)***

Giovannetti Equipment Sales, Woodland *Also called Half Moon Fruit & Produce Co* ***(P-5)***

Gipson Hoffman & Pancione A..........D.......310 556-4660
1901 Avenue Of The Stars # 1100 Los Angeles (90067) ***(P-23097)***

Girardi & Keese (PA)..........D.......213 977-0211
1126 Wilshire Blvd Los Angeles (90017) ***(P-23098)***

Girardi and Keefe..........D.......213 489-5330
1126 Wilshire Blvd Los Angeles (90017) ***(P-10883)***

Girl Scouts Heart Central Cal..........C.......916 452-9181
6601 Elvas Ave Sacramento (95819) ***(P-25161)***

Girl Scouts Northern Cal (PA)..........D.......510 562-8470
1650 Harbor Bay Pkwy # 100 Alameda (94502) ***(P-25162)***

Girl Scts Sn Diego-Imprl Cncl (PA)..........C.......619 610-0751
1231 Upas St San Diego (92103) ***(P-25163)***

Girl Scuts Greater Los Angeles (PA)..........C.......626 677-2200
801 S Grand Ave Ste 300 Los Angeles (90017) ***(P-25164)***

Girl Scuts San Grgonio Council (PA)..........D.......909 307-6555
1751 Plum Ln Redlands (92374) ***(P-25165)***

Girls and Boys Club Grdn Grove, Garden Grove *Also called Boys Grls Clubs Grdn Grove Inc* ***(P-25115)***

GIRLS REPUBLIC, Chino Hills *Also called Boys Republic* ***(P-24438)***

Giroux Glass Inc (PA)..........C.......213 747-7406
850 W Wash Blvd Ste 200 Los Angeles (90015) ***(P-3405)***

Giti Tire (usa) Ltd (HQ)..........D.......909 527-8800
10404 6th St Rancho Cucamonga (91730) ***(P-6691)***

Giumarra Bros Fruit Co Inc (PA)..........D.......213 627-2900
1601 E Olympic Blvd # 408 Los Angeles (90021) ***(P-8689)***

Giumarra Companies, Escondido *Also called Rio Vista Ventures LLC* ***(P-8448)***

Giumarra Company, The, Reedley *Also called Rio Vista Ventures LLC* ***(P-8449)***

Giumarra Farms Inc..........D.......661 395-7000
11220 Edison Hwy Edison (93220) ***(P-18)***

Giumarra International Berry, Los Angeles *Also called Giumarra Bros Fruit Co Inc* ***(P-8689)***

Giumarra Vineyards Corporation..........D.......661 395-7071
11220 Edison Hwy Bakersfield (93307) ***(P-145)***

Giumarra Vineyards Corporation (PA)..........B.......661 395-7000
11220 Edison Hwy Edison (93220) ***(P-146)***

Giusti Farms LLC..........E.......650 726-9221
1800 Higgins Canyon Rd Half Moon Bay (94019) ***(P-58)***

Giva Inc..........D.......408 260-9000
1030 E El Camino Real Sunnyvale (94087) ***(P-15179)***

Give Something Back Inc (PA)..........D.......800 261-2619
7730 Pardee Ln Ste A Oakland (94621) ***(P-8081)***

Give Something Back Off Sups, Oakland *Also called Give Something Back Inc* ***(P-8081)***

Givens Farms, Goleta *Also called Givens John* ***(P-59)***

Givens John..........D.......805 964-4477
1133 N Fairview Ave Goleta (93117) ***(P-59)***

GK Management Co Inc (PA)..........C.......310 204-2050
5150 Overland Ave Culver City (90230) ***(P-11481)***

GK Management Co Inc..........C.......310 204-2050
5150 Overland Ave Culver City (90230) ***(P-11482)***

GK Management Co Inc..........E.......619 437-1777
299 Prospect Pl Coronado (92118) ***(P-11483)***

GK Management Co Inc..........D.......818 705-8834
6540 Wilbur Ave Reseda (91335) ***(P-11484)***

GK Management Co Inc..........D.......310 836-1812
3975 Overland Ave Culver City (90232) ***(P-11027)***

Gkk Corporation..........D.......619 398-0215
1775 Hancock St Ste 150 San Diego (92110) ***(P-26049)***

Gkk Corporation (PA)..........D.......949 250-1500
2355 Main St Ste 220 Irvine (92614) ***(P-26050)***

Gkkworks, Irvine *Also called Gkk Corporation* ***(P-26050)***

GL, San Diego *Also called Garrad Hassan America Inc* ***(P-25699)***

GL Nemirow Inc..........D.......818 562-9433
2550 N Hollywood Way Burbank (91505) ***(P-13834)***

GLad Entertainment Inc (PA)..........D.......559 292-9000
4055 N Chestnut Ave Fresno (93726) ***(P-19178)***

Glad I'M Not Driving.com, Rialto *Also called Ptr Group Inc* ***(P-27006)***

Glad-A-Way Gardens Inc..........C.......805 938-0569
2669 E Clark Ave Santa Maria (93455) ***(P-261)***

Gladiator Security Services, Ontario *Also called Mazar Corp* ***(P-16729)***

Gladiolus Holdings LLC..........D.......530 622-3400
1040 Marshall Way Placerville (95667) ***(P-20455)***

Glamour Industries Co..........B.......323 728-2999
2220 Gaspar Ave Commerce (90040) ***(P-8170)***

Glaser Weil Fink Jacobs (PA)..........C.......310 553-3000
10250 Constellation Blvd # 1900 Los Angeles (90067) ***(P-23099)***

Glaspy & Glaspy A Prof Corp..........E.......408 279-8844
100 Pringle Ave Ste 750 Walnut Creek (94596) ***(P-23100)***

Glass Lewis & Co LLC (HQ)..........D.......415 678-4110
255 California St # 1100 San Francisco (94111) ***(P-26524)***

Glass Fab Tempering Sv, Tracy *Also called Glassfab Tempering Svcs Inc* ***(P-27738)***

Glass Pak Inc..........D.......707 207-0400
5825 Old School Rd Pleasanton (94588) ***(P-5208)***

Glassfab Tempering Svcs Inc (PA)..........D.......209 229-1060
1448 Mariani Ct Tracy (95376) ***(P-27738)***

Glaxosmithkline LLC..........E.......858 260-5900
3366 N Torrey Pines Ct La Jolla (92037) ***(P-8171)***

Glaza, Los Angeles *Also called Greater Los Angeles Zoo Assn* ***(P-24785)***

Glen Alpine Building Svcs Inc..........D.......510 582-7400
24685 Oneil Ave Hayward (94544) ***(P-14277)***

Glen Annie Golf Club..........D.......805 968-6400
405 Glen Annie Rd Goleta (93117) ***(P-18715)***

Glen Beverly Laboratories Inc..........D.......714 848-5777
7711 Center Ave Ste 100 Huntington Beach (92647) ***(P-25016)***

Glenborough LLC (PA)..........D.......650 343-9300
400 S El Camino Real # 1100 San Mateo (94402) ***(P-11485)***

Glendale Adventist Medical Ctr..........E.......818 409-8379
281 Harvey Dr Unit B Glendale (91206) ***(P-22301)***

Glendale Adventist Medical Ctr (HQ)..........A.......818 409-8000
1509 Wilson Ter Glendale (91206) ***(P-21426)***

Glendale Associates Ltd..........D.......818 246-6737
100 W Broadway Ste 100 # 100 Glendale (91210) ***(P-10884)***

Glendale Eye Medical Group..........D.......818 956-1010
500 N Cntl Ave Ste 400 Glendale (91203) ***(P-19483)***

Glendale Eye Medical Group (PA)..........D.......818 956-1010
607 N Central Ave Ste 203 Glendale (91203) ***(P-19484)***

Glendale Healthcare Center..........D.......818 246-5516
1208 S Central Ave Glendale (91204) ***(P-20456)***

Glendale Medical Offices, Glendale *Also called Kaiser Foundation Hospitals* ***(P-19601)***

Glendale Orange St Med Offs, Glendale *Also called Kaiser Foundation Hospitals* ***(P-19562)***

Glendale Super-Sport Club, Glendale *Also called 24 Hour Fitness Usa Inc* ***(P-18559)***

Glendale Water & Power, Glendale *Also called City of Glendale* ***(P-6017)***

Glendale YMCA Swim School, Glendale *Also called Young Mens Chrstn Assoc Gndl* ***(P-25352)***

Glendora Country Club..........D.......626 335-4051
2400 Country Club Dr Glendora (91741) ***(P-18928)***

Glenhaven Healthcare LLC..........D.......818 240-6720
212 W Chevy Chase Dr Glendale (91204) ***(P-22807)***

Glenn A Rick Engrg & Dev Co (PA)..........C.......619 291-0708
5620 Friars Rd San Diego (92110) ***(P-25715)***

Glenn Building Services Inc..........D.......626 398-8000
1148 N Lake Ave Apt 1 Pasadena (91104) ***(P-14278)***

Glenn Cnty Humn Resource Agcy..........C.......530 934-6510
420 E Laurel St Willows (95988) ***(P-24185)***

Glenn Cnty Plg Pub Works Agcy..........D.......530 934-6541
777 N Colusa St Willows (95988) ***(P-1768)***

Glenn County Health Svcs Agcy, Willows *Also called County of Glenn* ***(P-22770)***

Glenn County Humn Resorce Agcy, Willows *Also called County of Glenn* ***(P-23643)***

Glenn County Office Education..........D.......530 865-1145
676 E Walker St Fl 2 Orland (95963) ***(P-24325)***

Glenn E Porter..........E.......661 615-1500
3955 Coffee Rd Bakersfield (93308) ***(P-10356)***

Glenn E Thomas Company Inc..........D.......562 426-5111
2100 E Spring St Long Beach (90755) ***(P-17763)***

GLENN E THOMAS DODGE CHRIYSLAR, Long Beach *Also called Glenn E Thomas Company Inc* ***(P-17763)***

Glenn Medical Center Inc..........D.......530 934-4681
1133 W Sycamore St Willows (95988) ***(P-21427)***

Glenn-Colusa Irrigation Dst (PA)..........D.......530 934-8881
344 E Laurel St Willows (95988) ***(P-6555)***

Glenoaks Convalescent Hosp LP..........D.......818 240-4300
409 W Glenoaks Blvd Glendale (91202) ***(P-21428)***

Glenrock Group..........D.......408 323-9900
1000 Old Quarry Rd San Jose (95123) ***(P-18929)***

Glentrans, Glendale *Also called Hemodialysis Inc* ***(P-22477)***

Glenview Assisted Living LLP..........E.......760 704-6800
1950 Calle Barcelona Carlsbad (92009) ***(P-22808)***

Glenwood Care Center, Oxnard *Also called Glenwood Corporation* ***(P-20457)***

Glenwood Corporation..........D.......805 983-0305
1300 N C St Oxnard (93030) ***(P-20457)***

Glenwood Gardens..........B.......661 587-0221
350 Calloway Dr Unit A1 Bakersfield (93312) ***(P-20458)***

Glenwood Village Cmnty Assn..........D.......949 855-1800
26840 Aliso Viejo Pkwy # 100 Aliso Viejo (92656) ***(P-25166)***

Gless Ranch Inc (PA)..........E.......951 780-8458
18541 Van Buren Blvd Riverside (92508) ***(P-693)***

Glidewell Laboratories, Newport Beach *Also called James R Glidewell Dental* ***(P-22170)***

Glint Inc..........D.......650 817-7240
1100 Island Dr Ste 101 Redwood City (94065) ***(P-16138)***

Global 360 Inc..........D.......510 263-4800
1080 Marina Village Pkwy # 300 Alameda (94501) ***(P-26872)***

Global Accents Inc..........C.......310 639-2600
19808 Normandie Ave Torrance (90502) ***(P-6766)***

Global Ascent Inc..........E.......714 930-6860
36 Waterworks Way Irvine (92618) ***(P-17188)***

Global Asylum Incorporated..........E.......323 850-1214
440 W Los Feliz Rd Glendale (91204) ***(P-18056)***

Global Bakeries Inc..........D.......818 896-0525
13336 Paxton St Pacoima (91331) ***(P-8797)***

Global Blue Dvbe Inc..........D.......916 632-2583
5930 Price Ave McClellan (95652) ***(P-16269)***

Mergent e-mail: customerrelations@mergent.com
1314
2019 Directory of California
Wholesalers and Services Companies
(P-0000) Products & Services Section entry number
(PA)=Parent Co (HQ)=Headquarters (DH)=Div Headquarters

Global Building Services Inc......B......209 858-9501
17618 Murphy Pkwy Lathrop (95330) ***(P-27929)***
Global Building Services Inc (PA)......A......661 288-5733
25129 The Old Rd Ste 102 Stevenson Ranch (91381) ***(P-14279)***
Global Business Solutions Inc......B......714 257-1488
600 Anton Blvd Ste 1050 Costa Mesa (92626) ***(P-16385)***
Global Care Travel, San Diego *Also called Customzed Svcs Admnstrtors Inc* ***(P-10599)***
Global Check Service......C......619 449-5150
1524 Graves Ave Ste C El Cajon (92021) ***(P-17189)***
Global Debt Management LLC (PA)......D......949 825-7800
18881 Von Karman Ave # 1500 Irvine (92612) ***(P-17190)***
Global Dev Strategies Inc......D......858 408-1173
9985 Businesspark Ave A San Diego (92131) ***(P-17948)***
Global Domains International......E......760 602-3000
701 Palomar Airport Rd # 300 Carlsbad (92011) ***(P-5570)***
Global Dosimetry Solutions, Irvine *Also called Mirion Technologies Gds Inc* ***(P-26715)***
Global Eagle Entertainment Inc......C......949 608-8700
2941 Alton Pkwy Irvine (92606) ***(P-18057)***
Global Emergency Road Svc LLC......E......818 518-1166
9908 San Fernando Rd Pacoima (91331) ***(P-3802)***
Global Entertainment Inds Inc......D......818 567-0000
2948 N Ontario St Burbank (91504) ***(P-3526)***
Global Exprnce Specialists Inc......D......562 370-1500
5560 Katella Ave Cypress (90630) ***(P-17191)***
Global Exprnce Specialists Inc......D......818 638-5959
500 N Brand Blvd Ste 1860 Glendale (91203) ***(P-17192)***
Global Exprnce Specialists Inc......C......619 498-6300
491 C St Chula Vista (91910) ***(P-17193)***
Global Fibernet, Van Nuys *Also called Airespring Inc* ***(P-5445)***
Global Futures Exch & Trdg Co......D......818 996-0401
303 17th St Santa Monica (90402) ***(P-10045)***
Global Garments, Los Angeles *Also called Design Collection Inc* ***(P-8225)***
Global Ground Automation Inc......D......201 293-4900
1051 E Hillsdale Blvd Foster City (94404) ***(P-7754)***
Global Holdings Inc......C......818 905-6000
1230 Rosecrans Ave # 660 Manhattan Beach (90266) ***(P-11981)***
Global Horizons Inc......B......310 234-8475
468 N Camden Dr Ste 200 Beverly Hills (90210) ***(P-14627)***
Global Industry Analysts Inc......A......408 528-9966
6150 Hellyer Ave Ste 100 San Jose (95138) ***(P-26525)***
Global Infotech Corporation......A......408 567-0600
2890 Zanker Rd Ste 202 San Jose (95134) ***(P-27739)***
Global Innovation Partner, Los Angeles *Also called Cbre Global Investors LLC* ***(P-27185)***
Global Innovation Partners LLC......D......650 233-3600
188 The Embarcadero # 700 San Francisco (94105) ***(P-17194)***
Global Language Solutions LLC......D......949 798-1400
19800 Macarthur Blvd Irvine (92612) ***(P-17195)***
Global Mail Inc......C......310 735-0800
921 W Artesia Blvd Compton (90220) ***(P-5074)***
Global Management Company LLC......D......323 261-8114
3150 E Pico Blvd Los Angeles (90023) ***(P-27246)***
Global Med Services Inc......A......562 207-6970
11818 South St Ste 201a Cerritos (90703) ***(P-22302)***
Global Meddata Inc......D......650 369-9734
735 Industrial Rd Ste 203 San Carlos (94070) ***(P-22809)***
Global Network Travel, Glendale *Also called Goway Travel Inc* ***(P-4937)***
Global Nurses Online Inc......D......310 306-2760
5301 Beethoven St Ste 200 Los Angeles (90066) ***(P-14628)***
Global Paratransit Inc......B......310 715-7550
400 W Compton Blvd Gardena (90248) ***(P-3803)***
Global Plastics Inc......C......951 657-5466
145 Malbert St Perris (92570) ***(P-7978)***
Global Power Group Inc (PA)......D......619 579-1221
12060 Woodside Ave Lakeside (92040) ***(P-2591)***
Global Reach 18 Inc (PA)......D......310 203-5850
10100 Santa Monica Blvd # 900 Los Angeles (90067) ***(P-12061)***
Global Realty Group, Granada Hills *Also called Global Work Group LLC* ***(P-27247)***
Global Risk MGT Solutions LLC......C......949 759-8500
660 Nwport Ctr Dr Ste 600 Newport Beach (92660) ***(P-16225)***
Global Software Resources Inc (PA)......E......925 249-2200
4447 Stoneridge Dr Ste 1 Pleasanton (94588) ***(P-16386)***
Global Solutions Integration......D......949 307-1849
26632 Towne Centre Dr # 300 Foothill Ranch (92610) ***(P-25716)***
Global Staffing Inc......C......303 451-5602
5301 Beethoven St Ste 101 Los Angeles (90066) ***(P-14629)***
Global Stainless Supply......B......310 525-1865
17006 S Figueroa St Gardena (90248) ***(P-7276)***
Global Touchpoints Inc......D......916 878-5954
3005 Douglas Blvd Ste 108 Roseville (95661) ***(P-15180)***
Global USA Green Card......D......415 915-4151
201 Spear St Ste 1100 San Francisco (94105) ***(P-23101)***
Global Work Group LLC......D......424 220-9994
17224 San Fernando Granada Hills (91344) ***(P-27247)***
Global-Dining Inc California......C......310 576-9922
1212 3rd Street Promenade Santa Monica (90401) ***(P-26873)***
Globalenglish Corporation (PA)......C......425 868-0271
2000 Sierra Point Pkwy # 300 Brisbane (94005) ***(P-5571)***
Globalex Corporation......D......310 593-4833
2100 Abbot Kinney Blvd A Venice (90291) ***(P-15693)***
Globallogic Inc (PA)......C......408 273-8900
1741 Tech Dr Ste 400 San Jose (95110) ***(P-15181)***
Globalways Inc (PA)......D......510 580-1974
42808 Christy St Ste 202 Fremont (94538) ***(P-16387)***
Globe Shoes, El Segundo *Also called Osata Enterprises Inc* ***(P-8364)***
Globecast America Incorporated (HQ)......D......310 845-3900
10525 Washington Blvd Culver City (90232) ***(P-5918)***
Gloria Ferrer, Sonoma *Also called Freixenet Usa Inc* ***(P-9045)***
Glovia Inc......C......310 563-7000
2250 E Imperial Hwy # 200 El Segundo (90245) ***(P-15182)***
Glovis America Inc (HQ)......D......714 435-2960
17305 Von Karman Ave # 200 Irvine (92614) ***(P-5075)***
Glu Mobile Inc (PA)......C......415 800-6100
875 Howard St Ste 100 San Francisco (94103) ***(P-15183)***
GM Cruise LLC (HQ)......D......415 335-4097
1201 Bryant St San Francisco (94103) ***(P-3804)***
GMAC Insurance, Ontario *Also called National General Insurance Co* ***(P-10383)***
Gmg Janitorial Inc......C......415 642-2100
70 Dorman Ave Ste 2 San Francisco (94124) ***(P-14280)***
Gmg Stone Inc......E......619 258-6899
7988 Stromesa Ct San Diego (92126) ***(P-2999)***
Gmh Inc......E......805 485-1410
561 Kinetic Dr Ste A Oxnard (93030) ***(P-17895)***
GMI Building Services Inc......C......858 279-6262
8001 Vickers St San Diego (92111) ***(P-14281)***
Gms Janitorial Services Inc......D......858 569-6009
8690 Aero Dr Ste 115 San Diego (92123) ***(P-14282)***
Go Get Em Inc......D......702 985-5637
45248 Trevor Ave Lancaster (93534) ***(P-16899)***
Go West Holdings LLC......C......888 670-0080
795 Folsom St San Francisco (94107) ***(P-17196)***
Go West Tours Inc (PA)......E......415 837-0154
790 Eddy St San Francisco (94109) ***(P-4970)***
Go-Staff Inc......A......760 730-8520
9878 Complex Dr Oceanside (92054) ***(P-14630)***
Go-Staff Inc......A......657 242-9350
240 W Lincoln Ave Anaheim (92805) ***(P-14631)***
Go2 Systems Inc......D......949 553-0800
18400 Von Karman Ave Fl 9 Irvine (92612) ***(P-16226)***
Go2systems, Irvine *Also called Go2 Systems Inc* ***(P-16226)***
Gobig Inc......E......415 513-3029
338 Main St Unit 5c San Francisco (94105) ***(P-15967)***
Goetzman Group Inc (PA)......D......818 595-1112
21700 Oxnard St Ste 1540 Woodland Hills (91367) ***(P-27248)***
Goforth & Marti (PA)......D......951 684-0870
110 W A St Ste 140 San Diego (92101) ***(P-6723)***
Gogii, Marina Del Rey *Also called Textplus Inc* ***(P-5421)***
Goglanian Bakeries Inc (HQ)......B......714 549-1524
3401 W Segerstrom Ave Santa Ana (92704) ***(P-8798)***
Goguardian, Hermosa Beach *Also called Liminex Inc* ***(P-15259)***
Gold Bond Building Products, Richmond *Also called New Ngc Inc* ***(P-7984)***
Gold Coast Broadcasting, Ventura *Also called Kkzz 1590* ***(P-5734)***
Gold Coast Design Inc......D......619 574-0111
7667 Vickers St San Diego (92111) ***(P-2443)***
Gold Coast Farms LLC......E......559 564-6316
32701 Road 204 Woodlake (93286) ***(P-262)***
Gold Coast Ingredients Inc......D......323 724-8935
2429 Yates Ave Commerce (90040) ***(P-8799)***
Gold Coast Tours, Fullerton *Also called Hot Dogger Tours Inc* ***(P-3899)***
Gold Country Casino, Oroville *Also called Tyme Maidu Tribe-Berry Creek* ***(P-13351)***
Gold Country Health Center Inc (PA)......C......530 621-1100
4301 Golden Center Dr Placerville (95667) ***(P-24784)***
Gold Country Management Inc......D......916 929-3003
1825 Bell St Ste 100 Sacramento (95825) ***(P-11486)***
Gold Cross Ambulance, Los Angeles *Also called Schaefer Ambulance Service Inc* ***(P-3843)***
Gold Hill Grange No 326......D......916 645-3605
1514 5th St Lincoln (95648) ***(P-25167)***
Gold Parent LP......A......310 954-0444
11111 Santa Monica Blvd Los Angeles (90025) ***(P-9957)***
Gold River Racquet Club, Gold River *Also called Spare-Time Inc* ***(P-19057)***
Gold Star Foods Inc (PA)......C......909 843-9600
3781 E Airport Dr Ontario (91761) ***(P-8490)***
Gold Tree Inc......D......562 801-0218
11643 E Telg Rd St 204 Santa Fe Springs (90670) ***(P-27249)***
Gold's Gym, Redondo Beach *Also called Muscle Improvement Inc* ***(P-18634)***
Gold's Gym, Modesto *Also called Fitness Evolution* ***(P-18600)***
Gold's Gym, Vacaville *Also called Maximum Fitness LLC* ***(P-18630)***
Golda & I Chocolatiers Inc......D......949 660-9581
23052 Alicia Pkwy Ste H Mission Viejo (92692) ***(P-8800)***
Goldberg and Solovy Foods Inc, Vernon *Also called Palisades Ranch Inc* ***(P-8439)***
Golden, Irvine *Also called Atria Senior Living Group Inc* ***(P-26769)***
Golden 1 Credit Union......C......877 465-3361
1282 Stabler Ln Ste 640 Yuba City (95993) ***(P-9635)***
Golden 1 Credit Union (PA)......B......916 732-2900
8945 Cal Center Dr Sacramento (95826) ***(P-9636)***
Golden 1 Credit Union......D......530 251-0205
2942 Main St Susanville (96130) ***(P-9637)***
Golden Acorn Casino & Trvl Ctr, Campo *Also called Campo Band Missions Indians* ***(P-18781)***
Golden Acres Farms......E......760 399-1923
87770 62nd Ave Thermal (92274) ***(P-60)***
Golden Age Nutrition Program, Watsonville *Also called Community Bridges* ***(P-23600)***
Golden Bear Rest Assn LLC......E......415 227-8660
760 2nd St San Francisco (94107) ***(P-24959)***
Golden Bridge Intl Group......D......626 968-8229
727 9th Ave City of Industry (91745) ***(P-5076)***
Golden Care Inc......D......818 763-6275
6120 Vineland Ave North Hollywood (91606) ***(P-21083)***
Golden Coast Cnstr Restoration......D......916 955-7461
4811 Chippendale Dr # 301 Sacramento (95841) ***(P-1536)***
Golden Cross Care II Inc......D......559 268-3023
1233 A St Fresno (93706) ***(P-20459)***
Golden Cross Care Inc......C......626 791-1948
1450 N Fair Oaks Ave Pasadena (91103) ***(P-20460)***
Golden Cross Health Care, Pasadena *Also called Golden Cross Care Inc* ***(P-20460)***
Golden Cross Hlth Care Fresno, Fresno *Also called Golden Cross Care II Inc* ***(P-20459)***

ALPHABETIC

Employee Codes: A=Over 500 employees, B=251-500
C=101-250, D=51-100, E=50
2019 Directory of California
Wholesalers and Services Companies
© Mergent Inc. 1-800-342-5647
1315

Golden Door Properties LLC....C....760 744-5777
777 Deer Springs Rd San Marcos (92069) *(P-12606)*
Golden Eagle Insurance Corp (HQ)....C....619 744-6000
525 B St Ste 1300 San Diego (92101) *(P-10357)*
Golden Eagle Moving Svcs Inc....D....909 946-7655
1450 N Benson Ave Unit B Upland (91786) *(P-4187)*
Golden Empire Concrete Pdts....D....661 833-4490
8261 Mccutchen Rd Bakersfield (93311) *(P-3257)*
Golden Empire Convalescent Hos....C....530 273-1316
121 Dorsey Dr Grass Valley (95945) *(P-21429)*
Golden Empire Mortgage Inc....D....626 967-3236
664 Shoppers Ln Ste A Covina (91723) *(P-9808)*
Golden Empire Mortgage Inc....D....760 256-3593
420 Barstow Rd Barstow (92311) *(P-9809)*
Golden Empire Mortgage Inc (PA)....D....661 328-1600
1200 Discovery Dr Ste 300 Bakersfield (93309) *(P-9810)*
Golden Empire Mortgage Inc (PA)....D....661 328-1600
2130 Chester Ave Bakersfield (93301) *(P-9811)*
Golden Empire Transit District (PA)....C....661 869-2438
1830 Golden State Ave Bakersfield (93301) *(P-3658)*
Golden Gate....D....415 455-2000
101 E Sir Francis Drake Larkspur (94939) *(P-5216)*
Golden Gate Brdg Hwy & Transpo (PA)....C....415 921-5858
Toll Plz San Francisco (94129) *(P-5217)*
Golden Gate Bridge High....A....415 457-3110
1011 Andersen Dr San Rafael (94901) *(P-5218)*
Golden Gate Capitol....B....415 983-2700
1 Embarcadero Ctr # 3900 San Francisco (94111) *(P-27740)*
Golden Gate Ferry, Larkspur *Also called Golden Gate (P-5216)*
Golden Gate Fields, Albany *Also called Pacific Racing Association (P-18542)*
Golden Gate Nat Prks Cnsrvancy, San Rafael *Also called Golden Gate Nat Prks Cnsrvancy (P-27930)*
Golden Gate Nat Prks Cnsrvancy....D....415 785-4787
1600 Los Gamos Dr San Rafael (94903) *(P-27930)*
Golden Gate Nat Prks Cnsrvancy (PA)....D....415 561-3000
Fort Mason Bldg 201 San Francisco (94123) *(P-27931)*
Golden Gate Regional Ctr Inc (PA)....C....415 546-9222
1355 Market St Ste 220 San Francisco (94103) *(P-23822)*
Golden Gate Regional Ctr Inc....D....650 574-9232
3130 La Selva St Ste 202 San Mateo (94403) *(P-23823)*
Golden Gate Scnic Stmship Corp....E....415 901-5249
Shed C Pier 45 St Pier San Francisco (94133) *(P-4716)*
Golden Gate Section, San Francisco *Also called National Council Negro Women (P-25445)*
Golden Gate Transit, San Rafael *Also called Golden Gate Bridge High (P-5218)*
Golden Gtwy Tennis & Swim CLB, San Francisco *Also called Bay Club Holdings III LLC (P-19107)*
Golden Hotel LLC....D....714 739-5600
7762 Beach Blvd Buena Park (90620) *(P-12607)*
Golden Hotels Ltd Partnership....C....949 833-2770
18700 Macarthur Blvd Irvine (92612) *(P-12608)*
Golden Hour Data Systems Inc....C....858 768-2500
10052 Mesa Ridge Ct # 200 San Diego (92121) *(P-5077)*
Golden International....A....213 628-1388
424 S Los Angeles St # 2 Los Angeles (90013) *(P-12229)*
Golden Living LLC....D....559 237-8377
1715 S Cedar Ave Fresno (93702) *(P-20461)*
Golden Living LLC....D....818 893-6385
9541 Van Nuys Blvd Panorama City (91402) *(P-21084)*
Golden Living LLC....D....559 834-2542
1306 E Sumner Ave Fowler (93625) *(P-20462)*
Golden Living LLC....D....949 642-0387
340 Victoria St Costa Mesa (92627) *(P-20463)*
Golden Living LLC....D....707 546-0471
1221 Rosemarie Ln Stockton (95207) *(P-20464)*
Golden Living LLC....D....818 249-3925
2123 Verdugo Blvd Montrose (91020) *(P-21085)*
Golden Living LLC....D....559 275-4785
925 N Cornelia Ave Fresno (93706) *(P-20465)*
Golden Living LLC....D....209 745-1537
144 F St Galt (95632) *(P-22303)*
Golden Living LLC....D....415 563-0565
1477 Grove St San Francisco (94117) *(P-20466)*
Golden Living LLC....D....707 255-6060
705 Trancas St NAPA (94558) *(P-21086)*
Golden Living LLC....C....209 533-2500
19929 Greenley Rd Sonora (95370) *(P-21087)*
Golden Living LLC....D....209 529-0516
515 E Orangeburg Ave Modesto (95350) *(P-21088)*
Golden Living LLC....D....408 356-8136
14966 Terreno De Flores Los Gatos (95032) *(P-21089)*
Golden Living LLC....D....562 598-2477
3000 N Gate Rd Seal Beach (90740) *(P-21090)*
Golden Living LLC....D....661 323-2894
3601 San Dimas St Bakersfield (93301) *(P-20467)*
Golden Living LLC....D....805 494-4949
6700 Sepulveda Blvd Van Nuys (91411) *(P-22304)*
Golden Living LLC....D....805 983-0305
1300 N C St Oxnard (93030) *(P-20468)*
Golden Living LLC....D....805 642-1736
5445 Everglades St Ventura (93003) *(P-20469)*
Golden Living LLC....D....209 368-0693
950 S Fairmont Ave Lodi (95240) *(P-20470)*
Golden Living LLC....D....707 546-0471
4650 Hoen Ave Santa Rosa (95405) *(P-20471)*
Golden Living LLC....D....626 962-3368
850 S Sunkist Ave West Covina (91790) *(P-20472)*
Golden Living LLC....D....707 763-4109
217 Lakeville St Apt 3 Petaluma (94952) *(P-20473)*
Golden Living LLC....D....559 673-9278
1700 Howard Rd Madera (93637) *(P-21091)*
Golden Living LLC....C....408 923-7232
401 Ridge Vista Ave San Jose (95127) *(P-20474)*
Golden Living LLC....D....949 496-5786
35410 Del Rey Capistrano Beach (92624) *(P-20475)*
Golden Living LLC....D....530 241-6756
1836 Gold St Redding (96001) *(P-21092)*
Golden Living LLC....D....559 222-4807
3510 E Shields Ave Fresno (93726) *(P-20476)*
Golden Living LLC....D....559 486-4433
2715 Fresno St Fresno (93721) *(P-21093)*
Golden Living LLC....D....559 299-2591
111 Barstow Ave Clovis (93612) *(P-20477)*
Golden Living LLC....D....951 600-4640
24100 Monroe Ave Murrieta (92562) *(P-23824)*
Golden Living LLC....D....559 227-5383
3672 N 1st St Fresno (93726) *(P-20478)*
Golden Living LLC....D....559 638-3577
1090 E Dinuba Ave Reedley (93654) *(P-20479)*
Golden Living LLC....E....408 255-5555
5555 Prospect Rd Ofc San Jose (95129) *(P-24540)*
Golden Living LLC....C....209 548-0318
1900 Coffee Rd Modesto (95355) *(P-20480)*
Golden Living LLC....D....408 356-9151
350 De Soto Dr Los Gatos (95032) *(P-20481)*
Golden Living LLC....D....559 227-4063
3408 E Shields Ave Fresno (93726) *(P-21094)*
Golden Living LLC....D....209 466-3522
2740 N California St Stockton (95204) *(P-20482)*
Golden Living LLC....D....707 938-1096
678 2nd St W Sonoma (95476) *(P-20483)*
Golden Living LLC....D....530 343-6084
188 Cohasset Ln Chico (95926) *(P-20484)*
Golden Living LLC....D....209 722-6231
3169 M St Merced (95348) *(P-21095)*
Golden Living LLC....D....760 446-3591
1131 N China Lake Blvd Ridgecrest (93555) *(P-22305)*
Golden Living LLC....D....559 875-6501
2550 9th St Sanger (93657) *(P-21096)*
Golden Living LLC....D....209 862-2862
709 N St Newman (95360) *(P-20485)*
Golden Livingcenter, Sonoma *Also called Golden Living LLC (P-20483)*
Golden Livingcenter - Chateau, Stockton *Also called Golden Living LLC (P-20464)*
Golden Livingcenter - Clovis, Clovis *Also called Golden Living LLC (P-20477)*
Golden Livingcenter - Fresno, Fresno *Also called Golden Living LLC (P-21093)*
Golden Livingcenter - Galt, Galt *Also called Golden Living LLC (P-22303)*
Golden Livingcenter - Hylond, Fresno *Also called Golden Living LLC (P-21094)*
Golden Livingcenter - NAPA, NAPA *Also called Golden Living LLC (P-21086)*
Golden Livingcenter - Petaluma, Petaluma *Also called Golden Living LLC (P-20473)*
Golden Livingcenter - Portside, Stockton *Also called Golden Living LLC (P-20482)*
Golden Livingcenter - Redding, Redding *Also called Golden Living LLC (P-21092)*
Golden Livingcenter - Reedley, Reedley *Also called Golden Living LLC (P-20479)*
Golden Livingcenter - San Jose, San Jose *Also called Golden Living LLC (P-20474)*
Golden Livingcenter - Sanger, Sanger *Also called Golden Living LLC (P-21096)*
Golden Livingctr-Country View, Fresno *Also called Golden Living LLC (P-20465)*
Golden Lvngcenter - Santa Rosa, Santa Rosa *Also called Golden Living LLC (P-20471)*
Golden Lvngcnter - Bakersfield, Bakersfield *Also called Golden Living LLC (P-20467)*
Golden N-Life Diamite Intl Inc (PA)....D....510 651-0405
3500 Gateway Blvd Fremont (94538) *(P-8172)*
Golden Pacific Bancorp Inc (PA)....D....916 444-2450
1409 28th St Sacramento (95816) *(P-11953)*
Golden Peterbilt, Porterville *Also called E M Tharp Inc (P-6591)*
Golden Pond LP....E....916 369-8967
3415 Mayhew Rd Ofc Sacramento (95827) *(P-24541)*
Golden Pond Retirement Cmnty, Sacramento *Also called Golden Pond LP (P-24541)*
Golden Queen Mining Co LLC....C....661 824-4300
2818 Silver Queen Rd Mojave (93501) *(P-1005)*
Golden Rain Foundation (PA)....D....925 988-7700
1001 Golden Rain Rd Walnut Creek (94595) *(P-11487)*
Golden Rain Foundation....D....562 493-9581
1661 Golden Rain Rd Seal Beach (90740) *(P-19485)*
Golden Rain Foundation....B....925 988-7800
800 Rockview Dr Walnut Creek (94595) *(P-25168)*
Golden State Care Center, Baldwin Park *Also called Golden State Habilitation Conv (P-20486)*
Golden State Collision Centers....D....916 772-1666
841 Galleria Blvd Roseville (95678) *(P-17723)*
Golden State Colonial Convales, North Hollywood *Also called Silverscreen Healthcare Inc (P-20766)*
Golden State Crrctional Fcilty, Mc Farland *Also called Geo Group Inc (P-26869)*
Golden State Drilling Inc....D....661 589-0730
3500 Fruitvale Ave Bakersfield (93308) *(P-1037)*
Golden State Fence, Anaheim *Also called Fenceworks Inc (P-3518)*
Golden State Fence, Santa Paula *Also called Fenceworks Inc (P-3520)*
Golden State Fence Co., Riverside *Also called Fenceworks Inc (P-3519)*
Golden State Fruit, Lodi *Also called Calfornia Fruit Exchange LLC (P-8648)*
Golden State Habilitation Conv (PA)....B....626 962-3274
1758 Big Dalton Ave Baldwin Park (91706) *(P-20486)*
Golden State Health Ctrs Inc (PA)....C....818 385-3200
13347 Ventura Blvd Sherman Oaks (91423) *(P-20487)*
Golden State Health Ctrs Inc....C....626 579-0310
5522 Gracewood Ave Temple City (91780) *(P-21097)*
Golden State Health Ctrs Inc....C....818 882-8233
21820 Craggy View St Chatsworth (91311) *(P-21098)*

Mergent e-mail: customerrelations@mergent.com
1316
2019 Directory of California
Wholesalers and Services Companies
(P-0000) Products & Services Section entry number
(PA)=Parent Co (HQ)=Headquarters (DH)=Div Headquarters

Golden State Health Ctrs Inc ....C....818 834-5082
12220 Foothill Blvd Sylmar (91342) (P-21956)
Golden State Herbs (PA) ....E....760 342-7117
60125 Polk St Thermal (92274) (P-263)
Golden State Landscaping, Livermore Also called J Redfern Inc (P-863)
Golden State Lumber Inc ....C....209 234-7700
3033 S Airport Way Stockton (95206) (P-6824)
Golden State Medical Supply ....D....805 477-8966
5247 Camino Ruiz Camarillo (93012) (P-8033)
Golden State Mutl Lf Insur Co (PA) ....D....713 526-4361
1999 W Adams Blvd Los Angeles (90018) (P-10136)
Golden State Plastering ....D....559 439-3920
7082 N Harrison Ave Fresno (93650) (P-6895)
Golden State Warriors LLC ....D....510 986-2200
1011 Broadway Oakland (94607) (P-18519)
Golden State Water Company ....D....714 535-7711
1920 W Corporate Way Anaheim (92801) (P-6257)
Golden State Water Company (HQ) ....C....909 394-3600
630 E Foothill Blvd San Dimas (91773) (P-6258)
Golden State Water Company ....D....909 394-3600
630 E Foothill Blvd San Dimas (91773) (P-6259)
Golden State Water Company ....E....805 583-6400
600 W Los Angeles Ave Simi Valley (93065) (P-6260)
Golden State Water Company ....E....909 866-4678
42020 Garstin Dr Big Bear Lake (92315) (P-6038)
Golden State West Valley ....C....818 348-8422
7057 Shoup Ave Canoga Park (91307) (P-20488)
Golden Valley Citrus Inc ....D....559 568-1768
19875 Meredith Dr Strathmore (93267) (P-519)
Golden Valley Health Centers (PA) ....A....209 383-1848
737 W Childs Ave Merced (95341) (P-22584)
Golden Valley Health Centers ....D....209 383-5871
797 W Childs Ave Merced (95341) (P-22585)
Golden Vly Occpational Therapy, Oroville Also called Oroville Hospital (P-20191)
Golden West Custom WD Shutters ....E....949 951-0600
20561 Pascal Way Lake Forest (92630) (P-8034)
Golden West Packg Group LLC (PA) ....B....404 345-8365
8333 24th Ave Sacramento (95826) (P-11982)
Golden West Trading Inc ....C....323 581-3663
4401 S Downey Rd Vernon (90058) (P-8616)
Goldenpark LLC ....D....562 863-5555
16209 Paramount Blvd # 214 Paramount (90723) (P-12609)
Goldenram, Costa Mesa Also called Upgradedetect Inc (P-7125)
Goldfield Stage Company, El Cajon Also called McClintock Enterprises Inc (P-3890)
Goldman Sachs & Co ....C....415 393-7500
555 California St # 4500 San Francisco (94104) (P-9958)
Goldman Sachs & Co ....C....310 407-5700
2121 Avenue Stars 2600 Los Angeles (90067) (P-9959)
Goldman Avram ....D....925 275-3000
1855 Gateway Blvd Ste 750 Concord (94520) (P-26874)
Goldman Sachs, San Francisco Also called Goldman Sachs & Co (P-9958)
Goldman Sachs, Los Angeles Also called Goldman Sachs & Co (P-9959)
Goldrich & Kest Industries LLC (PA) ....A....310 204-2050
5150 Overland Ave Culver City (90230) (P-11877)
Goldrichkest (PA) ....B....310 204-2050
5150 Overland Ave Culver City (90230) (P-11878)
Goldrush Getaways, Citrus Heights Also called Travelmasters Inc (P-4956)
Golds Gym, Northridge Also called Musclebound Inc (P-18635)
Golds Gym International Inc ....D....626 304-1133
39 S Altadena Dr Pasadena (91107) (P-18605)
Golds Gym San Jose, San Jose Also called McCall Gym Group Inc (P-18631)
Goldsmith Construction Co Inc ....E....562 595-5975
2683 Lime Ave Signal Hill (90755) (P-3258)
Goldstar, Irvine Also called Spireon Inc (P-4375)
Goldstar Hlthcr Cntr of Chtswr ....C....818 882-8233
145 S Fairfax Ave Ste 200 Los Angeles (90036) (P-21099)
Goleta Hhg Hotel Dev LP ....D....805 562-5996
6878 Hollister Ave Goleta (93117) (P-12610)
Goleta Valley Athletic Club, Goleta Also called Millenium Athletic Club LLc (P-18632)
Goleta Valley Cottage Hospital ....B....805 681-6468
351 S Patterson Ave Santa Barbara (93111) (P-21430)
Golf & Tennis Pro Shop Inc ....D....650 600-5200
1751 E Bayshore Rd East Palo Alto (94303) (P-19179)
Golf Club At Boulder Ridge, San Jose Also called Glenrock Group (P-18929)
Golf Club At Roddy Ranch, Antioch Also called Roddy Ranch Pbc LLC (P-19018)
Golf Club At Terra Lago, The, Indio Also called Lb Hills Golf Club LLC (P-18727)
Golf Investment LLC (PA) ....D....949 498-6604
200 Avenida La Pata San Clemente (92673) (P-18930)
Golf Pro Shop, Riverside Also called Canyon Crest Country Club Inc (P-18883)
Golf Pro. Shop, Diablo Also called Diablo Country Club (P-18915)
Gomez Farm Labor Contg Inc ....D....760 399-1994
62610 Monroe St Thermal (92274) (P-650)
Gong's Ventures, Sanger Also called Gongs Market of Sanger Inc (P-10885)
Gongs Market of Sanger Inc (PA) ....E....559 875-5576
1825 Academy Ave Sanger (93657) (P-10885)
Gonsalves & Santucci Inc (PA) ....A....925 685-6799
5141 Commercial Cir Concord (94520) (P-3259)
Gonsalves & Santucci Inc ....C....707 745-5019
5141 Commercial Cir Concord (94520) (P-3375)
Gonzales Enterprises Inc ....C....530 343-8725
495 Ryan Ave Chico (95973) (P-8262)
Gonzales Painting Corp ....D....951 214-6400
14437 Meridian Pkwy Riverside (92518) (P-2444)
Gonzales Salvador Labor Contrs ....D....209 745-2223
217 4th St Galt (95632) (P-651)
Gonzalez Barba Enterprises ....E....323 233-7995
1575 E 46th St Los Angeles (90011) (P-5078)

Gonzalez Management Co Inc ....D....818 485-0596
10147 San Fernando Rd Pacoima (91331) (P-26875)
Gonzalez/Goodale Architects ....D....626 568-1428
135 W Green St Ste 200 Pasadena (91105) (P-26051)
Good Deal Insurance Services ....D....626 275-6795
2140 S Hacienda Blvd A Hacienda Heights (91745) (P-10637)
Good Eggs Inc ....E....415 483-7344
901 Rankin St San Francisco (94124) (P-8531)
Good Neighbor Pharmacy, Fresno Also called Northwest Medical Group Inc (P-19724)
Good Samaritan Hospital ....B....661 399-4461
901 Olive Dr Bakersfield (93308) (P-21431)
Good Samaritan Hospital (PA) ....C....213 977-2121
1225 Wilshire Blvd Los Angeles (90017) (P-21432)
Good Samaritan Hospital LP (HQ) ....A....408 559-2011
2425 Samaritan Dr San Jose (95124) (P-21433)
Good Samaritan Hospital LP ....C....408 356-4111
15891 Los Gtos Almaden Rd Los Gatos (95032) (P-21434)
Good Samaritan Hospital Aux ....A....213 977-2121
1225 Wilshire Blvd Los Angeles (90017) (P-19486)
GOOD SAMARITAN REHAB AND CARE, Stockton Also called Stockton Edson Healthcare
Corp (P-21224)
Good Samaritan Shelter ....D....805 346-8185
245 Inger Dr Ste 103b Santa Maria (93454) (P-23825)
Good Shepherd Communities, Porterville Also called Good Shepherd Lutheran Hm of
W (P-24542)
Good Shepherd Health Care Ce ....D....310 451-4809
1131 Arizona Ave Santa Monica (90401) (P-20489)
Good Shepherd Lutheran Hm of W (PA) ....D....559 791-2000
119 N Main St Porterville (93257) (P-24542)
Good Sports Plus Ltd ....B....310 671-4400
370 Amapola Ave Ste 208 Torrance (90501) (P-15184)
Good Technology Corporation (HQ) ....C....408 352-9102
3001 Bishop Dr Ste 400 San Ramon (94583) (P-15185)
Good Works LLC ....D....626 584-8130
1250 E Walnut St Ste 220 Pasadena (91106) (P-22306)
Goodall's Charter Bus Company, San Diego Also called Cusa Gcbs LLC (P-4969)
Goodby Silverstein & Partners, San Francisco Also called Goodby Slverstein Partners
Inc (P-13835)
Goodby Slverstein Partners Inc ....C....415 392-0669
720 California St San Francisco (94108) (P-13835)
Goodfellow Bros California LLC ....B....925 245-2111
50 Contractors St Livermore (94551) (P-1172)
Goodhire, Redwood City Also called Inflection Risk Solutions LLC (P-16147)
Goodland, Goleta Also called Khp III Goleta LLC (P-12808)
Goodman Food Products Inc (PA) ....C....310 674-3180
200 E Beach Ave Fl 1 Inglewood (90302) (P-8408)
Goodman Group Inc ....D....562 596-5561
3902 Katella Ave Los Alamitos (90720) (P-20490)
Goodman Manufacturing Co LP ....B....951 304-7402
41670 Reagan Way Murrieta (92562) (P-7649)
Goodman Manufacturing Co LP ....B....858 569-1715
3562 Ruffin Rd San Diego (92123) (P-7650)
Goodman North America LLC ....D....949 407-0100
18201 Von Karman Ave Irvine (92612) (P-11488)
Goodman Usa Inc ....D....408 329-5400
605 W California Ave Sunnyvale (94086) (P-19487)
Goodrich Lax A Cal Ltd Partnr ....D....626 254-9988
310 W Longden Ave Arcadia (91007) (P-12611)
Goodridge Usa Inc (HQ) ....D....310 533-1924
529 Van Ness Ave Torrance (90501) (P-6643)
Goodwill Inds Orange Cnty Cal ....C....714 754-7808
2910 W Garry Ave Santa Ana (92704) (P-24186)
Goodwill Inds S Centl Cal ....E....661 377-0191
1115 Olive Dr Bakersfield (93308) (P-24187)
Goodwill Inds San Diego Cnty ....B....760 806-7670
3841 Plaza Dr Ste 902 Oceanside (92056) (P-25424)
Goodwill Industries of Sacrame ....E....916 331-0237
8031 Watt Ave Sacramento (95843) (P-25425)
Goodwill Industrs of San Franc ....D....650 556-9709
1270 Oddstad Dr Redwood City (94063) (P-24188)
Goodwill of Silicon Valley (PA) ....D....408 998-5774
1080 N 7th St San Jose (95112) (P-14859)
Goodwill Srvng The Ppl of Sthr (PA) ....D....562 435-3411
800 W Pacific Coast Hwy Long Beach (90806) (P-17197)
Goodwin Ammonia Company ....D....714 894-0531
12361 Monarch St Garden Grove (92841) (P-4567)
Goodwin Procter LLP ....D....213 426-2500
601 S Figueroa St # 4100 Los Angeles (90017) (P-23102)
Google Checkout, Mountain View Also called Google Payment Corp (P-17198)
Google Fiber Inc (HQ) ....D....650 253-0000
1600 Amphitheatre Pkwy Mountain View (94043) (P-5572)
Google International LLC (HQ) ....D....650 253-0000
1600 Amphitheatre Pkwy Mountain View (94043) (P-5573)
Google LLC (HQ) ....C....650 253-0000
1600 Amphitheatre Pkwy Mountain View (94043) (P-15186)
Google LLC ....D....650 253-7323
1945 Charleston Rd Mountain View (94043) (P-16227)
Google Payment Corp ....E....650 253-0000
1600 Amphitheatre Pkwy Mountain View (94043) (P-17198)
Goproto, San Diego Also called Higgs Fletcher & Mack Llp (P-23129)
Gordian Medical, Irvine Also called American Medical Tech Inc (P-7151)
Gordian Medical Inc ....B....714 556-0200
17595 Cartwright Rd Irvine (92614) (P-7182)
Gordon Edelstein Krepack Gr ....E....213 739-7000
3580 Wilshire Blvd # 1800 Los Angeles (90010) (P-23103)
Gordon & Schwenkmeyer Inc ....D....916 569-1740
1860 Howe Ave Ste 300 Sacramento (95825) (P-17199)

Employee Codes: A=Over 500 employees, B=251-500
C=101-250, D=51-100, E=50

2019 Directory of California
Wholesalers and Services Companies

© Mergent Inc. 1-800-342-5647

1317

Gordon Betty Moore Foundation ....D....650 213-3000
1661 Page Mill Rd Palo Alto (94304) ***(P-25169)***
Gordon E Btty I More Fundation ....D....650 213-3000
1661 Page Mill Rd Palo Alto (94304) ***(P-27741)***
Gordon Edelstein & Krepack, Los Angeles *Also called Gordon Edelstein Krepack Gr* ***(P-23103)***
Gordon Lane Convalescent Hosp ....D....714 879-7301
1821 E Chapman Ave Fullerton (92831) ***(P-21435)***
Gordon Rees Sclly Mnskhani LLP ....D....916 830-6900
655 University Ave # 200 Sacramento (95825) ***(P-23104)***
Gordon Rees Sclly Mnskhani LLP ....D....949 255-6950
2211 Michelson Dr Irvine (92612) ***(P-23105)***
Gordon Rees Sclly Mnskhani LLP (PA) ....B....415 986-5900
275 Battery St Ste 2000 San Francisco (94111) ***(P-23106)***
Gordon Rees Sclly Mnskhani LLP ....D....213 576-5000
633 W 5th St Fl 52 Los Angeles (90071) ***(P-23107)***
Gordon Rees Sclly Mnskhani LLP ....D....619 696-6700
101 W Broadway Ste 1600 San Diego (92101) ***(P-23108)***
Gordon Rees Sclly Mnskhani LLP ....D....415 986-5900
101 W Broadway Ste 2000 San Diego (92101) ***(P-23109)***
Gores Group LLC (PA) ....D....310 209-3010
9800 Wilshire Blvd Beverly Hills (90212) ***(P-9960)***
Gores Norment Holdings Inc ....C....310 209-3010
10877 Wilshire Blvd # 1805 Los Angeles (90024) ***(P-11983)***
Gorilla Tech Americas Inc ....D....925 365-1161
2678 Bishop Dr Ste 290 San Ramon (94583) ***(P-27250)***
Got Appraisals, San Ramon *Also called AMR Appraisals Inc* ***(P-11213)***
Gothic Ground Management, Valencia *Also called Gothic Landscaping Inc* ***(P-847)***
Gothic Grounds Mgmt, Valencia *Also called Gothic Landscaping Inc* ***(P-757)***
Gothic Landscaping Inc (PA) ....C....661 257-1266
27502 Avenue Scott Valencia (91355) ***(P-847)***
Gothic Landscaping Inc ....B....661 257-5085
27413 Tourney Rd Ste 200 Valencia (91355) ***(P-757)***
Gould Evans P C ....D....415 503-1411
95 Brady St San Francisco (94103) ***(P-26052)***
Gourmet Foods ....D....510 887-0340
2557 Barrington Ct Hayward (94545) ***(P-8409)***
Gourmet Foods Inc (PA) ....D....310 632-3300
2910 E Harcourt St Compton (90221) ***(P-8410)***
Gourmet India Food Company LLC ....D....562 698-9763
12220 Rivera Rd Ste A Whittier (90606) ***(P-8801)***
Gourmet Specialties Inc ....D....323 587-1734
2120 E 25th St Vernon (90058) ***(P-8690)***
Gourmet Trading Company, Redondo Beach *Also called Nzg Specialties Inc* ***(P-8436)***
Gourmets Fresh Pasta ....D....626 798-0841
950 N Fair Oaks Ave Pasadena (91103) ***(P-8802)***
Government Technology, Folsom *Also called Erepublic Inc* ***(P-17155)***
Governmentjobscom Inc ....C....310 426-6304
300 Continental Blvd # 565 El Segundo (90245) ***(P-15694)***
Governors Office Plg & RES, Sacramento *Also called The Executive Office of* ***(P-26474)***
Goway Travel Inc ....D....800 810-3687
505 N Brand Blvd Ste 810 Glendale (91203) ***(P-4937)***
GPA Technologies Inc ....D....805 643-7878
2368 Eastman Ave Ste 8 Ventura (93003) ***(P-25717)***
Gps Flyers ....D....951 588-7777
527 Prospect Ave Hermosa Beach (90254) ***(P-27251)***
Gps Painting Wallcovering Inc ....C....714 730-8904
1307 E Saint Gertrude Pl C Santa Ana (92705) ***(P-2445)***
Gr Hardester LLC ....C....707 987-2325
21088 Calistoga Rd Middletown (95461) ***(P-12163)***
Gracenote Inc (HQ) ....D....510 428-7200
2000 Powell St Ste 1500 Emeryville (94608) ***(P-15187)***
Gradient Engineers Inc ....D....949 477-0555
17781 Cowan Ste 140 Irvine (92614) ***(P-25718)***
Graham Concrete Cnstr Inc ....D....559 292-6571
1323 Dayton Ave Ste 103 Clovis (93612) ***(P-3260)***
Graham Contractors Inc ....E....408 293-9516
860 Lonus St San Jose (95126) ***(P-1769)***
Graham Packaging Company LP ....C....209 572-5187
4500 Finch Rd Modesto (95357) ***(P-9221)***
Graham-Prewett Inc ....E....559 291-3741
2773 N Bus Park Ave # 101 Fresno (93727) ***(P-3161)***
Grainger 732, San Jose *Also called WW Grainger Inc* ***(P-7403)***
Granada Healthcre & Rehab Cntr ....D....707 443-1627
2885 Harris St Eureka (95503) ***(P-21100)***
Granada Hills Care Center, Granada Hills *Also called Granada Hlls Convalescent Hosp* ***(P-20491)***
Granada Hlls Convalescent Hosp ....D....818 891-1745
16123 Chatsworth St Granada Hills (91344) ***(P-20491)***
Granada Hotel, San Francisco *Also called Broadmoor Hotel* ***(P-12405)***
Grancare LLC ....B....510 232-5945
13484 San Pablo Ave San Pablo (94806) ***(P-20492)***
Grancell Village, Reseda *Also called Los Angles Jewish HM For Aging* ***(P-20603)***
Grand Auto Care ....E....626 331-8390
744 N Grand Ave Covina (91724) ***(P-17764)***
Grand Auto Repair, Covina *Also called Grand Auto Care* ***(P-17764)***
Grand Central Station, Livermore *Also called All-Guard Alarm Systems Inc* ***(P-2505)***
Grand Del Mar Resort LP ....A....858 314-2000
5300 Grand Del Mar Ct San Diego (92130) ***(P-12612)***
Grand Events, Modesto *Also called Central Valley Party Supply* ***(P-14485)***
Grand Hotel The, Sunnyvale *Also called Selvi-Vidovich LP* ***(P-13205)***
Grand Hyatt San Francisco, San Francisco *Also called Hyatt Corporation* ***(P-12748)***
Grand Intelligence LLC ....D....408 954-7368
2880 Zanker Rd Ste 203 San Jose (95134) ***(P-15188)***
Grand Pacific Carlsbad Ht LP ....B....760 827-2400
5480 Grand Pacific Dr Carlsbad (92008) ***(P-12613)***
Grand Pacific Resorts Inc ....C....760 431-8500
5900 Pasteur Ct Ste 200 Carlsbad (92008) ***(P-17200)***
Grand Pacific Resorts Inc (PA) ....C....760 431-8500
5900 Pasteur Ct Ste 200 Carlsbad (92008) ***(P-11489)***
Grand Pacific Resorts Svcs LP ....C....760 431-8500
5900 Pasteur Ct Ste 200 Carlsbad (92008) ***(P-12614)***
Grand Park Convalescent Hosp ....C....213 382-7315
2312 W 8th St Los Angeles (90057) ***(P-20493)***
Grand Performances ....D....213 687-2190
350 S Grand Ave Ste A4 Los Angeles (90071) ***(P-17201)***
Grand Supercenter Inc ....D....562 318-3451
8550 Chetle Ave Ste B Whittier (90606) ***(P-8411)***
Grand Terrace Care Center ....D....909 825-5221
12000 Mount Vernon Ave Grand Terrace (92313) ***(P-20494)***
Grand Valley Health Care Ctr ....C....818 786-3470
13524 Sherman Way Van Nuys (91405) ***(P-20495)***
Grand View Geranium Grdns Inc ....D....310 217-0490
18307 Central Ave Carson (90746) ***(P-264)***
Grand View Research Inc ....E....415 349-0058
201 Spear St Ste 1100 San Francisco (94105) ***(P-27252)***
Grand Vista Hotel, Simi Valley *Also called Simi West Inc* ***(P-13229)***
Grandcare Health Services LLC (PA) ....C....866 554-2447
2555 E Colorado Blvd Fl 4 Pasadena (91107) ***(P-22307)***
Grandcare Home Health Services, Pasadena *Also called Msj Healthcare LLC* ***(P-22370)***
Grande Colonial, La Jolla *Also called Fargo Colonial LLC* ***(P-12570)***
Grani Installation Inc (PA) ....D....714 898-0441
5411 Commercial Dr Huntington Beach (92649) ***(P-1537)***
Granit-Bayashi 2 A Joint Ventr ....D....831 724-1011
585 W Beach St Watsonville (95076) ***(P-1922)***
Granit-Bayashi 3 A Joint Ventr ....E....831 724-1011
585 W Beach St Watsonville (95076) ***(P-1770)***
Granite Bay Golf Club ....C....916 791-5379
9600 Golf Club Dr Granite Bay (95746) ***(P-18931)***
Granite Construction Company (HQ) ....C....831 724-1011
585 W Beach St Watsonville (95076) ***(P-1771)***
Granite Construction Company ....C....661 399-3361
3005 James Rd Bakersfield (93308) ***(P-1772)***
Granite Construction Company ....B....760 775-7500
38000 Monroe St Indio (92203) ***(P-1773)***
Granite Construction Company ....C....805 964-9951
5335 Debbie Rd Santa Barbara (93111) ***(P-1774)***
Granite Construction Company ....D....916 855-4400
4001 Bradshaw Rd Sacramento (95827) ***(P-2035)***
Granite Construction Company ....D....661 854-3051
21541 E Bear Mtn Blvd Arvin (93203) ***(P-1775)***
Granite Construction Company ....C....661 726-4447
213 E Avenue M Lancaster (93535) ***(P-1776)***
Granite Construction Company ....C....408 327-7000
715 Comstock St Santa Clara (95054) ***(P-1777)***
Granite Construction Company ....C....559 441-5700
2716 S Granite Ct Fresno (93706) ***(P-1778)***
Granite Construction Inc ....C....760 337-3030
2095 Us Highway 111 El Centro (92243) ***(P-1779)***
Granite Construction Inc (PA) ....C....831 724-1011
585 W Beach St Watsonville (95076) ***(P-1880)***
Granite Construction Inc ....D....831 657-1700
5 Justin Ct Monterey (93940) ***(P-1780)***
Granite Construction Inc ....D....916 855-4495
4291 Bradshaw Rd Sacramento (95827) ***(P-1781)***
Granite Construction Inc ....D....707 467-4100
1324 S State St Ukiah (95482) ***(P-1782)***
Granite Construction Inc ....D....831 763-5595
25485 Iverson Rd Gonzales (93926) ***(P-1783)***
Granite Construction Inc ....D....831 335-3445
1800 Felton Quarry Rd Felton (95018) ***(P-1784)***
Granite Escrow Services ....D....310 288-0110
439 N Canon Dr Ste 220 Beverly Hills (90210) ***(P-9685)***
Granite Hills Healthcare ....D....619 447-1020
1340 E Madison Ave El Cajon (92021) ***(P-20496)***
Granite Hlls Convalescent Hosp, El Cajon *Also called Care With Dignity Healthcare* ***(P-20287)***
Granite Rock Co (PA) ....D....831 768-2000
350 Technology Dr Watsonville (95076) ***(P-1091)***
Granite Rock Co ....C....831 768-2330
1900 Quarry Rd Aromas (95004) ***(P-1785)***
Granite Rock Co ....C....831 392-3780
End Of Quarry Rd Aromas (95004) ***(P-6896)***
Granite Rock Co ....D....831 768-2300
Quarry Rd Aromas (95004) ***(P-1092)***
Granite Rock Co ....B....650 869-3370
355 Blomquist St Redwood City (94063) ***(P-1786)***
Granite Solutions Groupe Inc ....C....415 963-3999
235 Montgomery St Ste 430 San Francisco (94104) ***(P-14632)***
Granlbakken Ski Racquet Resort, Tahoe City *Also called Granlibakken Management Co Ltd* ***(P-12615)***
Granlibakken Management Co Ltd ....D....800 543-3221
725 Granlibakken Rd Tahoe City (96145) ***(P-12615)***
Granlund Candies, Yucaipa *Also called B B G Management Group* ***(P-8543)***
Grant & Weber (PA) ....C....818 878-7700
26610 Agoura Rd Ste 209 Calabasas (91302) ***(P-14005)***
Grant & Weber Travel, Calabasas *Also called Grant & Weber* ***(P-14005)***
Grant Construction Inc ....C....661 588-4586
7702 Meany Ave Ste 103 Bakersfield (93308) ***(P-3038)***
Grant Thornton LLP ....D....415 986-3900
101 California St # 2700 San Francisco (94111) ***(P-26206)***
Grant Thornton LLP ....E....213 627-1717
1000 Wilshire Blvd # 300 Los Angeles (90017) ***(P-26207)***
Grant Thornton LLP ....E....408 275-9000
10 Almaden Blvd Ste 800 San Jose (95113) ***(P-26208)***
Grant Thornton LLP ....D....213 627-1717
515 S Flower St Ste 700 Los Angeles (90071) ***(P-26209)***

Mergent e-mail: customerrelations@mergent.com
1318
2019 Directory of California
Wholesalers and Services Companies
(P-0000) Products & Services Section entry number
(PA)=Parent Co (HQ)=Headquarters (DH)=Div Headquarters

Grant Thornton LLP......C......858 704-8000
12220 El Camino Real San Diego (92130) ***(P-26210)***
Grant-Cuesta Nursing Center, Mountain View *Also called Covenant Care California LLC* ***(P-21361)***
Grants Custom Cabinets......C......805 466-9680
7310 Kingsbury Rd Templeton (93465) ***(P-1173)***
Grants Landscape Services Inc......D......714 444-1903
3046 Orange Ave Santa Ana (92707) ***(P-848)***
Granville Cafe, Glendale *Also called Granville Glendale Inc* ***(P-26876)***
Granville Glendale Inc......D......818 550-0472
807 Americana Way Glendale (91210) ***(P-26876)***
Granville Homes Inc......D......559 268-2000
1396 W Herndon Ave # 101 Fresno (93711) ***(P-1174)***
Granville Hotel Corp......C......562 863-5555
13111 Sycamore Dr Norwalk (90650) ***(P-12616)***
Graphic Orb Inc......D......310 967-2350
8687 Melrose Ave Ste 8 West Hollywood (90069) ***(P-27253)***
Grass Valley LLC......D......530 272-1055
150 Sutton Way Ofc Grass Valley (95945) ***(P-24543)***
Grasshopper House LLC......C......310 589-2880
6428 Meadows Ct Malibu (90265) ***(P-22586)***
Graybar Electric Company Inc......C......909 451-4300
1370 Valley Vista Dr # 100 Diamond Bar (91765) ***(P-7362)***
Graybar Electric Company Inc......D......925 557-3000
3089 Whipple Rd Union City (94587) ***(P-7363)***
Graybill Medical Group Inc (PA)......C......866 228-2236
332 S Juniper St Ste 100 Escondido (92025) ***(P-19488)***
Graycon Inc......E......626 961-9640
232 S 8th Ave City of Industry (91746) ***(P-2222)***
Grayline of San Francisco, San Francisco *Also called Blue Bus Tours LLC* ***(P-19113)***
Graymeta Inc......E......855 202-2270
350 Via Las Brisas # 230 Newbury Park (91320) ***(P-16388)***
Graypay LLC......D......818 387-6735
6345 Balboa Blvd Ste 115 Encino (91316) ***(P-15695)***
Grayson Service Inc......C......661 589-5444
1845 Greeley Rd Bakersfield (93314) ***(P-1061)***
Grc Electric Inc......D......818 242-9891
675 S Glenwood Pl Burbank (91506) ***(P-2592)***
Great Amercn Seafood Import Co, Carson *Also called Southwind Foods LLC* ***(P-8602)***
Great American Insurance Co......D......323 937-8600
5750 Wilshire Blvd 360 Los Angeles (90036) ***(P-10358)***
Great American Insurance Co......C......213 430-4300
725 S Figueroa St # 3400 Los Angeles (90017) ***(P-10359)***
Great American Music Hall......E......415 885-0750
859 Ofarrell St San Francisco (94109) ***(P-18369)***
Great Destinations Inc......D......949 667-9401
25510 Commercentre Dr Lake Forest (92630) ***(P-27254)***
Great Lakes E & I/ Inquip JV......D......805 687-2007
6558 Lonetree Blvd Rocklin (95765) ***(P-2036)***
Great Scott Tree Service Inc (PA)......C......714 826-1750
10761 Court Ave Stanton (90680) ***(P-974)***
Great Western Bancorp Inc......B......213 622-1895
706 S Hill St Los Angeles (90014) ***(P-9461)***
Great Western Distributing Svc, Los Angeles *Also called Gils Distributing Service* ***(P-13973)***
Great Western Hotels Corp......E......760 446-6543
1050 N Norma St Ridgecrest (93555) ***(P-12617)***
Great Western Wind Energy LLC......D......888 903-6926
15445 Innovation Dr San Diego (92128) ***(P-6039)***
Great Wstn Cnvlescent Hosp Inc......C......818 248-6856
2635 Honolulu Ave Montrose (91020) ***(P-21101)***
Greater Alarm Company Inc (HQ)......D......949 474-0555
3750 Schaufele Ave # 200 Long Beach (90808) ***(P-2593)***
GREATER EL MONTE COMMUNITY HOSPITAL, El Monte *Also called Ahm Gemch Inc* ***(P-21270)***
Greater Los Angeles Agency......D......323 478-8000
2239 Norwalk Ave Los Angeles (90041) ***(P-23826)***
Greater Los Angeles Zoo Assn......D......323 644-4200
5333 Zoo Dr Los Angeles (90027) ***(P-24785)***
Greater Sacramento Sur......D......916 929-7229
2288 Auburn Blvd Ste 201 Sacramento (95821) ***(P-22587)***
Greater Sacramento Surgery Ctr, Sacramento *Also called Greater Sacramento Sur* ***(P-22587)***
Greater San Diego AC Co Inc......C......619 469-7818
3883 Ruffin Rd Ste C San Diego (92123) ***(P-2223)***
Greater South Bay Area HM Hlth......E......310 329-4835
18726 S Wstn Ave Ste 409 Gardena (90248) ***(P-22308)***
Greater South Bay Home Health, Gardena *Also called Greater South Bay Area HM Hlth* ***(P-22308)***
Greater Vallejo Recreation Dst......C......707 648-4600
395 Amador St Vallejo (94590) ***(P-19180)***
Greater Valley Medical Group (PA)......B......818 838-4500
11600 Indian Hills Rd # 300 Mission Hills (91345) ***(P-22588)***
Greatwide Dedicated Transport, Vernon *Also called Greatwide Logistics Svcs LLC* ***(P-5079)***
Greatwide Logistics Svcs LLC......D......323 268-7100
4310 Bandini Blvd Vernon (90058) ***(P-5079)***
Gree International Inc......C......415 409-5159
275 Battery St Ste 1700 San Francisco (94111) ***(P-15189)***
Gree International Entrmt Inc......C......415 409-5200
185 Berry St Ste 590 San Francisco (94107) ***(P-15190)***
Green Acres Lodge, Rosemead *Also called Longwood Management Corp* ***(P-20599)***
Green Acres Nursery & Sup LLC......D......916 782-2273
604 Sutter St Folsom (95630) ***(P-7703)***
Green Again Ldscpg & Con Inc......D......650 368-9304
851 Charter St Redwood City (94063) ***(P-849)***
Green Convergence (PA)......D......661 491-5111
28490 Wstnghuse Pl Ste 16 Valencia (91355) ***(P-7626)***
Green Diamond Resource Company......D......707 668-4400
900 Riverside Rd Korbel (95550) ***(P-991)***
Green Dot Corporation (PA)......C......626 765-2000
3465 E Foothill Blvd # 100 Pasadena (91107) ***(P-9714)***
Green Energy Innovations, Santa Fe Springs *Also called Sfadia Inc* ***(P-2732)***
Green Equity Investors III L P......A......310 954-0444
11111 Santa Monica Blvd # 2000 Los Angeles (90025) ***(P-9961)***
Green Farms Inc......B......858 831-7701
2652 Long Beach Ave Los Angeles (90058) ***(P-8691)***
Green Farms Inc (PA)......C......213 747-4411
2652 Long Beach Ave Ste 2 Los Angeles (90058) ***(P-8692)***
Green Glusk Field Clama & Mach......C......310 553-3610
1900 Avenue Of The Stars 21f Los Angeles (90067) ***(P-23110)***
Green Hasson & Janks LLP......C......310 873-1600
10990 Wilshire Blvd Fl 16 Los Angeles (90024) ***(P-26211)***
Green Hills Retirement Center, Millbrae *Also called Hillsdale Group LP* ***(P-21113)***
Green Hills Software Inc (PA)......C......805 965-6044
30 W Sola St Santa Barbara (93101) ***(P-15696)***
Green Planet 21 Inc (PA)......E......510 873-8777
336 Adeline St Oakland (94607) ***(P-7979)***
Green Ridge Services LLC......D......925 245-5500
6185 Industrial Way Livermore (94551) ***(P-6040)***
Green River Golf Corporation......D......714 970-8411
5215 Green River Rd Corona (92880) ***(P-18716)***
Green River Golf Course, Corona *Also called Green River Golf Corporation* ***(P-18716)***
Green Scene Landscape Inc......D......818 280-0420
21220 Devonshire St # 102 Chatsworth (91311) ***(P-850)***
Green Thumb International Inc......D......818 340-6400
21812 Sherman Way Canoga Park (91303) ***(P-9136)***
Green Thumb Nursery, Canoga Park *Also called Super Garden Centers Inc* ***(P-9167)***
Green Thumb Produce......C......951 849-4711
2648 W Ramsey St Banning (92220) ***(P-8693)***
Green Tortoise Adventure Trvl......D......415 834-1000
494 Broadway San Francisco (94133) ***(P-3898)***
Green Tree Capital LP......D......760 245-3461
14173 Green Tree Blvd Victorville (92395) ***(P-12618)***
Green Tree Inn, Victorville *Also called Lee-Victorville Hotel Corp* ***(P-12846)***
Green Tree Inn, Victorville *Also called Green Tree Capital LP* ***(P-12618)***
Green Tree Nursery......E......209 874-9100
23979 Lake Rd La Grange (95329) ***(P-9137)***
Green Trucking, Tulare *Also called Darrell L Green Inc* ***(P-4341)***
Green Valley Corporation (PA)......E......408 287-0246
777 N 1st St Fl 5 San Jose (95112) ***(P-1538)***
Green Valley Country Club......D......707 864-1101
35 Country Club Dr Fairfield (94534) ***(P-18932)***
Green Valley Security Inc......D......916 797-4058
6049 Douglas Blvd Ste 28 Granite Bay (95746) ***(P-16665)***
Green Wave Ingredients Inc......E......562 207-9770
14821 Northam St La Mirada (90638) ***(P-8173)***
Greenall, Suisun City *Also called E B Stone & Son Inc* ***(P-9078)***
Greenball Corp (PA)......E......714 782-3060
222 S Harbor Blvd Ste 700 Anaheim (92805) ***(P-6692)***
Greenberg Traurig LLP......D......415 655-1300
4 Embarcadero Ctr # 3000 San Francisco (94111) ***(P-23111)***
Greenberg Traurig LLP......D......310 586-7708
1840 Century Park E # 1900 Los Angeles (90067) ***(P-23112)***
Greenberg Traurig LLP......D......650 328-8500
1900 University Ave Fl 5 East Palo Alto (94303) ***(P-23113)***
Greenberg Traurig LLP......D......949 732-6500
3161 Michelson Dr # 1000 Irvine (92612) ***(P-23114)***
Greenbrea Care Center, Greenbrae *Also called Ocadian Care Centers LLC* ***(P-20675)***
Greenbriar Homes Communities......D......510 497-8200
4340 Stevens Creek Blvd # 240 San Jose (95129) ***(P-1340)***
Greenbriar Homes Community, Fremont *Also called Greenbriar Management Company* ***(P-11490)***
Greenbriar Management Company......D......510 497-8200
43160 Osgood Rd Fremont (94539) ***(P-11490)***
Greenbrier Lawn Tree Exprt Co......D......619 469-8720
3616 Bancroft Dr Spring Valley (91977) ***(P-851)***
Greencycle US Holding Inc (HQ)......D......858 677-0884
4686 Mercury St San Diego (92111) ***(P-11984)***
Greene Rdvsky Maloney Share LP......D......415 981-1400
4 Embarcadero Ctr # 4000 San Francisco (94111) ***(P-23115)***
Greenheart Farms Inc (PA)......B......805 481-2234
902 Zenon Way Arroyo Grande (93420) ***(P-345)***
Greenland US Consulting Inc......D......213 362-9300
515 S Figueroa St # 1703 Los Angeles (90071) ***(P-1341)***
Greenlaw Grupe Jr Operating Co, Angels Camp *Also called Motherlode Investors LLC* ***(P-18739)***
Greenleaf, Brisbane *Also called Oakville Produce Partners LLC* ***(P-8711)***
Greenleaf Paper Products......D......949 348-0048
26431 Crown Valley Pkwy # 150 Mission Viejo (92691) ***(P-8107)***
Greenpath Recovery Recycl Svcs, Colton *Also called Greenpath Recovery West Inc* ***(P-7980)***
Greenpath Recovery West Inc......D......909 954-0686
330 W Citrus St Ste 250 Colton (92324) ***(P-7980)***
Greenridge Senior Care......C......510 758-9600
2150 Pyramid Dr El Sobrante (94803) ***(P-24544)***
Greens Group Inc......C......949 829-4902
9289 Research Dr Irvine (92618) ***(P-12619)***
Greensoft Technology Inc......C......323 254-5961
155 S El Molino Ave # 100 Pasadena (91101) ***(P-16139)***
Greenspire LLC......D......310 477-7686
11620 Wilshire Blvd # 410 Los Angeles (90025) ***(P-27255)***
Greenteam of San Jose, San Jose *Also called Waste Connections Cal Inc* ***(P-6509)***
Greentree Property MGT Inc......E......415 347-8600
600 California St Fl 19 San Francisco (94108) ***(P-10886)***
Greenwalds Autobody Frameworks (PA)......D......619 477-2600
1814 Roosevelt Ave National City (91950) ***(P-17724)***

ALPHABETIC

Employee Codes: A=Over 500 employees, B=251-500
C=101-250, D=51-100, E=50
2019 Directory of California
Wholesalers and Services Companies
© Mergent Inc. 1-800-342-5647
1319

Greenwaste Recovery Inc ....E....408 283-4804
565 Charles St San Jose (95112) *(P-6405)*
Greenwaste Recovery Inc (PA) ....D....408 283-4800
625 Charles St San Jose (95112) *(P-6406)*
Greenway Arts Alliance Inc ....D....323 655-7679
544 N Fairfax Ave Los Angeles (90036) *(P-18370)*
Greenwood & Hall, Los Angeles *Also called Pcs Link Inc (P-27820)*
Greenwood Holdings LLC ....D....619 299-6633
3888 Greenwood St San Diego (92110) *(P-12620)*
Grefco Dicaperl, Torrance *Also called Dicaperl Corporation (P-1102)*
Greg H Carpenter Concrete Inc ....E....209 367-4224
955 N Guild Ave Lodi (95240) *(P-3261)*
Grega Brooke Sra ....E....707 938-3362
18501 Riverside Dr Sonoma (95476) *(P-11491)*
Gregg Dilling and Testing, Martinez *Also called Gregg Drilling & Testing Inc (P-3352)*
Gregg Drilling LLC (PA) ....D....562 427-6899
2726 Walnut Ave Signal Hill (90755) *(P-3350)*
Gregg Drilling LLC ....D....925 313-5800
950 Howe Rd Martinez (94553) *(P-3351)*
Gregg Drilling & Testing Inc ....D....925 313-5800
950 Howe Rd Martinez (94553) *(P-3352)*
Gregg Drilling & Testing Inc (PA) ....D....562 427-6899
2726 Walnut Ave Signal Hill (90755) *(P-3527)*
Gregg Electric Inc ....C....909 983-1794
608 W Emporia St Ontario (91762) *(P-2594)*
Greka Inc ....C....805 347-8700
1791 Sinton Rd Santa Maria (93458) *(P-1009)*
Gresham Savage Nolan & Tilden (PA) ....D....619 794-0050
550 E Hospitality Ln # 300 San Bernardino (92408) *(P-23116)*
Grey Direct-E Marketing, San Francisco *Also called G2 Direct and Digital (P-15174)*
Greybor Medical Transportation ....E....213 250-4444
119 Belmont Ave Ste 107 Los Angeles (90026) *(P-3805)*
Greyhound Lines Inc ....C....559 268-1829
1033 Broadway St Fresno (93721) *(P-3878)*
Greyhound Lines Inc ....B....213 629-8400
1716 E 7th St Los Angeles (90021) *(P-3954)*
Greyhound Lines Inc ....E....209 466-3568
121 S Center St Stockton (95202) *(P-4840)*
Greystar Management Svcs LP ....B....818 596-2180
6320 Canoga Ave Ste 1512 Woodland Hills (91367) *(P-11492)*
Greystar Management Svcs LP ....B....949 705-0010
17885 Von Karman Ave Irvine (92614) *(P-26877)*
Greystone Homes Inc ....C....925 242-0811
6121 Bollinger Canyon Rd # 500 San Ramon (94583) *(P-1175)*
Greystone Plastering Inc ....D....408 298-5934
1716 Stone Ave Ste B San Jose (95125) *(P-2889)*
Greystripe Incorporated ....C....415 644-1702
30699 Russell Ranch Rd # 250 Westlake Village (91362) *(P-13836)*
Grht Inc ....D....323 873-6393
14818 Raymer St Van Nuys (91405) *(P-9222)*
Grid Net Inc (PA) ....D....415 872-5097
126 S Park St San Francisco (94107) *(P-15191)*
Gridgain Systems Inc ....C....650 241-2281
1065 E Hillsdale Blvd Foster City (94404) *(P-17202)*
Gridley Packing Inc ....C....530 846-3753
1366 Larkin Rd Gridley (95948) *(P-520)*
Griffin Group LLC (PA) ....C....415 892-4569
4 Rebelo Ln Ste D Novato (94947) *(P-26878)*
Griffin Slr Management Inc ....D....310 270-4031
9454 Wilshire Blvd # 700 Beverly Hills (90212) *(P-26879)*
Griffin Technology LLC (HQ) ....D....615 399-7000
6001 Oak Cyn Irvine (92618) *(P-7484)*
Griffith Company (PA) ....D....714 984-5500
3050 E Birch St Brea (92821) *(P-1787)*
Griffith Company ....D....562 929-1128
12200 Bloomfield Ave Santa Fe Springs (90670) *(P-1788)*
Griffith Park Healthcare Ctr, Glendale *Also called Griffith Pk Rhbltation Ctr LLC (P-20497)*
Griffith Pk Rhbltation Ctr LLC ....D....818 845-8507
201 Allen Ave Glendale (91201) *(P-20497)*
Grifols Biologicals LLC ....B....323 255-2221
2410 Lillyvale Ave Los Angeles (90032) *(P-4568)*
Grifols Diagnstc Solutions Inc (HQ) ....C....323 225-2221
4560 Horton St Emeryville (94608) *(P-22095)*
Grifols Shared Svcs N Amer Inc (HQ) ....C....323 225-2221
2410 Lillyvale Ave Los Angeles (90032) *(P-8174)*
Grill On The Alley The Inc ....A....323 856-5530
6801 Hollywood Blvd Los Angeles (90028) *(P-17203)*
Grill Recording Studio ....D....510 531-4351
4770 San Pablo Ave Ste C Emeryville (94608) *(P-17204)*
Grimmway Enterprises Inc ....D....661 854-6240
12020 Malaga Rd Arvin (93203) *(P-1402)*
Grimmway Enterprises Inc ....C....760 344-0204
2171 W Bannister Rd Brawley (92227) *(P-17765)*
Grimmway Enterprises Inc ....C....661 393-3320
6101 S Zerker Rd Shafter (93263) *(P-521)*
Grimmway Enterprises Inc ....B....661 854-6250
830 Sycamore Rd Arvin (93203) *(P-522)*
Grimmway Enterprises Inc ....D....661 854-6200
11412 Malaga Rd Arvin (93203) *(P-523)*
Grimmway Enterprises Inc ....C....661 845-5200
6900 Mountain View Rd Bakersfield (93307) *(P-524)*
Grimmway Enterprises Inc ....B....661 399-0844
6301 S Zerker Rd Shafter (93263) *(P-346)*
Grimmway Enterprises Inc ....B....661 845-3758
12000 Main St Lamont (93241) *(P-8694)*
Grimmway Farms, Arvin *Also called Grimmway Enterprises Inc (P-523)*
Grimmway Farms, Bakersfield *Also called Grimmway Enterprises Inc (P-524)*
Grimmway Farms ....D....760 356-2513
2105 Anderholt Rd Holtville (92250) *(P-347)*
Grimmway Frozen Foods, Arvin *Also called Grimmway Enterprises Inc (P-522)*
Gringteam Inc ....C....858 485-4145
14455 Penasquitos Dr San Diego (92129) *(P-12621)*
Gringteam Inc ....B....909 605-4222
222 N Vineyard Ave Ontario (91764) *(P-12622)*
Gringteam Inc ....B....408 453-4000
2050 Gateway Pl San Jose (95110) *(P-12623)*
Gringteam Inc ....C....661 426-7919
3100 Camino Del Rio Ct Bakersfield (93308) *(P-12624)*
Gringteam Inc ....C....714 825-3333
201 E Macarthur Blvd Santa Ana (92707) *(P-12625)*
Gringteam Inc ....B....916 929-8855
2001 Point West Way Sacramento (95815) *(P-12626)*
Gringteam Inc ....B....209 526-6000
1150 9th St Frnt Modesto (95354) *(P-12627)*
Gringteam Inc ....B....619 297-5466
7450 Hazard Center Dr San Diego (92108) *(P-12628)*
Gringteam Inc ....C....650 344-5500
835 Airport Blvd Burlingame (94010) *(P-12629)*
Gringteam Inc ....D....949 661-1100
34402 Pacific Coast Hwy Dana Point (92624) *(P-12630)*
Gripp, Temecula *Also called Bbk Performance Inc (P-6626)*
Griswald Industries, Perris *Also called Griswold Industries (P-7850)*
Griswold Industries ....D....951 657-1718
24100 Water Ave Perris (92570) *(P-7850)*
Grisworld Real Estate MGT (PA) ....D....858 597-6100
5703 Oberlin Dr Ste 300 San Diego (92121) *(P-11493)*
Grizzard Cmmncations Group Inc ....D....818 543-1315
2 N Lake Ave Pasadena (91101) *(P-13837)*
Grm Information MGT Services ....E....562 373-9000
8500 Mercury Ln Pico Rivera (90660) *(P-26880)*
Grm Information MGT Svcs Inc ....D....562 373-9000
8500 Mercury Ln Pico Rivera (90660) *(P-26881)*
Grobstein Horwath & Co ....D....818 501-5200
15233 Ventura Blvd Fl 9 Van Nuys (91403) *(P-26212)*
Grobstein, Horwath & Company, Van Nuys *Also called Grobstein Horwath & Co (P-26212)*
Grocers Specialty Company (HQ) ....E....323 264-5200
5200 Sheila St Commerce (90040) *(P-8412)*
Grolink Plant Company Inc (PA) ....C....805 984-7958
4107 W Gonzales Rd Oxnard (93036) *(P-9138)*
Gross Convalescent Hospital ....D....209 334-3760
321 W Turner Rd Lodi (95240) *(P-20498)*
Grosslight Insurance Inc ....D....310 473-9611
1333 Westwood Blvd # 200 Los Angeles (90024) *(P-10638)*
Grossmont Center Management, La Mesa *Also called Grossmont Shopping Center Co (P-10887)*
Grossmont Grdns Rtrement Cmnty, La Mesa *Also called Healthcare Group (P-24557)*
Grossmont Home Hlth & Hospice, La Mesa *Also called Grossmont Hospital Corporation (P-21437)*
Grossmont Hospital Corporation (HQ) ....A....619 740-6000
5555 Grossmont Center Dr La Mesa (91942) *(P-21436)*
Grossmont Hospital Corporation ....C....619 667-1900
8881 Fletcher Pkwy # 105 La Mesa (91942) *(P-21437)*
Grossmont Shopping Center Co ....D....619 465-2900
5500 Grsmnt Ctr Dr # 213 La Mesa (91942) *(P-10887)*
Grossmont-Cuyamaca Community ....D....619 644-7684
8800 Grossmont College Dr El Cajon (92020) *(P-25170)*
Grosvenor Properties Ltd ....C....650 873-3200
380 S Airport Blvd South San Francisco (94080) *(P-12631)*
Grosvenor Visalia Associates ....D....559 651-5000
9000 W Airport Dr Visalia (93277) *(P-12632)*
Ground Maintenance Services, Thousand Oaks *Also called Kevin Persons Inc (P-763)*
Groundwork Open Source Inc ....D....415 992-4500
333 Bryant St Ste 100 San Francisco (94107) *(P-16228)*
Groundworks Inc ....D....925 513-0300
2145 Elkins Way Ste C Brentwood (94513) *(P-3262)*
Group Avantica Inc ....B....650 248-9678
2680 Bayshore Pkwy # 416 Mountain View (94043) *(P-15192)*
Group Delphi, Alameda *Also called Delphi Productions Inc (P-13816)*
Groupe Development Associates ....D....209 473-6000
3255 W March Ln Fl 4 Stockton (95219) *(P-11879)*
Groupware Technology Inc (PA) ....E....408 540-0090
541 Division St Campbell (95008) *(P-15968)*
Grove - Design District, The, San Francisco *Also called Ps24 Inc (P-27005)*
Grove Lumber & Bldg Sups Inc (PA) ....C....909 947-0277
1300 S Campus Ave Ontario (91761) *(P-6825)*
Grover Landscape Services Inc ....D....209 545-4401
6224 Stoddard Rd Modesto (95356) *(P-265)*
Grower Direct Nut Company Inc ....E....209 883-4890
2288 Geer Rd Hughson (95326) *(P-525)*
Growers Company Inc ....D....831 424-3850
21570 Potter Rd Salinas (93908) *(P-14633)*
Growers Express LLC (PA) ....B....831 757-9951
150 Main St Ste 210 Salinas (93901) *(P-8695)*
Growers Street Cooling LLC ....D....831 424-2929
1080 Growers St Salinas (93901) *(P-526)*
Growers Transplanting Inc (HQ) ....D....831 449-3440
360 Espinosa Rd Salinas (93907) *(P-313)*
Growing Company Inc ....D....916 379-9088
4 Wayne Ct Ste 3 Sacramento (95829) *(P-852)*
Growith Inc ....D....805 650-6650
1069 Camero Way Fremont (94539) *(P-2224)*
Grubb Co Inc ....D....510 339-0400
1960 Mountain Blvd Oakland (94611) *(P-11494)*
Gruen Assoc Archtects Planners, Los Angeles *Also called Gruen Associates (P-26053)*
Gruen Associates ....D....323 937-4270
6330 San Vicente Blvd # 200 Los Angeles (90048) *(P-26053)*
Grupe Company (PA) ....D....209 473-6000
3255 W March Ln Ste 400 Stockton (95219) *(P-11495)*

Mergent e-mail: customerrelations@mergent.com
1320
2019 Directory of California Wholesalers and Services Companies
(P-0000) Products & Services Section entry number
(PA)=Parent Co (HQ)=Headquarters (DH)=Div Headquarters

Grupe Dev Companynorthern Cal....C....209 473-6000
3255 W March Ln Ste 400 Stockton (95219) ***(P-1342)***
Grupe Properties Co....E....209 956-7885
2944 W Swain Rd Stockton (95219) ***(P-4569)***
Grupoex, La Mirada *Also called Mejico Express Inc* ***(P-4842)***
Gs Brothers Inc (PA)....C....310 833-1369
2215 N Gaffey St San Pedro (90731) ***(P-853)***
GS Levine Insurance Svcs Inc....D....858 481-8692
10505 Sorrento Valley Rd # 200 San Diego (92121) ***(P-10639)***
Gs1 Group Inc....D....626 510-6384
70 S Lake Ave Ste 945 Pasadena (91101) ***(P-16666)***
Gsa Design Inc....C....818 241-2558
4551 San Fernando Rd # 102 Glendale (91204) ***(P-17205)***
GSC Logistics Inc (PA)....C....510 844-3700
530 Water St Fl 5 Oakland (94607) ***(P-4348)***
GSE Construction Company Inc....D....925 447-0292
6950 Preston Ave Livermore (94551) ***(P-1789)***
GSe Construction Company Inc (PA)....C....925 447-0292
6950 Preston Ave Livermore (94551) ***(P-1923)***
Gsf Builders, Anaheim *Also called Gsf Enterprises Inc* ***(P-1539)***
Gsf Enterprises Inc....D....714 524-9500
700 N Valley St Ste B Anaheim (92801) ***(P-1539)***
Gsg Associates Inc....D....626 585-1808
1010 E Union St Ste 203 Pasadena (91106) ***(P-26882)***
Gsico, Foothill Ranch *Also called Global Solutions Integration* ***(P-25716)***
Gt Diamond, Irvine *Also called General Tool Inc* ***(P-7849)***
Gt Nexus Inc (HQ)....D....510 808-2222
1111 Broadway 5f Oakland (94607) ***(P-5574)***
GTE, Santa Monica *Also called Verizon Communications Inc* ***(P-5670)***
Gtech, Santa Fe Springs *Also called Igt Global Solutions Corp* ***(P-19188)***
GTS, Chico *Also called Gas Transmission Systems Inc* ***(P-25701)***
Gtt Communications (mp) Inc....D....714 327-2000
555 Anton Blvd Ste 200 Costa Mesa (92626) ***(P-27742)***
Gtt Communications (mp) Inc (HQ)....C....925 201-2500
6700 Koll Center Pkwy Pleasanton (94566) ***(P-5575)***
Gtxcel Inc....D....800 609-8994
2855 Telg Ave Ste 600 Berkeley (94705) ***(P-15193)***
Guarachi Wine Partners Inc....D....818 225-5100
22837 Ventura Blvd # 300 Woodland Hills (91364) ***(P-9047)***
Guarantee Real Estate....E....559 650-6030
756 W Shaw Ave Ste 105 Fresno (93704) ***(P-11496)***
Guarantee Real Estate Corp....D....559 321-6040
180 W Bullard Ave Ste 101 Clovis (93612) ***(P-11497)***
Guarantee Real Estate Corp....D....559 431-8600
6710 N West Ave Ste 108 Fresno (93711) ***(P-11498)***
Guaranteed Rate Inc....C....760 310-6008
1455 Frazee Rd Ste 500 San Diego (92108) ***(P-9812)***
Guard Force International Inc....E....512 296-0316
11566 Brookrun Ct Riverside (92505) ***(P-16900)***
Guard Management Inc....A....858 279-8282
8001 Vickers St San Diego (92111) ***(P-16667)***
Guard Systems District 1, Monterey Park *Also called Guard-Systems Inc* ***(P-16671)***
Guard-Systems Inc (PA)....A....626 443-0031
1190 Monterey Pass Rd Monterey Park (91754) ***(P-16668)***
Guard-Systems Inc....B....909 947-5400
1910 S Archibald Ave M2 Ontario (91761) ***(P-16669)***
Guard-Systems Inc....B....323 881-6711
1190 Monterey Pass Rd Monterey Park (91754) ***(P-16670)***
Guard-Systems Inc....B....323 881-6715
1190 Monterey Pass Rd Monterey Park (91754) ***(P-16671)***
Guardant Health Inc....B....855 698-8887
505 Penobscot Dr Redwood City (94063) ***(P-22096)***
Guardco Security Services....D....209 723-4273
1360 W 18th St Merced (95340) ***(P-16672)***
Guardian Computer Support....C....925 251-8800
7075 Commerce Cir Ste D Pleasanton (94588) ***(P-16287)***
Guardian Eagle Security Inc....B....888 990-0002
11400 W Olympic Blvd Fl 2 Los Angeles (90064) ***(P-16673)***
Guardian General Insur Svcs, Glendale *Also called Ggis Insurance Services Inc* ***(P-10636)***
Guardian National Inc....E....800 700-1467
20361 Prairie St Ste 1 Chatsworth (91311) ***(P-16674)***
Guardian National Security, Chatsworth *Also called Guardian National Inc* ***(P-16674)***
Guardian Rehabilitation Hosp....D....323 930-4815
533 S Fairfax Ave Los Angeles (90036) ***(P-21102)***
Guardian Security Agency, Concord *Also called Delta Personnel Services Inc* ***(P-16629)***
Guardians of The Los Angeles....D....310 479-2468
10780 Santa Monica Blvd # 225 Los Angeles (90025) ***(P-20499)***
Guardnow Inc (PA)....E....877 482-7366
18663 Ventura Blvd # 217 Tarzana (91356) ***(P-16675)***
Guardsmark LLC....B....925 484-4412
4713 1st St Ste 215 Pleasanton (94566) ***(P-16676)***
Guardsmark LLC....D....310 522-9603
1225 W 190th St Ste 280 Gardena (90248) ***(P-16677)***
Guardsmark LLC....C....310 287-3103
3000 S Robertson Blvd # 150 Los Angeles (90034) ***(P-16678)***
Guardsmark LLC (HQ)....C....714 619-9700
1551 N Tustin Ave Ste 650 Santa Ana (92705) ***(P-16679)***
Guardsmark LLC....B....415 956-6070
350 Sansome St San Francisco (94104) ***(P-16680)***
Guardsmark LLC....C....415 898-9022
505 Alexis Ct NAPA (94558) ***(P-16681)***
Guardsmark LLC....C....818 841-0288
101 S 1st St Ste 408 Burbank (91502) ***(P-16682)***
Guardsmark LLC....C....510 562-7606
100 Hegenberger Rd # 130 Oakland (94621) ***(P-16683)***
Guardsmark LLC....C....800 238-5878
4970 El Camino Real Los Altos (94022) ***(P-16684)***
Guardsmark LLC....C....661 325-5906
5300 Lennox Ave Ste 102 Bakersfield (93309) ***(P-16685)***
Guardsmark LLC....C....858 499-0025
5095 Murphy Canyon Rd # 301 San Diego (92123) ***(P-16686)***
Guardsmark LLC....C....559 243-1217
600 W Shaw Ave Ste 200 Fresno (93704) ***(P-16687)***
Guardsmark LLC....C....818 841-0288
101 S 1st St Ste 408 Burbank (91502) ***(P-16688)***
Guardsmark LLC....C....831 769-8981
30 E San Joaquin St # 204 Salinas (93901) ***(P-16689)***
Guardsmark LLC....C....650 685-2400
533 Airport Blvd Ste 303 Burlingame (94010) ***(P-16690)***
Guardsmark LLC....C....650 652-9130
1601 Bayshore Hwy Ste 350 Burlingame (94010) ***(P-16691)***
Guardsmark LLC....C....818 841-0288
101 S 1st St Ste 408 Burbank (91502) ***(P-16692)***
Guardsmark LLC....B....909 989-5345
2900 Adams St Ste C10a Riverside (92504) ***(P-16693)***
Guava Holdings LLC....E....530 671-0550
1220 Plumas St Yuba City (95991) ***(P-22022)***
Guavus Inc (HQ)....D....650 243-3400
2860 Junction Ave San Jose (95134) ***(P-15697)***
Guck Ariba....C....650 390-1445
807 Eleventh Ave Sunnyvale (94089) ***(P-15698)***
Gudgel Roofing Inc....E....916 387-6900
5321 84th St Sacramento (95826) ***(P-3162)***
Guerra Nut Shelling Company....D....831 637-4471
190 Hillcrest Rd Hollister (95023) ***(P-527)***
Guidance Center (PA)....C....562 595-1159
1301 Pine Ave Long Beach (90813) ***(P-22589)***
Guidance Software Inc (HQ)....C....626 229-9191
1055 E Colo Blvd Ste 400 Pasadena (91106) ***(P-15699)***
Guidance Solutions Inc....E....310 754-4000
4134 Del Rey Ave Marina Del Rey (90292) ***(P-16229)***
Guide Dogs For Blind Inc (PA)....C....415 499-4000
350 Los Ranchitos Rd San Rafael (94903) ***(P-628)***
Guidebook Inc (PA)....D....650 319-7233
340 Bryant St Ste 400 San Francisco (94107) ***(P-15194)***
Guided Discoveries Inc....E....951 659-6062
26800 Saunders Meadows Rd Idyllwild (92549) ***(P-13450)***
Guidewire Software Inc (PA)....C....650 357-9100
1001 E Hillsdale Blvd # 8 Foster City (94404) ***(P-15700)***
Guild Mortgage Company....E....916 486-6257
3626 Fair Oaks Blvd Sacramento (95864) ***(P-9885)***
Guild, The, Hawthorne *Also called Los Angeles Guild LLC* ***(P-27306)***
Guillen Electric Company Inc....E....909 480-3915
1485 Andrew Dr Ste D Claremont (91711) ***(P-2595)***
Guinn Corporation....D....661 325-6109
6533 Rosedale Hwy Bakersfield (93308) ***(P-3428)***
Gulf- California Broadcast Co....C....760 773-0342
31276 Dunham Way Thousand Palms (92276) ***(P-5796)***
Gulfstream Aerospace Corp GA....A....562 420-1818
4150 E Donald Douglas Dr Long Beach (90808) ***(P-25719)***
Gumbiner Savett Inc CPA....D....310 828-9798
1723 Cloverfield Blvd Santa Monica (90404) ***(P-10888)***
Gumbiner, Savett, Finkel, Fing, Santa Monica *Also called Gumbiner Savett Inc CPA* ***(P-10888)***
Gunderson Dettmer Stough Ville (PA)....C....650 321-2400
550 Allerton St Redwood City (94063) ***(P-23117)***
Gursey Schneider & Co LLC (PA)....D....310 552-0960
1888 Century Park E # 900 Los Angeles (90067) ***(P-26213)***
Guru Denim LLC (HQ)....C....323 266-3072
1888 Rosecrans Ave # 1000 Manhattan Beach (90266) ***(P-8304)***
Gustine Mini Storage, Gustine *Also called Andersen Nut Company* ***(P-493)***
Gusto, San Francisco *Also called Zenpayroll Inc* ***(P-15900)***
Guthy-Renker Direct, Santa Monica *Also called Guthy-Renker LLC* ***(P-8036)***
Guthy-Renker LLC (PA)....D....760 773-9022
100 N Pacific Coast Hwy # 1600 El Segundo (90245) ***(P-8035)***
Guthy-Renker LLC....D....949 454-1400
25892 Towne Centre Dr Foothill Ranch (92610) ***(P-17206)***
Guthy-Renker LLC....D....310 581-6250
3340 Ocean Park Blvd Fl 2 Santa Monica (90405) ***(P-8036)***
Guy George....E....831 728-2410
315 2nd St Ste A Watsonville (95076) ***(P-101)***
Guy Yocom Construction Inc (PA)....C....951 284-3456
3299 Horseless Carriage R Norco (92860) ***(P-3263)***
Gva Enterprises Inc (PA)....D....213 484-0510
316 S Westlake Ave Los Angeles (90057) ***(P-21103)***
Gva Enterprises Inc....D....213 484-0784
415 S Union Ave Los Angeles (90017) ***(P-20500)***
Gvs Italy....D....424 382-4343
8616 La Tijera Blvd Los Angeles (90045) ***(P-7277)***
Gyneclgic Onclogy Plvic Srgery, Los Gatos *Also called Sutter Health* ***(P-25260)***
Gypsum Contractors Inc....E....949 340-9100
23785 El Toro Rd Ste 135 Lake Forest (92630) ***(P-2890)***
Gypsum Dry Wall Supply Co....E....408 993-9710
2049 Senter Rd San Jose (95112) ***(P-8037)***
H & D Construction, El Cajon *Also called Steve Duich Inc* ***(P-3331)***
H & D Electric....B....916 332-0794
5237 Walnut Ave Ste 100 Sacramento (95841) ***(P-2596)***
H & F Grain Farms LLC....D....805 754-4449
1181 S Wolff Rd Oxnard (93033) ***(P-27743)***
H & H Transportation LLC....D....951 817-2300
300 El Sobrante Rd Corona (92879) ***(P-4188)***
H & H Truck Terminal, Victorville *Also called Hartwick & Hand Inc* ***(P-4019)***
H & K Abouaf Corporation....D....310 393-1282
9100 S Sepulveda Blvd # 1 Los Angeles (90045) ***(P-22309)***
H & N Fish Company, Vernon *Also called H & N Foods International Inc* ***(P-8576)***
H & N Foods International Inc (HQ)....C....323 586-9300
5580 S Alameda St Vernon (90058) ***(P-8576)***

ALPHABETIC

H & R Accounts Inc ....D....619 819-8844
3131 Camino Del Rio N San Diego (92108) ***(P-15195)***
H & R Block, San Francisco *Also called H&R Block Inc* ***(P-13708)***
H & R Block Inc ....D....805 349-9266
401 N Broadway Ste B Santa Maria (93454) ***(P-13706)***
H & R Block Inc ....C....707 643-1856
4300 Sonoma Blvd Ste 600 Vallejo (94589) ***(P-13707)***
H & R Gunlund Ranches Inc ....C....559 864-8186
3510 W Saginaw Ave Caruthers (93609) ***(P-147)***
H A Bowen Electric Inc ....D....510 483-0500
2055 Williams St San Leandro (94577) ***(P-2597)***
H and H Drug Stores Inc ....D....209 931-5200
4692 E Waterloo Rd Stockton (95215) ***(P-8038)***
H B, San Francisco *Also called Hassard Bonnington LLP* ***(P-23125)***
H B J Corporation ....D....707 333-7066
5806 Frontier Way Carmichael (95608) ***(P-2891)***
H C C S Inc ....D....916 454-5752
4700 Elvas Ave Sacramento (95819) ***(P-20501)***
H C I, Norco *Also called Hci Inc* ***(P-1924)***
H C I, Corona *Also called Hardwood Creations* ***(P-3040)***
H C Olsen Cnstr Co Inc ....D....626 359-8900
710 Los Angeles Ave Monrovia (91016) ***(P-1403)***
H C S, Newport Beach *Also called Healthcare Cost Solutions Inc* ***(P-26216)***
H C T Inc ....B....619 224-1234
1441 Quivira Rd San Diego (92109) ***(P-12633)***
H D G Associates ....C....805 963-0744
1111 E Cabrillo Blvd Santa Barbara (93103) ***(P-12634)***
H D R, Los Angeles *Also called HDR Architecture Inc* ***(P-25724)***
H D S I Managment ....E....323 231-1104
3460 S Broadway Los Angeles (90007) ***(P-10889)***
H D Smith LLC ....D....310 641-1885
1370 E Victoria St Carson (90746) ***(P-8175)***
H E L P Inc ....D....951 922-2305
53 S 6th St Banning (92220) ***(P-23827)***
H F Cox Inc (PA) ....D....661 366-3236
118 Cox Transport Way Bakersfield (93307) ***(P-4189)***
H H M I, Stanford *Also called Howard Hughes Medical Inst* ***(P-26378)***
H L Moe Co Inc (PA) ....C....818 572-2100
526 Commercial St Glendale (91203) ***(P-2225)***
H M C, Chula Vista *Also called Heartland Meat Company Inc* ***(P-8618)***
H M E, Carlsbad *Also called H M Electronics Inc* ***(P-7485)***
H M Electronics Inc (PA) ....B....858 535-6000
2848 Whiptail Loop Carlsbad (92010) ***(P-7485)***
H M H Engineers ....D....408 487-2200
1570 Oakland Rd San Jose (95131) ***(P-25720)***
H Naraghi Farms, Escalon *Also called Noralco Inc* ***(P-548)***
H O K, San Francisco *Also called Hellmuth Obata & Kassabaum Inc* ***(P-26057)***
H P Sears Co Inc ....D....661 325-5981
2000 18th St Bakersfield (93301) ***(P-14006)***
H Rauvel Inc (PA) ....D....310 604-0060
1710 E Sepulveda Blvd Carson (90745) ***(P-4570)***
H T V, Studio City *Also called High Technology Video Inc* ***(P-18195)***
H U S D Maintenance Operation ....D....510 784-2666
24400 Amador St Hayward (94544) ***(P-14283)***
H V Welker Co Inc ....D....408 263-4400
970 S Milpitas Blvd Milpitas (95035) ***(P-3104)***
H&E Equipment Services Inc ....C....714 522-6590
14241 Alondra Blvd La Mirada (90638) ***(P-14507)***
H&H Resolution LLC ....D....408 362-2293
151 Bernal Rd Ste 6 San Jose (95119) ***(P-14007)***
H&R Block Inc ....E....415 441-2666
1745 Van Ness Ave San Francisco (94109) ***(P-13708)***
H. T. Harvey & Associates, Los Gatos *Also called Triple Hs Inc* ***(P-27891)***
H.G. Fenton Company, San Diego *Also called Fenton Scripps Landing LLC* ***(P-11018)***
H.U.G. Company, Hayward *Also called Gourmet Foods* ***(P-8409)***
H2 Hotel LLC ....D....707 431-2202
219 Healdsburg Ave Healdsburg (95448) ***(P-12635)***
H2 Wellness Incorporated ....D....310 362-1888
11999 San Vicente Blvd Los Angeles (90049) ***(P-15701)***
H2c2 & Associates Inc (PA) ....E....510 562-6181
6925 San Leandro St Oakland (94621) ***(P-1540)***
Ha-Le Aloha Convalescent Hosp, Ceres *Also called Mark One Corporation* ***(P-21151)***
Haaker Equipment Company (PA) ....D....909 542-0800
2070 N White Ave La Verne (91750) ***(P-6596)***
Haas Factory Outlet, Anaheim *Also called Machining Time Savers Inc* ***(P-7766)***
Habenicht & Howlett A Corp ....D....415 824-7040
25 Patterson St San Francisco (94124) ***(P-3406)***
Habitat For Humanity of Greate ....E....310 323-4663
8739 Artesia Blvd Bellflower (90706) ***(P-24786)***
Habitat Rstration Sciences Inc (PA) ....D....760 479-4210
1217 Distribution Way Vista (92081) ***(P-854)***
Habitat Rstration Sciences Inc ....E....916 408-2990
3888 Cincinnati Ave Rocklin (95765) ***(P-855)***
Hacienda Golf Club ....D....562 694-1081
718 East Rd La Habra Heights (90631) ***(P-18933)***
Hacienda Health Care, Hanford *Also called Hacienda Rehabilitation & Heal* ***(P-20503)***
Hacienda Involved Parent Staff ....D....408 535-6259
1290 Kimberly Dr San Jose (95118) ***(P-25171)***
Hacienda Rehabilitation & Heal (PA) ....C....714 778-0221
1440 S State College Blvd 2a Anaheim (92806) ***(P-20502)***
Hacienda Rehabilitation & Heal ....C....559 582-9221
361 E Grangeville Blvd Hanford (93230) ***(P-20503)***
Hackerearth Inc ....C....650 461-4192
38350 Fremont Blvd Fremont (94536) ***(P-15196)***
Hackerone Inc (PA) ....D....415 891-0777
300 Montgomery St # 1200 San Francisco (94104) ***(P-16140)***
Hackney Electric Inc (PA) ....D....949 264-4000
23286 Arroyo Vis Rcho STA Marg (92688) ***(P-2598)***

Hagen Streiff Newton Oshiro ....E....925 941-1050
1990 N Calif Blvd Ste 320 Walnut Creek (94596) ***(P-26214)***
Haggin Oaks Golf Shop, Sacramento *Also called Morton Golf LLC* ***(P-18738)***
Hahn & Hahn LLP ....D....626 796-9123
301 E Colo Blvd Ste 900 Pasadena (91101) ***(P-23118)***
Haider Spine Ctr Med Group Inc ....E....951 413-0200
6276 River Crest Dr Ste A Riverside (92507) ***(P-19489)***
Haight Brown & Bonesteel LLP (PA) ....D....213 542-8000
555 S Flower St Ste 4500 Los Angeles (90071) ***(P-23119)***
Haight Gdnr Holland & Knight, San Francisco *Also called Holland & Knight LLP* ***(P-23134)***
Hailwood Inc ....D....805 487-4981
5755 Valentine Rd Ste 203 Ventura (93003) ***(P-10890)***
Hair Fashion Inc ....D....310 274-0851
348 N Beverly Dr Beverly Hills (90210) ***(P-13661)***
Haircutters ....D....562 690-2217
1230 W Imperial Hwy Ste A La Habra (90631) ***(P-13685)***
Haiyi Hotels Worldwide, San Francisco *Also called Apic Hotels Group LLC* ***(P-12326)***
Hakes Sash & Door Inc ....C....951 674-2414
31945 Corydon St Lake Elsinore (92530) ***(P-3039)***
Hal Hays Construction Inc (PA) ....C....951 369-1008
4181 Latham St Riverside (92501) ***(P-1404)***
Hal-Mar-Jac Enterprises ....C....415 467-1470
1044 Potrero Cir Suisun City (94585) ***(P-16694)***
Halbert Brothers Inc ....D....626 913-1800
17400 Chestnut St City of Industry (91748) ***(P-4349)***
Haldeman Inc ....E....323 726-7011
2937 Tanager Ave Commerce (90040) ***(P-2226)***
Haleakala Ranch LLC ....E....530 529-6651
9923 Tyler Rd Gerber (96035) ***(P-450)***
Half Moon Bay Golf Links, Half Moon Bay *Also called Ocean Links Corporation* ***(P-18742)***
Half Moon Bay Golf Links, Half Moon Bay *Also called Ocean Colony Partners LLC* ***(P-11900)***
Half Moon Bay Lodge ....E....650 726-9000
2400 Cabrillo Hwy S Half Moon Bay (94019) ***(P-12636)***
Half Moon Fruit & Produce Co (PA) ....D....530 662-1727
403 Court St Woodland (95695) ***(P-5)***
Half Moon Fruity and Prod Co, Woodland *Also called B E Giovannetti & Sons* ***(P-1)***
Hall AG Enterprises Inc ....C....559 846-7360
759 S Madera Ave Kerman (93630) ***(P-652)***
Hall AG Services, Kerman *Also called Hall AG Enterprises Inc* ***(P-652)***
Hall Ambulance Service Inc ....D....661 322-8741
2001 O St O Bakersfield (93301) ***(P-3806)***
Hall Ambulance Service Inc (PA) ....D....661 322-8741
1001 21st St Bakersfield (93301) ***(P-3807)***
Hall Capital Partners LLC (PA) ....D....415 288-0544
1 Maritime Plz Fl 5 San Francisco (94111) ***(P-10086)***
Hall Company ....D....209 364-0070
44328 W Nees Ave Firebaugh (93622) ***(P-348)***
Hall Management Corp ....A....559 846-7382
759 S Madera Ave Kerman (93630) ***(P-26883)***
Hall Windsor ....D....213 383-1547
1415 James M Wood Blvd Los Angeles (90015) ***(P-24545)***
Hall Wines LLC ....E....707 967-2626
401 Saint Helena Hwy S Saint Helena (94574) ***(P-9048)***
Halliburton Company ....D....661 393-8111
34722 7th Standard Rd Bakersfield (93314) ***(P-1062)***
Hallmark Channel, Studio City *Also called Crown Media United States LLC* ***(P-5897)***
Hallmark Distributing, Indio *Also called Triangle Distributing Co* ***(P-9030)***
Hallmark Inn, Davis *Also called Davis Hallmark Partnership* ***(P-12514)***
Hallmark Rehabilitation GP LLC ....A....949 282-5900
27442 Portola Pkwy # 200 El Toro (92610) ***(P-23828)***
Halo ....E....925 473-4642
4916 Chism Way Antioch (94531) ***(P-25426)***
Halo Unlimted Inc ....D....714 692-2270
1867 California Ave # 101 Corona (92881) ***(P-22810)***
Halstead Partnership ....D....916 830-8000
2850 Gateway Oaks Dr # 450 Sacramento (95833) ***(P-10891)***
Hamann Construction ....D....619 440-7424
1000 Pioneer Way El Cajon (92020) ***(P-1405)***
Hamblin's Auto & Body Shop, Riverside *Also called Hamblins Bdy Pnt Frame Sp Inc* ***(P-17766)***
Hamblins Bdy Pnt Frame Sp Inc ....D....951 689-8440
7590 Cypress Ave Riverside (92503) ***(P-17766)***
Hamburger Home ....D....213 637-5000
3701 Wilshire Blvd # 900 Los Angeles (90010) ***(P-1176)***
Hamburger Home (PA) ....D....323 876-0550
7120 Franklin Ave Los Angeles (90046) ***(P-24546)***
Hamburger Home ....C....818 980-3200
5900 Sepulvda Blvd Van Nuys (91411) ***(P-24547)***
Hamilton and Dillon Elc Inc ....D....209 529-6292
1128 Reno Ave Modesto (95351) ***(P-2599)***
Hamilton Brwart Insur Agcy LLC ....D....909 920-3250
1282 W Arrow Hwy Upland (91786) ***(P-10640)***
Hamilton Families ....D....415 409-2100
1631 Hayes St San Francisco (94117) ***(P-23829)***
Hamilton Family Ranch ....D....760 728-1358
2562 Doville Ranch Rd Fallbrook (92028) ***(P-205)***
Hamilton Partners ....D....650 347-8800
1301 Shoreway Rd Ste 250 Burlingame (94010) ***(P-27256)***
Hamlow Ranches Inc ....E....209 632-2873
4018 Swanson Rd Denair (95316) ***(P-218)***
Hammel Green & Abrahamson Inc ....D....916 787-5100
1200 R St Ste 100 Sacramento (95811) ***(P-26054)***
Hammer Down Davila Cnstr ....D....559 864-2001
2338 W Erie St Caruthers (93609) ***(P-1287)***
Hammonds Ranch Inc ....D....209 364-6185
47375 W Dakota Ave Firebaugh (93622) ***(P-349)***

Mergent e-mail: customerrelations@mergent.com
1322
2019 Directory of California
Wholesalers and Services Companies
(P-0000) Products & Services Section entry number
(PA)=Parent Co (HQ)=Headquarters (DH)=Div Headquarters

Hampstead Lafayette Hotel LLC...E...619 296-2101
2223 El Cajon Blvd San Diego (92104) **(P-12637)**
Hampton Inn, San Diego *Also called Boykin Mgt Co Ltd Lblty Co* **(P-12393)**
Hampton Inn, Elk Grove *Also called Dominion International Inc* **(P-12537)**
Hampton Inn, Santa Ana *Also called Pacifica Hiorange LP* **(P-13005)**
Hampton Inn, Garden Grove *Also called Stonebridge McWhinney LLC* **(P-13284)**
Hampton Inn, Aliso Viejo *Also called Sunstone Hotel Properties Inc* **(P-13305)**
Hampton Inn Norco Corona North...D...951 279-1111
1530 Hamner Ave Norco (92860) **(P-12638)**
Hampton Inn San Diego-Downtown, San Diego *Also called Dimension Development Two LLC* **(P-12523)**
Hampton Products Intl Corp (PA)...D...949 472-4256
50 Icon Foothill Ranch (92610) **(P-7589)**
Hana Commercial Finance Inc...D...213 240-1234
1000 Wilshire Blvd Fl 20 Los Angeles (90017) **(P-9740)**
Hana Financial Inc (PA)...D...213 240-1234
1000 Wilshire Blvd Fl 20 Los Angeles (90017) **(P-14508)**
Hancock Pk Rhblitation Ctr LLC...C...323 937-4860
505 N La Brea Ave Los Angeles (90036) **(P-20504)**
Handlery Hotels Inc...C...415 781-7800
351 Geary St San Francisco (94102) **(P-12639)**
Handlery Hotels Inc...C...415 781-4550
950 Hotel Cir N San Diego (92108) **(P-12640)**
Handlery Union Square Hotel, San Francisco *Also called Handlery Hotels Inc* **(P-12639)**
Hands-On Mobile Americas Inc (PA)...E...415 580-6400
208 Utah St Ste 300 San Francisco (94103) **(P-15969)**
Handshake, San Francisco *Also called Stryder Corp* **(P-15869)**
Handyman Connection...E...714 288-0077
1740 W Katella Ave Ste G Orange (92867) **(P-13747)**
Hanergy Holding America Inc...B...650 288-3722
1350 Bayshore Hwy Ste 825 Burlingame (94010) **(P-6041)**
Hanford Adult School, Hanford *Also called Hanford Joint Un High Schl Dst* **(P-23830)**
Hanford Community Hospital (HQ)...A...559 582-9000
115 Mall Dr Hanford (93230) **(P-21438)**
Hanford Hotels LLC...C...714 210-0400
17542 17th St Ste 450 Tustin (92780) **(P-12641)**
Hanford Joint Un High Schl Dst...D...559 583-5905
905 Campus Dr Hanford (93230) **(P-23830)**
Hanford Nursing Rehabilitation, Hanford *Also called Mission Medical Entps Inc* **(P-20647)**
Hangtown Knnel CLB Plcrvlle CA...D...530 622-4867
100 Placerville Dr Placerville (95667) **(P-629)**
Hanil Development Inc...E...213 387-0111
3680 Wilshire Blvd B01 Los Angeles (90010) **(P-11944)**
Hanin Federal Credit Union (PA)...E...213 368-9000
3700 Wilshire Blvd # 104 Los Angeles (90010) **(P-9560)**
Hanjin Global Logistics, Carson *Also called Hanjin Transportation Co Ltd* **(P-5080)**
Hanjin Shipping Co Ltd...A...201 291-4600
301 Hanjin Rd Long Beach (90802) **(P-4754)**
Hanjin Transportation Co Ltd...D...310 522-5030
1111 E Watson Center Rd A Carson (90745) **(P-5080)**
Hank Fisher Properties Inc...C...916 447-4444
2701 Capitol Ave Sacramento (95816) **(P-24548)**
Hank Fisher Properties Inc (PA)...C...916 485-1441
641 Fulton Ave Ste 200 Sacramento (95825) **(P-11028)**
Hank Fisher Properties Inc...D...916 921-1970
641 Feature Dr Apt 233 Sacramento (95825) **(P-21104)**
Hankey Group, Los Angeles *Also called Nowcom Corporation* **(P-16435)**
Hanks Inc...D...909 350-8365
13866 Slover Ave Fontana (92337) **(P-4018)**
Hanley Wood Mkt Intelligence (HQ)...D...714 540-8500
555 Anton Blvd Ste 950 Costa Mesa (92626) **(P-26526)**
Hanley Wood Mkt Intelligence (PA)...C...714 540-8500
555 Anton Blvd Ste 950 Costa Mesa (92626) **(P-27744)**
Hanmi Bank (HQ)...C...213 382-2200
3660 Wilshire Blvd Ph A Los Angeles (90010) **(P-9462)**
Hanna Brophy Mac Lean Mc Ale (PA)...E...510 839-1180
1956 Webster St Ste 450 Oakland (94612) **(P-23120)**
Hannam Chain Super 1 Market, Los Angeles *Also called Hannam Chain USA Inc* **(P-7135)**
Hannam Chain USA Inc (PA)...C...213 382-2922
2740 W Olympic Blvd Los Angeles (90006) **(P-7135)**
Hanover Builders Inc...E...818 706-2279
141 Duesenberg Dr Ste 6 Westlake Village (91362) **(P-1177)**
Hans Technologies Inc...D...510 464-8018
1300 Clay St Ste 600 Oakland (94612) **(P-2037)**
Hansen Adkins Auto Trnspt Inc (PA)...A...562 430-4100
3552 Green Ave Los Alamitos (90720) **(P-4190)**
Hansen Bros Enterprises (PA)...D...530 273-3100
11727 La Barr Meadows Rd Grass Valley (95949) **(P-1093)**
Hansen Equipment Company LLC...E...559 992-3111
7124 Whitley Ave Corcoran (93212) **(P-694)**
Hansen Icc LLC...D...760 268-7299
2111 Palomar Airport Rd Carlsbad (92011) **(P-26215)**
Hansen Information Tech, Rancho Cordova *Also called Infor (us) Inc* **(P-15711)**
Hansen Ranches...D...559 992-3111
7124 Whitley Ave Corcoran (93212) **(P-350)**
Hansol Goldpoint LLC...D...714 594-5073
12792 Valley View St # 211 Garden Grove (92845) **(P-5081)**
Hanson Bridgett LLP...E...916 442-3333
500 Capitol Mall Ste 1500 Sacramento (95814) **(P-23121)**
Hanson Bridgett LLP (PA)...B...415 543-2055
425 Market St Fl 26 San Francisco (94105) **(P-23122)**
Hanson Distributing Company (PA)...C...626 224-9800
975 W 8th St Azusa (91702) **(P-6644)**
Hanson Distributing Company...C...626 357-5241
975 W 8th St Azusa (91702) **(P-6645)**
Hapag-Lloyd (america) LLC...E...510 251-8405
180 Grand Ave Ste 1535 Oakland (94612) **(P-5082)**
Happy Camp Chamber Commerce...E...530 493-2900
35 Davis Rd Happy Camp (96039) **(P-24960)**
Happy Money, Costa Mesa *Also called Payoff Inc* **(P-9726)**
Happy Pet Co...E...707 586-8660
5813 Skylane Blvd Windsor (95492) **(P-602)**
Hara, San Mateo *Also called Tunari Corp Inc* **(P-15514)**
Haralambos Beverage Company...C...909 307-1777
26717 Palmetto Ave Redlands (92374) **(P-8999)**
Haralambos Beverage Company (PA)...C...562 347-4300
2300 Pellissier Pl City of Industry (90601) **(P-9000)**
Harbin Hot Springs, Middletown *Also called Heart Consciousness Church* **(P-13476)**
Harbor Bay Club Inc...D...510 521-5414
200 Packet Landing Rd Alameda (94502) **(P-18606)**
Harbor Building Services...D...310 320-2966
2701 Plaza Del Amo # 706 Torrance (90503) **(P-14284)**
Harbor Corporate Park, Santa Ana *Also called Kaiser Foundation Hospitals* **(P-19586)**
Harbor Department, San Pedro *Also called City of Los Angeles* **(P-4726)**
Harbor Developmental Disabilit...C...310 540-1711
21231 Hawthorne Blvd Torrance (90503) **(P-24787)**
Harbor Diesel and Eqp Inc...D...562 591-5665
537 W Anaheim St Long Beach (90813) **(P-7755)**
Harbor Distributing LLC (HQ)...C...714 933-2400
5901 Bolsa Ave Huntington Beach (92647) **(P-9001)**
Harbor Distributing LLC...B...310 538-5483
16407 S Main St Gardena (90248) **(P-9002)**
Harbor Distributing Co, Gardena *Also called Harbor Distributing LLC* **(P-9002)**
Harbor Freight Tools, Calabasas *Also called Central Purchasing LLC* **(P-7843)**
Harbor Fuel Dock...D...650 726-4419
1 Johnson Pier Half Moon Bay (94019) **(P-4749)**
Harbor Glen Care Center...D...626 963-7531
1033 E Arrow Hwy Glendora (91740) **(P-20505)**
Harbor Health Care Inc...C...562 866-7054
16917 Clark Ave Bellflower (90706) **(P-24549)**
Harbor Health Systems LLC...D...949 273-7020
3501 Jamboree Rd Ste 3000 Newport Beach (92660) **(P-22811)**
Harbor Industrial Services...D...310 522-1193
211 N Marine Ave Wilmington (90744) **(P-14441)**
Harbor Island Hotel Group LP...D...805 658-1212
1050 Schooner Dr Ventura (93001) **(P-12642)**
Harbor Pipe and Steel Inc...C...951 369-3990
1495 Columbia Ave Bldg 10 Riverside (92507) **(P-7278)**
Harbor Post Accute Care Center, Torrance *Also called Geri Care Inc* **(P-20454)**
Harbor Regional Center, Torrance *Also called Harbor Developmental Disabilit* **(P-24787)**
Harbor Ucla Med Foundation, Torrance *Also called Harbor-Ucla Med Foundation Inc* **(P-26884)**
Harbor View Community Svcs Ctr, Long Beach *Also called Sunbridge Healthcare LLC* **(P-20965)**
Harbor View Hotel Ventures LLC...D...619 239-6800
1646 Front St San Diego (92101) **(P-12643)**
Harbor View Hotels Inc...D...650 340-8500
600 Airport Blvd Burlingame (94010) **(P-12644)**
Harbor View House, San Pedro *Also called Healthview Inc* **(P-24558)**
Harbor View Inn, Santa Barbara *Also called Beach Motel Partners Ltd* **(P-12364)**
Harbor View Rehabilitation Ctr, Long Beach *Also called Sunbridge Harbor View* **(P-20790)**
Harbor Villa Care Center...D...714 635-8131
861 S Harbor Blvd Anaheim (92805) **(P-21105)**
Harbor Village II, Costa Mesa *Also called Independent Options* **(P-23854)**
Harbor's Insurance, Eureka *Also called Shaw & Petersen Insurance Inc* **(P-10773)**
Harbor-Cla Med Ctr Dept Srgery...D...310 222-2701
1000 W Carson St 25 Torrance (90502) **(P-21439)**
Harbor-Ucla Med Foundation Inc (PA)...D...310 222-5015
21840 S Norm Ave Torrance (90502) **(P-26884)**
Harbor-Ucla Medical Center...A...310 222-2345
1000 W Carson St 2 Torrance (90502) **(P-21440)**
Hard Rock Hotel, San Diego *Also called T-12 Three LLC* **(P-13319)**
Hard Rock Hotel Palm Springs, Palm Springs *Also called Kittridge Hotels & Resorts LLC* **(P-12818)**
Hardage Group of Companies...D...714 579-3200
3100 E Imperial Hwy Brea (92821) **(P-12645)**
Hardage Investments Inc...E...510 795-1200
39150 Cedar Blvd Newark (94560) **(P-10892)**
Hardcore Skateparks Inc...C...909 949-1601
285 N Benson Ave Upland (91786) **(P-18802)**
Hardesty LLC (PA)...E...949 407-6625
19800 Macar Boule Ste 820 Irvine (92612) **(P-14634)**
Harding & Associates, San Jose *Also called Harding Mktg Cmmunications Inc* **(P-14116)**
Harding Mktg Cmmunications Inc (PA)...D...408 345-4545
377 S Daniel Way San Jose (95128) **(P-14116)**
Hardisty Construction Administ...D...619 245-6828
410 W 30th St Ste A National City (91950) **(P-1541)**
Hardrock Tile & Marble Inc...D...714 282-1766
23151 Verdugo Dr Ste 111 Laguna Hills (92653) **(P-2809)**
Hardwood Creations (PA)...D...714 674-0527
1560 N Maple St Corona (92880) **(P-3040)**
Hardy & Harper Inc...E...714 444-1851
1312 E Warner Ave Santa Ana (92705) **(P-1790)**
Hardy Diagnostics (PA)...B...805 346-2766
1430 W Mccoy Ln Santa Maria (93455) **(P-7183)**
Hardy Window Company (PA)...C...714 996-1807
1639 E Miraloma Ave Placentia (92870) **(P-6826)**
Harelson Mechanical Inc...D...916 386-2586
3899 Security Park Dr Rancho Cordova (95742) **(P-3471)**
Haringa Inc (PA)...D...800 499-9991
14422 Best Ave Santa Fe Springs (90670) **(P-17207)**
Harkins Theatres Inc...D...909 627-8010
3100 Chino Ave Chino Hills (91709) **(P-18302)**

Employee Codes: A=Over 500 employees, B=251-500 C=101-250, D=51-100, E=50
2019 Directory of California Wholesalers and Services Companies
© Mergent Inc. 1-800-342-5647
1323

Harley Ellis Devereaux Corp...D.......415 981-2345
417 Montgomery St Ste 400 San Francisco (94104) ***(P-26055)***
Harmonium Inc (PA)...C.......858 684-3080
9245 Activity Rd Ste 200 San Diego (92126) ***(P-24326)***
Harmony Escrow Inc...D.......949 474-1134
17100 Gillette Ave Irvine (92614) ***(P-11499)***
Harmony Home Health LLC...D.......916 933-9777
2500 Ranch Rd Ste 104 Placerville (95667) ***(P-22310)***
Harmony Homecare, Placerville *Also called Harmony Home Health LLC* ***(P-22310)***
Harold E Nutter Inc (PA)...D.......916 334-4343
5930 Rosebud Ln Sacramento (95841) ***(P-2600)***
Harold E Nutter & Son, Sacramento *Also called Harold E Nutter Inc* ***(P-2600)***
Harold Jones Landscape Inc...E.......805 582-7443
530 New Los Angeles Ave Moorpark (93021) ***(P-758)***
Harold L Karpman MD, Beverly Hills *Also called Cardivsclr Mdcl Grp of Sthrn* ***(P-19349)***
Harper Construction Co Inc (PA)...C.......619 233-7900
2241 Kettner Blvd Ste 300 San Diego (92101) ***(P-1542)***
Harper Mechanical Contrs LLC...D.......619 543-1296
1011 Camino Del Rio S San Diego (92108) ***(P-7136)***
Harper's Model Homes Services, Davis *Also called Harpers Model Home Maintenance* ***(P-14285)***
Harpers Model Home Maintenance...D.......916 335-0282
1949 5th St Ste 108 Davis (95616) ***(P-14285)***
Harpo Entertainment Group, West Hollywood *Also called Harpo Productions Inc* ***(P-18058)***
Harpo Inc...D.......312 633-1000
1041 N Formosa Ave West Hollywood (90046) ***(P-18371)***
Harpo Productions Inc...C.......312 633-1000
1041 N Formosa Ave West Hollywood (90046) ***(P-18058)***
Harpo Studios, West Hollywood *Also called Harpo Inc* ***(P-18371)***
Harrah's, Valley Center *Also called Caesars Entrtnment Oprting Inc* ***(P-19117)***
Harrington Industrial Plas LLC (HQ)...D.......909 597-8641
14480 Yorba Ave Chino (91710) ***(P-7627)***
Harris & Associates Inc...D.......949 655-3900
22 Executive Park Ste 200 Irvine (92614) ***(P-25721)***
Harris & Associates Inc (PA)...C.......925 827-4900
1401 Wllw Pca Rd 500 Concord (94520) ***(P-25722)***
Harris & Associates Cnstr MGT, Concord *Also called Harris & Associates Inc* ***(P-25722)***
Harris & Ruth Painting Contg (PA)...D.......626 960-4004
2107 W San Bernardino Rd West Covina (91790) ***(P-2446)***
Harris & Sloan Consulting...E.......916 921-2800
2295 Gateway Oaks Dr # 165 Sacramento (95833) ***(P-27745)***
Harris Construction Co Inc...C.......559 251-0301
5286 E Home Ave Fresno (93727) ***(P-1543)***
Harris Corporation...B.......626 584-4527
1400 S Shamrock Ave Monrovia (91016) ***(P-25723)***
Harris Direct...D.......818 357-2040
21250 Califa St Ste 114 Woodland Hills (91367) ***(P-17208)***
Harris Farm Horse Division, Coalinga *Also called Harris Farms Inc* ***(P-351)***
Harris Farms Inc...E.......559 884-2203
27366 W Oakland Ave Coalinga (93210) ***(P-351)***
Harris Farms Inc...B.......559 935-0717
24505 W Dorris Ave Coalinga (93210) ***(P-352)***
Harris Farms Inc...B.......559 884-2477
23300 W Oakland Ave Coalinga (93210) ***(P-353)***
Harris Freeman & Co Inc (PA)...B.......714 765-1190
3110 E Miraloma Ave Anaheim (92806) ***(P-8803)***
Harris L Woods Elec Contr...D.......562 945-8751
9214 Norwalk Blvd Santa Fe Springs (90670) ***(P-2601)***
Harris Moran, Davis *Also called Hmclause Inc* ***(P-26377)***
Harris Mycfo Inc...D.......480 348-7725
2200 Geng Rd Ste 100 Palo Alto (94303) ***(P-27257)***
Harris Rebar Northern Cal Inc...C.......925 373-0733
355 S Vasco Rd Livermore (94550) ***(P-3376)***
Harris Stockwell (PA)...E.......310 277-6669
3580 Wilshire Blvd Fl 19 Los Angeles (90010) ***(P-23123)***
Harris Tea Company, Anaheim *Also called Harris Freeman & Co Inc* ***(P-8803)***
Harris Woolf Cal Almonds LLC (PA)...C.......559 884-2147
26060 Colusa Ave Coalinga (93210) ***(P-528)***
Harrison Drywall Inc...E.......415 821-9584
447 10th St San Francisco (94103) ***(P-2892)***
Harrison Nichols Co Ltd...C.......626 337-5020
501 W Foothill Blvd Azusa (91702) ***(P-4350)***
Harrison, E J & Sons Recycling, Ventura *Also called E J Harrison & Sons Inc* ***(P-6389)***
Harry Group Inc...D.......310 631-9646
2839 E El Presidio St Carson (90810) ***(P-5083)***
Harry's Auto Collision, Los Angeles *Also called Harrys Auto Body Inc* ***(P-17725)***
Harrys Auto Body Inc...D.......323 933-4600
1013 S La Brea Ave Los Angeles (90019) ***(P-17725)***
Hart Howerton Ltd (PA)...D.......415 439-2200
1 Union St Fl 3 San Francisco (94111) ***(P-759)***
Hart King Coldren A Prof Corp...D.......714 432-8700
4 Hutton Cntre Dr Ste 900 Santa Ana (92707) ***(P-23124)***
Harte Hanks Inc...D.......210 829-9000
2337 W Commonwealth Ave Fullerton (92833) ***(P-4571)***
Harte-Hanks Direct Mail/Califo...D.......714 738-5478
2337 W Commonwealth Ave Fullerton (92833) ***(P-14045)***
Harte-Hnks Mkt Intlligence Inc (PA)...C.......858 450-1667
15015 Ave Of Science # 110 San Diego (92128) ***(P-16141)***
Hartford Casualty Insurance Co...A.......415 836-4800
101 Montgomery St # 2700 San Francisco (94104) ***(P-10360)***
Hartford Fire Insurance Co...B.......916 294-1000
12009 Foundation Pl # 100 Gold River (95670) ***(P-10641)***
Hartford Fire Insurance Co...C.......213 452-5179
777 S Figueroa St Ste 700 Los Angeles (90017) ***(P-10642)***
Hartman Industries...D.......909 428-0114
14933 Whittram Ave Fontana (92335) ***(P-7279)***
Hartmann Studios Inc (HQ)...C.......510 232-5030
1150 Brickyard Cove Rd Point Richmond (94801) ***(P-17209)***
Hartmann Studios Incorporated...C.......510 232-5030
70 W Ohio Ave Ste H Richmond (94804) ***(P-17210)***
Hartwick & Hand Inc (PA)...D.......760 245-1666
16953 N D St Victorville (92394) ***(P-4019)***
Hartwig Realty Inc (PA)...D.......661 948-8424
43912 20th St W Lancaster (93534) ***(P-11500)***
Harvard Grand Inv Inc A Cal...D.......310 513-7560
2 Civic Plaza Dr Carson (90745) ***(P-12230)***
Harvest Facility Holdings LP...D.......909 793-8691
10 Terracina Blvd Ofc Redlands (92373) ***(P-11029)***
Harvest Food Distributors, National City *Also called Harvest Meat Company Inc* ***(P-8617)***
Harvest Landscape Entps Inc...C.......714 693-8100
2339 N Batavia St Orange (92865) ***(P-856)***
Harvest Landscape Maintenance, Orange *Also called Harvest Landscape Entps Inc* ***(P-856)***
Harvest Management Sub LLC...A.......805 543-0187
1299 Briarwood Dr San Luis Obispo (93401) ***(P-24550)***
Harvest Meat Company Inc (HQ)...D.......619 477-0185
1022 Bay Marina Dr # 106 National City (91950) ***(P-8617)***
Harvest of The Sea, Los Angeles *Also called Ore-Cal Corp* ***(P-8588)***
Harvest Small Business Fin LLC...D.......949 446-8683
24422 Avenida De Carlota Laguna Hills (92653) ***(P-9886)***
Harvest Technical Service Inc...C.......925 937-4874
1839 Ygnacio Valley Rd # 390 Walnut Creek (94598) ***(P-14635)***
Harvest V Citizens Patrol...C.......951 926-9763
25098 Avenida Valencia Homeland (92548) ***(P-16695)***
Harvey Inc...C.......858 769-4000
9455 Ridgehaven Ct # 200 San Diego (92123) ***(P-1544)***
Harvey General Contracting, San Diego *Also called Harvey Inc* ***(P-1544)***
Harveys Industries Inc...D.......714 277-4700
724 N Poinsettia St Santa Ana (92701) ***(P-8305)***
Hasc, Los Angeles *Also called Hospital Assn Southern Cal* ***(P-24789)***
Haskell Company (inc)...C.......925 960-1815
478 Lindbergh Ave Livermore (94551) ***(P-1406)***
Hassard Bonnington LLP (PA)...D.......415 288-9800
275 Battery St Ste 1600 San Francisco (94111) ***(P-23125)***
Hat Creek Cnstr & Mtls Inc (PA)...E.......530 335-5501
24339 State Highway 89 Burney (96013) ***(P-2038)***
Hatchbeauty Products LLC (PA)...D.......310 396-7070
10951 W Pico Blvd Ste 300 Los Angeles (90064) ***(P-8176)***
Hatfield Inc...E.......415 802-8635
5 3rd St Ste 525 San Francisco (94103) ***(P-13709)***
Hathaway Children and Family, Pacoima *Also called Hathaway-Sycamores Chld Fam Sv* ***(P-24551)***
Hathaway Dinwiddie Cnstr Co...D.......415 986-2718
565 Laurelwood Rd Santa Clara (95054) ***(P-1545)***
Hathaway Dinwiddie Cnstr Co...B.......415 986-2718
275 Battery St Ste 300 San Francisco (94111) ***(P-1546)***
Hathaway Dinwiddie Cnstr Group...D.......408 988-4200
565 Laurelwood Rd Santa Clara (95054) ***(P-10893)***
Hathaway Dinwiddie Cnstr Group (PA)...B.......415 986-2718
275 Battery St Ste 300 San Francisco (94111) ***(P-1547)***
Hathaway Resource Center...E.......323 837-0838
5701 S Eastrn Ave Ste 550 Los Angeles (90040) ***(P-23831)***
Hathaway-Sycamores Chld Fam Sv...D.......818 897-1766
12502 Van Nuys Blvd # 120 Pacoima (91331) ***(P-24551)***
Hathaway-Sycamores Chld Fam Sv...D.......323 257-9600
840 N Avenue 66 Los Angeles (90042) ***(P-24552)***
Hathaway-Sycamores Chld Fam Sv...B.......661 942-5749
44738 Sierra Hwy Lancaster (93534) ***(P-24553)***
Hathaway-Sycamores Chld Fam Sv...D.......323 733-0322
3741 Stocker St Ste 101 View Park (90008) ***(P-24554)***
Hathaway-Sycamores Chld Fam Sv (PA)...D.......626 395-7100
100 W Walnut St Ste 375 Pasadena (91124) ***(P-24555)***
Haulaway Storage Cntrs Inc...A.......800 826-9040
11292 Western Ave Stanton (90680) ***(P-4572)***
Havas Formula LLC...D.......619 234-0345
1215 Cushman Ave San Diego (92110) ***(P-27555)***
Havasu Landing Casino (PA)...D.......760 858-5380
1 Main St Needles (92363) ***(P-12646)***
Haven Engineering Inc...E.......888 838-3868
25 Kearny St Ste 304 San Francisco (94108) ***(P-5084)***
Hawaii Parent Corp...B.......415 263-3660
600 Montgomery St Fl 32 San Francisco (94111) ***(P-12062)***
Hawaiian Airlines Inc...D.......310 417-1677
200 World Way Ste 9 Los Angeles (90045) ***(P-4784)***
Hawaiian Gardens Casino...A.......562 860-5887
11871 Carson St Hawaiian Gardens (90716) ***(P-12647)***
Hawaiian Hotels & Resorts Inc...D.......805 480-0052
2830 Borchard Rd Newbury Park (91320) ***(P-12648)***
Hawk Transportation Inc...D.......800 709-4295
15238 Arrow Blvd Fontana (92335) ***(P-4191)***
Hawker Pacific Aerospace...B.......818 765-6201
11240 Sherman Way Sun Valley (91352) ***(P-17949)***
Haworth Inc...D.......408 262-6400
931 Cadillac Ct Milpitas (95035) ***(P-6724)***
Hawthorn Suites, Anaheim *Also called Sunstone Hotel Investors LLC* ***(P-13299)***
Hawthorne Cat, San Diego *Also called Hawthorne Machinery Co* ***(P-14442)***
Hawthorne Convalescent Center, Hawthorne *Also called Wilshire Hlth & Cmnty Svcs Inc* ***(P-21258)***
Hawthorne Healthcare...D.......310 679-9732
11630 Grevillea Ave Hawthorne (90250) ***(P-20506)***
Hawthorne Lift Systems, Fontana *Also called Naumann/Hobbs Material* ***(P-7778)***
Hawthorne Lift Systems, San Marcos *Also called Naumann/Hobbs Material* ***(P-7779)***
Hawthorne Machinery Co (PA)...C.......858 674-7000
16945 Camino San Bernardo San Diego (92127) ***(P-14442)***
Hawthorne Machinery Co (HQ)...D.......858 674-7000
16945 Camino San Bernardo San Diego (92127) ***(P-14443)***

Hawthorne Machinery Co........D.......858 674-7000
16945 Camino San Bernardo San Diego (92127) *(P-17767)*
Hawthorne Machinery Co........D.......858 974-6800
8050 Othello Ave San Diego (92111) *(P-7677)*
Hay House Inc (PA)........D.......760 431-7695
2776 Loker Ave W Carlsbad (92010) *(P-9114)*
Hay Kuhn Inc........E.......760 353-0124
1880 Jeffrey Rd El Centro (92243) *(P-9223)*
Hayday Farms Inc........D.......760 922-4713
15500 S Commercial St Blythe (92225) *(P-25)*
Hayes Mansion Conference Ctr........C.......408 226-3200
200 Edenvale Ave San Jose (95136) *(P-12649)*
Hayes Welding Inc (PA)........D.......760 246-4878
12522 Violet Rd Adelanto (92301) *(P-17923)*
Haynes and Boone LLP........D.......650 687-8800
525 University Ave # 400 Palo Alto (94301) *(P-23126)*
Haynes Building Service LLC........C.......626 359-6100
16027 Arrow Hwy Ste I Baldwin Park (91706) *(P-14286)*
Haynes Family Programs Inc........C.......909 593-2581
233 Baseline Rd La Verne (91750) *(P-24556)*
Hayward Active Club, Hayward *Also called 24 Hour Fitness Usa Inc (P-18570)*
Hayward Area Recreation Pkdist........D.......510 881-6700
1099 E St Hayward (94541) *(P-20154)*
Hayward Area Recreation Pkdist........E.......510 317-2300
1401 Golf Course Rd Hayward (94541) *(P-18717)*
Hayward Area Recreation Pkdist........D.......510 881-6750
1099 E St Rear Hayward (94541) *(P-4573)*
Hayward Baker Inc........D.......805 933-1331
1780 E Lemonwood Dr Santa Paula (93060) *(P-3528)*
Hayward Convalescent Hospital, Hayward *Also called Hillsdale Group LP (P-21114)*
Hayward Hills Health Care Ctr, Hayward *Also called Mariner Health Care Inc (P-20621)*
Hayward Manufacturing, Hayward *Also called Intarcia Therapeutics Inc (P-26384)*
Hayward Police Officers Assn........D.......510 293-7207
300 W Winton Ave Hayward (94544) *(P-25060)*
Hayward Sisters Hospital (HQ)........A.......510 264-4000
27200 Calaroga Ave Hayward (94545) *(P-21441)*
Hazard Construction Company........D.......858 587-3600
6465 Marindustry Dr San Diego (92121) *(P-1881)*
Hazel Creek Assisted Living, Orangevale *Also called Summerville At Hazel Creek LLC (P-24689)*
Hazel Hawkins Memorial Hosp, Hollister *Also called San Benito Health Care Dst (P-21702)*
Hazens Investment LLC........B.......310 642-1111
6101 W Century Blvd Los Angeles (90045) *(P-12650)*
HB Healthcare Associates LLC........D.......714 887-0144
18811 Florida St Huntington Beach (92648) *(P-20507)*
HB Parkco Construction Inc (PA)........B.......714 444-1441
3190 Arprt Loop Dr Ste F Costa Mesa (92626) *(P-3264)*
Hba Incorporated........D.......714 635-8602
421 E Cerritos Ave Anaheim (92805) *(P-2810)*
Hba International, Santa Monica *Also called Hirsch/Bedner Intl Inc (P-17221)*
Hbe Corporation........E.......805 641-1305
147 N Brent St Ventura (93003) *(P-1548)*
Hbe Rental, Grass Valley *Also called Hansen Bros Enterprises (P-1093)*
HCA Inc........C.......408 729-2801
225 N Jackson Ave San Jose (95116) *(P-21442)*
HCA Inc........C.......949 496-1122
654 Camino De Los Mares San Clemente (92673) *(P-21443)*
HCC Investors LLC........C.......858 759-7200
18550 Seven Bridges Rd Rancho Santa Fe (92091) *(P-18934)*
HCC Surety Group, Los Angeles *Also called American Contrs Indemnity Co (P-10421)*
Hci, Chowchilla *Also called Winnresidential Ltd Partnr (P-11143)*
Hci Inc (HQ)........B.......951 520-4200
3166 Hrseless Carriage Rd Norco (92860) *(P-1924)*
Hci Systems Inc (PA)........E.......909 628-7773
1354 S Parkside Pl Ontario (91761) *(P-2602)*
Hcis, Ontario *Also called Hci Systems Inc (P-2602)*
Hcl America Inc (HQ)........C.......408 733-0480
330 Potrero Ave Sunnyvale (94085) *(P-16270)*
Hcl Finance Inc (PA)........C.......408 845-9035
2560 Mission College Blvd Santa Clara (95054) *(P-9813)*
Hco Holding I Corporation (HQ)........D.......323 583-5000
999 N Pacific Coast Hwy El Segundo (90245) *(P-11985)*
Hcp Inc (PA)........D.......949 407-0700
1920 Main St Ste 1200 Irvine (92614) *(P-12164)*
Hcr Manorcare Med Svcs Fla LLC........C.......925 274-1325
1975 Tice Valley Blvd Walnut Creek (94595) *(P-20508)*
Hcr Manorcare Med Svcs Fla LLC........C.......714 241-9800
11680 Warner Ave Fountain Valley (92708) *(P-20509)*
Hcr Manorcare Med Svcs Fla LLC........C.......916 967-2929
7807 Uplands Way Citrus Heights (95610) *(P-20510)*
Hcr Manorcare Med Svcs Fla LLC........C.......951 925-9171
1717 W Stetson Ave Hemet (92545) *(P-20511)*
Hcr Manorcare Med Svcs Fla LLC........D.......408 735-7200
1150 Tilton Dr Sunnyvale (94087) *(P-20512)*
Hcr Manorcare Med Svcs Fla LLC........C.......925 975-5000
1226 Rossmoor Pkwy Walnut Creek (94595) *(P-20513)*
Hcr Manorcare Med Svcs Fla LLC........D.......760 944-0331
944 Regal Rd Encinitas (92024) *(P-20514)*
Hcs Holdco LLC (HQ)........C.......949 349-1200
27071 Aliso Creek Rd # 100 Aliso Viejo (92656) *(P-22311)*
Hct Packaging Inc (PA)........C.......310 260-7680
2800 28th St Ste 240 Santa Monica (90405) *(P-17211)*
Hd Supply Inc........D.......800 431-3000
101 Rverview Pkwy Ste 100 Santee (92071) *(P-4020)*
Hd Supply Construction Supply........D.......707 863-8282
1995 W Cordelia Rd Fairfield (94534) *(P-7590)*
Hd Supply Construction Supply........E.......408 428-2000
595 Brennan St San Jose (95131) *(P-7591)*
Hdd Construction, Caruthers *Also called Hammer Down Davila Cnstr (P-1287)*
HDR Architecture Inc........D.......626 584-1700
350 S Grand Ave Ste 2900 Los Angeles (90071) *(P-25724)*
HDR Architecture Inc........D.......415 546-4242
201 California St # 1500 San Francisco (94111) *(P-25725)*
HDR Engineering Inc........C.......714 730-2300
3230 El Camino Real # 200 Irvine (92602) *(P-25726)*
HDR Engineering Inc........D.......619 231-4865
401 B St Ste 1110 San Diego (92101) *(P-25727)*
HDR Engineering Inc........E.......858 712-8400
8690 Balboa Ave Ste 200 San Diego (92123) *(P-27258)*
HDR Engineering Inc........C.......626 584-1700
350 S Grand Ave Ste 2900 Los Angeles (90071) *(P-27259)*
HDR Engineering Inc........D.......925 974-2500
100 Pringle Ave Ste 400 Walnut Creek (94596) *(P-25728)*
HDR Engineering Inc........D.......415 546-4200
201 California St # 1500 San Francisco (94111) *(P-27260)*
HDR Engineering Inc........D.......916 564-4214
2379 Gateway Oaks Dr # 200 Sacramento (95833) *(P-25729)*
HDR Engineering Inc........D.......909 626-0967
431 W Baseline Rd Claremont (91711) *(P-25730)*
HDR Engineering Inc........D.......916 817-4700
2365 Iron Point Rd # 300 Folsom (95630) *(P-27261)*
HDR Environmental Ope........D.......858 712-8400
8690 Balboa Ave Ste 200 San Diego (92123) *(P-26056)*
HDR/Cardno Entrix Joint Ventr........D.......916 817-4700
2365 Iron Point Rd # 300 Folsom (95630) *(P-25731)*
Hdsi Management Inc (PA)........D.......323 231-1104
3460 S Broadway Los Angeles (90007) *(P-11501)*
HE Julien & Associates Inc........E.......805 488-8342
2275 E Hueneme Rd Oxnard (93033) *(P-857)*
Head Start, Quincy *Also called Sierra Cscade Fmly Opprtnities (P-24381)*
Head Start Child Dev Cncil Inc........C.......209 832-7844
2105 N Tracy Blvd Tracy (95376) *(P-24327)*
Head Start Program, Long Beach *Also called Charles Drew Univ Mdcine Scnce (P-24279)*
Headquarters, Los Angeles *Also called Nationwide Legal LLC (P-23281)*
Headstart, Watsonville *Also called Encompass Community Services (P-23787)*
Headstart Nursery Inc (PA)........D.......408 842-3030
4860 Monterey Rd Gilroy (95020) *(P-9139)*
Headstrong Corporation........D.......408 732-8700
150 Mathilda Pl Ste 200 Sunnyvale (94086) *(P-16389)*
Healdsburg Dist Hosp Rehab Svc........D.......707 433-9150
1540 Healdsburg Ave Healdsburg (95448) *(P-10203)*
Healdsburg District Hospital, Healdsburg *Also called North Sonoma County Hosp Dst (P-21605)*
Health & Human Services, San Diego *Also called County of San Diego (P-23721)*
Health & Human Services, Fallbrook *Also called County of San Diego (P-23722)*
Health & Human Services, Oceanside *Also called County of San Diego (P-23725)*
Health & Human Services, Auburn *Also called County of Placer (P-23703)*
Health & Human Services, Auburn *Also called County of Placer (P-22553)*
Health & Human Services, San Diego *Also called County of San Diego (P-21943)*
Health & Rehabilitation Center........E.......408 377-9275
2065 Los Gatos Almaden Rd San Jose (95124) *(P-20515)*
Health Advocates LLC........B.......818 995-9500
14721 Califa St Van Nuys (91411) *(P-24788)*
Health and Human Service, Crescent City *Also called County of Del Norte (P-24766)*
Health and Human Service Agcy, San Diego *Also called County of San Diego (P-23723)*
Health and Human Services, Sacramento *Also called County of Sacramento (P-23716)*
Health and Human Services, San Diego *Also called County of San Diego (P-23728)*
Health and Human Services Agcy, San Diego *Also called County of San Diego (P-23727)*
Health and Social Services, Fairfield *Also called County of Solano (P-23744)*
Health By Design........E.......916 974-3322
3029 La Via Way Sacramento (95825) *(P-22312)*
Health Care Agency, Santa Ana *Also called County of Orange (P-22073)*
Health Care Developers, Hesperia *Also called Foremost Healthcare Centers (P-11020)*
Health Care Group, San Diego *Also called L C C H Associates Inc (P-21131)*
Health Care Investments Inc........C.......310 323-3194
1140 W Rosecrans Ave Gardena (90247) *(P-20516)*
Health Care Resource Group, Buena Park *Also called Vsa & Associates Inc (P-25991)*
Health Care Workers Union (PA)........C.......510 251-1250
560 Thomas L Berkley Way Oakland (94612) *(P-10894)*
Health Comp Administrators (PA)........C.......559 499-2450
621 Santa Fe Ave Fresno (93721) *(P-10643)*
Health Department, Salinas *Also called County of Monterey (P-24770)*
Health Department, NAPA *Also called County of NAPA (P-22552)*
Health Educ Economic Devlpmnt........D.......510 604-6143
304 Coral Reef Rd Alameda (94501) *(P-27262)*
Health Educatn Psychiatry Offs, Los Angeles *Also called Kaiser Foundation Hospitals (P-22602)*
Health Entps Lf Long Plan........B.......818 654-0330
5805 Sepulveda Blvd Van Nuys (91411) *(P-22313)*
Health Entps Life-Long Plans, Van Nuys *Also called Health Entps Lf Long Plan (P-22313)*
Health Fitness America, Irvine *Also called Equinox-76th Street Inc (P-20175)*
Health Information Partners........C.......949 261-5000
4041 Macarthur Blvd # 360 Newport Beach (92660) *(P-21106)*
Health Link Medi Van........D.......310 981-9500
6053 W Century Blvd # 900 Los Angeles (90045) *(P-5227)*
Health Net Inc (HQ)........C.......818 676-6000
21650 Oxnard St Fl 25 Woodland Hills (91367) *(P-10204)*
Health Net Inc........C.......818 543-9037
101 N Brand Blvd Ste 1500 Glendale (91203) *(P-10205)*
Health Net Inc........B.......916 935-3520
12033 Foundation Pl Gold River (95670) *(P-10206)*
Health Net California Inc (HQ)........C.......818 676-6775
21281 Burbank Blvd Fl 4 Woodland Hills (91367) *(P-10207)*

ALPHABETIC

Employee Codes: A=Over 500 employees, B=251-500
C=101-250, D=51-100, E=50
2019 Directory of California
Wholesalers and Services Companies
© Mergent Inc. 1-800-342-5647
1325

Health Net California Inc ....B....510 465-9600
155 Grand Ave Lbby Oakland (94612) *(P-10208)*
Health Net Cmnty Solutions Inc ....C....800 675-6110
11971 Foundation Pl Gold River (95670) *(P-19490)*
Health Net Community Solutions ....D....818 676-6000
21650 Oxnard St Fl 25 Woodland Hills (91367) *(P-10209)*
Health Net Federal Svcs LLC (HQ) ....A....916 935-5000
2025 Aerojet Rd Rancho Cordova (95742) *(P-10210)*
Health Net Life Insurance Co ....C....800 865-6288
21281 Burbank Blvd Woodland Hills (91367) *(P-10211)*
Health Plan of San Joaquin ....C....209 942-6300
7751 S Manthey Rd French Camp (95231) *(P-10212)*
Health Plan of San Mateo, South San Francisco *Also called San Mateo Health Commission (P-22878)*
Health Quest, NAPA *Also called Back Street Fitness Inc (P-18576)*
Health Resources Corp ....B....714 754-5454
2701 S Bristol St Santa Ana (92704) *(P-21444)*
Health Services Dept, Palos Verdes Peninsu *Also called County of Los Angeles (P-21352)*
Health Services Dept, Los Angeles *Also called County of Los Angeles (P-21354)*
Health Services, Dept of, Acton *Also called County of Los Angeles (P-22011)*
Health Services, Dept of, Commerce *Also called County of Los Angeles (P-24768)*
Health Services, Dept of, Downey *Also called County of Los Angeles (P-22546)*
Health Services, Dept of, Los Angeles *Also called County of Los Angeles (P-21353)*
Health Services, Dept of, Los Angeles *Also called County of Los Angeles (P-19411)*
Health Services, Dept of, Los Angeles *Also called County of Los Angeles (P-22547)*
Health Services, Dept of, Torrance *Also called County of Los Angeles (P-8165)*
Health Services, Dept of, City of Industry *Also called County of Los Angeles (P-23673)*
Health Services, Dept of, Wilmington *Also called County of Los Angeles (P-19414)*
Health Source Staffing Inc ....D....619 220-8044
438 Camino San Diego (92108) *(P-22314)*
Health South Tustin Rehab Hosp ....C....714 832-9200
14851 Yorba St Tustin (92780) *(P-23832)*
Health System, San Mateo *Also called County of San Mateo (P-22556)*
Health System Medical Network, Beverly Hills *Also called Cedars-Sinai Medical Center (P-21306)*
Health Trust (PA) ....D....408 513-8700
3180 Newberry Dr Ste 200 San Jose (95118) *(P-25017)*
Health Valley Foods Inc ....B....626 334-3241
16007 Cmino De La Cantera Irwindale (91702) *(P-8804)*
Healthcare Barton System (PA) ....A....530 541-3420
2170 South Ave South Lake Tahoe (96150) *(P-21445)*
Healthcare Barton System ....E....530 543-5685
2170 South Ave South Lake Tahoe (96150) *(P-21446)*
Healthcare California ....D....559 243-9990
6327 N Fresno St Ste 104 Fresno (93710) *(P-22315)*
Healthcare Centre of Fresno, Fresno *Also called Fresno Skilled Nursing (P-20440)*
Healthcare Centre of Fresno ....C....559 268-5361
1665 M St Fresno (93721) *(P-22023)*
Healthcare Cost Solutions Inc ....D....949 721-2795
1200 Newprt Cntr Dr 190 Newport Beach (92660) *(P-26216)*
Healthcare Ctr of Downey LLC ....C....562 869-0978
12023 Lakewood Blvd Downey (90242) *(P-20517)*
Healthcare Group, Escondido *Also called Las Villas Del Norte (P-20576)*
Healthcare Group ....C....619 463-0281
5480 Marengo Ave Ste 619 La Mesa (91942) *(P-24557)*
Healthcare Investments II LLC ....D....310 638-9377
2001 Terra Ln Arcadia (91007) *(P-20518)*
Healthcare MGT Partners LLC ....B....949 263-8620
20 Executive Park Ste 155 Irvine (92614) *(P-26885)*
Healthcare MGT Systems Inc (PA) ....C....619 521-9641
900 Lane Ave Ste 190 Chula Vista (91914) *(P-20519)*
Healthcare MGT Systems Inc ....D....951 654-9347
980 W 7th St San Jacinto (92582) *(P-20520)*
Healthcare Partners LLC ....D....714 995-1000
1236 N Magnolia Ave Anaheim (92801) *(P-22812)*
Healthcare Partners LLC ....D....562 304-2100
3932 Long Beach Blvd Long Beach (90807) *(P-19491)*
Healthcare Partners LLC ....D....562 429-2473
4910 Airport Plaza Dr Long Beach (90815) *(P-22813)*
Healthcare Partners LLC ....B....562 988-7000
2600 Redondo Ave Ste 405 Long Beach (90806) *(P-19492)*
Healthcare Partners LLC ....E....714 964-6229
3501 S Harbor Blvd # 100 Santa Ana (92704) *(P-22814)*
Healthcare Partners Med Group, Long Beach *Also called Healthcare Partners LLC (P-19491)*
Healthcare Partners Med Group, Montebello *Also called Davita Medical Management LLC (P-19431)*
Healthcare Partners Med Group, El Monte *Also called Davita Medical Management LLC (P-19432)*
Healthcare Partners Med Group, El Segundo *Also called Davita Medical Management LLC (P-19433)*
Healthcare Pathways Management ....D....831 373-1111
5 Mandeville Cct Monterey (93940) *(P-22316)*
Healthcare Services, French Camp *Also called San Joaquin General Hospital (P-21707)*
Healthcare Services Group Inc ....A....562 494-7939
5199 E Pacific Coast Hwy # 402 Long Beach (90804) *(P-27932)*
Healthcare System 2000 ....D....714 899-2000
9191 Westminster Ave Garden Grove (92844) *(P-19493)*
Healthcomp ....B....559 499-2450
621 Santa Fe Ave Fresno (93721) *(P-10644)*
Healthcomp Administrators, Fresno *Also called Healthcomp (P-10644)*
Healthfirst Medical Group Inc (PA) ....E....562 949-9328
13440 Imperial Hwy Santa Fe Springs (90670) *(P-22590)*
Healthfusion Holdings Inc (HQ) ....D....858 523-2120
100 N Rios Ave Solana Beach (92075) *(P-11986)*
Healthnet California Inc ....D....562 598-4043
1661 Golden Rain Rd Seal Beach (90740) *(P-10213)*
Healthnet Seniority Plus, Seal Beach *Also called Healthnet California Inc (P-10213)*
Healthpocket Inc ....D....800 984-8015
444 Castro St Ste 710 Mountain View (94041) *(P-10165)*
Healthpointe Medical Group Inc (PA) ....D....714 956-2663
16702 Valley View Ave La Mirada (90638) *(P-19494)*
Healthright 360 ....D....909 624-1233
845 E Arrow Hwy Pomona (91767) *(P-23833)*
Healthsmart Management Service ....D....714 947-8600
10855 Bus Ctr Dr Ste C Cypress (90630) *(P-10645)*
Healthsmart Pacific Inc (PA) ....A....562 595-1911
180 E Ocean Blvd Ste 650 Long Beach (90802) *(P-21447)*
HealthSouth, Tustin *Also called Encompass Health Corporation (P-22575)*
HealthSouth, Bakersfield *Also called Encompass Health Corporation (P-24517)*
HealthSouth, Oakland *Also called Encompass Health Corporation (P-22020)*
Healthsport Ltd A Ltd Partnr (PA) ....C....707 822-3488
300 Dr Martin Luther Arcata (95521) *(P-18607)*
Healthsport-Arcata, Arcata *Also called Healthsport Ltd A Ltd Partnr (P-18607)*
Healthstream Inc ....B....800 733-8737
9605 Scranton Rd Ste 200 San Diego (92121) *(P-15702)*
Healthview Inc (PA) ....C....310 547-3341
921 S Beacon St San Pedro (90731) *(P-24558)*
Healthview Inc ....E....562 468-0136
12750 Center Court Dr S # 410 Cerritos (90703) *(P-24559)*
Healthy Beginnings French Camp ....D....209 468-6147
500 W Hospital Rd French Camp (95231) *(P-19495)*
Heallth Sanitation Services, Santa Maria *Also called Valley Garbage Rubbish Co Inc (P-6505)*
Hearn Construction, Vacaville *Also called Hearn Enterprise Inc (P-3529)*
Hearn Enterprise Inc (PA) ....C....707 446-5467
536 Davis St Vacaville (95688) *(P-3529)*
Hearsay Social Inc (PA) ....D....888 990-3777
185 Berry St Ste 3800 San Francisco (94107) *(P-15703)*
Hearst Communications Inc ....B....805 375-3121
2323 Teller Rd Newbury Park (91320) *(P-5919)*
Hearst Stations Inc ....D....831 758-8888
238 John St Salinas (93901) *(P-5797)*
Heart Consciousness Church (PA) ....C....707 987-2477
18424 Harbin Springs Rd Middletown (95461) *(P-13476)*
Heartflow Inc (PA) ....D....650 241-1221
1400 Seaport Blvd Bldg B Redwood City (94063) *(P-15970)*
Hearthstone Inc ....D....818 385-0005
24151 Ventura Blvd Calabasas (91302) *(P-10087)*
Heartland Express Inc Iowa ....E....319 626-3600
10131 Redwood Ave Fontana (92335) *(P-4192)*
Heartland Meat Company Inc ....D....619 407-3668
3461 Main St Chula Vista (91911) *(P-8618)*
Heartland Opportunity Ctr Inc (PA) ....D....559 674-4521
4567 N Marty Ave Fresno (93722) *(P-24189)*
Heartland Payment Systems LLC ....D....650 678-2824
548 Shorebird Cir # 3101 Redwood City (94065) *(P-17212)*
Heartland Payment Systems LLC ....D....909 609-1836
35804 Octopus Ln Wildomar (92595) *(P-17213)*
Heartland Payment Systems LLC ....D....707 338-0510
1007 W College Ave Ste B Santa Rosa (95401) *(P-17214)*
Heartland Payment Systems LLC ....D....424 247-8521
207 S Broadway Redondo Beach (90277) *(P-17215)*
Heartland Payment Systems LLC ....D....925 360-3258
2225 Buena Vista Ave A Walnut Creek (94597) *(P-17216)*
Heartland Payment Systems LLC ....D....916 844-9548
5325 Elkhorn Blvd Sacramento (95842) *(P-17217)*
Heartland Payment Systems Inc ....D....760 324-0133
510 Cerritos Way Cathedral City (92234) *(P-17218)*
Heartland Payment Systems Inc ....D....415 518-4810
1460 Golden Gate Ave # 5 San Francisco (94115) *(P-17219)*
HEARTLAND PAYMENT SYSTEMS, INC., San Francisco *Also called Heartland Payment Systems Inc (P-17219)*
Heat, San Francisco *Also called Hvsf Transition LLC (P-13841)*
Heat Software, Newport Beach *Also called Heat Waves LLC (P-15197)*
Heat Waves LLC ....C....323 753-8441
1015 Campanile Newport Beach (92660) *(P-15197)*
Heather Ann Creations, Costa Mesa *Also called Alfreds Pictures Frames Inc (P-16990)*
Heavenly Construction Inc ....D....408 723-4954
370 Umbarger Rd Ste A San Jose (95111) *(P-3530)*
Heavenly Greens, San Jose *Also called Heavenly Construction Inc (P-3530)*
Heaviland Enterprises Inc (PA) ....C....760 598-7065
2180 La Mirada Dr Vista (92081) *(P-858)*
Heavy Load Transfer LLC ....D....310 816-0260
18735 S Ferris Pl Rancho Dominguez (90220) *(P-4021)*
Hebrew Home For Aged Disabled ....A....415 334-2500
302 Silver Ave San Francisco (94112) *(P-20521)*
Heffernan Group, San Francisco *Also called Heffernan Insurance Brokers (P-10646)*
Heffernan Insurance Brokers ....E....800 829-9996
180 Howard St Ste 200 San Francisco (94105) *(P-10646)*
HEI Irvine LLC ....D....949 553-8332
2120 Main St Irvine (92614) *(P-12651)*
HEI Long Beach LLC ....C....562 983-3400
701 W Ocean Blvd Long Beach (90831) *(P-12652)*
HEI Mission Valley LP ....C....619 299-2729
901 Camino Del Rio S San Diego (92108) *(P-12653)*
Heidi Corporation ....D....626 333-6317
727 N Vernon Ave Azusa (91702) *(P-1288)*
Height Brown and Bonesteel ....D....213 241-0900
555 S Flower St Ste 4500 Los Angeles (90071) *(P-23127)*
Heilind Electronics Inc ....D....559 651-0168
700 N Plaza Dr Visalia (93291) *(P-7486)*
Heimark Distributing, Santa Fe Springs *Also called Triangle Distributing Co (P-9029)*

Mergent e-mail: customerrelations@mergent.com
1326
2019 Directory of California
Wholesalers and Services Companies
(P-0000) Products & Services Section entry number
(PA)=Parent Co (HQ)=Headquarters (DH)=Div Headquarters

Heinaman Contract Glazing Inc (PA) ... E ... 949 587-0266
26981 Vista Ter Ste E Lake Forest (92630) ***(P-3531)***

Helen Evans Home For Children, Hacienda Heights *Also called Care Associates Inc* ***(P-24451)***

Helen Woodward Animal Center (PA) ... D ... 858 756-4117
6461 El Apajo Rancho Santa Fe (92067) ***(P-25427)***

Helinet Aviation Services LLC (PA) ... D ... 818 902-0229
16303 Waterman Dr Van Nuys (91406) ***(P-18059)***

Helios Healthcare LLC ... C ... 916 482-0465
2540 Carmichael Way Carmichael (95608) ***(P-20522)***

Helios Healthcare LLC ... C ... 831 449-1515
350 Iris Dr Salinas (93906) ***(P-20523)***

Helios Healthcare LLC ... C ... 530 345-1306
587 Rio Lindo Ave Chico (95926) ***(P-21107)***

Helios Healthcare LLC ... C ... 707 644-7401
2200 Tuolumne St Vallejo (94589) ***(P-21108)***

Helix Healthcare Inc ... B ... 619 465-4411
7050 Parkway Dr La Mesa (91942) ***(P-21957)***

Helix Holdings I LLC ... D ... 415 805-3360
1 Circle Star Way Fl 2 San Carlos (94070) ***(P-26375)***

Helix Opco LLC ... C ... 415 805-3360
1 Circle Star Way Fl 2 San Carlos (94070) ***(P-26376)***

Helix Water District (PA) ... C ... 619 466-0585
7811 University Ave La Mesa (91942) ***(P-6261)***

Helix Water District ... D ... 619 596-3860
1233 Vernon Way El Cajon (92020) ***(P-6262)***

Hellman & Friedman Capital IV ... E ... 415 788-5111
1 Maritime Plz Ste 1200 San Francisco (94111) ***(P-12231)***

Hellmann Wrldwide Lgistics Inc ... D ... 310 847-4600
2270 E 220th St Long Beach (90810) ***(P-5085)***

Hellmann Wrldwide Lgistics Inc ... E ... 310 847-4600
2270 E 220th St Carson (90810) ***(P-5086)***

Hellmuth Obata & Kassabaum Inc (HQ) ... C ... 415 243-0555
1 Bush St Ste 200 San Francisco (94104) ***(P-26057)***

Hellmuth Obata & Kassabaum Inc ... E ... 310 838-9555
9530 Jefferson Blvd Culver City (90232) ***(P-26058)***

Hellosign, San Francisco *Also called Jn Projects Inc* ***(P-13755)***

Helloworld Travel Svcs USA Inc ... D ... 310 535-1000
6171 W Century Blvd # 160 Los Angeles (90045) ***(P-4938)***

Helm Management Co (PA) ... D ... 619 589-6222
4668 Nebo Dr Ste A La Mesa (91941) ***(P-11502)***

Helm Technical Services, El Dorado Hills *Also called G R Helm Inc* ***(P-14856)***

Helm, The, La Mesa *Also called Helm Management Co* ***(P-11502)***

Helmet House Inc (PA) ... D ... 800 421-7247
26855 Malibu Hills Rd Calabasas Hills (91301) ***(P-8263)***

Help At Home Inc ... D ... 916 933-9050
4535 Mcuri Flat Rd Ste 2h Placerville (95667) ***(P-23834)***

Help For The Hurting Inc ... D ... 909 796-4222
2205 S Artesia St San Bernardino (92408) ***(P-23835)***

Help Group West (PA) ... C ... 818 781-0360
13130 Burbank Blvd Sherman Oaks (91401) ***(P-22591)***

Help Hospitalized Veterans II ... D ... 951 926-4500
36585 Penfield Ln Winchester (92596) ***(P-23836)***

Help Unlmted Personnel Svc Inc ... C ... 805 962-4646
319 E Carrillo St Ste 102 Santa Barbara (93101) ***(P-22317)***

Helping Hands of Westminster, Westminster *Also called Helping Hands Sanctuary of Ida* ***(P-20525)***

Helping Hands Pantry, San Bernardino *Also called Help For The Hurting Inc* ***(P-23835)***

Helping Hands Sanctuary of Ida ... C ... 805 687-6651
3880 Via Lucero Santa Barbara (93110) ***(P-20524)***

Helping Hands Sanctuary of Ida ... D ... 714 892-6686
240 Hospital Cir Westminster (92683) ***(P-20525)***

Helping Hearts Foundation Inc ... D ... 916 368-7200
3050 Fite Cir Ste 108 Sacramento (95827) ***(P-24560)***

Helpline Youth Counseling (PA) ... E ... 562 273-0722
14181 Telegraph Rd Whittier (90604) ***(P-23837)***

Heluna Health, City of Industry *Also called Public Hlth Fndation Entps Inc* ***(P-25226)***

Hemacare Corporation (PA) ... C ... 818 986-3883
15350 Sherman Way Van Nuys (91406) ***(P-22815)***

Hemar & Rousso Attys At Law, Encino *Also called Hemar Rousso & Heald L L P* ***(P-23128)***

Hemar Rousso & Heald L L P ... E ... 818 501-3800
15910 Ventura Blvd # 1201 Encino (91436) ***(P-23128)***

Hemet Valley Ambulance, Hemet *Also called American Medical Response Inc* ***(P-3766)***

Hemet Valley Imaging Med Group (PA) ... D ... 951 925-6537
3292 E Florida Ave Ste F Hemet (92544) ***(P-19496)***

Hemington Landscape Svcs Inc ... D ... 530 677-9290
4170 Business Dr Cameron Park (95682) ***(P-859)***

Hemming Morse LLP (PA) ... D ... 415 836-4000
1390 Willow Pass Rd # 410 Concord (94520) ***(P-26217)***

Hemodialysis Inc (PA) ... C ... 818 500-8736
710 W Wilson Ave Glendale (91203) ***(P-22477)***

Hemodialysis Inc ... E ... 818 365-6961
14901 Rinaldi St Ste 100 Mission Hills (91345) ***(P-22478)***

Hendrickson Truck Lines Inc ... C ... 916 387-9614
7080 Florin Perkins Rd Sacramento (95828) ***(P-4193)***

Hendrickson Trucking Inc ... B ... 916 387-9614
7080 Florin Perkins Rd Sacramento (95828) ***(P-4194)***

Henkel Corporation ... C ... 925 458-8086
2850 Willow Pass Rd Bay Point (94565) ***(P-25732)***

Henkels & McCoy Inc ... B ... 909 517-3011
2840 Ficus St Pomona (91766) ***(P-1925)***

Henkels & McCoy Inc ... D ... 909 590-8419
2840 Ficus St Pomona (91766) ***(P-1926)***

Henrietta Weill Memorial Child (PA) ... D ... 661 322-1021
3628 Stockdale Hwy Bakersfield (93309) ***(P-22592)***

Henry Avocado Corporation (PA) ... D ... 760 745-6632
2208 Harmony Grove Rd Escondido (92029) ***(P-236)***

Henry Broadcasting Co ... E ... 415 285-1133
2277 Jerrold Ave San Francisco (94124) ***(P-5720)***

Henry Bros Electronics Inc ... C ... 714 525-4350
1511 E Orangethorpe Ave A Fullerton (92831) ***(P-15971)***

Henry Hibino Farms ... D ... 831 757-3081
106 Rico St Salinas (93907) ***(P-61)***

Henry J Kaiser Fmly Foundation (PA) ... C ... 650 854-9400
185 Berry St Ste 2000 San Francisco (94107) ***(P-12078)***

Henry Mayo Newhall Mem Hlth ... A ... 661 253-8000
23845 Mcbean Pkwy Valencia (91355) ***(P-21448)***

Henry Mayo Newhall Mem Hosp ... D ... 661 253-8112
23845 Mcbean Pkwy Valencia (91355) ***(P-19497)***

Henry Mayo Newhall Mem Hosp (PA) ... A ... 661 253-8000
23845 Mcbean Pkwy Valencia (91355) ***(P-21449)***

Henry Mayo Newhall Mem Hosp ... B ... 661 253-8227
23845 Mcbean Pkwy Santa Clarita (91355) ***(P-22816)***

Henry Samueli School Engrg, Irvine *Also called University California Irvine* ***(P-26484)***

Henry Wine Group LLC (HQ) ... B ... 707 745-8500
4301 Industrial Way Benicia (94510) ***(P-9049)***

Henry Wine Group of C.A., The, Benicia *Also called Henry Wine Group LLC* ***(P-9049)***

Henry's Pub, Berkeley *Also called Hotel Durant A Ltd Partnership* ***(P-12724)***

Henrymayo Newhall Mem Hosp, Valencia *Also called Henry Mayo Newhall Mem Hlth* ***(P-21448)***

Hensel Phelps Construction Co ... D ... 858 266-7979
5271 Viewridge Ct Frnt San Diego (92123) ***(P-1549)***

Hensel Phelps Construction Co ... C ... 408 452-1800
226 Airport Pkwy Ste 150 San Jose (95110) ***(P-1550)***

Hensel Phelps Construction Co ... D ... 619 544-6828
9404 Genesee Ave Ste 140 La Jolla (92037) ***(P-1551)***

Hensel Phlps Grnte Hngr JV ... C ... 949 852-0111
18850 Von Kamon 100 Irvine (92612) ***(P-1552)***

Henson Recording Studio, Los Angeles *Also called Jim Henson Company Inc* ***(P-18066)***

Hentrel Greathouse Foundation ... D ... 302 513-4056
127 S 1st Ave Barstow (92311) ***(P-25172)***

Henwood Energy Services Inc (HQ) ... C ... 916 955-6031
2379 Gateway Oaks Dr # 110 Sacramento (95833) ***(P-25733)***

Heppner Hardwoods Inc ... D ... 626 969-7983
555 W Danlee St Azusa (91702) ***(P-6827)***

Herald Christian Health Center (PA) ... D ... 626 286-8700
8841 Garvey Ave Rosemead (91770) ***(P-19498)***

Herb Thyme Farm Inc ... D ... 603 542-3690
7909 Crossway Dr Pico Rivera (90660) ***(P-26)***

Herbalife Intl Amer Inc (HQ) ... B ... 213 745-0500
800 W Olympic Blvd # 406 Los Angeles (90015) ***(P-8177)***

Herbert Malarkey Roofing Co ... D ... 562 806-8000
9301 Garfield Ave South Gate (90280) ***(P-3163)***

Herbs Pool Service Inc ... D ... 415 479-4040
3769 Redwood Hwy San Rafael (94903) ***(P-17220)***

Herc Rentals 9638, Carson *Also called Herc Rentals Inc* ***(P-14510)***

Herc Rentals 9643, Bakersfield *Also called Herc Rentals Inc* ***(P-14511)***

Herc Rentals 9741, Rohnert Park *Also called Herc Rentals Inc* ***(P-14509)***

Herc Rentals 9748, Benicia *Also called Herc Rentals Inc* ***(P-14512)***

Herc Rentals Inc ... D ... 707 586-6491
5500 Commerce Blvd Rohnert Park (94928) ***(P-14509)***

Herc Rentals Inc ... E ... 310 233-5000
22422 S Alameda St Carson (90810) ***(P-14510)***

Herc Rentals Inc ... C ... 661 392-3661
6315 Snow Rd Bakersfield (93308) ***(P-14511)***

Herc Rentals Inc ... E ... 707 747-4444
5251 Industrial Way Benicia (94510) ***(P-14512)***

Herc Rentals Inc ... C ... 510 633-2040
7727 Oakport St Oakland (94621) ***(P-14513)***

Herc Rentals Prosolutions, Oakland *Also called Herc Rentals Inc* ***(P-14513)***

Herca Construction Services, Perris *Also called Herca Telecomm Services Inc* ***(P-7678)***

Herca Telecomm Services Inc ... D ... 951 940-5941
18610 Beck St Perris (92570) ***(P-7678)***

Hercules Capital Inc (PA) ... D ... 650 289-3060
400 Hamilton Ave Ste 310 Palo Alto (94301) ***(P-12232)***

Hercules Fitness ... E ... 510 724-2900
600 Alfred Nobel Dr Hercules (94547) ***(P-18608)***

Here Films ... E ... 310 806-4288
10990 Wilshire Blvd Los Angeles (90024) ***(P-27746)***

Here Media Inc (PA) ... D ... 310 806-4288
10990 Wilshire Blvd Fl 18 Los Angeles (90024) ***(P-5576)***

Heritage 1 Window and Building ... C ... 916 481-5030
4300 Jetway Ct North Highlands (95660) ***(P-6828)***

Heritage Bank of Commerce (HQ) ... C ... 408 947-6900
150 Almaden Blvd Lbby San Jose (95113) ***(P-9463)***

Heritage California Aco, Northridge *Also called Regal Medical Group Inc* ***(P-25038)***

Heritage Community Credit Un (PA) ... D ... 916 364-1700
10399 Old Placerville Rd Sacramento (95827) ***(P-9561)***

Heritage Community Credit Un ... E ... 916 364-1700
10399 Old Clasaville Rd Rancho Cordova (95670) ***(P-9562)***

Heritage Conalescent Hospital, Sacramento *Also called Horizon West Inc* ***(P-20534)***

Heritage Estates-Livermore, Livermore *Also called Leisure Care LLC* ***(P-11052)***

Heritage Gardens Hlth Care Ctr, Loma Linda *Also called Heritage Health Care Inc* ***(P-20526)***

Heritage Golf Group Inc ... D ... 661 254-4401
27330 Tourney Rd Valencia (91355) ***(P-18718)***

Heritage Golf Group LLC ... D ... 949 369-6226
990 Avenida Talega San Clemente (92673) ***(P-18719)***

Heritage Health Care, Lancaster *Also called High Desert Med Corp A Med Grp* ***(P-19500)***

Heritage Health Care Inc ... C ... 909 796-0216
25271 Barton Rd Loma Linda (92354) ***(P-20526)***

Heritage House, Camarillo *Also called Wilshire Health and Cmnty Svcs* ***(P-24725)***

Heritage Indemnity Company ... D ... 303 987-5500
23 Pasteur Irvine (92618) ***(P-10361)***

Heritage Inn, Ridgecrest *Also called Great Western Hotels Corp* ***(P-12617)***

Heritage Interests LLC (PA) ... D ... 916 481-5030
4300 Jetway Ct North Highlands (95660) ***(P-3041)***

Employee Codes: A=Over 500 employees, B=251-500
C=101-250, D=51-100, E=50
2019 Directory of California
Wholesalers and Services Companies
© Mergent Inc. 1-800-342-5647
1327

Heritage Land Company Inc ....E....209 444-1700
111 N Zuckerman Rd Stockton (95206) ***(P-266)***
Heritage Landscape Inc ....C....818 999-2041
7949 Deering Ave Canoga Park (91304) ***(P-760)***
Heritage Manor Inc ....D....626 573-3141
610 N Garfield Ave Monterey Park (91754) ***(P-20527)***
Heritage Medical Group ....C....760 956-1286
12370 Hesperia Rd Ste 6 Victorville (92395) ***(P-22817)***
Heritage Medical Group (PA) ....D....661 327-4411
4580 California Ave Bakersfield (93309) ***(P-19499)***
Heritage One Carpentry Inc ....C....530 345-6622
2107 Forest Ave Ste 100 Chico (95928) ***(P-6829)***
Heritage One Door and Building ....D....916 481-5030
4300 Jetway Ct North Highlands (95660) ***(P-6830)***
HERITAGE POINTE, Mission Viejo *Also called Jewish Home For The Aging of O* ***(P-24569)***
Heritage Provider Network Inc (PA) ....A....818 654-3461
8510 Balboa Blvd Ste 285 Northridge (91325) ***(P-25018)***
Heritage Psychiatric Health, Oakland *Also called Telecare Corporation* ***(P-21991)***
Heritage Senior Care Inc ....D....800 562-2734
15428 Civic Dr Ste 345 Victorville (92392) ***(P-22318)***
Heritage, The, San Francisco *Also called San Francisco Ladies Protecti* ***(P-24665)***
Herman Health Care Center ....D....408 269-0701
2295 Plummer Ave San Jose (95125) ***(P-20528)***
Herman Sanitarium ....C....408 269-0701
2295 Plummer Ave San Jose (95125) ***(P-20529)***
Herman Weissker Inc (HQ) ....C....951 826-8800
1645 Brown Ave Riverside (92509) ***(P-1927)***
Hermitage Hlthcr Mnkn Mnr ....C....410 651-0011
400 Circle Dr Angwin (94508) ***(P-21109)***
Hero, San Diego *Also called Renovate America Inc* ***(P-15404)***
Herren Enterprises Inc ....D....949 951-1666
23091 Terra Dr Laguna Hills (92653) ***(P-3808)***
Herrero Builders Incorporated (PA) ....C....415 824-7675
2100 Oakdale Ave San Francisco (94124) ***(P-1407)***
Herrick Hospital, Berkeley *Also called Surgery Center of Alta Bates* ***(P-19955)***
Herring Broadcasting Company ....E....858 270-6900
4757 Morena Blvd San Diego (92117) ***(P-5798)***
Herring Networks Inc ....C....858 270-6900
4757 Morena Blvd San Diego (92117) ***(P-5799)***
Hertz Claim Management Corp ....D....626 296-4760
2923 Bradley St Ste 190 Pasadena (91107) ***(P-17639)***
Hertz Corporation ....E....818 997-0414
2627 N Hollywood Way # 8 Burbank (91505) ***(P-17640)***
Hertz Corporation ....D....408 450-6025
1000 Walsh Ave Santa Clara (95050) ***(P-17641)***
Hertz Corporation ....D....925 680-0316
30 S Buchanan Cir Pacheco (94553) ***(P-17642)***
Hertz Corporation ....D....650 624-6391
177 S Airport Blvd South San Francisco (94080) ***(P-17643)***
Hertz Corporation ....D....818 569-6900
3111 N Kenwood St Burbank (91505) ***(P-17644)***
Herzog Contracting Corp ....A....619 849-6990
2155 Hancock St San Diego (92110) ***(P-3532)***
HEs Transportation Svcs Inc ....E....510 783-6100
3623 Munster St Hayward (94545) ***(P-5087)***
Hesperia Senior Living LLC ....D....760 244-5579
17581 Sultana St Hesperia (92345) ***(P-24561)***
Hetrosys LLC ....D....408 270-0240
3858 Carrera Ct San Jose (95148) ***(P-27747)***
Hewitt and Canfield Cnstr Inc ....D....805 522-4426
495 E Easy St Ste A Simi Valley (93065) ***(P-3042)***
HEWLETT FOUNDATION, Menlo Park *Also called Hewlett Wlliam Flora Fndation* ***(P-25428)***
Hewlett Packard ....A....650 857-1501
3000 Hanover St Palo Alto (94304) ***(P-15198)***
Hewlett Packard Enterprise Co ....D....916 786-8000
8000 Foothills Blvd Roseville (95747) ***(P-15704)***
Hewlett Packard Enterprise Co (PA) ....C....650 687-5817
3000 Hanover St Palo Alto (94304) ***(P-15705)***
Hewlett Wlliam Flora Fndation ....D....650 234-4500
2121 Sand Hill Rd Menlo Park (94025) ***(P-25428)***
Hfrm II Inc (PA) ....B....530 242-2010
2051 Hilltop Dr Ste A18 Redding (96002) ***(P-10895)***
HFS Concepts 4 Inc ....E....562 424-1720
3229 E Spring St Ste 330 Long Beach (90806) ***(P-26059)***
HG Fenton Company ....D....619 400-0120
7577 Mission Valley Rd # 200 San Diego (92108) ***(P-11030)***
Hga Architects and Engineers, Sacramento *Also called Hammel Green & Abrahamson Inc* ***(P-26054)***
Hggc LLC (PA) ....B....650 321-4910
1950 University Ave # 350 East Palo Alto (94303) ***(P-15199)***
Hgt, Ontario *Also called Hub Group Trucking Inc* ***(P-4023)***
HHC Trs Portsmouth LLC ....D....760 322-6000
888 E Tahquitz Canyon Way Palm Springs (92262) ***(P-12654)***
Hhlp San Diego Lessee LLC ....D....619 446-3000
530 Broadway San Diego (92101) ***(P-12655)***
HHS Communications Inc ....D....909 230-5170
2042 S Grove Ave Ontario (91761) ***(P-2603)***
Hhsa Data Center, Sacramento *Also called Califrnia Hlth Humn Srvcs Agcy* ***(P-16102)***
HI Anaheim LLC ....D....714 533-1500
100 W Katella Ave Anaheim (92802) ***(P-12656)***
HI Desert Hospital, Lancaster *Also called County of Los Angeles* ***(P-19413)***
HI Fresno Hospitality LLC ....D....559 233-6650
1055 Van Ness Ave Fresno (93721) ***(P-12657)***
HI Lo Motel, Edgewood *Also called Siskiyou Development Company* ***(P-13231)***
Hi-Desert Medical Center, Yucca Valley *Also called Hi-Desert Mem Hlth Care Dst* ***(P-21450)***
Hi-Desert Mem Hlth Care Dst (PA) ....D....760 820-9229
6530 Lcontenpa Rd Ste 100 Yucca Valley (92284) ***(P-21450)***

Hi-TEC Sports Usa Inc (HQ) ....D....209 545-1111
5990 Sepulvda Blvd # 600 Van Nuys (91411) ***(P-8358)***
Hibrid Home LLC ....C....844 442-7431
10025 Mesa Rim Rd San Diego (92121) ***(P-2227)***
Hibshman Trading Corporation ....D....909 581-1800
9843 6th St Ste 103 Rancho Cucamonga (91730) ***(P-8306)***
Hid Global Safe Inc ....D....408 453-1008
3590 N 1st St Ste 320 San Jose (95134) ***(P-15972)***
Hidden Valley Golf Course, Hidden Valley Lake *Also called Hidden Valley Lake Association* ***(P-25173)***
Hidden Valley Lake Association (PA) ....D....707 987-3146
18174 Hidden Valley Rd Hidden Valley Lake (95467) ***(P-25173)***
Hidden Valley Mvg & Stor Inc (PA) ....D....602 252-7800
1218 Pacific Oaks Pl Escondido (92029) ***(P-4351)***
Hidden Villa Ranch, Norco *Also called Luberski Inc* ***(P-8535)***
Hidden Villa Ranch Produce Inc ....B....714 680-3447
310 N Harbor Blvd Ste 205 Fullerton (92832) ***(P-8532)***
Higard Farms LLC ....D....831 753-5982
6 Quail Run Cir Salinas (93907) ***(P-354)***
Higgs Fletcher & Mack Llp ....C....619 236-1551
401 W A St Ste 2600 San Diego (92101) ***(P-23129)***
High Caliber Line, Irwindale *Also called Calibre International LLC* ***(P-27545)***
High Country Lumber Inc (PA) ....E....760 873-5874
444 S Main St Bishop (93514) ***(P-6831)***
High Desert, Victorville *Also called Southern California Edison Co* ***(P-6140)***
High Desert Med Corp A Med Grp (PA) ....C....661 945-5984
43839 15th St W Lancaster (93534) ***(P-19500)***
High Desert Partnership ....B....760 946-5414
17500 Mana Rd Apple Valley (92307) ***(P-26527)***
High Desert Phoenix ....E....661 547-5630
42980 Staffordshire Dr Lancaster (93534) ***(P-19181)***
High Dsert Ptent Care Svcs LLC ....D....760 956-4150
17095 Main St Hesperia (92345) ***(P-19501)***
High End Development Inc ....D....925 687-2540
665 Stone Rd Benicia (94510) ***(P-3533)***
HIGH HAVEN, Los Angeles *Also called Broadview Inc* ***(P-20270)***
High Performance Wall Systems, Redding *Also called Redding Drywall Systems Inc* ***(P-2946)***
High Plains Ranch LLC (PA) ....C....559 583-1277
2911 Hanford Armona Rd Hanford (93230) ***(P-415)***
High Ridge Brands, La Palma *Also called Dr Fresh LLC* ***(P-8166)***
High Ridge Wind LLC ....A....888 903-6926
15445 Innovation Dr San Diego (92128) ***(P-6042)***
High Road Program (PA) ....D....805 497-8800
250 N Westlake Blvd # 210 Westlake Village (91362) ***(P-23838)***
High St Car Wash Lube & Oil, Oakland *Also called High Street Hand Car Wash Inc* ***(P-17862)***
High Street Hand Car Wash Inc ....D....510 536-4333
569 High St Oakland (94601) ***(P-17862)***
High Summit LLC ....E....925 605-2900
6909 Las Positas Rd Ste D Livermore (94551) ***(P-17795)***
High Technology Video Inc ....D....323 969-8822
10900 Ventura Blvd Studio City (91604) ***(P-18195)***
High Tide and Green Grass Inc ....D....805 981-8722
2401 W Vineyard Ave Oxnard (93036) ***(P-18720)***
High Valley Lodge, Sunland *Also called P R N Convalescent Hospital* ***(P-20685)***
High-Light Electric Inc ....D....951 352-9646
6942 Ed Perkic St Riverside (92504) ***(P-2604)***
Highcom Security Services ....D....510 893-7600
1900 Webster St Ste B Oakland (94612) ***(P-16696)***
Highland Care Center Redlands, Redlands *Also called AG Redlands LLC* ***(P-20981)***
Highland Head Start, Highland *Also called County of San Bernardino* ***(P-24309)***
Highland Hosp Hghland Wellness, Oakland *Also called Alameda Health System* ***(P-21276)***
Highland Lumber Sales Inc ....D....714 778-2293
300 E Santa Ana St Anaheim (92805) ***(P-6832)***
HIGHLAND PALMS HEALTHCARE CENT, Highland *Also called Cedar Holdings LLC* ***(P-20294)***
Highland Park Skilled Nursing ....D....323 254-6125
5125 Monte Vista St Los Angeles (90042) ***(P-20530)***
Highlands Inn Inc ....C....831 620-1234
120 Highland Dr Carmel (93923) ***(P-12658)***
Highlands Inn Investors II LP ....B....831 624-3801
120 Highland Dr Carmel (93923) ***(P-12659)***
Highmark Capital Management ....D....800 582-4734
350 California St Fl 22 San Francisco (94104) ***(P-10088)***
Highpoint Productions Inc ....D....818 728-7600
13400 Rverside Dr Ste 300 Sherman Oaks (91423) ***(P-18060)***
Hightail, San Mateo *Also called Open Text Inc* ***(P-15331)***
Highway Patrol, Woodland Hills *Also called West Valley Area Squad Club* ***(P-24858)***
Hignell Incorporated ....D....530 345-1965
1836 Laburnum Ave Chico (95926) ***(P-11031)***
Hikvision USA Inc (HQ) ....C....909 895-0400
18639 Railroad St City of Industry (91748) ***(P-16901)***
Hilary A Brodie MD PHD ....D....916 734-3744
2521 Stockton Blvd 7200 Sacramento (95817) ***(P-19502)***
Hilbers Inc ....D....530 673-2947
1210 Stabler Ln Yuba City (95993) ***(P-1553)***
HILBERS CONTRACTORS & ENGINEER, Yuba City *Also called Hilbers Inc* ***(P-1553)***
Hildreth Farm Incorporated ....D....707 462-0648
1520 Rddick Cunningham Rd Ukiah (95482) ***(P-219)***
Hill & Knowlton Strategies LLC ....D....415 281-7120
60 Green St San Francisco (94111) ***(P-27556)***
Hill Brothers Chemical Company (PA) ....C....714 998-8800
1675 N Main St Orange (92867) ***(P-8928)***
Hill Cress Home, San Bernardino *Also called Care Tech Inc* ***(P-20286)***
Hill Farrer & Burrill ....D....213 620-0460
300 S Grand Ave Fl 37 Los Angeles (90071) ***(P-23130)***

Mergent e-mail: customerrelations@mergent.com
1328
2019 Directory of California
Wholesalers and Services Companies
(P-0000) Products & Services Section entry number
(PA)=Parent Co (HQ)=Headquarters (DH)=Div Headquarters

Hill Physicians Med Group Inc (PA)....B....800 445-5747
2409 Camino Ramon San Ramon (94583) ***(P-19503)***
Hillcrest AC & Shtmtl, Bakersfield *Also called Hillcrest Sheet Metal Inc* ***(P-3164)***
Hillcrest Care Inc....D....909 882-2965
4280 Cypress Dr San Bernardino (92407) ***(P-21110)***
Hillcrest Cnvalescent Hosp Inc....C....323 636-3462
3401 Cedar Ave Long Beach (90807) ***(P-21111)***
Hillcrest Contracting Inc....D....951 273-9600
1467 Circle City Dr Corona (92879) ***(P-1791)***
Hillcrest Country Club....C....310 553-8911
10000 W Pico Blvd Los Angeles (90064) ***(P-18935)***
Hillcrest Manor Sanitarium, National City *Also called Imaginative Horizons Inc* ***(P-20541)***
Hillcrest Senior Housing Corp....B....650 757-1737
35 Hillcrest Dr Daly City (94014) ***(P-1289)***
Hillcrest Sheet Metal Inc....D....661 335-1500
2324 Perseus Ct Bakersfield (93308) ***(P-3164)***
Hilldale Habilitation Center, La Mesa *Also called Razavi Corporation* ***(P-20716)***
Hillendale Home Care, Walnut Creek *Also called Caswell Bay Inc* ***(P-22258)***
Hillhaven Convalescent Hosp, Burlingame *Also called Kindred Healthcare Operating* ***(P-22028)***
Hills Flat Lumber Co (PA)....D....530 273-6171
380 Railroad Ave Grass Valley (95945) ***(P-2605)***
Hills Wldg & Engrg Contr Inc....D....661 746-5400
22038 Stockdale Hwy Bakersfield (93314) ***(P-1063)***
Hillsborough, Modesto *Also called Woodside Group Inc* ***(P-9866)***
Hillsdale Group LP....D....818 623-2170
12750 Riverside Dr North Hollywood (91607) ***(P-21112)***
Hillsdale Group LP....E....650 742-9150
1201 Broadway Ofc Millbrae (94030) ***(P-21113)***
Hillsdale Group LP....D....510 538-3866
1832 B St Hayward (94541) ***(P-21114)***
Hillside Auto Salvage, Riverside *Also called Team Truck Dismantling Inc* ***(P-6704)***
Hillside Care Center, San Rafael *Also called Cal-Coast Healthcare Inc* ***(P-20279)***
Hillside Contractor, Santa Ana *Also called South Coast Stone Paving* ***(P-1852)***
Hillside Enterprises, Long Beach *Also called Association For Retarded* ***(P-24154)***
Hillside Hospital, San Diego *Also called San Miguel Hospital Assn* ***(P-21711)***
Hillside House Inc....D....805 687-4818
1235 Veronica Springs Rd Santa Barbara (93105) ***(P-20933)***
Hillside Mem Pk & Mortuary, Los Angeles *Also called Temple Israel of Hollywood* ***(P-13700)***
Hillsides....B....323 254-2274
940 Avenue 64 Pasadena (91105) ***(P-24562)***
Hilltop Family YMCA, Richmond *Also called Young MNS Chrstn Assn of E Bay* ***(P-25363)***
Hilltop Manor, Auburn *Also called Horizon West Healthcare Inc* ***(P-21115)***
Hilltop Ranch Inc....C....209 874-1875
13890 Looney Rd Ballico (95303) ***(P-529)***
Hilltop Securities Inc....E....800 765-2200
8350 Wilshire Blvd Beverly Hills (90211) ***(P-9962)***
Hilltop Trading, Ballico *Also called Hilltop Ranch Inc* ***(P-529)***
Hilltown Packing Co Inc....B....831 784-1931
9 Harris Pl A Salinas (93901) ***(P-530)***
Hillview Acres....D....714 694-2828
23091 Mill Creek Dr Laguna Hills (92653) ***(P-24563)***
Hillview Acres Childrens Home, Laguna Hills *Also called Hillview Acres* ***(P-24563)***
Hillview Convalescent Hospital....E....408 779-3633
530 W Dunne Ave Morgan Hill (95037) ***(P-20531)***
Hillview Mental Health Center....D....818 896-1161
12450 Van Nuys Blvd # 200 Pacoima (91331) ***(P-22593)***
HILMAR HEALTH CENTER, Livingston *Also called Livingston Community Health* ***(P-19655)***
Hilton, Santa Barbara *Also called Park Hotels & Resorts Inc* ***(P-13018)***
Hilton, San Diego *Also called Ww San Diego Harbor Island LLC* ***(P-13422)***
Hilton, San Diego *Also called Park Hotels & Resorts Inc* ***(P-13021)***
Hilton, La Jolla *Also called Torreyana Grille* ***(P-13333)***
Hilton, Sacramento *Also called Shri Sidhi Vinayaka Hotel Inc* ***(P-13224)***
Hilton, Oakland *Also called Park Hotels & Resorts Inc* ***(P-13023)***
Hilton, La Jolla *Also called Park Hotels & Resorts Inc* ***(P-13024)***
Hilton, Pasadena *Also called Park Hotels & Resorts Inc* ***(P-13027)***
Hilton, Milpitas *Also called Bre Select Hotels Oper LLC* ***(P-12397)***
Hilton, Mountain View *Also called Camino Real Group LLC* ***(P-12422)***
Hilton, Anaheim *Also called Makar Anaheim LLC* ***(P-12871)***
Hilton, Beverly Hills *Also called Park Hotels & Resorts Inc* ***(P-13030)***
Hilton, South Lake Tahoe *Also called Park Hotels & Resorts Inc* ***(P-13031)***
Hilton, Ontario *Also called Park Hotels & Resorts Inc* ***(P-13036)***
Hilton, San Gabriel *Also called Park Hotels & Resorts Inc* ***(P-13037)***
Hilton, Redding *Also called Win River Hotel Corporation* ***(P-13400)***
Hilton, Emeryville *Also called Rljhgn Emeryville Lessee LP* ***(P-13134)***
Hilton, Costa Mesa *Also called Park Hotels & Resorts Inc* ***(P-13039)***
Hilton, Long Beach *Also called Merritt Hospitality LLC* ***(P-12922)***
Hilton, San Diego *Also called Lho Mssion Bay Rsie Lessee Inc* ***(P-12850)***
Hilton, Oxnard *Also called T M Mian & Associates Inc* ***(P-13318)***
Hilton, Huntington Beach *Also called Waterfront Hotel LLC* ***(P-13382)***
Hilton, Monterey *Also called Ocean Park Hotels Inc* ***(P-12971)***
Hilton, Los Angeles *Also called Fortuna Enterprises LP* ***(P-12582)***
Hilton, San Jose *Also called West Hotel Partners LP* ***(P-13388)***
Hilton, Santa Clara *Also called Ontario Airport Hotel Corp* ***(P-12986)***
Hilton, Irvine *Also called Interstate Hotels Resorts Inc* ***(P-26900)***
Hilton, Valencia *Also called Ocean Park Hotels Inc* ***(P-12972)***
Hilton Checkers Los Angeles, Los Angeles *Also called Chsp Trs Los Angeles LLC* ***(P-12458)***
Hilton Concord, Concord *Also called Vwi Concord LLC* ***(P-13371)***
Hilton El Segundo LLC....D....310 726-0100
2100 E Mariposa Ave El Segundo (90245) ***(P-12660)***
Hilton Garded, San Diego *Also called SD Stadium Hotel LLC* ***(P-13197)***
Hilton Garden Hotel, Foster City *Also called Hilton Garden In San Mateo* ***(P-12661)***
Hilton Garden In San Mateo....D....650 522-9000
2000 Bridgepointe Pkwy Foster City (94404) ***(P-12661)***
Hilton Garden Inn, San Diego *Also called M4dev LLC* ***(P-12867)***
Hilton Garden Inn....D....510 346-5533
510 Lewelling Blvd San Leandro (94579) ***(P-12662)***
Hilton Garden Inn Calabasas, Calabasas *Also called T M Mian & Associates Inc* ***(P-13317)***
Hilton Garden Inn Carlsbad Bch, Carlsbad *Also called Interstate Hotels Resorts Inc* ***(P-26896)***
Hilton Garden Inn Emeryville, Emeryville *Also called Rlj Hgn Emeryville Lessee LP* ***(P-13480)***
Hilton Garden Inn Monterey, Monterey *Also called 1000 Aguajito Op Co LLC* ***(P-12286)***
Hilton Garden Inn Palo Alto, Palo Alto *Also called Palmetto Hospitality* ***(P-13015)***
Hilton Garden Inn Pismo, Pismo Beach *Also called Castlblack Pismo Bch Owner LLC* ***(P-12438)***
Hilton Garden Inn Sacremento, Sacramento *Also called Apple Hospitality Reit Inc* ***(P-12328)***
Hilton Garden Inn San, South San Francisco *Also called Larkspur Hsptality Dev MGT LLC* ***(P-12838)***
Hilton Garden Inn Santa, Goleta *Also called Goleta Hhg Hotel Dev LP* ***(P-12610)***
Hilton Garden Inns MGT LLC....C....760 476-0800
6450 Carlsbad Blvd Carlsbad (92011) ***(P-12663)***
Hilton Garden Inns MGT LLC....D....310 726-0100
2100 E Mariposa Ave El Segundo (90245) ***(P-12664)***
Hilton Garden Inns MGT LLC....E....925 292-2000
2801 Constitution Dr Fl 2 Livermore (94551) ***(P-12665)***
Hilton Hotel Long Beach, Long Beach *Also called Lb Funding LLC* ***(P-12843)***
Hilton Hotels, Long Beach *Also called HEI Long Beach LLC* ***(P-12652)***
Hilton Hotels, Ontario *Also called Park Hotels & Resorts Inc* ***(P-13026)***
Hilton Irvine, Irvine *Also called Equistar Irvine Company LLC* ***(P-12560)***
Hilton Los Angles Universal Cy....B....818 506-2500
555 Unversal Hollywood Dr Universal City (91608) ***(P-12666)***
Hilton Los Angls/Nversal Cy Ht, Universal City *Also called Sun Hill Properties Inc* ***(P-13286)***
Hilton Newark Sremont, Monrovia *Also called SM Broadway Corp* ***(P-12187)***
Hilton Pasadena, Pasadena *Also called Amstar/Davidson Robles LLC* ***(P-12319)***
Hilton Port Los Angls-San Pdro, San Pedro *Also called Meristar San Pedro Hilton LLC* ***(P-12920)***
Hilton Resort In Palm Spring, Palm Springs *Also called Walters Family Partnership* ***(P-13378)***
Hilton Resort Palm Springs....C....760 320-6868
400 E Tahquitz Canyon Way Palm Springs (92262) ***(P-12667)***
Hilton Sacramento Arden West, Sacramento *Also called Whgca LLC* ***(P-13399)***
Hilton Sacramento Arden West, Sacramento *Also called Interstate Hotels Resorts Inc* ***(P-12779)***
Hilton San Diego/Del Mar, Del Mar *Also called Ws Hdm LLC* ***(P-13419)***
Hilton San Diego/Del Mar, Del Mar *Also called Sunstone Durante LLC* ***(P-13292)***
Hilton San Francisco, Burlingame *Also called Harbor View Hotels Inc* ***(P-12644)***
Hilton San Francisco Fincl Dst....E....415 433-6600
750 Kearny St San Francisco (94108) ***(P-12668)***
Hilton San Jose and Towers, Los Angeles *Also called West Hotel Partners LP* ***(P-13387)***
Hilton Santa Clara, Santa Clara *Also called Stanford Hotels Corporation* ***(P-13262)***
Hilton Santa Cruz/Scotts Vly, Scotts Valley *Also called Inn At Scotts Valley LLC* ***(P-12763)***
Hilton Universal Hotel....D....818 506-2500
555 Unversal Hollywood Dr Universal City (91608) ***(P-12669)***
Hilton Wdlnd Hlls / Los Angles, Woodland Hills *Also called Canoga Hotel Corporation* ***(P-12424)***
Hilton Woodland Hills & Towers....C....818 595-1000
6360 Canoga Ave Woodland Hills (91367) ***(P-12670)***
Hiltonm Grdn Inn Lax El Sgundo, El Segundo *Also called Hilton El Segundo LLC* ***(P-12660)***
Hinds Hospice (PA)....C....559 674-0407
2490 W Shaw Ave Ste 100a Fresno (93711) ***(P-23839)***
Hinerfeld-Ward Inc....D....310 842-7929
8931 Ellis Ave Ste B1 Los Angeles (90034) ***(P-1178)***
Hines Gs Properties Inc....E....415 982-6200
101 California St # 1000 San Francisco (94111) ***(P-11880)***
Hines Horticulture Inc....B....760 723-1500
2500 Rainbow Valley Blvd Fallbrook (92028) ***(P-9140)***
Hines Interests Ltd Partnr....C....650 518-6139
1 Hacker Way Bldg 10 Menlo Park (94025) ***(P-11503)***
Hines Nurseries LLC....D....602 254-2831
22941 Mill Creek Dr Laguna Hills (92653) ***(P-9141)***
Hino Motors Mfg USA Inc....C....951 727-0286
4550 Wineville Ave Mira Loma (91752) ***(P-6646)***
Hinode, Woodland *Also called Sunfoods LLC* ***(P-8463)***
Hinshaw & Culbertson LLP....D....213 680-2800
633 W 5th St Ste 4700 Los Angeles (90071) ***(P-23131)***
Hinttech Inc....C....415 874-3200
505 Montgomery St Fl 11 San Francisco (94111) ***(P-27748)***
Hired Hand Home Care....C....707 575-4700
2901 Cleveland Ave # 203 Santa Rosa (95403) ***(P-22319)***
Hired Hands Inc....C....707 265-6400
1754 2nd St Ste D NAPA (94559) ***(P-14636)***
Hireforces, San Jose *Also called Incline Incorporated* ***(P-14646)***
Hireright, Irvine *Also called Corporate Risk Hldings III Inc* ***(P-17102)***
Hireright LLC (HQ)....C....949 428-5800
3349 Michelson Dr Ste 150 Irvine (92612) ***(P-16230)***
Hirsch Electronics LLC....D....949 250-8888
1900 Carnegie Ave Ste B Santa Ana (92705) ***(P-7487)***
Hirsch/Bedner Intl Inc (PA)....D....310 829-9087
3216 Nebraska Ave Santa Monica (90404) ***(P-17221)***
Hirschfeld Kraemer LLP (PA)....E....415 835-9000
505 Montgomery St Fl 13 San Francisco (94111) ***(P-23132)***
Hirsh Inc....E....213 622-9441
860 S Los Angeles St # 900 Los Angeles (90014) ***(P-1064)***
HIS KIDS RANCH, Potrero *Also called Rancho De Sus Ninos Inc* ***(P-24641)***

ALPHABETIC

Employee Codes: A=Over 500 employees, B=251-500
C=101-250, D=51-100, E=50
2019 Directory of California
Wholesalers and Services Companies
© Mergent Inc. 1-800-342-5647
1329

His Manna Inc ....C......831 423-5515
 150 Felker St Ste B Santa Cruz (95060) (P-27263)
His Passion Inc ....E......800 760-6389
 17195 Newhope St Ste 201 Fountain Valley (92708) (P-22320)
HISPANIC CONCILIO OF SAN MATEO, Redwood City Also called El Concilio San Mateo Cnty
Inc (P-23784)
Historic Mission Inn Corp ....B......951 784-0300
 3649 Mission Inn Ave Riverside (92501) (P-12671)
Historic Tours of America, San Diego Also called Old Town Trlley Turs San Diego (P-4974)
Historic TW Inc ....E......818 954-3096
 106 Disney Productions Burbank (91521) (P-18061)
Historical Properties Inc (PA) ....D......619 230-8417
 311 Island Ave San Diego (92101) (P-12672)
Historical Soc Centinela Vly ....B......310 649-6272
 7634 Midfield Ave Los Angeles (90045) (P-24885)
Hit Portfolio I Misc Trs LLC ....C......323 656-1234
 8401 W Sunset Blvd Los Angeles (90069) (P-12673)
Hit Portfolio I Misc Trs LLC ....B......909 240-9526
 3500 Market St Riverside (92501) (P-12674)
Hit Portfolio I Misc Trs LLC ....A......415 788-1234
 50 Drumm St San Francisco (94111) (P-12675)
Hit Portfolio I Misc Trs LLC ....B......925 743-1882
 2323 San Ramon Vly Blvd San Ramon (94583) (P-12676)
Hit Portfolio I Misc Trs LLC ....B......562 432-0161
 200 S Pine Ave Long Beach (90802) (P-12677)
Hit Portfolio I Misc Trs LLC ....B......831 372-1234
 1 Old Golf Course Rd Monterey (93940) (P-12678)
Hit Portfolio I Misc Trs LLC ....B......949 975-1234
 17900 Jamboree Rd Irvine (92614) (P-12679)
Hit Portfolio I Misc Trs LLC ....B......760 341-1000
 44600 Indian Wells Ln Indian Wells (92210) (P-12680)
Hit Portfolio I Misc Trs LLC ....B......949 729-1234
 1107 Jamboree Rd Newport Beach (92660) (P-12681)
Hit Portfolio I Misc Trs LLC ....B......408 453-3006
 55 E Brokaw Rd San Jose (95112) (P-12682)
Hit Portfolio I Misc Trs LLC ....A......415 788-1234
 5 Embarcadero Ctr San Francisco (94111) (P-12683)
Hit Portfolio I Misc Trs LLC ....C......619 849-1234
 600 F St San Diego (92101) (P-12684)
Hit Portfolio I NTC Trs LP ....E......310 333-0888
 2135 E El Segundo Blvd El Segundo (90245) (P-12685)
Hit Portfolio II NTC Trs LP ....E......760 431-9399
 5835 Owens Ave Carlsbad (92008) (P-12686)
Hit Portfolio II Trs LLC ....C......714 938-1111
 400 N State College Blvd Orange (92868) (P-12687)
Hitachi High Tech Amer Inc ....D......925 218-2800
 5960 Inglewood Dr Ste 200 Pleasanton (94588) (P-7488)
Hitachi Vantara Corporation ....C......858 537-3000
 15231 Ave Of Science # 100 San Diego (92128) (P-7056)
Hive Tech Gurus Incorporated ....E......323 445-1770
 510 Strtford Ct Unit 204a Del Mar (92014) (P-5577)
Hkf Inc (PA) ....B......323 225-1318
 5983 Smithway St Commerce (90040) (P-7651)
Hks Inc ....D......310 788-7700
 10880 Wilshire Blvd # 1850 Los Angeles (90024) (P-26060)
Hks Architects Inc ....E......415 356-3800
 500 Howard St Fl 4 San Francisco (94105) (P-26061)
Hlw Corp ....E......310 838-7100
 11166 Venice Blvd Culver City (90232) (P-17817)
Hmbl LLC ....C......323 656-8090
 8400 W Sunset Blvd Ste 3a West Hollywood (90069) (P-12688)
HMC Architects, Ontario Also called HMC Group (P-26062)
HMC Group (PA) ....C......909 989-9979
 3546 Concours Ontario (91764) (P-26062)
HMC Group ....D......909 980-8058
 2930 Inland Empire Blvd # 100 Ontario (91764) (P-26063)
Hmclause Inc (HQ) ....C......800 320-4672
 260 Cousteau Pl Ste 210 Davis (95618) (P-267)
Hmclause Inc ....D......530 747-3235
 9241 Mace Blvd Davis (95618) (P-26377)
Hmclause Inc ....D......530 713-5838
 42 Glenshire Ln Chico (95973) (P-268)
HMH BUILDERS, Sacramento Also called Swinerton Builders Hc (P-1665)
Hmi Associates Inc ....C......818 887-6800
 6800 Owensmouth Ave # 330 Canoga Park (91303) (P-16697)
Hmi Industrial Contractors Inc, Rancho Cordova Also called Harelson Mechanical
Inc (P-3471)
HMS Agricultural Corporation ....D......760 347-2335
 46247 Arabia St Indio (92201) (P-11504)
HMS Construction Inc (PA) ....D......760 727-9808
 2885 Scott St Vista (92081) (P-3353)
Hmt Electric Inc ....D......858 458-9771
 2340 Meyers Ave Escondido (92029) (P-2606)
Hmwc Cpas & Business Advisors ....D......714 505-9000
 17501 17th St Ste 100 Tustin (92780) (P-26218)
Hntb Corporation ....D......213 403-1000
 601 W 5th St Ste 1000 Los Angeles (90071) (P-25734)
Hntb Corporation ....D......714 460-1600
 200 Sandpointe Ave # 200 Santa Ana (92707) (P-25735)
Hntb Corporation ....D......949 460-1700
 36 Executive Park Ste 200 Irvine (92614) (P-25736)
Hntb Gerwick Water Solutions ....C......714 460-1600
 200 Sandpointe Ave Santa Ana (92707) (P-25737)
Hntb-Gerwick JV ....D......510 839-8972
 1300 Clay St Fl 7 Oakland (94612) (P-26064)
Hoag Memorial Hospital Presbt (PA) ....A......949 764-4624
 1 Hoag Dr Newport Beach (92663) (P-21451)
Hoag Memorial Hospital Presbt ....A......949 764-4624
 16200 Sand Canyon Ave Irvine (92618) (P-21452)

Hob Entertainment LLC ....C......714 778-2583
 1350 Disneyland Dr Anaheim (92802) (P-18436)
Hob Entertainment LLC ....C......323 848-5100
 8430 W Sunset Blvd West Hollywood (90069) (P-18437)
Hob Entertainment LLC ....C......619 299-2583
 1055 5th Ave San Diego (92101) (P-18438)
Hob Entertainment LLC (HQ) ....C......323 769-4600
 7060 Hollywood Blvd Los Angeles (90028) (P-18439)
Hoban Management, El Cajon Also called Thomas J Hoban (P-11795)
Hobbs Herder Advertising ....D......800 999-6090
 419 Main St Huntington Beach (92648) (P-13838)
Hobbs/Herder Training, Huntington Beach Also called Hobbs Herder Advertising (P-13838)
Hobby Lobby Stores Inc ....D......209 829-1807
 1301 W Pacheco Blvd Ste B Los Banos (93635) (P-17222)
Hochiki America Corporation ....C......714 522-2246
 7051 Village Dr Ste 100 Buena Park (90621) (P-7364)
Hodges Electric Inc ....E......559 298-5533
 1239 Hoblitt Ave Clovis (93612) (P-2607)
Hoem & Associates Inc ....D......650 871-5194
 951 Linden Ave South San Francisco (94080) (P-3105)
Hoffman Agency (PA) ....D......408 286-2611
 325 S 1st St Ste 300 San Jose (95113) (P-27557)
Hoffman Concrete Company Inc ....E......951 372-8333
 102 E Grand Blvd Corona (92879) (P-3265)
Hoffman Farms, Tulare Also called Nielsens Creamery (P-423)
Hoffman Hospice of The Valley ....D......661 410-1010
 8501 Brimhall Rd Bldg 100 Bakersfield (93312) (P-20934)
Hoffman Southwest Corp ....E......714 630-0404
 1183 N Kraemer Pl Anaheim (92806) (P-17950)
Hoffman Southwest Corp ....D......909 397-0567
 8930 Center Ave Rancho Cucamonga (91730) (P-17951)
Hoffman Texas Inc ....E......661 257-9200
 24971 Avenue Stanford Valencia (91355) (P-17952)
Hoffmann House, Citrus Heights Also called Paradise Oaks Youth Services (P-23958)
Hok Group Inc ....C......415 243-0555
 1 Bush St Ste 200 San Francisco (94104) (P-26065)
Hok Group Inc ....C......310 838-9555
 9530 Jefferson Blvd Culver City (90232) (P-26066)
Holbrook Construction Inc ....D......714 523-1150
 9814 Norwalk Blvd Ste 200 Santa Fe Springs (90670) (P-1554)
Holdrege Kull Consultimg Engr ....D......530 894-2487
 48 Bellarmine Ct Ste 40 Chico (95928) (P-25738)
Holiday Garden SF Corp ....E......714 533-3555
 1700 S Clementine St Anaheim (92802) (P-12689)
Holiday Inn, Los Angeles Also called Packard Realty Inc (P-13011)
Holiday Inn, Victorville Also called Victorvlle Trsure Holdings LLC (P-13368)
Holiday Inn, La Mirada Also called Sunstone Hotel Investors LLC (P-13294)
Holiday Inn, Burbank Also called JP Allen Extended Stay (P-12793)
Holiday Inn, Torrance Also called Six Continents Hotels Inc (P-13233)
Holiday Inn, Los Angeles Also called Brisam Lax (de) LLC (P-12402)
Holiday Inn, Marina Del Rey Also called Washington Inn LLC (P-13380)
Holiday Inn, Van Nuys Also called Six Continents Hotels Inc (P-13234)
Holiday Inn, San Diego Also called Sunstone Hotel Investors LLC (P-13297)
Holiday Inn, North Hollywood Also called Rio Vista Development Company (P-13124)
Holiday Inn, San Francisco Also called Intercontinental Hotels Group (P-12768)
Holiday Inn, Los Angeles Also called Six Continents Hotels Inc (P-13235)
Holiday Inn, Concord Also called Montclair Hotels Mb LLC (P-12939)
Holiday Inn, Stockton Also called Best Western Plus-Heritage Inn (P-12376)
Holiday Inn, Oakland Also called Tucson Hotels LP (P-13347)
Holiday Inn, Oceanside Also called Ocean Holiday LP (P-12969)
Holiday Inn, Torrance Also called Intercontinental Hotels Group (P-12769)
Holiday Inn, San Diego Also called Manas Hospitality LLC (P-12873)
Holiday Inn, Torrance Also called Six Continents Hotels Inc (P-13236)
Holiday Inn, San Francisco Also called Intercntnntal Ht Group Rsurces (P-12764)
Holiday Inn, San Diego Also called Six Continents Hotels Inc (P-13237)
Holiday Inn, Goleta Also called Intercontinental Hotels Group (P-12771)
Holiday Inn, Sacramento Also called Tucson Hotels LP (P-13348)
Holiday Inn, Anaheim Also called Conestoga Hotel (P-12483)
Holiday Inn, San Diego Also called Jck Hotels LLC (P-12789)
Holiday Inn, San Francisco Also called Intercontinental Hotels Group (P-12772)
Holiday Inn, Santa Ana Also called S W K Properties LLC (P-13157)
Holiday Inn, Anaheim Also called Hpt Trs Ihg-2 Inc (P-12735)
Holiday Inn, Beverly Hills Also called Ggwh LLC (P-12604)
Holiday Inn, Long Beach Also called Yhb Long Beach LLC (P-13433)
Holiday Inn, West Hollywood Also called Hmbl LLC (P-12688)
Holiday Inn, Dublin Also called Trevi Partners A Calif LP (P-13342)
Holiday Inn, Valencia Also called Ocean Park Hotels Mmex LLC (P-12973)
Holiday Inn, Bakersfield Also called Newport Hospitality Group Inc (P-12954)
Holiday Inn, San Diego Also called Narven Enterprises Inc (P-12950)
Holiday Inn, San Diego Also called San Diego Farah Partners (P-13168)
Holiday Inn, San Diego Also called Win Time Ltd (P-13401)
Holiday Inn, Laguna Hills Also called Laguna Hills Hotel Dev Ventr (P-12832)
Holiday Inn, Visalia Also called Grosvenor Visalia Associates (P-12632)
Holiday Inn, San Francisco Also called Todays Hotel Corporation (P-13330)
Holiday Inn, Anaheim Also called Dkn Hotel LLC (P-12530)
Holiday Inn, Palmdale Also called Palmdale Resort Inc (P-13014)
Holiday Inn, Buena Park Also called Uniwell Corporation (P-13355)
Holiday Inn, San Jose Also called San Jose Airport Hotel LLC (P-13176)
Holiday Inn, Willows Also called Kumar Hotels Inc (P-12823)
Holiday Inn, Diamond Bar Also called Oak Creek LP (P-12966)
Holiday Inn, Santa Maria Also called Santa Maria Hotel Corp (P-13188)

Mergent e-mail: customerrelations@mergent.com
1330

2019 Directory of California
Wholesalers and Services Companies

(P-0000) Products & Services Section entry number
(PA)=Parent Co (HQ)=Headquarters (DH)=Div Headquarters

Holiday Inn, National City *Also called Six Continents Hotels Inc* ***(P-13240)***
Holiday Inn, Sacramento *Also called Tucson Hotels LP* ***(P-13349)***
Holiday Inn, Los Angeles *Also called Remington Hotel Corporation* ***(P-13109)***
Holiday Inn & Suites Annaheim..........D.......714 535-0300
1240 S Walnut St Anaheim (92802) ***(P-12690)***
Holiday Inn Express Merced..........D.......209 383-0333
730 Motel Dr Merced (95341) ***(P-12691)***
Holiday Inn Hotel Torrance..........C.......310 781-9100
19800 S Vermont Ave Torrance (90502) ***(P-12692)***
Holiday Inn Resort At Lodge, Big Bear Lake *Also called Pacific Snow Valley Resort LLC* ***(P-13004)***
Holiday Inn Rncho Bernardo LLC..........D.......858 485-6530
17065 W Bernardo Dr San Diego (92127) ***(P-12693)***
Holiday Manor Care Center, Upland *Also called Sela Healthcare Inc* ***(P-20752)***
Holiday Meat & Provision Corp..........C.......310 674-0541
405 Centinela Ave Inglewood (90302) ***(P-8619)***
Holistic Approach HM Hlth Care, Stockton *Also called Holistic Approach Inc* ***(P-14637)***
Holistic Approach Inc..........D.......209 956-7050
4505 Precissi Ln Ste B Stockton (95207) ***(P-14637)***
Holland & Knight LLP..........D.......213 896-2400
400 S Hope St Ste 800 Los Angeles (90071) ***(P-23133)***
Holland & Knight LLP..........E.......415 743-6900
50 California St Ste 2800 San Francisco (94111) ***(P-23134)***
Holland America Flowers LLC..........D.......805 343-4004
808 Albert Way Arroyo Grande (93420) ***(P-269)***
Holland Flower Market Inc (PA)..........D.......213 627-9900
755 Wall St Ste 7g Los Angeles (90014) ***(P-9142)***
Hollandia Dairy Inc (PA)..........C.......760 744-3222
622 E Mission Rd San Marcos (92069) ***(P-416)***
Hollandia Produce LP..........C.......805 684-8739
1545 Santa Monica Rd Carpinteria (93013) ***(P-314)***
Hollenbeck Home For The Aged, Newhall *Also called Hollenbeck Palms* ***(P-24564)***
Hollenbeck Palms..........C.......323 263-6195
24431 Lyons Ave Apt 336 Newhall (91321) ***(P-24564)***
Holliday Rock Co Inc (PA)..........D.......909 982-1553
1401 N Benson Ave Upland (91786) ***(P-6897)***
Hollingshead Management, Los Angeles *Also called Proland Property Managment LLC* ***(P-11686)***
Hollins Schechter A Prof Corp..........D.......714 558-9119
1851 E 1st St Ste 600 Santa Ana (92705) ***(P-23135)***
Hollister Process Service..........E.......831 634-1479
341 Tres Pinos Rd Ste 201 Hollister (95023) ***(P-17223)***
Hollyway Cleaners, Los Angeles *Also called Valetor Inc* ***(P-13571)***
Hollywood Cmnty Hosp Hollywood, Los Angeles *Also called Hollywood Community Hospital M* ***(P-21453)***
Hollywood Community Hospital M..........C.......323 462-2271
6245 De Longpre Ave Los Angeles (90028) ***(P-21453)***
Hollywood Health System Inc..........D.......323 662-3731
4640 Lankershim Blvd # 100 North Hollywood (91602) ***(P-22321)***
Hollywood Hills, Los Angeles *Also called Forest Lawn Memorial-Park Assn* ***(P-11942)***
Hollywood Home Health Services, North Hollywood *Also called Hollywood Health System Inc* ***(P-22321)***
Hollywood Medical Center LP..........A.......213 413-3000
1300 N Vermont Ave Los Angeles (90027) ***(P-21454)***
Hollywood Mental Health Center..........D.......323 769-6100
1224 Vine St Los Angeles (90038) ***(P-22594)***
Hollywood Presbyterian Med Ctr, Los Angeles *Also called Hollywood Medical Center LP* ***(P-21454)***
Hollywood Presbyterian Med Ctr, Los Angeles *Also called Cha Hollywood Medical Ctr LP* ***(P-21311)***
Hollywood Rntals Prod Svcs LLC (PA)..........D.......818 407-7800
5300 Melrose Ave Los Angeles (90038) ***(P-18196)***
Hollywood Roosevelt Hotel, Los Angeles *Also called Roosevelt Hotel LLC* ***(P-13136)***
Hollywood Spa Inc..........E.......323 464-0445
5636 Vineland Ave North Hollywood (91601) ***(P-18609)***
Hollywood Spa, The, North Hollywood *Also called Hollywood Spa Inc* ***(P-18609)***
Hollywood Sports Park LLC..........D.......562 867-9600
9030 Somerset Blvd Bellflower (90706) ***(P-17224)***
Hollywood Standard LLC..........C.......323 822-3111
8300 W Sunset Blvd Los Angeles (90069) ***(P-12694)***
Holman Family Counseling Inc (PA)..........D.......818 704-1444
9451 Corbin Ave Ste 100 Northridge (91324) ***(P-20178)***
Holman Group, The, Northridge *Also called Holman Family Counseling Inc* ***(P-20178)***
Holmes & Narver Inc (HQ)..........C.......714 567-2400
999 W Town And Country Rd Orange (92868) ***(P-25739)***
Holmes Body Shop Inc (PA)..........D.......626 795-6447
466 Foothill Blvd La Canada Flintridge (91011) ***(P-17726)***
Holt CA, Pleasant Grove *Also called Holt of California* ***(P-7679)***
Holt of California (HQ)..........C.......916 991-8200
7310 Pacific Ave Pleasant Grove (95668) ***(P-7679)***
Holt of California..........C.......916 373-4100
3850 Channel Dr West Sacramento (95691) ***(P-7680)***
Holt of California..........C.......209 462-3660
1234 W Charter Way Stockton (95206) ***(P-7681)***
Holthouse Carlin Van Trigt LLP..........D.......626 243-5100
350 W Colo Blvd Fl 5 Flr 5 Pasadena (91105) ***(P-26219)***
Holthouse Carlin Van Trigt LLP..........D.......805 374-8555
400 W Ventura Blvd # 250 Camarillo (93010) ***(P-26220)***
Holthouse Carlin Van Trigt LLP..........D.......818 849-3140
15760 Ventura Blvd # 1700 Encino (91436) ***(P-26221)***
Holthouse Carlin Van Trigt LLP..........D.......714 361-7600
18565 Jamboree Rd Ste 400 Irvine (92612) ***(P-26222)***
Holthouse Carlin Van Trigt LLP (PA)..........C.......310 477-5551
11444 W Olympic Blvd # 11 Los Angeles (90064) ***(P-26223)***
Holy Cross Cemetary & Masoleum, Culver City *Also called Roman Cath Arch of Los Angels* ***(P-13694)***
Holy Cross Cemetery, Daly City *Also called Roman Catholic Archdiocese of* ***(P-11947)***
Holzmueller Corporation..........E.......415 826-8383
1000 25th St San Francisco (94107) ***(P-14514)***
Holzmueller Productions, San Francisco *Also called Holzmueller Corporation* ***(P-14514)***
Home Away Inc..........D.......559 642-3121
54432 Road 432 Bass Lake (93604) ***(P-12695)***
Home Box Office Inc..........D.......310 382-3000
2500 Broadway Ste 400 Santa Monica (90404) ***(P-5920)***
Home Building, Corona *Also called Ryland Hmes Inlnd Empire Cstmr* ***(P-1228)***
Home Capital Group..........D.......626 331-4213
948 N Grand Ave Covina (91724) ***(P-9814)***
Home Care America-San Marino, Pasadena *Also called Home Care of America Inc* ***(P-22322)***
Home Care of America Inc..........D.......626 309-7696
1122 E Green St 10 Pasadena (91106) ***(P-22322)***
Home Carpet Investment Inc (PA)..........D.......619 262-8040
730 Design Ct Ste 401 Chula Vista (91911) ***(P-3106)***
Home Comfort USA, Anaheim *Also called Ken Starr Inc* ***(P-2249)***
Home Community Lending, Santa Clara *Also called Hcl Finance Inc* ***(P-9813)***
Home Depot USA Inc..........D.......209 835-5133
1400 E Pescadero Ave Tracy (95304) ***(P-4574)***
Home Depot, The, Tracy *Also called Home Depot USA Inc* ***(P-4574)***
Home Entertainment Div, Los Angeles *Also called Fox Inc* ***(P-5792)***
Home Express Delivery Svc LLC..........A.......949 715-9844
230 Diamond St Laguna Beach (92651) ***(P-5088)***
Home Franchise Concepts LLC (PA)..........D.......949 404-1100
19000 Macarthur Blvd # 100 Irvine (92612) ***(P-3266)***
Home Guiding Hands Corporation (PA)..........B.......619 938-2850
1908 Friendship Dr Ste A El Cajon (92020) ***(P-24565)***
Home Health Brownsville, Brownsville *Also called Sutter North Med Foundation* ***(P-19993)***
Home Health Care Management (PA)..........D.......530 343-0727
1398 Ridgewood Dr Chico (95973) ***(P-22323)***
Home Health Plus, Santa Clara *Also called In Home Health Inc* ***(P-22341)***
Home Health Plus, West Covina *Also called In Home Health Inc* ***(P-22342)***
Home Helpers, Redding *Also called Thom Sharon & G Enterprises* ***(P-22436)***
Home Helpers San Mateo County..........D.......650 532-3122
655 Miramontes St Half Moon Bay (94019) ***(P-22324)***
Home Improvement Company Inc..........E.......760 744-4840
1585 Creek St San Marcos (92078) ***(P-3534)***
Home Instead Senior Care, San Jose *Also called South Bay Senior Solutions Inc* ***(P-22422)***
Home Instead Senior Care, Fresno *Also called P K B Investments Inc* ***(P-27385)***
Home Instead Senior Care, Vista *Also called Sherpaul Corporation* ***(P-22417)***
Home Instead Senior Care, Palm Desert *Also called Ambiente Enterprises Inc* ***(P-22218)***
Home Instead Senior Care, Long Beach *Also called Coastal Cmnty Senior Care LLC* ***(P-22265)***
Home Instead Senior Care, Redlands *Also called Safely Home* ***(P-22409)***
Home Instead Senior Care, Torrance *Also called Burdette De Cock Inc* ***(P-22243)***
Home Instead Senior Care, Azusa *Also called Seracada* ***(P-22414)***
Home Instead Senior Care, Santa Barbara *Also called S B C Senior Care Inc* ***(P-22408)***
Home Instead Senior Care, Los Angeles *Also called Tender Home Healthcare Inc* ***(P-22433)***
Home Instead Senior Care, Victorville *Also called Branlyn Prominence Inc* ***(P-22239)***
Home Instead Senior Care, Rancho Cucamonga *Also called Branlyn Prominence Inc* ***(P-22240)***
Home Instead Senior Care..........D.......858 277-3722
9665 Gran Rdge Dr Ste 250 San Diego (92123) ***(P-22325)***
Home Instead Senior Care..........D.......916 920-2273
11160 Sun Center Dr Rancho Cordova (95670) ***(P-22326)***
Home Instead Senior Care..........C.......805 577-0926
1720 E Los Angeles Ave H Simi Valley (93065) ***(P-22327)***
Home Instead Senior Care..........E.......619 460-6222
5360 Jackson Dr Ste 120 La Mesa (91942) ***(P-22328)***
Home Instead Senior Care..........E.......707 678-2005
405 Court St Woodland (95695) ***(P-22329)***
Home Instead Senior Care..........D.......510 686-9940
26 Carmello Rd Walnut Creek (94597) ***(P-22330)***
Home Instead Senior Care..........E.......949 347-6767
28570 Marguerite Pkwy # 221 Mission Viejo (92692) ***(P-22331)***
Home Organizers Inc..........A.......562 699-9945
3860 Capitol Ave City of Industry (90601) ***(P-3043)***
Home Port Inc..........D.......408 377-4134
5030 Union Ave San Jose (95124) ***(P-11148)***
HOMEBOY BAKERY, Los Angeles *Also called Homeboy Industries* ***(P-23840)***
Homeboy Industries (PA)..........B.......323 526-1254
130 Bruno St Los Angeles (90012) ***(P-23840)***
Homebridge Inc..........B.......415 255-2079
1035 Market St Ste L1 San Francisco (94103) ***(P-23841)***
Homebridge Financial Services..........A.......818 981-0606
15301 Ventura Blvd Sherman Oaks (91403) ***(P-9887)***
Homecare Professionals Inc..........D.......925 215-1214
1849 Willow Pass Rd # 305 Concord (94520) ***(P-22332)***
Homefrst Svcs Santa Clara Cnty..........C.......408 539-2100
507 Valley Way Milpitas (95035) ***(P-23842)***
Homegrown Natural Foods Inc..........D.......510 558-7500
1610 5th St Berkeley (94710) ***(P-8413)***
Homeguard Incorporated (PA)..........D.......408 993-1900
510 Madera Ave San Jose (95112) ***(P-14151)***
Homeland Housewares LLC..........D.......310 996-7200
11601 Wilshire Blvd Fl 23 Los Angeles (90025) ***(P-7418)***
Homeland Security Services Inc..........B.......714 956-2200
31805 Temecula Pkwy Temecula (92592) ***(P-16902)***
Homelegance Inc..........D.......510 933-6888
48200 Fremont Blvd Fremont (94538) ***(P-6725)***
Homeless Prenatal Program..........E.......415 546-6756
33 Middle Point Rd San Francisco (94124) ***(P-23843)***
Homeowners Association, Helendale *Also called Silver Lakes Association* ***(P-25251)***

Employee Codes: A=Over 500 employees, B=251-500
C=101-250, D=51-100, E=50
2019 Directory of California
Wholesalers and Services Companies
© Mergent Inc. 1-800-342-5647
1331

Homepointe Property Management, Sacramento *Also called Ram Commercial Enterprises Inc* ***(P-11701)***
Homeq Servicing Corporation (HQ)....A....916 339-6192
4837 Watt Ave North Highlands (95660) ***(P-9815)***
Homerun.com, San Francisco *Also called Demand Chain Inc* ***(P-7035)***
Homestar Systems Inc....D....415 694-6000
230 California St Ste 510 San Francisco (94111) ***(P-16390)***
Homestead of Fair Oaks, Fair Oaks *Also called Eskaton Properties Inc* ***(P-20409)***
Homestore Apartments & Rentals, Santa Clara *Also called Move Sales Inc* ***(P-13759)***
Hometown Buffet 261, Cerritos *Also called Hometown Buffet Inc* ***(P-13748)***
Hometown Buffet Inc....D....562 402-8307
11471 South St Cerritos (90703) ***(P-13748)***
Homewatch Caregivers, Carlsbad *Also called North Coast Home Care Inc* ***(P-22373)***
Homewatch Caregivers, Los Angeles *Also called South Bay Senior Services Inc* ***(P-22421)***
Homewood Care Center, San Jose *Also called Ocadian Care Centers LLC* ***(P-20677)***
Homewood Mountain Resort, Homewood *Also called Homewood Village Resorts LLC* ***(P-12697)***
Homewood Suites, Fairfield *Also called Hotel NAPA II Opco LP* ***(P-12729)***
Homewood Suites Anaheim Resort, Anaheim *Also called Npl Anaheim Investments LLC* ***(P-12964)***
Homewood Suites Hilton Sfo, Brisbane *Also called Sage Hospitality Resources LLC* ***(P-13162)***
Homewood Suites Libery Station, San Diego *Also called Liberty Station Hhg Hotel LP* ***(P-12854)***
Homewood Suites Management LLC....E....510 663-2700
1103 Embarcadero Oakland (94606) ***(P-12696)***
Homewood Suites Redondo, Redondo Beach *Also called Trcf Redondo LLC* ***(P-13340)***
Homewood Suites San Diego Hote, San Diego *Also called SD Hotel Circle LLC* ***(P-13196)***
Homewood Village Resorts LLC....E....530 525-2992
5145 W Lake Blvd Homewood (96141) ***(P-12697)***
Hon Hai Precision Indust Ltd....D....714 988-9388
500 S Kraemer Blvd # 100 Brea (92821) ***(P-7057)***
Hon Hai Precision Industry, San Jose *Also called Nsg Technology Inc* ***(P-17906)***
Honda Performance Dev Inc....D....661 294-7300
25145 Anza Dr Santa Clarita (91355) ***(P-17863)***
Honda R&D Americas Inc....E....818 345-7922
7514 Reseda Blvd Reseda (91335) ***(P-26528)***
Honey Flower Holdings LLC....C....951 351-2800
3688 Nye Ave Riverside (92505) ***(P-20532)***
Honey Lake Hospice Inc....D....530 257-3137
60 S Lassen St Susanville (96130) ***(P-7184)***
Honeybook Inc....D....770 403-9234
539 Bryant St Ste 200 San Francisco (94107) ***(P-15200)***
Honeymoon Real Estate LP....D....310 277-5221
9400 W Olympic Blvd Beverly Hills (90212) ***(P-12698)***
Honeyville Inc....D....909 980-9500
11600 Dayton Dr Rancho Cucamonga (91730) ***(P-4489)***
Honeywell, Lompoc *Also called Kbrwyle Tech Solutions LLC* ***(P-5986)***
Honeywell Authorized Dealer, Palm Springs *Also called Desert Air Conditioning Inc* ***(P-3149)***
Honeywell Authorized Dealer, Berkeley *Also called L J Kruse Co* ***(P-2254)***
Honeywell Authorized Dealer, Chatsworth *Also called All Tmperatures Controlled Inc* ***(P-2098)***
Honeywell Authorized Dealer, North Hollywood *Also called Circulating Air Inc* ***(P-2160)***
Honeywell Authorized Dealer, Sylmar *Also called Tri-Signal Integration Inc* ***(P-2770)***
Honeywell Authorized Dealer, San Jose *Also called J & J Air Conditioning Inc* ***(P-2238)***
Honeywell Authorized Dealer, Corona *Also called LDI Mechanical Inc* ***(P-2259)***
Honeywell Authorized Dealer, Santa Clara *Also called Environmental Systems Inc* ***(P-2202)***
Honeywell Authorized Dealer, Fresno *Also called Linkus Enterprises LLC* ***(P-1948)***
Honeywell Authorized Dealer, Riverside *Also called 20/20 Plumbing & Heating Inc* ***(P-2076)***
HONEYWELL AUTHORIZED DEALER, Fullerton *Also called C & L Refrigeration Corp* ***(P-2152)***
Honeywell Authorized Dealer, Anaheim *Also called Control Air Conditioning Corp* ***(P-2170)***
Honeywell Authorized Dealer, San Diego *Also called Greater San Diego AC Co Inc* ***(P-2223)***
HONEYWELL AUTHORIZED DEALER, San Diego *Also called Pacific Rim Mech Contrs Inc* ***(P-2304)***
Honeywell Authorized Dealer, Rocklin *Also called Brower Mechanical Inc* ***(P-17890)***
Honeywell Authorized Dealer, Hollister *Also called San Benito Htg & Shtmtl Inc* ***(P-2347)***
Honeywell Authorized Dealer, Corona *Also called Multi Mechanical Inc* ***(P-2285)***
Honeywell Authorized Dealer, Yuba City *Also called R B Spencer Inc* ***(P-2325)***
Honeywell Authorized Dealer, Pleasanton *Also called Sunbelt Controls Inc* ***(P-17897)***
Honeywell Authorized Dealer, Paramount *Also called Reliable Energy Management Inc* ***(P-2335)***
Honeywell International Inc....D....650 918-3229
1099 Sneath Ln San Bruno (94066) ***(P-7058)***
Honeywell International Inc....C....714 796-7500
514 S Lyon St Santa Ana (92701) ***(P-7652)***
Honeywell International Inc....D....916 923-7851
1740 Creekside Oaks 150 Sacramento (95833) ***(P-16903)***
Honeywell International Inc....E....714 283-0110
1635 N Batavia St Orange (92867) ***(P-7365)***
Honeywell International Inc....E....408 962-2000
1349 Moffett Park Dr Sunnyvale (94089) ***(P-7489)***
Honeywell International Inc....D....408 986-8200
487 Mathew St Santa Clara (95050) ***(P-7490)***
Hong Kong & Shanghai Banking....D....213 626-2460
770 Wilshire Blvd Ste 800 Los Angeles (90017) ***(P-9663)***
Hong Kong & Shanghai Hotels....D....310 551-2888
9882 Santa Monica Blvd Beverly Hills (90212) ***(P-12699)***
Hong Kong Bank, Los Angeles *Also called Hong Kong & Shanghai Banking* ***(P-9663)***
Honk Technologies Inc....D....800 979-3162
2251 Barry Ave Los Angeles (90064) ***(P-4992)***

Honolulu Freight Service (PA)....E....323 887-6777
1400 Date St Montebello (90640) ***(P-5089)***
Honor Rancho Station, Valencia *Also called Southern California Gas Co* ***(P-6176)***
Hood & Strong LLP (PA)....D....415 781-0793
275 Battery St Ste 900 San Francisco (94111) ***(P-26224)***
Hoover Institution....C....650 723-0603
434 Galvez Mall Stanford (94305) ***(P-17225)***
Hope Contra Costa, Pittsburg *Also called Lincoln Child Center Inc* ***(P-24579)***
Hope Hse For Mltple Hndicapped (PA)....C....626 443-1313
4215 Peck Rd El Monte (91732) ***(P-24566)***
Hope of Valley Mission....E....661 673-5951
19379 Soledad Canyon Rd Santa Clarita (91351) ***(P-22595)***
Hope of Valley Rescue Mission....D....818 392-0020
11076 Norris Ave Pacoima (91331) ***(P-23844)***
Hope Services....D....831 455-4940
19055 Portola Dr Salinas (93908) ***(P-24190)***
Hope Services (PA)....E....408 284-2850
30 Las Colinas Ln San Jose (95119) ***(P-24191)***
Hopkins & Carley A Law Corp (PA)....D....408 286-9800
70 S 1st St San Jose (95113) ***(P-23136)***
Hopland Band Pomo Indians Inc....C....707 744-1395
13101 Nokomis Rd Hopland (95449) ***(P-19182)***
Hopland Band Pomo Indians Inc (PA)....D....707 472-2100
3000 Shanel Rd Hopland (95449) ***(P-25429)***
Horizon Actuarial Services LLC....D....818 691-2000
5200 Lankershim Blvd North Hollywood (91601) ***(P-27264)***
Horizon Beverage Company....D....510 465-2212
8380 Pardee Dr Oakland (94621) ***(P-9003)***
Horizon Beverage Company LP....D....510 465-2212
8380 Pardee Dr Oakland (94621) ***(P-9004)***
Horizon Dental Grp, El Cajon *Also called Anthony P Garofalo A Dental* ***(P-20110)***
Horizon For Hmwners Asscations, Mammoth Lakes *Also called Horizons 4 Condominiums Inc* ***(P-25174)***
Horizon Media Inc....C....310 282-0909
1888 Century Park E # 700 Los Angeles (90067) ***(P-13839)***
Horizon Pharmaceutical LLC (HQ)....D....415 408-6200
7 Hamilton Landing # 100 Novato (94949) ***(P-26621)***
Horizon Solar Power, Hemet *Also called Lpsh Holdings Inc* ***(P-2269)***
Horizon Systems, Sunnyvale *Also called Horizon Technologies Inc* ***(P-7059)***
Horizon Technologies Inc....C....408 733-1530
1270 Oakmead Pkwy Ste 115 Sunnyvale (94085) ***(P-7059)***
Horizon West, Monterey *Also called Monterey Pines Sklld Nursg Fac* ***(P-20652)***
Horizon West Inc....C....916 488-8601
3529 Walnut Ave Carmichael (95608) ***(P-20533)***
Horizon West Inc....D....916 331-4590
5255 Hemlock St Sacramento (95841) ***(P-20534)***
Horizon West Inc....D....530 889-8122
3388 Bell Rd Auburn (95603) ***(P-26704)***
Horizon West Healthcare Inc....C....916 782-1238
1161 Cirby Way Roseville (95661) ***(P-22024)***
Horizon West Healthcare Inc (HQ)....D....916 624-6230
4020 Sierra College Blvd # 190 Rocklin (95677) ***(P-20535)***
Horizon West Healthcare Inc....C....707 462-1436
1162 S Dora St Ukiah (95482) ***(P-20536)***
Horizon West Healthcare Inc....C....530 885-7511
12225 Shale Ridge Ln Auburn (95602) ***(P-21115)***
Horizons 4 Condominiums Inc....D....760 934-6779
2113 Meridan Blvd Mammoth Lakes (93546) ***(P-25174)***
Horizons Adult Day Health Care....D....619 474-1822
1035 Harbison Ave National City (91950) ***(P-22818)***
Horn Group Inc....E....415 905-4000
101 Montgomery St Fl 15 San Francisco (94104) ***(P-13840)***
Hornberger Worstell Assoc Inc....E....415 391-1080
170 Maiden Ln Ste 600 San Francisco (94108) ***(P-26067)***
Hornberger, Mark R, San Francisco *Also called Hornberger Worstell Assoc Inc* ***(P-26067)***
Hornblower Cruises & Event, San Francisco *Also called Hornblower Yachts LLC* ***(P-4719)***
Hornblower Cruises & Events, San Diego *Also called Hornblower Yachts Inc* ***(P-4717)***
Hornblower Yachts Inc....C....619 686-8700
2825 5th Ave San Diego (92103) ***(P-4717)***
Hornblower Yachts Inc....C....619 234-8687
2825 5th Ave San Diego (92103) ***(P-27265)***
Hornblower Yachts LLC....D....916 446-1185
200 Marina Blvd Berkeley (94710) ***(P-4718)***
Hornblower Yachts LLC (PA)....C....415 788-8866
On The Embarcadero Pier 3 St Pier San Francisco (94111) ***(P-4719)***
Horner-Halleher Holding Co (PA)....C....562 944-8885
9303 Greenleaf Ave Santa Fe Springs (90670) ***(P-6767)***
Hornitos Telephone Co....D....608 831-1000
2896 Bear Vly Hornitos (95325) ***(P-5578)***
Horsemen Inc....D....714 847-4243
16911 Algonquin St Huntington Beach (92649) ***(P-16698)***
Hort Tech Inc....C....760 360-9000
78355 Darby Rd Bermuda Dunes (92203) ***(P-860)***
Horton Grand Hotel, San Diego *Also called Historical Properties Inc* ***(P-12672)***
Hortonworks Inc (PA)....A....408 916-4121
5470 Great America Pkwy Santa Clara (95054) ***(P-15706)***
Hoshall Corporation....E....916 987-1995
6608 Folsom Auburn Rd # 4 Folsom (95630) ***(P-13662)***
Hoshall Designer Group, Folsom *Also called Hoshall Corporation* ***(P-13662)***
Hospice & Home Health of E Bay....C....510 632-4390
333 Hegenberger Rd # 700 Oakland (94621) ***(P-22333)***
Hospice and Palliative Care....D....925 945-8924
2849 Miranda Ave Alamo (94507) ***(P-20935)***
Hospice By Bay (PA)....C....415 927-2273
17 E Sir Francis Drake Bl Larkspur (94939) ***(P-22334)***
HOSPICE CARING PROJECT, Scotts Valley *Also called Hospice of Santa Cruz County* ***(P-22337)***
Hospice Caring Project, Watsonville *Also called Hospice of Santa Cruz County* ***(P-22338)***

Mergent e-mail: customerrelations@mergent.com
1332
2019 Directory of California
Wholesalers and Services Companies
(P-0000) Products & Services Section entry number
(PA)=Parent Co (HQ)=Headquarters (DH)=Div Headquarters

Hospice Cheers....D....626 799-2727
625 Fair Oaks Ave Ste 229 South Pasadena (91030) *(P-22335)*
Hospice of Foothills (PA)....D....530 272-5739
11270 Rough And Ready Hwy Grass Valley (95945) *(P-22336)*
Hospice of Humboldt Inc (PA)....D....707 445-8443
3327 Timber Fall Ct Eureka (95503) *(P-22596)*
Hospice of Marin, Larkspur *Also called Hospice By Bay (P-22334)*
Hospice of San Joaquin....D....209 957-3888
3888 Pacific Ave Stockton (95204) *(P-20537)*
Hospice of Santa Cruz County (PA)....C....831 430-3000
940 Disc Dr Scotts Valley (95066) *(P-22337)*
Hospice of Santa Cruz County....D....831 430-3000
65 Neilson St Ste 121 Watsonville (95076) *(P-22338)*
Hospice of The East Bay, Alamo *Also called Hospice and Palliative Care (P-20935)*
Hospital Assn Southern Cal (PA)....D....213 347-2002
515 S Figueroa St # 1300 Los Angeles (90071) *(P-24789)*
Hospital Business Services Inc....C....909 235-4400
3300 E Guasti Rd Ontario (91761) *(P-17226)*
HOSPITAL COPORATION OF AMERICA, San Jose *Also called Good Samaritan Hospital LP (P-21433)*
HOSPITAL COPORATION OF AMERICA, Thousand Oaks *Also called Los Robles Hospital & Med Ctr (P-21571)*
Hospital of Barstow Inc....C....760 256-1761
820 E Mountain View St Barstow (92311) *(P-21455)*
Hospital of Community (HQ)....A....831 624-5311
23625 Holman Hwy Monterey (93940) *(P-22025)*
Hospitality Ventures MGT LLC....D....415 499-9222
101 Mcinnis Pkwy San Rafael (94903) *(P-12700)*
Hospitlity Fcsed Solutions Inc....D....562 424-1720
3229 E Spring St Ste 200 Long Beach (90806) *(P-26068)*
Host Hotels & Resorts Inc....C....415 775-7555
1250 Columbus Ave San Francisco (94133) *(P-12701)*
Host Hotels & Resorts Inc....C....619 232-1234
1 Market Pl San Diego (92101) *(P-12702)*
Host Hotels & Resorts LP....D....949 640-4000
900 Newport Center Dr Newport Beach (92660) *(P-12703)*
Host Hotels & Resorts LP....D....619 692-3800
8757 Rio San Diego Dr San Diego (92108) *(P-12704)*
Host Hotels & Resorts LP....D....650 347-1234
1333 Bayshore Hwy Burlingame (94010) *(P-12705)*
Host Hotels & Resorts LP....D....760 341-2211
74855 Country Club Dr Palm Desert (92260) *(P-12706)*
Host Hotels & Resorts LP....D....619 291-2900
1380 Harbor Island Dr San Diego (92101) *(P-12707)*
Host Hotels & Resorts LP....D....415 896-1600
55 4th St San Francisco (94103) *(P-12708)*
Host Hotels & Resorts LP....D....650 692-9100
1800 Old Bayshore Hwy Burlingame (94010) *(P-12709)*
Host Hotels & Resorts LP....D....310 823-1700
4375 Admiralty Way Venice (90292) *(P-12710)*
Host Hotels & Resorts LP....D....714 957-1100
500 Anton Blvd Costa Mesa (92626) *(P-12711)*
Host Hotels & Resorts LP....D....949 854-4500
500 Bayview Cir Newport Beach (92660) *(P-12712)*
Host Hotels & Resorts LP....D....310 216-5858
5400 W Century Blvd Los Angeles (90045) *(P-12713)*
Host Hotels & Resorts LP....D....310 546-7511
1400 Park View Ave Manhattan Beach (90266) *(P-12714)*
Host Hotels & Resorts LP....D....310 301-3000
4100 Admiralty Way Marina Del Rey (90292) *(P-12715)*
Host International Inc....C....408 294-1702
1661 Airport Blvd Ste 3e San Jose (95110) *(P-12716)*
Host International Inc....C....619 231-5100
3835 N Harbor Dr San Diego (92101) *(P-12717)*
Hostmark Investors Ltd Partnr....D....408 330-0001
4949 Great America Pkwy Santa Clara (95054) *(P-26886)*
Hot Dogger Tours Inc....C....714 988-4088
223 Imperial Hwy Ste 165 Fullerton (92835) *(P-3899)*
Hot Line Construction Inc....B....925 634-9333
9020 Brentwood Blvd Ste H Brentwood (94513) *(P-2608)*
Hotbox, Campbell *Also called Streamray Inc (P-18468)*
Hotdoodle.com, Fremont *Also called Metabyte Inc (P-16425)*
Hotel Adventures LLC....D....714 730-7717
17662 Irvine Blvd Ste 4 Tustin (92780) *(P-12718)*
Hotel Angeleno, Los Angeles *Also called Ascot Hotel LP (P-12337)*
Hotel Bel-Air, Los Angeles *Also called Kava Holdings Inc (P-12801)*
Hotel Britton, San Francisco *Also called Reneson Hotels Inc (P-13116)*
Hotel Casa Del Mar, Santa Monica *Also called Et Whitehall Seascape LLC (P-12565)*
Hotel Circle Inn & Suites....E....619 851-6800
2201 Hotel Cir S San Diego (92108) *(P-12719)*
Hotel Circle Property LLC....B....619 291-7131
500 Hotel Cir N San Diego (92108) *(P-12720)*
Hotel Contracting Services Inc....D....916 865-4204
2140 Prof Dr Ste 150 Roseville (95661) *(P-12721)*
Hotel De Anza, San Jose *Also called Saratoga Capital Inc (P-13192)*
Hotel Del Coronado LP....D....619 522-8011
1500 Orange Ave Coronado (92118) *(P-12722)*
Hotel Diamond....E....530 893-3100
220 W 4th St Chico (95928) *(P-12723)*
Hotel Durant A Ltd Partnership....D....510 845-8981
2600 Durant Ave Berkeley (94704) *(P-12724)*
Hotel Griffon, San Francisco *Also called Embarcadero Inn Associates (P-12556)*
Hotel Healdsburg (PA)....D....707 431-2800
25 Matheson St Healdsburg (95448) *(P-12725)*
Hotel Healdsburg....D....707 922-5399
317 Healdsburg Ave Healdsburg (95448) *(P-12726)*
Hotel Indigo Los Angles Dwntwn, Los Angeles *Also called Metropolis Hotel MGT LLC (P-12925)*
Hotel Indigo San Diego, San Diego *Also called Intercontinental Hotels Group (P-12767)*
Hotel Kabuki, San Francisco *Also called Bre/Japantown Owner LLC (P-12398)*
Hotel La Jolla....D....858 459-0261
7955 La Jolla Shores Dr La Jolla (92037) *(P-12727)*
Hotel Laguna, Aliso Viejo *Also called Andersen Hotels Inc (P-12325)*
Hotel Mac Restaurant Inc....E....510 233-0576
50 Washington Ave Richmond (94801) *(P-12728)*
Hotel Managers Group Llc....B....858 673-1534
11590 W Bernardo Ct # 211 San Diego (92127) *(P-26887)*
Hotel Marmonte, Santa Barbara *Also called H D G Associates (P-12634)*
Hotel Maya, Long Beach *Also called Queensbay Hotel LLC (P-13089)*
Hotel Menage, Anaheim *Also called Newport Hotel Capital LLC (P-12955)*
Hotel Moneco, San Francisco *Also called Kimpton Hotel & Rest Group LLC (P-26919)*
Hotel NAPA II Opco LP....E....707 863-0300
4755 Business Center Dr Fairfield (94534) *(P-12729)*
Hotel Nikko San Francisco Inc....B....415 394-1111
222 Mason St San Francisco (94102) *(P-12730)*
Hotel On Huntington Beach, Huntington Beach *Also called R C Hotels Inc (P-13090)*
Hotel Pacific, Monterey *Also called Columbia Hospitality Inc (P-12476)*
Hotel Palomar, Los Angeles *Also called Behringer Harvard Wilshire Blv (P-12366)*
Hotel Portofino, Redondo Beach *Also called Portofino Hotel Partners LP (P-13075)*
Hotel Sfitel San Francisco Bay, Redwood City *Also called French Redwood Inc (P-12592)*
Hotel Sofitel, Redwood City *Also called Accor Bus & Leisure N Amer LLC (P-12303)*
Hotel Solamar, San Diego *Also called Souldriver Lessee Inc (P-13248)*
Hotel Tonight Inc (PA)....D....800 208-2949
901 Market St Ste 310 San Francisco (94103) *(P-12731)*
Hotel Triton, San Francisco *Also called Dcp Jl Triton Sf LLC (P-12517)*
Hotel Vitale, San Francisco *Also called Mission Stuart Ht Partners LLC (P-12931)*
Hotel Whitcomb....D....415 626-8000
1231 Market St San Francisco (94103) *(P-12732)*
Hotel Zoe, San Francisco *Also called Creedence Lessee LLC (P-12498)*
Hotline Telecommunications (PA)....D....909 593-6575
528 Bethany Cir Claremont (91711) *(P-2609)*
Hotrollergirl Productions....D....530 521-2745
11890 Silver Spur St Ojai (93023) *(P-18520)*
Hotwire Inc....C....415 645-7350
114 Sansome St Ste 400 San Francisco (94104) *(P-5579)*
Houalla Enterprises Ltd....D....949 515-4350
2610 Avon St Newport Beach (92663) *(P-1555)*
Houchin Blood Services (PA)....D....661 323-4222
11515 Bolthouse Dr Bakersfield (93311) *(P-22819)*
Houchin Blood Services....D....661 327-8541
11515 Bolthouse Dr Bakersfield (93311) *(P-22820)*
Houdini Inc....C....714 228-4406
6311 Knott Ave Buena Park (90620) *(P-4575)*
Houlihan Lokey Inc (PA)....B....310 788-5200
10250 Constellation Blvd # 5 Los Angeles (90067) *(P-10089)*
House of Air LLC....D....415 345-9675
926 Mason St San Francisco (94129) *(P-19183)*
House of Blues, Los Angeles *Also called Hob Entertainment LLC (P-18439)*
House of Blues Concerts Inc (HQ)....C....323 769-4977
6255 W Sunset Blvd Fl 16 Los Angeles (90028) *(P-18440)*
Housing Athrty of The Cnty of....D....831 454-9455
2160 41st Ave Capitola (95010) *(P-11505)*
Housing Division, Sunnyvale *Also called City of Sunnyvale (P-13474)*
Housing Services, San Luis Obispo *Also called Cal Poly Corporation (P-13438)*
Houston Salem Inc....E....310 719-7004
217 E 157th St Gardena (90248) *(P-8307)*
Houweling Nurseries Oxnard Inc....B....805 488-8832
645 Laguna Rd Camarillo (93012) *(P-8414)*
Houweling's Tomatoes, Camarillo *Also called Houweling Nurseries Oxnard Inc (P-8414)*
Houzz Inc (PA)....D....650 326-3000
285 Hamilton Ave Fl 4 Palo Alto (94301) *(P-15201)*
Hovlid Skilled Nursing....E....530 846-9065
240 Spruce St Gridley (95948) *(P-20538)*
Howard CDM....E....562 427-4124
3750 Long Beach Blvd Long Beach (90807) *(P-1179)*
Howard Construction, Long Beach *Also called Howard CDM (P-1179)*
Howard Contracting Inc....E....562 596-2969
12354 Carson St Hawaiian Gardens (90716) *(P-3429)*
Howard Fischer Associates Inc....E....408 374-0580
10020 N De Anza Blvd # 101 Cupertino (95014) *(P-14638)*
Howard Frank R Memorial Hosp, Willits *Also called Willits Hospital Inc (P-21918)*
Howard Hughes Medical Inst....D....650 725-8252
279 Campus Dr Rm B202 Stanford (94305) *(P-26378)*
Howard Hughes Medical Inst....C....415 476-9668
1550 4th St Rm 190 San Francisco (94143) *(P-26379)*
Howard Johnson, Anaheim *Also called Northwest Hotel Corporation (P-12963)*
Howard Johnson (PA)....C....714 776-6120
1380 S Harbor Blvd Anaheim (92802) *(P-12733)*
Howard Roofing Company Inc....D....909 622-5598
245 N Mountain View Ave Pomona (91767) *(P-3165)*
Howard Training Center (PA)....D....209 538-2431
1424 Stonum Rd Modesto (95351) *(P-24192)*
Howards Appliances Inc....D....626 288-4010
5102 Industry Ave Pico Rivera (90660) *(P-4576)*
Howards Warehouse & Svc Ctr, Pico Rivera *Also called Howards Appliances Inc (P-4576)*
Howe Community Center....E....916 927-3802
2201 Cottage Way Sacramento (95825) *(P-19184)*
Howe Electric Construction Inc....C....559 255-8992
4682 E Olive Ave Fresno (93702) *(P-2610)*
Howroyd-Wright Emplymnt Agcy (HQ)....C....818 240-8688
327 W Broadway Glendale (91204) *(P-14639)*
Howroyd-Wright Emplymnt Agcy....C....818 240-8688
325 W Broadway Glendale (91204) *(P-14640)*

ALPHABETIC

Hoya Corporation...C.......858 309-6050
4255 Ruffin Rd San Diego (92123) ***(P-7235)***
Hoya San Diego, San Diego *Also called Hoya Corporation* ***(P-7235)***
Hoyt Roofs Inc...E.......714 632-3939
1809 N Orangethorpe Park Norco (92860) ***(P-3166)***
Hoyu America Co...D.......714 230-3000
6265 Phyllis Dr Cypress (90630) ***(P-8178)***
HP Capital LLC...D.......858 753-8486
3111 Camino Del Rio N San Diego (92108) ***(P-27266)***
HP Communications Inc...C.......951 572-1200
13341 Temescal Canyon Rd Corona (92883) ***(P-1928)***
HP Pavillion At San Jose, San Jose *Also called San Jose Sharks LLC* ***(P-18534)***
HP Sears Co., Bakersfield *Also called H P Sears Co Inc* ***(P-14006)***
Hpa-USA, Compton *Also called Hydroprocessing Associates LLC* ***(P-17228)***
HPM Construction LLC...D.......949 474-9170
17911 Mitchell S Irvine (92614) ***(P-1556)***
Hpp Food Services, Wilmington *Also called Icpk Corporation* ***(P-8415)***
Hps Mechanical Inc (PA)...C.......661 397-2121
3100 E Belle Ter Bakersfield (93307) ***(P-2228)***
Hps Plumbing Service Inc...B.......661 324-2121
3100 E Belle Ter Bakersfield (93307) ***(P-1929)***
Hpt Trs Ihg-2 Inc...D.......408 241-9305
481 El Camino Real Santa Clara (95050) ***(P-12734)***
Hpt Trs Ihg-2 Inc...D.......714 748-7777
1915 S Manchester Ave Anaheim (92802) ***(P-12735)***
Hpt Trs Ihg-2 Inc...D.......310 642-7500
5985 W Century Blvd Los Angeles (90045) ***(P-12736)***
Hpt Trs Ihg-2 Inc...B.......310 318-8888
300 N Harbor Dr Redondo Beach (90277) ***(P-12737)***
Hpt Trs Ihg-2 Inc...E.......408 745-1515
900 Hamlin Ct Sunnyvale (94089) ***(P-12738)***
Hqp, San Diego *Also called Community Clinics Hlth Netwrk* ***(P-25011)***
Hr Mission Commons Fc 5183...D.......909 793-8691
10 Terracina Blvd Redlands (92373) ***(P-24567)***
Hrc Fertility, Pasadena *Also called Huntington Reprodctve Ctr Inc* ***(P-19507)***
Hrd Aero Systems Inc...D.......661 295-0670
25555 Avenue Stanford Valencia (91355) ***(P-17953)***
Hrd Aero Systems Inc (PA)...C.......661 295-0670
25555 Avenue Stanford Valencia (91355) ***(P-17954)***
Hrd Oxygens, Valencia *Also called Hrd Aero Systems Inc* ***(P-17953)***
Hrl Laboratories LLC...B.......310 317-5000
3011 Malibu Canyon Rd Malibu (90265) ***(P-26622)***
Hrn Services, Citrus Heights *Also called Accountable Health Staff Inc* ***(P-14566)***
Hronis Inc A California Corp (PA)...D.......661 725-2503
10443 Hronis Rd Delano (93215) ***(P-206)***
Hronopoulos...E.......619 237-6161
110 W A St Ste 900 San Diego (92101) ***(P-26888)***
HRP Capital Inc...D.......951 676-0171
27699 Jefferson Ave # 201 Temecula (92590) ***(P-26889)***
Hsbc Bank USA NA, Los Angeles *Also called Hsbc Business Credit (usa)* ***(P-9506)***
Hsbc Business Credit (usa)...D.......213 553-8089
660 S Figueroa St Los Angeles (90017) ***(P-9506)***
Hsbc Finance Corporation...C.......408 796-3600
1420 El Paseo De Saratoga San Jose (95130) ***(P-9507)***
Hsbc Finance Corporation...A.......909 623-3355
931 Corporate Center Dr Pomona (91768) ***(P-9715)***
Hsbc Finance Corporation...B.......818 999-9175
21801 Ventura Bouelvard Woodland Hills (91364) ***(P-9816)***
Hsbc Finance Corporation...C.......213 628-8167
725 N Broadway Los Angeles (90012) ***(P-9508)***
Hsf Programme, San Francisco *Also called San Francisco Health Authority* ***(P-25040)***
Hsn LLC...C.......909 349-2600
13423 Santa Ana Ave Fontana (92337) ***(P-4577)***
Hssc, Santa Rosa *Also called Sonoma County Humane Society* ***(P-633)***
Hst Lessee Boston LLC...D.......619 692-2255
1380 Harbor Island Dr San Diego (92101) ***(P-12739)***
Hst Lessee San Diego LP...B.......619 291-2900
1380 Harbor Island Dr San Diego (92101) ***(P-12740)***
Hsu Foundation, Arcata *Also called Humboldt State University Spon* ***(P-27749)***
Huawei Enterprise USA Inc...D.......408 394-4295
20400 Stevens Creek Blvd Cupertino (95014) ***(P-5580)***
Hub Construction Spc Inc (PA)...E.......909 889-0161
379 S I St San Bernardino (92410) ***(P-14515)***
Hub Construction Spc Inc...E.......909 947-4669
1856 S Bon View Ave Ontario (91761) ***(P-7682)***
Hub Construction Sups & Eqp, San Bernardino *Also called Hub Construction Spc Inc* ***(P-14515)***
Hub Group Trucking Inc...B.......909 770-8950
13867 Valley Blvd Fontana (92335) ***(P-4022)***
Hub Group Trucking Inc...C.......951 693-9813
3801 E Guasti Rd Ontario (91761) ***(P-4023)***
Hub Intrntional Insur Svcs Inc...D.......916 974-7800
3636 American River Dr # 200 Sacramento (95864) ***(P-10647)***
Hub Intrntional Insur Svcs Inc...D.......559 447-4600
548 W Cromwell Ave # 101 Fresno (93711) ***(P-10648)***
Hub Intrntional Insur Svcs Inc...D.......805 682-2571
40 E Alamar Ave Santa Barbara (93105) ***(P-10649)***
HUB-LIMITED WORKSHOP, Los Angeles *Also called Mid Cities Assn Retarded Ctzns* ***(P-24207)***
Hubb Systems LLC...D.......510 865-9100
12305 Crosthwaite Cir Poway (92064) ***(P-15973)***
Hubbard Iron Doors Inc...E.......323 724-6500
7407 Telegraph Rd Montebello (90640) ***(P-7280)***
Huckleberry Youth Programs Inc (PA)...D.......415 668-2622
3310 Geary Blvd San Francisco (94118) ***(P-23845)***
Hudson Gardens, Pasadena *Also called Aah Hudson LP* ***(P-10972)***
Hudson Pacific Properties Inc (PA)...D.......310 445-5700
11601 Wilshire Blvd Fl 6 Los Angeles (90025) ***(P-12165)***
Hudson Ranch Power I LLC...D.......858 509-0150
12250 El Camino Real # 280 San Diego (92130) ***(P-6043)***
Hudson Tchmart Cmmerce Ctr LLC...D.......408 451-4440
5201 Great America Pkwy Santa Clara (95054) ***(P-10896)***
Hudson, H Claude Cmplte Hlth, Los Angeles *Also called County of Los Angeles* ***(P-19412)***
Hueston Hennigan LLP...D.......213 788-4340
523 W 6th St Ste 400 Los Angeles (90014) ***(P-23137)***
Hughes Research Laboratories, Malibu *Also called Hrl Laboratories LLC* ***(P-26622)***
Hugo Alonso Inc...E.......619 660-6255
2820 Via Orange Way Ste J Spring Valley (91978) ***(P-1408)***
Huitt - Zollars Inc...E.......949 988-5815
2603 Main St Ste 400 Irvine (92614) ***(P-26130)***
Hulk Construction...D.......714 701-9458
4352 Lakeview Ave Yorba Linda (92886) ***(P-3454)***
Hulu LLC...A.......888 631-4858
12312 W Olympic Boulev Los Angeles (90064) ***(P-5581)***
Hulu LLC (PA)...C.......310 571-4700
2500 Broadway Ste 200 Santa Monica (90404) ***(P-5800)***
Human Options Inc...E.......949 757-3635
1901 Newport Blvd Ste 240 Costa Mesa (92627) ***(P-23846)***
Human Options Inc (PA)...D.......949 737-5242
5540 Trabuco Rd Ste 100 Irvine (92620) ***(P-23847)***
Human Potential Cons LLC...D.......310 756-1560
500 E Carson Plaza Dr # 127 Carson (90746) ***(P-27593)***
Human Resource Solutions, Chico *Also called Roy Carrington Inc* ***(P-14748)***
Human Resources, Anaheim *Also called Interstate Electronics Corp* ***(P-27280)***
Human Resources, Santa Barbara *Also called Santa Barbara County of* ***(P-24029)***
Human Resources Department, Redwood City *Also called County of San Mateo* ***(P-26832)***
Human Resources Department, Redwood City *Also called County of San Mateo* ***(P-26833)***
Human Resources Department, Covina *Also called Citrus Valley Medical Ctr Inc* ***(P-21323)***
Human Services Agency, Belmont *Also called County of San Mateo* ***(P-23739)***
Human Services Association (PA)...D.......562 806-5400
6800 Florence Ave Bell (90201) ***(P-25019)***
Human Services Department, Yreka *Also called County of Siskiyou* ***(P-23743)***
Human Services Dept, Oakland *Also called City of Oakland* ***(P-23582)***
Human Services Dept, Delano *Also called County of Kern* ***(P-23650)***
Human Services Dept, Bakersfield *Also called County of Kern* ***(P-24767)***
Human Services Systems, San Bernardino *Also called County of San Bernardino* ***(P-23717)***
Human Services Systems, San Bernardino *Also called County of San Bernardino* ***(P-24308)***
Human Touch LLC...D.......562 426-8700
4600 E Conant St Long Beach (90808) ***(P-6726)***
Human Touch Home Health...C.......424 247-8165
3629 N Sepulveda Blvd Manhattan Beach (90266) ***(P-22339)***
HUMANE SOCIETY AND S P C A OF, Santa Rosa *Also called Humane Society Sonoma County* ***(P-25431)***
Humane Society Silicon Valley...D.......408 262-2133
901 Ames Ave Milpitas (95035) ***(P-25430)***
Humane Society Sonoma County (PA)...D.......707 542-0882
5345 Highway 12 Santa Rosa (95407) ***(P-25431)***
Humangood (PA)...D.......602 906-4024
6120 Stoneridge Mall Rd Pleasanton (94588) ***(P-21116)***
Humanitycom Inc...E.......415 230-0108
50 Osgood Pl Ste 330 San Francisco (94133) ***(P-15202)***
Humboldt Commnty Accss Resrc...D.......707 443-7077
1707 E St Ste 2 Eureka (95501) ***(P-23848)***
Humboldt County Mental Health, Eureka *Also called County of Humboldt* ***(P-22544)***
Humboldt Open Door Clinic, Arcata *Also called Open Door Community Hlth Ctrs* ***(P-22625)***
Humboldt Redwood Company LLC (HQ)...B.......707 764-4472
125 Main St Scotia (95565) ***(P-6833)***
Humboldt Senior Resource Ctr (PA)...C.......707 443-9747
1910 California St Eureka (95501) ***(P-23849)***
Humboldt State University Spon...D.......707 826-4189
1 Harpst St Arcata (95521) ***(P-27749)***
Humboldt Yacht Club...D.......707 443-1469
2479 Wrigley Rd Eureka (95503) ***(P-18936)***
Hume Lake Christian Camps Inc...D.......559 305-7770
64144 Hume Lake Rd Ofc Miramonte (93628) ***(P-13451)***
Humetrix Inc...E.......858 259-8987
1155 Camino Del Mar Ste 5 Del Mar (92014) ***(P-27267)***
Humnit Hotel At Lax LLC...D.......424 702-1234
6225 W Century Blvd Los Angeles (90045) ***(P-12741)***
Humphrey Plumbing Inc...D.......209 634-4626
880 S Kilroy Rd Turlock (95380) ***(P-2229)***
Humphreys Half Moon Inn, San Diego *Also called Bartell Hotels* ***(P-12353)***
Hunsaker & Assoc Irvine Inc (PA)...D.......949 583-1010
3 Hughes Irvine (92618) ***(P-25740)***
Hunt Ortmann Palffy Nieves...E.......626 440-5200
301 N Lake Ave Fl 7 Pasadena (91101) ***(P-23138)***
Hunt Convenience Stores LLC...E.......916 383-4868
5750 S Watt Ave Sacramento (95829) ***(P-26890)***
Hunt Enterprises Inc...C.......310 325-1496
2270 Sepulveda Blvd # 50 Torrance (90501) ***(P-11506)***
Hunter Advertising Mail Co, San Leandro *Also called Kp LLC* ***(P-14049)***
Hunter Easterday Corporation...C.......714 238-3400
1475 N Hundley St Anaheim (92806) ***(P-14287)***
Hunter Realty Inc...C.......805 346-8688
2605 S Miller St Ste 101 Santa Maria (93455) ***(P-11507)***
Hunter-La Purisima Corp...D.......661 616-0600
5060 California Ave # 640 Bakersfield (93309) ***(P-27750)***
Hunting Energy Services Inc...D.......661 633-4272
4900 California Ave 100a Bakersfield (93309) ***(P-1065)***
Hunting-Vinson, Bakersfield *Also called Hunting Energy Services Inc* ***(P-1065)***
Huntington Ambltry Surg Ctr...E.......626 229-8999
625 S Fair Oaks Ave Pasadena (91105) ***(P-19504)***
Huntington Bch Cnvlescent Hosp...B.......714 847-3515
18811 Florida St Huntington Beach (92648) ***(P-20539)***

Mergent e-mail: customerrelations@mergent.com
1334
2019 Directory of California
Wholesalers and Services Companies
(P-0000) Products & Services Section entry number
(PA)=Parent Co (HQ)=Headquarters (DH)=Div Headquarters

Huntington Beach Car Wash, Huntington Beach *Also called Russell Fisher Partnership (P-17838)*
Huntington Beach Cmnty Clinic, Huntington Beach *Also called Huntington Beach Commnty Clinc (P-19505)*
Huntington Beach Commnty Clinc ....C....714 847-4222
8041 Newman Ave Huntington Beach (92647) *(P-19505)*
Huntington Beach Hospital, Huntington Beach *Also called Prime Hlthcare Hntngton Bch (P-21663)*
Huntington Care LLC ....B....877 405-6990
2555 E Colo Blvd Ste 400h Pasadena (91107) *(P-22340)*
Huntington Care, Inc., Pasadena *Also called Huntington Care LLC (P-22340)*
Huntington Child Care Center, Los Angeles *Also called Casa Dscanso Convalescent Hosp (P-27580)*
Huntington Extended Care Ctr, Pasadena *Also called Pasadena Hospital Assn Ltd (P-20696)*
Huntington Hospital ....A....626 397-5000
100 W California Blvd Pasadena (91105) *(P-21456)*
Huntington Hotel Company ....D....858 756-1131
5951 Linea Del Cielo Rancho Santa Fe (92067) *(P-12742)*
Huntington Med Pathology Group, Pasadena *Also called Pasadena Cyto Pathology Lab (P-21636)*
Huntington Med Res Institutes ....D....626 397-5804
734 Fairmount Ave Pasadena (91105) *(P-26623)*
Huntington Memorial Hospital, Pasadena *Also called Pasadena Hospital Assn Ltd (P-21637)*
Huntington Memory Care Cmnty, Alhambra *Also called Silverado Senior Living Inc (P-21212)*
Huntington Otptent Surgery Ctr ....D....626 535-2434
625 S Fair Oaks Ave # 380 Pasadena (91105) *(P-19506)*
Huntington Park Nursing Center, Huntington Park *Also called Covenant Care California LLC (P-20344)*
HUNTINGTON PARK POLICE DEPARTM, Huntington Park *Also called Huntington Pk Police League (P-23850)*
Huntington Pk Police League ....D....323 584-6254
6542 Miles Ave Huntington Park (90255) *(P-23850)*
Huntington Reprodctve Ctr Inc (PA) ....E....626 204-9699
135 S Rosemead Blvd Pasadena (91107) *(P-19507)*
Huntington Rsdntial Rtrment Ht, Torrance *Also called Longwood Management Inc (P-11059)*
HUNTINGTON VALLEY HEALTHCARE C, Huntington Beach *Also called Douglas Fir Holdings LLC (P-20378)*
Huntleigh USA Corporation ....D....619 231-8111
3707 N Harbor Dr A-110 San Diego (92101) *(P-4893)*
Huntley Hotel Santa Monica Bch, Santa Monica *Also called Second Street Corporation (P-13202)*
Hunton Andrews Kurth LLP ....D....415 975-3700
50 California St Ste 1700 San Francisco (94111) *(P-23139)*
Hunton Andrews Kurth LLP ....D....213 532-2000
550 S Hope St Ste 2000 Los Angeles (90071) *(P-23140)*
Huntsman Architectural Group (PA) ....D....415 394-1212
50 California St Fl 7 San Francisco (94111) *(P-26069)*
Huoyen International Inc ....D....714 635-9000
1500 S Raymond Ave Fullerton (92831) *(P-12743)*
Huppe Landscape Company Inc (HQ) ....D....916 784-7666
9350 Viking Pl Roseville (95747) *(P-761)*
Hurley Construction Inc ....D....916 446-7599
1801 I St Ste 200 Sacramento (95811) *(P-1290)*
Huskies Lessee LLC ....B....415 392-7755
450 Powell St San Francisco (94102) *(P-12744)*
Hustle Digital Inc ....E....310 882-2680
12777 W Jefferson Blvd Los Angeles (90066) *(P-17227)*
Hustler Casino, Gardena *Also called El Dorado Enterprises Inc (P-12552)*
Hutchinson & Bloodgood LLP (PA) ....C....818 637-5000
550 N Brand Blvd Fl 14 Glendale (91203) *(P-26225)*
Hutchison Corporation ....D....310 763-7991
6107 Obispo Ave Long Beach (90805) *(P-2893)*
Huttig Building Products Inc ....D....916 383-3721
8120 Pwr Rdge Rd Bldg 100 Sacramento (95826) *(P-6834)*
Huttig Sash & Door Co, Sacramento *Also called Huttig Building Products Inc (P-6834)*
Hvac Installation and Repair, Los Angeles *Also called Precise Air Systems Inc (P-2316)*
Hvantage Technologies Inc ....D....818 661-6301
6700 Fllbrook Ave Ste 222 West Hills (91307) *(P-15203)*
Hvi Cat Canyon Inc ....C....805 621-5800
2617 E Clark Ave Santa Maria (93455) *(P-1066)*
Hvsf Transition LLC ....D....415 477-1999
1100 Sansome St San Francisco (94111) *(P-13841)*
Hwe Mechanical, Bakersfield *Also called Hills Wldg & Engrg Contr Inc (P-1063)*
Hwn Mariposa Associates LLC ....D....310 478-8757
11150 Santa Monica Blvd # 760 Los Angeles (90025) *(P-1343)*
Hy-Lond Hlth Care Cnter-Merced, Merced *Also called Avalon Care Cen (P-20242)*
Hy-Lond Hlth Care Cntr-Modesto, Modesto *Also called Avalon Care Center - Modesto (P-20245)*
Hy-Tech Tile Inc ....C....951 788-0550
1355 Palmyrita Ave Riverside (92507) *(P-3107)*
Hyatt Carmel Highlands, Carmel *Also called Highlands Inn Inc (P-12658)*
Hyatt Coporation As Agent of B ....D....760 603-6851
7100 Aviara Resort Dr Carlsbad (92011) *(P-12745)*
Hyatt Corporation ....B....530 562-3900
4001 Northstar Dr Truckee (96161) *(P-12746)*
Hyatt Corporation ....B....312 750-1234
6225 W Century Blvd Los Angeles (90045) *(P-12747)*
Hyatt Corporation ....B....415 848-6050
345 Stockton St San Francisco (94108) *(P-12748)*
Hyatt Corporation As Agent O ....B....714 750-1234
11999 Harbor Blvd Garden Grove (92840) *(P-12749)*
Hyatt Equities LLC ....B....408 993-1234
1740 N 1st St San Jose (95112) *(P-12750)*
Hyatt Fisherman's Wharf, San Francisco *Also called Chsp Trs Fisherman Wharf LLC (P-12457)*
Hyatt Grand Champion Resort, Indian Wells *Also called Hit Portfolio I Misc Trs LLC (P-12680)*
Hyatt Hotel, Monterey *Also called Classic Riverdale Inc (P-12466)*
Hyatt Hotel, Carmel *Also called Highlands Inn Investors II LP (P-12659)*
Hyatt Hotel, Los Angeles *Also called Hit Portfolio I Misc Trs LLC (P-12673)*
Hyatt Hotel, San Francisco *Also called Hit Portfolio I Misc Trs LLC (P-12675)*
Hyatt Hotel, Long Beach *Also called Hit Portfolio I Misc Trs LLC (P-12677)*
Hyatt Hotel, San Jose *Also called Hyatt Equities LLC (P-12750)*
Hyatt Hotel, Irvine *Also called Hit Portfolio I Misc Trs LLC (P-12679)*
Hyatt Hotel, Newport Beach *Also called Hit Portfolio I Misc Trs LLC (P-12681)*
Hyatt Hotel, Los Angeles *Also called Jwmcc Limited Partnership (P-12796)*
Hyatt Hotel, Monterey *Also called Classic Rsdence Mgt Ltd Partnr (P-12467)*
Hyatt Hotel, San Diego *Also called Manchester Grand Resorts LP (P-12874)*
Hyatt Hotel, Westlake Village *Also called Swvp Westlake LLC (P-13312)*
Hyatt Hotels Management Corp ....C....661 799-1234
24500 Town Center Dr Valencia (91355) *(P-12751)*
Hyatt Hotels Management Corp ....B....858 552-1234
3777 Lajolla Village Dr San Diego (92122) *(P-12752)*
Hyatt Hotels Management Corp ....C....760 322-9000
285 N Palm Canyon Dr Palm Springs (92262) *(P-12753)*
Hyatt Hotels Management Corp ....B....650 352-1234
4219 El Camino Real Palo Alto (94306) *(P-12754)*
Hyatt Hotels Management Corp ....B....831 372-1234
1 Old Golf Course Rd Monterey (93940) *(P-12755)*
Hyatt House Rancho Cordova, Rancho Cordova *Also called Select Hotels Group LLC (P-13204)*
Hyatt House San Ramon, San Ramon *Also called Hit Portfolio I Misc Trs LLC (P-12676)*
Hyatt Los Angeles Airport, Los Angeles *Also called Hyatt Corporation (P-12747)*
Hyatt Pl Fremont/Silicon Vly, Fremont *Also called Select Hotels Group LLC (P-13203)*
Hyatt Place San Jose Hotel, San Jose *Also called West San Crlos Ht Partners LLC (P-13390)*
Hyatt Regency Mission Bay Spa, San Diego *Also called H C T Inc (P-12633)*
Hyatt Regency Monterey, Monterey *Also called Hit Portfolio I Misc Trs LLC (P-12678)*
Hyatt Regency Orange County, Garden Grove *Also called Hyatt Corporation As Agent O (P-12749)*
Hyatt Regency Sacramento, Sacramento *Also called Capitol Regency LLC (P-12426)*
Hyatt Regency San Francisco Ht, San Francisco *Also called Hit Portfolio I Misc Trs LLC (P-12683)*
Hyatt Regency Santa Clara ....D....408 200-1234
5101 Great America Pkwy Santa Clara (95054) *(P-12756)*
Hyatt Rgncy San Frncisco Arprt, Burlingame *Also called Host Hotels & Resorts LP (P-12705)*
Hyatt Vacation Ownership Inc ....D....310 285-0990
9615 Brighton Way M180 Beverly Hills (90210) *(P-11508)*
Hyatt Vineyard Creek Ht & Spa, Santa Rosa *Also called Noble Aew Vineyard Creek LLC (P-12959)*
Hyatt Westlake Plaza Hotel, Westlake Village *Also called Sky Court USA Inc (P-13242)*
Hybrid Promotions LLC (PA) ....C....714 952-3866
10711 Walker St Cypress (90630) *(P-8264)*
Hyde Park Convalescent Hosp ....E....323 753-1354
6520 West Blvd Los Angeles (90043) *(P-20540)*
Hydrafacial Company, The, Long Beach *Also called Edge Systems LLC (P-7178)*
Hydratech LLC (HQ) ....D....559 233-0876
1331 S West Ave Fresno (93706) *(P-17955)*
Hydraulx, Los Angeles *Also called Avongard Products USa Ltd (P-18179)*
Hydro Chem Industrial Services, Pittsburg *Also called Hydrochem LLC (P-14288)*
Hydro Power Service, Sacramento *Also called HDR Engineering Inc (P-25729)*
Hydro Tek Systems Inc ....D....909 799-9222
2353 Almond Ave Redlands (92374) *(P-7887)*
Hydro-Pressure Systems, North Hollywood *Also called Woods Maintenance Services Inc (P-3613)*
Hydrochem LLC ....D....925 432-1749
901 Loveridge Rd 592 Pittsburg (94565) *(P-14288)*
Hydrochempsc, Torrance *Also called PSC Industrial Outsourcing LP (P-17975)*
Hydrochempsc, Gilroy *Also called PSC Industrial Outsourcing LP (P-6545)*
Hydrochempsc, San Ardo *Also called PSC Industrial Outsourcing LP (P-4051)*
Hydroprocessing Associates LLC ....E....310 667-6456
19122 S Santa Fe Ave Compton (90221) *(P-17228)*
Hydrox Properties Xii LLC ....D....510 262-7200
3170 Hilltop Mall Rd Richmond (94806) *(P-10897)*
Hyland Software Inc ....D....949 242-3100
2355 Main St Ste 100 Irvine (92614) *(P-15204)*
Hylton Security Inc ....C....916 442-1000
1015 2nd St Fl 2 Sacramento (95814) *(P-16699)*
Hypergrid Inc ....D....650 316-5524
110 Baytech Dr San Jose (95134) *(P-15205)*
Hyperloop One, Los Angeles *Also called Hyperloop Technologies Inc (P-5228)*
Hyperloop Technologies Inc ....C....213 800-3270
2159 Bay St Los Angeles (90021) *(P-5228)*
Hypermedia Systems Inc ....D....213 452-6731
101 N Pacific Coast Hwy El Segundo (90245) *(P-16391)*
Hyrian LLC ....C....212 590-2567
2355 Westwood Blvd Los Angeles (90064) *(P-14641)*
Hyundai Atver Tlmtics Amer Inc ....D....949 381-6000
10550 Talbert Ave Fl 2 Fountain Valley (92708) *(P-15206)*
Hyundai Capital America (HQ) ....D....714 965-3000
3161 Michelson Dr # 1900 Irvine (92612) *(P-9716)*
Hyundai Finance, Irvine *Also called Hyundai Capital America (P-9716)*
Hyundai Motor America (HQ) ....B....714 965-3000
10550 Talbert Ave Fountain Valley (92708) *(P-9717)*
Hyve Solutions Corporation (HQ) ....A....855 869-6873
44201 Nobel Dr Fremont (94538) *(P-16142)*

Employee Codes: A=Over 500 employees, B=251-500
C=101-250, D=51-100, E=50
2019 Directory of California
Wholesalers and Services Companies
© Mergent Inc. 1-800-342-5647
1335

I A C, Poway *Also called Intelligent Automation Corp (P-25749)*
I A C, Irvine *Also called Irvine APT Communities LP (P-11035)*
I B S, Roseville *Also called Iptor Supply Chain Systems USA (P-15234)*
I C Class Components Corp (PA)....D....310 539-5500
23605 Telo Ave Torrance (90505) *(P-7491)*
I C M, Los Angeles *Also called International Creative Mgt Inc (P-18373)*
I C M, Los Angeles *Also called International Creative MGT Inc (P-18374)*
I C S, San Francisco *Also called Integrated Clg Solutions Inc (P-14290)*
I C S I, Berkeley *Also called Interntional Cmpt Science Inst (P-26626)*
I C W, San Diego *Also called Insurance Company of West (P-10363)*
I Cann, Los Angeles *Also called Internet Corp For Assigned Nam (P-15982)*
I Cypress Company....A....831 649-8500
2700 17 Mile Dr Ste 3500 Pebble Beach (93953) *(P-12757)*
I Cypress Company (PA)....A....831 647-7500
1700 17 Mile Dr Pebble Beach (93953) *(P-12758)*
I D Property Corporation....C....213 625-0100
1001 Wilshire Blvd # 100 Los Angeles (90017) *(P-11509)*
I G F, Long Beach *Also called International Garment Finisher (P-13610)*
I Hot Leads....D....714 960-8028
19671 Beach Blvd Ste 204 Huntington Beach (92648) *(P-16143)*
I I D, Imperial *Also called Imperial Irrigation District (P-6044)*
I L S West Inc....E....714 505-7530
17501 17th St Ste 100 Tustin (92780) *(P-26226)*
I Lan Systems Inc....D....626 304-9021
237 S Raymond Ave Alhambra (91801) *(P-15974)*
I M A C A, Bishop *Also called Inyo Mono Advcts Fr Cmmnty Act (P-24791)*
I M T, Sherman Oaks *Also called Investors MGT Tr RE Group Inc (P-11034)*
I Mean It Creative Inc....E....310 287-1000
1643 Buckingham Rd Los Angeles (90019) *(P-13842)*
I N C Builders Inc....B....760 352-4200
1560 Ocotillo Dr Ste L El Centro (92243) *(P-14860)*
I N G, Compton *Also called Newport Apparel Corporation (P-8326)*
I P I, Los Angeles *Also called Imperial Parking Industries (P-17688)*
I P S, Mentone *Also called International Paving Svcs Inc (P-1792)*
I P S Services Inc....D....909 305-0250
627 E Foothill Blvd San Dimas (91773) *(P-22597)*
I Pwlc Inc....D....760 630-0231
408 Olive Ave Vista (92083) *(P-762)*
I S A Contracting Svcs Inc....A....559 659-1080
958 O St Firebaugh (93622) *(P-478)*
I S D, Los Angeles *Also called IDS Real Estate Group (P-11511)*
I T C, Citrus Heights *Also called Itc Srvice Group Acqsition LLC (P-27757)*
I T P, Burbank *Also called Information Tech Partners Inc (P-16395)*
I T S, Long Beach *Also called International Trnsp Svc (P-4727)*
I Wmi....B....562 977-4906
17100 Pioneer Blvd # 230 Artesia (90701) *(P-1557)*
I2c Inc....B....650 480-5222
1300 Island Dr Ste 105 Redwood City (94065) *(P-7060)*
IA Lodging NAPA Solano Trs LLC....C....707 253-8600
3425 Solano Ave NAPA (94558) *(P-12759)*
Iaba, Los Angeles *Also called Institute For Applied Behavior (P-20181)*
Iaba, Camarillo *Also called Institute For Applied Behavior (P-20182)*
IAC Publishing LLC....D....510 985-7400
555 12th St Ste 300 Oakland (94607) *(P-5582)*
IAC Search & Media Inc (HQ)....C....510 985-7400
555 12th St Ste 500 Oakland (94607) *(P-16231)*
Iap West Inc....D....310 667-9720
20036 S Via Baron Rancho Dominguez (90220) *(P-6647)*
Iap World Services Inc....D....650 604-0451
567 Dugan South Akron Rd Mountain View (94035) *(P-27594)*
Iap World Services Inc....B....760 380-6772
510 S Loop 1st St Bldg T Fort Irwin (92310) *(P-27595)*
Iapmo, Ontario *Also called International Assoc of Plmbng (P-24963)*
Iapmo Research and Testing Inc (HQ)....D....909 472-4100
5001 E Philadelphia St Ontario (91761) *(P-24961)*
Ias Administrations Inc....D....323 953-3490
1311 N New Hampshire Ave Los Angeles (90027) *(P-24790)*
Iasco (PA)....B....707 252-3522
1833 Castenada Dr Burlingame (94010) *(P-14861)*
Ibackup.com, Calabasas *Also called Idrive Inc (P-16392)*
Ibaset Inc....D....949 598-5200
27442 Portola Pkwy # 300 Foothill Ranch (92610) *(P-27751)*
Ibaset Federal Services LLC (PA)....D....949 598-5200
27442 Portola Pkwy # 300 Foothill Ranch (92610) *(P-15207)*
Ibftech Inc....D....424 217-8010
343 Main St El Segundo (90245) *(P-14642)*
Ibis Biosciences Inc....C....760 476-3200
2251 Faraday Ave Ste 150 Carlsbad (92008) *(P-26380)*
Ibisworld Inc (HQ)....D....800 330-3772
11755 Wilshire Blvd # 1100 Los Angeles (90025) *(P-26529)*
IBM, Agoura Hills *Also called International Bus Mchs Corp (P-15981)*
IBM, San Jose *Also called International Bus Mchs Corp (P-15230)*
IBM, San Francisco *Also called International Bus Mchs Corp (P-6963)*
IBM, Santa Clara *Also called International Bus Mchs Corp (P-16402)*
IBM, Costa Mesa *Also called International Bus Mchs Corp (P-16403)*
IBM, Emeryville *Also called International Bus Mchs Corp (P-16404)*
IBM, Foster City *Also called International Bus Mchs Corp (P-16405)*
IBM, San Jose *Also called International Bus Mchs Corp (P-6964)*
IBM, San Jose *Also called International Bus Mchs Corp (P-26386)*
IBM, San Ramon *Also called International Bus Mchs Corp (P-27278)*
Ibs Interprit Inc (PA)....C....760 268-7299
5860 El Camino Real Carlsbad (92008) *(P-15208)*
Ibuypower, City of Industry *Also called American Future Tech Corp (P-7005)*
Ic BP III Holdings Xii LLC....D....415 549-5054
1 Sansome St Ste 1500 San Francisco (94104) *(P-11510)*
Ic BP III Holdings Xv LLC....E....415 273-4250
1 Sansome St Fl 15 San Francisco (94104) *(P-11174)*
Ic Compliance LLC (PA)....A....650 378-4150
1065 E Hillsdale Blvd # 300 Foster City (94404) *(P-15209)*
Icallfirst....D....808 557-9299
18141 Beach Blvd Ste 290 Huntington Beach (92648) *(P-5583)*
Icarus Fuel Services US Corp....D....310 417-0124
7251 World Way W Los Angeles (90045) *(P-4894)*
Icat Logistics Inc....D....310 884-5923
11 Wandering Rill Irvine (92603) *(P-5090)*
ICC, Fontana *Also called Inland Cc Inc (P-3267)*
Ice, Brea *Also called Intercontinental Exchange Inc (P-10048)*
Ice Center Enterprises LLC....D....510 604-8878
10123 N Wolfe Rd Ste 1020 Cupertino (95014) *(P-19185)*
Ice Center, The, Cupertino *Also called Ice Center Enterprises LLC (P-19185)*
Ice Delivery Systems Inc....C....408 640-4625
6920 Santa Teresa Blvd # 206 San Jose (95119) *(P-4024)*
Ice Specialty Entrmt Inc (PA)....C....310 899-3889
409 Santa Monica Blvd E Santa Monica (90401) *(P-19186)*
Ice Station Valencia L L C....D....661 775-8686
27745 Smyth Dr Valencia (91355) *(P-19187)*
Iceoplex, Santa Monica *Also called Ice Specialty Entrmt Inc (P-19186)*
Icf Consulting Group Inc....A....703 934-3000
101 Lucas Valley Rd # 249 San Rafael (94903) *(P-27268)*
Icf Jones & Stokes Inc....D....949 333-6600
1 Ada Ste 100 Irvine (92618) *(P-27269)*
ICI Enterprises Inc....D....562 989-7715
790 E Willow St Ste 150 Long Beach (90806) *(P-24193)*
ICI Services Corporation....B....805 988-3210
1000 Town Center Dr # 225 Oxnard (93036) *(P-25741)*
Ickler Electric Corporation....E....858 486-1585
13250 Kirkham Way Poway (92064) *(P-2611)*
Icom Mechanical Inc....C....408 292-4968
477 Burke St San Jose (95112) *(P-2230)*
Icon Design and Display Inc....D....707 284-3400
645 4th St Ste 212 Santa Rosa (95404) *(P-17229)*
Icon Exposure Inc....D....323 933-1666
5450 Wilshire Blvd Los Angeles (90036) *(P-16960)*
Icon Media Direct Inc (PA)....D....818 995-6400
5910 Lemona Ave Van Nuys (91411) *(P-13843)*
Iconic Chronicles Magazine LLC....D....707 712-2097
5120 Monetta Ln Sacramento (95835) *(P-9115)*
Icpk Corporation....D....310 830-8020
1130 W C St Wilmington (90744) *(P-8415)*
Ics Integrated Comm Systems....D....408 491-6000
6680 Via Del Oro San Jose (95119) *(P-2612)*
Ics Professional Services Inc....C....714 868-3900
7755 Center Ave Fl 11 Huntington Beach (92647) *(P-3108)*
Ics-CA North, Roseville *Also called Industrial Container Services (P-7851)*
Ictp, Anaheim *Also called Ray W Choi (P-27419)*
Icw Group Holdings Inc (PA)....D....858 350-2400
15025 Innovation Dr San Diego (92128) *(P-10362)*
Icw Valencia LLC....D....858 350-2600
11455 El Camino Real San Diego (92130) *(P-10898)*
Icygen LLC....D....510 540-7122
940 Dwight Way Ste 13b Berkeley (94710) *(P-15975)*
ID Analytics LLC....C....858 312-6200
15253 Ave Of Science San Diego (92128) *(P-16904)*
ID On Demand, Santa Ana *Also called Idondemand Inc (P-15976)*
Idaptive LLC....C....669 444-5400
3300 Tannery Way Santa Clara (95054) *(P-15210)*
Idc Technologies Inc (PA)....D....408 376-0212
920 Hillview Ct Ste 250 Milpitas (95035) *(P-14643)*
Idea Travel Company....A....650 948-0207
13145 Byrd Ln Ste 101 Los Altos Hills (94022) *(P-4939)*
Ideal Home Sales, Lafayette *Also called Rate Is Low (P-9853)*
Ideal Products LLC....E....818 217-2574
14724 Ventura Blvd Fl 200 Sherman Oaks (91403) *(P-13749)*
Ideal Program Services Inc....D....323 296-2255
3970 W Martin Luther King Los Angeles (90008) *(P-23851)*
Ideal Transit Inc....E....626 448-2690
13404 Waco St Baldwin Park (91706) *(P-3659)*
Idealab Holdings LLC (PA)....A....626 585-6900
130 W Union St Pasadena (91103) *(P-12233)*
Idec Corporation (HQ)....D....408 747-0550
1175 Elko Dr Sunnyvale (94089) *(P-7492)*
Ideo LP....C....650 289-3400
780 High St Palo Alto (94301) *(P-17230)*
Ideo LP (PA)....C....650 289-3400
150 Forest Ave Palo Alto (94301) *(P-14117)*
Ideo LP....D....415 615-5000
28 The Embarcadero Annex San Francisco (94105) *(P-17231)*
Idexx Reference Labs Inc....E....949 477-2840
1370 Reynolds Ave Ste 109 Irvine (92614) *(P-22097)*
Idexx Reference Labs Inc....C....916 372-4200
2825 Kovr Dr West Sacramento (95605) *(P-22098)*
Idle Acres Convalescent Hosp, El Monte *Also called Sabu Enterprises Inc (P-21201)*
Idondemand Inc....B....415 200-4546
1900 Carnegie Ave Ste B Santa Ana (92705) *(P-15976)*
Idrive Inc....D....818 594-5972
26115 Mureau Rd Ste A Calabasas (91302) *(P-16392)*
IDS, Pasadena *Also called Interprsnal Dvlpmntal Fclttors (P-23866)*
IDS Inc....D....855 997-7437
20335 Ventura Blvd # 210 Woodland Hills (91364) *(P-4940)*
IDS Real Estate Group (PA)....D....213 627-9937
515 S Figueroa St Fl 16 Los Angeles (90071) *(P-11511)*
Idun Pharmaceuticals Inc....E....858 622-3000
9380 Judicial Dr San Diego (92121) *(P-26624)*
IEC, Commerce *Also called Interstate Electric Co Inc (P-7137)*

Mergent e-mail: customerrelations@mergent.com
1336
2019 Directory of California
Wholesalers and Services Companies
(P-0000) Products & Services Section entry number
(PA)=Parent Co (HQ)=Headquarters (DH)=Div Headquarters

Iehp, Rancho Cucamonga *Also called Inland Empire Health Plan* ***(P-10166)***
Ies Engineering, Bakersfield *Also called Innovative Engrg Systems Inc* ***(P-25747)***
Iest Family Farms ....D......559 674-9417
14576 Avenue 14 Madera (93637) ***(P-417)***
If Live LLC (PA) ....D......323 957-6868
2254 S Sepulveda Blvd Los Angeles (90064) ***(P-18062)***
Ifwe Inc (HQ) ....D......415 946-1850
848 Battery St San Francisco (94111) ***(P-15707)***
Ignite Health LLC (PA) ....C......949 861-3200
7535 Irvine Center Dr # 200 Irvine (92618) ***(P-13844)***
Ignited LLC (PA) ....C......310 773-3100
2150 Park Pl Ste 100 El Segundo (90245) ***(P-13845)***
Ignition Creative LLC ....D......310 315-6300
12959 Coral Tree Pl Los Angeles (90066) ***(P-18063)***
Igo Medical Group A Med Corp (PA) ....D......858 455-7520
9339 Genesee Ave Ste 220 San Diego (92121) ***(P-19508)***
Igotchu Inc ....D......818 987-1699
4712 Admiralty Way # 997 Marina Del Rey (90292) ***(P-16905)***
Igt Global Solutions Corp ....D......562 946-9922
10415 Slusher Dr Ste 1 Santa Fe Springs (90670) ***(P-19188)***
Iheartcommunications Inc ....B......415 975-5555
340 Townsend St Fl 4 San Francisco (94107) ***(P-5721)***
Iheartcommunications Inc ....D......951 684-1992
2030 Iowa Ave Ste A Riverside (92507) ***(P-5722)***
Iheartcommunications Inc ....D......559 230-4300
83 E Shaw Ave Ste 150 Fresno (93710) ***(P-5723)***
Iheartcommunications Inc ....B......858 522-5547
9660 Gran Rdge Dr Ste 100 San Diego (92123) ***(P-5724)***
Iheartcommunications Inc ....D......858 292-2000
9660 Gran Rdge Dr Ste 200 San Diego (92123) ***(P-5725)***
Iheartcommunications Inc ....D......818 846-0029
3400 W Olive Ave Ste 550 Burbank (91505) ***(P-5726)***
Iheartcommunications Inc ....C......916 929-5325
1545 River Park Dr # 500 Sacramento (95815) ***(P-5727)***
Iheartcommunications Inc ....D......661 942-1268
352 E Avenue K4 Lancaster (93535) ***(P-5728)***
Iheartcommunications Inc ....D......916 929-5325
1440 Ethan Way Sacramento (95825) ***(P-5729)***
Ihg Management (maryland) LLC ....C......310 642-7500
5985 W Century Blvd Los Angeles (90045) ***(P-12760)***
Ihi, Roseville *Also called Intercare Holdings Insur Svcs* ***(P-10653)***
Ihms (sf) LLC ....C......415 781-5555
340 Stockton St San Francisco (94108) ***(P-12761)***
Ihr Grnbuck Rncho Ccmnga Ventr, Rancho Cucamonga *Also called Aloft Ontario-Rancho Cucamonga* ***(P-12314)***
IHSS Consortium, The, San Francisco *Also called Homebridge Inc* ***(P-23841)***
Ikano Communications Inc (PA) ....D......801 924-0900
9221 Corbin Ave Ste 260 Northridge (91324) ***(P-16144)***
IKEA Purchasing Svcs US Inc ....B......818 841-3500
600 N San Fernando Blvd Burbank (91502) ***(P-26891)***
Ikes Landscaping & Maintenance ....D......530 758-1698
2700 Tiber Ave Davis (95616) ***(P-861)***
Illumina-Redwood City, Foster City *Also called Verinata Health Inc* ***(P-26489)***
Illumio Inc ....C......669 800-5000
160 San Gabriel Dr Sunnyvale (94086) ***(P-15211)***
Ilm Group, The, Ontario *Also called Industrial Labor MGT Group Inc* ***(P-14648)***
Ilwu Local 46, Port Hueneme *Also called Interntional Longshore Whse Un* ***(P-14651)***
Image 1st, Gardena *Also called Image First Healthcre Lndry Sp* ***(P-13609)***
Image 2000 (PA) ....E......818 781-2200
26037 Huntington Ln Valencia (91355) ***(P-17956)***
Image Business Forms, El Segundo *Also called Ibftech Inc* ***(P-14642)***
Image Entertainment Inc (HQ) ....D......818 407-9100
6320 Canoga Ave Ste 790 Woodland Hills (91367) ***(P-18239)***
Image First Healthcre Lndry Sp ....C......310 819-1463
17818 S Figueroa St Gardena (90248) ***(P-13609)***
Image IV Systems Inc (PA) ....D......323 849-3049
512 S Varney St Burbank (91502) ***(P-6960)***
Image of California Inc (PA) ....D......213 896-0039
655 E 30th St Los Angeles (90011) ***(P-14097)***
Image Options ....C......949 586-7665
80 Icon Foothill Ranch (92610) ***(P-13974)***
Image Source, San Bernardino *Also called Copier Source Inc* ***(P-6957)***
Imageologist, Inglewood *Also called Gelshmal Enterprises LLC* ***(P-6943)***
Imagescan Inc ....D......626 844-2050
390 S Fair Oaks Ave Pasadena (91105) ***(P-16145)***
Imagestat Corporation ....C......310 392-1100
2950 28th St Santa Monica (90405) ***(P-7061)***
Imageware Systems Inc (PA) ....D......858 673-8600
10815 Rncho Brnrdo Rd 3 # 310 San Diego (92127) ***(P-15708)***
Imaginary Forces LLC (PA) ....D......323 957-6868
2254 S Sepulveda Blvd Los Angeles (90064) ***(P-18064)***
Imaginative Horizons Inc ....D......619 477-1176
1889 National City Blvd National City (91950) ***(P-20541)***
Imaging Hlthcare Spcalists LLC ....D......619 229-2299
6386 Alvarado Ct San Diego (92120) ***(P-26705)***
Imaging Hlthcare Spcalists LLC (PA) ....D......619 295-9729
150 W Washington St San Diego (92103) ***(P-19509)***
Imaging Technologies Group LLC ....E......310 638-2500
5220 Pacific Concourse Dr Los Angeles (90045) ***(P-8082)***
Imax Corporation (HQ) ....D......310 255-5500
12582 Millennium Los Angeles (90094) ***(P-18197)***
Imca Capital, Los Angeles *Also called Imperial Mridian Companies Inc* ***(P-14516)***
Imerys Filtration Minerals, Lompoc *Also called Imerys Minerals California Inc* ***(P-1100)***
Imerys Filtration Minerals Inc (HQ) ....E......805 562-0200
1732 N 1st St Ste 450 San Jose (95112) ***(P-1103)***
Imerys Minerals California Inc ....B......805 736-1221
2500 Miguelito Canyon Rd Lompoc (93436) ***(P-1100)***
Imerys Minerals California Inc (HQ) ....D......805 736-1221
2500 San Miguelito Rd Lompoc (93436) ***(P-1104)***
IMG (PA) ....E......714 974-1700
4560 Dorinda Rd Yorba Linda (92887) ***(P-17232)***
Immanuel Baptist Cruch ....D......909 862-6641
28355 Baseline St Highland (92346) ***(P-24328)***
Immanuel Baptist Day School, Highland *Also called Immanuel Baptist Cruch* ***(P-24328)***
Immersion Medical Inc ....D......408 467-1900
50 Rio Robles San Jose (95134) ***(P-23141)***
Immigration Voice ....D......408 204-2200
3561 Homestead Rd 375 Santa Clara (95051) ***(P-12096)***
Imobile LLC ....B......209 833-6757
2613 Naglee Rd Tracy (95304) ***(P-5409)***
Imobile LLC ....B......909 599-8822
875 W Arrow Hwy San Dimas (91773) ***(P-5584)***
Imp, Los Angeles *Also called International Marine Pdts Inc* ***(P-8578)***
Imp Foods Inc ....D......510 429-4600
1650 Delta Ct Hayward (94544) ***(P-8577)***
Impac Mortgage Corp ....B......949 475-3600
19500 Jamboree Rd Irvine (92612) ***(P-9817)***
Impac Mortgage Holdings Inc (PA) ....A......949 475-3600
19500 Jamboree Rd Irvine (92612) ***(P-12166)***
Impac Secured Assets Corp ....D......949 475-3600
19500 Jamboree Rd Irvine (92612) ***(P-12097)***
Impact Assessment Inc ....D......858 459-0142
2166 Avenida De La Playa F La Jolla (92037) ***(P-26381)***
IMPACT BUSINESS SERVICE, Redwood City *Also called Community Gatepath* ***(P-23603)***
Impact Destinations & Events ....E......415 766-4170
1005 Market St Unit 402 San Francisco (94103) ***(P-13750)***
Impact DRG Alcohol Trtmnt Ctr, Pasadena *Also called Principles Inc* ***(P-22654)***
Impact Events, San Francisco *Also called Impact Destinations & Events* ***(P-13750)***
Impact Group LLC ....D......925 327-7322
7133 Koll Center Pkwy Pleasanton (94566) ***(P-8416)***
Impact Logistics ....E......909 937-9035
1155 S Milliken Ave Ste I Ontario (91761) ***(P-14644)***
Impact Solutions LLC ....E......760 231-0450
3604 Ocean Ranch Blvd Oceanside (92056) ***(P-14645)***
Imperial Capital Group LLC (PA) ....D......310 246-3700
2000 Ave Of The Los Angeles (90067) ***(P-9963)***
Imperial Capital LLC (PA) ....D......310 246-3700
10100 Santa Monica Blvd # 2400 Los Angeles (90067) ***(P-9964)***
Imperial Care Center, Studio City *Also called Longwood Management Corp* ***(P-21143)***
Imperial Cfs Inc ....E......310 768-8188
1000 Francisco St Torrance (90502) ***(P-4676)***
Imperial Convalescent, La Mirada *Also called Life Care Centers America Inc* ***(P-20585)***
Imperial County Behavioral HLT ....E......760 482-2149
2695 S 4th St El Centro (92243) ***(P-22598)***
Imperial County Mental Health, El Centro *Also called County of Imperial* ***(P-22545)***
Imperial County Probation Off, El Centro *Also called County of Imperial* ***(P-23645)***
Imperial Crest Healthcare Ctr, Hawthorne *Also called Longwood Management Corp* ***(P-20597)***
Imperial Irrgtion Dst Wtr Dept, Imperial *Also called Imperial Irrigation District* ***(P-6556)***
Imperial Irrigation District (PA) ....A......800 303-7756
333 E Barioni Blvd Imperial (92251) ***(P-6044)***
Imperial Irrigation District ....B......760 339-9220
333 E Barioni Blvd Imperial (92251) ***(P-6556)***
Imperial Irrigation District ....C......760 398-5811
81600 58th Ave La Quinta (92253) ***(P-6197)***
Imperial Irrigation District ....D......760 339-9800
2151 W Adams Ave El Centro (92243) ***(P-6183)***
Imperial Mridian Companies Inc ....D......310 447-3460
11901 Santa Monica Blvd # 338 Los Angeles (90025) ***(P-14516)***
Imperial Parking (us) LLC ....A......415 495-3909
1740 Cesar Chavez Fl 2 San Francisco (94124) ***(P-17684)***
Imperial Parking (us) LLC ....D......650 871-5423
195 N Access Rd South San Francisco (94080) ***(P-17685)***
Imperial Parking (us) LLC ....E......650 724-4309
360 Oak Rd Ste 1 Stanford (94305) ***(P-17686)***
Imperial Parking (us) LLC ....E......510 382-2140
7801 Earhart Rd Oakland (94621) ***(P-17687)***
Imperial Parking Industries (PA) ....D......323 651-5588
6404 Wilshire Blvd B Los Angeles (90048) ***(P-17688)***
Imperial Pipe & Supply, Shafter *Also called Bps Supply Group* ***(P-7263)***
Imperial Project Inc ....D......310 671-3263
1947 S Myrtle Ave Monrovia (91016) ***(P-18441)***
Imperva Inc (PA) ....C......650 345-9000
3400 Bridge Pkwy Ste 200 Redwood City (94065) ***(P-15212)***
Import Collection (PA) ....D......818 782-3060
7885 Nelson Rd Panorama City (91402) ***(P-9224)***
Import Direct, Van Nuys *Also called E & S International Entps Inc* ***(P-7412)***
Import Whl Univ Fund Raising, Torrance *Also called Gdf Parent LLC* ***(P-17182)***
Importers Software, Santa Clara *Also called Laxmi Group Inc* ***(P-15255)***
Impossible Foods Inc (PA) ....D......650 461-4385
400 Saginaw Dr Redwood City (94063) ***(P-8417)***
IMS, Sacramento *Also called Innovative Maint Solutions Inc* ***(P-2235)***
IMS, Marina Del Rey *Also called International Mgt Systems* ***(P-27755)***
IMS, Woodland Hills *Also called Innovative Merch Solutions LLC* ***(P-17239)***
IMS Recycling Services Inc (PA) ....D......619 231-2521
2697 Main St San Diego (92113) ***(P-6407)***
In & Out Car Wash Inc ....E......619 316-8492
3615 Monte Real Escondido (92029) ***(P-17818)***
In Home Health Inc ....C......408 986-8160
2005 De La Cruz Blvd # 271 Santa Clara (95050) ***(P-22341)***
In Home Health Inc ....D......419 254-7841
1000 Lakes Dr Ste 200 West Covina (91790) ***(P-22342)***
In Shape Health Club ....E......760 381-1200
14601 Valley Center Dr Victorville (92395) ***(P-22821)***

ALPHABETIC

Employee Codes: A=Over 500 employees, B=251-500
C=101-250, D=51-100, E=50
2019 Directory of California
Wholesalers and Services Companies
© Mergent Inc. 1-800-342-5647
1337

In Shape Health Clubs, Stockton *Also called In Shape Management Company* ***(P-18610)***
In Shape Management Company ... B ... 209 472-2231
6 S El Dorado St Stockton (95202) ***(P-18610)***
IN TOUCH LEADERSHIP PROJECT, Los Angeles *Also called Saint Justin Education Fu* ***(P-24835)***
In-Shape City, Stockton *Also called In-Shape Health Clubs LLC* ***(P-18611)***
In-Shape Health Clubs LLC (PA) ... E ... 209 472-2231
6 S El Dorado St Ste 700 Stockton (95202) ***(P-18611)***
In-Shape Health Clubs LLC ... C ... 209 836-2504
101 S Tracy Blvd Tracy (95376) ***(P-18612)***
In2vision Programs LLC ... D ... 562 789-8888
13601 Whittier Blvd Whittier (90605) ***(P-23852)***
Inamar, San Diego *Also called Chubb US Holding Inc* ***(P-10584)***
Inc J-Network, Huntington Beach *Also called Glen Beverly Laboratories Inc* ***(P-25016)***
Incare Dme ... D ... 818 582-1016
15446 Sherman Way Apt 319 Van Nuys (91406) ***(P-22822)***
Inclin Inc ... D ... 650 961-3422
2655 Campus Dr Ste 100 San Mateo (94403) ***(P-26382)***
Incline Incorporated ... C ... 408 454-1140
560 S Winchester Blvd # 500 San Jose (95128) ***(P-14646)***
Inclusion Services LLC ... C ... 562 945-2000
13225 Philadelphia St E Whittier (90601) ***(P-23853)***
Inclusive Cmnty Resources LLC ... C ... 510 981-8115
2855 Telegraph Ave Ste Ll Berkeley (94705) ***(P-24194)***
Incom Mechanical Inc ... D ... 707 586-0511
975 Transport Way Ste 5 Petaluma (94954) ***(P-2231)***
Incube Labs LLC (PA) ... D ... 408 457-3700
2051 Ringwood Ave San Jose (95131) ***(P-12234)***
Indemnity Company California (HQ) ... D ... 949 263-3300
17771 Cowan Ste 100 Irvine (92614) ***(P-10429)***
Independa Inc ... E ... 800 815-7829
11455 El Camino Real # 365 San Diego (92130) ***(P-15977)***
Independence At Home Iah, Long Beach *Also called Senior Care* ***(P-10310)***
Independent Construction Co, Concord *Also called D A McCosker Construction Co* ***(P-1754)***
Independent Electric Sup Inc (HQ) ... C ... 510 877-9850
2001 Marina Blvd San Leandro (94577) ***(P-7366)***
Independent Options ... D ... 714 434-1175
2532 Santa Catalina Dr # 104 Costa Mesa (92626) ***(P-23854)***
Independent Options Inc ... C ... 858 598-5260
8555 Aero Dr San Diego (92123) ***(P-24568)***
Independent Quality Care Inc ... D ... 415 479-1230
40 Professional Ctr Pkwy San Rafael (94903) ***(P-21117)***
Independent Quality Care Inc (PA) ... D ... 925 855-0881
3 Crow Canyon Ct San Ramon (94583) ***(P-21118)***
Independent Quality Care Inc ... D ... 510 836-3677
2910 Mcclure St Oakland (94609) ***(P-21119)***
Independent Quality Care Inc ... D ... 925 284-5544
3721 Mt Diablo Blvd Lafayette (94549) ***(P-21120)***
Independent Roofing Cons, Santa Ana *Also called IRC Technologies Inc* ***(P-3167)***
Independent Trading Company, San Clemente *Also called Brad Rambo & Associates Inc* ***(P-8250)***
Indepndnt Asstd Lvng & Memory, Arcadia *Also called Arcadia Gardens MGT Corp* ***(P-20916)***
Indevia Accounting Inc ... D ... 858 450-2981
2667 Camino Del Rio S # 101 San Diego (92108) ***(P-26227)***
Index Fresh Inc (PA) ... D ... 909 877-0999
3880 Lemon St Ste 210 Riverside (92501) ***(P-8696)***
Indian Health Council (PA) ... D ... 760 749-1410
50100 Golsh Rd Valley Center (92082) ***(P-24962)***
Indian Hills Golf Club, Riverside *Also called Banquet Facilities* ***(P-13719)***
Indian Hlth Ctr Snta Clara Vly ... C ... 408 445-3400
1333 Meridian Ave San Jose (95125) ***(P-19510)***
Indian River Transport Co ... B ... 209 664-0456
8444 W Doe Ave Visalia (93291) ***(P-4195)***
Indian Valley Golf Club Inc ... E ... 415 897-1118
3035 Novato Blvd Novato (94947) ***(P-18721)***
Indian Valley Health Care Dist ... D ... 530 284-7191
184 Hot Springs Rd Greenville (95947) ***(P-21457)***
Indian Valley Hospital, Greenville *Also called Indian Valley Health Care Dist* ***(P-21457)***
Indian Wells Country Club Inc ... D ... 760 345-2561
46000 Club Dr Indian Wells (92210) ***(P-18937)***
Indian Wells Golf Resort, Indian Wells *Also called Troon Golf LLC* ***(P-27070)***
Indian Wells Resort Hotel ... E ... 760 345-6466
76661 Us Highway 111 Indian Wells (92210) ***(P-12762)***
Indian Wells Vly Surgery Ctr, Ridgecrest *Also called Drummond Medical Group Inc* ***(P-19450)***
Indiana Adhc, Los Angeles *Also called Altamed Health Services Corp* ***(P-19281)***
Indigo Hospitality Management ... E ... 310 787-7795
1817 N Sepulveda Blvd Manhattan Beach (90266) ***(P-27270)***
Indigo Hotels, Manhattan Beach *Also called Indigo Hospitality Management* ***(P-27270)***
Indio Family Care Center, Indio *Also called County of Riverside* ***(P-19422)***
Indio Hlthcare Wllness Ctr LLC ... D ... 760 347-6000
82262 Valencia Ave Indio (92201) ***(P-20542)***
Indio Medical Offices, Indio *Also called Kaiser Foundation Hospitals* ***(P-19563)***
Indium Software Inc ... C ... 408 501-8844
1250 Oakmead Pkwy Ste 210 Sunnyvale (94085) ***(P-15709)***
Individuals Now ... D ... 707 544-3299
2447 Summerfield Rd Santa Rosa (95405) ***(P-23855)***
Indosys Corporation ... C ... 408 705-1953
3315 San Felipe Rd Ste 37 San Jose (95135) ***(P-14647)***
Inductive Automation LLC ... D ... 800 266-7798
90 Blue Ravine Rd Folsom (95630) ***(P-27271)***
Inductors Inc ... E ... 949 623-2460
140 Technology Dr Ste 500 Irvine (92618) ***(P-7493)***
Indus Corporation ... D ... 415 202-1830
1275 Columbus Ave San Francisco (94133) ***(P-15213)***
Indus Light & Magic (vanco) LL ... D ... 415 292-4671
1110 Gorgas Ave San Francisco (94129) ***(P-17957)***
Indus Technology Inc ... C ... 619 299-2555
2243 San Diego Ave # 200 San Diego (92110) ***(P-25742)***
Industrial Coml Systems Inc ... C ... 760 300-4094
1165 Joshua Way Vista (92081) ***(P-2232)***
Industrial Container Services ... D ... 916 781-2775
749 Galleria Blvd Roseville (95678) ***(P-7851)***
Industrial Grwth Partners V LP ... C ... 415 882-4550
101 Mission St Ste 1500 San Francisco (94105) ***(P-11987)***
Industrial Labor MGT Group Inc ... C ... 323 582-4100
647 E E St Ste 105 Ontario (91764) ***(P-14648)***
Industrial Masonry Inc ... D ... 951 284-0251
3299 Horse Carri Rd Ste H Norco (92860) ***(P-2811)***
Industrial Metal Supply Co, Sun Valley *Also called Norman Industrial Mtls Inc* ***(P-7293)***
Industrial Metal Supply Co Eba, San Diego *Also called Norman Industrial Mtls Inc* ***(P-7294)***
Industrial Parts Depot LLC (HQ) ... D ... 310 530-1900
23231 Normandie Ave Torrance (90501) ***(P-7756)***
Industrial Stitchtech Inc ... C ... 818 361-6319
520 Library St San Fernando (91340) ***(P-17233)***
INDUSTRIAL SUPPORT SYSTEMS, Fontana *Also called Fontana Resources At Work* ***(P-24184)***
Industrial Valco Inc (PA) ... E ... 310 635-0711
3135 E Ana St Compton (90221) ***(P-7852)***
Industry Events ... E ... 310 834-3422
25501 Narbonne Ave Lomita (90717) ***(P-18783)***
Industry Station, City of Industry *Also called Southern California Gas Co* ***(P-6168)***
Indvls ... E ... 818 703-3855
9 Macarthur Pl Unit 2306 Santa Ana (92707) ***(P-27272)***
Indyme Solutions LLC ... E ... 858 268-0717
8295 Aero Pl Ste 260 San Diego (92123) ***(P-27933)***
Indyne ... D ... 805 606-0664
300 W Point Ave El Granada (94018) ***(P-25020)***
Indyne Inc ... A ... 805 606-7225
1036 California Blvd # 11013 Vandenberg Afb (93437) ***(P-27596)***
Inegrated Care Communities, Moreno Valley *Also called Integrted Care Communities Inc* ***(P-20545)***
Infant Hring Scrning Spcalists, Corona *Also called Halo Unlimted Inc* ***(P-22810)***
Infant/Toddler Consort, Oakland *Also called California Child Care Resourc* ***(P-23522)***
Infantino, San Diego *Also called Blue Box Opco LLC* ***(P-7947)***
Infertlity Gynclogy Obstetrics, San Diego *Also called Igo Medical Group A Med Corp* ***(P-19508)***
Infineon Raceway, Sonoma *Also called Speedway Sonoma LLC* ***(P-18545)***
Infineon Tech Americas Corp ... A ... 310 726-8000
222 Kansas St El Segundo (90245) ***(P-26228)***
Infinex Investments Inc ... D ... 707 927-3578
550 Gateway Dr NAPA (94558) ***(P-10090)***
Infinite Home Health Inc ... D ... 818 888-7772
22151 Ventura Blvd # 102 Woodland Hills (91364) ***(P-22343)***
Infinite Technologies Inc (PA) ... D ... 916 987-3261
1264 Hawks Flight Ct # 210 El Dorado Hills (95762) ***(P-25743)***
Infinity Broadcasting Corp Cal ... D ... 323 936-5784
5670 Wilshire Blvd # 200 Los Angeles (90036) ***(P-5730)***
Infinity Care of East LA ... D ... 323 261-8108
101 S Fickett St Los Angeles (90033) ***(P-20543)***
Infinity Drywall Contg Inc ... D ... 714 634-2255
225 S Loara St Anaheim (92802) ***(P-2894)***
Infinity Energy Inc ... C ... 916 474-4723
1108 Tinker Rd Ste 150 Rocklin (95765) ***(P-2233)***
Infinity Metals Inc ... E ... 562 697-8826
600 E Lambert Rd La Habra (90631) ***(P-7281)***
Infinity Nurses Care Inc ... D ... 510 713-8892
39159 Paseo Padre Pkwy # 111 Fremont (94538) ***(P-14862)***
Infinity Service Group Inc ... D ... 909 466-6237
9155 Archibald Ave # 302 Rancho Cucamonga (91730) ***(P-2234)***
Infinity Staffing Service ... B ... 831 638-0360
710 Kirkpatric Ct Hollister (95023) ***(P-14863)***
Inflection LLC ... C ... 650 618-9910
555 Twin Dolphin Dr # 200 Redwood City (94065) ***(P-16146)***
Inflection Risk Solutions LLC ... E ... 650 618-9910
555 Twin Dolphin Dr Redwood City (94065) ***(P-16147)***
Influxdata Inc ... C ... 415 295-1901
799 Market St Ste 4 San Francisco (94103) ***(P-17234)***
Info Plus International, San Mateo *Also called Ip International Inc* ***(P-16409)***
Infogain Corporation (PA) ... C ... 408 355-6000
485 Alberto Way Ste 100 Los Gatos (95032) ***(P-16393)***
Infogen Labs Inc ... D ... 818 825-5024
18223 Charlton Ln Porter Ranch (91326) ***(P-16394)***
Infogroup Inc ... D ... 650 389-0700
951 Mariners Island Blvd # 130 San Mateo (94404) ***(P-14046)***
Infonet Services Corporation ... A ... 310 335-2600
1320 E Franklin Ave El Segundo (90245) ***(P-4578)***
Infonet Services Corporation (HQ) ... A ... 310 335-2859
2160 E Grand Ave El Segundo (90245) ***(P-5585)***
Infor (us) Inc ... C ... 678 319-8000
26250 Entp Way Ste 220 Lake Forest (92630) ***(P-15710)***
Infor (us) Inc ... C ... 916 921-0883
11000 Olson Dr Ste 201 Rancho Cordova (95670) ***(P-15711)***
Informa Research Services Inc (HQ) ... C ... 818 880-8877
26565 Agoura Rd Ste 300 Calabasas (91302) ***(P-27273)***
Informatica LLC (HQ) ... C ... 650 385-5000
2100 Seaport Blvd Redwood City (94063) ***(P-15712)***
Information & Referral Fed Los ... D ... 626 350-1841
526 W Las Tunas Dr San Gabriel (91776) ***(P-13751)***
Information Management Svcs, Downey *Also called Rancho Los Amigos Nationa* ***(P-23980)***
Information Services, Santa Cruz *Also called Santa Cruz County of* ***(P-16175)***
Information Services Dept, Fresno *Also called Community Hospitals Centl Cal* ***(P-16106)***
Information Services Dept, Redwood City *Also called County of San Mateo* ***(P-27926)***
Information Systems & Services, Sonora *Also called County of Tuolumne* ***(P-16112)***

Mergent e-mail: customerrelations@mergent.com
1338
2019 Directory of California
Wholesalers and Services Companies
(P-0000) Products & Services Section entry number
(PA)=Parent Co (HQ)=Headquarters (DH)=Div Headquarters

Information Systems Department, Santa Rosa *Also called County of Sonoma* ***(P-16111)***
Information Systems Labs Inc (PA)............E.......858 535-9680
12900 Brookprinter Pl # 800 Poway (92064) ***(P-25744)***
Information Tech Partners Inc............D.......800 789-7487
3003 N San Fernando Blvd Burbank (91504) ***(P-16395)***
Information Technology, Los Angeles *Also called Los Angeles Unified School Dst* ***(P-16289)***
Information Technology Agency, Los Angeles *Also called Los Angeles Unified School Dst* ***(P-16152)***
Informative Research (PA)............E.......714 638-2855
13030 Euclid St Ste 209 Garden Grove (92843) ***(P-14038)***
Infosoft Inc............D.......408 659-4326
7891 Westwood Dr Ste 113 Gilroy (95020) ***(P-27752)***
Infotech Consulting, San Francisco *Also called Brad Miller* ***(P-27170)***
Infrascale Inc............C.......310 878-2621
999 N Pacific Coast Hwy # 100 El Segundo (90245) ***(P-7062)***
Infrastructure Engrg Corp............E.......760 529-0795
301 Mission Ave Ste 202 Oceanside (92054) ***(P-25745)***
Ingenio Inc............C.......415 248-4000
182 Howard St 826 San Francisco (94105) ***(P-5586)***
Ingenio LLC............D.......415 992-8218
182 Howard St 826 San Francisco (94105) ***(P-17235)***
Ingenium Technologies Corp............D.......858 227-4422
5665 Oberlin Dr Ste 202 San Diego (92121) ***(P-25746)***
Inglewood Child Dev Ctr, Inglewood *Also called Inglewood Unified School Dst* ***(P-24329)***
Inglewood Health Care Center, Inglewood *Also called Mariner Health Care Inc* ***(P-20616)***
Inglewood Meadows Kbs LP............D.......310 820-4888
1 S Locust St Inglewood (90301) ***(P-11032)***
Inglewood Unified School Dst............D.......310 419-2691
401 S Inglewood Ave Inglewood (90301) ***(P-24329)***
Ingram Micro Inc (HQ)............A.......714 566-1000
3351 Michelson Dr Ste 100 Irvine (92612) ***(P-7063)***
Ingram Publisher Services Inc............D.......510 528-1444
1700 4th St Berkeley (94710) ***(P-9116)***
Ingredients Online, La Mirada *Also called Green Wave Ingredients Inc* ***(P-8173)***
Inhouseit Inc............D.......949 660-5655
3193 Red Hill Ave Costa Mesa (92626) ***(P-16288)***
Inhouselender.com, Santa Ana *Also called Affiliated Funding Corporation* ***(P-9869)***
Initial Security, Santa Fe Springs *Also called Alliedbarton Security Svcs LLC* ***(P-16554)***
Inkling Systems Inc............D.......415 975-4420
343 Sansome St Fl 8 San Francisco (94104) ***(P-27274)***
Inko Industrial Corporation............D.......408 830-1040
695 Vaqueros Ave Sunnyvale (94085) ***(P-16148)***
Inland Bhavioral Hlth Svcs Inc (PA)............D.......909 881-6146
1963 N E St San Bernardino (92405) ***(P-22823)***
Inland Business Machines Inc (HQ)............D.......916 928-0770
1326 N Market Blvd Sacramento (95834) ***(P-17958)***
Inland Cc Inc............C.......909 355-1318
13820 Slover Ave Fontana (92337) ***(P-3267)***
Inland Christian Home Inc............C.......909 395-9322
1950 S Mountain Ave Ofc Ontario (91762) ***(P-20544)***
Inland Cnties Regional Ctr Inc (PA)............D.......909 890-3000
1365 S Waterman Ave San Bernardino (92408) ***(P-26892)***
Inland Cold Storage, Bloomington *Also called Lineage Logistics Holdings LLC* ***(P-4357)***
Inland Empire Chapter-Assn of............D.......512 478-9000
4200 Concours Ste 360 Ontario (91764) ***(P-25432)***
Inland Empire Hauling, Corona *Also called USA Waste of California Inc* ***(P-6491)***
Inland Empire Health Plan............B.......866 228-4347
805 W 2nd St Ste C San Bernardino (92410) ***(P-10214)***
Inland Empire Health Plan (PA)............A.......909 890-2000
10801 6th St Ste 120 Rancho Cucamonga (91730) ***(P-10166)***
Inland Empire RE Solutions............D.......909 476-1000
8794 19th St Alta Loma (91701) ***(P-11512)***
Inland Empire Real Estate............E.......909 944-2070
8010 Haven Ave Rancho Cucamonga (91730) ***(P-11513)***
INLAND EMPIRE SURF SOCCER CLUB, San Bernardino *Also called Alliance Fc* ***(P-25377)***
Inland Empire Therapy Provider (PA)............D.......909 985-7905
1150 N Mountain Ave # 214 Upland (91786) ***(P-20179)***
Inland Empire Utilities Agency............D.......909 993-1755
12811 6th St Rancho Cucamonga (91739) ***(P-6263)***
Inland Empire Utilities Agency (PA)............D.......909 993-1600
6075 Kimball Ave Chino (91708) ***(P-6264)***
Inland Empire Utilities Agency............D.......909 993-1600
9400 Cherry Ave Fontana (92335) ***(P-6265)***
Inland Empre 66ers Bsebll CLB............C.......909 888-9922
280 S E St San Bernardino (92401) ***(P-18521)***
Inland Erosion Control Svcs............D.......951 301-8334
42181 Avenida Alvarado A Temecula (92590) ***(P-3430)***
Inland Eye Inst Med Group Inc (PA)............D.......909 825-3425
1900 E Washington St Colton (92324) ***(P-19511)***
Inland Hand Therapy & Rehab, Upland *Also called Mountain View Physical Therapy* ***(P-20190)***
Inland Hlth Org of So Cal (HQ)............E.......909 335-7171
1980 Orange Tree Ln # 200 Redlands (92374) ***(P-19512)***
Inland Inspections Consulting............E.......951 697-1000
7338 Sycamore Canyon Blvd Riverside (92508) ***(P-17236)***
Inland Kenworth (us) Inc (HQ)............C.......909 823-9955
9730 Cherry Ave Fontana (92335) ***(P-6597)***
Inland Pacific Ballet, Montclair *Also called Foundation For Dance Education* ***(P-18333)***
INLAND REGIONAL CENTER, San Bernardino *Also called Inland Cnties Regional Ctr Inc* ***(P-26892)***
Inland Star Dist Ctrs Inc (PA)............D.......559 237-2052
3146 S Chestnut Ave Fresno (93725) ***(P-4196)***
Inland Valley Business and Com............D.......951 378-5316
40335 Winchester Rd Temecula (92591) ***(P-25433)***
INLAND VALLEY CARE & REHAB CTR, Pomona *Also called Inland Valley Partners LLC* ***(P-20180)***
Inland Valley Cnstr Co Inc............D.......909 875-2112
18382 Slover Ave Bloomington (92316) ***(P-1344)***
Inland Valley Drug & Alcohol (PA)............D.......909 932-1069
1260 E Arrow Hwy Upland (91786) ***(P-23856)***
Inland Valley Partners LLC............C.......909 623-7100
250 W Artesia St Pomona (91768) ***(P-20180)***
Inland Vly Rgional Med Ctr Inc (HQ)............D.......951 677-1111
36485 Inland Valley Dr Wildomar (92595) ***(P-21458)***
Inland-Metro Services Inc............D.......909 373-6810
1059 W 14th St Upland (91786) ***(P-17237)***
Inman Spinosa & Buchan Inc............D.......310 519-1080
28901 S Wstn Ave Ste 139 Rancho Palos Verdes (90275) ***(P-11514)***
Inn At Rancho Santa Fe, The, Rancho Santa Fe *Also called Huntington Hotel Company* ***(P-12742)***
Inn At Scotts Valley LLC............D.......831 440-1000
6001 La Madrona Dr Scotts Valley (95060) ***(P-12763)***
Inner Circle Entertainment............D.......415 693-0777
464 Monterey Ave Ste A Los Gatos (95030) ***(P-8563)***
Inner Space Constructors Div, Long Beach *Also called Hutchison Corporation* ***(P-2893)***
Inner-City Express, San Jose *Also called Ice Delivery Systems Inc* ***(P-4024)***
Innerasia Travel Group, San Francisco *Also called Geographic Expeditions Inc* ***(P-4936)***
Innocean Wrldwide Americas LLC (HQ)............D.......714 861-5200
180 5th St Ste 200 Huntington Beach (92648) ***(P-13846)***
Innopath Software Inc (PA)............D.......408 962-9200
333 W El Camino Real # 290 Sunnyvale (94087) ***(P-15214)***
Innova Solutions Inc............C.......408 889-2020
3211 Scott Blvd Ste 202 Santa Clara (95054) ***(P-16396)***
Innovasystems Intl LLC............D.......619 955-5890
850 Beech St Unit 1006 San Diego (92101) ***(P-15215)***
Innovasystems Intl LLC (PA)............D.......619 756-6500
2385 Northside Dr Ste 300 San Diego (92108) ***(P-15216)***
Innovated Packaging Company............C.......510 713-3560
38505 Cherry St Ste C Newark (94560) ***(P-17238)***
Innovations Building Svcs LLC............D.......323 787-6068
402 S Orange Ave Apt D Monterey Park (91755) ***(P-14289)***
Innovative Artists Talent Agny (PA)............D.......310 656-0400
1505 10th St Santa Monica (90401) ***(P-18372)***
Innovative Bus Partnerships............E.......760 243-2229
17191 Jasmine St Victorville (92395) ***(P-21121)***
Innovative Cnstr Solutions............C.......714 893-6366
4011 W Chandler Ave Santa Ana (92704) ***(P-27597)***
Innovative Drywall Systems Inc............D.......760 743-0331
116 Market Pl Escondido (92029) ***(P-2895)***
Innovative Education MGT Inc............C.......530 295-3566
1166 Broadway Ste Q Placerville (95667) ***(P-26893)***
Innovative Engrg Systems Inc (PA)............D.......661 381-7800
8800 Crippen St Bakersfield (93311) ***(P-25747)***
Innovative Maint Solutions Inc............C.......916 568-1400
725 Del Paso Rd Sacramento (95834) ***(P-2235)***
Innovative Medical Solutions............D.......714 505-7070
3002 Dow Ave Ste 110 Tustin (92780) ***(P-17959)***
Innovative Merch Solutions LLC............C.......818 936-7800
21215 Burbank Blvd Woodland Hills (91367) ***(P-17239)***
Innovative Silicon Inc............D.......408 572-8700
4800 Great America Pkwy # 500 Santa Clara (95054) ***(P-17240)***
Innovative Sleep Centers Inc............D.......415 927-4990
1050 Northgate Dr Ste 250 San Rafael (94903) ***(P-19513)***
Innovative Staffing Resources, Tustin *Also called Innovtive Scntfic Slutions Inc* ***(P-14649)***
Innovel Solutions Inc............D.......707 748-1940
521 Stone Rd Benicia (94510) ***(P-5091)***
Innovel Solutions Inc............A.......661 721-5910
1700 Schuster Rd Delano (93215) ***(P-5092)***
Innovo Azteca Apparel Inc............D.......323 837-3700
5901 S Eastern Ave 104 Commerce (90040) ***(P-8227)***
Innovtive Emplyee Slutions Inc............A.......858 715-5100
9665 Gran Rdge Dr Ste 420 San Diego (92123) ***(P-26229)***
Innovtive Scntfic Slutions Inc............C.......714 508-8620
17581 Irvine Blvd Ste 202 Tustin (92780) ***(P-14649)***
Inns of Monterey, Monterey *Also called Columbia Hospitality Inc* ***(P-12475)***
Innsuites Hotels, San Diego *Also called Hampstead Lafayette Hotel LLC* ***(P-12637)***
Inova Diagnostics Inc (HQ)............B.......858 586-9900
9900 Old Grove Rd San Diego (92131) ***(P-26383)***
Inovative Packaging, Newark *Also called Integrated Pkg & Crating Svcs* ***(P-5209)***
Inoxpa USA Inc............B.......707 585-3900
3721 Santa Rosa Ave B4 Santa Rosa (95407) ***(P-7757)***
Inqbrands Inc............D.......909 390-7788
1801 E Holt Blvd Unit 101 Ontario (91761) ***(P-16397)***
Inreach Internet LLC (HQ)............D.......888 467-3224
4635 Georgetown Pl Stockton (95207) ***(P-5587)***
Insco Dico Group , The, Irvine *Also called Developers Surety Indemnity Co* ***(P-10426)***
Insco Insurance Services Inc (HQ)............D.......949 797-9243
17771 Cowan Ste 100 Irvine (92614) ***(P-10650)***
Inseego North America LLC (HQ)............D.......541 685-9045
9605 Scranton Rd Ste 300 San Diego (92121) ***(P-15978)***
Inside Outdoors Foundation............C.......714 708-3885
8755 Santiago Canyon Rd Silverado (92676) ***(P-23857)***
Inside Source Inc (PA)............D.......650 508-9101
985 Industrial Rd Ste 101 San Carlos (94070) ***(P-6727)***
Inside Source/Young, San Carlos *Also called Inside Source Inc* ***(P-6727)***
Insidesalescom Inc............D.......385 207-7252
1269 Deep Creek Rd Livermore (94550) ***(P-15713)***
Insideview Technologies Inc............C.......415 728-9309
444 De Haro St Ste 210 San Francisco (94107) ***(P-7064)***
Insight Health Corp (HQ)............E.......877 566-6500
23725 Birtcher Dr Ste 200 Lake Forest (92630) ***(P-22026)***
Insight Imaging, Lake Forest *Also called Insight Health Corp* ***(P-22026)***
Insight Investments LLC (HQ)............C.......714 939-2300
611 Anton Blvd Ste 700 Costa Mesa (92626) ***(P-16275)***

ALPHABETIC

Employee Codes: A=Over 500 employees, B=251-500
C=101-250, D=51-100, E=50
2019 Directory of California
Wholesalers and Services Companies
© Mergent Inc. 1-800-342-5647
1339

Insignia/Esg Ht Partners Inc (HQ) ....B....310 765-2600
11150 Santa Monica Blvd # 220 Los Angeles (90025) ***(P-10899)***
Insikt Inc ....D....415 391-2431
333 Bush St Ste 1700 San Francisco (94104) ***(P-17241)***
Insite Digestive Health Care ....C....408 471-2222
200 Jose Figueres Ave San Jose (95116) ***(P-19514)***
Insituform Technologies LLC ....E....714 724-2324
19000 Macarthur Blvd # 800 Irvine (92612) ***(P-1930)***
Insomniac Inc ....D....323 874-7020
9441 W Olympic Blvd Beverly Hills (90212) ***(P-18442)***
Insomniac Holdings LLC ....C....323 874-7020
9441 W Olympic Blvd Beverly Hills (90212) ***(P-18443)***
Inspection and Testing, Anaheim *Also called Emery Smith Laboratories Inc* ***(P-25659)***
Inspectorate America Corp ....C....800 424-0099
3401 Jack Northrop Ave Hawthorne (90250) ***(P-17242)***
Insperity Inc ....D....909 569-1000
1440 Bridgegate Dr # 200 Diamond Bar (91765) ***(P-27275)***
Inspira Inc ....D....408 247-9500
4125 Blackford Ave # 255 San Jose (95117) ***(P-15217)***
Inspiria Inc (PA) ....D....949 206-0606
25741 Atl Ocn Dr Ste A Lake Forest (92630) ***(P-25748)***
Installmonetizer, San Jose *Also called Big Bulb Ideas Inc* ***(P-15024)***
Instant Systems Inc ....D....510 657-8100
40211 Dolerita Ave Fremont (94539) ***(P-15218)***
Instantly, Encino *Also called Survey Sampling Intl LLC* ***(P-26568)***
Instantsys, Fremont *Also called Instant Systems Inc* ***(P-15218)***
Instart Labs, Palo Alto *Also called Instart Logic Inc* ***(P-15219)***
Instart Logic Inc ....D....888 418-5044
450 Lambert Ave Palo Alto (94306) ***(P-15219)***
Instill Corporation ....C....650 645-2600
777 Mariners Island Blvd # 400 San Mateo (94404) ***(P-15220)***
Instittional Property Advisors, Calabasas *Also called Marcus Mllchap RE Inv Svcs Inc* ***(P-11586)***
Institute Applied Bhvior Anlis, Tarzana *Also called Institute For Applied Behavior* ***(P-20183)***
Institute For Applied Behavior (PA) ....C....310 649-0499
5777 W Century Blvd # 675 Los Angeles (90045) ***(P-20181)***
Institute For Applied Behavior ....C....805 987-5886
2310 E Ponderosa Dr Ste 1 Camarillo (93010) ***(P-20182)***
Institute For Applied Behavior ....D....818 881-1933
19510 Ventura Blvd # 204 Tarzana (91356) ***(P-20183)***
Institute For Bhvoral Hlth Inc ....B....909 289-1041
1905 Bus Ctr Dr S Ste 100 San Bernardino (92408) ***(P-22824)***
INSTITUTE FOR CAREER DEVELOPME, San Jose *Also called Goodwill of Silicon Valley* ***(P-14859)***
Institute For Eductl Therapy ....E....831 457-1207
1007 University Ave Berkeley (94710) ***(P-24195)***
Institute For Health & Healing ....E....415 600-3503
2300 California St # 101 San Francisco (94115) ***(P-21459)***
Institute For Humn Social Dev (PA) ....D....650 871-5613
155 Bovet Rd Ste 300 San Mateo (94402) ***(P-24330)***
Institute For La Jolla ....C....858 752-6500
9420 Athena Cir La Jolla (92037) ***(P-26625)***
Institute For Multicultural ....D....818 240-4311
121 W Lexington Dr Glendale (91203) ***(P-27753)***
Institute For One World Health ....E....650 392-2510
600 California St Fl 11 San Francisco (94108) ***(P-18613)***
Institute For Wildlife Studies (PA) ....E....707 822-4258
835 3rd St Eureka (95501) ***(P-25175)***
Institute LLC ....E....408 782-7101
14830 Foothill Ave Morgan Hill (95037) ***(P-18722)***
Institute On Aging ....C....510 536-3377
2100 Embarcadero Ste 101 Oakland (94606) ***(P-21122)***
Institute On Aging ....D....415 600-2690
3698 California St San Francisco (94118) ***(P-23858)***
Institute On Aging (PA) ....D....415 750-4101
3575 Geary Blvd San Francisco (94118) ***(P-23859)***
Institutional Financing Svcs, Benicia *Also called Americas Lemonade Stand Inc* ***(P-17000)***
Insul Acoustics Inc ....C....323 686-2670
1432 Chico Ave El Monte (91733) ***(P-2896)***
Insulectro (PA) ....D....949 587-3200
20362 Windrow Dr Ste 100 Lake Forest (92630) ***(P-7494)***
Insulfoam, Dixon *Also called Carlisle Construction Mtls Inc* ***(P-6923)***
Insurance Auto Auctions Inc ....D....818 487-2222
7245 Laurel Canyon Blvd # 5 North Hollywood (91605) ***(P-6598)***
Insurance Company of West (HQ) ....C....858 350-2400
15025 Innovation Dr San Diego (92128) ***(P-10363)***
Insurance Dentists Amer Idoa, Campbell *Also called Dentistat Inc* ***(P-27214)***
Insurance Services Amercn LLC ....D....805 981-2220
300 E Esplanade Dr # 2100 Oxnard (93036) ***(P-10651)***
Insurance Services Office Inc ....B....415 874-4361
388 Market St Ste 750 San Francisco (94111) ***(P-16232)***
Insure Express Insurance Svc, Calabasas *Also called Cartel Marketing Inc* ***(P-10579)***
Intapp Inc (PA) ....C....650 852-0400
200 Portage Ave Palo Alto (94306) ***(P-15714)***
Intarcia Therapeutics Inc ....D....510 782-7800
24650 Industrial Blvd Hayward (94545) ***(P-26384)***
Intech Mechanical Company LLC ....C....916 797-4900
7501 Galilee Rd Roseville (95678) ***(P-2236)***
Integra Telecom Inc ....D....408 758-7700
101 Metro Dr San Jose (95110) ***(P-17243)***
Integral Development Corp (PA) ....C....650 424-4500
850 Hansen Way Palo Alto (94304) ***(P-15715)***
Integral Engineering, Palo Alto *Also called Integral Development Corp* ***(P-15715)***
Integral Senior Living LLC (PA) ....B....760 547-2863
2333 State St Ste 300 Carlsbad (92008) ***(P-11033)***
Integrated Behavioral Hlth Inc ....D....714 442-4150
3070 Bristol St Ste 350 Costa Mesa (92626) ***(P-22825)***
Integrated Clg Solutions Inc ....E....415 821-6757
3043 Mission St San Francisco (94110) ***(P-14290)***
Integrated Decision Systems ....D....310 954-5530
11150 W Olympic Blvd # 600 Los Angeles (90064) ***(P-15979)***
Integrated Dynmc Solutions Inc ....E....818 707-8797
31194 La Baya Dr Ste 203 Westlake Village (91362) ***(P-15221)***
Integrated Mech Systems Inc ....E....626 446-1854
2390 Bateman Ave Duarte (91010) ***(P-2237)***
Integrated Medical Specialists, San Diego *Also called Genesis Healthcare Partners PC* ***(P-22581)***
Integrated Office Tech LLC (PA) ....D....562 236-9200
12150 Mora Dr Ste 2 Santa Fe Springs (90670) ***(P-6961)***
Integrated Parcel Network ....B....714 278-6100
1706 W Orangethorpe Ave Fullerton (92833) ***(P-4420)***
Integrated Pkg & Crating Svcs ....E....510 745-8180
38505 Cherry St Newark (94560) ***(P-5209)***
Integrated Trnsp Svcs Inc ....D....310 553-6060
9740 W Pico Blvd Los Angeles (90035) ***(P-3809)***
Integrex Innovations, Tustin *Also called Integrium LLC* ***(P-26385)***
Integrits Corporation (PA) ....E....858 300-1600
5205 Kearny Villa Way # 200 San Diego (92123) ***(P-16398)***
Integrity Healthcare Services ....D....760 432-9811
425 W 5th Ave Ste 101 Escondido (92025) ***(P-22344)***
Integrity Management Entps, San Diego *Also called Gerwend Enterprises Inc* ***(P-27591)***
Integrity Management Svcs Inc ....C....805 238-0905
141 W Dana St Ste 100 Nipomo (93444) ***(P-14291)***
Integrity Rebar Placers ....C....951 696-6843
1345 Nandina Ave Perris (92571) ***(P-3377)***
Integrium LLC (PA) ....D....714 541-5591
14351 Myford Rd Ste A Tustin (92780) ***(P-26385)***
Integro USA Inc ....E....626 795-9000
115 N El Molino Ave Pasadena (91101) ***(P-10652)***
Integrted Care Communities Inc ....E....951 243-3837
11751 Davis St Moreno Valley (92557) ***(P-20545)***
Integrus LLC ....D....714 547-9500
1430 Village Way Ste K Santa Ana (92705) ***(P-6962)***
INTEL Corporation ....C....503 696-8080
2200 Mission College Blvd Santa Clara (95054) ***(P-15222)***
Intel Media Inc ....B....408 765-0063
2200 Mission College Blvd Santa Clara (95054) ***(P-5921)***
Intelex Systems Inc ....D....818 518-1100
6320 Canoga Ave Ste 1546 Woodland Hills (91367) ***(P-15223)***
Intelisys Inc ....D....800 615-8330
1318 Redwood Way Ste 120 Petaluma (94954) ***(P-27276)***
Intell Set, Long Beach *Also called Intelsat US LLC* ***(P-5983)***
Intellectsoft LLC ....C....650 300-4335
721 Colorado Ave Ste 101 Palo Alto (94303) ***(P-15224)***
Intellectual Ventures LLC ....B....650 941-1330
200 California Ave # 200 Palo Alto (94306) ***(P-26894)***
Intellicus Tech Pvt Ltd ....D....408 213-3314
720 University Ave # 130 Los Gatos (95032) ***(P-15980)***
Intelligent Automation Corp ....E....858 679-4140
13475 Danielson St # 100 Poway (92064) ***(P-25749)***
Intelliguard Security Services ....C....510 547-7656
4663 Harbord Dr Oakland (94618) ***(P-16700)***
Intellipro Group Inc ....B....408 200-9891
3120 Scott Blvd 301 Santa Clara (95054) ***(P-16399)***
Intellirisk Management Corp ....E....818 575-5400
31229 Cedar Valley Dr Westlake Village (91362) ***(P-14008)***
Intelliswift Software Inc (PA) ....C....510 490-9240
39600 Balentine Dr # 200 Newark (94560) ***(P-15225)***
Intellisync Corporation (HQ) ....D....650 625-2185
313 Fairchild Dr Mountain View (94043) ***(P-15226)***
Intelpeer Cloud Cmmnctions LLC ....C....650 525-9200
155 Bovet Rd Ste 405 San Mateo (94402) ***(P-5588)***
Intelsat US LLC ....C....310 525-5500
1600 Forbes Way Long Beach (90810) ***(P-5983)***
Inter Community Hospital, Covina *Also called Citrus Valley Medical Ctr Inc* ***(P-21325)***
Inter Community Hospital, Covina *Also called Citrus Vly Hlth Partners Inc* ***(P-26807)***
Inter Con Security Inc ....E....619 523-0291
2801 Camino Del Rio S 300h San Diego (92108) ***(P-27277)***
Inter Con Systems, Pasadena *Also called Inter-Con Investigators Inc* ***(P-16701)***
Inter Valley Pool Supply Inc ....D....626 969-5657
1415 E 3rd St Pomona (91766) ***(P-7931)***
Inter-City Cleaners ....D....650 875-9200
438 S Airport Blvd South San Francisco (94080) ***(P-13566)***
Inter-Con Investigators Inc ....D....626 535-2200
210 S De Lacey Ave Pasadena (91105) ***(P-16701)***
Inter-Con Security Systems Inc (PA) ....C....626 535-2200
210 S De Lacey Ave # 200 Pasadena (91105) ***(P-16702)***
Inter-Rail Trnspt Nshville LLC ....D....510 231-2744
861 Wharf St Richmond (94804) ***(P-5229)***
Inter-Rail Trnspt Nshville LLC ....D....707 746-1695
3800 Industrial Way Benicia (94510) ***(P-5230)***
Inter-State Oil Co (PA) ....D....916 457-6572
8221 Alpine Ave Sacramento (95826) ***(P-8962)***
Inter-Valley Health Plan Inc ....D....909 623-6333
300 S Park Ave Ste 300 # 300 Pomona (91766) ***(P-10215)***
Inter/Media Advertising, Woodland Hills *Also called Inter/Media Time Buying Corp* ***(P-13847)***
Inter/Media Time Buying Corp (PA) ....E....818 995-1455
22120 Clarendon St # 300 Woodland Hills (91367) ***(P-13847)***
Interact Pmti Inc (PA) ....D....805 658-5600
260 Maple Ct Ste 210 Ventura (93003) ***(P-25750)***
Interactivate Inc ....D....619 814-1999
707 Broadway Ste 1000 San Diego (92101) ***(P-16400)***
Interactive Data Corporation ....C....510 266-6000
919 E Hillsdale Blvd # 200 Foster City (94404) ***(P-10125)***
Interactive Data Corporation ....D....310 664-2500
2901 28th St Ste 300 Santa Monica (90405) ***(P-15227)***

Mergent e-mail: customerrelations@mergent.com
1340
2019 Directory of California Wholesalers and Services Companies
(P-0000) Products & Services Section entry number
(PA)=Parent Co (HQ)=Headquarters (DH)=Div Headquarters

Interactive Med Specialists..........D.......415 472-4204
252 Waterside Cir San Rafael (94903) ***(P-14864)***
Interactive Media Holdings (HQ)..........D.......949 861-8888
4 Park Plz Ste 1500 Irvine (92614) ***(P-13848)***
Interactive Solutions Inc (HQ)..........D.......510 214-9002
283 4th St Ste 301 Oakland (94607) ***(P-15716)***
Interana Inc..........D.......844 426-4678
305 Walnut St Ste 300 Redwood City (94063) ***(P-15228)***
Interbake Foods LLC..........D.......213 484-8161
1910 W Temple St Los Angeles (90026) ***(P-8805)***
Intercare Holdings Insur Svcs, Rocklin *Also called Pacific Secured Equities Inc* ***(P-27386)***
Intercare Holdings Insur Svcs..........B.......916 677-2500
3010 Lava Ridge Ct # 110 Roseville (95661) ***(P-10653)***
Intercare Therapy Inc..........C.......323 866-1880
4221 Wilshire Blvd 300a Los Angeles (90010) ***(P-20184)***
Intercntnntal Ht Group Rsurces..........B.......415 771-9000
1300 Columbus Ave San Francisco (94133) ***(P-12764)***
Intercom Inc..........B.......831 920-7088
55 2nd St Ste 400 San Francisco (94105) ***(P-15229)***
Intercommunity Care Centers..........C.......562 427-8915
2626 Grand Ave Long Beach (90815) ***(P-20546)***
Intercommunity Child..........D.......562 692-0383
10155 Colima Rd Whittier (90603) ***(P-23860)***
Intercommunity Dialysis Center, Whittier *Also called Intercommunity Dialysis Svcs* ***(P-22479)***
Intercommunity Dialysis Svcs..........E.......562 696-1841
12455 Washington Blvd Whittier (90602) ***(P-22479)***
Intercontinental Exchange Inc (HQ)..........B.......770 857-4700
1415 Moonstone Brea (92821) ***(P-10048)***
Intercontinental Hotels..........C.......415 616-6500
888 Howard St San Francisco (94103) ***(P-12765)***
Intercontinental Hotels Group..........C.......949 863-1999
17941 Von Karman Ave Irvine (92614) ***(P-12766)***
Intercontinental Hotels Group..........D.......619 727-4000
509 9th Ave San Diego (92101) ***(P-12767)***
Intercontinental Hotels Group..........C.......415 626-6103
50 8th St San Francisco (94103) ***(P-12768)***
Intercontinental Hotels Group..........D.......310 781-9100
19800 S Vermont Ave Torrance (90502) ***(P-12769)***
Intercontinental Hotels Group..........C.......415 398-8900
480 Sutter St San Francisco (94108) ***(P-12770)***
Intercontinental Hotels Group..........D.......805 964-6241
5650 Calle Real Goleta (93117) ***(P-12771)***
Intercontinental Hotels Group..........E.......415 409-4600
550 N Point St San Francisco (94133) ***(P-12772)***
Intercontinental Hotels Group..........D.......949 863-1999
17941 Von Karman Ave Irvine (92614) ***(P-12773)***
Intercontinental Hotels Group..........C.......909 930-5555
2280 S Haven Ave Ontario (91761) ***(P-12774)***
Intercontinental Mark Hopkins, San Francisco *Also called One Nob Hill Associates LLC* ***(P-12985)***
Intercontinental San Francisco, San Francisco *Also called Cdc San Francisco LLC* ***(P-12444)***
Intercontntl Hotels Grp Resour, Los Angeles *Also called Crowne Plaza Lax LLC* ***(P-12502)***
Interdent Inc (HQ)..........D.......310 765-2400
9800 S La Cienega Blvd # 800 Inglewood (90301) ***(P-20117)***
Interdent Service Corporation (HQ)..........E.......310 765-2400
9800 S La Cienega Blvd # 800 Inglewood (90301) ***(P-20118)***
INTERFACE CHILDREN FAMILY SERV, Camarillo *Also called Interface Community* ***(P-23861)***
Interface Community (PA)..........D.......805 485-6114
4001 Mission Oaks Blvd Camarillo (93012) ***(P-23861)***
Interface Rehab Inc..........A.......714 646-8300
774 S Placentia Ave # 200 Placentia (92870) ***(P-20185)***
Interfaith Community Svcs Inc..........D.......760 489-6380
550 W Washington Ave B Escondido (92025) ***(P-23862)***
Intergro Rehab Service..........D.......714 901-4200
1922 N Broadway Santa Ana (92706) ***(P-20186)***
Interhealth Corp (PA)..........A.......562 698-0811
12401 Washington Blvd Whittier (90602) ***(P-21460)***
Interhealth Services Inc (HQ)..........D.......562 698-0811
12401 Washington Blvd Whittier (90602) ***(P-22345)***
Interim Inc..........C.......831 754-3838
339 Pajaro St Ste B Salinas (93901) ***(P-27934)***
Interim Assisited Care of Nort..........D.......530 722-1530
373 Smile Pl Redding (96001) ***(P-22346)***
Interim Hlthcare Nthrn Cal Inc (PA)..........B.......530 221-1300
1647 Court St Redding (96001) ***(P-22347)***
Interim Services, Bakersfield *Also called Rncmba Inc* ***(P-14905)***
Interim Services, Redding *Also called Interim Assisited Care of Nort* ***(P-22346)***
Interim Services, Salinas *Also called Interim Inc* ***(P-27934)***
Interior Electric Incorporated..........D.......714 771-9098
747 N Main St Orange (92868) ***(P-2613)***
Interior Experts General Bldrs..........D.......909 203-4922
4534 Carter Ct Chino (91710) ***(P-2897)***
Interior Office Solutions Inc (PA)..........E.......949 724-9444
17800 Mitchell N Irvine (92614) ***(P-17244)***
Interior Office Solutions Inc..........E.......310 726-9067
444 S Flower St Ste 200 Los Angeles (90071) ***(P-17245)***
Interior Rmoval Specialist Inc..........C.......323 357-6900
8990 Atlantic Ave South Gate (90280) ***(P-3455)***
Interior Specialists Inc (HQ)..........D.......760 929-6700
1630 Faraday Ave Carlsbad (92008) ***(P-3109)***
Interior Specialists Inc..........D.......530 885-0632
9300 Hubbard Rd Auburn (95602) ***(P-3110)***
Interiors By Linda..........E.......760 341-9651
49585 Brian Ct La Quinta (92253) ***(P-17246)***
Interket Enterprise, Fremont *Also called Unitek Inc* ***(P-16070)***
Interlab Inc..........E.......619 302-3095
636 Broadway Ste 322 San Diego (92101) ***(P-7244)***
Interlink..........C.......310 734-1499
10940 Wilshire Blvd Los Angeles (90024) ***(P-9760)***
Interlink Company The, Los Angeles *Also called Interlink* ***(P-9760)***
Intermedia Holdings Inc (PA)..........D.......650 641-4000
825 E Middlefield Rd Mountain View (94043) ***(P-16401)***
Internal Associates Med Group, Culver City *Also called Gardner Neurologic Orthopedic* ***(P-26867)***
Internal Mdcine Rsdncy Affairs..........D.......916 734-7080
4150 V St Ste 3116 Sacramento (95817) ***(P-25021)***
Internal Services Department, Los Angeles *Also called County of Los Angeles* ***(P-26173)***
Internal Services Dept, Los Angeles *Also called County of Los Angeles* ***(P-17104)***
International Advisors LLC..........D.......497 961-7988
31248 Oak Crest Dr Westlake Village (91361) ***(P-27754)***
International Alliance Thea..........D.......805 898-0442
P.O. Box 413 Santa Barbara (93102) ***(P-25061)***
International Almond Exchange..........E.......831 728-4534
144 W Lake Ave Watsonville (95076) ***(P-190)***
International Assn of Plmbing, Ontario *Also called Iapmo Research and Testing Inc* ***(P-24961)***
International Assoc of Machini..........E.......760 326-7048
1303 S Highway 95 Needles (92363) ***(P-25062)***
International Assoc of Plmbng (PA)..........D.......909 472-4100
4755 E Philadelphia St Ontario (91761) ***(P-24963)***
International Bay Clubs LLC (PA)..........B.......949 645-5000
1221 W Coast Hwy Ste 145 Newport Beach (92663) ***(P-18938)***
International Brthrhd of Elctr (PA)..........D.......707 452-2700
30 Orange Tree Cir Vacaville (95687) ***(P-25063)***
International Bus Mchs Corp..........D.......914 499-1900
30501 Agoura Rd Ste 100 Agoura Hills (91301) ***(P-15981)***
International Bus Mchs Corp..........A.......408 463-2000
555 Bailey Ave San Jose (95141) ***(P-15230)***
International Bus Mchs Corp..........C.......415 545-4747
425 Market St San Francisco (94105) ***(P-6963)***
International Bus Mchs Corp..........A.......408 850-8999
2350 Mission College Blvd Santa Clara (95054) ***(P-16402)***
International Bus Mchs Corp..........B.......714 327-3501
1540 Scenic Ave Costa Mesa (92626) ***(P-16403)***
International Bus Mchs Corp..........B.......510 652-6700
1480 64th St Ste 200 Emeryville (94608) ***(P-16404)***
International Bus Mchs Corp..........B.......800 426-4968
1001 E Hillsdale Blvd Foster City (94404) ***(P-16405)***
International Bus Mchs Corp..........C.......408 452-4800
2077 Gateway Pl San Jose (95110) ***(P-6964)***
International Bus Mchs Corp..........B.......408 927-1080
650 Harry Rd San Jose (95120) ***(P-26386)***
International Bus Mchs Corp..........C.......925 277-5000
4000 Executive Pkwy # 300 San Ramon (94583) ***(P-27278)***
International Creative Mgt Inc (HQ)..........C.......310 550-4000
10250 Constellation Blvd Los Angeles (90067) ***(P-18373)***
International Creative MGT Inc..........C.......310 550-4000
10250 Constellation Blvd # 1 Los Angeles (90067) ***(P-18374)***
International Delicacies..........E.......510 669-2444
2100 Atlas Rd Ste F Richmond (94806) ***(P-8806)***
International Design Services..........D.......323 662-3963
2437 Micheltorena St Los Angeles (90039) ***(P-25751)***
International Fdn For Korea Un..........B.......213 550-2182
3435 Wilshire Blvd # 480 Los Angeles (90010) ***(P-17247)***
International Fmly Entrmt Inc (HQ)..........C.......818 560-1000
3800 W Alameda Ave Burbank (91505) ***(P-5922)***
International Garment Finisher..........D.......562 983-7400
2144 W Gaylord St Long Beach (90813) ***(P-13610)***
International Home Mortgage..........D.......562 945-7753
13601 Whittier Blvd # 311 Whittier (90605) ***(P-9818)***
International House..........C.......510 642-9490
2299 Piedmont Ave Ste 535 Berkeley (94720) ***(P-13440)***
INTERNATIONAL HOUSE AT U C BER, Berkeley *Also called International House* ***(P-13440)***
International Industrial Park..........D.......858 623-9000
5440 Morehouse Dr # 4000 San Diego (92121) ***(P-12063)***
International Inst Los Angeles (PA)..........D.......323 224-3800
3845 Selig Pl Los Angeles (90031) ***(P-23863)***
International Litigation Svcs..........E.......888 313-4457
65 Enterprise Aliso Viejo (92656) ***(P-6965)***
International Longshoremens..........D.......209 464-1827
22 N Union St Stockton (95205) ***(P-25064)***
International Marine Pdts Inc (HQ)..........E.......213 893-6123
500 E 7th St Los Angeles (90014) ***(P-8578)***
International Media Group Inc..........D.......310 478-1818
1990 S Bundy Dr Ste 850 Los Angeles (90025) ***(P-5801)***
International Medical Corps (PA)..........D.......310 826-7800
12400 Wilshire Blvd # 1500 Los Angeles (90025) ***(P-23864)***
International Mgt Systems..........D.......310 822-2022
4640 Admiralty Way # 500 Marina Del Rey (90292) ***(P-27755)***
International Missing Persons..........D.......714 827-1947
609 S Broder St Anaheim (92804) ***(P-13752)***
International Paper, Livermore *Also called Veritiv Operating Company* ***(P-7818)***
International Paper, La Mirada *Also called Veritiv Operating Company* ***(P-8130)***
International Paving Svcs Inc..........D.......909 794-2101
1199 Opal Ave Mentone (92359) ***(P-1792)***
International Spt Science Assn..........E.......805 745-8111
1015 Mark Ave Carpinteria (93013) ***(P-19189)***
International Thermoproducts..........E.......619 562-7001
11015 Mission Park Ct Santee (92071) ***(P-7758)***
International Toy Inc..........E.......949 333-3777
17682 Cowan Ste 100 Irvine (92614) ***(P-7952)***
International Trnsp Svc (HQ)..........C.......562 435-7781
1281 Pier G Way Long Beach (90802) ***(P-4727)***
Internationl TV Media Wireless, Bay Point *Also called Caribbean South Amercn Council* ***(P-4933)***

ALPHABETIC

Employee Codes: A=Over 500 employees, B=251-500
C=101-250, D=51-100, E=50
2019 Directory of California
Wholesalers and Services Companies
© Mergent Inc. 1-800-342-5647
1341

Internavia, San Diego *Also called Pacific Marine Dev Corp* ***(P-25861)***
Internet Archive ....C....415 561-6767
300 Funston Ave San Francisco (94118) ***(P-16233)***
Internet Blueprint Inc ....E....714 673-6000
1177 Warner Ave Tustin (92780) ***(P-15231)***
Internet Booking Agencycom Inc ....B....949 673-7707
232 Via Eboli Newport Beach (92663) ***(P-14650)***
Internet Brands Inc (PA) ....C....310 280-4000
909 N Pacific Coast Hwy # 11 El Segundo (90245) ***(P-16149)***
Internet Corp For Assigned Nam (PA) ....C....310 823-9358
12025 Waterfront Dr # 300 Los Angeles (90094) ***(P-15982)***
Internet Escrow Services Inc ....D....888 511-8600
180 Montgomery St Ste 650 San Francisco (94104) ***(P-11515)***
Internet Marketing Assn Inc ....D....949 443-9300
10 Mar Del Rey San Clemente (92673) ***(P-27279)***
Internet Security Systems Inc ....C....661 296-5752
28350 Tamarack Ln Santa Clarita (91390) ***(P-15232)***
Internet-Journals LLC ....D....510 665-1200
2100 Milvia St Ste 300 Berkeley (94704) ***(P-16406)***
Interntional Cmpt Science Inst ....E....510 643-9153
1947 Center St Ste 600 Berkeley (94704) ***(P-26626)***
Interntional Disposal Corp Cal ....D....408 945-2802
1601 Dixon Landing Rd Milpitas (95035) ***(P-6408)***
Interntional Longshore Whse Un ....D....805 488-2944
Bldng 608 Port Heneme Hbr Port Hueneme (93041) ***(P-14651)***
Interntional Pet Sups Dist Inc ....D....858 453-7845
10850 Via Frontera San Diego (92127) ***(P-9225)***
Interntional Un Oper Engineers ....E....626 792-2519
150 Corson St Pasadena (91103) ***(P-25065)***
Interntional Un Oper Engineers (PA) ....D....916 444-6880
1121 L St Ste 401 Sacramento (95814) ***(P-25066)***
Interntnal Arospc Coatings Inc ....C....760 246-1651
13640 Phantom St Victorville (92394) ***(P-4895)***
Interntnal Prnsrance Assoc LLC ....E....415 223-5548
504 Redwood Blvd Ste 240e Novato (94947) ***(P-10654)***
Interntnal Pvment Slutions Inc ....D....909 794-2101
1209 Van Buren St Ste 3 Thermal (92274) ***(P-3268)***
Interntnal Rscue Committee Inc ....D....619 641-7510
5348 University Ave # 205 San Diego (92105) ***(P-23865)***
Interntonal Win Treatments Inc (PA) ....D....562 236-2120
12301 Hawkins St Santa Fe Springs (90670) ***(P-6768)***
Intero Real Estate Services ....D....408 848-8400
790 1st St Gilroy (95020) ***(P-11516)***
Intero Real Estate Svcs Inc ....D....408 741-1600
12900 Saratoga Ave Saratoga (95070) ***(P-11517)***
Intero Real Estate Svcs Inc ....D....562 861-7242
8255 Firestone Blvd # 200 Downey (90241) ***(P-11518)***
Intero Real Estate Svcs Inc ....D....510 489-8989
32145 Alvarado Niles Rd # 101 Union City (94587) ***(P-11519)***
Intero Real Estate Svcs Inc ....C....408 574-5000
5890 Silver Creek Vly Rd San Jose (95138) ***(P-11520)***
Intero Real Estate Svcs Inc ....E....408 558-3600
1900 Camden Ave San Jose (95124) ***(P-11521)***
Intero Silicon Valley, San Jose *Also called Intero Real Estate Svcs Inc* ***(P-11521)***
Interpac Distribution Center, Woodland *Also called Interpac Technologies Inc* ***(P-17248)***
Interpac Technologies Inc ....D....530 662-6363
260 N Pioneer Ave Woodland (95776) ***(P-17248)***
Interpacific Group Inc ....A....415 442-0711
576 Beale St San Francisco (94105) ***(P-26230)***
Interpoltex, Jamul *Also called Poltex Company Inc* ***(P-15370)***
Interprsnal Dvlpmntal Fclttors ....D....626 793-8967
891 Worcester Ave Apt 3 Pasadena (91104) ***(P-23866)***
Interpublic Group of Companies, Los Angeles *Also called Dailey & Associates* ***(P-13808)***
Interstate Btry San Diego Inc ....E....858 790-8244
9345 Cabot Dr San Diego (92126) ***(P-6648)***
Interstate Con Pmpg Co Inc ....D....209 983-3092
11180 Vallejo Ct French Camp (95231) ***(P-3269)***
Interstate Electric Co Inc (PA) ....D....323 724-0420
2240 Yates Ave Commerce (90040) ***(P-7137)***
Interstate Electronics Corp ....A....714 758-0500
708 E Vermont Ave Anaheim (92805) ***(P-27280)***
Interstate Electronics Corp ....D....858 552-9500
3033 Science Park Rd San Diego (92121) ***(P-15983)***
Interstate Foods Inc ....C....310 635-0426
310 S Long Beach Blvd Compton (90221) ***(P-8533)***
Interstate Fuel Systems Inc ....D....916 457-6572
8221 Alpine Ave Sacramento (95826) ***(P-8963)***
Interstate Hotels Resorts Inc ....D....949 783-2500
4685 Macarthur Ct Ste 480 Newport Beach (92660) ***(P-26895)***
Interstate Hotels Resorts Inc ....C....415 362-5500
2500 Mason St San Francisco (94133) ***(P-12775)***
Interstate Hotels Resorts Inc ....C....213 617-1133
333 S Figueroa St Los Angeles (90071) ***(P-12776)***
Interstate Hotels Resorts Inc ....D....760 476-0800
6450 Carlsbad Blvd Carlsbad (92011) ***(P-26896)***
Interstate Hotels Resorts Inc ....B....213 624-1000
404 S Figueroa St 418a Los Angeles (90071) ***(P-12777)***
Interstate Hotels Resorts Inc ....C....760 322-7000
67 967 Vst Chno At Lndau Palm Springs (92263) ***(P-26897)***
Interstate Hotels Resorts Inc ....C....925 934-2500
1345 Treat Blvd Walnut Creek (94597) ***(P-26898)***
Interstate Hotels Resorts Inc ....D....510 843-3000
41 Tunnel Rd Berkeley (94705) ***(P-26899)***
Interstate Hotels Resorts Inc ....C....510 489-2200
32083 Alvarado Niles Rd Union City (94587) ***(P-12778)***
Interstate Hotels Resorts Inc ....C....916 922-4700
2200 Harvard St Sacramento (95815) ***(P-12779)***
Interstate Hotels Resorts Inc ....C....949 833-9999
18800 Macarthur Blvd Irvine (92612) ***(P-26900)***
Interstate Meat & Provision ....D....323 838-9400
6114 Scott Way Commerce (90040) ***(P-8491)***
Interstate Plastics, Sacramento *Also called Dongalen Enterprises Inc* ***(P-8914)***
Interstate Protective Services ....D....818 995-6664
20548 Ventura Blvd # 118 Woodland Hills (91364) ***(P-16703)***
Interstate Rhbltation Svcs LLC (PA) ....C....818 244-5656
333 E Glenoaks Blvd # 204 Glendale (91207) ***(P-20187)***
Interstate Truck Center LLC (PA) ....D....209 944-5821
2110 S Sinclair Ave Stockton (95215) ***(P-6599)***
Interstellar Inc (PA) ....D....415 598-0346
292 Ivy St Ste E San Francisco (94102) ***(P-26901)***
Intertek Caleb Brett, Signal Hill *Also called Intertek USA Inc* ***(P-17250)***
Intertek Group Inc ....D....949 448-4100
25800 Commercentre Dr Lake Forest (92630) ***(P-26706)***
Intertek Pharmaceutical Svcs, San Diego *Also called Intertek USA Inc* ***(P-26708)***
Intertek Testing Svcs NA Inc ....D....949 448-4100
25800 Commercentre Dr Lake Forest (92630) ***(P-26707)***
Intertek Testing Svcs NA Inc ....D....949 349-1684
25791 Commercentre Dr Lake Forest (92630) ***(P-17249)***
Intertek USA Inc ....D....858 558-2599
10420 Wateridge Cir San Diego (92121) ***(P-26708)***
Intertek USA Inc ....E....562 494-4999
1941 Freeman Ave Ste A Signal Hill (90755) ***(P-17250)***
Intertrend Communications Inc ....D....562 733-1888
228 E Broadway Long Beach (90802) ***(P-13849)***
Intertrust Technologies Corp (HQ) ....C....408 616-1600
920 Stewart Dr Sunnyvale (94085) ***(P-15233)***
Intervalley Pools, Pomona *Also called Inter Valley Pool Supply Inc* ***(P-7931)***
Intervec Phoenix Travel Club ....C....828 728-5287
1456 Seacoast Dr Unit 4a Imperial Beach (91932) ***(P-18939)***
Interviewing Service Amer Inc ....D....626 979-4140
200 S Grfield Ave Ste 302 Alhambra (91801) ***(P-26530)***
Interviewing Service Amer LLC (PA) ....C....818 989-1044
15400 Sherman Way Ste 400 Van Nuys (91406) ***(P-26531)***
Interwall Dev Systems Inc ....D....949 553-9102
17401 Armstrong Ave Irvine (92614) ***(P-2898)***
Interwest Insurance Svcs LLC (PA) ....C....916 488-3100
8950 Cal Center Dr Bldg 3 Sacramento (95826) ***(P-10655)***
Interwest Insurance Svcs LLC ....D....530 895-1010
1357 E Lassen Ave Ste 100 Chico (95973) ***(P-10656)***
Intex Recreation Corp ....D....310 549-1846
4001 Via Oro Ave Ste 210 Long Beach (90810) ***(P-6728)***
Intex Recreation Corp (PA) ....D....310 549-5400
4001 Via Oro Ave Ste 210 Long Beach (90810) ***(P-7932)***
Intex Recreation Corp ....C....310 549-5400
1665 Hughes Way Long Beach (90810) ***(P-10900)***
Intouch Health, Goleta *Also called Intouch Technologies Inc* ***(P-15717)***
Intouch Technologies Inc (PA) ....B....805 562-8686
7402 Hollister Ave Goleta (93117) ***(P-15717)***
Intrade Industries Inc (PA) ....D....559 274-9877
2559 S East Ave Fresno (93706) ***(P-4693)***
Intratek Computer Inc ....B....949 334-4200
9950 Irvine Center Dr Irvine (92618) ***(P-16407)***
Intravas Inc ....D....760 650-4040
6300 Yarrow Dr Carlsbad (92011) ***(P-27281)***
Intrepid Healthcare Svcs Inc, North Hollywood *Also called IPC Healthcare Inc* ***(P-19515)***
Intrepid Security Solutions ....E....855 379-2223
1999 S Bascom Ave Ste 700 Campbell (95008) ***(P-16906)***
Intrinsik Envmtl Sciences Inc ....D....310 392-6462
1608 Pacific Ave Ste 201 Venice (90291) ***(P-27756)***
Intuit Financial Services, Redwood City *Also called Digital Insight Corporation* ***(P-16217)***
Intuit Inc (PA) ....D....650 944-6000
2700 Coast Ave Mountain View (94043) ***(P-15718)***
Intuit Inc ....C....650 944-6000
2700 Coast Ave Bldg 7 Mountain View (94043) ***(P-15719)***
Intuit Inc ....C....650 944-6000
2535 Garcia Ave Mountain View (94043) ***(P-15720)***
Intuit Inc ....C....650 944-2840
141 Corona Way Portola Valley (94028) ***(P-15721)***
Intuit Inc ....C....650 944-6000
180 Jefferson Dr Menlo Park (94025) ***(P-15722)***
Intuit Inc ....B....858 215-8000
7545 Torrey Santa Fe Rd San Diego (92129) ***(P-15723)***
Inveserve Corporation ....D....626 458-3435
123 S Chapel Ave Alhambra (91801) ***(P-11522)***
Invesmart Inc ....D....408 961-2800
55 Almaden Blvd Ste 800 San Jose (95113) ***(P-10657)***
Investlinc Group LLC (PA) ....D....310 997-0580
1230 Rosecrans Ave # 600 Manhattan Beach (90266) ***(P-17251)***
Investlinc Group, The, Manhattan Beach *Also called Investlinc Group LLC* ***(P-17251)***
Investment Banking, Los Angeles *Also called J Alexander Investments Inc* ***(P-12064)***
Investment Concepts Inc (PA) ....C....714 283-5800
1667 E Lincoln Ave Orange (92865) ***(P-11881)***
Investment Real Estate, San Jose *Also called Zell Associates Inc* ***(P-10043)***
Investment Tech Group Inc ....C....310 216-6777
400 Crprate Pinte Ste 855 Culver City (90230) ***(P-9965)***
Investors Capital MGT Group ....B....310 553-5175
10390 Santa Monica Blvd Los Angeles (90025) ***(P-26902)***
Investors MGT Tr RE Group Inc (PA) ....E....818 784-4700
15303 Ventura Blvd # 200 Sherman Oaks (91403) ***(P-11034)***
Invitae Corporation (PA) ....D....415 374-7782
1400 16th St San Francisco (94103) ***(P-26709)***
Invitation Homes ....D....805 372-2900
465 N Halstead St Ste 150 Pasadena (91107) ***(P-10901)***
Inyo Mono Advcts Fr Cmmnty Act (PA) ....D....760 873-8557
137 E South St Bishop (93514) ***(P-24791)***
Inyo Sheriff Office, Independence *Also called Sheriffs Offices* ***(P-23382)***
Inzunza Real Estate Inc ....D....951 544-8801
25310 Madison Ave Ste 101 Murrieta (92562) ***(P-11523)***

Iogear, Irvine *Also called Aten Technology Inc (P-7011)*
Ion Media Networks Inc...E...818 953-7193
2531 Nina St Pasadena (91107) ***(P-5802)***
Ionics Altrpure Wtr Crparation...D...562 948-2188
7777 Industry Ave Pico Rivera (90660) ***(P-8807)***
Iotec, Santa Fe Springs *Also called Integrated Office Tech LLC (P-6961)*
Ip Access International...E...949 655-1000
31831 Cmno Capistrno 300a San Juan Capistrano (92675) ***(P-16408)***
Ip Infusion Inc (HQ)...D...408 400-1900
3965 Freedom Cir Ste 200 Santa Clara (95054) ***(P-15984)***
Ip International Inc...E...650 403-7800
1510 Fashion Island Blvd # 104 San Mateo (94404) ***(P-16409)***
Ipass Inc...D...650 232-4100
15241 Laguna Canyon Rd # 100 Irvine (92618) ***(P-15985)***
Ipass Inc (PA)...D...650 232-4100
3800 Bridge Pkwy Redwood City (94065) ***(P-5589)***
Ipayment Inc (HQ)...D...212 802-7200
30721 Russell Ranch Rd # 200 Westlake Village (91362) ***(P-17252)***
IPC (usa) Inc (HQ)...D...949 648-5600
4 Hutton Cntre Dr Ste 700 Santa Ana (92707) ***(P-8964)***
IPC Healthcare Inc (HQ)...D...888 447-2362
4605 Lankershim Blvd North Hollywood (91602) ***(P-19515)***
Ipd, Torrance *Also called Industrial Parts Depot LLC (P-7756)*
Ipitek Inc...C...760 438-1010
2461 Impala Dr Carlsbad (92010) ***(P-2614)***
Ipolipo Inc...D...408 916-5290
440 N Wolfe Rd Sunnyvale (94085) ***(P-15724)***
Ips, Woodland Hills *Also called Interstate Protective Services (P-16703)*
Ips Group Inc (PA)...D...858 404-0607
7737 Kenamar Ct San Diego (92121) ***(P-5984)***
Ipsos Otx Corporation (HQ)...C...310 736-3400
300 Crprate Pinte Ste 500 Culver City (90230) ***(P-26532)***
Ipsos Public Affairs Inc...C...559 451-2820
3402 N Blackstone Ave Fresno (93726) ***(P-26533)***
Ipsy, San Mateo *Also called Personlized Buty Discovery Inc (P-13667)*
Iptor Supply Chain Systems USA (HQ)...C...916 542-2820
915 Highland Pointe Dr # 250 Roseville (95678) ***(P-15234)***
Iq Pipeline LLC...D...858 483-7400
1550 Hotel Cir N Ste 270 San Diego (92108) ***(P-14865)***
Iqa Solutions Inc...D...562 420-1000
4089 E Conant St Long Beach (90808) ***(P-25752)***
Iqms (PA)...C...805 227-1122
2231 Wisteria Ln Paso Robles (93446) ***(P-15235)***
Iqtalent Partners LLC...D...888 501-4787
171 Main St Ste 284 Los Altos (94022) ***(P-14652)***
Ira Services Inc...C...650 593-2221
1160 Industrial Rd Ste 1 San Carlos (94070) ***(P-12098)***
Irby Construction Company...D...760 344-4478
100 W Keystone Rd Brawley (92227) ***(P-1931)***
IRC Technologies Inc (PA)...D...949 476-8626
2901 Pullman St Santa Ana (92705) ***(P-3167)***
Irdeto Usa Inc (HQ)...D...760 268-7299
3255 Scott Blvd Ste 3-101 Santa Clara (95054) ***(P-15236)***
Irell & Manella LLP (PA)...B...310 277-1010
1800 Avenue Of The Stars # 900 Los Angeles (90067) ***(P-23142)***
Irell & Manella LLP...D...949 760-0991
840 Nwport Ctr Dr Ste 400 Newport Beach (92660) ***(P-23143)***
Irell & Manella LLP...B...213 620-1555
1800 Avenue Of The Stars # 900 Los Angeles (90067) ***(P-23144)***
Irene Swindell's Adult Day Car, San Francisco *Also called Institute On Aging (P-23858)*
Irise (PA)...D...800 556-0399
2381 Rosecrans Ave # 100 El Segundo (90245) ***(P-15237)***
Irish Communication Company (HQ)...D...626 288-6170
2649 Stingle Ave Rosemead (91770) ***(P-1932)***
Irish Construction (HQ)...C...626 288-8530
2641 River Ave Rosemead (91770) ***(P-1933)***
Irish Construction...D...408 612-8440
19490 Monterey St Morgan Hill (95037) ***(P-1934)***
Irish Construction...D...619 713-1991
1329 Sweetwater Ln Spring Valley (91977) ***(P-1935)***
Irish Construction...D...209 576-8766
1028 Marchy Ln Ceres (95307) ***(P-1936)***
Iron Law Inc (PA)...D...844 476-6529
663 S Rancho Santa Fe Rd San Marcos (92078) ***(P-23145)***
Iron Mountain Assurance Corp, Milpitas *Also called Iron Mountain Fulfillment (P-14047)*
Iron Mountain Fulfillment (HQ)...E...408 945-1600
565 Sinclair Frontage Rd Milpitas (95035) ***(P-14047)***
Iron Mountain Incorporated...D...510 798-6387
30481 Whipple Rd Union City (94587) ***(P-16907)***
Iron Mountain Incorporated...D...661 775-9008
28751 Witherspoon Pkwy Valencia (91355) ***(P-4677)***
Iron Mountain Incorporated...D...562 345-6900
P.O. Box 7877 Newport Beach (92658) ***(P-4678)***
Iron Mountain Info MGT LLC...D...714 526-0916
12958 Midway Pl Cerritos (90703) ***(P-4679)***
Iron Workers Local 433...E...909 884-5500
252 Hillcrest Ave San Bernardino (92408) ***(P-12099)***
Ironclad Security Services Inc...D...408 773-2800
3561 Homestead Rd Ste 600 Santa Clara (95051) ***(P-16704)***
Ironworkers Union, Pasadena *Also called Ironwrker Emplyees Beneft Corp (P-12100)*
Ironwrker Emplyees Beneft Corp...D...626 792-7337
131 N El Molino Ave # 330 Pasadena (91101) ***(P-12100)***
Irp Lax Hotel LLC...C...310 645-4600
9750 Airport Blvd Los Angeles (90045) ***(P-12780)***
Irri-Scape Construction Inc...D...951 694-6936
20182 Carancho Rd Temecula (92590) ***(P-862)***
Irvine APT Communities LP (HQ)...C...949 720-5600
110 Innovation Dr Irvine (92617) ***(P-11035)***
Irvine Company LLC...D...949 653-5300
1 Golf Club Dr Irvine (92618) ***(P-25434)***
Irvine Company Office Property, Newport Beach *Also called Irvine Eastgate Office II LLC (P-12167)*
Irvine Eastgate Office II LLC...A...949 720-2000
550 Newport Center Dr Newport Beach (92660) ***(P-12167)***
Irvine Medical Center, Orange *Also called University California Irvine (P-21887)*
Irvine Police Department, Irvine *Also called City of Irvine (P-25010)*
Irvine Ranch Water District (PA)...C...949 453-5300
15600 Sand Canyon Ave Irvine (92618) ***(P-6266)***
Irvine Ranch Water District...C...949 453-5300
3512 Michelson Dr Irvine (92612) ***(P-6267)***
Irvine Regional Hospital, Anaheim *Also called Tenet Healthsystem Medical (P-21855)*
Irvine Technology Corporation...C...714 445-2624
17900 Von Karman Ave # 100 Irvine (92614) ***(P-14653)***
Irvine Unified School Distict...D...949 936-5300
100 Nightmist Irvine (92618) ***(P-3938)***
Irvine Valencia Growers...D...949 936-8000
11501 Jeffrey Rd Irvine (92602) ***(P-237)***
Irwin Naturals...D...310 306-3636
5310 Beethoven St Los Angeles (90066) ***(P-8179)***
Irwindale 6000, Irwindale *Also called Southern California Edison Co (P-6127)*
ISA, Van Nuys *Also called Interviewing Service Amer LLC (P-26531)*
Isaac Fair Corporation...D...858 369-8000
3661 Valley Centre Dr San Diego (92130) ***(P-15238)***
Isabel Garreton Inc (PA)...C...310 833-7768
770 Miraflores San Pedro (90731) ***(P-8308)***
Iscs Inc...C...408 362-3000
100 Great Oaks Blvd # 100 San Jose (95119) ***(P-15239)***
ISE Labs Inc...E...510 687-2500
46800 Bayside Pkwy Fremont (94538) ***(P-26710)***
ISE Labs Inc (HQ)...C...510 687-2500
46800 Bayside Pkwy Fremont (94538) ***(P-26711)***
Isearch Media LLC...D...415 358-0882
1710 S Amphlett Blvd # 320 San Mateo (94402) ***(P-13850)***
Iserve Residential Lending LLC...D...858 486-4169
16745 W Bernardo Dr # 100 San Diego (92127) ***(P-9819)***
Ishares, San Francisco *Also called Blackrock Instnl Tr Nat Assn (P-12030)*
Isheriff Inc...C...650 412-4300
555 Twin Dolphin Dr Redwood City (94065) ***(P-15240)***
ISI Inspection Services Inc...D...510 986-1157
1798 University Ave Berkeley (94703) ***(P-17253)***
ISI Inspection Services Inc (PA)...D...510 900-2101
1798 University Ave Berkeley (94703) ***(P-17254)***
Islamic Relief USA...D...714 676-1300
6131 Orangethorpe Ave # 450 Buena Park (90620) ***(P-23867)***
Island Hospitality MGT LLC...E...408 720-1000
750 Lakeway Dr Sunnyvale (94085) ***(P-12781)***
Island Hospitality MGT LLC...D...650 574-4700
2000 Winward Way San Mateo (94404) ***(P-12782)***
Island Hospitality MGT LLC...D...408 720-8893
1080 Stewart Dr Sunnyvale (94085) ***(P-12783)***
Island Hospitality MGT LLC...E...909 937-6788
2025 Convention Ctr Way Ontario (91764) ***(P-12784)***
Island Hospitality MGT LLC...D...650 591-8600
400 Concourse Dr Belmont (94002) ***(P-12785)***
Island Pacific Supermarket, City of Industry *Also called Abacus Business Capital Inc (P-8369)*
Islands Restaurant & Lounge, San Diego *Also called Crown Plaza SD (P-12501)*
Isolutecom Inc (PA)...E...805 498-6259
9 Northam Ave Newbury Park (91320) ***(P-15725)***
Isotis Orthobiologics Inc...C...949 595-8710
2 Goodyear Ste A Irvine (92618) ***(P-26387)***
Ispace Inc...C...310 563-3800
2381 Rosecrans Ave # 110 El Segundo (90245) ***(P-16410)***
Israel Discount Bank New York...C...213 861-6440
888 S Figueroa St Ste 550 Los Angeles (90017) ***(P-9464)***
Israel Pops Orchestra...E...818 343-6450
4841 Alonzo Ave Encino (91316) ***(P-18444)***
ISS Facility Services Inc...B...650 593-9774
40563 Encyclopedia Cir Fremont (94538) ***(P-14292)***
Issa, Carpinteria *Also called International Spt Science Assn (P-19189)*
Ists Worldwide Inc...C...510 794-1400
2201 Walnut Ave Ste 210 Fremont (94538) ***(P-16411)***
Isyndicate Inc...D...415 896-1900
455 9th St San Francisco (94103) ***(P-16234)***
Isys Solutions Inc...D...714 521-7656
2601 Saturn St Ste 302 Brea (92821) ***(P-27282)***
It Is Written, Riverside *Also called Adventist Media Center Inc (P-18339)*
Ita Group Inc...C...415 277-3200
455 Market St Ste 1450 San Francisco (94105) ***(P-27283)***
Italent Corporation (PA)...C...408 496-6200
27 Devine St Ste 20 San Jose (95110) ***(P-16412)***
Italent Digital, San Jose *Also called Italent Corporation (P-16412)*
Italfoods Inc...D...650 873-2640
205 Shaw Rd South San Francisco (94080) ***(P-8808)***
Itc Srvice Group Acqsition LLC (PA)...E...877 370-4482
7777 Greenback Ln Ste 201 Citrus Heights (95610) ***(P-27757)***
Itco Solutions Inc...B...650 367-0514
1003 Whitehall Ln Redwood City (94061) ***(P-16413)***
Itd Print Solutions, Los Angeles *Also called Imaging Technologies Group LLC (P-8082)*
Itek Services Inc...D...949 770-4835
25501 Arctic Ocean Dr Lake Forest (92630) ***(P-16414)***
Itera Software, Irvine *Also called Vision Solutions Inc (P-16528)*
Ito Farms, Westminster *Also called B & E Farms Inc (P-91)*
Itrenew Inc (HQ)...E...408 744-9600
8356 Central Ave Newark (94560) ***(P-16415)***
Itron Inc...A...510 844-2800
1111 Broadway Ste 1800 Oakland (94607) ***(P-2615)***

Employee Codes: A=Over 500 employees, B=251-500
C=101-250, D=51-100, E=50
2019 Directory of California
Wholesalers and Services Companies
© Mergent Inc. 1-800-342-5647
1343

ALPHABETIC

Itron Networked Solutions Inc (HQ).....B.....669 770-4000
230 W Tasman Dr San Jose (95134) *(P-5985)*
Its Technologies Logistics LLC.....D.....209 460-6023
6540 Austin Rd Stockton (95215) *(P-5231)*
Iunlimited Incorporated.....C.....916 218-6198
7801 Folsom Blvd Ste 203 Sacramento (95826) *(P-16705)*
Iuoe Local 39, Sacramento *Also called Iuoe Sttonary Engineers Lcl 39 (P-25067)*
Iuoe Sttonary Engineers Lcl 39.....E.....916 928-0399
1620 N Market Blvd Sacramento (95834) *(P-25067)*
IVBCF, Temecula *Also called Inland Valley Business and Com (P-25433)*
Ivie McNeill Wyatt A Prof Law.....E.....213 489-0028
444 S Flower St Ste 1800 Los Angeles (90071) *(P-23146)*
Ivo Wall Experts Inc.....D.....323 246-4026
5359 Sheila St Commerce (90040) *(P-2899)*
Ivy Insurance Group Inc (PA).....D.....626 566-2116
411 E Huntington Dr # 203 Arcadia (91006) *(P-10364)*
Ivy Realty.....E.....213 386-8888
611 S Wilton Pl Los Angeles (90005) *(P-11524)*
Iw Golf Club, Inc, Indian Wells *Also called Indian Wells Country Club Inc (P-18937)*
Iw Group (PA).....D.....310 289-5500
6300 Wilshire Blvd # 2150 Los Angeles (90048) *(P-13851)*
Iworks Us Inc.....D.....323 278-8363
2501 S Malt Ave Commerce (90040) *(P-3378)*
Ixia, Santa Clara *Also called Net Optics Inc (P-15774)*
Ixos Software Inc (PA).....D.....949 784-8000
8717 Research Dr Irvine (92618) *(P-7065)*
Ixsystems Inc (PA).....D.....408 943-4100
2490 Kruse Dr San Jose (95131) *(P-15726)*
Izmocars, San Francisco *Also called Homestar Systems Inc (P-16390)*
Izt Mortgage Inc (PA).....E.....925 946-1858
3011 Citrus Cir Ste 202 Walnut Creek (94598) *(P-9888)*
J & D Meat Company.....C.....559 445-1123
4671 E Edgar Ave Fresno (93725) *(P-8809)*
J & E Private Security Corp.....D.....909 594-1111
3227 Producer Way Ste 110 Pomona (91768) *(P-16706)*
J & J Acoustics Inc.....C.....408 275-9255
2260 De La Cruz Blvd Santa Clara (95050) *(P-2900)*
J & J Air Conditioning Inc.....D.....408 920-0662
1086 N 11th St San Jose (95112) *(P-2238)*
J & J Farms.....E.....559 659-1457
36245 W Ashlan Ave Firebaugh (93622) *(P-355)*
J & J Productions Incorporated.....E.....714 535-0951
1775 E Lincoln Ave # 205 Anaheim (92805) *(P-17255)*
J & L Collections Services Inc.....D.....800 481-6006
651 N Cherokee Ln Ste B2 Lodi (95240) *(P-14009)*
J & M Inc.....E.....925 724-0300
6700 National Dr Livermore (94550) *(P-1937)*
J & O'S Commercial Tire Center, Richmond *Also called Rubber Dust Inc (P-17750)*
J & P Financial Inc (PA).....E.....760 738-9000
330 W Felicita Ave Ste E1 Escondido (92025) *(P-9889)*
J & P Solari.....D.....209 931-1765
6302 Foppiano Ln Stockton (95212) *(P-220)*
J & R Debenedetto Orchards Inc.....D.....559 665-1712
26393 Road 22 1/2 Chowchilla (93610) *(P-695)*
J & S Farm.....D.....559 308-0294
803 W Kimball Ave Visalia (93277) *(P-356)*
J A Contracting Inc.....B.....559 733-4865
2209 W Tulare Ave Visalia (93277) *(P-653)*
J Alexander Investments Inc (PA).....D.....213 687-8400
922 S Barrington Ave A Los Angeles (90049) *(P-12064)*
J and J Wall Baking Co Inc.....D.....916 381-1410
8806 Fruitridge Rd Sacramento (95826) *(P-8492)*
J B A, Pasadena *Also called B Jacqueline and Assoc Inc (P-15015)*
J B Bostick Company Inc (PA).....D.....714 238-2121
2870 E La Cresta Ave Anaheim (92806) *(P-1793)*
J B Company.....D.....916 929-3003
1825 Bell St Ste 100 Sacramento (95825) *(P-1558)*
J B Hunt Transport Inc.....C.....909 466-5361
11559 Jersey Blvd Rancho Cucamonga (91730) *(P-4197)*
J B Hunt Transport Svcs Inc.....B.....619 230-0054
1620 5th Ave San Diego (92101) *(P-5232)*
J B J Distributing, Fullerton *Also called Veg-Land Inc (P-4491)*
J B Laquindanum & Associates.....E.....707 648-0501
2608 Springs Rd Vallejo (94591) *(P-13710)*
J Baron Inc.....D.....949 451-1200
5299 Alton Pkwy Irvine (92604) *(P-11525)*
J Brand Holdings LLC.....D.....212 228-8181
1318 E 7th St Ste 260 Los Angeles (90021) *(P-11988)*
J C C, San Rafael *Also called Bernard Osher Marin Jewish Com (P-23510)*
J C Entertainment Ltg Svcs Inc.....D.....818 252-7481
5435 W San Fernando Rd Los Angeles (90039) *(P-18375)*
J C French & Company.....D.....909 596-1423
2984 1st St Ste L La Verne (91750) *(P-2447)*
J C Sales, Vernon *Also called Shims Bargain Inc (P-9258)*
J C Towing Inc.....D.....619 429-1492
2501 Faivre St Chula Vista (91911) *(P-17864)*
J Craig Venter Institute Inc (PA).....B.....301 795-7000
4120 Capricorn Ln La Jolla (92037) *(P-26627)*
J Crecelius Inc.....D.....209 883-4826
5043 N Montpelier Rd Denair (95316) *(P-357)*
J D L Motor Express.....D.....619 232-6136
1250 Delevan Dr San Diego (92102) *(P-4025)*
J D Rush Company Inc (HQ).....C.....661 392-1900
5900 E Lerdo Hwy Shafter (93263) *(P-12101)*
J G Boswell Company.....D.....559 992-2141
710 Bainum Ave Corcoran (93212) *(P-531)*
J G Boswell Company.....C.....661 327-7721
21101 Bear Mountain Blvd Bakersfield (93311) *(P-13)*
J G Boswell Company.....B.....559 992-5141
28001 S Dairy Ave Corcoran (93212) *(P-14)*
J G Construction, Chino *Also called June A Grothe Construction Inc (P-1569)*
J G Golfing Enterprises Inc.....E.....909 885-2414
1494 S Waterman Ave San Bernardino (92408) *(P-18723)*
J Gelt Corporation.....E.....619 424-8181
1424 30th St Ste C San Diego (92154) *(P-23868)*
J Ginger Masonry LP (PA).....B.....951 688-5050
8188 Lincoln Ave Ste 100 Riverside (92504) *(P-2812)*
J H Maddocks Photography.....D.....818 842-7150
40 E Verdugo Ave Burbank (91502) *(P-16961)*
J H Meek & Sons Inc.....E.....530 662-1106
22075 County Road 99 Woodland (95695) *(P-358)*
J H Synder Co LLC.....D.....323 857-5546
5757 Wilshire Blvd Ph 30 Los Angeles (90036) *(P-11526)*
J Harris Sim Inc (PA).....D.....858 437-0190
9685 Via Excelencia # 200 San Diego (92126) *(P-1794)*
J I Miller, Granada Hills *Also called James I Miller (P-603)*
J I T Supply, Norco *Also called JIT Corporation (P-7495)*
J I T Transportation, Milpitas *Also called Dga Services Inc (P-4343)*
J L S Concrete Pumping Inc.....D.....805 643-0766
2055 N Ventura Ave Ventura (93001) *(P-3270)*
J M A, San Mateo *Also called Judy Madrigal & Associates Inc (P-19522)*
J M C International LLC.....E.....559 256-1300
1470 W Herndon Ave # 100 Fresno (93711) *(P-1559)*
J M Carden Sprinkler Co Inc.....D.....323 258-8300
2909 Fletcher Dr Los Angeles (90065) *(P-2239)*
J M Electric, Salinas *Also called Jensco Inc (P-2618)*
J M Equipment Company Inc (PA).....D.....209 522-3271
321 Spreckels Ave Manteca (95336) *(P-14517)*
J M Equipment Company Inc.....E.....559 233-0187
3751 E Calwa Ave Fresno (93725) *(P-7683)*
J M K C Express, Carson *Also called Harry Group Inc (P-5083)*
J M K Investments Inc (PA).....D.....408 249-2500
100 Saratoga Ave Ste 300 Santa Clara (95051) *(P-11527)*
J M V B Inc.....D.....714 288-9797
12118 Severn Way Riverside (92503) *(P-2448)*
J Marchini & Son Inc.....D.....559 665-2944
12000 Le Grand Rd Le Grand (95333) *(P-359)*
J Marchini & Son Inc.....D.....559 665-9710
8736 Minturn Rd Le Grand (95333) *(P-62)*
J P Carroll Co Inc.....D.....323 660-9230
5707 Milton Ave Whittier (90601) *(P-2449)*
J P Consulting.....E.....707 747-4800
4690 E 2nd St Ste 3 Benicia (94510) *(P-27284)*
J P H Consulting Inc (PA).....E.....323 934-5660
1101 Crenshaw Blvd Los Angeles (90019) *(P-20547)*
J P H Consulting Inc.....C.....323 934-5660
4515 Huntington Dr S Los Angeles (90032) *(P-20548)*
J P Original Corp (PA).....D.....626 839-4300
19101 E Walnut Dr N City of Industry (91748) *(P-8359)*
J P Witherow Roofing Company.....D.....619 297-4701
1083 N Cuyamaca St El Cajon (92020) *(P-3168)*
J Paul Getty Trust.....D.....310 440-7325
1200 Getty Center Dr # 400 Los Angeles (90049) *(P-26534)*
J Perez Associates Inc (PA).....D.....562 801-5397
10833 Valley View St # 200 Cypress (90630) *(P-3535)*
J R Industries, Westlake Village *Also called Jri Inc (P-7497)*
J R Pierce Plumbing Company.....D.....510 483-5473
14481 Wicks Blvd San Leandro (94577) *(P-2240)*
J R Roberts Corp (HQ).....D.....916 729-5600
7745 Greenback Ln Ste 300 Citrus Heights (95610) *(P-1560)*
J R Roberts Enterprises Inc.....C.....916 729-5600
7745 Greenback Ln Ste 300 Citrus Heights (95610) *(P-1561)*
J Redfern Inc.....C.....925 371-3300
164 N L St Livermore (94550) *(P-863)*
J Rivera Associates Inc.....D.....415 617-5660
139 S Guild Ave Lodi (95240) *(P-27935)*
J Robert Echter.....E.....760 436-0188
1150 Quail Gardens Dr Encinitas (92024) *(P-270)*
J Robert Scott Inc (PA).....C.....310 659-4910
500 N Oak St Inglewood (90302) *(P-8228)*
J T R Company Inc (PA).....D.....408 975-7733
1102 S 3rd St San Jose (95112) *(P-8180)*
J T R Company Inc.....E.....408 293-3272
1102 S 3rd St San Jose (95112) *(P-4579)*
J Vineyards & Winery, Healdsburg *Also called E & J Gallo Winery (P-142)*
J Vitale Landscape & Maint.....D.....619 938-2435
8801 Cottonwood Ave Santee (92071) *(P-864)*
J W Floor Covering Inc (PA).....C.....858 536-8565
9881 Carroll Centre Rd San Diego (92126) *(P-3111)*
J Walter Thompson USA LLC.....D.....415 268-5555
303 2nd St San Francisco (94107) *(P-13852)*
J Waters Inc.....E.....831 424-1946
75 San Miguel Ave Ste 5 Salinas (93901) *(P-16707)*
J&L Teamworks, Lodi *Also called J & L Collections Services Inc (P-14009)*
J&M Keystone Inc.....D.....619 466-9876
2709 Via Orange Way Ste A Spring Valley (91978) *(P-13579)*
J&R Fleet Services LLC.....D.....909 820-7000
210 Saint Katherine Dr La Canada Flintridge (91011) *(P-17768)*
J. Perez & Associates, Cypress *Also called J Perez Associates Inc (P-3535)*
J2 Cloud Services LLC (HQ).....D.....323 860-9200
6922 Hollywood Blvd # 500 Los Angeles (90028) *(P-5684)*
J2 Cloud Services, Inc., Los Angeles *Also called J2 Cloud Services LLC (P-5684)*
J2 Global Inc (PA).....C.....323 860-9200
6922 Hollywood Blvd # 500 Los Angeles (90028) *(P-5685)*
J5 Infrastructure Partners LLC.....D.....949 299-5258
2030 Main St Ste 200 Irvine (92614) *(P-5410)*

Mergent e-mail: customerrelations@mergent.com
1344
2019 Directory of California
Wholesalers and Services Companies
(P-0000) Products & Services Section entry number
(PA)=Parent Co (HQ)=Headquarters (DH)=Div Headquarters

J5th LLC ......D......619 487-1200
356 6th Ave San Diego (92101) *(P-12786)*

Ja Automation & Control LLC ......E......619 661-2591
6965 Cmino Mqladora Ste H San Diego (92154) *(P-7759)*

Jabez Building Services Inc ......D......714 776-7705
2094 Orange Ave Costa Mesa (92627) *(P-14293)*

Jabil Silver Creek Inc (HQ) ......C......669 255-2900
5981 Optical Ct San Jose (95138) *(P-17924)*

Jack Engle & Co (PA) ......D......323 589-8111
8440 S Alameda St Los Angeles (90001) *(P-7981)*

Jack H Caldwell & Sons Inc ......D......323 589-4008
4035 E 52nd St Maywood (90270) *(P-8697)*

Jack Jones Trucking Inc ......D......909 456-2500
1090 E Belmont St Ontario (91761) *(P-4026)*

Jack Kramer Club ......E......310 326-4404
11 Montecillo Dr Rlling HLS Est (90274) *(P-18940)*

Jack Morton Worldwide Inc ......D......310 967-2400
1840 Century Park E # 1800 Los Angeles (90067) *(P-13853)*

Jack Nadel Inc (PA) ......D......310 815-2600
8701 Bellanca Ave Los Angeles (90045) *(P-27285)*

Jack Nadel International, Los Angeles *Also called Jack Nadel Inc (P-27285)*

Jack Neal & Son Inc ......C......707 963-7303
360 Lafata St Saint Helena (94574) *(P-148)*

Jack P Selman ......D......714 639-9860
144 N Orange St Orange (92866) *(P-26070)*

Jack Parker Corp ......C......760 770-5000
4200 E Palm Canyon Dr Palm Springs (92264) *(P-12787)*

Jack Rubin & Sons Inc (PA) ......E......310 635-5407
13103 S Alameda St Compton (90222) *(P-7282)*

Jackie Hoofring ......E......818 961-7272
3390 Auto Mall Dr Westlake Village (91362) *(P-14654)*

Jackovics Enterprises Inc (PA) ......C......415 348-6377
150 Nellen Ave Ste 250 Corte Madera (94925) *(P-18614)*

Jackoway Tyreman Wertheimer Au ......D......310 553-0305
1925 Century Park E Fl 2 Los Angeles (90067) *(P-23147)*

Jacks Car Wash 3 ......D......559 438-8201
6745 N West Ave Fresno (93711) *(P-17819)*

Jackson Demarco Tidus Peter (PA) ......D......949 752-8585
2030 Main St Ste 1200 Irvine (92614) *(P-23148)*

Jackson & Blanc ......C......858 831-7900
7929 Arjons Dr San Diego (92126) *(P-2241)*

Jackson Construction (PA) ......E......916 381-8113
155 Cadillac Dr Sacramento (95825) *(P-1409)*

Jackson Family Wines Inc ......C......415 819-0301
1190 Kittyhawk Blvd Ste A Santa Rosa (95403) *(P-9050)*

Jackson National Life Insur Co ......D......310 899-7900
401 Wilshire Blvd # 1200 Santa Monica (90401) *(P-10137)*

Jackson Shrub Supply Inc ......D......818 982-0100
11505 Vanowen St North Hollywood (91605) *(P-18198)*

Jackson Tull Chrtred Engineers ......E......310 658-2132
550 Continental Blvd # 195 El Segundo (90245) *(P-15986)*

Jacksons Hardware Inc ......D......415 870-4083
435 Du Bois St San Rafael (94901) *(P-7592)*

Jacmar Companies, The, Alhambra *Also called Pacific Ventures Ltd (P-26974)*

Jacmar Ddc LLC ......D......916 372-9795
3057 Promenade St West Sacramento (95691) *(P-8810)*

Jacmar Food Service Dist, West Sacramento *Also called Jacmar Ddc LLC (P-8810)*

Jacob Health Care Center, San Diego *Also called Premier Management Company (P-22397)*

Jacob Stern & Sons Inc (PA) ......D......805 565-4532
1464 E Valley Rd Santa Barbara (93108) *(P-8929)*

Jacobs Atcs Fema A Joint Ventr ......D......571 218-1115
155 N Lake Ave Fl 5 Pasadena (91101) *(P-25753)*

Jacobs Civil Inc. ......D......310 847-2500
1500 Hughes Way Ste B400 Long Beach (90810) *(P-25754)*

Jacobs Consultancy Inc. ......D......650 579-7722
555 Airport Blvd Ste 300 Burlingame (94010) *(P-27758)*

Jacobs Cshman San Diego Fd Bnk ......E......858 527-1419
9850 Distribution Ave San Diego (92121) *(P-23869)*

Jacobs Engineering Company ......A......626 449-2171
1111 S Arroyo Pkwy Pasadena (91105) *(P-25755)*

Jacobs Engineering Group Inc ......D......925 423-7564
4435 First St Livermore (94551) *(P-1562)*

Jacobs Engineering Group Inc ......D......949 224-7585
2600 Michelson Dr Ste 500 Irvine (92612) *(P-25756)*

Jacobs Engineering Group Inc ......D......661 275-5685
37528 Morning Cir Palmdale (93550) *(P-25757)*

Jacobs Engineering Group Inc ......D......925 356-3900
2300 Clayton Rd Concord (94520) *(P-25758)*

Jacobs Engineering Group Inc ......D......310 847-2500
1500 Hughes Way Ste B400 Long Beach (90810) *(P-25759)*

Jacobs Engineering Group Inc ......D......909 974-2700
3257 E Guasti Rd Ste 130 Ontario (91761) *(P-25760)*

Jacobs Engineering Group Inc ......D......408 995-3257
95 S Market St Ste 300 San Jose (95113) *(P-25761)*

Jacobs Engineering Group Inc ......C......213 362-4336
1000 Wilshire Blvd # 2100 Los Angeles (90017) *(P-25762)*

Jacobs Engineering Group Inc ......D......626 578-3500
1111 S Arroyo Pkwy Pasadena (91105) *(P-2039)*

Jacobs Engineering Inc (HQ) ......D......626 578-3500
155 N Lake Ave Pasadena (91101) *(P-25763)*

Jacobs Farm/Del Cabo Inc ......D......650 827-1133
390 Swift Ave Ste 8 South San Francisco (94080) *(P-360)*

Jacobs Farm/Del Cabo Inc ......C......831 460-3500
144 Holm Rd Spc 42 Watsonville (95076) *(P-4027)*

Jacobs Field Svcs N Amer Inc ......C......949 224-7585
2600 Michelson Dr Ste 500 Irvine (92612) *(P-2040)*

Jacobs International Ltd Inc ......B......626 578-3500
155 N Lake Ave Pasadena (91101) *(P-25764)*

Jacobs Project Management Co ......D......949 224-7695
2600 Michelson Dr Ste 500 Irvine (92612) *(P-25765)*

Jacobs Project Management Co ......D......510 457-2436
300 Frank H Ogawa Plz Oakland (94612) *(P-27286)*

Jacobs Technology Inc ......D......760 446-7084
1550 N Norma St Ridgecrest (93555) *(P-25766)*

Jacobs Technology Inc ......E......650 604-5946
M S 213 15 Mountain View (94035) *(P-25767)*

Jacobs Technology Inc ......C......760 446-1549
1550 N Norma St Ridgecrest (93555) *(P-25768)*

Jacobs Tree Specialist Inc ......C......559 639-7138
2209 W Tulare Ave Visalia (93277) *(P-654)*

Jacobsson Engrg Cnstr Inc ......D......760 345-8700
72310 Varner Rd Thousand Palms (92276) *(P-1795)*

Jacobus Consulting Inc ......E......949 727-0720
15375 Barranca Pkwy B202 Irvine (92618) *(P-27287)*

Jade Inc ......D......818 365-7137
11126 Sepulveda Blvd B Mission Hills (91345) *(P-2901)*

Jag Framing Inc ......E......818 822-7110
16741 Los Alimos St Granada Hills (91344) *(P-3044)*

Jag Professional Services Inc ......D......310 945-5648
2008 Walnut Ave Manhattan Beach (90266) *(P-27759)*

Jag Software Inc ......D......408 262-0572
2235 Skyline Dr Milpitas (95035) *(P-7066)*

Jagpreet Enterprises Inc ......C......510 336-8376
25823 Clawiter Rd Hayward (94545) *(P-8811)*

Jaguar Computer Systems Inc ......E......951 273-7950
4135 Indus Way Riverside (92503) *(P-7067)*

Jake Hey Incorporated ......C......323 856-5280
257 S Lake St Burbank (91502) *(P-16962)*

Jakes Crawfish & Seafood, Sacramento *Also called Pacific Sea Food Co Inc (P-8592)*

Jakks Sales Corporation ......E......424 268-9444
2951 28th St Ste 51 Santa Monica (90405) *(P-7953)*

Jakov P Dulcich & Sons ......C......661 792-6360
31956 Peterson Rd Mc Farland (93250) *(P-149)*

Jal Berry Farms LLC ......D......831 763-7200
1767 San Juan Rd Aromas (95004) *(P-102)*

Jalmar Properties Inc (PA) ......E......310 207-8481
12121 Wilshire Blvd # 1120 Los Angeles (90025) *(P-11528)*

Jalux Americas Inc (HQ) ......A......310 524-1000
390 N Pacific Coast Hwy # 2000 El Segundo (90245) *(P-14518)*

JAM Industries Inc ......D......310 254-0300
2101 E Via Arado Compton (90220) *(P-4580)*

Jam Warehouse, Compton *Also called JAM Industries Inc (P-4580)*

Jamboor Medical Corporation ......D......760 241-8063
12675 Hesperia Rd Victorville (92395) *(P-22480)*

Jamboree Management, Laguna Hills *Also called Jamboree Realty Corp (P-11529)*

Jamboree Realty Corp (PA) ......C......949 380-0300
22982 Mill Creek Dr Laguna Hills (92653) *(P-11529)*

Jamcracker Inc. ......E......408 496-5500
4677 Old Ironsides Dr # 450 Santa Clara (95054) *(P-5590)*

James A Kiley MD, Folsom *Also called Dignity Health (P-19443)*

James B Branch Inc (PA) ......E......818 765-3521
4367 Clybourn Ave Toluca Lake (91602) *(P-4352)*

James C Jenkins Insur Svc Inc ......C......925 798-3334
1390 Willow Pass Rd Concord (94520) *(P-10658)*

James D Tate MD ......D......530 225-8710
2888 Eureka Way Ste 200 Redding (96001) *(P-19516)*

James E Roberts-Obayashi Corp ......C......925 820-0600
20 Oak Ct Danville (94526) *(P-1291)*

James Fedor Masonry Inc ......D......760 772-3036
54859 Bodine Dr Thermal (92274) *(P-2813)*

James G Parker Insurance Assoc (PA) ......D......559 222-7722
1753 E Fir Ave Fresno (93720) *(P-10659)*

James H Cowan & Associates Inc ......D......310 457-2574
5126 Clareton Dr Ste 200 Agoura Hills (91301) *(P-865)*

James Hardie Building Pdts Inc (HQ) ......C......949 348-1800
26300 La Alameda Ste 400 Mission Viejo (92691) *(P-6835)*

James Hardie Building Pdts Inc ......C......909 355-6500
10901 Elm Ave Fontana (92337) *(P-6836)*

James I Miller ......E......818 363-7444
17659 Chatsworth St Granada Hills (91344) *(P-603)*

James J Stevinson A Corp (PA) ......E......209 632-1681
25079 River Rd Stevinson (95374) *(P-418)*

James McCutcheon ......E......661 867-1810
17521 Walker Basin Rd Caliente (93518) *(P-1292)*

James McMinn Inc ......E......909 514-1231
21801 Barton Rd Ste B Grand Terrace (92313) *(P-1796)*

James Metals, Riverside *Also called Harbor Pipe and Steel Inc (P-7278)*

James R Glidewell Dental ......A......800 411-9723
2181 Dupont Dr Irvine (92612) *(P-22169)*

James R Glidewell Dental (PA) ......A......949 440-2600
4141 Macarthur Blvd Newport Beach (92660) *(P-22170)*

James-Timec International ......E......707 642-2222
155 Corporate Pl Vallejo (94590) *(P-2041)*

Jameshardie, Mission Viejo *Also called James Hardie Building Pdts Inc (P-6835)*

Jameson Properties Co Inc ......E......213 487-3770
3530 Wilshire Blvd # 600 Los Angeles (90010) *(P-10902)*

Jamison Childrens Home ......D......661 334-3500
1010 Shalimar Dr Bakersfield (93306) *(P-23870)*

Jamm Management LLC ......E......510 437-5200
2447 Stanford Way Antioch (94531) *(P-6649)*

Jan, North Hollywood *Also called Japanese Assistance Netwrk Inc (P-17256)*

Jan Marini Skin Research Inc ......D......408 620-3600
5883 Rue Ferrari Ste 175 San Jose (95138) *(P-8181)*

Jan Pro Clg Systems Sthern Cal ......E......714 220-0500
2401 E Katella Ave # 525 Anaheim (92806) *(P-14294)*

Jane McClurg ......D......559 834-3080
4584 E Floral Ave Selma (93662) *(P-150)*

Janet Hilton ......D......310 851-7200
990 W 190th St Ste 300 Torrance (90502) *(P-10660)*

Employee Codes: A=Over 500 employees, B=251-500
C=101-250, D=51-100, E=50

2019 Directory of California
Wholesalers and Services Companies

© Mergent Inc. 1-800-342-5647

1345

Janet K Hartzler MD ....D....760 340-3937
72057 Dinah Shore Dr D Rancho Mirage (92270) ***(P-19517)***
Janico Building Maintenance ....B....714 444-4339
3001 Red Hill Ave 2-221 Costa Mesa (92626) ***(P-14295)***
Janitorial, Santa Barbara *Also called Master Clean USA Inc* ***(P-14314)***
Janitorial Equipment Svcs Inc ....D....951 205-8937
11752 Garden Grove Blvd # 100 Garden Grove (92843) ***(P-14296)***
Janssen Alzheimer Immunothera ....D....650 794-2500
700 Gateway Blvd South San Francisco (94080) ***(P-26388)***
Janus Corporation (PA) ....D....925 969-9200
1081 Shary Cir Concord (94518) ***(P-3536)***
Janus Corporation ....E....951 479-0700
2025 Tandem Norco (92860) ***(P-3537)***
Janus Et Cie (PA) ....C....310 601-2908
12310 Greenstone Ave Santa Fe Springs (90670) ***(P-6729)***
Janus of Santa Cruz ....D....831 462-1060
200 7th Ave Ste 150 Santa Cruz (95062) ***(P-23871)***
Japan Airlines Co Ltd ....D....310 607-2305
300 Continental Blvd # 620 El Segundo (90245) ***(P-4941)***
Japanese Assistance Netwrk Inc ....B....818 505-6080
11135 Magnolia Blvd # 140 North Hollywood (91601) ***(P-17256)***
Japanese Cmnty Youth Council (PA) ....D....415 202-7905
2012 Pine St San Francisco (94115) ***(P-24792)***
Japanese Retirement Home, Los Angeles *Also called Senior Keiro Health Care* ***(P-24670)***
Jaqui Foundation Inc ....E....510 562-4721
675 Hegenberger Rd # 209 Oakland (94621) ***(P-27936)***
Jarka Enterprises Inc ....D....916 491-6180
1059 Vine St Ste 108 Sacramento (95811) ***(P-3538)***
Jaroth Inc ....C....925 553-3650
2001 Crow Canyon Rd # 200 San Ramon (94583) ***(P-2616)***
Jarrow Formulas Inc (PA) ....D....310 204-6936
1824 S Robertson Blvd Los Angeles (90035) ***(P-8182)***
JAS Pacific ....C....909 605-7777
201 N Euclid Ave Ste A Upland (91786) ***(P-25769)***
Jason Proctor Trnsp Co ....E....559 992-1767
2375 Dairy Ave Corcoran (93212) ***(P-3810)***
Javelin Logistics Company Inc ....C....800 577-1060
7447 Morton Ave Ste A Newark (94560) ***(P-4581)***
Javelin Logistics Corporation (PA) ....E....510 795-7287
7447 Morton Ave Ste A Newark (94560) ***(P-4353)***
Jay Fisher Farms Inc ....E....805 735-1598
2251 W Central Ave Lompoc (93436) ***(P-63)***
Jay's Catering, Garden Grove *Also called Mastroianni Family Entps Ltd* ***(P-13757)***
Jayasinghe Medical Group Inc (PA) ....D....562 267-7000
200 S Beach Blvd Ste A2 La Habra (90631) ***(P-19518)***
Jaylaneentertainment Corp ....D....707 820-2773
585 Fernando Dr Novato (94945) ***(P-13947)***
Jaynes Corporation California ....C....619 233-4080
111 Elm St Fl 4 San Diego (92101) ***(P-1563)***
Jazzercise Inc (PA) ....D....760 476-1750
2460 Impala Dr Carlsbad (92010) ***(P-18615)***
JB Dental Supply Co Inc (PA) ....C....310 202-8855
17000 Kingsview Ave Carson (90746) ***(P-7185)***
JB Finish Inc ....D....760 342-6300
82750 Atlantic St Indio (92203) ***(P-3045)***
JB Partners Group Inc ....C....818 668-8201
18375 Ventura Blvd Tarzana (91356) ***(P-11530)***
JB Upland Ltd Liability Co ....E....909 944-5456
9087 Arrow Rte Ste 140 Rancho Cucamonga (91730) ***(P-27288)***
Jbhunt Transport, San Diego *Also called J B Hunt Transport Svcs Inc* ***(P-5232)***
Jbs International Inc ....D....650 373-4900
555 Airport Blvd Ste 400 Burlingame (94010) ***(P-26628)***
Jbsprotection, Fontana *Also called Jones Bold Security Inc* ***(P-16708)***
JC Foodservice Inc (PA) ....D....626 299-3800
415 S Atlantic Blvd Monterey Park (91754) ***(P-7138)***
JC Party Rentals Inc ....D....818 765-4819
11562 Vanowen St North Hollywood (91605) ***(P-14519)***
JC Penney, Buena Park *Also called JC Penney Corporation Inc* ***(P-4582)***
JC Penney Corporation Inc ....C....714 523-6558
6800 Valley View St Buena Park (90620) ***(P-4582)***
JC Resorts Inn ....D....858 487-0700
17550 Bernardo Oaks Dr San Diego (92128) ***(P-12788)***
JC Resorts LLC ....B....949 376-2779
1555 S Coast Hwy Laguna Beach (92651) ***(P-26903)***
JC Resorts LLC ....D....760 944-1936
1275 Quail Gardens Dr Encinitas (92024) ***(P-26904)***
JC Sales, Commerce *Also called Shims Bargain Inc* ***(P-1433)***
Jck Hotels LLC ....D....858 635-5566
9888 Mira Mesa Blvd San Diego (92131) ***(P-12789)***
Jct Company LLC ....E....949 589-2021
29736 Avenida&Bandera Rancho Santa Margari (92688) ***(P-2242)***
Jcv Inc ....E....714 871-2007
1118 W Orangethorpe Ave Fullerton (92833) ***(P-2902)***
JD Food, Fresno *Also called J & D Meat Company* ***(P-8809)***
JD Group, San Diego *Also called Brokerage Lgstics Slutions Inc* ***(P-5021)***
JD Miller Construction Inc ....E....951 471-3513
506 W Graham Ave Ste 202 Lake Elsinore (92530) ***(P-2450)***
JD Power (HQ) ....C....714 621-6200
3200 Park Center Dr Fl 13 Costa Mesa (92626) ***(P-26535)***
JD Power ....B....805 418-8000
30870 Russell Ranch Rd Westlake Village (91362) ***(P-26536)***
JD Wesson & Associates Inc ....D....707 255-8667
3212 Jefferson St Ste 206 NAPA (94558) ***(P-17257)***
Jdf Construction Inc ....E....714 526-1120
201 Gemini Ave Brea (92821) ***(P-1180)***
JE Williams Trucking Inc ....E....406 248-7397
1875 Century Park E # 600 Los Angeles (90067) ***(P-4198)***
Jean Mart Inc ....D....323 752-7775
6700 Avalon Blvd Los Angeles (90003) ***(P-8309)***

Jeanne Jugan, A Residence, San Pedro *Also called Little Sisters The Poor of La* ***(P-20594)***
Jeep Gear, Irvine *Also called Alcone Marketing Group Inc* ***(P-13791)***
Jeeva Corp ....E....909 238-4073
750 E E St Unit B Ontario (91764) ***(P-2617)***
Jeff Carpenter Inc ....D....951 657-5115
1380 W Oleander Ave Perris (92571) ***(P-3431)***
Jeff Kerber Pool Plst Inc ....B....909 465-0677
166 San Lorenzo St Pomona (91766) ***(P-3539)***
Jeff Stover Inc ....D....530 345-9427
260 Cohasset Rd Ste 190 Chico (95926) ***(P-18616)***
Jeff Tracy Inc ....E....949 582-0877
15375 Barranca Pkwy A110 Irvine (92618) ***(P-2243)***
Jeffco Painting & Coating Inc ....D....707 562-1900
1260 Railroad Ave Vallejo (94592) ***(P-2451)***
Jeffer Mngels Btlr Mtchell LLP (PA) ....C....310 203-8080
1900 Avenue Of The Stars Los Angeles (90067) ***(P-23149)***
Jeffer Mngels Btlr Mtchell LLP ....D....415 398-8080
2 Embarcadero Ctr Fl 5 San Francisco (94111) ***(P-23150)***
Jefferies LLC ....D....310 445-1199
11100 Santa Monica Blvd # 12 Los Angeles (90025) ***(P-9966)***
Jefferson California Congress ....D....760 331-5500
6225 El Camino Real Carlsbad (92009) ***(P-25176)***
Jeffrey Pine Holdings LLC ....D....619 442-0544
622 S Anza St El Cajon (92020) ***(P-20549)***
Jeffrey Rome & Associates ....D....949 760-3929
131 Innovation Dr Ste 100 Irvine (92617) ***(P-26071)***
Jeld-Wen Inc ....B....760 597-4201
2760 Progress St Ste B Vista (92081) ***(P-6837)***
Jeld-Wen Windows, Vista *Also called Jeld-Wen Inc* ***(P-6837)***
Jelight Company Inc ....D....949 380-8774
2 Mason Irvine (92618) ***(P-7367)***
Jemtown Inc ....E....916 315-0555
6818 Five Star Blvd Rocklin (95677) ***(P-17820)***
Jenco Productions Inc (PA) ....C....909 381-9453
401 S J St San Bernardino (92410) ***(P-17258)***
Jencor Door and Trim Inc ....E....661 251-8161
26845 Oak Ave Ste 12 Canyon Country (91351) ***(P-3046)***
Jenkins Gales & Martinez Inc ....D....310 645-0561
6033 W Century Blvd # 601 Los Angeles (90045) ***(P-26905)***
Jenkins Poultry Farms, Farmington *Also called Pleasant Valley Farms* ***(P-624)***
Jenny Craig Inc (HQ) ....C....760 696-4000
5770 Fleet St Carlsbad (92008) ***(P-13753)***
Jenny Craig Wght Loss Ctrs Inc (HQ) ....C....760 696-4000
5770 Fleet St Carlsbad (92008) ***(P-13754)***
Jensco Inc ....E....831 422-7819
400 Griffin St Salinas (93901) ***(P-2618)***
Jensen Corp Landscape Contr ....C....408 446-4881
1983 Concourse Dr San Jose (95131) ***(P-866)***
Jensen Corp Landscape Contrs, San Jose *Also called Jensen Landscape Services Inc* ***(P-868)***
Jensen Corporate Holdings Inc (PA) ....C....408 446-1118
1983 Concourse Dr San Jose (95131) ***(P-867)***
Jensen Enterprises Inc ....D....916 992-8301
5400 Raley Blvd Sacramento (95838) ***(P-6933)***
Jensen Landscape Services Inc ....C....408 446-1118
1983 Concourse Dr San Jose (95131) ***(P-868)***
Jensen Precast, Sacramento *Also called Jensen Enterprises Inc* ***(P-6933)***
Jeopardy Productions Inc ....C....310 244-8855
10202 Washington Blvd Culver City (90232) ***(P-18065)***
Jeppesen Dataplan Inc ....C....408 961-2825
225 W Santa Clara St # 1600 San Jose (95113) ***(P-16235)***
Jeremiah Phillips LLC ....C....650 697-7733
863 Malcolm Rd Burlingame (94010) ***(P-4028)***
Jerry Leigh Entertainment AP, Panorama City *Also called Leigh Jerry California Inc* ***(P-8315)***
Jerry Melton & Sons Cnstr, Taft *Also called Jerry Melton & Sons Cnstr* ***(P-1067)***
Jerry Melton & Sons Cnstr ....D....661 765-5546
100 Jamison Ln Taft (93268) ***(P-1067)***
Jerry S Powell MD ....D....916 734-5959
4501 X St Sacramento (95817) ***(P-19519)***
Jerry Thompson & Sons Pntg Inc ....C....415 454-1500
3 Simms St San Rafael (94901) ***(P-2452)***
Jesse Alexander Transport ....D....760 669-0379
9338 Azurite Ave Hesperia (92344) ***(P-5233)***
Jesse Lee Group Inc ....D....510 351-3700
300 Crprate Pinte Ste 550 Culver City (90230) ***(P-26906)***
Jesse Lee Group Inc ....C....209 832-2273
2586 Buthmann Ave Tracy (95376) ***(P-26907)***
Jessica Cosmetics Intl Inc ....D....818 759-1050
13209 Saticoy St North Hollywood (91605) ***(P-8183)***
Jessica's Cosmetics, North Hollywood *Also called Jessica Cosmetics Intl Inc* ***(P-8183)***
Jet Advertising, El Segundo *Also called Your Man Tours Inc* ***(P-4985)***
Jet Airways of India Inc ....D....650 762-2345
111 Anza Blvd Ste 300 Burlingame (94010) ***(P-4785)***
Jet Center Los Angeles, Hawthorne *Also called Advanced Air LLC* ***(P-4855)***
Jet Delivery Inc (PA) ....D....800 716-7177
2169 Wright Ave La Verne (91750) ***(P-4421)***
Jet Edge International LLC ....D....818 442-0096
16700 Roscoe Blvd Hngr C Van Nuys (91406) ***(P-4860)***
Jet Sets, North Hollywood *Also called M Gaw Inc* ***(P-3546)***
Jet Source Inc ....D....760 438-0877
2056 Palomar Airport Rd Carlsbad (92011) ***(P-4896)***
Jetblue Airways Corporation ....D....718 286-7900
2627 N Hollywood Way Burbank (91505) ***(P-4786)***
Jetblue Airways Corporation ....D....510 381-1369
130 Alan Shepard Way M Oakland (94621) ***(P-4787)***
Jetblue Airways Corporation ....D....619 725-0807
3835 N Harbor Dr Ste 108 San Diego (92101) ***(P-4788)***
Jetmore International, South El Monte *Also called Jetworld Inc* ***(P-6600)***

Jetmore Wind LLC.....A.....888 903-6926
15445 Innovation Dr San Diego (92128) ***(P-6045)***
Jetro Cash and Carry Entps LLC.....D.....916 492-2305
1275 Vine St Sacramento (95811) ***(P-8418)***
Jetro Cash and Carry Entps LLC.....C.....714 666-8211
1265 N Kraemer Blvd Anaheim (92806) ***(P-8493)***
Jetro Cash and Carry Entps LLC.....D.....415 920-2888
2045 Evans Ave San Francisco (94124) ***(P-8620)***
Jetro Cash and Carry Entps LLC.....D.....323 964-1200
5333 W Jefferson Blvd Los Angeles (90016) ***(P-9005)***
Jetro Holdings LLC.....C.....858 564-0466
7466 Carroll Rd Ste 100 San Diego (92121) ***(P-7139)***
Jetro Holdings LLC.....C.....213 516-0301
1611 E Washington Blvd Los Angeles (90021) ***(P-7140)***
Jetsuite Inc (PA).....C.....949 892-4300
18952 Macarthur Blvd # 200 Irvine (92612) ***(P-4861)***
Jett Pro Line Maintenance Inc (PA).....D.....909 980-0552
2910 Inland Empire Blvd # 102 Ontario (91764) ***(P-4897)***
Jetworld Inc.....C.....626 448-0150
2656 Chico Ave South El Monte (91733) ***(P-6600)***
Jewis Vocational & Counseling.....D.....415 391-3600
225 Bush St Ste 400 San Francisco (94104) ***(P-24196)***
Jewish Cmnty Fndn of (PA).....B.....323 761-8700
6505 Wilshire Blvd Los Angeles (90048) ***(P-25177)***
Jewish Community Ctr Long Bch.....C.....562 426-7601
3801 E Willow St Long Beach (90815) ***(P-23872)***
Jewish Community Fedrtn San Fr (PA).....D.....415 777-0411
121 Steuart St Fl 7 San Francisco (94105) ***(P-24793)***
Jewish Family and Chld Svcs (PA).....B.....415 449-1200
2150 Post St San Francisco (94115) ***(P-23873)***
Jewish Family Svc Los Angeles (PA).....E.....323 761-8800
3580 Wilshire Blvd Los Angeles (90010) ***(P-25022)***
Jewish Family Svc Los Angeles.....D.....818 984-0276
12821 Victory Blvd North Hollywood (91606) ***(P-23874)***
Jewish Family Svc Los Angeles.....E.....323 937-5900
330 N Fairfax Ave Los Angeles (90036) ***(P-23875)***
Jewish Family Svc San Diego (PA).....D.....858 637-3000
8804 Balboa Ave San Diego (92123) ***(P-23876)***
Jewish Fmly & Cmnty Svcs E Bay (PA).....D.....510 704-7475
2484 Shattuck Ave Ste 210 Berkeley (94704) ***(P-23877)***
Jewish Free Loan Association, Los Angeles *Also called Jewish Family Svc Los Angeles **(P-25022)***
Jewish Home For The Aging of O.....C.....949 364-0010
27356 Bellogente Mission Viejo (92691) ***(P-24569)***
Jewish Senior Living Group.....D.....415 562-2600
302 Silver Ave San Francisco (94112) ***(P-11036)***
Jewish Vocational Services (PA).....E.....323 761-8888
6505 Wilshire Blvd # 200 Los Angeles (90048) ***(P-24197)***
Jezowski & Markel Contrs Inc.....C.....714 978-2222
749 N Poplar St Orange (92868) ***(P-3271)***
JF Shea Construction Inc.....D.....530 246-4292
17400 Clear Creek Rd Redding (96001) ***(P-1181)***
JF Shea Construction Inc.....D.....949 526-8792
2 Ada Ste 200 Irvine (92618) ***(P-1182)***
JF Shea Construction Inc.....E.....909 594-0998
675 Brea Canyon Rd Ste 8 Walnut (91789) ***(P-1183)***
JF Shea Construction Inc.....B.....408 225-1475
6130 Monterey Hwy Ofc San Jose (95138) ***(P-1184)***
JF Shea Construction Inc.....C.....925 245-3660
2580 Shea Center Dr Livermore (94551) ***(P-1185)***
Jfc International Inc (HQ).....C.....323 721-6100
7101 E Slauson Ave Commerce (90040) ***(P-8812)***
Jfc International Inc.....C.....323 721-6900
7101 E Slauson Ave Commerce (90040) ***(P-8813)***
JFCS/EAST BAY, Berkeley *Also called Jewish Fmly & Cmnty Svcs E Bay **(P-23877)***
Jfe Shoji Trade America Inc (HQ).....D.....562 637-3500
301 E Ocean Blvd Ste 1750 Long Beach (90802) ***(P-7283)***
Jfm, Lakeside *Also called Johnson Finch & McClure Cnstr **(P-3540)***
Jfp Company, Norco *Also called Anna Corporation **(P-2420)***
Jfrog Inc (PA).....D.....408 329-1540
270 E Caribbean Dr Sunnyvale (94089) ***(P-15241)***
JH Bryant Jr Inc (PA).....E.....310 532-1840
17217 S Broadway Gardena (90248) ***(P-1410)***
Jh Capital Partners LP.....E.....415 364-0300
451 Jackson St San Francisco (94111) ***(P-12235)***
Jhc Investment Inc.....D.....714 751-2400
7 Hutton Centre Dr Santa Ana (92707) ***(P-12790)***
Jhp Produce Inc.....D.....213 627-1093
1601 E Olympic Blvd # 200 Los Angeles (90021) ***(P-8698)***
Jiangsu Juwang Info Tech Co (PA).....D.....510 967-3729
195 Recino St Fremont (94539) ***(P-15242)***
Jifflenow, Sunnyvale *Also called Ipolipo Inc **(P-15724)***
Jiffy Lube, Los Alamitos *Also called Alamitos Enterprises LLC **(P-17846)***
Jillians San Francisco CA.....D.....415 369-6100
101 4th St Ste 170 San Francisco (94103) ***(P-17259)***
Jim & Doug Carters Automotive.....E.....818 842-5702
2612 N Hollywood Way Burbank (91505) ***(P-17689)***
Jim Aartman Inc (PA).....C.....209 599-5066
805 S Locust Ave Ripon (95366) ***(P-4029)***
Jim Aartman Milk Transport, Ripon *Also called Jim Aartman Inc **(P-4029)***
Jim Henson Company Inc (PA).....D.....323 856-6680
1416 N La Brea Ave Los Angeles (90028) ***(P-18066)***
Jim Murphy & Associates, Santa Rosa *Also called Murphy-True Inc **(P-1598)***
Jimenez Nursery Inc.....D.....805 684-7955
3800 Via Real Carpinteria (93013) ***(P-271)***
Jimenez Nursery and Landscapes, Carpinteria *Also called Jimenez Nursery Inc **(P-271)***
Jimmy Kimmel Live, Los Angeles *Also called ABC Cable Networks Group **(P-5689)***
Jimmys Fashions.....E.....818 790-8932
3135 Chadney Dr Glendale (91206) ***(P-17260)***
Jims Steel Supply LLC.....E.....661 324-6514
3530 Buck Owens Blvd Bakersfield (93308) ***(P-8039)***
Jims Supply Co Inc (PA).....D.....661 324-6514
3530 Buck Owens Blvd Bakersfield (93308) ***(P-7284)***
Jinx Inc.....D.....888 546-9266
13465 Gregg St Poway (92064) ***(P-7954)***
Jinx Hackwear/Jinx.com, Poway *Also called Jinx Inc **(P-7954)***
Jipc Management Inc.....A.....949 916-2000
22342 Avenida Empresa # 220 Rcho STA Marg (92688) ***(P-26908)***
JIT Corporation.....D.....805 238-5000
2790 Valley View Ave Norco (92860) ***(P-7495)***
Jj Fisher Construction Inc.....D.....805 723-5220
261 W Dana St Ste 100 Nipomo (93444) ***(P-1797)***
Jj Grand Hotel.....D.....213 383-3000
620 S Harvard Blvd Los Angeles (90005) ***(P-12791)***
JJ Mac Intyre Co Inc (PA).....C.....951 898-4300
4160 Temescal Canyon Rd Corona (92883) ***(P-14010)***
JJ Rios Farm Services Inc.....D.....209 333-7467
4890 E Acampo Rd Acampo (95220) ***(P-655)***
JJR Enterprises Inc (PA).....D.....916 363-2666
10491 Old Placerville Rd # 150 Sacramento (95827) ***(P-17905)***
Jk Consultants.....E.....209 532-7772
160 Station Way Unit 102 Arroyo Grande (93421) ***(P-27760)***
Jk Imaging Ltd.....D.....310 755-6848
17239 S Main St Gardena (90248) ***(P-6944)***
JKB Corporation.....E.....562 905-3477
561 S Walnut St La Habra (90631) ***(P-3272)***
Jkf Auto Service Inc.....D.....916 315-0555
6818 Five Star Blvd Rocklin (95677) ***(P-17821)***
Jla Home, Woodland *Also called E & E Co Ltd **(P-1158)***
Jla Home, Woodland *Also called E & E Co Ltd **(P-6757)***
Jla Home, Fremont *Also called E & E Co Ltd **(P-6758)***
Jlg Harvesting Inc.....B.....831 422-7871
27 Zabala Rd Salinas (93908) ***(P-532)***
Jlp Landscape Contracting.....E.....707 526-6285
901 7th St Santa Rosa (95404) ***(P-869)***
Jls Environmental Services Inc.....D.....916 660-1525
3460 Swetzer Rd Loomis (95650) ***(P-27598)***
JM Driver LLC.....D.....855 596-9832
10620 Treena St Ste 224 San Diego (92131) ***(P-15243)***
JM Roofing Company Inc.....D.....805 966-3696
534 E Ortega St Santa Barbara (93103) ***(P-3169)***
JM Streamline Inc.....D.....530 272-6806
154 Scandling Ave Grass Valley (95945) ***(P-1564)***
Jma Investments Ltd.....D.....916 685-1355
9265 Beatty Dr Sacramento (95826) ***(P-870)***
Jmac Lending Inc.....D.....949 390-2688
2510 Redhill Ave Santa Ana (92705) ***(P-9718)***
JMB Construction Inc.....D.....650 267-5300
132 S Maple Ave South San Francisco (94080) ***(P-1938)***
Jmbm, Los Angeles *Also called Jeffer Mngels Btlr Mtchell LLP **(P-23149)***
Jme Inc (PA).....D.....201 896-8600
527 Prk Ave San Fernando San Fernando (91340) ***(P-7368)***
Jmg Security Systems Inc.....D.....714 545-8882
17150 Newhope St Ste 109 Fountain Valley (92708) ***(P-2619)***
JMJ Financial Group (PA).....E.....949 340-6336
26800 Aliso Viejo Pkwy # 200 Aliso Viejo (92656) ***(P-9820)***
JMS Realtors Ltd (PA).....C.....559 490-1500
575 E Alluvial Ave # 101 Fresno (93720) ***(P-11531)***
Jmt Charitable Foundation.....D.....415 974-6000
1 Market Ste 620 San Francisco (94105) ***(P-26231)***
Jn Projects Inc.....D.....415 766-0273
301 Howard St Ste 200 San Francisco (94105) ***(P-13755)***
Jnr Inc.....D.....949 476-2788
19900 Macarthur Blvd # 700 Irvine (92612) ***(P-27289)***
Joan Kroc Center, Mission Viejo *Also called St Vincent De Paul Vlg Inc **(P-25470)***
Joan Young Co Realtors, Westlake Village *Also called Young Realtors **(P-11843)***
Job Options Incorporated.....A.....909 890-4612
1110 S Washington Ave San Bernardino (92408) ***(P-13634)***
Jobs Plus, Chico *Also called Caminar **(P-22515)***
Jobs Plus, San Ramon *Also called Plus Group Inc **(P-14694)***
Jobvite Inc.....D.....650 376-7200
1300 S El Camino Real # 400 San Mateo (94402) ***(P-27290)***
Joe & Mary Mottino YMCA, Oceanside *Also called YMCA of San Diego County **(P-25305)***
Joe Canpagna.....D.....619 222-0555
2830 Shelter Island Dr San Diego (92106) ***(P-11532)***
Joe Heidrick Enterprises Inc.....E.....530 662-2339
36826 County Road 24 Woodland (95695) ***(P-8)***
Joe L Coelho Inc.....E.....209 667-2676
18637 E Bradbury Rd Turlock (95380) ***(P-4199)***
Joe Lunardi Electric Inc.....D.....707 823-2129
5334 Sebastopol Rd Santa Rosa (95407) ***(P-2620)***
Joe Pucci & Sons Seafoods, Hayward *Also called Blue River Seafood Inc **(P-8571)***
Joe's Auto Parks, Los Angeles *Also called L and R Auto Parks Inc **(P-17690)***
Joerns LLC (HQ).....C.....800 966-6662
19748 Dearborn St Chatsworth (91311) ***(P-7186)***
Joes Sweeping Inc.....D.....562 929-4344
11914 Front St Norwalk (90650) ***(P-6409)***
Joguru Inc.....D.....855 526-4332
2600 El Camino Real Ste 4 Palo Alto (94306) ***(P-4971)***
Johann B Garovi.....E.....415 898-1801
109 Pinheiro Cir Novato (94945) ***(P-1882)***
Johannes Flowers Inc.....D.....805 684-5686
4990 Foothill Rd Carpinteria (93013) ***(P-272)***
John A Maida Enterprises.....E.....408 254-3100
P.O. Box 6144 San Jose (95150) ***(P-8083)***
John Aguilar & Company Inc.....D.....209 546-0171
1505 Navy Dr Stockton (95206) ***(P-4030)***

Employee Codes: A=Over 500 employees, B=251-500
C=101-250, D=51-100, E=50
2019 Directory of California
Wholesalers and Services Companies
© Mergent Inc. 1-800-342-5647
1347

John Alden Life Insurance Co.......D.......818 595-7600
20950 Warner Center Ln A Woodland Hills (91367) ***(P-10138)***
John Brink General Contractor.......E.......530 583-2005
1760 W Lake Blvd Ste 3 Tahoe City (96145) ***(P-1798)***
John C Fremont Healthcare Dst.......C.......209 966-3631
5189 Hospital Rd Mariposa (95338) ***(P-21461)***
John Collins Co Inc.......D.......818 227-2190
5155 Cedarwood Rd Mgr Bonita (91902) ***(P-11037)***
John Deere Authorized Dealer, Fresno *Also called Vucovich Inc* ***(P-7717)***
John Deere Authorized Dealer, Manteca *Also called J M Equipment Company Inc* ***(P-14517)***
John Deere Authorized Dealer, Poway *Also called Bay City Equipment Inds Inc* ***(P-7337)***
John Deere Authorized Dealer, Firebaugh *Also called Thomason Tractor Co California* ***(P-7714)***
John Deere Authorized Dealer, Visalia *Also called Lawrence Tractor Coinc* ***(P-7705)***
John Deere Authorized Dealer, Colton *Also called A-Z Bus Sales Inc* ***(P-6570)***
John Deere Authorized Dealer, Lakeside *Also called Rdo Construction Equipment Co* ***(P-14455)***
John Deere Authorized Dealer, Sacramento *Also called Pape Machinery Inc* ***(P-7685)***
John Deere Authorized Dealer, Riverside *Also called Complete Coach Works* ***(P-17857)***
John Deere Authorized Dealer, Riverside *Also called Rdo Construction Equipment Co* ***(P-7710)***
John F Dmingue Attorney At Law.......C.......408 591-5180
10 Almaden Blvd Ste 1100 San Jose (95113) ***(P-23151)***
John F Kennedy Memorial Hosp.......A.......760 347-6191
47111 Monroe St Indio (92201) ***(P-21462)***
John F Knnedy Mem Hosp Emrgncy, Indio *Also called John F Kennedy Memorial Hosp* ***(P-21462)***
John F Otto Inc.......C.......916 441-6870
1717 2nd St Sacramento (95811) ***(P-1565)***
John G Shipley.......D.......714 626-2000
100 W Valencia Mesa Dr # 201 Fullerton (92835) ***(P-11533)***
John Gore Organization Inc.......D.......650 340-0469
255 S B St San Mateo (94401) ***(P-18376)***
John Grizzle Farming.......E.......760 356-4381
1395 Bonds Corner Rd Holtville (92250) ***(P-361)***
John H Kautz Farms.......E.......209 334-4786
5490 Bear Creek Rd Lodi (95240) ***(P-463)***
John Hancock, Irvine *Also called Signature Resources Insurance* ***(P-10774)***
John Hancock Life Insur Co USA (HQ).......A.......213 689-0813
865 S Figueroa St # 3320 Los Angeles (90017) ***(P-17261)***
John J Maguire DDS.......D.......213 740-6462
39340 Fremont Blvd Fremont (94538) ***(P-20119)***
John Jackson Masonry.......D.......916 381-8021
5691 Power Inn Rd Ste B Sacramento (95824) ***(P-2814)***
John Jory Corporation (PA).......B.......714 279-7901
2180 N Glassell St Orange (92865) ***(P-2903)***
John Kenney Construction Inc.......D.......805 884-1579
619 E Montecito St Santa Barbara (93103) ***(P-3273)***
John L Ginger Masonry Inc.......D.......951 688-5050
8188 Lincoln Ave Ste 100 Riverside (92504) ***(P-2815)***
John M Adams Jr MD.......D.......310 829-2663
1301 20th St Ste 150 Santa Monica (90404) ***(P-19520)***
John M Frank Construction Inc.......D.......714 210-3600
913 E 4th St Santa Ana (92701) ***(P-1566)***
John M Frank Service Group, Santa Ana *Also called John M Frank Construction Inc* ***(P-1566)***
John Muir Behavioral Hlth Ctr.......C.......925 674-4100
2740 Grant St Concord (94520) ***(P-21958)***
John Muir Health.......A.......925 692-5600
5003 Commercial Cir Concord (94520) ***(P-21463)***
John Muir Health.......A.......925 952-2887
380 Civic Dr Ste 100 Pleasant Hill (94523) ***(P-21464)***
John Muir Health (PA).......A.......925 947-4449
1601 Ygnacio Valley Rd Walnut Creek (94598) ***(P-21465)***
John Muir Health.......E.......925 947-5300
1981 N Broadway Ste 180 Walnut Creek (94596) ***(P-21466)***
John Muir Health.......A.......925 939-3000
1601 Ygnacio Valley Rd Walnut Creek (94598) ***(P-21467)***
John Muir Health.......A.......925 682-8200
2540 East St Concord (94520) ***(P-21468)***
John Muir Med Ctr Cncord Cmpus, Concord *Also called John Muir Health* ***(P-21468)***
JOHN MUIR MEDICAL CENTER, Walnut Creek *Also called John Muir Physician Network* ***(P-21472)***
John Muir Medical Center, Walnut Creek *Also called John Muir Health* ***(P-21467)***
John Muir Physician Network.......A.......925 952-2701
112 La Casa Via Ste 300 Walnut Creek (94598) ***(P-21469)***
John Muir Physician Network.......A.......925 685-0843
91 Gregory Ln Ste 15 Pleasant Hill (94523) ***(P-21470)***
John Muir Physician Network.......A.......925 682-8200
2540 East St Concord (94520) ***(P-21471)***
John Muir Physician Network (PA).......A.......925 296-9700
1450 Treat Blvd Walnut Creek (94597) ***(P-21472)***
John Muir Physician Network.......B.......925 939-3000
1601 Ygnacio Valley Rd Walnut Creek (94598) ***(P-21473)***
John Muir Physician Network.......E.......925 838-4633
1505 Saint Alphonsus Way Alamo (94507) ***(P-19521)***
John Muir Physician Network.......A.......925 674-2200
2720 Grant St Concord (94520) ***(P-21474)***
John Paul USA (PA).......D.......415 905-6088
49 Stevenson St Ste 575 San Francisco (94105) ***(P-14866)***
John Plane Construction Inc.......C.......415 468-0555
661 Hayne Rd Hillsborough (94010) ***(P-1567)***
John S Meek Company Inc.......D.......310 830-6323
14732 S Maple Ave Gardena (90248) ***(P-2042)***
John Shannon Mc Gee Co Inc.......E.......562 789-1777
8190 Byron Rd Whittier (90606) ***(P-7369)***
John Stewart Company.......D.......707 676-5660
191 Heritage Ln Dixon (95620) ***(P-11534)***
John Stewart Company.......E.......213 787-2700
888 S Figueroa St Ste 700 Los Angeles (90017) ***(P-11535)***
John Stewart Company.......C.......415 345-4400
2451 Meadowview Rd Sacramento (95832) ***(P-11038)***
John Stewart Company (PA).......D.......213 833-1860
1388 Sutter St Ste 1100 San Francisco (94109) ***(P-11536)***
John Tillman Company, Compton *Also called Blake H Brown Inc* ***(P-7732)***
John Wayne Airport, Costa Mesa *Also called County of Orange* ***(P-4884)***
John Wayne Institute For Ctr.......C.......310 449-5253
2200 Santa Monica Blvd Santa Monica (90404) ***(P-26629)***
John's Incredible Pizza Co, Rcho STA Marg *Also called Jipc Management Inc* ***(P-26908)***
John's Pet Products, San Jose *Also called Johns Dog Food Distributing* ***(P-8814)***
Johnre Care LLC.......D.......951 658-6374
461 E Johnston Ave Hemet (92543) ***(P-20550)***
Johns Dog Food Distributing.......D.......408 275-1943
1633 Monterey Hwy San Jose (95112) ***(P-8814)***
Johnsen Construction Inc.......D.......530 642-2123
6448 Capitol Ave Diamond Springs (95619) ***(P-3274)***
Johnson & Johnson Pistaccios.......E.......818 242-7853
1720 Ben Lomond Dr Glendale (91202) ***(P-27)***
Johnson & Turner Painting Co.......E.......714 828-8282
8241 Electric Ave Stanton (90680) ***(P-2453)***
Johnson Air, Clovis *Also called Ladell Inc* ***(P-2256)***
Johnson Cntrls SEC Sltions LLC.......C.......818 428-6669
104 E Graham Pl Burbank (91502) ***(P-16908)***
Johnson Cntrls SEC Sltions LLC.......D.......951 787-0420
1120 Palmyrita Ave # 280 Riverside (92507) ***(P-16909)***
Johnson Cntrls SEC Sltions LLC.......C.......561 988-3600
3870 Murphy Canyon Rd # 140 San Diego (92123) ***(P-16910)***
Johnson Cntrls SEC Sltions LLC.......D.......650 634-9000
150 N Hill Dr Ste 3 Brisbane (94005) ***(P-16911)***
Johnson Cntrls SEC Sltions LLC.......D.......510 246-2862
3825 Bay Center Pl B Hayward (94545) ***(P-16912)***
Johnson Cntrls SEC Sltions LLC.......C.......714 223-2300
7565 Irvine Center Dr # 100 Irvine (92618) ***(P-16913)***
Johnson Contrls Authorized Dlr, Pleasant Hill *Also called Controlco* ***(P-7743)***
Johnson Controls.......D.......805 642-0366
1868 Palma Dr Ventura (93003) ***(P-2244)***
Johnson Controls.......C.......562 405-3817
12728 Shoemaker Ave Santa Fe Springs (90670) ***(P-16914)***
Johnson Controls.......D.......707 578-3212
3077 Wiljan Ct Ste B Santa Rosa (95407) ***(P-2245)***
Johnson Controls Inc.......D.......805 522-5555
1757 Tapo Canyon Rd # 120 Simi Valley (93063) ***(P-7496)***
Johnson Controls Inc.......D.......707 546-3042
2226 Northpoint Pkwy Santa Rosa (95407) ***(P-25770)***
Johnson Fain Inc.......D.......323 224-6000
1201 N Broadway Los Angeles (90012) ***(P-26072)***
Johnson Finch & McClure Cnstr (PA).......C.......619 938-9727
9749 Cactus St Lakeside (92040) ***(P-3540)***
Johnson La Follette.......D.......714 558-7008
2677 N Main St Ste 901 Santa Ana (92705) ***(P-23152)***
Johnson Machinery Co (PA).......C.......951 686-4560
800 E La Cadena Dr Riverside (92507) ***(P-7684)***
Johnson Ranch Racquet Club, Roseville *Also called Spare-Time Inc* ***(P-19056)***
Johnson Service Group Inc.......A.......408 728-9510
950 S Bascom Ave San Jose (95128) ***(P-10903)***
Johnson/Johnson, Glendale *Also called Johnson & Johnson Pistaccios* ***(P-27)***
Johnston Farms.......D.......661 366-3201
13031 E Packinghouse Rd Edison (93220) ***(P-19)***
Johnston Vacuum Tank Service, Taft *Also called Watkins Construction Co Inc* ***(P-2000)***
Joie, Vernon *Also called Dutch LLC* ***(P-8299)***
Joie, Vernon *Also called Collected Group Company LLC* ***(P-8296)***
Joie De Vivre Hospitality LLC.......A.......408 335-1700
210 E Main St Los Gatos (95030) ***(P-2621)***
Joie De Vivre Hospitality LLC (PA).......E.......415 835-0300
1750 Geary Blvd San Francisco (94115) ***(P-26909)***
Joie De Vivre Hospitality LLC.......D.......415 986-2000
386 Geary St San Francisco (94102) ***(P-26910)***
Joie De Vivre Hospitality LLC.......D.......650 879-1100
2001 Rossi Rd Pescadero (94060) ***(P-26911)***
Joie De Vivre Hospitality Inc.......D.......408 738-0500
910 E Fremont Ave Sunnyvale (94087) ***(P-12792)***
JOINT POWERS AGENCY, Irvine *Also called San Joaquin Hills Transporttn* ***(P-1845)***
Jolly Roger Inn, Anaheim *Also called Edward Thomas Companies* ***(P-12549)***
Jomar Industries Inc.......E.......323 770-0505
1500 W 139th St Gardena (90249) ***(P-17262)***
Jon K Takata Corporation (PA).......D.......510 315-5400
4142 Point Eden Way Hayward (94545) ***(P-23878)***
Jon Wayne Construction, Vista *Also called Jwc Construction Inc* ***(P-1294)***
Jonair Services LLC.......D.......310 529-5482
9800 S Sepulveda Blvd Los Angeles (90045) ***(P-4862)***
Jonathan Beach Club, Santa Monica *Also called Jonathan Club* ***(P-18941)***
Jonathan Club (PA).......B.......213 624-0881
545 S Figueroa St Los Angeles (90071) ***(P-25178)***
Jonathan Club.......C.......310 393-9245
850 Palisades Beach Rd Santa Monica (90403) ***(P-18941)***
Jonbec Care Incorporated (PA).......D.......909 798-4003
1711 Plum Ln Redlands (92374) ***(P-20936)***
Jonce Thomas Construction Co.......E.......510 657-7171
3390 Seldon Ct Fremont (94539) ***(P-3047)***
Jones & Jones MGT Group Inc.......C.......818 594-0019
8220 Topanga Canyon Blvd Canoga Park (91304) ***(P-11039)***
Jones Bold Security Inc.......D.......562 316-6552
7520 Sleepy Creek Ave Fontana (92336) ***(P-16708)***
Jones Covey Group, Rancho Cucamonga *Also called Jones/Covey Group Incorporated* ***(P-3541)***

Jones Day Limited Partnership......D......213 489-3939
555 S Flower St Fl 50 Los Angeles (90071) ***(P-17263)***
Jones Day Limited Partnership......D......858 314-1200
4655 Executive Dr # 1500 San Diego (92121) ***(P-23153)***
Jones Day Limited Partnership......D......949 851-3939
3161 Michelson Dr Ste 800 Irvine (92612) ***(P-23154)***
Jones Day Limited Partnership......D......650 739-3955
1755 Embarcadero Rd # 101 Palo Alto (94303) ***(P-23155)***
Jones Lang La Salle......D......213 239-6000
515 S Flower St Fl 13 Los Angeles (90071) ***(P-12168)***
Jones Lang Lasalle Inc......C......415 395-4900
4444 Mkt St Ste 1100 San Francisco (94111) ***(P-11537)***
Jones Lang Lsalle Americas Inc......C......949 296-3600
2211 Michelson Dr Irvine (92612) ***(P-10091)***
Jones Lumber Company Inc......D......323 564-6656
10711 Alameda St Lynwood (90262) ***(P-6838)***
Jones Sign Co Inc......C......858 569-1400
9025 Balboa Ave Ste 150 San Diego (92123) ***(P-7141)***
Jones Valley Resorts, Redding *Also called Shasta Lake Resorts LP* ***(P-19236)***
Jones/Covey Group Incorporated......D......888 972-7581
9595 Lucas Ranch Rd # 100 Rancho Cucamonga (91730) ***(P-3541)***
Joni and Friends (PA)......D......818 707-5664
30009 Ladyface Ct Agoura (91301) ***(P-23879)***
Jonset Corporation......D......949 551-5151
16251 Construction Cir W Irvine (92606) ***(P-6542)***
Jopari Solutions Inc......D......925 459-5200
1855 Gateway Blvd Ste 500 Concord (94520) ***(P-17264)***
Jordana Cosmetics Corporation......D......323 589-5625
2035 E 49th St Vernon (90058) ***(P-8184)***
Jordano's Food Service, Santa Barbara *Also called Jordanos Inc* ***(P-9006)***
Jordanos Inc (PA)......C......805 964-0611
550 S Patterson Ave Santa Barbara (93111) ***(P-9006)***
Jorge Pimental Diaz......C......661 344-5139
348 Manzanita Dr Delano (93215) ***(P-656)***
Jorgensen & Co, Fresno *Also called Jorgensen & Sons Inc* ***(P-8040)***
Jorgensen & Sons Inc (PA)......D......559 268-6241
2467 Foundry Park Ave Fresno (93706) ***(P-8040)***
Jose Vramontes......E......209 810-5384
14345 N Highway 88 Lodi (95240) ***(P-362)***
Joseph A Foroosh Dental Corp (PA)......D......760 241-3336
12640 Hesperia Rd Ste A Victorville (92395) ***(P-20120)***
Joseph C Sansone Company (PA)......D......818 226-3400
21300 Victory Blvd # 300 Woodland Hills (91367) ***(P-23156)***
Joseph Cozza Salon Inc (PA)......D......415 433-3030
25 Egret Way Mill Valley (94941) ***(P-13663)***
Joseph Dipuzo......E......760 325-1200
601 E Tahquitz Canyon Way # 120 Palm Springs (92262) ***(P-13492)***
Joseph Farms Cheese, Atwater *Also called Gallo Cattle Co A Ltd Partnr* ***(P-414)***
Joseph J Albanese Inc......A......408 727-5700
851 Martin Ave Santa Clara (95050) ***(P-3275)***
Joseph Jensen Filtration Plant, Granada Hills *Also called Metropolitan Water District* ***(P-6283)***
Joseph T Ryerson & Son Inc......D......323 267-6000
4310 Bandini Blvd Vernon (90058) ***(P-7285)***
Josephine's Personnel Services, San Jose *Also called Josephines Prof Staffing* ***(P-14655)***
Josephines Prof Staffing (PA)......C......408 943-0111
2158 Ringwood Ave San Jose (95131) ***(P-14655)***
Joshua House, Newport Beach *Also called National Therapeutic Svcs Inc* ***(P-22621)***
Joshua J Bodenstadt CPA A Prof......E......858 642-5050
4225 Executive Sq Ste 900 La Jolla (92037) ***(P-26232)***
Joyent Inc......C......415 400-0600
655 Montgomery St # 1600 San Francisco (94111) ***(P-16416)***
Joyride Coffee Distrs LLC......D......718 841-7206
1485 Yosemite Ave San Francisco (94124) ***(P-8815)***
JP Allen Inc......B......818 841-4770
150 E Angeleno Ave Burbank (91502) ***(P-11040)***
JP Allen Extended Stay......E......818 841-4770
150 E Angeleno Ave Burbank (91502) ***(P-12793)***
JP Allen Extended Stay (PA)......D......818 956-0202
450 Pioneer Dr Glendale (91203) ***(P-12794)***
JP Morgan Securities LLC......D......310 201-2693
14061 Mercado Dr Del Mar (92014) ***(P-9967)***
JP Motorsports Inc......D......818 381-8313
11582 Sheldon St Sun Valley (91352) ***(P-3811)***
Jpa Landscape & Cnstr Inc......D......925 960-9602
256 Boeing Ct Livermore (94551) ***(P-871)***
Jpi Development Group Inc......D......951 973-7680
41205 Golden Gate Cir Murrieta (92562) ***(P-2246)***
Jpmorgan Chase Bank Nat Assn......C......707 864-4700
5095 Business Center Dr Fairfield (94534) ***(P-9348)***
Jpmorgan Chase Bank Nat Assn......C......949 429-6071
1995 Santa Ana Ave Costa Mesa (92627) ***(P-17265)***
Jpmorgan Chase Bank Nat Assn......D......626 795-5177
860 E Colorado Blvd Pasadena (91101) ***(P-9349)***
Jpmorgan Chase Bank Nat Assn......C......805 482-2902
502 Las Posas Rd Camarillo (93010) ***(P-17266)***
Jpmorgan Chase Bank Nat Assn......E......818 763-7343
12051 Ventura Blvd Studio City (91604) ***(P-9350)***
Jpmorgan Chase Bank Nat Assn......D......626 919-3129
100 S Vincent Ave Fl 1 West Covina (91790) ***(P-9351)***
Jpmorgan Chase Bank Nat Assn......C......858 605-3300
10790 Rancho Bernardo Rd San Diego (92127) ***(P-17267)***
Jpmorgan Chase Bank Nat Assn......E......619 424-8197
1100 Palm Ave Imperial Beach (91932) ***(P-9509)***
Jpmorgan Chase Bank Nat Assn......A......209 460-2888
400 E Main St Fl 2 Stockton (95202) ***(P-9524)***
Jpmorgan Xign Corporation......D......925 469-9446
7077 Koll Center Pkwy Pleasanton (94566) ***(P-26233)***
Jr Construction Inc......D......858 505-4760
8123 Engineer Rd San Diego (92111) ***(P-1568)***
JR Filanc Cnstr Co Inc (PA)......D......760 941-7130
740 N Andreasen Dr Escondido (92029) ***(P-1939)***
JR Perce Plbg Inc Sacramento......C......916 434-9554
3610 Cincinnati Ave Rocklin (95765) ***(P-2247)***
JR Simplot Company......E......559 659-2033
35836 W Bullard Ave Firebaugh (93622) ***(P-9080)***
Jri Inc......E......818 706-2424
31280 La Baya Dr Westlake Village (91362) ***(P-7497)***
JS Homen Trucking Inc......D......209 723-9559
4224 Turlock Rd Snelling (95369) ***(P-4031)***
Js Hospitality Group LLC......D......805 988-3600
600 E Esplanade Dr Oxnard (93036) ***(P-12795)***
JS International Shipg Corp (PA)......D......650 697-3963
1535 Rollins Rd Ste B Burlingame (94010) ***(P-5093)***
JS Real Estate Prpts Inc......D......310 856-6868
134 W 168th St Gardena (90248) ***(P-3379)***
Js Tamers Inc......E......323 609-4101
468 N Camden Dr Ste 200 Beverly Hills (90210) ***(P-11538)***
Jsi Shipping, Burlingame *Also called JS International Shipg Corp* ***(P-5093)***
Jsl Technologies Inc......D......805 985-7700
1701 Pacific Ave Ste 270 Oxnard (93033) ***(P-25771)***
JT Wimsatt Contg Co Inc (PA)......D......661 775-8090
28064 Avenue Stanford B Valencia (91355) ***(P-3276)***
Jt3 LLC......A......661 277-4900
190 S Wolfe Ave Bldg 1260 Edwards (93524) ***(P-25772)***
Jtb Americas Ltd (HQ)......D......310 303-3750
19700 Mariner Ave Torrance (90503) ***(P-4942)***
Juan Lopez......D......619 428-3138
3065 Beyer Blvd Ste B106 San Diego (92154) ***(P-1186)***
Judson Enterprises Inc (PA)......B......916 596-6721
2440 Gold River Rd # 100 Rancho Cordova (95670) ***(P-1293)***
Judy Madrigal & Associates Inc......A......650 873-3444
2000 Alameda De Las Pulga San Mateo (94403) ***(P-19522)***
Jules and Associates Inc......D......213 362-5600
515 S Figueroa St # 1900 Los Angeles (90071) ***(P-14520)***
Julio Gonzalez......D......310 310-4055
1417 S Fairfax Ave Apt 4 Los Angeles (90019) ***(P-27761)***
Julius Steve Construction Inc......E......949 369-7820
230 Calle Pintoresco San Clemente (92672) ***(P-1411)***
Jump Dance Convention, North Hollywood *Also called Break Floor Productions LLC* ***(P-18346)***
Jumpshot Inc......D......415 212-9250
333 Bryant St Ste 240 San Francisco (94107) ***(P-15244)***
Jumpstart Games Inc......D......424 645-4311
500 W 190th St Ste 300 Gardena (90248) ***(P-15245)***
June A Grothe Construction Inc......D......909 993-9393
15632 El Prado Rd Chino (91710) ***(P-1569)***
June Group LLC......D......858 450-4290
9444 Waples St Ste 100 San Diego (92121) ***(P-14867)***
Jungle Fun & Adventure, Concord *Also called Leisure Planet* ***(P-19195)***
Juniper Hotel, Cupertino *Also called Cupertino Lessee LLC* ***(P-12505)***
Juniper Networks Inc......A......408 745-2000
1137 Innovation Way B Sunnyvale (94089) ***(P-15987)***
Juniper Networks Inc......D......805 880-2000
6868 Cortona Dr Ste C Goleta (93117) ***(P-15988)***
Juniper Networks Inc......D......916 503-1593
1215 K St Fl 17 Sacramento (95814) ***(P-15989)***
Juniper Networks Inc......A......888 586-4737
1133 Innovation Way A Sunnyvale (94089) ***(P-15990)***
Juniper Rock Corporation......B......949 500-1797
26000 Commercentre Dr Lake Forest (92630) ***(P-1089)***
Jurlique Hlistic Skin Care Inc (PA)......E......914 998-8800
1411 5th St Ste 501 Santa Monica (90401) ***(P-13664)***
Jurupa Stadium Cinema 14, Riverside *Also called Edwards Theatres Circuit Inc* ***(P-18287)***
Just Desserts, Fairfield *Also called New Desserts Inc* ***(P-8838)***
Just Mortgage Inc......C......562 908-5000
8577 Haven Ave Ste 306 Rancho Cucamonga (91730) ***(P-9821)***
Justice California Department......A......916 324-5039
1300 I St Ste 720 Sacramento (95814) ***(P-27762)***
Justman Packaging & Display......D......323 728-8888
5819 Telegraph Rd Commerce (90040) ***(P-7142)***
Juvenile Hall, Indio *Also called County of Riverside* ***(P-24482)***
Juvenile Justice Division Cal......B......805 485-7951
3100 Wright Rd Camarillo (93010) ***(P-26912)***
Jvc Americas Corp......D......714 527-7500
5665 Corporate Ave Cypress (90630) ***(P-17883)***
Jvc Americas Corp......D......562 463-8110
11925 Pike St Santa Fe Springs (90670) ***(P-17884)***
Jvc Company of America, Cypress *Also called Jvc Americas Corp* ***(P-17883)***
Jvc Service & Engineering, Santa Fe Springs *Also called Jvc Americas Corp* ***(P-17884)***
Jvckenwood USA Corporation (HQ)......C......310 639-9000
2201 E Dominguez St Long Beach (90810) ***(P-7419)***
JVSLA, Los Angeles *Also called Jewish Vocational Services* ***(P-24197)***
JW Marriott Desert, Palm Desert *Also called Host Hotels & Resorts LP* ***(P-12706)***
JW Marriott Le Merigot, Santa Monica *Also called C W Hotels Ltd* ***(P-12415)***
Jwc Construction Inc (PA)......E......760 727-2494
2580 Fortune Way Vista (92081) ***(P-1294)***
Jwc Construction Inc......E......949 252-2107
4570 Campus Dr Newport Beach (92660) ***(P-1295)***
Jwch Institute Inc......D......562 867-7999
14371 Clark Ave Bellflower (90706) ***(P-22826)***
Jwch Institute Inc......D......323 562-5813
6912 Ajax Ave Bell (90201) ***(P-26630)***
Jwch Institute Inc......D......562 281-0306
12360 Firestone Blvd Norwalk (90650) ***(P-26631)***

ALPHABETIC

Employee Codes: A=Over 500 employees, B=251-500
C=101-250, D=51-100, E=50
2019 Directory of California
Wholesalers and Services Companies
© Mergent Inc. 1-800-342-5647
1349

JWdangelo Company Inc ....E.......562 690-1000
601 S Harbor Blvd La Habra (90631) ***(P-7888)***
Jwmcc Limited Partnership ....B.......310 277-1234
2151 Avenue Of The Stars Los Angeles (90067) ***(P-12796)***
Jyg Concrete Construction Inc ....C.......661 607-0337
24841 Avenue Tibbitts Valencia (91355) ***(P-3277)***
K & P Janitorial Services ....D.......310 540-8878
412 S Pacific Coast Hwy # 200 Redondo Beach (90277) ***(P-14297)***
K & S Air Conditioning Inc ....C.......714 685-0077
143 E Meats Ave Orange (92865) ***(P-2248)***
K & S Auto, Truck & Tractor, Bay Point *Also called K & S Towing & Transport* ***(P-27291)***
K & S Towing & Transport ....D.......925 709-0759
2780 Willow Pass Rd Bay Point (94565) ***(P-27291)***
K A Associates Inc ....C.......310 556-2721
1800 Avenue Of The Stars # 200 Los Angeles (90067) ***(P-9968)***
K A R Construction Inc ....D.......909 988-5054
1306 Brooks St Ontario (91762) ***(P-3278)***
K Automotive Distributors (PA) ....D.......818 988-1550
14650 Calvert St Van Nuys (91411) ***(P-6650)***
K B I, Anaheim *Also called Kinsbursky Bros Supply Inc* ***(P-7982)***
K C C, El Segundo *Also called Carson Kurtzman Consultants* ***(P-22973)***
K E, Irvine *Also called Kite Electric Inc* ***(P-2625)***
K E M A, Oakland *Also called Dnv GL Energy Insights USA Inc* ***(P-27707)***
K E S, San Diego *Also called Koam Engineering Systems Inc* ***(P-15992)***
K G O T V News Bureau ....D.......510 451-4772
520 3rd St Ste 200 Oakland (94607) ***(P-5731)***
K G S Electronics, Arcadia *Also called Gar Enterprises* ***(P-7051)***
K G Walters Cnstr Co Inc ....D.......707 527-9968
195 Concourse Blvd Ste A Santa Rosa (95403) ***(P-2043)***
K Hovnanian, Irvine *Also called K Hovnanian Companies Cal Inc* ***(P-1187)***
K Hovnanian Companies Cal Inc (HQ) ....D.......714 368-4500
400 Exchange Ste 200 Irvine (92602) ***(P-1187)***
K K R, Menlo Park *Also called Kohlberg Kravis Roberts Co LP* ***(P-12239)***
K K W Trucking Inc (PA) ....B.......909 869-1200
3100 Pomona Blvd Pomona (91768) ***(P-4200)***
K Line America Inc ....E.......714 861-5000
950 S Coast Dr Ste 178 Costa Mesa (92626) ***(P-4698)***
K O X R, Oxnard *Also called Koxr Spanish Radio* ***(P-5735)***
K P F F Consulting Engineers, Los Angeles *Also called Kpff Inc* ***(P-25787)***
K R Anderson Inc (PA) ....D.......408 825-1800
18330 Sutter Blvd Morgan Hill (95037) ***(P-8930)***
K R G, Valencia *Also called Krg Technologies Inc* ***(P-15252)***
K S B W- T V, Salinas *Also called Hearst Stations Inc* ***(P-5797)***
K S Fabrication & Machine Inc ....C.......661 617-1700
6205 District Blvd Bakersfield (93313) ***(P-1940)***
K S I, Bakersfield *Also called KS Industries LP* ***(P-1944)***
K S S C - F M, Los Angeles *Also called Entravsion Communications Corp* ***(P-5785)***
K S S J Radio-101.9 FM City, Sacramento *Also called Entercom Communications Corp* ***(P-5714)***
K T A Construction Inc ....D.......619 562-9464
1920 Cordell Ct Ste 105 El Cajon (92020) ***(P-1941)***
K T Lucky Co Inc ....D.......626 579-7272
10925 Schmidt Rd El Monte (91733) ***(P-8816)***
K T T V-Fox 11, Los Angeles *Also called Fox Television Stations Inc* ***(P-5794)***
K T W Productions Inc ....A.......714 685-0428
6303 E Cedarbrooks Rd Orange (92867) ***(P-6769)***
K Tech Security & Protect Svc ....C.......619 858-5832
665 Alvin St San Diego (92114) ***(P-16709)***
K W K Trucking Inc ....C.......714 791-7928
6131 Manorfield Dr Huntington Beach (92648) ***(P-4032)***
K W P H Enterprises ....B.......559 443-5900
2911 E Tulare St Fresno (93721) ***(P-3812)***
K X T V Channel 10, Sacramento *Also called Kxtv Inc* ***(P-5819)***
K Y L D, San Francisco *Also called Iheartcommunications Inc* ***(P-5721)***
K&B Electric LLC ....C.......951 808-9501
290 Corporate Terrace Cir # 200 Corona (92879) ***(P-25773)***
K&B Engineering, Corona *Also called K&B Electric LLC* ***(P-25773)***
K&B Engineering ....C.......951 808-9501
290 Corporate Terrace Cir Corona (92879) ***(P-25774)***
K&I International Trade Inc ....E.......312 766-1848
3592 Rosemead Blvd # 220 Rosemead (91770) ***(P-6730)***
K&L Gates LLP ....D.......415 882-8200
55 2nd St Ste 1700 San Francisco (94105) ***(P-23157)***
K&L Gates LLP ....E.......310 552-5000
10100 Santa Monica Blvd # 700 Los Angeles (90067) ***(P-23158)***
K&L Gates LLP ....D.......415 249-1000
4 Embarcadero Ctr Lbby 10 San Francisco (94111) ***(P-23159)***
K&M Construction ....D.......831 643-2819
642 Pine Ave Pacific Grove (93950) ***(P-1296)***
K&S, Orange *Also called K & S Air Conditioning Inc* ***(P-2248)***
K-Designers, Rancho Cordova *Also called Judson Enterprises Inc* ***(P-1293)***
K-Fed Mutual Holding Company ....C.......626 339-9663
1359 N Grand Ave Covina (91724) ***(P-11954)***
K-Love Radio Network, Rocklin *Also called Educational Media Foundation* ***(P-5709)***
K-Micro Inc ....D.......310 442-3200
1618 Stanford St Santa Monica (90404) ***(P-7068)***
K/P LLC ....E.......510 614-7800
13947 Washington Ave San Leandro (94578) ***(P-14048)***
K2 Industrial Services Inc ....E.......562 624-5800
2375 W Esther St Long Beach (90813) ***(P-17268)***
Ka Management Inc ....D.......858 404-6080
5820 Oberlin Dr Ste 201 San Diego (92121) ***(P-26913)***
Kaa Design Group Inc ....D.......310 821-1400
4201 Redwood Ave Los Angeles (90066) ***(P-26073)***
Kabam Inc (HQ) ....D.......604 256-0054
575 Market St Ste 2450 San Francisco (94105) ***(P-15246)***
Kabc 790 Talk Radio, Los Angeles *Also called Cumulus Intrmdate Holdings Inc* ***(P-5707)***
Kabler Construction Svcs Inc ....E.......415 888-8812
467 Miller Ave Mill Valley (94941) ***(P-27292)***
Kad Engineering, Yucaipa *Also called Kad Paving Company* ***(P-1799)***
Kad Paving Company ....D.......909 790-3366
32147 Dunlap Blvd Ste K Yucaipa (92399) ***(P-1799)***
Kaden Cash LLC ....E.......818 714-4665
15845 Jackson Dr Fontana (92336) ***(P-18445)***
Kadena Pacific Inc ....E.......951 990-7865
3421 Gato Ct Ste A Riverside (92507) ***(P-1570)***
Kaercher Campbell Associate In ....C.......310 556-1900
600 Corporate Pointe # 1010 Culver City (90230) ***(P-10661)***
Kagan Capital Management Inc ....D.......831 624-1536
126 Clock Tower Pl Carmel (93923) ***(P-10092)***
Kaidan Hospitality LP ....D.......530 221-8700
1830 Hilltop Dr Redding (96002) ***(P-12797)***
Kaimanu Outrigger Canoe Club ....D.......510 895-0435
13424 Doolittle Dr San Leandro (94577) ***(P-19190)***
Kainos Home & Training Ctr ....E.......650 361-1355
2761 Fair Oaks Ave Ste A Redwood City (94063) ***(P-23880)***
Kainos Work Activity Ctr, Redwood City *Also called Kainos Home & Training Ctr* ***(P-23880)***
Kaiser Foundation Health Plan, San Diego *Also called Southern Cal Prmnnte Med Group* ***(P-10313)***
Kaiser Foundation Health Plan, Union City *Also called Kaiser Foundation Hospitals* ***(P-10216)***
Kaiser Foundation Health Plan, San Francisco *Also called Kaiser Foundation Hospitals* ***(P-10217)***
Kaiser Foundation Health Plan, Pasadena *Also called Kaiser Foundation Hospitals* ***(P-10218)***
Kaiser Foundation Health Plan, Vallejo *Also called Kaiser Foundation Hospitals* ***(P-10219)***
Kaiser Foundation Health Plan, Vernon *Also called Kaiser Foundation Hospitals* ***(P-21490)***
Kaiser Foundation Health Plan, San Rafael *Also called Kaiser Foundation Hospitals* ***(P-10220)***
Kaiser Foundation Health Plan, Los Angeles *Also called Kaiser Foundation Hospitals* ***(P-10221)***
Kaiser Foundation Health Plan, Oakland *Also called Kaiser Foundation Hospitals* ***(P-10222)***
Kaiser Foundation Health Plan, Fresno *Also called Kaiser Foundation Hospitals* ***(P-10223)***
Kaiser Foundation Health Plan, Elk Grove *Also called Kaiser Foundation Hospitals* ***(P-10224)***
Kaiser Foundation Health Plan, Victorville *Also called Kaiser Foundation Hospitals* ***(P-10225)***
Kaiser Foundation Health Plan, San Diego *Also called Kaiser Foundation Hospitals* ***(P-10226)***
Kaiser Foundation Health Plan, San Diego *Also called Kaiser Foundation Hospitals* ***(P-10227)***
Kaiser Foundation Health Plan, Temecula *Also called Kaiser Foundation Hospitals* ***(P-10228)***
Kaiser Foundation Health Plan, Mission Hills *Also called Kaiser Foundation Hospitals* ***(P-10229)***
Kaiser Foundation Health Plan, Panorama City *Also called Kaiser Foundation Hospitals* ***(P-10230)***
Kaiser Foundation Health Plan, Hayward *Also called Kaiser Foundation Hospitals* ***(P-10231)***
Kaiser Foundation Health Plan, Los Angeles *Also called Kaiser Foundation Hospitals* ***(P-10232)***
Kaiser Foundation Health Plan, Anaheim *Also called Kaiser Foundation Hospitals* ***(P-10235)***
Kaiser Foundation Health Plan, Campbell *Also called Kaiser Foundation Hospitals* ***(P-19610)***
Kaiser Foundation Health Plan, Walnut Creek *Also called Kaiser Foundation Hospitals* ***(P-10236)***
Kaiser Foundation Health Plan, Clovis *Also called Kaiser Foundation Hospitals* ***(P-10237)***
Kaiser Foundation Health Plan, Woodland Hills *Also called Kaiser Foundation Hospitals* ***(P-10238)***
Kaiser Foundation Health Plan, Roseville *Also called Kaiser Foundation Hospitals* ***(P-10239)***
Kaiser Foundation Health Plan, Oakhurst *Also called Kaiser Foundation Hospitals* ***(P-10240)***
Kaiser Foundation Health Plan, Ontario *Also called Kaiser Foundation Hospitals* ***(P-10241)***
Kaiser Foundation Health Plan, Palm Desert *Also called Kaiser Foundation Hospitals* ***(P-10242)***
Kaiser Foundation Health Plan, Ventura *Also called Kaiser Foundation Hospitals* ***(P-10243)***
Kaiser Foundation Health Plan, Santa Ana *Also called Kaiser Foundation Hospitals* ***(P-10244)***
Kaiser Foundation Health Plan, San Bernardino *Also called Kaiser Foundation Hospitals* ***(P-10245)***
Kaiser Foundation Health Plan, Corona *Also called Kaiser Foundation Hospitals* ***(P-22827)***
Kaiser Foundation Health Plan, Chino *Also called Kaiser Foundation Hospitals* ***(P-10246)***
Kaiser Foundation Health Plan, Daly City *Also called Kaiser Foundation Hospitals* ***(P-10247)***
Kaiser Foundation Health Plan, Union City *Also called Kaiser Foundation Hospitals* ***(P-10248)***
Kaiser Foundation Health Plan, Tracy *Also called Kaiser Foundation Hospitals* ***(P-10249)***
Kaiser Foundation Health Plan, San Bruno *Also called Kaiser Foundation Hospitals* ***(P-10250)***
Kaiser Foundation Health Plan, Santa Rosa *Also called Kaiser Foundation Hospitals* ***(P-10251)***
Kaiser Foundation Health Plan, Santa Rosa *Also called Kaiser Foundation Hospitals* ***(P-10252)***
Kaiser Foundation Health Plan, Modesto *Also called Kaiser Foundation Hospitals* ***(P-10253)***
Kaiser Foundation Health Plan, Rohnert Park *Also called Kaiser Foundation Hospitals* ***(P-10254)***
Kaiser Foundation Health Plan, Alameda *Also called Kaiser Foundation Hospitals* ***(P-10255)***
Kaiser Foundation Health Plan, Oakland *Also called Kaiser Foundation Hospitals* ***(P-10256)***
Kaiser Foundation Health Plan, Bellflower *Also called Kaiser Foundation Hospitals* ***(P-10257)***
Kaiser Foundation Health Plan, Selma *Also called Kaiser Foundation Hospitals* ***(P-10258)***
Kaiser Foundation Health Plan, Orange *Also called Kaiser Foundation Hospitals* ***(P-10259)***

Mergent e-mail: customerrelations@mergent.com
1350
2019 Directory of California Wholesalers and Services Companies
(P-0000) Products & Services Section entry number
(PA)=Parent Co (HQ)=Headquarters (DH)=Div Headquarters

Kaiser Foundation Health Plan, Palm Springs *Also called Kaiser Foundation Hospitals* ***(P-10260)***
Kaiser Foundation Health Plan, Torrance *Also called Kaiser Foundation Hospitals* ***(P-10261)***
Kaiser Foundation Health Plan, Thousand Oaks *Also called Kaiser Foundation Hospitals* ***(P-10262)***
Kaiser Foundation Health Plan, Simi Valley *Also called Kaiser Foundation Hospitals* ***(P-10263)***
Kaiser Foundation Health Plan, San Juan Capistrano *Also called Kaiser Foundation Hospitals* ***(P-10264)***
Kaiser Foundation Health Plan, Fontana *Also called Kaiser Foundation Hospitals* ***(P-10265)***
Kaiser Foundation Health Plan, Downey *Also called Kaiser Foundation Hospitals* ***(P-10266)***
Kaiser Foundation Health Plan, San Jose *Also called Kaiser Foundation Hospitals* ***(P-21516)***
Kaiser Foundation Health Plan, North Hollywood *Also called Kaiser Foundation Hospitals* ***(P-10268)***
Kaiser Foundation Health Plan, Los Angeles *Also called Kaiser Foundation Hospitals* ***(P-21520)***
Kaiser Foundation Health Plan, Fresno *Also called Kaiser Foundation Hospitals* ***(P-21521)***
Kaiser Foundation Health Plan, Modesto *Also called Kaiser Foundation Hospitals* ***(P-10269)***
Kaiser Foundation Health Plan, Orange *Also called Kaiser Foundation Hospitals* ***(P-10270)***
Kaiser Foundation Hospital......E......510 752-6295
4501 Broadway Oakland (94611) ***(P-22348)***
Kaiser Foundation Hospitals......C......714 279-4675
411 N Lakeview Ave Anaheim (92807) ***(P-19523)***
Kaiser Foundation Hospitals......C......949 262-5780
6 Willard Irvine (92604) ***(P-21475)***
Kaiser Foundation Hospitals......B......619 662-5107
4650 Palm Ave San Diego (92154) ***(P-12102)***
Kaiser Foundation Hospitals......D......510 675-5777
30116 Eigenbrodt Way Union City (94587) ***(P-10216)***
Kaiser Foundation Hospitals......A......408 361-2100
50 Great Oaks Blvd San Jose (95119) ***(P-22349)***
Kaiser Foundation Hospitals......C......949 425-3150
24502 Pacific Park Dr Aliso Viejo (92656) ***(P-19524)***
Kaiser Foundation Hospitals......D......619 542-7210
8889 Rio San Diego Dr San Diego (92108) ***(P-19525)***
Kaiser Foundation Hospitals......C......916 746-3937
1680 E Roseville Pkwy Roseville (95661) ***(P-21476)***
Kaiser Foundation Hospitals......A......707 393-4000
401 Bicentennial Way Santa Rosa (95403) ***(P-19526)***
Kaiser Foundation Hospitals......A......619 528-5888
4647 Zion Ave San Diego (92120) ***(P-12103)***
Kaiser Foundation Hospitals......A......818 719-2000
5601 De Soto Ave Woodland Hills (91367) ***(P-21477)***
Kaiser Foundation Hospitals......C......925 813-6500
4501 Sand Creek Rd Antioch (94531) ***(P-19527)***
Kaiser Foundation Hospitals......C......661 726-2500
43112 15th St W Lancaster (93534) ***(P-21478)***
Kaiser Foundation Hospitals......D......714 741-3448
12100 Euclid St Garden Grove (92840) ***(P-19528)***
Kaiser Foundation Hospitals......D......323 783-4011
4867 W Sunset Blvd Los Angeles (90027) ***(P-21479)***
Kaiser Foundation Hospitals......D......925 906-2380
320 Lennon Ln Walnut Creek (94598) ***(P-21480)***
Kaiser Foundation Hospitals......D......415 833-2616
2350 Geary Blvd Fl 2 San Francisco (94115) ***(P-10217)***
Kaiser Foundation Hospitals......A......925 295-4145
710 S Broadway Walnut Creek (94596) ***(P-22599)***
Kaiser Foundation Hospitals......A......626 851-1011
1011 Baldwin Park Blvd Baldwin Park (91706) ***(P-21481)***
Kaiser Foundation Hospitals......C......925 372-1000
200 Muir Rd Martinez (94553) ***(P-12104)***
Kaiser Foundation Hospitals......A......510 752-1000
3600 Broadway Oakland (94611) ***(P-19529)***
Kaiser Foundation Hospitals......B......562 657-9000
9333 Imperial Hwy Downey (90242) ***(P-21482)***
Kaiser Foundation Hospitals......A......415 833-2000
2425 Geary Blvd San Francisco (94115) ***(P-19530)***
Kaiser Foundation Hospitals (HQ)......C......510 271-6611
1 Kaiser Plz Oakland (94612) ***(P-21483)***
Kaiser Foundation Hospitals......E......626 405-5000
393 E Walnut St Pasadena (91188) ***(P-10218)***
Kaiser Foundation Hospitals......A......562 461-3000
9400 Rosecrans Ave Bellflower (90706) ***(P-21484)***
Kaiser Foundation Hospitals......A......510 752-1000
280 W Macarthur Blvd Oakland (94611) ***(P-21485)***
Kaiser Foundation Hospitals......D......707 645-2720
1761 Broadway St Ste 210 Vallejo (94589) ***(P-10219)***
Kaiser Foundation Hospitals......D......909 394-2530
1255 W Arrow Hwy San Dimas (91773) ***(P-21486)***
Kaiser Foundation Hospitals......D......888 750-0036
1301 California St Redlands (92374) ***(P-19531)***
Kaiser Foundation Hospitals......D......714 672-5100
1900 E Lambert Rd Brea (92821) ***(P-19532)***
Kaiser Foundation Hospitals......A......415 444-2000
99 Montecillo Rd San Rafael (94903) ***(P-19533)***
Kaiser Foundation Hospitals......D......619 528-2583
4405 Vandever Ave Fl 5 San Diego (92120) ***(P-21487)***
Kaiser Foundation Hospitals......B......510 307-1500
901 Nevin Ave Richmond (94801) ***(P-19534)***
Kaiser Foundation Hospitals......A......323 857-2000
6041 Cadillac Ave Los Angeles (90034) ***(P-19535)***
Kaiser Foundation Hospitals......A......818 375-2000
13651 Willard St Panorama City (91402) ***(P-21488)***
Kaiser Foundation Hospitals......B......408 972-6010
280 Hospital Pkwy San Jose (95119) ***(P-21489)***
Kaiser Foundation Hospitals......D......323 264-4310
3355 E 26th St Vernon (90058) ***(P-21490)***
Kaiser Foundation Hospitals......C......909 609-3800
17284 Slover Ave Fontana (92337) ***(P-19536)***
Kaiser Foundation Hospitals......D......415 444-3522
820 Las Gallinas Ave San Rafael (94903) ***(P-10220)***
Kaiser Foundation Hospitals......D......800 954-8000
1550 W Manchester Ave Los Angeles (90047) ***(P-10221)***
Kaiser Foundation Hospitals......D......510 752-7864
255 W Macarthur Blvd Oakland (94611) ***(P-10222)***
Kaiser Foundation Hospitals......D......559 448-4555
4785 N 1st St Fresno (93726) ***(P-10223)***
Kaiser Foundation Hospitals......D......916 544-6000
10305 Promenade Pkwy Elk Grove (95757) ***(P-10224)***
Kaiser Foundation Hospitals......D......888 750-0036
14011 Park Ave Victorville (92392) ***(P-10225)***
Kaiser Foundation Hospitals......D......619 528-5000
17140 Bernardo Center Dr San Diego (92128) ***(P-10226)***
Kaiser Foundation Hospitals......D......619 528-5000
5893 Copley Dr San Diego (92111) ***(P-10227)***
Kaiser Foundation Hospitals......D......866 984-7483
27309 Madison Ave Temecula (92590) ***(P-10228)***
Kaiser Foundation Hospitals......D......888 778-5000
11001 Sepulveda Blvd Mission Hills (91345) ***(P-10229)***
Kaiser Foundation Hospitals......D......818 375-2028
8001 Ventura Canyon Ave Panorama City (91402) ***(P-10230)***
Kaiser Foundation Hospitals......D......510 454-1000
27303 Sleepy Hollow Ave S Hayward (94545) ***(P-10231)***
Kaiser Foundation Hospitals......D......800 954-8000
5620 Mesmer Ave Los Angeles (90230) ***(P-10232)***
Kaiser Foundation Hospitals......A......707 624-4000
1 Quality Dr Vacaville (95688) ***(P-19537)***
Kaiser Foundation Hospitals......A......209 839-3200
2185 W Grant Line Rd Tracy (95377) ***(P-19538)***
Kaiser Foundation Hospitals......A......510 675-4010
3555 Whipple Rd Union City (94587) ***(P-19539)***
Kaiser Foundation Hospitals......A......888 750-0036
10850 Arrow Rte Rancho Cucamonga (91730) ***(P-19540)***
Kaiser Foundation Hospitals......A......888 988-2800
5475 E La Palma Ave Anaheim (92807) ***(P-19541)***
Kaiser Foundation Hospitals......A......877 524-7373
3733 San Dimas St Bakersfield (93301) ***(P-19542)***
Kaiser Foundation Hospitals......A......888 988-2800
3460 E La Palma Ave Anaheim (92806) ***(P-19543)***
Kaiser Foundation Hospitals......B......661 395-3000
2615 Chester Ave Bakersfield (93301) ***(P-21491)***
Kaiser Foundation Hospitals......A......877 524-7373
2531 Chester Ave Bakersfield (93301) ***(P-19544)***
Kaiser Foundation Hospitals......A......661 337-7160
2620 Chester Ave Bakersfield (93301) ***(P-19545)***
Kaiser Foundation Hospitals......A......877 524-7373
1200 Discovery Dr Bakersfield (93309) ***(P-19546)***
Kaiser Foundation Hospitals......A......800 823-4040
10820 183rd St Cerritos (90703) ***(P-19547)***
Kaiser Foundation Hospitals......A......888 515-3500
2620 Las Posas Rd Camarillo (93010) ***(P-19548)***
Kaiser Foundation Hospitals......A......877 524-7373
8800 Ming Ave Bakersfield (93311) ***(P-19549)***
Kaiser Foundation Hospitals......A......562 463-4377
12801 Crossroads Pkwy S City of Industry (91746) ***(P-19550)***
Kaiser Foundation Hospitals......A......800 823-4040
9449 Imperial Hwy Downey (90242) ***(P-19551)***
Kaiser Foundation Hospitals......A......442 281-5000
2185 Citracado Pkwy Escondido (92029) ***(P-19552)***
Kaiser Foundation Hospitals......A......800 780-1277
1336 Bridgegate Dr Diamond Bar (91765) ***(P-19553)***
Kaiser Foundation Hospitals......A......760 739-3000
555 E Valley Pkwy Escondido (92025) ***(P-19554)***
Kaiser Foundation Hospitals......A......800 823-4040
9353 Imperial Hwy Downey (90242) ***(P-19555)***
Kaiser Foundation Hospitals......A......707 427-4000
1550 Gateway Blvd Fairfield (94533) ***(P-19556)***
Kaiser Foundation Hospitals......A......800 922-2000
26882 Towne Centre Dr # 1 Foothill Ranch (92610) ***(P-19557)***
Kaiser Foundation Hospitals......A......866 205-3595
9310 Sierra Ave Fontana (92335) ***(P-19558)***
Kaiser Foundation Hospitals......A......916 986-4178
285 Palladio Pkwy Folsom (95630) ***(P-19559)***
Kaiser Foundation Hospitals......A......800 780-1230
18600 S Figueroa St Gardena (90248) ***(P-19560)***
Kaiser Foundation Hospitals......A......818 832-7200
10605 Balboa Blvd Ste 330 Granada Hills (91344) ***(P-19561)***
Kaiser Foundation Hospitals......A......800 954-8000
501 N Orange St Glendale (91203) ***(P-19562)***
Kaiser Foundation Hospitals......A......866 984-7483
46900 Monroe St Indio (92201) ***(P-19563)***
Kaiser Foundation Hospitals......B......661 949-5000
1600 W Avenue J Lancaster (93534) ***(P-21492)***
Kaiser Foundation Hospitals......A......619 528-5000
3875 Avocado Blvd La Mesa (91941) ***(P-19564)***
Kaiser Foundation Hospitals......A......916 543-5153
1900 Dresden Dr Lincoln (95648) ***(P-19565)***
Kaiser Foundation Hospitals......A......661 951-0070
44444 20th St W Lancaster (93534) ***(P-19566)***
Kaiser Foundation Hospitals......A......310 325-6542
2081 Palos Verdes Dr N Lomita (90717) ***(P-19567)***
Kaiser Foundation Hospitals......C......424 251-7000
2040 Pacific Coast Hwy Lomita (90717) ***(P-22600)***
Kaiser Foundation Hospitals......A......310 604-5700
3830 Martin Luther King Lynwood (90262) ***(P-19568)***
Kaiser Foundation Hospitals......A......209 735-5000
4601 Dale Rd Modesto (95356) ***(P-19569)***

ALPHABETIC

Kaiser Foundation Hospitals ....A.......888 778-5000
5250 Lankershim Blvd North Hollywood (91601) ***(P-19570)***
Kaiser Foundation Hospitals ....A.......209 735-5000
4125 Bangs Ave Modesto (95356) ***(P-19571)***
Kaiser Foundation Hospitals ....A.......562 807-6100
12501 Imperial Hwy Norwalk (90650) ***(P-19572)***
Kaiser Foundation Hospitals ....A.......909 724-5000
2295 S Vineyard Ave Ontario (91761) ***(P-19573)***
Kaiser Foundation Hospitals ....A.......888 515-3500
2200 E Gonzales Rd Oxnard (93036) ***(P-19574)***
Kaiser Foundation Hospitals ....A.......800 777-1256
73733 Fred Waring Dr Palm Desert (92260) ***(P-19575)***
Kaiser Foundation Hospitals ....A.......805 988-6300
2103 E Gonzales Rd Oxnard (93036) ***(P-19576)***
Kaiser Foundation Hospitals ....A.......510 243-4000
1301 Pinole Valley Rd Pinole (94564) ***(P-19577)***
Kaiser Foundation Hospitals ....A.......866 984-7483
University Park Ctr Palm Desert (92211) ***(P-19578)***
Kaiser Foundation Hospitals ....A.......951 248-4000
5225 Canyon Crest Dr Riverside (92507) ***(P-19579)***
Kaiser Foundation Hospitals ....A.......866 984-7483
14305 Meridian Pkwy Riverside (92518) ***(P-19580)***
Kaiser Foundation Hospitals ....A.......858 847-3500
3851 Shaw Ridge Rd San Diego (92130) ***(P-19581)***
Kaiser Foundation Hospitals ....A.......858 502-1350
4510 Viewridge Ave San Diego (92123) ***(P-19582)***
Kaiser Foundation Hospitals ....A.......650 358-7000
1000 Franklin Pkwy San Mateo (94403) ***(P-19583)***
Kaiser Foundation Hospitals ....C.......858 573-0090
7035 Convoy Ct San Diego (92111) ***(P-22601)***
Kaiser Foundation Hospitals ....A.......510 454-1000
2500 Merced St San Leandro (94577) ***(P-19584)***
Kaiser Foundation Hospitals ....A.......925 244-7600
2300 Camino Ramon San Ramon (94583) ***(P-19585)***
Kaiser Foundation Hospitals ....A.......714 223-2606
3601 S Harbor Blvd Santa Ana (92704) ***(P-19586)***
Kaiser Foundation Hospitals ....A.......888 778-5000
26415 Carl Boyer Dr Santa Clarita (91350) ***(P-19587)***
Kaiser Foundation Hospitals ....A.......888 515-3500
145 Hodencamp Rd Thousand Oaks (91360) ***(P-19588)***
Kaiser Foundation Hospitals ....A.......408 851-1000
1263 E Arques Ave Sunnyvale (94085) ***(P-19589)***
Kaiser Foundation Hospitals ....A.......888 515-3500
322 E Thousand Oaks Blvd Thousand Oaks (91360) ***(P-19590)***
Kaiser Foundation Hospitals ....A.......888 988-2800
2521 Michelle Dr Tustin (92780) ***(P-19591)***
Kaiser Foundation Hospitals ....B.......925 598-2799
5820 Owens Dr Bldg E-2 Pleasanton (94588) ***(P-21493)***
Kaiser Foundation Hospitals ....A.......408 972-7000
250 Hospital Pkwy San Jose (95119) ***(P-19592)***
Kaiser Foundation Hospitals ....A.......650 299-2000
1100 Veterans Blvd Redwood City (94063) ***(P-19593)***
Kaiser Foundation Hospitals ....A.......925 295-4000
1425 S Main St Walnut Creek (94596) ***(P-19594)***
Kaiser Foundation Hospitals ....E.......323 881-5516
5119 Pomona Blvd Los Angeles (90022) ***(P-12105)***
Kaiser Foundation Hospitals ....A.......310 325-5111
25825 Vermont Ave Harbor City (90710) ***(P-19595)***
Kaiser Foundation Hospitals ....C.......415 833-9688
601 Van Ness Ave Ste 2008 San Francisco (94102) ***(P-19596)***
Kaiser Foundation Hospitals ....D.......916 973-5000
1650 Response Rd Sacramento (95815) ***(P-21494)***
Kaiser Foundation Hospitals ....A.......909 427-5000
9961 Sierra Ave Fontana (92335) ***(P-19597)***
Kaiser Foundation Hospitals ....B.......619 641-4663
10990 San Dego Mission Rd San Diego (92108) ***(P-21495)***
Kaiser Foundation Hospitals ....E.......619 528-5000
8080 Parkway Dr La Mesa (91942) ***(P-21496)***
Kaiser Foundation Hospitals ....E.......661 398-5011
3501 Stockdale Hwy Bakersfield (93309) ***(P-21497)***
Kaiser Foundation Hospitals ....E.......408 945-2900
770 E Calaveras Blvd Milpitas (95035) ***(P-19598)***
Kaiser Foundation Hospitals ....A.......510 987-1000
1950 Franklin St Oakland (94612) ***(P-19599)***
Kaiser Foundation Hospitals ....E.......951 601-6174
12815 Heacock St Moreno Valley (92553) ***(P-12106)***
Kaiser Foundation Hospitals ....E.......951 353-2000
36450 Inland Valley Dr # 204 Wildomar (92595) ***(P-21498)***
Kaiser Foundation Hospitals ....E.......714 562-3420
5 Centerpointe Dr La Palma (90623) ***(P-19600)***
Kaiser Foundation Hospitals ....E.......818 552-3000
444 W Glenoaks Blvd Glendale (91202) ***(P-19601)***
Kaiser Foundation Hospitals ....E.......626 440-5639
3280 E Foothill Blvd Pasadena (91107) ***(P-19602)***
Kaiser Foundation Hospitals ....E.......714 685-3520
22550 Savi Ranch Pkwy Yorba Linda (92887) ***(P-19603)***
Kaiser Foundation Hospitals ....E.......619 528-5000
1630 E Main St El Cajon (92021) ***(P-21499)***
Kaiser Foundation Hospitals ....E.......858 573-0299
7060 Clairemont Mesa Blvd San Diego (92111) ***(P-19604)***
Kaiser Foundation Hospitals ....D.......323 562-6400
7825 Atlantic Ave Cudahy (90201) ***(P-21500)***
Kaiser Foundation Hospitals ....E.......619 528-5000
250 Travelodge Dr El Cajon (92020) ***(P-21501)***
Kaiser Foundation Hospitals ....E.......619 528-5000
732 N Broadway Escondido (92025) ***(P-19605)***
Kaiser Foundation Hospitals ....E.......866 319-4269
1249 S Sunset Ave West Covina (91790) ***(P-21502)***
Kaiser Foundation Hospitals ....E.......530 757-7100
1955 Cowell Blvd Davis (95618) ***(P-19606)***
Kaiser Foundation Hospitals ....E.......310 517-2956
15446 S Western Ave Gardena (90249) ***(P-21503)***
Kaiser Foundation Hospitals ....E.......818 592-3100
21263 Erwin St Woodland Hills (91367) ***(P-21504)***
Kaiser Foundation Hospitals ....E.......916 631-3088
10725 International Dr Rancho Cordova (95670) ***(P-10233)***
Kaiser Foundation Hospitals ....E.......707 765-3900
3900 Lakeville Hwy Petaluma (94954) ***(P-21505)***
Kaiser Foundation Hospitals ....E.......415 899-7400
97 San Marin Dr Novato (94945) ***(P-21506)***
Kaiser Foundation Hospitals ....E.......707 624-4000
1 Quality Dr Vacaville (95688) ***(P-10234)***
Kaiser Foundation Hospitals ....A.......510 678-4000
27400 Hesperian Blvd Hayward (94545) ***(P-19607)***
Kaiser Foundation Hospitals ....C.......650 903-3000
555 Castro St Fl 3 Mountain View (94041) ***(P-21507)***
Kaiser Foundation Hospitals ....C.......916 784-4000
1001 Riverside Ave Roseville (95678) ***(P-19608)***
Kaiser Foundation Hospitals ....D.......714 284-6634
1011 S East St Fl 1 Anaheim (92805) ***(P-10235)***
Kaiser Foundation Hospitals ....A.......925 906-2000
501 Lennon Ln Walnut Creek (94598) ***(P-21508)***
Kaiser Foundation Hospitals ....B.......925 847-5000
7601 Stoneridge Dr Pleasanton (94588) ***(P-21509)***
Kaiser Foundation Hospitals ....C.......916 817-5200
2155 Iron Point Rd Folsom (95630) ***(P-19609)***
Kaiser Foundation Hospitals ....D.......408 871-6500
220 E Hacienda Ave Campbell (95008) ***(P-19610)***
Kaiser Foundation Hospitals ....B.......510 891-3400
2000 Brdwy Oakland (94612) ***(P-21510)***
Kaiser Foundation Hospitals ....C.......661 334-2020
5055 California Ave # 110 Bakersfield (93309) ***(P-21511)***
Kaiser Foundation Hospitals ....D.......925 926-3000
25 N Via Monte Walnut Creek (94598) ***(P-10236)***
Kaiser Foundation Hospitals ....A.......650 742-2000
1200 El Camino Real South San Francisco (94080) ***(P-19611)***
Kaiser Foundation Hospitals ....C.......323 298-3300
5105 W Goldleaf Cir Los Angeles (90056) ***(P-22602)***
Kaiser Foundation Hospitals ....A.......916 688-2000
6600 Bruceville Rd Sacramento (95823) ***(P-19612)***
Kaiser Foundation Hospitals ....C.......925 779-5000
3400 Delta Fair Blvd Antioch (94509) ***(P-22603)***
Kaiser Foundation Hospitals ....B.......510 248-3000
39400 Paseo Padre Pkwy Fremont (94538) ***(P-19613)***
Kaiser Foundation Hospitals ....C.......707 258-2500
3285 Claremont Way NAPA (94558) ***(P-12107)***
Kaiser Foundation Hospitals ....A.......707 651-1000
975 Sereno Dr Vallejo (94589) ***(P-21512)***
Kaiser Foundation Hospitals ....C.......213 580-7200
765 W College St Los Angeles (90012) ***(P-21959)***
Kaiser Foundation Hospitals ....E.......866 340-5974
12470 Whittier Blvd Whittier (90602) ***(P-21513)***
Kaiser Foundation Hospitals ....D.......661 222-2323
27107 Tourney Rd Santa Clarita (91355) ***(P-19614)***
Kaiser Foundation Hospitals ....D.......559 324-5100
2071 Herndon Ave Clovis (93611) ***(P-10237)***
Kaiser Foundation Hospitals ....D.......888 515-3500
21263 Erwin St Woodland Hills (91367) ***(P-10238)***
Kaiser Foundation Hospitals ....D.......916 784-4050
1840 Sierra Gardens Dr Roseville (95661) ***(P-10239)***
Kaiser Foundation Hospitals ....D.......559 658-8388
40595 Westlake Dr Oakhurst (93644) ***(P-10240)***
Kaiser Foundation Hospitals ....D.......888 750-0036
2295 S Vineyard Ave Ontario (91761) ***(P-10241)***
Kaiser Foundation Hospitals ....D.......760 360-1475
42575 Washington St Palm Desert (92211) ***(P-10242)***
Kaiser Foundation Hospitals ....D.......888 515-3500
888 S Hill Rd Ventura (93003) ***(P-10243)***
Kaiser Foundation Hospitals ....D.......888 988-2800
3401 S Harbor Blvd Santa Ana (92704) ***(P-10244)***
Kaiser Foundation Hospitals ....D.......888 750-0036
1717 Date Pike San Bernardino (92404) ***(P-10245)***
Kaiser Foundation Hospitals ....D.......866 984-7483
2055 Kellogg Ave Corona (92879) ***(P-22827)***
Kaiser Foundation Hospitals ....D.......888 750-0036
11911 Central Ave Chino (91710) ***(P-10246)***
Kaiser Foundation Hospitals ....D.......650 301-5860
395 Hickey Blvd Daly City (94015) ***(P-10247)***
Kaiser Foundation Hospitals ....D.......510 675-2170
3553 Whipple Rd Union City (94587) ***(P-10248)***
Kaiser Foundation Hospitals ....D.......209 832-6339
2417 Naglee Rd Tracy (95304) ***(P-10249)***
Kaiser Foundation Hospitals ....D.......650 742-2100
901 El Camino Real San Bruno (94066) ***(P-10250)***
Kaiser Foundation Hospitals ....D.......707 571-3835
3554 Round Barn Blvd Santa Rosa (95403) ***(P-10251)***
Kaiser Foundation Hospitals ....D.......707 393-4033
3925 Old Redwood Hwy Santa Rosa (95403) ***(P-10252)***
Kaiser Foundation Hospitals ....D.......855 268-4096
1320 Standiford Ave Modesto (95350) ***(P-10253)***
Kaiser Foundation Hospitals ....D.......707 206-3000
5900 State Farm Dr # 100 Rohnert Park (94928) ***(P-10254)***
Kaiser Foundation Hospitals ....D.......510 752-1190
2417 Central Ave Alameda (94501) ***(P-10255)***
Kaiser Foundation Hospitals ....D.......510 251-0121
969 Broadway Oakland (94607) ***(P-10256)***
Kaiser Foundation Hospitals ....D.......562 461-3084
9333 Rosecrans Ave Bellflower (90706) ***(P-10257)***
Kaiser Foundation Hospitals ....D.......559 898-6000
2651 Highland Ave Selma (93662) ***(P-10258)***

Kaiser Foundation Hospitals ....D......714 748-7622
  4201 W Chapman Ave Orange (92868) *(P-10259)*
Kaiser Foundation Hospitals ....D......866 370-1942
  1717 E Vista Chino Ste B2 Palm Springs (92262) *(P-10260)*
Kaiser Foundation Hospitals ....D......800 780-1230
  20790 Madrona Ave Torrance (90503) *(P-10261)*
Kaiser Foundation Hospitals ....D......888 515-3500
  365 E Hillcrest Dr Thousand Oaks (91360) *(P-10262)*
Kaiser Foundation Hospitals ....D......888 515-3500
  3900 Alamo St Simi Valley (93063) *(P-10263)*
Kaiser Foundation Hospitals ....D......888 988-2800
  30400 Camino Capistrano San Juan Capistrano (92675) *(P-10264)*
Kaiser Foundation Hospitals ....D......909 427-3910
  9961 Sierra Ave Fontana (92335) *(P-10265)*
Kaiser Foundation Hospitals ....D......562 622-4190
  12200 Bellflower Blvd Downey (90242) *(P-10266)*
Kaiser Foundation Hospitals ....D......619 409-6405
  3955 Bonita Rd Bonita (91902) *(P-21514)*
Kaiser Foundation Hospitals ....D......805 482-0707
  5259 Mission Oaks Blvd Camarillo (93012) *(P-10267)*
Kaiser Foundation Hospitals ....A......951 353-2000
  10800 Magnolia Ave Riverside (92505) *(P-19615)*
Kaiser Foundation Hospitals ....A......909 427-5521
  789 E Cooley Dr Colton (92324) *(P-12108)*
Kaiser Foundation Hospitals ....A......209 825-3700
  1777 W Yosemite Ave Manteca (95337) *(P-21515)*
Kaiser Foundation Hospitals ....C......408 972-3000
  250 Hospital Pkwy Bldg D San Jose (95119) *(P-19616)*
Kaiser Foundation Hospitals ....A......415 833-2000
  2425 Geary Blvd San Francisco (94115) *(P-19617)*
Kaiser Foundation Hospitals ....B......951 243-0811
  27300 Iris Ave Moreno Valley (92555) *(P-19618)*
Kaiser Foundation Hospitals ....D......408 972-3376
  5755 Cottle Rd San Jose (95123) *(P-21516)*
Kaiser Foundation Hospitals ....D......818 503-7082
  11666 Sherman Way North Hollywood (91605) *(P-10268)*
Kaiser Foundation Hospitals ....C......408 972-6700
  275 Hospital Pkwy 765a San Jose (95119) *(P-21517)*
Kaiser Foundation Hospitals ....B......310 419-3303
  110 N La Brea Ave Inglewood (90301) *(P-19619)*
Kaiser Foundation Hospitals ....B......626 440-5659
  1055 E Colo Blvd Ste 100 Pasadena (91106) *(P-21518)*
Kaiser Foundation Hospitals ....A......916 784-4000
  1600 Eureka Rd Roseville (95661) *(P-21519)*
Kaiser Foundation Hospitals ....E......800 954-8000
  4867 W Sunset Blvd Los Angeles (90027) *(P-21520)*
Kaiser Foundation Hospitals ....A......559 448-4500
  7300 N Fresno St Fresno (93720) *(P-21521)*
Kaiser Foundation Hospitals ....A......559 448-4500
  7300 N Fresno St Fresno (93720) *(P-19620)*
Kaiser Foundation Hospitals ....B......888 750-0036
  250 W San Jose Ave Claremont (91711) *(P-21522)*
Kaiser Foundation Hospitals ....C......760 931-4228
  6860 Avenida Encinas Carlsbad (92011) *(P-19621)*
Kaiser Foundation Hospitals ....C......916 525-6300
  7300 Wyndham Dr Sacramento (95823) *(P-21523)*
Kaiser Foundation Hospitals ....D......310 513-6707
  23621 Main St Carson (90745) *(P-22604)*
Kaiser Foundation Hospitals ....C......209 476-3101
  7373 West Ln Stockton (95210) *(P-21524)*
Kaiser Foundation Hospitals ....D......209 557-1000
  1625 I St Modesto (95354) *(P-10269)*
Kaiser Foundation Hospitals ....D......888 988-2800
  200 N Lewis St Fl 1 Orange (92868) *(P-10270)*
Kaiser Foundation Hospitals ....A......408 851-1000
  710 Lawrence Expy Santa Clara (95051) *(P-21525)*
Kaiser Foundation Hospitals ....A......866 984-7483
  182 Granite St Corona (92879) *(P-12109)*
Kaiser Foundation Hospitals ....B......949 932-5000
  6640 Alton Pkwy Irvine (92618) *(P-12110)*
Kaiser Foundation Hospitals ....E......714 967-4700
  1900 E 4th St Santa Ana (92705) *(P-10271)*
Kaiser Fundation Hlth Plan Inc (PA) ....B......510 271-5800
  1 Kaiser Plz Oakland (94612) *(P-10272)*
Kaiser Fundation Hlth Plan Inc ....D......510 752-7644
  3801 Howe St Oakland (94611) *(P-10273)*
Kaiser Fundation Hlth Plan Inc ....D......510 271-5800
  4460 Hacienda Dr Pleasanton (94588) *(P-10274)*
Kaiser Fundation Hlth Plan Inc ....D......510 987-2255
  1950 Franklin St Fl 3 Oakland (94612) *(P-10275)*
Kaiser Group Holdings Inc ....D......510 419-6000
  2101 Webster St Ste 1000 Oakland (94612) *(P-25775)*
Kaiser Hlth Plan Asset MGT Inc ....E......510 271-5910
  1 Kaiser Plz Ste 1333 Oakland (94612) *(P-26914)*
Kaiser Manteca Medical Office ....C......209 825-3700
  1721 W Yosemite Ave Manteca (95337) *(P-22099)*
Kaiser Med Clinic ....C......650 903-2103
  555 Castro St Mountain View (94041) *(P-19622)*
Kaiser Med Security Services ....D......415 833-3683
  2241 Geary Blvd San Francisco (94115) *(P-16710)*
Kaiser Mental Health Center, Los Angeles *Also called Kaiser Foundation Hospitals (P-21959)*
Kaiser Permanente, San Jose *Also called Kaiser Foundation Hospitals (P-22349)*
Kaiser Permanente, San Diego *Also called Southern Cal Prmnnte Med Group (P-19907)*
Kaiser Permanente, San Diego *Also called Kaiser Foundation Hospitals (P-12103)*
Kaiser Permanente, Woodland Hills *Also called Kaiser Foundation Hospitals (P-21477)*
Kaiser Permanente, Lancaster *Also called Kaiser Foundation Hospitals (P-21478)*
Kaiser Permanente, Garden Grove *Also called Kaiser Foundation Hospitals (P-19528)*
Kaiser Permanente, Los Angeles *Also called Kaiser Foundation Hospitals (P-21479)*
Kaiser Permanente, Walnut Creek *Also called Kaiser Foundation Hospitals (P-22599)*

Kaiser Permanente, Baldwin Park *Also called Kaiser Foundation Hospitals (P-21481)*
Kaiser Permanente, Oakland *Also called Kaiser Foundation Hospitals (P-21483)*
Kaiser Permanente, Bellflower *Also called Kaiser Foundation Hospitals (P-21484)*
Kaiser Permanente, Oakland *Also called Kaiser Foundation Hospitals (P-21485)*
Kaiser Permanente, San Dimas *Also called Kaiser Foundation Hospitals (P-21486)*
Kaiser Permanente, Redlands *Also called Kaiser Foundation Hospitals (P-19531)*
Kaiser Permanente, Brea *Also called Kaiser Foundation Hospitals (P-19532)*
Kaiser Permanente, San Rafael *Also called Kaiser Foundation Hospitals (P-19533)*
Kaiser Permanente, Pasadena *Also called Southern Cal Prmnnte Med Group (P-10317)*
Kaiser Permanente, San Diego *Also called Kaiser Foundation Hospitals (P-21487)*
Kaiser Permanente, Richmond *Also called Kaiser Foundation Hospitals (P-19534)*
Kaiser Permanente, Panorama City *Also called Kaiser Foundation Hospitals (P-21488)*
Kaiser Permanente, San Jose *Also called Kaiser Foundation Hospitals (P-19592)*
Kaiser Permanente, Redwood City *Also called Kaiser Foundation Hospitals (P-19593)*
Kaiser Permanente, Walnut Creek *Also called Kaiser Foundation Hospitals (P-19594)*
Kaiser Permanente, Los Angeles *Also called Kaiser Foundation Hospitals (P-12105)*
Kaiser Permanente, Harbor City *Also called Kaiser Foundation Hospitals (P-19595)*
Kaiser Permanente, Sacramento *Also called Kaiser Foundation Hospitals (P-21494)*
Kaiser Permanente, Fontana *Also called Kaiser Foundation Hospitals (P-19597)*
Kaiser Permanente, West Covina *Also called Kaiser Foundation Hospitals (P-21502)*
Kaiser Permanente, Walnut Creek *Also called Kaiser Foundation Hospitals (P-21508)*
Kaiser Permanente, Pleasanton *Also called Kaiser Foundation Hospitals (P-21509)*
KAISER PERMANENTE, Oakland *Also called Kaiser Hlth Plan Asset MGT Inc (P-26914)*
Kaiser Permanente, Bakersfield *Also called Kaiser Foundation Hospitals (P-21511)*
Kaiser Permanente, South San Francisco *Also called Kaiser Foundation Hospitals (P-19611)*
Kaiser Permanente, Antioch *Also called Kaiser Foundation Hospitals (P-22603)*
Kaiser Permanente, Fremont *Also called Kaiser Foundation Hospitals (P-19613)*
Kaiser Permanente, NAPA *Also called Kaiser Foundation Hospitals (P-12107)*
Kaiser Permanente, Whittier *Also called Kaiser Foundation Hospitals (P-21513)*
Kaiser Permanente, Santa Clarita *Also called Kaiser Foundation Hospitals (P-19614)*
Kaiser Permanente, Colton *Also called Kaiser Foundation Hospitals (P-12108)*
Kaiser Permanente, San Francisco *Also called Kaiser Foundation Hospitals (P-19617)*
Kaiser Permanente, Inglewood *Also called Kaiser Foundation Hospitals (P-19619)*
Kaiser Permanente, Pasadena *Also called Kaiser Foundation Hospitals (P-21518)*
Kaiser Permanente, Downey *Also called Southern Cal Prmnnte Med Group (P-10320)*
Kaiser Permanente, Roseville *Also called Kaiser Foundation Hospitals (P-21519)*
Kaiser Permanente, Fresno *Also called Kaiser Foundation Hospitals (P-19620)*
Kaiser Permanente, Claremont *Also called Kaiser Foundation Hospitals (P-21522)*
Kaiser Permanente, Carson *Also called Kaiser Foundation Hospitals (P-22604)*
Kaiser Permanente, Stockton *Also called Kaiser Foundation Hospitals (P-21524)*
Kaiser Permanente, Santa Ana *Also called Kaiser Foundation Hospitals (P-10271)*
Kaiser Permanente ....D......510 450-2109
  3505 Broadway Oakland (94611) *(P-21526)*
Kaiser Permanente Admin H ....C......559 448-4405
  P.O. Box 12766 Oakland (94604) *(P-10276)*
Kaiser Permanente Advice, Sacramento *Also called Kaiser Foundation Hospitals (P-21523)*
Kaiser Permanente Division RES, Oakland *Also called Kaiser Foundation Hospitals (P-21510)*
Kaiser Permanente Eye, Roseville *Also called Kaiser Foundation Hospitals (P-21476)*
Kaiser Permanente Kearny, San Diego *Also called Kaiser Foundation Hospitals (P-19582)*
Kaiser Permanente Member Svcs, Palm Desert *Also called Kaiser Foundation Hospitals (P-19575)*
Kaiser Permanente Moreno, Moreno Valley *Also called Kaiser Foundation Hospitals (P-19618)*
Kaiser Permanente San, San Francisco *Also called Kaiser Foundation Hospitals (P-19530)*
Kaiser Permanente San, San Mateo *Also called Kaiser Foundation Hospitals (P-19583)*
Kaiser Permanente San, San Leandro *Also called Kaiser Foundation Hospitals (P-19584)*
Kaiser Permanente San, San Jose *Also called Kaiser Foundation Hospitals (P-21517)*
Kaiser Permanente San Fran, San Francisco *Also called Kaiser Foundation Hospitals (P-19596)*
Kaiser Permanente San Jose, San Jose *Also called Kaiser Foundation Hospitals (P-19616)*
Kaiser Permanente Santa, Santa Rosa *Also called Kaiser Foundation Hospitals (P-19526)*
Kaiser Permanente Santa, Santa Clara *Also called Kaiser Foundation Hospitals (P-21525)*
Kaiser Permanente South, Sacramento *Also called Kaiser Foundation Hospitals (P-19612)*
Kaiser Permanente West, Los Angeles *Also called Kaiser Foundation Hospitals (P-19535)*
Kaiser Perminente, Folsom *Also called Kaiser Foundation Hospitals (P-19609)*
Kaiser Prmanente Internet Svcs, Pleasanton *Also called Kaiser Foundation Hospitals (P-21493)*
Kaiser Prmnente Downey Med Ctr, Downey *Also called Kaiser Foundation Hospitals (P-21482)*
Kaiser Prmnnte Antioch Med Ctr, Antioch *Also called Kaiser Foundation Hospitals (P-19527)*
Kaiser Prmnnte Hayward Med Ctr, Hayward *Also called Kaiser Foundation Hospitals (P-19607)*
Kaiser Prmnnte Manteca Med Ctr, Manteca *Also called Kaiser Foundation Hospitals (P-21515)*
Kaiser Prmnnte Modesto Med Ctr, Modesto *Also called Permanente Medical Group Inc (P-10300)*
Kaiser Prmnnte Psadena Med Off, Pasadena *Also called Kaiser Foundation Hospitals (P-19602)*
Kaiser Prmnnte Vallejo Med Ctr, Vallejo *Also called Kaiser Foundation Hospitals (P-21512)*
Kaiser Radiology ....D......559 448-5541
  7300 N Fresno St Fresno (93720) *(P-22100)*
Kaiserair Inc (PA) ....C......510 569-9622
  8735 Earhart Rd Oakland (94621) *(P-8965)*
Kaizen Staffing, San Diego *Also called Payrollingcom Corp (P-26269)*
Kajima Construction Svcs Inc ....E......323 269-0020
  250 E 1st St Ste 400 Los Angeles (90012) *(P-1412)*

Employee Codes: A=Over 500 employees, B=251-500
C=101-250, D=51-100, E=50
2019 Directory of California
Wholesalers and Services Companies
© Mergent Inc. 1-800-342-5647
1353

Kajima International, Los Angeles *Also called Kajima Construction Svcs Inc* ***(P-1412)***
Kal Krishnan Consulting Svcs (PA)..............................D.......510 893-3500
800 S Figueroa St # 1210 Los Angeles (90017) ***(P-26915)***
Kal Tool Co, Baldwin Park *Also called G K Tool Corp* ***(P-7588)***
Kaleidioscope Stadium Cinema, Mission Viejo *Also called Edwards Theatres Circuit Inc* ***(P-18290)***
Kallidus Inc..............................D.......877 554-2176
425 Market St Ste 2200 San Francisco (94105) ***(P-15247)***
Kalpana LLC (PA)..............................B.......949 610-8200
620 Newport Center Dr # 1600 Newport Beach (92660) ***(P-12798)***
Kalpana LLC..............................C.......619 543-9000
901 Camino Del Rio S San Diego (92108) ***(P-12799)***
Kaman Industrial Tech Corp..............................E.......909 390-7919
910 S Wanamaker Ave Ontario (91761) ***(P-7853)***
Kamiya, Kenneth M Insurance, Torrance *Also called Charles M Kamiya and Sons Inc* ***(P-10581)***
Kamps Company..............................C.......209 823-8924
1262 Dupont Ct Manteca (95336) ***(P-14868)***
Kamunity Properties (PA)..............................E.......805 682-5008
3760 State St Santa Barbara (93105) ***(P-11041)***
Kan-Di-Ki LLC (PA)..............................C.......818 549-1880
2820 N Ontario St Burbank (91504) ***(P-22101)***
Kana Pipeline Inc..............................D.......714 986-1400
12620 Magnolia Ave Riverside (92503) ***(P-1942)***
Kana Software Inc (HQ)..............................D.......650 614-8300
2550 Walsh Ave Ste 120 Santa Clara (95051) ***(P-15727)***
Kandarian Agri Enterprises..............................C.......559 834-1501
116 W Adams Ave Fowler (93625) ***(P-151)***
Kane & Finkel LLC..............................D.......415 777-4990
534 4th St San Francisco (94107) ***(P-13854)***
Kane Fnkle Hlthcare Cmmnctions, San Francisco *Also called Kane & Finkel LLC* ***(P-13854)***
Kaney Foods, San Luis Obispo *Also called Amk Foodservices Inc* ***(P-8380)***
Kang Family Partners LLC..............................C.......805 688-1000
555 Mcmurray Rd Buellton (93427) ***(P-12800)***
Kanopy Insurance Center LLC..............................C.......877 513-2434
545 N Mountain Ave # 205 Upland (91786) ***(P-10502)***
Kapl Inc..............................B.......714 991-9543
1126 N Brookhurst St Anaheim (92801) ***(P-26389)***
Karam Bath..............................E.......559 864-3868
1673 W Kamm Ave Caruthers (93609) ***(P-152)***
Karcher Environmental Inc (PA)..............................C.......714 385-1490
2300 E Orangewood Ave Anaheim (92806) ***(P-3542)***
Karma Inc..............................C.......209 239-1222
410 Eastwood Ave Manteca (95336) ***(P-20551)***
Karsyn Construction Inc..............................D.......559 271-2900
2740 N Sunnyside Ave Fresno (93727) ***(P-1571)***
Kasdan Smnds Riley Vaughan LLP (PA)..............................D.......949 851-9000
19900 Macarthur Blvd # 850 Irvine (92612) ***(P-23160)***
Kash Apparel LLC..............................D.......213 747-8885
1437 E 20th St Los Angeles (90011) ***(P-8310)***
Kaspick & Co LLC (HQ)..............................D.......650 585-4100
203 Redwood Shores Pkwy # 300 Redwood City (94065) ***(P-27293)***
Katana Racing Inc (PA)..............................C.......562 977-8565
14407 Alondra Blvd La Mirada (90638) ***(P-6651)***
Katana Racing Whl & Tire Distr, La Mirada *Also called Katana Racing Inc* ***(P-6651)***
Kate Somerville Holdings LLC (HQ)..............................D.......323 655-4170
144 S Beverly Dr Ste 500 Beverly Hills (90212) ***(P-8185)***
Kate Summerville, Beverly Hills *Also called Skin Health Experts Medic* ***(P-22679)***
Katella Properties..............................C.......562 596-5561
3902 Katella Ave Los Alamitos (90720) ***(P-20552)***
Katerra Inc (PA)..............................D.......650 422-3572
2494 Sand Hill Rd Ste 100 Menlo Park (94025) ***(P-1068)***
Katherine Bousson..............................D.......510 582-1166
1015 Palisade St Hayward (94542) ***(P-19191)***
Katten Muchin Rosenman LLP..............................C.......310 788-4498
515 S Flower St Los Angeles (90071) ***(P-23161)***
Katten Muchin Rosenman LLP..............................C.......415 360-5444
1999 Harrison St Ste 700 Oakland (94612) ***(P-23162)***
Katten Muchin Rosenman LLP..............................C.......310 788-4400
2029 Century Park E # 2600 Los Angeles (90067) ***(P-23163)***
Katz Media Group Inc..............................D.......323 966-5000
5700 Wilshire Blvd # 100 Los Angeles (90036) ***(P-27763)***
Katzkin Leather Inc (PA)..............................C.......323 725-1243
6868 W Acco St Montebello (90640) ***(P-9226)***
Kaufman & Broad, Los Angeles *Also called Kaufman and Broad Limited* ***(P-1345)***
Kaufman & Broad, Los Angeles *Also called Kbsa Inc* ***(P-1347)***
Kaufman and Broad Limited..............................C.......310 231-4000
10990 Wilshire Blvd Fl 7 Los Angeles (90024) ***(P-1345)***
Kaufman Properties, Woodland Hills *Also called 7410 Woodman Avenue LLC* ***(P-10970)***
Kautz Ironstone Vineyards, Murphys *Also called Kautz Vineyards Inc* ***(P-153)***
Kautz Vineyards Inc (PA)..............................D.......209 728-1251
1894 6 Mile Rd Murphys (95247) ***(P-153)***
Kava Holdings Inc (PA)..............................B.......310 472-1211
701 Stone Canyon Rd Los Angeles (90077) ***(P-12801)***
Kavaliro, Petaluma *Also called AB Closing Corporation* ***(P-14562)***
Kawahara Nursery Inc..............................C.......408 779-2400
698 Burnett Ave Morgan Hill (95037) ***(P-273)***
Kawai America Corporation (HQ)..............................E.......310 631-1771
2055 E University Dr Compton (90220) ***(P-8041)***
Kawasaki Motors Corp USA (HQ)..............................B.......949 837-4683
26972 Burbank Foothill Ranch (92610) ***(P-6601)***
Kaweah Delta Health Care Dst..............................C.......559 591-5513
355 Monte Vista Dr Dinuba (93618) ***(P-21527)***
Kaweah Delta Health Care Dst (PA)..............................A.......559 624-2000
400 W Mineral King Ave Visalia (93291) ***(P-21528)***
Kaweah Delta Medical Center, Visalia *Also called Kaweah Delta Health Care Dst* ***(P-21528)***
Kaweah Dlta Hlth Care Dst Gild..............................C.......559 624-3100
4945 W Cypress Ave Visalia (93277) ***(P-22828)***
Kaweah Dlta Hlth Care Dst Gild..............................C.......559 592-7300
1014 San Juan Ave Ste A Exeter (93221) ***(P-22829)***
Kaweah Dlta Hlth Care Dst Gild..............................C.......559 592-7128
1014 San Juan Ave Exeter (93221) ***(P-19623)***
Kaweah Dlta Hlth Care Dst Gild..............................C.......559 624-4800
1110 S Ben Maddox Way Visalia (93292) ***(P-19624)***
Kawela One LLC..............................D.......650 843-5000
3000 El Camino Real Palo Alto (94306) ***(P-23164)***
Kay Dix Inc..............................E.......916 776-1701
14400 Andrus Island Rd Isleton (95641) ***(P-221)***
Kayne Anderson Rudni..............................D.......310 229-9260
1800 Avenue Of The Stars # 200 Los Angeles (90067) ***(P-12040)***
Kaza Azteca America Inc..............................C.......818 241-5400
3900 W Alameda Ave # 1200 Burbank (91505) ***(P-5803)***
Kazan McClain Satterley &..............................C.......877 995-6372
55 Harrison St Ste 400 Oakland (94607) ***(P-23165)***
Kazarian/Jewett Inc..............................E.......562 594-5927
6621 Pcf Cast Hwy Ste 120 Long Beach (90803) ***(P-1413)***
Kazeon Systems Inc..............................D.......650 641-8100
2841 Mission College Blvd Santa Clara (95054) ***(P-15248)***
KB Home (PA)..............................D.......310 231-4000
10990 Wilshire Blvd Fl 5 Los Angeles (90024) ***(P-10430)***
KB Home Coastal Inc..............................D.......310 231-4000
10990 Wilshire Blvd Fl 7 Los Angeles (90024) ***(P-1346)***
KB Home Grater Los Angeles Inc (HQ)..............................D.......310 231-4000
10990 Wilshire Blvd # 700 Los Angeles (90024) ***(P-1188)***
KB Home South Bay Inc..............................C.......925 983-2500
5000 Executive Pkwy # 125 San Ramon (94583) ***(P-1297)***
Kbak TV Channel 29 CBS..............................D.......661 327-7955
1901 Westwind Dr Bakersfield (93301) ***(P-5804)***
Kbaktv, Bakersfield *Also called Fisher Communications Inc* ***(P-5791)***
Kbl Group International Ltd..............................E.......562 699-9995
9142 9150 Norwalk Blvd Santa Fe Springs (90670) ***(P-8311)***
Kbl International, Santa Fe Springs *Also called Kbl Group International Ltd* ***(P-8311)***
Kbm Building Services, San Diego *Also called Kbm Fclity Sltons Holdings LLC* ***(P-14298)***
Kbm Fclity Sltons Holdings LLC..............................B.......858 467-0202
7976 Engineer Rd Ste 200 San Diego (92111) ***(P-14298)***
Kbrwyle Tech Solutions LLC..............................C.......760 255-8322
850 E Main St Barstow (92311) ***(P-25776)***
Kbrwyle Tech Solutions LLC..............................B.......805 734-2982
Vanonbrg Air Frc Bldg 660 Lompoc (93438) ***(P-5986)***
Kbsa Inc..............................D.......310 231-4000
10990 Wilshire Blvd 7th Los Angeles (90024) ***(P-1347)***
Kbzt Broadcasting, San Diego *Also called Abe Entercom Holdings LLC* ***(P-5690)***
Kc Services, Buena Park *Also called Korean Community Services Inc* ***(P-23885)***
Kcao, Hanford *Also called Kings Community Action O* ***(P-23882)***
Kcb Builders, Long Beach *Also called Kazarian/Jewett Inc* ***(P-1413)***
Kcb Towers Inc..............................D.......909 862-0322
27260 Meines St Highland (92346) ***(P-3380)***
Kcba Fox TV 35, Salinas *Also called Cowles California Media Co* ***(P-5780)***
Kcbs News Radio 74..............................D.......415 765-4112
865 Battery St San Francisco (94111) ***(P-5732)***
Kcetlink (PA)..............................C.......747 201-5000
2900 W Alameda Ave # 600 Burbank (91505) ***(P-5805)***
Kci Environmental Inc..............................E.......805 543-3311
207 Suburban Rd Ste 6 San Luis Obispo (93401) ***(P-27937)***
KCRW FM RADIO, Santa Monica *Also called Kcrw Foundation Inc* ***(P-24794)***
Kcrw Foundation Inc..............................D.......310 450-5183
1900 Pico Blvd Santa Monica (90405) ***(P-24794)***
KCS Electric Inc..............................D.......623 551-1500
1585 N Harmony Cir Anaheim (92807) ***(P-2622)***
Kcsm TV & Radio, San Mateo *Also called San Mateo County Community* ***(P-5836)***
Kdc Construction, West Sacramento *Also called Cirks Construction Inc* ***(P-1504)***
Kdc Inc (HQ)..............................C.......714 828-7000
4462 Corporate Center Dr Los Alamitos (90720) ***(P-2623)***
Kdc Systems, Los Alamitos *Also called Kdc Inc* ***(P-2623)***
Kdfcfm Radio, San Francisco *Also called Bonneville International Corp* ***(P-5693)***
Kdg Construction Consulting, Glendale *Also called Kennard Development Group* ***(P-1298)***
KDI Elements..............................C.......760 345-9933
79431 Country Club Dr Bermuda Dunes (92203) ***(P-3000)***
Kds Marketing..............................C.......818 240-7000
965 N Todd Ave Azusa (91702) ***(P-17269)***
Kds Printing and Packaging Inc..............................E.......909 770-5400
13397 Marlay Ave Ste A Fontana (92337) ***(P-17270)***
Kdtv, San Jose *Also called Univision Television Group Inc* ***(P-5845)***
Kearn Alternative Care Inc (PA)..............................B.......661 631-2036
2029 21st St Bakersfield (93301) ***(P-22350)***
Kearny Mesa Convalescent Hosp, San Diego *Also called Linda Vista Manor Inc* ***(P-20593)***
Keating Dental Arts Inc..............................C.......949 955-2100
16881 Hale Ave Ste A Irvine (92606) ***(P-22171)***
Keb Keb Magic Clown..............................D.......916 369-6054
637 Germaine Dr Galt (95632) ***(P-19192)***
Kec Engineering..............................C.......951 734-3010
200 N Sherman Ave Corona (92882) ***(P-1800)***
Keck Hospital of Usc..............................D.......800 872-2273
1500 San Pablo St Los Angeles (90033) ***(P-21529)***
Kedren Acute Psychia Hospit An, Los Angeles *Also called Kedren Community Hlth Ctr Inc* ***(P-21960)***
Kedren Community Hlth Ctr Inc..............................C.......323 524-0634
3800 S Figueroa St Los Angeles (90037) ***(P-23881)***
Kedren Community Hlth Ctr Inc (PA)..............................B.......323 233-0425
4211 Avalon Blvd Los Angeles (90011) ***(P-21960)***
Keeco LLC (PA)..............................D.......510 324-8800
30736 Wiegman Rd Hayward (94544) ***(P-6770)***
Keefe Plumbing Services, Glendale *Also called H L Moe Co Inc* ***(P-2225)***
Keen Account, Union City *Also called Buffalo Distribution* ***(P-8346)***

Mergent e-mail: customerrelations@mergent.com
1354
2019 Directory of California
Wholesalers and Services Companies
(P-0000) Products & Services Section entry number
(PA)=Parent Co (HQ)=Headquarters (DH)=Div Headquarters

Keenan & Associates ....D....650 306-0616
1791 Broadway St Ste 200 Redwood City (94063) ***(P-10662)***
Keenan & Associates (HQ) ....B....310 212-3344
2355 Crenshaw Blvd # 200 Torrance (90501) ***(P-10663)***
Keenan & Associates ....D....707 268-1616
626 H St Eureka (95501) ***(P-10664)***
Keenan & Associates ....D....951 788-0330
3550 Vine St Ste 200 Riverside (92507) ***(P-10665)***
Keenan & Associates ....D....916 858-2981
2868 Prospect Park Dr # 600 Rancho Cordova (95670) ***(P-10666)***
Keenan & Associates ....E....408 441-0754
1740 Tech Dr Ste 300 San Jose (95110) ***(P-10667)***
Keenan & Associates ....D....949 940-1760
901 Calle Amanecer # 200 San Clemente (92673) ***(P-10668)***
Keenan Farms Inc ....D....559 945-1400
31510 Plymouth Ave Kettleman City (93239) ***(P-191)***
Keenan Hopkins Suder & Stowell (PA) ....D....714 695-3670
5109 E La Palma Ave Ste A Anaheim (92807) ***(P-2904)***
Keenan Hopkins Suder & Stowell ....D....714 695-3670
5109 E La Palma Ave Ste A Anaheim (92807) ***(P-1572)***
Keeney Truck Lines Inc ....E....323 589-3231
3500 Fruitland Ave Maywood (90270) ***(P-4033)***
Keep Truckin Inc (PA) ....E....855 434-3564
370 Townsend St San Francisco (94107) ***(P-15249)***
Keesal Young Logan A Prof Corp (PA) ....D....562 436-2000
400 Oceangate Ste 1400 Long Beach (90802) ***(P-23166)***
Kehe Distributors LLC ....B....714 255-4600
6 Pointe Dr Ste 300 Brea (92821) ***(P-8817)***
Keiro Nursing Home ....C....323 276-5700
2221 Lincoln Park Ave Los Angeles (90031) ***(P-21530)***
Keiro Senior Health Care, Los Angeles *Also called Keiro Services* ***(P-26916)***
Keiro Services ....B....213 873-5700
420 E 3rd St Ste 1000 Los Angeles (90013) ***(P-26916)***
Keisers Holdings LLC ....D....559 265-4700
411 S West Ave Fresno (93706) ***(P-18617)***
Keith Development Corporation ....E....707 528-8703
2777 Cleveland Ave # 109 Santa Rosa (95403) ***(P-11882)***
Keith T Kusunis MD ....D....909 469-9494
91767 N Orange Grv Ave Pomona (91767) ***(P-22605)***
Keiwit Infrastructure West Co, Fairfield *Also called Kiewit Corporation* ***(P-1574)***
Keker and Van Nest LLP ....D....415 391-5400
633 Battery St Bsmt 91 San Francisco (94111) ***(P-23167)***
Keller William Realty, Visalia *Also called Beethoven Holdings Inc* ***(P-11235)***
Keller Williams Realtors, Visalia *Also called Keller Williams Realty Inc* ***(P-11544)***
Keller Williams Realtors, Auburn *Also called East Hall Investors Inc* ***(P-12222)***
Keller Williams Realtors, Carmel Valley *Also called Keller Williams Realty* ***(P-11539)***
Keller Williams Realtors, Covina *Also called Keller Williams Realty* ***(P-11540)***
Keller Williams Realtors, Torrance *Also called Keller Williams Realty* ***(P-11541)***
Keller Williams Realtors, Victorville *Also called Keller Williams Realty* ***(P-11542)***
Keller Williams Realtors, Granite Bay *Also called Williams Keller Realty* ***(P-11835)***
Keller Williams Realtors, Corona *Also called Pro Group Inc* ***(P-11681)***
Keller Williams Realtors, Chino Hills *Also called Ch Market Center Inc* ***(P-11311)***
Keller Williams Realtors, Riverside *Also called Keller Williams Realty* ***(P-11543)***
Keller Williams Realty ....D....831 622-6200
39 Calle De Los Ositos Carmel Valley (93924) ***(P-11539)***
Keller Williams Realty ....D....626 384-2803
100 N Citrus Ave Covina (91723) ***(P-11540)***
Keller Williams Realty ....B....310 375-3511
23670 Hawthorne Blvd # 100 Torrance (90505) ***(P-11541)***
Keller Williams Realty ....D....760 951-5242
12530 Hesperia Rd Ste 110 Victorville (92395) ***(P-11542)***
Keller Williams Realty ....E....951 215-0787
7898 Mission Grove Pkwy S # 102 Riverside (92508) ***(P-11543)***
Keller Williams Realty Inc ....D....559 636-1235
400 E Main St Visalia (93291) ***(P-11544)***
Keller Wllams Rlty Bvrly Hills ....D....310 432-6400
439 N Canon Dr Ste 300 Beverly Hills (90210) ***(P-11545)***
Kelley Drye & Warren LLP ....C....310 712-6100
10100 Santa Monica Blvd Los Angeles (90067) ***(P-23168)***
Kellogg Andlson Accntancy Corp (PA) ....D....818 971-5100
21700 Oxnard St Ste 800 Woodland Hills (91367) ***(P-26234)***
Kellwood Company LLC ....C....626 934-4133
1307 E Temple Ave City of Industry (91746) ***(P-8265)***
Kellwood Company LLC ....C....626 934-4155
13085 Temple Ave City of Industry (91746) ***(P-8312)***
Kelly Moses Floors ....E....951 296-5147
27430 Bostik Ct Ste 101 Temecula (92590) ***(P-3001)***
Kelly Paper Company (HQ) ....E....909 859-8200
288 Brea Canyon Rd Walnut (91789) ***(P-8070)***
Kellytoy Worldwide Inc ....D....323 923-1300
4811 S Alameda St Vernon (90058) ***(P-7955)***
Kelomar Inc ....C....760 344-5253
3949 Austin Rd Brawley (92227) ***(P-64)***
Kelpien Health Care, Montebello *Also called Beverly Community Hosp Assn* ***(P-21301)***
Kelvin Hildebrand Inc ....E....831 768-9104
6 Lewis Rd Royal Oaks (95076) ***(P-4034)***
Kemp Bros Construction Inc ....E....562 236-5000
10135 Geary Ave Santa Fe Springs (90670) ***(P-1414)***
Kemper Insurance, Glendale *Also called Arthur J Gallagher & Co* ***(P-10544)***
Kemper Insurance, Visalia *Also called Mitchell Buckman Inc* ***(P-10693)***
Kemper Insurance, Kingsburg *Also called Van Beurden Insurance Svcs Inc* ***(P-10822)***
Kemper Insurance, Los Angeles *Also called Grosslight Insurance Inc* ***(P-10638)***
Kemper Insurance, Irvine *Also called USI South Coast* ***(P-10820)***
Kemper Insurance, Sacramento *Also called Interwest Insurance Svcs LLC* ***(P-10655)***
Kemper Insurance, Lafayette *Also called Arthur J Gallagher & Co* ***(P-10547)***
Ken Blanchard Companies, The, Escondido *Also called Blanchard Training and Dev Inc* ***(P-27163)***
Ken Grody Ford, Buena Park *Also called Ted Ford Jones Inc* ***(P-17788)***
Ken Real Estate Lease Ltd ....D....714 778-1700
900 S Disneyland Dr Anaheim (92802) ***(P-12802)***
Ken Starr Inc ....D....714 632-8789
1120 N Tustin Ave Anaheim (92807) ***(P-2249)***
Kenan Advantage Group Inc ....D....323 582-3778
2709 E 37th St Vernon (90058) ***(P-4201)***
Kendal Floral Supply LLC (PA) ....D....760 431-4910
1960 Kellogg Ave Carlsbad (92008) ***(P-9143)***
Kendal North Bouquet Co, Carlsbad *Also called Kendal Floral Supply LLC* ***(P-9143)***
Kendall Farms LP ....E....760 731-0681
4230 White Lilac Rd Fallbrook (92028) ***(P-274)***
Kendrick Co The, Seal Beach *Also called Kendrick Construction Services* ***(P-1415)***
Kendrick Construction Services ....D....562 546-0200
3010 Old Ranch Pkwy # 470 Seal Beach (90740) ***(P-1415)***
Kenedco Inc ....D....951 699-9339
29363 Rancho Cal Rd Temecula (92591) ***(P-17271)***
Kenmore Residence Club, San Francisco *Also called Monroe Residence Club* ***(P-11080)***
Kennard Development Group ....E....818 241-0800
520 N Central Ave Ste 715 Glendale (91203) ***(P-1298)***
Kennedy Athletic Club (PA) ....D....805 466-6775
3534 El Camino Real Atascadero (93422) ***(P-18618)***
Kennedy Care Center, Los Angeles *Also called BV General Inc* ***(P-21026)***
Kennedy Care Center ....D....323 651-0043
619 N Fairfax Ave Los Angeles (90036) ***(P-21123)***
Kennedy Care Ctr Kosher Certif, Los Angeles *Also called Kennedy Care Center* ***(P-21123)***
Kennedy Club Fitness ....D....805 781-3488
188 Tank Farm Rd San Luis Obispo (93401) ***(P-18619)***
Kennedy Pipeline Company ....D....949 380-8363
61 Argonaut Laguna Hills (92656) ***(P-1943)***
Kennedy-Wilson Inc (PA) ....C....310 887-6400
151 El Camino Dr Beverly Hills (90212) ***(P-11546)***
Kennedy/Jenks Consultants Inc (PA) ....D....415 243-2150
303 2nd St Ste 300s San Francisco (94107) ***(P-25777)***
Kenneth Brdwick Intr Dsgns Inc ....D....310 274-9999
1615 Westwood Blvd # 201 Los Angeles (90024) ***(P-17272)***
Kenneth Corp ....A....714 537-5160
12601 Garden Grove Blvd Garden Grove (92843) ***(P-21531)***
Kenneth Norris Cancer Hospital, Los Angeles *Also called Tenet Health Systems Norris* ***(P-21851)***
Kenneth P Slaught Inc ....E....805 962-8989
200 E Carrillo St Ste 200 # 200 Santa Barbara (93101) ***(P-11547)***
Kenny Pabst ....E....562 439-2147
248 Redondo Ave Long Beach (90803) ***(P-11548)***
Kenshoo Inc (HQ) ....C....877 536-7462
22 4th St Fl 7 San Francisco (94103) ***(P-27294)***
Kensington Agency Inc ....E....619 280-6993
8469 La Mesa Blvd La Mesa (91942) ***(P-14869)***
Kensington Nursing Agency, La Mesa *Also called Kensington Agency Inc* ***(P-14869)***
Kensington Place, Walnut Creek *Also called Argonaut Kensington Associates* ***(P-23487)***
Kent Daniels & Associates Inc ....C....626 859-5018
680 Brea Canyon Rd # 258 Walnut (91789) ***(P-14656)***
Kentfield Rehabilation Hosp, Kentfield *Also called 1125 Sir Francis Drake Bouleva* ***(P-21994)***
Kentina, Temecula *Also called Sft Realty Galway Downs LLC* ***(P-11760)***
Kentmaster Mfg Co Inc (PA) ....E....626 359-8888
1801 S Mountain Ave Monrovia (91016) ***(P-7760)***
Kenwood Service Center West, Cerritos *Also called Usaco Service Corp* ***(P-17918)***
Kenyon Construction Inc ....B....925 371-8102
63 Trevarno Rd D Livermore (94551) ***(P-3279)***
Kenyon Construction Inc ....D....559 277-5645
4667 N Blythe Ave Fresno (93722) ***(P-2905)***
Kenyon Construction Inc ....C....916 514-9502
3223 E St North Highlands (95660) ***(P-2906)***
Kenyon Plastering, North Highlands *Also called Kenyon Construction Inc* ***(P-2906)***
Kenyon Plastream, Livermore *Also called Kenyon Construction Inc* ***(P-3279)***
Keolis Transit America Inc ....C....818 616-5254
14663 Keswick St Van Nuys (91405) ***(P-3660)***
Keolis Transit America Inc ....D....559 621-5783
4488 N Blackstone Ave Fresno (93726) ***(P-3661)***
Keolis Transit America Inc ....D....661 341-3910
660 W Avenue L Lancaster (93534) ***(P-3662)***
Keolis Transit America Inc (HQ) ....E....310 981-9500
6053 W Century Blvd # 900 Los Angeles (90045) ***(P-3813)***
Kerber Bros Inc ....C....562 921-3447
14006 Gracebee Ave Norwalk (90650) ***(P-3543)***
Kerdus Plastering Inc ....C....951 272-6720
575 6th St Norco (92860) ***(P-2907)***
Kerlan-Jobe Orthopedic Clinic (PA) ....D....310 665-7200
6801 Park Ter Ste 500 Los Angeles (90045) ***(P-19625)***
Kerman Telephone Co ....D....559 846-4954
811 S Madera Ave Kerman (93630) ***(P-5591)***
Kermantelnet Internet Service ....D....559 842-2223
811 S Madera Ave Kerman (93630) ***(P-5592)***
Kern 2008 Cmnty Partners LP ....D....559 651-3559
1219 N Plaza Dr Visalia (93291) ***(P-1299)***
Kern Alternative Care Inc ....C....661 631-2036
2029 21st St Bakersfield (93301) ***(P-22351)***
Kern Around Clock Foundation ....E....661 324-3221
5251 Office Park Dr # 400 Bakersfield (93309) ***(P-26917)***
Kern Cnty Mntal Hlth Child Sys ....D....661 868-8300
1111 Columbus St Ste 3000 Bakersfield (93305) ***(P-20937)***
Kern County Hospital Authority ....A....661 326-2102
1700 Mount Vernon Ave Bakersfield (93306) ***(P-21532)***
Kern County Water Agency ....D....661 634-1512
811 Nadine Ln Bakersfield (93308) ***(P-6268)***
Kern Direct Marketing, Woodland Hills *Also called Kern Organization Inc* ***(P-13855)***
Kern Family Helathcare, Bakersfield *Also called Kern Health Systems Inc* ***(P-19626)***

Employee Codes: A=Over 500 employees, B=251-500
C=101-250, D=51-100, E=50
2019 Directory of California
Wholesalers and Services Companies
© Mergent Inc. 1-800-342-5647
1355

Kern Federal Credit Union, Bakersfield *Also called Kern Member Insurance Services* ***(P-9564)***
Kern Federal Credit Union.......D.......661 327-9461
1717 Truxtun Ave Bakersfield (93301) ***(P-9563)***
Kern Health Systems Inc.......D.......661 664-5000
9700 Stockdale Hwy Bakersfield (93311) ***(P-19626)***
Kern Member Insurance Services.......E.......661 327-9461
1717 Truxtun Ave Bakersfield (93301) ***(P-9564)***
Kern Organization Inc.......D.......818 703-8775
20955 Warner Center Ln Woodland Hills (91367) ***(P-13855)***
Kern Rdlgy Imaging Systems Inc (PA).......C.......661 326-9600
2301 Bahamas Dr Bakersfield (93309) ***(P-19627)***
Kern Regional Center (PA).......C.......661 327-8531
3200 N Sillect Ave Bakersfield (93308) ***(P-24795)***
Kern Ridge Growers LLC.......B.......661 854-3141
25429 Barbara St Arvin (93203) ***(P-533)***
Kern River Co Generation Co.......D.......661 392-2663
Sw China Grade Loop Bakersfield (93308) ***(P-6046)***
KERN RIVER HEALTH CENTER, Bakersfield *Also called Clinica Sierra Vista* ***(P-19388)***
Kern River Outfitters, Bayside *Also called O A Outfitting Inc* ***(P-19210)***
Kern River Tours Inc.......D.......760 379-4616
2712 Mayfair Rd Lake Isabella (93240) ***(P-19193)***
Kern Schools Federal Credit Un (PA).......D.......661 833-7900
11500 Bolthouse Dr Bakersfield (93311) ***(P-9565)***
Kern Security Corporation.......D.......661 363-6874
2701 Fruitvale Ave Bakersfield (93308) ***(P-16915)***
Kern Security Systems, Bakersfield *Also called Kern Security Corporation* ***(P-16915)***
Kern Steel Fabrication Inc (PA).......D.......661 327-9588
627 Williams St Bakersfield (93305) ***(P-3381)***
Kern Valley Hosp Foundation (PA).......B.......760 379-2681
6412 Laurel Ave Lake Isabella (93240) ***(P-21533)***
Kernen Construction.......D.......707 826-8686
2350 Glendale Dr McKinleyville (95519) ***(P-1416)***
Kerria, Auburn *Also called Westview Heath Care Center* ***(P-20888)***
Kertel Communications Inc (HQ).......D.......559 432-5800
7600 N Palm Ave Ste 101 Fresno (93711) ***(P-2624)***
Kesari Hospitality LLC.......D.......619 298-1291
445 Hotel Cir S San Diego (92108) ***(P-12803)***
Kesq TV, Thousand Palms *Also called Gulf- California Broadcast Co* ***(P-5796)***
Ketchum Incorporated.......D.......310 437-2600
12777 W Jefferson Blvd # 120 Los Angeles (90066) ***(P-27558)***
Ketchum Incorporated.......D.......415 984-6100
1050 Battery St San Francisco (94111) ***(P-27559)***
Ketchum YMCA, Los Angeles *Also called Young Mens Chrstn Assn of La* ***(P-25347)***
Kevcomp Inc.......D.......562 423-3028
4300 Long Beach Blvd # 720 Long Beach (90807) ***(P-25778)***
Kevcomp Engineering, Long Beach *Also called Kevcomp Inc* ***(P-25778)***
Kevin Holubowski LLC.......C.......310 908-6542
7462 Denrock Ave Los Angeles (90045) ***(P-24796)***
Kevin Persons Inc.......E.......805 371-8746
2977 Los Feliz Dr Thousand Oaks (91362) ***(P-763)***
Key Environmental Services, Los Angeles *Also called The Teecor Group Inc* ***(P-3593)***
Key Inn & Suites, Tustin *Also called Key Inn Ltd A Cal Ltd Partnr* ***(P-12804)***
Key Inn Ltd A Cal Ltd Partnr.......E.......714 832-3220
1611 El Camino Real Tustin (92780) ***(P-12804)***
Key Largo Casino, Newport Beach *Also called Ambassador Gaming Inc* ***(P-19094)***
Keypoint Credit Union (PA).......C.......408 731-4100
2805 Bowers Ave Ste 105 Santa Clara (95051) ***(P-9638)***
Keypoint Credit Union.......C.......408 562-7011
2805 Bowers Ave Ste 105 Santa Clara (95051) ***(P-9639)***
Keystone Automotive Inds Inc.......D.......909 986-4586
2530 Lindsey Privado Dr C Ontario (91761) ***(P-6652)***
Keystone Marketing Specialists, Irvine *Also called Ksm Marketing Inc* ***(P-17282)***
Keystone NPS LLC (HQ).......D.......909 633-6354
11980 Mount Vernon Ave Grand Terrace (92313) ***(P-24797)***
Keystone PCF Property MGT Inc (PA).......D.......949 833-2600
16775 Von Karman Ave # 100 Irvine (92606) ***(P-11549)***
Keystone Schools-Ramona, Grand Terrace *Also called Keystone NPS LLC* ***(P-24797)***
Keyt Television, Santa Barbara *Also called Smith Broadcasting Group Inc* ***(P-5838)***
Kf Bella Vista Health Care, Ontario *Also called Bella Vista Healthcare Center* ***(P-20259)***
Kf Community Care LLC.......C.......626 357-3207
2335 Mountain Ave Duarte (91010) ***(P-21124)***
Kf Ontario Healthcare LLC.......E.......909 984-6713
1661 S Euclid Ave Ontario (91762) ***(P-21125)***
Kf Sunray LLC.......D.......323 734-2171
3210 W Pico Blvd Los Angeles (90019) ***(P-21126)***
Kfa LLP.......D.......310 399-7975
1625 Olympic Blvd Santa Monica (90404) ***(P-26074)***
Kfco Inc.......C.......310 441-2483
12100 W Washington Blvd Los Angeles (90066) ***(P-4035)***
Kfi.......E.......415 956-9812
1 Sansome St Fl 32 San Francisco (94104) ***(P-26918)***
Kfjc FM, Los Altos Hills *Also called Footh-De Anza Commun Colleg Di* ***(P-5719)***
Kforce Inc.......D.......858 550-1645
4510 Executive Dr Ste 325 San Diego (92121) ***(P-14657)***
Kfox, Los Angeles *Also called FM Seoul Bang Song Inc* ***(P-5718)***
Kfsn Television LLC.......C.......559 442-1170
1777 G St Fresno (93706) ***(P-5806)***
Kftv.......D.......559 222-2121
601 W Univision Plz Fresno (93704) ***(P-5807)***
KG Berry Farms LLC.......C.......805 680-6751
1660 Philbric Rd Santa Maria (93454) ***(P-363)***
KG Oldco Inc (HQ).......E.......408 980-8550
2270 Martin Ave Santa Clara (95050) ***(P-15991)***
Kgo 810am, San Francisco *Also called San Francisco Radio Assets LLC* ***(P-5753)***
Kgo Television Inc.......C.......415 954-7777
900 Front St San Francisco (94111) ***(P-5808)***

Kgtv, San Diego *Also called EW Scripps Company* ***(P-5790)***
Kh Construction, Fresno *Also called Nevocal Enterprises Inc* ***(P-1095)***
Khan Academy Inc.......D.......650 336-5426
1200 Villa St Ste 200 Mountain View (94041) ***(P-15728)***
Khanna Entps - II Ltd Partnr.......C.......916 338-5800
5321 Date Ave Sacramento (95841) ***(P-12805)***
Khatri Inc.......E.......209 576-1481
1608 Sunrise Ave Ste 6 Modesto (95350) ***(P-12806)***
Khatri Properties, Modesto *Also called Khatri Inc* ***(P-12806)***
Kheir, Los Angeles *Also called Korean Health Education* ***(P-23886)***
Khop, Stockton *Also called Cumulus Intrmdate Holdings Inc* ***(P-5708)***
Khp II San Diego Hotel LLC (PA).......D.......619 515-3000
1047 5th Ave San Diego (92101) ***(P-12807)***
Khp III Goleta LLC.......D.......805 964-6241
5650 Calle Real Goleta (93117) ***(P-12808)***
Khs & S Contractors, Anaheim *Also called Keenan Hopkins Suder & Stowell* ***(P-2904)***
Khsl TV, Chico *Also called Catamount Broadcasting of Chic* ***(P-5772)***
Khss Contractors, Anaheim *Also called Keenan Hopkins Suder & Stowell* ***(P-1572)***
Kicu TV 36, San Jose *Also called TV 36* ***(P-5842)***
Kid Helping Kids, Santa Barbara *Also called San Marcos Kids Helpng Kids FN* ***(P-25237)***
Kid Iq 24 Hr Childcare.......D.......310 492-3037
4451 E Sierra Madre Ave Fresno (93726) ***(P-24331)***
Kid Stock Inc.......D.......415 753-3737
1539 Funston Ave San Francisco (94122) ***(P-18377)***
Kidango Inc.......D.......408 297-9044
730 Empey Way San Jose (95128) ***(P-22830)***
Kidango Inc.......D.......510 494-9601
4700 Calaveras Ave Fremont (94538) ***(P-24332)***
Kidney Center Inc.......C.......805 433-7777
50 Moreland Rd Simi Valley (93065) ***(P-22481)***
Kidney Dialysis Center Verdugo, Simi Valley *Also called Kidney Center Inc* ***(P-22481)***
Kids First Foundation.......C.......760 631-7550
1025 Service Pl Ste 103 Vista (92084) ***(P-24570)***
Kids First Foundation.......D.......760 631-7550
993 S Santa Fe Ave Ste C Vista (92083) ***(P-24571)***
Kids Klub Care Centers Inc (PA).......D.......626 795-2501
380 S Raymond Ave Pasadena (91105) ***(P-24333)***
Kids Klub Pasadena, Pasadena *Also called Kids Klub Care Centers Inc* ***(P-24333)***
Kids N Things Inc (PA).......D.......805 522-1011
4221 Cochran St Simi Valley (93063) ***(P-24334)***
Kids Overcoming LLC.......D.......415 748-8052
40029 St Ste 204 Oakland (94609) ***(P-22352)***
Kids World Preschool, Temecula *Also called McCusker Enterprises Inc* ***(P-24347)***
Kids' Club YMCA Oxford School, Berkeley *Also called Young MNS Chrstn Assn of E Bay* ***(P-25361)***
Kidspace A Prticipatory Museum.......D.......626 449-9144
480 N Arroyo Blvd Pasadena (91103) ***(P-24886)***
Kie Con, Antioch *Also called Kiewit Infrastructure West Co* ***(P-1804)***
Kie-Con Inc.......D.......925 754-9494
3551 Wilbur Ave Antioch (94509) ***(P-1573)***
Kieckhafer Schiffer & Co LLP (PA).......E.......949 250-3900
6201 Oak Cyn Ste 200 Irvine (92618) ***(P-26235)***
Kier & Wright Civil ENGrs&srvy (PA).......D.......408 727-6665
3350 Scott Blvd Bldg 22 Santa Clara (95054) ***(P-25779)***
Kier & Wright Civil ENGrs&srvy.......E.......925 245-8788
2850 Collier Canyon Rd Livermore (94551) ***(P-26131)***
Kier Wrght Cvil Engineers Survy, Santa Clara *Also called Kier & Wright Civil ENGrs&srvy* ***(P-25779)***
Kiewit Corporation.......D.......707 439-7300
4650 Business Center Dr Fairfield (94534) ***(P-1574)***
Kiewit Corporation.......D.......907 222-9350
10704 Shoemaker Ave Santa Fe Springs (90670) ***(P-1575)***
Kiewit Infrastructure West Co.......D.......360 693-1478
12700 Stowe Dr Ste 180 Poway (92064) ***(P-1883)***
Kiewit Infrastructure West Co.......D.......510 452-1400
1111 Broadway Oakland (94607) ***(P-1801)***
Kiewit Infrastructure West Co.......D.......925 462-1088
3200 Busch Rd Pleasanton (94566) ***(P-1802)***
Kiewit Infrastructure West Co.......C.......562 946-1816
10704 Shoemaker Ave Santa Fe Springs (90670) ***(P-1803)***
Kiewit Infrastructure West Co.......E.......925 754-9494
3551 Wilbur Ave Antioch (94509) ***(P-1804)***
Kifm Smooth Jazz 981 Inc.......C.......619 297-3698
1615 Murray Canyon Rd San Diego (92108) ***(P-5733)***
Kiid, Roseville *Also called Walt Disney Company* ***(P-5762)***
Kilcrew Productions.......D.......619 564-2080
32811 Wesley St Wildomar (92595) ***(P-17273)***
Kilpatrick Twnsend Stckton LLP.......C.......925 472-5000
2175 N California Blvd Walnut Creek (94596) ***(P-23169)***
Kilroy Realty LP.......D.......949 788-1200
2211 Michelson Dr Ste 330 Irvine (92612) ***(P-11550)***
Kilroy Realty LP.......C.......415 243-8803
100 1st St Ste 250 San Francisco (94105) ***(P-11551)***
Kilroy Realty Corporation (PA).......D.......310 481-8400
12200 W Olympic Blvd # 200 Los Angeles (90064) ***(P-12169)***
Kim Chong.......D.......323 581-4700
2105 E 25th St Los Angeles (90058) ***(P-17274)***
Klma W Medical Center.......D.......530 625-4114
535 Airport Rd Hoopa (95546) ***(P-22606)***
Kimball Tirey & St John LLP (PA).......D.......619 234-1690
7676 Hazard Center Dr # 900 San Diego (92108) ***(P-23170)***
Kimberlite Corporation.......D.......209 948-2551
3728 Imperial Way Stockton (95215) ***(P-16916)***
Kimberlite Corporation (PA).......D.......559 264-9730
3621 W Beechwood Ave Fresno (93711) ***(P-16917)***
Kimberly Care Center Inc.......D.......805 925-8877
820 W Cook St Santa Maria (93458) ***(P-20553)***

Mergent e-mail: customerrelations@mergent.com
1356
2019 Directory of California
Wholesalers and Services Companies
(P-0000) Products & Services Section entry number
(PA)=Parent Co (HQ)=Headquarters (DH)=Div Headquarters

Kimco Staffing Services Inc ....A.....925 256-3132
1801 Oakland Blvd Ste 220 Walnut Creek (94596) *(P-22831)*
Kimley-Horn and Associates Inc ....D.....619 234-9411
401 B St Ste 600 San Diego (92101) *(P-25780)*
Kimpton Hotel & Rest Group LLC ....D.....415 885-2500
405 Taylor St San Francisco (94102) *(P-12809)*
Kimpton Hotel & Rest Group LLC (HQ) ....D.....415 397-5572
222 Kearny St Ste 200 San Francisco (94108) *(P-12810)*
Kimpton Hotel & Rest Group LLC ....C.....415 397-7720
221 Powell St San Francisco (94102) *(P-12811)*
Kimpton Hotel & Rest Group LLC ....D.....415 561-1100
425 N Point St San Francisco (94133) *(P-12812)*
Kimpton Hotel & Rest Group LLC ....D.....415 561-1111
2455 Mason St San Francisco (94133) *(P-12813)*
Kimpton Hotel & Rest Group LLC ....D.....415 292-0100
501 Geary St San Francisco (94102) *(P-26919)*
Kincaid & Decker Inc (PA) ....D.....818 785-1528
15800 Straden St Van Nuys (91406) *(P-6771)*
Kincaid Industries Inc ....D.....760 343-5457
31065 Plantation Dr Thousand Palms (92276) *(P-2250)*
Kind Homecare Inc ....D.....888 885-5463
3705 Haven Ave Ste 104 Menlo Park (94025) *(P-22353)*
Kinder Mrgan Enrgy Partners LP ....E.....310 518-7700
2000 E Sepulveda Blvd Carson (90810) *(P-4680)*
Kinder Mrgan Enrgy Partners LP ....E.....909 873-5100
2319 S Riverside Ave Bloomington (92316) *(P-4926)*
Kinder Mrgan Lqds Trminals LLC ....D.....415 467-8107
950 Tunnel Ave Brisbane (94005) *(P-4681)*
Kinder Mrgan Lqds Trminals LLC ....D.....619 283-6511
9950 San Diego Mission Rd San Diego (92108) *(P-6151)*
Kinder Mrgan Lqds Trminals LLC ....D.....408 435-7399
2150 Kruse Dr San Jose (95131) *(P-4682)*
Kindercare Education LLC ....D.....925 824-0267
3280 Crow Canyon Rd San Ramon (94583) *(P-24335)*
Kindercare Learning Ctrs LLC ....C.....562 961-8882
5251 E Las Lomas St Long Beach (90815) *(P-24336)*
Kindred Healthcare Inc ....D.....408 261-6943
4030 Moorpark Ave Ste 251 San Jose (95117) *(P-21534)*
Kindred Healthcare Oper Inc ....C.....925 692-5886
1800 Adobe St Concord (94520) *(P-20554)*
Kindred Healthcare Oper Inc ....D.....916 454-5752
4700 Elvas Ave Sacramento (95819) *(P-20555)*
Kindred Healthcare Oper Inc ....C.....916 457-6521
3500 Folsom Blvd Sacramento (95816) *(P-21127)*
Kindred Healthcare Oper Inc ....D.....805 487-7840
2641 S C St Oxnard (93033) *(P-21128)*
Kindred Healthcare Oper Inc ....D.....714 529-6842
875 N Brea Blvd Brea (92821) *(P-20556)*
Kindred Healthcare Oper Inc ....C.....502 596-7300
1940 El Cajon Blvd San Diego (92104) *(P-22027)*
Kindred Healthcare Oper Inc ....C.....909 862-0611
7534 Palm Ave Highland (92346) *(P-20557)*
Kindred Healthcare Oper Inc ....C.....650 962-6000
145 E Dana St Mountain View (94041) *(P-21535)*
Kindred Healthcare Oper Inc ....D.....925 443-1800
76 Fenton St Livermore (94550) *(P-20558)*
Kindred Healthcare Oper Inc ....B.....510 357-8300
2800 Benedict Dr San Leandro (94577) *(P-21536)*
Kindred Healthcare Oper Inc ....C.....760 471-2986
1586 W San Marcos Blvd San Marcos (92078) *(P-20559)*
Kindred Healthcare Oper Inc ....D.....831 424-8072
720 E Romie Ln Salinas (93901) *(P-20560)*
Kindred Healthcare Oper Inc ....D.....415 922-5085
2121 Pine St San Francisco (94115) *(P-20561)*
Kindred Healthcare Oper Inc ....C.....415 566-1200
1575 7th Ave San Francisco (94122) *(P-21537)*
Kindred Healthcare Oper Inc ....B.....909 391-0333
550 N Monterey Ave Ontario (91764) *(P-21538)*
Kindred Healthcare Operating ....B.....650 697-1865
1609 Trousdale Dr Burlingame (94010) *(P-22028)*
Kindred Healthcare Operating ....C.....661 872-2121
2211 Mount Vernon Ave Bakersfield (93306) *(P-20562)*
Kindred Healthcare Operating ....C.....916 351-9151
223 Fargo Way Folsom (95630) *(P-20563)*
Kindred Healthcare Operating ....B.....310 642-0325
5525 W Slauson Ave Los Angeles (90056) *(P-21539)*
Kindred Healthcare Operating ....D.....951 688-8200
9020 Garfield St Riverside (92503) *(P-21129)*
Kindred Hospital, San Leandro *Also called Kindred Healthcare Oper Inc (P-21536)*
Kindred Hospital - Brea, Brea *Also called Kindred Healthcare Oper Inc (P-20556)*
Kindred Hospital - Rancho, Rancho Cucamonga *Also called Knd Development 55 LLC (P-21542)*
Kindred Hospital La Mirada, La Mirada *Also called Southern Cal Spcialty Care Inc (P-21765)*
Kindred Hospital La Mirata, West Covina *Also called Southern Cal Spcialty Care Inc (P-21763)*
Kindred Hospital-Westminster ....B.....714 372-3014
200 Hospital Cir Westminster (92683) *(P-21540)*
Kindred Nrsing Hlthcre- Bybrry, Concord *Also called Kindred Healthcare Oper Inc (P-20554)*
Kindred Nursing, San Francisco *Also called Kindred Healthcare Oper Inc (P-20561)*
Kindred Nursing and Reha, San Rafael *Also called Kindred Nursing Centers W LLC (P-21541)*
Kindred Nursing Centers W LLC ....D.....510 521-5600
516 Willow St Alameda (94501) *(P-20564)*
Kindred Nursing Centers W LLC ....D.....415 456-7170
1601 5th Ave San Rafael (94901) *(P-21541)*
Kindred Nursing Centers W LLC ....C.....530 243-6317
2120 Benton Dr Redding (96003) *(P-20565)*
Kindred Nursing Centers W LLC ....C.....209 957-4539
1517 Knickerbocker Dr Stockton (95210) *(P-20566)*

Kindred Nursing Centers W LLC ....C.....415 673-8405
1359 Pine St San Francisco (94109) *(P-22607)*
Kindred Nursng & Healthcare, Livermore *Also called Kindred Healthcare Oper Inc (P-20558)*
Kindred Transitional, Stockton *Also called Kindred Nursing Centers W LLC (P-20566)*
Kindred Transitional Care, Alameda *Also called Kindred Nursing Centers W LLC (P-20564)*
Kindred Transitional Care, Redding *Also called Kindred Nursing Centers W LLC (P-20565)*
Kindred Transitional Care, San Francisco *Also called Kindred Nursing Centers W LLC (P-22607)*
Kinecta Alternative Fin (HQ) ....D.....310 538-2242
1440 Rosecrans Ave Manhattan Beach (90266) *(P-9686)*
Kinecta Federal Credit Union (PA) ....C.....310 643-5400
1440 Rosecrans Ave Manhattan Beach (90266) *(P-9566)*
Kinemed Inc ....D.....510 655-6525
40 Lincoln Ave Piedmont (94611) *(P-26390)*
Kinemetrics Inc (HQ) ....D.....626 795-2220
222 Vista Ave Pasadena (91107) *(P-25781)*
Kinetic Systems Inc ....E.....949 502-4856
1620 S Sunkist St Anaheim (92806) *(P-2251)*
Kineticom Inc (PA) ....D.....619 330-3100
8885 Rio San Diego Dr # 210 San Diego (92108) *(P-14658)*
Kinetics Mechanical Svc Inc ....D.....925 245-6200
6336 Patterson Pass Rd H Livermore (94550) *(P-2252)*
King & Spalding LLP ....B.....415 318-1200
101 2nd St Ste 2300 San Francisco (94105) *(P-23171)*
King Equipment LLC ....D.....909 986-5300
1690 Ashley Way Colton (92324) *(P-14444)*
King George Cabbage, Watsonville *Also called Guy George (P-101)*
King Harbor Sports Center, Redondo Beach *Also called Sport Center Fitness Inc (P-18667)*
King Hlmes Ptrno Berliner LLP ....E.....310 282-8989
1900 Avenue Of The Stars # 25 Los Angeles (90067) *(P-23172)*
King Janitorial Equipment Svcs, Garden Grove *Also called Janitorial Equipment Svcs Inc (P-14296)*
King Monster Inc ....D.....661 253-3000
27451 Tourney Rd Ste 140 Valencia (91355) *(P-11552)*
KING RELOCATION SERVICES, Santa Fe Springs *Also called Van King & Storage Inc (P-4085)*
King Relocation Services, Santa Fe Springs *Also called Van King & Storage Inc (P-4652)*
King Security Services Inc ....A.....415 556-5464
1159 7th St Novato (94945) *(P-16711)*
King Ventures ....C.....805 544-4444
285 Bridge St San Luis Obispo (93401) *(P-11883)*
King-Reynolds Ventures LLC ....D.....650 879-2136
2001 Rossi Rd Pescadero (94060) *(P-17275)*
Kingcom(us) LLC (HQ) ....C.....424 744-5697
3100 Ocean Park Blvd Santa Monica (90405) *(P-15729)*
Kingdom Express Inc ....D.....310 258-0900
18640 Crenshaw Blvd Torrance (90504) *(P-4202)*
Kingledon Inc ....D.....805 643-6000
2055 Harbor Blvd Ventura (93001) *(P-12814)*
Kings Arena Ltd Partnership ....D.....916 928-0000
1 Sports Pkwy Sacramento (95834) *(P-18522)*
Kings Casino Management Corp ....B.....916 560-4405
6510 Antelope Rd Citrus Heights (95621) *(P-19194)*
Kings Community Action O (PA) ....D.....559 582-4386
1130 N 11th Ave Hanford (93230) *(P-23882)*
Kings County Probation Dept., Hanford *Also called County of Kings (P-23652)*
Kings County Truck Lines (HQ) ....C.....559 686-2857
754 S Blackstone St Tulare (93274) *(P-4203)*
Kings Credit Services ....D.....559 322-2550
96 Shaw Ave Ste 221 Clovis (93612) *(P-14011)*
Kings Inn Hotel & Grille, San Diego *Also called Kings Inn Hotel San Diego (P-12815)*
Kings Inn Hotel San Diego ....D.....619 297-2231
1333 Hotel Cir S San Diego (92108) *(P-12815)*
Kings Jewelry and Loan, Los Angeles *Also called Kings Pawnshop (P-9890)*
Kings Nrsing Rhabilitaion Hosp, Hanford *Also called Wilshire Hlth & Cmnty Svcs Inc (P-21259)*
Kings Nrsing Rhabilitation Ctr, Hanford *Also called Mission Medical Entps Inc (P-20648)*
Kings Pawnshop ....D.....213 383-5555
800 S Vermont Ave Los Angeles (90005) *(P-9890)*
Kings Rehabilitation Center (PA) ....D.....559 582-9234
490 E Hanford Armona Rd Hanford (93230) *(P-23883)*
Kings River Conservation Dst ....D.....559 237-5567
4886 E Jensen Ave Fresno (93725) *(P-27938)*
Kings Seafood Company LLC ....D.....909 803-1280
12427 N Mainstreet Rancho Cucamonga (91739) *(P-8579)*
Kings Seafood Company LLC ....D.....714 793-1177
7691 Edinger Ave Huntington Beach (92647) *(P-8580)*
Kings Seafood Company LLC ....D.....714 771-6655
1521 W Katella Ave Orange (92867) *(P-8581)*
Kings View ....E.....209 357-0321
100 Airpark Rd Atwater (95301) *(P-24198)*
Kings View ....D.....559 582-9307
289 E 8th St Hanford (93230) *(P-22608)*
Kings View Work Experience Ctr ....E.....209 826-8118
703 I St Los Banos (93635) *(P-10167)*
Kingsburg Apple Packers Inc ....B.....559 897-5132
10363 Davis Ave Kingsburg (93631) *(P-8699)*
Kingsburg Apple Partners LP ....D.....559 897-5132
10363 Davis Ave Kingsburg (93631) *(P-222)*
Kingsburg Center, Kingsburg *Also called Sunbridge Care Entps W LLC (P-20789)*
Kingsburg Center, Kingsburg *Also called Sunbridge Care Entps W Inc (P-20788)*
Kingsburg Orchards, Kingsburg *Also called Kingsburg Apple Packers Inc (P-8699)*
Kingsley Apartments ....D.....323 666-8862
1345 N Kingsley Dr Los Angeles (90027) *(P-11042)*
Kingsley Court Apartments, Los Angeles *Also called Kingsley Apartments (P-11042)*
Kingsley Manor, Los Angeles *Also called Front Porch Communities (P-20441)*

Employee Codes: A=Over 500 employees, B=251-500
C=101-250, D=51-100, E=50

2019 Directory of California
Wholesalers and Services Companies

© Mergent Inc. 1-800-342-5647

1357

Kingspan Light & Air LLC ....C.......714 540-8950
401 Goetz Ave Santa Ana (92707) *(P-3170)*
Kingsview Corp ....D.......209 533-6245
2 S Green St Sonora (95370) *(P-22609)*
Kinsale Holdings Inc ....C.......415 400-2600
475 Sansome St Ste 570 San Francisco (94111) *(P-8186)*
Kinsbursky Bros Supply Inc (PA) ....D.......714 738-8516
125 E Commercial St Ste A Anaheim (92801) *(P-7982)*
Kinship Center ....D.......714 979-2365
18302 Irvine Blvd Ste 300 Tustin (92780) *(P-23884)*
Kintera Inc (HQ) ....D.......858 795-3000
9605 Scranton Rd Ste 200 San Diego (92121) *(P-15730)*
Kintetsu Enterprises ....D.......213 687-2000
328 E 1st St Los Angeles (90012) *(P-26920)*
Kintetsu Enterprises Co Amer, Torrance *Also called Kintetsu Enterprises Co Amer (P-12816)*
Kintetsu Enterprises Co Amer (HQ) ....C.......310 782-9300
21241 S Wstn Ave Ste 100 Torrance (90501) *(P-12816)*
Kintetsu Enterprises Co Amer ....D.......213 617-2000
328 E 1st St Los Angeles (90012) *(P-12817)*
Kipp Foundation ....C.......415 399-1556
135 Main St Ste 1700 San Francisco (94105) *(P-24798)*
Kirkhill Aircraft Parts Co (PA) ....C.......714 223-5400
3120 Enterprise St Brea (92821) *(P-7907)*
Kirkhill Aircraft Parts Co ....D.......714 223-5400
3101 Enterprise St Brea (92821) *(P-7908)*
Kirkhill Rubber Company ....D.......562 803-1117
2500 E Thompson St Long Beach (90805) *(P-7854)*
Kirkland & Ellis LLP ....A.......650 852-9131
3330 Hillview Ave Palo Alto (94304) *(P-23173)*
Kirkland & Ellis LLP ....C.......415 439-1400
555 California St # 2700 San Francisco (94104) *(P-23174)*
Kirkpatrick Ldscpg Svcs Inc ....C.......760 347-6926
43752 Jackson St Indio (92201) *(P-872)*
Kirschenman Enterprises Inc ....D.......661 366-5736
10100 Digiorgio Rd Bakersfield (93307) *(P-364)*
Kirschenman Enterprises Sls LP ....B.......661 366-5736
12826 Edison Hwy Edison (93220) *(P-17276)*
Kirschenman Packing Inc ....C.......661 366-5736
12826 Edison Hwy Edison (93220) *(P-534)*
Kisco Senior Living LLC ....D.......415 664-6264
1601 19th Ave Ofc San Francisco (94122) *(P-26921)*
Kisco Senior Living LLC ....D.......415 491-1935
275 Los Ranchitos Rd San Rafael (94903) *(P-11043)*
Kisco Senior Living LLC ....D.......714 872-9785
1731 W Medical Center Dr Anaheim (92801) *(P-11044)*
Kisco Senior Living LLC ....D.......949 888-2250
21952 Buena Suerte Rcho STA Marg (92688) *(P-11045)*
Kisco Senior Living LLC ....D.......559 449-8070
1100 E Spruce Ave Ofc Fresno (93720) *(P-11046)*
Kisco Senior Living LLC ....D.......707 585-1800
1350 Oak View Cir Rohnert Park (94928) *(P-11047)*
Kisco Senior Living LLC ....E.......650 948-7337
1174 Los Altos Ave Ofc Los Altos (94022) *(P-11048)*
Kissito Health Care Inc ....D.......510 582-8311
442 Sunset Blvd Hayward (94541) *(P-22354)*
Kissito Health Case Inc ....D.......925 689-9222
3318 Willow Pass Rd Concord (94519) *(P-22355)*
Kissito Health Case Inc ....D.......510 357-4015
368 Juana Ave San Leandro (94577) *(P-22356)*
Kissito Health Case Inc ....C.......209 524-4817
1310 W Granger Ave Modesto (95350) *(P-20567)*
Kit Carson Nursing & Rehab, Jackson *Also called Tutera Group Inc (P-24702)*
Kitayama Bros Inc ....D.......831 722-2912
481 San Andreas Rd Watsonville (95076) *(P-275)*
Kitayama Brothers Inc ....D.......831 722-8118
481 San Andreas Rd Watsonville (95076) *(P-276)*
Kitayama Flowers, Watsonville *Also called Kitayama Brothers Inc (P-276)*
Kitchen Mart Inc ....D.......916 315-3535
4381 Granite Dr Ste C Rocklin (95677) *(P-1189)*
Kite Electric Inc ....C.......949 380-7471
2 Thomas Irvine (92618) *(P-2625)*
Kite Pharma Inc (HQ) ....C.......310 824-9999
2400 Broadway Ste 100 Santa Monica (90404) *(P-26391)*
Kitson Landscape MGT Inc ....D.......805 681-9460
5787 Thornwood Dr Goleta (93117) *(P-873)*
Kittridge Gardens, Reseda *Also called GK Management Co Inc (P-11484)*
Kittridge Hotels & Resorts LLC ....D.......760 325-9676
150 S Indian Canyon Dr Palm Springs (92262) *(P-12818)*
Kiwanis International Inc ....D.......209 578-1448
3201 Canterbury Ct Modesto (95350) *(P-25179)*
Kjc Operating Company ....C.......760 762-5562
41100 Us Highway 395 Boron (93516) *(P-6047)*
Kkzz 1590 ....E.......805 289-1400
2284 S Victoria Ave 2g Ventura (93003) *(P-5734)*
Kl Cutting Service Inc ....C.......213 742-9001
2250 Maple Ave Los Angeles (90011) *(P-13635)*
Klassen Corporation (PA) ....D.......661 327-0875
2021 Westwind Dr Bakersfield (93301) *(P-1576)*
Klein Denatale Goldner Et Al (PA) ....D.......661 401-7755
4550 California Ave Fl 2 Bakersfield (93309) *(P-23175)*
Klein Denatale Goldner Cooper, Bakersfield *Also called Klein Denatale Goldner Et Al (P-23175)*
Klein Foods Inc ....D.......707 431-1533
11455 Old Redwood Hwy Healdsburg (95448) *(P-154)*
Klein-Testan-Brundo ....E.......714 245-8888
1851 E 1st St Ste 100 Santa Ana (92705) *(P-23176)*
Kleiner Prkins Cfeld Byers LLC (PA) ....C.......650 233-2750
2750 Sand Hill Rd Menlo Park (94025) *(P-12236)*
Kleinfelder Inc (HQ) ....C.......619 831-4600
550 W C St Ste 1200 San Diego (92101) *(P-25782)*
Kleinfelder Inc ....D.......559 486-0750
5125 N Gates Ave Ste 102 Fresno (93722) *(P-25783)*
Kleinfelder Inc ....D.......925 484-1700
6700 Koll Center Pkwy # 120 Pleasanton (94566) *(P-25784)*
Kleinfelder Inc ....D.......951 801-3681
3880 Lemon St Ste 300 Riverside (92501) *(P-27764)*
Kleinfelder Inc ....D.......916 366-1701
2882 Prospect Park Dr # 200 Rancho Cordova (95670) *(P-25785)*
Kleinfelder Associates ....A.......619 831-4600
550 W C St Ste 1200 San Diego (92101) *(P-27765)*
Kleinpartners Capital Corp ....B.......310 426-2055
400 Continental Blvd # 600 El Segundo (90245) *(P-12237)*
Klh Consulting Inc ....D.......707 575-9986
2324 Bethards Dr Santa Rosa (95405) *(P-27766)*
Klink Citrus Association ....C.......559 798-1881
32921 Road 159 Ivanhoe (93235) *(P-535)*
Klink Citrus Exchange, Ivanhoe *Also called Klink Citrus Association (P-535)*
Klm Management Company ....D.......626 330-3479
14120 Valley Blvd City of Industry (91746) *(P-8523)*
Klm Orthotic Laboratories Inc ....D.......661 295-2600
28280 Alta Vista Ave Valencia (91355) *(P-7187)*
Kloeckner Metals Corporation ....D.......562 906-2020
9804 Norwalk Blvd Ste 8 Santa Fe Springs (90670) *(P-7286)*
Kloeckner Metals Corporation ....E.......562 906-2020
9804 Norwalk Blvd Bldg A Santa Fe Springs (90670) *(P-7287)*
Kloeckner Metals Corporation ....D.......559 688-7980
2000 S O St Tulare (93274) *(P-7288)*
Kloudgin, Sunnyvale *Also called Enterprise Signal Inc (P-15669)*
Kls Air Express Inc (PA) ....D.......916 857-6305
2870 Gold Tailings Ct Rancho Cordova (95670) *(P-5094)*
Klx Aerospace Solutions, Carson *Also called Klx Inc (P-7909)*
Klx Inc ....D.......559 684-1037
3645 S K St Tulare (93274) *(P-4204)*
Klx Inc ....C.......310 900-1300
1351 Charles Willard St Carson (90746) *(P-7909)*
Km Fresno Investors LLC ....E.......323 556-6600
6222 Wilshire Blvd # 650 Los Angeles (90048) *(P-12238)*
Km Industrial Inc ....C.......562 786-6200
2375 W Esther St Long Beach (90813) *(P-14299)*
KMA Emergency Services Inc ....D.......510 614-1420
14275 Wicks Blvd San Leandro (94577) *(P-3814)*
Kmax TV, West Sacramento *Also called Sacramento Television Stns Inc (P-5835)*
KMD Architects (PA) ....D.......415 398-5191
417 Montgomery St Ste 200 San Francisco (94104) *(P-26075)*
Kmir-Tv6, Palm Desert *Also called Entravsion Communications Corp (P-5786)*
Kml Enterprises Career Dev LLC ....C.......714 221-3100
1900 S State College Blvd Anaheim (92806) *(P-16417)*
Kmph Fox 26 ....C.......559 255-2600
5111 E Mckinley Ave Fresno (93727) *(P-5809)*
Kms Fishermans Wharf LP ....C.......415 561-1100
425 N Point St San Francisco (94133) *(P-12819)*
Knd Development 55 LLC ....D.......909 581-6400
10841 White Oak Ave Rancho Cucamonga (91730) *(P-21542)*
Knet TV ....E.......323 469-5638
5757 Wilshire Blvd # 470 Los Angeles (90036) *(P-5810)*
Kniesels Auto Collision Center ....E.......916 315-8888
4680 Pacific St Rocklin (95677) *(P-6653)*
Knight Port Services, Compton *Also called Knight Transportation Inc (P-4205)*
Knight Transportation Inc ....C.......888 549-7802
2960 E Victoria St Compton (90221) *(P-4205)*
Knight-Calabasas LLC (PA) ....D.......818 222-3200
4515 Park Entrada Calabasas (91302) *(P-18942)*
Knight-Calabasas LLC ....D.......415 453-4940
333 Biscayne Dr San Rafael (94901) *(P-18943)*
Knight-Swift Trnsp Hldings Inc ....D.......209 858-1630
901 Darcy Pkwy Lathrop (95330) *(P-4206)*
Knight-Swift Trnsp Hldings Inc ....D.......559 441-0340
2797 S Orange Ave Fresno (93725) *(P-4207)*
Knight-Swift Trnsp Hldings Inc ....D.......951 360-0130
11888 Mission Blvd Mira Loma (91752) *(P-4208)*
Knight-Swift Trnsp Hldings Inc ....D.......619 671-0588
6933 Calle De Linea Chula Vista (91911) *(P-4209)*
Knights of Columbus ....D.......408 262-6609
871 Founders Ln Milpitas (95035) *(P-25435)*
Knights of Columbus ....C.......408 371-1531
2211 Shamrock Dr Campbell (95008) *(P-25180)*
Knights of Columbus ....C.......805 525-7810
1344 Magnolia Dr Santa Paula (93060) *(P-25181)*
Kno Inc ....D.......408 844-8120
2200 Mission College Blvd Santa Clara (95054) *(P-15731)*
Knobbe Martens Olson Bear LLP (PA) ....B.......949 760-0404
2040 Main St Fl 14 Irvine (92614) *(P-23177)*
Knolls Convalescent Hospital (PA) ....C.......760 245-5361
16890 Green Tree Blvd Victorville (92395) *(P-20568)*
Knolls Convalescent Hospital ....D.......760 245-6477
14973 Hesperia Rd Victorville (92395) *(P-20569)*
Knolls West Enterprise ....D.......760 245-0107
16890 Green Tree Blvd Victorville (92395) *(P-24572)*
Knolls West Post Acute LLC ....D.......760 245-5361
16890 Green Tree Blvd Victorville (92395) *(P-21130)*
Knolls West Residential Care, Victorville *Also called Knolls West Enterprise (P-24572)*
Knollwood Center, Riverside *Also called Knollwood Psychiatric and Chem (P-21961)*
Knollwood Psychiatric and Chem ....D.......951 275-8400
5900 Brockton Ave Riverside (92506) *(P-21961)*
KNOLLWOOD PSYCHIATRIC CENTER, Riverside *Also called Behavioral Health Resources (P-21929)*
Knott's Berry Farm Hotel, Buena Park *Also called Knotts Berry Farm LLC (P-12820)*
Knotts Berry Farm LLC ....C.......714 995-1111
7675 Crescent Ave Buena Park (90620) *(P-12820)*

Mergent e-mail: customerrelations@mergent.com
1358
2019 Directory of California
Wholesalers and Services Companies
(P-0000) Products & Services Section entry number
(PA)=Parent Co (HQ)=Headquarters (DH)=Div Headquarters

Knova Software Inc (HQ).....E.....408 863-5800
10201 Torre Ave Ste 350 Cupertino (95014) ***(P-15732)***
Knox Attorney Service Inc (PA).....C.....619 233-9700
2250 4th Ave Ste 200 San Diego (92101) ***(P-23178)***
Knox Services, San Diego *Also called Knox Attorney Service Inc* ***(P-23178)***
Knox Services LLC (PA).....D.....714 479-1650
1522 Brookhollow Dr Ste 3 Santa Ana (92705) ***(P-14090)***
Knudtson Building Maint Svc, Sherman Oaks *Also called Adhei Enterprises Inc* ***(P-14180)***
Koam Engineering Systems Inc.....C.....858 292-0922
7807 Convoy Ct Ste 200 San Diego (92111) ***(P-15992)***
Kobata Growers Inc (PA).....D.....310 323-0662
17622 Van Ness Ave Torrance (90504) ***(P-277)***
Kobey Corporation Inc (PA).....D.....619 523-2700
3740 Sports Arena Blvd # 2 San Diego (92110) ***(P-17277)***
Kobey Swap Meet At Spt Arena, San Diego *Also called Kobey Corporation Inc* ***(P-17277)***
Koce-TV Foundation.....D.....714 241-4100
3080 Bristol St Ste 400 Costa Mesa (92626) ***(P-5811)***
Koch-Armstrong General Engrg.....D.....619 561-2005
15315 Olde Highway 80 El Cajon (92021) ***(P-25786)***
Kodiak Roofing & Waterproofing, Roseville *Also called Dwayne Nash Industries Inc* ***(P-3151)***
Koeller Nbker Crlson Hluck LLP (PA).....D.....949 864-3400
3 Park Plz Ste 1500 Irvine (92614) ***(P-23179)***
Kofax Inc (PA).....B.....949 783-1000
15211 Laguna Canyon Rd Irvine (92618) ***(P-15250)***
Koffler Elec Mech Apprts Repai.....D.....510 567-0630
527 Whitney St San Leandro (94577) ***(P-7370)***
Kogoam, San Diego *Also called Iheartcommunications Inc* ***(P-5724)***
Kohlberg Kravis Roberts Co LP.....D.....650 233-6560
2800 Sand Hill Rd Ste 200 Menlo Park (94025) ***(P-12239)***
Kohls Corporation.....A.....909 382-4300
890 E Mill St San Bernardino (92408) ***(P-9227)***
Koit, San Francisco *Also called Bonneville International Corp* ***(P-5694)***
Kojenov Arkadi Nilovich.....E.....916 718-1790
5335 Hackberry Ln Sacramento (95841) ***(P-5095)***
Kole Imports.....D.....310 834-0004
24600 Main St Carson (90745) ***(P-9228)***
Koll Management Services Inc.....A.....949 833-3030
4343 Von Karman Ave Newport Beach (92660) ***(P-11553)***
Kollstar Golf Company, Newport Beach *Also called Kollwood Golf Operating LP* ***(P-18724)***
Kollwood Golf Operating LP.....B.....949 833-3025
4343 Von Karman Ave Newport Beach (92660) ***(P-18724)***
Kommonwealth Inc.....E.....310 278-7328
6420 Wilshire Blvd Los Angeles (90048) ***(P-8360)***
Kona Kai Resort Hotel, San Diego *Also called Westgroup Kona Kai LLC* ***(P-19086)***
Konami Digital Entrmt Inc (HQ).....D.....310 220-8100
2381 Rosecrans Ave # 200 El Segundo (90245) ***(P-15733)***
Kondaur Capital Corporation (PA).....C.....714 352-2038
333 S Anita Dr Ste 400 Orange (92868) ***(P-9822)***
Kone Inc.....D.....858 578-5100
9850 Businesspark Ave San Diego (92131) ***(P-17960)***
Kong Inc.....E.....415 754-9283
251 Post St Ste 200 San Francisco (94108) ***(P-15251)***
Konica Minolta Business Soluti.....D.....909 824-2000
1831 Commercenter W San Bernardino (92408) ***(P-6966)***
Konica Minolta Business Soluti.....E.....310 214-6696
879 W 190th St Ste 200 Gardena (90248) ***(P-6967)***
Kono Farms Incorporated.....C.....760 397-7110
87481 Avenue 74 Thermal (92274) ***(P-65)***
KONOCTI TRANSPORTATION SERVICE, Lakeport *Also called People Services Inc* ***(P-24628)***
Konocti Vista Casino (PA).....C.....707 262-1900
2755 Mission Rancheria Rd Lakeport (95453) ***(P-12821)***
Konoike-Pacific California Inc (HQ).....D.....310 518-1000
1420 Coil Ave Wilmington (90744) ***(P-4504)***
Koos Manufacturing Inc.....A.....323 249-1000
2741 Seminole Ave South Gate (90280) ***(P-17278)***
Kopy Kat Attorney Service, Brea *Also called V A Anderson Enterprises Inc* ***(P-17555)***
Kor Hotel Groups Inc.....D.....310 309-8066
530 Pico Blvd Santa Monica (90405) ***(P-26922)***
Koram Insurance Center Inc.....D.....323 660-1000
3807 Wilshire Blvd # 400 Los Angeles (90010) ***(P-10669)***
Kore1 Inc.....D.....949 706-6990
530 Technology Ste 150 Irvine (92618) ***(P-16418)***
Korea Tchnlgy Cmmnications USA.....C.....213 381-0061
10645 W Vanowen St Burbank (91505) ***(P-16918)***
Korean Air Lines Co Ltd.....C.....310 646-4866
380 World Way Ste S4 Los Angeles (90045) ***(P-4789)***
Korean Airlines.....C.....310 417-5294
380 World Way Los Angeles (90045) ***(P-4790)***
Korean Airlines Co Ltd.....C.....310 410-2000
6101 W Imperial Hwy Los Angeles (90045) ***(P-4791)***
Korean Arln Crgo Reservations, Los Angeles *Also called Korean Airlines Co Ltd* ***(P-4791)***
Korean Community Services Inc.....E.....714 527-6561
8633 Knott Ave Buena Park (90620) ***(P-23885)***
Korean Health Education (PA).....D.....213 427-4000
3727 W 6th St Ste 210 Los Angeles (90020) ***(P-23886)***
Koreatown Youth and Cmnty Ctr (PA).....D.....213 365-7400
3727 W 6th St Ste 300 Los Angeles (90020) ***(P-23887)***
KORN FERRY, Los Angeles *Also called Korn/Ferry International* ***(P-27295)***
Korn/Ferry International (PA).....C.....310 552-1834
1900 Avenue Stars Los Angeles (90067) ***(P-27295)***
Kos-USA.....D.....213 747-2591
3434 S Broadway Los Angeles (90007) ***(P-8313)***
Kositch Enterprises Inc.....D.....510 657-4460
5700 Boscell Cmn Fremont (94538) ***(P-2626)***
Kotobuki-Ya Inc.....D.....650 344-7955
314 Lang Rd Burlingame (94010) ***(P-3663)***

Kountable Inc.....D.....310 613-5481
321 Pacific Ave Fl 3 San Francisco (94111) ***(P-17279)***
Koury Engrg Tstg & Insptn.....D.....310 851-8685
14280 Euclid Ave Chino (91710) ***(P-17280)***
Kovel/Fuller LLC.....D.....310 841-4444
9925 Jefferson Blvd Culver City (90232) ***(P-13856)***
Koxr Spanish Radio.....E.....805 487-0444
200 S A St Ste 400 Oxnard (93030) ***(P-5735)***
Kozuki Farming Inc.....D.....559 646-2652
16518 E Adams Ave Parlier (93648) ***(P-223)***
Kp LLC.....C.....510 346-0729
13951 Washington Ave San Leandro (94578) ***(P-14049)***
Kp LLC.....D.....510 614-7800
13951 Washington Ave San Leandro (94578) ***(P-14050)***
Kpac, Wilmington *Also called Konoike-Pacific California Inc* ***(P-4504)***
Kpbs TV, San Diego *Also called San Diego State University* ***(P-5752)***
Kpc Group LLC (PA).....C.....951 782-8812
6800 Indiana Ave Ste 130 Riverside (92506) ***(P-27296)***
Kpc Healthcare Inc.....B.....714 800-1919
2701 S Bristol St Santa Ana (92704) ***(P-21543)***
Kpcb, Menlo Park *Also called Kleiner Prkins Cfeld Byers LLC* ***(P-12236)***
Kpff Inc.....C.....310 665-1536
700 S Flower St Ste 2100 Los Angeles (90017) ***(P-25787)***
Kpff Inc.....D.....562 437-9100
400 Oceangate Ste 500 Long Beach (90802) ***(P-25788)***
Kpff Inc.....D.....415 989-1004
45 Fremont St Fl 28 San Francisco (94105) ***(P-25789)***
Kpff Consulting Engineers, San Francisco *Also called Kpff Inc* ***(P-25789)***
Kpisoft Inc.....D.....415 439-5228
50 California St Ste 1500 San Francisco (94111) ***(P-15734)***
Kpmg LLP.....E.....310 273-2770
9171 Wilshire Blvd # 500 Beverly Hills (90210) ***(P-26236)***
Kpmg LLP.....C.....858 750-7100
4655 Executive Dr # 1100 San Diego (92121) ***(P-26237)***
Kpmg LLP.....E.....415 963-5100
55 2nd St Ste 1400 San Francisco (94105) ***(P-26238)***
Kpmg LLP.....D.....703 286-8175
550 S Hope St Ste 1500 Los Angeles (90071) ***(P-26239)***
Kpmg LLP.....A.....212 758-9700
550 S Hope St Ste 1500 Los Angeles (90071) ***(P-26240)***
Kpmg LLP.....E.....925 946-1300
2175 N Calif Blvd # 1000 Walnut Creek (94596) ***(P-26241)***
Kpmg LLP.....C.....916 448-4700
500 Capitol Mall Ste 2100 Sacramento (95814) ***(P-26242)***
Kpmg LLP.....E.....818 227-6900
21700 Oxnard St Ste 1800 Woodland Hills (91367) ***(P-26243)***
Kpower Sup McRswitch Inverters, Irvine *Also called Zippy Usa Inc* ***(P-7405)***
Kprs Construction Services Inc (PA).....D.....714 672-0800
2850 Saturn St Ste 110 Brea (92821) ***(P-1577)***
Kpwr Inc.....D.....818 953-4200
2600 W Olive Ave Ste 850 Burbank (91505) ***(P-5736)***
Kpwr Power 106, Burbank *Also called Kpwr Inc* ***(P-5736)***
Kpwr Radio LLC.....C.....562 745-2300
9550 Firestone Blvd # 105 Downey (90241) ***(P-17281)***
Kpxn-TV, Pasadena *Also called Ion Media Networks Inc* ***(P-5802)***
Kqed Inc (PA).....B.....415 864-2000
2601 Mariposa St San Francisco (94110) ***(P-5812)***
Kqed Public Media, San Francisco *Also called Kqed Inc* ***(P-5812)***
Kradjian Importing Company Inc (PA).....D.....818 502-1313
5018 San Fernando Rd Glendale (91204) ***(P-8818)***
Kraft & Kennedy Inc.....D.....415 956-4000
1 Post St Ste 2600 San Francisco (94104) ***(P-15993)***
Kraft Heinz Foods Company.....B.....925 469-0057
5000 Hopyard Rd Ste 235 Pleasanton (94588) ***(P-8819)***
Kraft Heinz Foods Company.....E.....559 499-5300
1055 E North Ave Fresno (93725) ***(P-8820)***
Kramer-Wilson Company Inc (PA).....C.....818 760-0880
6345 Balboa Blvd Ste 190 Encino (91316) ***(P-10365)***
Kranem Corporation.....C.....650 319-6743
560 S Winchester Blvd San Jose (95128) ***(P-15735)***
Kranz & Assoc Holdings LLC.....D.....650 854-4400
830 Menlo Ave Ste 100 Menlo Park (94025) ***(P-26244)***
Kratos Tech Trning Sltions Inc (HQ).....C.....858 812-7300
10680 Treena St Fl 6 San Diego (92131) ***(P-15736)***
Kravitz Investment Svcs Inc.....D.....818 995-6100
16030 Ventura Blvd # 200 Encino (91436) ***(P-10093)***
Krayden, Morgan Hill *Also called K R Anderson Inc* ***(P-8930)***
Krazan & Associates (PA).....D.....559 348-2200
215 W Dakota Ave Clovis (93612) ***(P-27767)***
KRC Builders Incorporated.....D.....916 417-1200
6141 W 4th St Rio Linda (95673) ***(P-3048)***
KRC Equipment LLC.....D.....760 744-1036
700 N Twin Oaks Valley Rd San Marcos (92069) ***(P-7704)***
KRC Los Altos, Los Altos *Also called Kisco Senior Living LLC* ***(P-11048)***
KRC Santa Margarita, Rcho STA Marg *Also called Kisco Senior Living LLC* ***(P-11045)***
Krca Television Inc, Burbank *Also called Krca Television LLC* ***(P-5813)***
Krca Television LLC.....C.....818 563-5722
1845 W Empire Ave Burbank (91504) ***(P-5813)***
Krcr TV, Redding *Also called California Oregon Broadcasting* ***(P-5771)***
Krcx 99 9 FM Tricolor, Sacramento *Also called Entravsion Communications Corp* ***(P-5715)***
Kretek International Inc (HQ).....D.....805 531-8888
5449 Endeavour Ct Moorpark (93021) ***(P-9184)***
Krg Technologies Inc.....A.....661 257-9967
25000 Ave Stnford Ste 243 Valencia (91355) ***(P-15252)***
Krikorian Premiere Theatre LLC.....C.....626 305-7469
410 S Myrtle Ave Monrovia (91016) ***(P-18303)***
Krikorian Premiere Theatre LLC.....C.....760 945-7469
25 Main St Vista (92083) ***(P-18304)***

ALPHABETIC

Employee Codes: A=Over 500 employees, B=251-500
C=101-250, D=51-100, E=50
2019 Directory of California
Wholesalers and Services Companies
© Mergent Inc. 1-800-342-5647
1359

Krikorian Premiere Theatre LLC....D....562 205-3456
8540 Whittier Blvd Pico Rivera (90660) ***(P-18305)***
Krishnmrti Foundation of Amer (PA)....E....805 646-2726
134 Besant Rd Ojai (93023) ***(P-12079)***
Krlh-AM 590-AM, Glendale *Also called Salem Media Group Inc* ***(P-5751)***
Krm Risk Management Svcs Inc....D....559 277-4800
4270 W Richert Ave # 101 Fresno (93722) ***(P-26923)***
Kroeker Inc....C....559 237-3764
4627 S Chestnut Ave Fresno (93725) ***(P-3456)***
Kron, San Francisco *Also called Nexstar Broadcasting Inc* ***(P-5829)***
Kron-TV, San Francisco *Also called Chronicle Broadcasting Co* ***(P-5778)***
Kron-TV, San Francisco *Also called Young Brdcstg of San Francisco* ***(P-5854)***
Kronick Moskovitz Tiedemann (PA)....D....916 321-4500
400 Capitol Mall Fl 27 Sacramento (95814) ***(P-23180)***
Kronos Foods Corp....D....559 674-4445
2401 W Almond Ave Madera (93637) ***(P-8821)***
Kronos Incorporated....D....800 580-7374
240 Commerce Irvine (92602) ***(P-15737)***
Kropa Realty....E....925 937-4040
3093 Citrus Cir Ste 150 Walnut Creek (94598) ***(P-11554)***
Kros-Wise....D....619 223-1980
3111 Camino Del Rio N San Diego (92108) ***(P-27768)***
Krth Radio 101 FM, Los Angeles *Also called Infinity Broadcasting Corp Cal* ***(P-5730)***
Krty Ltd A Cal Ltd Partnr....E....408 293-8030
750 Story Rd San Jose (95122) ***(P-5737)***
Krzr 103 7 FM, Fresno *Also called Iheartcommunications Inc* ***(P-5723)***
KS Fabrication & Machine, Bakersfield *Also called K S Fabrication & Machine Inc* ***(P-1940)***
KS Industries LP (PA)....A....661 617-1700
6205 District Blvd Bakersfield (93313) ***(P-1944)***
Ksby Communications Inc....D....805 541-6666
1772 Calle Joaquin San Luis Obispo (93405) ***(P-5814)***
Ksee, Fresno *Also called Nexstar Broadcasting Inc* ***(P-5828)***
Kseg-FM, Sacramento *Also called Entercom Communications Corp* ***(P-5712)***
KSFCU, Bakersfield *Also called Kern Schools Federal Credit Un* ***(P-9565)***
Ksi Corp (PA)....D....650 952-0815
839 Mitten Rd San Bruno (94066) ***(P-5096)***
Ksi Corp....D....650 952-0815
839 Mitten Rd Ste 200 Burlingame (94010) ***(P-5097)***
Ksi Engineering Inc....E....661 617-1700
6205 District Blvd Bakersfield (93313) ***(P-25790)***
Ksl II Mngement Operations LLC....D....760 564-8000
50905 Avenida Bermudas La Quinta (92253) ***(P-26924)***
KSL Media Inc....C....212 468-3395
15910 Ventura Blvd # 900 Encino (91436) ***(P-13975)***
Ksl Resorts Hotel Del Coronado....D....619 435-6611
1500 Orange Ave Coronado (92118) ***(P-12822)***
Ksm Healthcare Inc....D....818 242-1183
1400 W Glenoaks Blvd Glendale (91201) ***(P-20570)***
Ksm Marketing Inc....C....949 597-2222
10 Holland Irvine (92618) ***(P-17282)***
Kswb, Los Angeles *Also called Bonneville International Corp* ***(P-5692)***
Kswb Inc....D....858 492-9269
7191 Engineer Rd San Diego (92111) ***(P-5815)***
KT&c USA, Burbank *Also called Korea Tchnlgy Cmmnications USA* ***(P-16918)***
Ktff, Brisbane *Also called Lincoln Television Inc* ***(P-5821)***
Ktgy Group Inc....E....510 463-2097
1814 Franklin St Ste 400 Oakland (94612) ***(P-26076)***
Ktgy Group Inc (PA)....D....949 851-2133
17911 Von Karman Ave # 250 Irvine (92614) ***(P-26077)***
Ktgy Group Inc....E....310 394-2625
12555 W Jefferson Blvd # 100 Los Angeles (90066) ***(P-26078)***
Ktsf Channel 26....E....415 467-6397
100 Valley Dr Brisbane (94005) ***(P-5816)***
Ktvu Partnership Inc....C....510 834-1212
2 Jack London Sq Oakland (94607) ***(P-5817)***
Ktvu Television Fox 2, Oakland *Also called Ktvu Partnership Inc* ***(P-5817)***
Ktxl-Fox 40, Sacramento *Also called Channel 40 Inc* ***(P-5777)***
Ku Kyoung....C....510 582-2765
19960 Santa Maria Ave Castro Valley (94546) ***(P-20571)***
Kuehne + Nagel Inc....D....510 785-0555
2660 W Winton Ave Hayward (94545) ***(P-4583)***
Kuehne + Nagel Inc....E....415 656-4100
150 W Hill Pl Brisbane (94005) ***(P-5098)***
Kuehne + Nagel Inc....D....909 574-2300
9425 Nevada St Redlands (92374) ***(P-4584)***
Kugga Inc....D....925 639-0721
1841 Sunnyvale Ave Walnut Creek (94597) ***(P-15253)***
Kuic Inc....D....707 446-0200
555 Mason St Ste 245 Vacaville (95688) ***(P-5738)***
Kuic-FM, Vacaville *Also called Kuic Inc* ***(P-5738)***
Kuleto's, San Francisco *Also called Kimpton Hotel & Rest Group LLC* ***(P-12811)***
Kumar Hotels Inc....C....530 934-8900
545 N Humboldt Ave Willows (95988) ***(P-12823)***
Kunde Estate Winery, Kenwood *Also called Arthur Kunde & Sons Inc* ***(P-681)***
Kurt Meiswinkel Inc....E....650 344-7200
1407 E 3rd Ave San Mateo (94401) ***(P-2908)***
Kusc Radio....E....213 225-7400
1149 S Hill St Ste H100 Los Angeles (90015) ***(P-5739)***
Kushner & Associates, Calabasas *Also called Custom Tours Inc* ***(P-4987)***
Kusi TV Channel 51, San Diego *Also called McKinnon Broadcasting Company* ***(P-5823)***
Kusumoto Farms....D....408 927-8348
6535 Stonehill Dr San Jose (95120) ***(P-103)***
Kut From The Kloth, City of Industry *Also called Swatfame Inc* ***(P-8337)***
Kutir Corporation....E....510 402-4526
37600 Central Ct Ste 280 Newark (94560) ***(P-15994)***
Kvea-Tv-Channel 52, Burbank *Also called Estrella Communications Inc* ***(P-5789)***
Kvie Inc (PA)....D....916 929-5843
2030 W El Camino Ave # 100 Sacramento (95833) ***(P-5818)***
Kvie Channel 6, Sacramento *Also called Kvie Inc* ***(P-5818)***
Kvl Holdings Inc (PA)....E....831 678-2132
37700 Foothill Rd Soledad (93960) ***(P-155)***
Kw International Inc....D....310 747-1380
18511 S Broadwick St Rancho Dominguez (90220) ***(P-5099)***
Kw International Inc....B....213 703-6914
18724 S Broadwick St Rancho Dominguez (90220) ***(P-4683)***
Kwan Wo Ironworks Inc....C....415 822-9628
31628 Hayman St Hayward (94544) ***(P-3382)***
Kwik Wash Laundries, Union City *Also called CSC Serviceworks Holdings Inc* ***(P-13559)***
Kxtv Inc....C....916 441-2345
400 Broadway Sacramento (95818) ***(P-5819)***
Kya Services LLC....E....714 659-6476
1522 Brookhollow Dr Ste 3 Santa Ana (92705) ***(P-3112)***
Kyakamena Sklled Nrsing Fcilty, Berkeley *Also called Sanhyd Inc* ***(P-20746)***
KYCC, Los Angeles *Also called Koreatown Youth and Cmnty Ctr* ***(P-23887)***
Kyocera Dcment Sltons Amer Inc....D....925 849-3300
1855 Gateway Blvd Ste 400 Concord (94520) ***(P-6968)***
Kyocera International Inc....E....714 428-3600
3565 Cadillac Ave Costa Mesa (92626) ***(P-7498)***
Kyocera International Inc....D....310 647-2805
222 N Pacific Coast Hwy El Segundo (90245) ***(P-6945)***
Kyocera Technology Development, Concord *Also called Kyocera Dcment Sltons Amer Inc* ***(P-6968)***
KYOLIC, Mission Viejo *Also called Wakunaga of America Co Ltd* ***(P-8221)***
Kyoto Grand Hotel, Los Angeles *Also called 120 South Los Angeles Street H* ***(P-12287)***
Kyoto Grand Hotel and Gardens, Los Angeles *Also called Crestline Hotels & Resorts Inc* ***(P-12499)***
Kyriba Corp (HQ)....E....858 210-3560
9620 Towne Cntre Dr 200 San Diego (92121) ***(P-15738)***
Kysmet Security & Patrol Inc....E....831 710-2425
21 W Laurel Dr Ste 49 Salinas (93906) ***(P-16712)***
Kzsu 90.1 FM, Stanford *Also called Leland Stanford Junior Univ* ***(P-5741)***
L & J Farms Caraccioli LLC....E....831 675-7901
27905 Corda Rd Gonzales (93926) ***(P-365)***
L & L Logic and Logistics LP....E....707 795-2475
6 Hamilton Landing # 250 Novato (94949) ***(P-8361)***
L & L Nursery Supply Inc (PA)....C....909 591-0461
2552 Shenandoah Way San Bernardino (92407) ***(P-9081)***
L & O Aliso Viejo LLC....D....949 643-6700
50 Enterprise Aliso Viejo (92656) ***(P-18620)***
L & R Distributors Inc....B....909 980-3807
9292 9th St Rancho Cucamonga (91730) ***(P-8229)***
L & S Investment Co Inc....D....760 245-3461
14173 Green Tree Blvd Victorville (92395) ***(P-12824)***
L & T Meat Co....D....323 262-2815
3050 E 11th St Los Angeles (90023) ***(P-8494)***
L & W Supply Corporation....E....858 627-0811
7750 Convoy Ct San Diego (92111) ***(P-6898)***
L & W Supply Corporation....D....510 429-8003
31625 Hayman St Hayward (94544) ***(P-6899)***
L A Commercial Group Inc (PA)....D....818 551-6800
317 S Brand Blvd Glendale (91204) ***(P-14012)***
L A County Hospital, Torrance *Also called County of Los Angeles* ***(P-19410)***
L A Cstm AP & Promotions Inc (PA)....D....562 595-1770
2680 Temple Ave Long Beach (90806) ***(P-8266)***
L A Fitness Intl LLC....D....805 289-9907
1760 S Victoria Ave Ventura (93003) ***(P-18621)***
L A Fitness Sports Clubs, Ventura *Also called L A Fitness Intl LLC* ***(P-18621)***
L A Fitness Sports Clubs, San Diego *Also called Fitness International LLC* ***(P-18602)***
L A Girl, Ontario *Also called Beauty 21 Cosmetics Inc* ***(P-8146)***
L A Hearne Company (PA)....D....831 385-5441
512 Metz Rd King City (93930) ***(P-9082)***
L A Inflight Service Company, Gardena *Also called World Service West* ***(P-4922)***
L A Kings, Los Angeles *Also called Los Angles Kings Hockey CLB LP* ***(P-18528)***
L A P F C U, Van Nuys *Also called Los Angeles Police Credit Un* ***(P-9640)***
L A Party Rents Inc....D....818 989-4300
13520 Saticoy St Van Nuys (91402) ***(P-14521)***
L A Philharmonic, Los Angeles *Also called Los Angeles Philharmonic Assn* ***(P-18449)***
L A Rubber Co, Los Angeles *Also called Mechanical Drives Co* ***(P-7858)***
L A S Transportation Inc....B....559 264-6583
250 E Belmont Ave Fresno (93701) ***(P-4210)***
L A Services Inc....E....310 838-0408
9405 Jefferson Blvd Culver City (90232) ***(P-2253)***
L A Swikard Inc....C....858 408-3700
9520 Candida St San Diego (92126) ***(P-874)***
L A U S D, Pico Rivera *Also called Los Angeles Unified School Dst* ***(P-17303)***
L and R Auto Parks Inc....C....213 784-3018
707 Wilshire Blvd # 4300 Los Angeles (90017) ***(P-17690)***
L B C Holdings U S A Corp (PA)....C....650 873-0750
362 E Grand Ave South San Francisco (94080) ***(P-4943)***
L B Construction, Roseville *Also called Lancaster Burns Cnstr Inc* ***(P-2909)***
L Barrios & Associates Inc....E....626 960-2934
302 E Fthill Blvd Ste 101 San Dimas (91773) ***(P-875)***
L C C H Associates Inc....E....858 565-4424
4311 3rd Ave B San Diego (92103) ***(P-21131)***
L E Cooke Co....C....559 732-9146
26333 Road 140 Visalia (93292) ***(P-278)***
L E Coppersmith Inc (PA)....D....310 607-8000
525 S Douglas St Ste 100 El Segundo (90245) ***(P-5100)***
L E Coppersmith Inc....D....310 607-8000
525 S Douglas St El Segundo (90245) ***(P-5101)***
L I Metal Systems....E....562 948-5950
9041 Bermudez St Pico Rivera (90660) ***(P-3171)***
L J B, Irvine *Also called Tanvex Biopharma Usa Inc* ***(P-26470)***

Mergent e-mail: customerrelations@mergent.com
1360
2019 Directory of California
Wholesalers and Services Companies
(P-0000) Products & Services Section entry number
(PA)=Parent Co (HQ)=Headquarters (DH)=Div Headquarters

L J Kruse Co....D....510 644-0260
920 Pardee St Berkeley (94710) *(P-2254)*
L J T Flowers Inc....805 310-6036
2425 Bonita School Rd Nipomo (93444) *(P-279)*
L J Trucking USA....D....323 469-9663
120 S Anderson St Los Angeles (90033) *(P-4211)*
L L V A R E, Redlands *Also called Loma Linda Vet Association For (P-25191)*
L Lyon Distributing Inc....E....909 798-7129
254 W Stuart Ave Redlands (92374) *(P-17283)*
L R Investment Company....D....213 627-8211
515 S Flower St Ste 3200 Los Angeles (90071) *(P-17691)*
L S A Associates Inc (PA)....C....949 553-0666
20 Executive Park Ste 200 Irvine (92614) *(P-27769)*
L Tech Network Services Inc....D....562 222-1121
9926 Pioneer Blvd Ste 101 Santa Fe Springs (90670) *(P-2627)*
L W Roth Insurance Agency....D....916 721-6273
6060 Sunrise Vista Dr Citrus Heights (95610) *(P-24964)*
L&D Farm Labor....E....760 408-6311
53762 Sapphire Ln Coachella (92236) *(P-657)*
L&G Cable Construction....D....714 630-6174
2776 E Miraloma Ave Anaheim (92806) *(P-3544)*
L&H Airco LLC....D....916 677-1000
2530 Warren Dr Rocklin (95677) *(P-2255)*
L&T Staffing Inc (PA)....B....714 558-1821
950 W 17th St Ste E Santa Ana (92706) *(P-14659)*
L'Auberge Del Mar, Del Mar *Also called Lhoberge Lessee Inc (P-12852)*
L'Ermitage Hotel, Beverly Hills *Also called Raffles Lrmitage Beverly Hills (P-13096)*
L-3 Communications Maripro Inc, Goleta *Also called L3 Maripro Inc (P-25791)*
L-O Coronado Hotel Inc....A....619 435-6611
1500 Orange Ave Coronado (92118) *(P-12825)*
L-O Soma Hotel Inc....B....415 974-6400
50 3rd St San Francisco (94103) *(P-12826)*
L.A. Care Health Plan, Los Angeles *Also called Local Initiative Health Author (P-10279)*
L.A. Cold Storage, Los Angeles *Also called Standard-Southern Corporation (P-4511)*
L.A. Gay & Lesbian Center, Los Angeles *Also called Los Angeles Lgbt Center (P-24803)*
L.A.cO., Whittier *Also called County Santtn Dist 2 of La Co (P-6535)*
L3 Applied Technologies Inc....C....510 577-7100
2700 Merced St San Leandro (94577) *(P-26392)*
L3 Maripro Inc....D....805 683-3881
1522 Cook Pl Goleta (93117) *(P-25791)*
L3 Technologies Inc....D....858 623-6513
10770 Wtridge Cir Ste 200 San Diego (92121) *(P-5987)*
L3 Technologies Inc....D....760 375-0390
117 S Gold Canyon St Ridgecrest (93555) *(P-15995)*
La Asociacion Nacional Pro Per....B....213 202-5900
1452 W Temple St Ste 100 Los Angeles (90026) *(P-23888)*
La Asociacion Nacional Pro Per (PA)....A....626 564-1988
234 E Colo Blvd Ste 300 Pasadena (91101) *(P-23889)*
La Belle Days Spas and Salons, Palo Alto *Also called Beauty Bazar Inc (P-13647)*
La Bonne Vie Inc....D....805 773-5003
2723 Shell Beach Rd Shell Beach (93449) *(P-18622)*
La Boulange, San Francisco *Also called Bay Bread LLC (P-8760)*
La Boxing Franchise Corp....C....714 668-0911
1241 E Dyer Rd Ste 100 Santa Ana (92705) *(P-18623)*
La Canada Flintridge Cntry CLB....D....818 790-0611
5500 Godbey Dr La Canada (91011) *(P-18944)*
La Cantina Doors Inc....E....888 221-0141
1875 Ord Way Oceanside (92056) *(P-6934)*
La Casa Mental Health Center, Long Beach *Also called Telecare Corporation (P-21981)*
La Casa Mhrc, Long Beach *Also called Telecare Corporation (P-21980)*
La Checker Cab Co, Van Nuys *Also called Checker Cab Co (P-3865)*
La Cienega Associates....D....310 854-0071
8500 Beverly Blvd Ste 501 Los Angeles (90048) *(P-11555)*
La Clinica De La Raza Inc....C....510 535-6300
1515 Fruitvale Ave Oakland (94601) *(P-19628)*
La Clinica De La Raza Inc....B....707 556-8100
243 Georgia St Vallejo (94590) *(P-19629)*
La Clinica De La Raza Inc....C....510 535-4700
3050 E 16th St Oakland (94601) *(P-20121)*
La Clinica De La Raza Inc....C....510 535-6200
1601 Fruitvale Ave Oakland (94601) *(P-19630)*
La Clinica De La Raza Inc....C....925 431-1250
337 E Leland Rd Pittsburg (94565) *(P-20122)*
La Costa Glen, Carlsbad *Also called Continuing Lf Communities LLC (P-14591)*
La Costa Limousine (PA)....D....760 438-4455
2770 Loker Ave W Carlsbad (92010) *(P-3815)*
La Costa Resort & Spa, Carlsbad *Also called Lc Trs Inc (P-12844)*
La County High Desert Hlth Sys....B....661 945-8461
44900 60th St W Lancaster (93536) *(P-19631)*
LA COUNTY MUSEUM OF ART, Los Angeles *Also called Museum Associates (P-24891)*
La County Probation, Whittier *Also called County of Los Angeles (P-23665)*
La Cumbre Country Club....D....805 687-2421
4015 Via Laguna Santa Barbara (93110) *(P-18945)*
La Curacao, Vernon *Also called Adir International LLC (P-1371)*
La Department Water and Power....D....661 824-7900
17031 State Highway 14 Mojave (93501) *(P-6198)*
La Familia Counseling Center....D....916 452-3601
5523 34th St Sacramento (95820) *(P-23890)*
La Fitness, Mission Viejo *Also called Fitness International LLC (P-18601)*
La Follette Johnson De Haas (PA)....C....213 426-3600
865 S Figueroa St # 3200 Los Angeles (90017) *(P-23181)*
La Grande Farm....D....530 473-5923
P.O. Box 370 Williams (95987) *(P-66)*
La Habra Villa....D....714 529-1697
220 Newport Center Dr # 11 Newport Beach (92660) *(P-24573)*
La Hotel Venture LLC....B....213 617-1133
333 S Figueroa St Los Angeles (90071) *(P-12827)*
LA Hydro-Jet Rooter Svc Inc....D....818 768-4225
10639 Wixom St Sun Valley (91352) *(P-17961)*
La Hydrojet, Sun Valley *Also called LA Hydro-Jet Rooter Svc Inc (P-17961)*
LA Impact....D....323 869-6874
5700 S Eastern Ave Commerce (90040) *(P-17284)*
La Inc Convention Vistors Bur....D....213 236-2301
333 S Hope St Ste 1800 Los Angeles (90071) *(P-17285)*
La Joie Construction, San Mateo *Also called La Joie Jerry (P-26925)*
La Joie Jerry....E....650 375-1808
418 Sonora Dr San Mateo (94402) *(P-26925)*
La Jolla Bch & Tennis CLB Inc (PA)....C....858 454-7126
2000 Spindrift Dr La Jolla (92037) *(P-18946)*
La Jolla Bch & Tennis CLB Inc....C....858 459-8271
8110 Camino Del Oro La Jolla (92037) *(P-12828)*
La Jolla Country Club Inc....C....858 454-9601
7301 High Ave La Jolla (92037) *(P-18947)*
La Jolla Cove Hotel & Motel....D....858 459-2621
1155 Coast Blvd La Jolla (92037) *(P-12829)*
La Jolla Cove Motel, La Jolla *Also called La Jolla Cove Hotel & Motel (P-12829)*
La Jolla Group Inc....D....949 428-2800
14350 Myford Rd Irvine (92606) *(P-17286)*
La Jolla Inst For Allergy & Im, La Jolla *Also called Institute For La Jolla (P-26625)*
La Jolla Nrsing Rhbltation Ctr, La Jolla *Also called Covenant Care La Jolla LLC (P-20355)*
La Jolla Nurses Home Care....C....858 454-9339
2223 Avenida De La Playa La Jolla (92037) *(P-14660)*
La Jolla Orthopaedic....D....858 657-0055
4120 La Jolla Village Dr La Jolla (92037) *(P-19632)*
La Jolla Pharmaceutical Co (PA)....C....858 207-4264
4550 Towne Centre Ct San Diego (92121) *(P-26393)*
LA JOLLA PLAYHOUSE, La Jolla *Also called Theat and Arts Found of San Di (P-25268)*
La Jolla Village Towers 500....D....858 646-7700
8515 Costa Verde Blvd Ofc San Diego (92122) *(P-20572)*
La Jolla YMCA, La Jolla *Also called YMCA of San Diego County (P-25294)*
La Lakers, El Segundo *Also called Los Angeles Lakers Inc (P-18525)*
La Laser Center Pc Cpmc....D....310 446-4400
10884 Santa Monica Blvd # 300 Los Angeles (90025) *(P-19633)*
La Live Properties LLC....E....213 763-7700
800 W Olympic Blvd # 305 Los Angeles (90015) *(P-18378)*
La Maestra Community Clinic, San Diego *Also called La Maestra Family Clinic Inc (P-19635)*
La Maestra Community Hlth Ctrs, San Diego *Also called La Maestra Family Clinic Inc (P-19637)*
La Maestra Family Clinic Inc....D....619 280-1105
165 S 1st St El Cajon (92019) *(P-19634)*
La Maestra Family Clinic Inc....D....619 280-4213
4060 Fairmount Ave San Diego (92105) *(P-19635)*
La Maestra Family Clinic Inc....D....619 501-1235
4305 University Ave # 120 San Diego (92105) *(P-19636)*
La Maestra Family Clinic Inc (PA)....C....619 584-1612
4060 Fairmount Ave San Diego (92105) *(P-19637)*
La Mancha Development, Los Angeles *Also called A M S Partnership (P-11851)*
La Mesa Disposal, Signal Hill *Also called Edco Disposal Corporation Inc (P-6393)*
La Mesa Health Care Center....C....619 465-1313
3780 Massachusetts Ave La Mesa (91941) *(P-21132)*
La Mesa Internal Medical Group, La Mesa *Also called La Mesa Intrnl Mdc Mdcl Gr (P-19638)*
La Mesa Intrnl Mdc Mdcl Gr....E....619 460-4050
5111 Garfield St La Mesa (91941) *(P-19638)*
La Mesa Lions Club....D....619 469-9988
4387 Summit Dr La Mesa (91941) *(P-25182)*
La Mesa Medical Offices, La Mesa *Also called Kaiser Foundation Hospitals (P-21496)*
La Metro Hauling, Long Beach *Also called USA Waste of California Inc (P-6497)*
La Mirada Country Club, La Mirada *Also called American Golf Corporation (P-18683)*
La Mirage, San Diego *Also called Regency Hill Associates (P-11107)*
La Palma Care Center....D....714 772-7480
1130 W La Palma Ave Anaheim (92801) *(P-20573)*
La Palma Farms Inc....D....805 928-2333
1445 Jason Way Santa Maria (93455) *(P-9083)*
La Palma Hospital Medical Ctr....B....714 670-7400
7901 Walker St La Palma (90623) *(P-21544)*
LA PALMA INTERCOMMUNITY HOSPITAL, La Palma *Also called La Palma Hospital Medical Ctr (P-21544)*
La Palma Medical Offices, La Palma *Also called Kaiser Foundation Hospitals (P-19600)*
La Palma Nursing Center, Long Beach *Also called 1130 W La Palma Ave Inc (P-20214)*
La Palma Nursing Center, Anaheim *Also called La Palma Care Center (P-20573)*
La Paz Geropsychiatric Center, Paramount *Also called Telecare Corporation (P-21989)*
La Peer Health Systems, Beverly Hills *Also called La Peer Surgery Center LLC (P-19639)*
La Peer Surgery Center LLC....D....310 360-9119
8920 Wilshire Blvd # 101 Beverly Hills (90211) *(P-19639)*
La Petite Baleen Inc....D....650 588-7665
434 San Mateo Ave San Bruno (94066) *(P-18624)*
La Petite Baleen Swim School, San Bruno *Also called La Petite Baleen Inc (P-18624)*
La Posta Band Mission Indians, Boulevard *Also called La Posta Casino (P-12830)*
La Posta Casino....C....619 824-4100
777 Crestwood Rd Boulevard (91905) *(P-12830)*
La Provence Inc....D....760 736-3299
1370 W San Marcos Blvd # 130 San Marcos (92078) *(P-8822)*
La Provence Bakery, San Marcos *Also called La Provence Inc (P-8822)*
La Puerta....E....619 696-3466
560 4th Ave San Diego (92101) *(P-25183)*
La Quinta Country Club....D....760 564-4151
77750 Avenue 50 La Quinta (92253) *(P-18948)*
La Quinta Inn, Los Angeles *Also called Lq Management LLC (P-12864)*
La Quinta Inn, San Francisco *Also called Mile Post Properties LLC (P-12928)*
La Quinta Resort & Club, La Quinta *Also called Lqr Property LLC (P-12865)*
La Rinconada Country Club Inc (PA)....D....408 395-4181
14595 Clearview Dr Los Gatos (95032) *(P-18949)*

ALPHABETIC

Employee Codes: A=Over 500 employees, B=251-500
C=101-250, D=51-100, E=50
2019 Directory of California
Wholesalers and Services Companies
© Mergent Inc. 1-800-342-5647
1361

LA RINCONADA GOLF AND COUNTRY, Los Gatos *Also called La Rinconada Country Club Inc* ***(P-18949)***
La Salette Rehab Convlesc Hos, Stockton *Also called Mariner Health Care Inc* ***(P-20627)***
La Salle Apartments ....D....415 647-0607
30 Whitfield Ct Ste 1 San Francisco (94124) ***(P-11049)***
La Salle Preservation, San Francisco *Also called La Salle Apartments* ***(P-11049)***
La Sierra Care Center, Merced *Also called CF Merced La Sierra LLC* ***(P-20302)***
LA Specialty Produce Co (PA) ....B....562 741-2200
13527 Orden Dr Santa Fe Springs (90670) ***(P-8700)***
La Sports Arena, Los Angeles *Also called Los Angeles Mem Coliseum Comm* ***(P-25440)***
LA Sports Properties Inc ....C....213 742-7500
1212 S Flower St Fl 5 Los Angeles (90015) ***(P-18523)***
La Steel Services Inc ....E....951 393-2013
1760 California Ave # 201 Corona (92881) ***(P-3383)***
La Tavola LLC (PA) ....D....707 257-3358
2655 Napa Valley Corp Dr NAPA (94558) ***(P-13532)***
La Tortilla Factory Inc (PA) ....B....707 586-4000
3300 Westwind Blvd Santa Rosa (95403) ***(P-8823)***
La Verne Nursery Inc ....D....805 521-0111
3653 Center St Piru (93040) ***(P-280)***
La Vida Del Mar Associates, Solana Beach *Also called Senior Resource Group LLC* ***(P-24671)***
La Vida Mltispecialty Med Ctrs ....D....213 765-7500
1400 S Grand Ave Los Angeles (90015) ***(P-19640)***
La Voie & Sons Construction ....E....916 408-6900
1061 Nichols Ct Rocklin (95765) ***(P-26926)***
La Works, Irwindale *Also called East San Gbriel Vly Consortium* ***(P-3788)***
Laaco Ltd (PA) ....C....213 622-1254
431 W 7th St Los Angeles (90014) ***(P-11175)***
Laaco Ltd ....D....310 823-4567
4469 Admiralty Way Marina Del Rey (90292) ***(P-18950)***
LAAPOA, Los Angeles *Also called Los Angeles Airport Peace Offc* ***(P-25193)***
Lab-Gistics LLC ....C....650 309-2627
885 Pacific Ave San Jose (95126) ***(P-26394)***
Labaya Beachcomber LP ....E....805 278-6688
3101 Sturgis Rd Oxnard (93030) ***(P-17727)***
Labcyte Inc (PA) ....D....408 747-2000
170 Rose Orchard Way # 200 San Jose (95134) ***(P-26395)***
Labite, Los Angeles *Also called Kfco Inc* ***(P-4035)***
Labmed Partners ....E....949 242-9925
5000 Birch St Newport Beach (92660) ***(P-27297)***
LABOR EMPLOYMENT & TRAINING, Cerritos *Also called Uaw-Lbor Emplyment Trning Corp* ***(P-14789)***
Labor Finders Staffing, Fresno *Also called Labor Fnders of The Palm Bches* ***(P-14870)***
Labor Fnders of The Palm Bches ....D....559 221-2023
4325 N Blackstone Ave Fresno (93726) ***(P-14870)***
Labor One Inc ....D....559 430-4202
575 Minnewawa Ave Ste 3 Clovis (93612) ***(P-658)***
Labor Ready, Yuba City *Also called Trueblue Inc* ***(P-14925)***
Labor Ready, Santa Barbara *Also called Trueblue Inc* ***(P-14926)***
Labor Ready Inc ....E....760 433-4980
1405 Carmelo Dr 5112 Oceanside (92054) ***(P-14871)***
Laboratory Corporation America ....D....818 361-7089
14901 Rinaldi St Ste 203 Mission Hills (91345) ***(P-22102)***
Laboratory Corporation America ....D....510 635-4555
10930 Bigge St San Leandro (94577) ***(P-22103)***
Laboratory Specialty Gases ....C....619 234-6060
2506 Market St San Diego (92102) ***(P-7761)***
Laborers Funds Administrative (PA) ....C....707 864-2800
220 Campus Ln Fairfield (94534) ***(P-25068)***
Laborers Trust Funds Nthrn Cal, Fairfield *Also called Laborers Funds Administrative* ***(P-25068)***
Labratory, San Francisco *Also called Permanente Medical Group Inc* ***(P-21639)***
Labrent.com, Santa Clara *Also called Everett Basham* ***(P-5556)***
Lac Club, Los Angeles *Also called Los Angles Clippers Foundation* ***(P-27307)***
Lac Usc Medical Center ....C....323 226-7858
1200 N State St Rm 5250 Los Angeles (90033) ***(P-21545)***
LACERA, Pasadena *Also called Los Angeles Cnty Emp Retiremnt* ***(P-10487)***
Laclinica, Pittsburg *Also called La Clinica De La Raza Inc* ***(P-20122)***
Lacma, Los Angeles *Also called Los Angeles Cnty Mseum of Art* ***(P-24889)***
Lacmta, Los Angeles *Also called Los Angeles County MTA* ***(P-3676)***
Laco Associates (PA) ....E....707 443-5054
21 W 4th St Eureka (95501) ***(P-25792)***
Lacolina Jr High CA Congress O ....D....805 967-4506
4025 Foothill Rd Santa Barbara (93110) ***(P-25184)***
Laconstructora Co Inc ....E....760 439-7686
2030 Broadway Oceanside (92054) ***(P-1190)***
Lacuesta Farming Inc ....D....805 349-1940
1141 Tama Ln Santa Maria (93455) ***(P-104)***
Lacumbre Senior Living, Santa Barbara *Also called Helping Hands Sanctuary of Ida* ***(P-20524)***
Ladas & Parry LLP ....E....323 934-2300
5670 Wilshire Blvd # 2100 Los Angeles (90036) ***(P-23182)***
Ladd Construction Co, Redding *Also called Roy E Ladd Inc* ***(P-1844)***
Ladell Inc ....E....559 650-2000
605 N Halifax Ave Clovis (93611) ***(P-2256)***
Ladera Ranch, San Juan Capistrano *Also called Rancho Mission Viejo LLC* ***(P-11703)***
Ladwp, Independence *Also called Los Angeles Dept Wtr & Pwr* ***(P-6275)***
Ladwp, Los Angeles *Also called Los Angeles Dept Wtr & Pwr* ***(P-6276)***
Ladwp, Los Angeles *Also called Los Angeles Dept Wtr & Pwr* ***(P-6050)***
Lafaltte Rhbilitation Care Ctr ....D....209 466-2066
537 E Fulton St Stockton (95204) ***(P-20574)***
Lafayette Car Wash, Lafayette *Also called Prestige Car Wash Lafayette LP* ***(P-17836)***
Lafayette Park Hotel Corp (PA) ....B....650 330-8888
1100 Alma St Ste 106 Menlo Park (94025) ***(P-12831)***
Lafayette Textile Inds LLC ....D....323 264-2212
2051 E 55th St Vernon (90058) ***(P-8230)***
Laguna Bch Golf Bnglow Vlg LLC ....E....949 499-2271
31106 Coast Hwy Laguna Beach (92651) ***(P-451)***
Laguna Bch Golf Bnglow Vlg LLC ....D....949 499-2271
31106 Coast Hwy Laguna Beach (92651) ***(P-18725)***
Laguna Country Mart Ltd Inc ....E....310 826-5635
12410 Santa Monica Blvd Los Angeles (90025) ***(P-10904)***
Laguna Creek Racquet Club, Elk Grove *Also called Spare-Time Inc* ***(P-19058)***
Laguna Hills Hotel Dev Ventr ....D....949 586-5000
25205 La Paz Rd Laguna Hills (92653) ***(P-12832)***
Laguna Hills Surgery Center, Laguna Hills *Also called Cirrus Health II LP* ***(P-19382)***
Laguna Niguel Racquet Club, Laguna Niguel *Also called Spearman Clubs Inc* ***(P-19240)***
Laguna Playhouse (PA) ....C....949 497-2787
606 Laguna Canyon Rd Laguna Beach (92651) ***(P-18379)***
Laguna Woods Golf Club ....E....949 597-4336
24122 Moulton Pkwy Laguna Hills (92637) ***(P-18951)***
Laguna Woods Village ....A....949 597-4267
24351 El Toro Rd Laguna Woods (92637) ***(P-11556)***
Laguna Woods Village Golf Club, Laguna Hills *Also called Laguna Woods Golf Club* ***(P-18951)***
Lahontan Golf Club ....C....530 550-2400
12700 Lodgetrail Dr Truckee (96161) ***(P-18952)***
Laidlaw Education Services, San Bernardino *Also called First Student Inc* ***(P-3928)***
Laidlaw Education Services, Santa Ana *Also called First Student Inc* ***(P-3933)***
Laidlaw Educational Services, Palm Springs *Also called First Student Inc* ***(P-3926)***
Laidlaw Transit Services, Madera *Also called First Student Inc* ***(P-3935)***
Lake Arrowhead Cmnty Svcs Dst ....E....909 337-6395
6727 Arrowhead Lake Rd Hesperia (92345) ***(P-24799)***
Lake Arrwhead Rsort Oprtor Inc (HQ) ....C....909 336-1511
27984 Hwy 189 Lake Arrowhead (92352) ***(P-12833)***
Lake Balboa Care Center, Van Nuys *Also called Van Nuys Care Center Inc* ***(P-21245)***
Lake Bowl, Folsom *Also called Folsom Recreation Corp* ***(P-18488)***
Lake Cnty Trbal Hlth Cnsortium ....D....707 263-8382
925 Bevins Ct Lakeport (95453) ***(P-20123)***
Lake County Home Loans ....E....707 462-4000
350 E Gobbi St Ukiah (95482) ***(P-9823)***
Lake Elsinore Unified Schl Dst ....D....951 253-7830
21641 Bundy Canyon Rd Wildomar (92595) ***(P-3939)***
Lake Elsinore Unified Schl Dst ....D....951 253-7091
565 Chaney St Lake Elsinore (92530) ***(P-24337)***
Lake Elsn SC Trans, Wildomar *Also called Lake Elsinore Unified Schl Dst* ***(P-3939)***
Lake Forest Ll Master Homeown ....D....949 586-0860
24752 Toledo Ln Lake Forest (92630) ***(P-25185)***
Lake Forest Nursing Center, Lake Forest *Also called Life Care Centers America Inc* ***(P-20584)***
Lake Hemet Municipal Wtr Dst (PA) ....D....951 927-1816
26385 Fairview Ave Hemet (92544) ***(P-6269)***
Lake Merced Golf & Country CLB ....D....650 755-2233
2300 Junipero Serra Blvd Daly City (94015) ***(P-18953)***
Lake Merritt Hotel Associates ....E....510 832-2300
1800 Madison St Oakland (94612) ***(P-1300)***
Lake Mission Viejo Association ....D....949 770-1313
22555 Olympiad Rd Mission Viejo (92692) ***(P-25186)***
Lake Natoma Inn, Folsom *Also called Lake Natoma Lodging LP* ***(P-12834)***
Lake Natoma Lodging LP ....D....916 351-1500
702 Gold Lake Dr Folsom (95630) ***(P-12834)***
Lake of The Pines Association ....E....530 268-1141
11665 Lakeshore N Auburn (95602) ***(P-25187)***
LAKE OF THE PINES HOMEOWNERS, Auburn *Also called Lake of The Pines Association* ***(P-25187)***
Lake Park Retirment Residence, Oakland *Also called Califrnia-Nevada Methdst Homes* ***(P-21030)***
Lake Piru Marina, Valencia *Also called Pyramid Enterprises Inc* ***(P-19219)***
Lake San Marcos Resort, San Marcos *Also called Citizens Development Corp* ***(P-18889)***
Lake Tahoe Resort Hotel, South Lake Tahoe *Also called Roppongi-Tahoe Lp A Californi* ***(P-13137)***
Lake Tahoe Secret Witness ....D....530 541-6800
1051 Al Tahoe Blvd South Lake Tahoe (96150) ***(P-16713)***
Lake Wildwood Association ....C....530 432-1152
11255 Cottontail Way Penn Valley (95946) ***(P-25188)***
LAKE WILDWOOD GOLF COURSE., Penn Valley *Also called Lake Wildwood Association* ***(P-25188)***
Lakenor Auto Salvage, Santa Fe Springs *Also called Cadnchev Inc* ***(P-6702)***
Lakes Country Club Assn Inc (PA) ....B....760 568-4321
161 Old Ranch Rd Palm Desert (92211) ***(P-18954)***
Lakes Country Club, The, Palm Desert *Also called Lakes Country Club Assn Inc* ***(P-18954)***
Lakeside Fire Protection Dst ....D....619 390-2350
12216 Lakeside Ave Lakeside (92040) ***(P-17287)***
Lakeside Golf Club ....D....818 984-0601
4500 W Lakeside Dr Burbank (91505) ***(P-18726)***
Lakeside Grill, The, Yountville *Also called Vintners Golf Club* ***(P-18777)***
Lakeside Medical Systems, Northridge *Also called Lakeside Systems Inc* ***(P-26927)***
Lakeside Systems Inc ....A....866 654-3471
8510 Balboa Blvd Ste 150 Northridge (91325) ***(P-26927)***
Lakeside Tax & Financial Svcs ....D....619 561-2681
9748 Los Coches Rd Ste 3 Lakeside (92040) ***(P-17288)***
Lakeview Medical Offices, Anaheim *Also called Kaiser Foundation Hospitals* ***(P-19523)***
Lakeview Senior Center, Irvine *Also called City of Irvine* ***(P-23579)***
Lakewood Cerritos Dental Ctr ....D....562 860-0388
5819 Adenmoor Ave Lakewood (90713) ***(P-20124)***
Lakewood Country Club, Lakewood *Also called American Golf Corporation* ***(P-18681)***
Lakewood Healthcare Center, Downey *Also called Healthcare Ctr of Downey LLC* ***(P-20517)***
Lakewood Manor North Inc ....D....213 380-9175
831 S Lake St Los Angeles (90057) ***(P-20575)***

Mergent e-mail: customerrelations@mergent.com
1362
2019 Directory of California
Wholesalers and Services Companies
(P-0000) Products & Services Section entry number
(PA)=Parent Co (HQ)=Headquarters (DH)=Div Headquarters

Lakewood Mem Pk Fnrl Svcs Inc ....E....209 883-4465
900 Santa Fe Ave Hughson (95326) *(P-11945)*
Lakewood Memorial Pk & Fnrl HM, Hughson *Also called Alderwoods (delaware) Inc (P-11938)*
Lakewood Memorial Pk & Fnrl HM, Hughson *Also called Lakewood Mem Pk Fnrl Svcs Inc (P-11945)*
Lakewood Park Health Center, Downey *Also called Mental Hlth Cnvlscent Svcs Inc (P-20642)*
Lakewood Park Health Center (PA) ....B....562 869-0978
12023 Lakewood Blvd Downey (90242) *(P-17289)*
Lakewood Regional Medical Ctr, Lakewood *Also called Tenet Healthsystem Medical (P-20000)*
Lakewood South Car Wash LLC ....E....562 430-4975
11031 Alamitos Ave Los Alamitos (90720) *(P-17822)*
Lakewood Y M C A Gymnastics, Lakewood *Also called Young Mens Chrstn Assc Gr L B (P-25333)*
Lakin Tire of Calif, Santa Fe Springs *Also called Lakin Tire West Incorporated (P-6693)*
Lakin Tire West Incorporated (PA) ....D....562 802-2752
15305 Spring Ave Santa Fe Springs (90670) *(P-6693)*
Lakos, Fresno *Also called Claude Laval Corporation (P-7742)*
Lamanuzzi & Pantaleo LLC (PA) ....D....559 432-3170
11767 Road 27 1/2 Madera (93637) *(P-156)*
Lamesa City Public Works, La Mesa *Also called City of La Mesa (P-1742)*
Lamon Construction Company Inc ....E....530 671-1370
871 Von Geldern Way Yuba City (95991) *(P-1578)*
Lamoure's Cleaners & Laundry, Fresno *Also called Lamoures Inc (P-13487)*
Lamoures Inc (PA) ....D....559 264-0241
729 E Divisadero St Fresno (93721) *(P-13487)*
Lamp Inc ....C....213 488-9559
2116 Arlington Ave Lbby Los Angeles (90018) *(P-24574)*
Lamp Community, Los Angeles *Also called Lamp Inc (P-24574)*
Lamp Liter Associates ....D....559 733-4328
3130 W Main St Ste A Visalia (93291) *(P-12835)*
Lamp Liter Inn, Visalia *Also called Lamp Liter Associates (P-12835)*
Lancashire Group Incorporated ....B....510 792-9384
37053 Cherry St Ste 210 Newark (94560) *(P-27298)*
Lancaster Burns Cnstr Inc ....C....916 624-8404
8655 Washington Blvd Roseville (95678) *(P-2909)*
Lancaster Comm Svcs Fndtn ....D....661 723-6230
46008 7th St W Lancaster (93534) *(P-17769)*
Lancaster Crdlgy Med Group Inc (PA) ....D....661 726-3058
43847 Heaton Ave Ste B Lancaster (93534) *(P-19641)*
Lancaster Jethawks ....D....661 726-5400
45116 Valley Central Way Lancaster (93536) *(P-18955)*
Land & Personnel Management, Kerman *Also called Hall Management Corp (P-26883)*
Land Design Consultants Inc ....D....626 578-7000
2700 E Foothill Blvd # 200 Pasadena (91107) *(P-27770)*
Land Disposition Company, Irvine *Also called NRLL LLC (P-12251)*
Land Forms Landscape Cnstr, Irvine *Also called Jeff Tracy Inc (P-2243)*
Land Home Financial Svcs Inc (PA) ....E....925 676-7038
1355 Willow Way Ste 250 Concord (94520) *(P-9824)*
Land Scapes, Costa Mesa *Also called Dwiw Inc (P-833)*
Land Services Landscape Contrs ....D....510 656-8101
901 Brown Rd Fremont (94539) *(P-11884)*
Landcare Logic, San Diego *Also called Shoreline Land Care Inc (P-939)*
Landcare USA LLC ....D....949 559-7771
216 N Clara St Santa Ana (92703) *(P-876)*
Landcare USA LLC ....D....760 747-1174
770 Metcalf St Escondido (92025) *(P-877)*
Landcare USA LLC ....C....805 520-9394
1196 Patricia Ave Simi Valley (93065) *(P-878)*
Landcare USA LLC ....D....707 836-1460
930 Shiloh Rd Bldg 44-B Windsor (95492) *(P-879)*
Landcare USA LLC ....C....714 936-9512
15606 Cornet St Santa Fe Springs (90670) *(P-880)*
Landcare USA LLC ....D....310 719-1008
1315 W 130th St Gardena (90247) *(P-881)*
Landcare USA LLC ....D....310 354-1520
4134 Temple City Blvd Rosemead (91770) *(P-882)*
Landcare USA LLC ....C....310 354-1520
1323 W 130th St Gardena (90247) *(P-883)*
Landcare USA LLC ....D....916 635-0936
3213 Fitzgerald Rd Rancho Cordova (95742) *(P-884)*
Landcare USA LLC ....C....858 453-1755
5248 Governor Dr San Diego (92122) *(P-885)*
Landcare USA LLC ....C....818 346-7552
7755 Deering Ave Canoga Park (91304) *(P-886)*
Landcare USA LLC ....D....408 727-4099
85 Old Tully Rd San Jose (95111) *(P-887)*
Landco ....D....818 612-0118
7333 Clybourn Ave Sun Valley (91352) *(P-888)*
Landesign Cnstr & Maint Inc ....D....707 578-2657
1328 Airport Blvd Santa Rosa (95403) *(P-889)*
Landforce Express Corporation ....C....760 843-7839
17201 N D St Victorville (92394) *(P-4212)*
Landmark Event Staffing ....A....714 293-4248
4790 Irvine Blvd Ste 105 Irvine (92620) *(P-16714)*
Landmark Event Staffing ....A....510 632-9000
1965 Adams Ave San Leandro (94577) *(P-14872)*
Landmark Health LLC ....B....253 394-2566
7755 Center Ave Ste 630 Huntington Beach (92647) *(P-22357)*
Landmark Healthcare Svcs Inc (HQ) ....C....800 638-4557
1610 Arden Way Ste 280 Sacramento (95815) *(P-20155)*
Landmark Hotels LLC ....C....949 640-5040
312 Broadway St Ste 204 Laguna Beach (92651) *(P-12836)*
Landmark Medical Center, Pomona *Also called Landmark Medical Services Inc (P-21962)*
Landmark Medical Services Inc ....D....909 593-2585
2030 N Garey Ave Pomona (91767) *(P-21962)*
Landmark Princess, Laguna Beach *Also called Landmark Hotels LLC (P-12836)*
Landmark Protection Inc ....B....408 293-6300
675 N 1st St Ste 620 San Jose (95112) *(P-8267)*
Landmark Realty Center, Rancho Palos Verdes *Also called Inman Spinosa & Buchan Inc (P-11514)*
Landmark Services Inc ....D....714 547-6308
410 N Fairview St Santa Ana (92703) *(P-14300)*
Landmark Theatres, Los Angeles *Also called Silver Cinemas Acquisition Co (P-18321)*
Landor Associates Intl Ltd (HQ) ....C....415 365-1700
1001 Front St San Francisco (94111) *(P-14118)*
Landsberg Los Angeles Div 1001, Montebello *Also called Orora Packaging Solutions (P-8121)*
Landsberg Orora, Buena Park *Also called Orora Packaging Solutions (P-8118)*
Landsberg San Diego Div 1007, San Marcos *Also called Orora North America (P-8116)*
Landscape Center, Riverside *Also called B & B Nurseries Inc (P-9124)*
Landscape Development Inc (PA) ....B....661 295-1970
28447 Witherspoon Pkwy Valencia (91355) *(P-890)*
Lane Stuart Company LLC ....D....805 553-9562
740 Lucille Ct Moorpark (93021) *(P-11557)*
Lane Winpak Inc (HQ) ....D....909 386-1762
998 S Sierra Way San Bernardino (92408) *(P-9229)*
Lang Richert & Patch ....E....559 228-6700
5200 N Palm Ave Ste 401 Fresno (93704) *(P-23183)*
Langdon Wilson International (PA) ....E....213 250-1186
1055 Wilshire Blvd # 1500 Los Angeles (90017) *(P-26079)*
Langdon Wlson Arch Plg Intrors, Los Angeles *Also called Langdon Wilson International (P-26079)*
Langetwins Inc ....D....209 339-4055
1298 E Jahant Rd Acampo (95220) *(P-157)*
Langham Hotels International, Pasadena *Also called Langham Hotels Pacific Corp (P-12837)*
Langham Hotels Pacific Corp ....D....617 451-1900
1401 S Oak Knoll Ave Pasadena (91106) *(P-12837)*
Langham Huntington Hotel & Spa, Pasadena *Also called Pacific Huntington Hotel Corp (P-13003)*
Language Line Services Inc (HQ) ....D....800 752-6096
1 Lower Ragsdale Dr # 2 Monterey (93940) *(P-17290)*
Language Weaver Inc ....D....310 437-7300
6060 Center Dr Ste 150 Los Angeles (90045) *(P-15254)*
Lani, Irvine *Also called Loan Administration Netwrk Inc (P-14663)*
Lansing Farming Co, Fresno *Also called Woolf Farming Co Cal Inc (P-395)*
Lansing Mall Ltd Partnership ....E....510 782-3527
1 Southland Mall Hayward (94545) *(P-10905)*
Lansing Mall Ltd Partnership ....D....818 885-9700
9301 Tampa Ave Ofc Northridge (91324) *(P-10906)*
Lanting Hay Dealer Inc ....D....909 563-5601
9032 Merrill Ave Ontario (91762) *(P-9084)*
Lantz Security Systems Inc ....B....805 496-5775
101 N Westlake Blvd # 200 Westlake Village (91362) *(P-16715)*
Lantz Security Systems Inc ....C....818 871-0193
4111 Las Virgenes Rd # 202 Calabasas (91302) *(P-16919)*
Lantz Security Systems Inc (PA) ....D....661 949-3565
43440 Sahuayo St Lancaster (93535) *(P-16716)*
Lanwave Technology Inc ....D....408 253-3883
20111 Stevens Creek Blvd # 260 Cupertino (95014) *(P-25793)*
Lanza Vineyards Inc ....E....707 864-0730
4756 Suisun Valley Rd Fairfield (94534) *(P-158)*
Lapham Company Inc ....D....510 531-6000
4844 Telegraph Ave Oakland (94609) *(P-11558)*
Lapham Company Management, Oakland *Also called Lapham Company Inc (P-11558)*
Larchmont Radiology Med Group ....D....213 483-5953
2010 Wilshire Blvd # 409 Los Angeles (90057) *(P-19642)*
Laren D Tan MD ....D....909 558-4444
11234 Anderson St Loma Linda (92354) *(P-19643)*
Largo Concrete Inc ....A....909 981-7844
1690 W Foothill Blvd B Upland (91786) *(P-3280)*
Largo Concrete Inc ....A....408 874-2500
891 W Hamilton Ave Campbell (95008) *(P-3281)*
Largo Concrete Inc ....C....619 356-2142
1650 Hotel Cir N San Diego (92108) *(P-1191)*
Lark Avenue Car Wash ....D....408 371-2565
5005 Almaden Expy San Jose (95118) *(P-17823)*
Lark Avenue Car Wash ....D....408 377-2525
981 E Hamilton Ave Campbell (95008) *(P-17824)*
LARK Industries Inc (HQ) ....D....714 701-4200
4900 E Hunter Ave Anaheim (92807) *(P-17291)*
Larkin Leasing Inc ....D....714 528-3232
674 N Batavia St Orange (92868) *(P-1945)*
Larkspur Hsptality Dev MGT LLC ....D....650 872-1515
670 Gateway Blvd South San Francisco (94080) *(P-12838)*
Larrabee Brothrs Distribtng Co ....D....805 922-2108
815 S Blosser Rd Santa Maria (93458) *(P-9007)*
Larry Blair Realtor ....E....650 991-5267
2488 Junipero Serra Blvd Daly City (94015) *(P-11559)*
Larry Jacinto Construction Inc ....D....909 794-2151
9555 N Wabash Ave Redlands (92374) *(P-1805)*
Larry Jacinto Farming Inc ....D....909 794-2276
9555 N Wabash Ave Redlands (92374) *(P-696)*
Larsen Supply Co (PA) ....D....562 698-0731
12055 Slauson Ave Santa Fe Springs (90670) *(P-7628)*
Larson, Drake Sales, Thermal *Also called Drake Larson Ranchs (P-141)*
Larsons Studios, Los Angeles *Also called Lgh Digital Media Inc (P-18068)*
Las Brisas, San Luis Obispo *Also called Harvest Management Sub LLC (P-24550)*
Las Cumbres Observatory Global ....E....805 880-1600
6740 Cortona Dr Ste 102 Goleta (93117) *(P-26632)*
Las Flores Convalescent Hosp, Gardena *Also called Gardena Flores Inc (P-20447)*
Las Islas Family Med Group PC ....D....805 385-8662
325 W Chnnel Islands Blvd Oxnard (93033) *(P-19644)*

ALPHABETIC

Employee Codes: A=Over 500 employees, B=251-500
C=101-250, D=51-100, E=50
2019 Directory of California
Wholesalers and Services Companies
© Mergent Inc. 1-800-342-5647
1363

Las Posas Club Inc....D....805 482-1811
230 Ramona Pl Camarillo (93010) ***(P-18956)***
Las Posas Country Club....D....805 482-4518
955 Fairway Dr Camarillo (93010) ***(P-18957)***
Las Posas Road Medical Offices, Camarillo *Also called Kaiser Foundation Hospitals* ***(P-19548)***
Las Vegas / LA Express Inc (PA)....C....909 972-3100
1000 S Cucamonga Ave Ontario (91761) ***(P-4213)***
Las Villas De Carlsbad, San Diego *Also called Villas De Carlsbad Ltd A Cali* ***(P-24714)***
Las Villas De Carlsbad, Carlsbad *Also called Villas De Carlsbad Ltd A Cali* ***(P-24715)***
Las Villas Del Norte....D....760 741-1047
1325 Las Villas Way Escondido (92026) ***(P-20576)***
Las Virgenes Municipal Wtr Dst....C....818 251-2100
4232 Las Virgenes Rd Lbby Calabasas (91302) ***(P-6270)***
Lasaltte Hlth Rhbilitation Ctr, Stockton *Also called Five Star Quality Care Inc* ***(P-20430)***
Lasco, Santa Fe Springs *Also called Larsen Supply Co* ***(P-7628)***
Laser Electric Inc....E....760 658-6626
2250 Micro Pl 200 Escondido (92029) ***(P-2628)***
Laserfiche Document Imaging, Long Beach *Also called Compulink Management Ctr Inc* ***(P-15635)***
Lasertech Computer Distr Inc....D....626 435-2800
139 N Sunset Ave City of Industry (91744) ***(P-7069)***
Lassen Canyon Nursery Inc....D....530 938-4720
14735 Big Springs Rd Weed (96094) ***(P-105)***
Lassen Canyon Nursery Inc....D....209 599-7777
11651 Palm Ln Ripon (95366) ***(P-106)***
Lassen Canyon Nursery Inc (PA)....C....530 223-1075
1300 Salmon Creek Rd Redding (96003) ***(P-8419)***
Lassen Hse Assisted Living LLC....E....530 529-2900
705 Luther Rd Red Bluff (96080) ***(P-24575)***
Lassen Land Co....E....530 865-7676
320 E South St Orland (95963) ***(P-697)***
Lassen Medical Group Inc (PA)....D....530 527-0414
2450 Sster Mary Clumba Dr Red Bluff (96080) ***(P-19645)***
Lassen's, Ali Success System, Carlsbad *Also called Lassens Ali Leads Club* ***(P-24965)***
Lassens Ali Leads Club (PA)....D....760 434-3761
2644 Madison St Carlsbad (92008) ***(P-24965)***
Lassley Enterprises Inc....E....559 226-4300
1289 E Shaw Ave Fresno (93710) ***(P-11050)***
Last Frontier Healthcare Dst....C....530 233-5131
228 W Mcdowell Ave Alturas (96101) ***(P-21546)***
Lastline Inc....C....805 456-7075
6950 Hollister Ave # 101 Goleta (93117) ***(P-15739)***
Latara Enterprise Inc (PA)....C....909 623-9301
1716 W Holt Ave Pomona (91768) ***(P-22104)***
Latara Enterprise Inc....D....661 665-9780
9610 Stockdale Hwy Bakersfield (93311) ***(P-22105)***
Latara Enterprise Inc....D....760 256-3450
705 E Virginia Way Ste D Barstow (92311) ***(P-22106)***
Lateral Designs Inc....D....415 847-6618
639 Front St Fl 3 San Francisco (94111) ***(P-14119)***
Latham & Watkins LLP....C....650 328-4600
140 Scott Dr Menlo Park (94025) ***(P-23184)***
Latham & Watkins LLP....B....714 755-8288
1722 Skyhill Way Santa Ana (92705) ***(P-23185)***
Latham & Watkins LLP....B....818 753-5000
111 Univrsal Hllywd 257 Universal City (91608) ***(P-23186)***
Latham & Watkins LLP (PA)....A....213 485-1234
355 S Grand Ave Ste 1000 Los Angeles (90071) ***(P-23187)***
Latham & Watkins LLP....D....213 891-7108
555 W 5th St Ste 800 Los Angeles (90013) ***(P-23188)***
Latham & Watkins LLP....C....714 540-1235
650 Town Center Dr # 2000 Costa Mesa (92626) ***(P-23189)***
Latham & Watkins LLP....C....213 891-1200
520 S Grand Ave Ste 200 Los Angeles (90071) ***(P-23190)***
Latham & Watkins LLP....C....415 391-0600
505 Montgomery St # 1900 San Francisco (94111) ***(P-23191)***
Lathrop & Gage LLP....D....310 789-4600
1888 Century Park E # 1000 Los Angeles (90067) ***(P-23192)***
Latino Commission On Alcohol (PA)....E....650 244-1444
1001 Sneath Ln Ste 307 San Bruno (94066) ***(P-22610)***
Lattice Engines Inc (PA)....D....877 460-0010
1820 Gateway Dr Ste 200 San Mateo (94404) ***(P-16419)***
Laugh Factory Inc....D....562 495-2844
151 S Pine Ave Long Beach (90802) ***(P-25436)***
Laughlin Falbo Levy Moresi LLP (PA)....D....510 628-0496
555 12th St Ste 1900 Oakland (94607) ***(P-23193)***
Launch Media Inc (HQ)....C....310 593-6152
25 Taylor St San Francisco (94102) ***(P-5593)***
Launchpad Communications, Anaheim *Also called Consumer Resource Network LLC* ***(P-27199)***
Lauras House....D....949 361-3775
999 Corporate Dr Ste 225 Mission Viejo (92694) ***(P-23891)***
Laurel Convelescent Center, Fontana *Also called Sun Mar Management Services* ***(P-27050)***
Laurel Labor Services Inc....D....805 928-0113
727 Richmind Ct Santa Maria (93455) ***(P-14661)***
Laurel Park, Pomona *Also called Genesis Healthcare Corporation* ***(P-20451)***
Laurence-Hovenier Inc....C....951 736-2990
179 N Maple St Corona (92880) ***(P-3049)***
Lav Hotel Corp....C....858 454-0771
1132 Prospect St La Jolla (92037) ***(P-12839)***
Lava Beds National Monuments....E....530 667-2282
1 Indian Wells Hqtrs Tulelake (96134) ***(P-25437)***
Lavante Inc....E....408 754-1410
5225 Hellyer Ave Ste 200 San Jose (95138) ***(P-15740)***
Lavine Lofgren Morris Engelb....E....858 455-1200
4180 La Jolla Village Dr # 300 La Jolla (92037) ***(P-26245)***
Law Crossing (PA)....D....626 243-1801
175 S Lake Ave Unit 200 Pasadena (91101) ***(P-24199)***
Law Enforcement Officers Inc....C....855 477-3536
24000 Alicia Pkwy 17-229 Mission Viejo (92691) ***(P-16920)***
Law Offices Berglund & Johnson (PA)....D....951 276-4783
21550 Oxnard St Ste 900 Woodland Hills (91367) ***(P-23194)***
Law Offices Juan J. Dominguez, Los Angeles *Also called Dominguez Firm Inc* ***(P-23050)***
Law Offices of James F. Holtz, San Diego *Also called Artiano Shinoff Abed* ***(P-22923)***
Law Offices of Thomas W....C....858 883-2000
14286 Danielson St # 103 Poway (92064) ***(P-23195)***
Law School Financial Inc....C....626 243-1800
175 S Lake Ave Unit 200 Pasadena (91101) ***(P-9697)***
Law School Loans, Pasadena *Also called Law School Financial Inc* ***(P-9697)***
Lawinfocom Inc....D....760 510-3000
5901 Priestly Dr Ste 200 Carlsbad (92008) ***(P-15741)***
Lawndale Healthcare & Wellness....D....310 679-3344
15100 Prairie Ave Lawndale (90260) ***(P-20577)***
Lawnman II Inc....D....916 739-1420
4300 82nd St Ste C Sacramento (95826) ***(P-891)***
Lawrence B Bonas Company....D....714 668-5250
3197 Arprt Loop Dr Ste C Costa Mesa (92626) ***(P-2454)***
Lawrence Berkeley National Lab, Emeryville *Also called University California Berkeley* ***(P-26670)***
Lawrence Berkeley National Lab, Berkeley *Also called United States Dept of Energy* ***(P-26668)***
Lawrence Berkeley National Lab....A....510 486-5111
1 Cyclotron Rd 50-4133 Berkeley (94720) ***(P-22107)***
Lawrence Family Jewish Commu (PA)....C....858 362-1144
4126 Executive Dr La Jolla (92037) ***(P-24800)***
Lawrence Livermore NA....A....925 422-1100
7000 East Ave Livermore (94550) ***(P-25438)***
Lawrence Livermore Nat Lab, San Francisco *Also called Energy Livermore Off US Dept* ***(P-26617)***
Lawrence Livermore Nat Lab, San Jose *Also called Energy Livermore Off US Dept* ***(P-26618)***
Lawrence Livermore Nat Lab, Livermore *Also called United States Dept of Energy* ***(P-26480)***
Lawrence Tractor Coinc (PA)....D....559 734-7406
2436 E Valley Oaks Dr Visalia (93292) ***(P-7705)***
Lawson Mechanical Contractors (PA)....D....916 381-5000
6090 S Watt Ave Sacramento (95829) ***(P-2257)***
Lawson Roofing Co Inc....D....415 285-1661
1495 Tennessee St San Francisco (94107) ***(P-3172)***
Lawyers Title Company....D....858 650-3900
4542 Ruffner St Ste 200 San Diego (92111) ***(P-10464)***
Lawyers Title Company (HQ)....E....818 767-0425
7530 N Glenoaks Blvd Burbank (91504) ***(P-10465)***
Lawyers Title Insurance Corp....D....949 223-5575
18551 Von Karman Ave # 100 Irvine (92612) ***(P-10466)***
Lax Hospitality LP....C....310 670-9000
6225 W Century Blvd Los Angeles (90045) ***(P-12840)***
Lax Hotel Ventures LLC....E....310 645-4600
9750 Airport Blvd Los Angeles (90045) ***(P-12841)***
Lax International Service Ctr....D....310 337-8764
5800 W Century Blvd Los Angeles (90009) ***(P-17292)***
Lax Plaza Hotel....C....310 902-2202
6333 Bristol Pkwy Culver City (90230) ***(P-12842)***
LAX Wheel Refinishing Inc....D....323 269-1484
1520 Spence St Los Angeles (90023) ***(P-6654)***
Lax-C Inc....E....323 343-9000
1100 N Main St Los Angeles (90012) ***(P-8420)***
Laxmi Group Inc....D....408 329-7733
4699 Old Ironsides Dr # 100 Santa Clara (95054) ***(P-15255)***
Layfield USA Corporation (HQ)....D....619 562-1200
2500 Sweetwater Springs B Spring Valley (91978) ***(P-3545)***
Layne Christensen Company....C....909 390-2833
1717 W Park Ave Redlands (92373) ***(P-27771)***
Layton-Belling & Associates, Irvine *Also called Lba Inc* ***(P-27299)***
Lazar Landscape Design & Cnstr....D....510 444-5195
2884 Ettie St Oakland (94608) ***(P-764)***
Lazer Electric Inc....D....714 777-4233
4701 E Hunter Ave Anaheim (92807) ***(P-2629)***
Laztrans Inc....E....661 833-3783
5200 District Blvd Bakersfield (93313) ***(P-4214)***
Lb Funding LLC....D....562 983-3400
701 W Ocean Blvd Long Beach (90831) ***(P-12843)***
Lb Hills Golf Club LLC....D....760 775-2000
84000 Terra Lago Pkwy Indio (92203) ***(P-18727)***
Lba Inc (PA)....C....949 833-0400
3347 Michelson Dr Ste 200 Irvine (92612) ***(P-27299)***
Lba Realty Fund III - III LLC....D....949 833-0400
3347 Michelson Dr Ste 200 Irvine (92612) ***(P-12170)***
Lba Realty LLC (PA)....E....949 833-0400
3347 Michelson Dr Ste 200 Irvine (92612) ***(P-11560)***
Lba Rlty Fund I-Company IV LLC....D....949 955-9321
3347 Michelson Dr Ste 950 Irvine (92612) ***(P-12171)***
LBC Inc....D....805 581-1068
1881 Duncan St Simi Valley (93065) ***(P-3173)***
LBC Mundial Corporation (HQ)....D....650 873-0750
3563 Inv Blvd Ste 3 Hayward (94545) ***(P-4841)***
LBC North America, Hayward *Also called LBC Mundial Corporation* ***(P-4841)***
Lbi Media Inc....B....818 729-5316
1845 W Empire Ave Burbank (91504) ***(P-5740)***
Lbs Financial Credit Union....D....714 893-5111
1401 Quail St Ste 130 Newport Beach (92660) ***(P-9698)***
Lbs Financial Credit Union (PA)....C....562 598-9007
5505 Garden Grove Blvd # 500 Westminster (92683) ***(P-9699)***
Lc Trs Inc....A....760 438-9111
2100 Costa Del Mar Rd Carlsbad (92009) ***(P-12844)***

Mergent e-mail: customerrelations@mergent.com
1364
2019 Directory of California Wholesalers and Services Companies
(P-0000) Products & Services Section entry number
(PA)=Parent Co (HQ)=Headquarters (DH)=Div Headquarters

Ld Products Inc.....C.....562 986-6940
3700 Cover St Long Beach (90808) *(P-7070)*
LDI Mechanical Inc.....E.....916 361-3925
3760 Happy Ln Sacramento (95827) *(P-2258)*
LDI Mechanical Inc (PA).....C.....951 340-9685
1587 E Bentley Dr Corona (92879) *(P-2259)*
LDI Transportation Inc.....D.....909 620-7001
200 Erie St Pomona (91768) *(P-4354)*
Ldla Clothing LLC.....D.....323 312-2805
13071 Temple Ave La Puente (91746) *(P-8314)*
Le Bleu Chateau Inc.....E.....818 843-3141
1900 Grismer Ave Burbank (91504) *(P-24576)*
Le Courier, Burbank *Also called Tidavater Inc (P-17511)*
Le Crochet By Saro Inc (PA).....E.....818 846-3314
3333 W Pacific Ave Burbank (91505) *(P-6772)*
Le Merdien Dlfina Santa Monica, Santa Monica *Also called Blue Devils Lessee LLC (P-12389)*
Le Meridian Hotel, San Francisco *Also called Chesapeake Lodging Trust (P-12451)*
Le Montrose Hotel.....D.....310 855-1115
900 Hammond St Apt 434 West Hollywood (90069) *(P-12845)*
Le Montrose Suite Hotel, West Hollywood *Also called Le Montrose Hotel (P-12845)*
Le Parc Suite Hotel, West Hollywood *Also called Ols Hotels & Resorts LP (P-12980)*
Le Parker Meridien Palm Sprng, Palm Springs *Also called Jack Parker Corp (P-12787)*
Le Vecke Corporation (PA).....D.....951 681-8600
10810 Inland Ave Mira Loma (91752) *(P-9008)*
Le Vecke Group, Mira Loma *Also called Le Vecke Corporation (P-9008)*
Lead Staffing Corporation.....C.....800 928-5561
216 S Citrus St Ste 397 West Covina (91791) *(P-20188)*
Leader Drug Store, Torrance *Also called Little Company Mary Hospital (P-21556)*
Leader Emergency Vehicles, South El Monte *Also called Leader Industries Inc (P-3816)*
Leader Industries Inc.....C.....626 575-0880
10941 Weaver Ave South El Monte (91733) *(P-3816)*
Leadhealthstaff, Tarzana *Also called Advanced Medical Placement (P-24729)*
Leadstack Inc.....D.....628 200-3063
1390 Market St Ste 200 San Francisco (94102) *(P-14662)*
Leaf Commercial Capital Inc.....E.....866 219-7924
1100 Town & Country Rd Orange (92868) *(P-27300)*
Leaf Group Ltd (PA).....C.....310 656-6253
1655 26th St Santa Monica (90404) *(P-13948)*
League of California Cities (PA).....D.....916 658-8200
1400 K St Fl 4 Sacramento (95814) *(P-27560)*
League of Wmen Voters Whittier.....E.....562 947-5818
10011 Melgar Dr Whittier (90603) *(P-25371)*
Leantaas Inc.....D.....650 409-3501
469 El Camino Real # 100 Santa Clara (95050) *(P-15256)*
Lear Capital Inc.....D.....310 571-0190
1990 S Bundy Dr Ste 600 Los Angeles (90025) *(P-9969)*
LEARN, Whittier *Also called Rio Hondo Education Consortium (P-23998)*
Learner Financial, Walnut Creek *Also called Mechanics Bank (P-11955)*
Learning Services Corporation.....E.....760 746-3223
2335 Bear Valley Pkwy Escondido (92027) *(P-22611)*
Learning Services Corporation.....E.....408 848-4379
10855 De Bruin Way Gilroy (95020) *(P-22612)*
Learning Services Northern Cal, Gilroy *Also called Learning Services Corporation (P-22612)*
Learning Tree Pre-School, Tujunga *Also called Crescenta-Canada YMCA (P-25147)*
Leasing Equipment, San Francisco *Also called Atel Capital Group (P-9753)*
Leavitt Group Enterprises Inc.....C.....707 465-6508
785 E Washington Blvd # 4 Crescent City (95531) *(P-10670)*
Leavy Brothers Incorporated.....D.....916 773-5636
4117 Elverta Rd Ste 102 Antelope (95843) *(P-2910)*
Led Global LLC.....D.....917 921-4315
1010 Wilshire Blvd Los Angeles (90017) *(P-2260)*
Ledcor CMI Inc.....D.....602 595-3017
6405 Mira Mesa Blvd # 100 San Diego (92121) *(P-1417)*
Ledcor Management Services Inc.....E.....858 527-6400
6405 Mira Mesa Blvd Ste 1 San Diego (92121) *(P-26928)*
Ledesma & Meyer Cnstr Co Inc.....D.....909 297-1100
9441 Haven Ave Rancho Cucamonga (91730) *(P-1579)*
Ledesma & Meyer Dev Inc.....D.....909 476-0590
9441 Haven Ave Rancho Cucamonga (91730) *(P-26929)*
Ledra Brands Inc.....D.....714 259-9959
15774 Gateway Cir Tustin (92780) *(P-6773)*
Ledson Winery & Vineyards, Santa Rosa *Also called Steven N Ledson (P-1239)*
Lee Burkhart Liu Inc (PA).....D.....310 829-2249
5510 Lincoln Blvd Ste 250 Playa Vista (90094) *(P-26080)*
Lee Hong Degerman Kang.....D.....949 250-9954
3501 Jamboree Rd Ste 6000 Newport Beach (92660) *(P-23196)*
Lee & Assoc Comm Real Est Svcs.....E.....909 989-7771
3535 Inland Empire Blvd Ontario (91764) *(P-11561)*
Lee & Associates Coml RE Svcs, Ontario *Also called Lee & Assoc Comm Real Est Svcs (P-11561)*
Lee & Associates Coml RE Svcs (PA).....E.....949 727-1200
7700 Irvine Center Dr # 600 Irvine (92618) *(P-11562)*
Lee & Associates Realty Group.....E.....949 724-1000
100 Bayview Cir Ste 600 Newport Beach (92660) *(P-11563)*
Lee & Ro Inc (PA).....E.....626 912-3391
1199 Fullerton Rd City of Industry (91748) *(P-25794)*
Lee Bros Foodservices Inc (PA).....C.....408 275-0700
660 E Gish Rd San Jose (95112) *(P-8421)*
Lee Industrial Catering, San Jose *Also called Lee Bros Foodservices Inc (P-8421)*
Lee Jennings Target Ex Inc (PA).....C.....909 868-1040
1465 E Franklin Ave Pomona (91766) *(P-4036)*
Lee Johnson.....C.....858 481-4411
14750 El Camino Real Del Mar (92014) *(P-21133)*
Lee Mar Aquarium & Pet Sups, Vista *Also called Lee-Mar Aquarium & Pet Sups (P-9230)*
LEE& Associates, Newport Beach *Also called Lee & Associates Realty Group (P-11563)*
Lee-Mar Aquarium & Pet Sups.....D.....760 727-1300
2459 Dogwood Way Vista (92081) *(P-9230)*
Lee-Victorville Hotel Corp.....C.....760 245-3461
14173 Green Tree Blvd Victorville (92395) *(P-12846)*
Leed Electric Inc.....D.....562 270-9500
13138 Arctic Cir Santa Fe Springs (90670) *(P-2630)*
Leed International LLC.....E.....650 861-7883
1583 Shanghai Cir San Jose (95131) *(P-27772)*
Leekilpatrick Management Inc.....D.....818 500-9631
324 S Myrtle Ave Monrovia (91016) *(P-27301)*
Leemah Electronics Inc.....C.....415 394-1288
1080 Sansome St San Francisco (94111) *(P-6048)*
Leerink Partners LLC.....D.....800 778-1164
255 California St Fl 12 San Francisco (94111) *(P-9970)*
Lees Maintenance Service Inc.....B.....818 988-6644
14740 Keswick St Van Nuys (91405) *(P-14301)*
Legacy and Nursing Rehab.....D.....925 228-8383
1790 Muir Rd Martinez (94553) *(P-23892)*
Legacy Farms LLC.....C.....714 736-1800
6625 Caballero Blvd Buena Park (90620) *(P-8701)*
Legacy Frames.....D.....310 537-4210
11220 Wright Rd Lynwood (90262) *(P-7499)*
Legacy Global Logistics Svcs, San Jose *Also called Legacy Transportation Svcs Inc (P-4355)*
Legacy Healthcare Center LLC.....D.....626 798-0558
1570 N Fair Oaks Ave Pasadena (91103) *(P-22832)*
Legacy Marketing Group (PA).....C.....707 778-8638
2090 Marina Ave Petaluma (94954) *(P-27302)*
Legacy Mech & Enrgy Svcs Inc.....D.....925 820-6938
3130 Crow Canyon Pl # 410 San Ramon (94583) *(P-2261)*
Legacy Partners Hollywood.....D.....949 930-7706
1600 Vine St Los Angeles (90028) *(P-11051)*
Legacy Partners Limited Inc.....D.....760 747-2711
738 W Washington Ave A Escondido (92025) *(P-1806)*
Legacy Paving, Escondido *Also called Legacy Partners Limited Inc (P-1806)*
Legacy Prtners Residential Inc.....B.....949 930-6600
5141 California Ave # 100 Irvine (92617) *(P-26930)*
Legacy Prtners Residential Inc (PA).....C.....650 571-2250
4000 E 3rd Ave Ste 600 Foster City (94404) *(P-26931)*
Legacy Tile and Stone Inc.....E.....951 296-1096
26825 Jefferson Ave Ste D Murrieta (92562) *(P-3002)*
Legacy Transportation Svcs Inc (PA).....C.....408 294-9800
935 Mclaughlin Ave San Jose (95122) *(P-4355)*
Legacy Vulcan LLC.....E.....909 875-1150
2400 W Highland Ave San Bernardino (92407) *(P-1094)*
Legal Aid Society of San Diego (PA).....E.....619 263-1872
110 S Euclid Ave San Diego (92114) *(P-23197)*
Legal Enterprise, Calabasas *Also called Litigtion Rsrces of America-CA (P-17297)*
Legal Recovery Law Offices Inc.....D.....619 275-4001
5030 Camino De La Siesta # 340 San Diego (92108) *(P-23198)*
Legal Solutions Holdings Inc.....C.....800 244-3495
955 Overland Ct Ste 200 San Dimas (91773) *(P-23199)*
Legally Yours LLC.....C.....909 396-7200
750 N Diamond Bar Blvd # 224 Diamond Bar (91765) *(P-23200)*
Legalmatchcom (PA).....E.....415 946-0800
395 Oyster Point Blvd South San Francisco (94080) *(P-23201)*
Legalzoomcom Inc (HQ).....B.....323 962-8600
101 N Brand Blvd Fl 11 Glendale (91203) *(P-23202)*
Legend Merchant Group Inc.....E.....415 957-9555
201 Mission St Ste 230 San Francisco (94105) *(P-17293)*
Legend Transpotation, Yuba City *Also called New Legend Inc (P-4235)*
Legend3d Inc.....D.....858 793-4420
1500 N El Centro Ave # 100 Los Angeles (90028) *(P-18067)*
Leggett & Platt Incorporated.....D.....510 487-8063
31023 Huntwood Ave Hayward (94544) *(P-13976)*
Legion Corporation.....D.....800 750-0062
784 Geary St San Francisco (94109) *(P-16717)*
Legions Protective Svcs LLC.....E.....310 819-8881
17201 S Figueroa St Gardena (90248) *(P-16718)*
Legislative Counsel Tstg Off, Sacramento *Also called Office of The Legislative Coun (P-27810)*
Legislative Data Center, Sacramento *Also called Office of The Legislative Coun (P-5414)*
Legoland California LLC.....B.....760 918-5346
1 Legoland Dr Carlsbad (92008) *(P-18803)*
Legrande Affaire, Santa Clara *Also called Restivo Enterprises (P-3835)*
Legrande Affaire Inc.....C.....408 988-4884
651 Aldo Ave Santa Clara (95054) *(P-3817)*
Lehar Sales Co.....D.....510 465-3255
150 Chestnut St Oakland (94607) *(P-8534)*
Lehman Brothers, Los Angeles *Also called Barclays Capital Inc (P-9917)*
Lehr, Sacramento *Also called Stommel Inc (P-2748)*
Lei AG Seattle, Los Angeles *Also called Lowe Enterprises Inc (P-11570)*
Leichtag Assisted Living, Encinitas *Also called San Diego Hebrew Homes (P-20738)*
Leidos Inc.....C.....858 826-9090
2985 Scott St Vista (92081) *(P-26396)*
Leidos Inc.....B.....858 826-5552
4035 Hancock St San Diego (92110) *(P-26397)*
Leidos Inc.....D.....310 791-9671
1874 S Pacific Coast Hwy Redondo Beach (90277) *(P-26398)*
Leidos Inc.....C.....858 535-4499
9455 Towne Centre Dr # 200 San Diego (92121) *(P-26399)*
Leidos Inc.....C.....703 676-4300
10260 Campus Point Dr C San Diego (92121) *(P-26400)*
Leidos Inc.....B.....858 826-7670
1550 N Norma St Ridgecrest (93555) *(P-16150)*
Leidos Inc.....C.....858 826-9416
4161 Campus Point Ct San Diego (92121) *(P-26401)*

ALPHABETIC

Employee Codes: A=Over 500 employees, B=251-500
C=101-250, D=51-100, E=50
2019 Directory of California
Wholesalers and Services Companies
© Mergent Inc. 1-800-342-5647
1365

Leidos Inc.....D.....714 257-6400
590 W Central Ave Ste I Brea (92821) ***(P-26402)***
Leidos Inc.....C.....310 524-3134
300 N Sepulveda Blvd El Segundo (90245) ***(P-26403)***
Leidos Inc.....D.....858 826-6616
10740 Thornmint Rd San Diego (92127) ***(P-26404)***
Leidos Inc.....D.....510 428-2550
2000 Powell St Ste 1090 Emeryville (94608) ***(P-26405)***
Leidos Inc.....B.....858 826-6000
1299 Prospect St La Jolla (92037) ***(P-26406)***
Leidos Inc.....D.....858 826-6000
4065 Hancock St San Diego (92110) ***(P-26407)***
Leidos Inc.....C.....858 826-7129
10010 Campus Point Dr San Diego (92121) ***(P-26408)***
Leidos Inc.....D.....510 466-7138
505 14th St Ste 900 Oakland (94612) ***(P-26409)***
Leidos Inc.....D.....910 574-4597
N Depo Rd Bldg 4530 Fort Irwin (92310) ***(P-26410)***
Leidos Engineering LLC.....D.....714 257-6400
590 W Central Ave Ste I Brea (92821) ***(P-25795)***
Leidos Engineering LLC.....D.....858 826-6000
4161 Campus Point Ct E San Diego (92121) ***(P-25796)***
Leidos Engrg & Sciences LLC.....D.....619 542-3130
1330 30th St Ste A San Diego (92154) ***(P-26411)***
Leigh Jerry California Inc (PA).....A.....818 909-6200
7860 Nelson Rd Panorama City (91402) ***(P-8315)***
Leight Sales Co Inc.....D.....310 223-1000
1611 S Catalina Ave L45 Redondo Beach (90277) ***(P-7593)***
Leighton & Associates, Irvine *Also called Gradient Engineers Inc* ***(P-25718)***
Leighton and Associates Inc (PA).....D.....949 250-1421
17781 Cowan Irvine (92614) ***(P-27773)***
Leighton Group Inc (PA).....B.....949 477-4040
17781 Cowan Irvine (92614) ***(P-27599)***
Leighton Group Inc.....C.....760 776-4192
75450 Gerald Ford Dr Palm Desert (92211) ***(P-25023)***
Leisure Care, Livermore *Also called Livermore Snior Lving Assoc LP* ***(P-11990)***
Leisure Care LLC.....C.....925 371-2300
800 E Stanley Blvd Livermore (94550) ***(P-11052)***
Leisure Care Inc.....D.....949 645-6833
1455 Superior Ave Newport Beach (92663) ***(P-11053)***
Leisure Care LLC.....D.....818 713-0900
8138 Woodlake Ave Canoga Park (91304) ***(P-20938)***
Leisure Care LLC.....E.....714 974-1616
380 S Anaheim Hills Rd Anaheim (92807) ***(P-24577)***
Leisure Care LLC.....D.....559 434-1237
9525 N Fort Washington Rd Fresno (93730) ***(P-24578)***
Leisure Court Nursing Center, Anaheim *Also called 1135 N Leisure Ct Inc* ***(P-20215)***
Leisure Glen Convalescent Ctr, Glendale *Also called Buena Ventura Care Center Inc* ***(P-21024)***
Leisure Planet.....C.....925 687-4386
1975 Diamond Blvd Concord (94520) ***(P-19195)***
Leisure Sports Inc.....B.....925 942-6301
4670 Willow Rd Ste 100 Pleasanton (94588) ***(P-11989)***
Leisure Sports Inc.....C.....510 226-8500
46650 Landing Pkwy Fremont (94538) ***(P-18625)***
Leisure Sports Inc.....B.....925 938-3058
2805 Jones Rd Walnut Creek (94597) ***(P-12847)***
Leisure Village Association.....D.....805 484-2861
200 Leisure Village Dr Camarillo (93012) ***(P-25189)***
Leisure World Pharmacy, Seal Beach *Also called Tenet Healthsystem Medical* ***(P-20002)***
Leisure World Resales, Laguna Hills *Also called Professional Community MGT Cal* ***(P-11685)***
LEK Consulting LLC.....D.....310 209-9800
1100 Glendon Ave Ste 2100 Los Angeles (90024) ***(P-27303)***
Leland Health Care Services, Hemet *Also called Physicians For Healthy Hospita* ***(P-21644)***
Leland House, San Francisco *Also called Catholic Chrts Cyo Archdiocs* ***(P-23540)***
Leland Stanford Junior Univ.....C.....650 723-6254
1070 Arastradero Rd # 100 Palo Alto (94304) ***(P-26537)***
Leland Stanford Junior Univ.....D.....650 725-4868
551 Srra Mall Mem Adtrium Memorial Auditorium Stanford (94305) ***(P-5741)***
Leland Stanford Junior Univ.....D.....650 723-7863
1201 Welch Rd Stanford (94305) ***(P-19646)***
Leland Stanford Junior Univ.....E.....650 723-2997
328 Lomita Dr Palo Alto (94305) ***(P-21547)***
Leland Stanford Junior Univ.....C.....650 723-5548
3373 Hillview Ave Palo Alto (94304) ***(P-22833)***
Leland Stanford Junior Univ.....D.....650 723-4150
Melcode 4020 Bldg 540 Stanford (94305) ***(P-26633)***
Leland Stanford Junior Univ.....C.....650 723-2021
326 Galvez St Stanford (94305) ***(P-25190)***
Leland Stanford Junior Univ.....B.....650 723-7546
476 Lomita Mall Palo Alto (94305) ***(P-26538)***
Leland Stanford Junior Univ.....D.....650 723-9633
711 Serra St Stanford (94305) ***(P-2631)***
Leland Stanford Junior Univ.....A.....650 725-2377
820 Quarry Rd Palo Alto (94304) ***(P-21548)***
Leland Stanford Junior Univ.....A.....650 723-4000
2680 Hanover St Palo Alto (94304) ***(P-21549)***
Leland Stanford Junior Univ.....C.....650 723-0107
450 Via Palou Mall Stanford (94305) ***(P-26634)***
Leland Stanford Junior Univ.....C.....650 724-8899
397 Panama Mall Ste 360 Stanford (94305) ***(P-26635)***
Leland Stanford Junior Univ.....D.....650 725-4416
211 Quarry Rd N229 Palo Alto (94304) ***(P-19647)***
Leland Stanford Junior Univ.....A.....650 725-4617
1000 Welch Rd Palo Alto (94304) ***(P-21550)***
Leland Stanford Junior Univ.....A.....650 725-2386
473 Via Ortega Stanford (94305) ***(P-21551)***
Leland Stanford Junior Univ.....A.....650 725-6127
243 Panama St Stanford (94305) ***(P-21552)***
Leland Stanford Junior Univ.....D.....650 723-0821
870 Campus Dr Stanford (94305) ***(P-19648)***
Leland Stanford Junior Univ.....A.....650 723-4000
300 Pasteur Dr Stanford (94305) ***(P-21553)***
Leland Stanford Junior Univ.....D.....650 723-4733
1201 Welch Rd Palo Alto (94305) ***(P-26636)***
Lemo USA Inc.....D.....707 206-3700
635 Park Ct Rohnert Park (94928) ***(P-7500)***
Lemore Transportation Inc (PA).....D.....925 689-6444
1420 Royal Industrial Way Concord (94520) ***(P-4215)***
Lender Processing Services Inc.....D.....626 808-9000
3100 New York Dr Ste 200 Pasadena (91107) ***(P-16151)***
Lendingclub Asset MGT LLC.....B.....415 632-5600
71 Stevenson St Ste 300 San Francisco (94105) ***(P-9891)***
Lendingclub Corporation (PA).....D.....415 632-5600
71 Stevenson St Ste 300 San Francisco (94105) ***(P-9741)***
Lendlease US Construction Inc.....D.....213 430-4660
800 W 6th St Ste 1600 Los Angeles (90017) ***(P-26932)***
Lendup, San Francisco *Also called Flurish Inc* ***(P-9711)***
Lenlyn Limited Which Will Do B (HQ).....D.....310 417-3432
6151 W Century Blvd Los Angeles (90045) ***(P-9687)***
Lennar, Rancho Santa Fe *Also called HCC Investors LLC* ***(P-18934)***
Lennar Builders, Aliso Viejo *Also called Lennar Homes California Inc* ***(P-1192)***
Lennar Corporation.....D.....949 349-8000
25 Enterprise Ste 400 Aliso Viejo (92656) ***(P-1348)***
Lennar Homes Inc.....C.....916 517-4950
3788 Edington Dr Rancho Cordova (95742) ***(P-1349)***
Lennar Homes Inc.....C.....951 739-0267
980 Montecito Dr Ste 300 Corona (92879) ***(P-1350)***
Lennar Homes California Inc (HQ).....C.....949 349-8000
25 Enterprise Ste 400 Aliso Viejo (92656) ***(P-1192)***
Lennar Multi Family Community, Aliso Viejo *Also called LMC Hollywood Highland* ***(P-1582)***
Lennar Partners of Los Angeles (PA).....E.....949 885-8500
4350 Von Karman Ave # 200 Newport Beach (92660) ***(P-17294)***
Lennox Industries Inc.....C.....818 739-1616
19801 Nordhoff Pl Ste 109 Chatsworth (91311) ***(P-7653)***
Lenore John & Co (PA).....C.....619 232-6136
1250 Delevan Dr San Diego (92102) ***(P-8824)***
Lenox Financial Mortgage Corp.....C.....949 428-5100
200 Sandpointe Ave # 800 Santa Ana (92707) ***(P-9825)***
Leo A Daly Company, Sacramento *Also called Leo A Daly Company* ***(P-26083)***
Leo A Daly Company.....D.....213 627-9300
550 S Hope St Ste 2700 Los Angeles (90071) ***(P-26081)***
Leo A Daly Company.....D.....213 533-8855
550 S Hope St Ste 2700 Los Angeles (90071) ***(P-26082)***
Leo A Daly Company.....D.....916 564-3259
2150 River Plaza Dr Sacramento (95833) ***(P-26083)***
Leo Daly Company, Los Angeles *Also called Leo A Daly Company* ***(P-26081)***
Leo J Ryan Child Care Ctr, South San Francisco *Also called Peninsula Family Service* ***(P-23965)***
Leon Chien Corp.....D.....626 964-8302
17843 Colima Rd City of Industry (91748) ***(P-9826)***
Leonard Anthony Valenti Inc.....D.....408 848-9688
9110 Marcella Ave Gilroy (95020) ***(P-892)***
Leonard Chaidez Inc.....D.....714 279-8173
2298 N Batavia St Orange (92865) ***(P-975)***
Leonard Chaidez Tree Service, Orange *Also called Leonard Chaidez Inc* ***(P-975)***
Leonards Carpet Service Inc.....E.....858 453-9525
6767 Nancy Ridge Dr San Diego (92121) ***(P-3282)***
Leonid M Glosman DDS A D.....D.....818 989-2400
7864 Van Nuys Blvd Panorama City (91402) ***(P-20125)***
Lereta LLC (PA).....B.....626 543-1765
1123 Park View Dr Covina (91724) ***(P-9971)***
Leroy Durbin.....D.....562 531-2001
14620 Lakewood Blvd Bellflower (90706) ***(P-11564)***
Leroy Haynes Center, La Verne *Also called Haynes Family Programs Inc* ***(P-24556)***
Les Kelley Family Health Ctr.....D.....310 319-4700
1920 Colorado Ave Santa Monica (90404) ***(P-19649)***
Lescure Company Inc.....D.....925 283-2528
2301 Arnold Industrial Wa Concord (94520) ***(P-2262)***
Lesley Foundation.....D.....650 726-4888
701 Arnold Way Bldg A Half Moon Bay (94019) ***(P-27774)***
Level 10 Construction LP.....C.....408 747-5000
1050 Entp Way Ste 250 Sunnyvale (94089) ***(P-1580)***
Level 9 Security Services.....E.....562 949-7180
9020 Slauson Ave Ste 206 Pico Rivera (90660) ***(P-16719)***
Level 99, Gardena *Also called Phoenix Textile Inc* ***(P-8235)***
Level Four Business MGT LLC.....E.....310 914-1600
11812 San Vicente Blvd # 400 Los Angeles (90049) ***(P-27775)***
Level-It Installations Ltd.....E.....604 942-2022
2443 Fillmore St San Francisco (94115) ***(P-1581)***
Lever Inc.....D.....415 458-2731
989 Market St Ste 500 San Francisco (94103) ***(P-15257)***
Levin and Simes.....E.....415 426-3000
353 Sacramento St # 2000 San Francisco (94111) ***(P-23203)***
Levin-Richmond Terminal Corp.....D.....510 232-4422
402 Wright Ave Richmond (94804) ***(P-4728)***
Levy Cncessions At Staples Ctr, Los Angeles *Also called Levy Prmium Fdsrvice Ltd Prtnr* ***(P-1418)***
Levy Prmium Fdsrvice Ltd Prtnr.....D.....213 742-7867
1111 S Figueroa St Los Angeles (90015) ***(P-1418)***
Lewis & Taylor LLC.....C.....415 781-3496
440 Bryant St San Francisco (94107) ***(P-14302)***
Lewis & Taylor Bldg Svc Contrs, San Francisco *Also called Lewis & Taylor LLC* ***(P-14302)***
Lewis Brsbois Bsgard Smith LLP.....D.....213 250-1800
633 W 5th St Ste 4000 Los Angeles (90071) ***(P-23204)***
Lewis Brsbois Bsgard Smith LLP.....D.....951 252-6150
28765 Single Oak Dr Ste 1 Temecula (92590) ***(P-23205)***

Lewis Brsbois Bsgard Smith LLP (PA) ....A....213 250-1800
633 W 5th St Ste 4000 Los Angeles (90071) ***(P-23206)***
Lewis Brsbois Bsgard Smith LLP ....D....619 233-1006
701 B St Ste 1900 San Diego (92101) ***(P-23207)***
Lewis Brsbois Bsgard Smith LLP ....D....714 545-6015
650 Town Center Dr # 1400 Costa Mesa (92626) ***(P-23208)***
Lewis Brsbois Bsgard Smith LLP ....C....415 362-2580
333 Bush St San Francisco (94104) ***(P-23209)***
Lewis Brsbois Bsgard Smith LLP ....E....909 387-1130
650 E Hospitality Ln # 600 San Bernardino (92408) ***(P-23210)***
Lewis Companies (PA) ....B....909 985-0971
1156 N Mountain Ave Upland (91786) ***(P-1351)***
Lewis Marenstein Wicke Sherwin ....E....818 703-6000
20750 Ventura Blvd # 400 Woodland Hills (91364) ***(P-23211)***
Lewis P C Jackson ....E....415 394-9400
50 California St Ste 900 San Francisco (94111) ***(P-23212)***
Lewis P C Jackson ....D....213 689-0404
725 S Figueroa St # 2500 Los Angeles (90017) ***(P-23213)***
Lewis PR Inc (HQ) ....D....415 432-2400
111 Sutter St Ste 850 San Francisco (94104) ***(P-27561)***
Lewis-Goetz and Company Inc ....D....916 366-9340
10182 Croydon Way Sacramento (95827) ***(P-7855)***
Lexani Wheel Corporation ....C....951 808-4220
2380 Railroad St Ste 101 Corona (92880) ***(P-6655)***
Lexington Associates Inc (PA) ....D....415 332-8500
1 Harbor Dr Ste 105 Sausalito (94965) ***(P-11054)***
Lexington Scenery & Props Inc ....C....818 768-5768
12800 Rangoon St Arleta (91331) ***(P-3050)***
Lexisnexis, Los Angeles *Also called Relx Inc* ***(P-16245)***
Lexisnexis Courtlink Inc ....C....425 974-5000
2101 K St Sacramento (95816) ***(P-25024)***
Lexmar Distribution Inc ....C....909 620-7001
200 Erie St Pomona (91768) ***(P-4216)***
Lexxiom Inc ....B....909 481-2536
7945 Cartilla Ave A Rancho Cucamonga (91730) ***(P-26933)***
Lfk Law ....D....310 300-8464
9595 Wilshire Blvd Beverly Hills (90212) ***(P-23214)***
Lg Display America Inc ....E....760 692-0900
2791 Loker Ave W Carlsbad (92010) ***(P-7501)***
Lg Display America Inc (HQ) ....D....408 350-0190
2540 N 1st St Ste 400 San Jose (95131) ***(P-7502)***
Lge Electrical Sales Inc ....B....408 379-8568
7866 Convoy Ct San Diego (92111) ***(P-7371)***
Lgh Digital Media Inc ....E....323 469-3986
6520 W Sunset Blvd Los Angeles (90028) ***(P-18068)***
Lh Indian Wells Operating LLC ....C....760 341-2200
4500 Indian Wells Ln Indian Wells (92210) ***(P-12848)***
Lh Universal Operating LLC ....B....818 980-1212
333 Unversal Hollywood Dr Universal City (91608) ***(P-12849)***
Lho Mssion Bay Rsie Lessee Inc ....B....619 276-4010
1775 E Mission Bay Dr San Diego (92109) ***(P-12850)***
Lho Santa Cruz One Lesse Inc ....C....831 475-5600
1 Chaminade Ln Santa Cruz (95065) ***(P-12851)***
Lhoberge Lessee Inc ....C....858 259-1515
1540 Camino Del Mar Del Mar (92014) ***(P-12852)***
Liberman Broadcasting Inc (PA) ....D....818 729-5300
1845 W Empire Ave Burbank (91504) ***(P-5742)***
Liberty Ambulance, Ridgecrest *Also called Poulin Corporation* ***(P-12260)***
Liberty Ambulance LLC ....D....562 741-6230
9441 Washburn Rd Downey (90242) ***(P-3818)***
Liberty American Mortgage Corp (PA) ....D....916 780-3000
193 Blue Ravine Rd # 240 Folsom (95630) ***(P-9892)***
Liberty Dental Plan Cal Inc ....B....949 223-0007
340 Commerce Ste 100 Irvine (92602) ***(P-10277)***
Liberty Dental Plan Nevada Inc ....D....888 703-6999
340 Commerce Irvine (92602) ***(P-10278)***
Liberty Energy, South Lake Tahoe *Also called Algonquin Power and Utilities* ***(P-2504)***
Liberty Energy, South Lake Tahoe *Also called Liberty Utlties Clpeco Elc LLC* ***(P-6049)***
Liberty Glove Inc (PA) ....E....909 595-2992
433 Cheryl Ln City of Industry (91789) ***(P-8042)***
Liberty Glove & Safety Co, City of Industry *Also called Liberty Glove Inc* ***(P-8042)***
Liberty Hardware Mfg Corp ....D....909 605-2300
5555 Jurupa St Ontario (91761) ***(P-7594)***
Liberty Healthcare of Oklahoma ....D....408 532-7677
4463 San Felipe Rd Ofc San Jose (95135) ***(P-20578)***
Liberty Investments Exchange, Pasadena *Also called Arts Elegance Inc* ***(P-8001)***
Liberty Landscaping Inc ....D....951 683-2999
5212 El Rivino Rd Riverside (92509) ***(P-765)***
Liberty Mutual Insurance Co ....C....310 316-9428
19200 Von Karman Ave # 200 Irvine (92612) ***(P-10671)***
Liberty Mutual Insurance Co ....C....415 957-1175
101 Mission St Ste 740 San Francisco (94105) ***(P-10366)***
Liberty Mutual Insurance Co ....C....916 294-9518
13405 Folsom Blvd Ste 200 Folsom (95630) ***(P-10672)***
Liberty Mutual Insurance Co ....D....909 476-6688
3633 Inland Empire Blvd # 280 Ontario (91764) ***(P-10367)***
Liberty Mutual Insurance Co ....C....714 937-1400
790 The City Dr S Ste 200 Orange (92868) ***(P-10368)***
Liberty Mutual Insurance Co ....C....781 740-1920
20500 Belshaw Ave Carson (90746) ***(P-10369)***
Liberty Mutual Insurance Co ....B....916 564-1792
1750 Howe Ave Ste 450 Sacramento (95825) ***(P-10370)***
Liberty Packing Company LLC (PA) ....D....209 826-7100
724 Main St Woodland (95695) ***(P-8702)***
Liberty Station Hhg Hotel LP ....D....619 221-1900
2592 Laning Rd San Diego (92106) ***(P-12853)***
Liberty Station Hhg Hotel LP ....E....619 222-0500
2576 Laning Rd San Diego (92106) ***(P-12854)***
Liberty Utilities Pk Wtr Corp (HQ) ....D....562 923-0711
9750 Washburn Rd Downey (90241) ***(P-6271)***
Liberty Utlties Clpeco Elc LLC ....D....800 782-2506
933 Eloise Ave South Lake Tahoe (96150) ***(P-6049)***
Libsource LLC ....C....323 852-1083
10390 Santa Monica Blvd Los Angeles (90025) ***(P-26934)***
Licensale Inc ....D....604 681-6888
900 Bush St Apt 205 San Francisco (94109) ***(P-12138)***
Lieberman RES Worldwide LLC (PA) ....C....310 553-0550
1900 Ave Of The Sts 160 Los Angeles (90067) ***(P-26539)***
Lieff Cabraser Heimann & (PA) ....C....415 788-0245
275 Battery St Ste 2800 San Francisco (94111) ***(P-23215)***
Life Alert Emergency Response (PA) ....C....800 247-0000
16027 Ventura Blvd # 400 Encino (91436) ***(P-16921)***
Life Care Center of Bellflower, Bellflower *Also called Life Care Centers America Inc* ***(P-20586)***
Life Care Center of La Habra, La Habra *Also called Life Care Centers America Inc* ***(P-20579)***
Life Care Center of Norwalk, Norwalk *Also called Life Care Centers America Inc* ***(P-20587)***
Life Care Center San Gabriel, San Gabriel *Also called Life Care Centers America Inc* ***(P-20582)***
Life Care Centers America Inc ....D....562 690-0852
1233 W La Habra Blvd La Habra (90631) ***(P-20579)***
Life Care Centers America Inc ....C....760 724-8222
304 N Melrose Dr Vista (92083) ***(P-21134)***
Life Care Centers America Inc ....D....562 943-7156
11926 La Mirada Blvd La Mirada (90638) ***(P-20580)***
Life Care Centers America Inc ....C....562 947-8691
12200 La Mirada Blvd La Mirada (90638) ***(P-20581)***
Life Care Centers America Inc ....D....626 289-5365
909 W Santa Anita Ave San Gabriel (91776) ***(P-20582)***
Life Care Centers America Inc ....C....760 741-6109
1980 Felicita Rd Escondido (92025) ***(P-20583)***
Life Care Centers America Inc ....C....949 380-9380
25652 Old Trabuco Rd Lake Forest (92630) ***(P-20584)***
Life Care Centers America Inc ....C....562 943-7156
11926 La Mirada Blvd La Mirada (90638) ***(P-20585)***
Life Care Centers America Inc ....D....562 867-1761
16910 Woodruff Ave Bellflower (90706) ***(P-20586)***
Life Care Centers America Inc ....D....562 921-6624
12350 Rosecrans Ave Norwalk (90650) ***(P-20587)***
Life Care Centers America Inc ....B....760 252-2515
27555 Rimrock Rd Barstow (92311) ***(P-20588)***
Life Care Centers of Escondido, Escondido *Also called Life Care Centers America Inc* ***(P-20583)***
Life Cycle Engineering Inc ....D....619 785-5990
2535 Camino Del Rio S # 250 San Diego (92108) ***(P-14303)***
Life Enchancing Therapies, Upland *Also called Inland Empire Therapy Provider* ***(P-20179)***
Life Gnerations Healthcare LLC ....D....619 449-5555
8778 Cuyamaca St Santee (92071) ***(P-21135)***
Life Gnerations Healthcare LLC ....C....619 460-2330
7800 Parkway Dr La Mesa (91942) ***(P-20589)***
Life Ivf Center, Irvine *Also called Frank D Yelian MD PC* ***(P-19475)***
Life Line Screening Amer Ltd ....B....626 797-9774
2854 Casitas Ave Altadena (91001) ***(P-22834)***
Life Optons Vctnal Rsource Ctr (PA) ....C....805 735-3428
116 N I St Lompoc (93436) ***(P-23893)***
Life Steps Foundation Inc ....C....805 474-8431
1431 Pomeroy Rd Arroyo Grande (93420) ***(P-23894)***
Life Steps Foundation Inc ....D....562 436-0751
500 E 4th St Long Beach (90802) ***(P-23895)***
Life Steps Foundation Inc ....D....805 549-0150
1107 Johnson Ave San Luis Obispo (93401) ***(P-23896)***
Lifecare Assurance Company, Woodland Hills *Also called 21st Century Lf & Hlth Co Inc* ***(P-10154)***
Lifecare Assurance Company ....C....818 887-4436
21600 Oxnard St Fl 16 Woodland Hills (91367) ***(P-10168)***
Lifecare Health, Cerritos *Also called Healthview Inc* ***(P-24559)***
Lifecare Solutions, Pasadena *Also called Founders Healthcare LLC* ***(P-22300)***
Lifecare Systems Inc ....C....310 540-7676
4101 Torrance Blvd Torrance (90503) ***(P-20590)***
Lifehouse Inc (PA) ....D....415 472-2373
899 Northgate Dr Ste 500 San Rafael (94903) ***(P-23897)***
Lifeline Ambulance, Montebello *Also called Eastwestproto Inc* ***(P-3789)***
Lifeline Medical Transport, Ventura *Also called Ojai Ambulance Inc* ***(P-3827)***
Lifelong Medical Care (PA) ....E....510 704-6010
2344 6th St Berkeley (94710) ***(P-19650)***
Lifemoves (PA) ....E....650 685-5880
181 Constitution Dr Menlo Park (94025) ***(P-23898)***
Lifepoint Health Inc ....C....760 326-7100
1401 Bailey Ave Needles (92363) ***(P-21554)***
Lifeproof, San Diego *Also called Treefrog Developments Inc* ***(P-8063)***
Liferay Inc (PA) ....D....877 543-3729
1400 Montefino Ave # 100 Diamond Bar (91765) ***(P-15996)***
Lifesigns Now (PA) ....B....323 550-4210
2222 Laverna Ave Fl 1 Los Angeles (90041) ***(P-17295)***
Lifespan Care Management Agcy, Santa Cruz *Also called Lifespan Inc* ***(P-24801)***
Lifespan Inc ....D....831 469-4900
600 Frederick St Santa Cruz (95062) ***(P-24801)***
Lifestream, San Bernardino *Also called Blood Bank of San Bernardino A* ***(P-22747)***
Lifestreet Corporation ....D....650 508-2220
981 Industrial Rd Ste F San Carlos (94070) ***(P-9231)***
Lifestreet Media, San Carlos *Also called Lifestreet Corporation* ***(P-9231)***
Lifestyles Senior Housing Man ....D....916 714-3755
9325 E Stockton Blvd Elk Grove (95624) ***(P-23899)***
Lifetech Resources LLC ....E....818 885-1199
700 Science Dr Moorpark (93021) ***(P-8187)***
Lifetime Entrmt Svcs LLC ....D....310 556-7500
2049 Century Park E # 840 Los Angeles (90067) ***(P-5820)***
Lifetime TV Network, Los Angeles *Also called Lifetime Entrmt Svcs LLC* ***(P-5820)***

ALPHABETIC

Employee Codes: A=Over 500 employees, B=251-500
C=101-250, D=51-100, E=50
2019 Directory of California
Wholesalers and Services Companies
© Mergent Inc. 1-800-342-5647
1367

Lifetouch Inc.......D.......916 535-7733
7916 Alta Sunrise Ln Citrus Heights (95610) ***(P-13640)***
Lifetouch Nat Schl Studios Inc.......E.......510 293-1818
30351 Huntwood Ave Hayward (94544) ***(P-13641)***
Lifetouch Portrait Studios Inc.......E.......858 693-9197
9770 Carroll Centre Rd C San Diego (92126) ***(P-13642)***
Light House Group, The, Pacific Palisades *Also called Lighthouse Capital Funding* ***(P-12240)***
Light Rail, Sacramento *Also called Sacramento Regional Trnst Dist* ***(P-3955)***
Lightbeam Power Company Gridle.......D.......800 696-7114
100 Century Center Ct # 100 San Jose (95112) ***(P-1946)***
Lightbeam Pwr Gridley Main LLC.......D.......800 696-7114
100 Century Center Ct # 100 San Jose (95112) ***(P-1947)***
Lightbend Inc.......D.......877 989-7372
625 Market St Ste 1000 San Francisco (94105) ***(P-15258)***
Lightbrdge Hspice Plltive Care, San Diego *Also called Lightbridge Hospice LLC* ***(P-22029)***
Lightbridge Hospice LLC.......D.......858 458-2992
6155 Cornerstone Ct E San Diego (92121) ***(P-22029)***
Lightcrest LLC.......E.......888 320-8495
1112 Montana Ave Ste 705 Santa Monica (90403) ***(P-15997)***
Lighthouse Capital Funding.......E.......310 230-8335
15332 Antioch St Ste 540 Pacific Palisades (90272) ***(P-12240)***
Lighthouse Healthcare Ctr LLC.......D.......323 564-4461
2222 Santa Ana S Los Angeles (90059) ***(P-20591)***
Lighthouse Living Services (PA).......D.......916 454-4381
3600 Power Inn Rd Ste H Sacramento (95826) ***(P-23900)***
Lighting Department, Burbank *Also called Walt Disney Company* ***(P-5849)***
Lightwaves 2020 Inc.......E.......408 503-8888
1323 Great Mall Dr Milpitas (95035) ***(P-26412)***
Lilien LLC (HQ).......E.......415 389-7500
17 E Sir Francis Dr # 110 Larkspur (94939) ***(P-15998)***
Lily Holdings LLC.......D.......559 222-4807
3510 E Shields Ave Fresno (93726) ***(P-20592)***
Limbach Company LP.......C.......714 653-7000
1709 Apollo Ct Seal Beach (90740) ***(P-2263)***
Liminex Inc.......D.......310 963-3031
200 N Supulveda Blvd Ste Hermosa Beach (90254) ***(P-15259)***
Limoneira Company (PA).......C.......805 525-5541
1141 Cummings Rd Ofc Santa Paula (93060) ***(P-536)***
Linardos Enterprises Inc.......D.......415 644-0827
75 Broadway San Francisco (94111) ***(P-27304)***
Lincoln (PA).......D.......510 273-4700
1266 14th St Oakland (94607) ***(P-22613)***
Lincoln Child Center.......C.......510 531-3111
1266 14th St Oakland (94607) ***(P-25439)***
Lincoln Child Center Inc.......D.......925 521-1270
51 Marina Blvd Pittsburg (94565) ***(P-24579)***
Lincoln Glen Manor.......C.......408 267-1492
2671 Plummer Ave Ste A San Jose (95125) ***(P-21136)***
LINCOLN GLEN SKILLED NURSING, San Jose *Also called Lincoln Glen Manor* ***(P-21136)***
Lincoln Hills Golf Club.......E.......916 543-9200
1005 Sun City Ln Lincoln (95648) ***(P-18728)***
Lincoln Mariners Assoc Ltd.......D.......619 225-1473
4392 W Point Loma Blvd San Diego (92107) ***(P-11055)***
Lincoln Medical Offices, Lincoln *Also called Kaiser Foundation Hospitals* ***(P-19565)***
Lincoln Plaza Hotel Inc.......D.......626 571-8818
123 S Lincoln Ave Monterey Park (91755) ***(P-12855)***
Lincoln Products, City of Industry *Also called Ferguson Enterprises Inc* ***(P-7618)***
Lincoln School Bus Trnsp.......D.......209 953-8596
6749 Harrisburg Pl Stockton (95207) ***(P-3879)***
Lincoln Television Inc.......D.......415 468-2626
100 Valley Dr Brisbane (94005) ***(P-5821)***
Lincoln Training Center and RE.......D.......626 442-0621
2643 Loma Ave South El Monte (91733) ***(P-24200)***
Lincoln Witt Mercury.......D.......760 233-3333
728 N Escondido Blvd Escondido (92025) ***(P-17770)***
Linda Beach Coop Pre-School.......E.......510 547-4432
400 Highland Ave Piedmont (94611) ***(P-24338)***
Linda Loma Univ Hlth Care (HQ).......D.......909 558-2806
11370 Anderson St # 3900 Loma Linda (92350) ***(P-21555)***
Linda Loma Univ Hlth Care.......C.......909 558-2851
11370 Anderson St # 2100 Loma Linda (92354) ***(P-19651)***
Linda Loma Univ Hlth Care (PA).......A.......909 558-4729
11175 Campus St Loma Linda (92350) ***(P-19652)***
Linda Loma Univ Hlth Care.......C.......909 558-2840
11370 Anderson St # 3950 Loma Linda (92354) ***(P-19653)***
Linda Mar Care Center, Pacifica *Also called Pacifica Linda Mar Inc* ***(P-20688)***
Linda Placentia-Yorba.......D.......714 985-8775
1301 E Orangethorpe Ave Placentia (92870) ***(P-4585)***
Linda Terra Farms (PA).......C.......559 867-3473
5494 W Mount Whitney Ave Riverdale (93656) ***(P-403)***
Linda Valley Care Center, Loma Linda *Also called Chancellor Hlth Care Cal I Inc* ***(P-21036)***
LINDA VISTA HEALTH CARE CENTER, San Diego *Also called San Diego Family Care* ***(P-19842)***
Linda Vista Manor Inc.......C.......858 278-8121
7675 Family Cir San Diego (92111) ***(P-20593)***
Linda Yorba Water District (PA).......D.......714 701-3000
1717 E Miraloma Ave Placentia (92870) ***(P-6272)***
Lindamood-Bell Lrng Processes (PA).......C.......805 541-3836
406 Higuera St Ste 120 San Luis Obispo (93401) ***(P-24339)***
Lindbergh Parking Inc.......C.......619 291-1508
3705 N Harbor Dr San Diego (92101) ***(P-17692)***
Lindburgh Child Development, Costa Mesa *Also called Orange Cnty Sprntndent Schools* ***(P-24361)***
Linden Center.......D.......213 251-8226
816 N Fairfax Ave Los Angeles (90046) ***(P-21963)***
LINDEN CENTER BUSINESS OFC, Los Angeles *Also called Linden Center* ***(P-21963)***
Linden Crest Surgery Center.......D.......310 601-3900
9735 Wilshire Blvd # 100 Beverly Hills (90212) ***(P-19654)***
Linden Lab, San Francisco *Also called Linden Research Inc* ***(P-15260)***
Linden Nut, Stockton *Also called Pearl Crop Inc* ***(P-553)***
Linden Optometry A Prof Corp.......D.......323 681-5678
477 E Colorado Blvd Pasadena (91101) ***(P-20158)***
Linden Research Inc.......B.......415 243-9000
945 Battery St San Francisco (94111) ***(P-15260)***
Lindhurst Dental Clinic.......E.......530 743-4614
4941 Olivehurst Ave Olivehurst (95961) ***(P-20126)***
Lindhurst Family Health Center, Olivehurst *Also called Ampla Health* ***(P-19289)***
Lindley Fire Protection Co.......E.......714 535-5761
2220 E Via Burton Anaheim (92806) ***(P-2264)***
Lindo Hanna & Abbott, Chico *Also called Interwest Insurance Svcs LLC* ***(P-10656)***
Lindquist LLP (PA).......D.......925 277-9100
5000 Executive Pkwy # 400 San Ramon (94583) ***(P-26246)***
Lindsay Fruit Company LLC.......D.......559 562-1327
247 N Mount Vernon Ave Lindsay (93247) ***(P-17296)***
Lindsay Transportation.......C.......707 374-6800
180 River Rd Rio Vista (94571) ***(P-7762)***
Lindsay Trnsp Solutions, Rio Vista *Also called Lindsay Transportation* ***(P-7762)***
Lindsay Wildlife Museum.......D.......925 935-1978
1931 1st Ave Walnut Creek (94597) ***(P-24887)***
Line Hotel, The, Los Angeles *Also called Sydell Hotels LLC* ***(P-13314)***
Lineage Logistics LLC.......C.......323 583-3163
2045 E Vernon Ave Vernon (90058) ***(P-4505)***
Lineage Logistics LLC.......E.......951 360-7970
3251 De Forest Cir Ste C Mira Loma (91752) ***(P-4506)***
Lineage Logistics Holdings LLC (PA).......C.......800 678-7271
1 Park Plz Ste 550 Irvine (92614) ***(P-4507)***
Lineage Logistics Holdings LLC.......A.......909 433-3100
1 Park Plz Ste 550 Irvine (92614) ***(P-4356)***
Lineage Logistics Holdings LLC.......A.......909 874-1200
2551 S Lilac Ave Bloomington (92316) ***(P-4357)***
Lineage Logistics Icm LLC.......C.......972 462-0042
1 Park Plz Ste 550 Irvine (92614) ***(P-4508)***
Linear Industries Ltd (PA).......D.......626 303-1130
1850 Enterprise Way Monrovia (91016) ***(P-7856)***
Liner Law, Los Angeles *Also called Liner LLP* ***(P-23216)***
Liner LLP.......C.......310 500-3500
1100 Glendon Ave 14th Los Angeles (90024) ***(P-23216)***
Ling's, South El Monte *Also called Out of Shell LLC* ***(P-1426)***
Linkedin Corporation (HQ).......C.......650 687-3600
1000 W Maude Ave Sunnyvale (94085) ***(P-16236)***
Links Sgn Lngg Intrprtng, Shrd, Long Beach *Also called Goodwill Srvng The Ppl of Sthr* ***(P-17197)***
Linksys LLC.......C.......310 751-5100
12045 Waterfront Dr Playa Vista (90094) ***(P-7503)***
Linksys LLC (HQ).......B.......949 270-8500
131 Theory Irvine (92617) ***(P-7504)***
Linkus Enterprises LLC.......B.......559 256-6600
5595 W San Madele Ave Fresno (93722) ***(P-1948)***
Linkus Enterprises LLC (PA).......C.......530 229-9197
18631 Lloyd Ln Anderson (96007) ***(P-1949)***
Linnco LLC.......A.......661 616-3900
5201 Truxtun Ave Bakersfield (93309) ***(P-1024)***
Linne Entertainment LLC.......E.......213 425-1146
1250 N June St Apt 305 Los Angeles (90038) ***(P-18069)***
Linquest Corporation (PA).......C.......323 924-1600
5140 W Goldleaf Cir # 400 Los Angeles (90056) ***(P-25797)***
Linwood Grdns Convalescent Ctr, Visalia *Also called Far West Inc* ***(P-20424)***
Linwood Nursery, La Grange *Also called Green Tree Nursery* ***(P-9137)***
Lion Brothers Farms-Newstone, Madera *Also called Lion Raisins Inc* ***(P-366)***
Lion Creek Crossing V, Oakland *Also called Lion Creek Senior Housing Part* ***(P-11565)***
Lion Creek Senior Housing Part.......D.......510 878-9120
6710 Lion Way Oakland (94621) ***(P-11565)***
Lion Raisins Inc.......C.......559 662-8686
12555 Road 9 Madera (93637) ***(P-366)***
Lion-Vallen Ltd Partnership.......E.......760 385-4885
22 Area Aven A Bldg 2234 Camp Pendleton (92055) ***(P-26935)***
Lionakis.......C.......949 955-1919
20371 Irvine Ave Ste 120 Newport Beach (92660) ***(P-25798)***
Lionakis (PA).......C.......916 558-1901
1919 19th St Sacramento (95811) ***(P-25799)***
Lions Gate Entertainment Inc (HQ).......D.......310 449-9200
2700 Colorado Ave Ste 200 Santa Monica (90404) ***(P-18070)***
Lions Gate Films Inc.......C.......310 449-9200
2700 Colorado Ave Ste 200 Santa Monica (90404) ***(P-18071)***
Lionsgate Ht & Conference Ctr.......D.......916 643-6222
3410 Westover St McClellan (95652) ***(P-12856)***
Lipman Insur Admnistrators Inc (PA).......D.......510 796-4676
39420 Liberty St Ste 260 Fremont (94538) ***(P-10486)***
Lippin Group Inc (PA).......E.......323 965-1990
6100 Wilshire Blvd # 400 Los Angeles (90048) ***(P-27562)***
Liquid Investments Inc (PA).......C.......858 509-8510
3840 Via De La Valle # 300 Del Mar (92014) ***(P-9009)***
Liquidate Direct LLC.......E.......800 750-7617
2929 Washington Blvd Fl 2 Marina Del Rey (90292) ***(P-15999)***
Liquidity Services Inc.......D.......714 738-6446
741 E Ball Rd Ste 200 Anaheim (92805) ***(P-8268)***
Lisi Inc (PA).......C.......650 348-4131
1600 W Hillsdale Blvd # 100 San Mateo (94402) ***(P-10673)***
Lisi Inc.......D.......714 460-5153
2677 N Main St Ste 350 Santa Ana (92705) ***(P-10503)***
Lisi Aerospace North Amer Inc (HQ).......A.......310 326-8110
2602 Skypark Dr Torrance (90505) ***(P-4586)***
Lite Solar Corp.......C.......562 256-1249
3553 Atlantic Ave Long Beach (90807) ***(P-2265)***
Lite-On Inc (HQ).......E.......408 946-4873
720 S Hillview Dr Milpitas (95035) ***(P-7505)***

Mergent e-mail: customerrelations@mergent.com
1368
2019 Directory of California Wholesalers and Services Companies
(P-0000) Products & Services Section entry number
(PA)=Parent Co (HQ)=Headquarters (DH)=Div Headquarters

Lite-On Sales and Dist Inc ....D....510 687-1800
726 S Hillview Dr Milpitas (95035) ***(P-7071)***
Lite-On U S A, Milpitas *Also called Lite-On Inc* ***(P-7505)***
Lithia Automotive Group Inc ....E....209 956-6500
1020 S Beckman Rd Lodi (95240) ***(P-17865)***
Lithia Motors Inc ....E....209 956-1930
3077 E Hammer Ln Stockton (95212) ***(P-17771)***
Lithium Technologies LLC (PA) ....D....415 757-3100
1 Pier Ste 1 # 1 San Francisco (94111) ***(P-15742)***
Litigtion Rsrces of America-CA (PA) ....D....818 878-9227
4232-1 Las Virgenes Rd Calabasas (91302) ***(P-17297)***
Little Citizens Schools Inc ....D....323 732-1212
4256 S Western Ave Los Angeles (90062) ***(P-24340)***
Little Co Mary Hosp Pavilion, Torrance *Also called Providence Health System* ***(P-12122)***
Little Company Mary Hospital ....A....310 540-7676
4101 Torrance Blvd Torrance (90503) ***(P-21556)***
Little Giant Bldg Maint Inc ....C....415 508-0282
15 Brooks Pl Pacifica (94044) ***(P-14304)***
Little Mary Amblatory Care Ctr, Torrance *Also called Del AMO Diagnostic Center* ***(P-22565)***
Little Peoples ....D....951 849-1959
39514 Brookside Ave Cherry Valley (92223) ***(P-24580)***
Little Peoples World Inc ....E....951 845-8367
39514 Brookside Ave Cherry Valley (92223) ***(P-24581)***
Little River Inn Inc ....D....707 937-5942
7901 N Highway 1 Little River (95456) ***(P-12857)***
Little River Inn and Golf Crse, Little River *Also called Little River Inn Inc* ***(P-12857)***
Little Sister's Truck Wash, Fallbrook *Also called Little Sisters Truck Wash Inc* ***(P-17829)***
Little Sisters of Poor ....C....415 751-6510
300 Lake St San Francisco (94118) ***(P-24582)***
Little Sisters The Poor of La ....D....310 548-0625
2100 S Western Ave San Pedro (90732) ***(P-20594)***
Little Sisters Truck Wash Inc ....D....760 343-3448
72189 Varner Rd Thousand Palms (92276) ***(P-17825)***
Little Sisters Truck Wash Inc ....D....760 947-4448
8899 Three Flags Ave Oak Hills (92344) ***(P-17826)***
Little Sisters Truck Wash Inc ....D....909 549-1862
14264 Valley Blvd Fontana (92335) ***(P-17827)***
Little Sisters Truck Wash Inc ....D....760 253-2277
2960 Lenwood Rd Barstow (92311) ***(P-17828)***
Little Sisters Truck Wash Inc (PA) ....D....760 731-3170
25 Rolling View Ln Fallbrook (92028) ***(P-17829)***
Little Tokyo Service Center (PA) ....C....213 473-3003
231 E 3rd St Ste G106 Los Angeles (90013) ***(P-23901)***
Littler Mendelson PC (PA) ....B....415 433-1940
333 Bush St Fl 34 San Francisco (94104) ***(P-23217)***
Live International, Santa Monica *Also called Artisan Pictures Inc* ***(P-8018)***
Live Media LLC ....E....951 279-8877
1580 Magnolia Ave Corona (92879) ***(P-18446)***
Live Nation Entertainment Inc ....D....323 468-1160
6255 W Sunset Blvd Fl 16 Los Angeles (90028) ***(P-18447)***
Live Nation Entertainment Inc ....D....213 639-6178
7060 Hollywood Blvd Ste 2 Los Angeles (90028) ***(P-18380)***
Live Nation Entertainment Inc ....D....323 462-4785
151 El Camino Dr Fl 3 Beverly Hills (90212) ***(P-17298)***
Live Nation Entertainment Inc (PA) ....C....310 867-7000
9348 Civic Center Dr Lbby Beverly Hills (90210) ***(P-17299)***
Live Nation Merchandise Inc (HQ) ....E....415 247-7400
450 Mission St Ste 300 San Francisco (94105) ***(P-9232)***
Live Nation Worldwide Inc ....C....323 966-5066
6500 Wilshire Blvd # 200 Los Angeles (90048) ***(P-18381)***
Live Nation Worldwide Inc ....A....310 867-7000
9348 Civic Center Dr Lbby Beverly Hills (90210) ***(P-18382)***
Live Oak Rehab, San Gabriel *Also called Longwood Management Corp* ***(P-21144)***
Live Pos, La Jolla *Also called CSS Holdings Inc* ***(P-15090)***
Liveoffice LLC ....D....877 253-2793
900 Corporate Pointe Culver City (90230) ***(P-15743)***
Livermore Area Rcration Pk Dst ....C....925 373-5700
71 Trevarno Rd Livermore (94551) ***(P-19196)***
Livermore Area Rcration Pk Dst (PA) ....B....925 373-5700
4444 East Ave Livermore (94550) ***(P-19197)***
Livermore Casino, Livermore *Also called Sidjon Corporation* ***(P-13225)***
Livermore Snior Lving Assoc LP ....E....925 371-2300
900 E Stanley Blvd # 383 Livermore (94550) ***(P-11990)***
Livermore VA Medical Center, Livermore *Also called Veterans Health Administration* ***(P-20077)***
Livermore Valley Tennis Club ....D....925 443-7700
2000 Arroyo Rd Livermore (94550) ***(P-18626)***
Livescribe Inc ....E....503 290-4029
930 Roosevelt Irvine (92620) ***(P-7072)***
Livetime Software Inc ....E....415 905-4009
276 Avocado St Apt C102 Costa Mesa (92627) ***(P-15744)***
Livevox Inc (PA) ....D....415 671-6000
655 Montgomery St # 1190 San Francisco (94111) ***(P-27776)***
Livhome Inc (PA) ....A....800 807-5854
5670 Wilshire Blvd # 500 Los Angeles (90036) ***(P-22358)***
Living Centers, Vallejo *Also called Empres Financial Services LLC* ***(P-20392)***
Living Colors Inc ....D....818 893-5068
16026 Rayen St North Hills (91343) ***(P-2455)***
Living Desert ....C....760 346-5694
47900 Portola Ave Palm Desert (92260) ***(P-24930)***
Living Doll, La Puente *Also called Ldla Clothing LLC* ***(P-8314)***
Living Opportunities MGT Co ....C....323 589-5956
6900 Seville Ave Huntington Park (90255) ***(P-11056)***
Livingston Community Health ....C....209 394-7913
1140 Main St Livingston (95334) ***(P-19655)***
Livingston Mem Vna Hlth Corp ....C....805 642-0239
1996 Eastman Ave Ste 101 Ventura (93003) ***(P-26936)***
Livingston Mem Vst Nrs Associa, Ventura *Also called Livingston Mem Vna Hlth Corp* ***(P-26936)***
Livingston Ranch, Livingston *Also called E & J Gallo Winery* ***(P-686)***
Lj Distributors Inc ....D....562 229-7660
12840 Leyva St Norwalk (90650) ***(P-8703)***
LJ Walch Co Inc ....D....925 449-9252
6600 Preston Ave Livermore (94551) ***(P-7910)***
LJC Construction Inc ....D....209 668-2700
712 W Harding Rd Turlock (95380) ***(P-3174)***
LL Frank Work Center, Los Angeles *Also called Abilityfirst* ***(P-23456)***
LLC Brewer Crane ....D....619 390-8252
12570 Highway 67 Bldg 10 Lakeside (92040) ***(P-14445)***
Llieche, Loma Linda *Also called Loma Linda - Inland Empire C* ***(P-21559)***
Lloyd Pest Control Co (PA) ....C....619 298-9865
935 Sherman St San Diego (92110) ***(P-14152)***
Lloyd Pest Control Co ....E....714 979-6021
566 E Dyer Rd Santa Ana (92707) ***(P-14153)***
Lloyd W Aubry Co Inc (PA) ....D....510 732-9038
2148 Dunn Rd Hayward (94545) ***(P-3472)***
LLP Downey Brand ....D....775 329-5900
621 Capitol Mall Fl 18 Sacramento (95814) ***(P-23218)***
LLP Locke Lord ....C....415 318-8800
101 Montgomery St # 1950 San Francisco (94104) ***(P-23219)***
LLP Locke Lord ....C....213 485-1500
300 S Grand Ave Ste 2600 Los Angeles (90071) ***(P-23220)***
LLP Locke Lord ....D....949 423-2100
660 Nwport Ctr Dr Ste 900 Newport Beach (92660) ***(P-23221)***
LLP Mayer Brown ....A....650 331-2000
2 Palo Alto Sq Ste 300 Palo Alto (94306) ***(P-23222)***
LLP Mayer Brown ....C....213 229-9500
350 S Grand Ave Ste 2500 Los Angeles (90071) ***(P-23223)***
LLP Moss Adams ....D....916 503-8100
2882 Prospect Park Dr # 300 Rancho Cordova (95670) ***(P-26247)***
LLP Moss Adams ....D....818 577-1822
21700 Oxnard St Ste 300 Woodland Hills (91367) ***(P-26248)***
LLP Moss Adams ....E....209 955-6100
3121 W March Ln Ste 100 Stockton (95219) ***(P-26249)***
LLP Moss Adams ....C....415 956-1500
101 2nd St Ste 900 San Francisco (94105) ***(P-26250)***
LLP Moss Adams ....C....408 369-2400
635 Campbell Tech Pkwy # 100 Campbell (95008) ***(P-26251)***
LLP Moss Adams ....D....707 224-4001
1000 Main St NAPA (94559) ***(P-27305)***
LLP Moss Adams ....E....949 221-4000
2040 Main St Ste 900 Irvine (92614) ***(P-26252)***
LLP Moss Adams ....D....858 627-1400
4747 Executive Dr # 1300 San Diego (92121) ***(P-26253)***
LLP Robins Kaplan ....D....310 552-0130
2049 Century Park E # 3400 Los Angeles (90067) ***(P-23224)***
Llu Advntist Hlth Sciences Ctr ....D....909 558-4386
101 E Redlands Blvd San Bernardino (92408) ***(P-19656)***
Llu Center For Fertility, Loma Linda *Also called Linda Loma Univ Hlth Care* ***(P-19653)***
Llumc, Loma Linda *Also called Loma Linda University Med Ctr* ***(P-21561)***
Lmb Mortgage Services Inc ....C....310 348-6800
4859 W Slauson Ave # 405 Los Angeles (90056) ***(P-9827)***
LMC Hollywood Highland ....B....949 448-1600
95 Enterprise Ste 200 Aliso Viejo (92656) ***(P-1582)***
LMC West Inc ....E....209 869-0144
5300 Claus Rd Riverbank (95367) ***(P-7763)***
Lmno Cable Group, Encino *Also called Lmno Productions Inc* ***(P-18072)***
Lmno Productions Inc ....C....818 995-5555
15821 Ventura Blvd # 320 Encino (91436) ***(P-18072)***
LMS Corporation ....E....310 641-4222
300 Crprate Pinte Ste 301 Culver City (90230) ***(P-17300)***
LN Curtis and Sons (PA) ....D....510 839-5111
1800 Peralta St Oakland (94607) ***(P-7889)***
Lo Bue Bros Inc ....C....559 562-6367
713 E Hermosa St Lindsay (93247) ***(P-537)***
Lo Bue Bros East, Lindsay *Also called Lo Bue Bros Inc* ***(P-537)***
Loan Administration Netwrk Inc ....D....949 752-5246
18952 Macarthur Blvd # 315 Irvine (92612) ***(P-14663)***
Loan Depot Group, Woodland Hills *Also called Realty Alliance Inc* ***(P-9905)***
Loan Now ....D....714 352-2250
3100 S Harbor Blvd # 180 Santa Ana (92704) ***(P-9719)***
Loandepotcom LLC ....A....760 797-6000
901 N Palm Canyon Dr Palm Springs (92262) ***(P-9828)***
Loandepotcom LLC (PA) ....A....949 474-1322
26642 Towne Centre Dr Foothill Ranch (92610) ***(P-9829)***
Lobel Financial Corporation (PA) ....D....714 995-3333
1150 N Magnolia Ave Anaheim (92801) ***(P-9720)***
Local 250 Health Care Wkrs Un, Oakland *Also called Health Care Workers Union* ***(P-10894)***
Local 442, Santa Barbara *Also called International Alliance Thea* ***(P-25061)***
Local Corporation (PA) ....D....949 784-0800
7555 Irvine Center Dr Irvine (92618) ***(P-13857)***
Local Initiative Health Author ....A....213 694-1250
1055 W 7th St Fl 10 Los Angeles (90017) ***(P-10279)***
Local Media San Diego LLC ....D....858 888-7000
6160 Cornerstone Ct E # 150 San Diego (92121) ***(P-5743)***
Local.com, Irvine *Also called Local Corporation* ***(P-13857)***
Location Labs Inc ....D....510 601-7012
2100 Powell St Fl 14 Emeryville (94608) ***(P-15261)***
Location Services LLC (PA) ....D....800 588-0097
2365 Iron Point Rd # 160 Folsom (95630) ***(P-5234)***
Locator Services Inc ....C....619 229-6100
4616 Mission Gorge Pl San Diego (92120) ***(P-16720)***
Lockheed Martin Corporation ....C....415 402-0406
255 California St Ste 400 San Francisco (94111) ***(P-25800)***
Lockheed Martin Government Ser ....E....323 721-6979
500 N Via Val Verde Montebello (90640) ***(P-16420)***

ALPHABETIC

Lockheed Martin Orincon Corp (HQ) ....C....858 455-5530
10325 Meanley Dr San Diego (92131) ***(P-15262)***
Lockton Companies LLC- Pacifi (HQ) ....B....213 689-0500
725 S Figueroa St Fl 35 Los Angeles (90017) ***(P-10674)***
Lockton Insurance Brokers, Los Angeles *Also called Lockton Companies LLC-Pacifi* ***(P-10674)***
Locums Unlimited LLC ....B....619 550-3763
4141 Jutland Dr Ste 305 San Diego (92117) ***(P-20189)***
Lodge At Tiburon, The, Belvedere Tiburon *Also called Tiburon Hotel LLC* ***(P-13326)***
Lodge At Torrey Pines Partners ....B....858 550-3908
998 W Mission Bay Dr San Diego (92109) ***(P-12858)***
Lodge Inn and Health Center, Chico *Also called Terraces Retirement Community* ***(P-24696)***
Lodgen Lacher Golditch Sard ....E....818 783-0570
16530 Ventura Blvd # 305 Encino (91436) ***(P-26254)***
Lodgeworks LP ....D....707 690-9800
1230 1st St NAPA (94559) ***(P-12859)***
Lodi Development Inc ....E....209 367-7600
1420 S Mills Ave Ste E Lodi (95242) ***(P-11885)***
Lodi Memorial Hosp Assn Inc (HQ) ....A....209 334-3411
975 S Fairmont Ave Lodi (95240) ***(P-21557)***
Lodi Memorial Hosp Assn Inc ....E....209 339-7583
1200 W Vine St Lodi (95240) ***(P-21558)***
Lodi Memorial Hosp Assn Inc ....C....209 333-3100
800 S Lower Sacramento Rd Lodi (95242) ***(P-19657)***
Lodi Unified School District ....D....209 331-7181
1305 E Vine St Lodi (95240) ***(P-14305)***
Lodi Unified School District ....C....209 331-7169
820 S Cuff Ave Lodi (95240) ***(P-3940)***
Loeb & Loeb LLP (PA) ....C....310 282-2000
10100 Santa Monica Blvd # 2200 Los Angeles (90067) ***(P-23225)***
Loews Coronado Bay Resort, Coronado *Also called 51st St & 8th Ave Corp* ***(P-12296)***
Loews Corporation ....B....619 424-4000
4000 Coronado Bay Rd Coronado (92118) ***(P-23226)***
Loews Hollywood Hotel LLC ....B....323 450-2235
1755 N Highland Ave Hollywood (90028) ***(P-12860)***
Loews Regency San Francisco, San Francisco *Also called San Francisco Hotel Group LLC* ***(P-13174)***
Loews Santa Monica Beach Hotel, Santa Monica *Also called Dtrs Santa Monica LLC* ***(P-12543)***
Loewy Enterprises ....D....323 726-3838
500 Burning Tree Rd Fullerton (92833) ***(P-8704)***
Logcap IV - Task Order 7, Fort Irwin *Also called Dyncorp International LLC* ***(P-4887)***
Logicmonitor Inc (PA) ....C....805 617-3884
820 State St Fl 5 Santa Barbara (93101) ***(P-16237)***
Logictier Inc ....C....650 235-6600
7 41st Ave 76 San Mateo (94403) ***(P-16421)***
Logility Inc ....D....858 565-4238
4885 Greencraig Ln 200 San Diego (92123) ***(P-15263)***
Login Consulting Services Inc ....D....310 607-9091
300 Continental Blvd # 530 El Segundo (90245) ***(P-16422)***
Logistical Support LLC ....C....818 341-3344
20409 Prairie St Chatsworth (91311) ***(P-7911)***
Logistics Team, Walnut *Also called Amerifreight Inc* ***(P-4529)***
Logitech Ice At San Jose ....E....408 279-6000
1500 S 10th St San Jose (95112) ***(P-19198)***
Logix Development Corporation ....D....888 505-6449
473 Post St Camarillo (93010) ***(P-15264)***
Logix Federal Credit Union (PA) ....C....888 718-5328
2340 N Hollywood Way Burbank (91505) ***(P-9567)***
Loglogic Inc ....C....408 215-5900
110 Rose Orchard Way San Jose (95134) ***(P-15265)***
Logo Design Pros, San Francisco *Also called Lateral Designs Inc* ***(P-14119)***
Logo Expressions, Ontario *Also called Dennis Foland Inc* ***(P-8027)***
Logomark Inc ....C....714 675-6100
1201 Bell Ave Tustin (92780) ***(P-9233)***
Lois Lauer Realty ....C....909 748-7000
1998 Orange Tree Ln Redlands (92374) ***(P-11566)***
Loma Cleaning Service, Fremont *Also called ISS Facility Services Inc* ***(P-14292)***
Loma Linda - Inland Empire C ....C....909 651-5832
11175 Campus St Csp 11006 11006 Csp Loma Linda (92354) ***(P-21559)***
Loma Linda Catering Center, Loma Linda *Also called Loma Linda University Med Ctr* ***(P-21562)***
Loma Linda Community Hospital, Loma Linda *Also called Loma Linda University Med Ctr* ***(P-21565)***
Loma Linda Faculty Med Group, Loma Linda *Also called Linda Loma Univ Hlth Care* ***(P-19651)***
Loma Linda Healthcare Sys 605, Loma Linda *Also called Veterans Health Administration* ***(P-20078)***
Loma Linda Pharmacy, Loma Linda *Also called Loma Linda University Med Ctr* ***(P-21564)***
Loma Linda University ....D....909 558-6422
1911 W Park Ave Redlands (92373) ***(P-19658)***
Loma Linda University Med Ctr ....C....909 558-2100
11370 Anderson St 2100 Loma Linda (92350) ***(P-21560)***
Loma Linda University Med Ctr (HQ) ....A....909 558-4000
11234 Anderson St Loma Linda (92354) ***(P-21561)***
Loma Linda University Med Ctr ....D....909 558-8244
11175 Campus St Loma Linda (92350) ***(P-21562)***
Loma Linda University Med Ctr ....B....909 558-9275
1710 Barton Rd Redlands (92373) ***(P-21563)***
Loma Linda University Med Ctr ....C....909 558-4216
11223 Campus St Loma Linda (92354) ***(P-21564)***
Loma Linda University Med Ctr ....C....909 558-3096
11265 Mountain View Ave E Loma Linda (92354) ***(P-22359)***
Loma Linda University Med Ctr ....C....909 796-0167
25333 Barton Rd Loma Linda (92350) ***(P-21565)***
Loma Linda University Med Ctr ....A....877 558-6248
11234 Anderson St Loma Linda (92354) ***(P-19659)***
Loma Linda Vet Association For ....D....909 583-6250
710 Brookside Ave Ste 2 Redlands (92373) ***(P-25191)***
Loma Riviera Community Assn ....D....619 224-1313
9610 Waples St San Diego (92121) ***(P-25192)***
Loma Vista Nursery ....D....714 779-5583
18272 Bastanchury Rd Yorba Linda (92886) ***(P-9144)***
Loma Vista Nursery 2, Yorba Linda *Also called Loma Vista Nursery* ***(P-9144)***
Lomas Santa Fe Country Club, Solana Beach *Also called American Golf Corporation* ***(P-18826)***
Lombardo Diamnd Core Drlg Inc ....D....408 727-7922
2225 De La Cruz Blvd Santa Clara (95050) ***(P-3283)***
Lombardy Holdings Inc (PA) ....C....951 808-4550
151 Kalmus Dr Ste F6 Costa Mesa (92626) ***(P-1950)***
Lomita Care Center, Lomita *Also called Lomita Verde Inc* ***(P-21137)***
Lomita Medical Offices, Lomita *Also called Kaiser Foundation Hospitals* ***(P-19567)***
Lomita Verde Inc ....D....310 325-1970
1955 Lomita Blvd Lomita (90717) ***(P-21137)***
Lompoc Act, Lompoc *Also called Transitions - Mental Hlth Assn* ***(P-22699)***
Lompoc Convlsnt Care Ctr, Lompoc *Also called Lompoc Valley Medical Center* ***(P-21138)***
Lompoc Family YMCA, Lompoc *Also called Channel Islands Young Mens Ch* ***(P-25130)***
Lompoc Honda Body Shop, Lompoc *Also called Zikakis Auto Holdings LLC* ***(P-17747)***
LOMPOC SKILLED CARE CENTER, Lompoc *Also called Lompoc Valley Medical Center* ***(P-21566)***
Lompoc Skilled Nursing & Rehab, Lompoc *Also called Ghc of Lompoc LLC* ***(P-22583)***
Lompoc Valley Medical Center (PA) ....A....805 737-3300
1515 E Ocean Ave Lompoc (93436) ***(P-21566)***
Lompoc Valley Medical Center ....C....805 736-3466
216 N 3rd St Lompoc (93436) ***(P-21138)***
Lone Cypress Company LLC ....A....831 624-3811
17 Mile Dr Pebble Beach (93953) ***(P-12861)***
Lone Cypress Company LLC ....D....831 625-8507
1567 Cypress Dr Pebble Beach (93953) ***(P-18958)***
Lone Oak Farms ....C....559 583-1277
2911 Hanford Armona Rd Hanford (93230) ***(P-367)***
Lone Tree Convalescent Hosp ....C....925 754-0470
4001 Lone Tree Way Antioch (94509) ***(P-20595)***
LONE TREE GOLF COURSE, Antioch *Also called Antioch Public Golf Corp* ***(P-18686)***
Lonestar Sierra LLC ....C....866 575-5680
1820 W Orangewood Ave Orange (92868) ***(P-7857)***
Long & Levit LLP ....E....415 397-2222
465 California St Ste 500 San Francisco (94104) ***(P-23227)***
Long Bch Convention Entrmt Ctr, Long Beach *Also called City of Long Beach* ***(P-17079)***
Long Bch Museum Art Foundation ....D....562 439-2119
2300 E Ocean Blvd Long Beach (90803) ***(P-24888)***
Long Bch Unfied Schl Dst Lbusd, Long Beach *Also called Long Beach Unified School Dst* ***(P-14664)***
Long Beach Airport, Long Beach *Also called City of Long Beach* ***(P-4877)***
Long Beach Behavioral Health U ....D....310 221-6336
3200 Long Beach Blvd Long Beach (90807) ***(P-22835)***
Long Beach Cap, Long Beach *Also called Long Beach Cmnty Action Partnr* ***(P-24802)***
Long Beach Care Center Inc ....C....562 426-6141
2615 Grand Ave Long Beach (90815) ***(P-20596)***
Long Beach City College Whse, Long Beach *Also called Long Beach Cmnty College Dst* ***(P-4587)***
Long Beach City Fleet Services, Long Beach *Also called City of Long Beach* ***(P-17757)***
Long Beach Cmnty Action Partnr ....C....562 216-4600
117 W Victoria St Long Beach (90805) ***(P-24802)***
Long Beach Cmnty College Dst ....A....562 938-4291
1855 Walnut Ave Long Beach (90806) ***(P-4587)***
Long Beach Convention Center, Long Beach *Also called Smg Holdings Inc* ***(P-10945)***
Long Beach Cty Flt Svc Ofc, Long Beach *Also called City of Long Beach* ***(P-22978)***
Long Beach Day Nursery ....E....562 421-1488
3965 N Bellflower Blvd Long Beach (90808) ***(P-24341)***
Long Beach Golden Sails Inc ....D....562 596-1631
23545 Crenshaw Blvd # 100 Torrance (90505) ***(P-12862)***
Long Beach Hilton, The, Long Beach *Also called World Trade Ctr Ht Assoc Ltd* ***(P-13418)***
Long Beach Investment Group ....E....562 595-7277
2041 Pacific Coast Hwy Lomita (90717) ***(P-9830)***
Long Beach Marriott, Long Beach *Also called Ruffin Hotel Corp of Cal* ***(P-13153)***
Long Beach Memorial Med Ctr (HQ) ....A....562 933-2000
2801 Atlantic Ave Fl 2 Long Beach (90806) ***(P-21567)***
Long Beach Pain Center, Long Beach *Also called Healthsmart Pacific Inc* ***(P-21447)***
Long Beach Public Transit, Long Beach *Also called Long Beach Public Trnsp Co* ***(P-3665)***
Long Beach Public Trnsp Co ....B....562 591-2301
1300 Gardenia Ave Long Beach (90813) ***(P-3664)***
Long Beach Public Trnsp Co (PA) ....A....562 591-8753
1963 E Anaheim St Long Beach (90813) ***(P-3665)***
Long Beach Public Trnsp Co ....D....562 591-8753
1963 E Anaheim St Long Beach (90813) ***(P-3666)***
Long Beach Stadium Cinemas 26, Long Beach *Also called Edwards Theatres Circuit Inc* ***(P-18294)***
Long Beach Unified School Dst ....A....562 491-1281
999 Atlantic Ave Fl 3 Long Beach (90813) ***(P-14664)***
Long Beach Unified School Dst ....D....562 426-6176
2700 Pine Ave Long Beach (90806) ***(P-3941)***
Long Beach Unified School Dst ....C....562 997-7550
2425 Webster Ave Long Beach (90810) ***(P-14306)***
Long Beach Unified School Dst ....A....562 493-3596
3351 Val Verde Ave Long Beach (90808) ***(P-17301)***
Long Beach Yacht Club ....D....562 598-9401
6201 E Appian Way Long Beach (90803) ***(P-18959)***
Long Dragon Financial Service, Arcadia *Also called Long Dragon Realty Co Inc* ***(P-11567)***
Long Dragon Realty Co Inc ....C....626 309-7999
2633 S Baldwin Ave Arcadia (91007) ***(P-11567)***

Mergent e-mail: customerrelations@mergent.com
1370
2019 Directory of California Wholesalers and Services Companies
(P-0000) Products & Services Section entry number
(PA)=Parent Co (HQ)=Headquarters (DH)=Div Headquarters

Long Point Development LLC....A....310 265-2800
100 Terranea Way Rancho Palos Verdes (90275) **(P-12863)**
Long Swimming Pool Steel Inc....E....714 524-8172
3920 E Coronado St # 205 Anaheim (92807) **(P-3384)**
Long-Lok Fasteners Corporation....E....310 667-4200
20501 Belshaw Ave Carson (90746) **(P-7595)**
LONGSHOREMEN'S & WAREHOUSEMENS, Stockton *Also called International Longshoremens* **(P-25064)**
Longust Distributing LLC....E....480 820-6244
1206 N Miller St Unit A Anaheim (92806) **(P-6774)**
Longwood Management, San Dimas *Also called San Dimas Retirement Center* **(P-11109)**
Longwood Management Corp....C....310 679-1461
11834 Inglewood Ave Hawthorne (90250) **(P-20597)**
Longwood Management Corp....D....323 735-5146
2000 W Washington Blvd Los Angeles (90018) **(P-21139)**
Longwood Management Corp....E....818 781-6348
6728 Sepulveda Blvd Van Nuys (91411) **(P-11057)**
Longwood Management Corp....D....562 693-5240
7716 Pickering Ave Whittier (90602) **(P-21568)**
Longwood Management Corp....D....818 246-7174
605 W Broadway Glendale (91204) **(P-21140)**
Longwood Management Corp....D....818 881-7414
7836 Reseda Blvd Reseda (91335) **(P-21569)**
Longwood Management Corp....D....818 360-1864
17922 San Frnando Msn Granada Hills (91344) **(P-20598)**
Longwood Management Corp....D....626 280-2293
8101 Hill Dr Rosemead (91770) **(P-20599)**
Longwood Management Corp....C....626 280-4820
8035 Hill Dr Rosemead (91770) **(P-20600)**
Longwood Management Corp....D....323 737-7778
2190 W Adams Blvd Los Angeles (90018) **(P-21141)**
Longwood Management Corp....C....213 382-8461
1240 S Hoover St Los Angeles (90006) **(P-21142)**
Longwood Management Corp....C....818 980-8200
11429 Ventura Blvd Studio City (91604) **(P-21143)**
Longwood Management Corp....D....818 884-7100
895 E Pasadena St Pomona (91767) **(P-11058)**
Longwood Management Corp....E....323 933-1560
1900 S Longwood Ave Los Angeles (90016) **(P-20601)**
Longwood Management Corp....D....626 289-3763
537 W Live Oak St San Gabriel (91776) **(P-21144)**
Longwood Management Corp....D....714 962-5531
9925 La Alameda Ave Fountain Valley (92708) **(P-24583)**
Longwood Management Corp....C....562 432-5751
1913 E 5th St Long Beach (90802) **(P-21145)**
Longwood Management Inc....D....310 370-5828
20920 Earl St Ofc Torrance (90503) **(P-11059)**
Longwood Manor....C....323 935-1157
4853 W Washington Blvd Los Angeles (90016) **(P-20602)**
Longwood Manor Convalescent HM, Los Angeles *Also called Longwood Manor* **(P-20602)**
Loofs Lite A Line....E....562 436-2978
2500 Long Beach Blvd Long Beach (90806) **(P-18784)**
Lookout Productions LLC....E....310 408-5687
3748 W 9th St Apt 403 Los Angeles (90019) **(P-18073)**
Loomis Armored Us Inc....D....408 273-1101
897 Wrigley Way Milpitas (95035) **(P-16721)**
Loomis Armored Us LLC....D....619 232-5106
3555 Aero Ct San Diego (92123) **(P-16722)**
Loomis Armored Us LLC....D....916 441-1091
315 12th St Sacramento (95814) **(P-16723)**
Loomworks Apparel, Irvine *Also called Delta Galil USA Inc* **(P-8298)**
Loon LLC....C....310 625-3449
100 Mayfield Ave Mountain View (94043) **(P-17302)**
Looney Bins Inc (PA)....D....818 485-8200
12153 Montague St Pacoima (91331) **(P-6410)**
Lopez & Associates Engineers, El Monte *Also called R and L Lopez Associates Inc* **(P-25883)**
Lopez Canyon Landfill....C....818 834-5122
11950 Lopez Canyon Rd Sylmar (91342) **(P-6411)**
Lopez Harvesting....D....559 568-2553
24079 Avenue 196 Strathmore (93267) **(P-479)**
Lorber Greenfield & Polito LLP (PA)....D....858 486-6757
13985 Stowe Dr Poway (92064) **(P-23228)**
LOreal Usa Inc....C....510 548-0130
1848 4th St Berkeley (94710) **(P-8188)**
Loretta Lima Trnsp Corp....D....626 330-5517
240 S 6th Ave City of Industry (91746) **(P-4217)**
Loring Smart Roast Inc....D....707 526-7215
3200 Dutton Ave Ste 413 Santa Rosa (95407) **(P-7764)**
Loring Ward Advisor Services, San Jose *Also called Lwi Financial Inc* **(P-10094)**
Los Adobes De Maria, Santa Maria *Also called Peoples Self-Help Housing Corp* **(P-27821)**
Los Alamitos Hemo Dialysis Ctr, Los Alamitos *Also called Los Almtos Hmodialysis Ctr Inc* **(P-22482)**
Los Alamitos Medical Ctr Inc (HQ)....A....714 826-6400
3751 Katella Ave Los Alamitos (90720) **(P-21570)**
Los Almtos Hmodialysis Ctr Inc....D....562 426-8881
3810 Katella Ave Los Alamitos (90720) **(P-22482)**
Los Altos Center, Los Altos *Also called Palo Alto Medical Foundation* **(P-19750)**
Los Altos Food Products Inc....C....626 330-6555
450 Baldwin Park Blvd City of Industry (91746) **(P-8524)**
Los Altos Golf and Country CLB....D....650 947-3100
1560 Country Club Dr Los Altos (94024) **(P-18960)**
Los Altos YMCA, Long Beach *Also called Young Mens Chrstn Assc Gr L B* **(P-25334)**
Los Alts Sub-Acute Rhbltn, Los Altos *Also called Covenant Care California LLC* **(P-20353)**
Los Amigos Country Club Inc....D....562 923-9696
7295 Quill Dr Downey (90242) **(P-18961)**
Los Amigos Golf Course, Downey *Also called Los Amigos Country Club Inc* **(P-18961)**
Los Angeles 2024 Exploratory....E....310 407-0539
10960 Wilshire Blvd Los Angeles (90024) **(P-18962)**
Los Angeles Airport Peace Offc....B....310 242-5218
6080 Center Dr Fl 6 Los Angeles (90045) **(P-25193)**
Los Angeles Angels of Anaheim, Anaheim *Also called Angels Baseball LP* **(P-18505)**
Los Angeles Athletic Club Inc....C....213 625-2211
431 W 7th St Los Angeles (90014) **(P-18627)**
Los Angeles Auto Auction, Rosemead *Also called Cox Automotive Inc* **(P-6584)**
Los Angeles Bio Med RES Inst....E....310 222-3604
1124 W Carson St Rm 5l2 Torrance (90502) **(P-26540)**
Los Angeles Branch, Los Angeles *Also called Federal Rsrve Bnk San Frncisco* **(P-9274)**
Los Angeles Branch, Commerce *Also called Jfc International Inc* **(P-8813)**
Los Angeles Cardiology Assoc (PA)....D....213 977-0419
1245 Wilshire Blvd # 703 Los Angeles (90017) **(P-19660)**
Los Angeles Center For Alcohol (PA)....D....562 906-2676
11015 Bloomfield Ave Santa Fe Springs (90670) **(P-22614)**
Los Angeles Chargers, Costa Mesa *Also called Chargers Football Company LLC* **(P-18514)**
Los Angeles Chmber Orchstra....D....213 622-7001
350 S Figueroa St Ste 183 Los Angeles (90071) **(P-18448)**
Los Angeles City Hauling, Sun Valley *Also called USA Waste of California Inc* **(P-6489)**
Los Angeles Clippers, Los Angeles *Also called LA Sports Properties Inc* **(P-18523)**
Los Angeles Cnty Dev Svc Fndtn....C....213 383-1300
3303 Wilshire Blvd # 700 Los Angeles (90010) **(P-22836)**
Los Angeles Cnty Economic Dev, Los Angeles *Also called Economic Dev Corp of La County* **(P-27713)**
Los Angeles Cnty Emp Retiremnt (PA)....B....626 564-6000
300 N Lake Ave Ste 720 Pasadena (91101) **(P-10487)**
Los Angeles Cnty Mseum of Art....D....323 857-6000
5905 Wilshire Blvd Los Angeles (90036) **(P-24889)**
Los Angeles Cnty Mtro Trnspt, Los Angeles *Also called Los Angeles County MTA* **(P-3671)**
Los Angeles Cold Storage, Los Angeles *Also called Standard-Southern Corporation* **(P-4512)**
Los Angeles Cold Storage Co, Los Angeles *Also called Standard-Southern Corporation* **(P-4510)**
Los Angeles Community Hospital, Los Angeles *Also called Alta Hospitals System LLC* **(P-21279)**
Los Angeles Conven and Exh....B....213 741-1151
1201 S Figueroa St Los Angeles (90015) **(P-10907)**
Los Angeles Convention Center, Los Angeles *Also called AEG Management Lacc LLC* **(P-26750)**
Los Angeles Country Club....C....310 276-6104
10101 Wilshire Blvd Los Angeles (90024) **(P-18963)**
Los Angeles County, Pacoima *Also called County of Los Angeles* **(P-19415)**
Los Angeles County Bar Assn (PA)....D....213 627-2727
1055 W 7th St Ste 2700 Los Angeles (90017) **(P-25025)**
Los Angeles County Fair Assn (PA)....B....909 623-3111
1101 W Mckinley Ave Pomona (91768) **(P-19199)**
Los Angeles County Health Svc....E....310 763-2244
1108 N Oleander Ave Compton (90222) **(P-19661)**
Los Angeles County Hospital, Los Angeles *Also called Lac Usc Medical Center* **(P-21545)**
Los Angeles County MTA....C....213 922-6308
9201 Canoga Ave Chatsworth (91311) **(P-3667)**
Los Angeles County MTA....C....213 922-5887
900 Lyon St Los Angeles (90012) **(P-3668)**
Los Angeles County MTA....C....213 922-6301
1130 E 6th St Los Angeles (90021) **(P-3669)**
Los Angeles County MTA....B....213 922-6203
630 W Avenue 28 Los Angeles (90065) **(P-3670)**
Los Angeles County MTA....C....213 922-6202
1 Gateway Plz Los Angeles (90012) **(P-3671)**
Los Angeles County MTA (PA)....A....323 466-3876
1 Gateway Plz Fl 25 Los Angeles (90012) **(P-3672)**
Los Angeles County MTA....A....213 922-6207
8800 Santa Monica Blvd Los Angeles (90069) **(P-3673)**
Los Angeles County MTA....B....213 922-6215
11900 Branford St Sun Valley (91352) **(P-3674)**
Los Angeles County MTA....B....213 533-1506
720 E 15th St Los Angeles (90021) **(P-3675)**
Los Angeles County MTA....C....213 922-5012
470 Bauchet St Los Angeles (90012) **(P-3676)**
Los Angeles County MTA....C....310 392-8636
100 Sunset Ave Venice (90291) **(P-3677)**
Los Angeles County MTA....C....213 244-6783
818 W 7th St Ste 500 Los Angeles (90017) **(P-3678)**
Los Angeles County MTA....C....213 626-4455
320 S Santa Fe Ave Los Angeles (90013) **(P-3679)**
Los Angeles County Pub Works, South Gate *Also called County of Los Angeles* **(P-22777)**
Los Angeles Cty Rnch Los Amgos....A....562 385-7111
7601 Imperial Hwy Downey (90242) **(P-20939)**
Los Angeles Dept Convetion Tou, Los Angeles *Also called Los Angeles Conven and Exh* **(P-10907)**
Los Angeles Dept Wtr & Pwr....A....323 256-8079
4030 Crenshaw Blvd Los Angeles (90008) **(P-6273)**
Los Angeles Dept Wtr & Pwr....A....213 367-1342
11801 Sheldon St Sun Valley (91352) **(P-6274)**
Los Angeles Dept Wtr & Pwr....A....760 878-2156
201 S Webster St Independence (93526) **(P-6275)**
Los Angeles Dept Wtr & Pwr (PA)....C....213 367-4211
111 N Hope St Los Angeles (90012) **(P-6276)**
Los Angeles Dept Wtr & Pwr....D....213 367-4211
111 N Hope St Los Angeles (90012) **(P-6050)**
Los Angeles Dept Wtr & Pwr....A....213 367-5706
1141 W 2nd St Bldg D Los Angeles (90012) **(P-6277)**
Los Angeles Dept Wtr & Pwr....D....310 524-8500
12700 Vista Del Mar Playa Del Rey (90293) **(P-6199)**
Los Angeles Deseret Industries, Los Angeles *Also called Corp of Church of Christ Ld St* **(P-17921)**

ALPHABETIC

Los Angeles District Office, Glendale *Also called State Compensation Insur Fund (P-10405)*
Los Angeles Dodgers LLC ....A....323 224-1507
1000 Vin Scully Ave Los Angeles (90090) ***(P-18524)***
Los Angeles Dr-In Theatre Co, Montclair *Also called Mission Drive-In Theatre Co (P-18328)*
Los Angeles Engineering Inc ....C....626 869-1400
633 N Barranca Ave Covina (91723) ***(P-25801)***
Los Angeles Equestrian Center ....D....818 840-9063
480 W Riverside Dr Burbank (91506) ***(P-630)***
Los Angeles Federal Credit Un (PA) ....D....818 242-8640
300 S Glendale Ave # 100 Glendale (91205) ***(P-9568)***
Los Angeles Free Clinic (PA) ....B....323 653-8622
8405 Beverly Blvd Los Angeles (90048) ***(P-19662)***
Los Angeles Free Clinic ....D....323 653-8622
8405 Beverly Blvd Los Angeles (90048) ***(P-19663)***
Los Angeles Freightliner, Fontana *Also called Los Angeles Truck Centers LLC (P-6602)*
Los Angeles Guild LLC ....C....323 733-5033
3437 W El Segundo Blvd Hawthorne (90250) ***(P-27306)***
Los Angeles Job Corps ....C....213 748-0135
1020 S Olive St Los Angeles (90015) ***(P-24201)***
Los Angeles Junction Rlwy Co ....E....323 277-2004
4433 Exchange Ave Vernon (90058) ***(P-3634)***
Los Angeles Lakers Inc ....C....310 426-6000
2275 E Mariposa Ave El Segundo (90245) ***(P-18525)***
Los Angeles Lawyer Magazine, Los Angeles *Also called Los Angeles County Bar Assn (P-25025)*
Los Angeles Lgbt Center (PA) ....C....323 993-7618
1625 Schrader Blvd Los Angeles (90028) ***(P-24803)***
Los Angeles Magazine, Los Angeles *Also called Emmis Publishing Corporation (P-9113)*
Los Angeles Marriott Downtown, Los Angeles *Also called La Hotel Venture LLC (P-12827)*
Los Angeles Mem Coliseum Comm ....B....213 747-7111
3911 S Figueroa St Los Angeles (90037) ***(P-25440)***
Los Angeles Mission Inc (PA) ....D....213 629-1227
303 E 5th St Los Angeles (90013) ***(P-24584)***
Los Angeles Orphan Asylum Inc ....C....323 283-9311
7600 Graves Ave Rosemead (91770) ***(P-24585)***
Los Angeles Orphans Home Soc (HQ) ....C....323 463-2119
815 N El Centro Ave Los Angeles (90038) ***(P-24586)***
Los Angeles Philharmonic Assn (PA) ....A....213 972-7300
151 S Grand Ave Los Angeles (90012) ***(P-18449)***
Los Angeles Police Command ....B....877 275-5273
100 W 1st St Los Angeles (90012) ***(P-25441)***
Los Angeles Police Credit Un (PA) ....C....818 787-6520
16150 Sherman Way Van Nuys (91406) ***(P-9640)***
Los Angeles Rams LLC (PA) ....D....314 982-7267
29899 Agoura Rd Agoura Hills (91301) ***(P-18526)***
Los Angeles Regional Food Bank ....C....323 234-3030
1734 E 41st St Vernon (90058) ***(P-23902)***
Los Angeles Regional Office, Pasadena *Also called Employee Benefits Security ADM (P-10485)*
Los Angeles Residential Comm F ....D....661 296-8636
29890 Bouquet Canyon Rd Santa Clarita (91390) ***(P-24587)***
Los Angeles Royal Vista Golf C ....D....909 595-7471
20055 Colima Rd Walnut (91789) ***(P-18964)***
Los Angeles Rubber Company (PA) ....D....323 263-4131
2915 E Washington Blvd Los Angeles (90023) ***(P-7372)***
Los Angeles SEC National (PA) ....E....323 651-2930
543 N Fairfax Ave Los Angeles (90036) ***(P-23903)***
Los Angeles Senior Citizen ....D....310 271-9670
1425 S Wooster St Los Angeles (90035) ***(P-11060)***
Los Angeles South Bay Dst Off, Long Beach *Also called Rehabilitation California Dept (P-23990)*
Los Angeles Terminal, Los Angeles *Also called El Pas-Los Angles Lmsne Ex Inc (P-3895)*
Los Angeles Truck Centers LLC ....C....909 510-4000
13800 Valley Blvd Fontana (92335) ***(P-6602)***
Los Angeles Turf Club Inc (HQ) ....C....626 574-6330
285 W Huntington Dr Arcadia (91007) ***(P-18540)***
Los Angeles Unified School Dst ....B....818 997-2640
6651 Balboa Blvd Van Nuys (91406) ***(P-22615)***
Los Angeles Unified School Dst ....C....213 485-3691
200 N Main St Ste 1400 Los Angeles (90012) ***(P-16289)***
Los Angeles Unified School Dst ....C....818 365-9645
11450 Sharp Ave Mission Hills (91345) ***(P-24202)***
Los Angeles Unified School Dst ....C....323 753-3175
816 W 51st St Los Angeles (90037) ***(P-25194)***
Los Angeles Unified School Dst ....D....323 939-7322
1212 Queen Anne Pl Los Angeles (90019) ***(P-24342)***
Los Angeles Unified School Dst ....A....213 847-6911
200 N Main St Ste 1400 Los Angeles (90012) ***(P-16152)***
Los Angeles Unified School Dst ....C....213 739-5600
1157 S Berendo St Los Angeles (90006) ***(P-23904)***
Los Angeles Unified School Dst ....C....310 258-2000
8810 Emerson Ave Los Angeles (90045) ***(P-23905)***
Los Angeles Unified School Dst ....D....562 654-9007
8525 Rex Rd Pico Rivera (90660) ***(P-17303)***
Los Angeles Unified School Dst ....E....310 808-1500
17729 S Figueroa St Gardena (90248) ***(P-14307)***
Los Angeles Unified School Dst ....C....310 518-1128
1468 N Marine Ave Wilmington (90744) ***(P-23906)***
Los Angeles World Airports (PA) ....C....310 646-7911
6320 W 96th St Los Angeles (90045) ***(P-4898)***
Los Angeles World Airports ....D....909 544-5490
1230 Tower St Ontario (91761) ***(P-4899)***
Los Angles Ambulatory Care Ctr, Los Angeles *Also called Veterans Health Administration (P-20083)*
Los Angles Arbretum Foundation ....D....626 821-3222
301 N Baldwin Ave Arcadia (91007) ***(P-24931)***
Los Angles Area Chmber Cmmerce ....D....213 580-7500
350 S Bixel St Los Angeles (90017) ***(P-24966)***
Los Angles Child Gdance Clinic (PA) ....C....323 373-2400
3031 S Vermont Ave Los Angeles (90007) ***(P-23907)***
Los Angles Clippers Foundation ....D....213 742-7555
1111 S Figueroa St # 1100 Los Angeles (90015) ***(P-27307)***
Los Angles Cllege Chiropractic, Whittier *Also called S CA University Hlth Sciences (P-20156)*
Los Angles Cnsrvtion Corps Inc (PA) ....D....213 362-9000
1400 N Spring St Los Angeles (90012) ***(P-14873)***
Los Angles Cnty Cntl Jail Hosp, Los Angeles *Also called County of Los Angeles (P-21355)*
Los Angles Cnty Employees Assn ....D....213 368-8660
1545 Wilshire Blvd Los Angeles (90017) ***(P-25069)***
Los Angles Dst Off Policy Svcs, Monterey Park *Also called State Compensation Insur Fund (P-10411)*
Los Angles Homecare Pediatrics, Los Angeles *Also called Maxim Healthcare Services Inc (P-22364)*
Los Angles Jewish HM For Aging (PA) ....B....818 774-3000
7150 Tampa Ave Reseda (91335) ***(P-20603)***
Los Angles Jewish HM For Aging ....B....818 774-3000
18855 Victory Blvd Reseda (91335) ***(P-20604)***
Los Angles Kings Hockey CLB LP ....C....310 535-4502
555 N Nash St El Segundo (90245) ***(P-18527)***
Los Angles Kings Hockey CLB LP (PA) ....C....888 546-4752
800 W Olympic Blvd Los Angeles (90015) ***(P-18528)***
Los Angles Ryal Vsta Golf Crse, Walnut *Also called Los Angeles Royal Vista Golf C (P-18964)*
Los Angles Trism Convention Bd (PA) ....E....213 624-7300
333 S Hope St Ste 1800 Los Angeles (90071) ***(P-17304)***
Los Angles Universal Preschool ....C....213 416-1200
515 S Figueroa St Ste 900 Los Angeles (90071) ***(P-24343)***
Los Banos Nursing and Rehab, Los Banos *Also called Para & Palli Inc (P-20691)*
Los Banos School District, Los Banos *Also called Facilities Operation and Trnsp (P-3922)*
Los Defensores Inc ....E....310 519-4050
20101 Hamilton Ave # 300 Torrance (90502) ***(P-13858)***
Los Dos Valles Harvstg & Pkg ....C....805 739-1688
2365 Westgate Rd Santa Maria (93455) ***(P-480)***
Los Gatos Meadows, Los Gatos *Also called Episcopal Senior Communities (P-24519)*
Los Padres Bank, Solvang *Also called Pacific Western Bank (P-9478)*
Los Palos Convalescent Hosp, San Pedro *Also called San Pedro Convalescent HM Inc (P-20744)*
Los Posadas Service Center, Camarillo *Also called Telecare Corporation (P-21986)*
Los Prietos Boys Camp ....D....805 692-1750
3900 Paradise Rd Santa Barbara (93105) ***(P-24588)***
Los Robles Bank ....D....805 373-6763
33 W Thousand Oaks Blvd Thousand Oaks (91360) ***(P-9465)***
Los Robles Hospital & Med Ctr (HQ) ....D....805 497-2727
215 W Janss Rd Thousand Oaks (91360) ***(P-21571)***
Los Serranos Golf & Cntry CLB, Chino Hills *Also called Los Serranos Golf Club (P-18729)*
Los Serranos Golf Club ....C....909 597-1769
15656 Yorba Ave Chino Hills (91709) ***(P-18729)***
Los Verdes Golf Course, Rancho Palos Verdes *Also called American Golf Corporation (P-18840)*
Los Verdes Golf Curse, Rancho Palos Verdes *Also called Los Verdes MNS Golf Cntry CLB (P-18730)*
Los Verdes MNS Golf Cntry CLB ....E....310 377-7370
7000 Los Verdes Dr Ste 1 Rancho Palos Verdes (90275) ***(P-18730)***
Lost Canyons Golf Course, Simi Valley *Also called Big Sky Country Club LLC (P-18688)*
Lotus Communications Corp (PA) ....D....323 512-2225
3301 Barham Blvd Ste 200 Los Angeles (90068) ***(P-5744)***
Lotus Interworks Inc ....C....310 442-3330
10801 National Blvd # 500 Los Angeles (90064) ***(P-27308)***
Lou Bozigian ....D....661 948-4737
5900 Alleppo Ln Palmdale (93551) ***(P-11568)***
Louie Almeida & Settler (PA) ....D....818 461-9559
303 N Glenoaks Blvd # 400 Burbank (91502) ***(P-23229)***
Louis Luskin & Sons Inc ....D....323 938-5142
6004 Venice Blvd Los Angeles (90034) ***(P-2266)***
Louis Wurth and Company (HQ) ....D....714 529-1771
895 Columbia St Brea (92821) ***(P-7596)***
Lounge 22 LLC (PA) ....D....818 502-0700
211 N Brand Blvd Glendale (91203) ***(P-14522)***
Loup Logistics Company ....C....661 370-4341
2121 S Browning Rd Delano (93215) ***(P-5102)***
LOVARC, Lompoc *Also called Life Optons Vctnal Rsource Ctr (P-23893)*
Lovazzano Mechanical Inc ....D....650 367-6216
189 Constitution Dr Menlo Park (94025) ***(P-2267)***
Lovco Construction Inc ....C....562 595-1601
1300 E Burnett St Signal Hill (90755) ***(P-3432)***
Love Lifted US Youth Services ....E....818 471-0594
6356 Van Nuys Blvd # 229 Van Nuys (91401) ***(P-18628)***
Lovely Living Homecare ....D....909 625-7999
112 Harvard Ave Claremont (91711) ***(P-22360)***
Low Ball & Lynch A Prof Corp (PA) ....D....415 981-6630
505 Montgomery St Fl 7 San Francisco (94111) ***(P-23230)***
Low Cost Insurance, Northridge *Also called 1-800-4-insure Insurance Svcs (P-10506)*
Lowcom LLC ....C....213 408-0080
818 W 7th St Ste 700 Los Angeles (90017) ***(P-13859)***
Lowe Enterprises Inc ....C....310 820-6661
11777 San Vicente Blvd # 900 Los Angeles (90049) ***(P-11569)***
Lowe Enterprises Inc (PA) ....C....310 820-6661
11777 San Vicente Blvd # 900 Los Angeles (90049) ***(P-11570)***
Lowe Enterprises Coml Group, Los Angeles *Also called Lowe Enterprises RE Group (P-11887)*
Lowe Enterprises Inc ....D....310 820-6661
11777 San Vincente Blvd S Los Angeles (90049) ***(P-11886)***
Lowe Enterprises RE Group ....D....310 820-6661
11777 San Vicente Blvd # 900 Los Angeles (90049) ***(P-11887)***

Lowenstein Sandler LLP ....E.......650 433-5800
390 Lytton Ave Palo Alto (94301) ***(P-23231)***

Lowermybills, Los Angeles *Also called Lmb Mortgage Services Inc* ***(P-9827)***

Lowermybills, Inc. ....D.......310 348-6800
12181 Bluff Creek Dr Playa Vista (90094) ***(P-16238)***

Lowermybills.com, Playa Vista *Also called Lowermybills, Inc.* ***(P-16238)***

Loyal Svc Unt Spec Team, Long Beach *Also called Michael McCarthy* ***(P-16732)***

Loyal3 Holdings Inc ....D.......415 981-0700
150 California St Ste 400 San Francisco (94111) ***(P-17305)***

Loyalton At Rancho Solano ....D.......707 425-3588
3350 Cherry Hills Ct Ofc Fairfield (94534) ***(P-24589)***

Loyda Yu Real Estate Inc ....D.......619 475-7777
860 Kuhn Dr Ste 200 Chula Vista (91914) ***(P-11571)***

Loyola Marymount University ....C.......310 338-2866
1 Lmu Dr Ste 100 Los Angeles (90045) ***(P-5745)***

Lozano Car Wash, Mountain View *Also called Lozano Inc* ***(P-17830)***

Lozano Inc ....C.......650 941-0590
2690 W El Camino Real Mountain View (94040) ***(P-17830)***

Lozano Plumbing Services Inc ....C.......951 683-4840
3615 Presley Ave Riverside (92507) ***(P-2268)***

Lozano Smith LLP ....C.......559 431-5600
7404 N Spalding Ave Fresno (93720) ***(P-23232)***

Lozano Smith A Prof Corp (PA) ....D.......559 431-5600
7404 N Spalding Ave Fresno (93720) ***(P-23233)***

LPA Inc (PA) ....C.......949 261-1001
5161 California Ave # 100 Irvine (92617) ***(P-26084)***

LPA Inc ....C.......408 780-7200
60 S Market St Ste 150 San Jose (95113) ***(P-26085)***

Lpa Insurance Agency Inc ....D.......916 286-7850
4030 Truxel Rd Ste B Sacramento (95834) ***(P-15745)***

Lpas Inc ....D.......916 443-0335
2484 Natomas Park Dr # 100 Sacramento (95833) ***(P-26086)***

Lpcc, Camarillo *Also called Las Posas Country Club* ***(P-18957)***

Lpl Holdings Inc (HQ) ....D.......858 450-9606
4707 Executive Dr San Diego (92121) ***(P-9972)***

Lpsh Holdings Inc ....A.......951 926-1176
3570 W Florida Ave # 168 Hemet (92545) ***(P-2269)***

Lq Management LLC ....D.......310 645-2200
5249 W Century Blvd Los Angeles (90045) ***(P-12864)***

Lqr Property LLC ....C.......760 564-4111
49499 Eisenhower Dr La Quinta (92253) ***(P-12865)***

Lres Corporation (PA) ....D.......714 520-5737
765 The City Dr S Ste 300 Orange (92868) ***(P-11572)***

Lrw Investments LLC ....D.......310 337-1944
9700 Bellanca Ave Los Angeles (90045) ***(P-17693)***

LS Farms LLC ....B.......661 792-3192
29794 Schuster Rd Mc Farland (93250) ***(P-368)***

Lsf Central Cal Adult Svcs, Arroyo Grande *Also called Life Steps Foundation Inc* ***(P-23894)***

Lsf9 Cypress Holdings LLC ....A.......714 380-3127
2741 Walnut Ave Ste 200 Tustin (92780) ***(P-6935)***

Ltc Pharmacy, San Diego *Also called Pharmerica Long-Term Care LLC* ***(P-8204)***

Ltc Pharmacy, Riverside *Also called Pharmerica Long-Term Care LLC* ***(P-8205)***

Ltd Eyewear, Chatsworth *Also called Atlantic Optical Co Inc* ***(P-7233)***

Luberski Inc ....D.......951 271-3866
1811 Mountain Ave Norco (92860) ***(P-8535)***

Lucas Digital Ltd (HQ) ....B.......415 258-2000
3155 Kerner Blvd San Rafael (94901) ***(P-18383)***

Lucasfilm Coml Productions, San Francisco *Also called Lucasfilm Ltd LLC* ***(P-18074)***

Lucasfilm Ltd LLC (HQ) ....C.......415 623-1000
1110 Gorgas Ave Bldg C-Hr San Francisco (94129) ***(P-18074)***

Lucich Santos Farms ....C.......209 892-6500
12631 Rogers Rd Patterson (95363) ***(P-369)***

Lucid Design Group Inc ....D.......510 907-0400
304 12th St Ste 3c Oakland (94607) ***(P-16000)***

Lucid Vr Inc ....D.......408 391-0506
4500 Great America Pkwy Santa Clara (95054) ***(P-15266)***

Lucile Packard Childrens Hosp ....D.......650 321-2545
730 Welch Rd Ste B Palo Alto (94304) ***(P-22030)***

Lucile Packard Childrens Hosp ....E.......650 736-4089
1520 Page Mill Rd Palo Alto (94304) ***(P-22031)***

Lucile Salter Packard Chil ....C.......925 277-7550
5601 Norris Canyon Rd # 230 San Ramon (94583) ***(P-19664)***

Lucile Salter Packard Chil (PA) ....C.......650 497-8000
725 Welch Rd Palo Alto (94304) ***(P-22032)***

Lucile Salter Packard Chil ....C.......650 723-5791
300 Pasteur Dr Stanford (94305) ***(P-22033)***

Lucile Salter Packard Chil ....B.......650 736-4030
725 Welch Rd Palo Alto (94304) ***(P-27939)***

Lucky Chances Inc ....A.......650 758-2237
1700 Hillside Blvd Colma (94014) ***(P-19200)***

Lucky Chances Casino, Colma *Also called Lucky Chances Inc* ***(P-19200)***

Lucky Farms Inc ....D.......909 799-6688
1194 E Brier Dr San Bernardino (92408) ***(P-67)***

Lucky Installations ....E.......562 948-5950
9041 Bermudez St Pico Rivera (90660) ***(P-3175)***

Lucky Lady Card Room, San Diego *Also called California Club Lucky Lady* ***(P-12420)***

Lucky Strike Entertainment LLC ....D.......818 933-3752
6801 Hollywood Blvd # 143 Los Angeles (90028) ***(P-18492)***

Lucky Strike Entertainment LLC ....C.......818 933-0872
15260 Ventura Blvd # 1110 Sherman Oaks (91403) ***(P-18493)***

Lucky Strike Entertainment LLC ....D.......248 374-3420
20 City Blvd W Ste G2 Orange (92868) ***(P-18494)***

Lufkin Industries LLC ....D.......661 746-0030
31127 Coberly Rd Shafter (93263) ***(P-7765)***

Lufthnsa Crgo Aktngesellschaft ....C.......310 242-2590
5721 W Imperial Hwy Los Angeles (90045) ***(P-4792)***

Luis Esparza Services Inc ....B.......661 766-2344
183 Hwy 33 Maricopa (93252) ***(P-14665)***

Lukenbill Enterprises ....D.......916 454-2400
3600 Power Inn Rd Ste H Sacramento (95826) ***(P-4793)***

Luma Pictures Inc ....C.......310 888-8738
1424 2nd St Santa Monica (90401) ***(P-18199)***

Lumberyard Plaza Mall, Los Angeles *Also called Laguna Country Mart Ltd Inc* ***(P-10904)***

Lumens LLC (HQ) ....D.......916 444-5585
2020 L St Ste Ll10 Sacramento (95811) ***(P-7373)***

Lumetra Healthcare Solutions ....E.......415 677-2000
550 Kearny St Ste 300 San Francisco (94108) ***(P-27777)***

Lumina At Home, Los Angeles *Also called Lumina Healthcare LLC* ***(P-22361)***

Lumina Healthcare LLC (PA) ....D.......888 958-6462
5220 Pacific Concourse Dr Los Angeles (90045) ***(P-22361)***

Luminance, Commerce *Also called American De Rosa Lamparts LLC* ***(P-7328)***

Luminar Technologies Inc ....D.......626 629-8686
1891 Page Mill Rd 200 Palo Alto (94304) ***(P-26637)***

Lunares, San Francisco *Also called Sunday Bazaar Inc* ***(P-6789)***

Lunarpages, La Habra *Also called Add2net Inc* ***(P-16305)***

Lund Construction Co ....C.......916 344-5800
5302 Roseville Rd North Highlands (95660) ***(P-25802)***

Lund Equipment LP ....E.......916 344-5800
5302 Roseville Rd North Highlands (95660) ***(P-1807)***

Lundblade Builders, Eureka *Also called Fred H Lundblade Jr* ***(P-10879)***

Lundstrom & Associates Inc ....E.......619 641-5900
4804 Sunrise Hills Dr El Cajon (92020) ***(P-25803)***

Luppen and Hawley Inc ....C.......916 456-7831
6330 N Point Way Sacramento (95831) ***(P-2270)***

Lupton Excavation Inc ....D.......916 387-1104
8467 Florin Rd Sacramento (95828) ***(P-3433)***

Lusamerica Foods Inc (PA) ....D.......408 294-6622
16480 Railroad Ave Morgan Hill (95037) ***(P-8582)***

Lusive Decor ....E.......323 227-9207
3400 Medford St Los Angeles (90063) ***(P-27778)***

Luth Research Inc (PA) ....B.......619 234-5884
1365 4th Ave San Diego (92101) ***(P-26541)***

Luther Burbank Corporation ....D.......949 428-8043
20 Pacifica Ste 600 Irvine (92618) ***(P-9510)***

Luther Burbank Mem Foundation ....D.......707 546-3600
50 Mark West Springs Rd Santa Rosa (95403) ***(P-18384)***

Luther Burbank Savings (HQ) ....E.......707 578-9216
500 3rd St Santa Rosa (95401) ***(P-9535)***

Lutheran Health Facility, Burbank *Also called Front Porch Communities & Svcs* ***(P-21074)***

Lutrel Trucking Inc ....D.......661 397-9756
12856 Old River Rd Bakersfield (93311) ***(P-5103)***

Luxar Tech Inc ....C.......408 835-2551
42840 Christy St Ste 231 Fremont (94538) ***(P-5594)***

Luxe City Center, Los Angeles *Also called Emerik Hotel Corp* ***(P-12558)***

Luxe Light and Home, Los Angeles *Also called Lusive Decor* ***(P-27778)***

Luxe Sunset Boulevard Hotel, Los Angeles *Also called E H Summit Inc* ***(P-12544)***

Luxera Inc ....E.......510 456-7690
39300 Civic Center Dr # 140 Fremont (94538) ***(P-14308)***

Luxn Inc ....D.......408 213-7437
580 Maude Ct Sunnyvale (94085) ***(P-5988)***

Luxor Cabs Inc ....D.......415 282-4141
2230 Jerrold Ave San Francisco (94124) ***(P-3866)***

Lwi Financial Inc ....D.......408 260-3100
10 Almaden Blvd Fl 15 San Jose (95113) ***(P-10094)***

Lydia C Gonzalez ....E.......650 299-4707
1400 Veterans Blvd Redwood City (94063) ***(P-23908)***

Lyft Inc (PA) ....B.......415 230-2905
185 Berry St Ste 5000 San Francisco (94107) ***(P-3819)***

Lyle Company ....D.......916 266-7000
3140 Gold Camp Dr Ste 30 Rancho Cordova (95670) ***(P-27779)***

Lyles Diversified Inc (PA) ....B.......559 441-1900
1210 W Olive Ave Fresno (93728) ***(P-1951)***

Lymi Inc (PA) ....D.......213 434-2772
2263 E Vernon Ave Vernon (90058) ***(P-8316)***

Lynberg & Watkins A Prof Corp (PA) ....E.......213 624-8700
1150 S Olive St Fl 18 Los Angeles (90015) ***(P-23234)***

Lynberg & Watkins Attys At Law, Los Angeles *Also called Lynberg & Watkins A Prof Corp* ***(P-23234)***

Lynch Ambulance Service, Anaheim *Also called Filyn Corporation* ***(P-3794)***

Lynch Creek Medical Management, Petaluma *Also called Crocodile Bay Lodge* ***(P-13439)***

Lynch Gilardi & Grummer LLP ....E.......415 397-2800
170 Columbus Ave Fl 5 San Francisco (94133) ***(P-23235)***

Lyngso Garden Materials Inc ....E.......650 364-1730
345 Shoreway Rd San Carlos (94070) ***(P-6900)***

Lynup Corporation ....D.......858 207-4610
16875 W Bernardo Dr # 110 San Diego (92127) ***(P-27309)***

Lynwood Developmental Care ....D.......310 764-2023
14925 S Atlantic Ave Compton (90221) ***(P-21146)***

Lynwood Medical Offices, Lynwood *Also called Kaiser Foundation Hospitals* ***(P-19568)***

Lynx Software Technologies Inc (PA) ....D.......408 979-3900
855 Embedded Way San Jose (95138) ***(P-15746)***

Lynx Technology, San Diego *Also called JM Driver LLC* ***(P-15243)***

Lyon & Associates Realtors, Sacramento *Also called William L Lyon & Assoc Inc* ***(P-11833)***

Lyon Promenade LLC ....E.......949 252-9101
4901 Birch St Newport Beach (92660) ***(P-1352)***

Lyon Real Estate ....D.......916 355-7000
150 Natoma Station Dr # 300 Folsom (95630) ***(P-11573)***

Lyon Realtors, Fair Oaks *Also called William L Lyon & Assoc Inc* ***(P-11834)***

Lyon Realty ....C.......916 962-0111
8814 Madison Ave Fair Oaks (95628) ***(P-11574)***

Lyon Realty ....C.......530 295-4444
4340 Golden Center Dr A Placerville (95667) ***(P-11176)***

Lyon Realty (PA) ....A.......916 574-8800
2280 Del Paso Rd Ste 100 Sacramento (95834) ***(P-11575)***

Lyons Security Service Inc ....D.......714 401-4850
P.O. Box 18955 Anaheim (92817) ***(P-16922)***

Employee Codes: A=Over 500 employees, B=251-500
C=101-250, D=51-100, E=50
2019 Directory of California Wholesalers and Services Companies
© Mergent Inc. 1-800-342-5647
1373

Lyons Security Service Inc.....D.......916 925-9667
655 University Ave # 240 Sacramento (95825) *(P-16724)*
Lytton Garden II, Palo Alto *Also called Community Housing Inc (P-24473)*
Lytton Rancheria.....A.......510 215-7888
13255 San Pablo Ave San Pablo (94806) *(P-19201)*
M & A Mortgage Inc.....D.......714 560-1970
1600 N Broadway Ste 1020 Santa Ana (92706) *(P-9893)*
M & C, Los Angeles *Also called Murchison & Cumming LLP (P-23277)*
M & E Technical Services L L C (PA).....D.......256 964-6486
3601 Bayview Dr Manhattan Beach (90266) *(P-27600)*
M & G Jewelers Inc.....D.......909 989-2929
10823 Edison Ct Rancho Cucamonga (91730) *(P-17920)*
M & H Realty Partners LP.....D.......415 693-9000
353 Sacramento St Fl 21 San Francisco (94111) *(P-12241)*
M & J Seafood Company Inc.....D.......562 529-2786
6859 Walthall Way Paramount (90723) *(P-8583)*
M & L Plumbing Co Inc.....E.......559 291-5525
3540 N Duke Ave Fresno (93727) *(P-2271)*
M & M Distributors, Los Angeles *Also called Wiemar Distributors Inc (P-8747)*
M & M Electric, Sacramento *Also called May-Han Electric Inc (P-2638)*
M & M Enterprises.....D.......530 347-3238
3732 Hacienda Rd Cottonwood (96022) *(P-992)*
M & M Interiors Inc.....C.......951 279-9535
3410 La Sierra Ave Ste F Riverside (92503) *(P-1583)*
M & M Plumbing Inc.....D.......951 354-5388
6782 Columbus St Riverside (92504) *(P-2272)*
M & R Joint Venture Electrical.....D.......909 598-7700
231 Benton Ct Walnut (91789) *(P-2632)*
M & S Acquisition Corporation (PA).....C.......213 385-1515
707 Wilshire Blvd # 5200 Los Angeles (90017) *(P-11576)*
M & S Security Services Inc.....D.......661 397-9616
2900 L St Bakersfield (93301) *(P-16725)*
M & S SUPPLY CO, Eureka *Also called McMurray & Sons Inc (P-3178)*
M & S Trading Inc.....D.......714 241-7190
15778 Gateway Cir Tustin (92780) *(P-8269)*
M & T Calf Ranch.....D.......559 686-7663
14998 Avenue 192 Tulare (93274) *(P-400)*
M A A C Project, Chula Vista *Also called Metropolitan Area Advisory Com (P-24204)*
M A C, Northridge *Also called Mikuni American Corporation (P-6658)*
M Arthur Gensler Jr Assoc Inc.....E.......408 885-8100
225 W Santa Clara St San Jose (95113) *(P-26087)*
M Arthur Gensler Jr Assoc Inc (PA).....B.......415 433-3700
45 Fremont St Ste 1500 San Francisco (94105) *(P-26088)*
M Arthur Gensler Jr Assoc Inc.....C.......510 625-7400
2101 Webster St Ste 2000 Oakland (94612) *(P-26089)*
M Arthur Gensler Jr Assoc Inc.....C.......213 927-3600
500 S Figueroa St Los Angeles (90071) *(P-26090)*
M Arthur Gensler Jr Assoc Inc.....D.......949 863-9434
4675 Macarthur Ct Ste 100 Newport Beach (92660) *(P-26091)*
M B, San Jose *Also called Marquez Brothers Intl Inc (P-8424)*
M B M, Pleasanton *Also called Meadowbrook Meat Company Inc (P-8496)*
M Bar C Construction Inc.....D.......760 744-4131
674 Rancheros Dr San Marcos (92069) *(P-3385)*
M Block & Sons Inc.....C.......909 335-6684
26875 Pioneer Ave Redlands (92374) *(P-4588)*
M C, Los Angeles *Also called Muir-Chase Plumbing Co Inc (P-2284)*
M C Builder Corp.....E.......760 323-8010
1251 Montalvo Way Ste L Palm Springs (92262) *(P-2456)*
M C C, Brea *Also called Mercury Casualty Company (P-10371)*
M Caratan Inc (PA).....C.......661 725-2566
33787 Cecil Ave Delano (93215) *(P-159)*
M Caratan Inc.....C.......661 725-1777
33787 Cecil Ave Delano (93215) *(P-160)*
M E Nollkamper Inc (PA).....E.......951 737-9300
940 Manor Way Corona (92882) *(P-27310)*
M F Maher Inc.....D.......707 552-2774
490 Ryder St Vallejo (94590) *(P-1808)*
M F Salta Co Inc (PA).....D.......562 421-2512
20 Executive Park Ste 150 Irvine (92614) *(P-27311)*
M Gaw Inc.....D.......818 503-7997
6910 Farmdale Ave North Hollywood (91605) *(P-3546)*
M H Deyoung Memorial, San Francisco *Also called Corportion of Fine Arts Mseums (P-24877)*
M H Podell Company (PA).....D.......415 296-8800
22 Battery St Ste 404 Burlingame (94010) *(P-11888)*
M I G, Berkeley *Also called Moore Iacofano Goltsman Inc (P-27794)*
M I I, Bakersfield *Also called Mechanical Industries Inc (P-3387)*
M J D Concrete Works, Agoura Hills *Also called Mjd Construction Corp (P-1207)*
M K H Inc.....D.......818 882-9274
8870 Tampa Ave Northridge (91324) *(P-17831)*
M K S Construction Inc.....C.......916 446-2521
471 Bannon St Sacramento (95811) *(P-1193)*
M K Technical Services Inc.....E.......408 528-0401
4349 San Felipe Rd San Jose (95135) *(P-14874)*
M L Stern & Co LLC (HQ).....C.......323 658-4400
8350 Wilshire Blvd Fl 1 Beverly Hills (90211) *(P-9973)*
M M C, Covina *Also called Davita Magan Management Inc (P-19429)*
M M Direct Marketing Inc.....B.......714 265-4100
14271 Corporate Dr Garden Grove (92843) *(P-14051)*
M M Fab Inc.....D.......310 763-3800
2300 E Gladwick St Compton (90220) *(P-8231)*
M Network Television Inc.....E.......818 756-5150
6007 Sepulveda Blvd Van Nuys (91411) *(P-5822)*
M O C Insurance Services, San Francisco *Also called Maroevich OShea & Coghlan (P-10678)*
M O Dion & Sons Inc (PA).....D.......562 432-3946
1543 W 16th St Long Beach (90813) *(P-8966)*
M P Environmental Services, Bakersfield *Also called M P Vacuum Truck Service (P-6412)*
M P M & Associates Inc.....D.......818 708-9676
7011 Hayvenhurst Ave F Van Nuys (91406) *(P-1584)*
M P O Inc (HQ).....D.......562 628-1007
3760 Kilroy Airport Way # 5 Long Beach (90806) *(P-8189)*
M P Vacuum Truck Service (PA).....C.......661 393-1151
3400 Manor St Bakersfield (93308) *(P-6412)*
M R S, American Canyon *Also called Medical Receivables Solutions (P-27333)*
M S, Pleasant Hill *Also called Mark Scott Construction Inc (P-1587)*
M S E Enterprises Inc (PA).....D.......818 223-3500
23622 Calabasas Rd # 200 Calabasas (91302) *(P-11577)*
M S International Inc (PA).....B.......714 685-7500
2095 N Batavia St Orange (92865) *(P-6901)*
M Squared Consulting, San Francisco *Also called Collabrus Inc (P-26171)*
M Squared Consulting Inc (HQ).....C.......415 391-1038
111 Sutter St Ste 900 San Francisco (94104) *(P-27312)*
M T C, Los Angeles *Also called Mutual Trading Co Inc (P-8831)*
M T C, San Francisco *Also called Metropolitan Trnsp Comm (P-3682)*
M T C, City of Industry *Also called Micro-Technology Concepts Inc (P-7079)*
M T C Holdings (HQ).....E.......912 651-4000
3 Embarcadero Ctr Ste 550 San Francisco (94111) *(P-4729)*
M T D, Santa Barbara *Also called Santa Barbara Metro Trnst Dst (P-3720)*
M T M & M Inc.....D.......626 445-2922
3333 Peck Rd Monrovia (91016) *(P-14446)*
M T R, Newark *Also called Membrane Technology & RES Inc (P-26415)*
M V E, Modesto *Also called Mve Inc (P-25836)*
M V Transportation.....C.......831 373-1395
1375 Britain Ave Salinas (93901) *(P-5235)*
M V Transportation.....C.......760 255-3330
1612 State St Barstow (92311) *(P-5236)*
M X R, San Diego *Also called Merry X-Ray Chemical Corp (P-7192)*
M Z T, Santa Ana *Also called Macro-Z-Technology Company (P-1809)*
M&C Hotel Interests Inc.....D.......310 399-9344
530 Pico Blvd Santa Monica (90405) *(P-12866)*
M&G Duravent Inc.....B.......800 835-4429
877 Cotting Ct Vacaville (95688) *(P-4589)*
M&M Asset Management Gnl.....D.......310 769-6669
2936 W El Segundo Blvd Gardena (90249) *(P-11061)*
M-E Engineers Inc.....D.......310 842-8700
600 Wilshire Blvd # 1200 Los Angeles (90017) *(P-25804)*
M-N-Z Janitorial Services Inc.....C.......323 851-4115
2109 W Burbank Blvd Burbank (91506) *(P-14309)*
M4 Wind Services Inc.....D.......562 981-7797
4020 Long Beach Blvd Fl 2 Long Beach (90807) *(P-27940)*
M4dev LLC.....D.......619 696-6300
2137 Pacific Hwy Ste A San Diego (92101) *(P-12867)*
M7 Builders LLC.....E.......916 317-3529
4225 Northgate Blvd Sacramento (95834) *(P-1353)*
MA Laboratories Inc.....D.......626 820-8988
18725 San Jose Ave City of Industry (91748) *(P-26413)*
MA Labs, City of Industry *Also called MA Laboratories Inc (P-26413)*
MA Steiner Construction Inc.....D.......916 988-6300
2210 Plaza Dr Ste 300 Rocklin (95765) *(P-1419)*
Maac Project, Chula Vista *Also called Metropolitan Area Advisory Com (P-24206)*
Maac Project Cwbh, San Diego *Also called Metropolitan Area Advisory Com (P-24205)*
MAAP, Sacramento *Also called Mexican Amrcn Alcoholism Progr (P-23920)*
Mabie Marketing Group Inc.....C.......858 279-5585
8352 Clairemont Mesa Blvd San Diego (92111) *(P-17306)*
Mac Kenzie Warehouse, San Francisco *Also called S F Auto Parts Whse Inc (P-6671)*
Macarthur Transit Community.....C.......415 989-1111
345 Spear St Ste 700 San Francisco (94105) *(P-1194)*
Maccarthy House, San Jose *Also called Momentum For Mental Health (P-24808)*
Macdonald Housing Partners LP.....E.......510 620-0865
350 Macdonald Ave Ste 100 Richmond (94801) *(P-11578)*
Macdonald Mott Group Inc.....D.......323 903-4100
3699 Crenshaw Blvd Los Angeles (90016) *(P-25805)*
Macdonald Mott Group Inc.....D.......925 469-8010
12647 Alcosta Blvd San Ramon (94583) *(P-25806)*
Macdonald Mott LLC.....D.......408 321-5900
3103 N 1st St Bldg B San Jose (95134) *(P-25807)*
Macdonald Mott LLC.....D.......916 399-0580
2495 Natomas Park Dr # 530 Sacramento (95833) *(P-25808)*
Macerich Company (PA).....D.......310 394-6000
401 Wilshire Blvd Ste 700 Santa Monica (90401) *(P-12172)*
Macerich Company.....E.......562 861-9233
251 Stonewood St Downey (90241) *(P-10908)*
Macerich Company.....D.......310 474-5940
10800 W Pico Blvd Ste 312 Los Angeles (90064) *(P-11579)*
Macfarlane Partners LLC (PA).....D.......415 356-2500
201 Spear St Ste 1000 San Francisco (94105) *(P-12041)*
Machado & Sons Cnstr Inc.....E.......209 632-5260
1000 S Kilroy Rd Turlock (95380) *(P-1195)*
Machine Tools Supply, Costa Mesa *Also called Mt Supply Inc (P-7861)*
Machine Zone Inc (PA).....D.......650 320-1678
1050 Page Mill Rd Palo Alto (94304) *(P-15267)*
Machining Time Savers Inc.....D.......714 635-7373
1338 S State College Pkwy Anaheim (92806) *(P-7766)*
Machintel Corporation.....D.......617 517-3090
4225 Executive Sq Ste 955 La Jolla (92037) *(P-13860)*
Macias Gini & OConnell LLP (PA).....D.......916 928-4600
3000 S St Ste 300 Sacramento (95816) *(P-26255)*
Mackay Smps Cvil Engineers Inc (PA).....D.......925 416-1790
5142 Franklin Dr Ste C Pleasanton (94588) *(P-25809)*
Mackenzie Landscape A Cal Corp.....D.......951 679-5477
33380 Bailey Park Blvd Menifee (92584) *(P-893)*
Macmurray Pacific, San Francisco *Also called Wildenradt-Mcmurray Inc (P-7609)*
Macpherson's, Emeryville *Also called Art Supply Enterprises Inc (P-9196)*

Macqurie Arcft Lsg Svcs US Inc..........D......415 829-6600
2 Embarcadero Ctr Ste 200 San Francisco (94111) *(P-14523)*
Macro-Pro Inc (PA)..........C......562 595-0900
2400 Grand Ave Long Beach (90815) *(P-17307)*
Macro-Z-Technology Company (PA)..........D......714 564-1130
841 E Washington Ave Santa Ana (92701) *(P-1809)*
Macronix America Inc (HQ)..........D......408 262-8887
680 N Mccarthy Blvd # 200 Milpitas (95035) *(P-7506)*
Macsei Industries Corporation..........D......323 233-7864
1784 E Vernon Ave Vernon (90058) *(P-8621)*
Macys Inc..........D......916 373-0333
6200 Franklin Blvd Sacramento (95824) *(P-4684)*
Mad Dog Express Inc (PA)..........D......650 588-1900
299 Lawrence Ave South San Francisco (94080) *(P-4037)*
Mad Dogg Athletics Inc (PA)..........C......310 823-7008
2111 Narcissus Ct Venice (90291) *(P-8317)*
MAD RIVER COMMUNITY HOSPITAL, Arcata *Also called American Hospital Mgt Corp (P-21283)*
Madden Corporation..........D......714 922-1670
733 W Taft Ave Orange (92865) *(P-17308)*
Maddox Dairy LLC..........D......559 867-3545
3899 W Davis Ave Riverdale (93656) *(P-419)*
Maddox Dairy A Ltd Partnership (PA)..........D......559 867-3545
3899 W Davis Ave Riverdale (93656) *(P-420)*
Maddox Dairy A Ltd Partnership..........E......559 867-4457
7285 W Davis Ave Riverdale (93656) *(P-421)*
Maddox Dairy A Ltd Partnership..........D......559 866-5624
12863 W Kamm Ave Riverdale (93656) *(P-422)*
Made In USA Foundation Inc..........E......310 623-3872
11950 San Vicente Blvd # 220 Los Angeles (90049) *(P-25195)*
Mader News Inc..........D......818 551-5000
913 Ruberta Ave Glendale (91201) *(P-9117)*
Madera Cnty Bhvioral Hlth Svcs..........C......559 673-3508
209 E 7th St Madera (93638) *(P-22616)*
Madera Community Hospital..........C......559 675-5530
1210 E Almond Ave Ste A Madera (93637) *(P-21572)*
Madera Community Hospital..........C......559 665-3768
285 Hospital Dr Chowchilla (93610) *(P-21573)*
Madera Community Hospital (PA)..........B......559 675-5555
1250 E Almond Ave Madera (93637) *(P-21574)*
Madera Convalescent Hospital (PA)..........C......559 673-9228
517 S A St Madera (93638) *(P-20605)*
Madera Convalescent Hospital..........D......209 723-8814
1255 B St Merced (95341) *(P-21964)*
Madera Convalescent Hospital..........C......209 723-2911
510 W 26th St Merced (95340) *(P-21147)*
Madera Convalescent Hospital..........D......530 885-7051
260 Racetrack St Auburn (95603) *(P-21148)*
Madera County Probation Dept, Madera *Also called County of Los Angeles (P-23688)*
Madera County Road Department, Madera *Also called County of Madera (P-17858)*
Madera Private Security Patrol..........D......559 662-1546
910 W Yosemite Ave Madera (93637) *(P-16726)*
Madera Quality Nut, Madera *Also called Ready Roast Nut Company LLC (P-557)*
Maderas Golf Club..........D......858 451-8100
17750 Old Coach Rd Poway (92064) *(P-18731)*
Madison Care Center LLC..........D......619 444-1107
1391 E Madison Ave El Cajon (92021) *(P-20606)*
Madison Club Owners Assn..........C......760 777-9320
53035 Meriwether Way La Quinta (92253) *(P-18732)*
Madison Club, The, La Quinta *Also called Madison Club Owners Assn (P-18732)*
Madison Materials..........D......714 664-0159
1035 E 4th St Santa Ana (92701) *(P-6413)*
Madison Radiology Med Group..........D......626 793-8189
65 N Madison Ave Ste M250 Pasadena (91101) *(P-19665)*
Madison Square Building, Oakland *Also called San Francisco Bay Area Rapid (P-3714)*
Madrona Mnr Wine Cntry Inn..........D......707 433-4231
1001 Westside Rd Healdsburg (95448) *(P-12868)*
Madrone Vineyard Management, Sonoma *Also called Clarbec Inc (P-136)*
Maersk Inc..........D......714 428-5500
555 Anton Blvd Ste 300 Costa Mesa (92626) *(P-5104)*
Maersk Line, Costa Mesa *Also called Maersk Inc (P-5104)*
Mafab Inc (PA)..........D......714 893-0551
1925 Century Park E # 650 Los Angeles (90067) *(P-11991)*
Magagnini, Newark *Also called Intelliswift Software Inc (P-15225)*
Magana Labor Services Inc..........C......805 524-0446
2896 W Telegraph Rd Fillmore (93015) *(P-14666)*
Magarro Farms..........D......949 859-6506
23322 Peralta Dr Ste 3 Laguna Hills (92653) *(P-538)*
Magave Tequila Inc..........E......415 515-3536
6 Park Pl Belvedere Tiburon (94920) *(P-9051)*
Magdalena Ecke Family YMCA, Encinitas *Also called YMCA of San Diego County (P-25298)*
MAGELLAN HEALTH, San Diego *Also called Aurora Behavioral Health Care (P-21924)*
Maggiora Bros Drilling Inc (PA)..........D......831 724-1338
595 Airport Blvd Watsonville (95076) *(P-3354)*
Magic 92.5, San Diego *Also called Local Media San Diego LLC (P-5743)*
Magic Bullet, Los Angeles *Also called Homeland Housewares LLC (P-7418)*
Magic International, Santa Monica *Also called Mens Apparel Guild In Cal Inc (P-24967)*
Magic Mountain LLC..........B......661 255-4100
26101 Magic Mountain Pkwy Valencia (91355) *(P-18385)*
Magic Workforce Solutions LLC..........A......310 246-6153
9100 Wilsh Blvd Ste 700e Beverly Hills (90212) *(P-27563)*
Magma Design Automation Inc (HQ)..........B......408 565-7500
1650 Tech Dr Ste 100 San Jose (95110) *(P-15268)*
Magnell Associate Inc..........C......626 271-1420
9997 Rose Hills Rd Whittier (90601) *(P-4590)*
Magnell Associate Inc (HQ)..........C......626 271-9700
17560 Rowland St City of Industry (91748) *(P-7073)*
Magnell Associate Inc..........D......626 271-1580
18045 Rowland St City of Industry (91748) *(P-7074)*
Magnesite Specialties Inc..........E......858 578-4186
8686 Production Ave Ste A San Diego (92121) *(P-3113)*
Magnetic Imaging Affilates..........D......510 204-1820
5730 Telegraph Ave Oakland (94609) *(P-22108)*
Magnetika Inc (PA)..........D......310 527-8100
2041 W 139th St Gardena (90249) *(P-7374)*
MAGNOLIA CONVALESCENT HOSPITAL, Riverside *Also called Magnolia Rhbltion Nursing Ctr (P-21149)*
Magnolia Eductl RES Foundation (PA)..........D......714 892-5066
250 E 1st St Ste 1500 Los Angeles (90012) *(P-24804)*
Magnolia Grdns Convalescent HM, Granada Hills *Also called Longwood Management Corp (P-20598)*
Magnolia of Millbrae Inc..........D......650 697-7700
201 Chadbourne Ave Millbrae (94030) *(P-24590)*
Magnolia Post Acute Care, El Cajon *Also called Magnolia Special Care Center (P-20940)*
Magnolia Rhbltion Nursing Ctr..........C......951 688-4321
8133 Magnolia Ave Riverside (92504) *(P-21149)*
MAGNOLIA SCIENCE ACADEMY, Los Angeles *Also called Magnolia Eductl RES Foundation (P-24804)*
Magnolia Special Care Center..........D......619 442-8826
635 S Magnolia Ave El Cajon (92020) *(P-20940)*
Magnolia Ventures Ltd..........D......213 389-6900
4032 Wilshire Blvd Fl 6 Los Angeles (90010) *(P-17309)*
Magnum Drywall Inc..........D......510 979-0420
42027 Boscell Rd Fremont (94538) *(P-2911)*
Magnum USA, Van Nuys *Also called Hi-TEC Sports Usa Inc (P-8358)*
Magnus Security..........E......619 546-7789
2667 Camino Del Rio S San Diego (92108) *(P-16727)*
Magnussens Dodge Crysler Jeep..........D......530 885-2900
1901 Grass Valley Hwy Auburn (95603) *(P-17772)*
Maguire Aviation, Van Nuys *Also called 16700 Roscoe Associates LLC (P-18815)*
Maguire Aviation Group LLC..........E......818 989-2300
7155 Valjean Ave Van Nuys (91406) *(P-4863)*
Maguire Properties Twr 17 LLC..........D......310 857-1100
1733 Ocean Ave Fl 4 Santa Monica (90401) *(P-12173)*
Maher M F Concrete Cnstr, Vallejo *Also called M F Maher Inc (P-1808)*
MAI Systems, Lake Forest *Also called Infor (us) Inc (P-15710)*
Maida Specialties Co, San Jose *Also called John A Maida Enterprises (P-8083)*
Mail Boxes Etc, San Diego *Also called UPS Store Inc (P-17552)*
Mailmark Enterprises LLC..........E......818 407-0660
8587 Canoga Ave Canoga Park (91304) *(P-14052)*
Main Electric Supply Co LLC (PA)..........D......949 833-3052
3600 W Segerstrom Ave Santa Ana (92704) *(P-7375)*
Main Electric Supply Co LLC..........D......951 784-2900
461 Main St Riverside (92501) *(P-7376)*
Main Frame Construction, Santa Clarita *Also called Santa Clarita Valley Bldrs Inc (P-3074)*
Main Freight Sfo, South San Francisco *Also called Andrews Air Corporation (P-5007)*
Main Hospital, San Jose *Also called HCA Inc (P-21442)*
Main Street Fibers Inc..........D......909 986-6310
608 E Main St Ontario (91761) *(P-6414)*
Main Street Specialty Surgery..........D......714 704-1900
280 S Mn St Ste 100 Orange (92868) *(P-21575)*
Mainfreight Inc (HQ)..........D......310 900-1974
1400 Glenn Curtiss St Carson (90746) *(P-5105)*
Maintech Incorporated..........C......714 921-8000
2401 N Glassell St Orange (92865) *(P-15269)*
Maintenance, Long Beach *Also called Long Beach Unified School Dst (P-14306)*
Maintenance & Operation Dept, Montebello *Also called Montebello Unified School (P-14327)*
Maintenance & Operations, Lodi *Also called Lodi Unified School District (P-14305)*
Maintenance & Trnsp Fcilty, Irvine *Also called Irvine Unified School Distict (P-3938)*
Maintenance Department, Petaluma *Also called Transportation California Dept (P-1863)*
Maintenance Department, Fresno *Also called Fresno Unified School District (P-14270)*
Maintenance Dept, Gardena *Also called Los Angeles Unified School Dst (P-14307)*
Maintenance Dept, Brea *Also called City of Brea (P-27581)*
Maintenance Service For The Cy..........D......510 865-3778
1616 Fortmann Way Alameda (94501) *(P-14310)*
Maintenance Staff Inc..........A......562 493-3982
122 W 8th St Long Beach (90813) *(P-14311)*
Maintenance Unit, San Diego *Also called San Diego Unified School Dst (P-14375)*
Majestic Industry Hills LLC..........B......626 810-4455
1 Industry Hills Pkwy City of Industry (91744) *(P-12869)*
Majestic Industry Hills LLC (PA)..........A......562 692-9581
1 Industry Hills Pkwy City of Industry (91744) *(P-12870)*
Majestic Terminal Services Inc..........D......909 937-2580
2300 E Airport Dr Ontario (91761) *(P-3889)*
Majesty One Properties Inc..........C......909 980-8000
6249 Quartz St Rancho Cucamonga (91701) *(P-11580)*
Major Transportation Svcs Inc..........E......559 485-5949
3342 N Weber Ave Fresno (93722) *(P-4218)*
Makallon La Jolla Properties, Newport Beach *Also called Makar Properties LLC (P-11889)*
Makar Anaheim LLC..........A......714 740-4431
777 W Convention Way Anaheim (92802) *(P-12871)*
Makar Properties LLC (PA)..........A......949 255-1100
4100 Macarthur Blvd # 150 Newport Beach (92660) *(P-11889)*
Maker Studios Inc (HQ)..........C......310 606-2182
3515 Eastham Dr Culver City (90232) *(P-18450)*
Making Waves Education Program (PA)..........C......510 237-3434
3220 Blume Dr Ste 250 San Pablo (94806) *(P-12111)*
Makita USA Inc (HQ)..........C......714 522-8088
14930 Northam St La Mirada (90638) *(P-7597)*
Malaga Bank Fsb (HQ)..........D......310 375-9000
2514 Via Tejon Palos Verdes Estates (90274) *(P-9525)*
Malaga Financial Corporation (PA)..........D......310 375-9000
2514 Via Tejon Palos Verdes Estates (90274) *(P-9536)*

ALPHABETIC

Employee Codes: A=Over 500 employees, B=251-500
C=101-250, D=51-100, E=50
2019 Directory of California
Wholesalers and Services Companies
© Mergent Inc. 1-800-342-5647
1375

Malco Maintenance Inc....D....714 630-0194
3703 E Melville Way Anaheim (92806) ***(P-3547)***
Malco Services, Anaheim *Also called Malco Maintenance Inc* ***(P-3547)***
Malco Services Inc....D....714 630-0194
3703 E Melville Way Anaheim (92806) ***(P-27313)***
Malcolm & Cisneros A Law Corp....C....949 252-1039
2112 Business Center Dr # 200 Irvine (92612) ***(P-23236)***
Malcolm Cisneros, Irvine *Also called Malcolm & Cisneros A Law Corp* ***(P-23236)***
Malcolm Drilling Company Inc (PA)....C....415 901-4400
92 Natoma St Ste 400 San Francisco (94105) ***(P-3548)***
MALDEF, Los Angeles *Also called Mexican American Legal Defense* ***(P-23250)***
Malibu Beach Inn, Malibu *Also called Mbipch LLC* ***(P-12916)***
Malibu Canyon Ldscp & Maint....D....805 523-2676
2046 Tierra Rejada Rd Moorpark (93021) ***(P-766)***
Malibu Castle, Aliso Viejo *Also called Apex Parks Group LLC* ***(P-19099)***
Malibu Castle....E....210 341-6663
27061 Aliso Creek Rd # 100 Aliso Viejo (92656) ***(P-18804)***
Malibu Conference Center Inc....B....818 889-6440
327 Latigo Canyon Rd Malibu (90265) ***(P-10909)***
Malibu Country Club, Malibu *Also called California Fuji International* ***(P-18691)***
Malibu Design Group....E....323 271-1700
5445 Jillson St Commerce (90040) ***(P-8318)***
Malibu Grand Prix 51, Newport Beach *Also called Festival Fun Parks LLC* ***(P-18800)***
Malibu Lagoon Museum, Malibu *Also called Parks and Recreation Cal Dept* ***(P-24899)***
Malibu Limousine Service, Marina Del Rey *Also called Executive Network Entps Inc* ***(P-3793)***
Malibu Realty Inc....E....310 457-5124
23838 Pacific Coast Hwy Malibu (90265) ***(P-11581)***
Malibu Realty Property MGT, Malibu *Also called Malibu Realty Inc* ***(P-11581)***
Malikco LLC....E....925 974-3555
2121 N Calif Blvd Ste 290 Walnut Creek (94596) ***(P-15747)***
Malka Communications Group Inc....E....818 239-4431
15260 Ventura Blvd Sherman Oaks (91403) ***(P-27941)***
Mallcraft Inc....E....626 765-9100
2225 Windsor Ave Altadena (91001) ***(P-1585)***
Malloy Orchards Inc....C....530 695-1861
925 Koch Ln Live Oak (95953) ***(P-224)***
Maloof Sport Entertainment, Sacramento *Also called Kings Arena Ltd Partnership* ***(P-18522)***
Mamco Inc (PA)....C....951 776-9300
764 Ramona Expy Ste C Perris (92571) ***(P-1810)***
Mammoth Hospital, Mammoth Lakes *Also called Southern Mono Healthcare Dst* ***(P-21770)***
Mammoth Mountain Inn, Mammoth Lakes *Also called Mammoth Mountain Ski Area LLC* ***(P-12872)***
Mammoth Mountain Lake Corp....B....760 934-2571
10001 Minaret Rd Mammoth Lakes (93546) ***(P-13452)***
Mammoth Mountain Ski Area LLC (HQ)....B....760 934-2571
10001 Minaret Rd Mammoth Lakes (93546) ***(P-12872)***
Mamone James M, Roseville *Also called Sutter Health* ***(P-19959)***
Managed Care Systems Kern Cnty....D....661 716-7100
5251 Office Park Dr # 405 Bakersfield (93309) ***(P-10675)***
Managed Health Network....A....714 934-5519
7755 Center Ave Ste 700 Huntington Beach (92647) ***(P-10280)***
Managed Health Network (HQ)....B....415 460-8168
2370 Kerner Blvd San Rafael (94901) ***(P-10281)***
Managed Health Network....A....510 620-6143
2370 Kerner Blvd San Rafael (94901) ***(P-10282)***
Managed Homecare Inc....E....951 341-0782
2520 Redhill Ave Santa Ana (92705) ***(P-22362)***
Management Associates, Saint Helena *Also called Silverado Orchards* ***(P-11114)***
Management Success, Monrovia *Also called Leekilpatrick Management Inc* ***(P-27301)***
Management Tech Consulting LLC....D....323 851-5008
7738 Skyhill Dr Los Angeles (90068) ***(P-27780)***
Management Trust Assn Inc....C....805 496-5514
100 E Thousand Oaks Blvd Thousand Oaks (91360) ***(P-12112)***
Management Trust Assn Inc....C....858 547-4373
9815 Carroll Canyon Rd San Diego (92131) ***(P-12113)***
Management Trust Assn Inc....C....951 694-1758
4160 Temescal Canyon Rd # 202 Corona (92883) ***(P-12114)***
Management Trust Assn Inc (PA)....D....714 285-2626
15661 Red Hill Ave # 201 Tustin (92780) ***(P-12115)***
Management Trust Assn Inc....C....562 926-3372
12607 Hiddencreek Way R Cerritos (90703) ***(P-27314)***
Management Trust, The, Tustin *Also called Management Trust Assn Inc* ***(P-12115)***
Manas Hospitality LLC....E....619 298-1291
445 Hotel Cir S San Diego (92108) ***(P-12873)***
Manatt Phelps & Phillips LLP....E....714 371-2500
695 Town Center Dr # 1400 Costa Mesa (92626) ***(P-23237)***
Manchester Band Pomo Indians....D....707 882-2788
24 Mamie Laiwa Dr Point Arena (95468) ***(P-23909)***
Manchester Center, Fresno *Also called US Property Group Inc* ***(P-10958)***
Manchester Grand Resorts LP....A....619 232-1234
1 Market Pl Fl 33 San Diego (92101) ***(P-12874)***
Manchester Point Arena, Point Arena *Also called Manchester Band Pomo Indians* ***(P-23909)***
Manchster Mnor Cnvlescent Hosp....D....323 753-1789
837 W Manchester Ave Los Angeles (90044) ***(P-21150)***
Mandalay Baseball Properties, Los Angeles *Also called Mandalay Sports Entrmt LLC* ***(P-18529)***
Mandalay Sports Entrmt LLC (PA)....D....323 549-4300
4751 Wilshire Blvd Fl 3 Los Angeles (90010) ***(P-18529)***
Manduka LLC (HQ)....E....310 426-1495
2121 Park Pl Ste 250 El Segundo (90245) ***(P-7933)***
Mangan Inc (PA)....D....310 835-8080
3901 Via Oro Ave Long Beach (90810) ***(P-25810)***
Mangold Property Management....D....831 372-1338
575 Calle Principal Monterey (93940) ***(P-11582)***
Mangrove Lab & X-Ray, Chico *Also called Mangrove Medical Group* ***(P-19666)***
Mangrove Medical Group....E....530 345-0064
1040 Mangrove Ave Chico (95926) ***(P-19666)***
MANHATTAN COUNTRY CLUB, Manhattan Beach *Also called 1334 Partners LP* ***(P-18814)***
Manheim Riverside Auto Auction, Riverside *Also called Cox Automotive Inc* ***(P-6587)***
Manheim San Diego, Oceanside *Also called Cox Automotive Inc* ***(P-6588)***
Manhole Adjusting Contrs Inc....E....323 725-1387
9500 Beverly Rd Pico Rivera (90660) ***(P-1811)***
Maniflo Money Exchange Inc....D....619 434-7200
1442 Highland Ave National City (91950) ***(P-9688)***
Mann Lake Ltd....E....530 662-4061
500 Santa Anita Dr Woodland (95776) ***(P-9085)***
Mann Packing Co Inc (HQ)....B....831 422-7405
1333 Schilling Pl Salinas (93901) ***(P-539)***
Mann's Theatres, Los Angeles *Also called Weststar Cinemas Inc* ***(P-18323)***
Manning Gardens Inc....E....559 834-2586
2113 E Manning Ave Fresno (93725) ***(P-20607)***
Manning Gardens Care Ctr Inc....D....559 834-2586
2113 E Manning Ave Fresno (93725) ***(P-20608)***
Manning Grdns Cnvalescent Hosp, Fresno *Also called Manning Gardens Inc* ***(P-20607)***
Manning Kass Ellrod Ram Trestr (PA)....C....213 624-6900
801 S Figueroa St Fl 15 Los Angeles (90017) ***(P-23238)***
Mannkind Corporation (PA)....C....818 661-5000
30930 Russell Ranch Rd # 300 Westlake Village (91362) ***(P-26414)***
Manor At Santa Teresita Hosp, Duarte *Also called Santa Teresita Inc* ***(P-21722)***
Manor Bell L P....D....707 526-9782
790 Sonoma Ave Santa Rosa (95404) ***(P-1354)***
Manor Care, Fountain Valley *Also called Hcr Manorcare Med Svcs Fla LLC* ***(P-20509)***
Manor Care, Citrus Heights *Also called Hcr Manorcare Med Svcs Fla LLC* ***(P-20510)***
Manor Care, Sunnyvale *Also called Hcr Manorcare Med Svcs Fla LLC* ***(P-20512)***
Manorcare Health Services, Walnut Creek *Also called Hcr Manorcare Med Svcs Fla LLC* ***(P-20508)***
Manorcare Health Svcs Hemet, Hemet *Also called Hcr Manorcare Med Svcs Fla LLC* ***(P-20511)***
Manorcare Health Svcs Rossmoor, Walnut Creek *Also called Hcr Manorcare Med Svcs Fla LLC* ***(P-20513)***
Manorcare Hlth Svcs Encinitas, Encinitas *Also called Hcr Manorcare Med Svcs Fla LLC* ***(P-20514)***
Manpower, San Diego *Also called United States Dept of Navy* ***(P-14928)***
Manpower, San Diego *Also called CPM Ltd Inc* ***(P-14844)***
Mansion Hospitality Services....D....916 643-6222
3410 Westover St McClellan (95652) ***(P-27315)***
Manteca Care Rhabilitation Ctr, Manteca *Also called Karma Inc* ***(P-20551)***
Mantech International Corp....C....858 492-9938
8328 Clairemont Mesa Blvd San Diego (92111) ***(P-16001)***
Mantech International Corp....C....310 765-9324
615 N Nash St Ste 200 El Segundo (90245) ***(P-16002)***
Mantech Systems Engrg Corp....D....858 292-9000
8328 Clairemont Mesa Blvd # 100 San Diego (92111) ***(P-27781)***
Manufacturers Bank (HQ)....C....213 489-6200
515 S Figueroa St Fl 4 Los Angeles (90071) ***(P-9511)***
Manufacturing Facility, Davis *Also called Schilling Robotics LLC* ***(P-25905)***
Manufacturing Solutions Inc (PA)....B....714 453-0100
1738 N Neville St Orange (92865) ***(P-26937)***
MAOF, Montebello *Also called Mexican Amrcn Oprtnty Fndation* ***(P-23921)***
Maof Commerce, Commerce *Also called Mexican Amrcn Oprtnty Fndation* ***(P-23922)***
Map Cargo Global Logistics (PA)....D....310 297-8300
2501 Santa Fe Ave Redondo Beach (90278) ***(P-5106)***
Mapp Digital Us LLC....C....619 295-1856
9276 Scranton Rd Ste 500 San Diego (92121) ***(P-27316)***
Mapr Data Technologies, Santa Clara *Also called Mapr Technologies Inc* ***(P-15270)***
Mapr Technologies Inc (PA)....B....408 914-2390
4555 Great America Pkwy # 201 Santa Clara (95054) ***(P-15270)***
Mar-Kell Seal, Irvine *Also called Quadion LLC* ***(P-10107)***
Marathon General Inc....D....760 738-9714
1728 Mission Rd Escondido (92029) ***(P-1812)***
Marathon Industries Inc....C....661 286-1520
25597 Springbrook Ave Santa Clarita (91350) ***(P-6603)***
Marathon Land Inc (PA)....C....805 488-3585
2599 E Hueneme Rd Oxnard (93033) ***(P-281)***
Marathon Truck Bodies, Santa Clarita *Also called Marathon Industries Inc* ***(P-6603)***
Maravilla Foundation (PA)....D....323 721-4162
5729 Union Pacific Ave Commerce (90022) ***(P-25196)***
Marbella Country Club....C....949 248-3700
30800 Golf Club Dr San Juan Capistrano (92675) ***(P-18965)***
Marbella Golf & Country Club....C....949 248-3700
30800 Golf Club Dr San Juan Capistrano (92675) ***(P-18966)***
Marblewest Inc....E....714 847-6472
7421 Vincent Cir Huntington Beach (92648) ***(P-3003)***
Marbleworks, Huntington Beach *Also called Marblewest Inc* ***(P-3003)***
Marborg Industries (PA)....C....805 963-1852
728 E Yanonali St Santa Barbara (93103) ***(P-6415)***
March International Inc....E....909 821-5128
1249 S Dmnd Bar Blvd 20 Diamond Bar (91765) ***(P-2044)***
Marchini Inc....E....209 389-4566
12006 Le Grand Rd Le Grand (95333) ***(P-370)***
Marco Crane & Rigging Co....D....619 938-8080
10168 Channel Rd Lakeside (92040) ***(P-14447)***
Marco Roofing, Fremont *Also called Milan Corporation* ***(P-3180)***
Marcolin USA Inc....D....415 383-6348
6 Janet Way Apt 116 Belvedere Tiburon (94920) ***(P-7236)***
Marcos Auto Body Inc (PA)....D....626 286-5691
1390 E Palm St Altadena (91001) ***(P-17728)***
Marcum LLP....D....415 543-6900
303 2nd St Ste 950 San Francisco (94107) ***(P-26256)***
Marcum LLP....D....310 432-7400
2049 Century Park E # 300 Los Angeles (90067) ***(P-26257)***
Marcus & Millichap Capitl Corp....E....818 212-2250
23975 Park Sorrento # 400 Calabasas (91302) ***(P-11583)***

Marcus & Millichap Real Estate....................E.......415 391-9220
750 Battery St Fl 5 San Francisco (94111) ***(P-11584)***
Marcus Buckingham Company....................D.......323 302-9810
8350 Wilshire Blvd # 200 Beverly Hills (90211) ***(P-27317)***
Marcus Millichap Reis Nev Inc....................D.......650 494-1400
23975 Park Sorrento # 400 Calabasas (91302) ***(P-11585)***
Marcus Mllchap RE Inv Svcs Inc (HQ)....................E.......818 212-2250
23975 Park Sorrento # 400 Calabasas (91302) ***(P-11586)***
Mardx Diagnostics Inc....................D.......760 929-0500
5919 Farnsworth Ct Carlsbad (92008) ***(P-7188)***
Mare Island Outpatient Clinic, Vallejo *Also called Veterans Health Administration* ***(P-20058)***
Marelich Mechanical Co Inc (HQ)....................D.......510 785-5500
24041 Amador St Hayward (94544) ***(P-2273)***
Margate Construction Inc....................C.......310 830-8610
25007 Figueroa St Carson (90745) ***(P-1952)***
Marginpoint (PA)....................D.......949 766-9933
23046 Avnida De La Crlota Carlota Laguna Hills (92653) ***(P-27318)***
Marguerite Gardens, La Canada Flintridge *Also called California Peo Home* ***(P-24449)***
Mariadb Usa Inc....................D.......847 562-9000
350 Bay St Ste 100-319 San Francisco (94133) ***(P-7075)***
Mariak Industries Inc....................B.......310 661-4400
575 W Manville St Rancho Dominguez (90220) ***(P-6775)***
Mariak Window Fashion, Rancho Dominguez *Also called Mariak Industries Inc* ***(P-6775)***
Marian Extended Care Cntr, Santa Maria *Also called Dignity Health* ***(P-20377)***
Marian Home Care and Hospice, Santa Maria *Also called Dignity Health* ***(P-22285)***
Marian Hospital Homecare, Arroyo Grande *Also called Dignity Health* ***(P-22284)***
Marian Regional Medical Center, Santa Maria *Also called Dignity Health* ***(P-21369)***
Marian West, Santa Maria *Also called Dignity Health* ***(P-21390)***
Mariani Nut Company Inc (PA)....................C.......530 795-3311
709 Dutton St Winters (95694) ***(P-192)***
Mariani Nut Company Inc....................D.......530 795-2225
12 Baker St Winters (95694) ***(P-193)***
Mariani Packing Co Inc (PA)....................B.......707 452-2800
500 Crocker Dr Vacaville (95688) ***(P-540)***
Marianis Inn & Restaurant....................C.......408 243-0312
2500 El Camino Real Santa Clara (95051) ***(P-12875)***
Marianne Frostig Center (PA)....................E.......626 791-1255
971 N Altadena Dr Pasadena (91107) ***(P-25026)***
Maricopa Packers, Bakersfield *Also called Sun Pacific Maricopa* ***(P-570)***
Marie Cllender Wholesalers Inc....................D.......951 737-6760
170 E Rincon St Corona (92879) ***(P-8495)***
Marika Group Inc....................D.......858 537-5300
8960 Carroll Way San Diego (92121) ***(P-8319)***
Marin Airporter Inc....................D.......415 884-2878
1455 N Hamilton Pkwy Novato (94949) ***(P-3880)***
Marin Airporter Chrtr & Tours, San Rafael *Also called Marin Airporter Inc* ***(P-3680)***
Marin Airporter Inc (PA)....................D.......415 256-8833
8 Lovell Ave San Rafael (94901) ***(P-3680)***
Marin City Library, Sausalito *Also called County of Marin* ***(P-23689)***
Marin Clean Energy....................D.......415 464-6028
1125 Tamalpais Ave San Rafael (94901) ***(P-6051)***
Marin Cnvlscent Rhbltion Hosp....................D.......415 435-4554
30 Hacienda Dr Belvedere Tiburon (94920) ***(P-20609)***
Marin Community Clinic....................D.......415 448-1500
9 Commercial Blvd Ste 100 Novato (94949) ***(P-19667)***
Marin Community Clinics, Novato *Also called Marin Community Clinic* ***(P-19667)***
Marin Country Club Inc....................D.......415 382-6700
500 Country Club Dr Novato (94949) ***(P-18967)***
Marin County Sart Program....................D.......415 892-1628
655 Canyon Rd Novato (94947) ***(P-21965)***
Marin County Welfare Dept, San Rafael *Also called County of Marin* ***(P-23690)***
Marin General Hospital....................A.......415 925-7000
250 Bon Air Rd Kentfield (94904) ***(P-21576)***
Marin Horizon School Inc....................E.......415 388-8408
305 Montford Ave Mill Valley (94941) ***(P-24344)***
Marin Humane Society....................D.......415 883-4621
171 Bel Marin Keys Blvd Novato (94949) ***(P-25442)***
Marin Industrial Distributors, San Rafael *Also called Jacksons Hardware Inc* ***(P-7592)***
Marin Labor Services....................C.......805 525-7730
277 Country View Ct Santa Paula (93060) ***(P-659)***
Marin Municipal Water District (PA)....................C.......415 945-1455
220 Nellen Ave Corte Madera (94925) ***(P-6278)***
Marin Resource Recovery Center, San Rafael *Also called Marin Sanitary Service* ***(P-6416)***
Marin Sanitary Service (PA)....................D.......415 456-2601
1050 Andersen Dr San Rafael (94901) ***(P-6416)***
Marin Snior Crdnting Cncil Inc....................D.......415 454-0964
930 Tamalpais Ave San Rafael (94901) ***(P-23910)***
Marin Software Incorporated (PA)....................C.......415 399-2580
123 Mission St Fl 27 San Francisco (94105) ***(P-16153)***
Marina Auto Body Shop Inc....................E.......310 822-6615
721 Washington Blvd Marina Del Rey (90292) ***(P-17729)***
Marina Autobody, Marina Del Rey *Also called Williamson Enterprises Inc* ***(P-17745)***
Marina Care Center, Culver City *Also called D K Fortune & Associates Inc* ***(P-21057)***
Marina City Club LP A Cali....................C.......310 822-0611
4333 Admiralty Way Marina Del Rey (90292) ***(P-11062)***
Marina Convalescent Center, Fremont *Also called C J Health Services Inc* ***(P-20277)***
Marina Del Rey Hospital....................A.......310 823-8911
4650 Lincoln Blvd Marina Del Rey (90292) ***(P-21577)***
Marina Inn, San Leandro *Also called Apple Inns Inc* ***(P-12329)***
Marina International Hotel, Venice *Also called Outrigger Hotels Hawaii* ***(P-12989)***
Marina International Hotel, Marina Del Rey *Also called Al Anwa USA Incorporated* ***(P-12310)***
Marina Landscape Inc....................D.......714 939-6600
3707 W Garden Grove Blvd Orange (92868) ***(P-767)***
Marina Landscape Maint Inc....................B.......714 939-6600
1900 S Lewis St Anaheim (92805) ***(P-768)***
Marine Avenue Adult Center, Wilmington *Also called Los Angeles Unified School Dst* ***(P-23906)***
Marine Band San Diego....................E.......619 524-1754
1400 Russell Ave San Diego (92140) ***(P-18451)***
Marine Corps United States....................A.......760 725-1304
Camp Pendleton Oceanside (92055) ***(P-22034)***
Marine Corps United States....................E.......760 430-4709
A St Bldg 1341 Camp Pendleton (92055) ***(P-12876)***
Marine Corps Community Svcs, San Diego *Also called Business and Support Services* ***(P-19115)***
Marine Mammal Center (PA)....................E.......415 339-0430
2000 Bunker Rd Sausalito (94965) ***(P-604)***
Marine Room Restaurant, La Jolla *Also called La Jolla Bch & Tennis CLB Inc* ***(P-18946)***
Marine Technical Services Inc....................D.......310 549-8030
211 N Marine Ave Wilmington (90744) ***(P-17310)***
Marine World/Africa USA, Vallejo *Also called City of Vallejo* ***(P-18794)***
Mariner, San Jose *Also called Health & Rehabilitation Center* ***(P-20515)***
Mariner Health Care Inc....................D.......310 371-4628
4109 Emerald St Torrance (90503) ***(P-20610)***
Mariner Health Care Inc....................C.......510 792-3743
39022 Presidio Way Fremont (94538) ***(P-20611)***
Mariner Health Care Inc....................C.......408 842-9311
8170 Murray Ave Gilroy (95020) ***(P-20612)***
Mariner Health Care Inc....................C.......408 298-3950
2065 Forest Ave San Jose (95128) ***(P-20613)***
Mariner Health Care Inc....................C.......916 422-4825
7400 24th St Sacramento (95822) ***(P-20614)***
Mariner Health Care Inc....................C.......510 232-5945
13484 San Pablo Ave San Pablo (94806) ***(P-20615)***
Mariner Health Care Inc....................C.......310 677-9114
100 S Hillcrest Blvd Inglewood (90301) ***(P-20616)***
Mariner Health Care Inc....................D.......323 665-1185
3032 Rowena Ave Los Angeles (90039) ***(P-20617)***
Mariner Health Care Inc....................C.......530 756-1800
1850 E 8th St Davis (95616) ***(P-20618)***
Mariner Health Care Inc....................C.......818 246-5677
430 N Glendale Ave Glendale (91206) ***(P-20619)***
Mariner Health Care Inc....................D.......831 475-6323
675 24th Ave Santa Cruz (95062) ***(P-20620)***
Mariner Health Care Inc....................D.......510 538-4424
1768 B St Hayward (94541) ***(P-20621)***
Mariner Health Care Inc....................C.......510 785-2880
19700 Hesperian Blvd Hayward (94541) ***(P-20622)***
Mariner Health Care Inc....................D.......562 942-7019
8925 Mines Ave Pico Rivera (90660) ***(P-20623)***
Mariner Health Care Inc....................D.......415 479-3610
45 Professional Ctr Pkwy San Rafael (94903) ***(P-20624)***
Mariner Health Care Inc....................D.......408 377-9275
2065 Los Gatos Almaden Rd San Jose (95124) ***(P-20625)***
Mariner Health Care Inc....................D.......510 261-5200
3025 High St Oakland (94619) ***(P-20626)***
Mariner Health Care Inc....................C.......209 466-2066
537 E Fulton St Stockton (95204) ***(P-20627)***
Mariner Health Care Inc....................D.......818 985-5990
13000 Victory Blvd North Hollywood (91606) ***(P-20628)***
Mariner Health Care Inc....................D.......818 957-0850
3050 Montrose Ave La Crescenta (91214) ***(P-20629)***
Mariner Health Care Inc....................C.......916 481-5500
3400 Alta Arden Expy Sacramento (95825) ***(P-20630)***
Mariner Square Athletic Inc....................D.......510 523-8011
2227 Mariner Square Loop Alameda (94501) ***(P-18629)***
Mariner Systems Inc (PA)....................D.......305 266-7255
114 C Ave Coronado (92118) ***(P-17311)***
Mariner's Point Golf Course, Foster City *Also called Vb Golf LLC* ***(P-18775)***
Mariners Cove Apartments, San Diego *Also called Lincoln Mariners Assoc Ltd* ***(P-11055)***
Marines Memorial Association....................C.......415 673-6672
609 Sutter St San Francisco (94102) ***(P-25197)***
MARINES' MEMORIAL CLUB & HOTEL, San Francisco *Also called Marines Memorial Association* ***(P-25197)***
Marinow Harry MD Facs Inc....................E.......562 430-3561
3742 Katella Ave Ste 401 Los Alamitos (90720) ***(P-19668)***
Mariposa Horticultural Entps, Irwindale *Also called Mariposa Landscapes Inc* ***(P-894)***
Mariposa Landscapes Inc (PA)....................D.......626 960-0196
6232 Santos Diaz St Irwindale (91702) ***(P-894)***
Maritzcx Research LLC....................D.......310 783-4300
20285 S Wstn Ave Ste 101 Torrance (90501) ***(P-4972)***
Maritzcx Research LLC....................A.......310 525-1300
3901 Via Oro Ave Ste 200 Long Beach (90810) ***(P-26542)***
Mariz Berry Farms....................C.......805 981-9908
1650 E Gonzales Rd Oxnard (93036) ***(P-107)***
Mark 1 Mortgage Corporation (PA)....................E.......714 752-5700
1342 E Chapman Ave Orange (92866) ***(P-9894)***
Mark Clemons....................C.......760 361-1531
4584 Adobe Rd Twentynine Palms (92277) ***(P-4219)***
Mark Diversified Inc....................E.......916 923-6275
650 Howe Ave Ste 1045 Sacramento (95825) ***(P-1586)***
Mark E Jacobson M D....................D.......707 571-4022
1260 N Dutton Ave Ste 230 Santa Rosa (95401) ***(P-19669)***
Mark Garcia....................D.......707 446-4529
5131 Ellsworth Rd Ste B Vacaville (95688) ***(P-14312)***
Mark H Leibenhaut MD....................E.......916 454-6600
2800 L St Ste 110 Sacramento (95816) ***(P-19670)***
Mark Herzog & Company Inc....................D.......818 762-4640
4640 Lankershim Blvd North Hollywood (91602) ***(P-18075)***
Mark III Construction Inc (PA)....................D.......916 381-8080
5101 Florin Perkins Rd Sacramento (95826) ***(P-2633)***
Mark III Dvlpers Dsgn/Builders, Sacramento *Also called Mark III Construction Inc* ***(P-2633)***
Mark Land Electric Inc....................D.......818 883-5110
7876 Deering Ave Canoga Park (91304) ***(P-2634)***
Mark One Corporation....................E.......209 537-4581
1711 Richland Ave Ceres (95307) ***(P-21151)***

ALPHABETIC

Employee Codes: A=Over 500 employees, B=251-500
C=101-250, D=51-100, E=50
2019 Directory of California
Wholesalers and Services Companies
© Mergent Inc. 1-800-342-5647
1377

Mark R Eggen Construction Inc ....E....949 661-2674
34145 Pacific Coast Hwy # 325 Dana Point (92629) ***(P-1196)***
Mark Roberts, Santa Ana *Also called Celmol Inc* ***(P-9202)***
Mark Scott Construction Inc ....D....209 982-0502
241 Frank West Cir # 200 Stockton (95206) ***(P-1301)***
Mark Scott Construction Inc (PA) ....E....925 944-0502
2835 Contra Costa Blvd Pleasant Hill (94523) ***(P-1587)***
Mark Twain Conv. Hospital, San Andreas *Also called Avalon Care Center* ***(P-20243)***
Mark Twain Medical Center (HQ) ....C....209 754-3521
768 Mountain Ranch Rd San Andreas (95249) ***(P-21578)***
Mark Twain Medical Center ....B....209 754-1487
768 Mountain Ranch Rd San Andreas (95249) ***(P-21579)***
MARK TWAIN ST JOSEPH'S HOSPITAL, San Andreas *Also called Mark Twain Medical Center* ***(P-21578)***
Mark Twain St Josephs Hospital, San Andreas *Also called Dignity Health* ***(P-21384)***
Markel Corp ....B....818 595-0600
21600 Oxnard St Ste 900 Woodland Hills (91367) ***(P-10676)***
Markel West Inc ....E....818 595-0600
21600 Oxnard St Ste 400 Woodland Hills (91367) ***(P-10677)***
Marker Hotel, The, San Francisco *Also called Geary Darling Lessee Inc* ***(P-12600)***
Market Centre, Livermore *Also called Unified Grocers Inc* ***(P-8476)***
Market Hall Foods, Oakland *Also called Pasta Shop* ***(P-8847)***
Market Scan Info Systems Inc (PA) ....C....805 823-4258
815b Camarillo Springs Rd Camarillo (93012) ***(P-15271)***
Market Smart Inc ....D....925 846-6237
6900 Koll Center Pkwy # 406 Pleasanton (94566) ***(P-8422)***
Market Tech Media Corporation ....D....661 257-4745
27220 Turnberry Ln # 190 Valencia (91355) ***(P-14120)***
Marketbridge Corp ....D....240 752-1800
601 Montgomery St Ste 650 San Francisco (94111) ***(P-27319)***
Marketing Department, San Francisco *Also called Morrison & Foerster LLP* ***(P-23272)***
Marketing Professionals Inc ....B....714 578-0500
5100 E La Palma Ave # 116 Anaheim (92807) ***(P-27320)***
Marketing Sales & Dist Div, Fontana *Also called Weyerhaeuser Company* ***(P-6873)***
Marketlive Inc ....C....707 780-1600
617 2nd St Ste D Petaluma (94952) ***(P-16154)***
Marketo Inc (HQ) ....C....650 376-2300
901 Mariners Island Blvd San Mateo (94404) ***(P-15272)***
Marketshare Inc (PA) ....D....408 262-0677
2001 Tarob Ct Milpitas (95035) ***(P-13927)***
Marketwatch Inc (HQ) ....D....415 439-6400
201 California St Fl 13 San Francisco (94111) ***(P-16956)***
Marketwire Inc (HQ) ....D....310 765-3200
100 N Pacific Coast Hwy El Segundo (90245) ***(P-16957)***
Marklogic Corporation (PA) ....C....650 655-2300
999 Skyway Rd Ste 200 San Carlos (94070) ***(P-15273)***
Markmonitor Holdings Inc ....B....415 278-8400
425 Market St Ste 500 San Francisco (94105) ***(P-15274)***
Markmonitor Inc (HQ) ....D....415 278-8400
50 California St Ste 200 San Francisco (94111) ***(P-16423)***
Markstein Bev Co Sacramento ....C....916 920-3911
60 Main Ave Sacramento (95838) ***(P-9010)***
Markstein Beverage Co ....C....760 744-9100
505 S Pacific St San Marcos (92078) ***(P-9011)***
Markstein Beverage Company, Sacramento *Also called Markstein Bev Co Sacramento* ***(P-9010)***
Marksys LLC ....D....916 745-4883
3725 Cincinnati Ave # 200 Rocklin (95765) ***(P-27321)***
Markwins Beauty Products Inc ....D....909 595-8898
22067 Ferrero City of Industry (91789) ***(P-8190)***
Marland Co LP ....E....213 614-6171
444 S Flower St Ste 1200 Los Angeles (90071) ***(P-207)***
Marlin Equity Partners LLC (PA) ....D....310 364-0100
338 Pier Ave Hermosa Beach (90254) ***(P-10095)***
Marlin Equity Partners III LP (PA) ....C....310 364-0100
338 Pier Ave Hermosa Beach (90254) ***(P-12242)***
Marlinda Imperial Hospital, Pasadena *Also called Two Palms Nursing Center Inc* ***(P-21233)***
Marlinda Management Inc (PA) ....C....310 638-6691
3351 E Imperial Hwy Lynwood (90262) ***(P-21152)***
Marlora Investments LLC ....D....562 494-3311
3801 E Anaheim St Long Beach (90804) ***(P-20631)***
MARLORA POST ACCUTE REHABLITAT, Long Beach *Also called Marlora Investments LLC* ***(P-20631)***
Marmalade LLC ....E....310 317-4242
3894 Cross Creek Rd Malibu (90265) ***(P-17312)***
Marmalade Cafes, Malibu *Also called Marmalade LLC* ***(P-17312)***
Marmol Radziner ....D....310 826-6222
12210 Nebraska Ave Los Angeles (90025) ***(P-26092)***
Marna Health Services Inc ....D....909 882-2965
4280 Cypress Dr San Bernardino (92407) ***(P-21153)***
Marne Construction Inc ....D....714 935-0995
749 N Poplar St Orange (92868) ***(P-3284)***
Maroevich OShea & Coghlan ....D....415 957-0600
44 Montgomery St Ste 1700 San Francisco (94104) ***(P-10678)***
Marotto Corporation ....B....818 775-0320
9524 Topanga Canyon Blvd Chatsworth (91311) ***(P-14313)***
Marquee Fire Protection (PA) ....D....916 641-7997
710 W Stadium Ln Sacramento (95834) ***(P-2274)***
Marques Pipeline Inc ....E....916 923-3434
7225 26th St Sacramento (95834) ***(P-25811)***
Marquez Brothers Advg Agcy ....D....408 960-2700
5801 Rue Ferrari San Jose (95138) ***(P-17313)***
Marquez Brothers Entps Inc ....C....626 330-3310
15480 Valley Blvd City of Industry (91746) ***(P-8423)***
Marquez Brothers Intl Inc (PA) ....C....408 960-2700
5801 Rue Ferrari San Jose (95138) ***(P-8424)***
Marquez Brothers Intl Inc ....D....323 722-8103
1329 W Olympic Blvd Montebello (90640) ***(P-8425)***
Marquez Brothers Intl Inc ....C....559 584-8000
179 S 11th Ave Hanford (93230) ***(P-8426)***
Marrakesh Management Corp ....E....760 568-2688
47000 Marrakesh Dr Palm Desert (92260) ***(P-11587)***
Marriot Courtyard ....E....415 775-1103
580 Beach St San Francisco (94133) ***(P-12877)***
Marriott, Riverside *Also called Sunstone Hotel Management Inc* ***(P-13301)***
Marriott, San Diego *Also called Host Hotels & Resorts LP* ***(P-12704)***
Marriott, Santa Monica *Also called Cwgp Limited Partnership* ***(P-12508)***
Marriott, San Jose *Also called Host International Inc* ***(P-12716)***
Marriott, San Diego *Also called Hhlp San Diego Lessee LLC* ***(P-12655)***
Marriott, Visalia *Also called Welcome Group Management LLC* ***(P-13385)***
Marriott, Pleasanton *Also called Pleasanton Project Owner LLC* ***(P-13071)***
Marriott, Newport Beach *Also called Wj Newport LLC* ***(P-13414)***
Marriott, NAPA *Also called Sunstone Hotel Investors LLC* ***(P-13298)***
Marriott, Burbank *Also called Shc Burbank II LLC* ***(P-13213)***
Marriott, Newport Beach *Also called Host Hotels & Resorts LP* ***(P-12712)***
Marriott, Lake Arrowhead *Also called Lake Arrwhead Rsort Oprtor Inc* ***(P-12833)***
Marriott, Santa Monica *Also called Windsor Capital Group Inc* ***(P-13406)***
Marriott, Fullerton *Also called Merritt Hospitality LLC* ***(P-12923)***
Marriott, Oakland *Also called Cim/Oakland City Center LLC* ***(P-12460)***
Marriott, Baldwin Park *Also called Ols Hotels & Resorts LLC* ***(P-12979)***
Marriott, Pleasanton *Also called Pyramid Advisors LLC* ***(P-13084)***
Marriott, Manhattan Beach *Also called Host Hotels & Resorts LP* ***(P-12714)***
Marriott, Marina Del Rey *Also called Host Hotels & Resorts LP* ***(P-12715)***
Marriott, Riverside *Also called Windsor Capital Group Inc* ***(P-13412)***
Marriott, Walnut Creek *Also called Windsor Capital Group Inc* ***(P-13413)***
Marriott Burbank, Burbank *Also called AWH Burbank Hotel LLC* ***(P-12343)***
Marriott Burbank, Burbank *Also called Spire Concessions LLC* ***(P-13255)***
Marriott Fisherman's Wharf, San Francisco *Also called Host Hotels & Resorts Inc* ***(P-12701)***
Marriott Foundation For People ....D....510 834-4700
344 Thomas L Berkley Way Oakland (94612) ***(P-24203)***
Marriott Grand Residence ....B....530 542-8400
1001 Heavenly Village Way South Lake Tahoe (96150) ***(P-12878)***
Marriott Hotels & Resorts ....D....510 451-4000
1001 Broadway Oakland (94607) ***(P-12879)***
Marriott International Inc ....C....760 431-9399
5835 Owens Ave Carlsbad (92008) ***(P-12880)***
Marriott International Inc ....C....714 209-6586
4381 Myra Ave Cypress (90630) ***(P-12881)***
Marriott International Inc ....B....310 337-2800
9620 Airport Blvd Los Angeles (90045) ***(P-12882)***
Marriott International Inc ....C....858 523-1700
11966 El Camino Real San Diego (92130) ***(P-12883)***
Marriott International Inc ....A....310 641-5700
5855 W Century Blvd Los Angeles (90045) ***(P-12884)***
Marriott International Inc ....D....415 947-0700
299 2nd St San Francisco (94105) ***(P-12885)***
Marriott International Inc ....D....619 831-0225
900 Bayfront Ct San Diego (92101) ***(P-12886)***
Marriott International Inc ....C....510 413-3700
46100 Landing Pkwy Fremont (94538) ***(P-12887)***
Marriott International Inc ....B....949 724-3606
18000 Von Karman Ave Irvine (92612) ***(P-12888)***
Marriott International Inc ....B....858 587-1414
4240 La Jolla Village Dr La Jolla (92037) ***(P-12889)***
Marriott International Inc ....D....858 587-1770
5852 Stadium St San Diego (92122) ***(P-12890)***
Marriott International Inc ....C....760 776-0050
38305 Cook St Palm Desert (92211) ***(P-12891)***
Marriott International Inc ....C....310 333-0888
2135 E El Segundo Blvd El Segundo (90245) ***(P-12892)***
Marriott International Inc ....C....858 278-2100
5400 Kearny Mesa Rd San Diego (92111) ***(P-12893)***
Marriott International Inc ....C....562 425-5210
4700 Airport Plaza Dr Long Beach (90815) ***(P-12894)***
Marriott International Inc ....C....909 937-6788
2025 Convention Ctr Way Ontario (91764) ***(P-12895)***
Marriott International Inc ....C....818 887-4800
21850 Oxnard St Woodland Hills (91367) ***(P-12896)***
Marriott International Inc ....C....951 371-0107
1015 Montecito Dr Corona (92879) ***(P-12897)***
Marriott International Inc ....C....310 322-0700
2000 E Mariposa Ave El Segundo (90245) ***(P-12898)***
Marriott International Inc ....C....310 725-9696
14400 Aviation Blvd Hawthorne (90250) ***(P-12899)***
Marriott International Inc ....C....415 989-3500
905 California St San Francisco (94108) ***(P-12900)***
Marriott International Inc ....C....510 657-4600
39802 Cedar Blvd Newark (94560) ***(P-12901)***
Marriott International Inc ....C....562 595-0909
4111 E Willow St Long Beach (90815) ***(P-12902)***
Marriott International Inc ....C....707 935-6600
1325 Broadway Sonoma (95476) ***(P-12903)***
Marriott International Inc ....C....714 545-5261
3130 S Harbor Blvd # 500 Santa Ana (92704) ***(P-12904)***
Marriott International Inc ....C....925 689-1010
700 Ellinwood Way Pleasant Hill (94523) ***(P-12905)***
Marriott International Inc (PA) ....D....415 929-2030
500 Post St San Francisco (94102) ***(P-12906)***
Marriott International Inc ....C....213 284-3862
900 W Olympic Blvd Los Angeles (90015) ***(P-12907)***
Marriott International Inc ....C....650 692-9100
1800 Old Bayshore Hwy Burlingame (94010) ***(P-12908)***
Marriott International Inc ....D....619 831-0224
900 Bayfront Ct San Diego (92101) ***(P-12909)***

Marriott Los Angeles Downtown, Los Angeles *Also called Interstate Hotels Resorts Inc (P-12776)*
Marriott Rsrts Hspitality Corp........D.......760 779-1200
1091 Pinehurst Ln Palm Desert (92260) ***(P-12910)***
Marriott San Dego Gslamp Qrter, San Diego *Also called San Diego Hotel Company LLC (P-13169)*
Marriotts Newport Coast Villa........D.......949 464-6000
23000 Newport Coast Dr Newport Beach (92657) ***(P-12911)***
Marriotts Shadow Ridge........D.......760 674-2600
9003 Shadow Ridge Rd Palm Desert (92211) ***(P-12912)***
Marrow Meadows, Walnut *Also called M & R Joint Venture Electrical (P-2632)*
Marsh & McLennan Agency LLC........D.......949 544-8460
1 Polaris Way Ste 300 Aliso Viejo (92656) ***(P-10679)***
Marsh & McLennan Agency LLC........D.......415 243-4160
201 California St Ste 900 San Francisco (94111) ***(P-10680)***
Marsh & McLennan Agency LLC........C.......858 457-3414
9171 Towne Centre Dr # 500 San Diego (92122) ***(P-10681)***
Marsh & McLennan Companies Inc........D.......213 346-5555
777 S Figueroa St # 2200 Los Angeles (90017) ***(P-10682)***
Marsh Consulting Group........D.......239 433-5500
2626 Summer Ranch Rd Paso Robles (93446) ***(P-17314)***
Marsh USA Inc........D.......415 743-8000
345 California St # 1300 San Francisco (94104) ***(P-10683)***
Marsh USA Inc........D.......408 467-5600
1735 Tech Dr Ste 790 San Jose (95110) ***(P-10684)***
Marshall Hospital, Placerville *Also called Marshall Medical Center (P-21581)*
Marshall Medical Center........C.......916 933-2273
1100 Marshall Way El Dorado Hills (95762) ***(P-21580)***
Marshall Medical Center (PA)........A.......530 622-1441
1100 Marshall Way Placerville (95667) ***(P-21581)***
Marshall S Ezralow & Assoc, Calabasas *Also called M S E Enterprises Inc (P-11577)*
Marshall, Spector MD, San Gabriel *Also called Facey Medical Foundation (P-22806)*
Martech Medical Products Inc........C.......215 256-8833
565 Clara Nofal Rd Calexico (92231) ***(P-19671)***
Marthas Village & Kitchen........D.......760 347-4741
83791 Date Ave Indio (92201) ***(P-23911)***
Marticus Electric Inc........D.......916 368-2186
9266 Beatty Dr Ste D Sacramento (95826) ***(P-2635)***
Martin AC Partners Inc........C.......213 683-1900
444 S Flower St Ste 1200 Los Angeles (90071) ***(P-26093)***
Martin Associates Group Inc (PA)........D.......213 483-6490
950 S Grand Ave Fl 4 Los Angeles (90015) ***(P-25812)***
Martin ATI-AC Inc (PA)........D.......925 648-8800
4750 Willow Rd Ste 250 Pleasanton (94588) ***(P-26094)***
Martin Bros/Marcowall Inc (PA)........C.......310 532-5335
17104 S Figueroa St Gardena (90248) ***(P-2912)***
Martin Brothers Construction (PA)........D.......916 386-1600
8801 Folsom Blvd Ste 260 Sacramento (95826) ***(P-1813)***
MARTIN DE PORRES HOUSE, San Francisco *Also called MD P Foundation Inc (P-23913)*
Martin Integrated Systems........D.......714 998-9100
2330 N Pacific St Orange (92865) ***(P-2913)***
Martin Lther King/Drew Med Ctr........D.......310 773-4926
1670 E 120th St Los Angeles (90059) ***(P-19672)***
Martin Lthr Kng Chldr Ctr, Pittsburg *Also called State Preschool (P-24386)*
Martin Resorts Inc (PA)........B.......805 545-7900
1201 Palm St San Luis Obispo (93408) ***(P-12913)***
Martin, John A & Associates, Los Angeles *Also called Martin Associates Group Inc (P-25812)*
Martin-Brower Company LLC........C.......209 466-2980
4704 Fite Ct Stockton (95215) ***(P-8427)***
Martina Landscape Inc........D.......408 871-8800
811 Camden Ave Campbell (95008) ***(P-895)***
Martinez Farms Inc........B.......619 661-6571
2433 Cactus Rd San Diego (92154) ***(P-282)***
Martinez Medical Offices, Martinez *Also called Kaiser Foundation Hospitals (P-12104)*
Martis Camp Club........B.......530 550-6000
7951 Fleur Du Lac Ct Truckee (96161) ***(P-23912)***
Martrac, Fresno *Also called UPS Ground Freight Inc (P-4286)*
Marty Franich Leasing Co........E.......831 724-2463
555 Auto Center Dr Watsonville (95076) ***(P-17656)***
Marty's Cutting Service, Vernon *Also called Martys Cutting Inc (P-17315)*
Martys Cutting Inc........D.......323 582-5758
2615 Fruitland Ave Vernon (90058) ***(P-17315)***
Maruchan Inc........D.......949 789-2300
15800 Laguna Canyon Rd Irvine (92618) ***(P-4591)***
Mary and Friends........C.......562 691-1575
1101 Farrington Dr La Habra (90631) ***(P-24591)***
Mary Grahams Childrens Shelter, French Camp *Also called County of San Joaquin (P-23731)*
Mary Hlth SCK Cnvlscnt &NRsng........D.......805 498-3644
2929 Theresa Dr Newbury Park (91320) ***(P-20632)***
Marycrest Manor........D.......310 838-2778
10664 Saint James Dr Culver City (90230) ***(P-21154)***
Marymount Villa LLC........D.......510 895-5007
345 Davis St Ofc San Leandro (94577) ***(P-20941)***
Marysville Care Center, Marysville *Also called Marysvlle Nrsing Rehab Ctr LLC (P-20633)*
Marysville Post-Acute, Marysville *Also called Melon Holdings LLC (P-20641)*
Marysvlle Nrsing Rehab Ctr LLC........D.......530 742-7311
1617 Ramirez St Marysville (95901) ***(P-20633)***
Maryvale........D.......626 280-6510
7600 Graves Ave Rosemead (91770) ***(P-24592)***
Maryvale Day Care Center........C.......626 357-1514
2502 Huntington Dr Duarte (91010) ***(P-24345)***
Maryvale Day Care Center (PA)........C.......626 280-6511
7600 Graves Ave Rosemead (91770) ***(P-24346)***
Maryvale Edcatn Fmly Rsrce Ctr, Duarte *Also called Maryvale Day Care Center (P-24345)*
MARYVALE EDUCATIONAL DAY CARE, Rosemead *Also called Maryvale Day Care Center (P-24346)*
Masa Trucking Co........E.......310 329-1567
231 W 135th St Los Angeles (90061) ***(P-4358)***
Masa's, San Francisco *Also called San Francisco Hotel Associates (P-13173)*
MASADA HOMES, Gardena *Also called Counseling and Research Assoc (P-24477)*
Masada Homes Foster Fmly Agcy, Lancaster *Also called Counseling and Research Assoc (P-24478)*
Masco, San Jose *Also called Topbuild Services Group Corp (P-3595)*
Mashburn Trnsp Svcs Inc........C.......661 763-5724
1423 Kern St Taft (93268) ***(P-4220)***
Masker Painting, Oakland *Also called George E Masker Inc (P-2441)*
Mason McDuffie Mortgage Corp (PA)........D.......925 242-4400
2010 Crow Canyon Pl # 400 San Ramon (94583) ***(P-9831)***
Mason Street Opco LLC........A.......415 772-5000
950 Mason St San Francisco (94108) ***(P-12914)***
Mason-Mcduffie Real Estate Inc........D.......510 705-8611
2095 Rose St Ste 100 Berkeley (94709) ***(P-11588)***
Mason-Mcduffie Real Estate Inc........D.......925 932-1000
2051 Mt Diablo Blvd Walnut Creek (94596) ***(P-11589)***
Mason-Mcduffie Real Estate Inc........D.......925 776-2740
5887 Lone Tree Way Ste A Antioch (94531) ***(P-11590)***
Mason-Mcduffie Real Estate Inc........E.......510 886-7511
21060 Redwood Rd Ste 100 Castro Valley (94546) ***(P-11591)***
Mason-Mcduffie Real Estate Inc........D.......510 834-2010
3320 Grand Ave Oakland (94610) ***(P-11592)***
Mason-Mcduffie Real Estate Inc........D.......925 734-5000
5950 Stoneridge Dr Pleasanton (94588) ***(P-11593)***
Mason-West Inc........E.......619 226-8253
3910 Chapman St Ste D San Diego (92110) ***(P-7767)***
Masonic Home For Adults, Union City *Also called Masonic Homes of California (P-24594)*
Masonic Homes of California (PA)........B.......415 776-7000
1111 California St San Francisco (94108) ***(P-24593)***
Masonic Homes of California........B.......510 441-3700
34400 Mission Blvd Union City (94587) ***(P-24594)***
Masonic Homes of California........D.......626 251-2200
3823 N Reeder Ave Covina (91724) ***(P-24595)***
Masonry Concepts Inc........D.......562 802-3700
15408 Cornet St Santa Fe Springs (90670) ***(P-2816)***
Mass Electric Construction Co........D.......800 933-6322
1925 Wright Ave Ste D La Verne (91750) ***(P-2636)***
Massachusetts Mutl Lf Insur Co........D.......323 965-6339
8383 Wilshire Blvd # 600 Beverly Hills (90211) ***(P-10139)***
Massage Place........C.......310 204-3004
2516 Overland Ave Los Angeles (90064) ***(P-13756)***
Massdrop Inc........D.......415 340-2999
710 Sansome St San Francisco (94111) ***(P-27782)***
Massmutual, Beverly Hills *Also called Massachusetts Mutl Lf Insur Co (P-10139)*
Massnexus, Studio City *Also called Dpr Holdings LLC (P-11975)*
Massolo Trucking LLC (PA)........E.......831 424-7205
18765 Gould Rd Salinas (93908) ***(P-4038)***
Master Clean USA Inc........E.......805 681-0950
5511 Ekwill St Ste D Santa Barbara (93111) ***(P-14314)***
Master Design Drywall Inc........C.......760 480-9001
360 S Spruce St Escondido (92025) ***(P-2914)***
Master Disposal Co........E.......626 444-6789
1980 S Reservoir St Pomona (91766) ***(P-6417)***
Master Drywall Inc........C.......707 448-8659
6727 Bucktown Ln Vacaville (95688) ***(P-2915)***
Master Lightning SEC Solutions........D.......310 419-2915
545 N Mountain Ave # 207 Upland (91786) ***(P-16728)***
Master Roofing Systems Inc........D.......415 407-4450
52 S Linden Ave Ste 5 South San Francisco (94080) ***(P-3176)***
Master-Chef's Linen Rental, Los Angeles *Also called American Textile Maint Co (P-13506)*
Masters Electric Telcom, Riverside *Also called T S J Elec Communications Inc (P-2761)*
Masterserv Inc........E.......818 356-4602
560 Library St San Fernando (91340) ***(P-2275)***
Mastersev, San Fernando *Also called Masterserv Inc (P-2275)*
Mastroianni Family Entps Ltd........D.......310 952-1700
10581 Garden Grove Blvd Garden Grove (92843) ***(P-13757)***
Masudas Landscape Services........D.......408 379-7100
423 Salmar Ave Campbell (95008) ***(P-769)***
Mat Express, San Diego *Also called MAT Parcel Express Inc (P-4039)*
MAT Parcel Express Inc (PA)........D.......619 849-9600
2719 Kurtz St Ste C San Diego (92110) ***(P-4039)***
Matagrano Inc........C.......650 829-4829
440 Forbes Blvd South San Francisco (94080) ***(P-9012)***
Matched Care Gvrs Cntns Care, Atherton *Also called Matched Caregivers Inc (P-22363)*
Matched Caregivers Inc........C.......408 560-2382
1800 El Camino Real Ste B Atherton (94027) ***(P-22363)***
Mater Misericordiae Hospital (PA)........A.......209 564-5000
333 Mercy Ave Merced (95340) ***(P-21582)***
Material Handling Supply Inc (HQ)........D.......562 921-7715
12900 Firestone Blvd Santa Fe Springs (90670) ***(P-7768)***
Material Transport, Sacramento *Also called Pacific Coast Trnsp Svcs Inc (P-5239)*
Materials Marketing........D.......949 729-9881
250 Baker St Ste 100 Costa Mesa (92626) ***(P-27322)***
Matheny Sars Linkert Jaime LLP........D.......916 978-3434
3638 American River Dr Sacramento (95864) ***(P-23239)***
Mather Aviation LLC (PA)........D.......916 364-4711
10360 Macready Ave Mather (95655) ***(P-4900)***
Matheson Fast Freight Inc........D.......209 342-0184
9785 Goethe Rd Sacramento (95827) ***(P-4221)***
Matheson Fast Freight Inc (HQ)........D.......916 686-4600
9780 Dino Dr Elk Grove (95624) ***(P-4222)***
Matheson Trucking Inc (PA)........E.......916 685-2330
9785 Goethe Rd Sacramento (95827) ***(P-4223)***

ALPHABETIC

Employee Codes: A=Over 500 employees, B=251-500
C=101-250, D=51-100, E=50
2019 Directory of California
Wholesalers and Services Companies
© Mergent Inc. 1-800-342-5647
1379

Mathews & Clark Communications, Sunnyvale *Also called Positea Inv & Pub Relations (P-27570)*

Matich Corporation (PA) ....D......909 382-7400
1596 E Harry Shepard Blvd San Bernardino (92408) *(P-1814)*

Matich Corporation ....E......951 849-8280
13984 Apache Trl Cabazon (92230) *(P-1815)*

Matrix Aviation Services Inc ....C......310 337-3037
6171 W Century Blvd Ste 1 Los Angeles (90045) *(P-4993)*

Matrix Environmental Inc ....D......562 236-2704
2330 Cherry Indus Cir Long Beach (90805) *(P-3549)*

Matrix Group International Inc ....D......626 960-6205
1520 W Cameron Ave West Covina (91790) *(P-1197)*

Matrix Industries Inc ....B......562 236-2700
2330 E Cherry Indus Cir Long Beach (90805) *(P-3550)*

Matrix Institute On Addictions (PA) ....D......310 478-6006
1849 Sawtelle Blvd # 670 Los Angeles (90025) *(P-22035)*

Matrix Service Inc ....D......714 289-4419
500 W Collins Ave Orange (92867) *(P-1953)*

Matrix Surfaces Inc ....D......714 696-5449
5449 E La Palma Ave Anaheim (92807) *(P-3004)*

Matson Alarm Co Inc (PA) ....E......559 438-8000
581 W Fallbrook Ave # 100 Fresno (93711) *(P-2637)*

Matson Navigation Company Inc (HQ) ....C......510 628-4000
555 12th St Fl 7 Oakland (94607) *(P-4700)*

Matsui Nursery Inc (PA) ....D......831 422-6433
1645 Old Stage Rd Salinas (93908) *(P-283)*

Matsushita International Corp (PA) ....D......949 498-1000
1141 Via Callejon San Clemente (92673) *(P-12243)*

Matt Construction Corporation (PA) ....C......562 903-2277
9814 Norwalk Blvd Ste 100 Santa Fe Springs (90670) *(P-27323)*

Matt-Colombo A Joint Venture ....D......562 903-2277
9814 Norwalk Blvd Ste 100 Santa Fe Springs (90670) *(P-1588)*

Mattel Toy Company ....A......310 252-2357
333 Continental Blvd El Segundo (90245) *(P-7956)*

Matthew Burns ....D......209 676-4940
617 Flower Dr Folsom (95630) *(P-1589)*

Matthews International Corp. ....E......951 654-9123
580 S State St Ste 8 San Jacinto (92583) *(P-17962)*

Matthews Real Estate Inv Svcs, El Segundo *Also called Matthews Retail Group Inc (P-11594)*

Matthews Retail Group Inc ....D......866 889-0550
841 Apollo St Ste 150 El Segundo (90245) *(P-11594)*

Mattress Liqidation, Rancho Cucamonga *Also called Hibshman Trading Corporation (P-8306)*

Matus International Inc ....C......562 435-5200
1120 De Forest Ave Long Beach (90813) *(P-5107)*

Maud Booth Family Center, North Hollywood *Also called Volunteers of Amer Los Angeles (P-24122)*

Maverick Hotel Partners LLC ....B......415 655-9526
2 Embarcadero Ctr Fl 8 San Francisco (94111) *(P-26938)*

Max Group Corporation (PA) ....D......626 935-0050
17011 Green Dr City of Industry (91745) *(P-7076)*

Max Leather ....E......310 841-6990
8533 Washington Blvd Culver City (90232) *(P-9234)*

Max Mri Imaging Inc (PA) ....E......818 382-2220
17530 Ventura Blvd # 105 Encino (91316) *(P-22109)*

Max Sommers Real Estate ....D......310 560-1499
615 Esplanade Unit 312 Redondo Beach (90277) *(P-11595)*

Max Sportsters Inc ....E......408 446-8330
10050 N Foothill Blvd # 200 Cupertino (95014) *(P-26939)*

Max/Mr Imaging Inc ....D......818 382-2220
17530 Ventura Blvd # 105 Encino (91316) *(P-22110)*

Maxco Supply Inc (PA) ....C......559 646-8449
605 S Zediker Ave Parlier (93648) *(P-8108)*

Maxco Supply Inc ....D......559 646-6700
8419 Di Giorgio Rd Lamont (93241) *(P-8109)*

Maxgen Energy Services Corp ....B......714 908-5266
1690 Scenic Ave Costa Mesa (92626) *(P-6192)*

Maxim Crane Works LP ....C......209 464-7635
2373 S Mariposa Rd Stockton (95205) *(P-14448)*

Maxim Healthcare Services Inc ....B......408 914-7478
631 River Oaks Pkwy San Jose (95134) *(P-14875)*

Maxim Healthcare Services Inc ....A......805 278-4593
500 E Esplanade Dr Oxnard (93036) *(P-14876)*

Maxim Healthcare Services Inc ....C......323 937-9410
4221 Wilshire Blvd # 130 Los Angeles (90010) *(P-22364)*

Maxim Healthcare Services Inc ....B......951 684-4148
1845 Bus Ctr Dr Ste 112 San Bernardino (92408) *(P-14877)*

Maxim Planning Group ....D......818 425-4343
1214 E Colorado Blvd Pasadena (91106) *(P-27783)*

Maxim Services Ltd Inc ....D......925 969-1907
2470 Estand Way Pleasant Hill (94523) *(P-14315)*

Maximum Fitness LLC ....E......707 447-0606
135 Dobbins St Vacaville (95688) *(P-18630)*

Maximus Inc ....D......916 673-2175
625 Coolidge Dr Ste 100 Folsom (95630) *(P-27324)*

Maximus Inc ....D......916 364-6610
3130 Kilgore Rd Ste 100 Rancho Cordova (95670) *(P-22365)*

Maximus Inc ....E......916 673-4162
625 Coolidge Dr Ste 100 Folsom (95630) *(P-27325)*

Maximus CA Healthy Family, Folsom *Also called Maximus Inc (P-27324)*

Maximus Holdings Inc ....A......650 935-9500
2475 Hanover St Palo Alto (94304) *(P-15748)*

Maximus Real Estate Partners ....D......415 584-4832
1 Maritime Plz Ste 1900 San Francisco (94111) *(P-11177)*

Maxon Lift Corporation ....C......562 464-0099
11921 Slauson Ave Santa Fe Springs (90670) *(P-7769)*

Maxonic Inc ....D......408 739-4900
2542 S Bascom Ave Ste 190 Campbell (95008) *(P-16424)*

Maxplore Technologies Inc ....D......925 621-1400
4450 Rosewood Dr Ste 200 Pleasanton (94588) *(P-15275)*

Maxson Young Assoc Inc ....C......415 228-6400
180 Montgomery St # 2100 San Francisco (94104) *(P-10685)*

Maxus USA ....A......323 202-4650
6300 Wilshire Blvd # 720 Los Angeles (90048) *(P-27942)*

Maxwell Hotel, The, San Francisco *Also called Joie De Vivre Hospitality LLC (P-26910)*

Maxwell Petersen Associates ....E......714 230-3150
13950 Milton Ave Ste 200 Westminster (92683) *(P-27326)*

Maxx Metals Inc ....D......650 654-1500
355 Quarry Rd San Carlos (94070) *(P-7289)*

Maxzone Vehicle Lighting Corp (HQ) ....E......909 822-3288
15889 Slover Ave Unit A Fontana (92337) *(P-6656)*

May-Han Electric Inc ....D......916 929-0150
1600 Auburn Blvd Sacramento (95815) *(P-2638)*

Mayacama Golf Club LLC ....C......707 569-2900
1240 Mayacama Club Dr Santa Rosa (95403) *(P-18968)*

Mayacama Industries, Ukiah *Also called Ukiah Vly Assn For Hbilitation (P-24241)*

Mayer Associates ....D......310 274-5553
9090 Wilshire Blvd Fl 3 Beverly Hills (90211) *(P-11063)*

Mayer Brown & Platt, Los Angeles *Also called LLP Mayer Brown (P-23223)*

Mayesh Wholesale Florist Inc (PA) ....E......310 342-0980
5401 W 104th St Los Angeles (90045) *(P-9145)*

Mayfair Hotel ....D......213 484-9789
1430 Amherst Ave Apt 5 Los Angeles (90025) *(P-12915)*

Mayfield Equipment Company (PA) ....D......707 462-2404
235 E Perkins St Ukiah (95482) *(P-7706)*

Mayfield Robotics, Redwood City *Also called Robert Bosch Start-Up Pltfm NA (P-15415)*

Maynard Cooper & Gale PC ....C......415 704-7433
600 Montgomery St # 2600 San Francisco (94111) *(P-23240)*

Mayor Office, Pasadena *Also called City of Pasadena (P-14212)*

Mayor West Coast LLC ....E......424 221-5229
335 E Albertoni St 200-867 Carson (90746) *(P-4040)*

Mayoral Bros ....B......707 693-9111
420 Hillcrest Cir Dixon (95620) *(P-660)*

Maywood Acres Health Care Ctr, Oxnard *Also called Kindred Healthcare Oper Inc (P-21128)*

Maywood Acres Healthcare, Oxnard *Also called Milwood Healthcare Inc (P-10914)*

Maywood Halthcare Wellness Ctr ....E......323 560-0720
6025 Pine Ave Maywood (90270) *(P-20634)*

Mazar Corp ....D......909 292-8269
3200 E Guasti Rd Ste 100 Ontario (91761) *(P-16729)*

Mazda Research & Dev of N Amer ....D......949 852-8898
1421 Reynolds Ave Irvine (92614) *(P-25813)*

Mazzetti Inc (PA) ....E......415 362-3266
220 Montgomery St Ste 650 San Francisco (94104) *(P-25814)*

Mazzetti GBA, San Francisco *Also called Mazzetti Inc (P-25814)*

MB Coatings Inc ....D......714 625-2118
571 N Poplar St Ste G Orange (92868) *(P-17316)*

MB Herzog Electric Inc ....C......562 531-2002
15709 Illinois Ave Paramount (90723) *(P-2639)*

MB Landscaping & Nursery Inc ....D......310 965-1923
20300 Figueroa St Carson (90745) *(P-9146)*

Mbari, Moss Landing *Also called Monterey Bay Aquarium RES Inst (P-26419)*

MBC Systems, Santa Ana *Also called Medical Network Inc (P-26942)*

Mbe, Pasadena *Also called Ttg Engineers (P-25962)*

Mbh Architects Inc ....C......510 865-8663
960 Atlantic Ave Alameda (94501) *(P-26095)*

Mbh Enterprises Inc ....D......510 302-6680
1430 Franklin St Ste 201 Oakland (94612) *(P-7077)*

MBI, Stockton *Also called Midstate Barrier Inc (P-1820)*

Mbipch LLC ....D......310 456-6444
22211 Pacific Coast Hwy Malibu (90265) *(P-12916)*

MBK Laguna, Irvine *Also called MBK Real Estate Companies (P-11596)*

MBK Real Estate Companies ....E......949 789-8300
4 Park Plz Ste 1000 Irvine (92614) *(P-11596)*

MBK Real Estate Ltd A Calfor ....D......831 438-7533
100 Lockewood Ln Scotts Valley (95066) *(P-11064)*

MBK Real Estate Ltd A Calfor (HQ) ....D......949 789-8300
4 Park Plz Ste 1000 Irvine (92614) *(P-11597)*

MBK Real Estate Ltd A Califor ....E......310 399-3227
2107 Ocean Ave Ofc Santa Monica (90405) *(P-11065)*

MBK Senior Living LLC ....D......951 506-5555
41780 Btterfield Stage Rd Temecula (92592) *(P-21155)*

Mbp Land LLC ....D......619 291-5720
595 Hotel Cir S San Diego (92108) *(P-12917)*

Mbs Equipment Company (PA) ....D......310 558-3100
1600 Rosecrans Ave 4b Manhattan Beach (90266) *(P-18200)*

Mc Graw Commercial Insur Svc ....D......714 939-9875
8185 E Kaiser Blvd Anaheim (92808) *(P-10686)*

Mc Graw Commercial Insur Svc (PA) ....D......650 780-4800
3601 Haven Ave Menlo Park (94025) *(P-10687)*

Mc Graw Insurance Services Co ....D......650 780-4800
2200 Geng Rd Ste 200 Palo Alto (94303) *(P-10688)*

Mc Laughlin Mine, Lower Lake *Also called Barrick Gold Corporation (P-1004)*

Mc Namara Dodge Ney Beatt (PA) ....D......925 939-5330
3480 Buskirk Ave Ste 250 Pleasant Hill (94523) *(P-23241)*

MCA Music, Universal City *Also called Universal Studios Company LLC (P-18145)*

McAfee Inc ....D......858 967-2342
6707 Barnhurst Dr San Diego (92117) *(P-15749)*

McAfee LLC (HQ) ....C......888 847-8766
2821 Mission College Blvd Santa Clara (95054) *(P-15750)*

McAfee Finance 2 LLC ....A......888 847-8766
2821 Mission College Blvd Santa Clara (95054) *(P-15751)*

McAfee Security LLC ....A......866 622-3911
2821 Mission College Blvd Santa Clara (95054) *(P-15752)*

McAlister Institute For Treat (PA) ....C......619 442-0277
1400 N Johnson Ave # 101 El Cajon (92020) *(P-22617)*

Mergent e-mail: customerrelations@mergent.com
1380

2019 Directory of California
Wholesalers and Services Companies

(P-0000) Products & Services Section entry number
(PA)=Parent Co (HQ)=Headquarters (DH)=Div Headquarters

McAlister Institute For Treat D 760 726-4451
3923 Waring Rd Oceanside (92056) ***(P-22618)***

McAsd, La Jolla *Also called Museum Cntmprary Art San Diego* ***(P-24892)***

MCB-Cjs LLC D 714 230-3600
5312 Bolsa Ave Huntington Beach (92649) ***(P-27327)***

McCain Inc (HQ) C 760 727-8100
2365 Oak Ridge Way Vista (92081) ***(P-7770)***

McCall Gym Group Inc (PA) D 408 271-2416
1893 Monterey Hwy Ste 250 San Jose (95112) ***(P-18631)***

McCallum Theatre, Palm Desert *Also called Friends of Cultural Center Inc* ***(P-18367)***

McCampbell Analytical Inc D 925 252-9262
1534 Willow Pass Rd Pittsburg (94565) ***(P-26712)***

McCann World Group Inc (PA) D 415 262-5500
653 Front St San Francisco (94111) ***(P-13861)***

McCann-Erickson Corporation (HQ) D 415 348-5600
135 Main St Fl 21 San Francisco (94105) ***(P-13862)***

McCann-Erickson Usa Inc C 415 262-5600
600 Battery St Fl 1 San Francisco (94111) ***(P-26543)***

McCarthy Bldg Companies Inc B 949 851-8383
20401 Sw Birch St Ste 200 Newport Beach (92660) ***(P-1590)***

McCarthy Bldg Companies Inc D 949 851-8383
20401 Sw Birch St Ste 300 Newport Beach (92660) ***(P-1591)***

McCarthy Construction, Lawndale *Also called McCarthy Framing Construction* ***(P-3051)***

McCarthy Framing Construction D 310 219-3038
15133 Grevillea Ave Lawndale (90260) ***(P-3051)***

McClatchy Company A 916 321-1941
2100 Q St Sacramento (95816) ***(P-27943)***

McClellan Business Park LLC D 916 965-7100
3140 Peacekeeper Way McClellan (95652) ***(P-27328)***

McClellan Facilities Svcs LLC D 916 965-7100
3140 Peacekeeper Way McClellan (95652) ***(P-10910)***

McClellan Hospitality Svcs LLC D 916 965-7100
3140 Peacekeeper Way Mcclellan (95652) ***(P-12918)***

McClenahan Pest Control Inc E 650 326-8781
1 Arastradero Rd Portola Valley (94028) ***(P-14154)***

McClenahan S P Co Tree Service, Portola Valley *Also called SP McClenahan Co* ***(P-978)***

McClintock Enterprises Inc D 619 579-5300
777 Gable Way El Cajon (92020) ***(P-3890)***

McClone Construction Company C 559 431-9411
4340 Product Dr Cameron Park (95682) ***(P-1198)***

McClure Convalescent Hospital, Oakland *Also called Independent Quality Care Inc* ***(P-21119)***

McCollisters Trnsp Group Inc D 909 428-5700
10672 Jasmine St Fontana (92337) ***(P-4359)***

McCormack Roofng Constrctn & E D 714 777-4040
1260 N Hancock St Ste 108 Anaheim (92807) ***(P-3177)***

McCormick Barstow, Fresno *Also called McCormick Barstow Shepprd Wayt* ***(P-23242)***

McCormick Barstow Shepprd Wayt (PA) C 559 433-1300
7647 N Fresno St Fresno (93720) ***(P-23242)***

McCoy's Patrol Service, Suisun City *Also called Hal-Mar-Jac Enterprises* ***(P-16694)***

McCuen Construction Inc (PA) E 916 652-7824
3269 Swetzer Rd Loomis (95650) ***(P-1592)***

McCullough Construction D 707 825-1014
57 Alder Grove Rd Arcata (95521) ***(P-1816)***

McCusker Enterprises Inc D 951 699-9777
29879 Santiago Rd Temecula (92592) ***(P-24347)***

McCutcheon Enterprises Inc D 559 864-3200
604 W Nebraska Ave Fresno (93706) ***(P-161)***

McDermott Will & Emery LLP Inc C 310 277-4110
2049 Century Park E Fl 38 Los Angeles (90067) ***(P-23243)***

McDermott Will & Emery LLP Inc D 949 757-7165
4 Park Plz Ste 1700 Irvine (92614) ***(P-23244)***

McE, San Rafael *Also called Marin Clean Energy* ***(P-6051)***

McE Corporation (PA) D 925 803-4111
4000 Industrial Way Concord (94520) ***(P-1817)***

McElvany Inc D 209 826-1102
13343 Johnson Rd Los Banos (93635) ***(P-1954)***

McFadden Farm E 707 743-1122
16000 Powerhouse Rd Potter Valley (95469) ***(P-6)***

McGee Company, Whittier *Also called John Shannon Mc Gee Co Inc* ***(P-7369)***

McGrath Rentcorp D 925 453-3312
5700 Las Positas Rd Livermore (94551) ***(P-14524)***

McGrath Rentcorp C 877 221-2813
5700 Las Positas Rd Livermore (94551) ***(P-7771)***

McGrath Rentcorp (PA) C 925 606-9200
5700 Las Positas Rd Livermore (94551) ***(P-7772)***

McGraw Insurance Services, Anaheim *Also called Mc Graw Commercial Insur Svc* ***(P-10686)***

McGreever and Danlee Very, Azusa *Also called Morris National Inc* ***(P-8830)***

McGuire and Hester (PA) B 510 632-7676
2810 Harbor Bay Pkwy Alameda (94502) ***(P-1955)***

McGuire Contracting Inc D 909 357-1200
16579 Slover Ave Fontana (92337) ***(P-3285)***

McGuire Talent Inc D 909 527-7006
8608 Utica Ave Ste 220 Rancho Cucamonga (91730) ***(P-18386)***

McGuirewoods LLP D 310 315-8200
1800 Century Park E Fl 8 Los Angeles (90067) ***(P-23245)***

Mch, Madera *Also called Madera Community Hospital* ***(P-21574)***

Mch Electric Inc (PA) D 209 835-9755
7693 Longard Rd Livermore (94551) ***(P-2640)***

McHc, Ukiah *Also called Mendocino Cmnty Hlth Clnic Inc* ***(P-19684)***

McHenry Bowl Inc E 209 571-2695
3700 Mchenry Ave Modesto (95356) ***(P-18495)***

McHenry Medical Group Inc D 209 577-3388
1541 Florida Ave Ste 200 Modesto (95350) ***(P-19673)***

MCI Communications Svcs Inc C 213 625-1005
700 S Flower St Ste 1600 Los Angeles (90017) ***(P-5595)***

McIntyre Company (PA) D 909 962-6322
2817 E Cedar St Ste 200 Ontario (91761) ***(P-3386)***

McIntyre Vineyards, Carmel *Also called Monterey Pacific Inc* ***(P-701)***

McKann World Group, San Francisco *Also called McCann-Erickson Usa Inc* ***(P-26543)***

McKee Electric, Bakersfield *Also called Surgener Electric Inc* ***(P-2756)***

McKesson Corporation D 951 686-3575
6969 Brockton Ave Ste B Riverside (92506) ***(P-8191)***

McKesson Corporation D 510 666-0854
3000 Colby St Berkeley (94705) ***(P-8192)***

McKesson Corporation C 562 463-2100
9501 Norwalk Blvd Santa Fe Springs (90670) ***(P-8193)***

McKesson Corporation D 916 636-8700
11000 Trade Center Dr Rancho Cordova (95670) ***(P-8194)***

McKesson Corporation C 916 372-3655
3775 Seaport Blvd West Sacramento (95691) ***(P-8195)***

McKesson Corporation (PA) A 415 983-8300
1 Post St Fl 18 San Francisco (94104) ***(P-8196)***

McKesson Drug, Santa Fe Springs *Also called McKesson Corporation* ***(P-8193)***

McKesson Drug, West Sacramento *Also called McKesson Corporation* ***(P-8195)***

McKesson Medical-Surgical Inc D 800 767-6339
16043 El Prado Rd Chino (91708) ***(P-7189)***

McKesson Medical-Surgical Inc D 805 375-8800
1525 Rnch Conejo Blvd # 104 Newbury Park (91320) ***(P-7190)***

McKesson Ptent Care Sltons Inc (HQ) D 412 507-0077
9235 Activity Rd Ste 105 San Diego (92126) ***(P-22837)***

McKinley Childrens Center Inc (PA) C 909 599-1227
762 Cypress St San Dimas (91773) ***(P-24596)***

McKinley Equipment Corporation (PA) D 800 770-6094
17611 Armstrong Ave Irvine (92614) ***(P-7773)***

McKinley Home Foundation D 909 599-1227
762 Cypress St San Dimas (91773) ***(P-24805)***

McKinley Park Care Center D 916 452-3592
3700 H St Sacramento (95816) ***(P-21583)***

McKinley Plaza LLC D 619 405-6307
2401 E Division St National City (91950) ***(P-26940)***

McKinnon Broadcasting Company (HQ) C 858 571-5151
4575 Viewridge Ave San Diego (92123) ***(P-5823)***

McKinnon Publishing Company A 858 571-5151
4575 Viewridge Ave San Diego (92123) ***(P-5824)***

McKinsey & Company Inc E 424 249-1000
2000 Avenue Of The Stars # 800 Los Angeles (90067) ***(P-27329)***

McKinsey & Company Inc B 415 981-0250
555 California St # 4800 San Francisco (94104) ***(P-27330)***

McKinsey & Company Inc D 650 494-6262
3075 Hansen Way Bldg A Palo Alto (94304) ***(P-27331)***

McKool Smith Hennigan D 213 694-1200
300 S Grand Ave Ste 2900 Los Angeles (90071) ***(P-23246)***

McKowskis Maint Systems Inc D 619 269-4600
10979 San Dego Mission Rd San Diego (92108) ***(P-14316)***

McLane Company Inc C 209 221-7500
800 E Pescadero Ave Tracy (95304) ***(P-8428)***

McLane/Pacific Inc B 209 725-2500
3876 E Childs Ave Merced (95341) ***(P-8429)***

MCM Construction Inc (PA) D 916 334-1221
6413 32nd St North Highlands (95660) ***(P-1884)***

MCM Construction Inc D 310 549-9207
708 Pier A St Wilmington (90744) ***(P-3286)***

MCM Construction Inc C 909 875-0533
19010 Slover Ave Bloomington (92316) ***(P-1885)***

McM Partners Inc D 925 463-9500
6111 Johnson Ct Ste 110 Pleasanton (94588) ***(P-11598)***

McManis Faulkner A Prof Corp E 408 279-8700
50 W San Fernando St # 1000 San Jose (95113) ***(P-23247)***

McMillan Data Cmmnications Inc D 415 826-5100
1950 Cesar Chavez San Francisco (94124) ***(P-2641)***

McMillan Electric B 415 826-5100
1950 Cesar Chavez San Francisco (94124) ***(P-2642)***

McMillan Farm Management C 951 676-2045
29379 Rancho California R Temecula (92591) ***(P-26941)***

McMillin Communities Inc A 951 506-3303
41687 Temeku Dr Temecula (92591) ***(P-1199)***

McMillin Communities Inc (PA) A 619 561-5275
2750 Womble Rd Ste 200 San Diego (92106) ***(P-12244)***

McMillin Companies LLC (PA) D 619 477-4117
2750 Womble Rd Ste 200 San Diego (92106) ***(P-12245)***

McMillin Construction Svcs LP E 619 477-4170
2750 Womble Rd San Diego (92106) ***(P-1200)***

McMillin Escrow, Bonita *Also called McMillin RE & Mrtg Co Inc* ***(P-11599)***

McMillin Homes, San Diego *Also called McMillin Companies LLC* ***(P-12245)***

McMillin Homes, San Diego *Also called McMillin Management Svcs LP* ***(P-12042)***

McMillin Management Svcs LP (HQ) C 619 477-4117
2750 Womble Rd Ste 200 San Diego (92106) ***(P-12042)***

McMillin RE & Mrtg Co Inc (PA) D 619 475-0233
4210 Bonita Rd Ste B Bonita (91902) ***(P-11599)***

McMillin RE & Mrtg Co Inc D 619 422-4500
320 E H St Chula Vista (91910) ***(P-11600)***

McMillin Realty, San Diego *Also called McMillin Communities Inc* ***(P-12244)***

McMurray & Sons Inc (PA) D 707 443-3088
1818 Allard Ave Eureka (95503) ***(P-3178)***

McMurray Stern, Santa Fe Springs *Also called Gatehouse Msi LLC* ***(P-3037)***

MCP Industries Inc D 562 944-5511
10039 Norwalk Blvd Santa Fe Springs (90670) ***(P-8931)***

MCR Printing and Packg Corp C 619 488-3012
8830 Siempre Viva Rd San Diego (92154) ***(P-4592)***

MCS, Bakersfield *Also called Managed Care Systems Kern Cnty* ***(P-10675)***

McWong Envmtl & Enrgy Group E 916 371-8080
1921 Arena Blvd Sacramento (95834) ***(P-27784)***

MD Imaging Inc A Prof Med Corp D 530 243-1249
2020 Court St Redding (96001) ***(P-19674)***

MD P Foundation Inc C 415 552-0240
225 Potrero Ave San Francisco (94103) ***(P-23913)***

Mda US Systems LLC, Pasadena *Also called Ssl Robotics LLC* ***(P-25924)***

ALPHABETIC

Mdcc, Covina *Also called Mohan Dialysis Ctr of Covina* ***(P-22484)***
Mddr Inc.......C.......714 792-1993
555 Vanguard Way Brea (92821) ***(P-2276)***
MDE Electric Company Inc.......E.......415 552-2500
2166 Palou Ave San Francisco (94124) ***(P-2643)***
Mdr Inc.......D.......707 750-5376
511 E Channel Rd Benicia (94510) ***(P-25815)***
Mds Consulting (PA).......D.......949 251-8821
17320 Red Hill Ave # 350 Irvine (92614) ***(P-25816)***
ME and ME Inc.......D.......818 891-0197
14536 Roscoe Blvd Ste 112 Van Nuys (91402) ***(P-14878)***
ME Fox & Company Inc.......D.......408 435-8510
128 Component Dr San Jose (95131) ***(P-9013)***
Mea Digital Worx LLC.......E.......619 238-8923
530 B St Ste 1900 San Diego (92101) ***(P-13863)***
Meadow Club.......D.......415 453-3274
1001 Bolinas Rd Fairfax (94930) ***(P-18969)***
Meadow Glen Apartments, Sacramento *Also called John Stewart Company* ***(P-11038)***
Meadow View Manor Inc.......D.......530 272-2273
396 Dorsey Dr Grass Valley (95945) ***(P-20635)***
Meadowbrook Bhavioral Hlth Ctr, Los Angeles *Also called Genesis Healthcare Corporation* ***(P-20450)***
Meadowbrook Convalescent Hosp.......D.......951 658-2293
461 E Johnston Ave Hemet (92543) ***(P-24597)***
Meadowbrook Meat Company Inc.......D.......252 985-7200
5675 Sunol Blvd Pleasanton (94566) ***(P-8496)***
Meadowbrook Senior Living.......D.......818 991-3544
5217 Chesebro Rd Agoura Hills (91301) ***(P-23914)***
Meadowbrook Village Christian.......C.......760 746-2500
100 Holland Gln Escondido (92026) ***(P-24598)***
Meadowood Care Center, Stockton *Also called Meadowood Hlth Rehabilitation* ***(P-20636)***
Meadowood Hlth Rehabilitation.......B.......209 956-3444
3110 Wagner Heights Rd Stockton (95209) ***(P-20636)***
Meadowood Nursing Center, Clearlake *Also called Vindra Inc* ***(P-20866)***
Meadows Nappa Valley Care Ctr, NAPA *Also called California Odd Fellows* ***(P-10998)***
Meadows of NAPA Valley, NAPA *Also called California Odd Fellows* ***(P-10997)***
Meadows Senior Living, The, Elk Grove *Also called Lifestyles Senior Housing Man* ***(P-23899)***
MEALS ON WHEELS, San Diego *Also called Meals-On-Wheels Grtr Sn Diego* ***(P-23918)***
Meals On Wheels Diablo Region (PA).......D.......925 937-8311
1300 Civic Dr Fl 1 Walnut Creek (94596) ***(P-23915)***
Meals On Wheels-The Health Tr.......E.......408 961-9870
1400 Parkmoor Ave Ste 230 San Jose (95126) ***(P-23916)***
Meals On Whels San Frncsco Inc.......E.......415 920-1111
1375 Fairfax Ave San Francisco (94124) ***(P-23917)***
Meals-On-Wheels Grtr Sn Diego (PA).......D.......619 260-6110
2254 San Diego Ave # 200 San Diego (92110) ***(P-23918)***
Meany Wilson L P.......E.......415 905-5300
4 Embarcadero Ctr # 3330 San Francisco (94111) ***(P-11890)***
Mearsk, San Pedro *Also called APM Terminals Pacific LLC* ***(P-5011)***
Meathead Movers.......D.......805 349-8000
101 W Canon Perdido St Santa Maria (93454) ***(P-4224)***
Meathead Movers Inc.......D.......805 496-1416
300 Rolling Oaks Dr Thousand Oaks (91361) ***(P-4225)***
Meathead Movers Inc.......D.......805 541-4285
3600 S Higuera St San Luis Obispo (93401) ***(P-4226)***
Meathead Movers Inc (PA).......D.......805 544-6328
3600 S Higuera St San Luis Obispo (93401) ***(P-4227)***
Meathead Movers Inc.......D.......805 437-5100
412 Calle San Pablo Camarillo (93012) ***(P-4228)***
Meathead Movers Inc.......D.......805 966-6328
1524 State St Santa Barbara (93101) ***(P-4229)***
Mec International LLC.......C.......415 866-4497
1515 Tessa Ave Sacramento (95815) ***(P-25817)***
Mechanical Drives and Belting, Los Angeles *Also called Los Angeles Rubber Company* ***(P-7372)***
Mechanical Drives Co (PA).......D.......323 263-4131
2915 E Washington Blvd Los Angeles (90023) ***(P-7858)***
Mechanical Industries Inc.......E.......661 634-9477
314 Yampa St Bakersfield (93307) ***(P-3387)***
Mechanics Bank (HQ).......C.......800 797-6324
1111 Civic Dr Walnut Creek (94596) ***(P-9512)***
Mechanics Bank.......B.......855 272-2886
18400 Von Karman Ave Irvine (92612) ***(P-9721)***
Mechanics Bank.......D.......925 934-1601
590 Ygnacio Valley Rd # 210 Walnut Creek (94596) ***(P-11955)***
Mechanics Bank.......D.......510 741-7545
P.O. Box 5610 Hercules (94547) ***(P-9466)***
Med Focus/California Radiology, Santa Monica *Also called Stephen B Meisel MD A Med Corp* ***(P-19947)***
Med Staffing LLC.......E.......510 795-0114
1860 Mowry Ave Ste 302 Fremont (94538) ***(P-14879)***
Med-Data Incorporated.......D.......916 771-1362
3741 Douglas Blvd Ste 170 Roseville (95661) ***(P-26258)***
Med-Legal LLC.......C.......626 653-5160
4401 Atlantic Ave Long Beach (90807) ***(P-23248)***
Med-Life Ambulance Services.......D.......818 242-1785
4304 Alger St Los Angeles (90039) ***(P-3820)***
Medallia Inc (PA).......C.......650 321-3000
450 Concar Dr San Mateo (94402) ***(P-15753)***
Medallion Cnstr Clean-Up, Mountain View *Also called Service By Medallion* ***(P-14384)***
Medallion Landscape MGT Inc (PA).......D.......408 782-7500
10 San Bruno Ave Morgan Hill (95037) ***(P-770)***
Medamerica Billing Svcs Inc (HQ).......D.......209 491-7710
1601 Cummins Dr Ste D Modesto (95358) ***(P-26259)***
Medasend Biomedical Inc (PA).......C.......800 200-3581
1402 Daisy Ave Long Beach (90813) ***(P-22838)***
Medata Inc (PA).......D.......714 918-1310
5 Peters Canyon Rd # 250 Irvine (92606) ***(P-15754)***
Medex Pratice Solutions Inc.......D.......209 845-1346
4725 Enterprise Way Ste 1 Modesto (95356) ***(P-26260)***
Medfocus Radiology Network, Santa Monica *Also called Stephen B Meisel MD PC* ***(P-19946)***
Medi-Flight Northern Cal, Modesto *Also called Sutter Central Vly Hospitals* ***(P-4866)***
Medi-Van Ambulette, Los Angeles *Also called Health Link Medi Van* ***(P-5227)***
Media All Stars Inc.......D.......858 300-9600
8525 Gibbs Dr Ste 206 San Diego (92123) ***(P-17317)***
Media Arts Lab, Los Angeles *Also called Tbwa Worldwide Inc* ***(P-13909)***
Media Design Group, Los Angeles *Also called Revenue Frontier LLC* ***(P-13982)***
Media Services, Los Angeles *Also called Oberman Tivoli & Pickert Inc* ***(P-16025)***
Media Temple Inc.......C.......877 578-4000
6060 Center Dr Fl 5 Los Angeles (90045) ***(P-5596)***
Media Vntures Entrmt Group LLC.......E.......310 260-3171
1547 14th St Santa Monica (90404) ***(P-18076)***
Mediabrands Worldwide Inc.......B.......323 370-8000
5700 Wilshire Blvd # 400 Los Angeles (90036) ***(P-13977)***
Mediaplatform Inc.......D.......310 909-8410
8383 Wilshire Blvd # 460 Beverly Hills (90211) ***(P-18077)***
Mediaplex Inc (HQ).......D.......818 575-4500
30699 Russell Ranch Rd # 250 Westlake Village (91362) ***(P-13864)***
Medic Ambulance Service Inc (PA).......C.......707 644-1761
506 Couch St Vallejo (94590) ***(P-3821)***
Medical Billing Services, Monrovia *Also called California Business Bureau Inc* ***(P-13994)***
Medical Care Professionals.......D.......650 583-9898
363 El Cmino Real Ste 215 South San Francisco (94080) ***(P-20637)***
Medical Center, San Diego *Also called University Cal San Diego* ***(P-21878)***
Medical Center, San Bernardino *Also called Far West Inc* ***(P-20426)***
Medical Center, Ventura *Also called County of Ventura* ***(P-23758)***
Medical Centre, Sacramento *Also called University California Davis* ***(P-21883)***
Medical Couriers Inc.......D.......916 452-5700
176 Otto Cir Sacramento (95822) ***(P-4422)***
Medical Couriers Inc.......D.......650 872-1144
1611 Neptune Dr San Leandro (94577) ***(P-4423)***
Medical Diagnostic.......D.......714 841-2273
17682 Beach Blvd Ste 103 Huntington Beach (92647) ***(P-21156)***
Medical Ex Courier Systems, Orange *Also called Mx Courier Systems Inc* ***(P-17341)***
Medical Examiner, San Diego *Also called County of San Diego* ***(P-21357)***
Medical Examiner Forensic Ctr, San Diego *Also called County of San Diego* ***(P-22780)***
Medical Eye Services Inc.......D.......714 619-4660
345 Baker St Costa Mesa (92626) ***(P-10689)***
Medical Group Bverly Hills Inc (PA).......E.......310 385-3200
200 N Robertson Blvd Beverly Hills (90211) ***(P-19675)***
Medical Group Bverly Hills Inc.......E.......310 247-4646
250 N Robertson Blvd # 603 Beverly Hills (90211) ***(P-19676)***
Medical Hill Rehabilitation, Oakland *Also called Ocadian Care Centers LLC* ***(P-20674)***
Medical HM Care Professionals, Redding *Also called Medical Home Specialists Inc* ***(P-14880)***
Medical Home Specialists Inc.......C.......530 226-5577
2115 Churn Creek Rd Redding (96002) ***(P-14880)***
Medical Inst of Little Co Mary, Torrance *Also called Lifecare Systems Inc* ***(P-20590)***
Medical Insurance Exchange Cal.......D.......510 596-4935
6250 Claremont Ave Oakland (94618) ***(P-10690)***
Medical Investment Co.......C.......818 360-1003
16553 Rinaldi St Granada Hills (91344) ***(P-21157)***
Medical Management Cons Inc.......A.......858 587-0609
6046 Cornerstone Ct W San Diego (92121) ***(P-27332)***
Medical Management Cons Inc (PA).......E.......310 659-3835
8150 Beverly Blvd Los Angeles (90048) ***(P-14881)***
Medical Network Inc.......D.......949 863-0022
1809 E Dyer Rd Ste 311 Santa Ana (92705) ***(P-26942)***
Medical Receivables Solutions.......E.......707 980-6733
101 W American Canyon Rd American Canyon (94503) ***(P-27333)***
Medical Specialties Managers.......C.......714 571-5000
1 City Blvd W Ste 1100 Orange (92868) ***(P-27334)***
Medical Specialty Billing, Orange *Also called Medical Specialties Managers* ***(P-27334)***
Medical Support Services, Los Angeles *Also called MSS Nurses Registry Inc* ***(P-14885)***
Medical Support Services.......D.......323 860-7994
6660 W Sunset Blvd Ste J Los Angeles (90028) ***(P-14882)***
Medical Transcription Billing.......A.......800 869-3700
405 Kenyon St Ste 300 San Diego (92110) ***(P-15755)***
Medicl Imgng Ctr of Southrn CA.......D.......310 829-9788
2811 Wilshire Blvd # 100 Santa Monica (90403) ***(P-19677)***
Medico Professional Linen Svc, Los Angeles *Also called American Textile Maint Co* ***(P-13503)***
Medicrest of California 1.......D.......909 626-1294
5119 Bandera St Montclair (91763) ***(P-20638)***
Medidata Solutions Inc.......C.......415 295-4300
343 Sansome St Ste 1400 San Francisco (94104) ***(P-26638)***
Medimpact Hlthcare Systems Inc (HQ).......A.......858 566-2727
10181 Scripps Gateway Ct San Diego (92131) ***(P-25027)***
Medina Construction, Riverside *Also called Bens Asphalt & Maint Co Inc* ***(P-1731)***
Mediscan Diagnostic Svcs LLC.......D.......818 758-4224
21050 Califa St Ste 100 Woodland Hills (91367) ***(P-22839)***
Mediscan Staffing Services, Woodland Hills *Also called Mediscan Diagnostic Svcs LLC* ***(P-22839)***
Mediscan Staffing Services, Woodland Hills *Also called New Mediscan II LLC* ***(P-22847)***
Meditab Software Inc.......C.......510 632-2021
333 Hegenberger Rd # 800 Oakland (94621) ***(P-15756)***
Medley Communications Inc.......D.......760 294-4579
255 N Ash St Escondido (92027) ***(P-2644)***
Medley Communications Inc (PA).......C.......951 245-5200
43015 Black Deer Loop # 203 Temecula (92590) ***(P-2645)***
Medlin Development.......E.......909 825-5296
320 Tropicana Ranch Rd Colton (92324) ***(P-896)***

Mergent e-mail: customerrelations@mergent.com
1382
2019 Directory of California
Wholesalers and Services Companies
(P-0000) Products & Services Section entry number
(PA)=Parent Co (HQ)=Headquarters (DH)=Div Headquarters

Mednax Inc ....C 310 375-7172
23441 Madison St Ste 215 Torrance (90505) *(P-19678)*
Medpoint Management ....E 818 702-0100
6400 Canoga Ave Ste 163 Woodland Hills (91367) *(P-19679)*
Medric, Burlingame *Also called Acumen LLC (P-15909)*
Medsphere Systems Corporation (PA) ....D 760 692-3700
1903 Wright Pl Ste 120 Carlsbad (92008) *(P-27335)*
Medstar LLC ....D 916 669-0550
20 Busneca Pk Way Ste 100 Sacramento (95828) *(P-3822)*
Medstop Medical, North Hollywood *Also called Morigon Technologies LLC (P-7194)*
Medusind Solutions Inc (HQ) ....A 949 240-8895
31103 Rancho Viejo Rd San Juan Capistrano (92675) *(P-17318)*
Mee Industries Inc ....D 626 359-4550
16021 Adelante St Irwindale (91702) *(P-459)*
Meek's, Rocklin *Also called Cha-Dor Realty (P-6815)*
Meeting Services Inc ....D 858 348-0100
10895 Thornmint Rd Ste A San Diego (92127) *(P-14525)*
Mega Appraisers Inc ....A 818 246-7370
14724 Ventura Blvd # 800 Sherman Oaks (91403) *(P-17319)*
Mega Builders, Chatsworth *Also called A I T Development Corp (P-1107)*
Mega Farm Labor Services Inc ....C 661 229-8077
110 S Montclair St # 103 Bakersfield (93309) *(P-14667)*
Mega Mail Mall Inc ....E 888 998-6245
128 Avenida Del Mar San Clemente (92672) *(P-10911)*
Mega Professional Intl ....D 408 946-1500
995 Montague Expy Ste 121 Milpitas (95035) *(P-15276)*
Megapath, Pleasanton *Also called Gtt Communications (mp) Inc (P-5575)*
Megapath Cloud Company LLC (PA) ....D 925 201-2500
6800 Koll Center Pkwy Pleasanton (94566) *(P-5597)*
Megapath Group Inc (HQ) ....C 408 952-6400
2510 Zanker Rd San Jose (95131) *(P-5598)*
Megapath Group Inc ....C 408 324-1353
2510 Zanker Rd San Jose (95131) *(P-5599)*
Megapath Inc (PA) ....D 877 611-6342
6800 Koll Center Pkwy # 200 Pleasanton (94566) *(P-5600)*
Mehrdad Razavi, San Rafael *Also called Innovative Sleep Centers Inc (P-19513)*
Meiko America Inc ....D 951 360-0281
12300 Riverside Dr Eastvale (91752) *(P-4593)*
Mejico Express Inc (PA) ....C 714 690-8300
14849 Firestone Blvd Fl 1 La Mirada (90638) *(P-4842)*
Mek Escondido LLC ....D 760 747-0430
421 E Mission Ave Escondido (92025) *(P-20639)*
Mek Norwood Pines LLC ....D 916 922-7177
500 Jessie Ave Sacramento (95838) *(P-20640)*
Mekanism Inc (PA) ....D 415 908-4000
640 2nd St Fl 3 San Francisco (94107) *(P-13865)*
Meks's Auto Body, Concord *Also called Mike Roses Auto Body Inc (P-17730)*
Mekwus Solar Energy ....D 510 731-4134
20283 Santa Maria Ave # 2103 Castro Valley (94546) *(P-6184)*
Mel Bernie and Company Inc (PA) ....C 818 841-1928
3000 W Empire Ave Burbank (91504) *(P-8010)*
Mel Bernie and Company Inc ....C 818 841-1928
3000 W Empire Ave Burbank (91504) *(P-8320)*
Melano Enterprises, Oceanside *Also called Mellano & Co (P-9148)*
Melissa Bradley RE Inc ....D 415 388-5113
206 E Blithedale Ave Mill Valley (94941) *(P-11601)*
Melissa Bradley RE Inc ....D 707 258-3900
3249 Browns Valley Rd NAPA (94558) *(P-11602)*
Melissa Bradley RE Inc ....D 707 536-0888
1401 4th St Santa Rosa (95404) *(P-11603)*
Melissa Bradley RE Inc ....D 415 435-2705
1690 Tiburon Blvd Belvedere Tiburon (94920) *(P-11604)*
Melissa Bradley RE Inc ....D 415 209-1000
1701 Novato Blvd Ste 100 Novato (94947) *(P-11605)*
Melissa Bradley RE Inc ....D 415 485-4300
44 Bolinas Rd Fairfax (94930) *(P-11606)*
Melissas World Variety Produce, Vernon *Also called World Variety Produce Inc (P-8749)*
Mellano & Co (PA) ....B 213 622-0796
766 Wall St Los Angeles (90014) *(P-9147)*
Mellano & Co ....C 760 433-9550
734 Wilshire Rd Oceanside (92057) *(P-9148)*
Mellano Enterprises, Los Angeles *Also called Mellano & Co (P-9147)*
Mellennia Holdings, Los Angeles *Also called Millennia Holdings Inc (P-27348)*
Mellor, Anna B MD, Torrance *Also called South Bay Family Medical Group (P-19897)*
Melmet Steven J Law Ofc ....D 949 263-1000
2912 Daimler St Santa Ana (92705) *(P-23249)*
Melo Concrete Construction ....D 408 842-3484
5820 Obata Way Gilroy (95020) *(P-3287)*
Melon Holdings LLC ....D 530 742-7311
1617 Ramirez St Marysville (95901) *(P-20641)*
Melos Plst Lthg & Drywall ....D 559 237-0028
2038 E Jensen Ave Fresno (93706) *(P-2916)*
Meltwater News US Inc (HQ) ....D 415 829-5900
225 Bush St Ste 1000 San Francisco (94104) *(P-16958)*
Membrane Technology & RES Inc (PA) ....D 650 328-2228
39630 Eureka Dr Newark (94560) *(P-26415)*
Memeged Tevuot Shemesh (PA) ....C 866 575-1211
5550 Topanga Canyon Blvd # 280 Woodland Hills (91367) *(P-2277)*
Memo Scaffolding Inc ....D 562 404-8600
12722 Carmenita Rd Santa Fe Springs (90670) *(P-3551)*
Memon Aamir ....E 818 339-8810
20832 Roscoe Blvd Ste 207 Winnetka (91306) *(P-16730)*
Memor Ortho Surgic Group A M ....D 562 424-6666
2760 Atlantic Ave Long Beach (90806) *(P-19680)*
Memorex Products Inc ....C 562 653-2800
17777 Center Court Dr N S Cerritos (90703) *(P-7420)*
Memorial Center, Bakersfield *Also called Bakersfield Memorial Hospital (P-21294)*
Memorial Counseling Assoc Inc ....D 562 961-0155
4525 E Atherton St Long Beach (90815) *(P-19681)*
Memorial Healthtec Labratories ....A 714 962-4677
9920 Talbert Ave Fountain Valley (92708) *(P-26416)*
MEMORIAL HOSPITAL OF GARDENA, Gardena *Also called Gardena Hospital LP (P-21425)*
Memorial Medical Center, Modesto *Also called Sutter Central Vly Hospitals (P-21800)*
Memorial Promptcare Medical Gr (PA) ....E 714 891-9008
15464 Goldenwest St Westminster (92683) *(P-19682)*
Memorial Psychiatric Hlth Svcs ....E 562 494-9243
4525 E Atherton St Long Beach (90815) *(P-19683)*
Memorialcare Surgical Center A ....D 714 369-1100
18111 Brookhurst St # 3200 Fountain Valley (92708) *(P-21584)*
Memory To Go ....D 310 446-0111
10801 National Blvd # 101 Los Angeles (90064) *(P-7078)*
Memsql Inc (PA) ....E 855 463-6775
534 4th St San Francisco (94107) *(P-15277)*
Mendelsohn/Zien Advg LLC ....D 310 444-1990
11901 Santa Monica Blvd # 618 Los Angeles (90025) *(P-13866)*
Mendes Calf Ranch ....D 559 688-4708
13356 Avenue 168 Tipton (93272) *(P-397)*
Mendicino Cast Otptent Surgery, Fort Bragg *Also called Mendocino Coast District Hosp (P-21586)*
Mendocino Cmnty Hlth Clnic Inc (PA) ....C 707 468-1010
333 Laws Ave Ukiah (95482) *(P-19684)*
Mendocino Coast Clinics Inc ....D 707 964-1251
205 South St Fort Bragg (95437) *(P-22619)*
Mendocino Coast District Hosp (PA) ....B 707 961-1234
700 River Dr Fort Bragg (95437) *(P-21585)*
Mendocino Coast District Hosp ....C 707 961-4736
700 River Dr Fort Bragg (95437) *(P-21586)*
Mendocino Forest Pdts Co LLC ....C 707 468-1431
850 Kunzler Ranch Rd Ukiah (95482) *(P-6839)*
Mendocino Forest Pdts Co LLC (PA) ....B 707 620-2961
3700 Old Redwood Hwy # 200 Santa Rosa (95403) *(P-6840)*
Mendocino Forest Pdts Co LLC ....D 707 485-6800
6375 N State St Calpella (95418) *(P-6841)*
Mendocino Forest Pdts Co LLC ....D 707 620-2961
6500 Durable Mill Rd Calpella (95418) *(P-8043)*
Mendocino Hotel & Grdn Suites, Mendocino *Also called Mendocino Hotel & Resort Corp (P-12919)*
Mendocino Hotel & Resort Corp ....D 707 937-0511
45080 Main St Mendocino (95460) *(P-12919)*
Mendocino Railway ....C 707 964-6371
100 W Laurel St Fort Bragg (95437) *(P-5108)*
Mendocino Redwood Company LLC (PA) ....B 707 463-5110
850 Kunzler Ranch Rd Ukiah (95482) *(P-993)*
Mendocino Transit Authority ....D 707 462-1422
111 Boatyard Dr Fort Bragg (95437) *(P-3681)*
Mendoza Farms Inc ....E 805 352-1070
527 W Fesler St Apt A Santa Maria (93458) *(P-108)*
Menemsha Cnstr Solutions, Torrance *Also called Menemsha Development Group Inc (P-1593)*
Menemsha Development Group Inc (PA) ....C 310 676-6591
20521 Earl St Torrance (90503) *(P-1593)*
Menifee Lakes Country Club, Ontario *Also called Menifee Management Corp (P-18970)*
Menifee Management Corp ....D 951 672-4824
3200 E Guasti Rd Ste 100 Ontario (91761) *(P-18970)*
Menifee Valley Hospital Center, Sun City *Also called Physicians For Healthy Hospita (P-21643)*
Menke & Associates Inc (PA) ....D 415 362-5200
1 Kaiser Plz Ste 505 Oakland (94612) *(P-27785)*
Menlo Circus Club ....D 650 322-4616
190 Park Ln Atherton (94027) *(P-18971)*
Menlo Gateway Inc ....D 650 356-2900
303 Vintage Park Dr # 250 Foster City (94404) *(P-11149)*
Menlo Med Clinic A Med Corp ....C 650 498-6500
1300 Crane St Menlo Park (94025) *(P-19685)*
Menlo Park VA Medical Center, Menlo Park *Also called Veterans Health Administration (P-20079)*
Menlo Park-Atherton Education (PA) ....D 650 325-0100
181 Encinal Ave Atherton (94027) *(P-25443)*
Mens Apparel Guild In Cal Inc ....D 310 857-7500
2901 28th St Ste 100 Santa Monica (90405) *(P-24967)*
Mental Health Amer Los Angeles ....D 562 437-6717
456 Elm Ave Long Beach (90802) *(P-23919)*
Mental Health Assn Orange Cnty, Orange *Also called Orange County Association (P-25032)*
Mental Health California Dept ....B 707 449-6504
1600 California Dr Vacaville (95696) *(P-21966)*
Mental Health Department, Oakland *Also called La Clinica De La Raza Inc (P-19630)*
Mental Health Dept, Van Nuys *Also called Los Angeles Unified School Dst (P-22615)*
Mental Health Dept of, Arcadia *Also called County of Los Angeles (P-23677)*
Mental Health Dept of, Artesia *Also called County of Los Angeles (P-22548)*
Mental Health Dept of, Long Beach *Also called County of Los Angeles (P-19416)*
Mental Health Services, Stockton *Also called County of San Joaquin (P-22554)*
Mental Health Services, Red Bluff *Also called County of Tehama (P-23752)*
Mental Hlth Cnvlscent Svcs Inc ....B 562 869-0978
12023 Lakewood Blvd Downey (90242) *(P-20642)*
Mental Hlth Sbstnce Abuse Svcs, Auburn *Also called County of Placer (P-23704)*
Mental Hlth Svcs For Kngs Cnty, Hanford *Also called Kings View (P-22608)*
Mentor Media (usa) Sup ....D 909 930-0800
3768 Milliken Ave Ste A Eastvale (91752) *(P-26943)*
Mentor Worldwide LLC ....B 805 681-6000
5425 Hollister Ave Santa Barbara (93111) *(P-7191)*
Menzies Aviation (texas) Inc ....D 909 937-3998
1049 S Vineyard Ave Ontario (91761) *(P-4901)*
Mera Software Services Inc ....A 415 513-6401
2350 Mission College Blvd Santa Clara (95054) *(P-15278)*

ALPHABETIC

Employee Codes: A=Over 500 employees, B=251-500
C=101-250, D=51-100, E=50
2019 Directory of California
Wholesalers and Services Companies
© Mergent Inc. 1-800-342-5647
1383

Merabi & Sons LLC.....C.....818 817-0006
14545 Friar St Ste 101 Van Nuys (91411) ***(P-12174)***
Mercado Latino Inc (PA).....D.....626 333-6862
245 Baldwin Park Blvd City of Industry (91746) ***(P-8430)***
Mercado Latino Inc.....E.....510 475-5500
33430 Western Ave Union City (94587) ***(P-8431)***
Merced Convalescent Hospital, Merced *Also called Madera Convalescent Hospital* ***(P-21147)***
Merced Irrigation District (PA).....E.....209 722-5761
744 W 20th St Merced (95340) ***(P-6052)***
Merced Irrigation District.....C.....209 722-2719
3321 Franklin Rd Merced (95348) ***(P-6557)***
Merced School Employees F C U (PA).....D.....209 383-5550
1021 Olivewood Dr Merced (95348) ***(P-9569)***
Merced Transportation Company.....D.....209 384-2575
300 Grogan Ave Merced (95341) ***(P-3942)***
Mercedes Diaz Homes Inc.....D.....562 945-4576
7239 Washington Ave # 100 Whittier (90602) ***(P-1201)***
Mercer (us) Inc.....C.....213 346-2200
777 S Figueroa St # 2400 Los Angeles (90017) ***(P-27336)***
Mercer (us) Inc.....C.....415 743-8700
4 Embarcadero Ctr Lbby 4 # 4 San Francisco (94111) ***(P-27337)***
Mercer (us) Inc.....D.....949 222-1300
17901 Von Karman Ave # 1100 Irvine (92614) ***(P-27338)***
Mercer Global Securities LLC.....D.....805 565-1681
1801 E Cabrillo Blvd A Santa Barbara (93108) ***(P-10096)***
Mercer Health & Benefits LLC.....D.....415 743-8751
3 Embarcadero Ctr San Francisco (94111) ***(P-27339)***
Merchant of Tennis Inc.....C.....310 855-1946
1118 S La Cienega Blvd Los Angeles (90035) ***(P-17320)***
Merchant Services, Irvine *Also called Universal Card Inc* ***(P-17547)***
Merchant Services Inc (PA).....B.....817 725-0900
1 S Van Ness Ave Fl 5 San Francisco (94103) ***(P-16155)***
Merchant Valley Corporation.....C.....916 786-7227
1808 Avondale Dr Roseville (95747) ***(P-17321)***
Merchants Bank California N A.....D.....310 549-4350
1 Civic Plaza Dr Ste 100 Carson (90745) ***(P-9352)***
Merchants Building Maint Co.....B.....714 973-9272
1639 E Edinger Ave Ste C Santa Ana (92705) ***(P-14317)***
Merchants Building Maint Co (PA).....D.....323 881-6701
1190 Monterey Pass Rd Monterey Park (91754) ***(P-14318)***
Merchants Building Maint Co.....B.....858 455-0163
9555 Dist Ave 102 San Diego (92121) ***(P-14319)***
Merchants Building Maint Co.....C.....909 622-8260
1995 W Holt Ave Pomona (91768) ***(P-14320)***
Merchants Building Maint Co.....C.....323 881-8902
606 Monterey Paca Rd 20 Ste 202 Monterey Park (91754) ***(P-14321)***
Merchsource LLC.....D.....800 374-2744
7755 Irvine Center Dr Irvine (92618) ***(P-7957)***
Mercies Home (PA).....E.....661 832-3424
910 S Real Rd Bakersfield (93309) ***(P-24348)***
Mercury Air Cargo Inc (HQ).....C.....310 258-6100
6040 Avion Dr Ste 200 Los Angeles (90045) ***(P-4902)***
Mercury Casualty Company (HQ).....A.....323 937-1060
555 W Imperial Hwy Brea (92821) ***(P-10371)***
Mercury Defense Systems Inc (HQ).....D.....714 898-8200
10855 Bus Ctr Dr Bldg A Cypress (90630) ***(P-16156)***
Mercury General Corporation (PA).....D.....323 937-1060
4484 Wilshire Blvd Los Angeles (90010) ***(P-10372)***
Mercury Insurance Broker, Santa Monica *Also called Mercury Insurance Company* ***(P-10375)***
Mercury Insurance Company.....D.....714 671-6700
555 W Imperial Hwy Brea (92821) ***(P-10373)***
Mercury Insurance Company.....D.....916 353-4859
104 Woodmere Rd Folsom (95630) ***(P-10374)***
Mercury Insurance Company.....D.....310 451-4943
1433 Santa Monica Blvd Santa Monica (90404) ***(P-10375)***
Mercury Insurance Company.....D.....714 255-5000
1700 Greenbriar Ln Brea (92821) ***(P-10376)***
Mercury Insurance Company (HQ).....C.....323 937-1060
4484 Wilshire Blvd Los Angeles (90010) ***(P-10377)***
Mercury Insurance Company.....D.....858 694-4100
9635 Gran Rdge Dr Ste 200 San Diego (92123) ***(P-10378)***
Mercury Insurance Company.....D.....661 291-6470
27200 Tourney Rd Ste 400 Valencia (91355) ***(P-10379)***
Mercury Insurance Group, Folsom *Also called Mercury Insurance Company* ***(P-10374)***
Mercury Insurance Services LLC.....A.....323 937-1060
4484 Wilshire Blvd Los Angeles (90010) ***(P-10380)***
Mercury Interactive LLC (HQ).....B.....650 857-1501
3000 Hanover St Palo Alto (94304) ***(P-15757)***
Mercury Mailing Systems Inc.....D.....323 730-0307
2727 Exposition Blvd Los Angeles (90018) ***(P-14053)***
Mercury Messenger Service Inc.....E.....818 989-3115
16735 Saticoy St Ste 104 Van Nuys (91406) ***(P-17322)***
Mercury Systems, Cypress *Also called Mercury Defense Systems Inc* ***(P-16156)***
Mercury World Cargo, Los Angeles *Also called Mercury Air Cargo Inc* ***(P-4902)***
Mercy Air Tri-County LLC.....C.....909 829-1051
1670 Miro Way Rialto (92376) ***(P-4864)***
Mercy Foundation North.....D.....530 247-3424
2625 Edith Ave Ste E Redding (96001) ***(P-22840)***
Mercy General Hospital, Sacramento *Also called Mercy HM Svcs A Cal Ltd Partnr* ***(P-21590)***
Mercy General Hospital, Sacramento *Also called Dignity Health* ***(P-22078)***
Mercy General Hospital Bus Off, Sacramento *Also called Dignity Health* ***(P-21386)***
Mercy HM Svcs A Cal Ltd Partnr.....C.....661 632-5234
2215 Truxtun Ave Bakersfield (93301) ***(P-21587)***
Mercy HM Svcs A Cal Ltd Partnr (HQ).....A.....530 225-6000
2175 Rosaline Ave Ste A Redding (96001) ***(P-21588)***
Mercy HM Svcs A Cal Ltd Partnr.....B.....530 225-6000
2175 Rosaline Ave Ste A Redding (96001) ***(P-19686)***
Mercy HM Svcs A Cal Ltd Partnr.....B.....530 926-6111
914 Pine St Mount Shasta (96067) ***(P-21589)***
Mercy HM Svcs A Cal Ltd Partnr.....A.....916 453-4545
4001 J St Sacramento (95819) ***(P-21590)***
Mercy HM Svcs A Cal Ltd Partnr.....B.....209 564-4200
2740 M St Merced (95340) ***(P-21591)***
Mercy HM Svcs A Cal Ltd Partnr.....D.....530 245-4070
1544 Market St Redding (96001) ***(P-22366)***
MERCY HOSPITAL, San Francisco *Also called St Marys Med Ctr Foundation* ***(P-21789)***
Mercy Hospital, San Francisco *Also called Dignity Health* ***(P-21377)***
Mercy Hospital, Bakersfield *Also called Dignity Health* ***(P-21394)***
Mercy House Living Centers.....C.....714 836-7188
807 N Garfield St Santa Ana (92701) ***(P-24968)***
Mercy Housing Calif Xxv, Sacramento *Also called Mercy Housing California Xxvi* ***(P-11607)***
Mercy Housing California Xxvi.....D.....916 414-4400
2512 River Plaza Dr Sacramento (95833) ***(P-11607)***
Mercy Hse Trnstnal Living Ctrs, Santa Ana *Also called Mercy House Living Centers* ***(P-24968)***
Mercy Hsing California Xxxiv.....D.....415 503-0816
66 9th St San Francisco (94103) ***(P-11066)***
Mercy Medical, Red Bluff *Also called Lassen Medical Group Inc* ***(P-19645)***
Mercy Medical Center, Merced *Also called Mercy HM Svcs A Cal Ltd Partnr* ***(P-21591)***
Mercy Medical Center - Redding, Redding *Also called Mercy HM Svcs A Cal Ltd Partnr* ***(P-21588)***
MERCY MEDICAL CENTER MERCED, Merced *Also called Mater Misericordiae Hospital* ***(P-21582)***
Mercy Medical Center Redding, Redding *Also called Dignity Health* ***(P-21381)***
Mercy Retirement and Care Ctr.....C.....510 534-8540
3431 Foothill Blvd Oakland (94601) ***(P-24599)***
Mercy San Juan Med Trauma Ctr, Carmichael *Also called Dignity Health* ***(P-21371)***
Mercy San Juan Medical Center, Carmichael *Also called Dignity Health* ***(P-21379)***
Meredith Baer & Associates, South Gate *Also called Meribear Productions Inc* ***(P-17323)***
Meribear Productions Inc.....D.....310 204-5353
4100 Ardmore Ave South Gate (90280) ***(P-17323)***
Merical LLC (PA).....D.....714 238-7225
2995 E Miraloma Ave Anaheim (92806) ***(P-17324)***
Merical LLC.....B.....714 283-9551
233 E Bristol Ln Orange (92865) ***(P-17325)***
Merical/Vita-Pak, Orange *Also called Merical LLC* ***(P-17325)***
Meridian Gold Inc.....C.....209 785-3222
4461 Rock Creek Rd Copperopolis (95228) ***(P-1006)***
Meridian Holdings.....D.....805 539-2752
2580 El Camino Real Atascadero (93422) ***(P-7629)***
Meridian Industrial Trust.....D.....415 281-3900
455 Market St Ste 1700 San Francisco (94105) ***(P-12175)***
Meridian Knwldge Solutions LLC.....D.....913 985-9625
80 Iron Pont Cir Ste 100 Folsom (95630) ***(P-27340)***
Meridian Management Group.....C.....415 434-9700
1145 Bush St San Francisco (94109) ***(P-11608)***
Meridian Medical Offices, Riverside *Also called Kaiser Foundation Hospitals* ***(P-19580)***
Meridian Rack & Pinion Inc.....C.....858 587-8777
6740 Cobra Way Ste 200 San Diego (92121) ***(P-6657)***
Meridian Textiles Inc (PA).....D.....323 869-5700
6415 Canning St Commerce (90040) ***(P-8232)***
Meridian Vineyards, Paso Robles *Also called Treasury Wine Estates Americas* ***(P-180)***
Meridian World Travel, Menlo Park *Also called Peninsula World Travel LLC* ***(P-4946)***
Meringcarson Holdings (PA).....D.....916 441-0571
1700 I St Ste 210 Sacramento (95811) ***(P-13867)***
Meristar San Pedro Hilton LLC.....C.....310 514-3344
2800 Via Cabrillo Marina San Pedro (90731) ***(P-12920)***
Merit Logistics LLC.....A.....949 481-0685
33332 Valle Rd Ste 100 San Juan Capistrano (92675) ***(P-5109)***
Merit Property Management Inc, Irvine *Also called Firstservice Residential* ***(P-11467)***
Merit Technologies LLC.....D.....858 623-9800
10509 Vista Sorrento Pkwy # 420 San Diego (92121) ***(P-27341)***
Meritage Resort LLC.....B.....707 251-1900
875 Bordeaux Way NAPA (94558) ***(P-12921)***
Meritage Resort and Spa, The, NAPA *Also called Meritage Resort LLC* ***(P-12921)***
Meriwest Credit Union (PA).....C.....408 363-3200
5615 Chesbro Ave Ste 100 San Jose (95123) ***(P-9570)***
Merli Concrete Pumping, Gardena *Also called Stefan Merli Plastering Co Inc* ***(P-3330)***
Merlin Global Services LLC.....C.....904 305-9559
380 Stevens Ave Ste 305 Solana Beach (92075) ***(P-4865)***
Merlin Securities LLC.....D.....415 848-0269
45 Fremont St Ste 3000 San Francisco (94105) ***(P-9974)***
Merlot Film Productions Inc.....C.....323 575-2906
7800 Beverly Blvd Los Angeles (90036) ***(P-18078)***
Meroform Systems USA, Tustin *Also called Absolute Exhibits Inc* ***(P-16977)***
Merridian Neuro Care.....E.....949 263-6630
18a Journey Ste 200 Aliso Viejo (92656) ***(P-19687)***
Merrill Gardens.....D.....510 790-1645
2860 Country Dr Ofc Fremont (94536) ***(P-11150)***
Merrill Gardens At Bankers Hl, San Diego *Also called Merrill Gardens LLC* ***(P-11069)***
Merrill Gardens LLC.....D.....707 447-7496
799 Yellowstone Dr Vacaville (95687) ***(P-11609)***
Merrill Gardens LLC.....D.....707 553-2698
350 Locust Dr Apt L215 Vallejo (94591) ***(P-11067)***
Merrill Gardens LLC.....D.....707 585-7878
4855 Snyder Ln Apt 152 Rohnert Park (94928) ***(P-11068)***
Merrill Gardens LLC.....D.....619 961-4990
2567 2nd Ave San Diego (92103) ***(P-11069)***
Merrill Gardens LLC.....D.....714 842-6569
17200 Goldenwest St # 101 Huntington Beach (92647) ***(P-11070)***
Merrill Gardens LLC.....D.....408 370-6431
2115 Winchester Blvd Campbell (95008) ***(P-11071)***
Merrill Gardens LLC.....D.....760 414-9880
3500 Lake Blvd Oceanside (92056) ***(P-11072)***

Mergent e-mail: customerrelations@mergent.com
1384
2019 Directory of California
Wholesalers and Services Companies
(P-0000) Products & Services Section entry number
(PA)=Parent Co (HQ)=Headquarters (DH)=Div Headquarters

Merrill Gardens LLC ....D 805 310-4102
1220 Suey Rd Bldg A Santa Maria (93454) *(P-11073)*
Merrill Gardens LLC ....D 707 996-7101
800 Oregon St Sonoma (95476) *(P-11074)*
Merrill Gardens LLC ....D 209 823-0164
430 N Union Rd Manteca (95337) *(P-11075)*
Merrill Gardens LLC ....D 562 693-0505
13250 Philadelphia St Ofc Whittier (90601) *(P-11076)*
Merrill Gardns At Chateau Whit, Whittier *Also called Merrill Gardens LLC (P-11076)*
Merrill Lynch Pierce Fenner ....D 650 473-7888
333 Middlefield Rd Menlo Park (94025) *(P-9975)*
Merrill Lynch Pierce Fenner ....D 818 528-7809
16830 Ventura Blvd # 601 Encino (91436) *(P-9976)*
Merrill Lynch Pierce Fenner ....E 310 858-1500
9560 Wilshire Blvd Fl 3 Beverly Hills (90212) *(P-9977)*
Merrill Lynch Pierce Fenner ....D 818 528-7800
16830 Ventura Blvd # 601 Encino (91436) *(P-9978)*
Merrill Lynch Pierce Fenner ....D 650 842-2440
3075b Hansen Way Palo Alto (94304) *(P-9979)*
Merrill Lynch Pierce Fenner ....E 661 802-0764
730 Patricia Dr San Luis Obispo (93405) *(P-9980)*
Merrill Lynch Pierce Fenner ....C 949 467-3760
520 Newport Center Dr # 1900 Newport Beach (92660) *(P-9981)*
Merrill Lynch Pierce Fenner ....D 626 304-1596
800 E Colo Blvd Ste 400 Pasadena (91101) *(P-9895)*
Merrill Lynch Pierce Fenner ....C 800 964-5182
300 E Esplanade Dr Oxnard (93036) *(P-9982)*
Merrill Lynch Pierce Fenner ....C 650 473-7888
333 Middlefield Rd # 202 Menlo Park (94025) *(P-9983)*
Merrill Lynch Pierce Fenner ....C 619 699-3700
701 B St Ste 2350 San Diego (92101) *(P-9984)*
Merrill Lynch Pierce Fenner ....E 408 283-3000
50 W San Fernando St 16 San Jose (95113) *(P-9985)*
Merrill Lynch Pierce Fenner ....D 714 257-4400
145 S State College Blvd # 300 Brea (92821) *(P-10046)*
Merrill Lynch Pierce Fenner ....C 310 407-3900
2049 Century Park E # 1100 Los Angeles (90067) *(P-9986)*
Merrill Lynch Pierce Fenner ....D 925 945-4800
1331 N Calif Blvd Ste 400 Walnut Creek (94596) *(P-9987)*
Merrill Lynch Pierce Fenner ....E 415 274-7000
101 California St Fl 24 San Francisco (94111) *(P-9988)*
Merrill Lynch Pierce Fenner ....D 626 844-8500
800 E Colo Blvd Ste 400 Pasadena (91101) *(P-10047)*
Merrill Lynch Pierce Fenner ....D 949 859-2900
100 Spectrum Center Dr # 1100 Irvine (92618) *(P-9989)*
Merrill Lynch Pierce Fenner ....D 858 456-3600
7825 Fay Ave Ste 300 La Jolla (92037) *(P-9990)*
Merrill Lynch Wealth MGT, Pasadena *Also called Merrill Lynch Pierce Fenner (P-9895)*
Merritt Hawkins & Assoc LLC (HQ) ....C 858 792-0711
12400 High Bluff Dr San Diego (92130) *(P-14883)*
Merritt Hospitality LLC ....C 562 983-3400
701 W Ocean Blvd Long Beach (90831) *(P-12922)*
Merritt Hospitality LLC ....C 714 738-7800
2701 Nutwood Ave Fullerton (92831) *(P-12923)*
Merry X-Ray Chemical Corp (PA) ....C 858 565-4472
4909 Murphy Canyon Rd # 120 San Diego (92123) *(P-7192)*
Meruelo Enterprises, Downey *Also called Cantamar Property MGT Inc (P-11264)*
Mesa Cnsld Wtr Dst Imprv Corp (PA) ....D 949 631-1200
1965 Placentia Ave Costa Mesa (92627) *(P-6279)*
Mesa Cold Strg 4145, Fullerton *Also called US Foods Inc (P-8894)*
Mesa Contracting Corporation ....C 714 974-7300
22845 Savi Ranch Pkwy D Yorba Linda (92887) *(P-1818)*
Mesa Counselling ....E 909 421-9301
850 E Foothill Blvd Rialto (92376) *(P-27342)*
Mesa Distributing Coinc (HQ) ....C 858 452-2300
3840 Via De La Valle # 300 Del Mar (92014) *(P-9014)*
Mesa Energy Systems Inc (HQ) ....C 949 460-0460
2 Cromwell Irvine (92618) *(P-2278)*
Mesa Energy Systems Inc ....D 559 277-7900
3980 N Chestnut Ave Fresno (93726) *(P-2279)*
Mesa Energy Systems Inc ....C 818 756-0500
16130 Sherman Way Van Nuys (91406) *(P-2280)*
Mesa Management Inc ....D 949 851-0995
1451 Quail St Ste 201 Newport Beach (92660) *(P-11610)*
Mesa Pointe Stadium 12, Costa Mesa *Also called Edwards Theatres Circuit Inc (P-18288)*
Mesa Properties GP ....D 949 857-1905
25 Mauchly Ste 305 Irvine (92618) *(P-12924)*
Mesa Verde Convalescent Hosp ....C 949 548-5584
661 Center St Costa Mesa (92627) *(P-20643)*
Mesa Verde Country Club ....C 714 549-0377
3000 Club House Rd Costa Mesa (92626) *(P-18972)*
Mesa Verde Partners ....D 714 540-7500
1701 Golf Course Dr Costa Mesa (92626) *(P-18733)*
Mesa Verde Prosecute Care, Costa Mesa *Also called Mesa Verde Convalescent Hosp (P-20643)*
Mesa Vineyard Management Inc ....D 805 925-7200
2570 Prell Rd Santa Maria (93454) *(P-698)*
Mesa Vineyard Management Inc (PA) ....D 805 434-4100
110 Gibson Rd Templeton (93465) *(P-699)*
Mesa Water District, Costa Mesa *Also called Mesa Cnsld Wtr Dst Imprv Corp (P-6279)*
Mesquite Golf & Cntry CLB Corp ....E 760 323-9377
2700 E Mesquite Ave Ofc Palm Springs (92264) *(P-19202)*
Message Broadcastcom LLC ....E 949 428-3111
4685 Macarthur Ct Ste 250 Newport Beach (92660) *(P-17326)*
Message Center Communication ....E 858 974-7419
6779 Mesa Ridge Rd # 100 San Diego (92121) *(P-17327)*
Messagesolution Inc ....D 408 383-0100
1851 Mccarthy Blvd # 105 Milpitas (95035) *(P-16157)*

Messenger Express (PA) ....C 213 614-0475
5435 Cahuenga Blvd Ste C North Hollywood (91601) *(P-4424)*
Messenger Express ....D 858 550-1400
10671 Roselle St Ste 200 San Diego (92121) *(P-4425)*
Metabyte Inc ....D 510 405-1117
39300 Civic Center Dr # 260 Fremont (94538) *(P-16425)*
Metagenics Inc (HQ) ....C 949 366-0818
25 Enterprise Ste 200 Aliso Viejo (92656) *(P-8197)*
Metagenics Inc ....D 800 692-9400
100 Avenida La Pata San Clemente (92673) *(P-8198)*
Metaswitch Networks ....E 415 513-1500
1751 Harbor Bay Pkwy # 125 Alameda (94502) *(P-15279)*
Method Studios LLC ....C 310 434-6500
3401 Exposition Blvd Santa Monica (90404) *(P-18079)*
Methodist Hosp Southern Cal (PA) ....A 626 898-8000
300 W Huntington Dr Arcadia (91007) *(P-21592)*
Methodist Hospital of S CA ....D 626 574-3755
300 W Huntington Dr Arcadia (91007) *(P-21593)*
Methodist Hospital Sacramento, Sacramento *Also called Dignity Health (P-21385)*
Metier Ltd ....D 707 546-9300
1083 Vine St Ste 511 Healdsburg (95448) *(P-16426)*
MetLife, San Francisco *Also called Metropolitan Life Insur Co (P-10691)*
Metric Equipment Sales Inc ....D 510 264-0887
25841 Industrial Blvd # 200 Hayward (94545) *(P-7507)*
Metrick Property Management, San Francisco *Also called Blackrock Holdco 2 Inc (P-11245)*
Metricstream Inc (PA) ....C 650 620-2900
2479 E Byshore Rd Ste 260 Palo Alto (94303) *(P-15758)*
Metricus Inc ....C 650 328-2500
P.O. Box 458 Palo Alto (94302) *(P-17328)*
Metro Bldrs & Engineers Group, Newport Beach *Also called Houalla Enterprises Ltd (P-1555)*
Metro Building Maintenance, Los Angeles *Also called US Metro Group Inc (P-14423)*
Metro City, Sherman Oaks *Also called Metro Home Loan Inc (P-9832)*
Metro Home Loan Inc ....D 818 461-9840
15301 Ventura Blvd D300 Sherman Oaks (91403) *(P-9832)*
Metro One Telecom Inc ....C 626 337-8100
4900 Rivergrade Rd B210 Irwindale (91706) *(P-13868)*
Metro Pcs, Los Angeles *Also called Richards Group Inc (P-13892)*
Metro Service South Inc ....D 310 995-8950
3605 Cahuenga Blvd W Los Angeles (90068) *(P-14322)*
Metro-Goldwyn-Mayer Inc (HQ) ....B 310 449-3000
245 N Beverly Dr Beverly Hills (90210) *(P-18080)*
Metrolink, Los Angeles *Also called Southern Cal Rgional Rail Auth (P-3730)*
Metrolux 14 Theatres, Los Angeles *Also called Metrolux Theatres (P-18240)*
Metrolux Theatres ....D 310 858-2800
8727 W 3rd St Los Angeles (90048) *(P-18240)*
Metromile Inc (PA) ....D 888 244-1702
690 Folsom St Ste 200 San Francisco (94107) *(P-10381)*
Metron Incorporated ....E 858 792-8904
12250 El Camino Real # 260 San Diego (92130) *(P-27343)*
Metron-Athene Inc (PA) ....D 949 588-5757
23046 Avnida De La Crlota Carlota Laguna Hills (92653) *(P-15280)*
Metropcs-Fremont, Fremont *Also called T-Mobile Usa Inc (P-5418)*
Metropcs-Modesto, Modesto *Also called T-Mobile Usa Inc (P-5419)*
Metropcs-Van Ness, San Francisco *Also called T-Mobile Usa Inc (P-5420)*
Metroplex Theatres LLC ....A 310 856-1270
2275 W 190th St Ste 201 Torrance (90504) *(P-18306)*
Metroplitan Oakland Intl Arprt, Oakland *Also called Port Dept City of Oakland (P-4905)*
Metropolis Hotel MGT LLC ....C 213 683-4855
899 Francisco St Los Angeles (90017) *(P-12925)*
Metropolitan Area Advisory Com (PA) ....D 619 426-3595
1355 Third Ave Chula Vista (91911) *(P-24204)*
Metropolitan Area Advisory Com ....B 619 255-7284
1102 Cesar E Chavez Pkwy San Diego (92113) *(P-24205)*
Metropolitan Area Advisory Com ....C 619 420-8981
1355 Third Ave Chula Vista (91911) *(P-24206)*
Metropolitan Club ....D 415 673-0600
640 Sutter St San Francisco (94102) *(P-18973)*
Metropolitan Dst Private SEC ....D 661 942-3999
44262 Division St Ste A Lancaster (93535) *(P-16731)*
Metropolitan Elec Cnstr Inc ....C 415 642-3000
2400 3rd St San Francisco (94107) *(P-2646)*
Metropolitan Life Insur Co ....B 415 536-1065
425 Market St Ste 960 San Francisco (94105) *(P-10691)*
Metropolitan Marketing Inc (PA) ....D 909 620-5083
6320 Canoga Ave Ste 1630 Woodland Hills (91367) *(P-27344)*
Metropolitan Trnsp Comm (PA) ....C 415 778-6700
375 Beale St Ste 800 San Francisco (94105) *(P-3682)*
Metropolitan Waste Disposal, Paramount *Also called Calmet Inc (P-6368)*
Metropolitan Water District ....E 909 890-3776
1820 Commercenter Cir San Bernardino (92408) *(P-6280)*
Metropolitan Water District ....E 951 688-5672
18250 La Sierra Ave Riverside (92503) *(P-6281)*
Metropolitan Water District ....C 760 663-4911
33740 Borel Rd Winchester (92596) *(P-6282)*
Metropolitan Water District ....D 818 368-3731
13100 Balboa Blvd Granada Hills (91344) *(P-6283)*
Metropolitan Water District ....B 909 593-7474
700 Moreno Ave La Verne (91750) *(P-6284)*
Metropolitan Water District ....A 213 217-6667
700 N Alameda St Ste 1 Los Angeles (90012) *(P-6558)*
Metropolitan Water District ....D 951 926-7095
33752 Newport Rd Winchester (92596) *(P-6285)*
Metropolitan Water District ....D 951 780-1511
550 E Alessandro Blvd Riverside (92508) *(P-6286)*
Metropolitan Water District ....A 310 832-6106
2300 Palos Verdes Dr N Rllng HLS Est (90274) *(P-6287)*

ALPHABETIC

Metropolitan Water District...D....951 926-1501
33740 Borel Rd Winchester (92596) ***(P-6288)***
Metropolitan Water Lavern, La Verne *Also called Metropolitan Water District* ***(P-6284)***
Metropower Inc...D....562 305-9617
941 Grand Ave Long Beach (90804) ***(P-2647)***
Metropro Road Services Inc (PA)...D....714 556-7600
2550 S Garnsey St Santa Ana (92707) ***(P-17866)***
Mets//, Manhattan Beach *Also called M & E Technical Services L L C* ***(P-27600)***
Meus, Cypress *Also called Mitsubishi Electric Us Inc* ***(P-3473)***
Mexican American Legal Defense (PA)...D....213 629-2512
634 S Spring St Ste 1100 Los Angeles (90014) ***(P-23250)***
Mexican Amrcn Alcoholism Progr (PA)...D....916 394-2320
4241 Florin Rd Ste 110 Sacramento (95823) ***(P-23920)***
Mexican Amrcn Oprtnty Fndation (PA)...D....323 890-9600
401 N Garfield Ave Montebello (90640) ***(P-23921)***
Mexican Amrcn Oprtnty Fndation...E....323 588-7320
2650 Zoe Ave Fl 3 Huntington Park (90255) ***(P-24349)***
Mexican Amrcn Oprtnty Fndation...D....323 890-1555
5657 E Washington Blvd Commerce (90040) ***(P-23922)***
Mexican Heritg Ctr Gallery Inc...D....209 969-9306
111 S Sutter St Stockton (95202) ***(P-24890)***
Meyer Coatings Inc...E....714 467-4600
1844 W Bus Ctr Dr Ornge Orange (92867) ***(P-2457)***
Meyer Corporation US...D....707 399-2100
2001 Meyer Way Fairfield (94533) ***(P-6776)***
Meyer Properties Corp (PA)...D....949 862-0500
4320 Von Karman Ave Newport Beach (92660) ***(P-11891)***
Meyers Nave Riback Silver & (PA)...C....510 351-4300
555 12th St Ste 1500 Oakland (94607) ***(P-23251)***
Meyers Earthwork Inc...D....530 365-8858
4150 Fig Tree Ln Redding (96002) ***(P-3434)***
Meyers Farming, Firebaugh *Also called Oxford Farms Inc* ***(P-704)***
Meyers Group, Costa Mesa *Also called Hanley Wood Mkt Intelligence* ***(P-26526)***
Meyers Research LLC...D....714 619-7800
3200 Bristol St Ste 640 Costa Mesa (92626) ***(P-26544)***
Mf Daily Oxnard Ranch Partnr...E....805 646-5633
1033 E Ojai Ave Ojai (93023) ***(P-18734)***
Mf Services Company LLC (HQ)...D....949 474-5800
4350 Von Karman Ave # 400 Newport Beach (92660) ***(P-27345)***
Mfi Recovery Center (PA)...C....951 683-6596
5870 Arlington Ave # 103 Riverside (92504) ***(P-22620)***
Mfw Partners...E....858 454-8857
1120 Silverado St La Jolla (92037) ***(P-10912)***
MGA Entertainment Inc (PA)...B....818 894-2525
16300 Roscoe Blvd Ste 150 Van Nuys (91406) ***(P-7958)***
MGA Healthcare California Inc...E....310 324-5591
879 W 190th St Ste 700 Gardena (90248) ***(P-14884)***
Mgb Construction Inc...C....951 342-0303
91 Commercial Ave Riverside (92507) ***(P-1819)***
Mgd Inc (PA)...D....209 955-0535
3525 W Benjamin Holt Dr Stockton (95219) ***(P-11077)***
Mge Underground Inc...D....805 238-3510
816 26th St Paso Robles (93446) ***(P-1956)***
Mggb Inc...C....714 226-0520
10841 Noel St Ste 110 Los Alamitos (90720) ***(P-25818)***
Mgh Corporation...E....323 754-1408
1202 W 101st St Los Angeles (90044) ***(P-24600)***
Mgi, Newark *Also called Mickwee Group Inc* ***(P-17329)***
MGM, Beverly Hills *Also called Metro-Goldwyn-Mayer Inc* ***(P-18080)***
MGM and Ua Services Company...A....310 449-3000
245 N Beverly Dr Beverly Hills (90210) ***(P-27944)***
MGM Drywall Inc...D....408 292-4085
1050 Coml St Ste 102 San Jose (95112) ***(P-2917)***
Mgr Services Inc...D....909 981-4466
1425 W Foothill Blvd # 300 Upland (91786) ***(P-11611)***
MGT Industries Inc...D....310 324-3152
19034 S Vermont Ave Gardena (90248) ***(P-26944)***
Mhh Holdings Inc...C....949 651-9903
5653 Alton Pkwy Irvine (92618) ***(P-8825)***
Mhh Holdings Inc...D....626 744-9370
415 S Lake Ave Ste 108 Pasadena (91101) ***(P-8826)***
Mhn Government Services LLC...C....916 294-4941
2370 Kerner Blvd San Rafael (94901) ***(P-23923)***
Mhn Services...A....415 460-8300
2370 Kerner Blvd San Rafael (94901) ***(P-10283)***
MHRP Resort Inc...D....760 249-5808
24510 Highway 2 Wrightwood (92397) ***(P-12926)***
MHS, Fresno *Also called Turn Behavioral Hlth Svcs Inc* ***(P-22703)***
MHS Customer Service Inc...D....858 695-2151
7586 Trade St Ste C San Diego (92121) ***(P-14668)***
Mhx LLC...D....800 234-2098
22707 Wilmington Ave Carson (90745) ***(P-5110)***
Mias Fashion Mfg Co Inc...B....562 906-1060
12623 Cisneros Ln Santa Fe Springs (90670) ***(P-8321)***
Michael A Meczka...E....310 670-4824
5757 W Century Blvd # 120 Los Angeles (90045) ***(P-26545)***
Michael B Mayock Inc...D....415 456-9306
1945 Francisco Blvd E # 31 San Rafael (94901) ***(P-2918)***
Michael Baker Jr Inc...D....805 383-3373
5051 Verdugo Way Ste 300 Camarillo (93012) ***(P-25819)***
Michael Baker Intl Inc...C....510 879-0950
1 Kaiser Plz Ste 1150 Oakland (94612) ***(P-25820)***
Michael Baker Intl Inc...D....916 361-8384
2729 Prospect Park Dr # 220 Rancho Cordova (95670) ***(P-27786)***
Michael Baker Intl Inc...D....858 453-3602
9755 Clairemont Mesa Blvd San Diego (92124) ***(P-27787)***
Michael Baker Intl Inc...E....909 974-4900
3300 E Guasti Rd Ste 100 Ontario (91761) ***(P-27788)***
Michael Baker Intl Inc...D....951 676-8042
40810 County Center Dr # 100 Temecula (92591) ***(P-25821)***
Michael Bruington...E....831 663-1772
9 Soledad Dr Ste E Monterey (93940) ***(P-1202)***
Michael Cardellini...E....415 243-8400
650 California St Fl 14 San Francisco (94108) ***(P-25822)***
Michael Dusi Trucking Inc...D....805 237-9499
3230 Rverside Ave Ste 220 Paso Robles (93446) ***(P-4230)***
Michael Jon Designs, Vernon *Also called Morgan Fabrics Corporation* ***(P-8234)***
Michael Madden Co Inc...D....800 834-6248
2815 Warner Ave Irvine (92606) ***(P-8110)***
Michael Maguire & Associates...E....714 435-7500
611 Anton Blvd Ste 900 Costa Mesa (92626) ***(P-10692)***
Michael McCarthy...E....310 800-5367
3233 E Broadway Long Beach (90803) ***(P-16732)***
Michael P Byko DDS A Prof Corp (PA)...D....909 888-7817
164 W Hospitality Ln # 14 San Bernardino (92408) ***(P-20127)***
Michael Reyes...C....909 444-0120
577 N D St Ste 111a14 San Bernardino (92401) ***(P-1594)***
Michael S Duffy Sr Do Inc...D....619 461-3717
1501 5th Ave Ste 100 San Diego (92101) ***(P-19688)***
Michael SD Nagatini...D....559 738-7502
5400 W Hillsdale Ave Visalia (93291) ***(P-19689)***
Michael Sullivan & Assoc LLP...C....310 337-4480
400 Continental Blvd # 250 El Segundo (90245) ***(P-23252)***
Michael W Morgan...E....760 344-5253
3949 Austin Rd Brawley (92227) ***(P-68)***
Michael-Antonio Studio, Montclair *Also called E M S Trading Inc* ***(P-8354)***
Michaels Stores Inc...C....661 951-3500
3501 W Avenue H Lancaster (93536) ***(P-9235)***
Michaels Trnsp Svc Inc...D....707 674-6013
140 Yolano Dr Vallejo (94589) ***(P-3891)***
Michaelson Connor & Boul (PA)...D....714 230-3600
5312 Bolsa Ave Huntington Beach (92649) ***(P-27346)***
Micheli Farms Inc...E....530 695-9022
6005 Highway 99 Live Oak (95953) ***(P-225)***
Michelle Pasternak, Los Angeles *Also called SM 10000 Property LLC* ***(P-11919)***
Michelson Laboratories Inc (PA)...D....562 928-0553
6280 Chalet Dr Commerce (90040) ***(P-26713)***
Mickey Wall Painting Inc...E....209 669-0557
250 East Ave Turlock (95380) ***(P-2458)***
Mickwee Group Inc...D....510 651-5527
5600 Mowry School Rd # 230 Newark (94560) ***(P-17329)***
Micon Construction Cal Inc...D....714 666-0203
1616 Sierra Madre Cir Placentia (92870) ***(P-1595)***
Micro Holding Corp...A....415 788-5111
1 Maritime Plz Fl 12 San Francisco (94111) ***(P-16158)***
Micro P Technologies, El Segundo *Also called Pcm Sales Inc* ***(P-7089)***
Micro-Mechanics Inc...E....408 779-2927
465 Woodview Ave Morgan Hill (95037) ***(P-7508)***
Micro-Pro Microfilming Svcs, Long Beach *Also called Macro-Pro Inc* ***(P-17307)***
Micro-Technology Concepts Inc...D....626 839-6800
17837 Rowland St City of Industry (91748) ***(P-7079)***
Microbial Diseases Laboratory, Richmond *Also called Department Health Care Svcs* ***(P-22075)***
Microbiology & Qulty Assoc Inc...E....925 288-1400
2341 Stanwell Dr Concord (94520) ***(P-26639)***
Microconstants Inc...E....858 652-4600
9050 Camino Santa Fe San Diego (92121) ***(P-26417)***
Microfinancial Incorporated...C....805 367-8900
2801 Townsgate Rd Westlake Village (91361) ***(P-14526)***
Microlease, Hayward *Also called Metric Equipment Sales Inc* ***(P-7507)***
Microlease Inc (HQ)...D....866 520-0200
6060 Sepulveda Blvd Van Nuys (91411) ***(P-14527)***
Microsoft Corporation...D....650 964-7200
680 Vaqueros Ave Sunnyvale (94085) ***(P-15759)***
Microsoft Corporation...D....619 849-5872
7007 Friars Rd San Diego (92108) ***(P-15760)***
Microsoft Corporation...C....650 693-1009
1020 Entp Way Bldg B Sunnyvale (94089) ***(P-15761)***
Microsoft Corporation...C....949 263-3000
3 Park Plz Ste 1800 Irvine (92614) ***(P-15762)***
Microsoft Corporation...D....213 806-7300
13031 W Jefferson Blvd # 200 Playa Vista (90094) ***(P-15763)***
Microsoft Corporation...C....415 972-6400
555 California St Ste 200 San Francisco (94104) ***(P-15764)***
Microsoft Corporation...D....408 987-9608
2045 Lafayette St Santa Clara (95050) ***(P-15765)***
Microtek Lab Inc (HQ)...C....310 687-5823
13337 South St Cerritos (90703) ***(P-6969)***
Microtel Computer Systems Inc...D....626 839-6038
5545 Daniels St Chino (91710) ***(P-16427)***
Mid Century Insurance Company...C....323 932-7116
4680 Wilshire Blvd Los Angeles (90010) ***(P-10382)***
Mid Cities Assn Retarded Ctzns (PA)...D....310 537-4510
14208 Towne Ave Los Angeles (90061) ***(P-24207)***
MID PENN HOUSING, Saratoga *Also called Saratoga Court Inc* ***(P-11154)***
Mid Rckland Imging Prtners Inc (HQ)...E....310 445-2800
1510 Cotner Ave Los Angeles (90025) ***(P-22111)***
Mid State Steel Erection (PA)...D....209 464-9497
1916 Cherokee Rd Stockton (95205) ***(P-3388)***
Mid Valley Labor Services Inc...B....559 661-6390
19358 Avenue 18 1/2 Madera (93637) ***(P-14669)***
Mid Valley Packaging & Sup Co, Fowler *Also called Gahvejian Enterprises Inc* ***(P-8103)***
Mid Valley Plastering Inc...B....209 858-9766
15300 Mckinley Ave Lathrop (95330) ***(P-2919)***
Mid Vlley Racquetball Athc CLB...C....818 705-6500
18420 Hart St Reseda (91335) ***(P-18974)***

Mergent e-mail: customerrelations@mergent.com
1386
2019 Directory of California
Wholesalers and Services Companies
(P-0000) Products & Services Section entry number
(PA)=Parent Co (HQ)=Headquarters (DH)=Div Headquarters

ALPHABETIC SECTION
Mind Research Institute

Mid Wilshire Health Care Ctr ....D....213 483-9921
676 S Bonnie Brae St Los Angeles (90057) *(P-20644)*
Mid-Peninsula Roofing Inc ....D....650 375-7850
1326 Marsten Rd Burlingame (94010) *(P-3179)*
Mid-Peninsula Tyrella Corp (PA) ....D....650 299-8000
658 Bair Island Rd # 300 Redwood City (94063) *(P-11078)*
Mid-Valley Athletic Club, Reseda *Also called Mid Vlley Racquetball Athc CLB (P-18974)*
Mid-Valley Y M C A, Van Nuys *Also called Young Mens Chrstn Assn of La (P-25340)*
Mida Industries Inc ....C....562 616-1020
6101 Obispo Ave Long Beach (90805) *(P-14323)*
Midas Express Los Angeles Inc ....C....310 609-0366
11854 Alameda St Lynwood (90262) *(P-4594)*
Midland Credit Management Inc (HQ) ....A....877 240-2377
3111 Camino Del Rio N San Diego (92108) *(P-9742)*
Midland Express Credit LLC ....D....800 961-3904
2037 W Bullard Ave # 316 Fresno (93711) *(P-27347)*
Midmark Diagnostics Group, Gardena *Also called Brentwood Medical Tech Corp (P-7168)*
Midnight Auto Recycling LLC ....E....909 884-5308
434 E 6th St San Bernardino (92410) *(P-7983)*
Midnight Mission (PA) ....D....213 624-9258
601 S San Pedro St Los Angeles (90014) *(P-25198)*
Midnight Snack LP ....E....310 202-1470
4182 Irving Pl Culver City (90232) *(P-26945)*
Midnite Air Corp ....E....310 330-2300
8801 Bellanca Ave Los Angeles (90045) *(P-4843)*
Midnite Air Corp (HQ) ....D....310 910-9199
5001 Arprt Plz Dr Ste 250 Long Beach (90815) *(P-4844)*
Midokura USA Inc ....E....888 512-0460
315 Montgomery St Fl 8 San Francisco (94104) *(P-15281)*
Midori Landscape Inc ....D....714 751-8792
3231 S Main St Santa Ana (92707) *(P-897)*
Midori Landscaping, Santa Ana *Also called Midori Landscape Inc (P-897)*
MIDPEN HOUSING, Foster City *Also called Menlo Gateway Inc (P-11149)*
MIDPEN HOUSING, San Jose *Also called Vivente 1 Inc (P-11155)*
Midpen Housing Corporation ....B....650 356-2900
303 Vintage Park Dr # 250 Foster City (94404) *(P-11892)*
Midpen Resident Services Corp ....B....650 356-2965
303 Vintage Park Dr # 250 Foster City (94404) *(P-11151)*
Midpeninsul Rgnl Opn Sp ....D....650 691-1200
330 Distel Cir Los Altos (94022) *(P-27945)*
Midstate Barrier Inc ....D....209 944-9565
3291 S Highway 99 Stockton (95215) *(P-1820)*
Midstate Construction Corp ....D....707 762-3200
1180 Holm Rd Ste A Petaluma (94954) *(P-1203)*
Midway Car Rental, North Hollywood *Also called Midway Rent A Car Inc (P-17657)*
Midway Clinic Cars, Los Angeles *Also called Midway Rent A Car Inc (P-17645)*
Midway International Inc ....E....562 921-2255
13131 166th St Cerritos (90703) *(P-9236)*
Midway Rent A Car Inc ....C....818 985-9770
4201 Lankershim Blvd North Hollywood (91602) *(P-17657)*
Midway Rent A Car Inc ....D....310 445-4355
1800 S Sepulveda Blvd Los Angeles (90025) *(P-17645)*
Midwest Enviromental Control ....E....661 255-0722
22430 13th St Santa Clarita (91321) *(P-26418)*
Mig Management Services LLC ....D....949 474-5800
660 Newport Center Dr Newport Beach (92660) *(P-26946)*
Mighty Enterprises Inc ....D....310 516-7478
19706 Normandie Ave Torrance (90502) *(P-7774)*
Mighty Leaf Tea ....D....415 491-2650
100 Smith Ranch Rd # 120 San Rafael (94903) *(P-8827)*
Mighty USA, Torrance *Also called Mighty Enterprises Inc (P-7774)*
Miguel Ramos ....D....831 761-9941
196 San Andreas Rd Watsonville (95076) *(P-452)*
Mikado Best Western Hotel, North Hollywood *Also called Mikado Hotels Inc (P-12927)*
Mikado Hotels Inc ....E....818 763-9141
12600 Riverside Dr North Hollywood (91607) *(P-12927)*
Mikaelian & Sons Inc ....C....559 591-6324
10368 Avenue 400 Dinuba (93618) *(P-69)*
Mike Brown Electric Co ....D....707 792-8100
561a Mercantile Dr Cotati (94931) *(P-2648)*
Mike Campbell & Associates Ltd ....A....626 369-3981
10907 Downey Ave Ste 203 Downey (90241) *(P-4509)*
Mike Campbell Assoc Logictics, Downey *Also called Mike Campbell & Associates Ltd (P-4509)*
Mike Champlin ....D....925 961-1004
4374 Contractors Cmn Livermore (94551) *(P-2459)*
Mike Champlin Painting, Livermore *Also called Mike Champlin (P-2459)*
Mike Diamond Plumbing Inc (PA) ....D....310 838-6197
9405 Jefferson Blvd Culver City (90232) *(P-2281)*
Mike Jensen Farms ....C....559 897-4192
13138 S Bethel Ave Kingsburg (93631) *(P-226)*
Mike McCall Landscape Inc ....C....925 363-8100
4749 Clayton Rd Concord (94521) *(P-898)*
Mike Parker Landscape, Santa Ana *Also called Mpl Enterprises Inc (P-903)*
Mike Roses Auto Body Inc ....E....925 686-1739
2001 Fremont St Concord (94520) *(P-17730)*
Mike Rovner Construction Inc ....C....949 458-1562
22600 Lambert St Lake Forest (92630) *(P-26947)*
Mike Rovner Construction Inc (PA) ....B....805 584-5961
5400 Tech Cir Moorpark (93021) *(P-1204)*
Miken Clothing, Commerce *Also called Miken Sales Inc (P-8322)*
Miken Sales Inc (PA) ....D....323 266-2560
7230 Oxford Way Commerce (90040) *(P-8322)*
Mikuni American Corporation (HQ) ....D....310 676-0522
8910 Mikuni Ave Northridge (91324) *(P-6658)*
Milan Corporation ....E....510 656-6400
43230 Osgood Rd Fremont (94539) *(P-3180)*
Milauskas Eye Institute, Rancho Mirage *Also called Outpatnt Eye Srgry Ctr of Dsrt (P-19740)*
Milco Constructors Inc ....E....562 595-1977
3930b Cherry Ave Long Beach (90807) *(P-2045)*
Mile Post Properties LLC ....D....415 673-4711
1050 Van Ness Ave San Francisco (94109) *(P-12928)*
Mile Square Golf Course ....C....714 962-5541
10401 Warner Ave Fountain Valley (92708) *(P-18735)*
Miles Construction Group Inc ....E....951 260-2504
42020 Winchester Rd Temecula (92590) *(P-1205)*
Milestone Health Care Center, Costa Mesa *Also called Newport Sbacute Healthcare Ctr (P-20660)*
Milestone Hospice ....C....310 782-1177
1500 Crenshaw Blvd # 200 Torrance (90501) *(P-20942)*
Milestone Technologies Inc (PA) ....C....510 651-2454
3101 Skyway Ct Fremont (94539) *(P-16003)*
Milestone Topco Inc (HQ) ....A....650 376-2300
901 Mariners Island Blvd San Mateo (94404) *(P-11992)*
Milestones Adult Dev Ctr ....D....707 644-0464
1 Florida St Vallejo (94590) *(P-23924)*
Milestones of Development Inc ....D....707 644-0496
1 Florida St Vallejo (94590) *(P-20943)*
Milhous Feed ....C....530 292-3242
24077 State Highway 49 Nevada City (95959) *(P-9086)*
Milken Family Foundation ....C....310 570-4800
1250 4th St Fl 1 Santa Monica (90401) *(P-25199)*
Milken Institute ....E....310 570-4600
1250 4th St Fl 2 Santa Monica (90401) *(P-26640)*
Mill Creek Manor, Mentone *Also called Nice Avenue LLC (P-20661)*
Mill Valley Parks & Recreation, Mill Valley *Also called City of Mill Valley (P-19136)*
Mill Valley Refuse Service Inc ....D....415 457-2287
112 Front St San Rafael (94901) *(P-6418)*
Millbrae Racquet Club ....D....650 583-4345
301 Santa Paula Ave Millbrae (94030) *(P-18975)*
Millbrae Serra Sanitarium ....C....650 697-8386
150 Serra Ave Millbrae (94030) *(P-21158)*
Millbrae Srra Cnvalescent Hosp, Millbrae *Also called Millbrae Serra Sanitarium (P-21158)*
Millbrae Wcp Hotel II LLC ....E....650 443-5500
401 E Millbrae Ave Millbrae (94030) *(P-12929)*
Millenia Development ....E....951 660-5691
929 Bettina Way San Jacinto (92582) *(P-1206)*
Millenium Athletic Club LLc ....D....805 562-3845
170 Los Carneros Way Goleta (93117) *(P-18632)*
Millennia Holdings Inc ....D....213 252-1230
3731 Wilshire Blvd # 618 Los Angeles (90010) *(P-27348)*
Millennia Stainless Inc ....D....562 946-3545
10016 Romandel Ave Santa Fe Springs (90670) *(P-7859)*
Millennial Brands LLC (PA) ....D....866 938-4806
2000 Crow Canyon Pl # 300 San Ramon (94583) *(P-8362)*
Millennium Alarm Systems Inc (PA) ....E....310 337-1108
5777 W Century Blvd # 1755 Los Angeles (90045) *(P-16923)*
Millennium Biltmore Hotel, Los Angeles *Also called Whb Corporation (P-13398)*
Millennium Engrg Integration ....D....703 413-7750
350 N Akron Rd Moffett Field (94035) *(P-25823)*
Millennium Health LLC (PA) ....B....877 451-3534
16981 Via Tazon Ste F San Diego (92127) *(P-26714)*
Millennium Transportation Inc ....D....714 956-7882
3164 E La Palma Ave Ste D Anaheim (92806) *(P-5111)*
Miller Starr & Regalia A Pro (PA) ....D....925 935-9400
1331 N Calif Blvd Ste 500 Walnut Creek (94596) *(P-23253)*
Miller & Associates LLP ....D....310 315-1100
2530 Wilshire Blvd Fl 1 Santa Monica (90403) *(P-23254)*
Miller Children's Hospital, Long Beach *Also called Long Beach Memorial Med Ctr (P-21567)*
Miller Environmental Inc ....C....714 385-0099
1130 W Trenton Ave Orange (92867) *(P-3457)*
Millers Progressive Care, Riverside *Also called Wilmon Corporation (P-20894)*
Millie and Severson Inc ....D....562 493-3611
3601 Serpentine Dr Los Alamitos (90720) *(P-1420)*
Milliman Inc ....E....415 403-1333
650 California St Fl 21 San Francisco (94108) *(P-27946)*
Millmens Local 1496 ....E....559 275-8676
6190 N Cecelia Ave Fresno (93722) *(P-25070)*
Mills Corporation ....D....909 484-8300
1 Mills Cir Ste 1 # 1 Ontario (91764) *(P-10913)*
Mills-Peninsula Health HM Care, San Mateo *Also called Alliance Hospital Services (P-22213)*
Millsap Degnan & Assoc Inc ....D....415 472-4244
4280 Redwood Hwy Ste 10 San Rafael (94903) *(P-25824)*
Millward Brown LLC ....E....310 309-3352
2425 Olympic Blvd 240e Santa Monica (90404) *(P-26546)*
Millwork Holdings, Irvine *Also called Alton Irvine Inc (P-6708)*
Milo Wind Project LLC ....D....888 903-6926
15445 Innovation Dr San Diego (92128) *(P-6053)*
Milpitas Medical Offices, Milpitas *Also called Kaiser Foundation Hospitals (P-19598)*
Milspec Industries Inc (HQ) ....D....213 680-9690
5825 Greenwood Ave Commerce (90040) *(P-7598)*
Milt & Michael Master Dry Clrs, Burbank *Also called Shadkor Inc (P-13569)*
Miltenyi Biotec Inc (HQ) ....D....530 745-2800
2303 Lindbergh St Auburn (95602) *(P-7193)*
Milwood Healthcare Inc ....D....626 274-4345
2641 S C St Oxnard (93033) *(P-10914)*
Mimg Medical Management LLC ....D....949 282-1600
26522 La Alameda Ste 120 Mission Viejo (92691) *(P-26948)*
Minami Tamaki LLP ....E....415 788-9000
360 Post St Fl 8 San Francisco (94108) *(P-23255)*
Mind Dragon Inc ....E....877 367-6060
36002 Pansy St Winchester (92596) *(P-27789)*
Mind Over Eye, El Segundo *Also called Source Interlink Media LLC (P-15467)*
Mind Research Institute ....C....949 345-8700
111 Academy Ste 100 Irvine (92617) *(P-26641)*

ALPHABETIC

Employee Codes: A=Over 500 employees, B=251-500
C=101-250, D=51-100, E=50
2019 Directory of California
Wholesalers and Services Companies
© Mergent Inc. 1-800-342-5647
1387

Mindbody Inc (PA) ....C.......877 755-4279
4051 Broad St Ste 220 San Luis Obispo (93401) ***(P-16159)***
Mindfull Body ....D.......415 931-2639
2876 California St San Francisco (94115) ***(P-19203)***
Mindless Entertainment, North Hollywood *Also called 51 Minds Entertainment LLC* ***(P-18417)***
Mindsource Inc ....D.......650 314-6400
555 Clyde Ave Ste 100 Mountain View (94043) ***(P-15282)***
Mindwave Software, San Diego *Also called Isaac Fair Corporation* ***(P-15238)***
Mindworks Press, Costa Mesa *Also called Amen Clinics Inc A Med Corp* ***(P-22060)***
Mine Fashion, Los Angeles *Also called Edgemine Inc* ***(P-8300)***
Minegar Contracting Inc ....E.......760 598-5001
925 Poinsettia Ave Ste 10 Vista (92081) ***(P-3288)***
Miners Inn, The, Mariposa *Also called Ponderosa Enterprises* ***(P-13072)***
Minerva Networks Inc (PA) ....D.......800 806-9594
2150 Gold St Alviso (95002) ***(P-15283)***
Mineta San Jose Intl Arprt, San Jose *Also called City of San Jose* ***(P-4880)***
Ming Medical Offices, Bakersfield *Also called Kaiser Foundation Hospitals* ***(P-19549)***
Minilec Service Inc ....E.......818 341-1125
9207 Deering Ave Ste A Chatsworth (91311) ***(P-17885)***
Minilec Service-Los Angeles BR, Chatsworth *Also called Minilec Service Inc* ***(P-17885)***
Miniluxe Inc ....D.......424 442-1630
11965 San Vicente Blvd Los Angeles (90049) ***(P-13665)***
Minimalisms Inc ....D.......415 309-3108
49 Missouri St Apt 10 San Francisco (94107) ***(P-17330)***
Minka Group, Corona *Also called Minka Lighting Inc* ***(P-7377)***
Minka Lighting Inc (PA) ....D.......951 735-9220
1151 Bradford Cir Corona (92882) ***(P-7377)***
Minolta Business Systems, Gardena *Also called Konica Minolta Business Soluti* ***(P-6967)***
Minority Aids Project Inc ....D.......323 936-4949
5147 W Jefferson Blvd Los Angeles (90016) ***(P-23925)***
Minshew Brothers Stl Cnstr Inc ....C.......619 561-5700
12578 Vigilante Rd Lakeside (92040) ***(P-1421)***
Mintie Corporation (PA) ....D.......323 225-4111
1114 N San Fernando Rd Los Angeles (90065) ***(P-14324)***
Mintie Technologies, Los Angeles *Also called Mintie Corporation* ***(P-14324)***
Mintz Levin Cohn Ferris GL ....D.......858 314-1500
3580 Carmel Mountain Rd # 300 San Diego (92130) ***(P-23256)***
Mira Mesa Stadium 18, San Diego *Also called Edwards Theatres Circuit Inc* ***(P-18291)***
Mirabella Farms Inc ....D.......559 237-4495
5551 S Orange Ave Fresno (93725) ***(P-162)***
Miracle Home Health Agency ....E.......562 653-0668
13146 Mungo Ct Rancho Cucamonga (91739) ***(P-22367)***
Mirada, Long Beach *Also called Motion Theory Inc* ***(P-14122)***
Mirada Hills Rehb & Conva, La Mirada *Also called Life Care Centers America Inc* ***(P-20581)***
Miramar Ford Truck Sales Inc ....D.......619 272-5340
6066 Miramar Rd San Diego (92121) ***(P-6604)***
Miramar Hotel, Santa Barbara *Also called Morgans Hotel Group LLC* ***(P-12942)***
Miramar Transportation Inc ....D.......858 693-0071
9340 Cabot Dr Ste I San Diego (92126) ***(P-5112)***
Miramar Truck Center, San Diego *Also called Transwest San Diego LLC* ***(P-4380)***
Miramax Film Ny LLC ....D.......310 409-4321
1901 Avenue Of The Stars # 2000 Los Angeles (90067) ***(P-18081)***
Miramed Global Services Inc ....A.......805 277-1017
199 E Thsand Oaks Blvd Thousand Oaks (91360) ***(P-27790)***
Miramnte High Schl Parents CLB ....C.......925 280-3965
750 Moraga Way Orinda (94563) ***(P-24806)***
Miramonte Enterprises LLC ....C.......951 658-9441
275 N San Jacinto St Hemet (92543) ***(P-20645)***
Mirion Technologies Gds Inc (HQ) ....C.......949 419-1000
2652 Mcgaw Ave Irvine (92614) ***(P-26715)***
Mirixa Corporation ....D.......510 596-3000
5915 Hollis St Ste 201 Emeryville (94608) ***(P-17331)***
Mirnavseh Inc ....D.......858 335-2470
8436 Florissant Ct San Diego (92129) ***(P-15284)***
Mirum Inc ....C.......619 237-5552
350 10th Ave Ste 1200 San Diego (92101) ***(P-14121)***
Mis Sciences Corp ....C.......818 847-0213
2550 N Hollywood Way Burbank (91505) ***(P-5601)***
Mishima Foods USA Inc (PA) ....D.......310 787-1533
2340 Plaza Del Amo # 105 Torrance (90501) ***(P-8432)***
Mission Ambulance Inc ....D.......951 272-2300
1055 E 3rd St Corona (92879) ***(P-3823)***
MISSION BARGAIN CENTER, Oxnard *Also called Rescue Mission Alliance* ***(P-25454)***
MISSION BAY AQUATIC CENTER, San Diego *Also called Associated Students San Diego* ***(P-25382)***
Mission Beverage Co (HQ) ....C.......323 266-6238
550 S Mission Rd Los Angeles (90033) ***(P-9015)***
Mission Car Wash ....E.......707 537-2040
59 Mission Cir Santa Rosa (95409) ***(P-17832)***
Mission Car Wash & Quik Lube, Santa Rosa *Also called Mission Car Wash* ***(P-17832)***
MISSION CARE CENTER, Riverside *Also called Riverside Equities LLC* ***(P-20726)***
Mission Care Center, Rosemead *Also called Ensign Group Inc* ***(P-20400)***
Mission Cmmons Rtrment Rsdence, Redlands *Also called Harvest Facility Holdings LP* ***(P-11029)***
Mission Community Hospital, Panorama City *Also called Deanco Healthcare LLC* ***(P-21952)***
Mission Courier Inc ....D.......916 484-1992
3204 Orange Grove Ave North Highlands (95660) ***(P-17332)***
Mission Critical Tech Inc ....E.......310 246-4455
2041 Rosecrans Ave # 220 El Segundo (90245) ***(P-15285)***
Mission Crmchael Halthcare Ctr, Carmichael *Also called SSC Carmichael Operating Co LP* ***(P-20775)***
Mission De La Casa, San Jose *Also called Careage Inc* ***(P-20289)***
Mission Drive-In Theatre Co ....D.......909 465-9219
4407 State St Montclair (91763) ***(P-18328)***

MISSION ELECTRIC COMPANY, Fremont *Also called Kositch Enterprises Inc* ***(P-2626)***
Mission Energy Holding Company ....A.......949 752-5588
2600 Michelson Dr # 1700 Irvine (92612) ***(P-11993)***
Mission Federal Credit Union (PA) ....A.......858 546-2184
5785 Oberlin Dr Ste 312 San Diego (92121) ***(P-9571)***
Mission Federal Services LLC (PA) ....C.......858 524-2850
10325 Meanley Dr San Diego (92131) ***(P-9572)***
Mission Hills Country Club Inc ....C.......760 324-9400
34600 Mission Hills Dr Rancho Mirage (92270) ***(P-18976)***
MISSION HILLS HEALTHCARE CENTE, San Diego *Also called Mission Hills Healthcare Inc* ***(P-20646)***
Mission Hills Healthcare Inc ....D.......619 297-4086
4033 6th Ave San Diego (92103) ***(P-20646)***
Mission Hills Mortgage Bankers, Irvine *Also called Mission Hills Mortgage Corp* ***(P-9896)***
Mission Hills Mortgage Corp (HQ) ....C.......714 972-3832
18500 Von Karman Ave # 1100 Irvine (92612) ***(P-9896)***
Mission Hills Post Acute Care ....D.......619 297-4484
3680 Reynard Way San Diego (92103) ***(P-24601)***
Mission Hills Senior Living ....D.......760 770-7737
34560 Bob Hope Dr Rancho Mirage (92270) ***(P-24602)***
Mission Hosp Regional Med Ctr (PA) ....A.......949 364-1400
27700 Medical Center Rd Mission Viejo (92691) ***(P-21594)***
Mission Hospice & HM Care Inc (PA) ....C.......650 554-1000
1670 S Amphlett Blvd # 300 San Mateo (94402) ***(P-25444)***
Mission Inn Hotel and Spa, The, Riverside *Also called Historic Mission Inn Corp* ***(P-12671)***
Mission Internal Med Group Inc ....C.......949 364-3570
26800 Crown Valley Pkwy # 103 Mission Viejo (92691) ***(P-19690)***
Mission Internal Med Group Inc ....C.......949 364-6559
26800 Crown Valley Pkwy # 103 Mission Viejo (92691) ***(P-19691)***
Mission Internal Med Group Inc ....C.......949 364-3605
27882 Forbes Rd Ste 110 Laguna Niguel (92677) ***(P-19692)***
Mission Landscape Service ....D.......909 947-7290
952 E Francis St Ontario (91761) ***(P-899)***
Mission Ldscp Companies Inc ....C.......714 545-9962
536 E Dyer Rd Santa Ana (92707) ***(P-900)***
Mission Linen & Uniform Svc, Oceanside *Also called Mission Linen Supply* ***(P-13533)***
Mission Linen & Uniform Svc, Sacramento *Also called Mission Linen Supply* ***(P-13535)***
Mission Linen & Uniform Svc, Salinas *Also called Mission Linen Supply* ***(P-13536)***
Mission Linen & Uniform Svc, Fresno *Also called Mission Linen Supply* ***(P-13538)***
Mission Linen & Uniform Svc, Oxnard *Also called Mission Linen Supply* ***(P-13539)***
Mission Linen & Uniform Svc, Union City *Also called Mission Linen Supply* ***(P-13540)***
Mission Linen & Uniform Svc, Salinas *Also called Mission Linen Supply* ***(P-13611)***
Mission Linen & Uniform Svc, Santa Barbara *Also called Mission Linen Supply* ***(P-13541)***
Mission Linen & Uniform Svc, Chico *Also called Mission Linen Supply* ***(P-13542)***
Mission Linen & Uniform Svc, Salinas *Also called Mission Linen Supply* ***(P-13543)***
Mission Linen & Uniform Svc, Lancaster *Also called Mission Linen Supply* ***(P-13544)***
Mission Linen & Uniform Svc, Sacramento *Also called Mission Linen Supply* ***(P-13545)***
Mission Linen & Uniform Svc, Santa Maria *Also called Mission Linen Supply* ***(P-13546)***
Mission Linen & Uniform Svc, Chino *Also called Mission Linen Supply* ***(P-13547)***
Mission Linen Supply ....C.......760 757-9099
2727 Industry St Oceanside (92054) ***(P-13533)***
Mission Linen Supply ....E.......805 772-4451
399 Errol St Morro Bay (93442) ***(P-13534)***
Mission Linen Supply ....C.......916 423-3179
7520 Reese Rd Sacramento (95828) ***(P-13535)***
Mission Linen Supply ....D.......831 424-1707
315 Kern St Salinas (93905) ***(P-13536)***
Mission Linen Supply ....D.......707 443-8681
1401 Summer St Eureka (95501) ***(P-13537)***
Mission Linen Supply ....D.......559 268-0647
2555 S Orange Ave Fresno (93725) ***(P-13538)***
Mission Linen Supply ....D.......805 485-6794
505 Maulhardt Ave Oxnard (93030) ***(P-13539)***
Mission Linen Supply ....C.......510 429-7305
30305 Union City Blvd Union City (94587) ***(P-13540)***
Mission Linen Supply ....C.......831 424-1753
435 W Market St Salinas (93901) ***(P-13611)***
Mission Linen Supply ....E.......805 962-7687
712 E Montecito St Santa Barbara (93103) ***(P-13541)***
Mission Linen Supply ....E.......530 342-4110
1340 W 7th St Chico (95928) ***(P-13542)***
Mission Linen Supply ....D.......831 375-2491
435 W Market St Salinas (93901) ***(P-13543)***
Mission Linen Supply ....D.......661 948-5051
619 W Avenue I Lancaster (93534) ***(P-13544)***
Mission Linen Supply ....C.......916 423-3135
7524 Reese Rd Sacramento (95828) ***(P-13545)***
Mission Linen Supply ....D.......805 922-3579
602 S Western Ave Santa Maria (93458) ***(P-13546)***
Mission Linen Supply ....B.......909 393-5589
5400 Alton Way Chino (91710) ***(P-13547)***
Mission Linen Supply & Svcs, Eureka *Also called Mission Linen Supply* ***(P-13537)***
Mission Medical Entps Inc ....C.......559 582-2871
1007 W Lacey Blvd Hanford (93230) ***(P-20647)***
Mission Medical Entps Inc ....D.......559 582-4414
851 Leslie Ln Hanford (93230) ***(P-20648)***
Mission Neighborhood Hlth Ctr, San Francisco *Also called Mission Neighborhood Hlth Ctr* ***(P-19693)***
Mission Neighborhood Hlth Ctr (PA) ....C.......415 552-3870
240 Shotwell St San Francisco (94110) ***(P-19693)***
Mission Oaks Hospital, Los Gatos *Also called Good Samaritan Hospital LP* ***(P-21434)***
Mission Oaks Recreation Pk Dst ....D.......916 488-2810
3344 Mission Ave Carmichael (95608) ***(P-24807)***
Mission Peak Orthopedics ....D.......510 797-3933
5924 Stoneridge Dr # 200 Pleasanton (94588) ***(P-19694)***
Mission Pets Inc ....E.......415 904-9914
986 Mission St Fl 5 San Francisco (94103) ***(P-9237)***

Mergent e-mail: customerrelations@mergent.com
1388
2019 Directory of California
Wholesalers and Services Companies
(P-0000) Products & Services Section entry number
(PA)=Parent Co (HQ)=Headquarters (DH)=Div Headquarters

Mission Pines Apts, Martinez *Also called Braddock & Logan Inc* ***(P-10989)***
Mission Produce Inc......D......805 981-3650
3803 Dufau Rd Oxnard (93033) ***(P-8705)***
Mission Ranch Inc......E......831 624-6436
26270 Dolores St Carmel (93923) ***(P-12930)***
Mission Security and Patrol......D......805 899-3039
27 W Anapamu St Ste 141 Santa Barbara (93101) ***(P-16733)***
Mission Skilled Nursing Home, Santa Clara *Also called Covenant Care California LLC* ***(P-20340)***
Mission Stuart Ht Partners LLC......C......415 278-3700
8 Mission St San Francisco (94105) ***(P-12931)***
Mission Terrace, Santa Barbara *Also called Cliff View Terrace Inc* ***(P-24472)***
Mission Trail Wste Systems Inc......D......408 727-5365
1060 Richard Ave Santa Clara (95050) ***(P-4041)***
Mission Truck Sales......D......408 436-2920
780 E Brokaw Rd San Jose (95112) ***(P-17658)***
Mission Valley Bancorp......D......818 394-2300
9116 Sunland Blvd Sun Valley (91352) ***(P-11956)***
Mission Valley Ht Operator Inc......D......619 291-5720
595 Hotel Cir S San Diego (92108) ***(P-12932)***
Mission Valley Hts Surgery Ctr......D......619 291-3737
7485 Mission Valley Rd # 106 San Diego (92108) ***(P-19695)***
Mission Valley Truck Center, San Jose *Also called Mission Truck Sales* ***(P-17658)***
Mission Valley V A, San Diego *Also called Veterans Health Administration* ***(P-20074)***
Mission Valley YMCA, San Diego *Also called YMCA of San Diego County* ***(P-25303)***
Mission Viejo Country Club......C......949 582-1550
26200 Country Club Dr Mission Viejo (92691) ***(P-18977)***
Mission View Health Center, San Luis Obispo *Also called Compass Health Inc* ***(P-21041)***
Mission Villa LLC......E......650 756-1995
995 E Market St Daly City (94014) ***(P-24603)***
Mission Vlla Alzhmers Rsidence......E......408 559-8301
3333 S Bascom Ave Campbell (95008) ***(P-24604)***
Mist Systems Inc......D......408 326-0346
1601 S De Anza Blvd # 248 Cupertino (95014) ***(P-16004)***
Mistras Group Inc......D......661 829-1192
21215 Kratzmeyer Rd A Bakersfield (93314) ***(P-25825)***
Mistras Group Inc......D......562 597-3932
2230 E Artesia Blvd Long Beach (90805) ***(P-26716)***
Mistras Group Inc......D......323 583-1653
8427 Atlantic Ave Cudahy (90201) ***(P-25826)***
Mistras Group Inc......E......707 746-5870
6170 Egret Ct Benicia (94510) ***(P-26717)***
Mistras Impro, Bakersfield *Also called Mistras Group Inc* ***(P-25825)***
Mitch Brown Construction Inc......D......559 781-6389
14200 Road 284 Porterville (93257) ***(P-2046)***
Mitchell Buckman Inc (PA)......D......559 733-1181
500 N Santa Fe St Visalia (93292) ***(P-10693)***
Mitchell Concrete, Rancho Cordova *Also called Mitchell Jones Concrete Inc* ***(P-3289)***
Mitchell Engineering......E......415 227-1040
1395 Evans Ave San Francisco (94124) ***(P-3435)***
Mitchell International Inc (HQ)......C......858 368-7000
6220 Greenwich Dr San Diego (92122) ***(P-15286)***
Mitchell Jones Concrete Inc......C......916 638-6870
3185 Fitzgerald Rd Rancho Cordova (95742) ***(P-3289)***
Mitchell Silberberg Knupp LLP (PA)......C......310 312-2000
11377 W Olympic Blvd Fl 2 Los Angeles (90064) ***(P-23257)***
Mitchell Vineyard Management, Saint Helena *Also called Mitchell Vineyards LLC* ***(P-700)***
Mitchell Vineyards LLC......D......707 963-7050
1831 Sarahs Way Saint Helena (94574) ***(P-700)***
Mitchells Group Home, Los Angeles *Also called Mgh Corporation* ***(P-24600)***
Mithun Inc......D......415 956-0688
660 Market St Ste 300 San Francisco (94104) ***(P-25028)***
Mitsuba Corporation......D......909 374-2631
2509 Reata Pl Diamond Bar (91765) ***(P-7080)***
Mitsubishi Electric Us Inc (HQ)......C......714 220-2500
5900 Katella Ave Ste A Cypress (90630) ***(P-3473)***
Mitsubishi Electric Us Inc......D......714 934-5300
7345 Orangewood Ave Garden Grove (92841) ***(P-7509)***
Mitsubishi Materials USA Corp (HQ)......E......714 352-6100
11250 Slater Ave Fountain Valley (92708) ***(P-7860)***
Mitsubishi Motors Cr Amer Inc (HQ)......B......714 799-4730
6400 Katella Ave Cypress (90630) ***(P-9722)***
Mitsubishi Warehouse Cal Corp......D......310 886-5500
3040 E Victoria St Compton (90221) ***(P-4595)***
Mitsui & Co (usa) Inc......D......213 896-1100
601 S Figueroa St # 1900 Los Angeles (90017) ***(P-7290)***
Mitsui USA, Los Angeles *Also called Mitsui & Co (usa) Inc* ***(P-7290)***
Mitzel Company, Santa Ana *Also called Ralph D Mitzel Inc* ***(P-14454)***
Miyako Hotels......D......213 617-2000
328 E 1st St Ste 510 Los Angeles (90012) ***(P-12933)***
Mizuho Securities USA Inc......D......415 268-5500
3 Embarcadero Ctr # 1620 San Francisco (94111) ***(P-9991)***
Mj Star-Lite Inc......E......818 717-0834
9232 Independence Ave Chatsworth (91311) ***(P-2649)***
MJB Partners LLC......D......909 623-2481
651 N Main St Pomona (91768) ***(P-20649)***
Mjd Construction Corp......D......818 575-9864
28244 Dorothy Dr Agoura Hills (91301) ***(P-1207)***
Mjp Empire Inc (PA)......B......714 564-7900
1682 Langley Ave Fl 2 Irvine (92614) ***(P-2460)***
Mjus LLC (fka Mindjet Llc)......D......415 229-4344
275 Battery St Ste 1000 San Francisco (94111) ***(P-15766)***
Mkni, Visalia *Also called Morgan Kleppe & Nash* ***(P-10695)***
ML Electricworks Inc......D......951 687-5078
11325 Magnolia Ave Riverside (92505) ***(P-2650)***
ML Prior Inc......C......626 653-5160
955 Berrand Ct Ste 200 San Dimas (91773) ***(P-23258)***
Mladen Buntich Cnstr Co Inc......D......909 920-9977
1500 W 9th St Upland (91786) ***(P-1957)***
Mlim Holdings LLC......A......619 299-3131
350 Camino De La Reina San Diego (92108) ***(P-11994)***
Mlslistings Inc......D......408 874-0200
740 Kifer Rd Sunnyvale (94086) ***(P-27349)***
Mm Advertising, Cypress *Also called Money Mailer LLC* ***(P-14054)***
Mma Renewable Ventures LLC......D......415 229-8817
44 Montgomery St Ste 2200 San Francisco (94104) ***(P-7630)***
MMC, San Diego *Also called Medical Management Cons Inc* ***(P-27332)***
MMC, Los Angeles *Also called Medical Management Cons Inc* ***(P-14881)***
Mmi Services Inc......C......661 589-9366
4042 Patton Way Bakersfield (93308) ***(P-1069)***
MNS Engineers Inc (PA)......D......805 692-6921
201 N Calle Cesar Santa Barbara (93103) ***(P-25827)***
MNX, Long Beach *Also called Midnite Air Corp* ***(P-4844)***
Mobica US Inc......A......650 450-6654
2570 N 1st St Fl 2 San Jose (95131) ***(P-16005)***
Mobile Application, Santa Clara *Also called Soundhound Inc* ***(P-15466)***
Mobile Hm Communities of Amer (PA)......C......408 279-5200
1122 Willow St Ste 200 San Jose (95125) ***(P-11158)***
Mobile Modular, Livermore *Also called McGrath Rentcorp* ***(P-7771)***
Mobile Programming LLC (PA)......D......310 584-6300
30300 Agoura Rd Ste 140 Agoura Hills (91301) ***(P-15287)***
Mobileiron Inc (PA)......C......650 919-8100
401 E Middlefield Rd Mountain View (94043) ***(P-15767)***
Mobilenet Services Inc (PA)......C......949 951-4444
18 Morgan Ste 200 Irvine (92618) ***(P-25828)***
Mobilitie Investments III LLC......C......877 999-7070
2955 Red Hill Ave Ste 200 Costa Mesa (92626) ***(P-5602)***
Mobilitie Services LLC......B......877 999-7070
660 Newport Center Dr Newport Beach (92660) ***(P-5603)***
Mobilityware, Irvine *Also called Upstanding LLC* ***(P-15886)***
Mobilityware Inc......D......949 788-9900
440 Exchange Ste 100 Irvine (92602) ***(P-15288)***
Mobilygen Corporation......D......408 601-1000
160 Rio Robles San Jose (95134) ***(P-7510)***
Mobis Parts America LLC (HQ)......D......786 515-1101
10550 Talbert Ave Fl 4 Fountain Valley (92708) ***(P-6605)***
Mobis Wholesale, Carpinteria *Also called Ocean Breeze International* ***(P-288)***
Mobitv Inc......D......510 981-1303
1900 Powell St Ste 900 Emeryville (94608) ***(P-5604)***
Mobley Enterprises Inc......D......209 726-9190
2260 Cooper Ave Ste F Merced (95348) ***(P-14325)***
Mobpartner Inc......D......650 300-6388
4151 Mddlfield Rd Ste 100 San Francisco (94103) ***(P-13928)***
Moc Products Company Inc......D......510 635-1230
9840 Kitty Ln Oakland (94603) ***(P-17867)***
Mocana Corporation......D......415 617-0055
111 W Evelyn Ave Ste 210 Sunnyvale (94086) ***(P-16160)***
Mocean, Burbank *Also called Cmp Film & Design Burbank LLC* ***(P-27549)***
Mocean LLC......C......310 481-0808
2440 S Sepulveda Blvd # 150 Los Angeles (90064) ***(P-16161)***
Mocha, Oakland *Also called Museum of Childrens Art* ***(P-19206)***
Mochahost.com, San Jose *Also called Mochanin LLC* ***(P-16162)***
Mochanin LLC......D......408 432-7259
2880 Zanker Rd Ste 203 San Jose (95134) ***(P-16162)***
Mocse Federal Credit Union......D......209 572-3600
3600 Coffee Rd Modesto (95355) ***(P-9573)***
Mod Vid Film, Glendale *Also called Modern Videofilm Inc* ***(P-18201)***
Modani Furniture, West Hollywood *Also called Modani Los Angeles LLC* ***(P-6731)***
Modani Los Angeles LLC......E......310 652-2323
8873 W Sunset Blvd West Hollywood (90069) ***(P-6731)***
Modern Building Inc......E......530 891-4533
3083 Southgate Ln Chico (95928) ***(P-1422)***
Modern Button Company of Cal......E......213 747-7431
3957 S Hill St Los Angeles (90037) ***(P-8233)***
Modern Dev Co A Ltd Partnr......D......949 646-6400
7900 All America City Way Paramount (90723) ***(P-17333)***
Modern Hr Inc......B......310 270-9800
9000 W Sunset Blvd # 900 West Hollywood (90069) ***(P-27350)***
Modern Parking Inc......D......310 821-1081
14110 Palawan Way Marina Del Rey (90292) ***(P-17694)***
Modern Videofilm Inc......C......818 637-6800
1733 Flower St Glendale (91201) ***(P-18201)***
Modern Videofilm Inc (PA)......C......818 840-1700
2300 W Empire Ave Burbank (91504) ***(P-18202)***
Modesto Court Room Inc......D......209 577-1060
2012 Mchenry Ave Modesto (95350) ***(P-18978)***
Modesto Hospitality LLC......C......209 526-6000
1150 9th St Modesto (95354) ***(P-12934)***
Modesto Hospitality Lessee LLC......D......209 526-6000
1150 9th St Ste C Modesto (95354) ***(P-12935)***
Modesto Imaging Center, Modesto *Also called Radnet Management Inc* ***(P-27008)***
Modesto Industrial Elec Co Inc (PA)......C......209 495-1597
1417 Coldwell Ave Modesto (95350) ***(P-2651)***
Modesto Irrigation District......B......209 526-7563
1231 11th St Modesto (95354) ***(P-6054)***
Modesto Irrigation District (PA)......C......209 526-7337
1231 11th St Modesto (95354) ***(P-6055)***
Modesto Irrigation District......B......209 526-7373
929 Woodland Ave Modesto (95351) ***(P-6056)***
Modesto Medical Offices, Modesto *Also called Kaiser Foundation Hospitals* ***(P-19569)***
Modesto Wstewater Trtmnt Plant......D......209 577-5300
1221 Sutter Ave Modesto (95351) ***(P-6419)***
Modoc County ADM Svcs, Alturas *Also called County of Modoc* ***(P-23693)***
MODOC MEDICAL CENTER, Alturas *Also called Last Frontier Healthcare Dst* ***(P-21546)***

ALPHABETIC

Modrine Limited ... D ... 213 269-5466
750 N Diamond Bar Blvd Diamond Bar (91765) ***(P-15289)***

Modular Systems Inc ... D ... 805 963-9350
800 Garden St Ste K Santa Barbara (93101) ***(P-11612)***

Moffatt & Nichol ... E ... 925 944-5411
2185 N Calif Blvd Ste 500 Walnut Creek (94596) ***(P-25829)***

Moffatt & Nichol ... E ... 510 645-1238
2185 N Calif Blvd Ste 500 Walnut Creek (94596) ***(P-25830)***

Moffatt & Nichol ... D ... 562 426-9551
3780 Kilroy Arprt Way # 600 Long Beach (90806) ***(P-25831)***

Moffitt H C Hospital ... C ... 415 476-1000
505 Parnassus Ave San Francisco (94143) ***(P-21595)***

Mofo, San Francisco *Also called Morrison & Foerster LLP* ***(P-23271)***

Mogannam and Whalen Med Corp (PA) ... E ... 213 622-6010
1000 S Hope St Ste 101 Los Angeles (90015) ***(P-23926)***

Mohan Dialysis Center Industry ... D ... 626 333-3801
15757 E Valley Blvd City of Industry (91744) ***(P-22483)***

Mohan Dialysis Ctr of Covina ... D ... 626 859-2522
158 W College St Covina (91723) ***(P-22484)***

Mojo Networks Inc (PA) ... D ... 650 961-1111
5453 Great America Pkwy Santa Clara (95054) ***(P-15290)***

Mola Inc ... C ... 323 582-0088
2957 E 46th St Vernon (90058) ***(P-8323)***

Mold Testing and Inspection ... D ... 760 643-1834
4785 Sequoia Pl Oceanside (92057) ***(P-17334)***

Molecular Bioproducts Inc (HQ) ... C ... 858 453-7551
9389 Waples St San Diego (92121) ***(P-6420)***

Molecular Bioproducts Inc ... C ... 707 762-6689
2200 S Mcdowell Blvd Ext Petaluma (94954) ***(P-7245)***

Molecule Labs Inc ... E ... 714 892-3133
524 Stone Rd # 107 Benicia (94510) ***(P-27351)***

Molina Healthcare Inc ... B ... 858 614-1580
9275 Sky Park Ct Ste 400 San Diego (92123) ***(P-22841)***

Molina Healthcare Inc ... C ... 909 546-7116
790 E Foothill Blvd Rialto (92376) ***(P-19696)***

Molina Healthcare Inc ... B ... 310 221-3031
1500 Hughes Way Long Beach (90810) ***(P-10284)***

Molina Healthcare Inc (PA) ... A ... 562 435-3666
200 Oceangate Ste 100 Long Beach (90802) ***(P-19697)***

Molina Healthcare Inc ... B ... 562 435-3666
1 Golden Shore Long Beach (90802) ***(P-22842)***

Molina Healthcare California ... C ... 800 526-8196
200 Oceangate Ste 100 Long Beach (90802) ***(P-19698)***

Molina Healthcare of Californi ... A ... 562 435-3666
200 Oceangate Ste 100 Long Beach (90802) ***(P-10169)***

Molly Maid, La Verne *Also called Steve and Beth Chaput* ***(P-14401)***

Molly Maid ... E ... 949 367-8000
24412 Muirlands Blvd A Lake Forest (92630) ***(P-14326)***

Momentous Insurance Brkg Inc ... D ... 818 933-2700
5990 Sepulvda Blvd # 550 Van Nuys (91411) ***(P-10694)***

Momentum For Mental Health ... D ... 408 261-7777
2001 The Alameda San Jose (95126) ***(P-24808)***

Moms Orange County ... E ... 714 972-2610
1128 W Santa Ana Blvd Santa Ana (92703) ***(P-22368)***

Monarch Bay Golf Resort ... D ... 510 895-2162
13800 Monarch Bay Dr San Leandro (94577) ***(P-18736)***

Monarch Beach Golf Links (HQ) ... D ... 949 240-8247
50 Monarch Beach Resort N Dana Point (92629) ***(P-18737)***

Monarch Healthcare A Medical (HQ) ... D ... 949 923-3200
11 Technology Dr Irvine (92618) ***(P-19699)***

Monarch Landscape Holdings LLC (PA) ... C ... 213 816-1750
550 S Hope St Ste 1675 Los Angeles (90071) ***(P-901)***

Monarch Nut Company LLC ... C ... 661 725-6458
786 Road 188 Delano (93215) ***(P-541)***

Monarch Place Piedmont LLC ... C ... 510 658-9266
4500 Gilbert St Oakland (94611) ***(P-24605)***

Monarchy Diamond Inc ... B ... 213 924-1161
550 S Hill St Ste 1088 Los Angeles (90013) ***(P-1105)***

Monark LP ... D ... 310 769-6669
2804 W El Segundo Blvd Gardena (90249) ***(P-11079)***

Mondelez Global LLC ... D ... 909 605-0140
5815 Clark St Ontario (91761) ***(P-8828)***

Mondrian Hotel, Los Angeles *Also called Morgans Hotel Group MGT LLC* ***(P-12943)***

Money Mailer LLC (PA) ... C ... 714 889-3800
6261 Katella Ave Ste 200 Cypress (90630) ***(P-14054)***

Moneyline Lending Services, Irvine *Also called Genpact Mortgage Services Inc* ***(P-9807)***

Monico Alloys Inc (PA) ... D ... 310 928-0168
3039 E Ana St Compton (90221) ***(P-7291)***

Monique Suraci ... D ... 951 677-8111
41885 Ivy St Murrieta (92562) ***(P-18633)***

Monitise Americas Inc ... D ... 415 526-7000
1 Embrcdero Cntre Fl 9 Flr 9 San Francisco (94111) ***(P-15291)***

Mono Nation ... D ... 559 877-2450
58288 Road 225 North Fork (93643) ***(P-23927)***

Mono Wind Casino ... D ... 559 855-4350
37302 Rancheria Ln Auberry (93602) ***(P-12936)***

Monoprice Inc (HQ) ... C ... 909 989-6887
1 Pointe Dr Ste 400 Brea (92821) ***(P-8044)***

Monoprice.com, Brea *Also called Monoprice Inc* ***(P-8044)***

Monroe Operations LLC ... C ... 714 288-0872
811 N Ranch Wood Trl Orange (92869) ***(P-22036)***

Monroe Residence Club ... D ... 415 771-9119
1499 Sutter St San Francisco (94109) ***(P-11080)***

Monrovia Convalescent Hospital ... D ... 626 359-6618
1220 Huntington Dr Duarte (91010) ***(P-21159)***

Monrovia Growes, Azusa *Also called Monrovia Nursery Company* ***(P-284)***

Monrovia Health Center ... D ... 626 256-1600
330 W Maple Ave Monrovia (91016) ***(P-19700)***

Monrovia Memorial Hospital, Monrovia *Also called Alakor Healthcare LLC* ***(P-21275)***

Monrovia Nursery Company (PA) ... A ... 626 334-9321
817 E Monrovia Pl Azusa (91702) ***(P-284)***

Monrovia Ranch Market, Victorville *Also called E & T Foods Inc* ***(P-449)***

Monrovia Service Center, Monrovia *Also called Southern California Edison Co* ***(P-6116)***

Mons Viridis Llc ... D ... 415 297-6765
960 Jackson St San Francisco (94133) ***(P-5605)***

Monsanto, Woodland *Also called Seminis Vegetable Seeds Inc* ***(P-9099)***

Monsanto Company ... B ... 530 669-6224
37437 State Highway 16 Woodland (95695) ***(P-8706)***

Monster Inc (PA) ... B ... 415 840-2000
601 Gateway Blvd Ste 900 South San Francisco (94080) ***(P-8045)***

Monster Energy Company (HQ) ... C ... 951 739-6200
1 Monster Way Corona (92879) ***(P-8829)***

Monster Mechanical Inc ... D ... 408 727-8362
1855 Norman Ave Campbell (95008) ***(P-2282)***

Monster Products, South San Francisco *Also called Monster Inc* ***(P-8045)***

Montage Beverly Hills, Beverly Hills *Also called Montage Hotels & Resorts LLC* ***(P-12937)***

Montage Health ... A ... 831 625-4821
P.O. Box Hh Monterey (93942) ***(P-19701)***

Montage Health (PA) ... A ... 831 625-4830
23625 Holman Hwy Monterey (93940) ***(P-26949)***

Montage Hotels & Resorts LLC ... B ... 310 499-4199
225 N Canon Dr Beverly Hills (90210) ***(P-12937)***

Montage Hotels & Resorts LLC (PA) ... A ... 949 715-5002
3 Ada Ste 100 Irvine (92618) ***(P-12938)***

Montage Laguna Beach, Irvine *Also called Montage Hotels & Resorts LLC* ***(P-12938)***

Montalvo Association ... D ... 408 961-5800
15400 Montalvo Rd Saratoga (95070) ***(P-24932)***

Montana Investigation, San Francisco *Also called Black Bear Security Services* ***(P-16583)***

Montavista Software LLC (HQ) ... C ... 408 572-8000
2315 N 1st St Fl 4 San Jose (95131) ***(P-15768)***

MONTCLAIR HOSPITAL MEDICAL CENTER, Montclair *Also called Prime Healthcare Svcs III LLC* ***(P-21661)***

Montclair Hotels Mb LLC ... D ... 925 687-5500
1050 Burnett Ave Concord (94520) ***(P-12939)***

Montclair Mnor Cnvlescent Hosp, Montclair *Also called Medicrest of California 1* ***(P-20638)***

Montclair Physical Therapy, Claremont *Also called Pomona Valley Hospital Med Ctr* ***(P-21654)***

Monte Nido & Affiliates, Calabasas *Also called Monte Nido Residential Ctr LLC* ***(P-24606)***

Monte Nido & Affiliates, Malibu *Also called Monte Nido Residential Ctr LLC* ***(P-22369)***

Monte Nido Residential Ctr LLC ... C ... 818 457-9958
514 Live Oak Circle Dr Calabasas (91302) ***(P-24606)***

Monte Nido Residential Ctr LLC (PA) ... D ... 310 457-9958
23815 Stuart Ranch Rd Malibu (90265) ***(P-22369)***

Monte Vista Grove Homes ... D ... 626 796-6135
2889 San Pasqual St Pasadena (91107) ***(P-24607)***

Monte Vista Retirement Lodge ... D ... 619 465-1331
2211 Massachusetts Ave Lemon Grove (91945) ***(P-11081)***

Monte Vista School, Redding *Also called County of Shasta* ***(P-24310)***

Monte Vista Village, Lemon Grove *Also called Monte Vista Retirement Lodge* ***(P-11081)***

Monte Vsta Mem Schlrship Assoc ... E ... 831 722-8178
2 School Way Watsonville (95076) ***(P-27791)***

Montebello School Transportion ... D ... 323 887-7900
505 S Greenwood Ave Montebello (90640) ***(P-3943)***

Montebello Transit ... C ... 323 887-4600
400 S Taylor Ave Montebello (90640) ***(P-3683)***

Montebello Unified School ... D ... 323 887-2140
500 Hendricks St Fl 2 Montebello (90640) ***(P-14327)***

Montecito Country Club Inc ... D ... 805 969-0800
920 Summit Rd Santa Barbara (93108) ***(P-18979)***

Montecito Family YMCA, Santa Barbara *Also called Channel Islands Young Mens Ch* ***(P-25133)***

Montecito Fire Protection Dst ... E ... 805 969-7762
595 San Ysidro Rd Santa Barbara (93108) ***(P-25200)***

Montecito Retirement Assn ... B ... 805 969-8011
300 Hot Springs Rd Santa Barbara (93108) ***(P-20650)***

Montecito Sequoia Inc ... D ... 559 565-3388
8000 Generals Hwy Kings Canyon Nationa (93633) ***(P-12940)***

Montecito Sequoia Lodge, Kings Canyon Nationa *Also called Montecito Sequoia Inc* ***(P-12940)***

Montego Heights Lodge, Walnut Creek *Also called Atria Senior Living Group Inc* ***(P-24427)***

Montenay Pacific Power, Long Beach *Also called Veolia Es Waste-To-Energy Inc* ***(P-6506)***

Monterey Bay Acadamy Laundry ... D ... 831 728-1481
675 Beach Dr Watsonville (95076) ***(P-13488)***

Monterey Bay Aqar Foundation (PA) ... C ... 831 648-4800
886 Cannery Row Monterey (93940) ***(P-24933)***

Monterey Bay Aquarium RES Inst ... C ... 831 775-1700
7700 Sandholdt Rd Moss Landing (95039) ***(P-26419)***

Monterey Bay Bouquet Acquisit ... C ... 831 786-2700
481 San Andreas Rd Watsonville (95076) ***(P-9149)***

Monterey Bay Masonry Inc ... E ... 408 289-8295
333 Phelan Ave San Jose (95112) ***(P-2817)***

Monterey Beach Hotel, Monterey *Also called Zhg Inc* ***(P-13436)***

Monterey Construction Company, Salinas *Also called Reegs Inc* ***(P-1311)***

Monterey Country Club, Palm Desert *Also called American Golf Corporation* ***(P-18843)***

Monterey County Office Educatn ... D ... 831 755-0324
901 Blanco Cir Salinas (93901) ***(P-26547)***

Monterey County Public Works, Salinas *Also called County of Monterey* ***(P-1753)***

Monterey County Sheriffs Dept, Salinas *Also called County of Monterey* ***(P-25412)***

Monterey Credit Union (PA) ... D ... 831 647-1000
501 E Franklin St Monterey (93940) ***(P-9641)***

Monterey Dental Group ... D ... 831 373-3068
333 El Dorado St Monterey (93940) ***(P-20128)***

Monterey Financial Svcs Inc (PA) ... C ... 760 639-3500
4095 Avenida De La Plata Oceanside (92056) ***(P-9723)***

Mergent e-mail: customerrelations@mergent.com
1390
2019 Directory of California
Wholesalers and Services Companies
(P-0000) Products & Services Section entry number
(PA)=Parent Co (HQ)=Headquarters (DH)=Div Headquarters

Monterey Healthcare & Wellness ....D....626 280-3220
1267 San Gabriel Blvd Rosemead (91770) *(P-20651)*
Monterey Marriott, Monterey *Also called San Carlos Associates Ltd (P-13166)*
Monterey Mechanical Co (PA) ....E....510 632-3173
8275 San Leandro St Oakland (94621) *(P-2047)*
Monterey Mushrooms Inc (PA) ....E....831 763-5300
260 Westgate Dr Watsonville (95076) *(P-315)*
Monterey Mushrooms Inc ....B....408 779-4191
642 Hale Ave Morgan Hill (95037) *(P-316)*
Monterey Mushrooms Inc ....A....831 728-8300
777 Maher Ct Royal Oaks (95076) *(P-317)*
Monterey Mushrooms-Morgan Hill, Morgan Hill *Also called Monterey Mushrooms Inc (P-316)*
Monterey One Water (PA) ....D....831 372-3367
5 Harris Ct Bldg D Monterey (93940) *(P-6323)*
Monterey Pacific Inc (PA) ....E....831 678-4845
169 The Crossroads Blvd Carmel (93923) *(P-701)*
Monterey Park Branch, Monterey Park *Also called Cathay Bank (P-9425)*
MONTEREY PARK HOSPITAL, Monterey Park *Also called Monterey Park Hospital (P-21596)*
Monterey Park Hospital ....C....626 570-9000
900 S Atlantic Blvd Monterey Park (91754) *(P-21596)*
Monterey Peninsula Country CLB ....C....831 373-1556
3000 Club Rd Pebble Beach (93953) *(P-18980)*
Monterey Peninsula Dntl Group ....D....831 373-3068
333 El Dorado St Monterey (93940) *(P-20129)*
Monterey Peninsula Hospital ....E....831 373-0924
576 Hartnell St Ste 260 Monterey (93940) *(P-21597)*
Monterey Pines Sklld Nursg Fac ....D....831 373-3716
1501 Skyline Dr Monterey (93940) *(P-20652)*
Monterey Pk Convalescent Hosp ....D....626 280-0280
416 N Garfield Ave Monterey Park (91754) *(P-21160)*
Monterey Plaza Hotel & Spa, Monterey *Also called Monterey Plaza Ht Ltd Partnr (P-12941)*
Monterey Plaza Ht Ltd Partnr ....B....800 334-3999
400 Cannery Row Monterey (93940) *(P-12941)*
Monterey Rgional Waste MGT Dst ....C....831 384-5313
14201 Del Monte Blvd Marina (93933) *(P-6421)*
Monterey-Salinas Transit Corp ....C....831 754-2804
1375 Burton Ave Salinas (93901) *(P-3881)*
Montessori Learning Commons (PA) ....D....916 444-7786
1123 D St Sacramento (95814) *(P-24350)*
Montessori On The Lake, Lake Forest *Also called Environments For Learning Inc (P-24319)*
Montetisea Framing, Denair *Also called J Crecelius Inc (P-357)*
Montgomery Tank Lines, South Gate *Also called Quality Carriers Inc (P-4248)*
Montpelier Nut Company Inc (PA) ....D....209 566-9084
1518 K St Modesto (95354) *(P-8564)*
Montpelier Orchards MGT Co Inc ....E....209 883-4079
4931 S Montpelier Rd Denair (95316) *(P-542)*
Montrenes Financial Svcs Inc ....D....562 795-0450
27 Montpellier Newport Beach (92660) *(P-17335)*
Montrose Envmtl Group Inc ....B....925 680-4300
2825 Verne Roberts Cir Antioch (94509) *(P-26718)*
Montrose Envmtl Group Inc (PA) ....D....949 988-3500
1 Park Plz Ste 1000 Irvine (92614) *(P-27792)*
Montrose Envmtl Group Inc ....A....714 332-8646
1631 E Saint Andrew Pl Santa Ana (92705) *(P-27793)*
Monument Construction Inc ....D....408 778-1350
16200 Vineyard Blvd # 100 Morgan Hill (95037) *(P-902)*
Monument Security Inc ....C....510 430-3540
24301 Suthland Dr Ste 312 Hayward (94545) *(P-16734)*
Monument Security Inc (PA) ....C....916 564-4234
4926 43rd St Ste 10 McClellan (95652) *(P-16735)*
Moog Inc ....D....650 210-9000
2581 Leghorn St Mountain View (94043) *(P-25832)*
Moon Mountain Farms LLC ....E....805 521-1742
3846 E Telegraph Rd Fillmore (93015) *(P-371)*
Mooney Farms ....E....530 899-2661
1220 Fortress St Chico (95973) *(P-543)*
Moonlight Companies, Reedley *Also called Moonlight Packing Corporation (P-8707)*
Moonlight Packing Corporation (PA) ....C....559 638-7799
17719 E Huntsman Ave Reedley (93654) *(P-8707)*
Moonstone Hotel Properties, Cambria *Also called Moonstone Management Corp (P-11613)*
Moonstone Management Corp (PA) ....C....805 927-4200
2905 Burton Dr Cambria (93428) *(P-11613)*
Moor Products, Mission Viejo *Also called Greenleaf Paper Products (P-8107)*
Moore Business Forms, Walnut Creek *Also called R R Donnelley & Sons Company (P-3623)*
Moore Business Forms, Temecula *Also called RR Donnelley & Sons Company (P-8088)*
Moore Iacofano Goltsman Inc (PA) ....D....510 845-7549
800 Hearst Ave Berkeley (94710) *(P-27794)*
Moore Law Group A Prof Corp ....D....714 431-2000
3710 S Susan St Ste 210 Santa Ana (92704) *(P-23259)*
Moore Twining Associates Inc (PA) ....D....559 268-7021
2527 Fresno St Fresno (93721) *(P-26719)*
Moorefield Construction Inc (PA) ....D....714 972-0700
600 N Tustin Ave Ste 210 Santa Ana (92705) *(P-1596)*
Mooretown Rancheria ....B....530 533-3885
3 Alverda Dr Oroville (95966) *(P-18785)*
Mooretown Rancheria (PA) ....E....530 533-3625
1 Alverda Dr Oroville (95966) *(P-19204)*
Moorpark Active Adult Center, Moorpark *Also called City of Moorpark (P-23581)*
Moose Family Center 545, Santa Cruz *Also called Moose International Inc (P-25201)*
Moose International Inc ....C....831 438-1817
2470 El Rancho Dr Santa Cruz (95060) *(P-25201)*
Moov Corporation ....C....877 666-8932
123 Mission St Ste 1000 San Francisco (94105) *(P-15292)*
Moovweb, San Francisco *Also called Moov Corporation (P-15292)*
Mopar Enterprises ....D....858 492-1123
1710 Dornoch Ct Ste A San Diego (92154) *(P-14055)*
Morada Produce Company LP ....A....209 546-0426
500 N Jack Tone Rd Stockton (95215) *(P-544)*
Moraga Cntry CLB Hmowners Assn ....D....925 376-2200
1600 Saint Andrews Dr Moraga (94556) *(P-18981)*
Morale Welfare Recreation Fund ....C....831 242-6631
4260 Gigling Rd Seaside (93955) *(P-24809)*
More Truck Lines Inc ....D....951 371-6673
1776 All American Way Corona (92879) *(P-4042)*
MORE WORKSHOP, Placerville *Also called Mother Lode Rehabilit (P-24608)*
Moreland PCF Snoqualmie LLC ....C....661 322-1081
5060 California Ave # 1150 Bakersfield (93309) *(P-11893)*
Moreno & Associates Inc ....D....408 924-0353
1260 Birchwood Dr Sunnyvale (94089) *(P-14328)*
Moreno Valley Family Hlth Ctr, Moreno Valley *Also called Community Health Systems Inc (P-19398)*
Moreno Valley Heacock Med Offs, Moreno Valley *Also called Kaiser Foundation Hospitals (P-12106)*
Morgan Lewis & Bockius LLP ....A....415 393-2000
1 Market St Ste 500 San Francisco (94105) *(P-23260)*
Morgan Lewis & Bockius LLP ....D....650 843-4000
1400 Page Mill Rd Palo Alto (94304) *(P-23261)*
Morgan Lewis & Bockius LLP ....C....949 399-7000
600 Anton Blvd Ste 1800 Costa Mesa (92626) *(P-23262)*
Morgan Lewis & Bockius LLP ....C....213 612-2500
300 S Grand Ave Ste 2200 Los Angeles (90071) *(P-23263)*
Morgan Lewis & Bockius LLP ....B....415 442-1000
1 Market Plz Lbby 1 # 1 San Francisco (94105) *(P-23264)*
Morgan Lewis & Bockius LLP ....C....213 612-2500
300 S Grand Ave Ste 2200 Los Angeles (90071) *(P-23265)*
Morgan Creek Productions (PA) ....D....310 432-4848
10351 Santa Monica Blvd # 200 Los Angeles (90025) *(P-18241)*
Morgan Fabrics Corporation (PA) ....D....323 583-9981
4265 Exchange Ave Vernon (90058) *(P-8234)*
Morgan Farm LLC ....D....831 726-5120
201 Vista Dr Watsonville (95076) *(P-109)*
Morgan Kleppe & Nash ....D....559 732-3436
501 N Church St Visalia (93291) *(P-10695)*
Morgan Linen Service, Los Angeles *Also called Morgan Services Inc (P-13548)*
Morgan Services Inc ....D....213 485-9666
905 Yale St Los Angeles (90012) *(P-13548)*
Morgan Stanley, San Francisco *Also called TransMontaigne PDT Svcs LLC (P-5248)*
Morgan Stanley ....D....949 760-2440
800 Nwport Ctr Dr Ste 500 Newport Beach (92660) *(P-10097)*
Morgan Stanley ....D....626 405-9313
55 S Lake Ave Ste 800 Pasadena (91101) *(P-9992)*
Morgan Stanley ....E....858 597-7777
4350 La Jolla Village Dr # 1000 San Diego (92122) *(P-9993)*
Morgan Stanley ....D....949 809-1200
1901 Main St Ste 700 Irvine (92614) *(P-9994)*
Morgan Stanley & Co LLC ....E....916 444-8041
407 Capitol Mall Ste 1900 Sacramento (95814) *(P-9995)*
Morgan Stanley & Co LLC ....E....559 431-5900
5250 N Palm Ave Ste 321 Fresno (93704) *(P-9996)*
Morgan Stanley & Co LLC ....D....714 836-5181
2677 N Main St Fl 10 Santa Ana (92705) *(P-9997)*
Morgan Stanley & Co LLC ....D....619 236-1331
101 W Broadway Ste 1800 San Diego (92101) *(P-9998)*
Morgan Stanley & Co LLC ....D....661 663-8100
9100 Ming Ave Ste 205 Bakersfield (93311) *(P-9999)*
Morgan Stanley & Co LLC ....D....510 839-8080
1999 Harrison St Ste 2200 Oakland (94612) *(P-10000)*
Morgan Stanley & Co LLC ....D....650 340-6550
216 Lorton Ave Burlingame (94010) *(P-10001)*
Morgan Stanley & Co LLC ....D....310 319-5200
1453 3rd St Ste 200 Santa Monica (90401) *(P-10002)*
Morgan Stanley & Co LLC ....D....408 947-2200
225 W Santa Clara St # 900 San Jose (95113) *(P-10003)*
Morgan Stanley & Co LLC ....C....310 285-4800
9665 Wilshire Blvd # 600 Beverly Hills (90212) *(P-10004)*
Morgan Stanley & Co LLC ....B....415 693-6000
101 California St Fl 3 San Francisco (94111) *(P-10005)*
Morgans Hotel Group LLC ....C....805 969-2203
1555 S Jameson Ln Santa Barbara (93108) *(P-12942)*
Morgans Hotel Group MGT LLC ....C....323 650-8999
8440 W Sunset Blvd Los Angeles (90069) *(P-12943)*
Morgans Hotel Group MGT LLC ....C....415 775-4700
495 Geary St San Francisco (94102) *(P-12944)*
Morigon Technologies LLC ....E....818 764-8880
7615 Fulton Ave North Hollywood (91605) *(P-7194)*
Morley Construction, Santa Monica *Also called MSC Service Co (P-26261)*
Morley Construction Company (HQ) ....D....310 399-1600
3330 Ocean Park Blvd # 101 Santa Monica (90405) *(P-3290)*
Morning Star Company The, Woodland *Also called Liberty Packing Company LLC (P-8702)*
Morningside Community Assn ....D....760 328-3323
82 Mayfair Dr Rancho Mirage (92270) *(P-25202)*
Morningside Corecare Assoc LP ....C....650 854-5600
2180 Sand Hill Rd Ste 200 Menlo Park (94025) *(P-20653)*
Morningside of Fullerton, Fullerton *Also called Corecare I I I (P-24476)*
Morphosis Architects ....D....310 453-2247
3440 Wesley St Culver City (90232) *(P-26096)*
Morphotrak LLC (HQ) ....C....714 238-2000
5515 E La Palma Ave # 100 Anaheim (92807) *(P-16006)*
Morris Distributing Inc ....D....707 769-7294
3800a Lakeville Hwy Petaluma (94954) *(P-9016)*
Morris Grritano Insur Agcy Inc ....D....805 543-6887
1122 Laurel Ln San Luis Obispo (93401) *(P-10696)*
Morris National Inc (HQ) ....D....626 385-2000
760 N Mckeever Ave Azusa (91702) *(P-8830)*

ALPHABETIC

Employee Codes: A=Over 500 employees, B=251-500
C=101-250, D=51-100, E=50
2019 Directory of California
Wholesalers and Services Companies
© Mergent Inc. 1-800-342-5647
1391

Morris Polich & Purdy LLP (PA)....D....213 891-9100
1055 W 7th St Ste 2400 Los Angeles (90017) ***(P-23266)***
Morrison & Foerster LLP....C....858 720-5100
12531 High Bluff Dr # 100 San Diego (92130) ***(P-23267)***
Morrison & Foerster LLP....B....650 813-5600
755 Page Mill Rd Ste A100 Palo Alto (94304) ***(P-23268)***
Morrison & Foerster LLP....E....925 295-3300
425 Market St Fl 32 San Francisco (94105) ***(P-23269)***
Morrison & Foerster - Library, Palo Alto *Also called Morrison & Foerster LLP* ***(P-23268)***
Morrison & Foerster LLP....C....213 892-5200
707 Wilshire Blvd # 6000 Los Angeles (90017) ***(P-23270)***
Morrison & Foerster LLP (PA)....B....415 268-7000
425 Market St Fl 30 San Francisco (94105) ***(P-23271)***
Morrison & Foerster LLP....C....415 268-7178
425 Market St Fl 32 San Francisco (94105) ***(P-23272)***
Morrison Concrete Inc....E....562 802-1450
14114 Rosecrans Ave Ste C Santa Fe Springs (90670) ***(P-3291)***
Morrison Health Care, Palm Springs *Also called Morrison MGT Specialists Inc* ***(P-26950)***
Morrison Landscaping Inc....E....714 571-0455
1225 E Wakeham Ave Santa Ana (92705) ***(P-7323)***
Morrison MGT Specialists, Fresno *Also called Morrison MGT Specialists Inc* ***(P-22843)***
Morrison MGT Specialists Inc....C....559 459-6449
2823 Fresno St Fresno (93721) ***(P-22843)***
Morrison MGT Specialists Inc....D....760 323-6296
1150 N Indian Canyon Dr Palm Springs (92262) ***(P-26950)***
Morrison MGT Specialists Inc....D....530 332-7557
1531 Esplanade Chico (95926) ***(P-26951)***
Morrison MGT Specialists Inc....D....818 364-4219
14445 Olive View Dr Sylmar (91342) ***(P-26952)***
Morro Bay Public Works....D....805 772-6261
955 Shasta Ave Morro Bay (93442) ***(P-1821)***
Morrow-Meadows Corporation (PA)....A....858 974-3650
231 Benton Ct City of Industry (91789) ***(P-2652)***
Morrow-Meadows Corporation....C....510 562-1980
1050 Bing St San Carlos (94070) ***(P-2653)***
Morse Court Apartments, Sunnyvale *Also called Mp Morse Court Associates* ***(P-11152)***
Mortgage Capital Assoc Inc....D....310 477-6877
11150 W Olympic Blvd # 1160 Los Angeles (90064) ***(P-9833)***
Mortgage Capital Partners Inc....D....310 295-2900
12400 Wilshire Blvd # 900 Los Angeles (90025) ***(P-9834)***
Mortgage Corp America Inc....D....805 582-2220
2315 Kuehner Dr Ste 115 Simi Valley (93063) ***(P-9897)***
Mortgage Corp of America, Simi Valley *Also called Mortgage Corp America Inc* ***(P-9897)***
Mortgage Fax Inc....D....714 899-2656
18685 Main St Ste 101 Huntington Beach (92648) ***(P-14039)***
Mortgage Works Financial, Redlands *Also called Mountain West Financial Inc* ***(P-9835)***
Morton & Pitalo Inc (PA)....D....916 984-7621
75 Iron Point Cir Ste 120 Folsom (95630) ***(P-25833)***
Morton Bakar Center, Alameda *Also called Garfield Nursing Home Inc* ***(P-20448)***
Morton Bakar Center, Hayward *Also called Telecare Corporation* ***(P-21983)***
Morton Golf LLC....D....916 481-4653
3645 Fulton Ave Sacramento (95821) ***(P-18738)***
Mosaic....D....858 397-2261
10991 Via Banco San Diego (92126) ***(P-26953)***
Mosaic Quest, San Diego *Also called Mosaic* ***(P-26953)***
Moschip Semiconductor Tech USA....C....408 737-7141
840 N Hillview Dr Milpitas (95035) ***(P-7511)***
Moskow, Lonnie J MD, Laguna Hills *Also called South County Orthopedic Specia* ***(P-19899)***
Moss & Company Inc (PA)....D....310 453-0911
15300 Ventura Blvd # 418 Sherman Oaks (91403) ***(P-11614)***
Moss Landing Marine Labs....C....831 771-4400
8272 Moss Landing Rd Moss Landing (95039) ***(P-22112)***
Moss Landing Power Plant, Moss Landing *Also called Dynegy Moss Landing LLC* ***(P-6028)***
Motech Americas LLC....B....302 451-7500
1300 Valley Vista Dr # 207 Diamond Bar (91765) ***(P-26420)***
Motel 6 Operating LP....D....310 419-1234
5101 W Century Blvd Inglewood (90304) ***(P-12945)***
Mother Lode Rehabilit....C....530 622-4848
399 Placerville Dr Placerville (95667) ***(P-24608)***
Motherlode Investors LLC....D....209 736-8112
711 Mccauley Ranch Rd Angels Camp (95222) ***(P-18739)***
Motiga Inc....D....425 748-8509
100 Rdwood Shres Pkwy 4 Redwood City (94065) ***(P-15293)***
Motion Math Inc....C....415 590-2961
582 Market St Ste 511 San Francisco (94104) ***(P-15294)***
Motion Pcture Hlth Wlfare Fund....C....818 769-0007
11365 Ventura Blvd # 300 Studio City (91604) ***(P-10488)***
Motion Picture and TV Fund (PA)....A....818 876-1777
23388 Mulholland Dr # 200 Woodland Hills (91364) ***(P-21598)***
Motion Picture and TV Fund....D....310 231-3000
1950 Sawtelle Blvd # 130 Los Angeles (90025) ***(P-21599)***
Motion Picture Assn Amer Inc (PA)....C....818 995-6600
15301 Ventura Blvd Bldg E Sherman Oaks (91403) ***(P-24969)***
Motion Picture Industry Plans....C....818 769-0007
11365 Ventura Blvd # 300 Studio City (91604) ***(P-10489)***
Motion Solutions, Aliso Viejo *Also called Bearing Engineers Inc* ***(P-7839)***
Motion Theory Inc....C....310 396-9433
444 W Ocean Blvd Ste 1400 Long Beach (90802) ***(P-14122)***
Motivational Fulfillment, Chino *Also called Motivational Marketing Inc* ***(P-17336)***
Motivational Marketing Inc....B....909 517-2200
15820 Euclid Ave Chino (91708) ***(P-17336)***
Motivational Systems Inc (PA)....D....619 474-8246
2200 Cleveland Ave National City (91950) ***(P-14123)***
Motive Energy Inc (PA)....D....714 888-2525
125 E Coml St Bldg B Anaheim (92801) ***(P-7378)***
Motive Nation, Downey *Also called Rockview Dairies Inc* ***(P-8861)***
Motorola Mobility LLC....D....858 455-1500
6450 Sequence Dr San Diego (92121) ***(P-7512)***
Motorola Solutions Inc....D....650 318-3200
805 E Middlefield Rd Mountain View (94043) ***(P-15295)***
Moulton Logistics Management (PA)....D....818 997-1800
7850 Ruffner Ave Van Nuys (91406) ***(P-17337)***
Moulton Niguel Water (PA)....D....949 831-2500
27500 La Paz Rd Laguna Niguel (92677) ***(P-6289)***
Mount Diablo Medical Center, Concord *Also called John Muir Physician Network* ***(P-21471)***
Mount Hermon Association Inc (PA)....D....831 335-4466
37 Conference Dr Mount Hermon (95041) ***(P-13453)***
Mount Miguel Covenant Village, Spring Valley *Also called Evangelical Covenant Church* ***(P-24524)***
Mount Rbdoux Convalescent Hosp....C....951 681-2200
6401 33rd St Riverside (92509) ***(P-20654)***
Mount San Jacinto Win Pk Auth....D....760 325-1449
1 Tramway Rd Palm Springs (92262) ***(P-19205)***
Mount Shasta Resort, Mount Shasta *Also called Siskiyou Lake Golf Resort Inc* ***(P-18764)***
Mount View Hotel, Calistoga *Also called Mv Hospitality Inc* ***(P-18636)***
Mount View Spa, Calistoga *Also called Spa Partners Inc* ***(P-18658)***
Mount Woodson Country Club, Ramona *Also called Spe Go Holdings Inc* ***(P-19059)***
Mountain Cascade Inc (PA)....C....925 373-8370
555 Exchange Ct Livermore (94550) ***(P-1958)***
Mountain Comm Hlth Cre Dist....C....530 623-5541
410 N Taylor St Weaverville (96093) ***(P-21600)***
Mountain Comm Hlth Cre Dist (PA)....C....530 623-5541
60 Easter Ave Weaverville (96093) ***(P-21601)***
Mountain Empire Fmly Medicine, Campo *Also called Mountain Hlth & Cmnty Svcs Inc* ***(P-19702)***
Mountain Gate Country Club, Los Angeles *Also called American Golf Corporation* ***(P-18830)***
Mountain Gear Corporation....C....626 851-2488
4889 4th St Irwindale (91706) ***(P-8270)***
Mountain High Resort Assoc LLC....A....760 249-5808
24512 Highway 2 Wrightwood (92397) ***(P-11615)***
Mountain High Ski Resort, Wrightwood *Also called MHRP Resort Inc* ***(P-12926)***
Mountain Hlth & Cmnty Svcs Inc (PA)....D....619 478-5311
1388 Buckman Springs Rd Campo (91906) ***(P-19702)***
Mountain Lakes Senior Living, Redding *Also called Northstar Senior Living Inc* ***(P-26965)***
Mountain Meadow Mushrooms Inc....D....760 749-1201
26948 N Broadway Escondido (92026) ***(P-318)***
Mountain Play Association....E....415 383-1100
1556 4th St B San Rafael (94901) ***(P-18387)***
Mountain Retreat Incorporated....D....925 838-7780
111 Deerwood Rd Ste 100 San Ramon (94583) ***(P-11894)***
MOUNTAIN SHADOWS COMMUNITY HOM, Escondido *Also called Mountain Shadows Support Group* ***(P-20944)***
Mountain Shadows Support Group (PA)....C....760 743-3714
2067 W El Norte Pkwy Escondido (92026) ***(P-20944)***
Mountain Springs Kirkwood LLC....C....209 258-6000
1501 Kirkwood Meadows Dr Kirkwood (95646) ***(P-12946)***
Mountain Top Comm Svcs LLC....E....909 798-4400
1902 Orange Tree Ln Redlands (92374) ***(P-27795)***
Mountain Valley Child and Fami....C....530 265-9057
24077 State Highway 49 Nevada City (95959) ***(P-20945)***
Mountain Valley Express Co Inc (PA)....D....209 823-2168
6750 Longe St Ste 100 Stockton (95206) ***(P-4231)***
Mountain Valley Express Co Inc....C....562 630-5500
7701 Rosecrans Ave Paramount (90723) ***(P-5113)***
Mountain View AG Services Inc....A....559 528-6004
13281 Avenue 416 Orosi (93647) ***(P-661)***
Mountain View Child Care Inc....C....818 252-5863
10716 La Tuna Canyon Rd Sun Valley (91352) ***(P-24351)***
Mountain View Child Care Inc (PA)....B....909 796-6915
1720 Mountain View Ave Loma Linda (92354) ***(P-21602)***
Mountain View Cnvalescent Hosp....E....818 367-1033
13333 Fenton Ave Sylmar (91342) ***(P-20655)***
Mountain View Healthcare Ctr, Mountain View *Also called Balboa Enterprises Inc* ***(P-20255)***
Mountain View Physical Therapy....D....909 949-6235
299 W Fthill Blvd Ste 200 Upland (91786) ***(P-20190)***
Mountain View Sport Club, Mountain View *Also called 24 Hour Fitness Usa Inc* ***(P-18568)***
Mountain West Financial Inc (PA)....B....909 793-1500
1209 Nevada St Ste 200 Redlands (92374) ***(P-9835)***
Mountain-Pacific Financial (PA)....D....858 456-8420
1010 Prospect St Ste 300 La Jolla (92037) ***(P-11616)***
Mountains Community Hosp Fndtn....C....909 336-3651
29101 Hospital Rd Lake Arrowhead (92352) ***(P-21603)***
Mountasia Family Fun Center, Santa Clarita *Also called Mountasia of Santa Clarita* ***(P-13758)***
Mountasia Family Fun Center....D....661 253-4386
21516 Golden Triangle Rd Santa Clarita (91350) ***(P-18805)***
Mountasia of Santa Clarita....D....661 253-4386
21516 Golden Triangle Rd Santa Clarita (91350) ***(P-13758)***
Mounting Systems Inc....D....916 374-8872
180 Promenade Cir Ste 300 Sacramento (95834) ***(P-2283)***
Move Inc....C....818 701-0012
8428 Calvin Ave Northridge (91324) ***(P-11617)***
Move Inc (HQ)....B....408 558-7100
3315 Scott Blvd Ste 250 Santa Clara (95054) ***(P-11618)***
Move Co....C....805 557-2300
30700 Russell Ranch Rd # 100 Westlake Village (91362) ***(P-11619)***
Move Sales Inc (HQ)....D....805 557-2300
3315 Scott Blvd Ste 250 Santa Clara (95054) ***(P-13759)***
Mover Services Inc....E....310 868-5143
721 E Compton Blvd Rancho Dominguez (90220) ***(P-3552)***
Movie Movers, West Hollywood *Also called Quixote Mm LLC* ***(P-18213)***
Movieclips.com, Los Angeles *Also called Zefr Inc* ***(P-18172)***
Movies Anywhere LLC....D....818 560-0038
500 S Buena Vista St Burbank (91521) ***(P-18252)***

Mergent e-mail: customerrelations@mergent.com
1392
2019 Directory of California Wholesalers and Services Companies
(P-0000) Products & Services Section entry number
(PA)=Parent Co (HQ)=Headquarters (DH)=Div Headquarters

Moving Solutions Inc .... C 408 920-0110
7093 Central Ave Newark (94560) (P-4360)
Movoto LLC .... D 888 766-8686
1900 S Norfolk St Ste 310 San Mateo (94403) (P-11620)
Mowery Thomason Inc .... C 714 666-1717
1225 N Red Gum St Anaheim (92806) (P-2920)
Moya Farm Labor Services, Reedley Also called Moya Juan Farm Labor Services (P-662)
Moya Juan Farm Labor Services .... C 559 638-9498
7919 S Alta Ave Reedley (93654) (P-662)
Moyes Custom Furniture Inc .... E 714 729-0234
3431 E La Palma Ave Ste 3 Anaheim (92806) (P-17922)
Moyles Central Vly Hlth Care (PA) .... B 559 688-0288
999 N M St Tulare (93274) (P-20656)
Moyles Central Vly Hlth Care .... C 559 782-1509
1100 W Morton Ave Porterville (93257) (P-20657)
Moyles Health Care Inc .... A 559 686-1601
604 E Merritt Ave Tulare (93274) (P-21161)
Mozilla Corporation (HQ) .... B 650 903-0800
331 E Evelyn Ave Ste 100 Mountain View (94041) (P-16007)
Mozingo Construction Inc .... E 209 848-0160
751 Wakefield Ct Oakdale (95361) (P-3436)
Mp Aero LLC .... D 818 901-9828
7701 Woodley Ave Van Nuys (91406) (P-3553)
Mp Environmental Services Inc (PA) .... C 800 458-3036
3400 Manor St Bakersfield (93308) (P-6422)
Mp Holdings, McClellan Also called McClellan Business Park LLC (P-27328)
Mp Mine Operations LLC .... C 702 277-0848
67750 Bailey Rd Mountain Pass (92366) (P-1101)
Mp Morse Court Associates .... D 408 734-9442
825 Morse Ave Sunnyvale (94085) (P-11152)
Mp Shoreline Assoc Ltd Partnr .... E 650 966-1327
460 N Shoreline Blvd Mountain View (94043) (P-11082)
Mp Tice Oaks Associates A CA .... D 650 356-2976
2150 Valley Blvd Walnut Creek (94595) (P-11621)
Mpc Productions LLC .... D 310 418-8115
12035 Killion St Sherman Oaks (91401) (P-18452)
Mpcc, Pebble Beach Also called Monterey Peninsula Country CLB (P-18980)
Mpic, Milpitas Also called Mega Professional Intl (P-15276)
Mpl Enterprises Inc .... D 714 545-1717
2302 S Susan St Santa Ana (92704) (P-903)
Mpower Communications Corp (HQ) .... D 866 699-8242
515 S Flower St Los Angeles (90071) (P-5606)
Mpp Brea Div 6079, Brea Also called Orora Packaging Solutions (P-8119)
Mpp Fullerton Div 6061, Fullerton Also called Orora Packaging Solutions (P-8122)
Mpp San Diego Div 6064, San Marcos Also called Orora North America (P-8114)
MPS Security, Murrieta Also called National Bus Invstigations Inc (P-17343)
Mq Power, Carson Also called Multiquip Inc (P-7379)
Mr Clean Maintenance Services, Bloomington Also called Chiro Inc (P-7884)
Mr Cool, Fresno Also called Donald P Dick AC Inc (P-2187)
Mr Copy Inc (HQ) .... D 858 573-6300
5657 Copley Dr San Diego (92111) (P-6970)
Mr Mailer, Baldwin Park Also called All Direct Mail Services Inc (P-14041)
Mr Rooter, Fremont Also called Growith Inc (P-2224)
Mr Rooter, Ventura Also called D S R Inc (P-17942)
MRC, Moorpark Also called Mike Rovner Construction Inc (P-1204)
Mrc, Smart Tech Solutions, San Diego Also called Mr Copy Inc (P-6970)
Mrca Fire Division .... E 818 880-4752
1670 Las Virgenes Cyn Rd Calabasas (91302) (P-25203)
Mrt Inc .... E 949 348-2292
19781 Pauling Foothill Ranch (92610) (P-14056)
Mrwpca, Monterey Also called Monterey One Water (P-6323)
Ms Bubbles Inc (PA) .... D 323 544-0300
2731 S Alameda St Los Angeles (90058) (P-8324)
Msas Cargo International, Brisbane Also called Dhl Supply Chain (usa) (P-5044)
Msblous LLC .... D 909 929-9689
11671 Dayton Dr Rancho Cucamonga (91730) (P-4596)
MSC Chatsworth .... D 818 718-7696
9324 Corbin Ave Northridge (91324) (P-8046)
MSC Metalworking, City of Industry Also called Rutland Tool & Supply Co (P-7868)
MSC Service Co .... D 310 399-1600
3330 Ocean Park Blvd # 101 Santa Monica (90405) (P-26261)
Mscsoftware Corporation (HQ) .... C 714 540-8900
4675 Macarthur Ct Ste 900 Newport Beach (92660) (P-15769)
Mscsoftware Corporation .... B 714 540-8900
4675 Macarthur Ct Ste 900 Newport Beach (92660) (P-16008)
Msd Capital LP .... D 310 458-3600
100 Wilshire Blvd # 1450 Santa Monica (90401) (P-12246)
MSEFCU, Merced Also called Merced School Employees F C U (P-9569)
Mshift Inc .... E 408 437-2740
39899 Balentine Dr # 235 Newark (94560) (P-15296)
MSI, Santa Barbara Also called Modular Systems Inc (P-11612)
MSI, Orange Also called M S International Inc (P-6901)
MSI Computer Corp (HQ) .... D 626 913-0828
901 Canada Ct City of Industry (91748) (P-7081)
MSI Invntory Srvce-Los Angeles, Covina Also called Accu-Count Inventory Svcs Inc (P-16982)
MSI PRODUCTION SERVICES, San Diego Also called Meeting Services Inc (P-14525)
Msj Healthcare LLC .... E 818 244-8446
2555 E Colorado Blvd Fl 4 Pasadena (91107) (P-22370)
Msl Electric Inc .... D 714 693-4837
4938 E La Palma Ave Anaheim (92807) (P-2654)
Msla Management LLC .... C 626 824-6020
1294 E Colorado Blvd Pasadena (91106) (P-27796)
Msr Hotels & Resorts Inc .... D 408 496-6400
2885 Lakeside Dr Santa Clara (95054) (P-12947)

MSS Nurses Registry Inc .... D 323 467-5717
6660 W Sunset Blvd Ste J Los Angeles (90028) (P-14885)
Mt Diablo Center, Pleasant Hill Also called Choice In Aging (P-22530)
Mt Diablo Heart Health Center, Concord Also called John Muir Physician Network (P-21474)
Mt Diablo Medical Center, Walnut Creek Also called John Muir Physician Network (P-21473)
Mt Eden Nursery Co Inc (PA) .... E 408 213-5777
2124 Bering Dr San Jose (95131) (P-11178)
Mt Hamilton Grange .... D 408 513-5528
2840 Aborn Rd San Jose (95135) (P-24810)
Mt Miquel Covenant Village .... C 619 479-4790
325 Kempton St Spring Valley (91977) (P-21162)
Mt Rubidoux Convalescent Hosp, San Bernardino Also called Waterman Convalescent Hospital (P-20876)
Mt Sinai Mem Pk & Mortuary, Los Angeles Also called Sinai Temple (P-13698)
Mt Supply Inc (HQ) .... C 800 938-6658
3505 Cadillac Ave Ste K2 Costa Mesa (92626) (P-7861)
Mt View Apartments LLC .... D 925 866-8429
3170 Crow Canyon Pl # 165 San Ramon (94583) (P-11083)
MT&i, Oceanside Also called Mold Testing and Inspection (P-17334)
Mtc Direct Inc (PA) .... C 626 839-6800
17837 Rowland St City of Industry (91748) (P-7082)
Mtc Distributing (PA) .... C 209 523-6449
4900 Stoddard Rd Modesto (95356) (P-9185)
Mtc Financial Inc .... E 949 252-8300
17100 Gillette Ave Irvine (92614) (P-12116)
Mtc Transportation, Twentynine Palms Also called Mark Clemons (P-4219)
Mtc Worldwide Corp .... C 626 839-6800
17837 Rowland St City of Industry (91748) (P-7083)
Mthuron Inc .... D 925 932-4101
1903 Rutan Dr Livermore (94551) (P-3005)
MTI, San Diego Also called Merit Technologies LLC (P-27341)
Mtm & Thomasville Co .... D 626 934-1112
16035 Phoenix Dr City of Industry (91745) (P-1597)
Mtv Networks, Los Angeles Also called Viacom Networks (P-18151)
Muehlhan Certifed Coatings Inc .... C 707 639-4414
2320 Cordelia Rd Fairfield (94534) (P-3554)
Mueller Grooming & Pet Sups, Sacramento Also called Mueller Pet Medical Center (P-605)
Mueller Pet Medical Center .... E 916 428-9202
7625 Freeport Blvd Sacramento (95832) (P-605)
Mufg Americas Leasing Corp (HQ) .... D 213 488-3700
445 S Figueroa St # 2700 Los Angeles (90071) (P-14528)
Mufg Bank Ltd .... D 213 488-3700
777 S Figueroa St Ste 600 Los Angeles (90017) (P-9513)
Mufg Union Bank Foundation .... A 213 236-5000
445 S Figueroa St Ste 710 Los Angeles (90071) (P-9467)
Mufg Union Bank National Assn (HQ) .... A 415 705-7000
400 California St Fl 14 San Francisco (94104) (P-9353)
Mufg Union Bank National Assn .... E 213 972-5500
120 S San Pedro St Los Angeles (90012) (P-9354)
Mufg Union Bank National Assn .... D 805 564-6410
20 E Carrillo St Santa Barbara (93101) (P-9355)
Mufg Union Bank National Assn .... D 310 550-6522
9460 Wilshire Blvd # 200 Beverly Hills (90212) (P-9356)
Mufg Union Bank National Assn .... D 619 230-4666
1201 5th Ave San Diego (92101) (P-9357)
Mufg Union Bank National Assn .... D 213 312-4500
900 S Main St Los Angeles (90015) (P-9358)
Mufg Union Bank National Assn .... E 310 354-4700
15800 S Western Ave Gardena (90247) (P-9359)
Mufg Union Bank National Assn .... D 510 891-2495
460 Hegenberger Rd Fl 3 Oakland (94621) (P-9360)
Muir Labs .... B 925 947-3335
1601 Ygnacio Valley Rd Walnut Creek (94598) (P-22113)
Muir Orthopedic Specialists .... C 925 939-8585
2405 Shadelands Dr # 210 Walnut Creek (94598) (P-19703)
Muir-Chase Plumbing Co Inc .... D 818 500-1940
4530 Brazil St Ste 1 Los Angeles (90039) (P-2284)
Muirlab, Walnut Creek Also called Muir Labs (P-22113)
Mulechain Inc .... D 888 456-8881
2901 W Coast Hwy Ste 200 Newport Beach (92663) (P-4043)
Mulen, Seal Beach Also called P2f Holdings (P-9240)
Mulesoft Inc .... A 415 229-2009
50 Fremont St Ste 300 San Francisco (94105) (P-15770)
Mulhearn .... D 562 860-2443
11306 183rd St Ste 101 Cerritos (90703) (P-11622)
Mulhearn Group, Hacienda Heights Also called Berkshire Hattaway Home Servcs (P-11239)
Mulholland SEC & Patrol Inc .... B 818 755-0202
11454 San Vicente Blvd Fl Los Angeles (90049) (P-16736)
Mullahey Chevrolet Inc .... E 714 871-2545
11899 Woodruff Ave Downey (90241) (P-17731)
Mullen & Henzell LLP .... E 805 966-1501
112 E Victoria St Santa Barbara (93101) (P-23273)
Muller Ranch LLC .... D 530 662-0105
15810 County Road 95 Woodland (95695) (P-2)
Muller-Ing-Gateway LLC .... D 951 687-2900
23521 Paseo De Valencia # 200 Laguna Hills (92653) (P-10915)
Mulligan Family Fun Center, Murrieta Also called Mulligan Ltd A Cal Ltd Partnr (P-18807)
Mulligan Family Fun Center, Los Alamitos Also called Mulligan Limited (P-18806)
Mulligan Limited .... C 714 484-6799
4281 Katella Ave Ste 228 Los Alamitos (90720) (P-12080)
Mulligan Limited (PA) .... D 714 484-6799
4281 Katella Ave Ste 228 Los Alamitos (90720) (P-18806)
Mulligan Ltd A Cal Ltd Partnr .... D 951 696-9696
24950 Madison Ave Murrieta (92562) (P-18807)
Mullikin Medical Center, Stockton Also called Caremark Rx LLC (P-19352)
Mullin TBG Insur Agcy Svcs LLC .... C 310 203-8770
100 N Pacific Coast Hwy El Segundo (90245) (P-10697)
Mullintbg, El Segundo Also called Mullin TBG Insur Agcy Svcs LLC (P-10697)

Employee Codes: A=Over 500 employees, B=251-500
C=101-250, D=51-100, E=50

2019 Directory of California
Wholesalers and Services Companies

© Mergent Inc. 1-800-342-5647

1393

Mulroses Usa Inc ....D....213 489-1761
741 S San Pedro St Los Angeles (90014) ***(P-285)***
Multax Systems Inc (PA) ....C....310 379-8398
2512 Artesia Blvd 300c Redondo Beach (90278) ***(P-25834)***
Multi Mechanical Inc ....D....714 632-7404
469 Blaine St Corona (92879) ***(P-2285)***
Multi Specialty Group Practice, Yuba City *Also called Sutter North Med Foundation* ***(P-19991)***
Multi Specialty Medical Svc, Visalia *Also called Visalia Medical Clinic Inc* ***(P-20088)***
Multi-Pak Corporation ....D....818 709-0508
20131 Bahama St Chatsworth (91311) ***(P-17338)***
Multimodal Esquer Inc ....D....619 710-0477
8856 Siempre Viva Rd San Diego (92154) ***(P-4232)***
Multipak, Chatsworth *Also called Multi-Pak Corporation* ***(P-17338)***
Multipoint Wireless LLC ....E....714 262-4172
2549 Eastbluff Dr Ste 474 Newport Beach (92660) ***(P-25835)***
MULTIPURPOSE SENIOR SERVICES P, Ukiah *Also called Community Care Management Corp* ***(P-23602)***
Multiquip Inc (HQ) ....B....310 537-3700
18910 Wilmington Ave Carson (90746) ***(P-7379)***
Multiven Inc ....E....408 828-2715
303 Twin Dolphin Dr # 600 Redwood City (94065) ***(P-16428)***
Multivision Inc (HQ) ....D....510 740-5600
66 Franklin St Fl 3 Oakland (94607) ***(P-17339)***
Munger Tolles & Olson LLP ....C....213 683-9100
350 S Grand Ave Fl 50 Los Angeles (90071) ***(P-23274)***
Munger Bros LLC ....A....661 721-0390
786 Road 188 Delano (93215) ***(P-238)***
Munger Farm, Delano *Also called Munger Bros LLC* ***(P-238)***
Munger Farms, Delano *Also called Monarch Nut Company LLC* ***(P-541)***
Munger Tolles Olson Foundation (PA) ....B....213 683-9100
350 S Grand Ave 50 Los Angeles (90071) ***(P-23275)***
Munger Tolles Olson Foundation ....E....415 512-4000
560 Mission St Fl 27 San Francisco (94105) ***(P-23276)***
Muni-Fed Energy Inc ....E....714 321-3346
192 N Marina Dr Long Beach (90803) ***(P-2286)***
Municipal Svcs Agency, Sacramento *Also called County of Sacramento* ***(P-1876)***
Muniservices LLC (HQ) ....C....800 800-8181
7625 N Palm Ave Ste 108 Fresno (93711) ***(P-27352)***
Mural, San Francisco *Also called Tactivos Inc* ***(P-5651)***
Muranaka Farm ....C....805 529-0201
11018 W Los Angeles Ave Moorpark (93021) ***(P-70)***
Murchison & Cumming LLP (PA) ....D....213 623-7400
801 S Grand Ave Ste 900 Los Angeles (90017) ***(P-23277)***
Murcor Inc ....C....909 623-4001
740 Corp Ctr Dr Pomona (91768) ***(P-11623)***
Murphy (PA) ....D....415 788-1900
88 Kearny St Fl 10 San Francisco (94108) ***(P-23278)***
Murphy McKay & Associates Inc ....E....925 283-9555
3468 Mt Diablo Blvd B108 Lafayette (94549) ***(P-16429)***
Murphy OBrien Inc ....D....310 453-2539
11444 W Olympic Blvd # 600 Los Angeles (90064) ***(P-27564)***
Murphy-True Inc ....D....707 576-7337
464 Kenwood Ct Ste B Santa Rosa (95407) ***(P-1598)***
Murray Company, E Rncho Dmngz *Also called Murray Plumbing and Htg Corp* ***(P-2287)***
Murray Plumbing and Htg Corp (PA) ....A....310 637-1500
18414 S Santa Fe Ave E Rncho Dmngz (90221) ***(P-2287)***
Murrieta Day Spa, Murrieta *Also called Monique Suraci* ***(P-18633)***
Murrieta Gardens Senior Living ....D....951 600-7676
18878 E Armstead St Azusa (91702) ***(P-20946)***
Murrietta Circuits ....D....714 970-2430
5000 E Landon Dr Anaheim (92807) ***(P-2655)***
Murtaugh Myer Nlson Trglia LLP ....D....949 794-4000
2603 Main St Ste 900 Irvine (92614) ***(P-23279)***
Muscle Improvement Inc ....D....310 374-5522
200 N Harbor Dr Redondo Beach (90277) ***(P-18634)***
Musclebound Inc (PA) ....B....818 349-0123
19835 Nordhoff St Northridge (91324) ***(P-18635)***
Muscolino Inventory Svc Inc ....E....209 576-8469
1620 N Carptr Rd Ste D50 Modesto (95351) ***(P-17340)***
Muse Concrete Contractors Inc ....D....530 226-5151
8599 Commercial Way Redding (96002) ***(P-1822)***
Museum Associates ....B....323 857-6172
5905 Wilshire Blvd Los Angeles (90036) ***(P-24891)***
Museum Cntmprary Art San Diego (PA) ....D....858 454-3541
700 Prospect St La Jolla (92037) ***(P-24892)***
Museum of Childrens Art ....E....510 465-8770
1221 Broadway Oakland (94612) ***(P-19206)***
Museum of Contemporary Art (PA) ....C....213 626-6222
250 S Grand Ave Los Angeles (90012) ***(P-24893)***
Museum of Latin American Art ....E....562 437-1689
628 Alamitos Ave Long Beach (90802) ***(P-24894)***
Music Center, Los Angeles *Also called Performing Arts Center of La C* ***(P-18393)***
Music Circus, Sacramento *Also called Broadway Sacramento* ***(P-18348)***
Music Collective LLC ....E....818 508-3303
12711 Ventura Blvd # 110 Studio City (91604) ***(P-18203)***
Music Intllgnce Neuro Dev Inst, Irvine *Also called Mind Research Institute* ***(P-26641)***
Musick Peeler & Garrett LLP (PA) ....C....213 629-7600
624 S Grand Ave Ste 2000 Los Angeles (90017) ***(P-23280)***
Musicmatch Inc ....C....858 485-4300
16935 W Bernardo Dr # 270 San Diego (92127) ***(P-15771)***
Muth Development Co Inc ....D....714 527-2239
11100 Beach Blvd Stanton (90680) ***(P-10916)***
Mutual Assist Network Del Paso (PA) ....E....916 927-7694
811 Grand Ave Ste A Sacramento (95838) ***(P-23928)***
Mutual Trading Co Inc (HQ) ....C....213 626-9458
431 Crocker St Los Angeles (90013) ***(P-8831)***
Mv Hospitality Inc ....E....707 942-6877
1457 Lincoln Ave Calistoga (94515) ***(P-18636)***
Mv Medical Management ....D....323 257-7637
1860 Colo Blvd Ste 200 Los Angeles (90041) ***(P-27353)***
Mv Transportation Inc ....D....323 666-0856
13690 Vaughn St San Fernando (91340) ***(P-3684)***
Mv Transportation Inc ....C....510 351-1603
1944 Williams St San Leandro (94577) ***(P-3824)***
Mv Transportation Inc ....D....818 409-3387
1242 Los Angeles St Glendale (91204) ***(P-3685)***
Mv Transportation Inc ....D....209 547-7879
1250 S Wilson Way Ste A1 Stockton (95205) ***(P-3686)***
Mv Transportation Inc ....D....209 339-1972
24 S Sacramento St Lodi (95240) ***(P-3687)***
Mv Transportation Inc ....D....805 557-7372
265 S Rancho Rd Thousand Oaks (91361) ***(P-3688)***
Mv Transportation Inc ....D....707 446-5573
479 Mason St Ste 221 Vacaville (95688) ***(P-3689)***
Mv Transportation Inc ....D....562 790-8642
7231 Rosecrans Ave Paramount (90723) ***(P-5237)***
Mve Inc (PA) ....D....209 526-4214
1117 L St Modesto (95354) ***(P-25836)***
Mve + Partners Inc (PA) ....D....949 809-3388
1900 Main St Ste 800 Irvine (92614) ***(P-26097)***
Mvf World Wide Services, Burbank *Also called Modern Videofilm Inc* ***(P-18202)***
Mvp Partners, Santa Ana *Also called Colton Real Estate Group* ***(P-11167)***
Mw Partners ....D....949 705-0682
201 Sandpointe Ave # 200 Santa Ana (92707) ***(P-27354)***
Mw U.S., San Francisco *Also called Exyte US Inc* ***(P-25679)***
Mw2 Consulting LLC ....D....408 573-6310
981 Manor Way Los Altos (94024) ***(P-27355)***
MWH Americas Inc ....D....805 683-2409
437 2nd St Solvang (93463) ***(P-25837)***
MWH Americas Inc ....C....626 386-1100
750 Royal Oaks Dr Ste 100 Monrovia (91016) ***(P-25838)***
MWH Americas Inc ....D....415 430-1800
44 Montgomery St Ste 1400 San Francisco (94104) ***(P-25839)***
MWH Americas Inc ....D....626 796-9141
618 Michillinda Ave # 200 Arcadia (91007) ***(P-25840)***
Mws Precision Wire Inds Inc ....D....818 991-8553
31200 Cedar Valley Dr Westlake Village (91362) ***(P-7292)***
Mws Wire Industries, Westlake Village *Also called Mws Precision Wire Inds Inc* ***(P-7292)***
Mx Courier Systems Inc ....E....714 288-8622
990 N Tustin St Orange (92867) ***(P-17341)***
Mxb Battery Operations LP ....D....415 230-8000
717 Battery St San Francisco (94111) ***(P-25204)***
Mxic, Milpitas *Also called Macronix America Inc* ***(P-7506)***
My Choice Inhome Care LLC ....D....951 244-8770
31610 Rr Cyn Rd Ste 4 Canyon Lake (92587) ***(P-22371)***
My Day Counts, Anaheim *Also called Orange Cnty Adult Achvment Ctr* ***(P-17375)***
My Express Freight, Beverly Hills *Also called G Katen Partners Ltd Lblty Co* ***(P-5068)***
My Kids Dentist ....B....951 600-1062
24635 Madison Ave Ste E Murrieta (92562) ***(P-20130)***
My Office Inc ....D....858 549-6700
6060 Nncy Rdge Dr Ste 100 San Diego (92121) ***(P-3555)***
My Points.com, San Francisco *Also called Mypointscom LLC* ***(P-13869)***
My Wireless, Santa Ana *Also called B-Per Electronic Inc* ***(P-5299)***
Mya Systems Inc ....E....877 679-0952
27 Maiden Ln Ste 300 San Francisco (94108) ***(P-14670)***
Mycase, San Diego *Also called Appfolio Inc* ***(P-15587)***
Myers & Sons Construction LP ....C....916 283-9950
4600 Northgate Blvd # 100 Sacramento (95834) ***(P-1823)***
Myers Capital Partners LLC ....E....626 568-1398
450 S Marengo Ave Pasadena (91101) ***(P-10006)***
Myers FSI, Ontario *Also called Myers Power Products Inc* ***(P-7380)***
Myers Power Products Inc (PA) ....C....909 923-1800
2950 E Philadelphia St Ontario (91761) ***(P-7380)***
Myers Tire Supply Dist Inc ....D....602 233-1037
107 Exchange Pl Pomona (91768) ***(P-6659)***
Myers Tire Supply Division, Pomona *Also called Myers Tire Supply Dist Inc* ***(P-6659)***
Mygrant Glass Company Inc (PA) ....E....510 785-4360
3271 Arden Rd Hayward (94545) ***(P-6660)***
Myinternetservicescom LLC ....D....213 256-0575
1010 E Union St Ste 125 Pasadena (91106) ***(P-5607)***
Myoscience Inc ....E....510 933-1500
46400 Fremont Blvd Fremont (94538) ***(P-27797)***
Mypointscom LLC (HQ) ....D....415 615-1100
44 Montgomery St Ste 1050 San Francisco (94104) ***(P-13869)***
Myra Investment and Dev Corp ....D....209 834-2343
47 W 6th St Tracy (95376) ***(P-12176)***
Myriad Flowers International ....D....805 684-8079
4601 Foothill Rd Carpinteria (93013) ***(P-286)***
Mystic Inc (PA) ....D....213 746-8538
2444 Porter St Los Angeles (90021) ***(P-8325)***
MYYOGAWORKS, Culver City *Also called Yogaworks Inc* ***(P-18678)***
Mza Events Inc (PA) ....E....213 201-1348
3550 Wilshire Blvd # 1012 Los Angeles (90010) ***(P-17342)***
N & S Tractor Co (PA) ....D....209 383-5888
600 S St 59 Merced (95341) ***(P-17963)***
N A Aricent Inc ....D....408 324-1800
226 Airport Pkwy Ste 595 San Jose (95110) ***(P-15297)***
N A C O, Groveland *Also called Thousand Trails Inc* ***(P-13469)***
N A T C, Pleasanton *Also called North American Title Co Inc* ***(P-10467)***
N A Tomatobank ....D....626 759-9200
901 S Baldwin Ave Arcadia (91007) ***(P-9514)***
N Compass International Inc ....C....323 785-1700
8223 Santa Monica Blvd West Hollywood (90046) ***(P-27356)***

Mergent e-mail: customerrelations@mergent.com
1394
2019 Directory of California
Wholesalers and Services Companies
(P-0000) Products & Services Section entry number
(PA)=Parent Co (HQ)=Headquarters (DH)=Div Headquarters

N G A Associates ....E....760 726-4015
205 W Alvarado St Fallbrook (92028) *(P-10917)*
N G I, Brea *Also called The Nevell Group Inc (P-1673)*
N H A, San Diego *Also called Neighborhood House Association (P-23930)*
N I D, Grass Valley *Also called Nevada Irrigation District (P-6559)*
N Model Inc (PA) ....C....650 610-4600
777 Mariners Island Blvd San Mateo (94404) *(P-15298)*
N N R, Carson *Also called Nnr Global Logistics USA Inc (P-5122)*
N Qiagen Amercn Holdings Inc (HQ) ....C....800 426-8157
27220 Turnberry Ln # 200 Valencia (91355) *(P-8199)*
N S B N Investments Llc ....D....310 273-2501
9454 Wilshire Blvd Fl 4 Beverly Hills (90212) *(P-12247)*
N Th Degree, Foothill Ranch *Also called Nth Degree Inc (P-17362)*
N V H, San Leandro *Also called N V Heathorn Inc (P-2288)*
N V Heathorn Inc ....D....510 569-9100
1155 Beecher St San Leandro (94577) *(P-2288)*
N V Landscape Inc ....D....661 286-8888
24400 Walnut St Ste D Newhall (91321) *(P-904)*
N-U Enterprise, Irvine *Also called Ancca Corporation (P-2843)*
Nabisco, Ontario *Also called Mondelez Global LLC (P-8828)*
Nabors Well Services Co ....C....661 588-6140
1025 Earthmover Ct Bakersfield (93314) *(P-1038)*
Nabors Well Services Co ....B....661 589-3970
7515 Rosedale Hwy Bakersfield (93308) *(P-1070)*
Nabors Well Services Co ....C....310 639-7074
19431 S Santa Fe Ave Compton (90221) *(P-1071)*
Nabors Well Services Co ....D....661 392-7668
1954 James Rd Bakersfield (93308) *(P-1072)*
Nadel Inc (PA) ....D....310 826-2100
1990 S Bundy Dr Ste 400 Los Angeles (90025) *(P-26098)*
Nafithat Alsharq, La Mesa *Also called Abbood Zeyad (P-25494)*
NAFTA Distributors ....E....909 605-7515
5120 Santa Ana St Ontario (91761) *(P-8433)*
Nafta Shoes Inc ....D....626 369-9681
14632 Nelson Ave City of Industry (91744) *(P-13686)*
Nagra, San Francisco *Also called Opentv Inc (P-15790)*
Nagra Usa Inc ....E....310 335-5225
485 Clyde Ave Mountain View (94043) *(P-7775)*
Nagra Usa Inc (HQ) ....D....310 335-5225
841 Apollo St Ste 300 El Segundo (90245) *(P-7776)*
Naht Care At, San Diego *Also called Neighborhood House Association (P-23931)*
Nail Emporium ....E....714 779-9889
1221 N Lakeview Ave Anaheim (92807) *(P-7890)*
Nail Emporium Beauty Supply, Anaheim *Also called Nail Emporium (P-7890)*
Nakase Brothers Wholesale Nurs (PA) ....D....949 855-4388
9441 Krepp Dr Huntington Beach (92646) *(P-9150)*
Nakase Brothers Wholesale Nurs ....C....949 855-4388
20621 Lake Forest Dr Lake Forest (92630) *(P-9151)*
Nalco Company LLC ....D....925 957-9720
1320 Arnold Dr Ste 246 Martinez (94553) *(P-8932)*
Nallatech Inc ....D....805 383-8997
741 Flynn Rd Camarillo (93012) *(P-7513)*
Namasta Inc ....E....650 591-3639
2313 Hastings Dr Belmont (94002) *(P-18982)*
Namm, Carlsbad *Also called National Assn Mus Mrchants Inc (P-24970)*
Nan Fang Dist Group Inc ....D....510 297-5382
2100 Williams St San Leandro (94577) *(P-7777)*
Nan McKay and Associates Inc ....D....619 258-1855
1810 Gillespie Way # 202 El Cajon (92020) *(P-27357)*
Nancy Smith Construction Inc ....E....510 923-1671
47 Yorkshire Dr Oakland (94618) *(P-1302)*
Nanolab Technologies Inc (PA) ....D....408 433-3320
1708 Mccarthy Blvd Milpitas (95035) *(P-26720)*
Nanthealth Inc (HQ) ....D....310 883-1300
9920 Jefferson Blvd Culver City (90232) *(P-16009)*
Nantmobile LLC ....C....310 883-7888
9920 Jefferson Blvd Culver City (90232) *(P-15299)*
Nantworks LLC (PA) ....D....310 883-1300
9920 Jefferson Blvd Culver City (90232) *(P-16010)*
NAPA Auto Parts, NAPA *Also called County of NAPA (P-23695)*
NAPA County Juvenile Probation, NAPA *Also called County of NAPA (P-23696)*
NAPA Es Leasing LLC ....C....707 253-9540
1075 California Blvd NAPA (94559) *(P-12948)*
NAPA Golf Associates LLC ....D....707 257-1900
2555 Jameson Canyon Rd NAPA (94558) *(P-18983)*
NAPA Nursing Center Inc ....C....707 257-0931
3275 Villa Ln NAPA (94558) *(P-20658)*
NAPA Sanitation District ....E....707 254-9231
1515 Soscol Ferry Rd NAPA (94558) *(P-6324)*
NAPA Solano Cmnty Blood Ctr, Fairfield *Also called Blood Centers of Pacific (P-22749)*
NAPA State Hospital, NAPA *Also called Califrnia Dept State Hospitals (P-21933)*
NAPA Sunrise Rotary Club Inc ....D....707 257-9564
P.O. Box 5324 NAPA (94581) *(P-25205)*
NAPA Valley Country Club ....D....707 252-1111
3385 Hagen Rd NAPA (94558) *(P-18984)*
NAPA Valley Lodge LP ....D....707 875-3525
103 Coast Highway 1 Bodega Bay (94923) *(P-12949)*
NAPA Valley Marriott, NAPA *Also called IA Lodging NAPA Solano Trs LLC (P-12759)*
NAPA VALLEY MEDICAL CENTER, NAPA *Also called Queen of Valley Medical Center (P-21679)*
NAPA Valley PSI Inc ....D....707 255-0177
651 Trabajo Ln NAPA (94559) *(P-24208)*
NAPA Valley Railroad Co, NAPA *Also called NAPA Valley Wine Train LLC (P-19207)*
NAPA Valley Wine Train LLC (HQ) ....C....707 253-2160
1275 Mckinstry St NAPA (94559) *(P-19207)*
NAPA West, Five Points *Also called ATI Machinery Inc (P-7700)*
Napastyle Inc (PA) ....E....707 251-5100
360 Industrial Ct Ste A NAPA (94558) *(P-13949)*
Narven Enterprises Inc ....D....619 239-2261
1430 7th Ave Ste B San Diego (92101) *(P-12950)*
Nasdaq Inc ....C....510 705-8951
4300 Bohannon Dr Ste 110 Menlo Park (94025) *(P-26954)*
Nasser Company Inc (PA) ....D....714 279-2100
22720 Savi Ranch Pkwy Yorba Linda (92887) *(P-8434)*
Nasser Company of Arizona, Yorba Linda *Also called Nasser Company Inc (P-8434)*
Nat Geo TV, Los Angeles *Also called Fox Networks Group Inc (P-5914)*
Nat L Eggert Operations Center, El Cajon *Also called Helix Water District (P-6262)*
Nat Sim Corp ....D....818 705-3131
7405 Woodley Ave Van Nuys (91406) *(P-8084)*
NAT'L ASSN FOR HISPANIC ELDERL, Pasadena *Also called La Asociacion Nacional Pro Per (P-23889)*
Natera Inc (PA) ....C....650 249-9090
201 Industrial Rd Ste 410 San Carlos (94070) *(P-22114)*
National Air Inc ....C....619 299-2500
2053 Kurtz St San Diego (92110) *(P-2289)*
National Air and Energy, San Diego *Also called National Air Inc (P-2289)*
National Air Cargo Inc ....D....310 662-4766
222 N Sepulveda Blvd # 2000 El Segundo (90245) *(P-5114)*
National Apartment Flrg LLC ....D....800 773-6904
3205 Ocean Park Blvd # 180 Santa Monica (90405) *(P-3114)*
National Assn For Hispanic, Los Angeles *Also called La Asociacion Nacional Pro Per (P-23888)*
National Assn Ltr Carriers ....B....805 543-7329
4251 S Higuera St San Luis Obispo (93401) *(P-25071)*
National Assn Ltr Carriers ....B....415 362-0214
2310 Mason St Fl 4 San Francisco (94133) *(P-25072)*
National Assn Ltr Crrers BR 52, San Luis Obispo *Also called National Assn Ltr Carriers (P-25071)*
National Assn Mus Mrchants Inc ....D....760 438-8001
5790 Armada Dr Carlsbad (92008) *(P-24970)*
National Association For Self, Citrus Heights *Also called L W Roth Insurance Agency (P-24964)*
National Builder Services Inc ....D....714 634-7800
3835 E Thousand Oaks Blvd R Westlake Village (91362) *(P-14886)*
National Bus Invstigations Inc ....D....951 677-3500
25020 Las Brisas Rd Ste A Murrieta (92562) *(P-17343)*
National Business Group Inc (PA) ....D....818 221-6000
15319 Chatsworth St Mission Hills (91345) *(P-14449)*
National Cble Cmmnications LLC ....D....310 231-0745
11150 Santa Monica Blvd # 900 Los Angeles (90025) *(P-13978)*
National Cement, Duarte *Also called United Hauling Corp (P-17618)*
National Center On Deafness ....D....818 677-2054
18111 Nordhoff St Northridge (91330) *(P-23929)*
National Cmnty Renaissance Cal (PA) ....D....909 483-2444
9421 Haven Ave Rancho Cucamonga (91730) *(P-11895)*
National Cnstr Rentals Inc (HQ) ....D....818 221-6000
15319 Chatsworth St Mission Hills (91345) *(P-14529)*
National Commercial Services ....D....818 701-4400
6644 Valjean Ave Ste 100 Van Nuys (91406) *(P-14013)*
National Community Renaissance (PA) ....D....909 483-2444
9421 Haven Ave Ste 100 Rancho Cucamonga (91730) *(P-13477)*
National Construction & Maint ....E....909 888-7042
23846 Sunnymead Blvd # 10 Moreno Valley (92553) *(P-1599)*
National Council Negro Women ....D....415 564-4153
784 Cole St San Francisco (94117) *(P-25445)*
National Credit Industries Inc ....D....626 967-4355
1100 Via Verde San Dimas (91773) *(P-9898)*
National Custom Packing Inc ....E....831 724-2026
13526 Blackie Rd Castroville (95012) *(P-545)*
National Distribution Agcy Inc (HQ) ....D....510 487-6226
7025 Central Ave Newark (94560) *(P-4597)*
National Distribution Centers ....D....909 390-5696
5140 Santa Ana St Ontario (91761) *(P-5115)*
National Distribution Services ....D....951 739-2400
340 N Grant Ave Corona (92882) *(P-8047)*
National Ecnomic RES Assoc Inc ....D....213 346-3000
777 S Figueroa St # 1950 Los Angeles (90017) *(P-26548)*
National Employee Benefits LLC ....C....877 778-8330
3200 E Guasti Rd Ste 100 Ontario (91761) *(P-27358)*
National Everclean Svcs Inc ....D....877 532-5326
28632 Roadside Dr Ste 275 Agoura Hills (91301) *(P-26721)*
National Fail Safe Inc ....E....562 493-5447
6442 Industry Way Westminster (92683) *(P-2656)*
National Fail-Safe SEC Systems, Westminster *Also called National Fail Safe Inc (P-2656)*
National Film Laboratories ....C....323 466-0281
900 Glenneyre St Laguna Beach (92651) *(P-18204)*
National Fitness Testing, Los Angeles *Also called Young Mens Chrstn Assn of La (P-25345)*
National Fncl Srvcs Cnsrtm LLC ....D....650 572-2872
3161 Los Prados St San Mateo (94403) *(P-27359)*
National General Insurance Co ....D....909 944-8085
3633 Inland Empire Blvd # 700 Ontario (91764) *(P-10383)*
National Genetics Institute ....C....310 996-6610
2440 S Sepulveda Blvd # 235 Los Angeles (90064) *(P-22115)*
NATIONAL GOLF PROPERTIES, San Juan Capistrano *Also called Marbella Country Club (P-18965)*
National Golf Properties Inc ....D....415 488-4030
5800 Sir Francis Drake San Geronimo (94963) *(P-18985)*
National Hospitality LLC ....D....805 688-8000
400 Alisal Rd Solvang (93463) *(P-12951)*
National Hot Rod Association (PA) ....C....626 914-4761
2035 E Financial Way Glendora (91741) *(P-18541)*
National Insurance Associates, Solana Beach *Also called National Insurance Housing (P-27798)*

ALPHABETIC

Employee Codes: A=Over 500 employees, B=251-500
C=101-250, D=51-100, E=50
2019 Directory of California
Wholesalers and Services Companies
© Mergent Inc. 1-800-342-5647
1395

National Insurance Housing....D....800 550-1911
265 Santa Helena Ste 210 Solana Beach (92075) ***(P-27798)***
National Lgal Studies Inst Inc....E....951 653-4240
23962 Alssndro Blvd Ste P Moreno Valley (92553) ***(P-17344)***
National Link Incorporated....D....909 670-1900
2235 Auto Centre Dr Glendora (91740) ***(P-6971)***
National Liquidators....E....949 631-6715
2715 W Coast Hwy Newport Beach (92663) ***(P-7934)***
National Marine Fisheries Svc....C....858 546-7081
8604 La Jolla Shores Dr La Jolla (92037) ***(P-26421)***
National Mentor Inc....D....909 483-2505
9166 Anaheim Pl Ste 200 Rancho Cucamonga (91730) ***(P-24209)***
National Mentor Inc....E....661 387-1000
2131 Mars Ct Bakersfield (93308) ***(P-24811)***
National Monitoring Center, Lake Forest *Also called Advanced Protection Inds Inc* ***(P-16870)***
National Notary Association....C....818 739-4071
9350 De Soto Ave Chatsworth (91311) ***(P-25029)***
NATIONAL NURSES UNITED, Oakland *Also called California Nurses Association* ***(P-25004)***
National Organic Packing, Riverside *Also called Blue Banner Company Inc* ***(P-495)***
National Organization of....C....800 489-0210
18663 Ventura Blvd Tarzana (91356) ***(P-22844)***
National Parking & Valet, Monterey *Also called Pacific Parking & Valet LLC* ***(P-6544)***
National Paving Company Inc....D....951 369-1332
4361 Fort Dr Riverside (92509) ***(P-1824)***
National Planning Corporation....C....800 881-7174
100 N Pacific Coast Hwy # 1800 El Segundo (90245) ***(P-9724)***
National Product Services LLC....E....562 594-8206
1005 Marvista Ave Seal Beach (90740) ***(P-27565)***
National Public Safety....D....619 401-9431
490 N Magnolia Ave El Cajon (92020) ***(P-16737)***
National Railroad Pass Corp....A....925 335-5180
601 Marina Vista Ave Martinez (94553) ***(P-3620)***
National Railroad Pass Corp....C....619 239-9989
1050 Kettner Blvd Ste 1 San Diego (92101) ***(P-3621)***
National Rehab, San Diego *Also called McKesson Ptent Care Sltons Inc* ***(P-22837)***
National Rent A Car, Oakland *Also called National Rental (us) Inc* ***(P-17646)***
National Rent A Car, Santa Clara *Also called National Rental (us) Inc* ***(P-17647)***
National Rental (us) Inc....D....510 877-4507
7600 Earhart Rd Ste 4 Oakland (94621) ***(P-17646)***
National Rental (us) Inc....D....408 492-0501
2752 De La Cruz Blvd Santa Clara (95050) ***(P-17647)***
National Research Group Inc....B....323 817-2000
6255 W Sunset Blvd Fl 19 Los Angeles (90028) ***(P-26549)***
National Retail Trnsp Inc....D....310 605-3777
355 W Carob St Compton (90220) ***(P-4233)***
National Rtrement Partners Inc (PA)....D....949 488-8726
34700 Pacific Coast Hwy Capistrano Beach (92624) ***(P-10698)***
National Safe, Fullerton *Also called Henry Bros Electronics Inc* ***(P-15971)***
National Safety Services....E....714 679-9118
3400 Avenue Of The Arts Costa Mesa (92626) ***(P-27799)***
National Security, San Diego *Also called Leidos Inc* ***(P-26407)***
National Security Industries....B....916 779-0640
1217 Del Paso Blvd Ste A Sacramento (95815) ***(P-16924)***
National Security Industries....B....831 425-2052
501 Mission St Ste 1a Santa Cruz (95060) ***(P-16738)***
National Security Santa Cruz, Santa Cruz *Also called National Security Industries* ***(P-16738)***
National Security Tech LLC....D....925 960-2500
161 S Vasco Rd Ste A Livermore (94551) ***(P-25841)***
National Surety Corporation....A....415 899-2000
1465 N Mcdowell Blvd # 100 Petaluma (94954) ***(P-10431)***
National Technical Systems Inc....E....510 578-3500
41039 Boyce Rd Fremont (94538) ***(P-25842)***
National Teleconsultants Inc....C....818 265-4400
550 N Brand Blvd Fl 17 Glendale (91203) ***(P-25843)***
National Therapeutic Svcs Inc (PA)....D....866 311-0003
3822 Campus Dr Ste 100 Newport Beach (92660) ***(P-22621)***
National Tube & Steel, Mission Hills *Also called National Business Group Inc* ***(P-14449)***
National Veterinary Assoc Inc....D....707 462-8625
2300 N State St Ukiah (95482) ***(P-606)***
National Veterinary Assoc Inc (PA)....C....805 777-7722
29229 Canwood St Ste 100 Agoura Hills (91301) ***(P-607)***
NationaLease, San Diego *Also called Miramar Ford Truck Sales Inc* ***(P-6604)***
Nationbuilder, Los Angeles *Also called 3dna Corp* ***(P-14950)***
Nationl Medcl Assn Comp Health....D....619 231-9300
3177 Ocean View Blvd San Diego (92113) ***(P-22622)***
Nations Capital Group LLC....E....818 793-2050
5353 Balboa Blvd Ste 300 Encino (91316) ***(P-9743)***
Nations Direct Lender & In....C....800 969-7779
160 S Old Springs Rd # 260 Anaheim (92808) ***(P-17345)***
Nations Petroleum Cal LLC....D....661 387-6402
9600 Ming Ave Ste 300 Bakersfield (93311) ***(P-1045)***
Nations Surgery Center, Encino *Also called Nations Capital Group LLC* ***(P-9743)***
Nationwide Environmental Svcs, Norwalk *Also called Joes Sweeping Inc* ***(P-6409)***
Nationwide Funding LLC....E....949 679-3600
5520 Trabuco Rd Ste 100 Irvine (92620) ***(P-9761)***
Nationwide Guard Services Inc....D....909 608-1112
9327 Fairway View Pl # 200 Rancho Cucamonga (91730) ***(P-16739)***
Nationwide Legal LLC (PA)....D....213 249-9999
1609 James M Wood Blvd Los Angeles (90015) ***(P-23281)***
Nationwide Theatres Corp (HQ)....D....310 657-8420
120 N Robertson Blvd Fl 3 Los Angeles (90048) ***(P-18329)***
Nationwide Theatres Corp....D....562 421-8448
2500 Carson St Lakewood (90712) ***(P-18496)***
Nationwide Trans Inc (PA)....D....909 355-3211
1633 S Campus Ave Ontario (91761) ***(P-5116)***
Native American Health Ctr Inc (PA)....D....510 535-4400
2950 International Blvd Oakland (94601) ***(P-19704)***
Native Sons Landscaping Inc....E....925 837-8175
25 Beta Ct Ste L San Ramon (94583) ***(P-905)***
Natividad Medical Center....A....831 755-4111
1441 Constitution Blvd Salinas (93906) ***(P-21604)***
Natomas Marketplace 16, Sacramento *Also called Regal Cinemas Inc* ***(P-18317)***
Natomas Racquet Club, Sacramento *Also called Spare-Time Inc* ***(P-18666)***
Natural Health Trends Corp....D....310 541-0888
609 Deep Valley Dr # 390 Rllng HLS Est (90274) ***(P-22845)***
Natural History Museum of Los....B....213 763-3442
900 Exposition Blvd Los Angeles (90007) ***(P-24895)***
Natural Rsrces Def Council Inc....D....310 434-2300
1314 2nd St Santa Monica (90401) ***(P-25206)***
Naturally Aged Flooring, Moorpark *Also called Ace Floor Co Inc* ***(P-3093)***
Naturebridge....D....415 332-5771
1033 Fort Cronkhite Sausalito (94965) ***(P-25446)***
Natures Image Inc....D....949 680-4400
20361 Hermana Cir Lake Forest (92630) ***(P-771)***
Natures Produce Company....D....323 235-4343
3305 Bandini Blvd Vernon (90058) ***(P-8708)***
Naumann/Hobbs Material....C....909 427-0125
8575 Cherry Ave Fontana (92335) ***(P-7778)***
Naumann/Hobbs Material....C....858 207-6274
1600 E Mission Rd San Marcos (92069) ***(P-7779)***
Naumes Inc....E....530 743-2055
3792 Feather River Blvd Olivehurst (95961) ***(P-287)***
Naval Coating Inc....C....619 234-8366
3475 E St San Diego (92102) ***(P-3556)***
Naval Dental Center, San Diego *Also called United States Dept of Navy* ***(P-20023)***
Naval Fac Eng Cmmd SW Wrkng CA....D....619 532-1158
1220 Pacific Hwy San Diego (92132) ***(P-25844)***
Naval Hospital Lemoore, Lemoore *Also called United States Dept of Navy* ***(P-21869)***
Naval Medical Center, San Diego *Also called United States Dept of Navy* ***(P-21870)***
Naval Medical Clinic, Port Hueneme *Also called United States Dept of Navy* ***(P-20026)***
Naval Research, San Diego *Also called United States Dept of Navy* ***(P-26481)***
Naval Research Lab, Monterey *Also called United States Dept of Navy* ***(P-26482)***
Navigant Consulting Inc....D....213 452-4516
300 S Grand Ave Ste 3850 Los Angeles (90071) ***(P-27360)***
Navigant Cymetrix Corporation....C....424 201-6300
1515 W 190th St Ste 350 Gardena (90248) ***(P-26955)***
Navigate Biopharma Svcs Inc....C....866 992-4939
1890 Rutherford Rd Carlsbad (92008) ***(P-26642)***
Navis Holdings LLC....C....510 267-5000
55 Harrison St Ste 600 Oakland (94607) ***(P-15300)***
Navisite LLC....E....408 965-9000
2805 Lafayette St Santa Clara (95050) ***(P-5608)***
Navitas LLC....E....415 883-8116
15 Pamaron Way Novato (94949) ***(P-8832)***
Navitas Naturals, Novato *Also called Navitas LLC* ***(P-8832)***
Navmedwest, San Diego *Also called United States Dept of Navy* ***(P-20027)***
Navy Bachelor Quarters, Ridgecrest *Also called Navy Exchange Service Command* ***(P-13478)***
Navy Exchange Service Command....D....760 939-8681
1395 Hussey Rd Ridgecrest (93555) ***(P-13478)***
Navy Exchange Service Command....C....909 517-2640
4250 Eucalyptus Ave Chino (91710) ***(P-4598)***
Navy Federal Credit Union....C....888 842-6328
2040 Harbison Dr Vacaville (95687) ***(P-9574)***
Navy Hospital, Lemoore *Also called United States Dept of Navy* ***(P-21868)***
Nazareth House, Fresno *Also called Congregation of Poor Sisters* ***(P-24474)***
Nazareth House, San Rafael *Also called Sisters of Nazareth* ***(P-21218)***
Nazareth House, San Diego *Also called Poor Sisters of Nazareth of SA* ***(P-24632)***
Nazzareno Electric Co Inc....D....714 712-4744
1250 E Gene Autry Way Anaheim (92805) ***(P-2657)***
Nb Enterprises & Dist Inc....D....866 216-1515
603 Wilshire Blvd Los Angeles (90017) ***(P-26956)***
NBBJ LP....E....213 243-3333
523 W 6th St Ste 300 Los Angeles (90014) ***(P-26099)***
NBC 7/Channel 39, San Diego *Also called Station Venture Operations LP* ***(P-5839)***
NBC Consulting Inc....D....310 798-5000
2110 Artesia Blvd Ste 323 Redondo Beach (90278) ***(P-27361)***
NBC Subsidiary (knbc-Tv) LLC....C....818 684-5746
100 Universal City Plz Universal City (91608) ***(P-5825)***
NBC Universal Inc....C....818 260-5746
3000 W Alameda Ave Burbank (91523) ***(P-5826)***
Nbccat Corp....D....209 858-0283
1044 Madruga Rd Lathrop (95330) ***(P-17796)***
NC Fit Inc....D....408 910-6748
647 N Santa Cruz Ave C Los Gatos (95030) ***(P-18637)***
NC Interactive LLC....D....650 393-2200
1900 S Norfolk St Ste 125 San Mateo (94403) ***(P-15772)***
NC Interactive LLC....D....512 623-8700
1 Polaris Way Ste 110 Aliso Viejo (92656) ***(P-16430)***
Nca,, Los Angeles *Also called National Cble Cmmnications LLC* ***(P-13978)***
Ncc Group Inc (HQ)....D....415 268-9300
123 Mission St Ste 1020 San Francisco (94105) ***(P-16431)***
Ncca Diagnostics Medical Group, Sacramento *Also called Northern California Cardiology* ***(P-19723)***
Ncircle Network Security Inc (HQ)....D....415 625-5900
101 2nd St Ste 400 San Francisco (94105) ***(P-15301)***
Ncire, San Francisco *Also called Northern California Institute* ***(P-24816)***
NCJW LA, Los Angeles *Also called Los Angeles SEC National* ***(P-23903)***
NCM, Moreno Valley *Also called National Construction & Maint* ***(P-1599)***
Ncompass International, West Hollywood *Also called N Compass International Inc* ***(P-27356)***
Ncpa, Roseville *Also called Northern California Power Agcy* ***(P-6057)***
Ncpa- Plant 1, Middletown *Also called Northern California Power Agcy* ***(P-6058)***

Ncsoft, Aliso Viejo *Also called NC Interactive LLC* ***(P-16430)***
Nctd, Oceanside *Also called North County Transit District* ***(P-3690)***
ND Systems Inc........D.......408 776-0085
5750 Hellyer Ave San Jose (95138) ***(P-13979)***
Ndga, Santa Clara *Also called Bandai Namco Entrmt Amer Inc* ***(P-7946)***
Nds Americas Inc (HQ)........D.......714 434-2100
3500 Hyland Ave Costa Mesa (92626) ***(P-5923)***
Nds Surgical Imaging LLC........C.......408 776-0085
5750 Hellyer Ave San Jose (95138) ***(P-7195)***
Ndti, Ridgecrest *Also called New Directions Tech Inc* ***(P-16018)***
Neal Electric Corp (HQ)........D.......858 513-2525
2790 Business Park Dr Vista (92081) ***(P-2658)***
Neal Trucking Inc........D.......951 685-5048
9749 Bellegrave Ave Riverside (92509) ***(P-4044)***
Neals Janitorial Service........E.......408 271-9944
1588 Calco Creek Dr San Jose (95127) ***(P-14329)***
Near-Cal Corp........E.......951 245-5400
512 Chaney St Lake Elsinore (92530) ***(P-1600)***
Neardata Inc........D.......818 249-2469
4502 Dyer St Ste 103 La Crescenta (91214) ***(P-27362)***
Neardata Systems, La Crescenta *Also called Neardata Inc* ***(P-27362)***
Nebula Inc........D.......650 539-9900
1100 La Avenida St Mountain View (94043) ***(P-26422)***
Nebula Systems, Mountain View *Also called Nebula Inc* ***(P-26422)***
Ned E Dunphy........D.......661 395-1000
4550 California Ave Fl 2 Bakersfield (93309) ***(P-23282)***
Ned L Webster Concrete Cnstr........D.......805 529-4900
8800 Grimes Canyon Rd Moorpark (93021) ***(P-3292)***
Nederlander of California Inc........E.......323 468-1700
6233 Hollywood Blvd Fl 2 Los Angeles (90028) ***(P-10918)***
Neese Inc........E.......707 544-4444
588 Roseland Ave Santa Rosa (95407) ***(P-3867)***
Nefab Packaging West LLC........D.......408 678-2516
8477 Central Ave Newark (94560) ***(P-17346)***
Neff Construction, Ontario *Also called Southtown Industrial Park* ***(P-10950)***
Neg Operations LLC........C.......310 777-1940
401 Wilshire Blvd # 1070 Santa Monica (90401) ***(P-18205)***
Nehemiah Construction Inc........E.......707 746-6815
12150 Tributary Ln P Rancho Cordova (95670) ***(P-1825)***
Nehemiah Progressive Housing D........D.......916 231-1999
424 N 7th St Ste 250 Sacramento (95811) ***(P-11896)***
Neighborhood Healthcare........D.......951 225-6400
41840 Enterprise Cir N Temecula (92590) ***(P-22846)***
Neighborhood Healthcare (PA)........A.......760 520-8372
425 N Date St Ste 203 Escondido (92025) ***(P-19705)***
Neighborhood Healthcare........D.......619 440-2751
855 E Madison Ave El Cajon (92020) ***(P-19706)***
Neighborhood Healthcare........D.......760 737-2000
460 N Elm St Escondido (92025) ***(P-19707)***
Neighborhood House Association........D.......619 262-8199
4111 Home Ave Ste F San Diego (92105) ***(P-24352)***
Neighborhood House Association (PA)........B.......858 715-2642
5660 Copley Dr San Diego (92111) ***(P-23930)***
Neighborhood House Association........E.......619 527-1287
4425 Federal Blvd Ste 24 San Diego (92102) ***(P-23931)***
Neighborhood House Association........D.......619 263-7761
841 S 41st St San Diego (92113) ***(P-23932)***
Neighborhood Hse Assoc Fmily, San Diego *Also called Neighborhood House Association* ***(P-23932)***
Neighborhood Preservation Div, Stockton *Also called County of San Joaquin* ***(P-24772)***
Neil Dymott Frank McFall........C.......619 238-1712
110 W A St San Diego (92101) ***(P-23283)***
Neil Bassetti Farms........E.......831 674-2040
41715 Espinosa Rd Greenfield (93927) ***(P-71)***
Neil Dymott Perkins Brown, San Diego *Also called Neil Dymott Frank McFall* ***(P-23283)***
Neilson Marketing Services, Laguna Hills *Also called Nms Data Inc* ***(P-27804)***
Nelson Shelton & Associates........C.......310 271-2229
355 N Canon Dr Beverly Hills (90210) ***(P-11624)***
Nelson & Associates Inc........D.......562 921-4423
12816 Leffingwell Ave Santa Fe Springs (90670) ***(P-7381)***
Nelson Moving & Storage Inc........E.......949 582-0380
25742 Atlantic Ocean Dr Lake Forest (92630) ***(P-4234)***
Nelson North American, Lake Forest *Also called Nelson Moving & Storage Inc* ***(P-4234)***
Nelson, Shelton, & Associates, Beverly Hills *Also called Nelson Shelton & Associates* ***(P-11624)***
Neo Tech, Chatsworth *Also called Oncore Manufacturing LLC* ***(P-25853)***
Neogov, El Segundo *Also called Governmentjobscom Inc* ***(P-15694)***
Neonatal Medical Assoc Inc........B.......562 933-8100
1022 E Tehachapi Dr Long Beach (90807) ***(P-19708)***
Neonroots LLC........C.......310 907-9210
8560 W Sunset Blvd # 500 West Hollywood (90069) ***(P-15773)***
Neopets Inc........E.......818 551-4338
412 W Broadway Ste 303 Glendale (91204) ***(P-5609)***
Neostyle Eyewear Corporation........D.......760 305-4004
2651 La Mirada Dr Ste 150 Vista (92081) ***(P-7237)***
Neovia Logistics Dist LP........C.......626 359-4500
600 Live Oak Ave Irwindale (91706) ***(P-5117)***
Nep Group Inc........E.......951 279-8877
1580 Magnolia Ave Corona (92879) ***(P-18082)***
Nep Group Inc........D.......412 423-1354
7635 Airport Bus Pkwy Van Nuys (91406) ***(P-18083)***
Nephrology, Los Angeles *Also called Cedars-Sinai Medical Center* ***(P-19359)***
Neps Worldwide, La Mirada *Also called Northeast Protective Svcs Inc* ***(P-16744)***
Neptune Management Corporation........D.......510 797-2269
4065 Mowry Ave Fremont (94538) ***(P-13691)***
Neptune Management Corporation........D.......916 771-5300
9650 Fairway Dr 120 Roseville (95678) ***(P-13692)***
Ner Precious Metals Inc........D.......213 489-1549
10660 Wilshire Blvd Los Angeles (90024) ***(P-8011)***
Nest Labs Inc (HQ)........D.......650 331-1127
3400 Hillview Ave Palo Alto (94304) ***(P-7514)***
Nestle Dreyers Ice Cream Co........C.......909 595-0677
351 Cheryl Ln Walnut (91789) ***(P-8525)***
Nestle Ice Cream Company........A.......661 398-3500
7301 District Blvd Bakersfield (93313) ***(P-8526)***
Nestle Usa Inc........C.......408 846-6892
6205 Engel Way Gilroy (95020) ***(P-8527)***
Nestle Waters North Amer Inc........C.......714 532-6220
619 N Main St Orange (92868) ***(P-8833)***
Nestle Waters North Amer Inc........C.......951 572-4600
14020 Elm St Cabazon (92230) ***(P-8834)***
Nestle Waters North Amer Inc........D.......818 349-9201
9400 Mason Ave Chatsworth (91311) ***(P-8835)***
Nestle Waters North Amer Inc........D.......925 294-7720
7480 Las Positas Rd Livermore (94551) ***(P-8836)***
Nestor Enterprises LLC........E.......209 727-5711
13852 E Peltier Rd Acampo (95220) ***(P-163)***
Nestwise LLC........B.......855 444-6378
9785 Towne Centre Dr San Diego (92121) ***(P-17347)***
Net Eternity, Redding *Also called Alexandria Clayton* ***(P-15911)***
Net Express........D.......510 887-4395
32 Snyder Way Fremont (94536) ***(P-16011)***
Net Optics Inc........D.......408 737-7777
5301 Stevens Creek Blvd Santa Clara (95051) ***(P-15774)***
Net4site LLC........D.......408 427-3004
3350 Scott Blvd Bldg 34b Santa Clara (95054) ***(P-27363)***
Netafim Irrigation Inc (HQ)........C.......559 453-6800
5470 E Home Ave Fresno (93727) ***(P-7707)***
Netapp Inc........C.......949 754-6600
300 Spectrum Center Dr # 900 Irvine (92618) ***(P-16012)***
Netapp Inc........C.......408 822-3402
1299 Orleans Dr Sunnyvale (94089) ***(P-16013)***
Netapp Inc........C.......818 227-5025
6320 Canoga Ave Ste 1500 Woodland Hills (91367) ***(P-16014)***
Netapp Inc........C.......408 419-5301
1345 Crossman Ave Sunnyvale (94089) ***(P-16015)***
Netapp Inc........C.......408 822-3803
3334 Meadowlands Ln San Jose (95135) ***(P-16016)***
Netball America Inc........E.......949 307-4455
4686 Oceano Cir Huntington Beach (92649) ***(P-17348)***
Netbase Solutions Inc (PA)........D.......650 810-2100
3960 Freedom Cir 201 Santa Clara (95054) ***(P-27364)***
Netcontinuum Inc........D.......408 961-5600
1454 Almaden Valley Dr San Jose (95120) ***(P-16925)***
Netcube Systems Inc........D.......650 862-7858
1275 Arbor Ave Los Altos (94024) ***(P-15775)***
Netease Information Tech Corp........D.......415 612-7866
2000 Sierra Point Pkwy # 800 Brisbane (94005) ***(P-15302)***
Netflix Inc........A.......408 540-3700
121 Albright Way Los Gatos (95032) ***(P-18330)***
Netflix Inc (PA)........C.......408 540-3700
100 Winchester Cir Los Gatos (95032) ***(P-18331)***
NETGEAR, Carlsbad *Also called Arlo Technologies Inc* ***(P-16874)***
Netline Corporation (PA)........D.......408 374-4200
750 University Ave # 200 Los Gatos (95032) ***(P-27365)***
Netlinx Publishing Solutions, Sacramento *Also called System Integrators Inc* ***(P-16063)***
Netnow........B.......408 370-0425
41 Heritage Village Ln Campbell (95008) ***(P-5610)***
Netpace Inc........D.......925 543-7760
5000 Executive Pkwy # 530 San Ramon (94583) ***(P-16432)***
Netpolarity Inc........B.......408 971-1100
900 E Campbell Ave Campbell (95008) ***(P-14671)***
Netronix Integration Inc (PA)........D.......408 573-1444
2170 Paragon Dr San Jose (95131) ***(P-2659)***
Netskope Inc........D.......800 979-6988
270 3rd St Los Altos (94022) ***(P-15303)***
Netsource Inc........D.......415 831-3681
5955 Geary Blvd San Francisco (94121) ***(P-14672)***
Netsuite Inc (HQ)........C.......650 627-1000
2955 Campus Dr Ste 100 San Mateo (94403) ***(P-15776)***
Netversant - Silicon Vly Inc (PA)........C.......510 771-1200
47811 Warm Springs Blvd Fremont (94539) ***(P-2660)***
Network Automation Inc........E.......213 738-1700
3530 Wilshire Blvd # 1800 Los Angeles (90010) ***(P-15777)***
Network Capital Funding Corp (PA)........B.......949 442-0060
5 Park Plz Ste 800 Irvine (92614) ***(P-9836)***
Network Global Logistics LLC........C.......888 285-7447
13479 Valley Blvd Fontana (92335) ***(P-4845)***
Network Intgrtion Partners Inc........D.......909 919-2800
11981 Jack Benny Dr # 103 Rancho Cucamonga (91739) ***(P-16017)***
Network Management Group Inc (PA)........C.......323 263-2632
1100 S Flower St Ste 3110 Los Angeles (90015) ***(P-26957)***
Network Medical Management Inc........C.......626 282-0288
1668 S Grfeld Ave Ste 100 Alhambra (91801) ***(P-26958)***
Network of One, Culver City *Also called Roundup Media LLC* ***(P-13895)***
Networked Insurance Agents LLC........C.......800 682-8476
443 Crown Point Cir Ste A Grass Valley (95945) ***(P-10699)***
Netzero Inc (HQ)........C.......805 418-2000
21301 Burbank Blvd Fl 3 Woodland Hills (91367) ***(P-15304)***
Neuberg Nuberg Importers Group........E.......800 832-2742
6001 Santa Monica Blvd Los Angeles (90038) ***(P-6777)***
Neudesic LLC (PA)........C.......949 754-4500
200 Spectrum Center Dr # 2000 Irvine (92618) ***(P-16433)***
Neuintel LLC (PA)........D.......949 625-6117
20 Pacifica Ste 1000 Irvine (92618) ***(P-15305)***
Neuro Drinks, Sherman Oaks *Also called Neurobrands LLC* ***(P-8837)***

ALPHABETIC

Employee Codes: A=Over 500 employees, B=251-500 C=101-250, D=51-100, E=50
2019 Directory of California Wholesalers and Services Companies
© Mergent Inc. 1-800-342-5647
1397

Neurobrands LLC....C.......310 393-6444
15303 Ventura Blvd # 675 Sherman Oaks (91403) ***(P-8837)***
Neuron Esb, Irvine *Also called Neudesic LLC* ***(P-16433)***
Neuropace Inc....D.......650 237-2700
455 Bernardo Ave Mountain View (94043) ***(P-26423)***
Neurosurgery, Eureka *Also called St Joseph Hospital* ***(P-21780)***
Nevada County Behavioral Hlth....E.......530 265-1450
500 Crown Point Cir # 120 Grass Valley (95945) ***(P-22623)***
Nevada Irrigation District (PA)....C.......530 273-6185
1036 W Main St Grass Valley (95945) ***(P-6559)***
Nevada Republic Electric N Inc....C.......916 294-0140
11855 White Rock Rd Rancho Cordova (95742) ***(P-2661)***
Nevada Truck & Trailer Repair, West Sacramento *Also called Fredericksen Tank Lines Inc* ***(P-4180)***
Neversoft Entertainment Inc....C.......818 610-4100
21255 Burbank Blvd # 600 Woodland Hills (91367) ***(P-15306)***
Neville Alleyne MD, Oceanside *Also called Tri City Orthopedic Sgy & Mdcl* ***(P-20011)***
Nevin Levy LLP A Partnership....D.......415 800-5770
50 California St Ste 1500 San Francisco (94111) ***(P-11625)***
Nevins Adams Properties, Santa Barbara *Also called Nevins-Adams Properties Inc* ***(P-10919)***
Nevins-Adams Properties Inc (PA)....C.......805 963-2884
920 Garden St Ste A Santa Barbara (93101) ***(P-10919)***
Nevocal Enterprises Inc....D.......559 277-0700
5320 N Barcus Ave Fresno (93722) ***(P-1095)***
New Advances For People Disabi....D.......661 327-0188
1120 21st St Bakersfield (93301) ***(P-24812)***
New Age Electric Inc....D.......408 279-8787
1085 N 11th St San Jose (95112) ***(P-2662)***
New Alliance Insurance Brokers....E.......424 205-6700
3700 Santa Fe Ave Ste 300 Long Beach (90810) ***(P-10700)***
New American Funding, Tustin *Also called Broker Solutions Inc* ***(P-27173)***
New Bi US Gaming LLC....D.......858 592-2472
10920 Via Frontera # 420 San Diego (92127) ***(P-15778)***
New Bridge Foundation Inc....D.......510 548-7270
2323 Hearst Ave Berkeley (94709) ***(P-23933)***
New Bridge Foundation Inc....D.......510 548-7270
1820 Scenic Ave Berkeley (94709) ***(P-22037)***
New Bthny Rsdntl CRE&sklld....D.......209 827-8933
1441 Berkeley Dr Los Banos (93635) ***(P-24609)***
New CAM Commerce Solutions LLC....D.......714 338-0200
5555 Garden Grove Blvd # 100 Westminster (92683) ***(P-15779)***
New Century Farms....E.......805 928-2333
1445 Jason Way Santa Maria (93455) ***(P-702)***
New Century Insurance Services (PA)....E.......626 300-9000
16 N 2nd St Alhambra (91801) ***(P-10701)***
New Century Media Corp....E.......562 695-1000
2727 Pellissier Pl City of Industry (90601) ***(P-8048)***
New Century Science & Tech....D.......626 581-5500
18031 Cortney Ct City of Industry (91748) ***(P-7935)***
New Cingular Wireless Svcs Inc....D.......562 924-0000
P.O. Box 68055 Artesia (90702) ***(P-5611)***
New Cingular Wireless Svcs Inc....D.......562 941-6422
9830 Norwalk Blvd Ste 100 Santa Fe Springs (90670) ***(P-5411)***
New Civic Company Ltd....C.......415 986-1668
870 Market St Ste 1168 San Francisco (94102) ***(P-12248)***
New Colusa Indian Bingo....B.......530 458-8844
3770 State Highway 45 Colusa (95932) ***(P-19208)***
NEW COVENANT CARE CENTER OF DI, Dinuba *Also called New Covenant Care of Dinuba* ***(P-20659)***
New Covenant Care of Dinuba....D.......559 591-3300
1730 S College Ave Dinuba (93618) ***(P-20659)***
New Crew Production Corp....C.......323 234-8880
200 W 138th St Los Angeles (90061) ***(P-17349)***
New Day Staffing Inc....C.......619 481-5400
5920 Friars Rd Ste 104 San Diego (92108) ***(P-14887)***
New Deal Studios Inc....D.......310 578-9929
1812 W Burbank Blvd Burbank (91506) ***(P-18206)***
New Desserts Inc....D.......415 780-6860
5000 Fulton Dr Fairfield (94534) ***(P-8838)***
New Directions Inc (PA)....D.......310 914-4045
11303 Wilshire Blvd Los Angeles (90025) ***(P-23934)***
New Directions For Veterans, Los Angeles *Also called New Directions Inc* ***(P-23934)***
New Directions Tech Inc (PA)....D.......760 384-2444
137 W Drummond Ave Ste A Ridgecrest (93555) ***(P-16018)***
New Discovery Inc....D.......925 783-6613
1475 Clubhouse Dr Byron (94505) ***(P-18986)***
New Discovery Inc....D.......925 634-0505
2600 Cherry Hills Dr Byron (94505) ***(P-18740)***
New Dream Network LLC (PA)....D.......626 644-9466
135 S State College Blvd Brea (92821) ***(P-5612)***
New Dream Network LLC....D.......323 375-3842
707 Wilshire Blvd # 5050 Los Angeles (90017) ***(P-5613)***
New Earth Enterprises Inc....D.......760 942-1298
3790 Manchester Ave Encinitas (92024) ***(P-906)***
New Economics For Women (PA)....D.......213 483-2060
303 Loma Dr Los Angeles (90017) ***(P-23935)***
New England Financial, Woodland Hills *Also called Russon Financial Services Inc* ***(P-27435)***
New England Shtmtl Works Inc....C.......559 268-7375
2731 S Cherry Ave Fresno (93706) ***(P-25845)***
New Figueroa Hotel Inc....D.......213 627-8971
1000 S Hope St Apt 201 Los Angeles (90015) ***(P-12952)***
New Global Telecom Inc....D.......213 489-3708
624 S Grand Ave Ste 2900 Los Angeles (90017) ***(P-17350)***
New Haven Youth Fmly Svcs Inc....C.......760 630-4060
P.O. Box 1199 Vista (92085) ***(P-23936)***
New Home Company Inc (PA)....D.......949 382-7800
85 Enterprise Ste 450 Aliso Viejo (92656) ***(P-1355)***
New Home Feed, Oakland *Also called Zillow Group Inc* ***(P-16202)***
New Home Professionals....C.......925 556-1555
6500 Dublin Blvd Ste 201 Dublin (94568) ***(P-11626)***
New Hope Care Center, Tracy *Also called Jesse Lee Group Inc* ***(P-26907)***
New Hope Harvesting LLC....D.......805 478-4469
918 Nita Ct Santa Maria (93454) ***(P-481)***
New Image Emrgncy Shltr (PA)....C.......562 983-7289
1008 E 59th St Los Angeles (90001) ***(P-23937)***
New Image Landscape Company....D.......510 226-9191
3250 Darby Cmn Fremont (94539) ***(P-907)***
New Legend Inc....C.......530 674-3100
1235 Oswald Rd Yuba City (95991) ***(P-4235)***
New Mediscan II LLC....D.......866 758-4224
21050 Califa St 100 Woodland Hills (91367) ***(P-22847)***
New Ngc Inc....E.......510 234-6745
1040 Canal Blvd Richmond (94804) ***(P-7984)***
New Paradigm Productions Inc (PA)....D.......415 924-8000
39 Mesa St Ste 212 San Francisco (94129) ***(P-18084)***
New Port Orthopedic Institute....D.......949 722-5071
19582 Beach Blvd Ste 118 Huntington Beach (92648) ***(P-19709)***
New Pride Corporation....E.......310 631-7000
2757 E Del Amo Blvd Compton (90221) ***(P-17749)***
New Regency Productions Inc (PA)....D.......310 369-8300
10201 W Pico Blvd Bldg 12 Los Angeles (90064) ***(P-18085)***
New Relic Inc (PA)....C.......650 777-7600
188 Spear St Ste 1200 San Francisco (94105) ***(P-15780)***
New Solar Incorporated....E.......888 886-0103
1525 Mccarthy Blvd Milpitas (95035) ***(P-26959)***
New Start Home Health Care Inc....C.......818 665-7898
21515 Vanowen St Ste 205 Canoga Park (91303) ***(P-23938)***
New Stockton Poultry Inc....E.......209 466-1952
302 S San Joaquin St Stockton (95203) ***(P-8536)***
New View Landscape Inc....D.......818 222-8972
24860 Calabasas Rd Calabasas (91302) ***(P-908)***
New Visa Health Services Inc....B.......760 723-0053
3414 Preakness Ct Fallbrook (92028) ***(P-21163)***
New Vista Behavioral Health....D.......949 284-0095
1901 Newport Blvd Ste 200 Costa Mesa (92627) ***(P-24813)***
New Vista Health Services....C.......310 477-5501
1516 Sawtelle Blvd Los Angeles (90025) ***(P-21164)***
New Vista Health Services....C.......818 352-1421
8647 Fenwick St Sunland (91040) ***(P-21165)***
New Vista Pst Act Care Cntr, Los Angeles *Also called New Vista Health Services* ***(P-21164)***
New Vsta Nrsing Rhbltation Ctr, Sunland *Also called New Vista Health Services* ***(P-21165)***
New Wave Entertainment, Burbank *Also called NW Entertainment Inc* ***(P-18087)***
New Wave Transport, Santa Fe Springs *Also called Gold Tree Inc* ***(P-27249)***
New Way Landscape & Tree Svcs....C.......858 505-8300
7485 Ronson Rd San Diego (92111) ***(P-909)***
New Way LLC....D.......925 688-1520
1130 Burnett Ave Ste G Concord (94520) ***(P-24610)***
New West Partitions....C.......916 456-8365
2550 Sutterville Rd Sacramento (95820) ***(P-2921)***
New York Life Insurance Co....B.......650 571-1220
1300 S El Cmno Real 400 San Mateo (94402) ***(P-10702)***
New York Life Insurance Co....D.......925 809-7020
191 Sand Creek Rd Ste 200 Brentwood (94513) ***(P-10140)***
New York Life Insurance Co....D.......714 255-5100
675 Placentia Ave Ste 250 Brea (92821) ***(P-10703)***
New York Life Insurance Co....D.......805 898-7625
3757 State St Ste 310 Santa Barbara (93105) ***(P-10704)***
New York Life Insurance Co....D.......818 662-7500
801 N Brand Blvd Glendale (91203) ***(P-10705)***
New York Life Insurance Co....D.......408 392-9782
1731 Tech Dr Ste 400 San Jose (95110) ***(P-10706)***
New York Life Insurance Co....D.......559 447-3900
205 E Rver Pk Cir Ste 250 Fresno (93720) ***(P-10707)***
New York Life Insurance Co....D.......951 354-2094
4204 Riverwalk Pkwy # 200 Riverside (92505) ***(P-10141)***
New York Life Insurance Co....D.......949 797-2400
2020 Main St Ste 1200 Irvine (92614) ***(P-10708)***
New York Life Insurance Co....E.......415 393-6060
425 Market St Fl 16 San Francisco (94105) ***(P-10709)***
New York Life Insurance Co....D.......916 774-6200
2999 Douglas Blvd Ste 350 Roseville (95661) ***(P-10710)***
New York Life Insurance Co....C.......858 623-8600
4365 Executive Dr Ste 800 San Diego (92121) ***(P-10711)***
New York Life Insurance Co....D.......415 999-9576
2633 Camino Ramon Ste 525 San Ramon (94583) ***(P-10712)***
New York Life Insurance Co....E.......805 656-4598
300 E Esplanade Dr # 2050 Oxnard (93036) ***(P-10713)***
New York Life Insurance Co....E.......323 782-3000
6300 Wilshire Blvd # 1900 Los Angeles (90048) ***(P-10714)***
New York Life Insurance Co....D.......559 447-3900
7112 N Fresno St Ste 100 Fresno (93720) ***(P-10715)***
New York Life Insurance Co....D.......909 305-6500
140 Via Verde Ste 200 San Dimas (91773) ***(P-10716)***
New-Jack Industries Inc....B.......310 297-3605
2613 Manhattan Beach Blvd # 100 Redondo Beach (90278) ***(P-16740)***
Newark Courtyard By Marriott....D.......510 792-5200
34905 Newark Blvd Newark (94560) ***(P-12953)***
NEWARK CRISIS CENTER, Newark *Also called Second Chance Inc* ***(P-24036)***
Neway Packaging Corp (PA)....D.......602 454-9000
1973 E Via Arado Rancho Dominguez (90220) ***(P-8111)***
Newbury Park Clinic, Newbury Park *Also called Timothy Everitt* ***(P-20210)***
Newco Distributors Inc....D.......909 291-2240
9060 Rochester Ave Rancho Cucamonga (91730) ***(P-9087)***
Newcomb Academy, Long Beach *Also called Long Beach Unified School Dst* ***(P-17301)***
Newland Group Inc (PA)....E.......858 455-7503
4790 Eastgate Mall # 150 San Diego (92121) ***(P-11897)***

Mergent e-mail: customerrelations@mergent.com
1398
2019 Directory of California
Wholesalers and Services Companies
(P-0000) Products & Services Section entry number
(PA)=Parent Co (HQ)=Headquarters (DH)=Div Headquarters

Newland Northwest, San Diego *Also called Newland Group Inc* ***(P-11897)***
Newland Real Estate Group LLC (HQ).....D.....858 455-7503
4790 Eastgate Mall # 150 San Diego (92121) ***(P-10098)***
Newma Garris Gilmo + Partne I.....D.....949 756-0818
3100 Bristol St Ste 400 Costa Mesa (92626) ***(P-26100)***
Newmark & Company RE Inc.....D.....714 667-8252
1551 N Tustin Ave Ste 300 Santa Ana (92705) ***(P-27366)***
Newmark & Company RE Inc.....D.....949 608-2000
4675 Macarthur Ct # 1600 Newport Beach (92660) ***(P-11627)***
Newmark Grubb Knight Frank, Santa Ana *Also called Newmark & Company RE Inc* ***(P-27366)***
Newmark Grubb Knight Frank, Newport Beach *Also called Newmark & Company RE Inc* ***(P-11627)***
Newmeyer & Dillion LLP (PA).....C.....949 854-7000
895 Dove St Fl 5 Newport Beach (92660) ***(P-23284)***
Newport Academy, Orange *Also called Monroe Operations LLC* ***(P-22036)***
Newport Apparel Corporation (PA).....D.....310 605-1900
1215 W Walnut St Compton (90220) ***(P-8326)***
Newport Bay Hospital, Newport Beach *Also called Beacon Healthcare Services* ***(P-21927)***
Newport Bch Marriott Ht & Spa, Newport Beach *Also called Host Hotels & Resorts LP* ***(P-12703)***
Newport Beach Country Club Inc.....D.....949 644-9550
1 Clubhouse Dr Newport Beach (92660) ***(P-18987)***
Newport Beach Orthopedic Inst.....D.....949 722-7038
22 Corporate Plaza Dr Newport Beach (92660) ***(P-19710)***
Newport Beach Surgery Ctr LLC.....C.....949 631-0988
361 Hospital Rd Ste 124 Newport Beach (92663) ***(P-19711)***
Newport Ch International LLC (PA).....D.....714 572-8881
1100 W Town And Country R Orange (92868) ***(P-7985)***
Newport Diagnostic Center Inc (PA).....D.....949 760-3025
1605 Avocado Ave Newport Beach (92660) ***(P-22116)***
Newport Diversified Inc.....C.....562 921-4359
13963 Alondra Blvd Santa Fe Springs (90670) ***(P-17351)***
Newport Diversified Inc.....D.....619 449-7800
1286 Fletcher Pkwy El Cajon (92020) ***(P-17352)***
Newport Fmly Mdcne/A Med Group.....D.....949 644-1025
520 Superior Ave Newport Beach (92663) ***(P-19712)***
Newport Group Inc (PA).....C.....925 328-4540
1350 Treat Blvd Ste 300 Walnut Creek (94597) ***(P-26960)***
Newport Harbor Radiology Assoc.....D.....949 721-8191
360 San Miguel Dr # 105106 Newport Beach (92660) ***(P-19713)***
Newport Hospitality Group Inc.....C.....661 323-1900
801 Truxtun Ave Bakersfield (93301) ***(P-12954)***
Newport Hotel Capital LLC.....C.....714 758-0900
1221 S Harbor Blvd Anaheim (92805) ***(P-12955)***
Newport Imaging Center, Newport Beach *Also called Newport Harbor Radiology Assoc* ***(P-19713)***
Newport Meat Company, Irvine *Also called Newport Meat Southern Cal Inc* ***(P-8622)***
Newport Meat Southern Cal Inc.....C.....949 399-4200
16691 Hale Ave Irvine (92606) ***(P-8622)***
Newport Mesa Memory Care Cmnty, Costa Mesa *Also called Silverado Senior Living Inc* ***(P-21211)***
Newport Pacific Capital Co Inc (PA).....C.....949 852-5575
17300 Red Hill Ave # 280 Irvine (92614) ***(P-11628)***
Newport Radio Surgery Center, Newport Beach *Also called Newport Diagnostic Center Inc* ***(P-22116)***
Newport Sbacute Healthcare Ctr.....C.....949 642-1974
2570 Newport Blvd Costa Mesa (92627) ***(P-20660)***
Newport Television LLC.....C.....559 761-0243
4880 N 1st St Fresno (93726) ***(P-18388)***
Newport Television LLC.....D.....661 283-1700
2120 L St Bakersfield (93301) ***(P-5827)***
Newshire Investment, Los Angeles *Also called Otts Asia* ***(P-12256)***
Newstar Fresh Foods LLC.....D.....831 758-7800
126 Sun St Salinas (93901) ***(P-546)***
Newstar Fresh Foods LLC (PA).....C.....888 782-7220
850 Work St Ste 101 Salinas (93901) ***(P-547)***
Newsways Distributors, Los Angeles *Also called Newsways Services Inc* ***(P-9118)***
Newsways Services Inc.....C.....323 258-6000
1324 Cypress Ave Los Angeles (90065) ***(P-9118)***
Newton Softed Inc.....E.....949 396-6192
2807 Mcgaw Ave Irvine (92614) ***(P-27800)***
Newval Chemical, Orange *Also called Marne Construction Inc* ***(P-3284)***
Newwest Funding, Downey *Also called Newwest Mortgage Company* ***(P-9899)***
Newwest Mortgage Company.....D.....562 861-8393
8255 Firestone Blvd # 101 Downey (90241) ***(P-9899)***
Nex Systems, Stockton *Also called Designers LLC* ***(P-13577)***
Nexa Technologies Inc (HQ).....D.....972 590-8669
18552 Macarthur Blvd # 100 Irvine (92612) ***(P-15307)***
Nexant Inc (PA).....D.....415 369-1000
101 2nd St Ste 1000 San Francisco (94105) ***(P-27801)***
Nexcare Collaborative (PA).....E.....818 907-0322
15477 Ventura Blvd Sherman Oaks (91403) ***(P-23939)***
Nexenta Systems Inc.....C.....408 791-3341
2025 Gateway Pl Ste 160 San Jose (95110) ***(P-15781)***
Nexgenix Inc (PA).....B.....714 665-6240
2 Peters Canyon Rd # 200 Irvine (92606) ***(P-15308)***
Nexinfo Solutions Inc.....E.....714 368-1452
8502 E Chapman Ave # 364 Orange (92869) ***(P-7084)***
Nexsentio Inc.....D.....408 392-9249
1346 Ridder Park Dr San Jose (95131) ***(P-14330)***
Nexstar Broadcasting Inc.....C.....559 222-2411
5035 E Mckinley Ave Fresno (93727) ***(P-5828)***
Nexstar Broadcasting Inc.....B.....415 441-4444
900 Front St Ste 300 San Francisco (94111) ***(P-5829)***
Nexstar Digital LLC.....D.....310 971-9300
12777 W Jefferson Blvd Los Angeles (90066) ***(P-13870)***
Next Door Sltons To Dom Vlence.....D.....408 279-2962
234 E Gish Rd Ste 200 San Jose (95112) ***(P-24814)***
Next Image Medical Inc (PA).....D.....858 847-9185
3390 Carmel Mountain Rd # 150 San Diego (92121) ***(P-27367)***
Next Issue Media LLC (PA).....D.....650 521-5151
1 Apple Park Way Cupertino (95014) ***(P-17353)***
Next Management LLC.....E.....323 782-0038
8447 Wilshire Blvd # 301 Beverly Hills (90211) ***(P-27368)***
Next Management Co, Beverly Hills *Also called Next Management LLC* ***(P-27368)***
Next Move, Sacramento *Also called Sacramento Area Emerg Housing* ***(P-24001)***
Next Venture Inc.....D.....818 637-2888
560 Rverdale Drv Glendale Glendale (91204) ***(P-1601)***
Nextdoorcom Inc.....D.....415 236-0000
875 Stevenson St Ste 100 San Francisco (94103) ***(P-24815)***
Nextel Communications Inc.....D.....323 290-2400
1810 W Slauson Ave Ste G Los Angeles (90047) ***(P-5412)***
Nextel Communications Inc.....D.....925 682-2355
272 Sun Valley Mall Concord (94520) ***(P-5413)***
Nextgen Healthcare Inc (PA).....C.....949 255-2600
18111 Von Karman Ave Irvine (92612) ***(P-15782)***
Nextgen Healthcare Info System (HQ).....D.....949 255-2600
18111 Von Karman Ave Irvine (92612) ***(P-15309)***
Nextpoint Inc (PA).....D.....310 360-5904
8750 Wilshire Blvd 300e Beverly Hills (90211) ***(P-5614)***
NFFE-IAM 2152, Needles *Also called International Assoc of Machini* ***(P-25062)***
Nfl Network, Culver City *Also called Nfl Properties LLC* ***(P-18389)***
Nfl Properties LLC.....B.....310 840-4635
10950 Wash Blvd Ste 100 Culver City (90232) ***(P-18389)***
Nfp Advisors, Simi Valley *Also called Nfp Property & Casualty Svcs* ***(P-27369)***
Nfp Property & Casualty Svcs.....E.....805 579-1900
2450 Tapo St Simi Valley (93063) ***(P-27369)***
NGL, Fontana *Also called Network Global Logistics LLC* ***(P-4845)***
NGS Fish House, Rancho Cucamonga *Also called Kings Seafood Company LLC* ***(P-8579)***
Ngs Group Inc.....D.....323 735-1700
4152 W Washington Blvd Los Angeles (90018) ***(P-8839)***
Nguyen, Myhanh MD, Sunnyvale *Also called Sutter Health* ***(P-19976)***
Nhca Inc.....C.....310 519-8200
2330 Grand Ave Long Beach (90815) ***(P-12956)***
Nhr Newco Holdings LLC (HQ).....C.....805 964-9975
6500 Hollister Ave # 210 Santa Barbara (93117) ***(P-7085)***
Nhra, Glendora *Also called National Hot Rod Association* ***(P-18541)***
Ni Ki Cruz LLC.....D.....408 332-7616
5255 Stevens Creek Blvd Santa Clara (95051) ***(P-27370)***
Niacc-Avitech Technologies Inc (PA).....D.....559 291-2500
245 W Dakota Ave Clovis (93612) ***(P-17964)***
Nibbelink Masonry Cnstr Corp.....D.....661 948-7859
2010 W Avenue K Lancaster (93536) ***(P-2818)***
Nibbi Bros Associates Inc.....C.....415 863-1820
1000 Brannan St Ste 102 San Francisco (94103) ***(P-1303)***
Nibbi Bros Concrete, San Francisco *Also called Nibbi Bros Associates Inc* ***(P-1303)***
Nic Partners, Rancho Cucamonga *Also called Network Intgrtion Partners Inc* ***(P-16017)***
Nice Avenue LLC.....D.....909 794-1189
2278 Nice Ave Mentone (92359) ***(P-20661)***
Nicholas A Stevens, Burlingame *Also called M H Podell Company* ***(P-11888)***
Nicholas B Macy Dvm.....D.....831 475-5400
2585 Soquel Dr Santa Cruz (95065) ***(P-608)***
Nicholas Grant Corporation.....D.....619 390-3900
12570 Highway 67 Lakeside (92040) ***(P-1826)***
Nicholas Lane Contractors Inc.....B.....714 630-7630
1157 N Red Gum St Anaheim (92806) ***(P-1208)***
Nichols Inst Reference Labs (HQ).....A.....949 728-4000
33608 Ortega Hwy San Juan Capistrano (92675) ***(P-22117)***
Nichols Lumber & Hardware Co.....D.....626 960-4802
13470 Dalewood St Baldwin Park (91706) ***(P-6842)***
Nichols Melburg Rossetto Assoc (PA).....E.....530 222-3300
300 Knollcrest Dr Redding (96002) ***(P-26101)***
Nick and MO, Irwindale *Also called Wor International Inc* ***(P-8283)***
Nicks Cove Inc.....D.....415 663-1033
23240 Ca 1 Marshall (94940) ***(P-12957)***
Nicola International Inc.....C.....818 767-1133
11119 Dora St Sun Valley (91352) ***(P-8840)***
Nicolaides Fink Thorpe Michael.....D.....415 745-3778
101 Montgomery St # 2300 San Francisco (94104) ***(P-23285)***
Nicole Pttrson Crt Rprting LLC.....E.....559 400-2407
545 E Alluvial Ave # 109 Fresno (93720) ***(P-23286)***
Nidek Incorporated.....E.....510 226-5700
47651 Westinghouse Dr Fremont (94539) ***(P-7238)***
Nielsen Claritas Inc.....B.....858 622-0800
9444 Waples St Ste 280 San Diego (92121) ***(P-15310)***
Nielsen Company (us) LLC.....B.....323 817-2000
6255 W Sunset Blvd Fl 20 Los Angeles (90028) ***(P-26550)***
Nielsen Company (us) LLC.....C.....858 677-9542
5375 Mira Sorrento Pl # 400 San Diego (92121) ***(P-26551)***
Nielsen Company (us) LLC.....D.....323 462-0050
6255 W Sunset Blvd Fl 19 Los Angeles (90028) ***(P-26552)***
Nielsen Media Research, Los Angeles *Also called Nielsen Company (us) LLC* ***(P-26550)***
Nielsen Mobile LLC (HQ).....C.....917 435-9301
1010 Battery St San Francisco (94111) ***(P-17354)***
Nielsens Creamery (PA).....D.....559 686-4744
21346 Road 140 Tulare (93274) ***(P-423)***
Nieves Landscape Inc.....C.....714 835-7332
1629 E Edinger Ave Santa Ana (92705) ***(P-910)***
Nifty Thrift, Concord *Also called Futures Explored* ***(P-23819)***
Nigal Inc (PA).....D.....619 428-5051
561 E San Ysidro Blvd A San Ysidro (92173) ***(P-5686)***
Nightingale Vantagemed Corp (HQ).....D.....916 638-4744
10670 White Rock Rd Rancho Cordova (95670) ***(P-15783)***
Nightrider Overnite Copy Svc, San Francisco *Also called Ricoh Usa Inc* ***(P-6979)***

ALPHABETIC

Employee Codes: A=Over 500 employees, B=251-500
C=101-250, D=51-100, E=50
2019 Directory of California
Wholesalers and Services Companies
© Mergent Inc. 1-800-342-5647
1399

Nightrider Overnite Copy Svc, Oakland *Also called Ricoh Usa Inc* ***(P-6981)***
Nihon Kohden America Inc (HQ)....D....949 580-1555
15353 Barranca Pkwy Irvine (92618) ***(P-7196)***
Nijjar Realty Inc (PA)....D....626 575-0062
4900 Santa Anita Ave 2b El Monte (91731) ***(P-11629)***
Nikewoman....E....408 942-6457
447 Great Mall Dr Milpitas (95035) ***(P-8363)***
Nikken Global Inc (HQ)....C....949 789-2000
2 Corporate Park Ste 100 Irvine (92606) ***(P-7891)***
Nikon Precision Inc (HQ)....C....650 508-4674
1399 Shoreway Rd Belmont (94002) ***(P-7780)***
Nines Restaurant....D....925 516-3413
100 Summerset Dr Brentwood (94513) ***(P-27371)***
Ninos Latino Unidos FSA....D....562 801-5454
10016 Pioneer Blvd # 123 Santa Fe Springs (90670) ***(P-24611)***
Ninth House Inc....E....612 339-0927
1 Montgomery St Ste 2200 San Francisco (94104) ***(P-24210)***
Ninth House Network, San Francisco *Also called Ninth House Inc* ***(P-24210)***
Ninyo & Moore Geotechnical (PA)....D....858 576-1000
5710 Ruffin Rd San Diego (92123) ***(P-27802)***
Ninyo & Moore Geotechnical....D....949 753-7070
475 Goddard Ste 200 Irvine (92618) ***(P-27803)***
Nipomo Dial A Ride....D....805 929-2881
179 Cross St San Luis Obispo (93401) ***(P-3825)***
Nippon Ex Nec Lgstics Amer Inc....D....310 604-6100
18615 S Ferris Pl Rancho Dominguez (90220) ***(P-4045)***
Nippon Express USA Inc....E....310 532-6300
970 Francisco St Torrance (90502) ***(P-5118)***
Nippon Express USA Inc....D....310 532-6300
300 Westmont Dr San Pedro (90731) ***(P-5119)***
Nippon Express USA Inc....D....310 535-7200
2233 E Grand Ave El Segundo (90245) ***(P-5120)***
Nippon Travel Agency Amer Inc....D....310 768-1817
1411 W 190th St Ste 650 Gardena (90248) ***(P-4944)***
Nippon Travel Agency PCF Inc (HQ)....D....310 768-0017
1025 W 190th St Ste 300 Gardena (90248) ***(P-4945)***
Nissan North America Inc....D....916 920-4712
3939 N Freeway Blvd Sacramento (95834) ***(P-4599)***
Nissan of Stockton, Lodi *Also called Lithia Automotive Group Inc* ***(P-17865)***
Nissen Vineyard Services Inc....D....707 963-3480
1226 Spring St Saint Helena (94574) ***(P-703)***
Nissin Intl Trnspt USA Inc (HQ)....E....310 222-8500
1540 W 190th St Torrance (90501) ***(P-5121)***
Nitai Partners Inc....D....855 879-2847
1761 Reichert Way Chula Vista (91913) ***(P-15311)***
Nitro Software Inc....C....415 632-4894
20 California St Ste 400 San Francisco (94111) ***(P-15312)***
Nittany Lion Landscaping Inc....D....714 635-1788
14770 Firestone Blvd # 203 La Mirada (90638) ***(P-911)***
Nitto Avecia Pharma Services (PA)....D....949 951-4425
10 Vanderbilt Irvine (92618) ***(P-26722)***
Nitto Denko Technical Corp....D....760 435-7011
501 Via Del Monte Oceanside (92058) ***(P-26553)***
Nix Neighborhood Lending, Manhattan Beach *Also called Kinecta Alternative Fin* ***(P-9686)***
Nixon Inc (PA)....C....760 944-0900
701 S Coast Highway 101 Encinitas (92024) ***(P-8012)***
Nixon Peabody LLP....C....415 984-8200
1 Embarcadero Ctr Fl 18 San Francisco (94111) ***(P-23287)***
Nixon Peabody LLP....D....213 629-6000
555 W 5th St Fl 30 Los Angeles (90013) ***(P-23288)***
Nixon Watches, Encinitas *Also called Nixon Inc* ***(P-8012)***
Nl Services, La Mirada *Also called Nittany Lion Landscaping Inc* ***(P-911)***
NLc Enterprises Incorporated....E....562 693-3590
15710 Leffingwell Rd Whittier (90604) ***(P-17355)***
Nliven, San Diego *Also called Defenseweb Technologies Inc* ***(P-16343)***
Nlsi, Moreno Valley *Also called National Lgal Studies Inst Inc* ***(P-17344)***
Nlyte Software Americas Ltd (HQ)....C....650 561-8200
2800 Campus Dr Ste 135 San Mateo (94403) ***(P-15784)***
Nmi Holdings Inc....B....855 530-6642
2100 Powell St Fl 12th Emeryville (94608) ***(P-10432)***
Nmi Industrial Holdings Inc....D....916 635-7030
8503 Weyand Ave Sacramento (95828) ***(P-25846)***
Nmms Twin Peaks LLC....D....818 710-6100
5850 Canoga Ave Ste 650 Woodland Hills (91367) ***(P-11630)***
NMN Construction Inc....D....707 763-6981
1077 Lakeville St Petaluma (94952) ***(P-3293)***
Nmr Design, Redding *Also called Nichols Melburg Rossetto Assoc* ***(P-26101)***
Nms Data Inc....E....949 472-2700
23172 Plaza Pointe Dr # 205 Laguna Hills (92653) ***(P-27804)***
Nms Management Inc....D....619 425-0440
155 W 35th St Ste A National City (91950) ***(P-14331)***
Nms Properties Inc....D....310 475-7600
1430 5th St Ste 101 Santa Monica (90401) ***(P-11631)***
Nmwd, Novato *Also called North Marin Water District* ***(P-6290)***
Nna Insurance Services, Chatsworth *Also called Nna Services LLC* ***(P-17356)***
NNA Insurance Services....C....818 739-4071
9350 De Soto Ave Chatsworth (91311) ***(P-10717)***
Nna Services, Chatsworth *Also called National Notary Association* ***(P-25029)***
NNA Services....C....818 739-4071
9350 De Soto Ave Chatsworth (91311) ***(P-25030)***
Nna Services LLC....C....818 739-4071
9350 De Soto Ave Chatsworth (91311) ***(P-17356)***
Nnj Services Inc....C....858 550-7900
9610 Waples St San Diego (92121) ***(P-11632)***
Nnn Realty Investors LLC....B....714 667-8252
19700 Fairchild Ste 300 Irvine (92612) ***(P-12249)***
Nnncc Ranch....D....559 626-4890
7602 Monson Ave Orange Cove (93646) ***(P-17357)***
Nnr Global Logistics USA Inc....C....310 357-2100
21023 Main St Ste D Carson (90745) ***(P-5122)***
No Barriers....D....707 451-1947
479 Mason St Ste 325 Vacaville (95688) ***(P-23940)***
No More Dirt Inc....C....415 821-6757
1699 Valencia St San Francisco (94110) ***(P-14332)***
No Ordinary Moments Inc....C....714 848-3800
16742 Gothard St Ste 115 Huntington Beach (92647) ***(P-22372)***
No Shnacks Inc....E....909 293-8747
7480 Harvard Ct Fontana (92336) ***(P-26961)***
Noah Concrete Corporation....D....408 842-7211
5900 Rossi Ln Gilroy (95020) ***(P-3294)***
Nob Hill Properties Inc....B....415 474-5400
1075 California St San Francisco (94108) ***(P-12958)***
Noble Aew Vineyard Creek LLC....D....707 284-1234
170 Railroad St Santa Rosa (95401) ***(P-12959)***
Noble Americas Enrgy Solutions, San Diego *Also called Calpine Energy Solutions LLC* ***(P-6180)***
Noble Credit Union (PA)....E....559 252-5000
2580 W Shaw Ln Frnt Fresno (93711) ***(P-9575)***
Noble Energy, Seal Beach *Also called Samedan Oil Corporation* ***(P-1028)***
Noble Rents Inc....D....855 767-4424
8314 Slauson Ave Pico Rivera (90660) ***(P-14450)***
Noble Tower Preservation LP....D....510 444-5228
1515 Lakeside Dr Oakland (94612) ***(P-11633)***
Noble/Utah Long Beach LLC....C....562 436-3000
333 E Ocean Blvd Long Beach (90802) ***(P-12960)***
Noblesse Oblige Inc....A....760 353-3336
2015 Silsbee Rd El Centro (92243) ***(P-482)***
Nohl Ranch Inn, Anaheim *Also called Leisure Care LLC* ***(P-24577)***
Noiro West LLC....C....619 819-6620
701 A St San Diego (92101) ***(P-12961)***
Noland Hamerly Etienne (PA)....E....831 372-7525
333 Salinas St Salinas (93901) ***(P-23289)***
Nolte Associates, Sacramento *Also called Nv5 Inc* ***(P-25849)***
Nolte, George S & Associates, San Diego *Also called Nv5 Inc* ***(P-25850)***
Nominum Inc (HQ)....E....650 381-6000
3355 Scott Blvd Fl 3 Santa Clara (95054) ***(P-15313)***
Nomura Securities Intl Inc....B....415 445-3831
425 California St # 2600 San Francisco (94104) ***(P-10007)***
Nongshim America Inc (HQ)....C....909 481-3698
12155 6th St Rancho Cucamonga (91730) ***(P-8435)***
Noodle Analytics Inc....D....415 412-2139
604 Mission St Fl 9 Flr 9 Oakland (94605) ***(P-15314)***
Noodle.ai, Oakland *Also called Noodle Analytics Inc* ***(P-15314)***
Nor-Cal Beverage Co Inc (PA)....B....916 372-0600
2150 Stone Blvd West Sacramento (95691) ***(P-9017)***
Nor-Cal Beverage Co Inc....C....714 526-8600
1226 N Olive St Anaheim (92801) ***(P-17358)***
Nor-Cal Medical Temps, Belvedere Tiburon *Also called Pharmacy Temps Inc* ***(P-14890)***
Nor-Cal Moving Services (PA)....C....510 371-4942
3129 Corporate Pl Hayward (94545) ***(P-4361)***
Nor-Cal Moving Services....D....408 954-1175
560 E Trimble Rd San Jose (95131) ***(P-4362)***
Nor-Cal Pipeline Services....D....530 673-3886
1875 S River Rd West Sacramento (95691) ***(P-1959)***
Nor-Cal Produce Inc....C....916 373-0830
2995 Oates St West Sacramento (95691) ***(P-8709)***
Nor-Wall Inc (PA)....E....707 445-5445
518 W Clark St Eureka (95501) ***(P-18988)***
Nora Lighting Inc....D....800 686-6672
6505 Gayhart St Commerce (90040) ***(P-7382)***
Noralco Inc....C....209 551-4545
20001 Mchenry Ave Escalon (95320) ***(P-548)***
Norcal Inc....C....714 224-3949
1400 Moonstone Brea (92821) ***(P-3052)***
Norcal Ambulance Services, Oakland *Also called North Star Emergency Svcs Inc* ***(P-3826)***
Norcal Beverage Co, Anaheim *Also called Nor-Cal Beverage Co Inc* ***(P-17358)***
Norcal Care Centers Inc....D....925 757-8787
1210 A St Antioch (94509) ***(P-21166)***
Norcal Gold Inc....E....916 984-8778
2340 E Bidwell St Folsom (95630) ***(P-11634)***
Norcal Inc....C....714 224-3949
1400 Moonstone Brea (92821) ***(P-3053)***
Norcal Mutual Insurance Co (PA)....B....415 397-9703
575 Market St Fl 10 San Francisco (94105) ***(P-10718)***
Norcal Painters Inc....D....415 566-6800
60 29th St 241 San Francisco (94110) ***(P-2461)***
Norco Auto Wash, Fountain Valley *Also called Norco Hills Car Wash* ***(P-17833)***
Norco Fire Department....A....951 737-8097
3902 Hillside Ave Norco (92860) ***(P-10490)***
Norco Hills Car Wash....E....951 279-4398
18020 Magnolia St Fountain Valley (92708) ***(P-17833)***
Norco Ranch Inc (HQ)....B....951 737-6735
12005 Cabernet Dr Fontana (92337) ***(P-433)***
Nordby Construction Co....E....707 526-4500
1550 Airport Blvd Ste 101 Santa Rosa (95403) ***(P-1602)***
Nordby Wine Caves, Santa Rosa *Also called Nordby Construction Co* ***(P-1602)***
Nordic Industries Inc....D....530 742-7124
1437 Furneaux Rd Olivehurst (95961) ***(P-2048)***
Nordic Security Services, Newport Beach *Also called Dansk Enterprises Inc* ***(P-16626)***
Nordic/Great Lakes E&I JV....D....530 742-7124
1437 Furneaux Rd Olivehurst (95961) ***(P-2049)***
Nordman Cormany Hair & Compton....C....805 485-1000
1000 Town Center Dr Fl 6 Oxnard (93036) ***(P-23290)***
Nordstrom, South Gate *Also called Rick Studer* ***(P-4252)***
Nordstrom Inc....B....909 390-1040
1600 S Milliken Ave Ontario (91761) ***(P-4600)***

Noritsu America Corporation (HQ)......C......714 521-9040
6900 Noritsu Ave Buena Park (90620) ***(P-6946)***
Noritz America Corporation (HQ)......D......714 433-2905
11160 Grace Ave Fountain Valley (92708) ***(P-7654)***
Norland Group......C......408 855-8255
3350 Scott Blvd Ste 6501 Santa Clara (95054) ***(P-16434)***
Norlyn Builders Newport Beach, Newport Beach *Also called Leisure Care Inc* ***(P-11053)***
Norman Fox & Co (PA)......D......626 581-5600
14970 Don Julian Rd City of Industry (91746) ***(P-8933)***
Norman Charter, Santa Fe Springs *Also called Norman International Inc* ***(P-6778)***
Norman Industrial Mtls Inc (PA)......B......818 729-3333
8300 San Fernando Rd Sun Valley (91352) ***(P-7293)***
Norman Industrial Mtls Inc......E......858 277-8200
7550 Ronson Rd San Diego (92111) ***(P-7294)***
Norman International Inc......D......562 946-0420
12301 Hawkins St Santa Fe Springs (90670) ***(P-6778)***
Norman S Wright Mech Eqp Corp (PA)......D......415 467-7600
99 S Hill Dr Ste A Brisbane (94005) ***(P-7655)***
Normand/Wlshire Rtrment Ht Inc......D......818 373-5429
6700 Sepulveda Blvd Van Nuys (91411) ***(P-11084)***
Normandie Casino & Showroom, Rancho Palos Verdes *Also called Normandie Club LP* ***(P-19209)***
Normandie Club LP......A......310 352-3486
57 Via Malona Rancho Palos Verdes (90275) ***(P-19209)***
Normandin Auto Brokers......D......408 266-2824
900 Cptl Expy Aut Mall San Jose (95136) ***(P-6606)***
Normandin Chrysler Jeep, San Jose *Also called Normandins* ***(P-17773)***
Normandins......C......877 330-0391
900 Cptl Expy Aut Mall San Jose (95136) ***(P-17773)***
Normans Nursery Inc (PA)......E......626 285-9795
8665 Duarte Rd San Gabriel (91775) ***(P-9152)***
Normans Nursery Inc......C......209 887-2033
6250 N Escalon Bellota Rd Linden (95236) ***(P-9153)***
Norogachi Construction Inc/CA......D......916 236-4201
600 Industrial Dr Ste 100 Galt (95632) ***(P-2922)***
Norse Dairy Systems, Los Angeles *Also called Interbake Foods LLC* ***(P-8805)***
Nortech Waste LLC......C......916 645-5230
3033 Fiddyment Rd Roseville (95747) ***(P-6423)***
North Amercn Science Assoc Inc......D......949 951-3110
9 Morgan Irvine (92618) ***(P-26723)***
North American Acceptance Corp......C......714 868-3195
3191 Red Hill Ave Ste 100 Costa Mesa (92626) ***(P-9725)***
North American Cinemas Inc......B......707 571-1412
409 Aviation Blvd Santa Rosa (95403) ***(P-18307)***
North American Health Care......D......530 662-9193
625 Cottonwood St Woodland (95695) ***(P-26962)***
North American Health Care Inc (PA)......C......949 240-2423
5150 E A Palma Ave 206 Anaheim (92807) ***(P-26963)***
North American Med MGT Cal Inc (HQ)......D......909 605-8000
3281 E Guasti Rd Fl 7 Ontario (91761) ***(P-26964)***
North American Security Inc......B......310 630-4840
550 E Carson Plaza Dr # 222 Carson (90746) ***(P-16741)***
North American Studio Alliance, Belmont *Also called Namasta Inc* ***(P-18982)***
North American Title Co Inc......D......925 399-3000
6612 Owens Dr 100 Pleasanton (94588) ***(P-10467)***
North American Van Lines, Corona *Also called South Coast Logistics* ***(P-4373)***
North American Van Lines, Newark *Also called Moving Solutions Inc* ***(P-4360)***
North Amrcn SEC Invstgtons Inc......B......323 634-1911
550 E Carson Plaza Dr Carson (90746) ***(P-16742)***
NORTH AREA COMMUNITY MENTAL HE, Sacramento *Also called Terkensha Associates Inc* ***(P-24084)***
North Bay Auto Auction, Fairfield *Also called Wind River Enterprises Inc* ***(P-6614)***
North Bay Construction Inc......D......707 283-0093
431 Payran St Petaluma (94952) ***(P-1827)***
North Bay Construction Inc......E......707 836-8500
930 Shiloh Rd Bldg 46 Windsor (95492) ***(P-3295)***
North Bay Developmental (PA)......D......707 256-1224
10 Executive Ct Ste A NAPA (94558) ***(P-24211)***
North Bay Distribution Inc......D......707 450-1219
2029 E Monte Vista Ave Vacaville (95688) ***(P-8271)***
North Bay Distribution Inc (PA)......D......707 452-9984
2050 Cessna Dr Vacaville (95688) ***(P-4601)***
North Bay Eye Assoc A Med Corp......D......707 206-0849
50 Professional Center Dr # 210 Rohnert Park (94928) ***(P-19714)***
North Bay Eye Assoc Med Group, Rohnert Park *Also called North Bay Eye Assoc A Med Corp* ***(P-19714)***
North Bay Pool and Spa, Monrovia *Also called Vivopools LLC* ***(P-17574)***
North Bay Regional Center, NAPA *Also called North Bay Developmental* ***(P-24211)***
North Brook Nursing and Rehab, Willits *Also called Ensign Willits LLC* ***(P-21064)***
North Coast Cleaning Services......E......707 269-0838
211 7th St Eureka (95501) ***(P-14333)***
North Coast Fabricators Inc......E......707 822-4629
4801 West End Rd Arcata (95521) ***(P-1423)***
North Coast Fisheries LLC......D......707 579-0679
2255 Challenger Way # 101 Santa Rosa (95407) ***(P-8584)***
North Coast Home Care Inc......D......760 260-8700
5731 Palmer Way Ste F Carlsbad (92010) ***(P-22373)***
North Coast Presbyterian Ch......D......760 753-2535
1831 S El Camino Real Encinitas (92024) ***(P-24353)***
North Coast Surgery Center......D......760 940-0997
3903 Waring Rd Oceanside (92056) ***(P-22624)***
North Counties Drywall Inc......E......707 996-0198
20563 Broadway Sonoma (95476) ***(P-2923)***
North County Health Prj Inc (PA)......C......760 736-6755
150 Valpreda Rd Frnt San Marcos (92069) ***(P-19715)***
North County Ob-Gyn Med Group (PA)......E......858 453-0753
9850 Genesee Ave Ste 600 La Jolla (92037) ***(P-19716)***
North County Services, San Marcos *Also called North County Health Prj Inc* ***(P-19715)***
North County Transit District (PA)......C......760 966-6500
810 Mission Ave Oceanside (92054) ***(P-3690)***
North Hollywood Medical Offs, North Hollywood *Also called Kaiser Foundation Hospitals* ***(P-19570)***
North La County Regional Ctr (PA)......B......818 778-1900
15400 Sherman Way Ste 170 Van Nuys (91406) ***(P-27805)***
North La County Regional Ctr......D......661 945-6761
43210 Gingham Ave Ste 6 Lancaster (93535) ***(P-27806)***
North Marin Water District (PA)......E......415 897-4133
999 Rush Creek Pl Novato (94945) ***(P-6290)***
North Modesto Kiwanis Club, Modesto *Also called Kiwanis International Inc* ***(P-25179)***
North Orange Cnty Fmly Y M C A, Fullerton *Also called YMCA of North Orange County* ***(P-25292)***
North Orange Coast Pntg Inc......D......951 279-2694
3969 Sierra Ave Norco (92860) ***(P-2462)***
North Orange County Svc Ctr, Fullerton *Also called Southern California Edison Co* ***(P-6122)***
North Pacific Resources Inc......D......206 676-3828
333 S Grand Ave Ste 4200 Los Angeles (90071) ***(P-8585)***
North Pt Hlth Wellness Ctr LLC......D......559 320-2200
668 E Bullard Ave Fresno (93710) ***(P-20662)***
North Ranch Country Club......C......818 889-3531
4761 Valley Spring Dr Westlake Village (91362) ***(P-18989)***
North Ridge Country Club......D......916 967-5717
7600 Madison Ave Fair Oaks (95628) ***(P-18990)***
North River Ranch LLC......E......714 556-6244
3601 W Pendleton Ave Santa Ana (92704) ***(P-110)***
North San Jose Job Center, San Jose *Also called Work2future Foundation* ***(P-24252)***
North Shore Greenhouses Inc......C......760 397-0400
82900 Johnson St Thermal (92274) ***(P-319)***
North Shore Investment Inc......D......707 464-6151
1280 Marshall St Crescent City (95531) ***(P-20663)***
North Shore Living Herbs, Thermal *Also called North Shore Greenhouses Inc* ***(P-319)***
North Sonoma County Hosp Dst......C......707 431-6500
1375 University St Healdsburg (95448) ***(P-21605)***
North Star Building Maint Inc......D......805 518-0417
2828 Cochran St Ste 214 Simi Valley (93065) ***(P-14334)***
North Star Emergency Svcs Inc......D......510 452-3400
2537 Willow St Oakland (94607) ***(P-3826)***
North State Elec Contrs Inc......D......916 572-0571
11415 Sunrise Gold Cir # 1 Rancho Cordova (95742) ***(P-2663)***
North State Imaging, Chico *Also called North State Radiology* ***(P-19717)***
North State Radiology......E......530 898-0504
1702 Esplanade Chico (95926) ***(P-19717)***
North State Security Inc......D......530 243-0295
1970 Hartnell Ave Redding (96002) ***(P-16743)***
North Valley Construction Inc......D......925 373-1246
4010 Raymond Rd Livermore (94551) ***(P-3557)***
North Valley Nursing Center, Tujunga *Also called Sun Mar Management Services* ***(P-27052)***
North Valley Occupational Ctr, Mission Hills *Also called Los Angeles Unified School Dst* ***(P-24202)***
North West Learning Center......E......559 228-3057
3485 W Ashcroft Ave Fresno (93722) ***(P-24354)***
North Wind Cnstr Svcs LLC......D......916 333-3015
730 Howe Ave Ste 700 Sacramento (95825) ***(P-1209)***
Northbay Healthcare Corp (PA)......C......707 646-5000
1200 B Gale Wilson Blvd Fairfield (94533) ***(P-21606)***
Northbay Healthcare Group (PA)......A......707 646-5000
1200 B Gale Wilson Blvd Fairfield (94533) ***(P-21607)***
Northbay Healthcare System, Fairfield *Also called Northbay Healthcare Corp* ***(P-21606)***
Northbay Medical Center, Fairfield *Also called Northbay Healthcare Group* ***(P-21607)***
Northcoast Childrens Services......D......530 629-2283
730 Hwy 96 Willow Creek (95573) ***(P-23941)***
Northcountry Clinic......D......707 822-2481
785 18th St Arcata (95521) ***(P-19718)***
Northeast Community Clinic......D......323 373-9400
3751 S Harvard Blvd Los Angeles (90018) ***(P-19719)***
Northeast Community Clinics, Los Angeles *Also called La Vida Mltispecialty Med Ctrs* ***(P-19640)***
Northeast Protective Svcs Inc......D......800 577-0899
16040 Peppertree Ln La Mirada (90638) ***(P-16744)***
Northeast Valley Health Corp......D......818 340-3570
7107 Remmet Ave Canoga Park (91303) ***(P-22848)***
Northeast Valley Health Corp......D......818 432-4400
7223 Fair Ave Sun Valley (91352) ***(P-22849)***
Northeast Valley Health Corp (PA)......D......818 898-1388
1172 N Maclay Ave San Fernando (91340) ***(P-23942)***
Northeast Valley Health Corp......D......818 365-8086
1600 San Fernando Rd San Fernando (91340) ***(P-19720)***
Northeast Valley Health Corp......D......818 896-0531
12756 Van Nuys Blvd Pacoima (91331) ***(P-19721)***
Northeastern Rur Hlth Clinics (PA)......D......530 251-5000
1850 Spring Ridge Dr Susanville (96130) ***(P-19722)***
Northern CA Cngrgtnl Rtmt......C......831 624-1281
8545 Carmel Valley Rd Carmel (93923) ***(P-21167)***
Northern CA Retiredd Ofcrs......C......707 432-1200
2600 Estates Dr Fairfield (94533) ***(P-24612)***
Northern Cal Rehabilitation, Redding *Also called Ocadian Care Centers LLC* ***(P-20673)***
Northern Cal Ret Clks-Emp Fund......C......925 746-7530
190 N Wiget Ln Ste 110 Walnut Creek (94598) ***(P-12117)***
Northern Cal Yuth Fmly Prgrams (PA)......D......530 893-2316
2577 California Park Dr Chico (95928) ***(P-23943)***
Northern California Cardiology (PA)......D......916 733-1788
5301 F St Ste 117 Sacramento (95819) ***(P-19723)***
Northern California Hlth Care......D......530 223-2332
16201 Plateau Cir Redding (96001) ***(P-22374)***
Northern California Inalliance......C......530 633-9695
411 4th St Wheatland (95692) ***(P-23944)***

Employee Codes: A=Over 500 employees, B=251-500
C=101-250, D=51-100, E=50
2019 Directory of California
Wholesalers and Services Companies
© Mergent Inc. 1-800-342-5647
1401

Northern California Inalliance (PA) ....C....916 381-1300
6950 21st Ave Sacramento (95820) ***(P-23945)***
Northern California Institute ....B....415 750-6954
4150 Clement St San Francisco (94121) ***(P-24816)***
Northern California Mkt Area, Sacramento *Also called Veritiv Operating Company* ***(P-8131)***
Northern California Power Agcy (PA) ....D....916 781-3636
651 Commerce Dr Roseville (95678) ***(P-6057)***
Northern California Power Agcy ....D....707 987-2381
12000 Ridge Rd Middletown (95461) ***(P-6058)***
Northern California Presbyteri ....D....415 464-1767
501 Via Casitas Ofc Greenbrae (94904) ***(P-21168)***
Northern California Presbyteri ....B....415 922-9700
1400 Geary Blvd San Francisco (94109) ***(P-20664)***
Northern California Region, San Mateo *Also called Securitas SEC Svcs USA Inc* ***(P-16936)***
Northern California Region, Stockton *Also called Securitas SEC Svcs USA Inc* ***(P-16789)***
Northern California Region, Fresno *Also called Securitas SEC Svcs USA Inc* ***(P-16790)***
Northern California Region, Redding *Also called Securitas SEC Svcs USA Inc* ***(P-16795)***
Northern California Region, Petaluma *Also called Securitas SEC Svcs USA Inc* ***(P-16798)***
Northern California Region, Eureka *Also called Securitas SEC Svcs USA Inc* ***(P-16800)***
Northern California Region, Palm Desert *Also called Securitas SEC Svcs USA Inc* ***(P-16803)***
Northern California Region, Salinas *Also called Securitas SEC Svcs USA Inc* ***(P-16804)***
Northern California Region, Oakland *Also called Securitas SEC Svcs USA Inc* ***(P-16805)***
Northern California Regional, Sacramento *Also called Granite Construction Company* ***(P-2035)***
Northern California Rehab ....C....530 246-9000
2801 Eureka Way Redding (96001) ***(P-21608)***
Northern Cnstr & Operations, Escondido *Also called San Diego Gas & Electric Co* ***(P-6202)***
Northern Division, Pittsburg *Also called Arb Inc* ***(P-4530)***
Northern Hydro, Big Creek *Also called Southern California Edison Co* ***(P-6115)***
Northern Inyo Healthcare Dst ....B....760 873-5811
150 Pioneer Ln Bishop (93514) ***(P-21609)***
Northern Inyo Hospital, Bishop *Also called Northern Inyo Healthcare Dst* ***(P-21609)***
Northern Mono Chamber Commerce ....E....530 208-6078
115281 Us Highway 395 Topaz (96133) ***(P-24971)***
Northern Queen Inc ....D....530 265-4492
400 Railroad Ave Nevada City (95959) ***(P-12962)***
Northern Queen Inn, Nevada City *Also called Northern Queen Inc* ***(P-12962)***
Northern Reg. Sub Base, Bakersfield *Also called Southern California Gas Co* ***(P-6165)***
Northern Rfrigerated Trnsp Inc (PA) ....C....209 664-3800
2700 W Main St Turlock (95380) ***(P-4236)***
Northern Trust Company ....E....310 282-3800
2049 Century Park E # 3600 Los Angeles (90067) ***(P-9361)***
Northern Valley Catholic Socia ....C....530 241-0552
2400 Washington Ave Redding (96001) ***(P-23946)***
Northern Vly Indian Hlth Inc ....D....530 896-9400
845 W East Ave Chico (95926) ***(P-20131)***
Northern Vly Indian Hlth Inc ....D....530 661-4400
175 W Court St Woodland (95695) ***(P-21967)***
Northgate Branch, San Rafael *Also called Bank of Marin* ***(P-9413)***
Northgate Care Center ....D....415 479-1230
40 Professional Ctr Pkwy San Rafael (94903) ***(P-21169)***
Northgate Convalescent Hosp, San Rafael *Also called Independent Quality Care Inc* ***(P-21117)***
Northgate Ter Cmnty Partner LP ....E....510 465-9346
550 24th St Oakland (94612) ***(P-11635)***
Northgate Terrace Apts ....D....530 671-2026
1290 Northgate Dr Apt 48 Yuba City (95991) ***(P-11085)***
Northland Control Systems Inc (PA) ....D....510 226-1015
1533 California Cir Milpitas (95035) ***(P-2664)***
Northpoint Day Treatment Sch, Northridge *Also called Child and Family Guidance Ctr* ***(P-22528)***
Northpointe Apartment Homes, Long Beach *Also called Parwood Preservation LP* ***(P-11664)***
Northpointe Healthcare Centre, Fresno *Also called North Pt Hlth Wellness Ctr LLC* ***(P-20662)***
Northridge 07 A LLC ....D....818 505-6777
12411 Ventura Blvd Studio City (91604) ***(P-10920)***
Northridge Fashion Center, Northridge *Also called Lansing Mall Ltd Partnership* ***(P-10906)***
Northridge Fashion Center 10, Northridge *Also called Pacific Theaters* ***(P-18254)***
Northridge Nursing Center, Reseda *Also called Longwood Management Corp* ***(P-21569)***
Northrop Grumman Federal Cr Un (PA) ....D....310 808-4000
879 W 190th St Ste 800 Gardena (90248) ***(P-9642)***
Northrop Grumman Systems Corp ....B....310 556-4911
6411 W Imperial Hwy Los Angeles (90045) ***(P-17359)***
Northrop Grumman Systems Corp ....B....858 514-0400
9326 Spectrum Center Blvd San Diego (92123) ***(P-15315)***
Northrop Grumman Systems Corp ....A....858 592-3000
1 Rancho Carmel Dr San Diego (92128) ***(P-26424)***
Northrop Grumman Systems Corp ....C....650 604-6056
P.O. Box 81 Moffett Field (94035) ***(P-16019)***
Northrop Grumman Systems Corp ....D....805 987-9739
5161 Verdugo Way Camarillo (93012) ***(P-16020)***
Northstar, Irvine *Also called Custom Business Solutions Inc* ***(P-6958)***
Northstar Contg Group Inc ....D....714 639-7600
13320 Cambridge St Santa Fe Springs (90670) ***(P-3458)***
Northstar Contg Group Inc (HQ) ....D....510 491-1330
2614-20 Barrington Ct Hayward (94545) ***(P-3558)***
Northstar Dem & Remediation LP (HQ) ....C....714 672-3500
404 N Berry St Brea (92821) ***(P-3459)***
Northstar Senior Living Inc ....A....530 242-8300
2334 Washington Ave Ste A Redding (96001) ***(P-26965)***
Northstar Technology Corp (PA) ....C....949 788-0738
32 Mauchly Ste C Irvine (92618) ***(P-15316)***
Northstar-At-Tahoe, Truckee *Also called Trimont Land Company* ***(P-11802)***
Northstate Plastering Inc ....D....707 207-0950
2210 Cordelia Rd Fairfield (94534) ***(P-3296)***
Northwest Excavating Inc ....D....818 349-5861
18201 Napa St Northridge (91325) ***(P-14451)***
Northwest Hotel Corporation (PA) ....D....714 776-6120
1380 S Harbor Blvd Anaheim (92802) ***(P-12963)***
Northwest Insurance Agency ....D....707 573-1300
418 B St Ste 100 Santa Rosa (95401) ***(P-10719)***
Northwest Landscape Maint Co ....E....408 298-6489
283 Kinney Dr San Jose (95112) ***(P-912)***
Northwest Medical Group Inc ....D....559 271-6302
7355 N Palm Ave Ste 100 Fresno (93711) ***(P-19724)***
Northwest Medical Pharmacy, Fresno *Also called Northwest Physicians Med Group* ***(P-19725)***
Northwest Physicians Med Group ....D....559 271-6370
7355 N Palm Ave Ste 100 Fresno (93711) ***(P-19725)***
Northwest Staffing Resources ....A....916 960-2668
701 University Ave # 120 Sacramento (95825) ***(P-14673)***
Northwestern Bell Telephones, City of Industry *Also called Unical Enterprises Inc* ***(P-7124)***
Northwestern Mutl Fincl Netwrk (PA) ....C....619 234-3111
4225 Executive Sq La Jolla (92037) ***(P-10720)***
NORTON SCIENCE AND LANGUAGE AC, Apple Valley *Also called High Desert Partnership* ***(P-26527)***
Norton Simon Museum ....D....626 449-6840
411 W Colorado Blvd Pasadena (91105) ***(P-24896)***
Norwalk Community Hospital ....D....562 863-4763
13222 Bloomfield Ave Norwalk (90650) ***(P-21610)***
Norwalk La Mirada Unif ....D....714 521-0970
15135 Escalona Rd La Mirada (90638) ***(P-25031)***
Norwalk Marriott Hotel, Paramount *Also called Goldenpark LLC* ***(P-12609)***
Norwalk Meadows Nursing Ctr LP ....C....562 864-2541
10625 Leffingwell Rd Norwalk (90650) ***(P-20665)***
Norwalk Medical Offices, Norwalk *Also called Kaiser Foundation Hospitals* ***(P-19572)***
Norwalk Transit System ....D....562 929-5550
12650 Imperial Hwy Norwalk (90650) ***(P-3691)***
Norwest Venture Partners VI LP ....D....650 289-2243
525 University Ave # 800 Palo Alto (94301) ***(P-12250)***
Nossaman LLP (PA) ....D....213 612-7800
777 S Figueroa St # 3400 Los Angeles (90017) ***(P-23291)***
Nossaman LLP ....D....760 918-0500
1925 Palomar Oaks Way # 220 Carlsbad (92008) ***(P-23292)***
Nossaman LLP ....E....415 398-3600
50 California St Ste 3400 San Francisco (94111) ***(P-23293)***
Nossaman LLP ....E....949 833-7800
18101 Von Karman Ave # 1800 Irvine (92612) ***(P-23294)***
Not Your Daughters Jeans, Vernon *Also called Nydj Apparel LLC* ***(P-8327)***
Notellage Corporation ....E....323 257-8151
4681 Eagle Rock Blvd Los Angeles (90041) ***(P-21170)***
Notthoff Engineering, Huntington Beach *Also called AMG Huntington Beach LLC* ***(P-25535)***
Nourmand & Associates ....E....310 274-4000
421 N Beverly Dr Ste 200 Beverly Hills (90210) ***(P-11636)***
Nova ATL Elc A Joint Ventr ....D....707 265-1100
185 Devlin Rd NAPA (94558) ***(P-2050)***
Nova Brink A Joint Venture ....D....707 265-1100
185 Devlin Rd NAPA (94558) ***(P-2051)***
Nova Container Freight Station, Carson *Also called H Rauvel Inc* ***(P-4570)***
Nova Group Inc ....C....707 265-1100
185 Devlin Rd NAPA (94558) ***(P-1960)***
Nova Grp Inc -Obayashi Corp A ....E....707 265-1116
185 Devlin Rd NAPA (94558) ***(P-1961)***
Nova Lane Constructors A JV ....D....707 265-1100
185 Devlin Rd NAPA (94558) ***(P-2052)***
Nova Ortho-Med Inc (PA) ....E....310 352-3600
1470 Beachey Pl Carson (90746) ***(P-7197)***
Nova Plumbing Inc ....C....714 556-6682
3111 W Central Ave Santa Ana (92704) ***(P-2290)***
Nova-Cpf Inc ....C....707 257-3200
7411 Napa Vallejo Hwy NAPA (94558) ***(P-1962)***
Nova/Tic Gov Proj JV ....C....707 257-3200
185 Devlin Rd NAPA (94558) ***(P-1963)***
Novalogic Inc (PA) ....D....818 880-1997
27489 Agoura Rd Ste 300 Agoura Hills (91301) ***(P-15317)***
Novariant Inc (PA) ....D....510 933-4800
46610 Landing Pkwy Fremont (94538) ***(P-25847)***
Novartis Institut ....D....858 812-1976
10675 John J Hopkins Dr San Diego (92121) ***(P-26643)***
Novastar Post Inc ....D....323 467-5020
23466 Hatteras St Woodland Hills (91367) ***(P-18086)***
Novatime Technology Inc (HQ) ....D....909 895-8100
9680 Haven Ave Ste 200 Rancho Cucamonga (91730) ***(P-14674)***
Novato Fire Protection Dist ....D....415 878-2690
95 Rowland Way Novato (94945) ***(P-17360)***
Novato Healthcare Center LLC ....C....415 897-6161
1565 Hill Rd Novato (94947) ***(P-20666)***
Novato Medical Offices, Novato *Also called Kaiser Foundation Hospitals* ***(P-21506)***
Novo Construction Inc (PA) ....C....650 701-1500
1460 Obrien Dr Menlo Park (94025) ***(P-1603)***
Novo Engineering Inc (PA) ....D....760 598-6686
1350 Specialty Dr Ste A Vista (92081) ***(P-25848)***
Novo Nordisk Biotech, Davis *Also called Novozymes Inc* ***(P-26554)***
Novogradac and Co LLP ....E....415 356-8000
246 1st St Ste 500 San Francisco (94105) ***(P-26262)***
Novozymes Inc (HQ) ....D....530 757-8100
1445 Drew Ave Davis (95618) ***(P-26554)***
Novozymes Us Inc ....A....530 757-8100
1445 Drew Ave Davis (95618) ***(P-11995)***
Now Medical Services Inc ....D....310 479-4520
1641 1/2 Westwood Blvd Los Angeles (90024) ***(P-14888)***
Nowcom Corporation ....D....323 938-6449
4751 Wilshire Blvd # 205 Los Angeles (90010) ***(P-16435)***

Mergent e-mail: customerrelations@mergent.com
1402
2019 Directory of California Wholesalers and Services Companies
(P-0000) Products & Services Section entry number
(PA)=Parent Co (HQ)=Headquarters (DH)=Div Headquarters

Nowher Partners LLC	D	818 857-3366
26767 Agoura Rd Ste A Calabasas (91302) *(P-8841)*		
Npario Inc	D	650 461-9696
350 Cambridge Ave Ste 330 Palo Alto (94306) *(P-15318)*		
Nph Medical Services	D	530 899-2255
555 Flying V St Ste 5 Chico (95928) *(P-14675)*		
Nphase LLC	D	312 577-1650
6195 Lusk Blvd Ste 200 San Diego (92121) *(P-5989)*		
Npl Anaheim Investments LLC	D	714 750-2010
2010 S Harbor Blvd Anaheim (92802) *(P-12964)*		
NPS Marketing	B	916 941-5510
3381 Sage Rose Ln Placerville (95667) *(P-27372)*		
Nr 2 Group Inc	E	626 251-6681
1561 Chapin Unit C Baldwin Park (91706) *(P-4046)*		
NRC Environmental Services Inc	D	562 432-1304
3777 Long Beach Blvd Long Beach (90807) *(P-6424)*		
NRC Environmental Services Inc (HQ)	D	510 749-1390
1605 Ferry Pt Alameda (94501) *(P-6543)*		
Nrea-TRC 711 LLC	C	213 488-3500
711 S Hope St Los Angeles (90017) *(P-12965)*		
NRG California South LP	D	909 899-7241
8996 Etiwanda Ave Rancho Cucamonga (91739) *(P-6059)*		
NRG Clean Power Inc	E	818 444-2020
7012 Owensmouth Ave Canoga Park (91303) *(P-6060)*		
NRG El Segundo Operations Inc	D	310 615-6344
301 Vista Del Mar El Segundo (90245) *(P-6061)*		
NRG Energy Inc	D	415 255-8105
455 Golden Gate Ave San Francisco (94102) *(P-6062)*		
NRG Energy Inc	D	913 689-3904
3201 Wilbur Ave Antioch (94509) *(P-6063)*		
NRG Power Inc	D	714 424-6484
3011 S Shannon St Santa Ana (92704) *(P-2665)*		
Nrhc, Susanville Also called Northeastern Rur Hlth Clinics (P-19722)		
Nri Distribution, Los Angeles Also called Nri Usa LLC (P-5123)		
Nri Usa LLC (PA)	D	323 345-6456
13200 S Broadway Los Angeles (90061) *(P-5123)*		
Nri Usa LLC	D	323 345-6456
227 E Compton Blvd Gardena (90248) *(P-5124)*		
NRLL LLC	E	949 768-7777
1 Mauchly Irvine (92618) *(P-12251)*		
Nrp Holding Co Inc (PA)	C	949 583-1000
1 Mauchly Irvine (92618) *(P-11996)*		
Nrt, Concord Also called Goldman Avram (P-26874)		
Nrt Commercial Utah LLC	D	626 449-5222
42 S Pasadena Ave Pasadena (91105) *(P-11637)*		
Nsbn, Los Angeles Also called Cliftonlarsonallen LLP (P-26168)		
Nsg Technology Inc	B	408 547-8700
1705 Junction Ct Ste 200 San Jose (95112) *(P-17906)*		
Nsv International Corp	D	562 438-3836
1250 E 29th St Signal Hill (90755) *(P-6661)*		
Nsw Real Estate Holdings LLC	D	415 467-7600
99 S Hill Dr Ste A Brisbane (94005) *(P-11638)*		
Nt Sunset Inc	E	510 420-3772
2220 Livingston St # 201 Oakland (94606) *(P-26644)*		
Nta America, Gardena Also called Nippon Travel Agency Amer Inc (P-4944)		
Nta Pacific, Gardena Also called Nippon Travel Agency PCF Inc (P-4945)		
Ntent Inc	D	760 930-7600
1808 Aston Ave Ste 170 Carlsbad (92008) *(P-15319)*		
Nth Connect Telecom Inc	D	408 922-0800
2371 Bering Dr San Jose (95131) *(P-17361)*		
Nth Degree Inc	E	714 734-4155
27092 Burbank Foothill Ranch (92610) *(P-17362)*		
NTN Buzztime Inc (PA)	D	760 438-7400
2231 Rutherford Rd # 200 Carlsbad (92008) *(P-5830)*		
Ntrepid Corporation	D	800 921-2414
10201 Wtridge Cir Ste 300 San Diego (92121) *(P-26966)*		
Ntrepid LLC	D	858 866-1309
10201 Wtridge Cir Ste 300 San Diego (92121) *(P-16436)*		
Ntrust Infotech Inc	D	562 207-1600
230 Commerce Ste 180 Irvine (92602) *(P-15785)*		
NTS It Care Inc	C	408 480-4083
1605 S Main St Ste 125 Milpitas (95035) *(P-15320)*		
NTS Silicon Valley, Fremont Also called National Technical Systems Inc (P-25842)		
NTS Technical Systems	D	909 382-2360
3505 E 3rd St San Bernardino (92408) *(P-26724)*		
NTS Technical Systems	C	714 998-4351
1536 E Valencia Dr Fullerton (92831) *(P-26725)*		
NTS Technical Systems	D	661 259-8184
20970 Centre Pointe Pkwy Santa Clarita (91350) *(P-27807)*		
Ntt Data Inc	D	213 228-2500
1000 Corporate Center Dr # 140 Monterey Park (91754) *(P-16021)*		
Ntt Data Services Corporation	D	310 342-3200
6701 Center Dr W Ste 1000 Los Angeles (90045) *(P-16271)*		
Nu Flow America Inc (PA)	D	619 275-9130
7710 Kenamar Ct San Diego (92121) *(P-2291)*		
Nu Horizons Electronics Corp	E	408 946-4154
890 N Mccarthy Blvd San Jose (95131) *(P-7515)*		
Nuance Communications Inc	C	781 565-5000
1198 E Arques Ave Sunnyvale (94085) *(P-15786)*		
Nuance Communications Inc	C	650 847-0000
1005 Hamilton Ct Menlo Park (94025) *(P-15321)*		
Nucompass Mobility Svcs LLC (PA)	D	925 734-3434
6800 Koll Center Pkwy Pleasanton (94566) *(P-17363)*		
Nucourse Distribution Inc	D	866 655-4366
22342 Avenida Empresa # 200 Rcho STA Marg (92688) *(P-7516)*		
Nuevacare LLC	D	650 396-3596
2100 Geng Rd Ste 210 Palo Alto (94303) *(P-20667)*		
Nuevo Amnecer Latino Chld Svcs (PA)	D	323 720-9951
5400 Pomona Blvd Los Angeles (90022) *(P-23947)*		

Nugget Market Inc	C	530 662-5479
157 Main St Woodland (95695) *(P-4602)*		
Nugget Mkts Pharmacy, Woodland Also called Nugget Market Inc (P-4602)		
Nulaid Foods (PA)	D	209 599-2121
200 W 5th St Ripon (95366) *(P-8537)*		
Numbers Only Inc	D	408 689-7258
4320 Stevens Creek Blvd San Jose (95129) *(P-16437)*		
Numero Uno Market	D	323 231-9403
4373 S Vermont Ave Los Angeles (90037) *(P-12252)*		
Numero Uno Market	D	213 381-1734
9127 S Figueroa St Los Angeles (90003) *(P-12253)*		
Nuna Health, San Francisco Also called Nuna Incorporated (P-15322)		
Nuna Incorporated	D	415 942-5200
650 Townsend St Ste 425 San Francisco (94103) *(P-15322)*		
Nunes Company Inc (PA)	E	831 751-7510
925 Johnson Ave Salinas (93901) *(P-8710)*		
Nunes Cooling Inc	E	831 751-7510
925 Johnson Ave Salinas (93901) *(P-549)*		
Nurlogic Design Inc (HQ)	D	858 455-7570
5580 Morehouse Dr San Diego (92121) *(P-16022)*		
Nurse Providers Inc	A	650 992-8559
355 Gellert Blvd Ste 110 Daly City (94015) *(P-14676)*		
Nursecore Management Svcs LLC	D	805 938-7660
1010 S Broadway Santa Maria (93454) *(P-24613)*		
Nursefinders LLC (HQ)	C	858 314-7427
12400 High Bluff Dr San Diego (92130) *(P-14677)*		
Nurses & Prof Hlth Care, Chico Also called Nph Medical Services (P-14675)		
Nurses Internet Staffing Svcs (PA)	C	323 720-9900
6055 E Wash Blvd Ste 409 Commerce (90040) *(P-14678)*		
Nurses Tuch HM Hlth Prvder Inc	E	818 500-4877
135 S Jackson St Ste 100 Glendale (91205) *(P-22375)*		
Nursing & Rehab At Home	D	650 286-4272
1660 S Amphlett Blvd # 112 San Mateo (94402) *(P-22376)*		
Nursing Registry, Daly City Also called Nurse Providers Inc (P-14676)		
Nurturing Tots Inc	D	818 996-1602
3784 Winford Dr Tarzana (91356) *(P-24355)*		
Nushake Inc	D	209 239-8616
319 S Parallel Ave Ripon (95366) *(P-3181)*		
Nushake Roofing, Ripon Also called Nushake Inc (P-3181)		
Nussbaum, Barry Company, Solana Beach Also called BNC Real Estate (P-11248)		
Nutanix Inc (PA)	D	408 216-8360
1740 Tech Dr Ste 150 San Jose (95110) *(P-15323)*		
Nutec Enterprises Inc	D	661 287-3200
24200 Magic Mountain Pkwy # 105 Valencia (91355) *(P-11639)*		
Nutra-Figs, Fresno Also called San Joaquin Figs Inc (P-564)		
Nutrien AG Solutions Inc	D	760 355-1133
305 Larsen Rd Imperial (92251) *(P-9088)*		
Nutrien AG Solutions Inc	D	805 922-5848
1335 W Main St Santa Maria (93458) *(P-9089)*		
Nutrien AG Solutions Inc	E	559 884-6010
21929 S Lassen Five Points (93624) *(P-9090)*		
Nutrien AG Solutions Inc	D	831 757-5391
1143 Terven Ave Salinas (93901) *(P-9091)*		
Nutririon Services, Santa Ana Also called Santa Ana Unified School Dst (P-22879)		
Nutrition Service Division, Long Beach Also called Women Infant & Children (P-24134)		
Nutrition Services, San Bernardino Also called San Bernardino City Unf School (P-22873)		
Nuvi Global	A	559 306-2646
518 W Henderson Ave Apt 9 Porterville (93257) *(P-7198)*		
Nuvision Fincl Federal Cr Un (PA)	C	714 375-8000
7812 Edinger Ave Ste 100 Huntington Beach (92647) *(P-9576)*		
Nuvo TV, Glendale Also called Sitv Inc (P-5837)		
Nuvoton Technology Corp Amer	D	408 544-1718
2727 N 1st St San Jose (95134) *(P-7517)*		
Nuworld Business Systems, Cerritos Also called Young Systems Corporation (P-6994)		
Nv5 Inc (HQ)	D	916 641-9100
2525 Natomas Park Dr # 300 Sacramento (95833) *(P-25849)*		
Nv5 Inc	C	858 385-0500
15092 Avenue Of Science # 200 San Diego (92128) *(P-25850)*		
Nv5 Inc	D	916 641-9100
2495 Natomas Park Dr # 300 Sacramento (95833) *(P-25851)*		
NW Entertainment Inc (PA)	D	818 295-5000
2660 W Olive Ave Burbank (91505) *(P-18087)*		
NW Manor Community Partners LP	D	714 662-5565
17782 Sky Park Cir Irvine (92614) *(P-11898)*		
NW Packaging LLC (PA)	D	909 706-3627
1201 E Lexington Ave Pomona (91766) *(P-9238)*		
Nwp Services Corporation (HQ)	C	949 253-2500
535 Anton Blvd Ste 1100 Costa Mesa (92626) *(P-15787)*		
NY Transport Inc	D	909 355-9832
14998 Washington Dr Fontana (92335) *(P-4237)*		
Nydj Apparel LLC	C	323 581-9040
5401 S Soto St Vernon (90058) *(P-8327)*		
Nygard Inc	D	310 776-8900
14401 S San Pedro St Gardena (90248) *(P-8328)*		
Nyse Arca Inc	B	415 393-4000
115 Sansome St San Francisco (94104) *(P-10049)*		
Nzg Specialties Inc (PA)	D	310 216-7575
2580 Santa Fe Ave Redondo Beach (90278) *(P-8436)*		
O & R, Glendale Also called Rev Enterprises (P-16773)		
O & S Holdings LLC	E	310 207-8600
11611 San Vicente Blvd Los Angeles (90049) *(P-11899)*		
O A Outfitting Inc	D	707 498-2917
6602 Wofford Heights Blvd Bayside (95524) *(P-19210)*		
O C Jones & Sons Inc (PA)	C	510 526-3424
1520 4th St Berkeley (94710) *(P-1828)*		
O C Jones & Sons Inc	D	510 663-6911
155 Filbert St Ste 209 Oakland (94607) *(P-27808)*		

Employee Codes: A=Over 500 employees, B=251-500
C=101-250, D=51-100, E=50

2019 Directory of California
Wholesalers and Services Companies

© Mergent Inc. 1-800-342-5647

1403

O C McDonald Co Inc ....C....408 295-2182
1150 W San Carlos St San Jose (95126) **(P-2292)**
O C P T, Orange *Also called Orange Children & Parents* **(P-24360)**
O C Sailing Club Inc ....D....510 843-4200
1 Spinnaker Way Berkeley (94710) **(P-19211)**
O E C Shipg Los Angeles Inc ....E....562 926-7186
13100 Alondra Blvd # 100 Cerritos (90703) **(P-5125)**
O H I, Irvine *Also called European Hotl Invstrs of CA* **(P-12567)**
O P I Products Inc (HQ) ....B....818 759-8688
13034 Saticoy St North Hollywood (91605) **(P-7892)**
O'Connor Hospital Pedia Center, San Jose *Also called OConnor Hospital* **(P-21612)**
O'Connor Wound Care Clinic, San Jose *Also called OConnor Hospital* **(P-21613)**
O'Neill Vintners & Distillers, Larkspur *Also called ONeill Beverages Co LLC* **(P-164)**
O.H. Kruse Grain and Milling, Goshen *Also called Western Milling LLC* **(P-9103)**
O1 Communications Inc ....D....888 444-1111
4359 Town Center Blvd # 217 El Dorado Hills (95762) **(P-5615)**
O2 Micro Inc ....D....408 987-5920
3118 Patrick Henry Dr Santa Clara (95054) **(P-16023)**
O2a, Paso Robles *Also called Omega 2 Alpha Services LLC* **(P-27373)**
Oak Creek LP ....D....909 860-5440
21725 Gateway Center Dr Diamond Bar (91765) **(P-12966)**
Oak Creek Apartments ....E....650 327-1600
1600 Sand Hill Rd Palo Alto (94304) **(P-11086)**
Oak Creek Golf Club, Irvine *Also called Irvine Company LLC* **(P-25434)**
Oak Distribution, Los Angeles *Also called Oak Paper Products Co Inc* **(P-8112)**
Oak Grove Center, Murrieta *Also called Oak Grove Inst Foundation Inc* **(P-19726)**
Oak Grove Inst Foundation Inc ....B....951 238-6022
1251 N A St Perris (92570) **(P-453)**
Oak Grove Inst Foundation Inc (PA) ....B....951 677-5599
24275 Jefferson Ave Murrieta (92562) **(P-19726)**
Oak Harbor Freight Lines Inc ....D....510 608-8841
6700 Smith Ave Newark (94560) **(P-4238)**
Oak Harbor Freight Lines Inc ....D....916 371-3960
832 F St West Sacramento (95605) **(P-4239)**
Oak Hill Capital Partners LP ....A....650 234-0500
2775 Sand Hill Rd Ste 220 Menlo Park (94025) **(P-22377)**
Oak Knoll Convalescent Center ....D....707 778-8686
450 Hayes Ln Petaluma (94952) **(P-20668)**
Oak Paper Products Co Inc (PA) ....C....323 268-0507
3686 E Olympic Blvd Los Angeles (90023) **(P-8112)**
Oak River Rehabilitation ....C....530 365-0025
3300 Franklin St Anderson (96007) **(P-20669)**
Oak Springs Nursery Inc ....D....818 367-5832
13761 Eldridge Ave Sylmar (91342) **(P-6560)**
Oak Street Physical Therapy, Lomita *Also called Kaiser Foundation Hospitals* **(P-22600)**
Oak Valley Golf Club, Beaumont *Also called California Oak Valley Golf* **(P-18692)**
Oak Valley Hospital District (HQ) ....B....209 847-3011
350 S Oak Ave Oakdale (95361) **(P-21611)**
Oak Valley Hotel LLC ....D....619 297-1101
2270 Hotel Cir N San Diego (92108) **(P-12967)**
Oak View Snoma Hlls Apartments, Rohnert Park *Also called Kisco Senior Living LLC* **(P-11047)**
Oakdale Golf and Country Club ....D....209 847-2984
243 N Stearns Rd Oakdale (95361) **(P-18991)**
Oakdale Heights MGT Corp (PA) ....B....530 222-6797
250 Hemsted Dr Ste 100 Redding (96002) **(P-11087)**
Oakdale Heights Senior Living ....E....661 663-9671
3209 Brookside Dr Bakersfield (93311) **(P-20670)**
Oakdale Irrgtion Dst Fing Corp ....D....209 847-0341
1205 E F St Oakdale (95361) **(P-6291)**
Oakdale Memorial Park (PA) ....D....626 335-0281
1401 S Grand Ave Glendora (91740) **(P-11946)**
Oakhurst Country Club, Clayton *Also called American Golf Corporation* **(P-18837)**
OAKHURST HEALTHCARE & WELLNESS, Oakhurst *Also called Oakhurst Skilled Nursing Welln* **(P-20671)**
Oakhurst Industries Inc ....D....510 265-2400
3265 Investment Blvd Hayward (94545) **(P-8437)**
Oakhurst Skilled Nursing Welln ....D....559 683-2244
40131 Highway 49 Oakhurst (93644) **(P-20671)**
Oakland Athletics, Oakland *Also called Athletics Investment Group LLC* **(P-18507)**
Oakland District Office, Oakland *Also called State Compensation Insur Fund* **(P-10397)**
Oakland Healthcare & Wellness ....C....323 330-6572
3030 Webster St Oakland (94609) **(P-20672)**
Oakland Ice Center, Oakland *Also called City of Oakland* **(P-19139)**
Oakland Medical Center, Oakland *Also called Kaiser Foundation Hospitals* **(P-19529)**
Oakland Mrtime Spport Svcs Inc ....E....510 868-1005
11 Burma Rd Oakland (94607) **(P-4750)**
Oakland Museum of California ....D....510 318-8400
1000 Oak St Oakland (94607) **(P-24897)**
Oakland Pallet Company Inc (PA) ....C....510 278-1291
2500 Grant Ave San Lorenzo (94580) **(P-6843)**
Oakland Private Industry Counc ....D....510 768-4400
268 Grand Ave Oakland (94610) **(P-24212)**
Oakland Public Education Fund ....D....510 221-6968
520 3rd St Ste 109 Oakland (94607) **(P-12081)**
Oakland Shops/Annex, Oakland *Also called San Francisco Bay Area Rapid* **(P-3712)**
Oakland Unified School Dst ....C....510 535-2717
955 High St Oakland (94601) **(P-14335)**
Oakland V A Outpatient Clinic, Oakland *Also called Veterans Health Administration* **(P-20065)**
Oakland Zoo In Knowland Park, Oakland *Also called East Bay Btncal Zoological Soc* **(P-19162)**
Oakmont Country Club ....C....818 542-4260
3100 Country Club Dr Glendale (91208) **(P-18992)**
Oakmont Golf Club Inc (PA) ....D....707 538-2454
7025 Oakmont Dr Santa Rosa (95409) **(P-18741)**
Oakridge Care Center, Oakland *Also called A T Associates Inc* **(P-20977)**
Oakridge Landscape Inc (PA) ....E....661 295-7228
28064 Avenue Stanford K Valencia (91355) **(P-464)**
Oaks Diagnostics Inc (PA) ....D....310 855-0035
6310 San Vicente Blvd Los Angeles (90048) **(P-19727)**
Oaks Post Acute, The, Petaluma *Also called Trestles Holdings LLC* **(P-12013)**
Oaks, The, Petaluma *Also called Oak Knoll Convalescent Center* **(P-20668)**
Oaktree Capital Management LP (HQ) ....C....213 830-6300
333 S Grand Ave Ste 2800 Los Angeles (90071) **(P-10099)**
Oaktree Holdings Inc ....A....213 830-6300
333 S Grand Ave Ste 2800 Los Angeles (90071) **(P-12254)**
Oaktree Real Estate Opportunit ....A....213 830-6300
333 S Grand Ave Fl 28 Los Angeles (90071) **(P-11640)**
Oaktree Strategic Income LLC ....A....213 830-6300
333 S Grand Ave Fl 28 Los Angeles (90071) **(P-17364)**
Oakview Convalescent Hospital ....E....818 352-4426
9166 Tujunga Canyon Blvd Tujunga (91042) **(P-21171)**
Oakville Produce Partners LLC ....C....415 647-2991
453 Valley Dr Brisbane (94005) **(P-8711)**
Oakwood Apartments, Woodland Hills *Also called R & B Realty Group* **(P-11102)**
Oakwood Apts, Marina Del Rey *Also called R & B Realty Group* **(P-11103)**
Oakwood Athletic Club, Lafayette *Also called Clubsport San Ramon LLC* **(P-18587)**
Oakwood Garden Apts, Los Angeles *Also called R & B Realty Group* **(P-11101)**
Oakwood Gardens Care Center, Fresno *Also called Lily Holdings LLC* **(P-20592)**
Oakwood Village, Auburn *Also called Horizon West Inc* **(P-26704)**
Oakwood Worldwide, Los Angeles *Also called R & B Realty Group LP* **(P-11698)**
Oasis Brands Inc ....D....540 658-2830
6700 Artesia Blvd Buena Park (90620) **(P-8113)**
Oasis Country Club, Palm Desert *Also called Oasis Palm Dsert Hmowners Assn* **(P-18993)**
Oasis IPA, Palm Springs *Also called Desert Medical Group Inc* **(P-19437)**
Oasis Mental Health Trtmnt Ctr ....C....760 863-8609
47915 Oasis St Indio (92201) **(P-21968)**
Oasis Palm Dsert Hmowners Assn ....D....760 345-5661
42330 Casbah Way Palm Desert (92211) **(P-18993)**
Oasis Repower LLC ....A....888 903-6926
15445 Innovation Dr San Diego (92128) **(P-6064)**
Oasis Technology Inc ....D....805 445-4833
601 E Daily Dr Ste 226 Camarillo (93010) **(P-16024)**
Oates Buzz Enterprises ....D....916 381-3600
555 Capitol Mall Ste 900 Sacramento (95814) **(P-10921)**
Oatey Supply Chain Svcs Inc ....E....510 797-4677
6600 Smith Ave Newark (94560) **(P-7631)**
Ob Usa Inc ....C....213 465-4876
13152 Imperial Hwy Santa Fe Springs (90670) **(P-9018)**
Oberman Tivoli & Pickert Inc ....C....310 440-9600
500 S Sepulveda Blvd # 500 Los Angeles (90049) **(P-16025)**
Obey Clothing, Irvine *Also called One 3 Two Inc* **(P-8329)**
Objective Systems Integrators (HQ) ....E....916 467-1500
2365 Iron Point Rd # 170 Folsom (95630) **(P-15324)**
Oblong Industries Inc (PA) ....C....213 683-8863
923 E 3rd St Ste 111 Los Angeles (90013) **(P-15325)**
OBryant Electric Inc ....C....818 407-1986
9314 Eton Ave Chatsworth (91311) **(P-2666)**
Obscura Digital Incorporated ....E....415 227-9979
14 Louisiana St San Francisco (94107) **(P-13950)**
Observatories of The Carnegie, Pasadena *Also called Carnegie Institution Wash* **(P-26606)**
Oc 405 Partners Joint Venture ....D....858 251-2200
3100 W Lake Center Dr # 200 Santa Ana (92704) **(P-1886)**
Oc Accessories LLC ....D....949 229-2410
1968 S Coast Hwy Ste 195 Laguna Beach (92651) **(P-17365)**
OC Communications Inc (PA) ....C....916 686-3700
2204 Kausen Dr Ste 100 Elk Grove (95758) **(P-5924)**
Oc Engineering ....D....714 667-3212
300 N Flower St Santa Ana (92703) **(P-25852)**
Oc Food Bank, Garden Grove *Also called Community Action Partnershi* **(P-23595)**
Oc IV A California LP ....E....925 734-5800
4511 Willow Rd Ste 1 Pleasanton (94588) **(P-17774)**
OC Special Events SEC Inc ....C....714 541-4111
1232 Village Way Ste K Santa Ana (92705) **(P-16745)**
Oc Waste & Recycling, Santa Ana *Also called County of Orange* **(P-6385)**
Ocadian Care Centers LLC ....C....530 246-9000
2801 Eureka Way Redding (96001) **(P-20673)**
Ocadian Care Centers LLC ....D....510 832-3222
475 29th St Oakland (94609) **(P-20674)**
Ocadian Care Centers LLC ....D....415 461-9700
1220 S Eliseo Dr Greenbrae (94904) **(P-20675)**
Ocadian Care Centers LLC ....D....415 499-1000
1550 Silveira Pkwy San Rafael (94903) **(P-20676)**
Ocadian Care Centers LLC ....E....408 295-2665
75 N 13th St San Jose (95112) **(P-20677)**
Ocb Riverside, Riverside *Also called American Reprographics Co LLC* **(P-14076)**
Occidental Area Health Center, Guerneville *Also called West County Health Centers Inc* **(P-20096)**
Occidental Cnty Sanitation Dst ....D....707 547-1900
404 Aviation Blvd Santa Rosa (95403) **(P-6325)**
Occupational Health Services, Mountain View *Also called El Camino Hospital* **(P-22019)**
Occupational Medicine, Salinas *Also called Natividad Medical Center* **(P-21604)**
Occupational Therapy Training, Torrance *Also called Special Service For Groups Inc* **(P-24844)**
Occupnl Urgnt Care Hlth Syst ....B....916 374-4600
750 Riverpoint Dr West Sacramento (95605) **(P-22850)**
Ocean Avenue LLC ....B....310 576-7777
101 Wilshire Blvd Santa Monica (90401) **(P-12968)**
Ocean Blue Envmtl Svcs Inc (PA) ....D....562 624-4120
925 W Esther St Long Beach (90813) **(P-4047)**
Ocean Breeze International ....D....805 684-1747
3910 Via Real Carpinteria (93013) **(P-288)**

Ocean Breeze Manufacturing ....D....323 586-8760
1961 Hawkins Cir Los Angeles (90001) *(P-17366)*
Ocean Colony Partners LLC ....C....650 726-5764
2450 Cabrillo Hwy S # 200 Half Moon Bay (94019) *(P-11900)*
Ocean Dream, Commerce *Also called Malibu Design Group (P-8318)*
Ocean Fresh Fish Seafood Mktg, Los Angeles *Also called Ocean Group Inc (P-8586)*
Ocean Group Inc (PA) ....D....213 622-3677
1100 S Santa Fe Ave Los Angeles (90021) *(P-8586)*
Ocean Holiday LP ....D....760 231-7000
1401 Carmelo Dr Oceanside (92054) *(P-12969)*
Ocean House Retirement Inn, Santa Monica *Also called MBK Real Estate Ltd A Califor (P-11065)*
Ocean Knight Shipping Inc ....C....310 885-3388
19516 S Susana Rd # 101 Compton (90221) *(P-5126)*
Ocean Links Corporation ....D....650 726-1800
2 Miramontes Point Rd Half Moon Bay (94019) *(P-18742)*
Ocean Mist Farming Company (PA) ....C....831 633-2144
10855 Ocean Mist Pkwy A Castroville (95012) *(P-72)*
Ocean Mist Farms, Castroville *Also called California Artichoke & Vegetab (P-499)*
Ocean Mist Farms, Castroville *Also called Ocean Mist Farming Company (P-72)*
Ocean Park Community Center ....D....310 828-6717
1447 16th St Santa Monica (90404) *(P-27809)*
Ocean Park Community Center ....D....310 450-0650
1751 Cloverfield Blvd Santa Monica (90404) *(P-23948)*
Ocean Park Health Center ....E....415 753-8100
1351 24th Ave San Francisco (94122) *(P-19728)*
Ocean Park Hotels Inc (PA) ....B....805 544-0812
9777 Blue Larkspur Ln # 102 Monterey (93940) *(P-12970)*
Ocean Park Hotels Inc ....C....831 373-6141
1000 Aguajito Rd Monterey (93940) *(P-12971)*
Ocean Park Hotels Inc ....D....661 284-3200
27710 The Old Rd Valencia (91355) *(P-12972)*
Ocean Park Hotels Mmex LLC ....E....661 284-2101
27513 Wayne Mills Pl Valencia (91355) *(P-12973)*
Ocean Queen 87 Inc ....E....323 585-1200
4511 Everett Ave Vernon (90058) *(P-8587)*
Ocean Service, San Diego *Also called Overseas Service Corporation (P-27950)*
Ocean View Flowers LLC ....C....800 736-5608
1105 Union Sugar Ave Lompoc (93436) *(P-289)*
Ocean View Manor LP ....D....805 781-3088
3533 Empleo St San Luis Obispo (93401) *(P-11179)*
Ocean View Manor Apartments, San Luis Obispo *Also called Ocean View Manor LP (P-11179)*
Oceans Eleven Casino ....B....760 439-6988
121 Brooks St Oceanside (92054) *(P-12974)*
Oceanside Hlthcare Stffing Inc ....C....213 503-5649
2216 El Camino Rela 211 Santa Clarita (91350) *(P-22851)*
Oceanside Laundry LLC ....D....831 722-4358
675 Beach Dr Watsonville (95076) *(P-13560)*
Oceanside Lifeguards ....D....760 435-4500
300 N Coast Hwy Oceanside (92054) *(P-19212)*
Oceanview Produce Company ....D....805 488-6401
3000 E Hueneme Rd Oxnard (93033) *(P-73)*
Oceanx LLC (HQ) ....D....310 774-4088
100 N Pacific Coast Hwy El Segundo (90245) *(P-17367)*
Ocm Real Estate Opportunities ....A....213 830-6300
333 S Grand Ave Fl 28 Los Angeles (90071) *(P-12255)*
Ocmban, Irvine *Also called Ocmbc Inc (P-9837)*
Ocmbc Inc ....D....714 479-0999
19000 Macarthur Blvd # 200 Irvine (92612) *(P-9837)*
OConnell Landscape Maint Inc ....E....760 630-4963
4600 Leisure Village Way Oceanside (92056) *(P-913)*
OConner Woods A California ....D....209 956-3400
3400 Wagner Heights Rd Stockton (95209) *(P-11088)*
Oconnor Hospital, San Jose *Also called OConnor Imaging Med Group Inc (P-19729)*
OConnor Hospital ....D....408 947-2929
2039 Forest Ave San Jose (95128) *(P-21612)*
OConnor Hospital (HQ) ....A....408 947-2500
2105 Forest Ave San Jose (95128) *(P-21613)*
OConnor Imaging Med Group Inc ....D....408 947-2992
2105 Forest Ave San Jose (95128) *(P-19729)*
OConnor Pest Control Visalia ....D....559 366-4853
1728 W Prospect Ave Visalia (93291) *(P-14155)*
OConnor Woods Housing Corp ....D....209 956-3400
3400 Wagner Heights Rd Stockton (95209) *(P-11089)*
Ocsi.co, Oakland *Also called Outsource Consulting Svcs Inc (P-14683)*
Octa, Orange *Also called Orange County Trnsp Auth (P-3695)*
Odd Fellow-Rebekah Chld HM Cal (PA) ....C....408 846-2100
290 I O O F Ave Gilroy (95020) *(P-24614)*
Odd Fellow-Rebekah Chld HM Cal ....D....831 775-0348
1260 S Main St Ste 101 Salinas (93901) *(P-24615)*
Odd Fellows Home California ....B....408 741-7100
14500 Fruitvale Ave # 3000 Saratoga (95070) *(P-24616)*
Oddworld Inhabitants Inc ....D....805 503-3000
869 Monterey St San Luis Obispo (93401) *(P-15788)*
Odesus Inc (PA) ....D....310 473-4600
11766 Wilshire Blvd # 400 Los Angeles (90025) *(P-16438)*
Odona Central Security Inc ....C....323 728-8818
71 N San Gabriel Blvd Pasadena (91107) *(P-16746)*
Ods Technologies LP ....C....310 242-9400
6701 Center Dr W Ste 160 Los Angeles (90045) *(P-5831)*
Odu-Usa Inc (HQ) ....D....805 484-0540
300 Camarillo Ranch Rd A Camarillo (93012) *(P-7518)*
Odyssey Environmental Services, Lodi *Also called Odyssey Landscaping Co Inc (P-3297)*
Odyssey Healthcare Inc ....D....714 245-7420
525 Cabrillo Park Dr # 150 Santa Ana (92701) *(P-20678)*
Odyssey Healthcare Inc ....D....408 626-4868
1500 E Hamilton Ave # 212 Campbell (95008) *(P-20679)*
Odyssey Healthcare Inc ....D....858 565-2499
9444 Balboa Ave Ste 290 San Diego (92123) *(P-22378)*
Odyssey Healthcare Inc ....E....760 674-0066
74350 Country Club Dr Palm Desert (92260) *(P-21172)*
Odyssey Healthcare Inc ....D....760 241-7044
17290 Jasmine St Ste 104 Victorville (92395) *(P-22379)*
Odyssey Landscaping Co Inc ....D....209 369-6197
5400 W Highway 12 Lodi (95242) *(P-3297)*
Odyssey Telecorp Inc ....C....650 470-7550
550 Lytton Ave Fl 2 Palo Alto (94301) *(P-5616)*
Oec Group, Cerritos *Also called O E C Shipg Los Angeles Inc (P-5125)*
Oel/Hhh Inc ....D....818 246-6050
1833 Victory Blvd Glendale (91201) *(P-26102)*
OES Equipment LLC (PA) ....D....510 284-1900
37421 Centralmont Pl Fremont (94536) *(P-14530)*
Office Cmnty Inv Infrstructure, San Francisco *Also called Successor To San Francisco (P-27871)*
Office Depot Inc ....D....916 927-0171
4720 Northgate Blvd Sacramento (95834) *(P-6972)*
Office Movers Inc ....E....408 254-5010
4020 Nelson Ave Ste 200 Concord (94520) *(P-4363)*
Office of Child Development ....D....310 842-4230
10800 Farragut Dr Culver City (90230) *(P-24356)*
Office of Inspector General, Los Angeles *Also called Los Angeles County MTA (P-3678)*
Office of Nutritional Services, Visalia *Also called Visalia Unified School Dst (P-24111)*
Office of The Legislative Coun ....B....916 341-8708
1100 J St Fl 7 Sacramento (95814) *(P-5414)*
Office of The Legislative Coun ....A....916 445-3796
925 L St Ste 900 Sacramento (95814) *(P-27810)*
Office On Aging, ADRC Of River, Riverside *Also called County of Riverside (P-23713)*
Office Star Products, Ontario *Also called Blumenthal Distributing Inc (P-6712)*
Office Team, Menlo Park *Also called Robert Half International Inc (P-14740)*
Office Team, San Ramon *Also called Robert Half International Inc (P-14745)*
OfficeMax Incorporated ....D....951 485-9353
7300 Chapman Ave Garden Grove (92841) *(P-4603)*
Officeteam, Irvine *Also called Robert Half International Inc (P-14741)*
Officeworks Inc ....D....510 444-2161
300 Frank H Ste 269 Oakland (94612) *(P-14679)*
Officeworks Inc ....D....951 784-2534
11801 Pierce St Fl 2 Riverside (92505) *(P-14680)*
Official Police Garage Assn of ....A....805 624-0572
67 W Boulder Creek Rd Simi Valley (93065) *(P-4747)*
Offshore Crane & Service Co (PA) ....D....805 648-3348
1375 N Olive St Ste A Ventura (93001) *(P-14452)*
Ofi Markesa International, Vernon *Also called Orient Fisheries Inc (P-8589)*
Ogilvy & Mather Worldwide Inc ....D....310 280-2200
2425 Olympic Blvd 2200w Santa Monica (90404) *(P-13871)*
Ogilvy Pub Rltons Wrldwide Inc ....D....916 231-7700
1530 J St Sacramento (95814) *(P-27566)*
Ogletree Deakins Nash Smoak ....D....415 442-4810
1 Market St Ste 1300 San Francisco (94105) *(P-23295)*
OGrady Paving Inc ....C....650 966-1926
2513 Wyandotte St Mountain View (94043) *(P-1829)*
OH My Green Inc ....D....650 989-8181
1845 Rollins Rd Burlingame (94010) *(P-8842)*
OHagin Manufacturing LLC ....E....707 872-3620
210 Classic Ct Ste 100 Rohnert Park (94928) *(P-2293)*
OHagins Inc ....D....707 303-3660
210 Classic Ct Ste 100 Rohnert Park (94928) *(P-2294)*
Ohana Partners Inc (PA) ....D....408 856-3232
454 S Abbott Ave Milpitas (95035) *(P-14531)*
Ohi Resort Hotels LLC ....D....714 867-5555
12021 Harbor Blvd Garden Grove (92840) *(P-12975)*
Ohl, Redlands *Also called Geodis Logistics LLC (P-4564)*
Oil Changers, Pleasanton *Also called Oc IV A California LP (P-17774)*
Oil Well Service Company (PA) ....C....562 612-0600
10840 Norwalk Blvd Santa Fe Springs (90670) *(P-1073)*
Oilfield Electric & Motor, Ventura *Also called Oilfield Electric Company (P-2667)*
Oilfield Electric Company ....D....805 648-3131
1801 N Ventura Ave Ventura (93001) *(P-2667)*
Oj Insulation LP ....D....408 842-6315
5820 Obata Way Unit B Gilroy (95020) *(P-2924)*
Oj Insulation LP ....E....760 839-3200
2061 Albergrov Ave Escondido (92029) *(P-2925)*
Oj Insulation LP ....D....760 200-4343
78 015 Wildcat Dr Palm Desert (92211) *(P-2926)*
Oj Insulation LP (PA) ....C....626 812-6070
600 S Vincent Ave Azusa (91702) *(P-2927)*
Oj Insulation & Fireplaces, Escondido *Also called Oj Insulation LP (P-2925)*
Ojai Ambulance Inc ....E....805 653-9111
632 E Thompson Blvd Ventura (93001) *(P-3827)*
Ojai Raptor Center ....D....805 649-6884
370 Baldwin Rd Ojai (93023) *(P-631)*
Ojai Valley Community Hospital, Ojai *Also called Community Memorial Health Sys (P-21342)*
Ojai Valley Inn & Spa, Ojai *Also called Ovis Llc (P-12991)*
Ojai Valley Inn Golf Course ....A....805 646-2420
905 Country Club Rd Ojai (93023) *(P-12976)*
Ojai Valley Spa, Ojai *Also called Ojai Valley Inn Golf Course (P-12976)*
OK Produce, Fresno *Also called Charlies Enterprises (P-8652)*
Okabe International Inc (PA) ....E....415 921-0808
1739 Buchanan St Ste B San Francisco (94115) *(P-4973)*
Okta Inc (PA) ....C....888 722-7871
301 Brannan St Fl 1 San Francisco (94107) *(P-15326)*
Olam Americas Inc (HQ) ....A....559 447-1390
25 Union Pl Ste 3 Fresno (93720) *(P-550)*
Olam Spces Vgtable Ingredients, Fresno *Also called Olam West Coast Inc (P-551)*

ALPHABETIC

Employee Codes: A=Over 500 employees, B=251-500
C=101-250, D=51-100, E=50
2019 Directory of California
Wholesalers and Services Companies
© Mergent Inc. 1-800-342-5647
1405

Olam West Coast Inc (HQ) .... C 559 447-1390
205 E Rver Pk Cir Ste 310 Fresno (93720) ***(P-551)***
Old Dominion Freight Line Inc .... C 323 725-3400
1225 Washington Blvd Montebello (90640) ***(P-4240)***
Old Globe Theatre .... B 619 234-5623
1363 Old Globe Way San Diego (92101) ***(P-18390)***
Old Republic Contractors Ins .... D 626 683-5200
225 S Lake Ave Ste 900 Pasadena (91101) ***(P-10721)***
Old Republic HM Protection Inc .... B 925 866-1500
2 Annabel Ln Ste 112 San Ramon (94583) ***(P-10722)***
Old Republic Title Company .... A 818 240-1936
101 N Brand Blvd Ste 1400 Glendale (91203) ***(P-10468)***
Old Republic Title Company .... E 831 757-8051
584 S Main St Salinas (93901) ***(P-10469)***
Old Spaghetti Factory, The, Rancho Mirage *Also called Osf International Inc* ***(P-8844)***
Old Town Fmly Hospitality Corp .... C 619 246-8010
4962 Concannon Ct San Diego (92130) ***(P-12977)***
Old Town Gallery of Fine Art, Auburn *Also called Auburn Old Town Gallery* ***(P-19105)***
Old Town Trlley Turs San Diego .... D 619 298-8687
2115 Kurtz St San Diego (92110) ***(P-4974)***
Olde Thompson Inc .... C 800 827-1565
3250 Camino Del Sol Oxnard (93030) ***(P-6779)***
Oldenkamp Trucking Inc (PA) .... D 661 833-3400
13535 S Union Ave Bakersfield (93307) ***(P-4048)***
Older Adults Care Management (PA) .... C 650 329-1411
881 Fremont Ave Ste A2 Los Altos (94024) ***(P-23949)***
Ole Health .... E 707 254-1770
1100 Trancas St Ste 300 NAPA (94558) ***(P-19730)***
Oleander Holdings LLC .... D 916 331-4590
5255 Hemlock St Sacramento (95841) ***(P-20680)***
Olen Commercial Realty Corp .... B 949 644-6536
7 Corporate Plaza Dr Newport Beach (92660) ***(P-10922)***
Olen Companies, The, Newport Beach *Also called Olen Residential Realty Corp* ***(P-1304)***
Olen Residential Realty, Newport Beach *Also called Olen Commercial Realty Corp* ***(P-10922)***
Olen Residential Realty Corp (HQ) .... D 949 644-6536
7 Corporate Plaza Dr Newport Beach (92660) ***(P-1304)***
Olive Crest .... D 760 341-8507
73700 Dinah Shore Dr # 101 Palm Desert (92211) ***(P-24617)***
Olive Crest .... D 562 216-8841
917 Pine Ave Long Beach (90813) ***(P-24618)***
Olive Crest (PA) .... B 714 543-5437
2130 E 4th St Ste 200 Santa Ana (92705) ***(P-24619)***
Olive Crest Op, Long Beach *Also called Olive Crest* ***(P-24618)***
Olive Grove Retirement Resort .... D 951 687-2241
7858 California Ave Riverside (92504) ***(P-11090)***
Olive Hill Greenhouses .... D 760 728-4596
3508 Olive Hill Rd Fallbrook (92028) ***(P-290)***
Olive Knolls Christian School .... D 661 393-3566
6201 Fruitvale Ave Bakersfield (93308) ***(P-24357)***
Olive Ridge Post Acute Care, Oroville *Also called Evergreen At Oroville LLC* ***(P-20417)***
Olive View-Ucla Medical Center (PA) .... D 818 364-1555
14445 Olive View Dr Sylmar (91342) ***(P-19731)***
Olive View/Ucla Education & .... D 818 364-3434
14445 Olive View Dr Sylmar (91342) ***(P-26645)***
Olive Vista, Center, Pomona *Also called Genesis Healthcare Corporation* ***(P-20452)***
Olivenhain Municipal Water Dst .... D 760 753-6466
1966 Olivenhain Rd Encinitas (92024) ***(P-6292)***
Oliver & Company Inc .... D 510 412-9090
1300 S 51st St Richmond (94804) ***(P-1604)***
Olivermcmillan LLC (HQ) .... D 619 321-1111
733 8th Ave San Diego (92101) ***(P-11901)***
Olivet International Inc (PA) .... C 951 681-8888
11015 Hopkins St Mira Loma (91752) ***(P-8049)***
Olivieri Enterprises LP .... C 916 791-7857
210 Estates Dr Ste 200 Roseville (95678) ***(P-3054)***
Ols Hotels & Resorts LLC (PA) .... A 818 905-8280
16000 Ventura Blvd # 1010 Encino (91436) ***(P-12978)***
Ols Hotels & Resorts LLC .... A 626 962-6000
14635 Bldwin Pk Towne Ctr Baldwin Park (91706) ***(P-12979)***
Ols Hotels & Resorts LP .... C 310 855-1115
733 W Knoll Dr West Hollywood (90069) ***(P-12980)***
Olson & Assoc .... D 714 878-6649
3448 Lupine Cir Ste 102 Costa Mesa (92626) ***(P-16439)***
Olson Company LLC (PA) .... D 562 596-4770
3010 Old Ranch Pkwy # 100 Seal Beach (90740) ***(P-1210)***
Olson Company, The, Seal Beach *Also called Olson Urban Housing LLC* ***(P-11902)***
Olson Homes, Seal Beach *Also called Olson Company LLC* ***(P-1210)***
Olson Urban Housing LLC .... D 562 596-4770
3010 Old Ranch Pkwy # 100 Seal Beach (90740) ***(P-11902)***
Oltmans Construction Co (PA) .... D 562 948-4242
10005 Mission Mill Rd Whittier (90601) ***(P-1424)***
Oltmans Investment Company .... E 562 948-4242
10005 Mission Mill Rd Whittier (90601) ***(P-10923)***
Oltmans Property Management, Whittier *Also called Oltmans Investment Company* ***(P-10923)***
Olympia Convalescent Hospital .... C 213 487-3000
1100 S Alvarado St Los Angeles (90006) ***(P-21173)***
Olympia Health Care LLC .... A 323 938-3161
5900 W Olympic Blvd Los Angeles (90036) ***(P-21614)***
Olympia Medical Center, Los Angeles *Also called Olympia Health Care LLC* ***(P-21614)***
Olympic Circle Sailing Club, Berkeley *Also called O C Sailing Club Inc* ***(P-19211)***
Olympic Club (PA) .... B 415 345-5100
524 Post St San Francisco (94102) ***(P-25207)***
Olympic Construction, Roseville *Also called Olivieri Enterprises LP* ***(P-3054)***
Olympic Frt & Vegatable Distr, Los Angeles *Also called Coast Citrus Distributors* ***(P-8658)***
Olympic Investors Ltd .... D 925 322-8996
1908 Olympic Blvd Walnut Creek (94596) ***(P-18994)***
Olympic Security, Bellflower *Also called Advent Securities Investments* ***(P-9912)***
Olympix Fitness LLC .... D 562 366-4600
4101 E Olympic Plz Long Beach (90803) ***(P-18638)***
Olympus Adhc Inc .... E 310 572-7272
11613 Washington Pl Los Angeles (90066) ***(P-24358)***
Olympus Adult Day Hlthcare Ctr, Los Angeles *Also called Olympus Adhc Inc* ***(P-24358)***
Olympus America Inc .... C 949 466-3548
23342 Madero Mission Viejo (92691) ***(P-7199)***
OLYMPUS AMERICA INC., Mission Viejo *Also called Olympus America Inc* ***(P-7199)***
Olympus Building Services Inc .... A 760 750-4629
441 La Moree Rd San Marcos (92078) ***(P-27601)***
Olympus Power LLC .... C 661 393-6885
34759 Lencioni Ave Bakersfield (93308) ***(P-6065)***
Omar Orozco .... D 530 723-0849
816 Gibson Rd Woodland (95695) ***(P-663)***
Omar Orozco's Contracting, Woodland *Also called Omar Orozco* ***(P-663)***
Omega 2 Alpha Services LLC .... D 805 610-2249
935 Riverside Ave Ste 23 Paso Robles (93446) ***(P-27373)***
Omega Insurance Services .... E 714 973-0311
721 S Parker St Ste 300 Orange (92868) ***(P-10723)***
Omega Management Services, Corning *Also called Omega Waste Management Inc* ***(P-27374)***
Omega Moulding West LLC .... C 323 261-3510
5500 Lindbergh Ln Bell (90201) ***(P-6780)***
Omega Security Services & Cons .... D 818 831-1100
10611 Garden Grove Ave # 2 Northridge (91326) ***(P-16747)***
Omega Walnut Inc .... E 530 865-0136
7233 County Road 24 Orland (95963) ***(P-552)***
Omega Waste Management Inc .... D 530 824-1890
957 Colusa St Corning (96021) ***(P-27374)***
Omega/Cinema Props Inc .... D 323 466-8201
5857 Santa Monica Blvd Los Angeles (90038) ***(P-18207)***
Omelet LLC (PA) .... D 213 427-6400
3540 Hayden Ave Culver City (90232) ***(P-13872)***
OMelveny & Myers LLP (PA) .... A 213 430-6000
400 S Hope St Fl 19 Los Angeles (90071) ***(P-23296)***
OMelveny & Myers LLP .... C 949 760-9600
610 Nwport Ctr Dr Fl 17 Flr 17 Newport Beach (92660) ***(P-23297)***
OMelveny & Myers LLP .... C 310 553-6700
1999 Avenue Of The Stars # 600 Los Angeles (90067) ***(P-23298)***
OMelveny & Myers LLP .... C 650 473-2600
2765 Sand Hill Rd Menlo Park (94025) ***(P-23299)***
OMelveny & Myers LLP .... C 415 984-8700
2 Embarcadero Ctr Fl 28 San Francisco (94111) ***(P-23300)***
Omni Consulting Group LLP .... D 530 750-5199
3531 Mono Pl Ste 100 Davis (95618) ***(P-27375)***
Omni Family Health (PA) .... D 661 459-1900
4900 California Ave 400b Bakersfield (93309) ***(P-19732)***
Omni Hotels Corporation .... B 760 568-2727
41000 Bob Hope Dr Rancho Mirage (92270) ***(P-12981)***
Omni Hotels Corporation .... B 619 231-6664
675 L St San Diego (92101) ***(P-12982)***
Omni Hotels Corporation .... B 415 677-9494
500 California St San Francisco (94104) ***(P-12983)***
Omni Hotels Corporation .... C 213 617-3300
251 S Olive St Fl 1 Los Angeles (90012) ***(P-12984)***
Omni Research Group, Davis *Also called Omni Consulting Group LLP* ***(P-27375)***
Omni Seals, Inc., Rancho Cucamonga *Also called Smith International Inc* ***(P-1079)***
Omni Ventures Group Llc .... D 510 384-1033
300 Pasadena Ave South Pasadena (91030) ***(P-11997)***
Omni Womens Hlth Med Group Inc .... D 559 441-4271
2550 Merced St Fresno (93721) ***(P-19733)***
Omni-Temp Refrigeration, Downey *Also called Omniment Industries Inc* ***(P-2295)***
Omnia Italian Design Inc .... C 909 393-4400
4900 Edison Ave Chino (91710) ***(P-6732)***
Omnicare Inc .... D 510 293-9663
20967 Cabot Blvd Hayward (94545) ***(P-8200)***
Omniduct, Buena Park *Also called ECB Corp* ***(P-2194)***
Omnikron Systems Inc .... D 818 591-7890
20920 Warner Center Ln A Woodland Hills (91367) ***(P-16440)***
Omniment Industries Inc (PA) .... C 562 923-9660
9300 Hall Rd Downey (90241) ***(P-2295)***
Omninet Twin Towers Gp LLC .... E 310 300-4100
9420 Wilshire Blvd # 400 Beverly Hills (90212) ***(P-11641)***
Omninet Twin Towers LP .... E 310 300-4110
9420 Wilshire Blvd # 400 Beverly Hills (90212) ***(P-11642)***
Omniteam Inc .... C 562 923-9660
9300 Hall Rd Downey (90241) ***(P-7663)***
Omnitrans Inc .... B 909 383-1680
234 S I St San Bernardino (92410) ***(P-24620)***
Omnitrans Inc .... C 909 379-7100
4748 Arrow Hwy Montclair (91763) ***(P-3692)***
Omnitrans Access, San Bernardino *Also called Omnitrans Inc* ***(P-24620)***
Omniupdate Inc .... D 805 484-9400
1320 Flynn Rd Ste 100 Camarillo (93012) ***(P-15327)***
On Call Consulting, Thousand Oaks *Also called Miramed Global Services Inc* ***(P-27790)***
On Central Realty Inc .... B 323 543-8500
1648 Colorado Blvd Los Angeles (90041) ***(P-11643)***
On Lok Inc .... D 415 292-8888
1333 Bush St San Francisco (94109) ***(P-19734)***
On Lok Life Ways, Fremont *Also called On Lok Senior Health Services* ***(P-10286)***
On Lok Lifeways, San Francisco *Also called On Lok Senior Health Services* ***(P-10285)***
On Lok Senior Health Services (PA) .... A 415 292-8888
1333 Bush St San Francisco (94109) ***(P-10285)***
On Lok Senior Health Services .... E 510 249-2700
3683 Peralta Blvd Fremont (94536) ***(P-10286)***
On My Own Indepedent Living .... D 707 938-9156
920 1st St W Sonoma (95476) ***(P-21174)***

On The Move ... E ... 707 251-9432
780 Lincoln Ave NAPA (94558) ***(P-24817)***
On Trac Overhead Door Co Inc ... E ... 909 799-8555
1430 Richardson St San Bernardino (92408) ***(P-3055)***
On-Scene Security Services Inc ... E ... 661 263-2343
P.O. Box 800147 Santa Clarita (91380) ***(P-16748)***
On-Site Lasermedic Corporation (PA) ... D ... 818 775-9111
21540 Prairie St Ste D Chatsworth (91311) ***(P-16290)***
On-Site Manager Inc (HQ) ... E ... 866 266-7483
307 Orchard Cy Dr Ste 110 Campbell (95008) ***(P-17368)***
On-Time AC & Htg Inc (PA) ... D ... 925 598-1911
7020 Commerce Dr Ste C Pleasanton (94588) ***(P-2296)***
On24 Inc (PA) ... B ... 877 202-9599
50 Beale St Ste 800 San Francisco (94105) ***(P-15789)***
Ona, Irvine *Also called Canon Solutions America Inc* ***(P-7737)***
Onboardiq Inc ... E ... 480 433-1197
625 Market St Ste 500 San Francisco (94105) ***(P-16239)***
Oncore Manufacturing LLC (HQ) ... A ... 818 734-6500
9340 Owensmouth Ave Chatsworth (91311) ***(P-25853)***
One 3 Two Inc ... C ... 949 596-8400
17353 Derian Ave Irvine (92614) ***(P-8329)***
One California Plaza, Los Angeles *Also called Hill Farrer & Burrill* ***(P-23130)***
One Call Medical Inc ... D ... 818 346-8700
8501 Fllbrook Ave Ste 100 Canoga Park (91304) ***(P-27376)***
One Call Plumber Goleta ... D ... 805 284-0441
140 Nectarine Ave Apt 4 Goleta (93117) ***(P-13760)***
One Call Plumber Santa Barbara ... D ... 805 364-6337
1016 Cliff Dr Apt 309 Santa Barbara (93109) ***(P-2297)***
One Diversified LLC ... D ... 408 969-1972
3275 Edward Ave Santa Clara (95054) ***(P-27811)***
One Embarcadero Center Venture ... D ... 415 772-0700
4 Embarcadero Ctr Ste 1 San Francisco (94111) ***(P-12177)***
One Flynn Center, San Francisco *Also called Flynn Industries Inc* ***(P-258)***
One K Studios LLC ... E ... 818 531-3800
3400 W Olive Ave Ste 300 Burbank (91505) ***(P-14124)***
One Legal Inc ... D ... 213 617-1212
350 S Figueroa St Ste 385 Los Angeles (90071) ***(P-17369)***
One Main Financial Services ... C ... 626 335-0617
1121 E Alosta Ave Azusa (91702) ***(P-27377)***
One Main Financial Services ... C ... 707 546-5162
711 Stony Point Rd Santa Rosa (95407) ***(P-27378)***
One Medical Group, San Francisco *Also called 1life Healthcare Inc* ***(P-22720)***
One Medical Group Inc (PA) ... C ... 415 578-3100
130 Sutter St Fl 2 San Francisco (94104) ***(P-19735)***
One Medical Group Inc ... D ... 415 529-4522
3885 24th St San Francisco (94114) ***(P-19736)***
One Nob Hill Associates LLC ... D ... 415 392-3434
999 California St San Francisco (94108) ***(P-12985)***
One Planet Ops Inc (PA) ... C ... 925 983-2800
1820 Bonanza St Ste 200 Walnut Creek (94596) ***(P-13873)***
One Silver Serve Inc ... E ... 818 995-6444
17835 Ventura Blvd # 108 Encino (91316) ***(P-27602)***
One Stop Program, Los Angeles *Also called Uaw-Lbor Emplyment Trning Corp* ***(P-14788)***
One Town Center Associates LLC ... E ... 714 435-2100
3315 Fairview Rd Costa Mesa (92626) ***(P-10924)***
One Work Place, San Francisco *Also called One Workplace L Ferrari LLC* ***(P-27603)***
One Workplace L Ferrari, San Francisco *Also called One Workplace L Ferrari LLC* ***(P-6733)***
One Workplace L Ferrari LLC ... E ... 415 357-2200
475 Brannan St San Francisco (94107) ***(P-6733)***
One Workplace L Ferrari LLC ... D ... 415 357-2200
475 Brannan St Ste 210 San Francisco (94107) ***(P-27603)***
One10 LLC ... D ... 415 398-3534
180 Montgomery St San Francisco (94104) ***(P-27379)***
One10 LLC ... D ... 415 844-2200
735 Battery St Fl 1 San Francisco (94111) ***(P-27380)***
Onebill Software Inc ... D ... 844 462-7638
3080 Olcott St Ste D230 Santa Clara (95054) ***(P-15328)***
Onebody Inc ... D ... 510 285-2000
2000 Powell St Ste 555 Emeryville (94608) ***(P-22380)***
Onecalifornia Bank, Oakland *Also called Beneficial State Bank* ***(P-9496)***
Onegeneration (PA) ... D ... 818 708-6625
17400 Victory Blvd Van Nuys (91406) ***(P-23950)***
Onehealth Solutions Inc ... D ... 858 947-6333
420 Stevens Ave Ste 200 Solana Beach (92075) ***(P-16441)***
ONeill Beverages Co LLC (PA) ... D ... 844 825-6600
101 Larkspur Landing Cir Larkspur (94939) ***(P-164)***
Onelegacy ... C ... 213 229-5600
221 S Figueroa St Ste 500 Los Angeles (90012) ***(P-22852)***
Onelegacy (PA) ... D ... 213 625-0665
221 S Figueroa St Ste 500 Los Angeles (90012) ***(P-22853)***
Onemain Holdings Inc ... C ... 209 869-8030
2401 Claribel Rd Ste C Riverbank (95367) ***(P-9838)***
Onemain Holdings Inc ... C ... 909 392-5578
2278 Foothill Blvd La Verne (91750) ***(P-10100)***
Onemain Holdings Inc ... C ... 951 245-5029
31712 Casino Dr Ste 6a Lake Elsinore (92530) ***(P-9839)***
Onemarket Network LLC (HQ) ... C ... 415 638-9868
835 Market St Ste 700 Los Angeles (90067) ***(P-16026)***
Oneoc (PA) ... D ... 714 953-5757
1901 E 4th St Ste 100 Santa Ana (92705) ***(P-25447)***
Oneunited Bank ... D ... 323 295-3381
3683 Crenshaw Blvd Los Angeles (90016) ***(P-9468)***
Onewest Bank, Culver City *Also called CIT Bank NA* ***(P-9313)***
Onewest Bank NA ... D ... 562 433-0971
3500 E 7th St Long Beach (90804) ***(P-9526)***
Online Communications Inc ... C ... 916 652-7253
3291 Swetzer Rd Loomis (95650) ***(P-2668)***
Online Energy LLC ... E ... 510 583-0091
20885 Redwood Rd Unit 405 Castro Valley (94546) ***(P-7781)***
Online Energy Uv Systems, Castro Valley *Also called Online Energy LLC* ***(P-7781)***
Online Technical Services Inc (PA) ... E ... 408 378-1100
1901 S Bascom Ave Ste 840 Campbell (95008) ***(P-14681)***
Onrad Inc ... D ... 800 848-5876
1770 Iowa Ave Ste 280 Riverside (92507) ***(P-26967)***
Onrad Medical Group, Riverside *Also called Onrad Inc* ***(P-26967)***
Onsite Consulting LLC ... D ... 323 401-3190
5042 Wilshire Blvd # 135 Los Angeles (90036) ***(P-27812)***
Onsite Health Inc (PA) ... D ... 949 305-2253
85 Argonaut Ste 220 Aliso Viejo (92656) ***(P-22854)***
Onsolve LLC ... D ... 858 724-1200
3398 Carmel Mountain Rd # 100 San Diego (92121) ***(P-15329)***
Ontario Airport Hotel Corp ... C ... 408 562-6709
4949 Great America Pkwy Santa Clara (95054) ***(P-12986)***
Ontario Community Hospital, Ontario *Also called Kindred Healthcare Oper Inc* ***(P-21538)***
Ontario Convention Center, Ontario *Also called Smg Food and Beverage LLC* ***(P-17473)***
Ontario Convention Center Corp ... C ... 909 937-3000
2000 E Convention Ctr Way Ontario (91764) ***(P-17370)***
Ontario Distribution Center, Ontario *Also called National Distribution Centers* ***(P-5115)***
Ontario Health Educatn Co Inc ... E ... 951 817-8553
3130 Sedona Ct Ontario (91764) ***(P-22381)***
Ontario Healthcare Center, Ontario *Also called Kf Ontario Healthcare LLC* ***(P-21125)***
Ontario Mills Shopping Center, Ontario *Also called Mills Corporation* ***(P-10913)***
Ontario Montclar Sch Dist Food ... C ... 909 930-6360
1525 S Bon View Ave Ontario (91761) ***(P-22855)***
Ontario Refrigeration Svc Inc (PA) ... C ... 909 984-2771
635 S Mountain Ave Ontario (91762) ***(P-2298)***
Ontario Vineyard Medical Offs, Ontario *Also called Kaiser Foundation Hospitals* ***(P-19573)***
Ontario-Don, Ontario *Also called Synnex Corporation* ***(P-4638)***
Ontel Security Services Inc ... D ... 209 521-0200
708 L St Modesto (95354) ***(P-16749)***
Ontic Engineering and Mfg Inc (HQ) ... B ... 818 678-6555
20400 Plummer St Chatsworth (91311) ***(P-7912)***
Ontrac, Santa Maria *Also called Express Messenger Systems Inc* ***(P-4404)***
Ontrac, Compton *Also called Express Messenger Systems Inc* ***(P-4406)***
Ontrac, South San Francisco *Also called Express Messenger Systems Inc* ***(P-4407)***
Ontrac, Fresno *Also called Express Messenger Systems Inc* ***(P-4409)***
Oocl (usa) Inc ... D ... 408 576-6543
2700 Zanker Rd Ste 200 San Jose (95134) ***(P-5127)***
Oocl (usa) Inc ... D ... 562 499-2600
111 W Ocean Blvd Ste 1800 Long Beach (90802) ***(P-5128)***
Oocl (usa) Inc ... D ... 562 499-2600
17777 Center Court Dr N # 500 Cerritos (90703) ***(P-5129)***
Ooma Inc (PA) ... C ... 650 566-6600
525 Almanor Ave Ste 200 Sunnyvale (94085) ***(P-5617)***
Ooyala Inc (HQ) ... C ... 650 961-3400
2099 Gateway Pl Ste 600 San Jose (95110) ***(P-15330)***
Op Bancorp ... C ... 213 892-9999
1000 Wilshire Blvd # 500 Los Angeles (90017) ***(P-9469)***
Opal Fry and Son ... E ... 661 858-2523
Maricopa Hwy Bakersfield (93307) ***(P-74)***
Opal Soft Inc ... D ... 408 267-2211
1288 Kifer Rd Ste 201 Sunnyvale (94086) ***(P-16442)***
Opallios Inc ... E ... 408 769-4594
4633 Old Ironsides Dr # 315 Santa Clara (95054) ***(P-27813)***
Opalsoft, Sunnyvale *Also called Opal Soft Inc* ***(P-16442)***
Oparc ... D ... 909 598-8055
355 S Lemon Ave Ste J Walnut (91789) ***(P-23951)***
Oparc (PA) ... E ... 909 982-4090
9029 Vernon Ave Montclair (91763) ***(P-24213)***
Open Door Community Hlth Ctrs ... D ... 707 826-8610
770 10th St Arcata (95521) ***(P-22625)***
Open Door Community Hlth Ctrs (PA) ... D ... 707 826-8642
670 9th St Ste 203cfo Arcata (95521) ***(P-22626)***
Open Harbor Inc ... D ... 650 413-4200
1123 Industrial Rd San Francisco (94111) ***(P-27381)***
Open Text Inc (HQ) ... C ... 650 645-3000
2950 S Delaware St San Mateo (94403) ***(P-15331)***
Openpopcom Inc (PA) ... D ... 714 249-7044
5422 Beach Blvd Buena Park (90621) ***(P-27814)***
Opentable Inc (HQ) ... C ... 415 344-4200
1 Montgomery St Ste 700 San Francisco (94104) ***(P-17371)***
Opentv Inc (HQ) ... C ... 415 962-5000
275 Sacramento St Ste Sl1 San Francisco (94111) ***(P-15790)***
Openx Technologies Inc (HQ) ... D ... 855 673-6948
888 E Walnut St Fl 2 Pasadena (91101) ***(P-13874)***
Opera San Jose Inc ... D ... 408 437-4450
2149 Paragon Dr San Jose (95131) ***(P-18391)***
Operating Engineers Funds Inc (PA) ... C ... 866 400-5200
100 Corson St Ste 222 Pasadena (91103) ***(P-12118)***
Operating Engineers Loca ... C ... 408 782-9803
325 Digital Dr Morgan Hill (95037) ***(P-25854)***
Operation Samahan Inc ... C ... 619 477-4451
10737 Camino Ruiz Ste 235 San Diego (92126) ***(P-19737)***
Operation Technology Inc (PA) ... D ... 949 462-0100
17 Goodyear Ste 100 Irvine (92618) ***(P-15332)***
Operations, Los Angeles *Also called Wells Fargo Bank NA* ***(P-9380)***
Operations Control Center, Oakland *Also called San Francisco Bay Area Rapid* ***(P-3707)***
Operations/Risk Group, Pasadena *Also called Parsons Constructors Inc* ***(P-26980)***
Operatix Inc ... D ... 408 332-5796
111 N Market St Ste 300 San Jose (95113) ***(P-27382)***
Opex Communications Inc ... E ... 562 968-5420
3777 Long Beach Blvd # 400 Long Beach (90807) ***(P-5618)***
Opinion Dynamics Corp Fla Inc ... D ... 510 444-5050
1999 Harrison St Ste 1250 Oakland (94612) ***(P-27383)***
Oplink Communications Inc (HQ) ... D ... 510 933-7200
46360 Fremont Blvd Fremont (94538) ***(P-5990)***
Oprah Winfrey Network, West Hollywood *Also called Own LLC* ***(P-5925)***

ALPHABETIC

Employee Codes: A=Over 500 employees, B=251-500
C=101-250, D=51-100, E=50
2019 Directory of California
Wholesalers and Services Companies
© Mergent Inc. 1-800-342-5647
1407

Opsec Specialized Protection ....D....661 942-3999
44262 Division St Ste A Lancaster (93535) *(P-16750)*
Opswat Inc (PA) ....D....415 590-7300
398 Kansas St San Francisco (94103) *(P-15333)*
Optec Displays Inc ....D....626 369-7188
1700 S De Soto Pl Ste A Ontario (91761) *(P-7143)*
Optics Laboratory Inc ....D....626 350-1926
9480 Telstar Ave Ste 3 El Monte (91731) *(P-22118)*
Optim, Pleasanton Also called Unchained Labs *(P-22153)*
Optima Building Services Maint ....D....707 586-6640
210 Mountain View Ave Santa Rosa (95407) *(P-14336)*
Optima Mortgage Corporation ....D....714 389-4650
2081 Bus Ctr Dr Ste 230 Irvine (92612) *(P-9840)*
Optima Network Services Inc (HQ) ....D....305 599-1800
15345 Fairfield Ranch Rd # 225 Chino Hills (91709) *(P-27947)*
Optima Tax Relief LLC ....C....714 361-4636
3100 S Harbor Blvd # 250 Santa Ana (92704) *(P-13711)*
Optimal Health Services Inc ....D....661 393-4483
1315 Boughton Dr Bakersfield (93308) *(P-22382)*
Optimal Hospice Care, Bakersfield Also called Optimal Hospice Foundation *(P-22383)*
Optimal Hospice Foundation ....D....562 494-7687
3200 E 19th St Signal Hill (90755) *(P-20947)*
Optimal Hospice Foundation ....C....661 716-4000
1675 Chester Ave Ste 401 Bakersfield (93301) *(P-22383)*
Optimizely Inc (PA) ....B....415 376-4598
631 Howard St Ste 100 San Francisco (94105) *(P-15334)*
Optimum Inc (PA) ....E....909 990-0767
17890 Valley Blvd Ste A Bloomington (92316) *(P-25855)*
Optimum Con Fundations USA Inc ....D....877 212-7994
6258 Rustic Ln Jurupa Valley (92509) *(P-3298)*
Optimum Cx LLC ....C....805 922-2999
1288 W Mccoy Ln Ste C Santa Maria (93455) *(P-17372)*
Optimum Solutions Group LLC ....C....415 954-7100
419 Ponderosa Ct Lafayette (94549) *(P-15791)*
Optimus Ventures LLC ....E....888 881-5969
143 Selby Ln Atherton (94027) *(P-7519)*
Optio Solutions LLC ....C....800 360-2827
1444 N Mcdowell Blvd Petaluma (94954) *(P-14014)*
Option Care Home Care Inc ....D....818 351-3000
9401 Chivers Ave Sun Valley (91352) *(P-22384)*
Option One Home Med Eqp Inc ....C....909 478-5413
1220 Research Dr Ste A Redlands (92374) *(P-14435)*
Options Family of Services ....E....805 462-8544
5755 Valentina Ave Atascadero (93422) *(P-22627)*
Options For Learning ....D....626 308-2411
2001 Elm St Alhambra (91803) *(P-24359)*
Optisource Technologies Inc ....E....714 288-0825
1855 W Katella Ave # 170 Orange (92867) *(P-14091)*
Optumrx Inc ....B....760 804-2399
2858 Loker Ave E Ste 100 Carlsbad (92010) *(P-10287)*
Optumrx Inc (HQ) ....B....714 825-3600
2300 Main St Irvine (92614) *(P-10288)*
Opus Bank ....C....714 578-7500
200 W Commonwealth Ave Fullerton (92832) *(P-9515)*
Opus Inspection Inc ....D....714 999-6727
1410 S Acacia Ave Ste A Fullerton (92831) *(P-15335)*
Opya Inc ....D....650 931-6300
1720 S Amphlett Blvd # 110 San Mateo (94402) *(P-22628)*
Ora Pacific Regional Field Off ....D....949 608-2907
19701 Fairchild Irvine (92612) *(P-17373)*
Oracle, San Mateo Also called Netsuite Inc *(P-15776)*
Oracle America Inc ....C....408 276-4300
4220 Network Cir Santa Clara (95054) *(P-15792)*
Oracle America Inc ....D....415 908-3609
475 Sansome St Fl 15 San Francisco (94111) *(P-15793)*
Oracle America Inc ....C....408 276-3331
4120 Network Cir Santa Clara (95054) *(P-15336)*
Oracle America Inc ....D....925 694-3314
5815 Owens Dr Pleasanton (94588) *(P-15794)*
Oracle America Inc ....B....408 635-3072
80 Railroad Ave Milpitas (95035) *(P-15795)*
Oracle America Inc ....D....858 625-5044
9540 Towne Centre Dr San Diego (92121) *(P-15796)*
Oracle America Inc ....C....408 276-7534
4230 Leonard Stocking Dr Santa Clara (95054) *(P-15797)*
Oracle America Inc ....D....800 633-0584
500 Oracle Pkwy Redwood City (94065) *(P-7086)*
Oracle Corp ....A....650 506-7000
17901 Von Karman Ave # 800 Irvine (92614) *(P-27948)*
Oracle Corporation ....C....713 654-0919
279 Barnes Rd Tustin (92782) *(P-15798)*
Oracle Corporation ....B....650 607-5402
214 Clarence Ave Sunnyvale (94086) *(P-15799)*
Oracle Corporation ....B....650 678-3612
1408 Antigua Ln Foster City (94404) *(P-15800)*
Oracle Corporation ....B....408 421-2890
1490 Newhall St Santa Clara (95050) *(P-15801)*
Oracle Corporation ....B....408 276-5552
231 Kerry Dr Santa Clara (95050) *(P-15802)*
Oracle Corporation ....B....408 276-3822
3084 Thurman Dr San Jose (95148) *(P-15803)*
Oracle Corporation ....C....858 202-0648
9515 Towne Centre Dr San Diego (92121) *(P-15804)*
Oracle Corporation ....B....650 506-9864
3532 Eastin Pl Santa Clara (95051) *(P-15805)*
Oracle Corporation ....B....408 390-8623
372 Calero Ave San Jose (95123) *(P-15806)*
Oracle Corporation ....C....415 402-7200
475 Sansome St Fl 15 San Francisco (94111) *(P-15807)*

Oracle Corporation ....B....916 435-8342
6224 Hummingbird Ln Rocklin (95765) *(P-15808)*
Oracle Corporation ....B....877 767-2253
5805 Owens Dr Pleasanton (94588) *(P-15809)*
Oracle Corporation ....B....925 694-6258
3925 Emerald Isle Ln San Jose (95135) *(P-15810)*
Oracle Corporation ....B....510 471-6971
5863 Carmel Way Union City (94587) *(P-15811)*
Oracle Corporation ....B....310 258-7500
5750 Hannum Ave Ste 200 Culver City (90230) *(P-15812)*
Oracle Corporation ....B....310 343-7405
200 N Pacific Coast Hwy # 400 El Segundo (90245) *(P-15813)*
Oracle Corporation ....B....916 315-3500
1001 Sunset Blvd Rocklin (95765) *(P-15814)*
Oracle Corporation (PA) ....A....650 506-7000
500 Oracle Pkwy Redwood City (94065) *(P-16443)*
Oracle Systems Corporation ....D....818 817-2900
200 N Pacific Coast Hwy # 400 El Segundo (90245) *(P-15815)*
Oracle Systems Corporation ....D....650 506-8648
102 Santa Barbara Ave Daly City (94014) *(P-15816)*
Oracle Systems Corporation ....B....650 654-7606
301 Island Pkwy Belmont (94002) *(P-15817)*
Oracle Systems Corporation ....C....650 506-6780
500 Oracle Pwky San Mateo (94403) *(P-15818)*
Oracle Systems Corporation ....B....650 506-0300
10 Twin Dolphin Dr Redwood City (94065) *(P-15819)*
Oracle Systems Corporation (HQ) ....A....650 506-7000
500 Oracle Pkwy Redwood City (94065) *(P-16444)*
Oracle Systems Corporation ....B....925 694-3000
5840 Owens Dr Pleasanton (94588) *(P-15820)*
Oracle Systems Corporation ....D....949 224-1000
2010 Main St Ste 450 Irvine (92614) *(P-15821)*
Oracle Systems Corporation ....B....949 623-9460
17901 Von Karman Ave # 800 Irvine (92614) *(P-15822)*
Oracle Taleo LLC ....A....925 452-3000
4140 Dublin Blvd Ste 400 Dublin (94568) *(P-15823)*
Orange Belt Adventures, Visalia Also called Orange Belt Stages *(P-3900)*
Orange Belt Stages (PA) ....D....559 733-4408
2134 E Mineral King Ave Visalia (93292) *(P-3900)*
Orange Cast Title Southern Cal (PA) ....D....714 558-2836
1551 N Tustin Ave Ste 300 Santa Ana (92705) *(P-17374)*
Orange Cast Title Southern Cal ....D....714 822-3211
2411 W La Palma Ave # 300 Anaheim (92801) *(P-10470)*
Orange Children & Parents ....D....714 639-4000
1063 N Glassell St Orange (92867) *(P-24360)*
Orange Cnty Adult Achvment Ctr ....C....714 744-5301
225 W Carl Karcher Way Anaheim (92801) *(P-17375)*
Orange Cnty Conservation Corps ....D....714 451-1301
1853 N Raymond Ave Anaheim (92801) *(P-24214)*
Orange Cnty George M Raymond N, Orange Also called Raymond Group *(P-27012)*
Orange Cnty Sprntndent Schools ....D....949 650-2506
220 23rd St Costa Mesa (92627) *(P-24361)*
Orange Coast Building Services ....C....714 453-6300
2191 S Dupont Dr Anaheim (92806) *(P-1425)*
Orange Coast Ctr For Surgl Cr, Fountain Valley Also called Memorialcare Surgical Center A *(P-21584)*
Orange Coast Masonry Acquisit ....D....714 538-4386
601 N Batavia St Orange (92868) *(P-2819)*
Orange Coast Memorial Med Ctr (HQ) ....D....714 378-7000
9920 Talbert Ave Fountain Valley (92708) *(P-21615)*
Orange Coast Service Center, Westminster Also called Southern California Edison Co *(P-6135)*
Orange County Association (PA) ....D....714 547-7559
822 W Town And Country Rd Orange (92868) *(P-25032)*
Orange County Child Abuse ....D....714 543-4333
2390 E Orangewood Ave # 300 Anaheim (92806) *(P-23952)*
Orange County Cncl Bsa (PA) ....D....714 546-4990
1211 E Dyer Rd Ste 100 Santa Ana (92705) *(P-25208)*
Orange County Dept Education ....A....714 730-7301
300 S C St Tustin (92780) *(P-26968)*
Orange County Employees Retir ....D....714 558-6200
2223 S Wellington Ave Santa Ana (92701) *(P-12043)*
Orange County Head Start (PA) ....D....714 241-8920
2501 Pullman St Ste 100 Santa Ana (92705) *(P-24362)*
Orange County Head Start ....C....714 761-4967
9200 W Pacific Pl Anaheim (92804) *(P-24363)*
Orange County Health Auth ....B....714 246-8500
505 City Pkwy W Orange (92868) *(P-25033)*
Orange County Health Care Agcy ....B....714 568-5683
405 W 5th St Ste 700 Santa Ana (92701) *(P-25034)*
Orange County One Stop Center ....D....714 241-4900
5405 Grdn Rd Blvd Ste 100 Westminster (92683) *(P-14682)*
Orange County Plst Co Inc ....C....714 957-1971
3191 Arprt Loop Dr Ste B1 Costa Mesa (92626) *(P-2928)*
Orange County Produce LLC ....D....949 451-0880
11405 Jeffrey Rd Irvine (92602) *(P-111)*
Orange County Royale Convlscnt ....D....949 458-6346
23228 Madero Mission Viejo (92691) *(P-21616)*
Orange County Royale Convlscnt (PA) ....B....714 546-6450
1030 W Warner Ave Santa Ana (92707) *(P-21175)*
Orange County Sanitation (PA) ....A....714 962-2411
10844 Ellis Ave Fountain Valley (92708) *(P-6425)*
Orange County Sanitation ....C....714 962-2411
22212 Brookhurst St Huntington Beach (92646) *(P-6326)*
Orange County Service Center, San Clemente Also called San Diego Gas & Electric Co *(P-6187)*
Orange County Services Inc ....E....714 541-9753
3022 N Hesperian St Santa Ana (92706) *(P-2299)*

Mergent e-mail: customerrelations@mergent.com
1408

2019 Directory of California
Wholesalers and Services Companies

(P-0000) Products & Services Section entry number
(PA)=Parent Co (HQ)=Headquarters (DH)=Div Headquarters

ORANGE COUNTY TRANSIT DISTRICT, Orange *Also called Orange County Trnsp Auth* **(P-3694)**
Orange County Trnsp Auth.....A.....714 560-6282
11790 Cardinal Cir Garden Grove (92843) **(P-3693)**
Orange County Trnsp Auth (PA).....B.....714 636-7433
550 S Main St Orange (92868) **(P-3694)**
Orange County Trnsp Auth.....A.....714 999-1726
600 S Main St Ste 910 Orange (92868) **(P-3695)**
Orange County-Irvine Med Ctr, Irvine *Also called Kaiser Foundation Hospitals* **(P-12110)**
Orange Countys Credit Union (PA).....C.....714 755-5900
1721 E Saint Andrew Pl Santa Ana (92705) **(P-9577)**
Orange Courier Inc.....B.....714 384-3600
3731 W Warner Ave Santa Ana (92704) **(P-17376)**
Orange Cove Health Center, Orange Cove *Also called United Health Ctrs San Joaquin* **(P-22706)**
Orange Healthcare & Wellness.....C.....714 633-3568
920 W La Veta Ave Orange (92868) **(P-20681)**
Orange Labs, San Francisco *Also called France Telecom RES & Dev LLC* **(P-26518)**
Orange Pacific Plumbing Inc.....D.....714 992-4547
801 Panorama Rd Fullerton (92831) **(P-2300)**
Orange Silicon Valley.....D.....415 243-1500
60 Spear St Ste 1100 San Francisco (94105) **(P-27815)**
Orangepeople LLC.....D.....949 535-1308
300 Spectrum Center Dr Irvine (92618) **(P-27949)**
Orangetree Convalescent Hosp.....C.....951 785-6060
4000 Harrison St Riverside (92503) **(P-21617)**
Orangewood Foundation.....D.....714 619-0200
1575 E 17th St Santa Ana (92705) **(P-23953)**
Orbital Sciences Corporation.....B.....703 406-5000
2401 E El Segundo Blvd # 200 El Segundo (90245) **(P-26425)**
Orchard - Post Acute Care Ctr.....A.....562 693-7701
12385 Washington Blvd Whittier (90606) **(P-20682)**
Orchard Holdings Group Inc.....C.....949 502-8300
1 Venture Ste 300 Irvine (92618) **(P-11644)**
Orchard Horror Film LLC.....E.....212 203-6147
15715 Woodvale Rd Encino (91436) **(P-18453)**
Orchard Hospital.....C.....530 846-9000
240 Spruce St Gridley (95948) **(P-21618)**
Orchard Hotel, San Francisco *Also called Orchard International Group* **(P-12987)**
Orchard International Group (PA).....D.....415 362-8878
665 Bush St San Francisco (94108) **(P-12987)**
Orchard Medical Offices, Downey *Also called Kaiser Foundation Hospitals* **(P-19551)**
Orchard Park, Clovis *Also called Regent Assisted Living Inc* **(P-24650)**
Orchid MPS.....D.....714 549-9203
3233 W Harvard St Santa Ana (92704) **(P-7200)**
Orco Block, Stanton *Also called Muth Development Co Inc* **(P-10916)**
Orcutt Lions Club.....D.....805 937-0158
126 S Broadway St Orcutt (93455) **(P-25448)**
Ore-Cal Corp (PA).....D.....213 623-8493
634 Crocker St Los Angeles (90021) **(P-8588)**
Oregon PCF Bldg Pdts Calif Inc.....D.....916 381-8051
8185 Signal Ct Ste A Sacramento (95824) **(P-6844)**
Oregon PCF Bldg Pdts Maple Inc.....C.....909 627-4043
2401 E Philadelphia St Ontario (91761) **(P-6845)**
Oren's Replay, Van Nuys *Also called Factory 2-U Import Export Inc* **(P-8303)**
Orenda Center.....D.....707 565-7450
1430 Neotomas Ave Santa Rosa (95405) **(P-22629)**
Orepac Building Products, Sacramento *Also called Oregon PCF Bldg Pdts Calif Inc* **(P-6844)**
Orepac Millwork Products, Ontario *Also called Oregon PCF Bldg Pdts Maple Inc* **(P-6845)**
Oreq Corporation.....E.....951 296-5076
42306 Remington Ave Temecula (92590) **(P-26969)**
Organic Inc.....D.....310 543-4600
390 Amapola Ave Ste 8 Torrance (90501) **(P-16445)**
Organic Inc (HQ).....C.....415 581-5300
600 California St Fl 8 San Francisco (94108) **(P-16446)**
Organic & Sustainable Buty Inc.....E.....310 815-8201
5933 Bowcroft St Los Angeles (90016) **(P-13666)**
Organic Affinity LLC.....D.....801 870-7433
3980 Hopevale Dr Sherman Oaks (91403) **(P-7520)**
Organic Holdings Inc.....B.....415 581-5300
600 California St Fl 8 San Francisco (94108) **(P-13875)**
Organic On, San Francisco *Also called Organic Holdings Inc* **(P-13875)**
Organic Pastures Dairy Co LLC.....E.....559 846-9732
7221 S Jameson Ave Fresno (93706) **(P-424)**
Organovo Holdings Inc (PA).....D.....858 224-1000
6275 Nncy Rdge Dr Ste 110 San Diego (92121) **(P-26426)**
Organztion Amrcn Kdaly Edctors.....E.....310 441-3555
10801 National Blvd # 590 Los Angeles (90064) **(P-25449)**
Orient Fisheries Inc.....D.....323 588-4185
1912 E Vernon Ave Ste 110 Vernon (90058) **(P-8589)**
Oriental Motor USA Corporation (HQ).....D.....310 715-3300
570 Alaska Ave Torrance (90503) **(P-7383)**
Oriental Trading Co, Richmond *Also called Ctc Food International Inc* **(P-8782)**
Origaudio, Fountain Valley *Also called Forty Four Group LLC* **(P-13831)**
Origin Systems Inc.....B.....650 628-1500
209 Redwood Shores Pkwy Redwood City (94065) **(P-15337)**
Original Mowbrays Tree Svc Inc (PA).....C.....909 383-7009
1845 Bus Ctr Dr Ste 215 San Bernardino (92408) **(P-976)**
Original Petes Pizza Inc.....E.....916 442-6770
2001 J St Sacramento (95811) **(P-12139)**
Original Seatbeltbag , The, Santa Ana *Also called Harveys Industries Inc* **(P-8305)**
Original Sid Blackman Plbg Inc.....D.....760 352-3632
1160 S 2nd St El Centro (92243) **(P-2301)**
Orinda Convalescent Hospital.....D.....925 254-6500
11 Altarinda Rd Orinda (94563) **(P-21176)**
Orinda Country Club.....D.....925 254-4313
315 Camino Sobrante Orinda (94563) **(P-18995)**
Orion - Rand, Simi Valley *Also called Rand Medical Billing Inc* **(P-26280)**
Orion Construction Corporation.....D.....760 597-9660
2185 La Mirada Dr Vista (92081) **(P-1964)**
Orion Pictures Corporation.....A.....310 449-3000
245 N Beverly Dr Beverly Hills (90210) **(P-18088)**
Orion Security, San Jose *Also called Yosh Enterprises Inc* **(P-16863)**
Oritz Corporation (PA).....C.....650 692-8000
1555 Old Bayshore Hwy # 400 Burlingame (94010) **(P-8623)**
Ormat Nevada Inc.....E.....760 353-8200
947 Dogwood Rd Heber (92249) **(P-6200)**
Ormesa LLC.....D.....760 356-3020
3300 E Evan Hewes Hwy Holtville (92250) **(P-6066)**
Orora North America.....D.....760 510-7170
664 N Twin Oaks Valley Rd San Marcos (92069) **(P-8114)**
Orora North America.....C.....626 284-9524
3201 W Mission Rd Alhambra (91803) **(P-8115)**
Orora North America.....D.....760 510-7000
664 N Twin Oaks Valley Rd San Marcos (92069) **(P-8116)**
Orora North America.....C.....714 562-6002
6200 Caballero Blvd Buena Park (90620) **(P-8117)**
Orora Packaging Solutions (HQ).....D.....714 562-6000
6600 Valley View St Buena Park (90620) **(P-8118)**
Orora Packaging Solutions.....D.....714 984-2300
3200 Enterprise St Brea (92821) **(P-8119)**
Orora Packaging Solutions.....D.....510 487-1211
33463 Western Ave Union City (94587) **(P-8120)**
Orora Packaging Solutions.....C.....323 832-2000
1640 S Greenwood Ave Montebello (90640) **(P-8121)**
Orora Packaging Solutions.....C.....714 278-6000
1901 E Rosslynn Ave Fullerton (92831) **(P-8122)**
Orora Packaging Solutions.....D.....714 773-0124
1911 E Rosslynn Ave Fullerton (92831) **(P-8123)**
Oroville Hosp Post Acute Ctr, Oroville *Also called 1000 Executive Parkway LLC* **(P-20213)**
Oroville Hospital (PA).....A.....530 533-8500
2767 Olive Hwy Oroville (95966) **(P-21619)**
Oroville Hospital.....D.....530 538-8700
2353 Myers St Ste B Oroville (95966) **(P-20191)**
Oroville Internal Meds Group.....E.....530 538-3171
2721 Olive Hwy Ste 12 Oroville (95966) **(P-19738)**
Orrick Hrrington Sutcliffe LLP (PA).....C.....415 773-5700
405 Howard St San Francisco (94105) **(P-23301)**
Orrick Hrrington Sutcliffe LLP.....C.....650 614-7400
1000 Marsh Rd Menlo Park (94025) **(P-23302)**
Orrick Hrrington Sutcliffe LLP.....C.....650 614-7454
1020 Marsh Rd Menlo Park (94025) **(P-23303)**
Orrick Hrrington Sutcliffe LLP.....C.....213 629-2020
777 S Figueroa St # 3200 Los Angeles (90017) **(P-23304)**
Orrick Hrrington Sutcliffe LLP.....D.....916 447-9200
400 Capitol Mall Ste 3000 Sacramento (95814) **(P-23305)**
Ortega Elementary Pto.....D.....650 738-6670
1283 Terra Nova Blvd Pacifica (94044) **(P-25209)**
Ortega High School, Lake Elsinore *Also called Lake Elsinore Unified Schl Dst* **(P-24337)**
Orthocad, San Jose *Also called Cadent Inc* **(P-15924)**
Orthopaedic Hospital (PA).....C.....213 742-1000
403 W Adams Blvd Los Angeles (90007) **(P-21620)**
Orthopaedic Inst For Children, Los Angeles *Also called Orthopaedic Hospital* **(P-21620)**
Orthopedic Consultants (PA).....E.....818 788-7343
16311 Ventura Blvd # 800 Encino (91436) **(P-19739)**
Orthopedics Department, Los Angeles *Also called Southern Cal Prmnnte Med Group* **(P-19912)**
Ortiz Asphalt Paving Inc.....E.....951 966-7060
16588 Farmington St Hesperia (92345) **(P-1830)**
Ortiz Enterprises Incorporated (PA).....D.....949 753-1414
6 Cushing Ste 200 Irvine (92618) **(P-1831)**
Orwick Fresh Foods Inc.....E.....909 985-5604
7940 Cherry Ave Ste 203 Fontana (92336) **(P-8843)**
Osage Hlthcare Wellness Centre, Inglewood *Also called Centinela Sklld Nrsng & Wllnss* **(P-20298)**
Osata Enterprises Inc.....D.....310 297-1550
225 S Aviation Blvd El Segundo (90245) **(P-8364)**
Oscar Valero.....E.....530 668-4342
1685 Jones St Woodland (95776) **(P-372)**
Osf International Inc.....D.....760 341-5600
71743 Highway 111 Rancho Mirage (92270) **(P-8844)**
Oshman Family Jewish Cmnty Ctr.....C.....650 223-8700
3921 Fabian Way Palo Alto (94303) **(P-23954)**
Oshyn Inc.....D.....213 483-1770
100 W Broadway Ste 330 Long Beach (90802) **(P-16163)**
OSI, Folsom *Also called Objective Systems Integrators* **(P-15324)**
OSI Digital Inc.....E.....949 724-8300
2525 Main St Ste 350 Irvine (92614) **(P-16447)**
OSI Software, San Leandro *Also called Osisoft LLC* **(P-15338)**
Osisoft LLC (PA).....B.....510 297-5800
1600 Alvarado St San Leandro (94577) **(P-15338)**
Osram Opto Semiconductors Inc.....D.....408 588-3800
1150 Kifer Rd Ste 100 Sunnyvale (94086) **(P-7521)**
Osram Opto Semiconductors Inc (HQ).....E.....408 962-3736
1150 Kifer Rd Ste 100 Sunnyvale (94086) **(P-7522)**
Osscim Inc.....E.....714 680-0015
172 E Orangethorpe Ave Placentia (92870) **(P-3182)**
Ost Crane Service, Ventura *Also called Ost Trucks and Cranes Inc* **(P-17377)**
Ost Trucks and Cranes Inc.....D.....805 643-9963
2951 N Ventura Ave Ventura (93001) **(P-17377)**
Ostcs, Covina *Also called Outsource Testing Inc* **(P-27816)**
Ostendo Technologies Inc (PA).....D.....760 710-3003
6185 Paseo Del Norte # 200 Carlsbad (92011) **(P-26427)**
Osterhout Design Group, San Francisco *Also called Osterhout Group Inc* **(P-17378)**
Osterhout Group Inc.....E.....415 644-4000
153 Townsend St Ste 570 San Francisco (94107) **(P-17378)**

ALPHABETIC

Employee Codes: A=Over 500 employees, B=251-500
C=101-250, D=51-100, E=50
2019 Directory of California
Wholesalers and Services Companies
© Mergent Inc. 1-800-342-5647
1409

OTasty Foods Inc..........D.......626 330-1229
160 S Hacienda Blvd City of Industry (91745) ***(P-8438)***
Otay Lakes Road Branch, Chula Vista *Also called Citibank National Association* ***(P-9331)***
Otay Mesa Medical Offices, San Diego *Also called Kaiser Foundation Hospitals* ***(P-12102)***
Otay Water District..........C.......619 670-2222
2554 Swetwater Sprng Blvd Spring Valley (91978) ***(P-6293)***
Otb Acquisition LLC..........C.......520 458-0540
770 S Brea Blvd Ste 227 Brea (92821) ***(P-12988)***
Otis Elevator Company..........E.......323 342-4500
2701 Media Center Dr # 2 Los Angeles (90065) ***(P-7782)***
Otis Elevator Company..........E.......714 758-9593
711 E Ball Rd Ste 200 Anaheim (92805) ***(P-17965)***
Otis Elevator Company..........C.......415 546-0880
444 Spear St Ste 100 San Francisco (94105) ***(P-17966)***
Otis Elevator Intl Inc..........D.......510 874-5129
1358 14th St Oakland (94607) ***(P-3474)***
Otismed Corporation..........D.......510 786-3171
1600 Harbor Bay Pkwy # 200 Alameda (94502) ***(P-7201)***
Otr Global LLC..........E.......415 675-7660
155 Montgomery St Ste 501 San Francisco (94104) ***(P-26555)***
Otto Cap, Ontario *Also called Otto International Inc* ***(P-8272)***
Otto Construction, Sacramento *Also called John F Otto Inc* ***(P-1565)***
Otto International Inc (PA)..........E.......909 937-1998
3550 Jurupa St Ste A Ontario (91761) ***(P-8272)***
Otts Asia..........D.......562 259-3447
10015 Baring Cross St Los Angeles (90044) ***(P-12256)***
Ouch Systems, West Sacramento *Also called Occupnl Urgnt Care Hlth Syst* ***(P-22850)***
Oum & Co LLP (PA)..........D.......415 434-3744
601 California St # 1800 San Francisco (94108) ***(P-26263)***
Our Alchemy LLC (PA)..........D.......310 893-6289
5900 Wilshire Blvd Fl 18 Los Angeles (90036) ***(P-18253)***
Our House, Vallejo *Also called Crestwood Behavioral Hlth Inc* ***(P-21948)***
Our House Residential Care Ctr..........D.......559 674-8670
109 E Central Ave Madera (93638) ***(P-21177)***
Our Lady of Fatima Villa Inc..........D.......408 741-2950
20400 Srtoga Los Gatos Rd Saratoga (95070) ***(P-20683)***
Our Lady of Grace P T G..........E.......619 466-0055
2766 Navajo Rd El Cajon (92020) ***(P-17379)***
Our Watch..........D.......714 897-1022
12832 Valley View St # 211 Garden Grove (92845) ***(P-22385)***
Our Way, Oceanside *Also called E R I T Inc* ***(P-24513)***
Out of Shell LLC..........C.......626 401-1923
9658 Remer St South El Monte (91733) ***(P-1426)***
Outcast Agency LLC..........C.......415 392-8282
100 Montgomery St # 1200 San Francisco (94104) ***(P-27567)***
Outfront Media Inc..........C.......408 457-0111
2635 N 1st St Ste 236 San Jose (95134) ***(P-13929)***
Outfront Media LLC..........D.......510 527-3350
1695 Eastshore Hwy Berkeley (94710) ***(P-13930)***
Outlook Amusements Inc..........C.......818 433-3800
2900 W Alameda Ave # 400 Burbank (91505) ***(P-16448)***
Outpatient Rehabilitation Svcs, Walnut Creek *Also called John Muir Health* ***(P-21466)***
Outpatnt Eye Srgry Ctr of Dsrt..........E.......760 340-3937
72057 Dinah Shore Dr D1 Rancho Mirage (92270) ***(P-19740)***
Outreach & Escort Inc (PA)..........D.......408 678-8585
2221 Oakland Rd Ste 200 San Jose (95131) ***(P-3696)***
Outrigger Hotels Hawaii..........D.......310 301-2000
4200 Admiralty Way Venice (90292) ***(P-12989)***
Outrigger Hotels Hawaii..........D.......323 491-9015
8462 W Sunset Blvd West Hollywood (90069) ***(P-12990)***
Outside Lines Inc..........E.......714 637-4747
2150 S Towne Cntre Pl 1 Anaheim (92806) ***(P-772)***
Outsource Consulting Svcs Inc (PA)..........D.......510 986-0686
505 14th St Ste 900 Oakland (94612) ***(P-14683)***
Outsource Testing Inc..........D.......909 592-8898
1278 Center Court Dr Covina (91724) ***(P-27816)***
Ovations Fanfare..........D.......714 708-1880
88 Fair Dr Costa Mesa (92626) ***(P-26970)***
Over 60 Health Center, Berkeley *Also called Lifelong Medical Care* ***(P-19650)***
Overaa Construction, Richmond *Also called C Overaa & Co* ***(P-1382)***
Overaa Construction, San Pablo *Also called C Overaa & Co* ***(P-1383)***
Overhead Door Corporation..........D.......714 680-0600
1617 N Orangethorpe Way Anaheim (92801) ***(P-3056)***
Overland Pacific & Cutler LLC (PA)..........D.......562 429-9391
3750 Schaufele Ave # 150 Long Beach (90808) ***(P-17380)***
Overmiller Inc..........D.......925 798-2122
195 Mason Cir Concord (94520) ***(P-17967)***
Overseas Service Corporation..........C.......858 408-0751
8221 Arjons Dr Ste B2 San Diego (92126) ***(P-27950)***
Overseenet (PA)..........C.......213 408-0080
550 S Hope St Ste 200 Los Angeles (90071) ***(P-13876)***
Overton Security Services Inc..........C.......510 791-7380
39300 Civic Center Dr # 370 Fremont (94538) ***(P-16751)***
Ovis Llc..........A.......805 646-5511
905 Country Club Rd Ojai (93023) ***(P-12991)***
Owen & Company..........D.......916 993-2700
1455 Response Rd Ste 260 Sacramento (95815) ***(P-10724)***
Owens & Minor Inc..........D.......909 944-2100
5125 Ontario Mills Pkwy Ontario (91764) ***(P-7202)***
Owens & Minor Inc..........D.......209 833-4600
18520 Stanford Rd Tracy (95377) ***(P-7203)***
Owens Corning Sales LLC..........B.......408 235-1351
960 Central Expy Santa Clara (95050) ***(P-6925)***
Owl Companies (PA)..........A.......949 797-2000
2465 Campus Dr Irvine (92612) ***(P-24215)***
Owl Education and Training..........A.......949 797-2000
2465 Campus Dr Irvine (92612) ***(P-24216)***
Own LLC..........C.......323 602-5500
1041 N Formosa Ave West Hollywood (90046) ***(P-5925)***
Ownit Mortgage Solutions Inc..........B.......513 872-6922
4360 Park Terrace Dr # 100 Westlake Village (91361) ***(P-9841)***
Oxford Farms Inc..........E.......559 659-3033
901 N St Ste 103 Firebaugh (93622) ***(P-704)***
Oxford Palace Hotel..........D.......213 382-7756
745 S Oxford Ave Los Angeles (90005) ***(P-12992)***
Oxford Suites Chico, Chico *Also called Baney Corporation* ***(P-12351)***
Oxgord Incorporated..........C.......800 221-0718
16325 S Avalon Blvd Gardena (90248) ***(P-9239)***
Oxnard 2103 East Gonzales Road, Oxnard *Also called Kaiser Foundation Hospitals* ***(P-19576)***
Oxnard 2200 East Gonzales, Oxnard *Also called Kaiser Foundation Hospitals* ***(P-19574)***
Oxnard Beach Hotel LP..........E.......805 488-6560
350 E Port Hueneme Rd Port Hueneme (93041) ***(P-12993)***
Oxnard Family Circle Adhc, Oxnard *Also called Family Circle Inc* ***(P-23795)***
Oxnard Manor Healthcare Ctr LP..........D.......805 983-0324
1400 W Gonzales Rd Oxnard (93036) ***(P-20684)***
Oxnard Perfrmn Arts & Convtn..........E.......805 486-2424
800 Hobson Way Oxnard (93030) ***(P-17381)***
Oxnard Veterans Center, Oxnard *Also called Veterans Health Administration* ***(P-20072)***
OXY USA Inc..........C.......661 869-8000
9600 Ming Ave Ste 300 Bakersfield (93311) ***(P-1025)***
P & A Holdings Inc (PA)..........D.......619 233-3522
636 Broadway Ste 310 San Diego (92101) ***(P-11957)***
P & D Consultants Inc (HQ)..........E.......714 835-4447
999 W Town And Country Rd Orange (92868) ***(P-25856)***
P & P Agrilabor..........D.......831 679-2307
Highway 101 Floretta Rd Chualar (93925) ***(P-14684)***
P & R Paper Supply Co Inc (PA)..........C.......909 389-1811
1898 E Colton Ave Redlands (92374) ***(P-8124)***
P A C E, Los Angeles *Also called Pacific Asian Consortm Emplymn* ***(P-24217)***
P A T H, Los Angeles *Also called People Assisting Homeless* ***(P-23968)***
P B C Pavers Inc..........D.......714 278-0488
1560 W Lambert Rd Brea (92821) ***(P-2463)***
P B I, Long Beach *Also called Pbi-Birkenwald Market Eqp Inc* ***(P-7144)***
P C A, Livermore *Also called Pen-Cal Administrators Inc* ***(P-26984)***
P C A Farm Management LLC..........A.......661 720-2400
1901 S Lexington St Delano (93215) ***(P-705)***
P C I & Associates, San Diego *Also called PCI Collections Inc* ***(P-14015)***
P C M, Foothill Ranch *Also called Professional Community MGT Cal* ***(P-11682)***
P C S, Concord *Also called Patriot Contract Services LLC* ***(P-4699)***
P C S C, Torrance *Also called Ttik Inc* ***(P-16948)***
P H B Contracting Inc..........C.......760 347-7290
43180 Sunburst St Indio (92201) ***(P-2929)***
P H I, South San Francisco *Also called Peking Handicraft Inc* ***(P-6782)***
P H Ranch Inc..........E.......209 358-5111
6335 Oakdale Rd Winton (95388) ***(P-425)***
P H S Management Group (PA)..........E.......714 547-7551
721 N Eckhoff St Orange (92868) ***(P-27384)***
P J J Enterprises Inc..........D.......619 232-6136
1250 Delevan Dr San Diego (92102) ***(P-14532)***
P J Video Services Inc..........D.......714 705-6088
630 The City Dr S Ste 100 Orange (92868) ***(P-18089)***
P J'S Construction Supplies, Fremont *Also called PJs Lumber Inc* ***(P-6853)***
P K B Investments Inc..........C.......559 243-1224
745 E Locust Ave Ste 105 Fresno (93720) ***(P-27385)***
P M B, San Diego *Also called Pacific Medical Buildings LP* ***(P-11647)***
P M C A, Burlingame *Also called Provident Mrtg Cpitl Assoc Inc* ***(P-9850)***
P Monterey LP..........D.......831 250-6159
200 Glenwood Cir Ste A50 Monterey (93940) ***(P-24621)***
P Murphy & Associates Inc..........C.......818 841-2002
359 E Magnolia Blvd Ste G Burbank (91502) ***(P-15339)***
P R N Convalescent Hospital..........D.......818 352-3158
7912 Topley Ln Sunland (91040) ***(P-20685)***
P R P, Costa Mesa *Also called Profit Recovery Partners LLC* ***(P-27826)***
P W C, San Dimas *Also called Pacific W Space Cmmnctions Inc* ***(P-1966)***
P& JP Brokerage LLC..........E.......310 801-9707
15301 Ventura Blvd Ste P2 Sherman Oaks (91403) ***(P-5130)***
P-Cove Enterprises Inc..........D.......818 341-1101
8745 Remmet Ave Canoga Park (91304) ***(P-16027)***
P-Wave Holdings LLC..........A.......310 209-3010
10877 Wilshire Blvd Los Angeles (90024) ***(P-12257)***
P2f Holdings..........D.......562 296-1055
1760 Apollo Ct Seal Beach (90740) ***(P-9240)***
P2s Engineering, Long Beach *Also called P2s Inc* ***(P-25857)***
P2s Inc..........C.......562 497-2999
5000 E Spring St Ste 800 Long Beach (90815) ***(P-25857)***
P8ge Consulting Inc..........E.......310 666-2301
8406 Beverly Blvd Los Angeles (90048) ***(P-27817)***
Paat & Kimmel Development Inc..........D.......909 315-8074
1490 S Vineyard Ave Ste D Ontario (91761) ***(P-1605)***
Pac West Land Care Inc..........C.......760 630-0231
408 Olive Ave Vista (92083) ***(P-914)***
Pac-12 Enteprises LLC..........C.......415 580-4200
360 3rd St Ste 300 San Francisco (94107) ***(P-13951)***
Pacbell, San Francisco *Also called Pacific Bell Telephone Company* ***(P-5619)***
Paccar Leasing Corporation..........C.......559 268-4344
2892 E Jensen Ave Fresno (93706) ***(P-17606)***
Pace Inc..........D.......925 602-0900
2301 Arnold Industrial Wa Concord (94520) ***(P-2930)***
Pace Administrator To Work, Los Angeles *Also called Pacific Asian Consortm Emplymn* ***(P-23955)***
Pace Drywall, Concord *Also called Pace Inc* ***(P-2930)***
Pace Supply Corp (PA)..........D.......707 755-2499
6000 State Farm Dr # 200 Rohnert Park (94928) ***(P-7632)***

Mergent e-mail: customerrelations@mergent.com
1410
2019 Directory of California Wholesalers and Services Companies
(P-0000) Products & Services Section entry number
(PA)=Parent Co (HQ)=Headquarters (DH)=Div Headquarters

Pacheco Brothers Gardening Inc (PA)..........D.......510 732-6330
20973 Cabot Blvd Hayward (94545) ***(P-773)***
Pachinko World Inc..........C.......714 895-7772
5912 Bolsa Ave Ste 108 Huntington Beach (92649) ***(P-18786)***
Pachulski Stang Zehl Jones LLP (PA)..........D.......310 277-6910
10100 Santa Monica Blvd # 1100 Los Angeles (90067) ***(P-23306)***
Pacific Airworks Group LLC..........D.......909 815-7012
255 S Leland Norton Way San Bernardino (92408) ***(P-25858)***
Pacific American Fish Co Inc (PA)..........B.......323 319-1551
5525 S Santa Fe Ave Vernon (90058) ***(P-8590)***
Pacific Aquascape Inc..........D.......714 481-7260
18685 Main St Ste 101 Huntington Beach (92648) ***(P-3559)***
Pacific Asian Consortm Emplymn..........D.......213 989-3228
1055 Wilshire Blvd # 1475 Los Angeles (90017) ***(P-23955)***
Pacific Asian Consortm Emplymn (PA)..........C.......213 353-3982
1055 Wilshire Blvd Ste 14 Los Angeles (90017) ***(P-24217)***
Pacific Aviation Corporation (PA)..........C.......310 646-4015
380 World Way Ste S31 Los Angeles (90045) ***(P-4903)***
Pacific Bay Lending Group..........D.......714 367-5125
1 Centerpointe Dr Ste 330 La Palma (90623) ***(P-9900)***
Pacific Bay Properties (PA)..........E.......949 440-7200
4041 Macarthur Blvd # 500 Newport Beach (92660) ***(P-1211)***
Pacific Beach House LLC (PA)..........D.......650 712-0220
4100 Cabrillo Hwy N Half Moon Bay (94019) ***(P-12994)***
Pacific Bell Telephone Company (HQ)..........A.......415 542-9000
430 Bush St Fl 3 San Francisco (94108) ***(P-5619)***
Pacific Boring Incorporated..........E.......559 864-9444
1985 W Mountain View Ave Caruthers (93609) ***(P-3355)***
Pacific Building Group..........D.......858 552-0600
13541 Stoney Creek Rd San Diego (92129) ***(P-2931)***
Pacific Building Group (PA)..........C.......858 552-0600
9752 Aspen Creek Ct # 100 San Diego (92126) ***(P-1606)***
Pacific Building Maint Inc (PA)..........D.......805 642-0214
1601 Ives Ave Ste E Oxnard (93033) ***(P-14337)***
Pacific Cambria Inc..........D.......805 927-6114
2905 Burton Dr Cambria (93428) ***(P-12995)***
Pacific Capital Companies LLC..........C.......800 583-3015
11620 Wilshire Blvd Los Angeles (90025) ***(P-9762)***
Pacific Care Inc..........D.......562 494-6500
1903 Redondo Ave Long Beach (90755) ***(P-22386)***
Pacific Cast Bnkers Bancshares (PA)..........D.......415 399-1900
1676 N Calif Blvd Ste 300 Walnut Creek (94596) ***(P-9470)***
Pacific Cast Sightseeing Tours, Anaheim *Also called Coach Usa Inc* ***(P-4967)***
Pacific Centrex Services Inc..........D.......818 623-2300
114 E Haley St Ste A Santa Barbara (93101) ***(P-5620)***
Pacific Cheese Co Inc (PA)..........C.......510 784-8800
21090 Cabot Blvd Hayward (94545) ***(P-8528)***
Pacific Chemical Dist Corp (HQ)..........D.......714 521-7161
6250 Caballero Blvd Buena Park (90620) ***(P-4685)***
Pacific Choice Seafood Company..........B.......707 442-2981
1 Commercial St Eureka (95501) ***(P-8591)***
Pacific Cities Management Inc (PA)..........D.......916 348-1188
6056 Rutland Dr Ste 1 Carmichael (95608) ***(P-11645)***
Pacific City Hotel LLC..........B.......714 698-6100
21080 Pacific Coast Hwy Huntington Beach (92648) ***(P-12996)***
Pacific Civil & Strl Cons LLC..........E.......916 421-1000
7415 Greenhaven Dr # 100 Sacramento (95831) ***(P-25859)***
Pacific Clay Products Inc..........C.......661 857-1401
14741 Lake St Lake Elsinore (92530) ***(P-6902)***
Pacific Cleaning Service Inc..........E.......949 829-8790
3334 Pacific Coast Hwy # 205 Corona Del Mar (92625) ***(P-14338)***
Pacific Clinics..........D.......562 949-8455
11721 Telegraph Rd Ste A Santa Fe Springs (90670) ***(P-22630)***
Pacific Clinics Foundation..........D.......626 796-3453
855 N Orange Grove Blvd Pasadena (91103) ***(P-23956)***
Pacific Club (PA)..........D.......949 955-1123
4110 Macarthur Blvd Newport Beach (92660) ***(P-18996)***
Pacific Coast Bankers Bank..........D.......415 399-1900
1676 N Calif Blvd Ste 300 Walnut Creek (94596) ***(P-9471)***
Pacific Coast Care Center, Salinas *Also called Kindred Healthcare Oper Inc* ***(P-20560)***
Pacific Coast Companies Inc..........C.......916 631-6500
10600 White Rock Rd # 100 Rancho Cordova (95670) ***(P-17382)***
Pacific Coast Container Inc (PA)..........C.......510 346-6100
432 Estudillo Ave Ste 1 San Leandro (94577) ***(P-5238)***
Pacific Coast Drum Company..........D.......626 443-3096
2200 Rosemead Blvd 2204 El Monte (91733) ***(P-7862)***
Pacific Coast Equipment Co Inc (PA)..........E.......714 630-5957
3839 E Coronado St Anaheim (92807) ***(P-3475)***
Pacific Coast Lacquer, Los Angeles *Also called Berg Lacquer Co* ***(P-9188)***
Pacific Coast Ldscp MGT Inc..........D.......925 513-2310
3960 Holway Dr Byron (94514) ***(P-774)***
Pacific Coast Manor, Capitola *Also called Covenant Care LLC* ***(P-20335)***
Pacific Coast Nursery Inc..........D.......714 630-4868
2885 E La Cresta Ave Anaheim (92806) ***(P-9154)***
Pacific Coast Produce Inc..........E.......805 240-3385
950 Mountain View Ave # 1 Oxnard (93030) ***(P-8712)***
Pacific Coast Producers..........B.......209 365-9982
650 S Guild Ave Lodi (95240) ***(P-17383)***
Pacific Coast Services Inc..........A.......209 956-2532
3202 W March Ln Ste D Stockton (95219) ***(P-22387)***
Pacific Coast Sightseeing Tour..........C.......714 507-1157
2001 S Manchester Ave Anaheim (92802) ***(P-4975)***
Pacific Coast Supply LLC..........D.......805 434-4800
626 N Main St Templeton (93465) ***(P-6846)***
Pacific Coast Supply LLC..........C.......916 481-2220
4290 Roseville Rd North Highlands (95660) ***(P-6847)***
Pacific Coast Supply LLC (HQ)..........C.......916 971-2301
4290 Roseville Rd North Highlands (95660) ***(P-6848)***
Pacific Coast Sweeping, Rancho Santa Margari *Also called Wendt Landscape Services Inc* ***(P-961)***
Pacific Coast Trnsp Svcs Inc..........E.......916 266-5300
7500 San Joaquin St Sacramento (95820) ***(P-5239)***
Pacific Coast Truck and Whse (PA)..........E.......619 661-5451
692 Anita St Chula Vista (91911) ***(P-6662)***
Pacific Coast Warehouse Co, Newark *Also called National Distribution Agcy Inc* ***(P-4597)***
Pacific Communications Assoc..........E.......925 634-1203
761 2nd St Brentwood (94513) ***(P-27818)***
Pacific Compensation Insur Co..........C.......818 575-8500
1 Baxter Way Ste 170 Westlake Village (91362) ***(P-10384)***
Pacific Concept Laundry, Los Angeles *Also called E & C Fashion Inc* ***(P-17143)***
Pacific Concrete Specialties..........D.......209 358-0741
101 Business Park Way Atwater (95301) ***(P-3299)***
Pacific Contours Corporation (PA)..........D.......714 693-1260
5340 E Hunter Ave Anaheim (92807) ***(P-7913)***
Pacific Crossing LLC..........C.......949 679-2588
95 Argonaut Ste 100 Aliso Viejo (92656) ***(P-16028)***
Pacific Cycle Inc..........E.......909 481-5613
9282 Pittsburgh Ave Rancho Cucamonga (91730) ***(P-4604)***
Pacific Cycle P Finished Goods, Rancho Cucamonga *Also called Pacific Cycle Inc* ***(P-4604)***
Pacific Dental Services Llc (PA)..........B.......714 845-8500
17000 Red Hill Ave Irvine (92614) ***(P-20132)***
Pacific Design Directions Inc..........E.......714 685-7766
8171 E Kaiser Blvd Anaheim (92808) ***(P-1212)***
Pacific Dining Food Svc MGT, Fremont *Also called Page Front Catering* ***(P-7893)***
Pacific Eagle Holdings Corp..........D.......415 398-2473
353 Sacramento St Ste 360 San Francisco (94111) ***(P-10925)***
Pacific Earth Resources (PA)..........D.......805 986-8277
305 Hueneme Rd Camarillo (93012) ***(P-291)***
Pacific Eastern Intl Pdts..........D.......714 538-3434
12551 Barrett Ln Santa Ana (92705) ***(P-9241)***
Pacific Eastern Intl Pdts I, Santa Ana *Also called Pacific Eastern Intl Pdts* ***(P-9241)***
Pacific Echo Inc..........D.......310 539-1822
23540 Telo Ave Torrance (90505) ***(P-7863)***
Pacific Energy Fuels Company..........A.......415 973-8200
77 Beale St Ste 100 San Francisco (94105) ***(P-6158)***
Pacific Engineering Builders..........D.......650 557-1238
1009 Terra Nova Blvd Pacifica (94044) ***(P-1607)***
Pacific Equities Captl..........D.......310 477-5300
1640 S Sepulveda Blvd # 308 Los Angeles (90025) ***(P-11180)***
Pacific Event Productions Inc (PA)..........C.......858 458-9908
6989 Corte Santa Fe San Diego (92121) ***(P-13761)***
Pacific Excavation Inc..........D.......916 686-2800
9796 Kent St Elk Grove (95624) ***(P-3437)***
Pacific Exteriors, Garden Grove *Also called Quail Engineering Inc* ***(P-1839)***
Pacific Exteriors Inc..........D.......714 265-1998
13911 Enterprise Dr Ste B Garden Grove (92843) ***(P-2932)***
Pacific Eye Associated Inc..........D.......415 923-3007
2100 Webster St Ste 214 San Francisco (94115) ***(P-19741)***
Pacific Fire Safety, Pomona *Also called Ferguson Fire Fabrication Inc* ***(P-7624)***
Pacific Foods & Dist Inc..........D.......714 547-0787
3431 W Carriage Dr Santa Ana (92704) ***(P-8845)***
Pacific Fresh Sea Food Company (HQ)..........C.......916 419-5500
1420 National Dr Sacramento (95834) ***(P-8497)***
Pacific Fresh Seafood Company, Wilmington *Also called Pacific Sea Food Co Inc* ***(P-8593)***
Pacific Frnsic Psychlogy Assoc..........D.......925 253-3111
9261 Folsom Blvd Ste 300 Sacramento (95826) ***(P-22631)***
Pacific Gardens, Santa Clara *Also called Community Home Partners LLC* ***(P-20921)***
Pacific Gardens Hlth Care Ctr, Fresno *Also called Covenant Care California LLC* ***(P-20345)***
Pacific Gas and Electric Co..........D.......415 973-7000
425 Beck Ave Fairfield (94533) ***(P-6067)***
Pacific Gas and Electric Co (HQ)..........A.......415 973-7000
77 Beale St San Francisco (94105) ***(P-6068)***
Pacific Gas and Electric Co..........C.......916 375-5005
885 Embarcadero Dr West Sacramento (95605) ***(P-6069)***
Pacific Gas and Electric Co..........B.......530 742-3251
530 E St Marysville (95901) ***(P-6070)***
Pacific Gas and Electric Co..........D.......510 450-5744
4525 Hollis St Oakland (94608) ***(P-6071)***
Pacific Gas and Electric Co..........B.......510 784-3253
24300 Clawiter Rd Hayward (94545) ***(P-6159)***
Pacific Gas and Electric Co..........B.......559 268-2868
650 O St Fresno (93721) ***(P-6072)***
Pacific Gas and Electric Co..........E.......707 765-5118
210 Corona Rd Petaluma (94954) ***(P-6073)***
Pacific Gas and Electric Co..........C.......530 477-3245
788 Taylorville Rd Grass Valley (95949) ***(P-6074)***
Pacific Gas and Electric Co..........C.......800 756-7243
111 Stony Cir Santa Rosa (95401) ***(P-6075)***
Pacific Gas and Electric Co..........C.......530 894-4739
460 Rio Lindo Ave Chico (95926) ***(P-6160)***
Pacific Gas and Electric Co..........D.......925 676-0948
4690 Evora Rd Concord (94520) ***(P-6076)***
Pacific Gas and Electric Co..........E.......530 621-7237
4636 Missouri Flat Rd Placerville (95667) ***(P-6077)***
Pacific Gas and Electric Co..........A.......805 506-5280
9 Mi Nw Of Avila Bch Avila Beach (93424) ***(P-6078)***
Pacific Gas and Electric Co..........C.......530 365-7672
3600 Meadow View Dr Redding (96002) ***(P-6079)***
Pacific Gas and Electric Co..........E.......530 889-3102
12840 Bill Clark Way Auburn (95602) ***(P-6080)***
Pacific Gas and Electric Co..........D.......925 674-6305
1850 Gateway Blvd Ste 800 Concord (94520) ***(P-6081)***
Pacific Gas and Electric Co..........E.......831 648-3231
2311 Garden Rd Monterey (93940) ***(P-6082)***
Pacific Gas and Electric Co..........C.......510 770-2025
42105 Boyce Rd Fremont (94538) ***(P-6083)***
Pacific Gas and Electric Co..........D.......707 444-0700
1000 King Salmon Ave Eureka (95503) ***(P-6084)***

ALPHABETIC

Employee Codes: A=Over 500 employees, B=251-500
C=101-250, D=51-100, E=50
2019 Directory of California
Wholesalers and Services Companies
© Mergent Inc. 1-800-342-5647
1411

Pacific Gas and Electric Co ....E....559 855-6112
33755 Old Mill Rd Auberry (93602) ***(P-6085)***
Pacific Gas and Electric Co ....C....650 755-1236
450 Eastmoor Ave Daly City (94015) ***(P-6086)***
Pacific Gas and Electric Co ....E....209 576-6636
1524 N Carpenter Rd Modesto (95351) ***(P-6087)***
Pacific Gas and Electric Co ....D....209 942-1787
3136 Boeing Way Stockton (95206) ***(P-6088)***
Pacific Gas and Electric Co ....D....805 773-6109
800 Price Canyon Rd Pismo Beach (93449) ***(P-6089)***
Pacific Gas and Electric Co ....C....925 373-2623
3797 1st St Livermore (94551) ***(P-6090)***
Pacific Gas and Electric Co ....B....530 757-5803
316 L St Davis (95616) ***(P-6091)***
Pacific Gas and Electric Co ....B....415 695-3513
2180 Harrison St San Francisco (94110) ***(P-6092)***
Pacific Gas and Electric Co ....D....408 945-6215
66 Ranch Dr Milpitas (95035) ***(P-6093)***
Pacific Gas and Electric Co ....D....209 295-2651
28570 Tiger Creek Rd Pioneer (95666) ***(P-6094)***
Pacific Gas and Electric Co ....D....661 398-5918
4201 Arrow St Bakersfield (93308) ***(P-6095)***
Pacific Gas and Electric Co ....D....805 434-4418
160 Cow Meadow Pl Templeton (93465) ***(P-6096)***
Pacific Gas and Electric Co ....D....415 973-8089
245 Market St Ste 104 San Francisco (94105) ***(P-6161)***
Pacific Gas Turbine Center LLC ....C....858 877-2910
7007 Consolidated Way San Diego (92121) ***(P-17968)***
Pacific Golf & Country Club ....D....949 498-6604
200 Avenida La Pata San Clemente (92673) ***(P-18997)***
Pacific Grain & Foods LLC (PA) ....C....559 276-2580
4067 W Shaw Ave Ste 116 Fresno (93722) ***(P-8906)***
Pacific Grain and Foods, Fresno *Also called Pacific Grain & Foods LLC* ***(P-8906)***
Pacific Green Landscape Inc (PA) ....C....619 390-1546
8834 Winter Gardens Blvd Lakeside (92040) ***(P-915)***
Pacific Groservice Inc ....B....408 727-4826
567 Cinnabar St San Jose (95110) ***(P-9186)***
Pacific Grove Aslmar Oper Corp ....C....831 372-8016
800 Asilomar Blvd Pacific Grove (93950) ***(P-12997)***
Pacific Grove Cnvalescent Hosp ....D....831 375-2695
200 Lighthouse Ave Pacific Grove (93950) ***(P-21178)***
Pacific Grove Hospital, Riverside *Also called Vista Behavioral Health Inc* ***(P-21993)***
Pacific Growth Equities LLC ....D....415 274-6800
1 Bush St Fl 17 San Francisco (94104) ***(P-10008)***
Pacific Gtwy Wrkfrce Prtnr Inc ....E....562 570-3700
3447 Atlantic Ave Long Beach (90807) ***(P-14685)***
Pacific Harbor Line Inc (HQ) ....C....310 834-4594
705 N Henry Ford Ave Wilmington (90744) ***(P-3622)***
Pacific Haven Convalescent HM, Garden Grove *Also called Pacific Haven Convalescent HM* ***(P-21179)***
Pacific Haven Convalescent HM ....D....714 534-1942
12072 Trask Ave Garden Grove (92843) ***(P-21179)***
Pacific Health and Welness, Redondo Beach *Also called NBC Consulting Inc* ***(P-27361)***
Pacific Health Corporation ....B....714 619-7797
3699 Wilshire Blvd # 540 Los Angeles (90010) ***(P-21621)***
Pacific Home Works Inc ....C....310 781-3012
20725 S Wstn Ave Ste 100 Torrance (90501) ***(P-3560)***
Pacific Homecare Services, Stockton *Also called Pacific Coast Services Inc* ***(P-22387)***
Pacific Homes Foundation ....D....818 729-8106
303 N Lennox Glenoaks1000 # 1000 Burbank (91502) ***(P-21180)***
Pacific Hotel Dev Ventr LP ....C....650 347-8260
625 El Camino Real Palo Alto (94301) ***(P-12998)***
Pacific Hotel Management LLC ....C....510 547-7888
1603 Powell St Emeryville (94608) ***(P-12999)***
Pacific Hotel Management LLC ....C....510 262-0700
3150 Garrity Way Richmond (94806) ***(P-13000)***
Pacific Hotel Management LLC ....B....650 328-2800
625 El Camino Real Palo Alto (94301) ***(P-13001)***
Pacific Hotel Management Inc ....C....949 608-1091
4545 Macarthur Blvd Newport Beach (92660) ***(P-13002)***
Pacific Housing Management (PA) ....D....714 508-1777
945 Katella St Laguna Beach (92651) ***(P-11646)***
Pacific Huntington Hotel Corp ....A....626 568-3900
1401 S Oak Knoll Ave Pasadena (91106) ***(P-13003)***
Pacific Hydrotech Corporation ....C....951 943-8803
314 E 3rd St Perris (92570) ***(P-25860)***
Pacific Indemnity Company ....B....213 622-2334
555 S Flower St Ste 300 Los Angeles (90071) ***(P-10725)***
Pacific Inn, The, Seal Beach *Also called Saga Seal Co Ltd* ***(P-13160)***
Pacific Inptient Med Group Inc ....D....415 485-8824
9 Jeffrey Ct Novato (94945) ***(P-19742)***
Pacific Insulation, Commerce *Also called Farwest Insulation Contracting* ***(P-2883)***
Pacific Interior Design, Anaheim *Also called Pacific Design Directions Inc* ***(P-1212)***
Pacific Interior Medicine, San Francisco *Also called Arlene Keller MD* ***(P-19303)***
Pacific International Mktg, Salinas *Also called Pacific Intl Vgetable Mktg Inc* ***(P-8713)***
Pacific Intl Vgetable Mktg Inc (PA) ....D....831 422-3745
740 Airport Blvd Salinas (93901) ***(P-8713)***
Pacific Investment MGT Co LLC (HQ) ....C....949 720-6000
650 Newport Center Dr Newport Beach (92660) ***(P-10101)***
Pacific Labor Services Inc ....E....805 488-4625
5690 Cypress Rd Oxnard (93033) ***(P-13441)***
Pacific Lath & Plaster, Escondido *Also called Master Design Drywall Inc* ***(P-2914)***
Pacific Legal Foundation (PA) ....D....916 419-7111
930 G St Sacramento (95814) ***(P-23307)***
Pacific Leisure Management, San Francisco *Also called Okabe International Inc* ***(P-4973)***
Pacific Life & Annuity Company ....A....949 219-3011
700 Newport Center Dr Newport Beach (92660) ***(P-10142)***
Pacific Life Global Funding ....D....949 219-3011
700 Newport Center Dr Newport Beach (92660) ***(P-9744)***
Pacific Lighting Mfr Inc ....D....310 327-7711
2329 E Pacifica Pl Compton (90220) ***(P-7384)***
Pacific Lighting Mfr Inc ....D....310 327-7711
2329 E Pacifica Pl Rancho Dominguez (90220) ***(P-7385)***
Pacific Line Clean-Up Inc ....C....949 348-0245
27601 Forbes Rd Ste 29 Laguna Niguel (92677) ***(P-3561)***
Pacific Lodge Boy's Home, Woodland Hills *Also called Pacific Lodge Youth Services* ***(P-24622)***
Pacific Lodge Youth Services ....C....818 347-1577
4900 Serrania Ave Woodland Hills (91364) ***(P-24622)***
Pacific Logistics Corp (PA) ....C....562 478-4700
7255 Rosemead Blvd Pico Rivera (90660) ***(P-5131)***
Pacific Maintenance Svcs Inc ....C....909 793-7111
1902 Verde Vista Dr Redlands (92373) ***(P-14339)***
Pacific Marine Credit Union (PA) ....C....760 430-7511
1278 Rocky Point Dr Oceanside (92056) ***(P-9578)***
Pacific Marine Dev Corp ....E....760 593-9138
11956 Bernardo Plaza Dr San Diego (92128) ***(P-25861)***
Pacific Medical Inc (PA) ....C....800 726-9180
1700 N Chrisman Rd Tracy (95304) ***(P-17384)***
Pacific Medical Buildings LP ....D....858 794-1900
3394 Carmel Mountain Rd # 200 San Diego (92121) ***(P-11647)***
Pacific Mercantile Bank (HQ) ....E....714 438-2500
949 S Coast Dr Ste 300 Costa Mesa (92626) ***(P-9472)***
Pacific Metro Electric Inc ....D....209 939-3222
3150 E Fremont St Stockton (95205) ***(P-2669)***
Pacific Metro LLC (PA) ....B....408 201-5000
18715 Madrone Pkwy Morgan Hill (95037) ***(P-9242)***
Pacific Monarch Resorts Inc ....D....949 228-1396
7 Grenada St Laguna Niguel (92677) ***(P-11648)***
Pacific Monarch Resorts Inc (PA) ....D....949 609-2400
4000 Macarthur Blvd # 600 Newport Beach (92660) ***(P-11649)***
Pacific Mortgage Resources, Walnut Creek *Also called Diablo Realty Inc* ***(P-11399)***
Pacific Occptnal Medicine Svcs ....E....562 997-2290
2776 Pacific Ave Long Beach (90806) ***(P-21622)***
Pacific Outdoor Living, Sun Valley *Also called Pro Ponds West Inc* ***(P-779)***
Pacific Outdoor Living, Sun Valley *Also called Pacific Pavingstone Inc* ***(P-3300)***
Pacific Palms Healthcare LLC ....D....562 433-6791
1020 Termino Ave Long Beach (90804) ***(P-22388)***
Pacific Paper Converting Inc (PA) ....D....323 888-1330
6023 Bandini Blvd Los Angeles (90040) ***(P-8125)***
Pacific Park, Santa Monica *Also called Santa Monica Amusements LLC* ***(P-18809)***
Pacific Park Management ....D....415 440-4840
1300 Fillmore St San Francisco (94115) ***(P-26971)***
Pacific Parking & Valet LLC ....C....831 646-0426
2560 Garden Rd Ste 109 Monterey (93940) ***(P-6544)***
Pacific Partners MGT Svcs Inc ....D....650 358-5804
1051 E Hillsdale Blvd Foster City (94404) ***(P-26972)***
Pacific Partners MSI, Foster City *Also called Pacific Partners MGT Svcs Inc* ***(P-26972)***
Pacific Parts International, Canoga Park *Also called Richard Huetter Inc* ***(P-6670)***
Pacific Pavingstone Inc ....C....818 244-4000
8309 Tujunga Ave Unit 201 Sun Valley (91352) ***(P-3300)***
Pacific Pharma Inc ....A....714 246-4600
18600 Von Karman Ave Irvine (92612) ***(P-8201)***
Pacific Pioneer Insur Group, Cypress *Also called Pacific Pioneer Insur Group* ***(P-10726)***
Pacific Pioneer Insur Group (PA) ....C....714 228-7888
6363 Katella Ave Cypress (90630) ***(P-10726)***
Pacific Plms Conference Resort, City of Industry *Also called Majestic Industry Hills LLC* ***(P-12869)***
Pacific Plms Conference Resort, City of Industry *Also called Majestic Industry Hills LLC* ***(P-12870)***
Pacific Premier Bank (HQ) ....C....714 431-4000
17901 Von Karman Ave Irvine (92614) ***(P-9473)***
Pacific Premier Bank ....D....213 626-0085
333 S Grand Ave Los Angeles (90071) ***(P-9474)***
Pacific Process Systems Inc (PA) ....D....661 321-9681
7401 Rosedale Hwy Bakersfield (93308) ***(P-1074)***
Pacific Production Plumbing (PA) ....E....951 509-3100
1584 Pioneer Way El Cajon (92020) ***(P-2302)***
Pacific Program/Design Managem ....D....626 440-2000
100 W Walnut St Pasadena (91124) ***(P-26973)***
Pacific Properties Realty, Hawthorne *Also called Argon Enterprises Inc* ***(P-11220)***
Pacific Protection Services ....D....818 313-9369
22144 Clarendon St # 110 Woodland Hills (91367) ***(P-16752)***
Pacific Pulmonary Services Co, Petaluma *Also called Braden Partners LP A Calif* ***(P-22238)***
Pacific Racing Association ....C....510 559-7300
1100 Eastshore Hwy Albany (94710) ***(P-18542)***
Pacific Rebar Inc ....D....909 984-7199
501 S Oaks Ave Ontario (91762) ***(P-3389)***
Pacific Regional Laboratory SW, Irvine *Also called Ora Pacific Regional Field Off* ***(P-17373)***
Pacific Rehabilitation & Wel ....D....707 443-9767
2211 Harrison Ave Eureka (95501) ***(P-20686)***
Pacific Relocation Consultants, Long Beach *Also called Overland Pacific & Cutler LLC* ***(P-17380)***
Pacific Restoration Group Inc ....E....951 940-6069
325 E Ellis Ave Perris (92570) ***(P-775)***
Pacific Retirement Svcs Inc ....C....530 753-1450
1515 Shasta Dr Ofc Davis (95616) ***(P-24623)***
Pacific Rim Contractors Inc ....D....714 641-7380
1315 E Saint Andrew Pl B Santa Ana (92705) ***(P-2933)***
Pacific Rim Mech Contrs Inc ....D....714 285-2600
1701 E Edinger Ave Ste F2 Santa Ana (92705) ***(P-2303)***
Pacific Rim Mech Contrs Inc (PA) ....B....858 974-6500
7655 Convoy Ct San Diego (92111) ***(P-2304)***
Pacific Rim Realty Group ....E....805 553-9562
740 Lucille Ct Moorpark (93021) ***(P-11650)***

Mergent e-mail: customerrelations@mergent.com
1412
2019 Directory of California
Wholesalers and Services Companies
(P-0000) Products & Services Section entry number
(PA)=Parent Co (HQ)=Headquarters (DH)=Div Headquarters

Pacific Rim Resources Srch....C....714 638-0307
14148 Brookhurst St Garden Grove (92843) ***(P-14686)***
Pacific Royal Group....C....510 200-2993
5500 Stewart Ave Ste 113 Fremont (94538) ***(P-9243)***
Pacific Sd/Pcfic Arbor Nrsries, Camarillo *Also called Pacific Earth Resources* ***(P-291)***
Pacific Sea Food Co Inc....D....916 419-5500
1420 National Dr Sacramento (95834) ***(P-8592)***
Pacific Sea Food Co Inc....E....310 835-4343
605 Flint Ave Wilmington (90744) ***(P-8593)***
Pacific Seafood Sacramento, Sacramento *Also called Pacific Fresh Sea Food Company* ***(P-8497)***
Pacific Secured Equities Inc....B....916 677-2500
6020 West Oaks Blvd # 100 Rocklin (95765) ***(P-27386)***
Pacific Service Credit Union (PA)....D....888 858-6878
3000 Clayton Rd Concord (94519) ***(P-9579)***
Pacific Shores Masonry....E....951 371-8550
1369 Walker Ln Corona (92879) ***(P-2820)***
Pacific Shores Med Group Inc (PA)....D....562 590-0345
1043 Elm Ave Ste 104 Long Beach (90813) ***(P-19743)***
Pacific Slope Tree Coop Inc....E....415 663-1300
11201 State Rte One 201 Point Reyes Station (94956) ***(P-977)***
Pacific Snow Valley Resort LLC....D....909 866-3121
40650 Village Dr Big Bear Lake (92315) ***(P-13004)***
Pacific Southwest, Long Beach *Also called Foss Maritime Company* ***(P-4697)***
Pacific Southwest Cnstr & Eqp....D....619 445-5190
2308 Shaylene Way Alpine (91901) ***(P-1965)***
Pacific Southwest Instruments, Corona *Also called Pacwest Instrument Labs Inc* ***(P-17969)***
Pacific Spanish Network Inc....D....619 427-6323
296 H St Ste 300 Chula Vista (91910) ***(P-5746)***
Pacific Specialty Insurance Co....E....650 780-4800
2200 Geng Rd Ste 200 Palo Alto (94303) ***(P-10727)***
Pacific State Bancorp....D....209 870-3214
1899 W March Ln Stockton (95207) ***(P-9527)***
Pacific States Industries Inc....C....707 894-4242
31401 Mccray Rd Cloverdale (95425) ***(P-6849)***
Pacific States Industries Inc....D....408 779-7354
10 Madrone Ave Morgan Hill (95037) ***(P-6850)***
Pacific Steel Casting Co LLC....B....510 558-2283
1333 2nd St Berkeley (94710) ***(P-7295)***
Pacific Sthwest Structures Inc....C....619 469-2323
7845 Lemon Grove Way A Lemon Grove (91945) ***(P-3301)***
Pacific Structures Inc (PA)....C....415 970-5434
3004 16th St Fl 2 San Francisco (94103) ***(P-3302)***
Pacific Structures Cnstr Inc....E....740 480-4133
101 State Pl Ste E Escondido (92029) ***(P-3303)***
Pacific Sttes Envmtl Cntrs Inc....E....925 803-4333
11555 Dublin Blvd Dublin (94568) ***(P-1608)***
Pacific Suites Hotel, Santa Monica *Also called Windsor Capital Group Inc* ***(P-13403)***
Pacific Sun Labor....D....760 556-5085
350 G St Brawley (92227) ***(P-664)***
Pacific Supply, Santa Ana *Also called Beacon Sales Acquisition Inc* ***(P-6920)***
Pacific Symphony....D....714 755-5788
17620 Fitch Ste 100 Irvine (92614) ***(P-18454)***
Pacific Systems Interiors Inc....C....310 436-6820
190 E Arrow Hwy Ste D San Dimas (91773) ***(P-2934)***
Pacific Tank Lines Inc....D....951 680-1900
5230 Wilson St Ste A Riverside (92509) ***(P-6155)***
Pacific Telemanagement Svcs, San Ramon *Also called Jaroth Inc* ***(P-2616)***
Pacific Terrace, San Diego *Also called Bartell Hotels* ***(P-12355)***
Pacific Terrace Inn, Coronado *Also called El Cordova Hotel* ***(P-12551)***
Pacific Theaters....D....818 501-5121
9400 Shirley Ave Northridge (91324) ***(P-18254)***
Pacific Theaters Inc (PA)....C....310 657-8420
120 N Robertson Blvd Fl 3 Los Angeles (90048) ***(P-18308)***
Pacific Theaters Inc....D....310 607-0007
831 S Nash St El Segundo (90245) ***(P-18309)***
Pacific Theaters Inc....D....562 634-1183
4821 Del Amo Blvd Lakewood (90712) ***(P-18310)***
Pacific Theatres Entrtmt Corp (HQ)....D....310 659-9432
120 N Robertson Blvd Fl 3 Los Angeles (90048) ***(P-18311)***
Pacific Thtres Cmmerce Theatre, Commerce *Also called Commerce Center Theatres* ***(P-18283)***
Pacific Towboat & Salvage Co, Long Beach *Also called Foss Maritime Co Inc* ***(P-4746)***
Pacific Towing, Stockton *Also called Covey Auto Express Inc* ***(P-17859)***
Pacific Toxicology Labs....D....818 598-3110
9348 De Soto Ave Chatsworth (91311) ***(P-26726)***
Pacific Trellis Fruit LLC (PA)....C....323 859-9600
2301 E 7th St Ste C200 Los Angeles (90023) ***(P-8714)***
Pacific Union Club....D....415 775-1234
1000 California St San Francisco (94108) ***(P-25210)***
Pacific Union Co....D....415 789-8686
1550 Tiburon Blvd Ste U Belvedere (94920) ***(P-11651)***
Pacific Union Co....D....415 474-6600
1699 Van Ness Ave San Francisco (94109) ***(P-11652)***
Pacific Union Homes Inc (PA)....D....925 314-3800
675 Hartz Ave Ste 300 Danville (94526) ***(P-11903)***
Pacific Union Intl Inc....B....415 461-8686
23 Ross Cmn Ross (94957) ***(P-11653)***
Pacific Union Intl Inc....A....707 934-2300
135 W Napa St Ste 200 Sonoma (95476) ***(P-9901)***
Pacific Union Intl Inc....B....510 338-1379
1900 Mountain Blvd # 102 Oakland (94611) ***(P-11654)***
Pacific Union RE Group (HQ)....D....415 929-7100
1699 Van Ness Ave 2 San Francisco (94109) ***(P-11655)***
Pacific Union Residental Brkg....D....510 339-6460
1900 Mountain Blvd # 102 Oakland (94611) ***(P-11656)***
Pacific Utlity Instllation Inc....D....714 970-6430
1585 N Harmony Cir Anaheim (92807) ***(P-2670)***
Pacific Ventures Ltd....C....626 576-0737
2200 W Valley Blvd Alhambra (91803) ***(P-26974)***
Pacific View Companies, La Mesa *Also called Pvcc Inc* ***(P-10929)***
Pacific Vision Services Inc....D....909 824-6090
1900 E Washington St Colton (92324) ***(P-20159)***
Pacific W Space Cmmnctions Inc....D....909 592-4321
900 W Gladstone St San Dimas (91773) ***(P-1966)***
Pacific West Corporation (PA)....D....515 270-8181
10369 Regis Ct Rancho Cucamonga (91730) ***(P-16449)***
Pacific West Lath & Plaster....E....916 329-9028
6853 Mccomber St Sacramento (95828) ***(P-2935)***
Pacific West Security Inc....D....801 748-1034
1587 Schallenberger Rd San Jose (95131) ***(P-16926)***
Pacific West Tree Service, Vista *Also called Pac West Land Care Inc* ***(P-914)***
Pacific Western Bank....C....213 430-7000
818 W 7th St Ste 220 Los Angeles (90017) ***(P-9475)***
Pacific Western Bank....B....858 756-3023
6110 El Tordo Rancho Santa Fe (92067) ***(P-9362)***
Pacific Western Bank....E....310 996-9100
11150 W Olympic Blvd # 100 Los Angeles (90064) ***(P-9476)***
Pacific Western Bank....C....760 432-1350
900 Canterbury Pl Ste 300 Escondido (92025) ***(P-9363)***
Pacific Western Bank....D....760 918-2469
5900 La Place Ct Ste 200 Carlsbad (92008) ***(P-9364)***
Pacific Western Bank....D....619 562-6400
9955 Mission Gorge Rd Santee (92071) ***(P-9477)***
Pacific Western Bank....D....858 436-3500
12481 High Bluff Dr # 350 San Diego (92130) ***(P-9365)***
Pacific Western Bank....D....760 432-1100
900 Cantebury Pl Ste 300 Escondido (92025) ***(P-9366)***
Pacific Western Bank....C....805 688-6644
610 Alamo Pintado Rd Solvang (93463) ***(P-9478)***
Pacific Western Sales (PA)....D....714 572-6730
2980 Enterprise St Ste A Brea (92821) ***(P-9244)***
Pacific Wine Distributors Inc....D....626 471-9997
15751 Tapia St Irwindale (91706) ***(P-4049)***
Pacifica Care Center....C....650 355-5622
385 Esplanade Ave Pacifica (94044) ***(P-20687)***
Pacifica Companies LLC (PA)....D....619 296-9000
1775 Hancock St Ste 200 San Diego (92110) ***(P-12178)***
Pacifica Consulting Services, Culver City *Also called Servicon Systems Inc* ***(P-27604)***
Pacifica Crossroads, San Ramon *Also called Pacifica Reflections* ***(P-1356)***
Pacifica Health and Medical....C....619 688-1848
2650 Cmino Del Rio N 21 San Diego (92108) ***(P-13762)***
Pacifica Hiorange LP....D....714 556-3838
2720 Hotel Ter Santa Ana (92705) ***(P-13005)***
Pacifica Hospital of Valley, Sun Valley *Also called Pacifica of Valley Corporation* ***(P-21623)***
Pacifica Hosts Inc....C....310 670-9000
6225 W Century Blvd Los Angeles (90045) ***(P-13006)***
Pacifica Hotel & Conference Ce....C....310 649-1776
6161 W Centinela Ave Culver City (90230) ***(P-13007)***
Pacifica Hotel Company....C....619 221-8000
1551 Shelter Island Dr San Diego (92106) ***(P-13008)***
Pacifica Hotel Company (HQ)....E....805 957-0095
39 Argonaut Aliso Viejo (92656) ***(P-11657)***
Pacifica Hotel Company....E....650 726-9000
2400 Cabrillo Hwy S Half Moon Bay (94019) ***(P-13009)***
Pacifica Katie Avenue LLC....D....619 296-9000
1775 Hancock St Ste 100 San Diego (92110) ***(P-26556)***
Pacifica Linda Mar Inc....D....650 359-4800
751 San Pedro Terrace Rd Pacifica (94044) ***(P-20688)***
Pacifica Nursing & Rehab Ctr, Pacifica *Also called Pacifica Care Center* ***(P-20687)***
Pacifica of Valley Corporation....A....818 767-3310
9449 San Fernando Rd Sun Valley (91352) ***(P-21623)***
Pacifica Reflections....E....925 275-9800
405 Reflections Cir San Ramon (94583) ***(P-1356)***
Pacifica San Jose LP....C....619 296-9000
1775 Hancock St Ste 100 San Diego (92110) ***(P-13010)***
Pacifica Services Inc....D....626 405-0131
106 S Mentor Ave Ste 200 Pasadena (91106) ***(P-25862)***
Pacificare, Concord *Also called United Behavioral Health* ***(P-10323)***
Pacificare Dental....C....661 631-8613
3110 W Lake Center Dr Santa Ana (92704) ***(P-10289)***
Pacificare Health Plan Admin (HQ)....B....714 825-5200
3120 W Lake Center Dr Santa Ana (92704) ***(P-10290)***
Pacificare Health Systems, Huntington Beach *Also called Unitedhealth Group Inc* ***(P-10324)***
Pacificare Health Systems, Cypress *Also called Unitedhealth Group Inc* ***(P-10325)***
Pacificare Health Systems LLC (HQ)....A....714 952-1121
5995 Plaza Dr Cypress (90630) ***(P-10291)***
Pacificare of California, Cypress *Also called Uhc of California* ***(P-10322)***
Pacificdental Benefits Inc (PA)....C....925 363-6000
2300 Clayton Rd Ste 1000 Concord (94520) ***(P-10292)***
Paciolan LLC (HQ)....D....949 476-2050
5171 California Ave # 200 Irvine (92617) ***(P-15824)***
Pacira Pharmaceuticals Inc....B....858 625-2424
10578 Science Center Dr San Diego (92121) ***(P-8202)***
Pack & Crate Services Inc....E....760 737-6893
238 N Quince St Escondido (92025) ***(P-4364)***
Packaging Innovators LLC....D....925 371-2000
6650 National Dr Livermore (94550) ***(P-8126)***
Packaging Manufacturing Inc....C....619 498-9199
6425 Randolph St Commerce (90040) ***(P-9245)***
Packard Childrens Hlth Aliance....D....650 497-8000
725 Welch Rd Palo Alto (94304) ***(P-19744)***
Packard Hospitality Group LLC....C....858 277-4305
9555 Chesapeake Dr # 202 San Diego (92123) ***(P-26975)***
Packard Medical Group Inc....D....650 724-3637
770 Welch Rd Palo Alto (94304) ***(P-19745)***

ALPHABETIC

Employee Codes: A=Over 500 employees, B=251-500
C=101-250, D=51-100, E=50
2019 Directory of California
Wholesalers and Services Companies
© Mergent Inc. 1-800-342-5647
1413

Packard Realty Inc...D.......310 649-5151
9901 S La Cienega Blvd Los Angeles (90045) ***(P-13011)***
Packet Design Inc...D.......408 490-1000
1 Almaden Blvd Ste 1150 San Jose (95113) ***(P-15340)***
Packetvideo Corporation (HQ)...D.......858 731-5300
10350 Science Center Dr San Diego (92121) ***(P-15341)***
PacLease, Fresno *Also called Paccar Leasing Corporation* ***(P-17606)***
Paclo, Pico Rivera *Also called Pacific Logistics Corp* ***(P-5131)***
Pactiv LLC...C.......559 251-7351
5370 E Home Ave Fresno (93727) ***(P-9246)***
Pactiv LLC...D.......530 529-3340
1 Diamond Ave Red Bluff (96080) ***(P-9247)***
Pactron...D.......408 329-5500
3000 Patrick Henry Dr Santa Clara (95054) ***(P-16450)***
Pacwend Inc...D.......209 577-6690
1308 Kansas Ave Ste 6 Modesto (95351) ***(P-26976)***
Pacwend III Inc...D.......209 577-6690
1308 Kansas Ave Ste 6 Modesto (95351) ***(P-26977)***
Pacwest Instrument Labs Inc...D.......951 737-0790
1721 Railroad St Corona (92880) ***(P-17969)***
Padi Americas Inc...C.......949 858-7234
30151 Tomas Rcho STA Marg (92688) ***(P-25035)***
Padilla Construction Company...C.......714 685-8500
205 W Bristol Ln Orange (92865) ***(P-2936)***
Padilla Farm Labor Inc...C.......559 562-1166
20486 Road 196 Lindsay (93247) ***(P-208)***
Padre Associates Inc...D.......661 829-2686
3500 Coffee Rd Ste B Bakersfield (93308) ***(P-25863)***
Padre Dam Municipal Water Dst (PA)...D.......619 258-4617
9300 Fanita Pkwy Santee (92071) ***(P-6294)***
Padres LP...A.......619 795-5000
100 Park Blvd Petco Park San Diego (92101) ***(P-18530)***
Pafco, Vernon *Also called Pacific American Fish Co Inc* ***(P-8590)***
Paganini Companies, San Francisco *Also called Paganini Electric Corporation* ***(P-2671)***
Paganini Electric Corporation...C.......415 575-3900
190 Hubbell St Ste 200 San Francisco (94107) ***(P-2671)***
Page Front Catering...D.......408 406-8487
34793 Ardentech Ct Fremont (94555) ***(P-7893)***
Pagerduty Inc (PA)...D.......650 989-2965
600 Townsend St Ste 200e San Francisco (94103) ***(P-5991)***
Paglia & Associates Cnstr...D.......714 982-5151
2790 E Regal Park Dr Anaheim (92806) ***(P-1213)***
Pahc Apartments Inc...E.......650 321-9709
2595 E Byshore Rd Ste 200 Palo Alto (94303) ***(P-11091)***
Pain Management Specialists PC...E.......805 544-7246
1551 Bishop St Ste 230 San Luis Obispo (93401) ***(P-19746)***
Paiute Palace Casino, Bishop *Also called Bishop Paiute Gaming Corp* ***(P-19111)***
Pajaro Valley Greenhouses (PA)...D.......831 722-2773
90 Hecker Pass Rd Watsonville (95076) ***(P-9155)***
Pajaro Valley Prevntn & Studen...D.......831 728-6445
335 E Lake Ave Watsonville (95076) ***(P-23957)***
Pak West Paper & Packaging, Santa Ana *Also called Blower-Dempsay Corporation* ***(P-9197)***
Paklab, Chino *Also called Universal Packg Systems Inc* ***(P-4646)***
Pala Band of Mission Indians...C.......760 207-2603
3478 Sunset Dr Fallbrook (92028) ***(P-18455)***
Pala Casino Spa & Resort...A.......760 510-5100
11154 Highway 76 Pala (92059) ***(P-13012)***
Pala Mesa Limited Partnership...C.......760 728-5881
2001 Old Highway 395 Fallbrook (92028) ***(P-13013)***
Pala Mesa Resort, Fallbrook *Also called Pala Mesa Limited Partnership* ***(P-13013)***
Palace Business Solutions, Santa Cruz *Also called Trowbridge Enterprises* ***(P-8091)***
Palace Entertainment Inc (HQ)...E.......949 261-0404
4590 Macarthur Blvd # 400 Newport Beach (92660) ***(P-19213)***
Palace of The Legion Honor, San Francisco *Also called Corportion of Fine Arts Mseums* ***(P-24876)***
Palace Park, Irvine *Also called Festival Fun Parks LLC* ***(P-19173)***
Paladin Eastside Services Inc...D.......323 890-0180
111 S Grfield Ave Ste 101 Montebello (90640) ***(P-24624)***
Paladin Home Care...E.......510 526-2273
555 Pierce St Ste Cml 4 Albany (94706) ***(P-21181)***
Paladin Private Security, Sacramento *Also called Paladin Prtction Spcalists Inc* ***(P-16753)***
Paladin Prtction Spcalists Inc...C.......916 331-3175
320 Commerce Cir Sacramento (95815) ***(P-16753)***
Paladin Realty Partners LLC (PA)...E.......310 914-2410
10880 Wilshire Blvd Los Angeles (90024) ***(P-11658)***
Palantir Technologies Inc (PA)...C.......650 815-0200
100 Hamilton Ave Ste 300 Palo Alto (94301) ***(P-15342)***
Palantir Usg Inc (HQ)...C.......650 815-0200
635 Waverley St Palo Alto (94301) ***(P-15343)***
Palcare Inc...E.......650 340-1289
945 California Dr Burlingame (94010) ***(P-24364)***
Palecek Imports Inc (PA)...D.......510 236-7730
601 Parr Blvd Richmond (94801) ***(P-6734)***
Palisades Interactive, Santa Monica *Also called Palisades Media Group Inc* ***(P-13980)***
Palisades Media Group Inc (PA)...D.......310 564-5400
1601 Cloverf Blvd 6000n Santa Monica (90404) ***(P-13980)***
Palisades Optimist Foundation...D.......310 454-4111
15312 Whitfield Ave Pacific Palisades (90272) ***(P-25211)***
Palisades Ranch Inc...B.......323 581-6161
5925 Alcoa Ave Vernon (90058) ***(P-8439)***
Pall Fortebio LLC...D.......650 322-1360
47661 Fremont Blvd Fremont (94538) ***(P-26428)***
Palm Canyon Resort & Spa, Palm Springs *Also called Diamond Resorts LLC* ***(P-12521)***
Palm Desert Community Assn, Palm Desert *Also called Sun City Palm Dsert Cmnty Assn* ***(P-25254)***
Palm Desert Greens Association...D.......760 346-8005
73750 Country Club Dr Palm Desert (92260) ***(P-25212)***
Palm Desert Medical Offices, Palm Desert *Also called Kaiser Foundation Hospitals* ***(P-19578)***
Palm Desert Town Center, Palm Desert *Also called West Ville Palm Desert* ***(P-10962)***
Palm Drive Healthcare District, Sebastopol *Also called County of Sonoma* ***(P-21359)***
Palm Dsert Rcrtl Fclities Corp...D.......760 346-0015
38995 Desert Willow Dr Palm Desert (92260) ***(P-18998)***
Palm Garden Hotel, Thousand Oaks *Also called Ventu Park LLC* ***(P-13365)***
Palm Grdns Rsdntial Care Fclty...E.......530 661-0574
240 Palm Ave Woodland (95695) ***(P-24625)***
Palm Grove Health Care, Torrance *Also called Unified Inv Programs Inc* ***(P-22898)***
Palm Harbor Residency LP...C.......562 595-4551
3501 Cedar Ave Long Beach (90807) ***(P-21182)***
PALM SPRINGS AERIAL TRAMWAY, Palm Springs *Also called Mount San Jacinto Win Pk Auth* ***(P-19205)***
Palm Springs Art Museum Inc...D.......760 322-4800
101 N Museum Dr Palm Springs (92262) ***(P-24898)***
Palm Springs Convention Center, Palm Springs *Also called Smg Holdings Inc* ***(P-27456)***
Palm Springs Disposal Services...D.......760 327-1351
4690 E Mesquite Ave Palm Springs (92264) ***(P-6426)***
Palm Springs Health Care Ctr, Palm Springs *Also called Five Star Quality Care Inc* ***(P-26859)***
Palm Springs Renaissance, Palm Springs *Also called Remington Hotel Corporation* ***(P-13108)***
Palm Sprng Riviera Resorts Spa, Palm Springs *Also called Riviera Reincarnate LLC* ***(P-13133)***
Palm Ter Hlth Care Rhblitation, Laguna Hills *Also called Gate Three Healthcare LLC* ***(P-24538)***
Palm Terrace Care Center, Riverside *Also called T C H P Inc* ***(P-20837)***
Palmcrest Grand Care Ctr Inc...D.......562 595-4551
3501 Cedar Ave Long Beach (90807) ***(P-20689)***
Palmcrest North Convalescent, Long Beach *Also called Palm Harbor Residency LP* ***(P-21182)***
Palmdale Area, Lancaster *Also called Granite Construction Company* ***(P-1776)***
Palmdale Center For Pain MGT...E.......661 267-6876
819 Auto Center Dr Palmdale (93551) ***(P-19747)***
Palmdale Med Mental Hlth Svcs, Santa Clarita *Also called American Health Services LLC* ***(P-19285)***
Palmdale Resort Inc...E.......661 947-8055
38630 5th St W Palmdale (93551) ***(P-13014)***
Palmdale Water District...D.......661 947-4111
2029 E Avenue Q Palmdale (93550) ***(P-6295)***
Palmdale Womans Club...D.......661 266-3008
2141 E Avenue Q Palmdale (93550) ***(P-13763)***
Palmetto Hospitality...E.......650 843-0795
4216 El Camino Real Palo Alto (94306) ***(P-13015)***
Palo Alpo Medical Foudation, Palo Alto *Also called Sutter Health* ***(P-19978)***
Palo Alto Clinic, Palo Alto *Also called Palo Alto Medical Foundation* ***(P-19749)***
Palo Alto Commons...D.......650 320-8626
4075 El Camino Way Palo Alto (94306) ***(P-24626)***
Palo Alto Community Child Care...D.......650 855-9828
890 Escondido Rd Stanford (94305) ***(P-24365)***
Palo Alto Egg and Food Svc Co...E.......510 456-2420
6691 Clark Ave Newark (94560) ***(P-8440)***
Palo Alto Family Y M C A...E.......650 856-9622
3412 Ross Rd Palo Alto (94303) ***(P-25213)***
Palo Alto Food Company, Newark *Also called Palo Alto Egg and Food Svc Co* ***(P-8440)***
Palo Alto Hills Golf An...D.......650 948-1800
3000 Alexis Dr Palo Alto (94304) ***(P-13764)***
Palo Alto Med Fndtion STA Cruz...A.......831 458-5670
2025 Soquel Ave Santa Cruz (95062) ***(P-21624)***
Palo Alto Medical Clinic...E.......650 321-4121
795 El Camino Real Palo Alto (94301) ***(P-19748)***
Palo Alto Medical Foundation (HQ)...A.......650 321-4121
795 El Camino Real Palo Alto (94301) ***(P-19749)***
Palo Alto Medical Foundation...D.......650 254-5200
370 Distel Cir Los Altos (94022) ***(P-19750)***
Palo Alto Medical Foundation...D.......408 730-4390
201 Old San Francisco Rd Sunnyvale (94086) ***(P-19751)***
Palo Alto Medical Foundation...D.......408 524-5900
1085 W El Camino Real Sunnyvale (94087) ***(P-19752)***
Palo Alto Medical Foundation...D.......408 739-6000
701 E El Camino Real Mountain View (94040) ***(P-19753)***
Palo Alto Medical Foundation...E.......650 326-8120
795 El Camino Real Palo Alto (94301) ***(P-26429)***
Palo Alto Nursing Center, Palo Alto *Also called Covenant Care California LLC* ***(P-20338)***
Palo Alto Research Center Inc...C.......650 812-4000
3333 Coyote Hill Rd Palo Alto (94304) ***(P-26430)***
Palo Alto VA Medical Center, Palo Alto *Also called Veterans Health Administration* ***(P-20064)***
Palo Alto Vineyard MGT LLC...D.......707 996-7725
50 Adobe Canyon Rd Kenwood (95452) ***(P-665)***
Palo Alto Vterans Inst For RES...C.......650 858-3970
3801 Miran Ave Bldg 101a Palo Alto (94304) ***(P-26646)***
Palo Verde Health Care Dst...C.......760 922-4115
250 N 1st St Blythe (92225) ***(P-21625)***
Palo Verde Hospital, Blythe *Also called Palo Verde Health Care Dst* ***(P-21625)***
Palo Verde Hospital Assn...C.......760 922-4115
250 N 1st St Blythe (92225) ***(P-21626)***
Palo Verde Irrigation District...D.......760 922-3144
180 W 14th Ave Blythe (92225) ***(P-6561)***
Palomar Gem & Mineral Club...D.......760 743-0809
2120 Mission Rd Ste 260 Escondido (92029) ***(P-18999)***
Palomar Health...B.......858 675-5360
555 E Valley Pkwy 6 Escondido (92025) ***(P-21627)***
Palomar Health...A.......760 739-3000
2185 Citracado Pkwy Escondido (92029) ***(P-21628)***
Palomar Health...B.......858 613-4000
15615 Pomerado Rd Poway (92064) ***(P-21629)***

Mergent e-mail: customerrelations@mergent.com
1414
2019 Directory of California
Wholesalers and Services Companies
(P-0000) Products & Services Section entry number
(PA)=Parent Co (HQ)=Headquarters (DH)=Div Headquarters

Palomar Health D.....858 613-4000
15615 Pomerado Rd Poway (92064) ***(P-22172)***
Palomar Health Downtown Campus, Escondido *Also called Kaiser Foundation Hospitals* ***(P-19554)***
Palomar Health Technology Inc (PA) C.....442 281-5000
456 E Grand Ave Escondido (92025) ***(P-21630)***
Palomar Medical Center, Escondido *Also called Palomar Health Technology Inc* ***(P-21630)***
Palomar Medical Center, Escondido *Also called Kaiser Foundation Hospitals* ***(P-19552)***
Palomar Medical Center, Escondido *Also called Palomar Health* ***(P-21628)***
Palomar San Diego, San Diego *Also called Khp II San Diego Hotel LLC* ***(P-12807)***
Palomar Vista Healthcare Ctr, Escondido *Also called Ensign Group Inc* ***(P-20399)***
Palomar Vista Healthcare Ctr, Escondido *Also called West Escondido Healthcare LLC* ***(P-20883)***
Paloras Corporation D.....650 440-7663
228 Hamilton Ave Fl 3 Palo Alto (94301) ***(P-27387)***
Palos Verdes Beach & Athc CLB D.....310 375-8777
389 Paseo Del Mar Palos Verdes Estates (90274) ***(P-19000)***
Palos Verdes Bowl, Torrance *Also called Crenshaw Bowling* ***(P-18487)***
Palp Inc C.....562 599-5841
2230 Lemon Ave Long Beach (90806) ***(P-1832)***
Palumbo Lawyers LLP (PA) D.....949 442-0300
15635 Alton Pkwy Ste 300 Irvine (92618) ***(P-23308)***
Pam's Delivery Svc & Nat Msgnr, Orange *Also called Madden Corporation* ***(P-17308)***
Pama Management Co E.....951 929-0340
123 N Inez St Ste 16 Hemet (92543) ***(P-26978)***
Pamc Ltd (PA) A.....213 624-8411
531 W College St Los Angeles (90012) ***(P-21631)***
Pamc Health Foundation, Los Angeles *Also called Pamc Ltd* ***(P-21631)***
Pamona Valley Physical Therapy, Claremont *Also called Pomona Valley Hospital Med Ctr* ***(P-20196)***
Pamona Vallley Hospital, Pomona *Also called Pomona Valley Hospital Med Ctr* ***(P-22038)***
Pan American Bank Fsb B.....949 224-1917
18191 Von Karman Ave # 300 Irvine (92612) ***(P-9528)***
Pan Pacific Petroleum Co Inc (PA) B.....562 928-0100
9302 Garfield Ave South Gate (90280) ***(P-4241)***
Pan Pacific Petroleum Co Inc D.....661 589-3200
1850 Coffee Rd Bakersfield (93308) ***(P-4242)***
Pan Pacific San Diego, San Diego *Also called Pan Pcfic Htels Rsrts Amer Inc* ***(P-13016)***
Pan Pcfic Htels Rsrts Amer Inc B.....619 239-4500
400 W Broadway San Diego (92101) ***(P-13016)***
Pan-Pacific Mechanical LLC (PA) C.....949 474-9170
18250 Euclid St Fountain Valley (92708) ***(P-2305)***
Pan-Pacific Mechanical LLC A.....650 561-8810
1205 Chrysler Dr Menlo Park (94025) ***(P-2306)***
Pan-Pacific Mechanical LLC C.....858 764-2464
11622 El Camino Real San Diego (92130) ***(P-2307)***
Pan-Pacific Plumbing & Mech, San Diego *Also called Pan-Pacific Mechanical LLC* ***(P-2307)***
Pana-Pacific, Fresno *Also called Brix Group Inc* ***(P-7451)***
Panalpina Inc E.....650 825-3036
401 E Grand Ave South San Francisco (94080) ***(P-5132)***
Panalpina Inc D.....310 819-4060
19900 S Vermont Ave Ste A Torrance (90502) ***(P-5133)***
Panama-Buena Vista Un Schl Dst B.....661 397-2205
5901 Schirra Ct Bakersfield (93313) ***(P-14340)***
Panama-Buena Vista Un Schl Dst D.....661 831-7879
4200 Ashe Rd Bakersfield (93313) ***(P-4605)***
Panaroma Gardens, Panorama City *Also called Ensign Group Inc* ***(P-20396)***
Panasas Inc (PA) D.....408 215-6800
969 W Maude Ave Sunnyvale (94085) ***(P-15344)***
Panasonic C.....949 581-0661
26160 Enterprise Way Lake Forest (92630) ***(P-7421)***
Panasonic Avionics Corporation D.....949 472-2376
26211 Enterprise Way Lake Forest (92630) ***(P-25864)***
Panasonic Avionics Corporation (HQ) B.....949 672-2000
26200 Enterprise Way Lake Forest (92630) ***(P-25865)***
Panasonic Broadcast TV Systems, Los Angeles *Also called Panasonic Corp North America* ***(P-7422)***
Panasonic Corp North America C.....323 436-3500
3330 Chnga Blvd W Ste 505 Los Angeles (90068) ***(P-7422)***
Panasonic Corp North America E.....619 661-1134
2055 Sanyo Ave San Diego (92154) ***(P-7423)***
Panasonic Corp North America D.....201 348-7000
2033 Gateway Pl Ste 200 San Jose (95110) ***(P-7424)***
Panasonic Corp North America C.....408 861-3900
10900 N Tantau Ave 200 Cupertino (95014) ***(P-26431)***
Panasonic Corp North America D.....619 661-1134
2055 Sanyo Ave San Diego (92154) ***(P-7425)***
Panattoni Development Co Inc (PA) D.....916 381-1561
20411 Sw Birch St Ste 200 Newport Beach (92660) ***(P-11659)***
Panavision Group, Woodland Hills *Also called Panavision Inc* ***(P-14533)***
Panavision Inc (PA) B.....818 316-1000
6101 Variel Ave Woodland Hills (91367) ***(P-14533)***
Pancan, Manhattan Beach *Also called Pancreatic Cancr Actn Netwrk I* ***(P-22856)***
Pancreatic Cancr Actn Netwrk I (PA) C.....310 725-0025
1500 Rosecrans Ave # 200 Manhattan Beach (90266) ***(P-22856)***
Pandol & Sons E.....661 725-3755
401 Road 192 Delano (93215) ***(P-165)***
Pandol Bros Inc (PA) C.....661 725-3755
33150 Pond Rd Delano (93215) ***(P-8715)***
Pandora Media Inc B.....424 653-6803
3000 Ocean Park Blvd # 3050 Santa Monica (90405) ***(P-5747)***
Pandora Media Inc (PA) C.....510 451-4100
2101 Webster St Ste 1650 Oakland (94612) ***(P-5748)***
Pangea Corporation E.....949 443-0666
34145 Pacific Coast Hwy Dana Point (92629) ***(P-27951)***
Panoche Water District E.....209 364-6136
52027 W Althea Ave Firebaugh (93622) ***(P-6562)***

Panorama Community Hospital E.....818 787-2222
14850 Roscoe Blvd Panorama City (91402) ***(P-21632)***
Panorama Madows Nursing Ctr LP D.....818 894-5707
14857 Roscoe Blvd Panorama City (91402) ***(P-20690)***
Panorama Park Apts D.....661 325-4047
401 W Columbus St Apt 64 Bakersfield (93301) ***(P-11092)***
Panther Custom Wheels, Chino *Also called Prestige Autotech Corporation* ***(P-6666)***
Panzura Inc D.....408 457-8504
695 Campbell Tech Pkwy # 225 Campbell (95008) ***(P-16029)***
Pape Machinery Inc D.....916 922-7181
2850 El Centro Rd Sacramento (95833) ***(P-7685)***
Pape Material Handling Inc D.....510 659-4100
47132 Kato Rd Fremont (94538) ***(P-7783)***
Pape Trucks Inc D.....559 268-4344
2892 E Jensen Ave Fresno (93706) ***(P-17775)***
Pape' Kenworth, Fresno *Also called Pape Trucks Inc* ***(P-17775)***
Paper Company, The, Irvine *Also called Michael Madden Co Inc* ***(P-8110)***
Paper Cutters, Los Angeles *Also called Pacific Paper Converting Inc* ***(P-8125)***
Paper Mart Indus & Ret Packg, Orange *Also called Frick Paper Company* ***(P-8102)***
Papercraft Los Angeles, Cerritos *Also called Bunzl Usa Inc* ***(P-8097)***
Papich Construction Co Inc (PA) C.....805 473-3016
398 Sunrise Ter Arroyo Grande (93420) ***(P-1833)***
Pappas Telecasting Company, Fresno *Also called Kmph Fox 26* ***(P-5809)***
Par Electrical Contractors Inc D.....760 291-1192
525 Corporate Dr Escondido (92029) ***(P-2672)***
Par Electrical Contractors Inc D.....909 854-2880
11276 5th St Ste 100 Rancho Cucamonga (91730) ***(P-2673)***
Par Electrical Contractors Inc D.....707 693-1237
1416 Midway Rd Vacaville (95688) ***(P-2674)***
PAR SERVICES, Culver City *Also called Exceptional Chld Foundation* ***(P-24182)***
Par Services, Culver City *Also called Exceptional Chld Foundation* ***(P-24183)***
Para & Palli Inc D.....209 826-0790
931 Idaho Ave Los Banos (93635) ***(P-20691)***
Para Los Ninos C.....213 623-3942
845 E 6th St Los Angeles (90021) ***(P-24366)***
Paracelsus Los Angeles Comm C.....323 267-0477
4081 E Olympic Blvd Los Angeles (90023) ***(P-21633)***
Paradigm Industries Inc D.....310 965-1900
13344 S Main St Ste C Los Angeles (90061) ***(P-17385)***
Paradigm Information Services D.....858 693-6115
10755 F Scrps Pwy Pkwy424 San Diego (92131) ***(P-27952)***
Paradigm Music LLC (PA) D.....310 288-8000
360 N Crescent Dr Beverly Hills (90210) ***(P-18392)***
Paradigm Staffing Solutions E.....510 663-7860
1970 Broadway Ste 615 Oakland (94612) ***(P-14687)***
Paradise Ambulance Service, Chico *Also called First Responder Ems Inc* ***(P-3796)***
Paradise Building Services C.....909 399-0707
9664 Hermosa Ave Rancho Cucamonga (91730) ***(P-14341)***
Paradise Electric Inc D.....619 449-4141
697 Greenfield Dr El Cajon (92021) ***(P-2675)***
Paradise Lessee Inc B.....858 274-4630
1404 Vacation Rd San Diego (92109) ***(P-13017)***
Paradise Oaks Youth Services D.....916 725-7182
7806 Uplands Way A Citrus Heights (95610) ***(P-23958)***
Paradise Point Resort, San Diego *Also called Westgroup San Diego Associates* ***(P-13391)***
Paradise Point Resort & Spa, San Diego *Also called Paradise Lessee Inc* ***(P-13017)***
Paradise Ridge Fmly Resources, Paradise *Also called Youth For Change* ***(P-24139)***
Paradise Solid Waste, Paradise *Also called USA Waste of California Inc* ***(P-6499)***
Paradise Valley Estates, Fairfield *Also called Northern CA Retiredd Ofcrs* ***(P-24612)***
Paradise Valley Hospital (PA) A.....619 470-4100
2400 E 4th St National City (91950) ***(P-21634)***
Paradise Valley Hospital D.....619 472-7474
180 Otay Lakes Rd Ste 100 Bonita (91902) ***(P-22389)***
Paradise Vly Hlth Care Ctr Inc D.....619 470-6700
2575 E 8th St National City (91950) ***(P-20692)***
Paragon Coml Bldg Maint Inc D.....916 334-8801
6731 32nd St Ste J North Highlands (95660) ***(P-14342)***
Paragon Health & Rehab CT E.....559 638-3578
1090 E Dinuba Ave Reedley (93654) ***(P-22632)***
Paragon Industries Inc C.....760 898-4716
19305 White Sage Trl Desert Hot Springs (92241) ***(P-3006)***
Paragon Industries Inc D.....714 778-8453
1235 S State College Blvd Anaheim (92806) ***(P-6903)***
Paragon Partners Ltd (PA) D.....714 379-3376
5660 Katella Ave Ste 100 Cypress (90630) ***(P-27819)***
Paragon Personel Services, Brea *Also called Sunshine Clearing Corporation* ***(P-14772)***
Paragon Plastics Co Div, Chino *Also called Consolidated Plastics Corp* ***(P-8913)***
Paragon Real Estate Group D.....415 323-4066
350 Rhode Island St San Francisco (94103) ***(P-11660)***
Paragon Textiles Inc D.....310 323-7500
13003 S Figueroa St Los Angeles (90061) ***(P-8330)***
Parallax Capital Partners LLC (PA) D.....949 296-4800
23332 Mill Creek Dr # 155 Laguna Hills (92653) ***(P-12065)***
Paramount, San Francisco *Also called Third & Mission Associates LLC* ***(P-11794)***
Paramount Bldg Solutions LLC C.....951 272-4001
2045 California Ave # 101 Corona (92881) ***(P-14343)***
Paramount Bldg Solutions LLC C.....916 564-4102
4741 Pell Dr Ste 3 Sacramento (95838) ***(P-1609)***
Paramount Citrus, Delano *Also called Wonderful Company LLC* ***(P-211)***
Paramount Citrus Packing Co, Delano *Also called Wonderful Citrus Packing LLC* ***(P-589)***
Paramount Convalescent Group D.....562 634-6895
8558 Rosecrans Ave Paramount (90723) ***(P-21183)***
Paramount Equity Mortgage LLC C.....916 290-9999
10888 White Rock Rd Rancho Cordova (95670) ***(P-9842)***
Paramount Equity Mortgage LLC D.....916 290-9999
4200 Douglas Blvd Granite Bay (95746) ***(P-9843)***

Paramount Equity Mortgage LLC.....C.....916 290-9999
22 Executive Park Ste 100 Irvine (92614) ***(P-9844)***
Paramount Export Company.....D.....858 452-8101
5875 Lamas St San Diego (92122) ***(P-8716)***
Paramount Farming, Shafter *Also called Wonderful Orchards LLC* ***(P-197)***
Paramount Pictures, Los Angeles *Also called Paramount Television Service* ***(P-18091)***
Paramount Pictures Corporation (HQ).....A.....323 956-5000
5555 Melrose Ave Los Angeles (90038) ***(P-18090)***
Paramount Properties, Beverly Hills *Also called Rodeo Realty Inc* ***(P-11739)***
Paramount Properties, Woodland Hills *Also called Rodeo Realty Inc* ***(P-11742)***
Paramount Properties Encino BR, Encino *Also called Rodeo Realty Inc* ***(P-11737)***
Paramount Restyling Auto Inc (PA).....D.....909 781-6492
1410 E Holt Blvd Ontario (91761) ***(P-6663)***
Paramount Studios, Los Angeles *Also called Paramount Pictures Corporation* ***(P-18090)***
Paramount Swap Meet, Paramount *Also called Modern Dev Co A Ltd Partnr* ***(P-17333)***
Paramount Television Service.....A.....323 956-5000
5555 Melrose Ave Rm 204 Los Angeles (90038) ***(P-18091)***
Paramount Theatre of Arts Inc.....D.....510 893-2300
2025 Broadway Oakland (94612) ***(P-10926)***
Paramount Trnsp Systems Inc (PA).....E.....760 510-7979
1350 Grand Ave San Marcos (92078) ***(P-5134)***
Paramout Farms, Lost Hills *Also called Roll Properties Intl Inc* ***(P-12263)***
Paramunt Contrs Developers Inc.....E.....323 464-7050
6464 W Sunset Blvd # 700 Los Angeles (90028) ***(P-11661)***
Paramunt Madows Nursing Ctr LP.....D.....562 531-0990
7039 Alondra Blvd Paramount (90723) ***(P-26979)***
Parasec Incorporated (PA).....D.....916 576-7000
2804 Gateway Oaks Dr # 100 Sacramento (95833) ***(P-23309)***
Parasoft Corporation (PA).....E.....626 256-3680
101 E Huntington Dr Fl 2 Monrovia (91016) ***(P-7087)***
Paratransit Incorporated (PA).....C.....916 429-2009
2501 Florin Rd Sacramento (95822) ***(P-3828)***
Paratransit Incorporated.....C.....209 522-2300
3300 Tully Rd Modesto (95350) ***(P-3829)***
Parc, Palo Alto *Also called Palo Alto Research Center Inc* ***(P-26430)***
Parc 55 Hotel, San Francisco *Also called Rp/Kinetic Parc 55 Owner LLC* ***(P-13145)***
Parc Management LLC.....A.....925 609-1364
1950 Waterworld Pkwy Concord (94520) ***(P-19214)***
Parc Specialty Contractors.....D.....916 992-5405
1400 Vinci Ave Sacramento (95838) ***(P-3562)***
Parca, Burlingame *Also called Partners and Advocates* ***(P-23959)***
Parcell Steel Corp (PA).....C.....951 471-3200
26365 Earthmover Cir Corona (92883) ***(P-3390)***
Parchment Inc.....D.....480 719-1646
3000 Lava Ridge Ct # 210 Roseville (95661) ***(P-17386)***
Pardee Homes.....E.....858 259-6390
12220 El Camino Real # 300 San Diego (92130) ***(P-11904)***
Pardee Homes (HQ).....D.....310 955-3100
177 E Colo Blvd Ste 550 Pasadena (91105) ***(P-11905)***
Pardee Tree Nursery.....D.....760 630-5400
30970 Via Puerta Del Sol Oceanside (92057) ***(P-9156)***
Parenthood of Planned.....D.....415 821-1282
1650 Valencia St San Francisco (94110) ***(P-25214)***
Parenthood of Planned.....D.....707 527-7656
1140 Sonoma Ave Ste 3 Santa Rosa (95405) ***(P-22633)***
Parenthood of Planned (PA).....D.....619 881-4500
1075 Camino Del Rio S # 100 San Diego (92108) ***(P-22634)***
Parenthood of Planned.....D.....951 222-3101
12900 Frederick St Ste C Moreno Valley (92553) ***(P-22635)***
Parenthood of Planned.....D.....530 351-7100
2935 Bechelli Ln Redding (96002) ***(P-22636)***
Parents United, San Jose *Also called Giarretto Institute* ***(P-23821)***
Pareto Networks Inc.....C.....877 727-8020
1183 Bordeaux Dr Ste 22 Sunnyvale (94089) ***(P-5621)***
Parexel International Corp.....C.....818 254-7076
1560 E Chevy Chase Dr # 140 Glendale (91206) ***(P-26432)***
Paribas Asset Management Inc.....D.....415 772-1300
1 Front St Fl 23 San Francisco (94111) ***(P-9664)***
Paris Blues Inc (PA).....D.....310 605-2000
2397 Miguel Miranda Ave Duarte (91010) ***(P-11998)***
Pariveda Solutions Inc.....C.....415 946-6100
201 California St # 1250 San Francisco (94111) ***(P-16030)***
Park and Recreation, San Diego *Also called City of San Diego* ***(P-22010)***
Park and Recreation, Folsom *Also called City of Folsom* ***(P-19130)***
Park Central Hotel Fresno, Fresno *Also called Park Inn By Readisson Fresno* ***(P-13045)***
Park Central Ht San Francisco, San Francisco *Also called Viva Soma Lessee Inc* ***(P-27087)***
Park Cleaners Inc (PA).....D.....626 281-5942
419 Mcgroarty St San Gabriel (91776) ***(P-13549)***
Park Cntl Care Rhblitation Ctr.....D.....510 797-5300
2100 Parkside Dr Fremont (94536) ***(P-20693)***
Park Disposal Service, Buena Park *Also called Edco Disposal Corporation Inc* ***(P-6394)***
Park Hotels & Resorts Inc.....B.....805 564-4333
633 E Cabrillo Blvd Santa Barbara (93103) ***(P-13018)***
Park Hotels & Resorts Inc.....D.....408 942-0400
901 E Calaveras Blvd Milpitas (95035) ***(P-13019)***
Park Hotels & Resorts Inc.....D.....714 990-6000
900 E Birch St Brea (92821) ***(P-13020)***
Park Hotels & Resorts Inc.....B.....619 276-4010
1775 E Mission Bay Dr San Diego (92109) ***(P-13021)***
Park Hotels & Resorts Inc.....B.....415 771-1400
333 Ofarrell St San Francisco (94102) ***(P-13022)***
Park Hotels & Resorts Inc.....C.....510 635-5000
1 Hegenberger Rd Oakland (94621) ***(P-13023)***
Park Hotels & Resorts Inc.....E.....858 450-4569
10950 N Torrey Pines Rd La Jolla (92037) ***(P-13024)***
Park Hotels & Resorts Inc.....D.....707 253-9540
1075 California Blvd NAPA (94559) ***(P-13025)***
Park Hotels & Resorts Inc.....C.....909 980-3420
700 N Haven Ave Ontario (91764) ***(P-13026)***
Park Hotels & Resorts Inc.....C.....626 577-1000
168 S Los Robles Ave Pasadena (91101) ***(P-13027)***
Park Hotels & Resorts Inc.....B.....415 392-8000
55 Cyril Magnin St San Francisco (94102) ***(P-13028)***
Park Hotels & Resorts Inc.....D.....626 915-3441
1211 E Garvey St Covina (91724) ***(P-13029)***
Park Hotels & Resorts Inc.....C.....310 415-3340
9876 Wilshire Blvd Beverly Hills (90210) ***(P-13030)***
Park Hotels & Resorts Inc.....C.....530 543-2126
4130 Lake Tahoe Blvd South Lake Tahoe (96150) ***(P-13031)***
Park Hotels & Resorts Inc.....C.....650 342-4600
150 Anza Blvd Burlingame (94010) ***(P-13032)***
Park Hotels & Resorts Inc.....C.....626 445-8525
211 E Huntington Dr Arcadia (91006) ***(P-13033)***
Park Hotels & Resorts Inc.....D.....562 861-1900
8425 Firestone Blvd Downey (90241) ***(P-13034)***
Park Hotels & Resorts Inc.....D.....714 739-5600
7762 Beach Blvd Buena Park (90620) ***(P-13035)***
Park Hotels & Resorts Inc.....C.....909 980-0400
700 N Haven Ave Ontario (91764) ***(P-13036)***
Park Hotels & Resorts Inc.....C.....626 270-2700
225 W Valley Blvd San Gabriel (91776) ***(P-13037)***
Park Hotels & Resorts Inc.....C.....949 553-8332
2120 Main St Irvine (92614) ***(P-13038)***
Park Hotels & Resorts Inc.....B.....714 540-7000
3050 Bristol St Costa Mesa (92626) ***(P-13039)***
Park Hotels & Resorts Inc.....D.....415 771-1400
333 Ofarrell St San Francisco (94102) ***(P-13040)***
Park Hotels & Resorts Inc.....D.....714 632-1221
3100 E Frontera St Anaheim (92806) ***(P-13041)***
Park Hotels & Resorts Inc.....D.....650 589-3400
250 Gateway Blvd South San Francisco (94080) ***(P-13042)***
Park Hotels & Resorts Inc.....E.....530 541-6122
901 Ski Run Blvd South Lake Tahoe (96150) ***(P-13043)***
Park Hyatt Aviara Resort, Carlsbad *Also called Aviara Resort Associates* ***(P-12342)***
Park Inn, Anaheim *Also called Badalian Enterprises Inc* ***(P-12349)***
Park Inn By Radisson.....D.....559 226-2200
3737 N Blackstone Ave Fresno (93726) ***(P-13044)***
Park Inn By Readisson Fresno.....D.....559 226-2200
3737 N Blackstone Ave Fresno (93726) ***(P-13045)***
Park Labrea Management, Los Angeles *Also called Plb Management LLC* ***(P-11098)***
Park Landscape Maint 1-2-3-4, Rcho STA Marg *Also called Park Landscape Maintenance* ***(P-916)***
Park Landscape Maintenance (PA).....B.....949 546-8300
22421 Gilberto Ste A Rcho STA Marg (92688) ***(P-916)***
Park Lane A Classic Residenc, Monterey *Also called Classic Park Lane Partnership* ***(P-11002)***
Park Lane, The, Monterey *Also called P Monterey LP* ***(P-24621)***
Park Maintenance, Torrance *Also called City of Torrance* ***(P-19143)***
Park Manor Suites, San Diego *Also called Gentry Associates LLC* ***(P-12601)***
Park Marino Convalescent Ctr.....E.....626 463-4105
2585 E Washington Blvd Pasadena (91107) ***(P-21184)***
Park n Fly Inc.....D.....310 417-3566
6351 W Century Blvd Los Angeles (90045) ***(P-17695)***
Park Newport Apartments, Newport Beach *Also called Park Newport Ltd* ***(P-11093)***
Park Newport Ltd (PA).....D.....949 644-1900
1 Park Newport Newport Beach (92660) ***(P-11093)***
Park One Lax, Los Angeles *Also called Park n Fly Inc* ***(P-17695)***
PARK PASEO, Glendale *Also called Cal Southern Presbt Homes* ***(P-10995)***
Park Place Ford LLC.....D.....909 946-5555
555 W Foothill Blvd Upland (91786) ***(P-17776)***
Park Plaza Hotel.....E.....510 635-5300
150 Hegenberger Rd Oakland (94621) ***(P-13046)***
Park Regency Inc.....D.....818 363-6116
10146 Balboa Blvd Granada Hills (91344) ***(P-11662)***
Park Shadelands Medical Offs, Walnut Creek *Also called Kaiser Foundation Hospitals* ***(P-21480)***
Park Uniform Rentals, San Gabriel *Also called Park Cleaners Inc* ***(P-13549)***
Park View Gardens, Santa Rosa *Also called Ensign Group Inc* ***(P-20398)***
PARK VISTA AT MORNINGSIDE, Fullerton *Also called Corecare V A Cal Ltd Partnr* ***(P-20324)***
Park West Rescom Inc.....C.....949 546-8300
22421 Gilberto Rcho STA Marg (92688) ***(P-917)***
Parkco Building Company.....D.....714 444-1441
3190 Airport Loop Dr F Costa Mesa (92626) ***(P-1610)***
Parker Landscape Dev Inc.....E.....916 383-4071
6011 Franklin Blvd Sacramento (95824) ***(P-776)***
Parker Milliken Clark OHar.....D.....818 784-8087
555 S Flower St Fl 30 Los Angeles (90071) ***(P-23310)***
Parker Stanbury LLP (PA).....D.....619 528-1259
444 S Flower St Ste 1900 Los Angeles (90071) ***(P-23311)***
Parker Station, Woodland Hills *Also called Guarachi Wine Partners Inc* ***(P-9047)***
Parkers Retirement Residence, Fountain Valley *Also called Longwood Management Corp* ***(P-24583)***
Parkhurst Terrace.....D.....831 685-0800
100 Parkhurst Cir Aptos (95003) ***(P-1305)***
Parking Company of America.....D.....562 862-2118
523 W 6th St Ste 528 Los Angeles (90014) ***(P-17696)***
Parking Concepts Inc.....B.....949 752-5558
12 Mauchly Ste I Irvine (92618) ***(P-17387)***
Parking Concepts Inc.....E.....310 208-1611
1036 Broxton Ave Los Angeles (90024) ***(P-17697)***
Parking Concepts Inc.....E.....213 746-5764
1801 Georgia St Los Angeles (90015) ***(P-17698)***
Parking Concepts Inc.....C.....310 821-1081
14110 Palawan Way Venice (90292) ***(P-17699)***

Parking Concepts Inc .... E 213 623-2661
800 Wilshire Blvd Los Angeles (90017) **(P-17700)**
Parking Concepts Inc .... D 310 322-5008
12001 Vista Del Mar Playa Del Rey (90293) **(P-17701)**
Parking Network Inc .... C 213 613-1500
350 S Figueroa St Ste 420 Los Angeles (90071) **(P-3563)**
Parking Spot, The, Los Angeles *Also called Prg Parking Century LLC* **(P-17703)**
Parking Spot, The, Los Angeles *Also called Tps Parking Management LLC* **(P-17708)**
Parkinsons Institute .... D 800 786-2958
675 Almanor Ave Ste 101 Sunnyvale (94085) **(P-26647)**
Parkmerced Investors LLC .... E 877 243-5544
3711 19th Ave San Francisco (94132) **(P-14534)**
Parks & Recreation, Commerce *Also called City of Commerce* **(P-19127)**
Parks & Recreation Dept, Los Angeles *Also called City of Los Angeles* **(P-24873)**
Parks & Recreation Dept, Spring Valley *Also called County of San Diego* **(P-23726)**
Parks & Recreation Dept, Los Angeles *Also called City of Los Angeles* **(P-13448)**
Parks and Recreation Cal Dept .... E 209 763-5121
2000 Camanche Rd Ofc Ione (95640) **(P-19215)**
Parks and Recreation Cal Dept .... D 310 456-8432
23200 Pacific Coast Hwy Malibu (90265) **(P-24899)**
Parks and Recreation Dept, Pomona *Also called County of Los Angeles* **(P-18699)**
Parks Department, Redwood City *Also called County of San Mateo* **(P-13463)**
Parks Recreation Libraries, Orange *Also called City of Orange* **(P-19140)**
Parks-Rcreation-Community Svcs, Irvine *Also called City of Irvine* **(P-19134)**
Parkside Lending LLC .... D 415 771-3700
180 Redwood St Ste 250 San Francisco (94102) **(P-10009)**
Parkside Special Care Center .... D 619 442-7744
444 W Lexington Ave El Cajon (92020) **(P-20694)**
PARKTREE COMMUNITY HEALTH CENT, Pomona *Also called Pomona Community Health Center* **(P-25037)**
Parkview Cmnty Hosp Med Ctr .... A 951 354-7404
3865 Jackson St Riverside (92503) **(P-21635)**
Parkview Jlian Cnvlescent Hosp .... D 661 831-9150
1801 Julian Ave Bakersfield (93304) **(P-20695)**
Parkway Apartments LLC .... E 925 866-8429
3170 Crow Canyon Pl # 165 San Ramon (94583) **(P-11094)**
Parkwood Landscape Maint Inc .... D 818 988-9677
16443 Hart St Van Nuys (91406) **(P-918)**
Parma Management Co Inc .... E 858 457-4999
6390 Greenwich Dr Ste 150 San Diego (92122) **(P-11663)**
Parole Unit Office, Eureka *Also called Correctons Rhbltation Cal Dept* **(P-23618)**
Parpro Holdings Co Ltd .... C 619 498-9004
9355 Airway Rd Ste 4 San Diego (92154) **(P-11999)**
Parsec Inc .... A 323 268-5011
4940 Sheila St Commerce (90040) **(P-5240)**
Parsec Inc .... D 323 276-3116
750 Lamar St Los Angeles (90031) **(P-5241)**
Parsons Brnckrhoff Hldings Inc .... D 916 567-2500
2329 Oakes Dr Ste 200 Sacramento (95833) **(P-27388)**
Parsons Constructors Inc .... A 626 440-2000
100 W Walnut St Pasadena (91124) **(P-26980)**
Parsons Corporation (PA) .... A 626 440-2000
100 W Walnut St Pasadena (91124) **(P-2053)**
Parsons Corporation .... C 714 562-5725
1 Centerpointe Dr Ste 210 La Palma (90623) **(P-2054)**
Parsons Corporation .... D 415 490-2400
44 Montgomery St Ste 880 San Francisco (94104) **(P-1834)**
Parsons Corporation .... D 626 440-2000
100 W San Fernando St # 450 San Jose (95113) **(P-1835)**
Parsons Engrg Science Inc (HQ) .... B 626 440-2000
100 W Walnut St Pasadena (91124) **(P-25866)**
Parsons Government Svcs Inc (HQ) .... B 626 440-2000
100 W Walnut St Pasadena (91124) **(P-25867)**
Parsons Government Svcs Inc .... D 925 313-3217
2000 Marina Vista Ave Martinez (94553) **(P-25868)**
Parsons Government Svcs Inc (HQ) .... D 949 768-8161
25531 Commercentre Dr Lake Forest (92630) **(P-26433)**
Parsons Government Svcs Inc .... B 619 685-0085
525 B St Ste 1600 San Diego (92101) **(P-25869)**
Parsons Gvrnment Svcs Intl Inc .... B 626 440-6000
100 W Walnut St Pasadena (91124) **(P-1611)**
Parsons Project Services Inc .... C 626 440-4000
100 W Walnut St Pasadena (91124) **(P-1427)**
Parsons Services Company .... A 626 440-2000
100 W Walnut St Pasadena (91124) **(P-25870)**
Parsons Technical Services Inc .... D 626 440-3998
100 W Walnut St Pasadena (91124) **(P-25871)**
Parsons Wtr Infrastructure Inc .... A 626 440-7000
100 W Walnut St Pasadena (91124) **(P-25872)**
Parthenon DCS Holdings LLC .... A 925 960-4800
4 Embarcadero Ctr San Francisco (94111) **(P-26981)**
Participant Channel Inc .... D 310 550-7715
331 Foothill Rd Fl 3 Beverly Hills (90210) **(P-5832)**
Participant Media LLC (PA) .... D 310 550-5100
331 Foothill Rd Fl 3 Beverly Hills (90210) **(P-18092)**
Partitions Installation Inc .... D 562 207-9868
13021 Leffingwell Ave Santa Fe Springs (90670) **(P-3564)**
Partner Assessment Corporation (PA) .... C 800 419-4923
2154 Torrance Blvd # 200 Torrance (90501) **(P-25873)**
Partner Engineering & Science, Torrance *Also called Partner Assessment Corporation* **(P-25873)**
Partner Hero Inc .... E 888 968-2767
1001 Avenida Pico C260 San Clemente (92673) **(P-17388)**
Partners and Advocates .... D 650 312-0730
800 Airport Blvd Ste 320 Burlingame (94010) **(P-23959)**
Partners Capital Group Inc (PA) .... D 949 916-3900
201 Sandpointe Ave # 500 Santa Ana (92707) **(P-17389)**
Partners For Community Access .... D 510 558-6700
708 Gilman St Berkeley (94710) **(P-23960)**
Partners In Leadership LLC (HQ) .... D 951 694-5596
27555 Ynez Rd Ste 300 Temecula (92591) **(P-27389)**
Partners In Leadership Interme (PA) .... D 951 506-6878
27555 Ynez Rd Temecula (92591) **(P-27390)**
Partners Information Tech Inc (HQ) .... D 714 736-4487
7101 Village Dr Buena Park (90621) **(P-16451)**
Partners Risk Specialists .... E 619 326-0840
6136 Mission Gorge Rd # 125 San Diego (92120) **(P-27953)**
Partnership Health Plan Cal .... B 707 863-4100
4665 Business Center Dr Fairfield (94534) **(P-10293)**
Partos Agency LLC .... D 310 458-7800
227 Broadway Ste 204 Santa Monica (90401) **(P-17390)**
Partos Company, The, Santa Monica *Also called Partos Agency LLC* **(P-17390)**
Parts .... D 916 371-3115
2445 Evergreen Ave West Sacramento (95691) **(P-17607)**
Partschannel Inc .... E 562 654-3400
8905 Rex Rd Pico Rivera (90660) **(P-6664)**
Partsearch Technologies Inc .... E 661 257-7700
25158 Avenue Stanford Santa Clarita (91355) **(P-7523)**
Party Pantry Garden Room .... E 714 899-0626
12777 Knott St Garden Grove (92841) **(P-13765)**
Parwood Preservation LP .... D 562 531-7880
5441 N Paramount Blvd Long Beach (90805) **(P-11664)**
Paryroll Department, Redwood City *Also called Verity Health System Cal Inc* **(P-21899)**
Pasadena Baking Co .... E 626 796-5093
70 W Pal Meto Ave Pasadena (91105) **(P-8846)**
Pasadena Billing Associates .... D 626 795-6596
225 S Lake Ave Ste 535 Pasadena (91101) **(P-26264)**
Pasadena Center Operating Co .... C 626 795-9311
300 E Green St Pasadena (91101) **(P-17391)**
Pasadena Child Dev Assoc Inc .... D 626 793-7350
620 N Lake Ave Pasadena (91101) **(P-22637)**
Pasadena Child Development Ass .... D 626 793-7350
620 N Lake Ave Pasadena (91101) **(P-23961)**
Pasadena Chld Training Soc .... C 626 798-0853
2933 El Nido Dr Altadena (91001) **(P-24627)**
PASADENA CONVENTION CENTER, Pasadena *Also called Pasadena Center Operating Co* **(P-17391)**
Pasadena Cyto Pathology Lab .... B 626 397-8616
100 W Calif Blvd Fl 3 Pasadena (91105) **(P-21636)**
Pasadena Hospital Assn Ltd (PA) .... A 626 397-5000
100 W California Blvd Pasadena (91105) **(P-21637)**
Pasadena Hospital Assn Ltd .... D 626 397-3322
716 S Fair Oaks Ave Pasadena (91105) **(P-20696)**
Pasadena Hotel Dev Ventr LP .... D 626 449-4000
303 Cordova St Pasadena (91101) **(P-13047)**
Pasadena Humane Society .... D 626 792-7151
361 S Raymond Ave Pasadena (91105) **(P-25450)**
Pasadena Madows Nursing Ctr LP .... D 626 796-1103
150 Bellefontaine St Pasadena (91105) **(P-20697)**
Pasadena Model Railroad Club .... D 323 222-1718
5458 Alhambra Ave Los Angeles (90032) **(P-19001)**
Pasadena Rbles Acquisition LLC .... D 626 577-1000
168 S Los Robles Ave Pasadena (91101) **(P-13048)**
Pasadena Rehabilitation Inst, Pasadena *Also called Algos Inc A Medical Corp* **(P-22500)**
Pasadena Sport Club, Pasadena *Also called 24 Hour Fitness Usa Inc* **(P-18552)**
Pasadena Vision, Pasadena *Also called Linden Optometry A Prof Corp* **(P-20158)**
Pasea Hotel & Spa, Huntington Beach *Also called Pacific City Hotel LLC* **(P-12996)**
Paseo Vlg Hsing Partners LP .... E 714 991-9172
1115 N Citron St Anaheim (92801) **(P-11095)**
Pasha Distribution Svcs LLC .... D 714 889-2460
3010 Old Ranch Pkwy # 220 Seal Beach (90740) **(P-5135)**
Pasha Freight, San Rafael *Also called Pasha Group* **(P-5136)**
Pasha Group (PA) .... B 415 927-6400
4040 Civic Center Dr # 350 San Rafael (94903) **(P-5136)**
Pasha Group .... C 310 735-0952
19020 S Dminguez Hills Dr Compton (90220) **(P-5137)**
Pasha Hawaii Trnspt Lines LLC .... D 510 271-1400
1425 Maritime St Oakland (94607) **(P-4701)**
Pasha Hawaii Trnspt Lines LLC (PA) .... C 415 927-6400
4040 Civic Center Dr # 350 San Rafael (94903) **(P-4706)**
Pasha Stevedoring Terminals LP .... E 310 233-2006
802 S Fries Ave Wilmington (90744) **(P-4730)**
Pasha Stevedoring Terminals LP .... E 415 927-6353
802 S Fries Ave Wilmington (90744) **(P-4702)**
Paskenta Band Nomlaki Indians .... B 530 528-3500
2655 Everett Freeman Way Corning (96021) **(P-13049)**
Paso Robles Hotel, Paso Robles *Also called Paso Robles Inn LLC* **(P-13050)**
Paso Robles Inn LLC .... D 805 238-2660
1103 Spring St Paso Robles (93446) **(P-13050)**
Paso Robles Tank - Brown-Minne (PA) .... D 805 227-1641
825 26th St Paso Robles (93446) **(P-3391)**
Passages, Malibu *Also called Grasshopper House LLC* **(P-22586)**
Passco Companies LLC (PA) .... D 949 442-1000
2050 Main St Ste 650 Irvine (92614) **(P-11665)**
Passprt Accept Fclty Los Angel .... D 323 460-4811
1425 N Cherokee Ave Los Angeles (90093) **(P-17392)**
Pasta Shop (PA) .... D 510 250-6005
5655 College Ave Ste 201 Oakland (94618) **(P-8847)**
Patel Brothers Inc .... C 510 590-6914
693 Hillcrest Ter Fremont (94539) **(P-26982)**
Patelco Credit Union .... D 925 785-9487
310 Hartz Ave Danville (94526) **(P-9643)**
Patelco Credit Union (PA) .... C 800 358-8228
5050 Hopyard Rd Pleasanton (94588) **(P-9580)**
Patenaude & Felix A Prof Corp (PA) .... D 858 244-7600
4545 Murphy Canyon Rd # 3 San Diego (92123) **(P-23312)**

ALPHABETIC

Employee Codes: A=Over 500 employees, B=251-500
C=101-250, D=51-100, E=50
2019 Directory of California
Wholesalers and Services Companies
© Mergent Inc. 1-800-342-5647
1417

Pater Digintas Inc......D......831 624-1875
23795 Holman Hwy Monterey (93940) ***(P-20698)***
Pathfinder Health Inc......C......714 636-5649
10051 Lampson Ave Garden Grove (92840) ***(P-22390)***
Pathfinder Services, Folsom *Also called Location Services LLC* ***(P-5234)***
Pathnostics, Irvine *Also called Cap Diagnostics LLC* ***(P-22064)***
Pathpoint......D......805 782-8890
11491 Los Osos Valley Rd San Luis Obispo (93405) ***(P-24218)***
Pathway Capital Management LP (PA)......D......949 622-1000
18575 Jamboree Rd Ste 700 Irvine (92612) ***(P-26983)***
Pathway Inc......D......909 890-1070
287 W Orange Show Ln San Bernardino (92408) ***(P-23962)***
Pathway Society......E......408 244-1834
102 S 11th St San Jose (95112) ***(P-22638)***
Pathway To Choices Inc......D......510 724-9044
751 Belmont Way Pinole (94564) ***(P-23963)***
Pathways, Oakland *Also called Hospice & Home Health of E Bay* ***(P-22333)***
Pathways Home Health......E......650 634-0133
395 Oyster Point Blvd # 128 South San Francisco (94080) ***(P-22857)***
Pathways La (PA)......E......213 427-2700
3325 Wilshire Blvd # 1100 Los Angeles (90010) ***(P-23964)***
Patient Business Services, Escondido *Also called Palomar Health* ***(P-21627)***
Patientpop Inc......D......844 487-8399
214 Wilshire Blvd Santa Monica (90401) ***(P-15825)***
Patients Hospital......D......530 225-8700
2900 Eureka Way Redding (96001) ***(P-21638)***
Patientsafe Solutions Inc (PA)......D......858 746-3100
9330 Scranton Rd San Diego (92121) ***(P-15345)***
Patina Freight Inc......C......909 444-1025
525 S Lemon Ave Walnut (91789) ***(P-4606)***
Patra Corporation (PA)......C......415 595-9987
1107 Inv Blvd Ste 100 El Dorado Hills (95762) ***(P-10143)***
Patreon Inc......D......415 967-2735
600 Townsend St Ste 500 San Francisco (94103) ***(P-15346)***
Patric Communications Inc (PA)......D......619 579-2898
33 Hammond Ste 201 Irvine (92618) ***(P-2676)***
Patrick Dean Bryan......D......530 273-5484
12481 Lttle Deer Creek Ln Nevada City (95959) ***(P-3565)***
Patrick Industries Inc......C......909 350-4440
13414 Slover Ave Fontana (92337) ***(P-6904)***
Patrick K Willis Company Inc......B......800 398-6480
5118 Rbert J Mathews Pkwy El Dorado Hills (95762) ***(P-17393)***
Patricks Construction Clean-Up......D......916 452-5495
7851 14th Ave Sacramento (95826) ***(P-2055)***
Patriot Brokerage Inc......D......910 227-4142
7840 Foothill Blvd Ste H Sunland (91040) ***(P-5138)***
Patriot Contract Services LLC......B......925 296-2000
1320 Willow Pass Rd # 485 Concord (94520) ***(P-4699)***
Patrol Masters Inc......C......714 426-2526
1651 E 4th St Ste 150 Santa Ana (92701) ***(P-16754)***
Patron Solutions LLC......C......949 823-1700
5171 California Ave # 200 Irvine (92617) ***(P-15826)***
Pattern Energy Group LP (PA)......D......415 283-4000
Bay 3 Pier 1 San Francisco (94111) ***(P-6097)***
Pattern Renewables 2 LP......C......415 283-4000
Bay 3 Pier 1 San Francisco (94111) ***(P-2308)***
Patterson Dental 426, El Segundo *Also called Patterson Dental Supply Inc* ***(P-7204)***
Patterson Dental 454, Roseville *Also called Patterson Dental Supply Inc* ***(P-7205)***
Patterson Dental 590, Dinuba *Also called Patterson Dental Supply Inc* ***(P-7206)***
Patterson Dental Supply Inc......D......310 426-3100
185 S Douglas St Ste 100 El Segundo (90245) ***(P-7204)***
Patterson Dental Supply Inc......D......916 780-5100
1030 Winding Creek Rd # 150 Roseville (95678) ***(P-7205)***
Patterson Dental Supply Inc......D......559 595-1450
800 Monte Vista Dr Dinuba (93618) ***(P-7206)***
Patterson Dental Supply Inc......E......818 435-1368
9200 Oakdale Ave Ste 500 Chatsworth (91311) ***(P-15347)***
Patterson Ritner Lockwood (PA)......D......818 241-8001
620 N Brand Blvd Fl 3 Glendale (91203) ***(P-23313)***
Patton Air Conditioning, Fresno *Also called Patton Sheet Metal Works Inc* ***(P-3183)***
Patton Sales Corp (PA)......C......909 988-0661
1095 E California St Ontario (91761) ***(P-7296)***
Patton Sheet Metal Works Inc......E......559 486-5222
272 N Palm Ave Fresno (93701) ***(P-3183)***
Patton State Hospital, Patton *Also called Califrnia Dept State Hospitals* ***(P-21934)***
Patton's Steel, Ontario *Also called Patton Sales Corp* ***(P-7296)***
Paul Calvo and Company......E......626 814-8000
1619 W Garvey Ave N # 201 West Covina (91790) ***(P-11666)***
Paul Graham Drilling & Svc Co......C......707 374-5123
2500 Airport Rd Rio Vista (94571) ***(P-1039)***
Paul Hastings LLP......D......714 668-6200
695 Town Center Dr # 120 Costa Mesa (92626) ***(P-23314)***
Paul Hastings LLP......C......714 668-6200
695 Town Center Dr # 120 Costa Mesa (92626) ***(P-23315)***
Paul Hastings LLP (PA)......C......213 683-6000
515 S Flower St Fl 25 Los Angeles (90071) ***(P-23316)***
Paul Hastings LLP......D......858 458-3000
4747 Executive Dr # 1200 San Diego (92121) ***(P-23317)***
Paul Hastings LLP......C......415 856-7000
101 California St San Francisco (94111) ***(P-23318)***
Paul Hastings LLP......C......650 320-1800
1117 California Ave Palo Alto (94304) ***(P-23319)***
Paul Kagan Associates, Carmel *Also called Kagan Capital Management Inc* ***(P-10092)***
Paul Maurer Company......D......714 231-8241
16081 Warren Ln Huntington Beach (92649) ***(P-19216)***
Paul Maurer Shows, Huntington Beach *Also called Paul Maurer Company* ***(P-19216)***
Paul Mitchell John Systems (PA)......D......310 248-3888
20705 Centre Pointe Pkwy Santa Clarita (91350) ***(P-8203)***
Paul Pietrzyk......E......209 726-5034
1142 Acapulco Ct Merced (95348) ***(P-2937)***
Paul Trucking, Watsonville *Also called Amar Transportation Inc* ***(P-4096)***
Paul Williams Tile Co Inc......D......760 772-7440
77570 Springfield Ln K Palm Desert (92211) ***(P-3007)***
Pauls Drywall, Merced *Also called Paul Pietrzyk* ***(P-2937)***
Paulus Engineering Inc......D......714 632-3322
2871 E Coronado St Anaheim (92806) ***(P-1967)***
Pauma Band of Mission Indians......B......760 742-2177
777 Pauma Reservation Rd Pauma Valley (92061) ***(P-13051)***
Pauma Valley Country Club......D......760 742-1230
15835 Pauma Valley Dr Pauma Valley (92061) ***(P-19002)***
Pave-Tech Inc......E......760 727-8700
2231 La Mirada Dr Vista (92081) ***(P-1836)***
Pavement Recycling Systems Inc (PA)......C......951 682-1091
10240 San Sevaine Way Jurupa Valley (91752) ***(P-7986)***
Pavex Construction Company, Redwood City *Also called Granite Rock Co* ***(P-1786)***
Pavigym America Corp......D......858 414-8624
1902 Wright Pl Fl 2 Carlsbad (92008) ***(P-6781)***
Pavilion At Sunny Hills......C......714 992-5701
2222 N Harbor Blvd Fullerton (92835) ***(P-20699)***
Pavilion Surgery Center LLC......D......714 744-8850
1140 W La Veta Ave Orange (92868) ***(P-19754)***
Pavir, Palo Alto *Also called Palo Alto Vterans Inst For RES* ***(P-26646)***
Pavletich Elc Cmmnications Inc (PA)......D......661 589-9473
6308 Seven Seas Ave Bakersfield (93308) ***(P-2677)***
Paxata Inc......D......650 542-7897
1800 Seaport Blvd Fl 3 Redwood City (94063) ***(P-15827)***
Paxvax Inc......E......858 450-9595
3985 Sorrento Valley Blvd A San Diego (92121) ***(P-26434)***
Paychex Inc......D......559 432-1100
9 E River Park Pl E # 210 Fresno (93720) ***(P-26265)***
Paychex Inc......D......858 547-2920
10150 Meanley Dr Ste 200 San Diego (92131) ***(P-26266)***
Paychex Inc......E......951 682-6100
1420 Iowa Ave Ste 100 Riverside (92507) ***(P-26267)***
Paychex Inc......D......310 338-7900
300 Crprate Pinte Ste 150 Culver City (90230) ***(P-26268)***
Paychex Benefit Tech Inc......C......800 322-7292
2385 Northside Dr Ste 100 San Diego (92108) ***(P-5622)***
Paycycle Inc......D......866 729-2925
210 Portage Ave Palo Alto (94306) ***(P-5623)***
Paydarfar Industries Inc......D......949 481-3267
26054 Acero Mission Viejo (92691) ***(P-7088)***
Payden and Rygel (PA)......C......213 625-1900
333 S Grand Ave Ste 3200 Los Angeles (90071) ***(P-10102)***
Payless Patio & Rockery, San Jose *Also called County Building Materials Inc* ***(P-6819)***
Paylocity Holding Corporation......B......847 956-4850
2107 Livingston St Oakland (94606) ***(P-15828)***
Payment Processing Inc......C......510 795-2290
8200 Central Ave Newark (94560) ***(P-15348)***
Payne & Fears LLP (PA)......D......949 851-1101
4 Park Plz Ste 1100 Irvine (92614) ***(P-23320)***
Payne Brothers Ranches......D......530 662-2354
13330 County Road 102 Woodland (95776) ***(P-75)***
Payne, E L Company, Los Angeles *Also called E L Payne Heating Company* ***(P-2192)***
Payoff Inc......D......949 430-0630
3200 Park Center Dr # 800 Costa Mesa (92626) ***(P-9726)***
Paypal Inc (HQ)......C......877 981-2163
2211 N 1st St San Jose (95131) ***(P-5624)***
Paypal Holdings Inc (PA)......C......408 967-1000
2211 N 1st St San Jose (95131) ***(P-5625)***
Paypros, Newark *Also called Payment Processing Inc* ***(P-15348)***
Payroll Dept., Chico *Also called Enloe Medical Center* ***(P-19461)***
Payrollingcom Corp......E......858 866-2626
4626 Albuquerque St Uppr San Diego (92109) ***(P-26269)***
Pb Car Movers......D......310 283-2741
5510 W 120th St Hawthorne (90250) ***(P-17394)***
Pbc Companies, Brea *Also called Peterson Bros Contruction Inc* ***(P-3307)***
Pbfy Flexible Packaging, Brea *Also called Pacific Western Sales* ***(P-9244)***
Pbi-Birkenwald Market Eqp Inc (PA)......E......562 595-4785
2667 Gundry Ave Long Beach (90755) ***(P-7144)***
PBM Maintenance Corp......B......818 771-1100
8523 Lankershim Blvd Sun Valley (91352) ***(P-14344)***
Pbms Inc......D......213 386-2552
1909 Wilshire Blvd Los Angeles (90057) ***(P-14345)***
Pbp Hotel LLC......D......619 881-6900
1515 Hotel Cir S San Diego (92108) ***(P-11906)***
PBR Twin Peaks, Woodland Hills *Also called Nmms Twin Peaks LLC* ***(P-11630)***
Pbs Socal, Costa Mesa *Also called Koce-TV Foundation* ***(P-5811)***
PC Mechanical Inc......E......805 925-2888
2803 Industrial Pkwy Santa Maria (93455) ***(P-1075)***
PC World Corp (PA)......C......240 855-8988
2017 Merkley Ave West Sacramento (95691) ***(P-5626)***
PCA, Los Angeles *Also called Beres Consulting* ***(P-24945)***
Pcamp, Los Angeles *Also called Parking Company of America* ***(P-17696)***
PCC Northwest, San Leandro *Also called Pacific Coast Container Inc* ***(P-5238)***
Pccp LLC (PA)......D......415 732-7645
555 California St # 3450 San Francisco (94104) ***(P-12179)***
Pcg Technology Consulting, Sacramento *Also called Public Consulting Group Inc* ***(P-27411)***
Pcha, Palo Alto *Also called Packard Childrens Hlth Aliance* ***(P-19744)***
PCI, San Diego *Also called Project Concern International* ***(P-24974)***
PCI Collections Inc......B......619 595-3114
402 W Broadway Fl 4 San Diego (92101) ***(P-14015)***
PCL Construction Services Inc......C......818 246-3481
500 N Brand Blvd Ste 1500 Glendale (91203) ***(P-1612)***
PCL Industrial Services Inc......B......661 832-3995
1500 S Union Ave Bakersfield (93307) ***(P-1428)***

ALPHABETIC SECTION | Pennymac, Agoura Hills

Pcm, Laguna Woods *Also called Professional Community MGT Cal (P-11684)*
Pcm, Foothill Ranch *Also called Professional Community MGT Cal (P-11153)*
Pcm Sales Inc (HQ)....................C....310 354-5600
1940 E Mariposa Ave El Segundo (90245) ***(P-7089)***
Pcs Link Inc....................B....949 655-5000
12424 Wilshire Blvd # 1030 Los Angeles (90025) ***(P-27820)***
Pcs Mobile Solutions LLC....................D....323 567-2490
3534 Tweedy Blvd South Gate (90280) ***(P-5627)***
Pcs Property Managment LLC....................C....310 231-1000
11859 Wilshire Blvd # 600 Los Angeles (90025) ***(P-11667)***
Pcs1, Santa Barbara *Also called Pacific Centrex Services Inc (P-5620)*
Pcv Murcor Real Estate Svcs, Pomona *Also called Murcor Inc (P-11623)*
Pcwc, Ontario *Also called Chino-Pacific Warehouse Corp (P-4540)*
Pd Liquidation Inc....................C....818 772-0100
21350 Lassen St Chatsworth (91311) ***(P-9248)***
PDC Capital Group LLC....................D....866 500-8550
250 Fischer Ave Costa Mesa (92626) ***(P-11907)***
Pdf Solutions Inc (PA)....................E....408 280-7900
333 W San Carlos St San Jose (95110) ***(P-15349)***
PDM Steel Service Centers....................D....408 988-3000
3500 Bassett St Santa Clara (95054) ***(P-7297)***
PDM Steel Service Centers....................E....559 442-1410
4005 E Church Ave Fresno (93725) ***(P-7298)***
PDM Steel Service Centers (HQ)....................D....209 943-0555
3535 E Myrtle St Stockton (95205) ***(P-7299)***
PDM Steel Service Centers....................D....209 234-0548
936 Performance Dr Stockton (95206) ***(P-7300)***
PDQ Automatic Transm Parts Inc....................D....916 681-7701
8380 Tiogawoods Dr Sacramento (95828) ***(P-17753)***
Pdrfc, Palm Desert *Also called Palm Dsert Rcrtl Fclities Corp (P-18998)*
Pds, Irvine *Also called Pacific Dental Services Llc (P-20132)*
Pds Tech Inc....................A....408 916-4848
1798 Tech Dr Ste 130 San Jose (95110) ***(P-14688)***
Pds Tech Inc....................A....805 418-9862
370 N Wstlake Blvd Stw120 Stw Westlake Village (91362) ***(P-16452)***
Pds Tech Inc....................D....214 647-9600
3100 S Harbor Blvd # 135 Santa Ana (92704) ***(P-14689)***
Peace Action West (PA)....................E....510 830-3600
2201 Broadway Ste 321 Oakland (94612) ***(P-25372)***
Peace Keepers Private Security....................D....925 978-4140
2734b Delta Fair Blvd Antioch (94509) ***(P-16755)***
Peace Officrs For A Grn Envirn....................E....951 824-7705
21800 Barton Rd Ste 108 Grand Terrace (92313) ***(P-3566)***
Peaceful Hearts Home Care Inc....................D....951 541-9343
387 Magnolia Ave Ste 103 Corona (92879) ***(P-22391)***
Peach Inc....................C....323 654-2333
1311 N Highland Ave Los Angeles (90028) ***(P-4426)***
Peach Tree Healthcare....................D....530 749-3242
5730 Packard Ave Ste 500 Marysville (95901) ***(P-19755)***
Peachwood Medical Group Clovis....................D....559 324-6200
275 W Herndon Ave Clovis (93612) ***(P-19756)***
Peacock Gap Golf & Country CLB, San Rafael *Also called Knight-Calabasas LLC (P-18943)*
Peacock Stes Resort Ltd Partnr....................D....714 535-8255
1745 S Anaheim Blvd Anaheim (92805) ***(P-13052)***
Pearce Services LLC (HQ)....................E....805 237-7480
3720 La Cruz Way Paso Robles (93446) ***(P-1968)***
Pearl Crop Inc (PA)....................D....209 808-7575
1550 Industrial Dr Stockton (95206) ***(P-553)***
Pearlman Borska & Wax LLP (PA)....................D....818 501-4343
15910 Ventura Blvd Fl 18 Encino (91436) ***(P-23321)***
Pearson Dental Supplies Inc (PA)....................C....818 362-2600
13161 Telfair Ave Sylmar (91342) ***(P-7207)***
Pearson Realty (PA)....................D....559 432-6200
7480 N Palm Ave Ste 101 Fresno (93711) ***(P-11668)***
Pearson Surgical Supply Co, Sylmar *Also called Pearson Dental Supplies Inc (P-7207)*
Pebble Bch Resrt Co DBA Lone C (PA)....................C....831 647-7500
2700 17 Mile Dr Pebble Beach (93953) ***(P-13053)***
Pebble Beach Company, Pebble Beach *Also called I Cypress Company (P-12758)*
Pebble Beach Resorts, Pebble Beach *Also called Pebble Bch Resrt Co DBA Lone C (P-13053)*
Pechanga Development Corp....................A....951 695-4655
45000 Pechanga Pkwy Temecula (92592) ***(P-13054)***
Pechanga Resort & Casino, Temecula *Also called Pechanga Development Corp (P-13054)*
Peci, San Francisco *Also called Clearesult Consulting Inc (P-27689)*
Peck & Hiller Company....................D....707 258-8800
870 Napa Vally Corp Way NAPA (94558) ***(P-3304)***
Pecs, Rancho Cucamonga *Also called Professnal Elec Cnstr Svcs Inc (P-2687)*
Pedestal Capital II LLC....................D....562 863-5555
13111 Sycamore Dr Norwalk (90650) ***(P-12258)***
Pedi Center, Bakersfield *Also called Dignity Health (P-21393)*
Pediatric & Family Medical Ctr....................C....213 342-3325
1530 S Olive St Los Angeles (90015) ***(P-22639)***
Pediatric Cancer Research, Orange *Also called Childrens Healthcare Cal (P-19376)*
Pediatric Physical Rehab Clnc....................E....559 353-6130
9300 Valley Childrens Pl Madera (93636) ***(P-22640)***
Pediatric Therapy Network....................D....310 328-0276
1815 W 213th St Ste 100 Torrance (90501) ***(P-22641)***
Peeble Beach Resort, Pebble Beach *Also called I Cypress Company (P-12757)*
Peed Equipment Company....................E....951 657-0900
43466 Business Park Dr Temecula (92590) ***(P-14453)***
Peekay Investments Prpts LLC....................E....714 403-1923
901 N China Lake Blvd Ridgecrest (93555) ***(P-13055)***
Peerless Building Maint Co, Chatsworth *Also called Tuttle Family Enterprises Inc (P-14412)*
Peerless Building Maint Inc....................D....530 222-6369
4665 Mountain Lakes Blvd Redding (96003) ***(P-14346)***
Peerless Maintenance Service....................B....714 871-3380
1100 S Euclid St La Habra (90631) ***(P-14347)***
Peeters Transportation Co....................E....800 356-5877
451 Eccles Ave South San Francisco (94080) ***(P-4365)***
Peeters/Mayflower, South San Francisco *Also called Peeters Transportation Co (P-4365)*
Pegasus Building Svcs Co Inc (PA)....................B....562 961-1998
2343 Mira Mar Ave Long Beach (90815) ***(P-14348)***
Pegasus Home Health Care A CA....................D....818 551-1932
132 N Artsakh St Glendale (91206) ***(P-22392)***
Pegasus Home Health Services, Glendale *Also called Pegasus Home Health Care A CA (P-22392)*
Pegasus Maritime Inc....................D....714 728-8565
535 N Brand Blvd Ste 400 Glendale (91203) ***(P-5139)***
Pegasus Risk Management Inc (PA)....................D....209 574-2800
642 Galaxy Way Modesto (95356) ***(P-10728)***
Pegasus Squire Inc....................D....866 208-6837
12021 Wilshire Blvd Ste 7 Los Angeles (90025) ***(P-16453)***
Peggs Company Inc (PA)....................D....253 584-9548
4851 Felspar St Riverside (92509) ***(P-17970)***
Peking Handicraft Inc (PA)....................C....650 871-3788
1388 San Mateo Ave South San Francisco (94080) ***(P-6782)***
Pelco By Schneider Electric, Chino *Also called Schneider Electric Usa Inc (P-4630)*
Pelomar Family YMCA, Escondido *Also called YMCA of San Diego County (P-25296)*
Pemer Packing Co Inc....................A....831 758-8586
20260 Spence Rd Salinas (93908) ***(P-14690)***
Pen-Cal Administrators Inc....................D....925 251-3400
7633 Suthfront Rd Ste 120 Livermore (94551) ***(P-26984)***
Pena Grading & Demolition Inc....................E....818 768-5202
11253 Vinedale St Sun Valley (91352) ***(P-1837)***
Pena Trucking, Sun Valley *Also called Pena Grading & Demolition Inc (P-1837)*
Pena's Recycling Center, Cutler *Also called Penas Disposal Inc (P-6427)*
Penas Disposal Inc....................D....559 528-3909
12094 Avenue 408 Cutler (93615) ***(P-6427)***
Pendleton Farms....................D....760 754-2359
307 Wilshire Rd Oceanside (92057) ***(P-112)***
Penguin Computing Inc (HQ)....................D....415 954-2800
45800 Northport Loop W Fremont (94538) ***(P-7090)***
Penhall Company....................D....510 357-8810
13750 Catalina St San Leandro (94577) ***(P-3305)***
Penhall Company (HQ)....................D....714 772-6450
2121 W Crescent Ave Ste A Anaheim (92801) ***(P-2821)***
Penhall San Leandro 153, San Leandro *Also called Penhall Company (P-3305)*
Peninou French Ldry & Clrs Inc (PA)....................D....800 392-2532
101 S Maple Ave South San Francisco (94080) ***(P-13636)***
Peninsula Beverly Hill's, Beverly Hills *Also called Belvedere Hotel Partnership (P-12368)*
Peninsula Beverly Hills, The, Beverly Hills *Also called Belvedere Partnership (P-12369)*
Peninsula Community Foundation....................D....650 358-9369
1700 S El Camino Real # 300 San Mateo (94402) ***(P-12082)***
Peninsula Crrdor Jint Pwers Bd....................C....650 508-6200
1250 San Carlos Ave San Carlos (94070) ***(P-3697)***
Peninsula Custom Homes Inc....................D....650 574-0241
1401 Old County Rd San Carlos (94070) ***(P-1214)***
Peninsula Family Service (PA)....................B....650 403-4300
24 2nd Ave San Mateo (94401) ***(P-24367)***
Peninsula Family Service....................D....650 952-6848
1200 Miller Ave South San Francisco (94080) ***(P-23965)***
Peninsula Family YMCA Sunshine, San Diego *Also called YMCA of San Diego County (P-25300)*
Peninsula Jewish Community Ctr....................C....650 212-7522
800 Foster City Blvd Foster City (94404) ***(P-23966)***
Peninsula Pathology Associates, South San Francisco *Also called Pennisula Pthlogists Med Group (P-22119)*
Peninsula Regent, The, San Mateo *Also called Bay Area Senior Services Inc (P-23503)*
Peninsula Volunteers Inc (PA)....................E....650 326-0665
800 Middle Ave Menlo Park (94025) ***(P-23967)***
Peninsula Womens Health (PA)....................E....650 692-3818
1828 El Camino Real Ste 8 Burlingame (94010) ***(P-19757)***
Peninsula World Travel LLC (PA)....................E....650 328-2030
825 Santa Cruz Ave Menlo Park (94025) ***(P-4946)***
Peninsula YMCA, San Mateo *Also called Young Mens Christian Assoc SF (P-25323)*
Penney Lawn Service Inc....................D....661 587-4788
4000 Allen Rd Bakersfield (93314) ***(P-919)***
Pennisula Pthlogists Med Group....................D....650 616-2940
393 E Grand Ave Ste I South San Francisco (94080) ***(P-22119)***
Pennmar, El Monte *Also called San Gbriel Vly Cnvlescent Hosp (P-21971)*
Penny Lane Centers (PA)....................B....818 892-3423
15305 Rayen St North Hills (91343) ***(P-24818)***
Penny Lane Centers....................C....818 892-3423
15317 Rayen St North Hills (91343) ***(P-24819)***
Penny Lane Centers....................C....818 892-3423
15317 Rayen St North Hills (91343) ***(P-24820)***
Penny Lane Centers....................C....562 903-4135
10330 Pioneer Blvd # 290 Santa Fe Springs (90670) ***(P-24821)***
Penny Lane Centers....................C....818 892-3423
15331 Rayen St North Hills (91343) ***(P-24822)***
Penny Lane Centers....................C....818 892-1112
15302 Rayen St North Hills (91343) ***(P-24823)***
Penny Lane Centers....................C....818 892-3423
15256 Acre St North Hills (91343) ***(P-24824)***
Penny Lane Centers....................C....818 892-3423
1020 E Palmdale Blvd Palmdale (93550) ***(P-24825)***
Penny Lane Centers....................C....323 318-9960
2450 S Atl Blvd Ste 101 Commerce (90040) ***(P-24826)***
Penny Lane Centers....................C....661 274-0770
43520 Division St Lancaster (93535) ***(P-24827)***
Penny Lawn Service, Bakersfield *Also called Penney Lawn Service Inc (P-919)*
Penny Roofing Company....................E....323 731-5424
2501 Exposition Blvd Los Angeles (90018) ***(P-3184)***
Pennymac, Agoura Hills *Also called Private Nat Mrtg Acptance LLC (P-9847)*

ALPHABETIC

Pennymac Corp....A....818 878-8416
27001 Agoura Rd Agoura Hills (91301) ***(P-9902)***
Pennymac Financial Svcs Inc....A....949 341-0020
36 Discovery Irvine (92618) ***(P-27391)***
Pension Administrators Inc (PA)....C....949 253-4080
17701 Mitchell N Irvine (92614) ***(P-14057)***
Penske Automotive Group Inc....E....415 492-1922
17 Woodland Ave San Rafael (94901) ***(P-17608)***
Penske Automotive Group Inc....E....408 293-7688
803 S 1st St San Jose (95110) ***(P-17609)***
Penske Logistics LLC....D....800 529-6531
2090 Etiwanda Ave Ontario (91761) ***(P-4243)***
Penske Media Corporation (PA)....D....310 321-5000
11175 Santa Monica Blvd Los Angeles (90025) ***(P-13952)***
Penske Truck Leasing Co LP....E....213 628-1255
2300 E Olympic Blvd Los Angeles (90021) ***(P-17610)***
Penske Truck Leasing Co LP....D....310 327-3116
19646 Figueroa St Long Beach (90745) ***(P-17611)***
Penske Truck Rental Inc....E....818 718-2536
11200 Peoria St Sun Valley (91352) ***(P-17612)***
Pentair Equipment Protection, San Diego *Also called Schroff Inc* ***(P-17909)***
Pentech Financial Services Inc (PA)....D....408 879-2200
75 E Santa Clara St # 1100 San Jose (95113) ***(P-9763)***
Pentech Funding Services, San Jose *Also called Pentech Financial Services Inc* ***(P-9763)***
Pentel of America Ltd (HQ)....C....310 320-3831
2715 Columbia St Torrance (90503) ***(P-8085)***
Pentel of America Ltd....E....909 975-2200
4000 E Airport Dr Ste C Ontario (91761) ***(P-8086)***
Penterman Farming Co Inc....D....707 967-9977
3851 Chiles Pope Vly Rd Saint Helena (94574) ***(P-706)***
Pentron Clinical Tech LLC....D....203 265-7397
1717 W Collins Ave Orange (92867) ***(P-22120)***
Penwal Industries Inc....D....909 466-1555
10611 Acacia St Rancho Cucamonga (91730) ***(P-1613)***
People Assisting Homeless....C....323 644-2216
340 N Madison Ave Los Angeles (90004) ***(P-23968)***
People Center Inc....E....781 864-1232
2443 Fillmore St San Francisco (94115) ***(P-15829)***
People Coordinated Services (PA)....D....323 735-1231
1221 S Western Ave Los Angeles (90006) ***(P-24828)***
People Creating Success Inc....D....661 225-9700
1607 E Palmdale Blvd H Palmdale (93550) ***(P-23969)***
People Creating Success Inc....C....805 644-9480
380 Arneill Rd Camarillo (93010) ***(P-19758)***
People Creating Success Inc (PA)....B....805 375-9222
2585 Teller Rd Newbury Park (91320) ***(P-21185)***
People Onesource, Long Beach *Also called Covenant Industries Inc* ***(P-14593)***
People Science Inc....E....888 924-1004
951 Mariners Island Blvd San Mateo (94404) ***(P-14691)***
People Services Inc (PA)....D....707 263-3810
4195 Lakeshore Blvd Lakeport (95453) ***(P-24628)***
People's Place, Torrance *Also called Topwin Corporation* ***(P-8280)***
Peoples Care Inc....C....760 962-1900
13901 Amargosa Rd Ste 101 Victorville (92392) ***(P-22393)***
Peoples Care Inc....C....562 320-0174
7355 Greenleaf Ave Whittier (90602) ***(P-24368)***
Peoples Choice Home (PA)....D....949 494-6167
7515 Irvine Center Dr Irvine (92618) ***(P-9845)***
Peoples Choice Staffing Inc....D....951 735-0550
4218 Green River Rd # 101 Corona (92880) ***(P-14692)***
Peoples Self-Help Housing Corp....D....805 349-9341
1026 W Boone St Santa Maria (93458) ***(P-27821)***
Peopleware Technical Resources....D....310 640-2406
302 W Grand Ave Ste 4 El Segundo (90245) ***(P-14693)***
Pep Boys Manny Moe Jack of Cal....E....562 908-4400
11456 Washington Blvd Whittier (90606) ***(P-17777)***
Pep Creations, San Diego *Also called Pacific Event Productions Inc* ***(P-13761)***
Pepper Tree Inn....D....530 583-3711
645 N Lake Blvd Tahoe City (96145) ***(P-13056)***
Pepper Tree Motel....D....909 988-2646
1241 E Holt Blvd Ontario (91761) ***(P-13057)***
Pepperjam LLC....C....760 585-7150
408 Cassidy St Ste 101 Oceanside (92054) ***(P-15350)***
Peppermill Casinos Inc....C....925 671-7711
4021 Port Chicago Hwy Concord (94520) ***(P-13058)***
Peppermint Ridge (PA)....D....951 273-7320
825 Magnolia Ave Corona (92879) ***(P-24629)***
Pepsi-Cola Metro Btlg Co Inc....D....707 535-4560
3029 Coffey Ln Santa Rosa (95403) ***(P-8848)***
Pepsi-Cola Metro Btlg Co Inc....C....209 557-5100
200 River Rd Modesto (95351) ***(P-4607)***
Pepsi-Cola Metro Btlg Co Inc....C....707 746-5404
4701 Park Rd Benicia (94510) ***(P-4608)***
Pepsi-Cola Metro Btlg Co Inc....C....626 338-5531
4416 Azusa Canyon Rd Baldwin Park (91706) ***(P-8849)***
Pepsi-Cola Metro Btlg Co Inc....C....818 898-3829
1200 Arroyo St San Fernando (91340) ***(P-8850)***
Pepsi-Cola Metro Btlg Co Inc....D....415 206-7400
200 Jennings St San Francisco (94124) ***(P-8851)***
Pepsi-Cola Metro Btlg Co Inc....B....951 697-3200
6659 Sycamore Canyon Blvd Riverside (92507) ***(P-7664)***
Pepsico Inc....C....626 338-5531
4416 Azusa Canyon Rd Baldwin Park (91706) ***(P-8565)***
Peralta Pharmacy, Oakland *Also called Sutter Health* ***(P-8214)***
Pereira & ODell LLC (PA)....D....415 284-9916
215 2nd St Ste 100 San Francisco (94105) ***(P-13877)***
Perez Contracting LLC....C....661 399-2700
12620 Snow Rd Bakersfield (93314) ***(P-707)***
Perfect Bar LLC....D....866 628-8548
3931 Sorrento Valley Blvd San Diego (92121) ***(P-8852)***
Perfect Foods, San Diego *Also called Perfect Bar LLC* ***(P-8852)***
Perfect Workout Inc (PA)....D....949 943-7281
150 N El Camino Real Encinitas (92024) ***(P-18639)***
Perfect World Entrmt Inc....C....650 590-7700
101 Redwood Shr Pkwy # 400 Redwood City (94065) ***(P-15351)***
Perfection Glass Inc....E....951 674-0240
554 3rd St Lake Elsinore (92530) ***(P-3407)***
Performance Building Services....C....949 364-4364
22642 Lambert St Ste 409 Lake Forest (92630) ***(P-14349)***
Performance Cleanroom Services, Lake Forest *Also called Performance Building Services* ***(P-14349)***
Performance Contracting Inc....E....925 273-3800
1943 Rutan Dr Livermore (94551) ***(P-1429)***
Performance Designed Pdts LLC (HQ)....D....323 234-9911
2300 W Empire Ave # 600 Burbank (91504) ***(P-7959)***
Performance Food Group Inc....D....800 697-7662
16639 Gale Ave City of Industry (91745) ***(P-8441)***
Performance Food Group Inc....C....831 462-4400
1047 17th Ave Santa Cruz (95062) ***(P-8442)***
Performance Roma Southern Cal, City of Industry *Also called Performance Food Group Inc* ***(P-8441)***
Performance Sheets LLC....C....626 333-0195
440 Baldwin Park Blvd City of Industry (91746) ***(P-3185)***
PERFORMANCE TEAM FREIGHT SYSTEM, INC., Santa Fe Springs *Also called Performance Team Frt Sys Inc* ***(P-4609)***
Performance Team Frt Sys Inc....D....562 741-1300
12816 Shoemaker Ave Santa Fe Springs (90670) ***(P-4609)***
Performance Team Frt Sys Inc....C....801 301-1732
1651 California St Ste A Redlands (92374) ***(P-17395)***
Performance Team Frt Sys Inc....C....310 241-4100
401 Westmont Dr San Pedro (90731) ***(P-4610)***
Performance Team Frt Sys Inc....D....562 345-2200
1331 Torrance Blvd Torrance (90501) ***(P-5140)***
Performance Team Frt Sys Inc....C....424 358-6943
1651 California St Redlands (92374) ***(P-5141)***
Performance Team LLC (PA)....C....562 345-2200
2240 E Maple Ave El Segundo (90245) ***(P-5142)***
Performance Tech Partners LLC....C....800 787-4143
11341 Gold Ex Dr Ste 160 Gold River (95670) ***(P-16454)***
Performance Warehouse Co....D....916 920-2221
901 Arden Way Sacramento (95815) ***(P-6665)***
Performant Financial Corp (PA)....D....925 960-4800
333 N Canyons Pkwy # 100 Livermore (94551) ***(P-16240)***
Performant Recovery Inc....C....209 858-3500
17080 S Harlan Rd Lathrop (95330) ***(P-14016)***
Performant Recovery Inc (HQ)....C....209 858-3994
333 N Canyons Pkwy # 100 Livermore (94551) ***(P-14017)***
Performant Technologies Inc....B....925 960-4800
333 N Canyons Pkwy # 100 Livermore (94551) ***(P-10103)***
Performing Arts Center of La C....C....213 972-7211
135 N Grand Ave Los Angeles (90012) ***(P-18393)***
Performnce Foodservice-Ledyard, Santa Cruz *Also called Performance Food Group Inc* ***(P-8442)***
Perillo Industries Inc....E....805 498-9838
2150 Anchor Ct Ste A Newbury Park (91320) ***(P-7524)***
Perkins Coie LLP....D....415 725-1313
3150 Porter Dr Palo Alto (94304) ***(P-23322)***
Perkins Coie LLP....D....310 788-9900
1620 26th St Ste 600s Santa Monica (90404) ***(P-23323)***
Perkins Coie LLP....E....415 344-7000
505 Howard St Ste 1000 San Francisco (94105) ***(P-23324)***
Perkins Pntg & Cstm Coatings, San Diego *Also called William M Perkins Company Inc* ***(P-2492)***
Perkowitz & Ruth Architects, Long Beach *Also called Rdc-S111 Inc* ***(P-26105)***
Perkstreet Financial Inc....E....978 801-1177
1100 La Avenida St Ste A Mountain View (94043) ***(P-27392)***
Perlegen Sciences Inc....C....650 625-4500
35473 Dumbarton Ct Newark (94560) ***(P-26435)***
Permanente Federation LLC....D....510 625-6920
1 Kaiser Plz Fl 27 Oakland (94612) ***(P-27393)***
Permanente Medical Group, Mountain View *Also called Kaiser Foundation Hospitals* ***(P-21507)***
Permanente Medical Group Inc....D....559 448-4500
7300 N Fresno St Fresno (93720) ***(P-19759)***
Permanente Medical Group Inc....D....916 688-2055
6600 Bruceville Rd Sacramento (95823) ***(P-19760)***
Permanente Medical Group Inc....D....650 742-2100
901 El Camino Real San Bruno (94066) ***(P-19761)***
Permanente Medical Group Inc....D....707 393-4000
3558 Round Barn Blvd Santa Rosa (95403) ***(P-19762)***
Permanente Medical Group Inc....D....415 833-2000
2425 Geary Blvd San Francisco (94115) ***(P-21639)***
Permanente Medical Group Inc....D....408 972-6883
275 Hospital Pkwy Ste 470 San Jose (95119) ***(P-19763)***
Permanente Medical Group Inc....D....925 372-1000
200 Muir Rd Martinez (94553) ***(P-19764)***
Permanente Medical Group Inc....D....510 752-1000
3779 Piedmont Ave Oakland (94611) ***(P-19765)***
Permanente Medical Group Inc....D....510 248-3000
39400 Paseo Padre Pkwy Fremont (94538) ***(P-19766)***
Permanente Medical Group Inc....D....408 945-2900
770 E Calaveras Blvd Milpitas (95035) ***(P-19767)***
Permanente Medical Group Inc....D....925 813-6149
4501 Sand Creek Rd Antioch (94531) ***(P-19768)***
Permanente Medical Group Inc....D....650 827-6500
220 Oyster Point Blvd South San Francisco (94080) ***(P-10294)***
Permanente Medical Group Inc....D....650 299-2000
1150 Veterans Blvd Redwood City (94063) ***(P-19769)***

Permanente Medical Group Inc ....D....650 299-2015
910 Marshall St Redwood City (94063) *(P-19770)*
Permanente Medical Group Inc ....D....510 231-5406
914 Marina Way S Richmond (94804) *(P-19771)*
Permanente Medical Group Inc ....D....510 454-1000
2500 Merced St San Leandro (94577) *(P-19772)*
Permanente Medical Group Inc ....D....650 598-2852
900 Veterans Blvd Ste 400 Redwood City (94063) *(P-10295)*
Permanente Medical Group Inc (HQ) ....B....866 858-2226
1950 Franklin St Fl 18th Oakland (94612) *(P-22858)*
Permanente Medical Group Inc ....D....415 444-2000
99 Montecillo Rd San Rafael (94903) *(P-19773)*
Permanente Medical Group Inc ....D....925 906-2000
320 Lennon Ln Walnut Creek (94598) *(P-19774)*
Permanente Medical Group Inc ....D....415 209-2444
100 Rowland Way Ste 125 Novato (94945) *(P-19775)*
Permanente Medical Group Inc ....D....415 899-7400
97 San Marin Dr Novato (94945) *(P-19776)*
Permanente Medical Group Inc ....D....510 559-5119
1725 Eastshore Hwy Berkeley (94710) *(P-10296)*
Permanente Medical Group Inc ....D....916 784-4000
1600 Eureka Rd Roseville (95661) *(P-19777)*
Permanente Medical Group Inc ....C....415 833-2000
2238 Geary Blvd San Francisco (94115) *(P-10297)*
Permanente Medical Group Inc ....D....510 559-5338
1750 2nd St Berkeley (94710) *(P-19778)*
Permanente Medical Group Inc ....D....707 765-3900
3900 Lakeville Hwy Petaluma (94954) *(P-19779)*
Permanente Medical Group Inc ....E....707 427-4000
1550 Gateway Blvd Fairfield (94533) *(P-10298)*
Permanente Medical Group Inc ....D....510 675-4010
3555 Whipple Rd Union City (94587) *(P-10299)*
Permanente Medical Group Inc ....D....925 243-2600
3000 Las Positas Rd Livermore (94551) *(P-19780)*
Permanente Medical Group Inc ....D....650 358-7000
1000 Franklin Pkwy San Mateo (94403) *(P-19781)*
Permanente Medical Group Inc ....D....209 735-5000
4601 Dale Rd Modesto (95356) *(P-10300)*
Permanente Medical Group Inc ....D....707 765-3930
1617 Broadway St Vallejo (94590) *(P-19782)*
Permanente Medical Group Inc ....D....510 625-6262
1800 Harrison St Fl 7th Oakland (94612) *(P-19783)*
Permanente Medical Group Inc ....D....510 752-1190
235 W Macarthur Blvd Oakland (94611) *(P-19784)*
Permanente Medical Group Inc ....D....209 476-3737
7373 West Ln Stockton (95210) *(P-19785)*
Permanente Medical Group Inc ....E....209 476-2000
1305 Tommydon St Stockton (95210) *(P-19786)*
Permanente Medical Group Inc ....C....916 631-3000
10725 International Dr Rancho Cordova (95670) *(P-19787)*
Permanente Medical Group Inc ....D....650 301-5860
395 Hickey Blvd Fl 1 Daly City (94015) *(P-19788)*
Permanentee Medical Group, Roseville *Also called Kaiser Foundation Hospitals (P-19608)*
Permits Today LLC ....D....626 585-2931
140 S Lake Ave Ste 323 Pasadena (91101) *(P-17396)*
Pernixdata Inc ....D....408 724-8413
1740 Tech Dr Ste 150 San Jose (95110) *(P-15352)*
Perona Langer Beck A Prof Corp ....D....562 426-6155
300 E San Antonio Dr Long Beach (90807) *(P-23325)*
Perr & Knight Inc (PA) ....D....310 230-9339
401 Wilshire Blvd Ste 300 Santa Monica (90401) *(P-10729)*
Perris Valley Cmnty Hosp LLC (PA) ....B....951 436-5000
2224 Medical Center Dr Perris (92571) *(P-21640)*
Perris Valley Cmnty Hosp LLC ....C....909 581-6400
10841 White Oak Ave Rancho Cucamonga (91730) *(P-21641)*
Perry & Shaw Inc ....D....619 390-6500
9029 Park Plaza Dr # 104 La Mesa (91942) *(P-25874)*
Perry Coast Construction Inc ....C....951 774-0677
14457 Meridian Pkwy Riverside (92518) *(P-1614)*
Perry Floor Systems Inc ....D....909 949-1211
963 Seaboard Ct Upland (91786) *(P-3306)*
Perry-Smith LLP ....D....916 441-1000
400 Capitol Mall Ste 1400 Sacramento (95814) *(P-26270)*
Persistant Systems, Santa Clara *Also called Persistent Tlcom Solutions Inc (P-15354)*
Persistent Systems Inc (HQ) ....D....408 216-7010
2055 Laurelwood Rd # 210 Santa Clara (95054) *(P-15353)*
Persistent Tlcom Solutions Inc ....E....408 216-7010
2055 Laurelwood Rd # 210 Santa Clara (95054) *(P-15354)*
Personagraph Corporation ....D....408 616-1600
920 Stewart Dr Ste 100 Sunnyvale (94085) *(P-15355)*
PERSONAL CARE SERVICES, Santa Barbara *Also called Visiting Care & Companions Inc (P-22444)*
Personal Protective Svcs Inc (PA) ....D....650 344-3302
398 Beach Rd Fl 2 Burlingame (94010) *(P-16756)*
Personalis Inc ....D....650 752-1300
1330 Obrien Dr Menlo Park (94025) *(P-26436)*
Personlized Buty Discovery Inc (PA) ....D....888 769-4526
201 Baldwin Ave Fl 2 San Mateo (94401) *(P-13667)*
Personlzed Hmcare Hmmaker Agcy ....D....916 979-4975
4700 Northgate Blvd Sacramento (95834) *(P-22394)*
Personnel Preference Inc ....C....530 938-3909
150 Boles St Ste A Weed (96094) *(P-14889)*
Perspecta Engineering Inc ....D....408 961-3250
1315 Dell Ave Campbell (95008) *(P-16031)*
Perterman, San Jose *Also called Durham School Services (P-3913)*
Perverted Jstice Fundation Inc ....C....310 910-9380
703 Pier Ave Ste B154 Hermosa Beach (90254) *(P-12083)*
Pescadero Conservation Aliance ....E....650 879-1441
4100 Cabrillo Hwy Pescadero (94060) *(P-25215)*
Pescatore, San Francisco *Also called Kimpton Hotel & Rest Group LLC (P-12813)*
PET POURRI, Milpitas *Also called Humane Society Silicon Valley (P-25430)*
Petalon Landscape MGT Inc ....D....408 453-3998
1766 Rogers Ave San Jose (95112) *(P-920)*
Petaluma Health Center Inc ....B....707 559-7500
1179 N Mcdowell Blvd A Petaluma (94954) *(P-19789)*
Petaluma Medical Offices, Petaluma *Also called Kaiser Foundation Hospitals (P-21505)*
Petaluma Valley Hospital, Petaluma *Also called Srm Alliance Hospital Services (P-21773)*
Petaluma Valley Hospital, Petaluma *Also called St Joseph Health System (P-21777)*
Petco Animal Supplies Inc (HQ) ....B....858 453-7845
10850 Via Frontera San Diego (92127) *(P-632)*
Pete Santellan ....C....559 564-3748
176 S Valencia Blvd Ste C Woodlake (93286) *(P-666)*
Peter H Mattson & Co Inc ....D....650 356-2500
343 Hatch Dr Foster City (94404) *(P-26437)*
Peter J Wolk MD ....E....530 534-6517
2721 Olive Hwy Oroville (95966) *(P-19790)*
Peter Kiewit Sons Inc ....C....909 962-6001
1925 Wright Ave Ste C La Verne (91750) *(P-1838)*
Petersen Builders Inc ....E....707 838-3035
7706 Bell Rd Ste A Windsor (95492) *(P-1215)*
Petersen-Dean Inc ....D....661 254-3322
21616 Golden Triangle Rd # 101 Santa Clarita (91350) *(P-3186)*
Petersen-Dean Inc ....E....707 469-7470
1705 Enterprise Dr Fairfield (94533) *(P-3187)*
Petersen-Dean Inc ....C....714 629-9670
2210 S Dupont Dr Anaheim (92806) *(P-3188)*
Petersen-Dean Commercial Inc ....C....707 469-7470
1705 Enterprise Dr Fairfield (94533) *(P-3189)*
Petersendean, Fairfield *Also called Petersen-Dean Commercial Inc (P-3189)*
Petersendean, Santa Clarita *Also called Petersen-Dean Inc (P-3186)*
Petersendean, Anaheim *Also called Petersen-Dean Inc (P-3188)*
Peterson Bros Construction, Brea *Also called P B C Pavers Inc (P-2463)*
Peterson Bros Contruction Inc ....A....714 278-0488
1560 W Lambert Rd Brea (92821) *(P-3307)*
Peterson Cat, San Leandro *Also called Peterson Machinery Co (P-17907)*
Peterson Family Inc ....D....559 897-5064
38694 Road 16 Kingsburg (93631) *(P-227)*
Peterson Machinery Co (PA) ....D....541 302-9199
955 Marina Blvd San Leandro (94577) *(P-17907)*
Peterson Painting Inc ....B....925 455-5864
5750 La Ribera St Livermore (94550) *(P-2464)*
Petes Connection Inc ....E....760 723-1972
407 Ranger Rd Fallbrook (92028) *(P-5926)*
Petit Ermitage, West Hollywood *Also called Valadon Hotel LLC (P-13363)*
Petrelli Electric Inc ....D....661 268-7312
11615 Davenport Rd Agua Dulce (91390) *(P-2678)*
Petrochem Insulation Inc ....C....310 638-6663
19010 S Alameda St Compton (90221) *(P-2938)*
Petrol Advertising Inc ....D....323 644-3720
443 N Varney St Burbank (91502) *(P-13878)*
Petroleum Sales Inc ....D....415 256-1600
2066 Redwood Hwy Greenbrae (94904) *(P-1026)*
Petroquip, Santa Ana *Also called G W Maintenance Inc (P-7848)*
Pets Unlimited ....C....415 563-6700
2343 Fillmore St San Francisco (94115) *(P-25451)*
Petti Kohn Ingrassia & L PR Co ....D....310 649-5772
11622 El Camino Real San Diego (92130) *(P-23326)*
Pf West LLC ....C....415 479-9600
101 Lucas Valley Rd # 150 San Rafael (94903) *(P-18640)*
Pfitech, Costa Mesa *Also called Precise Fit Limited One LLC (P-14696)*
Pfl Security, Rancho Mirage *Also called Protect-For-Less Security Svcs (P-16929)*
Pfyffer Associates Inc ....E....831 423-8572
2611 Mission St Santa Cruz (95060) *(P-76)*
PG&e, Fairfield *Also called Pacific Gas and Electric Co (P-6067)*
PG&E, San Francisco *Also called Pacific Gas and Electric Co (P-6068)*
PG&e, West Sacramento *Also called Pacific Gas and Electric Co (P-6069)*
PG&e, Marysville *Also called Pacific Gas and Electric Co (P-6070)*
PG&e, Hayward *Also called Pacific Gas and Electric Co (P-6159)*
PG&e, Fresno *Also called Pacific Gas and Electric Co (P-6072)*
PG&e, Petaluma *Also called Pacific Gas and Electric Co (P-6073)*
PG&e, Grass Valley *Also called Pacific Gas and Electric Co (P-6074)*
PG&e, Chico *Also called Pacific Gas and Electric Co (P-6160)*
PG&e, Concord *Also called Pacific Gas and Electric Co (P-6076)*
PG&e, Placerville *Also called Pacific Gas and Electric Co (P-6077)*
PG&e, Avila Beach *Also called Pacific Gas and Electric Co (P-6078)*
PG&e, Redding *Also called Pacific Gas and Electric Co (P-6079)*
PG&e, Auburn *Also called Pacific Gas and Electric Co (P-6080)*
PG&e, Concord *Also called Pacific Gas and Electric Co (P-6081)*
PG&e, San Francisco *Also called Pacific Energy Fuels Company (P-6158)*
PG&e, Monterey *Also called Pacific Gas and Electric Co (P-6082)*
PG&e, Fremont *Also called Pacific Gas and Electric Co (P-6083)*
PG&e, Eureka *Also called Pacific Gas and Electric Co (P-6084)*
PG&e, Auberry *Also called Pacific Gas and Electric Co (P-6085)*
PG&e, Daly City *Also called Pacific Gas and Electric Co (P-6086)*
PG&e, Modesto *Also called Pacific Gas and Electric Co (P-6087)*
PG&e, Stockton *Also called Pacific Gas and Electric Co (P-6088)*
PG&e, Pismo Beach *Also called Pacific Gas and Electric Co (P-6089)*
PG&e, Livermore *Also called Pacific Gas and Electric Co (P-6090)*
PG&e, Davis *Also called Pacific Gas and Electric Co (P-6091)*
PG&e, San Francisco *Also called Pacific Gas and Electric Co (P-6092)*
PG&e, Milpitas *Also called Pacific Gas and Electric Co (P-6093)*
PG&e, Pioneer *Also called Pacific Gas and Electric Co (P-6094)*
PG&e, Bakersfield *Also called Pacific Gas and Electric Co (P-6095)*

ALPHABETIC

PG&e, Templeton *Also called Pacific Gas and Electric Co* ***(P-6096)***
PG&e, San Francisco *Also called Pacific Gas and Electric Co* ***(P-6161)***
PG&e Capital LLC ....B....415 321-4600
1 Market San Francisco (94105) ***(P-27394)***
PG&e Corporation (PA) ....C....415 973-1000
77 Beale St San Francisco (94105) ***(P-6185)***
Pgande ....E....209 942-1745
10901 E Highway 120 Manteca (95336) ***(P-24972)***
PGS 360, City of Industry *Also called Prime Global Solutions Inc* ***(P-5148)***
Phacil Inc ....A....415 901-1600
601 California St # 1710 San Francisco (94108) ***(P-15356)***
Phamatech Incorporated ....C....858 643-5555
15175 Innovation Dr San Diego (92128) ***(P-26727)***
Pharmacy At Cares, The, Sacramento *Also called Cares Community Health* ***(P-19356)***
Pharmacy Temps Inc ....E....415 459-5211
2125 Paradise Dr Belvedere Tiburon (94920) ***(P-14890)***
Pharmerica Long-Term Care LLC ....C....858 537-9374
8930 Activity Rd Ste K San Diego (92126) ***(P-8204)***
Pharmerica Long-Term Care LLC ....D....951 784-1616
1130 Palmyrita Ave # 350 Riverside (92507) ***(P-8205)***
Phase 3 Communications Inc ....D....408 946-9011
224 N 27th St Ste B San Jose (95116) ***(P-2679)***
PHD Marketing Inc ....D....909 620-1000
1373 Ridgeway St Pomona (91768) ***(P-9249)***
Phelan & Taylor Produce Co ....C....805 489-2413
1860 Pacific Coast Hwy Oceano (93445) ***(P-554)***
Phelps Group ....E....310 752-4400
12121 W Bluff Dr Ste 200 Playa Vista (90094) ***(P-13879)***
Phenomenon Mktg & Entrmt LLC (PA) ....D....323 648-4000
5900 Wilshire Blvd Fl 28 Los Angeles (90036) ***(P-27395)***
PHF II Burbank LLC ....C....818 843-6000
2500 N Hollywood Way Burbank (91505) ***(P-13059)***
PHF Ruby LLC ....C....415 885-4700
2620 Jones St San Francisco (94133) ***(P-13060)***
Phfe Wic Program ....C....626 856-6650
12871 Schabarum Ave Irwindale (91706) ***(P-23970)***
Phg Engineering Services LLC ....D....714 283-8288
180 N Rverview Dr Ste 165 Anaheim (92808) ***(P-25875)***
PHH, Hemet *Also called Physicians For Healthy Hospita* ***(P-21642)***
PHI Delta Theta Inc ....E....818 885-9940
17740 Halsted St Northridge (91325) ***(P-13479)***
Phifactor Technologies LLC ....D....424 234-9494
6415 Surfside Way Malibu (90265) ***(P-22121)***
Phihong USA Corp (HQ) ....D....510 445-0100
47800 Fremont Blvd Fremont (94538) ***(P-7091)***
Philip DAmato Racing LLC ....D....949 830-7027
28202 Palmada Mission Viejo (92692) ***(P-18543)***
Philip West Industrial Service, Long Beach *Also called PSC Industrial Outsourcing LP* ***(P-6431)***
Philippine Airlines ....D....310 646-1981
11001 Aviation Blvd Los Angeles (90045) ***(P-4794)***
Philippine Airlines Inc ....C....415 217-3100
447 Sutter St Ste 200 San Francisco (94108) ***(P-4795)***
Philips Hlthcare Infrmtics Inc (HQ) ....C....650 293-2300
4430 Rosewood Dr Ste 200 Pleasanton (94588) ***(P-15357)***
Philips Medical Systems Clevel ....D....949 699-2300
1 Marconi Irvine (92618) ***(P-7208)***
Phillips & Assoc Law Offs PC ....D....510 464-8040
1300 Clay St Ste 600 Oakland (94612) ***(P-23327)***
Phillips Farms ....E....559 798-1871
33771 Road 156 Visalia (93292) ***(P-228)***
Phillips Plywood Co Inc ....D....818 897-7736
13599 Desmond St Pacoima (91331) ***(P-6851)***
Phillips Steel Company ....E....562 435-7571
1368 W Anaheim St Long Beach (90813) ***(P-7301)***
Philmont Management Inc ....D....213 380-0159
3450 Wilshire Blvd # 850 Los Angeles (90010) ***(P-1615)***
Philotic Inc ....D....510 730-1740
524 3rd St San Francisco (94107) ***(P-15358)***
Phoenix American Incorporated (PA) ....D....415 485-4500
2401 Kerner Blvd San Rafael (94901) ***(P-5927)***
Phoenix Engineering Co Inc ....D....310 532-1134
550 E Carson Plaza Dr # 112 Carson (90746) ***(P-14891)***
Phoenix Home Lf Mutl Insur Co, Hemet *Also called Anka Behavioral Health Inc* ***(P-10527)***
Phoenix House Orange County ....D....714 953-9373
1207 E Fruit St Santa Ana (92701) ***(P-24630)***
Phoenix Houses Los Angeles Inc ....D....818 686-3000
11600 Eldridge Ave Lake View Terrace (91342) ***(P-24631)***
PHOENIX HSE FNDTN, INC. & AF, Lake View Terrace *Also called Phoenix Houses Los Angeles Inc* ***(P-24631)***
Phoenix International, Torrance *Also called CH Robinson Freight Svcs Ltd* ***(P-5031)***
Phoenix Intl Holdings Inc ....C....619 207-0871
127 Press Ln Chula Vista (91910) ***(P-17397)***
Phoenix Personnel, Carson *Also called Phoenix Engineering Co Inc* ***(P-14891)***
Phoenix Satellite TV US Inc ....E....626 388-1188
3810 Durbin St Baldwin Park (91706) ***(P-5928)***
Phoenix Textile Inc ....D....213 239-9640
910 S Los Angeles St Los Angeles (90015) ***(P-17398)***
Phoenix Textile Inc (PA) ....D....310 715-7090
14600 S Broadway Gardena (90248) ***(P-8235)***
Phone App Company, The, Hermosa Beach *Also called Southbay Website Design LLC* ***(P-16181)***
Phone Ware Inc ....B....858 530-8550
8902 Activity Rd Ste A San Diego (92126) ***(P-17399)***
Photo TLC Inc ....C....415 462-0010
3925 Cypress Dr Petaluma (94954) ***(P-16963)***
Photocenter Imaging, Burbank *Also called J H Maddocks Photography* ***(P-16961)***

Phs / Mwa (HQ) ....E....950 695-1008
42355 Rio Nedo Temecula (92590) ***(P-4904)***
Phs Staffing, Los Angeles *Also called Premier Healthcare Svcs LLC* ***(P-14698)***
Phs/Mwa Aviation Services, Temecula *Also called Phs / Mwa* ***(P-4904)***
Phtl, San Rafael *Also called Pasha Hawaii Trnspt Lines LLC* ***(P-4706)***
PhyCor, Temecula *Also called HRP Capital Inc* ***(P-26889)***
Physical Distribution Svc Inc (PA) ....D....323 881-0886
16000 Heron Ave La Mirada (90638) ***(P-4611)***
Physical Optics Corporation (PA) ....C....310 320-3088
1845 W 205th St Torrance (90501) ***(P-26438)***
Physical Rehabilitation Netwrk ....E....408 570-0510
2833 Junction Ave Ste 206 San Jose (95134) ***(P-20192)***
Physical Rhbltation Netwrk LLC (PA) ....D....760 931-8310
3025 Corte Del Nogal Carlsbad (92011) ***(P-20193)***
Physical Therapy Hand Ctrs Inc (PA) ....D....760 294-9800
540 S Andreasen Dr Ste C Escondido (92029) ***(P-20194)***
Physical Therapy Hand Ctrs Inc ....E....760 233-9655
1815 E Valley Pkwy Ste 5 Escondido (92027) ***(P-20195)***
Physical Therapy Unit, Burbank *Also called Therapeutic Associates Inc* ***(P-20207)***
Physical/Occupational Therapy, Madera *Also called Pediatric Physical Rehab Clnc* ***(P-22640)***
Physician Assoc San Gabriel ....C....626 817-8300
199 S Los Robles Ave Pasadena (91101) ***(P-10301)***
Physician Management Group Inc ....C....858 309-6300
3860 Calle Fortunada # 210 San Diego (92123) ***(P-26985)***
PHYSICIAN OFFICE SUPPORT SERVI, Torrance *Also called Torrance Memorial Medical Ctr* ***(P-21859)***
Physician Weblink of Cal (HQ) ....C....949 923-3201
7 Technology Dr Irvine (92618) ***(P-26986)***
Physicians Automated Lab Inc (HQ) ....D....661 325-0744
820 34th St Ste 102 Bakersfield (93301) ***(P-22122)***
Physicians Choice LLC ....D....818 340-9988
21860 Burbank Blvd # 120 Woodland Hills (91367) ***(P-26271)***
Physicians Choice HM Hlth Inc ....E....310 793-1616
3220 Sepulveda Blvd # 100 Torrance (90505) ***(P-22395)***
Physicians For Healthy Hospita (PA) ....D....951 652-2811
1117 E Devonshire Ave Hemet (92543) ***(P-21642)***
Physicians For Healthy Hospita ....B....951 679-8888
28400 Mccall Blvd Sun City (92585) ***(P-21643)***
Physicians For Healthy Hospita ....C....951 652-2811
371 N Weston Pl Hemet (92543) ***(P-21644)***
Physicians For Healthy Hospita ....C....951 652-2811
1280 S Buena Vista St San Jacinto (92583) ***(P-21645)***
Physicians Referral Service, Lancaster *Also called Lancaster Crdlgy Med Group Inc* ***(P-19641)***
Piano Disc, Sacramento *Also called Burgett Incorporated* ***(P-8021)***
Piazza Trucking, South Gate *Also called Samuel J Piazza & Son Inc* ***(P-4370)***
Piccadilly Hospitality LLC ....E....559 348-5520
2305 W Shaw Ave Fresno (93711) ***(P-13061)***
Piccadilly Inn Airport, Fresno *Also called Art Piccadilly Shaw LLC* ***(P-12335)***
Piccadilly Inn Shaw, Fresno *Also called Art Piccadilly Shaw LLC* ***(P-12334)***
Piccadilly Inn Shaw, Fresno *Also called Piccadilly Hospitality LLC* ***(P-13061)***
Pick Pull Auto Dismantling Inc (HQ) ....E....916 689-2000
10850 Gold Center Dr # 325 Rancho Cordova (95670) ***(P-6703)***
Pick-A-Part, Monrovia *Also called M T M & M Inc* ***(P-14446)***
Pick-A-Part Auto Wrecking ....D....559 485-3071
9445 Cambridge St Cypress (90630) ***(P-7987)***
Pickford Realty Inc ....D....805 782-6000
1015 Nipomo St Ste 100 San Luis Obispo (93401) ***(P-11669)***
Pickwick Hotel The, San Francisco *Also called Yhb San Francisco LLC* ***(P-13434)***
Pico Cleaner Inc (PA) ....D....310 274-2431
9150 W Pico Blvd Los Angeles (90035) ***(P-13567)***
Pico Party Rents, Los Angeles *Also called Pico Rents Inc* ***(P-14535)***
Pico Rents Inc ....D....310 275-9431
13414 S Figueroa St Los Angeles (90061) ***(P-14535)***
PICO WOOSTER SENIOR HOUSING, Los Angeles *Also called Los Angeles Senior Citizen* ***(P-11060)***
Picsart Inc ....D....415 757-6800
351 California St Ste 650 San Francisco (94104) ***(P-15359)***
Picture It On Canvas Inc ....D....858 679-1200
1800 Seaport Blvd Redwood City (94063) ***(P-16964)***
Pie Town Productions Inc ....C....818 255-9300
5433 Laurel Canyon Blvd North Hollywood (91607) ***(P-18093)***
Piedmont Gardens, Oakland *Also called American Baptist Homes of West* ***(P-24416)***
Piedmont Transfer & Storage ....E....408 288-5600
1555 S 7th St Ste A San Jose (95112) ***(P-4244)***
Piege Co (PA) ....C....818 727-9100
20120 Plummer St Chatsworth (91311) ***(P-8273)***
Piehl, Joel J DDS, Hawthorne *Also called Schnierow Dental Care* ***(P-20136)***
Pier 2620 Ht Fishermans Wharf, San Francisco *Also called PHF Ruby LLC* ***(P-13060)***
Pier 39 Limited Partnership (PA) ....D....415 705-5500
Beach Embarcadero Level 3 San Francisco (94133) ***(P-10927)***
Pier Pont Hotel LP ....E....805 643-6144
550 San Jon Rd Ventura (93001) ***(P-13062)***
Pier Restaurant, San Francisco *Also called Blue and Gold Fleet* ***(P-4710)***
Pierce Brothers (HQ) ....D....818 763-9121
10621 Victory Blvd North Hollywood (91606) ***(P-13693)***
Pierce Enterprises, El Monte *Also called Wgg Enterprises Inc* ***(P-2982)***
Piercey Automotive Group, Irvine *Also called Piercey Management Svcs Inc* ***(P-26987)***
Piercey Management Svcs Inc (PA) ....D....949 379-3701
16901 Millikan Ave Irvine (92606) ***(P-26987)***
Pierpont Inn Inc ....E....805 643-0245
550 San Jon Rd Ventura (93001) ***(P-13063)***
Pierre Landscape Inc ....C....818 373-0023
5455 2nd St Irwindale (91706) ***(P-777)***
Pierry Inc (PA) ....E....800 860-7953
557 Grand St Redwood City (94062) ***(P-15830)***

Mergent e-mail: customerrelations@mergent.com
1422
2019 Directory of California
Wholesalers and Services Companies
(P-0000) Products & Services Section entry number
(PA)=Parent Co (HQ)=Headquarters (DH)=Div Headquarters

Pih Health, Whittier *Also called Interhealth Corp* ***(P-21460)***
Pih Health Hospital - Downey ....A....562 698-0811
11500 Brookshire Ave Downey (90241) ***(P-21646)***
Pih Health Hospital - Whitti ....B....626 357-6876
122 N Primrose Ave Apt A Monrovia (91016) ***(P-21647)***
Pih Health Hospital - Whitti ....A....562 904-5482
11500 Brookshire Ave Downey (90241) ***(P-21648)***
Pih Health Hospital - Whittier (PA) ....A....562 698-0811
12401 Washington Blvd Whittier (90602) ***(P-21649)***
Pih Home Health Services, Whittier *Also called Pih Health Hospital - Whittier* ***(P-21649)***
Pilgrim Haven Retirement Home, Los Altos *Also called American Baptist Homes of West* ***(P-20991)***
Pilgrim Operations LLC ....B....818 478-4500
12020 Chanl Blvd Ste 200 North Hollywood (91607) ***(P-6947)***
Pilgrim Place Beauty Salon, Claremont *Also called Pilgrim Place In Claremont* ***(P-13668)***
Pilgrim Place In Claremont (PA) ....C....909 399-5500
625 Mayflower Rd Claremont (91711) ***(P-21186)***
Pilgrim Place In Claremont ....C....909 621-9581
721 Harrison Ave Claremont (91711) ***(P-13668)***
Pillar Data Systems Inc ....B....408 503-4000
2840 Junction Ave San Jose (95134) ***(P-15831)***
Pillsbury Winthrop Shaw ....C....415 983-1000
4 Embarcadero Ctr # 2100 San Francisco (94111) ***(P-23328)***
Pillsbury Winthrop Shaw ....C....213 488-7100
725 S Figueroa St # 2900 Los Angeles (90017) ***(P-23329)***
Pillsbury Winthrop Shaw ....C....415 983-1865
29 Eucalyptus Rd Berkeley (94705) ***(P-23330)***
Pillsbury Winthrop Shaw ....B....415 983-1075
50 Fremont St Ste 522 San Francisco (94105) ***(P-23331)***
Pillsbury Winthrop Shaw ....C....650 233-4500
2550 Hanover St Palo Alto (94304) ***(P-23332)***
Pilot Freight Services, San Diego *Also called Miramar Transportation Inc* ***(P-5112)***
Pilot Painting & Construction ....D....714 229-5900
5555 Corporate Ave Cypress (90630) ***(P-2465)***
Pimco, Newport Beach *Also called Pacific Investment MGT Co LLC* ***(P-10101)***
Pimco Funds Distribution Co ....B....949 720-4761
840 Nwport Ctr Dr Ste 100 Newport Beach (92660) ***(P-12044)***
Pina Vineyard Management LLC ....E....707 944-2229
7960 Silverado Trl NAPA (94558) ***(P-708)***
Pinamar LLC ....D....925 243-8979
6909 Las Positas Rd Ste D Livermore (94551) ***(P-14536)***
Pinasco Mechinical, Stockton *Also called Pinasco Plumbing & Heating Inc* ***(P-2309)***
Pinasco Plumbing & Heating Inc ....E....209 463-7793
2145 E Taylor St Stockton (95205) ***(P-2309)***
Pindler & Pindler Inc (PA) ....D....805 531-9090
11910 Poindexter Ave Moorpark (93021) ***(P-8236)***
Pine & Powell Partners LLC ....D....415 989-3500
905 California St San Francisco (94108) ***(P-13064)***
Pine Company, Culver City *Also called Pine Data Processing Inc* ***(P-16164)***
Pine Crest, Maywood *Also called Maywood Halthcare Wellness Ctr* ***(P-20634)***
Pine Data Processing Inc ....D....310 815-5700
10559 Jefferson Blvd Culver City (90232) ***(P-16164)***
Pine Grove Healthcare ....D....626 285-3131
126 N San Gabriel Blvd San Gabriel (91775) ***(P-20700)***
PINE KNOLL PUBLICATIONS, Redlands *Also called Study Tapes* ***(P-18127)***
Pine Mountain Lake Association (PA) ....C....209 962-4080
19228 Pine Mountain Dr Groveland (95321) ***(P-25216)***
Pine Tree Lumber Company LP (PA) ....D....760 745-0411
707 N Andreasen Dr Escondido (92029) ***(P-6852)***
Pine View Center, Paradise *Also called Sunbridge Paradise Rhblttn Ctr* ***(P-20792)***
Pinedridge Care Ctr, San Rafael *Also called Mariner Health Care Inc* ***(P-20624)***
Pinegrove Hlthcare Wllness Ctr, San Gabriel *Also called Fernview Convalescent Hospital* ***(P-20427)***
Pinelands Preservation Inc ....D....609 703-0359
4501 Auburn Blvd Ste 201 Sacramento (95841) ***(P-921)***
Piner's Medical Supply, NAPA *Also called Piners Nursing Home Inc* ***(P-20701)***
Piners Nursing Home Inc ....D....707 224-7925
1800 Pueblo Ave NAPA (94558) ***(P-20701)***
Pinery LLC ....D....858 675-3575
13701 Highland Valley Rd Escondido (92025) ***(P-994)***
Pines At Plcrvlle Hlthcare Ctr, Placerville *Also called Gladiolus Holdings LLC* ***(P-20455)***
Pink Diamonds, Vernon *Also called Stone Blue Inc* ***(P-13622)***
Pinnacle 1617 LLC ....E....619 239-9600
1617 1st Ave San Diego (92101) ***(P-13065)***
Pinnacle Builders Inc ....B....916 372-5000
1911 Douglas Blvd Ste 85 Roseville (95661) ***(P-1216)***
Pinnacle Communication Svcs, Glendale *Also called Pinnacle Networking Svcs Inc* ***(P-2680)***
Pinnacle Contracting Corp ....E....818 888-6548
21800 Burbank Blvd # 210 Woodland Hills (91367) ***(P-1616)***
Pinnacle Document Systems (PA) ....D....925 417-8400
470 Boulder Ct Ste 100 Pleasanton (94566) ***(P-6973)***
Pinnacle Electrical Svcs Inc ....D....818 241-6009
730 Fairmont Ave Ste 100 Glendale (91203) ***(P-27822)***
Pinnacle Escrow Company, Northridge *Also called Pinnacle Estate Properties* ***(P-11670)***
Pinnacle Estate Properties (PA) ....C....818 993-4707
9137 Reseda Blvd Northridge (91324) ***(P-11670)***
Pinnacle Funding Group Inc ....E....925 552-5302
2092 Omega Rd Ste H San Ramon (94583) ***(P-9903)***
Pinnacle Networking Services, Glendale *Also called Pinnacle Electrical Svcs Inc* ***(P-27822)***
Pinnacle Networking Svcs Inc ....D....818 241-6009
730 Fairmont Ave Glendale (91203) ***(P-2680)***
Pinnacle Rvrside Hspitality LP ....C....951 784-8000
3400 Market St Riverside (92501) ***(P-13066)***
Pinnacle Telecom Inc (PA) ....E....916 426-1000
8100 Sierra College Blvd Roseville (95661) ***(P-16032)***
Pinnacle Travel Services LLC ....C....310 414-1787
390 N Pacific Coast Hwy El Segundo (90245) ***(P-4947)***
Pinner Construction Co Inc (PA) ....D....714 490-4000
1255 S Lewis St Anaheim (92805) ***(P-1617)***
Pinole Assisted Living Cmnty ....D....510 758-1122
2850 Estates Ave Pinole (94564) ***(P-11096)***
Pinole Medical Offices, Pinole *Also called Kaiser Foundation Hospitals* ***(P-19577)***
Pinole Senior Center ....D....510 724-9800
2500 Charles St Pinole (94564) ***(P-23971)***
PINOLE SENIOR VILLAGE, Pinole *Also called Pinole Assisted Living Cmnty* ***(P-11096)***
Pinsetters Inc ....D....916 488-7545
2600 Watt Ave Sacramento (95821) ***(P-18497)***
Pinterest Inc (PA) ....B....650 561-5407
808 Brannan St San Francisco (94103) ***(P-16241)***
Pioneer Health Care Services ....C....925 631-9100
1640 School St Ste 100 Moraga (94556) ***(P-26988)***
Pioneer House, Sacramento *Also called Cathedral Pioneer Church Homes* ***(P-20293)***
Pioneer Medical Group Inc ....D....562 862-2775
11411 Brookshire Ave # 108 Downey (90241) ***(P-19791)***
Pioneer Medical Group Inc ....D....562 229-0902
16510 Bloomfield Ave Cerritos (90703) ***(P-22859)***
Pioneer Sands LLC ....D....949 728-0171
31302 Ortega Hwy San Juan Capistrano (92675) ***(P-1097)***
Pioneer Square Hotel Company ....E....415 346-2323
1940 Fillmore St San Francisco (94115) ***(P-13067)***
Pioneer Theatres Inc ....C....310 532-8183
2500 Redondo Beach Blvd Torrance (90504) ***(P-17400)***
Pioneer Towers Rhf Partners LP ....E....916 443-6548
515 P St Ofc Sacramento (95814) ***(P-11097)***
Pioneers Mem Healthcare Dst (PA) ....A....760 351-3333
207 W Legion Rd Brawley (92227) ***(P-21650)***
Pioneers Memorial Hospital, Brawley *Also called Pioneers Mem Healthcare Dst* ***(P-21650)***
Pipe Dream Products, Chatsworth *Also called Pd Liquidation Inc* ***(P-9248)***
Pipe Restoration Inc ....E....714 564-7600
3122 W Alpine St Santa Ana (92704) ***(P-2310)***
Pipeline Plumbing, Norco *Also called F J Hoover Plumbing Inc* ***(P-2205)***
Pipeline Restoration Plumbing ....E....714 957-5836
2700 S Main St Ste E Santa Ana (92707) ***(P-2311)***
Pircher Nichols & Meeks (PA) ....D....310 201-0132
1925 Century Park E # 1700 Los Angeles (90067) ***(P-23333)***
Pismo Beach Athletic Club ....E....805 773-3011
1751 Price St Pismo Beach (93449) ***(P-18641)***
Pismo Coast Village Inc ....D....805 773-1811
165 S Dolliver St Pismo Beach (93449) ***(P-13068)***
Piston Agency, San Diego *Also called Mea Digital Worx LLC* ***(P-13863)***
Pit River Casino, Burney *Also called Pit River Tribal Council* ***(P-19217)***
Pit River Health Service Inc (PA) ....D....530 335-3651
36977 Park Ave Burney (96013) ***(P-22860)***
Pit River Health Services, Burney *Also called Pit River Tribal Council* ***(P-19792)***
Pit River Tribal Council ....D....530 335-3651
36977 Park Ave Burney (96013) ***(P-19792)***
Pit River Tribal Council ....D....530 335-2334
20265 Tamarack Ave Burney (96013) ***(P-19217)***
Pitco Foods, San Jose *Also called Pacific Groservice Inc* ***(P-9186)***
Pitco Foods, San Jose *Also called Pittsburg Wholesale Groc Inc* ***(P-8444)***
Pitman Family Farms (PA) ....D....559 875-9300
1075 North Ave Sanger (93657) ***(P-373)***
Pitman Farms, Sanger *Also called Pitman Family Farms* ***(P-373)***
Pitney Bowes Presort Svcs Inc ....C....310 763-4615
18550 S Broadwick St Compton (90220) ***(P-17401)***
Pitney Bowes Presort Svcs Inc ....D....415 468-1660
125 Valley Dr Brisbane (94005) ***(P-17402)***
Pitts & Bachmann Realtors Inc ....D....805 963-1391
1436 State St Santa Barbara (93101) ***(P-11671)***
Pittsburg Care Center Ltd ....E....925 432-3831
535 School St Pittsburg (94565) ***(P-20702)***
Pittsburg Skilled Nursing ....D....925 808-6540
535 School St Pittsburg (94565) ***(P-20703)***
Pittsburg Wholesale Groc Inc ....D....916 372-7772
1670 Overland Ct West Sacramento (95691) ***(P-8443)***
Pittsburg Wholesale Groc Inc (PA) ....C....916 372-7772
567 Cinnabar St San Jose (95110) ***(P-8444)***
Piveg Inc ....C....858 436-3070
10455 Sorrento Valley Rd # 101 San Diego (92121) ***(P-8445)***
Pivot Interiors Inc ....D....949 988-5400
3200 Park Center Dr # 100 Costa Mesa (92626) ***(P-2681)***
Pivot Systems Inc ....C....408 435-1000
4320 Stevens Creek Blvd San Jose (95129) ***(P-15360)***
Pivot Technology Solutions Ltd ....A....647 788-2034
11988 El Camino Real San Diego (92130) ***(P-16455)***
Pivotal Labs, San Francisco *Also called Pivotal Software Inc* ***(P-15361)***
Pivotal Software Inc (HQ) ....C....415 777-4868
875 Howard St Fl 5 San Francisco (94103) ***(P-15361)***
Pivotcloud Inc ....E....408 475-6090
1230 Midas Way Ste 210 Sunnyvale (94085) ***(P-15362)***
Pixar ....A....510 922-3000
1200 Park Ave Emeryville (94608) ***(P-18094)***
Pixar Animation Studios, Emeryville *Also called Pixar* ***(P-18094)***
Pixelmags Inc ....D....310 598-7303
1800 Century Park E # 600 Los Angeles (90067) ***(P-15363)***
Pixelogic Media Partners LLC ....C....818 861-2001
4000 W Alameda Ave # 110 Burbank (91505) ***(P-18208)***
Pixim Inc ....D....650 934-0550
1730 N 1st St San Jose (95112) ***(P-16033)***
Pixior LLC (PA) ....D....323 721-2221
5901 S Eastern Ave Commerce (90040) ***(P-17403)***
Pjbs Holdings Inc (PA) ....D....661 822-5273
1401 Goodrick Dr Tehachapi (93561) ***(P-6428)***
PJs Lumber Inc ....C....510 743-5300
45055 Fremont Blvd Fremont (94538) ***(P-6853)***

ALPHABETIC

Employee Codes: A=Over 500 employees, B=251-500
C=101-250, D=51-100, E=50
2019 Directory of California
Wholesalers and Services Companies
© Mergent Inc. 1-800-342-5647
1423

Pk Autobody Inc.....E.....559 298-9691
361 N Minnewawa Ave Clovis (93612) ***(P-17732)***
Pk Management LLC.....B.....818 808-0600
15301 Ventura Blvd # 570 Sherman Oaks (91403) ***(P-26989)***
Pk Nevada LLC.....E.....310 255-0025
1317 5th St Fl 2 Santa Monica (90401) ***(P-11672)***
Pkf Certif Pub Accts A Prof (PA).....D.....818 630-7630
550 N Brand Blvd Ste 950 Glendale (91203) ***(P-26272)***
Pkl Services Inc.....C.....858 679-1755
14265 Danielson St C1 Poway (92064) ***(P-17971)***
Place Asian Amrcn Rcovery Svcs, San Jose *Also called Asian Amercn Recovery Svcs Inc* ***(P-21996)***
Placentia Linda Hospital, Placentia *Also called Tenet Healthsystem Medical* ***(P-22054)***
Placer Co Bar Association (PA).....B.....916 557-9181
P.O. Box 4598 Auburn (95604) ***(P-25036)***
Placer County ADM Svcs.....C.....530 886-5401
2962 Richardson Dr Auburn (95603) ***(P-27954)***
Placer County Water Agency (PA).....C.....530 823-4850
144 Ferguson Rd Auburn (95603) ***(P-6098)***
Placer County- Adult Sys Care.....D.....530 886-2974
11533 C Ave Auburn (95603) ***(P-22642)***
Placer Insurance, Roseville *Also called Premiere Agency of California* ***(P-10738)***
Placervlle Pnes Cnvlscent Hosp.....C.....530 622-3400
1040 Marshall Way Placerville (95667) ***(P-21187)***
Plaid Inc.....C.....415 799-1354
85 2nd St Ste 400 San Francisco (94105) ***(P-16242)***
Plan Member Financial Corp.....D.....800 874-6910
6187 Carpinteria Ave Carpinteria (93013) ***(P-10104)***
Plan-It Interactive Inc (PA).....E.....707 752-6010
150 W Industrial Way Benicia (94510) ***(P-13766)***
Plan-It Life Inc.....D.....951 742-7561
5729 Vista Del Caballero Riverside (92509) ***(P-23972)***
Planet Fitness, San Rafael *Also called Pf West LLC* ***(P-18640)***
Planet Group Inc.....D.....402 491-3560
5796 Armada Dr Ste 300 Carlsbad (92008) ***(P-16034)***
Planet Labs Inc (PA).....D.....415 829-3313
346 9th St San Francisco (94103) ***(P-16165)***
Planetout Inc (HQ).....E.....415 834-6500
795 Folsom St Fl 1 San Francisco (94107) ***(P-5628)***
Planmember Services, Carpinteria *Also called Plan Member Financial Corp* ***(P-10104)***
Planned Parenthood Federation.....D.....949 548-8830
601 W 19th St Ste B Costa Mesa (92627) ***(P-22643)***
Planned Parenthood Federation.....D.....916 446-5247
555 Capitol Mall Ste 510 Sacramento (95814) ***(P-22644)***
Planned Parenthood Los Angeles (PA).....D.....213 284-3200
400 W 30th St Los Angeles (90007) ***(P-22645)***
Planned Parenthood Mar Monte (PA).....D.....831 373-1709
316 N Main St Ste 100 Salinas (93901) ***(P-22646)***
Planned Parenthood Shasta-Paci, Concord *Also called Planned Prnthod Shst-Dblo Inc* ***(P-22648)***
Planned Parenthood/Orange and (PA).....C.....714 633-6373
700 S Tustin St Fl 1 Orange (92866) ***(P-22647)***
Planned Prnthod Shst-Dblo Inc (PA).....E.....925 676-0300
2185 Pacheco St Concord (94520) ***(P-22648)***
Planned Prnthod Cal Cntl Cast (PA).....D.....805 963-2445
518 Garden St Santa Barbara (93101) ***(P-22649)***
Planned Prnthood Mar Monte Inc.....C.....408 287-7529
1691 The Alameda San Jose (95126) ***(P-22650)***
Planned Prnthood Mar Monte Inc (PA).....D.....408 287-7532
1691 The Alameda San Jose (95126) ***(P-22651)***
Planned Prnthood Mar Monte Inc.....D.....949 768-3643
26302 La Paz Rd 200 Mission Viejo (92691) ***(P-22652)***
Planning and Public Works Agcy, Willows *Also called County of Glenn* ***(P-1748)***
Planprescriber Inc.....B.....650 584-2700
440 E Middlefield Rd Mountain View (94043) ***(P-10730)***
Plant Maintenance Inc.....C.....925 228-3285
1330 Arnold Dr Ste 147 Martinez (94553) ***(P-14892)***
Plant Sciences Inc.....E.....530 398-4042
234 Juniper Knoll Rd Macdoel (96058) ***(P-9157)***
Plant Source Inc.....E.....760 743-7743
2029 Sycamore Dr San Marcos (92069) ***(P-9158)***
Plant Tape Usa Inc.....E.....831 455-2255
1 Harris Rd Fl 1 # 1 Salinas (93908) ***(P-465)***
Plantasia Inc.....D.....310 375-0387
2550 Via Tejon Ste 3f Palos Verdes Estates (90274) ***(P-922)***
Plantasia Landscaping, Palos Verdes Estates *Also called Plantasia Inc* ***(P-922)***
Plantation Golf Club Inc.....D.....760 775-3688
50994 Monroe St Indio (92201) ***(P-19003)***
Plantel Nurseries Inc.....B.....805 349-8952
2775 E Clark Ave Santa Maria (93455) ***(P-9159)***
Planters Hay Inc.....D.....760 344-0620
1295 E St 78 Brawley (92227) ***(P-9092)***
Plasma Collection Centers Inc.....C.....323 441-7720
2410 Lillyvale Ave Los Angeles (90032) ***(P-22861)***
Plastiflex Company Inc (HQ).....C.....619 662-8792
601 E Palomar St Ste 424 Chula Vista (91911) ***(P-17404)***
Platinum Clg Indianapolis LLC.....B.....310 584-8000
1522 2nd St Santa Monica (90401) ***(P-14350)***
Platinum Construction Inc.....D.....714 527-0700
865 S East St Anaheim (92805) ***(P-1618)***
Platinum Empire Group Inc.....C.....310 821-5888
3521 Lomita Blvd Ste 202b Torrance (90505) ***(P-14893)***
Platinum Equity, Beverly Hills *Also called Finn Holding Corporation* ***(P-4705)***
Platinum Equity Partners Inc.....C.....714 444-3100
3131 S Standard Ave Santa Ana (92705) ***(P-17733)***
Platinum Facilities Services.....C.....408 998-9004
1530 Oakland Rd Ste 120 San Jose (95112) ***(P-14351)***
Platinum Group Companies Inc (PA).....C.....818 721-3800
22560 La Quilla Dr Chatsworth (91311) ***(P-12000)***
Platinum Healthcare Staffing, Torrance *Also called Platinum Empire Group Inc* ***(P-14893)***
Platinum Landscape Inc.....C.....760 200-3673
42575 Melanie Pl Ste C Palm Desert (92211) ***(P-778)***
Platinum Protection Group Inc.....D.....800 824-1097
8018 E Santa Ana Cyn Rd Anaheim (92808) ***(P-16757)***
Platinum Roofing Inc.....D.....408 280-5028
1900 Dobbin Dr San Jose (95133) ***(P-3190)***
Platinum Strands Salon.....D.....714 532-2633
3443 E Chapman Ave Orange (92869) ***(P-13669)***
Platinum Visual Systems, Corona *Also called ABC School Equipment Inc* ***(P-7239)***
Platt Security Services, Long Beach *Also called Platt Security Systems Inc* ***(P-16758)***
Platt Security Systems Inc.....C.....562 986-4484
3275 E Grant St Ste D Long Beach (90755) ***(P-16758)***
Playboy Enterprises Inc (PA).....D.....310 424-1800
9346 Civic Center Dr # 200 Beverly Hills (90210) ***(P-18095)***
Playboy Entrmt Group Inc (HQ).....C.....323 276-4000
2300 W Empire Ave Burbank (91504) ***(P-18096)***
Playboy Magazine, Beverly Hills *Also called Playboy Enterprises Inc* ***(P-18095)***
Playhaven LLC.....E.....310 308-9668
1447 2nd St Ste 200 Santa Monica (90401) ***(P-15364)***
Playmar Inc.....D.....408 324-1930
2502 Channing Ave San Jose (95131) ***(P-6905)***
Playphone Inc (PA).....D.....408 261-6200
100 Mathilda Pl Ste 160 Sunnyvale (94086) ***(P-15365)***
Playspan LLC.....E.....408 617-9155
2900 Gordon Ave Ste 201 Santa Clara (95051) ***(P-9745)***
Playtika Santa Monica LLC.....C.....310 622-7380
2701 Ocean Park Blvd # 220 Santa Monica (90405) ***(P-18787)***
Playworks Education Energized (PA).....E.....510 893-4180
380 Washington St Oakland (94607) ***(P-19218)***
Playwrights Foundation Inc.....D.....415 626-2176
1616 16th St Ste 350 San Francisco (94103) ***(P-18394)***
Plaza De La Raza Child Develop.....D.....323 224-1788
225 N Avenue 25 Los Angeles (90031) ***(P-24369)***
Plaza De La Raza Child Develop.....D.....562 695-1070
6411 Norwalk Blvd Whittier (90606) ***(P-24370)***
Plaza De La Raza Child Develop (PA).....D.....562 776-1301
13300 Crssrds Pkwy N 44 La Puente (91746) ***(P-24371)***
Plaza Hand Carwash Inc.....E.....951 697-4420
23100 Alssndro Blvd Ste B Moreno Valley (92553) ***(P-17834)***
Plaza Home Mortgage Inc (PA).....E.....858 346-1200
4820 Eastgate Mall # 100 San Diego (92121) ***(P-9846)***
Plaza Manor Preservation LP.....A.....619 475-2125
2615 E Plaza Blvd National City (91950) ***(P-11673)***
Plaza Suites.....D.....408 748-9800
3100 Lakeside Dr Santa Clara (95054) ***(P-13069)***
Plb Management LLC.....E.....323 549-5400
6200 W 3rd St Los Angeles (90036) ***(P-11098)***
PLD Enterprises Inc.....D.....213 626-4444
440 Stanford Ave Los Angeles (90013) ***(P-8594)***
PLD Enterprises Inc (PA).....D.....310 547-3366
1621 W 25th St Ste 228 San Pedro (90732) ***(P-8595)***
Plda Inc.....D.....408 273-4528
2570 N 1st St 218 San Jose (95131) ***(P-11181)***
Pleasant Canyon Hotel Inc.....E.....925 847-0535
11920 Dublin Canyon Rd Pleasanton (94588) ***(P-13070)***
Pleasant Care, Alameda *Also called Emmanuel Cnvlscent Hosp Almeda* ***(P-21062)***
Pleasant Care of Vista.....C.....760 945-3033
247 E Bobier Dr Vista (92084) ***(P-20704)***
Pleasant Hawaiian Holiday, Westlake Village *Also called Pleasant Holidays LLC* ***(P-4976)***
Pleasant Hl Byshore Dspsal Inc.....C.....925 685-4711
441 N Buchanan Cir Pacheco (94553) ***(P-6429)***
Pleasant Holidays LLC (HQ).....B.....818 991-3390
2404 Townsgate Rd Westlake Village (91361) ***(P-4976)***
Pleasant Valley Farms (PA).....D.....209 886-1000
30636 E Carter Rd Farmington (95230) ***(P-624)***
Pleasant Valley Flowers Inc.....B.....805 986-2776
3132 E Pleasant Valley Rd Oxnard (93033) ***(P-320)***
Pleasant View Convalescent Hos.....C.....408 253-9034
22590 Voss Ave Cupertino (95014) ***(P-21188)***
Pleasanton Hilton Hotel, Pleasanton *Also called American Property Management* ***(P-12316)***
Pleasanton Project Owner LLC.....D.....925 847-7592
11950 Dublin Canyon Rd Pleasanton (94588) ***(P-13071)***
Pleasanton Unified School Dst.....C.....925 462-5500
4665 Bernal Ave Pleasanton (94566) ***(P-14125)***
Pleasantview Industries Inc.....D.....661 296-6700
27921 Urbandale Ave Saugus (91350) ***(P-22653)***
Pledge Insurance Brokerage.....D.....323 588-0223
2865 E Florence Ave Huntington Park (90255) ***(P-10731)***
Plex Systems Inc.....C.....248 391-8001
4305 Hacienda Dr Ste 500 Pleasanton (94588) ***(P-16166)***
Plexicor Inc (PA).....E.....714 918-8700
3598 Cadillac Ave Costa Mesa (92626) ***(P-16927)***
Plivo Inc (PA).....D.....415 758-3659
201 Mission St Ste 230 San Francisco (94105) ***(P-5629)***
Plivo US, San Francisco *Also called Plivo Inc* ***(P-5629)***
Plott Family Care Center, Riverside *Also called Mount Rbdoux Convalescent Hosp* ***(P-20654)***
Plott Family Care Centers, Riverside *Also called Orangetree Convalescent Hosp* ***(P-21617)***
Plott Family Home Care, San Bernardino *Also called Plott Management Co* ***(P-20705)***
Plott Management Co.....D.....909 883-0288
264 E 18th St San Bernardino (92404) ***(P-20705)***
Plowboy Landscapes Inc.....D.....805 643-4966
2190 N Ventura Ave Ventura (93001) ***(P-923)***
Plug & Play LLC.....C.....408 524-1400
440 N Wolfe Rd Sunnyvale (94085) ***(P-12259)***
Plug Connection Inc.....D.....760 631-0992
2627 Ramona Dr Vista (92084) ***(P-292)***
Plugandplaytechcenter.com, Sunnyvale *Also called Plug & Play LLC* ***(P-12259)***

Plum Healthcare Group LLC ....D 909 793-2609
1620 W Fern Ave Redlands (92373) ***(P-17405)***

Plum Healthcare Group LLC (PA) ....D 760 471-0388
100 E San Marcos Blvd # 200 San Marcos (92069) ***(P-20706)***

Plum Healthcare Group LLC ....D 408 998-8447
1990 Fruitdale Ave San Jose (95128) ***(P-20707)***

Plum Healthcare Group LLC ....C 619 873-2500
1391 E Madison Ave El Cajon (92021) ***(P-20708)***

Plumas District Hospital (PA) ....C 530 283-2121
1065 Bucks Lake Rd Quincy (95971) ***(P-21651)***

Plumas District Hospital ....C 530 283-0650
1045 Bucks Lake Rd Quincy (95971) ***(P-19793)***

Plumas Rural Services ....D 530 283-2725
711 E Main St Quincy (95971) ***(P-23973)***

Plumb Tech Inc ....D 310 322-4925
1242 E Maple Ave El Segundo (90245) ***(P-2312)***

Plumbing, San Jose *Also called Aqualine Piping Inc* ***(P-2125)***

Plumbing Master, Riverside *Also called Lozano Plumbing Services Inc* ***(P-2268)***

Plumbing Piping & Cnstr Inc ....D 714 821-0490
5950 Lakeshore Dr Cypress (90630) ***(P-2313)***

Plumbing Systems West Inc ....D 909 794-3823
31491 Outer Highway 10 Redlands (92373) ***(P-2314)***

PLUMBING WORLD, Long Beach *Also called Columbia Specialty Company Inc* ***(P-2164)***

Plummer Vlg Preservation LP ....D 818 891-0646
15450 Plummer St North Hills (91343) ***(P-11099)***

Plumpjack The, Olympic Valley *Also called Cncml A California Ltd Partnr* ***(P-12471)***

Plus Group Inc ....D 925 831-8551
2551 Sn Rmn Vlly Blvd 2 San Ramon (94583) ***(P-14694)***

Plx Technology Inc ....C 408 435-7400
1320 Ridder Park Dr San Jose (95131) ***(P-15832)***

Ply Gem Pacific Windows Corp ....D 951 272-1300
235 Radio Rd Corona (92879) ***(P-6854)***

Plymouth Square, Stockton *Also called Stockton Congregational Home* ***(P-24687)***

Plymouth Square, Stockton *Also called Retirement Housing Foundation* ***(P-11732)***

Plymouth Village, Redlands *Also called American Baptist Homes of West* ***(P-20990)***

Pm2net, Irvine *Also called Newton Softed Inc* ***(P-27800)***

PMBC, Costa Mesa *Also called Pacific Mercantile Bank* ***(P-9472)***

Pmd Industries Inc ....E 949 222-0999
703 Randolph Ave Costa Mesa (92626) ***(P-2682)***

Pmk-Bnc Inc (PA) ....C 310 854-0455
1840 Century Park E # 1400 Los Angeles (90067) ***(P-27568)***

Pmk-Bnc Inc ....E 310 854-4800
8687 Melrose Ave Fl 8th Los Angeles (90069) ***(P-27569)***

Pmt Crdit Risk Trnsf Tr 2015-1 ....C 818 224-7028
3043 Townsgate Rd Westlake Village (91361) ***(P-12119)***

Pmt Crdit Risk Trnsf Tr 2015-2 ....C 818 224-7442
3043 Townsgate Rd Westlake Village (91361) ***(P-12120)***

Pmt Issuer Trust - Fmsr ....C 818 224-7028
3043 Townsgate Rd Westlake Village (91361) ***(P-12180)***

PNC, San Francisco *Also called Esurance Insurance Svcs Inc* ***(P-10615)***

Pnc Inc ....D 619 713-2278
2533 Folex Way Spring Valley (91978) ***(P-8624)***

PNC Bank National Association ....D 818 880-3300
26901 Agoura Rd Ste 200 Calabasas (91301) ***(P-27396)***

PNC Bank National Association ....D 626 432-4500
2 N Lake Ave Ste 440 Pasadena (91101) ***(P-9367)***

PNC Bank National Association ....D 626 351-2211
465 N Halstead St Ste 160 Pasadena (91107) ***(P-9368)***

Pnmac Gmsr Issuer Trust ....A 818 746-2271
3043 Townsgate Rd Westlake Village (91361) ***(P-12121)***

Point Blue Cnservation Science, Petaluma *Also called Point Reyes Bird Observator* ***(P-25452)***

Point Loma Convalescent Hosp ....C 619 224-4141
3202 Duke St San Diego (92110) ***(P-20709)***

Point Loma Post Acute Care Ctr, San Diego *Also called Point Loma Rhblitation Ctr LLC* ***(P-20710)***

Point Loma Rhblitation Ctr LLC ....C 619 224-4141
3202 Duke St San Diego (92110) ***(P-20710)***

Point of View Inc ....D 909 860-0705
947 N Del Sol Ln Diamond Bar (91765) ***(P-15366)***

Point One Elec Systems Inc ....D 925 667-2935
6751 Southfront Rd Livermore (94551) ***(P-2683)***

Point Reyes Bird Observator ....D 415 868-0371
3820 Cypress Dr Ste 11 Petaluma (94954) ***(P-25452)***

Point Reyes Bird Observatory ....D 707 781-2555
3820 Cypress Dr Ste 11 Petaluma (94954) ***(P-26648)***

Point360 ....D 818 556-5700
1133 N Hollywood Way Burbank (91505) ***(P-18209)***

Point360 (PA) ....C 818 565-1400
2701 Media Center Dr Los Angeles (90065) ***(P-18210)***

Pointdirect Transport Inc ....D 909 371-0837
10858 Almond Ave Fontana (92337) ***(P-5143)***

Pointe At Lantern Crest, The, Santee *Also called Santee Senior Retirement Com* ***(P-24034)***

Pointspeed Inc ....D 650 638-3720
135 Wyndham Dr Portola Valley (94028) ***(P-16456)***

Poison Spyder Customs Inc ....A 951 849-5911
1177 W Lincoln St Ste 100 Banning (92220) ***(P-17868)***

Polar Tankers Inc (HQ) ....D 562 388-1400
300 Oceangate Long Beach (90802) ***(P-4703)***

Polarion Software Inc ....D 877 572-4005
1001 Marina Village Pkwy # 403 Alameda (94501) ***(P-15833)***

Polaris Building Maintenance ....D 650 964-9400
2580 Wyandotte St Ste E Mountain View (94043) ***(P-14352)***

Polaris Home Care LLC ....D 408 400-7020
830 Stewart Dr Ste 214 Sunnyvale (94085) ***(P-22396)***

Polaris Networks Incorporated ....D 408 625-7273
14856 Holden Way San Jose (95124) ***(P-15367)***

Polaris Research & Development ....D 415 777-3229
390 4th St Fl 1 San Francisco (94107) ***(P-27823)***

Polaris Wireless Inc ....E 408 492-8900
301 N Whisman Rd Mountain View (94043) ***(P-15368)***

Polestar Labs Inc ....D 760 480-2600
1223 Pacific Oaks Pl # 102 Escondido (92029) ***(P-7209)***

Polexis Inc ....D 858 812-7300
10680 Treena St Fl 6 San Diego (92131) ***(P-15369)***

Police Department, Oakland *Also called San Francisco Bay Area Rapid* ***(P-3713)***

Police Department, Berkeley *Also called City of Berkeley* ***(P-26165)***

Policeone Academy, San Francisco *Also called Praetorian Group* ***(P-16458)***

Poliseek Ais Insur Sltions Inc ....D 866 480-7335
17785 Center Court Dr N # 250 Cerritos (90703) ***(P-10732)***

Pollard Crnert Crwford Stevens ....E 626 793-4440
35 N Lake Ave Ste 500 Pasadena (91101) ***(P-23334)***

Polsinelli LLP, Los Angeles *Also called Polsinelli PC* ***(P-23335)***

Polsinelli PC ....D 310 556-1801
2049 Century Park E Los Angeles (90067) ***(P-23335)***

Poltex Company Inc ....D 619 669-1846
14748 Wild Colt Pl Jamul (91935) ***(P-15370)***

Polycomp Administrative Svcs ....E 916 773-3480
3000 Lava Ridge Ct # 130 Roseville (95661) ***(P-10733)***

Polymer Technology Group, The, Berkeley *Also called DSM Biomedical Inc* ***(P-26355)***

Polypeptide Laboratories Inc (HQ) ....D 310 782-3569
365 Maple Ave Torrance (90503) ***(P-22123)***

Polypeptide Labs San Diego LLC ....D 858 408-0808
9395 Cabot Dr San Diego (92126) ***(P-26439)***

Polyvore Inc ....D 650 968-1195
701 First Ave Sunnyvale (94089) ***(P-9250)***

Pomerado Hospital, Poway *Also called Palomar Health* ***(P-21629)***

Pomerado Hospital, Poway *Also called Palomar Health* ***(P-22172)***

Pomerado Operations LLC ....D 858 487-6242
12696 Monte Vista Rd Poway (92064) ***(P-20711)***

Pomeroy Rcrtion Rhbltation Ctr (PA) ....C 415 665-4100
207 Skyline Blvd San Francisco (94132) ***(P-23974)***

Pomona City Refuse Collection, Pomona *Also called City of Pomona* ***(P-6376)***

Pomona College ....C 909 621-8000
333 N College Way Claremont (91711) ***(P-14058)***

Pomona Community Health Center ....D 909 630-7927
1450 E Holt Ave Pomona (91767) ***(P-25037)***

Pomona Housing Partners LP ....E 909 622-1010
1731 W Holt Ave Pomona (91768) ***(P-11674)***

Pomona Intergenerational, Pomona *Also called Pomona Housing Partners LP* ***(P-11674)***

Pomona Valley Harley-Davidson, Montclair *Also called Pomona Valley Motorcycles Inc* ***(P-17972)***

Pomona Valley Hospital Med Ctr (PA) ....A 909 865-9500
1798 N Garey Ave Pomona (91767) ***(P-21652)***

Pomona Valley Hospital Med Ctr ....A 909 865-9104
1601 Monte Vista Ave Claremont (91711) ***(P-21653)***

Pomona Valley Hospital Med Ctr ....C 909 865-9700
1798 N Garey Ave Pomona (91767) ***(P-22038)***

Pomona Valley Hospital Med Ctr ....D 909 621-7956
1775 Monte Vista Ave Claremont (91711) ***(P-20196)***

Pomona Valley Hospital Med Ctr ....A 909 865-9977
1601 Monte Vista Ave # 270 Claremont (91711) ***(P-21654)***

Pomona Valley Motorcycles Inc ....D 909 981-9500
8710 Central Ave Montclair (91763) ***(P-17972)***

Pomona Valley Workshop (PA) ....D 909 624-3555
4650 Brooks St Montclair (91763) ***(P-24219)***

Pomona Vista Care Center, Pomona *Also called MJB Partners LLC* ***(P-20649)***

Poms & Assoc Insur Brks Inc (PA) ....D 818 449-9300
5700 Canoga Ave Ste 400 Woodland Hills (91367) ***(P-10734)***

Pomwonderful LLC (HQ) ....C 310 966-5800
11444 W Olympic Blvd Los Angeles (90064) ***(P-8853)***

Pomwonderful LLC ....C 310 966-5800
900 Airport Blvd Mendota (93640) ***(P-8854)***

Ponder Environmental Svcs Inc (PA) ....D 707 748-7775
4563 E 2nd St Benicia (94510) ***(P-27824)***

Ponderosa Builders Inc ....A 714 434-9494
3300 W Macarthur Blvd Santa Ana (92704) ***(P-14353)***

Ponderosa Electric Inc ....D 949 253-3100
17155 Von Karman Ave # 101 Irvine (92614) ***(P-2684)***

Ponderosa Enterprises (PA) ....E 209 742-7777
5181 Hwy 49 N Mariposa (95338) ***(P-13072)***

Ponderosa Mobile Estates, San Francisco *Also called Marcus & Millichap Real Estate* ***(P-11584)***

Ponte Vineyard Inn ....D 951 587-6688
35001 Rancho Cal Rd Temecula (92591) ***(P-13073)***

Ponto Nursery Inc ....D 760 724-6003
2545 Ramona Dr Vista (92084) ***(P-9160)***

Pool Pals Division, Temecula *Also called Oreq Corporation* ***(P-26969)***

Poor Sisters of Nazareth of SA ....D 619 563-0480
6333 Rancho Mission Rd San Diego (92108) ***(P-24632)***

Pop Media Networks LLC (HQ) ....D 323 856-4000
5510 Lincoln Blvd Ste 400 Playa Vista (90094) ***(P-18456)***

Pop-Tent Inc ....D 949 313-7160
34221 Golden Lantern St # 202 Dana Point (92629) ***(P-13880)***

Poppy Hills Inc ....D 831 625-1513
3200 Lopez Rd Pebble Beach (93953) ***(P-18743)***

Poppy Ridge Golf Course, Livermore *Also called Poppy Ridge Inc* ***(P-18744)***

Poppy Ridge Inc ....D 925 456-8229
4280 Greenville Rd Livermore (94550) ***(P-18744)***

Poppy State Express Inc ....D 209 664-3950
2700 W Main St Turlock (95380) ***(P-4245)***

POPS, Manhattan Beach *Also called Puttin On Productions Corp* ***(P-18101)***

Por La Mar Nursery, Santa Barbara *Also called W J Griffin Inc* ***(P-9177)***

Porchlight Inc ....D 562 989-5100
3800 Kilroy Airport Way Long Beach (90806) ***(P-21189)***

Employee Codes: A=Over 500 employees, B=251-500
C=101-250, D=51-100, E=50
2019 Directory of California
Wholesalers and Services Companies
© Mergent Inc. 1-800-342-5647
1425

Porrey Pines Bank Inc....B....510 899-7500
1951 Webster St Oakland (94612) ***(P-9369)***
Port Dept City of Oakland (PA)....B....510 627-1100
530 Water St Fl 3 Oakland (94607) ***(P-4731)***
Port Dept City of Oakland....C....510 563-3300
1 Airport Dr Ste 45 Oakland (94621) ***(P-4905)***
Port Logistics Group Inc....C....310 669-2551
19801 S Santa Fe Ave Compton (90221) ***(P-4366)***
Port Logistics Group Inc....D....909 839-5901
501 Cheryl Ln Bldg 10 City of Industry (91789) ***(P-4367)***
Port Logistics Group Inc....B....626 330-1300
15530 Salt Lake Ave City of Industry (91745) ***(P-5144)***
Port of Long Bch Employees CLB....B....562 590-4102
4801 Airport Plaza Dr Long Beach (90815) ***(P-25073)***
Port of Los Angeles, Wilmington *Also called City of Los Angeles* ***(P-3950)***
Port of Oakland, Oakland *Also called Port Dept City of Oakland* ***(P-4731)***
Port of Sacramento, West Sacramento *Also called Sacramento-Yolo Port District* ***(P-4733)***
PORT OF SAN DIEGO, San Diego *Also called San Diego Unified Port Dst* ***(P-4736)***
PORT OF STOCKTON, Stockton *Also called Stockton Port District* ***(P-4741)***
Port Royal Marina, Torrance *Also called California Yacht Marina Inc* ***(P-4748)***
Portellus Inc....D....949 250-9600
2522 Chambers Rd Ste 100 Tustin (92780) ***(P-15834)***
Porteous Enterprises Inc....C....310 549-9180
12801 Leffingwell Ave Santa Fe Springs (90670) ***(P-7599)***
Porter Construction Co Inc....C....831 455-3020
18931 Portola Dr Ste A Salinas (93908) ***(P-1217)***
Porter Crispin & LLC Bogusky....C....305 859-2070
2110 Colorado Ave Ste 200 Santa Monica (90404) ***(P-13881)***
Porter Ranch Development Co....D....323 655-7330
8383 Wilshire Blvd # 700 Beverly Hills (90211) ***(P-1357)***
Porter Valley Catering, Northridge *Also called Porter Valley Country Club* ***(P-19004)***
Porter Valley Country Club....C....818 360-1071
19216 Singing Hills Dr Northridge (91326) ***(P-19004)***
Portermatt Electric Inc....D....714 596-8788
5431 Production Dr Huntington Beach (92649) ***(P-2685)***
Porterville Annex, Porterville *Also called Family Healthcare Network* ***(P-19470)***
Porterville Convalescent Hosp, Porterville *Also called Moyles Central Vly Hlth Care* ***(P-20657)***
Porterville Developmental Ctr, Porterville *Also called Developmental Svcs Cal Dept* ***(P-20375)***
Porterville Sheltered Workshop....D....559 684-9168
1853 E Cross Ave Tulare (93274) ***(P-7210)***
Portfolio Hotels & Resorts LLC....E....831 375-2411
700 Munras Ave Monterey (93940) ***(P-13074)***
Porto Vista Hotel, San Diego *Also called 1835 Columbia Street LP* ***(P-12290)***
Portofino Hotel Partners LP....C....310 379-8481
260 Portofino Way Redondo Beach (90277) ***(P-13075)***
Portofino Inn & Suites Anaheim....A....714 782-7600
1831 S Harbor Blvd Anaheim (92802) ***(P-13076)***
Portola Hotel & Spa, Monterey *Also called Custom House Hotel LP* ***(P-12507)***
Ports America Inc....D....510 749-7400
1601 Harbor Bay Pkwy # 150 Alameda (94502) ***(P-4732)***
Posada Royale Hotel & Suites....E....805 584-6300
1775 Madera Rd Simi Valley (93065) ***(P-13077)***
Posca Brothers Dental Lab....D....562 427-1811
641 W Willow St Long Beach (90806) ***(P-22173)***
Posh Bagel Inc (PA)....D....408 980-8451
445 Nelo St Santa Clara (95054) ***(P-8855)***
Posh Bakery Inc....C....408 980-8451
445 Nelo St Santa Clara (95054) ***(P-8856)***
Positea Inv & Pub Relations....E....408 736-1120
710 Lakeway Dr Sunnyvale (94085) ***(P-27570)***
Positive Choice Wellness Ctr, San Diego *Also called Kaiser Foundation Hospitals* ***(P-22601)***
Positive Option Family Service (PA)....D....916 973-2838
2400 Glendale Ln Ste H Sacramento (95825) ***(P-23975)***
Positive Solution Staffing LLC....C....909 606-7512
15949 Oak Hill Dr Chino Hills (91709) ***(P-14695)***
Positron Public Safety, Roseville *Also called West Safety* ***(P-17589)***
Post Alarm Systems (PA)....D....626 446-7159
47 E Saint Joseph St Arcadia (91006) ***(P-16928)***
Post Alarm Systems Patrol Svcs, Arcadia *Also called Post Alarm Systems* ***(P-16928)***
Post Factory, Orange *Also called P J Video Services Inc* ***(P-18089)***
Post Group Inc (PA)....C....323 462-2300
1415 N Cahuenga Blvd Los Angeles (90028) ***(P-18211)***
Post Modern Edit LLC....D....310 396-7375
4551 Glencoe Ave Ste 210 Marina Del Rey (90292) ***(P-18097)***
Post Modern Edit LLC (PA)....D....949 608-8700
2941 Alton Pkwy Irvine (92606) ***(P-18098)***
Post Street Renaissance....B....415 563-0303
545 Post St San Francisco (94102) ***(P-13078)***
Post Surgical Recovery Center, Huntington Beach *Also called Friedman Professional Mgt Co* ***(P-19478)***
Postaer Rubin and Associates (PA)....C....310 394-4000
2525 Colorado Ave Ste 100 Santa Monica (90404) ***(P-13882)***
Postman Inc....D....415 796-6470
595 Market St Ste 1130 San Francisco (94105) ***(P-15371)***
Postmates Inc (PA)....C....800 882-6106
201 3rd St Fl 2 San Francisco (94103) ***(P-5242)***
Potawot Health Clinic, Arcata *Also called United Indian Health Svcs Inc* ***(P-20019)***
Potential Industries Inc (PA)....C....310 807-4466
922 E E St Wilmington (90744) ***(P-6430)***
Potter Roemer LLC (HQ)....D....626 855-4890
17451 Hurley St City of Industry (91744) ***(P-6855)***
Poulin Corporation (PA)....D....760 375-6531
111 S Mahan St Ridgecrest (93555) ***(P-12260)***
Poumtjack Hotels, NAPA *Also called Carneros Inn LLC* ***(P-12431)***
Pounce Consulting Inc....C....714 774-3500
6080 Center Dr Ste 600 Los Angeles (90045) ***(P-16457)***
Poundex Associates Corporation....D....909 444-5878
21490 Baker Pkwy City of Industry (91789) ***(P-6735)***
Powell Works Inc....B....909 861-6699
17807 Maclaren St Ste B La Puente (91744) ***(P-7784)***
Power 106 Radio....D....818 953-4200
2600 W Olive Ave Fl 8 Burbank (91505) ***(P-5749)***
Power Engineers Incorporated....D....714 507-2700
731 E Ball Rd Ste 100 Anaheim (92805) ***(P-25876)***
Power Engineers Incorporated....D....925 372-9284
218 Loreto Ct Martinez (94553) ***(P-25877)***
Power Factors LLC....D....415 299-7448
80 E Sir Francis Drake Bl Larkspur (94939) ***(P-7092)***
Power Generation Entps Inc....C....818 484-8550
11411 Cumpston St Ste 104 North Hollywood (91601) ***(P-7785)***
Power Logistics, Stockton *Also called Exel N Amercn Logistics Inc* ***(P-4502)***
Power Plant, Glendale *Also called City of Glendale* ***(P-6018)***
Power Plus, Perris *Also called SR Bray LLC* ***(P-14546)***
Power Plus, Anaheim *Also called SR Bray LLC* ***(P-2740)***
Power Plus LLC....D....714 507-1881
1210 N Red Gum St Anaheim (92806) ***(P-7386)***
Power Plus Solutions Corp....E....714 507-1881
1210 N Red Gum St Anaheim (92806) ***(P-2686)***
Powerhouse Building Inc....D....415 446-0188
4320 Redwood Hwy Ste 200 San Rafael (94903) ***(P-3308)***
Powerhouse Realty Inc....D....323 562-7777
3452 E Florence Ave Huntington Park (90255) ***(P-11675)***
Powerlight, Richmond *Also called Sunpower Corporation Systems* ***(P-2375)***
Powerplant Mint Spcialists Inc....C....714 427-6900
2900 Bristol St Ste H202 Costa Mesa (92626) ***(P-2056)***
Powerreviews Oc LLC....D....415 315-9208
180 Montgomery St # 1800 San Francisco (94104) ***(P-15372)***
Powerschool Group LLC (HQ)....C....916 288-1636
150 Parkshore Dr Folsom (95630) ***(P-15835)***
Ppc Enterprises Inc....C....951 354-5402
5920 Rickenbacker Ave Riverside (92504) ***(P-2315)***
Pphm Inc....D....714 508-6100
14282 Franklin Ave Tustin (92780) ***(P-8206)***
Ppic, San Francisco *Also called Public Policy Institute Cal* ***(P-24975)***
Ppm Real Estate Inc....D....510 758-5636
3575 San Pablo Dam Rd El Sobrante (94803) ***(P-11676)***
Ppmc, Corona *Also called Primary Provider MGT Co Inc* ***(P-26993)***
Pponext Inc....B....888 446-6098
1501 Hughes Way Ste 400 Long Beach (90810) ***(P-22862)***
Pps Parking Inc....A....949 223-8707
1800 E Garry Ave Ste 107 Santa Ana (92705) ***(P-13767)***
PR Rancho Hotel LLC....D....916 638-4141
11260 Point East Dr Rancho Cordova (95742) ***(P-13079)***
Practice Fusion Inc (PA)....D....415 346-7700
731 Market St Ste 400 San Francisco (94103) ***(P-15373)***
Practice Wares Inc....E....916 526-2674
2377 Gold Meadow Way Gold River (95670) ***(P-7211)***
Practicewares Dental Supply, Gold River *Also called Practice Wares Inc* ***(P-7211)***
Praetorian Event Services, Petaluma *Also called Praetorian USA* ***(P-13768)***
Praetorian Group (PA)....E....415 962-8310
200 Green St Ste 200 # 200 San Francisco (94111) ***(P-16458)***
Praetorian USA....D....707 780-8020
925 Lakeville St 129 Petaluma (94952) ***(P-13768)***
Prajin 1 Stop Distributors Inc (PA)....E....323 395-5302
5701 Pacific Blvd 5711 Huntington Park (90255) ***(P-8050)***
Prajin Discount Distributors, Huntington Park *Also called Prajin 1 Stop Distributors Inc* ***(P-8050)***
Pramira Inc....C....800 678-1169
1422 Edinger Ave Ste 250 Tustin (92780) ***(P-16459)***
Prana Living LLC (HQ)....D....866 915-6457
3209 Lionshead Ave Carlsbad (92010) ***(P-8274)***
Praxair Inc....D....562 983-2100
2300 E Pacific Coast Hwy Wilmington (90744) ***(P-8934)***
Praxair Inc....D....562 427-0099
2677 Signal Pkwy Long Beach (90755) ***(P-7786)***
PRBO, Petaluma *Also called Point Reyes Bird Observatory* ***(P-26648)***
PRC Builders Inc....D....949 529-7011
26616 Mission St San Juan Capistrano (92675) ***(P-1306)***
Prdctions N Fremantle Amer Inc (HQ)....D....818 748-1100
2900 W Alameda Ave # 800 Burbank (91505) ***(P-18395)***
Pre Con Industries Inc....D....805 928-3397
4340 Viewridge Ave Ste B San Diego (92123) ***(P-2939)***
Pre Con Industries Inc....E....805 481-7305
950 Riata Ln Nipomo (93444) ***(P-3057)***
Pre Con Industries Inc....D....760 499-6176
917 W Inyokern Rd Ste C Ridgecrest (93555) ***(P-2940)***
Pre Con Industries Inc....E....805 345-3147
514 Work St Salinas (93901) ***(P-26990)***
Pre-Employcom....D....800 300-1821
3655 Meadow View Dr Redding (96002) ***(P-16759)***
Pre-Employcom Inc....D....530 378-7680
3615 Meadow View Dr Redding (96002) ***(P-16760)***
Precept Inc (HQ)....D....949 955-1430
130 Theory Ste 200 Irvine (92617) ***(P-10735)***
Precept Group The, Irvine *Also called Precept Inc* ***(P-10735)***
Precious Enterprises Inc....D....408 265-2226
14130 Douglass Ln Saratoga (95070) ***(P-24372)***
Precise Air Systems Inc....D....818 240-1737
5467 W San Fernando Rd Los Angeles (90039) ***(P-2316)***
Precise Auto Protection, Azusa *Also called Precise Enterprises LLC* ***(P-27397)***
Precise Distribution Inc....E....951 367-1037
12215 Holly St Riverside (92509) ***(P-4612)***

Mergent e-mail: customerrelations@mergent.com
1426
2019 Directory of California
Wholesalers and Services Companies
(P-0000) Products & Services Section entry number
(PA)=Parent Co (HQ)=Headquarters (DH)=Div Headquarters

Precise Enterprises LLC ....E....818 599-6450
751 W 9th St Azusa (91702) ***(P-27397)***
Precise Fit Limited One LLC ....B....310 824-1800
959 Suth Cast Dr Ste 200 Costa Mesa (92626) ***(P-14696)***
Preciseq Inc ....D....310 709-6094
11601 Wilshire Blvd Fl 5 Los Angeles (90025) ***(P-16460)***
Precision Auto Body, Reseda *Also called Auto Body Management Inc* ***(P-17712)***
Precision Auto Detailing LLC ....D....650 992-9775
700 Serramonte Blvd Colma (94014) ***(P-17835)***
Precision Framing Inc ....B....916 791-7464
1504 Eureka Rd Ste 160 Roseville (95661) ***(P-3058)***
Precision Home Care LLC ....D....916 749-4051
2450 Venture Oaks Way # 225 Sacramento (95833) ***(P-23976)***
Precision Ideo Inc ....B....650 688-3400
150 Forest Ave Palo Alto (94301) ***(P-17406)***
Precision Medical Products Inc ....D....573 474-9302
2217 Plaza Dr Rocklin (95765) ***(P-19794)***
Precision Relocation Inc ....C....714 690-9344
16055 Heron Ave Ste B La Mirada (90638) ***(P-4368)***
Precision Television Inc ....D....925 825-5296
2350 Stanwell Dr Concord (94520) ***(P-17886)***
Precision Toxicology LLC ....D....800 635-6901
4215 Sorrento Valley Blvd San Diego (92121) ***(P-22124)***
Precision TV, Concord *Also called Precision Television Inc* ***(P-17886)***
Predentials, Oakland *Also called Mason-Mcduffie Real Estate Inc* ***(P-11592)***
Predicate Logic Inc (PA) ....D....858 715-0100
6498 Weathers Pl Ste 200 San Diego (92121) ***(P-25878)***
Predicine Inc ....E....650 300-2188
3555 Arden Rd Hayward (94545) ***(P-19795)***
Preferred Brokers Inc (PA) ....D....661 836-2345
9100 Ming Ave Ste 100 Bakersfield (93311) ***(P-11677)***
Preferred Construction Co Inc ....D....714 630-3004
5199 E Pacific Coast Hwy Long Beach (90804) ***(P-1619)***
Preferred Employers Insur Co ....D....619 688-3900
9797 Aero Dr Ste 200 San Diego (92123) ***(P-10736)***
Preferred Financial, San Ramon *Also called A D Bilich Inc* ***(P-9767)***
Preferred Hlthcare Rgistry Inc ....C....800 787-6787
9089 Clairemont Mesa Blvd # 200 San Diego (92123) ***(P-14697)***
Preferred Insulation Contrs (PA) ....D....951 735-3725
1691 Jenks Dr Corona (92880) ***(P-3567)***
Preferred Plumbing and Drain, North Highlands *Also called AAA Drain Patrol* ***(P-2082)***
Preferred Produce, Salinas *Also called Elioco Produce Inc* ***(P-644)***
Preferred Valet Parking LLC ....E....619 233-7275
2568 Violet St San Diego (92105) ***(P-17702)***
Pregis LLC ....D....510 404-1360
33340 Central Ave Union City (94587) ***(P-9251)***
Prellis Mortgage Company, Granada Hills *Also called C21 Peak* ***(P-11259)***
Prelude Systems Inc (PA) ....C....949 208-7126
5 Corporate Park Ste 140 Irvine (92606) ***(P-16461)***
Preludesys, Irvine *Also called Prelude Systems Inc* ***(P-16461)***
Premier America Credit Union (PA) ....C....818 772-4000
19867 Prairie St Lbby Chatsworth (91311) ***(P-9644)***
Premier Auto W Covina LLC ....D....626 858-7202
777 W Orangethorpe Ave Placentia (92870) ***(P-17778)***
Premier Building Maint Svcs, Los Angeles *Also called Pbms Inc* ***(P-14345)***
Premier Business Centers, Irvine *Also called Premier Office Centers LLC* ***(P-17408)***
Premier Care Center For Palm, Palm Springs *Also called Ensign Palm I LLC* ***(P-20402)***
Premier Commercial Bancorp ....D....714 978-2400
2400 E Katella Ave # 125 Anaheim (92806) ***(P-9479)***
Premier Dealer Services Inc ....D....858 810-1700
9449 Balboa Ave Ste 300 San Diego (92123) ***(P-10737)***
Premier Disp & Exhibits Inc (PA) ....D....562 431-2731
11261 Warland Dr Cypress (90630) ***(P-17407)***
Premier Drywall, Salinas *Also called Pre Con Industries Inc* ***(P-26990)***
Premier Drywall ....D....805 928-3397
725 Oak St Santa Maria (93454) ***(P-2941)***
Premier Exec Solutions Inc ....E....310 989-9925
269 S Beverly Dr Ste 981 Beverly Hills (90212) ***(P-27825)***
Premier Floor Care Inc (PA) ....C....925 679-4901
390 Carrol Ct Ste C Brentwood (94513) ***(P-14354)***
Premier Golf Properties LP ....D....619 442-9891
3121 Willow Glen Dr El Cajon (92019) ***(P-18745)***
Premier Healthcare Svcs LLC (HQ) ....C....626 204-7930
815 Colorado Blvd Ste 400 Los Angeles (90041) ***(P-14698)***
Premier Hlthcare Solutions Inc ....B....858 569-8629
12225 El Camino Real San Diego (92130) ***(P-26991)***
Premier IMS Insurance Services, San Diego *Also called Premier Hlthcare Solutions Inc* ***(P-26991)***
Premier Insite Group Inc ....D....562 741-5018
111 W Ocean Blvd Ste 400 Long Beach (90802) ***(P-14699)***
Premier Mailing Inc ....E....562 408-2134
14522 Garfield Ave Paramount (90723) ***(P-14059)***
Premier Mailing Services, Paramount *Also called Premier Mailing Inc* ***(P-14059)***
Premier Management Company (PA) ....D....310 286-3074
1141 S Beverly Dr Fl 3 Los Angeles (90035) ***(P-26273)***
Premier Management Company ....E....619 582-5168
4075 54th St San Diego (92105) ***(P-22397)***
Premier Meat Company, Vernon *Also called Wayne Provision Co Inc* ***(P-8633)***
Premier Medical Transport Inc ....D....888 353-9556
260 N Palm St 200 Brea (92821) ***(P-5145)***
Premier Medical Trnsp Inc ....D....909 433-3939
575 Maple Ct Ste A Colton (92324) ***(P-3830)***
Premier Mushrooms LP (PA) ....C....530 458-2700
2880 Niagara Ave Colusa (95932) ***(P-8717)***
Premier Mushrooms LP ....C....530 458-2700
2847 Niagara Ave Colusa (95932) ***(P-321)***
Premier Nursing Services Inc (PA) ....A....562 437-4313
444 W Ocean Blvd Ste 1050 Long Beach (90802) ***(P-14700)***
Premier Office Centers LLC (PA) ....E....949 253-4616
2102 Business Center Dr Irvine (92612) ***(P-17408)***
Premier Packaging/Assembly, Santa Fe Springs *Also called Haringa Inc* ***(P-17207)***
Premier Plumbing Company, Riverside *Also called Ppc Enterprises Inc* ***(P-2315)***
Premier Pools and Spas Lp (PA) ....D....916 852-0223
11250 Pyrites Way Gold River (95670) ***(P-3568)***
Premier Residential Svcs LLC ....D....760 773-4081
43100 Cook St Ste 101 Palm Desert (92211) ***(P-13769)***
Premier Source LLC ....D....415 349-2010
999 Bayhill Dr Fl 3 San Bruno (94066) ***(P-26649)***
Premier Tile & Marble ....D....310 516-1712
15000 S Main St Gardena (90248) ***(P-3008)***
Premier Valley Inc (PA) ....D....209 847-6111
1414 E F St Bldg A Oakdale (95361) ***(P-11678)***
Premiere Agency of California ....D....916 784-1008
5 Sierra Gate Plz Fl 2nd Roseville (95678) ***(P-10738)***
Premiere Financial ....D....760 518-5034
6498 Willow Pl Carlsbad (92011) ***(P-10105)***
Premiere Packing, Shafter *Also called Grimmway Enterprises Inc* ***(P-346)***
Premiere Properties, Carlsbad *Also called Premiere Financial* ***(P-10105)***
Premiere Radio Network Inc (HQ) ....C....818 377-5300
15260 Ventura Blvd # 400 Sherman Oaks (91403) ***(P-18396)***
Premium Harvesting, Salinas *Also called Premium Packing Inc* ***(P-483)***
Premium Packing Inc ....C....831 443-6855
449 Harrison Rd Salinas (93907) ***(P-483)***
Premium Rock Drywall Inc ....D....818 676-3350
31348 Via Colinas Ste 103 Westlake Village (91362) ***(P-2942)***
Premium Trnsp Svcs Inc (PA) ....C....310 816-0260
18735 S Ferris Pl Rancho Dominguez (90220) ***(P-5146)***
Prentice Hall Legal Fincl Svcs, Sacramento *Also called Corporation Service Company* ***(P-14229)***
Presbyterian Inter Cmnty Hosp, Whittier *Also called Interhealth Services Inc* ***(P-22345)***
Preschool Service, San Bernardino *Also called County of San Bernardino* ***(P-24307)***
Prescott Companies (PA) ....E....760 634-4700
5950 La Place Ct Ste 200 Carlsbad (92008) ***(P-11679)***
Prescott Hotel, The, San Francisco *Also called Post Street Renaissance* ***(P-13078)***
Prescription Solutions, Carlsbad *Also called Optumrx Inc* ***(P-10287)***
Prescription Solutions, Irvine *Also called Optumrx Inc* ***(P-10288)***
Prescription Solutions ....A....760 804-2370
2858 Loker Ave E Ste 100 Carlsbad (92010) ***(P-27398)***
Preserve Golf Club Inc ....E....831 620-6871
1 Rancho San Carlos Rd Carmel (93923) ***(P-18746)***
Presidian Hotel, Visalia *Also called Viscamar LLC* ***(P-13370)***
Presidio Community YMCA, San Francisco *Also called Young Mens Christian Assoc SF* ***(P-25322)***
Presidio Components Inc ....C....858 578-9390
7169 Construction Ct San Diego (92121) ***(P-7525)***
Presidio Hotel Group LLC ....D....916 631-7500
10713 White Rock Rd Rancho Cordova (95670) ***(P-13080)***
Presidio Wealth Management LLC ....E....415 449-2500
101 California St # 2400 San Francisco (94111) ***(P-10106)***
Presido YMCA, San Francisco *Also called Young Mens Christian Assnsf* ***(P-25318)***
Prestige Asstd Lvng in Chico, Chico *Also called Caldwell Ventures LLC* ***(P-20280)***
Prestige Auto Collision Inc ....D....949 470-6031
23726 Via Fabricante Mission Viejo (92691) ***(P-17734)***
Prestige Autotech Corporation ....E....909 627-6411
4975 Edison Ave Chino (91710) ***(P-6666)***
Prestige Car Wash Lafayette LP ....E....925 283-1190
3319 Mt Diablo Blvd Lafayette (94549) ***(P-17836)***
Prestige Concrete ....D....858 679-2772
13507 Midland Rd Poway (92064) ***(P-3309)***
Prestige Gunite California Inc ....E....909 276-9096
18300 Wood Edge Ln Riverside (92504) ***(P-3310)***
Prestige Preschools Inc (PA) ....D....818 957-1170
3795 La Crescenta Ave # 200 Glendale (91208) ***(P-24373)***
Prestige Protection, San Ramon *Also called Universal Protection Svc LP* ***(P-16845)***
Prestige Sales II LLC ....D....714 632-8020
1038 E Bastanchury Rd Fullerton (92835) ***(P-8857)***
Prestige Security Service Inc ....B....310 670-5999
5855 Green Valley Cir # 207 Culver City (90230) ***(P-16761)***
Prestige Too Auto Body Inc ....E....310 787-8852
11899 Woodruff Ave Downey (90241) ***(P-17735)***
Preston Pipelines Inc (PA) ....C....408 262-1418
133 Bothelo Ave Milpitas (95035) ***(P-1969)***
Preston Pipelines Inc A Cal ....B....408 262-6989
133 Bothelo Ave Milpitas (95035) ***(P-1970)***
Preston Wynne Spa Inc ....D....408 741-1750
14567 Big Basin Way A2 Saratoga (95070) ***(P-18642)***
Prevent Life Safety Svcs Inc ....E....925 667-2088
1410 Stealth St Livermore (94551) ***(P-17409)***
Prevention Institute ....D....510 444-4133
221 Oak St Ste A Oakland (94607) ***(P-27399)***
Prg (california) Inc ....E....818 252-2600
1245 Aviation Pl San Fernando (91340) ***(P-18099)***
Prg Parking Century LLC ....D....310 642-0947
5701 W Century Blvd Los Angeles (90045) ***(P-17703)***
Prh Pro Inc ....C....714 510-7226
13089 Peyton Dr Ste C362 Chino Hills (91709) ***(P-7864)***
PRI Medical Technologies Inc (HQ) ....D....818 394-2800
10939 Pendleton St Sun Valley (91352) ***(P-7212)***
Pribuss Engineering Inc ....D....650 588-0447
523 Mayfair Ave South San Francisco (94080) ***(P-2317)***
Price Associates ....E....818 995-9216
15760 Ventura Blvd # 1100 Encino (91436) ***(P-23336)***
Price Law Group A Prof Corp (PA) ....C....818 995-4540
15760 Ventura Blvd # 1100 Encino (91436) ***(P-23337)***
Price Postel and Parma LLP ....D....805 962-0011
200 E Carrillo St Ste 400 Santa Barbara (93101) ***(P-23338)***

Employee Codes: A=Over 500 employees, B=251-500
C=101-250, D=51-100, E=50
2019 Directory of California
Wholesalers and Services Companies
© Mergent Inc. 1-800-342-5647
1427

Price Spider, Irvine *Also called Neuintel LLC* ***(P-15305)***
Price, Stuart, Encino *Also called Price Associates* ***(P-23336)***
Pricemetrix Usa Inc.......E.......714 357-6192
3 Bridgeport Rd Newport Coast (92657) ***(P-16167)***
Pricewaterhousecoopers LLP.......B.......949 437-5200
2020 Main St Ste 400 Irvine (92614) ***(P-26274)***
Pricewaterhousecoopers LLP.......A.......408 817-3700
488 Almaden Blvd Ste 1800 San Jose (95110) ***(P-26275)***
Pricewaterhousecoopers LLP.......B.......858 677-2400
5375 Mira Sorrento Pl San Diego (92121) ***(P-26276)***
Pricewaterhousecoopers LLP.......D.......916 930-8100
400 Capitol Mall Ste 600 Sacramento (95814) ***(P-26277)***
Pricewaterhousecoopers LLP.......B.......415 498-5000
3 Embarcadero Ctr Fl 20 San Francisco (94111) ***(P-26278)***
Pride Auto Body, Van Nuys *Also called Pride Collision Centers Inc* ***(P-17736)***
Pride Collision Centers Inc (PA).......D.......818 909-0660
7950 Haskell Ave Van Nuys (91406) ***(P-17736)***
Pride Industries (PA).......C.......916 788-2100
10030 Foothills Blvd Roseville (95747) ***(P-4686)***
Pride Industries.......C.......805 985-8481
Cbc Base Bldg 19 43rd St Port Hueneme (93041) ***(P-1307)***
Pride Industries.......C.......530 888-0331
13080 Earhart Ave Auburn (95602) ***(P-24220)***
Pride Industries.......D.......530 477-1832
12451 Loma Rica Dr Grass Valley (95945) ***(P-24221)***
Pride Industries.......D.......916 334-5415
3608 Madison Ave Ste 43 North Highlands (95660) ***(P-24222)***
Pride Industries.......C.......916 649-9499
1281 National Dr Sacramento (95834) ***(P-27955)***
Prima Royale, Pasadena *Also called Prima Royale Enterprises Ltd* ***(P-8365)***
Prima Royale Enterprises Ltd.......D.......626 960-8388
150 S Los Robles Ave # 100 Pasadena (91101) ***(P-8365)***
Primal Elements Inc.......D.......714 899-0757
18062 Redondo Cir Huntington Beach (92648) ***(P-8207)***
Primary Care Assod Med Group (PA).......D.......760 471-7505
1635 Lake San Marcos Dr # 201 San Marcos (92078) ***(P-26992)***
Primary Color Systems Corp.......C.......310 841-0250
401 Coral Cir El Segundo (90245) ***(P-14098)***
Primary Critical Care Medical.......D.......818 847-9950
620 N Brand Blvd Ste 500 Glendale (91203) ***(P-19796)***
Primary Eyecare Network, Alameda *Also called Abb/Con-Cise Optical Group LLC* ***(P-7231)***
Primary Freight Services Inc (PA).......D.......310 635-3000
6545 Caballero Blvd Buena Park (90620) ***(P-5147)***
Primary Provider MGT Co Inc (PA).......C.......951 280-7700
2115 Compton Ave Ste 301 Corona (92881) ***(P-26993)***
Prime Administration LLC.......A.......323 549-7155
357 S Curson Ave Los Angeles (90036) ***(P-12181)***
Prime Clinical Systems (PA).......D.......626 449-1705
3675 Huntington Dr Ste A Pasadena (91107) ***(P-15374)***
Prime Communications LP.......D.......951 253-3304
29273 Central Ave Lake Elsinore (92532) ***(P-5630)***
Prime Focus North America Inc (HQ).......D.......323 461-7887
5750 Hannum Ave Ste 100 Culver City (90230) ***(P-18212)***
Prime Focus World, Culver City *Also called Prime Focus North America Inc* ***(P-18212)***
Prime Global Solutions Inc (PA).......D.......800 424-7746
15801 E Valley Blvd City of Industry (91744) ***(P-5148)***
Prime Group, Los Angeles *Also called Prime Administration LLC* ***(P-12181)***
Prime Health Care Svcs Grdn Gr.......B.......714 537-5160
12601 Garden Grove Blvd Garden Grove (92843) ***(P-21655)***
Prime Healthcare Anaheim LLC.......A.......714 827-3000
3033 W Orange Ave Anaheim (92804) ***(P-21656)***
Prime Healthcare Centinela LLC.......A.......310 673-4660
555 E Hardy St Inglewood (90301) ***(P-21657)***
Prime Healthcare Services, Ontario *Also called Bio-Med Services Inc* ***(P-22742)***
Prime Healthcare Services.......A.......530 244-5400
1100 Butte St Redding (96001) ***(P-21658)***
Prime Healthcare Services - Sh.......A.......818 981-7111
4929 Van Nuys Blvd Sherman Oaks (91403) ***(P-27400)***
Prime Healthcare Servs Sh.......A.......530 244-5458
1450 Liberty St Redding (96001) ***(P-21659)***
Prime Healthcare Svcs II LLC.......B.......818 981-7111
4929 Van Nuys Blvd Sherman Oaks (91403) ***(P-21660)***
Prime Healthcare Svcs III LLC (HQ).......C.......909 625-5411
5000 San Bernardino St Montclair (91763) ***(P-21661)***
Prime Healthcare-San Dimas LLC.......B.......909 599-6811
1350 W Covina Blvd San Dimas (91773) ***(P-21662)***
Prime Hlthcare Hntngton Bch.......B.......714 843-5000
17772 Beach Blvd Huntington Beach (92647) ***(P-21663)***
Prime International Security.......D.......310 670-4565
1630 Centinela Ave # 209 Inglewood (90302) ***(P-16762)***
Prime Security, Inglewood *Also called Prime International Security* ***(P-16762)***
Prime Stop, Moreno Valley *Also called Plaza Hand Carwash Inc* ***(P-17834)***
Prime Tech Cabinets Inc.......C.......714 558-4837
2652 White Rd Irvine (92614) ***(P-3059)***
Prime Time Athletic Club Inc.......D.......650 204-3662
1730 Rollins Rd Burlingame (94010) ***(P-18643)***
Prime Time International, Coachella *Also called Sun and Sands Enterprises LLC* ***(P-83)***
Prime-Line Products Company (PA).......B.......909 887-8118
26950 San Bernardino Ave Redlands (92374) ***(P-7600)***
Primecare Quality HM Care Inc.......D.......949 681-3515
2372 Morse Ave Irvine (92614) ***(P-1218)***
Primeco Painting & Cnstr.......D.......760 967-8278
220 Oceanside Blvd Oceanside (92054) ***(P-2466)***
Primed MGT Consulting Svcs Inc.......B.......925 327-6710
2409 Camino Ramon San Ramon (94583) ***(P-26994)***
Primerica Financial Svcs Inc.......D.......951 695-4325
27470 Jefferson Ave 5a Temecula (92590) ***(P-10739)***
Primerica Life Insurance Co.......C.......650 323-2554
260 Sheridan Ave Ste B42 Palo Alto (94306) ***(P-10740)***
Primerica Life Insurance Co.......C.......661 947-9070
41307 12th St W Ste 200 Palmdale (93551) ***(P-10741)***
Primerica Life Insurance Co.......C.......951 652-6190
175 N Cawston Ave Hemet (92545) ***(P-10742)***
Primetime International Inc.......D.......760 399-4166
86705 Avenue 54 Ste A Coachella (92236) ***(P-8718)***
Primex Clinical Labs Inc (PA).......D.......818 779-0496
16742 Stagg St Ste 120 Van Nuys (91406) ***(P-22125)***
Primitive Logic Inc.......D.......415 391-8080
704 Sansome St San Francisco (94111) ***(P-16035)***
Primm Valley Golf Club.......D.......702 679-5509
1 Yates Wells Rd Nipton (92364) ***(P-18747)***
Primoris Services Corporation.......B.......949 598-9242
26000 Commercentre Dr Lake Forest (92630) ***(P-1971)***
Primrose Alzheimers Living (PA).......E.......707 568-4355
726 College Ave Santa Rosa (95404) ***(P-24633)***
Primrose Alzheimers Living.......E.......707 578-8360
2080 Guerneville Rd Santa Rosa (95403) ***(P-24634)***
Primrose Alzheimers Living.......D.......916 392-3510
7707 Rush River Dr Sacramento (95831) ***(P-24635)***
Primrose Sacramento, Sacramento *Also called Primrose Alzheimers Living* ***(P-24635)***
Primus Group Inc (PA).......E.......805 922-0055
2810 Industrial Pkwy Santa Maria (93455) ***(P-27401)***
Primus Labs, Santa Maria *Also called Primus Group Inc* ***(P-27401)***
Primus Pipe and Tube Inc (HQ).......D.......562 808-8000
5855 Obispo Ave Long Beach (90805) ***(P-7302)***
Princess Cruise Lines Ltd.......A.......661 753-2291
P.O. Box 966 Santa Clarita (91380) ***(P-4948)***
Princess Cruise Lines Ltd (HQ).......A.......661 753-0000
24305 Town Center Dr Santa Clarita (91355) ***(P-4708)***
Princess Cruises, Santa Clarita *Also called Princess Cruise Lines Ltd* ***(P-4948)***
Princess Cruises, Santa Clarita *Also called Princess Cruise Lines Ltd* ***(P-4708)***
Princess Cruises and Tours Inc (HQ).......A.......206 336-6000
24305 Town Center Dr # 200 Valencia (91355) ***(P-4949)***
Principal Financial Group Inc.......D.......818 243-7141
500 N Brand Blvd Ste 1800 Glendale (91203) ***(P-10144)***
Principal Financial Group Inc.......D.......559 261-2000
1350 E Spruce Ave Ste 100 Fresno (93720) ***(P-10145)***
Principles Inc (PA).......D.......323 681-2575
1680 N Fair Oaks Ave Pasadena (91103) ***(P-22654)***
Prindle Decker & Amaro LLP (PA).......D.......562 436-3946
310 Golden Shore Fl 4 Long Beach (90802) ***(P-23339)***
Printful Inc.......D.......818 351-7181
19749 Dearborn St Chatsworth (91311) ***(P-16965)***
Printing Inds Assn Suthern Cal.......D.......323 728-9500
5800 S Eastrn Ave Ste 400 Commerce (90040) ***(P-24973)***
Printing Technology Inc.......C.......818 576-9220
21001 Nordhoff St Chatsworth (91311) ***(P-7865)***
Priority 1 Warehousing Inc (PA).......D.......209 824-8876
2577 W Yosemite Ave Manteca (95337) ***(P-4613)***
Priority Building Services LLC.......B.......714 255-2940
521 Mercury Ln Brea (92821) ***(P-14355)***
Priority Cooling, Firebaugh *Also called Tri-State AG Inc* ***(P-6552)***
Priority Dispatch Service Inc.......D.......408 400-3860
309 Laurelwood Rd Ste 10 Santa Clara (95054) ***(P-4427)***
Priority Landscape Services, Brea *Also called Priority Building Services LLC* ***(P-14355)***
Priority One Med Trnspt Inc (PA).......D.......909 948-4400
9327 Fairway View Pl # 300 Rancho Cucamonga (91730) ***(P-3831)***
Priority One Support, Irvine *Also called Alorica Inc* ***(P-16084)***
Prism Electronics Corp (PA).......E.......408 778-7050
900 Lightpost Way 100 Morgan Hill (95037) ***(P-7526)***
Prison Industry Authority-Pia.......D.......559 386-6060
1 Kings Way Avenal (93204) ***(P-23340)***
Pritchett Rapf and Associates.......D.......310 456-6771
23732 Malibu Rd Malibu (90265) ***(P-11680)***
Private Industry Cncl Slno Cty (PA).......E.......707 864-3370
320 Campus Ln Ste A Fairfield (94534) ***(P-14701)***
Private Label Pc LLC.......C.......626 965-8686
748 Epperson Dr Ste B City of Industry (91748) ***(P-7093)***
Private Medical-Care Inc.......C.......562 924-8311
12898 Towne Center Dr Cerritos (90703) ***(P-10302)***
Private Nat Mrtg Accptance LLC (HQ).......A.......818 224-7401
6101 Condor Dr Agoura Hills (91301) ***(P-9847)***
Privilege International Inc.......D.......323 585-0777
2323 Firestone Blvd South Gate (90280) ***(P-6736)***
Priyo Inc.......E.......408 248-2507
605 Tumbleweed Cmn Fremont (94539) ***(P-15375)***
Prize Proz.......E.......909 509-8600
1500 S Hellman Ave Ontario (91761) ***(P-27402)***
Prn LLC (HQ).......D.......415 805-2525
600 Montgomery St # 1800 San Francisco (94111) ***(P-15376)***
Prn Ambulance LLC.......B.......818 810-3600
8928 Sepulveda Blvd North Hills (91343) ***(P-3832)***
Prn Radio Networks, Sherman Oaks *Also called Premiere Radio Network Inc* ***(P-18396)***
Pro Act LLC.......D.......831 655-4250
40 Ragsdale Dr Ste 200 Monterey (93940) ***(P-8719)***
Pro America Premium Tools, Baldwin Park *Also called American Kal Enterprises Inc* ***(P-7574)***
Pro Building Maintenance Inc.......C.......951 279-3386
149 N Maple St Ste H Corona (92880) ***(P-14356)***
Pro Care 2000 Home Health Care, Long Beach *Also called Pacific Care Inc* ***(P-22386)***
Pro Group Inc.......C.......951 271-3000
4160 Temescal Canyon Rd # 500 Corona (92883) ***(P-11681)***
Pro Loaders Inc (PA).......C.......909 355-5531
14032 Santa Ana Ave Fontana (92337) ***(P-5149)***
Pro Pacific Fresh, Durham *Also called Chico Produce Inc* ***(P-8653)***
Pro Ponds West Inc.......D.......818 244-4000
8309 Tujunga Ave Unit 201 Sun Valley (91352) ***(P-779)***

Mergent e-mail: customerrelations@mergent.com
1428
2019 Directory of California
Wholesalers and Services Companies
(P-0000) Products & Services Section entry number
(PA)=Parent Co (HQ)=Headquarters (DH)=Div Headquarters

Pro Scape Inc ....E....760 480-1544
510 Venture St Escondido (92029) ***(P-924)***

Pro Specialties Group Inc ....D....858 541-1100
4863 Shawline St Ste D San Diego (92111) ***(P-9252)***

Pro TEC Manufacturing, Canoga Park *Also called T M P Inc* ***(P-8279)***

Pro Unlimited Inc ....E....650 344-1099
1350 Bayshore Hwy Ste 350 Burlingame (94010) ***(P-26995)***

Pro-Craft Construction Inc ....D....909 790-5222
31597 Outer Highway 10 B Redlands (92373) ***(P-2318)***

Pro-Med Hlth Care Admnistrator ....D....909 932-1045
4150 Concours Ste 100 Ontario (91764) ***(P-26996)***

Pro-Tech Design & Mfg Inc ....D....562 207-1680
14561 Marquardt Ave Santa Fe Springs (90670) ***(P-17410)***

Pro-Tek Consulting (PA) ....C....805 807-5571
21300 Victory Blvd # 240 Woodland Hills (91367) ***(P-16462)***

Pro-Wash Inc ....D....323 756-6000
9117 S Main St Los Angeles (90003) ***(P-13561)***

Proactiv, El Segundo *Also called Guthy-Renker LLC* ***(P-8035)***

Proactive Bus Solutions Inc ....C....510 302-0120
428 13th St Fl 5 Oakland (94612) ***(P-26997)***

Proactive Risk Management Inc ....D....213 840-8856
1111 S Grand Ave Apt 611 Los Angeles (90015) ***(P-26998)***

Probation, Red Bluff *Also called County of Tehama* ***(P-23753)***

Probation Department, Fresno *Also called County of Fresno* ***(P-23638)***

Probation Department, Pasadena *Also called County of Los Angeles* ***(P-23653)***

Probation Department, Lancaster *Also called County of Los Angeles* ***(P-23655)***

Probation Department, Redwood City *Also called County of San Mateo* ***(P-23734)***

Probation Department, San Mateo *Also called County of San Mateo* ***(P-23735)***

Probation Department, San Mateo *Also called County of San Mateo* ***(P-23736)***

Probation Department, Clovis *Also called County of Fresno* ***(P-23639)***

Probation Department, Sacramento *Also called Sacramento County Off Educatn* ***(P-24003)***

Probation Department, Los Angeles *Also called County of Los Angeles* ***(P-23667)***

Probation Department, East Palo Alto *Also called County of San Mateo* ***(P-23737)***

Probation Department, Downey *Also called County of Los Angeles* ***(P-23684)***

Probation Department, San Mateo *Also called County of San Mateo* ***(P-23740)***

Probation Department, Redwood City *Also called County of San Mateo* ***(P-23741)***

Probation Dept, San Diego *Also called County of San Diego* ***(P-23724)***

Probation Dept, Anaheim *Also called County of Orange* ***(P-23698)***

Probation Dept, Westminster *Also called County of Orange* ***(P-23699)***

Probation Dept, Los Angeles *Also called County of Los Angeles* ***(P-23664)***

Probation Dept, Rancho Cucamonga *Also called County of San Bernardino* ***(P-23718)***

Probation Dept, Santa Barbara *Also called Santa Barbara County of* ***(P-24025)***

Probation Dept, Santa Maria *Also called Santa Barbara County of* ***(P-24026)***

Probation Dept, Santa Monica *Also called County of Los Angeles* ***(P-23675)***

Probation Dept, Van Nuys *Also called County of Los Angeles* ***(P-23676)***

Probation Dept, Los Angeles *Also called County of Los Angeles* ***(P-23678)***

Probation Dept, Los Angeles *Also called County of Los Angeles* ***(P-23681)***

Probation Dept, Compton *Also called County of Los Angeles* ***(P-23682)***

Probation Dept, Pasadena *Also called County of Los Angeles* ***(P-23683)***

Probation Dept, San Jose *Also called Santa Clara County of* ***(P-24031)***

Probation Dept, Auburn *Also called County of Placer* ***(P-23705)***

Probation Dept, Santa Barbara *Also called Santa Barbara County of* ***(P-24028)***

Probation Dept-Juvenile, Bakersfield *Also called County of Kern* ***(P-23646)***

Probation Dept-Juvenile Div, Morgan Hill *Also called Santa Clara County of* ***(P-24667)***

Probe Information Services Inc ....C....916 676-1826
6375 Auburn Blvd Citrus Heights (95621) ***(P-16763)***

Prober & Raphael A Law Corp ....D....818 227-0100
20750 Ventura Blvd # 100 Woodland Hills (91364) ***(P-23341)***

Prober & Raphael, ALC, Woodland Hills *Also called Prober & Raphael A Law Corp* ***(P-23341)***

Procall Solutions Inc ....C....800 733-9675
20 Ragsdale Dr Ste 100 Monterey (93940) ***(P-17411)***

Procel Temporary Services Inc ....B....310 372-0560
222 W 6th St Ste 370 San Pedro (90731) ***(P-14894)***

Procera Networks Inc (HQ) ....D....510 230-2777
2055 Junction Ave Ste 105 San Jose (95131) ***(P-15377)***

Processing Office, Corcoran *Also called J G Boswell Company* ***(P-531)***

Processweaver Inc ....D....888 932-8373
5201 Great America Pkwy # 300 Santa Clara (95054) ***(P-15378)***

Procida Landscape Inc ....C....916 387-5296
8465 Specialty Cir Sacramento (95828) ***(P-925)***

Procore Technologies Inc (PA) ....C....866 477-6267
6309 Carpinteria Ave Carpinteria (93013) ***(P-15379)***

Procter & Gamble Distrg LLC ....B....209 538-3987
1992 Rockefeller Dr Ceres (95307) ***(P-8935)***

Procter & Gamble Distrg LLC ....B....925 867-4900
2010 Crow Canyon Pl # 230 San Ramon (94583) ***(P-8936)***

Prodata Research, San Diego *Also called Soleil Communications LLC* ***(P-26566)***

Proday Co ....D....517 980-1362
2122 Union St San Francisco (94123) ***(P-13953)***

Prodege LLC (PA) ....D....310 294-9599
100 N Pacific Coast Hwy # 800 El Segundo (90245) ***(P-15380)***

Produce Company ....C....310 508-7760
16809 Bellflower Blvd # 32 Bellflower (90706) ***(P-8720)***

Produce Exchange Incorporated (HQ) ....D....925 454-8700
7407 Southfront Rd Livermore (94551) ***(P-8721)***

Producer -Writers Guild ....D....818 846-1015
2900 W Alameda Ave # 1100 Burbank (91505) ***(P-10491)***

Producers Dairy Foods Inc (PA) ....C....559 264-6583
250 E Belmont Ave Fresno (93701) ***(P-8498)***

Produces Dairy, Fresno *Also called L A S Transportation Inc* ***(P-4210)***

Product Development Corp (PA) ....C....831 333-1100
30 Ragsdale Dr Ste 101 Monterey (93940) ***(P-17412)***

Product Partners, Santa Monica *Also called Beachbody LLC* ***(P-13936)***

Product Quality Partners Inc ....D....925 484-6491
450 Main St Ste 207 Pleasanton (94566) ***(P-16463)***

Product Slingshot Inc ....D....760 929-9380
2221 Rutherford Rd Carlsbad (92008) ***(P-27403)***

Production Delivery Svcs Inc ....D....562 777-0060
12133 Greenstone Ave Santa Fe Springs (90670) ***(P-4246)***

PRODUCTION FACILITIES UNLIMITE, La Puente *Also called San Gabriel Vly Training Ctr* ***(P-24226)***

Production Framing Inc ....D....916 978-2843
2000 Opportunity Dr # 140 Roseville (95678) ***(P-3060)***

Production Framing Systems Inc (PA) ....C....916 978-2888
2000 Opportunity Dr # 140 Roseville (95678) ***(P-3061)***

Production Plus Plumbing Inc ....C....760 597-0235
2472 Grand Ave Vista (92081) ***(P-2319)***

Production Special Events Svcs ....E....818 831-5326
17326 Devonshire St Northridge (91325) ***(P-18397)***

Production Transport, Santa Fe Springs *Also called Production Delivery Svcs Inc* ***(P-4246)***

Productos Chata, Chula Vista *Also called Culinary Hispanic Foods Inc* ***(P-8783)***

Profed Mortgage, Rancho Cucamonga *Also called Provident Savings Bank* ***(P-9851)***

Professional Building Maint, Sun Valley *Also called PBM Maintenance Corp* ***(P-14344)***

Professional Bureau of Collect ....C....916 685-3399
9675 Elk Grove Florin Rd Elk Grove (95624) ***(P-14018)***

Professional Community MGT Cal (PA) ....E....800 369-7260
27051 Towne Centre Dr # 200 Foothill Ranch (92610) ***(P-11682)***

Professional Community MGT Cal ....E....951 845-2191
850 Country Club Dr Banning (92220) ***(P-11683)***

Professional Community MGT Cal ....C....949 206-0580
24351 El Toro Rd Laguna Woods (92637) ***(P-11684)***

Professional Community MGT Cal ....D....949 768-7261
27051 Towne Centre Dr # 200 Foothill Ranch (92610) ***(P-11153)***

Professional Community MGT Cal ....C....949 597-4200
23522 Paseo De Valencia Laguna Hills (92653) ***(P-11685)***

Professional Construction Svcs, Rancho Cucamonga *Also called Rwc Enterprises Inc* ***(P-25898)***

Professional Exchange Svc ....E....559 229-6249
4747 N 1st St Ste 140 Fresno (93726) ***(P-17413)***

Professional Golf MGT LLC ....D....760 564-0804
49155 Vista Estrella La Quinta (92253) ***(P-26999)***

Professional Health Tech ....D....858 449-1599
8131 Calle Del Cielo La Jolla (92037) ***(P-19797)***

Professional Hospital Sup Inc (HQ) ....A....951 699-5000
42500 Winchester Rd Temecula (92590) ***(P-7213)***

Professional Insur Assoc Inc (PA) ....E....650 592-7333
1100 Industrial Rd Ste 3 San Carlos (94070) ***(P-10743)***

Professional Janitorial Svc ....E....310 410-1452
234 Eucalyptus Dr B El Segundo (90245) ***(P-14357)***

Professional Maint Systems, San Diego *Also called Professional Maint Systems Inc* ***(P-14358)***

Professional Maint Systems Inc ....A....619 276-1150
4912 Naples St San Diego (92110) ***(P-14358)***

Professional Medical MGT, Hemet *Also called Hemet Valley Imaging Med Group* ***(P-19496)***

Professional Parking (PA) ....C....714 722-0242
2799 E 21st St Signal Hill (90755) ***(P-17704)***

Professional Produce ....D....323 277-1550
2570 E 25th St Los Angeles (90058) ***(P-8722)***

Professional Security Cons (PA) ....C....310 207-7729
11454 San Vicente Blvd # 2 Los Angeles (90049) ***(P-16764)***

Professional Services Company, San Francisco *Also called Shenyang Zhong Yi Tin-Plating* ***(P-10937)***

Professional Staffing, Granada Hills *Also called PS National Inc* ***(P-14708)***

Professional Staffing Associat, Downey *Also called Rancho Los Amigos Nationa* ***(P-23981)***

Professional Svcs Med Group, Huntington Park *Also called All Care Medical Group Inc* ***(P-19271)***

Professionals Choice Sport ....D....619 873-1100
2025 Gillespie Way # 106 El Cajon (92020) ***(P-9093)***

Professnal Cmmnctons Netwrk LP (PA) ....E....951 275-9149
6774 Magnolia Ave Riverside (92506) ***(P-17414)***

Professnal Creer Placementscom ....E....415 615-0688
1990 N Calif Blvd Fl 8 Walnut Creek (94596) ***(P-14702)***

Professnal Elec Cnstr Svcs Inc ....C....909 373-4100
9112 Santa Anita Ave Rancho Cucamonga (91730) ***(P-2687)***

Professnal Ldscp Solutions Inc ....E....916 424-3815
6108 27th St Ste C Sacramento (95822) ***(P-780)***

Professnal Rgistry Netwrk Corp ....C....714 394-4071
20132 Canyon Dr Yorba Linda (92886) ***(P-14703)***

Professonal Technical SEC Svcs ....B....510 645-9200
1970 Broadway Ste 840 Oakland (94612) ***(P-16765)***

Professonal Tele Answering Svc, Chatsworth *Also called Seven One Inc* ***(P-17468)***

Professsional Insurance, San Carlos *Also called Professional Insur Assoc Inc* ***(P-10743)***

Proficient LLC ....D....310 519-8200
601 S Palos Verdes St San Pedro (90731) ***(P-13081)***

Proficio Inc (PA) ....E....800 779-5042
3264 Grey Hawk Ct Carlsbad (92010) ***(P-7094)***

Profile of Santa Cruz ....D....831 479-0393
2045 40th Ave Ste B Capitola (95010) ***(P-14704)***

Profit Recovery Partners LLC ....D....949 851-2777
2995 Red Hill Ave Ste 200 Costa Mesa (92626) ***(P-27826)***

Progauge Technologies Inc ....E....661 392-9600
2331 Cepheus Ct Bakersfield (93308) ***(P-7787)***

Progenity Inc (PA) ....C....760 494-1555
4330 La Jolla Village Dr # 200 San Diego (92122) ***(P-22126)***

Progress Foundation ....D....415 553-3100
52 Dore St San Francisco (94103) ***(P-25217)***

Progress Glass Co Inc (PA) ....C....415 824-7040
25 Patterson St San Francisco (94124) ***(P-3408)***

Progress House Inc (PA) ....D....530 626-9240
2844 Coloma St Ste A&B Placerville (95667) ***(P-24636)***

Employee Codes: A=Over 500 employees, B=251-500
C=101-250, D=51-100, E=50
2019 Directory of California
Wholesalers and Services Companies
© Mergent Inc. 1-800-342-5647
1429

PROGRESSIN DRYWALL, Lancaster *Also called Excel Contractors Inc* ***(P-1162)***
Progressive Computing LLC..........D.......858 707-0707
3615 Krny Vlla Rd Ste 105 San Diego (92123) ***(P-15381)***
Progressive Corporation..........D.......626 232-1540
2470 Via Mariposa San Dimas (91773) ***(P-10385)***
Progressive Corporation..........D.......440 461-5000
150 N Hill Dr Ste 9 Brisbane (94005) ***(P-10386)***
Progressive Floor Covering Inc..........E.......714 213-8805
924 S Highland Ave Fullerton (92832) ***(P-3115)***
Progressive Insurance, San Dimas *Also called Progressive Corporation* ***(P-10385)***
Progressive Insurance, Brisbane *Also called Progressive Corporation* ***(P-10386)***
Progressive Management Systems, West Covina *Also called RM Galicia Inc* ***(P-14021)***
Progressive Marketing Group, Commerce *Also called Progressive Produce LLC* ***(P-8723)***
Progressive Power Group Inc..........E.......714 899-2300
12552 Western Ave Garden Grove (92841) ***(P-2320)***
Progressive Produce LLC (HQ)..........C.......323 890-8100
5790 Peachtree St Commerce (90040) ***(P-8723)***
Progressive Roofing, Stockton *Also called Progressive Services Inc* ***(P-3191)***
Progressive Services Inc..........D.......209 824-2837
3832 S Highway 99 Ste A Stockton (95215) ***(P-3191)***
Progressive Solutions, San Jose *Also called Sarpa-Feldman Enterprises Inc* ***(P-17458)***
Progressive Sub-Acute Care..........C.......408 378-8875
13425 Sousa Ln Saratoga (95070) ***(P-22039)***
Progressive Trnsp Svcs Inc..........D.......510 268-3776
19500 S Alameda St Compton (90221) ***(P-7866)***
Progrssive Employment Concepts (PA)..........D.......916 723-3112
6060 Sunrise Vista Dr # 1875 Citrus Heights (95610) ***(P-24223)***
Project Air Force, Santa Monica *Also called Air Force US Dept of* ***(P-26586)***
Project Boat Holdings LLC..........A.......310 712-1850
360 N Crescent Dr Bldg S Beverly Hills (90210) ***(P-12001)***
Project Concern International (PA)..........D.......858 279-9690
5151 Murphy Canyon Rd # 320 San Diego (92123) ***(P-24974)***
Project Consulting Specialists..........E.......650 265-2400
425 N Whisman Rd Ste 600 Mountain View (94043) ***(P-27827)***
Project Design Consultants..........D.......619 235-6471
701 B St Ste 800 San Diego (92101) ***(P-27828)***
Project Go Incorporated..........E.......916 782-3443
801 Vernon St Roseville (95678) ***(P-3569)***
Project Management Institute..........D.......760 458-6198
8895 Towne Centre Dr San Diego (92122) ***(P-27000)***
Project Open Hand (PA)..........D.......415 292-3400
730 Polk St Fl 3 San Francisco (94109) ***(P-23977)***
Project Six..........D.......818 781-0360
13130 Burbank Blvd Sherman Oaks (91401) ***(P-17415)***
Proland Property Managment LLC (PA)..........D.......213 738-8175
2510 W 7th St Fl 2 Los Angeles (90057) ***(P-11686)***
Prolifics Inc (HQ)..........B.......212 267-7722
24025 Park Sorrento # 405 Calabasas (91302) ***(P-16464)***
Prolifics Testing Inc..........D.......925 485-9535
24025 Park Sorrento # 405 Calabasas (91302) ***(P-15382)***
Prolinx Services Inc..........D.......408 689-5777
2033 Gateway Pl Ste 500 San Jose (95110) ***(P-14705)***
Prologic Rdmption Slutions Inc (PA)..........A.......310 322-7774
2121 Rosecrans Ave El Segundo (90245) ***(P-17416)***
Prologis Inc (PA)..........B.......415 394-9000
Bay 1 Pier 1 San Francisco (94111) ***(P-12182)***
Prologis LP (HQ)..........B.......415 394-9000
Bay 1 Pier 1 San Francisco (94111) ***(P-12183)***
Prologue Films (PA)..........E.......310 589-9090
534 Victoria Ave Venice (90291) ***(P-14126)***
Promab Biotechnologies Inc..........D.......510 860-4615
2600 Hilltop Dr San Pablo (94806) ***(P-26440)***
Promed Hlth Care Admnistrators..........D.......909 932-1045
9302 Pttsbrgh Ave Ste 220 Rancho Cucamonga (91730) ***(P-19798)***
Promesa Behavioral Health..........D.......209 725-3114
2815 G St Merced (95340) ***(P-24637)***
Promesa Behavioral Health (PA)..........C.......559 439-5437
7120 N Marks Ave Fresno (93711) ***(P-24638)***
Prometheus RE Group Inc (PA)..........C.......650 931-3400
1900 S Norfolk St Ste 150 San Mateo (94403) ***(P-11687)***
Promise Hosp E Los Angeles LP..........B.......562 531-3110
16453 Colorado Ave Paramount (90723) ***(P-21664)***
Promise Technology Inc..........D.......408 228-1400
580 Cottonwood Dr Milpitas (95035) ***(P-7095)***
Promo Shop Inc (PA)..........D.......310 821-1780
5420 Mcconnell Ave Los Angeles (90066) ***(P-27404)***
Promote Media LP..........D.......323 433-7950
8484 Wilshire Blvd # 630 Beverly Hills (90211) ***(P-27405)***
Prompt Care, Westminster *Also called Memorial Promptcare Medical Gr* ***(P-19682)***
Proof of Concept Poc Lab, Sunnyvale *Also called Juniper Networks Inc* ***(P-15987)***
Proofpoint Inc (PA)..........C.......408 517-4710
892 Ross Dr Sunnyvale (94089) ***(P-15383)***
Proove Medical Labs Inc..........C.......949 427-5303
15326 Elton Pkwy Irvine (92618) ***(P-22127)***
Propak Logistics Inc..........D.......559 782-8696
1300 S F St Porterville (93257) ***(P-17973)***
Propane Transport Service Inc..........C.......209 823-8005
903 W Center St Ste 7 Manteca (95337) ***(P-4050)***
Propath Inc..........E.......949 341-8000
17891 Cartwright Rd # 100 Irvine (92614) ***(P-1308)***
Propel Software Corporation..........C.......408 571-6300
1010 Rincon Cir San Jose (95131) ***(P-16465)***
Property I D, Los Angeles *Also called I D Property Corporation* ***(P-11509)***
Property Insight..........C.......909 876-6505
202 E Airport Dr Ste 210 San Bernardino (92408) ***(P-10928)***
Property Maintenance Company (PA)..........C.......408 297-7849
255 W Julian St Ste 301 San Jose (95110) ***(P-14359)***
Property Management, Riverside *Also called Real Estate California Dept* ***(P-11715)***
Property Management Assoc Inc (PA)..........C.......323 295-2000
6011 Bristol Pkwy Culver City (90230) ***(P-11688)***
Property Management Cons (PA)..........E.......858 485-9811
11717 Bernardo Plaza Ct # 220 San Diego (92128) ***(P-11689)***
Propertyplus Insur Agcy Inc..........A.......818 432-2640
21820 Burbank Blvd # 130 Woodland Hills (91367) ***(P-10744)***
Prophet Brand Strategy (PA)..........E.......415 677-0909
1 Bush St Fl 7 San Francisco (94104) ***(P-27406)***
Proponent, Brea *Also called Kirkhill Aircraft Parts Co* ***(P-7907)***
Propulsion Controls Engrg (PA)..........D.......619 235-0961
1620 Rigel St San Diego (92113) ***(P-17974)***
Pros Incorporated..........D.......661 589-5400
3400 Patton Way Bakersfield (93308) ***(P-1076)***
Proscape Landscape, Signal Hill *Also called Fenderscape Inc* ***(P-841)***
Prosciento Inc..........C.......619 427-1300
855 Third Ave Ste 3340 Chula Vista (91911) ***(P-26441)***
Proskauer Rose LLP..........D.......310 557-2900
2049 Century Park E # 3200 Los Angeles (90067) ***(P-23342)***
Prosoft Technology Inc (HQ)..........D.......661 716-5100
9201 Camino Media Ste 200 Bakersfield (93311) ***(P-5992)***
Prospance Inc (PA)..........D.......925 415-2394
4221 Bus Ctr Dr Ste 1 Fremont (94538) ***(P-15384)***
Prospect Enterprises Inc (PA)..........C.......213 599-5700
625 Kohler St Los Angeles (90021) ***(P-8596)***
Prospect Medical Group Inc (HQ)..........B.......714 796-5900
1920 E 17th St Ste 200 Santa Ana (92705) ***(P-27001)***
Prospect Medical Holdings Inc (PA)..........D.......310 943-4500
3415 S Sepulveda Blvd # 9 Los Angeles (90034) ***(P-19799)***
Prospect Medical Systems Inc (HQ)..........C.......714 667-8156
600 City Pkwy W Ste 800 Orange (92868) ***(P-27002)***
Prosper Funding LLC..........C.......415 593-5400
101 2nd St Fl 15 San Francisco (94105) ***(P-9746)***
Prosper Marketplace Inc (PA)..........D.......415 593-5400
221 Main St Fl 3 San Francisco (94105) ***(P-9904)***
Prostavar Rx, Los Angeles *Also called Superbalife International LLC* ***(P-8213)***
Prosum Inc (PA)..........D.......310 404-1545
2201 Park Pl Ste 102 El Segundo (90245) ***(P-16168)***
Prosum Technology Services, El Segundo *Also called Prosum Inc* ***(P-16168)***
Protec Association Services (PA)..........C.......858 569-1080
10180 Willow Creek Rd San Diego (92131) ***(P-14360)***
Protec Building Services, San Diego *Also called Protec Association Services* ***(P-14360)***
Protech Construction, Anaheim *Also called Paglia & Associates Cnstr* ***(P-1213)***
Protect-For-Less Security Svcs..........E.......760 343-1192
72877 Dinah Shore Dr Rancho Mirage (92270) ***(P-16929)***
Protect-US..........C.......714 721-8127
12397 Lewis St Ste 202 Garden Grove (92840) ***(P-16766)***
Protected Outcomes Corporation..........D.......203 545-9565
9663 Santa Monica Blvd Beverly Hills (90210) ***(P-16767)***
Protection Specialists..........B.......818 503-1306
6841 Whitsett Ave Apt 104 North Hollywood (91605) ***(P-16768)***
Protege Builders Inc..........E.......916 825-8478
4306 Pinell St Sacramento (95838) ***(P-3062)***
Prothena Biosciences Inc..........E.......650 837-8550
331 Oyster Point Blvd South San Francisco (94080) ***(P-26650)***
Protiviti Inc..........D.......415 402-3663
2613 Camino Ramon San Ramon (94583) ***(P-27407)***
Protiviti Inc (HQ)..........D.......650 234-6000
2884 Sand Hill Rd Ste 200 Menlo Park (94025) ***(P-27408)***
Protiviti Inc..........D.......213 327-1400
400 S Hope St Ste 900 Los Angeles (90071) ***(P-27409)***
Protosource Corporation..........D.......559 490-8600
2511 W Shaw Ave Ste 102 Fresno (93711) ***(P-16169)***
Prototypes Centers For Innov..........C.......213 542-3838
1000 N Alameda St Ste 390 Los Angeles (90012) ***(P-23978)***
Prototypes Women's Center, Pomona *Also called Healthright 360* ***(P-23833)***
Protravel International LLC..........D.......310 271-9566
9171 Wilshire Blvd # 428 Beverly Hills (90210) ***(P-4950)***
Proven Solutions Inc..........D.......310 933-4544
11150 Santa Monica Blvd # 1060 Los Angeles (90025) ***(P-14706)***
Providence Health & Services F..........A.......818 843-5111
501 S Buena Vista St Burbank (91505) ***(P-21665)***
Providence Health & Services S..........D.......310 832-3311
1300 W 7th St San Pedro (90732) ***(P-21666)***
Providence Health & Svcs - Ore..........B.......510 444-0839
540 23rd St Oakland (94612) ***(P-21667)***
Providence Health & Svcs - Ore..........B.......818 365-8051
15031 Rinaldi St Mission Hills (91345) ***(P-21668)***
Providence Health System..........A.......818 898-4530
15031 Rinaldi St Mission Hills (91345) ***(P-19800)***
Providence Health System..........A.......818 898-4561
15031 Rinaldi St Mission Hills (91345) ***(P-21669)***
Providence Health System..........A.......310 376-9474
20929 Hawthorne Blvd Torrance (90503) ***(P-19801)***
Providence Health System..........A.......310 832-3311
1300 W 7th St San Pedro (90732) ***(P-21670)***
Providence Health System..........A.......818 843-5111
501 S Buena Vista St Burbank (91505) ***(P-21671)***
Providence Health System..........D.......310 514-5270
1322 W 6th St San Pedro (90732) ***(P-21672)***
Providence Health System..........C.......310 543-5900
4320 Maricopa St Torrance (90503) ***(P-12122)***
Providence Health System..........C.......310 370-5895
3551 Voyager St Ste 201 Torrance (90503) ***(P-12123)***
Providence Health System..........C.......818 846-8141
511 S Buena Vista St Burbank (91505) ***(P-12124)***
Providence Health System..........A.......310 530-3800
2601 Airport Dr Ste 230 Torrance (90505) ***(P-21673)***
Providence Health System..........C.......310 370-5895
4101 Torrance Blvd Torrance (90503) ***(P-22398)***

Mergent e-mail: customerrelations@mergent.com
1430
2019 Directory of California
Wholesalers and Services Companies
(P-0000) Products & Services Section entry number
(PA)=Parent Co (HQ)=Headquarters (DH)=Div Headquarters

Providence Health System............C......310 303-6970
4101 Torrance Blvd Torrance (90503) ***(P-27003)***
Providence Holy Cross (PA)............D......818 365-8051
15031 Rinaldi St Mission Hills (91345) ***(P-21674)***
Providence Holy Cross Med Ctr, Mission Hills *Also called Providence Health System* ***(P-21669)***
Providence Holy Cross Med Ctr, Mission Hills *Also called Providence Health & Svcs - Ore* ***(P-21668)***
Providence Little Company of M, San Pedro *Also called Providence Health & Services S* ***(P-21666)***
Providence Seminars Inc............D......760 827-2100
6349 Palomar Oaks Ct Carlsbad (92011) ***(P-27410)***
Providence Service Corporation............E......661 765-7025
1021 4th St Taft (93268) ***(P-22655)***
Providence Speech Hearing Ctr............E......714 639-4990
1301 W Providence Ave Orange (92868) ***(P-22656)***
Providence St Johns Hlth Ctr............B......310 829-6562
2121 Santa Monica Blvd Santa Monica (90404) ***(P-21675)***
Providence St Joseph Med Ctr, Burbank *Also called Therapeutic Associates Inc* ***(P-22055)***
Providence Tarzana Medical Ctr............A......818 881-0800
18321 Clark St Tarzana (91356) ***(P-21676)***
Provident Bank, Riverside *Also called Provident Savings Bank LLC* ***(P-9480)***
Provident Bank, Riverside *Also called Provident Savings Bank* ***(P-9530)***
Provident Credit Union (PA)............C......650 508-0300
303 Twin Dolphin Dr # 303 Redwood City (94065) ***(P-9645)***
Provident Financial Management............D......310 282-0477
3130 Wilshire Blvd # 600 Santa Monica (90403) ***(P-27004)***
Provident Fincl Holdings Inc............D......916 709-3257
9245 Laguna Springs Dr # 13 Elk Grove (95758) ***(P-9848)***
Provident Funding Assoc LP (PA)............E......650 652-1300
851 Traeger Ave Ste 100 San Bruno (94066) ***(P-9849)***
Provident Group Crown Pnte LLC............D......951 737-7482
737 Magnolia Ave Ofc Corona (92879) ***(P-11100)***
Provident Mrtg Cpitl Assoc Inc............A......650 652-1300
1633 Bayshore Hwy Ste 155 Burlingame (94010) ***(P-9850)***
Provident Savings Bank (HQ)............D......951 782-6177
6570 Magnolia Ave Riverside (92506) ***(P-9529)***
Provident Savings Bank............D......951 686-6060
6674 Brockton Ave Riverside (92506) ***(P-9530)***
Provident Savings Bank............E......909 484-6286
10370 Commerce Center Dr # 200 Rancho Cucamonga (91730) ***(P-9851)***
Provident Savings Bank LLC............D......951 686-6060
3756 Central Ave Riverside (92506) ***(P-9480)***
Providian Leasing, Diamond Bar *Also called Providian Staffing Corporation* ***(P-14707)***
Providian Staffing Corporation (PA)............A......909 598-9099
1249 S Diamond Bar Blvd Diamond Bar (91765) ***(P-14707)***
Providnce All STS Subacute LLC............D......510 481-3200
1652 Mono Ave San Leandro (94578) ***(P-20712)***
Providnce Holy Cross Fundation, Burbank *Also called Providence Health & Services F* ***(P-21665)***
Proview Advanced Solutions Inc............D......949 752-2484
130 Theory Ste 200 Irvine (92617) ***(P-10745)***
Provoast Automation Controls (PA)............D......858 748-2237
12635 Danielson Ct # 205 Poway (92064) ***(P-7788)***
Prowall Lath and Plaster............D......760 480-9001
360 S Spruce St Escondido (92025) ***(P-2943)***
Proxim Wireless Corporation............C......408 383-7600
2114 Ringwood Ave San Jose (95131) ***(P-26557)***
Prs/Roebbelen JV............E......916 641-0324
4811 Tunis Rd Sacramento (95835) ***(P-1620)***
Prsi, Jurupa Valley *Also called Pavement Recycling Systems Inc* ***(P-7986)***
Prudential, Encino *Also called Burkshire Has A Way Home Servc* ***(P-11253)***
Prudential, Pleasanton *Also called McM Partners Inc* ***(P-11598)***
Prudential, San Diego *Also called Joe Canpagna* ***(P-11532)***
Prudential, San Luis Obispo *Also called Pickford Realty Inc* ***(P-11669)***
Prudential, Thousand Oaks *Also called Gemmm Corp* ***(P-11479)***
Prudential, Berkeley *Also called Mason-Mcduffie Real Estate Inc* ***(P-11588)***
Prudential, Walnut Creek *Also called Mason-Mcduffie Real Estate Inc* ***(P-11589)***
Prudential, Santa Maria *Also called Hunter Realty Inc* ***(P-11507)***
Prudential, Chula Vista *Also called Coronado Financial Corp* ***(P-11385)***
Prudential, Antioch *Also called Mason-Mcduffie Real Estate Inc* ***(P-11590)***
Prudential, Rancho Cucamonga *Also called Empire Estates Inc* ***(P-11419)***
Prudential, Valencia *Also called Nutec Enterprises Inc* ***(P-11639)***
Prudential 24 Hour Real Estate............D......562 861-7257
8635 Florence Ave Ste 101 Downey (90240) ***(P-11690)***
Prudential CA Realty............D......510 487-6088
39275 Mssion Blvd Ste 103 Fremont (94539) ***(P-11691)***
Prudential California Realty............E......818 993-8900
9003 Reseda Blvd Ste 105 Northridge (91324) ***(P-11692)***
Prudential California Realty............D......415 664-9400
677 Portola Dr San Francisco (94127) ***(P-11693)***
Prudential California Realty............D......858 487-3520
976 Main St Ste A Ramona (92065) ***(P-11694)***
Prudential Cleanroom Services, Milpitas *Also called Prudential Overall Supply* ***(P-13616)***
Prudential Cleanroom Services, Commerce *Also called Prudential Overall Supply* ***(P-13617)***
Prudential Dust Control, Riverside *Also called Prudential Overall Supply* ***(P-13614)***
Prudential Insur Co of Amer............E......949 440-5300
3333 Michelson Dr Ste 820 Irvine (92612) ***(P-10746)***
Prudential Insur Co of Amer............D......415 398-7310
4 Embarcadero Ctr # 2700 San Francisco (94111) ***(P-10747)***
Prudential Insur Co of Amer............E......818 990-2122
15303 Ventura Blvd # 1550 Sherman Oaks (91403) ***(P-10748)***
Prudential Insur Co of Amer............D......415 486-3050
180 Montgomery St # 1900 San Francisco (94104) ***(P-10303)***
Prudential Insur Co of Amer............D......818 901-0028
5990 Sepulvda Blvd # 300 Van Nuys (91411) ***(P-10749)***
Prudential Malibu Realty, Malibu *Also called Terra Coastal Properties Inc* ***(P-11790)***
Prudential Norcal Realty, Carmichael *Also called Diez & Leis RE Group Inc* ***(P-11400)***
Prudential Overall Supply............D......323 724-4888
6920 Bandini Blvd Commerce (90040) ***(P-13612)***
Prudential Overall Supply (PA)............D......949 250-4855
1661 Alton Pkwy Irvine (92606) ***(P-13613)***
Prudential Overall Supply............C......951 687-0440
6997 Jurupa Ave Riverside (92504) ***(P-13614)***
Prudential Overall Supply............D......760 727-7163
2485 Ash St Vista (92081) ***(P-13615)***
Prudential Overall Supply............D......408 719-0886
1437 N Milpitas Blvd Milpitas (95035) ***(P-13616)***
Prudential Overall Supply............D......323 722-0636
6948 Bandini Blvd Commerce (90040) ***(P-13617)***
Prudential Overall Supply............D......559 264-8231
1260 E North Ave Fresno (93725) ***(P-13618)***
Prudential Overall Supply............D......805 529-0833
5300 Gabbert Rd Moorpark (93021) ***(P-13550)***
Prudential RE Affiliates Inc, Irvine *Also called Brer Affiliates LLC* ***(P-12134)***
Prudential Realty Corp............D......415 566-9800
1430 Taraval St San Francisco (94116) ***(P-11695)***
Prudential Security Services, Los Angeles *Also called Eastside Group Corporation* ***(P-16636)***
Pruitthealth Inc............E......626 810-5567
1982 Camwood Ave City of Industry (91748) ***(P-21190)***
Prutel Joint Venture............A......949 240-2000
1 Ritz Carlton Dr Dana Point (92629) ***(P-13082)***
PS Arts............E......310 586-1017
6701 Center Dr W Ste 550 Los Angeles (90045) ***(P-27829)***
PS Business Parks Inc (PA)............D......818 244-8080
701 Western Ave Glendale (91201) ***(P-12184)***
PS Business Parks LP............D......818 244-8080
701 Western Ave Glendale (91201) ***(P-11696)***
PS Development Corporation............D......818 340-0965
21625 Prairie St Chatsworth (91311) ***(P-2688)***
PS Environmental Svcs Inc............D......310 373-6259
23775 Madison St Torrance (90505) ***(P-17417)***
PS National Inc............B......818 366-1300
17645 Chatsworth St Granada Hills (91344) ***(P-14708)***
PS Partners III Ltd............C......818 244-8080
701 Western Ave Ste 200 Glendale (91201) ***(P-4614)***
Ps2 (PA)............D......310 243-2980
17903 S Hobart Blvd Gardena (90248) ***(P-2467)***
Ps24 Inc............D......415 834-5105
65 Division St San Francisco (94103) ***(P-27005)***
Psav, Cerritos *Also called Audio Visual Headquarters* ***(P-14474)***
Psav Holdings LLC............A......562 366-0138
111 W Ocean Blvd Ste 1110 Long Beach (90802) ***(P-14537)***
PSC Industrial Outsourcing LP............C......310 325-1600
19340 Van Ness Ave Torrance (90501) ***(P-17975)***
PSC Industrial Outsourcing LP............D......562 997-6000
1661 E 32nd St Long Beach (90807) ***(P-6431)***
PSC Industrial Outsourcing LP............D......831 635-0220
5780 Obata Way Ste A Gilroy (95020) ***(P-6545)***
PSC Industrial Outsourcing LP............D......831 627-2595
62117 Railroad Ave San Ardo (93450) ***(P-4051)***
PSG Fencing Corporation (PA)............C......831 726-2002
6630 Monterey Rd Gilroy (95020) ***(P-3570)***
PSI Fire............E......408 842-9308
820 Eschenburg Dr Gilroy (95020) ***(P-15385)***
Psi3g Inc............D......916 803-2879
2979 Promenade St Ste 100 West Sacramento (95691) ***(P-6783)***
Psinapse Technology Ltd............D......925 225-0400
1063 Serpentine Ln Ste A Pleasanton (94566) ***(P-14709)***
Pslq Inc............D......951 795-4260
28910 Rancho California R Temecula (92590) ***(P-1309)***
Psomas............C......714 751-7373
3 Hutton Cntre Dr Ste 200 Santa Ana (92707) ***(P-26132)***
Psomas............E......760 843-5700
14369 Park Ave Ste 101b Victorville (92392) ***(P-26133)***
Psomas (PA)............C......213 223-1400
555 S Flower St Ste 4300 Los Angeles (90071) ***(P-26134)***
Psomas............C......916 788-8122
1075 Crkside Rdg Dr # 200 Roseville (95678) ***(P-25879)***
Psychemedics Corporation............D......310 216-7776
5832 Uplander Way Culver City (90230) ***(P-26728)***
Psychiatric Ctrs At San Diego (PA)............D......619 528-4600
4542 Ruffner St Ste 200 San Diego (92111) ***(P-19802)***
Psychiatric Health Facility, Placerville *Also called County of El Dorado* ***(P-21942)***
Psychiatric Solutions Inc............C......626 286-1191
4619 Rosemead Blvd Rosemead (91770) ***(P-22657)***
Psychiatric Solutions Inc............C......916 288-0300
8001 Bruceville Rd Sacramento (95823) ***(P-19803)***
Psychiatric Solutions Inc............C......916 489-3336
4250 Auburn Blvd Sacramento (95841) ***(P-21969)***
Psychiatric Solutions Inc............C......510 796-1100
39001 Sundale Dr Fremont (94538) ***(P-19804)***
Psychiatric Solutions Inc............C......951 789-4405
17241 Van Buren Blvd Riverside (92504) ***(P-19805)***
Psynergy Programs Inc............D......408 776-0422
18225 Hale Ave Morgan Hill (95037) ***(P-24639)***
Pszyjw, Los Angeles *Also called Pachulski Stang Zehl Jones LLP* ***(P-23306)***
Pt Gaming LLC............A......323 260-5060
235 Oregon St El Segundo (90245) ***(P-13083)***
Pt Logistics Inc............E......831 728-4535
144 W Lake Ave Ste B Watsonville (95076) ***(P-4052)***
Pta CA Cngrss of Parnts Tchrs............D......714 836-2700
3030 N Hesperian St Santa Ana (92706) ***(P-25218)***
Pta CA Congress of Parents............E......818 340-6700
5014 Serrania Ave Woodland Hills (91364) ***(P-25219)***

ALPHABETIC

Pta California Cong P A S Elem..........E.......925 606-4700
5280 Irene Way Livermore (94550) ***(P-25220)***
Pta California Congress of Par..........D.......310 328-3100
21514 Halldale Ave Torrance (90501) ***(P-25221)***
Ptac Carmel Valley Mid School..........D.......858 481-8221
3800 Mykonos Ln San Diego (92130) ***(P-25222)***
Ptac Rail Ranch Elem School..........D.......951 696-1404
25030 Via Santee Murrieta (92563) ***(P-25223)***
Pti, Chatsworth *Also called Printing Technology Inc* ***(P-7865)***
Pti Solutions, Roseville *Also called Pinnacle Telecom Inc* ***(P-16032)***
Ptr Group Inc..........E.......951 965-1822
652 S Joyce Ave Rialto (92376) ***(P-27006)***
Pts Staffing Solutions..........C.......949 268-4000
2860 Michelle Ste 150 Irvine (92606) ***(P-14710)***
Ptsi Managed Services Inc..........D.......626 440-3118
100 W Walnut St Pasadena (91124) ***(P-25880)***
Pub Works/Community Dev, Santa Barbara *Also called Santa Barbara City of* ***(P-17456)***
Public Bell Inc..........D.......818 396-1675
11277 Garden Grove Blvd # 200 Garden Grove (92843) ***(P-15386)***
Public Communications Svcs Inc..........C.......310 231-1000
11859 Wilshire Blvd # 600 Los Angeles (90025) ***(P-5631)***
Public Consulting Group Inc..........D.......916 565-8090
2150 River Plaza Dr # 380 Sacramento (95833) ***(P-27411)***
Public Counsel..........D.......213 385-2977
610 S Ardmore Ave Los Angeles (90005) ***(P-23343)***
Public Defender, Fullerton *Also called County of Orange* ***(P-23004)***
Public Defender, Compton *Also called County of Los Angeles* ***(P-23001)***
Public Defender Administration, Los Angeles *Also called County of Los Angeles* ***(P-23000)***
Public Defender's Office, Fresno *Also called County of Fresno* ***(P-22995)***
Public Defender's Office, Sacramento *Also called County of Sacramento* ***(P-23006)***
Public Defender- Main Office, Riverside *Also called County of Riverside* ***(P-23005)***
Public Defenders Office, Los Angeles *Also called County of Los Angeles* ***(P-22997)***
Public Employees Retirement..........B.......916 795-3400
400 Q St Sacramento (95811) ***(P-10492)***
Public Health California Dept..........C.......213 620-6160
320 W 4th St Ste 830 Los Angeles (90013) ***(P-19806)***
Public Health California Dept..........C.......661 835-4668
2400 Wible Rd Ste 14 Bakersfield (93304) ***(P-19807)***
Public Health California Dept..........C.......510 412-1502
850 Marina Bay Pkwy F175 Richmond (94804) ***(P-19808)***
Public Health Department, El Centro *Also called County of Imperial* ***(P-22771)***
Public Health Dept, Santa Barbara *Also called Santa Barbara County of* ***(P-22880)***
Public Health Dept, San Jose *Also called Santa Clara County of* ***(P-19853)***
Public Health Di, Lakeport *Also called County Lake Health Services* ***(P-25013)***
Public Health Institute (PA)..........A.......510 285-5500
555 12th St Ste 1050 Oakland (94607) ***(P-26651)***
Public Health Nursing Service, Sacramento *Also called County of Sacramento* ***(P-20333)***
Public Hlth Fndation Entps Inc..........C.......626 856-6600
12781 Schabarum Ave Irwindale (91706) ***(P-22863)***
Public Hlth Fndation Entps Inc..........C.......562 801-2323
8666 Whittier Blvd Pico Rivera (90660) ***(P-22864)***
Public Hlth Fndation Entps Inc..........C.......323 263-0262
277 S Atlantic Blvd Los Angeles (90022) ***(P-25224)***
Public Hlth Fndation Entps Inc..........C.......323 733-9381
1649 W Washington Blvd Los Angeles (90007) ***(P-22865)***
Public Hlth Fndation Entps Inc..........C.......310 320-5215
1640 W Carson St Ste G Torrance (90501) ***(P-25225)***
Public Hlth Fndation Entps Inc..........C.......626 856-6618
12781 Shama Rd El Monte (91732) ***(P-22866)***
Public Hlth Fndation Entps Inc (PA)..........A.......800 201-7320
13300 Crssrds Pkwy N City of Industry (91746) ***(P-25226)***
Public Investment Corporation..........C.......310 451-5227
4340 Eucalyptus Ave Chino (91710) ***(P-11908)***
Public Policy Institute Cal (PA)..........D.......415 291-4400
500 Washington St Ste 600 San Francisco (94111) ***(P-24975)***
Public Security Inc..........E.......323 293-9884
3860 Crenshaw Blvd # 223 Los Angeles (90008) ***(P-16769)***
Public Service Yard, Glendale *Also called City of Glendale* ***(P-6223)***
Public Services, Coronado *Also called City of Coronado* ***(P-6182)***
Public Social Service, Norco *Also called County of Riverside* ***(P-23706)***
Public Social Services, Moreno Valley *Also called County of Riverside* ***(P-19419)***
Public Social Services, Lake Elsinore *Also called County of Riverside* ***(P-23708)***
Public Social Services, Lake Elsinore *Also called County of Riverside* ***(P-23711)***
Public Social Services, Los Angeles *Also called County of Los Angeles* ***(P-23671)***
Public Social Services, Canyon Country *Also called County of Los Angeles* ***(P-10483)***
Public Social Services, Norwalk *Also called County of Los Angeles* ***(P-23679)***
Public Storage (PA)..........C.......818 244-8080
701 Western Ave Glendale (91201) ***(P-12185)***
Public Storage Prpts IV Ltd..........D.......818 244-8080
701 Western Ave Glendale (91201) ***(P-4615)***
Public Storage Prpts Xviii Inc..........D.......818 244-8080
701 Western Ave Ste 200 Glendale (91201) ***(P-4616)***
Public Work Dept, Burlingame *Also called Street and Sewer Yard Corp* ***(P-6331)***
Public Works, Imperial *Also called County of Imperial* ***(P-1749)***
Public Works, Corona *Also called City of Corona* ***(P-6196)***
Public Works and Highway Dept, Burlingame *Also called City of Burlingame* ***(P-1739)***
Public Works Department, Morgan Hill *Also called City of Morgan Hill* ***(P-27686)***
Public Works Department, Woodland *Also called City of Woodland* ***(P-27582)***
Public Works Department, Woodland *Also called City of Woodland* ***(P-25616)***
Public Works Dept, Los Angeles *Also called City of Los Angeles* ***(P-25612)***
Public Works Dept, Hayward *Also called City of Alameda* ***(P-1746)***
Public Works Dept, Auburn *Also called County of Placer* ***(P-25629)***
Public Works Dept, Palmdale *Also called City of Palmdale* ***(P-14211)***
Public Works Engineering Div, Daly City *Also called City of Daly City* ***(P-25610)***
Public Works Office, Vacaville *Also called City of Vacaville* ***(P-25615)***
Public Works Operations, Modesto *Also called County of Stanislaus* ***(P-6534)***
Public Works Superintendent, Alameda *Also called Maintenance Service For The Cy* ***(P-14310)***
Public Works, Dept of, Palmdale *Also called County of Los Angeles* ***(P-1750)***
Public Works, Dept of, Los Angeles *Also called County of Los Angeles* ***(P-1751)***
Publis Works, Lomita *Also called City of Lomita* ***(P-6224)***
Pubmatic Inc (PA)..........D.......650 351-9162
305 Main St Fl 1 Redwood City (94063) ***(P-13883)***
Puente Hills Landfill, Whittier *Also called County Santtn Dist 2 of La Co* ***(P-6386)***
Pullan Enterprises, Anaheim *Also called Rapid Plumbing Inc* ***(P-2329)***
Pulmonary Medicine Assoc..........D.......916 733-5040
2801 K St Ste 500 Sacramento (95816) ***(P-19809)***
Pulp Studio Incorporated (PA)..........D.......310 815-4999
2100 W 139th St Gardena (90249) ***(P-14127)***
Pulse Secure LLC (HQ)..........D.......408 372-9600
2700 Zanker Rd Ste 200 San Jose (95134) ***(P-15387)***
Pulse-Link Inc..........D.......760 448-4690
2730 Loker Ave W Carlsbad (92010) ***(P-26442)***
Pulte Home Company LLC..........D.......925 249-3200
6210 Stoneridge Mall Rd Pleasanton (94588) ***(P-1219)***
Punch Studio LLC (PA)..........C.......310 390-9900
6025 W Slauson Ave Culver City (90230) ***(P-8087)***
Punctus Temporis Translations..........E.......510 309-0888
5201 Great America Pkwy Santa Clara (95054) ***(P-17418)***
Pupil Transportation, Whittier *Also called County of Los Angeles* ***(P-3912)***
Puratos Bakery Supply, Rancho Cucamonga *Also called Puratos Corporation* ***(P-4490)***
Puratos Corporation..........D.......909 484-1312
11167 White Birch Dr Rancho Cucamonga (91730) ***(P-4490)***
Purcell-Murray Company Inc (PA)..........D.......415 468-6620
999 Skyway Rd Ste 100 San Carlos (94070) ***(P-7633)***
Purchasing & Warehouse, Bakersfield *Also called Panama-Buena Vista Un Schl Dst* ***(P-4605)***
Purchasing Department, Redlands *Also called City of Redlands* ***(P-6377)***
Purchasing Department, Ventura *Also called Community Mem HSP/Sn Benua* ***(P-21340)***
Pure Beauty-A Freeman Company, Union City *Also called Purebeauty Inc* ***(P-7894)***
Pure Luxury Limousine Service..........C.......800 626-5466
4246 Petaluma Blvd N Petaluma (94952) ***(P-3833)***
Pure Luxury Worldwide Trnsp, Petaluma *Also called Pure Luxury Limousine Service* ***(P-3833)***
Purebeauty Inc..........E.......510 477-7950
32920 Alvarado Niles Rd # 220 Union City (94587) ***(P-7894)***
Puregear, Irwindale *Also called Superior Communications Inc* ***(P-7548)***
Purolator International Inc..........D.......650 871-7075
775 W Manville St Compton (90220) ***(P-5150)***
Puronics Retail Services Inc..........D.......925 456-7000
5775 Las Positas Rd Livermore (94551) ***(P-2321)***
Puronics Water Systems Inc..........D.......925 456-7000
5775 Las Positas Rd Livermore (94551) ***(P-7634)***
Purosil Division, Santa Fe Springs *Also called MCP Industries Inc* ***(P-8931)***
Purple Language Services Co..........C.......916 435-8216
595 Menlo Dr Rocklin (95765) ***(P-18100)***
Puttin On Productions Corp..........E.......310 546-5544
2010 N Sepulveda Blvd A Manhattan Beach (90266) ***(P-18101)***
Pvcc Inc (PA)..........D.......619 463-4040
8100 La Mesa Blvd Ste 101 La Mesa (91942) ***(P-10929)***
Pvhmc, Pomona *Also called Pomona Valley Hospital Med Ctr* ***(P-21652)***
PW Gillibrand Co Inc..........D.......805 526-2195
4537 Ish Dr Simi Valley (93063) ***(P-1098)***
Pw Jade LLC..........D.......707 843-5192
1825 4th St Santa Rosa (95404) ***(P-22399)***
PW Stephens Envmtl Inc (PA)..........D.......714 892-2028
15201 Pipeline Ln Ste B Huntington Beach (92649) ***(P-3571)***
PW Stephens Envmtl Inc..........D.......510 651-9506
4047 Clipper Ct Fremont (94538) ***(P-3572)***
PWC STRategy& (us) LLC..........C.......415 498-5000
3 Embarcadero Ctr Fl 20 San Francisco (94111) ***(P-27412)***
Pws Inc (PA)..........D.......323 721-8832
12020 Garfield Ave South Gate (90280) ***(P-7895)***
PWS Holdings LLC..........C.......323 721-8832
6500 Flotilla St Commerce (90040) ***(P-7896)***
Pyj V A California Ltd Partnr..........D.......805 495-8437
4812 Lakeview Canyon Rd Westlake Village (91361) ***(P-18748)***
Pyramid Advisors LLC..........D.......925 847-6000
11950 Dublin Canyon Rd Pleasanton (94588) ***(P-13084)***
Pyramid Alternatives Inc (PA)..........E.......650 355-8787
480 Manor Pl Pacifica (94044) ***(P-22658)***
Pyramid Enterprises Inc (PA)..........D.......661 702-1420
28368 Constellation Rd # 380 Valencia (91355) ***(P-19219)***
Pyramid Flowers Inc..........C.......805 382-8070
3813 Doris Ave Oxnard (93030) ***(P-293)***
Pyramid Logistics Services Inc (PA)..........D.......714 903-2600
14650 Hoover St Westminster (92683) ***(P-4247)***
Pyramid Painting Inc..........E.......650 903-9791
2925 Bayview Dr Fremont (94538) ***(P-2468)***
Pyramid Peak Corporation..........D.......949 769-8600
450 Nwport Ctr Dr Ste 650 Newport Beach (92660) ***(P-12261)***
Pyramid Produce Inc..........C.......661 366-5736
12826 Edison Hwy Bakersfield (93307) ***(P-667)***
Pyro-Comm Systems Inc (PA)..........C.......714 902-8000
15531 Container Ln Huntington Beach (92649) ***(P-2689)***
Q Analysts LLC (PA)..........D.......408 907-8500
4320 Stevens Creek Blvd # 130 San Jose (95129) ***(P-27413)***
Q B C, Los Angeles *Also called Qualified Blling Cllctions LLC* ***(P-14020)***
Q L P Inc..........E.......805 579-0440
2285 Ward Ave Simi Valley (93065) ***(P-7387)***

Mergent e-mail: customerrelations@mergent.com
1432
2019 Directory of California
Wholesalers and Services Companies
(P-0000) Products & Services Section entry number
(PA)=Parent Co (HQ)=Headquarters (DH)=Div Headquarters

Q S H Properties Inc...D.......714 957-9200
2701 Hotel Ter Santa Ana (92705) ***(P-13085)***
Q S I, South San Francisco *Also called Quality Systems Installations* ***(P-3573)***
Q S San Luis Obispo LP...E.......805 541-5001
1631 Monterey St San Luis Obispo (93401) ***(P-13086)***
Qad Inc (PA)...C.......805 566-6000
100 Innovation Pl Santa Barbara (93108) ***(P-15836)***
Qal Affiliate Inc...E.......408 238-5111
2680 S White Rd Ste 150 San Jose (95148) ***(P-11697)***
Qantas Vctons Nwmans Vacations, Los Angeles *Also called Helloworld Travel Svcs USA Inc* ***(P-4938)***
Qbe First Insurance Agency Inc...B.......949 206-6200
9800 Muirlands Blvd Irvine (92618) ***(P-10750)***
Qbi LLC (PA)...D.......818 594-4900
21031 Ventura Blvd # 1200 Woodland Hills (91364) ***(P-26279)***
Qc Wall Systems, Rancho Murieta *Also called Energy Store of California Inc* ***(P-2201)***
Qcommission, San Mateo *Also called Cellarstone Inc* ***(P-16324)***
Qct LLC...A.......510 270-6111
1010 Rincon Cir San Jose (95131) ***(P-16036)***
Qlm Consulting Inc...E.......415 331-9292
2400 Bridgeway Ste 290 Sausalito (94965) ***(P-27414)***
Qmadix Inc...D.......818 988-4300
14350 Arminta St Panorama City (91402) ***(P-7527)***
Qng Inc...D.......480 330-3804
2809 Whipple Rd Union City (94587) ***(P-7528)***
Qre Operating LLC...C.......213 225-5900
707 Wilshire Blvd # 4600 Los Angeles (90017) ***(P-1046)***
Qsolv Inc...C.......408 429-0918
440 N Wolfe Rd Ste 26 Sunnyvale (94085) ***(P-16037)***
Qtc Management Inc (HQ)...C.......800 260-1515
924 Overland Ct San Dimas (91773) ***(P-22867)***
Qtc Mdcal Group Inc A Med Corp...A.......800 260-1515
21700 Copley Dr Ste 200 Diamond Bar (91765) ***(P-22868)***
Quad Knopf Inc (PA)...E.......559 733-0440
901 E Main St Visalia (93292) ***(P-25881)***
Quad/Graphics Inc...C.......916 371-9500
1201 Shore St West Sacramento (95691) ***(P-13884)***
Quadion LLC...A.......714 546-0994
17651 Armstrong Ave Irvine (92614) ***(P-10107)***
Quadra Productions Inc...C.......310 244-1234
10202 Washington Blvd Culver City (90232) ***(P-18102)***
Quadramed Corporation...A.......951 736-6290
800 S Main St Corona (92882) ***(P-14019)***
Quadrant Components Inc...D.......510 656-9988
46567 Fremont Blvd Fremont (94538) ***(P-7096)***
Quadriga Inc...D.......650 270-6326
555 Clfornia Ave Ste 4925 San Francisco (94104) ***(P-15388)***
Quadrix Information Tech Inc...E.......424 603-2140
10736 Jefferson Blvd # 132 Culver City (90230) ***(P-27830)***
Quadrixit, Culver City *Also called Quadrix Information Tech Inc* ***(P-27830)***
Quail Engineering Inc...E.......714 636-0612
11372 Trask Ave Ste 110 Garden Grove (92843) ***(P-1839)***
Quail H Farms LLC...A.......209 394-8001
5301 Robin Ave Livingston (95334) ***(P-28)***
Quail Hill Investments Inc...C.......408 978-9000
1124 Meridian Ave San Jose (95125) ***(P-12186)***
Quail Lodge Inc...C.......831 624-1581
8205 Valley Greens Dr Carmel (93923) ***(P-13087)***
Quail Park Retirement Village...D.......559 624-3500
4520 W Cypress Ave Visalia (93277) ***(P-20948)***
Quail Ridge Senior Living, Grass Valley *Also called Grass Valley LLC* ***(P-24543)***
Quails Inn Motel, San Marcos *Also called San Marcos Caterers Inc* ***(P-13179)***
Quailty Inn of Barstow, Barstow *Also called Darensburg Roghair & Renier* ***(P-12512)***
Quake City Caps, Los Angeles *Also called Quake City Casuals Inc* ***(P-8275)***
Quake City Casuals Inc...C.......213 746-0540
1800 S Flower St Los Angeles (90015) ***(P-8275)***
Quakehold, Vista *Also called Ready America Inc* ***(P-8052)***
QUAKER GARDENS, Stanton *Also called California Friends Homes* ***(P-24448)***
Quaker Oats Company...E.......714 526-8800
2501 E Orangethorpe Ave Fullerton (92831) ***(P-4617)***
Quaker Pet Group Inc...D.......415 721-7400
160 Mitchell Blvd San Rafael (94903) ***(P-9253)***
Qualcomm International Inc (HQ)...A.......858 587-1121
5775 Morehouse Dr San Diego (92121) ***(P-12140)***
Qualfax Inc...D.......562 988-1272
3605 Long Beach Blvd # 428 Long Beach (90807) ***(P-17419)***
Qualia Collection Services, Petaluma *Also called Optio Solutions LLC* ***(P-14014)***
Qualified Benefits, Woodland Hills *Also called Qbi LLC* ***(P-26279)***
Qualified Benefits Inc...E.......818 594-4900
21021 Ventura Blvd # 100 Woodland Hills (91364) ***(P-10751)***
Qualified Blling Cllctions LLC...C.......323 556-3470
4601 Wilshire Blvd Fl 3 Los Angeles (90010) ***(P-14020)***
Quality Auto Craft Inc...A.......925 426-0120
3295 Bernal Ave Ste B Pleasanton (94566) ***(P-17779)***
Quality Carriers Inc...D.......800 282-2031
5042 Cecelia St South Gate (90280) ***(P-4248)***
Quality Childrens Services (PA)...C.......760 942-3433
6108 Innovation Way Carlsbad (92009) ***(P-24374)***
Quality Claims Management Corp...D.......619 450-8600
2763 Camino Del Rio S San Diego (92108) ***(P-10752)***
Quality Coast Incorporated...E.......619 443-9192
2462 Main St Ste H Chula Vista (91911) ***(P-14361)***
Quality Construction, Tarzana *Also called Zohar Construction Inc* ***(P-1262)***
Quality Electrical Services, Costa Mesa *Also called Edward Straling* ***(P-2569)***
Quality Group Homes Inc...C.......916 930-0066
250 Dos Rios St Ste A1 Sacramento (95811) ***(P-1220)***
Quality Home Loans...C.......818 206-6600
27001 Agoura Rd Ste 200 Agoura Hills (91301) ***(P-9852)***
Quality Hotel Airport, Arcadia *Also called Goodrich Lax A Cal Ltd Partnr* ***(P-12611)***
Quality In-Hmecare Specialists...D.......530 303-3477
1166 Broadway Ste T Placerville (95667) ***(P-22400)***
Quality Inn, San Luis Obispo *Also called Q S San Luis Obispo LP* ***(P-13086)***
Quality Inn, Santa Ana *Also called Q S H Properties Inc* ***(P-13085)***
Quality Inv Prpts Scrmento LLC...D.......916 679-2100
1100 N Market Blvd Sacramento (95834) ***(P-16170)***
Quality Laminating, Pacoima *Also called Phillips Plywood Co Inc* ***(P-6851)***
Quality Loan Service Corp...B.......619 645-7711
2763 Camino Del Rio S San Diego (92108) ***(P-12125)***
Quality Long Term Care Nev Inc...D.......818 361-0191
14122 Hubbard St Sylmar (91342) ***(P-20713)***
Quality Management, Stanford *Also called Stanford Health Care* ***(P-21790)***
Quality Marine, Los Angeles *Also called Allaquaria LLC* ***(P-9193)***
Quality Planning Corporation...D.......415 369-0707
388 Market St Ste 750 San Francisco (94111) ***(P-27415)***
Quality Plus Auto Parts Inc...E.......619 424-9991
1333 30th St Ste C San Diego (92154) ***(P-6667)***
Quality Production Svcs Inc...D.......310 406-3350
18711 S Broadwick St Compton (90220) ***(P-2944)***
Quality Reinforcing Inc...D.......858 748-8400
13275 Gregg St Poway (92064) ***(P-3392)***
Quality Systems Installations...D.......650 875-9000
212 Shaw Rd Ste 3 South San Francisco (94080) ***(P-3573)***
Quality Tech Svcs Sacramento, Sacramento *Also called Quality Inv Prpts Scrmento LLC* ***(P-16170)***
Quality Techniques Engrg Cnstr, Rocklin *Also called Quality Telecom Consultants* ***(P-1972)***
Quality Telecom Consultants (PA)...D.......916 315-0500
3740 Cincinnati Ave Rocklin (95765) ***(P-1972)***
Quality Temp Staffing, Granada Hills *Also called Siracusa Enterprises Inc* ***(P-14760)***
Quality Wall Systems Inc...D.......951 739-4409
104 S Maple St Corona (92880) ***(P-2945)***
Qualitylogic Inc (PA)...C.......805 531-9030
2245 1st St Ste 103 Simi Valley (93065) ***(P-27831)***
Qualstaff Resources, San Diego *Also called June Group LLC* ***(P-14867)***
Qualys Inc (PA)...C.......650 801-6100
919 E Hillsdale Blvd Fl 4 Foster City (94404) ***(P-15389)***
Quantcast Corporation (PA)...D.......800 293-5706
795 Folsom St Fl 5 San Francisco (94107) ***(P-15390)***
Quantos Payroll, Los Angeles *Also called Film Payroll Services Inc* ***(P-26204)***
Quantros Inc (PA)...D.......408 957-3300
691 S Milpitas Blvd # 100 Milpitas (95035) ***(P-15391)***
Quantum Corporation (PA)...B.......408 944-4000
224 Airport Pkwy Ste 550 San Jose (95110) ***(P-26443)***
Quantum Secure, Inc., San Jose *Also called Hid Global Safe Inc* ***(P-15972)***
Quantum Solutions Inc...E.......818 577-4555
5146 Douglas Fir Rd # 205 Calabasas (91302) ***(P-16466)***
Quantum Technologies Inc...C.......949 399-4500
25242 Arctic Ocean Dr Lake Forest (92630) ***(P-1027)***
Quantum3d Government Systems, Milpitas *Also called Cg2 Inc* ***(P-26611)***
Quarry At La Quinta Inc (PA)...D.......760 777-1100
41865 Boardwalk Ste 214 Palm Desert (92211) ***(P-18749)***
Quarry Collection, Huntington Beach *Also called GBI Tile & Stone Inc* ***(P-6894)***
Quartus Engineering Inc (PA)...D.......858 875-6000
9689 Towne Centre Dr San Diego (92121) ***(P-25882)***
Quartz Logistics Inc...D.......626 606-2001
780 Nogales St Ste D City of Industry (91748) ***(P-5151)***
Qubera Solutions Inc...E.......650 294-4460
676 Gail Ave Apt 26 Sunnyvale (94086) ***(P-16467)***
Quechan Gaming Commission, Winterhaven *Also called Quechan Indian Tribe* ***(P-19220)***
Quechan Indian Tribe...B.......760 572-2413
350 Picacho Rd Winterhaven (92283) ***(P-19220)***
Queen Anne Early Education Ctr, Los Angeles *Also called Los Angeles Unified School Dst* ***(P-24342)***
Queen Mary Hotel, Long Beach *Also called RMS Foundation Inc* ***(P-13135)***
Queen Mary, The, Long Beach *Also called Urban Commons Queensway LLC* ***(P-13358)***
Queen of Angels Hollywood Pres...A.......213 413-3000
1300 N Vermont Ave Los Angeles (90027) ***(P-21677)***
Queen of The Valley Campus, West Covina *Also called Citrus Vly Hlth Partners Inc* ***(P-19383)***
Queen of The Valley Hospital, West Covina *Also called Citrus Valley Medical Ctr Inc* ***(P-21324)***
Queen of Valley Hospital...A.......626 962-4011
1115 S Sunset Ave West Covina (91790) ***(P-21678)***
Queen of Valley Medical Center (HQ)...A.......707 252-4411
1000 Trancas St NAPA (94558) ***(P-21679)***
Queensbay Hotel LLC (PA)...C.......562 628-0625
444 W Ocean Blvd Long Beach (90802) ***(P-13088)***
Queensbay Hotel LLC...D.......562 481-3910
700 Queensway Dr Long Beach (90802) ***(P-13089)***
Queenscare Fmly Clinics-Eastsd, Los Angeles *Also called Queenscare Health Centers* ***(P-19810)***
Queenscare Health Centers...D.......323 780-4510
4816 E 3rd St Los Angeles (90022) ***(P-19810)***
Queenscare Health Centers...D.......323 644-6180
4618 Fountain Ave Los Angeles (90029) ***(P-19811)***
Quercus Ranch, Kelseyville *Also called BT Holdings Inc* ***(P-215)***
Quest Components Inc...E.......626 333-5858
14711 Clark Ave City of Industry (91745) ***(P-7529)***
Quest Dgnstics Clncal Labs Inc...B.......408 975-1015
2369 Bering Dr San Jose (95131) ***(P-22128)***
Quest Dgnstics Clncal Labs Inc...B.......661 964-6582
26081 Avenue Hall 150 Valencia (91355) ***(P-22129)***
Quest Diagn Nichols Inst Valen, Valencia *Also called Specialty Laboratories Inc* ***(P-22148)***
Quest Diagnostics, West Hills *Also called Unilab Corporation* ***(P-22154)***
Quest Diagnostics Incorporated...B.......925 687-2514
401 Gregory Ln Ste 146 Pleasant Hill (94523) ***(P-22130)***

ALPHABETIC

Employee Codes: A=Over 500 employees, B=251-500
C=101-250, D=51-100, E=50
2019 Directory of California
Wholesalers and Services Companies
© Mergent Inc. 1-800-342-5647
1433

Quest Diagnostics Incorporated ....B....949 728-4235
33608 Ortega Hwy Mission Viejo (92675) ***(P-22131)***
Quest Diagnostics Incorporated ....D....559 438-2893
1275 E Spruce Ave Ste 102 Fresno (93720) ***(P-22132)***
Quest Group (PA) ....D....949 585-0111
2621 White Rd Irvine (92614) ***(P-8051)***
Quest Intl Monitor Svc Inc (PA) ....D....949 581-9900
60 Parker Irvine (92618) ***(P-16291)***
Quest Media & Supplies Inc (PA) ....D....916 338-7070
9000 Fthills Blvd Ste 100 Roseville (95747) ***(P-16038)***
Quest Software Inc ....D....415 373-2222
118 2nd St Fl 6 San Francisco (94105) ***(P-15837)***
Quest Software Inc (HQ) ....A....949 754-8000
4 Polaris Way Aliso Viejo (92656) ***(P-16039)***
Quest Software Inc ....D....949 754-8000
4 Polaris Way Aliso Viejo (92656) ***(P-15838)***
Questmark, Ontario *Also called Centimark Corporation* ***(P-3134)***
Quetico LLC (PA) ....D....909 628-6200
5521 Schaefer Ave Chino (91710) ***(P-9254)***
Quick Systems Inc ....E....702 335-3574
5042 Wilshire Blvd # 28533 Los Angeles (90036) ***(P-2322)***
Quick-N-Ezee Indian Foods, Hayward *Also called Jagpreet Enterprises Inc* ***(P-8811)***
Quicken Inc ....C....650 564-3399
3760 Haven Ave Menlo Park (94025) ***(P-15392)***
Quicken Sub, LLC, Menlo Park *Also called Quicken Inc* ***(P-15392)***
Quicksilver Delivery Inc ....D....415 431-1600
129 Kissling St San Francisco (94103) ***(P-17420)***
Quicksilver Delivery Service, San Francisco *Also called Quicksilver Delivery Inc* ***(P-17420)***
Quigley-Simpson La, Los Angeles *Also called Quigly-Simpson Heppelwhite Inc* ***(P-13885)***
Quigly-Simpson Heppelwhite Inc ....C....310 996-5800
11601 Wilshire Blvd Fl 7 Los Angeles (90025) ***(P-13885)***
Quik Pick Express LLC ....C....310 763-3000
1021 E 233rd St Carson (90745) ***(P-5152)***
Quincy Family Medicine, Quincy *Also called Plumas District Hospital* ***(P-19793)***
Quinn Company ....D....818 767-7171
13275 Golden State Rd Sylmar (91342) ***(P-7686)***
Quinn Company ....D....661 393-5800
2200 Pegasus Dr Bakersfield (93308) ***(P-7687)***
Quinn Company ....D....805 485-2171
801 Del Norte Blvd Oxnard (93030) ***(P-7688)***
Quinn Company ....D....805 925-8611
1655 Carlotti Dr Santa Maria (93454) ***(P-7689)***
Quinn Emanuel Urquhart ....E....415 875-6600
50 California St Ste 2200 San Francisco (94111) ***(P-23344)***
Quinn Emanuel Urquhart ....D....650 801-5000
555 Twin Dolphin Dr Fl 5 Redwood City (94065) ***(P-23345)***
Quinn Emanuel Urquhart (PA) ....B....213 443-3000
865 S Figueroa St Fl 10 Los Angeles (90017) ***(P-23346)***
Quinn Group Inc ....D....805 485-2171
801 Del Norte Blvd Oxnard (93030) ***(P-7708)***
Quinn Group Inc ....C....661 393-5800
2200 Pegasus Dr Bakersfield (93308) ***(P-7709)***
Quinn Group Inc ....A....831 758-8461
1300 Abbott St Salinas (93901) ***(P-7690)***
Quinn Lift Inc ....D....831 758-4086
1300 Abbott St Salinas (93901) ***(P-7789)***
Quinn Shepherd Machinery ....B....562 463-6000
10006 Rose Hills Rd City of Industry (90601) ***(P-7691)***
Quinstar Technology Inc ....D....310 320-1111
24085 Garnier St Torrance (90505) ***(P-7530)***
Quinstreet Inc (PA) ....E....650 578-7700
950 Tower Ln Ste 600 Foster City (94404) ***(P-17421)***
Quintiles Pacific Incorporated (HQ) ....E....650 567-2000
448 E Middlefield Rd Mountain View (94043) ***(P-26558)***
Quiring Corporation ....D....559 432-2800
5118 E Clinton Way # 201 Fresno (93727) ***(P-1621)***
Quiring General LLC ....D....559 432-2800
5118 E Clinton Way # 201 Fresno (93727) ***(P-1622)***
Quixote Mm LLC ....E....323 851-5030
1011 N Fuller Ave Ste B West Hollywood (90046) ***(P-18213)***
Quixote Production Vehicles, West Hollywood *Also called Quixote Studios LLC* ***(P-14538)***
Quixote Studios LLC (PA) ....E....323 851-5030
1011 N Fuller Ave West Hollywood (90046) ***(P-14538)***
Quixote Studios LLC ....E....818 252-7722
11473 Penrose St Sun Valley (91352) ***(P-17660)***
Qumu Inc ....D....650 396-8530
1100 Grundy Ln Ste 110 San Bruno (94066) ***(P-15839)***
Quora Inc ....E....650 485-2464
650 Castro St Ste 450 Mountain View (94041) ***(P-16243)***
Quotient Technology Inc (PA) ....C....650 605-4600
400 Logue Ave Mountain View (94043) ***(P-13981)***
Quova Inc ....D....650 965-2898
401 Castro St Fl 3 Mountain View (94041) ***(P-27832)***
Quovera Inc (PA) ....C....650 691-0114
788 Stone Ln Palo Alto (94303) ***(P-27833)***
Quovera Inc ....E....949 224-3825
19800 Macarthur Blvd Irvine (92612) ***(P-27834)***
Qupid Shoe, Walnut *Also called East Lion Corporation* ***(P-8355)***
Quri Inc ....E....415 413-0100
655 Montgomery St Lbby 1 San Francisco (94111) ***(P-26559)***
Qw Media International LLC ....E....949 200-4616
620 Newport Center Dr # 11 Newport Beach (92660) ***(P-13954)***
Qwest Corporation ....D....925 974-4908
1350 Treat Blvd Ste 200 Walnut Creek (94597) ***(P-5632)***
Qy Research Inc ....D....626 295-2442
17890 Castleton St City of Industry (91748) ***(P-27416)***
R T A, Riverside *Also called Riverside Transit Agency* ***(P-3699)***
R & A Painting Inc ....D....916 688-3955
11730 Sheldon Lake Dr Elk Grove (95624) ***(P-2469)***
R & B Realty Group ....D....323 851-3450
3600 Barham Blvd Los Angeles (90068) ***(P-11101)***
R & B Realty Group ....D....818 710-5400
22122 Victory Blvd Woodland Hills (91367) ***(P-11102)***
R & B Realty Group ....D....310 751-4545
4111 Via Marina Marina Del Rey (90292) ***(P-11103)***
R & B Realty Group LP ....A....310 478-1021
2222 Corinth Ave Los Angeles (90064) ***(P-11698)***
R & B Reinforcing Steel Corp ....D....909 591-1726
13581 5th St Chino (91710) ***(P-3393)***
R & B Wholesale Distrs Inc (PA) ....C....909 230-5400
2350 S Milliken Ave Ontario (91761) ***(P-7426)***
R & D Leasing Inc ....D....559 924-1276
19101 Kent Ave Lemoore (93245) ***(P-14539)***
R & G Enterprises ....C....559 781-1351
627 N Main St Porterville (93257) ***(P-484)***
R & N Packing Co ....C....209 364-6101
47920 W Nees Ave Firebaugh (93622) ***(P-555)***
R & R Electric ....E....310 785-0288
2029 Century Park E A4 Los Angeles (90067) ***(P-2690)***
R & R Maher Cnstr Co Inc ....D....707 552-0330
1324 Lemon St Vallejo (94590) ***(P-3311)***
R & R Mechanical Contrs Inc ....D....619 449-9900
1400 N Johnson Ave # 114 El Cajon (92020) ***(P-2323)***
R & R Profession ....C....760 754-9020
2216 S El Camino Real # 211 Oceanside (92054) ***(P-20197)***
R & S Floor Covering, Riverside *Also called R&S Carpet Services Inc* ***(P-6784)***
R & S Investments LLC ....D....415 591-2700
1 Bush St Fl 9 San Francisco (94104) ***(P-12045)***
R & V Management Corporation ....D....619 429-3305
768 Hollister St San Diego (92154) ***(P-27007)***
R A Schreiber Plumbing ....E....619 659-3101
2358 Tavern Rd Alpine (91901) ***(P-2324)***
R and L Lopez Associates Inc (PA) ....D....626 336-9655
3649 Tyler Ave El Monte (91731) ***(P-25883)***
R and R Labor Inc ....B....831 638-0290
710 Kirkpatric Ct Hollister (95023) ***(P-668)***
R and R Prof Hlthcare Staffing, Santa Clarita *Also called Oceanside Hlthcare Stffing Inc* ***(P-22851)***
R and R Professional Medical, Oceanside *Also called R & R Profession* ***(P-20197)***
R B International Inc (PA) ....E....626 357-7652
13450 Brooks Dr Ste B Baldwin Park (91706) ***(P-7790)***
R B Spencer Inc ....D....530 674-8307
1188 Hassett Ave Yuba City (95991) ***(P-2325)***
R C H, San Francisco *Also called Pomeroy Rcrtion Rhbltation Ctr* ***(P-23974)***
R C Hotels Inc ....D....714 891-0123
7667 Center Ave Huntington Beach (92647) ***(P-13090)***
R C I Enterprises Inc ....E....310 370-5900
3848 Del Amo Blvd Ste 301 Torrance (90503) ***(P-7246)***
R C I Image Systems, Torrance *Also called R C I Enterprises Inc* ***(P-7246)***
R C O Reforesting, Yreka *Also called RCO Reforesting Inc* ***(P-999)***
R C Roberts & Co (PA) ....C....415 456-8600
801 A St San Rafael (94901) ***(P-11159)***
R D S Unlimited Inc ....E....619 443-0221
14372 Olde Highway 80 E El Cajon (92021) ***(P-3063)***
R DS For Healthcare ....E....209 333-2115
1420 W Kettleman Ln N5 Lodi (95242) ***(P-20198)***
R E Cuddie Co ....E....408 998-1250
1751 Junction Ave San Jose (95112) ***(P-3116)***
R E Maher Inc ....D....707 642-3907
4545 Hess Rd American Canyon (94503) ***(P-3312)***
R F Macdonald Co (PA) ....C....510 784-0110
25920 Eden Landing Rd Hayward (94545) ***(P-7791)***
R F R Corporation ....D....800 346-7663
3310 Verdugo Rd Los Angeles (90065) ***(P-11909)***
R Fellen Inc ....D....559 233-6248
2939 S Peach Ave Fresno (93725) ***(P-20714)***
R G Canning Enterprises Inc ....C....323 560-7469
4515 E 59th Pl Maywood (90270) ***(P-17422)***
R G Vanderweil Engineers LLP ....C....562 256-8623
3760 Kilroy Airport Way # 230 Long Beach (90806) ***(P-25884)***
R H D, Corona *Also called Ranch House Doors Inc* ***(P-3065)***
R H O Capital Partners Inc ....E....650 463-0300
525 University Ave # 1350 Palo Alto (94301) ***(P-12262)***
R H Phillips Inc (HQ) ....C....530 757-5557
26836 County Road 12a Esparto (95627) ***(P-166)***
R H Phillips Vineyard, Esparto *Also called R H Phillips Inc* ***(P-166)***
R Haupt Roofing Construction ....E....310 515-9709
1305 W 132nd St Fl 2 Gardena (90247) ***(P-3192)***
R J Dailey Construction Co ....D....650 948-5196
401 1st St Los Altos (94022) ***(P-1221)***
R J Daum Construction Co (PA) ....C....714 894-4300
11581 Monarch St Garden Grove (92841) ***(P-1623)***
R J M Construction Inc ....E....909 794-8853
224 Donna Dr Redlands (92374) ***(P-1624)***
R Joy Inc ....D....530 832-5760
1584 Wolf Meadows Ln Portola (96122) ***(P-25885)***
R K I, Union City *Also called Rki Instruments Inc* ***(P-7795)***
R K Properties, Long Beach *Also called Rance King Properties Inc* ***(P-11106)***
R L G, San Mateo *Also called Research Libraries Group Inc* ***(P-16247)***
R L Jones-San Diego Inc (PA) ....D....760 357-3177
1778 Zinetta Rd Ste A Calexico (92231) ***(P-5153)***
R L Jones-San Diego Inc ....D....760 357-0140
1778 Zinetta Rd Ste A1 Calexico (92231) ***(P-5154)***
R L Klein & Associates ....D....562 427-5577
3553 Atlantic Ave Ste A Long Beach (90807) ***(P-14895)***
R L Safety Inc ....E....408 557-0887
2157 Cherrystone Dr San Jose (95128) ***(P-23979)***

Mergent e-mail: customerrelations@mergent.com
1434
2019 Directory of California Wholesalers and Services Companies
(P-0000) Products & Services Section entry number
(PA)=Parent Co (HQ)=Headquarters (DH)=Div Headquarters

R M A Group Inc (PA)....D....909 980-6096
12130 Santa Margarita Ct Rancho Cucamonga (91730) ***(P-25886)***
R M B Packaging Co Inc....E....818 998-0658
9667 Canoga Ave Chatsworth (91311) ***(P-9255)***
R M B SEC Cnslting Invstgtions, Fountain Valley *Also called Bell Private Security Inc* ***(P-16582)***
R M Harris Company Inc....D....925 335-3000
1000 Howe Rd Ste 200 Martinez (94553) ***(P-1887)***
R M Matovu Memorial....E....412 337-5975
327 Consuelo Dr Santa Barbara (93110) ***(P-21680)***
R Mc Closkey Insurance Agency....C....949 223-8100
4001 Macarthur Blvd # 300 Newport Beach (92660) ***(P-10753)***
R Mora Farm Labor....E....661 746-2858
930 5th St Wasco (93280) ***(P-669)***
R N D Enterprises, Lancaster *Also called BDR Industries Inc* ***(P-5857)***
R N Priority Nursing Service....D....760 635-7776
P.O. Box 234216 Encinitas (92023) ***(P-14711)***
R Navarro Landscape Services....D....562 690-6414
359 West Rd La Habra Heights (90631) ***(P-926)***
R P Direct, Santa Monica *Also called Postaer Rubin and Associates* ***(P-13882)***
R P M C Travel, Calabasas *Also called Rpmc Inc* ***(P-27571)***
R P S Resort Corp....C....760 327-8311
1600 N Indian Canyon Dr Palm Springs (92262) ***(P-13091)***
R Q Construction Inc....C....760 477-1199
3194 Lionshead Ave Carlsbad (92010) ***(P-1430)***
R R Donnelley & Sons Company....E....310 784-8485
18915 S Laurel Park Rd Rancho Dominguez (90220) ***(P-14060)***
R R Donnelley & Sons Company....E....925 951-1320
1646 N Calif Blvd Ste 510 Walnut Creek (94596) ***(P-3623)***
R Ranch Market....A....714 573-1182
1112 Walnut Ave Tustin (92780) ***(P-454)***
R S A Laboratories, Santa Clara *Also called Rsa Security LLC* ***(P-15419)***
R S I Insurance Brokers Inc (PA)....D....714 546-6616
2801 Bristol St Ste 200 Costa Mesa (92626) ***(P-10754)***
R S P, Commerce *Also called Rolled Steel Products Corp* ***(P-7310)***
R S Software India Limited....D....408 382-1200
1900 Mccarthy Blvd # 103 Milpitas (95035) ***(P-16468)***
R Stanley Security Service....D....661 634-9283
403 18th St Bakersfield (93301) ***(P-16770)***
R Systems Inc (HQ)....C....916 939-9696
5000 Windplay Dr Ste 5 El Dorado Hills (95762) ***(P-16469)***
R T C NURSERY, Ramona *Also called Unyeway Inc* ***(P-24242)***
R T Framing Corporation....D....805 496-3985
299 W Hillcrest Dr # 212 Thousand Oaks (91360) ***(P-3064)***
R T I, Sunnyvale *Also called Real-Time Innovations Inc* ***(P-15398)***
R W Garcia Co Inc (PA)....E....408 287-4616
100 Enterprise Way Scotts Valley (95066) ***(P-8566)***
R W Lyall & Company Inc (HQ)....C....951 270-1500
2665 Research Dr Corona (92882) ***(P-1047)***
R W Zant Co (PA)....D....323 980-5457
1470 E 4th St Los Angeles (90033) ***(P-8625)***
R&M USA Inc....D....408 945-6626
840 Yosemite Way Milpitas (95035) ***(P-7531)***
R&S Carpet Services Inc....D....909 740-6645
1485 Spruce St Ste C106 Riverside (92507) ***(P-6784)***
R-Bros Painting Inc....E....408 291-6820
707 W Hedding St San Jose (95110) ***(P-2470)***
R2c Group, San Francisco *Also called Respond 2 LLC* ***(P-18108)***
R2g Enterprises Inc....D....510 489-6218
31154 San Benito St Hayward (94544) ***(P-3193)***
R3 Strategic Support Group Inc....D....800 418-2040
1050 B Ave Ste A Coronado (92118) ***(P-27417)***
Ra Hughes Enterprises In....E....619 390-4880
9316 Abraham Way Santee (92071) ***(P-2326)***
RABBIT HAVEN THE, Scotts Valley *Also called Ava The Rabbit Haven Inc* ***(P-27652)***
Rabobank National Association....C....831 422-6642
301 Main St Salinas (93901) ***(P-9481)***
Race Street Fish & Poultry, San Jose *Also called Race Street Foods Inc* ***(P-8538)***
Race Street Foods Inc (PA)....D....408 294-6161
967 W Hedding St San Jose (95126) ***(P-8538)***
Racelegal Com....E....619 265-8159
315 Fourth Ave Chula Vista (91910) ***(P-25453)***
Racquet Club of Irvine....D....949 786-3000
5 Ethel Coplen Way Ste 5 # 5 Irvine (92612) ***(P-19005)***
Racquetball World, Canoga Park *Also called Bay Clubs Inc* ***(P-18857)***
Radar Medical Systems Inc....D....440 337-9521
1510 Cotner Ave Los Angeles (90025) ***(P-27956)***
Radford Alexander Corporation....D....310 523-2555
14700 S Avalon Blvd Gardena (90248) ***(P-4053)***
Radford Studio Center Inc....B....818 655-5000
4024 Radford Ave Studio City (91604) ***(P-18398)***
Radiabeam Technologies LLC....E....310 822-5845
1717 Stuart St Santa Clara (95054) ***(P-26652)***
Radiant Logic Inc....D....415 209-6800
75 Rowland Way Ste 300 Novato (94945) ***(P-15393)***
Radiant Services Corp (PA)....C....310 327-6300
651 W Knox St Gardena (90248) ***(P-13489)***
Radiation Medical Group Inc (PA)....E....619 220-4100
9333 Genesee Ave Ste 300 San Diego (92121) ***(P-19812)***
Radica Enterprises Ltd....D....310 252-2000
333 Continental Blvd El Segundo (90245) ***(P-7960)***
Radica USA, El Segundo *Also called Radica Enterprises Ltd* ***(P-7960)***
Radio Station, Los Angeles *Also called Loyola Marymount University* ***(P-5745)***
RADIO STATION KFBS, La Mirada *Also called Far East Broadcasting Co Inc* ***(P-5717)***
Radio Time, San Francisco *Also called Tunein Inc* ***(P-5758)***
Radiology Department Cal Hosp....E....213 742-5840
1338 S Hope St Fl 4 Los Angeles (90015) ***(P-19813)***
Radiometer America Inc (HQ)....C....800 736-0600
250 S Kraemer Blvd Ms Brea (92821) ***(P-7214)***
Radison Hotel Newport Beach, Newport Beach *Also called Pacific Hotel Management Inc* ***(P-13002)***
Radisson Hotel At Usc....C....213 748-4141
3540 S Figueroa St Los Angeles (90007) ***(P-13092)***
Radisson Hotel La Westside, Culver City *Also called Pacifica Hotel & Conference Ce* ***(P-13007)***
Radisson Hotel Phoenix Cy Ctr, Anaheim *Also called Sunshine Midtown LLC* ***(P-13290)***
Radisson Hotel Santa Maria....D....805 928-8000
3455 Skyway Dr Santa Maria (93455) ***(P-13093)***
Radisson Ht Fishermans Wharf....D....415 392-6700
250 Beach St San Francisco (94133) ***(P-13094)***
Radisson Ht Frsno Cnfrence Ctr, Fresno *Also called HI Fresno Hospitality LLC* ***(P-12657)***
Radisson Inn, Los Angeles *Also called Pacifica Hosts Inc* ***(P-13006)***
Radisson Inn, Berkeley *Also called Boykin Mgt Co Ltd Lblty Co* ***(P-12394)***
Radisson Inn, Los Angeles *Also called Radisson Hotel At Usc* ***(P-13092)***
Radisson Inn, Westlake Village *Also called Amgreen-Karena Ht Partnr Ltd* ***(P-12318)***
Radisson Inn, Sunnyvale *Also called S R H H Inc* ***(P-13156)***
Radisson Inn, San Diego *Also called Rancho Bernardo Partners Ltd* ***(P-13099)***
Radisson Inn, Union City *Also called Interstate Hotels Resorts Inc* ***(P-12778)***
Radisson Inn, Agoura Hills *Also called Ww Lbv Inc* ***(P-13421)***
Radisson Inn, Los Angeles *Also called Lax Hospitality LP* ***(P-12840)***
Radisson Inn, Los Angeles *Also called Radlax Gateway Hotel LLC* ***(P-13095)***
Radisson Inn, San Bernardino *Also called First Hotels International Inc* ***(P-12575)***
Radisson Plaza Hotel Inn, San Jose *Also called Silicon Valley Hwang LLC* ***(P-13227)***
Radisson Suites Anaheim, Buena Park *Also called Golden Hotel LLC* ***(P-12607)***
Radix Textile Inc....D....323 234-1667
750 E Jefferson Blvd Los Angeles (90011) ***(P-8237)***
Radlax Gateway Hotel LLC....B....310 670-9000
6225 W Century Blvd Los Angeles (90045) ***(P-13095)***
Radleys....E....310 765-2223
3780 Wilshire Blvd Los Angeles (90010) ***(P-18103)***
Radnet Inc (PA)....C....310 445-2800
1510 Cotner Ave Los Angeles (90025) ***(P-22133)***
Radnet Management Inc....D....209 524-6800
157 E Coolidge Ave Modesto (95350) ***(P-27008)***
Radnet Management Inc....D....323 549-3000
8750 Wilshire Blvd # 100 Beverly Hills (90211) ***(P-27009)***
Radonich Corp....E....408 275-8888
886 Faulstich Ct San Jose (95112) ***(P-2691)***
Rady Childrens Hosp & Hlth Ctr (PA)....A....858 576-1700
3020 Childrens Way San Diego (92123) ***(P-22040)***
Rady Chld Hospital-San Diego....A....858 966-6795
8001 Frost St San Diego (92123) ***(P-22041)***
Rady Chld Hospital-San Diego (HQ)....A....858 576-1700
3020 Childrens Way San Diego (92123) ***(P-21681)***
Rady Chld Hospital-San Diego....D....858 966-5833
8022 Birmingham Dr # 22 San Diego (92123) ***(P-27010)***
Rafael Convalescent Hospital....C....415 479-3450
234 N San Pedro Rd San Rafael (94903) ***(P-21191)***
Raffles Lrmitage Beverly Hills....C....310 278-3344
9291 Burton Way Beverly Hills (90210) ***(P-13096)***
Raging Waters San Dimas 703, San Dimas *Also called Festival Fun Parks LLC* ***(P-7928)***
Raging Wire, Sacramento *Also called Ragingwire Data Centers Inc* ***(P-16272)***
Ragingwire Data Centers Inc (HQ)....B....916 286-3000
1200 Striker Ave Sacramento (95834) ***(P-16272)***
Rahf IV Casa Panorama LP....E....216 621-6060
14555 Osborne St Panorama City (91402) ***(P-11104)***
Rahf IV Grove LP....E....216 621-6060
227 W H St Ontario (91762) ***(P-11105)***
Rail Delivery Services Inc....D....909 355-4100
8600 Banana Ave Fontana (92335) ***(P-4054)***
Railpros Inc (PA)....D....714 734-8765
1 Ada Ste 200 Irvine (92618) ***(P-25887)***
Railpros Field Services....E....877 315-0513
1 Ada Ste 200 Irvine (92618) ***(P-17423)***
Railroad Technology, Sacramento *Also called Macdonald Mott LLC* ***(P-25808)***
Railway Distributing Inc (PA)....E....408 280-7625
675 Emory St San Jose (95110) ***(P-6906)***
Rain Bird Corporation....D....619 661-4493
2475-A Paseo De Las Ameri San Diego (92154) ***(P-6563)***
Rain Bird Distribution Corp....D....626 963-9311
1000 W Sierra Madre Ave Azusa (91702) ***(P-2057)***
Rain Creek Baking, Madera *Also called Kronos Foods Corp* ***(P-8821)***
Rain For Rent, Bakersfield *Also called Western Oilfields Supply Co* ***(P-14555)***
Rainbow - Brite Indus Svcs LLC....D....559 925-2580
463 E Salmon River Dr Fresno (93730) ***(P-14362)***
Rainbow Agricultural Services, Ukiah *Also called Mayfield Equipment Company* ***(P-7706)***
Rainbow Camp Inc....E....310 456-3066
26619 Marigold Ct Calabasas (91302) ***(P-19221)***
Rainbow Disposal Co Inc (HQ)....C....714 847-3581
17121 Nichols Ln Huntington Beach (92647) ***(P-6432)***
Rainbow Farms, Denair *Also called Valley Fresh Foods Inc* ***(P-436)***
Rainbow Home Care Services....D....714 544-8070
1560 Brookhollow Dr # 100 Santa Ana (92705) ***(P-22401)***
Rainbow Municipal Water Dst....E....760 728-1178
3707 Old Highway 395 Fallbrook (92028) ***(P-6296)***
Rainbow Properties Inc....D....323 562-0730
4812 Ostrom Ave Lakewood (90713) ***(P-11699)***
Rainbow Ranches Inc....C....661 858-2266
13650 Copus Rd Bakersfield (93313) ***(P-374)***
Rainbow Realty Corporation....D....949 770-9626
24221 Paseo De Valencia Laguna Woods (92637) ***(P-11700)***
Rainbow Refuse Recycling, Huntington Beach *Also called Rainbow Disposal Co Inc* ***(P-6432)***

ALPHABETIC

Employee Codes: A=Over 500 employees, B=251-500
C=101-250, D=51-100, E=50
2019 Directory of California
Wholesalers and Services Companies
© Mergent Inc. 1-800-342-5647
1435

Rainbow Sandals Inc.....E.....949 276-4431
900 Calle Negocio San Clemente (92673) *(P-8366)*
Rainbow Transfer Recycling.....C.....714 847-5818
17121 Nichols Ln Huntington Beach (92647) *(P-6433)*
Rainbow Vending & Distributing, San Diego *Also called Canteen Vending - San Diego (P-8544)*
Rainbow Wtrprfing Restoration.....C.....415 641-1578
600 Treat Ave San Francisco (94110) *(P-3574)*
Raincross Hospitality Corp (PA).....D.....951 346-4700
3637 5th St Riverside (92501) *(P-13770)*
Raines Law Group LLP.....E.....310 440-4100
9720 Wilshire Blvd Fl 5 Beverly Hills (90212) *(P-23347)*
Rainforest Qa Inc.....C.....650 866-1407
600 Battery St Fl 2 San Francisco (94111) *(P-15394)*
Rainier Financial Group LLC.....E.....310 335-9200
2321 Rosecrans Ave # 4270 El Segundo (90245) *(P-27418)*
Rainmaker Systems Inc.....C.....408 659-1800
1821 S Bascom Ave Ste 385 Campbell (95008) *(P-27011)*
Raintree Systems Inc.....D.....951 252-9400
27307 Via Industria Temecula (92590) *(P-15395)*
Raiser Senior Services LLC.....D.....650 342-4106
601 Laurel Ave Apt 903 San Mateo (94401) *(P-24640)*
Raison D'Etre Bakery, South San Francisco *Also called Ashbury Market Inc (P-8757)*
Rakon America LLC.....A.....847 930-5100
7600 Dublin Blvd Ste 220 Dublin (94568) *(P-7532)*
Rakstar Production, Los Angeles *Also called Entertainment & Sports Today (P-5783)*
Rakworx Inc.....C.....949 215-1362
17 Hammond Ste 404 Irvine (92618) *(P-16292)*
Raleigh Enterprises Inc (PA).....C.....310 899-8900
5300 Melrose Ave Fl 4 Los Angeles (90038) *(P-13097)*
Raleigh Enterprises Inc.....C.....323 466-3111
5300 Melrose Ave Fl 3 Los Angeles (90038) *(P-18214)*
Raleigh Holdings, Los Angeles *Also called Raleigh Enterprises Inc (P-13097)*
Raleigh Studios, Los Angeles *Also called Raleigh Enterprises Inc (P-18214)*
Ralison International Inc.....E.....909 393-0008
15328 Central Ave Chino (91710) *(P-7988)*
Ralph Collazo Packing Inc.....D.....760 353-0856
72 E Main St Ste A Heber (92249) *(P-17424)*
Ralph D Mitzel Inc.....D.....714 554-4745
1520 N Fairview St Santa Ana (92706) *(P-14454)*
Ralphs 00134, Glendale *Also called Ralphs Grocery Company (P-4618)*
Ralphs 00173, Downey *Also called Ralphs Grocery Company (P-4622)*
Ralphs 6, Encino *Also called Ralphs Grocery Company (P-4621)*
Ralphs 96, Pasadena *Also called Ralphs Grocery Company (P-4623)*
Ralphs Grocery Company.....C.....818 549-0035
211 N Glendale Ave Glendale (91206) *(P-4618)*
Ralphs Grocery Company.....A.....310 637-1101
4841-45 San Fernando W Los Angeles (90039) *(P-4619)*
Ralphs Grocery Company.....D.....562 633-0830
13525 Lakewood Blvd Downey (90242) *(P-4620)*
Ralphs Grocery Company.....C.....818 345-6882
17840 Ventura Blvd Encino (91316) *(P-4621)*
Ralphs Grocery Company.....D.....562 869-2042
9200 Lakewood Blvd Downey (90240) *(P-4622)*
Ralphs Grocery Company.....D.....626 793-7480
160 N Lake Ave Pasadena (91101) *(P-4623)*
Ram Commercial Enterprises Inc.....E.....916 429-1205
5896 S Land Park Dr Sacramento (95822) *(P-11701)*
Ram Mechanical Inc.....D.....209 531-9155
3506 Moore Rd Ceres (95307) *(P-2327)*
Ramada Clock Tower Inn, Ventura *Also called Clocktower Inn (P-12468)*
Ramada Inn, Fresno *Also called Fresno Hotel Partners LP (P-12594)*
Ramada Inn, Sunnyvale *Also called Executive Inn Inc (P-12569)*
Ramada Inn, San Diego *Also called Royal Hospitality Incorporated (P-13143)*
Ramada Inn, San Diego *Also called Trigild International Inc (P-13346)*
Ramada Inn, Hawthorne *Also called Calhot Illinios LLC (P-12418)*
Ramada Inn, Redondo Beach *Also called D & W LLC (P-12511)*
Ramada Inn University, Fresno *Also called Shaw Hospitality Group Inc (P-13212)*
Ramada Plaza Ht Anaheim Resort.....C.....714 991-6868
515 W Katella Ave Anaheim (92802) *(P-13098)*
Ramada Plz Ht San Dego/ Ht Cir, San Diego *Also called G5 Global Partners Ix LLC (P-12595)*
Ramboll Environ, Irvine *Also called Ramboll US Corporation (P-27957)*
Ramboll Environ US Corporation.....D.....510 655-7400
2200 Powell St Ste 700 Emeryville (94608) *(P-27835)*
Ramboll Environ US Corporation.....D.....949 261-5151
5 Park Plz Ste 500 Irvine (92614) *(P-27836)*
Ramboll Environment & Health, Irvine *Also called Ramboll Environ US Corporation (P-27836)*
Ramboll US Corporation.....E.....949 798-3604
18100 Von Karman Ave # 600 Irvine (92612) *(P-27957)*
Ramcar Batteries Inc.....E.....323 726-1212
2700 Carrier Ave Commerce (90040) *(P-6668)*
Ramcast Ornamental Sup Co Inc (PA).....C.....323 585-1625
2201 Firestone Blvd Los Angeles (90002) *(P-7303)*
Ramco Employment Services, Oxnard *Also called Ramco Enterprises LP (P-556)*
Ramco Enterprises LP.....A.....805 922-9888
325 Plaza Dr Ste 1 Santa Maria (93454) *(P-14712)*
Ramco Enterprises LP.....A.....831 722-3370
585 Auto Center Dr Watsonville (95076) *(P-14713)*
Ramco Enterprises LP.....A.....805 486-9328
520 E 3rd St Ste B Oxnard (93030) *(P-556)*
Ramkade Insurance Services.....D.....818 444-1340
21550 Oxnard St Ste 500 Woodland Hills (91367) *(P-10755)*
Ramona Care Center Inc.....C.....626 442-5721
11900 Ramona Blvd El Monte (91732) *(P-20715)*
Ramona Community Services Corp (HQ).....C.....951 658-9288
890 W Stetson Ave Ste A Hemet (92543) *(P-22402)*
Ramona Nrsing Rhbilitation Ctr, El Monte *Also called Ramona Care Center Inc (P-20715)*
Ramona Rehabilitation and Post.....C.....951 652-0011
485 W Johnston Ave Hemet (92543) *(P-21682)*
Ramona Vna & Hospice, Hemet *Also called Ramona Community Services Corp (P-22402)*
Ramos Oil Co Inc (PA).....D.....916 371-2570
1515 S River Rd West Sacramento (95691) *(P-8945)*
Ramos Orchards.....D.....530 795-4748
9192 Boyce Rd Winters (95694) *(P-194)*
Rams Hill Country Club.....D.....760 767-4259
1881 Rams Hill Rd Borrego Springs (92004) *(P-19006)*
Ramsell Public Health Rx LLC.....D.....510 587-2600
200 Webster St Ste 300 Oakland (94607) *(P-10756)*
Ramsey-Shilling Residential RE.....D.....323 851-5512
3360 Barham Blvd Los Angeles (90068) *(P-11702)*
Ramsgate Engineering Inc.....D.....661 392-0050
2331 Cepheus Ct Bakersfield (93308) *(P-25888)*
Rance King Properties Inc (PA).....C.....562 240-1000
3737 E Broadway Long Beach (90803) *(P-11106)*
Ranch At Laguna Beach, The, Laguna Beach *Also called Laguna Bch Golf Bnglow Vlg LLC (P-451)*
Ranch At Little Hills, The, San Ramon *Also called Concessionaires Urban Park (P-19151)*
Ranch Golf Club.....D.....408 270-0557
4601 Hill Top View Ln San Jose (95138) *(P-18750)*
Ranch Hand Entertainment Inc.....D.....612 396-2632
11333 Moorpark St Pmb 441 Studio City (91602) *(P-18104)*
Ranch House Doors Inc.....D.....951 278-2884
1527 Pomona Rd Corona (92880) *(P-3065)*
Ranch Winery, The, Saint Helena *Also called E & J Gallo Winery (P-27708)*
Ranching Shop, Corcoran *Also called J G Boswell Company (P-14)*
Rancho Bernardo Golf Club.....D.....858 487-1134
17550 Bernardo Oaks Dr San Diego (92128) *(P-19007)*
Rancho Bernardo Partners Ltd.....D.....858 451-6600
11520 W Bernardo Ct San Diego (92127) *(P-13099)*
Rancho California Landscaping.....E.....310 768-1680
13801 S Western Ave Gardena (90249) *(P-927)*
Rancho California Water Dst (PA).....C.....951 296-6900
42135 Winchester Rd Temecula (92590) *(P-6297)*
Rancho Ccamonga Cmnty Hosp LLC.....C.....909 581-6400
10841 White Oak Ave Rancho Cucamonga (91730) *(P-21683)*
Rancho Clinic Rancho San Diego, La Mesa *Also called Scripps Health (P-19865)*
Rancho Cordova Medical Offices, Rancho Cordova *Also called Kaiser Foundation Hospitals (P-10233)*
Rancho Cucamonga Family YMCA, Rancho Cucamonga *Also called West End Yung MNS Christn Assn (P-25285)*
Rancho Cucamonga Medical Offs, Rancho Cucamonga *Also called Kaiser Foundation Hospitals (P-19540)*
Rancho Cucamonga Sport Club, Rancho Cucamonga *Also called 24 Hour Fitness Usa Inc (P-18553)*
Rancho De Sus Ninos Inc.....D.....619 661-9232
P.O. Box 360 Potrero (91963) *(P-24641)*
Rancho Del Oro Ldscp Maint Inc.....D.....760 726-0215
4167 Avenida De La Plata Oceanside (92056) *(P-781)*
Rancho Foods Inc.....D.....323 585-0503
2528 E 37th St Vernon (90058) *(P-8626)*
Rancho Jurupa Park.....E.....951 684-7032
4800 Crestmore Rd Riverside (92509) *(P-19222)*
Rancho La Quinta Country Club, La Quinta *Also called TD Desert Dev Ltd Partnr (P-11929)*
Rancho Laguna Farms LLC.....D.....805 925-7805
2410 W Main St Santa Maria (93458) *(P-375)*
Rancho Leonero Resort.....E.....760 438-2905
5671 Palmer Way Ste E Carlsbad (92010) *(P-13100)*
Rancho Los Amigos Nationa.....B.....562 401-7111
7601 Imperial Hwy Downey (90242) *(P-23980)*
Rancho Los Amigos Nationa.....A.....562 401-7111
7601 Imperial Hwy Downey (90242) *(P-23981)*
Rancho Los Amigos Nationa.....B.....562 401-7266
12852 Erickson Ave Downey (90242) *(P-23982)*
Rancho Los Amigos Nationa (PA).....D.....562 401-7111
7601 Imperial Hwy Downey (90242) *(P-23983)*
Rancho Mission Viejo LLC (PA).....D.....949 240-3363
28811 Ortega Hwy San Juan Capistrano (92675) *(P-11703)*
Rancho Murieta Country Club.....D.....916 354-2400
7000 Alameda Dr Rancho Murieta (95683) *(P-19008)*
Rancho Niguel Dental Group.....E.....949 249-4180
30140 Town Center Dr Laguna Niguel (92677) *(P-20133)*
Rancho Pacific Electric Inc.....E.....909 476-1022
9063 Santa Anita Ave Rancho Cucamonga (91730) *(P-2692)*
Rancho Penasquitos Sport Club, San Diego *Also called 24 Hour Fitness Usa Inc (P-18569)*
Rancho Physical Therapy Inc.....C.....760 752-1011
277 Rancheros Dr San Marcos (92069) *(P-20199)*
Rancho Physical Therapy Inc (PA).....C.....951 696-9353
24630 Washington Ave # 200 Murrieta (92562) *(P-20200)*
Rancho Research Institute.....C.....562 401-8111
7601 Imperial Hwy Downey (90242) *(P-26653)*
Rancho Salinas Packing Inc.....C.....831 758-3624
2376 Alisal Rd Salinas (93908) *(P-670)*
Rancho San Antonio Boys HM Inc (PA).....D.....818 882-6400
21000 Plummer St Chatsworth (91311) *(P-24642)*
Rancho San Antonio Medical Ctr, Rancho Cucamonga *Also called San Antonio Community Hospital (P-21700)*
Rancho San Antonio Retirement.....B.....650 265-2637
23500 Cristo Rey Dr Cupertino (95014) *(P-24643)*
Rancho San Diego Cinema 16, El Cajon *Also called Edwards Theatres Circuit Inc (P-18289)*
Rancho San Diego Medical Offs, La Mesa *Also called Kaiser Foundation Hospitals (P-19564)*
Rancho San Joaquin Golf Course, Irvine *Also called American Golf Corporation (P-18828)*

Mergent e-mail: customerrelations@mergent.com
1436
2019 Directory of California Wholesalers and Services Companies
(P-0000) Products & Services Section entry number
(PA)=Parent Co (HQ)=Headquarters (DH)=Div Headquarters

Rancho Santa Ana Botanic Grdn ...... D......909 625-8767
1500 N College Ave Claremont (91711) *(P-24934)*
Rancho Santa Fe, Rancho Santa Fe *Also called Pacific Western Bank* *(P-9362)*
Rancho Santa Fe Association A ...... D......858 756-1182
5827 Viadelacumere Rancho Santa Fe (92067) *(P-19009)*
Rancho Santa Fe Protective Svc ...... E......760 433-8887
1991 Village Park Way # 100 Encinitas (92024) *(P-16771)*
Rancho Sante Fe Golf Club, Rancho Santa Fe *Also called Rancho Santa Fe Association A* *(P-19009)*
Rancho Simi Recreation Pk Dst (PA) ...... D......805 584-4400
4201 Guardian St Simi Valley (93063) *(P-19223)*
Rancho Speciality Hospital, Rancho Cucamonga *Also called Rancho Ccamonga Cmnty Hosp LLC* *(P-21683)*
Rancho Springs Medical Center, Murrieta *Also called Southwest Healthcare Sys Aux* *(P-21772)*
Rancho Valencia Resort ...... B......858 756-1123
5921 Valencia Cir Rancho Santa Fe (92067) *(P-13101)*
Rancho Vista Health Center ...... C......760 941-1480
200 Grapevine Rd Apt 15 Vista (92083) *(P-20949)*
Rancho West Landscape ...... E......951 301-3979
39140 Pala Vista Dr Temecula (92591) *(P-928)*
Rancho Wholesale, Chino *Also called Redwood Products Chino Inc* *(P-6856)*
Ranchwood Contractors Inc ...... D......209 826-6200
923 E Pacheco Blvd Los Banos (93635) *(P-1625)*
Rancon Real Estate Corporation (PA) ...... D......951 677-1800
27740 Jefferson Ave # 100 Temecula (92590) *(P-11704)*
Rand Medical Billing Inc ...... D......805 578-8300
1633 Erringer Rd Fl 1 Simi Valley (93065) *(P-26280)*
Rand Technology LLC (PA) ...... D......949 255-5700
15225 Alton Pkwy Unit 100 Irvine (92618) *(P-7533)*
Randall Mc-Anany Company ...... D......310 822-3344
4935 Mcconnell Ave Ste 20 Los Angeles (90066) *(P-2471)*
Randazzo Enterprises Inc ...... D......831 633-4420
13550 Blackie Rd Castroville (95012) *(P-3460)*
Rando AAA Hvac Inc ...... E......408 293-4717
1712 Stone Ave Ste 1 San Jose (95125) *(P-2328)*
Randstad Finance & Accounting, Burlingame *Also called Randstad Professionals Us LLC* *(P-14714)*
Randstad North America Inc ...... C......559 297-0054
7014 N Cedar Ave Fresno (93720) *(P-14896)*
Randstad North America Inc ...... C......559 582-2700
106 E 7th St Hanford (93230) *(P-14897)*
Randstad North America Inc ...... C......559 592-6700
1110 W Visalia Rd Ste 116 Exeter (93221) *(P-14898)*
Randstad North America Inc ...... C......415 397-3384
27 Maiden Ln Ste 202 San Francisco (94108) *(P-14899)*
Randstad Professionals Us LLC ...... C......650 343-5111
111 Anza Blvd Ste 202 Burlingame (94010) *(P-14714)*
Randstad Technologies LP ...... D......619 798-7300
8880 Rio San Diego Dr # 107 San Diego (92108) *(P-16470)*
Range Generation Next LLC ...... D......310 647-9438
105 13th St Bldg 6525 Vandenberg Afb (93437) *(P-25889)*
Range Generation Next LLC ...... E......310 647-9438
Pillar Point Air Sta El Granada (94018) *(P-27837)*
Ranger Pipelines Incorporated ...... D......415 822-3700
1790 Yosemite Ave San Francisco (94124) *(P-1973)*
Ranker Inc ...... E......323 782-1448
6420 Wilshire Blvd # 880 Los Angeles (90048) *(P-13886)*
Ranscapes Inc ...... E......866 883-9297
30 Hughes Ste 209 Irvine (92618) *(P-14363)*
Ransome Company ...... E......510 686-9900
1933 Williams St San Leandro (94577) *(P-1626)*
Raphaels Party Rentals Inc (PA) ...... E......858 444-1692
8606 Miramar Rd San Diego (92126) *(P-14540)*
Rapid Plumbing Inc (PA) ...... D......714 695-1800
3840 E Miraloma Ave Anaheim (92806) *(P-2329)*
Rapid Product Dev Group Inc ...... C......760 703-5770
300 W Grand Ave Escondido (92025) *(P-27838)*
Rapid Solutions Consulting LLC ...... E......415 226-1131
1900 S Norfolk St Ste 350 San Mateo (94403) *(P-15396)*
Rapiscan Systems Inc ...... E......310 978-1457
2805 Columbia St Torrance (90503) *(P-16930)*
Rapp Worldwide Inc ...... D......310 563-7200
12777 W Jefferson Blvd Los Angeles (90066) *(P-13887)*
Rappi Inc ...... B......347 740-4824
353 Mission St Fl 14 San Francisco (94105) *(P-4428)*
Ras, Sacramento *Also called Mark H Leibenhaut MD* *(P-19670)*
Ras Management Inc (PA) ...... E......510 727-1800
4545 Crow Canyon Pl Castro Valley (94552) *(P-4624)*
Rashman Corporation ...... D......818 993-3030
8600 Wilbur Ave Northridge (91324) *(P-7897)*
Ratcliff Architects ...... D......510 899-6400
5856 Doyle St Emeryville (94608) *(P-26103)*
Rate Is Low ...... E......925 299-9364
3744 Mt Diablo Blvd # 205 Lafayette (94549) *(P-9853)*
Rava Ranches Inc ...... D......831 385-3285
700 Airport Rd King City (93930) *(P-455)*
Raven Biotechnologies Inc ...... D......650 624-2600
1 Corporate Dr South San Francisco (94080) *(P-26444)*
Ravenswood Family Health Ctr, East Palo Alto *Also called South Cnty Cmnty Hlth Ctr Inc* *(P-22887)*
Ravenswood Solutions Inc ...... D......650 241-3661
3065 Skyway Ct Fremont (94539) *(P-16040)*
Ravig Inc ...... D......925 526-1234
510 Garcia Ave Ste E Pittsburg (94565) *(P-7097)*
Rawitser Golf Shop Mike ...... E......408 441-4653
1560 Oakland Rd San Jose (95131) *(P-18751)*

Rawlings Mechanical Corp (PA) ...... D......323 875-2040
11615 Pendleton St Sun Valley (91352) *(P-2330)*
Ray Stone, Sacramento *Also called Brunswick Corner Partnership* *(P-11251)*
Ray W Choi ...... D......714 783-1000
731 E Ball Rd Ste 100 Anaheim (92805) *(P-27419)*
Rayco Electric, Rancho Cordova *Also called Rci Electric Inc* *(P-2694)*
Raycon Construction Inc ...... E......805 525-5256
1795 E Lemonwood Dr Santa Paula (93060) *(P-2822)*
Raycon Environmental Cnstr ...... E......805 955-0900
882 Patriot Dr Ste G Moorpark (93021) *(P-3575)*
Raylee Electric ...... E......916 408-7556
1202 Tarapin Ln Lincoln (95648) *(P-2693)*
Raymak Automotive Inc ...... E......310 329-8910
15600 S Main St Gardena (90248) *(P-17780)*
Raymond Brown Company, San Francisco *Also called Walter E McGuire RE Inc* *(P-11821)*
Raymond Group (PA) ...... D......714 771-7670
520 W Walnut Ave Orange (92868) *(P-27012)*
Raymond Handling Concepts Corp (HQ) ...... D......510 745-7500
41400 Boyce Rd Fremont (94538) *(P-17976)*
Raymond Handling Solutions Inc (HQ) ...... C......562 944-8067
9939 Norwalk Blvd Santa Fe Springs (90670) *(P-7792)*
Raymond Handling Solutions Inc ...... D......909 930-9399
4602 E Brickell St Ontario (91761) *(P-7793)*
Rayner Equipment Systems, Sacramento *Also called California Pavement Maint Inc* *(P-1736)*
Raytheon Command and Control ...... E......714 446-3232
2000 E El Segundo Blvd El Segundo (90245) *(P-7534)*
Raytheon Command and Control (HQ) ...... A......714 446-3118
1801 Hughes Dr Fullerton (92833) *(P-7535)*
Raytheon Company ...... C......858 455-9741
9985 Pcf Hts Blvd Ste 200 San Diego (92121) *(P-25890)*
Raytheon Company ...... C......310 647-9438
2000 E El Segundo Blvd El Segundo (90245) *(P-25891)*
Raytheon Company ...... D......805 562-2941
75 Coromar Dr Goleta (93117) *(P-17425)*
Raytheon Company ...... B......760 386-2572
988 Inner Loop Rd Fort Irwin (92310) *(P-17908)*
Rayv Inc ...... E......310 600-2959
6380 Wilshire Blvd # 1006 Los Angeles (90048) *(P-16041)*
Razavi Corporation ...... D......619 465-8010
7979 La Mesa Blvd La Mesa (91942) *(P-20716)*
Razor USA LLC (PA) ...... D......562 345-6000
12723 166th St Cerritos (90703) *(P-7936)*
RB Anglers Club ...... D......858 487-6484
12578 Cresta Pl San Diego (92128) *(P-19010)*
Rbb Architects Inc (PA) ...... D......310 479-1473
10980 Wilshire Blvd Los Angeles (90024) *(P-26104)*
Rbc Capital Markets LLC ...... E......310 273-7600
9665 Wilshire Blvd Fl 4 Beverly Hills (90212) *(P-10010)*
Rbi Bearings, Baldwin Park *Also called R B International Inc* *(P-7790)*
RC Construction Services, Rialto *Also called Robert Clapper Cnstr Svcs Inc* *(P-1633)*
RC Packing LLC ...... B......831 675-0308
26769 El Camino Real Gonzales (93926) *(P-485)*
RC Wendt Painting Inc ...... C......714 960-2700
21612 Surveyor Cir Huntington Beach (92646) *(P-2472)*
RCA Properties, Paso Robles *Also called RE Max Parkside Real Estate* *(P-11707)*
RCAC, West Sacramento *Also called Rural Cmnty Assistance Corp* *(P-23999)*
Rcb Corporation (PA) ...... D......916 567-2600
2485 Natomas Park Dr # 100 Sacramento (95833) *(P-9482)*
Rcc Facility Incorporated ...... D......510 658-2041
210 40th Street Way Oakland (94611) *(P-21192)*
Rci, Irvine *Also called Racquet Club of Irvine* *(P-19005)*
Rci Electric Inc ...... D......916 858-8000
3144 Fitzgerald Rd Rancho Cordova (95742) *(P-2694)*
RCO Reforesting Inc ...... E......530 842-7647
1332 Fairlane Rd Ste A Yreka (96097) *(P-999)*
Rcr Companies, Riverside *Also called Rcr Plumbing and Mech Inc* *(P-2331)*
Rcr Plumbing and Mech Inc (PA) ...... C......951 371-5000
12620 Magnolia Ave Riverside (92503) *(P-2331)*
Rcs World Travel, Ventura *Also called Registration Ctrl Systems Inc* *(P-17426)*
Rcsn Inc ...... C......714 965-0244
10221 Slater Ave Ste 214 Fountain Valley (92708) *(P-14715)*
Rcwd, Temecula *Also called Rancho California Water Dst* *(P-6297)*
Rdc-S111 Inc (PA) ...... D......562 628-8000
245 E 3rd St Long Beach (90802) *(P-26105)*
Rdi Engineering, Monterey Park *Also called Roque Development and Inv* *(P-25896)*
Rdl Reference Laboratory, Los Angeles *Also called Rheumatology Diagnostics Lab* *(P-22137)*
RDM Electric Co Inc ...... D......909 591-0990
13867 Redwood Ave Chino (91710) *(P-2695)*
Rdo Construction Equipment Co ...... D......619 443-3758
10108 Riverford Rd Lakeside (92040) *(P-14455)*
Rdo Construction Equipment Co ...... E......951 778-3700
20 Iowa Ave Riverside (92507) *(P-7710)*
Rdo Vermeer LLC ...... D......916 643-0999
3980 Research Dr Sacramento (95838) *(P-7692)*
Rdp Acquisition Company ...... B......510 652-8187
5929 College Ave Oakland (94618) *(P-26560)*
Rdr Builders LP ...... D......209 368-7561
1806 W Kettleman Ln Ste F Lodi (95242) *(P-1310)*
Rdr Production Builders, Lodi *Also called Rdr Builders LP* *(P-1310)*
RE Barren Ridge 1 LLC ...... C......415 675-1500
300 California St Fl 7 San Francisco (94104) *(P-6099)*
RE Infolink, Sunnyvale *Also called Mlslistings Inc* *(P-27349)*
RE La Mesa LLC ...... D......415 675-1500
300 California St Fl 8 San Francisco (94104) *(P-2058)*
RE Max 2000 Realty, City of Industry *Also called Leon Chien Corp* *(P-9826)*
RE Max Advantage ...... D......800 247-4200
648 Yerington Ln Lincoln (95648) *(P-11705)*

Employee Codes: A=Over 500 employees, B=251-500
C=101-250, D=51-100, E=50

2019 Directory of California
Wholesalers and Services Companies

© Mergent Inc. 1-800-342-5647

1437

A
L
P
H
A
B
E
T
I
C

RE Max All Cities Lk Arrowhead ....E.......909 337-6111
28200 Highway 189 Lake Arrowhead (92352) ***(P-11706)***
RE Max Parkside Real Estate ....D.......805 239-3310
711 12th St Paso Robles (93446) ***(P-11707)***
RE Max Westlake Investments, Daly City *Also called Casbn Investment Inc* ***(P-11270)***
RE Milano Plumbing Corp ....E.......925 500-1372
4881 Sunrise Dr Ste B Martinez (94553) ***(P-2332)***
Re/Max, Westlake Village *Also called Remax Olson* ***(P-11730)***
Re/Max, Los Alamitos *Also called College Park Realty Inc* ***(P-11367)***
Re/Max, Sacramento *Also called Remax Gold* ***(P-11728)***
Re/Max, Upland *Also called Diamond Ridge Corporation* ***(P-9799)***
Re/Max, Yorba Linda *Also called Yorba Properties Corp* ***(P-11841)***
Re/Max, Irvine *Also called J Baron Inc* ***(P-11525)***
Re/Max, Lincoln *Also called RE Max Advantage* ***(P-11705)***
Re/Max, Ventura *Also called Evans/Sipes Inc* ***(P-11423)***
Re/Max, La Jolla *Also called Mountain-Pacific Financial* ***(P-11616)***
Re/Max, Cypress *Also called Riphagen & Bullerdick Inc* ***(P-11734)***
Re/Max, Folsom *Also called Norcal Gold Inc* ***(P-11634)***
Re/Max, Costa Mesa *Also called Remax Metro Inc* ***(P-11729)***
Re/Max ....E.......661 616-4040
201 New Stine Rd Ste 300 Bakersfield (93309) ***(P-11708)***
Re/Max LLC ....E.......303 770-5531
1071 E 16th St Upland (91784) ***(P-11709)***
Re/Max Beach Cities Realty Mar ....C.......310 376-2225
400 S Sepulveda Blvd # 100 Manhattan Beach (90266) ***(P-11710)***
Re/Max Magic ....E.......661 616-4040
11420 Ming Ave Ste 530 Bakersfield (93311) ***(P-11711)***
RE/Max of Valencia Inc (PA) ....C.......661 255-2650
25101 The Old Rd Santa Clarita (91381) ***(P-11712)***
Re/Max Plos Vrdes Rlty / Exces ....E.......310 541-5224
450 Silver Spur Rd Rancho Palos Verdes (90275) ***(P-11713)***
Re/Maxcc, Walnut Creek *Also called C C Connection Inc* ***(P-11257)***
Reach Fitness Club ....D.......650 327-3224
1235 Radio Rd Ste 120 Redwood City (94065) ***(P-18644)***
Reach Out West End ....D.......909 982-8641
1126 W Foothill Blvd # 250 Upland (91786) ***(P-24829)***
REACH Project (PA) ....D.......925 754-3673
1915 D St Antioch (94509) ***(P-22659)***
Reaching For Independence Inc ....D.......707 725-9010
609 14th St Fortuna (95540) ***(P-24830)***
Reachlocal Inc (HQ) ....C.......818 274-0260
21700 Oxnard St Ste 1600 Woodland Hills (91367) ***(P-13888)***
Reading and Beyond ....D.......559 840-1068
4670 E Butler Ave Fresno (93702) ***(P-25227)***
Reading Entertainment Inc (HQ) ....D.......213 235-2226
500 Citadel Dr Ste 300 Commerce (90040) ***(P-18312)***
Reading International Inc ....E.......951 696-7045
41090 California Oaks Rd Murrieta (92562) ***(P-18313)***
Reading International Inc ....D.......858 207-2606
11620 Carmel Mountain Rd San Diego (92128) ***(P-18314)***
Reading International Inc ....A.......916 442-0985
2508 Land Park Dr Sacramento (95818) ***(P-18315)***
Reading International Inc (PA) ....C.......213 235-2240
5995 Sepulveda Blvd Fl 3 Culver City (90230) ***(P-18316)***
Reading Partners ....D.......408 945-5720
600 Valley Way Milpitas (95035) ***(P-23984)***
Ready America Inc (PA) ....D.......760 295-0234
1399 Specialty Dr Vista (92081) ***(P-8052)***
Ready Roast Nut Company LLC (PA) ....D.......559 661-1696
2805 Falcon Dr Madera (93637) ***(P-557)***
Readylink Inc ....D.......760 343-7000
72030 Metroplex Dr Thousand Palms (92276) ***(P-14716)***
Readylink Healthcare ....D.......760 343-7000
72030 Metroplex Dr Thousand Palms (92276) ***(P-14717)***
Real Estate America Inc ....D.......510 594-3100
2000 Powell St Ste 100 Emeryville (94608) ***(P-11714)***
Real Estate California Dept ....D.......951 715-0130
3737 Main St Ofc Riverside (92501) ***(P-11715)***
Real Estate Digital LLC ....C.......800 234-2139
27081 Aliso Creek Rd # 200 Aliso Viejo (92656) ***(P-15397)***
Real Estate Equity Exchange ....D.......415 992-4200
650 California St Fl 18 San Francisco (94108) ***(P-9854)***
Real Estate Image Inc ....C.......714 502-3900
1415 S Acacia Ave Fullerton (92831) ***(P-14061)***
Real Good Food Company LLC ....C.......909 744-0073
A11 N Maryland Ave 201 Glendale (91206) ***(P-8858)***
Real Human Svcs & Workforce, Crescent City *Also called Del Norte Workforce Center* ***(P-24178)***
Real Property Systems Inc ....C.......760 243-1143
1443 E Washington Blvd Pasadena (91104) ***(P-11716)***
Real Software Systems LLC (PA) ....D.......818 313-8000
21255 Burbank Blvd # 220 Woodland Hills (91367) ***(P-15840)***
Real Time Information Svcs Inc ....E.......559 222-9400
191 W Shaw Ave Ste 106 Fresno (93704) ***(P-14900)***
Real Time Logic Inc ....D.......858 812-7300
4820 Estgate Mall Ste 200 San Diego (92121) ***(P-16042)***
Real Time Staffing Services ....D.......805 882-2200
301 Mentor Dr 210 Santa Barbara (93111) ***(P-14718)***
Real-Time Innovations Inc ....D.......408 990-7400
232 E Java Dr Sunnyvale (94089) ***(P-15398)***
Real-Time Staffing Services, Fresno *Also called Real Time Information Svcs Inc* ***(P-14900)***
Realdefense LLC ....D.......310 693-5935
1541 Ocean Ave Ste 200 Santa Monica (90401) ***(P-16931)***
Really Likeable People Inc ....E.......760 431-5577
2251 Las Palmas Dr Carlsbad (92011) ***(P-8367)***
Realm, Milpitas *Also called R&M USA Inc* ***(P-7531)***
Realogy Holdings Corp ....B.......707 284-1111
3554 Round Barn Blvd Santa Rosa (95403) ***(P-11717)***
Realsuite SM, Santa Clara *Also called Move Inc* ***(P-11618)***
Realtor Sfr Green ....E.......858 488-4090
4090 Mission Blvd San Diego (92109) ***(P-11718)***
Realty Alliance Inc ....D.......818 610-0080
20812 Ventura Blvd # 101 Woodland Hills (91364) ***(P-9905)***
Realty Concepts, Fresno *Also called JMS Realtors Ltd* ***(P-11531)***
Realty Executives, Escondido *Also called J & P Financial Inc* ***(P-9889)***
Realty Executives ....C.......661 286-8600
26650 The Old Rd Ste 300 Valencia (91381) ***(P-11719)***
Realty Group San Diego, Carlsbad *Also called Richard Realty Group Inc* ***(P-11733)***
Realty One Group Inc ....D.......951 565-8105
19322 Jesse Ln Riverside (92508) ***(P-11720)***
Realty One Group Solution, Valencia *Also called King Monster Inc* ***(P-11552)***
Realty World, Wheatland *Also called Wheatland School District* ***(P-11832)***
Reaume and Associates Inc ....D.......310 398-5768
11527 W Washington Blvd Los Angeles (90066) ***(P-25892)***
Reaume, E M & Associates, Los Angeles *Also called Reaume and Associates Inc* ***(P-25892)***
Rebar Engineering Inc ....C.......562 946-2461
10706 Painter Ave Santa Fe Springs (90670) ***(P-3394)***
Rebecca Terley ....D.......562 925-4252
9028 Rose St Bellflower (90706) ***(P-20717)***
REBEKAH CHILDREN'S SERVICES, Gilroy *Also called Odd Fellow-Rebekah Chld HM Cal* ***(P-24614)***
Rebekah Children's Services, Salinas *Also called Odd Fellow-Rebekah Chld HM Cal* ***(P-24615)***
Rec Center ....C.......415 831-6818
501 Stanyan St San Francisco (94117) ***(P-7937)***
Reche Cyn Regional Rehab Ctr, Colton *Also called Reche Cyn Rhblitation Hlth Ctr* ***(P-20718)***
Reche Cyn Rhblitation Hlth Ctr ....B.......909 370-4411
1350 Reche Canyon Rd Colton (92324) ***(P-20718)***
Reciprocity Inc ....E.......415 851-8667
3043 Mission St San Francisco (94110) ***(P-15399)***
Recology Inc (PA) ....D.......415 875-1000
50 California St Ste 2400 San Francisco (94111) ***(P-6434)***
Recology Inc ....D.......415 330-1300
Tunnel Ave And Beatty Rd San Francisco (94134) ***(P-6435)***
Recology Inc ....D.......916 379-3300
245 N 1st St Dixon (95620) ***(P-6436)***
Recology Inc ....D.......415 970-1582
100 Cargo Way San Francisco (94124) ***(P-6437)***
Recology Inc ....D.......530 533-5868
2720 S 5th Ave Oroville (95965) ***(P-6438)***
Recology Inc ....C.......415 330-1400
501 Tunnel Ave San Francisco (94134) ***(P-6439)***
Recology Los Altos ....D.......650 961-8044
650 Martin Ave Santa Clara (95050) ***(P-6440)***
Recology San Francisco ....C.......415 468-1752
501 Tunnel Ave San Francisco (94134) ***(P-6441)***
Recology San Mateo County ....D.......650 595-3900
225 Shoreway Rd San Carlos (94070) ***(P-6442)***
Recology South Valley (HQ) ....D.......408 842-3358
1351 Pacheco Pass Hwy Gilroy (95020) ***(P-6443)***
Recology Sunset Scavenger, San Francisco *Also called Sunset Scavenger Company* ***(P-6480)***
Recology Sustainable Crushing, San Francisco *Also called Recology Inc* ***(P-6437)***
Recology Vacaville Solano ....D.......707 448-2945
1 Town Sq Ste 200 Vacaville (95688) ***(P-6444)***
Recology Vallejo (HQ) ....C.......707 552-3110
2021 Broadway St Vallejo (94589) ***(P-6445)***
Recology Yuba-Sutter ....D.......530 743-6933
3001 N Levee Rd Marysville (95901) ***(P-6446)***
Recon Environmental Inc (PA) ....D.......619 308-9333
1927 5th Ave Ste 200 San Diego (92101) ***(P-27839)***
Records Center/Storage, Oakland *Also called San Francisco Bay Area Rapid* ***(P-3708)***
Recovery Place Inc ....D.......954 200-8308
5000 E Spring St Ste 650 Long Beach (90815) ***(P-22042)***
Recovery Solutions Santa Ana, Santa Ana *Also called CRC Health Corporate* ***(P-22563)***
Recp Cy Oxnard LLC ....D.......805 604-7527
600 E Esplanade Dr Oxnard (93036) ***(P-13102)***
Recp Rl Oxnard LLC ....C.......805 278-2200
2101 W Vineyard Ave Oxnard (93036) ***(P-13103)***
Recp/Wndsor Scramento Ventr LP ....D.......916 455-6800
4422 Y St Sacramento (95817) ***(P-13104)***
Recreation Complex, South Lake Tahoe *Also called City of South Lake Tahoe* ***(P-19142)***
Recreation Dept, Coronado *Also called City of Coronado* ***(P-19129)***
Recreation Park Golf Course 18, Long Beach *Also called American Golf Corporation* ***(P-18682)***
Recurrent Energy LLC (HQ) ....D.......415 956-3168
3000 Oak Rd Ste 300 Walnut Creek (94597) ***(P-2333)***
Recurve Inc ....D.......510 540-4860
220 Montgomery St Ste 820 San Francisco (94104) ***(P-17896)***
Recycle Waste, Santa Clara *Also called Mission Trail Wste Systems Inc* ***(P-4041)***
Recycled Wood Products, Pomona *Also called Rwp Transfer Inc* ***(P-8056)***
Recycler Core Company Inc ....D.......951 276-1687
2727 Kansas Ave Riverside (92507) ***(P-6669)***
Recyclers I Electronic ....D.......317 522-1414
7815 N Palm Ave Ste 140 Fresno (93711) ***(P-6447)***
Recycling Industries Inc ....D.......916 452-3961
4741 Watt Ave North Highlands (95660) ***(P-6448)***
Red and White Fleet, San Francisco *Also called Golden Gate Scnic Stmship Corp* ***(P-4716)***
Red Blossom Farms, Salinas *Also called Red Blossom Sales Inc* ***(P-376)***
Red Blossom Sales Inc ....B.......805 349-9404
865 Black Rd Santa Maria (93458) ***(P-113)***
Red Blossom Sales Inc (PA) ....A.......805 686-4747
400 W Ventura Blvd # 140 Camarillo (93010) ***(P-114)***

Mergent e-mail: customerrelations@mergent.com
1438
2019 Directory of California Wholesalers and Services Companies
(P-0000) Products & Services Section entry number
(PA)=Parent Co (HQ)=Headquarters (DH)=Div Headquarters

Red Blossom Sales Inc .... A 831 751-9169
9 Harris Pl Salinas (93901) *(P-376)*
Red Bull Distribution Co Inc (HQ) .... D 916 515-3501
1740 Stewart St Santa Monica (90404) *(P-8859)*
Red Carpet Car Wash, Visalia *Also called Bowie Enterprises (P-17803)*
Red Carpet Car Wash, Fresno *Also called Bowie Enterprises (P-17804)*
Red Carpet Car Wash, Clovis *Also called Bowie Enterprises (P-17805)*
Red Carpet Car Wash, Fresno *Also called Bowie Enterprises (P-17853)*
Red Chamber Co (PA) .... B 323 234-9000
1912 E Vernon Ave Vernon (90058) *(P-8597)*
Red Condor Inc .... D 707 569-7419
1300 Valley House Dr # 115 Rohnert Park (94928) *(P-15400)*
Red Earth Casino, Thermal *Also called Torres-Martinez (P-13332)*
Red Earth Casino .... C 760 395-1200
3089 Norm Niver Rd Thermal (92274) *(P-13105)*
Red Hawk Casino, Placerville *Also called Shingle Sprng Trbal Gming Auth (P-19237)*
Red Hawk Fire & SEC CA Inc .... D 510 438-1300
4384 Enterprise Pl Fremont (94538) *(P-2696)*
Red Hawk Fire & SEC CA Inc .... C 714 685-8100
1640 N Batavia St Orange (92867) *(P-2697)*
Red Hawk Fire & SEC CA Inc (HQ) .... D 818 683-1500
7605 N San Fernando Rd Los Angeles (90065) *(P-2698)*
Red Hawk Fire & SEC CA Inc .... D 760 233-9787
920 S Andreasen Dr # 102 Escondido (92029) *(P-2699)*
Red Hill Country Club .... D 909 982-1358
8358 Red Hl Cntry Clb Dr Rancho Cucamonga (91730) *(P-19011)*
Red Interactive Agency LLC (PA) .... D 310 399-4242
3420 Ocean Park Blvd # 3080 Santa Monica (90405) *(P-13889)*
Red Lion Hotel Redding, Redding *Also called Kaidan Hospitality LP (P-12797)*
Red One - PSI Joint Ventr LLC .... E 559 772-8264
310 W Murray Ave Visalia (93291) *(P-1627)*
Red Peak Group LLC .... D 818 222-7762
23975 Park Sorrento # 410 Calabasas (91302) *(P-27420)*
Red Pocket Inc .... D 888 993-3888
2060d E Avenida De Los Thousand Oaks (91362) *(P-5633)*
Red Pocket Mobile, Thousand Oaks *Also called Red Pocket Inc (P-5633)*
Red Pointe Roofing LP (PA) .... D 714 685-0010
1814 N Neville St Orange (92865) *(P-3194)*
Red Pointe Roofing LP .... D 818 998-3857
9542 Topanga Canyon Blvd Chatsworth (91311) *(P-3195)*
Red Sky Interactive .... C 415 430-3200
201 Mission St Fl 8 San Francisco (94105) *(P-13890)*
Red Tail Golf Assoc, Rancho Santa Fe *Also called Farms Golf Club Inc (P-18923)*
Red Top Rice Growers .... E 530 868-5975
3200 8th St Biggs (95917) *(P-558)*
Redbarn Pet Products Inc (PA) .... C 562 495-7315
3229 E Spring St Ste 310 Long Beach (90806) *(P-9256)*
Redbarn Premium Pet Products, Long Beach *Also called Redbarn Pet Products Inc (P-9256)*
Redbull Distribution Co Colo, Santa Monica *Also called Red Bull Distribution Co Inc (P-8859)*
Redding Aero Enterprises Inc .... D 530 224-2300
3775 Flight Ave Ste 100 Redding (96002) *(P-3698)*
Redding Bank of Commerce (HQ) .... D 530 224-7355
1951 Churn Creek Rd Redding (96002) *(P-9370)*
Redding District Office, Redding *Also called State Compensation Insur Fund (P-10399)*
Redding Drywall Systems Inc .... E 530 222-8767
3092 Crossroads Dr Redding (96003) *(P-2946)*
Redding Family Medicine Assoc .... E 530 244-4907
2510 Airpark Dr Ste 201 Redding (96001) *(P-19814)*
Redding Jet Center, Redding *Also called Redding Aero Enterprises Inc (P-3698)*
Redding Medical Group, Redding *Also called David Civalier MD Inc (P-19427)*
Redding Medical Home Care, Redding *Also called Tenet Healthsystem Medical (P-22434)*
Redding Pathologists Lab (PA) .... C 530 225-8050
1725 Gold St Redding (96001) *(P-19815)*
Redding Pathologists Lab .... D 530 225-8050
2036 Railroad Ave Redding (96001) *(P-22134)*
Redding Ranch Indian Hlth CL, Redding *Also called Redding Rancheria (P-22869)*
Redding Rancheria (PA) .... D 530 225-8979
2000 Redding Rancheria Rd Redding (96001) *(P-13106)*
Redding Rancheria .... D 530 224-2700
1441 Liberty St Redding (96001) *(P-22869)*
Redding Tree Growers Corp .... D 559 594-9299
18985 Avenue 256 Apt A Exeter (93221) *(P-1000)*
Redding V A Outpatient Clinic, Redding *Also called Veterans Health Administration (P-20063)*
Redding Veterans Home, The, Redding *Also called Veterans Affairs Cal Dept (P-20856)*
Redevelopment Agency of The Ci .... D 707 421-7309
701 Civic Center Blvd Suisun City (94585) *(P-27840)*
Redfin Corporation .... B 206 340-8794
655 Montgomery St # 1430 San Francisco (94111) *(P-11721)*
Redgate Memorial Hospital, Long Beach *Also called Behavioral Health Services Inc (P-23506)*
Redhill Group Inc .... D 949 752-5900
18010 Sky Park Cir # 275 Irvine (92614) *(P-26561)*
Redhill Towing & Autobody .... D 415 456-8943
428 Irwin St San Rafael (94901) *(P-17869)*
Redhorse Constructors Inc .... D 415 492-2020
36 Professional Ctr Pkwy San Rafael (94903) *(P-1222)*
Redis Labs Inc .... D 415 930-9666
700 E El Camino Real # 250 Mountain View (94040) *(P-15401)*
Redlands Cmnty Hosp Foundation .... C 909 793-1382
1875 Barton Rd Redlands (92373) *(P-21193)*
Redlands Community Hospital, Redlands *Also called RHS Corp (P-27018)*
Redlands Community Hospital (PA) .... D 909 335-5500
350 Terracina Blvd Redlands (92373) *(P-21684)*
Redlands Country Club .... D 909 793-2661
1749 Garden St Redlands (92373) *(P-19012)*
Redlands Division, Redlands *Also called American Med (P-3745)*
Redlands Employment Services .... B 951 688-0083
4295 Jurupa St Ste 110 Ontario (91761) *(P-14719)*
Redlands Foothill Groves .... E 909 793-2164
304 9th St Redlands (92374) *(P-559)*
Redlands Ford Inc .... D 909 793-3211
1121 W Colton Ave Redlands (92374) *(P-17737)*
Redlands Health Care Group, Redlands *Also called Plum Healthcare Group LLC (P-17405)*
REDLANDS HEALTHCARE CENTER, Redlands *Also called Ash Holdings LLC (P-20236)*
Redlands Recycling, Riverside *Also called Riverside Scrap Ir & Met Corp (P-7989)*
Redlands Staffing Services, Ontario *Also called Redlands Employment Services (P-14719)*
Redman Container, Carson *Also called Calko Transport Company Inc (P-4335)*
Redrocks Fumigation, San Jose *Also called Homeguard Incorporated (P-14151)*
Redseal Inc .... D 408 641-2200
940 Stewart Dr Ste 101 Sunnyvale (94085) *(P-15841)*
Redstone Print & Mail Inc .... D 916 318-6450
910 Riverside Pkwy Ste 40 West Sacramento (95605) *(P-27421)*
Redwood, Culver City *Also called Uproxx Media Group Inc (P-6003)*
Redwood Bridge Club .... D 619 296-4274
3111 6th Ave San Diego (92103) *(P-19224)*
Redwood Building Maint Co .... D 707 782-9100
1364 N Mcdowell Blvd B Petaluma (94954) *(P-14364)*
Redwood Coast Medical Services (PA) .... E 707 884-1721
46900 Ocean Dr Gualala (95445) *(P-19816)*
Redwood Coast Regional (PA) .... D 707 462-3832
1116 Airport Park Blvd Ukiah (95482) *(P-23985)*
Redwood Coast Regional .... E 707 445-0893
525 2nd St Ste 300 Eureka (95501) *(P-23986)*
REDWOOD COAST REGIONAL CENTER, Ukiah *Also called Redwood Coast Regional (P-23985)*
Redwood Coast Regional Center, Eureka *Also called Redwood Coast Regional (P-23986)*
Redwood Coast Seniors Inc .... D 707 964-0443
490 N Harold St Fort Bragg (95437) *(P-23987)*
Redwood Community Services (PA) .... C 707 467-2000
631 S Orchard Ave Ukiah (95482) *(P-23988)*
Redwood Convalescent Hospital .... D 510 537-8848
22103 Redwood Rd Castro Valley (94546) *(P-21194)*
Redwood Credit Union .... C 800 479-7928
1129 S Cloverdale Blvd A Cloverdale (95425) *(P-9581)*
Redwood Credit Union (PA) .... C 707 545-4000
3033 Cleveland Ave # 100 Santa Rosa (95403) *(P-9582)*
Redwood Elderlink & Homelink, Escondido *Also called Redwood Elderlink Scph (P-24644)*
Redwood Elderlink Scph .... B 760 480-1030
710 W 13th Ave Escondido (92025) *(P-24644)*
Redwood Electric Group Inc (PA) .... A 707 451-7348
2775 Northwestern Pkwy Santa Clara (95051) *(P-2700)*
Redwood Empir .... D 707 586-5533
3400 Standish Ave Santa Rosa (95407) *(P-6449)*
Redwood Empire Addctons Prgram, Santa Rosa *Also called Drug Abuse Alternatives Center (P-22569)*
Redwood Empire Division, Cloverdale *Also called Pacific States Industries Inc (P-6849)*
Redwood Empire Ice Oprtons LLC (PA) .... D 707 546-7147
1667 W Steele Ln Santa Rosa (95403) *(P-19225)*
Redwood Empire Packing Inc .... C 707 462-5521
8801 Old River Rd Ukiah (95482) *(P-560)*
Redwood Empire Vineyard Mgt .... D 707 857-3401
22000 Geyserville Ave Geyserville (95441) *(P-709)*
Redwood Empire Whl Lbr Pdts, Morgan Hill *Also called Pacific States Industries Inc (P-6850)*
Redwood Health Club (PA) .... D 707 468-0441
3101 S State St Ukiah (95482) *(P-18645)*
Redwood Healthcare Staffing .... D 619 238-4180
600 B St Ste 1570 San Diego (92101) *(P-14901)*
Redwood Memorial Hosp Fortuna (PA) .... C 707 725-7327
3300 Renner Dr Fortuna (95540) *(P-21685)*
Redwood Painting Co Inc .... C 925 432-4500
620 W 10th St Pittsburg (94565) *(P-2473)*
Redwood Products Chino Inc .... D 909 923-5656
9301 Remington Ave Chino (91710) *(P-6856)*
Redwood Regional Medical Group, Santa Rosa *Also called Sotoyome Medical Building LLC (P-10947)*
Redwood Regional Medical Group .... D 707 463-3636
1165 S Dora St Bldg H Ukiah (95482) *(P-19817)*
Redwood Regional Medical Group (PA) .... D 707 525-4080
990 Sonoma Ave Ste 15 Santa Rosa (95404) *(P-22135)*
Redwood Regional Oncology Ctr, Santa Rosa *Also called Redwood Regional Medical Group (P-22135)*
Redwood Senior Homes & Svcs, Escondido *Also called Cal Southern Presbt Homes (P-24446)*
Redwood Town Court, Escondido *Also called Cal Southern Presbt Homes (P-24447)*
Redwood Toxicology Lab Inc .... C 707 577-7958
3650 Westwind Blvd Santa Rosa (95403) *(P-22136)*
Redwood Valley Industrial Park .... D 707 485-8766
8800 West Rd Redwood Valley (95470) *(P-4625)*
Redwoods, The, Mill Valley *Also called The Redwoods A Cmnty Seniors (P-24697)*
Reed Brothers Security, Oakland *Also called Security Central Inc (P-17988)*
Reed Smith LLP .... D 415 659-5964
2 Embarcadero Ctr Fl 20 San Francisco (94111) *(P-23348)*
Reed Smith LLP .... C 213 457-8000
355 S Grand Ave Ste 2900 Los Angeles (90071) *(P-23349)*
Reed Smith LLP .... C 415 543-8700
101 2nd St Ste 1800 San Francisco (94105) *(P-23350)*
Reed Smith LLP .... C 415 543-8700
2 Embarcadero Ctr Fl 21 San Francisco (94111) *(P-23351)*

ALPHABETIC

Employee Codes: A=Over 500 employees, B=251-500
C=101-250, D=51-100, E=50
2019 Directory of California
Wholesalers and Services Companies
© Mergent Inc. 1-800-342-5647
1439

Reed Thomas Company Inc......D......714 558-7691
1025 N Santiago St Santa Ana (92701) ***(P-3438)***
Reef, Carlsbad *Also called South Cone Inc* ***(P-8368)***
Reegs Inc......D......831 455-7931
88 Monterey Salinas Hwy A Salinas (93908) ***(P-1311)***
Reel Security California Inc......D......818 928-4737
15303 Ventura Blvd # 1080 Sherman Oaks (91403) ***(P-16772)***
Reeve Trucking Company Inc (PA)......D......209 948-4061
5050 Carpenter Rd Stockton (95215) ***(P-4249)***
Reeve-Knight Construction Inc......D......916 786-5112
128 Ascot Dr Roseville (95661) ***(P-1628)***
Reeves Tractor Service Inc......D......714 692-4020
5455 Blue Ridge Dr Yorba Linda (92887) ***(P-1840)***
Referral Realty Cupertino, Cupertino *Also called Z & M Associates Inc* ***(P-11844)***
Referral Realty Inc......D......408 996-8100
1601 S De Anza Blvd # 150 Cupertino (95014) ***(P-11722)***
Reflections and Enclave Hoa, Irvine *Also called Keystone PCF Property MGT Inc* ***(P-11549)***
Reflektion Inc (PA)......E......650 293-0800
777 Mariners Island Blvd # 510 San Mateo (94404) ***(P-15402)***
Reformation, The, Vernon *Also called Lymi Inc* ***(P-8316)***
Refrigeration Hdwr Sup Corp......E......818 768-3636
9021 Norris Ave Sun Valley (91352) ***(P-7665)***
Refugee Resettlement, San Diego *Also called Catholic Charities Diocese San* ***(P-23533)***
Refuse Department, Lemoore *Also called City of Lemoore* ***(P-6375)***
Regal Cinemas Inc......D......916 419-0205
3561 Truxel Rd Sacramento (95834) ***(P-18317)***
Regal Cinemas Inc......D......310 544-3042
550 Deep Valley Dr # 339 Rllng HLS Est (90274) ***(P-18318)***
Regal Medical Group Inc (PA)......D......818 654-3400
8510 Balboa Blvd Ste 275 Northridge (91325) ***(P-25038)***
Regatta Tropicals Ltd (PA)......D......805 473-1320
1742 Manhattan Ave Ste C Grover Beach (93433) ***(P-8724)***
Regency, San Jose *Also called Liberty Healthcare of Oklahoma* ***(P-20578)***
Regency Caterers By Hyatt, San Diego *Also called Hyatt Hotels Management Corp* ***(P-12752)***
Regency Centers LP......A......760 724-9795
40 Main St Vista (92083) ***(P-20719)***
Regency Enterprises, Los Angeles *Also called New Regency Productions Inc* ***(P-18085)***
Regency Enterprises Inc (PA)......B......818 901-0255
9261 Jordan Ave Chatsworth (91311) ***(P-7388)***
Regency Fire Protection Inc......D......818 982-0126
7651 Densmore Ave Van Nuys (91406) ***(P-2334)***
Regency Health Services, Covina *Also called Covina Rehabilitation Center* ***(P-20358)***
Regency Hill Associates......D......619 281-5200
6560 Ambrosia Dr San Diego (92124) ***(P-11107)***
Regency Inn, Bakersfield *Also called Days Inn Bakersfield* ***(P-12516)***
Regency Inn, Costa Mesa *Also called US Hotel and Resort MGT Inc* ***(P-13360)***
Regency Lighting, Chatsworth *Also called Regency Enterprises Inc* ***(P-7388)***
Regency Oaks Care Center......C......562 498-3368
3850 E Esther St Long Beach (90804) ***(P-20720)***
Regency Park, Pasadena *Also called Zenith Health Care* ***(P-11845)***
Regency Park El Molino, Pasadena *Also called Regency Park Senior Living Inc* ***(P-11723)***
Regency Park Oak Knoll, Pasadena *Also called Regency Park Senior Living Inc* ***(P-24645)***
Regency Park Senior Living Inc......D......626 396-4911
255 S Oak Knoll Ave Pasadena (91101) ***(P-24645)***
Regency Park Senior Living Inc......D......626 578-0460
245 S El Molino Ave Pasadena (91101) ***(P-11723)***
Regency Theatres Inc......E......818 224-3825
26901 Agoura Rd Ste 150 Agoura Hills (91301) ***(P-18319)***
Regenesis Bioremediation Pdts (PA)......E......949 366-8000
1011 Calle Sombra San Clemente (92673) ***(P-27841)***
Regent Aerospace Corporation (PA)......C......661 257-3000
28110 Harrison Pkwy Valencia (91355) ***(P-3576)***
Regent Assisted Living Inc......D......626 332-3344
150 S Grand Ave Ofc West Covina (91791) ***(P-24646)***
Regent Assisted Living Inc......E......661 663-8400
8100 Westwold Dr Ofc Bakersfield (93311) ***(P-24647)***
Regent Assisted Living Inc......D......209 491-0800
2325 St Pauls Way Modesto (95355) ***(P-24648)***
Regent Assisted Living Inc......D......831 459-8400
80 Front St Santa Cruz (95060) ***(P-24649)***
Regent Assisted Living Inc......D......559 325-8400
675 W Alluvial Ave Ofc Clovis (93611) ***(P-24650)***
Regent At Laurel Springs, Bakersfield *Also called Regent Assisted Living Inc* ***(P-24647)***
Regent Court, Modesto *Also called Regent Assisted Living Inc* ***(P-24648)***
Regent Senior Living W Covina, West Covina *Also called Regent Assisted Living Inc* ***(P-24646)***
Regent Worldwide Sales LLC......E......310 806-4288
10990 Wilshire Blvd Los Angeles (90024) ***(P-18105)***
Regents Point, Irvine *Also called Cal Southern Presbt Homes* ***(P-10992)***
Region Dev & Affairs Off, Salinas *Also called Planned Parenthood Mar Monte* ***(P-22646)***
Regional Center, Chico *Also called Far Northern Coordinating Coun* ***(P-23803)***
Regional Center For Devlpmtnly, Lancaster *Also called North La County Regional Ctr* ***(P-27806)***
Regional Center of E Bay Inc......C......510 383-1200
7677 Oakport St Ste 300 Oakland (94621) ***(P-23989)***
Regional Connector Constrs......E......951 368-6400
1995 Agua Mansa Rd Riverside (92509) ***(P-1223)***
Regional Investment & MGT LLC......E......310 821-1945
4640 Admiralty Way # 1050 Marina Del Rey (90292) ***(P-1312)***
Regional Medical Ctr San Jose, San Jose *Also called San Jose Medical Systems Lp* ***(P-21709)***
Regional Office, Redlands *Also called Southern California Gas Co* ***(P-6167)***
Regional Transportation Comm, San Diego *Also called San Diego Assn Governments* ***(P-24978)***
Regional Youth Svcs N Vly Schl, Victor *Also called Victor Treatment Centers Inc* ***(P-24710)***

Regis Corporation......E......310 274-8791
9403 Santa Monica Blvd Beverly Hills (90210) ***(P-13670)***
Registrar of Voters, Santa Ana *Also called County of Orange* ***(P-25370)***
Registration Ctrl Systems Inc (PA)......D......805 654-0171
1833 Portola Rd Unit B Ventura (93003) ***(P-17426)***
Registry Monitoring Ins Srvcs......C......800 400-4924
5388 Sterling Center Dr Westlake Village (91361) ***(P-11724)***
Registry Network Inc (PA)......C......760 966-3700
1207 Carlsbad Village Dr X Carlsbad (92008) ***(P-14902)***
Regulus Therapeutics Inc......D......858 202-6300
10614 Science Center Dr San Diego (92121) ***(P-26654)***
Rehab Associates, Long Beach *Also called Eric D Feldman MD Inc* ***(P-19463)***
Rehab West Inc......E......619 518-3710
277 Rancheros Dr Ste 190 San Marcos (92069) ***(P-10757)***
Rehabilitation California Dept......E......562 422-8325
4300 Long Beach Blvd # 200 Long Beach (90807) ***(P-23990)***
Rehabilitation Center, Lodi *Also called Lodi Memorial Hosp Assn Inc* ***(P-19657)***
Rehablitation Inst Orange Cnty, Orange *Also called Rehabltation Inst Southern Cal* ***(P-22660)***
Rehabltation Inst Southern Cal (PA)......C......714 633-7400
1800 E La Veta Ave Orange (92866) ***(P-22660)***
Rehabltion Cntre of Bvrly Hlls......C......323 782-1500
580 S San Vicente Blvd Los Angeles (90048) ***(P-20721)***
Rehabltion Cntre of Bkrsfield, Bakersfield *Also called Bakersfield Healthcare* ***(P-20254)***
Rehabworks At Freedom Village, Lake Forest *Also called Freedom Village Healthcare Ctr* ***(P-20438)***
Reichardt Duck Farm Inc......D......707 762-6314
3770 Middle Two Rock Rd Petaluma (94952) ***(P-444)***
Reichert Lengfeld Ltd Partnr......D......510 845-1077
725 Folger Ave Albany (94710) ***(P-13107)***
Reid & Helly......D......951 682-1771
3880 Lemon St Fl 5 Riverside (92501) ***(P-23352)***
Reign Accessories Inc......E......310 297-6400
4000 Redondo Beach Ave Redondo Beach (90278) ***(P-27013)***
Reilly Worldwide Inc......E......310 449-4065
3000 Olympic Blvd Santa Monica (90404) ***(P-18106)***
Reinhardt Roofing Inc......D......510 713-7014
19258 Donna Ct Morgan Hill (95037) ***(P-3196)***
Reiter Affl Companies LLC......C......805 925-8577
124 Carmen Ln Ste A Santa Maria (93458) ***(P-115)***
Reiter Affl Companies LLC......D......831 786-4244
140 Westridge Dr Watsonville (95076) ***(P-116)***
Reiter Affl Companies LLC (PA)......E......805 483-1000
730 S A St Oxnard (93030) ***(P-117)***
Reiter Berry Watsonville, Watsonville *Also called Reiter Affl Companies LLC* ***(P-116)***
Related Technologies Inc......D......916 357-5900
81 Blue Ravine Rd Ste 230 Folsom (95630) ***(P-15403)***
Relational Investors LLC......D......858 704-3333
12400 High Bluff Dr # 600 San Diego (92130) ***(P-10108)***
Relationedge LLC......C......858 451-4665
10120 Pacific Heights Blv San Diego (92121) ***(P-16244)***
Releasepoint, Claremont *Also called Western Feld Invstigations Inc* ***(P-16261)***
Reliable Caregivers Inc......C......415 436-0100
1700 California St # 400 San Francisco (94109) ***(P-22403)***
Reliable Carriers Inc......E......818 252-6400
9122 Glenoaks Blvd Sun Valley (91352) ***(P-4250)***
Reliable Co, Glendale *Also called Coinmach Corporation* ***(P-13558)***
Reliable Container, Santa Fe Springs *Also called Georgia-Pacific LLC* ***(P-8105)***
Reliable Energy Management Inc......D......562 984-5511
7201 Rosecrans Ave Paramount (90723) ***(P-2335)***
Reliable Gardens Inc......D......818 904-9801
7837 Burnet Ave Van Nuys (91405) ***(P-929)***
Reliable Graphics, Van Nuys *Also called ARC Document Solutions Inc* ***(P-14081)***
Reliable Health Care Svcs Inc......E......310 397-2229
5705 Sepulveda Blvd Culver City (90230) ***(P-14903)***
Reliable Interiors Inc......C......951 371-3390
104 S Maple St Corona (92880) ***(P-27014)***
Reliable Moving & Storage, Arvin *Also called Bakersfield Moving & Storage* ***(P-4331)***
Reliable Nursing Solutions......D......760 946-9191
16057 Kamana Rd Ste B Apple Valley (92307) ***(P-14720)***
Reliable Wholesale Lumber Inc (PA)......D......714 848-8222
7600 Redondo Cir Huntington Beach (92648) ***(P-6857)***
Reliance Company, Los Angeles *Also called Zastrow Construction Inc* ***(P-1328)***
Reliance Intermodal Inc......D......209 946-0200
1919 Martin Luther King Stockton (95210) ***(P-8446)***
Reliance Media Works Vfx Inc......E......818 557-7333
1800 Vine St Los Angeles (90028) ***(P-18215)***
Reliance Steel & Aluminum Co (PA)......D......213 687-7700
350 S Grand Ave Ste 5100 Los Angeles (90071) ***(P-7304)***
Reliance Steel & Aluminum Co......D......510 476-4400
33201 Western Ave Union City (94587) ***(P-7305)***
Reliance Steel & Aluminum Co......D......562 695-0467
9351 Norwalk Blvd Santa Fe Springs (90670) ***(P-7306)***
Reliance Steel & Aluminum Co......C......714 736-4800
15090 Northam St La Mirada (90638) ***(P-7307)***
Reliance Steel & Aluminum Co......C......323 583-6111
2537 E 27th St Vernon (90058) ***(P-7308)***
Reliance Steel & Aluminum Co......D......562 944-3322
12034 Greenstone Ave Santa Fe Springs (90670) ***(P-7309)***
Reliance Steel Company, Vernon *Also called Reliance Steel & Aluminum Co* ***(P-7308)***
Relibale Carriers, Sun Valley *Also called Reliable Carriers Inc* ***(P-4250)***
Religious Technology Center......D......323 663-3258
1710 Ivar Ave Ste 1100 Los Angeles (90028) ***(P-12141)***
Rels LLC......A......949 214-1000
40 Pacifica Ste 900 Irvine (92618) ***(P-11725)***
Rels Valuation, Irvine *Also called Rels LLC* ***(P-11725)***
Relx Inc......D......213 627-1130
555 W 5th St Ste 4500 Los Angeles (90013) ***(P-16245)***
REM Eye Wear, Sun Valley *Also called REM Optical Company Inc* ***(P-7247)***

REM Optical Company Inc.....D.....818 504-3950
10941 La Tuna Canyon Rd Sun Valley (91352) **(P-7247)**
Remax Accord, Pleasanton *Also called S&J Stadtler Inc* **(P-11751)**
Remax Active Realty.....E.....510 505-1660
4056 Decoto Rd Fremont (94555) **(P-11726)**
Remax Active Teal State, Fremont *Also called Remax Active Realty* **(P-11726)**
Remax All Stars Realty.....D.....951 739-4000
765 N Main St Corona (92880) **(P-11727)**
Remax Champions Real Estate, Upland *Also called Re/Max LLC* **(P-11709)**
Remax College Park Realty, Long Beach *Also called College Park Realty Inc* **(P-11368)**
Remax Estate Properties, Rancho Palos Verdes *Also called Re/Max Plos Vrdes Rlty / Exces* **(P-11713)**
Remax Gold.....D.....916 609-2800
3620 Fair Oaks Blvd # 300 Sacramento (95864) **(P-11728)**
Remax Legends, Alta Loma *Also called Inland Empire RE Solutions* **(P-11512)**
Remax Metro Inc.....D.....714 557-2544
150 Paularino Ave Ste 125 Costa Mesa (92626) **(P-11729)**
Remax Olson.....D.....805 267-4929
30699 Russell Ranch Rd Westlake Village (91362) **(P-11730)**
Remax Value Properties, San Jose *Also called Quail Hill Investments Inc* **(P-12186)**
Remax VIP, Bell Gardens *Also called Auchante Inc* **(P-11225)**
Remedy Intelligent Staffing, Aliso Viejo *Also called Remedytemp Inc* **(P-14904)**
Remedytemp Inc (HQ).....C.....949 425-7600
101 Enterprise Ste 100 Aliso Viejo (92656) **(P-14904)**
Remington Club I & II, San Diego *Also called Five Star Quality Care Inc* **(P-20433)**
Remington Hotel Corporation.....D.....760 322-6000
888 E Tahquitz Canyon Way Palm Springs (92262) **(P-13108)**
Remington Hotel Corporation.....A.....310 553-6561
1150 S Beverly Dr Los Angeles (90035) **(P-13109)**
Remington Ldging Hsptality LLC.....A.....877 932-5333
6526 Yount St Yountville (94599) **(P-13110)**
Remote Control Productions Inc (PA).....E.....310 260-0171
1547 14th St Santa Monica (90404) **(P-18107)**
Renaissance Clubsport, Walnut Creek *Also called Leisure Sports Inc* **(P-12847)**
Renaissance Hotel Clubsport.....D.....949 643-6700
50 Enterprise Aliso Viejo (92656) **(P-13111)**
Renaissance Hotel Holdings Inc.....D.....707 935-6600
1325 Broadway Sonoma (95476) **(P-13112)**
Renaissance Hotel Operating Co.....A.....760 773-4444
44400 Indian Wells Ln Indian Wells (92210) **(P-13113)**
Renaissance Indian Wells, Indian Wells *Also called Renaissance Hotel Operating Co* **(P-13113)**
Renaissance Palm Springs, Palm Springs *Also called HHC Trs Portsmouth LLC* **(P-12654)**
Renaissance Palm Springs Hotel, Palm Springs *Also called Crestline Hotels & Resorts LLC* **(P-12500)**
Renaissnce Clbsport Aliso Vejo, Aliso Viejo *Also called L & O Aliso Viejo LLC* **(P-18620)**
Renaissnce Esmralda Resort Spa.....D.....760 773-4444
44400 Indian Wells Ln Indian Wells (92210) **(P-13114)**
Renal Center, Orange *Also called St Joseph Hospital of Orange* **(P-21783)**
Renal Treatment Ctrs - Cal Inc.....D.....714 990-0110
595 Tamarack Ave Ste A Brea (92821) **(P-22485)**
Renal Treatment Ctrs - Cal Inc.....D.....949 930-6882
15271 Laguna Canyon Rd Irvine (92618) **(P-22486)**
Reneson Hotels Inc (PA).....D.....650 449-5353
2700 Junipero Serra Blvd Daly City (94015) **(P-13115)**
Reneson Hotels Inc.....C.....415 621-7001
112 7th St San Francisco (94103) **(P-13116)**
Renn Transportation Inc.....D.....408 842-3545
8845 Forest St Gilroy (95020) **(P-4251)**
Reno Tenco, Boron *Also called Rio Tinto Minerals Inc* **(P-1010)**
Renova Energy Corp.....E.....760 568-3413
75181 Mediterranean Palm Desert (92211) **(P-2336)**
Renovate America Inc.....C.....858 605-5333
15073 Ave Of Science # 200 San Diego (92128) **(P-15404)**
Renovo Solutions LLC.....B.....714 599-7969
4 Executive Cir Ste 185 Irvine (92614) **(P-27015)**
Rent.com, Los Angeles *Also called Viva Group Inc* **(P-11138)**
Renteria Santiago J Farm Labo.....C.....661 792-0052
137 W Kern Ave Mc Farland (93250) **(P-14721)**
Rentjuice Corporation.....D.....415 376-0369
225 Bush St Ste 1100 San Francisco (94104) **(P-5634)**
Rentokil North America Inc.....D.....562 802-2238
15415 Marquardt Ave Santa Fe Springs (90670) **(P-9094)**
Rentpayment.com, Walnut Creek *Also called Yapstone Inc* **(P-17601)**
Renty LLC.....E.....858 560-0066
8025 Clairemont Mesa Blvd San Diego (92111) **(P-3834)**
REO World Inc.....D.....949 478-8000
170 Nwport Ctr Dr Ste 150 Newport Beach (92660) **(P-12046)**
Replanet LLC.....D.....909 980-1203
9910 6th St Rancho Cucamonga (91730) **(P-6450)**
Reprints Desk Inc.....D.....310 477-0354
15821 Ventura Blvd # 165 Encino (91436) **(P-16246)**
Reproductive Ptnr Med Grp Inc (PA).....E.....310 318-3010
510 N Prospect Ave # 202 Redondo Beach (90277) **(P-19818)**
Reproductive Science Center.....D.....925 867-1800
100 Park Pl Ste 200 San Ramon (94583) **(P-19819)**
Reproductive Science Ctr Bay, San Ramon *Also called Reproductive Science Center* **(P-19819)**
Republic Document Management (PA).....D.....909 718-1421
660 N Diamond Bar Blvd # 258 Diamond Bar (91765) **(P-23353)**
Republic Electric Inc.....D.....916 294-0140
3820 Happy Ln Sacramento (95827) **(P-2701)**
Republic Electric West Inc.....D.....916 294-0140
3820 Happy Ln Sacramento (95827) **(P-2702)**
Republic Indemnity Co Amer.....D.....415 981-3200
100 Pine St Fl 14 San Francisco (94111) **(P-10387)**
Republic Indemnity Company Cal.....C.....818 990-9860
15821 Ventura Blvd # 370 Encino (91436) **(P-10388)**
Republic Indemnity Company of (HQ).....C.....818 990-9860
15821 Ventura Blvd # 370 Encino (91436) **(P-10389)**
Republic Master Chefs Textile, Long Beach *Also called American Textile Maint Co* **(P-13505)**
Republic Services, Salinas *Also called BFI Waste Systems N Amer Inc* **(P-6356)**
Republic Services Inc.....E.....909 370-3377
2059 E Steel Rd Colton (92324) **(P-6451)**
Republic Services Inc.....D.....310 527-6980
1449 W Rosecrans Ave Gardena (90249) **(P-6452)**
Republic Services Inc.....D.....805 385-8060
111 S Del Norte Blvd Oxnard (93030) **(P-6453)**
Republic Svcs Vsco Rd Landfill.....E.....925 447-0491
4001 N Vasco Rd Livermore (94551) **(P-7427)**
Republic Uniform, Long Beach *Also called American Textile Maint Co* **(P-13504)**
Reputation Impression LLC.....D.....858 633-4500
9245 Activity Rd Ste 106 San Diego (92126) **(P-27422)**
Reputation Management Cons Inc.....D.....949 682-7906
1720 E Garry Ave Ste 103 Santa Ana (92705) **(P-27423)**
Reputationcom Inc (PA).....C.....650 381-3056
1400 A Sport Blvd Ste 401 Redwood City (94063) **(P-16932)**
RES-Care Inc.....D.....800 707-8781
17291 Irvine Blvd Ste 150 Tustin (92780) **(P-22404)**
RES-Care Inc.....C.....818 637-7727
611 S Central Ave Glendale (91204) **(P-20950)**
RES-Care California Inc.....E.....626 334-7862
200 W Paramount St Azusa (91702) **(P-20951)**
Res.net, Lake Forest *Also called US Real Estate Services Inc* **(P-11808)**
Rescom Services Inc.....D.....760 930-3900
1637 Kings Way Vista (92084) **(P-930)**
Rescue Agency Pub Beneft LLC (PA).....D.....619 231-7555
2437 Morena Blvd San Diego (92110) **(P-13891)**
Rescue Children Inc.....E.....559 268-1123
335 G St Fresno (93706) **(P-23991)**
Rescue Concrete Inc.....D.....916 852-2400
9275 Beatty Dr Sacramento (95826) **(P-3313)**
Rescue Mission Alliance (PA).....D.....805 487-1234
315 N A St Oxnard (93030) **(P-25454)**
Rescue Mission Alliance.....E.....805 201-4341
125 S Harrison Ave Oxnard (93030) **(P-22870)**
Rescue Rooter, Hayward *Also called American Residential Svcs LLC* **(P-2114)**
Rescue Rooter, Orange *Also called American Residential Svcs LLC* **(P-2115)**
Rescue Rooter, Sylmar *Also called American Residential Svcs LLC* **(P-2116)**
Rescue Rooter Bay Area North, San Leandro *Also called American Residential Svcs LLC* **(P-2113)**
Rescue Rooter Bay Area South, San Jose *Also called American Residential Svcs LLC* **(P-17932)**
Rescue Rotter, Riverside *Also called American Residential Svcs LLC* **(P-2112)**
Research, San Diego *Also called Sun Pharmaceuticals Inc* **(P-26462)**
Research & Dev & Mfg Site, San Diego *Also called Pacira Pharmaceuticals Inc* **(P-8202)**
Research Affiliates Capital LP.....D.....949 325-8700
620 Nwport Ctr Dr Ste 900 Newport Beach (92660) **(P-10109)**
Research Affiliates LLC.....D.....949 325-8700
620 Nwport Ctr Dr Ste 900 Newport Beach (92660) **(P-10110)**
Research Libraries Group Inc.....D.....650 288-1288
777 Mariners Island Blvd # 550 San Mateo (94404) **(P-16247)**
Research of America.....C.....916 443-4722
1232 Q St Ste 100 Sacramento (95811) **(P-16171)**
Research Triangle Institute.....D.....510 849-4942
2150 Shattuck Ave Ste 800 Berkeley (94704) **(P-27424)**
Reservation Ranch (PA).....C.....707 487-3516
356 Sarina Rd N Smith River (95567) **(P-13117)**
Reserve At Spanos Park, The, Stockton *Also called American Golf Corporation* **(P-18831)**
Reserve Club.....D.....760 674-2222
49400 Desert Butte Trl Indian Wells (92210) **(P-19013)**
Residence In Anaheim, Anaheim *Also called Holiday Garden SF Corp* **(P-12689)**
Residence Inn By Mariott, San Diego *Also called J5th LLC* **(P-12786)**
Residence Inn By Marriot Lax/C, Los Angeles *Also called Svi Lax LLC* **(P-13309)**
Residence Inn By Marriott, Oxnard *Also called Windsor Capital Group Inc* **(P-13402)**
Residence Inn By Marriott, Pleasanton *Also called Pleasant Canyon Hotel Inc* **(P-13070)**
Residence Inn By Marriott, San Diego *Also called Marriott International Inc* **(P-12909)**
Residence Inn By Marriott, San Diego *Also called Marriott International Inc* **(P-12890)**
Residence Inn By Marriott, San Mateo *Also called Island Hospitality MGT LLC* **(P-12782)**
Residence Inn By Marriott, Ontario *Also called Island Hospitality MGT LLC* **(P-12784)**
Residence Inn By Marriott, El Segundo *Also called Marriott International Inc* **(P-12892)**
Residence Inn By Marriott, San Diego *Also called Marriott International Inc* **(P-12893)**
Residence Inn By Marriott, Ontario *Also called Marriott International Inc* **(P-12895)**
Residence Inn By Marriott, Corona *Also called Marriott International Inc* **(P-12897)**
Residence Inn By Marriott, Los Angeles *Also called Sunstone Hotel Properties Inc* **(P-13303)**
Residence Inn By Marriott, Manhattan Beach *Also called Sunstone Hotel Properties Inc* **(P-13304)**
Residence Inn By Marriott, Pleasant Hill *Also called Marriott International Inc* **(P-12905)**
Residence Inn By Marriott, Los Angeles *Also called Beverly Sunstone Hills LLC* **(P-12382)**
Residence Inn By Marriott, La Mirada *Also called B S A Partners* **(P-12348)**
Residence Inn By Marriott.....D.....559 222-8900
5322 N Diana St Fresno (93710) **(P-13118)**
Residence Inn By Marriott.....D.....714 533-3555
1700 S Clementine St Anaheim (92802) **(P-13119)**
Residence Inn By Marriott.....D.....714 996-0555
700 W Kimberly Ave Placentia (92870) **(P-13120)**
Residence Inn By Marriott.....D.....858 673-1900
11002 Rancho Carmel Dr San Diego (92128) **(P-13121)**
Residence Inn La Lax El Segndo, El Segundo *Also called Hit Portfolio I NTC Trs LP* **(P-12685)**

A
L
P
H
A
B
E
T
I
C

Employee Codes: A=Over 500 employees, B=251-500
C=101-250, D=51-100, E=50
2019 Directory of California
Wholesalers and Services Companies
© Mergent Inc. 1-800-342-5647
1441

Residence Mutual Insurance Co ....D....949 724-9402
2172 Dupont Dr Ste 220 Irvine (92612) ***(P-10390)***
Resident Group Services Inc (PA) ....C....714 630-5300
1156 N Grove St Anaheim (92806) ***(P-931)***
Residential Bancorp (PA) ....D....330 499-8333
22632 Goln Spgs Dr Ste 20 Diamond Bar (91765) ***(P-9855)***
Residential Design Service, Anaheim *Also called LARK Industries Inc* ***(P-17291)***
Residential Fire Systems Inc ....D....714 666-8450
8085 E Crystal Dr Anaheim (92807) ***(P-2337)***
Residential Mortgage Ctr 39, El Segundo *Also called City National Bank* ***(P-9340)***
Residential Wall Systems, Corona *Also called Quality Wall Systems Inc* ***(P-2945)***
Residnce By Mria San Dego Cntl, San Diego *Also called Rt Sd-Denver LP* ***(P-13150)***
Residnce Inn By Mrriott Irvine ....D....949 380-3000
10 Morgan Irvine (92618) ***(P-13122)***
Residnce Inn By Mrriott Oxnard, Oxnard *Also called Recp Rl Oxnard LLC* ***(P-13103)***
Residnce Inn By Mrrott Stckton, Stockton *Also called Castlehill Properties Inc* ***(P-12439)***
Residncy Prgram Natividad Hosp, Salinas *Also called County of Monterey* ***(P-21356)***
Residntial Alzheimers Care Inc ....C....858 565-4424
9619 Chesapeake Dr # 103 San Diego (92123) ***(P-27016)***
Resmex Partners LLC ....E....415 440-2737
438 Geary St San Francisco (94102) ***(P-17427)***
Resolution Economics Group LLC (PA) ....D....310 275-9137
1925 Century Park E Fl 15 Los Angeles (90067) ***(P-27842)***
Resolve Systems LLC (PA) ....D....949 325-0120
2302 Martin Ste 225 Irvine (92612) ***(P-15405)***
Resonate Inc (PA) ....C....408 545-5500
90 Great Oaks Blvd # 205 San Jose (95119) ***(P-15406)***
Resort At Pelican Hill LLC ....C....949 467-6800
22701 Pelican Hill Rd S Newport Coast (92657) ***(P-13123)***
Resort At Squaw Creek, Alpine Meadows *Also called Squaw Creek Associates LLC* ***(P-13257)***
Resort Campground Intl, Lytle Creek *Also called Burlingame Industries Inc* ***(P-13460)***
Resort Parking Services Inc ....C....760 328-4041
39755 Berkey Dr B Palm Desert (92211) ***(P-17705)***
Resort Procomm Inc ....D....858 866-6280
9550 Waples St Ste 105 San Diego (92121) ***(P-27425)***
Resortime.com, Carlsbad *Also called Grand Pacific Resorts Inc* ***(P-17200)***
Resource Collection Inc ....A....310 219-3272
3771 W 242nd St Ste 205 Torrance (90505) ***(P-14365)***
Resource Connection of Amador (PA) ....D....209 754-3114
444 E Saint Charles St San Andreas (95249) ***(P-23992)***
Resource Connection of Amador ....D....209 223-7685
430 Sutter Hill Rd Sutter Creek (95685) ***(P-23993)***
Resource Connection, The, San Andreas *Also called Resource Connection of Amador* ***(P-23992)***
Resource Environmental Inc ....D....562 468-7000
6634 Schilling Ave Long Beach (90805) ***(P-1629)***
Resource Management Group Inc (PA) ....D....858 677-0884
4686 Mercury St San Diego (92111) ***(P-5155)***
Resource Rfrral Child Care Dev ....E....559 673-9173
1225 Gill Ave Madera (93637) ***(P-23994)***
Resource Staffing Group, Sacramento *Also called Northwest Staffing Resources* ***(P-14673)***
Resources Connection Inc ....D....714 430-6550
695 Town Center Dr # 600 Costa Mesa (92626) ***(P-27426)***
Resources Connection Inc (PA) ....A....714 430-6400
17101 Armstrong Ave # 100 Irvine (92614) ***(P-27427)***
Resources Connection LLC (HQ) ....D....714 430-6400
17101 Armstrong Ave # 100 Irvine (92614) ***(P-14722)***
Resources Global Professionals, Irvine *Also called Resources Connection LLC* ***(P-14722)***
Resources Global Professionals, Costa Mesa *Also called Resources Connection Inc* ***(P-27426)***
RESPITE SERVICE, Yuba City *Also called Tri County Respite Care Svc* ***(P-24095)***
Respond 2 LLC ....D....415 398-4200
727 Ansome St San Francisco (94111) ***(P-18108)***
Response 1 Medical Staffing ....C....916 932-0430
1101 Inv Blvd Ste 140 El Dorado Hills (95762) ***(P-14723)***
Responselogix Inc ....C....408 220-6505
2001 Gateway Pl Ste 750w San Jose (95110) ***(P-27017)***
Responsible Med Solutions Corp ....E....951 308-0024
41715 Winchester Rd # 101 Temecula (92590) ***(P-19820)***
Responsys Inc (HQ) ....C....650 745-1700
1100 Grundy Ln Ste 300 San Bruno (94066) ***(P-15407)***
Responsys.com, San Bruno *Also called Responsys Inc* ***(P-15407)***
Restaurant Depot, Sacramento *Also called Jetro Cash and Carry Entps LLC* ***(P-8418)***
Restaurant Depot, San Francisco *Also called Jetro Cash and Carry Entps LLC* ***(P-8620)***
Restaurant Depot ....E....714 378-3535
17332 Gothard St Huntington Beach (92647) ***(P-8447)***
Restaurant Depot LLC ....C....408 344-0107
520 Brennan St San Jose (95131) ***(P-8499)***
Restaurant Depot LLC ....C....714 666-9205
1265 N Kraemer Blvd Anaheim (92806) ***(P-9019)***
Restaurant Depot LLC ....C....626 744-0204
180 N San Gabriel Blvd Pasadena (91107) ***(P-8500)***
Restaurant Depot LLC ....D....310 516-7400
19901 Hamilton Ave Ste A Torrance (90502) ***(P-9020)***
Restaurant Depot LLC ....C....415 920-2888
2045 Evans Ave San Francisco (94124) ***(P-9021)***
Restaurant Depot LLC ....C....323 964-1220
5333 W Jefferson Blvd Los Angeles (90016) ***(P-9022)***
Restaurant Depot LLC ....C....510 628-0600
400 High St Oakland (94601) ***(P-8501)***
Restaurant Depot LLC ....C....714 378-3535
17332 Gothard St Huntington Beach (92647) ***(P-8502)***
Restaurant Depot LLC ....D....562 634-6771
2300 E 68th St Long Beach (90805) ***(P-8503)***
Restaurant Depot LLC ....C....818 376-7687
15853 Strathern St Van Nuys (91406) ***(P-9023)***
Restaurant In A Box Llc ....E....800 676-1281
3191 Red Hill Ave Costa Mesa (92626) ***(P-15408)***
Restec Contractors Inc ....D....510 670-0100
22955 Kidder St Hayward (94545) ***(P-3577)***
Restivo Enterprises ....D....408 988-4884
2590 Lafayette St Santa Clara (95050) ***(P-3835)***
Restoration Management Company, Hayward *Also called Jon K Takata Corporation* ***(P-23878)***
Restoration Resources, Rocklin *Also called Sierra View Landscape Inc* ***(P-940)***
Restoration Resources Hrs, Rocklin *Also called Habitat Rstration Sciences Inc* ***(P-855)***
Restore Motion, Foothill Ranch *Also called Team Makena LLC* ***(P-7221)***
Result Group Inc ....D....480 777-7130
2603 Main St Ste 710 Irvine (92614) ***(P-16043)***
Retail Pro International LLC ....D....916 605-7200
400 Plaza Dr Ste 200 Folsom (95630) ***(P-15409)***
Retail Pro Software, Folsom *Also called Retail Pro International LLC* ***(P-15409)***
Retail Services & Systems Inc ....D....916 984-6923
2765 E Bidwell St Folsom (95630) ***(P-27843)***
Retail Services & Systems Inc ....D....805 494-0108
394 N Moorpark Rd Thousand Oaks (91360) ***(P-27844)***
Retail Services Wis Corp ....D....951 653-1472
13800 Heacock St D135c Moreno Valley (92553) ***(P-17428)***
Retail Services Wis Corp ....D....626 288-1200
9080 Telstar Ave Ste 313 El Monte (91731) ***(P-17429)***
Retail Services Wis Corp ....C....916 485-3427
3800 Watt Ave Ste 101 Sacramento (95821) ***(P-17430)***
Retail Services Wis Corp ....D....714 637-3431
1838 N Tustin St Ste A Orange (92865) ***(P-17431)***
Retail Services Wis Corp ....E....818 772-4969
21354 Nordhoff St Ste 108 Chatsworth (91311) ***(P-17432)***
Retail Services Wis Corp ....D....818 407-2680
19420 Business Center Dr Northridge (91324) ***(P-17433)***
Retail Services Wis Corp ....D....805 644-5422
1932 Eastman Ave Ventura (93003) ***(P-17434)***
Retailnext Inc (PA) ....D....408 884-2162
60 S Market St Ste 1000 San Jose (95113) ***(P-15410)***
Retailnext Inc ....C....408 298-2585
845 Market St Ste 450 San Francisco (94103) ***(P-26562)***
Retinal Consultants Inc (PA) ....D....916 454-4861
3939 J St Ste 106 Sacramento (95819) ***(P-19821)***
Retirement Housing Foundation (PA) ....D....562 257-5100
911 N Studebaker Rd # 100 Long Beach (90815) ***(P-11731)***
Retirement Housing Foundation ....C....530 823-6131
750 Auburn Ravine Rd Auburn (95603) ***(P-24651)***
Retirement Housing Foundation ....D....209 466-4341
1319 N Madison St Ofc Stockton (95202) ***(P-11732)***
Retirement Lf Care Communities ....D....510 505-0555
3800 Walnut Ave Apt 401 Fremont (94538) ***(P-24652)***
Retreat & Conference Center ....E....707 252-3810
4401 Redwood Rd NAPA (94558) ***(P-13771)***
Retronix International Inc ....D....949 388-6930
65 Enterprise Aliso Viejo (92656) ***(P-17977)***
Retronix Semiconductors, Aliso Viejo *Also called Retronix International Inc* ***(P-17977)***
Rett Inc ....D....619 231-0403
402 W Broadway Ste 400 San Diego (92101) ***(P-14133)***
Reuben H Fleet Science Center ....C....619 238-1233
1875 El Prado San Diego (92101) ***(P-24900)***
Reutlinger Community ....C....925 964-2062
4000 Camino Tassajara Danville (94506) ***(P-23995)***
REUTLINGER COMMUNITY FOR JEWIS, Danville *Also called Reutlinger Community* ***(P-23995)***
Rev Enterprises ....E....818 551-7111
417 Arden Ave Ste 103 Glendale (91203) ***(P-16773)***
Revchem Composites Inc (PA) ....D....909 877-8477
2720 S Willow Ave B Bloomington (92316) ***(P-6926)***
Revchem Plastics, Bloomington *Also called Revchem Composites Inc* ***(P-6926)***
Reveal Imaging, Vista *Also called Leidos Inc* ***(P-26396)***
Revel Travel At Altour, Beverly Hills *Also called Revel Travel Service Inc* ***(P-4951)***
Revel Travel Service Inc ....D....310 553-5555
449 S Beverly Dr Ste 101 Beverly Hills (90212) ***(P-4951)***
Revenue Frontier LLC ....D....310 584-9200
6922 Hollywood Blvd 2 Los Angeles (90028) ***(P-13982)***
Revenue, Dept of, San Jose *Also called Santa Clara County of* ***(P-14022)***
Review Boost, Carlsbad *Also called Intravas Inc* ***(P-27281)***
Revjet ....C....650 508-2215
981 Industrial Rd Ste F San Carlos (94070) ***(P-15842)***
Revlon Professional, San Diego *Also called Creative Nail Design Inc* ***(P-13651)***
Revo Payments, Venice *Also called Globalex Corporation* ***(P-15693)***
Revolt Media and Tv LLC ....C....323 645-3000
1800 N Highland Ave Fl 7 Los Angeles (90028) ***(P-5833)***
Revolution Studios Dist Co LP (PA) ....D....310 255-7000
225 Santa Monica Blvd # 900 Santa Monica (90401) ***(P-18242)***
Rew Inc ....D....805 541-1308
973 Higuera St Ste A San Luis Obispo (93401) ***(P-10304)***
Rew Inc, Riverside *Also called Roy E Whitehead Inc* ***(P-3069)***
Rex Moore Group Inc ....B....916 372-1300
6001 Outfall Cir Sacramento (95828) ***(P-2703)***
Rex More Elec Contrs Engineers (PA) ....A....916 372-1300
6001 Outfall Cir Sacramento (95828) ***(P-2704)***
Rex More Elec Contrs Engineers ....D....559 294-1300
5803 E Harvard Ave Fresno (93727) ***(P-2705)***
Rex More Elec Contrs Engineers ....D....510 785-1300
6001 Outfall Cir Sacramento (95828) ***(P-2706)***
Rey Con Construction Inc ....C....805 525-8134
1795 E Lemonwood Dr Santa Paula (93060) ***(P-3314)***
Rey-Crest Roofg Waterproofing, Los Angeles *Also called Rey-Crest Roofg Waterproofing* ***(P-3578)***

Mergent e-mail: customerrelations@mergent.com
1442
2019 Directory of California
Wholesalers and Services Companies
(P-0000) Products & Services Section entry number
(PA)=Parent Co (HQ)=Headquarters (DH)=Div Headquarters

Rey-Crest Roofg Waterproofing....D....323 257-9329
3065 Verdugo Rd Los Angeles (90065) ***(P-3578)***
Reyes Coca-Cola Bottling LLC....D....818 362-4307
12925 Bradley Ave Sylmar (91342) ***(P-8860)***
Reyes Holdings LLC....B....858 452-2300
8870 Liquid Ct San Diego (92121) ***(P-10011)***
Reynen & Bardis Construction (PA)....C....916 366-3665
10630 Mather Blvd Mather (95655) ***(P-1224)***
Reynolds Cleaning Services Inc....C....650 599-0202
1472 Oddstad Dr Redwood City (94063) ***(P-14366)***
Reynolds Health Industries....D....562 591-7621
1201 Walnut Ave Long Beach (90813) ***(P-21195)***
RFI Communications SEC Systems, San Jose *Also called RFI Enterprises Inc* ***(P-2707)***
RFI Enterprises Inc (PA)....D....408 298-5400
360 Turtle Creek Ct San Jose (95125) ***(P-2707)***
Rfid Corporation....C....925 473-9978
701 Willow Pass Rd Ste 10 Pittsburg (94565) ***(P-13551)***
Rfid Textile Services Inc....C....714 998-6109
1575 N Case St Orange (92867) ***(P-13619)***
Rfid Textile Services Inc....D....909 623-5135
300 E Commercial St Pomona (91767) ***(P-13552)***
Rfid Textile Services Inc....D....408 840-7504
8190 Murray Ave Gilroy (95020) ***(P-13620)***
Rfj Corporation....D....415 824-6890
930 Innes Ave San Francisco (94124) ***(P-2947)***
Rfj Meiswinkel, San Francisco *Also called Rfj Corporation* ***(P-2947)***
Rggd Inc (PA)....D....323 581-6617
4950 S Santa Fe Ave Vernon (90058) ***(P-8053)***
Rgis LLC....D....661 827-9195
5500 Ming Ave Ste 185 Bakersfield (93309) ***(P-17435)***
Rgis LLC....D....805 644-0454
1787 Mesa Verde Ave Ventura (93003) ***(P-17436)***
Rgis LLC....D....916 387-9692
8801 Folsom Blvd Ste 173 Sacramento (95826) ***(P-17437)***
Rgis LLC....C....248 651-2511
500 E Olive Ave Ste 240 Burbank (91501) ***(P-17438)***
Rgis LLC....D....925 829-2875
7567 Amador Valley Blvd Dublin (94568) ***(P-17439)***
Rgis LLC....D....408 243-9141
4320 Stevens Creek Blvd San Jose (95129) ***(P-17440)***
Rgis LLC....D....661 702-8987
25115 Avenue Stanford Valencia (91355) ***(P-17441)***
Rgis LLC....D....530 898-1015
20 Landing Cir Ste 100 Chico (95973) ***(P-17442)***
Rgis LLC....D....626 974-4841
1041 W Badillo St Covina (91722) ***(P-17443)***
Rgis LLC....D....559 224-5898
1322 E Shaw Ave Ste 170 Fresno (93710) ***(P-17444)***
Rgis LLC....D....714 541-1431
2000 E 4th St Ste 350 Santa Ana (92705) ***(P-17445)***
Rgis LLC....C....650 757-6770
2171 Junipero Serra Blvd # 400 Daly City (94014) ***(P-17446)***
Rgnext, Vandenberg Afb *Also called Range Generation Next LLC* ***(P-25889)***
Rgnext, El Granada *Also called Range Generation Next LLC* ***(P-27837)***
Rgs Services, Anaheim *Also called Resident Group Services Inc* ***(P-931)***
Rh, Alamo *Also called Round Hill Country Club* ***(P-19021)***
Rh Framing Inc....C....831 759-8860
815 Quail Ridge Ln Salinas (93908) ***(P-3066)***
Rhc Equipment LLC....E....530 892-1918
5237 Mallard Estates Rd Chico (95973) ***(P-1630)***
Rhcc, Fremont *Also called Raymond Handling Concepts Corp* ***(P-17976)***
Rheumatology Diagnostics Lab....D....310 253-5455
10755 Venice Blvd Los Angeles (90034) ***(P-22137)***
Rhf Plymouth Tower....D....951 248-0456
3401 Lemon St Ofc Riverside (92501) ***(P-24653)***
Rhi, Santa Rosa *Also called Richard Hancock Inc* ***(P-3067)***
Rhino Building Services Inc....C....858 455-1440
6650 Flanders Dr Ste K San Diego (92121) ***(P-14367)***
Rhino Ready Mix Trucking Inc (PA)....E....661 679-3643
3701 Pegasus Dr Ste 126 Bakersfield (93308) ***(P-4055)***
RHO Chem LLC (HQ)....E....323 776-6234
425 Isis Ave Inglewood (90301) ***(P-6546)***
RHODA GOLDMAN PLAZA, San Francisco *Also called Scott Street Senior Housing Co* ***(P-20953)***
Rhodes Retail Services Inc....D....916 714-9233
8603 Excelsior Rd Elk Grove (95624) ***(P-27428)***
RHS Corp....A....909 335-5500
350 Terracina Blvd Redlands (92373) ***(P-27018)***
Rhythm & Hues Studios, El Segundo *Also called Rhythm and Hues Inc* ***(P-18109)***
Rhythm and Hues Inc (PA)....D....310 448-7500
2100 E Grand Ave Ste A El Segundo (90245) ***(P-18109)***
Rhythmone LLC....D....650 961-9024
800 W El Camino Real Mountain View (94040) ***(P-15411)***
Rhythmone LLC (HQ)....D....415 655-1450
601 Montgomery St Fl 16 San Francisco (94111) ***(P-5635)***
RIA FINANCIAL SERVICE, Buena Park *Also called Continental Exch Solutions Inc* ***(P-9677)***
Riad Adoumie MD....D....310 373-6864
23560 Madison St Ste 110 Torrance (90505) ***(P-19822)***
Rialto Bioenergy Facility LLC....C....760 436-8870
5780 Fleet St Ste 310 Carlsbad (92008) ***(P-25893)***
RICA, Encino *Also called Republic Indemnity Company Cal* ***(P-10388)***
Rice Drywall Inc....D....714 543-5400
919 E 6th St Santa Ana (92701) ***(P-2948)***
Rich Meiers Landscaping Inc (PA)....D....661 723-2220
652 W Avenue L14 Lancaster (93534) ***(P-782)***
Richard Bagdasarian Inc....D....760 396-2168
65500 Lincoln St Mecca (92254) ***(P-167)***
Richard Burns MD....D....951 296-9300
41637 Margarita Rd # 100 Temecula (92591) ***(P-19823)***
Richard H Vila, Richmond *Also called Vila Construction Co* ***(P-1693)***
Richard Hancock Inc....E....707 528-4900
1029 3rd St Santa Rosa (95404) ***(P-3067)***
Richard Huetter Inc....D....818 700-8001
21050 Osborne St Canoga Park (91304) ***(P-6670)***
Richard Iest Dairy, Madera *Also called Iest Family Farms* ***(P-417)***
Richard Iest Dairy Inc....D....559 673-2635
13507 Road 17 Madera (93637) ***(P-29)***
Richard J Mendoza Inc....D....415 644-0180
501 2nd St Ste 330 San Francisco (94107) ***(P-10391)***
Richard J Metz MD Inc....E....310 553-3189
2080 Century Park E # 1609 Los Angeles (90067) ***(P-19824)***
Richard Joy Engineering, Portola *Also called R Joy Inc* ***(P-25885)***
Richard K Newman and Assoc Inc (PA)....E....661 634-1130
121 Monterey St Bakersfield (93305) ***(P-13553)***
Richard Realty Group Inc....D....760 603-8377
2792 Gateway Rd Ste 103 Carlsbad (92009) ***(P-11733)***
Richard Shames MD....D....415 388-0456
25 Mitchell Blvd Ste 8 San Rafael (94903) ***(P-19825)***
Richard Swanson Inc....D....209 632-3883
17659 Swanson Rd Delhi (95315) ***(P-195)***
Richard Wilson Wellington....D....626 812-7881
1025 N Todd Ave Azusa (91702) ***(P-294)***
Richards Watson & Gershon PC (PA)....C....213 626-8484
355 S Grand Ave Fl 40 Los Angeles (90071) ***(P-23354)***
Richards Group Inc....C....214 891-5700
888 S Figueroa St # 1400 Los Angeles (90017) ***(P-13892)***
Richards Grove Saralees Vinyrd....D....707 837-9200
1998 Jones Rd Windsor (95492) ***(P-168)***
Richmond American Homes....E....818 908-3267
16600 Sherman Way Ste 180 Van Nuys (91406) ***(P-1225)***
Richmond Area Mlt-Services Inc....D....415 392-4453
720 Sacramento St San Francisco (94108) ***(P-22661)***
Richmond Area Mlt-Services Inc....D....415 800-0699
3120 Mission St San Francisco (94110) ***(P-22662)***
Richmond Area Mlt-Services Inc....D....415 689-5662
1375 Mission St San Francisco (94103) ***(P-22663)***
Richmond Area Mlt-Services Inc....D....415 579-3021
1282 Market St San Francisco (94102) ***(P-22664)***
Richmond Area Mlt-Services Inc (PA)....D....415 800-0699
639 14th Ave San Francisco (94118) ***(P-22665)***
Richmond Country Club....D....510 231-2241
1 Markovich Ln Richmond (94806) ***(P-19014)***
Richmond District YMCA, San Francisco *Also called Young Mens Christian Assoc SF* ***(P-25325)***
Richmond Dst Neighborhood Ctr (PA)....D....415 751-6600
741 30th Ave San Francisco (94121) ***(P-23996)***
Richmond Peak Quality, Richmond *Also called Richmond Wholesale Meat Co* ***(P-8627)***
Richmond Plastering Inc....E....562 924-4202
12102 Centralia Rd Ste B Hawaiian Gardens (90716) ***(P-2949)***
Richmond Repair Shop, Richmond *Also called San Francisco Bay Area Rapid* ***(P-3709)***
Richmond Rescue Mission (PA)....D....510 215-4555
2114 Macdonald Ave Richmond (94801) ***(P-23997)***
Richmond Sanitary Service Inc (HQ)....C....510 262-7100
3260 Blume Dr Ste 100 Richmond (94806) ***(P-6547)***
Richmond Wholesale Meat Co....D....510 233-5111
2920 Regatta Blvd Richmond (94804) ***(P-8627)***
Richmond Yard Tower, Richmond *Also called San Francisco Bay Area Rapid* ***(P-3711)***
Rick Engineering Company, San Diego *Also called Glenn A Rick Engrg & Dev Co* ***(P-25715)***
Rick H Hitch Plastering Inc....C....916 334-3591
3306 Orange Grove Ave North Highlands (95660) ***(P-2950)***
Rick Hamm Construction Inc....D....714 532-0815
201 W Carleton Ave Orange (92867) ***(P-1841)***
Rick Solomon Enterprises Inc (PA)....D....310 280-3700
8460 Higuera St Culver City (90232) ***(P-8276)***
Rick Studer....E....323 357-1720
2610 Wisconsin Ave South Gate (90280) ***(P-4252)***
Rick Weiss New Hope Apartments....E....310 395-1026
1637 Appian Way Santa Monica (90401) ***(P-11108)***
Ricoh Business Solutions, Huntington Beach *Also called Ricoh Usa Inc* ***(P-6977)***
Ricoh Usa Inc....D....916 638-3333
3046 Prospect Park Dr # 100 Rancho Cordova (95670) ***(P-6974)***
Ricoh Usa Inc....D....415 733-5600
333 Bush St Ste 2500 San Francisco (94104) ***(P-6975)***
Ricoh Usa Inc....E....818 294-8601
9430 Topanga Canyon Blvd # 100 Chatsworth (91311) ***(P-6976)***
Ricoh Usa Inc....E....714 396-0568
17011 Beach Blvd Ste 1000 Huntington Beach (92647) ***(P-6977)***
Ricoh Usa Inc....D....213 629-1838
6330 Variel Ave Woodland Hills (91367) ***(P-6978)***
Ricoh Usa Inc....D....415 392-6850
333 Bush St Ste 2500 San Francisco (94104) ***(P-6979)***
Ricoh Usa Inc....E....818 703-0265
21820 Burbank Blvd # 229 Woodland Hills (91367) ***(P-6980)***
Ricoh Usa Inc....E....510 839-6399
1300 Clay St Ste 165 Oakland (94612) ***(P-6981)***
Ricoh Usa Inc....C....925 988-4000
1320 Willow Pass Rd Concord (94520) ***(P-6982)***
Ricoh Usa Inc....D....949 225-2300
16969 Von Karman Ave Irvine (92606) ***(P-6983)***
RIDE ON TRANSPORTATION, San Luis Obispo *Also called United Cerebral Palsy Assoc of* ***(P-24851)***
Rideout Memorial Hospital (HQ)....A....530 749-4416
726 4th St Marysville (95901) ***(P-21686)***
Ridgecrest Regional Hospital....B....760 499-7260
1011 N China Lake Blvd Ridgecrest (93555) ***(P-19826)***

ALPHABETIC

Ridgecrest Regional Hospital (PA).....D.....760 446-3551
1081 N China Lake Blvd Ridgecrest (93555) ***(P-21687)***
Ridgeside Construction Inc.....D.....909 218-7593
4345 E Lowell St Ste A Ontario (91761) ***(P-1226)***
Ridgeside Finishing, Ontario *Also called Ridgeside Construction Inc* ***(P-1226)***
Ridgetop Energy LLC.....E.....661 822-2400
7021 Oak Creek Rd Mojave (93501) ***(P-6100)***
Ridgway, Santa Rosa *Also called Finley Swim Center* ***(P-19175)***
Right At Home, Santa Rosa *Also called Pw Jade LLC* ***(P-22399)***
Right At Home, Pasadena *Also called Good Works LLC* ***(P-22306)***
Right At Home.....D.....310 313-0600
3435 Ocean Park Blvd # 110 Santa Monica (90405) ***(P-22405)***
Right Choice A Health Care.....B.....626 335-1318
620 S Glendora Ave Ste A Glendora (91740) ***(P-14724)***
Right Choice In-Home Care Inc.....A.....818 836-6001
7104 Owensmouth Ave Canoga Park (91303) ***(P-22406)***
Right Stuff Health Club, The, Campbell *Also called SIM Investment Corporation* ***(P-18651)***
Right Stuff Health Club, The, San Jose *Also called SIM Investment Corporation* ***(P-18652)***
Rightpoint Consulting LLC.....C.....310 451-4619
1453 3rd Street Promenade Santa Monica (90401) ***(P-16471)***
Rightscale Inc (PA).....D.....805 500-4164
402 E Gutierrez St Santa Barbara (93101) ***(P-15412)***
Riivos Inc.....D.....415 813-1840
130 Battery St Fl 3 San Francisco (94111) ***(P-2708)***
Rika Corporation.....D.....949 830-9050
332 W Brenna Ln Orange (92867) ***(P-3395)***
Rinaldi Convalescent Hospital, Granada Hills *Also called Medical Investment Co* ***(P-21157)***
Rinaldi Tile & Marble, Royal Oaks *Also called Gino Rinaldi Inc* ***(P-2998)***
Rincon Pacific LLC.....D.....805 986-8806
1312 Del Norte Rd Camarillo (93010) ***(P-118)***
Ringadoc, San Francisco *Also called Practice Fusion Inc* ***(P-15373)***
Ringcentral Inc (PA).....D.....650 472-4100
20 Davis Dr Belmont (94002) ***(P-16172)***
Rinks Anaheim Ice, The, Anaheim *Also called Anaheim Ice* ***(P-19096)***
Rio Bravo Ranch Shop.....E.....661 872-5050
15701 Highway 178 Bakersfield (93306) ***(P-456)***
Rio Bravo Rocklin, Lincoln *Also called Rocklin Power Investors LP* ***(P-6101)***
Rio Hndo Sbcute Nrsing Ctr LLC.....C.....323 838-5915
273 E Beverly Blvd Montebello (90640) ***(P-20722)***
Rio Hondo Community Dev Corp.....D.....626 401-2784
11706 Ramona Blvd Ste 107 El Monte (91732) ***(P-24831)***
Rio Hondo Convalescent Hosp, Montebello *Also called Rio Hndo Sbcute Nrsing Ctr LLC* ***(P-20722)***
Rio Hondo Education Consortium.....C.....562 945-0150
7200 Greenleaf Ave # 300 Whittier (90602) ***(P-23998)***
Rio Mesa Farms LLC.....D.....831 728-1965
75 Sakata Ln Watsonville (95076) ***(P-119)***
Rio Seo, San Diego *Also called Riosoft Holdings Inc* ***(P-15413)***
Rio Tinto Minerals Inc.....C.....760 762-7121
14486 Borax Rd Boron (93516) ***(P-1010)***
Rio Vista Development Company (PA).....C.....818 980-8000
4222 Vineland Ave North Hollywood (91602) ***(P-13124)***
Rio Vista Ventures LLC (PA).....E.....760 480-8502
15651 Old Milky Way Escondido (92027) ***(P-8448)***
Rio Vista Ventures LLC.....E.....559 897-6730
3646 Avenue 416 Reedley (93654) ***(P-8449)***
Riolo Transportation Inc.....C.....760 729-4405
2725 Jefferson St Ste 2d Carlsbad (92008) ***(P-5243)***
Rios Farming Company LLC.....C.....707 965-2587
3851 Chiles Pope Vly Rd Saint Helena (94574) ***(P-169)***
Riosoft Holdings Inc.....E.....858 529-5005
9255 Towne Centre Dr # 750 San Diego (92121) ***(P-15413)***
Riot Games Inc (HQ).....C.....310 828-7953
12333 W Olympic Blvd Los Angeles (90064) ***(P-15414)***
Riphagen & Bullerdick Inc.....E.....714 763-2100
5925 Ball Rd Cypress (90630) ***(P-11734)***
Rippling, San Francisco *Also called People Center Inc* ***(P-15829)***
Rls Electrical Contrs Inc.....E.....951 688-8049
7330 Sycamore Canyon Blvd # 1 Riverside (92508) ***(P-2709)***
Risk Management, San Bernardino *Also called Llu Advntist Hlth Sciences Ctr* ***(P-19656)***
Risk Management Solutions Inc (HQ).....C.....510 505-2500
7575 Gateway Blvd Newark (94560) ***(P-12142)***
Riskalyze Inc.....D.....530 748-1660
373 Elm Ave Auburn (95603) ***(P-16472)***
Ritchie Plumbing Inc.....C.....949 709-7575
11320 Lombardy Ln Moreno Valley (92557) ***(P-2338)***
Rite of Pass Athl Trai Cent.....C.....209 736-4500
10400 Fricot City Rd San Andreas (95249) ***(P-24654)***
Rite Way Enterprises.....E.....818 376-6960
7131 Valjean Ave Van Nuys (91406) ***(P-5156)***
Rite-Way Meat Packers Inc.....D.....323 826-2144
5151 Alcoa Ave Vernon (90058) ***(P-8628)***
Ritz Carlton, Rancho Mirage *Also called Ritz-Carlton Hotel Company LLC* ***(P-13126)***
Ritz Carlton Rancho Mirage, Rancho Mirage *Also called Ritz-Carlton Hotel Company LLC* ***(P-13130)***
Ritz Companies, Irvine *Also called Savoy Contractors Group Inc* ***(P-1230)***
Ritz-Carlton Halfmoon Bay, Half Moon Bay *Also called Bre Diamond Hotel LLC* ***(P-12396)***
Ritz-Carlton Hotel Company LLC.....B.....415 781-9000
690 Market St San Francisco (94104) ***(P-13125)***
Ritz-Carlton Hotel Company LLC.....B.....760 321-8282
68900 Frank Sinatra Dr Rancho Mirage (92270) ***(P-13126)***
Ritz-Carlton Hotel Company LLC.....B.....949 240-5020
1 Ritz Carlton Dr Dana Point (92629) ***(P-13127)***
Ritz-Carlton Hotel Company LLC.....A.....301 547-4700
8301 Hollister Ave Santa Barbara (93117) ***(P-13128)***
Ritz-Carlton Hotel Company LLC.....B.....415 773-6168
600 Stockton St San Francisco (94108) ***(P-13129)***
Ritz-Carlton Hotel Company LLC.....B.....760 321-8282
68900 Frank Sinatra Dr Rancho Mirage (92270) ***(P-13130)***
Ritz-Carlton Ht Marina Del Rey, Venice *Also called Host Hotels & Resorts LP* ***(P-12710)***
Ritz-Carlton Laguna Niguel, Dana Point *Also called Prutel Joint Venture* ***(P-13082)***
Ritz-Carlton Marina Del Rey.....D.....310 823-1700
4375 Admiralty Way Marina Del Rey (90292) ***(P-13131)***
Ritz-Carlton San Francisco, San Francisco *Also called Ritz-Carlton Hotel Company LLC* ***(P-13129)***
River Bend Nursing Home Inc.....D.....916 371-1890
2215 Oakmont Way West Sacramento (95691) ***(P-20723)***
River City Auto Recovery Inc.....D.....916 851-1100
3401 Fitzgerald Rd Rancho Cordova (95742) ***(P-17447)***
River City Bank, Sacramento *Also called Rcb Corporation* ***(P-9482)***
River City Bank (HQ).....D.....916 567-2600
2485 Natomas Park Dr # 100 Sacramento (95833) ***(P-9483)***
River Cy Basbal Inv Group LLC (PA).....D.....916 376-4700
400 Ball Park Dr West Sacramento (95691) ***(P-18531)***
River Cy Geoprofessionals Inc.....D.....916 372-1434
3050 Industrial Blvd West Sacramento (95691) ***(P-25894)***
River Island Country Club Inc.....D.....559 781-2917
31989 River Island Dr Porterville (93257) ***(P-19015)***
River Maid Land Co A Cal Ll (PA).....B.....209 369-3586
6011 E Pine St Lodi (95240) ***(P-561)***
River Oak Center For Children.....C.....916 226-2800
9412 Big Horn Blvd Ste 6 Elk Grove (95758) ***(P-20201)***
River Oak Center For Children (PA).....C.....916 609-5100
5445 Laurel Hills Dr Sacramento (95841) ***(P-22666)***
River Oak Center For Children.....D.....916 550-5600
5445 Laurel Hills Dr Sacramento (95841) ***(P-21196)***
River Ranch Fresh Foods LLC (HQ).....B.....831 758-1390
911 Blanco Cir Ste B Salinas (93901) ***(P-8725)***
River Ridge Farms Inc.....D.....805 647-6880
3135 Los Angeles Ave Oxnard (93036) ***(P-295)***
River Ridge Golf Club, Oxnard *Also called High Tide and Green Grass Inc* ***(P-18720)***
River Ridge Golf Club.....D.....805 981-8724
2401 W Vineyard Ave Oxnard (93036) ***(P-19016)***
River Ridge Gulf Course, Oxnard *Also called City of Oxnard* ***(P-18696)***
River Rock Casino, Geyserville *Also called River Rock Entertainment Auth* ***(P-13132)***
River Rock Entertainment Auth.....A.....707 857-2777
3250 Highway 128 Geyserville (95441) ***(P-13132)***
River Rock Equipment LLC.....D.....916 791-1609
216 Kenroy Ln Roseville (95678) ***(P-12002)***
Rivera Sanitarium Inc.....D.....562 949-2591
7246 Rosemead Blvd Pico Rivera (90660) ***(P-20724)***
Riverside Aditorium Events Ctr, Riverside *Also called Raincross Hospitality Corp* ***(P-13770)***
Riverside Auto Auction, Anaheim *Also called Califrnia Auto Dalers Exch LLC* ***(P-6580)***
Riverside Bhvral Heathcare Ctr, Riverside *Also called Riverside Sanitarium LLC* ***(P-20728)***
Riverside Care Inc.....C.....951 683-7111
4301 Caroline Ct Riverside (92506) ***(P-20725)***
Riverside Cmnty Hlth Systems (HQ).....D.....951 788-3000
4445 Magnolia Ave Fl 6 Riverside (92501) ***(P-21688)***
Riverside Cnty Probation Dept, Riverside *Also called County of Riverside* ***(P-23714)***
Riverside Cnty Rgional Med Ctr, Riverside *Also called Riverside University Health* ***(P-21690)***
Riverside Cnvalescent Hosp Inc (PA).....D.....530 343-5595
375 Cohasset Rd Chico (95926) ***(P-21197)***
Riverside Community Hospital, Riverside *Also called Riverside Cmnty Hlth Systems* ***(P-21688)***
Riverside Community Hospital, Riverside *Also called Riverside Healthcare System LP* ***(P-21689)***
Riverside Companion Services, San Bernardino *Also called Maxim Healthcare Services Inc* ***(P-14877)***
RIVERSIDE CONVALESCENT HOSPIT, Chico *Also called Riverside Cnvalescent Hosp Inc* ***(P-21197)***
Riverside Convention Center, Riverside *Also called Entrepreneurial Hospitality* ***(P-17152)***
Riverside Convention Center, Riverside *Also called City of Riverside* ***(P-17081)***
Riverside County Flood Control.....C.....951 955-1200
1995 Market St Riverside (92501) ***(P-27958)***
Riverside Dialysis Center.....E.....951 682-2700
4361 Latham St Ste 100 Riverside (92501) ***(P-22487)***
Riverside District Office, Riverside *Also called State Compensation Insur Fund* ***(P-10408)***
Riverside Equities LLC.....D.....951 688-2222
8487 Magnolia Ave Riverside (92504) ***(P-20726)***
Riverside Health Care Corp.....D.....209 523-5667
1611 Scenic Dr Modesto (95355) ***(P-21198)***
Riverside Health Care Corp (PA).....D.....530 897-5100
1469 Humboldt Rd Ste 175 Chico (95928) ***(P-21199)***
Riverside Health Care Corp.....D.....916 446-2506
1090 Rio Ln Sacramento (95822) ***(P-20727)***
Riverside Healthcare System LP.....A.....951 788-3000
4445 Magnolia Ave Riverside (92501) ***(P-21689)***
Riverside Marriott, Riverside *Also called Pinnacle Rvrside Hspitality LP* ***(P-13066)***
Riverside Med Clnic Ptient Ctr, Riverside *Also called Riverside Medical Clinic Inc* ***(P-19828)***
Riverside Medical Center, Riverside *Also called Kaiser Foundation Hospitals* ***(P-19615)***
Riverside Medical Clinic Inc.....B.....951 683-6370
7117 Brockton Ave Riverside (92506) ***(P-19827)***
Riverside Medical Clinic Inc (PA).....B.....951 683-6370
3660 Arlington Ave Riverside (92506) ***(P-19828)***
Riverside Nursery & Ldscp Inc.....D.....559 275-1891
4763 W Spruce Ave Ste 111 Fresno (93722) ***(P-9161)***
Riverside Research Institute.....E.....949 631-0107
3333 W Coast Hwy Ste 101 Newport Beach (92663) ***(P-26655)***
Riverside Sanitarium LLC.....D.....951 684-7701
4580 Palm Ave Riverside (92501) ***(P-20728)***
Riverside Scrap Ir & Met Corp (PA).....E.....951 686-2120
2993 6th St Riverside (92507) ***(P-7989)***

Riverside Transit Agency (PA).....B.....951 565-5000
1825 3rd St Riverside (92507) *(P-3699)*
Riverside University Health (PA).....D.....951 358-5000
4065 County Circle Dr Riverside (92503) *(P-21690)*
Riverside University Health.....A.....951 486-4000
26520 Cactus Ave Moreno Valley (92555) *(P-21691)*
Riverside-San Bernardino (PA).....D.....951 849-4761
11555 1/2 Potrero Rd Banning (92220) *(P-22667)*
Riverside-San Bernardino.....D.....951 654-0803
607 Donna Way San Jacinto (92583) *(P-19829)*
Riverview Golf and Country CLB.....D.....530 224-2254
4200 Bechelli Ln Redding (96002) *(P-19017)*
Riverwalk PST-Cute Rhblitation, Mission Viejo *Also called Rock Canyon Healthcare Inc (P-21200)*
Riviera Finance of Texas Inc (PA).....C.....310 540-3993
220 Avenue I Redondo Beach (90277) *(P-9747)*
Riviera Health Care Center, Pico Rivera *Also called Riviera Nursing & Conva (P-20729)*
Riviera Nursing & Conva.....C.....562 806-2576
8203 Telegraph Rd Pico Rivera (90660) *(P-20729)*
Riviera Partners LLC (PA).....D.....877 748-4372
141 10th St San Francisco (94103) *(P-27429)*
Riviera Reincarnate LLC.....D.....760 327-8311
1600 N Indian Canyon Dr Palm Springs (92262) *(P-13133)*
Rivio Inc.....E.....408 653-4400
2500 Augustine Dr Ste 100 Santa Clara (95054) *(P-5636)*
Rizal Community Center, Sacramento *Also called Southgate Recreation & Pk Dst (P-24062)*
RJ Allen Inc.....D.....714 539-1022
10392 Stanford Ave Garden Grove (92840) *(P-14456)*
RJ Noble Company (PA).....C.....714 637-1550
15505 E Lincoln Ave Orange (92865) *(P-1842)*
Rjb Enterprises Inc.....E.....714 484-3101
2579 W Woodland Dr Anaheim (92801) *(P-2710)*
Rjms Corporation (PA).....D.....510 675-0500
6999 Southfront Rd Livermore (94551) *(P-7794)*
RJN Investigations Inc.....D.....951 686-7638
360 E 1st St Ste 696 Tustin (92780) *(P-16774)*
RJP Construction & Painting (PA).....D.....949 707-5449
22600 Lambert St Ste 807 Lake Forest (92630) *(P-2474)*
RJS & Associates Inc.....C.....510 670-9111
1675 Sabre St Hayward (94545) *(P-3315)*
Rjt Compuquest Inc (PA).....B.....310 378-6666
222 N Pacific Coast Hwy El Segundo (90245) *(P-16473)*
RK Electric Inc.....C.....510 580-2850
42021 Osgood Rd Fremont (94539) *(P-2711)*
Rk Logistics Group Inc (PA).....D.....408 942-8107
41707 Christy St Fremont (94538) *(P-5157)*
Rki Instruments Inc (PA).....D.....510 441-5656
33248 Central Ave Union City (94587) *(P-7795)*
Rl Properties, Albany *Also called Reichert Lengfeld Ltd Partnr (P-13107)*
Rlh Fire Protection, Bakersfield *Also called CMA Fire Protection (P-2163)*
Rlj Hgn Emeryville Lessee LP.....D.....510 658-9300
1800 Powell St Emeryville (94608) *(P-13480)*
Rljhgn Emeryville Lessee LP.....C.....510 658-9300
1800 Powell St Emeryville (94608) *(P-13134)*
RM Galicia Inc.....C.....626 813-6200
1521 W Cameron Ave # 100 West Covina (91790) *(P-14021)*
RMA Group, Rancho Cucamonga *Also called R M A Group Inc (P-25886)*
RMC Painting & Restoration, Burlingame *Also called Robert Meuschke Company Inc (P-2475)*
RMC Transport, Riverside *Also called Bledsoe Masonry Inc (P-2798)*
Rmd Group Inc.....B.....562 866-9288
2311 E South St Long Beach (90805) *(P-27430)*
Rmg Recycling, San Diego *Also called Resource Management Group Inc (P-5155)*
Rmi International Inc.....D.....310 781-6768
1919 Torrance Blvd Torrance (90501) *(P-16775)*
Rmis, Westlake Village *Also called Registry Monitoring Ins Srvcs (P-11724)*
Rmkr, Campbell *Also called Rainmaker Systems Inc (P-27011)*
RMR Construction Company.....C.....415 647-0884
2424 Oakdale Ave San Francisco (94124) *(P-1631)*
RMR Inc (PA).....D.....805 928-4013
2311 S Oakley Ave Ste C Santa Maria (93455) *(P-3316)*
RMS Foundation Inc.....A.....562 435-3511
1126 Queens Hwy Long Beach (90802) *(P-13135)*
RMS Group Inc.....D.....714 373-4882
17802 Mitchell N Irvine (92614) *(P-1632)*
Rmt Landscape Contractors Inc.....E.....510 568-3208
421 Pendleton Way Oakland (94621) *(P-932)*
Rnc Capital Management LLC.....D.....310 477-6543
11601 Wilshire Blvd Ph Los Angeles (90025) *(P-10111)*
Rnc Genter Capital Management, Los Angeles *Also called Rnc Capital Management LLC (P-10111)*
Rncmba Inc.....C.....661 395-1700
4801 Truxtun Ave Bakersfield (93309) *(P-14905)*
Road Dept, San Andreas *Also called County of Calaveras (P-23632)*
Road Safety Inc.....C.....916 543-4600
4335 Pacific St Ste A Rocklin (95677) *(P-17448)*
Roadex America Inc.....D.....310 878-9800
1515 W 178th St Gardena (90248) *(P-5158)*
Roadium Open Air Market, Torrance *Also called Pioneer Theatres Inc (P-17400)*
Roadrunner Shuttle, Camarillo *Also called Airport Connection Inc (P-3637)*
Roadstar Trucking Inc.....D.....510 487-2404
30527 San Antonio St Hayward (94544) *(P-4056)*
Robbins Geller Rudman Dowd LLP (PA).....B.....619 231-1058
655 W Broadway Ste 1900 San Diego (92101) *(P-23355)*
Robert A Bothman Inc (PA).....C.....408 279-2277
2690 Scott Blvd Santa Clara (95050) *(P-3317)*
Robert A Hall.....D.....707 837-8564
9769 Dawn Way Windsor (95492) *(P-14906)*
Robert Alves Farms Inc.....D.....559 896-3309
10642 E Dinuba Ave Selma (93662) *(P-170)*
Robert Bosch Start-Up Pltfm NA.....E.....248 876-6430
400 Convention Way Redwood City (94063) *(P-15415)*
Robert C Hamilton.....D.....626 794-4103
1760 N Fair Oaks Ave Pasadena (91103) *(P-24655)*
Robert Cecchini Inc.....D.....925 634-4400
5301 Orwood Rd Brentwood (94513) *(P-77)*
Robert Clapper Cnstr Svcs Inc.....D.....909 829-3688
2223 N Locust Ave Rialto (92377) *(P-1633)*
Robert Consl Englekirk Strctrl (PA).....D.....323 733-6673
2116 Arlington Ave Lbby Los Angeles (90018) *(P-25895)*
Robert Half International Inc.....D.....408 961-2975
10 Almaden Blvd Ste 900 San Jose (95113) *(P-14725)*
Robert Half International Inc.....D.....213 270-6731
865 S Figueroa St # 2600 Los Angeles (90017) *(P-14726)*
Robert Half International Inc.....D.....415 434-2429
50 California St Ste 1000 San Francisco (94111) *(P-14727)*
Robert Half International Inc.....D.....510 744-6486
39141 Civic Center Dr # 205 Fremont (94538) *(P-14728)*
Robert Half International Inc.....D.....831 241-9042
4 Lower Ragsdale Dr # 101 Monterey (93940) *(P-14729)*
Robert Half International Inc.....D.....714 450-9838
1 City Blvd W Ste 1115 Orange (92868) *(P-14730)*
Robert Half International Inc (PA).....D.....650 234-6000
2884 Sand Hill Rd Ste 200 Menlo Park (94025) *(P-14907)*
Robert Half International Inc.....D.....925 930-7766
3000 Oak Rd Walnut Creek (94597) *(P-14731)*
Robert Half International Inc.....D.....951 779-9081
2280 Market St Ste 220 Riverside (92501) *(P-14732)*
Robert Half International Inc.....D.....916 852-1705
3100 Zinfandel Dr Ste 260 Rancho Cordova (95670) *(P-14733)*
Robert Half International Inc.....E.....408 293-8611
10 Almaden Blvd Ste 900 San Jose (95113) *(P-14734)*
Robert Half International Inc.....D.....888 744-9202
4225 Executive Sq Ste 300 La Jolla (92037) *(P-14735)*
Robert Half International Inc.....C.....415 434-1900
50 California St Ste 1000 San Francisco (94111) *(P-14736)*
Robert Half International Inc.....E.....650 574-8200
1850 Gateway Dr Ste 200 San Mateo (94404) *(P-14737)*
Robert Half International Inc.....D.....650 234-6000
2884 Sand Hill Rd Ste 200 Menlo Park (94025) *(P-14738)*
Robert Half International Inc.....D.....650 234-6000
2884 Sand Hill Rd Ste 200 Menlo Park (94025) *(P-14739)*
Robert Half International Inc.....D.....650 234-6000
2884 Sand Hill Rd Ste 200 Menlo Park (94025) *(P-14740)*
Robert Half International Inc.....D.....949 476-3199
18200 Von Karman Ave # 800 Irvine (92612) *(P-14741)*
Robert Half International Inc.....D.....626 463-2037
790 E Colo Blvd Ste 650 Pasadena (91101) *(P-14742)*
Robert Half International Inc.....D.....310 719-1400
990 W 190th St Ste 290 Torrance (90502) *(P-14743)*
Robert Half International Inc.....D.....650 812-9790
3600 W Byshore Rd Ste 103 Palo Alto (94303) *(P-14744)*
Robert Half International Inc.....E.....925 913-1000
2613 Camino Ramon San Ramon (94583) *(P-14745)*
Robert Half MGT Resources.....E.....510 271-0910
1999 Harrison St Ste 1100 Oakland (94612) *(P-27431)*
Robert Heely Construction, Bakersfield *Also called Robert Heely Construction LP (P-1974)*
Robert Heely Construction LP (PA).....B.....661 617-1400
5401 Woodmere Dr Bakersfield (93313) *(P-1974)*
Robert J Echter Foxpoint Farms, Encinitas *Also called J Robert Echter (P-270)*
Robert Kaufman Co Inc (PA).....C.....310 538-3482
129 W 132nd St Los Angeles (90061) *(P-8238)*
Robert Kaufman Co Inc.....E.....310 538-3482
135 W 132nd St Los Angeles (90061) *(P-8239)*
Robert Kaufman Fabrics, Los Angeles *Also called Robert Kaufman Co Inc (P-8238)*
Robert Kinsella Inc.....D.....949 453-9533
15375 Barranca Pkwy G107 Irvine (92618) *(P-8450)*
Robert Meuschke Company Inc.....E.....650 342-3993
1039 Edwards Rd Burlingame (94010) *(P-2475)*
Robert Moreno Insurance Svcs.....C.....714 525-5168
22860 Savi Ranch Pkwy Yorba Linda (92887) *(P-10758)*
Robert Morken Construction.....E.....530 386-1512
1300 Regency Way Ste 59 Kings Beach (96143) *(P-1227)*
Robert Quintero Labor Contg.....E.....559 732-6954
1827 S Bardo St Visalia (93277) *(P-14746)*
Robert Sknner Filtration Plant, Winchester *Also called Metropolitan Water District (P-6288)*
Robert Young Family Ltd Partnr.....D.....707 433-3228
4950 Red Winery Rd Geyserville (95441) *(P-710)*
Robert Young Vineyards, Geyserville *Also called Robert Young Family Ltd Partnr (P-710)*
Robert's Lumber, Bloomington *Also called Roberts Lumber Sales Inc (P-6858)*
Robertas Labor Contracting.....B.....831 678-8176
137 Main St Soledad (93960) *(P-14747)*
Roberts & Associates Inc.....D.....951 727-4357
8175 Limonite Ave Ste A1 Riverside (92509) *(P-22407)*
Roberts Lumber Sales Inc.....D.....909 350-9164
2661 S Lilac Ave Bloomington (92316) *(P-6858)*
Robertson Piper Management LLC.....C.....650 625-8333
963 Fremont Ave Los Altos (94024) *(P-27432)*
Robin K.....D.....323 235-5152
4731 Fruitland Ave Vernon (90058) *(P-8331)*
Robinsn Clgne Rsn Shpr Dvs Inc.....D.....619 338-4060
620 Nwport Ctr Dr Ste 700 San Diego (92101) *(P-23356)*
Robinson & Sons.....D.....530 265-5844
293 Lower Grass Valley Rd # 201 Nevada City (95959) *(P-401)*
Robinson and Enterprises, Nevada City *Also called Robinson & Sons (P-401)*
Robinson and Wood Inc.....D.....408 298-7120
160 W Santa Clara St # 1000 San Jose (95113) *(P-23357)*

ALPHABETIC

Employee Codes: A=Over 500 employees, B=251-500
C=101-250, D=51-100, E=50
2019 Directory of California
Wholesalers and Services Companies
© Mergent Inc. 1-800-342-5647
1445

Robinson Company Contrs Inc.....D.....619 697-6040
8871 Troy St Spring Valley (91977) ***(P-2339)***
Robinson Electric, Spring Valley *Also called Robinson Company Contrs Inc* ***(P-2339)***
Robinson Fresh, Torrance *Also called C H Robinson Intl Inc* ***(P-5022)***
Robinson Ranch Golf LLC.....C.....818 885-0599
27734 Sand Canyon Rd Santa Clarita (91387) ***(P-18752)***
Roboca Technology.....C.....561 501-3999
245 E Main St Ste 115 Alhambra (91801) ***(P-15416)***
Rocha Transportation, Modesto *Also called Ed Rocha Livestock Trnsp Inc* ***(P-4135)***
Rocha, Jill B MD, Ventura *Also called West Ventura Family Care Ctr* ***(P-20099)***
Roche Molecular Systems Inc.....C.....510 814-2800
1145 Atlantic Ave Ste 100 Alameda (94501) ***(P-26445)***
Roche Molecular Systems Inc (HQ).....B.....925 730-8000
4300 Hacienda Dr Pleasanton (94588) ***(P-26446)***
Rock Canyon Healthcare Inc.....B.....949 487-9500
27101 Puerta Real Ste 450 Mission Viejo (92691) ***(P-21200)***
Rock Paper Scissors LLC.....E.....310 586-0600
2308 Broadway Santa Monica (90404) ***(P-18110)***
Rock-It Cargo USA LLC.....D.....310 455-1900
120 N Topanga Canyon Blvd # 215 Topanga (90290) ***(P-5159)***
Rock-It Cargo USA LLC.....C.....310 410-0935
5343 W Imperial Hwy # 900 Los Angeles (90045) ***(P-5160)***
Rockefeller Group Dev Corp.....D.....949 468-1800
4 Park Plz Ste 840 Irvine (92614) ***(P-11910)***
Rocket Dog Brands, San Ramon *Also called Millennial Brands LLC* ***(P-8362)***
Rocket Farms Inc (PA).....C.....800 227-5229
2651 Cabrillo Hwy N Half Moon Bay (94019) ***(P-296)***
Rocket Farms Herbs Inc.....B.....562 340-5108
370 Espinosa Rd Salinas (93907) ***(P-377)***
Rocket Fuel Inc (HQ).....C.....650 595-1300
2000 Seaport Blvd Ste 400 Redwood City (94063) ***(P-16474)***
Rocket Smog Inc.....D.....310 390-7664
11413 W Washington Blvd Los Angeles (90066) ***(P-17781)***
Rockey Murata Landscaping.....D.....562 921-3210
15417 Cornet St Santa Fe Springs (90670) ***(P-783)***
Rockley Photonics Inc (HQ).....D.....626 304-9960
234 E Colo Blvd Ste 600 Pasadena (91101) ***(P-15417)***
Rocklin Power Investors LP.....D.....916 645-3383
3100 Thunder Valley Ct Lincoln (95648) ***(P-6101)***
Rockport ADM Svcs LLC.....D.....323 223-3441
4585 N Figueroa St Los Angeles (90065) ***(P-20730)***
Rockport ADM Svcs LLC (PA).....D.....323 330-6500
5900 Wilshire Blvd # 1600 Los Angeles (90036) ***(P-27433)***
Rockport Healthcare Services, Los Angeles *Also called Rockport ADM Svcs LLC* ***(P-27433)***
Rockstar San Diego.....C.....760 929-0700
2200 Faraday Ave Ste 200 Carlsbad (92008) ***(P-16173)***
Rockview Dairies Inc (PA).....D.....562 927-5511
7011 Stewart And Gray Rd Downey (90241) ***(P-8861)***
Rocky Coast Builders Inc.....D.....760 489-7770
135 Market Pl Escondido (92029) ***(P-3068)***
Rocky Packaging Solution Inc (PA).....E.....909 591-3331
13980 Mountain Ave Chino (91710) ***(P-9257)***
Rocky Point Care Center, Lakeport *Also called Windflower Holdings LLC* ***(P-20895)***
Rockyou Inc (PA).....D.....415 580-6400
1111 Broadway Ste 300 Oakland (94607) ***(P-16248)***
Rockyou Media, Oakland *Also called Rockyou Inc* ***(P-16248)***
Rocology South Bay, Santa Clara *Also called Recology Los Altos* ***(P-6440)***
Rodbat Security Services, Torrance *Also called Rmi International Inc* ***(P-16775)***
Rodda Electric Inc (PA).....D.....925 240-6024
380 Carrol Ct Ste L Brentwood (94513) ***(P-2340)***
Roddy Ranch Pbc LLC.....D.....925 978-4653
1 Tour Way Antioch (94531) ***(P-19018)***
Rodeo Realty Inc.....D.....818 986-7300
15300 Ventura Blvd # 101 Sherman Oaks (91403) ***(P-11735)***
Rodeo Realty Inc.....D.....310 873-0100
11940 San Vicente Blvd Los Angeles (90049) ***(P-11736)***
Rodeo Realty Inc.....D.....818 285-3700
17501 Ventura Blvd Encino (91316) ***(P-11737)***
Rodeo Realty Inc.....D.....818 308-8273
12345 Ventura Blvd Ste A Studio City (91604) ***(P-11738)***
Rodeo Realty Inc (PA).....D.....818 349-9997
9171 Wilshire Blvd # 321 Beverly Hills (90210) ***(P-11739)***
Rodeo Realty Inc.....D.....818 349-9997
9338 Reseda Blvd Ste 102 Northridge (91324) ***(P-11740)***
Rodeo Realty Inc.....D.....818 657-4609
23901 Calabasas Rd # 1050 Calabasas (91302) ***(P-11741)***
Rodeo Realty Inc.....D.....818 999-2030
21031 Ventura Blvd # 100 Woodland Hills (91364) ***(P-11742)***
Rodeway Inn, Tahoe City *Also called Pepper Tree Inn* ***(P-13056)***
Rodgers Security Service Inc.....C.....310 684-3016
8726 S Sepulveda Blvd Los Angeles (90045) ***(P-16776)***
Rodgers Trucking Co, San Leandro *Also called Frank Ghiglione Inc* ***(P-4015)***
Rodgz Farm Labor Contg LLC.....D.....530 329-8403
4422 College Way Olivehurst (95961) ***(P-671)***
Rodin & Co Inc.....D.....818 358-3427
7411 Laurel Canyon Blvd # 10 North Hollywood (91605) ***(P-2476)***
Rodney Strong Vineyards, Healdsburg *Also called Klein Foods Inc* ***(P-154)***
Roe Holdings LLC.....D.....310 559-9222
8437 Warner Dr Culver City (90232) ***(P-13893)***
Roebbelen Construction Inc.....D.....916 939-4000
1241 Hawks Flight Ct El Dorado Hills (95762) ***(P-1634)***
Roebbelen Contracting Inc.....B.....916 939-4000
1241 Hawks Flight Ct El Dorado Hills (95762) ***(P-1635)***
Rogan Building Services Inc.....E.....951 248-1261
1531 7th St Riverside (92507) ***(P-14368)***
Roger L Crumley MD Inc.....E.....714 456-5750
101 City Dr S Bldg 56 5 Orange (92868) ***(P-19830)***

Rogers Poultry Co (PA).....C.....323 585-0802
2020 E 67th St Los Angeles (90001) ***(P-8539)***
Rogers Trucking, San Leandro *Also called Frank Ghiglione Inc* ***(P-4016)***
Roi Communications Inc (PA).....D.....831 430-0170
5274 Scotts Valley Dr # 107 Scotts Valley (95066) ***(P-27845)***
Rokstad Power Corp.....E.....888 310-8830
8825 Aero Dr Ste 305 San Diego (92123) ***(P-7389)***
Roku Inc (PA).....B.....408 556-9040
150 Winchester Cir Los Gatos (95032) ***(P-5929)***
Roland Corporation US (HQ).....C.....323 890-3700
5100 S Eastern Ave Los Angeles (90040) ***(P-8054)***
Roland Dga Corporation (HQ).....C.....949 727-2100
15363 Barranca Pkwy Irvine (92618) ***(P-7098)***
Roll Properties Intl Inc.....C.....661 797-6500
13646 Highway 33 Lost Hills (93249) ***(P-12263)***
Rolled Steel Products Corp (PA).....D.....323 723-8836
2187 Garfield Ave Commerce (90040) ***(P-7310)***
Rolling Hills Casino, Corning *Also called Paskenta Band Nomlaki Indians* ***(P-13049)***
Rolling Hills Club, Novato *Also called Tennis Everyone Incorporated* ***(P-19067)***
Rolling Hills Estates City of, Rllng HLS Est *Also called Rolling Hlls Esttes Tennis CLB* ***(P-19226)***
Rolling Hlls Esttes Tennis CLB.....E.....310 541-4585
25851 Hawthorne Blvd Rllng HLS Est (90275) ***(P-19226)***
Rolo Logistics, Pico Rivera *Also called Rolo Transportation Company* ***(P-4057)***
Rolo Transportation Company.....D.....562 463-1440
9935 Beverly Blvd Pico Rivera (90660) ***(P-4057)***
Roma Food Enterprises Inc.....D.....800 233-6211
6211 Las Positas Rd Livermore (94551) ***(P-8862)***
Roma of Northern California, Livermore *Also called Roma Food Enterprises Inc* ***(P-8862)***
Romach LLC.....D.....805 378-1174
2956 Sparrow Dr Fullerton (92835) ***(P-7390)***
Roman Cath Arch of Los Angels.....E.....310 836-5500
5835 W Slauson Ave Culver City (90230) ***(P-13694)***
Roman Cath Arch of Los Angels.....A.....805 687-8811
199 N Hope Ave Santa Barbara (93110) ***(P-13695)***
Roman Catholic Archdiocese of.....D.....650 756-2060
1500 Old Mission Rd Daly City (94014) ***(P-11947)***
Roman Cthlic Bishp of San Jose.....A.....833 304-0763
22555 Cristo Rey Dr Los Altos (94024) ***(P-11948)***
Roman Cthlic Bshp of Snta Rosa.....C.....707 528-8712
987 Airway Ct Santa Rosa (95403) ***(P-24832)***
Romark Logistics of California.....D.....909 356-5600
13521 Santa Ana Ave Ste A Fontana (92337) ***(P-4626)***
ROMERO CONSTRUCTION, Escondido *Also called Romero General Cnstr Corp* ***(P-1843)***
Romero General Cnstr Corp.....C.....760 489-8412
2150 N Centre City Pkwy I Escondido (92026) ***(P-1843)***
Romex Textiles Inc (PA).....E.....213 749-9090
785 E 14th Pl Los Angeles (90021) ***(P-8240)***
Ron D & Shelley N Horn.....E.....559 834-2118
3719 E Floral Ave Fresno (93725) ***(P-171)***
Ron Filice Enterprises Inc.....E.....408 294-0477
738 N 1st St Ste 202 San Jose (95112) ***(P-10759)***
Ron Nurss Inc.....D.....916 631-9761
11290 Sunrise Park Dr B Rancho Cordova (95742) ***(P-3318)***
Ron's Pharmacy Services, San Diego *Also called Belville Enterprises Inc* ***(P-19322)***
Ronald J Lemieux Assoc Law Off.....D.....562 375-0095
4195 N Viking Way Ste E Long Beach (90808) ***(P-23358)***
Ronald L Wolfe & Assoc Inc.....E.....805 964-6770
173 Chapel St Santa Barbara (93111) ***(P-11743)***
Ronald Reagan Building, Los Angeles *Also called Ucla Health System* ***(P-20017)***
Ronald Reagan Presdntl Library, Simi Valley *Also called Ronald Reagan Presidential* ***(P-24901)***
Ronald Reagan Presidential.....D.....805 522-2977
40 Presidential Dr # 200 Simi Valley (93065) ***(P-24901)***
Ronald Reagan Ucla Medical Ctr, Los Angeles *Also called University Cal Los Angeles* ***(P-21877)***
Ronco Inventions LLC (PA).....C.....800 486-1806
21344 Superior St Chatsworth (91311) ***(P-6785)***
Rongcheng Trading LLC.....E.....626 338-1090
19319 Arenth Ave City of Industry (91748) ***(P-8629)***
Ronsin Photocopy Inc (PA).....D.....909 594-5995
215 Lemon Creek Dr Walnut (91789) ***(P-17449)***
Roofing Constructors Inc.....C.....415 648-6472
15002 Wicks Blvd San Leandro (94577) ***(P-3197)***
Roofing Supply Group LLC.....D.....424 269-7330
14128 Kornblum Ave Hawthorne (90250) ***(P-6927)***
Roofing Wholesale Co Inc.....E.....619 287-7600
8674 Jamacha Rd Spring Valley (91977) ***(P-6928)***
Roofing Wholesale Co Inc.....D.....909 825-8440
118 Commercial Rd San Bernardino (92408) ***(P-6929)***
Roosevelt Hotel LLC.....C.....323 466-7000
7000 Hollywood Blvd Los Angeles (90028) ***(P-13136)***
Roost, Sausalito *Also called Gate Five Group LLC* ***(P-6763)***
Rooster Run Golf Club Inc.....E.....707 778-1211
2301 E Washington St Petaluma (94954) ***(P-18753)***
Rope Partner Inc.....D.....831 460-9448
125 Mcpherson St Ste B Santa Cruz (95060) ***(P-7867)***
Ropers Majeski Kohn & Bentley, Redwood City *Also called Ropers Majeski Kohn Bentley* ***(P-23359)***
Ropers Majeski Kohn Bentley (PA).....D.....650 364-8200
1001 Marshall St Fl 3 Redwood City (94063) ***(P-23359)***
Ropes & Gray LLP.....B.....415 315-6300
3 Embarcadero Ctr Ste 300 San Francisco (94111) ***(P-23360)***
Ropes & Gray LLP.....D.....650 617-4000
1900 University Ave # 600 East Palo Alto (94303) ***(P-23361)***
Roppongi-Tahoe Lp A Californi.....C.....530 544-5400
4130 Lake Tahoe Blvd South Lake Tahoe (96150) ***(P-13137)***

Mergent e-mail: customerrelations@mergent.com
1446
2019 Directory of California Wholesalers and Services Companies
(P-0000) Products & Services Section entry number
(PA)=Parent Co (HQ)=Headquarters (DH)=Div Headquarters

Roque Development and Inv .... D 626 427-9077
227 E Pomona Blvd Ste B Monterey Park (91755) *(P-25896)*
Rore Inc (PA) .... D 858 404-7393
5151 Shoreham Pl Ste 260 San Diego (92122) *(P-1636)*
Rory V Parker .... C 510 595-5543
818 27th St Ste 101 Oakland (94607) *(P-16777)*
Rosanna Inc .... C 714 751-5100
3350 Avenue Of The Arts Costa Mesa (92626) *(P-13138)*
Rosano Partners .... E 213 802-0300
700 S Flower St Ste 2526 Los Angeles (90017) *(P-11744)*
Rosary Academy Parent Council .... D 714 879-6302
1340 N Acacia Ave Fullerton (92831) *(P-25228)*
Roscoe Real Estate Ltd Partnr .... D 310 260-7500
1819 Ocean Ave Santa Monica (90401) *(P-13139)*
Rose & Kindel Grayling .... C 916 441-1034
1414 K St Ste 220 Sacramento (95814) *(P-24833)*
Rose & Shore Inc .... B 323 826-2144
5151 Alcoa Ave Vernon (90058) *(P-17450)*
Rose Bowl Aquatics Center .... D 626 564-0330
360 N Arroyo Blvd Pasadena (91103) *(P-19019)*
Rose Brand Wipers Inc .... D 818 505-6290
11440 Sheldon St Sun Valley (91352) *(P-18399)*
Rose Garden Convalescent Ctr, Pasadena *Also called David Ross Inc (P-20367)*
Rose Hills Co, Whittier *Also called Rose Hills Mortuary Inc (P-13696)*
Rose Hills Company (HQ) .... A 562 699-0921
3888 Workman Mill Rd Whittier (90601) *(P-11949)*
Rose Hills Holdings Corp (PA) .... A 562 699-0921
3888 Workman Mill Rd Whittier (90601) *(P-11950)*
Rose Hills Mem Pk & Mortuary, Whittier *Also called Rose Hills Company (P-11949)*
Rose Hills Mem Pk & Mortuary, Whittier *Also called Rose Hills Holdings Corp (P-11950)*
Rose Hills Mortuary Inc .... A 562 699-0921
3888 Workman Mill Rd Whittier (90601) *(P-13696)*
Rose International Inc .... C 636 812-4000
450 N Brand Blvd Fl 6 Glendale (91203) *(P-15418)*
Rose International Inc .... C 636 812-4000
4000 Executive Pkwy # 150 San Ramon (94583) *(P-27846)*
Rose International Inc .... E 636 812-4000
18952 Macarthur Blvd # 440 Irvine (92612) *(P-27847)*
Rose Thompson Company .... D 760 736-6020
949 Cassou Rd San Marcos (92069) *(P-297)*
Roseburg Forest Products Co .... C 530 938-2721
98 Mill St Weed (96094) *(P-6859)*
Rosecrans Care Center, Gardena *Also called Health Care Investments Inc (P-20516)*
Rosemary Childrens Services (PA) .... C 626 844-3033
36 S Kinneloa Ave 200 Pasadena (91107) *(P-24656)*
Rosemont Media LLC .... E 858 200-0044
1010 Turquoise St Ste 201 San Diego (92109) *(P-13894)*
Rosen Electronics LLC .... D 951 898-9808
1120 California Ave Corona (92881) *(P-8055)*
Rosendin Electric Inc (PA) .... A 408 286-2800
880 Mabury Rd San Jose (95133) *(P-2712)*
Rosendin Electric Inc .... A 714 739-1334
1730 S Anaheim Way Anaheim (92805) *(P-2713)*
Rosendin Electric Inc .... A 408 321-2200
2698 Orchard Pkwy San Jose (95134) *(P-2714)*
Rosendin Electric Inc .... C 415 495-9300
2121 Oakdale Ave San Francisco (94124) *(P-2715)*
Rosendin Electric Inc .... A 415 495-9300
1001 Potrero Ave San Francisco (94110) *(P-2716)*
ROSENER HOUSE, Menlo Park *Also called Peninsula Volunteers Inc (P-23967)*
Rosenthal Group, The, Venice *Also called Trg Inc (P-11800)*
Roseryan Inc .... D 510 456-3056
35473 Dumbarton Ct Newark (94560) *(P-26281)*
Roseville Care Center, Roseville *Also called Crocus Holdings LLC (P-20363)*
Roseville Convalescent Hosp, Roseville *Also called Horizon West Healthcare Inc (P-22024)*
Roseville Foothils and Jct, Roseville *Also called Wells Fargo Bank National Assn (P-9391)*
Roseville Imaging, Roseville *Also called Sutter Health (P-22151)*
Roseville Sportworld Inc .... D 916 783-8550
1009 Orlando Ave Roseville (95661) *(P-19227)*
Roseville Towne Place Suites .... D 916 782-2232
10569 Fairway Dr Roseville (95678) *(P-13140)*
Rosewood Convalescent Hospital, Pleasant Hill *Also called Dreamctchers Empwerment Netwrk (P-24509)*
Rosewood Hotels & Resorts LLC .... B 650 561-1500
2825 Sand Hill Rd Menlo Park (94025) *(P-13141)*
Rosewood Rehabilitation, Carmichael *Also called Carmichael Care Inc (P-20290)*
Rosewood Retirement Community, Bakersfield *Also called American Baptist Homes of West (P-20989)*
Rosewood Sand Hill Hotel, Menlo Park *Also called Rosewood Hotels & Resorts LLC (P-13141)*
Ross F Carroll Inc .... E 209 848-5959
8873 Warnerville Rd Oakdale (95361) *(P-25897)*
Ross Valley Homes Inc .... D 415 461-2300
501 Via Casitas Greenbrae (94904) *(P-20952)*
Rossi Hamerslough Reishchl & .... D 408 244-4570
1960 The Alameda Ste 200 San Jose (95126) *(P-23362)*
Rossin Steel Inc .... C 619 656-9200
2660 Cactus Rd San Diego (92154) *(P-7311)*
Rossmoor, Walnut Creek *Also called Golden Rain Foundation (P-11487)*
Rossmoor Carwash, Los Alamitos *Also called Lakewood South Car Wash LLC (P-17822)*
Rotary CLB PCF Grove Char Fund .... D 831 372-3877
706 Forest Ave Pacific Grove (93950) *(P-19020)*
Rotary Club, Palo Cedro *Also called Rotary International (P-25229)*
ROTARY CLUB OF NAPA SUNRISE OF, NAPA *Also called NAPA Sunrise Rotary Club (P-25205)*
Rotary International .... D 530 547-5272
9839 Meadowlark Way Palo Cedro (96073) *(P-25229)*

Roth Capital Partners LLC (PA) .... D 800 678-9147
888 San Clemente Dr # 400 Newport Beach (92660) *(P-10012)*
Roth Staffing Companies LP (PA) .... D 714 939-8600
450 N State College Blvd Orange (92868) *(P-14908)*
Rothfleisch Ranches Inc .... D 760 344-1819
129 S El Cerrito Dr Brawley (92227) *(P-711)*
Roto Rooter Plumbing & Drain S .... E 951 658-8541
2141 Industrial Ct Ste B Vista (92081) *(P-17978)*
Roto-Rooter, Anaheim *Also called Hoffman Southwest Corp (P-17950)*
Roto-Rooter, Concord *Also called Overmiller Inc (P-17967)*
Roto-Rooter, Livermore *Also called Sanact Inc (P-17982)*
Roto-Rooter, Rancho Cucamonga *Also called Hoffman Southwest Corp (P-17951)*
Roto-Rooter Services Company .... D 650 322-2366
220 Demeter St East Palo Alto (94303) *(P-17979)*
Rotorcraft Support Inc .... D 818 997-7667
16425 Hart St Van Nuys (91406) *(P-4906)*
Rouche O Edgar DDS, Riverside *Also called American Dntl Partners of Cal (P-20108)*
Round Hill Country Club .... E 925 934-8211
3169 Roundhill Rd Alamo (94507) *(P-19021)*
Round Hill Enterprises .... C 925 934-8211
3169 Roundhill Rd Alamo (94507) *(P-19022)*
Round Hill Golf & Country Club, Alamo *Also called Round Hill Enterprises (P-19022)*
Round Valley Indian Health Ctr .... D 707 983-6182
Hwy 162 Biggar Ln Covelo (95428) *(P-19831)*
Roundabout Entertainment Inc .... D 818 842-9300
217 S Lake St Burbank (91502) *(P-18111)*
Roundup Media LLC .... E 310 841-2366
5895 Blackwelder St Culver City (90232) *(P-13895)*
Rounsevile Rehabilitation Ctr, Oakland *Also called Rcc Facility Incorporated (P-21192)*
Rountree Plumbing and Htg Inc .... D 650 298-0300
1624 Santa Clara Dr 130 Roseville (95661) *(P-2341)*
Roux Associates Inc .... D 562 446-8600
5150 E Pacific Coast Hwy # 450 Long Beach (90804) *(P-27848)*
Row Management Ltd Inc .... C 310 887-3671
499 N Canon Dr Beverly Hills (90210) *(P-11745)*
Rowan Incorporated .... D 760 692-0700
2778 Loker Ave W Carlsbad (92010) *(P-2717)*
Rowan Electric, Carlsbad *Also called Rowan Incorporated (P-2717)*
Rowland Convalescent Hosp Inc .... D 626 967-2741
330 W Rowland St Covina (91723) *(P-20731)*
ROWLAND, THE, Covina *Also called Rowland Convalescent Hosp Inc (P-20731)*
Roy C Shannon MD, Oroville *Also called Oroville Internal Meds Group (P-19738)*
Roy Carrington Inc .... D 530 893-2100
2460 Ceres Ave Chico (95926) *(P-14748)*
Roy E Ladd Inc .... E 530 241-6102
3724 Sunlight Ct Redding (96001) *(P-1844)*
Roy E Whitehead Inc .... D 951 682-1490
2245 Via Cerro Riverside (92509) *(P-3069)*
Roy Jorgensen Associates Inc .... D 310 468-2478
19001 S Western Ave Torrance (90501) *(P-14369)*
Roy Miller Freight Lines LLC (PA) .... D 714 632-5511
3165 E Coronado St Anaheim (92806) *(P-4058)*
Royal Airline Linen Inc .... D 310 677-9885
125 N Ash Ave Inglewood (90301) *(P-13490)*
Royal Ambulance Inc .... D 510 568-6161
14472 Wicks Blvd San Leandro (94577) *(P-3836)*
Royal Care Skilled Nursing Ctr, Long Beach *Also called Covenant Care California LLC (P-20342)*
Royal Coach Tours (PA) .... C 408 279-4801
630 Stockton Ave San Jose (95126) *(P-3901)*
Royal Convalescent Hospital .... D 760 344-5431
320 Cattle Call Dr Brawley (92227) *(P-20732)*
Royal Crest Building Maint .... E 714 562-5034
8601 Roland St Ste E Buena Park (90621) *(P-14370)*
Royal Crest Healthcare, Covina *Also called Cruz Hoffstetter LLC (P-17116)*
Royal Crown Enterprises Inc .... D 626 854-8080
780 Epperson Dr City of Industry (91748) *(P-8863)*
Royal Express Inc (PA) .... C 559 272-3500
3545 E Date Ave Fresno (93725) *(P-4369)*
Royal Glass Company Inc .... D 408 969-0444
3200 De La Cruz Blvd Santa Clara (95054) *(P-3409)*
Royal Gorge Crss Cntry Ski Rst, Soda Springs *Also called Royal Gorge Nordic Ski Resort (P-13142)*
Royal Gorge Nordic Ski Resort (PA) .... D 530 426-3871
9411 Hillside Rd Soda Springs (95728) *(P-13142)*
Royal Hospitality Incorporated .... D 858 278-0800
5550 Kearny Mesa Rd San Diego (92111) *(P-13143)*
Royal Investigation Patrol Inc .... D 510 352-6800
2950 Merced St Ste 108 San Leandro (94577) *(P-16778)*
Royal Laundry, South San Francisco *Also called American Etc Inc (P-13482)*
Royal Mountain King, Copperopolis *Also called Meridian Gold Inc (P-1006)*
Royal Oaks, Duarte *Also called Cal Southern Presbt Homes (P-10996)*
Royal Oaks Care Center, Arcadia *Also called Healthcare Investments II LLC (P-20518)*
Royal Oaks Enterprises Inc .... E 408 779-2362
15480 Watsonville Rd Morgan Hill (95037) *(P-322)*
Royal Oaks Manor, Duarte *Also called Begroup (P-20258)*
Royal Oaks Mushroom, Morgan Hill *Also called Royal Oaks Enterprises Inc (P-322)*
Royal Packing Dcf .... D 559 945-2537
32839 S Lassen Ave Huron (93234) *(P-78)*
Royal Paper Corp (PA) .... D 562 903-9030
10232 Palm Dr Santa Fe Springs (90670) *(P-8127)*
Royal Plywood Company LLC .... D 916 386-9873
6003 88th St Ste 100 Sacramento (95828) *(P-6860)*
Royal Plywood Company LLC (PA) .... D 562 404-2989
14171 Park Pl Cerritos (90703) *(P-6861)*
Royal Poultry, Vernon *Also called Golden West Trading Inc (P-8616)*

Employee Codes: A=Over 500 employees, B=251-500
C=101-250, D=51-100, E=50
2019 Directory of California
Wholesalers and Services Companies
© Mergent Inc. 1-800-342-5647
1447

Royal Roofing & Cnstr Co..............D.......714 764-1100
1144 N Armando St Anaheim (92806) *(P-3198)*
Royal Roofing Construction Co, Placentia *Also called Osscim Inc (P-3182)*
Royal Scandinavian Inn, Solvang *Also called National Hospitality LLC (P-12951)*
Royal Specialty Undwrt Inc..............D.......818 922-6700
15303 Ventura Blvd # 500 Sherman Oaks (91403) *(P-10392)*
Royal Supply Midwest, Santa Fe Springs *Also called Royal Paper Corp (P-8127)*
Royal Terrace Healthcare..............D.......626 256-4654
1340 Highland Ave Duarte (91010) *(P-20733)*
Royal Truck Body, Carson *Also called Fortress Resources LLC (P-17760)*
Royal Trucking, Concord *Also called Lemore Transportation Inc (P-4215)*
Royal West Drywall Inc..............D.......951 271-4600
2008 2nd St Norco (92860) *(P-2951)*
Royale Hlth Care Mission Viejo, Mission Viejo *Also called Orange County Royale Convlscnt (P-21616)*
Royalty Tours..............E.......408 279-4801
630 Stockton Ave San Jose (95126) *(P-4977)*
Royce Corporation (PA)..............D.......209 545-0789
4970 Salida Blvd Salida (95368) *(P-14156)*
Rp Automotive Inc (PA)..............C.......626 430-9011
2010 E Garvey Ave S West Covina (91791) *(P-17782)*
Rp Realty Partners LLC..............E.......310 207-6990
990 W 8th St Ste 600 Los Angeles (90017) *(P-10930)*
Rp Scs Wsd Hotel LLC..............D.......619 398-3020
421 W B St San Diego (92101) *(P-13144)*
Rp/Kinetic Parc 55 Owner LLC..............B.......415 392-8000
55 Cyril Magnin St San Francisco (94102) *(P-13145)*
RPC Old Town Avenue Owner LLC..............D.......619 299-7400
3900 Old Town Ave San Diego (92110) *(P-13146)*
RPC Old Town Jefferson..............D.......619 725-4221
2435 Jefferson St San Diego (92110) *(P-13147)*
Rpd Hotels 18 LLC (PA)..............A.......213 746-1531
2361 Rosecrans Ave # 150 El Segundo (90245) *(P-13148)*
RPM Consolidated Services Inc (PA)..............D.......714 388-3500
1901 Raymer Ave Fullerton (92833) *(P-4627)*
RPM Mechanical - A Joint Ventr..............D.......858 565-4131
2919 E Victoria St Compton (90221) *(P-2342)*
RPM Transportation Inc (HQ)..............C.......714 388-3500
11660 Arroyo Ave Santa Ana (92705) *(P-4253)*
Rpmc Inc (PA)..............D.......818 222-7762
23975 Park Sorrento # 410 Calabasas (91302) *(P-27571)*
Rpx Corporation (HQ)..............D.......866 779-7641
1 Market Plz Lbby Bl-100 San Francisco (94105) *(P-12143)*
Rq Construction LLC..............C.......760 631-7707
3194 Lionshead Ave Carlsbad (92010) *(P-1431)*
RR Donnelley, Rancho Dominguez *Also called R R Donnelley & Sons Company (P-14060)*
RR Donnelley & Sons Company..............D.......951 296-2890
40610 County Center Dr Temecula (92591) *(P-8088)*
RRI, Downey *Also called Rancho Research Institute (P-26653)*
Rrm Construction Inc..............E.......562 440-3539
9135 Cord Ave Downey (90240) *(P-1313)*
Rrm Design Group (PA)..............D.......805 439-0442
3765 S Higuera St Ste 102 San Luis Obispo (93401) *(P-26106)*
Rromeo Corporation..............D.......714 640-3800
535 Anton Blvd Ste 200 Costa Mesa (92626) *(P-27019)*
Rruff-Rocklin Residents Unite..............E.......415 806-2778
3031 St Rocklin (95765) *(P-25230)*
Rs Calibration Services Inc..............E.......925 462-4217
1047 Serpentine Ln # 500 Pleasanton (94566) *(P-17980)*
Rsa Films Inc (PA)..............D.......310 659-1577
634 N La Peer Dr West Hollywood (90069) *(P-18112)*
Rsa Security LLC..............C.......650 529-9992
2831 Mission College Blvd Santa Clara (95054) *(P-15419)*
RSC Associates Inc (PA)..............C.......530 893-8228
3120 Cohasset Rd Ste 5 Chico (95973) *(P-11746)*
Rse, Sacramento *Also called Runyon Saltzman Inc (P-13897)*
Rsf Protective Services, Encinitas *Also called Rancho Santa Fe Protective Svc (P-16771)*
RSI Professional Cab Solutions..............C.......909 614-2900
11350 Riverside Dr Frnt Mira Loma (91752) *(P-3070)*
RSM US LLP..............D.......415 848-5300
44 Montgomery St Ste 3900 San Francisco (94104) *(P-26282)*
RSM US LLP..............D.......949 255-6500
18401 Von Karman Ave # 500 Irvine (92612) *(P-26283)*
RSM US LLP..............D.......408 572-4440
100 W San Fernando St San Jose (95113) *(P-26284)*
Rss, Los Angeles *Also called Rodgers Security Service Inc (P-16776)*
Rsui Group, Sherman Oaks *Also called Royal Specialty Undwrt Inc (P-10392)*
Rt Pasad Hotel Partners LP..............C.......626 403-7600
180 N Fair Oaks Ave Pasadena (91103) *(P-13149)*
Rt Sd-Denver LP..............E.......858 278-2100
5400 Kearny Mesa Rd San Diego (92111) *(P-13150)*
RTC, Los Angeles *Also called Religious Technology Center (P-12141)*
RTC Aerospace, Chatsworth *Also called Logistical Support LLC (P-7911)*
Rte Enterprises Inc..............D.......818 999-5300
21530 Roscoe Blvd Canoga Park (91304) *(P-2477)*
Ruan..............D.......209 634-4928
830 W Glenwood Ave Turlock (95380) *(P-4059)*
Ruann Dairy, Riverdale *Also called Maddox Dairy A Ltd Partnership (P-421)*
Rubber Dust Inc (PA)..............D.......510 237-6344
533 S 13th St Richmond (94804) *(P-17750)*
Rubicon B Hacienda LLC..............D.......424 290-5000
525 N Pacific Coast Hwy El Segundo (90245) *(P-13151)*
Rubicon B Hacienda LLC..............D.......424 290-5555
475 N Pacific Coast Hwy El Segundo (90245) *(P-13152)*
Rubicon Corporation America..............E.......818 765-2001
10425 Oklahoma Ave Chatsworth (91311) *(P-11747)*
Rubicon Enterprises Inc..............C.......510 235-1516
2500 Bissell Ave Richmond (94804) *(P-14371)*
RUBICON PROGRAMS, Richmond *Also called Rubicon Enterprises Inc (P-14371)*
Rubicon Programs Incorporated (PA)..............D.......510 235-1516
2500 Bissell Ave Richmond (94804) *(P-14372)*
Rubicon Project Inc (PA)..............C.......310 207-0272
12181 Bluff Creek Dr Fl 4 Los Angeles (90094) *(P-13896)*
Rubicon Realty, Chatsworth *Also called Rubicon Corporation America (P-11747)*
Rubidoux Family Care Center, Riverside *Also called County of Riverside (P-19418)*
Ruby Creek Resources..............E.......212 671-0404
1835 W Olympic Blvd Los Angeles (90006) *(P-27434)*
Ruby Hill Golf Club LLC..............D.......925 417-5840
3400 W Ruby Hill Dr Pleasanton (94566) *(P-18754)*
Ruby Sky, Los Gatos *Also called Inner Circle Entertainment (P-8563)*
Ruckus Wireless Inc (HQ)..............C.......650 265-4200
350 W Java Dr Sunnyvale (94089) *(P-5637)*
Ruder, Michael MD, Palo Alto *Also called Cardic Arithmias (P-19347)*
Rudolph and Sletten Inc (HQ)..............D.......650 216-3600
2 Circle Star Way Fl 4 San Carlos (94070) *(P-1637)*
Rudy Carrillo Drywall Inc..............D.......818 841-2011
1913 W Magnolia Blvd Burbank (91506) *(P-2952)*
Ruffin Hotel Corp of Cal..............B.......562 425-5210
4700 Airport Plaza Dr Long Beach (90815) *(P-13153)*
Rugby Laboratories Inc (HQ)..............D.......951 270-1400
311 Bonnie Cir Corona (92880) *(P-8208)*
Rugged Engineered Pdts Sector, San Diego *Also called Epsilon Systems Solutions Inc (P-25673)*
Ruhs-Emergency Department, Moreno Valley *Also called Riverside University Health (P-21691)*
Ruiteng Internet Technology Co..............C.......302 597-7438
18351 Colima Rd 255 Rowland Heights (91748) *(P-16174)*
Runa Hr Holdings Inc..............D.......562 883-3546
3067 E 1st St Long Beach (90803) *(P-15420)*
Running Creek Casino..............C.......707 275-9209
635 E State Highway 20 Upper Lake (95485) *(P-13154)*
Runyon Saltzman Inc..............D.......916 446-9900
2020 L St Ste 100 Sacramento (95811) *(P-13897)*
Rural Cmnty Assistance Corp (PA)..............D.......916 447-2854
3120 Freeboard Dr Ste 201 West Sacramento (95691) *(P-23999)*
Rural/Metro Corporation..............C.......510 266-0885
2364 W Winton Ave Hayward (94545) *(P-3837)*
Rural/Metro Corporation..............C.......888 876-0740
1345 Vander Way San Jose (95112) *(P-3838)*
Rural/Metro San Diego Inc..............D.......619 280-6060
10405 San Diego Mission R San Diego (92108) *(P-3839)*
Russell Fisher Partnership..............E.......714 842-4453
16061 Beach Blvd Huntington Beach (92647) *(P-17837)*
Russell Fisher Partnership (PA)..............D.......909 930-5420
18971 Beach Blvd Huntington Beach (92648) *(P-17838)*
Russell Mechanical Inc..............D.......916 635-2522
3251 Monier Cir Ste A Rancho Cordova (95742) *(P-2343)*
Russian River Health Center..............E.......707 869-2849
16319 3rd St Guerneville (95446) *(P-19832)*
Russon Financial Services Inc..............D.......818 999-2800
19935 Ventura Blvd # 100 Woodland Hills (91364) *(P-27435)*
Rustic Canyon Group LLC..............D.......310 998-8000
201 Santa Monica Blvd # 500 Santa Monica (90401) *(P-12264)*
Rustic Canyon Partners, Santa Monica *Also called Rustic Canyon Group LLC (P-12264)*
Rutan & Tucker LLP (PA)..............C.......714 641-5100
611 Anton Blvd Ste 1400 Costa Mesa (92626) *(P-23363)*
Ruth Barajas..............E.......415 977-6949
965 Mission St Ste 520 San Francisco (94103) *(P-24000)*
Rutherford Co Inc (PA)..............D.......323 666-5284
2107 Crystal St Los Angeles (90039) *(P-2953)*
Rutland Tool & Supply Co (HQ)..............C.......562 566-5000
2225 Workman Mill Rd City of Industry (90601) *(P-7868)*
Rutledge Claims Management Inc..............D.......858 883-2000
14286 Danielson St # 103 Poway (92064) *(P-10760)*
Ruuhwa Dann and Associates Inc..............D.......909 467-4800
1541 Brooks St Ontario (91762) *(P-6454)*
Rvtlzation Anaheim II Partners..............D.......714 520-4041
1515 S Calle Del Mar Anaheim (92802) *(P-11748)*
RW Lynch Co Inc (PA)..............D.......925 837-3877
2333 San Ramon Valley Blv San Ramon (94583) *(P-13898)*
RW&g, Los Angeles *Also called Richards Watson & Gershon PC (P-23354)*
Rwc Enterprises Inc..............E.......909 373-4100
9130 Santa Anita Ave Rancho Cucamonga (91730) *(P-25898)*
Rwp Transfer Inc..............E.......909 868-6882
1313 E Phillips Blvd Pomona (91766) *(P-8056)*
Rwr Homes Inc (PA)..............D.......805 413-1792
1014 S Westlake Blvd # 14 Westlake Village (91361) *(P-11911)*
Rx Pro Health LLC..............A.......858 369-4050
12400 High Bluff Dr San Diego (92130) *(P-14909)*
Ryan Herco Flow Solutions, Burbank *Also called Ryan Herco Products Corp (P-7635)*
Ryan Herco Products Corp (HQ)..............D.......818 841-1141
3010 N San Fernando Blvd Burbank (91504) *(P-7635)*
Ryans Express Trnsp Svcs Inc (PA)..............D.......310 219-2960
19500 Mariner Ave Torrance (90503) *(P-3902)*
Ryde Hotel LLC..............E.......916 776-1318
14340 State Highway 160 Walnut Grove (95690) *(P-13155)*
Ryde Motel, Walnut Grove *Also called Ryde Hotel LLC (P-13155)*
Rydek Eletronics LLC..............D.......310 641-9800
898 N Pacific Coast Hwy # 475 El Segundo (90245) *(P-14749)*
Ryder Integrated Logistics Inc..............E.......818 701-9332
19133 Parthenia St Northridge (91324) *(P-17613)*
Ryder Truck Rental Inc..............C.......415 285-0756
2700 3rd St San Francisco (94107) *(P-17614)*
Ryder Truck Rental Inc..............D.......562 921-0033
13630 Firestone Blvd Santa Fe Springs (90670) *(P-17615)*
Ryder Truck Rental Inc..............D.......909 980-5084
9608 Santa Anita Ave Rancho Cucamonga (91730) *(P-17616)*

Mergent e-mail: customerrelations@mergent.com
1448
2019 Directory of California
Wholesalers and Services Companies
(P-0000) Products & Services Section entry number
(PA)=Parent Co (HQ)=Headquarters (DH)=Div Headquarters

Rye Electric Inc....D....949 441-0545
3940 Electric Ave Laguna Hills (92653) ***(P-2718)***
Ryland Hmes Inlnd Empire Cstmr....D....951 273-3473
1250 Corona Pointe Ct # 100 Corona (92879) ***(P-1228)***
Ryland Homes, Carlsbad *Also called Calatlantic Group Inc* ***(P-1333)***
Ryland Homes of Texas Inc....C....805 367-3800
15360 Barranca Pkwy Irvine (92618) ***(P-1358)***
Ryot Corp....D....323 356-1787
11995 Bluff Creek Dr Playa Vista (90094) ***(P-14128)***
S & J, Los Angeles *Also called Sam Jung USA Inc* ***(P-8241)***
S & J Ranches LLC....D....559 437-2600
39639 Avenue 10 Madera (93636) ***(P-562)***
S & M Moving Systems, Santa Fe Springs *Also called Van Torrance & Storage Company* ***(P-4386)***
S & M Moving Systems....D....510 497-2300
48551 Warm Springs Blvd Fremont (94539) ***(P-4254)***
S & S Construction Co, Beverly Hills *Also called Shapell Industries LLC* ***(P-11915)***
S & S Construction Services, El Monte *Also called S & S Rent-A-Fence Inc* ***(P-14542)***
S & S Portable Services Inc....D....626 967-9300
4511 Rowland Ave El Monte (91731) ***(P-14541)***
S & S Ranch Inc....D....559 655-3491
904 S Lyon Ave Mendota (93640) ***(P-466)***
S & S Rent-A-Fence Inc....D....818 896-7710
4511 Rowland Ave El Monte (91731) ***(P-14542)***
S & S Tool & Supply Inc (PA)....D....925 313-0360
2700 Maxwell Way Fairfield (94534) ***(P-7869)***
S A Cali-U Acoustics Inc....D....805 376-9300
1111 Rancho Conejo Blvd # 501 Thousand Oaks (91320) ***(P-2954)***
S A Camp Companies (PA)....E....661 399-4451
17876 Zerker Rd Bakersfield (93308) ***(P-7711)***
S A Camp Pump Company....D....661 399-2976
17876 Zerker Rd Bakersfield (93308) ***(P-17981)***
S A S, Concord *Also called Bay Alarm Company* ***(P-2517)***
S A S, Millbrae *Also called Trans World Maintenance Inc* ***(P-2487)***
S and R Towing Inc (PA)....E....760 722-6686
1060 Airport Rd Oceanside (92058) ***(P-17870)***
S and S Supplies and Solutions, Fairfield *Also called S & S Tool & Supply Inc* ***(P-7869)***
S B C, Fresno *Also called AT&T Services Inc* ***(P-5476)***
S B C, Monterey *Also called AT&T Services Inc* ***(P-5483)***
S B C Senior Care Inc....D....805 560-6995
101 W Anapamu St Ste C Santa Barbara (93101) ***(P-22408)***
S B Communications, Hawthorne *Also called South Bay Rgonal Pub Comm Auth* ***(P-5995)***
S B M, McClellan *Also called Sbm Site Services LLC* ***(P-14378)***
S C A, Victorville *Also called Comav Technical Services LLC* ***(P-4882)***
S C A G, Los Angeles *Also called Cal Southern Assn Governments* ***(P-27668)***
S C L, Gardena *Also called Schumacher Cargo Logistics Inc* ***(P-5163)***
S C P M G, Fontana *Also called Southern Cal Prmnnte Med Group* ***(P-21762)***
S C P M G, Colton *Also called Southern Cal Prmnnte Med Group* ***(P-19913)***
S C P M G, El Cajon *Also called Southern Cal Prmnnte Med Group* ***(P-19915)***
S C P M G, Anaheim *Also called Southern Cal Prmnnte Med Group* ***(P-19916)***
S C P M G, San Juan Capistrano *Also called Southern Cal Prmnnte Med Group* ***(P-19917)***
S C P M G, Yorba Linda *Also called Southern Cal Prmnnte Med Group* ***(P-19918)***
S C P M G, Santa Ana *Also called Southern Cal Prmnnte Med Group* ***(P-19919)***
S C P M G, San Diego *Also called Southern Cal Prmnnte Med Group* ***(P-19920)***
S C P M G, Escondido *Also called Southern Cal Prmnnte Med Group* ***(P-19921)***
S C P M G, San Dimas *Also called Southern Cal Prmnnte Med Group* ***(P-10318)***
S C P M G, Cudahy *Also called Southern Cal Prmnnte Med Group* ***(P-19922)***
S C P M G, Woodland Hills *Also called Southern Cal Prmnnte Med Group* ***(P-19923)***
S C P M G, Santa Clarita *Also called Southern Cal Prmnnte Med Group* ***(P-19924)***
S C S, North Highlands *Also called Security Contractor Svcs Inc* ***(P-6936)***
S C Security Inc....E....661 251-6999
26752 Oak Ave Ste C Santa Clarita (91351) ***(P-16779)***
S C Tile and Surfaces, El Cajon *Also called S C Tile Company Inc* ***(P-3009)***
S C Tile Company Inc....E....619 669-1575
606 S Marshall Ave El Cajon (92020) ***(P-3009)***
S C Yamamoto, La Habra *Also called Shinsuke Clifford Yamamoto* ***(P-938)***
S CA University Hlth Sciences....E....562 947-8755
P.O. Box 1166 Whittier (90609) ***(P-20156)***
S D I, Lakeside *Also called Standard Drywall Inc* ***(P-2962)***
S D O A, San Diego *Also called San Diego Orthopaedic Associat* ***(P-19844)***
S D Property Management Inc....D....323 658-7990
14937 Delano St Van Nuys (91411) ***(P-11749)***
S D Y S, San Diego *Also called San Diego Youth Services Inc* ***(P-24012)***
S E C C Corporation....D....760 246-6218
16224 Koala Rd Adelanto (92301) ***(P-1975)***
S E O P Inc....C....949 682-7906
1621 Alton Pkwy Ste 150 Irvine (92606) ***(P-27436)***
S E Pipe Line Construction Co....D....562 868-9771
11832 Bloomfield Ave Santa Fe Springs (90670) ***(P-1976)***
S F Auto Parts Whse Inc....D....415 255-0115
6000 3rd St San Francisco (94124) ***(P-6671)***
S F Broadcasting of Wisconsin....C....310 586-2410
2425 Olympic Blvd Santa Monica (90404) ***(P-5834)***
S G D Enterprises....E....323 658-1047
14937 Delano St Van Nuys (91411) ***(P-933)***
S G I, Pasadena *Also called Seville Group* ***(P-27027)***
S G S Produce, Los Angeles *Also called Shapiro-Gilman-Shandler Co* ***(P-8730)***
S H E, Visalia *Also called Self Help Enterprises* ***(P-25247)***
S I J Inc....E....951 304-9444
26035 Jefferson Ave Murrieta (92562) ***(P-3071)***
S J Amoroso Cnstr Co Inc (PA)....B....650 654-1900
390 Bridge Pkwy Redwood City (94065) ***(P-1638)***
S J General Building Maint....D....408 392-0800
919 Berryessa Rd Ste 10 San Jose (95133) ***(P-14373)***
S J S Link International Inc (PA)....E....310 860-7666
468 N Camden Dr Ste 311 Beverly Hills (90210) ***(P-8504)***
S J W, San Jose *Also called San Jose Water Company* ***(P-6306)***
S K & A Information Svcs Inc (HQ)....D....949 476-2051
2601 Main St Ste 650 Irvine (92614) ***(P-26563)***
S K S Enterprises Inc (PA)....D....209 599-4095
11830 French Camp Rd Manteca (95336) ***(P-434)***
S L G G Consulting Group LLC (PA)....C....310 477-3924
10960 Wilshire Blvd # 1100 Los Angeles (90024) ***(P-26285)***
S L H C C Inc....E....916 457-6521
3500 Folsom Blvd Sacramento (95816) ***(P-20734)***
S L S Hotel, Los Angeles *Also called Sbehg 465 S La Cienega LLC* ***(P-13194)***
S M C, Simi Valley *Also called Smart Living Company* ***(P-9259)***
S M G, San Francisco *Also called Smg Holdings Inc* ***(P-10944)***
S M U D, Sacramento *Also called Sacramento Municpl Utility Dst* ***(P-6102)***
S O S CLUB, Modesto *Also called Sportsmen of Stanislaus Inc* ***(P-18668)***
S P R E Inc....D....510 222-8340
3223 Blume Dr Richmond (94806) ***(P-11750)***
S P Richards Company....D....951 681-3114
10235 San Sevaine Way # 120 Mira Loma (91752) ***(P-8089)***
S P Thomas Co of Northern Cal (PA)....D....916 786-2040
1201 Plumber Way Ste 112 Roseville (95678) ***(P-11912)***
S R H H Inc....E....408 247-0800
1085 E El Camino Real Sunnyvale (94087) ***(P-13156)***
S R I C B I....D....650 859-4865
333 Ravenswood Ave Menlo Park (94025) ***(P-27849)***
S R J, San Clemente *Also called Julius Steve Construction Inc* ***(P-1411)***
S R Mutual Funds, City of Industry *Also called California Country Club* ***(P-18879)***
S S 8, Milpitas *Also called Ss8 Networks Inc* ***(P-5998)***
S S F, South San Francisco *Also called Ssf Imported Auto Parts LLC* ***(P-6677)***
S S I, Oxnard *Also called Synectic Solutions Inc* ***(P-16497)***
S S W Mechanical Cnstr Inc....C....760 327-1481
670 S Oleander Rd Palm Springs (92264) ***(P-2344)***
S Stamoules Inc....A....559 655-9777
904 S Lyon Ave Mendota (93640) ***(P-563)***
S T L, Sacramento *Also called Sacramento Theatrical Ltg Ltd* ***(P-18400)***
S Taylor Construction Inc....C....310 291-4505
23905 Clinton Keith Rd Wildomar (92595) ***(P-1229)***
S W Construction Inc....C....714 978-7871
1145 E Stanford Ct Anaheim (92805) ***(P-3072)***
S W K Properties LLC....D....714 481-6300
2726 S Grand Ave Lbby Santa Ana (92705) ***(P-13157)***
S W K Properties LLC (PA)....D....213 383-9204
3807 Wilshire Blvd # 1226 Los Angeles (90010) ***(P-27020)***
S W P T X Inc....C....714 564-7900
1682 Langley Ave Irvine (92614) ***(P-2478)***
S&B Surgery Center II, Rllng HLS Est *Also called Spalding Srgcl Ctr of Bvrly Hl* ***(P-19930)***
S&E Gourmet Cuts Inc....C....909 370-0155
379 Industrial Rd San Bernardino (92408) ***(P-8567)***
S&F Management Company LLC (PA)....D....310 385-1090
9200 W Sunset Blvd # 700 West Hollywood (90069) ***(P-20735)***
S&J Stadtler Inc....B....925 847-8900
5980 Stoneridge Dr # 122 Pleasanton (94588) ***(P-11751)***
S&P Global Inc....C....831 393-6044
1566 Moffett St Salinas (93905) ***(P-10112)***
S&W Seed Company (PA)....E....559 884-2535
106 K St Fl 3 Sacramento (95814) ***(P-30)***
S.p Richards, Mira Loma *Also called S P Richards Company* ***(P-8089)***
SA Camp Pump and Drilling Co, Bakersfield *Also called S A Camp Pump Company* ***(P-17981)***
SA Photonics Inc....D....408 560-3500
120 Knowles Dr Los Gatos (95032) ***(P-27850)***
SA Recycling LLC....D....619 238-6740
3055 Commercial St San Diego (92113) ***(P-6455)***
SA Recycling LLC....D....323 564-5601
10313 S Alameda St Los Angeles (90002) ***(P-6456)***
SA Recycling LLC....D....805 483-0512
780 E Easy St Simi Valley (93065) ***(P-6457)***
SA Recycling LLC....D....714 667-7898
2006 W 5th St Santa Ana (92703) ***(P-6458)***
SA Recycling LLC....D....323 875-2520
9754 San Fernando Rd Sun Valley (91352) ***(P-6459)***
SA Recycling LLC....D....559 688-0271
2525 S K St Tulare (93274) ***(P-6460)***
SA Recycling LLC....D....805 486-7525
521 N Rice Ave Oxnard (93030) ***(P-6461)***
SA Recycling LLC....D....626 359-5815
2495 Buena Vista St Duarte (91010) ***(P-6462)***
SA Recycling LLC....D....323 723-8327
1540 S Greenwood Ave Montebello (90640) ***(P-6463)***
SA Recycling LLC....D....559 237-6677
3489 S Chestnut Ave Fresno (93725) ***(P-6464)***
SA Recycling LLC....D....760 391-5591
48100 Harrison St Coachella (92236) ***(P-6465)***
SA Recycling LLC....D....626 444-9530
12301 Valley Blvd El Monte (91732) ***(P-6466)***
SA Recycling LLC....D....661 327-3559
2000 E Brundage Ln Bakersfield (93307) ***(P-6467)***
SA Recycling LLC....D....909 622-3337
11614 Eastend Ave Chino (91710) ***(P-6468)***
SA Recycling LLC (PA)....C....714 632-2000
2411 N Glassell St Orange (92865) ***(P-7990)***
SA Recycling LLC....D....661 723-1383
42353 8th St E Lancaster (93535) ***(P-6469)***
SA Recycling LLC....D....909 825-1662
790 E M St Colton (92324) ***(P-6470)***
SA Recycling LLC....D....714 632-2000
3202 Main St San Diego (92113) ***(P-6471)***

ALPHABETIC

Employee Codes: A=Over 500 employees, B=251-500 C=101-250, D=51-100, E=50
2019 Directory of California Wholesalers and Services Companies
© Mergent Inc. 1-800-342-5647
1449

SA Technologies Inc (PA)....D....408 400-3900
5201 Great America Pkwy # 457 Santa Clara (95054) ***(P-14750)***
Sa-Tech, Oxnard *Also called Systems Application & Tech Inc* ***(P-25937)***
Saa Sierra Programs LLC....D....530 541-1244
130 Fallen Leaf Rd South Lake Tahoe (96150) ***(P-25231)***
Saalex Corp (PA)....C....805 482-1070
811 Camarillo Springs Rd A Camarillo (93012) ***(P-25899)***
Saalex Solutions, Camarillo *Also called Saalex Corp* ***(P-25899)***
Saama Technologies Inc (PA)....C....408 371-1900
900 E Hamilton Ave Campbell (95008) ***(P-15421)***
Saarman Construction Ltd....C....415 749-2700
683 Mcallister St San Francisco (94102) ***(P-1314)***
Saatchi & Saatchi N Amer Inc....C....310 437-2500
13031 W Jefferson Blvd Los Angeles (90094) ***(P-13899)***
Sab Pacific, San Diego *Also called All Stars* ***(P-3483)***
Saba Software Inc (PA)....D....877 722-2101
4120 Dublin Blvd Ste 200 Dublin (94568) ***(P-15843)***
Sabah International Inc (HQ)....D....925 463-0431
5925 Stoneridge Dr Pleasanton (94588) ***(P-2719)***
Saban Brands LLC (HQ)....D....310 557-5230
10100 Santa Monica Blvd # 500 Los Angeles (90067) ***(P-27437)***
Saban Community Clinic, Los Angeles *Also called Los Angeles Free Clinic* ***(P-19662)***
Saban Research Institute, The, Los Angeles *Also called Childrens Hospital Los Angeles* ***(P-26613)***
Saber, Murrieta *Also called South Coast Piering Inc* ***(P-1657)***
Saber Plumbing Inc....D....760 480-5716
325 Market Pl Escondido (92029) ***(P-2345)***
Sabu Enterprises Inc....E....626 443-1351
5044 Buffington Rd El Monte (91732) ***(P-21201)***
Sac Health System (PA)....D....909 382-7100
1455 3rd Ave San Bernardino (92408) ***(P-20134)***
Sac International Steel Inc (PA)....D....323 232-2467
6130 Avalon Blvd Los Angeles (90003) ***(P-7312)***
Sac River Outfitters....D....530 275-3500
1403 Edgewood Dr Redding (96003) ***(P-19228)***
Sac Val Waste Disposal, Sacramento *Also called USA Waste of California Inc* ***(P-4077)***
Saccani Distributing Company....D....916 441-0213
2600 5th St Sacramento (95818) ***(P-9024)***
Sackett National Holdings Inc....D....866 834-6242
2605 Camino Del Rio S # 400 San Diego (92108) ***(P-27438)***
Sacramento 49er, Sacramento *Also called Sacramnto Forty Niner Trvl Plz* ***(P-13159)***
Sacramento Area Emerg Housing (PA)....E....916 454-2120
2925 34th St Sacramento (95817) ***(P-24001)***
Sacramento Area Sewer District (PA)....B....916 876-6000
10060 Goethe Rd Sacramento (95827) ***(P-6472)***
Sacramento Childrens Home....D....916 927-5059
1217 Del Paso Blvd Ste B Sacramento (95815) ***(P-24657)***
Sacramento Childrens Home (PA)....C....916 452-3981
2750 Sutterville Rd Sacramento (95820) ***(P-24658)***
Sacramento Chinese Community S....C....916 442-4228
420 I St Ste 5 Sacramento (95814) ***(P-24002)***
Sacramento County Off Educatn....E....916 875-0300
9750 Bus Park Dr Ste 220 Sacramento (95827) ***(P-24003)***
Sacramento County Water Agency....D....916 874-6851
827 7th St Ste 301 Sacramento (95814) ***(P-6298)***
Sacramento Credit Union (PA)....D....916 444-6070
800 H St Ste 100 Sacramento (95814) ***(P-9646)***
Sacramento Cy Unified Schl Dst (PA)....B....916 643-7400
5735 47th Ave Sacramento (95824) ***(P-25232)***
Sacramento District Office, Sacramento *Also called State Compensation Insur Fund* ***(P-10406)***
Sacramento Div, West Sacramento *Also called Quad/Graphics Inc* ***(P-13884)***
Sacramento Ear Nose & Throat (PA)....D....916 736-3399
1111 Expo Blvd Bldg 700 Sacramento (95815) ***(P-19833)***
Sacramento Employement & Train....C....916 263-3800
925 Del Paso Blvd Ste 100 Sacramento (95815) ***(P-24224)***
Sacramento Employement & Train (PA)....C....916 263-3800
925 Del Paso Blvd Ste 100 Sacramento (95815) ***(P-24225)***
Sacramento Harness Association....D....916 239-4040
1600 Exposition Blvd Sacramento (95815) ***(P-24976)***
Sacramento Hotel Partners LLC....D....916 326-5000
100 Capitol Mall Sacramento (95814) ***(P-13158)***
Sacramento Kenworth, Sacramento *Also called Ssmb Pacific Holding Co Inc* ***(P-6611)***
Sacramento Loaves & Fishes (PA)....D....916 446-0874
1351 N C St Ste 22 Sacramento (95811) ***(P-24004)***
Sacramento Mental Hlth Clinic, Mather *Also called Veterans Health Administration* ***(P-20061)***
Sacramento Municpl Utility Dst (PA)....A....916 452-3211
6201 S St Sacramento (95817) ***(P-6102)***
Sacramento Municpl Utility Dst....A....916 452-3211
6201 S St Sacramento (95817) ***(P-6103)***
Sacramento Municpl Utility Dst....A....916 452-3211
6201 S St Sacramento (95817) ***(P-17797)***
Sacramento Municpl Utility Dst....D....916 732-5155
6301 S St Sacramento (95817) ***(P-6104)***
Sacramento Municpl Utility Dst....B....916 732-5616
6201 S St Sacramento (95817) ***(P-6105)***
Sacramento Operating Co LP....C....916 422-4825
7400 24th St Sacramento (95822) ***(P-20736)***
Sacramento Packing Inc (PA)....E....530 671-4488
833 Tudor Rd Yuba City (95991) ***(P-229)***
Sacramento Post-Acute, Sacramento *Also called Oleander Holdings LLC* ***(P-20680)***
Sacramento Prestige Gunite Inc....E....916 723-0404
8634 Antelope North Rd Antelope (95843) ***(P-3319)***
Sacramento Reg Co Sanit Dist (PA)....A....916 876-6000
10060 Goethe Rd Sacramento (95827) ***(P-6548)***
Sacramento Reg Co Sanit Dist....B....916 875-9000
8521 Laguna Station Rd Elk Grove (95758) ***(P-6327)***
Sacramento Regional Trnst Dist (PA)....A....916 726-2877
1400 29th St Sacramento (95816) ***(P-3700)***
Sacramento Regional Trnst Dist....C....916 321-2800
1400 29th St Sacramento (95816) ***(P-3701)***
Sacramento Regional Trnst Dist....C....916 869-8611
2700 Academy Way Sacramento (95815) ***(P-3955)***
Sacramento River Cats Baseball....E....916 376-4700
400 Ball Park Dr West Sacramento (95691) ***(P-18532)***
Sacramento Suburban Water Dst....D....916 972-7171
3701 Marconi Ave Ste 100 Sacramento (95821) ***(P-6299)***
Sacramento Suburban Water Dst....D....916 972-7171
3701 Marconi Ave Ste 100 Sacramento (95821) ***(P-6300)***
Sacramento Television Stns Inc (HQ)....C....916 374-1452
2713 Kovr Dr West Sacramento (95605) ***(P-5835)***
Sacramento Theatrical Ltg Ltd....D....916 447-3258
950 Richards Blvd Sacramento (95811) ***(P-18400)***
Sacramento V A Medical Center, Mather *Also called Veterans Health Administration* ***(P-20076)***
Sacramento Valley Region 2, Gold River *Also called California Dept Fish Wildlife* ***(P-13447)***
Sacramento Yolo Cnty Mosquito....D....916 685-1022
8631 Bond Rd Elk Grove (95624) ***(P-6549)***
Sacramento Zoological Society....E....916 808-5888
3930 W Land Park Dr Sacramento (95822) ***(P-24935)***
Sacramento-Yolo Port District....C....916 371-8000
1110 W Capitol Ave West Sacramento (95691) ***(P-4733)***
Sacramnto Forty Niner Trvl Plz....C....916 927-4774
2828 El Centro Rd Sacramento (95833) ***(P-13159)***
Sacramnto Hsing Rdvlpment Agcy....C....916 440-1376
630 I St Fl 3 Sacramento (95814) ***(P-10761)***
Sacramnto Mtro A Qulty MGT Dst....D....916 874-4800
777 12th St Ste 300 Sacramento (95814) ***(P-27851)***
Sacramnto Ntiv Amercn Hlth Ctr....C....916 341-0575
2020 J St Sacramento (95811) ***(P-19834)***
Sacromento Eductn Readng Lions....E....916 228-2219
10461 Old Plza Vlle 130 Sacramento (95827) ***(P-25233)***
Sada Systems Inc....C....818 766-2400
5250 Lankershim Blvd # 620 North Hollywood (91601) ***(P-16475)***
Sadaf Foods, Vernon *Also called Soofer Co Inc* ***(P-8870)***
Saddle Back Valley YMCA, Mission Viejo *Also called Young Mens Chrstn Assn Orange* ***(P-25351)***
Saddle Corp (PA)....D....949 589-3422
23531 Ridge Route Dr C Laguna Hills (92653) ***(P-3579)***
Saddleback Dialysis, Laguna Hills *Also called Dva Renal Healthcare Inc* ***(P-22474)***
Saddleback Mem Med Lab Svcs, Laguna Hills *Also called Saddleback Memorial Med Ctr* ***(P-22138)***
Saddleback Memorial Hospital, San Clemente *Also called San Clemente Medical Ctr LLC* ***(P-21703)***
Saddleback Memorial Med Ctr (HQ)....A....949 837-4500
24451 Health Center Dr # 1 Laguna Hills (92653) ***(P-21692)***
Saddleback Memorial Med Ctr....C....949 452-3405
24411 Health Center Dr Laguna Hills (92653) ***(P-22138)***
Saddleback Valley Service Ctr, Irvine *Also called Southern California Edison Co* ***(P-6133)***
Saddleback Vly....D....949 586-1234
25631 Peter A Hartman Way Mission Viejo (92691) ***(P-19023)***
Saddleback Waterproofing, Laguna Hills *Also called Saddle Corp* ***(P-3579)***
Saddlemen, Compton *Also called Bst Enterprises Inc* ***(P-6628)***
Sadie Rose Baking Co....D....858 831-0290
8926 Ware Ct San Diego (92121) ***(P-8864)***
Saehan Bank (PA)....E....213 368-7700
3200 Wilshire Blvd # 700 Los Angeles (90010) ***(P-9484)***
Safari Harvstg & Farming LLC....B....805 925-2600
313 Plaza Dr Ste B12 Santa Maria (93454) ***(P-378)***
Safc Carlsbad Inc....D....760 710-6100
6219 El Camino Real Carlsbad (92009) ***(P-26656)***
Safe America Credit Union (PA)....D....925 734-4111
6001 Gibraltar Dr Pleasanton (94588) ***(P-9583)***
Safe Credit Union (PA)....C....916 979-7233
2295 Iron Point Rd # 100 Folsom (95630) ***(P-9647)***
Safe Credit Union....C....916 979-7233
2295 Iron Point Rd # 100 Folsom (95630) ***(P-9648)***
Safe Credit Union....E....916 979-7233
9055 Woodcreek Oaks Blvd # 150 Roseville (95747) ***(P-9584)***
Safe Harbor Intl Relief....E....949 858-6786
30615 Avnida De Las Flres Rancho Santa Margari (92688) ***(P-24834)***
Safe Harbor Treatment Cen....E....949 645-1026
722 Superba Ave Venice (90291) ***(P-22668)***
Safe Refuge....D....562 987-5722
1041 Redondo Ave Long Beach (90804) ***(P-24659)***
Safe Security Inc....B....925 830-4777
2440 Camino Ramon Ste 200 San Ramon (94583) ***(P-16933)***
Safe-Guard Products Intl LLC....D....800 742-7896
18100 Von Karman Ave # 150 Irvine (92612) ***(P-10762)***
Safeco Door & Hardware Inc....D....510 429-4768
31054 San Antonio St Hayward (94544) ***(P-3410)***
Safeco Glass, Hayward *Also called Safeco Door & Hardware Inc* ***(P-3410)***
Safeco Insurance Company Amer....C....818 956-4250
330 N Brand Blvd Ste 680 Glendale (91203) ***(P-10763)***
Safeguard Business Systems Inc....C....805 486-9769
414 N A St Oxnard (93030) ***(P-8090)***
Safeguard Health Enterprises (HQ)....B....949 425-4300
95 Enterprise Ste 100 Aliso Viejo (92656) ***(P-10305)***
Safelite Autoglass, Sacramento *Also called Safelite Fulfillment Inc* ***(P-17752)***
Safelite Fulfillment Inc....D....916 442-4715
261 Richards Blvd Sacramento (95811) ***(P-17752)***
Safely Home....D....909 370-0343
461 Tennessee St Ste O Redlands (92373) ***(P-22409)***
Safetraces Inc....C....925 398-8985
6111 Johnson Ct Ste 200 Pleasanton (94588) ***(P-15422)***

Safety Dynamics, Oakland *Also called Intelliguard Security Services (P-16700)*
Safety Security Patrol LLC ....D....909 888-7778
560 N Arrowhead Ave 3b San Bernardino (92401) *(P-16780)*
Safeway Stores Incorporated ....D....408 719-9460
750 Walsh Ave Santa Clara (95050) *(P-1639)*
Safeway Stores Incorporated ....B....209 833-4700
16900 W Schulte Rd Tracy (95377) *(P-4628)*
Safran, Anaheim *Also called Morphotrak LLC (P-16006)*
Safway Services LP ....E....650 652-9255
1660 Gilbreth Rd Burlingame (94010) *(P-7693)*
Safway Services LP ....E....707 745-2000
4072b Teal Ct Benicia (94510) *(P-7694)*
Sag- Aftra Federal ....D....818 562-3400
134 N Kenwood St Burbank (91505) *(P-9585)*
Sag-Aftra Foundation ....E....323 549-6708
5757 Wilshire Blvd Ph 1 Los Angeles (90036) *(P-25074)*
Saga Seal Co Ltd ....D....562 493-7501
600 Marina Dr Seal Beach (90740) *(P-13160)*
Sagan Systems Inc ....D....650 387-8485
201 California St # 1300 San Francisco (94111) *(P-15423)*
Sage Behavior Services Inc ....D....714 773-0077
505 E Commonwealth Ave Fullerton (92832) *(P-21970)*
Sage Electric Company ....D....818 718-9080
9144 Owensmouth Ave Chatsworth (91311) *(P-2720)*
Sage Hospitality Resources LLC ....D....626 357-5211
700 W Huntington Dr Monrovia (91016) *(P-13161)*
Sage Hospitality Resources LLC ....D....650 589-1600
2000 Shoreline Ct Brisbane (94005) *(P-13162)*
Sage Intacct Inc (HQ) ....E....408 878-0900
300 Park Ave Ste 1400 San Jose (95110) *(P-16476)*
Sage Software Inc ....D....949 753-1222
7595 Irvine Center Dr # 200 Irvine (92618) *(P-16249)*
Sage Software Inc ....C....650 579-3628
1380 Tatan Trail Rd Burlingame (94010) *(P-15844)*
Sage Software Holdings Inc (HQ) ....B....866 530-7243
6561 Irvine Center Dr Irvine (92618) *(P-15845)*
Sage Staffing Consultants Inc (PA) ....C....661 254-4026
27441 Tourney Rd Ste 150 Valencia (91355) *(P-14910)*
Sahara, Artesia *Also called South Asian Help Referral Agcy (P-24056)*
Sahargun Mechanical, Stockton *Also called Sahargun Plumbing Inc (P-2346)*
Sahargun Plumbing Inc ....D....209 474-2611
2216 Stewart St Stockton (95205) *(P-2346)*
Saia Inc ....C....916 483-8331
1508 Wyant Way Sacramento (95864) *(P-4255)*
Saia Motor Freight Line LLC ....E....916 690-8417
9119 Elkmont Dr Elk Grove (95624) *(P-4256)*
Saia Motor Freight Line LLC ....D....323 277-2880
2550 E 28th St Vernon (90058) *(P-4257)*
Saia Motor Freight Line LLC ....D....510 347-6890
1755 Aurora Dr San Leandro (94577) *(P-4258)*
Saia S Reno Barbara K, Sacramento *Also called Saia Inc (P-4255)*
Saic, San Diego *Also called Leidos Inc (P-26400)*
Saic, San Diego *Also called Science Applications Intl Corp (P-16045)*
Saic, San Diego *Also called Science Applications Intl Corp (P-16046)*
Saic, Oakland *Also called Leidos Inc (P-26409)*
Saic Government Solutions, San Diego *Also called Science Applications Intl Corp (P-16478)*
Saiful/Bouquet Con Stru Eng (PA) ....D....626 304-2616
155 N Lake Ave Fl 6 Pasadena (91101) *(P-25900)*
Saint Agnes HM Hlth & Hospice, Fresno *Also called Trinity Home Health Svcs Inc (P-22439)*
Saint Agnes Med Providers Inc ....D....559 435-2630
1379 E Herndon Ave Fresno (93720) *(P-22871)*
Saint Agnes Medical Center (HQ) ....A....559 450-3000
1303 E Herndon Ave Fresno (93720) *(P-21693)*
Saint Baldricks Foundation, Simi Valley *Also called Vickie Lobello (P-25480)*
SAINT BARNABAS SENIOR SERVICES, Los Angeles *Also called St Barnabas Senior Center of L (P-24067)*
Saint Claires Nursing Ctr LLC ....C....916 392-4440
6248 66th Ave Sacramento (95823) *(P-20737)*
Saint Francis Memorial Hosp (HQ) ....A....415 353-6000
900 Hyde St San Francisco (94109) *(P-21694)*
Saint Helena Hosp Clearlake, Clearlake *Also called Adventist Health Clearlake (P-21263)*
Saint Jhns Hlth Ctr Foundation ....C....310 315-6111
2200 Santa Monica Blvd Santa Monica (90404) *(P-19835)*
Saint Jhns Hlth Ctr Foundation ....D....310 829-5511
2121 Santa Monica Blvd Santa Monica (90404) *(P-24375)*
Saint Jhns Hlth Ctr Foundation ....B....310 829-8970
2020 Santa Monica Blvd 3rdfl3 Santa Monica (90404) *(P-21695)*
SAINT JOHN'S WELL CHILD CENTER, Los Angeles *Also called St Johns Well Child (P-20138)*
Saint Johns Child Fmly Dev Ctr, Santa Monica *Also called Saint Jhns Hlth Ctr Foundation (P-24375)*
SAINT JOSEPH CENTER VOLUNTEER, Venice *Also called St Joseph Center (P-24068)*
Saint Joseph Hlth Sys HM Hlth, Anaheim *Also called St Joseph Home Health Network (P-22426)*
Saint Joseph Hlth Sys Hospice, Anaheim *Also called St Joseph Hospice (P-24069)*
Saint Joseph Home Care Network ....D....707 206-9124
1165 Montgomery Dr Santa Rosa (95405) *(P-24660)*
Saint Justin Education Fu ....D....323 221-3400
2415 Shoredale Ave Los Angeles (90031) *(P-24835)*
Saint Louise Hospital ....B....408 848-2000
9400 N Name Uno Gilroy (95020) *(P-21696)*
Saint Mary Medical Center, Long Beach *Also called Dignity Health (P-21376)*
Saint Nicolas Vineyard, Soledad *Also called Kvl Holdings Inc (P-155)*
Saint-Joseph Home Health ....E....408 244-5488
1525 Mccarthy Blvd # 208 Milpitas (95035) *(P-22872)*

Sajahtera Inc ....A....310 276-2251
9641 Sunset Blvd Beverly Hills (90210) *(P-13163)*
Sakata Seed America Inc (HQ) ....D....408 778-7758
18095 Serene Dr Morgan Hill (95037) *(P-9095)*
Sakura Finetek USA Inc (HQ) ....C....310 972-7800
1750 W 214th St Torrance (90501) *(P-7215)*
Salad Time Farms, Baldwin Park *Also called Tanimura & Antle Inc (P-577)*
Saladinos Inc (PA) ....C....559 271-3700
3325 W Figarden Dr Fresno (93711) *(P-8451)*
Salas OBrien Engineers Inc (PA) ....E....408 282-1500
305 S 11th St San Jose (95112) *(P-25901)*
Salazar Labor Contracting ....D....760 746-0805
957 Sugarloaf Dr Escondido (92026) *(P-672)*
Salem Christian Homes Inc (PA) ....C....909 614-0575
6921 Edison Ave Ste A Chino (91710) *(P-24661)*
Salem Media Group Inc (PA) ....C....805 987-0400
4880 Santa Rosa Rd Camarillo (93012) *(P-5750)*
Salem Media Group Inc ....D....818 956-5254
701 N Brand Blvd Ste 550 Glendale (91203) *(P-5751)*
Salesforcecom Inc (PA) ....A....415 901-7000
1 Market Ste 300 San Francisco (94105) *(P-15846)*
Salesforcecom Foundation ....C....800 667-6389
The Landmark One St The Landma San Francisco (94105) *(P-5638)*
Salesian Boys and Girls Club ....D....415 397-3068
680 Filbert St San Francisco (94133) *(P-19024)*
Salestar LLC (PA) ....D....510 637-4700
300 Lakeside Dr Fl 11 Oakland (94612) *(P-7099)*
Salient Global Technologies, Pittsburg *Also called Ravig Inc (P-7097)*
Salinas Disposal Service, Hayward *Also called USA Waste of California Inc (P-6504)*
Salinas Disposal Service, Salinas *Also called USA Waste of California Inc (P-6500)*
Salinas Med Mngt Srvcs Org Inc ....D....831 751-7070
355 Abbott St Ste 100 Salinas (93901) *(P-19836)*
Salinas Urgent Care, Salinas *Also called Salinas Valley Memorial Hlthca (P-21699)*
Salinas Valley Medical Clinic ....B....831 424-7389
236 San Jose St Salinas (93901) *(P-19837)*
Salinas Valley Memorial Hlthca ....B....831 759-3236
440 E Romie Ln Salinas (93901) *(P-21697)*
Salinas Valley Memorial Hlthca ....B....831 884-5048
5 Lower Ragsdle Dr 102 Monterey (93940) *(P-19838)*
Salinas Valley Memorial Hlthca (PA) ....D....831 757-4333
450 E Romie Ln Salinas (93901) *(P-21698)*
Salinas Valley Memorial Hlthca ....B....831 757-3041
611 Abbott St Ste 101 Salinas (93901) *(P-22043)*
Salinas Valley Memorial Hlthca ....B....831 755-7880
558 Abbott St Salinas (93901) *(P-21699)*
Salinas Valley Memorial Hosp, Salinas *Also called Salinas Valley Memorial Hlthca (P-21698)*
Salinas Valley Prime Care Med, Salinas *Also called Salinas Med Mngt Srvcs Org Inc (P-19836)*
Salomon Smith Barney, El Segundo *Also called Citigroup Global Markets Inc (P-9931)*
Salomon Smith Barney, Sacramento *Also called Citigroup Global Markets Inc (P-9932)*
Salomon Smith Barney, Fresno *Also called Citigroup Global Markets Inc (P-9937)*
Salon Lujon Inc ....D....714 738-1882
216 N Harbor Blvd Fullerton (92832) *(P-13671)*
Salon Media Group Inc (PA) ....D....415 870-7566
870 Market St Ste 442 San Francisco (94102) *(P-16250)*
Salon Technique ....E....714 871-4247
101 N Harbor Blvd Fullerton (92832) *(P-13772)*
Salon-Salon ....D....209 571-3500
1700 Mchenry Ave Ste 29 Modesto (95350) *(P-13672)*
Salson Logistics Inc ....C....310 328-6800
1331 Torrance Blvd Torrance (90501) *(P-5244)*
Salt Catering, Los Angeles *Also called Salt of Earth Productions Inc (P-17451)*
Salt Lake Hotel Associates LP (PA) ....C....415 397-5572
222 Kearny St Ste 200 San Francisco (94108) *(P-13164)*
Salt of Earth Productions Inc ....C....818 399-1860
1437 S Robertson Blvd Los Angeles (90035) *(P-17451)*
Saltzburg Ray & Bergman LLP ....C....310 481-6700
12121 Wilshire Blvd # 600 Los Angeles (90025) *(P-23364)*
Salu Beauty Inc ....D....916 475-1400
11344 Coloma Rd Ste 725 Gold River (95670) *(P-25039)*
Salu.net, Gold River *Also called Salu Beauty Inc (P-25039)*
Salud Para La Gente ....C....831 728-0222
195 Aviation Way Ste 200 Watsonville (95076) *(P-19839)*
Salud Para La Gnte Hlth Clinic, Watsonville *Also called Salud Para La Gente (P-19839)*
Salutary Sports Clubs Inc ....E....530 677-5705
4242 Sports Club Dr Shingle Springs (95682) *(P-18646)*
Salvador Martinez ....C....559 781-5150
2049 N Newcomb St Porterville (93257) *(P-673)*
Salvation Army (HQ) ....C....562 491-8464
180 E Ocean Blvd Ste 500 Long Beach (90802) *(P-24005)*
Salvation Army ....D....661 325-8626
200 19th St Bakersfield (93301) *(P-22669)*
Salvation Army ....E....213 484-0772
2737 W Sunset Blvd Los Angeles (90026) *(P-24006)*
Salvation Army ....D....209 466-3871
1247 S Wilson Way Stockton (95205) *(P-22670)*
Salvation Army ....D....858 279-1100
2799 Health Center Dr San Diego (92123) *(P-24662)*
Salvation Army ....D....415 643-8000
154 Oshaughnessy Blvd San Francisco (94127) *(P-24663)*
Salvation Army ....B....619 269-1404
6845 University Ave San Diego (92115) *(P-18647)*
Salvation Army ....D....916 563-3700
3755 N Freeway Blvd Sacramento (95834) *(P-24836)*
Salvation Army Glden State Div (PA) ....D....415 553-3500
832 Folsom St Fl 6 San Francisco (94107) *(P-24007)*
Salvation Army Residences Inc ....D....213 553-3273
900 James M Wood Blvd Los Angeles (90015) *(P-24008)*

ALPHABETIC

Employee Codes: A=Over 500 employees, B=251-500
C=101-250, D=51-100, E=50
2019 Directory of California
Wholesalers and Services Companies
© Mergent Inc. 1-800-342-5647
1451

Sam Hill & Sons Inc ....E....805 620-0828
2627 Beene Rd Ventura (93003) ***(P-1977)***
Sam Jung USA Inc ....D....323 231-0811
843 E 31st St Los Angeles (90011) ***(P-8241)***
Sam Kholi Transport, Fontana *Also called Defenders Trnsp Svcs Inc* ***(P-5040)***
Sam Trans, South San Francisco *Also called San Mateo County Transit Dst* ***(P-3719)***
Sam Trans, San Carlos *Also called San Mateo County Transit Dst* ***(P-3956)***
Samaritan Imaging Center ....A....213 977-2140
1245 Wilshire Blvd # 205 Los Angeles (90017) ***(P-22139)***
Samaritan Village Inc ....C....209 883-3212
7700 Fox Rd Hughson (95326) ***(P-24009)***
Samarkand Retirement Community, Santa Barbara *Also called Evangelical Covenant Church* ***(P-24525)***
Samba TV, San Francisco *Also called Free Stream Media Corp* ***(P-9218)***
Sambazon Inc (PA) ....D....877 726-2296
209 Avenida Fabricante # 200 San Clemente (92672) ***(P-8726)***
Sambreel Services LLC ....E....760 266-5090
5857 Owens Ave Ste 300 Carlsbad (92008) ***(P-15424)***
Same Swim LLC ....D....323 582-2588
2333 E 49th St Vernon (90058) ***(P-8332)***
Samedan Oil Corporation ....B....661 319-5038
1360 Landing Ave Seal Beach (90740) ***(P-1028)***
Samiyatex, Los Angeles *Also called Paragon Textiles Inc* ***(P-8330)***
Samsung Electronics Amer Inc ....D....310 537-7000
18600 S Broadwick St Rancho Dominguez (90220) ***(P-7428)***
Samsung Electronics Amer Inc ....A....650 210-1000
665 Clyde Ave Mountain View (94043) ***(P-7536)***
Samsung International Inc (HQ) ....E....619 671-6859
333 H St Ste 6000 Chula Vista (91910) ***(P-7537)***
Samsung Research America Inc (HQ) ....E....408 544-5700
665 Clyde Ave Mountain View (94043) ***(P-26447)***
Samsung SDS America Inc ....D....408 638-8800
2665 N 1st St Ste 110 San Jose (95134) ***(P-15425)***
Samsung Semiconductor Inc (HQ) ....C....408 544-4000
3655 N 1st St San Jose (95134) ***(P-7538)***
Samuel J Piazza & Son Inc (PA) ....D....323 357-1999
9001 Rayo Ave South Gate (90280) ***(P-4370)***
Samy Co, Cypress *Also called Hoyu America Co* ***(P-8178)***
San Andreas Regional Center (PA) ....C....408 374-9960
6203 San Ignacio Ave # 110 San Jose (95119) ***(P-24010)***
SAN ANTONIO COMMUNITY HOSPITAL, Rancho Cucamonga *Also called Assistance League Foothill Com* ***(P-24740)***
San Antonio Community Hospital ....E....909 948-8000
7777 Milliken Ave Ste A Rancho Cucamonga (91730) ***(P-21700)***
San Antonio Regional Hospital (PA) ....A....909 985-2811
999 San Bernardino Rd Upland (91786) ***(P-21701)***
San Benito Health Care Dst (PA) ....B....831 637-5711
911 Sunset Dr Ste A Hollister (95023) ***(P-21702)***
San Benito Htg & Shtmtl Inc ....D....831 637-1112
1771 San Felipe Rd Hollister (95023) ***(P-2347)***
San Bernabe Vineyards ....D....831 385-4897
53001 Oasis Rd King City (93930) ***(P-172)***
San Bernardino California City (PA) ....B....909 384-7272
290 N D St San Bernardino (92401) ***(P-23365)***
San Bernardino California City ....D....909 384-5111
300 N D St Fl 3 San Bernardino (92418) ***(P-24977)***
San Bernardino Care Company ....C....909 884-4781
467 E Gilbert St San Bernardino (92404) ***(P-21202)***
San Bernardino City Unf School ....C....909 388-6100
956 W 9th St San Bernardino (92411) ***(P-14374)***
San Bernardino City Unf School ....D....909 388-6307
303 S K St San Bernardino (92410) ***(P-24376)***
San Bernardino City Unf School ....D....909 881-8000
1257 Northpark Blvd San Bernardino (92407) ***(P-22873)***
San Bernardino Family YMCA, San Bernardino *Also called YMCA of East Valley* ***(P-25290)***
San Bernardino Golf Club, San Bernardino *Also called J G Golfing Enterprises Inc* ***(P-18723)***
San Bernardino Hilton (HQ) ....C....909 889-0133
285 E Hospitality Ln San Bernardino (92408) ***(P-13165)***
San Bernardino Med Group Inc (PA) ....C....909 883-8611
1700 N Waterman Ave San Bernardino (92404) ***(P-19840)***
San Bernardino Mtns Wildlife ....E....909 226-6189
29450 Pine Ridge Dr Cedar Glen (92321) ***(P-446)***
San Bernardino Parole Unit 14, San Bernardino *Also called Correctons Rhbltation Cal Dept* ***(P-23619)***
San Bernardino Symphony ....D....909 381-5388
198 N Arrowhead Ave 2b San Bernardino (92408) ***(P-18457)***
San Brnrdino Pub Emplyees Assn ....E....909 386-1260
433 N Sierra Way San Bernardino (92410) ***(P-25075)***
San Carlos Associates Ltd ....C....831 649-4234
350 Calle Principal Monterey (93940) ***(P-13166)***
San Clemente Medical Ctr LLC ....B....949 496-1122
654 Camino De Los Mares San Clemente (92673) ***(P-21703)***
San Clemente Villas By Sea ....D....949 489-3400
660 Camino De Los Mares San Clemente (92673) ***(P-24664)***
San Dego Cnty Rgnal Arprt Auth (PA) ....D....619 400-2400
3225 N Harbor Dr Fl 3 San Diego (92101) ***(P-4907)***
San Dego Cnty Rgnal Arprt Auth ....C....619 400-2404
2320 Stillwater Rd San Diego (92101) ***(P-4908)***
San Dego Cnvntion Ctr Corp Inc (PA) ....D....619 525-5000
111 W Harbor Dr San Diego (92101) ***(P-10931)***
San Dego Mission Vly Hilton Ht, San Diego *Also called Kalpana LLC* ***(P-12799)***
San Dego Mrrott Marquis Marina ....E....301 380-3000
333 W Harbor Dr San Diego (92101) ***(P-13167)***
San Dego Ntural History Museum, San Diego *Also called San Dego Soc of Ntural History* ***(P-24902)***
San Dego Soc of Ntural History ....D....619 232-3821
1788 El Prado San Diego (92101) ***(P-24902)***

San Diego Aerospace Museum ....D....619 258-1221
335 Kenney St El Cajon (92020) ***(P-24903)***
San Diego Arcft Carier Museum ....C....619 544-9600
910 N Harbor Dr San Diego (92101) ***(P-24904)***
San Diego Assn Governments (PA) ....B....619 699-1900
401 B St Ste 800 San Diego (92101) ***(P-24978)***
San Diego Bay Area Elc Inc ....D....858 748-2060
13100 Kirkham Way Ste 205 Poway (92064) ***(P-2721)***
San Diego Blood Bank (PA) ....C....619 296-6393
3636 Gtwy Ctr Ave Ste 100 San Diego (92102) ***(P-22874)***
San Diego Blood Bank ....C....619 441-1804
776 Arnele Ave El Cajon (92020) ***(P-22875)***
San Diego Blood Bnk Foundation, San Diego *Also called San Diego Blood Bank* ***(P-22874)***
San Diego Car Accident Lawyers ....E....858 201-4178
Maple St San Diego (92104) ***(P-17452)***
San Diego Cemetery Assn ....D....858 453-2121
5600 Carroll Canyon Rd San Diego (92121) ***(P-13697)***
San Diego Center For Children (PA) ....D....858 277-9550
3002 Armstrong St San Diego (92111) ***(P-21203)***
San Diego Choices, San Diego *Also called Telecare Corporation* ***(P-21985)***
San Diego CLD Stg 4140, National City *Also called US Foods Inc* ***(P-8898)***
San Diego Coastl Med Group Inc ....C....760 901-5259
2201 Mission Ave Oceanside (92058) ***(P-22876)***
San Diego Community Hsing Corp ....C....619 527-4633
230 Catania St San Diego (92113) ***(P-27852)***
San Diego Composites Inc ....D....858 751-0450
9220 Activity Rd Ste 100 San Diego (92126) ***(P-25902)***
San Diego Correctional Fcilty, San Diego *Also called Corecivic Inc* ***(P-27583)***
San Diego Country Club Inc ....D....619 422-8895
88 L St Chula Vista (91911) ***(P-19025)***
San Diego Country Estates Assn ....C....760 789-3788
24157 San Vicente Rd Ramona (92065) ***(P-25234)***
San Diego County Credit Union (PA) ....C....877 732-2848
6545 Sequence Dr San Diego (92121) ***(P-9649)***
San Diego County Employees Ret ....D....619 515-6800
2275 Rio Bonito Way # 100 San Diego (92108) ***(P-25076)***
San Diego County Water Auth (PA) ....B....858 522-6600
4677 Overland Ave San Diego (92123) ***(P-6301)***
San Diego County Water Auth ....D....760 480-1991
610 W 5th Ave Escondido (92025) ***(P-6302)***
San Diego Diagnstc Radlgy Medi (PA) ....D....858 565-6328
8745 Aero Dr Ste 200 San Diego (92123) ***(P-19841)***
San Diego District Office, San Diego *Also called State Compensation Insur Fund* ***(P-10400)***
San Diego Family Care (PA) ....D....858 279-0925
6973 Linda Vista Rd San Diego (92111) ***(P-19842)***
San Diego Family Care ....C....619 563-0250
4290 Polk Ave San Diego (92105) ***(P-22877)***
San Diego Family Housing LLC ....B....858 874-8100
3360 Murray Ridge Rd San Diego (92123) ***(P-25455)***
San Diego Farah Partners ....E....619 239-2261
1430 7th Ave Ste B San Diego (92101) ***(P-13168)***
San Diego Fish Market, San Diego *Also called Top of Market* ***(P-27064)***
San Diego Gas & Electric Co (HQ) ....C....619 696-2000
8326 Century Park Ct San Diego (92123) ***(P-6186)***
San Diego Gas & Electric Co ....C....800 411-7343
990 Bay Blvd Chula Vista (91911) ***(P-6152)***
San Diego Gas & Electric Co ....E....949 361-8090
662 Camino De Los Mares San Clemente (92673) ***(P-6187)***
San Diego Gas & Electric Co ....C....760 438-6200
5016 Carlsbad Blvd Carlsbad (92008) ***(P-6201)***
San Diego Gas & Electric Co ....B....760 432-5885
571 Enterprise St Escondido (92029) ***(P-6202)***
San Diego Gas & Electric Co ....C....619 699-1018
701 33rd St San Diego (92102) ***(P-6203)***
San Diego Gulls Hockey CLB LLC ....D....619 359-4700
7676 Hazard Center Dr San Diego (92108) ***(P-19229)***
San Diego Harbor Excursion, Coronado *Also called Star & Crescent Boat Company* ***(P-4721)***
San Diego Hbr Excursions Inc ....D....619 234-4111
1050 N Harbor Dr San Diego (92101) ***(P-2059)***
San Diego Hebrew Homes (PA) ....C....760 942-2695
211 Saxony Rd Encinitas (92024) ***(P-20738)***
San Diego Hospice ....A....619 688-1600
2400 Historic Decatur Rd # 107 San Diego (92106) ***(P-22410)***
San Diego Hospice & Institute, San Diego *Also called San Diego Hospice* ***(P-22410)***
San Diego Hotel Company LLC ....C....619 696-0234
660 K St San Diego (92101) ***(P-13169)***
San Diego Hotel Lease LLC ....C....619 446-3000
530 Broadway San Diego (92101) ***(P-13170)***
San Diego Humane Soc & Spca ....D....619 299-7012
5500 Gaines St San Diego (92110) ***(P-25456)***
San Diego Imaging - Chula Vist (PA) ....D....858 565-0950
8745 Aero Dr Ste 200 San Diego (92123) ***(P-19843)***
San Diego Land Systems ....E....858 558-0542
8720 Miramar Pl San Diego (92121) ***(P-784)***
San Diego Lesbian Gay Bisexu ....E....619 692-2077
3909 Centre St San Diego (92103) ***(P-24011)***
San Diego Lessee LLC ....C....619 297-5466
7450 Hazard Center Dr San Diego (92108) ***(P-13171)***
San Diego Marriott Mission Vly, San Diego *Also called Ws Mmv Hotel LLC* ***(P-13420)***
San Diego Med Svcs Entp LLC ....B....619 280-6060
10405 Sn Diego Mn Rd 20 San Diego (92108) ***(P-3840)***
San Diego Messenger Inc ....E....858 514-8866
4848 Ronson Ct Ste G San Diego (92111) ***(P-4429)***
San Diego Metro Trnst Sys ....A....619 231-1466
1255 Imperial Ave # 1000 San Diego (92101) ***(P-3702)***
San Diego Metropolitan Cr Un (PA) ....D....619 297-4835
9212 Balboa Ave San Diego (92123) ***(P-9650)***
San Diego Mission Vly Hilton, San Diego *Also called HEI Mission Valley LP* ***(P-12653)***

San Diego Mortgage & RE....E....619 334-7779
9461 Grsmnt Smt Dr Ste D La Mesa (91941) ***(P-11752)***
San Diego Museum of Art....D....619 696-1971
1450 El Prado San Diego (92101) ***(P-24905)***
San Diego Old Town, San Diego *Also called RPC Old Town Jefferson* ***(P-13147)***
San Diego Opera Association (PA)....E....619 232-7636
233 A St Ste 500 San Diego (92101) ***(P-18401)***
San Diego Orthopaedic Associat....D....619 299-8500
4060 4th Ave Ste 700 San Diego (92103) ***(P-19844)***
San Diego Padres, San Diego *Also called Padres LP* ***(P-18530)***
San Diego Pathologists Medical (PA)....C....619 297-4012
7592 Metro Dr Ste 406 San Diego (92108) ***(P-19845)***
San Diego Recyling Inc....B....619 287-7555
6670 Federal Blvd Lemon Grove (91945) ***(P-6473)***
San Diego Region, San Diego *Also called Water Resources Control Bd Cal* ***(P-24990)***
San Diego Regional Ctr For Dev, National City *Also called San Diego-Imperial* ***(P-24013)***
San Diego Rescue Mission Inc (PA)....D....619 819-1880
120 Elm St San Diego (92101) ***(P-24837)***
San Diego Sheraton Corporation....A....619 291-6400
1590 Harbor Island Dr San Diego (92101) ***(P-13172)***
San Diego State University....D....619 594-1515
5200 Campanile Dr San Diego (92182) ***(P-5752)***
San Diego Supercomputer Center, La Jolla *Also called University Cal San Diego* ***(P-16195)***
San Diego Symphony Orchestra....C....619 235-0800
1245 7th Ave San Diego (92101) ***(P-18458)***
San Diego Testing Engineers....D....858 715-5800
7895 Convoy Ct Ste 18 San Diego (92111) ***(P-25903)***
San Diego Theatres Inc....C....619 615-4000
1100 3rd Ave San Diego (92101) ***(P-10932)***
San Diego Tourism Authority (PA)....D....619 232-3101
750 B St Ste 1500 San Diego (92101) ***(P-17453)***
San Diego Transit Corporation (PA)....A....619 238-0100
100 16th St San Diego (92101) ***(P-3703)***
San Diego Transit Corporation....B....619 238-0100
100 16th St San Diego (92101) ***(P-3704)***
San Diego Trolley Inc....B....619 595-4933
1341 Commercial St San Diego (92113) ***(P-3705)***
San Diego Unified Hbr Police, San Diego *Also called San Diego Unified Port Dst* ***(P-4735)***
San Diego Unified Port Dst....C....619 686-6200
1400 Tidelands Ave National City (91950) ***(P-4734)***
San Diego Unified Port Dst....C....619 686-6585
3380 N Harbor Dr San Diego (92101) ***(P-4735)***
San Diego Unified Port Dst (PA)....C....619 686-6200
3165 Pacific Hwy San Diego (92101) ***(P-4736)***
San Diego Unified School Dst....A....858 627-7130
4860 Ruffner St San Diego (92111) ***(P-14375)***
San Diego Welders Supply, San Diego *Also called Westair Gases & Equipment Inc* ***(P-7821)***
San Diego Wild Animal Park, Escondido *Also called Zoological Society San Diego* ***(P-24938)***
San Diego Youth Services Inc (PA)....D....619 221-8600
3255 Wing St Ste 550 San Diego (92110) ***(P-24012)***
San Diego Zoo, San Diego *Also called Zoological Society San Diego* ***(P-24939)***
San Diego-Imperial....D....619 336-6600
2727 Hoover Ave National City (91950) ***(P-24013)***
San Diego-Imperial Council (PA)....E....619 294-3806
1207 Upas St San Diego (92103) ***(P-25235)***
San Diego-Imperial Counties De (PA)....B....858 576-2996
4355 Ruffin Rd Ste 220 San Diego (92123) ***(P-24014)***
San Diego-Imperial Counties De....D....760 736-1200
1370 W Sn Mrcos Blvd # 100 San Marcos (92078) ***(P-24015)***
San Dimas Bushnell Building, Rosemead *Also called Southern California Edison Co* ***(P-6129)***
SAN DIMAS COMMUNITY HOSPITAL, San Dimas *Also called Prime Healthcare-San Dimas LLC* ***(P-21662)***
San Dimas Golf Inc....D....909 599-8486
1400 Avenida Entrada San Dimas (91773) ***(P-19026)***
San Dimas Luggage Company....D....909 510-8820
2095 S Archibald Ave Ontario (91761) ***(P-8057)***
San Dimas Medical Group Inc....D....661 663-4800
100 Old River Rd Bakersfield (93311) ***(P-19846)***
San Dimas Retirement Center (PA)....D....909 599-8441
834 W Arrow Hwy San Dimas (91773) ***(P-11109)***
San Fernando City of Inc....D....818 832-2400
10605 Balboa Blvd Ste 100 Granada Hills (91344) ***(P-22671)***
San Fernando Health Center, San Fernando *Also called Northeast Valley Health Corp* ***(P-19720)***
San Fernando Juvenile Hall, Sylmar *Also called County of Los Angeles* ***(P-24480)***
San Fernando Valley Community (PA)....B....818 901-4830
16360 Roscoe Blvd Fl 2 Van Nuys (91406) ***(P-22672)***
San Fernando Valley Interfaith, Van Nuys *Also called County of Los Angeles* ***(P-23672)***
San Francisco City & County....D....415 695-5660
1520 Oakdale Ave San Francisco (94124) ***(P-24016)***
San Francisco 49ers, Santa Clara *Also called Forty Niners Football Co LLC* ***(P-18517)***
San Francisco Aids Foundation (PA)....D....415 487-3000
1035 Market St Ste 400 San Francisco (94103) ***(P-24017)***
San Francisco Ballet Assn....C....415 865-2000
455 Franklin St San Francisco (94102) ***(P-18402)***
San Francisco Bay, San Francisco *Also called Charolais Care V Inc* ***(P-22263)***
San Francisco Bay AR Tran Assn....C....510 501-5318
915 San Antonio Ave Alameda (94501) ***(P-25457)***
San Francisco Bay Area Councl....D....510 577-9000
1001 Davis St San Leandro (94577) ***(P-25236)***
San Francisco Bay Area Rapid....E....510 464-6000
1330 Broadway Oakland (94612) ***(P-3706)***
San Francisco Bay Area Rapid....D....510 834-1297
800 Madison St Oakland (94607) ***(P-3707)***
San Francisco Bay Area Rapid....C....510 464-6126
300 Lakeside Dr 23 Oakland (94612) ***(P-3708)***
San Francisco Bay Area Rapid....C....510 233-6848
1101 13th St Richmond (94801) ***(P-3709)***
San Francisco Bay Area Rapid (PA)....B....510 464-6000
300 Lakeside Dr Oakland (94604) ***(P-3710)***
San Francisco Bay Area Rapid....D....510 233-7444
1101 13th St Richmond (94801) ***(P-3711)***
San Francisco Bay Area Rapid....A....510 286-2893
601 E 8th St Oakland (94606) ***(P-3712)***
San Francisco Bay Area Rapid....D....510 464-7000
800 Madison St Oakland (94607) ***(P-3713)***
San Francisco Bay Area Rapid....C....510 464-6000
300 Lakeside Dr Fl 17 Oakland (94612) ***(P-3714)***
San Francisco City & County....D....415 356-2700
617 Mission St San Francisco (94105) ***(P-24018)***
San Francisco City & County....D....415 356-2700
617 Mission St San Francisco (94105) ***(P-24019)***
San Francisco City & County....C....415 550-4600
200 Paul Ave B San Francisco (94124) ***(P-17798)***
San Francisco City Clinic....D....415 487-5500
356 7th St San Francisco (94103) ***(P-22673)***
San Francisco District Office, San Francisco *Also called California Dept Rehabilitation* ***(P-14581)***
San Francisco Federal Cr Un (PA)....D....415 775-5377
770 Golden Gate Ave Fl 1 San Francisco (94102) ***(P-9586)***
San Francisco Fertility Ctrs....D....415 834-3000
55 Francisco St Ste 300 San Francisco (94133) ***(P-19847)***
San Francisco Food Bank....D....415 282-1900
900 Pennsylvania Ave San Francisco (94107) ***(P-24020)***
San Francisco Forty Niners....D....408 562-4949
4949 Mrie P Debartolo Way Santa Clara (95054) ***(P-12003)***
San Francisco Forty Niners (PA)....C....408 562-4949
4949 Mrie P Debartolo Way Santa Clara (95054) ***(P-18533)***
San Francisco Foundation....D....415 733-8500
1 Embarcadero Ctr # 1400 San Francisco (94111) ***(P-17454)***
San Francisco General Hospital, San Francisco *Also called Gastroenterology Division* ***(P-19481)***
San Francisco General Hospital, San Francisco *Also called City & County of San Francisco* ***(P-21326)***
San Francisco Health Authority (PA)....D....415 615-4407
50 Beale St Fl 12 San Francisco (94105) ***(P-25040)***
San Francisco Hilton & Towers, San Francisco *Also called Park Hotels & Resorts Inc* ***(P-13022)***
San Francisco Hotel Associates....D....415 392-4666
650 Bush St San Francisco (94108) ***(P-13173)***
San Francisco Hotel Group LLC....C....415 276-9888
222 Sansome St San Francisco (94104) ***(P-13174)***
San Francisco Ladies Protecti....D....415 931-3136
3400 Laguna St San Francisco (94123) ***(P-24665)***
San Francisco Marriott Marquis, San Francisco *Also called Host Hotels & Resorts LP* ***(P-12708)***
San Francisco Marriott Un Sq, San Francisco *Also called Intercontinental Hotels Group* ***(P-12770)***
San Francisco Meritime N H P....D....415 561-7000
Fort Myson Ctr Bldg E265 San Francisco (94123) ***(P-24906)***
San Francisco Museum Modrn Art (PA)....B....415 357-4035
151 3rd St San Francisco (94103) ***(P-24907)***
San Francisco Opera Assn....A....415 861-4008
301 Van Ness Ave San Francisco (94102) ***(P-18403)***
San Francisco Partclr Cncl Sct....D....415 255-3525
525 5th St San Francisco (94107) ***(P-24021)***
San Francisco Public Schools, San Francisco *Also called San Francisco City & County* ***(P-24016)***
San Francisco Radio Assets LLC (HQ)....C....415 216-1300
750 Battery St Fl 2 San Francisco (94111) ***(P-5753)***
San Francisco Reinsurance Co....D....415 899-2000
1465 N Mcdowell Blvd Petaluma (94954) ***(P-10170)***
San Francisco Residential Care, San Francisco *Also called Self-Help For Elderly* ***(P-24040)***
San Francisco Sightseeing, San Francisco *Also called Franciscan Lines Inc* ***(P-3798)***
San Francisco Symphony Inc (PA)....B....415 552-8000
201 Van Ness Ave San Francisco (94102) ***(P-18459)***
San Francisco Tennis Club....D....415 777-9000
645 5th St San Francisco (94107) ***(P-18648)***
San Francisco Towers, San Francisco *Also called Covia Communities* ***(P-24490)***
San Francisco Travel Assn....D....415 974-6900
1 Front St Ste 2900 San Francisco (94111) ***(P-17455)***
San Francisco Vamc, San Francisco *Also called Veterans Health Administration* ***(P-20066)***
San Francisco Zoological Soc....C....415 753-7080
1 Zoo Rd San Francisco (94132) ***(P-19230)***
San Franciso Campus For Jewish, San Francisco *Also called Hebrew Home For Aged Disabled* ***(P-20521)***
San Fransisco Speciality Prod, Santa Fe Springs *Also called LA Specialty Produce Co* ***(P-8700)***
San Frncsco Econ Oprtnty Cncil....C....415 749-3798
1426 Fillmore St Ste 301 San Francisco (94115) ***(P-24838)***
San Frncsco Mrtime Nat Pk Assn (PA)....E....415 561-6662
Fort Mason Fl 2 Bldg E San Francisco (94123) ***(P-24908)***
San Frncsco North/Petaluma KOA....E....707 763-1492
20 Rainsville Rd Petaluma (94952) ***(P-13467)***
San Frnndo Vly Intrfith Cuncil....C....818 885-5220
8956 Vanalden Ave Northridge (91324) ***(P-24839)***
San Gabriel Ambulatory Sugery....A....626 300-5300
207 S Santa Anita St G16 San Gabriel (91776) ***(P-19848)***
San Gabriel Childrens Ctr Inc (PA)....D....626 859-2089
2200 E Route 66 Ste 100 Glendora (91740) ***(P-24022)***
San Gabriel Childrens Ctr Inc....D....626 859-2089
4740 N Grand Ave Covina (91724) ***(P-24666)***

ALPHABETIC

Employee Codes: A=Over 500 employees, B=251-500
C=101-250, D=51-100, E=50
2019 Directory of California
Wholesalers and Services Companies
© Mergent Inc. 1-800-342-5647
1453

San Gabriel Convalescent Ctr, Rosemead *Also called Longwood Management Corp* ***(P-20600)***
San Gabriel Country Club......D......626 287-9671
350 E Hermosa Dr San Gabriel (91775) ***(P-19027)***
San Gabriel Nursery and Flor (PA)......D......626 286-0787
632 S San Gabriel Blvd San Gabriel (91776) ***(P-298)***
San Gabriel Transit Inc......D......626 430-3650
14913 Ramona Blvd Baldwin Park (91706) ***(P-3868)***
San Gabriel Transit Inc (PA)......C......626 258-1310
3650 Rockwell Ave El Monte (91731) ***(P-3715)***
San Gabriel Transit Inc......D......818 771-0374
7955 San Fernando Rd Sun Valley (91352) ***(P-3869)***
San Gabriel Valley Cab Co, El Monte *Also called San Gabriel Transit Inc* ***(P-3715)***
San Gabriel Valley Water Assn......D......626 815-1305
725 N Azusa Ave Azusa (91702) ***(P-6303)***
San Gabriel Valley Water Co (PA)......C......626 448-6183
11142 Garvey Ave El Monte (91733) ***(P-6304)***
San Gabriel Valley Water Co......D......909 822-2201
8440 Nuevo Ave Fontana (92335) ***(P-6305)***
San Gabriel Vly Training Ctr (PA)......D......626 330-3185
400 S Covina Blvd La Puente (91746) ***(P-24226)***
San Gabriel-Pomona Valley Hlg, Baldwin Park *Also called USA Waste of California Inc* ***(P-6492)***
SAN GABRIEL/POMONA REGIONAL CE, Pomona *Also called San Gabriel/Pomona Valleys* ***(P-24023)***
San Gabriel/Pomona Valleys......B......909 620-7722
75 Rancho Camino Dr Pomona (91766) ***(P-24023)***
San Gbriel Vly Cnvlescent Hosp......D......626 401-1557
3938 Cogswell Rd El Monte (91732) ***(P-21971)***
San Gbriel Vly Med Ctr Fndtion......A......626 289-5454
438 W Las Tunas Dr San Gabriel (91776) ***(P-21704)***
San Geronimo Golf Course, San Geronimo *Also called National Golf Properties Inc* ***(P-18985)***
San Gorgonio Memorial Hospital (PA)......C......951 845-1121
600 N Highland Sprng Ave Banning (92220) ***(P-21705)***
San Gorgonio Memorial Hospital......D......760 656-2251
1751 N Sunrise Way Ste G Palm Springs (92262) ***(P-22674)***
San Jacinto Healthcare, Hemet *Also called Miramonte Enterprises LLC* ***(P-20645)***
San Joaquin Beverage, Stockton *Also called Dbi Beverage San Joaquin* ***(P-8991)***
San Joaquin Cnty Aging & Commu......C......209 468-9455
102 S San Joaquin St Stockton (95202) ***(P-24024)***
San Joaquin Community Hospital, Bakersfield *Also called Kaiser Foundation Hospitals* ***(P-21491)***
San Joaquin Community Hospital (PA)......A......661 395-3000
2615 Chester Ave Bakersfield (93301) ***(P-21706)***
San Joaquin Country Club......D......559 439-3483
3484 W Bluff Ave Fresno (93711) ***(P-19028)***
San Joaquin County Adult Svcs, Stockton *Also called County of San Joaquin* ***(P-23730)***
San Joaquin County Operations, Stockton *Also called American Medical Response West* ***(P-3770)***
San Joaquin Figs Inc......E......559 224-4492
3564 N Hazel Ave Fresno (93722) ***(P-564)***
San Joaquin Gardens, Fresno *Also called American Baptist Homes of West* ***(P-24415)***
San Joaquin General Hospital......A......209 468-6000
500 W Hospital Rd French Camp (95231) ***(P-21707)***
San Joaquin General Hospital......C......209 468-6000
500 W Hospital Rd French Camp (95231) ***(P-21708)***
San Joaquin Hills Transporttn (PA)......D......949 754-3400
125 Pacifica Ste 100 Irvine (92618) ***(P-1845)***
San Joaquin Regional Trnst Dst......C......209 948-5566
421 E Weber Ave Stockton (95202) ***(P-3716)***
San Joaquin Val UNI Air Pol (PA)......C......559 230-6000
1990 E Gettysburg Ave Fresno (93726) ***(P-27853)***
San Joaquin Val UNI Air Pol......D......209 497-1000
2700 M St Ste 275 Bakersfield (93301) ***(P-27854)***
San Joaquin Valley A P C D......D......559 230-6000
1990 E Gettysburg Ave Fresno (93726) ***(P-27855)***
San Joaquin Valley Intergrp......E......559 856-0559
6048 E Cimarron Ave Fresno (93727) ***(P-25458)***
San Joaquin Valley Railroad Co......C......559 592-1857
221 N F St Exeter (93221) ***(P-3624)***
San Joaquin Valley Rehabili (HQ)......B......559 436-3600
7173 N Sharon Ave Fresno (93720) ***(P-22675)***
San Jose Airport Garden Hotel......D......408 793-3300
1740 N 1st St San Jose (95112) ***(P-13175)***
San Jose Airport Hotel LLC......C......408 793-3939
1740 N 1st St San Jose (95112) ***(P-13176)***
San Jose Arena Management LLC......C......510 623-7200
44388 Old Warm Sprng Blvd Fremont (94538) ***(P-27021)***
San Jose Chld Discovery Museum......D......408 298-5437
180 Woz Way San Jose (95110) ***(P-24909)***
San Jose Conservation Corps......C......408 283-7171
2650 Senter Rd San Jose (95111) ***(P-24227)***
San Jose Country Club......D......408 258-4901
15571 Alum Rock Ave San Jose (95127) ***(P-19029)***
San Jose District Office, San Jose *Also called State Compensation Insur Fund* ***(P-10398)***
San Jose Fairmont Lessee LLC......B......408 998-1900
170 S Market St Lbby San Jose (95113) ***(P-13177)***
SAN JOSE FOOTHILL FAMILY, San Jose *Also called Foothill Health Center Inc* ***(P-19474)***
San Jose Hlthcare Wellness Ctr, San Jose *Also called San Joses Healthcare & Well* ***(P-20739)***
San Jose Lessee LLC......D......408 453-4000
2050 Gateway Pl San Jose (95110) ***(P-13178)***
San Jose Medical Group / MGT, San Jose *Also called Verity Medical Foundation* ***(P-20056)***
San Jose Medical Systems Lp......A......408 259-5000
225 N Jackson Ave San Jose (95116) ***(P-21709)***
San Jose Municipal Golf Course, San Jose *Also called Rawitser Golf Shop Mike* ***(P-18751)***
San Jose Museum of Art Assn......D......408 271-6840
110 S Market St San Jose (95113) ***(P-24910)***
San Jose Redevelopment Agency......C......408 535-8500
200 E Santa Clara St 14th San Jose (95113) ***(P-27856)***
San Jose Sharks LLC......C......408 999-6810
525 W Santa Clara St San Jose (95113) ***(P-18534)***
San Jose Silicon Valley Cham......D......408 291-5250
101 W Santa Clara St San Jose (95113) ***(P-24979)***
San Jose State University......E......408 924-1000
1 Washington Sq San Jose (95112) ***(P-19849)***
San Jose Surgical Supply Inc (PA)......E......408 293-9033
902 S Bascom Ave San Jose (95128) ***(P-7216)***
San Jose Water Company (HQ)......C......408 288-5314
110 W Taylor St San Jose (95110) ***(P-6306)***
San Jose Water Company......C......408 298-0364
1221 S Bascom Ave San Jose (95128) ***(P-6307)***
San Joses Healthcare & Well......D......408 295-2665
75 N 13th St San Jose (95112) ***(P-20739)***
San Juan Golf Inc......E......949 493-1167
32120 San Juan Creek Rd San Juan Capistrano (92675) ***(P-18755)***
San Juan Hill Country Club, San Juan Capistrano *Also called San Juan Golf Inc* ***(P-18755)***
San Juan Oaks LLC......D......831 636-6113
3825 Union Rd Hollister (95023) ***(P-18756)***
San Juan Oaks Golf Club, Hollister *Also called San Juan Oaks LLC* ***(P-18756)***
San Leandro Healthcare Center, San Leandro *Also called Kissito Health Case Inc* ***(P-22356)***
San Leandro Healthcare Center......D......510 357-4015
368 Juana Ave San Leandro (94577) ***(P-20740)***
San Leandro Hospital LP......B......510 357-6500
13855 E 14th St San Leandro (94578) ***(P-21710)***
San Leandro Surgery Center Lt......D......510 276-2800
15035 E 14th St San Leandro (94578) ***(P-19850)***
San Lndro Care Rhblitation Ctr, San Leandro *Also called Sunbridge Healthcare LLC* ***(P-20967)***
San Lorenzo 0119, San Lorenzo *Also called Wells Fargo Bank National Assn* ***(P-9396)***
San Lorenzo Village Shopg Ctr, San Mateo *Also called David D Bohannon Organization* ***(P-10866)***
San Luis Ambulance Service Inc......C......805 543-2626
3546 S Higuera St San Luis Obispo (93401) ***(P-3841)***
San Luis Care Center, Newman *Also called Avalon Care Ctr - Newman LLC* ***(P-20249)***
San Luis Dlta-Mendota Wtr Auth......D......209 835-2593
15990 Kelso Rd Byron (94514) ***(P-6564)***
San Luis Obispo Cnty Frm Inc (PA)......C......805 543-3751
224 Tank Farm Rd San Luis Obispo (93401) ***(P-9096)***
San Luis Obispo Golf......C......805 543-3400
255 Country Club Dr San Luis Obispo (93401) ***(P-19030)***
San Luis Obispo Regional......D......805 781-4465
179 Cross St Ste A San Luis Obispo (93401) ***(P-3717)***
San Luis Obispo VA Cboc, San Luis Obispo *Also called Veterans Health Administration* ***(P-20060)***
San Luis Physical Therapy (PA)......E......805 788-0805
1106 Walnut St 110 San Luis Obispo (93401) ***(P-20202)***
San Luis Sports Physical Therp, San Luis Obispo *Also called San Luis Physical Therapy* ***(P-20202)***
San Manuel Indian Bingo Casino (PA)......A......909 864-5050
777 San Manuel Blvd Highland (92346) ***(P-19231)***
San Marcos Caterers Inc......D......760 744-0120
1025 La Bonita Dr San Marcos (92078) ***(P-13179)***
San Marcos Kids Helpng Kids FN......C......800 659-6411
4750 Hollister Ave Santa Barbara (93110) ***(P-25237)***
SAN MARCOS MECHANICAL, Vista *Also called Industrial Coml Systems Inc* ***(P-2232)***
San Marcos Operating Co LP......D......760 471-2986
1586 W Square Marcos Blvd San Marcos (92078) ***(P-20741)***
San Marcos Stadium Cinema 18, San Marcos *Also called Edwards Theatres Circuit Inc* ***(P-18295)***
San Marcos Unified School Dst......D......760 752-1252
255 Pico Ave Ste 250 San Marcos (92069) ***(P-24377)***
San Marino Manor......E......626 446-5263
6812 Oak Ave San Gabriel (91775) ***(P-21204)***
San Marino Plastering Inc......A......714 693-7840
4501 E La Palma Ave # 200 Anaheim (92807) ***(P-2955)***
San Mateo Cnty Expo Fair Assn......E......650 574-3247
2495 S Delaware St San Mateo (94403) ***(P-19232)***
San Mateo Cnty Pub Hlth Clinic......E......650 301-8600
380 90th St Daly City (94015) ***(P-22676)***
San Mateo County Community......D......650 574-6586
1700 W Hillsdale Blvd San Mateo (94402) ***(P-5836)***
SAN MATEO COUNTY EXPO CENTER, San Mateo *Also called San Mateo Cnty Expo Fair Assn* ***(P-19232)***
San Mateo County Transit Dst (PA)......C......650 508-6200
1250 San Carlos Ave San Carlos (94070) ***(P-3718)***
San Mateo County Transit Dst......B......650 588-4860
301 N Access Rd South San Francisco (94080) ***(P-3719)***
San Mateo County Transit Dst......C......650 508-6412
501 Pico Blvd San Carlos (94070) ***(P-3956)***
San Mateo Credit Union (PA)......D......650 363-1725
350 Convention Way # 300 Redwood City (94063) ***(P-9651)***
San Mateo Credit Union......C......650 363-1725
1515 S El Camino Real # 100 San Mateo (94402) ***(P-9652)***
San Mateo Head Start Program, San Mateo *Also called Institute For Humn Social Dev* ***(P-24330)***
San Mateo Health Commission......C......650 616-0050
801 Gateway Blvd Ste 100 South San Francisco (94080) ***(P-22878)***
San Mateo Healthcare & Wellnes......D......650 692-3758
1100 Trousdale Dr Burlingame (94010) ***(P-20742)***
San Mateo Marriott, San Mateo *Also called Atrium Plaza LLC* ***(P-12340)***
San Mateo Sport Club, Burlingame *Also called 24 Hour Fitness Usa Inc* ***(P-18563)***

Mergent e-mail: customerrelations@mergent.com
1454
2019 Directory of California
Wholesalers and Services Companies
(P-0000) Products & Services Section entry number
(PA)=Parent Co (HQ)=Headquarters (DH)=Div Headquarters

San Miguel Hospital Assn....C....619 297-2251
1940 El Cajon Blvd San Diego (92104) **(P-21711)**
San Miguel Produce Inc....B....805 488-0981
4444 Navalair Rd Oxnard (93033) **(P-79)**
San Miguel Villa, Concord *Also called Tranquility Incorporated* **(P-21230)**
San Onfre Nclear Gnerating Stn, San Clemente *Also called Southern California Edison Co* **(P-6123)**
San Pablo Healthcare....C....510 235-3720
13328 San Pablo Ave San Pablo (94806) **(P-20743)**
San Pablo Lodge 43....D....707 642-1391
342 Georgia St Vallejo (94590) **(P-25238)**
San Pedro Convalescent HM Inc....D....310 832-6431
1430 W 6th St San Pedro (90732) **(P-20744)**
San Pedro Hospital Pavilion, San Pedro *Also called Providence Health System* **(P-21672)**
San Pedro Peninsula Hospital, San Pedro *Also called Providence Health System* **(P-21670)**
San Psqual Band Mssion Indians....B....760 291-5500
16300 Nyemii Pass Rd Valley Center (92082) **(P-13180)**
San Psqual Csino Dev Group Inc....E....760 291-5500
16300 Nyemii Pass Rd Valley Center (92082) **(P-13181)**
San Rafael Hillcrest LLC....D....415 479-8800
1010 Northgate Dr San Rafael (94903) **(P-13182)**
San Rafael Rock Quarry Inc (HQ)....D....415 459-7740
1000 Point San Pedro Rd San Rafael (94901) **(P-1090)**
San Ramon Medical Offices, San Ramon *Also called Kaiser Foundation Hospitals* **(P-19585)**
San Ramon Regional Med Ctr LLC....A....925 275-9200
6001 Norris Canyon Rd San Ramon (94583) **(P-21712)**
San Salvador Pre-School, Colton *Also called Colton Joint Unified Schl Dst* **(P-24298)**
San Tomas Convalescent Hosp, San Jose *Also called Aquinas Corporation* **(P-20233)**
San Val Alarm System, Thousand Palms *Also called San Val Corp* **(P-785)**
San Val Corp (PA)....B....760 346-3999
72203 Adelaid St Thousand Palms (92276) **(P-785)**
San Vicente Hospital....D....323 930-1040
6000 San Vicente Blvd Los Angeles (90036) **(P-21713)**
San Vicente Inn & Golf Club, Ramona *Also called San Diego Country Estates Assn* **(P-25234)**
San Ysidro Bb Property LLC....C....805 969-5046
900 San Ysidro Ln Santa Barbara (93108) **(P-13183)**
San Ysidro Health Center, San Ysidro *Also called Centro De Salud De La* **(P-22526)**
San-Mar Construction Co Inc....C....714 693-5400
4875 E La Palma Ave # 601 Anaheim (92807) **(P-3073)**
Sanact Inc (PA)....C....510 483-2324
5717 Brisa St Livermore (94550) **(P-17982)**
Sanborn Theatres Inc....D....909 296-9728
41090 Calif Oaks Rd Murrieta (92562) **(P-18320)**
Sanco Pipelines Incorporated....E....408 377-2793
727 University Ave Los Gatos (95032) **(P-1978)**
Sanctuary, The, Redwood City *Also called Bay Clubs Inc* **(P-18578)**
Sand Canyon Corporation (HQ)....D....949 727-9425
7595 Irvine Center Dr # 100 Irvine (92618) **(P-9906)**
Sand Canyon LLC....D....949 551-2560
11 Strawberry Farm Rd Irvine (92612) **(P-18757)**
Sand Dollar Holdings Inc (PA)....D....619 477-0185
1022 Bay Marina Dr # 106 National City (91950) **(P-8630)**
Sandbar Solar and Electric, Santa Cruz *Also called Santa Cruz Westside Elc Inc* **(P-2722)**
Sanderlings, Aptos *Also called Seascape Resort Ltd A Calif* **(P-13200)**
Sanders & Wohrman Corporation....C....714 919-0446
709 N Poplar St Orange (92868) **(P-2479)**
Sandhurst Convales Grp Ltd A....E....310 675-3304
13922 Cerise Ave Hawthorne (90250) **(P-20745)**
Sandis Civil Engineers (PA)....D....408 636-0900
1700 Winchester Blvd Campbell (95008) **(P-26135)**
Sandisk LLC....C....408 801-1000
951 Sandisk Dr Milpitas (95035) **(P-27439)**
Sandm San Dego Mrriott Del Mar....A....858 523-1700
11966 El Camino Real San Diego (92130) **(P-13184)**
Sandoval Brothers Inc....D....831 678-1465
36503 Mile End Rd Soledad (93960) **(P-14751)**
Sandoval Labor Contractor, Williams *Also called Elvira Sandoval* **(P-14611)**
Sandrini Farms....D....661 792-3192
29794 Schuster Rd Mc Farland (93250) **(P-173)**
Sands Rv Resort, San Rafael *Also called R C Roberts & Co* **(P-11159)**
Sandwich Spot (PA)....D....916 492-2613
1630 18th St Sacramento (95811) **(P-13185)**
Sanford Burnham Prebys Medical (PA)....A....858 795-5000
10901 N Torrey Pines Rd La Jolla (92037) **(P-26657)**
Sangamo Therapeutics Inc (PA)....C....510 970-6000
501 Canal Blvd Richmond (94804) **(P-26448)**
Sangiacomo Vineyards, Sonoma *Also called V Sangiacomo & Sons* **(P-181)**
Sanhyd Inc....D....510 843-2131
2131 Carleton St Berkeley (94704) **(P-20746)**
Sanitary Fill, San Francisco *Also called Recology Inc* **(P-6439)**
Sanitation, Simi Valley *Also called Golden State Water Company* **(P-6260)**
Sanitation Districts....A....562 908-4288
1955 Workman Mill Rd Whittier (90601) **(P-6474)**
Sankara Eye Foundation USA....E....408 456-0555
1900 Mccarthy Blvd # 302 Milpitas (95035) **(P-25459)**
Sansa Technology LLC....E....866 204-3710
6990 Village Pkwy Dublin (94568) **(P-26449)**
Sansei Gardens Inc....C....510 226-9191
3250 Darby Cmn Fremont (94539) **(P-934)**
Sansum Clinic (PA)....D....805 681-7700
470 S Patterson Ave Santa Barbara (93111) **(P-19851)**
Sansum Clinic....E....805 682-6507
509 E Montecito St # 200 Santa Barbara (93103) **(P-22411)**
Santa Ana City of....E....714 565-2600
1000 E Santa Ana Blvd # 108 Santa Ana (92701) **(P-14752)**
Santa Ana Country Club....D....714 556-3000
20382 Newport Blvd Santa Ana (92707) **(P-19031)**
Santa Ana District Office, Santa Ana *Also called State Compensation Insur Fund* **(P-10395)**
Santa Ana Police Officers Assn....A....714 836-1211
1607 N Sycamore St Santa Ana (92701) **(P-25460)**
Santa Ana Radiology Center....D....714 835-6055
1100 N Tustin Ave Ste A Santa Ana (92705) **(P-19852)**
Santa Ana Unified School Dst....D....714 431-1900
1749 Carnegie Ave Santa Ana (92705) **(P-22879)**
Santa Anita Associates (PA)....D....626 447-2764
405 S Santa Anita Ave Arcadia (91006) **(P-18758)**
Santa Anita Convalescent Hospi....C....626 579-0310
5522 Gracewood Ave Temple City (91780) **(P-20747)**
Santa Anita Family Young....D....626 359-9244
501 S Mountain Ave Monrovia (91016) **(P-24228)**
Santa Anita Golf Course, Arcadia *Also called Santa Anita Associates* **(P-18758)**
Santa Anita Park, Arcadia *Also called Los Angeles Turf Club Inc* **(P-18540)**
Santa Barbara City of....D....805 962-6464
1100 Anacapa St Dept 3 Santa Barbara (93101) **(P-4978)**
Santa Barbara Airbus....E....805 964-7759
750 Technology Dr Goleta (93117) **(P-3842)**
Santa Barbara Athletic CLB Inc....D....805 966-6147
520 Castillo St Santa Barbara (93101) **(P-19032)**
Santa Barbara City of....C....805 564-5485
630 Garden St Santa Barbara (93101) **(P-17456)**
Santa Barbara Cnty Social Svcs, Santa Maria *Also called Santa Barbara Cottage Hospital* **(P-21716)**
Santa Barbara Convalescent Ctr, Santa Barbara *Also called California Convalescent Hosp* **(P-21027)**
Santa Barbara Cottage Care Ctr, Santa Barbara *Also called Cottage Care Center* **(P-21345)**
Santa Barbara Cottage Hospital, Santa Barbara *Also called Cottage Health* **(P-21346)**
Santa Barbara Cottage Hospital....A....805 569-7367
400 W Pueblo St Santa Barbara (93105) **(P-21714)**
Santa Barbara Cottage Hospital (PA)....D....805 682-7111
400 W Pueblo St Santa Barbara (93105) **(P-21715)**
Santa Barbara Cottage Hospital....C....805 346-7135
2125 Centerpointe Pkwy Santa Maria (93455) **(P-21716)**
Santa Barbara County of....B....805 882-3700
117 E Carrillo St Santa Barbara (93101) **(P-24025)**
Santa Barbara County of....C....805 614-1550
1410 S Broadway Ste L Santa Maria (93454) **(P-24026)**
Santa Barbara County of....D....805 681-5100
345 Camino Del Remedio Santa Barbara (93110) **(P-22880)**
Santa Barbara County of....C....805 737-7080
1100 W Laurel Ave Lompoc (93436) **(P-24027)**
Santa Barbara County of....E....805 346-7540
312 E Cook St Ste D Santa Maria (93454) **(P-23366)**
Santa Barbara County of....D....805 884-1600
429 N San Antonio Rd Santa Barbara (93110) **(P-24028)**
Santa Barbara County of....C....866 901-3212
4 E Carrillo St Santa Barbara (93101) **(P-24029)**
Santa Barbara Fabricare Inc....E....805 963-6677
14 W Gutierrez St Santa Barbara (93101) **(P-13568)**
Santa Barbara Family YMCA, Santa Barbara *Also called Channel Islands Young Mens Ch* **(P-25132)**
Santa Barbara Farms LLC (PA)....D....805 736-9776
1200 Union Sugar Ave Lompoc (93436) **(P-80)**
Santa Barbara Metro Trnst Dst (PA)....D....805 963-3364
550 Olive St Santa Barbara (93101) **(P-3720)**
Santa Barbara Museum....D....805 682-4711
2559 Puesta Del Sol Santa Barbara (93105) **(P-24911)**
Santa Barbara Museum of Art (PA)....D....805 963-4364
1130 State St Santa Barbara (93101) **(P-24912)**
Santa Barbara PC Users Group....E....805 964-5411
462 S San Marcos Rd Santa Barbara (93111) **(P-17457)**
Santa Barbara San Luis Obispo....C....800 421-2560
4050 Calle Real Santa Barbara (93110) **(P-10171)**
Santa Barbara Service Center, Goleta *Also called Southern California Edison Co* **(P-6131)**
Santa Barbara Trnsp Corp (HQ)....D....805 681-8355
6414 Hollister Ave Goleta (93117) **(P-3944)**
Santa Barbara Trnsp Corp....D....805 928-0402
1331 Jason Way Santa Maria (93455) **(P-3945)**
Santa Barbra Cttge Hsptl....B....805 569-7224
400 W Pueblo St Santa Barbara (93105) **(P-22140)**
Santa Brbara Zlgcal Foundation....C....805 962-1673
500 Ninos Dr Santa Barbara (93103) **(P-24936)**
Santa Catalina Island Company (PA)....D....310 510-2000
150 Metropole Ave Avalon (90704) **(P-4979)**
Santa Clara County of....D....408 435-2000
2314 N 1st St San Jose (95131) **(P-24030)**
Santa Clara Arques Med Offs, Sunnyvale *Also called Kaiser Foundation Hospitals* **(P-19589)**
Santa Clara Cnty Fderal Cr Un (PA)....C....408 282-0700
1641 N 1st St Ste 245 San Jose (95112) **(P-9587)**
Santa Clara County of....A....408 792-2704
3180 Newberry Dr Ste 150 San Jose (95118) **(P-23367)**
Santa Clara County of....D....408 201-7600
19050 Malaguerra Ave Morgan Hill (95037) **(P-24667)**
Santa Clara County of....C....408 885-7200
2325 Enborg Ln Fl 4 San Jose (95128) **(P-26286)**
Santa Clara County of....E....408 885-6818
2325 Enborg Ln Ste 380 San Jose (95128) **(P-21717)**
Santa Clara County of....C....408 355-2200
298 Garden Hill Dr Los Gatos (95032) **(P-19233)**
Santa Clara County of....D....408 282-3200
1555 Berger Dr Fl 1 San Jose (95112) **(P-14022)**
Santa Clara County of....C....408 435-2111
2314 N 1st St San Jose (95131) **(P-24031)**
Santa Clara County of....D....408 792-5680
976 Lenzen Ave Ste 1800 San Jose (95126) **(P-19853)**
Santa Clara County of....C....408 885-7354
751 S Bascom Ave Fl 4 San Jose (95128) **(P-26287)**

Employee Codes: A=Over 500 employees, B=251-500
C=101-250, D=51-100, E=50
2019 Directory of California
Wholesalers and Services Companies
© Mergent Inc. 1-800-342-5647
1455

Santa Clara Hilton, The, Santa Clara *Also called Hostmark Investors Ltd Partnr* ***(P-26886)***
Santa Clara Tenant Corp ....D....408 496-6400
2885 Lakeside Dr Santa Clara (95054) ***(P-13186)***
Santa Clara Valley Corporation ....D....408 947-1100
715 N 1st St Ste 27 San Jose (95112) ***(P-14376)***
Santa Clara Valley Health & Ho, San Jose *Also called Santa Clara County of* ***(P-21717)***
Santa Clara Valley Medical Ctr ....B....408 885-6300
2400 Moorpark Ave San Jose (95128) ***(P-19854)***
Santa Clara Valley Medical Ctr ....A....408 885-5730
2220 Moorpark Ave San Jose (95128) ***(P-22881)***
Santa Clara Valley Medical Ctr (PA) ....B....408 885-5000
751 S Bascom Ave San Jose (95128) ***(P-21718)***
Santa Clara Valley Trnsp Auth (PA) ....A....408 321-2300
3331 N 1st St San Jose (95134) ***(P-3721)***
Santa Clara Valley Trnsp Auth ....C....408 321-5559
3331 N 1st St Bldg B San Jose (95134) ***(P-3722)***
Santa Clara Valley Trnsp Auth ....B....408 321-5555
3331 N 1st St San Jose (95134) ***(P-3882)***
Santa Clara Valley Water (PA) ....A....408 265-2600
5750 Almaden Expy San Jose (95118) ***(P-6308)***
Santa Clara Valley Water ....D....408 395-8121
400 More Ave Los Gatos (95032) ***(P-6309)***
Santa Clara Vlly Health/Hosptl, San Jose *Also called Santa Clara County of* ***(P-26287)***
Santa Clara Vly Job Career Ctr ....D....805 933-8300
725 E Main St Ste 101 Santa Paula (93060) ***(P-14753)***
Santa Clara Vngard Booster CLB ....E....408 727-5532
1795 Space Park Dr Santa Clara (95054) ***(P-25239)***
Santa Clara Woman's Club Adobe, Santa Clara *Also called Santa Clara Womens Club* ***(P-19033)***
Santa Clara Womens Club ....D....408 246-8000
3260 The Alameda Santa Clara (95050) ***(P-19033)***
Santa Clarita City of ....B....661 294-1287
28250 Constellation Rd Santa Clarita (91355) ***(P-3883)***
Santa Clarita City of ....B....661 284-1423
23920 Valencia Blvd # 300 Santa Clarita (91355) ***(P-19234)***
Santa Clarita Athletic Club ....D....661 255-3365
23942 Lyons Ave Ste 106 Newhall (91321) ***(P-18649)***
Santa Clarita Concrete ....E....661 252-2012
16164 Sierra Hwy Santa Clarita (91390) ***(P-3320)***
Santa Clarita Convalescent HM, Newhall *Also called Valencia Health Care Inc* ***(P-21242)***
Santa Clarita Hauling/Blue, Santa Clarita *Also called USA Waste of California Inc* ***(P-6502)***
Santa Clarita Health Care Assn (PA) ....D....661 253-8000
23845 Mcbean Pkwy Santa Clarita (91355) ***(P-27022)***
Santa Clarita Health Care Ctr, Santa Clarita *Also called Henry Mayo Newhall Mem Hosp* ***(P-22816)***
Santa Clarita Interiors Inc ....D....661 253-0861
25682 Springbrook Ave # 130 Santa Clarita (91350) ***(P-3396)***
Santa Clarita Medical Group ....E....661 255-6802
25775 Mcbean Pkwy Ste 209 Valencia (91355) ***(P-19855)***
Santa Clarita Swim Club, Valencia *Also called Academy Swim Club* ***(P-18817)***
Santa Clarita Valley Bldrs Inc ....C....661 295-6722
24307 Magic Mountain Pkwy # 122 Santa Clarita (91355) ***(P-3074)***
SANTA CLARITA VALLEY SENIOR CE, Santa Clarita *Also called Santa Clarita Vlly Cmmtt Aging* ***(P-24032)***
Santa Clarita Vlly Cmmtt Aging ....D....661 259-9444
22900 Market St Santa Clarita (91321) ***(P-24032)***
Santa Cruz County of ....E....831 763-8400
1430 Freedom Blvd Ste D Watsonville (95076) ***(P-19856)***
Santa Cruz County of ....D....831 454-2030
701 Ocean St Rm 530 Santa Cruz (95060) ***(P-16175)***
Santa Cruz County Symphony ....E....831 462-0553
307 Church St Santa Cruz (95060) ***(P-18460)***
Santa Cruz Hotel Associates ....C....831 426-4330
175 W Cliff Dr Santa Cruz (95060) ***(P-13187)***
Santa Cruz Medical Foundation (HQ) ....D....831 458-5537
2025 Soquel Ave Santa Cruz (95062) ***(P-19857)***
Santa Cruz Metro ....B....831 426-6080
135 Aviation Way Ste 2 Watsonville (95076) ***(P-3723)***
Santa Cruz Metro Trnst Dst ....D....831 469-1954
110 Vernon St Ste B Santa Cruz (95060) ***(P-3884)***
Santa Cruz Montessori School ....E....831 476-1646
6230 Soquel Dr Aptos (95003) ***(P-24378)***
Santa Cruz Seaside Company (PA) ....B....831 423-5590
400 Beach St Santa Cruz (95060) ***(P-18808)***
Santa Cruz Westside Elc Inc ....D....831 469-8888
2119 Delaware Ave Santa Cruz (95060) ***(P-2722)***
Santa Fe Pacific Pipeline, Bloomington *Also called Kinder Mrgan Enrgy Partners LP* ***(P-4926)***
Santa For Hirecom, Newport Beach *Also called Internet Booking Agencycom Inc* ***(P-14650)***
Santa Lucia Preserve Company ....D....831 620-6760
1 Rancho San Carlos Rd Carmel (93923) ***(P-19034)***
Santa Margarita Water District (PA) ....D....949 459-6400
26111 Antonio Pkwy Rcho STA Marg (92688) ***(P-6310)***
Santa Margarita Water District ....C....949 459-6400
26101 Antonio Pkwy Rcho STA Marg (92688) ***(P-6311)***
Santa Margarita YMCA Garrison, Oceanside *Also called YMCA of San Diego County* ***(P-25306)***
SANTA MARIA CARE CENTER, Santa Maria *Also called Kimberly Care Center Inc* ***(P-20553)***
Santa Maria Cinema 10, Santa Maria *Also called Edwards Theatres Circuit Inc* ***(P-18301)***
Santa Maria Hotel Corp ....D....805 928-6000
2100 N Broadway Santa Maria (93454) ***(P-13188)***
Santa Maria Valley YMCA ....C....805 937-8521
3400 Skyway Dr Santa Maria (93455) ***(P-25240)***
Santa Mnica Mntins Trils Cncil ....D....818 222-4531
24735 Mulholland Hwy Woodland Hills (91302) ***(P-25241)***
Santa Mnica Wlshire Imging LLC ....E....323 549-3055
5455 Wilshire Blvd Los Angeles (90036) ***(P-22141)***
Santa Monica City of ....B....310 451-5444
1334 5th St Santa Monica (90401) ***(P-3885)***
Santa Monica Amusements LLC ....B....310 451-9641
380 Santa Monica Pier Santa Monica (90401) ***(P-18809)***
Santa Monica Bay Physcians ....C....310 459-2363
881 Alma Real Dr Ste 214 Pacific Palisades (90272) ***(P-19858)***
Santa Monica Bay Physicians He (PA) ....D....310 417-5900
5767 W Century Blvd Los Angeles (90045) ***(P-19859)***
Santa Monica Bay Womens Club ....E....310 395-1308
1210 4th St Santa Monica (90401) ***(P-25461)***
Santa Monica City of ....D....310 399-5865
2802 4th St Santa Monica (90405) ***(P-24379)***
Santa Monica City of ....E....310 458-8551
1855 Main St Santa Monica (90401) ***(P-10933)***
Santa Monica Express Inc ....D....310 458-6000
11150 W Olympic Blvd # 150 Los Angeles (90064) ***(P-4060)***
Santa Monica Hotel Owner LLC ....C....310 395-3332
1707 4th St Santa Monica (90401) ***(P-13189)***
Santa Monica Hsr Ltd Partnr ....C....310 395-3332
1707 4th St Santa Monica (90401) ***(P-13190)***
Santa Monica Orthopedic (PA) ....D....310 315-2018
2020 Santa Monica Blvd # 230 Santa Monica (90404) ***(P-19860)***
Santa Monica Outpatient Center, Santa Monica *Also called Childrens Hospital Los Angeles* ***(P-19378)***
Santa Monica Rhf Housing Inc (PA) ....D....562 257-5100
911 N Studebaker Rd Long Beach (90815) ***(P-11110)***
Santa Monica Seafood Company ....C....310 393-5244
1000 Wilshire Blvd Santa Monica (90401) ***(P-8598)***
Santa Monica Sport Club, Santa Monica *Also called 24 Hour Fitness Usa Inc* ***(P-18561)***
Santa Monica Ucla Medical Ctr, Santa Monica *Also called University Cal Los Angeles* ***(P-21876)***
Santa Paula Hospital, Santa Paula *Also called Ventura County Medical Center* ***(P-20052)***
Santa Paula Water Works Ltd ....D....562 923-0711
9750 Washburn Rd Downey (90241) ***(P-12004)***
Santa Rosa & Sonoma Co Real Es ....E....707 524-1124
1057 College Ave Santa Rosa (95404) ***(P-11753)***
Santa Rosa Berry Farms LLC ....B....805 981-3060
3500 Camino Ave Ste 250 Oxnard (93030) ***(P-120)***
Santa Rosa Clinic, Santa Rosa *Also called Veterans Health Administration* ***(P-20069)***
Santa Rosa Community Hlth Ctrs (PA) ....C....707 547-2222
3569 Round Barn Cir Santa Rosa (95403) ***(P-24033)***
Santa Rosa Convalescent Hosp, Santa Rosa *Also called Ashley Ltc Inc* ***(P-20237)***
Santa Rosa Dental Group ....D....707 545-0944
1820 Sonoma Ave Ste 80 Santa Rosa (95405) ***(P-20135)***
Santa Rosa Golf & Country Club ....D....707 546-3485
333 Country Club Dr Santa Rosa (95401) ***(P-19035)***
Santa Rosa Memorial Hospital (HQ) ....A....707 546-3210
1165 Montgomery Dr Santa Rosa (95405) ***(P-21719)***
Santa Rosa Radiology Med Group (PA) ....E....707 546-4062
121 Sotoyome St Santa Rosa (95405) ***(P-22142)***
Santa Rosa Rnchria Gaming Comm ....D....559 924-6948
17225 Jersey Ave Lemoore (93245) ***(P-18461)***
Santa Rosa Surgery Center LP ....D....707 575-5831
1111 Sonoma Ave Ste 214 Santa Rosa (95405) ***(P-21720)***
Santa Teresa Conv Hospital ....D....562 948-1961
9140 Verner St Pico Rivera (90660) ***(P-21721)***
Santa Teresa Golf Center, San Jose *Also called Santa Teresa Golf Club* ***(P-18759)***
Santa Teresa Golf Club ....D....408 225-2650
260 Bernal Rd San Jose (95119) ***(P-18759)***
Santa Teresita Inc (PA) ....B....626 359-3243
819 Buena Vista St Duarte (91010) ***(P-21722)***
Santa Ynez Valley Cottage Hosp ....D....805 688-6431
2050 Viborg Rd Solvang (93463) ***(P-21723)***
Santa Ynez Valley Marriott, Buellton *Also called Kang Family Partners LLC* ***(P-12800)***
Santaluz Club Inc ....C....858 759-3120
8170 Caminito Santaluz E San Diego (92127) ***(P-19036)***
Santana Concrete ....D....909 421-2218
18241 Slover Ave Bloomington (92316) ***(P-3321)***
Santana Row Hotel Partners LP ....C....408 551-0010
355 Santana Row Ste 1010 San Jose (95128) ***(P-13191)***
Sante Community Physicians, Fresno *Also called Sante Health System Inc* ***(P-10172)***
Sante Health System Inc (PA) ....D....559 228-5400
7370 N Palm Ave Ste 101 Fresno (93711) ***(P-10172)***
Santee Senior Retirement Com ....C....619 955-0901
400 Lantern Crest Way Santee (92071) ***(P-24034)***
Santee Systems Services II ....D....323 445-0044
229 E Gage Ave Los Angeles (90003) ***(P-24035)***
Santee Systems Services II LL ....E....323 445-0044
229 E Gage Ave Los Angeles (90003) ***(P-18650)***
Santellan Farm Labor Contr, Woodlake *Also called Pete Santellan* ***(P-666)***
Santen Incorporated ....D....415 268-9100
6401 Hollis St Ste 125 Emeryville (94608) ***(P-26658)***
Sants Clair Alcohol Meth Prog, San Jose *Also called Central Valley Clinic Inc* ***(P-22523)***
Sanyo Denki America Inc (HQ) ....D....310 783-5400
468 Amapola Ave Torrance (90501) ***(P-7100)***
Sanyo Foods Corp America ....C....714 730-1611
12442 Tustin Ranch Rd Tustin (92782) ***(P-19037)***
Sanzaru Games Inc ....E....650 312-1000
1065 E Hillsdale Blvd Foster City (94404) ***(P-15426)***
Sap Labs LLC ....D....650 849-4000
3475 Deer Creek Rd Palo Alto (94304) ***(P-15427)***
Sap Labs LLC (HQ) ....B....650 849-4000
3410 Hillview Ave Palo Alto (94304) ***(P-15428)***
Sap, Oracle, Service Provider, West Sacramento *Also called PC World Corp* ***(P-5626)***
Sapho Inc ....D....650 597-2746
1150 Bayhill Dr Ste 325 San Bruno (94066) ***(P-15429)***
SARA, Cypress *Also called Scientific Applications & RES* ***(P-26450)***
Sarabian Farms, Sanger *Also called Virginia Sarabian* ***(P-231)***

Mergent e-mail: customerrelations@mergent.com
1456
2019 Directory of California Wholesalers and Services Companies
(P-0000) Products & Services Section entry number
(PA)=Parent Co (HQ)=Headquarters (DH)=Div Headquarters

Sarah Elizabeth Treusdell....................E......661 949-0131
921 W Avenue J Ste C Lancaster (93534) *(P-22677)*
Saratech, Mission Viejo *Also called Paydarfar Industries Inc (P-7088)*
Saratoga Capital Inc....................D......408 286-1000
233 W Santa Clara St San Jose (95113) *(P-13192)*
Saratoga Court Inc....................D......408 866-1392
18855 Cox Ave Saratoga (95070) *(P-11154)*
Saratoga Retirement Community, Saratoga *Also called Odd Fellows Home California (P-24616)*
Sarco Inc....................E......949 888-5548
30412 Esperanza Rcho STA Marg (92688) *(P-7539)*
Saroyan Lumber and Moulding Co, Huntington Park *Also called Saroyan Lumber Company Inc (P-6862)*
Saroyan Lumber Company Inc (PA)....................D......800 624-9309
6230 S Alameda St Huntington Park (90255) *(P-6862)*
Sarpa-Feldman Enterprises Inc....................D......408 982-1790
650 N King Rd San Jose (95133) *(P-17458)*
Sas Entertainment Partners Inc....................E......213 400-1901
6224 Greenleaf Ave Whittier (90601) *(P-18462)*
Sas Institute Inc....................D......949 250-9999
1148 N Lemon St Orange (92867) *(P-15847)*
Sat, Sacramento *Also called Lpa Insurance Agency Inc (P-15745)*
Satellite Dialysis, Modesto *Also called Satellite Healthcare Inc (P-22488)*
Satellite Dialysis Centers, San Jose *Also called Satellite Healthcare Inc (P-22489)*
Satellite First Communities LP (PA)....................D......510 647-0700
1835 Alcatraz Ave Berkeley (94703) *(P-11111)*
Satellite Healthcare Inc....................D......209 578-0691
3500 Coffee Rd Ste 21 Modesto (95355) *(P-22488)*
Satellite Healthcare Inc (PA)....................D......650 404-3600
300 Santana Row Ste 300 # 300 San Jose (95128) *(P-22489)*
Satellite Healthcare Inc....................D......408 258-8720
2121 Alexian Dr Ste 118 San Jose (95116) *(P-22490)*
Satellite Management Co (PA)....................C......714 558-2411
1010 E Chestnut Ave Santa Ana (92701) *(P-11754)*
Satellite Office, Van Nuys *Also called Southern Cal Orthpd Inst LP (P-19902)*
Satellite Pros, Ontario *Also called Jeeva Corp (P-2617)*
Sather Installation, Murrieta *Also called SI Inc (P-3076)*
Saticoy Country Club....................D......805 647-1153
4450 Clubhouse Dr Somis (93066) *(P-19038)*
Saticoy Fruit Exchange, Santa Paula *Also called Saticoy Lemon Association (P-565)*
Saticoy Fruit Exchange, Ventura *Also called Saticoy Lemon Association (P-209)*
Saticoy Lemon Association (PA)....................D......805 654-6500
103 N Peck Rd Santa Paula (93060) *(P-565)*
Saticoy Lemon Association....................D......805 654-6500
7560 Bristol Rd Ventura (93003) *(P-209)*
Saticoy Lemon Association....................C......805 654-6543
600 E 3rd St Oxnard (93030) *(P-24980)*
Satmetrix Systems Inc (PA)....................D......650 227-8300
1820 Gateway Dr Ste 300 San Mateo (94404) *(P-15430)*
Saturn Electric Inc....................E......858 271-4100
7552 Trade St Ste A San Diego (92121) *(P-2723)*
Sauce Labs Inc (PA)....................D......415 946-1117
116 New Montgomery St # 3 San Francisco (94105) *(P-16044)*
Saugus Division, Santa Clarita *Also called NTS Technical Systems (P-27807)*
Savala Equipment Company Inc (PA)....................D......949 552-1859
16402 Construction Cir E Irvine (92606) *(P-14457)*
Savala Equipment Rentals, Irvine *Also called Savala Equipment Company Inc (P-14457)*
Savant Construction Inc....................D......909 614-4300
13830 Mountain Ave Chino (91710) *(P-1640)*
Save Our Sunol....................D......925 862-2263
2934 Kilkare Rd Sunol (94586) *(P-25242)*
Save Queen LLC....................B......562 435-3511
429 Shoreline Village Dr I Long Beach (90802) *(P-13193)*
Savings Bank Mendocino County (PA)....................C......707 462-6613
200 N School St Ukiah (95482) *(P-9485)*
Saviynt Inc (PA)....................C......310 641-1664
1301 E El Segundo Blvd El Segundo (90245) *(P-27440)*
Savoy Contractors Group Inc....................C......949 753-1919
8905 Research Dr Irvine (92618) *(P-1230)*
Savvius Inc (HQ)....................D......925 937-3200
1340 Treat Blvd Ste 500 Walnut Creek (94597) *(P-15431)*
Sawmill, Ukiah *Also called Mendocino Forest Pdts Co LLC (P-6839)*
Sawyers Heating & AC....................D......209 416-7700
5272 Jerusalem Ct Ste D Modesto (95356) *(P-2348)*
Saylor Lane Healthcare Center, Sacramento *Also called Kindred Healthcare Oper Inc (P-21127)*
Saylor Lane Healthcare Center, Sacramento *Also called S L H C C Inc (P-20734)*
Sb Group Us Inc....................D......650 562-8110
1 Circle Star Way Fl 1 # 1 San Carlos (94070) *(P-10113)*
Sb Product Group LLC....................C......650 562-8221
1 Circle Star Way Fl 3 San Carlos (94070) *(P-2724)*
Sbb Roofing Inc (PA)....................C......323 254-2888
3310 Verdugo Rd Los Angeles (90065) *(P-3199)*
SBC, San Diego *Also called AT&T Services Inc (P-5471)*
SBC, San Ramon *Also called AT&T Services Inc (P-5470)*
SBC, Monterey *Also called AT&T Services Inc (P-5473)*
SBC, Jackson *Also called AT&T Services Inc (P-5475)*
SBC, Anaheim *Also called AT&T Services Inc (P-5478)*
SBC, San Diego *Also called AT&T Services Inc (P-5479)*
SBC, Paso Robles *Also called AT&T Services Inc (P-5481)*
SBC, Riverside *Also called AT&T Services Inc (P-5482)*
SBC, Mountain View *Also called AT&T Services Inc (P-5484)*
SBC, Pasadena *Also called AT&T Services Inc (P-5486)*
SBC, Bakersfield *Also called AT&T Services Inc (P-27648)*
SBC, Los Angeles *Also called AT&T Services Inc (P-5487)*
SBC, Santa Rosa *Also called AT&T Services Inc (P-5492)*
SBC, Los Angeles *Also called AT&T Services Inc (P-5495)*
SBC, San Jose *Also called AT&T Services Inc (P-5496)*
SBC, San Francisco *Also called AT&T Services Inc (P-5497)*
SBC, Fremont *Also called AT&T Services Inc (P-5498)*
SBC, Buena Park *Also called AT&T Services Inc (P-5500)*
SBC, Concord *Also called AT&T Services Inc (P-5501)*
SBC, Sacramento *Also called AT&T Services Inc (P-5504)*
SBC, Oceanside *Also called AT&T Services Inc (P-5505)*
SBC, Sacramento *Also called AT&T Services Inc (P-5506)*
SBC, Concord *Also called AT&T Services Inc (P-5507)*
SBC, San Diego *Also called AT&T Services Inc (P-5508)*
SBC, Escondido *Also called AT&T Services Inc (P-5509)*
SBC, Alhambra *Also called AT&T Services Inc (P-5512)*
SBC, San Jose *Also called AT&T Services Inc (P-5515)*
SBC, Oakland *Also called AT&T Services Inc (P-5516)*
SBC Communications, Rancho Cordova *Also called AT&T Services Inc (P-5491)*
SBE Contracting....................E......714 544-5066
17256 Red Hill Ave Irvine (92614) *(P-2725)*
SBE Hotel Group LLC....................D......323 655-8000
8000 Beverly Blvd Los Angeles (90048) *(P-12265)*
Sbehg 465 S La Cienega LLC....................B......310 247-0400
465 S La Cienega Blvd Los Angeles (90048) *(P-13194)*
Sbm Management Services LP....................B......866 855-2211
5241 Arnold Ave McClellan (95652) *(P-14377)*
Sbm Site Services LLC (PA)....................A......916 922-7600
5241 Arnold Ave McClellan (95652) *(P-14378)*
SBMC, Ukiah *Also called Savings Bank Mendocino County (P-9485)*
SBP, La Jolla *Also called Sanford Burnham Prebys Medical (P-26657)*
SBPEA, San Bernardino *Also called San Brnrdino Pub Emplyees Assn (P-25075)*
Sbrm Inc (PA)....................D......760 480-0208
2342 Meyers Ave Escondido (92029) *(P-14379)*
Sbrpstc, San Jose *Also called South Bay Regl Public Safety T (P-24231)*
SBSA, Redwood City *Also called Silicon Valley Clean Water (P-6328)*
Sbsbtc, National City *Also called South Bay Sand Blasting and Ta (P-17989)*
SC Builders Inc (PA)....................D......408 328-0688
910 Thompson Pl Sunnyvale (94085) *(P-1641)*
SC Fuels, Orange *Also called Southern Counties Oil Co (P-8946)*
SC Harp El Segundo LLC....................D......310 322-0999
1985 E Grand Ave El Segundo (90245) *(P-13195)*
SC Wright Construction Inc....................B......619 698-6909
3838 Camino Del Rio Nth S San Diego (92108) *(P-25904)*
Sca Enterprises Inc (PA)....................C......818 845-7621
3817 W Magnolia Blvd Burbank (91505) *(P-17459)*
Scalelab LLC....................E......310 526-7524
10351 Santa Monica Blvd # 404 Los Angeles (90025) *(P-18113)*
Scalematrix Holdings Inc....................D......888 349-9994
5775 Kearny Villa Rd San Diego (92123) *(P-16477)*
Scan, Long Beach *Also called Porchlight Inc (P-21189)*
Scan California Management Co....................A......562 989-5100
3800 Kilroy Airport Way Long Beach (90806) *(P-10306)*
Scan Group (PA)....................B......562 308-2733
3800 Kilroy Arprt Way # 100 Long Beach (90806) *(P-10307)*
Scan Health Plan, Long Beach *Also called Senior Care (P-10309)*
Scan-Vino LLC (PA)....................D......209 931-3570
5463 Cherokee Rd Stockton (95215) *(P-4259)*
Scandia Amusement Park, Ontario *Also called Scandia Recreation Centers (P-18788)*
Scandia Family Fun Center, Sacramento *Also called Scandia Sports Inc (P-19235)*
Scandia Recreation Centers....................D......909 390-3092
1155 S Wanamaker Ave Ontario (91761) *(P-18788)*
Scandia Sports Inc....................E......916 331-5757
5070 Hillsdale Blvd Sacramento (95842) *(P-19235)*
Scantibodies Clinical Lab Inc....................E......866 249-1212
9236 Abraham Way Santee (92071) *(P-22143)*
Scarborough Farms Inc....................C......805 483-9113
731 Pacific Ave Oxnard (93030) *(P-81)*
Scat Enterprises Inc....................D......310 370-5501
1400 Kingsdale Ave Redondo Beach (90278) *(P-6672)*
Scattergood Generation Plant, Playa Del Rey *Also called Los Angeles Dept Wtr & Pwr (P-6199)*
SCC Acquisitions Inc....................C......949 777-4000
2392 Morse Ave Irvine (92614) *(P-11913)*
SCC ESA Dept of Risk Mgmt....................D......408 441-4207
2310 N 1st St Ste 202 San Jose (95131) *(P-10764)*
SCCH Inc....................D......562 494-5188
1880 Dawson Ave Signal Hill (90755) *(P-27023)*
Scci, Orcutt *Also called Spiess Construction Co Inc (P-1983)*
SCE, Rosemead *Also called Southern California Edison Co (P-6113)*
SCE Eastern Hydro Division....................D......760 873-0767
4000 Bishop Creek Rd Bishop (93514) *(P-6106)*
SCE FCU, Baldwin Park *Also called SCE Federal Credit Union (P-9588)*
SCE Federal Credit Union (PA)....................C......626 960-6888
12701 Schabarum Ave Baldwin Park (91706) *(P-9588)*
Scene7 Inc....................D......415 506-6000
6 Hamilton Landing # 150 Novato (94949) *(P-15432)*
Scenic Circle Care Center, Modesto *Also called Riverside Health Care Corp (P-21198)*
Scenic Route Inc....................E......818 896-6006
13516 Desmond St Pacoima (91331) *(P-3580)*
Scga Golf Course MGT Inc....................D......951 677-7446
39500 Robrt Trnt Jnes Pkw Murrieta (92563) *(P-18760)*
Schaefer Ambulance Service Inc (PA)....................D......323 469-1473
4627 Beverly Blvd Los Angeles (90004) *(P-3843)*
Schaefer Ambulance Service Inc....................E......760 353-3380
905 S Imperial Ave El Centro (92243) *(P-3844)*

Employee Codes: A=Over 500 employees, B=251-500
C=101-250, D=51-100, E=50
2019 Directory of California
Wholesalers and Services Companies
© Mergent Inc. 1-800-342-5647
1457

Schaefer Ambulance Service Inc ....D.......626 333-4533
324 N Towne Ave Pomona (91767) ***(P-3845)***
Schaefer Mary-Judith ....D.......562 634-3164
7202 Petterson Ln Paramount (90723) ***(P-3581)***
Schaefer Parking Lot Service, Paramount *Also called Schaefer Mary-Judith* ***(P-3581)***
Schafer Bros Trnsf Pano Movers (PA) ....D.......310 835-7231
1981 E 213th St Carson (90810) ***(P-4629)***
Schafer Logistics, Carson *Also called Schafer Bros Trnsf Pano Movers* ***(P-4629)***
Schaper Construction Inc (PA) ....D.......408 437-0337
1177 N 15th St San Jose (95112) ***(P-2480)***
Scharp's Oasis House, Los Angeles *Also called South Cntl Heatlh & Rehab Prog* ***(P-22683)***
Scheid Vineyards Cal Inc ....D.......831 385-4801
305 Hilltown Rd Salinas (93908) ***(P-174)***
Scheid Vineyards Inc (PA) ....D.......310 301-1555
305 Hilltown Rd Salinas (93908) ***(P-175)***
Scheid Vineyards Inc ....C.......707 433-1858
373 Healdsburg Ave Healdsburg (95448) ***(P-176)***
Schenker Inc ....D.......650 745-3000
380 Littlefield Ave South San Francisco (94080) ***(P-5161)***
Scherzer International Corp (PA) ....D.......818 227-2770
21650 Oxnard St Ste 300 Woodland Hills (91367) ***(P-17460)***
Schetter Electric, Sacramento *Also called M K S Construction Inc* ***(P-1193)***
Schetter Electric Inc (PA) ....D.......916 446-2521
471 Bannon St Sacramento (95811) ***(P-2726)***
Schick Moving & Storage Co (PA) ....C.......714 731-5500
2721 Michelle Dr Tustin (92780) ***(P-4371)***
Schilling Paradise Corp ....C.......619 449-4141
697 Greenfield Dr El Cajon (92021) ***(P-1979)***
Schilling Robotics LLC ....D.......530 753-6718
201 Cousteau Pl Davis (95618) ***(P-25905)***
Schindler Elevator Corporation ....D.......310 785-9775
2000 Avenue Of The Stars Los Angeles (90067) ***(P-17983)***
Schindler Elevator Corporation ....C.......818 336-3000
16450 Fthill Blvd Ste 200 Sylmar (91342) ***(P-17984)***
Schirmer Fire Protection Eng ....D.......213 630-2020
707 Wilshire Blvd # 2600 Los Angeles (90017) ***(P-10765)***
Schlumberger Technology Corp ....D.......661 864-4750
2841 Pegasus Dr Bakersfield (93308) ***(P-1077)***
Schlumberger Technology Corp ....D.......714 379-7332
12131 Industry St Garden Grove (92841) ***(P-1078)***
Schlumberger Well Services, Bakersfield *Also called Schlumberger Technology Corp* ***(P-1077)***
Schmidt Fire Protection Co Inc ....D.......858 279-6122
4760 Murphy Canyon Rd # 100 San Diego (92123) ***(P-2349)***
Schmidt Phyllis MD Corporation ....A.......213 613-1163
711 W College St Los Angeles (90012) ***(P-21724)***
Schmitt House, El Monte *Also called Hope Hse For Mltple Hndicapped* ***(P-24566)***
Schneider Electric 600, Pleasanton *Also called Schneider Electric Usa Inc* ***(P-7391)***
Schneider Electric 650, Diamond Bar *Also called Schneider Electric Usa Inc* ***(P-7392)***
Schneider Electric Usa Inc ....D.......925 462-0986
6160 Stoneridge Mall Rd # 200 Pleasanton (94588) ***(P-7391)***
Schneider Electric Usa Inc ....D.......909 612-5400
21680 Gateway Center Dr # 300 Diamond Bar (91765) ***(P-7392)***
Schneider Electric Usa Inc ....D.......909 438-2295
14725 Monte Vista Ave Chino (91710) ***(P-4630)***
Schneider National Inc ....C.......661 858-1031
4193 Industrial Pkwy Dr Lebec (93243) ***(P-4260)***
Schneider National Inc ....C.......909 574-2165
14392 Valley Blvd Fontana (92335) ***(P-5162)***
Schnierow Dental Care ....E.......310 377-6453
13450 Hawthorne Blvd Hawthorne (90250) ***(P-20136)***
Schnitzer Steel Industries Inc ....D.......510 444-3919
1101 Embarcadero W Oakland (94607) ***(P-7991)***
Scholastic Book Fairs Inc ....D.......714 237-1100
2890 E White Star Ave Anaheim (92806) ***(P-9119)***
Scholastic Book Fairs Inc ....D.......510 771-1700
42001 Christy St Fremont (94538) ***(P-9120)***
Scholls, Bloomington *Also called Distribution Alternatives Inc* ***(P-4549)***
School Innovations Achievement (PA) ....D.......916 933-2290
5200 Golden Foothill Pkwy El Dorado Hills (95762) ***(P-15848)***
School of Hope, San Bernardino *Also called Assoc For Retarded Citizens* ***(P-24153)***
School Portraits By Kranz ....D.......714 545-1775
9992 Center Dr Villa Park (92861) ***(P-13643)***
Schools Financial Credit Union (PA) ....C.......916 569-5400
1485 Response Rd Ste 126 Sacramento (95815) ***(P-9653)***
Schoolsfirst Federal Credit Un (PA) ....B.......714 258-4000
2115 N Broadway Santa Ana (92706) ***(P-9589)***
Schoolsfirst Federal Credit Un ....D.......800 462-8328
8865 Foothill Blvd Rancho Cucamonga (91730) ***(P-457)***
Schoolsfirst Federal Credit Un ....C.......714 258-4000
15442 Newport Ave Tustin (92780) ***(P-9590)***
Schoolwires Inc ....D.......626 974-7600
645 S Barranca St West Covina (91791) ***(P-5993)***
Schramsberg Vineyards Company ....E.......707 942-4558
1400 Schramsberg Rd Calistoga (94515) ***(P-177)***
Schricker, Oceanside *Also called Central Indiana Hdwr Co Inc* ***(P-7582)***
Schrimp, Roger Attorney, Oakdale *Also called Damrell Nelson Schrimp Pall* ***(P-23019)***
Schroff Inc ....C.......858 740-2400
7328 Trade St San Diego (92121) ***(P-17909)***
Schryver Med Sls & Mktg LLC ....C.......303 371-0073
526 Mccormick St San Leandro (94577) ***(P-22144)***
Schryver Med Sls & Mktg LLC ....D.......303 459-8160
1845 N Case St Orange (92865) ***(P-22145)***
Schryver Med Sls & Mktg LLC ....D.......303 459-8150
310 N Cluff Ave Ste 212 Lodi (95240) ***(P-22146)***
Schuff Steel Company ....C.......209 938-0869
2324 Navy Dr Stockton (95206) ***(P-3397)***
Schulte Ranches ....D.......805 563-0821
Rr 1 Box 228 Goleta (93117) ***(P-379)***
Schumacher Cargo Logistics Inc (PA) ....D.......562 408-6677
550 W 135th St Gardena (90248) ***(P-5163)***
Schwager Davis Inc ....C.......408 281-9300
198 Hillsdale Ave San Jose (95136) ***(P-2060)***
Schweizer Rena ....D.......818 501-7100
15720 Ventura Blvd # 100 Encino (91436) ***(P-11755)***
SCI, North Hollywood *Also called Pierce Brothers* ***(P-13693)***
SCI, Corona Del Mar *Also called Service Corp International* ***(P-11759)***
SCI, Oceanside *Also called Service Corp International* ***(P-11951)***
Sci Inc ....D.......951 245-7511
18501 Collier Ave B106 Lake Elsinore (92530) ***(P-3322)***
SCI Corp ....D.......650 578-1142
303 Vintage Park Dr # 220 Foster City (94404) ***(P-14380)***
Scico, Avalon *Also called Santa Catalina Island Company* ***(P-4979)***
Scicon Technologies Corp (PA) ....D.......661 295-8630
27525 Newhall Ranch Rd # 2 Valencia (91355) ***(P-25906)***
Scicon Technologies Corp ....D.......949 252-1341
1300 Quail St Ste 208 Newport Beach (92660) ***(P-25907)***
Science Applications Intl Corp ....D.......703 676-4300
4015 Hancock St Ste 1000 San Diego (92110) ***(P-16478)***
Science Applications Intl Corp ....A.......858 826-3061
4015 Hancock St San Diego (92110) ***(P-16045)***
Science Applications Intl Corp ....B.......858 826-6000
4242 Campus Point Ct San Diego (92121) ***(P-16046)***
Scientific Applications & RES (PA) ....D.......714 828-1465
6300 Gateway Dr Cypress (90630) ***(P-26450)***
Scientific Concepts Inc ....B.......650 578-1142
303 Vintage Park Dr # 220 Foster City (94404) ***(P-17985)***
Scihp, Santa Rosa *Also called Sonoma County Indian Health PR* ***(P-19896)***
Scils, Petaluma *Also called Sonoma Cnty Ind Living Skills* ***(P-24680)***
Sciots Tract Association ....D.......530 753-5219
937 Chestnut Ln Davis (95616) ***(P-25243)***
Sclarc, Los Angeles *Also called South Central Los* ***(P-24842)***
Scmg, San Diego *Also called Sharp Community Medical Group* ***(P-25041)***
Scmh, Whittier *Also called Southern California Mtl Hdlg* ***(P-7802)***
SCMS, Aptos *Also called Santa Cruz Montessori School* ***(P-24378)***
Scope Seven LLC ....D.......310 220-3939
2201 Park Pl Ste 100 El Segundo (90245) ***(P-8058)***
Scopely Inc (PA) ....C.......323 400-6618
3530 Hayden Ave Ste A Culver City (90232) ***(P-15849)***
Scorpio Enterprises ....D.......562 946-9464
12556 Mccann Dr Santa Fe Springs (90670) ***(P-2350)***
Scorpion Athc Booster CLB Inc ....E.......805 482-2005
300 E Esplanade Dr # 250 Oxnard (93036) ***(P-25244)***
Scorpion Design LLC ....A.......661 702-0100
27750 Entertainment Dr Valencia (91355) ***(P-13900)***
Scott A Porter Prof Corp ....D.......916 929-1481
350 University Ave # 200 Sacramento (95825) ***(P-23368)***
Scott J Witlin Atty, Los Angeles *Also called Proskauer Rose LLP* ***(P-23342)***
Scott Jacks DDS Inc ....C.......323 564-2444
4444 Tweedy Blvd South Gate (90280) ***(P-20137)***
Scott Place Associates ....D.......650 345-8222
60 31st Ave San Mateo (94403) ***(P-11756)***
Scott Silva Concrete Inc ....D.......916 859-0593
11374 Gold Dredge Way Rancho Cordova (95742) ***(P-3323)***
Scott Street Senior Housing Co ....C.......415 345-5083
2180 Post St San Francisco (94115) ***(P-20953)***
Scott's Glass Service, Carson *Also called Scotts Labor Leasing Co Inc* ***(P-14754)***
Scottel Voice & Data Inc ....C.......310 737-7300
6100 Center Dr Ste 720 Los Angeles (90045) ***(P-17910)***
Scottish American Insurance (PA) ....D.......714 550-5050
2002 E Mcfadden Ave # 100 Santa Ana (92705) ***(P-10766)***
Scotts Labor Leasing Co Inc ....D.......310 835-8388
22560 Lucerne St Carson (90745) ***(P-14754)***
Scotts Plant Service Co ....D.......209 545-0903
6206 Carver Rd Modesto (95356) ***(P-935)***
SCR, Costa Mesa *Also called South Coast Repertory Inc* ***(P-18405)***
SCR, Irvine *Also called Redhill Group Inc* ***(P-26561)***
Screamline Investment Corp (PA) ....C.......323 201-0114
2130 S Tubeway Ave Commerce (90040) ***(P-4980)***
Screen Actors Guild - American ....C.......818 954-9400
3601 W Olive Ave Fl 2 Burbank (91505) ***(P-10493)***
Screen Actors Guild-Producers, Burbank *Also called Screen Actors Guild - American* ***(P-10493)***
Screen Gems-EMI Music Inc ....E.......310 586-2700
2700 Colorado Ave Ste 100 Santa Monica (90404) ***(P-17461)***
Screen Spe Usa LLC (HQ) ....C.......408 523-9140
820 Kifer Rd Ste B Sunnyvale (94086) ***(P-7540)***
Scribd Inc ....D.......415 896-9890
333 Bush St Ste 2400 San Francisco (94104) ***(P-16251)***
Scrip Advantage Inc ....D.......559 320-0052
4273 W Richert Ave # 110 Fresno (93722) ***(P-17462)***
Scripps Ambulatory Surgery Ctr, Encinitas *Also called Scripps Health* ***(P-21726)***
Scripps Aquarium, La Jolla *Also called Birch Aquarium At Scripps* ***(P-24925)***
Scripps Clinic ....C.......858 794-1250
12395 El Camino Real San Diego (92130) ***(P-21725)***
Scripps Clinic - Encinatas, Encinitas *Also called Scripps Health* ***(P-19867)***
Scripps Clinic Carmel Valley ....B.......858 554-8096
10666 N Torrey Pines Rd La Jolla (92037) ***(P-19861)***
Scripps Clinic Foundation ....A.......858 554-9000
12395 El Camino Real San Diego (92130) ***(P-27024)***
Scripps Clinic Medical Group ....B.......858 554-9606
10666 N Torrey Pines Rd La Jolla (92037) ***(P-19862)***
Scripps Del Mar, San Diego *Also called Scripps Health* ***(P-22678)***

Mergent e-mail: customerrelations@mergent.com
1458
2019 Directory of California
Wholesalers and Services Companies
(P-0000) Products & Services Section entry number
(PA)=Parent Co (HQ)=Headquarters (DH)=Div Headquarters

Scripps Dialasys Inc (PA)...E...619 453-9070
9870 Genesee Ave La Jolla (92037) ***(P-19863)***
Scripps Dialysis Center, La Jolla *Also called Scripps Dialasys Inc* ***(P-19863)***
Scripps Green Hospital, La Jolla *Also called Scripps Health* ***(P-21733)***
Scripps Health...D...760 753-8413
320 Santa Fe Dr Ste 310 Encinitas (92024) ***(P-21726)***
Scripps Health...B...760 806-9263
122 Civic Center Dr # 101 Vista (92084) ***(P-20748)***
Scripps Health...D...858 622-9076
10140 Campus Point Dr San Diego (92121) ***(P-19864)***
Scripps Health...D...619 294-8111
4077 5th Ave San Diego (92103) ***(P-21727)***
Scripps Health...C...619 862-6600
237 Church Ave Chula Vista (91910) ***(P-20203)***
Scripps Health...C...858 678-6966
10010 Campus Point Dr San Diego (92121) ***(P-25245)***
Scripps Health...C...858 657-4218
10790 Rancho Bernardo Rd San Diego (92127) ***(P-20749)***
Scripps Health...B...858 271-9770
15004 Innovation Dr San Diego (92128) ***(P-21728)***
Scripps Health...B...619 245-2350
7565 Mission Valley Rd # 200 San Diego (92108) ***(P-22882)***
Scripps Health...C...760 479-3900
477 N El Camino Real A208 Encinitas (92024) ***(P-21729)***
Scripps Health...C...760 753-6501
354 Santa Fe Dr Encinitas (92024) ***(P-21730)***
Scripps Health...D...619 670-5400
10862 Calle Verde La Mesa (91941) ***(P-19865)***
Scripps Health...A...619 691-7000
435 H St Chula Vista (91910) ***(P-21731)***
Scripps Health (PA)...A...800 727-4777
10140 Campus Point Dr Ax415 San Diego (92121) ***(P-21732)***
Scripps Health...B...858 455-9100
10666 N Torrey Pines Rd La Jolla (92037) ***(P-21733)***
Scripps Health...B...858 292-4211
7910 Frost St Ste 320 San Diego (92123) ***(P-19866)***
Scripps Health...B...619 294-8111
4077 Fifth Ave San Diego (92103) ***(P-21734)***
Scripps Health...D...760 633-6915
310 Santa Fe Dr Ste 200 Encinitas (92024) ***(P-19867)***
Scripps Health...B...858 764-3000
3811 Valley Centre Dr San Diego (92130) ***(P-22412)***
Scripps Health...C...800 727-4777
10666 N Torrey Pines Rd La Jolla (92037) ***(P-21735)***
Scripps Health...C...760 806-5700
488 E Valley Pkwy Ste 411 Escondido (92025) ***(P-19868)***
Scripps Health...C...858 452-1279
9850 Genesee Ave Ste 900 La Jolla (92037) ***(P-25246)***
Scripps Health...B...858 458-5100
9834 Genesee Ave Ste 311 La Jolla (92037) ***(P-19869)***
Scripps Health...C...858 626-5200
9850 Genesee Ave Ste 620 La Jolla (92037) ***(P-19870)***
Scripps Health...B...858 626-6150
9888 Genesee Ave La Jolla (92037) ***(P-21736)***
Scripps Health...D...858 554-8892
10666 N Torrey Pines Rd La Jolla (92037) ***(P-19871)***
Scripps Health...D...858 554-9489
10666 N Torrey Pines Rd La Jolla (92037) ***(P-19872)***
Scripps Health...C...760 901-5200
3998 Vista Way Ste E Oceanside (92056) ***(P-19873)***
Scripps Health...C...858 626-4123
9888 Genesee Ave La Jolla (92037) ***(P-21737)***
Scripps Health...D...858 784-5888
10790 Rancho Bernardo Rd San Diego (92127) ***(P-19874)***
Scripps Health...C...858 652-5504
10550 N Torrey Pines Rd La Jolla (92037) ***(P-26451)***
Scripps Health...C...858 794-0160
3811 Valley Centre Dr San Diego (92130) ***(P-22678)***
Scripps Mem Hosp - Encinatas, Encinitas *Also called Scripps Health* ***(P-21730)***
Scripps Mem Hosp - La Jolla, La Jolla *Also called Scripps Health* ***(P-21737)***
Scripps Mem Hospital-La Jolla, La Jolla *Also called Scripps Health* ***(P-21736)***
Scripps Memorial Hospitals...D...858 450-4481
9834 Genesee Ave Ste 328 La Jolla (92037) ***(P-21738)***
Scripps Mercy Hospital, San Diego *Also called Scripps Health* ***(P-21727)***
Scripps Mercy Hospital, San Diego *Also called Scripps Health* ***(P-21734)***
Scripps Mercy Hospital...D...619 294-8111
4077 5th Ave Mer35 San Diego (92103) ***(P-21739)***
Scripps Mercy Hospitals, Chula Vista *Also called Scripps Health* ***(P-21731)***
Scripps Rancho Bernardo, San Diego *Also called Scripps Health* ***(P-21728)***
Scripps Research Institute (PA)...D...858 784-1000
10550 N Torrey Pines Rd La Jolla (92037) ***(P-26659)***
Scripps Shared Services, San Diego *Also called Scripps Health* ***(P-20749)***
Scripps Torrey Pines, La Jolla *Also called Scripps Health* ***(P-21735)***
Scripps Whttier Dbetes Program, San Diego *Also called Scripps Health* ***(P-19864)***
Script To Screen Inc...D...714 558-3287
200 N Tustin Ave Ste 200 # 200 Santa Ana (92705) ***(P-18114)***
Scripto, Ontario *Also called Calico Brands Inc* ***(P-9201)***
Scst Inc (PA)...D...619 280-4321
6280 Riverdale St San Diego (92120) ***(P-26729)***
Scv Facilities Services...D...310 803-4588
1907 W 75th St Los Angeles (90047) ***(P-14381)***
SCVMC, San Jose *Also called Santa Clara Valley Medical Ctr* ***(P-21718)***
Scwa, Sacramento *Also called Sacramento County Water Agency* ***(P-6298)***
SCWD, Laguna Beach *Also called South Coast Water District* ***(P-6314)***
SD Deacon Corp California...D...916 969-0900
7745 Greenback Ln Ste 250 Citrus Heights (95610) ***(P-1642)***
SD Hotel Circle LLC...D...619 881-6800
2201 Hotel Cir S San Diego (92108) ***(P-13196)***
SD Sports MDCne&fmly Hlth Cntr...D...619 229-3910
6699 Alvarado Rd Ste 2100 San Diego (92120) ***(P-19875)***
SD Squared North America Ltd...C...650 721-1158
600 California St Fl 11 San Francisco (94108) ***(P-15433)***
SD Stadium Hotel LLC...D...858 278-9300
3805 Murphy Canyon Rd San Diego (92123) ***(P-13197)***
Sdcraa, San Diego *Also called San Dego Cnty Rgnal Arprt Auth* ***(P-4907)***
Sdg Enterprises...D...805 777-7978
822 Hampshire Rd Ste H Westlake Village (91361) ***(P-2351)***
SDG&E, San Diego *Also called San Diego Gas & Electric Co* ***(P-6186)***
Sdi Media USA, Los Angeles *Also called SDI Media USA Inc* ***(P-18115)***
SDI Media USA Inc (HQ)...D...323 602-5455
6060 Center Dr Ste 100 Los Angeles (90045) ***(P-18115)***
Sdj General Partnership...D...805 582-3200
2125 N Madera Rd Ste C Simi Valley (93065) ***(P-10934)***
Sdl, Los Angeles *Also called Language Weaver Inc* ***(P-15254)***
SDS, San Diego *Also called Strategic Data Systems* ***(P-16060)***
SE San Diego Hotel LLC...D...619 515-3000
1047 5th Ave San Diego (92101) ***(P-13198)***
SE Scher Corporation...A...408 844-0772
1585 The Alameda San Jose (95126) ***(P-14911)***
SE Scher Corporation...A...858 546-8300
2525 Camino Del Rio S San Diego (92108) ***(P-14755)***
SE Scher Corporation...B...916 632-1363
6731 Five Star Blvd Ste C Rocklin (95677) ***(P-14756)***
Sea Breeze Collision, Tustin *Also called Sterling Collision Center LLC* ***(P-17744)***
Sea Breeze Financial Services (PA)...E...949 223-9700
18191 Von Karman Ave # 150 Irvine (92612) ***(P-9856)***
Sea Breeze Health Care Inc...C...714 847-9671
7781 Garfield Ave Huntington Beach (92648) ***(P-20750)***
Sea Breeze Mortgage Services, Irvine *Also called Sea Breeze Financial Services* ***(P-9856)***
Sea Catch Seafoods, El Monte *Also called Atlanta Seafoods LLC* ***(P-8570)***
Sea Cliff Health Care, Huntington Beach *Also called Huntington Bch Cnvlescent Hosp* ***(P-20539)***
Sea Cliff Healthcare Center, Huntington Beach *Also called HB Healthcare Associates LLC* ***(P-20507)***
Sea View Medical Group Inc...D...805 373-5781
1901 Solar Dr Ste 265 Oxnard (93036) ***(P-22883)***
Sea West Cast Gard Fdral Cr Un (PA)...D...510 568-4100
8750 Mountain Blvd Oakland (94605) ***(P-9591)***
Sea Win Inc...E...213 688-2899
526 Stanford Ave Los Angeles (90013) ***(P-8599)***
Sea-Air International Inc...D...310 338-0778
11222 S La Cienega Blvd # 100 Inglewood (90304) ***(P-5164)***
Sea-Logix LLC...D...510 271-1400
1425 Maritime St Oakland (94607) ***(P-4261)***
Sea-Logix LLC (HQ)...D...415 927-6400
4040 Civic Center Dr # 350 San Rafael (94903) ***(P-4262)***
Seaboard Corporation...B...806 435-5935
10350 Hritg Pk Dr Ste 111 Santa Fe Springs (90670) ***(P-404)***
Seaboard Produce Distrs Inc...D...805 981-8001
710 Del Norte Blvd Oxnard (93030) ***(P-7712)***
Seabreeze Management Comp, Aliso Viejo *Also called Glenwood Village Cmnty Assn* ***(P-25166)***
Seabreeze Management Company (PA)...D...949 855-1800
26840 Aliso Viejo Pkwy # 100 Aliso Viejo (92656) ***(P-27025)***
Seacastle Inc...D...925 480-3000
4000 Executive Pkwy # 240 San Ramon (94583) ***(P-14543)***
Seacliff Country Club, Huntington Beach *Also called American Golf Corporation* ***(P-18835)***
Seacliff Inn Inc...D...831 661-4671
7500 Old Dominion Ct Aptos (95003) ***(P-13199)***
Seacoast Commerce Bank (HQ)...D...858 432-7000
11939 Rancho Bernardo Rd # 200 San Diego (92128) ***(P-9486)***
Seacrest Convalescent Hosp Inc...D...310 833-3526
1416 W 6th St San Pedro (90732) ***(P-20751)***
Seafus Corporation...E...415 584-6100
1365 Lowrie Ave South San Francisco (94080) ***(P-14382)***
Seal Electric Inc...C...619 449-7323
1162 Greenfield Dr El Cajon (92021) ***(P-2727)***
Sealant Systems International...D...805 489-0490
125 Venture Dr Ste 210 San Luis Obispo (93401) ***(P-6694)***
Sealaska Envmtl Svcs LLC...D...619 564-8329
3838 Camino Del Rio N # 240 San Diego (92108) ***(P-27857)***
Seaman Nurseries Inc...D...559 665-1860
336 Robertson Blvd Ste A Chowchilla (93610) ***(P-467)***
Sean P OConnor...D...949 851-7323
1900 Main St Ste 700 Irvine (92614) ***(P-23369)***
Seapassion Logistics Inc...D...562 907-4300
20450 E Walnut Dr N Walnut (91789) ***(P-5165)***
Seaport Fish Company, Wilmington *Also called Star Fisheries* ***(P-8604)***
SEAPORT MEAT COMPANY, Spring Valley *Also called Pnc Inc* ***(P-8624)***
Search Agency Inc (PA)...D...310 582-5700
11150 W Olym Blvd Ste 600 Los Angeles (90064) ***(P-13901)***
Search Engine Optimization Inc...D...760 929-0039
5841 Edison Pl Ste 140 Carlsbad (92008) ***(P-17463)***
Search Optics LLC (PA)...D...858 678-0707
5770 Oberlin Dr San Diego (92121) ***(P-27441)***
Searles Valley Minerals Inc...A...760 372-2259
80201 Trona Rd Trona (93562) ***(P-1099)***
Sears, Benicia *Also called Innovel Solutions Inc* ***(P-5091)***
Sears, Delano *Also called Innovel Solutions Inc* ***(P-5092)***
Sears Roebuck and Co...D...951 719-3528
40680 Winchester Rd Temecula (92591) ***(P-17871)***
Sears Roebuck and Co...D...530 751-4628
1235 Colusa Ave Yuba City (95991) ***(P-17872)***
Sears Roebuck and Co...C...714 256-7328
100 Brea Mall Brea (92821) ***(P-17986)***

ALPHABETIC

Employee Codes: A=Over 500 employees, B=251-500
C=101-250, D=51-100, E=50
2019 Directory of California
Wholesalers and Services Companies
© Mergent Inc. 1-800-342-5647
1459

Sears Roebuck and Co........C.......909 390-4210
5691 E Philadelphia St Ontario (91761) *(P-17987)*
Sears Roebuck and Co........C.......619 590-3812
1406 N Johnson Ave El Cajon (92020) *(P-17911)*
Sears Auto Center, Yuba City *Also called Sears Roebuck and Co (P-17872)*
Sears Home Imprv Pdts Inc........D.......858 790-7721
9586 Dist Ave Ste F San Diego (92121) *(P-1231)*
Sears Service Center, El Cajon *Also called Sears Roebuck and Co (P-17911)*
Seascape Golf Club, Aptos *Also called American Golf Corporation (P-18842)*
Seascape Resort Ltd A Calif........B.......831 662-7120
19 Seascape Vlg Aptos (95003) *(P-13200)*
Seaside Hotel Lessee Inc........C.......310 260-7500
1819 Ocean Ave Santa Monica (90401) *(P-17464)*
Seaside Laguna Inn & Suites........D.......949 494-9717
1661 S Coast Hwy Laguna Beach (92651) *(P-13201)*
Seaside Rfrigerated Trnspt Inc (PA)........E.......510 732-0472
7041 Las Positas Rd Ste H Livermore (94551) *(P-4263)*
Season Produce Co Inc........B.......213 689-0008
1601 E Olympic Blvd # 315 Los Angeles (90021) *(P-8727)*
Seasons........D.......562 691-1200
200 W Whittier Blvd La Habra (90631) *(P-24668)*
Seatech Consulting Group Inc........E.......310 356-6828
609 Deep Valley Dr # 200 Rllng HLS Est (90274) *(P-16479)*
Seaver International........D.......707 291-4929
4169 Green Valley Schl Rd Sebastopol (95472) *(P-16480)*
Seaview Hlthcre & Rehab Ctr LL........D.......707 443-5668
6400 Purdue Dr Eureka (95503) *(P-24669)*
Seaview Industries........E.......714 957-5073
2501 Harbor Blvd Costa Mesa (92626) *(P-17465)*
Seaworld Global Logistics........B.......310 208-9488
1421 Barry Ave Apt 5 Los Angeles (90025) *(P-5166)*
Sebastian, Kerman *Also called Kerman Telephone Co (P-5591)*
Sebastian, Fresno *Also called Kertel Communications Inc (P-2624)*
Sebastian Enterprises Inc (PA)........C.......559 946-4954
811 S Madera Ave Kerman (93630) *(P-5639)*
Sebastopol Rifle & Pistol Club........D.......707 824-0184
343 Flynn St Sebastopol (95472) *(P-19039)*
SEC Pac Inc........D.......925 938-9200
1555 Riviera Ave Ste E Walnut Creek (94596) *(P-11757)*
Seca Eqp Removal & Dismantle........E.......209 543-1600
684 Bitritto Ct Modesto (95356) *(P-3461)*
Seca Eqp Removal & Dismantling, Modesto *Also called Seca Eqp Removal & Dismantle (P-3461)*
Secom International (PA)........D.......310 641-1290
9610 Bellanca Ave Los Angeles (90045) *(P-16047)*
Second Chance Inc (PA)........E.......510 792-4357
6330 Thornton Ave Ste B Newark (94560) *(P-24036)*
Second Harvest Food........D.......949 653-2900
8014 Marine Way Irvine (92618) *(P-24037)*
Second Harvest Food Bank (PA)........E.......408 266-8866
750 Curtner Ave San Jose (95125) *(P-24038)*
Second Image National LLC........D.......909 445-8080
700 E Bonita Ave Pomona (91767) *(P-14099)*
Second Image National LLC (PA)........C.......800 229-7477
170 E Arrow Hwy San Dimas (91773) *(P-14092)*
Second Opinion Med Grp Inc........D.......805 496-4315
2876 Sycamore Dr Ste 305 Simi Valley (93065) *(P-10308)*
Second Street Corporation........C.......310 394-5454
1111 2nd St Santa Monica (90403) *(P-13202)*
Secova Inc........C.......714 384-0530
3090 Bristol St Ste 200 Costa Mesa (92626) *(P-27442)*
Secova Eservices Inc (HQ)........D.......714 384-0655
3090 Bristol St Ste 200 Costa Mesa (92626) *(P-27443)*
Secret Charm LLC (PA)........B.......213 742-7744
1433 Walnut St Los Angeles (90011) *(P-8333)*
Secrom Inc........D.......310 830-4010
345 E Carson St Carson (90745) *(P-21205)*
Sectek Inc........D.......650 604-1785
Bldg 15 Mountain View (94035) *(P-16934)*
Sectran Armored Truck Service, Pico Rivera *Also called Sectran Security Incorporated (P-16781)*
Sectran Security Incorporated (PA)........C.......562 948-1446
7633 Industry Ave Pico Rivera (90660) *(P-16781)*
Secure Limousine, Whittier *Also called Secure Transportation Co Inc (P-3846)*
Secure Net Alliance........E.......818 848-4900
601 S Glenoaks Blvd # 409 Burbank (91502) *(P-16782)*
Secure Nursing Service Inc........B.......213 736-6771
3333 Wilshire Blvd # 625 Los Angeles (90010) *(P-14757)*
Secure One Data Solutions LLC........E.......562 924-7056
11090 Artesia Blvd Ste D Cerritos (90703) *(P-16176)*
Secure Transportation Co Inc (PA)........C.......562 941-0107
13111 Meyer Rd Whittier (90605) *(P-3846)*
Secure Transportation Co Inc........D.......858 790-3958
9557 Candida St San Diego (92126) *(P-5245)*
Secure Transportation Company........D.......951 737-7300
12785 Magnolia Ave # 102 Riverside (92503) *(P-3847)*
Secureauth Corporation (PA)........D.......949 777-6959
8845 Irvine Center Dr # 200 Irvine (92618) *(P-15434)*
Securecom Inc........E.......916 638-2855
4822 Golden Foothill Pkwy El Dorado Hills (95762) *(P-2728)*
Securelion Security, Newark *Also called Courtesy Security Inc (P-16617)*
Securitas Critical Infrastruct........A.......858 560-0448
3914 Murphy Canyon Rd A120 San Diego (92123) *(P-16783)*
Securitas Critical Infrastruct........A.......310 817-2177
1835 W Orangewood Ave # 250 Orange (92868) *(P-16784)*
Securitas Critical Infrastruct........A.......805 685-1100
Rm 117 Bldg 7525 Vandenberg Afb (93437) *(P-16785)*
Securitas Critical Infrastruct........A.......310 426-3300
360 N Pacific Coast Hwy El Segundo (90245) *(P-16786)*
Securitas Electronic SEC Inc........D.......858 812-7349
7002 Convoy Ct San Diego (92111) *(P-16935)*
Securitas SEC Svcs USA Inc........C.......805 650-6285
5700 Ralston St Ventura (93003) *(P-16787)*
Securitas SEC Svcs USA Inc........C.......650 358-1556
1650 Borel Pl Ste 227 San Mateo (94402) *(P-16936)*
Securitas SEC Svcs USA Inc........C.......916 564-2009
2045 Hurley Way Sacramento (95825) *(P-16788)*
Securitas SEC Svcs USA Inc........C.......209 943-1401
3115 W March Ln Ste A Stockton (95219) *(P-16789)*
Securitas SEC Svcs USA Inc........C.......559 221-2302
155 E Shaw Ave Ste 315 Fresno (93710) *(P-16790)*
Securitas SEC Svcs USA Inc........C.......571 321-0913
750 Terrado Plz Ste 107 Covina (91723) *(P-16791)*
Securitas SEC Svcs USA Inc........C.......510 568-6818
425 Bush St Ste 400 San Francisco (94108) *(P-16792)*
Securitas SEC Svcs USA Inc........D.......909 974-3160
430 N Vineyard Ave # 335 Ontario (91764) *(P-16793)*
Securitas SEC Svcs USA Inc........C.......760 353-8177
2344 S 2nd St Ste C El Centro (92243) *(P-16794)*
Securitas SEC Svcs USA Inc........D.......530 245-0256
2415 Larkspur Ln Ste B Redding (96002) *(P-16795)*
Securitas SEC Svcs USA Inc........C.......619 641-0049
1550 Hotel Cir N Ste 440 San Diego (92108) *(P-16796)*
Securitas SEC Svcs USA Inc........B.......818 706-4909
4330 Park Terrace Dr Westlake Village (91361) *(P-16797)*
Securitas SEC Svcs USA Inc........C.......707 586-1393
1304 Sthpint Blvd Ste 110 Petaluma (94954) *(P-16798)*
Securitas SEC Svcs USA Inc........C.......805 967-8987
5276 Hollister Ave # 204 Goleta (93111) *(P-16799)*
Securitas SEC Svcs USA Inc........D.......707 445-5463
1606 Koster St Ste A Eureka (95501) *(P-16800)*
Securitas SEC Svcs USA Inc........C.......916 569-4500
2045 Hurley Way Ste 175 Sacramento (95825) *(P-16801)*
Securitas SEC Svcs USA Inc........C.......951 676-3954
27450 Ynez Rd Ste 315 Temecula (92591) *(P-16802)*
Securitas SEC Svcs USA Inc........C.......559 221-2302
43-00 Cook St Ste 100 Palm Desert (92211) *(P-16803)*
Securitas SEC Svcs USA Inc........C.......831 444-9607
1611 Bunker Hill Way # 100 Salinas (93906) *(P-16804)*
Securitas SEC Svcs USA Inc........C.......925 746-0552
7677 Oakport St Ste 725 Oakland (94621) *(P-16805)*
Securitas SEC Svcs USA Inc........C.......909 865-4356
1101 W Mckinley Ave Pomona (91768) *(P-16806)*
Securitas SEC Svcs USA Inc........C.......323 832-9074
6055 E Wash Blvd Ste 155 Commerce (90040) *(P-16807)*
Securitas SEC Svcs USA Inc........C.......213 580-8825
1055 Wilshire Blvd Los Angeles (90017) *(P-16808)*
Securitas SEC Svcs USA Inc........C.......562 427-2737
1500 W Carson St Ste 109 Long Beach (90810) *(P-16809)*
Securitas SEC Svcs USA Inc........C.......310 787-0747
400 Crenshaw Blvd Ste 200 Torrance (90503) *(P-16810)*
Securitas SEC Svcs USA Inc........C.......714 385-9745
2870 Skypark Dr Ste 315 Torrance (90505) *(P-16811)*
Securitas SEC Svcs USA Inc........C.......760 245-1915
15428 Civic Dr Ste 305 Victorville (92392) *(P-16812)*
Securitas SEC Svcs USA Inc........C.......818 891-0458
16909 Parthenia St # 202 Northridge (91343) *(P-16813)*
Securitas SEC Svcs USA Inc........C.......818 706-6800
4330 Park Terrace Dr Westlake Village (91361) *(P-16814)*
Securitech Security Services........C.......213 387-5050
2733 N San Fernando Rd Los Angeles (90065) *(P-16815)*
Security Alarm Fing Entps Inc........D.......925 830-4786
2440 Camino Ramon Ste 200 San Ramon (94583) *(P-16937)*
Security America Inc........D.......310 532-0121
7120 Hayvenhurst Ave # 201 Van Nuys (91406) *(P-16816)*
Security California Bancorp........D.......951 368-2265
3403 10th St Ste 830 Riverside (92501) *(P-11958)*
Security Central Inc........D.......510 652-2477
4432 Telegraph Ave Oakland (94609) *(P-17988)*
Security Company, Burbank *Also called Secure Net Alliance (P-16782)*
Security Contractor Svcs Inc (PA)........D.......916 338-4200
5339 Jackson St North Highlands (95660) *(P-6936)*
Security Indust Spcialists Inc (PA)........C.......310 215-5100
6071 Bristol Pkwy Culver City (90230) *(P-16817)*
Security Nat Mstr Holdg Co LLC (PA)........C.......707 442-2818
323 5th St Eureka (95501) *(P-9857)*
Security On-Demand Inc........E.......858 563-5655
12121 Scripps Summit Dr # 320 San Diego (92131) *(P-16048)*
Security On-Site Services Inc........D.......916 988-6500
2210 Plaza Dr Ste 300 Rocklin (95765) *(P-16938)*
Security One Inc........D.......800 778-3017
1859 Streiff Ln Santa Rosa (95403) *(P-16818)*
Security Pacific Home Loans, Westlake Village *Also called Ownit Mortgage Solutions Inc (P-9841)*
Security Pacific RE Brkg, Richmond *Also called S P R E Inc (P-11750)*
Security Pacific RE Brkg........D.......510 245-9901
292 Violet Rd Hercules (94547) *(P-11758)*
Security Pacific Real Estate, Walnut Creek *Also called SEC Pac Inc (P-11757)*
Security Paving Company Inc (PA)........D.......818 362-9200
13170 Telfair Ave Sylmar (91342) *(P-1846)*
Security Signal Devices Inc (PA)........E.......800 888-0444
1740 N Lemon St Anaheim (92801) *(P-16939)*
Security Specialists, San Fernando *Also called Tyan Inc (P-16841)*
Secuto Music, Burbank *Also called Roundabout Entertainment Inc (P-18111)*
Sedgwick Claims MGT Svcs Inc........D.......626 568-1415
3280 E Foothill Blvd # 350 Pasadena (91107) *(P-10767)*
Sedgwick Claims MGT Svcs Inc........C.......818 591-9444
24025 Park Sorrento # 200 Calabasas (91302) *(P-10768)*

Sedgwick Claims MGT Svcs Inc....D....510 302-3000
2101 Webster St Oakland (94612) *(P-10769)*
Sedgwick Claims MGT Svcs Inc....D....916 568-7394
1851 Heritage Ln Sacramento (95815) *(P-10770)*
Seecon Built Homes Inc....D....925 671-7711
4021 Port Chicago Hwy Concord (94520) *(P-11914)*
Seed Dynamics Inc....D....831 424-1177
1081b Harkins Rd Salinas (93901) *(P-566)*
Seeds of Change Inc....C....310 764-7700
2555 S Dominguez Hills Dr Rancho Dominguez (90220) *(P-9097)*
Seeley Brothers, Brea *Also called Norcal Inc (P-3053)*
Seeley Brothers, Brea *Also called Norcal Inc (P-3052)*
Seems Plumbing Co Inc....E....310 297-4969
5400 W Rosecrans Ave Lowr Hawthorne (90250) *(P-2352)*
Sefnco Communications Inc....D....530 338-2460
9714 Tanqueray Ct Ste A Redding (96003) *(P-5994)*
Sega Entertainment USA Inc....D....909 987-4263
12777 W Jefferson Blvd # 100 Los Angeles (90066) *(P-18789)*
Sega of America Inc....C....415 701-6000
350 Rhode Island St # 400 San Francisco (94103) *(P-7101)*
Seguin Mreau NAPA Coperage Inc....D....707 252-3408
151 Camino Dorado NAPA (94558) *(P-7870)*
Segura Enterprises Inc....D....805 349-0550
1011 W Mccoy Ln Santa Maria (93455) *(P-16819)*
Segura Security Services, Santa Maria *Also called Segura Enterprises Inc (P-16819)*
Seibo LLC (PA)....D....310 465-1700
425 Via Corta Ste 304 Palos Verdes Estates (90274) *(P-18216)*
Seidner-Miller Automotive Inc....E....909 394-3500
1253 S Lone Hill Ave Glendora (91740) *(P-17783)*
Seiler LLP (PA)....C....650 365-4646
3 Lagoon Dr Ste 400 Redwood City (94065) *(P-26288)*
Seiler LLP....D....415 392-2123
220 Montgomery St Ste 300 San Francisco (94104) *(P-26289)*
Seirra Telephone, Oakhurst *Also called Sierra Tel Cmmunications Group (P-5643)*
SEIU Local 1021....C....510 350-9811
447 29th St Oakland (94609) *(P-674)*
Seiu Local 2015....C....213 985-0384
2910 Beverly Blvd Los Angeles (90057) *(P-25077)*
Seiu Local 721....D....213 368-8660
1545 Wilshire Blvd # 100 Los Angeles (90017) *(P-25078)*
Seiu Uhw-West, Commerce *Also called Seiu United Healthcare Workers (P-25080)*
Seiu United Healthcare Workers (PA)....C....510 251-1250
560 Thomas L Berkley Way Oakland (94612) *(P-25079)*
Seiu United Healthcare Workers....E....323 734-8399
5480 Ferguson Dr Commerce (90022) *(P-25080)*
Sela Healthcare Inc (PA)....C....909 985-1981
867 E 11th St Upland (91786) *(P-20752)*
Select Data Inc....C....714 577-1000
4155 E La Palma Ave # 250 Anaheim (92807) *(P-15435)*
Select Harvest Usa LLC (PA)....D....209 668-2471
14827 W Harding Rd Turlock (95380) *(P-8910)*
Select Home Care....D....805 777-3855
2393 Townsgate Rd Ste 100 Westlake Village (91361) *(P-22413)*
Select Hotels Group LLC....E....510 623-6000
3101 W Warren Ave Fremont (94538) *(P-13203)*
Select Hotels Group LLC....E....916 638-4141
11260 Point East Dr Rancho Cordova (95742) *(P-13204)*
Select Personnel Services, Santa Barbara *Also called Select Temporaries LLC (P-14758)*
Select Staffing, Santa Barbara *Also called Real Time Staffing Services (P-14718)*
Select Staffing, Santa Barbara *Also called Employbridge LLC (P-14849)*
Select Temporaries LLC (HQ)....D....805 882-2200
3820 State St Santa Barbara (93105) *(P-14758)*
Selecta Products Inc (PA)....661 823-7050
1200 E Tehachapi Blvd Tehachapi (93561) *(P-7393)*
Selecta Switch, Tehachapi *Also called Selecta Products Inc (P-7393)*
Selectforce, Irvine *Also called Accurate Background LLC (P-16206)*
Selectquote Insurance Services (PA)....C....415 543-7338
595 Market St Fl 10 San Francisco (94105) *(P-10771)*
Selex Inc (PA)....D....707 836-8836
442 Longfellow St Livermore (94550) *(P-3582)*
Selex Inc....D....707 836-8836
930 Shiloh Rd Windsor (95492) *(P-3583)*
Self Help Enterprises (PA)....D....559 651-1000
8445 W Elowin Ct Visalia (93291) *(P-25247)*
Self Serve Auto Dismantlers (PA)....C....714 630-8901
3200 E Frontera St Anaheim (92806) *(P-6475)*
Self-Aid Workshop, Glendale *Also called Camble Center (P-24162)*
Self-Help For Elderly....D....415 391-3843
777 Stockton St Ste 110 San Francisco (94108) *(P-24039)*
Self-Help For Elderly (PA)....C....415 677-7600
731 Sansome St Ste 100 San Francisco (94111) *(P-24040)*
Self-Help For Elderly....D....408 873-1183
940 S Stelling Rd Cupertino (95014) *(P-24041)*
Selig Construction Corp....E....530 893-5898
337 Huss Dr Chico (95928) *(P-1232)*
Selligent Inc (HQ)....D....650 421-4200
1300 Island Dr Ste 200 Redwood City (94065) *(P-16049)*
Selma Portuguese Azorian Assn....E....559 896-2508
1245 Nebraska Ave Selma (93662) *(P-24042)*
Seltzer Caplan McMahon (PA)....C....619 685-3003
750 B St Ste 2100 San Diego (92101) *(P-23370)*
Selu College, Inglewood *Also called Beckett Enterprise (P-27159)*
Selvi-Vidovich LP....D....408 720-8500
865 W El Camino Real Sunnyvale (94087) *(P-13205)*
Selzer Home Loans, Ukiah *Also called Lake County Home Loans (P-9823)*
Sema, Diamond Bar *Also called Specialty Equipment Mkt Assn (P-24984)*
Sema Construction Inc....D....949 330-4300
6 Orchard Ste 150 Irvine (92618) *(P-1888)*
Semans Communications (PA)....D....650 529-9984
112 Stonegate Rd Portola Vally (94028) *(P-2729)*
Semantic Ai Inc (PA)....D....619 222-4050
4922 N Harbor Dr San Diego (92106) *(P-16050)*
Semantic Research, San Diego *Also called Semantic Ai Inc (P-16050)*
Semi (PA)....C....408 943-6900
673 S Milpitas Blvd Milpitas (95035) *(P-24981)*
Semifreddi's Bakery, Alameda *Also called Semifreddis Inc (P-8865)*
Semifreddis Inc (PA)....C....510 596-9930
1980 N Loop Rd Alameda (94502) *(P-8865)*
Seminis Inc....D....831 623-4554
500 Lucy Brown Rd San Juan Bautista (95045) *(P-26452)*
Seminis Inc (HQ)....B....805 485-7317
2700 Camino Del Sol Oxnard (93030) *(P-26453)*
Seminis Vegetable Seeds Inc (HQ)....A....855 733-3834
2700 Camino Del Sol Oxnard (93030) *(P-9098)*
Seminis Vegetable Seeds Inc....E....530 669-6903
37437 State Highway 16 Woodland (95695) *(P-9099)*
Sempra Energy (PA)....A....619 696-2000
488 8th Ave San Diego (92101) *(P-6193)*
Sempra Energy....A....619 696-2000
9305 Lightwave Ave San Diego (92123) *(P-6107)*
Sempra Energy Global Entps....A....619 696-2000
101 Ash St San Diego (92101) *(P-6162)*
Sempra Energy International (HQ)....A....619 696-2000
101 Ash St San Diego (92101) *(P-6108)*
Sempra Energy Utilities, San Diego *Also called Sempra Energy International (P-6108)*
Sendbird, San Mateo *Also called Smile Family Inc (P-15455)*
Sendmail Inc (HQ)....D....510 594-5400
892 Ross Dr Sunnyvale (94089) *(P-5640)*
Sendme Inc....D....415 978-9504
150 Spear St Ste 1400 San Francisco (94105) *(P-5641)*
Sendmemobile.com, San Francisco *Also called Sendme Inc (P-5641)*
Seneca Center, Fremont *Also called Seneca Family of Agencies (P-24043)*
Seneca Family of Agencies....D....510 226-6180
40950 Chapel Way Fremont (94538) *(P-24043)*
Seneca Family of Agency, Tustin *Also called Kinship Center (P-23884)*
Seneca Healthcare District....D....530 258-1977
199 Reynolds Rd Chester (96020) *(P-19876)*
Seneca Healthcare District (PA)....C....530 258-2151
130 Brentwood Dr Chester (96020) *(P-21740)*
Seneca Hospital Almanor Clinic, Chester *Also called Seneca Healthcare District (P-19876)*
Senegence International, Foothill Ranch *Also called Sgii Inc (P-8209)*
Senior Assisted Living Comm Ch, Pleasant Hill *Also called Carlton Senior Living (P-22256)*
Senior Care (PA)....A....562 989-5100
3800 Kilroy Airport Way Long Beach (90806) *(P-10309)*
Senior Care....D....562 492-9878
2501 Cherry Ave Ste 380 Long Beach (90755) *(P-10310)*
Senior Care Inc....C....619 928-5644
4960 Mills St La Mesa (91942) *(P-20954)*
Senior Care Inc....C....619 817-8855
3423 Channel Way San Diego (92110) *(P-20955)*
Senior Companions At Home....E....650 364-1265
650 El Camino Real Ste E Redwood City (94063) *(P-24044)*
Senior Helpers South Coast, Fountain Valley *Also called His Passion Inc (P-22320)*
Senior Keiro Health Care....D....323 263-9651
325 S Boyle Ave Los Angeles (90033) *(P-24670)*
Senior Living Solutions LLC....C....408 385-1835
1725 S Bascom Ave Apt 105 Campbell (95008) *(P-20956)*
SENIOR NUTRITION, Fort Bragg *Also called Redwood Coast Seniors Inc (P-23987)*
SENIOR NUTRITION PROGRAM, Los Angeles *Also called People Coordinated Services (P-24828)*
Senior Resource Group LLC....E....858 519-0890
850 Del Mar Downs Rd # 338 Solana Beach (92075) *(P-24671)*
Senior Services, Oxnard *Also called City of Oxnard (P-23584)*
Senomyx Inc....D....858 646-8300
4767 Nexus Center Dr San Diego (92121) *(P-26454)*
Sensity Systems Inc (HQ)....D....408 841-4200
1237 E Arques Ave Sunnyvale (94085) *(P-27858)*
Sentek Consulting Inc....C....619 543-9550
2811 Nimitz Blvd Ste G San Diego (92106) *(P-16481)*
Sentek Global, San Diego *Also called Sentek Consulting Inc (P-16481)*
Sentient Technologies USA LLC....E....415 422-9886
1 California St Ste 2300 San Francisco (94111) *(P-15436)*
Sentinel Acqstion Holdings Inc....A....310 201-4100
2000 Avenue Of The Stars Los Angeles (90067) *(P-15437)*
Sentinel Monitoring Corp (HQ)....C....949 453-1550
220 Technology Dr Ste 200 Irvine (92618) *(P-16940)*
Sentinel Offender Services LLC (PA)....D....949 453-1550
201 Technology Dr Irvine (92618) *(P-16941)*
Sepulveda Ambulatory Care, North Hills *Also called Veterans Health Administration (P-20075)*
Sequel Contractors Inc....E....562 802-7227
13546 Imperial Hwy Santa Fe Springs (90670) *(P-1847)*
Sequenom Inc (HQ)....D....858 202-9000
3595 John Hopkins Ct San Diego (92121) *(P-26455)*
Sequenom Center For Molecular....B....858 202-9051
3595 John Hopkins Ct San Diego (92121) *(P-22147)*
Sequenom Laboratories, San Diego *Also called Sequenom Center For Molecular (P-22147)*
Sequoia Adrc LP....D....650 364-5504
650 Main St Redwood City (94063) *(P-24045)*
Sequoia Alchol DRG Rcovery Ctr, Redwood City *Also called Sequoia Adrc LP (P-24045)*
Sequoia Beverage Company LP....C....559 651-2444
2122 N Plaza Dr Visalia (93291) *(P-9025)*
Sequoia Bnefits Insur Svcs LLC....D....650 369-0200
1850 Gateway Dr Ste 600 San Mateo (94404) *(P-27444)*

ALPHABETIC

Employee Codes: A=Over 500 employees, B=251-500
C=101-250, D=51-100, E=50
2019 Directory of California
Wholesalers and Services Companies
© Mergent Inc. 1-800-342-5647
1461

Sequoia Capital Operations LLC ....D......650 854-3927
  2800 Sand Hill Rd Ste 100 Menlo Park (94025) *(P-12266)*
Sequoia Concepts Inc ....D......818 409-6000
  28632 Roadside Dr Ste 110 Agoura Hills (91301) *(P-14023)*
Sequoia Enterprises Inc ....D......559 592-9455
  150 W Pine St Exeter (93221) *(P-8728)*
Sequoia Environmental Svcs Inc ....D......949 480-4742
  1 University Dr Aliso Viejo (92656) *(P-786)*
Sequoia Financial Services, Agoura Hills Also called Sequoia Concepts Inc *(P-14023)*
Sequoia Health Services (HQ) ....D......650 369-5811
  170 Alameda De Las Pulgas Redwood City (94062) *(P-21741)*
SEQUOIA HOSPITAL, Redwood City Also called Sequoia Health Services *(P-21741)*
Sequoia Insurance Company (HQ) ....D......831 655-9612
  31 Upper Ragsdale Dr Monterey (93940) *(P-10393)*
Sequoia Insurance Company ....D......916 933-9524
  P.O. Box 1510 Monterey (93942) *(P-10772)*
Sequoia Orange, Exeter Also called Sequoia Enterprises Inc *(P-8728)*
Sequoia Orange Co Inc (PA) ....D......559 592-9455
  150 W Pine St Exeter (93221) *(P-567)*
Sequoia Regional Cancer Center ....C......559 624-3000
  602 W Willow Ave Visalia (93291) *(P-22044)*
Sequoia Residential Funding ....D......415 389-7373
  1 Belvedere Pl Ste 330 Mill Valley (94941) *(P-9748)*
Sequoia Retail Systems Inc (HQ) ....D......650 237-9000
  660 W Dana St Mountain View (94041) *(P-15438)*
Sequoia Senior Solutions Inc ....D......707 263-3070
  825 S Main St Lakeport (95453) *(P-24046)*
Sequoia Senior Solutions Inc ....D......707 621-9235
  205 W Clay St Ukiah (95482) *(P-24047)*
Sequoia Surgical Center LP ....E......925 935-6700
  2405 Shadelands Dr # 200 Walnut Creek (94598) *(P-19877)*
Sequoia Surgical Pavilion, Walnut Creek Also called Sequoia Surgical Center LP *(P-19877)*
Sequoia Wood Country Club ....D......209 795-1000
  1000 Cypress Point Dr Arnold (95223) *(P-19040)*
Sequos-San Frncsco Residential, San Francisco Also called Northern California Presbyteri *(P-20664)*
Seracada ....E......626 486-0800
  709 E Lavender Way Azusa (91702) *(P-22414)*
Serco Inc ....C......858 569-8979
  9350 Waxie Way Ste 400 San Diego (92123) *(P-25908)*
Serec Entertainment LLC ....E......626 893-0600
  1671 N Rocky Rd Upland (91784) *(P-7601)*
Serene Ast LLC (HQ) ....D......408 986-8544
  3211 Scott Blvd Ste 201 Santa Clara (95054) *(P-16482)*
Serfin Funds Transfer (PA) ....D......626 457-3070
  1000 S Fremont Ave A-O Alhambra (91803) *(P-9689)*
Serimian M S D L Ranch ....E......559 896-1517
  10463 S Del Rey Ave Selma (93662) *(P-380)*
Serpico Landscaping Inc ....E......510 293-0341
  1764 National Ave Hayward (94545) *(P-936)*
Serra Community Med Clinic Inc ....C......818 768-3000
  9375 San Fernando Rd Sun Valley (91352) *(P-19878)*
Serra Medical Clinic Inc ....D......818 768-3000
  9375 San Fernando Rd Sun Valley (91352) *(P-19879)*
Serrania Charter Elementary, Woodland Hills Also called Pta CA Congress of Parents *(P-25219)*
Serrano Associates LLC ....D......916 939-3333
  5005 Serrano Pkwy El Dorado Hills (95762) *(P-19041)*
Serrano Country Club, El Dorado Hills Also called Serrano Associates LLC *(P-19041)*
Serrano Country Club Inc ....C......916 933-5005
  5005 Serrano Pkwy P El Dorado Hills (95762) *(P-19042)*
Serrano Covalescent Hospital ....D......323 465-2106
  5401 Fountain Ave Los Angeles (90029) *(P-20753)*
Serrano Electric Inc ....E......408 986-1570
  1705 Russell Ave Santa Clara (95054) *(P-2730)*
Serrano Hotel, San Francisco Also called Kimpton Hotel & Rest Group LLC *(P-12809)*
Serrato-Mcdermott Inc ....D......510 656-6233
  43815 S Grimmer Blvd Fremont (94538) *(P-6673)*
Servexo ....E......323 527-9994
  879 W 190th St Ste 400 Gardena (90248) *(P-16820)*
Servexo Protective Service, Gardena Also called Servexo *(P-16820)*
Servi-Tech Controls Inc (PA) ....D......559 264-6679
  2612 N Bus Park Ave # 101 Fresno (93727) *(P-2353)*
Servi-Tek Inc ....B......858 638-7735
  3970 Sorrento Valley Blvd San Diego (92121) *(P-14383)*
Servi-Tek Janitorial Services, San Diego Also called Servi-Tek Inc *(P-14383)*
Service 1st Electrical Svcs ....E......714 630-9699
  1092 N Armando St Anaheim (92806) *(P-2731)*
Service By Medallion ....B......650 625-1010
  411 Clyde Ave Mountain View (94043) *(P-14384)*
Service Champions, Pleasanton Also called On-Time AC & Htg Inc *(P-2296)*
Service Cleaning and Maint, Los Angeles Also called Service Parking Corporation *(P-17706)*
Service Container Company LLC ....D......858 391-7344
  1754 Carr Rd Ste 204 Calexico (92231) *(P-17466)*
Service Corp International ....D......949 644-2700
  3500 Pacific View Dr Corona Del Mar (92625) *(P-11759)*
Service Corp International ....D......760 754-6600
  1999 S El Camino Real Oceanside (92054) *(P-11951)*
Service Employee Intl Un, Los Angeles Also called Los Angles Cnty Employees Assn *(P-25069)*
Service Employees Intl Union, San Jose Also called Service Workers Local 715 *(P-25081)*
Service First Contractors ....E......714 573-2200
  2510 N Grand Ave Ste 110 Santa Ana (92705) *(P-1643)*
Service Genius Los Angeles Inc ....D......818 200-3379
  9761 Variel Ave Chatsworth (91311) *(P-2354)*
Service Hospitality LLC ....D......925 566-8820
  1050 Burnett Ave Concord (94520) *(P-13206)*
Service King Cllision Repr Ctr, Oakland Also called Service King Holdings LLC *(P-17738)*

Service King Cllision Repr Ctr, San Diego Also called Service King Holdings LLC *(P-17739)*
Service King Cllision Repr Ctr, Fountain Valley Also called Service King Holdings LLC *(P-17740)*
Service King Holdings LLC ....D......510 562-9650
  7801 Oakport St Oakland (94621) *(P-17738)*
Service King Holdings LLC ....D......619 219-3927
  4660 Alvarado Canyon Rd San Diego (92120) *(P-17739)*
Service King Holdings LLC ....D......714 962-2600
  18065 Euclid St Fountain Valley (92708) *(P-17740)*
Service King Paint & Body LLC ....C......925 301-8481
  6080 Dublin Blvd Dublin (94568) *(P-17741)*
Service Lathing Company ....E......510 483-9732
  1090 139th Ave San Leandro (94578) *(P-2956)*
Service Master Industries Inc ....D......760 480-0208
  2342 Meyers Ave Escondido (92029) *(P-17467)*
Service Parking Corporation ....D......323 851-2416
  3800 Barham Blvd Ste P1 Los Angeles (90068) *(P-17706)*
Service Quality, Concord Also called Customer Loyalty Builders Inc *(P-27209)*
Service Solutions Group LLC ....D......626 960-9390
  5367 2nd St Irwindale (91706) *(P-17912)*
Service Transport Inc ....D......951 403-3464
  29991 Cyn Hls Rd Ste 137 Lake Elsinore (92532) *(P-4372)*
Service Workers Local 715 (PA) ....D......408 678-3300
  2302 Zanker Rd San Jose (95131) *(P-25081)*
ServiceMaster, South San Francisco Also called Seafus Corporation *(P-14382)*
ServiceMaster, Merced Also called Mobley Enterprises Inc *(P-14325)*
ServiceMaster, Merced Also called Culver-Melin Enterprises *(P-14244)*
ServiceMaster, Santa Maria Also called Skylstad-Schoelen Co Inc *(P-14393)*
ServiceMaster, Stockton Also called Wtmg Inc *(P-14428)*
ServiceMaster Company LLC ....D......760 298-7001
  1003 Hi Point St Los Angeles (90035) *(P-14385)*
ServiceMaster Company LLC ....C......714 245-1465
  216 N Clara St Santa Ana (92703) *(P-14386)*
Servicemax Inc (HQ) ....D......925 965-7859
  4450 Rosewood Dr Ste 200 Pleasanton (94588) *(P-15439)*
Servicmster Clean By Integrity, Oxnard Also called Pacific Building Maint Inc *(P-14337)*
Servicmster Cmplete Rstoration, Escondido Also called Sbrm Inc *(P-14379)*
Servico Building Maint Co ....D......707 935-1224
  13732b Carmel Ave Glen Ellen (95442) *(P-14387)*
Servicon Systems Inc ....A......310 970-0700
  3329 Jack Northrop Ave Hawthorne (90250) *(P-3324)*
Servicon Systems Inc (PA) ....A......310 204-5040
  3965 Landmark St Culver City (90232) *(P-27604)*
Serving Seniors (PA) ....D......619 235-6572
  525 14th St Ste 200 San Diego (92101) *(P-24048)*
Serving Seniors LLC ....D......916 372-9640
  2764 Rogue River Cir West Sacramento (95691) *(P-22415)*
Serviz Inc ....D......818 381-4826
  15303 Ventura Blvd # 1600 Sherman Oaks (91403) *(P-13773)*
SERVPRO Encino/Sherman Oaks, Encino Also called One Silver Serve Inc *(P-27602)*
SERVPRO of Mendocino ....E......707 462-3848
  3001 S State St Ste 5 Ukiah (95482) *(P-14388)*
SES, San Diego Also called Superior Envmtl Svcs Inc *(P-14404)*
Ses LLC ....A......949 727-3200
  26561 Rancho Pkwy S Lake Forest (92630) *(P-15440)*
Sesloc Federal Credit Union (PA) ....C......805 543-1816
  3855 Broad St San Luis Obispo (93401) *(P-9592)*
Set A Head Start Westside, Sacramento Also called Sacramento Employement & Train *(P-24224)*
Set Free Services Inc ....D......530 243-3373
  3300 Veda St Redding (96001) *(P-27445)*
Seta, Sacramento Also called Sacramento Employement & Train *(P-24225)*
Sethi Management Inc ....C......760 692-5288
  6100 Innovation Way Carlsbad (92009) *(P-27026)*
Sethi Management Inc ....D......760 652-4010
  183 Calle Magdalena # 101 Encinitas (92024) *(P-13207)*
Seti Institute ....C......650 961-6633
  189 Bernardo Ave 100 Mountain View (94043) *(P-26660)*
Seti Institute, The, Mountain View Also called Seti Institute *(P-26660)*
Seton Medical Center (HQ) ....A......650 992-4000
  1900 Sullivan Ave Daly City (94015) *(P-21742)*
Seton Medical Center ....C......650 563-7100
  600 Marine Blvd Moss Beach (94038) *(P-21743)*
Seton Medical Center ....D......650 992-4000
  1784 Sullivan Ave Ste 200 Daly City (94015) *(P-21744)*
Seton Medical Center Coastside, Moss Beach Also called Seton Medical Center *(P-21743)*
Setton Pstchio Terra Bella Inc (HQ) ....D......559 535-6050
  9370 Road 234 Terra Bella (93270) *(P-8866)*
Seven Hospitality, Irvine Also called State Group LLC *(P-27468)*
Seven Lakes Hm Assn Cntry CLB ....E......760 328-2695
  1 Desert Lakes Dr Palm Springs (92264) *(P-19043)*
Seven Licensing Company LLC ....D......323 881-0308
  801 S Figueroa St # 2500 Los Angeles (90017) *(P-8334)*
Seven Oaks Country Club ....C......661 664-6404
  2000 Grand Lakes Ave Bakersfield (93311) *(P-19044)*
Seven One Inc (PA) ....D......818 904-3435
  21540 Prairie St Ste E Chatsworth (91311) *(P-17468)*
Seven Resorts Inc (PA) ....B......949 588-7100
  9771 Irvine Center Dr Irvine (92618) *(P-13208)*
Seven Seas Associates LLC ....C......619 291-1300
  411 Hotel Cir S San Diego (92108) *(P-13209)*
Seven Seas Best Western, San Diego Also called Seven Seas Associates LLC *(P-13209)*
Seven7 Brands, Los Angeles Also called Seven Licensing Company LLC *(P-8334)*
Severson & Werson A Prof Corp ....D......415 398-3344
  1 Embarcadero Ctr Fl 26 San Francisco (94111) *(P-23371)*
Severson Group Incorporated (PA) ....D......562 493-3611
  3601 Serpentine Dr Los Alamitos (90720) *(P-1644)*

Seville Construction Svcs Inc ....D....626 204-0800
199 S Hudson Ave Pasadena (91101) ***(P-27446)***
Seville Group (PA) ....D....626 395-7474
199 S Hudson Ave Ste 101 Pasadena (91101) ***(P-27027)***
Sexy Hair Concepts ....D....800 848-3383
9232 Eton Ave Chatsworth (91311) ***(P-8242)***
Seyfarth Shaw LLP ....C....213 270-9600
333 S Hope St Ste 3900 Los Angeles (90071) ***(P-23372)***
Seyfarth Shaw LLP ....C....310 277-7200
2029 Century Park E # 3400 Los Angeles (90067) ***(P-23373)***
Seyfarth Shaw LLP ....D....415 397-2823
560 Mission St Fl 31 San Francisco (94105) ***(P-23374)***
Seymour Gale & Associates ....E....213 622-5361
4501 Cedros Ave Unit 118 Sherman Oaks (91403) ***(P-8335)***
Sezzo Labs Inc ....E....408 562-0081
313 Adeline Ave San Jose (95136) ***(P-16051)***
SF-MARIN FOOD BANK, San Francisco *Also called San Francisco Food Bank* ***(P-24020)***
Sf-Potrero Hill, San Francisco *Also called Citibank National Association* ***(P-9332)***
Sfadia Inc ....D....323 622-1930
10011 Pioneer Blvd Santa Fe Springs (90670) ***(P-2732)***
SFCU, Palo Alto *Also called Stanford Federal Credit Union* ***(P-9595)***
Sfd Partners LLC ....B....415 392-7755
450 Powell St San Francisco (94102) ***(P-13210)***
SFF, Sacramento *Also called Sierra Forever Families* ***(P-24050)***
Sfi 2365 Iron Point LLC ....E....415 395-9701
260 California St # 1100 San Francisco (94111) ***(P-10935)***
Sfi Carlsbad LLC ....E....415 395-9701
260 California St # 1100 San Francisco (94111) ***(P-10936)***
Sfmc, Lynwood *Also called St Francis Medical Center* ***(P-19936)***
Sfmoma Museum Store, San Francisco *Also called San Francisco Museum Modrn Art* ***(P-24907)***
Sfn Group Inc ....D....949 727-8500
114 Pacifica Ste 210 Irvine (92618) ***(P-14912)***
Sfn Group Inc ....C....530 222-3434
3050 Bictor Ave Ste A Redding (96002) ***(P-14913)***
Sfo Airporter Inc (PA) ....D....650 246-2734
160 S Linden Ave Ste 300 South San Francisco (94080) ***(P-3724)***
Sfo Airporter Inc ....D....415 495-3909
325 5th St San Francisco (94107) ***(P-3725)***
Sfo Shuttle Bus Company, Stanford *Also called Imperial Parking (us) LLC* ***(P-17686)***
Sfo Shuttle Bus Company, Oakland *Also called Imperial Parking (us) LLC* ***(P-17687)***
Sfo Shuttle Bus Inc ....C....650 877-0430
San Francisco Intl Arprt San Francisco (94128) ***(P-3726)***
Sfo-3 - San Francisco Full Svc, Brisbane *Also called Expeditors Intl Wash Inc* ***(P-5055)***
Sfpp LP (HQ) ....C....714 560-4400
1100 W Town And Country R Orange (92868) ***(P-4925)***
Sft Realty Galway Downs LLC ....D....951 232-1880
38801 Los Porralitos Temecula (92592) ***(P-11760)***
Sfusd Building Ground ....D....415 695-5508
834 Toland St San Francisco (94124) ***(P-14389)***
Sfusd Jrotc Brigade ....D....415 242-2546
2162 24th Ave San Francisco (94116) ***(P-15441)***
Sg Personnel LLC ....B....831 444-0523
420 Espinosa Rd Salinas (93907) ***(P-299)***
Sg Personnel LLC ....D....209 369-3018
5400 E Harney Ln Lodi (95240) ***(P-300)***
SGF Produce Holding Corp ....B....714 630-6292
701 W Kimberly Ave # 210 Placentia (92870) ***(P-8729)***
Sgii Inc ....C....949 521-6161
19651 Alter Foothill Ranch (92610) ***(P-8209)***
Sgokc, Beale Afb *Also called US Dept of the Air Force* ***(P-20038)***
SGS North America Inc ....D....408 588-0200
1759 S Main St Ste 116 Milpitas (95035) ***(P-26730)***
Shade Structures Inc ....B....714 427-6981
1085 N Main St Ste C Orange (92867) ***(P-3584)***
Shadkor Inc ....D....818 953-4627
4021 W Alameda Ave Burbank (91505) ***(P-13569)***
Shadow Animation LLC ....E....323 466-7771
940 N Mansfield Ave Los Angeles (90038) ***(P-18116)***
Shadow Hlls Cnvlscent Hosp Inc ....D....818 352-4438
10158 Sunland Blvd Sunland (91040) ***(P-20754)***
Shadow Mnt Rsort/Rcqut CL Tns, Palm Desert *Also called Destination Residences LLC* ***(P-12518)***
Shadowbrook Health Care Inc ....E....530 534-1353
1 Gilmore Ln Oroville (95966) ***(P-20755)***
Shady Canyon Golf Club Inc ....C....949 856-7000
100 Shady Canyon Dr Irvine (92603) ***(P-19045)***
Shaker Express, San Diego *Also called California Air Cartage Inc* ***(P-4777)***
Shalev Senior Living ....E....818 780-4808
6245 Matilija Ave Van Nuys (91401) ***(P-24672)***
Shamrock Center, Burbank *Also called Shamrock Plus Inc* ***(P-10013)***
Shamrock Companies, The, Anaheim *Also called Shamrock Supply Company Inc* ***(P-7602)***
Shamrock Plus Inc ....E....818 845-4444
4444 W Lakeside Dr Lbby Burbank (91505) ***(P-10013)***
Shamrock Supply Company Inc (PA) ....D....714 575-1800
3366 E La Palma Ave Anaheim (92806) ***(P-7602)***
Shamrock-Hostmark Palm Desrt ....D....760 340-6600
74700 Highway 111 Palm Desert (92260) ***(P-13211)***
Shannon Ranches Inc ....C....707 998-9656
12601 E Highway 20 Clearlake Oaks (95423) ***(P-27447)***
Shapell Inc ....D....925 735-4253
9000 S Gale Ridge Rd San Ramon (94582) ***(P-18761)***
Shapell Industries LLC (HQ) ....D....323 655-7330
8383 Wilshire Blvd # 700 Beverly Hills (90211) ***(P-11915)***
Shapell Industries LLC ....E....818 366-1132
11280 Corbin Ave Northridge (91326) ***(P-1233)***
Shapell's Home Center, Northridge *Also called Shapell Industries LLC* ***(P-1233)***
Shapiro Ben Basat Painting, Van Nuys *Also called C B B Z S Inc* ***(P-2426)***
Shapiro-Gilman-Shandler Co (PA) ....C....213 593-1200
739 Decatur St Los Angeles (90021) ***(P-8730)***
Shapp International Trdg Inc ....C....818 348-3000
6000 Reseda Blvd Tarzana (91356) ***(P-6863)***
Shapp Internatioonal, Tarzana *Also called Shapp International Trdg Inc* ***(P-6863)***
Shared Services, Torrance *Also called Securitas SEC Svcs USA Inc* ***(P-16810)***
Sharedata Inc ....D....408 490-2500
2465 Augustine Dr Santa Clara (95054) ***(P-15850)***
Sharedta/E Trade Bus Solutions, Santa Clara *Also called Sharedata Inc* ***(P-15850)***
Sharespost Inc ....D....800 279-7754
555 Montgomery St San Francisco (94111) ***(P-12005)***
Sharethis Inc (PA) ....E....650 641-0191
4005 Miranda Ave Ste 100 Palo Alto (94304) ***(P-13902)***
Sharf Woodward & Associates ....D....818 989-2200
5900 Sepulvda Blvd # 104 Van Nuys (91411) ***(P-14759)***
Shark's Ice, San Jose *Also called Logitech Ice At San Jose* ***(P-19198)***
Sharks Sports & Entrmt LLC ....A....408 287-7070
525 W Santa Clara St San Jose (95113) ***(P-18535)***
Sharon Care Center LLC ....C....323 655-2023
8167 W 3rd St Los Angeles (90048) ***(P-20756)***
Sharp Chula Vista Medical Ctr, Chula Vista *Also called Sharp Chula Vista Medical Ctr* ***(P-21745)***
Sharp Chula Vista Medical Ctr ....A....619 502-5800
751 Medical Center Ct Chula Vista (91911) ***(P-21745)***
Sharp Chula Vista Medical Ctr ....D....858 499-5150
8695 Spectrum Center Blvd San Diego (92123) ***(P-21746)***
Sharp Community Medical Group ....C....858 499-4525
8695 Spectrum Center Blvd San Diego (92123) ***(P-25041)***
Sharp Guard Services Inc ....A....213 739-1900
3450 Wilshire Blvd # 1000 Los Angeles (90010) ***(P-16821)***
Sharp Health Care, San Diego *Also called Sharp Healthcare* ***(P-21749)***
Sharp Health Plan ....D....858 499-8300
8520 Tech Way Ste 200 San Diego (92123) ***(P-10311)***
Sharp Healthcare ....C....619 398-2988
7910 Frost St Ste 280 San Diego (92123) ***(P-19880)***
Sharp Healthcare ....D....619 284-1400
3575 Euclid Ave San Diego (92105) ***(P-19881)***
Sharp Healthcare ....D....858 939-5434
8008 Frost St Ste 106 San Diego (92123) ***(P-21747)***
Sharp Healthcare ....D....619 442-0844
225 W Madison Ave Ste 1 El Cajon (92020) ***(P-19882)***
Sharp Healthcare (PA) ....A....858 499-4000
8695 Spectrum Center Blvd San Diego (92123) ***(P-21748)***
Sharp Healthcare ....C....619 446-1575
300 Fir St San Diego (92101) ***(P-19883)***
Sharp Healthcare ....D....858 653-6100
8901 Activity Rd San Diego (92126) ***(P-19884)***
Sharp Healthcare ....C....858 627-5152
3554 Ruffin Rd Ste Soca San Diego (92123) ***(P-21749)***
Sharp Healthcare ....D....760 806-5600
130 Cedar Rd Vista (92083) ***(P-21750)***
Sharp Healthcare ....D....858 541-4850
8080 Dagget St Ste 200 San Diego (92111) ***(P-22416)***
Sharp Healthcare ....C....858 499-2000
751 Medical Center Ct Chula Vista (91911) ***(P-20757)***
Sharp Healthcare ....D....858 616-8411
2020 Genesee Ave Fl 2 San Diego (92123) ***(P-19885)***
Sharp Healthcare ....D....858 621-4010
10670 Wexford St San Diego (92131) ***(P-21751)***
Sharp Healthcare ....D....800 827-4277
4510 Viewridge Ave San Diego (92123) ***(P-19886)***
Sharp Healthcare ....D....619 460-6200
8860 Center Dr Ste 450 La Mesa (91942) ***(P-19887)***
Sharp Healthcare ....D....858 616-8200
2020 Genesee Ave San Diego (92123) ***(P-19888)***
Sharp Home Care, San Diego *Also called Sharp Healthcare* ***(P-22416)***
Sharp Mary Birch H ....D....858 939-3400
3003 Health Center Dr San Diego (92123) ***(P-21752)***
Sharp McDonald Center ....A....858 637-6920
7989 Linda Vista Rd San Diego (92111) ***(P-22045)***
Sharp Memorial Hospital (HQ) ....A....858 939-3636
7901 Frost St San Diego (92123) ***(P-21753)***
Sharp Memorial Hospital ....C....858 278-4110
7850 Vista Hill Ave San Diego (92123) ***(P-21972)***
Sharp Mesa Vista Hospital, San Diego *Also called Sharp Memorial Hospital* ***(P-21972)***
Sharp Mission Park Medical Ctr, Vista *Also called Sharp Healthcare* ***(P-21750)***
Sharp Reece Stealy Med Group, San Diego *Also called Sharp Healthcare* ***(P-19886)***
Sharp Rees-Stealy, San Diego *Also called Sharp Healthcare* ***(P-21747)***
Sharp Rees-Stealy Div, San Diego *Also called Sharp Healthcare* ***(P-19883)***
SHARP REES-STEALY PHARMACY, San Diego *Also called Sharp Memorial Hospital* ***(P-21753)***
Sharp Rees-Stealy Pharmacy, San Diego *Also called Sharp Healthcare* ***(P-21748)***
Sharper Future ....D....415 297-6767
870 Market St Ste 1265 San Francisco (94102) ***(P-19889)***
Shartsis Friese LLP ....C....415 421-6500
1 Maritime Plz Fl 18 San Francisco (94111) ***(P-23375)***
Shason Inc (PA) ....D....323 269-6666
4940 Triggs St Ste B Commerce (90022) ***(P-8243)***
Shasta Blood Center, San Francisco *Also called Blood Centers of Pacific* ***(P-22748)***
Shasta Cattle Women, Cottonwood *Also called County of Shasta* ***(P-25143)***
Shasta Convalescent Center ....C....530 222-3630
3550 Churn Creek Rd Redding (96002) ***(P-21206)***
Shasta Convalescent Hospital, Redding *Also called Shasta Convalescent Center* ***(P-21206)***
Shasta County Calworks, Redding *Also called County of Shasta* ***(P-10484)***
Shasta County Head Start Child (PA) ....E....530 241-1036
375 Lake Blvd Ste 100 Redding (96003) ***(P-24380)***

ALPHABETIC

Employee Codes: A=Over 500 employees, B=251-500
C=101-250, D=51-100, E=50
2019 Directory of California
Wholesalers and Services Companies
© Mergent Inc. 1-800-342-5647
1463

Shasta Lake Resorts LP.......D.......209 785-3300
22300 Jones Vly Marina Dr Redding (96003) ***(P-19236)***
Shasta Landscaping Inc.......D.......760 744-6551
1340 Descanso Ave San Marcos (92069) ***(P-937)***
Shasta Livestock Auction Yard.......D.......530 347-3793
3917 Main St Cottonwood (96022) ***(P-8907)***
Shasta Produce Co, South San Francisco *Also called Andrighetto Produce Inc* ***(P-3487)***
Shasta Regional Med Ctr Srmc, Redding *Also called Prime Healthcare Services* ***(P-21658)***
Shasta-Trinity Ranger Unit, Redding *Also called Forestry and Fire Protection* ***(P-998)***
Shattuck Health Care Inc.......D.......510 665-2800
2829 Shattuck Ave Berkeley (94705) ***(P-20758)***
Shaw & Petersen Insurance Inc.......E.......707 443-0845
1313 5th St Eureka (95501) ***(P-10773)***
Shaw Bakers LLC.......D.......650 273-1440
320b Shaw Rd Ste B South San Francisco (94080) ***(P-8867)***
Shaw Construction, Fresno *Also called Shaws Strctures Unlimited Inc* ***(P-1432)***
Shaw Hospitality Group Inc.......D.......559 224-4040
324 E Shaw Ave Fresno (93710) ***(P-13212)***
Shawmut Design and Cnstr, Los Angeles *Also called Shawmut Woodworking & Sup Inc* ***(P-1645)***
Shawmut Woodworking & Sup Inc.......C.......323 602-1000
11390 W Olympic Blvd Fl 2 Los Angeles (90064) ***(P-1645)***
Shawnan, Downey *Also called Sialic Contractors Corporation* ***(P-1849)***
Shaws Strctures Unlimited Inc.......E.......559 275-3475
2573 W Cambridge Ave Fresno (93705) ***(P-1432)***
Shc Burbank II LLC.......C.......818 843-6000
2500 N Hollywood Way Burbank (91505) ***(P-13213)***
Shc Reference Laboratory, Palo Alto *Also called Stanford Health Care* ***(P-21793)***
SHe Manages Properties Inc (PA).......D.......619 291-6300
9340 Hazard Way Ste B2 San Diego (92123) ***(P-11761)***
Shea Convalescent Hospital, Whittier *Also called Longwood Management Corp* ***(P-21568)***
Shea Family Care Somerset, El Cajon *Also called Somerset Special Care Center* ***(P-20961)***
Shea Homes, Irvine *Also called JF Shea Construction Inc* ***(P-1182)***
SHEA HOMES, Rio Vista *Also called Trilogy Rio Vista* ***(P-1447)***
Shea Homes, San Jose *Also called JF Shea Construction Inc* ***(P-1184)***
Shea Homes, Livermore *Also called JF Shea Construction Inc* ***(P-1185)***
Shea Homes Arizona Ltd Partnr.......D.......909 594-9500
655 Brea Canyon Rd Walnut (91789) ***(P-11762)***
Shea Homes At Montage LLC.......D.......909 594-9500
655 Brea Canyon Rd Walnut (91789) ***(P-1234)***
Shea Homes Lmtd Partnership A (HQ).......E.......909 594-9500
655 Brea Canyon Rd Walnut (91789) ***(P-1235)***
Shea Homes Ltd Prtnershp, Walnut *Also called Vistancia Marketing LLC* ***(P-27517)***
Shea Homes Vantis LLC.......D.......909 594-9500
655 Brea Canyon Rd Walnut (91789) ***(P-1315)***
Shea Labagh Dobberstein Cpa (PA).......E.......415 731-0100
44 Montgomery St Ste 3200 San Francisco (94104) ***(P-26290)***
Shea Properties MGT Co Inc.......B.......949 389-7000
130 Vantis Dr Ste 200 Aliso Viejo (92656) ***(P-11763)***
Shed Media US Inc.......D.......323 904-4680
3800 Barham Blvd Ste 410 Los Angeles (90068) ***(P-13955)***
Sheedy Drayage Co (PA).......D.......415 648-7171
1215 Michigan St San Francisco (94107) ***(P-14458)***
Sheehan Construction Inc.......B.......707 603-2610
477 Devlin Rd Ste 108 NAPA (94558) ***(P-1236)***
Shekinah Inc.......E.......714 475-5460
7755 Center Ave Ste 1000 Huntington Beach (92647) ***(P-23376)***
Sheldon Mechanical Corporation.......D.......661 286-1361
26015 Avenue Hall Santa Clarita (91355) ***(P-2355)***
Sheldon Ranches.......D.......559 562-3978
25140 Burr Dr Lindsay (93247) ***(P-381)***
Shell Vacations LLC.......D.......415 441-7100
501 Post St San Francisco (94102) ***(P-27028)***
Shelter Inc (PA).......D.......925 335-0698
1333 Willow Pass Rd # 206 Concord (94520) ***(P-24049)***
Shelter Point Hotel & Marina, San Diego *Also called Pacifica Hotel Company* ***(P-13008)***
Shelter Pointe Hotel & Marina, San Diego *Also called Shelter Pointe LLC* ***(P-4751)***
Shelter Pointe LLC.......C.......619 221-8000
1551 Shelter Island Dr San Diego (92106) ***(P-4751)***
Shelton Construction Company.......D.......714 903-7853
5628 Spinnaker Bay Dr Long Beach (90803) ***(P-1848)***
Shen Zhen New World II LLC.......D.......818 980-1212
333 Universal Hollywood Dr Universal City (91608) ***(P-13214)***
Shenyang Zhong Yi Tin-Plating.......C.......415 788-2280
843 Clay St San Francisco (94108) ***(P-10937)***
Shepard Eye Center.......E.......805 925-2637
1418 E Main St Ste 110 Santa Maria (93454) ***(P-19890)***
Sheplace Design Center, San Francisco *Also called Bay West Shwplace Invstors LLC* ***(P-10856)***
Sheppard Mullin Richter (PA).......B.......213 620-1780
333 S Hope St Fl 43 Los Angeles (90071) ***(P-23377)***
Sheppard Mullin Richter.......D.......619 338-6500
12275 El Camino R Ste 200 San Diego (92130) ***(P-23378)***
Sheppard Mullin Richter.......D.......415 434-9100
4 Embarcadero Ctr # 1700 San Francisco (94111) ***(P-23379)***
Sheppard Mullin Richter.......D.......310 228-3700
1901 Avenue Of The Stars # 1600 Los Angeles (90067) ***(P-23380)***
Sheppard Mullin Richter.......D.......714 513-5100
650 Town Center Dr Fl 4 Costa Mesa (92626) ***(P-23381)***
Sheppard Mullin, Los Angeles *Also called Sheppard Mullin Richter* ***(P-23377)***
Sheraton, San Francisco *Also called Interstate Hotels Resorts Inc* ***(P-12775)***
Sheraton, Santa Monica *Also called M&C Hotel Interests Inc* ***(P-12866)***
Sheraton, Los Angeles *Also called Hazens Investment LLC* ***(P-12650)***
Sheraton, Emeryville *Also called Pacific Hotel Management LLC* ***(P-12999)***
Sheraton, San Diego *Also called Dimension Development Two LLC* ***(P-12524)***
Sheraton, Pasadena *Also called Dallas Union Hotel Inc* ***(P-12157)***
Sheraton, San Diego *Also called Hst Lessee Boston LLC* ***(P-12739)***
Sheraton, San Diego *Also called 8110 Aero Holding LLC* ***(P-12300)***
Sheraton, La Jolla *Also called Bartell Hotels* ***(P-12357)***
Sheraton, Palo Alto *Also called Pacific Hotel Management LLC* ***(P-13001)***
Sheraton Carlsbad Resort & Spa, Carlsbad *Also called Grand Pacific Carlsbad Ht LP* ***(P-12613)***
Sheraton Corporation.......B.......415 362-5500
2500 Mason St San Francisco (94133) ***(P-13215)***
Sheraton Corporation.......B.......310 642-1111
6101 W Century Blvd Los Angeles (90045) ***(P-13216)***
Sheraton Corporation.......B.......916 447-1700
1230 J St 13th Sacramento (95814) ***(P-13217)***
Sheraton Corporation.......B.......909 204-6100
11960 Foothill Blvd Rancho Cucamonga (91739) ***(P-13218)***
Sheraton Corporation.......B.......925 463-3330
5990 Stoneridge Mall Rd Pleasanton (94588) ***(P-13219)***
Sheraton Downtown Los Angeles, Los Angeles *Also called Nrea-TRC 711 LLC* ***(P-12965)***
Sheraton Grand Sacramento Ht, Sacramento *Also called Sheraton Corporation* ***(P-13217)***
Sheraton Gtwy Los Angeles Ht, Los Angeles *Also called Sheraton Corporation* ***(P-13216)***
Sheraton Hotel San Jose, Milpitas *Also called Cni Thl Ops LLC* ***(P-12472)***
Sheraton Hotel Sunnyvale, Sunnyvale *Also called Sunnyvale Sof-X Owner L P* ***(P-13288)***
Sheraton Hotel Sunnyvale, Sunnyvale *Also called W2005 New Cntury Ht Prtflio LP* ***(P-13375)***
Sheraton Htl San Diego Msn Vly.......D.......619 321-4602
1433 Camino Del Rio S San Diego (92108) ***(P-13220)***
Sheraton Ontario Airport Hotel, Los Angeles *Also called S W K Properties LLC* ***(P-27020)***
Sheraton Palo Alto, Palo Alto *Also called Pacific Hotel Dev Ventr LP* ***(P-12998)***
Sheraton Pasadena, Pasadena *Also called Pasadena Hotel Dev Ventr LP* ***(P-13047)***
Sheraton Pk Ht At Anheim Rsort, Anaheim *Also called Anaheim Hotel LLC* ***(P-12321)***
Sheraton San Diego Ht & Marina, San Diego *Also called Hst Lessee San Diego LP* ***(P-12740)***
Sheraton San Diego Ht & Marina, San Diego *Also called Host Hotels & Resorts LP* ***(P-12707)***
Sheraton San Diego Mission Vly, San Diego *Also called Sheraton Htl San Diego Msn Vly* ***(P-13220)***
Sheraton Sn Diego Htl Msn Vly, San Diego *Also called Ashford Trs Nickel LLC* ***(P-26767)***
Sheraton Sonoma Cnty Petaluma, Petaluma *Also called Sonoma Hotel Partners LP* ***(P-13247)***
Sheraton Suites San Diego, San Diego *Also called Noiro West LLC* ***(P-12961)***
Sheraton Universal Hotel, Universal City *Also called Shen Zhen New World II LLC* ***(P-13214)***
Sheraton Universal Hotel, North Hollywood *Also called SLC Operating Ltd Partnership* ***(P-13775)***
Sheraton Universal Hotel, Universal City *Also called Lh Universal Operating LLC* ***(P-12849)***
Sheriff's Dept, Elk Grove *Also called County of Sacramento* ***(P-27588)***
Sheriff's Dept, San Francisco *Also called City & County of San Francisco* ***(P-23574)***
Sheriffs Offices.......D.......760 878-0383
550 S Clay St Independence (93526) ***(P-23382)***
Sherman Oaks Health System.......D.......818 981-7111
4929 Van Nuys Blvd Sherman Oaks (91403) ***(P-21754)***
Sherman Oaks Hospital, Sherman Oaks *Also called Prime Healthcare Svcs II LLC* ***(P-21660)***
Sherman Security.......C.......909 941-4167
7218 Hermosa Ave Rancho Cucamonga (91701) ***(P-16822)***
Sherman Village Hlth Care Ctr, North Hollywood *Also called Hillsdale Group LP* ***(P-21112)***
Sherman Village Hlth Care Ctr, North Hollywood *Also called Coldwater Care Center LLC* ***(P-20319)***
Shermn-Lehr Cstm Tile Wrks Inc.......D.......916 386-0417
5691 Power Inn Rd Ste A Sacramento (95824) ***(P-3010)***
Sherpaul Corporation.......D.......760 639-6472
901 Hacienda Dr Ste B Vista (92081) ***(P-22417)***
Sherton Grdn Grove Anheim S Ht.......D.......714 703-8400
12221 Harbor Blvd Garden Grove (92840) ***(P-13221)***
Sherwood Country Club.......C.......805 496-3036
320 W Stafford Rd Thousand Oaks (91361) ***(P-19046)***
Sherwood Development Company (PA).......E.......805 496-1833
2300 Norfield Ct Thousand Oaks (91361) ***(P-11916)***
Sherwood Guest Home, Lynwood *Also called Marlinda Management Inc* ***(P-21152)***
Sherwood Healthcare Center, Sacramento *Also called H C C S Inc* ***(P-20501)***
Sherwood Mechanical Inc.......D.......858 679-3000
6630 Top Gun St San Diego (92121) ***(P-2356)***
Sherwood Oaks Enterprises.......D.......707 964-6333
130 Dana St Fort Bragg (95437) ***(P-20759)***
Sherwood Oaks Health Center, Fort Bragg *Also called Sherwood Oaks Enterprises* ***(P-20759)***
Sherwood Valley Rancheria.......D.......707 459-7330
100 Kawi Pl Willits (95490) ***(P-13222)***
Sherwood Vllley Rnchria Casino, Willits *Also called Sherwood Valley Rancheria* ***(P-13222)***
Shibui Apartments, Torrance *Also called Hunt Enterprises Inc* ***(P-11506)***
Shield Security Inc (HQ).......B.......714 210-1501
1551 N Tustin Ave Ste 650 Santa Ana (92705) ***(P-16823)***
Shield Security Inc.......C.......818 239-5800
21110 Vanowen St Canoga Park (91303) ***(P-16824)***
Shield Security Inc.......B.......562 283-1100
150 E Wardlow Rd Long Beach (90807) ***(P-16825)***
Shield Security Inc.......B.......909 920-1173
265 N Euclid Ave Upland (91786) ***(P-16826)***
Shields For Families (PA).......D.......323 242-5000
11601 S Western Ave Los Angeles (90047) ***(P-22046)***
Shields Nursing Centers Inc (PA).......C.......510 724-9911
606 Alfred Nobel Dr Hercules (94547) ***(P-20760)***
Shields Nursing Centers Inc.......D.......510 525-3212
3230 Carlson Blvd El Cerrito (94530) ***(P-20761)***
Shieldx Networks Inc.......E.......760 724-2700
4093 Oceanside Blvd Ste A Oceanside (92056) ***(P-15442)***

Mergent e-mail: customerrelations@mergent.com
1464
2019 Directory of California
Wholesalers and Services Companies
(P-0000) Products & Services Section entry number
(PA)=Parent Co (HQ)=Headquarters (DH)=Div Headquarters

Shift Technologies Inc...D...415 800-2038
2500 Market St San Francisco (94114) ***(P-6607)***
Shiftpixy Inc...E...949 207-7184
1 Venture Ste 150 Irvine (92618) ***(P-15443)***
Shih Yu-Lang Central YMCA, San Francisco *Also called Young Mens Christian Assoc SF* ***(P-25327)***
Shii LLC...E...909 354-8000
2151 E Cnvntn Ctr Way # 222 Ontario (91764) ***(P-11764)***
Shilpark Paint Automotive, Los Angeles *Also called Shilpark Paint Corporation* ***(P-9189)***
Shilpark Paint Corporation (PA)...D...323 732-7093
1640 S Vermont Ave Los Angeles (90006) ***(P-9189)***
Shimadzu Medical Systems USA, Long Beach *Also called Shimadzu Precision Instrs Inc* ***(P-7914)***
Shimadzu Precision Instrs Inc (HQ)...D...562 420-6226
3645 N Lakewood Blvd Long Beach (90808) ***(P-7914)***
Shimadzu Precision Instrs Inc...D...310 217-8855
20101 S Vermont Ave Torrance (90502) ***(P-7217)***
Shimano North Amer Holdg Inc (HQ)...C...949 951-5003
1 Holland Irvine (92618) ***(P-7938)***
Shimmick Construction Co Inc (HQ)...C...510 777-5000
8201 Edgewater Dr Ste 202 Oakland (94621) ***(P-2061)***
Shims Bargain Inc (PA)...D...323 881-0099
2600 S Soto St Vernon (90058) ***(P-9258)***
Shims Bargain Inc...C...323 726-8800
7030 E Slauson Ave Commerce (90040) ***(P-1433)***
Shine and Bright Hand Car Wash, Culver City *Also called Hlw Corp* ***(P-17817)***
Shingle Sprng Trbal Gming Auth...A...530 677-7000
1 Red Hawk Pkwy Placerville (95667) ***(P-19237)***
Shinsuke Clifford Yamamoto...D...714 992-5783
2031 Emery Ave La Habra (90631) ***(P-938)***
Shinwoo P&C Usa Inc...A...619 407-7164
2177 Britannia Blvd # 203 San Diego (92154) ***(P-17469)***
Shipbycom LLC...D...626 271-9800
218 Machlin Ct Walnut (91789) ***(P-4061)***
Shipco Transport Inc...D...562 295-2900
100 W Victoria St Long Beach (90805) ***(P-5167)***
Shipito, Hawthorne *Also called Eastbiz Corporation* ***(P-19165)***
Shiva-Shakthi, San Diego *Also called Marika Group Inc* ***(P-8319)***
Shlemmer and Algaze Associates, Irvine *Also called Shlemmer+algaze+associ* ***(P-25909)***
Shlemmer+algaze+associ (PA)...D...949 724-8958
18201 Von Karman Ave # 120 Irvine (92612) ***(P-25909)***
Shn Cnslting Engnrs-Geologists, Eureka *Also called Shn Consulting Engin* ***(P-25910)***
Shn Consulting Engin (PA)...D...707 441-8855
812 W Wabash Ave Eureka (95501) ***(P-25910)***
Sho-Air International Inc (PA)...E...949 476-9111
5401 Argosy Ave Ste 102 Huntington Beach (92649) ***(P-5168)***
Shoei Foods USA Inc...D...530 742-7866
1900 Feather River Blvd Olivehurst (95961) ***(P-8452)***
Shook & Waller Cnstr Inc...D...707 578-3933
7677 Bell Rd Ste 101 Windsor (95492) ***(P-3075)***
Shook Hardy & Bacon LLP...D...415 544-1900
1 Montgomery St Ste 2700 San Francisco (94104) ***(P-23383)***
Shooter & Butts Inc...E...925 460-5155
3768 Old Santa Rita Rd Pleasanton (94588) ***(P-787)***
Shopkick Inc...D...650 763-8727
2317 Broadway St Fl 3 Redwood City (94063) ***(P-15444)***
Shopper Inc...B...805 527-6700
3987 Heritage Oak Ct Simi Valley (93063) ***(P-7145)***
Shopping Center Mgt Corp...D...650 617-8234
660 Stanford Shopping Ctr Palo Alto (94304) ***(P-10938)***
Shoppingcom Inc...C...650 616-6500
8000 Marina Blvd Ste 500 Brisbane (94005) ***(P-16177)***
Shopzilla.com, Santa Monica *Also called Connexity Inc* ***(P-5537)***
Shore Hotel...D...310 458-1515
1515 Ocean Ave Santa Monica (90401) ***(P-13223)***
Shorebreeze Apartments, Mountain View *Also called Mp Shoreline Assoc Ltd Partnr* ***(P-11082)***
Shorecliff Properties, Pismo Beach *Also called T I C Hotels Inc* ***(P-13316)***
Shoreline Care Center, Oxnard *Also called Covenant Care California LLC* ***(P-20343)***
Shoreline Holdings Inc (PA)...C...562 498-6444
2505 Mira Mar Ave Long Beach (90815) ***(P-2733)***
Shoreline Land Care Inc...D...858 560-8555
7348 Trade St Ste B San Diego (92121) ***(P-939)***
Shoreline S Intermediate Care...C...510 523-8857
430 Willow St Alameda (94501) ***(P-20957)***
Shorenstein Company LLC...E...415 772-7000
235 Montgomery St Fl 15 San Francisco (94104) ***(P-10939)***
Shorenstein Properties LLC (PA)...C...415 772-7000
235 Montgomery St Fl 16 San Francisco (94104) ***(P-10940)***
Shores Restaurant, La Jolla *Also called La Jolla Bch & Tennis CLB Inc* ***(P-12828)***
Shoreview Preservation LP...D...415 647-6922
35 Lillian Ct San Francisco (94124) ***(P-11112)***
Shoring & Excavating, Santa Fe Springs *Also called Shoring Engineers* ***(P-3585)***
Shoring Engineers...D...562 944-9331
12645 Clark St Santa Fe Springs (90670) ***(P-3585)***
Shotspotter Inc...D...510 794-3100
7979 Gateway Blvd Ste 210 Newark (94560) ***(P-15851)***
Show Call Productions Inc...B...619 602-0656
5212 Lenore Dr San Diego (92115) ***(P-18404)***
Showa Marine Inc (PA)...D...213 627-4091
668 S Alameda St Ste A Los Angeles (90021) ***(P-8600)***
Showcase Installations, Santa Fe Springs *Also called Partitions Installation Inc* ***(P-3564)***
Showershapes, Ventura *Also called G W Surfaces* ***(P-3523)***
Showpad Inc (HQ)...B...415 800-2033
301 Howard St Ste 1800 San Francisco (94105) ***(P-16483)***
Showroom Interiors LLC...C...323 348-1551
1900 E 25th St Vernon (90058) ***(P-14544)***
Shri Sidhi Vinayaka Hotel Inc...C...855 922-5252
500 Leisure Ln Sacramento (95815) ***(P-13224)***
Shriner's Hospital, Los Angeles *Also called Shriners Hspitals For Children* ***(P-22047)***
Shriners Hspitals For Children...B...213 388-3151
3160 Geneva St Los Angeles (90020) ***(P-22047)***
Shriners Hspitals For Children...B...916 453-2050
2425 Stockton Blvd Sacramento (95817) ***(P-22048)***
Shriners Hspitals For Children...B...916 453-2000
2425 Stockton Blvd Sacramento (95817) ***(P-22049)***
Shuler, Kurt MD, Davis *Also called Sutter Health* ***(P-21834)***
Shusters Transportation Inc...D...707 459-4131
750 E Valley St Willits (95490) ***(P-4062)***
Shutterfly Inc (PA)...C...650 610-5200
2800 Bridge Pkwy Ste 100 Redwood City (94065) ***(P-16966)***
Shutters On The Beach, Santa Monica *Also called By The Blue Sea LLC* ***(P-12413)***
Shutters On The Beach, Santa Monica *Also called Edward Thomas Hospitality Corp* ***(P-12550)***
SI Inc...E...951 304-9444
26035 Jefferson Ave Murrieta (92562) ***(P-3076)***
Sia Engineering (usa) Inc...D...310 693-7108
7001 W Imperial Hwy Los Angeles (90045) ***(P-25911)***
Sialic Contractors Corporation...D...562 803-9977
12240 Woodruff Ave Downey (90241) ***(P-1849)***
SICK CHILD CARE CENTER, THE, San Jose *Also called Sjb Child Development Centers* ***(P-24382)***
Sideman & Bancroft LLP...D...415 392-1960
1 Embarcadero Ctr Ste 860 San Francisco (94111) ***(P-23384)***
Sidjon Corporation...D...925 606-6135
3571 1st St Livermore (94551) ***(P-13225)***
Sidley Austin LLP...D...650 565-7000
1001 Page Mill Rd Bldg 1 Palo Alto (94304) ***(P-23385)***
Sidley Austin LLP...B...650 565-7000
1001 Page Mill Rd Bldg 1 Palo Alto (94304) ***(P-23386)***
Siemens AG...C...650 969-9112
685 E Middlefield Rd Mountain View (94043) ***(P-25912)***
Siemens Industry Inc...B...510 783-6000
25821 Industrial Blvd # 300 Hayward (94545) ***(P-7394)***
Siemens Industry Inc...C...510 783-6000
25821 Industrial Blvd # 300 Hayward (94545) ***(P-7796)***
Siemens Industry Inc...D...909 627-6141
2420 S Reservoir St Pomona (91766) ***(P-7395)***
Siemens Industry Inc...D...858 693-8711
9835 Carroll Ctre Rd 10 San Diego (92126) ***(P-7797)***
Siemens Industry Inc...C...714 761-2200
6141 Katella Ave Cypress (90630) ***(P-7396)***
Siemens Industry Inc...D...916 371-2600
1585 Parkway Blvd West Sacramento (95691) ***(P-17913)***
Siemens Med Solutions USA Inc...B...650 694-5747
685 E Middlefield Rd Mountain View (94043) ***(P-7218)***
Siemens Mobility Inc...D...916 621-2700
5301 Price Ave McClellan (95652) ***(P-17784)***
Siemens PLM Software, Cypress *Also called Siemens Product Life Mgmt Sftw* ***(P-15445)***
Siemens Product Life Mgmt Sftw...D...714 952-6500
10824 Hope St Cypress (90630) ***(P-15445)***
Sierra At Taho Ski Resorts...E...530 659-7519
1111 Sierra At Tahoe Rd Twin Bridges (95735) ***(P-13226)***
Sierra Bancorp...C...559 449-8145
7029 N Ingram Ave Ste 101 Fresno (93650) ***(P-9487)***
Sierra Bay Contractors Inc...E...925 671-7711
4021 Port Chicago Hwy # 150 Concord (94520) ***(P-1434)***
Sierra Bookkeeping & Tax Svc...D...916 349-7610
5777 Madison Ave Ste 615 Sacramento (95841) ***(P-26291)***
Sierra Care Rehabilitation Ctr...D...916 782-3188
310 Oak Ridge Dr Roseville (95661) ***(P-20762)***
Sierra Cascade Blueberries...E...530 894-8728
12753 Doe Mill Rd Forest Ranch (95942) ***(P-121)***
Sierra Central Credit Union (PA)...D...530 671-3009
1351 Harter Pkwy Yuba City (95993) ***(P-9654)***
Sierra Club (PA)...C...415 977-5500
2101 Webster St Ste 1300 Oakland (94612) ***(P-25248)***
Sierra Club Books, Oakland *Also called Sierra Club* ***(P-25248)***
Sierra Cscade Fmly Opprtnities (PA)...C...530 283-1242
424 N Mill Creek Rd Quincy (95971) ***(P-24381)***
Sierra Disposal Service, South Lake Tahoe *Also called South Tahoe Refuse Co* ***(P-6478)***
Sierra Electric Co, San Francisco *Also called Stadtner Co Inc* ***(P-2744)***
Sierra Entertainment...E...530 666-9646
341 Industrial Way Woodland (95776) ***(P-3625)***
Sierra Equipment Leasing Inc...E...925 676-7300
1140 Suncast Ln El Dorado Hills (95762) ***(P-14545)***
Sierra Forest Products...C...559 535-4893
9000 Road 234 Terra Bella (93270) ***(P-6864)***
Sierra Forever Families...D...916 368-5114
8928 Volunteer Ln Ste 100 Sacramento (95826) ***(P-24050)***
Sierra Gold Nurseries Inc...D...530 674-1145
5320 Garden Hwy Yuba City (95991) ***(P-301)***
Sierra Group, Glendale *Also called Next Venture Inc* ***(P-1601)***
Sierra Health Services LLC...E...209 956-7725
2423 W March Ln Ste 100 Stockton (95207) ***(P-26292)***
Sierra Hills Care Center Inc...D...916 782-7007
1139 Cirby Way Roseville (95661) ***(P-20958)***
Sierra International McHy LLC...D...661 327-7073
1620 E Brundage Ln Frnt Bakersfield (93307) ***(P-7992)***
Sierra Lakes Golf Club...D...909 350-2500
16600 Clubhouse Dr Fontana (92336) ***(P-18762)***
Sierra Landscape & Maintenance...D...530 895-0263
546 Hickory St Chico (95928) ***(P-788)***
Sierra Lathing Company Inc...C...909 421-0211
1189 Leiske Dr Rialto (92376) ***(P-2957)***

ALPHABETIC

Employee Codes: A=Over 500 employees, B=251-500
C=101-250, D=51-100, E=50
2019 Directory of California
Wholesalers and Services Companies
© Mergent Inc. 1-800-342-5647
1465

Sierra Living Concepts Inc .... D 510 402-4906
46560 Fremont Blvd # 414 Fremont (94538) *(P-6786)*
Sierra Lobo Inc .... C 626 510-6340
465 N Halstead St Ste 130 Pasadena (91107) *(P-25913)*
Sierra Lodge 788, Oakhurst *Also called Sierra Masonic Association (P-25249)*
Sierra Lumber & Decking, San Jose *Also called Sierra Lumber Co (P-3077)*
Sierra Lumber Co .... C 408 286-7071
1711 Senter Rd San Jose (95112) *(P-3077)*
Sierra Manor Apts, Chico *Also called Hignell Incorporated (P-11031)*
Sierra Masonic Association .... D 559 683-7713
2166 Hwy 49 Oakhurst (93644) *(P-25249)*
Sierra Mountain Express, El Dorado Hills *Also called Sierra Equipment Leasing Inc (P-14545)*
Sierra Nevada Brewing Co .... C 510 647-3439
2031 4th St Berkeley (94710) *(P-9026)*
Sierra Nevada Corporation .... C 408 395-2004
985 University Ave Ste 4 Los Gatos (95032) *(P-25914)*
Sierra Nevada Home Care, Grass Valley *Also called Sierra Nevada Memorial Hm Care (P-22418)*
Sierra Nevada Memorial Hm Care .... D 530 274-6350
1020 Mccourtney Rd Ste A Grass Valley (95949) *(P-22418)*
Sierra Oaks Senior Living .... D 530 241-5100
1520 Collyer Dr Redding (96003) *(P-24673)*
Sierra Pacific 4117, Modesto *Also called US Foods Inc (P-8895)*
Sierra Pacific Development .... D 559 256-1300
1470 W Herndon Ave # 100 Fresno (93711) *(P-11917)*
Sierra Pacific Farms Inc (PA) .... D 951 699-9980
43406 Business Park Dr Temecula (92590) *(P-712)*
Sierra Pacific Htg & Air-Solar, Rancho Cordova *Also called Sierra PCF HM & Comfort Inc (P-7656)*
Sierra Pacific Mortgage Co Inc .... D 805 489-6060
104 Traffic Way Arroyo Grande (93420) *(P-9858)*
Sierra Pacific Mortgage Co Inc (PA) .... A 916 932-1700
1180 Iron Point Rd # 200 Folsom (95630) *(P-9859)*
Sierra Pacific Ortho .... C 559 256-5200
1630 E Herndon Ave Fresno (93720) *(P-19891)*
Sierra Pacific West Inc .... D 760 599-0755
2125 La Mirada Dr Vista (92081) *(P-1646)*
Sierra PCF HM & Comfort Inc .... D 916 638-0543
2550 Mercantile Dr Ste D Rancho Cordova (95742) *(P-7656)*
Sierra Recycling & Dem Inc .... D 661 327-7073
1620 E Brundage Ln Frnt Bakersfield (93307) *(P-3462)*
Sierra Systems Inc (PA) .... C 310 536-6288
222 N Pacific Coast Hwy El Segundo (90245) *(P-27448)*
Sierra Tel Business Systems, Oakhurst *Also called Sierra Tel Cmmunications Group (P-5642)*
Sierra Tel Cmmunications Group .... D 559 683-7777
40044 Highway 49 Ste C2 Oakhurst (93644) *(P-5642)*
Sierra Tel Cmmunications Group (PA) .... D 559 683-4611
49150 Road 426 Oakhurst (93644) *(P-5643)*
Sierra Telephone Company Inc .... D 559 683-4611
49150 Crane Valley Rd 426 Oakhurst (93644) *(P-5644)*
Sierra Transport Inc .... D 661 836-3166
12856 Old River Rd Bakersfield (93311) *(P-4063)*
Sierra Valley Rehab Center .... C 559 784-7375
301 W Putnam Ave Porterville (93257) *(P-21207)*
Sierra View Care Center, Baldwin Park *Also called Sierra View Care Holdings LLC (P-20763)*
Sierra View Care Holdings LLC .... D 626 960-1971
14318 Ohio St Baldwin Park (91706) *(P-20763)*
Sierra View Country Club .... D 916 782-3741
105 Alta Vista Ave Roseville (95678) *(P-19047)*
Sierra View District Hospital, Porterville *Also called Sierra View Local Hospital Dst (P-21755)*
Sierra View Dst Hosp Leag Inc (PA) .... C 559 784-1110
465 W Putnam Ave Porterville (93257) *(P-19892)*
Sierra View Homes .... C 559 637-2256
1155 E Springfield Ave Reedley (93654) *(P-20764)*
SIERRA VIEW HOMES RESIDENTIAL, Reedley *Also called Sierra View Homes (P-20764)*
Sierra View Landscape Inc .... E 916 408-2990
3888 Cincinnati Ave Rocklin (95765) *(P-940)*
Sierra View Local Hospital Dst .... B 559 781-7877
283 Pearson Dr Porterville (93257) *(P-21755)*
Sierra Vista 16 A LLC .... E 818 505-6777
12411 Ventura Blvd Studio City (91604) *(P-10941)*
Sierra Vista Extended Stay, Brea *Also called Otb Acquisition LLC (P-12988)*
Sierra Vista Family Medical .... D 805 582-4000
1227 E Los Angeles Ave Simi Valley (93065) *(P-22884)*
Sierra Vista Hospital, Sacramento *Also called Psychiatric Solutions Inc (P-19803)*
Sierra Vista Hospital Inc (HQ) .... A 805 546-7600
1010 Murray Ave San Luis Obispo (93405) *(P-21756)*
Sierra Vista Memory Care Cmnty, Azusa *Also called Silverado Senior Living Inc (P-21210)*
Sierra Vista Regional Med Ctr, San Luis Obispo *Also called Sierra Vista Hospital Inc (P-21756)*
Sierra Waste Transport Inc .... E 916 386-9937
6956 Florin Perkins Rd Sacramento (95828) *(P-5246)*
Sierra Weatherization Co Inc .... D 408 354-1900
43 E Main St Ste B Los Gatos (95030) *(P-13903)*
Sierra Wes Drywall Inc (PA) .... B 916 652-4491
3340 Swetzer Ct Ste A Loomis (95650) *(P-2958)*
Sierra West Construction Inc .... E 530 268-7614
24744 Connie Ct Auburn (95602) *(P-3078)*
Sierra West Home Care, Santa Monica *Also called Right At Home (P-22405)*
Sierra Wireless America Inc (HQ) .... D 760 444-5650
2738 Loker Ave W Ste A Carlsbad (92010) *(P-5415)*
Sierra-Cascade Nursery Inc (PA) .... B 530 254-6867
472-715 Johnson Rd Susanville (96130) *(P-302)*
Sift Science Inc .... D 415 882-7709
123 Mission St Fl 20 San Francisco (94105) *(P-15446)*

Sight Machine Inc .... D 888 461-5739
243 Vallejo St San Francisco (94111) *(P-15852)*
Sigma Investment Holdings LLC .... E 626 398-3098
2288 Villa Heights Rd Pasadena (91107) *(P-2062)*
Sigma Kappa Sorority .... D 510 540-9142
2409 Warring St Berkeley (94704) *(P-13481)*
Sigma Networks Inc .... C 408 876-4002
2191 Zanker Rd San Jose (95131) *(P-5645)*
Sigma Services Inc (PA) .... D 805 642-8377
2140 Eastman Ave Ste 110 Ventura (93003) *(P-1647)*
Sigmanet Inc (HQ) .... D 909 230-7500
4290 E Brickell St Ontario (91761) *(P-7102)*
Sigmaways Inc .... D 510 573-4208
39737 Paseo Padre Pkwy Fremont (94538) *(P-27449)*
Sign of Dove .... D 916 786-3277
707 Sunrise Ave Ofc Roseville (95661) *(P-11113)*
Signal 88 LLC .... A 714 713-5306
821 S Rockefeller Ave Ontario (91761) *(P-16827)*
Signal Pharmaceuticals LLC .... D 858 795-4700
10300 Campus Point Dr # 100 San Diego (92121) *(P-8210)*
Signaldemand Inc .... E 415 356-0800
101 Montgomery St Ste 400 San Francisco (94104) *(P-15447)*
Signature Athletic Club The, Carmichael *Also called Wenmat Inc (P-25483)*
Signature Building Maint Inc .... D 408 377-8066
1330 White Oaks Rd Campbell (95008) *(P-14390)*
Signature Consultants LLC .... D 310 229-5731
8560 W Sunset Blvd Los Angeles (90069) *(P-27859)*
Signature Flight Support Corp .... D 559 981-2490
3050 N Winery Ave Fresno (93703) *(P-4909)*
Signature Flight Support Corp .... D 650 877-6800
1052 N Access Rd San Francisco (94128) *(P-4910)*
Signature Flight Support Corp .... D 818 464-9500
7240 Hayvenhurst Ave Van Nuys (91406) *(P-4911)*
Signature Flight Support Corp .... D 562 997-0700
3333 E Spring St Ste 205 Long Beach (90806) *(P-4912)*
Signature Flooring Inc .... D 714 558-9200
701 N Hariton St Orange (92868) *(P-3117)*
Signature Floors, Orange *Also called Signature Flooring Inc (P-3117)*
Signature Painting & Cnstr Inc .... E 925 287-0444
1565 3rd Ave Walnut Creek (94597) *(P-2481)*
Signature Properties Inc .... D 925 463-1122
4670 Willow Rd Ste 200 Pleasanton (94588) *(P-11918)*
Signature Resources Insurance .... D 949 930-2400
19900 Macarthur Blvd # 920 Irvine (92612) *(P-10774)*
Signature Services .... D 949 851-9391
4425 Jamboree Rd Ste 250 Newport Beach (92660) *(P-10942)*
Signatures Sni, San Francisco *Also called Live Nation Merchandise Inc (P-9232)*
Signet Armorlite Inc (HQ) .... B 760 744-4000
5803 Newton Dr Ste A Carlsbad (92008) *(P-22885)*
Signet Testing Labs Inc (HQ) .... C 510 887-8484
3526 Breakwater Ct Hayward (94545) *(P-26731)*
Significant Cleaning Svcs LLC .... C 408 559-5959
1855 Hamilton Ave Ste 104 San Jose (95125) *(P-14391)*
Signode Industrial Group LLC .... D 209 931-0917
3901 Navone Rd Stockton (95215) *(P-7798)*
Signon San Diego, San Diego *Also called Copley Press Inc (P-15637)*
Sigue Corporation (PA) .... D 818 837-5939
13190 Telfair Ave Sylmar (91342) *(P-17470)*
Silent Valley Club Inc .... D 951 849-4501
46305 Poppet Flats Rd Banning (92220) *(P-13468)*
Silicon Prime Technologies Inc .... E 310 279-0222
4154 W 172nd St Torrance (90504) *(P-15448)*
Silicon Valley Bank .... D 818 382-2600
15260 Ventura Blvd # 1800 Sherman Oaks (91403) *(P-9371)*
Silicon Valley Bank (HQ) .... A 408 654-7400
3003 Tasman Dr Santa Clara (95054) *(P-9516)*
Silicon Valley Clean Water .... D 650 591-7121
1400 Radio Rd Redwood City (94065) *(P-6328)*
Silicon Valley Exec Netwrk .... A 408 746-5803
1336 Nelson Way Sunnyvale (94087) *(P-27860)*
Silicon Valley Hwang LLC .... C 408 452-0200
1471 N 4th St San Jose (95112) *(P-13227)*
Silicon Valley Mechanical Inc .... D 408 943-0380
2115 Ringwood Ave San Jose (95131) *(P-2357)*
Silicon Valley Monterey Bay Co .... D 209 965-3432
29211 Highway 108 Long Barn (95335) *(P-13454)*
Silicon Valley Office, Menlo Park *Also called Winston & Strawn LLP (P-23443)*
Silicon Valley Power, Santa Clara *Also called City of Santa Clara (P-6019)*
Silicon Vly Cmnty Foundation .... C 650 450-5400
2440 W El Camin Mountain View (94040) *(P-25250)*
Silicon Vly Educatn Foundation .... A 408 790-9400
1400 Parkmoor Ave Ste 200 San Jose (95126) *(P-24840)*
Silicon Vly SEC & Patrol Inc (PA) .... C 408 267-1539
1131 Luchessi Dr Ste 2 San Jose (95118) *(P-16828)*
Siliconsage Construction Inc .... C 408 916-3205
560 S Mathilda Ave Sunnyvale (94086) *(P-1316)*
Siliconsystems Inc .... D 949 900-9400
26840 Aliso Viejo Pkwy # 1 Aliso Viejo (92656) *(P-7397)*
Siliconware Usa Inc (HQ) .... E 408 573-5500
1735 Tech Dr Ste 300 Fl 3 San Jose (95110) *(P-7541)*
Silla Automotive LLC .... D 661 392-8880
1901 Mineral Ct Ste C Bakersfield (93308) *(P-6674)*
Sillcrest Nursing Home, San Bernardino *Also called Marna Health Services Inc (P-21153)*
Silliker Labs Group Inc .... E 714 226-0000
6360 Gateway Dr Cypress (90630) *(P-26732)*
Silman Construction, San Leandro *Also called Silman Venture Corporation (P-1435)*
Silman Venture Corporation (PA) .... C 510 347-4800
1600 Factor Ave San Leandro (94577) *(P-1435)*

Mergent e-mail: customerrelations@mergent.com
1466

2019 Directory of California
Wholesalers and Services Companies

(P-0000) Products & Services Section entry number
(PA)=Parent Co (HQ)=Headquarters (DH)=Div Headquarters

Silv Communication Inc ....D....213 381-7999
3460 Wilshire Blvd # 1100 Los Angeles (90010) ***(P-27861)***

Silva Artist Management,, Los Angeles *Also called Artist Silva Management LLC* ***(P-26766)***

Silva Farms LLC (PA) ....B....831 675-2327
111 Alpine Dr Gonzales (93926) ***(P-82)***

Silva Trucking Inc ....E....209 982-1114
36 W Mathews Rd French Camp (95231) ***(P-4064)***

Silver Cinemas Acquisition Co (PA) ....D....310 473-6701
2222 S Barrington Ave Los Angeles (90064) ***(P-18321)***

Silver Creek Home Owners ....E....408 559-1977
1935 Dry Creek Rd Ste 203 Campbell (95008) ***(P-27029)***

Silver Creek Industries Inc ....C....951 943-5393
2830 Barrett Ave Perris (92571) ***(P-1648)***

Silver Creek Vly Cntry CLB Inc ....C....408 239-5775
5460 Country Club Pkwy San Jose (95138) ***(P-19048)***

Silver Crk Vlly Ctry CLB HM Ow, Campbell *Also called Silver Creek Home Owners* ***(P-27029)***

Silver Fredman A Prof Law Corp ....E....310 556-2356
2029 Century Park E # 1900 Los Angeles (90067) ***(P-23387)***

Silver Lake Financial, San Francisco *Also called Silver Lake Partners II LP* ***(P-12068)***

Silver Lake Medical Center, Los Angeles *Also called Success Healthcare 1 LLC* ***(P-22428)***

Silver Lake Partners LP (PA) ....D....650 233-8120
2775 Sand Hill Rd Ste 100 Menlo Park (94025) ***(P-12066)***

Silver Lake Partners II LP ....D....408 454-4732
10080 N Wolfe Rd Sw3190 Cupertino (95014) ***(P-12067)***

Silver Lake Partners II LP ....C....415 293-4355
1 Market Plz San Francisco (94105) ***(P-12068)***

Silver Lakes Association ....D....760 245-1606
15273 Orchard Hill Ln Helendale (92342) ***(P-25251)***

Silver Rock Resort Golf Club ....D....760 777-8884
79179 Ahmanson Ln La Quinta (92253) ***(P-18763)***

Silver Service, San Andreas *Also called Mark Twain Medical Center* ***(P-21579)***

Silver Shield Security ....C....408 435-1111
2107 N 1st St Ste 100 San Jose (95131) ***(P-16829)***

Silver Spur Christian Camp ....D....209 928-4248
17301 Silver Spur Dr Tuolumne (95379) ***(P-13455)***

Silver Strand ....E....818 701-9707
8945 Fullbright Ave Chatsworth (91311) ***(P-3079)***

Silverado Bellingham LLC ....D....949 240-7200
6400 Oak Cyn Ste 200 Irvine (92618) ***(P-22419)***

Silverado Contractors Inc (PA) ....D....510 658-9960
2855 Mandela Pkwy Fl 2 Oakland (94608) ***(P-3463)***

Silverado Energy Company ....B....949 752-5588
18101 Von Karman Ave Irvine (92612) ***(P-6109)***

Silverado Orchards (PA) ....D....707 963-1461
601 Pope St Ofc Saint Helena (94574) ***(P-11114)***

Silverado Resort and Spa ....A....707 257-0200
1600 Atlas Peak Rd NAPA (94558) ***(P-19049)***

Silverado Rsort Svcs Group LLC ....B....707 257-0200
1600 Atlas Peak Rd NAPA (94558) ***(P-13228)***

Silverado Senior Living Inc ....D....424 257-6418
514 N Prospect Ave # 120 Redondo Beach (90277) ***(P-20765)***

Silverado Senior Living Inc ....D....650 226-8017
1301 Ralston Ave Ste A Belmont (94002) ***(P-21208)***

Silverado Senior Living Inc (PA) ....D....949 240-7200
6400 Oak Cyn Ste 200 Irvine (92618) ***(P-21209)***

Silverado Senior Living Inc ....D....626 650-9891
125 W Sierra Madre Ave Azusa (91702) ***(P-21210)***

Silverado Senior Living Inc ....D....949 945-0189
350 W Bay St Costa Mesa (92627) ***(P-21211)***

Silverado Senior Living Inc ....E....626 872-3941
1118 N Stoneman Ave Alhambra (91801) ***(P-21212)***

Silverado Senior Living Inc ....D....760 456-5137
1500 Borden Rd Escondido (92026) ***(P-21213)***

Silverado Senior Living Inc ....D....760 270-9917
335 Saxony Rd Encinitas (92024) ***(P-21214)***

Silverado Senior Living Inc ....D....657 888-5752
240 E 3rd St Tustin (92780) ***(P-21215)***

Silverado Senior Living Inc ....D....323 984-7313
330 N Hayworth Ave Los Angeles (90048) ***(P-21216)***

Silverado Senior Living Holdin ....A....949 240-7200
6400 Oak Cyn Ste 200 Irvine (92618) ***(P-24674)***

Silvergate San Marcos, San Marcos *Also called Americare Hlth Retirement Inc* ***(P-10852)***

Silverline Construction Inc ....C....310 464-8314
1421 W 132nd St Gardena (90249) ***(P-1649)***

Silverscreen Healthcare Inc ....C....909 793-1382
1875 Barton Rd Redlands (92373) ***(P-21217)***

Silverscreen Healthcare Inc ....D....818 763-8247
10830 Oxnard St North Hollywood (91606) ***(P-20766)***

Silverwood Landscape Cnstr Inc ....E....714 427-6134
2209 S Lyon St Santa Ana (92705) ***(P-941)***

SIM Investment Corporation (PA) ....B....408 874-0610
1600 W Campbell Ave Campbell (95008) ***(P-18651)***

SIM Investment Corporation ....D....408 445-3310
1329 Blossom Hill Rd San Jose (95118) ***(P-18652)***

Simas Floor Co Inc (PA) ....C....916 452-4933
3550 Power Inn Rd Sacramento (95826) ***(P-3118)***

Simas Floor Co Design Center, Sacramento *Also called Simas Floor Co Inc* ***(P-3118)***

Simbol Inc (PA) ....D....925 226-7400
6920 Koll Center Pkwy # 216 Pleasanton (94566) ***(P-26456)***

Simbol Materials, Pleasanton *Also called Simbol Inc* ***(P-26456)***

Simco Electronics (PA) ....D....408 734-9750
3131 Jay St Ste 100 Santa Clara (95054) ***(P-17914)***

Simi Hills Golf Course, Simi Valley *Also called American Golf Corporation* ***(P-18844)***

Simi Radiology & Imaging ....D....805 522-5978
4100 Guardian St Ste 205 Simi Valley (93063) ***(P-27450)***

Simi Valley Family YMCA, Simi Valley *Also called Young Mens Christian Asso* ***(P-19264)***

Simi Valley Plaza 10, Simi Valley *Also called Edwards Theatres Circuit Inc* ***(P-18300)***

Simi Vly Care & Rehabilitation, Simi Valley *Also called Chase Group Llc* ***(P-27190)***

Simi Vly Hosp & Hlth Care Svcs (HQ) ....D....805 955-6000
2975 Sycamore Dr Simi Valley (93065) ***(P-20204)***

Simi West Inc ....C....805 583-2000
999 Enchanted Way Simi Valley (93065) ***(P-13229)***

Simmons Construction Inc ....E....661 636-1321
19252 Flypath Way Bakersfield (93308) ***(P-1650)***

Simon and Gladstone A Prof, Marina Del Rey *Also called Berger Kahn* ***(P-22941)***

Simon Mrtn-Vgue Wnklstein Mris, San Francisco *Also called A Smwm California Corporation* ***(P-26017)***

Simone Fruit Co Inc ....D....559 275-1368
8008 W Shields Ave Fresno (93723) ***(P-568)***

Simoni & Massoni Farms ....E....925 634-2304
2510 Taylor Ln Byron (94514) ***(P-9)***

Simons Wholesale Bakery Inc ....E....714 259-0855
1901 Ritchey St Santa Ana (92705) ***(P-8868)***

Simple Luxuries LLC ....E....310 627-6514
1560 N Sycamore Ave Rialto (92376) ***(P-3325)***

Simplehuman LLC (PA) ....D....310 436-2250
19850 Magellan Dr Torrance (90502) ***(P-6787)***

Simpler Postage Inc (PA) ....D....408 915-0063
1 Montgomery St Ste 400 San Francisco (94104) ***(P-5169)***

Simplex Time Recorder 480, San Diego *Also called Simplex Time Recorder LLC* ***(P-2734)***

Simplex Time Recorder LLC ....D....858 740-0100
9855 Carroll Canyon Rd San Diego (92131) ***(P-2734)***

Simplot Growers Solutions, Firebaugh *Also called JR Simplot Company* ***(P-9080)***

Simpson & Simpson ....D....213 736-6664
633 W 5th St Ste 3320 Los Angeles (90071) ***(P-27030)***

Simpson Delmore and Greene LLP (PA) ....E....619 515-1194
600 W Broadway Ste 400 San Diego (92101) ***(P-23388)***

Simpson Gumpertz & Heger Inc ....D....415 495-3700
100 Pine St Ste 1600 San Francisco (94111) ***(P-25915)***

Simpson Gumpertz & Heger Inc ....C....510 835-0705
500 12th St Oakland (94607) ***(P-25916)***

Simpson Strong-Tie Intl Inc ....D....925 560-9000
5956 W Las Positas Blvd Pleasanton (94588) ***(P-7313)***

Simpson Thacher & Bartlett LLP ....C....650 251-5000
2475 Hanover St Palo Alto (94304) ***(P-23389)***

Sims Group USA Corporation ....D....408 494-4242
1900 Monterey Hwy San Jose (95112) ***(P-7993)***

Sims Group USA Corporation (HQ) ....D....510 412-5300
600 S 4th St Richmond (94804) ***(P-7994)***

Sims Group USA Corporation ....D....510 236-0606
600 S 4th St Richmond (94804) ***(P-7995)***

Sims/LMC Recyclers, San Jose *Also called Sims Group USA Corporation* ***(P-7993)***

Simsmetal America, Richmond *Also called Sims Group USA Corporation* ***(P-7994)***

Simulations Plus Inc (PA) ....D....661 723-7723
42505 10th St W Ste 103 Lancaster (93534) ***(P-16052)***

Sinai Temple ....C....323 469-6000
5950 Forest Lawn Dr Los Angeles (90068) ***(P-13698)***

Sinanian Development Inc ....D....818 996-9666
18980 Ventura Blvd # 200 Tarzana (91356) ***(P-1651)***

Sinclair Companies ....C....619 238-1818
1055 2nd Ave San Diego (92101) ***(P-13230)***

Sinclair Concrete ....D....916 663-0303
7205 Church St Penryn (95663) ***(P-3326)***

Sinecera Inc ....D....626 962-1087
5397 3rd St Irwindale (91706) ***(P-17471)***

Singapore Airlines Cargo Pte ....D....650 876-7363
710 Mcdonald Rd San Francisco (94128) ***(P-4796)***

Singapore Airlines Limited ....C....310 647-1922
222 N Pacific Coast Hwy # 1600 El Segundo (90245) ***(P-4797)***

Singerlewak LLP (PA) ....C....310 477-3924
10960 Wilshire Blvd Los Angeles (90024) ***(P-26293)***

Singerlewak LLP ....D....949 261-8600
2050 Main St Ste 700 Irvine (92614) ***(P-26294)***

Singerlewak LLP ....D....818 999-3924
21550 Oxnard St Ste 1000 Woodland Hills (91367) ***(P-26295)***

Singley Enterprises (PA) ....E....866 890-1776
121 Main Ave Sacramento (95838) ***(P-6865)***

Sioux City Ht & Conference Ctr, Escondido *Also called Choa Hope LLC* ***(P-12455)***

Sippi Anne Riverside Ranch LLP ....E....661 871-9697
18200 Highway 178 Bakersfield (93306) ***(P-24675)***

Sir Francis Drake Hotel, San Francisco *Also called Huskies Lessee LLC* ***(P-12744)***

Sir Francis Drake Hotel, San Francisco *Also called Sfd Partners LLC* ***(P-13210)***

Siracusa Enterprises Inc ....D....818 831-1130
17737 Chtswrth St Ste 200 Granada Hills (91344) ***(P-14760)***

Sirva Inc ....C....925 824-3109
2010 Crow Canyon Pl San Ramon (94583) ***(P-4264)***

Sisa, Mountain View *Also called Samsung Research America Inc* ***(P-26447)***

Sisco Family Connection, Milpitas *Also called Bright Horizons Chld Ctrs LLC* ***(P-24269)***

Siskiyou Development Company ....D....530 938-2731
88 S Weed Blvd Edgewood (96094) ***(P-13231)***

Siskiyou Hospital Inc ....B....530 842-4121
444 Bruce St Yreka (96097) ***(P-21757)***

Siskiyou Lake Golf Resort Inc ....D....530 926-3030
1000 Siskiyou Lake Blvd Mount Shasta (96067) ***(P-18764)***

Siskiyou Opportunity Center (PA) ....C....530 926-4698
1516 S Mount Shasta Blvd Mount Shasta (96067) ***(P-24229)***

Sissc, Ridgecrest *Also called Leidos Inc* ***(P-16150)***

Sisters of Nazareth ....D....415 479-8282
245 Nova Albion Way San Rafael (94903) ***(P-21218)***

Sisters of Nzareth Los Angeles ....D....310 839-2361
3333 Manning Ave Los Angeles (90064) ***(P-24676)***

Sisters of Soul (sos) Youth ....D....909 533-4889
937 Via Lata Ste 400 Colton (92324) ***(P-24982)***

Sita Ram LLC ....D....209 223-0211
200 S State Highway 49 Jackson (95642) ***(P-13232)***

Site 210, Pacheco *Also called Pleasant Hl Byshore Dspsal Inc* ***(P-6429)***

Employee Codes: A=Over 500 employees, B=251-500
C=101-250, D=51-100, E=50
2019 Directory of California
Wholesalers and Services Companies
© Mergent Inc. 1-800-342-5647
1467

Site 910, Santa Barbara *Also called BFI Waste Systems N Amer Inc* ***(P-6355)***
Site 916, Fremont *Also called BFI Waste Systems N Amer Inc* ***(P-6357)***
Site Crew Inc........B.......714 668-0100
3185 Airway Ave Ste G Costa Mesa (92626) ***(P-14392)***
Site L69, Milpitas *Also called Interntional Disposal Corp Cal* ***(P-6408)***
Site R45, Milpitas *Also called Browning-Ferris Industries LLC* ***(P-6361)***
Sitelite Holdings Inc........C.......949 265-6200
111 Theory Fl 2 Irvine (92617) ***(P-16484)***
Sitestuff Yardi Systems I (PA)........D.......805 966-3666
430 S Fairview Ave Goleta (93117) ***(P-27451)***
Sitoa........D.......916 444-0008
6900 Airport Blvd Sacramento (95837) ***(P-3870)***
Sitonit Seating Inc........C.......714 995-4800
6415 Katella Ave Cypress (90630) ***(P-6737)***
Sitrick Brincko Group LLC........D.......310 788-2850
1840 Century Park E # 800 Los Angeles (90067) ***(P-27452)***
Situs Holdings LLC........B.......415 374-2820
101 Montgomery St # 2250 San Francisco (94104) ***(P-12267)***
Sitv Inc........D.......323 317-9534
700 N Central Ave Ste 600 Glendale (91203) ***(P-5837)***
Six Continents Hotels Inc........D.......310 371-8525
19901 Prairie Ave Torrance (90503) ***(P-13233)***
Six Continents Hotels Inc........D.......818 989-5010
8244 Orion Ave Van Nuys (91406) ***(P-13234)***
Six Continents Hotels Inc........D.......213 748-1291
1020 S Figueroa St Los Angeles (90015) ***(P-13235)***
Six Continents Hotels Inc........C.......310 781-9100
19800 S Vermont Ave Torrance (90502) ***(P-13236)***
Six Continents Hotels Inc........D.......619 232-3861
1355 N Harbor Dr San Diego (92101) ***(P-13237)***
Six Continents Hotels Inc........D.......925 847-6000
11950 Dublin Canyon Rd # 609 Pleasanton (94588) ***(P-13238)***
Six Continents Hotels Inc........D.......619 795-4000
1110 A St San Diego (92101) ***(P-13239)***
Six Continents Hotels Inc........D.......619 474-2800
700 National City Blvd National City (91950) ***(P-13240)***
Six Flags Entertainment Corp........B.......916 924-3747
1600 Exposition Blvd Sacramento (95815) ***(P-18810)***
Six Flags Magic Mountain, Valencia *Also called Magic Mountain LLC* ***(P-18385)***
Six Point Harness........E.......323 462-3344
1759 Glendale Blvd Los Angeles (90026) ***(P-18217)***
Six Rivers National Bank (HQ)........D.......707 443-8400
402 F St Eureka (95501) ***(P-9372)***
Six Rivers Planned Parenthood........D.......707 442-5700
3225 Timber Fall Ct Eureka (95503) ***(P-24841)***
SJ Distributors Inc (PA)........D.......888 988-2328
625 Vista Way Milpitas (95035) ***(P-8505)***
Sj Hotel Manager LLC........D.......401 946-4600
350 W Santa Clara St San Jose (95113) ***(P-13241)***
Sjb Child Development Centers (PA)........C.......408 538-0200
1400 Parkmoor Ave Ste 220 San Jose (95126) ***(P-24382)***
SJHS SONOMA COUNTY, Santa Rosa *Also called Santa Rosa Memorial Hospital* ***(P-21719)***
Sjsu Foundation........A.......408 924-1410
210 N 4th St Ste 300 San Jose (95112) ***(P-25462)***
Sjvi, Fresno *Also called San Joaquin Valley Intergrp* ***(P-25458)***
SJW Group (PA)........B.......408 279-7800
110 W Taylor St San Jose (95110) ***(P-6312)***
Sk Hynix America Inc (HQ)........D.......408 232-8000
3101 N 1st St San Jose (95134) ***(P-7103)***
Sk Sanctuary Day Spa Salon LLC........E.......858 459-2400
6919 La Jolla Blvd La Jolla (92037) ***(P-18653)***
SK&a, Irvine *Also called S K & A Information Svcs Inc* ***(P-26563)***
Skadden Arps Slate Meagher & F........C.......213 687-5000
300 S Grand Ave Ste 3400 Los Angeles (90071) ***(P-23390)***
SKANSKA ROCKY MOUNTAIN DISTRICT, Riverside *Also called Skanska USA Civil West Rocky M* ***(P-2063)***
Skanska USA Civil West Rocky M (HQ)........D.......970 565-8000
1995 Agua Mansa Rd Riverside (92509) ***(P-2063)***
Skanska USA Cvil W Cal Dst Inc (HQ)........A.......951 684-5360
1995 Agua Mansa Rd Riverside (92509) ***(P-1850)***
Skanska-Rados A Joint Venture........D.......213 978-0600
11390 W Olympic Blvd Los Angeles (90064) ***(P-1851)***
Skate Enterprises Inc........D.......562 924-0911
12356 Central Ave Chino (91710) ***(P-19238)***
Skatetown, Roseville *Also called Roseville Sportworld Inc* ***(P-19227)***
Skava, San Francisco *Also called Kallidus Inc* ***(P-15247)***
Skeffington Enterprises Inc........D.......714 540-1700
2200 S Yale St Santa Ana (92704) ***(P-12006)***
Skidmore Owings & Merrill LLP........C.......415 981-1555
1 Front St Ste 2500 San Francisco (94111) ***(P-26107)***
Skidmore Owings & Merrill LLP........C.......310 651-9924
10100 Santa Monica Blvd Beverly Hills (90210) ***(P-26108)***
Skidmore Owings & Merrill LLP........C.......213 996-8366
555 W 5th St Fl 30 Los Angeles (90013) ***(P-26109)***
Skilled Healthcare LLC (HQ)........D.......949 282-5800
27442 Portola Pkwy # 200 Foothill Ranch (92610) ***(P-20767)***
Skilled Healthcare LLC........D.......323 663-3951
5154 W Sunset Blvd Los Angeles (90027) ***(P-20768)***
Skilled Nursing Facility, Taft *Also called West Side District Hospital* ***(P-21914)***
Skills Center Inc (PA)........D.......831 421-9900
220 Lincoln St Santa Cruz (95060) ***(P-24230)***
Skin Health Experts Medic........D.......310 623-6869
144 S Beverly Dr Ste 500 Beverly Hills (90212) ***(P-22679)***
Skirball Cultural Center........C.......310 440-4500
2701 N Sepulveda Blvd Los Angeles (90049) ***(P-24913)***
Skire Inc........D.......650 289-2600
500 Oracle Pkwy Redwood City (94065) ***(P-15449)***
Skitch, Redwood City *Also called Evernote Corporation* ***(P-5557)***
Skoll Foundation........E.......650 331-1031
250 University Ave Lbby Palo Alto (94301) ***(P-25463)***
Skunk Train, The, Fort Bragg *Also called Mendocino Railway* ***(P-5108)***
Sky Chefs Inc........C.......650 652-7886
1845 Rollins Rd Burlingame (94010) ***(P-4631)***
Sky Court USA Inc........C.......805 497-9991
880 S Westlake Blvd Westlake Village (91361) ***(P-13242)***
Sky High Sports, Woodland Hills *Also called Skyhigh Woodland Hills LLC* ***(P-19239)***
Sky King, Sacramento *Also called Lukenbill Enterprises* ***(P-4793)***
Sky Park Gardens Assisted........D.......916 422-5650
5510 Sky Pkwy Ofc Sacramento (95823) ***(P-24677)***
Sky Scan Satelite Systems........D.......909 322-1393
9994 Willowbrook Rd Riverside (92509) ***(P-5930)***
Sky West Golf Course, Hayward *Also called Hayward Area Recreation Pkdist* ***(P-18717)***
Sky Zone LLC (HQ)........D.......310 734-0300
1201 W 5th St Ste T340 Los Angeles (90017) ***(P-18463)***
Skyblue Sewing Manufacturing........E.......415 777-9978
960 Mission St Fl 2 San Francisco (94103) ***(P-17472)***
Skybox Security Inc (PA)........D.......408 441-8060
2077 Gateway Pl Ste 200 San Jose (95110) ***(P-16942)***
Skyhigh Networks Inc........D.......408 564-0278
900 E Hamilton Ave # 400 Campbell (95008) ***(P-16943)***
Skyhigh Woodland Hills LLC........D.......805 484-6300
6051 De Soto Ave Woodland Hills (91367) ***(P-19239)***
Skyhill Financial Inc........D.......714 657-3938
5772 Bolsa Ave Ste 100 Huntington Beach (92649) ***(P-11765)***
Skylar Film Studios LLC........C.......424 653-8902
13589 Mindanao Way # 11 Marina Del Rey (90292) ***(P-18218)***
Skylawn Memorial Park, Redwood City *Also called Chapel of Chimes* ***(P-11940)***
Skyles Insurance Agency........E.......916 361-9585
9840 Business Park Dr Sacramento (95827) ***(P-10775)***
Skylight Convalescent Center, Long Beach *Also called Reynolds Health Industries* ***(P-21195)***
Skylight Halthcare Systems Inc........D.......858 523-3700
10935 Vista Sorrento Pkwy # 350 San Diego (92130) ***(P-27453)***
Skyline Commercial Interiors (PA)........D.......415 908-1020
505 Sansome St Fl 7 San Francisco (94111) ***(P-1652)***
Skyline Construction, San Francisco *Also called Skyline Commercial Interiors* ***(P-1652)***
Skyline Consulting Group........C.......650 529-3455
13186 Skyline Blvd Woodside (94062) ***(P-27454)***
Skyline Health Care Center, San Jose *Also called Mariner Health Care Inc* ***(P-20613)***
Skyline Health Care Ctr, Los Angeles *Also called Mariner Health Care Inc* ***(P-20617)***
Skyline Healthcare & Wellness........D.......323 665-1185
3032 Rowena Ave Los Angeles (90039) ***(P-20769)***
Skyline Healthcare Center, Los Angeles *Also called Skyline Healthcare & Wellness* ***(P-20769)***
Skyline Place, Sonora *Also called Sonora Retirement Center Inc* ***(P-24681)***
Skylite Networks........D.......403 934-9349
43333 Osgood Rd Fremont (94539) ***(P-15450)***
Skylstad-Schoelen Co Inc........D.......805 349-0503
3130 Skyway Dr Ste 701 Santa Maria (93455) ***(P-14393)***
Skyone Federal Credit Union (PA)........D.......310 491-7500
14600 Aviation Blvd Hawthorne (90250) ***(P-9593)***
Skypark Inc........D.......650 875-6655
1000 San Mateo Ave San Bruno (94066) ***(P-13774)***
Skype Inc........D.......650 493-7900
1 Microsoft Way Redmond Palo Alto (94304) ***(P-5646)***
Skypower Holdings LLC........C.......323 860-4900
4700 Wilshire Blvd Los Angeles (90010) ***(P-2358)***
Skyslope Inc........D.......916 833-2390
825 K St Fl 2 Sacramento (95814) ***(P-16485)***
Skyva Construction Inc........E.......916 726-4999
5781 Old Antelope N Rd Antelope (95843) ***(P-1237)***
Skywest Airlines Inc........D.......951 926-9511
32128 Chagall Ct Winchester (92596) ***(P-4798)***
Skywest Airlines Inc........D.......951 600-9181
26818 Bahama Way Murrieta (92563) ***(P-4799)***
Slack Technologies Inc (PA)........C.......415 579-9153
500 Howard St San Francisco (94105) ***(P-15853)***
Slade Gorton & Co Inc........D.......714 676-4200
1 Centerpointe Dr Ste 311 La Palma (90623) ***(P-8601)***
Slade Industrial Landscape Inc........D.......818 885-1916
8838 Zelzah Ave Sherwood Forest (91325) ***(P-789)***
Slakey Brothers Inc........E.......408 494-0460
1480 Nicora Ave San Jose (95133) ***(P-7636)***
Slakey Brothers Inc........E.......209 556-1100
1001 Oates Ct Modesto (95358) ***(P-7314)***
Slate Creek Wind Project LLC........A.......888 903-6926
15445 Innovation Dr San Diego (92128) ***(P-6110)***
Slater Inc........D.......909 822-6800
11045 Rose Ave Fontana (92337) ***(P-2064)***
Slauson Plaza Med Group, Pico Rivera *Also called Altamed Health Services Corp* ***(P-22727)***
SLC Operating Ltd Partnership........B.......818 980-1212
333 Unversal Hollywood Dr North Hollywood (91608) ***(P-13775)***
Slch Inc (PA)........E.......626 798-0558
1920 N Fair Oaks Ave Pasadena (91103) ***(P-20770)***
Sleepy Giant Entertainment Inc........C.......949 464-7986
4 San Joaquin Plz Ste 200 Newport Beach (92660) ***(P-15451)***
Sleepy Giant Entertainment Inc........D.......714 460-4113
3501 Jamboree Rd Ste 5000 Newport Beach (92660) ***(P-18464)***
Slide Go, Redlands *Also called Prime-Line Products Company* ***(P-7600)***
Slideco Recreation Inc........D.......530 246-9550
151 N Boulder Dr Redding (96003) ***(P-18811)***
Sliding Door Co, The, Chatsworth *Also called Sliding Door Company* ***(P-3080)***
Sliding Door Company (PA)........D.......818 997-7855
20235 Bahama St Chatsworth (91311) ***(P-3080)***
SLM Services, Simi Valley *Also called Specialized Landscape MGT Svcs* ***(P-944)***
SLO TRANSITIONS, San Luis Obispo *Also called Transitions - Mental Hlth Assn* ***(P-24094)***
Slogcc, San Luis Obispo *Also called San Luis Obispo Golf* ***(P-19030)***

Mergent e-mail: customerrelations@mergent.com
1468
2019 Directory of California
Wholesalers and Services Companies
(P-0000) Products & Services Section entry number
(PA)=Parent Co (HQ)=Headquarters (DH)=Div Headquarters

Slorta, San Luis Obispo *Also called San Luis Obispo Regional* ***(P-3717)***
SM 10000 Property LLC....D....305 374-5700
10000 Santa Monica Blvd Los Angeles (90067) ***(P-11919)***
SM Broadway Corp....D....626 301-1198
710 S Myrtle Ave Ste 285 Monrovia (91016) ***(P-12187)***
SM International, Fremont *Also called S & M Moving Systems* ***(P-4254)***
SMA America, Rocklin *Also called SMA Solar Technology Amer LLC* ***(P-7542)***
SMA Builders Inc....E....818 994-8306
16134 Leadwell St Van Nuys (91406) ***(P-1238)***
SMA Solar Technology Amer LLC (HQ)....D....916 625-0870
6020 West Oaks Blvd Rocklin (95765) ***(P-7542)***
Smachines, Santa Clara *Also called Soft Machines Inc* ***(P-16053)***
Small Business Advertising Inc....E....818 262-8923
24009 Ventura Blvd # 245 Calabasas (91302) ***(P-13983)***
Smart & Final Stores Inc (PA)....B....323 869-7500
600 Citadel Dr Commerce (90040) ***(P-8453)***
Smart & Final Stores Inc....A....626 334-5189
303 E Foothill Blvd Azusa (91702) ***(P-8454)***
Smart & Final Stores LLC....D....858 268-2400
4439 Genesee Ave San Diego (92117) ***(P-8455)***
Smart & Final Stores LLC....D....858 270-8200
1260 Garnet Ave San Diego (92109) ***(P-8456)***
Smart & Final Stores LLC....D....619 523-3640
3315 Rosecrans St Ste B San Diego (92110) ***(P-8457)***
Smart & Final Stores LLC....D....760 726-7274
471 College Blvd Oceanside (92057) ***(P-8458)***
Smart & Final Stores LLC....D....619 291-8287
4175 Park Blvd San Diego (92103) ***(P-8459)***
Smart & Final Stores LLC....D....858 350-7900
659 Lomas Santa Fe Dr Solana Beach (92075) ***(P-8460)***
Smart Choice Investments Inc....D....310 944-6985
23332 Hawthorne Blvd # 203 Torrance (90505) ***(P-14761)***
Smart Energy Solar Inc....C....800 405-1978
1641 Comm St Corona (92880) ***(P-2359)***
Smart Energy Systems LLC (PA)....C....909 703-9609
19900 Macarthur Blvd Irvine (92612) ***(P-15452)***
Smart Energy Systems LLC....C....909 703-9609
Michelson Dr Ste 3370 Irvine (92612) ***(P-15453)***
Smart Energy USA, Corona *Also called Smart Energy Solar Inc* ***(P-2359)***
Smart Living Company (PA)....E....805 578-5500
4100 Guardian St Simi Valley (93063) ***(P-9259)***
Smart Management & Companies....B....916 392-3000
1501 Corp Way Ste 200 Sacramento (95831) ***(P-27031)***
Smart Software Tstg Solutions....D....833 778-7872
2450 Peralta Blvd Ste 202 Fremont (94536) ***(P-27862)***
Smart Systems Technologies (PA)....D....949 367-9375
9 Goodyear Irvine (92618) ***(P-6111)***
Smartcues Inc, Mountain View *Also called Spotcues Inc* ***(P-7109)***
Smartdrive Systems Inc (PA)....D....858 225-5550
4790 Estgate Mall Ste 200 San Diego (92121) ***(P-15454)***
Smartek21 LLC....B....650 617-3221
530 Lytton Ave Fl 2 Palo Alto (94301) ***(P-16486)***
Smartfinancial, Costa Mesa *Also called Cyber Technology LLC* ***(P-10601)***
Smartrevenuecom Inc....B....203 733-9156
101 Cooper St Ste 205 Santa Cruz (95060) ***(P-26564)***
Smartway Express Inc....C....559 272-3500
2660 S Railroad Ave Fresno (93725) ***(P-5170)***
Smartzip Analytics Inc (PA)....D....925 218-1900
4450 Rosewood Dr Ste 300 Pleasanton (94588) ***(P-27455)***
Smashon Inc....E....855 762-7466
1754 Tech Dr Ste 234 San Jose (95110) ***(P-16487)***
SMC Corporation of America....E....408 943-9600
2841 Junction Ave Ste 110 San Jose (95134) ***(P-7799)***
SMC Networks Inc (HQ)....D....949 679-8029
20 Mason Irvine (92618) ***(P-7104)***
Smci, Glendale *Also called Software Management Cons Inc* ***(P-16489)***
SMD Logistics Inc....C....831 758-5300
26710 Encinal Rd Salinas (93908) ***(P-5171)***
Smf Clinical Lab, Sacramento *Also called Sutter Health* ***(P-25263)***
Smg....B....209 937-7433
3445 S El Dorado St Stockton (95206) ***(P-27605)***
Smg Food and Beverage LLC (PA)....D....909 937-3000
2000 E Convention Ctr Way Ontario (91764) ***(P-17473)***
Smg Holdings Inc....D....310 432-2893
225 E Broadway 312 Glendale (91205) ***(P-10943)***
Smg Holdings Inc....C....650 738-8737
747 Howard St San Francisco (94103) ***(P-10944)***
Smg Holdings Inc....B....559 445-8100
848 M St Fl 2nd Fresno (93721) ***(P-17474)***
Smg Holdings Inc....D....760 325-6611
277 N Avenida Caballeros Palm Springs (92262) ***(P-27456)***
Smg Holdings Inc....D....562 499-7611
300 E Ocean Blvd Long Beach (90802) ***(P-10945)***
Smg Management Facility, Ontario *Also called Ontario Convention Center Corp* ***(P-17370)***
Smg Stockton, Stockton *Also called Smg* ***(P-27605)***
Smg Stone Company Inc....D....818 767-0000
8460 San Fernando Rd Sun Valley (91352) ***(P-2823)***
Smile Brands Group Inc (PA)....D....714 668-1300
100 Spectrum Center Dr # 1500 Irvine (92618) ***(P-27032)***
Smile Family Inc....D....727 771-3641
107 S Railroad Ave San Mateo (94401) ***(P-15455)***
Smile Housing Corporation....D....805 772-6066
800 Quintana Rd Ste 2c Morro Bay (93442) ***(P-22680)***
Smile Keepers, Inglewood *Also called Interdent Inc* ***(P-20117)***
Smile Wide Dental, Irvine *Also called Universal Care Inc* ***(P-22707)***
Smisc Holdings....E....707 938-8448
Hwy 121 Sonoma (95476) ***(P-18544)***
Smith & Sons Investment Co....E....949 646-9648
735 Ohms Way Costa Mesa (92627) ***(P-11766)***
Smith Barney, Los Angeles *Also called Citigroup Global Markets Inc* ***(P-9930)***
Smith Barney, Torrance *Also called Citigroup Global Markets Inc* ***(P-9934)***
Smith Barney, Irvine *Also called Citigroup Global Markets Inc* ***(P-9935)***
Smith Barney, La Jolla *Also called Citigroup Global Markets Inc* ***(P-9936)***
Smith Barney, Rllng HLS Est *Also called Citigroup Global Markets Inc* ***(P-9938)***
Smith Barneys, Menlo Park *Also called Citigroup Global Markets Inc* ***(P-9940)***
Smith Broadcasting Group Inc (PA)....C....805 965-0400
2315 Red Rose Way Santa Barbara (93109) ***(P-27033)***
Smith Broadcasting Group Inc....D....805 882-3933
730 Miramonte Dr Santa Barbara (93109) ***(P-5838)***
Smith Bros Inc (PA)....D....805 449-2841
2301 Townsgate Rd Ste A Westlake Village (91361) ***(P-3081)***
Smith Bros Finished Carpentry, Westlake Village *Also called Smith Bros Inc* ***(P-3081)***
Smith Brothers Restaurant Inc....D....626 577-2400
100 Corson St Lbby Pasadena (91103) ***(P-27034)***
Smith Coleman Inc....E....310 671-8271
707 N La Brea Ave Inglewood (90302) ***(P-11767)***
Smith Electric Service, Santa Maria *Also called Brannon Inc* ***(P-1381)***
Smith International Inc....C....909 906-7900
11031 Jersey Blvd Ste A Rancho Cucamonga (91730) ***(P-1079)***
Smith Micro Software Inc (PA)....C....949 362-5800
51 Columbia Aliso Viejo (92656) ***(P-15854)***
Smith Packing Inc....C....805 343-0329
680 S Simas Rd Santa Maria (93455) ***(P-9260)***
Smith Ranch....E....530 695-2521
1671 Campbell Rd Live Oak (95953) ***(P-230)***
Smith Residential Care Fcilty (PA)....D....559 584-8451
318 E 4th St Hanford (93230) ***(P-22420)***
Smith River Lucky 7 Casino....D....707 487-7777
350 N Indian Rd Smith River (95567) ***(P-13243)***
Smith-Emery Company (PA)....D....213 745-5312
781 E Washington Blvd Los Angeles (90021) ***(P-27457)***
Smith-Emery San Francisco Inc....C....415 642-7326
1940 Oakdale Ave San Francisco (94124) ***(P-17475)***
Smithgroup Inc....D....415 227-0100
301 Battery St San Francisco (94111) ***(P-26110)***
Smithgroup Inc....C....313 442-8351
301 Battery St Fl 7 San Francisco (94111) ***(P-26111)***
Smithgroupjjr, San Francisco *Also called Smithgroup Inc* ***(P-26111)***
Smoke Tree Inc....D....760 327-1221
1850 Smoke Tree Ln Palm Springs (92264) ***(P-13244)***
Smoke Tree Ranch, Palm Springs *Also called Smoke Tree Inc* ***(P-13244)***
Smokehouse Pet Products Inc....E....818 771-0181
11850 Sheldon St Sun Valley (91352) ***(P-8869)***
Smp Construction & Maint Inc (PA)....D....925 961-9012
1813 Rutan Dr Ste A Livermore (94551) ***(P-1653)***
SMS Transportation....D....310 527-9200
18516 S Broadway Gardena (90248) ***(P-23391)***
SMS Transportation Svcs Inc....C....213 489-5367
865 S Figueroa St # 2750 Los Angeles (90017) ***(P-3727)***
Smss, Foster City *Also called Sony Interactive Entrmt LLC* ***(P-17477)***
Smud Energy Services, Sacramento *Also called Sacramento Municpl Utility Dst* ***(P-6104)***
Smuk Inc....C....323 904-4680
3800 Barham Blvd Ste 410 Los Angeles (90068) ***(P-18117)***
Snackademic, San Francisco *Also called Cesar Chavez Student Center* ***(P-10863)***
Snap Inc (PA)....C....310 399-3339
2772 Dnald Douglas Loop N Santa Monica (90405) ***(P-15456)***
Snap Technologies Inc....E....626 585-6900
130 W Union St Pasadena (91103) ***(P-27458)***
Snap-On Incorporated....D....626 965-0668
19220 San Jose Ave City of Industry (91748) ***(P-7603)***
Snap-On Tools, City of Industry *Also called Snap-On Incorporated* ***(P-7603)***
SNAPCHAT, Santa Monica *Also called Snap Inc* ***(P-15456)***
Snapdocs Inc....E....415 967-0136
100 Montgomery St # 2400 San Francisco (94104) ***(P-15457)***
Snapdragon Place 1 LP....D....805 659-3791
702 County Square Dr Ventura (93003) ***(P-11115)***
Snaplogic Inc (PA)....C....888 494-1570
1825 S Grant St Ste 550 San Mateo (94402) ***(P-15855)***
Snb Corporation....C....310 457-9111
30765 Pacific Malibu (90265) ***(P-24051)***
Sneary Construction Inc....E....909 982-1833
1182 Monte Vista Ave # 2 Upland (91786) ***(P-2959)***
Snell & Wilmer LLP....C....714 427-7000
600 Anton Blvd Ste 1400 Costa Mesa (92626) ***(P-23392)***
Snelling Employment LLC....D....510 769-4400
2203 Harvbor Bay Pkwy Alameda (94502) ***(P-14762)***
Snf Management....D....310 385-1090
9200 W Sunset Blvd # 700 West Hollywood (90069) ***(P-27035)***
Snoopy's Galary and Gift Shop, Santa Rosa *Also called Redwood Empire Ice Oprtons LLC* ***(P-19225)***
Snoozie Shavings Inc (PA)....D....707 464-6186
525 Elk Valley Rd Crescent City (95531) ***(P-4265)***
Snow Creek Resort, Mammoth Lakes *Also called Snowcreek Property Management* ***(P-11768)***
Snow Summit Ski Corporation (PA)....A....909 866-5766
880 Summit Blvd Big Bear Lake (92315) ***(P-13245)***
Snowbounders Ski Club....D....714 892-4897
5402 Tattershall Ave Westminster (92683) ***(P-19050)***
Snowcreek Property Management....E....760 934-3333
1254 Old Mammoth Rd Mammoth Lakes (93546) ***(P-11768)***
Snowflake Computing Inc (PA)....D....844 766-9355
100 S Ellsworth Ave San Mateo (94401) ***(P-15458)***
Snowline Hspc Eldorado Cnty....C....916 817-2338
6520 Pleasant Valley Rd Diamond Springs (95619) ***(P-20959)***
Snowline Hspice El Dorado Cnty....C....530 621-7820
6520 Pleasant Valley Rd Diamond Springs (95619) ***(P-20960)***

ALPHABETIC

Employee Codes: A=Over 500 employees, B=251-500
C=101-250, D=51-100, E=50
2019 Directory of California
Wholesalers and Services Companies
© Mergent Inc. 1-800-342-5647
1469

Snyder Langston, Irvine *Also called Snyder Langston L P (P-1654)*
Snyder Langston L P..........D.......949 863-9200
17962 Cowan Irvine (92614) ***(P-1654)***
So CA Edison, Rosemead *Also called Southern California Edison Co (P-6141)*
So Cal Land Maintenance Inc..........D.......714 231-1454
2965 E Coronado St Anaheim (92806) ***(P-14394)***
So Cal Sandbags Inc..........D.......951 277-3404
12620 Bosley Ln Corona (92883) ***(P-7871)***
So Cal Ship Services..........D.......310 519-8411
971 S Seaside Ave San Pedro (90731) ***(P-4720)***
So Calif Stone Center, Encino *Also called Southern Cal Stone Ctr LLC (P-19926)*
So California Ventures Ltd..........D.......714 524-0021
1101 Richfield Rd Placentia (92870) ***(P-1655)***
So-Cal Strl Stl Fbrication Inc..........E.......909 877-1299
130 S Spruce Ave Rialto (92376) ***(P-3398)***
Soaprojects Inc (PA)..........D.......650 960-9900
495 N Whisman Rd Ste 100 Mountain View (94043) ***(P-27459)***
Soares Lumber Company, Gilroy *Also called PSG Fencing Corporation (P-3570)*
Sobaliving Llc..........E.......800 595-3803
22669 Pacific Coast Hwy Malibu (90265) ***(P-22886)***
Sobel Ross H Law Offices..........E.......310 788-8995
1875 Century Park E Los Angeles (90067) ***(P-23393)***
Sobel, Ross Howell, Los Angeles *Also called Sobel Ross H Law Offices (P-23393)*
Soboba Band Luiseno Indians..........A.......951 665-1000
23333 Soboba Rd San Jacinto (92583) ***(P-17476)***
Soboba Casino, San Jacinto *Also called Soboba Band Luiseno Indians (P-17476)*
Soboba Indian Health Clinic, San Jacinto *Also called Riverside-San Bernardino (P-19829)*
Sobol Philip A MD P C Inc..........E.......310 649-5894
8618 S Sepulveda Blvd # 130 Los Angeles (90045) ***(P-19893)***
SOBRIETY HOUSE, Long Beach *Also called Safe Refuge (P-24659)*
Soc Pathology Medical Group..........D.......310 225-3220
2374 E Pacifica Pl Rancho Dominguez (90220) ***(P-19894)***
Soc/General Services/Bpm..........D.......415 703-5341
455 Golden Gate Ave # 2600 San Francisco (94102) ***(P-27036)***
Socal Coatings Inc..........E.......619 660-5395
2820 Via Orange Way Ste J Spring Valley (91978) ***(P-2482)***
Socal Home Care-Givers Svcs, Tustin *Also called RES-Care Inc (P-22404)*
Socal Services Inc..........C.......858 453-1331
6336 Greenwich Dr Ste 100 San Diego (92122) ***(P-14763)***
Socal Sportsnet LLC..........A.......619 795-5000
100 Park Blvd San Diego (92101) ***(P-18465)***
Socal Staffing, San Diego *Also called Therastaff Inc (P-14921)*
Socal Uniform Rental, San Gabriel *Also called Cal Southern Services (P-13520)*
Sociable Labs Inc..........E.......415 225-8740
25 Division St San Mateo (94402) ***(P-16178)***
Social Advocates For Y..........C.......619 283-9624
4275 El Cajon Blvd # 101 San Diego (92105) ***(P-24052)***
SOCIAL ADVOCATES FOR YOUTH, Santa Rosa *Also called Individuals Now (P-23855)*
Social Advocates For Youth (PA)..........E.......805 928-1707
105 N Lincoln St Santa Maria (93458) ***(P-24053)***
Social Finance Inc (PA)..........C.......415 697-2049
1 Letterman Dr Ste 250 San Francisco (94129) ***(P-9907)***
Social Finance Inc..........B.......707 473-9889
375 Healdsburg Ave # 280 Healdsburg (95448) ***(P-9908)***
Social Hbltion Rlpse Prvntion, San Francisco *Also called Sharper Future (P-19889)*
SOCIAL INTEREST SOLUTIONS, Oakland *Also called Center To Promote Healthcare A (P-22760)*
Social Science Service Center..........D.......909 421-7120
18612 Santa Ana Ave Bloomington (92316) ***(P-22050)***
Social Service Dept- Admin, City of Industry *Also called County of Los Angeles (P-26831)*
Social Services Agency, Santa Ana *Also called County of Orange (P-23701)*
Social Services Agency, Orange *Also called County of Orange (P-23702)*
Social Services Dept, Lompoc *Also called Santa Barbara County of (P-24027)*
Social Services, Department of, Ukiah *Also called County of Mendocino (P-23691)*
Social Services, Dept of, Lancaster *Also called County of Los Angeles (P-23658)*
Social Studies School Service..........D.......310 839-2436
10200 Jefferson Blvd Culver City (90232) ***(P-7248)***
Social Vocational Services Inc..........D.......559 443-7119
1401 Fulton St Ste 510 Fresno (93721) ***(P-24678)***
Socialize Inc..........E.......415 529-4019
450 Townsend St 102 San Francisco (94107) ***(P-15856)***
Society For San Francisco..........C.......415 554-3000
201 Alabama St San Francisco (94103) ***(P-25464)***
Society of St Vincent (PA)..........D.......510 638-7600
2272 San Pablo Ave Oakland (94612) ***(P-25465)***
Society of St Vincent De (PA)..........D.......323 224-6280
210 N Avenue 21 Los Angeles (90031) ***(P-25466)***
Society6 LLC..........E.......310 394-6400
1655 26th St Santa Monica (90404) ***(P-16179)***
Socratic Technologies Inc (PA)..........D.......415 430-2200
208 Utah St Ste 350 San Francisco (94103) ***(P-26565)***
Sodexo Inc..........D.......818 952-2201
1812 Verdugo Blvd Fl 1 Glendale (91208) ***(P-27460)***
Sodexo Management Inc..........D.......925 325-9657
851 Howard St San Francisco (94103) ***(P-27037)***
Sodexo Management Inc..........D.......209 667-3634
1 University Cir Turlock (95382) ***(P-27038)***
Sodexo Operations LLC..........D.......831 582-3838
100 Campus Ctr Bldg 16 Seaside (93955) ***(P-27039)***
Sodexo Operations LLC..........D.......619 429-5692
1325 Iris Ave Bldg 181 Imperial Beach (91932) ***(P-14395)***
Soex Group, Vernon *Also called Soex West Usa LLC (P-8277)*
Soex West Usa LLC..........B.......323 264-8300
3294 E 26th St Vernon (90058) ***(P-8277)***
Soffietti Co..........D.......909 907-2277
236 W Orange Show San Bernardino (92408) ***(P-7604)***
Sofi, San Francisco *Also called Social Finance Inc (P-9907)*
Sofitel, Los Angeles *Also called Beverly Blvd Leaseco LLC (P-12380)*
Sofitel Los Angeles, Los Angeles *Also called Accor Corp (P-12304)*
Soft Machines Inc..........D.......408 969-0215
3920 Freedom Cir Santa Clara (95054) ***(P-16053)***
Softhq..........E.......858 658-9200
6494 Weathers Pl Ste 200 San Diego (92121) ***(P-16488)***
Softscript Inc..........A.......310 451-2110
2215 Campus Dr El Segundo (90245) ***(P-14134)***
Softsol Resources Inc (HQ)..........C.......510 824-2000
46755 Fremont Blvd Fremont (94538) ***(P-15459)***
Software Ag Inc..........C.......408 490-5300
2901 Tasman Dr Ste 219 Santa Clara (95054) ***(P-15857)***
Software AG of Virginia, Santa Clara *Also called Software Ag Inc (P-15857)*
Software AG Usa Inc..........C.......703 860-5050
1198 E Arques Ave Sunnyvale (94085) ***(P-15460)***
Software Dynamics Incorporated..........C.......818 992-3299
8501 Fllbrook Ave Ste 200 Canoga Park (91304) ***(P-16054)***
Software Management Cons Inc (PA)..........B.......818 240-3177
500 Nth Brn Blvd Ste 1100 Glendale (91203) ***(P-16489)***
Sohnen Barry As Co Trustee..........E.......562 946-3531
8945 Eice Rd Santa Fe Springs (90670) ***(P-12126)***
Sohnen Enterprises Inc (PA)..........E.......562 903-4957
13225 Marquardt Ave Santa Fe Springs (90670) ***(P-17887)***
Soiree Valet Parking Service..........C.......415 284-9700
1470 Howard St San Francisco (94103) ***(P-13776)***
Sol Transportation Inc..........E.......760 720-4327
2525 Ramona Dr Vista (92084) ***(P-3848)***
Solag Disposal Co, San Juan Capistrano *Also called Solag Incorporated (P-6476)*
Solag Incorporated..........D.......949 728-1206
31641 Ortege Hwy San Juan Capistrano (92675) ***(P-6476)***
Solairus Aviation, Petaluma *Also called Sunset Aviation LLC (P-4913)*
Solano County Mental Health..........E.......707 428-1131
9808 Venice Blvd Ste 700 Culver City (90232) ***(P-24054)***
Solano County Probation Dept, Fairfield *Also called County of Solano (P-23745)*
SOLANO FAMILY & CHILDREN'S SER, Fairfield *Also called Solano Family & Chld Council (P-24383)*
Solano Family & Chld Council..........D.......707 863-3950
421 Executive Ct N Fairfield (94534) ***(P-24383)***
Solano Garbage Company Inc..........D.......707 437-8900
2901 Industrial Ct Fairfield (94533) ***(P-6477)***
Solano Gateway Realty Inc (PA)..........D.......707 422-1725
2420 Martin Rd Ste 100 Fairfield (94534) ***(P-11769)***
Solano Irrigation District..........D.......707 448-6847
810 Vaca Valley Pkwy # 201 Vacaville (95688) ***(P-6565)***
Solano Pacific Corporation..........D.......707 745-6000
900 1st St Benicia (94510) ***(P-11770)***
Solano Regional Medical Group (PA)..........C.......707 426-3911
1234 Empire St Fairfield (94533) ***(P-19895)***
Solar Company Inc..........D.......510 888-9488
20861 Wilbeam Ave Ste 1 Castro Valley (94546) ***(P-2360)***
Solar Energy LLC..........D.......818 449-5816
21600 Oxnard St Ste 1200 Woodland Hills (91367) ***(P-2361)***
Solar Link International Inc..........C.......909 605-7789
4652 E Brickell St Ste A Ontario (91761) ***(P-7872)***
Solar Spectrum LLC..........B.......844 777-6527
150 Linden St Oakland (94607) ***(P-2362)***
Solaredge Technologies Inc..........B.......650 320-7695
2225 E Bayshore Rd Palo Alto (94303) ***(P-7398)***
Solari Enterprises Inc..........C.......714 282-2520
1507 W Yale Ave Orange (92867) ***(P-10946)***
Solaris Paper Inc..........C.......562 653-1680
13415 Carmenita Rd Santa Fe Springs (90670) ***(P-7996)***
Solarreserve Inc..........D.......310 315-2200
520 Broadway Fl 6 Santa Monica (90401) ***(P-6112)***
Solartis LLC..........C.......310 251-4861
1601 N Sepulveda Blvd Manhattan Beach (90266) ***(P-15461)***
Solcius LLC..........B.......951 772-0030
12155 Magnolia Ave 12b Riverside (92503) ***(P-2363)***
Solcom Inc..........B.......510 940-2490
24801 Huntwood Ave Hayward (94544) ***(P-1980)***
Solcom Communications Inc, Hayward *Also called Solcom Inc (P-1980)*
Solecon Industrial Contrs Inc..........D.......209 572-7390
1401 Mcwilliams Way Modesto (95351) ***(P-2364)***
Soledad Cmnty Hlth Care Dst..........D.......831 678-2462
612 Main St Soledad (93960) ***(P-20771)***
SOLEDAD MEDICAL GROUP, Soledad *Also called Soledad Cmnty Hlth Care Dst (P-20771)*
Soleeva Energy Inc..........D.......408 396-4954
1938 Junction Ave San Jose (95131) ***(P-2365)***
Soleil Communications LLC..........D.......619 624-2888
2655 Camino Dl Rio N 11 San Diego (92108) ***(P-26566)***
Solemnity Personnel..........E.......323 718-3979
2008 Camfiled Ave Commerce (90040) ***(P-14764)***
Solestage Inc..........E.......909 576-1309
17651 Railroad St City of Industry (91748) ***(P-16055)***
Solex Contracting Inc..........D.......951 308-1706
42146 Remington Ave Temecula (92590) ***(P-1981)***
Solheim Lutheran Home..........C.......323 257-7518
2236 Merton Ave Los Angeles (90041) ***(P-24679)***
Soli-Bond Inc..........E.......661 631-1633
4230 Foster Ave Bakersfield (93308) ***(P-1080)***
Solid Commerce, Marina Del Rey *Also called Liquidate Direct LLC (P-15999)*
Solid Drywall, Antelope *Also called Leavy Brothers Incorporated (P-2910)*
Solid Waste Services, San Marcos *Also called Edco Waste & Recycl Svcs Inc (P-6395)*
Solid Wastes of Willits Inc (PA)..........D.......707 459-4845
351 Franklin Ave Willits (95490) ***(P-4065)***
Solidcore Systems Inc (HQ)..........D.......408 387-8400
3965 Freedom Cir Santa Clara (95054) ***(P-15462)***
Soligent Distribution LLC (HQ)..........D.......707 992-3100
1400 N Mcdowell Blvd # 201 Petaluma (94954) ***(P-7543)***

Mergent e-mail: customerrelations@mergent.com
1470
2019 Directory of California
Wholesalers and Services Companies
(P-0000) Products & Services Section entry number
(PA)=Parent Co (HQ)=Headquarters (DH)=Div Headquarters

Solimar Farms Inc D 805 986-8806
1312 Del Norte Rd Camarillo (93010) ***(P-122)***

Solix Technologies Inc (PA) D 408 654-6446
4701 Patrick Henry Dr # 2001 Santa Clara (95054) ***(P-15463)***

Solo W-2 Inc C 925 680-0200
3478 Buskirk Ave Ste 1000 Pleasant Hill (94523) ***(P-27461)***

Solo Workforce, Pleasant Hill *Also called Solo W-2 Inc* ***(P-27461)***

Solomon Ward Sdnwurm Smith LLP D 619 231-0303
401 B St Ste 1200 San Diego (92101) ***(P-23394)***

Solopoint Solutions Inc D 714 708-3639
150 Paularino Ave Ste 282 Costa Mesa (92626) ***(P-25917)***

Solpac Inc C 619 296-6247
2424 Congress St San Diego (92110) ***(P-1656)***

Solpac Construction Inc C 619 296-6247
2424 Congress St San Diego (92110) ***(P-27040)***

Soltek Pacific, San Diego *Also called Solpac Inc* ***(P-1656)***

SOLTEK PACIFIC CONSTRUCTION CO, San Diego *Also called Solpac Construction Inc* ***(P-27040)***

Soltis Golf Incorporated D 909 822-7000
869 W 9th St Upland (91786) ***(P-2065)***

Solugenix Corporation (PA) D 866 749-7658
601 Valencia Ave Brea (92823) ***(P-27863)***

Solugenix Corporation D 866 749-7658
225 N Barranca St West Covina (91791) ***(P-16490)***

Solute (PA) D 619 224-2810
1660 Hotel Cir N Ste 600 San Diego (92108) ***(P-25918)***

Solute Consulting, San Diego *Also called Solute* ***(P-25918)***

Solution One Industries Inc D 254 702-7329
Ave G St Bldg 934 Fort Irwin (92310) ***(P-4632)***

Solutions 2 Go LLC D 949 825-7700
20091 Ellipse Foothill Ranch (92610) ***(P-7961)***

Solutionset LLC C 415 367-6300
100 Montgomery St # 1500 San Francisco (94104) ***(P-13904)***

Solve All Facility Services, Oceanside *Also called Bergensons Property Svcs Inc* ***(P-14200)***

Solve Healthcare Corporation (PA) D 949 891-0300
1300 Bristol St N Ste 285 Newport Beach (92660) ***(P-27864)***

Solver Inc E 310 691-5300
10780 Santa Monica Blvd # 370 Los Angeles (90025) ***(P-7105)***

Soma Surgicenter E 415 641-6889
1580 Valencia St San Francisco (94110) ***(P-21758)***

Somansa Technologies Inc D 408 297-1234
3003 N 1st St 301 San Jose (95134) ***(P-7106)***

Somerford Place, Fresno *Also called Fresno Heritage Partners* ***(P-24535)***

Somerford Place Encinitas, Encinitas *Also called Five Star Quality Care Inc* ***(P-24529)***

Somerford Place Fresno, Fresno *Also called Five Star Quality Care Inc* ***(P-20434)***

Somerford Place Stockton, Stockton *Also called Five Star Quality Care Inc* ***(P-22299)***

Somerset Special Care Center D 619 442-0245
151 Claydelle Ave El Cajon (92020) ***(P-20961)***

Somis Pacific AG Management, Temecula *Also called Sierra Pacific Farms Inc* ***(P-712)***

Sonata Software North Amer Inc (HQ) D 510 791-7220
2201 Walnut Ave Ste 180 Fremont (94538) ***(P-15464)***

Sonic Industries Inc C 310 532-8382
20030 Normandie Ave Torrance (90502) ***(P-25919)***

Sonic Solutions Holdings Inc B 408 562-8400
2830 De La Cruz Blvd Santa Clara (95050) ***(P-15858)***

Sonicocom Inc D 213 291-0475
2202 S Figueroa St Los Angeles (90007) ***(P-16491)***

Sonicwall Inc (PA) D 800 509-1265
1033 Mccarthy Blvd Milpitas (95035) ***(P-16056)***

Sonifi Solutions Inc C 650 752-1980
1065 E Hillsdale Blvd # 228 Foster City (94404) ***(P-5931)***

Sonitrol, San Jose *Also called Pacific West Security Inc* ***(P-16926)***

Sonitrol Security Systems, Fresno *Also called Kimberlite Corporation* ***(P-16917)***

Sonoma Cnty Ind Living Skills D 707 765-8444
1799 Pepper Rd Petaluma (94952) ***(P-24680)***

Sonoma County Airport Ex Inc D 707 837-8700
5807 Old Redwood Hwy Santa Rosa (95403) ***(P-3728)***

Sonoma County Data Processing, Santa Rosa *Also called County of Sonoma* ***(P-16110)***

Sonoma County Humane Society E 707 542-0882
5345 Highway 12 Santa Rosa (95407) ***(P-633)***

Sonoma County Indian Health PR (PA) C 707 521-4545
144 Stony Point Rd Santa Rosa (95401) ***(P-19896)***

Sonoma County Water Agency C 707 526-5370
404 Aviation Blvd Ste 0 Santa Rosa (95403) ***(P-6313)***

Sonoma Grapevines Inc (PA) D 707 542-5521
1919 Dennis Ln Santa Rosa (95403) ***(P-9162)***

Sonoma Hotel Operator Inc C 707 938-9000
100 Boyes Blvd Sonoma (95476) ***(P-13246)***

Sonoma Hotel Partners LP D 707 283-2888
745 Baywood Dr Petaluma (94954) ***(P-13247)***

Sonoma Life Support, Santa Rosa *Also called American Med Resp Amblnc Svc* ***(P-3750)***

Sonoma Technology Inc D 707 665-9900
1450 N Mcdowell Blvd Petaluma (94954) ***(P-27865)***

Sonoma Valley Health Care Dst (PA) B 707 935-5000
347 Andrieux St Sonoma (95476) ***(P-21759)***

SONOMA VALLEY HOSPITAL, Sonoma *Also called Sonoma Valley Health Care Dst* ***(P-21759)***

Sonoma Valley Womans Club D 707 938-8313
574 1st St E Sonoma (95476) ***(P-25252)***

Sonoma Vly Cnty Sanitation Dst C 707 547-1900
404 Aviation Blvd Santa Rosa (95403) ***(P-6329)***

Sonora Regional Medical Center, Sonora *Also called Adventist Health Sonora* ***(P-21264)***

Sonora Retirement Center Inc E 209 588-0373
12877 Sylva Ln Ofc Sonora (95370) ***(P-24681)***

Sonora Trade Company Inc D 619 878-5848
2127 Olympic Pkwy Chula Vista (91915) ***(P-9261)***

Sonoran Roofing Inc (PA) C 916 624-1080
4161 Citrus Ave Rocklin (95677) ***(P-3200)***

Sonshine Auto Body, Victorville *Also called Sonshine Collision Services* ***(P-17742)***

Sonshine Collision Services D 760 243-3185
17200 Jasmine St Victorville (92395) ***(P-17742)***

Sonshine North Autobody D 760 245-3183
17200 Jasmine St Victorville (92395) ***(P-17743)***

Sony Corporation of America C 650 655-8000
2207 Bridgepointe Pkwy Foster City (94404) ***(P-15465)***

Sony Dadc New Mdia Sltions Inc C 310 760-8500
4499 Glencoe Ave Marina Del Rey (90292) ***(P-18243)***

Sony Electronics Inc C 714 508-7634
14450 Myford Rd Irvine (92606) ***(P-18118)***

Sony Electronics Inc B 415 833-4796
835 Howard St San Francisco (94103) ***(P-18119)***

Sony Electronics Inc C 310 835-6121
2201 E Carson St Carson (90810) ***(P-7429)***

Sony Interactive Entrmt LLC (HQ) C 310 981-1500
2207 Bridgepointe Pkwy Foster City (94404) ***(P-17477)***

Sony Logistics, Carson *Also called Sony Electronics Inc* ***(P-7429)***

Sony Music Entertainment Inc C 310 272-2555
9830 Wilshire Blvd Beverly Hills (90212) ***(P-8059)***

Sony Pictures Entrmt Inc B 310 840-8000
9050 Washington Blvd Culver City (90232) ***(P-18120)***

Sony Pictures Entrmt Inc B 310 202-1234
9336 Washington Blvd Culver City (90232) ***(P-18466)***

Sony Pictures Entrmt Inc B 310 244-3558
6527 W 82nd St Los Angeles (90045) ***(P-18467)***

Sony Pictures Entrmt Inc (HQ) A 310 244-4000
10202 Washington Blvd Culver City (90232) ***(P-18121)***

Sony Pictures Imageworks Inc A 310 840-8000
9050 Washington Blvd Culver City (90232) ***(P-16180)***

Sony Pictures Studios, Culver City *Also called Sony Pictures Entrmt Inc* ***(P-18121)***

Sony Pictures Studios Inc B 310 244-4000
1250 S Beverly Glen Blvd # 112 Los Angeles (90024) ***(P-18122)***

Sony Pictures Television Inc (HQ) B 310 244-7625
10202 Washington Blvd Culver City (90232) ***(P-18123)***

Sony Publishers, Beverly Hills *Also called Sony Music Entertainment Inc* ***(P-8059)***

Soofer Co Inc D 323 234-6666
2828 S Alameda St Vernon (90058) ***(P-8870)***

Sophia Lyn Convalescent Hosp, Pasadena *Also called Slch Inc* ***(P-20770)***

Soren McAdam Christianson LLP D 909 798-2222
2068 Orange Tree Ln # 100 Redlands (92374) ***(P-26296)***

Soroptmist Intl Huntington Bch E 714 271-9305
212 Utica Ave Huntington Beach (92648) ***(P-17478)***

Soroptomist Intl Tahoe Sierra E 530 573-1657
3050 Lake Tahoe Blvd South Lake Tahoe (96150) ***(P-25467)***

Sorrento Therapeutics Inc (PA) C 858 203-4100
4955 Directors Pl San Diego (92121) ***(P-26457)***

SOS Hosting, El Segundo *Also called Infrascale Inc* ***(P-7062)***

SOS Metals Inc (HQ) C 310 217-8848
201 E Gardena Blvd Gardena (90248) ***(P-7997)***

SOS Security Incorporated C 310 392-9600
2601 Ocean Park Blvd # 208 Santa Monica (90405) ***(P-16830)***

SOS Security Incorporated C 510 782-4900
26250 Industrial Blvd # 48 Hayward (94545) ***(P-16831)***

SOS Security LLC D 310 859-8248
331 N Beverly Dr Ste 3 Beverly Hills (90210) ***(P-16832)***

Sosa Granite & Marble Inc E 925 373-7675
7701 Marathon Dr Livermore (94550) ***(P-3011)***

Sosa Tile Co, Livermore *Also called Sosa Granite & Marble Inc* ***(P-3011)***

Sothebys Intl Rlty Inc E 310 456-6431
23405 Pacific Coast Hwy Malibu (90265) ***(P-11771)***

Soto Company Inc D 949 493-9403
34275 Camino Capistrano A Capistrano Beach (92624) ***(P-942)***

Soto Food Service, Hacienda Heights *Also called Soto Provision Inc* ***(P-6788)***

Soto Provision Inc D 626 458-4600
488 Parriott Pl W Hacienda Heights (91745) ***(P-6788)***

Sotoyome Medical Building LLC D 707 525-4000
990 Sonoma Ave Ste 15 Santa Rosa (95404) ***(P-10947)***

Souldriver Lessee Inc D 619 819-9500
435 6th Ave San Diego (92101) ***(P-13248)***

Soule Park Golf Course, Ojai *Also called Mf Daily Oxnard Ranch Partnr* ***(P-18734)***

Sound Mind and Body Inc D 206 547-2706
117 Via Yella Newport Beach (92663) ***(P-18654)***

Sound Technologies Inc D 760 918-9626
5810 Van Allen Way Carlsbad (92008) ***(P-7219)***

Sound-Crete Contracting D 760 291-1240
530 Opper St Ste A Escondido (92029) ***(P-7695)***

Sound-Eklin, Carlsbad *Also called Sound Technologies Inc* ***(P-7219)***

Soundhound Inc (PA) D 408 441-3200
5400 Betsy Ross Dr Santa Clara (95054) ***(P-15466)***

Source 44 LLC C 877 916-6337
1921 Palomar Oaks Way # 205 Carlsbad (92008) ***(P-27866)***

Source Intelligence, Carlsbad *Also called Source 44 LLC* ***(P-27866)***

Source Interlink Media LLC D 310 531-9394
2221 Rosecrans Ave # 195 El Segundo (90245) ***(P-15467)***

Source Logistics Center Corp D 323 887-3884
812 Union St Montebello (90640) ***(P-5172)***

Source Rfrgn & Hvac Inc (PA) C 714 578-2300
800 E Orangethorpe Ave Anaheim (92801) ***(P-2366)***

Sourcewise D 408 350-3200
2115 The Alameda San Jose (95126) ***(P-24055)***

South Asian Help Referral Agcy E 562 402-4132
17100 Pioneer Blvd # 260 Artesia (90701) ***(P-24056)***

South Bay Airport Shuttle D 408 225-4444
14420 Union Ave San Jose (95124) ***(P-3729)***

South Bay Auto Auction D 310 719-2000
13210 S Normandie Ave Gardena (90249) ***(P-6608)***

SOUTH BAY CENTER FOR COMMUNITY, Wilmington *Also called South Bay Ctr For Counseling* ***(P-24058)***

Employee Codes: A=Over 500 employees, B=251-500 C=101-250, D=51-100, E=50
2019 Directory of California Wholesalers and Services Companies
© Mergent Inc. 1-800-342-5647
1471

South Bay Community Services ....C....619 420-3620
430 F St Chula Vista (91910) ***(P-24057)***
South Bay Construction Company, Campbell *Also called B C C S Inc* ***(P-1471)***
South Bay Ctr For Counseling ....D....310 414-2090
540 N Marine Ave Wilmington (90744) ***(P-24058)***
South Bay Drive In Theatre, San Diego *Also called De Anza Land & Leisure Corp* ***(P-18284)***
South Bay Family Medical Group ....D....310 378-2234
3105 Lomita Blvd Torrance (90505) ***(P-19897)***
South Bay Freight System LLC (PA) ....D....626 271-9800
900 Turnbull Canyon Rd City of Industry (91745) ***(P-5173)***
South Bay Group, City of Industry *Also called South Bay Freight System LLC* ***(P-5173)***
South Bay Historical RR Soc ....E....408 243-3969
1005 Railroad Ave Santa Clara (95050) ***(P-25468)***
South Bay Power Plant, Chula Vista *Also called San Diego Gas & Electric Co* ***(P-6152)***
South Bay Regl Public Safety T ....E....408 270-6494
560 Bailey Ave San Jose (95141) ***(P-24231)***
South Bay Rgonal Pub Comm Auth ....E....310 973-1802
4440 W Broadway Hawthorne (90250) ***(P-5995)***
South Bay Sand Blasting and Ta ....D....619 238-8338
326 W 30th St National City (91950) ***(P-17989)***
South Bay Senior Services Inc ....D....310 338-8558
8929 S Sepulveda Blvd # 314 Los Angeles (90045) ***(P-22421)***
South Bay Senior Solutions Inc ....D....408 370-6360
1660 Hamilton Ave Ste 204 San Jose (95125) ***(P-22422)***
South Bay Vlla Preservation LP ....D....310 516-7325
13111 S San Pedro St Los Angeles (90061) ***(P-11116)***
South Baylo Acupuncture Clinic, Los Angeles *Also called South Baylo University* ***(P-22681)***
South Baylo University ....C....213 387-2414
2727 W 6th St Los Angeles (90057) ***(P-22681)***
South Capitol Cottage ....D....951 662-3026
15054 Daisy Rd Adelanto (92301) ***(P-27867)***
South Central Family Hlth Ctr ....D....323 908-4200
4425 S Central Ave Los Angeles (90011) ***(P-19898)***
South Central Los (PA) ....C....213 744-7000
2500 S Western Ave Los Angeles (90018) ***(P-24842)***
South China Sheet Metal Inc ....D....323 225-1522
1740 Albion St Los Angeles (90031) ***(P-2367)***
South Cntl Heatlh & Rehab Prog ....D....310 667-4070
2620 Industry Way Lynwood (90262) ***(P-22682)***
South Cntl Heatlh & Rehab Prog ....D....323 751-2677
5201 S Vermont Ave Los Angeles (90037) ***(P-22683)***
South Cnty Cmnty Hlth Ctr Inc (PA) ....D....650 330-7407
1885 Bay Rd East Palo Alto (94303) ***(P-22887)***
South Coast Air Qulty MGT Dst (PA) ....A....909 396-2000
21865 Copley Dr Diamond Bar (91765) ***(P-27868)***
South Coast Auto Insurance, Huntington Beach *Also called Freeway Insurance* ***(P-10631)***
South Coast Childrens Soc Inc ....C....909 478-3377
24950 Redlands Blvd Loma Linda (92354) ***(P-24059)***
South Coast Childrens Soc Inc ....C....909 364-9788
11780 Central Ave Chino (91710) ***(P-24060)***
South Coast Concrete Cnstr ....E....951 351-7777
6770 Central Ave Ste B Riverside (92504) ***(P-3327)***
South Coast Fencing Center ....D....714 549-2946
3518 W Lake Center Dr C Santa Ana (92704) ***(P-3586)***
South Coast Health Wellness ....E....951 686-9001
4768 Palm Ave Riverside (92501) ***(P-20772)***
South Coast Logistics ....E....714 894-4744
4160 Temescal Canyon Rd # 311 Corona (92883) ***(P-4373)***
South Coast Mechanical Inc ....D....714 738-6644
2283 E Via Burton Anaheim (92806) ***(P-2368)***
South Coast Piering Inc ....D....800 922-2488
41357 Date St Murrieta (92562) ***(P-1657)***
South Coast Plaza LLC (PA) ....D....714 546-0110
3333 Bristol St Ofc Costa Mesa (92626) ***(P-10948)***
South Coast Plaza LLC ....D....714 435-2000
3333 Bristol St Ofc Costa Mesa (92626) ***(P-10949)***
South Coast Plaza Mall, Costa Mesa *Also called South Coast Plaza LLC* ***(P-10949)***
South Coast Plaza Village, Costa Mesa *Also called South Coast Plaza LLC* ***(P-10948)***
South Coast Repertory Inc ....D....714 708-5500
655 Town Center Dr Costa Mesa (92626) ***(P-18405)***
South Coast Stone Paving ....D....714 835-0258
2618 N Baker St Santa Ana (92706) ***(P-1852)***
South Coast Village, Santa Ana *Also called Edwards Theatres Circuit Inc* ***(P-18292)***
South Coast Water District (PA) ....D....949 499-4555
31592 West St Laguna Beach (92651) ***(P-6314)***
South Coast Westin Hotel Co ....D....714 540-2500
686 Anton Blvd Costa Mesa (92626) ***(P-13249)***
South Cone Inc ....C....760 431-2300
5935 Darwin Ct Carlsbad (92008) ***(P-8368)***
South County Housing Corp (PA) ....E....510 582-1460
16500 Monterey St Ste 120 Morgan Hill (95037) ***(P-11772)***
South County Orthopedic Specia ....D....949 586-3200
24331 El Toro Rd Ste 200 Laguna Hills (92637) ***(P-19899)***
South Feather Water & Pwr Agcy (PA) ....D....530 533-4578
2310 Oro Quincy Hwy Oroville (95966) ***(P-6566)***
South Gate Care Centers, South Gate *Also called Far West Inc* ***(P-20425)***
South Gate Dental Group, South Gate *Also called Castle Dental* ***(P-20113)***
South Hills Country Club ....D....626 339-1231
2655 S Citrus St West Covina (91791) ***(P-19051)***
South Market Child Care Inc ....D....415 820-3500
790 Folsom St San Francisco (94107) ***(P-24384)***
South Pasadena San Marino YMCA, South Pasadena *Also called Young Mens Chrstn Assn of La* ***(P-25341)***
South San Jquin Irrigation Dst ....D....209 249-4600
11011 E Highway 120 Manteca (95336) ***(P-6567)***
South Seas Imports, Compton *Also called M M Fab Inc* ***(P-8231)***
South Tahoe Public Utility Dst ....C....530 544-6474
1275 Meadow Crest Dr South Lake Tahoe (96150) ***(P-6330)***
South Tahoe Refuse Co ....D....530 541-5105
2140 Ruth Ave South Lake Tahoe (96150) ***(P-6478)***
South Valley Almond Co LLC ....C....661 391-9000
15443 Beech Ave Wasco (93280) ***(P-8911)***
South Valley Farms, Wasco *Also called South Valley Almond Co LLC* ***(P-8911)***
South Valley Plumbing Inc ....C....408 265-5566
3750 Charter Park Dr F San Jose (95136) ***(P-2369)***
South Valley School District, Fountain Valley *Also called Fountain Valley School Dst* ***(P-14268)***
South West Sun Solar Inc ....E....714 582-3909
13752 Harbor Blvd Garden Grove (92843) ***(P-7637)***
Southbay Sndblst & Tank Clg ....D....619 238-8338
3589 Dalbergia St San Diego (92113) ***(P-17990)***
SOUTHBAY TEEN CHALLENGE, Santa Clara *Also called Teen Challenge Norwestcal Nev* ***(P-24083)***
Southbay Website Design LLC ....D....310 370-4043
1601 Pcf Cast Hwy Ste 290 Hermosa Beach (90254) ***(P-16181)***
Southbourne Inc ....C....415 781-5555
340 Stockton St San Francisco (94108) ***(P-13250)***
Southcoast Dyeing & Finishing, Santa Ana *Also called Chroma Systems* ***(P-13575)***
Southcoast Heating and Air, Vista *Also called ARS American Residential* ***(P-2128)***
Southcoast Welding & Mfg LLC ....B....619 429-1337
2591 Faivre St Ste 1 Chula Vista (91911) ***(P-17925)***
Southeast Area Social Services ....E....562 946-2237
10400 Pioneer Blvd Ste 8 Santa Fe Springs (90670) ***(P-24061)***
SOUTHEAST INDUSTRIES, Downey *Also called ARC Los Angles Orange Counties* ***(P-24147)***
Southeastern Westminster, Westminster *Also called Southern California Edison Co* ***(P-6132)***
Southern Building Maint Inc ....D....213 598-7071
836 Crenshaw Blvd Ste 102 Los Angeles (90005) ***(P-14396)***
Southern CA Hlth & Rhbltn Prg ....C....310 631-8004
2610 Industry Way Ste A Lynwood (90262) ***(P-19900)***
Southern Cal Appraisal Co, Burbank *Also called Sca Enterprises Inc* ***(P-17459)***
Southern Cal Blldog Rescue Inc ....E....714 381-7691
2219 N Spurgeon St Santa Ana (92706) ***(P-25469)***
Southern Cal Halthcare Sys Inc ....A....310 836-7000
3828 Delmas Ter Culver City (90232) ***(P-21760)***
Southern Cal Hosp At Culver Cy, Culver City *Also called Southern Cal Halthcare Sys Inc* ***(P-21760)***
Southern Cal Maid Svc Crpt Clg ....D....310 675-0585
14909 Crenshaw Blvd # 209 Gardena (90249) ***(P-14397)***
Southern Cal Orthopedics, La Mirada *Also called Healthpointe Medical Group Inc* ***(P-19494)***
Southern Cal Orthpd Inst LP ....D....805 497-7015
375 Rolling Oaks Dr Thousand Oaks (91361) ***(P-19901)***
Southern Cal Orthpd Inst LP ....C....818 901-6600
6815 Noble Ave Frnt Frnt Van Nuys (91405) ***(P-19902)***
Southern Cal Orthpd Inst LP ....D....818 901-6600
6815 Noble Ave Ste 112 Westlake Village (91361) ***(P-19903)***
Southern Cal Orthpd Inst LP (PA) ....C....818 901-6600
6815 Noble Ave Van Nuys (91405) ***(P-19904)***
Southern Cal Pipe Trades ADM, Los Angeles *Also called Southern Cal Pipe Trades ADM* ***(P-12127)***
Southern Cal Pipe Trades ADM (PA) ....D....213 385-6161
501 Shatto Pl Ste 500 Los Angeles (90020) ***(P-12127)***
Southern Cal Prmnnte Med Group ....D....949 262-5780
6 Willard Irvine (92604) ***(P-19905)***
Southern Cal Prmnnte Med Group ....D....800 272-3500
13652 Cantara St Panorama City (91402) ***(P-10312)***
Southern Cal Prmnnte Med Group ....D....858 974-1000
5855 Copley Dr Ste 250 San Diego (92111) ***(P-10313)***
Southern Cal Prmnnte Med Group ....D....661 398-5085
3501 Stockdale Hwy Bakersfield (93309) ***(P-19906)***
Southern Cal Prmnnte Med Group ....D....619 528-5000
4647 Zion Ave San Diego (92120) ***(P-19907)***
Southern Cal Prmnnte Med Group ....B....866 984-7483
10800 Magnolia Ave Riverside (92505) ***(P-10314)***
Southern Cal Prmnnte Med Group ....D....310 604-5700
3830 Martin L King Jr Blv Lynwood (90262) ***(P-19908)***
Southern Cal Prmnnte Med Group ....D....661 290-3100
26415 Carl Boyer Dr Santa Clarita (91350) ***(P-21761)***
Southern Cal Prmnnte Med Group ....D....323 857-2000
6041 Cadillac Ave Los Angeles (90034) ***(P-19909)***
Southern Cal Prmnnte Med Group ....D....800 780-1230
25825 Vermont Ave Harbor City (90710) ***(P-19910)***
Southern Cal Prmnnte Med Group ....E....909 427-5000
9961 Sierra Ave Fontana (92335) ***(P-21762)***
Southern Cal Prmnnte Med Group ....D....323 783-5455
4841 Hollywood Blvd Los Angeles (90027) ***(P-19911)***
Southern Cal Prmnnte Med Group ....D....626 960-4844
1511 W Garvey Ave N West Covina (91790) ***(P-10315)***
Southern Cal Prmnnte Med Group ....D....714 734-4500
17542 17th St Ste 300 Tustin (92780) ***(P-10316)***
Southern Cal Prmnnte Med Group ....B....323 783-4893
4760 W Sunset Blvd Los Angeles (90027) ***(P-19912)***
Southern Cal Prmnnte Med Group (PA) ....D....626 405-5704
393 Walnut Dr Pasadena (91107) ***(P-10317)***
Southern Cal Prmnnte Med Group ....E....909 370-2501
789 E Cooley Dr Colton (92324) ***(P-19913)***
Southern Cal Prmnnte Med Group ....E....714 841-7293
18081 Beach Blvd Huntington Beach (92648) ***(P-19914)***
Southern Cal Prmnnte Med Group ....E....619 528-5000
1630 E Main St El Cajon (92021) ***(P-19915)***
Southern Cal Prmnnte Med Group ....E....714 279-4675
411 N Lakeview Ave Anaheim (92807) ***(P-19916)***
Southern Cal Prmnnte Med Group ....E....949 234-2139
30400 Camino Capistrano San Juan Capistrano (92675) ***(P-19917)***
Southern Cal Prmnnte Med Group ....E....714 685-3520
22550 Savi Ranch Pkwy Yorba Linda (92887) ***(P-19918)***

Southern Cal Prmnnte Med Group..........D.......714 967-4760
1900 E 4th St Santa Ana (92705) ***(P-19919)***
Southern Cal Prmnnte Med Group..........E.......619 516-6000
4405 Vandever Ave San Diego (92120) ***(P-19920)***
Southern Cal Prmnnte Med Group..........E.......760 839-7200
732 N Broadway Escondido (92025) ***(P-19921)***
Southern Cal Prmnnte Med Group..........E.......909 394-2505
1255 W Arrow Hwy San Dimas (91773) ***(P-10318)***
Southern Cal Prmnnte Med Group..........E.......323 562-6459
7825 Atlantic Ave Cudahy (90201) ***(P-19922)***
Southern Cal Prmnnte Med Group..........E.......818 592-3038
21263 Erwin St Woodland Hills (91367) ***(P-19923)***
Southern Cal Prmnnte Med Group..........E.......661 222-2150
27107 Tourney Rd Santa Clarita (91355) ***(P-19924)***
Southern Cal Prmnnte Med Group..........A.......619 528-5000
6860 Avenida Encinas Carlsbad (92011) ***(P-10319)***
Southern Cal Prmnnte Med Group..........A.......562 657-2200
9353 Imprl Hwy Grdn Med Downey (90242) ***(P-10320)***
Southern Cal Prmnnte Med Group..........B.......949 376-8619
23781 Maquina Mission Viejo (92691) ***(P-22888)***
Southern Cal Prmnnte Med Group..........D.......661 334-2020
5055 California Ave Bakersfield (93309) ***(P-19925)***
Southern Cal Rgional Rail Auth..........B.......213 452-0200
900 Wilshire Blvd # 1500 Los Angeles (90017) ***(P-3730)***
Southern Cal Spcialty Care Inc..........D.......626 339-5451
845 N Lark Ellen Ave West Covina (91791) ***(P-21763)***
Southern Cal Spcialty Care Inc..........C.......714 564-7800
1901 College Ave Santa Ana (92706) ***(P-21764)***
Southern Cal Spcialty Care Inc (HQ)..........D.......562 944-1900
14900 Imperial Hwy La Mirada (90638) ***(P-21765)***
Southern Cal Stone Ctr LLC..........D.......818 784-8975
5400 Balboa Blvd Ste 111 Encino (91316) ***(P-19926)***
Southern Cal Tele & Enrgy, Temecula *Also called Southern California Tele Co* ***(P-5647)***
Southern Calif Mtl Hdlg Co, Northridge *Also called Southern California Mtl Hdlg* ***(P-7800)***
Southern California / Hawa Reg, El Centro *Also called Securitas SEC Svcs USA Inc* ***(P-16794)***
Southern California / Hawa Reg, Goleta *Also called Securitas SEC Svcs USA Inc* ***(P-16799)***
Southern California / Hawa Reg, Pomona *Also called Securitas SEC Svcs USA Inc* ***(P-16806)***
Southern California / Hawa Reg, Commerce *Also called Securitas SEC Svcs USA Inc* ***(P-16807)***
Southern California / Hawa Reg, Los Angeles *Also called Securitas SEC Svcs USA Inc* ***(P-16808)***
Southern California / Hawa Reg, Long Beach *Also called Securitas SEC Svcs USA Inc* ***(P-16809)***
Southern California / Hawa Reg, Victorville *Also called Securitas SEC Svcs USA Inc* ***(P-16812)***
Southern California Alcohol An (PA)..........D.......562 923-4545
11500 Paramount Blvd Downey (90241) ***(P-22684)***
Southern California Car Transf..........D.......858 586-0006
11139 Roxboro Rd San Diego (92131) ***(P-5247)***
Southern California Carriers, Heber *Also called C S Transport Inc* ***(P-3985)***
Southern California Cen, Long Beach *Also called Memor Ortho Surgic Group A M* ***(P-19680)***
Southern California Document, Brea *Also called Document Proc Solutions Inc* ***(P-16119)***
Southern California Edison Co (HQ)..........A.......626 302-1212
2244 Walnut Grove Ave Rosemead (91770) ***(P-6113)***
Southern California Edison Co..........C.......626 543-8081
4900 Rivergrade Rd 2b1 Irwindale (91706) ***(P-6114)***
Southern California Edison Co..........C.......559 893-3611
54205 Mt Poplar Ave Big Creek (93605) ***(P-6115)***
Southern California Edison Co..........D.......626 303-8480
1440 S California Ave Monrovia (91016) ***(P-6116)***
Southern California Edison Co..........C.......760 873-0715
4000 Bishop Creek Rd Bishop (93514) ***(P-6117)***
Southern California Edison Co..........C.......714 934-0838
14799 Chestnut St Westminster (92683) ***(P-6118)***
Southern California Edison Co..........C.......559 893-2037
55481 Mt Poplar Big Creek (93605) ***(P-6119)***
Southern California Edison Co..........C.......626 302-5101
8380 Klingerman St Rosemead (91770) ***(P-6120)***
Southern California Edison Co..........C.......626 543-6093
4900 Rivergrade Rd Baldwin Park (91706) ***(P-6121)***
Southern California Edison Co..........D.......714 870-3225
1851 W Valencia Dr Fullerton (92833) ***(P-6122)***
Southern California Edison Co..........A.......949 368-2881
14300 Mesa Rd San Clemente (92672) ***(P-6123)***
Southern California Edison Co..........C.......626 302-1212
2131 Walnut Grove Ave Rosemead (91770) ***(P-6124)***
Southern California Edison Co..........C.......714 973-5481
1241 S Grand Ave Santa Ana (92705) ***(P-6125)***
Southern California Edison Co..........C.......818 999-1880
3589 Foothill Dr Thousand Oaks (91361) ***(P-6126)***
Southern California Edison Co..........E.......626 815-7296
6000 N Irwindale Ave A Irwindale (91702) ***(P-6127)***
Southern California Edison Co..........D.......909 469-0251
265 N East End Ave Pomona (91767) ***(P-6128)***
Southern California Edison Co..........D.......714 895-0488
1515 Walnut Grove Ave Rosemead (91770) ***(P-6129)***
Southern California Edison Co..........C.......310 608-5029
1924 E Cashdan St Compton (90220) ***(P-6130)***
Southern California Edison Co..........D.......805 683-5291
103 Love Pl Goleta (93117) ***(P-6131)***
Southern California Edison Co..........B.......714 895-0420
7300 Fenwick Ln Westminster (92683) ***(P-6132)***
Southern California Edison Co..........C.......949 587-5416
14155 Bake Pkwy Irvine (92618) ***(P-6133)***
Southern California Edison Co..........C.......626 633-3070
6042a N Irwindale Ave Irwindale (91702) ***(P-6134)***
Southern California Edison Co..........C.......714 895-0163
7333 Bolsa Ave Westminster (92683) ***(P-6135)***
Southern California Edison Co..........D.......626 814-4212
13025 Los Angeles St Irwindale (91706) ***(P-6136)***
Southern California Edison Co..........C.......909 592-3757
800 W Cienega Ave San Dimas (91773) ***(P-6137)***
Southern California Edison Co..........D.......562 903-3191
9901 Geary Ave Santa Fe Springs (90670) ***(P-6138)***
Southern California Edison Co..........B.......562 491-3803
125 Elm Ave Long Beach (90802) ***(P-6139)***
Southern California Edison Co..........C.......760 951-3242
12353 Hesperia Rd Victorville (92395) ***(P-6140)***
Southern California Edison Co..........C.......626 302-0530
1515 Walnut Grove Ave Rosemead (91770) ***(P-6141)***
Southern California Fleet Svc..........E.......951 272-8655
6726 Nicolett St Riverside (92504) ***(P-17785)***
Southern California Gas Co (HQ)..........C.......213 244-1200
555 W 5th St Los Angeles (90013) ***(P-6163)***
Southern California Gas Co..........D.......714 634-7221
1 Liberty Aliso Viejo (92656) ***(P-6164)***
Southern California Gas Co..........E.......661 399-4431
1510 N Chester Ave Bakersfield (93308) ***(P-6165)***
Southern California Gas Co..........B.......213 244-1200
1801 S Atlantic Blvd Monterey Park (91754) ***(P-6166)***
Southern California Gas Co..........B.......909 335-7802
1981 W Lugonia Ave Redlands (92374) ***(P-6167)***
Southern California Gas Co..........D.......213 244-1200
920 S Stimson Ave City of Industry (91745) ***(P-6168)***
Southern California Gas Co..........D.......213 244-1200
25200 Trumble Rd Romoland (92585) ***(P-6169)***
Southern California Gas Co..........D.......323 881-3587
333 E Main St Ste J Alhambra (91801) ***(P-6170)***
Southern California Gas Co..........D.......562 803-3341
6738 Bright Ave Whittier (90601) ***(P-6171)***
Southern California Gas Co..........D.......310 823-7945
8141 Gulana Ave Venice (90293) ***(P-6172)***
Southern California Gas Co..........C.......909 335-7941
155 S G St San Bernardino (92410) ***(P-6173)***
Southern California Gas Co..........C.......213 244-1200
1600 Corporate Center Dr Monterey Park (91754) ***(P-6174)***
Southern California Gas Co..........E.......562 803-7453
9240 Firestone Blvd Downey (90241) ***(P-6175)***
Southern California Gas Co..........A.......909 305-8297
1050 Overland Ct San Dimas (91773) ***(P-6156)***
Southern California Gas Co..........D.......800 427-2200
23130 Valencia Blvd Valencia (91355) ***(P-6176)***
Southern California Gas Co..........B.......818 701-2592
9400 Oakdale Ave Chatsworth (91311) ***(P-6153)***
Southern California Gas Tower..........B.......213 244-1200
555 W 5th St Los Angeles (90013) ***(P-6177)***
Southern California Golf Assn (PA)..........D.......818 980-3630
3740 Cahuenga Blvd North Hollywood (91604) ***(P-24983)***
Southern California Mar Assn..........D.......714 850-4004
3333 Fairview Rd Costa Mesa (92626) ***(P-17786)***
Southern California Mkt Area, Los Angeles *Also called Veritiv Operating Company* ***(P-8133)***
Southern California Mkt Area, Commerce *Also called Veritiv Operating Company* ***(P-8134)***
Southern California Mtl Hdlg..........D.......805 650-6000
19755 Bahama St Northridge (91324) ***(P-7800)***
Southern California Mtl Hdlg..........D.......818 349-1220
8124 Deering Ave Canoga Park (91304) ***(P-7801)***
Southern California Mtl Hdlg (HQ)..........C.......562 949-1006
12393 Slauson Ave Whittier (90606) ***(P-7802)***
Southern California Physicia..........D.......858 824-7000
6760 Top Gun St Ste 100 San Diego (92121) ***(P-27041)***
SOUTHERN CALIFORNIA PIPE TRADE, Los Angeles *Also called Defined Contribution Trust Fun* ***(P-12092)***
Southern California Regional, Indio *Also called Granite Construction Company* ***(P-1773)***
Southern California Tele Co (PA)..........D.......951 693-1880
27515 Enterprise Cir W Temecula (92590) ***(P-5647)***
Southern Clfrn Edsn - Prvt CHR, Rosemead *Also called Southern California Edison Co* ***(P-6124)***
Southern Contracting Company..........C.......760 744-0760
559 N Twin Oaks Valley Rd San Marcos (92069) ***(P-2735)***
Southern Counties Bldg Maint (PA)..........C.......805 928-9900
1035 N Armando St Ste F Anaheim (92806) ***(P-14398)***
Southern Counties Oil Co (PA)..........D.......714 744-7140
1800 W Katella Ave # 400 Orange (92867) ***(P-8946)***
Southern Fresh Prod Provs Inc..........D.......562 236-2784
11954 Washington Blvd Whittier (90606) ***(P-8731)***
Southern Glazers Wine..........B.......510 477-5500
33321 Dowe Ave Union City (94587) ***(P-9052)***
Southern Glazers Wine..........E.......951 274-2420
723 Palmyrita Ave Riverside (92507) ***(P-9053)***
Southern Glazers Wine..........C.......858 537-3912
10730 Scripps Ranch Blvd San Diego (92131) ***(P-9054)***
Southern Glazers Wine..........D.......408 750-3540
2320 Kruse Dr San Jose (95131) ***(P-9055)***
Southern Glazers Wine..........B.......562 926-2000
17101 Valley View Ave Cerritos (90703) ***(P-9056)***
Southern Hmbldt Cmnty Dst Hosp..........D.......707 923-3921
733 Cedar St Garberville (95542) ***(P-21766)***
Southern Humboldt Cmnty Clinic, Garberville *Also called Southern Hmbldt Cmnty Dst Hosp* ***(P-21766)***
Southern Humboldt Comm Hlth Cr..........D.......707 923-3925
733 Cedar St Garberville (95542) ***(P-21767)***
Southern Implants Inc..........C.......949 273-8505
5 Holland Ste 209 Irvine (92618) ***(P-27042)***
Southern Indian Health Council (PA)..........D.......619 445-1188
4058 Willows Rd Alpine (91901) ***(P-19927)***

ALPHABETIC

Southern Inyo Healthcare Dst....C....760 876-5501
501 E Locust St Lone Pine (93545) ***(P-20773)***
Southern Mnterey Cnty Mem Hosp (PA)....B....831 385-6000
300 Canal St King City (93930) ***(P-21768)***
Southern Mnterey Cnty Mem Hosp....C....831 674-0112
467 El Camino Real Greenfield (93927) ***(P-21769)***
Southern Mntrey Cnty Labor Sup, Greenfield *Also called Southern Mntrrey Cnty Lbor Sup* ***(P-675)***
Southern Mntrrey Cnty Lbor Sup....D....831 674-2727
44 El Camino Real Unit A Greenfield (93927) ***(P-675)***
Southern Mono Healthcare Dst....B....760 934-3311
85 Sierra Park Rd Mammoth Lakes (93546) ***(P-21770)***
Southern Pacific Railroad, Bakersfield *Also called Union Pacific Railroad Company* ***(P-3633)***
Southern Regional Office, Bakersfield *Also called San Joaquin Val UNI Air Pol* ***(P-27854)***
Southern Sierra Medical Clinic, Ridgecrest *Also called Ridgecrest Regional Hospital* ***(P-21687)***
Southgate Glass & Screen Inc (PA)....E....916 476-8396
6852 Franklin Blvd Sacramento (95823) ***(P-6937)***
Southgate Glass & Screen Inc....E....916 476-8396
6199 Warehouse Way Sacramento (95826) ***(P-6938)***
Southgate Recreation & Pk Dst....E....916 421-7275
7320 Florin Mall Dr Sacramento (95823) ***(P-24062)***
Southland Arthritis Osteo....E....951 672-1866
949 Calhoun Pl Ste F Hemet (92543) ***(P-19928)***
Southland Care, Mission Viejo *Also called Ensign Southland LLC* ***(P-20404)***
Southland Credit Union (PA)....D....562 862-6831
10701 Los Alamitos Blvd Los Alamitos (90720) ***(P-9655)***
Southland Credit Union....D....562 862-6831
8545 Florence Ave Downey (90240) ***(P-9656)***
Southland Electric Inc....D....858 634-5050
4950 Greencraig Ln San Diego (92123) ***(P-2736)***
Southland Industries (PA)....E....800 613-6240
7390 Lincoln Way Garden Grove (92841) ***(P-2370)***
Southland Industries....C....714 901-5800
12131 Western Ave Garden Grove (92841) ***(P-2371)***
Southland Integrated Svcs Inc (PA)....D....714 558-6009
1618 W 1st St Santa Ana (92703) ***(P-24843)***
Southland Lutheran Home, Norwalk *Also called Front Porch Communities & Svcs* ***(P-21075)***
Southland Mall, Hayward *Also called Lansing Mall Ltd Partnership* ***(P-10905)***
Southland Paving Inc....D....760 747-6895
361 N Hale Ave Escondido (92029) ***(P-3328)***
Southland Steel, Newport Beach *Also called Fallon Land Company Inc* ***(P-7273)***
Southland Technology Inc....D....858 694-0932
8053 Vickers St San Diego (92111) ***(P-7107)***
Southland Transit Inc (PA)....C....626 258-1310
3650 Rockwell Ave El Monte (91731) ***(P-3849)***
Southland Transit Co, Baldwin Park *Also called San Gabriel Transit Inc* ***(P-3868)***
Southtown Industrial Park....E....909 947-3768
1701 S Bon View Ave 104 Ontario (91761) ***(P-10950)***
Southwest Airlines Co....D....510 563-1000
1 Airport Dr Ste 25 Oakland (94621) ***(P-4800)***
Southwest Airlines Co....B....619 231-7345
3665 N Harbor Dr Ste 216 San Diego (92101) ***(P-4801)***
Southwest Airlines Co....D....310 665-5700
100 World Way Ste 328 Los Angeles (90045) ***(P-4802)***
Southwest Airlines Co....C....510 563-1234
10 Alan Shepard Way Oakland (94621) ***(P-4803)***
Southwest Construction Co Inc....D....760 728-4460
2909 Rainbow Valley Blvd Fallbrook (92028) ***(P-3329)***
Southwest Contractors (PA)....C....661 588-0484
3235 Unicorn Rd Bakersfield (93308) ***(P-1982)***
Southwest Convalesant, Hawthorne *Also called Windsor Gardens* ***(P-20901)***
Southwest Correctional Medical....D....831 641-3298
2511 Garden Rd Ste A160 Monterey (93940) ***(P-22685)***
Southwest Dealer Services Inc....C....925 753-0696
1001 G St Ste 113 Sacramento (95814) ***(P-17479)***
Southwest Express LLC....D....949 474-5038
1720 E Garry Ave Ste 107 Santa Ana (92705) ***(P-4066)***
Southwest Fsheries Science Ctr, La Jolla *Also called National Marine Fisheries Svc* ***(P-26421)***
Southwest Gas Corporation....D....760 951-4000
13471 Mariposa Rd Victorville (92395) ***(P-6178)***
Southwest General Contrs Inc....E....760 480-8747
912 S Andreasen Dr # 101 Escondido (92029) ***(P-7696)***
Southwest Healthcare Sys Aux....E....800 404-6627
38977 Sky Canyon Dr # 200 Murrieta (92563) ***(P-21771)***
Southwest Healthcare Sys Aux (HQ)....B....951 696-6000
25500 Medical Center Dr Murrieta (92562) ***(P-21772)***
Southwest Inspection and Tstg....D....562 941-2990
441 Commercial Way La Habra (90631) ***(P-17480)***
Southwest Inspection Testing, La Habra *Also called Southwest Inspection and Tstg* ***(P-17480)***
Southwest Landscape Inc....D....714 545-1084
2205 S Standard Ave Santa Ana (92707) ***(P-943)***
Southwest Material Hdlg Inc (PA)....C....951 727-0477
3725 Nobel Ct Mira Loma (91752) ***(P-7803)***
Southwest Rgnal Cncil Crpnters (PA)....E....213 385-1457
533 S Fremont Ave Fl 10 Los Angeles (90071) ***(P-25082)***
Southwest Toyota Lift, Mira Loma *Also called Southwest Material Hdlg Inc* ***(P-7803)***
Southwest Traders Incorporated....D....209 462-1607
4747 Frontier Way Stockton (95215) ***(P-8461)***
Southwest Traders Incorporated (PA)....C....951 699-7800
27565 Diaz Rd Temecula (92590) ***(P-8462)***
Southwest Transportation Agcy, Caruthers *Also called Fresno Cnty Sprntndent Schools* ***(P-3937)***
Southwest YMCA, Saratoga *Also called YMCA of Silicon Valley* ***(P-25488)***

Southwestern Artists Assn....E....619 232-3522
1770 Vlg Pl Gallery 23 23 Gallery San Diego (92101) ***(P-24914)***
Southwestern Orthpd Med Corp....E....562 803-0600
15901 Hawthorne Blvd Lawndale (90260) ***(P-19929)***
Southwestern Yacht Club Inc....E....619 222-0438
2702 Qualtrough St San Diego (92106) ***(P-19052)***
Southwind Foods LLC (PA)....D....323 262-8222
20644 S Fordyce Ave Carson (90810) ***(P-8602)***
Southwire Company LLC....D....909 989-2888
9199 Cleveland Ave # 100 Rancho Cucamonga (91730) ***(P-7399)***
Sovereign Capital MGT Group, San Diego *Also called Sovereign Capitl MGT Group Inc* ***(P-11773)***
Sovereign Capitl MGT Group Inc....A....619 294-8989
750 B St Ste 2397 San Diego (92101) ***(P-11773)***
Sovereign Health, Rancho Mirage *Also called Dual Diagnosis Trtmnt Ctr Inc* ***(P-22793)***
Sovereign Health of California, Los Angeles *Also called Dual Diagnosis Trtmnt Ctr Inc* ***(P-22080)***
Sovereign Health of California, San Clemente *Also called Dual Diagnosis Trtmnt Ctr Inc* ***(P-22570)***
SP McClenahan Co....D....650 326-8781
1 Arastradero Rd Portola Valley (94028) ***(P-978)***
Sp Plus Corporation....D....213 488-3100
3470 Wilshire Blvd # 400 Los Angeles (90010) ***(P-17707)***
Spa At Club Sport, San Ramon *Also called Clubsport San Ramon LLC* ***(P-18588)***
Spa Cas Palmas....E....760 836-3106
41000 Bob Hope Dr Rancho Mirage (92270) ***(P-18655)***
Spa Dreams....D....818 298-1120
6419 Hesperia Ave Reseda (91335) ***(P-18656)***
Spa Havens LP....C....760 945-2055
29402 Spa Haven Way Vista (92084) ***(P-18657)***
Spa Las Palmas of Marriot Intl, Rancho Mirage *Also called Spa Cas Palmas* ***(P-18655)***
Spa Partners Inc....E....707 942-5789
1457 Lincoln Ave Calistoga (94515) ***(P-18658)***
Spa Resort Casino, Palm Springs *Also called Agua Clnte Band Chilla Indians* ***(P-12308)***
Spa Resort Casino (PA)....A....888 999-1995
401 E Amado Rd Palm Springs (92262) ***(P-13251)***
Space Age Metal Products Inc....C....310 539-5500
23605 Telo Ave Torrance (90505) ***(P-7108)***
Space Components Division, San Diego *Also called Atk Space Systems Inc* ***(P-26594)***
Space Systems/Loral LLC (HQ)....D....650 852-7320
3825 Fabian Way Palo Alto (94303) ***(P-5996)***
Space Systems/Loral LLC....C....650 852-4000
1140 Hamilton Ct Menlo Park (94025) ***(P-4633)***
Spacer.com, Mountain View *Also called 500 Startups Management Co LLC* ***(P-12195)***
Spacetone Acoustics Inc....E....925 931-0749
1051 Serpentine Ln # 300 Pleasanton (94566) ***(P-2960)***
Spad Holdings LLC....D....805 496-9978
966 S Westlake Blvd Ste 4 Westlake Village (91361) ***(P-18659)***
Spad Holdings LLC....D....661 286-0229
24245 Magic Mountain Pkwy Valencia (91355) ***(P-18660)***
Spad Holdings LLC....E....714 993-6003
860 N Rose Dr Placentia (92870) ***(P-18661)***
Spad Holdings LLC....D....949 733-0473
14280 Culver Dr Ste B Irvine (92604) ***(P-18662)***
Spad Holdings LLC....D....818 710-7606
6100 Topanga Canyon Blvd # 1310 Woodland Hills (91367) ***(P-18663)***
Spad Holdings LLC....D....818 772-8900
19456 Nordhoff St Northridge (91324) ***(P-18664)***
Spad Holdings LLC....D....818 552-2027
601 N Brand Blvd Glendale (91203) ***(P-18665)***
Spalding Srgcl Ctr of Bvrly Hl....C....949 863-0022
27520 Hawthorne Blvd # 176 Rllng HLS Est (90274) ***(P-19930)***
Span Construction & Engrg Inc (PA)....D....559 661-1111
1841 Howard Rd Madera (93637) ***(P-1658)***
Spanish Hills Country Club (PA)....C....805 389-1644
999 Crestview Ave Camarillo (93010) ***(P-19053)***
Spanish Trils Girl Scout Cncil....E....909 627-2609
5007 Center St Chino (91710) ***(P-24063)***
Spare-Time Inc....D....916 983-9180
820 Halidon Way Folsom (95630) ***(P-19054)***
Spare-Time Inc....D....916 859-5910
11344 Coloma Rd Ste 350 Gold River (95670) ***(P-19055)***
Spare-Time Inc....D....916 782-2600
2501 Eureka Rd Roseville (95661) ***(P-19056)***
Spare-Time Inc....C....209 371-0241
429 W Lockeford St Lodi (95240) ***(P-18498)***
Spare-Time Inc....E....916 638-7001
2201 Gold Rush Dr Gold River (95670) ***(P-19057)***
Spare-Time Inc....D....916 649-0909
2450 Natomas Park Dr Sacramento (95833) ***(P-18666)***
Spare-Time Inc....D....916 859-5910
9570 Racquet Ct Elk Grove (95758) ***(P-19058)***
Spark Unlimited Inc....D....818 788-1005
40 E Verdugo Ave 2 Burbank (91502) ***(P-15468)***
Sparkle Uniform & Linen Svc, Bakersfield *Also called Richard K Newman and Assoc Inc* ***(P-13553)***
Sparkletts, Van Nuys *Also called Ds Services of America Inc* ***(P-8784)***
Sparkletts, Irwindale *Also called Ds Services of America Inc* ***(P-8785)***
Sparta Consulting Inc....B....916 985-0300
111 Woodmere Rd Ste 200 Folsom (95630) ***(P-16492)***
Sparxent Inc (PA)....E....949 222-2287
65 Enterprise Aliso Viejo (92656) ***(P-16057)***
Spc Building Services, Riverside *Also called J M V B Inc* ***(P-2448)***
Spe Go Holdings Inc....E....858 638-0672
16422 N Woodson Dr Ramona (92065) ***(P-19059)***
Spearman Clubs Inc (PA)....D....949 496-2070
23500 Clubhouse Dr Laguna Niguel (92677) ***(P-19240)***

Mergent e-mail: customerrelations@mergent.com
1474
2019 Directory of California
Wholesalers and Services Companies
(P-0000) Products & Services Section entry number
(PA)=Parent Co (HQ)=Headquarters (DH)=Div Headquarters

Spears Manufacturing Co (PA).....C.....818 364-1611
15853 Olden St Sylmar (91342) ***(P-7713)***
Spec Personnel LLC.....C.....408 727-8000
1900 La Fytte St Unit 125 Santa Clara (95050) ***(P-14765)***
Spec Services Inc.....D.....714 963-8077
10540 Talbert Ave 100e Fountain Valley (92708) ***(P-25920)***
Spec Services Inc (PA).....C.....714 963-8077
10540 Talbert Ave 100e Fountain Valley (92708) ***(P-25921)***
Special Dispatch Cal Inc.....D.....510 713-0300
8328 Central Ave Newark (94560) ***(P-4266)***
Special Dispatch Cal Inc (PA).....D.....714 521-8200
16330 Phoebe Ave La Mirada (90638) ***(P-4374)***
Special Events, Livermore *Also called Pinamar LLC* ***(P-14536)***
Special Events, Livermore *Also called High Summit LLC* ***(P-17795)***
Special Events Staffing.....A.....626 296-6771
1015 N Lake Ave Ste 205 Pasadena (91104) ***(P-14766)***
Special Home Needs.....D.....408 985-8666
1440 Jackson St Santa Clara (95050) ***(P-20962)***
Special Needs Network.....E.....323 291-7100
4401 Crenshaw Blvd # 215 Los Angeles (90043) ***(P-22051)***
Special Service Contrs Inc.....D.....805 227-1081
3580 Airport Rd Paso Robles (93446) ***(P-3587)***
Special Service For Groups Inc.....D.....310 323-6887
19401 S Vt Ave Ste A200 Torrance (90502) ***(P-24844)***
Special Service For Groups Inc (PA).....A.....213 368-1888
905 E 8th St Unit 1 Los Angeles (90021) ***(P-24232)***
Special Service For Groups Inc.....D.....213 620-5713
470 E 3rd St Ste D Los Angeles (90013) ***(P-24845)***
Specialized Landscape MGT Svcs.....D.....805 520-7590
4212 Peast Los Angeles Simi Valley (93063) ***(P-944)***
Specialized Laundry Svcs Inc.....C.....510 487-8297
33485 Western Ave Union City (94587) ***(P-13621)***
Specialty Center, Ridgecrest *Also called Ridgecrest Regional Hospital* ***(P-19826)***
Specialty Construction Inc.....D.....805 543-1706
645 Clarion Ct San Luis Obispo (93401) ***(P-2737)***
Specialty Equipment Mkt Assn (PA).....D.....909 396-0289
1575 Valley Vista Dr Diamond Bar (91765) ***(P-24984)***
Specialty Laboratories Inc (HQ).....A.....661 799-6543
27027 Tourney Rd Valencia (91355) ***(P-22148)***
Specialty Minerals Inc.....C.....760 248-5300
6565 Meridian Rd Lucerne Valley (92356) ***(P-1087)***
Specialty Produce, San Diego *Also called Tomatoes Extraordinaire Inc* ***(P-8738)***
Specialty Risk Services Inc.....D.....714 674-1000
1 Pointe Dr Ste 220 Brea (92821) ***(P-10776)***
Specialty Risk Services Inc.....C.....877 809-9478
6140 Stoneridge Mall Rd # 245 Pleasanton (94588) ***(P-10777)***
Specialty Sealing, Anaheim *Also called Boyd Corporation* ***(P-7842)***
Specialty Services, Arcadia *Also called Andover Maintenance Inc* ***(P-14195)***
Specialty Solid Waste & Recycl, Santa Clara *Also called Bay Counties Waste Svcs Inc* ***(P-6351)***
Specialty Steel Service, Stockton *Also called PDM Steel Service Centers* ***(P-7299)***
Specialty Steel Service Co Inc (HQ).....D.....916 771-4737
3300 Douglas Blvd Ste 128 Roseville (95661) ***(P-7315)***
Specialty Surg Ctr Beverly Hil.....D.....310 659-6333
8670 Wilshire Blvd # 301 Beverly Hills (90211) ***(P-19931)***
Specialty Surgical Centers.....E.....949 341-3499
15825 Laguna Canyon Rd # 200 Irvine (92618) ***(P-19932)***
Specialty Team Plastering Inc.....C.....805 966-3858
4652 Vintage Ranch Ln Santa Barbara (93110) ***(P-2961)***
Specialty Textile Services LLC.....D.....619 476-8750
1333 30th St Ste A San Diego (92154) ***(P-8244)***
Specilty Srgical Ctr Encino LP.....D.....310 659-6333
16501 Ventura Blvd # 103 Encino (91436) ***(P-19933)***
Specilzed Foster Care Pasadena, Pasadena *Also called County of Los Angeles* ***(P-22775)***
Specimen Contracting, Sunland *Also called Brightview Tree Company* ***(P-987)***
Spectacor Management Group.....B.....562 436-3636
300 E Ocean Blvd Long Beach (90802) ***(P-10951)***
Spectra, Santa Clara *Also called Spec Personnel LLC* ***(P-14765)***
Spectra Company.....C.....909 599-0760
2510 Supply St Pomona (91767) ***(P-2824)***
Spectra I California.....D.....310 835-0808
21818 S Wilmington Ave # 402 Carson (90810) ***(P-2738)***
Spectra Industrial Electric, Carson *Also called Spectra I California* ***(P-2738)***
Spectra Premium (usa) Corp.....D.....951 653-0640
2220 Almond Ave Redlands (92374) ***(P-6675)***
Spectrum Abatement, Orange *Also called United Spectrum Inc* ***(P-3599)***
Spectrum Community Services (PA).....D.....510 881-0300
2617 Barrington Ct Hayward (94545) ***(P-24064)***
Spectrum Credit Union.....C.....510 251-6000
500 12th St Ste 200 Oakland (94607) ***(P-9594)***
Spectrum Hotel Group LLC.....D.....949 471-8888
90 Pacifica Irvine (92618) ***(P-13252)***
Spectrum Hotel Group LLC.....D.....949 471-8888
90 Pacifica Irvine (92618) ***(P-13253)***
Spectrum Information Svcs LLC (PA).....D.....949 752-7070
16 Technology Dr Ste 107 Irvine (92618) ***(P-14062)***
Spectrum MGT Holdg Co LLC.....D.....714 657-1040
6021 Katella Ave Ste 100 Cypress (90630) ***(P-5932)***
Spectrum MGT Holdg Co LLC.....D.....951 260-3143
4077 W Stetson Ave Hemet (92545) ***(P-5933)***
Spectrum MGT Holdg Co LLC.....D.....626 857-1075
1041 E Route 66 Glendora (91740) ***(P-5934)***
Spectrum MGT Holdg Co LLC.....D.....951 587-8660
27555 Ynez Rd Ste 203 Temecula (92591) ***(P-5935)***
Spectrum MGT Holdg Co LLC.....D.....909 918-6972
1078 E Hospitality Ln D San Bernardino (92408) ***(P-5936)***
Spectrum MGT Holdg Co LLC.....D.....562 677-0228
17777 Center Court Dr N Cerritos (90703) ***(P-5937)***
Spectrum MGT Holdg Co LLC.....D.....714 871-2643
1565 S Harbor Blvd Fullerton (92832) ***(P-5938)***
Spectrum MGT Holdg Co LLC.....D.....562 372-4008
350 Stonewood St Downey (90241) ***(P-5939)***
Spectrum MGT Holdg Co LLC.....D.....818 700-6126
9260 Topanga Canyon Blvd Chatsworth (91311) ***(P-5940)***
Spectrum MGT Holdg Co LLC.....C.....714 657-1060
6021 Katella Ave Ste 100 Cypress (90630) ***(P-5941)***
Spectrum MGT Holdg Co LLC.....D.....714 903-4000
12040 Western Ave Garden Grove (92841) ***(P-5942)***
Spectrum MGT Holdg Co LLC.....D.....310 647-3000
550 Continental Blvd # 250 El Segundo (90245) ***(P-5943)***
Spectrum MGT Holdg Co LLC.....C.....760 340-2225
41725 Cook St Palm Desert (92211) ***(P-5944)***
Spectrum MGT Holdg Co LLC.....D.....909 821-8159
1500 Auto Center Dr Ontario (91761) ***(P-5945)***
Spectrum MGT Holdg Co LLC.....D.....714 414-1431
3430 E Miraloma Ave Anaheim (92806) ***(P-5946)***
Spectrum MGT Holdg Co LLC.....D.....951 571-8738
12625 Frederick St F10 Moreno Valley (92553) ***(P-5947)***
Spectrum Prof Staffing Inc.....C.....800 644-1150
13520 Evening Creek Dr N # 300 San Diego (92128) ***(P-14914)***
Spectrum Security Services Inc.....D.....714 542-9600
1633 E 4th St Ste 238 Santa Ana (92701) ***(P-16833)***
Spectrum Security Services Inc (PA).....C.....619 669-6660
13967 Campo Rd Ste 101 Jamul (91935) ***(P-16944)***
Spectrum Services Group Inc.....D.....916 760-7913
4600 Northgate Blvd # 120 Sacramento (95834) ***(P-27869)***
Speedway Sonoma LLC.....D.....707 938-8448
Hwy 37 N Sonoma (95476) ***(P-18545)***
Speedy Locksmith.....D.....760 439-5000
429 Avnida De La Estrella San Clemente (92672) ***(P-17991)***
Spencer Building Maintenance.....B.....916 922-1900
10457 Old Placerville Rd Sacramento (95827) ***(P-14399)***
Spencer Recovery Centers Inc (PA).....D.....949 376-3705
1316 S Coast Hwy Laguna Beach (92651) ***(P-22686)***
Sperasoft Inc.....B.....408 715-6615
2033 Gateway Pl Ste 500 San Jose (95110) ***(P-15469)***
Sperry Van Ness, Los Angeles *Also called Svn International Corp* ***(P-11782)***
Spf Capital Real Estate LLC.....D.....310 519-8200
601 S Palos Verdes St San Pedro (90731) ***(P-13254)***
Sph-Irvine LLC.....E.....949 833-1432
18952 Macarthur Blvd # 103 Irvine (92612) ***(P-19934)***
Spherion Staffing Group, Redding *Also called Sfn Group Inc* ***(P-14913)***
Spicers Paper Inc (HQ).....C.....562 698-1199
12310 Slauson Ave Santa Fe Springs (90670) ***(P-8071)***
Spidercloud Wireless Inc (HQ).....D.....408 567-9165
475 Sycamore Dr Milpitas (95035) ***(P-5997)***
Spieker Companies Inc (PA).....C.....650 968-2660
1020 Corp Way Ste 100 Palo Alto (94303) ***(P-11774)***
Spiess Construction Co Inc.....D.....805 937-5859
201 S Broadway St Ste 101 Orcutt (93455) ***(P-1983)***
Spigit Inc.....D.....855 774-4480
275 Battery St Ste 1000 San Francisco (94111) ***(P-15859)***
Spike Technologies Inc.....E.....408 410-0624
2386 Lacey Dr Milpitas (95035) ***(P-16058)***
Spilo Worldwide Inc.....D.....213 687-8600
233 Wilshire Blvd Ste 400 Santa Monica (90401) ***(P-7898)***
Spinecare Medical Group Inc.....D.....650 985-7500
455 Hickey Blvd Ste 310 Daly City (94015) ***(P-19935)***
Spiniello Companies.....D.....909 629-1000
2650 Pomona Blvd Pomona (91768) ***(P-1984)***
Spinning, Venice *Also called Mad Dogg Athletics Inc* ***(P-8317)***
Spinning Spur Wind Three LLC.....A.....858 521-3319
15445 Innovation Dr San Diego (92128) ***(P-6142)***
Spira-Loc, El Cajon *Also called University Mechanical &* ***(P-2392)***
Spiral Technology Inc.....D.....661 723-3148
229 E Avenue K8 Ste 105 Lancaster (93535) ***(P-25922)***
Spire Concessions LLC.....D.....818 843-6000
2500 N Hollywood Way Burbank (91505) ***(P-13255)***
Spireon Inc (PA).....C.....800 557-1449
16802 Aston Irvine (92606) ***(P-4375)***
Spirit of Woman of California.....D.....559 233-4353
327 W Belmont Ave Fresno (93728) ***(P-22687)***
Spiritual Direction.....E.....650 952-9456
164 San Luis Ave San Bruno (94066) ***(P-24065)***
Splash Fast Lube, Salinas *Also called Gieg Chevron LLC* ***(P-17816)***
Splash Swim School Inc.....E.....925 838-7946
2411 Old Crow Canyon Rd San Ramon (94583) ***(P-19241)***
Splunk Inc (PA).....C.....415 848-8400
270 Brannan St San Francisco (94107) ***(P-15860)***
Sport Center Fitness Inc.....D.....310 376-9443
819 N Harbor Dr Redondo Beach (90277) ***(P-18667)***
Sports Club of El Dorado, Shingle Springs *Also called Salutary Sports Clubs Inc* ***(P-18646)***
Sports Office, Oakland *Also called City of Oakland* ***(P-19138)***
Sportsmen of Stanislaus Inc.....D.....209 578-5801
819 Sunset Ave Modesto (95351) ***(P-18668)***
Sportsmens Lodge Hotel LLC.....C.....818 769-4700
12825 Ventura Blvd Studio City (91604) ***(P-13256)***
Sportvision Inc.....E.....510 736-2925
6657 Kaiser Dr Fremont (94555) ***(P-18124)***
Spot Free Car Wash, Escondido *Also called In & Out Car Wash Inc* ***(P-17818)***
Spotcues Inc.....A.....408 435-2700
1975 W El Cmno Real 301 Mountain View (94040) ***(P-7109)***
Spotlight 29 Casino, Coachella *Also called 29 Palms Enterprises Corp* ***(P-19089)***
Spreadtrum Cmmncations USA Inc.....D.....858 546-0895
10180 Telesis Ct Ste 500 San Diego (92121) ***(P-26458)***
Sprig Electric Co (PA).....C.....408 298-3134
1860 S 10th St San Jose (95112) ***(P-2739)***

Employee Codes: A=Over 500 employees, B=251-500
C=101-250, D=51-100, E=50
2019 Directory of California
Wholesalers and Services Companies
© Mergent Inc. 1-800-342-5647
1475

Spring Bioscience Corp.......A.......925 474-8463
4300 Hacienda Dr Pleasanton (94588) *(P-22149)*
Spring Hl Mnor Cnvlescent Hosp, Grass Valley *Also called Springhill Manor Rehabilitatio (P-21219)*
Spring Lake Village, Santa Rosa *Also called Covia Communities (P-24489)*
Spring Valley Lake Country CLB.......D.......760 245-5356
13229 Spring Valley Pkwy Victorville (92395) *(P-19060)*
Spring Valley Post Acute LLC.......C.......760 245-6477
14973 Hesperia Rd Victorville (92395) *(P-20774)*
Springboard Solutions LLC.......C.......951 779-7739
4351 Latham St Riverside (92501) *(P-27870)*
Springhill Manor Rehabilitatio.......E.......530 273-7247
355 Joerschke Dr Grass Valley (95945) *(P-21219)*
Springhill Suites, Atascadero *Also called Atascadero Hotel Partners LLC (P-12339)*
Springhill Suites, San Diego *Also called Marriott International Inc (P-12886)*
Springhill Suites Oceanside, Oceanside *Also called Gfp Oceanside Block 21 LLC (P-12603)*
Springhuse Manor Care Hlth Svc.......D.......714 671-7898
285 W Central Ave Ofc Brea (92821) *(P-24682)*
Springleaf Fincl Holdings LLC.......C.......909 796-1603
905 E Hospitality Ln B San Bernardino (92408) *(P-27462)*
Springleaf Fincl Holdings LLC.......C.......951 296-0135
26451 Ynez Rd Temecula (92591) *(P-27463)*
Springleaf Fincl Holdings LLC.......C.......760 241-1451
17140 Bear Valley Rd Victorville (92395) *(P-27464)*
Springs Ambulance Service Inc.......D.......760 883-5000
1111 Montalvo Way Palm Springs (92262) *(P-3850)*
Springs Club Inc.......D.......760 328-0254
1 Duke Dr Rancho Mirage (92270) *(P-19061)*
Springs Country Club, The, Rancho Mirage *Also called Springs Club Inc (P-19061)*
Sprinkles Cupcakes Inc.......D.......310 657-4102
5916 Bowcroft St Los Angeles (90016) *(P-1436)*
Sprint Communications Co LP.......E.......818 755-7100
111 Unversal Hollywood Dr Universal City (91608) *(P-5648)*
Sprint Communications Co LP.......D.......909 382-6030
1505 E Enterprise Dr San Bernardino (92408) *(P-5649)*
Sprint Corporation.......B.......949 748-3353
6591 Irvine Center Dr # 100 Irvine (92618) *(P-5416)*
Sprouts Farmers Market Inc.......C.......888 577-7688
280 De Berry St Colton (92324) *(P-4634)*
Spruce Technology Inc.......D.......925 415-8160
3516 Browntail Way San Ramon (94582) *(P-15470)*
Spurr Co., Paso Robles *Also called Dave Spurr Excavating Inc (P-3422)*
Spus7 235 Pine LP.......D.......231 683-4200
235 Pine St Ste 125 San Francisco (94104) *(P-12069)*
Spus7 Miami Acc LP.......E.......213 683-4200
515 S Flower St Ste 3100 Los Angeles (90071) *(P-12070)*
Spycher Brothers, Turlock *Also called Select Harvest Usa LLC (P-8910)*
Spyglass Hill Community Assn.......E.......949 855-1800
39 Argonaut Ste 100 Aliso Viejo (92656) *(P-25253)*
Sqa Services Inc.......B.......310 544-6888
550 Silver Spur Rd # 300 Rllng HLS Est (90275) *(P-27465)*
Squab Producers Calif Inc.......D.......209 537-4744
409 Primo Way Modesto (95358) *(P-8540)*
Squar Milner Peterson (PA).......C.......949 222-2999
4100 Nwport Pl Dr Ste 300 Newport Beach (92660) *(P-26297)*
Square Inc (PA).......E.......415 375-3176
1455 Market St Ste 600 San Francisco (94103) *(P-15861)*
Square Enix Inc.......C.......310 846-0400
999 N Pacific Coast Hwy # 3 El Segundo (90245) *(P-7110)*
Squaretrade Inc (HQ).......C.......415 541-1000
360 3rd St Fl 6 San Francisco (94107) *(P-10504)*
Squaw Creek Associates LLC.......A.......530 581-6624
400 Squaw Creek Rd Alpine Meadows (96146) *(P-13257)*
Squaw Valley Development Co (HQ).......D.......530 452-6985
1960 Squaw Valley Rd Olympic Valley (96146) *(P-13258)*
Squaw Valley Ski, Olympic Valley *Also called Squaw Valley Development Co (P-13258)*
Squaw Valley Ski Corporation (HQ).......C.......530 583-6985
1960 Squaw Valley Rd Olympic Valley (96146) *(P-13259)*
Squire Patton Boggs (us) LLP.......D.......213 624-2500
555 S Flower St Ste 3100 Los Angeles (90071) *(P-23395)*
Squire Patton Boggs (us) LLP.......C.......415 954-0334
275 Battery St Ste 2600 San Francisco (94111) *(P-23396)*
SR Bray LLC.......E.......951 436-2920
2750 N Perris Blvd Perris (92571) *(P-14546)*
SR Bray LLC (PA).......E.......714 765-7551
1210 N Red Gum St Anaheim (92806) *(P-2740)*
SR Freeman Inc.......D.......408 364-2200
2380 S Bascom Ave Ste 200 Campbell (95008) *(P-3082)*
Sra Oss Inc.......C.......408 855-8200
5201 Great America Pkwy # 419 Santa Clara (95054) *(P-15862)*
Srcsd, Sacramento *Also called Sacramento Reg Co Sanit Dist (P-6548)*
Srd Engineering Inc.......D.......714 630-2480
3578 E Enterprise Dr Anaheim (92807) *(P-1985)*
Srg Management LLC.......C.......858 792-9300
500 Stevens Ave Ste 100 Solana Beach (92075) *(P-27043)*
Srht Property Mgmt Co.......D.......213 683-0522
1317 E 7th St Los Angeles (90021) *(P-27044)*
SRI (PA).......E.......415 989-5363
100 Bush St Ste 1650 San Francisco (94104) *(P-9909)*
SRI International (PA).......A.......650 859-2000
333 Ravenswood Ave Menlo Park (94025) *(P-26661)*
SRI International.......C.......805 542-9330
4111 Broad St Ste 220 San Luis Obispo (93401) *(P-26662)*
SRK Global Consulting.......D.......310 295-2524
7225 Crescent Park W # 255 Los Angeles (90094) *(P-16493)*
Srm Alliance Hospital Services (PA).......B.......707 778-1111
400 N Mcdowell Blvd Petaluma (94954) *(P-21773)*
SRS Consulting Inc.......D.......510 252-0625
39465 Paseo Padre P Fremont (94538) *(P-16494)*
SRS Protection Inc.......D.......805 744-7122
2064 Eastman Ave Ste 110 Ventura (93003) *(P-16834)*
SS Heritage Inn Ontario LLC.......D.......909 937-5000
3595 E Guasti Rd Ontario (91761) *(P-13260)*
SS Hert Trucking Inc (PA).......E.......760 248-9327
33924 Old Woman Sprng Rd Lucerne Valley (92356) *(P-4267)*
Ss Skikos Incorporated.......D.......707 575-3000
1289 Sebastopol Rd Santa Rosa (95407) *(P-4376)*
SS TRAVEL, San Francisco *Also called San Francisco Travel Assn (P-17455)*
SS&c Advent, San Francisco *Also called Advent Software Inc (P-14967)*
Ss8 Networks Inc (PA).......C.......408 894-8400
750 Tasman Dr Milpitas (95035) *(P-5998)*
Ssa Containers Inc.......D.......206 623-0304
1521 Pier J Ave Long Beach (90802) *(P-4737)*
Ssa Marine Inc.......E.......562 983-1001
1521 Pier J Ave Long Beach (90802) *(P-4738)*
Ssa Pacific Inc.......D.......916 374-1866
2895 Industrial Blvd # 100 West Sacramento (95691) *(P-4739)*
Ssa Pacific Inc.......D.......310 833-9606
Outer Harbor Berth 54 55 San Pedro (90731) *(P-4740)*
Ssae 16 Professionals LLP.......D.......866 480-9485
3419 E Chapman Ave # 334 Orange (92869) *(P-26298)*
SSC Carmichael Operating Co LP.......D.......916 485-4793
3630 Mission Ave Carmichael (95608) *(P-20775)*
SSC Construction Inc.......C.......951 278-1177
4195 Chino Hills Pkwy Chino Hills (91709) *(P-25923)*
SSC Newport Beach Oper Co LP.......C.......949 642-8044
466 Flagship Rd Newport Beach (92663) *(P-20776)*
SSC Oakland Excell Oper Co LP.......D.......510 261-5200
3025 High St Oakland (94619) *(P-20777)*
SSC Pittsburg Operating Co LP.......A.......925 427-4444
2351 Loveridge Rd Pittsburg (94565) *(P-21220)*
SSC San Jose Operating Co LP.......D.......408 249-0344
340 Northlake Dr San Jose (95117) *(P-20778)*
Ssd Systems, Anaheim *Also called Security Signal Devices Inc (P-16939)*
SSE Merchandise, San Jose *Also called Sharks Sports & Entrmt LLC (P-18535)*
Ssf Imported Auto Parts LLC.......D.......310 782-8859
21175 Main St Ste A Carson (90745) *(P-6676)*
Ssf Imported Auto Parts LLC (HQ).......D.......800 203-9287
466 Forbes Blvd South San Francisco (94080) *(P-6677)*
SSG ADMINISTRATIVE OFFICES, Los Angeles *Also called Special Service For Groups Inc (P-24232)*
Ssi, Lathrop *Also called Super Store Industries (P-8878)*
Ssi, Rocklin *Also called Surveillance Systems (P-7549)*
Ssi, Valley Center *Also called Survival Systems Intl Inc (P-17993)*
Ssi, San Luis Obispo *Also called Sealant Systems International (P-6694)*
Ssinfotek Inc.......E.......949 732-3100
15615 Alton Pkwy Ste 450 Irvine (92618) *(P-16059)*
Ssjid, Manteca *Also called South San Jquin Irrigation Dst (P-6567)*
Ssl, Palo Alto *Also called Space Systems/Loral LLC (P-5996)*
Ssl Robotics LLC (HQ).......D.......626 296-1373
1250 Lincoln Ave Ste 100 Pasadena (91103) *(P-25924)*
Ssl Robotics LLC.......D.......626 296-1373
1250 Lincoln Ave Ste 100 Pasadena (91103) *(P-25925)*
Ssl Robotics LLC.......C.......626 296-1373
4398 Corporate Center Dr Los Alamitos (90720) *(P-25926)*
Ssmb Pacific Holding Co Inc (HQ).......D.......510 836-6100
1755 Adams Ave San Leandro (94577) *(P-6609)*
Ssmb Pacific Holding Co Inc.......D.......530 222-1212
20769 Industry Rd Anderson (96007) *(P-6610)*
Ssmb Pacific Holding Co Inc.......D.......916 371-3372
707 Display Way Sacramento (95838) *(P-6611)*
SSPCA, Sacramento *Also called The For Sacramento Society (P-25474)*
SST, Newark *Also called Shotspotter Inc (P-15851)*
Sstmas Y Aranda Eqpos Hdrlicos.......E.......619 245-4502
280 Campillo St Ste L Calexico (92231) *(P-7804)*
Ssw, Palm Springs *Also called S S W Mechanical Cnstr Inc (P-2344)*
St Andrews Children Center.......E.......949 651-0198
4400 Barranca Pkwy Irvine (92604) *(P-24385)*
St Andrews Health Care, Los Angeles *Also called Washington Enterprises 3 LLC (P-20875)*
ST ANNE'S HOME, San Francisco *Also called Little Sisters of Poor (P-24582)*
St Annes Maternity Home.......C.......213 381-2931
155 N Occidental Blvd Los Angeles (90026) *(P-24683)*
St Anthony Foundation (PA).......E.......415 241-2600
150 Golden Gate Ave San Francisco (94102) *(P-24066)*
St Baldricks Foundation Inc (PA).......D.......626 792-8247
1333 S Mayflower Ave Monrovia (91016) *(P-25042)*
St Barnabas Senior Center of L.......D.......213 388-4444
675 S Carondelet St Los Angeles (90057) *(P-24067)*
St Denis Electric Inc.......E.......805 343-9999
734 Ralcoa Way Arroyo Grande (93420) *(P-2741)*
St Edna Sbcute Cnvalescent Ctr, Santa Ana *Also called Covenant Care California LLC (P-20352)*
St Elizabeth Community Hosp (HQ).......D.......530 529-7760
2550 Sster Mary Clumba Dr Red Bluff (96080) *(P-21774)*
St Francis Electric Inc.......C.......510 639-0639
975 Carden St San Leandro (94577) *(P-2742)*
St Francis Electric LLC.......C.......510 750-8271
975 Carden St San Leandro (94577) *(P-2743)*
St Francis Extended Care Inc.......D.......510 785-3630
718 Bartlett Ave Hayward (94541) *(P-21221)*
St Francis Hts Convalescent.......D.......650 755-9515
35 Escuela Dr Daly City (94015) *(P-21222)*
St Francis Medical Center, Redwood City *Also called Verity Health System Cal Inc (P-21898)*
St Francis Medical Center (HQ).......C.......310 900-8900
3630 E Imperial Hwy Lynwood (90262) *(P-19936)*
St Francis Pavillion, Daly City *Also called Forte Enterprises Inc (P-26862)*

Mergent e-mail: customerrelations@mergent.com
1476
2019 Directory of California
Wholesalers and Services Companies
(P-0000) Products & Services Section entry number
(PA)=Parent Co (HQ)=Headquarters (DH)=Div Headquarters

St Francis Yacht Club ... C ... 415 563-6363
700 Marina Blvd San Francisco (94123) ***(P-19062)***

St George Whsng Trckg Cal Inc (HQ) ... D ... 310 764-4395
1650 S Central Ave Compton (90220) ***(P-4635)***

St Helena Hospital Clearlake, Clearlake *Also called Advintist Hlth Clearlake Hosp* ***(P-21269)***

St Helena Hospital (PA) ... A ... 707 963-1882
10 Woodland Rd Saint Helena (94574) ***(P-21775)***

St Helena Hospital Clearlake, Clearlake *Also called Adventist Health System/West* ***(P-19270)***

St John's Health Centre, Santa Monica *Also called Saint Jhns Hlth Ctr Foundation* ***(P-21695)***

St Johns Regional Medical Ctr, Oxnard *Also called Dignity Health* ***(P-21391)***

St Johns Retirement Village (PA) ... C ... 530 662-9674
135 Woodland Ave Woodland (95695) ***(P-21223)***

St Johns Well Child (PA) ... D ... 323 541-1600
808 W 58th St Los Angeles (90037) ***(P-20138)***

St Joseph Center ... D ... 310 396-6468
204 Hampton Dr Venice (90291) ***(P-24068)***

St Joseph Community Home Care ... D ... 209 478-9547
7400 Shoreline Dr Ste 4 Stockton (95219) ***(P-22423)***

St Joseph Health Per Care Svcs ... D ... 800 365-1110
1315 Corona Pointe Ct Corona (92879) ***(P-22424)***

St Joseph Health System ... D ... 714 992-3000
101 E Valencia Mesa Dr Fullerton (92835) ***(P-21776)***

St Joseph Health System ... E ... 707 443-9371
2280 Harrison Ave Ste B Eureka (95501) ***(P-19937)***

St Joseph Health System ... E ... 707 778-2505
400 N Mcdowell Blvd Fl 1 Petaluma (94954) ***(P-21777)***

St Joseph Heritage Med Group (PA) ... C ... 714 633-1011
2212 E 4th St Ste 201 Santa Ana (92705) ***(P-21778)***

St Joseph Home Health Network (HQ) ... D ... 714 712-9500
200 W Center St Promenade Anaheim (92805) ***(P-22425)***

St Joseph Home Health Network ... E ... 714 712-9559
200 W Center St Promenade Anaheim (92805) ***(P-22426)***

St Joseph Hospice ... D ... 714 712-7100
200 W Center St Promenade Anaheim (92805) ***(P-24069)***

St Joseph Hospital (PA) ... D ... 707 445-8121
2700 Dolbeer St Eureka (95501) ***(P-21779)***

St Joseph Hospital ... A ... 707 268-0190
2752 Harrison Ave Ste A Eureka (95501) ***(P-21780)***

St Joseph Hospital of Eureka ... A ... 707 445-8121
2700 Dolbeer St Eureka (95501) ***(P-21781)***

St Joseph Hospital of Orange (HQ) ... A ... 714 633-9111
1100 W Stewart Dr Orange (92868) ***(P-21782)***

St Joseph Hospital of Orange ... D ... 714 771-8037
1100 W Stewart Dr Orange (92868) ***(P-21783)***

St Joseph Surgery Center LP ... D ... 209 467-6316
1800 N California St # 1 Stockton (95204) ***(P-19938)***

St Josephs Med Ctr Stockton ... A ... 209 943-2000
1800 N California St Stockton (95204) ***(P-21784)***

St Josephs Medical Center ... C ... 209 943-2000
1800 N California St Stockton (95204) ***(P-21785)***

St Jude Heritage Medical Group ... C ... 714 528-4211
4300 Rose Dr Yorba Linda (92886) ***(P-19939)***

St Jude Hospital (HQ) ... A ... 714 871-3280
101 E Valencia Mesa Dr Fullerton (92835) ***(P-21786)***

St Jude Hospital ... A ... 714 992-3057
101 E Valencia Mesa Dr Fullerton (92835) ***(P-19940)***

St Jude Hospital Yorba Linda ... E ... 949 365-2492
27800 Medical Center Rd Mission Viejo (92691) ***(P-19941)***

St Jude Hospital Yorba Linda ... C ... 714 665-1797
11420 Warner Ave Fountain Valley (92708) ***(P-19942)***

St Jude Hospital Yorba Linda (PA) ... D ... 714 449-4800
251 Imperial Hwy Ste 481 Fullerton (92835) ***(P-27466)***

ST JUDE MEDICAL CENTER, Fullerton *Also called St Jude Hospital* ***(P-21786)***

St Jude Medical Ctr Purch Dept, Fullerton *Also called St Jude Hospital* ***(P-19940)***

St Louis Rams, Agoura Hills *Also called Los Angeles Rams LLC* ***(P-18526)***

St Luke Hlthcr & Rehab Ctr LL ... D ... 707 725-4467
2321 Newburg Rd Fortuna (95540) ***(P-20779)***

St Madeleine Sophies Center ... D ... 619 442-5129
2119 E Madison Ave El Cajon (92019) ***(P-24233)***

St Mary Medical Center (HQ) ... A ... 562 491-9000
1050 Linden Ave Long Beach (90813) ***(P-21787)***

St Mary Medical Center (PA) ... A ... 760 242-2311
18300 Us Highway 18 Apple Valley (92307) ***(P-21788)***

ST MARY'S SCHOOL OF NURSING, Long Beach *Also called St Mary Medical Center* ***(P-21787)***

St Marys Med Ctr Foundation ... A ... 415 668-1000
450 Stanyan St San Francisco (94117) ***(P-21789)***

St Michael Convalescent Hosp ... D ... 510 782-8424
25919 Gading Rd Hayward (94544) ***(P-20780)***

St Paul's Towers, Oakland *Also called Covia Communities* ***(P-24487)***

St Paul's Villa, National City *Also called St Pauls Episcopal Home Inc* ***(P-24686)***

St Pauls Episcopal Home Inc ... D ... 619 239-2097
2635 2nd Ave Ofc San Diego (92103) ***(P-24684)***

St Pauls Episcopal Home Inc ... D ... 619 239-8687
235 Nutmeg St San Diego (92103) ***(P-24685)***

St Pauls Episcopal Home Inc ... D ... 619 232-2996
2700 E 4th St National City (91950) ***(P-24686)***

St Regis Resort Monarch Beach, Dana Point *Also called Cph Monarch Hotel LLC* ***(P-12497)***

St Rose Hospital, Hayward *Also called Hayward Sisters Hospital* ***(P-21441)***

St Vincent De Paul, Oakland *Also called District Council DC* ***(P-23772)***

St Vincent De Paul of La, Los Angeles *Also called Society of St Vincent De* ***(P-25466)***

St Vincent De Paul Vlg Inc ... C ... 619 233-8500
28225 Driza Mission Viejo (92692) ***(P-25470)***

St Vincent Health Care, Pasadena *Also called Vincent Hayley Enterprises* ***(P-21249)***

St Vincent Senior Citizn Nutr (PA) ... D ... 213 484-7775
2131 W 3rd St Los Angeles (90057) ***(P-25043)***

St Vncent De Paul Bltmore Inc ... C ... 916 485-3482
3100 Norris Ave Sacramento (95821) ***(P-24070)***

St. Francis Medical Center, Lynwood *Also called Verity Health System Cal Inc* ***(P-21902)***

St. George Logistics, Compton *Also called St George Whsng Trckg Cal Inc* ***(P-4635)***

St. Johns Pleasant Valley Hosp, Camarillo *Also called Dignity Health* ***(P-21388)***

St. Louise Regional Hospital, Gilroy *Also called Verity Health System Cal Inc* ***(P-21900)***

St. Mary's Medical Center, San Francisco *Also called Dignity Health* ***(P-21392)***

STA, Thousand Palms *Also called Sunline Transit Agency* ***(P-3886)***

Staccato Communications Inc ... D ... 858 812-0981
6195 Lusk Blvd Ste 200 San Diego (92121) ***(P-17481)***

Stackla Inc ... D ... 415 528-4910
33 New Montgomery St San Francisco (94105) ***(P-15863)***

Stadtner Co Inc ... E ... 415 752-2850
3112 Geary Blvd San Francisco (94118) ***(P-2744)***

Staff Assistance Inc (PA) ... B ... 818 894-7879
72 Moody Ct Ste 100 Thousand Oaks (91360) ***(P-14767)***

Staff Assistance Inc ... B ... 805 371-9980
72 Moody Ct Ste 100 Thousand Oaks (91360) ***(P-14768)***

Staff Pro Inc ... C ... 619 544-1774
675 Convention Way San Diego (92101) ***(P-16835)***

Staff Pro Inc (PA) ... A ... 714 230-7200
15272 Jason Cir Huntington Beach (92649) ***(P-16945)***

Staff Today Incorporated ... C ... 800 928-5561
212 E Rowland St 313 Covina (91723) ***(P-14915)***

Staffchex Inc ... A ... 818 709-6100
20537 Devonshire St Chatsworth (91311) ***(P-14769)***

Staffing Home Care, San Bruno *Also called Staffing Specialists Intl* ***(P-22427)***

Staffing Solutions, Santa Ana *Also called L&T Staffing Inc* ***(P-14659)***

Staffing Solutions Inc ... D ... 408 980-9000
2142 Bering Dr San Jose (95131) ***(P-14770)***

Staffing Specialists Intl ... E ... 650 737-0777
2598 Olympic Dr San Bruno (94066) ***(P-22427)***

Stage 4 Solutions Incorporated ... E ... 408 868-9739
19200 Portos Dr Saratoga (95070) ***(P-27467)***

Stage II Design & Production, Corte Madera *Also called Stage II Inc* ***(P-17482)***

Stage II Inc ... E ... 415 285-8400
21 Channel Dr Corte Madera (94925) ***(P-17482)***

Stage Right Production Svcs, Agoura *Also called Up Stage Inc* ***(P-18150)***

Stagecoach Vineyards ... D ... 707 255-5459
1345 Hestia Way NAPA (94558) ***(P-178)***

Stagnaro Brothers Seafood Inc ... D ... 831 423-1188
320 Washington St Santa Cruz (95060) ***(P-8603)***

Stainless Stl Fabricators Inc ... D ... 714 739-9904
15120 Desman Rd La Mirada (90638) ***(P-7805)***

Stalker Software Inc ... E ... 415 569-2280
125 Park Pl Ste 210 Richmond (94801) ***(P-15864)***

Stamos Capital Partners LP ... D ... 650 233-5000
2498 Sand Hill Rd Menlo Park (94025) ***(P-10114)***

Stamoules Produce Co, Mendota *Also called S Stamoules Inc* ***(P-563)***

Stamoules Produce Company, Mendota *Also called S & S Ranch Inc* ***(P-466)***

Stampscom Inc (PA) ... A ... 310 482-5800
1990 E Grand Ave El Segundo (90245) ***(P-14063)***

Stan Farm, Modesto *Also called Stanislaus Farm Supply Company* ***(P-9100)***

Stan Tashman & Associates Inc ... A ... 310 460-7600
8675 Wash Blvd Ste 203 Culver City (90232) ***(P-27045)***

Stan Winston Inc ... D ... 818 782-0870
340 Parkside Dr San Fernando (91340) ***(P-18219)***

Stan Winston Studio, San Fernando *Also called Stan Winston Inc* ***(P-18219)***

Standard Cattle LLC ... D ... 559 693-1977
8105a S Lassen Ave San Joaquin (93660) ***(P-625)***

Standard Cattle Company, San Joaquin *Also called Standard Cattle LLC* ***(P-625)***

Standard Cattle LLC ... C ... 559 693-1977
729 E Jefferson Rd El Nido (95317) ***(P-8908)***

Standard Chartered Bank ... C ... 626 639-8000
601 S Figueroa St # 2775 Los Angeles (90017) ***(P-9488)***

Standard Drywall Inc (HQ) ... B ... 619 443-7034
9902 Channel Rd Lakeside (92040) ***(P-2962)***

Standard Hollywood Lessee LLC ... C ... 323 822-3102
8300 W Sunset Blvd Los Angeles (90069) ***(P-13261)***

Standard Hollywood, The, Los Angeles *Also called Standard Hollywood Lessee LLC* ***(P-13261)***

Standard Hotel, The, Los Angeles *Also called 550 Flower St Operations LLC* ***(P-12297)***

Standard Industries Inc ... E ... 209 242-5000
3301 Navone Rd Stockton (95215) ***(P-6930)***

Standard Industries Inc ... D ... 661 387-1110
6505 S Zerker Rd Shafter (93263) ***(P-6931)***

Standard Iron & Metals Co ... E ... 510 535-0222
4525 San Leandro St Oakland (94601) ***(P-7998)***

Standard Pacific Capital LLC ... E ... 415 352-7100
101 California St Fl 36 San Francisco (94111) ***(P-10014)***

Standard Pacific Homes, Carlsbad *Also called Calatlantic Group Inc* ***(P-1134)***

Standard Pacific Homes Ventura, Oxnard *Also called Calatlantic Group Inc* ***(P-1136)***

Standard Party Rentals, Richmond *Also called Hartmann Studios Incorporated* ***(P-17210)***

Standard Poors Fincl Svcs LLC ... E ... 415 371-5000
1 California St Fl 31 San Francisco (94111) ***(P-10115)***

Standard The, Los Angeles *Also called Hollywood Standard LLC* ***(P-12694)***

Standard-Southern Corporation ... D ... 213 624-1831
400 S Central Ave Los Angeles (90013) ***(P-4510)***

Standard-Southern Corporation ... C ... 213 624-1831
440 S Central Ave Los Angeles (90013) ***(P-4511)***

Standard-Southern Corporation ... D ... 213 624-1831
715 E 4th St Los Angeles (90013) ***(P-4512)***

Standardbearer Insur Co Ltd ... B ... 949 487-9500
27101 Puerta Real Ste 450 Mission Viejo (92691) ***(P-20781)***

STANFORD & LATHROP MEMORIAL HO, Sacramento *Also called Stanford Youth Solutions* ***(P-24846)***

Stanford Alumni Association, Stanford *Also called Leland Stanford Junior Univ* ***(P-25190)***

Stanford Cancer Center S Bay, San Jose *Also called Stanford Health Care* ***(P-21791)***

Stanford Court Hotel, San Francisco *Also called Pine & Powell Partners LLC* ***(P-13064)***
Stanford Court Nursing Center, La Mesa *Also called Life Gnerations Healthcare LLC* ***(P-20589)***
Stanford Crt Nrsing Cntr-Sntee, Santee *Also called Life Gnerations Healthcare LLC* ***(P-21135)***
Stanford Federal Credit Union (PA)..........D.......650 725-1000
1860 Embarcadero Rd # 200 Palo Alto (94303) ***(P-9595)***
Stanford Health Care..........A.......650 723-4000
300 Pasteur Dr Stanford (94305) ***(P-21790)***
Stanford Health Care..........A.......408 426-4900
2589 Samaritan Dr San Jose (95124) ***(P-21791)***
Stanford Health Care (HQ)..........A.......650 723-4000
300 Pasteur Dr Stanford (94305) ***(P-21792)***
Stanford Health Care..........A.......650 736-7844
3375 Hillview Ave Palo Alto (94304) ***(P-21793)***
Stanford Health Care Primary..........D.......650 723-6963
211 Quarry Rd Fl 3 Palo Alto (94304) ***(P-19943)***
Stanford Health Services, Palo Alto *Also called Stanford Health Care Primary* ***(P-19943)***
Stanford Hospital and Clinics..........A.......650 213-8360
1510 Page Mill Rd Ste 2 Palo Alto (94304) ***(P-21794)***
Stanford Hospitals and Clinics, Palo Alto *Also called Leland Stanford Junior Univ* ***(P-21548)***
Stanford Hotels Corporation..........C.......408 330-0001
4949 Great America Pkwy Santa Clara (95054) ***(P-13262)***
Stanford Hotels Corporation (PA)..........E.......415 398-3333
433 California St Ste 700 San Francisco (94104) ***(P-13263)***
Stanford Law Schl Off Fncl Aid..........D.......650 723-9247
Crown Quadrangle 559 Stanford (94305) ***(P-17483)***
STANFORD LINEAR ACCELERATOR CE, Stanford *Also called Stanford Univ Med Ctr Aux* ***(P-24071)***
Stanford Management Company..........D.......650 721-2200
635 Knight Way Stanford (94305) ***(P-27046)***
Stanford Medical Center, Stanford *Also called Stanford Health Care* ***(P-21792)***
Stanford Medical Center, Palo Alto *Also called Leland Stanford Junior Univ* ***(P-21549)***
Stanford Park Hotel..........C.......650 322-1234
100 El Camino Real Menlo Park (94025) ***(P-13264)***
Stanford Sierra Camp & Lodge, South Lake Tahoe *Also called Saa Sierra Programs LLC* ***(P-25231)***
Stanford Univ Earth Secinces, Stanford *Also called Leland Stanford Junior Univ* ***(P-26635)***
Stanford Univ Frman Spgli Inst..........C.......650 723-8681
616 Serra St Stanford (94305) ***(P-26663)***
Stanford Univ Med Ctr Aux..........B.......650 723-6636
300 Pasteur Dr Stanford (94305) ***(P-24071)***
Stanford University, Stanford *Also called Leland Stanford Junior Univ* ***(P-21551)***
Stanford University, Stanford *Also called Leland Stanford Junior Univ* ***(P-21552)***
Stanford University Med Ctr, Palo Alto *Also called Leland Stanford Junior Univ* ***(P-21550)***
Stanford University Medical, Stanford *Also called Leland Stanford Junior Univ* ***(P-21553)***
Stanford Youth Solutions (PA)..........D.......916 344-0199
8912 Volunteer Ln Sacramento (95826) ***(P-24846)***
Stanislaus County Police..........C.......209 529-9121
1325 Beverly Dr Modesto (95351) ***(P-24072)***
Stanislaus Farm Supply Company (PA)..........D.......209 538-7070
624 E Service Rd Modesto (95358) ***(P-9100)***
Stanislaus Medical Center, Modesto *Also called County of Stanislaus* ***(P-21360)***
Stanislaus Surgical Center, Modesto *Also called Stanislaus Surgical Hosp LLC* ***(P-21795)***
Stanislaus Surgical Hosp LLC (PA)..........C.......209 572-2700
1421 Oakdale Rd Modesto (95355) ***(P-21795)***
Stanislaus County Mental Hlth, Modesto *Also called County of Stanislaus* ***(P-22559)***
Stanley M Kirkpatrick MD..........E.......858 966-5855
3020 Childrens Way San Diego (92123) ***(P-19944)***
Stanley Pest Control, South El Monte *Also called Statewide Pest Control Co Inc* ***(P-14157)***
Stanley R Klein MD Facs Inc..........E.......310 373-6864
23451 Madison St Ste 300 Torrance (90505) ***(P-19945)***
Stanley Steemer Carpet Cleaner, San Diego *Also called Colt Services Inc* ***(P-13576)***
Stanley Steemer of Los Angles (PA)..........D.......626 791-9400
841 W Foothill Blvd Azusa (91702) ***(P-13580)***
Stansbury Hm Preservation Assn..........E.......530 895-3848
307 W 5th St Chico (95928) ***(P-24915)***
Stantec Arch & Engrg PC..........C.......949 923-6000
38 Technology Dr Ste 100 Irvine (92618) ***(P-25927)***
Stantec Arch & Engrg PC..........D.......415 882-9500
100 California St # 1000 San Francisco (94111) ***(P-25928)***
Stantec Architecture Inc..........C.......949 923-6000
38 Technology Dr Irvine (92618) ***(P-26112)***
Stantec Architecture Inc..........D.......626 796-9141
300 N Lake Ave Ste 400 Pasadena (91101) ***(P-26113)***
Stantec Architecture Inc..........D.......415 882-9500
100 California St # 1000 San Francisco (94111) ***(P-25929)***
Stantec Consulting Svcs Inc..........D.......916 773-8100
3875 Atherton Rd Rocklin (95765) ***(P-26114)***
Stantec Consulting Svcs Inc..........C.......925 627-4500
1340 Treat Blvd Ste 525 Walnut Creek (94597) ***(P-25930)***
Stantec Consulting Svcs Inc..........D.......805 963-9532
111 E Victoria St Santa Barbara (93101) ***(P-26136)***
Stantec Consulting Svcs Inc..........D.......626 796-9141
300 N Lake Ave Ste 400 Pasadena (91101) ***(P-25931)***
Stantec Consulting Svcs Inc..........C.......949 923-6000
38 Technology Dr Ste 100 Irvine (92618) ***(P-26115)***
Stantec Consulting Svcs Inc..........E.......916 924-8844
3301 C St Ste 1900 Sacramento (95816) ***(P-25932)***
Stantec Consulting Svcs Inc..........D.......415 882-9500
100 California St # 1000 San Francisco (94111) ***(P-25933)***
Stantec Energy & Resources Inc (HQ)..........C.......661 396-3770
5500 Ming Ave Ste 300 Bakersfield (93309) ***(P-26137)***
Stantec Holdings Del III Inc (HQ)..........C.......661 396-3770
5500 Ming Ave Ste 300 Bakersfield (93309) ***(P-12007)***
Stantru Reinforcing Steel, Fontana *Also called Stantru Resources Inc* ***(P-1437)***
Stantru Resources Inc..........D.......909 587-1441
11175 Redwood Ave Fontana (92337) ***(P-1437)***
Stapleton - Spence Packing Co (PA)..........C.......408 297-8815
1900 State Highway 99 Gridley (95948) ***(P-8871)***
Star & Crescent Boat Company (PA)..........E.......619 234-4111
1311 1st St Coronado (92118) ***(P-4721)***
Star - Lite Electric, Chatsworth *Also called Mj Star-Lite Inc* ***(P-2649)***
Star Brite Building Maint..........B.......562 988-2829
2688 Dawson Ave Long Beach (90755) ***(P-14400)***
Star Fabrics Inc (PA)..........D.......213 688-2871
1440 Walnut St Los Angeles (90011) ***(P-8245)***
Star Fisheries..........D.......310 549-4992
841 Watson Ave Wilmington (90744) ***(P-8604)***
Star Fisheries (PA)..........D.......310 832-8395
222 W 6th St Ste 500 San Pedro (90731) ***(P-8605)***
Star H-R..........A.......707 894-4404
105 E 1st St Cloverdale (95425) ***(P-14771)***
Star H-R (PA)..........A.......707 762-4447
3820 Cypress Dr Ste 2 Petaluma (94954) ***(P-14916)***
Star Inc..........C.......916 632-8407
4145 Delmar Ave Ste 1 Rocklin (95677) ***(P-24073)***
Star Laundry Services Inc..........D.......619 572-1009
3410 Main St San Diego (92113) ***(P-13637)***
Star Lax LLC..........C.......310 642-4500
150 S Doheny Dr Beverly Hills (90211) ***(P-17648)***
Star Nail International, Valencia *Also called Star Nail Products Inc* ***(P-8211)***
Star Nail Products Inc..........D.......661 257-3376
29120 Avenue Paine Valencia (91355) ***(P-8211)***
Star of California..........D.......805 379-1401
299 W Hillcrest Dr Thousand Oaks (91360) ***(P-22889)***
Star of California..........C.......805 466-1638
8834 Morro Rd Atascadero (93422) ***(P-22890)***
Star of California (PA)..........C.......805 644-7823
4880 Market St Ventura (93003) ***(P-22891)***
Star One Credit Union (PA)..........C.......408 543-5202
1306 Bordeaux Dr Sunnyvale (94089) ***(P-9596)***
Star Real Estate..........D.......714 500-3300
19440 Goldenwest St Huntington Beach (92648) ***(P-11775)***
Star Real Estate..........C.......714 731-3777
12651 Newport Ave Tustin (92780) ***(P-11776)***
Star Real Estate South County..........C.......949 389-0004
26711 Aliso Creek Rd 200a Aliso Viejo (92656) ***(P-11777)***
Star Scrap Metal Company Inc..........D.......562 921-5045
1509 S Bluff Rd Montebello (90640) ***(P-6479)***
Star Services, San Diego *Also called Star Laundry Services Inc* ***(P-13637)***
Star Staffing, Petaluma *Also called Star H-R* ***(P-14916)***
Star View Adolescent Center..........D.......310 373-4556
4025 W 226th St Torrance (90505) ***(P-21973)***
Star View Chldrn Fmly Srvcs..........D.......310 868-5379
1085 W Victoria St Compton (90220) ***(P-24074)***
Starco Group Inc..........D.......909 989-9898
9160 Hyssop Dr Rancho Cucamonga (91730) ***(P-17484)***
Stargate Digital, South Pasadena *Also called Stargate Films Inc* ***(P-18125)***
Stargate Films Inc..........D.......626 403-8403
1001 El Centro St South Pasadena (91030) ***(P-18125)***
Stark Services..........D.......818 985-2003
12444 Victory Blvd # 300 North Hollywood (91606) ***(P-16182)***
Starlight Educational Center, Westminster *Also called Westview Services Inc* ***(P-24249)***
Starlight International Ltd LP..........D.......562 439-5740
38 Saint Joseph Ave Long Beach (90803) ***(P-8212)***
Starlight Management Group..........D.......408 334-7456
1355 N 4th St San Jose (95112) ***(P-13265)***
Starline Tours Hollywood Inc..........D.......323 262-1114
2130 S Tubeway Ave Commerce (90040) ***(P-4981)***
Starline Tours Hollywood Inc (PA)..........D.......323 463-3333
6801 Hollywood Blvd # 221 Los Angeles (90028) ***(P-4982)***
Starpoint Property MGT LLC..........C.......310 247-0550
450 N Roxbury Dr Ste 1050 Beverly Hills (90210) ***(P-11778)***
Starpoint Surgery Center, Irvine *Also called Sph-Irvine LLC* ***(P-19934)***
Stars, San Leandro *Also called Subacute Trtmnt Adolescnt Reha* ***(P-22689)***
Stars Recreation Center LP..........E.......707 455-7827
155 Browns Valley Pkwy Vacaville (95688) ***(P-18499)***
Startel Corporation (PA)..........D.......949 863-8700
16 Goodyear B-125 Irvine (92618) ***(P-15471)***
Startup Farms Intl LLC..........B.......510 440-0110
45690 Northport Loop E Fremont (94538) ***(P-15472)***
Starvista..........C.......650 591-9623
610 Elm St Ste 212 San Carlos (94070) ***(P-24075)***
Starwest Botanicals Inc (PA)..........D.......916 638-8100
161 Main Ave Sacramento (95838) ***(P-8872)***
Starwood Hotel..........D.......310 641-7740
5990 Green Valley Cir Culver City (90230) ***(P-13266)***
Starwood Hotels & Resorts, Costa Mesa *Also called South Coast Westin Hotel Co* ***(P-13249)***
Starwood Hotels & Resorts, San Diego *Also called San Diego Sheraton Corporation* ***(P-13172)***
Starwood Hotels & Resorts, Culver City *Also called Starwood Hotel* ***(P-13266)***
Starwood Hotels & Resorts..........C.......909 484-2018
10480 4th St Rancho Cucamonga (91730) ***(P-13267)***
Starwood Hotels & Resorts..........C.......916 447-1700
1230 J St Sacramento (95814) ***(P-13268)***
Starwood Hotels & Resorts..........D.......415 777-5300
181 3rd St San Francisco (94103) ***(P-13269)***
Starwood Hotels & Resorts..........C.......415 479-8800
1010 Northgate Dr San Rafael (94903) ***(P-13270)***
Starwood Hotels & Resorts..........D.......650 692-6363
401 E Millbrae Ave Millbrae (94030) ***(P-13271)***
Starwood Hotels & Resorts..........C.......415 284-4000
125 3rd St San Francisco (94103) ***(P-13272)***

Mergent e-mail: customerrelations@mergent.com
1478
2019 Directory of California Wholesalers and Services Companies
(P-0000) Products & Services Section entry number
(PA)=Parent Co (HQ)=Headquarters (DH)=Div Headquarters

Starwood Hotels & Resorts ....C....619 239-2200
910 Broadway Cir San Diego (92101) *(P-13273)*
Starwood Htls & Rsrts Wrldwde ....C....310 208-8765
930 Hilgard Ave Los Angeles (90024) *(P-13274)*
Starwood Htls & Rsrts Wrldwde ....A....213 624-1000
404 S Figueroa St Los Angeles (90071) *(P-13275)*
Starwood Htls & Rsrts Wrldwde ....B....760 328-5955
71333 Dinah Shore Dr Rancho Mirage (92270) *(P-13276)*
Starwood Htls & Rsrts Wrldwde ....D....415 284-4049
125 3rd St San Francisco (94103) *(P-13277)*
Starwood Htls & Rsrts Wrldwde ....C....415 512-1111
2 New Montgomery St San Francisco (94105) *(P-13278)*
Starwood Htls & Rsrts Wrldwde ....C....323 798-1300
6250 Hollywood Blvd Los Angeles (90028) *(P-13279)*
Starwood Htls & Rsrts Wrldwde ....C....909 622-2220
601 W Mckinley Ave Pomona (91768) *(P-13280)*
Starwood Htls & Rsrts Wrldwde ....D....619 239-9600
1617 1st Ave San Diego (92101) *(P-13281)*
Starzz Management Services (PA) ....D....510 632-5533
528 Stonehaven Ct Hayward (94544) *(P-27047)*
Stat Registry Service, Long Beach *Also called Code America Inc (P-14589)*
State Bar of California (PA) ....B....415 538-2000
180 Howard St Fl Grnd San Francisco (94105) *(P-25044)*
State Bar of California ....B....213 765-1000
845 S Figueroa St Los Angeles (90017) *(P-25045)*
State Compensation Insur Fund (PA) ....D....888 782-8338
333 Bush St Fl 8 San Francisco (94104) *(P-10394)*
State Compensation Insur Fund ....B....714 565-5000
1750 E 4th St Fl 3 Santa Ana (92705) *(P-10395)*
State Compensation Insur Fund ....C....661 664-4000
9801 Camino Media Ste 101 Bakersfield (93311) *(P-10396)*
State Compensation Insur Fund ....C....510 577-3000
2955 Peralta Oaks Ct Oakland (94605) *(P-10397)*
State Compensation Insur Fund ....C....888 782-8338
333 W San Carlos St # 950 San Jose (95110) *(P-10398)*
State Compensation Insur Fund ....C....888 782-8338
364 Knollcrest Dr Redding (96002) *(P-10399)*
State Compensation Insur Fund ....B....888 782-8338
10105 Pacific Hgts Blvd San Diego (92121) *(P-10400)*
State Compensation Insur Fund ....B....559 433-2700
10 E Rver Pk Pl E Ste 110 Fresno (93720) *(P-10401)*
State Compensation Insur Fund ....C....213 576-7335
655 N Central Ave Ste 200 Glendale (91203) *(P-10402)*
State Compensation Insur Fund ....C....323 266-5551
655 N Central Ave Ste 200 Glendale (91203) *(P-10403)*
State Compensation Insur Fund ....C....888 782-8338
3247 W March Ln Ste 110 Stockton (95219) *(P-10404)*
State Compensation Insur Fund ....C....888 782-8338
655 N Central Ave Ste 200 Glendale (91203) *(P-10405)*
State Compensation Insur Fund ....B....916 924-5100
2275 Gateway Oaks Dr Sacramento (95833) *(P-10406)*
State Compensation Insur Fund ....D....707 443-9721
800 W Harris St Ste 37 Eureka (95503) *(P-10407)*
State Compensation Insur Fund ....C....888 782-8338
6301 Day St Riverside (92507) *(P-10408)*
State Compensation Insur Fund ....B....888 782-8338
2901 N Ventura Rd Ste 100 Oxnard (93036) *(P-10173)*
State Compensation Insur Fund ....C....925 523-5000
5880 Owens Dr Pleasanton (94588) *(P-10409)*
State Compensation Insur Fund ....C....888 782-8338
5890 Owens Dr Pleasanton (94588) *(P-10410)*
State Compensation Insur Fund ....C....323 266-5000
900 Corporate Center Dr Monterey Park (91754) *(P-10411)*
State Farm Fire and Cslty Co ....D....559 625-4330
5127 W Walnut Ave Visalia (93277) *(P-10778)*
State Farm Fire and Cslty Co ....B....707 588-6011
6400 State Farm Dr Rohnert Park (94928) *(P-10779)*
State Farm Insurance, Los Angeles *Also called State Farm Mutl Auto Insur Co (P-10780)*
State Farm Insurance, Encino *Also called State Farm Mutl Auto Insur Co (P-10781)*
State Farm Insurance, Visalia *Also called State Farm Fire and Cslty Co (P-10778)*
State Farm Insurance, Los Altos *Also called State Farm Mutl Auto Insur Co (P-10782)*
State Farm Insurance, Agoura Hills *Also called State Farm Mutl Auto Insur Co (P-10783)*
State Farm Insurance, Pinole *Also called State Farm Mutl Auto Insur Co (P-10784)*
State Farm Insurance, Long Beach *Also called State Farm Mutl Auto Insur Co (P-10785)*
State Farm Insurance, Fontana *Also called State Farm Mutl Auto Insur Co (P-10786)*
State Farm Insurance, Bakersfield *Also called State Farm Mutl Auto Insur Co (P-10787)*
State Farm Insurance, San Mateo *Also called State Farm Mutl Auto Insur Co (P-10788)*
State Farm Insurance, Irvine *Also called State Farm Mutl Auto Insur Co (P-10789)*
State Farm Insurance, Oakhurst *Also called State Farm Mutl Auto Insur Co (P-10790)*
State Farm Insurance, Woodland Hills *Also called State Farm Mutl Auto Insur Co (P-10791)*
State Farm Insurance, Pacific Palisades *Also called State Farm Mutl Auto Insur Co (P-10792)*
State Farm Insurance, Los Angeles *Also called State Farm Mutl Auto Insur Co (P-10793)*
State Farm Insurance, Bakersfield *Also called State Farm Mutl Auto Insur Co (P-10794)*
State Farm Insurance, Rohnert Park *Also called State Farm Fire and Cslty Co (P-10779)*
State Farm Mutl Auto Insur Co ....B....309 766-2311
12122 S Halldale Ave # 200 Los Angeles (90047) *(P-10780)*
State Farm Mutl Auto Insur Co ....D....818 849-5126
16656 Ventura Blvd # 203 Encino (91436) *(P-10781)*
State Farm Mutl Auto Insur Co ....D....650 694-6767
5050 El Camino Real # 108 Los Altos (94022) *(P-10782)*
State Farm Mutl Auto Insur Co ....D....818 597-4300
30125 Agoura Rd Ste 200 Agoura Hills (91301) *(P-10783)*
State Farm Mutl Auto Insur Co ....D....510 222-1102
1558 Fitzgerald Dr Pinole (94564) *(P-10784)*
State Farm Mutl Auto Insur Co ....D....310 632-9810
1705 E 10th St Apt 201 Long Beach (90813) *(P-10785)*
State Farm Mutl Auto Insur Co ....D....909 349-2050
17122 Slover Ave Ste 106 Fontana (92337) *(P-10786)*
State Farm Mutl Auto Insur Co ....D....661 324-4077
2019 24th St Bakersfield (93301) *(P-10787)*
State Farm Mutl Auto Insur Co ....D....650 345-3571
2555 Flores St Ste 175 San Mateo (94403) *(P-10788)*
State Farm Mutl Auto Insur Co ....D....309 766-2311
3351 Michelson Dr Ste 200 Irvine (92612) *(P-10789)*
State Farm Mutl Auto Insur Co ....D....559 683-3467
40315 Junction Dr Ste A Oakhurst (93644) *(P-10790)*
State Farm Mutl Auto Insur Co ....D....818 887-1060
5345 Fallbrook Ave Woodland Hills (91367) *(P-10791)*
State Farm Mutl Auto Insur Co ....D....310 454-0349
845 Via De La Paz Ste 12 Pacific Palisades (90272) *(P-10792)*
State Farm Mutl Auto Insur Co ....D....323 852-6868
8040 W 3rd St Los Angeles (90048) *(P-10793)*
State Farm Mutl Auto Insur Co ....D....661 664-9663
4600 Ashe Rd Ste 308 Bakersfield (93313) *(P-10794)*
STATE FUND, San Francisco *Also called State Compensation Insur Fund (P-10394)*
State Fund Office, Glendale *Also called State Compensation Insur Fund (P-10402)*
State Group LLC ....B....949 612-2879
36 Umbria Irvine (92618) *(P-27468)*
State Pipe & Supply Inc ....E....909 356-5670
2180 N Locust Ave Rialto (92377) *(P-7316)*
State Pipe & Supply Inc (HQ) ....D....909 877-9999
183 S Cedar Ave Rialto (92376) *(P-7317)*
State Preschool, Alhambra *Also called Options For Learning (P-24359)*
State Preschool ....E....925 473-4380
950 El Pueblo Ave Pittsburg (94565) *(P-24386)*
State Roofing Systems Inc ....D....510 317-1477
15444 Hesperian Blvd San Leandro (94578) *(P-3201)*
States Drawer Box Spc LLC ....D....714 744-4247
1482 N Batavia St Orange (92867) *(P-6866)*
States Logistics Services Inc ....C....714 523-1276
7221 Cate Dr Buena Park (90621) *(P-5174)*
States Logistics Services Inc (PA) ....C....714 521-6520
5650 Dolly Ave Buena Park (90621) *(P-4636)*
Statewide, Sacramento *Also called Domus Construction & Design (P-1157)*
Statewide Pest Control Co Inc (PA) ....C....626 443-2847
2555 Loma Ave South El Monte (91733) *(P-14157)*
Station Venture Operations LP ....D....619 231-3939
9680 Granite Ridge Dr San Diego (92123) *(P-5839)*
Stations, San Jose *Also called Andrian Inc (P-3486)*
Status Medical Management, Modesto *Also called Pegasus Risk Management Inc (P-10728)*
Stavatti Industries Ltd ....D....651 238-5369
1443 S Gage St San Bernardino (92408) *(P-1007)*
Staybridge Suites, San Diego *Also called Six Continents Hotels Inc (P-13239)*
Staybridge Suites, Sunnyvale *Also called Hpt Trs Ihg-2 Inc (P-12738)*
STC Netcom Inc (PA) ....D....951 685-8181
11611 Industry Ave Fontana (92337) *(P-2745)*
Steadfast Management Co Inc ....C....714 542-2229
15520 Tustin Village Way Tustin (92780) *(P-11117)*
Stearns Lending LLC (HQ) ....B....714 513-7777
4 Hutton Centre Dr Fl 10 Santa Ana (92707) *(P-9860)*
Steel House Inc ....C....310 773-3331
3644 Eastham Dr Culver City (90232) *(P-13905)*
Steele Canyon Golf Club Corp (PA) ....D....619 441-6900
3199 Stonefield Dr Jamul (91935) *(P-18765)*
Steele Cis LLC ....B....415 692-5000
1 Sansome St Ste 3500 San Francisco (94104) *(P-23397)*
Steele Corp SEC Advisory Svcs, San Francisco *Also called Firstcall (P-16647)*
Steelpoint Capital Partners LP ....D....858 764-8700
2081 Faraday Ave Carlsbad (92008) *(P-12268)*
Steelriver Infrastructure Fund (HQ) ....C....415 291-2200
1 Letterman Dr Bldg C San Francisco (94129) *(P-6179)*
Steelriver Infrasturcture Part (PA) ....C....415 512-1515
1 Harbor Dr Ste 101 Sausalito (94965) *(P-12008)*
Steeltech Construction Svcs ....D....714 630-2890
4081 E La Palma Ave Ste G Anaheim (92807) *(P-1438)*
Steelwave Inc (PA) ....C....650 571-2200
4000 E 3rd Ave Ste 500 Foster City (94404) *(P-11920)*
Steelwave Inc ....C....949 863-0390
2050 Main St Ste 230 Irvine (92614) *(P-11921)*
Steelwave LLC ....A....650 571-2200
4000 E 3rd Ave Ste 500 Foster City (94404) *(P-11922)*
Stefan Merli Plastering Co Inc (PA) ....D....310 323-0404
1230 W 130th St Gardena (90247) *(P-3330)*
Steger Inc ....E....714 974-4383
1938 N Batavia St Ste L Orange (92865) *(P-2483)*
Stein & Lubin LLP ....E....415 981-0550
600 Montgomery St Fl 14 San Francisco (94111) *(P-23398)*
Steinberg Architects (PA) ....D....408 295-5446
125 S Market St Ste 110 San Jose (95113) *(P-26116)*
Steinberg Group Architects, San Jose *Also called Steinberg Architects (P-26116)*
Steiny and Company Inc (PA) ....D....626 962-1055
221 N Ardmore Ave Los Angeles (90004) *(P-2746)*
Steiny and Company Inc ....C....213 382-2331
221 N Ardmore Ave Los Angeles (90004) *(P-2747)*
Stellar Distributing Inc ....B....559 664-8400
21801 Ave Ste 16 Madera (93637) *(P-8732)*
Stellar Group Incorporated ....D....209 549-0899
1035 Reno Ave Modesto (95351) *(P-7666)*
Stellar Microelectronics Inc ....C....661 775-3500
28454 Livingston Ave Valencia (91355) *(P-7544)*
Stellartech Research Corp (PA) ....D....408 331-3134
560 Cottonwood Dr Milpitas (95035) *(P-26459)*
Steno Employment Services Inc ....A....909 476-1404
8560 Vineyard Ave Ste 208 Rancho Cucamonga (91730) *(P-14917)*
Step, Sacramento *Also called Stratgies To Empwer People Inc (P-20963)*
Step House Recovery, Fountain Valley *Also called Stephouse Recovery Center (P-24076)*

ALPHABETIC

Employee Codes: A=Over 500 employees, B=251-500
C=101-250, D=51-100, E=50
2019 Directory of California
Wholesalers and Services Companies
© Mergent Inc. 1-800-342-5647
1479

Step Up On Second Street Inc (PA)....D....310 394-6889
1328 2nd St Ofc Santa Monica (90401) ***(P-25471)***
Stephen B Meisel MD PC....E....310 828-8843
2811 Wilshire Blvd # 900 Santa Monica (90403) ***(P-19946)***
Stephen B Meisel MD A Med Corp (HQ)....D....310 828-8843
2811 Wilshire Blvd # 900 Santa Monica (90403) ***(P-19947)***
Stephouse Recovery Center....D....714 394-3494
10529 Slater Ave Fountain Valley (92708) ***(P-24076)***
Stepping Stn Grwth Ctr Fr Chld....D....510 568-3331
311 Macarthur Blvd San Leandro (94577) ***(P-24234)***
Steptoe & Johnson LLP....E....213 439-9400
633 W 5th St Fl 7 Los Angeles (90071) ***(P-23399)***
Steren Electronics Intl LLC (PA)....D....800 266-3333
6920 Carroll Rd Ste 100 San Diego (92121) ***(P-7545)***
Steren Shop, San Diego *Also called Steren Electronics Intl LLC* ***(P-7545)***
Stereo D LLC....B....818 861-3100
3355 W Empire Ave Fl 1 Burbank (91504) ***(P-18220)***
Stereod, Burbank *Also called Stereo D LLC* ***(P-18220)***
Stericycle Comm Solutions Inc....D....888 370-6711
2255 Watt Ave Ste 50 Sacramento (95825) ***(P-17485)***
Stericycle Comm Solutions Inc....E....714 991-9595
612 S Harbor Blvd Anaheim (92805) ***(P-17486)***
Stericycles Envmtl Solutions, Rancho Cordova *Also called General Environmental* ***(P-17184)***
Sterile Proc Svcs Amer LLC....E....562 428-5858
2240 E Artesia Blvd Long Beach (90805) ***(P-17487)***
Sterling Asset Management, Fairfield *Also called Community Housing Opport* ***(P-26816)***
Sterling Brand, San Francisco *Also called Sterling Consulting Group LLC* ***(P-27469)***
Sterling Building Services, Anaheim *Also called Danlil Enterprise Inc* ***(P-14250)***
Sterling Collision Center LLC (PA)....D....714 259-1111
1111 Bell Ave Ste A Tustin (92780) ***(P-17744)***
Sterling Consulting Group LLC....D....415 248-7900
55 Union St Fl 3 San Francisco (94111) ***(P-27469)***
Sterling Court, San Mateo *Also called Fifty Peninsula Partners* ***(P-11019)***
Sterling Dry Cleaners, Los Angeles *Also called Sterling Westwood Inc* ***(P-13570)***
Sterling Hsa Inc....E....800 617-4729
475 14th St Ste 120 Oakland (94612) ***(P-17488)***
Sterling Inn, Victorville *Also called Sterling-Ase Ltd Partnership* ***(P-11118)***
Sterling Mktg & Fincl Corp....E....209 593-1140
4660 Spyres Way Ste 1 Modesto (95356) ***(P-27470)***
Sterling Pacific Meat Company, Commerce *Also called Interstate Meat & Provision* ***(P-8491)***
Sterling Plumbing Inc....D....714 641-5480
3111 W Central Ave Santa Ana (92704) ***(P-2372)***
Sterling Senior Communities, Temecula *Also called MBK Senior Living LLC* ***(P-21155)***
Sterling Westwood Inc....D....310 287-2431
3405 Overland Ave Los Angeles (90034) ***(P-13570)***
Sterling-Ase Ltd Partnership....C....760 951-9507
17738 Francesca Rd Victorville (92395) ***(P-11118)***
Steuber Corporation (PA)....D....310 632-8255
20425 S Susana Rd Long Beach (90810) ***(P-7146)***
Steve and Beth Chaput....E....909 596-9994
1025 Sentinel Dr Ste 103 La Verne (91750) ***(P-14401)***
Steve Beattie Inc....D....310 454-1786
1766 Westridge Rd Los Angeles (90049) ***(P-2484)***
Steve Beattie Painting, Los Angeles *Also called Steve Beattie Inc* ***(P-2484)***
Steve Duich Inc....E....619 444-6118
1369 N Magnolia Ave El Cajon (92020) ***(P-3331)***
Steve Manning Construction Inc....D....530 222-0810
5211 Churn Creek Rd Redding (96002) ***(P-1853)***
Steve Roberson....D....562 927-2626
7825 Florence Ave Downey (90240) ***(P-11779)***
Steve Silver Productions Inc....D....415 421-4284
678 Green St Ste 2 San Francisco (94133) ***(P-18406)***
Steven Engineering Inc....C....650 588-9200
230 Ryan Way South San Francisco (94080) ***(P-7873)***
Steven G Fogg MD....D....559 449-5010
1360 E Herndon Ave # 401 Fresno (93720) ***(P-19948)***
Steven Global Freight Services, Redondo Beach *Also called Stevens Global Logistics Inc* ***(P-5175)***
Steven N Ledson....D....707 537-3810
7335 Sonoma Hwy Santa Rosa (95409) ***(P-1239)***
Steven P Abelow MD....D....530 544-8033
2311 Lake Tahoe Blvd South Lake Tahoe (96150) ***(P-19949)***
Steven Rubinstein MD, Sunnyvale *Also called Palo Alto Medical Foundation* ***(P-19751)***
Steven Snyder, Hollister *Also called Hollister Process Service* ***(P-17223)***
Stevens Creek Quarry Inc (PA)....D....408 253-2512
12100 Stevens Canyon Rd Cupertino (95014) ***(P-1854)***
Stevens Global Logistics Inc (PA)....D....310 216-5645
3700 Redondo Beach Ave Redondo Beach (90278) ***(P-5175)***
Stevinson Ranch Golf Club, Stevinson *Also called Stevinson Ranch-Savannah GP* ***(P-18766)***
Stevinson Ranch-Savannah GP....D....209 668-8200
2700 Van Clief Rd Stevinson (95374) ***(P-18766)***
Stewardship Company LLC....C....831 620-6700
1 Rancho San Carlos Rd Carmel (93923) ***(P-27048)***
Stewart Enterprises Inc....E....858 453-2121
5600 Carroll Canyon Rd San Diego (92121) ***(P-13699)***
Stewart Title California Inc (HQ)....C....619 692-1600
7676 Hazard Center Dr # 1400 San Diego (92108) ***(P-10471)***
Stila Styles, Mira Loma *Also called Geodis Logistics LLC* ***(P-4566)***
Stjohn God Rtirement Care Ctr....C....323 731-0641
2468 S St Andrews Pl Los Angeles (90018) ***(P-20782)***
Stk International Inc....D....310 720-1277
6160 Peach Tree St Compton (90220) ***(P-7962)***
Stmicroelectronics Inc....C....408 452-8585
2755 Great America Way Santa Clara (95054) ***(P-7546)***
Stockbridge/Sbe Holdings LLC....A....323 655-8000
5900 Wilshire Blvd # 3100 Los Angeles (90036) ***(P-13282)***
Stockcross Financial Svcs Inc (PA)....E....800 993-2015
9464 Wilshire Blvd Beverly Hills (90212) ***(P-10015)***
Stockdale Country Club....D....661 832-0310
7001 Stockdale Hwy Bakersfield (93309) ***(P-19063)***
Stockdale Medical Offices, Bakersfield *Also called Kaiser Foundation Hospitals* ***(P-21497)***
Stocker & Allaire Inc....E....831 375-1890
21 Mandeville Ct Monterey (93940) ***(P-1240)***
Stockham Construction Inc....B....707 664-0945
475 Portal St Cotati (94931) ***(P-3083)***
Stockmar Industrial, Long Beach *Also called Elite Craftsman* ***(P-14256)***
Stockton Cardiology Medical Gr....D....209 824-1555
1148 Norman Dr Ste 3 Manteca (95336) ***(P-19950)***
Stockton Cardiology Medical Gr (PA)....E....209 994-5750
415 E Harding Way Ste D Stockton (95204) ***(P-19951)***
Stockton Congregational Home....D....209 466-4341
1319 N Madison St Ofc Stockton (95202) ***(P-24687)***
Stockton District Office, Stockton *Also called State Compensation Insur Fund* ***(P-10404)***
Stockton Edson Healthcare Corp....D....209 948-8762
1630 N Edison St Stockton (95204) ***(P-21224)***
Stockton Hilton Hotel, Stockton *Also called Stockton Hotel Ltd* ***(P-13283)***
Stockton Hotel Ltd....C....209 957-9090
2323 Grand Canal Blvd Stockton (95207) ***(P-13283)***
Stockton Orthpd Med Group Inc....E....209 948-1641
2545 W Hammer Ln Stockton (95209) ***(P-19952)***
Stockton Port District....D....209 946-0246
2201 W Washington St # 13 Stockton (95203) ***(P-4741)***
Stockton Scavengers Assn, Stockton *Also called USA Waste of California Inc* ***(P-4079)***
Stollwood Convalescent Hosp, Woodland *Also called St Johns Retirement Village* ***(P-21223)***
Stommel Inc (PA)....E....916 646-6626
4707 Northgate Blvd Sacramento (95834) ***(P-2748)***
Stomper Co Inc....D....510 574-0570
7799 Enterprise Dr Newark (94560) ***(P-3464)***
Stone & Youngberg LLC (PA)....C....415 445-2300
1 Ferry Plz San Francisco (94111) ***(P-10016)***
Stone Blue Inc....D....323 277-0008
2501 E 28th St Vernon (90058) ***(P-13622)***
Stone Bros Management (PA)....D....209 478-1791
5250 Claremont Ave Stockton (95207) ***(P-11923)***
Stone Entertainment, Costa Mesa *Also called Volcom LLC* ***(P-17575)***
Stone Land Company (PA)....D....559 947-3185
28521 Nevada Ave Stratford (93266) ***(P-15)***
Stone Ranch, Stratford *Also called Stone Land Company* ***(P-15)***
Stone Tree Landscape Corp....E....323 965-0944
5757 Wilshire Blvd # 505 Los Angeles (90036) ***(P-945)***
Stonebrae LP....D....510 728-7878
222 Country Club Dr Hayward (94542) ***(P-19064)***
Stonebridge McWhinney LLC....E....714 703-8800
11747 Harbor Blvd Garden Grove (92840) ***(P-13284)***
Stonebrook Convalescent Center....C....925 689-7457
4367 Concord Blvd Concord (94521) ***(P-20783)***
Stonebrook Health Care Center, Concord *Also called Stonebrook Convalescent Center* ***(P-20783)***
Stonehouse Restaurant, Santa Barbara *Also called San Ysidro Bb Property LLC* ***(P-13183)***
Stoneland, North Hollywood *Also called Arriaga Usa Inc* ***(P-6876)***
Stoneridge Creek Pleasanton, Pleasanton *Also called Conti Life Comm Plea LLC* ***(P-17100)***
Stoneriver Inc....B....714 705-8227
770 The Cy Dr S Ste 5000 Orange (92868) ***(P-15473)***
Stonesfair Financial Corp....D....650 347-0442
577 Airport Blvd Ste 700 Burlingame (94010) ***(P-11119)***
Stonesfair Management LLC (PA)....D....650 401-3810
577 Airport Blvd Ste 700 Burlingame (94010) ***(P-11780)***
Stonetree Golf LLC....E....415 209-6744
9 Stonetree Ln Novato (94945) ***(P-18767)***
Stonetree Management, Novato *Also called Stonetree Golf LLC* ***(P-18767)***
Stonewood Ctr Mall Office, Downey *Also called Macerich Company* ***(P-10908)***
Stop Hop Center, Carson *Also called Anschutz So Calif Sports Compl* ***(P-18506)***
Storage West, Los Angeles *Also called Laaco Ltd* ***(P-11175)***
Store & Online, City of Industry *Also called Solestage Inc* ***(P-16055)***
Store 17, Moorpark *Also called Prudential Overall Supply* ***(P-13550)***
Storer Transportation....D....209 644-5100
1909 S Argonaut St Stockton (95206) ***(P-3731)***
Storer Transportation Service (PA)....B....209 521-8250
3519 Mcdonald Ave Modesto (95358) ***(P-3892)***
Storer Travel Service, Modesto *Also called Storer Transportation Service* ***(P-3892)***
Stormgeo (HQ)....C....408 731-8600
140 Kifer Ct Sunnyvale (94086) ***(P-27959)***
Storquest Self Storage (HQ)....D....310 451-2130
201 Wilshire Blvd Ste 102 Santa Monica (90401) ***(P-4637)***
Story Teller, Universal City *Also called Amblin/Reliance Holding Co LLC* ***(P-18014)***
Storybots Inc....D....310 314-4394
4121 Redwood Ave Los Angeles (90066) ***(P-15474)***
Stradling Yocca Carlson & Raut (PA)....C....949 725-4000
660 Newport Center Dr # 1600 Newport Beach (92660) ***(P-23400)***
Stradling Yocca Carlson & Raut....C....916 449-2350
500 Capitol Mall Sacramento (95814) ***(P-23401)***
Straight Edge, Windsor *Also called Robert A Hall* ***(P-14906)***
Straight Lander Inc....D....323 337-9075
8335 W Sunset Blvd # 320 Los Angeles (90069) ***(P-27049)***
Straight Line Roofing & Cnstr....E....530 672-9995
3811 Dividend Dr Ste A Shingle Springs (95682) ***(P-3202)***
Strand Energy Company....C....562 944-9580
10350 Heritage Park Dr Santa Fe Springs (90670) ***(P-1029)***
Strands Finance, San Mateo *Also called Strands Labs Inc* ***(P-15476)***
Strands Inc A Delaware Corp....E....541 753-4426
999 Baker Way Ste 430 San Mateo (94404) ***(P-15475)***

Mergent e-mail: customerrelations@mergent.com
1480
2019 Directory of California Wholesalers and Services Companies
(P-0000) Products & Services Section entry number
(PA)=Parent Co (HQ)=Headquarters (DH)=Div Headquarters

Strands Labs Inc.....E.....415 398-4333
999 Baker Way Ste 430 San Mateo (94404) *(P-15476)*
Strata Information Group Inc.....D.....619 296-0170
3935 Harney St Ste 203 San Diego (92110) *(P-16495)*
Stratacare Llc.....C.....949 743-1200
17838 Gillette Ave Ste D Irvine (92614) *(P-15477)*
Stratcitycom LLC.....D.....408 858-0006
1317 Monterosso St Danville (94506) *(P-15865)*
Strategic Bus Insights Inc (PA).....D.....650 859-4600
333 Ravenswood Ave Menlo Park (94025) *(P-27471)*
Strategic Data Systems.....C.....619 546-7200
2020 Camino Del Rio N # 505 San Diego (92108) *(P-16060)*
Strategic Enlace Inc.....D.....714 256-8648
281 N Puente St Brea (92821) *(P-27472)*
Strategic Financial Group.....E.....949 622-7200
18191 Von Karman Ave # 100 Irvine (92612) *(P-10795)*
Strategic Insights Inc.....D.....858 452-7500
9191 Towne Centre Dr # 401 San Diego (92122) *(P-15866)*
Strategic Mechanical Inc.....C.....559 291-1952
4661 E Commerce Ave Fresno (93725) *(P-2373)*
Strategic Operations Inc.....C.....858 244-0559
4705 Ruffin Rd San Diego (92123) *(P-17489)*
Strategic Property Management.....D.....619 295-2211
2055 3rd Ave Ste 200 San Diego (92101) *(P-11781)*
Strategic Secuirty Services, Fremont *Also called Strategic Security Services (P-10126)*
Strategic Security Services.....C.....510 623-2355
48521 Warm Springs Blvd # 302 Fremont (94539) *(P-10126)*
Strategic Staffing Svcs Inc.....A.....818 248-0049
35 N Lake Ave Ste 140 Pasadena (91101) *(P-27473)*
Strategies For Change (PA).....D.....916 395-3552
4343 Williamsbourgh Dr Sacramento (95823) *(P-22688)*
Strategy Companion Corp.....D.....714 460-8398
3240 El Camino Real # 120 Irvine (92602) *(P-15867)*
Strategy For Water & Land Reso.....E.....949 572-3034
49 Donovan Irvine (92620) *(P-26460)*
Stratford, San Mateo *Also called Raiser Senior Services LLC (P-24640)*
Stratford School Inc.....D.....408 371-3020
220 Kensington Way Los Gatos (95032) *(P-24387)*
Stratford School Inc (PA).....E.....650 493-1151
870 N California Ave Palo Alto (94303) *(P-24388)*
Stratgies To Empwer People Inc (PA).....D.....916 679-1527
2330 Glendale Ln Sacramento (95825) *(P-20963)*
Stratham Homes Inc.....D.....949 833-1554
2201 Dupont Dr Ste 300 Irvine (92612) *(P-1317)*
Straub - Brutoco A Joint Ventr.....C.....760 414-9000
202 W College St Ste 201 Fallbrook (92028) *(P-1359)*
Straub Distributing Co Ltd (PA).....C.....714 779-4000
4633 E La Palma Ave Anaheim (92807) *(P-9027)*
Strawberry Farms Golf Club, Irvine *Also called Sand Canyon LLC (P-18757)*
Strawberry Farms Golf Club LLC.....D.....949 551-2560
11 Strawberry Farm Rd Irvine (92612) *(P-18768)*
Streamline Construction, Grass Valley *Also called JM Streamline Inc (P-1564)*
Streamline Finishes Inc.....D.....949 600-8964
26429 Rancho Pkwy S # 140 Lake Forest (92630) *(P-1659)*
Streamline Shippers Assn Inc (PA).....C.....323 271-3800
6279 E Slauson Ave # 303 Commerce (90040) *(P-24985)*
Streamray Inc.....B.....408 745-5449
910 E Hamilton Ave Fl 6 Campbell (95008) *(P-18468)*
Streamvector Inc.....D.....760 203-3257
940 Stewart Dr 212 Sunnyvale (94085) *(P-15478)*
Strech Plastics Incorporated.....E.....951 922-2224
900 John St Ste J Banning (92220) *(P-7915)*
Street and Sewer Yard Corp.....E.....650 696-7260
1361 N Carolan Ave Burlingame (94010) *(P-6331)*
Street Maintenance Department, Encinitas *Also called City of Encinitas (P-1741)*
Street Sidewalks St Tree Maint, Chino *Also called City of Chino (P-6531)*
Streets Street Tree Inquiries, Oxnard *Also called City of Oxnard (P-18793)*
Stress Relief Services.....D.....760 241-7472
12603 Mariposa Rd Victorville (92395) *(P-13285)*
Strevus Inc.....D.....415 704-8182
455 Market St Ste 1670 San Francisco (94105) *(P-15868)*
Stria, Bakersfield *Also called Technosocialworkcom LLC (P-16188)*
Striim Inc.....E.....425 894-1998
575 Middlefield Rd Palo Alto (94301) *(P-15479)*
Strikes Unlimited Inc.....D.....916 626-3600
5681 Lonetree Blvd Rocklin (95765) *(P-18500)*
Stripe Inc.....A.....888 963-8955
185 Berry St Ste 550 San Francisco (94107) *(P-16061)*
Stripe Payments Company, San Francisco *Also called Stripe Inc (P-16061)*
Strivr Labs Inc.....D.....650 656-9987
90 Middlefield Rd Ste 101 Menlo Park (94025) *(P-15480)*
Strlng Path Medcl Corp.....E.....562 799-8900
3030 Old Ranch Pkwy # 430 Seal Beach (90740) *(P-17873)*
Stronghold Engineering Inc (PA).....C.....951 684-9303
2000 Market St Riverside (92501) *(P-1660)*
Stroock & Stroock & Lavan LLP.....C.....310 556-5800
2029 Century Park E # 1800 Los Angeles (90067) *(P-23402)*
Structural Integrity Assoc Inc (PA).....D.....408 978-8200
5215 Hellyer Ave Ste 210 San Jose (95138) *(P-25934)*
Structure Cast, Bakersfield *Also called Golden Empire Concrete Pdts (P-3257)*
Structures West Inc.....D.....760 737-2349
300 W Grand Ave Ste 201 Escondido (92025) *(P-3332)*
Stryder Corp.....D.....415 981-8400
225 Bush St Fl 12 San Francisco (94104) *(P-15869)*
Stu Segall Productions Inc.....C.....858 974-8988
4705 Ruffin Rd San Diego (92123) *(P-18126)*
Stuart C. Gildred Family YMCA, Santa Ynez *Also called Channel Islands Young Mens Ch (P-25135)*
Stuart Lovett.....D.....510 444-0790
350 30th St Ste 208 Oakland (94609) *(P-19953)*
Stuart Rental Company, Milpitas *Also called Ohana Partners Inc (P-14531)*
Stubhub Inc (HQ).....D.....415 222-8400
199 Fremont St Fl 4 San Francisco (94105) *(P-16183)*
Stubhub.com, San Francisco *Also called Stubhub Inc (P-16183)*
Stucco Works Inc.....B.....916 383-6699
5451 Whse Way Ste 105 Sacramento (95826) *(P-2963)*
Student Government Associat.....C.....949 824-5547
D200 Student Center Irvine (92697) *(P-4952)*
Student Health Services, San Jose *Also called San Jose State University (P-19849)*
Student Movers Inc.....D.....303 296-0600
825 Chalcedony St San Diego (92109) *(P-4377)*
Student Transportation America, San Jose *Also called Student Trnsp Amer Inc (P-3851)*
Student Transportation America, Santa Maria *Also called Santa Barbara Trnsp Corp (P-3945)*
Student Trnsp Amer Inc.....D.....408 998-8275
1540 S 7th St San Jose (95112) *(P-3851)*
Student Un San Jose State Univ.....D.....408 924-6405
211 S. 9th Street San Jose (95192) *(P-25472)*
Student Union Building, San Jose *Also called Student Un San Jose State Univ (P-25472)*
Student Works Painting, Irvine *Also called S W P T X Inc (P-2478)*
Student Works Painting Inc.....B.....714 564-7900
1682 Langley Ave Irvine (92614) *(P-2485)*
Students of Associated.....D.....916 278-6216
6000 J St Sacramento (95819) *(P-24389)*
Studio 71 LP.....C.....323 370-1500
8383 Wilshire Blvd Ste 10 Beverly Hills (90211) *(P-13956)*
Studio By Clubsport, The, Danville *Also called 2 G Fitness LLC (P-18546)*
Studio Royale, Culver City *Also called GK Management Co Inc (P-11027)*
Study Tapes.....D.....909 792-0111
1341 Pine Knoll Cres Redlands (92373) *(P-18127)*
Study US Research Inst Inc.....D.....213 840-9575
1335 N La Brea Ave 2-205 Los Angeles (90028) *(P-26664)*
Stumbaugh & Associates Inc (PA).....D.....818 240-1627
3303 N San Fernando Blvd Burbank (91504) *(P-3588)*
Sturdy Oil Company.....D.....831 970-9897
721 Vertin Ave Salinas (93901) *(P-8967)*
Sturgeon & Son, Bakersfield *Also called Sturgeon Services Intl Inc (P-12009)*
Sturgeon Services Intl, Santa Maria *Also called Sturgeon Son Grading & Pav Inc (P-25935)*
Sturgeon Services Intl Inc (PA).....E.....661 322-4408
3511 Gilmore Ave Bakersfield (93308) *(P-12009)*
Sturgeon Son Grading & Pav Inc (PA).....C.....661 322-4408
3511 Gilmore Ave Bakersfield (93308) *(P-3439)*
Sturgeon Son Grading & Pav Inc.....C.....805 938-0618
6516 Cat Canyon Rd Santa Maria (93454) *(P-25935)*
Stussy Inc.....D.....949 474-9255
17426 Daimler St Irvine (92614) *(P-8278)*
Stutman Treister Glatt Prof Co, Los Angeles *Also called Stutman Trster Glatt Prof Corp (P-23403)*
Stutman Trster Glatt Prof Corp.....D.....310 228-5600
1901 Avenue Of The Ste 200 Los Angeles (90067) *(P-23403)*
Stv Architects Inc.....D.....213 482-9444
1055 W 7th St Ste 3150 Los Angeles (90017) *(P-26117)*
Stx Wireless Operations LLC.....A.....858 882-6000
5887 Copley Dr San Diego (92111) *(P-5417)*
Sub-Acute Saratoga Hospital, Saratoga *Also called Progressive Sub-Acute Care (P-22039)*
Subacute Chld Hosp Cal Inc.....D.....408 558-3644
3777 S Bascom Ave Campbell (95008) *(P-22052)*
Subacute Trtmnt Adolescnt Reha (PA).....D.....510 352-9200
545 Estudillo Ave San Leandro (94577) *(P-22689)*
Suburban Medical Center, Paramount *Also called Promise Hosp E Los Angeles LP (P-21664)*
Success Factors, South San Francisco *Also called Successfactors Inc (P-15481)*
Success Healthcare 1 LLC (PA).....A.....213 989-6100
1711 W Temple St Los Angeles (90026) *(P-22428)*
Success Strategies Inst Inc.....D.....949 721-6808
6 Executive Cir Ste 250 Irvine (92614) *(P-24235)*
Successfactors Inc (HQ).....C.....650 212-1296
1 Tower Pl Ste 1100 South San Francisco (94080) *(P-15481)*
Successor Agency To The Norco, Norco *Also called City of Norco (P-27687)*
Successor To San Francisco.....D.....415 749-2400
1 S Van Ness Ave Fl 5 San Francisco (94103) *(P-27871)*
Suddath Relo Sys of No CA.....D.....408 288-3030
2055 S 7th St San Jose (95112) *(P-4268)*
Suddath Relocation Systems of.....E.....904 858-1273
2020 S 10th St San Jose (95112) *(P-4269)*
Sudhakar Company International.....D.....909 879-2933
1450 N Fitzgerald Ave Rialto (92376) *(P-1855)*
Suds Car Wash Inc.....E.....916 673-6300
4620 Post St El Dorado Hills (95762) *(P-17839)*
Suez Wts Systems Usa Inc.....D.....408 360-5900
5900 Silvercreek Vly Rd San Jose (95138) *(P-7638)*
Suffolk Construction Co Inc.....D.....949 453-9400
550 S Hope St Ste 700 Los Angeles (90071) *(P-1661)*
Sufi, Fremont *Also called Startup Farms Intl LLC (P-15472)*
Sugar Bowl Corporation.....D.....530 426-9000
629 Sugar Bowl Rd Norden (95724) *(P-19242)*
Sugar Foods Corporation.....C.....818 768-7900
9500 El Dorado Ave Sun Valley (91352) *(P-17490)*
Sugar Foods Corporation.....D.....818 768-7900
9500 El Dorado Ave Sun Valley (91352) *(P-17491)*
Sugar Transport of The NW.....D.....209 931-3587
5463 Cherokee Rd Stockton (95215) *(P-4067)*
Sugar Workers Local 1.....B.....510 787-1676
641 Loring Ave Crockett (94525) *(P-25083)*
Sugarcrm Inc (PA).....C.....408 454-6900
10050 N Wolfe Rd Sw2130 Cupertino (95014) *(P-15482)*

ALPHABETIC

Employee Codes: A=Over 500 employees, B=251-500 C=101-250, D=51-100, E=50
2019 Directory of California Wholesalers and Services Companies
© Mergent Inc. 1-800-342-5647
1481

Suissa Miller Advertising LLC ....D......310 392-9666
8687 Melrose Ave West Hollywood (90069) *(P-13906)*
SUISUN REDEVELOPMENT AGENCY, Suisun City *Also called Redevelopment Agency of The Ci (P-27840)*
Suja Juice, Oceanside *Also called Suja Life LLC (P-8873)*
Suja Life LLC ....C......855 879-7852
3841 Ocean Ranch Blvd # 101 Oceanside (92056) *(P-8873)*
Sukut Construction LLC ....D......714 540-5351
4010 W Chandler Ave Santa Ana (92704) *(P-1986)*
Sukut Construction (PA) ....D......714 540-5351
4010 W Chandler Ave Santa Ana (92704) *(P-3440)*
Sullinovo ....C......619 260-1432
2750 Womble Rd Ste 100 San Diego (92106) *(P-6550)*
Sullivan & Cromwell LLP ....D......310 712-6600
1888 Century Park E # 2100 Los Angeles (90067) *(P-23404)*
Sullivan Moving & Storage (HQ) ....E......858 874-2600
5704 Copley Dr San Diego (92111) *(P-4270)*
Sullivancurtismonroe Insurance (PA) ....D......800 427-3253
1920 Main St Ste 600 Irvine (92614) *(P-27474)*
Sully-Miller Contracting Co (HQ) ....B......714 578-9600
135 S State College Blvd # 400 Brea (92821) *(P-1856)*
Suma Fruit Intl USA Inc ....E......559 875-5000
1810 Academy Ave Sanger (93657) *(P-569)*
Sumitomo Electric Device Innov ....D......408 232-9500
2355 Zanker Rd San Jose (95131) *(P-7547)*
Sumitomo Rubber North Amer Inc (HQ) ....D......909 466-1116
8656 Haven Ave Rancho Cucamonga (91730) *(P-6695)*
Summer Crest Apartments, National City *Also called Plaza Manor Preservation LP (P-11673)*
Summer House Inc (PA) ....D......530 662-8493
206 5th St Woodland (95695) *(P-24688)*
Summer Systems Inc ....D......661 257-4419
28942 Hancock Pkwy Valencia (91355) *(P-1662)*
Summerfield Suites By Hyatt, Belmont *Also called Island Hospitality MGT LLC (P-12785)*
Summerhill Construction Co ....E......925 244-7520
3000 Executive Pkwy # 450 San Ramon (94583) *(P-1241)*
Summerhill Homes, San Ramon *Also called Summerhill Construction Co (P-1241)*
Summerville At Hazel Creek LLC ....A......916 988-7901
6125 Hazel Ave Orangevale (95662) *(P-24689)*
Summerville Senior Living Inc ....D......562 943-3724
10615 Jordan Rd Whittier (90603) *(P-11120)*
Summerville Senior Living Inc ....D......818 341-2552
20801 Devonshire St Chatsworth (91311) *(P-11121)*
Summit Building Services Inc ....D......925 827-9500
1128 Willow Pass Ct Concord (94520) *(P-14402)*
Summit Electric, Santa Rosa *Also called Summit Technology Group Inc (P-2749)*
Summit Hr Worldwide Inc ....D......408 884-7100
220 Main St Ste 208a San Jose (95112) *(P-27475)*
Summit Technology Group Inc ....E......707 542-4773
2450c Bluebell Dr Ste C Santa Rosa (95403) *(P-2749)*
Summitpointe Golf Club, Milpitas *Also called American Golf Corporation (P-18838)*
Summitview Child Treatment Ctr ....E......530 644-2412
5036 Sunrey Rd Placerville (95667) *(P-24690)*
SUN & SAIL CLUB, Lake Forest *Also called Lake Forest LI Master Homeown (P-25185)*
Sun America, Los Angeles *Also called American Intl Group Inc (P-10496)*
Sun and Sands Enterprises LLC (PA) ....D......760 399-4278
86705 Avenue 54 Ste A Coachella (92236) *(P-83)*
Sun Basket Inc (PA) ....C......408 669-4418
1170 Olinder Ct San Jose (95122) *(P-24077)*
Sun Chlorella USA Corp ....D......310 891-0600
3305 Kashiwa St Torrance (90505) *(P-8874)*
SUN CITY GARDENS, Sun City *Also called Sun City Rhf Housing Inc (P-24691)*
Sun City Palm Dsert Cmnty Assn (PA) ....D......760 200-2100
38180 Del Webb Blvd Palm Desert (92211) *(P-25254)*
Sun City Rhf Housing Inc. ....D......951 679-2391
28500 Bradley Rd Sun City (92586) *(P-24691)*
Sun City Rsvlle Cmnty Assn Inc (PA) ....A......916 774-3880
7050 Del Webb Blvd Roseville (95747) *(P-18769)*
Sun Coast Gen Insur Agcy Inc ....D......949 768-1132
23042 Mill Creek Dr Laguna Hills (92653) *(P-10796)*
Sun Coast Merchandise Corp. ....C......323 720-9700
6315 Bandini Blvd Commerce (90040) *(P-8060)*
Sun Diego Charter, National City *Also called Sureride Charter Inc (P-3903)*
Sun Electric LP ....D......714 210-3744
2101 S Yale St Ste B Santa Ana (92704) *(P-2750)*
Sun Express, Fontana *Also called Hanks Inc (P-4018)*
Sun Haven Care Inc ....D......714 870-0060
201 E Bastanchury Rd Fullerton (92835) *(P-20784)*
Sun Healthcare Group Inc (HQ) ....B......949 255-7100
27442 Portola Pkwy # 200 Foothill Ranch (92610) *(P-19954)*
Sun Hill Properties Inc (HQ) ....B......818 506-2500
555 Unversal Hollywood Dr Universal City (91608) *(P-13286)*
Sun Innovations Inc. ....E......510 573-3913
43241 Osgood Rd Fremont (94539) *(P-26461)*
Sun Lakes Cntry Club Hmeownrs ....D......951 845-2135
850 Country Club Dr Banning (92220) *(P-25255)*
Sun Lakes Country Club, Banning *Also called Professional Community MGT Cal (P-11683)*
Sun Light & Power ....D......510 845-2997
1035 Folger Ave Berkeley (94710) *(P-17492)*
Sun Maid Growers, Kingsburg *Also called Sun-Maid Growers California (P-8877)*
Sun Mar Health Care, Rosemead *Also called Sun Mar Management Services (P-27051)*
Sun Mar Management Service, Monterey Park *Also called Monterey Pk Convalescent Hosp (P-21160)*
SUN MAR MANAGEMENT SERVICES, Anaheim *Also called Sun Mar Nursing Center Inc (P-21225)*
Sun Mar Management Services ....D......909 822-8066
7509 Laurel Ave Fontana (92336) *(P-27050)*

Sun Mar Management Services ....D......626 288-8353
3136 Del Mar Ave Rosemead (91770) *(P-27051)*
Sun Mar Management Services ....D......818 352-1454
7660 Wyngate St Tujunga (91042) *(P-27052)*
Sun Mar Management Services ....D......951 687-3842
8171 Magnolia Ave Riverside (92504) *(P-20785)*
Sun Mar Nursing Center Inc ....D......714 776-1720
1720 W Orange Ave Anaheim (92804) *(P-21225)*
Sun Microsystems, Santa Clara *Also called Oracle America Inc (P-15792)*
Sun Microsystems, Pleasanton *Also called Oracle America Inc (P-15794)*
Sun Microsystems, Milpitas *Also called Oracle America Inc (P-15795)*
Sun Microsystems, San Diego *Also called Oracle America Inc (P-15796)*
Sun Microsystems, Santa Clara *Also called Oracle America Inc (P-15797)*
Sun Oaks Tennis & Fitness, Redding *Also called Walsh Group Inc (P-19084)*
Sun Pacific Cold Storage, Bakersfield *Also called Exeter Packers Inc (P-4503)*
Sun Pacific Farming, Bakersfield *Also called 7th Standard Ranch Company (P-127)*
Sun Pacific Farming, Bakersfield *Also called Sun Pacific Marketing Coop Inc (P-8734)*
Sun Pacific Farming Coop Inc (PA) ....B......559 592-7121
1250 E Myer Ave Exeter (93221) *(P-713)*
Sun Pacific Maricopa ....B......661 847-1015
31452 Old River Rd Bakersfield (93311) *(P-570)*
Sun Pacific Marketing Coop Inc ....A......213 612-9957
33502 Lerdo Hwy Bakersfield (93308) *(P-27476)*
Sun Pacific Marketing Coop Inc (PA) ....A......213 612-9957
1095 E Green St Pasadena (91106) *(P-8733)*
Sun Pacific Marketing Coop Inc ....B......661 847-1015
31452 Old River Rd Bakersfield (93311) *(P-8734)*
Sun Pacific Packers, Exeter *Also called Exeter Packers Inc (P-511)*
Sun Pharmaceuticals Inc ....C......858 380-8865
13718 Sorbonne Ct San Diego (92128) *(P-26462)*
Sun Rich Fresh Foods USA Inc (HQ) ....D......951 735-3800
515 E Rincon St Corona (92879) *(P-571)*
Sun Ten Labs Liquidation Co ....D......949 587-0509
9250 Jeronimo Rd Irvine (92618) *(P-8875)*
Sun Valley Dairy, Sun Valley *Also called Svd Inc (P-8529)*
Sun Valley Group Inc (PA) ....B......707 822-2885
3160 Upper Bay Rd Arcata (95521) *(P-303)*
Sun Villa Inc ....C......559 784-6644
350 N Villa St Porterville (93257) *(P-20786)*
Sun West Mortgage Company Inc (PA) ....D......800 453-7884
18000 Studebaker Rd # 200 Cerritos (90703) *(P-9861)*
Sun West Wild Rice Facility ....E......530 868-5188
Vance Ave Biggs (95917) *(P-7)*
Sun World International Inc (PA) ....A......661 392-5000
16351 Driver Rd Bakersfield (93308) *(P-572)*
Sun World International LLC ....B......661 392-5000
5701 Truxtun Ave Ste 200 Bakersfield (93309) *(P-382)*
Sun World International Inc ....B......760 398-9300
52200 Industrial Way Coachella (92236) *(P-573)*
Sun-Air Convalescent Hospital, Panorama City *Also called Panorama Madows Nursing Ctr LP (P-20690)*
Sun-Maid Growers California (PA) ....A......559 897-6235
13525 S Bethel Ave Kingsburg (93631) *(P-8876)*
Sun-Maid Growers California ....B......559 897-8900
15628 E Nebraska Ave Kingsburg (93631) *(P-8877)*
Sun-Maid Growers California ....E......800 752-9277
4683 Chabot Dr Ste 100 Pleasanton (94588) *(P-179)*
SunAmerica Hsng Fnd 1071 ....C......310 772-6000
1 Sun America Ctr Fl 36 Los Angeles (90067) *(P-10952)*
SunAmerica Inc (HQ) ....A......310 772-6000
1 Sun America Ctr Fl 38 Los Angeles (90067) *(P-9666)*
SunAmerica Investments Inc (HQ) ....D......310 772-6000
1 Sun America Ctr Fl 37 Los Angeles (90067) *(P-27053)*
SunAmerica Investments Inc. ....C......310 772-6000
1 Sun America Ctr Fl 38 Los Angeles (90067) *(P-12047)*
Sunbelt Controls Inc. ....D......626 610-2340
735 N Todd Ave Azusa (91702) *(P-2374)*
Sunbelt Controls Inc. ....E......925 660-3900
4511 Willow Rd Ste 4 Pleasanton (94588) *(P-17897)*
Sunbelt Controls Inc (HQ) ....B......818 244-6571
6265 San Fernando Rd Glendale (91201) *(P-2751)*
Sunbelt Towing Inc (PA) ....D......619 297-8697
4370 Pacific Hwy San Diego (92110) *(P-17874)*
Sunberry Growers LLC. ....A......805 922-9888
2224 Westgate Rd Santa Maria (93455) *(P-8735)*
Sunbrdge Care Ctr - Bellflower, Bellflower *Also called Rebecca Terley (P-20717)*
Sunbridge Brittany Rehab Centr ....C......916 484-1393
3900 Garfield Ave Carmichael (95608) *(P-20787)*
Sunbridge Care Ctr - Grnd Ter, Grand Terrace *Also called Grand Terrace Care Center (P-20494)*
Sunbridge Care Ctr For Downey, Downey *Also called Sunbridge Healthcare LLC (P-20966)*
Sunbridge Care Entps W Inc ....D......559 897-5881
1101 Stroud Ave Kingsburg (93631) *(P-20788)*
Sunbridge Care Entps W LLC ....A......559 897-5881
1101 Stroud Ave Kingsburg (93631) *(P-20789)*
Sunbridge Elmhaven Care Center, Stockton *Also called Sunbridge Healthcare LLC (P-20791)*
Sunbridge Harbor View ....C......562 989-9907
490 W 14th St Long Beach (90813) *(P-20790)*
Sunbridge Healthcare LLC. ....D......209 477-4817
6940 Pacific Ave Stockton (95207) *(P-20791)*
Sunbridge Healthcare LLC. ....D......530 934-2834
320 N Crawford St Willows (95988) *(P-20964)*
Sunbridge Healthcare LLC. ....C......562 981-9392
850 E Wardlow Rd Long Beach (90807) *(P-20965)*
Sunbridge Healthcare LLC. ....C......562 869-2567
9300 Telegraph Rd Downey (90240) *(P-20966)*

Mergent e-mail: customerrelations@mergent.com
1482

2019 Directory of California
Wholesalers and Services Companies

(P-0000) Products & Services Section entry number
(PA)=Parent Co (HQ)=Headquarters (DH)=Div Headquarters

Sunbridge Healthcare LLC....D....510 352-2211
14766 Washington Ave San Leandro (94578) ***(P-20967)***

Sunbridge Paradise Rhblttn Ctr....D....530 872-3200
8777 Skyway Paradise (95969) ***(P-20792)***

Suncal, Irvine *Also called Argent Management LLC* ***(P-11219)***

Suncrest Nurseries Inc....D....831 728-2595
400 Casserly Rd Watsonville (95076) ***(P-9163)***

Sundance Construction Inc....C....714 437-0802
3500 W Lake Center Dr B Santa Ana (92704) ***(P-3084)***

Sundance Financial Inc....E....619 298-9877
2505 Congress St Ste 220 San Diego (92110) ***(P-11924)***

Sundance Natural Foods Company....E....760 945-9898
2231 Willowbrook Dr Oceanside (92056) ***(P-239)***

Sunday Bazaar Inc....D....415 621-0764
495 Barneveld Ave San Francisco (94124) ***(P-6789)***

Sundt Construction, Sacramento *Also called Halstead Partnership* ***(P-10891)***

Sunergy California LLC....E....916 550-5370
4741 Urbani Ave McClellan (95652) ***(P-7639)***

Sunfoods LLC (HQ)....D....530 661-1923
1620 E Kentucky Ave Woodland (95776) ***(P-8463)***

Sungard Bi-Tech Inc (HQ)....E....530 891-5281
890 Fortress St Chico (95973) ***(P-15483)***

Sungevity, Oakland *Also called Solar Spectrum LLC* ***(P-2362)***

Sunharbor Management LLC....E....760 356-1262
708 E 5th St Holtville (92250) ***(P-24692)***

Suning Cmmerce R D Ctr USA Inc....D....650 834-9800
845 Page Mill Rd Palo Alto (94304) ***(P-26567)***

Suning USA, Palo Alto *Also called Suning Cmmerce R D Ctr USA Inc* ***(P-26567)***

Sunkist Enterprises....D....650 347-3900
1308 Rollins Rd Burlingame (94010) ***(P-7605)***

Sunkist Growers Inc (PA)....C....661 290-8900
27770 Entertainment Dr # 120 Valencia (91355) ***(P-8736)***

Sunkist Growers Inc....C....909 983-9811
531 W Poplar Ave Tipton (93272) ***(P-574)***

Sunkist Growers Inc....C....559 752-4256
531 W Poplar Ave Tipton (93272) ***(P-575)***

Sunland Insurance Agency....A....559 251-7861
4961 E Kings Canyon Rd Fresno (93727) ***(P-10797)***

SUNLAND SHUTTERS, Long Beach *Also called Ta Chen International Inc* ***(P-7318)***

Sunline Transit Agency....C....760 972-4059
790 Vine Ave Coachella (92236) ***(P-3852)***

Sunline Transit Agency (PA)....C....760 343-3456
32505 Harry Oliver Trl Thousand Palms (92276) ***(P-3886)***

Sunlit Gardens, Murrieta *Also called Alta Loma Assisted Living LLC* ***(P-23470)***

Sunny Cal Adhc Inc....D....626 307-7772
8450 Valley Blvd Ste 121b Rosemead (91770) ***(P-24078)***

Sunny Retirement Home....C....408 454-5600
22445 Cupertino Rd Cupertino (95014) ***(P-21226)***

Sunny View Care Center, Los Angeles *Also called Longwood Management Corp* ***(P-21139)***

Sunnyside Convalescent Hosp, Fresno *Also called R Fellen Inc* ***(P-20714)***

Sunnyside Gardens....D....408 730-4070
1025 Carson Dr Sunnyvale (94086) ***(P-24693)***

Sunnyside Resort....D....530 583-7200
1850 W Lake Blvd Tahoe City (96145) ***(P-13287)***

Sunnyside Rhblttion Nrsing Ctr....C....310 320-4130
22617 S Vermont Ave Torrance (90502) ***(P-20793)***

Sunnyslope Tree Farm Inc....D....714 532-1440
1545 N Glassell St Orange (92867) ***(P-9164)***

Sunnyslope Trees, Orange *Also called Sunnyslope Tree Farm Inc* ***(P-9164)***

Sunnyvale Fluid Sys Tech Inc....E....510 933-2500
3393 W Warren Ave Fremont (94538) ***(P-7874)***

Sunnyvale Health Care, Sunnyvale *Also called Sunnyvale Healthcare Center* ***(P-20794)***

Sunnyvale Healthcare Center....D....408 245-8070
1291 S Bernardo Ave Sunnyvale (94087) ***(P-20794)***

Sunnyvale Sof-X Owner L P....E....408 542-8264
1100 N Mathilda Ave Sunnyvale (94089) ***(P-13288)***

Sunol Valley Golf Course, Pleasanton *Also called Sunol Vly Golf & Recreation Co* ***(P-18770)***

Sunol Vly Golf & Recreation Co....D....925 862-2404
5117 Mount Tam Cir Pleasanton (94588) ***(P-18770)***

Sunplus HM Care - Pleasant Hl, Pleasant Hill *Also called Accentcare Home Health Cal Inc* ***(P-22189)***

Sunplus HM Hlth - Newport Bch, Newport Beach *Also called Accentcare Home Health Cal Inc* ***(P-22193)***

Sunplus Home Care - Ontario, Ontario *Also called Accentcare Home Health Cal Inc* ***(P-22191)***

Sunplus Home Care - San Diego, San Diego *Also called Accentcare Home Health Cal Inc* ***(P-22192)***

Sunpower By Green Convergence, Valencia *Also called Green Convergence* ***(P-7626)***

Sunpower Corporation Systems (HQ)....D....510 260-8200
1414 Harbour Way S # 1901 Richmond (94804) ***(P-2375)***

Sunpro Solar Inc....D....951 678-7733
34859 Frederick St # 101 Wildomar (92595) ***(P-2376)***

Sunray Healthcare Center, Los Angeles *Also called Kf Sunray LLC* ***(P-21126)***

Sunridge Care & Rehabilitation, Salinas *Also called Helios Healthcare LLC* ***(P-20523)***

Sunridge Farms, Royal Oaks *Also called Falcon Trading Company* ***(P-8787)***

Sunridge Nurseries Inc....D....661 363-8463
441 Vineland Rd Bakersfield (93307) ***(P-468)***

Sunrise Assistd Lving of Wlnt, Walnut Creek *Also called Sunrise Senior Living LLC* ***(P-20814)***

Sunrise Asssted Lving San Mteo, San Mateo *Also called Sunrise Senior Living Inc* ***(P-20799)***

Sunrise At Alta Loma, Rancho Cucamonga *Also called Sunrise Senior Living Inc* ***(P-20795)***

Sunrise At Bonita, Chula Vista *Also called Sunrise Senior Living LLC* ***(P-20819)***

Sunrise At La Costa, Carlsbad *Also called Sunrise Senior Living LLC* ***(P-20818)***

Sunrise At Raincross Village, Riverside *Also called Sunrise Senior Living LLC* ***(P-20834)***

Sunrise At Sterling Canyon, Valencia *Also called Sunrise Senior Living Inc* ***(P-20803)***

Sunrise Brands LLC (PA)....E....323 780-8250
801 S Figueroa St # 2500 Los Angeles (90017) ***(P-8336)***

Sunrise Company, Palm Desert *Also called Sunrise Desert Partners* ***(P-11926)***

Sunrise Convalescent Hospital, Pasadena *Also called D & C Care Center Inc* ***(P-21056)***

Sunrise Delivery Service Inc....D....323 464-5121
13351 Riverside Dr 672d Sherman Oaks (91423) ***(P-4430)***

Sunrise Desert Partners....D....760 404-1280
300 Eagle Cir Palm Desert (92211) ***(P-11925)***

Sunrise Desert Partners (PA)....C....760 772-7227
300 Eagle Dance Cir Palm Desert (92211) ***(P-11926)***

Sunrise Farms LLC....D....707 778-6450
395 Liberty Rd Petaluma (94952) ***(P-8541)***

Sunrise Food Ministry....D....916 965-5431
5901 San Juan Ave Citrus Heights (95610) ***(P-24079)***

Sunrise Growers Inc (HQ)....B....714 630-2170
701 W Kimberly Ave # 210 Placentia (92870) ***(P-8737)***

Sunrise Growers-Frozsun Foods, Placentia *Also called Sunrise Growers Inc* ***(P-8737)***

Sunrise of Beverly Hills, Beverly Hills *Also called Sunrise Senior Living Inc* ***(P-20805)***

Sunrise of Carmichael, Carmichael *Also called Sunrise Senior Living Inc* ***(P-20810)***

Sunrise of Danville, Danville *Also called Sunrise Senior Living LLC* ***(P-20813)***

Sunrise of Fresno, Fresno *Also called Sunrise Senior Living LLC* ***(P-20825)***

Sunrise of Hemet, Hemet *Also called Sunrise Senior Living LLC* ***(P-20831)***

Sunrise of Hermosa Beach, Hermosa Beach *Also called Sunrise Senior Living LLC* ***(P-20817)***

Sunrise of La Palma, La Palma *Also called Sunrise Senior Living LLC* ***(P-20826)***

Sunrise of Mission Viejo, Mission Viejo *Also called Sunrise Senior Living LLC* ***(P-20816)***

Sunrise of Monterey, Monterey *Also called Sunrise Senior Living Inc* ***(P-20811)***

Sunrise of Oakland Hills, Moraga *Also called Sunrise Senior Living Inc* ***(P-20797)***

Sunrise of Palm Springs, Palm Springs *Also called Sunrise Senior Living LLC* ***(P-20828)***

Sunrise of Palo Alto, Beverly Hills *Also called Sunrise Senior Living Inc* ***(P-20802)***

Sunrise of Petaluma, Petaluma *Also called Sunrise Senior Living Inc* ***(P-20798)***

Sunrise of Petaluma....D....707 776-2885
815 Wood Sorrel Dr Petaluma (94954) ***(P-24694)***

Sunrise of Playa Vista, Los Angeles *Also called Sunrise Senior Living Inc* ***(P-20806)***

Sunrise of Rocklin, Rocklin *Also called Sunrise Senior Living LLC* ***(P-20832)***

Sunrise of Sacramento, Sacramento *Also called Sunrise Senior Living LLC* ***(P-20820)***

Sunrise of Santa Rosa, Santa Rosa *Also called Sunrise Senior Living Inc* ***(P-20812)***

Sunrise of Studio City, Studio City *Also called Sunrise Senior Living LLC* ***(P-20824)***

Sunrise of Sunnyvale, Sunnyvale *Also called Sunrise Senior Living LLC* ***(P-20822)***

Sunrise of Westlake Village, Westlake Village *Also called Sunrise Senior Living LLC* ***(P-20823)***

Sunrise of Woodland Hills, Encino *Also called Sunrise Senior Living Inc* ***(P-20801)***

Sunrise Plumbing & Mech Inc....E....562 424-0332
7581 Hazard Ave Ste C Westminster (92683) ***(P-2377)***

Sunrise Produce Company, Fullerton *Also called Loewy Enterprises* ***(P-8704)***

Sunrise Ranch....D....805 488-0813
3623 Etting Rd Oxnard (93033) ***(P-304)***

Sunrise Retirement Villa, Roseville *Also called Sign of Dove* ***(P-11113)***

Sunrise Retirement Villa....D....916 786-3277
707 Sunrise Ave Ofc Roseville (95661) ***(P-11122)***

Sunrise Senior Living Inc....D....909 941-3001
9519 Baseline Rd Rancho Cucamonga (91730) ***(P-20795)***

Sunrise Senior Living Inc....D....760 340-5999
72201 Country Club Dr Palm Desert (92210) ***(P-20796)***

Sunrise Senior Living Inc....D....510 531-7190
1600 Canyon Rd 103 Moraga (94556) ***(P-20797)***

Sunrise Senior Living Inc....D....707 776-2885
815 Wood Sorrel Dr Petaluma (94954) ***(P-20798)***

Sunrise Senior Living Inc....D....650 558-8555
955 S El Camino Real San Mateo (94402) ***(P-20799)***

Sunrise Senior Living Inc....D....562 594-5788
3840 Lampson Ave Seal Beach (90740) ***(P-20800)***

Sunrise Senior Living Inc....E....818 346-9046
5501 Newcastle Ave # 130 Encino (91316) ***(P-20801)***

Sunrise Senior Living Inc....D....650 326-1108
201 N Crescent Dr Apt 503 Beverly Hills (90210) ***(P-20802)***

Sunrise Senior Living Inc....D....661 253-3551
25815 Mcbean Pkwy Ofc Valencia (91355) ***(P-20803)***

Sunrise Senior Living Inc....D....949 234-3000
25421 Sea Bluffs Dr Dana Point (92629) ***(P-20804)***

Sunrise Senior Living Inc....D....310 274-4479
201 N Crescent Dr Beverly Hills (90210) ***(P-20805)***

Sunrise Senior Living Inc....D....310 437-7178
5555 Playa Vista Dr Los Angeles (90094) ***(P-20806)***

Sunrise Senior Living Inc....D....415 664-6264
1601 19th Ave San Francisco (94122) ***(P-20807)***

Sunrise Senior Living Inc....D....408 223-1312
4855 San Felipe Rd San Jose (95135) ***(P-20808)***

Sunrise Senior Living Inc....D....949 581-6111
24552 Paseo De Valencia Laguna Hills (92653) ***(P-20809)***

Sunrise Senior Living Inc....D....916 485-4500
5451 Fair Oaks Blvd Carmichael (95608) ***(P-20810)***

Sunrise Senior Living Inc....D....831 643-2400
1110 Carmelo St Monterey (93940) ***(P-20811)***

Sunrise Senior Living Inc....E....707 575-7503
3250 Chanate Rd Ofc Santa Rosa (95404) ***(P-20812)***

Sunrise Senior Living LLC....D....925 309-4178
1027 Diablo Rd Danville (94526) ***(P-20813)***

Sunrise Senior Living LLC....E....925 932-3500
2175 Ygnacio Valley Rd Walnut Creek (94598) ***(P-20814)***

Sunrise Senior Living LLC....D....818 886-1616
17650 Devonshire St Northridge (91325) ***(P-20815)***

Sunrise Senior Living LLC....D....949 582-2010
26151 Country Club Dr Mission Viejo (92691) ***(P-20816)***

ALPHABETIC

Employee Codes: A=Over 500 employees, B=251-500
C=101-250, D=51-100, E=50
2019 Directory of California
Wholesalers and Services Companies
© Mergent Inc. 1-800-342-5647
1483

Sunrise Senior Living LLC ... E ... 310 937-0959
1837 Pacific Coast Hwy Hermosa Beach (90254) ***(P-20817)***

Sunrise Senior Living LLC ... D ... 760 930-0060
7020 Manzanita St Carlsbad (92011) ***(P-20818)***

Sunrise Senior Living LLC ... D ... 619 470-2220
3302 Bonita Rd Chula Vista (91910) ***(P-20819)***

Sunrise Senior Living LLC ... E ... 916 486-0200
345 Munroe St Sacramento (95825) ***(P-20820)***

Sunrise Senior Living LLC ... D ... 303 410-0500
530 Water St Fl 5 Oakland (94607) ***(P-20821)***

Sunrise Senior Living LLC ... D ... 408 749-8600
633 S Knickerbocker Dr # 263 Sunnyvale (94087) ***(P-20822)***

Sunrise Senior Living LLC ... D ... 805 557-1100
3101 Townsgate Rd Westlake Village (91361) ***(P-20823)***

Sunrise Senior Living LLC ... D ... 818 505-8484
4610 Coldwater Canyon Ave Studio City (91604) ***(P-20824)***

Sunrise Senior Living LLC ... D ... 559 325-8170
7444 N Cedar Ave Fresno (93720) ***(P-20825)***

Sunrise Senior Living LLC ... D ... 714 739-8111
5321 La Palma Ave Fl 2 La Palma (90623) ***(P-20826)***

Sunrise Senior Living LLC ... D ... 949 248-8855
31741 Rancho Viejo Rd San Juan Capistrano (92675) ***(P-20827)***

Sunrise Senior Living LLC ... D ... 760 322-3444
1780 E Baristo Rd Palm Springs (92262) ***(P-20828)***

Sunrise Senior Living LLC ... D ... 650 654-9700
1301 Ralston Ave Ste A Belmont (94002) ***(P-20829)***

Sunrise Senior Living LLC ... D ... 805 388-8086
6000 Santa Rosa Rd Ofc Camarillo (93012) ***(P-20830)***

Sunrise Senior Living LLC ... D ... 951 929-5988
1177 S Palm Ave Hemet (92543) ***(P-20831)***

Sunrise Senior Living LLC ... D ... 916 632-3003
6100 Sierra College Blvd Rocklin (95677) ***(P-20832)***

Sunrise Senior Living LLC ... D ... 760 346-5420
41505 Carlotta Dr Palm Desert (92211) ***(P-20833)***

Sunrise Senior Living LLC ... D ... 951 785-1200
5232 Central Ave Riverside (92504) ***(P-20834)***

Sunrise Villa Ctr Head Start, Wasco *Also called Community Action Partnr Kern* ***(P-24299)***

Sunrize Staging Inc ... D ... 760 743-2043
1326 Mission Rd Escondido (92029) ***(P-3589)***

Sunrun Installation Svcs Inc ... A ... 408 746-3062
575 Dado St San Jose (95131) ***(P-2378)***

Sunrun Installation Svcs Inc (HQ) ... C ... 415 580-6900
775 Fiero Ln Ste 200 San Luis Obispo (93401) ***(P-2752)***

Sunscape Eyewear Inc ... D ... 949 553-0590
17526 Von Karman Ave A Irvine (92614) ***(P-8061)***

Sunset Aviation LLC (PA) ... E ... 707 775-2786
201 1st St Ste 307 Petaluma (94952) ***(P-4913)***

Sunset Building Maintance Inc ... E ... 408 727-3408
1920 Lafayette St Ste E Santa Clara (95050) ***(P-14403)***

Sunset Building Maintenance, Santa Clara *Also called Sunset Building Maintance Inc* ***(P-14403)***

Sunset Development Company, San Ramon *Also called Annabel Investment Company* ***(P-11855)***

Sunset Hills Country Club, Thousand Oaks *Also called American Golf Corporation* ***(P-18827)***

Sunset Landscape Maintenance ... D ... 949 455-4636
27201 Burbank El Toro (92610) ***(P-946)***

Sunset Linen Service, Santa Rosa *Also called City Towel & Dust Service Inc* ***(P-13527)***

Sunset Manor Convalescent Hosp, El Monte *Also called Gibralter Convalescent Hosp* ***(P-21082)***

Sunset Moulding Co ... D ... 530 695-3379
2200 Paseo Rd Live Oak (95953) ***(P-6867)***

Sunset Neighborhood Beacon Ctr, San Francisco *Also called Aspiranet* ***(P-24420)***

Sunset Pet Hospital Inc (PA) ... D ... 916 967-7768
7751 Sunset Ave Fair Oaks (95628) ***(P-609)***

Sunset Property Services, Irvine *Also called Jonset Corporation* ***(P-6542)***

Sunset Scavenger Company ... B ... 415 330-1300
250 Executive Park Blvd # 2100 San Francisco (94134) ***(P-6480)***

Sunset Station, Los Angeles *Also called Passprt Accept Fclty Los Angel* ***(P-17392)***

Sunset Tower Hotel LLC ... D ... 323 654-7100
8358 W Sunset Blvd Los Angeles (90069) ***(P-13289)***

Sunshine Clearing Corporation ... E ... 714 829-0273
1215 W Imperial Hwy # 210 Brea (92821) ***(P-14772)***

Sunshine Communications Inc ... C ... 619 448-7600
350 Cypress Ln Ste D El Cajon (92020) ***(P-2753)***

Sunshine Floral Inc ... D ... 805 684-1177
4595 Foothill Rd Carpinteria (93013) ***(P-9165)***

Sunshine Floral LLC ... D ... 805 982-8822
1070 S Rice Ave Ste 1 Oxnard (93033) ***(P-9166)***

Sunshine Metal Clad Inc ... D ... 661 366-0575
7201 Edison Hwy Bakersfield (93307) ***(P-2964)***

Sunshine Midtown LLC ... E ... 602 604-4900
631 W Katella Ave Anaheim (92802) ***(P-13290)***

Sunshine Villa Assisted Living, Santa Cruz *Also called Regent Assisted Living Inc* ***(P-24649)***

Sunstone Center Crt Lessee Inc ... C ... 949 382-4000
200 Spectrum Center Dr # 21 Irvine (92618) ***(P-13291)***

Sunstone Durante LLC ... C ... 858 792-5200
15575 Jimmy Durante Blvd Del Mar (92014) ***(P-13292)***

Sunstone Hotel Investors Inc (PA) ... E ... 949 330-4000
200 Spectrum Center Dr Irvine (92618) ***(P-12188)***

Sunstone Hotel Investors Inc ... C ... 310 215-1000
9801 Airport Blvd Los Angeles (90045) ***(P-13293)***

Sunstone Hotel Investors LLC ... C ... 714 739-8500
14299 Firestone Blvd La Mirada (90638) ***(P-13294)***

Sunstone Hotel Investors LLC ... C ... 661 267-6587
39375 5th St W Palmdale (93551) ***(P-13295)***

Sunstone Hotel Investors LLC ... D ... 310 830-9200
2 Civic Plaza Dr Carson (90745) ***(P-13296)***

Sunstone Hotel Investors LLC ... D ... 619 239-6171
1617 1st Ave Ste 16 San Diego (92101) ***(P-13297)***

Sunstone Hotel Investors LLC ... D ... 707 253-8600
3425 Solano Ave NAPA (94558) ***(P-13298)***

Sunstone Hotel Investors LLC ... C ... 714 635-5000
1752 S Clementine St Anaheim (92802) ***(P-13299)***

Sunstone Hotel Investors LLC (PA) ... D ... 949 330-4000
120 Vantis Dr Ste 350 Aliso Viejo (92656) ***(P-12269)***

Sunstone Hotel Investors LLC ... C ... 310 649-1400
6161 W Century Blvd Los Angeles (90045) ***(P-13300)***

Sunstone Hotel Management Inc ... C ... 951 784-8000
3400 Market St Riverside (92501) ***(P-13301)***

Sunstone Hotel Management Inc (PA) ... E ... 949 297-4183
120 Vantis Dr Ste 350 Aliso Viejo (92656) ***(P-13302)***

Sunstone Hotel Properties Inc ... D ... 310 228-4100
1177 S Beverly Dr Los Angeles (90035) ***(P-13303)***

Sunstone Hotel Properties Inc ... D ... 310 546-7627
1700 N Sepulveda Blvd Manhattan Beach (90266) ***(P-13304)***

Sunstone Hotel Properties Inc (HQ) ... C ... 949 330-4000
120 Vantis Dr Ste 350 Aliso Viejo (92656) ***(P-13305)***

Sunstone Ocean Lessee Inc ... B ... 949 382-4000
200 Spectrum Center Dr # 21 Irvine (92618) ***(P-13306)***

Sunstone Top Gun LLC ... D ... 858 453-0400
4550 La Jolla Village Dr San Diego (92122) ***(P-13307)***

Sunstone Top Gun Lessee Inc ... C ... 949 330-4000
4550 La Jolla Village Dr San Diego (92122) ***(P-13308)***

Sunsystem Technology LLC (PA) ... B ... 916 671-3351
2731 Citrus Rd Ste D Rancho Cordova (95742) ***(P-26463)***

Suntreat Packing & Shipping Co, Lindsay *Also called Acmpc California 3 LLC* ***(P-200)***

Suntreat Pkg Shipg A Ltd Prtnr ... C ... 559 562-4991
391 Oxford Ave Lindsay (93247) ***(P-5210)***

Sunvair Aerospace Group Inc (PA) ... D ... 661 294-3777
29145 The Old Rd Valencia (91355) ***(P-17992)***

Sunwest Bank (HQ) ... E ... 714 730-4441
2050 Main St Fl 3 Irvine (92614) ***(P-9489)***

Sunwest Electric Inc ... C ... 714 630-8700
3064 E Miraloma Ave Anaheim (92806) ***(P-2754)***

Super 8 Motel, San Francisco *Also called Chirag Hospitality Inc* ***(P-12454)***

Super Care Inc ... D ... 760 245-2034
12176 Industrial Blvd Victorville (92395) ***(P-7220)***

Super Color Labs, West Hollywood *Also called Super Photo Laboratory Inc* ***(P-16967)***

Super Garden Centers Inc ... E ... 818 348-9266
7659 Topanga Canyon Blvd Canoga Park (91304) ***(P-9167)***

Super Photo Laboratory Inc ... D ... 323 512-0247
979 N La Brea Ave West Hollywood (90038) ***(P-16967)***

Super Shuttle, Sun Valley *Also called Arcadia Transit Inc* ***(P-3639)***

Super Store Industries ... B ... 209 858-3365
16888 Mckinley Ave Lathrop (95330) ***(P-8878)***

Super Talent Technology Corp ... A ... 408 957-8133
2077 N Capitol Ave San Jose (95132) ***(P-7111)***

Superbalife International LLC ... D ... 310 553-7400
1171 S Robertson Blvd # 525 Los Angeles (90035) ***(P-8213)***

Superclean America, Palm Springs *Also called Joseph Dipuzo* ***(P-13492)***

Supercuts, Folsom *Also called Dager Corporation* ***(P-13652)***

Supercuts Admnistrative Office (PA) ... C ... 760 753-5543
7750 El Cmino Real Ste 2g Carlsbad (92009) ***(P-13673)***

Superior Automatic Sprnklr Co ... D ... 408 946-7272
4378 Enterprise St Fremont (94538) ***(P-2379)***

Superior Cattle Feeders LLC (PA) ... D ... 760 348-2218
551 S Industrial Ave Calipatria (92233) ***(P-398)***

Superior Communications Inc (PA) ... C ... 877 522-4727
5027 Irwindale Ave # 900 Irwindale (91706) ***(P-7548)***

Superior Construction Inc ... D ... 951 808-8780
265 N Joy St Corona (92879) ***(P-1242)***

Superior Contracting Corp ... E ... 831 757-1089
45 N Main St Salinas (93901) ***(P-2965)***

Superior Court Unit, Fresno *Also called County of Fresno* ***(P-22994)***

Superior Elec Mech & Plbg Inc ... B ... 909 357-9400
8613 Helms Ave Rancho Cucamonga (91730) ***(P-2755)***

Superior Envmtl Svcs Inc ... E ... 619 462-7079
6383 Lake Arrowhead Dr San Diego (92119) ***(P-14404)***

Superior Foods Inc ... D ... 831 728-3691
275 Westgate Dr Watsonville (95076) ***(P-8506)***

Superior Foods Companies, The, Watsonville *Also called Superior Foods Inc* ***(P-8506)***

Superior Fruit LLC ... C ... 805 485-2519
4324 E Vineyard Ave Oxnard (93036) ***(P-123)***

Superior Gunite (PA) ... C ... 818 896-9199
12306 Van Nuys Blvd Sylmar (91342) ***(P-3333)***

Superior Machining Mfg Co Inc ... D ... 714 529-6000
322 Oak Pl Brea (92821) ***(P-7806)***

Superior Masonry Walls Ltd ... D ... 909 370-1800
300 W Olive St Ste A Colton (92324) ***(P-2825)***

Superior Paving Company Inc ... D ... 951 739-9200
1880 N Delilah St Corona (92879) ***(P-1857)***

Superior Pntg Drywall Fnshings, Carmichael *Also called H B J Corporation* ***(P-2891)***

Superior Seafood Co, Los Angeles *Also called PLD Enterprises Inc* ***(P-8594)***

Superior Seafood Co, San Pedro *Also called PLD Enterprises Inc* ***(P-8595)***

Superior Services, Oceanside *Also called Superior Support Services Inc* ***(P-27054)***

Superior Sod I LP ... C ... 909 923-5068
17821 17th St Ste 165 Tustin (92780) ***(P-305)***

Superior Support Services Inc ... B ... 559 458-0507
702 Civic Center Dr Oceanside (92054) ***(P-27054)***

Superior Tile Co, San Leandro *Also called TRM Corporation* ***(P-3013)***

Superior Truck Lines Inc ... E ... 559 924-6418
527 F St Lemoore (93245) ***(P-4271)***

Superior Truck Lines Inc (PA) ... D ... 209 862-9430
1457 Main St Ste A Newman (95360) ***(P-4272)***

Mergent e-mail: customerrelations@mergent.com
1484
2019 Directory of California Wholesalers and Services Companies
(P-0000) Products & Services Section entry number
(PA)=Parent Co (HQ)=Headquarters (DH)=Div Headquarters

Superior Vision Services Inc (PA)....D....916 859-6218
11101 White Rock Rd # 150 Rancho Cordova (95670) ***(P-10321)***
Superior Wall Systems Inc....B....714 278-0000
1232 E Orangethorpe Ave Fullerton (92831) ***(P-2966)***
Supershuttle International Inc....C....909 944-2606
9559 Center Ave Ste F Rancho Cucamonga (91730) ***(P-3732)***
Supershuttle International Inc....D....916 648-2500
3100 Northgate Blvd Sacramento (95833) ***(P-3733)***
Supershuttle Los Angeles Inc....C....310 222-5500
531 Van Ness Ave Torrance (90501) ***(P-3734)***
Supershuttle Orange County Inc....B....310 222-5500
531 Van Ness Ave Torrance (90501) ***(P-3735)***
Supershuttle Sacramento, Sacramento *Also called Supershuttle International Inc* ***(P-3733)***
Supervalu, Commerce *Also called Unified Grocers Inc* ***(P-8474)***
Supply Change Services, Sacramento *Also called Sacramento Municpl Utility Dst* ***(P-6105)***
Supply Pro, San Diego *Also called Supplypro Inc* ***(P-7807)***
Supplypro Inc (PA)....D....858 587-6400
9401 Waples St Ste 150 San Diego (92121) ***(P-7807)***
Support Associates Inc....C....949 595-4379
22901 Mill Creek Dr Laguna Hills (92653) ***(P-27606)***
Support For Home Inc....E....530 792-8484
1333 Howe Ave Ste 206 Sacramento (95825) ***(P-1243)***
Supportcom Inc (PA)....D....650 556-9440
1200 Crossman Ave Ste 210 Sunnyvale (94089) ***(P-16184)***
Supreme Court United States....C....619 557-7149
101 W Broadway Ste 700 San Diego (92101) ***(P-24080)***
Sure Forming Systems Inc....E....562 598-6348
10602 Humbolt St Los Alamitos (90720) ***(P-3334)***
Sure Haven Inc....A....949 467-9213
1730 Pomona Ave Ste 3 Costa Mesa (92627) ***(P-22053)***
Sure Haven Addiction Treatment, Costa Mesa *Also called Sure Haven Inc* ***(P-22053)***
Surecraft Door and Hdwr Inc....C....760 737-2120
2875 Executive Pl Escondido (92029) ***(P-3085)***
Sureride Charter Inc....C....619 336-9200
522 W 8th St National City (91950) ***(P-3903)***
Surety West Logistics Inc....D....800 761-2551
980 9th St Fl 16 Sacramento (95814) ***(P-5176)***
Surety West Transportation, Sacramento *Also called Surety West Logistics Inc* ***(P-5176)***
Surf Sand Hotel, Laguna Beach *Also called JC Resorts LLC* ***(P-26903)***
Surface Pumps Inc (PA)....D....661 393-1545
3301 Unicorn Rd Bakersfield (93308) ***(P-7808)***
Surfside Race Place At Del Mar, Del Mar *Also called Del Mar Thoroughbred Club* ***(P-18539)***
Surgener Electric Inc....D....661 399-3321
1406 N Chester Ave Bakersfield (93308) ***(P-2756)***
Surgery Center of Alta Bates (HQ)....A....510 204-4444
2450 Ashby Ave Berkeley (94705) ***(P-21796)***
Surgery Center of Alta Bates....E....510 204-4411
2001 Dwight Way Berkeley (94704) ***(P-19955)***
Surgery Center of Alta Bates....D....510 204-1591
2001 Dwight Way Berkeley (94704) ***(P-19956)***
Surgery Center of Health South, Oakland *Also called EBSC LP* ***(P-19452)***
Surgical Care Affiliate....E....916 529-4590
2450 Venture Oaks Way # 120 Sacramento (95833) ***(P-26299)***
Surgical Staff Inc....C....916 444-4424
1523 G St Sacramento (95814) ***(P-14918)***
Surplus Line Association Cal....D....415 434-4900
12667 Alcosta Blvd # 450 San Ramon (94583) ***(P-24986)***
Surprise Valley Health Care Di....D....530 279-6111
741 N Main St Cedarville (96104) ***(P-21797)***
Surterre Properties Inc (PA)....C....949 717-7100
1400 Newport Center Dr # 100 Newport Beach (92660) ***(P-10953)***
Surveillance Systems....E....800 508-6981
4465 Granite Dr Ste 700 Rocklin (95677) ***(P-7549)***
Survey Junkie, Glendale *Also called Active Measure Inc* ***(P-26496)***
Survey Sampling Intl LLC....C....866 872-4006
16501 Ventura Blvd # 300 Encino (91436) ***(P-26568)***
Surveysavvy.com, San Diego *Also called Luth Research Inc* ***(P-26541)***
Survival Insurance Inc....C....818 565-1584
2550 N Hollywood Way # 120 Burbank (91505) ***(P-10798)***
Survival Insurance Brkg A Cal, Burbank *Also called Survival Insurance Inc* ***(P-10798)***
Survival Systems Intl Inc (PA)....D....760 749-6800
34140 Valley Center Rd Valley Center (92082) ***(P-17993)***
Survivalcave Inc....E....800 719-7650
10620 Treena St Ste 230 San Diego (92131) ***(P-8879)***
Sustainable Agriculture, Rancho Dominguez *Also called Seeds of Change Inc* ***(P-9097)***
Sutter Alhambra Surgery Center, Elk Grove *Also called Sutter Health* ***(P-21816)***
Sutter Amador Hospital (HQ)....B....209 223-7500
200 Mission Blvd Jackson (95642) ***(P-21798)***
Sutter Amador Hospital Lab, Jackson *Also called Sutter Hlth Scrmnto Sierra Reg* ***(P-19987)***
Sutter Auburn Faith Hospital, Auburn *Also called Sutter Health* ***(P-22690)***
Sutter Bay Hospitals (HQ)....A....415 600-6000
633 Folsom St Fl 5 San Francisco (94107) ***(P-21799)***
SUTTER C H S, Novato *Also called Sutter West Bay Hospitals* ***(P-21848)***
SUTTER C H S, Lakeport *Also called Sutter Lakeside Hospital* ***(P-21841)***
SUTTER C H S, Vallejo *Also called Sutter Solano Medical Center* ***(P-21845)***
Sutter C H S, Sacramento *Also called Sutter Health* ***(P-21824)***
SUTTER C H S, Jackson *Also called Sutter Amador Hospital* ***(P-21798)***
Sutter Central Vly Hospitals (HQ)....C....209 526-4500
1700 Coffee Rd Modesto (95355) ***(P-21800)***
Sutter Central Vly Hospitals....E....209 526-4500
1700 Coffee Rd Modesto (95355) ***(P-4866)***
Sutter Club Inc....D....916 442-0456
1220 9th St Sacramento (95814) ***(P-25256)***
Sutter Coast Hospital (HQ)....C....707 464-8511
800 E Washington Blvd Crescent City (95531) ***(P-21801)***
Sutter Davis Hospital, Davis *Also called Sutter Hlth Scrmnto Sierra Reg* ***(P-21837)***
Sutter Delta Medical Ctr Aux....D....925 779-7200
3901 Lone Tree Way Antioch (94509) ***(P-21802)***
Sutter Elk Grove Surgery Ctr, Elk Grove *Also called Sutter Health* ***(P-21819)***
Sutter Gould Med Foundation (PA)....E....209 948-5940
600 Coffee Rd Modesto (95355) ***(P-19957)***
Sutter Health, Santa Rosa *Also called Santa Rosa Surgery Center LP* ***(P-21720)***
Sutter Health, Sacramento *Also called Sutter Valley Med Foundation* ***(P-21847)***
Sutter Health....C....530 747-0389
2068 John Jones Rd # 100 Davis (95616) ***(P-19958)***
Sutter Health....C....916 733-1025
1625 Stockton Blvd # 207 Sacramento (95816) ***(P-21803)***
Sutter Health....C....916 797-4725
3 Medical Plaza Dr # 100 Roseville (95661) ***(P-19959)***
Sutter Health....D....925 371-3800
2950 Collier Canyon Rd Livermore (94551) ***(P-22892)***
Sutter Health....B....415 600-7034
P.O. Box 7999 San Francisco (94120) ***(P-21804)***
Sutter Health....C....650 853-2975
795 El Camino Real Palo Alto (94301) ***(P-19960)***
Sutter Health....C....916 733-9588
1020 29th St Ste 600 Sacramento (95816) ***(P-21805)***
Sutter Health....B....408 524-5952
2734 El Camino Real Santa Clara (95051) ***(P-19961)***
Sutter Health....B....530 757-5111
2000 Sutter Pl Davis (95616) ***(P-21806)***
Sutter Health....B....415 600-3311
633 Folsom St Fl 5 San Francisco (94107) ***(P-27477)***
Sutter Health....C....707 526-1800
510 Doyle Park Dr Santa Rosa (95405) ***(P-21807)***
Sutter Health....A....925 779-7273
3901 Lone Tree Way Antioch (94509) ***(P-21808)***
Sutter Health....B....415 345-0100
3468 California St San Francisco (94118) ***(P-21809)***
Sutter Health....C....209 366-2007
1335 S Fairmont Ave Lodi (95240) ***(P-21810)***
Sutter Health....C....209 223-5445
100 Mission Blvd Jackson (95642) ***(P-19962)***
Sutter Health....C....415 731-6300
595 Buckingham Way # 515 San Francisco (94132) ***(P-21811)***
Sutter Health....C....415 600-0110
1375 Sutter St San Francisco (94109) ***(P-21812)***
Sutter Health....C....831 458-6310
1301 Mission St Santa Cruz (95060) ***(P-25257)***
Sutter Health....C....916 797-4715
3 Medical Plaza Dr # 100 Roseville (95661) ***(P-21813)***
Sutter Health....C....530 750-5904
2030 Sutter Pl Ste 1000 Davis (95616) ***(P-21814)***
Sutter Health....C....916 691-5900
8170 Laguna Blvd Ste 210 Elk Grove (95758) ***(P-19963)***
Sutter Health....C....707 535-5600
110 Stony Point Rd # 200 Santa Rosa (95401) ***(P-21815)***
Sutter Health....C....916 455-8137
8170 Laguna Blvd Ste 103 Elk Grove (95758) ***(P-21816)***
Sutter Health....A....415 600-1020
2340 Clay St Rm 121 San Francisco (94115) ***(P-21817)***
Sutter Health....C....707 263-6885
5196 Hill Rd E Ste 300 Lakeport (95453) ***(P-19964)***
Sutter Health....C....916 262-9400
2725 Capitol Ave Sacramento (95816) ***(P-19965)***
Sutter Health....C....916 566-4819
2880 Gateway Oaks Dr # 220 Sacramento (95833) ***(P-21818)***
Sutter Health....B....831 458-6272
2950 Research Park Dr Soquel (95073) ***(P-25258)***
Sutter Health....A....916 544-5423
8200 Laguna Blvd Elk Grove (95758) ***(P-21819)***
Sutter Health....C....209 827-4866
520 W I St Los Banos (93635) ***(P-25259)***
Sutter Health....C....707 263-3520
5150 Hill Rd Ste E Lakeport (95453) ***(P-20150)***
Sutter Health....C....415 600-0140
1375 Sutter St Ste 208 San Francisco (94109) ***(P-21820)***
Sutter Health....A....415 600-4280
2015 Steiner St Fl 1 San Francisco (94115) ***(P-21821)***
Sutter Health....C....415 897-8495
100 Rowland Way Ste 210 Novato (94945) ***(P-21822)***
Sutter Health....C....408 523-3900
360 Dardanelli Ln Ste 2d Los Gatos (95032) ***(P-25260)***
Sutter Health....C....916 262-9414
2725 Capitol Ave Dept 304 Sacramento (95816) ***(P-19966)***
Sutter Health....A....916 646-8300
1500 Expo Pkwy Sacramento (95815) ***(P-19967)***
Sutter Health....B....510 547-2244
3875 Telegraph Ave Oakland (94609) ***(P-19968)***
Sutter Health....C....510 869-8777
3000 Telegraph Ave Oakland (94609) ***(P-19969)***
Sutter Health....B....916 887-0000
2825 Capitol Ave Sacramento (95816) ***(P-21823)***
Sutter Health (PA)....A....916 733-8800
2200 River Plaza Dr Sacramento (95833) ***(P-21824)***
Sutter Health....B....530 406-5600
475 Pioneer Ave Ste 400 Woodland (95776) ***(P-19970)***
Sutter Health....C....209 524-1211
600 Coffee Rd Modesto (95355) ***(P-21825)***
Sutter Health....D....916 454-8200
3707 Schriever Ave Mather (95655) ***(P-20835)***
Sutter Health....C....530 406-5600
475 Pioneer Ave Ste 100 Woodland (95776) ***(P-19971)***
Sutter Health....C....209 538-1733
2516 E Whitmore Ave Ceres (95307) ***(P-21826)***

ALPHABETIC

Employee Codes: A=Over 500 employees, B=251-500
C=101-250, D=51-100, E=50
2019 Directory of California
Wholesalers and Services Companies
© Mergent Inc. 1-800-342-5647
1485

Sutter Health ...C ...209 522-0146
3612 Dale Rd Modesto (95356) ***(P-19972)***
Sutter Health ...B ...916 691-5900
8170 Laguna Blvd Ste 220 Elk Grove (95758) ***(P-21827)***
Sutter Health ...D ...916 733-8133
5151 F St Sacramento (95819) ***(P-21828)***
Sutter Health ...C ...510 204-1591
2001 Dwight Way Berkeley (94704) ***(P-22150)***
Sutter Health ...C ...650 262-4262
50 S San Mateo Dr Ste 470 San Mateo (94401) ***(P-19973)***
Sutter Health ...C ...805 966-1600
25 W Micheltorena St Santa Barbara (93101) ***(P-19974)***
Sutter Health ...E ...831 477-3600
2880 Soquel Ave Ste 10 Santa Cruz (95062) ***(P-21829)***
Sutter Health ...C ...209 334-3333
999 S Fairmont Ave # 200 Lodi (95240) ***(P-19975)***
Sutter Health ...C ...408 733-4380
325 N Mathilda Ave Sunnyvale (94085) ***(P-19976)***
Sutter Health ...C ...707 263-6885
5196 Hill Rd E Ste 300 Lakeport (95453) ***(P-19977)***
Sutter Health ...B ...707 545-2255
4702 Hoen Ave Santa Rosa (95405) ***(P-21830)***
Sutter Health ...C ...650 853-2904
795 El Camino Real Palo Alto (94301) ***(P-19978)***
Sutter Health ...D ...916 784-2277
1640 E Roseville Pkwy Roseville (95661) ***(P-22151)***
Sutter Health ...D ...916 451-3344
3161 L St Sacramento (95816) ***(P-19979)***
Sutter Health ...C ...916 453-5955
1020 29th St Ste 570b Sacramento (95816) ***(P-19980)***
Sutter Health ...C ...415 647-8600
3555 Cesar Chavez San Francisco (94110) ***(P-19981)***
Sutter Health ...C ...510 618-5200
1651 Alvarado St San Leandro (94577) ***(P-20968)***
Sutter Health ...C ...530 749-3585
969 Plumas St Ste 103116 Yuba City (95991) ***(P-19982)***
Sutter Health ...C ...916 731-5672
P.O. Box 160100 Sacramento (95816) ***(P-21831)***
Sutter Health ...D ...916 797-4700
3 Medical Plaza Dr # 100 Roseville (95661) ***(P-19983)***
Sutter Health ...C ...831 458-5500
2880 Soquel Ave Santa Cruz (95062) ***(P-25261)***
Sutter Health ...C ...707 523-7253
2449 Summerfield Rd Santa Rosa (95405) ***(P-21832)***
Sutter Health ...B ...916 454-6747
8318 Ferguson Ave Sacramento (95828) ***(P-21833)***
Sutter Health ...C ...916 262-9456
2725 Capitol Ave Dept 404 Sacramento (95816) ***(P-19984)***
Sutter Health ...C ...530 750-5888
2030 Sutter Pl Ste 1300 Davis (95616) ***(P-21834)***
Sutter Health ...C ...415 602-5380
100 Rowland Way Novato (94945) ***(P-21835)***
Sutter Health ...C ...510 869-8835
3300 Webster St Ste 101 Oakland (94609) ***(P-8214)***
Sutter Health ...A ...530 888-4500
11775 Education St # 201 Auburn (95602) ***(P-22690)***
Sutter Health ...C ...916 286-6665
1025 Atlantic Ave Ste 100 Alameda (94501) ***(P-25262)***
Sutter Health ...B ...916 551-9550
2715 K St Ste A Sacramento (95816) ***(P-25263)***
Sutter Health At Work ...D ...916 565-8607
1014 N Market Blvd Ste 20 Sacramento (95834) ***(P-19985)***
Sutter Hlth At Work - Natomas, Sacramento *Also called Sutter Health At Work* ***(P-19985)***
Sutter Hlth Rhabilitation Svcs ...D ...916 733-3040
2801 L St Fl 3 Sacramento (95816) ***(P-24081)***
Sutter Hlth Scrmnto Sierra Reg ...A ...530 747-5010
2030 Sutter Pl Ste 2000 Davis (95616) ***(P-19986)***
Sutter Hlth Scrmnto Sierra Reg ...A ...209 223-7540
100 Mission Blvd Jackson (95642) ***(P-19987)***
Sutter Hlth Scrmnto Sierra Reg ...A ...916 733-7080
701 Howe Ave Ste F20 Sacramento (95825) ***(P-22893)***
Sutter Hlth Scrmnto Sierra Reg (HQ) ...B ...916 733-8800
2200 River Plaza Dr Sacramento (95833) ***(P-21836)***
Sutter Hlth Scrmnto Sierra Reg ...B ...530 756-6440
2000 Sutter Pl Davis (95616) ***(P-21837)***
Sutter Hlth Scrmnto Sierra Reg ...B ...916 454-2222
5151 F St Sacramento (95819) ***(P-21838)***
Sutter Hlth Scrmnto Sierra Reg ...D ...916 446-3100
1234 U St Sacramento (95818) ***(P-24082)***
Sutter Hlth Scrmnto Sierra Reg ...A ...916 781-1000
1 Medical Plaza Dr Roseville (95661) ***(P-21839)***
Sutter Hlth Scrmnto Sierra Reg ...A ...916 733-3095
2800 L St Sacramento (95816) ***(P-21840)***
Sutter Hlth Scrmnto Sierra Reg ...A ...530 406-5616
475 Pioneer Ave Ste 100 Woodland (95776) ***(P-19988)***
Sutter Home Winery Inc ...C ...707 963-5928
18655 Jacob Brack Rd Lodi (95242) ***(P-17493)***
Sutter Lakeside Hospital (HQ) ...B ...707 262-5000
5176 Hill Rd E Lakeport (95453) ***(P-21841)***
Sutter Maternity & Surgery Ctr ...C ...831 477-2200
2900 Chanticleer Ave Santa Cruz (95065) ***(P-21842)***
Sutter Med Group of Redwoods, Santa Rosa *Also called Sutter Health* ***(P-21807)***
Sutter Med Group of Redwoods ...D ...707 546-2788
3883 Airway Dr Ste 202 Santa Rosa (95403) ***(P-19989)***
Sutter Medical Center, Sacramento *Also called Sutter Health* ***(P-21823)***
Sutter Medical Center, Sacramento *Also called Sutter Hlth Scrmnto Sierra Reg* ***(P-21840)***
Sutter Medical Center, Woodland *Also called Sutter Hlth Scrmnto Sierra Reg* ***(P-19988)***
Sutter Medical Ctr Sacramento, Sacramento *Also called Sutter Hlth Rhabilitation Svcs* ***(P-24081)***
Sutter Medical Foundation ...A ...916 924-7764
1014 N Market Blvd Ste 20 Sacramento (95834) ***(P-20205)***
Sutter Memorial Hospital, Sacramento *Also called Sutter Hlth Scrmnto Sierra Reg* ***(P-21836)***
Sutter Memorial Hospital, Sacramento *Also called Sutter Hlth Scrmnto Sierra Reg* ***(P-21838)***
Sutter N Med Group A Prof Corp (PA) ...D ...530 749-3661
969 Plumas St Ste 205 Yuba City (95991) ***(P-19990)***
Sutter North Med Foundation (PA) ...C ...530 741-1300
969 Plumas St Yuba City (95991) ***(P-19991)***
Sutter North Med Foundation ...D ...530 749-3635
480 Plumas Blvd Yuba City (95991) ***(P-19992)***
Sutter North Med Foundation ...D ...530 675-1245
16911 Willow Glen Rd Brownsville (95919) ***(P-19993)***
Sutter North Med Foundation ...D ...530 749-3450
400 Plumas Blvd Ste 115 Yuba City (95991) ***(P-19994)***
Sutter Occupational Hlth Svcs, Roseville *Also called Sutter Health* ***(P-19983)***
Sutter Pacific Med Foundation, San Francisco *Also called Sutter Health* ***(P-21812)***
Sutter Pacific Med Foundation, Lakeport *Also called Sutter Health* ***(P-19977)***
Sutter Pacific Med Foundation, Santa Rosa *Also called Sutter Health* ***(P-21830)***
Sutter Physician Services (HQ) ...A ...916 854-6600
10470 Old Placrvl Rd # 100 Sacramento (95827) ***(P-27478)***
Sutter Regional Med Foundation ...D ...707 454-5800
770 Mason St Vacaville (95688) ***(P-19995)***
Sutter Roseville Medical Ctr, Roseville *Also called Sutter Hlth Scrmnto Sierra Reg* ***(P-21839)***
Sutter Roseville Medical Ctr ...A ...916 781-1000
1 Medical Plaza Dr Roseville (95661) ***(P-21843)***
Sutter Rsvlle Med Ctr Fndation ...A ...916 781-1000
1 Medical Plaza Dr Roseville (95661) ***(P-21844)***
Sutter Senior Care, Sacramento *Also called Sutter Hlth Scrmnto Sierra Reg* ***(P-24082)***
Sutter Solano Medical Center (HQ) ...A ...707 554-4444
300 Hospital Dr Vallejo (94589) ***(P-21845)***
Sutter Surgical Hospital N Vly ...C ...530 749-5700
455 Plumas Blvd Yuba City (95991) ***(P-21846)***
Sutter Valley Med Foundation (PA) ...A ...916 887-7122
2700 Gateway Oaks Dr Sacramento (95833) ***(P-21847)***
Sutter Vsiting Nurse Assn Hosp, Concord *Also called Sutter Vsting Nrse Assn Hspice* ***(P-22431)***
Sutter Vsting Nrse Assn Hspice ...D ...415 600-6200
1625 Van Ness Ave San Francisco (94109) ***(P-22429)***
Sutter Vsting Nrse Assn Hspice (HQ) ...E ...866 652-9178
1900 Powell St Ste 300 Emeryville (94608) ***(P-22430)***
Sutter Vsting Nrse Assn Hspice ...D ...510 618-5277
1651 Alvarado St San Leandro (94577) ***(P-20836)***
Sutter Vsting Nrse Assn Hspice ...D ...925 677-4250
5099 Commercial Cir # 20594520 Concord (94520) ***(P-22431)***
Sutter West Bay Hospitals (HQ) ...B ...415 209-1300
180 Rowland Way Novato (94945) ***(P-21848)***
Sutter West Foundation, Davis *Also called Sutter Hlth Scrmnto Sierra Reg* ***(P-19986)***
Sutter Yuba Mental Health Svcs, Yuba City *Also called County of Sutter* ***(P-22560)***
Suttles Plumbing & Mech Corp ...D ...818 718-9779
21541 Nordhoff St Ste C Chatsworth (91311) ***(P-2380)***
Sutter North Home Health, Yuba City *Also called Sutter North Med Foundation* ***(P-19994)***
Svb Financial Group (PA) ...D ...408 654-7400
3003 Tasman Dr Santa Clara (95054) ***(P-9490)***
Svcf, Mountain View *Also called Silicon Vly Cmnty Foundation* ***(P-25250)***
Svd Inc ...D ...818 504-1775
8088 San Fernando Rd Sun Valley (91352) ***(P-8529)***
Svi Lax LLC ...D ...310 281-0300
5933 W Century Blvd Los Angeles (90045) ***(P-13309)***
Svmc Precision Orthopedics, Salinas *Also called Salinas Valley Memorial Hlthca* ***(P-22043)***
Svn International Corp ...D ...310 979-0800
11999 San Vicente Blvd # 215 Los Angeles (90049) ***(P-11782)***
Swa Group (PA) ...C ...415 332-5100
2200 Bridgeway Sausalito (94965) ***(P-790)***
Swagbucks, El Segundo *Also called Prodege LLC* ***(P-15380)***
Swagelok Northern California, Fremont *Also called Sunnyvale Fluid Sys Tech Inc* ***(P-7874)***
Swaminatha Mahadevan MD ...D ...650 723-6576
701 Welch Rd Bldg C Palo Alto (94304) ***(P-19996)***
Swan Engineering Inc ...D ...916 474-5299
4470 Yankee Hill Rd # 200 Rocklin (95677) ***(P-3441)***
Swander Pace Capital LLC (PA) ...A ...415 477-8500
101 Mission St Ste 1900 San Francisco (94105) ***(P-27479)***
Swann Communications USA Inc ...D ...562 777-2551
12636 Clark St Santa Fe Springs (90670) ***(P-7112)***
Swanson Farms ...D ...209 667-2002
5213 W Main St Turlock (95380) ***(P-439)***
Swanton Berry Farms Inc ...E ...831 425-8919
25 Swanton Rd Davenport (95017) ***(P-383)***
Swatfame Inc (PA) ...B ...626 961-7928
16425 Gale Ave City of Industry (91745) ***(P-8337)***
Swayzer A-1 Sanitizing, Carson *Also called Swayzers Incorporated* ***(P-14405)***
Swayzers Incorporated ...D ...323 979-7223
1663 E Del Amo Blvd Carson (90746) ***(P-14405)***
Swca Incorporated ...D ...626 240-0587
51 W Dayton St Ste 100 Pasadena (91105) ***(P-27872)***
Swca Environmental Consultants, Pasadena *Also called Swca Incorporated* ***(P-27872)***
Sweda Company LLC ...C ...626 357-9999
17411 E Valley Blvd City of Industry (91744) ***(P-8013)***
Sweetwater Authority (PA) ...C ...619 422-8395
505 Garrett Ave Chula Vista (91910) ***(P-6315)***
Sweetwater Gardens Inc ...E ...707 937-4140
955 Ukiah Mendocino (95460) ***(P-18669)***
Sweis Inc (PA) ...C ...310 375-0558
23760 Hawthorne Blvd Torrance (90505) ***(P-7899)***
Swenson Developers and Contrs, San Jose *Also called Santa Clara Valley Corporation* ***(P-14376)***
Swenson, Barry Builder, San Jose *Also called Green Valley Corporation* ***(P-1538)***
Swift Courier Service, Concord *Also called Swift Worldwide Inc* ***(P-4273)***

Mergent e-mail: customerrelations@mergent.com
1486
2019 Directory of California
Wholesalers and Services Companies
(P-0000) Products & Services Section entry number
(PA)=Parent Co (HQ)=Headquarters (DH)=Div Headquarters

Swift Worldwide Inc (PA)....C....510 351-7949
1390 Willow Pass Rd # 420 Concord (94520) ***(P-4273)***
Swinerton Bldrs Pacific R....D....619 954-8011
16798 W Bernardo Dr San Diego (92127) ***(P-1663)***
Swinerton Builders (HQ)....C....415 421-2980
260 Townsend St San Francisco (94107) ***(P-1439)***
Swinerton Builders....D....213 896-3400
865 S Figueroa St # 3000 Los Angeles (90017) ***(P-1664)***
Swinerton Builders....D....858 622-4040
16798 W Bernardo Dr San Diego (92127) ***(P-1440)***
Swinerton Builders Hc....C....916 383-4825
15 Business Park Way # 101 Sacramento (95828) ***(P-1665)***
Swinerton Builders Inc....D....925 602-6400
2300 Clayton Rd Ste 800 Concord (94520) ***(P-1244)***
Swinerton Incorporated....D....925 689-2336
2300 Clayton Rd Ste 800 Concord (94520) ***(P-1318)***
Swinerton Incorporated (PA)....C....415 421-2980
260 Townsend St San Francisco (94107) ***(P-1666)***
Swinerton MGT & Consulting, San Francisco *Also called Swinerton Builders* ***(P-1439)***
Swinford Electric Inc....E....714 578-8888
1150 E Elm Ave Fullerton (92831) ***(P-2757)***
Swirl Inc....D....415 276-8300
101 Montgomery St San Francisco (94129) ***(P-13907)***
Swiss Dairy, City of Industry *Also called Dean Socal LLC* ***(P-8519)***
Swiss Hotel Group Inc....D....707 938-2884
18 W Spain St Sonoma (95476) ***(P-13310)***
Swiss Port Corp....B....310 417-0258
11001 Aviation Blvd Los Angeles (90045) ***(P-27607)***
Swiss RE America Holding Corp....E....858 485-5018
27412 Carino Cir Mission Viejo (92692) ***(P-10146)***
Swissport, Los Angeles *Also called Swiss Port Corp* ***(P-27607)***
Swissport Cargo Services LP....A....310 910-9541
11001 Aviation Blvd Los Angeles (90045) ***(P-4914)***
Swissport Fueling Inc....D....510 562-1701
1 Edward White Way Oakland (94621) ***(P-8968)***
Swissport Usa Inc....C....650 821-6220
San Francisco Intl Arprt San Francisco (94128) ***(P-4915)***
Swissport Usa Inc....B....310 345-1986
7025 W Imperial Hwy Los Angeles (90045) ***(P-4916)***
Swissport Usa Inc....C....571 214-7068
Delta Cargo Bldg 612 San Francisco (94128) ***(P-4917)***
Swissport Usa Inc....B....310 910-9560
11001 Aviation Blvd Los Angeles (90045) ***(P-4918)***
Switchfly Inc (PA)....D....415 541-9100
601 Montgomery St Fl 17 San Francisco (94111) ***(P-7113)***
Sws, Fullerton *Also called Superior Wall Systems Inc* ***(P-2966)***
Swt Stockton, Temecula *Also called Southwest Traders Incorporated* ***(P-8462)***
Swvp Del Mar Hotel LLC....C....858 481-5900
11915 El Camino Real San Diego (92130) ***(P-13311)***
Swvp Westlake LLC....C....805 557-1234
880 S Westlake Blvd Westlake Village (91361) ***(P-13312)***
Syapse Inc....D....650 924-1461
303 2nd St Ste S650 San Francisco (94107) ***(P-15870)***
Syar Industries Inc....D....707 643-3261
885 Lake Herman Rd Vallejo (94591) ***(P-1088)***
Syar Industries Inc....D....707 433-3366
13666 Healdsburg Ave Healdsburg (95448) ***(P-6907)***
Sycamore Cc Inc....D....760 451-3700
3742 Flowerwood Ln Fallbrook (92028) ***(P-19065)***
Sycamore Cogeneration Co (PA)....D....661 615-4630
1546 China Grade Loop Bakersfield (93308) ***(P-6143)***
SYCAMORE COURT APT, Newport Beach *Also called 10632 Bolsa Avenue LP* ***(P-10967)***
Sycamore Mineral Spring Resort....D....805 595-7302
1215 Avila Beach Dr San Luis Obispo (93405) ***(P-13313)***
Sycamore Park Care Center LLC....D....323 223-3441
4585 N Figueroa St Los Angeles (90065) ***(P-21227)***
SYCAMORE PARK CONVALESCENT HOSPITAL, Los Angeles *Also called Sycamore Park Care Center LLC* ***(P-21227)***
Sycamores School, Altadena *Also called Pasadena Chld Training Soc* ***(P-24627)***
Sycuan Casino....A....619 445-6002
5459 Casino Way El Cajon (92019) ***(P-19243)***
Sycuan Resort and Casino, El Cajon *Also called Sycuan Casino* ***(P-19243)***
Sydell Hotels LLC....C....213 381-7411
3515 Wilshire Blvd Los Angeles (90010) ***(P-13314)***
Sygma Network Inc....C....661 723-0405
46905 47th St W Lancaster (93536) ***(P-8880)***
Sygma Network Inc....C....209 932-5300
3741 Gold River Ln Stockton (95215) ***(P-8464)***
Sygma Network, The, Sun Valley *Also called Sugar Foods Corporation* ***(P-17490)***
Sylmar Hlth Rehabilitation Ctr, Sylmar *Also called Sylmar Hlth Rehabilitation Ctr* ***(P-21974)***
Sylmar Hlth Rehabilitation Ctr, Sylmar *Also called Golden State Health Ctrs Inc* ***(P-21956)***
Sylmar Hlth Rehabilitation Ctr....C....818 834-5082
12220 Foothill Blvd Sylmar (91342) ***(P-21974)***
Sylmark Group, Van Nuys *Also called Sylmark Inc* ***(P-27055)***
Sylmark Inc (PA)....D....818 217-2000
7821 Orion Ave Ste 200 Van Nuys (91406) ***(P-27055)***
Sylvester Roofing Company Inc....E....760 743-0048
2593 Auto Park Way Escondido (92029) ***(P-3203)***
Symantec Corporation (PA)....B....650 527-8000
350 Ellis St Mountain View (94043) ***(P-16496)***
Symitar Systems Inc....C....619 542-6700
8985 Balboa Ave San Diego (92123) ***(P-15484)***
Synagro West LLC....D....650 652-6531
1499 Bayshore Hwy Ste 111 Burlingame (94010) ***(P-27873)***
Synarc Reiscdronate, Newark *Also called Bioclinca* ***(P-26339)***
Synarc's, Newark *Also called Bioclinca* ***(P-15025)***
Synchronoss Technologies Inc....B....800 575-7606
60 S Market St Ste 700 San Jose (95113) ***(P-2758)***
Synctruck LLC....C....415 425-0447
415 Darrell Rd Hillsborough (94010) ***(P-4431)***
Synectic Solutions Inc (PA)....D....805 483-4800
1701 Pacific Ave Ste 260 Oxnard (93033) ***(P-16497)***
Synergex International Corp....D....916 635-7300
2330 Gold Meadow Way Gold River (95670) ***(P-15871)***
Synergy Companies, Hayward *Also called Eagle Systems Intl Inc* ***(P-2193)***
Synergy Environmental, Hayward *Also called American Synergy Asbestos Remo* ***(P-3484)***
Synergy Health Ast LLC (HQ)....D....858 586-1166
9020 Activity Rd Ste D San Diego (92126) ***(P-27480)***
Synergy Health North Amer Inc....D....562 428-5858
2240 E Artesia Blvd Long Beach (90805) ***(P-13554)***
Synermed....D....213 626-4556
711 W College St Fl 4 Los Angeles (90012) ***(P-27056)***
Synermed....C....216 406-2845
1200 Corp Ctr Dr Ste 200 Monterey Park (91754) ***(P-19997)***
Syngenta Seeds Inc....E....408 847-4242
5653 Monterey Frontage Rd Gilroy (95020) ***(P-9101)***
Syniverse Technologies LLC....C....408 324-1830
181 Metro Dr Ste 450 San Jose (95110) ***(P-16498)***
Synnex Corporation....D....909 923-8900
3655 E Philadelphia St Ontario (91761) ***(P-4638)***
Synnexxus LLC....E....714 933-4500
20251 Sw Acacia St # 200 Newport Beach (92660) ***(P-23405)***
Synopsys Inc (PA)....B....650 584-5000
690 E Middlefield Rd Mountain View (94043) ***(P-15872)***
Synopsys Inc....D....626 795-9101
199 S Los Robles Ave # 400 Pasadena (91101) ***(P-15873)***
Synoptek Inc (PA)....D....949 241-8600
19520 Jamboree Rd Ste 110 Irvine (92612) ***(P-16499)***
Synplicity Inc (HQ)....C....650 584-5000
690 E Middlefield Rd Mountain View (94043) ***(P-15874)***
Syntelesys Inc....E....323 859-2160
2550 Corp Pl Ste C108 Monterey Park (91754) ***(P-17888)***
Synteracthcr Inc (HQ)....B....760 268-8200
5909 Sea Otter Pl Ste 100 Carlsbad (92010) ***(P-26464)***
Synteracthcr Corporation (HQ)....B....760 268-8200
5909 Sea Otter Pl Ste 100 Carlsbad (92010) ***(P-26465)***
Synteracthcr Holdings Corp (PA)....B....760 268-8200
5909 Sea Otter Pl Ste 100 Carlsbad (92010) ***(P-26466)***
Synthetic Genomics Inc (HQ)....C....858 754-2900
11149 N Torrey Pines Rd La Jolla (92037) ***(P-26467)***
Sypartners LLC (HQ)....D....415 536-6600
475 Brannan St Ste 100 San Francisco (94107) ***(P-27874)***
Sysco Central California Inc....B....209 527-7700
136 Mariposa Rd Modesto (95354) ***(P-8465)***
Sysco Los Angeles Inc....A....909 595-9595
20701 Currier Rd Walnut (91789) ***(P-8466)***
Sysco Riverside Inc....B....951 601-5300
15750 Meridian Pkwy Riverside (92518) ***(P-8467)***
Sysco Sacramento Inc....B....916 275-2714
7062 Pacific Ave Pleasant Grove (95668) ***(P-8468)***
Sysco San Diego Inc....B....858 513-7300
12180 Kirkham Rd Poway (92064) ***(P-8469)***
Sysco San Francisco Inc (HQ)....A....510 226-3000
5900 Stewart Ave Fremont (94538) ***(P-8470)***
Sysco San Francisco Inc....C....831 771-5000
1622 Moffett St Salinas (93905) ***(P-8471)***
Sysco Ventura Inc....B....805 205-7000
3100 Sturgis Rd Oxnard (93030) ***(P-8472)***
Sysdig, Davis *Also called Draios Inc* ***(P-15119)***
Sysintelli Inc....C....858 271-1600
9466 Black Mountain Rd # 200 San Diego (92126) ***(P-15485)***
Syska & Hennessy Engineers Inc....D....310 312-0200
800 Crprate Pinte Ste 200 Culver City (90230) ***(P-25936)***
Sysorex USA (HQ)....D....415 389-7500
101 Larkspur Landing Cir # 120 Larkspur (94939) ***(P-16062)***
Syspro Impact Software Inc....C....714 437-1000
959 S Coast Dr Ste 100 Costa Mesa (92626) ***(P-7114)***
Systech Integrators Inc....C....408 441-2700
2050 Gateway Pl San Jose (95110) ***(P-16500)***
Systech Solutions Inc (PA)....D....818 550-9690
500 N Brand Blvd Ste 1900 Glendale (91203) ***(P-15486)***
Systechs, Orange *Also called Cruz Modular Inc* ***(P-4340)***
System Integrators Inc (HQ)....C....916 830-2400
1740 N Market Blvd Sacramento (95834) ***(P-16063)***
Systems America Public Sector, Walnut Creek *Also called Tryfacta Inc* ***(P-15513)***
Systems and Software Entps LLC (HQ)....D....714 854-8600
2929 E Imperial Hwy # 170 Brea (92821) ***(P-15487)***
Systems Application & Tech Inc....D....805 487-7373
1000 Town Center Dr # 110 Oxnard (93036) ***(P-25937)***
Systems Paving Inc (PA)....D....949 263-8301
1570 Brookhollow Dr Santa Ana (92705) ***(P-1858)***
Syzygy Technologies Inc....D....619 297-0970
1272 Calpella Ct Chula Vista (91913) ***(P-25938)***
T & P Farms....D....530 476-3038
1241 Putnam Way Arbuckle (95912) ***(P-3)***
T & R Painting & Drywall, Van Nuys *Also called Touch-Up Inc* ***(P-2971)***
T & R Painting Construction....C....818 779-3800
7116 Valjean Ave Van Nuys (91406) ***(P-2486)***
T & T Solutions Inc....D....818 676-1786
7018 Owensmouth Ave # 201 Canoga Park (91303) ***(P-16501)***
T & T Truck & Crane Service, Ventura *Also called Offshore Crane & Service Co* ***(P-14452)***
T & T Trucking Inc (PA)....C....800 692-3457
11396 N Hwy 99 Lodi (95240) ***(P-4274)***
T - Y Nursery Inc....C....760 742-2151
15335 Highway 76 Pauma Valley (92061) ***(P-9168)***
T and D Communications Inc (PA)....D....510 824-0010
6761 Sierra Ct Ste F Dublin (94568) ***(P-15488)***

Employee Codes: A=Over 500 employees, B=251-500
C=101-250, D=51-100, E=50
2019 Directory of California
Wholesalers and Services Companies
© Mergent Inc. 1-800-342-5647
1487

T and M Agricultural Svcs LLC.....C.....707 963-3330
493 Dowdell Ln Saint Helena (94574) ***(P-714)***
T B Penick & Sons Inc.....C.....951 719-1492
41892 Enterprise Cir S Temecula (92590) ***(P-1245)***
T B Penick & Sons Inc (PA).....C.....858 558-1800
15435 Innovation Dr # 100 San Diego (92128) ***(P-1441)***
T Boyer Company.....E.....949 642-2431
1656 Babcock St Costa Mesa (92627) ***(P-2759)***
T C Construction Company Inc.....C.....619 448-4560
10540 Prospect Ave Santee (92071) ***(P-1987)***
T C H P Inc.....D.....951 687-7330
11162 Palm Terrace Ln Riverside (92505) ***(P-20837)***
T C I, Redondo Beach *Also called Transportation Concept Inc* ***(P-3736)***
T C P, Santa Monica *Also called Tennenbaum Capitl Partners LLC* ***(P-12273)***
T C R Limited Partnership.....C.....310 645-1881
5440 W Century Blvd Los Angeles (90045) ***(P-17649)***
T C W Realty Fund VI.....C.....213 683-4200
515 S Flower St Fl 31 Los Angeles (90071) ***(P-12189)***
T D R, Turlock *Also called Turlock Dairy & Rfrgn Inc* ***(P-7716)***
T F Louderback Inc (PA).....C.....510 965-6120
700 National Ct Richmond (94804) ***(P-9028)***
T G T Enterprises Inc.....C.....858 413-0300
12650 Danielson Ct Poway (92064) ***(P-14064)***
T I C Hotels Inc.....D.....619 238-7577
555 W Ash St San Diego (92101) ***(P-13315)***
T I C Hotels Inc.....D.....805 773-4671
2555 Price St Pismo Beach (93449) ***(P-13316)***
T I D, Turlock *Also called Turlock Irrigation District* ***(P-6568)***
T L Fabrications LP.....D.....562 802-3980
2921 E Coronado St Anaheim (92806) ***(P-3399)***
T M B, San Fernando *Also called Jme Inc* ***(P-7368)***
T M Cobb Company.....D.....916 381-7330
8490 Rovana Cir Sacramento (95828) ***(P-6868)***
T M I, San Diego *Also called Toward Maximum Independence* ***(P-24090)***
T M Mian & Associates Inc.....D.....818 591-2300
24150 Park Sorrento Calabasas (91302) ***(P-13317)***
T M Mian & Associates Inc.....D.....805 983-8600
2000 Solar Dr Oxnard (93036) ***(P-13318)***
T M P Inc.....D.....818 718-1222
21051 Osborne St Canoga Park (91304) ***(P-8279)***
T M S, Campbell *Also called Telecmmnctons MGT Slutions Inc* ***(P-2764)***
T McGee Electric Inc.....D.....909 591-6461
2390 S Reservoir St Pomona (91766) ***(P-2760)***
T Points Inc.....E.....323 846-9176
350 W Mrtn Lthr King Jr Los Angeles (90037) ***(P-13638)***
T R L, Rancho Cucamonga *Also called TRL Systems Incorporated* ***(P-2771)***
T Royal Management (PA).....D.....559 447-9887
7419 N Cedar Ave Ste 102 Fresno (93720) ***(P-11783)***
T S J Elec Communications Inc.....D.....951 785-0921
7490 Jurupa Ave Riverside (92504) ***(P-2761)***
T T Miyasaka Inc.....B.....831 722-3871
209 Riverside Rd Watsonville (95076) ***(P-124)***
T U D, Sonora *Also called Tuolumne Utilities District* ***(P-6316)***
T W M Industries.....A.....925 866-1156
3131 Crow Canyon Pl San Ramon (94583) ***(P-12071)***
T W R Framing.....D.....951 279-2000
1661 Railroad St Corona (92880) ***(P-14773)***
T Y Lin International (HQ).....D.....415 291-3700
345 California St Fl 23 San Francisco (94104) ***(P-25939)***
T Y R, Seal Beach *Also called Tyr Sport Inc* ***(P-8340)***
T&C Roofing Inc.....D.....925 513-8463
2155 Elkins Way Ste H Brentwood (94513) ***(P-3204)***
T-12 Three LLC.....B.....619 702-3000
207 5th Ave San Diego (92101) ***(P-13319)***
T-Force Inc (PA).....D.....949 208-1527
4695 Macarthur Ct Newport Beach (92660) ***(P-27875)***
T-Mobile Usa Inc.....C.....510 797-8290
4095 Mowry Ave Fremont (94538) ***(P-5418)***
T-Mobile Usa Inc.....C.....209 529-0539
2225 Plaza Pkwy Ste I1b Modesto (95350) ***(P-5419)***
T-Mobile Usa Inc.....C.....415 440-5370
900 Van Ness Ave Ste 1 San Francisco (94109) ***(P-5420)***
T-N-T Grading, Escondido *Also called TNT Grading Inc* ***(P-1861)***
T.C.A.H, Sonora *Also called Watch Resources Inc* ***(P-24127)***
T.com Ontario Fc T-9479, Ontario *Also called Target Corporation* ***(P-4687)***
T.S.c, Altadena *Also called Tom Sawyer Camps Inc* ***(P-24394)***
T/O Printing, Westlake Village *Also called Thousand Oaks Prtg & Spc Inc* ***(P-17509)***
T25cl Entertainment LLC.....C.....951 308-2040
1074 55th St Oakland (94608) ***(P-18128)***
T2d Media, El Monte *Also called Dang Quinten* ***(P-5978)***
T3 Direct, Modesto *Also called Sterling Mktg & Fincl Corp* ***(P-27470)***
T3w Business Solutions Inc.....D.....619 298-0888
3921 Ampudia St San Diego (92110) ***(P-27057)***
Ta Chen International Inc (HQ).....C.....562 808-8000
5855 Obispo Ave Long Beach (90805) ***(P-7318)***
TA Industries Inc (PA).....D.....562 466-1000
11335 Greenstone Ave Santa Fe Springs (90670) ***(P-7640)***
Ta-Kai Home Care Inc.....D.....714 393-4586
22349 La Palma Ave # 105 Yorba Linda (92887) ***(P-22432)***
Taber Company Inc.....D.....714 543-7100
1442 Ritchey St Santa Ana (92705) ***(P-6869)***
Table Community Foudation.....D.....209 951-1753
3201 W Benjamin Holt Dr Stockton (95219) ***(P-25264)***
Table Mountain Casino.....A.....559 822-7777
8184 Table Mountain Rd Friant (93626) ***(P-13320)***
Tabletops Unlimited Inc (PA).....D.....310 549-6000
23000 Avalon Blvd Carson (90745) ***(P-6790)***
Tabula Inc.....D.....408 986-9140
1100 La Avenida St Ste A Mountain View (94043) ***(P-7550)***
TAC Rbo, Sacramento *Also called Surgical Care Affiliate* ***(P-26299)***
Tacer, Van Nuys *Also called Town & Country Event Rentals* ***(P-14549)***
Tachi Palace Hotel & Casino.....A.....559 924-7751
17225 Jersey Ave Lemoore (93245) ***(P-13321)***
Tachyon Inc.....E.....858 882-8108
9339 Carroll Park Dr # 150 San Diego (92121) ***(P-5650)***
Tacit Knowledge Inc.....D.....415 694-4322
27 Maiden Ln Fl 4 San Francisco (94108) ***(P-16502)***
Tacori Enterprises.....D.....818 863-1536
1736 Gardena Ave Glendale (91204) ***(P-8014)***
Tactical Engrg & Analis Inc (PA).....C.....858 573-9869
6050 Santo Rd Ste 250 San Diego (92124) ***(P-16503)***
Tactical Lgistic Solutions Inc.....D.....909 464-2813
13799 Monte Vista Ave Chino (91710) ***(P-4639)***
Tactical Telesolutions Inc.....C.....415 788-8808
2121 N California Blvd Walnut Creek (94596) ***(P-17494)***
Tactivos Inc.....D.....415 687-2501
303 2nd St Ste S200 San Francisco (94107) ***(P-5651)***
Tad Group LLC.....C.....949 476-3601
W Tower 5000 W Tow Newport Beach (92660) ***(P-16946)***
Tadin Inc.....D.....213 406-8880
3345 E Slauson Ave Vernon (90058) ***(P-8881)***
Tadin Herb & Tea Co., Vernon *Also called Tadin Inc* ***(P-8881)***
Tae Technologies Inc (PA).....C.....949 830-2117
19631 Pauling Foothill Ranch (92610) ***(P-26468)***
Taft Broadcasting Company LLC.....D.....951 413-2337
23755 Z St March ARB (92518) ***(P-18129)***
Taft College Children Center.....E.....661 763-7850
29 Emmons Park Dr Taft (93268) ***(P-24390)***
Taft Correctional Institution, Taft *Also called Geo Group Inc* ***(P-27590)***
Taft Electric Company (PA).....C.....805 642-0121
1694 Eastman Ave Ventura (93003) ***(P-2762)***
Taft Production Company.....D.....661 765-7194
950 Petroleum Club Rd Taft (93268) ***(P-1011)***
Tahoe Beach & Ski Club.....D.....530 541-6220
3601 Lake Tahoe Blvd South Lake Tahoe (96150) ***(P-13322)***
Tahoe Donner Golf Course Inc.....D.....530 587-9455
11509 Northwoods Blvd Truckee (96161) ***(P-18771)***
Tahoe Forest Hospital District.....C.....530 582-3277
10956 Donner Paca Rd Truckee (96161) ***(P-21849)***
Tahoe Forest Hospital District (PA).....A.....530 587-6011
10121 Pine Ave Truckee (96161) ***(P-21850)***
Tahoe Lake Partners LLC.....D.....707 255-9890
855 Bordeaux Way Ste 200 NAPA (94558) ***(P-11927)***
Tahoe Seasons Resort Time Inte.....C.....530 541-6700
3901 Saddle Rd South Lake Tahoe (96150) ***(P-11784)***
Tahoe Trcke Unfd Sch Dis Fincn.....D.....530 582-7630
11725 Donner Past Rd Truckee (96160) ***(P-27876)***
Tahoe Workx, Truckee *Also called Tahoe Forest Hospital District* ***(P-21849)***
Tahoe-Truckee Sanitation Agcy.....D.....530 587-2525
13720 Butterfield Dr Truckee (96161) ***(P-6332)***
Tai Seng Entertainment, South San Francisco *Also called U-2 Home Entertainment Inc* ***(P-7555)***
Tailbroom Media Grop, North Hollywood *Also called Pilgrim Operations LLC* ***(P-6947)***
Tailored Living Choices LLC.....C.....707 259-0526
1957 Sierra Ave NAPA (94558) ***(P-3590)***
Taisei Construction Corp (HQ).....D.....714 886-1530
970 W 190th St Ste 920 Torrance (90502) ***(P-1442)***
Tait Environmental Svcs Inc (PA).....D.....714 560-8200
701 Parkcenter Dr Santa Ana (92705) ***(P-3591)***
Takara Bio Usa Inc.....C.....650 919-7300
1290 Terra Bella Ave Mountain View (94043) ***(P-26469)***
Takeda California Inc.....C.....858 622-8528
10410 Science Center Dr San Diego (92121) ***(P-26665)***
Takenaka Partners LLC (PA).....E.....213 593-4011
801 S Figueroa St Ste 620 Los Angeles (90017) ***(P-10017)***
Talbot Insurance & Fincl Svcs, Santa Barbara *Also called Caesar and Seider Insur Svcs* ***(P-10570)***
Talco Plastics Inc (PA).....D.....951 531-2000
1000 W Rincon St Corona (92880) ***(P-6481)***
Talega Golf Club, San Clemente *Also called Heritage Golf Group LLC* ***(P-18719)***
Talend Inc (HQ).....D.....650 539-3200
800 Bridge Pkwy Ste 200 Redwood City (94065) ***(P-16064)***
Talent & Acquisition LLC.....D.....213 742-1972
100 W Broadway Ste 650 Long Beach (90802) ***(P-15489)***
Talent Space Inc.....D.....408 330-1900
2570 N 1st St Ste 400 San Jose (95131) ***(P-14774)***
Talentburst Inc.....C.....415 813-4011
575 Market St Ste 3025 San Francisco (94105) ***(P-17495)***
Talentscale LLC.....D.....951 744-0053
31805 Temecula Pkwy 204 Temecula (92592) ***(P-25940)***
Talentwave, Foster City *Also called Ic Compliance LLC* ***(P-15209)***
Talix Inc.....D.....628 220-3885
660 3rd St Ste 302 San Francisco (94107) ***(P-15875)***
Tall Pony Productions Inc.....C.....310 456-7495
300 Loma Metisse Rd Malibu (90265) ***(P-18130)***
Taller Technologies, San Francisco *Also called Quadriga Inc* ***(P-15388)***
Talley & Associates, Santa Fe Springs *Also called Talley Inc* ***(P-7551)***
Talley Farms.....C.....805 489-2508
2900 Lopez Dr Arroyo Grande (93420) ***(P-576)***
Talley Inc (PA).....C.....562 906-8000
12976 Sandoval St Santa Fe Springs (90670) ***(P-7551)***
Talley Transportation.....D.....559 673-9013
12325 Road 29 Madera (93638) ***(P-4068)***
Talon Executive Services Inc.....E.....714 434-7476
151 Kalmus Dr Ste A103 Costa Mesa (92626) ***(P-16947)***

Talon International Inc (PA) ....D....818 444-4100
21900 Burbank Blvd # 270 Woodland Hills (91367) ***(P-8246)***
Talview Inc ....C....510 227-8227
3260 Hillview Ave Palo Alto (94304) ***(P-16504)***
Tama Trading Company ....D....213 748-8262
1920 E 20th St Vernon (90058) ***(P-8882)***
Tamal Pais, Greenbrae *Also called Northern California Presbyteri* ***(P-21168)***
TAMALPAIS, Greenbrae *Also called Ross Valley Homes Inc* ***(P-20952)***
Tamalpais Creek, Novato *Also called Atria Senior Living Group Inc* ***(P-24429)***
Tamarack Bch Condo Owners Assn ....E....760 729-3500
3200 Carlsbad Blvd Carlsbad (92008) ***(P-25265)***
Tammi R James MD ....E....916 383-6783
7273 14th Ave Ste 120b Sacramento (95820) ***(P-19998)***
Tamo Inc ....E....909 803-1030
8545 Pecan Ave Rancho Cucamonga (91739) ***(P-4275)***
Tamtron Corporation (HQ) ....D....408 323-3303
6203 San Ignacio Ave # 110 San Jose (95119) ***(P-15490)***
Tan Jay-Nygard Outlet Store, Gardena *Also called Nygard Inc* ***(P-8328)***
Tanaka Farms ....D....949 653-2100
5380 University Dr Irvine (92612) ***(P-8883)***
Tangoe Inc ....D....858 452-6800
9920 Pcf Hts Blvd Ste 200 San Diego (92121) ***(P-15876)***
Tanimura & Antle, Salinas *Also called Plant Tape Usa Inc* ***(P-465)***
Tanimura & Antle Inc ....B....831 424-6100
4401 Foxdale St Baldwin Park (91706) ***(P-577)***
Tanimura & Antle Inc ....D....805 483-2358
761 Commercial Ave Oxnard (93030) ***(P-4640)***
Tanimura Antle Fresh Foods Inc (PA) ....D....831 455-2950
1 Harris Rd Salinas (93908) ***(P-84)***
Tanimura Brothers ....D....831 424-0841
81 Hitchcock Rd Salinas (93908) ***(P-10018)***
Tanner Mainstain Blatt & Gly ....D....310 446-2700
10866 Wilshire Blvd Fl 10 Los Angeles (90024) ***(P-26300)***
Tano Capital LLC ....E....650 212-0330
1 Franklin Pkwy San Mateo (94403) ***(P-12270)***
Tantra Lake Partners LP ....C....949 756-5959
18802 Bardeen Ave Irvine (92612) ***(P-11123)***
Tanvex Biopharma Usa Inc (PA) ....D....858 210-4100
2030 Main St Ste 600 Irvine (92614) ***(P-26470)***
Tao Mechanical Ltd ....E....925 447-5220
136 Wright Brothers Ave Livermore (94551) ***(P-2381)***
Taos Mountain LLC (PA) ....B....408 324-2800
121 Daggett Dr San Jose (95134) ***(P-16505)***
Tap Operating Co LLC ....A....310 900-5500
400 W Artesia Blvd Compton (90220) ***(P-6678)***
Tap Ram Reinforcing Inc ....D....562 484-0859
11658 Excelsior Dr Norwalk (90650) ***(P-3400)***
Tap Worldwide LLC (PA) ....A....310 900-5500
400 W Artesia Blvd Compton (90220) ***(P-6679)***
Tapestry Solutions Inc (HQ) ....C....858 503-1990
5643 Copley Dr San Diego (92111) ***(P-15491)***
Tapia Brothers Co, Maywood *Also called Tapia Enterprises Inc* ***(P-8473)***
Tapia Enterprises Inc (PA) ....D....323 560-7415
6067 District Blvd Maywood (90270) ***(P-8473)***
Tapia Farms ....E....661 256-4401
8425 W Ave 8 Rosamond (93560) ***(P-384)***
Tapjoy Inc (PA) ....D....415 766-6900
111 Sutter St Fl 12 San Francisco (94104) ***(P-13908)***
Tara, Lomita *Also called Torrance Amateur Rdo Assn Inc* ***(P-25475)***
Tarbel Realtors, Murrieta *Also called F M Tarbell Co* ***(P-11428)***
Tarbell Financial Corporation ....D....909 335-0750
1440 Industrial Park Ave Redlands (92374) ***(P-11785)***
Tarbell Financial Corporation (PA) ....D....714 972-0988
1403 N Tustin Ave Ste 380 Santa Ana (92705) ***(P-9910)***
Tarbell Realtors, Anaheim *Also called F M Tarbell Co* ***(P-11429)***
Tarbell Realtors, Anaheim *Also called F M Tarbell Co* ***(P-11430)***
Tarbell Realtors, Santa Ana *Also called F M Tarbell Co* ***(P-11431)***
Tarbell Realtors, Corona *Also called F M Tarbell Co* ***(P-11432)***
Tarbell Realtors, Laguna Hills *Also called F M Tarbell Co* ***(P-11433)***
Tarbell Realtors, Menifee *Also called F M Tarbell Co* ***(P-11434)***
Tarbell Realtors, Temecula *Also called F M Tarbell Co* ***(P-11435)***
Tarbell Realtors, Diamond Bar *Also called F M Tarbell Co* ***(P-11436)***
Tarbell Realtors, Irvine *Also called F M Tarbell Co* ***(P-11437)***
Tarbell Realtors, Irvine *Also called F M Tarbell Co* ***(P-11438)***
Tarbell Realtors, Palm Desert *Also called F M Tarbell Co* ***(P-11441)***
Tarbell Realtors, Upland *Also called F M Tarbell Co* ***(P-11442)***
Target Corporation ....C....909 937-5500
1505 S Haven Ave Ontario (91761) ***(P-4687)***
Target Corporation ....B....530 666-3705
2050 E Beamer St Woodland (95776) ***(P-4688)***
Target Corporation ....C....559 431-0104
7600 N Blackstone Ave Fresno (93720) ***(P-4689)***
TARGET CW, San Diego *Also called Wmbe Payrolling Inc* ***(P-14799)***
Target Specialty Products, Santa Fe Springs *Also called Rentokil North America Inc* ***(P-9094)***
Target Specialty Products, Santa Fe Springs *Also called Western Exterminator Company* ***(P-14164)***
Targus International LLC (PA) ....C....714 765-5555
1211 N Miller St Anaheim (92806) ***(P-9262)***
Tariff Building Associates LP (PA) ....D....415 397-5572
222 Kearny St Ste 200 San Francisco (94108) ***(P-10954)***
Tarpy Heating & Air ....E....619 485-3311
9723 Roe Dr Santee (92071) ***(P-2382)***
Tarpy Plumbing Heating and Air, Santee *Also called Tarpy Heating & Air* ***(P-2382)***
Tarra Landscape, Oakland *Also called Tree Sculpture Group* ***(P-949)***
Tarrant Apparel Group ....C....323 780-8250
801 S Figueroa St # 2500 Los Angeles (90017) ***(P-8338)***
Tarsadia Hotels, Newport Beach *Also called Uka LLC* ***(P-13352)***
Tarzana Treatment Centers Inc ....C....818 654-3815
422 W Rancho Vista Blvd C280 Palmdale (93551) ***(P-22691)***
Tarzana Treatment Centers Inc (PA) ....C....818 996-1051
18646 Oxnard St Tarzana (91356) ***(P-22692)***
Tarzana Treatment Centers Inc ....C....562 428-4111
5190 Atlantic Ave Lakewood (90805) ***(P-22693)***
Tarzana Treatment Centers Inc ....E....562 218-1868
2101 Magnolia Ave Long Beach (90806) ***(P-22694)***
Tarzana Treatment Centers Inc ....D....661 726-2630
44447 10th St W Lancaster (93534) ***(P-22695)***
Tarzana Treatment Ctr, Lancaster *Also called Tarzana Treatment Centers Inc* ***(P-22695)***
Tarzana Trtmnt Ctrs LNG Bch O, Lakewood *Also called Tarzana Treatment Centers Inc* ***(P-22693)***
Task Force For Reg Autostaff, Monrovia *Also called Trap* ***(P-17520)***
Taskus Inc (PA) ....E....888 400-8275
3221 Donald Douglas Santa Monica (90405) ***(P-16185)***
Taslimi Construction Co Inc ....D....310 447-3000
1805 Colorado Ave Santa Monica (90404) ***(P-1667)***
Tasq Technology Inc ....B....916 632-7600
8875 Washington Blvd A Roseville (95678) ***(P-9690)***
Tata America Intl Corp ....D....408 569-5845
5201 Great America Pkwy # 400 Santa Clara (95054) ***(P-16506)***
Tata Communications Amer Inc ....D....650 262-0004
700 Airport Blvd Ste 100 Burlingame (94010) ***(P-17496)***
Tata Consulting Services, Santa Clara *Also called Tata America Intl Corp* ***(P-16506)***
Tate Neurological Surgery, Redding *Also called James D Tate MD* ***(P-19516)***
Taulia Inc (PA) ....D....415 376-8280
250 Montgomery St Ste 400 San Francisco (94104) ***(P-15492)***
Tavant Technologies Inc (PA) ....D....408 519-5400
3965 Freedom Cir Ste 750 Santa Clara (95054) ***(P-15493)***
Tawa Services Inc (PA) ....C....714 521-8899
6281 Regio Ave Fl 2 Buena Park (90620) ***(P-8884)***
Tax and Financial Group, Newport Beach *Also called R Mc Closkey Insurance Agency* ***(P-10753)***
Tax Compliance Inc ....D....858 547-4100
10089 Willow Creek Rd # 300 San Diego (92131) ***(P-15494)***
Tax Problem Center, Los Angeles *Also called Authority Tax Services LLC* ***(P-17019)***
Tax Resolution Services, Co, Calabasas *Also called Danerica Enterprises Inc* ***(P-13737)***
Taxaudit.com, Folsom *Also called Taxresources Inc* ***(P-26301)***
Taxresources Inc (PA) ....C....877 369-7827
600 Coolidge Dr Ste 300 Folsom (95630) ***(P-26301)***
Taylor Bailey Inc ....D....707 967-8090
355 Lafata St Ste E Saint Helena (94574) ***(P-1668)***
Taylor Farms California Inc (HQ) ....E....831 754-0471
150 Main St Ste 500 Salinas (93901) ***(P-578)***
Taylor Fresh Foods Inc (PA) ....C....831 676-9023
150 Main St Ste 400 Salinas (93901) ***(P-579)***
Taylor Morrison California LLC ....C....949 341-1200
100 Spectrum Center Dr # 1450 Irvine (92618) ***(P-11928)***
Taylor Structures Inc ....D....707 499-6870
905 Cotting Ln Ste 100 Vacaville (95688) ***(P-1669)***
Taylored Services LLC (HQ) ....D....909 510-4800
1495 E Locust St Ontario (91761) ***(P-4641)***
Taylored Services Holdings LLC (HQ) ....D....909 510-4800
1495 E Locust St Ontario (91761) ***(P-5177)***
Taylored Svcs Parent Co Inc (PA) ....D....909 510-4800
1495 E Locust St Ontario (91761) ***(P-5178)***
TBG Insurance Services Corp ....B....310 203-8770
100 N Pacific Coast Hwy # 500 El Segundo (90245) ***(P-10799)***
Tbs, Costa Mesa *Also called Transprttion Brkg Spclists Inc* ***(P-4071)***
Tbwa Chiat/Day Inc ....D....310 305-5000
5353 Grosvenor Blvd Los Angeles (90066) ***(P-17497)***
Tbwa Worldwide Inc ....C....310 305-4400
12539 Beatrice St Los Angeles (90066) ***(P-13909)***
Tc Property Mgt A Californi ....D....530 666-5799
1224 Cottonwood St Ofc Woodland (95695) ***(P-12271)***
Tcal, San Diego *Also called Takeda California Inc* ***(P-26665)***
Tcb Industrial Inc (PA) ....C....209 571-0569
2955 Farrar Ave Modesto (95354) ***(P-1443)***
Tccsc, Los Angeles *Also called Tessie Clvland Cmnty Svcs Corp* ***(P-24086)***
Tcg Builders Inc ....E....408 321-6450
890 N Mccarthy Blvd # 100 Milpitas (95035) ***(P-1670)***
Tcg Software Services Inc ....E....714 665-6200
320 Commerce Ste 200 Irvine (92602) ***(P-15495)***
TCI Aluminum/North Inc ....D....510 786-3750
2353 Davis Ave Hayward (94545) ***(P-7319)***
Tcm Group LLC ....E....909 527-8580
3130 Inland Empire Blvd Ontario (91764) ***(P-27058)***
Tcmi Inc (PA) ....E....650 614-8200
250 Middlefield Rd Menlo Park (94025) ***(P-12272)***
Tcp Global Corporation (PA) ....D....858 909-2110
6695 Rasha St San Diego (92121) ***(P-9190)***
Tct Circuit Supply Inc ....D....714 644-9700
560 S Melrose St Placentia (92870) ***(P-7875)***
Tcv Management 2004 LLC ....E....650 614-8200
528 Ramona St Palo Alto (94301) ***(P-27059)***
Tcw Funds Management Inc ....A....213 244-0000
865 S Figueroa St # 2100 Los Angeles (90017) ***(P-10019)***
Tcw Group Inc (PA) ....B....213 244-0000
865 S Figueroa St # 1800 Los Angeles (90017) ***(P-10116)***
Tcw Value Added Ltd Partnr ....D....213 244-0000
865 S Figueroa St Los Angeles (90017) ***(P-12128)***
TD Desert Dev Ltd Partnr (HQ) ....C....760 777-1001
81570 Carboneras La Quinta (92253) ***(P-11929)***
Tdic, Sacramento *Also called Dentists Insurance Company* ***(P-10604)***

Employee Codes: A=Over 500 employees, B=251-500
C=101-250, D=51-100, E=50
2019 Directory of California
Wholesalers and Services Companies
© Mergent Inc. 1-800-342-5647
1489

TDS, Hornitos *Also called Hornitos Telephone Co* ***(P-5578)***
Teachers Insurance and Annuity, Redwood City *Also called Kaspick & Co LLC* ***(P-27293)***
Teale Data Center, Rancho Cordova *Also called Technology Services Cal Dept* ***(P-16187)***
Tealium Inc (PA) ....D....858 779-1344
11095 Torreyana Rd Fl 2 San Diego (92121) ***(P-16186)***
Team Dykspra (PA) ....D....951 898-6482
2315 California Ave Corona (92881) ***(P-17840)***
Team Finish Inc ....D....714 671-9190
155 Arovista Cir Ste A Brea (92821) ***(P-3335)***
Team Ghilotti Inc ....E....707 763-8700
2531 Petaluma Blvd S Petaluma (94952) ***(P-1859)***
Team Makena LLC (PA) ....D....949 474-1753
27051 Towne Centre Dr # 180 Foothill Ranch (92610) ***(P-7221)***
Team One, Los Angeles *Also called Team-One Emplyment Spclsts LLC* ***(P-14775)***
Team Post-Op Inc (HQ) ....D....949 253-5500
17256 Red Hill Ave Irvine (92614) ***(P-7222)***
Team Power Forklift, Fair Oaks *Also called Clarklift-West Inc* ***(P-7741)***
Team Risk MGT Strategies LLC ....A....877 767-8728
3131 Camino Del Rio N # 650 San Diego (92108) ***(P-27877)***
Team San Jose ....A....408 295-9600
408 Almaden Blvd San Jose (95110) ***(P-17498)***
Team Services, Burbank *Also called The Team Companies LLC* ***(P-26302)***
Team Spirit Realty Inc ....E....714 562-0404
6301 Beach Blvd Ste 225 Buena Park (90621) ***(P-11786)***
Team Superstores, Vallejo *Also called Teamross Inc* ***(P-17787)***
Team Tomato, Norwalk *Also called Lj Distributors Inc* ***(P-8703)***
Team Truck Dismantling Inc ....D....951 685-6744
3760 Pyrite St Riverside (92509) ***(P-6704)***
Team West Contracting Corp ....D....951 340-3426
2733 S Vista Ave Bloomington (92316) ***(P-2066)***
Team-One Emplyment Spclsts LLC ....A....310 481-4480
2999 Overland Ave Ste 212 Los Angeles (90064) ***(P-14775)***
Teamross Inc ....D....707 643-9000
301 Auto Mall Pkwy Vallejo (94591) ***(P-17787)***
Tecan Sp Inc ....D....626 962-0010
14180 Live Oak Ave Baldwin Park (91706) ***(P-7249)***
Tech Flex Package ....E....323 241-1800
12624 Daphne Ave Hawthorne (90250) ***(P-14129)***
Tech Knowledge Associates LLC ....D....714 735-3810
1 Centerpointe Dr Ste 200 La Palma (90623) ***(P-17994)***
Tech Mahindra (americas) Inc ....D....949 462-0640
23461 S Pointe Dr Ste 370 Laguna Hills (92653) ***(P-15496)***
Tech Museum of Innovation (PA) ....D....408 795-6116
201 S Market St San Jose (95113) ***(P-24916)***
Tech Museum of Innovation ....D....408 795-6168
145 W San Carlos St San Jose (95113) ***(P-24917)***
Tech Packaging Inc ....D....909 243-7047
9545 Santa Anita Ave A Rancho Cucamonga (91730) ***(P-9263)***
Tech Soup, San Francisco *Also called Techsoup Global* ***(P-25266)***
Tech Systems Inc ....C....714 523-5404
7372 Walnut Ave Ste J Buena Park (90620) ***(P-7552)***
Tech-Ed Networks Inc ....C....916 784-2005
10000 Allantown Dr # 175 Roseville (95678) ***(P-16507)***
Techaisle LLC ....E....408 253-4416
5053 Doyle Rd Ste 105 San Jose (95129) ***(P-26569)***
Techcon, Morgan Hill *Also called Monument Construction Inc* ***(P-902)***
Techexcel Inc (PA) ....D....925 871-3900
3675 Mt Diablo Blvd # 330 Lafayette (94549) ***(P-15497)***
Techflow Inc (PA) ....C....858 412-8000
9889 Willow Creek Rd San Diego (92131) ***(P-27608)***
Techlink Systems Inc (PA) ....B....415 732-7580
1 Post St Ste 300 San Francisco (94104) ***(P-14776)***
Techmate, San Francisco *Also called Convoy Inc* ***(P-16281)***
Techncolor Crative Svcs USA Inc (HQ) ....B....818 260-3800
6040 W Sunset Blvd Los Angeles (90028) ***(P-18221)***
Techncolor Crative Svcs USA Inc ....C....323 467-1244
6040 W Sunset Blvd Los Angeles (90028) ***(P-18222)***
Techncolor Vdocassette Mich Inc (HQ) ....B....805 445-1122
3233 Mission Oaks Blvd Camarillo (93012) ***(P-18223)***
Technical Services, Mountain View *Also called Northrop Grumman Systems Corp* ***(P-16019)***
Technical Temps Inc ....D....408 956-8256
1096 Pecten Ct Milpitas (95035) ***(P-14777)***
Technicolor Inc ....B....818 260-4577
2255 N Ontario St Ste 180 Burbank (91504) ***(P-16968)***
Technicolor Inc (HQ) ....D....805 445-1122
3233 Mission Oaks Blvd Camarillo (93012) ***(P-18224)***
Technicolor - Funimation Ent, Calexico *Also called Technicolor HM Entrmt Svcs Inc* ***(P-18225)***
Technicolor HM Entrmt Svcs Inc ....B....760 357-3372
1778 Zinetta Rd Ste F Calexico (92231) ***(P-18225)***
Technicolor HM Entrmt Svcs Inc ....B....909 974-2016
5491 E Philadelphia St Ontario (91761) ***(P-18226)***
Technicolor HM Entrmt Svcs Inc (HQ) ....B....805 445-1122
3233 Mission Oaks Blvd Camarillo (93012) ***(P-18227)***
Technicolor Hollywood, Los Angeles *Also called Technicolor Thomson Group* ***(P-18228)***
Technicolor Lab, Burbank *Also called Technicolor Inc* ***(P-16968)***
Technicolor New Media Inc ....E....818 480-5100
250 E Olive Ave Ste 300 Burbank (91502) ***(P-18131)***
Technicolor Thomson Group ....A....323 817-6600
6040 W Sunset Blvd Los Angeles (90028) ***(P-18228)***
Technicolor Thomson Group ....B....818 260-3600
2255 N Ontario St Ste 100 Burbank (91504) ***(P-18229)***
Technicolor Thomson Group ....B....909 974-2222
5491 E Philadelphia St Ontario (91761) ***(P-18230)***
Technicolor Thomson Group ....A....805 445-1122
3301 Mission Oaks Blvd Camarillo (93012) ***(P-18231)***
Technicolor Video Service, Camarillo *Also called Techncolor Vdocassette Mich Inc* ***(P-18223)***
Technicolor Video Services, Camarillo *Also called Technicolor HM Entrmt Svcs Inc* ***(P-18227)***
Technicon Design Corporation ....C....949 218-1300
26522 La Alameda Ste 150 Mission Viejo (92691) ***(P-17499)***
Techno Coatings Inc ....C....714 774-4671
795 Debra St Anaheim (92805) ***(P-1671)***
Technologent, Irvine *Also called Thomas Gallaway Corporation* ***(P-7115)***
Technology Associates EC Inc ....D....760 765-5275
3115 Melrose Dr Ste 110 Carlsbad (92010) ***(P-27481)***
Technology Credit Union ....D....408 467-2382
1562 S Bascom Ave San Jose (95125) ***(P-9657)***
Technology Credit Union ....D....408 467-2385
43848 Pcf Commons Blvd Fremont (94538) ***(P-9658)***
Technology Credit Union (PA) ....C....408 451-9111
2010 N 1st St Ste 200 San Jose (95131) ***(P-9659)***
Technology Credit Union ....D....650 326-6445
490 California Ave Palo Alto (94306) ***(P-9660)***
Technology Crossover Ventures, Menlo Park *Also called Tcmi Inc* ***(P-12272)***
Technology Resource Center Inc ....D....714 542-1004
2101 E 4th St Ste 130a Santa Ana (92705) ***(P-16508)***
Technology Services Cal Dept ....E....916 464-3747
10860 Gold Center Dr # 100 Rancho Cordova (95670) ***(P-16187)***
Technology Services Cal Dept (HQ) ....D....916 319-9223
1325 J St Ste 1600 Sacramento (95814) ***(P-16509)***
Technosocialworkcom LLC ....D....661 617-6601
4300 Resnik Ct Unit 103 Bakersfield (93313) ***(P-16188)***
Techsoup Global (PA) ....C....800 659-3579
435 Brannan St Ste 100 San Francisco (94107) ***(P-25266)***
Techstyles Sportswear, Hayward *Also called Bruml Management LLC* ***(P-8290)***
Tecolote Research Inc ....C....310 640-4700
2120 E Grand Ave Ste 200 El Segundo (90245) ***(P-27482)***
Tecom Industries Incorporated ....C....805 267-0100
375 Conejo Ridge Ave Thousand Oaks (91361) ***(P-7553)***
Tecta America Southern Cal Inc (HQ) ....E....714 973-6233
1217 E Wakeham Ave Santa Ana (92705) ***(P-3205)***
Tectura Corporation (PA) ....E....650 273-4249
951 Old County Rd 2-317 Belmont (94002) ***(P-16510)***
Ted Cooper/Cooper Industries ....E....408 358-3060
P.O. Box 36007 San Jose (95158) ***(P-947)***
Ted Ford Jones Inc (PA) ....C....714 521-3110
6211 Beach Blvd Buena Park (90621) ***(P-17788)***
Ted Jacob Engrg Group Inc (PA) ....D....510 763-4880
1763 Broadway Oakland (94612) ***(P-25941)***
Ted Levine Drum Co (PA) ....D....626 579-1084
1817 Chico Ave South El Monte (91733) ***(P-17995)***
Teecom ....D....510 337-2800
1333 Broadway Ste 601 Oakland (94612) ***(P-25942)***
Teen Challenge Norwestcal Nev ....D....408 703-2001
390 Mathew St Santa Clara (95050) ***(P-24083)***
Teg Staffing Inc ....A....619 260-2000
2355 Northside Dr Ste 200 San Diego (92108) ***(P-14778)***
Tegile Systems Inc ....C....510 791-7900
7999 Gateway Blvd Ste 120 Newark (94560) ***(P-26471)***
Tegp Inc ....A....619 584-3408
2375 Northside Dr Ste 360 San Diego (92108) ***(P-14919)***
Tegsco LLC ....D....415 575-2340
450 7th St San Francisco (94103) ***(P-17875)***
Tegtmeier Associates Inc ....D....530 872-7700
6701 Clark Rd Paradise (95969) ***(P-10955)***
Tehachapi Vly Healthcare Dst (PA) ....C....661 750-4848
305 S Robinson St Tehachapi (93561) ***(P-24847)***
Tehama Golf Club LLC ....D....831 622-2200
4 Tehama Carmel (93923) ***(P-19066)***
Teichert Construction, Sacramento *Also called A Teichert & Son Inc* ***(P-6874)***
Teichert/Great Lakes E&I JV ....D....916 484-3011
3500 American River Dr Sacramento (95864) ***(P-2067)***
Teixeira Farms Inc ....C....805 928-3801
2600 Bonita Lateral Rd Santa Maria (93458) ***(P-85)***
Tejon Ranch Co (PA) ....D....661 248-3000
4436 Lebec Rd Lebec (93243) ***(P-196)***
Tekever Corporation ....D....408 730-2617
5201 Great America Pkwy Santa Clara (95054) ***(P-15877)***
Tektetco ....D....707 822-9000
5251 Ericson Way Arcata (95521) ***(P-1444)***
Tekworks Inc ....D....877 835-9675
12742 Knott St Garden Grove (92841) ***(P-5652)***
Tekworks Inc (PA) ....C....858 668-1705
13000 Gregg St Ste B Poway (92064) ***(P-17500)***
Tel Tech Plus Inc ....E....760 510-1323
393 Enterprise St San Marcos (92078) ***(P-2763)***
Telacu, Commerce *Also called East Los Angeles Community Un* ***(P-9737)***
Telacu Industries Inc (HQ) ....E....323 721-1655
5400 E Olympic Blvd # 300 Commerce (90022) ***(P-9862)***
Telaflora LLC ....B....310 231-9199
11444 W Olympic Blvd Fl 4 Los Angeles (90064) ***(P-9169)***
Teldata, Santee *Also called Catania Hijar Corporation* ***(P-1905)***
Tele-Car Courier Service, Los Angeles *Also called Tele-Car Couriers Inc* ***(P-4432)***
Tele-Car Couriers Inc ....D....877 910-1313
4035 Eagle Rock Blvd Los Angeles (90065) ***(P-4432)***
Tele-Direct Communications ....D....916 348-2170
4741 Madison Ave Ste 200 Sacramento (95841) ***(P-17501)***
Tele-Interpreters LLC ....B....800 811-7881
1 Lower Ragsdale Dr # 2 Monterey (93940) ***(P-17502)***
Telecare Corporation ....D....714 361-6760
275 Baker St Costa Mesa (92626) ***(P-21975)***
Telecare Corporation ....D....510 895-5502
2050 Fairmont Dr San Leandro (94578) ***(P-21976)***
Telecare Corporation ....D....760 245-8837
16460 Victor St Victorville (92395) ***(P-21977)***
Telecare Corporation ....D....619 275-8000
1675 Morena Blvd Ste 100 San Diego (92110) ***(P-21978)***

Telecare Corporation (PA) ... E ... 510 337-7950
1080 Marina Village Pkwy # 100 Alameda (94501) ***(P-21979)***

Telecare Corporation ... D ... 562 630-8672
6060 N Paramount Blvd Long Beach (90805) ***(P-21980)***

Telecare Corporation ... C ... 562 634-9534
6060 N Paramount Blvd Long Beach (90805) ***(P-21981)***

Telecare Corporation ... C ... 510 261-9191
1451 28th Ave Oakland (94601) ***(P-21982)***

Telecare Corporation ... C ... 510 582-7676
494 Blossom Way Hayward (94541) ***(P-21983)***

Telecare Corporation ... C ... 510 352-9690
15200 Foothill Blvd San Leandro (94578) ***(P-21984)***

Telecare Corporation ... D ... 619 692-8225
3851 Rosecrans St San Diego (92110) ***(P-21985)***

Telecare Corporation ... D ... 805 383-3669
1756 S Lewis Rd Camarillo (93012) ***(P-21986)***

Telecare Corporation ... C ... 650 367-1890
200 Edmonds Rd Redwood City (94062) ***(P-21987)***

Telecare Corporation ... C ... 510 337-7950
1080 Marina Village Pkwy # 100 Alameda (94501) ***(P-21988)***

Telecare Corporation ... C ... 562 633-5111
8835 Vans St Paramount (90723) ***(P-21989)***

Telecare Corporation ... D ... 650 817-9070
300 Harbor Blvd E Belmont (94002) ***(P-21990)***

Telecare Corporation ... C ... 510 535-5115
2633 E 27th St Oakland (94601) ***(P-21991)***

Telecare Fsp, Belmont *Also called Telecare Corporation* ***(P-21990)***

Telecare La Step Down ... E ... 562 216-4900
4335 Atlantic Ave Long Beach (90807) ***(P-22696)***

Telecare Las Posadas ... D ... 805 383-3669
1756 S Lewis Rd Camarillo (93012) ***(P-22697)***

Telecmmnctons MGT Slutions Inc ... D ... 408 866-5495
570 Division St Campbell (95008) ***(P-2764)***

Telecntric Communications Intl ... D ... 562 906-2555
12070 Telg Rd Ste 107 Santa Fe Springs (90670) ***(P-17503)***

Telecom Evolutions LLC ... E ... 818 264-4400
9221 Corbin Ave Ste 260 Northridge (91324) ***(P-17504)***

Telecom Inc ... D ... 510 873-8283
2201 Broadway Ste 103 Oakland (94612) ***(P-17505)***

Telecom Technology Svcs Inc ... C ... 925 224-7812
7901 Stoneridge Dr # 500 Pleasanton (94588) ***(P-27878)***

Telecommunications Dept, Salinas *Also called County of Monterey* ***(P-17106)***

Telecommunications Division, Sacramento *Also called General Services Cal Dept* ***(P-25707)***

Telecontact Resource Services, Riverbank *Also called Econtactlive Inc* ***(P-17146)***

Teledyne Scientific Imaging LLC ... C ... 805 373-4979
5212 Verdugo Way Camarillo (93012) ***(P-26472)***

Teledyne Scientific Imaging LLC (HQ) ... C ... 805 373-4545
1049 Camino Dos Rios Thousand Oaks (91360) ***(P-26473)***

Teledyne Scientific Company, Thousand Oaks *Also called Teledyne Scientific Imaging LLC* ***(P-26473)***

Telegraph Hill Partners Invest (PA) ... E ... 415 765-6980
360 Post St Ste 601 San Francisco (94108) ***(P-27483)***

Teleinterpreters, Monterey *Also called Language Line Services Inc* ***(P-17290)***

Telemarketing, Fresno *Also called Fowler Packing Company Inc* ***(P-517)***

Telemedicine Corp ... E ... 888 472-2853
8920 Wilshire Blvd # 310 Beverly Hills (90211) ***(P-22894)***

Telenav Inc ... B ... 360 765-0058
4655 Great America Pkwy # 300 Santa Clara (95054) ***(P-27484)***

Telenet Voip Inc ... D ... 310 253-9000
850 N Park View Dr El Segundo (90245) ***(P-17915)***

Telepictures, Burbank *Also called Warner Bros Transatlantic Inc* ***(P-18251)***

Teleplan Service Solutions Inc ... D ... 916 677-4500
8875 Washington Blvd B Roseville (95678) ***(P-16293)***

Telescape, Los Angeles *Also called Truconnect Communications Inc* ***(P-5656)***

Telesis Community Credit Union (PA) ... D ... 818 885-1226
9301 Winnetka Ave Chatsworth (91311) ***(P-9597)***

Telesis Onion Co (PA) ... C ... 559 884-2441
3265 W Figarden Dr Fresno (93711) ***(P-86)***

Telesis Onion Co ... E ... 559 884-2441
21484 S Colusa Five Points (93624) ***(P-580)***

Telestar Consulting Inc ... E ... 310 748-0008
519 N Alta Dr Beverly Hills (90210) ***(P-27485)***

Telestream LLC (PA) ... D ... 530 470-1300
848 Gold Flat Rd Nevada City (95959) ***(P-15498)***

Telesys Software ... E ... 650 522-9922
1900 S Norfolk St Ste 221 San Mateo (94403) ***(P-15499)***

Teletrac Inc (HQ) ... D ... 714 897-0877
7391 Lincoln Way Garden Grove (92841) ***(P-5999)***

TELEVISION ACADEMY, North Hollywood *Also called Academy TV Arts & Sciences* ***(P-24993)***

Television Games Network, Los Angeles *Also called Ods Technologies LP* ***(P-5831)***

Telfer Oil Company (PA) ... D ... 925 228-1515
211 Foster St Martinez (94553) ***(P-1860)***

Telisimo International Corp ... B ... 619 325-1593
2330 Shelter Island Dr 210a San Diego (92106) ***(P-5653)***

Tell Steel Inc ... D ... 562 435-4826
2345 W 17th St Long Beach (90813) ***(P-7320)***

Telogis, Inc., Aliso Viejo *Also called Verizon Connect Telo Inc* ***(P-16197)***

Telstar Instruments (PA) ... D ... 925 671-2888
1717 Solano Way Ste 34 Concord (94520) ***(P-2765)***

Temalpakh Inc ... D ... 760 770-5778
979 S Gene Autry Trl Palm Springs (92264) ***(P-1672)***

Temarry Recycling Inc ... D ... 619 270-9453
476 Tecate Rd Tecate (91980) ***(P-6482)***

Temco, Laguna Beach *Also called C & B Delivery Services* ***(P-4534)***

Temco Logistics, Laguna Beach *Also called Home Express Delivery Svc LLC* ***(P-5088)***

Temecula 24 Hour Care, Temecula *Also called Responsible Med Solutions Corp* ***(P-19820)***

Temecula Stadium Cinemas 15, Temecula *Also called Edwards Theatres Circuit Inc* ***(P-18297)***

Temecula Valley Drywall Inc ... D ... 951 600-1742
41228 Raintree Ct Murrieta (92562) ***(P-2967)***

Temecula Valley Unified School ... B ... 951 695-7110
40516 Roripaugh Rd Temecula (92591) ***(P-3946)***

Temeku Hills, Temecula *Also called McMillin Communities Inc* ***(P-1199)***

Temp Unlimited LLC ... D ... 562 860-3340
11306 183rd St Ste 301 Cerritos (90703) ***(P-14920)***

Tempest Telecom Solutions LLC (PA) ... D ... 805 879-4800
136 W Canon Perdido St # 100 Santa Barbara (93101) ***(P-27879)***

Temple City Convalescent Hosp, Temple City *Also called Fran-Jom Inc* ***(P-21068)***

Temple City Youth Dev Fund ... D ... 626 548-5085
6415 N Muscatel Ave San Gabriel (91775) ***(P-25267)***

Temple Garden Homes Inc ... E ... 626 286-6408
5746 Loma Ave Temple City (91780) ***(P-24695)***

Temple Israel of Hollywood (PA) ... D ... 323 876-8330
7300 Hollywood Blvd Los Angeles (90046) ***(P-13700)***

Temple Park Convalescent Hosp ... D ... 213 380-2035
2411 W Temple St Los Angeles (90026) ***(P-21228)***

Templeton Franklin Intl Tr ... E ... 650 312-2000
1 Franklin Pkwy San Mateo (94403) ***(P-12048)***

Templo Calvario Cmnty Dev Corp ... D ... 714 543-3711
2501 W 5th St Santa Ana (92703) ***(P-24848)***

Templton Fgn Smaller Companies, San Mateo *Also called Templeton Franklin Intl Tr* ***(P-12048)***

Temporary Plant Cleaners, Martinez *Also called Plant Maintenance Inc* ***(P-14892)***

Temporary Staffing Union ... A ... 714 728-5186
19800 Macarthur Blvd Irvine (92612) ***(P-25084)***

Ten, El Segundo *Also called Enthusiast Network Inc* ***(P-5053)***

Ten Enthusiast Network LLC ... C ... 714 709-9021
1821 E Dyer Rd Ste 150 Santa Ana (92705) ***(P-9121)***

TEN ENTHUSIAST NETWORK, LLC, Santa Ana *Also called Ten Enthusiast Network LLC* ***(P-9121)***

Ten Publishing Media LLC (PA) ... C ... 310 531-9900
831 S Douglas St Ste 100 El Segundo (90245) ***(P-18232)***

Ten-X LLC ... A ... 800 793-6107
1301 Shoreway Rd Ste 425 Belmont (94002) ***(P-11787)***

Ten-X LLC ... B ... 949 609-5376
3050 S Del St Ste 201 San Mateo (94403) ***(P-11788)***

Tenaya Lodge, Fish Camp *Also called DNC Prks Resorts At Tenaya Inc* ***(P-12531)***

Tender Home Healthcare Inc ... D ... 323 466-2345
3550 Wilshire Blvd # 700 Los Angeles (90010) ***(P-22433)***

Tenderloin Housing Clinic Inc ... C ... 415 771-2427
472 Turk St San Francisco (94102) ***(P-22895)***

Tenderloin Housing Clinic Inc (PA) ... C ... 415 771-9850
126 Hyde St San Francisco (94102) ***(P-11789)***

Tenet, Palm Springs *Also called Desert Regional Med Ctr Inc* ***(P-21364)***

TENET, Santa Ana *Also called French Park Care Center* ***(P-20439)***

TENET, Modesto *Also called Doctors Med Ctr Modesto Inc* ***(P-21397)***

Tenet, Palm Springs *Also called Desert Regional Med Ctr Inc* ***(P-22017)***

Tenet Health System Hospital, Manteca *Also called Tenet Healthsystem Medical* ***(P-21854)***

Tenet Health Systems Norris ... B ... 323 865-3000
1441 Eastlake Ave Los Angeles (90089) ***(P-21851)***

Tenet Healthsystem Medical ... A ... 714 966-8191
13032 Earlham St Santa Ana (92705) ***(P-21852)***

Tenet Healthsystem Medical ... B ... 925 275-8303
414 Cliffside Dr Danville (94526) ***(P-19999)***

Tenet Healthsystem Medical ... A ... 562 531-2550
3700 South St Lakewood (90712) ***(P-20000)***

Tenet Healthsystem Medical ... A ... 562 531-2550
16331 Arthur St Cerritos (90703) ***(P-21853)***

Tenet Healthsystem Medical ... C ... 619 426-6310
330 Moss St Chula Vista (91911) ***(P-21992)***

Tenet Healthsystem Medical ... B ... 209 823-3111
1205 E North St Manteca (95336) ***(P-21854)***

Tenet Healthsystem Medical ... A ... 714 428-6800
1400 S Duglaca Rd Ste 250 Anaheim (92806) ***(P-21855)***

Tenet Healthsystem Medical ... D ... 530 222-1992
475 Knollcrest Dr Redding (96002) ***(P-22434)***

Tenet Healthsystem Medical ... A ... 805 546-7698
3751 Katella Ave Los Alamitos (90720) ***(P-20001)***

Tenet Healthsystem Medical ... B ... 714 993-2000
1301 N Rose Dr Placentia (92870) ***(P-22054)***

Tenet Healthsystem Medical ... D ... 562 493-9581
1661 Golden Rain Rd Seal Beach (90740) ***(P-20002)***

Tenet Healthsystem Medical ... A ... 408 378-6131
815 Pollard Rd Los Gatos (95032) ***(P-21856)***

Tenet Healthsystem Medical ... C ... 626 300-5500
1000 S Fremont Ave Unit 1 Alhambra (91803) ***(P-20003)***

Tennant Health Systems ... C ... 626 300-3500
1000 S Fremont Ave Unit 2 Alhambra (91803) ***(P-20004)***

Tennenbaum Capitl Partners LLC (HQ) ... D ... 310 566-1000
2951 28th St Ste 1000 Santa Monica (90405) ***(P-12273)***

Tennis Channel Inc (HQ) ... D ... 310 392-1920
2850 Ocean Park Blvd # 150 Santa Monica (90405) ***(P-18407)***

Tennis Everyone Incorporated ... D ... 415 897-2185
351 San Andreas Dr Novato (94945) ***(P-19067)***

Tennyson Electric Inc ... E ... 925 606-1038
7275 National Dr Livermore (94550) ***(P-2766)***

Tenpo Hardware, Ontario *Also called Ameriwest Industries Inc* ***(P-7575)***

Tensilica Inc (HQ) ... D ... 408 986-8000
3393 Octavius Dr Santa Clara (95054) ***(P-12144)***

Tepa Ec LLC (PA) ... D ... 719 596-8114
1022 South St Orland (95963) ***(P-25943)***

Tera Investments Inc ... E ... 530 753-7129
4810 Chiles Rd Davis (95618) ***(P-12274)***

ALPHABETIC

Employee Codes: A=Over 500 employees, B=251-500
C=101-250, D=51-100, E=50

2019 Directory of California
Wholesalers and Services Companies

© Mergent Inc. 1-800-342-5647
1491

Teraburst Networks Inc ....E.......408 400-4100
1289 Anvilwood Ave Sunnyvale (94089) ***(P-6000)***
Teradata Corporation ....A.......858 485-1220
17095 Via Del Campo San Diego (92127) ***(P-16511)***
Teresi Trucking LLC (PA) ....D.......209 368-2472
900 1/2 E Victor Rd Lodi (95240) ***(P-4276)***
Teris LLC (PA) ....D.......650 213-9922
2455 Faber Pl Ste 200 Palo Alto (94303) ***(P-16189)***
Teris LLC ....E.......619 231-3282
600 W Broadway Ste 300 San Diego (92101) ***(P-16190)***
Teris Bay Area, Palo Alto *Also called Teris LLC* ***(P-16189)***
Teris-Bay Area LLC ....D.......650 213-9922
2455 Faber Pl Ste 200 Palo Alto (94303) ***(P-23406)***
Terix Computer Service, Santa Clara *Also called Tusa Inc* ***(P-16297)***
Terkensha Associates Inc ....D.......916 922-9868
811 Grand Ave Ste D Sacramento (95838) ***(P-24084)***
Terminix Intl Co Ltd Partnr ....E.......818 972-2037
3055 N California St Burbank (91504) ***(P-14158)***
Terminix Intl Co Ltd Partnr ....D.......925 460-5063
6678 Owens Dr Ste 100 Pleasanton (94588) ***(P-14159)***
Terminix Intl Co Ltd Partnr ....E.......909 332-2479
649 S Waterman Ave Ste A San Bernardino (92408) ***(P-14160)***
Terminix Intl Co Ltd Partnr ....D.......818 361-1191
21113 Superior St Chatsworth (91311) ***(P-14161)***
Tero Tek International Inc (PA) ....D.......661 725-1135
1408 S Lexington St Delano (93215) ***(P-25944)***
Terra Coastal Properties Inc ....E.......310 457-2534
23405 Pacific Coast Hwy Malibu (90265) ***(P-11790)***
Terra Firma Farm Corp ....E.......530 795-2473
4713 Baker Rd Winters (95694) ***(P-87)***
Terra Firma Farms, Winters *Also called Terra Firma Farm Corp* ***(P-87)***
Terra Firma Landscape Company, San Diego *Also called L A Swikard Inc* ***(P-874)***
Terra Linda Farms 1 ....E.......559 867-3400
17625 S Marks Ave Riverdale (93656) ***(P-385)***
Terra Nova Counseling (PA) ....D.......916 344-0249
5750 Sunrise Blvd Ste 100 Citrus Heights (95610) ***(P-24085)***
Terra Pacific Landscape (HQ) ....D.......714 567-0177
1627 E Wilshire Ave Santa Ana (92705) ***(P-791)***
Terra Vista Management, San Diego *Also called Terra Vista Management Inc* ***(P-11791)***
Terra Vista Management Inc ....C.......858 581-4200
2211 Pacific Beach Dr San Diego (92109) ***(P-11791)***
Terracare Associates LLC ....D.......925 374-0060
921 Arnold Dr Martinez (94553) ***(P-27486)***
Terrace View Care Center, Fullerton *Also called Sun Haven Care Inc* ***(P-20784)***
Terraces At Par Marino, Pasadena *Also called Diversified Health Svcs Del* ***(P-24505)***
Terraces At Squaw Peak, Pleasanton *Also called Humangood* ***(P-21116)***
Terraces of Los Gatos Agei, Los Gatos *Also called American Baptist Homes of West* ***(P-20992)***
Terraces of Roseville, The, Roseville *Also called Westmont Living Inc* ***(P-24721)***
Terraces Retirement Community ....C.......530 894-1010
2850 Sierra Sunrise Ter Chico (95928) ***(P-24696)***
Terracina Meadows Apts ....E.......916 419-0925
4500 Tynebourne St F105 Sacramento (95834) ***(P-11124)***
Terranea Resort, Rancho Palos Verdes *Also called Long Point Development LLC* ***(P-12863)***
Terranomics, Burlingame *Also called Cushman & Wakefield Inc* ***(P-11389)***
Terranova Ranch Inc ....E.......559 866-5644
16729 W Floral Ave Helm (93627) ***(P-386)***
Terre Du Soleil Ltd ....B.......707 963-1211
180 Rutherford Hill Rd Rutherford (94573) ***(P-13323)***
Terry Hines & Assoc, Burbank *Also called GL Nemirow Inc* ***(P-13834)***
Terry Meyer ....D.......408 723-3300
1712 Meridian Ave Ste C San Jose (95125) ***(P-11792)***
Terry Tuell Concrete Inc ....D.......559 431-0812
287 W Fallbrook Ave # 105 Fresno (93711) ***(P-3336)***
Tesancia La Jlla Ht Spa Resort, La Jolla *Also called Destination Residences LLC* ***(P-13739)***
Teserra (PA) ....B.......760 340-9000
86100 Avenue 54 Coachella (92236) ***(P-3592)***
Tesi Investment Company LLC ....D.......619 224-3254
5005 N Harbor Dr San Diego (92106) ***(P-13324)***
Tesla Energy Operations Inc (HQ) ....A.......650 638-1028
3055 Clearview Way San Mateo (94402) ***(P-2383)***
Tessie Clvland Cmnty Svcs Corp ....D.......323 586-7333
8019 Compton Ave Ste 219 Los Angeles (90001) ***(P-24086)***
Test-Rite Products Corp (HQ) ....D.......909 605-9899
1900 Burgundy Pl Ontario (91761) ***(P-6791)***
Testamerica Laboratories Inc ....C.......949 261-1022
17461 Derian Ave Ste 100 Irvine (92614) ***(P-26733)***
Testamerica Laboratories Inc ....D.......916 373-5600
880 Riverside Pkwy West Sacramento (95605) ***(P-26734)***
Testequity LLC (PA) ....C.......805 498-9933
6100 Condor Dr Moorpark (93021) ***(P-17916)***
Testing and Selection, Sacramento *Also called Justice California Department* ***(P-27762)***
Testing Engineers San Diego, San Diego *Also called San Diego Testing Engineers* ***(P-25903)***
Teter LLP (PA) ....E.......559 437-0887
7535 N Palm Ave Ste 201 Fresno (93711) ***(P-25945)***
Tetra Tech Inc ....D.......619 525-7188
1230 Columbia St Ste 1000 San Diego (92101) ***(P-27487)***
Tetra Tech Inc ....D.......805 739-2600
3201 Airpark Dr Ste 108 Santa Maria (93455) ***(P-27880)***
Tetra Tech Inc ....D.......949 263-0846
17885 Von Karman Ave # 500 Irvine (92614) ***(P-25946)***
Tetra Tech Inc ....D.......949 809-5000
17885 Von Karman Ave # 500 Irvine (92614) ***(P-25947)***
Tetra Tech Bas Inc (HQ) ....D.......909 860-7777
1360 Valley Vista Dr Diamond Bar (91765) ***(P-25948)***
Tetra Tech Dpk, San Francisco *Also called Dpk Consulting* ***(P-27218)***
Tetra Tech Ec Inc ....D.......619 234-8690
1230 Columbia St Ste 750 San Diego (92101) ***(P-27881)***
Tetra Tech Ec Inc ....A.......916 852-8300
2969 Prospect Park Dr # 100 Rancho Cordova (95670) ***(P-27882)***
Tetra Tech Engrg & Arch Svcs, Irvine *Also called Tetra Tech Inc* ***(P-25947)***
Tetra Tech Executive Svcs Inc ....C.......626 470-2400
3475 E Foothill Blvd Pasadena (91107) ***(P-14779)***
Tetra Tech Nus Inc ....D.......412 921-7090
3475 E Foothill Blvd Pasadena (91107) ***(P-27883)***
Tetra Tech Technical Services ....C.......626 351-4664
3475 E Foothill Blvd Fl 3 Pasadena (91107) ***(P-25949)***
Teutonic Holdings LLC ....C.......818 264-4400
9221 Corbin Ave Ste 260 Northridge (91324) ***(P-16252)***
Texaco Inc ....B.......661 654-7000
9525 Camino Media Bakersfield (93311) ***(P-11793)***
Texas Farm, Santa Fe Springs *Also called Seaboard Corporation* ***(P-404)***
Texas Home Health America LP (PA) ....D.......972 201-3800
1455 Auto Center Dr # 200 Ontario (91761) ***(P-20206)***
Texas Instruments Sunnyvale ....E.......408 541-9900
165 Gibraltar Ct Sunnyvale (94089) ***(P-17506)***
Textainer Equipment Mgt US Ltd (HQ) ....D.......415 434-0551
650 California St Fl 16 San Francisco (94108) ***(P-14547)***
Textainer Group Holdings Ltd (HQ) ....D.......415 434-0551
650 California St Fl 16 San Francisco (94108) ***(P-27060)***
Textaner Eqp Income Fund II LP ....D.......415 434-0551
650 California St Fl 16 San Francisco (94108) ***(P-14548)***
Textplus Inc ....D.......424 272-0296
13160 Mindanao Way # 217 Marina Del Rey (90292) ***(P-5421)***
Textron Aviation Inc ....D.......916 929-5656
5850 Citation Way Sacramento (95837) ***(P-4919)***
Texture Specialties Inc ....E.......559 904-6047
295 Mccreary Ave Hanford (93230) ***(P-3401)***
Texxis Limited ....D.......213 631-3547
400 Spectrum Center Dr # 1 Irvine (92618) ***(P-15500)***
Tf Courier Inc ....D.......916 379-0708
8331 Demetre Ave Sacramento (95828) ***(P-4433)***
Tf Courier Inc ....D.......888 541-2965
7130 Miramar Rd Ste 400 San Diego (92121) ***(P-4434)***
Tf Courier Inc ....D.......714 888-1452
2051 Raymer Ave Ste A Fullerton (92833) ***(P-4435)***
Tf Courier Inc ....D.......214 560-9000
21760 Garcia Ln City of Industry (91789) ***(P-4436)***
Tgcon Inc (HQ) ....D.......925 449-5764
50 Contractors St Livermore (94551) ***(P-25950)***
Tharp Truck Rental Inc (PA) ....C.......559 782-5800
15243 Road 192 Porterville (93257) ***(P-17996)***
Tharpe & Howell (PA) ....D.......714 437-4900
15250 Ventura Blvd Fl 9 Sherman Oaks (91403) ***(P-23407)***
The Bay Club Hotel and Marina, San Diego *Also called Bay Club Hotel and Marina A C* ***(P-12360)***
The Boardwalk, El Cajon *Also called Newport Diversified Inc* ***(P-17352)***
The Broadmoore, San Francisco *Also called Broadmoor Hotel* ***(P-10990)***
The Charles Schwab Trust Co (HQ) ....E.......415 371-0518
425 Market St Fl 7 San Francisco (94105) ***(P-10020)***
The David Lcile Pckard Fndtion ....D.......650 917-7167
300 2nd St Los Altos (94022) ***(P-25473)***
The Designory Inc (HQ) ....C.......562 624-0200
211 E Ocean Blvd Ste 100 Long Beach (90802) ***(P-14130)***
The Eberly Company, Beverly Hills *Also called Charles & Cynthia Eberly Inc* ***(P-11001)***
The Executive Office of ....D.......916 322-2318
1400 10th St Rm 100 Sacramento (95814) ***(P-26474)***
The For Califo Cente ....C.......760 839-4138
340 N Escondido Blvd Escondido (92025) ***(P-24918)***
The For Hospital Committee (HQ) ....B.......925 847-3000
5555 W Las Positas Blvd Pleasanton (94588) ***(P-27061)***
The For Sacramento Society ....D.......916 383-7387
6201 Florin Perkins Rd Sacramento (95828) ***(P-25474)***
The For Valley Resource Center (PA) ....E.......951 766-8659
1285 N Santa Fe St Hemet (92543) ***(P-24236)***
The For Work Training Center ....E.......530 534-1112
1811 Kusel Rd Oroville (95966) ***(P-24237)***
The Golf Club of California, Fallbrook *Also called Sycamore Cc Inc* ***(P-19065)***
The Goodwin Company, Garden Grove *Also called Goodwin Ammonia Company* ***(P-4567)***
The Gray-Line Tours Company ....C.......323 463-3333
6541 Hollywood Blvd Los Angeles (90028) ***(P-3904)***
The Lodge At Torrey Pines, La Jolla *Also called Bh Partn A Calif Limit Partne* ***(P-12384)***
The Messenger Company, San Diego *Also called San Diego Messenger Inc* ***(P-4429)***
The National Food Lab LLC ....C.......925 828-1440
365 N Canyons Pkwy # 201 Livermore (94551) ***(P-26666)***
The Nevell Group Inc (PA) ....C.......714 579-7501
3001 Enterprise St # 200 Brea (92821) ***(P-1673)***
The Newly Wed, Culver City *Also called Avoca Productions Inc* ***(P-18022)***
The Orthopedic Institute of ....A.......213 977-2010
616 Witmer St Los Angeles (90017) ***(P-20005)***
The Peninsula Beverly Hills, Beverly Hills *Also called Hong Kong & Shanghai Hotels* ***(P-12699)***
The Pines Ltd ....C.......619 447-1880
1423 E Washington Ave El Cajon (92019) ***(P-11125)***
The Redwoods A Cmnty Seniors ....C.......415 383-2741
40 Camino Alto Ofc Mill Valley (94941) ***(P-24697)***
The Residence, Encino *Also called Actual Reality Pictures Inc* ***(P-11190)***
The Sterling Hotel, Sacramento *Also called Elizabethan Inn Associates LP* ***(P-12554)***
The Team Companies LLC (PA) ....D.......818 558-3261
901 W Alameda Ave Ste 100 Burbank (91506) ***(P-26302)***
The Teecor Group Inc ....D.......213 632-2350
1450 S Burlington Ave Los Angeles (90006) ***(P-3593)***
The Tristaff Group, San Diego *Also called Garich Inc* ***(P-14624)***
The Valley Club of Montecito ....E.......805 969-2215
1901 E Valley Rd Santa Barbara (93108) ***(P-19068)***
The Valley Inn, Holtville *Also called Sunharbor Management LLC* ***(P-24692)***

Mergent e-mail: customerrelations@mergent.com
1492
2019 Directory of California
Wholesalers and Services Companies
(P-0000) Products & Services Section entry number
(PA)=Parent Co (HQ)=Headquarters (DH)=Div Headquarters

The Villa Florence Hotel, San Francisco *Also called Florence Villa Hotel* ***(P-12578)***
The Woodbridge Golf Cntry CLB ....D....209 369-2371
800 E Woodbridge Rd Woodbridge (95258) ***(P-19069)***
Theat and Arts Found of San Di ....C....858 623-3366
2910 La Jolla Village Dr La Jolla (92093) ***(P-25268)***
Thefloorstore/Flor Stor, Laguna Hills *Also called Tom Ray Industries Inc* ***(P-6794)***
Thera Home Care, Redwood City *Also called Zb Rehab Staffing Inc* ***(P-14947)***
Therapak LLC (HQ) ....D....909 267-2000
651 Wharton Dr Claremont (91711) ***(P-7223)***
Therapeutic Associates Inc ....D....818 748-4900
181 S Buena Vista St Burbank (91505) ***(P-22055)***
Therapeutic Associates Inc ....D....818 843-5111
Saint Joseph Hospital Burbank (91505) ***(P-20207)***
Therapeutic Pathways Inc ....D....916 489-1376
2775 Cottage Way Ste 8 Sacramento (95825) ***(P-20208)***
Therapy & Rehabilitation Ctrs, Simi Valley *Also called Simi Vly Hosp & Hlth Care Svcs* ***(P-20204)***
Therapy For Kids Inc ....E....714 870-6116
233 Orangefair Mall Fullerton (92832) ***(P-20209)***
Therapy In Your Home O TP TS ....D....408 358-0201
147 Vista Del Monte Los Gatos (95030) ***(P-22435)***
Therastaff Inc ....C....858 569-7555
2355 Northside Dr Ste 140 San Diego (92108) ***(P-14921)***
Therm Pacific, Commerce *Also called Hkf Inc* ***(P-7651)***
Thermal Air, Anaheim *Also called General Engineering Wstn Inc* ***(P-2219)***
Thermal Mechanical ....D....408 988-8744
425 Aldo Ave Santa Clara (95054) ***(P-2384)***
Thermalair Inc (HQ) ....D....714 630-3200
1140 N Red Gum St Anaheim (92806) ***(P-2385)***
Thermasource LLC (PA) ....D....707 523-2960
150 Post St Ste 400 San Francisco (94108) ***(P-25951)***
Thermo Power Industries ....E....562 799-0087
10570 Humbolt St Los Alamitos (90720) ***(P-2968)***
THETRADEDESK, Ventura *Also called Trade Desk Inc* ***(P-15509)***
Thiara Sukhwant ....E....530 673-1581
1537 Atkinson Ct Yuba City (95993) ***(P-469)***
Thiara Orchards, Yuba City *Also called Thiara Sukhwant* ***(P-469)***
Thiel Capital LLC (PA) ....D....415 567-7360
1 Letterman Dr Ste 400 San Francisco (94129) ***(P-27488)***
Think Passenger Inc (PA) ....D....323 556-5400
12100 Wilshire Blvd # 1950 Los Angeles (90025) ***(P-15501)***
Think Together ....A....562 236-3835
12016 Telegraph Rd Santa Fe Springs (90670) ***(P-18670)***
Think Together ....A....909 723-1400
202 E Airport Dr Ste 200 San Bernardino (92408) ***(P-24391)***
Think Together ....A....626 373-2311
800 S Barranca Ave # 120 Covina (91723) ***(P-24392)***
Think Together ....A....951 571-9944
22620 Goldencrest Dr # 104 Moreno Valley (92553) ***(P-24393)***
Thinkom Solutions Inc ....C....310 371-5486
4881 W 145th St Hawthorne (90250) ***(P-6001)***
Thinkwell Group Inc ....D....818 333-3444
2710 Media Center Dr Los Angeles (90065) ***(P-18408)***
Third & Mission Associates LLC ....E....415 341-8457
680 Mission St San Francisco (94105) ***(P-11794)***
Thirdwave Technology Services ....E....310 563-2160
4054 Del Rey Ave Ste 207 Marina Del Rey (90292) ***(P-16294)***
Thismoment Inc ....C....415 200-4730
690 Market St Unit 1101 San Francisco (94104) ***(P-15502)***
Thoits Insurance Service Inc ....D....408 792-5400
444 Castro St Ste 200 Mountain View (94041) ***(P-10800)***
Thom Sharon & G Enterprises ....E....530 226-8350
2620 Larkspur Ln Ste N Redding (96002) ***(P-22436)***
Thoma Bravo LLC ....B....415 263-3660
600 Montgomery St Fl 32 San Francisco (94111) ***(P-12275)***
Thoma Electric Co, San Luis Obispo *Also called Thoma Electric Inc* ***(P-2767)***
Thoma Electric Inc ....D....805 543-3850
3562 Empleo St Ste C San Luis Obispo (93401) ***(P-2767)***
Thomas Crane and Trckg Co Inc ....E....562 592-2837
18851 Stewart Ln Huntington Beach (92648) ***(P-2068)***
Thomas Doll & Company, Walnut Creek *Also called Thomas Wirig Doll & Co Cpas* ***(P-26303)***
Thomas Edward Companies (PA) ....C....310 859-9366
9950 Santa Monica Blvd Beverly Hills (90212) ***(P-13325)***
Thomas Gallaway Corporation (PA) ....D....949 716-9500
100 Spectrum Center Dr # 700 Irvine (92618) ***(P-7115)***
Thomas J Hoban (PA) ....E....619 442-1665
215 W Lexington Ave El Cajon (92020) ***(P-11795)***
Thomas Kinkade Company, The, Morgan Hill *Also called Pacific Metro LLC* ***(P-9242)***
Thomas M Obinson Jr ....D....559 432-6200
7480 N Palm Ave Ste 101 Fresno (93711) ***(P-11796)***
Thomas Mark & Company Inc (PA) ....E....408 453-5373
2290 N 1st St Ste 304 San Jose (95131) ***(P-25952)***
Thomas Weisel Partners LLC (HQ) ....B....415 364-2500
1 Montgomery St Ste 3700 San Francisco (94104) ***(P-10021)***
Thomas Wirig Doll & Co Cpas ....D....925 939-2500
165 Lennon Ln Ste 200 Walnut Creek (94598) ***(P-26303)***
Thomason Tractor Co California ....E....559 659-2039
985 12th St Firebaugh (93622) ***(P-7714)***
Thompson & Colegate LLP ....E....951 682-5550
3610 14th St Lowr Riverside (92501) ***(P-23408)***
Thompson & Rich Crane Service ....E....209 465-3161
2373 E Mariposa Rd Stockton (95205) ***(P-17507)***
Thompson Builders Corporation ....C....415 456-8972
250 Bel Marin Keys Blvd A Novato (94949) ***(P-1319)***
Thompson Building Materials, Orange *Also called Valori Sand & Gravel Company* ***(P-6911)***
Thompson Building Materials, Fontana *Also called Valori Sand & Gravel Company* ***(P-6912)***
Thompson Building Mtls Inc ....E....619 287-9410
6618 Federal Blvd Lemon Grove (91945) ***(P-6908)***
Thompson Cnstr Sup Door Frame, Corona *Also called Fennel Inc* ***(P-3035)***
Thompson Coburn LLP ....B....310 282-2500
2029 Century Park E # 1900 Los Angeles (90067) ***(P-23409)***
Thompson Family Farms LLC ....E....714 848-7536
16478 Beach Blvd Ste 391 Westminster (92683) ***(P-387)***
Thomson Reuters (legal) Inc ....D....650 210-1900
2440 W El Camino Real Mountain View (94040) ***(P-27884)***
Thomson Reuters (legal) Inc ....D....415 344-6000
50 California St Ste 200 San Francisco (94111) ***(P-27885)***
Thomson Reuters (markets) LLC ....D....415 677-2500
1 Sansome St San Francisco (94104) ***(P-17508)***
Thor Inc (PA) ....D....310 727-1777
318 Avenue I Redondo Beach (90277) ***(P-14780)***
Thor Agency, Redondo Beach *Also called Thor Inc* ***(P-14780)***
Thor Group Inc (PA) ....E....310 727-1777
318 Avenue I Redondo Beach (90277) ***(P-14781)***
Thoreau Janitorial Svcs Inc ....C....310 822-8017
5120 W Goldleaf Cir # 10 Los Angeles (90056) ***(P-14406)***
Thoreau Services Nationwide, Los Angeles *Also called Thoreau Janitorial Svcs Inc* ***(P-14406)***
Thornton and Thomasetti, San Francisco *Also called Michael Cardellini* ***(P-25822)***
Thornton Tomasetti Inc ....D....415 365-6900
650 California St Fl 14 San Francisco (94108) ***(P-25953)***
Thorpe Design Inc ....D....925 634-0787
410 Beatrice St Ct Ste A Brentwood (94513) ***(P-2386)***
Thorsens Inc ....D....209 524-5296
2310 N Walnut Rd Turlock (95382) ***(P-3206)***
Thorsens Plumbing & AC, Turlock *Also called Thorsens Inc* ***(P-3206)***
Thorsnes Bartolotta & McGuire ....D....619 236-9363
2550 5th Ave Ste 1100 San Diego (92103) ***(P-23410)***
Thosand Oaks 145 Hodencamp, Thousand Oaks *Also called Kaiser Foundation Hospitals* ***(P-19588)***
Thoughtful Asia Limited, Sherman Oaks *Also called Thoughtful Media Group Inc* ***(P-13957)***
Thoughtful Media Group Inc ....D....818 465-7500
14724 Ventura Blvd # 1110 Sherman Oaks (91403) ***(P-13957)***
Thousand Oaks 322 E Thousand, Thousand Oaks *Also called Kaiser Foundation Hospitals* ***(P-19590)***
Thousand Oaks Health Care Ctr, Thousand Oaks *Also called Five Star Quality Care Inc* ***(P-20432)***
Thousand Oaks Prtg & Spc Inc ....C....818 706-8330
5334 Sterling Center Dr Westlake Village (91361) ***(P-17509)***
Thousand Oaks Service Center, Thousand Oaks *Also called Southern California Edison Co* ***(P-6126)***
Thousand Oaks Surgical Hosp LP ....D....805 777-7750
401 Rolling Oaks Dr Thousand Oaks (91361) ***(P-21857)***
Thousand Trails Inc ....E....209 962-0100
31191 Hardin Flat Rd Groveland (95321) ***(P-13469)***
Thousandeyes Inc (PA) ....D....415 513-4526
201 Mission St Ste 1700 San Francisco (94105) ***(P-15878)***
Threatmetrix Inc ....C....408 200-5700
160 W Santa Clara St # 1400 San Jose (95113) ***(P-15503)***
Three D Electric, Benicia *Also called Western Sun Enterprises Inc* ***(P-2788)***
Three Rivers Golf Course, Lawndale *Also called Alondra Golf Course Inc* ***(P-18680)***
Three Sons Inc ....D....562 801-4100
5201 Industry Ave Pico Rivera (90660) ***(P-8631)***
Three Way Logistics Inc (PA) ....D....408 748-3929
42505 Christy St Fremont (94538) ***(P-5179)***
Threesixty Group, Irvine *Also called Merchsource LLC* ***(P-7957)***
Threshold Digital Research Lab ....E....310 452-8885
1649 11th St Santa Monica (90404) ***(P-27489)***
Threshold Technologies Inc ....D....909 606-1666
8352 Kimball Ave Bldg F35 Chino (91708) ***(P-4920)***
Thrifty Car Rental, Newport Beach *Also called Thrifty Rent-A-Car System Inc* ***(P-17651)***
Thrifty Car Rental, Los Angeles *Also called T C R Limited Partnership* ***(P-17649)***
Thrifty Car Rental ....C....877 283-0898
780 Mcdonnell Rd Ste 1 San Francisco (94128) ***(P-17650)***
Thrifty Rent-A-Car System Inc ....E....949 757-0659
3500 Irvine Ave Newport Beach (92660) ***(P-17651)***
Thrive Support Services Inc ....E....925 682-2273
900 Court St Martinez (94553) ***(P-22437)***
Thunder Group Inc (PA) ....E....626 935-1605
780 Nogales St Ste C City of Industry (91748) ***(P-6792)***
Thunder Mountain Enterprises (PA) ....D....916 381-3400
9335 Elder Creek Rd Sacramento (95829) ***(P-3594)***
Thunder Valley Casino, Lincoln *Also called United Auburn Indian Community* ***(P-13353)***
Thunderbird Country Club ....D....760 328-2161
70737 Country Club Dr Rancho Mirage (92270) ***(P-19070)***
Thurston Martin H DDS Ms ....E....858 676-5010
11616 Iberia Pl San Diego (92128) ***(P-20139)***
Thyde Inc (PA) ....C....951 817-2300
300 El Sobrante Rd Corona (92879) ***(P-17510)***
Thyssenkrupp Elevator Corp ....D....510 476-1900
14400 Catalina St San Leandro (94577) ***(P-7809)***
Thyssenkrupp Elevator Corp ....E....510 476-1900
30984 Santana St Hayward (94544) ***(P-7810)***
Thyssenkrupp Elevator Corp ....D....619 596-7220
1965 Gillespie Way # 101 El Cajon (92020) ***(P-17997)***
Thyssenkrupp Elevator Corp ....D....818 847-2568
2850 N California St Burbank (91504) ***(P-7811)***
Thyssenkrupp Elevator Corp ....E....323 278-9888
16290 Shoemaker Ave Cerritos (90703) ***(P-17998)***
TI Limited LLC (PA) ....D....323 877-5991
20335 Ventura Blvd Woodland Hills (91364) ***(P-15879)***
Tibco Software Inc (HQ) ....C....650 846-1000
3307 Hillview Ave Palo Alto (94304) ***(P-15504)***
Tiburcio Vasquez Hlth Ctr Inc (PA) ....E....510 471-5880
33255 9th St Union City (94587) ***(P-20006)***

ALPHABETIC

Employee Codes: A=Over 500 employees, B=251-500
C=101-250, D=51-100, E=50
2019 Directory of California
Wholesalers and Services Companies
© Mergent Inc. 1-800-342-5647
1493

Tiburcio Vasquez Hlth Ctr Inc..........D.......510 471-5907
22331 Mission Blvd Hayward (94541) ***(P-20007)***
Tiburon Inc..........D.......858 799-7000
9477 Waples St Ste 100 San Diego (92121) ***(P-16065)***
Tiburon Hotel LLC..........D.......415 435-5996
1651 Tiburon Blvd Belvedere Tiburon (94920) ***(P-13326)***
Tiburon Peninsula Club Inc..........E.......415 789-7900
1600 Mar West St Belvedere Tiburon (94920) ***(P-19071)***
Tic, Panorama City *Also called Import Collection* ***(P-9224)***
Tic Hotels Inc..........E.......619 238-7577
555 W Ash St San Diego (92101) ***(P-13327)***
Tic World-Wide Corp..........D.......619 233-7500
555 W Ash St San Diego (92101) ***(P-13328)***
Tic Worldwide, San Diego *Also called Tic Hotels Inc* ***(P-13327)***
Tice Oaks Apartments, Walnut Creek *Also called Mp Tice Oaks Associates A CA* ***(P-11621)***
Ticketmaster Entertainment LLC..........A.......800 653-8000
8800 W Sunset Blvd West Hollywood (90069) ***(P-18409)***
Tickets.com, Inc., Costa Mesa *Also called Ticketscom LLC* ***(P-18410)***
Ticketscom LLC (HQ)..........E.......714 327-5400
535 Anton Blvd Ste 250 Costa Mesa (92626) ***(P-18410)***
Ticketswest, Irvine *Also called Paciolan LLC* ***(P-15824)***
Ticketweb LLC..........E.......415 901-0210
685 Market St Ste 200 San Francisco (94105) ***(P-19244)***
Ticor Title Company California..........E.......951 509-0211
4210 Riverwalk Pkwy # 200 Riverside (92505) ***(P-10472)***
Ticor Title Insurance Company (HQ)..........C.......616 302-3121
131 N El Molino Ave Pasadena (91101) ***(P-10473)***
Tidavater Inc..........C.......818 848-4151
2107 W Alameda Ave Burbank (91506) ***(P-17511)***
Tidebreak Inc..........D.......650 289-9869
958 San Leandro Ave # 500 Mountain View (94043) ***(P-7116)***
Tides Inc (PA)..........C.......415 561-6400
1014 Torney Ave Ste 1 San Francisco (94129) ***(P-24849)***
Tides Center..........C.......415 359-9401
124 Turk St San Francisco (94102) ***(P-13329)***
Tides Network..........D.......415 561-6400
The Prsdio 1014 Trney Ave San Francisco (94129) ***(P-24850)***
Tides Shared Spaces, San Francisco *Also called Tides Inc* ***(P-24849)***
Tidwell Excav Acquisition Inc..........D.......805 647-4707
1691 Los Angeles Ave Ventura (93004) ***(P-3442)***
Tierra Del Oro Girl Scout Cnsl..........D.......916 452-9174
6601 Elvas Ave Sacramento (95819) ***(P-25269)***
Tierra Del Sol Foundation (PA)..........C.......818 352-1419
9919 Sunland Blvd Sunland (91040) ***(P-24698)***
Tierra Del Sol Foundation..........D.......909 626-8301
250 W 1st St Ste 120 Claremont (91711) ***(P-19245)***
Tierra Del Soul, Claremont *Also called Tierra Del Sol Foundation* ***(P-19245)***
Tierra Oaks Golf Club Inc..........D.......530 275-0795
19700 La Crescenta Dr Redding (96003) ***(P-19072)***
Tierra Rejada Golf Course, Moorpark *Also called Donovan Bros Golf LLC* ***(P-18707)***
Tifanny Mulhearn Realtors, Cerritos *Also called Mulhearn* ***(P-11622)***
Tiffany Dale Inc (PA)..........D.......714 739-2700
14765 Industry Cir La Mirada (90638) ***(P-6793)***
Tiffanys Liu..........D.......415 644-0846
9465 Wilshire Blvd Beverly Hills (90212) ***(P-24087)***
Tiger Analytics LLC..........D.......408 508-4430
4701 Patrick Henry Dr Santa Clara (95054) ***(P-26570)***
Tiger Electric Inc (PA)..........D.......714 529-8061
650 N Berry St Brea (92821) ***(P-2768)***
Tiger Lines LLC (HQ)..........D.......209 334-4100
927 Black Diamond Way Lodi (95240) ***(P-4277)***
Tigerconnect..........E.......310 401-1820
2110 Broadway Santa Monica (90404) ***(P-16512)***
Tile West Inc (PA)..........D.......415 382-7550
11 Hamilton Dr Novato (94949) ***(P-3012)***
Tiller Constructors Partnr Inc..........D.......714 771-5600
306 W Katella Ave Ste A Orange (92867) ***(P-1674)***
Tillster Inc (PA)..........D.......858 784-0800
5959 Cornerstone Ct W # 100 San Diego (92121) ***(P-16513)***
Tim Hofer Inc..........C.......559 732-6676
148 N Akers St Visalia (93291) ***(P-14407)***
Tim Mello Construction..........E.......530 205-8588
464 Lamarque Ct Grass Valley (95945) ***(P-1246)***
Tim Paxins Pacific Excavation..........E.......916 686-2800
9796 Kent St Elk Grove (95624) ***(P-3443)***
TIMBER CREEK GOLF COURSE, Roseville *Also called Sun City Rsvlle Cmnty Assn Inc* ***(P-18769)***
Timber Ridge At Eureka, Eureka *Also called Western Living Concepts Inc* ***(P-24719)***
Timber Works Construction Inc..........C.......916 786-6666
7031 Roseville Rd Ste A Sacramento (95842) ***(P-1247)***
Timberlake Painting, Murrieta *Also called Temecula Valley Drywall Inc* ***(P-2967)***
Timco, Fontana *Also called Tst Inc* ***(P-4073)***
Time and Alarm Systems (PA)..........D.......951 685-1761
3828 Wacker Dr Mira Loma (91752) ***(P-2769)***
Time Financial Services, Woodland Hills *Also called Ramkade Insurance Services* ***(P-10755)***
Time Inc..........D.......415 982-5000
2 Embarcadero Ctr # 1900 San Francisco (94111) ***(P-13958)***
Time Inc..........C.......310 268-7200
11766 Wilshire Blvd # 1700 Los Angeles (90025) ***(P-13959)***
Time Warner, Burbank *Also called Historic TW Inc* ***(P-18061)***
Time Warner, Temecula *Also called Spectrum MGT Holdg Co LLC* ***(P-5935)***
Time Warner, San Bernardino *Also called Spectrum MGT Holdg Co LLC* ***(P-5936)***
Time Warner, Lancaster *Also called Warner Media LLC* ***(P-5966)***
Time Warner, Simi Valley *Also called Warner Media LLC* ***(P-5967)***
Time Warner, Cypress *Also called Spectrum MGT Holdg Co LLC* ***(P-5941)***
Time Warner, Garden Grove *Also called Spectrum MGT Holdg Co LLC* ***(P-5942)***
Time Warner, El Segundo *Also called Spectrum MGT Holdg Co LLC* ***(P-5943)***
Time Warner, Anaheim *Also called Spectrum MGT Holdg Co LLC* ***(P-5946)***
Time Warner Cable Entps LLC..........D.......818 972-0808
3500 W Olive Ave Ste 1000 Burbank (91505) ***(P-18132)***
Time Warner Cable Entps LLC..........C.......323 993-7076
1438 N Gower St Los Angeles (90028) ***(P-5948)***
Time Warner Cable Entps LLC..........A.......469 665-7735
550 Continental Blvd # 250 El Segundo (90245) ***(P-5949)***
Time Warner Cable Entps LLC..........C.......818 953-3283
3300 Warner Blvd Burbank (91505) ***(P-5950)***
Time Warner Cable Inc..........D.......619 346-4573
3051 Clairemont Dr San Diego (92117) ***(P-5951)***
Time Warner Cable Inc..........D.......888 892-2253
118 N 8th St Santa Paula (93060) ***(P-5952)***
Time Warner Cable Inc..........D.......805 214-1353
2323 Teller Rd Newbury Park (91320) ***(P-5953)***
Time Warner Cable Inc..........B.......858 695-3220
10450 Pacific Center Ct San Diego (92121) ***(P-5954)***
Time Warner Cable Inc..........D.......951 306-3117
660 W Acacia Ave Hemet (92543) ***(P-5955)***
Time Warner Cable Inc..........C.......424 529-6011
500 Lakewood Center Mall Lakewood (90712) ***(P-5956)***
Time Warner Cable Inc..........D.......626 705-7482
15255 Salt Lake Ave City of Industry (91745) ***(P-5957)***
Time Warner Cable Inc..........D.......760 256-3526
1881 W Main St Barstow (92311) ***(P-5958)***
Time Warner Cable Inc..........B.......323 993-8000
900 N Cahuenga Blvd Los Angeles (90038) ***(P-5959)***
Time Warner Cable Inc..........B.......858 695-3110
8949 Ware Ct San Diego (92121) ***(P-5960)***
Time Warner Cable Inc..........D.......760 335-4800
313 N 8th St El Centro (92243) ***(P-5961)***
Time Warner Media Sales, Cypress *Also called Spectrum MGT Holdg Co LLC* ***(P-5932)***
Timec Acquisitions Inc (HQ)..........A.......707 642-2222
155 Corporate Pl Vallejo (94590) ***(P-2069)***
Timec Companies Inc (HQ)..........B.......707 642-2222
155 Corporate Pl Vallejo (94590) ***(P-2070)***
Timelogic, Carlsbad *Also called Active Motif Inc* ***(P-26311)***
Timeshare Relief Inc..........C.......951 525-1539
15435 Park Point Ave # 106 Lake Elsinore (92532) ***(P-11849)***
Timmerman Starlite Trckg Inc..........D.......209 538-1706
3955 Starlite Dr Ceres (95307) ***(P-4278)***
Timothy Everitt..........E.......805 214-9933
1000 Newbury Rd Ste 135 Newbury Park (91320) ***(P-20210)***
Tinco Sheet Metal Inc..........D.......323 263-0511
958 N Eastern Ave Los Angeles (90063) ***(P-3207)***
Tintri Inc..........B.......650 810-8200
303 Ravendale Dr Mountain View (94043) ***(P-16253)***
Tire & Wheel Master Inc..........D.......209 465-9000
3745 Petersen Rd Stockton (95215) ***(P-6696)***
Tire Centers West LLC..........C.......909 854-1200
10516 Commerce Way # 875 Fontana (92337) ***(P-6697)***
Tireco Inc (PA)..........C.......310 767-7990
500 W 190th St Ste 100 Gardena (90248) ***(P-6698)***
Tishman Construction Corp Cal..........D.......213 542-6400
444 S Flower St Ste 2500 Los Angeles (90071) ***(P-27062)***
Titan Pulse Sciences Division, San Leandro *Also called Engility LLC* ***(P-25664)***
Titan Sheet Metal Inc..........C.......951 372-1362
180 Vander St Corona (92880) ***(P-3208)***
Titan Solar, Woodland Hills *Also called Memeged Tevuot Shemesh* ***(P-2277)***
Titan Solar Construction..........C.......866 575-1211
6711 Valjean Ave Van Nuys (91406) ***(P-2387)***
Title Boy, Venice *Also called Prologue Films* ***(P-14126)***
Title Records Inc..........D.......818 767-9610
8926 Sunland Blvd Sun Valley (91352) ***(P-11850)***
Tj Cross Engineers Inc..........C.......661 831-8782
200 New Stine Rd Ste 270 Bakersfield (93309) ***(P-25954)***
Tjd LLC..........C.......209 357-3420
1685 Shaffer Rd Atwater (95301) ***(P-21229)***
Tk Carsites Inc..........D.......714 937-1239
2975 Red Hill Ave Ste 175 Costa Mesa (92626) ***(P-15505)***
Tka, La Palma *Also called Tech Knowledge Associates LLC* ***(P-17994)***
TLC Child & Family Services (PA)..........C.......707 823-7300
1800 Gravenstein Hwy N Sebastopol (95472) ***(P-24699)***
TLC of Bay Area Inc..........D.......408 988-7667
991 Clyde Ave Santa Clara (95054) ***(P-20838)***
Tlcs Inc..........D.......916 441-0123
650 Howe Ave Ste 400 Sacramento (95825) ***(P-24088)***
Tlg, Newark *Also called Lancashire Group Incorporated* ***(P-27298)***
Tm Financial Forensics LLC (PA)..........E.......415 692-6350
2 Embarcadero Ctr # 2510 San Francisco (94111) ***(P-27886)***
Tm Motion Picture Eqp Rentals, Manhattan Beach *Also called Mbs Equipment Company* ***(P-18200)***
TMI, San Jose *Also called Traffic Management Inc* ***(P-17515)***
Tmp Worldwide Advertising & Co..........D.......818 539-2000
330 N Brand Blvd Ste 1050 Glendale (91203) ***(P-13910)***
Tms America, Torrance *Also called Total Management Svcs Amer Inc* ***(P-14782)***
TMT Industries Inc..........D.......909 493-3441
8978 Haven Ave Rancho Cucamonga (91730) ***(P-4279)***
Tmx Engineering LLC..........D.......714 641-5884
2141 S Standard Ave Santa Ana (92707) ***(P-25955)***
Tnci Operating Company LLC (HQ)..........D.......800 800-8400
114 E Haley St Ste I Santa Barbara (93101) ***(P-5654)***
TNT Express Worldwide, Los Angeles *Also called TNT USA Inc* ***(P-4846)***
TNT Grading Inc..........D.......760 736-4054
529 W 4th Ave B Escondido (92025) ***(P-1861)***
TNT Originals, Burbank *Also called Turner Broadcasting System Inc* ***(P-18138)***
TNT USA Inc..........D.......310 242-9700
8500 Osage Ave Los Angeles (90045) ***(P-4846)***

Mergent e-mail: customerrelations@mergent.com
1494
2019 Directory of California
Wholesalers and Services Companies
(P-0000) Products & Services Section entry number
(PA)=Parent Co (HQ)=Headquarters (DH)=Div Headquarters

To Help Everyone Health & Weln, Los Angeles *Also called Clinic Inc* ***(P-22532)***
Toad 1350..........E.......951 369-1350
2030 Iowa Ave Ste A Riverside (92507) ***(P-5754)***
Tobin Lucks, Woodland Hills *Also called Joseph C Sansone Company* ***(P-23156)***
Todays Hotel Corporation (PA)..........C.......415 441-4000
1500 Van Ness Ave San Francisco (94109) ***(P-13330)***
Todays Vi LLC..........D.......909 980-2200
4760 Mills Cir Ontario (91764) ***(P-13331)***
Tofasco of America Inc (PA)..........D.......909 392-8282
1661 Fairplex Dr La Verne (91750) ***(P-27063)***
Toiyabe Indian Health Prj Inc (PA)..........C.......760 873-8461
250 N See Vee Ln Bishop (93514) ***(P-20140)***
Tokai Intl Holdings Inc (PA)..........E.......909 930-5000
2055 S Haven Ave Ontario (91761) ***(P-12010)***
Tokio Marine Management Inc..........C.......626 568-7600
800 E Colorado Blvd Ste 8 Pasadena (91101) ***(P-10801)***
Toll Brothers Inc..........D.......925 855-0260
6800 Koll Center Pkwy # 320 Pleasanton (94566) ***(P-1248)***
Toll Brothers Division Office, Pleasanton *Also called Toll Brothers Inc* ***(P-1248)***
Toll Global Fwdg Scs USA Inc..........D.......951 360-8310
3355 Dulles Dr Mira Loma (91752) ***(P-5180)***
Tollhouse Hotel, Los Gatos *Also called Trevi Partners A Calif LP* ***(P-13341)***
Tom Ferry Your Coach, Irvine *Also called Success Strategies Inst Inc* ***(P-24235)***
Tom Hom Investment Corp..........D.......858 456-5000
7660 Fay Ave Ste H La Jolla (92037) ***(P-10956)***
Tom Malloy Corporation (PA)..........E.......310 327-5554
636 E Rosecrans Ave Los Angeles (90059) ***(P-7697)***
Tom Ray, Sacramento *Also called T M Cobb Company* ***(P-6868)***
Tom Ray Industries Inc..........D.......949 380-8333
23182 Alcalde Dr Ste G Laguna Hills (92653) ***(P-6794)***
Tom Sawyer Camps Inc..........C.......626 794-1156
707 W Woodbury Rd Ste F Altadena (91001) ***(P-24394)***
Tomarco Contractor Spc Inc (PA)..........D.......714 523-1771
14848 Northam St La Mirada (90638) ***(P-7606)***
Tomarco Fastening Systems, La Mirada *Also called Tomarco Contractor Spc Inc* ***(P-7606)***
Tomas Jewelry, Arcata *Also called Toucan Inc* ***(P-8015)***
Tomatoes Extraordinaire Inc..........C.......619 295-3172
1929 Hancock St Ste 150 San Diego (92110) ***(P-8738)***
Tommy Bahama Group Inc..........C.......805 482-8868
610 Ventura Blvd Ste 1340 Camarillo (93010) ***(P-17512)***
Tommy Bahama Group Inc..........C.......415 737-0400
1720 Redwood Hwy Spc A019 Corte Madera (94925) ***(P-17513)***
Tommy Gun Plastering Inc..........D.......909 795-9966
944 4th St Calimesa (92320) ***(P-2969)***
Tomra Recycling Network, Rancho Cucamonga *Also called Replanet LLC* ***(P-6450)***
Tonal Systems Inc..........D.......855 698-6625
325 Vermont St San Francisco (94103) ***(P-19246)***
Toner Supply USA Inc..........E.......818 504-6540
8055 Lankershim Blvd # 11 North Hollywood (91605) ***(P-7117)***
Toni & Guy Hairdressing (PA)..........D.......949 721-1666
1177 Newport Center Dr Newport Beach (92660) ***(P-13674)***
Tonner Hills Hsing Partners LP..........E.......949 263-8676
17701 Cowan Ste 200 Irvine (92614) ***(P-1320)***
Tonopah Solar Energy LLC..........D.......310 315-2200
520 Broadway Fl 6 Santa Monica (90401) ***(P-2388)***
Tony Gomez Tree Service..........D.......619 593-1552
700 N Johnson Ave Ste H El Cajon (92020) ***(P-979)***
Tony La Russas Animal RES Fnd..........D.......925 256-1273
2890 Mitchell Dr Walnut Creek (94598) ***(P-610)***
Tony Marquez Pool Plst Inc..........D.......818 833-5872
14960 Foothill Blvd Sylmar (91342) ***(P-2970)***
Tony R Crisalli Inc..........E.......951 727-0110
3468 Campbell St Riverside (92509) ***(P-14459)***
Tonys Express Inc (PA)..........C.......909 427-8700
10613 Jasmine St Fontana (92337) ***(P-4280)***
Tonys Fine Foods (HQ)..........B.......916 374-4000
3575 Reed Ave West Sacramento (95605) ***(P-8632)***
Too Good Gourmet Inc (PA)..........D.......510 317-8150
2380 Grant Ave San Lorenzo (94580) ***(P-8885)***
Toolwire Inc..........D.......925 227-8500
7031 Koll Center Pkwy # 220 Pleasanton (94566) ***(P-15506)***
Toolworks Inc..........B.......510 649-1322
3075 Adeline St Ste 230 Berkeley (94703) ***(P-24089)***
Toolworks Inc (PA)..........D.......415 733-0990
25 Kearny St Ste 400 San Francisco (94108) ***(P-24238)***
Toot Sweets Fine Desserts, Berkeley *Also called Toot Sweets Ltd* ***(P-8886)***
Toot Sweets Ltd (PA)..........E.......510 526-0610
1277 Gilman St Berkeley (94706) ***(P-8886)***
Top Finance Company, Chatsworth *Also called Platinum Group Companies Inc* ***(P-12000)***
Top of Market..........B.......619 234-4867
750 N Harbor Dr San Diego (92101) ***(P-27064)***
Top Priority Couriers Inc (PA)..........D.......951 781-1000
1257 Columbia Ave Ste D1 Riverside (92507) ***(P-4437)***
Top Seed Tennis Academy Inc..........D.......818 222-2782
23400 Park Sorrento Calabasas (91302) ***(P-19247)***
Top Tier Consulting..........D.......818 338-2121
21550 Oxnard St Fl 3 Woodland Hills (91367) ***(P-27490)***
Topa Berkeley Ltd..........D.......310 203-9199
1800 Avenue Of The Stars Los Angeles (90067) ***(P-11797)***
Topa Insurance Company (HQ)..........D.......310 201-0451
1800 Ave Of Stars # 1200 Los Angeles (90067) ***(P-10505)***
Topa Management Company (PA)..........C.......310 203-9199
1800 Avenue Of The Stars # 1400 Los Angeles (90067) ***(P-10957)***
Topanga Productions Inc..........E.......310 244-4000
10202 Wash Blvd Ste 1132 Culver City (90232) ***(P-18133)***
Topanga Villas Company..........D.......818 884-8017
5807 Topanga Canyon Blvd Woodland Hills (91367) ***(P-11126)***
Topbuild Services Group Corp..........D.......408 882-0411
1341 Old Oakland Rd San Jose (95112) ***(P-3595)***
Topco Sales, Simi Valley *Also called Wsm Investments LLC* ***(P-12148)***
Topdown Consulting Inc..........D.......888 644-8445
530 Divisadero St Ste 310 San Francisco (94117) ***(P-27491)***
Topgolf Media LLC (HQ)..........D.......214 377-0615
100 California St Ste 650 San Francisco (94111) ***(P-19248)***
Topica Inc..........D.......415 344-0800
1 Post St Ste 875 San Francisco (94104) ***(P-5655)***
Topocean Consolidation Service (PA)..........C.......562 908-1688
2727 Workman Mill Rd City of Industry (90601) ***(P-5181)***
Tops Auto Parks, Los Angeles *Also called Paramunt Contrs Developers Inc* ***(P-11661)***
Topson Downs California Inc (PA)..........C.......310 558-0300
3840 Watseka Ave Culver City (90232) ***(P-8339)***
Topstar Floral Inc..........E.......805 984-7972
4255 W Gonzales Rd Oxnard (93036) ***(P-306)***
Topwin Corporation (PA)..........D.......310 325-2255
1808 Abalone Ave Torrance (90501) ***(P-8280)***
Toro Enterprises Inc..........D.......805 483-4515
2101 Ventura Blvd Oxnard (93036) ***(P-1862)***
Toro Nursery Inc..........D.......310 715-1982
17585 Crenshaw Blvd Torrance (90504) ***(P-9170)***
Torrance Amateur Rdo Assn Inc..........E.......310 245-0989
2162 248th St Lomita (90717) ***(P-25475)***
Torrance Care Center West Inc..........C.......310 370-4561
4333 Torrance Blvd Torrance (90503) ***(P-20839)***
Torrance Health Assn Inc (PA)..........A.......310 325-9110
3330 Lomita Blvd Torrance (90505) ***(P-21858)***
Torrance Marriott Hotel, Torrance *Also called Xld Group LLC* ***(P-13432)***
Torrance Memorial Medical Ctr, Torrance *Also called Torrance Health Assn Inc* ***(P-21858)***
Torrance Memorial Medical Ctr (HQ)..........A.......310 325-9110
3330 Lomita Blvd Torrance (90505) ***(P-21859)***
Torrance Surgery Center LP..........A.......310 986-2005
23560 Crenshaw Blvd # 104 Torrance (90505) ***(P-20008)***
Torres Construction Corp (PA)..........D.......323 257-7460
1370 N El Molino Ave Pasadena (91104) ***(P-1445)***
Torres Fence Co Inc..........E.......559 237-4141
2357 S Orange Ave Fresno (93725) ***(P-3596)***
Torres General Inc..........D.......619 448-8900
9484 Mission Park Pl Santee (92071) ***(P-1249)***
Torres-Martinez..........C.......760 395-1200
3089 Norm Niver Rd Thermal (92274) ***(P-13332)***
Torrey Aat Point LLC..........D.......858 350-2600
11455 El Camino Real San Diego (92130) ***(P-12190)***
Torrey Pines Bank (HQ)..........C.......858 523-4600
12220 El Camino Real # 200 San Diego (92130) ***(P-9491)***
Torreyana Grille..........D.......858 558-1500
10950 N Torrey Pines Rd La Jolla (92037) ***(P-13333)***
Toscana, Palm Desert *Also called Sunrise Desert Partners* ***(P-11925)***
Toscana Country Club, Palm Desert *Also called Toscana Homes LP* ***(P-1321)***
Toscana Country Club Inc..........C.......760 404-1444
76009 Via Club Villa Indian Wells (92210) ***(P-19073)***
Toscana Homes LP..........E.......760 772-7227
300 Eagle Dance Cir Palm Desert (92211) ***(P-1321)***
Toscana Land LLC..........D.......760 772-7200
300 Eagle Dance Cir Palm Desert (92211) ***(P-11930)***
Toshiba Amer Bus Solutions Inc (HQ)..........B.......949 462-6000
25530 Commercentre Dr Lake Forest (92630) ***(P-6984)***
Toshiba Amer Elctrnic Cmpnents, San Jose *Also called Toshiba Memory America Inc* ***(P-7554)***
Toshiba Bus Solutions USA Inc (HQ)..........C.......949 462-6000
9740 Irvine Blvd Irvine (92618) ***(P-17917)***
Toshiba Education Center..........D.......949 583-3000
9740 Irvine Blvd Irvine (92618) ***(P-26571)***
Toshiba Medical Systems, Tustin *Also called Canon Medical Systems USA Inc* ***(P-7170)***
Toshiba Memory America Inc (HQ)..........C.......408 526-2400
2610 Orchard Pkwy San Jose (95134) ***(P-7554)***
Toshiba Memory America Inc..........E.......916 986-4707
35 Iron Point Cir Ste 100 Folsom (95630) ***(P-26475)***
Tosoh Bioscience Inc..........D.......650 615-4970
6000 Shoreline Ct Ste 101 South San Francisco (94080) ***(P-7224)***
Tosoh USA, South San Francisco *Also called Tosoh Bioscience Inc* ***(P-7224)***
Total Airport Services LLC..........D.......650 358-0144
3537 Branson Dr San Mateo (94403) ***(P-4921)***
Total Building Care Inc..........D.......562 467-8333
21228 Norwalk Blvd Hawaiian Gardens (90716) ***(P-1675)***
TOTAL CLEAN, La Verne *Also called Haaker Equipment Company* ***(P-6596)***
Total Education Solutions Inc (PA)..........A.......323 341-5580
625 Fair Oaks Ave Ste 300 South Pasadena (91030) ***(P-27887)***
Total Hr Management, Pasadena *Also called Strategic Staffing Svcs Inc* ***(P-27473)***
Total Immersion, Los Angeles *Also called Dfusion Software Inc* ***(P-15105)***
Total Intermodal Services Inc (PA)..........E.......562 427-6300
2396 E Sepulveda Blvd Long Beach (90810) ***(P-4742)***
Total Management Svcs Amer Inc..........E.......310 328-0867
21151 S Wstn Ave Ste 139 Torrance (90501) ***(P-14782)***
Total Professional Network..........D.......213 382-5550
3946 Wilshire Blvd Los Angeles (90010) ***(P-14783)***
Total Quality Maintenance Inc..........C.......650 846-4700
895 Commercial St Palo Alto (94303) ***(P-14408)***
Total Renal Care Inc..........E.......925 737-0120
5720 Stoneridge Mall Rd # 160 Pleasanton (94588) ***(P-22491)***
Total Renal Care Inc..........D.......949 930-6882
15271 Laguna Canyon Rd Irvine (92618) ***(P-22492)***
Total Renal Care Inc..........A.......707 556-3637
125 Corporate Pl Ste C Vallejo (94590) ***(P-22493)***
Total Renal Care Inc..........D.......760 947-7405
14135 Main St Ste 501 Hesperia (92345) ***(P-22494)***
Total Tire Recycling, Sacramento *Also called AAA Signs Inc* ***(P-17748)***
Total Trnsp & Dist Inc..........D.......310 603-0467
1551 E Victoria St Carson (90746) ***(P-4378)***

Employee Codes: A=Over 500 employees, B=251-500
C=101-250, D=51-100, E=50
2019 Directory of California
Wholesalers and Services Companies
© Mergent Inc. 1-800-342-5647
1495

Total Trnsp Logistics Inc...D.......951 360-9521
4325 Etiwanda Ave Ste A Mira Loma (91752) ***(P-4281)***
Total Woman...D.......714 993-6003
860 N Rose Dr Placentia (92870) ***(P-18671)***
Total Woman - Glendale, Glendale *Also called Spad Holdings LLC* ***(P-18665)***
Total Woman - Irvine, Irvine *Also called Spad Holdings LLC* ***(P-18662)***
Total Woman - Northridge, Northridge *Also called Spad Holdings LLC* ***(P-18664)***
Total Woman - Placentia, Placentia *Also called Spad Holdings LLC* ***(P-18661)***
Total Woman - Warner Center, Woodland Hills *Also called Spad Holdings LLC* ***(P-18663)***
Total Woman - Westlake Village, Westlake Village *Also called Spad Holdings LLC* ***(P-18659)***
Total-Western Inc...D.......661 589-5200
2811 Fruitvale Ave Ste A Bakersfield (93308) ***(P-1322)***
Total-Western Inc (HQ)...E.......562 220-1450
8049 Somerset Blvd Paramount (90723) ***(P-1081)***
Totally Kids Rhbilitation Hosp, Loma Linda *Also called Mountain View Child Care Inc* ***(P-21602)***
Totally Kids Spcalty Hlth Care, Sun Valley *Also called Mountain View Child Care Inc* ***(P-24351)***
Totten Tubes Inc (PA)...D.......626 812-0220
500 W Danlee St Azusa (91702) ***(P-7321)***
Toucan Inc (PA)...D.......707 822-6662
824 L St Unit 6 Arcata (95521) ***(P-8015)***
Touch-Up Inc...C.......818 994-6166
7116 Valjean Ave Van Nuys (91406) ***(P-2971)***
Touchstone Television Prod LLC (PA)...E.......323 671-5116
500 S Buena Vista St Burbank (91521) ***(P-18134)***
Tough2beat Auto Sales, Granada Hills *Also called Errama Trucking Company Inc* ***(P-4136)***
Tour Master, Calabasas Hills *Also called Helmet House Inc* ***(P-8263)***
Tourcoach Transportation, Commerce *Also called Screamline Investment Corp* ***(P-4980)***
Tourdates.com, San Francisco *Also called Launch Media Inc* ***(P-5593)***
Tournesol Siteworks LLC (PA)...D.......800 542-2282
2930 Faber St Union City (94587) ***(P-3597)***
Toward Maximum Independence (PA)...C.......858 467-0600
4740 Murphy Canyon Rd # 300 San Diego (92123) ***(P-24090)***
Towbes Group Inc (PA)...D.......805 962-2121
21 E Victoria St Ste 200 Santa Barbara (93101) ***(P-11931)***
Tower Car Wash, San Francisco *Also called Vladigor Investment Inc* ***(P-17842)***
Tower Energy Group (PA)...D.......310 538-8000
1983 W 190th St Ste 100 Torrance (90504) ***(P-8969)***
Tower Glass Inc...D.......619 596-6199
9570 Pathway St Ste A Santee (92071) ***(P-3411)***
Tower Hematology Oncology Medi...D.......310 888-8680
9090 Wilshire Blvd # 200 Beverly Hills (90211) ***(P-20009)***
Tower Park Marina, Lodi *Also called Westrec Marina Management Inc* ***(P-4752)***
Tower St John Imaging, Los Angeles *Also called Santa Mnica Wlshire Imging LLC* ***(P-22141)***
Tower- Imaging Roxanne, Beverly Hills *Also called Beverly Radiology Med Group* ***(P-19323)***
Towmaster Tire & Wheel, Anaheim *Also called Greenball Corp* ***(P-6692)***
Town & Country Event Rentals (PA)...B.......818 908-4211
7725 Airport Bus Pkwy Van Nuys (91406) ***(P-14549)***
Town & Country Event Rentals...B.......805 770-5729
1 N Calle Cesar Chavez # 7 Santa Barbara (93103) ***(P-17514)***
Town & Country Manor of The Ch...C.......714 547-7581
555 E Memory Ln Ofc Ofc Santa Ana (92706) ***(P-20840)***
Town & Country Roofing, Brentwood *Also called T&C Roofing Inc* ***(P-3204)***
Town Cats Morgan Hill Rescue...E.......408 779-5761
195 San Pedro Ave Ste B Morgan Hill (95037) ***(P-634)***
Towne Inc...D.......714 540-3095
3441 W Macarthur Blvd Santa Ana (92704) ***(P-14065)***
Towne Advertising, Santa Ana *Also called Towne Inc* ***(P-14065)***
Towne Construction Inc...D.......619 390-4557
12115 Lakeside Ave Lakeside (92040) ***(P-2972)***
TownePlace Suites...D.......408 370-4510
700 E Campbell Ave Campbell (95008) ***(P-13334)***
TownePlace Suites By Marriott, Campbell *Also called TownePlace Suites* ***(P-13334)***
Towns End Studios LLC...A.......415 802-7936
699 8th St San Francisco (94103) ***(P-15507)***
Toyo Tire USA Corp...E.......562 431-6502
2151 S Vintage Ave Ontario (91761) ***(P-6699)***
Toyon Research Corporation (PA)...D.......805 968-6787
6800 Cortona Dr Goleta (93117) ***(P-25956)***
Toyota Logistics Services...C.......619 531-0157
1340 Cesar E Chavez Pkwy San Diego (92113) ***(P-17876)***
Toyota Logistics Services (HQ)...C.......310 618-5009
19001 S Western Ave Torrance (90501) ***(P-17877)***
Toyota Logistics Services...B.......562 437-6767
785 Edison Ave Long Beach (90813) ***(P-17878)***
Toyota Material Hdlg Nthrn Cal, Livermore *Also called Rjms Corporation* ***(P-7794)***
Toyota Research Institute Inc...D.......703 231-6680
4440 El Camino Real Los Altos (94022) ***(P-26667)***
Toyota-Sunnyvale Inc (PA)...C.......408 245-6640
898 W El Camino Real Sunnyvale (94087) ***(P-17789)***
Toyotalift Inc (PA)...E.......619 562-5438
1850 John Towers Ave El Cajon (92020) ***(P-7812)***
TPC Stonebrea, Hayward *Also called Stonebrae LP* ***(P-19064)***
Tpd Dell Dios...E.......760 741-2888
1817 Avenida Del Diablo Escondido (92029) ***(P-24091)***
Tpg La Commerce LLC...D.......401 946-4600
5757 Telegraph Rd Commerce (90040) ***(P-13335)***
Tpg Reflections II LLC...D.......213 613-1900
515 S Flower St Los Angeles (90071) ***(P-11127)***
Tpg Sixth Street Partners LLC...C.......415 743-1500
345 California St Ste 330 San Francisco (94104) ***(P-10117)***
Tpg/Calstrs, Los Angeles *Also called Tpg Reflections II LLC* ***(P-11127)***
Tps Aviation Inc (PA)...C.......510 475-1010
1515 Crocker Ave Hayward (94544) ***(P-7916)***
Tps Parking Management LLC...D.......310 846-4747
9101 S Sepulveda Blvd Los Angeles (90045) ***(P-17708)***
Tpx Communications, Los Angeles *Also called US Telepacific Corp* ***(P-5659)***
Tr Big Sur Management LLC...E.......831 667-4212
48123 Highway 1 Big Sur (93920) ***(P-13336)***
Tr Warner Center LP...B.......818 887-4800
21850 Oxnard St Woodland Hills (91367) ***(P-13337)***
Trace3 Inc...D.......310 220-0164
2120 E Grand Ave Ste 145 El Segundo (90245) ***(P-27492)***
Trace3 LLC (PA)...D.......949 333-2300
7565 Irvine Center Dr Irvine (92618) ***(P-27493)***
Trackr Inc...D.......855 981-1690
7410 Hollister Ave Santa Barbara (93117) ***(P-15508)***
Tracy Bancshares Inc...D.......209 836-5111
1003 N Central Ave Tracy (95376) ***(P-9531)***
Tracy Dlta Solid Waste Mgt Inc...D.......209 835-0601
30703 S Macarthur Dr Tracy (95377) ***(P-6483)***
Tracy Industries, Ontario *Also called Genuine Parts Distributors* ***(P-6642)***
Tracy Interfaith Ministries...D.......209 836-5424
311 W Grant Line Rd Tracy (95376) ***(P-24092)***
Tracy Medical Offices, Tracy *Also called Kaiser Foundation Hospitals* ***(P-19538)***
Tracy Sutter Community Hosp...B.......209 835-1500
1420 N Tracy Blvd Tracy (95376) ***(P-21860)***
Tracy Trujillo MD...E.......925 838-6511
200 Porter Dr Ste 300 San Ramon (94583) ***(P-20010)***
Trade Desk Inc (PA)...D.......805 585-3434
42 N Chestnut St Ventura (93001) ***(P-15509)***
Trade Services E2002-031, El Monte *Also called Wells Fargo Bank National Assn* ***(P-9389)***
Tradebeam Inc...D.......650 653-4800
303 Twin Dolphin Dr # 600 Redwood City (94065) ***(P-16514)***
Tradecom Med Transcription Inc...C.......408 225-9200
363 Piercy Rd San Jose (95138) ***(P-7225)***
Trademark Concrete Systems (PA)...E.......714 970-8200
4561 E Eisenhower Cir Anaheim (92807) ***(P-3337)***
Tradeshift Holdings Inc (HQ)...D.......800 381-3585
612 Howard St Ste 100 San Francisco (94105) ***(P-12011)***
Tradesmen International LLC...D.......949 588-3280
15500 Rockfield Blvd Irvine (92618) ***(P-27065)***
Tradewind Seafood Inc...E.......805 483-8555
1505 Mountain View Ave Oxnard (93030) ***(P-8606)***
Tradewinds Lodge (PA)...D.......707 964-4761
400 S Main St Fort Bragg (95437) ***(P-13338)***
Tradewinds Lodge Partnership, Sacramento *Also called Tradewinds Partnership* ***(P-13339)***
Tradewinds Partnership...D.......916 333-5239
2920 Arden Way Ste F1 Sacramento (95825) ***(P-13339)***
Trading Financial Capital, Los Angeles *Also called Trading Financial Credit LLC* ***(P-9727)***
Trading Financial Credit LLC (PA)...E.......213 375-3113
3055 Wilshire Blvd # 530 Los Angeles (90010) ***(P-9727)***
Tradition Golf Club, La Quinta *Also called Chapman Golf Development LLC* ***(P-18887)***
Tradition Golf Club Associates...D.......760 564-3355
78505 Avenue 52 La Quinta (92253) ***(P-18772)***
Traditions Golf LLC...D.......408 323-5200
23600 Mckean Rd San Jose (95141) ***(P-18773)***
Traffic Management Inc...E.......877 763-5999
690 Quinn Ave San Jose (95112) ***(P-17515)***
Traffic Management Inc (PA)...C.......562 595-4278
2435 Lemon Ave Signal Hill (90755) ***(P-17516)***
Traffic Tech Inc...C.......800 396-2531
910 Hale Pl Ste 100 Chula Vista (91914) ***(P-5182)***
Trail Lines Inc...D.......562 758-6980
9415 Sorensen Ave Santa Fe Springs (90670) ***(P-4069)***
Trailblazer Technologies...D.......818 848-6500
4100 W Burbank Blvd Fl 3 Burbank (91505) ***(P-17517)***
Trailer Park Inc...D.......831 462-3271
4300 Soquel Dr Spc 90 Soquel (95073) ***(P-13470)***
Trailer Park Inc...D.......310 845-8400
6922 Hollywood Blvd # 1200 Los Angeles (90028) ***(P-13911)***
Trailer Park Inc (PA)...D.......310 845-3000
6922 Hollywood Blvd Fl 12 Los Angeles (90028) ***(P-13912)***
Traina Dried Fruit Inc...C.......209 892-5472
337 1/2 Lemon Ave Patterson (95363) ***(P-8887)***
Traina Foods, Patterson *Also called Traina Dried Fruit Inc* ***(P-8887)***
Training Toward Self Reliance...E.......916 442-8877
1446 Ethan Way 101 Sacramento (95825) ***(P-24093)***
Trams Inc (HQ)...D.......310 641-8726
5777 W Century Blvd # 1200 Los Angeles (90045) ***(P-16066)***
Trandes Corp...C.......619 398-0464
4250 Pacific Hwy Ste 209 San Diego (92110) ***(P-25957)***
Trane US Inc...D.......916 577-1100
4145 Delmar Ave Ste 2 Rocklin (95677) ***(P-7657)***
Tranquility Incorporated...C.......925 825-4280
1050 San Miguel Rd Concord (94518) ***(P-21230)***
Tranquilmoney Inc...D.......800 979-6739
5823 Ruddy Duck Ct Stockton (95207) ***(P-7118)***
Trans Globe Lighting, Valencia *Also called Bel Air Lighting Inc* ***(P-7338)***
Trans West Investigations Inc...D.......213 381-1500
3255 Wilshire Blvd Los Angeles (90010) ***(P-16836)***
Trans World Maintenance Inc...D.......650 455-2450
1590 Rollins Rd Millbrae (94030) ***(P-2487)***
Trans-Pak Incorporated...C.......310 618-6937
2601 S Garnsey St Santa Ana (92707) ***(P-17518)***
Trans-West Security Svcs Inc...B.......661 381-2900
8503 Crippen St Bakersfield (93311) ***(P-16837)***
Transamerica Cbo I Inc...D.......415 983-4000
600 Montgomery St Fl 16 San Francisco (94111) ***(P-10118)***
Transamerica Finance Corp...D.......714 778-5100
1731 W Medical Center Dr Anaheim (92801) ***(P-10147)***
Transamerica Intl Holdings...C.......415 983-4000
600 Montgomery St Fl 16 San Francisco (94111) ***(P-12012)***

Mergent e-mail: customerrelations@mergent.com
1496
2019 Directory of California
Wholesalers and Services Companies
(P-0000) Products & Services Section entry number
(PA)=Parent Co (HQ)=Headquarters (DH)=Div Headquarters

Transamerica Securities Sales ....D.......213 741-7702
1150 S Olive St Ste T25 Los Angeles (90015) ***(P-10022)***

Transamerican Auto Parts, Banning *Also called Poison Spyder Customs Inc* ***(P-17868)***

Transbay Fire Protection Inc (PA) ....E.......925 846-9484
2182 Rheem Dr Pleasanton (94588) ***(P-3476)***

Transcendent Security Services ....E.......562 850-3313
3553 Atl Ave Ste 1197 Long Beach (90807) ***(P-16838)***

Transcription Company, The, Burbank *Also called Trailblazer Technologies* ***(P-17517)***

Transdev Services Inc ....B.......626 357-7912
5640 Peck Rd Arcadia (91006) ***(P-3853)***

Transer America, Lake Elsinore *Also called Timeshare Relief Inc* ***(P-11849)***

Transforce Inc ....E.......209 952-2573
965 E Yosemite Ave Ste 7 Manteca (95336) ***(P-14922)***

Transiris Corporation ....D.......650 303-3495
555 Airport Blvd Ste 325 Burlingame (94010) ***(P-27494)***

Transit Air Cargo Inc ....D.......714 571-0393
2204 E 4th St Santa Ana (92705) ***(P-5183)***

Transitional Assistance Dept, Yucca Valley *Also called County of San Bernardino* ***(P-23720)***

Transitions - Mental Hlth Assn ....D.......805 614-4940
117 W Tunnell St Santa Maria (93458) ***(P-22698)***

Transitions - Mental Hlth Assn ....D.......805 865-1940
401 E Cypress Ave Lompoc (93436) ***(P-22699)***

Transitions - Mental Hlth Assn (PA) ....D.......805 540-6500
784 High St San Luis Obispo (93401) ***(P-24094)***

Transmerica Fincl Advisors Inc ....C.......213 741-7702
1150 S Olive St Ste T250 Los Angeles (90015) ***(P-10023)***

TransMontaigne PDT Svcs LLC ....B.......415 576-2000
555 California St # 2100 San Francisco (94104) ***(P-5248)***

Transmrcan Mling Flfllment Inc ....D.......760 745-5343
355 State Pl Escondido (92029) ***(P-14066)***

Transmrica Occidental Lf Insur (HQ) ....A.......213 742-2111
1150 S Olive St Fl 23 Los Angeles (90015) ***(P-10148)***

Transpac, Vacaville *Also called Valyria LLC* ***(P-6801)***

Transpacific Management Svc ....D.......714 285-2626
15661 Red Hill Ave # 205 Tustin (92780) ***(P-11798)***

Transpak Inc (PA) ....C.......408 254-0500
520 Marburg Way San Jose (95133) ***(P-17519)***

Transpak Inc ....D.......858 292-9094
8710 Avenida De La Fuente San Diego (92154) ***(P-5211)***

Transpak Los Angeles, Santa Ana *Also called Trans-Pak Incorporated* ***(P-17518)***

Transphorm Inc (PA) ....D.......805 456-1300
115 Castilian Dr Goleta (93117) ***(P-26476)***

Transport Drivers Inc ....B.......800 497-6345
620 N Dmnd Bar Blvd Ste B Diamond Bar (91765) ***(P-14923)***

Transport Drivers Inc ....C.......909 937-3312
2131 S Grove Ave Ste D Ontario (91761) ***(P-14924)***

Transport Express Inc ....D.......310 898-2000
19801 S Santa Fe Ave Compton (90221) ***(P-4379)***

Transportation, Lodi *Also called Lodi Unified School District* ***(P-3940)***

Transportation Bureau, Los Angeles *Also called County of Los Angeles* ***(P-5222)***

Transportation California Dept ....C.......707 762-6641
611 Payran St Petaluma (94952) ***(P-1863)***

Transportation California Dept ....C.......707 428-2031
2019 W Texas St Fairfield (94533) ***(P-1864)***

Transportation California Dept ....D.......530 225-3349
1490 George Dr Redding (96003) ***(P-948)***

Transportation California Dept ....C.......562 692-0823
1940 Workman Mill Rd Whittier (90601) ***(P-1865)***

Transportation Chrtr Svcs Inc ....E.......714 396-0346
1931 N Batavia St Orange (92865) ***(P-3905)***

Transportation Concept Inc ....D.......323 268-2202
1521 Kingsdale Ave Redondo Beach (90278) ***(P-3736)***

Transportation Department, Berkeley *Also called Berkeley Unified School Dst* ***(P-3909)***

Transportation Department, Sacramento *Also called Elk Grove Unified School Dst* ***(P-3921)***

Transportation Department, Long Beach *Also called Long Beach Unified School Dst* ***(P-3941)***

Transportation Dept, Ukiah *Also called County of Mendocino* ***(P-1752)***

Transportation Management LLC ....E.......310 524-1555
880 Apollo St Ste 235 El Segundo (90245) ***(P-4070)***

Transprttion Brkg Spclists Inc ....B.......714 754-4230
3151 Airway Ave Ste F208 Costa Mesa (92626) ***(P-4071)***

Transtar Automotive, Van Nuys *Also called Transtar Industries Inc* ***(P-6680)***

Transtar Industries Inc ....E.......818 785-2000
15010 Calvert St Van Nuys (91411) ***(P-6680)***

Transwest San Diego LLC ....B.......858 450-0707
6066 Miramar Rd San Diego (92121) ***(P-4380)***

Transwestern Corp Pointe LLC ....D.......310 642-1001
600 Crprate Pinte Ste 250 Culver City (90230) ***(P-11799)***

Tranzeal Inc ....E.......408 834-8711
2107 N 1st St Ste 500 San Jose (95131) ***(P-27495)***

Trap ....D.......626 572-5610
1833 S Mountain Ave Monrovia (91016) ***(P-17520)***

Trapac LLC (HQ) ....E.......310 513-1572
630 W Harry Bridges Blvd Wilmington (90744) ***(P-4743)***

Travel Store ....D.......714 529-1947
633 S Brea Blvd Brea (92821) ***(P-4953)***

Travel Store (PA) ....D.......310 575-5540
11601 Wilshire Blvd Los Angeles (90025) ***(P-4954)***

Travel Syndicate ....D.......818 297-9979
350 S Beverly Dr Ste 170 Beverly Hills (90212) ***(P-4955)***

Travelers Club Luggage Inc ....D.......714 523-8808
5911 Fresca Dr La Palma (90623) ***(P-8062)***

Travelers Indemnity Company ....C.......909 612-3000
21688 Gateway Center Dr # 300 Diamond Bar (91765) ***(P-10802)***

Travelers Insurance, Diamond Bar *Also called Travelers Indemnity Company* ***(P-10802)***

Travelers Insurance, Walnut Creek *Also called Travelers Property Cslty Corp* ***(P-10803)***

Travelers Insurance, Brea *Also called Travelers Property Cslty Corp* ***(P-10804)***

Travelers Property Cslty Corp ....B.......925 945-4000
401 Lennon Ln Walnut Creek (94598) ***(P-10803)***

Travelers Property Cslty Corp ....C.......714 671-8000
145 S State College Blvd # 240 Brea (92821) ***(P-10804)***

Travelmasters Inc ....E.......916 722-1648
8350 Auburn Blvd Ste 200 Citrus Heights (95610) ***(P-4956)***

Travelodge, Los Angeles *Also called Airport Century Inn* ***(P-12309)***

Travelstore, Los Angeles *Also called Travel Store* ***(P-4954)***

Travelzoo Usa Inc ....D.......650 316-6956
800 W El Camino Re Mountain View (94040) ***(P-13960)***

Travers Tree Service Inc ....E.......310 545-5816
1811 Lomita Blvd Lomita (90717) ***(P-980)***

Travidia Inc (PA) ....C.......530 343-6400
265 Airpark Blvd Ste 500 Chico (95973) ***(P-15880)***

Travis Credit Union ....B.......707 449-4000
1300 E Covell Blvd Davis (95616) ***(P-9598)***

Travis Credit Union ....B.......800 877-8328
1796 Tuolumne St Vallejo (94589) ***(P-9599)***

Travis Credit Union ....B.......800 877-8328
2095 Diamond Blvd Ste 115 Concord (94520) ***(P-9600)***

Travis Credit Union ....B.......800 877-8328
3263 Claremont Way NAPA (94558) ***(P-9601)***

Travis Credit Union (PA) ....B.......707 449-4000
1 Travis Way Vacaville (95687) ***(P-9602)***

Travis Credit Union ....B.......916 443-1446
1515 K St Sacramento (95814) ***(P-9603)***

Travis Credit Union ....B.......209 723-0732
1194 W Olive Ave Merced (95348) ***(P-9604)***

Travis Credit Union ....B.......925 777-0573
5819 Lone Tree Way Ste A Antioch (94531) ***(P-9605)***

Travis Credit Union ....B.......707 449-4000
11 Cernon St Vacaville (95688) ***(P-9606)***

Travis Credit Union ....B.......707 449-4000
2570 N Texas St Fairfield (94533) ***(P-9607)***

Travis Credit Union ....B.......800 877-8328
1372 E Main St Woodland (95776) ***(P-9608)***

Travis Credit Union ....B.......707 449-4000
2020 Harbison Dr Vacaville (95687) ***(P-9609)***

Travis James Watts ....C.......209 810-6159
9631 Harvey Rd Galt (95632) ***(P-388)***

TRC Pleasanton Dialysis Cntr, Pleasanton *Also called Total Renal Care Inc* ***(P-22491)***

TRC Solutions Inc (HQ) ....C.......949 753-0101
9685 Research Dr Ste 100 Irvine (92618) ***(P-27888)***

Trcf Redondo LLC ....E.......310 536-1209
2430 Marine Ave Redondo Beach (90278) ***(P-13340)***

Treadwell & Rollo Inc (HQ) ....E.......415 955-9040
555 Montgomery St # 1300 San Francisco (94111) ***(P-25958)***

Treasure Data Inc ....D.......866 899-5386
2565 Leghorn St Mountain View (94043) ***(P-15510)***

Treasurer/Tax Collector, Alturas *Also called County of Modoc* ***(P-17105)***

Treasury Wine Estates Americas ....C.......707 259-4500
555 Gateway Dr NAPA (94558) ***(P-9057)***

Treasury Wine Estates Americas ....C.......805 237-6000
7000 E Highway 46 Paso Robles (93446) ***(P-180)***

Tredence Inc (PA) ....C.......408 819-2336
1900 Camden Ave Ste 66 San Jose (95124) ***(P-26572)***

Tree Sculpture Group ....D.......510 562-4000
463 Roland Way Oakland (94621) ***(P-949)***

Treebeard Landscape Inc ....D.......619 697-8302
9917 Campo Rd Spring Valley (91977) ***(P-950)***

Treefrog Developments Inc ....D.......619 324-7755
15110 Ave Of Science San Diego (92128) ***(P-8063)***

Treeline and Associates ....D.......909 476-2757
9330 Baseline Rd Ste 106 Rancho Cucamonga (91701) ***(P-27496)***

Treeline Staffing ....E.......415 819-7195
100 Broadway San Francisco (94111) ***(P-14784)***

Treepeople Inc ....E.......818 753-4600
12601 Mulholland Dr Beverly Hills (90210) ***(P-981)***

Trees Apartments LLC ....D.......408 848-6400
7030 Eigleberry St Gilroy (95020) ***(P-11128)***

Trellisware Technologies Inc ....D.......858 753-1600
16516 Via Esprillo # 300 San Diego (92127) ***(P-5422)***

Trench Shoring Company, Los Angeles *Also called Tom Malloy Corporation* ***(P-7697)***

Trend Micro Incorporated ....D.......408 257-1500
10101 N De Anza Blvd Cupertino (95014) ***(P-7119)***

Trendex Corporation ....D.......818 407-9600
9353 Eton Ave Chatsworth (91311) ***(P-1676)***

Trendnet Inc (PA) ....D.......310 961-5500
20675 Manhattan Pl Torrance (90501) ***(P-7120)***

Trendsettah Usa Inc ....D.......888 775-4881
1420 S Highland Ave L203 Fullerton (92832) ***(P-8064)***

Trendshift LLC ....D.......866 644-8877
13274 Fiji Way Ste 250 Marina Del Rey (90292) ***(P-15511)***

Trendsource Inc ....D.......619 718-7467
4891 Pacific Hwy Ste 200 San Diego (92110) ***(P-26573)***

Trepco Imports & Dist Ltd ....E.......619 690-7999
11860 Cmnty Rd Ste 150 Poway (92064) ***(P-9187)***

Tressler LLP ....D.......949 336-1200
2 Park Plz Ste 1050 Irvine (92614) ***(P-23411)***

Trestles Holdings LLC ....D.......707 778-8686
450 Hayes Ln Petaluma (94952) ***(P-12013)***

Trevi Partners A Calif LP ....D.......408 395-7070
140 S Santa Cruz Ave Los Gatos (95030) ***(P-13341)***

Trevi Partners A Calif LP (HQ) ....D.......925 828-7750
6680 Regional St Dublin (94568) ***(P-13342)***

Trevi Partners A Calif LP ....D.......831 624-1841
3665 Rio Rd Carmel (93923) ***(P-13343)***

Trevi Partners A Calif LP (PA) ....C.......925 225-4000
5955 Coronado Ln Pleasanton (94588) ***(P-13344)***

Trex Partners LLC.......C.......858 646-5300
10455 Pacific Center Ct San Diego (92121) ***(P-12014)***
Trg Inc.......D.......310 396-6750
1350 Abbot Kinney Blvd # 101 Venice (90291) ***(P-11800)***
Tri - Star Win Coverings Inc.......E.......818 718-3188
19555 Prairie St Northridge (91324) ***(P-6795)***
Tri Ced Community Recycling, Union City *Also called Tri-City Economic Dev Corp **(P-6484)***
Tri City Emergency Med Group.......E.......760 439-1963
5050 Avenida Encinas # 200 Carlsbad (92008) ***(P-26304)***
Tri City Mental Health Center.......D.......909 784-3200
1900 Royalty Dr Pomona (91767) ***(P-22700)***
Tri City Orthopedic Sgy & Mdcl.......E.......760 724-9000
3905 Waring Rd Oceanside (92056) ***(P-20011)***
Tri Counties Bank (HQ).......D.......530 898-0300
63 Constitution Dr Chico (95973) ***(P-9517)***
Tri Counties Bank.......C.......650 583-8450
975 El Camino Real South San Francisco (94080) ***(P-9373)***
Tri Counties Bank.......D.......530 478-6001
305 Railroad Ave Ste 1 Nevada City (95959) ***(P-9518)***
Tri County Regional Center.......D.......805 485-3177
2220 E Gonzales Rd 210a Oxnard (93036) ***(P-20211)***
Tri County Respite Care Svc.......D.......530 755-3500
1215 Plumas St Ste 1600 Yuba City (95991) ***(P-24095)***
Tri Pointe Contractors LP (HQ).......D.......949 478-8600
5 Peters Canyon Rd # 100 Irvine (92606) ***(P-1360)***
Tri Pointe Homes Inc (HQ).......C.......949 438-1400
19520 Jamboree Rd Ste 300 Irvine (92612) ***(P-1323)***
Tri Tool Inc (PA).......C.......916 288-6100
3041 Sunrise Blvd Rancho Cordova (95742) ***(P-7813)***
Tri Valley Vegetable Harvstg.......D.......805 928-2727
123 N Depot St Santa Maria (93458) ***(P-486)***
Tri Valley Wholesale, Fairfield *Also called Tri-Valley Supply Inc **(P-6932)***
Tri-Ad Actuaries Inc.......C.......760 743-7555
221 W Crest St Ste 300 Escondido (92025) ***(P-10805)***
Tri-City Economic Dev Corp.......D.......510 429-8030
33377 Western Ave Union City (94587) ***(P-6484)***
Tri-City Health Center (PA).......C.......510 770-8040
39500 Liberty St Fremont (94538) ***(P-20012)***
Tri-City Home Care Services.......C.......760 940-5800
2095 W Vista Way Ste 220 Vista (92083) ***(P-22438)***
Tri-City Hospital District (PA).......A.......760 724-8411
4002 Vista Way Oceanside (92056) ***(P-21861)***
Tri-City Medical Center, Oceanside *Also called Tri-City Hospital District **(P-21861)***
Tri-Counties Association F (PA).......C.......805 962-7881
520 E Montecito St Santa Barbara (93103) ***(P-24096)***
Tri-Counties Association F.......C.......805 922-4640
1234 Fairway Dr A Santa Maria (93455) ***(P-25046)***
Tri-Counties Blood Bank, San Luis Obispo *Also called Vitalant **(P-22902)***
TRI-COUNTIES REGIONAL CENTER, Santa Barbara *Also called Tri-Counties Association F **(P-24096)***
Tri-Marine Fish Company LLC.......D.......310 547-1144
220 Cannery St San Pedro (90731) ***(P-8607)***
Tri-Marine Fishing MGT LLC.......E.......310 547-1144
220 Cannery St San Pedro (90731) ***(P-27066)***
Tri-Modal Dist Svcs Inc (PA).......C.......310 522-5506
2011 E Carson St Carson (90810) ***(P-4381)***
Tri-Mountain, Irwindale *Also called Mountain Gear Corporation **(P-8270)***
Tri-Power Group Inc.......D.......925 583-8200
617 N Mary Ave Sunnyvale (94085) ***(P-6002)***
Tri-Signal Integration Inc (PA).......D.......818 566-8558
15853 Monte St Ste 101 Sylmar (91342) ***(P-2770)***
Tri-Star Ccw Management L P.......D.......310 322-0999
1985 E Grand Ave El Segundo (90245) ***(P-13345)***
Tri-Star Drywall Lp.......D.......559 299-9858
2479 Burgan Ave Clovis (93611) ***(P-2973)***
Tri-State AG Inc.......D.......209 364-6185
47375 W Dakota Ave Firebaugh (93622) ***(P-6552)***
Tri-State Employment Svc Inc.......B.......310 521-9616
450 Westmont Dr San Pedro (90731) ***(P-14785)***
Tri-Tech Internet Services Inc.......E.......818 548-5400
3465 Ocean View Blvd Glendale (91208) ***(P-16254)***
Tri-Tech Logistics LLC.......C.......855 373-7049
3230 E Imperial Hwy # 140 Brea (92821) ***(P-5184)***
Tri-Tech Restoration Co Inc.......D.......818 565-3900
3301 N San Fernando Blvd Burbank (91504) ***(P-1446)***
Tri-Union Seafoods LLC (HQ).......D.......858 558-9662
2150 E Grand Ave El Segundo (90245) ***(P-8608)***
Tri-Valley Supply Inc (PA).......D.......707 469-7470
1705 Enterprise Dr Fairfield (94533) ***(P-6932)***
Tri-West Ltd (PA).......C.......562 692-9166
12005 Pike St Santa Fe Springs (90670) ***(P-6796)***
Triad Broadcasting Company (PA).......C.......831 655-6350
2511 Garden Rd Ste A104 Monterey (93940) ***(P-5755)***
Triad Homes Assoc.......D.......760 873-4273
873 N Main St Ste 150 Bishop (93514) ***(P-25959)***
Triad-Holmes Associates, Bishop *Also called Triad Homes Assoc **(P-25959)***
Triage Consulting Group (PA).......B.......415 512-9400
221 Main St Ste 1100 San Francisco (94105) ***(P-27497)***
Triage Entertainment Inc.......D.......310 417-4800
6701 Center Dr W Ste 300 Los Angeles (90045) ***(P-18135)***
Triage Partners LLC.......D.......562 634-0058
15717 Texaco Ave Paramount (90723) ***(P-16515)***
Triangle Distributing Co (PA).......C.......562 699-3424
12065 Pike St Santa Fe Springs (90670) ***(P-9029)***
Triangle Distributing Co.......D.......760 347-4052
82851 Avenue 45 Indio (92201) ***(P-9030)***
Trianim Health Services Inc.......D.......818 362-6882
27201 Tourney Rd Ste 115 Valencia (91355) ***(P-22896)***
Trianz Inc (HQ).......C.......408 387-5800
2350 Mission College Blvd Santa Clara (95054) ***(P-16516)***
Tribal Tektet, Arcata *Also called Tektetco **(P-1444)***
Tribeworx LLC.......D.......800 949-3432
4 San Joaquin Plz Ste 150 Newport Beach (92660) ***(P-15881)***
Tricks Gymnastic Inc (PA).......D.......916 791-4496
4070 Cavitt Stallman Rd Granite Bay (95746) ***(P-19249)***
Tricom Management Inc.......C.......714 630-2029
4025 E La Palma Ave # 101 Anaheim (92807) ***(P-27067)***
Tricor America Inc.......D.......310 676-0800
12441 Eucalyptus Ave 7 Hawthorne (90250) ***(P-5185)***
Tricor America Inc.......D.......714 701-9880
1465 N Brasher St Anaheim (92807) ***(P-4438)***
Tricor America Inc.......C.......916 371-1704
1690 Cebrian St West Sacramento (95691) ***(P-4439)***
Tricor America Inc.......C.......510 293-3960
3149 Diablo Ave Hayward (94545) ***(P-4847)***
Tricor California, West Sacramento *Also called Tricor America Inc **(P-4439)***
Tricor Entertainment Inc.......C.......626 282-5184
1613 Chelsea Rd San Marino (91108) ***(P-18136)***
Tricor International.......D.......650 877-3678
717 Airport Blvd South San Francisco (94080) ***(P-5186)***
Tricorp Construction Inc (PA).......D.......916 779-8010
1030 G St Sacramento (95814) ***(P-1677)***
Tricorp Hearn Construction, Sacramento *Also called Tricorp Construction Inc **(P-1677)***
Trident Capital Inc (PA).......C.......650 289-4400
400 S El Camino Real # 300 San Mateo (94402) ***(P-12276)***
Trident Dental Labratories, Hawthorne *Also called Trident Labs LLC **(P-22174)***
Trident Labs LLC.......C.......310 915-9121
12000 Aviation Blvd Hawthorne (90250) ***(P-22174)***
Trifecta Clinical, Los Angeles *Also called Trifecta Multimedia LLC **(P-16517)***
Trifecta Multimedia LLC (PA).......E.......626 355-1303
725 S Figueroa St # 4050 Los Angeles (90017) ***(P-16517)***
Trigild International Inc.......D.......619 291-6500
2151 Hotel Cir S San Diego (92108) ***(P-13346)***
Trilar Management Group.......C.......951 925-2021
1025 S Gilbert St Hemet (92543) ***(P-27068)***
Trilink Biotechnologies LLC.......D.......858 546-0004
9955 Mesa Rim Rd San Diego (92121) ***(P-26477)***
Trilliant Incorporated.......D.......650 204-5050
1100 Island Dr Ste 201 Redwood City (94065) ***(P-27889)***
Trilliant Networks Inc (PA).......D.......650 204-5050
1100 Island Dr Ste 201 Redwood City (94065) ***(P-17521)***
Trilogy Day Spa, Manhattan Beach *Also called Trilogy Squaw Spa LLC **(P-13675)***
Trilogy Financial Services Inc (PA).......C.......714 843-9977
17011 Beach Blvd Ste 800 Huntington Beach (92647) ***(P-17522)***
Trilogy Financial Services Inc.......E.......858 755-6696
12520 High Bluff Dr # 140 San Diego (92130) ***(P-17523)***
Trilogy Golf At La Quinta.......D.......760 771-0707
60151 Trilogy Pkwy La Quinta (92253) ***(P-18774)***
Trilogy Plumbing Inc (PA).......C.......714 441-2952
1525 S Sinclair St Anaheim (92806) ***(P-2389)***
Trilogy Realty Group Inc.......D.......937 206-0725
2025 N Mantle Ln Santa Ana (92705) ***(P-11801)***
Trilogy Rio Vista.......D.......707 374-1100
1200 Clubhouse Dr Rio Vista (94571) ***(P-1447)***
Trilogy Squaw Spa LLC.......E.......310 760-0044
451 Manhattan Beach Blvd Manhattan Beach (90266) ***(P-13675)***
Trim Tech Industries Inc.......E.......408 573-4514
1724 Ringwood Ave San Jose (95131) ***(P-6870)***
Trimarine Fish Group, San Pedro *Also called Tri-Marine Fishing MGT LLC **(P-27066)***
Trimark Operations Center.......D.......916 357-5970
2365 Iron Point Rd # 100 Folsom (95630) ***(P-27890)***
Trimark Raygal LLC.......D.......949 474-1000
210 Commerce Irvine (92602) ***(P-17524)***
Trimont Land Company (HQ).......B.......530 562-1010
5001 Northstar Dr Truckee (96161) ***(P-11802)***
Trinchero Family Estates, Lodi *Also called Sutter Home Winery Inc **(P-17493)***
Trinet Group Inc (PA).......C.......510 352-5000
1100 San Leandro Blvd # 300 San Leandro (94577) ***(P-14786)***
Trinity Brdcstg Netwrk Inc.......C.......714 665-3619
2442 Michelle Dr Tustin (92780) ***(P-5840)***
Trinity Broadcasting Network, Tustin *Also called Trinity Christian Center of SA **(P-5841)***
Trinity Building Services.......B.......650 873-2121
430 N Canal St Ste 2 South San Francisco (94080) ***(P-14409)***
Trinity Capital Corporation (HQ).......D.......415 956-5174
475 Sansome St Fl 19 San Francisco (94111) ***(P-9764)***
Trinity Care & Nutria, Cerritos *Also called Trinitycare LLC **(P-22440)***
Trinity Christian Center of SA (PA).......C.......714 665-3619
2442 Michelle Dr Tustin (92780) ***(P-5841)***
Trinity Christn Ctr Santa Ana, Tustin *Also called Trinity Brdcstg Netwrk Inc **(P-5840)***
Trinity Fresh Distribution LLC.......D.......916 714-7368
8200 Berry Ave Ste 140 Sacramento (95828) ***(P-8888)***
Trinity Fruit Packing Company.......C.......559 743-3913
18700 E South Ave Reedley (93654) ***(P-581)***
Trinity Health Systems.......D.......818 983-0103
13400 Sherman Way North Hollywood (91605) ***(P-21231)***
Trinity Health Systems.......D.......562 437-2797
723 E 9th St Long Beach (90813) ***(P-20841)***
Trinity Health Systems (PA).......D.......626 960-1971
14318 Ohio St Baldwin Park (91706) ***(P-20842)***
Trinity Home Care, Torrance *Also called Providence Health System **(P-22398)***
Trinity Home Health Svcs Inc.......D.......559 450-5112
6729 N Willow Ave Ste 103 Fresno (93710) ***(P-22439)***
Trinity Hospital, Weaverville *Also called Mountain Comm Hlth Cre Dist **(P-21600)***
Trinity Hospital, Weaverville *Also called Mountain Comm Hlth Cre Dist **(P-21601)***
Trinity Packing Company Inc.......B.......559 743-3913
18700 E South Ave Reedley (93654) ***(P-17525)***

Mergent e-mail: customerrelations@mergent.com
1498
2019 Directory of California
Wholesalers and Services Companies
(P-0000) Products & Services Section entry number
(PA)=Parent Co (HQ)=Headquarters (DH)=Div Headquarters

Trinity Plaza, Richmond *Also called Macdonald Housing Partners LP* ***(P-11578)***
Trinity Technology Group Inc ....D....916 779-0201
2015 J St Ste 105 Sacramento (95811) ***(P-16067)***
Trinity Youth Services (PA) ....D....909 980-4755
201 N Indian Hill Blvd # 201 Claremont (91711) ***(P-24700)***
Trinitycare LLC (PA) ....D....818 709-4221
13030 Alondra Blvd Cerritos (90703) ***(P-22440)***
Trinus Corporation ....E....818 246-1143
225 S Lake Ave Ste 1080 Pasadena (91101) ***(P-15512)***
Trion Worlds, Inc. ....B....650 631-9800
2400 Bridge Pkwy 100 Redwood City (94065) ***(P-15882)***
Triple A, Walnut Creek *Also called California State Automobile* ***(P-10345)***
Triple B Forwarders, Carson *Also called Triple B Forwarders Inc* ***(P-5187)***
Triple B Forwarders Inc (PA) ....C....310 604-5840
1511 Glenn Curtiss St Carson (90746) ***(P-5187)***
Triple E Trucking ....E....661 834-0071
1215 E White Ln Bakersfield (93307) ***(P-4072)***
Triple Hs Inc (PA) ....D....408 458-3200
983 University Ave Bldg D Los Gatos (95032) ***(P-27891)***
Triple R Transportation Inc ....D....661 725-6494
978 Rd 192 Delano (93215) ***(P-3854)***
Triple Ring Technologies Inc ....E....510 592-3000
39655 Eureka Dr Newark (94560) ***(P-27498)***
Triple-E Machinery Moving Inc ....D....626 444-1137
3301 Gilman Rd El Monte (91732) ***(P-4282)***
Triplecurve LLC ....D....855 874-2878
5716 Corsa Ave Ste 110 Westlake Village (91362) ***(P-27499)***
Tristaff Group, Fallbrook *Also called Garich Inc* ***(P-14625)***
Tristar Insurance Group Inc (PA) ....A....562 495-6600
100 Oceangate Ste 700 Long Beach (90802) ***(P-10412)***
Tristar Risk Management ....D....714 543-0700
203 N Golden Circle Dr # 200 Santa Ana (92705) ***(P-10806)***
Tristar Television Music Inc ....E....310 244-4000
10202 Washington Blvd Culver City (90232) ***(P-18411)***
Tristart Risk Management, Long Beach *Also called Tristar Insurance Group Inc* ***(P-10412)***
Triton Cont Intl Inc N Amer (HQ) ....D....415 956-6311
456 Montgomery St Ste 800 San Francisco (94104) ***(P-14460)***
Triton Logistics Corporation ....D....619 822-8832
706 Steffy Rd Ramona (92065) ***(P-5188)***
Triton Management Services LLC ....D....760 431-9911
1000 Aviara Dr Ste 300 Carlsbad (92011) ***(P-27069)***
Triton Media Group LLC (PA) ....A....323 290-6900
15303 Ventura Blvd # 1500 Sherman Oaks (91403) ***(P-5756)***
Triton Media Group LLC ....D....661 294-9000
8935 Lindblade St Culver City (90232) ***(P-5757)***
Triton Structural Concrete Inc ....C....858 866-2450
15435 Innovation Dr # 100 San Diego (92128) ***(P-1678)***
Triton Tower Inc (PA) ....D....916 375-8546
3200 Jefferson Blvd West Sacramento (95691) ***(P-1988)***
Triumph Protection Group Inc ....C....800 224-0286
853 Cotting Ct Ste D Vacaville (95688) ***(P-16839)***
Triunfo Public Facilities Corp ....D....805 658-4605
1001 Partridge Dr Ventura (93003) ***(P-6204)***
Trius Trucking Inc ....D....559 834-4000
4692 E Lincoln Ave Fowler (93625) ***(P-5189)***
Trivad Inc ....C....650 286-1086
1350 Bayshore Hwy Ste 450 Burlingame (94010) ***(P-7121)***
Triways Inc ....D....951 361-4840
11201 Iberia St Ste B Mira Loma (91752) ***(P-4382)***
TRL Systems Incorporated ....D....909 390-8392
9531 Milliken Ave Rancho Cucamonga (91730) ***(P-2771)***
TRM Corporation (PA) ....C....510 895-2700
2378 Polvorosa Ave San Leandro (94577) ***(P-3013)***
Trojan Professional Svcs Inc ....D....714 816-7169
4410 Cerritos Ave Los Alamitos (90720) ***(P-16255)***
Troon Golf LLC ....C....760 346-4653
44500 Indian Wells Ln Indian Wells (92210) ***(P-27070)***
Troop Real Estate Inc ....D....805 402-3028
4165 E Thousand Oaks Blvd # 100 Westlake Village (91362) ***(P-11803)***
Troop Real Estate Inc (PA) ....A....805 581-3200
3200 E Los Angeles Ave Simi Valley (93065) ***(P-11804)***
Trope & Trope, Los Angeles *Also called Trope and Trope LLP* ***(P-23412)***
Trope and Trope LLP ....D....323 879-2726
12121 Wilshire Blvd # 801 Los Angeles (90025) ***(P-23412)***
Tropical Plaza Nursery Inc ....D....714 998-4100
9642 Santiago Blvd Villa Park (92867) ***(P-951)***
Trotta Associates ....D....310 306-6866
13160 Mindanao Way # 100 Marina Del Rey (90292) ***(P-26574)***
Troutman Sanders LLP ....D....858 509-6000
11682 El Camino Real # 400 San Diego (92130) ***(P-23413)***
Troutman Sanders LLP ....D....415 477-5700
580 California St # 1100 San Francisco (94104) ***(P-23414)***
Trowbridge Enterprises (PA) ....D....831 476-3815
2606 Chanticleer Ave Santa Cruz (95065) ***(P-8091)***
Troxel Cycling & Fitness LLC ....C....858 587-7720
6222 Ferris Sq Ste A San Diego (92121) ***(P-7939)***
Troy Lee Designs LLC (PA) ....D....951 371-5219
155 E Rincon St Corona (92879) ***(P-7940)***
Troyer Contracting Company Inc ....D....562 944-6452
10122 Freeman Ave Santa Fe Springs (90670) ***(P-3598)***
Troygould PC ....D....310 553-4441
1801 Century Park E # 1600 Los Angeles (90067) ***(P-23415)***
Trs Staffing Solutions, Aliso Viejo *Also called Fluor Corporation* ***(P-25685)***
Tru Green Landcare Inc ....B....602 276-4311
5248 Governor Dr San Diego (92122) ***(P-952)***
Tru Green-Chemlawn, Riverside *Also called Trugreen Limited Partnership* ***(P-953)***
Truaire, Santa Fe Springs *Also called TA Industries Inc* ***(P-7640)***
Truck Terminal, Bakersfield *Also called Pan Pacific Petroleum Co Inc* ***(P-4242)***
Truck Underwriters Association (HQ) ....A....323 932-3200
4680 Wilshire Blvd Los Angeles (90010) ***(P-25047)***
Truck Underwriters Association ....A....323 932-3200
6303 Owensmouth Ave Fl 1 Woodland Hills (91367) ***(P-10149)***
Truckee Dnner Rcreation Pk Dst ....D....530 582-7720
8924 Donner Pass Rd Truckee (96161) ***(P-19250)***
Truckee Donner Pub Utly Dist F ....D....530 587-3896
11570 Donner Pass Rd Truckee (96161) ***(P-6144)***
TRUCKEE DONNER PUD, Truckee *Also called Truckee Donner Pub Utly Dist F* ***(P-6144)***
Truckee High School, Truckee *Also called Tahoe Trcke Unfd Sch Dis Fincn* ***(P-27876)***
Truconnect Communications Inc (PA) ....C....800 430-0443
1149 S Hill St Ste 400 Los Angeles (90015) ***(P-5656)***
True Air Mechanical Inc ....C....888 316-0642
4 Faraday Irvine (92618) ***(P-2390)***
True Home Heating and AC, Irvine *Also called True Air Mechanical Inc* ***(P-2390)***
True Investments LLC ....E....949 258-9720
2260 University Dr Newport Beach (92660) ***(P-12277)***
True North Ar LLC ....D....916 369-9850
10971 Sun Center Dr # 200 Rancho Cordova (95670) ***(P-14787)***
True Rate Insurance Agency Inc (PA) ....E....323 735-1600
2820 S Vermont Ave Ste 1 Los Angeles (90007) ***(P-10807)***
True Religion Brand Jeans, Manhattan Beach *Also called Guru Denim LLC* ***(P-8304)***
True Wrld Fods Los Angeles LLC ....D....323 846-3300
4200 S Alameda St Vernon (90058) ***(P-8609)***
True Wrld Fods San Frncsco LLC ....D....510 352-8140
1815 Williams St San Leandro (94577) ***(P-8610)***
Truebeck Construction Inc (PA) ....E....650 227-1957
201 Redwood Shores Pkwy # 125 Redwood City (94065) ***(P-1679)***
Trueblue Inc ....C....530 755-3291
1362 Colusa Hwy Yuba City (95993) ***(P-14925)***
Trueblue Inc ....E....805 963-5370
123 E Carrillo St Santa Barbara (93101) ***(P-14926)***
Truecar Inc (PA) ....E....800 200-2000
120 Broadway Ste 200 Santa Monica (90401) ***(P-13777)***
Truesdail Laboratories Inc ....E....714 730-6239
3337 Michelson Dr Irvine (92612) ***(P-26478)***
Truform Construction Corp ....E....714 630-7447
1041 N Shepard St Anaheim (92806) ***(P-3086)***
Trugreen, Santa Ana *Also called Landcare USA LLC* ***(P-876)***
Trugreen, Escondido *Also called Landcare USA LLC* ***(P-877)***
Trugreen, Simi Valley *Also called Landcare USA LLC* ***(P-878)***
Trugreen, Gardena *Also called Landcare USA LLC* ***(P-883)***
Trugreen, Rancho Cordova *Also called Landcare USA LLC* ***(P-884)***
Trugreen, San Diego *Also called Landcare USA LLC* ***(P-885)***
Trugreen, Canoga Park *Also called Landcare USA LLC* ***(P-886)***
Trugreen, San Jose *Also called Landcare USA LLC* ***(P-887)***
Trugreen Limited Partnership ....E....951 231-2760
1130 Palmyrita Ave # 300 Riverside (92507) ***(P-953)***
Trugreen Lndcare Michael Bogan, Santa Fe Springs *Also called Landcare USA LLC* ***(P-880)***
Truitt Oilfield Maint Corp ....B....661 871-4099
1051 James Rd Bakersfield (93308) ***(P-1082)***
Trulia Inc (HQ) ....B....415 648-4358
535 Mission St Fl 7 San Francisco (94105) ***(P-16191)***
Trumpia, Anaheim *Also called Docircle Inc* ***(P-5550)***
Trust Automation Inc ....D....805 544-0761
143 Suburban Rd Ste 100 San Luis Obispo (93401) ***(P-25960)***
Trust Company of The West, Los Angeles *Also called Tcw Group Inc* ***(P-10116)***
Trust Employee ADM & MGT, San Diego *Also called Team Risk MGT Strategies LLC* ***(P-27877)***
Trustarc Inc ....D....415 520-3400
835 Market St Ste 800 San Francisco (94103) ***(P-16518)***
Truste, San Francisco *Also called Trustarc Inc* ***(P-16518)***
Trustee Corps, Irvine *Also called Mtc Financial Inc* ***(P-12116)***
Truxtun Radiology Med Group LP ....C....661 325-6200
3940 San Dimas St Bakersfield (93301) ***(P-22152)***
Try Caviar, San Francisco *Also called Caviar Inc* ***(P-23545)***
Tryad Service Corporation ....D....661 391-1524
5900 E Lerdo Hwy Shafter (93263) ***(P-1083)***
Tryfacta Inc ....B....408 419-9200
2950 Buskirk Ave Ste 160 Walnut Creek (94597) ***(P-15513)***
Trz Holdings II Inc ....B....213 955-7170
725 S Figueroa St # 1850 Los Angeles (90017) ***(P-11805)***
Tscm Corporation ....D....714 841-1988
17791 Jamestown Ln Huntington Beach (92647) ***(P-14410)***
Tsg, San Diego *Also called Socal Services Inc* ***(P-14763)***
Tsi ....D....949 515-7800
789 W 20th St Costa Mesa (92627) ***(P-14411)***
Tsmc North America (HQ) ....C....408 382-8000
2851 Junction Ave San Jose (95134) ***(P-27500)***
Tst Inc ....D....310 835-0115
11601 Etiwanda Ave Fontana (92337) ***(P-4073)***
Tst Inc ....D....909 590-1098
11601 Etiwanda Ave Fontana (92337) ***(P-7999)***
Tsu Corporate Services, North Hollywood *Also called Toner Supply USA Inc* ***(P-7117)***
Ttg Engineers ....D....714 490-5555
222 S Harbor Blvd Ste 800 Anaheim (92805) ***(P-25961)***
Ttg Engineers (PA) ....C....626 463-2800
300 N Lake Ave Fl 14 Pasadena (91101) ***(P-25962)***
TTI, Milpitas *Also called Technical Temps Inc* ***(P-14777)***
TTI Technologies, Exeter *Also called Exeter Engineering Inc* ***(P-510)***
Ttik Inc (PA) ....D....310 303-3600
3541 Challenger St Torrance (90503) ***(P-16948)***
Ttp-US, San Marcos *Also called Tel Tech Plus Inc* ***(P-2763)***
Tts, Pleasanton *Also called Telecom Technology Svcs Inc* ***(P-27878)***
TTSA, Truckee *Also called Tahoe-Truckee Sanitation Agcy* ***(P-6332)***
Ttsi, Rancho Dominguez *Also called Premium Trnsp Svcs Inc* ***(P-5146)***

ALPHABETIC

Employee Codes: A=Over 500 employees, B=251-500
C=101-250, D=51-100, E=50
2019 Directory of California
Wholesalers and Services Companies
© Mergent Inc. 1-800-342-5647
1499

TTSR, Sacramento *Also called Training Toward Self Reliance* ***(P-24093)***
TTT West Coast Inc ....C.......818 972-0500
3000 W Alameda Ave # 125 Burbank (91505) ***(P-18137)***
Ttx Company ....B.......951 685-0158
10800 San Sevaine Way Mira Loma (91752) ***(P-5249)***
Tubemogul Inc ....D.......510 653-0126
1250 53rd St Ste 1 Emeryville (94608) ***(P-15883)***
Tucker Distributors ....E.......714 970-5742
5380 E Hunter Ave Anaheim (92807) ***(P-7658)***
Tucker Electric Corporation ....E.......818 426-7645
3365 Chestnut Ln Santa Rosa Valley (93012) ***(P-2772)***
Tucker Electrical, Santa Rosa Valley *Also called Tucker Electric Corporation* ***(P-2772)***
Tucker Ellis LLP ....D.......213 430-3400
1000 Wilshire Blvd # 1800 Los Angeles (90017) ***(P-23416)***
Tucker Sheet Metal Distr, Anaheim *Also called Tucker Distributors* ***(P-7658)***
Tucoemas Federal Credit Union (PA) ....D.......559 737-5900
5222 W Cypress Ave Visalia (93277) ***(P-9610)***
Tucoemas Federal Credit Union ....D.......559 429-7094
2300 W Whitendale Ave Visalia (93277) ***(P-9611)***
Tucson Hotels LP ....B.......510 658-9300
1800 Powell St Oakland (94608) ***(P-13347)***
Tucson Hotels LP ....C.......916 446-0100
300 J St Sacramento (95814) ***(P-13348)***
Tucson Hotels LP ....C.......916 446-0100
300 J St Sacramento (95814) ***(P-13349)***
Tucson Hotels LP ....C.......831 393-1115
1441 Canyon Del Rey Blvd Seaside (93955) ***(P-13350)***
Tudor Cnstr & Restoration, Elk Grove *Also called Bennathon Corp* ***(P-1479)***
Tulare Cnty Chld Care Home Edu ....D.......559 651-0247
7000 W Doe Ave Ste C Visalia (93291) ***(P-24395)***
Tulare Cty Trng Ctr Hndcpd ....D.......559 651-3683
8929 W Goshen Ave Visalia (93291) ***(P-24239)***
Tulare Home Care, Tulare *Also called Tulare Local Health Care Dst* ***(P-21862)***
Tulare Local Health Care Dst ....A.......559 685-3462
869 N Cherry St Tulare (93274) ***(P-21862)***
Tulare Nrsing Rhbilitation Ctr, Tulare *Also called Tulare Nrsing Rhblitation Hosp* ***(P-20843)***
Tulare Nrsing Rhblitation Hosp ....C.......559 686-8581
680 E Merritt Ave Tulare (93274) ***(P-20843)***
Tule River Indian Hlth Ctr Inc ....D.......559 784-2316
380 N Reservation Rd Porterville (93257) ***(P-22701)***
Tuls Cattle, Tulare *Also called M & T Calf Ranch* ***(P-400)***
Tum Yeto Inc ....E.......619 232-7523
2001 Commercial St San Diego (92113) ***(P-7941)***
Tumbleweed Day Camp, Los Angeles *Also called Tumbleweed Educational Entps* ***(P-19251)***
Tumbleweed Educational Entps ....C.......310 444-3232
1024 Hanley Ave Los Angeles (90049) ***(P-19251)***
Tumi Inc ....D.......408 244-6512
333 Santana Row Apt 230 San Jose (95128) ***(P-8065)***
Tunari Corp Inc ....D.......650 249-6740
2755 Campus Dr Ste 300 San Mateo (94403) ***(P-15514)***
Tunein Inc ....C.......650 319-7100
210 King St Fl 3 San Francisco (94107) ***(P-5758)***
Tuolomne Cnty Bhvrl Hlth, Sonora *Also called Kingsview Corp* ***(P-22609)***
Tuolumne City Inv Grp II LP ....E.......209 928-1567
18402 Tuolumne Rd Apt 31 Tuolumne (95379) ***(P-11129)***
Tuolumne Cy Senior Apartments, Tuolumne *Also called Tuolumne City Inv Grp II LP* ***(P-11129)***
Tuolumne Me-Wuk Indian ....D.......209 928-5400
18880 Cherry Valley Blvd Tuolumne (95379) ***(P-20013)***
Tuolumne Mewuk Indian Health, Tuolumne *Also called Tuolumne Me-Wuk Indian* ***(P-20013)***
Tuolumne Utilities District ....D.......209 532-5536
18885 Nugget Blvd Sonora (95370) ***(P-6316)***
Tupaz Day Care Services Inc ....D.......408 377-1622
3015 Union Ave San Jose (95124) ***(P-24097)***
Tupaz Homes LLC ....D.......408 377-1622
2038 Biarritz Pl San Jose (95138) ***(P-1250)***
Turbine Repair Services LLC (PA) ....D.......909 947-2256
1838 E Cedar St Ontario (91761) ***(P-17999)***
Turbo Data Systems Inc (PA) ....E.......714 573-5757
18302 Irvine Blvd Ste 200 Tustin (92780) ***(P-16192)***
Turbo Tires, Irwindale *Also called Turbo Wholesale Tires Inc* ***(P-6700)***
Turbo Wholesale Tires Inc (PA) ....A.......626 856-1400
5793 Martin Rd Irwindale (91706) ***(P-6700)***
Turbotax, San Diego *Also called Intuit Inc* ***(P-15723)***
Turelk Inc ....D.......858 633-8085
11622 El Camino Real # 100 San Diego (92130) ***(P-1680)***
Turelk Inc (PA) ....C.......310 835-3736
3700 Santa Fe Ave Ste 200 Long Beach (90810) ***(P-1681)***
Turelk San Diego, San Diego *Also called Turelk Inc* ***(P-1680)***
Turf Star Inc ....D.......760 772-3575
79253 Country Club Dr Bermuda Dunes (92203) ***(P-7715)***
Turfstar, Bermuda Dunes *Also called Turf Star Inc* ***(P-7715)***
Turk & Eddy Associates LP ....D.......415 474-6524
201 Eddy St San Francisco (94102) ***(P-11130)***
Turkey Creek Golf Club, Lincoln *Also called Clubcorp Usa Inc* ***(P-18698)***
Turlock Dairy & Rfrgn Inc ....D.......209 667-6455
1819 S Walnut Rd Turlock (95380) ***(P-7716)***
Turlock Diagnostic Center, Turlock *Also called Emanuel Medical Center Inc* ***(P-21407)***
Turlock Irrigation District (PA) ....C.......209 883-8222
333 E Canal Dr Turlock (95380) ***(P-25085)***
Turlock Irrigation District ....B.......209 883-8300
901 N Broadway Turlock (95380) ***(P-6568)***
Turlock Nrsing Rhabilation Ctr, Turlock *Also called Covenant Care California LLC* ***(P-20348)***
Turn Around Communications Inc ....C.......626 443-2400
4400 Temple City Blvd El Monte (91731) ***(P-1989)***
Turn Behavioral Hlth Svcs Inc (PA) ....D.......858 573-2600
9465 Farnham St San Diego (92123) ***(P-22702)***
Turn Behavioral Hlth Svcs Inc ....D.......559 264-7521
2550 W Clinton Ave Fresno (93705) ***(P-22703)***
Turn Inc (PA) ....C.......650 353-4399
901 Marshall St 200 Redwood City (94063) ***(P-13984)***
TURNABOUT SHOP, El Cerrito *Also called Berkeley Clinic Auxuillary* ***(P-25398)***
Turner Broadcasting System Inc ....E.......818 977-5452
3500 W Olive Ave Ste 1500 Burbank (91505) ***(P-18138)***
Turner Broadcasting System Inc ....D.......310 788-6767
1888 Century Park E # 1200 Los Angeles (90067) ***(P-5759)***
Turner Construction Company ....B.......714 940-9000
1900 S State College Blvd # 200 Anaheim (92806) ***(P-1682)***
Turner Construction Company ....D.......213 891-3000
555 S Flower St Ste 4220 Los Angeles (90071) ***(P-1251)***
Turner Construction Company ....D.......916 444-4421
2500 Venture Oaks Way # 200 Sacramento (95833) ***(P-1683)***
Turner Construction Company ....E.......510 267-8100
300 Frank H Ogawa Plz # 510 Oakland (94612) ***(P-1684)***
Turner Construction Company ....D.......415 705-8900
311 California St Ste 450 San Francisco (94104) ***(P-1685)***
Turner Construction Company ....D.......858 320-4040
15378 Ave Of Science # 100 San Diego (92128) ***(P-1686)***
Turner Construction Company ....D.......916 444-4421
2500 Venture Oaks Way # 200 Sacramento (95833) ***(P-1687)***
Turner Dockworth, San Francisco *Also called Destination Moon LP* ***(P-14111)***
Turner Security Systems Inc ....C.......559 486-3466
120 W Shields Ave Fresno (93705) ***(P-16840)***
Turner Techtronics Inc ....C.......949 724-1339
17845 Sky Park Cir Irvine (92614) ***(P-16295)***
Turner Techtronics Inc (PA) ....C.......818 973-1060
7675 N San Fernando Rd Burbank (91505) ***(P-16296)***
Turning Point Central Cal Inc ....E.......559 627-1490
711 N Court St Visalia (93291) ***(P-24098)***
Turning Point Cmnty Programs ....D.......916 393-1222
4600 47th Ave Ste 111 Sacramento (95824) ***(P-24701)***
Turning Point For God ....D.......619 258-3600
10007 Riverford Rd Lakeside (92040) ***(P-18412)***
Turning Point I S A, Sacramento *Also called Turning Point Cmnty Programs* ***(P-24701)***
Turning Point Ministries, Lakeside *Also called Turning Point For God* ***(P-18412)***
Turnupseed Electric Service ....D.......559 686-1541
1580 S K St Tulare (93274) ***(P-2773)***
Turtle Bay Exploration Park ....E.......530 243-4282
1335 Arboretum Dr Ste A Redding (96003) ***(P-24919)***
Turtle Entertainment America ....E.......818 861-7315
1212 Chestnut St Burbank (91506) ***(P-18469)***
Turtle Rock Cdc, Irvine *Also called Child Development Incorporated* ***(P-24286)***
Tusa Inc (PA) ....C.......888 848-3749
986 Walsh Ave Santa Clara (95050) ***(P-16297)***
Tuscan Inn, San Francisco *Also called Kms Fishermans Wharf LP* ***(P-12819)***
Tuscan Inn, San Francisco *Also called Kimpton Hotel & Rest Group LLC* ***(P-12812)***
Tuscan Inn, San Francisco *Also called 425 North Point Street LLC* ***(P-12292)***
Tustin Care Center Corp ....D.......714 832-6780
1051 Bryan Ave Tustin (92780) ***(P-20969)***
Tustin Executive Center, Tustin *Also called Southern Cal Prmnnte Med Group* ***(P-10316)***
Tustin Hcnda Memory Care Cmnty, Tustin *Also called Silverado Senior Living Inc* ***(P-21215)***
Tustin Ranch Golf Club, Tustin *Also called Crown Golf Properties LP* ***(P-27205)***
Tustin Ranch Golf Club, Tustin *Also called Sanyo Foods Corp America* ***(P-19037)***
Tustin Ranch Medical Offices, Tustin *Also called Kaiser Foundation Hospitals* ***(P-19591)***
Tutera Group Inc ....D.......209 223-2231
811 Court St Jackson (95642) ***(P-24702)***
Tutor Perini Corporation (PA) ....C.......818 362-8391
15901 Olden St Sylmar (91342) ***(P-1688)***
Tutor Perini/Zachry/Parsons ....D.......559 385-7025
1401 Fulton St Ste 400 Fresno (93721) ***(P-2071)***
Tutor-Saliba Corporation (HQ) ....D.......818 362-8391
15901 Olden St Sylmar (91342) ***(P-1689)***
Tuttle Family Enterprises Inc ....B.......818 534-2566
21020 Superior St Chatsworth (91311) ***(P-14412)***
Tuv Sud America Inc ....D.......858 546-3999
10040 Mesa Rim Rd San Diego (92121) ***(P-26735)***
TV 36 ....E.......408 953-3636
2102 Commerce Dr San Jose (95131) ***(P-5842)***
TV Group, San Diego *Also called Panasonic Corp North America* ***(P-7423)***
TV Guide Entrmt Group LLC ....D.......310 360-1441
2700 Colorado Ave Ste 200 Santa Monica (90404) ***(P-7430)***
Tvb (usa) Inc (HQ) ....E.......562 345-9871
15411 Blackburn Ave Norwalk (90650) ***(P-5962)***
Tvgla, Los Angeles *Also called Visionaire Group Inc* ***(P-13917)***
Tvguide.com, Playa Vista *Also called Pop Media Networks LLC* ***(P-18456)***
Tvu Networks Corporation (PA) ....D.......650 969-6732
857 Maude Ave Mountain View (94043) ***(P-5843)***
TW Security Corp (HQ) ....C.......949 932-1000
5 Park Plz Ste 400 Irvine (92614) ***(P-7122)***
TW Services Inc ....B.......714 441-2400
2751 E Chapman Ave # 204 Fullerton (92831) ***(P-5250)***
Twain Harte Horsemen ....D.......209 601-5585
23580 View Ln Columbia (95310) ***(P-25270)***
Twelve Bridges Golf Club, Lincoln *Also called Crstb Partners LLC* ***(P-18703)***
Twentieth Century Fox Home E (HQ) ....A.......310 369-1000
10201 W Pico Blvd Los Angeles (90064) ***(P-18139)***
Twentieth Cntury Fox Film Corp (HQ) ....D.......310 369-1000
10201 W Pico Blvd Los Angeles (90064) ***(P-18140)***
Twentieth Cntury Fox Intl Corp (HQ) ....B.......310 969-5300
10201 W Pico Blvd Bldg 1 Los Angeles (90064) ***(P-18244)***
Twenty Mile Productions LLC ....C.......412 251-0767
11833 Miss Ave Ste 101 Los Angeles (90025) ***(P-18470)***
Twenty4seven Hotels Corp ....B.......949 734-6400
520 Newport Center Dr # 520 Newport Beach (92660) ***(P-27071)***

Mergent e-mail: customerrelations@mergent.com
1500
2019 Directory of California
Wholesalers and Services Companies
(P-0000) Products & Services Section entry number
(PA)=Parent Co (HQ)=Headquarters (DH)=Div Headquarters

TWI- Techno West Inc .... D 714 635-4070
1391 S Allec St Anaheim (92805) *(P-2488)*
Twilight Haven .... D 559 251-8417
1717 S Winery Ave Fresno (93727) *(P-20844)*
Twilio Inc (PA) .... C 415 390-2337
375 Beale St Ste 300 San Francisco (94105) *(P-5423)*
Twin Cities Community Hosp Inc .... B 805 434-3500
1100 Las Tablas Rd Templeton (93465) *(P-20014)*
Twin Med LLC (PA) .... D 323 582-9900
11333 Greenstone Ave Santa Fe Springs (90670) *(P-7226)*
Twin Oaks Nrsing Rhblttion Ctr, Chico Also called Evergreen At Chico LLC *(P-20414)*
Twin Oaks Power LP (HQ) .... D 619 696-2034
101 Ash St Hq10b San Diego (92101) *(P-6145)*
Twining Inc (PA) .... D 562 426-3355
2883 E Spring St Ste 300 Long Beach (90806) *(P-26736)*
Twining Laboratories, Long Beach Also called Twining Inc *(P-26736)*
Twitch Interactive Inc .... A 415 919-5000
225 Bush St Ste 900 San Francisco (94104) *(P-5657)*
Twitter Inc (PA) .... C 415 222-9670
1355 Market St Ste 900 San Francisco (94103) *(P-16256)*
Two Harbors Enterprises Inc .... D 310 510-2000
150 Metropole Ave Avalon (90704) *(P-3737)*
Two Jinn Inc (PA) .... D 760 431-9911
1000 Aviara Dr Ste 300 Carlsbad (92011) *(P-17526)*
Two Palms Nursing Center Inc (PA) .... E 626 798-8991
2637 E Washington Blvd Pasadena (91107) *(P-21232)*
Two Palms Nursing Center Inc .... D 626 796-1103
150 Bellefontaine St Pasadena (91105) *(P-21233)*
Two Palms Nursing Center Inc .... D 323 681-4615
150 Bellefontaine St Pasadena (91105) *(P-21234)*
Two Pore Guys System Inc .... D 821 420-0710
101 Cooper St Santa Cruz (95060) *(P-16068)*
Two Rivers Demolition Inc .... D 916 638-6775
2620 Mercantile Dr 100 Rancho Cordova (95742) *(P-3465)*
Two Roads Prof Resources Inc .... C 714 901-3804
5122 Bolsa Ave Ste 112 Huntington Beach (92649) *(P-14927)*
TWR Enterprises Inc .... C 951 279-2000
1661 Railroad St Corona (92880) *(P-3087)*
Ty Investment Inc .... D 619 448-4242
1015 21st St Unit A Santa Monica (90403) *(P-19074)*
TY Lin International Group (PA) .... C 415 291-3700
345 California St Fl 23 San Francisco (94104) *(P-25963)*
Tyan Inc .... D 818 785-5831
1500 Glenoaks Blvd San Fernando (91340) *(P-16841)*
Tyan Computer Corporation .... D 510 651-8868
3288 Laurelview Ct Fremont (94538) *(P-7123)*
Tyler Bluff Wind Project LLC .... A 888 903-6926
15445 Innovation Dr San Diego (92128) *(P-6146)*
Tyler Palmieri Wiener .... D 949 851-9400
1900 Main St Ste 700 Irvine (92614) *(P-23417)*
Tyme Maidu Tribe-Berry Creek .... A 530 538-4560
4020 Olive Hwy Oroville (95966) *(P-13351)*
Tyr Sport Inc .... D 562 430-1380
1790 Apollo Ct Seal Beach (90740) *(P-8340)*
Tz Holdings LP .... A 949 719-2200
567 San Nicolas Dr # 120 Newport Beach (92660) *(P-15884)*
Tzippy Care Inc .... D 323 737-7778
2190 W Adams Blvd Los Angeles (90018) *(P-21235)*
U A L, Irvine Also called United Agribusiness League *(P-24987)*
U B C 200, Beverly Hills Also called Mufg Union Bank National Assn *(P-9356)*
U C Health Systems, Sacramento Also called U C Med Humn Rsrces Aplcat Svc *(P-21863)*
U C I Distribution Plus, Pasadena Also called United Couriers Inc *(P-4813)*
U C L Incorporated (PA) .... D 323 235-0099
620 S Hacienda Blvd City of Industry (91745) *(P-4283)*
U C L A Dermatology, Los Angeles Also called Gary Lask *(P-19480)*
U C Med Humn Rsrces Aplcat Svc .... D 916 734-5916
2730 Stockton Blvd # 21002500 Sacramento (95817) *(P-21863)*
U C P-UNITED CEREBAL PALSY ASS, Fresno Also called United Crbrl Plsy of Cntrl
CA *(P-24852)*
U C S F School of Dentistry .... E 415 476-5609
100 Buchanan St San Francisco (94102) *(P-20141)*
U F C Pension Trust Fund, Cypress Also called Cal Southern United Food *(P-10477)*
U F I, Los Angeles Also called United Fabrics Intl Inc *(P-8247)*
U Gym LLC .... D 951 808-3850
470 N Mckinley St Corona (92879) *(P-18672)*
U Gym LLC (PA) .... D 714 668-0911
1501 Quail St Ste 100 Newport Beach (92660) *(P-18673)*
U S Army Corps of Engineers .... D 916 557-7491
1645 Riverbank Rd West Sacramento (95605) *(P-25964)*
U S Army Corps of Engineers .... D 916 649-0133
2194 Ascot Ave Rio Linda (95673) *(P-25965)*
U S Army Corps of Engineers .... D 916 925-7001
3900 Roseville Rd North Highlands (95660) *(P-25966)*
U S Army Corps of Engineers .... D 415 289-3067
2100 Bridgeway Sausalito (94965) *(P-25967)*
U S C, Los Angeles Also called Usc Credit Union *(P-9616)*
U S Foods, La Mirada Also called US Foods Inc *(P-8481)*
U S GOVERNMENT, Tulelake Also called Lava Beds National Monuments *(P-25437)*
U S Mbile Wrless Cmmunications (PA) .... D 858 537-0709
8300 Juniper Creek Ln # 100 San Diego (92126) *(P-5424)*
U S Merchant Services, Newport Beach Also called Montrenes Financial Svcs Inc *(P-17335)*
U S Office & Industry Supply, Van Nuys Also called Nat Sim Corp *(P-8084)*
U S Perma Inc .... E 408 436-0600
1696 Rogers Ave San Jose (95112) *(P-3014)*
U S Private Protection SEC Inc .... C 310 301-0010
5555 Inglewood Blvd # 205 Culver City (90230) *(P-16842)*
U S Weatherford L P .... D 661 589-9483
2815 Fruitvale Ave Bakersfield (93308) *(P-1084)*

U S Xpress Inc .... C 760 768-6707
363 Nina Lee Rd Calexico (92231) *(P-4284)*
U T L A, Los Angeles Also called United Teachers-Los Angeles *(P-25088)*
U W G Northern California Div, Stockton Also called Unified Grocers Inc *(P-8475)*
U W G Southern California Div, Los Angeles Also called Unified Grocers Inc *(P-8530)*
U-2 Home Entertainment Inc .... E 650 871-8118
170 S Spruce Ave Ste 200 South San Francisco (94080) *(P-7555)*
U-Dub Productions, Palm Desert Also called Desert Television LLC *(P-5782)*
U-Haul Co of California (HQ) 800 528-0463
44511 S Grimmer Blvd Fremont (94538) *(P-17617)*
U. S. Grant Hotel, San Diego Also called American Prprty-Mnagement Corp *(P-12317)*
U.S. Trading Company, Hayward Also called Ustov Inc *(P-8484)*
Ua Galaxy Los Cerritos .... D 562 865-6499
4900 E 4th St Ontario (91764) *(P-18322)*
Ua Galaxy Los Cerritos 33, Ontario Also called Ua Galaxy Los Cerritos *(P-18322)*
Uaw-Lbor Emplyment Trning Corp .... C 323 730-7900
3965 S Vermont Ave Los Angeles (90037) *(P-14788)*
Uaw-Lbor Emplyment Trning Corp (PA) .... C 562 989-7700
11010 Artesia Blvd # 100 Cerritos (90703) *(P-14789)*
Uber Technologies Inc 832 610-0359
900 Arastradero Rd Bldg B Palo Alto (94304) *(P-16257)*
Ubi Soft Entertainment 415 547-4000
625 3rd St Fl 3 San Francisco (94107) *(P-18471)*
Ubics Inc 415 289-1400
1050 Bridgeway Sausalito (94965) *(P-15515)*
Ubiquity, San Francisco Also called Decimal Inc *(P-17126)*
UBS Financial Services Inc .... C 213 972-1511
777 S Figueroa St # 5100 Los Angeles (90017) *(P-10024)*
UBS Financial Services Inc .... D 310 274-8441
131 S Rodeo Dr Ste 200 Beverly Hills (90212) *(P-10025)*
UBS Financial Services Inc .... C 619 236-0460
600 W Broadway Ste 2100 San Diego (92101) *(P-10026)*
UBS Financial Services Inc 415 954-6700
555 California St # 3200 San Francisco (94104) *(P-10027)*
UBS Financial Services Inc 949 760-5308
888 San Clemente Dr # 300 Newport Beach (92660) *(P-10028)*
UBS Financial Services Inc .... E 916 648-7200
1610 Arden Way Ste 200 Sacramento (95815) *(P-10029)*
UBS Financial Services Inc .... D 415 398-6400
555 California St # 4650 San Francisco (94104) *(P-10030)*
UBS Financial Services Inc .... E 408 282-8402
50 W San Fernando St Fl 8 San Jose (95113) *(P-17527)*
UBS Financial Services Inc .... E 951 684-6300
3801 University Ave # 300 Riverside (92501) *(P-17528)*
UBS Financial Services Inc .... D 858 454-9181
1200 Prospect St Ste 100 La Jolla (92037) *(P-17529)*
UBS Financial Services Inc .... E 626 449-1501
200 S Los Robles Ave # 600 Pasadena (91101) *(P-17530)*
UBS Financial Services Inc .... D 415 398-6400
555 California St # 4650 San Francisco (94104) *(P-10031)*
UBS Securities LLC .... D 415 352-5650
555 California St # 4650 San Francisco (94104) *(P-10032)*
Uc David Home Care Services, Sacramento Also called Ucd Mc Home Care
Services *(P-27072)*
Uc Davis Health System (PA) 916 734-1000
4610 X St Sacramento (95817) *(P-20015)*
Uc Davis Medical Center, Sacramento Also called University California Davis *(P-21884)*
Uc Irvine Hlth Rgonal Burn Ctr, Orange Also called University California Irvine *(P-20032)*
Uc Irvine Medical Center, Orange Also called University California Irvine *(P-21886)*
Uc Regents 310 301-8777
300 Medical Plaza Los Angeles (90095) *(P-20016)*
Uc Riverside RES Economic Dev, Riverside Also called University Cal Riverside *(P-26575)*
Uca General Insurance, Cypress Also called United Chinese American Genera *(P-10809)*
Ucc Direct Services Inc .... D 818 662-4100
330 N Brand Blvd Ste 700 Glendale (91203) *(P-16193)*
UCCR, Petaluma Also called United Cmps Cnfrences Retreats *(P-13456)*
Ucd Mc Home Care Services .... C 916 734-2458
3630 Business Dr Sacramento (95820) *(P-27072)*
Ucd Recreation Hall .... D 530 752-6071
1 Shields Ave Davis (95616) *(P-19252)*
UCI Construction Inc .... D 661 587-0192
3900 Fruitvale Ave Bakersfield (93308) *(P-25968)*
UCI Family Health Center, Santa Ana Also called University California Irvine *(P-20033)*
Ucla Bookstore, Los Angeles Also called Associated Students UCLA *(P-24742)*
Ucla Copy Services .... E 310 794-6371
555 Westwood Plz Ste B Los Angeles (90095) *(P-14093)*
Ucla Foundation .... B 310 794-3193
10920 Wilshire Blvd # 200 Los Angeles (90024) *(P-12084)*
Ucla Health System .... D 310 825-9111
757 Westwood Plz Los Angeles (90095) *(P-20017)*
Ucla Health System Auxiliary .... A 310 267-4327
10920 Wilshire Blvd Los Angeles (90024) *(P-22441)*
Ucla Healthcare .... D 310 319-4560
1821 Wilshire Blvd Fl 6 Santa Monica (90403) *(P-21864)*
Ucla Marina Center .... D 310 825-3671
111 Deneve Dr Los Angeles (90095) *(P-19253)*
Ucla Mdcn SC Phrmclgy, Los Angeles Also called Associated Students UCLA *(P-19310)*
Ucla Medical Center, Los Angeles Also called University Cal Los Angeles *(P-21874)*
Ucla Medical Center, Sylmar Also called University Cal Los Angeles *(P-21875)*
Ucla Nrpsychtric Bhvioral Hlth, Los Angeles Also called Uc Regents *(P-20016)*
Ucla Primary Care Westlake, Westlake Village Also called University Cal Los
Angeles *(P-20028)*
Ucp Dronfield North, Sylmar Also called United Cp/S Chldrns Fndn La *(P-21237)*
Ucp Work Inc .... C 805 962-6699
2040 Alameda Padre Serra Santa Barbara (93103) *(P-25476)*

Employee Codes: A=Over 500 employees, B=251-500
C=101-250, D=51-100, E=50

2019 Directory of California
Wholesalers and Services Companies

© Mergent Inc. 1-800-342-5647

1501

Ucp Work Inc (PA).....C.....805 566-9000
5320 Carpinteria Ave G Carpinteria (93013) ***(P-24240)***
Ucr Botany and Plant Sciences.....D.....951 827-5133
3401 Watkins Dr Riverside (92507) ***(P-12085)***
Ucsd Healthcare.....D.....858 657-7105
355 Dickinson St 340 San Diego (92103) ***(P-22897)***
Ucsd Thornton Hospital, La Jolla *Also called University Cal San Diego* ***(P-21879)***
Ucsf Aids Health Project.....D.....415 476-6445
1930 Market St San Francisco (94102) ***(P-24099)***
Ucsf Benioff Chld Hosp Oakland, Oakland *Also called Childrens Hospotal & Research* ***(P-21319)***
Ucsf Medical Center, San Francisco *Also called University Cal San Francisco* ***(P-20029)***
Ucsf Medical Center At Mt Zion, San Francisco *Also called University Cal San Francisco* ***(P-21882)***
UDC, Anaheim *Also called Universal Dust Collector* ***(P-1448)***
Uec, Cypress *Also called United Exchange Corp* ***(P-17532)***
Uesugi Farms Inc (PA).....D.....408 842-1294
1020 State Highway 25 Gilroy (95020) ***(P-88)***
Ufc Gym, Newport Beach *Also called U Gym LLC* ***(P-18673)***
Ufcw & Employers Trust LLC (PA).....C.....800 552-2400
1000 Burnett Ave Ste 200 Concord (94520) ***(P-12129)***
Ufcw Local 770, Los Angeles *Also called United Food and Commercial* ***(P-25087)***
UFS International LLC.....C.....714 713-6311
16871 Millikan Ave Irvine (92606) ***(P-17531)***
Ugm Citatah Inc (PA).....C.....562 921-9549
13220 Cambridge St Santa Fe Springs (90670) ***(P-6909)***
Ugmc, Santa Fe Springs *Also called Ugm Citatah Inc* ***(P-6909)***
Uhc of California (HQ).....A.....714 952-1121
5995 Plaza Dr Cypress (90630) ***(P-10322)***
Uhp Healthcare, Inglewood *Also called Watts Health Foundation Inc* ***(P-20971)***
UHS, Chino *Also called Canyon Ridge Hospital Inc* ***(P-21937)***
UHS, Torrance *Also called Del AMO Hospital Inc* ***(P-21953)***
UHS Surgical Services, Sun Valley *Also called PRI Medical Technologies Inc* ***(P-7212)***
Uhs-Corona Inc (HQ).....A.....951 737-4343
800 S Main St Corona (92882) ***(P-21865)***
Uhs-Corona Inc.....C.....951 736-7200
730 Magnolia Ave Corona (92879) ***(P-22704)***
Uiprojects, Costa Mesa *Also called United Infrstrcture Prjcts Inc* ***(P-25969)***
Uka LLC.....E.....949 610-8000
620 Newport Center Dr # 1400 Newport Beach (92660) ***(P-13352)***
Ukiah Adventist Hospital (HQ).....B.....707 462-3111
275 Hospital Dr Ukiah (95482) ***(P-21866)***
Ukiah Adventist Hospital.....C.....707 462-3111
1120 S Dora St Ukiah (95482) ***(P-21867)***
Ukiah Convalescent Hospital, Ukiah *Also called Berryman Health Inc* ***(P-21008)***
Ukiah SC Transportation.....D.....707 463-5234
710 Maple Ave Ukiah (95482) ***(P-3947)***
Ukiah Valley Medical Center, Ukiah *Also called Ukiah Adventist Hospital* ***(P-21866)***
Ukiah Vly Assn For Hbilitation (PA).....D.....707 468-8824
990 S Dora St Ukiah (95482) ***(P-24241)***
Uline Inc.....D.....909 605-7090
2950 Jurupa St Ontario (91761) ***(P-9264)***
Ulta Beauty, Turlock *Also called Ulta Salon Cosmt Fragrance Inc* ***(P-13682)***
Ulta Beauty Inc.....C.....916 581-4121
117 Ferrari Ranch Rd Lincoln (95648) ***(P-13676)***
Ulta Beauty Inc.....C.....805 825-0093
755 E Betteravia Rd Santa Maria (93454) ***(P-13677)***
Ulta Beauty Inc.....C.....858 581-9003
4941 Clairemont Dr Ste B San Diego (92117) ***(P-13678)***
Ulta Beauty Inc.....C.....951 652-2966
2243 W Florida Ave Hemet (92545) ***(P-13679)***
Ulta Salon Cosmt Fragrance Inc.....C.....909 592-5393
1229 S Lone Hill Ave Glendora (91740) ***(P-13680)***
Ulta Salon Cosmt Fragrance Inc.....C.....661 664-1402
9000 Ming Ave Bakersfield (93311) ***(P-13681)***
Ulta Salon Cosmt Fragrance Inc.....C.....209 664-1725
2841 Countryside Dr Turlock (95380) ***(P-13682)***
Ulta Salon Cosmt Fragrance Inc.....C.....760 744-0853
185 S Las Posas Rd San Marcos (92078) ***(P-13683)***
Ultimate Communication Systems, Anaheim *Also called Rjb Enterprises Inc* ***(P-2710)***
Ultimate Construction Inc.....C.....562 633-3389
8811 Alonzo Blvd Long Beach (90805) ***(P-3088)***
Ultimate Creations LLC.....D.....559 221-4936
516 W Shaw Ave Ste 200 Fresno (93704) ***(P-12278)***
ULTIMATE DEMO, Pomona *Also called Ultimate Removal Inc* ***(P-3466)***
Ultimate Landscaping MGT.....D.....714 502-9711
700 E Sycamore St Anaheim (92805) ***(P-954)***
Ultimate Maintenance Svcs Inc.....E.....310 542-1474
4237 Redondo Beach Blvd Lawndale (90260) ***(P-14413)***
Ultimate Removal Inc.....C.....909 524-0800
2168 Pomona Blvd Pomona (91768) ***(P-3466)***
Ultimate Staffing Services, Orange *Also called Roth Staffing Companies LP* ***(P-14908)***
Ultimo Software Solutions Inc.....C.....408 943-1490
33268 Central Ave 2 Union City (94587) ***(P-15885)***
Ultra Solutions LLC.....E.....909 628-1778
1137 E Philadelphia St Ontario (91761) ***(P-7227)***
Ultradot Media.....D.....562 906-0737
9908 Bell Ranch Dr Santa Fe Springs (90670) ***(P-13961)***
Ultraex LLC.....D.....510 723-3760
2633 Barrington Ct Hayward (94545) ***(P-4440)***
Ultraex Inc.....D.....800 882-1000
2633 Barrington Ct Hayward (94545) ***(P-4848)***
Ultralink LLC.....C.....714 427-5500
535 Anton Blvd Ste 200 Costa Mesa (92626) ***(P-10150)***
Ultrasigns Electrical Advg, San Diego *Also called Jones Sign Co Inc* ***(P-7141)***
Ultraviolet Devices Inc.....D.....661 295-8140
26145 Technology Dr Valencia (91355) ***(P-7659)***
Ultrex Management Services (PA).....D.....805 783-1234
712 Fiero Ln Ste 33 San Luis Obispo (93401) ***(P-6985)***
Uma Enterprises Inc (PA).....C.....310 631-1166
350 W Apra St Compton (90220) ***(P-6797)***
Umi of Huntington Beach, Huntington Beach *Also called United Medical Imaging Inc* ***(P-20020)***
Umina Bros Inc (PA).....D.....213 622-9206
1601 E Olympic Blvd # 403 Los Angeles (90021) ***(P-8739)***
Umpqua Bank.....D.....818 385-1362
16501 Ventura Blvd Encino (91436) ***(P-9374)***
Umpqua Bank.....D.....619 668-5159
7777 Alvarado Rd Ste 515 La Mesa (91942) ***(P-9492)***
Ums Banking, Glendale *Also called United Merchant Svcs Cal Inc* ***(P-6986)***
UNAC/UHCP, San Dimas *Also called Associations of United Nurses* ***(P-25054)***
Unchained Labs (PA).....C.....925 587-9800
6870 Koll Center Pkwy # 20 Pleasanton (94566) ***(P-22153)***
Uncle Credit Union (PA).....D.....925 447-5001
2100 Las Positas Ct Livermore (94551) ***(P-9612)***
Undc, Sacramento *Also called Universal Network Dev Corp* ***(P-27892)***
Underground Cnstr Co Inc.....C.....707 746-8800
5145 Industrial Way Benicia (94510) ***(P-6188)***
Underground Elephant Inc.....D.....800 466-4178
808 J St San Diego (92101) ***(P-13913)***
Underwriters Laboratories Inc.....B.....248 427-5300
455 E Trimble Rd San Jose (95131) ***(P-26737)***
Underwriters Laboratories Inc.....B.....510 771-1000
47173 Benicia St Fremont (94538) ***(P-26738)***
Underwriters Laboratories Inc.....C.....408 754-6500
4510 Riding Club Ct Hayward (94542) ***(P-26739)***
Underwriters Laboratories Inc.....C.....408 493-9910
2191 Zanker Rd San Jose (95131) ***(P-26740)***
Unfi, Rocklin *Also called United Natural Foods West Inc* ***(P-8891)***
Unfi, Rocklin *Also called United Natural Foods Inc* ***(P-8890)***
UNI Hosiery Co Inc (PA).....C.....213 228-0100
1911 E Olympic Blvd Los Angeles (90021) ***(P-8281)***
Unical Aviation Inc (PA).....C.....909 348-1700
680 S Lemon Ave City of Industry (91789) ***(P-7917)***
Unical Enterprises Inc.....D.....626 965-5588
16960 Gale Ave City of Industry (91745) ***(P-7124)***
Unico Industrial Service Co (PA).....E.....707 736-8787
945 Tyler St Benicia (94510) ***(P-18000)***
Unico Mechanical Corp.....D.....707 745-4540
1209 Polk St Benicia (94510) ***(P-7814)***
Unifax Insurance Systems Inc.....D.....818 591-9800
26050 Mureau Rd Fl 2 Calabasas (91302) ***(P-10808)***
Unified Aircraft Services Inc (PA).....D.....909 877-0535
1571 S Lilac Ave Bloomington (92316) ***(P-5212)***
Unified Grocers Inc (HQ).....A.....323 264-5200
5200 Sheila St Commerce (90040) ***(P-8474)***
Unified Grocers Inc.....D.....323 232-6124
457 E Martin Luther King Los Angeles (90011) ***(P-8530)***
Unified Grocers Inc.....C.....209 931-1990
1990 Piccoli Rd Stockton (95215) ***(P-8475)***
Unified Grocers Inc.....D.....323 264-5200
455 N Canyons Pkwy Livermore (94551) ***(P-8476)***
Unified Inv Programs Inc (PA).....D.....310 782-1878
2368 Torrance Blvd # 200 Torrance (90501) ***(P-22898)***
Unified Teldata Inc.....D.....415 888-8940
126 Neider Ln Mill Valley (94941) ***(P-7556)***
Unified Valet Parking Inc.....D.....818 822-5807
99 S Chester Ave Fl 2 Pasadena (91106) ***(P-17709)***
Unifirst Corporation.....E.....209 941-8364
819 N Hunter St Stockton (95202) ***(P-13623)***
Unifirst Corporation.....E.....916 929-3766
4630 Beloit Dr Ste 40 Sacramento (95838) ***(P-13555)***
Unifirst Corporation.....D.....619 263-6116
4041 Market St San Diego (92102) ***(P-13624)***
Unifirst Corporation.....C.....909 390-8670
700 Etiwanda Ave Ste C Ontario (91761) ***(P-13625)***
Unifirst Corporation.....D.....559 233-0400
4730 E Commerce Ave Fresno (93725) ***(P-13626)***
Unifirst Corporation.....D.....408 297-8101
2016 Zanker Rd San Jose (95131) ***(P-13627)***
Uniform Accessories, Northridge *Also called Rashman Corporation* ***(P-7897)***
Unify Financial Federal Cr Un (PA).....D.....310 536-5000
1899 Western Way Ste 100 Torrance (90501) ***(P-9613)***
Uniglobe Travel Planner, Irvine *Also called Uniglobe Travel West Inc* ***(P-4957)***
Uniglobe Travel West Inc (PA).....D.....949 623-9000
18662 Macarthur Blvd # 100 Irvine (92612) ***(P-4957)***
Unigro, San Bernardino *Also called L & L Nursery Supply Inc* ***(P-9081)***
Unilab Corporation (HQ).....B.....818 737-6000
8401 Fallbrook Ave West Hills (91304) ***(P-22154)***
Unilab Corporation.....B.....408 927-8331
6475 Camden Ave Ste 104 San Jose (95120) ***(P-22155)***
Union 76, Los Angeles *Also called Kim Chong* ***(P-17274)***
Union Asphalt Inc.....D.....805 922-3551
1625 E Donovan Rd Santa Maria (93454) ***(P-4074)***
Union Bank, Los Angeles *Also called Bank of Tokyo Ltd* ***(P-9495)***
Union Building Maintenance, Commerce *Also called Uniserve Facilities Svcs Corp* ***(P-14414)***
Union City Medical Offices, Union City *Also called Kaiser Foundation Hospitals* ***(P-19539)***
Union Pacific, Delano *Also called Loup Logistics Company* ***(P-5102)***
Union Pacific Corporation.....A.....916 789-5311
9451 Atkinson St Ste 100 Roseville (95747) ***(P-3626)***
Union Pacific Railroad Company.....D.....805 286-5851
999 Paso Robles St Paso Robles (93446) ***(P-3627)***
Union Pacific Railroad Company.....C.....559 443-2244
3135 N Weber Ave Fresno (93705) ***(P-3628)***

Union Pacific Railroad Company ....D.......909 685-2710
2000 S Sycamore Ave Bloomington (92316) ***(P-3629)***
Union Pacific Railroad Company ....D.......916 789-5930
9391 Atkinson St Ste 100 Roseville (95747) ***(P-3630)***
Union Pacific Railroad Company ....D.......213 446-1900
4341 E Washington Blvd Commerce (90023) ***(P-3631)***
Union Pacific Railroad Company ....C.......916 789-6055
10031 Fthlls Blvd Ste 200 Roseville (95747) ***(P-3632)***
Union Pacific Railroad Company ....D.......661 321-4604
730 Sumner St Bakersfield (93305) ***(P-3633)***
Union Pan Asian Communities (PA) ....D.......619 232-6454
1031 25th St San Diego (92102) ***(P-24100)***
Union Sanitary District ....C.......510 477-7500
5072 Benson Rd Union City (94587) ***(P-6333)***
Union Supply Company, Rancho Dominguez *Also called Union Supply Group Inc* ***(P-8477)***
Union Supply Group Inc (PA) ....C.......310 603-8899
2301 E Pacifica Pl Rancho Dominguez (90220) ***(P-8477)***
Union Technology Corp (PA) ....E.......323 266-6871
718 Monterey Pass Rd Monterey Park (91754) ***(P-7557)***
Unique Carpets Ltd ....D.......951 352-8125
7360 Jurupa Ave Riverside (92504) ***(P-6798)***
Unique Scaffold, Concord *Also called Ernie & Sons Scaffolding* ***(P-3514)***
Unis LLC (PA) ....C.......909 839-2600
218 Machlin Ct Walnut (91789) ***(P-5190)***
Unis LLC ....D.......310 747-7388
19914 S Via Baron Rancho Dominguez (90220) ***(P-4642)***
Uniserve Facilities Svcs Corp (PA) ....B.......213 533-1000
2363 S Atlantic Blvd Commerce (90040) ***(P-14414)***
Uniserve Facilities Svcs Corp ....A.......310 440-6747
1200 Getty Center Dr Los Angeles (90049) ***(P-14415)***
Unish Corporation ....E.......408 708-9300
4300 Stevens Creek Blvd # 126 San Jose (95129) ***(P-16519)***
Unison, San Francisco *Also called Real Estate Equity Exchange* ***(P-9854)***
Unison Electric ....E.......714 375-5915
16652 Gemini Ln Huntington Beach (92647) ***(P-2774)***
Unisource Discovery LLC (PA) ....D.......888 248-0020
625 The City Dr S Ste 303 Orange (92868) ***(P-23418)***
Unisource Maint Sup Systems, La Palma *Also called Veritiv Operating Company* ***(P-8135)***
Unisource Packaging Inc ....C.......925 227-6000
4225 Hacienda Dr Ste A Pleasanton (94588) ***(P-8128)***
Unisource Solutions Inc (PA) ....C.......562 654-3500
8350 Rex Rd Pico Rivera (90660) ***(P-6738)***
Unisys Corporation ....A.......949 380-5000
9701 Jeronimo Rd Ste 100 Irvine (92618) ***(P-16069)***
Unitas Global LLC (PA) ....D.......213 785-6200
453 S Spring St Ste 201 Los Angeles (90013) ***(P-16194)***
Unitd Van Lines Agnt, Hayward *Also called Chipman Corporation* ***(P-4117)***
Unite Eurotherapy Inc ....D.......760 585-1800
2870 Whiptail Loop Carlsbad (92010) ***(P-8215)***
United Administrative Services, San Jose *Also called Chelbay Schuler & Chelbay* ***(P-10482)***
United Administrative Services ....C.......408 288-4400
6800 Santa Teresa Blvd # 100 San Jose (95119) ***(P-10494)***
United Agribusiness League (PA) ....E.......800 223-4590
54 Corporate Park Irvine (92606) ***(P-24987)***
United Airlines Inc ....C.......650 634-4209
United Airlines Mnt Optnb San Francisco (94128) ***(P-4804)***
United Airlines Inc ....C.......650 634-2468
2435 Whitman Way San Bruno (94066) ***(P-4805)***
United Airlines Inc ....C.......916 877-3002
6850 Airport Blvd Ste 34 Sacramento (95837) ***(P-4994)***
United Airlines Inc ....C.......310 342-8086
6018 Avion Dr Los Angeles (90045) ***(P-4806)***
United Airlines Inc ....D.......650 634-7800
Maintenance Operation Ctr San Francisco (94128) ***(P-4807)***
United Airlines Inc ....C.......619 692-3310
3835 N Harbor Dr Ste 115 San Diego (92101) ***(P-4808)***
United Airlines Inc ....B.......310 258-3319
7300 World Way W Rm 144 Los Angeles (90045) ***(P-4809)***
United Airlines Inc ....C.......650 634-4469
San Francisco Intl Arprt San Francisco (94128) ***(P-4810)***
United Airlines Inc ....D.......760 778-5690
3400 E Tahquitz Cyn 17 Palm Springs (92262) ***(P-4811)***
United Airlines Inc ....C.......650 634-2772
545 Mcdonald Rd 68305 San Francisco (94128) ***(P-4812)***
United Artists Productions Inc ....C.......310 449-3000
10250 Constellation Blvd # 19 Los Angeles (90067) ***(P-18245)***
United Artists Television Corp ....C.......310 449-3000
10250 Constellation Blvd # 27 Los Angeles (90067) ***(P-18246)***
United Auburn Indian Community ....A.......916 408-7777
1200 Athens Ave Lincoln (95648) ***(P-13353)***
United Behavioral Health ....C.......925 246-1343
2300 Clayton Rd Ste 1000 Concord (94520) ***(P-10323)***
United Behavioral Health ....D.......619 641-6800
3111 Cmino Del Rio N 50 San Diego (92108) ***(P-27073)***
United Behavioral Health (HQ) ....C.......415 547-1403
425 Market St Fl 18 San Francisco (94105) ***(P-27074)***
United Biosource LLC ....D.......415 293-1340
303 2nd St Ste S700 San Francisco (94107) ***(P-715)***
United Blood Services Ventura, San Luis Obispo *Also called Vitalant* ***(P-22901)***
United Brothers Concrete Inc ....C.......760 346-1013
41905 Boardwalk Ste K Palm Desert (92211) ***(P-3338)***
United Building Maint Inc ....C.......916 772-8101
8211 Sierra College Blvd Roseville (95661) ***(P-14416)***
United Building Services, Santa Ana *Also called Ponderosa Builders Inc* ***(P-14353)***
United California Glass & Door 415 824-8500
745 Cesar Chavez San Francisco (94124) ***(P-18001)***
United California Realty Inc ....D.......760 949-4040
12829 Bear Valley Rd Victorville (92392) ***(P-11806)***
United Care Homes, City of Industry *Also called Pruitthealth Inc* ***(P-21190)***
United Cargo Logistics, City of Industry *Also called U C L Incorporated* ***(P-4283)***
United Cerebral Palsy Assn San, Stockton *Also called United Cerebral Palsy Associat* ***(P-22056)***
United Cerebral Palsy Assn San (PA) ....C.......858 495-3155
8525 Gibbs Dr Ste 209 San Diego (92123) ***(P-25477)***
United Cerebral Palsy Assoc ....C.......949 333-6400
980 Roosevelt Ste 100 Irvine (92620) ***(P-24101)***
United Cerebral Palsy Assoc (PA) ....C.......209 956-0290
333 W Benjamin Holt Dr # 1 Stockton (95207) ***(P-25048)***
United Cerebral Palsy Assoc of ....D.......805 543-2039
3620 Sacramento Dr # 201 San Luis Obispo (93401) ***(P-24851)***
United Cerebral Palsy Associat ....C.......209 956-0295
333 W Benjamin Holt Dr # 1 Stockton (95207) ***(P-22056)***
United Chinese American Genera (PA) ....E.......714 228-7800
6363 Katella Ave Cypress (90630) ***(P-10809)***
United Cmps Cnfrences Retreats (PA) ....D.......707 762-3220
1304 Sthpint Blvd Ste 200 Petaluma (94954) ***(P-13456)***
United Com Serve ....D.......530 790-3000
1260 Williams Way Yuba City (95991) ***(P-20845)***
United Consortium, Valencia *Also called CC Wellness LLC* ***(P-8159)***
United Convalescent Facilities ....D.......626 629-6950
230 E Adams Blvd Los Angeles (90011) ***(P-21236)***
United Couriers Inc (HQ) ....C.......213 383-3611
3280 E Foothill Blvd Pasadena (91107) ***(P-4813)***
United Cp/S Chldrns Fndn La ....E.......805 494-1141
2170 N Westlake Blvd 22 Westlake Village (91362) ***(P-24102)***
United Cp/S Chldrns Fndn La ....D.......818 364-5911
13272 Dronfield Ave Sylmar (91342) ***(P-21237)***
United Cp/S Chldrns Fndn La ....C.......818 998-8755
11051 Old Snta Susna Pass Chatsworth (91311) ***(P-24703)***
United Cp/S Chldrns Fndn La ....D.......818 782-2211
6430 Independence Ave Woodland Hills (91367) ***(P-21238)***
United Cp/S Chldrns Fndn La ....D.......323 737-0303
2628 Brighton Ave Los Angeles (90018) ***(P-24103)***
United Cpitl Fncl Advisers LLC ....D.......949 999-8500
620 Nwport Ctr Dr Ste 500 Newport Beach (92660) ***(P-10119)***
United Crbrl Plsy of Cntrl CA (PA) ....E.......559 221-8272
4224 N Cedar Ave Fresno (93726) ***(P-24852)***
United Development Group Inc ....E.......858 244-0900
2805 Dickens St Ste 103 San Diego (92106) ***(P-11932)***
United El Segundo Inc (PA) ....D.......310 323-3992
4130 Cover St Long Beach (90808) ***(P-8970)***
United Exchange Corp (PA) ....D.......562 977-4500
5836 Corp Ave Ste 200 Cypress (90630) ***(P-17532)***
United Express Messengers Inc ....D.......310 261-2000
1801 Century Park E # 520 Los Angeles (90067) ***(P-17533)***
United Fabricare Supply Inc (PA) ....D.......310 886-3790
1237 W Walnut St Compton (90220) ***(P-7900)***
United Fabrics Intl Inc ....D.......213 749-8200
1723 S Central Ave Los Angeles (90021) ***(P-8247)***
United Facilities Inc ....E.......209 839-8051
25451 Mountain House Pkwy Tracy (95377) ***(P-4643)***
United Facilities Inc ....E.......951 685-7030
11618 Mulberry Ave Fontana (92337) ***(P-4644)***
United Families Inc (PA) ....D.......760 336-8922
1561 S 4th St El Centro (92243) ***(P-24104)***
United Family Care Inc (PA) ....C.......909 874-1679
8110 Mango Ave Ste 104 Fontana (92335) ***(P-20018)***
United Farm Workers America (PA) ....C.......661 822-5571
29700 Wdford Tehachapi Rd Keene (93531) ***(P-25086)***
United Floral Exchange Inc ....D.......760 597-1940
2834 La Mirada Dr Ste B Vista (92081) ***(P-9171)***
United Food and Commercial (PA) ....D.......213 487-7070
630 Shatto Pl Ste 300 Los Angeles (90005) ***(P-25087)***
United Guard Security Inc ....C.......310 881-2984
879 W 190th St Ste 510 Gardena (90248) ***(P-16843)***
United Hauling Corp ....D.......626 358-9417
2620 Buena Vista St Duarte (91010) ***(P-17618)***
United Health Ctrs San Joaquin (PA) ....B.......559 646-6618
650 S Zediker Ave Bldg 3 Parlier (93648) ***(P-22705)***
United Health Ctrs San Joaquin ....D.......559 626-4031
445 11th St Orange Cove (93646) ***(P-22706)***
United Health Systems Inc ....C.......530 662-9161
124 Walnut St Woodland (95695) ***(P-20846)***
United Imaging, Woodland Hills *Also called United Ribbon Company Inc* ***(P-6987)***
United Ind Taxi Drivers (PA) ....D.......323 462-1088
900 N Alvarado St Los Angeles (90026) ***(P-3871)***
United Independent Taxi Co ....E.......213 385-2227
900 N Alvarado St Los Angeles (90026) ***(P-3872)***
United Indian Health Svcs Inc (PA) ....C.......707 825-5000
1600 Weeot Way Arcata (95521) ***(P-20019)***
United Infrstrcture Prjcts Inc ....D.......949 310-0092
1041 W 18th St Ste B104 Costa Mesa (92627) ***(P-25969)***
United Insurance Company ....E.......323 869-9381
5601 E Slauson Ave # 105 Commerce (90040) ***(P-10810)***
United International, Novato *Also called Cellmark Inc* ***(P-8022)***
United Landscape Resource Inc ....D.......530 671-1029
5411 Colusa Hwy Yuba City (95993) ***(P-955)***
United Marble & Granite Inc ....D.......408 347-3300
2163 Martin Ave Santa Clara (95050) ***(P-6910)***
United Material Handling Inc ....D.......951 657-4900
1190 Harley Knox Blvd Perris (92571) ***(P-4645)***
United Medical Imaging Inc ....C.......714 843-6255
16161 Gothard St Ste C Huntington Beach (92647) ***(P-20020)***
United Medical Management Inc ....C.......909 886-5291
1680 N Waterman Ave San Bernardino (92404) ***(P-21239)***
United Merchant Svcs Cal Inc ....D.......818 246-6767
750 Fairmont Ave Ste 201 Glendale (91203) ***(P-6986)***
United Mfg Assembly Inc ....D.......510 490-1065
44169 Fremont Blvd Fremont (94538) ***(P-26741)***

ALPHABETIC

Employee Codes: A=Over 500 employees, B=251-500
C=101-250, D=51-100, E=50
2019 Directory of California
Wholesalers and Services Companies

1503

United Natural Foods Inc..........C.......831 462-5870
2450 17th Ave Ste 250 Santa Cruz (95062) ***(P-8889)***
United Natural Foods Inc..........D.......916 625-4100
1101 Sunset Blvd Rocklin (95765) ***(P-8890)***
United Natural Foods West Inc (HQ)..........B.......401 528-8634
1101 Sunset Blvd Rocklin (95765) ***(P-8891)***
United Network Info Svcs, Walnut *Also called Unis LLC* ***(P-5190)***
United Oil, Long Beach *Also called United El Segundo Inc* ***(P-8970)***
United Owners Services, Anaheim *Also called Tricom Management Inc* ***(P-27067)***
United Pacific Waste..........D.......562 699-7600
4334 San Gbriel Rver Pkwy Pico Rivera (90660) ***(P-6485)***
United Paradyne Corporation..........D.......805 734-2359
P.O. Box 5368 Santa Barbara (93150) ***(P-27075)***
United Parcel Service Inc..........A.......760 241-5540
14592 Palmdale Rd Victorville (92392) ***(P-17534)***
United Parcel Service Inc..........D.......800 742-5877
12745 Arroyo St Sylmar (91342) ***(P-4441)***
United Parcel Service Inc..........C.......650 737-3737
657 Forbes Blvd South San Francisco (94080) ***(P-4442)***
United Parcel Service Inc OH..........D.......858 541-2336
160 W Main St El Centro (92243) ***(P-4443)***
United Parcel Service Inc OH..........B.......760 325-1762
650 N Commercial Rd Palm Springs (92262) ***(P-4444)***
United Parcel Service Inc OH..........A.......678 339-3171
3331 Industrial Dr Ste C Santa Rosa (95403) ***(P-17535)***
United Parcel Service Inc OH..........C.......510 262-2338
1601 Atlas Rd Richmond (94806) ***(P-4445)***
United Parcel Service Inc OH..........C.......831 758-9112
1139 Madison Ln Salinas (93907) ***(P-4446)***
United Parcel Service Inc OH..........D.......800 742-5877
2800 W 227th St Torrance (90505) ***(P-4447)***
United Parcel Service Inc OH..........B.......323 837-1220
2747 Vail Ave Commerce (90040) ***(P-17536)***
United Parcel Service Inc OH..........D.......530 365-7850
6845 Eastside Rd Anderson (96007) ***(P-4448)***
United Parcel Service Inc OH..........C.......760 872-7661
2915 N Sierra Hwy Bishop (93514) ***(P-4449)***
United Parcel Service Inc OH..........C.......707 864-8200
5000 W Cordelia Rd Fairfield (94534) ***(P-4450)***
United Parcel Service Inc OH..........C.......800 742-5877
1400 Hil Mor Dr Ceres (95307) ***(P-4451)***
United Parcel Service Inc OH..........C.......916 373-4076
1380 Shore St West Sacramento (95691) ***(P-4452)***
United Parcel Service Inc OH..........B.......949 643-6634
22 Brookline Aliso Viejo (92656) ***(P-17537)***
United Parcel Service Inc OH..........C.......707 224-1205
2531 Napa Valley Corp Dr NAPA (94558) ***(P-4453)***
United Parcel Service Inc OH..........D.......916 373-4089
128 Shore St Sacramento (95829) ***(P-4454)***
United Parcel Service Inc OH..........B.......323 260-8957
3333 S Downey Rd Vernon (90058) ***(P-4849)***
United Parcel Service Inc OH..........B.......310 217-2646
17115 S Western Ave Gardena (90247) ***(P-4455)***
United Parcel Service Inc OH..........B.......408 291-2942
1999 S 7th St San Jose (95112) ***(P-4456)***
United Parcel Service Inc OH..........C.......951 928-5221
25283 Sherman Rd Sun City (92585) ***(P-4850)***
United Parcel Service Inc OH..........C.......209 944-5932
1724 Wawona St Manteca (95337) ***(P-4851)***
United Parcel Service Inc OH..........C.......415 252-4564
2222 17th St San Francisco (94103) ***(P-4457)***
United Parcel Service Inc OH..........C.......707 252-4560
1012 Sterling St Vallejo (94591) ***(P-4458)***
United Parcel Service Inc OH..........C.......858 455-8800
6060 Cornerstone Ct W San Diego (92121) ***(P-4459)***
United Parcel Service Inc OH..........C.......310 474-0019
10690 Santa Monica Blvd Los Angeles (90025) ***(P-4460)***
United Parcel Service Inc OH..........C.......949 643-6595
22 Brookline Aliso Viejo (92656) ***(P-4461)***
United Parcel Service Inc OH..........A.......909 974-7250
3221 E Jurupa Ontario (91764) ***(P-17538)***
United Parcel Service Inc OH..........D.......951 377-8253
22 Brookline Aliso Viejo (92656) ***(P-4462)***
United Parcel Service Inc OH..........C.......909 974-7190
Ontario Airport Ontario (91758) ***(P-4852)***
United Parcel Service Inc OH..........C.......800 828-8264
290 W Avenue L Lancaster (93534) ***(P-4463)***
United Parcel Service Inc OH..........C.......404 828-6000
16000 Arminta St Van Nuys (91406) ***(P-4464)***
United Parcel Service Inc OH..........C.......909 279-5111
7925 Ronson Rd San Diego (92111) ***(P-4465)***
United Parcel Service Inc OH..........C.......510 813-5662
8400 Pardee Dr Oakland (94621) ***(P-4466)***
United Parcel Service Inc OH..........B.......800 742-5877
1746 D St South Lake Tahoe (96150) ***(P-17539)***
United Parcel Service Inc OH..........C.......562 404-3236
13233 Moore St Cerritos (90703) ***(P-4467)***
United Parcel Service Inc OH..........A.......626 280-8012
201 W Garvey Ave Ste 102 Monterey Park (91754) ***(P-17540)***
United Parcel Service Inc OH..........C.......707 468-5481
259 Cherry St Ukiah (95482) ***(P-4468)***
United Parcel Service Inc OH..........A.......818 735-0945
4607 Lakeview Canyon Rd Westlake Village (91361) ***(P-17541)***
United Parcel Service Inc OH..........C.......831 757-6294
6 Upper Ragsdale Dr Monterey (93940) ***(P-4469)***
United Parcel Service Inc OH..........C.......801 973-3400
3601 Sacramento Dr San Luis Obispo (93401) ***(P-4470)***
United Parcel Service Inc OH..........C.......650 952-5200
3860 Cypress Dr Petaluma (94954) ***(P-4471)***
United Parcel Service Inc OH..........C.......925 689-6584
1970 Olivera Rd Concord (94520) ***(P-4472)***
United Parcel Service Inc OH..........C.......805 964-7848
505 Pine Ave Goleta (93117) ***(P-4473)***
United Parcel Service Inc OH..........C.......805 922-7851
309 Cooley Ln Santa Maria (93455) ***(P-4474)***
United Parcel Service Inc OH..........C.......209 736-0878
2342 Gun Club Rd Angels Camp (95222) ***(P-4475)***
United Parcel Service Inc OH..........C.......805 375-1832
1501 Rancho Conejo Blvd Newbury Park (91320) ***(P-4476)***
United Parcel Service Inc OH..........C.......650 952-5200
1355 Adams Ct Menlo Park (94025) ***(P-4477)***
United Parcel Service Inc OH..........A.......323 729-6762
3000 E Washington Blvd Los Angeles (90023) ***(P-4478)***
United Parcel Service Inc OH..........C.......619 482-8119
2300 Boswell Ct Chula Vista (91914) ***(P-4479)***
United Parcel Service Inc OH..........D.......559 651-7690
7401 W Sunnyview Ave Visalia (93291) ***(P-4480)***
United Parcel Service Inc OH..........C.......831 425-1054
251 Sylvania Ave Santa Cruz (95060) ***(P-4481)***
United Parcel Service Inc OH..........D.......909 974-7000
3140 Jurupa St Ontario (91761) ***(P-4482)***
United Parcel Service Inc OH..........C.......800 833-9943
4500 Norris Canyon Rd San Ramon (94583) ***(P-4483)***
United Parcel Service Inc OH..........B.......951 749-3400
11811 Landon Dr Mira Loma (91752) ***(P-17542)***
United Parcel Service Inc OH..........C.......805 642-6784
2559 Palma Dr Ventura (93003) ***(P-4484)***
United Parcel Service Inc OH..........B.......800 742-5877
48921 Warm Springs Blvd Fremont (94539) ***(P-17543)***
United Parcel Service Inc OH..........C.......626 814-6216
1100 Baldwin Park Blvd Baldwin Park (91706) ***(P-4485)***
United Parcel Service Inc OH..........C.......916 857-0311
3930 Kristi Ct Sacramento (95827) ***(P-4486)***
United Parcel Service Inc OH..........B.......866 553-1069
91 W Easy St Simi Valley (93065) ***(P-17544)***
United Paving Company, Corona *Also called Superior Paving Company Inc* ***(P-1857)***
United Payment Services Inc..........B.......866 886-4833
3537 Old Conejo Rd # 113 Newbury Park (91320) ***(P-17545)***
United Petrochemicals Inc..........D.......949 629-8736
3000 W Macarthur Blvd # 300 Santa Ana (92704) ***(P-8937)***
United Power Contractors Inc..........C.......760 735-8028
405 Maple St Ste A-103 Ramona (92065) ***(P-1990)***
United Pumping Service Inc..........D.......626 961-9326
14000 Valley Blvd City of Industry (91746) ***(P-4075)***
United Refrigeration Inc..........D.......310 204-2500
3573a Hayden Ave Culver City (90232) ***(P-7667)***
United Rentals North Amer Inc..........D.......209 948-9500
2911 E Fremont St Stockton (95205) ***(P-14550)***
United Rentals North Amer Inc..........C.......562 695-0748
3455 San Gbriel Rver Pkwy Pico Rivera (90660) ***(P-14551)***
United Ribbon Company Inc..........D.......818 716-1515
21201 Oxnard St Woodland Hills (91367) ***(P-6987)***
United Riggers & Erectors Inc (PA)..........C.......909 978-0400
4188 Valley Blvd Walnut (91789) ***(P-3477)***
United Road Towing Inc..........D.......909 923-6100
1516 S Bon View Ave Ontario (91761) ***(P-17879)***
United Road Towing Inc..........D.......909 798-4863
945 W Brockton Ave Redlands (92374) ***(P-17880)***
United Seal Coating Slurryseal..........D.......805 563-4922
3463 State St Ste 522 Santa Barbara (93105) ***(P-1690)***
United Service Tech Inc..........D.......714 224-1406
21801 Cactus Ave Ste A Riverside (92518) ***(P-18002)***
United Site Services Cal Inc (PA)..........D.......626 462-9110
242 Live Oak Ave Irwindale (91706) ***(P-14552)***
United Site Services Cal Inc..........C.......408 295-2263
3408 Hillcap Ave San Jose (95136) ***(P-14553)***
United Site Services Cal Inc..........E.......707 747-2810
1 Oak Rd Benicia (94510) ***(P-6486)***
United Spectrum Inc..........E.......714 283-1010
1910 N Lime St Orange (92865) ***(P-3599)***
United States Attorneys..........C.......213 894-2400
300 N Los Angeles St Lbby Los Angeles (90012) ***(P-23419)***
United States Cold Storage Cal, Bakersfield *Also called United States Cold Storage Inc* ***(P-4513)***
United States Cold Storage Inc..........D.......661 832-2653
6501 District Blvd Bakersfield (93313) ***(P-4513)***
United States Cold Storage Inc..........E.......559 686-1110
810 E Continental Ave Tulare (93274) ***(P-4514)***
United States Cold Storage Inc..........E.......559 237-6145
2003 S Cherry Ave Fresno (93721) ***(P-4515)***
United States Cold Storage Inc..........E.......209 835-2653
1400 N Macarthur Dr Ste A Tracy (95376) ***(P-4516)***
United States Dept of Energy..........A.......510 486-4000
1 Cyclotron Rd Berkeley (94720) ***(P-26668)***
United States Dept of Energy..........A.......510 486-4936
1 Cyclotron Rd Berkeley (94720) ***(P-26479)***
United States Dept of Energy..........A.......925 422-1100
7000 East Ave Livermore (94550) ***(P-26480)***
United States Dept of Navy..........C.......619 524-1069
32444 Echo Ln Fl 3 San Diego (92147) ***(P-14928)***
United States Dept of Navy..........A.......559 998-4201
937 Vista Pl Lemoore (93245) ***(P-21868)***
United States Dept of Navy..........A.......619 532-6397
8808 Balboa Ave San Diego (92123) ***(P-20021)***
United States Dept of Navy..........A.......619 532-8953
34800 Bob Wilson Dr # 409 San Diego (92134) ***(P-20022)***
United States Dept of Navy..........B.......619 556-8210
2310 Craven St San Diego (92136) ***(P-20023)***

Mergent e-mail: customerrelations@mergent.com
1504

2019 Directory of California
Wholesalers and Services Companies

(P-0000) Products & Services Section entry number
(PA)=Parent Co (HQ)=Headquarters (DH)=Div Headquarters

United States Dept of Navy........A.......559 998-4481
Bldg 937 Franklin Ave Lemoore (93246) ***(P-21869)***
United States Dept of Navy........A.......619 532-6400
34800 Bob Wilson Dr San Diego (92134) ***(P-21870)***
United States Dept of Navy........B.......760 830-2190
Us Naval Hosp Bldg 1145 Twentynine Palms (92278) ***(P-21871)***
United States Dept of Navy........A.......805 982-6392
162 1st St Port Hueneme (93043) ***(P-20024)***
United States Dept of Navy........E.......619 532-1897
937 N Harbor Dr San Diego (92132) ***(P-26481)***
United States Dept of Navy........B.......559 998-2894
937 Franklin Blvd Lemoore (93246) ***(P-21872)***
United States Dept of Navy........A.......619 532-7400
34730 Bob Wilson Dr San Diego (92134) ***(P-20025)***
United States Dept of Navy........A.......805 982-6370
162 1st St Bldg 1402 Port Hueneme (93043) ***(P-20026)***
United States Dept of Navy........A.......619 767-6592
4170 Norman Scott Rd San Diego (92136) ***(P-20027)***
United States Dept of Navy........D.......831 656-4613
7 Grace Hopper Ave Stop 2 Monterey (93943) ***(P-26482)***
United States Fdral Prbatn, San Jose *Also called Adminstrtive Office of US Crts* ***(P-23459)***
United States Fire Insur Co........D.......213 797-3100
777 S Figueroa St # 1500 Los Angeles (90017) ***(P-10811)***
United States Forest Service........E.......530 335-4103
17696 State Highway 89 Hat Creek (96040) ***(P-1001)***
United States Info Systems Inc........C.......845 353-9224
7621 Galilee Rd Roseville (95678) ***(P-2775)***
United States Marines Youth Fd........D.......805 967-7990
90 La Venta Dr Santa Barbara (93110) ***(P-25271)***
United States Pipe Fndry LLC........C.......510 441-5810
1295 Whipple Rd Union City (94587) ***(P-4927)***
United States Pony Clubs........D.......916 791-1223
7010 Hidden Valley Pl Granite Bay (95746) ***(P-19075)***
United States Probation Office, San Diego *Also called Adminstrtive Office of US Crts* ***(P-23460)***
United States Technical Svcs........C.......714 374-6300
16541 Gothard St Ste 214 Huntington Beach (92647) ***(P-16520)***
United Stationers, City of Industry *Also called Essendant Co* ***(P-8079)***
United Sttes Bowl Congress Inc........D.......530 527-9049
12895 Arbor Ln Red Bluff (96080) ***(P-18501)***
United Sttes Intrmdal Svcs LLC........D.......209 341-4045
502 E Whitmore Ave Modesto (95358) ***(P-5191)***
United Sttes Olympic Committee........E.......619 656-1500
2800 Olympic Pkwy Chula Vista (91915) ***(P-18536)***
United Svcs Amer Federal Cr Un (PA)........D.......858 831-8100
9999 Willow Creek Rd San Diego (92131) ***(P-9614)***
United Talent Agency LLC........B.......310 385-2800
1880 Century Park E # 711 Los Angeles (90067) ***(P-27501)***
United Taxi San Fernando Vly, Los Angeles *Also called United Ind Taxi Drivers* ***(P-3871)***
United Teachers-Los Angeles........D.......213 487-5560
3303 Wilshire Blvd Fl 10 Los Angeles (90010) ***(P-25088)***
United Technologies, Anaheim *Also called Otis Elevator Company* ***(P-17965)***
United Temp Services Inc........D.......408 472-4309
694 Albanese Cir San Jose (95111) ***(P-14790)***
United Van Lines, San Diego *Also called Sullivan Moving & Storage* ***(P-4270)***
United Van Lines, Fontana *Also called McCollisters Trnsp Group Inc* ***(P-4359)***
United Way Inc........C.......661 874-4288
44907 10th St W Lancaster (93534) ***(P-24853)***
United Way Inc (PA)........D.......213 808-6220
1150 S Olive St Ste T500 Los Angeles (90015) ***(P-24854)***
United Way of Bay Area (PA)........D.......415 808-4300
550 Kearny St Ste 1000 San Francisco (94108) ***(P-24105)***
UNITED WAY OF GREATER LOS ANGE, Los Angeles *Also called United Way Inc* ***(P-24854)***
UNITED WAY, THE, San Francisco *Also called United Way of Bay Area* ***(P-24105)***
Unitedhealth Group Inc........B.......714 969-9050
7891 Moonmist Cir Huntington Beach (92648) ***(P-10324)***
Unitedhealth Group Inc........D.......952 936-1300
5701 Katella Ave Cypress (90630) ***(P-10325)***
Unitedhealth Group Inc........B.......530 879-8251
2080 E 20th St Chico (95928) ***(P-10326)***
Unitek Inc........D.......510 623-8544
41350 Christy St Fremont (94538) ***(P-16070)***
Unitek Information Systems Inc (PA)........D.......510 249-1060
4670 Auto Mall Pkwy Fremont (94538) ***(P-16521)***
Unitek It Education, Fremont *Also called Unitek Information Systems Inc* ***(P-16521)***
Uniti Bank (PA)........D.......888 733-2599
6301 Beach Blvd Ste 100 Buena Park (90621) ***(P-9519)***
UNITIBANK, Buena Park *Also called Uniti Bank* ***(P-9519)***
Unity Biotechnology Inc........D.......650 416-1192
3280 Byshore Blvd Ste 100 Brisbane (94005) ***(P-26483)***
Unity Courier Service Inc (PA)........A.......323 255-9800
3231 Fletcher Dr Los Angeles (90065) ***(P-4487)***
Unity Courier Service Inc........D.......510 568-8890
1132 Beecher St San Leandro (94577) ***(P-17546)***
Unity SEC & Protective Svc........D.......323 695-7234
619 E Washington Blvd Pasadena (91104) ***(P-16844)***
Univar USA Inc........C.......323 727-7005
2600 Garfield Ave Commerce (90040) ***(P-8938)***
Univar USA Inc........D.......408 435-8649
2256 Junction Ave San Jose (95131) ***(P-8939)***
Univers of Calif San Diego Hs........A.......619 543-3713
200 W Arbor Dr 8201 San Diego (92103) ***(P-21873)***
Universal........D.......909 882-5337
4632 Acacia Ave San Bernardino (92407) ***(P-14417)***
Universal Accounts Inc........D.......626 356-7900
690 E Green St Ste 300 Pasadena (91101) ***(P-14024)***
Universal Asphalt Co Inc........E.......562 941-0201
10610 Painter Ave Santa Fe Springs (90670) ***(P-1866)***
Universal Bank (PA)........D.......626 854-2818
3455 S Nogales St Fl 2 West Covina (91792) ***(P-9532)***
Universal Bldg Svcs & Sup Co (PA)........C.......510 527-1078
3120 Pierce St Richmond (94804) ***(P-14418)***
Universal Bldg Svcs & Sup Co........C.......925 934-5533
421 N Buchanan Cir Pacheco (94553) ***(P-14419)***
Universal Bldg Svcs & Sup Co........C.......408 995-5111
430 Roberson Ln San Jose (95112) ***(P-14420)***
Universal Card Inc........B.......949 861-4000
9012 Research Dr Ste 200 Irvine (92618) ***(P-17547)***
Universal Care Inc (PA)........B.......562 424-6200
19762 Macarthur Blvd # 100 Irvine (92612) ***(P-22707)***
Universal City, Santa Monica *Also called Universal Studios Company LLC* ***(P-18149)***
Universal City Studios LLC (HQ)........D.......800 864-8377
100 Universal City Plz Universal City (91608) ***(P-18141)***
Universal Creative, Universal City *Also called Universal City Studios LLC* ***(P-18141)***
Universal Custom Courier, San Fernando *Also called Universal Mail Delivery Svc* ***(P-4076)***
Universal Custom Farming Co, Tranquillity *Also called Don Gragnani Farms* ***(P-336)***
Universal Cylinder Exch Inc........D.......714 744-1036
692 N Cypress St Ste B Orange (92867) ***(P-27960)***
Universal Dust Collector (PA)........D.......714 630-8588
1041 N Kraemer Pl Anaheim (92806) ***(P-1448)***
Universal Field Services Inc........E.......559 453-2901
1630 E Shaw Ave Ste 163 Fresno (93710) ***(P-2072)***
Universal Framing Products, Santa Clarita *Also called Universal Wood Moulding Inc* ***(P-6799)***
Universal General Builders........D.......650 591-3104
871 Industrial Rd Ste A San Carlos (94070) ***(P-25970)***
Universal Home Care Inc........C.......323 653-9222
151 N San Vicente Blvd Beverly Hills (90211) ***(P-22442)***
Universal Limousine & Trnsp Co........D.......916 361-5466
9944 Mills Station Rd C Sacramento (95827) ***(P-3855)***
Universal Mail Delivery Svc (PA)........D.......818 997-7531
501 S Brand Blvd Ste 4 San Fernando (91340) ***(P-4076)***
Universal McCann, San Francisco *Also called McCann World Group Inc* ***(P-13861)***
Universal Mus Group Hldngs Inc........A.......317 871-0319
21301 Burbank Blvd # 100 Woodland Hills (91367) ***(P-8066)***
Universal Mus Investments Inc (HQ)........D.......818 577-4700
2220 Colorado Ave Santa Monica (90404) ***(P-17548)***
Universal Music Group Inc (HQ)........D.......310 865-4000
2220 Colorado Ave Santa Monica (90404) ***(P-17549)***
Universal Music Group Inc........D.......310 865-4000
2220 Colorado Ave Santa Monica (90404) ***(P-18472)***
Universal Music Group Inc........E.......818 286-4000
10 Universal City Plz Universal City (91608) ***(P-17550)***
Universal Network Dev Corp (PA)........D.......916 475-1200
2555 3rd St Ste 112 Sacramento (95818) ***(P-27892)***
Universal Network Exchange, Burbank *Also called Unx Inc A Delaware Corp* ***(P-15516)***
Universal Packg Systems Inc........C.......909 517-2442
14570 Monte Vista Ave Chino (91710) ***(P-4646)***
Universal Paragon Corporation (PA)........B.......415 468-6676
150 Executive Park Blvd # 4000 San Francisco (94134) ***(P-13354)***
Universal Protection Svc LP........D.......805 496-4401
2415 San Ramon Vly Blvd San Ramon (94583) ***(P-16845)***
Universal Protection Svc LP........D.......562 981-5700
340 Golden Shore Ste 100 Long Beach (90802) ***(P-16846)***
Universal Protection Svc LP........D.......818 227-1240
21300 Victory Blvd # 230 Woodland Hills (91367) ***(P-16847)***
Universal Protection Svc LP (HQ)........C.......714 619-9700
1551 N Tustin Ave Ste 650 Santa Ana (92705) ***(P-16848)***
Universal Protection Svc LP........C.......415 759-5056
1208 Vicente St San Francisco (94116) ***(P-16849)***
Universal Self Storage........E.......951 206-5263
25980 Barton Rd Loma Linda (92354) ***(P-4647)***
Universal Services America LP (HQ)........D.......714 619-9700
1551 N Tustin Ave Santa Ana (92705) ***(P-16850)***
Universal Site Services Inc........D.......916 635-1122
3174 Luyung Dr Ste 3 Rancho Cordova (95742) ***(P-14421)***
Universal Site Services Inc (PA)........D.......800 647-9337
760 E Capitol Ave Milpitas (95035) ***(P-14422)***
Universal Space Lines Inc........D.......215 328-9130
1501 Quail St Ste 102 Newport Beach (92660) ***(P-25971)***
Universal Stdios Licensing Inc........C.......818 762-6284
100 Universal City Plz Universal City (91608) ***(P-12145)***
Universal Studios Inc........C.......818 262-4301
1295 Los Angeles St Ste 1 Glendale (91204) ***(P-18142)***
Universal Studios Inc........D.......818 753-0000
4123 Lankershim Blvd North Hollywood (91602) ***(P-18143)***
Universal Studios Inc........C.......818 777-2351
3900 Lankershim Blvd Studio City (91604) ***(P-18144)***
Universal Studios Company LLC........B.......818 622-4455
1000 Univ Studio Blvd 2 Universal City (91608) ***(P-18145)***
Universal Studios Company LLC (HQ)........C.......818 777-1000
100 Universal City Plz North Hollywood (91608) ***(P-18146)***
Universal Studios Company LLC........C.......818 777-1000
100 Universal City Plz # 3 Universal City (91608) ***(P-18147)***
Universal Studios Company LLC........C.......310 235-4749
2440 S Sepulveda Blvd # 100 Los Angeles (90064) ***(P-18148)***
Universal Studios Company LLC........D.......310 865-5000
2220 Colorado Ave Santa Monica (90404) ***(P-18149)***
Universal Studios Consmr Pdts, Universal City *Also called Universal Stdios Licensing Inc* ***(P-12145)***
Universal Wood Moulding Inc (PA)........E.......661 362-6262
21139 Centre Pointe Pkwy Santa Clarita (91350) ***(P-6799)***
Universe Holdings Dev Co LLC........E.......310 785-0077
350 S Beverly Dr Ste 210 Beverly Hills (90212) ***(P-11807)***
UNIVERSITY BOOKSTORE, Los Angeles *Also called California State Univ Aux Svcs* ***(P-26795)***

ALPHABETIC

University Cal Irvine Med Cent..........B.......714 456-5678
208 Giotto Irvine (92614) ***(P-22899)***
University Cal Los Angeles..........E.......805 494-6920
1250 Avanta Dr Ste 207 Westlake Village (91361) ***(P-20028)***
University Cal Los Angeles..........A.......310 825-0640
200 Ucla Medical Plz Los Angeles (90095) ***(P-21874)***
University Cal Los Angeles..........A.......818 364-1555
14445 Olive View Dr Sylmar (91342) ***(P-21875)***
University Cal Los Angeles..........A.......310 319-4000
1225 15th St Santa Monica (90404) ***(P-21876)***
University Cal Los Angeles..........A.......310 825-9111
757 Westwood Plz Los Angeles (90095) ***(P-21877)***
University Cal Riverside..........D.......951 827-4801
900 University Ave Riverside (92521) ***(P-26575)***
University Cal San Diego..........A.......619 543-6654
200 W Arbor Dr Frnt San Diego (92103) ***(P-21878)***
University Cal San Diego..........B.......858 534-5000
10100 Hopkins Dr La Jolla (92093) ***(P-16195)***
University Cal San Diego..........B.......858 657-7000
9300 Campus Point Dr La Jolla (92037) ***(P-21879)***
University Cal San Francisco..........D.......415 476-9000
500 Parnassus Ave San Francisco (94143) ***(P-26669)***
University Cal San Francisco..........A.......415 476-7000
401 Parnassus Ave San Francisco (94143) ***(P-21880)***
University Cal San Francisco..........E.......415 476-1611
400 Parnassus Ave A633 San Francisco (94143) ***(P-21881)***
University Cal San Francisco..........D.......415 353-3155
3330 Geary Blvd San Francisco (94118) ***(P-20029)***
University Cal San Francisco..........D.......510 987-0700
616 Forbes Blvd South San Francisco (94080) ***(P-4648)***
University Cal San Francisco..........B.......415 567-6600
1600 Divisadero St San Francisco (94143) ***(P-21882)***
University California Davis..........E.......916 734-2846
2315 Stockton Blvd # 6309 Sacramento (95817) ***(P-20030)***
University California Davis..........A.......916 734-3141
4400 V St Sacramento (95817) ***(P-21883)***
University California Davis..........C.......530 752-2300
Student House Ctr Davis (95616) ***(P-20031)***
University California Davis..........A.......916 734-2011
2450 48th St Ste 2401 Sacramento (95817) ***(P-21884)***
University California Davis..........A.......916 734-5113
4150 V St Ste 1200 Sacramento (95817) ***(P-21885)***
University California Irvine..........A.......714 456-6170
101 The City Dr S Bldg 1a Orange (92868) ***(P-20032)***
University California Irvine..........D.......714 480-2443
800 N Main St Santa Ana (92701) ***(P-20033)***
University California Irvine..........E.......949 646-2267
1640 Newport Blvd Ste 340 Costa Mesa (92627) ***(P-20034)***
University California Irvine..........A.......714 456-6011
101 The City Dr S Orange (92868) ***(P-21886)***
University California Irvine..........D.......949 824-2819
2220 Engineering Gateway Irvine (92697) ***(P-26484)***
University California Irvine..........A.......714 456-5558
200 S Manchester Ave # 400 Orange (92868) ***(P-21887)***
University California Berkeley..........A.......510 495-2490
5885 Hollis St Emeryville (94608) ***(P-26670)***
University California Berkeley..........B.......510 642-2000
2222 Bancroft Way Berkeley (94720) ***(P-20035)***
University Credit Union..........C.......310 477-6628
1500 S Sepulveda Blvd Los Angeles (90025) ***(P-9615)***
University Head Neck Surgeons, Orange *Also called Roger L Crumley MD Inc* ***(P-19830)***
University Health Services, Berkeley *Also called University California Berkeley* ***(P-20035)***
UNIVERSITY LEASE, Irvine *Also called California First National Bank* ***(P-9497)***
University Marelich Mech Inc..........C.......714 632-2600
1000 N Kraemer Pl Anaheim (92806) ***(P-2391)***
University Mechanical & (HQ)..........C.......619 956-2500
1168 Fesler St El Cajon (92020) ***(P-2392)***
University of CA Office, Oakland *Also called C/O Uc San Francisco* ***(P-26791)***
University of Pacific..........A.......209 946-2030
1040 E Stadium Dr Stockton (95204) ***(P-19254)***
University Park Healthcare Ctr, Los Angeles *Also called United Convalescent Facilities* ***(P-21236)***
University Retirement Cmnty, Davis *Also called Pacific Retirement Svcs Inc* ***(P-24623)***
University Southern California..........D.......626 457-4240
1000 S Fremont Ave Unit 7 Alhambra (91803) ***(P-26485)***
University Southern California..........A.......323 442-8500
1500 San Pablo St Los Angeles (90033) ***(P-21888)***
University Southern California..........D.......213 743-5339
849 W 34th St Ste 208 Los Angeles (90089) ***(P-20036)***
University Student Union Inc..........C.......323 343-2450
5151 State University Dr Los Angeles (90032) ***(P-17551)***
University Student Union of CA..........B.......818 677-2251
18111 Nordhoff St Northridge (91330) ***(P-25272)***
Univision 67, Monterey *Also called Entravsion Communications Corp* ***(P-5784)***
Univision Communications Inc..........C.......818 484-7399
655 N Central Ave # 2500 Glendale (91203) ***(P-5760)***
Univision Radio Inc..........E.......559 430-8500
601 W Univision Plz Fresno (93704) ***(P-5761)***
Univision Television Group Inc..........D.......559 222-2121
601 W Univision Plz Fresno (93704) ***(P-5844)***
Univision Television Group Inc..........D.......415 538-8000
1940 Zanker Rd San Jose (95112) ***(P-5845)***
Univision Television Group Inc..........E.......858 576-1919
5770 Ruffin Rd San Diego (92123) ***(P-5846)***
Uniwell Corporation..........C.......714 522-7000
7000 Beach Blvd Buena Park (90620) ***(P-13355)***
Uniwell Corporation..........D.......559 268-1000
2233 Ventura St Fresno (93721) ***(P-11933)***
Uniwell Fresno Hotel LLC..........D.......559 268-1000
2233 Ventura St Fresno (93721) ***(P-13356)***
Uniworld Boutique River Cruise, Encino *Also called Uniworld River Cruises Inc* ***(P-4983)***
Uniworld River Cruises Inc..........C.......818 382-2322
17323 Ventura Blvd # 300 Encino (91316) ***(P-4983)***
Unknown, Carlsbad *Also called Bomel Construction Co Inc* ***(P-1379)***
Unknown, Susanville *Also called Golden 1 Credit Union* ***(P-9637)***
Unlimited SEC Specialists Inc..........E.......877 310-4877
13636 Ventura Blvd # 206 Sherman Oaks (91423) ***(P-16851)***
Unocal Corporation (HQ)..........B.......310 726-7600
6001 Bollinger Canyon Rd San Ramon (94583) ***(P-1030)***
UNUM Life Insurance Co Amer..........C.......818 291-4739
655 N Central Ave Glendale (91203) ***(P-10812)***
Unumprovident, Glendale *Also called UNUM Life Insurance Co Amer* ***(P-10812)***
Unx Inc A Delaware Corp..........D.......818 333-3300
175 E Olive Ave Fl 2 Burbank (91502) ***(P-15516)***
Unyeway Inc (PA)..........D.......760 789-5960
2330 Main St Ste E Ramona (92065) ***(P-24242)***
Unyeway Inc..........D.......619 562-6330
11440 Riverside Dr Ste D Lakeside (92040) ***(P-24243)***
Up N Down Scaffold Company Inc (PA)..........D.......619 266-0542
5216 Naranja St San Diego (92114) ***(P-3600)***
Up Stage Inc..........E.......818 879-8781
30757 Canwood St Agoura (91301) ***(P-18150)***
Upac, San Diego *Also called Union Pan Asian Communities* ***(P-24100)***
Upgradedetect Inc (PA)..........D.......949 460-9000
3303 Harbor Blvd Ste D7 Costa Mesa (92626) ***(P-7125)***
Upham Hotel..........E.......805 962-0058
1404 De La Vina St # 93101 Santa Barbara (93101) ***(P-13357)***
Upland Community Care Inc..........D.......909 985-1903
1221 E Arrow Hwy Upland (91786) ***(P-21240)***
Upland Rehabilitation Care Ctr, Upland *Also called Upland Community Care Inc* ***(P-21240)***
Upland Valley Fun Center, Upland *Also called Apex Parks Group LLC* ***(P-19098)***
Upland Ymca-Valencia, Upland *Also called West End Yung MNS Christn Assn* ***(P-25284)***
Uplift Family Services (PA)..........D.......408 379-3790
251 Llewellyn Ave Campbell (95008) ***(P-24704)***
Uplift Family Services..........D.......408 379-3790
499 Loma Alta Ave Los Gatos (95030) ***(P-22708)***
Uplift Inc..........D.......844 257-5400
801 El Camino Real Menlo Park (94025) ***(P-27502)***
Uproxx Media Group Inc (PA)..........D.......310 424-2080
10381 Jefferson Blvd Culver City (90232) ***(P-6003)***
UPS, El Centro *Also called United Parcel Service Inc OH* ***(P-4443)***
UPS, Palm Springs *Also called United Parcel Service Inc OH* ***(P-4444)***
UPS, Santa Rosa *Also called United Parcel Service Inc OH* ***(P-17535)***
UPS, Richmond *Also called United Parcel Service Inc OH* ***(P-4445)***
UPS, Salinas *Also called United Parcel Service Inc OH* ***(P-4446)***
UPS, Torrance *Also called United Parcel Service Inc OH* ***(P-4447)***
UPS, Commerce *Also called United Parcel Service Inc OH* ***(P-17536)***
UPS, Anderson *Also called United Parcel Service Inc OH* ***(P-4448)***
UPS, Bishop *Also called United Parcel Service Inc OH* ***(P-4449)***
UPS, Fairfield *Also called United Parcel Service Inc OH* ***(P-4450)***
UPS, Ceres *Also called United Parcel Service Inc OH* ***(P-4451)***
UPS, West Sacramento *Also called United Parcel Service Inc OH* ***(P-4452)***
UPS, Aliso Viejo *Also called United Parcel Service Inc OH* ***(P-17537)***
UPS, NAPA *Also called United Parcel Service Inc OH* ***(P-4453)***
UPS, Sacramento *Also called United Parcel Service Inc OH* ***(P-4454)***
UPS, Vernon *Also called United Parcel Service Inc OH* ***(P-4849)***
UPS, Gardena *Also called United Parcel Service Inc OH* ***(P-4455)***
UPS, San Jose *Also called United Parcel Service Inc OH* ***(P-4456)***
UPS, Sun City *Also called United Parcel Service Inc OH* ***(P-4850)***
UPS, Manteca *Also called United Parcel Service Inc OH* ***(P-4851)***
UPS, Vallejo *Also called United Parcel Service Inc OH* ***(P-4458)***
UPS, San Diego *Also called United Parcel Service Inc OH* ***(P-4459)***
UPS, Los Angeles *Also called United Parcel Service Inc OH* ***(P-4460)***
UPS, Aliso Viejo *Also called United Parcel Service Inc OH* ***(P-4461)***
UPS, Ontario *Also called United Parcel Service Inc OH* ***(P-17538)***
UPS, Aliso Viejo *Also called United Parcel Service Inc OH* ***(P-4462)***
UPS, Ontario *Also called United Parcel Service Inc OH* ***(P-4852)***
UPS, Victorville *Also called United Parcel Service Inc* ***(P-17534)***
UPS, Sylmar *Also called United Parcel Service Inc* ***(P-4441)***
UPS, Lancaster *Also called United Parcel Service Inc OH* ***(P-4463)***
UPS, Van Nuys *Also called United Parcel Service Inc OH* ***(P-4464)***
UPS, San Diego *Also called United Parcel Service Inc OH* ***(P-4465)***
UPS, Oakland *Also called United Parcel Service Inc OH* ***(P-4466)***
UPS, South Lake Tahoe *Also called United Parcel Service Inc OH* ***(P-17539)***
UPS, Cerritos *Also called United Parcel Service Inc OH* ***(P-4467)***
UPS, Monterey Park *Also called United Parcel Service Inc OH* ***(P-17540)***
UPS, Ukiah *Also called United Parcel Service Inc OH* ***(P-4468)***
UPS, Westlake Village *Also called United Parcel Service Inc OH* ***(P-17541)***
UPS, Monterey *Also called United Parcel Service Inc OH* ***(P-4469)***
UPS, San Luis Obispo *Also called United Parcel Service Inc OH* ***(P-4470)***
UPS, Petaluma *Also called United Parcel Service Inc OH* ***(P-4471)***
UPS, Concord *Also called United Parcel Service Inc OH* ***(P-4472)***
UPS, Goleta *Also called United Parcel Service Inc OH* ***(P-4473)***
UPS, Santa Maria *Also called United Parcel Service Inc OH* ***(P-4474)***
UPS, Angels Camp *Also called United Parcel Service Inc OH* ***(P-4475)***
UPS, Newbury Park *Also called United Parcel Service Inc OH* ***(P-4476)***
UPS, Menlo Park *Also called United Parcel Service Inc OH* ***(P-4477)***
UPS, Los Angeles *Also called United Parcel Service Inc OH* ***(P-4478)***

ALPHABETIC SECTION
US Metro Group Inc

UPS, South San Francisco *Also called United Parcel Service Inc* ***(P-4442)***
UPS, Chula Vista *Also called United Parcel Service Inc OH* ***(P-4479)***
UPS, Visalia *Also called United Parcel Service Inc OH* ***(P-4480)***
UPS, Santa Cruz *Also called United Parcel Service Inc OH* ***(P-4481)***
UPS, Ontario *Also called United Parcel Service Inc OH* ***(P-4482)***
UPS, San Ramon *Also called United Parcel Service Inc OH* ***(P-4483)***
UPS, Mira Loma *Also called United Parcel Service Inc OH* ***(P-17542)***
UPS, Ventura *Also called United Parcel Service Inc OH* ***(P-4484)***
UPS, Fremont *Also called United Parcel Service Inc OH* ***(P-17543)***
UPS, Baldwin Park *Also called United Parcel Service Inc OH* ***(P-4485)***
UPS, Sacramento *Also called United Parcel Service Inc OH* ***(P-4486)***
UPS, Simi Valley *Also called United Parcel Service Inc OH* ***(P-17544)***
UPS Freight, Pico Rivera *Also called UPS Ground Freight Inc* ***(P-4293)***
UPS Freight Services Inc .... D 909 879-7400
2650 S Willow Ave Bloomington (92316) ***(P-4285)***
UPS Ground Freight Inc .... D 559 445-9010
4587 S Chestnut Ave Fresno (93725) ***(P-4286)***
UPS Ground Freight Inc .... D 661 395-9500
600 Williams St Bakersfield (93305) ***(P-4287)***
UPS Ground Freight Inc .... D 209 858-5095
1444 Lathrop Rd Lathrop (95330) ***(P-4288)***
UPS Ground Freight Inc .... D 951 361-1300
12455 Harvest Dr Eastvale (91752) ***(P-4289)***
UPS Ground Freight Inc .... D 707 526-1910
7 College Ave Santa Rosa (95401) ***(P-4290)***
UPS Ground Freight Inc .... D 408 400-0595
925 Morse Ave Sunnyvale (94089) ***(P-4291)***
UPS Ground Freight Inc .... D 831 751-0262
20760 Spence Rd Salinas (93908) ***(P-4292)***
UPS Ground Freight Inc .... D 562 801-1300
7754 Paramount Blvd Pico Rivera (90660) ***(P-4293)***
UPS Ground Freight Inc .... D 916 371-9101
900 E St West Sacramento (95605) ***(P-4294)***
UPS Ground Freight Inc .... D 866 372-5619
650 S Acacia Ave Fullerton (92831) ***(P-4295)***
UPS Store Inc (HQ) .... C 858 455-8800
6060 Cornerstone Ct W San Diego (92121) ***(P-17552)***
UPS Supply Chain Solutions Inc .... A 650 635-2693
550-3 Eccles Ave San Francisco (94101) ***(P-5192)***
UPS Supply Chain Solutions Inc .... C 310 404-2719
19701 Hamilton Ave # 250 Torrance (90502) ***(P-5193)***
UPS Supply Chain Solutions Inc .... E 650 875-8300
455 Forbes Blvd South San Francisco (94080) ***(P-5194)***
UPS Supply Chain Solutions Inc .... E 415 775-6644
601 Van Neca Ave Ste E San Francisco (94102) ***(P-4649)***
UPS Worldwide Logistics Inc .... C 310 673-7661
3600 W Century Blvd Inglewood (90303) ***(P-5195)***
Upstanding LLC .... C 949 788-9900
440 Exchange Ste 100 Irvine (92602) ***(P-15886)***
Upwind Blade Solutions Inc .... C 866 927-3142
2869 Historic Decatur Rd # 100 San Diego (92106) ***(P-18003)***
Upwork Global Inc .... E 650 316-7500
441 Logue Ave Mountain View (94043) ***(P-25049)***
Uquality Automotive Pdts Corp (PA) .... E 562 282-2888
16411 Shoemaker Ave Cerritos (90703) ***(P-6681)***
Urata & Sons Concrete Inc .... C 916 638-5364
3430 Luyung Dr Rancho Cordova (95742) ***(P-3339)***
Urban Commons Queensway LLC .... A 562 499-1611
1126 Queens Hwy Long Beach (90802) ***(P-13358)***
Urban Corps of San Diego .... C 619 235-6884
3127 Jefferson St San Diego (92110) ***(P-24244)***
Urban Painting Inc .... D 415 485-1130
40 Lisbon St San Rafael (94901) ***(P-2489)***
Urban Services YMCA, Oakland *Also called Young MNS Chrstn Assn of E Bay* ***(P-25353)***
Urban Sony Service Center, Irvine *Also called Sony Electronics Inc* ***(P-18118)***
Urban Trading Software Inc .... E 877 633-6171
21227 Foothill Blvd Hayward (94541) ***(P-15887)***
Urgent Care-Selma Dst Hosp, Selma *Also called Adventist Medical Center-Selma* ***(P-21268)***
Uribe Trucking Inc .... C 805 483-1125
542 Flynn Rd Camarillo (93012) ***(P-4383)***
Urology Assoc of Cen Cal .... D 559 321-2800
7014 N Whitney Ave Ste A Fresno (93720) ***(P-20037)***
URS Group Inc .... C 510 893-3600
300 Lakeside Dr Ste 400 Oakland (94612) ***(P-25972)***
URS Group Inc .... D 415 896-5858
300 Lakeside Dr Ste 400 Oakland (94612) ***(P-25973)***
URS Group Inc .... D 213 996-2200
915 Wilshire Blvd Ste 700 Los Angeles (90017) ***(P-25974)***
URS Group Inc .... D 909 980-4000
901 Via Piemonte Ste 500 Ontario (91764) ***(P-25975)***
URS Group Inc .... D 213 996-2200
915 Wilshire Blvd Ste 700 Los Angeles (90017) ***(P-25976)***
URS Group Inc .... D 925 446-3800
2300 Clayton Rd Ste 1400 Concord (94520) ***(P-25977)***
URS Group Inc .... D 805 964-6010
130 Robin Hill Rd Ste 100 Santa Barbara (93117) ***(P-25978)***
URS Group Inc .... D 916 679-2000
2020 L St Ste 400 Sacramento (95811) ***(P-25979)***
URS Group Inc .... D 408 297-9585
100 W San Fernando St # 200 San Jose (95113) ***(P-25980)***
URS Group Inc .... D 415 896-5858
300 Lakeside Dr Ste 400 Oakland (94612) ***(P-25981)***
URS Holdings Inc (HQ) .... B 415 774-2700
600 Montgomery St Fl 25 San Francisco (94111) ***(P-25982)***
URS-Gei Joint Venture .... E 510 874-3051
1333 Broadway Ste 800 Oakland (94612) ***(P-25983)***
US 3, Santa Ana *Also called Utility Systems Science* ***(P-15520)***

US Advisor LLC .... D 707 253-9953
600 Trancas St NAPA (94558) ***(P-12191)***
US Air Conditioning Distrs LLC .... D 626 854-0429
16900 Chestnut St City of Industry (91748) ***(P-7660)***
US Airforce Band of Golden W .... E 707 424-2263
551 Waldron St Bldg 240 Travis Afb (94535) ***(P-18473)***
US Airways, Los Angeles *Also called American Airlines Inc* ***(P-4771)***
US Airways, San Diego *Also called American Airlines Inc* ***(P-4772)***
US Airways, Los Angeles *Also called American Airlines Inc* ***(P-4773)***
US Army Corps of Engineers .... A 916 557-7490
1325 J St Frnt Sacramento (95814) ***(P-25984)***
US Army Corps of Engineers .... A 213 452-3967
915 Wilshire Blvd Ste 930 Los Angeles (90017) ***(P-25985)***
US Bank, Los Alamitos *Also called US Bank National Association* ***(P-9375)***
US Bank, San Diego *Also called US Bank National Association* ***(P-9376)***
US Bank National Association .... E 562 795-7520
10021 Bloomfield St Los Alamitos (90720) ***(P-9375)***
US Bank National Association .... D 619 744-2140
1420 Kettner Blvd Ste 101 San Diego (92101) ***(P-9376)***
US Bankcard Services Inc .... D 888 888-8872
17171 Gale Ave Ste 110 City of Industry (91745) ***(P-17553)***
US Best Repair Service Inc .... C 888 750-2378
2004 Mcgaw Ave Irvine (92614) ***(P-1252)***
US Best Repairs, Irvine *Also called US Best Repair Service Inc* ***(P-1252)***
US Credit Bancorp Inc .... D 310 829-2112
851 20th St Santa Monica (90403) ***(P-9863)***
US Data Management LLC (PA) .... C 888 231-0816
535 Chapala St Santa Barbara (93101) ***(P-16522)***
US Dept of the Air Force .... C 661 277-3030
35 N Wolfe Ave Edwards (93524) ***(P-6004)***
US Dept of the Air Force .... B 530 634-4839
15301 Warren Shingle Rd Marysville (95903) ***(P-21889)***
US Dept of the Air Force .... D 661 275-5410
10 E Saturn Dr Edwards (93524) ***(P-26486)***
US Dept of the Air Force .... D 530 634-4738
15301 Warren Shingle Rd Beale Afb (95903) ***(P-20038)***
US Elogistics Service Corp .... D 732 357-6665
1521 E Francis St Ontario (91761) ***(P-4650)***
US Elogistics Service Corp .... D 732 881-6606
13725 Pipeline Ave Chino (91710) ***(P-4651)***
US Family Care, Rialto *Also called Caremark Rx Inc* ***(P-19350)***
US Family Care, Hesperia *Also called Caremark Rx LLC* ***(P-19351)***
US Foods Inc .... C 951 256-2400
1283 Sherborn St Ste 102 Corona (92879) ***(P-8478)***
US Foods Inc .... B 760 599-6200
1201 Park Center Dr Vista (92081) ***(P-9265)***
US Foods Inc .... C 800 888-3147
1283 Sherborn St Ste 102 Corona (92879) ***(P-8892)***
US Foods Inc .... B 925 606-3525
300 Lawrence Dr Frnt Livermore (94551) ***(P-8479)***
US Foods Inc .... C 951 582-8500
1283 Sherborn St Ste 102 Corona (92879) ***(P-8893)***
US Foods Inc .... C 714 670-3500
15155 Northam St La Mirada (90638) ***(P-8480)***
US Foods Inc .... E 714 670-3500
15155 Northam St La Mirada (90638) ***(P-8481)***
US Foods Inc .... C 714 449-9990
700 S Raymond Ave Fullerton (92831) ***(P-8894)***
US Foods Inc .... C 209 572-2882
4300 Finch Rd Modesto (95357) ***(P-8895)***
US Foods Inc .... C 714 449-2880
1415 N Raymond Ave Anaheim (92801) ***(P-8896)***
US Foods Inc .... C 714 670-3500
15155 Northam St La Mirada (90638) ***(P-8897)***
US Foods Inc .... C 619 474-6525
1240 W 28th St National City (91950) ***(P-8898)***
US Foods Inc .... C 951 256-2400
1283 Sherborn St Ste 102 Corona (92879) ***(P-8899)***
US Foods International LLC .... D 310 515-2189
500 W 140th St Fl 2 Gardena (90248) ***(P-8482)***
US Grant Hotel Ventures LLC .... D 619 744-2007
326 Broadway San Diego (92101) ***(P-13359)***
US Green Building Council - .... D 818 621-4880
2879 Breezy Meadow Ln Corona (92883) ***(P-12086)***
US GREEN BUILDING COUNCIL INLA, Corona *Also called US Green Building Council - **(P-12086)***
US Home, Corona *Also called US Home Corporation* ***(P-1361)***
US Home Corporation .... E 951 817-3500
980 Montecito Dr 302 Corona (92879) ***(P-1361)***
US Hotel and Resort MGT Inc .... D 949 650-2988
2544 Newport Blvd Costa Mesa (92627) ***(P-13360)***
US Interactive Delaware .... C 408 863-7500
1270 Oakmead Pkwy Ste 318 Sunnyvale (94085) ***(P-13914)***
US Interactive Delaware (PA) .... C 408 863-7500
1270 Oakmead Pkwy Ste 318 Sunnyvale (94085) ***(P-25986)***
US International Media LLC (PA) .... D 310 482-6700
3415 S Sepulveda Blvd # 800 Los Angeles (90034) ***(P-13985)***
US Interstate Distrg Inc .... C 818 678-4592
21621 Nordhoff St Chatsworth (91311) ***(P-5658)***
US Lines LLC (HQ) .... D 714 751-3333
3501 Jamboree Rd Ste 300 Newport Beach (92660) ***(P-24988)***
US Loan Auditors LLC .... D 916 248-8625
7485 Rush Rver Dr Ste 710 Sacramento (95831) ***(P-26305)***
US Merchant Systems LLC .... D 877 432-8871
48073 Fremont Blvd Fremont (94538) ***(P-7558)***
US Merchants Fincl Group Inc .... C 909 923-3388
1625 Proforma Ave Ontario (91761) ***(P-17554)***
US Metro Group Inc .... A 213 382-6435
605 S Wilton Pl Los Angeles (90005) ***(P-14423)***

ALPHABETIC

Employee Codes: A=Over 500 employees, B=251-500
C=101-250, D=51-100, E=50
2019 Directory of California
Wholesalers and Services Companies

1507

US Naval Medical Clinical Lab, Port Hueneme *Also called United States Dept of Navy* ***(P-20024)***
US Outdoor, Los Angeles *Also called US International Media LLC* ***(P-13985)***
US Probation, San Diego *Also called Supreme Court United States* ***(P-24080)***
US Property Group Inc ....E....559 227-1901
1901 E Shields Ave # 203 Fresno (93726) ***(P-10958)***
US Real Estate Services Inc ....D....949 598-9920
25520 Commercentre Dr # 1 Lake Forest (92630) ***(P-11808)***
US Security Associates Inc ....C....209 476-7062
555 W Benjamin Holt Dr # 222 Stockton (95207) ***(P-16852)***
US Skillserve Inc (PA) ....A....562 930-0777
4115 E Broadway Ste A Long Beach (90803) ***(P-27076)***
US Skillserve Inc ....C....909 621-4751
9620 Fremont Ave Montclair (91763) ***(P-20847)***
US Small Cpitl Value Portfolio ....D....310 395-8005
1299 Ocean Ave Ste 150 Santa Monica (90401) ***(P-12049)***
US Telepacific Corp (HQ) ....E....866 699-8242
515 S Flower St Ste 4500 Los Angeles (90071) ***(P-5659)***
US Tournament Golf Ltd Lblty ....E....909 987-6695
5464 Topaz St Rancho Cucamonga (91701) ***(P-27503)***
USA Bouquet LLC ....D....800 878-9909
2834 La Mirada Dr Ste B Vista (92081) ***(P-9172)***
USA Fact Inc (PA) ....D....951 656-7800
6200 Box Springs Blvd B Riverside (92507) ***(P-27504)***
USA Federal Credit Union, San Diego *Also called United Svcs Amer Federal Cr Un* ***(P-9614)***
USA Multifamily Management ....C....916 773-6060
3200 Douglas Blvd Ste 200 Roseville (95661) ***(P-11809)***
USA Properties Fund Inc (PA) ....D....916 773-6060
3200 Douglas Blvd Ste 200 Roseville (95661) ***(P-11934)***
USA Staffing Inc ....D....805 269-2677
505 Higuera St San Luis Obispo (93401) ***(P-14929)***
USA Transport Inc ....E....559 783-3563
12191 Violet Rd Adelanto (92301) ***(P-4384)***
USA Travel Services LLC ....A....207 899-8803
714 Washington Blvd Marina Del Rey (90292) ***(P-25478)***
USA Truck Inc ....D....909 334-1406
5861 Pine Ave Ste A-2 Chino Hills (91709) ***(P-4296)***
USA Valet Parking LLC ....E....916 792-1055
980 9th St Ste 1620 Sacramento (95814) ***(P-13778)***
USA Waste of California Inc ....D....559 741-1766
26951 Road 140 Visalia (93292) ***(P-6487)***
USA Waste of California Inc ....D....916 379-0500
8491 Fruitridge Rd Sacramento (95826) ***(P-6488)***
USA Waste of California Inc ....D....818 252-3112
9081 Tujunga Ave Sun Valley (91352) ***(P-6489)***
USA Waste of California Inc (HQ) ....C....916 387-1400
11931 Foundation Pl # 200 Gold River (95670) ***(P-6490)***
USA Waste of California Inc ....C....916 379-2611
8761 Younger Creek Dr Sacramento (95828) ***(P-4077)***
USA Waste of California Inc ....C....831 384-4860
11240 Commercial Pkwy Castroville (95012) ***(P-4078)***
USA Waste of California Inc ....E....209 946-5721
1240 Navy Dr Stockton (95206) ***(P-4079)***
USA Waste of California Inc ....D....800 423-9986
800 S Temescal St Corona (92879) ***(P-6491)***
USA Waste of California Inc ....E....530 274-3090
13083 Grass Valley Ave Grass Valley (95945) ***(P-4080)***
USA Waste of California Inc ....D....626 856-1285
13970 Live Oak Ave Baldwin Park (91706) ***(P-6492)***
USA Waste of California Inc ....D....805 466-3636
8740 Pueblo Ave Ste B Atascadero (93422) ***(P-6493)***
USA Waste of California Inc ....D....619 596-5117
1001 W Bradley Ave El Cajon (92020) ***(P-6494)***
USA Waste of California Inc ....D....909 590-1793
13793 Redwood St Chino (91710) ***(P-6495)***
USA Waste of California Inc ....D....559 834-9151
4333 E Jefferson Ave Fresno (93725) ***(P-6496)***
USA Waste of California Inc ....D....310 830-7100
1970 E 213th St Long Beach (90810) ***(P-6497)***
USA Waste of California Inc ....D....310 763-8500
407 E El Segundo Blvd Compton (90222) ***(P-6498)***
USA Waste of California Inc ....D....530 877-2777
951 American Way Paradise (95969) ***(P-6499)***
USA Waste of California Inc ....D....831 754-2500
1120 Madison Ln Salinas (93907) ***(P-6500)***
USA Waste of California Inc ....D....559 834-4070
10725 W Goshen Ave Visalia (93291) ***(P-6501)***
USA Waste of California Inc ....D....661 259-2398
25772 Springbrook Ave Santa Clarita (91350) ***(P-6502)***
USA Waste of California Inc ....D....714 637-3010
1800 S Grand Ave Santa Ana (92705) ***(P-6503)***
USA Waste of California Inc ....D....831 384-5000
29331 Pacific St Hayward (94544) ***(P-6504)***
Usaco Service Corp ....C....562 483-8747
16205 Distribution Way Cerritos (90703) ***(P-17918)***
Usag Ansbach Financial MGT Div ....D....210 466-1376
420 Montgomery St San Francisco (94104) ***(P-27077)***
Usag Rheinland Pfalz Fincl MGT ....D....210 466-1376
420 Montgomery St San Francisco (94104) ***(P-27078)***
Usag Vicenza Italy Dmwr F M D ....D....210 466-1376
420 Montgomery St San Francisco (94104) ***(P-27079)***
Usag Wiesbaden Fincl MGT Div ....D....210 466-1376
420 Montgomery St San Francisco (94104) ***(P-27080)***
Usas Express International ....D....310 645-2313
420 Hindry Ave Ste G Inglewood (90301) ***(P-5196)***
USB Solarcity Master Tenant ....D....650 963-5693
393 Vintage Park Dr # 140 Foster City (94404) ***(P-12015)***
Usc Care Medical Group Inc ....D....323 442-5100
1510 San Pablo St Ste 649 Los Angeles (90033) ***(P-21890)***
Usc Credit Union ....D....213 821-7100
3720 S Flower St Los Angeles (90089) ***(P-9616)***
Usc Emergency Medicine Assoc ....D....323 226-6667
1200 N State St Ste 1011 Los Angeles (90033) ***(P-20039)***
Usc Institute For Neuroimaging ....C....323 442-7246
2001 N Soto St Ste 102 Los Angeles (90032) ***(P-20040)***
Usc MARk& Mary Steven Neuro, Los Angeles *Also called Usc Institute For Neuroimaging* ***(P-20040)***
Usc Shoah Fndn Inst For Visual ....D....213 740-6001
650 W 35th St Ste 114 Los Angeles (90089) ***(P-25479)***
Usc Srgcal Edcatn RES Fndation, Los Angeles *Also called Usc Surgeons Incorporated* ***(P-20041)***
Usc Student Health Center, Los Angeles *Also called University Southern California* ***(P-20036)***
Usc Surgeons Incorporated ....C....323 442-5910
1510 San Pablo St Ste 514 Los Angeles (90033) ***(P-20041)***
Usc University Hospital, Los Angeles *Also called University Southern California* ***(P-21888)***
Usc Verdugo Hills Hospital LLC ....A....818 790-7100
1812 Verdugo Blvd Glendale (91208) ***(P-21891)***
Usc Vrdugo Hlls Hosp Fundation (PA) ....B....800 872-2273
1812 Verdugo Blvd Glendale (91208) ***(P-21892)***
Uscb Inc ....D....213 387-6181
3535 Wilshire Blvd # 700 Los Angeles (90010) ***(P-14025)***
Uscb Inc (PA) ....C....213 985-2111
355 S Grand Ave Ste 3200 Los Angeles (90071) ***(P-14026)***
Uscb America, Los Angeles *Also called Uscb Inc* ***(P-14026)***
Uscf Caps Department Medicine, San Francisco *Also called University Cal San Francisco* ***(P-26669)***
Usd, Union City *Also called Union Sanitary District* ***(P-6333)***
USDA Forest Service ....D....951 680-1560
4955 Canyon Crest Dr Riverside (92507) ***(P-26487)***
USDA Forest Service ....D....530 626-1546
100 Forni Rd Placerville (95667) ***(P-1002)***
Usdm Life Science, Santa Barbara *Also called US Data Management LLC* ***(P-16522)***
User Zoom Inc ....D....408 533-8619
10 Almaden Blvd Ste 250 San Jose (95113) ***(P-15517)***
USF Import FWD Wh 4150, Corona *Also called US Foods Inc* ***(P-8899)***
USF Reddaway Inc ....C....562 923-0648
11937 Regentview Ave Downey (90241) ***(P-4297)***
USF-La Mirada 4150, La Mirada *Also called US Foods Inc* ***(P-8897)***
Usfi Inc ....D....310 768-1937
110 W Walnut St 221 Gardena (90248) ***(P-8483)***
USG Enterprises Inc ....D....310 827-2220
4325 Glencoe Ave Marina Del Rey (90292) ***(P-4722)***
USG Interiors LLC ....D....209 466-4636
2575 Loomis Rd Stockton (95205) ***(P-6871)***
Ushio America Inc (HQ) ....D....714 236-8600
5440 Cerritos Ave Cypress (90630) ***(P-7400)***
USI Insurance Services Nat ....D....925 988-1700
1350 Treat Blvd Ste 550 Walnut Creek (94597) ***(P-10813)***
USI Insurance Services Nat Inc ....D....707 769-2900
1039a N Mcdowell Blvd Petaluma (94954) ***(P-10814)***
USI Insurance Services Nat Inc ....D....559 666-2001
5200 N Palm Ave Ste 114 Fresno (93704) ***(P-10815)***
USI Insurance Services Nat Inc ....C....213 253-6700
777 S Figueroa St # 2100 Los Angeles (90017) ***(P-10816)***
USI Insurance Services Nat Inc ....C....916 589-8000
10940 White Rock Rd Rancho Cordova (95670) ***(P-10817)***
USI Insurance Services Nat Inc ....C....628 201-9001
201 Mission St Ste 1100 San Francisco (94105) ***(P-10818)***
USI of Southern California Ins ....E....818 251-3000
21700 Oxnard St Ste 1200 Woodland Hills (91367) ***(P-10819)***
USI South Coast ....D....949 790-9200
29a Technology Dr 200 Irvine (92618) ***(P-10820)***
Usl, Newport Beach *Also called Universal Space Lines Inc* ***(P-25971)***
USS Cal Builders Inc ....C....714 828-4882
8051 Main St Stanton (90680) ***(P-1691)***
UST Development Inc ....C....626 205-1123
2001 Elm Ct Ontario (91761) ***(P-5425)***
UST Global Inc (PA) ....D....949 716-8757
5 Polaris Way Aliso Viejo (92656) ***(P-15518)***
UST Telecom, Ontario *Also called UST Development Inc* ***(P-5425)***
Ustov Inc ....E....510 781-1818
21118 Cabot Blvd Hayward (94545) ***(P-8484)***
Ustream Inc ....D....415 489-9400
410 Townsend St Fl 4 San Francisco (94107) ***(P-5660)***
Usts, Huntington Beach *Also called United States Technical Svcs* ***(P-16520)***
Utah Pacific Construction Co ....E....951 677-9876
40940 Eleanora Way Murrieta (92562) ***(P-1991)***
Utblo Inc ....C....562 493-3664
11061 Los Alamitos Blvd Los Alamitos (90720) ***(P-12016)***
UTC Fire SEC Americas Corp Inc ....D....949 737-7800
2955 Red Hill Ave Ste 100 Costa Mesa (92626) ***(P-15519)***
Utc, Mas, Costa Mesa *Also called UTC Fire SEC Americas Corp Inc* ***(P-15519)***
Utdi, Mill Valley *Also called Unified Teldata Inc* ***(P-7556)***
Uti Leak Seekers ....D....323 724-0081
1398 Monterey Pass Rd Monterey Park (91754) ***(P-1992)***
Uti Underground Technology, Monterey Park *Also called Uti Leak Seekers* ***(P-1992)***
Utility Systems Science (PA) ....D....714 542-1004
601 Parkcenter Dr Ste 209 Santa Ana (92705) ***(P-15520)***
Utility Trailer Sales of S CA (PA) ....D....877 275-4887
15567 Valley Blvd Fontana (92335) ***(P-6612)***
Utility Tree Service LLC (HQ) ....E....530 226-0330
1884 Keystone Ct Ste A Redding (96003) ***(P-982)***
Utility Tree Service, Inc., Redding *Also called Utility Tree Service LLC* ***(P-982)***
Utility Tree Services, Goleta *Also called Asplundh Tree Expert Co* ***(P-966)***
Utility Trlr Sls of Centl Cal ....E....559 237-2001
2680 S East Ave Fresno (93706) ***(P-7815)***

Mergent e-mail: customerrelations@mergent.com
1508
2019 Directory of California
Wholesalers and Services Companies
(P-0000) Products & Services Section entry number
(PA)=Parent Co (HQ)=Headquarters (DH)=Div Headquarters

Utopia Lighting, Compton *Also called Pacific Lighting Mfr Inc* ***(P-7384)***
Utopia Lighting, Rancho Dominguez *Also called Pacific Lighting Mfr Inc* ***(P-7385)***
Uyeda Farm.....E.....831 722-6345
656 Lakeview Rd Watsonville (95076) ***(P-125)***
Uyematsu Inc.....D.....831 724-2200
1004 E Lake Ave Watsonville (95076) ***(P-126)***
V & L Produce Inc.....C.....323 589-3125
2550 E 25th St Vernon (90058) ***(P-8740)***
V A Anderson Enterprises Inc (PA).....D.....714 990-6100
400 Atlas St Brea (92821) ***(P-17555)***
V A Anderson Enterprises Inc.....D.....925 866-6150
2680 Bishop Dr Ste 140 San Ramon (94583) ***(P-14094)***
V and V Farms, Lodi *Also called Jose Vramontes* ***(P-362)***
V B Z, Richgrove *Also called Vincent B Zaninovich Sons Inc* ***(P-182)***
V Development Inc.....D.....925 634-8890
550 Harvest Park Dr Ste A Brentwood (94513) ***(P-1324)***
V G Carelli International Corp.....E.....310 247-8410
1 Park Plz Ste 600 Irvine (92614) ***(P-17556)***
V G Pacific Equities, Los Angeles *Also called Pacific Equities Captl* ***(P-11180)***
V G S, Salinas *Also called Vegetable Growers Supply Co* ***(P-9266)***
V I P Associates Inc (PA).....E.....831 646-1549
470 Camino El Estero Monterey (93940) ***(P-13361)***
V M S, Glendora *Also called Venue Management Systems Inc* ***(P-16853)***
V N A & Hospice Southern Calif, San Bernardino *Also called Vna Hospice & Pllatve Cre S CA* ***(P-22460)***
V P H, Van Nuys *Also called Valley Presbyterian Hospital* ***(P-21896)***
V P I, Camarillo *Also called Voice Print International LLC* ***(P-16200)***
V S N F Inc.....D.....916 452-6631
2120 Stockton Blvd Sacramento (95817) ***(P-20848)***
V S S, West Sacramento *Also called Vss International Inc* ***(P-1868)***
V Sangiacomo & Sons.....C.....707 938-5503
21543 Broadway Sonoma (95476) ***(P-181)***
V Troth Inc.....D.....661 948-4646
1801 W Avenue K Ste 101 Lancaster (93534) ***(P-11810)***
V Vcc Havens, Vista *Also called Vista Valley Country Club* ***(P-19083)***
V&V Farm Labor Contractor.....E.....209 599-4834
18396 S Wagner Ave Ripon (95366) ***(P-389)***
V-Tek Systems Corporation.....D.....909 396-5355
21045 Ridge Park Dr Yorba Linda (92886) ***(P-16071)***
V3 Electric Inc.....C.....916 597-2627
4925 Rj Mathews Pkwy 100 El Dorado Hills (95762) ***(P-2393)***
VA Hospital, Fresno *Also called Veterans Health Administration* ***(P-21903)***
VA HSR&d Center of Excellence, North Hills *Also called Veterans Health Administration* ***(P-20080)***
Vacation and Holiday Benefit F.....D.....213 385-6161
501 Shatto Pl Ste 5 Los Angeles (90020) ***(P-12130)***
Vacation Interval Realty, Newport Beach *Also called Pacific Monarch Resorts Inc* ***(P-11649)***
Vacaville Condolescent and Reh.....C.....707 449-8000
585 Nut Tree Ct Vacaville (95687) ***(P-14930)***
Vacaville Medical Center, Vacaville *Also called Kaiser Foundation Hospitals* ***(P-19537)***
Vacaville Psychiatric Program, Vacaville *Also called Mental Health California Dept* ***(P-21966)***
Vacavlle Cnvalescent Rehab Ctr.....C.....707 449-8000
585 Nut Tree Ct Vacaville (95687) ***(P-21241)***
Vaco Lajolla LLC.....D.....858 642-0000
4250 Executive Sq Ste 750 La Jolla (92037) ***(P-14791)***
Vaco Technology, La Jolla *Also called Vaco Lajolla LLC* ***(P-14791)***
Vadnais Trenchless Svcs Inc.....B.....858 550-1460
26000 Commercentre Dr Lake Forest (92630) ***(P-1993)***
Vadnais Trenchless Svcs Inc.....D.....858 550-1460
2130 La Mirada Dr Vista (92081) ***(P-1994)***
Vagabond Inn Corporation (HQ).....D.....213 284-7533
2361 Rosecrans Ave # 150 El Segundo (90245) ***(P-13362)***
Vagabond Inns, El Segundo *Also called Rpd Hotels 18 LLC* ***(P-13148)***
Val-Pro Inc.....D.....213 689-0844
1661 Mcgarry St Los Angeles (90021) ***(P-8741)***
Valadon Hotel LLC.....D.....310 854-1114
8822 Cynthia St West Hollywood (90069) ***(P-13363)***
Valassis Communications Inc.....D.....714 751-4006
1575 Corporate Dr Costa Mesa (92626) ***(P-14067)***
Valassis Direct Mail Inc.....D.....510 505-6500
6955 Mowry Ave Newark (94560) ***(P-14068)***
Valco Construction, Bakersfield *Also called Gilliam & Sons Inc* ***(P-3427)***
Vale Healthcare Center, San Pablo *Also called Mariner Health Care Inc* ***(P-20615)***
Vale Healthcare Center, San Pablo *Also called Grancare LLC* ***(P-20492)***
Valeant Biomedicals Inc (HQ).....D.....949 461-6000
1 Enterprise Aliso Viejo (92656) ***(P-8940)***
Valencia Bros Inc.....D.....760 353-2168
257 Maple Ave El Centro (92243) ***(P-3340)***
Valencia Brothers Concrete, El Centro *Also called Valencia Bros Inc* ***(P-3340)***
Valencia Country Club, Valencia *Also called Heritage Golf Group Inc* ***(P-18718)***
VALENCIA GARDENS HEALTH CARE CENTER, Riverside *Also called Riverside Care Inc* ***(P-20725)***
Valencia Health Care Inc.....D.....661 254-2425
23801 Newhall Ave Newhall (91321) ***(P-21242)***
Valencia Tree Landscape.....E.....805 965-4244
321 N Quarantina St Santa Barbara (93103) ***(P-792)***
Valente Concrete.....D.....951 279-2221
255 Benjamin Dr Corona (92879) ***(P-3341)***
Valentine Corporation.....E.....415 453-3732
111 Pelican Way San Rafael (94901) ***(P-3601)***
Valero Labor, Woodland *Also called Oscar Valero* ***(P-372)***
Valet Parking Svc A Cal Partnr (PA).....A.....323 465-5873
6933 Hollywood Blvd Los Angeles (90028) ***(P-17710)***
Valet Services, Bell Gardens *Also called Anitsa Inc* ***(P-13483)***
Valetor Inc.....E.....323 654-1271
8359 Santa Monica Blvd Los Angeles (90069) ***(P-13571)***
Valew Welding & Fabrication, Adelanto *Also called Hayes Welding Inc* ***(P-17923)***
Valgenesis Inc.....E.....510 445-0505
395 Oyster Point Blvd # 228 South San Francisco (94080) ***(P-7126)***
Valiant Integrated Services.....B.....858 277-6780
9333 Balboa Ave San Diego (92123) ***(P-24989)***
Validant, San Francisco *Also called Kinsale Holdings Inc* ***(P-8186)***
Validus Group Inc.....D.....949 457-7606
1 Orchard Ste 210 Lake Forest (92630) ***(P-14792)***
Valin Corporation (PA).....D.....408 730-9850
1941 Ringwood Ave San Jose (95131) ***(P-7816)***
Valle Sanit and Flood Contr Di.....D.....707 644-8949
450 Ryder St Vallejo (94590) ***(P-27893)***
Valle Verde Retirement Center, Santa Barbara *Also called American Baptist Homes of West* ***(P-10978)***
Valle Vista Convalescent Hosp, Escondido *Also called Covenant Care California LLC* ***(P-20351)***
Valle Vsta Cnvlescent Hosp Inc.....D.....760 745-1288
1025 W 2nd Ave Escondido (92025) ***(P-21243)***
Vallejo Garbage & Recycling, Vallejo *Also called Recology Vallejo* ***(P-6445)***
Valley Aggregate Transport Inc.....D.....530 821-2600
753 N George Wash Blvd Yuba City (95993) ***(P-4081)***
Valley Air District, Fresno *Also called San Joaquin Val UNI Air Pol* ***(P-27853)***
Valley Base Materials, Sylmar *Also called Security Paving Company Inc* ***(P-1846)***
Valley Bulk Inc.....D.....760 843-0574
17649 Turner Rd Victorville (92394) ***(P-4298)***
Valley Can.....E.....916 273-4890
921 11th St Ste 220 Sacramento (95814) ***(P-24855)***
Valley Care Center, Porterville *Also called Wescordon Incorporated* ***(P-20880)***
Valley Care Health System, The, Pleasanton *Also called The For Hospital Committee* ***(P-27061)***
Valley Care Olive View Med Ctr, Sylmar *Also called Olive View-Ucla Medical Center* ***(P-19731)***
Valley Careidence Opco LLC.....D.....559 784-8371
661 W Poplar Ave Porterville (93257) ***(P-20849)***
Valley Center Municipal.....D.....760 735-4500
29300 Valley Center Rd Valley Center (92082) ***(P-6317)***
Valley Center Municpl Wtr Dst.....D.....760 735-4500
29300 Valley Center Rd Valley Center (92082) ***(P-6334)***
Valley Child Guidance Clinic, Palmdale *Also called Child and Family Guidance Ctr* ***(P-22527)***
Valley Childrens Healthcare.....A.....559 353-3000
9300 Valley Childrens Pl Madera (93636) ***(P-20042)***
Valley Childrens Hospital.....C.....559 353-6425
9300 Valley Childrens Pl Madera (93636) ***(P-21893)***
Valley Childrens Hospital (PA).....A.....559 353-3000
9300 Valley Childrens Pl Madera (93636) ***(P-21894)***
Valley Clark Plbg & Htg Co Inc (PA).....D.....818 782-1047
7640 Gloria Ave Ste L Van Nuys (91406) ***(P-2394)***
Valley Cmnty Counseling Svcs (PA).....D.....209 956-4240
6707 Embarcadero Dr Stockton (95219) ***(P-24106)***
Valley Communications Inc (PA).....D.....916 349-7300
6921 Roseville Rd Sacramento (95842) ***(P-2776)***
Valley Community Health Center, Pleasanton *Also called Center Cnslng Edctn & Crisis* ***(P-23546)***
Valley Community Healthcare.....B.....818 763-8836
6801 Coldwater Canyon Ave 1b North Hollywood (91605) ***(P-20043)***
Valley Convalescent Hospital, Watsonville *Also called West Coast Hospitals Inc* ***(P-21253)***
Valley Couriers Inc (PA).....D.....818 591-2212
646 N San Fernando Rd Los Angeles (90065) ***(P-4082)***
Valley Detriot Diesel, Bakersfield *Also called Valley Power Systems Inc* ***(P-7817)***
Valley Drive-In Theatre, Santa Maria *Also called Cal Gran Theatres LLC* ***(P-18276)***
Valley Eye Center Group, Van Nuys *Also called George M Rajacich MD PC* ***(P-19482)***
Valley Farm Management Inc.....D.....831 678-1592
37500 Foothill Rd Soledad (93960) ***(P-716)***
Valley Fig Growers, Pleasanton *Also called Sun-Maid Growers California* ***(P-179)***
Valley Fig Growers.....E.....559 237-3893
2028 S 3rd St Fresno (93702) ***(P-582)***
Valley First Credit Union (PA).....D.....209 549-8511
1419 J St Modesto (95354) ***(P-9617)***
Valley Flowers Inc.....D.....805 684-6651
3920 Via Real Carpinteria (93013) ***(P-9173)***
Valley Fresh Foods Inc.....D.....209 669-5600
3600 E Linwood Ave Turlock (95380) ***(P-435)***
Valley Fresh Foods Inc.....D.....209 669-5510
1220 Hall Rd Denair (95316) ***(P-436)***
Valley Garbage Rubbish Co Inc.....D.....805 614-1131
1850 W Betteravia Rd Santa Maria (93455) ***(P-6505)***
Valley Health Care Systems Inc.....C.....916 505-4112
1300 National Dr Ste 140 Sacramento (95834) ***(P-14793)***
Valley Healthcare, San Bernardino *Also called United Medical Management Inc* ***(P-21239)***
Valley Healthcare Center LLC.....D.....559 251-7161
4840 E Tulare Ave Fresno (93727) ***(P-20850)***
Valley Healthcare Center LLC.....C.....559 251-7161
4840 E Tulare Ave Fresno (93727) ***(P-20851)***
Valley Healthcare Staffing, Sacramento *Also called Valley Health Care Systems Inc* ***(P-14793)***
Valley Hospital Medical Center (HQ).....B.....818 885-8500
18300 Roscoe Blvd Northridge (91325) ***(P-21895)***
Valley House Care Center, Santa Clara *Also called TLC of Bay Area Inc* ***(P-20838)***
Valley Hunt Club.....D.....626 793-7134
520 S Orange Grove Blvd Pasadena (91105) ***(P-25273)***
Valley Indoor Swap Meet, Woodland Hills *Also called Metropolitan Marketing Inc* ***(P-27344)***
Valley Industrial X-Ra.....C.....661 399-8497
3700 Pegasus Dr 100 Bakersfield (93308) ***(P-26742)***

Employee Codes: A=Over 500 employees, B=251-500
C=101-250, D=51-100, E=50
2019 Directory of California
Wholesalers and Services Companies
© Mergent Inc. 1-800-342-5647
1509

Valley Inventory Service Inc ....D......707 422-6050
  1180 Horizon Dr Ste B Fairfield (94533) *(P-17557)*
Valley Labor Service Inc ....D......559 591-5591
  39678 Road 84 Dinuba (93618) *(P-14794)*
Valley Landscaping & Maint Inc ....C......209 334-3659
  12900 N Lwer Scramento Rd Lodi (95242) *(P-956)*
Valley Light Industries Inc ....C......626 337-6200
  5360 Irwindale Ave Baldwin Park (91706) *(P-24245)*
Valley Management Services ....B......626 333-1243
  425 S Hacienda Blvd City of Industry (91745) *(P-27081)*
Valley Manor Convalescent Hosp, North Hollywood *Also called Golden Care Inc (P-21083)*
Valley Med Ctr Billing Dept, San Jose *Also called Santa Clara County of (P-26286)*
Valley Medical Group of Lompoc ....D......805 736-1253
  136 N 3rd St Lompoc (93436) *(P-20044)*
Valley Medical Trnsp LLC ....D......760 501-8929
  43612 Jackson St Ste 4 Indio (92201) *(P-3856)*
Valley Molding & Frame, North Hollywood *Also called Valley Wholesale Supply Corp (P-6800)*
Valley Mtn Regional Ctr Inc (PA) ....C......209 473-0951
  702 N Aurora St Stockton (95202) *(P-24107)*
Valley Mtn Regional Ctr Inc ....D......209 529-2626
  1620 Cummins Dr Modesto (95358) *(P-24705)*
Valley Northamerican, Concord *Also called Valley Relocation and Storage (P-4385)*
Valley Nurses ....D......714 549-2512
  1450 W 9th St Pomona (91766) *(P-20212)*
Valley Oak Dental Group ....D......209 823-9341
  1507 W Yosemite Ave Manteca (95337) *(P-20142)*
Valley Oaks Residential ....D......209 239-3244
  10623 E Highway 120 Manteca (95336) *(P-24108)*
VALLEY OASIS SHELTER, Lancaster *Also called Antelope Vly Dom Vlnce Council (P-23482)*
Valley Ob Gyn Medical Group ....E......909 580-6333
  400 N Pepper Ave Fl 6 Colton (92324) *(P-20045)*
Valley of California, Inc., Concord *Also called Coldwell Bnkr Residential Brkg (P-11350)*
Valley of Sun Cosmetics LLC ....C......310 327-9062
  535 Patrice Pl Gardena (90248) *(P-8216)*
Valley of The Sun Labs, Gardena *Also called Valley of Sun Cosmetics LLC (P-8216)*
Valley Pacific Concrete Inc ....C......951 672-6151
  27580 Tabb Ln Menifee (92584) *(P-3342)*
Valley Pacific Petro Svcs Inc ....C......661 746-7737
  9521 Enos Ln Bakersfield (93314) *(P-8971)*
Valley Palms Convalescent Hosp, North Hollywood *Also called Trinity Health Systems (P-21231)*
Valley Peterbilt, Stockton *Also called Interstate Truck Center LLC (P-6599)*
Valley Physical Theraphy, Escondido *Also called Physical Therapy Hand Ctrs Inc (P-20195)*
Valley Physicians Alliance ....D......559 538-3000
  255 E Rver Pk Cir Ste 240 Fresno (93720) *(P-27082)*
Valley Pinte Nursing Rehab Ctr ....E......510 538-8464
  20090 Stanton Ave Castro Valley (94546) *(P-24706)*
Valley Power System, City of Industry *Also called Valley Management Services (P-27081)*
Valley Power Systems Inc ....E......661 325-9001
  4000 Rosedale Hwy Bakersfield (93308) *(P-7817)*
Valley Presbyterian Hospital ....A......818 782-6600
  15107 Vanowen St Van Nuys (91405) *(P-21896)*
Valley Pride Inc ....D......760 398-1353
  86120 Tyler Ln Coachella (92236) *(P-487)*
Valley Pride Inc (PA) ....B......831 633-5883
  10855 Ocean Mist Pkwy D Castroville (95012) *(P-676)*
Valley Process Systems Inc ....D......408 261-1277
  3567 Benton St Ste 341 Santa Clara (95051) *(P-2395)*
Valley Productions Inc ....E......559 661-6121
  17247 La Canada Rd Madera (93636) *(P-17558)*
Valley Properties Inc ....D......818 360-3430
  10324 Balboa Blvd Lbby Granada Hills (91344) *(P-10959)*
Valley Radiology Consultants (PA) ....D......619 797-8248
  6185 Paseo Del Norte # 110 Carlsbad (92011) *(P-22156)*
Valley Relocation and Storage (PA) ....C......925 230-2025
  5000 Marsh Dr Concord (94520) *(P-4385)*
Valley Republic Bank ....D......661 371-2000
  5000 California Ave # 110 Bakersfield (93309) *(P-9493)*
Valley Rsrce Ctr For Retarded ....D......951 766-8659
  1285 N Santa Fe St Hemet (92543) *(P-24856)*
Valley Rubber & Gasket, Sacramento *Also called Lewis-Goetz and Company Inc (P-7855)*
Valley Sheet Metal Co, Marysville *Also called Frank M Booth Inc (P-25692)*
Valley Skilled Nursing Care, Sacramento *Also called V S N F Inc (P-20848)*
Valley Stre Frnt Jwsh Fmly Svc, North Hollywood *Also called Jewish Family Svc Los Angeles (P-23874)*
Valley Sun Mechanical Cnstr ....D......661 321-9070
  4205 Atlas Ct Bakersfield (93308) *(P-3602)*
Valley Sweet LLC ....D......559 686-3381
  222 N Garden St Ste 400 Visalia (93291) *(P-4517)*
Valley Teen Ranch ....D......559 437-1144
  2610 W Shaw Ln Ste 105 Fresno (93711) *(P-24707)*
Valley Toxicology Service Inc ....D......916 371-5440
  2401 Port St West Sacramento (95691) *(P-22157)*
Valley Transportation Inc (PA) ....D......559 266-6674
  2837 S East Ave Fresno (93725) *(P-4083)*
Valley US Inc ....D......408 260-7342
  888 Saratoga Ave Ste 201 San Jose (95129) *(P-16523)*
Valley View Care Center, Riverbank *Also called Valley West Health Care Inc (P-20854)*
Valley View Casino, Valley Center *Also called San Psqual Band Mssion Indians (P-13180)*
Valley View Casino, Valley Center *Also called San Psqual Csino Dev Group Inc (P-13181)*
Valley View Skilled Nursing, Ukiah *Also called Horizon West Healthcare Inc (P-20536)*
Valley View Sklled Nursing Ctr ....D......707 462-1436
  1162 S Dora St Ukiah (95482) *(P-20852)*
VALLEY VILLAGE, Santa Clara *Also called Church of Vly Rtrment Hmes Inc (P-24470)*
Valley Village (PA) ....D......818 587-9450
  20830 Sherman Way Winnetka (91306) *(P-24708)*

Valley Vista Nursing and Trans ....C......818 763-6275
  6120 Vineland Ave North Hollywood (91606) *(P-20853)*
Valley Water Proofing Inc ....D......408 985-7701
  825 Civic Center Dr Ste 6 Santa Clara (95050) *(P-3603)*
Valley West Care Center, Williams *Also called Valley West Health Care Inc (P-21244)*
Valley West Health Care Inc (PA) ....D......530 473-5321
  1224 E St Williams (95987) *(P-21244)*
Valley West Health Care Inc ....D......209 869-2569
  2649 Topeka St Riverbank (95367) *(P-20854)*
Valley Wholesale Drug Co LLC ....D......209 466-0131
  1401 W Fremont St Stockton (95203) *(P-8217)*
Valley Wholesale Supply Corp (PA) ....D......818 769-5656
  10708 Vanowen St North Hollywood (91605) *(P-6800)*
Valley Wide Beverage Company, Fresno *Also called Fresno Beverage Company Inc (P-8996)*
Valley Wide Recreation Pk Dst (PA) ....D......951 654-1505
  901 W Esplanade Ave San Jacinto (92582) *(P-19255)*
Valley-HI Country Club ....E......916 684-2120
  9595 Franklin Blvd Elk Grove (95758) *(P-19076)*
Valleycare Health, Livermore *Also called Valleycare Hospital Corp (P-20046)*
Valleycare Health System, Livermore *Also called For Hospital Committee (P-26860)*
Valleycare Hospital Corp (HQ) ....D......925 447-7000
  1111 E Stanley Blvd Livermore (94550) *(P-20046)*
Valleycrest Ldscp Maint Vcc ....E......800 466-8510
  24121 Ventura Blvd Calabasas (91302) *(P-793)*
Valleywide Construction Inc ....C......559 834-6212
  284 W Lester Ave Clovis (93619) *(P-1253)*
Valori Sand & Gravel Company (PA) ....D......714 637-0104
  141 W Taft Ave Orange (92865) *(P-6911)*
Valori Sand & Gravel Company ....C......909 350-3000
  11027 Cherry Ave Fontana (92337) *(P-6912)*
Vals Plumbing and Heating Inc ....D......831 424-1633
  413 Front St Salinas (93901) *(P-2396)*
Valtox Laboratories, West Sacramento *Also called Valley Toxicology Service Inc (P-22157)*
Valuation Concepts LLC ....D......818 812-6233
  16350 Ventura Blvd D140 Encino (91436) *(P-11811)*
Value Options-V B H, Cypress *Also called Valueoptions of California (P-10821)*
Value-Centered Solutions Inc ....E......510 662-3333
  2300 Stanwell Dr Ste A Concord (94520) *(P-27505)*
Valueoptions of California ....C......800 228-1286
  5665 Plaza Dr Ste 400 Cypress (90630) *(P-10821)*
Valverde Construction Inc ....D......562 906-1826
  10936 Shoemaker Ave Santa Fe Springs (90670) *(P-1995)*
Valvoline Instant Oil Change, Santa Fe Springs *Also called Valvoline International Inc (P-17881)*
Valvoline International Inc ....E......562 906-6200
  9520 John St Santa Fe Springs (90670) *(P-17881)*
Valyria LLC (HQ) ....D......707 452-0600
  1050 Aviator Dr Vacaville (95688) *(P-6801)*
Van Acker Cnstr Assoc Inc ....C......415 383-5589
  1060 Redwood Hwy Frntg Rd Mill Valley (94941) *(P-1254)*
Van Beurden Insurance Svcs Inc (PA) ....D......559 634-7125
  1600 Draper St Kingsburg (93631) *(P-10822)*
Van Daele Development Corp ....C......951 354-6800
  2900 Adams St Ste C25 Riverside (92504) *(P-1362)*
Van Daele Homes, Riverside *Also called Van Daele Development Corp (P-1362)*
Van De Pol Enterprises Inc (PA) ....D......209 465-3421
  4895 S Airport Way Stockton (95206) *(P-8972)*
Van Dyk Tank Lines Inc ....E......951 682-5000
  1800 S Riverside Ave Colton (92324) *(P-4084)*
Van Etten Suzumoto Becket LLP ....D......310 315-8284
  1620 26th St Ste 6000n Santa Monica (90404) *(P-27506)*
Van Groningen & Sons Inc ....B......209 982-5248
  15100 Jack Tone Rd Manteca (95336) *(P-390)*
Van Grow Jack S MD ....E......714 564-3300
  1140 W La Veta Ave # 640 Orange (92868) *(P-20047)*
Van Horn Youth Center, Riverside *Also called County of Riverside (P-23715)*
Van Inn II Inc (PA) ....D......510 548-6600
  25 Avenida De Orinda Orinda (94563) *(P-20855)*
Van King & Storage Inc (PA) ....D......562 921-0555
  13535 Larwin Cir Santa Fe Springs (90670) *(P-4085)*
Van King & Storage Inc ....E......562 921-0555
  13535 Larwin Cir Santa Fe Springs (90670) *(P-4652)*
Van Ness Hotel Inc ....D......415 673-4711
  1050 Van Ness Ave San Francisco (94109) *(P-13364)*
Van Nuys Airport, Van Nuys *Also called City of Los Angeles (P-4878)*
Van Nuys Care Center Inc ....D......818 343-0700
  16955 Vanowen St Van Nuys (91406) *(P-21245)*
Van Nuys Community Hospital, Van Nuys *Also called Alta Healthcare System LLC (P-24730)*
Van Nuys Health Care Center, Van Nuys *Also called Five Star Quality Care Inc (P-20431)*
Van Sark Inc ....D......415 362-5888
  1255 Battery St Ste 200 San Francisco (94111) *(P-6739)*
Van Torrance & Storage Company (PA) ....D......562 567-2100
  12128 Burke St Santa Fe Springs (90670) *(P-4386)*
Vanalden Ave School, Reseda *Also called West Valley Family YMCA (P-24398)*
Vance Corporation ....E......909 355-4333
  17761 Slover Ave Bloomington (92316) *(P-1867)*
Vancrest Construction Corp ....E......323 256-0011
  7171 N Figueroa St Los Angeles (90042) *(P-1692)*
Vandenberg Afb Child Care ....E......805 606-1555
  Summersill Bldg 11613 Lompoc (93437) *(P-24396)*
Vander Weerd General Cnstr ....D......559 688-1099
  837 Commercial Ave Tulare (93274) *(P-3444)*
Vandorpe Chou Associates Inc ....E......714 978-9780
  1845 W Orangewood Ave # 210 Orange (92868) *(P-25987)*
Vanguard Legato, San Leandro *Also called Vanguard Legato A Cal Corp (P-6740)*
Vanguard Legato A Cal Corp ....D......510 351-3333
  2121 Williams St San Leandro (94577) *(P-6740)*

Mergent e-mail: customerrelations@mergent.com
1510

2019 Directory of California
Wholesalers and Services Companies

(P-0000) Products & Services Section entry number
(PA)=Parent Co (HQ)=Headquarters (DH)=Div Headquarters

Vanguard Legato Group, San Jose *Also called Business Furn Solutions Inc* ***(P-6714)***
Vanguard Lgistics Svcs USA Inc (HQ)........D......310 847-3000
5000 Arprt Plz Dr Ste 200 Long Beach (90815) ***(P-5197)***
Vanguard Lgistics Svcs USA Inc........D......310 637-3700
2665 E Del Amo Blvd Compton (90221) ***(P-4653)***
Vanguard Resources Corp........D......858 336-7147
13816 Fontanelle Pl San Diego (92128) ***(P-27609)***
Vanir Construction MGT Inc (PA)........D......916 444-3700
4540 Duckhorn Dr Ste 300 Sacramento (95834) ***(P-27083)***
Vanpike Inc (PA)........D......858 453-1331
6336 Greenwich Dr Ste 100 San Diego (92122) ***(P-14931)***
Vantage Company, Orange *Also called W Corporation* ***(P-27907)***
Vantage Oncology LLC (HQ)........B......310 335-4000
1500 Rosecrans Ave # 400 Manhattan Beach (90266) ***(P-20048)***
Vantage Plaster & Drywall........D......760 345-3622
79607 Country Club Dr Bermuda Dunes (92203) ***(P-2974)***
Vantagepoint Capital Partners, San Bruno *Also called Vantagepoint Management Inc* ***(P-12279)***
Vantagepoint Management Inc (PA)........D......650 866-3100
1111 Bayhill Dr Ste 220 San Bruno (94066) ***(P-12279)***
Vantagepoint Venture Partners........D......650 866-3100
1001 Bayhill Dr Ste 300 San Bruno (94066) ***(P-12050)***
Vaquero Energy Incorporated........E......661 363-7240
15545 Hermosa Rd Bakersfield (93307) ***(P-1031)***
Vaquero Farms Inc........D......559 659-2790
43405 W Panoche Rd Firebaugh (93622) ***(P-391)***
Variations In Stone Inc........D......949 438-8337
360 La Perle Pl Costa Mesa (92627) ***(P-2826)***
Varis LLC........D......916 294-0860
3915 Security Park Dr B Rancho Cordova (95742) ***(P-27507)***
Varis LLC (PA)........C......916 294-0860
9245 Sierra College Blvd Roseville (95661) ***(P-27508)***
Varner Family Ltd Partnership (PA)........D......661 399-1163
5900 E Lerdo Hwy Shafter (93263) ***(P-12131)***
Varsity Contractors Inc........D......949 586-8283
24155 Laguna Hills Mall Laguna Hills (92653) ***(P-14424)***
Vasindas Around The Clock Care........E......661 395-5820
5251 Office Park Dr # 403 Bakersfield (93309) ***(P-24709)***
Vasko Electric Inc........D......916 568-7700
4300 Astoria St Sacramento (95838) ***(P-2777)***
Vasona Management Inc........D......510 413-0091
37390 Central Mont Pl Fremont (94538) ***(P-1255)***
Vasonic Construction, Fremont *Also called Vasona Management Inc* ***(P-1255)***
Vasquez Brothers Inc........D......831 678-8894
157 Kidder St Soledad (93960) ***(P-583)***
Vastek Inc........C......925 948-5701
1230 Columbia St Ste 1180 San Diego (92101) ***(P-17559)***
Vasto Valle Farms, Huron *Also called Dick Anderson & Sons Farming* ***(P-335)***
Vat Incorporated (HQ)........E......781 935-1446
655 River Oaks Pkwy San Jose (95134) ***(P-7876)***
Vauche Bank Berkshire Mortgage, Irvine *Also called Berkshire Mortgage Fin Corp* ***(P-9781)***
Vavrinek Trine Day & Co LLP (PA)........C......909 466-4410
10681 Fthill Blvd Ste 300 Rancho Cucamonga (91730) ***(P-26306)***
Vaxaville Medical Offices, Vacaville *Also called Kaiser Foundation Hospitals* ***(P-10234)***
Vaya, San Diego *Also called Vietnms-Mrcan Yuth Alance Corp* ***(P-25280)***
Vayan Marketing Group LLC........E......310 943-4990
10877 Wilshire Blvd Fl 12 Los Angeles (90024) ***(P-27509)***
Vb Golf LLC........D......650 573-7888
2401 E 3rd Ave Foster City (94404) ***(P-18775)***
Vbp Orange, San Francisco *Also called Venables/Bell & Partners LLC* ***(P-13915)***
VCA Animal Hospitals Inc........E......650 631-7400
501 Laurel St San Carlos (94070) ***(P-611)***
VCA Animal Hospitals Inc........E......916 652-5816
3901 Sierra College Blvd Loomis (95650) ***(P-612)***
VCA Animal Hospitals Inc (HQ)........C......310 571-6500
12401 W Olympic Blvd Los Angeles (90064) ***(P-613)***
VCA Antech Inc........B......310 207-0781
12401 W Olympic Blvd Los Angeles (90064) ***(P-614)***
VCA Desert Animal Hospitals........D......760 778-9999
4299 E Ramon Rd Palm Springs (92264) ***(P-615)***
VCA Engineering, Orange *Also called Vandorpe Chou Associates Inc* ***(P-25987)***
VCA Holly Street, San Carlos *Also called VCA Animal Hospitals Inc* ***(P-611)***
VCA Inc........D......310 473-2951
1818 S Sepulveda Blvd Los Angeles (90025) ***(P-616)***
VCA Inc........D......530 224-2200
2505 Hilltop Dr Redding (96002) ***(P-617)***
VCA Lmis Bsin Vterinary Clinic, Loomis *Also called VCA Animal Hospitals Inc* ***(P-612)***
VCA TLC Animal Hospital, Los Angeles *Also called VCA Animal Hospitals Inc* ***(P-613)***
VCA-Asher Animal Hospital, Redding *Also called VCA Inc* ***(P-617)***
Vcall, Beverly Hills *Also called Mediaplatform Inc* ***(P-18077)***
Vci Construction LLC (HQ)........D......909 946-0905
1921 W 11th St Ste A Upland (91786) ***(P-1996)***
Vci Event Technology Inc........C......714 772-2002
1261 S Simpson Cir Anaheim (92806) ***(P-14554)***
Veatch Carlson Grogan & Nelson........E......213 381-2861
1055 Wilshire Blvd Fl 11 Los Angeles (90017) ***(P-23420)***
Veba Administrators Inc........E......310 577-1444
4640 Admiralty Way Fl 9 Marina Del Rey (90292) ***(P-10823)***
Vector Resources Inc (PA)........C......310 436-1000
3530 Voyager St Torrance (90503) ***(P-2778)***
Vector Resources Inc........E......858 546-1014
9808 Waples St San Diego (92121) ***(P-25988)***
Vector Security Inc........D......323 224-6700
5411 Valley Blvd Los Angeles (90032) ***(P-2779)***
Vector Talent II LLC........A......415 293-5000
1 Market St Ste 2300 San Francisco (94105) ***(P-12072)***
Vector USA, San Diego *Also called Vector Resources Inc* ***(P-25988)***
Vectorusa, Torrance *Also called Vector Resources Inc* ***(P-2778)***
Veeva Systems Inc (PA)........C......925 452-6500
4280 Hacienda Dr Pleasanton (94588) ***(P-15888)***
Veg Land Sales Inc (PA)........D......714 871-6712
1518 E Valencia Dr Fullerton (92831) ***(P-8485)***
Veg-Fresh Farms LLC........C......800 422-5535
1400 W Rincon St Corona (92880) ***(P-8742)***
Veg-Land Inc........E......714 871-6712
1518 E Valencia Dr Fullerton (92831) ***(P-4491)***
Vegetable Growers Supply Co (PA)........E......831 759-4600
1360 Merrill St Salinas (93901) ***(P-9266)***
Vegiworks Inc........D......415 643-8686
2101 Jerrold Ave San Francisco (94124) ***(P-8743)***
Vehicle Accessory Center LLC........D......909 987-8237
10863 Jersey Blvd # 101 Rancho Cucamonga (91730) ***(P-6682)***
Velapoint LLC........D......877 434-1904
16802 Aston Irvine (92606) ***(P-10824)***
Velazquez Packing Inc........D......805 735-6477
124 N I St Lompoc (93436) ***(P-677)***
Veldhuis Dairy, Winton *Also called P H Ranch Inc* ***(P-425)***
Velocitel Rf Inc........C......949 809-4999
2415 Campus Dr Ste 200 Irvine (92612) ***(P-25989)***
Velocity Commercial Capitl LLC........E......818 532-3700
30699 Russell Ranch Rd Westlake Village (91362) ***(P-11812)***
Velocity Tech Solutions Inc........D......949 417-0260
111 Pacifica Ste 320 Irvine (92618) ***(P-16196)***
Venables/Bell & Partners LLC........C......415 288-3300
201 Post St Fl 2 San Francisco (94108) ***(P-13915)***
Venco Western Inc (PA)........C......805 981-2400
2400 Eastman Ave Oxnard (93030) ***(P-957)***
Vencore Inc........E......571 313-6000
2750 Womble Rd Ste 202 San Diego (92106) ***(P-27894)***
Vencore Svcs & Solutions Inc........E......408 961-3200
1315 Dell Ave Campbell (95008) ***(P-16072)***
Vendini Inc (PA)........D......415 693-9611
660 Market St Ste 400 San Francisco (94104) ***(P-15521)***
Vendor Direct Solutions LLC........C......213 362-5622
515 S Figueroa St # 1900 Los Angeles (90071) ***(P-27084)***
Venegas Farming LLC........E......805 529-5038
8002 Balcom Canyon Rd Somis (93066) ***(P-678)***
Vengroff Williams & Assoc Inc........C......714 889-6200
2099 S State College Blvd # 300 Anaheim (92806) ***(P-14027)***
Venice Family Clinic (PA)........D......310 664-7703
604 Rose Ave Venice (90291) ***(P-20049)***
Venice Family Clinic........C......310 392-8636
2509 Pico Blvd Santa Monica (90405) ***(P-20050)***
Venida Packing Company........C......559 592-2816
19823 Avenue 300 Exeter (93221) ***(P-5213)***
Ventage Senior Housing........E......949 631-3555
4000 Hilaria Way Newport Beach (92663) ***(P-11131)***
Ventana Inn & Spa, Big Sur *Also called 48123 CA Investors LLC* ***(P-12294)***
Ventrum LLC........D......510 304-0852
2033 Gateway Pl Ste 500 San Jose (95110) ***(P-16524)***
Ventu Park LLC........D......805 716-4200
495 N Ventu Park Rd Thousand Oaks (91320) ***(P-13365)***
Ventura Beach Marriott Hotel, Ventura *Also called Kingledon Inc* ***(P-12814)***
Ventura Cnty Council On Aging........D......805 986-1424
4917 S Rose Ave Oxnard (93033) ***(P-24109)***
Ventura Cnty Human Srvce, Oxnard *Also called County of Ventura* ***(P-24311)***
Ventura County Credit Union (PA)........D......805 477-4000
2575 Vista Del Mar Dr Ventura (93001) ***(P-9661)***
Ventura County Fire Department........E......805 389-9710
165 Durley Ave Camarillo (93010) ***(P-25274)***
Ventura County Hematology (PA)........E......805 485-8709
1700 N Rose Ave Ste 320 Oxnard (93030) ***(P-20051)***
Ventura County Lemon Coops........D......805 385-3345
P.O. Box 6986 Oxnard (93031) ***(P-584)***
Ventura County Medical Center........D......805 933-8600
845 N 10th St Ste 3 Santa Paula (93060) ***(P-20052)***
Ventura County Medical Center (PA)........C......805 652-6000
3291 Loma Vista Rd Ventura (93003) ***(P-20053)***
Ventura County Medical Center........D......805 652-6201
3291 Loma Vista Rd # 343 Ventura (93003) ***(P-20054)***
Ventura County Office Educatn........D......805 495-7037
1379 Oakridge Ct Thousand Oaks (91362) ***(P-25275)***
Ventura Family YMCA, Ventura *Also called Channel Islands Young Mens Ch* ***(P-25134)***
Ventura Hsptality Partners LLC........C......805 648-2100
450 Harbor Blvd Ventura (93001) ***(P-13366)***
Ventura Medical Management LLC........B......805 477-6220
2601 E Main St Ventura (93003) ***(P-27085)***
Ventura Pacific Co, Ventura *Also called Ventura County Lemon Coops* ***(P-584)***
Ventura Streets Dept........D......805 652-4515
336 San Jon Rd Ventura (93001) ***(P-1256)***
Ventura Transfer Company (PA)........D......310 549-1660
2418 E 223rd St Long Beach (90810) ***(P-4299)***
Ventura Yuth Crrctional Fcilty, Camarillo *Also called Juvenile Justice Division Cal* ***(P-26912)***
Venture Design Services Inc (PA)........C......714 765-3740
1051 S East St Anaheim (92805) ***(P-26488)***
Venture Design Services Inc........D......707 524-8368
451 Aviation Blvd Ste 215 Santa Rosa (95403) ***(P-17560)***
Venture Lath and Plaster, North Highlands *Also called Rick H Hitch Plastering Inc* ***(P-2950)***
Venture Pacific Tools Inc........D......949 475-5505
17152 Daimler St Irvine (92614) ***(P-7607)***
Venue Management Services Inc........B......626 445-6000
500 N 1st Ave Ste 4 Arcadia (91006) ***(P-27895)***
Venue Management Systems Inc........A......626 445-6000
2041 E Gladstone St Ste A Glendora (91740) ***(P-16853)***
Venus Group Inc........D......949 609-1299
25861 Wright Foothill Ranch (92610) ***(P-6802)***
Venus Textiles, Foothill Ranch *Also called Venus Group Inc* ***(P-6802)***

ALPHABETIC

Employee Codes: A=Over 500 employees, B=251-500
C=101-250, D=51-100, E=50

2019 Directory of California
Wholesalers and Services Companies

© Mergent Inc. 1-800-342-5647

1511

Venvest Ballard Inc..........D.......951 276-9744
3030 Myers St Riverside (92503) ***(P-2397)***
Veolia Es Waste-To-Energy Inc..........D.......562 436-0636
100 Pier S Ave Long Beach (90802) ***(P-6506)***
Ver Sales Inc (PA)..........D.......818 567-3000
2509 N Naomi St Burbank (91504) ***(P-7322)***
Veracyte Inc..........C.......650 243-6300
6000 Shoreline Ct Ste 300 South San Francisco (94080) ***(P-22158)***
Verance Corporation..........D.......858 202-2800
10089 Willow Creek Rd San Diego (92131) ***(P-26576)***
Verasa Management LLC..........D.......707 257-1800
1314 Mckinstry St NAPA (94559) ***(P-13367)***
Verdugo Hills Medical Assoc, Glendale *Also called Verdugo Hills Urgent Care Mg* ***(P-20055)***
Verdugo Hills Urgent Care Mg..........D.......818 241-4331
544 N Glendale Ave Glendale (91206) ***(P-20055)***
Verdugo Mental Health..........D.......818 244-7257
1540 E Colorado St Glendale (91205) ***(P-22709)***
Verdugo Vista Healthcare Ctr, La Crescenta *Also called Mariner Health Care Inc* ***(P-20629)***
Verdugo Vly Convalescent Hosp, Montrose *Also called Great Wstn Cnvlescent Hosp Inc* ***(P-21101)***
Veridiam Allied Swiss..........D.......760 941-1702
4645 North Ave Oceanside (92056) ***(P-27896)***
Verifi Inc..........D.......323 655-5789
8391 Beverly Blvd Ste 310 Los Angeles (90048) ***(P-27510)***
Verifone Inc..........D.......916 408-4900
1401 Aviation Blvd Lincoln (95648) ***(P-4654)***
Verinata Health Inc..........D.......650 632-1680
200 Lincoln Centre Dr Foster City (94404) ***(P-26489)***
Verint, Santa Clara *Also called Kana Software Inc* ***(P-15727)***
Verint Americas Inc..........D.......408 830-5400
2250 Walsh Ave Ste 120 Santa Clara (95050) ***(P-15522)***
Veritable Vegetable Inc..........D.......415 641-3500
1100 Cesar Chavez San Francisco (94124) ***(P-8744)***
Veritas Health Services Inc..........A.......909 464-8600
5451 Walnut Ave Chino (91710) ***(P-21897)***
Veritas Technologies LLC (HQ)..........C.......650 933-1000
500 E Middlefield Rd Mountain View (94043) ***(P-15523)***
Veritas US Inc..........C.......650 933-1000
500 E Middlefield Rd Mountain View (94043) ***(P-15524)***
Veritiv Operating Company..........C.......925 245-6075
7337 Las Positas Rd Livermore (94551) ***(P-7818)***
Veritiv Operating Company..........D.......559 268-0467
4395 S Minnewawa Ave # 101 Fresno (93725) ***(P-8129)***
Veritiv Operating Company..........D.......714 690-4000
15005 Northam St La Mirada (90638) ***(P-8130)***
Veritiv Operating Company..........D.......916 283-2160
1701 National Dr Ste 110 Sacramento (95834) ***(P-8131)***
Veritiv Operating Company..........D.......415 586-9160
345 Schwerin St San Francisco (94134) ***(P-8132)***
Veritiv Operating Company..........C.......310 527-3000
13217 S Figueroa St Los Angeles (90061) ***(P-8133)***
Veritiv Operating Company..........C.......323 725-3700
2600 Commerce Way Commerce (90040) ***(P-8134)***
Veritiv Operating Company..........B.......714 690-6600
20 Centerpointe Dr # 130 La Palma (90623) ***(P-8135)***
Verity Health System Cal Inc..........B.......310 900-8900
203 Redwood Shores Pkwy Redwood City (94065) ***(P-21898)***
Verity Health System Cal Inc..........C.......650 551-6507
203 Redwood Shores Pkwy # 700 Redwood City (94065) ***(P-21899)***
Verity Health System Cal Inc..........D.......408 848-2000
9400 N Name Uno Gilroy (95020) ***(P-21900)***
Verity Health System Cal Inc..........D.......310 900-2000
3680 E Imperial Hwy # 306 Lynwood (90262) ***(P-21901)***
Verity Health System Cal Inc..........A.......310 900-8900
3630 E Imperial Hwy Lynwood (90262) ***(P-21902)***
Verity Medical Foundation (HQ)..........D.......408 278-3000
400 Race St San Jose (95126) ***(P-20056)***
Verizon, Indio *Also called Frontier California Inc* ***(P-5561)***
Verizon, Torrance *Also called Cellco Partnership* ***(P-5306)***
Verizon, Livermore *Also called Cellco Partnership* ***(P-5307)***
Verizon, Costa Mesa *Also called Cellco Partnership* ***(P-5316)***
Verizon, Roseville *Also called Cellco Partnership* ***(P-5318)***
Verizon, Santa Maria *Also called Frontier California Inc* ***(P-5562)***
Verizon, Irvine *Also called Cellco Partnership* ***(P-5319)***
Verizon, Barstow *Also called Frontier California Inc* ***(P-5563)***
Verizon, Capitola *Also called Cellco Partnership* ***(P-5324)***
Verizon, Bakersfield *Also called Cellco Partnership* ***(P-5325)***
Verizon, Carlsbad *Also called Cellco Partnership* ***(P-5326)***
Verizon, Corte Madera *Also called Cellco Partnership* ***(P-5327)***
Verizon, El Cajon *Also called Cellco Partnership* ***(P-5328)***
Verizon, Fresno *Also called Cellco Partnership* ***(P-5329)***
Verizon, Cerritos *Also called Cellco Partnership* ***(P-5330)***
Verizon, Chico *Also called Cellco Partnership* ***(P-5331)***
Verizon, Corona *Also called Cellco Partnership* ***(P-5332)***
Verizon, Brea *Also called Cellco Partnership* ***(P-5334)***
Verizon, Rancho Cucamonga *Also called Frontier California Inc* ***(P-4017)***
Verizon, San Fernando *Also called Frontier California Inc* ***(P-5564)***
Verizon, Manteca *Also called Frontier California Inc* ***(P-5565)***
Verizon, Folsom *Also called Cellco Partnership* ***(P-5367)***
Verizon, San Francisco *Also called Cellco Partnership* ***(P-5383)***
Verizon, Whittier *Also called Cellco Partnership* ***(P-5384)***
Verizon, Hayward *Also called American Messaging Svcs LLC* ***(P-5447)***
Verizon, Laguna Niguel *Also called Cellco Partnership* ***(P-5388)***
Verizon, Westlake Village *Also called Frontier California Inc* ***(P-5566)***
Verizon, Exeter *Also called Frontier California Inc* ***(P-5567)***
Verizon, San Luis Obispo *Also called Cellco Partnership* ***(P-5393)***
Verizon, Fresno *Also called Frontier California Inc* ***(P-5408)***
Verizon Bus Netwrk Svcs Inc..........C.......916 779-5600
11080 White Rock Rd # 100 Rancho Cordova (95670) ***(P-5661)***
Verizon Bus Netwrk Svcs Inc..........C.......916 569-5999
1740 Creekside Oaks 200 Sacramento (95833) ***(P-5662)***
Verizon Bus Netwrk Svcs Inc..........D.......510 497-2500
4340 Solar Way Fremont (94538) ***(P-16273)***
Verizon Business, Los Angeles *Also called MCI Communications Svcs Inc* ***(P-5595)***
Verizon Business Global LLC..........D.......415 606-3621
1516 Stillwell Rd Apt F San Francisco (94129) ***(P-5663)***
Verizon Business Global LLC..........E.......951 653-4482
6177 River Crest Dr Ste B Riverside (92507) ***(P-5963)***
Verizon Business Global LLC..........D.......909 466-5633
800 W 6th St Ste 1150 Los Angeles (90017) ***(P-5664)***
Verizon Communications Inc..........C.......562 496-0288
5077 E Lew Davis St Long Beach (90808) ***(P-5665)***
Verizon Communications Inc..........D.......559 562-0000
180 N Mirage Ave Lindsay (93247) ***(P-27897)***
Verizon Communications Inc..........C.......760 245-0409
16461 Mojave Dr Victorville (92395) ***(P-5666)***
Verizon Communications Inc..........A.......805 988-5760
1800 Solar Dr Oxnard (93030) ***(P-14795)***
Verizon Communications Inc..........D.......310 315-7597
2001 Broadway Fl 1 Santa Monica (90404) ***(P-17561)***
Verizon Communications Inc..........C.......559 637-0204
1625 E Dinuba Ave Reedley (93654) ***(P-5667)***
Verizon Communications Inc..........C.......805 441-4001
994 Mill St San Luis Obispo (93401) ***(P-5668)***
Verizon Communications Inc..........C.......805 390-5417
2801 Townsgate Rd Ste 300 Westlake Village (91361) ***(P-17562)***
Verizon Communications Inc..........A.......818 438-1104
18442 Arminta St Reseda (91335) ***(P-17563)***
Verizon Communications Inc..........E.......661 328-2226
1220 Oak St Ste M Bakersfield (93304) ***(P-5669)***
Verizon Communications Inc..........C.......562 804-0354
9900 Flower St Bellflower (90706) ***(P-6005)***
Verizon Communications Inc..........B.......310 319-6148
2943 Exposition Blvd Santa Monica (90404) ***(P-5670)***
Verizon Communications Inc..........A.......909 421-5053
18850 Orange St Bloomington (92316) ***(P-17564)***
Verizon Communications Inc..........A.......213 330-2556
700 S Flower St Ste 1700 Los Angeles (90017) ***(P-17565)***
Verizon Communications Inc..........C.......818 388-8549
21306 Superior St Chatsworth (91311) ***(P-5671)***
Verizon Connect Nwf Inc..........D.......858 450-3245
9868 Scranton Rd Ste 1000 San Diego (92121) ***(P-15525)***
Verizon Connect Telo Inc (HQ)..........C.......949 389-5500
20 Enterprise Ste 100 Aliso Viejo (92656) ***(P-16197)***
Verizon Digital Media Svcs Inc (HQ)..........A.......310 396-7400
13031 W Jefferson Blvd # 900 Los Angeles (90094) ***(P-16525)***
Verizon Network Integration..........C.......562 903-7953
12905 Los Nietos Rd Santa Fe Springs (90670) ***(P-5672)***
Verizon New York Inc..........D.......909 481-7897
961 N Milliken Ave # 101 Ontario (91764) ***(P-7559)***
Verizon South Inc..........D.......805 681-8527
424 S Patterson Ave Goleta (93111) ***(P-5673)***
Verizon Wireless, Beaumont *Also called Cellco Partnership* ***(P-5304)***
Verizon Wireless, Castro Valley *Also called ABC Phones North Carolina Inc* ***(P-5256)***
Verizon Wireless, Temecula *Also called Cellco Partnership* ***(P-5305)***
Verizon Wireless, South Lake Tahoe *Also called ABC Phones North Carolina Inc* ***(P-5257)***
Verizon Wireless, Monterey *Also called Cellco Partnership* ***(P-5308)***
Verizon Wireless, Orange *Also called Cellco Partnership* ***(P-5309)***
Verizon Wireless, Brentwood *Also called Cellco Partnership* ***(P-5310)***
Verizon Wireless, Riverside *Also called Cellco Partnership* ***(P-5311)***
Verizon Wireless, Fresno *Also called Cellco Partnership* ***(P-5315)***
Verizon Wireless, Eastvale *Also called Cellco Partnership* ***(P-5317)***
Verizon Wireless, Watsonville *Also called Cellco Partnership* ***(P-5320)***
Verizon Wireless, La Habra *Also called Cellco Partnership* ***(P-5321)***
Verizon Wireless, Orange *Also called Cellco Partnership* ***(P-5322)***
Verizon Wireless, San Marcos *Also called Cellco Partnership* ***(P-5323)***
Verizon Wireless, Fremont *Also called Cellco Partnership* ***(P-5333)***
Verizon Wireless, Panorama City *Also called Cellco Partnership* ***(P-5337)***
Verizon Wireless, Ventura *Also called Cellco Partnership* ***(P-5338)***
Verizon Wireless, Encinitas *Also called Cellco Partnership* ***(P-5340)***
Verizon Wireless, Corona *Also called Cellco Partnership* ***(P-5341)***
Verizon Wireless, Burbank *Also called Cellco Partnership* ***(P-5343)***
Verizon Wireless, Baldwin Park *Also called Cellco Partnership* ***(P-5344)***
Verizon Wireless, Gilroy *Also called Cellco Partnership* ***(P-5345)***
Verizon Wireless, Pasadena *Also called Cellco Partnership* ***(P-5346)***
Verizon Wireless, Sacramento *Also called Cellco Partnership* ***(P-5347)***
Verizon Wireless, Rancho Mirage *Also called Cellco Partnership* ***(P-5348)***
Verizon Wireless, Milpitas *Also called Cellco Partnership* ***(P-5349)***
Verizon Wireless, Lake Forest *Also called Cellco Partnership* ***(P-5350)***
Verizon Wireless, San Francisco *Also called Cellco Partnership* ***(P-5351)***
Verizon Wireless, Turlock *Also called Cellco Partnership* ***(P-5352)***
Verizon Wireless, Encino *Also called Cellco Partnership* ***(P-5354)***
Verizon Wireless, Chula Vista *Also called Cellco Partnership* ***(P-5355)***
Verizon Wireless, Oakland *Also called Cellco Partnership* ***(P-5356)***
Verizon Wireless, Sacramento *Also called Cellco Partnership* ***(P-5358)***
Verizon Wireless, Downey *Also called Cellco Partnership* ***(P-5361)***
Verizon Wireless, Hesperia *Also called Cellco Partnership* ***(P-5362)***
Verizon Wireless, Clovis *Also called Cellco Partnership* ***(P-5363)***
Verizon Wireless, Palmdale *Also called Cellco Partnership* ***(P-5364)***

Verizon Wireless, Huntington Beach *Also called Cellco Partnership* **(P-5365)**
Verizon Wireless, Los Angeles *Also called Cellco Partnership* **(P-5366)**
Verizon Wireless, Modesto *Also called Cellco Partnership* **(P-5368)**
Verizon Wireless, Los Angeles *Also called Cellco Partnership* **(P-5369)**
Verizon Wireless, Carson *Also called Cellco Partnership* **(P-5370)**
Verizon Wireless, Hollywood *Also called Cellco Partnership* **(P-5371)**
Verizon Wireless, West Hollywood *Also called Cellco Partnership* **(P-5372)**
Verizon Wireless, San Francisco *Also called Cellco Partnership* **(P-5373)**
Verizon Wireless, Union City *Also called Cellco Partnership* **(P-5374)**
Verizon Wireless, Valencia *Also called Cellco Partnership* **(P-5375)**
Verizon Wireless, Cypress *Also called Cellco Partnership* **(P-5376)**
Verizon Wireless, El Centro *Also called Cellco Partnership* **(P-5377)**
Verizon Wireless, Simi Valley *Also called Cellco Partnership* **(P-5378)**
Verizon Wireless, Canoga Park *Also called Cellco Partnership* **(P-5379)**
Verizon Wireless, Santa Cruz *Also called Cellco Partnership* **(P-5380)**
Verizon Wireless, San Bernardino *Also called Cellco Partnership* **(P-5381)**
Verizon Wireless, Citrus Heights *Also called Cellco Partnership* **(P-5382)**
Verizon Wireless, San Diego *Also called Cellco Partnership* **(P-5385)**
Verizon Wireless, Chino *Also called Cellco Partnership* **(P-5386)**
Verizon Wireless, Yuba City *Also called Cellco Partnership* **(P-5387)**
Verizon Wireless, Santa Barbara *Also called Cellco Partnership* **(P-5389)**
Verizon Wireless, Santa Rosa *Also called Cellco Partnership* **(P-5390)**
Verizon Wireless, Palo Alto *Also called Cellco Partnership* **(P-5392)**
Verizon Wireless, Irvine *Also called 4g Wireless Inc* **(P-5255)**
Verizon Wireless, Santa Ana *Also called Cellco Partnership* **(P-5394)**
Verizon Wireless, Huntington Park *Also called Cellco Partnership* **(P-5974)**
Verizon Wireless, San Diego *Also called Cellco Partnership* **(P-5395)**
Verizon Wireless, Lancaster *Also called Cellco Partnership* **(P-5396)**
Verizon Wireless, Commerce *Also called Cellco Partnership* **(P-5398)**
Verizon Wireless, Pico Rivera *Also called Cellco Partnership* **(P-5399)**
Verizon Wireless Inc........C.......408 354-6374
15 Montebello Way Los Gatos (95030) **(P-5426)**
Verizon Wireless Premium Ret, Carlsbad *Also called 4g Wireless Inc* **(P-5435)**
Verizon Wreless Authorized Ret, Bell *Also called 4g Wireless Inc* **(P-5430)**
Verizon Wreless Authorized Ret, Dublin *Also called 4g Wireless Inc* **(P-5431)**
Verizon Wreless Authorized Ret, Los Angeles *Also called 4g Wireless Inc* **(P-5432)**
Verizon Wreless Authorized Ret, Los Angeles *Also called 4g Wireless Inc* **(P-5433)**
Verizon Wreless Authorized Ret, Escondido *Also called 4g Wireless Inc* **(P-5434)**
Verizon Wreless Authorized Ret, Perris *Also called 4g Wireless Inc* **(P-5436)**
Verizon Wreless Authorized Ret, Redondo Beach *Also called 4g Wireless Inc* **(P-5437)**
Verizon Wreless Authorized Ret, Long Beach *Also called 4g Wireless Inc* **(P-5438)**
Vermeer Pacific, Sacramento *Also called Rdo Vermeer LLC* **(P-7692)**
Vermont Care Center, Torrance *Also called Geri-Care II Inc* **(P-21080)**
Vernon Autoparts Inc........D.......323 249-7545
1559 W 134th St Gardena (90249) **(P-17799)**
Vernon Central Warehouse Inc........C.......323 234-2200
2050 E 38th St Vernon (90058) **(P-4387)**
Vernon Security Inc........D.......562 790-8993
15317 Parmnt Blvd Ste 201 Paramount (90723) **(P-16949)**
Vernon Transportation Company, Stockton *Also called John Aguilar & Company Inc* **(P-4030)**
Vernon Truck Wash Inc........C.......323 267-0706
3308 Bandini Blvd Vernon (90058) **(P-17841)**
Vernon Warehouse Co, Vernon *Also called Vernon Central Warehouse Inc* **(P-4387)**
Veros Credit LLC (PA)........D.......714 415-6185
2333 N Broadway Ste 400 Santa Ana (92706) **(P-9749)**
Versa Engineering & Tech Inc (PA)........D.......925 405-4505
1320 Willow Pass Rd # 500 Concord (94520) **(P-25990)**
Versa Products Inc (PA)........D.......310 353-7100
14105 Avalon Blvd Los Angeles (90061) **(P-6741)**
Versacheck, San Diego *Also called G7 Productivity Systems* **(P-15688)**
Versatables.com, Los Angeles *Also called Versa Products Inc* **(P-6741)**
Vertafore Fsc Inc........C.......800 433-2550
28038 Dorothy Dr Agoura Hills (91301) **(P-15526)**
Vertex Coatings Inc........D.......909 923-5795
1291 W State St Ontario (91762) **(P-2490)**
Vertex Phrmctcals San Dego LLC (HQ)........C.......858 404-6600
3215 Merryfield Row San Diego (92121) **(P-26490)**
Vertical Search Works Inc........D.......212 967-9502
1808 Aston Ave Ste 170 Carlsbad (92008) **(P-13916)**
Verticalresponse Inc........C.......866 683-7842
550 Kearny St Ste 710 San Francisco (94108) **(P-27511)**
Vertisystem Inc........C.......510 794-8099
39300 Civic Center Dr # 230 Fremont (94538) **(P-16073)**
Verve Music Group, Santa Monica *Also called Universal Music Group Inc* **(P-18472)**
Very Important Pet Vaccine Svc, Windsor *Also called Happy Pet Co* **(P-602)**
Vesta Luxury Home Staging, Vernon *Also called Showroom Interiors LLC* **(P-14544)**
Vestek Systems Inc (HQ)........D.......415 344-6000
425 Market St Fl 6 San Francisco (94105) **(P-16258)**
Veterans Affairs Cal Dept........C.......530 224-3300
3400 Knighton Rd Redding (96002) **(P-20856)**
Veterans Affairs Cal Dept........B.......916 653-2535
1227 O St Ste 105 Sacramento (95814) **(P-27898)**
Veterans Affairs Testing Off, Sacramento *Also called Veterans Affairs Cal Dept* **(P-27898)**
Veterans Affrs LNG Bch Hlthre........D.......562 826-8000
5901 E 7th St Long Beach (90822) **(P-20057)**
Veterans EZ Info Inc........C.......866 839-1329
1901 1st Ave Ste 192 San Diego (92101) **(P-27899)**
Veterans Health Administration........B.......858 552-7525
3350 La Jolla Village Dr San Diego (92161) **(P-20143)**
Veterans Health Administration........B.......707 562-8200
Walnut Ave Bldg 201 Vallejo (94589) **(P-20058)**
Veterans Health Administration........A.......310 478-3711
11301 Wilshire Blvd Los Angeles (90073) **(P-20059)**
Veterans Health Administration........A.......559 225-6100
2615 E Clinton Ave Fresno (93703) **(P-21903)**
Veterans Health Administration........B.......805 543-1233
1288 Morro St Ste 200 San Luis Obispo (93401) **(P-20060)**
Veterans Health Administration........B.......916 366-5427
10535 Hospital Way Mather (95655) **(P-20061)**
Veterans Health Administration........A.......559 225-6100
2615 E Clinton Ave Fresno (93703) **(P-20062)**
Veterans Health Administration........B.......530 226-7555
351 Hartnell Ave Redding (96002) **(P-20063)**
Veterans Health Administration........A.......650 493-5000
3801 Miranda Ave Bldg 101 Palo Alto (94304) **(P-20064)**
Veterans Health Administration........B.......510 267-7820
2221 Martin Luther King J Oakland (94612) **(P-20065)**
Veterans Health Administration........D.......415 750-2009
4150 Clement St 6205 San Francisco (94121) **(P-20066)**
Veterans Health Administration........B.......530 879-5000
280 Cohasset Rd Chico (95926) **(P-20067)**
Veterans Health Administration........B.......707 442-5335
727 E St Eureka (95501) **(P-20068)**
Veterans Health Administration........B.......707 570-3800
3315 Chanate Rd Santa Rosa (95404) **(P-20069)**
Veterans Health Administration........B.......619 409-1600
835 Third Ave Chula Vista (91911) **(P-20070)**
Veterans Health Administration........B.......760 745-2000
815 E Pennsylvania Ave Escondido (92025) **(P-20071)**
Veterans Health Administration........B.......805 983-6384
250 Citrus Grove Ln # 250 Oxnard (93036) **(P-20072)**
Veterans Health Administration........C.......818 895-9311
16111 Plummer St North Hills (91343) **(P-20073)**
Veterans Health Administration........B.......619 400-5000
8810 Rio San Diego Dr San Diego (92108) **(P-20074)**
Veterans Health Administration........A.......818 891-7711
16111 Plummer St North Hills (91343) **(P-20075)**
Veterans Health Administration........B.......916 843-7000
10535 Hospital Way Mather (95655) **(P-20076)**
Veterans Health Administration........B.......925 447-2560
4951 Arroyo Rd Livermore (94550) **(P-20077)**
Veterans Health Administration........A.......909 825-7084
11201 Benton St Loma Linda (92357) **(P-20078)**
Veterans Health Administration........A.......650 614-9997
795 Willow Rd Menlo Park (94025) **(P-20079)**
Veterans Health Administration........D.......818 895-9449
16111 Plummer St North Hills (91343) **(P-20080)**
Veterans Health Administration........C.......714 780-5400
1801 W Romneya Dr Ste 303 Anaheim (92801) **(P-20081)**
Veterans Health Administration........E.......661 632-1871
1801 Westwind Dr Bakersfield (93301) **(P-20082)**
Veterans Health Administration........C.......213 253-2677
351 E Temple St Los Angeles (90012) **(P-20083)**
Veterans Health Administration........B.......661 323-8387
1110 Golden Valley Fwy Bakersfield (93301) **(P-20084)**
Veterans Home Cal - Fresno........D.......559 493-4400
2811 W California Ave Fresno (93706) **(P-20857)**
Veterans Medical Research Fund........C.......858 642-3080
3350 La Jolla Village Dr San Diego (92161) **(P-25276)**
Veterans Village of San Diego, San Diego *Also called Vietnam Veterans of San Diego* **(P-25279)**
Veterinary Centers America VCA, Los Angeles *Also called Vicar Operating Inc* **(P-620)**
Veterinary Pharmaceuticals Inc........D.......559 582-6800
13159 Hanford Armona Rd Hanford (93230) **(P-8218)**
Veterinary Practice Assoc Inc........C.......949 833-9020
10435 Sorrento Valley Rd San Diego (92121) **(P-22710)**
Veterinary Service Inc........D.......951 328-4900
935 Palmyrita Ave Riverside (92507) **(P-7228)**
Veterinary Specialty Hospital, San Diego *Also called Veterinary Practice Assoc Inc* **(P-22710)**
Veterinary Surgical Associates........D.......650 696-8196
251 N Amphlett Blvd San Mateo (94401) **(P-20085)**
Veterinary Surgical Associates (PA)........C.......925 827-1777
1410 Monu Blvd Ste 100 Concord (94520) **(P-618)**
Veternary Med Srgcal Group Inc........D.......805 339-2290
2199 Sperry Ave Ventura (93003) **(P-619)**
Vetronix Crpration/Bosch Group, Santa Barbara *Also called Vetronix Sales Corporation* **(P-6683)**
Vetronix Sales Corporation........D.......805 966-2000
2030 Alameda Padre Serra Santa Barbara (93103) **(P-6683)**
Vexillum Inc........C.......916 218-3815
10636 Industrial Ave Roseville (95678) **(P-6147)**
Vfs Fire Protection Services, Orange *Also called Bernel Inc* **(P-2142)**
VFW Post 6476........C.......909 754-3828
1789 N 8th St Colton (92324) **(P-25277)**
Vh Property Corp........B.......310 303-3210
1 Ocean Trl Rancho Palos Verdes (90275) **(P-18776)**
VI At Palo Alto, Palo Alto *Also called Cc-Palo Alto Inc* **(P-20919)**
Via Adventures Inc (PA)........E.......209 384-1315
300 Grogan Ave Merced (95341) **(P-3906)**
Via Care Cmnty Hlth Ctr Inc........D.......323 268-9191
507 S Atlantic Blvd Los Angeles (90022) **(P-20086)**
Via Charter Lines, Merced *Also called Via Adventures Inc* **(P-3906)**
Via Communications Inc........C.......510 687-4650
940 Mission Ct Fremont (94539) **(P-26491)**
Via Embedded Store, Fremont *Also called Via Technologies Inc* **(P-7560)**
Via Magazine, San Francisco *Also called CA Ste Atom Assoc Intr-Ins Bur* **(P-10340)**
Via Technologies Inc........C.......510 683-3300
940 Mission Ct Fremont (94539) **(P-7560)**
Via Trading Corporation........D.......877 202-3616
2520 Industry Way Lynwood (90262) **(P-9267)**

ALPHABETIC

Via Verde Country Club, San Dimas *Also called San Dimas Golf Inc* ***(P-19026)***
Viacom Consumer Products Inc........E.......323 956-5634
5555 Melrose Ave Los Angeles (90038) ***(P-12146)***
Viacom Networks........A.......310 752-8000
1575 N Gower St Ste 100 Los Angeles (90028) ***(P-18151)***
Viacyte Inc........D.......858 455-3708
3550 General Atomics Ct B2-503 San Diego (92121) ***(P-26671)***
Viad Corp........D.......562 370-1500
5560 Katella Ave Cypress (90630) ***(P-17566)***
Vian Enterprises Inc........E.......530 885-1997
1501 Industrial Dr Auburn (95603) ***(P-17567)***
Viant, Irvine *Also called Interactive Media Holdings* ***(P-13848)***
Viant Technology LLC (HQ)........C.......949 861-8888
4 Park Plz Ste 1500 Irvine (92614) ***(P-13986)***
Viant US, Irvine *Also called Viant Technology LLC* ***(P-13986)***
Viaworld Advanced Products........D.......408 597-7051
920 Saratoga Ave Ste 103 San Jose (95129) ***(P-7608)***
Vibra Healthcare LLC........D.......559 325-5601
1315 Shaw Ave Ste 102 Clovis (93612) ***(P-21904)***
Vibra Healthcare LLC........D.......530 246-9000
2801 Eureka Way Redding (96001) ***(P-21905)***
Vibra Healthcare LLC........D.......559 436-3600
7173 N Sharon Ave Fresno (93720) ***(P-21906)***
Vibra Healthcare LLC........C.......619 260-8300
555 Washington St San Diego (92103) ***(P-21907)***
Vibra Hosp San Bernardino LLC........C.......909 473-1233
1760 W 16th St San Bernardino (92411) ***(P-21908)***
Vibra Hospital Northern Cal, Redding *Also called Vibra Healthcare LLC* ***(P-21905)***
Vibra Hospital of San Diego, San Diego *Also called Vibra Healthcare LLC* ***(P-21907)***
Vibra Hospital Sacramento LLC........C.......916 351-9151
330 Montrose Dr Folsom (95630) ***(P-21909)***
Vibra Hospital San Diego LLC........D.......619 260-8300
555 Washington St San Diego (92103) ***(P-21910)***
Vibrantcare Outpatient Rehab (PA)........D.......916 782-1212
2270 Douglas Blvd Ste 216 Roseville (95661) ***(P-22711)***
Vicar Operating Inc (HQ)........C.......310 571-6500
12401 W Olympic Blvd Los Angeles (90064) ***(P-620)***
Viceroy Santa Monica, Santa Monica *Also called Seaside Hotel Lessee Inc* ***(P-17464)***
Vickie Lobello........D.......805 750-2327
1333 S Mayflower Ave 40 Simi Valley (93063) ***(P-25480)***
Vicor Inc........D.......510 621-2000
855 Marina Bay Pkwy # 100 Richmond (94804) ***(P-16074)***
Victor Cmnty Support Svcs Inc........C.......530 273-2244
900 E Main St Ste 201 Grass Valley (95945) ***(P-27961)***
Victor Cmnty Support Svcs Inc (PA)........B.......530 893-0758
1360 E Lassen Ave Chico (95973) ***(P-22712)***
Victor Treatment Centers Inc........C.......209 340-7900
9150 E Hwy 12 Victor (95253) ***(P-24710)***
Victor Treatment Centers Inc........C.......707 360-1509
341 Irwin Ln Santa Rosa (95401) ***(P-24711)***
Victor Valley Moose Lodge No........C.......760 244-1808
10230 E Ave Hesperia (92345) ***(P-25278)***
Victoria Care Center........D.......805 642-1736
5445 Everglades St Ventura (93003) ***(P-20858)***
Victoria Island Farms........D.......209 465-5609
16021 E Hwy 4 Holt (95234) ***(P-392)***
Victoria Place Community Assn........D.......909 981-4131
195 N Euclid Ave Upland (91786) ***(P-25481)***
Victoria Post Acute Care........C.......619 440-5005
654 S Anza St El Cajon (92020) ***(P-21246)***
Victorian Inn, Monterey *Also called Columbia Hospitality Inc* ***(P-12477)***
Victorvlle Trsure Holdings LLC........D.......760 245-6565
15494 Palmdale Rd Victorville (92392) ***(P-13368)***
Victory Foam Inc (PA)........D.......949 474-0690
3 Holland Irvine (92618) ***(P-9268)***
Victory Pharma Inc........C.......858 720-4500
11682 El Camino Real # 250 San Diego (92130) ***(P-8219)***
Victory Studio, Burbank *Also called Warner Bros Entertainment Inc* ***(P-18160)***
Victus Group Inc........C.......559 429-8080
2350 W Shaw Ave Fresno (93711) ***(P-27086)***
Vid, Vista *Also called Vista Irrigation District* ***(P-6569)***
Vida Health Inc........D.......408 203-7959
100 Montgomery St Ste 750 San Francisco (94104) ***(P-15527)***
Vidal Sassoon Salon, Beverly Hills *Also called Regis Corporation* ***(P-13670)***
Vident........D.......714 221-6700
22705 Savi Ranch Pkwy # 100 Yorba Linda (92887) ***(P-7229)***
Video Products Distributors, Folsom *Also called VPD IV Inc* ***(P-18247)***
Video Vice Data Communications........B.......714 897-6300
12681 Pala Dr Garden Grove (92841) ***(P-6006)***
Videocam, Anaheim *Also called Vci Event Technology Inc* ***(P-14554)***
Vidhwan Inc (PA)........C.......408 289-8200
2 N Market St Ste 400 San Jose (95113) ***(P-27512)***
Vidhwan Inc........C.......408 521-0167
2 N Market St Ste 410 San Jose (95113) ***(P-15528)***
Viele & Sons Inc........D.......714 447-3663
1820 E Valencia Dr Fullerton (92831) ***(P-8486)***
Viele & Sons Instnl Groc, Fullerton *Also called Viele & Sons Inc* ***(P-8486)***
Vienna Convalescent Hospital........C.......209 368-7141
800 S Ham Ln Lodi (95242) ***(P-20859)***
Vietnam Veterans of San Diego (PA)........D.......619 497-0142
4141 Pacific Hwy San Diego (92110) ***(P-25279)***
VIETNAMESE COMMUNITY OF ORANGE, Santa Ana *Also called Southland Integrated Svcs Inc* ***(P-24843)***
Vietnms-Mrcan Yuth Alance Corp........E.......619 320-8292
7968 Arjons Dr Ste 109 San Diego (92126) ***(P-25280)***
View Heights Convalescent Hosp, Los Angeles *Also called Amada Enterprises Inc* ***(P-20229)***
VIEW PARK CONVALESCENT CENTER, Los Angeles *Also called Burlington Convalescent Hosp* ***(P-20275)***
View Park Convalescent Center, Los Angeles *Also called Burlington Convalescent Hosp* ***(P-20276)***
Viewray Technologies Inc........D.......650 252-0920
815 E Middlefield Rd Mountain View (94043) ***(P-7230)***
Viewsonic Corporation (PA)........C.......909 444-8888
10 Pointe Dr Ste 200 Brea (92821) ***(P-7127)***
Vignolo Farms Inc........C.......661 393-1431
33342 Dresser Ave Bakersfield (93308) ***(P-16)***
Viharas Group Inc........D.......310 537-6700
1919 W Artesia Blvd Compton (90220) ***(P-12051)***
Viking Asset Management LLC........A.......415 981-5300
505 Sansome St Ste 1275 San Francisco (94111) ***(P-10120)***
Viking Demolition, Glendale *Also called Viking Equipment Corp* ***(P-3467)***
Viking Equipment Corp........D.......818 500-9447
540 W Windsor Rd Glendale (91204) ***(P-3467)***
Viking Ocean Cruises, Woodland Hills *Also called Viking River Cruises Inc* ***(P-4958)***
Viking Office Products Inc (HQ)........B.......562 490-1000
3366 E Willow St Signal Hill (90755) ***(P-8092)***
Viking Pools LLC........E.......530 473-5319
121 Crawford Rd Williams (95987) ***(P-3604)***
Viking River Cruises Inc (HQ)........D.......818 227-1234
5700 Canoga Ave Ste 200 Woodland Hills (91367) ***(P-4958)***
Vila Construction Co........D.......510 236-9111
590 S 33rd St Richmond (94804) ***(P-1693)***
Villa Balboa Community Assoc........D.......949 450-1515
22 Mauchly Irvine (92618) ***(P-25281)***
Villa Convalescent Hosp Inc........D.......951 689-5788
8965 Magnolia Ave Riverside (92503) ***(P-20860)***
Villa De La Mar Inc........E.......562 494-5001
5001 E Anaheim St Long Beach (90804) ***(P-21247)***
Villa Del Rey Retirement Inn, Escondido *Also called Emeritus Corporation* ***(P-11012)***
Villa Fairmont Mental Hlth Ctr, San Leandro *Also called Telecare Corporation* ***(P-21984)***
Villa Gardens, Pasadena *Also called Front Porch Communities & Svcs* ***(P-24536)***
Villa La Esperanza LP........D.......805 781-3088
3533 Empleo St San Luis Obispo (93401) ***(P-1363)***
Villa Las Plmas Healthcare Ctr, El Cajon *Also called Jeffrey Pine Holdings LLC* ***(P-20549)***
Villa Las Posas, Camarillo *Also called Atria Senior Living Group Inc* ***(P-24425)***
Villa Maria Care Center, Long Beach *Also called Trinity Health Systems* ***(P-20841)***
Villa Maria Care Center, Baldwin Park *Also called Trinity Health Systems* ***(P-20842)***
Villa Marin Homeowners Assn........C.......415 499-8711
100 Thorndale Dr San Rafael (94903) ***(P-25282)***
VILLA MONTALVO, Saratoga *Also called Montalvo Association* ***(P-24932)***
Villa Mrin Rtrement Residences, San Rafael *Also called Villa Marin Homeowners Assn* ***(P-25282)***
Villa Oaks Convalescent Homes, Pasadena *Also called Voch Inc* ***(P-21252)***
Villa Pacific Contractors Inc........E.......714 850-1640
3303 Harbor Blvd Ste D6 Costa Mesa (92626) ***(P-2827)***
Villa Paseo Palms, Paso Robles *Also called Villa Paseo Senior Residences* ***(P-11132)***
Villa Paseo Senior Residences........D.......805 227-4588
2818 Ramada Dr Paso Robles (93446) ***(P-11132)***
VILLA RANCHO BERNARDO CARE CEN, San Diego *Also called Villa Rancho Brno Hlth Cr LLC* ***(P-20861)***
Villa Rancho Brno Hlth Cr LLC........C.......858 672-3900
15720 Bernardo Center Dr San Diego (92127) ***(P-20861)***
Villa Real Inc........D.......209 460-5069
421 S El Dorado St Ste D1 Stockton (95203) ***(P-27900)***
Villa Sclabrini Retirement Ctr, Sun Valley *Also called Fathers of St Charles* ***(P-11017)***
Villa Serena Healthcare Center........D.......562 437-2797
723 E 9th St Long Beach (90813) ***(P-20862)***
Villa Serra Corporation........D.......831 754-5532
1320 Padre Dr Apt 103 Salinas (93901) ***(P-11133)***
Villa Siena........D.......650 961-6484
1855 Miramonte Ave 117 Mountain View (94040) ***(P-21248)***
Villa Theresa Mobile Home Park, San Jose *Also called Barbaccia Properties* ***(P-11157)***
Villa Valencia Health Care Ctr, Laguna Hills *Also called Sunrise Senior Living Inc* ***(P-20809)***
Village 8, Westlake Village *Also called WF Cinema Holdings LP* ***(P-18324)***
Village At Granite Bay........D.......916 789-0326
8550 Barton Rd Granite Bay (95746) ***(P-24712)***
Village At Northridge........C.......818 514-4497
9222 Corbin Ave Northridge (91324) ***(P-24713)***
Village At Sydney Creek, San Luis Obispo *Also called Village Pacific Mgt Group* ***(P-20863)***
Village At Sydney Creek, San Luis Obispo *Also called Village Pacific Mgt Group* ***(P-20864)***
Village Club........E.......619 425-3333
429 Broadway Chula Vista (91910) ***(P-19256)***
Village Glen Apartments........D.......626 963-4575
633 S Pasadena Ave Apt 45 Glendora (91740) ***(P-11134)***
Village Integrated Svc Agcy, Long Beach *Also called Mental Health Amer Los Angeles* ***(P-23919)***
Village Nurseries Whl LLC (PA)........E.......714 279-3100
1589 N Main St Orange (92867) ***(P-9174)***
Village Nurseries Whl LLC........B.......916 993-2292
6901 Bradshaw Rd Sacramento (95829) ***(P-9175)***
Village Nurseries Whl LLC........C.......951 657-3940
20099 Santa Rosa Mine Rd Perris (92570) ***(P-9176)***
Village Pacific Mgt Group........D.......805 543-2350
1234 Laurel Ln San Luis Obispo (93401) ***(P-20863)***
Village Pacific Mgt Group (PA)........D.......805 543-2300
55 Broad St San Luis Obispo (93405) ***(P-20864)***
Village Square Healthcare Ctr, San Marcos *Also called San Marcos Operating Co LP* ***(P-20741)***
Village Square Nursing Center........C.......760 471-2986
1586 W San Marcos Blvd San Marcos (92078) ***(P-20865)***

VILLAGE WEST HEALTH CENTER, Riverside *Also called Air Force Village West Inc* ***(P-20223)***
Village West Yacht Club ....D....209 478-8992
6633 Embarcadero Dr Stockton (95219) ***(P-19077)***
Villagecraft Quality Furn, Santa Monica *Also called Century Finance Incorporated* ***(P-9790)***
Villages Golf and Country Club ....C....408 274-4400
5000 Cribari Ln San Jose (95135) ***(P-19078)***
Villages, The, San Jose *Also called Villages Golf and Country Club* ***(P-19078)***
Villageway Management Inc ....D....949 450-1515
23041 Ave De La Carlta # 270 Laguna Hills (92653) ***(P-11813)***
Villageway Property Management, Laguna Hills *Also called Villageway Management Inc* ***(P-11813)***
Villara Corporation (PA) ....B....916 646-2700
4700 Lang Ave McClellan (95652) ***(P-2398)***
Villara Corporation ....D....916 364-9370
9828 Bus Park Dr Ste A1 Sacramento (95827) ***(P-2399)***
Villara Corporation ....E....707 863-8222
5005 Fulton Dr Ste F Fairfield (94534) ***(P-3209)***
Villara Corporation ....D....209 824-1082
332 E Wetmore St Manteca (95337) ***(P-2400)***
Villara Corporation ....D....916 646-2222
4700 Lang Ave McClellan (95652) ***(P-2401)***
Villas De Carlsbad Ltd A Cali (PA) ....C....858 565-4424
9619 Chesapeake Dr # 103 San Diego (92123) ***(P-24714)***
Villas De Carlsbad Ltd A Cali ....E....760 434-7116
1088 Laguna Dr Carlsbad (92008) ***(P-24715)***
Vimark Inc ....D....707 857-3588
19500 Geyserville Ave Geyserville (95441) ***(P-717)***
Vimark Vineyards, Geyserville *Also called Vimark Inc* ***(P-717)***
Vimo Inc (PA) ....D....650 618-4600
1305 Terra Bella Ave Mountain View (94043) ***(P-27901)***
Vin Dibona Productions, Los Angeles *Also called Cara Communications Corp* ***(P-18030)***
Vina Holdings Inc ....D....714 622-5334
13800 Arizona St Westminster (92683) ***(P-22443)***
Vince Solutions (PA) ....D....510 432-0852
3910 Riverbend Ter Fremont (94555) ***(P-27513)***
Vincent B Zaninovich Sons Inc ....A....661 720-9031
20715 Ave 8 Richgrove (93261) ***(P-182)***
Vincent Contractors Inc ....B....714 693-1726
4501 E La Palma Ave # 200 Anaheim (92807) ***(P-2828)***
Vincent Hayley Enterprises ....D....626 398-8182
1810 N Fair Oaks Ave Pasadena (91103) ***(P-21249)***
Vincent V Zaninovich & Sons ....D....661 849-2613
2480 E Washington St Earlimart (93219) ***(P-183)***
Vinculums Services Inc ....C....949 783-3552
10 Pasteur Ste 100 Irvine (92618) ***(P-27902)***
Vindicia Inc ....C....650 264-4700
2988 Campus Dr Ste 300 San Mateo (94403) ***(P-15889)***
Vindra Inc ....D....707 994-7738
3805 Dexter Ln Clearlake (95422) ***(P-20866)***
Vine Transit, NAPA *Also called City of NAPA* ***(P-3876)***
Vineyard Plastering Inc ....E....909 357-3701
10335 Vineyard Dr Fontana (92337) ***(P-2975)***
Vino Farms Inc (PA) ....E....209 334-6975
1377 E Lodi Ave Lodi (95240) ***(P-718)***
Vino Farms Inc ....D....707 433-8241
10651 Eastside Rd Healdsburg (95448) ***(P-719)***
Vino Farms Inc ....C....916 775-4095
51375 S Netherlands Rd Clarksburg (95612) ***(P-393)***
Vino Farms LLC ....A....209 334-6975
1377 E Lodi Ave Lodi (95240) ***(P-9058)***
Vinod Kumar MD ....D....661 324-4100
5020 Commerce Dr Bakersfield (93309) ***(P-20087)***
Vinson & Elkins LLP ....C....650 617-8400
1841 Page Mill Rd Fl 2 Palo Alto (94304) ***(P-23421)***
Vinson & Elkins LLP ....C....415 979-6900
555 Mission St Ste 2000 San Francisco (94105) ***(P-23422)***
Vintage Associates Inc ....C....760 772-3673
78755 Darby Rd Bermuda Dunes (92203) ***(P-958)***
Vintage Club (PA) ....E....760 346-5566
75005 Vintage Dr W Indian Wells (92210) ***(P-19079)***
Vintage Club ....D....760 340-0500
75001 Vintage Dr W Indian Wells (92210) ***(P-19080)***
Vintage Club Master Assn Inc ....D....760 340-0500
75001 Vintage Dr W Indian Wells (92210) ***(P-25283)***
Vintage Design Inc (PA) ....D....714 974-4822
25200 Commercentre Dr Lake Forest (92630) ***(P-3119)***
Vintage Estates of Hayward, Hayward *Also called St Michael Convalescent Hosp* ***(P-20780)***
Vintage Faire Nrsng Rhbltn, Modesto *Also called Covenant Care California LLC* ***(P-21050)***
VINTAGE GARDENS, Fresno *Also called Central Cal Nikkei Foundation* ***(P-24460)***
Vintage Golden Gate, San Francisco *Also called Avalon Golden Gate LLC* ***(P-24433)***
Vintage Nursery, Bermuda Dunes *Also called Vintage Associates Inc* ***(P-958)***
Vintage Production California, Bakersfield *Also called California Resources Prod Corp* ***(P-1019)***
Vintage Senior Housing LLC ....B....805 583-3500
5300 E Los Angeles Ave Simi Valley (93063) ***(P-11135)***
Vintage Senior Living Corp ....D....949 364-6210
27783 Center Dr Mission Viejo (92692) ***(P-11136)***
Vintage Senior Management Inc ....A....818 954-9500
2721 W Willow St Burbank (91505) ***(P-24110)***
Vintage Senior Management Inc ....A....707 595-0009
91 Napa Rd Sonoma (95476) ***(P-11137)***
Vintage Silver Creek, San Jose *Also called Sunrise Senior Living Inc* ***(P-20808)***
Vintage Simi Hills, Simi Valley *Also called Vintage Senior Housing LLC* ***(P-11135)***
Vintage Wine Estates Inc (PA) ....C....877 289-9463
205 Concourse Blvd Santa Rosa (95403) ***(P-9059)***
Vintners Golf Club ....E....707 944-1992
7901 Solano Ave Yountville (94599) ***(P-18777)***
Vintners Inn ....D....707 575-7350
4350 Barnes Rd Santa Rosa (95403) ***(P-13369)***
Vintrust Inc ....E....877 846-8787
38 Keyes Ave Ste 200 San Francisco (94129) ***(P-4690)***
Vinwood Cellars Inc ....E....707 857-4011
18700 Geyserville Ave Geyserville (95441) ***(P-9060)***
VIP, Folsom *Also called Visionary Integration* ***(P-12017)***
VIP Tours of California Inc ....D....310 216-7507
9830 Bellanca Ave Los Angeles (90045) ***(P-4984)***
VIP Transport Inc ....E....951 272-3700
2703 Wardlow Rd Corona (92882) ***(P-4300)***
Vipstore USA Co ....B....626 934-7880
13674 Star Ruby Ave Corona (92880) ***(P-9269)***
Virco Inc (HQ) ....D....310 533-0474
2027 Harpers Way Torrance (90501) ***(P-6742)***
Virga Investment Property ....C....530 755-4409
430 S George Wash Blvd Yuba City (95993) ***(P-10960)***
Virgil Convalescent Hospital, Los Angeles *Also called Virgil Sntrium Cnvlescent Hosp* ***(P-20867)***
Virgil Sntrium Cnvlescent Hosp ....C....323 665-5793
975 N Virgil Ave Los Angeles (90029) ***(P-20867)***
Virgin America Inc (HQ) ....C....877 359-8474
555 Airport Blvd Burlingame (94010) ***(P-4814)***
Virgin Fish Inc (PA) ....C....310 391-6161
1000 Corporate Pointe # 150 Culver City (90230) ***(P-3857)***
Virgin Galactic LLC (HQ) ....D....562 384-4400
16555 Spcship Landing Way Mojave (93501) ***(P-5251)***
Virginia Country Club ....C....562 427-0924
4602 N Virginia Rd Long Beach (90807) ***(P-19081)***
Virginia Hardwood Company (PA) ....D....626 815-0540
1000 W Foothill Blvd Azusa (91702) ***(P-6872)***
Virginia Sarabian ....E....559 493-2900
2816 S Leonard Ave Sanger (93657) ***(P-231)***
Virident Systems Inc ....C....408 573-5000
1745 Tech Dr Ste 700 San Jose (95110) ***(P-26492)***
Virtium LLC ....D....949 888-2444
30052 Tomas Rcho STA Marg (92688) ***(P-16526)***
Virtual Instruments Corp ....D....408 579-4000
2331 Zanker Rd San Jose (95131) ***(P-16527)***
Visa USA Inc (HQ) ....C....650 432-3200
900 Metro Center Blvd Foster City (94404) ***(P-17568)***
Visalia Convention Center, Visalia *Also called City of Visalia* ***(P-17084)***
Visalia Country Club ....D....559 734-3733
625 N Ranch St Visalia (93291) ***(P-19082)***
Visalia Medical Clinic Inc (PA) ....B....559 733-5222
5400 W Hillsdale Ave Visalia (93291) ***(P-20088)***
Visalia Unified School Dst ....C....559 730-7871
801 N Mooney Blvd Visalia (93291) ***(P-24111)***
Visalia Youth Services, Visalia *Also called Turning Point Central Cal Inc* ***(P-24098)***
Viscamar LLC ....D....559 636-1111
300 S Court St Visalia (93291) ***(P-13370)***
Viscent Orthpd Solutions LLC (HQ) ....E....214 501-0180
2885 Loker Ave E Carlsbad (92010) ***(P-20089)***
Viscira LLC ....D....415 848-8010
200 Vallejo St San Francisco (94111) ***(P-7128)***
Viscomm Inc (PA) ....D....415 454-7191
35 Leveroni Ct Novato (94949) ***(P-16259)***
Visio Integ Profe LLC (HQ) ....D....916 985-9625
80 Iron Point Cir Ste 100 Folsom (95630) ***(P-27514)***
Vision Care Center (PA) ....D....559 486-2000
7075 N Sharon Ave Fresno (93720) ***(P-20090)***
Vision Care Center Central Cal, Fresno *Also called Vision Care Center* ***(P-20090)***
Vision Express/Wrag-Time Trnsp, Gardena *Also called Wrag-Time Air Freight Inc* ***(P-4307)***
Vision Fund International, Monrovia *Also called World Vision International* ***(P-25487)***
VISION FUND INTERNATIONAL, Monrovia *Also called Visionfund International* ***(P-17569)***
Vision Realty Managements, Beverly Hills *Also called Starpoint Property MGT LLC* ***(P-11778)***
Vision Service Plan (PA) ....A....916 851-5000
3333 Quality Dr Rancho Cordova (95670) ***(P-10327)***
Vision Solutions Inc (PA) ....D....949 253-6500
15300 Barranca Pkwy # 100 Irvine (92618) ***(P-15529)***
Vision Solutions Inc ....D....949 253-6500
15300 Barranca Pkwy # 100 Irvine (92618) ***(P-16528)***
Vision Tech Solutions LLC ....D....310 656-3100
222 N Pacific Coast Hwy # 1500 El Segundo (90245) ***(P-15530)***
Visionaire Group Inc ....D....310 823-1800
5340 Alla Rd Ste 100 Los Angeles (90066) ***(P-13917)***
Visionary Integration (PA) ....D....916 985-9625
80 Iron Point Cir Ste 100 Folsom (95630) ***(P-12017)***
Visionary Intgrtion Prfssonals, Folsom *Also called Visio Integ Profe LLC* ***(P-27514)***
Visionfund International ....D....626 303-8811
800 W Chestnut Ave Monrovia (91016) ***(P-17569)***
Visions Unlimited (PA) ....C....916 394-0800
6833 Stockton Blvd # 485 Sacramento (95823) ***(P-22713)***
Visionstar Inc ....D....213 387-3700
3435 Wilsh Blvd Ste 2120 Los Angeles (90010) ***(P-27515)***
Visit Anaheim, Anaheim *Also called Anaheim/Orange Cnty Visitor Bu* ***(P-17002)***
Visiting Angels, Chino *Also called Angels In Motion LLC* ***(P-22224)***
Visiting Angels Riverside Cnty, Riverside *Also called Roberts & Associates Inc* ***(P-22407)***
Visiting Care & Companions Inc ....D....805 690-6202
509 E Montecito St # 200 Santa Barbara (93103) ***(P-22444)***
Visiting Nrse Assn Orange Cnty (PA) ....D....949 263-4700
2520 Redhill Ave Santa Ana (92705) ***(P-22445)***
Visiting Nurse & Hospice Care, Santa Barbara *Also called Visiting Nurse & Hospice Care* ***(P-25050)***
Visiting Nurse & Hospice Care (PA) ....C....805 965-5555
509 E Montecito St # 200 Santa Barbara (93103) ***(P-25050)***

ALPHABETIC

Employee Codes: A=Over 500 employees, B=251-500
C=101-250, D=51-100, E=50
2019 Directory of California
Wholesalers and Services Companies
© Mergent Inc. 1-800-342-5647
1515

Visiting Nurse Associ......D......909 621-3961
150 W 1st St Ste 176 Claremont (91711) ***(P-22446)***
Visiting Nurse Association......D......831 385-1014
5 Lower Ragsdle Dr 102 Monterey (93940) ***(P-22447)***
Visiting Nurse Association of (HQ)......D......831 477-2600
2880 Soquel Ave Ste 10 Santa Cruz (95062) ***(P-25051)***
Visitng Nurse Assn Inlnd CNT (PA)......A......951 413-1200
6235 River Crest Dr Ste L Riverside (92507) ***(P-22448)***
Visitng Nurse Assn Inlnd CNT......C......760 346-3982
42600 Cook St Ste 202 Palm Desert (92211) ***(P-22449)***
Visitor Services & Facilities, San Jose *Also called City of San Jose* ***(P-24927)***
Visiworks Software, El Dorado Hills *Also called Dorado Software Inc* ***(P-15116)***
Visor, San Francisco *Also called Hatfield Inc* ***(P-13709)***
Vista Anglina Hsing Prtners LP......E......213 482-4718
418 E Edgeware Rd Los Angeles (90026) ***(P-11814)***
Vista Behavioral Health Inc......D......800 992-0901
5900 Brockton Ave Riverside (92506) ***(P-21993)***
Vista Care Group LLC (PA)......D......760 295-3900
1863 Devon Pl Vista (92084) ***(P-24112)***
Vista Community Clinic (PA)......B......760 631-5000
1000 Vale Terrace Dr Vista (92084) ***(P-20151)***
Vista Community Clinic......E......760 631-5030
134 Grapevine Rd Vista (92083) ***(P-20152)***
Vista Cove Care Center......D......805 525-7134
250 March St Santa Paula (93060) ***(P-21250)***
Vista Cove Care Center At Long......D......562 426-4461
3401 Cedar Ave Long Beach (90807) ***(P-20868)***
Vista Cove Care Ctr - Rialto......D......909 877-1361
1471 S Riverside Ave Rialto (92376) ***(P-20869)***
Vista Del Mar Child Fmly Svcs......B......310 836-1223
1533 Euclid St Santa Monica (90404) ***(P-24716)***
Vista Del Mar Health Centers, Vista *Also called Life Care Centers America Inc* ***(P-21134)***
Vista Gardens, Vista *Also called Vista Care Group LLC* ***(P-24112)***
Vista Hill Foundation......D......619 266-0166
4125 Alpha St San Diego (92113) ***(P-24113)***
Vista Hill Foundation (PA)......E......585 514-5100
8910 Clairemont Mesa Blvd San Diego (92123) ***(P-25052)***
Vista Home Health Service Inc......D......818 701-1877
343 E Palmdale Blvd Ste 4 Palmdale (93550) ***(P-22450)***
Vista Hospital Riverside, Rancho Cucamonga *Also called Perris Valley Cmnty Hosp LLC* ***(P-21641)***
Vista Hospital San Gabriel Vly, Baldwin Park *Also called Vista Specialty Hosp Cal LP* ***(P-21911)***
Vista Irrigation District......D......760 597-3100
1391 Engineer St Vista (92081) ***(P-6569)***
Vista Knoll Inc......D......760 630-2273
2000 Westwood Rd Vista (92083) ***(P-20870)***
Vista Knoll Spclzed Care Fclty, Vista *Also called Vista Woods Health Assoc LLC* ***(P-20872)***
VISTA PACIFICA CONVALESCENT CE, Riverside *Also called Vista Pacifica Enterprises Inc* ***(P-20871)***
Vista Pacifica Enterprises Inc (PA)......C......951 682-4833
3662 Pacific Ave Riverside (92509) ***(P-20871)***
Vista Pacifica Enterprises Inc......C......951 682-4867
3662 Pacific Ave Riverside (92509) ***(P-21251)***
Vista Pcifica Convalescent Ctr, Riverside *Also called Vista Pacifica Enterprises Inc* ***(P-21251)***
Vista Specialty Hosp Cal LP......C......626 388-2700
14148 Francisquito Ave Baldwin Park (91706) ***(P-21911)***
Vista Specialty Hosp Riverside, Perris *Also called Perris Valley Cmnty Hosp LLC* ***(P-21640)***
Vista Steel Co Inc......E......805 653-1189
331 W Lewis St Ventura (93001) ***(P-2073)***
Vista Sun Apartments, Orange *Also called Investment Concepts Inc* ***(P-11881)***
Vista Universal Inc (PA)......E......510 785-6166
2430 American Ave Hayward (94545) ***(P-14425)***
Vista Valencia Group Inc......E......661 255-4600
25545 Via Paladar Valencia (91355) ***(P-11815)***
Vista Valley Country Club......D......760 758-2800
29354 Vista Valley Dr Vista (92084) ***(P-19083)***
Vista Verde Farms......E......661 720-9733
11251 Melcher Rd Delano (93215) ***(P-8900)***
Vista Verde Farms Inc......D......559 992-3111
7124 Whitley Ave Corcoran (93212) ***(P-470)***
Vista Woods Health Assoc LLC......C......760 630-2273
2000 Westwood Rd Vista (92083) ***(P-20872)***
Vistage International Inc (PA)......C......858 523-6800
4840 Eastgate Mall San Diego (92121) ***(P-27516)***
Vistancia Marketing LLC......D......909 594-9500
655 Brea Canyon Rd Walnut (91789) ***(P-27517)***
Visual Concepts Entertainment......C......415 479-3634
10 Hamilton Landing Novato (94949) ***(P-15531)***
Visual Pak San Diego LLC......C......847 689-1000
2320 Paseo De Las Ave 2 San Diego (92154) ***(P-17570)***
Visualon Inc......C......408 645-6618
2590 N 1st St Ste 100 San Jose (95131) ***(P-15890)***
Vita North America, Yorba Linda *Also called Vident* ***(P-7229)***
Vital Express Inc......E......330 777-5450
4000 Macarthur Blvd Ste 6 Newport Beach (92660) ***(P-5252)***
Vital Farmland Holdings LLC......D......415 465-2400
3 Corte Las Casas Belvedere Tiburon (94920) ***(P-17571)***
Vitalant......C......510 785-9554
111 Review Way Hayward (94544) ***(P-22900)***
Vitalant......D......805 543-1077
4119 Broad St Ste 100 San Luis Obispo (93401) ***(P-22901)***
Vitalant......D......831 751-1993
4119 Broad St Ste 100 San Luis Obispo (93401) ***(P-22902)***
Vitas Healthcare Corp Cal......D......408 964-6800
670 N Mccarthy Blcvd 220 Milpitas (95035) ***(P-22451)***
Vitas Healthcare Corp Cal......D......916 925-7010
2710 Gateway Oaks Dr # 100 Sacramento (95833) ***(P-22452)***
Vitas Healthcare Corp Cal......D......925 930-9373
355 Lennon Ln Ste 150 Walnut Creek (94598) ***(P-22453)***
Vitas Healthcare Corp Cal......C......909 386-6000
7888 Mission Grove Pkwy S Riverside (92508) ***(P-22454)***
Vitas Healthcare Corp Cal......D......626 918-2273
1343 N Grand Ave Ste 100 Covina (91724) ***(P-22455)***
Vitas Healthcare Corp Cal......D......310 324-2273
990 W 190th St Ste 550 Torrance (90502) ***(P-22456)***
Vitas Healthcare Corp Cal......D......619 680-4400
9655 Gran Rdge Dr Ste 300 San Diego (92123) ***(P-22457)***
Vitas Healthcare Corp Cal......D......818 760-2273
16830 Ventura Blvd # 315 Encino (91436) ***(P-22458)***
Vitas Healthcare Corporation......D......805 437-2100
333 N Lantana St Ste 124 Camarillo (93010) ***(P-20970)***
Vitas Innovative Hospice Care, Milpitas *Also called Vitas Healthcare Corp Cal* ***(P-22451)***
Vitas Innovative Hospice Care, Riverside *Also called Vitas Healthcare Corp Cal* ***(P-22454)***
Vitas Innovative Hospice Care, San Diego *Also called Vitas Healthcare Corp Cal* ***(P-22457)***
Vitas Innovative Hospice Care, Encino *Also called Vitas Healthcare Corp Cal* ***(P-22458)***
Vitco Distributors Inc......D......909 355-1300
715 E California St Ontario (91761) ***(P-8136)***
Vitco Food Service, Ontario *Also called Vitco Distributors Inc* ***(P-8136)***
Vitesse LLC......A......650 543-4800
1601 Willow Rd Menlo Park (94025) ***(P-16198)***
Vitran Logistics Inc......D......909 972-3100
1000 S Cucamonga Ave Ontario (91761) ***(P-4655)***
Vitro LLC......D......619 234-0408
2305 Historic Decatur Rd # 205 San Diego (92106) ***(P-13918)***
Vitrorobertson LLC......D......619 234-0408
2305 Historic Decatur Rd San Diego (92106) ***(P-13919)***
Vituity, Emeryville *Also called Cep America LLC* ***(P-19370)***
Viva Group Inc......D......310 449-6400
11766 Wilshire Blvd # 300 Los Angeles (90025) ***(P-11138)***
Viva International, Belvedere Tiburon *Also called Marcolin USA Inc* ***(P-7236)***
Viva Life Science Inc......D......949 645-6100
350 Paularino Ave Costa Mesa (92626) ***(P-8220)***
Viva Soma Lessee Inc......A......415 974-6400
50 3rd St San Francisco (94103) ***(P-27087)***
Vivente 1 Inc......D......408 279-2706
2400 Enborg Ln San Jose (95128) ***(P-11155)***
Vivente 2 Inc......D......408 279-2706
5347 Dent Ave San Jose (95118) ***(P-11156)***
Vivid Solution......D......310 498-2559
5959 W Century Blvd Los Angeles (90045) ***(P-17572)***
Vivopools Inc......D......818 952-2121
825 S Primrose Ave Ste H Monrovia (91016) ***(P-17573)***
Vivopools LLC......D......888 702-8486
245 W Foothill Blvd Monrovia (91016) ***(P-17574)***
Vladigor Investment Inc......D......415 558-9274
1601 Mission St San Francisco (94103) ***(P-17842)***
Vlot Brothers, Chowchilla *Also called Case Vlott Cattle* ***(P-408)***
Vlot Brothers Dairy, Chowchilla *Also called Vlot Brothers Trucking Co Inc* ***(P-426)***
Vlot Brothers Trucking Co Inc......D......559 665-7399
3197 Avenue 21 Chowchilla (93610) ***(P-426)***
Vm Services Inc......E......714 678-5200
1051 S East St Anaheim (92805) ***(P-15532)***
Vm Services Inc (HQ)......C......510 744-3720
6701 Mowry Ave Newark (94560) ***(P-15533)***
Vmbc, Aliso Viejo *Also called Voice Mail Broadcasting Corp* ***(P-16199)***
Vmsg, Ventura *Also called Veternary Med Srgcal Group Inc* ***(P-619)***
Vmware Inc......C......650 427-2100
3400 Hillview Ave Palo Alto (94304) ***(P-15534)***
Vmware Inc (HQ)......C......650 427-5000
3401 Hillview Ave Palo Alto (94304) ***(P-15535)***
Vmware Inc......C......650 812-8200
3305 Hillview Ave Palo Alto (94304) ***(P-15536)***
Vn Home Health Care LP......D......408 998-0550
2528 Qume Dr Ste 7 San Jose (95131) ***(P-22459)***
Vna Home Health Systems, Santa Ana *Also called Visiting Nrse Assn Orange Cnty* ***(P-22445)***
Vna Hospice & Pllatve Cre S CA......C......909 384-0737
412 E Vanderbilt Way San Bernardino (92408) ***(P-22460)***
Vna Hospice & Pllatve Cre S CA (PA)......C......909 624-3574
412 E Vanderbilt Way San Bernardino (92408) ***(P-22461)***
Vna Private Duty Care, Claremont *Also called Visiting Nurse Associ* ***(P-22446)***
Vna Private Duty Care, San Bernardino *Also called Vna Hospice & Pllatve Cre S CA* ***(P-22461)***
Vnahnc, Emeryville *Also called Sutter Vsting Nrse Assn Hspice* ***(P-22430)***
Vnaic, Riverside *Also called Visitng Nurse Assn Inlnd CNT* ***(P-22448)***
Vocational Imprv Program Inc (PA)......C......909 483-5924
9210 Rochester Ave Rancho Cucamonga (91730) ***(P-24246)***
Vocational Visions......C......949 837-7280
26041 Pala Mission Viejo (92691) ***(P-24247)***
Voch Inc......D......626 798-1111
1920 N Fair Oaks Ave Pasadena (91103) ***(P-21252)***
Voice Mail Broadcasting Corp......D......714 437-0600
5 Columbia Aliso Viejo (92656) ***(P-16199)***
Voice Print International LLC (PA)......D......805 389-5200
160 Camino Ruiz Camarillo (93012) ***(P-16200)***
Voit Commercial Brokerage, Irvine *Also called Voit Development Manager Inc* ***(P-11935)***
Voit Development Manager Inc......D......949 851-5110
2020 Main St Ste 100 Irvine (92614) ***(P-11935)***
Voit Real Estate Services Lp......C......949 644-8648
101 Shipyard Way Ste A Newport Beach (92663) ***(P-11816)***
Volcano Communications Company (PA)......D......209 296-7502
20000 State Highway 88 Pine Grove (95665) ***(P-5674)***
Volcano Telephone Co., Pine Grove *Also called Volcano Vision Inc* ***(P-5964)***
Volcano Telephone Company, Pine Grove *Also called Volcano Communications Company* ***(P-5674)***

Mergent e-mail: customerrelations@mergent.com
1516
2019 Directory of California
Wholesalers and Services Companies
(P-0000) Products & Services Section entry number
(PA)=Parent Co (HQ)=Headquarters (DH)=Div Headquarters

Volcano Vision Inc ......C......209 296-2288
20000 State Highway 88 Pine Grove (95665) ***(P-5964)***
Volcom LLC ......C......949 646-2175
1725 Monrovia Ave Costa Mesa (92627) ***(P-8282)***
Volcom LLC (HQ) ......C......949 646-2175
1740 Monrovia Ave Costa Mesa (92627) ***(P-17575)***
Volkswagen South Coast ......D......657 231-5600
1450 Auto Mall Dr Santa Ana (92705) ***(P-17790)***
Voloagri Inc ......C......805 547-9391
3424 Roberto Ct San Luis Obispo (93401) ***(P-9102)***
Volt Management Corp ......C......310 316-8523
19191 S Vt Ave Ste 950 Torrance (90502) ***(P-14932)***
Volt Management Corp ......B......714 921-7460
2411 N Glassell St Orange (92865) ***(P-14933)***
Volt Management Corp ......C......858 576-3140
7676 Hazard Center Dr # 1000 San Diego (92108) ***(P-14934)***
Volt Management Corp ......C......858 578-0920
7676 Hazard Center Dr # 1000 San Diego (92108) ***(P-14935)***
Volt Management Corp ......C......559 435-1255
7330 N Palm Ave Ste 105 Fresno (93711) ***(P-14936)***
Volt Management Corp ......C......714 921-8800
2401 N Glassell St Orange (92865) ***(P-14937)***
Volt Management Corp ......D......916 923-0454
1544 Eureka Rd Ste 150 Roseville (95661) ***(P-14938)***
Volt Management Corp ......D......951 789-8133
1650 Iowa Ave Ste 140 Riverside (92507) ***(P-14939)***
Volt Management Corp ......C......209 952-5627
3558 Deer Park Dr 2 Stockton (95219) ***(P-14940)***
Volt Management Corp ......C......805 485-0506
1701 Solar Dr Ste 145 Oxnard (93030) ***(P-14941)***
Volt Telecom Group, Corona *Also called Volt Telecom Group Inc* ***(P-27903)***
Volt Telecom Group, Corona *Also called Volt Telecom Group Inc* ***(P-27904)***
Volt Telecom Group Inc ......E......800 548-6602
218 Helicopter Cir Corona (92880) ***(P-27903)***
Volt Telecom Group Inc ......C......951 493-8900
218 Helicopter Cir Corona (92880) ***(P-27904)***
Volt Temporary Services, Orange *Also called Volt Management Corp* ***(P-14933)***
Volt Workforce Solutions, Torrance *Also called Volt Management Corp* ***(P-14932)***
Volt Workforce Solutions, San Diego *Also called Volt Management Corp* ***(P-14934)***
Volt Workforce Solutions, San Diego *Also called Volt Management Corp* ***(P-14935)***
Volt Workforce Solutions, Fresno *Also called Volt Management Corp* ***(P-14936)***
Volt Workforce Solutions, Orange *Also called Volt Management Corp* ***(P-14937)***
Volt Workforce Solutions, Roseville *Also called Volt Management Corp* ***(P-14938)***
Volt Workforce Solutions, Riverside *Also called Volt Management Corp* ***(P-14939)***
Volt Workforce Solutions, Stockton *Also called Volt Management Corp* ***(P-14940)***
Volt Workforce Solutions, Oxnard *Also called Volt Management Corp* ***(P-14941)***
Volta Charging LLC ......D......888 264-2208
155 De Haro St San Francisco (94103) ***(P-13931)***
Volume Services Inc ......D......415 972-1500
24 Willie Mays Plz San Francisco (94107) ***(P-19257)***
Volume Services Inc ......D......323 644-6038
5333 Zoo Dr Los Angeles (90027) ***(P-19258)***
Volume Services Inc ......D......619 525-5800
111 W Harbor Dr San Diego (92101) ***(P-19259)***
Volume Services Inc ......D......951 245-9995
500 Diamond Dr Lake Elsinore (92530) ***(P-19260)***
VOLUNTEER CENTER ORANGE COUNTY, Santa Ana *Also called Oneoc* ***(P-25447)***
Volunteers of Amer Los Angeles ......C......818 764-8722
11512 Valerio St North Hollywood (91605) ***(P-24114)***
Volunteers of Amer Los Angeles ......C......818 834-9097
10896 Lehigh Ave Pacoima (91331) ***(P-24115)***
Volunteers of Amer Los Angeles ......C......323 780-3770
522 N Dangler Ave Los Angeles (90022) ***(P-24116)***
Volunteers of Amer Los Angeles ......C......626 337-9878
1760 W Cameron Ave # 104 West Covina (91790) ***(P-24117)***
Volunteers of Amer Los Angeles ......D......661 290-2829
25141 Avenida Rondel Valencia (91355) ***(P-24118)***
Volunteers of Amer Los Angeles ......C......818 352-5974
10819 Plainview Ave Tujunga (91042) ***(P-24119)***
Volunteers of Amer Los Angeles ......D......714 426-9834
2100 N Broadway Ste 300 Santa Ana (92706) ***(P-24120)***
Volunteers of Amer Los Angeles ......C......818 769-3617
6724 Tujunga Ave North Hollywood (91606) ***(P-24121)***
Volunteers of Amer Los Angeles ......E......818 506-0597
11243 Kittridge St North Hollywood (91606) ***(P-24122)***
Volunteers of Amer Los Angeles ......C......818 834-8957
12550 Van Nuys Blvd Pacoima (91331) ***(P-24123)***
Volunteers of America Inc ......C......609 877-2665
10626 Schirra Ave Mather (95655) ***(P-24124)***
Volunteers of America Greater ......C......510 663-4546
672 13th St Ste 100 Oakland (94612) ***(P-24125)***
Volunteers of America Greater (PA) ......D......916 265-3400
3434 Marconi Ave Ste A Sacramento (95821) ***(P-24126)***
Volutone LLC (PA) ......D......805 520-8500
170 W Cochran St Simi Valley (93065) ***(P-16950)***
Volutone Distributing Co., Simi Valley *Also called Volutone LLC* ***(P-16950)***
Vormetric Inc (HQ) ......D......408 433-6000
2860 Junction Ave San Jose (95134) ***(P-16529)***
Vorwaller & Brooks Inc ......D......760 262-6300
72182 Corporate Way Thousand Palms (92276) ***(P-1257)***
Voter Precinct Voter Reg Off, Norwalk *Also called County of Los Angeles* ***(P-16108)***
Votum Staffing Inc ......B......310 499-4902
515 W Whittier Blvd Montebello (90640) ***(P-14796)***
Vox Network Solutions Inc ......C......650 989-1000
8000 Marina Blvd Ste 130 Brisbane (94005) ***(P-27905)***
Voxify Inc ......D......510 545-3011
1151 Marina Village Pkwy Alameda (94501) ***(P-15537)***
VPD IV Inc (PA) ......C......916 605-1500
150 Parkshore Dr Folsom (95630) ***(P-18247)***
Vpet Usa Inc (PA) ......D......909 605-1668
12925 Marlay Ave Fontana (92337) ***(P-8915)***
Vpm Management Inc ......C......949 863-1500
2400 Main St Ste 201 Irvine (92614) ***(P-27088)***
Vps Companies Inc (PA) ......E......831 724-7551
310 Walker St Watsonville (95076) ***(P-8507)***
Vps Companies Inc ......E......831 633-4011
13526 Blackie Rd Castroville (95012) ***(P-8508)***
Vsa & Associates Inc (PA) ......D......562 698-2468
6571 Altura Blvd Ste 100 Buena Park (90620) ***(P-25991)***
VSC Sports Inc ......D......415 820-3525
750 Folsom St San Francisco (94107) ***(P-27906)***
Vsp Holding Company Inc ......D......916 851-5000
3333 Quality Dr Rancho Cordova (95670) ***(P-10328)***
Vss Compressor Service, Paramount *Also called Vss Sales Inc* ***(P-18004)***
Vss International Inc (HQ) ......D......916 373-1500
3785 Channel Dr West Sacramento (95691) ***(P-1868)***
Vss Monitoring Inc (HQ) ......C......408 585-6800
178 E Tasman Dr San Jose (95134) ***(P-5675)***
Vss Sales Inc (PA) ......D......562 630-0606
16220 Garfield Ave Paramount (90723) ***(P-18004)***
VT Milcom Inc ......D......619 424-9024
1660 Logan Ave Ste 2 San Diego (92113) ***(P-25992)***
Vtc Enterprises (PA) ......B......805 928-5000
2445 A St Santa Maria (93455) ***(P-24248)***
Vubiquity Inc ......C......818 526-5000
15301 Ventura Blvd Bldg E Sherman Oaks (91403) ***(P-18248)***
Vubiquity Holdings Inc (PA) ......C......818 526-5000
15301 Ventura Blvd # 3000 Sherman Oaks (91403) ***(P-5965)***
Vucovich Inc (PA) ......D......559 486-8020
4288 S Bagley Ave Fresno (93725) ***(P-7717)***
Vvd Comuunications, Garden Grove *Also called Video Vice Data Communications* ***(P-6006)***
Vwi Concord LLC ......C......925 827-2000
1970 Diamond Blvd Concord (94520) ***(P-13371)***
Vwise Inc ......D......949 716-1276
85 Enterprise Ste 320 Aliso Viejo (92656) ***(P-15538)***
VWR International LLC ......E......714 220-2615
6609 Mount Whitney Dr Buena Park (90620) ***(P-7250)***
VWR Scientific, Buena Park *Also called VWR International LLC* ***(P-7250)***
Vxi Global Solutions LLC (PA) ......A......213 739-4720
220 W 1st St Fl 3 Los Angeles (90012) ***(P-17576)***
Vyborny Vineyard Management ......D......707 944-9135
7327 Silverado Trl Rutherford (94573) ***(P-720)***
Vyshnavi Information Techn ......C......408 454-6218
2603 Camino Ramon Ste 200 San Ramon (94583) ***(P-15539)***
W A Rasic Cnstr Co Inc (PA) ......C......562 928-6111
4150 Long Beach Blvd Long Beach (90807) ***(P-1997)***
W B Starr Inc ......D......949 770-8835
20602 Canada Rd Lake Forest (92630) ***(P-959)***
W Bradley Electric Inc ......C......650 701-1502
501 Seaport Ct Ste 103a Redwood City (94063) ***(P-2780)***
W Bradley Electric Inc (PA) ......E......415 898-1400
90 Hill Rd Novato (94945) ***(P-2781)***
W Brown & Assc Property & Csu ......D......949 851-2060
19000 Macarthur Blvd Irvine (92612) ***(P-10825)***
W C I, Hollister *Also called Woltcom Inc* ***(P-2790)***
W Corporation ......C......714 532-8800
1643 W Orange Grove Ave Orange (92868) ***(P-27907)***
W Diamond Supply Co (HQ) ......D......909 859-8939
19321 E Walnut Dr N City of Industry (91748) ***(P-6803)***
W F Hayward Co ......D......530 303-3030
629 Main St Ste 101 Placerville (95667) ***(P-2976)***
W F Hayward Co (PA) ......D......310 532-9501
1264 W 130th St Gardena (90247) ***(P-2977)***
W G A, Irvine *Also called Western Growers Association* ***(P-24991)***
W G B, Tustin *Also called Wood Gutmann Bogart Insur Brkg* ***(P-10836)***
W G Warranty and Insur Svcs, Calabasas *Also called All Motorists Insurance Agency* ***(P-10513)***
W H C Inc ......D......916 927-9300
2240 Northrop Ave Sacramento (95825) ***(P-20873)***
W I C, Sutter Creek *Also called Resource Connection of Amador* ***(P-23993)***
W I S, Moreno Valley *Also called Retail Services Wis Corp* ***(P-17428)***
W I S, El Monte *Also called Retail Services Wis Corp* ***(P-17429)***
W J Griffin Inc ......C......805 683-5639
905 S Patterson Ave Santa Barbara (93111) ***(P-9177)***
W L Butler Construction Inc (PA) ......E......650 361-1270
735 Shasta St Redwood City (94063) ***(P-1694)***
W L Hickey Sons Inc ......C......408 736-4938
190 Commercial St Sunnyvale (94085) ***(P-2402)***
W Los Angeles ......B......310 208-8765
930 Hilgard Ave Los Angeles (90024) ***(P-13372)***
W M Klorman Construction Corp ......D......818 591-5969
23047 Ventura Blvd Fl 2 Woodland Hills (91364) ***(P-1695)***
W M Lyles Co (HQ) ......B......559 441-1900
1210 W Olive Ave Fresno (93728) ***(P-1998)***
W M Lyles Co ......E......661 387-1600
2810 Unicorn Rd Bakersfield (93308) ***(P-25993)***
W O R K, Carpinteria *Also called Ucp Work Inc* ***(P-24240)***
W R Hambrecht Co Inc (PA) ......D......415 551-8600
Bay 3 Pier 1 San Francisco (94111) ***(P-10033)***
W S B & Associates Inc ......D......510 444-6266
150 Executive Park Blvd # 4700 San Francisco (94134) ***(P-16854)***
W S B & Associates Inc (PA) ......D......415 864-3510
1390 Market St Ste 314 San Francisco (94102) ***(P-16855)***
W San Diego Hotel, San Diego *Also called Rp Scs Wsd Hotel LLC* ***(P-13144)***

ALPHABETIC

Employee Codes: A=Over 500 employees, B=251-500 C=101-250, D=51-100, E=50
2019 Directory of California Wholesalers and Services Companies
© Mergent Inc. 1-800-342-5647
1517

W Scott Bllard Dsign Arch Inc .... E 323 386-4740
1800 Century Park E # 600 Los Angeles (90067) ***(P-17577)***
W Why W Enterprises Inc .... D 626 969-4292
2671 Pomona Blvd Pomona (91768) ***(P-4388)***
W-Bel Age LLC .... D 310 854-1111
1020 N San Vicente Blvd West Hollywood (90069) ***(P-13373)***
W-Emerald LLC .... C 619 239-4500
400 W Broadway San Diego (92101) ***(P-13374)***
W2005 New Cntury Ht Prtflio LP .... D 408 745-6000
1100 N Mathilda Ave Sunnyvale (94089) ***(P-13375)***
W2005 Wyn Hotels LP .... D 323 887-8100
5757 Telegraph Rd Commerce (90040) ***(P-13376)***
Wachovia A Division Wells F .... A 415 571-2832
420 Montgomery St San Francisco (94104) ***(P-9377)***
Wad Productions Inc .... D 818 260-5673
3500 W Olive Ave Ste 1000 Burbank (91505) ***(P-18152)***
Waddell & Reed Inc .... D 714 437-7510
695 Town Center Dr # 200 Costa Mesa (92626) ***(P-10034)***
Wade & Lowe A Prof Corp (PA) .... D 909 483-6700
3200 Inland Empire Blvd # 160 Ontario (91764) ***(P-23423)***
Wagan Corporation .... E 510 471-9221
31088 San Clemente St Hayward (94544) ***(P-6684)***
Wageworks Inc (PA) .... C 650 577-5200
1100 Park Pl Fl 4 San Mateo (94403) ***(P-27518)***
Waggoners Trucking .... D 800 999-9097
801 Mcwane Blvd Port Hueneme (93043) ***(P-4301)***
Wagner Construction Co (PA) .... C 619 873-2160
12512 Ca 67 Lakeside (92040) ***(P-3343)***
Wagner Financials, Manhattan Beach *Also called GBS Financial Corp* ***(P-17181)***
Wagner Heights Nursing & Rehab, Stockton *Also called Covenant Care California LLC* ***(P-20337)***
Wagner Jacobson Brokerage Inc .... E 323 872-1636
16400 Ventura Blvd # 333 Encino (91436) ***(P-11817)***
Wags & Wiggles Dog Daycare LLC (PA) .... D 949 635-9655
23171 Arroyo Vis Rcho STA Marg (92688) ***(P-635)***
Wah Hung Intl McHy Inc .... D 323 263-3513
800 Monterey Pass Rd Monterey Park (91754) ***(P-6613)***
Wakunaga of America Co Ltd (HQ) .... D 949 855-2776
23501 Madero Mission Viejo (92691) ***(P-8221)***
Walk Through Video, McClellan *Also called Villara Corporation* ***(P-2398)***
Walker & Dunlop Inc .... D 301 215-5500
12100 Wilshire Blvd # 1500 Los Angeles (90025) ***(P-9864)***
Walker & Zanger Inc (PA) .... D 818 280-8300
16719 Schoenborn St North Hills (91343) ***(P-6913)***
Walker Advertising LLC .... E 310 519-4050
20101 Hamilton Ave # 300 Torrance (90502) ***(P-13920)***
Walker Communications Inc .... D 707 421-1300
521 Railroad Ave Suisun City (94585) ***(P-2782)***
Walkme Inc (HQ) .... D 855 492-5563
525 Market St Lbby San Francisco (94105) ***(P-15540)***
Walkup Melodia Kelly .... E 415 981-7210
650 California St Fl 26 San Francisco (94108) ***(P-23424)***
Walkup Law Office, San Francisco *Also called Walkup Melodia Kelly* ***(P-23424)***
Wall Systems Inc .... D 805 523-9091
11975 Discovery Ct Moorpark (93021) ***(P-2978)***
Wall Tech, Diamond Bar *Also called March International Inc* ***(P-2044)***
Wallace-Kuhl & Associates, West Sacramento *Also called River Cy Geoprofessionals Inc* ***(P-25894)***
Wallace-Kuhl Investments LLC (PA) .... D 916 372-1434
3050 Industrial Blvd West Sacramento (95691) ***(P-25994)***
Wallis Fashions Inc .... C 510 763-8018
1100 8th Ave Oakland (94606) ***(P-17578)***
Wally Park, Los Angeles *Also called Lrw Investments LLC* ***(P-17693)***
Walnut Country, Concord *Also called Cowell Homeowners Association* ***(P-25144)***
Walnut Creek Active Club, Walnut Creek *Also called 24 Hour Fitness Usa Inc* ***(P-18567)***
Walnut Creek Embassy Suites, Walnut Creek *Also called Ashford Trs Nickel LLC* ***(P-12338)***
Walnut Creek Spt & Fitnes CLB, Walnut Creek *Also called Olympic Investors Ltd* ***(P-18994)***
Walnut Manor Care Center, Anaheim *Also called Front Porch Communities* ***(P-21069)***
Walnut Valley Unified Schl Dst .... D 909 595-1261
880 S Lemon Ave Walnut (91789) ***(P-25482)***
Walnut Valley Water District .... D 909 595-7554
271 Brea Canyon Rd Walnut (91789) ***(P-6318)***
Walnut Whtney Cnvalescent Hosp .... C 916 488-8601
3529 Walnut Ave Carmichael (95608) ***(P-20874)***
Walnut Whtney Convalecent Hosp, Carmichael *Also called Horizon West Inc* ***(P-20533)***
Walong Marketing Inc (PA) .... D 714 670-8899
6281 Regio Ave Buena Park (90620) ***(P-8901)***
Walpert Center, Hayward *Also called ARC of Alameda County* ***(P-24149)***
Walsh Group Inc .... D 530 221-4405
3135 Agassi Ln Redding (96002) ***(P-19084)***
Walsh Vineyards Management Inc .... C 707 255-1650
1125 Golden Gate Dr NAPA (94558) ***(P-11818)***
Walsworth Franklin & Bevins, Orange *Also called Walswrth Frnklin Bevins McCall* ***(P-23425)***
Walswrth Frnklin Bevins McCall (PA) .... D 714 634-2522
1 City Blvd W Ste 500 Orange (92868) ***(P-23425)***
Walt Disney Company .... D 916 780-1470
8265 Sierra College Blvd # 21 Roseville (95661) ***(P-5762)***
Walt Disney Company .... B 818 544-5009
532 Paula Ave Glendale (91201) ***(P-5847)***
Walt Disney Company .... B 818 295-3134
914 N Victory Blvd Burbank (91502) ***(P-5848)***
Walt Disney Company .... D 818 560-1268
121 E Buena Vista Burbank (91521) ***(P-5849)***
Walt Disney Company .... A 818 567-5590
3900 W Alameda Ave Rm 845 Burbank (91505) ***(P-18474)***
Walt Disney Company .... A 818 544-6500
1133 Flower St Glendale (91201) ***(P-18812)***
Walt Disney Company .... B 714 781-4532
1313 S Harbor Blvd Anaheim (92802) ***(P-4656)***
Walt Disney Company .... C 818 553-7333
650 S Buenavista St Burbank (91501) ***(P-18813)***
Walt Disney Company .... C 714 781-4278
1598 S Harbor Blvd Anaheim (92802) ***(P-13377)***
Walt Disney Company .... B 818 460-6655
500 S Buena Vista St Burbank (91521) ***(P-5850)***
Walt Disney Company .... A 818 560-1000
500 S Buena Vista St Burbank (91521) ***(P-5851)***
Walt Disney Company (PA) .... A 818 560-1000
500 S Buena Vista St Burbank (91521) ***(P-5852)***
Walt Disney Company .... C 818 553-4222
601 Circle Seven Dr Glendale (91201) ***(P-18153)***
Walt Disney Company .... B 818 560-1000
350 S Buena Vista St Burbank (91521) ***(P-5853)***
Walt Disney Family Museum .... D 415 345-6800
104 Montgomery St San Francisco (94129) ***(P-24920)***
Walt Disney Imagineering (HQ) .... A 818 544-6500
1401 Flower St Glendale (91201) ***(P-18233)***
Walt Disney Pictures and TV .... D 818 560-1000
500 S Buena Vista St Burbank (91521) ***(P-18255)***
Walt Disney Records Direct (HQ) .... A 818 560-1000
500 S Buena Vista St Burbank (91521) ***(P-18154)***
Walt Disney Studios, Burbank *Also called Walt Disney Company* ***(P-5853)***
Walter & Wolf, Fremont *Also called Walters & Wolf Glass Company* ***(P-3412)***
Walter Anderson Plumbing Inc .... C 619 449-7646
1830 John Towers Ave El Cajon (92020) ***(P-2403)***
Walter E McGuire RE Inc .... C 650 348-0222
360 Primrose Rd Burlingame (94010) ***(P-11819)***
Walter E McGuire RE Inc (PA) .... B 415 929-1500
2001 Lombard St San Francisco (94123) ***(P-11820)***
Walter E McGuire RE Inc .... E 415 296-0123
17 Bluxome St San Francisco (94107) ***(P-11821)***
Walter J Conn & Associates .... D 213 683-0500
800 W 6th St Ste 600 Los Angeles (90017) ***(P-26118)***
Walter Voss Cynthia RE Max .... D 562 434-5980
6695 E Pacific Coast Hwy # 150 Long Beach (90803) ***(P-11822)***
Walters & Wolf Glass Company (PA) .... C 510 490-1115
41450 Boscell Rd Fremont (94538) ***(P-3412)***
Walters & Wolf Interiors (PA) .... D 415 243-9400
41450 Boscell Rd Fremont (94538) ***(P-3089)***
Walters Family Partnership .... C 760 320-6868
400 E Tahquitz Canyon Way Palm Springs (92262) ***(P-13378)***
Walters Wholesale Electric Co (HQ) .... E 562 988-3100
2825 Temple Ave Signal Hill (90755) ***(P-7401)***
Walters Wholesale Electric Co .... C 714 784-1900
200 N Berry St Brea (92821) ***(P-7402)***
Walton Electric Corporation .... D 909 981-5051
755 N Central Ave Upland (91786) ***(P-2783)***
Walton Engineering Inc .... D 916 372-1888
3900 Commerce Dr West Sacramento (95691) ***(P-3605)***
Walz Group LLC (HQ) .... C 951 491-6800
27398 Via Industria Temecula (92590) ***(P-15541)***
Walz Postal Solutions, Temecula *Also called Walz Group LLC* ***(P-15541)***
Wamc Company Inc (PA) .... D 858 454-2753
7420 Clairemont Mesa Blvd San Diego (92111) ***(P-11139)***
Wannajob Inc .... D 562 426-5272
2710 Saint Louis Ave Signal Hill (90755) ***(P-14942)***
War Memorial Prfrmg Art Ctr, San Francisco *Also called City & County of San Francisco* ***(P-18356)***
Ward Enterprises .... B 209 358-0445
2679 Buhach Rd Atwater (95301) ***(P-14426)***
Ward, E B, Brisbane *Also called Edward B Ward & Company Inc* ***(P-7646)***
Wardlow 2 LP (PA) .... D 562 432-8066
333 S Grand Ave Ste 4070 Los Angeles (90071) ***(P-18005)***
Ware Disposal Inc .... C 714 834-0234
1451 Manhattan Ave Fullerton (92831) ***(P-6507)***
Ware Malcomb (PA) .... C 949 660-9128
10 Edelman Irvine (92618) ***(P-26119)***
Warehouse, Lancaster *Also called Michaels Stores Inc* ***(P-9235)***
Warehouse, El Segundo *Also called Infonet Services Corporation* ***(P-4578)***
Warehouse and Distribution, Mira Loma *Also called Triways Inc* ***(P-4382)***
Warfighter & Family Services .... D 619 556-7168
2375 Recreation Way San Diego (92136) ***(P-17579)***
Warfighter & Family Services C, San Diego *Also called Warfighter & Family Services* ***(P-17579)***
Warmington Homes (PA) .... C 714 434-4435
3090 Pullman St Costa Mesa (92626) ***(P-1364)***
Warmington Homes .... D 949 679-3100
15615 Alton Pkwy Ste 150 Irvine (92618) ***(P-1365)***
Warmington Homes .... C 925 866-6700
2400 Camino Ramon Ste 234 San Ramon (94583) ***(P-1366)***
Warmington Residental, San Ramon *Also called Warmington Homes* ***(P-1366)***
Warmington Residential Cal Inc .... C 714 557-5511
3090 Pullman St Costa Mesa (92626) ***(P-1258)***
Warner Bros Consumer Pdts Inc (HQ) .... C 818 954-7980
4001 W Olive Ave Burbank (91505) ***(P-27908)***
Warner Bros Distributing Inc .... C 818 954-6000
4000 Warner Blvd Bldg 154 Burbank (91522) ***(P-27089)***
Warner Bros Domestic TV Dist, Burbank *Also called Warner Bros Entertainment Inc* ***(P-18158)***
Warner Bros Entertainment Inc .... C 818 954-1817
4000 Warner Blvd Burbank (91522) ***(P-18155)***
Warner Bros Entertainment Inc .... B 818 954-7232
4000 Warner Blvd Burbank (91522) ***(P-18156)***
Warner Bros Entertainment Inc .... C 818 954-3000
4000 Warner Blvd Burbank (91522) ***(P-18157)***

Mergent e-mail: customerrelations@mergent.com
1518
2019 Directory of California
Wholesalers and Services Companies
(P-0000) Products & Services Section entry number
(PA)=Parent Co (HQ)=Headquarters (DH)=Div Headquarters

Warner Bros Entertainment Inc.....C.....818 954-5301
4000 Warner Blvd Bldg 118 Burbank (91522) ***(P-18158)***
Warner Bros Entertainment Inc.....C.....818 954-6000
4000 Warner Blvd Burbank (91522) ***(P-18159)***
Warner Bros Entertainment Inc (HQ).....A.....818 954-6000
4000 Warner Blvd Burbank (91522) ***(P-18160)***
Warner Bros Entertainment Inc.....C.....818 954-3000
4000 Warner Blvd Burbank (91522) ***(P-18161)***
Warner Bros Entertainment Inc.....C.....818 954-2181
4000 Warner Blvd Bldg 30 Burbank (91522) ***(P-18162)***
Warner Bros Home Entrmt Inc (HQ).....D.....818 954-6000
4000 Warner Blvd Bldg 160 Burbank (91522) ***(P-18163)***
Warner Bros Intl TV Dist Inc.....D.....818 954-6000
4000 Warner Blvd Burbank (91522) ***(P-18164)***
Warner Bros Records Inc (HQ).....B.....818 846-9090
3300 Warner Blvd Burbank (91505) ***(P-17580)***
Warner Bros Studio Facilities, Burbank *Also called Warner Bros Entertainment Inc* ***(P-18157)***
Warner Bros Transatlantic Inc (HQ).....A.....818 977-0018
4000 Warner Blvd Burbank (91522) ***(P-18249)***
Warner Bros Transatlantic Inc.....A.....818 977-6384
3300 W Olive Ave Ste 200 Burbank (91505) ***(P-18250)***
Warner Bros Transatlantic Inc.....A.....818 972-0777
3500 W Olive Ave Ste 1000 Burbank (91505) ***(P-18251)***
Warner Bros. Legal Department, Burbank *Also called Warner Bros Entertainment Inc* ***(P-18156)***
Warner Bros. Paint Department, Burbank *Also called Warner Bros Entertainment Inc* ***(P-18155)***
Warner Brothers Studios.....D.....818 954-5000
4000 Warner Blvd Burbank (91522) ***(P-18165)***
Warner Center Marriott Hotel, Woodland Hills *Also called Tr Warner Center LP* ***(P-13337)***
Warner Media LLC.....D.....661 344-1546
2014 W Avenue K Lancaster (93536) ***(P-5966)***
Warner Media LLC.....D.....805 421-4467
2650 Tapo Canyon Rd Simi Valley (93063) ***(P-5967)***
Warner Pacific Insur Svcs Inc (PA).....C.....408 298-4049
32110 Agoura Rd Westlake Village (91361) ***(P-10826)***
Warner Villa, Woodland Hills *Also called Topanga Villas Company* ***(P-11126)***
Warren Auto De Mexico LLC.....D.....858 794-7947
517 S Cedros Ave Solana Beach (92075) ***(P-9270)***
Warren Distributing Inc (PA).....D.....562 789-3360
8737 Dice Rd Santa Fe Springs (90670) ***(P-6685)***
Warren Drye Kelley.....D.....310 712-6100
10100 Santa Monica Blvd # 1050 Los Angeles (90067) ***(P-23426)***
Warren E & P, Long Beach *Also called Warren E&P Inc* ***(P-8973)***
Warren E&P Inc.....D.....877 587-9494
400 Oceangate Ste 200 Long Beach (90802) ***(P-8973)***
Warren Knox Roofing, Santa Cruz *Also called Forever Firewood Inc* ***(P-3157)***
Warren Security Systems Inc.....E.....415 456-7034
1305 Francisco Blvd E San Rafael (94901) ***(P-16951)***
Warrior Custom Golf Inc (PA).....C.....949 699-2499
15 Mason Irvine (92618) ***(P-7942)***
Warrior Golf, Irvine *Also called Warrior Custom Golf Inc* ***(P-7942)***
Warwick California Corporation.....D.....415 992-3809
490 Geary St San Francisco (94102) ***(P-13379)***
Warwick Hotel San Francisco, San Francisco *Also called Warwick California Corporation* ***(P-13379)***
Wash Mltfmily Ldry Systems LLC (PA).....C.....310 643-8491
100 N Pacific Coast Hwy El Segundo (90245) ***(P-13562)***
Washington Enterprises 3 LLC.....D.....323 731-0861
2300 W Washington Blvd Los Angeles (90018) ***(P-20875)***
Washington Group, Del Mar *Also called Aecom Energy & Cnstr Inc* ***(P-1713)***
Washington Group, La Mirada *Also called Aecom Energy & Cnstr Inc* ***(P-25508)***
Washington Inn LLC.....D.....310 821-4455
737 Washington Blvd Marina Del Rey (90292) ***(P-13380)***
Washington Inventory Service (HQ).....C.....858 565-8111
9265 Sky Park Ct Ste 100 San Diego (92123) ***(P-17581)***
Washington Inventory Service.....D.....619 461-8198
7150 El Cajon Blvd San Diego (92115) ***(P-17582)***
Washington Iron Works, Gardena *Also called Washington Orna Ir Works Inc* ***(P-3606)***
Washington Mutual, Studio City *Also called Jpmorgan Chase Bank Nat Assn* ***(P-9350)***
Washington Orna Ir Works Inc (PA).....D.....310 327-8660
17926 S Broadway Gardena (90248) ***(P-3606)***
Washington Otptent Surgery Ctr, Fremont *Also called Washington Outpatient* ***(P-21912)***
Washington Outpatient.....D.....510 791-5374
2299 Mowry Ave Fl 1 Fremont (94538) ***(P-21912)***
Washington Township.....A.....510 797-3342
2000 Mowry Ave Fremont (94538) ***(P-21913)***
Wasser Filtration Inc.....D.....714 525-0630
1215 N Fee Ana St Anaheim (92807) ***(P-7819)***
Wasserman Comden & Casselman (PA).....D.....323 872-0995
5567 Reseda Blvd Ste 330 Tarzana (91356) ***(P-23427)***
Wasserman Media Group LLC (PA).....C.....310 407-0200
10900 Wilshire Blvd Los Angeles (90024) ***(P-27519)***
Waste Connections, Diamond Springs *Also called County of El Dorado* ***(P-6384)***
Waste Connections Cal Inc.....C.....408 752-8530
301 Carl Rd Sunnyvale (94089) ***(P-6508)***
Waste Connections Cal Inc (HQ).....C.....408 282-4400
1333 Oakland Rd San Jose (95112) ***(P-6509)***
Waste Management, Visalia *Also called USA Waste of California Inc* ***(P-6487)***
Waste Management, Gold River *Also called USA Waste of California Inc* ***(P-6490)***
Waste Management, Castroville *Also called Ajax Portable Services* ***(P-14469)***
Waste Management, Atascadero *Also called USA Waste of California Inc* ***(P-6493)***
Waste Management, El Cajon *Also called USA Waste of California Inc* ***(P-6494)***
Waste Management, Chino *Also called USA Waste of California Inc* ***(P-6495)***
Waste Management Cal Inc (HQ).....C.....877 836-6526
9081 Tujunga Ave Sun Valley (91352) ***(P-6510)***
Waste Management Cal Inc.....D.....619 596-5100
1001 W Bradley Ave El Cajon (92020) ***(P-6511)***
Waste Management Cal Inc.....D.....661 947-7197
1200 W City Ranch Rd Palmdale (93551) ***(P-6512)***
Waste Management Cal Inc.....D.....760 439-2824
2141 Oceanside Blvd Oceanside (92054) ***(P-6513)***
Waste Management Nevada County, Grass Valley *Also called USA Waste of California Inc* ***(P-4080)***
Waste Management Orange County, Santa Ana *Also called USA Waste of California Inc* ***(P-6503)***
Waste Managment, Corning *Also called Andersncttonwood Disposal Svcs* ***(P-3971)***
Waste MGT Collectn & Recycl.....C.....951 242-0421
17700 Indian St Moreno Valley (92551) ***(P-6514)***
Waste Mgt Collectn & Recycl.....C.....626 960-7551
5701 S Eastrn Ave Ste 300 Commerce (90040) ***(P-6515)***
Waste Mgt Collectn & Recycl.....C.....925 935-8900
2658 N Main St Walnut Creek (94597) ***(P-4086)***
Waste Mgt Collectn & Recycl.....D.....831 768-9505
1340 W Beach St Watsonville (95076) ***(P-6516)***
Waste MGT Collectn & Recycl.....D.....707 462-0210
219 Pudding Creek Rd Fort Bragg (95437) ***(P-6517)***
Waste MGT Collectn & Recycl.....D.....909 242-0421
17700 Indian St Moreno Valley (92551) ***(P-6518)***
Waste MGT Collectn & Recycl.....D.....707 462-0210
450 Orr Springs Rd Ukiah (95482) ***(P-6519)***
Waste MGT Collectn Recycl Inc.....B.....714 637-3010
1800 S Grand Ave Santa Ana (92705) ***(P-14461)***
Waste MGT Collectn Recycl Inc.....D.....949 451-2600
16122 Construction Cir E Irvine (92606) ***(P-6520)***
Waste MGT of Alameda Cnty (HQ).....A.....510 613-8710
172 98th Ave Oakland (94603) ***(P-6521)***
Waste MGT of Alameda Cnty.....D.....510 638-2303
2615 Davis St San Leandro (94577) ***(P-6522)***
Wastexperts Incorporated.....D.....925 484-1057
440 Boulder Ct Ste 200 Pleasanton (94566) ***(P-27090)***
Watch Resources Inc (PA).....D.....209 533-0510
12801 Cabezut Rd Sonora (95370) ***(P-24127)***
Watchit Media Inc.....C.....702 740-1700
655 Montgomery St # 1000 San Francisco (94111) ***(P-18166)***
Water & Power Department, Long Beach *Also called County of Los Angeles* ***(P-6233)***
Water & Sewer Service.....D.....925 828-8524
7051 Dublin Blvd Dublin (94568) ***(P-1999)***
Water Course Way, Palo Alto *Also called Watercourse Way* ***(P-13779)***
Water Division, Fresno *Also called City of Fresno* ***(P-6222)***
Water Drops Express Carwash, Santa Monica *Also called Alisam Oxnard Operating* ***(P-10849)***
Water Emergency Dispatch, Long Beach *Also called City of Long Beach* ***(P-6225)***
Water Heaters Only Inc.....D.....650 368-9998
3620 Haven Ave Redwood City (94063) ***(P-7431)***
Water Quality Control Plant, Palo Alto *Also called City of Palo Alto* ***(P-17080)***
Water Resources Cal Dept.....E.....916 324-3812
1416 9th St Rm 1225 Sacramento (95814) ***(P-16260)***
Water Resources Control Bd Cal.....D.....619 521-3010
2375 Northside Dr Ste 100 San Diego (92108) ***(P-24990)***
Water Resources Division, Livermore *Also called City of Livermore* ***(P-2023)***
Water Supply, Vacaville *Also called County of Solano* ***(P-6236)***
Water Svcs Operations & Repr, Oxnard *Also called City of Oxnard* ***(P-6228)***
Watercourse Way.....C.....650 462-2000
165 Channing Ave Palo Alto (94301) ***(P-13779)***
Waterfall Resort.....D.....805 879-3780
5951 Encina Rd Ste 207 Goleta (93117) ***(P-13381)***
Waterfront Hotel LLC.....B.....714 845-8000
21100 Pacific Coast Hwy Huntington Beach (92648) ***(P-13382)***
Waterfront Plaza Hotel LLC.....D.....510 836-3800
10 Washington St Oakland (94607) ***(P-13383)***
Waterhill Ltd.....E.....626 369-6828
140 N Orange Ave City of Industry (91744) ***(P-6743)***
Waterhouse Management Corp.....C.....916 772-4918
500 Giuseppe Ct Ste 2 Roseville (95678) ***(P-11160)***
Waterline Data Science Inc.....D.....650 868-4409
615 National Ave Ste 100 Mountain View (94043) ***(P-15542)***
Waterman Convalescent Hospital.....C.....951 681-2200
6401 33rd St Riverside (92509) ***(P-22057)***
Waterman Convalescent Hospital (PA).....C.....909 882-1215
1850 N Waterman Ave San Bernardino (92404) ***(P-20876)***
Watermark Rtrment Cmmnties Inc.....D.....760 346-5420
41505 Carlotta Dr Palm Desert (92211) ***(P-20877)***
Watermark Rtrment Cmmnties Inc.....D.....858 597-8000
3890 Nobel Dr San Diego (92122) ***(P-11823)***
Waters Edge Inc.....C.....510 748-4300
2401 Blanding Ave Alameda (94501) ***(P-20878)***
Waters Edge Lodge.....E.....510 769-6264
801 Island Dr Apt 267 Alameda (94502) ***(P-24717)***
Waters Edge Nursing Home, Alameda *Also called Waters Edge Inc* ***(P-20878)***
Waters Moving & Storage Inc.....D.....925 372-0914
37 Bridgehead Rd Martinez (94553) ***(P-4389)***
Waterworks Park, Redding *Also called Slideco Recreation Inc* ***(P-18811)***
Waterworld USA, Concord *Also called Parc Management LLC* ***(P-19214)***
Waterworld USA, Sacramento *Also called Six Flags Entertainment Corp* ***(P-18810)***
Watg, Irvine *Also called Wimberly Allison Tong Goo Inc* ***(P-26124)***
Watkin & Bortolussi Inc.....D.....415 453-4675
726 Alfred Nobel Dr Hercules (94547) ***(P-960)***
Watkins Construction Co Inc.....D.....661 763-5395
112 E Cedar St Taft (93268) ***(P-2000)***
Watlow Electric Mfg Co.....D.....408 776-6646
6781 Via Del Oro San Jose (95119) ***(P-25995)***

ALPHABETIC

Employee Codes: A=Over 500 employees, B=251-500 C=101-250, D=51-100, E=50
2019 Directory of California Wholesalers and Services Companies

1519

Watson Carton ....D.......408 979-9618
4178 Ross Ave San Jose (95124) ***(P-24857)***
Watson Cogeneration Co Inc ....D.......310 816-8100
22850 Wilmington Ave Carson (90745) ***(P-6148)***
Watson Contractors Inc ....D.......916 481-6293
3185 Longview Dr Sacramento (95821) ***(P-1449)***
Watsonville Coast Produce Inc ....C.......831 722-3851
275 Kearney Ext Frnt Watsonville (95076) ***(P-8745)***
Watsonville Health Clinic, Watsonville *Also called Santa Cruz County of* ***(P-19856)***
Watsonville Nursing Center, Watsonville *Also called CF Watsonville East LLC* ***(P-20305)***
Watsonville Post Acute Center, Watsonville *Also called CF Watsonville LLC* ***(P-20304)***
Watsonville Post Acute Center, Watsonville *Also called CF Watsonville West LLC* ***(P-20306)***
Watt Commercial Properties, Santa Monica *Also called Watt Properties Inc* ***(P-11936)***
Watt Properties Inc (PA) ....D.......310 314-2430
2716 Ocean Park Blvd # 2025 Santa Monica (90405) ***(P-11936)***
Watts Health Center, Los Angeles *Also called Watts Health Foundation Inc* ***(P-12132)***
Watts Health Foundation Inc (HQ) ....B.......310 424-2220
3405 W Imperial Hwy # 304 Inglewood (90303) ***(P-20971)***
Watts Health Foundation Inc ....B.......323 357-6688
10300 Compton Ave Los Angeles (90002) ***(P-12132)***
Watts Healthcare Corporation ....C.......323 241-1780
700 W Imperial Hwy Los Angeles (90044) ***(P-20091)***
Watts Healthcare Corporation (PA) ....C.......323 564-4331
10300 Compton Ave Los Angeles (90002) ***(P-20092)***
Watts Labor Community Action ....C.......323 563-5639
958 E 108th St Los Angeles (90059) ***(P-24128)***
Wave Plastic Surgery Ctr Inc ....B.......626 964-7788
18433 Colima Rd La Puente (91748) ***(P-20093)***
Wavestrong Inc ....D.......925 549-2882
5674 Stoneridge Dr # 225 Pleasanton (94588) ***(P-16075)***
Wawanesa General Insurance Co ....B.......619 285-6020
9050 Friars Rd Ste 200 San Diego (92108) ***(P-10413)***
Wawansea General Insurance, San Diego *Also called Wawanesa General Insurance Co* ***(P-10413)***
Wawona Packing Co LLC ....A.......559 528-4000
12133 Avenue 408 Cutler (93615) ***(P-585)***
Wawona Packing Co LLC ....B.......559 528-4699
12133 Avenue 408 Cutler (93615) ***(P-17583)***
Waxies Enterprises Inc ....C.......909 942-3100
905 Wineville Ave Ontario (91764) ***(P-7901)***
Waxies Enterprises Inc ....E.......925 454-2900
901 N Canyon Pkwy Livermore (94551) ***(P-7902)***
Way Cool Homecare Inc ....E.......619 444-3200
900 N Cuyamaca St Ste 201 El Cajon (92020) ***(P-22462)***
Way Forward Technology Inc ....E.......661 286-2769
28738 The Old Rd Valencia (91355) ***(P-15543)***
Waymakers (PA) ....D.......714 492-1010
1221 E Dyer Rd Ste 120 Santa Ana (92705) ***(P-24129)***
Wayne E Swisher Cem Contr Inc ....D.......925 757-3660
2620 E 18th St Antioch (94509) ***(P-3344)***
Wayne Maples Plumbing & Htg ....D.......707 445-2500
317 W Cedar St Eureka (95501) ***(P-2404)***
Wayne Perry Inc (PA) ....C.......714 826-0352
8281 Commonwealth Ave Buena Park (90621) ***(P-3607)***
Wayne Provision Co Inc (PA) ....D.......323 277-5888
5030 Gifford Ave Vernon (90058) ***(P-8633)***
Wayne R Kidder ....D.......805 967-6993
915 Via Los Padres Santa Barbara (93111) ***(P-20094)***
Waypoint Real Estate Group LLC ....D.......510 250-2200
1999 Harrison St Fl 22nd Oakland (94612) ***(P-11824)***
Wb Electric Inc ....D.......408 842-7911
30611 Road 400 Coarsegold (93614) ***(P-2784)***
Wca, Los Angeles *Also called West Coast Ambulance Corp* ***(P-3858)***
Wcct Global Inc (PA) ....D.......714 668-1500
5630 Cerritos Ave Cypress (90630) ***(P-26672)***
Wcg World, San Francisco *Also called Weisscomm Group Ltd* ***(P-27909)***
WCIRB, Oakland *Also called Workers Compensation* ***(P-10416)***
WCO Hotels Inc (HQ) ....D.......323 636-3251
1150 W Magic Way Anaheim (92802) ***(P-13384)***
WD Partners Inc ....E.......949 753-7676
16808 Armstrong Ave # 100 Irvine (92606) ***(P-26120)***
Wdc Explrtion Wells Holdg Corp ....C.......916 419-6043
1300 National Dr Ste 140 Sacramento (95834) ***(P-2001)***
Wdi, Santa Fe Springs *Also called Warren Distributing Inc* ***(P-6685)***
Wdm Group, San Diego *Also called White Digital Media Inc* ***(P-9122)***
Wdpt Film Distribution LLC ....C.......818 560-1000
500 S Buena Vista St Burbank (91521) ***(P-7561)***
We Care Day Care & Pre School ....D.......209 832-4072
1790 Sequoia Blvd Tracy (95376) ***(P-24397)***
We Pack It All, Duarte *Also called Bershtel Enterprises LLC* ***(P-17030)***
We See Dragons LLC ....C.......310 361-5700
1100 Glendon Ave Ste 1700 Los Angeles (90024) ***(P-16530)***
We Team Security Firm Inc ....D.......800 745-9051
12655 W Jefferson Blvd Los Angeles (90066) ***(P-16856)***
Wealth Educators Inc ....C.......310 623-9145
5209 Wilshire Blvd Los Angeles (90036) ***(P-27091)***
Wealthtv, San Diego *Also called Herring Broadcasting Company* ***(P-5798)***
Weatherford International LLC ....D.......805 781-3580
1880 Santa Barbara Ave # 220 San Luis Obispo (93401) ***(P-1085)***
Weatherford International LLC ....D.......661 587-9753
21728 Rosedale Hwy Bakersfield (93314) ***(P-1086)***
WEAVE, Sacramento *Also called WEAVE Incorporated* ***(P-14943)***
WEAVE Incorporated (PA) ....D.......916 448-2321
1900 K St Ste 200 Sacramento (95811) ***(P-14943)***
Web Traffic School, Oakland *Also called Interactive Solutions Inc* ***(P-15716)***
Webasto Charging Systems Inc (HQ) ....D.......626 415-4000
800 Royal Oaks Dr Ste 210 Monrovia (91016) ***(P-6686)***
Webb Sunrise Inc ....E.......619 220-7050
3320 Kemper St Ste 201 San Diego (92110) ***(P-9271)***
Webcor Builders, Alameda *Also called Webcor Construction LP* ***(P-1696)***
Webcor Construction LP (HQ) ....D.......510 748-1900
1751 Harbor Bay Pkwy # 200 Alameda (94502) ***(P-1696)***
Weber Distribution LLC (PA) ....B.......855 469-3237
13530 Rosecrans Ave Santa Fe Springs (90670) ***(P-4518)***
Weber Distribution Cwo, Rancho Cucamonga *Also called Weber Distribution Warehouses* ***(P-4657)***
Weber Distribution Warehouses ....E.......909 481-1600
9345 Santa Anita Ave B Rancho Cucamonga (91730) ***(P-4657)***
Weber Distribution Warehouses ....E.......562 404-9996
15301 Shoemaker Ave Norwalk (90650) ***(P-4658)***
Weber Logistics, Santa Fe Springs *Also called Weber Distribution LLC* ***(P-4518)***
Weber Shandwick ....D.......415 262-5600
600 Battery St Fl 1 San Francisco (94111) ***(P-27572)***
Webers Quality Meats Inc ....D.......510 635-9892
990 Carden St San Leandro (94577) ***(P-8634)***
Webex.com, San Jose *Also called Cisco Webex LLC* ***(P-17076)***
Webly Systems Inc ....E.......888 444-6400
2603 Camino Ramon Ste 200 San Ramon (94583) ***(P-17584)***
Webpass Inc ....D.......415 233-4100
267 8th St San Francisco (94103) ***(P-5676)***
Webster Investment Management, San Francisco *Also called Forward Management LLC* ***(P-10080)***
Webyog Inc ....C.......408 512-1434
2900 Gordon Ave 100-7p Santa Clara (95051) ***(P-15544)***
Weckworth Construction Co Inc ....D.......916 939-6636
3941 Park Dr Ste 20-373 El Dorado Hills (95762) ***(P-2785)***
Weckworth Electric Company, El Dorado Hills *Also called Weckworth Construction Co Inc* ***(P-2785)***
Weco - Us.ca. El Centro, El Centro *Also called Wilbur-Ellis Company LLC* ***(P-9106)***
Weco Aerospace Systems, Lincoln *Also called Weygandt & Associates* ***(P-18007)***
Weco Aerospace Systems, Lincoln *Also called Gdsa-Lincoln Inc* ***(P-17904)***
Wedbush Securities Inc (HQ) ....B.......213 688-8000
1000 Wilshire Blvd # 800 Los Angeles (90017) ***(P-10035)***
Wedgewood Hspitality Group Inc ....E.......951 491-8110
43385 Business Park Dr Temecula (92590) ***(P-13780)***
Wedgewood Inc (PA) ....D.......310 640-3070
2015 Manhattan Beach Blvd # 100 Redondo Beach (90278) ***(P-12280)***
Wedriveu Holdings Inc ....D.......650 579-5800
700 Airport Blvd Ste 250 Burlingame (94010) ***(P-14797)***
Weeks Drilling and Pump Co (PA) ....E.......707 823-3184
6100 Highway 12 Sebastopol (95472) ***(P-2405)***
Weeks Roses, Wasco *Also called Early Morning LLC* ***(P-256)***
WEI-Chuan USA Inc (PA) ....C.......323 587-2101
6655 Garfield Ave Bell Gardens (90201) ***(P-8509)***
Weil Gotshal & Manges LLP ....C.......650 802-3000
201 Redwood Shors Pkwy Redwood City (94065) ***(P-23428)***
Weinberg Roger & Resenfeld (PA) ....D.......510 337-1001
1001 Marina Village Pkwy # 200 Alameda (94501) ***(P-23429)***
Weingart Center Association ....C.......213 622-6359
566 S San Pedro St Los Angeles (90013) ***(P-24130)***
Weingart Center For Homeless, Los Angeles *Also called Weingart Center Association* ***(P-24130)***
Weingart-Lakewood Family YMCA, Lakewood *Also called Young Mens Chrstn Assc Gr L B* ***(P-25336)***
Weinstein Company LLC ....D.......424 204-4800
9100 Wilshire Blvd 700w Beverly Hills (90212) ***(P-18167)***
Weinstein Construction Corp ....E.......818 782-4000
15102 Raymer St Van Nuys (91405) ***(P-1697)***
Weintraub Tobin Chediak ....E.......310 858-7888
9665 Wilshire Blvd # 900 Beverly Hills (90212) ***(P-23430)***
Weintraub Tobin Chediak (PA) ....E.......916 558-6000
400 Capitol Mall Fl 11 Sacramento (95814) ***(P-23431)***
Weiss Associates, Emeryville *Also called Aguatierra Associates Inc* ***(P-27575)***
Weisscomm Group Ltd (PA) ....D.......415 362-5018
50 Francisco St Ste 400 San Francisco (94133) ***(P-27909)***
Weitz & Luxenberg PC ....D.......310 247-0921
1880 Century Park E # 700 Los Angeles (90067) ***(P-23432)***
Welcome Baby, Anaheim *Also called Orange County Child Abuse* ***(P-23952)***
Welcome Group Management LLC ....D.......310 378-6666
300 S Court St Visalia (93291) ***(P-13385)***
Weldlogic Inc ....D.......805 375-1670
2651 Lavery Ct Newbury Park (91320) ***(P-17926)***
Welfare Administration, Oroville *Also called County of Butte* ***(P-23629)***
Welfare Department, Sonora *Also called County of Tuolumne* ***(P-23754)***
Welfare Dept, Pomona *Also called City of Pomona* ***(P-24752)***
Welfare Dept Warehouse, Oroville *Also called County of Butte* ***(P-23630)***
Welk Group Inc (PA) ....B.......760 749-3000
8860 Lawrence Welk Dr Escondido (92026) ***(P-13386)***
Welk Music Group, Escondido *Also called Welk Group Inc* ***(P-13386)***
Welk Resort Center, San Marcos *Also called Welk Resort Group Inc* ***(P-11825)***
Welk Resort Group Inc (PA) ....E.......760 652-4913
300 Rancheros Dr Ste 450 San Marcos (92069) ***(P-11825)***
Welker Bros, Milpitas *Also called H V Welker Co Inc* ***(P-3104)***
Well Being Group Inc ....D.......559 432-3737
7075 N Howard St Ste 102 Fresno (93720) ***(P-22463)***
Well Within Spa ....D.......831 458-9355
417 Cedar St Santa Cruz (95060) ***(P-3608)***
Wellhead Electric Company Inc ....E.......916 447-5171
650 Bercut Dr Ste C Sacramento (95811) ***(P-6149)***
Wellington, The, Laguna Hills *Also called Birtcher/Aetna Laguna Hills* ***(P-10988)***
Wellmade Products, Merced *Also called WLMD* ***(P-3612)***
Wellpoint Inc ....C.......805 375-1605
319 N San Dimas Ave Ste F San Dimas (91773) ***(P-10151)***

Mergent e-mail: customerrelations@mergent.com
1520
2019 Directory of California
Wholesalers and Services Companies
(P-0000) Products & Services Section entry number
(PA)=Parent Co (HQ)=Headquarters (DH)=Div Headquarters

Wells & Bennett Realtors (PA)....D....510 531-7000
1451 Leimert Blvd Oakland (94602) ***(P-11826)***
Wells Fargo & Company (PA)....C....866 249-3302
420 Montgomery St Frnt San Francisco (94104) ***(P-9378)***
Wells Fargo Advisors, Los Angeles *Also called Wells Fargo Clearing Svcs LLC* ***(P-10036)***
Wells Fargo Advisors, San Francisco *Also called Wells Fargo Clearing Svcs LLC* ***(P-10037)***
Wells Fargo Advisors, La Jolla *Also called Wells Fargo Clearing Svcs LLC* ***(P-10038)***
Wells Fargo Advisors, Seal Beach *Also called Wells Fargo Clearing Svcs LLC* ***(P-10039)***
Wells Fargo Advisors, Woodland Hills *Also called Wells Fargo Clearing Svcs LLC* ***(P-10040)***
Wells Fargo Asset Management....B....415 396-8000
525 Market St Fl 10 San Francisco (94105) ***(P-12052)***
Wells Fargo Bank Ltd....D....213 253-6227
333 S Grand Ave Ste 500 Los Angeles (90071) ***(P-9379)***
Wells Fargo Bank NA....C....213 628-2251
333 S Hope St Ste D100 Los Angeles (90071) ***(P-9380)***
Wells Fargo Bank National Assn....E....818 766-7172
10225 Riverside Dr Toluca Lake (91602) ***(P-9381)***
Wells Fargo Bank National Assn....E....415 396-6267
120 Kearny St Ste 1750 San Francisco (94108) ***(P-9382)***
Wells Fargo Bank National Assn....D....415 396-6161
1 Montgomery St Ste 200 San Francisco (94104) ***(P-9383)***
Wells Fargo Bank National Assn....D....209 578-6810
1120 K St Modesto (95354) ***(P-9384)***
Wells Fargo Bank National Assn....E....408 998-3714
2170 Tully Rd San Jose (95122) ***(P-9385)***
Wells Fargo Bank National Assn....D....858 622-6958
4365 Executive Dr Fl 18 San Diego (92121) ***(P-9386)***
Wells Fargo Bank National Assn....D....707 259-5552
901 Main St NAPA (94559) ***(P-9387)***
Wells Fargo Bank National Assn....D....925 746-3718
1655 Grant St Concord (94520) ***(P-9388)***
Wells Fargo Bank National Assn....B....626 312-3006
9000 Flair Dr Fl 3 El Monte (91731) ***(P-9389)***
Wells Fargo Bank National Assn....A....858 454-0362
7714 Girard Ave La Jolla (92037) ***(P-9390)***
Wells Fargo Bank National Assn....D....916 724-2982
5007 Foothills Blvd Roseville (95747) ***(P-9391)***
Wells Fargo Bank National Assn....E....408 378-8155
60 W Hamilton Ave Campbell (95008) ***(P-9392)***
Wells Fargo Bank National Assn....B....415 777-9497
100 Spear St Ste 100 # 100 San Francisco (94105) ***(P-9393)***
Wells Fargo Bank National Assn....B....916 774-2249
1620 E Roseville Pkwy Roseville (95661) ***(P-9394)***
Wells Fargo Bank National Assn....C....626 573-1338
3440 Flair Dr El Monte (91731) ***(P-9395)***
Wells Fargo Bank National Assn....E....510 276-0875
16000 Hesperian Blvd San Lorenzo (94580) ***(P-9396)***
Wells Fargo Bank National Assn....D....510 792-3512
39265 Paseo Padre Pkwy Fremont (94538) ***(P-9397)***
Wells Fargo Bank National Assn....D....510 266-0595
950 Southland Dr Hayward (94545) ***(P-9398)***
Wells Fargo Bank National Assn....E....916 440-4570
2301 Watt Ave Sacramento (95825) ***(P-9399)***
Wells Fargo Bank National Assn....D....925 463-1983
5798 Stoneridge Mall Rd Pleasanton (94588) ***(P-9400)***
Wells Fargo Bank National Assn....D....310 831-0632
28350 S Western Ave Rancho Palos Verdes (90275) ***(P-9401)***
Wells Fargo Bank National Assn....C....415 222-6834
455 Market Fremont (94536) ***(P-9402)***
Wells Fargo Bank National Assn....D....805 541-0143
665 Marsh St San Luis Obispo (93401) ***(P-9403)***
Wells Fargo Bank National Assn....A....415 394-4021
420 Montgomery St Fl 6 San Francisco (94104) ***(P-9404)***
Wells Fargo Bank National Assn....D....510 530-3095
2220 Mountain Blvd # 160 Oakland (94611) ***(P-9405)***
Wells Fargo Bank National Assn....E....562 924-1616
18712 Gridley Rd Cerritos (90703) ***(P-9406)***
Wells Fargo Bank National Assn....B....510 745-5025
3440 Walnut Ave Fl 3 Fremont (94538) ***(P-9407)***
Wells Fargo Bank National Assn....C....310 285-5817
433 N Camden Dr Ste 1200 Beverly Hills (90210) ***(P-9408)***
Wells Fargo Capital Fin Inc (HQ)....C....310 453-7300
2450 Colo Ave 3000w 3rd 3000 3rd Santa Monica (90404) ***(P-17585)***
Wells Fargo Capital Fin LLC (HQ)....D....310 453-7300
2450 Colo Ave Ste 3000w Santa Monica (90404) ***(P-9765)***
Wells Fargo Clearing Svcs LLC....E....213 486-5200
777 S Figueroa St # 4700 Los Angeles (90017) ***(P-10036)***
Wells Fargo Clearing Svcs LLC....C....415 291-1200
555 California St # 2300 San Francisco (94104) ***(P-10037)***
Wells Fargo Clearing Svcs LLC....E....858 456-7706
888 Prospect St Ste 220 La Jolla (92037) ***(P-10038)***
Wells Fargo Clearing Svcs LLC....E....562 594-1220
3020 Old Ranch Pkwy # 190 Seal Beach (90740) ***(P-10039)***
Wells Fargo Clearing Svcs LLC....D....818 226-2222
5820 Canoga Ave Ste 100 Woodland Hills (91367) ***(P-10040)***
Wells Fargo Coml Dist Fin LLC....D....916 636-2020
3100 Zinfandel Dr Ste 255 Rancho Cordova (95670) ***(P-9750)***
Wells Fargo Dealer Svcs Inc (HQ)....B....949 727-1002
23 Pasteur Irvine (92618) ***(P-9728)***
Wells Fargo Home Mortgage Inc....E....916 782-2221
3010 Lava Ridge Ct # 150 Roseville (95661) ***(P-9409)***
Wells Fargo Home Mortgage Inc....B....760 603-7000
5540 Fermi Ct Fl 2002 Carlsbad (92008) ***(P-9865)***
Wells Fargo Intl Bond CIT....C....415 396-4943
525 Market St Fl 10 San Francisco (94105) ***(P-12053)***
Wells Fargo Securities LLC....D....415 645-0800
600 California St Fl 17 San Francisco (94108) ***(P-10041)***
Wells Hse Hspice Fundation Inc....D....714 952-3795
245 Cherry Ave Long Beach (90802) ***(P-20879)***
Wellspace Health (PA)....D....916 325-5556
1820 J St Sacramento (95811) ***(P-22714)***
WELLSPRING, Sacramento *Also called Positive Option Family Service* ***(P-23975)***
Wendel Rosen Black & Dean LLP (PA)....D....510 834-6600
1111 Broadway Fl 24 Oakland (94607) ***(P-23433)***
Wendt Landscape Services Inc....D....949 589-8680
29714 Avenida De Las Rancho Santa Margari (92688) ***(P-961)***
Wendy's, Modesto *Also called Pacwend III Inc* ***(P-26977)***
Wendy's, Modesto *Also called Pacwend Inc* ***(P-26976)***
Wenmat Inc....D....916 485-0714
6001 Fair Oaks Blvd Carmichael (95608) ***(P-25483)***
Wentworth Hauser & Violich Inc....D....415 981-6911
301 Battery St Fl 4 San Francisco (94111) ***(P-10121)***
Wenzlau Engineering Inc....D....310 604-3400
2950 E Harcourt St Compton (90221) ***(P-7562)***
WERM Investments LLC....E....213 627-8070
14242 Ventura Blvd # 212 Sherman Oaks (91423) ***(P-18475)***
Wermers Multi-Family Corp....C....858 535-1475
5120 Shoreham Pl Ste 150 San Diego (92122) ***(P-1325)***
Werner Enterprises Inc....E....909 823-5803
10251 Calabash Ave Fontana (92335) ***(P-4302)***
Wesco Aircraft, Valencia *Also called Falcon Aerospace Holdings LLC* ***(P-26857)***
Wesco Aircraft Hardware Corp (HQ)....B....661 775-7200
24911 Avenue Stanford Valencia (91355) ***(P-7918)***
Wesco Aircraft Hardware Corp....B....661 775-7200
27727 Avenue Scott Valencia (91355) ***(P-7919)***
Wesco Aircraft Holdings Inc (PA)....D....661 775-7200
24911 Avenue Stanford Valencia (91355) ***(P-27092)***
Wescom Central Credit Union (PA)....B....888 493-7266
123 S Marengo Ave Pasadena (91101) ***(P-9662)***
Wescom Holdings LLC (HQ)....D....888 493-7266
123 S Marengo Ave Pasadena (91101) ***(P-10827)***
Wescon Technology Inc....C....408 727-8818
4655 Old Ironsides Dr # 170 Santa Clara (95054) ***(P-16076)***
Wescordon Incorporated (PA)....C....559 784-8371
661 W Poplar Ave Porterville (93257) ***(P-20880)***
Weslar Inc....D....661 702-1362
28310 Constellation Rd Valencia (91355) ***(P-3090)***
Weslend Financial, Santa Ana *Also called Lenox Financial Mortgage Corp* ***(P-9825)***
Wesley Palms, San Diego *Also called Front Porch Communities* ***(P-11023)***
West Air Inc....D....559 454-7843
5005 E Andersen Ave Fresno (93727) ***(P-4853)***
West Anaheim Care Center, Anaheim *Also called West Anaheim Extended Care* ***(P-20881)***
West Anaheim Extended Care....C....714 821-1993
645 S Beach Blvd Anaheim (92804) ***(P-20881)***
WEST ANAHEIM MEDICAL CENTER, Anaheim *Also called Prime Healthcare Anaheim LLC* ***(P-21656)***
West Antlope Vly Hstorical Soc....D....661 945-5369
45026 11th St W Lancaster (93534) ***(P-24921)***
West Central Food Service, Norwalk *Also called West Central Produce Inc* ***(P-8746)***
West Central Produce Inc....B....213 629-3600
12840 Leyva St Norwalk (90650) ***(P-8746)***
West Cntinela Vly Care Ctr Inc....D....310 674-3216
950 S Flower St Inglewood (90301) ***(P-20882)***
West Coast AC Co Inc....C....619 561-8000
1155 Pioneer Way Ste 101 El Cajon (92020) ***(P-2406)***
West Coast Aggregate Supply....E....760 342-7598
92500 Airport Blvd Thermal (92274) ***(P-1096)***
West Coast Air Conditioning, Oxnard *Also called Gmh Inc* ***(P-17895)***
West Coast Ambulance Corp....C....310 435-1862
6739 S Victoria Ave Los Angeles (90043) ***(P-3858)***
West Coast Arborists Inc....E....909 783-6544
21718 Walnut Ave Grand Terrace (92313) ***(P-983)***
West Coast Aviation Svcs LLC (PA)....E....949 852-8340
19711 Campus Dr Ste 200 Santa Ana (92707) ***(P-27520)***
West Coast Charters, Santa Ana *Also called West Coast Aviation Svcs LLC* ***(P-27520)***
West Coast Childrens Center....E....510 269-9030
545 Ashbury Ave El Cerrito (94530) ***(P-20095)***
West Coast Construction, Riverside *Also called Perry Coast Construction Inc* ***(P-1614)***
West Coast Consulting LLC (PA)....C....949 250-4102
9233 Research Dr Ste 200 Irvine (92618) ***(P-15891)***
West Coast Contractors Inc....C....541 267-7689
2320 Courage Dr Ste 111 Fairfield (94533) ***(P-1698)***
West Coast Coupon Inc....E....818 341-2400
9400 Oso Ave Chatsworth (91311) ***(P-13987)***
West Coast Drywall & Co Inc....B....951 778-3592
1610 W Linden St Riverside (92507) ***(P-2979)***
West Coast Firestopping Inc....D....714 935-1104
1130 W Trenton Ave Orange (92867) ***(P-3609)***
West Coast Grape Farming Inc....A....209 538-3131
800 E Keyes Rd Ceres (95307) ***(P-721)***
West Coast Hospitals Inc....D....831 722-3581
919 Freedom Blvd Watsonville (95076) ***(P-21253)***
West Coast Interiors Inc....A....951 778-3592
1610 W Linden St Riverside (92507) ***(P-2491)***
West Coast Legal Service Inc....E....408 938-6520
1245 S Winchester Blvd # 208 San Jose (95128) ***(P-17586)***
West Coast Ltg & Enrgy Inc....D....951 296-0680
18550 Minthorn St Lake Elsinore (92530) ***(P-2786)***
West Coast Mailing & Dist, San Diego *Also called Mopar Enterprises* ***(P-14055)***
West Coast Maintenance Inc....D....310 324-2511
16312 S Main St Gardena (90248) ***(P-14427)***
West Coast Materials, Buena Park *Also called West Coast Sand and Gravel Inc* ***(P-6914)***
West Coast Painting, Riverside *Also called West Coast Interiors Inc* ***(P-2491)***
West Coast Physical Therapy, Laguna Niguel *Also called Mission Internal Med Group Inc* ***(P-19692)***
West Coast Prime Meats LLC....C....714 255-8560
344 Cliffwood Park St Brea (92821) ***(P-8635)***

ALPHABETIC

Employee Codes: A=Over 500 employees, B=251-500
C=101-250, D=51-100, E=50
2019 Directory of California
Wholesalers and Services Companies
© Mergent Inc. 1-800-342-5647
1521

West Coast Radiology Center, Santa Ana *Also called Santa Ana Radiology Center* ***(P-19852)***
West Coast Rags, Long Beach *Also called Coastal Closeouts Inc* ***(P-17091)***
West Coast Sand and Gravel Inc (PA)..........D.......714 522-0282
7282 Orangethorpe Ave Buena Park (90621) ***(P-6914)***
West Coast Santa Cruz Hotel, Santa Cruz *Also called Santa Cruz Hotel Associates* ***(P-13187)***
West Coast Storm Inc (PA)..........E.......909 890-5700
9701 Wilshire Blvd # 1000 Beverly Hills (90212) ***(P-27610)***
West Coast Turf (PA)..........E.......760 340-7300
42540 Melanie Pl Palm Desert (92211) ***(P-307)***
West Corporation..........C.......310 481-7878
170 N Church Ln Los Angeles (90049) ***(P-17587)***
West Corporation..........C.......949 294-2801
3063 W Chapman Ave # 2353 Orange (92868) ***(P-17588)***
West Cotton AG Management Inc..........C.......559 945-2511
15900 W Dorris Huron (93234) ***(P-722)***
West Countra Costa Youth Svcs (PA)..........D.......510 412-5647
263 S 20th St Richmond (94804) ***(P-24131)***
West County Health Centers Inc..........D.......707 869-2849
16312 3rd St Guerneville (95446) ***(P-20096)***
West County Resource Recovery..........E.......510 231-4200
101 Pittsburg Ave Richmond (94801) ***(P-6523)***
West County Trnsp Agcy..........C.......707 206-9988
367 W Robles Ave Santa Rosa (95407) ***(P-3738)***
West Covina Lanes, West Covina *Also called Bowlero Corp* ***(P-18482)***
West Covina Medical Clinic Inc (PA)..........C.......626 960-8614
1500 W West Covina Pkwy West Covina (91790) ***(P-20097)***
WEST COVINA PHYSICAL THERAPY, West Covina *Also called Doctors Hospital W Covina Inc* ***(P-21396)***
West Dermatology Med MGT Inc..........C.......909 793-3000
400 Newport Center Dr # 702 Newport Beach (92660) ***(P-20098)***
West End Yung MNS Christn Assn..........D.......909 946-6120
1150 E Foothill Blvd Upland (91786) ***(P-25284)***
West End Yung MNS Christn Assn..........D.......909 477-2780
11200 Baseline Rd Rancho Cucamonga (91701) ***(P-25285)***
West Escondido Healthcare LLC..........D.......760 746-0303
201 N Fig St Escondido (92025) ***(P-20883)***
West Flower Growers..........D.......805 488-0814
3623 Etting Rd Oxnard (93033) ***(P-308)***
West Health Care, Bonita *Also called Paradise Valley Hospital* ***(P-22389)***
West Hills Construction Inc..........E.......800 515-5270
423 Jenks Cir Ste 101 Corona (92880) ***(P-1450)***
West Hills Golf Associates..........E.......714 528-6400
1800 Carbon Canyon Rd Chino Hills (91709) ***(P-19085)***
West Hollywood Sport Club, West Hollywood *Also called 24 Hour Fitness Usa Inc* ***(P-18554)***
West Hotel Partners LP (PA)..........C.......310 477-3593
11828 La Grange Ave 200 Los Angeles (90025) ***(P-13387)***
West Hotel Partners LP..........C.......408 947-4450
300 Almaden Blvd San Jose (95110) ***(P-13388)***
West Inn & Suites LLC..........D.......760 448-4500
4970 Avenida Encinas Carlsbad (92008) ***(P-13389)***
West Interactive Services Corp..........D.......888 527-5225
100 Enterprise Way Scotts Valley (95066) ***(P-5687)***
West Lake Touchless Car Wash..........E.......650 992-5344
223 87th St Daly City (94015) ***(P-17843)***
West Los Angeles V A Med Ctr, Los Angeles *Also called Veterans Health Administration* ***(P-20059)***
West Medions, San Leandro *Also called KMA Emergency Services Inc* ***(P-3814)***
West Oahu Mall Associates..........E.......310 276-1290
1880 Century Park E # 810 Los Angeles (90067) ***(P-12192)***
West Oakland Health Center, Oakland *Also called West Oakland Health Council* ***(P-22715)***
West Oakland Health Council (PA)..........C.......510 835-9610
700 Adeline St Oakland (94607) ***(P-22715)***
West Pacific Medical Lab, Santa Fe Springs *Also called California Lab Sciences LLC* ***(P-26687)***
West Pacific Medical Lab LLC (PA)..........D.......818 773-9771
10200 Pioneer Blvd # 500 Santa Fe Springs (90670) ***(P-22159)***
West Pico Distributors LLC..........D.......323 586-9050
5201 S Downey Rd Vernon (90058) ***(P-8487)***
West Pico Foods Inc..........C.......323 586-9050
5201 S Downey Rd Vernon (90058) ***(P-8510)***
West Publishing Corporation..........C.......424 243-2100
800 Crprate Pinte Ste 150 Culver City (90230) ***(P-16077)***
West Riverside Veterinary Hosp..........E.......951 686-2242
5488 Mission Blvd Riverside (92509) ***(P-621)***
West Safety..........E.......514 340-3314
3009 Douglas Blvd Ste 300 Roseville (95661) ***(P-17589)***
West San Crlos Ht Partners LLC..........D.......408 998-0400
282 Almaden Blvd San Jose (95113) ***(P-13390)***
West Side District Hospital..........C.......805 763-4211
110 E North St Taft (93268) ***(P-21914)***
West Side Rehab Corporation..........C.......323 231-4174
1755 Kings Way Los Angeles (90069) ***(P-10961)***
West States Skanska Inc..........C.......970 565-4903
1995 Agua Mansa Rd Riverside (92509) ***(P-2002)***
West Unfied Cmmnctons Svcs Inc..........D.......925 988-7112
1676 N California Blvd Walnut Creek (94596) ***(P-17590)***
West Valley Area Squad Club..........C.......818 888-0980
5825 De Soto Ave Woodland Hills (91367) ***(P-24858)***
West Valley Christian Academy, Tracy *Also called We Care Day Care & Pre School* ***(P-24397)***
West Valley Cnstr Co Inc (PA)..........C.......408 371-5510
580 E Mcglincy Ln Campbell (95008) ***(P-2003)***
West Valley Engineering Inc..........D.......925 416-9707
3875 Hopyard Rd Ste 130 Pleasanton (94588) ***(P-14798)***
West Valley Engineering Inc (PA)..........D.......408 735-1420
390 Potrero Ave Sunnyvale (94085) ***(P-14944)***
West Valley Family YMCA..........C.......818 774-2840
18810 Vanowen St Reseda (91335) ***(P-24398)***
West Valley Jewish Cmnty Ctr..........D.......818 348-0048
22622 Vanowen St Canoga Park (91307) ***(P-19261)***
West Valley M R F, Fontana *Also called West Valley Manufacturing LLC* ***(P-6524)***
West Valley Manufacturing LLC..........C.......909 899-5501
13373 Napa St Fontana (92335) ***(P-6524)***
West Valley Staffing Group, Sunnyvale *Also called West Valley Engineering Inc* ***(P-14944)***
West Ventura Family Care Ctr..........D.......805 641-5620
133 W Santa Clara St Ventura (93001) ***(P-20099)***
West Ville Palm Desert..........E.......760 346-2121
72840 Highway 111 Ste 115 Palm Desert (92260) ***(P-10962)***
West Yost & Associates Inc (PA)..........D.......530 756-5905
2020 Res Pk Dr Ste 100 Davis (95618) ***(P-25996)***
West-Spec Partners..........E.......818 725-7000
20525 Nordhoff St Ste 42 Chatsworth (91311) ***(P-7877)***
Westair Gas and Equipment, San Diego *Also called Laboratory Specialty Gases* ***(P-7761)***
Westair Gases & Equipment Inc..........D.......619 474-0079
2300 Haffley Ave National City (91950) ***(P-7820)***
Westair Gases & Equipment Inc (PA)..........E.......866 937-8247
2506 Market St San Diego (92102) ***(P-7821)***
Westak International Sales Inc (HQ)..........C.......408 734-8686
1116 Elko Dr Sunnyvale (94089) ***(P-7563)***
Westar Capital Assoc II LLC..........A.......714 481-5160
949 S Coast Dr Costa Mesa (92626) ***(P-12281)***
Westar Manufacturing Inc..........D.......562 633-0581
13217 Laureldale Ave Downey (90242) ***(P-3610)***
Westar Marine Services, San Francisco *Also called Cross Link Inc* ***(P-4745)***
Westates Mechanical Corp Inc..........D.......510 635-9830
734 Whitney St San Leandro (94577) ***(P-2407)***
Westcal Management, Carmichael *Also called Pacific Cities Management Inc* ***(P-11645)***
Westcare California Inc (HQ)..........D.......559 251-4800
1900 N Gateway Blvd 100 Fresno (93727) ***(P-24718)***
Westchester Emerson Cmnty, Los Angeles *Also called Los Angeles Unified School Dst* ***(P-23905)***
Westcoast Childrens Clinic..........C.......510 269-9030
3301 E 12th St Ste 259 Oakland (94601) ***(P-22716)***
Westcoast Medial Imaging, Los Angeles *Also called Larchmont Radiology Med Group* ***(P-19642)***
Westcoast Performance Pdts USA..........D.......714 630-4411
3100 E Coronado St Anaheim (92806) ***(P-12193)***
Westcoast Warehousing LLC..........E.......310 537-9958
100 W Manville St Rancho Dominguez (90220) ***(P-4659)***
Westcoe Escrow Division, Riverside *Also called Westcoe Realtors Inc* ***(P-11827)***
Westcoe Realtors Inc..........D.......951 784-2500
7191 Magnolia Ave Riverside (92504) ***(P-11827)***
Westcor Construction of Cal..........C.......909 796-8900
2351 W Lugonia Ave Ste D Redlands (92374) ***(P-1259)***
Westcore Croydon, San Diego *Also called Westcore Delta LLC* ***(P-12282)***
Westcore Delta LLC..........D.......858 625-4100
4350 La Jolla Village Dr # 900 San Diego (92122) ***(P-12282)***
Westech Systems Inc..........D.......559 298-5237
827 Jefferson Ave Clovis (93612) ***(P-2787)***
Wested..........D.......510 302-4200
300 Lakeside Dr Fl 25th Oakland (94612) ***(P-26673)***
Wested..........D.......415 289-2300
180 Harbor Dr Ste 112 Sausalito (94965) ***(P-26674)***
Wested (PA)..........C.......415 565-3000
730 Harrison St Ste 500 San Francisco (94107) ***(P-26675)***
Wested..........C.......415 565-3000
730 Harrison St Ste 500 San Francisco (94107) ***(P-26676)***
Western Air & Refrigeration, Seal Beach *Also called Limbach Company LP* ***(P-2263)***
Western Alliance Bank, Oakland *Also called Porrey Pines Bank Inc* ***(P-9369)***
Western Alliance Bank..........D.......408 423-8500
55 Almaden Blvd Ste 200 San Jose (95113) ***(P-9494)***
Western Alliance Bank..........D.......415 230-4834
455 Market St Ste 1050 San Francisco (94105) ***(P-9520)***
Western Alliance Bank..........D.......949 222-0855
7545 Irvine Center Dr # 200 Irvine (92618) ***(P-9521)***
Western Allied Mechanical Inc..........C.......650 326-8290
1180 Obrien Dr Menlo Park (94025) ***(P-2408)***
Western Allied Service Company..........B.......562 941-3243
12046 Florence Ave Santa Fe Springs (90670) ***(P-17898)***
Western America Properties LLC..........D.......310 374-4381
111 N Sepulveda Blvd # 330 Manhattan Beach (90266) ***(P-11828)***
Western Area Security Services, Burbank *Also called Callan Management Corporation* ***(P-16881)***
Western Asset Core Plus..........D.......626 844-9400
385 E Colorado Blvd Pasadena (91101) ***(P-12054)***
Western Asset MGT Co LLC (HQ)..........E.......626 844-9265
385 E Colorado Blvd # 250 Pasadena (91101) ***(P-12055)***
Western Asset Mrtg Capitl Corp..........A.......626 844-9400
385 E Colorado Blvd Pasadena (91101) ***(P-12194)***
Western Building Materials Co (PA)..........D.......559 454-8500
4620 E Olive Ave Fresno (93702) ***(P-2980)***
WESTERN CITY MAGAZINE, Sacramento *Also called League of California Cities* ***(P-27560)***
Western Communications, Newbury Park *Also called Hearst Communications Inc* ***(P-5919)***
Western Concrete Pumping Inc (PA)..........D.......760 598-7855
2181 La Mirada Dr Vista (92081) ***(P-3345)***
Western Connection, Carol Rose, Vernon *Also called B Boston & Associates Inc* ***(P-8285)***
Western Convalescent Hospital, Los Angeles *Also called Tzippy Care Inc* ***(P-21235)***
Western Convelescence, Los Angeles *Also called Longwood Management Corp* ***(P-21141)***
Western Costume Leasing..........D.......818 760-0900
11041 Vanowen St North Hollywood (91605) ***(P-13781)***
Western Dental Services Inc (PA)..........B.......714 480-3000
530 S Main St Ste 600 Orange (92868) ***(P-20144)***

Mergent e-mail: customerrelations@mergent.com
1522

2019 Directory of California
Wholesalers and Services Companies

(P-0000) Products & Services Section entry number
(PA)=Parent Co (HQ)=Headquarters (DH)=Div Headquarters

Western Division Regional Off, Long Beach *Also called Southern California Edison Co* **(P-6139)**
Western Drug Medical Supply, Stockton *Also called H and H Drug Stores Inc* **(P-8038)**
Western Drywall Inc.....D.....209 847-6401
4981 Salida Blvd Salida (95368) **(P-2981)**
Western Energetix LLC.....C.....530 885-0401
2360 Lindbergh St Auburn (95602) **(P-8947)**
Western Exterminator Company.....D.....310 274-9244
3333 W Temple St Los Angeles (90026) **(P-14162)**
Western Exterminator Company.....E.....310 835-3513
1985 W Wardlow Rd Long Beach (90810) **(P-14163)**
Western Exterminator Company.....D.....562 802-2238
15415 Marquardt Ave Santa Fe Springs (90670) **(P-14164)**
Western Feld Invstigations Inc (PA).....D.....800 999-9589
405 W Foothill Blvd 204 Claremont (91711) **(P-16261)**
Western Freight Carrier Inc.....D.....909 357-1011
13819 Slover Ave Fontana (92337) **(P-5198)**
Western General Agency Inc.....D.....818 766-6500
12200 Sylvan St Ste 140 North Hollywood (91606) **(P-10828)**
Western General Holding Co (PA).....C.....818 880-9070
5230 Las Virgenes Rd # 100 Calabasas (91302) **(P-10414)**
Western General Insurance Co.....C.....818 880-9070
5230 Las Virgenes Rd Calabasas (91302) **(P-10415)**
Western Growers Association (PA).....C.....949 863-1000
15525 Sand Canyon Ave Irvine (92618) **(P-24991)**
Western Health Advantage.....D.....916 567-1950
2349 Gateway Oaks Dr # 100 Sacramento (95833) **(P-10174)**
Western Health Resources.....E.....559 537-2860
440 Greenfield Ave Ste B Hanford (93230) **(P-27521)**
Western Healthcare Center, Colton *Also called Western Healthcare Management* **(P-20884)**
Western Healthcare Management.....C.....909 824-1530
1700 E Washington St Colton (92324) **(P-20884)**
Western Hills Country Club, Chino Hills *Also called West Hills Golf Associates* **(P-19085)**
Western Hills Golf & Cntry CLB, Chino *Also called Donovan Golf Courses MGT* **(P-18709)**
Western Homes, Fresno *Also called Lassley Enterprises Inc* **(P-11050)**
Western Host Inc (PA).....E.....650 692-3500
1 Old Bayshore Hwy Millbrae (94030) **(P-17591)**
Western Insulfoam, Chino *Also called Carlisle Construction Mtls Inc* **(P-6922)**
Western Living Concepts Inc (PA).....E.....707 443-3000
2740 Timber Ridge Ln Ofc Eureka (95503) **(P-24719)**
Western Magnesite Inc.....E.....818 255-1150
11927 Sherman Rd Unit 1 North Hollywood (91605) **(P-3611)**
Western Meat Processors Inc.....E.....760 355-1175
502 E Barioni Blvd Imperial (92251) **(P-402)**
Western Med Assoc Med Group (PA).....D.....831 475-1111
1595 Soquel Dr Ste 330 Santa Cruz (95065) **(P-20100)**
Western Med Center-Santa Ana, Santa Ana *Also called Western Medical Center Aux* **(P-21915)**
Western Medical Center Aux (HQ).....C.....714 835-3555
1301 N Tustin Ave Santa Ana (92705) **(P-21915)**
Western Medical Management LLC.....E.....949 260-6575
3333 Michelson Dr Ste 735 Irvine (92612) **(P-27093)**
Western Messenger Service Inc.....C.....415 487-4229
75 Columbia Sq San Francisco (94103) **(P-4087)**
Western Milling LLC (HQ).....C.....559 302-1000
31120 West St Goshen (93227) **(P-9103)**
Western National Contractors.....D.....949 862-6200
8 Executive Cir Irvine (92614) **(P-27094)**
Western National Properties (PA).....C.....949 862-6200
8 Executive Cir Irvine (92614) **(P-1326)**
Western National Securities (PA).....C.....949 862-6200
8 Executive Cir Irvine (92614) **(P-11829)**
Western Nevada Supply Co.....C.....530 582-5009
10990 Industrial Way A Truckee (96161) **(P-7641)**
Western Oil & Spreading, Martinez *Also called Telfer Oil Company* **(P-1860)**
Western Oilfields Supply Co (PA).....C.....661 399-9124
3404 State Rd Bakersfield (93308) **(P-14555)**
Western Operations, Rancho Cucamonga *Also called Gentex Corporation* **(P-26373)**
Western Operations Center, Westlake Village *Also called Securitas SEC Svcs USA Inc* **(P-16797)**
Western Overseas Corporation (PA).....E.....562 985-0616
10731 Walker St Ste B Cypress (90630) **(P-5199)**
Western Pacific Distrg LLC.....C.....714 974-6837
341 W Meats Ave Orange (92865) **(P-6915)**
Western Paving Contractors Inc.....D.....626 338-7889
15533 Arrow Hwy Irwindale (91706) **(P-1869)**
Western PCF Crane & Eqp LLC (HQ).....D.....562 286-6618
8600 Calabash Ave Fontana (92335) **(P-14462)**
Western Precooling Systems (PA).....C.....510 656-2220
43990 Fremont Blvd Fremont (94538) **(P-586)**
Western Precooling Systems.....D.....805 486-6371
761 Commercial Ave Oxnard (93030) **(P-14556)**
Western Pump Inc (PA).....D.....619 239-9988
3235 F St San Diego (92102) **(P-18006)**
Western Region, Milpitas *Also called Xcerra Corporation* **(P-7566)**
Western Regional Office, Rancho Cordova *Also called Ducks Unlimited Inc* **(P-1003)**
Western Repacking Lllp.....D.....916 668-8443
2771 French Camp Rd Manteca (95336) **(P-17592)**
Western Rim Constructors Inc.....E.....760 489-4328
621 S Andreasen Dr Ste B Escondido (92029) **(P-1870)**
Western Rim Pipeline, Lakeside *Also called A M Ortega Construction Inc* **(P-2495)**
Western Roofing Service, San Leandro *Also called Roofing Constructors Inc* **(P-3197)**
Western Slope Health Care, Placerville *Also called Western Slope Health Center* **(P-20885)**
Western Slope Health Center.....D.....530 622-6842
3280 Washington St Placerville (95667) **(P-20885)**
Western Star Nurseries LLC.....E.....209 744-2552
9394 Robson Rd Galt (95632) **(P-9178)**
Western Star Trnsp LLC.....C.....310 605-1300
1065 E Walnut St Carson (90746) **(P-4303)**
Western States Affiliate, Los Angeles *Also called American Heart Association Inc* **(P-24995)**
Western States Fire Protection.....D.....916 924-1631
4740 Northgate Blvd # 150 Sacramento (95834) **(P-2409)**
Western States Info Netwrk Inc.....D.....916 263-1180
1825 Bell St Ste 205 Sacramento (95825) **(P-26677)**
Western Sun Enterprises Inc.....C.....707 748-2542
4690 E 2nd St Ste 4 Benicia (94510) **(P-2788)**
Western Tear-Off & Disposal.....D.....626 443-9984
10920 Grand Ave Temple City (91780) **(P-3210)**
Western Towing, San Diego *Also called Sunbelt Towing Inc* **(P-17874)**
Western Transit Systems Inc.....D.....949 515-0188
13591 Harbor Blvd Garden Grove (92843) **(P-3873)**
Western United Insurance Co.....C.....800 959-9842
3349 Michelson Dr Ste 100 Irvine (92612) **(P-10829)**
Western Waste Services, Temple City *Also called Western Tear-Off & Disposal* **(P-3210)**
Western Wine Services Inc (PA).....D.....800 999-8463
880 Hanna Dr American Canyon (94503) **(P-4660)**
Westfield LLC (HQ).....B.....813 926-4600
2049 Century Park E # 4000 Los Angeles (90067) **(P-10963)**
Westfield America Inc (HQ).....C.....310 478-4456
2049 Century Park E Fl 41 Los Angeles (90067) **(P-10964)**
Westfield America Ltd Partnr.....D.....310 478-4456
2049 Century Park E Fl 41 Los Angeles (90067) **(P-11937)**
Westfield America Ltd Partnr.....B.....310 277-3898
2049 Century Park E # 4100 Los Angeles (90067) **(P-10965)**
Westgage Grdn Convalescent Ctr, Visalia *Also called Far West Inc* **(P-21065)**
Westgate Cnstr & Maint Inc.....D.....707 208-5763
5045 Fulton Dr Ste D Fairfield (94534) **(P-1699)**
Westgate Gardens Care Center.....C.....559 733-0901
4525 W Tulare Ave Visalia (93277) **(P-20886)**
Westgate Hotel, San Diego *Also called Sinclair Companies* **(P-13230)**
Westgroup Kona Kai LLC.....D.....619 221-8000
1551 Shelter Island Dr San Diego (92106) **(P-19086)**
Westgroup San Diego Associates.....B.....858 274-4630
1404 Vacation Rd San Diego (92109) **(P-13391)**
Westin Bonaventure Ht & Suites, Los Angeles *Also called Interstate Hotels Resorts Inc* **(P-12777)**
Westin Desert Willow.....D.....760 636-7003
75 Willow Ridge Palm Desert (92260) **(P-13392)**
Westin Long Beach Hotel, The, Long Beach *Also called Noble/Utah Long Beach LLC* **(P-12960)**
Westin Los Angeles Airport, Los Angeles *Also called Host Hotels & Resorts LP* **(P-12713)**
Westin Pasadena, The, Pasadena *Also called Brookfield Dtla Fund Office* **(P-12406)**
Westin San Diego, San Diego *Also called Diamondrock San Dego Tnant LLC* **(P-12522)**
Westin San Diego, San Diego *Also called W-Emerald LLC* **(P-13374)**
Westin San Francisco Arprt Ht, Millbrae *Also called Western Host Inc* **(P-17591)**
Westlake Christian Terrace - E, Oakland *Also called Christian Church Homes* **(P-11317)**
Westlake Development Group LLC (PA).....D.....650 579-1010
520 S El Camino Real # 900 San Mateo (94402) **(P-10966)**
Westlake Development Group LLC.....D.....650 579-1010
520 El Camino Real Fl 9 Belmont (94002) **(P-27095)**
Westlake Financial Services, Los Angeles *Also called Westlake Services LLC* **(P-9766)**
Westlake Health Care Center.....C.....805 494-1233
1101 Crenshaw Blvd Los Angeles (90019) **(P-20887)**
Westlake Inn Hotel, Westlake Village *Also called Westlake Village Inn* **(P-13393)**
Westlake Nail Spa.....D.....650 994-7777
233 Lake Merced Blvd Daly City (94015) **(P-18674)**
Westlake Realty Group Inc (PA).....D.....650 579-1010
520 S El Camino Real # 900 San Mateo (94402) **(P-11830)**
Westlake Services LLC (PA).....C.....323 692-8800
4751 Wilshire Blvd # 100 Los Angeles (90010) **(P-9766)**
Westlake Village Apartments, Daly City *Also called Gerson Baker & Associates* **(P-11026)**
Westlake Village Golf Course, Westlake Village *Also called Pyj V A California Ltd Partnr* **(P-18748)**
Westlake Village Inn.....C.....818 889-0230
31943 Agoura Rd Westlake Village (91361) **(P-13393)**
Westland Floral, Carpinteria *Also called Westland Orchids Inc* **(P-9179)**
Westland Hotel Corporation.....E.....209 931-3131
4219 E Waterloo Rd Stockton (95215) **(P-13394)**
Westland Orchids Inc.....E.....805 684-1436
1400 Cravens Ln Carpinteria (93013) **(P-9179)**
Westland Trailer Mfg, Lodi *Also called Bjj Company LLC* **(P-4109)**
Westliving Management LLC (PA).....D.....760 602-5850
5800 Armada Dr Ste 100 Carlsbad (92008) **(P-24720)**
Westmed Ambulance.....D.....510 401-5420
14275 Wicks Blvd San Leandro (94577) **(P-3859)**
Westmed Ambulance Inc.....C.....310 456-3830
3872 Las Flores Canyon Rd Malibu (90265) **(P-3860)**
Westmed Ambulance Inc.....B.....310 219-1779
2537 Old San Pasqual Rd Escondido (92027) **(P-3861)**
Westminster Gardens.....D.....626 359-2571
1420 Santo Domingo Ave Duarte (91010) **(P-21254)**
Westminster Housing Parteners.....E.....714 891-3000
8140 13th St Westminster (92683) **(P-11831)**
Westminster Woods Camp & Confe.....E.....707 874-2426
6510 Bohemian Hwy Occidental (95465) **(P-13457)**
Westmont Living Inc.....B.....916 786-3277
707 Sunrise Ave Roseville (95661) **(P-24721)**
Westmont Living Inc (PA).....C.....858 456-1233
7660 Fay Ave Ste N La Jolla (92037) **(P-24722)**
Weston Solutions Inc.....D.....760 795-6900
5817 Dryden Pl Ste 101 Carlsbad (92008) **(P-26493)**
Westpac Materials, Orange *Also called Western Pacific Distrg LLC* **(P-6915)**
Westpoint Marketing Intl Inc.....D.....323 233-0233
5901 Avalon Blvd Los Angeles (90003) **(P-17593)**

A L P H A B E T I C

Employee Codes: A=Over 500 employees, B=251-500
C=101-250, D=51-100, E=50
2019 Directory of California
Wholesalers and Services Companies
© Mergent Inc. 1-800-342-5647
1523

Westport Capital Partners LLC......D.......310 294-1234
2121 Rosecrans Ave # 4325 El Segundo (90245) ***(P-12283)***
Westpost Berkeley LLC......D.......510 548-7920
200 Marina Blvd Berkeley (94710) ***(P-13395)***
Westrec Marina Management Inc......D.......209 369-1041
14900 W Highway 12 Frnt Lodi (95242) ***(P-4752)***
Westridge Golf Inc......D.......562 690-4200
1400 S La Habra Hills Dr La Habra (90631) ***(P-18778)***
Westrux International Inc......D.......909 825-5121
2200 E Steel Rd Colton (92324) ***(P-5200)***
Westside Childrens Center Inc......D.......310 846-4100
5721 W Slauson Ave # 140 Culver City (90230) ***(P-24399)***
Westside Health Center, Los Angeles *Also called Motion Picture and TV Fund* ***(P-21599)***
Westside Jewish Cmnty Ctr Inc (PA)......C.......323 938-2531
5870 W Olympic Blvd Los Angeles (90036) ***(P-24859)***
Westside Lodge......E.......415 864-1515
120 Page St San Francisco (94102) ***(P-24860)***
Westside Security Patrol, Bakersfield *Also called M & S Security Services Inc* ***(P-16725)***
Weststar Cinemas Inc......D.......323 461-3331
6801 Hollywood Blvd # 335 Los Angeles (90028) ***(P-18323)***
Weststar Marine Services Inc......C.......415 495-3191
50 Pier San Francisco (94158) ***(P-4755)***
Westview Cmnty Arts Program, Anaheim *Also called Westview Services Inc* ***(P-20889)***
Westview Healh Care Center......C.......530 885-7511
12225 Shale Ridge Ln Auburn (95602) ***(P-20888)***
Westview Services Inc......C.......714 956-4199
1701 S Euclid St Ste E Anaheim (92802) ***(P-20889)***
Westview Services Inc......D.......951 343-2356
11728 Magnolia Ave Ste D Riverside (92503) ***(P-27962)***
Westview Services Inc......D.......714 879-3980
626 W Commonwealth Ave Fullerton (92832) ***(P-24132)***
Westview Services Inc......D.......714 418-2090
9421 Edinger Ave Westminster (92683) ***(P-24249)***
Westward Hospitality MGT......D.......510 548-7920
200 Marina Blvd Berkeley (94710) ***(P-13396)***
Westwind Communications, Bakersfield *Also called Kbak TV Channel 29 CBS* ***(P-5804)***
Westwind Engineering Inc......C.......310 831-3454
553 N Pcfc Cst Hwy B179 Redondo Beach (90277) ***(P-25997)***
Westwind Engineering Inc......D.......310 831-3454
553 N Pcf Coastte B179 B Redondo Beach (90277) ***(P-25998)***
Westwind Enterprises Ltd (PA)......C.......408 998-8444
1515 The Alameda San Jose (95126) ***(P-11161)***
Westwind Equity Investors, Newport Beach *Also called Windjammer Capital Invstr III* ***(P-10042)***
Westwind Media, Burbank *Also called Westwind Studios LLC* ***(P-18169)***
Westwind Media Inc......D.......818 972-9000
100 W Alameda Ave Burbank (91502) ***(P-18168)***
Westwind Studios LLC......E.......818 972-9000
100 W Alameda Ave Burbank (91502) ***(P-18169)***
Westwood Healthcare Center LP......D.......310 826-0821
12121 Santa Monica Blvd Los Angeles (90025) ***(P-20890)***
Westwood Insurance Agency (HQ)......D.......818 990-9715
8407 Fllbrook Ave Ste 200 Canoga Park (91304) ***(P-10830)***
Westwood Marquis Hotel & Grdns, Los Angeles *Also called W Los Angeles* ***(P-13372)***
Wet (PA)......C.......818 769-6200
10847 Sherman Way Sun Valley (91352) ***(P-17594)***
Wetherby Asset Management......D.......415 399-9159
580 California St Fl 8 San Francisco (94104) ***(P-10122)***
Wetzel & Sons Moving and Stor......D.......818 890-0992
12400 Osborne St Pacoima (91331) ***(P-4390)***
Wetzel Trucking, Pacoima *Also called Wetzel & Sons Moving and Stor* ***(P-4390)***
Weyerhaeuser Company......D.......562 983-6589
800 Pier T Ave Long Beach (90802) ***(P-995)***
Weyerhaeuser Company......D.......909 877-6100
17400 Slover Ave Fontana (92337) ***(P-6873)***
Weygandt & Associates......E.......916 543-0431
1501 Avi Blvd Ste 100 Lincoln (95648) ***(P-18007)***
Weyrick Pacific, Templeton *Also called Pacific Coast Supply LLC* ***(P-6846)***
WF Cinema Holdings LP......E.......805 379-8966
180 Promenade Way Ste R Westlake Village (91362) ***(P-18324)***
Wfc Holdings LLC (HQ)......C.......415 396-7392
420 Montgomery St San Francisco (94104) ***(P-9410)***
Wfcf Technology E2040-030, Santa Monica *Also called Wells Fargo Capital Fin Inc* ***(P-17585)***
Wfg National Title Insur Co (PA)......D.......818 476-4000
700 N Brand Blvd Ste 1100 Glendale (91203) ***(P-10474)***
Wfs, Los Angeles *Also called Worldwide Flight Services Inc* ***(P-4815)***
Wg, Santa Fe Springs *Also called Ethosenergy Field Services LLC* ***(P-1058)***
Wga West Inc......D.......323 782-4512
7000 W 3rd St Los Angeles (90048) ***(P-13962)***
Wgg Enterprises Inc......C.......626 442-5493
11340 Stewart St El Monte (91731) ***(P-2982)***
Whaling Bar & Grill, La Jolla *Also called Lav Hotel Corp* ***(P-12839)***
Wham-O Inc......D.......818 963-4200
6301 Owensmouth Ave # 700 Woodland Hills (91367) ***(P-7963)***
Whatever It Takes Inc......E.......760 329-6000
10805 Palm Dr Desert Hot Springs (92240) ***(P-13397)***
Whb Corporation......A.......213 624-1011
506 S Grand Ave Los Angeles (90071) ***(P-13398)***
Wheatland School District......D.......530 633-3135
100 Wheatland Park Dr Wheatland (95692) ***(P-11832)***
Wheatland Wind Project LLC......A.......888 903-6926
15445 Innovation Dr San Diego (92128) ***(P-6150)***
Wheel of Fortune, Culver City *Also called Quadra Productions Inc* ***(P-18102)***
Wheeler and Company, Cupertino *Also called Max Sportsters Inc* ***(P-26939)***
Whelan Security Co......B.......310 343-8628
400 Continental Blvd El Segundo (90245) ***(P-16857)***
Whgca LLC......C.......916 922-4700
2200 Harvard St Sacramento (95815) ***(P-13399)***
Whiskey Girl......D.......619 236-1616
702 5th Ave San Diego (92101) ***(P-27096)***
WHISTLESTOP, San Rafael *Also called Marin Snior Crdnting Cncil Inc* ***(P-23910)***
Whitaker Welness Institute In......D.......949 851-1550
4321 Birch St Ste 100 Newport Beach (92660) ***(P-20101)***
White & Case LLP......C.......213 687-9655
555 S Flower St Ste 2700 Los Angeles (90071) ***(P-23434)***
White Blossom Care Center, San Jose *Also called Plum Healthcare Group LLC* ***(P-20707)***
White Cap 24, Fairfield *Also called Hd Supply Construction Supply* ***(P-7590)***
White Cap 35, San Jose *Also called Hd Supply Construction Supply* ***(P-7591)***
White Cap Construction Supply......A.......949 794-5300
1815 Ritchey St Santa Ana (92705) ***(P-7698)***
White Carnival LLC......E.......310 914-1600
11812 San Vicente Blvd # 4 Los Angeles (90049) ***(P-27097)***
White Digital Media Inc......C.......760 827-7800
3394 Carmel Mountain Rd # 250 San Diego (92121) ***(P-9122)***
White Hills Vineyard Ranc......D.......805 934-1986
8385 Graciosa Rd Santa Maria (93455) ***(P-723)***
White House Properties, Encino *Also called Schweizer Rena* ***(P-11755)***
White House Sales, Sacramento *Also called Chem Quip Inc* ***(P-7925)***
White Memorial Med Group Inc (PA)......D.......323 987-1300
1701 E Cesar E Chavez Ave # 510 Los Angeles (90033) ***(P-20102)***
White Memorial Medical Center (HQ)......A.......323 268-5000
1720 E Cesar E Chavez Ave Los Angeles (90033) ***(P-21916)***
White Rabbit Partners Inc......C.......310 975-1450
9000 W Sunset Blvd # 1500 West Hollywood (90069) ***(P-24723)***
White Sands of La Jolla Clinic, La Jolla *Also called Cal Southern Presbt Homes* ***(P-24445)***
Whitefield Medical Lab & Rdlgy, Pomona *Also called Whitefield Medical Lab Inc* ***(P-22160)***
Whitefield Medical Lab Inc (PA)......E.......909 625-2114
764 Indigo Ct Ste A Pomona (91767) ***(P-22160)***
Whitegold Solutions Inc......E.......415 456-4493
43 Fernwood Way Ste 210 San Rafael (94901) ***(P-16531)***
Whitehall Asset Management, Rohnert Park *Also called Emt LLC* ***(P-12159)***
Whitehat Security Inc......D.......408 343-8300
1741 Tech Dr Ste 300 San Jose (95110) ***(P-16532)***
Whiting Concrete Construction, Rancho Murieta *Also called Whiting Construction Inc* ***(P-3346)***
Whiting Construction Inc......D.......916 354-2756
7281 Lone Pine Dr Rancho Murieta (95683) ***(P-3346)***
Whiting-Turner Contracting Co......C.......818 879-8100
29209 Canwood St Ste 100 Agoura Hills (91301) ***(P-1700)***
Whiting-Turner Contracting Co......C.......213 310-7900
1000 Wilshire Blvd 1850 Los Angeles (90017) ***(P-1701)***
Whiting-Turner Contracting Co......E.......949 863-0800
250 Commerce Ste 150 Irvine (92602) ***(P-1702)***
Whitmire Distribution, Valencia *Also called Cardinal Health Inc* ***(P-8158)***
Whittier Active Club, Whittier *Also called 24 Hour Fitness Usa Inc* ***(P-18566)***
Whittier City Community Svcs, Whittier *Also called City of Whittier* ***(P-23586)***
Whittier Equipment Rentals......D.......562 863-0641
11832 Bloomfield Ave Santa Fe Springs (90670) ***(P-2004)***
Whittier Grand Hotel, Whittier *Also called Ghg Properties LLC* ***(P-12605)***
Whittier Hills Health Care Ctr, Whittier *Also called Ensign Group Inc* ***(P-20397)***
Whittier Hospital Med Ctr Inc......C.......562 945-3561
9080 Colima Rd Whittier (90605) ***(P-21917)***
Whittier Inst For Diabetes......D.......877 944-8843
10140 Campus Point Dr San Diego (92121) ***(P-26678)***
Whittier Service Center, Santa Fe Springs *Also called Southern California Edison Co* ***(P-6138)***
Who Dat Nation Trnsp LLC......D.......760 403-7237
13186 Rincon Rd Apple Valley (92308) ***(P-5253)***
Wholesale Air-Time Inc......E.......951 693-1880
27515 Enterprise Cir W Temecula (92590) ***(P-5677)***
Wholesale Fuels Inc......D.......661 327-4900
2200 E Brundage Ln Bakersfield (93307) ***(P-8974)***
Wholesale Solar Inc......D.......800 472-1142
412 N Mount Shasta Blvd Mount Shasta (96067) ***(P-2410)***
WI Spa LLC......E.......213 487-2700
2700 Wilshire Blvd Los Angeles (90057) ***(P-18675)***
Wic, Torrance *Also called Public Hlth Fndation Entps Inc* ***(P-25225)***
Wic, Bakersfield *Also called Public Health California Dept* ***(P-19807)***
Wic, El Monte *Also called Public Hlth Fndation Entps Inc* ***(P-22866)***
Wicoro Inc (HQ)......E.......626 962-4489
919 N Sunset Ave West Covina (91790) ***(P-21255)***
Wideorbit Inc (PA)......C.......415 675-6700
1160 Battery St Ste 300 San Francisco (94111) ***(P-15545)***
Wiemar Distributors Inc......D.......213 747-7036
1953 S Alameda St Los Angeles (90058) ***(P-8747)***
Wier Construction Corporation......E.......760 743-6776
16884 Old Survey Rd Escondido (92025) ***(P-1703)***
Wightman Enterprises Inc......D.......916 961-2959
8017 Sacramento St Fair Oaks (95628) ***(P-14945)***
Wikimedia Foundation Inc......C.......415 839-6885
1 Montgomery St Ste 1600 San Francisco (94104) ***(P-25484)***
Wilbur Packing Company Inc......B.......530 671-4911
1500 Eager Rd Live Oak (95953) ***(P-587)***
Wilbur-Ellis Company LLC......D.......559 866-5667
12550 S Colorado Ave Helm (93627) ***(P-9104)***
Wilbur-Ellis Company LLC (HQ)......B.......415 772-4000
345 California St Fl 27 San Francisco (94104) ***(P-9105)***
Wilbur-Ellis Company LLC......D.......760 352-2847
45 Danenberg Dr El Centro (92243) ***(P-9106)***
Wilbur-Ellis Company LLC......D.......831 422-6473
1427 Abbott St Salinas (93901) ***(P-9107)***
Wild Electric Incorporated......D.......559 251-7770
4626 E Olive Ave Fresno (93702) ***(P-2789)***
Wild Goose Storage Inc......D.......530 846-7350
2780 W Liberty Rd Gridley (95948) ***(P-6154)***

Mergent e-mail: customerrelations@mergent.com
1524
2019 Directory of California Wholesalers and Services Companies
(P-0000) Products & Services Section entry number
(PA)=Parent Co (HQ)=Headquarters (DH)=Div Headquarters

Wild Karma Inc..........B......510 639-9088
400 Estudillo Ave Ste 100 San Leandro (94577) *(P-20891)*
Wild Palms Hotel & Bar, Sunnyvale *Also called Joie De Vivre Hospitality Inc (P-12792)*
Wild Side West (PA)..........D......818 837-5000
311 Parkside Dr San Fernando (91340) *(P-14131)*
Wildenradt-Mcmurray Inc..........D......510 835-5500
568 7th St San Francisco (94103) *(P-7609)*
WILDHAVEN RANCH, Cedar Glen *Also called San Bernardino Mtns Wildlife (P-446)*
Wildlife Waystation..........E......818 899-5201
14831 Lttle Tjunga Cyn Rd Sylmar (91342) *(P-25485)*
Wildomar Medical Offices, Wildomar *Also called Kaiser Foundation Hospitals (P-21498)*
Wildside, San Fernando *Also called Wild Side West (P-14131)*
Wildwood Express..........E......559 805-3237
12416 Swanson Ave Kingsburg (93631) *(P-4304)*
Wiline Networks Inc (PA)..........E......888 494-5463
1164 Triton Dr Foster City (94404) *(P-5678)*
Wilkie Masonry Inc..........E......916 652-0118
4016 Hunter Oaks Ln Loomis (95650) *(P-2829)*
Will Perkins Inc..........C......213 270-8400
617 W 7th St Fl 12 Los Angeles (90017) *(P-26121)*
Will Perkins Inc..........D......415 856-3000
2 Bryant St Ste 300 San Francisco (94105) *(P-26122)*
Willamette Valley Trtmnt Ctr, Cupertino *Also called CRC Health Corporate (P-22564)*
Willdan Engineering..........D......714 978-8200
2401 E Katella Ave # 300 Anaheim (92806) *(P-25999)*
Willdan Group Inc (PA)..........D......800 424-9144
2401 E Katella Ave # 300 Anaheim (92806) *(P-26000)*
William Brammer..........C......760 746-6006
20505 San Pasqual Rd Escondido (92025) *(P-8748)*
William C Arterberry..........D......760 728-9096
40147 Calle Roxanne Fallbrook (92028) *(P-240)*
William E Heinselman..........E......916 920-0220
3303 Luyung Dr Rancho Cordova (95742) *(P-26001)*
William F Kellogg Corporation..........D......818 845-7455
475 W Riverside Dr 479dr Burbank (91506) *(P-7920)*
William H Warden III MD..........D......562 424-6666
2760 Atlantic Ave Long Beach (90806) *(P-20103)*
William Hzmlhlch Archtects Inc..........D......949 250-0607
2850 Redhill Ave Ste 200 Santa Ana (92705) *(P-26123)*
William L Lyon & Assoc Inc..........D......916 447-7878
2801 J St Sacramento (95816) *(P-11833)*
William L Lyon & Assoc Inc..........D......916 535-0356
8814 Madison Ave Fair Oaks (95628) *(P-11834)*
William Love Swimming Pool, Compton *Also called City of Compton (P-19128)*
William Lyon Fin Services, Newport Beach *Also called Duxford Financial Inc (P-9800)*
William Lyon Homes (PA)..........C......949 833-3600
4695 Macarthur Ct Ste 800 Newport Beach (92660) *(P-1367)*
William Lyon Homes Inc (HQ)..........D......949 833-3600
4695 Macarthur Ct Ste 800 Newport Beach (92660) *(P-1368)*
William M Perkins Company Inc (PA)..........E......619 236-0343
3148 Market St San Diego (92102) *(P-2492)*
William McGann MD..........D......415 221-0665
1 Shrader St Ste 650 San Francisco (94117) *(P-20104)*
William Morris Agency, Los Angeles *Also called William Morris Endeavor (P-18413)*
William Morris Consulting, Beverly Hills *Also called William Morris Endeavor (P-18414)*
William Morris Endeavor..........B......310 285-9000
2624 Military Ave Los Angeles (90064) *(P-18413)*
William Morris Endeavor..........B......310 285-9000
9601 Wilshire Blvd Fl 3 Beverly Hills (90210) *(P-18414)*
William Morris Endeavor En (HQ)..........C......310 285-9000
9601 Wilshire Blvd Fl 3 Beverly Hills (90210) *(P-18415)*
William S Hart Pony & Softball..........D......661 254-9780
23437 Valencia Blvd Valencia (91355) *(P-27910)*
William Warren Group Inc (PA)..........D......310 451-2130
201 Wilshire Blvd Ste 102 Santa Monica (90401) *(P-17619)*
Williams & Sons Masonry Inc..........D......619 443-1751
8531 Winter Gardens Blvd A Lakeside (92040) *(P-2830)*
Williams Keller Realty..........D......916 774-6700
7005 Boardwalk Dr Granite Bay (95746) *(P-11835)*
Williams Tank Lines (PA)..........D......209 944-5613
1477 Tillie Lewis Dr Stockton (95206) *(P-4305)*
Williamson Enterprises Inc..........D......310 822-6615
721 Washington Blvd Marina Del Rey (90292) *(P-17745)*
Willis Allen Real Estate (PA)..........E......858 459-4033
1131 Wall St La Jolla (92037) *(P-11836)*
Willis Allen Real Estate..........E......858 756-2444
6024 Pasco Delicias Rancho Santa Fe (92067) *(P-11837)*
Willis Insurance Svcs Cal Inc..........E......858 678-2000
4250 Executive Sq Ste 250 La Jolla (92037) *(P-10152)*
Willis Lease Finance Corp (PA)..........D......415 408-4700
773 San Marin Dr Ste 2215 Novato (94945) *(P-14557)*
Willis Towers Watson, San Francisco *Also called Wtw Delaware Holdings LLC (P-27526)*
Willis Towers Watson, San Diego *Also called Wtw Delaware Holdings LLC (P-27527)*
Willits Hospital Inc..........B......707 459-6801
1 Marcela Dr Willits (95490) *(P-21918)*
Willits Perpetual LLC..........D......818 668-6800
21600 Oxnard St Woodland Hills (91367) *(P-17595)*
Willits Seniors Inc..........D......707 459-6826
1501 Baechtel Rd Willits (95490) *(P-24133)*
WILLITS SOLID WASTES, Willits *Also called Solid Wastes of Willits Inc (P-4065)*
Willmark Cmmnties Univ Vlg Inc (PA)..........D......858 271-0582
9948 Hibert St Ste 210 San Diego (92131) *(P-11140)*
Willow Creek Care Center, Clovis *Also called Willow Creek Halthcare Ctr LLC (P-20893)*
Willow Creek Halthcare Ctr LLC..........A......559 323-6200
650 W Alluvial Ave Clovis (93611) *(P-20892)*
Willow Creek Halthcare Ctr LLC..........D......559 323-6200
650 W Alluvial Ave Clovis (93611) *(P-20893)*
Willow Creek Treatment Center, Santa Rosa *Also called Victor Treatment Centers Inc (P-24711)*
Willow Farms LLC..........D......805 647-0720
9452 Telephone Rd Pmb 142 Ventura (93004) *(P-394)*
Willow Garage Inc..........D......650 322-2584
921 E Charleston Rd Palo Alto (94303) *(P-26494)*
Willow Glen Hsing Partners LP..........E......408 267-7252
465 Willow Glen Way # 100 San Jose (95125) *(P-11838)*
Willow Glen Villa, San Jose *Also called Atria Senior Living Group Inc (P-24428)*
Willow Glen Villa A..........D......408 266-1660
1660 Gaton Dr San Jose (95125) *(P-11141)*
Willow Pass Healthcare Center, Concord *Also called Kissito Health Case Inc (P-22355)*
Willow Pass Hlth Care Ctr Inc..........D......925 689-9222
3318 Willow Pass Rd Concord (94519) *(P-22464)*
Willow Rock Center, San Leandro *Also called Telecare Corporation (P-21976)*
Willow Sprngs Alzhmrs Spcl Cr..........E......530 242-0654
191 Churn Creek Rd Redding (96003) *(P-24724)*
Willow Tree Convalescent Hosp, Oakland *Also called Willow Tree Nursing Center (P-21256)*
Willow Tree Nursing Center, Oakland *Also called Covenant Care California LLC (P-20341)*
Willow Tree Nursing Center..........D......510 261-2628
2124 57th Ave Oakland (94621) *(P-21256)*
Willowick Golf Course, Santa Ana *Also called Donovan Golf Courses MGT (P-18708)*
Willows Care Rhabilitation Ctr, Willows *Also called Sunbridge Healthcare LLC (P-20964)*
Wilmark Development, San Diego *Also called Wilmark Management Services (P-11839)*
Wilmark Management Services (PA)..........D......858 271-0583
9948 Hibert St Ste 210 San Diego (92131) *(P-11839)*
Wilmay Inc..........D......805 524-2603
893 Oak Ave Fillmore (93015) *(P-17596)*
Wilmer Cutler Pick Hale Dorr..........C......213 443-5300
350 S Grand Ave Ste 2100 Los Angeles (90071) *(P-23435)*
Wilmington Schll Bys & Grls CL, Wilmington *Also called Boys and Girls Clubs of The La (P-25110)*
Wilmon Corporation..........D......951 685-7474
8951 Granite Hill Dr Riverside (92509) *(P-20894)*
Wilmor & Sons Plumbing & Cnstr..........D......916 381-9114
8510 Thys Ct Sacramento (95828) *(P-2411)*
Wilner Klein Siegel..........E......310 550-4595
9601 Wilshire Blvd # 700 Beverly Hills (90210) *(P-23436)*
Wilshire Animal Hospital..........E......310 828-4587
2421 Wilshire Blvd Santa Monica (90403) *(P-622)*
Wilshire Associates Inc (PA)..........C......310 451-3051
1299 Ocean Ave Ste 700 Santa Monica (90401) *(P-27522)*
Wilshire Center Dental Group..........E......213 386-3336
3932 Wilshire Blvd # 102 Los Angeles (90010) *(P-20145)*
Wilshire Consumer Credit..........E......323 692-8585
4751 Wilshire Blvd Los Angeles (90010) *(P-9729)*
Wilshire Country Club..........D......323 934-6050
301 N Rossmore Ave Los Angeles (90004) *(P-19087)*
Wilshire Health and Cmnty Svcs..........D......805 434-3035
290 Heather Ct Templeton (93465) *(P-21257)*
Wilshire Health and Cmnty Svcs..........D......805 484-2777
903 Carmen Dr Camarillo (93010) *(P-24725)*
Wilshire Hlth & Cmnty Svcs Inc..........D......310 679-9732
11630 Grevillea Ave Hawthorne (90250) *(P-21258)*
Wilshire Hlth & Cmnty Svcs Inc..........D......559 582-4414
851 Leslie Ln Hanford (93230) *(P-21259)*
Wilshire Insurance Company..........E......661 940-7300
1206 W Avenue J Ste 100 Lancaster (93534) *(P-10831)*
Wilshire Nursing & Rehab, Templeton *Also called Wilshire Health and Cmnty Svcs (P-21257)*
Wilson Elser Moskowitz..........D......213 443-5100
555 S Flower St Ste 2900 Los Angeles (90071) *(P-23437)*
Wilson Hampton Pntg Contrs Inc..........D......714 772-5091
1524 W Mable St Anaheim (92802) *(P-2493)*
Wilson Sonsini Goodrich & Rosa..........C......858 350-2300
12235 El Camino Real # 200 San Diego (92130) *(P-23438)*
Wilson Sonsini Goodrich & Rosa (PA)..........A......650 493-9300
650 Page Mill Rd Palo Alto (94304) *(P-23439)*
Wilson Sonsini Goodrich & Rosa..........D......415 947-2000
1 Market Plz Fl 33 San Francisco (94105) *(P-23440)*
Wilson Stephen Construction Co, Anaheim *Also called S W Construction Inc (P-3072)*
Wilson Supply, Compton *Also called Dnow LP (P-4673)*
Wilson Turner Kosmo LLP..........D......619 236-9600
550 W C St Ste 1050 San Diego (92101) *(P-23441)*
Wimberly Allison Tong Goo Inc..........D......949 574-8500
300 Spectrum Center Dr # 500 Irvine (92618) *(P-26124)*
Wimer Construction..........E......818 848-0400
10855 Wimer Country Rd Sunland (91040) *(P-1704)*
Win River Hotel Corporation..........E......530 226-5111
5050 Bechelli Ln Redding (96002) *(P-13400)*
Win Time Ltd (PA)..........C......858 695-2300
9335 Kearny Mesa Rd San Diego (92126) *(P-13401)*
Win-Dor Inc (PA)..........C......714 576-2030
450 Delta Ave Brea (92821) *(P-3091)*
Win-River Resort & Casino..........B......530 243-3377
2100 Redding Rancheria Rd Redding (96001) *(P-19262)*
Winbond Electronics Corp Amer..........D......408 943-6666
2727 N 1st St San Jose (95134) *(P-7564)*
Wincere Inc..........C......408 841-4355
2350 Mission College Blvd # 290 Santa Clara (95054) *(P-16533)*
Winchester Mystery House LLC..........D......408 247-2101
525 S Winchester Blvd San Jose (95128) *(P-19263)*
Winco Dwl Industries Co, La Mirada *Also called Winco Industries Company (P-7903)*
Winco Industries Company..........E......562 926-5600
14950 Valley View Ave La Mirada (90638) *(P-7903)*
Wind River Enterprises Inc..........D......707 864-1040
250 Dittmer Rd Fairfield (94534) *(P-6614)*
Wind River Systems Inc (HQ)..........C......510 748-4100
500 Wind River Way Alameda (94501) *(P-15892)*

ALPHABETIC

Employee Codes: A=Over 500 employees, B=251-500
C=101-250, D=51-100, E=50

2019 Directory of California
Wholesalers and Services Companies

© Mergent Inc. 1-800-342-5647
1525

Wind River Systems Inc.....D.....858 824-3100
10505 Sorrento Valley Rd San Diego (92121) ***(P-15893)***
Windermere Real Estate East.....D.....760 568-2568
71691 Highway 111 Rancho Mirage (92270) ***(P-11840)***
Windes Inc (PA).....D.....562 435-1191
111 W Ocean Blvd Ste 22 Long Beach (90802) ***(P-26307)***
Windflower Holdings LLC.....D.....707 263-6101
625 16th St Lakeport (95453) ***(P-20895)***
Windham At Saint Agnes.....D.....559 449-8070
1100 E Spruce Ave Ofc Fresno (93720) ***(P-11142)***
Windjammer Capital Invstr III.....A.....949 706-9989
610 Newport Center Dr # 1100 Newport Beach (92660) ***(P-10042)***
Windjmmer Capitl Investors LLC (PA).....D.....949 706-9989
610 Newport Center Dr Newport Beach (92660) ***(P-12284)***
Windrow Earth Transport Inc.....E.....909 355-5531
14032 Santa Ana Ave Fontana (92337) ***(P-2074)***
Windsor Anaheim Healthcare (PA).....B.....714 826-8950
3415 W Ball Rd Anaheim (92804) ***(P-20896)***
Windsor Capital Group Inc.....D.....805 988-0627
2101 W Vineyard Ave Oxnard (93036) ***(P-13402)***
Windsor Capital Group Inc.....D.....310 566-1100
3250 Ocean Park Blvd # 350 Santa Monica (90405) ***(P-13403)***
Windsor Capital Group Inc.....D.....310 566-1100
3250 Ocean Park Blvd # 350 Santa Monica (90405) ***(P-13404)***
Windsor Capital Group Inc.....D.....209 577-3825
3250 Ocean Park Blvd # 350 Santa Monica (90405) ***(P-13405)***
Windsor Capital Group Inc.....D.....209 577-3825
3250 Ocean Park Blvd # 350 Santa Monica (90405) ***(P-13406)***
Windsor Capital Group Inc.....D.....714 990-6000
900 E Birch St Brea (92821) ***(P-13407)***
Windsor Capital Group Inc.....D.....951 676-5656
29345 Rancho California Temecula (92591) ***(P-13408)***
Windsor Capital Group Inc.....D.....310 566-1100
3250 Ocean Park Blvd # 350 Santa Monica (90405) ***(P-13409)***
Windsor Capital Group Inc.....D.....310 566-1100
3250 Ocean Park Blvd # 350 Santa Monica (90405) ***(P-13410)***
Windsor Capital Group Inc.....D.....714 241-3800
1325 E Dyer Rd Santa Ana (92705) ***(P-13411)***
Windsor Capital Group Inc.....D.....951 276-1200
1510 University Ave Riverside (92507) ***(P-13412)***
Windsor Capital Group Inc.....C.....925 934-2000
2355 N Main St Walnut Creek (94596) ***(P-13413)***
Windsor Capital Holet Group, Sacramento *Also called Recp/Wndsor Scramento Ventr LP **(P-13104)***
Windsor Convalescent.....C.....925 689-2266
3806 Clayton Rd Concord (94521) ***(P-20897)***
Windsor Convalescent.....C.....510 793-7222
2400 Parkside Dr Fremont (94536) ***(P-20898)***
Windsor Convalescent.....C.....831 424-0687
637 E Romie Ln Salinas (93901) ***(P-20899)***
Windsor Court/Stratford Place, Westminster *Also called Westminster Housing Parteners **(P-11831)***
Windsor Garden Conv Ctr Hwthrn, Hawthorne *Also called Sandhurst Convales Grp Ltd A **(P-20745)***
Windsor Gardens, Salinas *Also called Windsor Convalescent **(P-20899)***
Windsor Gardens.....D.....562 422-9219
4333 Torrance Blvd Torrance (90503) ***(P-20900)***
Windsor Gardens.....D.....310 675-3304
13922 Cerise Ave Hawthorne (90250) ***(P-20901)***
Windsor Gardens Convalescnt, National City *Also called Windsor Healthcare Management **(P-20904)***
Windsor Gardens Convalescnt.....D.....323 937-5466
915 Crenshaw Blvd Los Angeles (90019) ***(P-20902)***
Windsor Gardens Hea, North Hollywood *Also called Mariner Health Care Inc **(P-20628)***
Windsor Gardens Healthcare C.....C.....510 582-4636
1628 B St Hayward (94541) ***(P-21260)***
WINDSOR GARDENS OF FULLERTON, Fullerton *Also called Windsor Gardns Healthcare Cntr **(P-20903)***
Windsor Gardens of Long Beach, Torrance *Also called Windsor Gardens **(P-20900)***
Windsor Gardns Healthcare Cntr.....C.....714 871-6020
245 E Wilshire Ave Fullerton (92832) ***(P-20903)***
Windsor Golf Club Inc.....D.....707 838-7888
1340 19th Hole Dr Windsor (95492) ***(P-18779)***
Windsor Grdns Cnvlescent Ctr A, Anaheim *Also called Windsor Anaheim Healthcare **(P-20896)***
Windsor Healthcare Management.....C.....619 474-6741
220 E 24th St National City (91950) ***(P-20904)***
Windsor Manor, Glendale *Also called Cal Southern Presbt Homes **(P-10994)***
WINDSOR MANOR REHABILITATION CENTER OF CO, Concord *Also called Windsor Convalescent **(P-20897)***
Windsor Monterey Care Ctr LLC.....D.....831 373-2731
1575 Skyline Dr Monterey (93940) ***(P-21261)***
Windsor Palms Care Ctr Artesia, Artesia *Also called Windsor Twin Palms Hlthcare **(P-20906)***
Windsor Park Care Ctr Fremont, Fremont *Also called Windsor Convalescent **(P-20898)***
Windsor Rdge Rhblttion Ctr LLC.....D.....831 449-1515
350 Iris Dr Salinas (93906) ***(P-22717)***
Windsor Redwoods LP.....D.....707 526-1020
790 Sonoma Ave Santa Rosa (95404) ***(P-17597)***
Windsor Skyline Care Ctr LLC.....D.....831 449-5496
348 Iris Dr Salinas (93906) ***(P-20905)***
Windsor Twin Palms Hlthcare.....C.....562 865-0271
11900 Artesia Blvd Artesia (90701) ***(P-20906)***
Windsor Vallejo Care Center, Vallejo *Also called Helios Healthcare LLC **(P-21108)***
Windstar Capital Advisors.....C.....310 505-3720
10940 Wilshire Blvd Los Angeles (90024) ***(P-10123)***
Windwalker Security Patrol Inc.....D.....209 333-3953
23987 Nw Frontage Rd Acampo (95220) ***(P-16858)***
Wine Country Party & Events, Torrance *Also called Bright Event Rentals LLC **(P-14479)***
Wine Dept, Los Angeles *Also called Youngs Market Company LLC **(P-9068)***
Wine Group Inc.....D.....559 638-3511
2916 S Reed Ave Sanger (93657) ***(P-9061)***
Wine Warehouse, Commerce *Also called Ben Myerson Candy Co Inc **(P-9034)***
Wine Warehouse, Richmond *Also called Ben Myerson Candy Co Inc **(P-9035)***
Winegard Energy Inc.....D.....559 441-0243
2885 S Chestnut Ave Fresno (93725) ***(P-2983)***
Winegard Energy Inc.....D.....661 393-9467
2159 Zeus Ct Bakersfield (93308) ***(P-2984)***
Winegardner Masonry Inc.....E.....909 795-9711
32147 Dunlap Blvd Ste A Yucaipa (92399) ***(P-2831)***
Winery Exchange Inc (PA).....E.....415 382-6900
500 Redwood Blvd Ste 200 Novato (94947) ***(P-9062)***
Winfield Construction, Emeryville *Also called Alpha-Winfield Contractors Inc **(P-1113)***
Wing Aviation LLC.....D.....650 260-8170
100 Mayfield Ave Mountain View (94043) ***(P-4854)***
Wingert Grebing Brubaker & Jus.....D.....619 232-8151
600 W Broadway Ste 1200 San Diego (92101) ***(P-23442)***
Winiarski Management Inc.....D.....707 944-2020
5766 Silverado Trl NAPA (94558) ***(P-9063)***
Winmax Systems Corporation.....C.....408 894-9000
1900 Mccarthy Blvd # 301 Milpitas (95035) ***(P-15546)***
Winnarainbow Inc (PA).....E.....510 525-4304
1301 Henry St Berkeley (94709) ***(P-13458)***
Winners Only Inc.....C.....760 599-0300
1365 Park Center Dr Vista (92081) ***(P-6744)***
Winning Performance Pdts Inc.....E.....818 367-1041
13010 Bradley Ave Sylmar (91342) ***(P-17598)***
Winnresidential Ltd Partnr.....B.....559 435-3434
2350 W Shaw Ave Ste 148 Fresno (93711) ***(P-17620)***
Winnresidential Ltd Partnr.....B.....559 665-9600
255 Washington Rd Chowchilla (93610) ***(P-11143)***
Winsor House Compalessant.....D.....707 448-6458
101 S Orchard Ave Vacaville (95688) ***(P-20907)***
Winsor House Convalescent Hosp, Vacaville *Also called Winsor House Compalessant **(P-20907)***
Winston & Strawn LLP.....B.....650 858-6500
275 Middlefield Rd # 205 Menlo Park (94025) ***(P-23443)***
Winter Care Center Sacramento.....C.....916 922-8855
501 Jessie Ave Sacramento (95838) ***(P-20908)***
Winterthur U S Holdings Inc.....C.....213 228-0281
888 S Figueroa St Ste 570 Los Angeles (90017) ***(P-10832)***
Winton Ireland Strom & Green (PA).....D.....209 667-0995
627 E Canal Dr Turlock (95380) ***(P-10833)***
Winton-Ireland, Strom and Gr, Turlock *Also called Winton Ireland Strom & Green **(P-10833)***
Winward International Inc (PA).....D.....510 487-8686
42760 Albrae St Fremont (94538) ***(P-9180)***
Winward Silks, Fremont *Also called Winward International Inc **(P-9180)***
Winzler & Kelly.....D.....707 523-1010
2235 Mercury Way Ste 150 Santa Rosa (95407) ***(P-26002)***
Wipfli LLP.....D.....510 768-0066
505 14th St Ste 1220 Oakland (94612) ***(P-27523)***
Wipli HFS Consultants, Oakland *Also called Wipfli LLP **(P-27523)***
Wired Rite Electric, Burbank *Also called Grc Electric Inc **(P-2592)***
Wireless Lines, Los Angeles *Also called Cellular Palace Inc **(P-7460)***
Wireless Store Inc.....C.....916 206-3600
2217 10th St Sacramento (95818) ***(P-6007)***
Wirenetics Co, Valencia *Also called Circle W Enterprises Inc **(P-7346)***
Wirtz Qulty Installations Inc.....D.....858 569-3816
7932 Armour St San Diego (92111) ***(P-2832)***
Wirtz Tile & Stone Inc.....D.....858 569-3816
7932 Armour St San Diego (92111) ***(P-3120)***
Wis, San Diego *Also called Washington Inventory Service **(P-17581)***
Wis, San Diego *Also called Washington Inventory Service **(P-17582)***
Wisdom University.....D.....415 259-7122
35 Miller Ave Mill Valley (94941) ***(P-25486)***
Wise Commerce Inc.....D.....855 469-4737
1730 S El Camino Real # 500 San Mateo (94402) ***(P-15547)***
Wish I Ah Care Center Inc.....C.....559 855-2211
1665 M St Fresno (93721) ***(P-20909)***
Wish-Ah Skilled, Fresno *Also called Wish-I-Ah Skilled Nursing **(P-20911)***
Wish-I-Ah Hlthcre & Wellness.....D.....559 855-2211
1665 M St Fresno (93721) ***(P-20910)***
Wish-I-Ah Skilled Nursing.....C.....949 285-8859
1665 M St Fresno (93721) ***(P-20911)***
Wismettac Asian Foods Inc (HQ).....C.....562 802-1900
13409 Orden Dr Santa Fe Springs (90670) ***(P-8488)***
Wismettac Fresh Fish, Santa Fe Springs *Also called Wismettac Asian Foods Inc **(P-8488)***
Withrow Cattle.....D.....916 780-0364
5301 Pleasant Grove Rd Pleasant Grove (95668) ***(P-427)***
Withrow Dairy, Pleasant Grove *Also called Withrow Cattle **(P-427)***
Withrow Phrm & Hlth Spc Lab.....D.....323 721-4281
2235 Via Puerta Unit A Laguna Woods (92637) ***(P-8222)***
Wj Newport LLC.....C.....949 476-2001
4500 Macarthur Blvd Newport Beach (92660) ***(P-13414)***
Wjbradley Mortgage Capital, Newport Beach *Also called Emery Financial Inc **(P-9881)***
WL Butler Inc.....C.....650 361-1270
1629 Main St Redwood City (94063) ***(P-1327)***
Wlcac, Los Angeles *Also called Watts Labor Community Action **(P-24128)***
WLMD (PA).....C.....209 723-9120
1715 Kibby Rd Merced (95341) ***(P-3612)***
Wm B Saleh Co.....D.....559 255-2046
1364 N Jackson Ave Fresno (93703) ***(P-2494)***
Wm Bolthouse Farms Inc (HQ).....A.....661 366-7209
7200 E Brundage Ln Bakersfield (93307) ***(P-89)***

Mergent e-mail: customerrelations@mergent.com
1526
2019 Directory of California
Wholesalers and Services Companies
(P-0000) Products & Services Section entry number
(PA)=Parent Co (HQ)=Headquarters (DH)=Div Headquarters

Wm Healthcare Solutions Inc ....D....713 328-7350
4280 Bandini Blvd Vernon (90058) ***(P-6525)***
WM LYLES CO, Fresno *Also called Lyles Diversified Inc* ***(P-1951)***
WM LYLES CO, Fresno *Also called American Paving Co* ***(P-1719)***
Wm Michael Stemler Inc (PA) ....C....209 948-8483
3244 Brookside Rd Ste 200 Stockton (95219) ***(P-10834)***
Wm Michael Stemler Inc ....C....559 228-4144
7110 N Fresno St Ste 350 Fresno (93720) ***(P-10835)***
Wm ONeill Lath and Plst Corp ....E....408 329-1413
P.O. Box 60352 Sunnyvale (94088) ***(P-2985)***
Wm Recycle America LLC ....D....562 948-3888
8405 Loch Lomond Dr Pico Rivera (90660) ***(P-6526)***
Wm S Hart Pony & Softball, Valencia *Also called William S Hart Pony & Softball* ***(P-27910)***
Wm Vandergeest Landscape Care ....D....714 545-8432
3342 W Castor St Santa Ana (92704) ***(P-962)***
Wm Wireless Inc ....E....562 633-9288
6723 N Paramount Blvd Long Beach (90805) ***(P-5427)***
Wmbe Payrolling Inc ....D....858 810-3000
9475 Chesapeake Dr Ste A San Diego (92123) ***(P-14799)***
Wme Bi LLC ....D....877 592-2472
17075 Camino San Diego (92127) ***(P-15894)***
Wmk Office San Diego LLC (PA) ....D....858 569-4700
4780 Estgate Mall Ste 100 San Diego (92121) ***(P-6745)***
Wmk Sacramento LLC ....C....916 929-8855
2001 Point West Way Sacramento (95815) ***(P-13415)***
WMS Transportation, Ventura *Also called Sam Hill & Sons Inc* ***(P-1977)***
Wnc Housing LP ....E....714 662-5565
17782 Sky Park Cir Irvine (92614) ***(P-12285)***
Wolf Firm A Law Corporation ....D....949 720-9200
2955 Main St Ste 200 Irvine (92614) ***(P-23444)***
Wolfe & Associates, Santa Barbara *Also called Ronald L Wolfe & Assoc Inc* ***(P-11743)***
Wolfe Engineering, Inc., San Jose *Also called Jabil Silver Creek Inc* ***(P-17924)***
Wolfe Trucking Inc ....C....818 376-6960
7131 Valjean Ave Van Nuys (91406) ***(P-4306)***
Wolfsen Incorporated ....C....209 827-7700
1269 W I St Los Banos (93635) ***(P-17)***
Woltcom Inc ....C....831 638-4900
2300 Tech Pkwy Ste 8 Hollister (95023) ***(P-2790)***
Wolters Kluwer Corp Legal Svcs, Aliso Viejo *Also called Citizenhawk Inc* ***(P-26806)***
Womble Bond Dickinson (us) LLP ....C....408 720-8300
1841 Page Mill Rd Fl 2 Palo Alto (94304) ***(P-23445)***
Women Health Center (PA) ....D....530 891-1917
1469 Humboldt Rd Ste 200 Chico (95928) ***(P-22718)***
Women Infant & Children ....D....562 570-4228
2525 Grand Ave Long Beach (90815) ***(P-24134)***
Women' S Health, French Camp *Also called Healthy Beginnings French Camp* ***(P-19495)***
Women's Health Center, Colusa *Also called Colusa Regional Medical Center* ***(P-26815)***
Women's Health Center, Merced *Also called Golden Valley Health Centers* ***(P-22585)***
Women's Imaging Center, Redding *Also called MD Imaging Inc A Prof Med Corp* ***(P-19674)***
Womens Center-Youth Fmly Svcs (PA) ....C....209 941-2611
620 N San Joaquin St Stockton (95202) ***(P-24135)***
Womens Law Center ....D....714 667-1038
950 W 17th St Ste D Santa Ana (92706) ***(P-24136)***
Womens Trnstnal Living Ctr Inc ....E....714 992-1939
P.O. Box 916 Fullerton (92836) ***(P-24250)***
Wonderful Citrus Packing LLC ....D....805 525-3818
2707 W Telegraph Rd Fillmore (93015) ***(P-210)***
Wonderful Citrus Packing LLC ....D....559 798-3100
36445 Road 172 Visalia (93292) ***(P-588)***
Wonderful Citrus Packing LLC (HQ) ....B....661 720-2400
1901 S Lexington St Delano (93215) ***(P-589)***
Wonderful Citrus Packing LLC ....D....805 988-1456
710 Del Norte Blvd Oxnard (93030) ***(P-590)***
Wonderful Company LLC ....B....661 720-2400
1901 S Lexington St Delano (93215) ***(P-211)***
Wonderful Orchards LLC (HQ) ....C....661 399-4456
6801 E Lerdo Hwy Shafter (93263) ***(P-197)***
Wonderful Orchards LLC ....C....661 797-6400
13646 Highway 33 Lost Hills (93249) ***(P-198)***
Wonderfulpistachiosandalmonds, Lost Hills *Also called Wonderful Orchards LLC* ***(P-198)***
Wonderland Music Company Inc ....D....818 840-1671
500 S Buena Vista St Burbank (91521) ***(P-12147)***
Wondertreats Inc ....B....209 521-8881
2200 Lapham Dr Modesto (95354) ***(P-9272)***
Wonderware, Lake Forest *Also called Aveva Software LLC* ***(P-15919)***
Wonderware Corporation (HQ) ....B....949 727-3200
26561 Rancho Pkwy S Lake Forest (92630) ***(P-7129)***
Wood Bros Inc ....D....559 924-7715
14147 18th Ave Lemoore (93245) ***(P-2075)***
Wood Castle Construction Inc ....E....626 966-8600
770 W Golden Grove Way Covina (91722) ***(P-1260)***
Wood Environment & ....D....949 642-0245
121 Innovation Dr Ste 200 Irvine (92617) ***(P-26003)***
Wood Environment & ....C....510 663-4100
180 Grand Ave Fl 11 Oakland (94612) ***(P-26004)***
Wood Environment & ....D....323 889-5300
6001 Rickenbacker Rd Commerce (90040) ***(P-26005)***
Wood Gutmann Bogart Insur Brkg ....D....714 505-7000
15901 Red Hill Ave # 100 Tustin (92780) ***(P-10836)***
Wood Ranch Golf Club, Simi Valley *Also called American Golf Corporation* ***(P-18684)***
Wood Rodgers Inc (PA) ....C....916 341-7760
3301 C St Ste 100b Sacramento (95816) ***(P-26006)***
Wood Smith Henning Berman LLP (PA) ....E....310 481-7600
10960 Wilshire Blvd Fl 18 Los Angeles (90024) ***(P-23446)***
Woodbridge Glass Inc ....C....714 838-4444
14321 Myford Rd Tustin (92780) ***(P-3413)***
Woodbridge Village Association ....D....949 786-1800
31 Creek Rd Irvine (92604) ***(P-25286)***

Wooden Valley Farms, Fairfield *Also called Lanza Vineyards Inc* ***(P-158)***
Woodfin Suite Hotels LLC ....A....858 314-7910
12555 High Bluff Dr # 330 San Diego (92130) ***(P-13416)***
Woodfin Suites, Newark *Also called Hardage Investments Inc* ***(P-10892)***
Woodfin Suites Hotel Brea, Brea *Also called Hardage Group of Companies* ***(P-12645)***
Woodland Care Center LLC ....D....818 881-4540
7120 Corbin Ave Reseda (91335) ***(P-21262)***
Woodland Healthcare ....D....530 756-2364
2660 W Covell Blvd Davis (95616) ***(P-21919)***
Woodland Healthcare ....C....530 668-2600
1207 Fairchild Ct Woodland (95695) ***(P-21920)***
Woodland Jint Unified Schl Dst ....E....530 662-0201
25 Matmor Rd Woodland (95776) ***(P-3948)***
Woodland Lfyett Sklled Nursing, Lafayette *Also called Independent Quality Care Inc* ***(P-21120)***
Woodland Lfytte Cnvlscent Hosp, San Ramon *Also called Independent Quality Care Inc* ***(P-21118)***
Woodland Park Retirement Hotel, Pomona *Also called Longwood Management Corp* ***(P-11058)***
Woodland Residential Services ....D....530 419-0059
1381 E Gum Ave Woodland (95776) ***(P-11144)***
Woodland Swim Team Bosters CLB ....D....530 662-9783
155 West St Woodland (95695) ***(P-25287)***
Woodley Lakes Golf Course ....D....818 780-6886
6331 Woodley Ave Van Nuys (91406) ***(P-18780)***
Woodmart Window Coverings, Van Nuys *Also called Kincaid & Decker Inc* ***(P-6771)***
Woodmont Real Estate Svcs LP ....B....707 569-0582
3883 Airway Dr Santa Rosa (95403) ***(P-27963)***
Woodmont Realty Advisors Inc ....D....650 592-3960
1050 Ralston Ave Belmont (94002) ***(P-10495)***
Woodruff Spradlin & Smart ....D....714 558-7000
555 Anton Blvd Ste 1200 Costa Mesa (92626) ***(P-23447)***
Woodruff Convalescent Center, Bellflower *Also called Estrella Inc* ***(P-20412)***
Woodruff-Sawyer & Co (PA) ....C....415 391-2141
50 California St Fl 12 San Francisco (94111) ***(P-10837)***
Woods Electric Company, Santa Fe Springs *Also called Harris L Woods Elec Contr* ***(P-2601)***
Woods Maintenance Services Inc ....C....818 764-2515
7260 Atoll Ave North Hollywood (91605) ***(P-3613)***
Woodside Group Inc ....E....209 579-2030
3509 Coffee Rd Ste D10 Modesto (95355) ***(P-9866)***
Woodside Healthcare Center, Sacramento *Also called W H C Inc* ***(P-20873)***
Woodspear Properties (PA) ....E....760 761-4340
810 Los Vallecitos Blvd # 201 San Marcos (92069) ***(P-11145)***
Woolf Enterprises, Huron *Also called California Valley Land Co Inc* ***(P-460)***
Woolf Farming Co Cal Inc (PA) ....A....559 945-9292
7041 N Van Ness Blvd Fresno (93711) ***(P-395)***
Wor International Inc ....E....626 812-8888
15612 1st St Irwindale (91706) ***(P-8283)***
Word & Brown Insurance ....C....714 567-4398
721 S Parker St Ste 200 Orange (92868) ***(P-27098)***
Word and Brown, Orange *Also called Omega Insurance Services* ***(P-10723)***
Word and Brown Hearing Ctr, Orange *Also called Providence Speech Hearing Ctr* ***(P-22656)***
Wordsmart Corporation ....D....858 565-8068
10025 Mesa Rim Rd San Diego (92121) ***(P-15895)***
Work Force Services Inc ....C....661 327-5019
300 Truxtun Ave Bakersfield (93301) ***(P-14946)***
Work Force Staffing, Bakersfield *Also called Work Force Services Inc* ***(P-14946)***
Work Truck Solutions Inc ....D....855 987-4544
2485 Notre Dame Blvd Chico (95928) ***(P-16534)***
Work2fture - Yuth Training Ctr, San Jose *Also called Work2future Foundation* ***(P-24251)***
Work2future - Gilroy Job Ctr, Gilroy *Also called Work2future Foundation* ***(P-24253)***
Work2future Foundation ....C....408 794-1234
2072 Lucretia Ave San Jose (95122) ***(P-24251)***
Work2future Foundation ....C....408 216-6202
1901 Zanker Rd San Jose (95112) ***(P-24252)***
Work2future Foundation ....C....408 758-3477
379 Tomkins Ct Gilroy (95020) ***(P-24253)***
Workcare Inc ....C....714 978-7488
300 S Harbor Blvd Ste 600 Anaheim (92805) ***(P-27611)***
Workday Inc (PA) ....C....925 951-9000
6110 Stoneridge Mall Rd Pleasanton (94588) ***(P-15548)***
Workers Compensation (PA) ....C....888 229-2472
1221 Broadway Ste 900 Oakland (94612) ***(P-10416)***
Workforce, Santa Cruz *Also called His Manna Inc* ***(P-27263)***
Workforce Development Bureau, Long Beach *Also called Career Transition Center* ***(P-24163)***
Workforce Inv Bd Solano Cnty, Fairfield *Also called Private Industry Cncl Slno Cty* ***(P-14701)***
Workforce Investment- Admin, Merced *Also called County of Merced* ***(P-24174)***
Workforce Resource Center, Santa Maria *Also called Employment Dev Cal Dept* ***(P-14612)***
Workforcelogic ....D....707 939-4300
425 California St San Francisco (94104) ***(P-15549)***
Working Assets Long Distance, San Francisco *Also called Credo Mobile Inc* ***(P-5541)***
Working With Autism ....D....818 501-4240
16530 Ventura Blvd # 310 Encino (91436) ***(P-22719)***
Workmens Auto Insurance Co ....D....213 742-8700
714 W Olympic Blvd # 800 Los Angeles (90015) ***(P-10417)***
Workrite Uniform Company Inc (HQ) ....B....805 483-0175
1701 Lombard St Ste 200 Oxnard (93030) ***(P-13628)***
Works Floor & Wall, The, Palm Springs *Also called Temalpakh Inc* ***(P-1672)***
Workshare Technology Inc ....C....415 590-7700
650 California St Fl 7 San Francisco (94108) ***(P-15550)***
World Class Distribution Inc ....C....909 574-4140
2121 Boeing Way Stockton (95206) ***(P-4661)***
World Class Distribution Inc ....C....909 574-4140
800 S Shamrock Ave Monrovia (91016) ***(P-4662)***

ALPHABETIC

Employee Codes: A=Over 500 employees, B=251-500 C=101-250, D=51-100, E=50
2019 Directory of California Wholesalers and Services Companies
© Mergent Inc. 1-800-342-5647
1527

World Famous San Diego Zoo, San Diego *Also called Zoological Society San Diego* ***(P-24937)***
World For US, San Diego *Also called Mirnavseh Inc* ***(P-15284)***
World Gym Fitness Centers, Burbank *Also called Executive Fitness Management* ***(P-18597)***
World Mark By Trend West, Oceanside *Also called World Mark of Oceanside* ***(P-13417)***
World Mark of Oceanside....D....760 721-0890
1301 Carmelo Dr Oceanside (92054) ***(P-13417)***
World Private Security Inc....C....818 894-1800
16921 Parthenia St # 201 Northridge (91343) ***(P-16859)***
World Service West....C....310 538-7000
1812 W 135th St Gardena (90249) ***(P-4922)***
World Trade Ctr Ht Assoc Ltd....C....562 983-3400
701 W Ocean Blvd Long Beach (90831) ***(P-13418)***
World Tuned Radio, Oceanside *Also called CK Enterprises Inc* ***(P-17086)***
World Variety Produce Inc....B....800 588-0151
5325 S Soto St Vernon (90058) ***(P-8749)***
World Vision International (HQ)....C....626 303-8811
800 W Chestnut Ave Monrovia (91016) ***(P-25487)***
World Wide Technology Inc....E....310 537-8335
1165 W Walnut St Compton (90220) ***(P-7130)***
Worldlink East, Los Angeles *Also called Worldlink LLC* ***(P-17599)***
Worldlink LLC (PA)....D....323 866-5900
6100 Wilshire Blvd # 1400 Los Angeles (90048) ***(P-17599)***
Worldpac Inc (HQ)....C....510 742-8900
37137 Hickory St Newark (94560) ***(P-6687)***
Worldsite.ws, Carlsbad *Also called Global Domains International* ***(P-5570)***
Worldstage Inc (PA)....D....714 508-1858
1111 Bell Ave Ste A Tustin (92780) ***(P-27099)***
Worldway Airmail Center, Los Angeles *Also called Lax International Service Ctr* ***(P-17292)***
Worldwide Flight Services Inc....C....310 646-7510
5908 Avion Dr Los Angeles (90045) ***(P-4923)***
Worldwide Flight Services Inc....C....310 342-7830
5758 W Century Blvd Los Angeles (90045) ***(P-4815)***
Worldwide Ground Transportatio....D....408 727-0000
651 Aldo Ave Santa Clara (95054) ***(P-3862)***
Worldwide Holdings Inc (PA)....D....213 236-4500
725 S Figueroa St # 1900 Los Angeles (90017) ***(P-10838)***
Worldwide Intgrted Rsurces Inc....D....323 838-8938
7171 Telegraph Rd Montebello (90640) ***(P-7904)***
Worldwide Produce, Los Angeles *Also called Green Farms Inc* ***(P-8691)***
Worldwide Produce, Los Angeles *Also called Green Farms Inc* ***(P-8692)***
Worldwide Security Associates (HQ)....B....310 743-3000
10311 S La Cienega Blvd Los Angeles (90045) ***(P-16860)***
Worldwind Services LLC....D....661 822-4877
915 Tehachapi Wllw Spgs Tehachapi (93561) ***(P-2791)***
Worleyparsons Group Inc....B....626 803-9000
181 W Huntington Dr 100 Monrovia (91016) ***(P-26007)***
Worleyparsons Group Inc....B....610 855-2000
721 Charles E Young Dr S Los Angeles (90095) ***(P-26008)***
Worleyparsons Group Inc....B....626 440-7000
100 W Walnut Pasadena (91101) ***(P-26009)***
Worth Magazine, Malibu *Also called Curtco Publishing LLC* ***(P-13940)***
Worxsitehr Insur Solutions Inc....D....877 479-3591
5000 Parkway Calabasas # 302 Calabasas (91302) ***(P-10839)***
Would You Rather - Season 1, Burbank *Also called A Its Laugh Productions Inc* ***(P-18008)***
Woundco Holdings Inc....B....310 551-0101
10877 Wilshire Blvd Los Angeles (90024) ***(P-14436)***
Wow Party Rental Inc....D....714 367-3380
14575 Firestone Blvd La Mirada (90638) ***(P-14558)***
Wp Electric Communications Inc....E....909 606-3510
14198 Albers Way Chino (91710) ***(P-2792)***
Wpcs Intrntional-Suisun Cy Inc....D....916 624-1300
2208 Srra Madows Dr Ste B Rocklin (95677) ***(P-2793)***
Wpromote LLC (PA)....D....310 421-4844
2100 E Grand Ave Fl 1 El Segundo (90245) ***(P-27524)***
Wr Chavez Company, Poway *Also called Wr Chavez Construction Inc* ***(P-1705)***
Wr Chavez Construction Inc....D....858 375-2100
12125 Kear Pl Ste A Poway (92064) ***(P-1705)***
WR Forde Associates Inc....D....415 924-3072
984 Hensley St Richmond (94801) ***(P-1871)***
Wrag-Time Air Freight Inc (PA)....B....800 586-9701
596 W 135th St Gardena (90248) ***(P-4307)***
Wrap News Inc....E....424 248-0612
2260 S Centinela Ave # 150 Los Angeles (90064) ***(P-16959)***
Wrap, The, Los Angeles *Also called Wrap News Inc* ***(P-16959)***
Wright Finlay & Zak LLP....D....949 477-5050
4665 Macarthur Ct Ste 200 Newport Beach (92660) ***(P-23448)***
Wright Broadband Group Inc....D....858 362-0380
4413 La Jolla Village Dr San Diego (92122) ***(P-27911)***
Wright Contracting EPA, Santa Rosa *Also called Wright Contracting LLC* ***(P-1706)***
Wright Contracting LLC....D....707 528-1172
3020 Dutton Ave Santa Rosa (95407) ***(P-1706)***
Writers Guild America West Inc....C....323 951-4000
7000 W 3rd St Los Angeles (90048) ***(P-25089)***
Writing Company, Culver City *Also called Social Studies School Service* ***(P-7248)***
Written On My Skin LLC....E....312 504-5100
7119 W Sunset Blvd # 316 Los Angeles (90046) ***(P-18170)***
Wrs, Woodland *Also called Woodland Residential Services* ***(P-11144)***
Ws Hdm LLC....D....858 792-5200
15575 Jimmy Durante Blvd Del Mar (92014) ***(P-13419)***
Ws Mmv Hotel LLC....D....619 692-3800
8757 Rio San Diego Dr San Diego (92108) ***(P-13420)***
Wsa Group Inc (PA)....E....310 743-3000
19208 S Vermont Ave 200 Gardena (90248) ***(P-16861)***
WSH&b, Los Angeles *Also called Wood Smith Henning Berman LLP* ***(P-23446)***
Wsm Investments LLC....C....818 332-4600
3990b Heritage Oak Ct Simi Valley (93063) ***(P-12148)***
Wsp USA Buildings Inc....C....415 398-3833
405 Howard St Ste 500 San Francisco (94105) ***(P-26010)***
Wsp USA Inc....D....714 973-4880
1100 W Town And Cntry 2 Orange (92868) ***(P-26011)***
Wsp USA Inc....D....909 427-9166
16689 Foothill Blvd Fontana (92335) ***(P-27525)***
Wsp USA Inc....E....212 465-5000
444 S Flower St Ste 800 Los Angeles (90071) ***(P-26012)***
Wsp USA Inc....C....415 243-4600
425 Market St Fl 17 San Francisco (94105) ***(P-26013)***
Wsp USA Inc....D....909 888-1106
451 E Vanderbilt Way # 200 San Bernardino (92408) ***(P-26014)***
WTLC, Fullerton *Also called Womens Trnstnal Living Ctr Inc* ***(P-24250)***
Wtmg Inc (PA)....D....209 954-1599
2735 Teepee Dr Ste D Stockton (95205) ***(P-14428)***
Wtw Delaware Holdings LLC....C....415 733-4100
345 California St Fl 15 San Francisco (94104) ***(P-27526)***
Wtw Delaware Holdings LLC....D....858 523-5500
10955 Vista Sorrento Pkwy # 300 San Diego (92130) ***(P-27527)***
Wu Yee Child Care Center, San Francisco *Also called Wu Yee Childrens Services* ***(P-27964)***
Wu Yee Childrens Services....D....415 677-0100
880 Clay St San Francisco (94108) ***(P-24400)***
Wu Yee Childrens Services....D....415 677-0100
831 Broadway San Francisco (94133) ***(P-27964)***
Wurldtech Security Tech Ltd....D....604 669-6674
2623 Camino Ramon San Ramon (94583) ***(P-7565)***
Wurms Janitorial Service Inc....D....951 582-0003
544 Bateman Cir Corona (92880) ***(P-14429)***
Wurzel Landscape Maintenance....E....818 762-8653
3214 Oakdell Rd Studio City (91604) ***(P-963)***
WW Grainger Inc....C....408 432-8200
2261 Ringwood Ave San Jose (95131) ***(P-7403)***
WW Grainger Inc....C....951 727-2300
4700 Hamner Ave Eastvale (91752) ***(P-7878)***
Ww Lbv Inc....C....818 707-1220
30100 Agoura Rd Agoura Hills (91301) ***(P-13421)***
Ww San Diego Harbor Island LLC....C....619 291-6700
1960 Harbor Island Dr San Diego (92101) ***(P-13422)***
Wwl Vehicle Svcs Americas Inc....C....310 835-8806
500 E Water St Wilmington (90744) ***(P-4663)***
Wx Brands, Novato *Also called Winery Exchange Inc* ***(P-9062)***
Wyndgate Technologies....D....916 404-8400
4925 Robert J Mathews Pkw El Dorado Hills (95762) ***(P-16535)***
Wyndham Anaheim Garden Grove, Garden Grove *Also called Ohi Resort Hotels LLC* ***(P-12975)***
Wyndham Garden Fresno Airport, Fresno *Also called Fresno Airport Hotels LLC* ***(P-12593)***
Wyndham Garden Hotel, Commerce *Also called Wyndham International Inc* ***(P-13427)***
Wyndham Garden Pierpont Inn, Ventura *Also called Fpl LLC* ***(P-12590)***
Wyndham Garden San Jose Arprt, San Jose *Also called Starlight Management Group* ***(P-13265)***
Wyndham Hotels & Resorts, Carmel *Also called Wyndham International Inc* ***(P-13426)***
Wyndham Hotels & Resorts, Fullerton *Also called Anaheim Park Hotel* ***(P-12322)***
Wyndham Hotels & Resorts, Belmont *Also called Wyndham International Inc* ***(P-13429)***
Wyndham Hotels & Resorts, San Jose *Also called Wyndham International Inc* ***(P-13430)***
Wyndham International Inc....C....714 992-1700
222 W Houston Ave Fullerton (92832) ***(P-13423)***
Wyndham International Inc....C....760 322-6000
888 E Tahquitz Canyon Way Palm Springs (92262) ***(P-13424)***
Wyndham International Inc....C....619 239-4500
400 W Broadway San Diego (92101) ***(P-13425)***
Wyndham International Inc....C....831 625-9500
1 Old Ranch Rd Carmel (93923) ***(P-13426)***
Wyndham International Inc....D....323 887-4331
5757 Telegraph Rd Commerce (90040) ***(P-13427)***
Wyndham International Inc....D....714 751-5100
3350 Ave Of The Arts Costa Mesa (92626) ***(P-13428)***
Wyndham International Inc....E....650 591-8600
400 Concourse Dr Belmont (94002) ***(P-13429)***
Wyndham International Inc....C....408 451-3050
1350 N 1st St San Jose (95112) ***(P-13430)***
Wyndham Irvn-Orange Cnty Arprt....D....949 863-1999
17941 Von Karman Ave Irvine (92614) ***(P-27100)***
Wyndham San Dego At Emrald Plz, San Diego *Also called Wyndham International Inc* ***(P-13425)***
Wyndham San Jose, San Diego *Also called Pacifica San Jose LP* ***(P-13010)***
Wynne Systems Inc (HQ)....D....949 224-6300
2603 Main St Ste 710 Irvine (92614) ***(P-15551)***
Wynwood At The Palms, Loma Linda *Also called Brookdale Snior Lving Cmmnties* ***(P-21023)***
X M G M, Lathrop *Also called Nbccat Corp* ***(P-17796)***
X Prize Foundation Inc....E....310 741-4880
800 Crprate Pinte Ste 350 Culver City (90230) ***(P-24861)***
X-Act Finish & Trim Inc....D....951 582-9229
248 Glider Cir Corona (92880) ***(P-3092)***
X3 Management Services Inc....D....760 597-9336
2128 Auto Park Way Escondido (92029) ***(P-27912)***
Xad Inc....C....650 386-6867
189 Bernardo Ave 100 Mountain View (94043) ***(P-27528)***
Xamarin Inc (PA)....C....855 926-2746
1355 Market St 3 San Francisco (94103) ***(P-15552)***
Xanterra Parks & Resorts Inc....C....760 786-2345
Hwy 190 Death Valley (92328) ***(P-13431)***
Xantrion Incorporated....E....510 272-4701
651 Thomas L Berkley Way Oakland (94612) ***(P-16536)***
Xavient Digital, Simi Valley *Also called Xavient Info Systems Inc* ***(P-15896)***
Xavient Info Systems Inc....A....805 955-4111
2125 N Madera Rd Ste B Simi Valley (93065) ***(P-15896)***

Mergent e-mail: customerrelations@mergent.com
1528
2019 Directory of California Wholesalers and Services Companies
(P-0000) Products & Services Section entry number
(PA)=Parent Co (HQ)=Headquarters (DH)=Div Headquarters

Xavier Plumbing and Mech Inc........D.......909 883-9426
2606 Mira Monte Dr San Bernardino (92405) ***(P-2412)***
Xavor Corporation........D.......949 529-7372
300 Spectrum Center Dr # 400 Irvine (92618) ***(P-16537)***
Xceed Financial Credit Union (PA)........D.......800 932-8222
888 N Nash St El Segundo (90245) ***(P-9618)***
XCEL Mechanical Systems Inc........C.......310 660-0090
1710 W 130th St Gardena (90249) ***(P-2413)***
Xcelmobility Inc........D.......650 320-1728
2225 E Byshore Rd Ste 200 Palo Alto (94303) ***(P-15897)***
Xcerra Corporation........C.......408 635-4300
880 N Mccarthy Blvd # 100 Milpitas (95035) ***(P-7566)***
Xcite Steps Corp........C.......858 722-1948
3978 Sorrento Valley Blvd # 100 San Diego (92121) ***(P-20972)***
Xdbs Corporation........D.......302 566-3006
3501 Jack Northrop Ave Hawthorne (90250) ***(P-26577)***
Xdbsb2b, Hawthorne *Also called Xdbs Corporation* ***(P-26577)***
Xdimensional Technologies Inc........D.......714 672-8960
145 S State College Blvd # 160 Brea (92821) ***(P-16078)***
Xerox Corporation........D.......818 848-8676
914 S Victory Blvd Burbank (91502) ***(P-14095)***
Xerox Corporation........D.......310 526-3940
2118 Wilshire Blvd Santa Monica (90403) ***(P-6988)***
Xerox Corporation........D.......650 813-6787
478 Ferne Ave Palo Alto (94306) ***(P-6989)***
Xerox Corporation........D.......916 444-8100
560 J St 300 Sacramento (95814) ***(P-6990)***
Xerox Corporation........C.......650 813-7138
3333 Coyote Hill Rd Palo Alto (94304) ***(P-6991)***
Xerox Corporation........B.......714 565-1100
1851 E 1st St Ste 200 Santa Ana (92705) ***(P-6992)***
Xerox Corporation........C.......408 953-2700
2665 N 1st St Ste 200 San Jose (95134) ***(P-16298)***
Xerox Education Services LLC (HQ)........D.......310 830-9847
2277 E 220th St Long Beach (90810) ***(P-6993)***
Xi Enterprise Inc........D.......661 266-3200
2140 E Palmdale Blvd Palmdale (93550) ***(P-18676)***
Xl Construction Corporation........D.......916 282-2900
1810 13th St Ste 110 Sacramento (95811) ***(P-1261)***
Xl Construction Corporation........D.......408 240-6312
343 Sansome St Ste 505 San Francisco (94104) ***(P-1707)***
Xl Construction Corporation (PA)........C.......408 240-6000
851 Buckeye Ct Milpitas (95035) ***(P-1708)***
Xl Fire Protection Co (PA)........D.......714 554-6132
3022 N Hesperian St Santa Ana (92706) ***(P-2414)***
Xl Specialty Insurance Corp........D.......925 942-6142
1340 Treat Blvd Walnut Creek (94597) ***(P-10433)***
Xl Staffing Inc........C.......619 579-0442
450 Fletcher Pkwy Ste 204 El Cajon (92020) ***(P-14800)***
Xld Group LLC........D.......310 316-3636
3635 Fashion Way Torrance (90503) ***(P-13432)***
Xobee Networks Inc........D.......559 579-1300
7910 N Ingram Ave Ste 101 Fresno (93711) ***(P-5679)***
Xojet Inc (PA)........D.......650 594-6300
2000 Sierra Point Pkwy # 200 Brisbane (94005) ***(P-4924)***
Xoom Corporation........C.......415 777-4800
425 Market St Ste 1200 San Francisco (94105) ***(P-9691)***
Xoriant Corporation (PA)........C.......408 743-4400
1248 Reamwood Ave Sunnyvale (94089) ***(P-16538)***
Xoxo, City of Industry *Also called Kellwood Company LLC* ***(P-8265)***
Xoxo, City of Industry *Also called Kellwood Company LLC* ***(P-8312)***
Xp Power LLC........D.......209 267-1630
11383 Prospect Dr Jackson (95642) ***(P-7567)***
Xp Systems Corporation (HQ)........C.......805 532-9100
405 Science Dr Moorpark (93021) ***(P-16079)***
Xpo Enterprise Services Inc........C.......916 399-8291
3810 Hill Rd Lakeport (95453) ***(P-4308)***
Xpo Logistics Freight Inc........D.......209 983-8285
5475 S Airport Way Stockton (95206) ***(P-4309)***
Xpo Logistics Freight Inc........D.......408 435-3876
2171 Otoole Ave San Jose (95131) ***(P-4310)***
Xpo Logistics Freight Inc........E.......858 569-8921
4965 Convoy St San Diego (92111) ***(P-4311)***
Xpo Logistics Freight Inc........D.......559 485-1164
4195 E Central Ave Fresno (93725) ***(P-4312)***
Xpo Logistics Freight Inc........D.......831 758-8874
787 Airport Blvd Salinas (93901) ***(P-4313)***
Xpo Logistics Freight Inc........C.......818 890-2095
12466 Montague St Pacoima (91331) ***(P-4314)***
Xpo Logistics Freight Inc........D.......714 282-7717
2102 N Batavia St Orange (92865) ***(P-4315)***
Xpo Logistics Freight Inc........C.......916 399-8291
3516 Kiessig Ave Sacramento (95823) ***(P-4316)***
Xpo Logistics Freight Inc........D.......949 581-9030
20697 Prism Pl Lake Forest (92630) ***(P-4317)***
Xpo Logistics Freight Inc........C.......213 744-0664
1955 E Washington Blvd Los Angeles (90021) ***(P-4318)***
Xpo Logistics Freight Inc........D.......760 922-8538
12555 Mesa Dr Blythe (92225) ***(P-4319)***
Xpo Logistics Freight Inc........D.......707 584-0211
4095 S Moorland Ave Santa Rosa (95407) ***(P-4320)***
Xpo Logistics Freight Inc........C.......510 785-6920
2200 Claremont Ct Hayward (94545) ***(P-4321)***
Xpo Logistics Freight Inc........C.......951 685-1244
13364 Marlay Ave Fontana (92337) ***(P-4322)***
Xpo Logistics Freight Inc........C.......562 946-8331
12903 Lakeland Rd Santa Fe Springs (90670) ***(P-4323)***
Xpo Logistics Supply Chain Inc........C.......559 408-7951
3825 S Willow Ave Fresno (93725) ***(P-5201)***
Xpo Logistics Supply Chain Inc........C.......909 975-6300
5200a E Airport Dr Ontario (91761) ***(P-5202)***
Xqawesome Inc........C.......949 929-9622
20 Mason Ln Ladera Ranch (92694) ***(P-24254)***
Xtra Department Inc........D.......562 462-3800
12631 Imperial Hwy F106 Santa Fe Springs (90670) ***(P-27101)***
Xtraplus Corporation........D.......510 897-1890
39889 Eureka Dr Newark (94560) ***(P-7131)***
Xtreme Security Services Inc........E.......909 390-6818
337 N Vineyard Ave # 210 Ontario (91764) ***(P-16862)***
Xyka Inc........E.......408 340-1923
5201 Great America Pkwy # 320 Santa Clara (95054) ***(P-15553)***
Y & R, San Francisco *Also called Young & Rubicam Inc* ***(P-13921)***
Y & S Auto Body Shop, San Pedro *Also called Y & S Enterprises Inc* ***(P-17746)***
Y & S Enterprises Inc (PA)........E.......310 548-1120
1441 N Gaffey St San Pedro (90731) ***(P-17746)***
Y M C A, Berkeley *Also called Young MNS Chrstn Assn of E Bay* ***(P-24404)***
Y M C A Childcare Resource Ser, Oceanside *Also called YMCA of San Diego County* ***(P-25293)***
Y M C A Los Cerritos, Bellflower *Also called Young Mens Chrstn Assc Gr L B* ***(P-25335)***
Y M C A Metro Clinic, Berkeley *Also called Young MNS Chrstn Assn of E Bay* ***(P-25358)***
Y M C A The, Long Beach *Also called Young Mens Chrstn Assc Gr L B* ***(P-25339)***
Y M International Inc (PA)........C.......415 467-3888
165 Valley Dr Brisbane (94005) ***(P-17600)***
Y W C A of Sonoma County........E.......707 546-9922
811 3rd St Ste 100 Santa Rosa (95404) ***(P-25288)***
Y, THE, San Diego *Also called YMCA of San Diego County* ***(P-25295)***
Yagi Bros Inc........D.......209 394-7311
5614 Lincoln Blvd Livingston (95334) ***(P-31)***
Yagi Bros Produce, Livingston *Also called Yagi Bros Inc* ***(P-31)***
Yale/Chase Eqp & Svcs Inc (PA)........C.......562 463-8000
2615 Pellissier Pl City of Industry (90601) ***(P-7822)***
Yaley Enterprises Inc........E.......530 365-5252
7664 Avianca Dr Redding (96002) ***(P-8067)***
Yamaha Corporation of America (HQ)........B.......714 522-9011
6600 Orangethorpe Ave Buena Park (90620) ***(P-8068)***
Yamaha Motor Corporation USA (HQ)........B.......714 761-7300
6555 Katella Ave Cypress (90630) ***(P-7921)***
Yamaha Music Corporation U S A, Buena Park *Also called Yamaha Corporation of America* ***(P-8068)***
Yamamoto of Orient Inc (HQ)........C.......909 594-7356
122 Voyager St Pomona (91768) ***(P-8902)***
Yamamotoyama of America, Pomona *Also called Yamamoto of Orient Inc* ***(P-8902)***
Yancey Roofing, Sacramento *Also called Gudgel Roofing Inc* ***(P-3162)***
Yang C Park........D.......408 260-8066
3703 Payne Ave San Jose (95117) ***(P-14801)***
Yang Ming America Corporation........D.......626 782-9797
181 W Huntington Dr # 202 Monrovia (91016) ***(P-5203)***
Yapstone Inc (PA)........C.......866 289-5977
2121 N Calif Blvd Ste 400 Walnut Creek (94596) ***(P-17601)***
Yardi Systems Inc (PA)........B.......805 699-2040
430 S Fairview Ave Santa Barbara (93117) ***(P-15554)***
Yates & Associates, Santa Ana *Also called Scottish American Insurance* ***(P-10766)***
YC Cable Usa Inc (HQ)........D.......510 824-2788
44061 Nobel Dr Fremont (94538) ***(P-17602)***
Ycg LLC........D.......760 230-8016
566 Shanas Ln Encinitas (92024) ***(P-27913)***
Ycusd, Yuba City *Also called Yuba City Unified School* ***(P-24862)***
Ydesign Group LLC (PA)........E.......866 842-6209
1850 Mt Diablo Blvd # 510 Walnut Creek (94596) ***(P-7404)***
Year Round Landscape Maint Inc........E.......909 597-7734
15189 Sierra Bonita Ln Chino (91710) ***(P-964)***
Yee Yuen Linen Service, Los Angeles *Also called Yuen Yee Laundry & Cleaners* ***(P-13491)***
Yefllow Shttle Vtrans Sdan Svc, San Leandro *Also called A-Para Transit Corp* ***(P-3739)***
Yellow Cab Company Penninsula........C.......408 739-1234
7013 Realm Dr Ste A San Jose (95119) ***(P-3874)***
Yellow Cab Cooperative Inc........D.......415 333-3333
55 New Montgomery St # 208 San Francisco (94105) ***(P-3875)***
Yellow Cabs, San Jose *Also called Yellow Cab Company Penninsula* ***(P-3874)***
Yellow Jacket Drlg Svcs LLC........D.......909 989-8563
9460 Lucas Ranch Rd Rancho Cucamonga (91730) ***(P-3356)***
Yellow Radio Service, San Diego *Also called Administrative Services SD* ***(P-3864)***
Yellow Transportation, Hayward *Also called Yrc Inc* ***(P-4324)***
Yellow Transportation, Gardena *Also called Yrc Inc* ***(P-4325)***
Yellow Transportation, Tracy *Also called Yrc Inc* ***(P-5254)***
Yellowpagescom LLC (HQ)........B.......818 937-5500
611 N Brand Blvd Ste 500 Glendale (91203) ***(P-17603)***
Yelp Inc (PA)........D.......415 908-3801
140 New Montgomery St # 900 San Francisco (94105) ***(P-16262)***
Yes Videocom Inc (PA)........B.......408 907-7600
2805 Bowers Ave Ste 230 Santa Clara (95051) ***(P-18171)***
Yeshiva Rau Isacsohn Academy........C.......323 549-3170
540 N La Brea Ave Los Angeles (90036) ***(P-24401)***
Yeshivath Torath Emeth Academy, Los Angeles *Also called Yeshiva Rau Isacsohn Academy* ***(P-24401)***
Yew Bio-Pharm Group Inc........D.......626 401-9588
9460 Telstar Ave Ste 6 El Monte (91731) ***(P-996)***
Yf Art Holdings Gp LLC........A.......678 441-1400
9130 W Sunset Blvd Los Angeles (90069) ***(P-12018)***
Yhb Long Beach LLC........D.......562 597-4401
2640 N Lakewood Blvd Long Beach (90815) ***(P-13433)***
Yhb San Francisco LLC........D.......415 421-7500
85 5th St San Francisco (94103) ***(P-13434)***
Yliving, Walnut Creek *Also called Ydesign Group LLC* ***(P-7404)***
Ymarketing LLC........D.......714 545-2550
4000 Macarthur Blvd # 350 Newport Beach (92660) ***(P-27529)***

Employee Codes: A=Over 500 employees, B=251-500
C=101-250, D=51-100, E=50
2019 Directory of California
Wholesalers and Services Companies
© Mergent Inc. 1-800-342-5647
1529

YMCA, Burbank *Also called Young Mens Christian* ***(P-25317)***
YMCA, Los Angeles *Also called Young Mens Chrstn Assn of La* ***(P-25342)***
YMCA, San Francisco *Also called Young Mens Christian Assoc SF* ***(P-25326)***
YMCA, Fullerton *Also called Young Mens Chrstn Assn Orange* ***(P-25350)***
YMCA, San Francisco *Also called Bayview Hunters Point Y M C A* ***(P-25097)***
YMCA Child Care Resource Svcs, San Diego *Also called YMCA of San Diego County* ***(P-25301)***
YMCA Crescenta-Canada, La Canada *Also called Crescenta-Canada YMCA* ***(P-25146)***
YMCA Glb Grant, Long Beach *Also called Young Mens Chrstn Assc Gr L B* ***(P-25338)***
YMCA Head Start, Berkeley *Also called Young MNS Chrstn Assn of E Bay* ***(P-25359)***
YMCA Metro La Summit Park, Valencia *Also called Young Mens Chrstn Assn of La* ***(P-25344)***
YMCA Metro La-52nd St School, Los Angeles *Also called Los Angeles Unified School Dst* ***(P-25194)***
YMCA of East Bay, Oakland *Also called Young MNS Chrstn Assn of E Bay* ***(P-25356)***
YMCA of East Valley (PA)....C....909 798-9622
500 E Citrus Ave Redlands (92373) ***(P-25289)***
YMCA of East Valley....E....909 881-9622
808 E 21st St San Bernardino (92404) ***(P-25290)***
YMCA of East Valley....E....909 425-9622
7793 Central Ave Highland (92346) ***(P-25291)***
YMCA of North Orange County....D....714 879-9622
2000 Youth Way Fullerton (92835) ***(P-25292)***
YMCA of San Diego County....D....760 754-6042
1310 Union Plaza Ct # 200 Oceanside (92054) ***(P-25293)***
YMCA of San Diego County....C....858 453-3483
8355 Cliffridge Ave La Jolla (92037) ***(P-25294)***
YMCA of San Diego County (PA)....C....858 292-9622
3708 Ruffin Rd San Diego (92123) ***(P-25295)***
YMCA of San Diego County....B....760 745-7490
1050 N Broadway Escondido (92026) ***(P-25296)***
YMCA of San Diego County....D....619 464-1323
8881 Dallas St La Mesa (91942) ***(P-25297)***
YMCA of San Diego County....D....858 292-4034
200 Saxony Rd Encinitas (92024) ***(P-25298)***
YMCA of San Diego County....D....619 281-8313
2927 Meade Ave San Diego (92116) ***(P-25299)***
YMCA of San Diego County....D....619 226-8888
2150 Beryl St Ste 18 San Diego (92109) ***(P-25300)***
YMCA of San Diego County....C....619 521-3055
3333 Camino Del Rio S # 400 San Diego (92108) ***(P-25301)***
YMCA of San Diego County....E....760 765-0642
4761 Pine Hills Rd Julian (92036) ***(P-25302)***
YMCA of San Diego County....C....619 298-3576
5505 Friars Rd San Diego (92110) ***(P-25303)***
YMCA of San Diego County....D....619 449-9622
10123 Hoffman Ln Santee (92071) ***(P-25304)***
YMCA of San Diego County....D....760 758-0808
4701 Mesa Dr Oceanside (92056) ***(P-25305)***
YMCA of San Diego County....D....760 757-8270
333 Garrison St Oceanside (92054) ***(P-25306)***
YMCA of San Diego County....D....619 422-8068
50 Fourth Ave Chula Vista (91910) ***(P-25307)***
YMCA OF SAN FRANCISCO, San Francisco *Also called Young Mens Christian Assoc SF* ***(P-25324)***
YMCA of San Joaquin County....D....209 472-9622
2105 W March Ln Ste 1 Stockton (95207) ***(P-25308)***
YMCA of Santa Clara Valley, San Jose *Also called YMCA of Silicon Valley* ***(P-25313)***
YMCA of Silicon Valley (PA)....D....408 351-6400
80 Saratoga Ave Santa Clara (95051) ***(P-25309)***
YMCA of Silicon Valley....B....650 493-9622
1922 The Alameda Ste 300 San Jose (95126) ***(P-25310)***
YMCA of Silicon Valley....C....408 298-1717
1717 The Alameda San Jose (95126) ***(P-25311)***
YMCA of Silicon Valley....B....650 969-9622
2400 Grant Rd Mountain View (94040) ***(P-25312)***
YMCA of Silicon Valley....D....408 226-9622
5632 Santa Teresa Blvd San Jose (95123) ***(P-25313)***
YMCA of Silicon Valley....C....408 370-1877
13500 Quito Rd Saratoga (95070) ***(P-25488)***
YMCA of The Mid-Peninsula Inc....B....650 493-9622
1922 The Alameda Ste 300 San Jose (95126) ***(P-25314)***
YMCA of Westchester, Los Angeles *Also called Young Mens Chrstn Assn of La* ***(P-25343)***
YMCA Overnight Camp, Julian *Also called YMCA of San Diego County* ***(P-25302)***
YMCA Pre School Hillview, Richmond *Also called Young MNS Chrstn Assn of E Bay* ***(P-24403)***
YMCA Richmond Afterschool Ctr, San Francisco *Also called Young Mens Christian Assoc SF* ***(P-25328)***
YMCA Youth & Family Service, San Rafael *Also called Young Mens Christian Assnsf* ***(P-25319)***
YMCA Youth & Family Services, San Diego *Also called YMCA of San Diego County* ***(P-25299)***
YMCA Youth & Family Services....D....619 543-9850
4080 Centre St Ste 203 San Diego (92103) ***(P-25315)***
Ymcasf, San Rafael *Also called Young Mens Christian Assoc SF* ***(P-25330)***
Yodlee Inc (HQ)....C....650 980-3600
3600 Bridge Pkwy Ste 200 Redwood City (94065) ***(P-27530)***
Yoga Works Inc (HQ)....E....310 664-6470
5780 Uplander Way Culver City (90230) ***(P-18677)***
Yogaworks, Culver City *Also called Yoga Works Inc* ***(P-18677)***
Yogaworks Inc (PA)....D....310 664-6470
5780 Uplander Way Culver City (90230) ***(P-18678)***
Yokohl Valley Packing, Lindsay *Also called Lindsay Fruit Company LLC* ***(P-17296)***
Yolo Hospice Inc (PA)....D....530 758-5566
1909 Galileo Ct Ste A Davis (95618) ***(P-22465)***
Yorba Bena Ice Skting Bowl Ctr, San Francisco *Also called VSC Sports Inc* ***(P-27906)***
Yorba Linda Country Club, Yorba Linda *Also called American Golf Corporation* ***(P-18832)***
Yorba Linda Medical Offices, Yorba Linda *Also called Kaiser Foundation Hospitals* ***(P-19603)***
Yorba Park Medical Group, Santa Ana *Also called St Joseph Heritage Med Group* ***(P-21778)***
Yorba Properties Corp....D....714 777-5112
20459 Yorba Linda Blvd Yorba Linda (92886) ***(P-11841)***
York Hlthcare Wllness Cntre LP....D....323 254-3407
6071 York Blvd Los Angeles (90042) ***(P-20912)***
Yosemite Capital Mangagement, Tustin *Also called Hmwc Cpas & Business Advisors* ***(P-26218)***
Yosemite Concession Services, Yosemite Ntpk *Also called DNC Prks Rsrts At Yosemite Inc* ***(P-12532)***
Yosemite Farm Credit Aca (PA)....D....209 667-2366
806 W Monte Vista Ave Turlock (95382) ***(P-9700)***
Yosemite Lakes Owners Assn....D....559 658-7466
30250 Yosemite Springs Pk Coarsegold (93614) ***(P-25316)***
Yosemite Management Group LLC (PA)....D....209 379-2817
11128 Hwy 140 El Portal (95318) ***(P-13435)***
Yosemite Meat Company Inc....D....209 524-5117
601 Zeff Rd Modesto (95351) ***(P-4519)***
Yosemite Waters, Los Angeles *Also called Aab Water Company Inc* ***(P-6205)***
Yosh Enterprises Inc....B....408 287-4411
675 E Gish Rd San Jose (95112) ***(P-16863)***
Yoshimura Research & Dev Amer....D....909 628-4722
5420 Daniels St Ste A Chino (91710) ***(P-6688)***
You Consulting Group, Encinitas *Also called Ycg LLC* ***(P-27913)***
Youappi Inc....D....646 854-3390
2 Embarcadero Ctr # 2310 San Francisco (94111) ***(P-27531)***
Young & Rubicam Inc....C....415 882-0600
303 2nd St Ste N300 San Francisco (94107) ***(P-13921)***
Young Bae Fashions Inc....D....323 583-8684
4811 Hampton St Vernon (90058) ***(P-8341)***
Young Brdcstg of San Francisco....C....415 441-4444
900 Front St San Francisco (94111) ***(P-5854)***
Young Communications, San Francisco *Also called Young Electric Co* ***(P-2794)***
Young Dowlin L....E....760 397-4104
101 Clay St San Francisco (94111) ***(P-212)***
Young Electric Co....C....415 648-3355
195 Erie St San Francisco (94103) ***(P-2794)***
Young Estates....D....805 446-1800
971 S Westlke Blvd 100 Westlake Village (91361) ***(P-11842)***
Young Mens Christian (PA)....D....818 845-8551
321 E Magnolia Blvd Burbank (91502) ***(P-25317)***
Young Mens Christian Assn, South Pasadena *Also called Young Mens Chrstn Assn of La* ***(P-25348)***
Young Mens Christian Assnsf....D....415 447-9622
63 Funston Ave San Francisco (94129) ***(P-25318)***
Young Mens Christian Assnsf....C....415 459-9622
1115 3rd St San Rafael (94901) ***(P-25319)***
Young Mens Christian Asso....D....805 583-5338
3200 Cochran St Simi Valley (93065) ***(P-19264)***
Young Mens Christian Asso....D....805 523-7613
4031 N Moorpark Rd Thousand Oaks (91360) ***(P-25320)***
Young Mens Christian Assoc SF....D....415 831-4093
680 18th Ave San Francisco (94121) ***(P-25321)***
Young Mens Christian Assoc SF....D....415 447-9602
57 Post St San Francisco (94104) ***(P-25322)***
Young Mens Christian Assoc SF....C....650 286-9622
1877 S Grant St San Mateo (94402) ***(P-25323)***
Young Mens Christian Assoc SF (PA)....E....415 777-9622
50 California St Ste 650 San Francisco (94111) ***(P-25324)***
Young Mens Christian Assoc SF....D....415 666-9622
360 18th Ave San Francisco (94121) ***(P-25325)***
Young Mens Christian Assoc SF....D....415 957-9622
169 Steuart St San Francisco (94105) ***(P-25326)***
Young Mens Christian Assoc SF....D....415 885-0460
246 Eddy St San Francisco (94102) ***(P-25327)***
Young Mens Christian Assoc SF....D....415 752-0790
4545 Anza St San Francisco (94121) ***(P-25328)***
Young Mens Christian Assoc SF....D....415 883-9622
3 Hamilton Landing # 140 Novato (94949) ***(P-25329)***
Young Mens Christian Assoc SF....B....415 492-9622
1500 Los Gamos Dr San Rafael (94903) ***(P-25330)***
Young Mens Christian Associat....D....562 624-2376
525 E 7th St Long Beach (90813) ***(P-25331)***
Young Mens Christn Assn Orange....D....714 771-1287
2241 E Palmyra Ave Orange (92869) ***(P-25332)***
Young Mens Chrstn Assc Gr L B....D....562 272-4884
4116 South St Lakewood (90712) ***(P-25333)***
Young Mens Chrstn Assc Gr L B....B....562 596-3394
1720 N Bellflower Blvd Long Beach (90815) ***(P-25334)***
Young Mens Chrstn Assc Gr L B....D....562 925-1292
15530 Woodruff Ave Bellflower (90706) ***(P-25335)***
Young Mens Chrstn Assc Gr L B....C....562 425-7431
5835 Carson St Lakewood (90713) ***(P-25336)***
Young Mens Chrstn Assc Gr L B....D....562 423-0491
4949 Atlantic Ave Long Beach (90805) ***(P-25337)***
Young Mens Chrstn Assc Gr L B....D....562 423-0491
4949 Atlantic Ave Long Beach (90805) ***(P-25338)***
Young Mens Chrstn Assc Gr L B....D....562 633-0106
6125 Coke Ave Long Beach (90805) ***(P-25339)***
Young Mens Chrstn Assn of La....E....818 989-3800
6901 Lennox Ave Van Nuys (91405) ***(P-25340)***
Young Mens Chrstn Assn of La....D....626 799-9119
1605 Garfield Ave South Pasadena (91030) ***(P-25341)***
Young Mens Chrstn Assn of La (PA)....D....213 351-2256
625 S New Hampshire Ave Los Angeles (90005) ***(P-25342)***
Young Mens Chrstn Assn of La....E....310 216-9036
8015 S Sepulveda Blvd Los Angeles (90045) ***(P-25343)***

Mergent e-mail: customerrelations@mergent.com
1530

2019 Directory of California
Wholesalers and Services Companies

(P-0000) Products & Services Section entry number
(PA)=Parent Co (HQ)=Headquarters (DH)=Div Headquarters

Young Mens Chrstn Assn of La....C....661 253-3593
26147 Mcbean Pkwy Valencia (91355) *(P-25344)*
Young Mens Chrstn Assn of La....C....562 862-4201
11531 Downey Ave Downey (90241) *(P-24137)*
Young Mens Chrstn Assn of La....C....323 467-4161
1553 N Shrader Blvd Los Angeles (90028) *(P-25345)*
Young Mens Chrstn Assn of La....D....562 862-4201
11531 Downey Ave Downey (90241) *(P-25346)*
Young Mens Chrstn Assn of La....D....818 763-5126
5142 Tujunga Ave North Hollywood (91601) *(P-24402)*
Young Mens Chrstn Assn of La....D....213 624-2348
401 S Hope St Los Angeles (90071) *(P-25347)*
Young Mens Chrstn Assn of La....D....323 682-2147
1605 Garfield Ave South Pasadena (91030) *(P-25348)*
Young Mens Chrstn Assn Orange....D....949 642-9990
2300 University Dr Newport Beach (92660) *(P-25349)*
Young Mens Chrstn Assn Orange....D....714 879-9622
2000 Youth Way Fullerton (92835) *(P-25350)*
Young Mens Chrstn Assn Orange....D....949 859-9622
27341 Trabuco Cir Mission Viejo (92692) *(P-25351)*
Young Mens Chrstn Assoc Gndl....D....818 484-8256
140 N Louise St Glendale (91206) *(P-25352)*
Young MNS Chrstn Assn of E Bay....D....510 654-9622
3265 Market St Oakland (94608) *(P-25353)*
Young MNS Chrstn Assn of E Bay....D....925 687-8900
350 Civic Dr Pleasant Hill (94523) *(P-25354)*
Young MNS Chrstn Assn of E Bay....A....925 609-7971
1705 Thornwood Dr Concord (94521) *(P-25355)*
Young MNS Chrstn Assn of E Bay....A....510 451-8039
2350 Broadway Oakland (94612) *(P-25356)*
Young MNS Chrstn Assn of E Bay....D....510 601-8674
4727 San Pablo Ave Emeryville (94608) *(P-25357)*
Young MNS Chrstn Assn of E Bay....D....510 486-8400
2111 Mrtn Lthr King Jr Wa Berkeley (94704) *(P-25358)*
Young MNS Chrstn Assn of E Bay....D....510 848-9092
2009 10th St Berkeley (94710) *(P-25359)*
Young MNS Chrstn Assn of E Bay....C....510 848-9622
2001 Allston Way Berkeley (94704) *(P-25360)*
Young MNS Chrstn Assn of E Bay....A....510 223-7070
3800 Clark Rd Richmond (94803) *(P-24403)*
Young MNS Chrstn Assn of E Bay....D....510 526-2146
1130 Oxford St Berkeley (94707) *(P-25361)*
Young MNS Chrstn Assn of E Bay....A....510 644-6290
2241 Russell St Berkeley (94705) *(P-24404)*
Young MNS Chrstn Assn of E Bay....B....510 412-5647
263 S 20th St Richmond (94804) *(P-25362)*
Young MNS Chrstn Assn of E Bay....C....510 222-9622
4300 Lakeside Dr Richmond (94806) *(P-25363)*
Young MNS Chrstn Assn of E Bay....D....510 848-6800
2001 Allston Way Berkeley (94704) *(P-25364)*
Young MNS Chrstn Assn of E Bay....D....510 559-2090
1422 San Pablo Ave Berkeley (94702) *(P-25365)*
Young Realtors....D....805 497-0947
971 S Westlake Blvd # 100 Westlake Village (91361) *(P-11843)*
Young Systems Corporation....D....562 921-2256
13125 Midway Pl Cerritos (90703) *(P-6994)*
Young Womens Christian Assoc....C....323 295-4280
2501 W Vernon Ave Los Angeles (90008) *(P-25366)*
Young Womens Christian Associ....D....408 295-4011
375 S 3rd St San Jose (95112) *(P-25367)*
Young's Nursery, San Francisco *Also called Young Dowlin L (P-212)*
Youngs Holdings Inc (PA)....D....714 368-4615
14402 Franklin Ave Tustin (92780) *(P-9064)*
Youngs Market Company LLC (HQ)....B....800 317-6150
14402 Franklin Ave Tustin (92780) *(P-9065)*
Youngs Market Company LLC....D....408 782-3121
850 Jarvis Dr Morgan Hill (95037) *(P-9066)*
Youngs Market Company LLC....B....510 475-2200
5100 Franklin Dr Pleasanton (94588) *(P-9067)*
Youngs Market Company LLC....B....213 629-3929
500 S Central Ave Los Angeles (90013) *(P-9068)*
Youngs Market Company LLC....D....707 584-5170
256 Sutton Pl Ste 106 Santa Rosa (95407) *(P-9069)*
Youngs Market Company LLC....E....916 617-4402
3620 Industrial Blvd # 10 West Sacramento (95691) *(P-9070)*
Youngstown Grape Distrs Inc....C....559 638-2271
1625 G St Reedley (93654) *(P-591)*
Your Executive Solutions....A....562 388-4150
9054 Slauson Ave Pico Rivera (90660) *(P-14802)*
Your Man Tours Inc (HQ)....D....310 649-3820
100 N Pacific Coast Hwy # 1700 El Segundo (90245) *(P-4985)*
Your Man Tours Inc....D....513 772-4411
100 N Pacific Coast Hwy # 1700 El Segundo (90245) *(P-25489)*
Your Practice Online LLC....C....877 388-8569
4590 Macarthur Blvd # 500 Newport Beach (92660) *(P-5680)*
Your Way Fumigation Inc....D....951 699-9116
41880 Kalmia St Ste 170 Murrieta (92562) *(P-14165)*
Yourpeople Inc....A....415 798-9086
250 Brannan St 3 San Francisco (94107) *(P-10840)*
Youth For Change....D....530 605-1520
2400 Washington Ave Redding (96001) *(P-24138)*
Youth For Change (PA)....C....530 877-8187
5538 Skyway Paradise (95969) *(P-24139)*
Youth For Change....D....530 538-8347
2185 Baldwin Ave Oroville (95966) *(P-24140)*
Youth Homes Incorporated....D....925 933-2627
1159 Everett Ct Concord (94518) *(P-24726)*
Yrc Freight, Adelanto *Also called Yrc Inc (P-4694)*
Yrc Inc....D....510 783-7010
25555 Clawiter Rd Hayward (94545) *(P-4324)*
Yrc Inc....C....310 404-2221
15400 S Main St Gardena (90248) *(P-4325)*
Yrc Inc....D....760 246-0031
17401 Adelanto Rd Adelanto (92301) *(P-4694)*
Yrc Inc....D....916 371-4555
3210 52nd Ave Sacramento (95823) *(P-4326)*
Yrc Inc....C....209 833-1300
1535 E Pescadero Ave Tracy (95304) *(P-5254)*
Yrc Worldwide Inc....D....650 952-1112
201 Haskins Way South San Francisco (94080) *(P-4327)*
YREKA EMPLOYMENT SERVICES, Mount Shasta *Also called Siskiyou Opportunity Center (P-24229)*
Ytech, Monterey Park *Also called Syntelesys Inc (P-17888)*
Ytel Inc....D....800 382-4913
94 Icon Foothill Ranch (92610) *(P-15555)*
Yti, San Pedro *Also called Yusen Terminals LLC (P-4744)*
Yub Inc....C....650 265-7316
520 Logue Ave Mountain View (94043) *(P-16201)*
Yuba City Nursing & Rehab LLC....D....530 671-0550
1220 Plumas St Yuba City (95991) *(P-20913)*
Yuba City Post-Acute, Yuba City *Also called Guava Holdings LLC (P-22022)*
Yuba City Racquet Club Inc....D....530 673-6900
825 Jones Rd Yuba City (95991) *(P-19088)*
Yuba City Unified School....A....530 822-7601
750 N Palora Ave Yuba City (95991) *(P-24862)*
Yuba Community College Dst....D....530 788-0973
2088 N Beale Rd Marysville (95901) *(P-24141)*
Yuba County Planning Dept, Marysville *Also called County of Yuba (P-11867)*
Yuba County Probation Dept, Marysville *Also called County of Yuba (P-23760)*
Yucaipa Companies LLC (PA)....C....310 789-7200
9130 W Sunset Blvd Los Angeles (90069) *(P-27914)*
Yucaipa Valley Water District (PA)....D....909 797-5117
12770 2nd St Yucaipa (92399) *(P-6319)*
Yue Feng Inc....D....310 253-9795
145 S Fairfax Ave Los Angeles (90036) *(P-24142)*
Yuen SOO Benevolent Assn....C....209 464-3048
119 Chung Wah Ln Stockton (95202) *(P-25368)*
Yuen Yee Laundry & Cleaners....D....323 734-7205
2575 S Normandie Ave Los Angeles (90007) *(P-13491)*
Yuja Inc....C....888 257-2278
2168 Ringwood Ave San Jose (95131) *(P-15898)*
Yukevich / Cvanaugh A Law Corp (PA)....D....213 362-7777
355 S Grand Ave Fl 15 Los Angeles (90071) *(P-23449)*
Yuma Lakes Resort, Earp *Also called Colorado River Adventures Inc (P-13462)*
Yume Inc (HQ)....D....650 591-9400
601 Montgomery St # 1600 San Francisco (94111) *(P-13922)*
Yuneec USA Inc....D....855 284-8888
2275 Sampson Ave Ste 200 Corona (92879) *(P-7568)*
Yupana Inc....E....925 482-0657
5039 Commercial Cir Ste J Concord (94520) *(P-26015)*
Yusen Logistics Americas Inc....C....310 518-3008
2417 E Carson St Ste 100 Carson (90810) *(P-5204)*
Yusen Terminals LLC (HQ)....D....310 548-8000
701 New Dock St San Pedro (90731) *(P-4744)*
YWCA, Santa Rosa *Also called Y W C A of Sonoma County (P-25288)*
YWCA Contra Costa/Sacramento (PA)....D....925 372-4213
1320 Arnold Dr Ste 170 Martinez (94553) *(P-24143)*
YWCA SILICON VALLEY, San Jose *Also called Young Womens Christian Associ (P-25367)*
Z & M Associates Inc....D....408 996-8100
1601 S Danza Blvd Ste 150 Cupertino (95014) *(P-11844)*
Z Garcia Farm Labor, Arvin *Also called Edwardo Z Garcia (P-642)*
Z J'S Auto Body, Clovis *Also called Pk Autobody Inc (P-17732)*
Z Microsystems, San Diego *Also called Zmicro Inc (P-16081)*
Z Valet & Shuttle Service, Los Angeles *Also called Z Valet Inc (P-13782)*
Z Valet Inc....C....323 954-3700
4221 Wilshire Blvd 170-11 Los Angeles (90010) *(P-13782)*
Z-Best Concrete Inc....D....951 774-1870
2575 Main St Riverside (92501) *(P-3347)*
Z57 Inc (HQ)....D....858 623-5577
10045 Mesa Rim Rd San Diego (92121) *(P-13923)*
Zabin Industries Inc (PA)....D....213 749-1215
3957 S Hill St Ste A Los Angeles (90037) *(P-8248)*
Zadaonet....D....650 556-6377
685 Scofield Ave Apt 22 East Palo Alto (94303) *(P-5681)*
Zaharoni Holdings....E....310 297-9722
5400 W Rosecrans Ave Lowr Hawthorne (90250) *(P-27102)*
Zanker Road Landfill, San Jose *Also called Zanker Road Resource MGT Ltd (P-6527)*
Zanker Road Resource MGT Ltd....D....408 457-1189
675 Los Esteros Rd San Jose (95134) *(P-6527)*
Zantos Living Trust, Anaheim *Also called Westcoast Performance Pdts USA (P-12193)*
Zapier Inc....D....770 988-0633
548 Market St San Francisco (94104) *(P-15556)*
Zastrow Construction Inc....C....323 478-1956
3267 Verdugo Rd Los Angeles (90065) *(P-1328)*
Zb National Association....E....858 793-7400
11622 El Camino Real San Diego (92130) *(P-9411)*
Zb National Association....C....310 258-9300
100 Crprate Pinte Ste 110 Culver City (90230) *(P-9412)*
Zb Rehab Staffing Inc....D....650 396-2207
650 El Camino Real Ste M Redwood City (94063) *(P-14947)*
Zeeto Media, San Diego *Also called Zeetogroup LLC (P-13924)*
Zeetogroup LLC....D....888 771-9194
925 B St Fl 5 San Diego (92101) *(P-13924)*
Zefr Inc....C....310 392-3555
4101 Redwood Ave Los Angeles (90066) *(P-18172)*
Zeiter Eye Medical Group Inc (PA)....D....209 366-0446
255 E Weber Ave Stockton (95202) *(P-20105)*

ALPHABETIC

Zell Associates Inc (PA) .... D 408 978-1950
1777 Hamilton Ave # 1250 San Jose (95125) *(P-10043)*

Zelle Hofmann Voelbel Masn LLP .... E 415 693-0700
44 Montgomery St Ste 3400 San Francisco (94104) *(P-23450)*

Zellerbach Rehearsal Hall, San Francisco *Also called City & County of San Francisco (P-18355)*

Zelos Consulting LLC .... E 650 968-2881
2400 Wyandotte St B103 Mountain View (94043) *(P-27915)*

Zemarc Corporation (PA) .... E 323 721-5598
6431 Flotilla St Commerce (90040) *(P-7823)*

Zend Technologies Usa Inc .... C 408 253-8800
19200 Stevens Creek Blvd # 100 Cupertino (95014) *(P-15557)*

Zendesk Inc (PA) .... C 415 418-7506
1019 Market St San Francisco (94103) *(P-15899)*

Zenefits Ftw Insurance Svcs, San Francisco *Also called Yourpeople Inc (P-10840)*

Zenith A Fairfax Company, The, Woodland Hills *Also called Zenith Insurance Company (P-10418)*

Zenith Health Care .... D 626 578-0460
245 S El Molino Ave Pasadena (91101) *(P-11845)*

Zenith Infotech Limited .... C 510 687-1943
39675 Cedar Blvd Ste 240b Newark (94560) *(P-16080)*

Zenith Insurance Company (HQ) .... B 818 713-1000
21255 Califa St Woodland Hills (91367) *(P-10418)*

Zenith Insurance Company .... D 619 299-6252
7676 Hazard Center Dr # 1200 San Diego (92108) *(P-10419)*

Zenith Insurance Company .... D 925 460-0600
4460 Rosewood Dr Ste 300 Pleasanton (94588) *(P-10153)*

Zenith Talent Corporation .... C 844 467-2300
3315 San Felipe Rd Ste 37 San Jose (95135) *(P-14803)*

Zenpayroll Inc (PA) .... B 800 936-0383
525 20th St San Francisco (94107) *(P-15900)*

Zentek Corporation .... D 916 749-3610
3031 Stnfrd Rnch Rd 2 Rocklin (95765) *(P-15558)*

Zephyr Partners Re-LLC .... E 858 558-3650
700 2nd St Encinitas (92024) *(P-11846)*

Zephyr Real Estate, San Francisco *Also called Dppm Inc (P-11409)*

Zephyr River Expeditions Inc .... D 800 431-3636
22517 Parrotts Ferry Rd Columbia (95310) *(P-19265)*

Zephyr White Water Expeditions, Columbia *Also called Zephyr River Expeditions Inc (P-19265)*

Zerep Management Corporation .... D 626 961-6291
17445 Railroad St City of Industry (91748) *(P-6528)*

Zero Energy Contracting Inc .... C 626 701-3180
13850 Cerritos Corporate Cerritos (90703) *(P-2415)*

Zero Energy Contracting LLC .... D 626 701-3180
13850 Cerritos Corporate Cerritos (90703) *(P-2416)*

Zero Motorcycles Inc .... D 831 438-3500
380 El Pueblo Rd Scotts Valley (95066) *(P-6615)*

Zero Waste Solutions Inc .... C 925 270-3339
1850 Gateway Blvd # 1030 Concord (94520) *(P-27612)*

Zestfinance Inc .... D 323 450-3000
1377 N Serrano Ave Los Angeles (90027) *(P-15559)*

Zettler Components Inc (PA) .... C 949 831-5000
75 Columbia Orange (92868) *(P-7569)*

Zhg Inc .... D 831 394-3321
2600 Sand Dunes Dr Monterey (93940) *(P-13436)*

Ziffren B B F G-L S&C Fnd .... C 310 552-3388
1801 Century Park W Los Angeles (90067) *(P-23451)*

Zignal Labs Inc .... D 415 683-7871
600 California St Fl 18 San Francisco (94108) *(P-15560)*

Zikakis Auto Holdings LLC (PA) .... E 805 736-4595
1224 N H St Lompoc (93436) *(P-17747)*

Zikko Inc .... C 916 949-8989
6345 Auburn Blvd Ste C Citrus Heights (95621) *(P-4391)*

Zillionaire Empress Danielle B .... A 310 461-9923
8549 Wilshire Blvd # 817 Beverly Hills (90211) *(P-12056)*

Zillow Group Inc .... A 415 836-6760
4100 Redwood Rd Oakland (94619) *(P-16202)*

Zim Industries Inc .... D 661 393-9661
7212 Fruitvale Ave Bakersfield (93308) *(P-3357)*

Zimmer Gnsul Frsca Partnr Amer, Los Angeles *Also called Zimmer Gunsul (P-26125)*

Zimmer Gunsul .... D 213 617-1901
515 S Flower St Ste 3700 Los Angeles (90071) *(P-26125)*

Zimmerman Roofing Inc .... D 916 454-3667
3675 R St Sacramento (95816) *(P-3211)*

Zinio Systems Inc .... D 415 494-2700
114 Sansome St Fl 4 San Francisco (94104) *(P-15901)*

Ziontech Solutions Inc .... D 408 434-6001
1900 Mccarthy Blvd # 415 Milpitas (95035) *(P-16539)*

Zipline International Inc .... C 415 993-0604
529 Railroad Ave South San Francisco (94080) *(P-27532)*

Zippy Usa Inc .... D 949 366-9525
1 Morgan Irvine (92618) *(P-7405)*

Ziprecruiter Inc .... A 800 557-9015
604 Arizona Ave Santa Monica (90401) *(P-27533)*

Zipzoomfly, Newark *Also called Xtraplus Corporation (P-7131)*

Zl Technologies Inc (PA) .... E 408 240-8989
860 N Mccarthy Blvd # 100 Milpitas (95035) *(P-15561)*

Zmicro Inc (PA) .... D 858 831-7000
9820 Summers Ridge Rd San Diego (92121) *(P-16081)*

Zmodo Technology Corp Ltd .... A 217 903-5673
17870 Castleton St # 200 City of Industry (91748) *(P-7570)*

Zodax LP (PA) .... D 818 785-5626
14040 Arminta St Panorama City (91402) *(P-6804)*

Zodiac Inflight Innovations US, Brea *Also called Systems and Software Entps LLC (P-15487)*

Zoe Holding Company Inc .... C 415 421-4900
44 Montgomery St San Francisco (94104) *(P-27965)*

Zoel Holding Company Inc .... C 916 646-3100
2143 Hurley Way Sacramento (95825) *(P-14804)*

Zohar Construction Inc .... D 818 609-7473
4272 Pasadero Pl Tarzana (91356) *(P-1262)*

Zoic Inc .... C 310 838-0770
3582 Eastham Dr Culver City (90232) *(P-18173)*

Zoic Studios, Culver City *Also called Zoic Inc (P-18173)*

Zonare Medical Systems Inc .... D 650 230-2800
420 Bernardo Ave Mountain View (94043) *(P-26679)*

Zone24x7 Inc (PA) .... B 408 268-8589
3150 Almaden Expy Ste 234 San Jose (95118) *(P-15562)*

Zonneveld Dairies Inc .... D 559 923-4546
1560 Cerini Ave Laton (93242) *(P-428)*

Zonneveld Farms .... D 559 923-4546
1560 Cerini Ave Laton (93242) *(P-429)*

Zoological Society San Diego (PA) .... A 619 231-1515
2920 Zoo Dr San Diego (92101) *(P-24937)*

Zoological Society San Diego .... A 760 747-8702
15500 San Pasqual Vly Rd Escondido (92027) *(P-24938)*

Zoological Society San Diego .... A 619 744-3325
2920 Zoo Dr San Diego (92101) *(P-24939)*

Zoosk Inc (PA) .... D 415 728-9543
989 Market St Fl 5 San Francisco (94103) *(P-5682)*

Zs Associates Inc .... D 805 413-5900
2535 W Hillcrest Dr # 100 Thousand Oaks (91320) *(P-27534)*

Zs Associates Inc .... D 650 762-7800
400 S El Camino Real # 1500 San Mateo (94402) *(P-17604)*

Zs Associates Inc .... D 858 677-2200
4365 Executive Dr # 1530 San Diego (92121) *(P-27535)*

Zscaler Inc (PA) .... C 408 533-0288
110 Rose Orchard Way San Jose (95134) *(P-15902)*

Zspace Inc .... D 408 498-4050
490 De Guigne Dr Ste 200 Sunnyvale (94085) *(P-7406)*

Zumwalt Construction Inc .... D 559 252-1000
5520 E Lamona Ave Fresno (93727) *(P-1709)*

Zuora Inc (PA) .... B 800 425-1281
3050 S Del St Ste 301 San Mateo (94403) *(P-15903)*

Zurich American Insurance Co. .... D 213 270-0600
777 S Figueroa St Ste 400 Los Angeles (90017) *(P-10841)*

Zurich American Insurance Co. .... C 415 538-7100
525 Market St Ste 2900 San Francisco (94105) *(P-10842)*

Zvents Inc .... E 408 376-7346
199 Fremont St Fl 4 San Francisco (94105) *(P-13925)*

Zvrs, Rocklin *Also called Csdvrs LLC (P-17117)*

Zwicker & Associates PC .... C 925 689-7070
1320 Willow Paca Rd 730 Concord (94520) *(P-23452)*

Zws/ABS Joint Venture LLC .... D 510 461-1433
39899 Balentine Dr # 200 Newark (94560) *(P-14430)*

Zyme Solutions Inc (PA) .... D 650 585-2258
240 Twin Dolphin Dr Ste D Redwood City (94065) *(P-16263)*

Zymo Research Corp (PA) .... D 949 679-1190
17062 Murphy Ave Irvine (92614) *(P-26495)*

Zynga Inc (PA) .... C 855 449-9642
699 8th St San Francisco (94103) *(P-16203)*

Zyrion Inc .... D 408 524-7424
440 N Wolfe Rd Sunnyvale (94085) *(P-15904)*

Zyxel Communications Inc .... D 714 632-0882
1130 N Miller St Anaheim (92806) *(P-5683)*

Mergent e-mail: customerrelations@mergent.com
1532

2019 Directory of California
Wholesalers and Services Companies

(P-0000) Products & Services Section entry number
(PA)=Parent Co (HQ)=Headquarters (DH)=Div Headquarters

COUNTY/CITY CROSS-REFERENCE INDEX

Alameda
Alameda
Albany
Berkeley
Castro Valley
Dublin
Emeryville
Fremont
Hayward
Livermore
Newark
Oakland
Piedmont
Pleasanton
San Leandro
San Lorenzo
Sunol
Union City

Alpine
Kirkwood

Amador
Ione
Jackson
Pine Grove
Pioneer
Plymouth
Sutter Creek

Butte
Biggs
Chico
Durham
Forest Ranch
Gridley
Oroville
Paradise
Richvale

Calaveras
Angels Camp
Arnold
Bear Valley
Copperopolis
Murphys
San Andreas
Valley Springs

Colusa
Arbuckle
Colusa
Williams

Contra Costa
Alamo
Antioch
Bay Point
Brentwood
Byron
Clayton
Concord
Crockett
Danville
Diablo
El Cerrito
El Sobrante
Hercules
Lafayette
Martinez

Moraga
Oakley
Orinda
Pacheco
Pinole
Pittsburg
Pleasant Hill
Point Richmond
Richmond
San Pablo
San Ramon
Walnut Creek

Del Norte
Crescent City
Smith River

El Dorado
Cameron Park
Diamond Springs
El Dorado
El Dorado Hills
Garden Valley
Kelsey
Lotus
Placerville
Shingle Springs
South Lake Tahoe
Twin Bridges

Fresno
Auberry
Big Creek
Caruthers
Clovis
Coalinga
Del Rey
Firebaugh
Five Points
Fowler
Fresno
Friant
Helm
Huron
Kerman
Kingsburg
Lakeshore
Laton
Mendota
Miramonte
Orange Cove
Parlier
Reedley
Riverdale
San Joaquin
Sanger
Selma
Tollhouse
Tranquillity

Glenn
Orland
Willows

Humboldt
Arcata
Bayside
Blue Lake
Eureka
Fortuna

Garberville
Hoopa
Korbel
Loleta
McKinleyville
Scotia
Trinidad
Willow Creek

Imperial
Brawley
Calexico
Calipatria
El Centro
Heber
Holtville
Imperial
Winterhaven

Inyo
Bishop
Death Valley
Independence
Little Lake
Lone Pine

Kern
Arvin
Bakersfield
Boron
Buttonwillow
Caliente
California City
Delano
Edison
Edwards
Edwards Afb
Keene
Kernville
Lake Isabella
Lamont
Lebec
Lost Hills
Maricopa
Mc Farland
Mc Kittrick
Mojave
Ridgecrest
Rosamond
Shafter
Taft
Tehachapi
Wasco

Kings
Avenal
Corcoran
Hanford
Kettleman City
Lemoore
Stratford

Lake
Clearlake
Clearlake Oaks
Hidden Valley Lake
Kelseyville
Lakeport
Lower Lake
Middletown

Upper Lake

Lassen
Herlong
Susanville

Los Angeles
Acton
Agoura
Agoura Hills
Agua Dulce
Alhambra
Altadena
Arcadia
Arleta
Artesia
Avalon
Azusa
Baldwin Park
Bell
Bell Gardens
Bellflower
Beverly Hills
Burbank
Calabasas
Calabasas Hills
Canoga Park
Canyon Country
Carson
Cerritos
Chatsworth
City of Industry
Claremont
Commerce
Compton
Covina
Cudahy
Culver City
Diamond Bar
Downey
Duarte
E Rncho Dmngz
El Monte
El Segundo
Encino
Gardena
Glendale
Glendora
Granada Hills
Hacienda Heights
Harbor City
Hawaiian Gardens
Hawthorne
Hermosa Beach
Hollywood
Huntington Park
Inglewood
Irwindale
La Canada
La Canada Flintridge
La Crescenta
La Mirada
La Puente
La Verne
Lake View Terrace
Lakewood
Lancaster
Lawndale

Littlerock
Llano
Lomita
Long Beach
Los Angeles
Lynwood
Malibu
Manhattan Beach
Marina Del Rey
Maywood
Mission Hills
Monrovia
Montebello
Monterey Park
Montrose
Newhall
North Hills
North Hollywood
Northridge
Norwalk
Pacific Palisades
Pacoima
Palmdale
Palos Verdes Estates
Palos Verdes Peninsu
Panorama City
Paramount
Pasadena
Pico Rivera
Playa Del Rey
Playa Vista
Pls Vrds Pnsl
Pomona
Porter Ranch
Rancho Dominguez
Rancho Palos Verdes
Redondo Beach
Reseda
Rllng HLS Est
Rosemead
Rowland Heights
San Dimas
San Fernando
San Gabriel
San Marino
San Pedro
Santa Clarita
Santa Fe Springs
Santa Monica
Saugus
Sherman Oaks
Sherwood Forest
Signal Hill
South El Monte
South Gate
South Pasadena
Stevenson Ranch
Studio City
Sun Valley
Sunland
Sylmar
Tarzana
Temple City
Toluca Lake
Topanga
Torrance
Tujunga

Universal City
Valencia
Valley Village
Van Nuys
Venice
Vernon
View Park
Walnut
West Covina
West Hills
West Hollywood
Whittier
Wilmington
Winnetka
Woodland Hills

Madera

Bass Lake
Chowchilla
Coarsegold
Madera
North Fork
Oakhurst

Marin

Belvedere
Belvedere Tiburon
Bolinas
Corte Madera
Fairfax
Greenbrae
Kentfield
Larkspur
Marshall
Mill Valley
Novato
Point Reyes Station
Ross
San Geronimo
San Quentin
San Rafael
Sausalito

Mariposa

El Portal
Fish Camp
Hornitos
Mariposa
Yosemite Ntpk

Mendocino

Albion
Calpella
Caspar
Covelo
Fort Bragg
Gualala
Hopland
Little River
Mendocino
Point Arena
Potter Valley
Redwood Valley
Ukiah
Willits

Merced

Atwater
Ballico
Delhi
Dos Palos
El Nido
Gustine

Le Grand
Livingston
Los Banos
Merced
Snelling
Stevinson
Winton

Modoc

Alturas
Cedarville

Mono

Mammoth Lakes
Topaz

Monterey

Aromas
Big Sur
Carmel
Carmel Valley
Castroville
Chualar
Gonzales
Greenfield
King City
Marina
Monterey
Moss Landing
Pacific Grove
Pebble Beach
Salinas
San Ardo
Seaside
Soledad

Napa

American Canyon
Angwin
Calistoga
NAPA
Rutherford
Saint Helena
Yountville

Nevada

Grass Valley
Nevada City
Norden
Penn Valley
Soda Springs
Truckee

Orange

Aliso Viejo
Anaheim
Brea
Buena Park
Capistrano Beach
Corona Del Mar
Costa Mesa
Cypress
Dana Point
El Toro
Foothill Ranch
Fountain Valley
Fullerton
Garden Grove
Huntington Beach
Irvine
La Habra
La Habra Heights
La Palma

Ladera Ranch
Laguna Beach
Laguna Hills
Laguna Niguel
Laguna Woods
Lake Forest
Los Alamitos
Mission Viejo
Newport Beach
Newport Coast
Orange
Placentia
Rancho Santa Margari
Rcho STA Marg
San Clemente
San Juan Capistrano
Santa Ana
Seal Beach
Silverado
Stanton
Trabuco Canyon
Tustin
Villa Park
Westminster
Yorba Linda

Placer

Alpine Meadows
Auburn
Granite Bay
Homewood
Kings Beach
Lincoln
Loomis
Olympic Valley
Penryn
Rocklin
Roseville
Tahoe City

Plumas

Chester
Greenville
Portola
Quincy

Riverside

Anza
Banning
Beaumont
Bermuda Dunes
Blythe
Cabazon
Calimesa
Canyon Lake
Cathedral City
Cherry Valley
Coachella
Corona
Desert Hot Springs
Eastvale
Hemet
Homeland
Idyllwild
Indian Wells
Indio
Jurupa Valley
La Quinta
Lake Elsinore
March ARB
Mecca
Menifee

Mira Loma
Moreno Valley
Murrieta
Norco
Palm Desert
Palm Springs
Perris
Rancho Mirage
Riverside
Romoland
San Jacinto
Sun City
Temecula
Thermal
Thousand Palms
Wildomar
Winchester

Sacramento

Antelope
Carmichael
Citrus Heights
Courtland
Elk Grove
Fair Oaks
Folsom
Galt
Gold River
Isleton
Mather
McClellan
North Highlands
Orangevale
Rancho Cordova
Rancho Murieta
Rio Linda
Sacramento
Walnut Grove

San Benito

Hollister
San Juan Bautista

San Bernardino

Adelanto
Alta Loma
Apple Valley
Barstow
Big Bear City
Big Bear Lake
Bloomington
Blue Jay
Cedar Glen
Chino
Chino Hills
Colton
Earp
Etiwanda
Fontana
Fort Irwin
Grand Terrace
Helendale
Hesperia
Highland
Lake Arrowhead
Loma Linda
Lucerne Valley
Lytle Creek
Mentone
Montclair
Mountain Pass
Needles

Nipton
Oak Hills
Ontario
Parker Dam
Patton
Rancho Cucamonga
Redlands
Rialto
San Bernardino
Trona
Twentynine Palms
Upland
Victorville
Wrightwood
Yucaipa
Yucca Valley

San Diego

Alpine
Bonita
Bonsall
Borrego Springs
Boulevard
Camp Pendleton
Campo
Carlsbad
Chula Vista
Coronado
Del Mar
El Cajon
Encinitas
Escondido
Fallbrook
Imperial Beach
Jamul
Julian
La Jolla
La Mesa
Lakeside
Lemon Grove
National City
Oceanside
Pala
Pauma Valley
Potrero
Poway
Ramona
Rancho Santa Fe
San Diego
San Marcos
San Ysidro
Santee
Solana Beach
Spring Valley
Tecate
Valley Center
Vista

San Francisco

San Francisco

San Joaquin

Acampo
Escalon
Farmington
French Camp
Holt
Lathrop
Linden
Lodi
Manteca
Ripon

Stockton
Tracy
Victor
Woodbridge

San Luis Obispo
Arroyo Grande
Atascadero
Avila Beach
Cambria
Grover Beach
Los Osos
Morro Bay
Nipomo
Oceano
Paso Robles
Pismo Beach
San Luis Obispo
San Simeon
Shell Beach
Templeton

San Mateo
Atherton
Belmont
Brisbane
Burlingame
Colma
Daly City
El Granada
Foster City
Half Moon Bay
Hillsborough
Menlo Park
Millbrae
Moss Beach
Pacifica
Pescadero
Portola Valley
Portola Vally
Redwood City
San Bruno
San Carlos
San Francisco
San Mateo
South San Francisco
Woodside

Santa Barbara
Buellton
Carpinteria
Goleta
Guadalupe
Lompoc
Orcutt
Santa Barbara
Santa Maria
Santa Ynez
Solvang
Vandenberg Afb

Santa Clara
Alviso
Campbell
Cupertino
East Palo Alto
Gilroy
Los Altos
Los Altos Hills
Los Gatos
Milpitas
Moffett Field
Morgan Hill
Mountain View
Palo Alto
San Jose
San Martin
Santa Clara
Saratoga
Stanford
Sunnyvale

Santa Cruz
Aptos
Boulder Creek
Capitola
Davenport
Felton
Mount Hermon
Royal Oaks
Santa Cruz
Scotts Valley
Soquel
Watsonville

Shasta
Anderson
Burney
Cottonwood
Hat Creek
Palo Cedro
Redding

Sierra
Loyalton

Siskiyou
Edgewood
Etna
Happy Camp
Macdoel
Mount Shasta
Tulelake
Weed
Yreka

Solano
Benicia
Dixon
Fairfield
Rio Vista
Suisun City
Travis Afb
Vacaville
Vallejo

Sonoma
Bodega Bay
Cazadero
Cloverdale
Cotati
Fulton
Geyserville
Glen Ellen
Guerneville
Healdsburg
Kenwood
Occidental
Petaluma
Rohnert Park
Santa Rosa
Sebastopol
Sonoma
Windsor

Stanislaus
Ceres
Denair
Hickman
Hughson
Keyes
La Grange
Modesto
Newman
Oakdale
Patterson
Riverbank
Salida
Turlock
Waterford

Sutter
Live Oak
Meridian
Pleasant Grove
Yuba City

Tehama
Corning
Gerber
Red Bluff
Vina

Trinity
Weaverville

Tulare
Cutler
Dinuba
Earlimart
Exeter
Goshen
Ivanhoe
Kings Canyon Nationa
Lindsay
Orosi
Porterville
Richgrove
Strathmore
Terra Bella
Tipton
Traver
Tulare
Visalia

Woodlake

Tuolumne
Columbia
Groveland
Jamestown
Long Barn
Pinecrest
Sonora
Tuolumne

Ventura
Agoura Hills
Camarillo
Fillmore
Moorpark
Newbury Park
Oak View
Ojai
Oxnard
Piru
Port Hueneme
Santa Paula
Santa Rosa Valley
Simi Valley
Somis
Thousand Oaks
Ventura
Westlake Village

Yolo
Brooks
Clarksburg
Davis
El Macero
Esparto
Knights Landing
West Sacramento
Winters
Woodland

Yuba
Beale Afb
Brownsville
Marysville
Olivehurst
Wheatland

GEOGRAPHIC SECTION

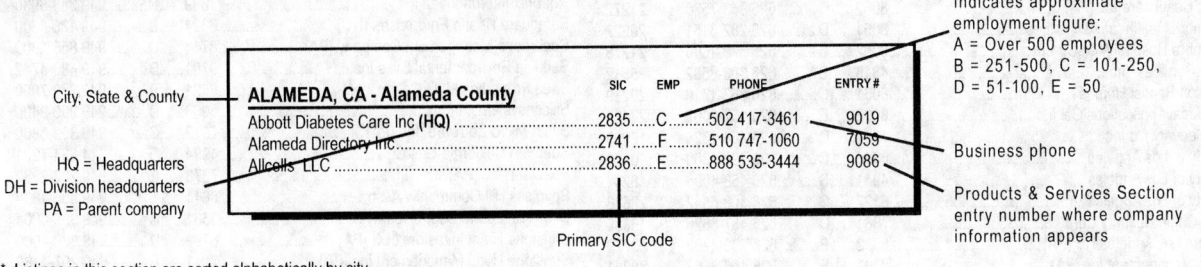

City, State & County → **ALAMEDA, CA - Alameda County**

	SIC	EMP	PHONE	ENTRY #
Abbott Diabetes Care Inc **(HQ)**	2835	C	502 417-3461	9019
Alameda Directory Inc	2741	F	510 747-1060	7059
Allcells LLC	2836	E	888 535-3444	9086

Indicates approximate employment figure:
A = Over 500 employees
B = 251-500, C = 101-250,
D = 51-100, E = 50

Business phone

Products & Services Section entry number where company information appears

HQ = Headquarters
DH = Division headquarters
PA = Parent company

Primary SIC code

* Listings in this section are sorted alphabetically by city.

* Listings within each city are sorted alphabetically by company name.

ACAMPO, CA - San Joaquin County

	SIC	EMP	PHONE	ENTRY #
JJ Rios Farm Services Inc	0761	D	209 333-7467	655
Langetwins Inc	0172	D	209 339-4055	157
Nestor Enterprises LLC	0172	E	209 727-5711	163
Windwalker Security Patrol Inc	7381	D	209 333-3953	16858

ACTON, CA - Los Angeles County

	SIC	EMP	PHONE	ENTRY #
County of Los Angeles	8069	D	661 223-8700	22011
Dedication & Everlasting Love	0752	D	661 269-4010	627
Delta Rescue Inc	8699	D	661 269-4010	25416

ADELANTO, CA - San Bernardino County

	SIC	EMP	PHONE	ENTRY #
Centerline Wood Products	5099	D	760 246-4530	8023
Cwp Cabinets Inc	1751	C	760 246-4530	3025
Geo Group Inc	8741	D	760 246-1171	26868
Hayes Welding Inc **(PA)**	7692	D	760 246-4878	17923
S E C C Corporation	1623	D	760 246-6218	1975
South Capitol Cottage	8748	D	951 662-3026	27867
USA Transport Inc	4214	E	559 783-3563	4384
Yrc Inc	4231	D	760 246-0031	4694

AGOURA, CA - Los Angeles County

	SIC	EMP	PHONE	ENTRY #
Abraham Jsha Hschl Dy Schl Wst	8351	D	818 707-2365	24256
Joni and Friends **(PA)**	8322	D	818 707-5664	23879
Up Stage Inc	7812	E	818 879-8781	18150

AGOURA HILLS, CA - Los Angeles County

	SIC	EMP	PHONE	ENTRY #
Amcal Communities Inc	6552	E	818 706-0694	11853
Amh Portfolio One LLC	6798	C	480 921-4600	12151
Davidson Hotel Partners Lp	7011	D	818 707-1220	12513
Ess	1711	D	888 303-6424	2204
First Student Inc	4151	D	818 707-2082	3932
International Bus Mchs Corp	7373	C	914 499-1900	15981
James H Cowan & Associates Inc	0782	D	310 457-2574	865
Los Angeles Rams LLC **(PA)**	7941	C	314 982-7267	18526
Meadowbrook Senior Living	8322	D	818 991-3544	23914
Mjd Construction Corp	1521	D	818 575-9864	1207
Mobile Programming LLC **(PA)**	7371	D	310 584-6300	15287
National Everclean Svcs Inc	8734	D	877 532-5326	26721
National Veterinary Assoc Inc **(PA)**	0742	C	805 777-7722	607
Novalogic Inc **(PA)**	7371	D	818 880-1997	15317
Pennymac Corp	6163	A	818 878-8416	9902
Private Nat Mrtg Accptance LLC **(HQ)**	6162	A	818 224-7401	9847
Quality Home Loans	6162	D	818 206-6600	9852
Regency Theatres Inc	7832	E	818 224-3825	18319
Sequoia Concepts Inc	7322	D	818 409-6000	14023
State Farm Mutl Auto Insur Co	6411	D	818 597-4300	10783
Vertafore Fsc Inc	7371	C	800 433-2550	15526
Whiting-Turner Contracting Co	1542	C	818 879-8100	1700
Ww Lbv Inc	7011	C	818 707-1220	13421
Coldwell Bankers Residential **(PA)**	6531	C	818 575-2660	11346

AGUA DULCE, CA - Los Angeles County

	SIC	EMP	PHONE	ENTRY #
Petrelli Electric Inc	1731	D	661 268-7312	2678

ALAMEDA, CA - Alameda County

	SIC	EMP	PHONE	ENTRY #
Abb/Con-Cise Optical Group LLC	5048	D	800 852-8089	7231
Abb/Con-Cise Optical Group LLC	5048	D	510 483-9400	7232
Absolutdata Technologies Inc	7389	D	510 748-9922	16976
Alameda Alliance For Health	6324	C	510 747-4555	10179
Alameda Bureau Elec Imprv Corp **(HQ)**	4911	D	510 748-3902	6011
Alameda Family Services	8351	D	510 629-6300	24263
Alameda Hlthcare & Wellnss Ctr	8051	D	510 523-8857	20224
Allcells LLC	8731	D	510 521-2600	26315
American Cancer Soc Cal Div **(PA)**	8733	D	510 893-7900	26589

	SIC	EMP	PHONE	ENTRY #
Bay Marine & Indus Sup LLC	5099	E	510 337-9122	8019
Bay View Rhbilitation Hosp LLC	8051	D	510 521-5600	20256
Berg Wlliam L Attorney At Law **(PA)**	8111	C	510 523-3200	22940
Bladium Inc **(PA)**	7991	D	510 814-4999	18581
Center For Ind Living Inc **(PA)**	8322	D	510 841-4776	23547
Chipman Corporation **(PA)**	4214	E	510 748-8700	4336
City Alameda Health Care Corp **(PA)**	8062	D	510 522-3700	21327
City Alameda Health Care Corp	8741	B	510 814-4000	26809
Club Nautique **(PA)**	7997	D	510 521-5544	18894
Delphi Productions Inc **(PA)**	7311	C	510 748-7494	13816
Diehard Security Solutions Inc	7381	C	510 995-8450	16630
Elder Care Alliance Camarillo	8361	D	510 769-2700	24516
Elder Care Alliance San Rafael	8051	D	510 769-2700	20387
Embarcadero Systems Corp	7371	C	510 749-7400	15135
Emmanuel Cnvlscent Hosp Almeda	8059	D	510 521-5765	21062
Family Stations Inc **(PA)**	4832	C	510 568-6200	5716
Frito-Lay North America Inc	5145	C	510 769-5000	8556
Garfield Nursing Home Inc	8051	C	510 582-7676	20448
Girl Scouts Northern Cal **(PA)**	8641	D	510 562-8470	25162
Global 360 Inc	8741	D	510 263-4800	26872
Harbor Bay Club Inc	7991	D	510 521-5414	18606
Health Educ Economic Devlpmnt	8742	D	510 604-6143	27262
Kaiser Foundation Hospitals	6324	C	510 752-1190	10255
Kindred Nursing Centers W LLC	8051	D	510 521-5600	20564
Maintenance Service For The Cy	7349	D	510 865-3778	14310
Mariner Square Athletic Inc	7991	D	510 523-8011	18629
Mbh Architects Inc	8712	C	510 865-8663	26095
McGuire and Hester **(PA)**	1623	B	510 632-7676	1955
Metaswitch Networks	7371	E	415 513-1500	15279
NRC Environmental Services Inc **(HQ)**	4959	C	510 749-1390	6543
Otismed Corporation	5047	D	510 786-3171	7201
Polarion Software Inc	7372	D	877 572-4005	15833
Ports America Inc	4491	D	510 749-7400	4732
Roche Molecular Systems Inc	8731	C	510 814-2800	26445
San Francisco Bay AR Tran Assn	8699	C	510 501-5318	25457
Semifreddis Inc **(PA)**	5149	C	510 596-9930	8865
Shoreline S Intermediate Care	8052	C	510 523-8857	20957
Snelling Employment LLC	7361	D	510 769-4400	14762
Sutter Health	8641	C	916 286-6665	25262
Telecare Corporation **(PA)**	8063	E	510 337-7950	21979
Telecare Corporation	8063	D	510 337-7950	21988
Voxify Inc	7371	C	510 545-3011	15537
Waters Edge Inc	8051	C	510 748-4300	20878
Waters Edge Lodge	8361	E	510 769-6264	24717
Webcor Construction LP **(DH)**	1542	D	510 748-1900	1696
Weinberg Roger & Resenfeld **(PA)**	8111	D	510 337-1001	23429
Wind River Systems Inc **(HQ)**	7372	C	510 748-4100	15892

ALAMO, CA - Contra Costa County

	SIC	EMP	PHONE	ENTRY #
Beta Healthcare Group **(PA)**	6351	D	925 838-6070	10423
Cintas Corporation	7213	D	925 743-1745	13522
Edgewood Properties **(PA)**	6513	D	925 838-2847	11011
Hospice and Palliative Care	8052	D	925 945-8924	20935
John Muir Physician Network	8011	E	925 838-4633	19521
Round Hill Country Club	7997	D	925 934-8211	19021
Round Hill Enterprises	7997	C	925 934-8211	19022

ALBANY, CA - Alameda County

	SIC	EMP	PHONE	ENTRY #
Pacific Racing Association	7948	C	510 559-7300	18542
Paladin Home Care	8059	E	510 526-2273	21181
Reichert Lengfeld Ltd Partnr	7011	D	510 845-1077	13107

ALBION, CA - Mendocino County

	SIC	EMP	PHONE	ENTRY #
Albion River Inn Incorporated	7011	D	707 937-1919	12312

GEOGRAPHIC

	SIC	EMP	PHONE	ENTRY #

ALHAMBRA, CA - Los Angeles County

	SIC	EMP	PHONE	ENTRY #
Ahmc Healthcare	8062	C	626 570-0612	21271
Ahmc Healthcare Inc	8099	A	626 248-3452	22724
Ahmc Healthcare Inc (PA)	8062	C	626 943-7526	21272
Alhambra Healthcare & Wellness	8051	D	626 282-3151	20227
Alhambra Hospital Med Ctr LP	8062	C	626 570-1606	21278
AT&T Services Inc	4813	B	626 308-8582	5512
Atherton Baptist Homes	8051	C	626 863-1710	20239
Bio-Mdcal Applications Cal Inc	8092	E	626 457-9002	22467
City Security Co Inc	7381	D	626 458-2325	16605
County of Los Angeles	6324	C	626 299-5300	10198
County of Los Angeles	4941	B	626 458-4000	6234
County of Los Angeles	8322	C	626 308-5542	23686
Drew Chain Security Corp	7381	D	626 457-8626	16632
Eastern Los Angeles RE (PA)	8322	B	626 299-4700	23779
Ethos Management Inc (PA)	8741	E	626 456-3669	26851
Evikecom Inc	5091	D	626 286-0360	7927
I Lan Systems Inc	7373	D	626 304-9021	15974
Interviewing Service Amer Inc	8732	D	626 979-4140	26530
Inveserve Corporation	6531	D	626 458-3435	11522
Network Medical Management Inc	8741	C	626 282-0288	26958
New Century Insurance Services (PA)	6411	E	626 300-9000	10701
Options For Learning	8351	D	626 308-2411	24359
Orora North America	5113	C	626 284-9524	8115
Pacific Ventures Ltd	8741	C	626 576-0737	26974
Roboca Technology	7371	C	561 501-3999	15416
Serfin Funds Transfer (PA)	6099	D	626 457-3070	9689
Silverado Senior Living Inc	8059	E	626 872-3941	21212
Southern California Gas Co	4924	D	323 881-3587	6170
Tenet Healthsystem Medical	8011	C	626 300-5500	20003
Tennant Health Systems	8011	C	626 300-3500	20004
University Southern California	8731	D	626 457-4240	26485

ALISO VIEJO, CA - Orange County

	SIC	EMP	PHONE	ENTRY #
AAA Accounting Services	8721	D	949 791-7368	26138
Aliso Viejo Golf Club Inc	7992	C	949 598-9200	18679
All Hnds Crwash Dtail Ctr Lube	7542	C	949 716-3600	17800
Ambry Genetics Corporation (DH)	8071	D	949 900-5500	22059
American Zettler Inc (HQ)	5065	C	949 360-5830	7437
Andersen Hotels Inc	7011	D	949 494-1151	12325
Apex Parks Group LLC (PA)	7996	C	949 349-8461	18790
Apex Parks Group LLC	7999	D	210 341-6663	19099
Basketball Marketing Co Inc	8742	D	866 866-1232	27154
Bearing Engineers Inc (PA)	5085	D	949 586-7442	7839
By Wind Inc	7371	D	949 385-6219	15042
Citizenhawk Inc	8741	D	949 427-3002	26806
Clarient Diagnostic Svcs Inc	8071	B	888 443-3310	22068
Concerto Healthcare Inc (PA)	8322	C	949 537-3400	23615
Covenant Care California LLC (HQ)	8051	E	949 349-1200	20350
Covenant Care Indiana Inc (DH)	8051	D	949 349-1200	20354
Cox Communications Inc	4841	D	949 716-2000	5890
Cresse Mark School of Baseball	7999	D	714 892-6145	19155
Datallegro Inc	5045	D	949 680-3000	7034
Diageo North America Inc	5182	D	949 421-3974	9038
Efuel LLC	5172	D	949 330-7145	8956
Facility Services Partners	8741	D	949 480-4090	26856
First Team RE - Orange Cnty	6531	D	949 389-0004	11466
Fluor Corporation	8711	D	949 349-2000	25685
Fluor Daniel Construction Co (DH)	1622	B	949 349-2000	1879
Fluor Enterprises Inc	1799	C	469 398-7000	3521
Fluor Enterprises Inc	5082	C	949 349-2000	7675
Fluor Industrial Services Inc	7349	A	949 439-2000	14267
Fluor Plant Services Intl Inc	8711	D	949 349-2000	25688
Fluoramec LLC (HQ)	8711	E	949 349-2000	25689
Geo Telecom	1623	E	949 362-0921	1921
Glenwood Village Cmnty Assn	8641	D	949 855-1800	25166
Hcs Holdco LLC (DH)	8082	C	949 349-1200	22311
International Litigation Svcs	5044	E	888 313-4457	6965
JMJ Financial Group (PA)	6162	C	949 340-6336	9820
Kaiser Foundation Hospitals	8011	C	949 425-3150	19524
L & O Aliso Viejo LLC	7991	D	949 643-6700	18620
Lennar Corporation	1531	D	949 349-8000	1348
Lennar Homes California Inc (DH)	1521	D	949 349-8000	1192
LMC Hollywood Highland	1542	B	949 448-1600	1582
Malibu Castle	7996	E	210 341-6663	18804
Marsh & McLennan Agency LLC	6411	D	949 544-8460	10679
Merridian Neuro Care	8011	D	949 263-6630	19687
Metagenics Inc (DH)	5122	C	949 366-0818	8197
NC Interactive LLC	7379	D	512 623-8700	16430
New Home Company Inc (PA)	1531	D	949 382-7800	1355
Onsite Health Inc (PA)	8099	D	949 305-2253	22854
Pacific Crossing LLC	7373	C	949 679-2588	16028
Pacifica Hotel Company (HQ)	6531	E	805 957-0095	11657
Quest Software Inc (HQ)	7373	A	949 754-8000	16039
Quest Software Inc	7372	D	949 754-8000	15838

	SIC	EMP	PHONE	ENTRY #
Real Estate Digital LLC	7371	C	800 234-2139	15397
Remedytemp Inc (DH)	7363	C	949 425-7600	14904
Renaissance Hotel Clubsport	7011	D	949 643-6700	13111
Retronix International Inc	7699	D	949 388-6930	17977
Safeguard Health Enterprises (HQ)	6324	B	949 425-4300	10305
Seabreeze Management Company (PA)	8741	D	949 855-1800	27025
Sequoia Environmental Svcs Inc	0781	D	949 480-4742	786
Shea Properties MGT Co Inc	6531	D	949 389-7000	11763
Siliconsystems Inc	5063	D	949 900-9400	7397
Smith Micro Software Inc (PA)	7372	C	949 362-5800	15854
Southern California Gas Co	4924	D	714 634-7221	6164
Sparxent Inc (PA)	7373	E	949 222-2287	16057
Spyglass Hill Community Assn	8641	E	949 855-1800	25253
Star Real Estate South County	6531	D	949 389-0004	11777
Sunstone Hotel Investors LLC (PA)	6799	D	949 330-4000	12269
Sunstone Hotel Management Inc (PA)	7011	D	949 297-4183	13302
Sunstone Hotel Properties Inc (DH)	7011	C	949 330-4000	13305
United Parcel Service Inc OH	7389	B	949 643-6634	17537
United Parcel Service Inc OH	4215	A	949 643-6595	4461
United Parcel Service Inc OH	4215	A	951 377-8253	4462
UST Global Inc (PA)	7371	C	949 716-8757	15518
Valeant Biomedicals Inc (DH)	5169	D	949 461-6000	8940
Verizon Connect Telo Inc (DH)	7374	C	949 389-5500	16197
Voice Mail Broadcasting Corp	7374	D	714 437-0600	16199
Vwise Inc	7371	C	949 716-1276	15538

ALPINE, CA - San Diego County

	SIC	EMP	PHONE	ENTRY #
Abhe & Svoboda Inc	1542	D	619 659-1320	1454
Alpine Convalescent Center Inc	8093	D	619 659-3120	22502
Pacific Southwest Cnstr & Eqp	1623	D	619 445-5190	1965
R A Schreiber Plumbing	1711	E	619 659-3101	2324
Southern Indian Health Council (PA)	8011	D	619 445-1188	19927

ALPINE MEADOWS, CA - Placer County

	SIC	EMP	PHONE	ENTRY #
Alpine Meadows Ski Area	7011	E	530 583-4232	12315
Squaw Creek Associates LLC	7011	A	530 581-6624	13257

ALTA LOMA, CA - San Bernardino County

	SIC	EMP	PHONE	ENTRY #
Expreal Inc	6531	D	909 373-4400	11426
Inland Empire RE Solutions	6531	D	909 476-1000	11512

ALTADENA, CA - Los Angeles County

	SIC	EMP	PHONE	ENTRY #
Altadena Town and Country Club	7997	D	626 345-9088	18825
Cutting Edge Protection I	7241	E	949 307-1596	13684
D C Golf A CA Partnership	7992	E	626 797-3821	18705
Five Acres-The Boys & Girls &	8361	B	626 798-6793	24528
Life Line Screening Amer Ltd	8099	B	626 797-9774	22834
Mallcraft Inc	1542	E	626 765-9100	1585
Marcos Auto Body Inc (PA)	7532	D	626 286-5691	17728
Pasadena Chld Training Soc	8361	C	626 798-0853	24627
Tom Sawyer Camps Inc	8351	C	626 794-1156	24394

ALTURAS, CA - Modoc County

	SIC	EMP	PHONE	ENTRY #
County of Modoc	7389	C	530 233-6223	17105
County of Modoc	8322	C	530 233-6501	23692
County of Modoc	8051	C	530 233-3416	20332
County of Modoc	8322	D	530 233-6400	23693
Ed Staub & Sons Petroleum Inc	5172	D	530 233-2610	8955
Last Frontier Healthcare Dst	8062	C	530 233-5131	21546

ALVISO, CA - Santa Clara County

	SIC	EMP	PHONE	ENTRY #
Acme Building Maintenance Co (DH)	7349	D	408 263-5911	14179
Bayscape Management Inc	8741	D	408 288-2940	26777
Gardner Family Hlth Netwrk Inc (PA)	8093	E	408 200-2291	22580
Minerva Networks Inc (PA)	7371	D	800 806-9594	15283

AMERICAN CANYON, CA - Napa County

	SIC	EMP	PHONE	ENTRY #
Biagi Bros Inc	4225	D	707 642-4412	4533
Bvk Gaming Inc	7999	D	707 644-8853	19116
Comcast Corporation	4841	D	707 266-7584	5873
Eagle Vnes Vnyrds Golf CLB LLC	7997	D	707 257-4470	18917
Ghilotti Construction Co Inc	1611	C	707 556-9145	1767
Medical Receivables Solutions	8742	E	707 980-6733	27333
R E Maher Inc	1771	D	707 642-3907	3312
Western Wine Services Inc (PA)	4225	D	800 999-8463	4660

ANAHEIM, CA - Orange County

	SIC	EMP	PHONE	ENTRY #
1135 N Leisure Ct Inc	8051	C	714 772-1353	20215
24 Hour Fitness Usa Inc	7991	E	714 525-9924	18557
3067 Orange Avenue LLC	8051	C	714 827-2440	20216
5 Day Business Forms Mfg Inc (PA)	5112	D	213 623-3577	8072
5 Day Business Forms Mfg Inc	5112	D	714 632-8674	8073
A & R Wholesale Distrs Inc	5145	D	714 777-7742	8542
A S I Corporation	7311	C	714 526-5533	13785
Aat Kings Tours USA Inc	4725	D	714 456-0505	4959
Above Hlth HM Care Sltions LLC	8082	D	714 585-2185	22185
Advantage Mailing LLC (PA)	7331	C	714 538-3881	14040
Advantage-Crown Sls & Mktg LLC (DH)	5141	A	714 780-3000	8377

Mergent email: customerrelations@mergent.com
1538

2019 Directory of California
Wholesalers and Services Companies

(P-0000) Products & Services Section entry number
(PA)=Parent Co (HQ)=Headquarters (DH)=Div Headquarters

Company	SIC	EMP	PHONE	ENTRY #
Adventure City Inc	7999	D	714 821-3311	19090
Aecom Global II LLC	8711	A	415 774-2700	25509
Agire Mortgage Corporation	6162	E	714 564-5821	9768
Air Mechanical Inc	1711	D	714 995-3947	2090
Albd Electric and Cable	1731	D	949 440-1216	2503
Alexanders Grand Salon	7231	D	714 282-6438	13644
Aliantel Inc	8748	D	714 829-1650	27631
Alsco Inc	7213	D	714 774-4165	13498
Altamed Health Services Corp	8011	C	714 635-0593	19277
Altamed Health Services Corp	8011	C	714 780-5690	19282
Americold Logistics LLC	4222	D	678 441-1468	4493
Amisub (Irvine Regional Hospi)	8062	A	949 916-7556	21285
Ampco Contracting Inc	4959	C	949 955-2255	6529
Anaheim Arena Management LLC	7941	A	714 704-2400	18503
Anaheim Arts Council	8412	C	714 868-6094	24863
Anaheim Ducks Hockey Club LLC (PA)	7941	C	714 940-2900	18504
Anaheim First Fmly Dntl Group	8741	D	714 999-5050	26760
Anaheim Global Medical Center	8062	B	714 533-6220	21287
Anaheim Harbor Medical Group (PA)	8011	C	714 533-4511	19290
Anaheim Hills Auto Body Inc	7532	D	714 632-8266	17711
Anaheim Hotel LLC	7011	D	714 750-1811	12321
Anaheim Ice	7999	D	714 535-7465	19096
Anaheim Medical Center	8011	D	714 774-1450	19291
Anaheim Park Inn and Camelot	7011	D	714 635-7275	12323
Anaheim Plaza Hotel Inc	7011	C	714 772-5900	12324
Anaheim Regional Medical Ctr	8062	A	714 774-1450	21288
Anaheim Regional Medical Ctr	8011	B	714 999-3847	19292
Anaheim Regional Medical Ctr (PA)	8069	E	714 774-1450	21995
Anaheim/Orange Cnty Visitor Bu (PA)	7389	D	714 765-8888	17002
Angels Baseball LP (PA)	7941	A	714 940-2000	18505
Apprendre Technologies Inc	7371	D	561 244-9917	14992
Arciero Brothers Inc	1771	C	714 238-6600	3215
Ardcore Senior Living	8361	D	714 974-2226	24419
Arizona Tile LLC	5032	C	714 978-6403	6875
Assocted Gstrntrlogy Med Group (PA)	8011	D	714 778-1300	19311
AT&T Corp	4812	D	714 284-3818	5278
AT&T Corp	4813	D	714 666-5504	5460
AT&T Services Inc	4813	C	210 886-4922	5478
AT&T Services Inc	4813	C	714 259-4441	5480
Avalon Building Maintenance (PA)	7349	C	714 693-2407	14199
B & B Specialties Inc	5072	D	714 985-3075	7579
Badalian Enterprises Inc	7011	D	714 635-4082	12349
Bcp Systems Inc	7378	D	714 202-3900	16278
Behavioral Health Works Inc	8099	D	800 249-1266	22741
Bell Pipe & Supply Co	5085	E	714 772-3200	7840
Best Interiors Inc (PA)	1742	C	714 490-7999	2850
Best Western Stovalls Inn	7011	E	714 776-4800	12377
Best Western Stovalls Inn (PA)	7011	D	714 956-4430	12378
Bethesda University California	6732	C	714 517-1945	12073
Boyd Corporation	5085	D	714 777-5995	7842
Bpo Management Services Inc (PA)	7371	D	714 972-2670	15033
Brady Company/Los Angeles Inc	1742	C	714 533-9850	2853
Brendan Tours (PA)	4725	C	818 428-6000	4964
Bridgford Marketing Company (DH)	5147	D	714 526-5533	8612
Broughton Hospitality Group (PA)	8741	C	714 908-4237	26786
Brownco Construction Co Inc	1542	D	714 935-9600	1486
Buena Vista Care Center Inc	8051	D	714 535-7264	20274
Bunzl Distribution Cal LLC (DH)	5113	D	714 688-1900	8095
Cal Mutual Inc	6162	D	888 700-4650	9784
Cal-State Auto Parts Inc (PA)	5013	C	714 630-5954	6629
California Private Trnsp Co LP	4785	D	714 637-9191	5214
California Safety Agency	7381	E	866 996-6990	16597
Califrnia Auto Dalers Exch LLC	5012	B	714 996-2400	6580
Carmel Architectural Sales	1761	D	714 630-7221	3133
Carrington Mrtg Holdings LLC	8741	D	888 267-0584	26797
Castle & Cooke Inc	6211	A	714 385-9641	9924
Cbre Inc	6531	C	714 939-2100	11276
Challenger Industries Inc	8748	D	714 630-4344	27683
Cinema City Theaters	7832	E	714 970-0865	18278
Cintas Corporation No 2	5199	D	714 288-8400	9206
City of Anaheim	6512	B	714 704-2400	10864
Clinica Sagrado Corazon	8011	E	714 491-7777	19387
Clp Resources Inc	7363	D	714 300-0510	14839
Coach Usa Inc	4725	C	714 978-8855	4967
Comfort California Inc	7011	D	714 750-3131	12480
Conestoga Hotel	7011	D	714 535-0300	12483
Consolidated Design West Inc	7336	D	714 999-1476	14106
Construction Customer Service	1521	E	714 701-1858	1147
Consumer Resource Network LLC	8742	B	800 291-4794	27199
Contiki US Holdings Inc	4725	D	714 935-0808	4968
Control AC Svc Corp	1711	D	714 777-8600	2169
Control Air Conditioning Corp (PA)	1711	C	714 777-8600	2170
Coordnted Dlvry Instlltion Inc	4212	D	714 501-4040	3996
Country Villa Service Corp (PA)	8741	D	310 574-3733	26823
County of Orange	8322	D	714 937-4500	23698
Coventry Court Health Center	8051	C	714 636-2800	20356
Crocker Group LLC	6531	D	714 221-5621	11388
Crossmark Inc	5141	D	714 464-6318	8397
D/K Mechanical Contractors Inc	1711	C	714 970-0180	2180
Danlil Enterprise Inc	7349	D	714 776-7705	14250
Danny Ryan Precision Contg Inc	1795	D	949 642-6664	3451
Development Resource Cons Inc (PA)	8711	D	714 685-6860	25642
Disney Enterprises Inc	7011	A	714 778-6600	12525
Disney Enterprises Inc	7011	B	714 999-0990	12526
Disneyland International	7996	C	714 781-4000	18797
Disneyland International	7011	B	714 956-6746	12527
Diversified Clinical Services	8099	D	714 579-8400	22790
Dkn Hotel LLC	7011	D	714 535-0300	12530
Dma Greencare Contracting Inc	0782	E	714 630-9470	829
Docircle Inc	4813	E	415 484-4221	5550
Dolphins Cove Resort Ltd	7011	D	714 980-0830	12536
Donahue Schriber Rlty Group LP (PA)	6512	C	714 283-3535	10871
Doubltree Suites By Hilton LLC	7011	C	714 750-3000	12542
Driver Spg	7389	E	855 300-4774	17139
DSV Solutions LLC	4789	D	714 630-0110	5223
Econo Air Conditioning Inc	1711	E	714 630-3090	2195
Ecotech Rfrgn & Hvac Inc	1711	D	888 833-8100	2196
Edge Mortgage Advisory Co LLC	8748	D	714 564-5800	27714
Edward Thomas Companies	7011	D	714 782-7500	12549
Eleganza Tiles Inc (PA)	1743	D	714 224-1700	2995
Emerald Landscape Services	0782	D	714 844-2200	836
Emercon Construction Inc (PA)	1521	D	714 630-9615	1161
Emery Smith Laboratories Inc	8711	D	714 238-6133	25659
Eps Corporate Holdings Inc	5074	D	714 635-3131	7615
Etherwan Systems Inc	7379	D	714 779-3800	16360
Evriholder Products LLC (HQ)	5023	E	714 490-7878	6761
Exactax Inc (PA)	7291	D	714 284-4802	13705
Express Messenger Systems Inc	4215	D	949 235-1400	4403
F M Tarbell Co	6531	D	714 772-8990	11429
F M Tarbell Co	6531	E	714 637-7240	11430
Family Tree Produce Inc	5148	C	714 693-5688	8676
Fci Lender Services Inc	7322	C	714 974-1945	14002
Fedex Freight Corporation	4213	D	714 996-8720	4152
Fedex Ground Package Sys Inc	4213	C	800 463-3339	4166
Fedex Ground Package Sys Inc	4213	D	800 463-3339	4167
Fenceworks Inc	1799	D	714 238-0091	3518
Filyn Corporation	4119	C	714 632-0225	3794
First Team RE - Orange Cnty	6531	D	714 974-9191	11465
Firstline Security Systems Inc (PA)	7382	C	714 937-1440	16897
Fjs Inc	7011	C	714 905-1050	12577
Fkc Partners A Cal Ltd Partnr	6531	E	714 528-9864	11469
Fortress Holding Group LLC	6719	D	714 202-8710	11977
Frank Gates Service Company	6331	C	800 994-4611	10355
Freeman Audio Visual LLC	7359	C	714 254-3400	14506
Freeman Expositions LLC	7389	C	714 254-3400	17174
Freight Management Inc	8742	D	714 632-1440	27242
Front Porch Communities	8059	C	714 776-7150	21069
G4s Secure Solutions USA Inc	7381	C	714 939-4900	16657
GBS Linens Inc (PA)	7213	D	714 778-6448	13531
General Engineering Wstn Inc (PA)	1711	D	714 630-3200	2219
Go-Staff Inc	7361	A	657 242-9350	14631
Golden State Water Company	4941	C	714 535-7711	6257
Greenball Corp (PA)	5014	E	714 782-3060	6692
Gsf Enterprises Inc	1542	D	714 524-9500	1539
Hacienda Rehabilitation & Heal (PA)	8051	C	714 778-0221	20502
Harbor Villa Care Center	8059	C	714 635-8131	21105
Harris Freeman & Co Inc (PA)	5149	B	714 765-1190	8803
Hba Incorporated	1741	D	714 635-8602	2810
Healthcare Partners LLC	8099	D	714 995-1000	22812
HI Anaheim LLC	7011	D	714 533-1500	12656
Highland Lumber Sales Inc	5031	D	714 778-2293	6832
Hob Entertainment LLC	7929	C	714 778-2583	18436
Hoffman Southwest Corp	7699	E	714 630-0404	17950
Holiday Garden SF Corp	7011	E	714 533-3555	12689
Holiday Inn & Suites Annaheim	7011	D	714 535-0300	12690
Howard Johnson (PA)	7011	C	714 776-6120	12733
Hpt Trs Ihg-2 Inc	7011	D	714 748-7777	12735
Hunter Easterday Corporation	7349	C	714 238-3400	14287
Infinity Drywall Contg Inc	1742	D	714 634-2255	2894
International Missing Persons	7299	D	714 827-1947	13752
Interstate Electronics Corp	8742	A	714 758-0500	27280
J & J Productions Incorporated	7389	E	714 535-0951	17255
J B Bostick Company Inc	1611	D	714 238-2121	1793
Jan Pro Clg Systems Sthern Cal	7349	E	714 220-0500	14294
Jetro Cash and Carry Entps LLC	5142	C	714 666-8211	8493
Kaiser Foundation Hospitals	8011	C	714 279-4675	19523
Kaiser Foundation Hospitals	8011	A	888 988-2800	19541
Kaiser Foundation Hospitals	8011	A	888 988-2800	19543
Kaiser Foundation Hospitals	6324	D	714 284-6634	10235
Kapl Inc	8731	B	714 991-9543	26389

Employment Codes: A=Over 500 employees, B=251-500,
C=101-250, D=51-100, E=50

2019 Directory of California
Wholesalers and Services Companies

© Mergent Inc. 1-800-342-5647
1539

Company	SIC	EMP	PHONE	ENTRY #
Karcher Environmental Inc (PA)	1799	C	714 385-1490	3542
KCS Electric Inc	1731	D	623 551-1500	2622
Keenan Hopkins Suder & Stowell (PA)	1742	D	714 695-3670	2904
Keenan Hopkins Suder & Stowell	1542	D	714 695-3670	1572
Ken Real Estate Lease Ltd	7011	D	714 778-1700	12802
Ken Starr Inc	1711	D	714 632-8789	2249
Kinetic Systems Inc	1711	E	949 502-4856	2251
Kinsbursky Bros Supply Inc (PA)	5093	D	714 738-8516	7982
Kisco Senior Living LLC	6513	D	714 872-9785	11044
Kml Enterprises Career Dev LLC	7379	C	714 221-3100	16417
L&G Cable Construction	1799	D	714 630-6174	3544
La Palma Care Center	8051	D	714 772-7480	20573
LARK Industries Inc (HQ)	7389	D	714 701-4200	17291
Lazer Electric Inc	1731	D	714 777-4233	2629
Leisure Care LLC	8361	E	714 974-1616	24577
Lindley Fire Protection Co	1711	E	714 535-5761	2264
Liquidity Services Inc	5136	D	714 738-6446	8268
Lobel Financial Corporation (PA)	6141	D	714 995-3333	9720
Long Swimming Pool Steel Inc	1791	E	714 524-8172	3384
Longust Distributing LLC	5023	E	480 820-6244	6774
Lyons Security Service Inc	7382	D	714 401-4850	16922
Machining Time Savers Inc	5084	D	714 635-7373	7766
Makar Anaheim LLC	7011	A	714 740-4431	12871
Malco Maintenance Inc	1799	D	714 630-0194	3547
Malco Services Inc	8742	D	714 630-0194	27313
Marina Landscape Maint Inc	0781	B	714 939-6600	768
Marketing Professionals Inc	8742	B	714 578-0500	27320
Matrix Surfaces Inc	1743	D	714 696-5449	3004
Mc Graw Commercial Insur Svc	6411	D	714 939-9875	10686
McCormack Roofng Constrctn & E	1761	D	714 777-4040	3177
Merical LLC (PA)	7389	D	714 238-7225	17324
Millennium Transportation Inc	4731	D	714 956-7882	5111
Morphotrak LLC (DH)	7373	C	714 238-2000	16006
Motive Energy Inc (PA)	5063	D	714 888-2525	7378
Mowery Thomason Inc	1742	C	714 666-1717	2920
Moyes Custom Furniture Inc	7641	E	714 729-0234	17922
Msl Electric Inc	1731	D	714 693-4837	2654
Murrietta Circuits	1731	D	714 970-2430	2655
Nail Emporium	5087	E	714 779-9889	7890
Nations Direct Lender & In	7389	C	800 969-7779	17345
Nazzareno Electric Co Inc	1731	D	714 712-4744	2657
Newport Hotel Capital LLC	7011	D	714 758-0900	12955
Nicholas Lane Contractors Inc	1521	B	714 630-7630	1208
Nor-Cal Beverage Co Inc	7389	C	714 526-8600	17358
North American Health Care Inc (PA)	8741	C	949 240-2423	26963
Northwest Hotel Corporation (PA)	7011	D	714 776-6120	12963
Npl Anaheim Investments LLC	7011	D	714 750-2010	12964
Orange Cast Title Southern Cal	6361	D	714 822-3211	10470
Orange Cnty Adult Achvment Ctr	7389	D	714 744-5301	17375
Orange Cnty Conservation Corps	8331	D	714 451-1301	24214
Orange Coast Building Services	1541	C	714 453-6300	1425
Orange County Child Abuse	8322	D	714 543-4333	23952
Orange County Head Start	8351	C	714 761-4967	24363
Otis Elevator Company	7699	E	714 758-9593	17965
Outside Lines Inc	0781	E	714 637-4747	772
Overhead Door Corporation	1751	D	714 680-0600	3056
Pacific Coast Equipment Co Inc (PA)	1796	E	714 630-5957	3475
Pacific Coast Nursery Inc	5193	D	714 630-4868	9154
Pacific Coast Sightseeing Tour	4725	C	714 507-1157	4975
Pacific Contours Corporation	5088	D	714 693-1260	7913
Pacific Design Directions Inc	1521	D	714 685-7766	1212
Pacific Utlty Instllation Inc	1731	D	714 970-6430	2670
Paglia & Associates Cnstr	1521	D	714 982-5151	1213
Paragon Industries Inc	5032	D	714 778-8453	6903
Park Hotels & Resorts Inc	7011	D	714 632-1221	13041
Paseo Vlg Hsing Partners LP	6513	E	714 991-9172	11095
Paulus Engineering Inc	1623	D	714 632-3322	1967
Peacock Stes Resort Ltd Partnr	7011	D	714 535-8255	13052
Penhall Company (DH)	1741	E	714 772-6450	2821
Petersen-Dean Inc	1761	C	714 629-9670	3188
Phg Engineering Services LLC	8711	D	714 283-8288	25875
Pinner Construction Co Inc (PA)	1542	D	714 490-4000	1617
Platinum Construction Inc	1542	D	714 527-0700	1618
Platinum Protection Group Inc	7381	D	800 824-1097	16757
Portofino Inn & Suites Anaheim	7011	A	714 782-7600	13076
Power Engineers Incorporated	8711	D	714 507-2700	25876
Power Plus LLC	5063	D	714 507-1881	7386
Power Plus Solutions Corp	1731	D	714 507-1881	2686
Premier Commercial Bancorp	6022	D	714 978-2400	9479
Prime Healthcare Anaheim LLC	8062	A	714 827-3000	21656
Ramada Plaza Ht Anaheim Resort	7011	C	714 991-6868	13098
Rapid Plumbing Inc (PA)	1711	D	714 695-1800	2329
Ray W Choi	8742	D	714 783-1000	27419
Residence Inn By Marriott	7011	D	714 533-3555	13119
Resident Group Services Inc (PA)	0782	C	714 630-5300	931
Residential Fire Systems Inc	1711	D	714 666-8450	2337
Restaurant Depot LLC	5181	C	714 666-9205	9019
Rjb Enterprises Inc	1731	E	714 484-3101	2710
Rosendin Electric Inc	1731	A	714 739-1334	2713
Roy Miller Freight Lines LLC (PA)	4212	D	714 632-5511	4058
Royal Roofing & Cnstr Co	1761	D	714 764-1100	3198
Rvtlzation Anaheim II Partners	6531	D	714 520-4041	11748
S W Construction Inc	1751	C	714 978-7871	3072
San Marino Plastering Inc	1742	D	714 693-7840	2955
San-Mar Construction Co Inc	1751	C	714 693-5400	3073
Scholastic Book Fairs Inc	5192	D	714 237-1100	9119
Security Signal Devices Inc (PA)	7382	E	800 888-0444	16939
Select Data Inc	7371	C	714 577-1000	15435
Self Serve Auto Dismantlers (PA)	4953	C	714 630-8901	6475
Service 1st Electrical Svcs	1731	E	714 630-9699	2731
Shamrock Supply Company Inc (PA)	5072	C	714 575-1800	7602
So Cal Land Maintenance Inc	7349	D	714 231-1454	14394
Source Rfrgn & Hvac Inc (PA)	1711	D	714 578-2300	2366
South Coast Mechanical Inc	1711	D	714 738-6644	2368
Southern Cal Prmnnte Med Group	8011	E	714 279-4675	19916
Southern Counties Bldg Maint (PA)	7349	E	805 928-9900	14398
Spectrum MGT Holdg Co LLC	4841	D	714 414-1431	5946
SR Bray LLC (PA)	1731	E	714 765-7551	2740
Srd Engineering Inc	1623	D	714 630-2480	1985
St Joseph Home Health Network (DH)	8082	D	714 712-9500	22425
St Joseph Home Health Network	8082	E	714 712-9559	22426
St Joseph Hospice	8322	D	714 712-7100	24069
Steeltech Construction Svcs	1541	D	714 630-2890	1438
Stericycle Comm Solutions Inc	7389	E	714 991-9595	17486
Straub Distributing Co Ltd (PA)	5181	C	714 779-4000	9027
Sun Mar Nursing Center Inc	8059	D	714 776-1720	21225
Sunshine Midtown LLC	7011	E	602 604-4900	13290
Sunstone Hotel Investors LLC	7011	E	714 635-5000	13299
Sunwest Electric Inc	1731	D	714 630-8700	2754
T L Fabrications LP	1791	D	562 802-3980	3399
Targus International LLC (PA)	5199	C	714 765-5555	9262
Techno Coatings Inc	1542	D	714 774-4671	1671
Tenet Healthsystem Medical	8062	A	714 428-6800	21855
Thermalair Inc (HQ)	1711	D	714 630-3200	2385
Trademark Concrete Systems (PA)	1771	E	714 970-8200	3337
Transamerica Finance Corp	6311	D	714 778-5100	10147
Tricom Management Inc	8741	D	714 630-2029	27067
Tricor America Inc	4215	D	714 701-9880	4438
Trilogy Plumbing Inc (PA)	1711	D	714 441-2952	2389
Truform Construction Corp	1751	E	714 630-7447	3086
Ttg Engineers	8711	D	714 490-5555	25961
Tucker Distributors	5075	E	714 970-5742	7658
Turner Construction Company	1542	D	714 940-9000	1682
TWI- Techno West Inc	1721	D	714 635-4070	2488
Ultimate Landscaping MGT	0782	D	714 502-9711	954
Universal Dust Collector (PA)	1541	D	714 630-8588	1448
University Marelich Mech Inc	1711	C	714 632-2600	2391
US Foods Inc	5149	C	714 449-2880	8896
Vci Event Technology Inc	7359	C	714 772-2002	14554
Vengroff Williams & Assoc Inc	7322	C	714 889-6200	14027
Venture Design Services Inc (PA)	8731	C	714 765-3740	26488
Veterans Health Administration	8011	E	714 780-5400	20081
Vincent Contractors Inc	1741	B	714 693-1726	2828
Vm Services Inc	7371	E	714 678-5200	15532
Walt Disney Company	4225	B	714 781-4532	4656
Walt Disney Company	7011	D	714 781-4278	13377
Wasser Filtration Inc	5084	D	714 525-0630	7819
WCO Hotels Inc (HQ)	7011	D	323 636-3251	13384
West Anaheim Extended Care	8051	C	714 821-1993	20881
Westcoast Performance Pdts USA	6798	D	714 630-4411	12193
Westview Services Inc	8051	C	714 956-4199	20889
Willdan Engineering	8711	D	714 978-8200	25999
Willdan Group Inc (PA)	8711	D	800 424-9144	26000
Wilson Hampton Pntg Contrs Inc	1721	D	714 772-5091	2493
Windsor Anaheim Healthcare (PA)	8051	B	714 826-8950	20896
Workcare Inc	8744	C	714 978-7488	27611
Zyxel Communications Inc	4813	D	714 632-0882	5683

ANDERSON, CA - Shasta County

Company	SIC	EMP	PHONE	ENTRY #
Bettendorf Enterprises Inc	4213	D	530 365-1937	4104
Davey Tree Surgery Company	0783	D	530 378-2674	971
Linkus Enterprises LLC (PA)	1623	C	530 229-9197	1949
Oak River Rehabilitation	8051	C	530 365-0025	20669
Ssmb Pacific Holding Co Inc	5012	D	530 222-1212	6610
United Parcel Service Inc OH	4215	D	530 365-7850	4448

ANGELS CAMP, CA - Calaveras County

Company	SIC	EMP	PHONE	ENTRY #
Motherlode Investors LLC	7992	D	209 736-8112	18739
United Parcel Service Inc OH	4215	C	209 736-0878	4475

Mergent email: customerrelations@mergent.com
1540
2019 Directory of California
Wholesale and Services Companies
(P-0000) Products & Services Section entry number
(PA)=Parent Co (HQ)=Headquarters (DH)=Div Headquarters

	SIC	EMP	PHONE	ENTRY #

ANGWIN, CA - Napa County

	SIC	EMP	PHONE	ENTRY #
Hermitage Hlthcr Mnkn Mnr	8059	C	410 651-0011	21109

ANTELOPE, CA - Sacramento County

	SIC	EMP	PHONE	ENTRY #
Leavy Brothers Incorporated	1742	D	916 773-5636	2910
Sacramento Prestige Gunite Inc	1771	E	916 723-0404	3319
Skyva Construction Inc	1521	E	916 726-4999	1237

ANTIOCH, CA - Contra Costa County

	SIC	EMP	PHONE	ENTRY #
Antioch Public Golf Corp	7992	D	925 706-4220	18686
Antioch Rotary Club	7997	E	925 757-1800	18847
AT&T Corp	4813	D	925 776-1200	5468
Banister Electrical Inc	1731	D	925 778-7801	2515
Better Homes and Gardens Mason	6531	D	925 776-2740	11241
Black Diamond Electric Inc	1731	D	925 777-3440	2523
City of Antioch	4959	D	925 779-6950	6530
Contra Costa ARC	8331	D	925 755-4925	24171
Contra Costa Newspapers Inc	5192	E	925 757-2525	9111
First Student Inc	4111	C	925 754-4878	3651
Freschi Air Systems Inc	1711	D	925 827-9761	2214
Halo	8699	E	925 473-4642	25426
Jamm Management LLC	5013	E	510 437-5200	6649
Kaiser Foundation Hospitals	8011	D	925 813-6500	19527
Kaiser Foundation Hospitals	8093	C	925 779-5000	22603
Kie-Con Inc	1542	D	925 754-9494	1573
Kiewit Infrastructure West Co	1611	E	925 754-9494	1804
Lone Tree Convalescent Hosp	8051	C	925 754-0470	20595
Mason-Mcduffie Real Estate Inc	6531	E	925 776-2740	11590
Montrose Envmtl Group Inc	8734	B	925 680-4300	26718
Norcal Care Centers Inc	8059	D	925 757-8787	21166
NRG Energy Inc	4911	D	913 689-3904	6063
Peace Keepers Private Security	7381	D	925 978-4140	16755
Permanente Medical Group Inc	8011	D	925 813-6149	19768
REACH Project (PA)	8093	D	925 754-3673	22659
Roddy Ranch Pbc LLC	7997	E	925 978-4653	19018
Sutter Delta Medical Ctr Aux	8062	D	925 779-7200	21802
Sutter Health	8062	A	925 779-7273	21808
Travis Credit Union	6061	B	925 777-0573	9605
Wayne E Swisher Cem Contr Inc	1771	D	925 757-3660	3344

ANZA, CA - Riverside County

	SIC	EMP	PHONE	ENTRY #
Cahuilla Creek Rest & Casino	7999	C	951 763-1200	19118

APPLE VALLEY, CA - San Bernardino County

	SIC	EMP	PHONE	ENTRY #
8520 Western Ave Inc	8059	C	714 828-8222	20974
Alpha Connection Group Home	8631	D	760 247-6370	25053
Apple Valley Golf Club	7997	C	760 242-3653	18848
Apple Vlley/ Vctrvlle Cnsrtium	7299	D	760 240-7000	13716
Automobile Club Southern Cal	8699	C	760 247-4110	25393
Front Porch Communities & Svcs	8051	D	760 240-5051	20442
High Desert Partnership	8732	B	760 946-5414	26527
Reliable Nursing Solutions	7361	D	760 946-9191	14720
St Mary Medical Center (PA)	8062	A	760 242-2311	21788
Who Dat Nation Trnsp LLC	4789	D	760 403-7237	5253

APTOS, CA - Santa Cruz County

	SIC	EMP	PHONE	ENTRY #
Aegis Senior Communities LLC	8082	E	831 684-2700	22207
American Golf Corporation	7997	D	831 688-3213	18842
Cabrillo College Children Ctr	8351	D	831 479-6352	24271
Dignity Health Med Foundation	8099	D	831 535-1560	22786
Easter Seals Central Cal	8322	D	831 684-2166	23778
First Alarm (PA)	1731	C	831 476-1111	2585
Parkhurst Terrace	1522	D	831 685-0800	1305
Santa Cruz Montessori School	8351	E	831 476-1646	24378
Seacliff Inn Inc	7011	D	831 661-4671	13199
Seascape Resort Ltd A Calif	7011	B	831 662-7120	13200

ARBUCKLE, CA - Colusa County

	SIC	EMP	PHONE	ENTRY #
Alsco - Geyer Irrigation Inc	5083	D	530 476-2253	7699
T & P Farms	0111	D	530 476-3038	3

ARCADIA, CA - Los Angeles County

	SIC	EMP	PHONE	ENTRY #
American Home Alarms Inc	1731	C	888 531-5065	2508
American Plus Bank (PA)	6021	E	626 821-9188	9275
Andover Maintenance Inc	7349	D	626 254-1651	14195
Arcadia Convalescent Hosp Inc (PA)	8059	C	323 681-1504	20997
Arcadia Gardens MGT Corp	8052	D	626 574-8571	20916
Arroyo Insurance Services Inc (PA)	6411	D	626 799-9532	10542
Avantra Real Estate Services	6531	E	626 357-7028	11229
Century 21 Ludecke Inc (PA)	6531	D	626 445-0123	11306
Chen Dvid MD Dgnstc Med Group	5047	D	626 566-3900	7174
Childrens Hospital Los Angeles	8062	D	626 795-7177	21316
City of Arcadia	4111	B	626 574-5435	3641
Coldwell Banker Residential RE	6531	D	626 445-5500	11343
Commercial Roofing Systems Inc	1761	D	626 359-5354	3141
Community Housing Options	8322	D	626 359-3300	23605
Country Villa Service Corp	8051	D	626 445-2421	20330

	SIC	EMP	PHONE	ENTRY #
County of Los Angeles	8322	E	626 821-5858	23677
Ego Inc	8721	C	626 447-0296	26189
Foothill Federal Credit Union (PA)	6061	E	626 445-0950	9559
Forta (PA)	8049	D	626 446-7027	20177
Fumai Industrial Inc	5065	D	626 272-1788	7481
Gar Enterprises (PA)	5045	C	626 574-1175	7051
George Fasching	7542	E	626 446-0654	17815
Goodrich Lax A Cal Ltd Partnr	7011	D	626 254-9988	12611
Healthcare Investments II LLC	8051	D	310 638-9377	20518
Ivy Insurance Group Inc (PA)	6331	D	626 566-2116	10364
Long Dragon Realty Co Inc	6531	D	626 309-7999	11567
Los Angeles Turf Club Inc (DH)	7948	C	626 574-6330	18540
Los Angles Arbretum Foundation	8422	D	626 821-3222	24931
Methodist Hosp Southern Cal (PA)	8062	A	626 898-8000	21592
Methodist Hospital of S CA	8062	C	626 574-3755	21593
MWH Americas Inc	8711	D	626 796-9141	25840
N A Tomatobank	6029	D	626 759-9200	9514
Park Hotels & Resorts Inc	7011	C	626 445-8525	13033
Post Alarm Systems (PA)	7382	D	626 446-7159	16928
Santa Anita Associates (PA)	7992	C	626 447-2764	18758
Transdev Services Inc	4119	B	626 357-7912	3853
Venue Management Services Inc	8748	E	626 445-6000	27895

ARCATA, CA - Humboldt County

	SIC	EMP	PHONE	ENTRY #
American Hospital Mgt Corp (PA)	8062	B	707 822-3621	21283
Aquatic Designing Inc	8711	E	707 822-4629	25542
Danco Builders Inc	1522	D	707 822-9000	1279
Danco Communities	6552	D	707 822-9000	11869
Healthsport Ltd A Ltd Partnr (PA)	7991	C	707 822-3488	18607
Humboldt State University Spon	8748	D	707 826-4189	27749
McCullough Construction	1611	D	707 825-1014	1816
North Coast Fabricators Inc	1541	E	707 822-4629	1423
Northcountry Clinic	8011	D	707 822-2481	19718
Open Door Community Hlth Ctrs	8093	D	707 826-8610	22625
Open Door Community Hlth Ctrs (PA)	8093	D	707 826-8642	22626
Sun Valley Group Inc (PA)	0181	B	707 822-2885	303
Tektetco	1541	D	707 822-9000	1444
Toucan Inc (PA)	5094	D	707 822-6662	8015
United Indian Health Svcs Inc (PA)	8011	C	707 825-5000	20019

ARLETA, CA - Los Angeles County

	SIC	EMP	PHONE	ENTRY #
Lexington Scenery & Props Inc	1751	C	818 768-5768	3050

ARNOLD, CA - Calaveras County

	SIC	EMP	PHONE	ENTRY #
Sequoia Wood Country Club	7997	D	209 795-1000	19040

AROMAS, CA - Monterey County

	SIC	EMP	PHONE	ENTRY #
Driscolls Inc	5148	E	831 763-5100	8672
Granite Rock Co	1611	C	831 768-2330	1785
Granite Rock Co	5032	C	831 392-3780	6896
Granite Rock Co	1442	C	831 768-2300	1092
Jal Berry Farms LLC	0171	D	831 763-7200	102

ARROYO GRANDE, CA - San Luis Obispo County

	SIC	EMP	PHONE	ENTRY #
Ameri-Kleen	7349	C	805 546-0706	14189
Ball Tagawa Growers	0181	E	805 481-7526	244
Bill Papich Construction Inc	1629	D	805 489-9420	2013
Community Action Partnership	8111	C	805 489-4026	22986
Compass Health Inc	8059	C	805 489-8137	21043
Cypress Ridge Golf Course	7992	C	805 474-7979	18704
Dignity Health	8082	C	805 489-4261	22284
Dignity Health	8062	B	805 473-7626	21374
Greenheart Farms Inc (PA)	0191	B	805 481-2234	345
Holland America Flowers LLC	0181	D	805 343-4004	269
Jk Consultants	8748	E	209 532-7772	27760
Life Steps Foundation Inc	8322	C	805 474-8431	23894
Papich Construction Co Inc (PA)	1611	C	805 473-3016	1833
Sierra Pacific Mortgage Co Inc	6162	D	805 489-6060	9858
St Denis Electric Inc	1731	E	805 343-9999	2741
Talley Farms	0723	C	805 489-2508	576

ARTESIA, CA - Los Angeles County

	SIC	EMP	PHONE	ENTRY #
Artesia Christian Home Inc	8059	C	562 865-5218	20999
County of Los Angeles	8093	E	562 402-0688	22548
E R G Home Health Provider	8082	D	562 403-1070	22289
Edwards Theatres Circuit Inc	7832	D	562 403-1133	18296
I Wmi	1542	B	562 977-4906	1557
New Cingular Wireless Svcs Inc	4813	D	562 924-0000	5611
South Asian Help Referral Agcy	8322	C	562 402-4132	24056
Windsor Twin Palms Hlthcare	8051	C	562 865-0271	20906

ARVIN, CA - Kern County

	SIC	EMP	PHONE	ENTRY #
Arvin-Edison Water Storage Dst (PA)	4971	E	661 854-5573	6553
Bakersfield Moving & Storage	4214	E	661 397-4521	4331
Edwardo Z Garcia	0761	C	661 854-5414	642
Evergreen Health Care LLC	8051	D	661 854-4475	20419
Granite Construction Company	1611	D	661 854-3051	1775
Grimmway Enterprises Inc	1541	D	661 854-6240	1402

G E O G R A P H I C

Employment Codes: A=Over 500 employees, B=251-500,
C=101-250, D=51-100, E=50

2019 Directory of California
Wholesalers and Services Companies

© Mergent Inc. 1-800-342-5647

1541

Company	SIC	EMP	PHONE	ENTRY #
Grimmway Enterprises Inc	0723	B	661 854-6250	522
Grimmway Enterprises Inc	0723	D	661 854-6200	523
Kern Ridge Growers LLC	0723	B	661 854-3141	533

ATASCADERO, CA - San Luis Obispo County

Company	SIC	EMP	PHONE	ENTRY #
Atascadero Hotel Partners LLC	7011	D	805 462-3500	12339
Califrnia Dept State Hospitals	8063	A	805 468-2000	21935
California Department of State	8063	A	805 468-2501	21936
Compass Health Inc	8059	A	805 466-9254	21044
Kennedy Athletic Club (PA)	7991	D	805 466-6775	18618
Meridian Holdings	5074	D	805 539-2752	7629
Options Family of Services	8093	E	805 462-8544	22627
Star of California	8099	C	805 466-1638	22890
USA Waste of California Inc	4953	C	805 466-3636	6493

ATHERTON, CA - San Mateo County

Company	SIC	EMP	PHONE	ENTRY #
Matched Caregivers Inc	8082	C	408 560-2382	22363
Menlo Circus Club	7997	D	650 322-4616	18971
Menlo Park-Atherton Education (PA)	8699	D	650 325-0100	25443
Optimus Ventures LLC	5065	E	888 881-5969	7519

ATWATER, CA - Merced County

Company	SIC	EMP	PHONE	ENTRY #
Castle Family Health Ctrs Inc (PA)	8093	D	209 381-2000	22520
Central Counties	8734	D	209 356-0355	26689
Gallo Cattle Co A Ltd Partnr	0241	B	209 394-7984	414
Gino/Giuseppe Inc	1771	D	209 358-0556	3256
Kings View	8331	E	209 357-0321	24198
Pacific Concrete Specialties	1771	D	209 358-0741	3299
Tjd LLC	8059	C	209 357-3420	21229
Ward Enterprises	7349	D	209 358-0445	14426

AUBERRY, CA - Fresno County

Company	SIC	EMP	PHONE	ENTRY #
Mono Wind Casino	7011	D	559 855-4350	12936
Pacific Gas and Electric Co	4911	E	559 855-6112	6085

AUBURN, CA - Placer County

Company	SIC	EMP	PHONE	ENTRY #
American Medical Response Inc	4119	E	530 887-9440	3768
Andregg Geomatics	8713	D	530 885-7072	26127
Auburn Oaks Care Center	8051	D	650 949-7777	20241
Auburn Old Town Gallery	7999	D	530 887-9150	19105
Auburn Placer Disposal Service	4953	D	530 885-3735	6350
California Envmtl Systems Inc	8711	D	530 820-3693	25587
Century Commercial Service	5063	E	530 823-1004	7344
Chapa-De Indian Health (PA)	8011	D	530 887-2800	19372
Coldwell Bnkr Residential Brkg	6531	D	530 823-7653	11349
Congrgtnal Ch Retirement Cmnty	6513	D	530 823-6131	11004
County of Placer	8322	D	530 886-1870	23703
County of Placer	8093	D	530 889-7215	22553
County of Placer	8711	C	530 889-7500	25629
County of Placer	8322	D	530 823-4300	23704
County of Placer	8322	C	530 889-7900	23705
Decker Landscaping Inc	0782	D	916 652-1780	821
East Hall Investors Inc	6799	D	530 328-1900	12222
Foothill Oaks Care Center Inc	8051	D	530 888-6257	20435
Horizon West Inc	8734	D	530 889-8122	26704
Horizon West Healthcare Inc	8059	C	530 885-7511	21115
Interior Specialists Inc	1752	D	530 885-0632	3110
Lake of The Pines Association	8641	E	530 268-1141	25187
Madera Convalescent Hospital	8059	D	530 885-7051	21148
Magnussens Dodge Crysler Jeep	7538	D	530 885-2900	17772
Miltenyi Biotec Inc (HQ)	5047	D	530 745-2800	7193
Pacific Gas and Electric Co	4911	E	530 889-3102	6080
Placer Co Bar Association (PA)	8621	B	916 557-9181	25036
Placer County ADM Svcs	8999	C	530 886-5401	27954
Placer County Water Agency (PA)	4911	D	530 823-4850	6098
Placer County- Adult Sys Care	8093	D	530 886-2974	22642
Pride Industries	8331	C	530 888-0331	24220
Retirement Housing Foundation	8361	D	530 823-6131	24651
Riskalyze Inc	7379	D	530 748-1660	16472
Sierra West Construction Inc	1751	E	530 268-7614	3078
Sutter Health	8093	A	530 888-4500	22690
Vian Enterprises Inc	7389	E	530 885-1997	17567
Western Energetix LLC	5171	C	530 885-0401	8947
Westview Healh Care Center	8051	A	530 885-7511	20888

AVALON, CA - Los Angeles County

Company	SIC	EMP	PHONE	ENTRY #
Catalina Business Entps Inc	7999	E	310 510-1600	19120
Catalina Glassbottom Boat Inc	4489	D	310 510-2888	4714
Santa Catalina Island Company (PA)	4725	D	310 510-2000	4979
Two Harbors Enterprises Inc	4111	D	310 510-2000	3737

AVENAL, CA - Kings County

Company	SIC	EMP	PHONE	ENTRY #
Prison Industry Authority-Pia	8111	D	559 386-6060	23340

AVILA BEACH, CA - San Luis Obispo County

Company	SIC	EMP	PHONE	ENTRY #
Pacific Gas and Electric Co	4911	A	805 506-5280	6078

AZUSA, CA - Los Angeles County

Company	SIC	EMP	PHONE	ENTRY #
Artistic Entrmt Svcs LLC	7929	D	626 334-9388	18423
Buena Vista Food Products Inc (DH)	5149	C	626 815-8859	8762
California Pediatric Fmly Svcs	8322	D	626 812-0055	23524
Cemex Cement Inc	5032	C	626 969-1747	6879
David L Amador Inc	1771	D	626 334-2011	3245
Hanson Distributing Company (PA)	5013	C	626 224-9800	6644
Hanson Distributing Company	5013	C	626 357-5241	6645
Harrison Nichols Co Ltd	4214	C	626 337-5020	4350
Heidi Corporation	1522	D	626 333-6317	1288
Heppner Hardwoods Inc	5031	D	626 969-7983	6827
Kds Marketing	7389	C	818 240-7000	17269
Monrovia Nursery Company (PA)	0181	A	626 334-9321	284
Morris National Inc (HQ)	5149	D	626 385-2000	8830
Murrieta Gardens Senior Living	8052	D	951 600-7676	20946
Oj Insulation LP (PA)	1742	C	626 812-6070	2927
One Main Financial Services	8742	D	626 335-0617	27377
Precise Enterprises LLC	8742	E	818 599-6450	27397
Rain Bird Distribution Corp	1629	D	626 963-9311	2057
RES-Care California Inc	8052	E	626 334-7862	20951
Richard Wilson Wellington	0181	D	626 812-7881	294
San Gabriel Valley Water Assn	4941	D	626 815-1305	6303
Seracada	8082	E	626 486-0800	22414
Silverado Senior Living Inc	8059	D	626 650-9801	21210
Smart & Final Stores Inc	5141	A	626 334-5189	8454
Stanley Steemer of Los Angles (PA)	7217	D	626 791-9400	13580
Sunbelt Controls Inc	1711	D	626 610-2340	2374
Totten Tubes Inc (PA)	5051	D	626 812-0220	7321
Virginia Hardwood Company (PA)	5031	D	626 815-0540	6872

BAKERSFIELD, CA - Kern County

Company	SIC	EMP	PHONE	ENTRY #
7th Standard Ranch Company	0172	B	661 399-0416	127
A-C Electric Company (PA)	1731	B	661 410-0000	2497
A-C Electric Company	8711	D	661 633-5368	25493
Accelerated Envmtl Svcs Inc	7349	D	661 765-4003	14177
Account Control Technology Inc	7322	E	661 395-5702	13989
Advance Beverage Co Inc	5181	D	661 833-3783	8976
Aera Energy LLC (HQ)	1381	A	661 665-5000	1032
Ag-Wise Enterprises Inc (PA)	0762	C	661 325-1567	679
Agape In Home Care Inc	8082	E	661 835-0364	22209
Agri-Mix Transport Inc	4212	C	661 833-6280	3969
Alaidandrew Corporation	8059	C	661 334-2200	20983
Allpro Industry Solutions LLC	4731	E	661 854-3613	5005
American Baptist Homes of West	8059	C	661 834-0620	20989
Ameripride Services Inc	7213	C	661 324-7941	13509
AMF Bowling Centers Inc	7933	E	661 324-4966	18478
Ancon Marine	7699	D	310 952-8160	17934
Anthony Vineyards Inc (PA)	0172	C	661 858-6211	129
Arrival Communications Inc (DH)	7389	D	661 322-7375	17011
Asbury Transportation Co	4213	D	661 327-2271	4101
AT&T Services Inc	4813	C	661 398-2000	5472
AT&T Services Inc	4813	B	661 327-6030	5477
AT&T Services Inc	8748	C	661 324-2046	27648
Automobile Club Southern Cal	8699	E	661 327-4661	25387
B & B Surplus Inc (PA)	5051	D	661 589-0381	7260
Baker Hughes A GE Company LLC	1389	D	661 387-1010	1049
Baker Hughes A GE Company LLC	1389	D	800 229-7447	1051
Baker Petrolite LLC	1389	D	661 325-4138	1052
Bakersfield Assc Rrtd Ctzns	8331	C	661 834-2272	24155
Bakersfield Country Club	7997	D	661 871-4000	18852
Bakersfield Family Med Group	8099	D	661 846-3605	22740
Bakersfield Healthcare	8051	A	661 872-2121	20254
Bakersfield Kitchen & Bath	1711	D	661 836-2284	2134
Bakersfield Memorial Hospital	8062	A	661 327-1792	21294
Bakersfield Symphony Orch	7929	D	661 323-7928	18424
Baymarr Constructors Inc (PA)	1771	D	661 395-1676	3221
Bc Laboratories Inc	8734	D	661 327-4911	26685
Beautitudes Beauty Supply LLC	5087	D	800 830-6076	7882
Behavioral H Bakersfield	8063	C	661 398-1800	21928
Berry Petroleum Company LLC (HQ)	1311	D	661 616-3900	1013
Better Way Services	8322	D	661 326-6444	23511
Biomat Usa Inc	8099	D	661 863-0621	22745
Bolthouse Farms	0161	A	661 366-7205	38
Boys Girls Clubs of Kern Cnty	8641	D	661 325-3730	25113
Braden Partners LP A Calif	5047	D	661 632-1979	7167
Braun Electric Company Inc (HQ)	1731	B	661 633-1451	2525
Bright House Networks LLC	4841	D	661 634-2200	5858
Brown Armstrong Accntancy Corp	8721	D	661 324-4971	26152
Burtch Trucking Inc	1611	D	661 399-1736	1734
Buttonwillow Warehouse Co Inc (HQ)	5191	D	661 695-6500	9077
Califia Farms LLC	0191	D	661 679-1000	328
California Physicians Service	6324	C	661 631-2277	10183
California Resources Prod Corp (HQ)	1311	D	661 869-8000	1019
California Water Service Co	4941	D	661 396-2400	6216
Cameron West Coast Inc	5082	D	661 837-4980	7671

Mergent email: customerrelations@mergent.com
1542

2019 Directory of California
Wholesalers and Services Companies

(P-0000) Products & Services Section entry number
(PA)=Parent Co (HQ)=Headquarters (DH)=Div Headquarters

Company	SIC	EMP	PHONE	ENTRY #
Car Wash Partners Inc	7542	C	661 837-9485	17807
Castle & Cooke California Inc	4953	E	661 664-6500	6370
Castle & Cooke Commercial CA	6552	D	661 665-1540	11864
Cbizmhm LLC	8721	E	661 325-7500	26161
Cellco Partnership	4812	D	661 827-8728	5325
Cellco Partnership	4899	D	661 663-9451	5973
Central Cardiology Med Clinic	8011	C	661 395-0000	19366
Centre For Neuro Skills (PA)	8093	C	661 872-3408	22525
Cintas Corporation No 3	7218	D	661 282-4300	13599
Citizens Business Bank	6022	D	661 281-0300	9436
City of Bakersfield	8322	C	661 852-7300	23576
CL Knox Inc	1389	D	661 837-0477	1054
Clifford & Brown A Prof Corp	8111	C	661 322-6023	22982
Clinica Sierra Vista	8099	E	661 326-6490	22768
Clinica Sierra Vista (PA)	8011	D	661 635-3050	19388
CMA Fire Protection (PA)	1711	D	661 322-9344	2163
Cni Thl Propco Fe LLC	7011	D	661 325-9700	12473
Community Action Partnr Kern	8399	D	661 336-0317	24761
Community Action Partnr Kern	8399	D	661 366-5953	24763
Community Action Partnr Kern (PA)	8322	E	661 336-5236	23599
Construction Specialty Svc Inc	1623	D	661 864-7573	1911
Contra Costa Electric Inc	1731	C	661 322-4036	2551
Core-Mark International Inc	5149	C	661 366-2673	8776
Core-Mark International Inc	5194	C	661 366-2673	9182
County of Kern	8322	A	661 868-4100	23646
County of Kern	8322	D	661 392-2010	23647
County of Kern	8322	D	661 336-6800	23648
County of Kern	8011	E	661 868-8360	19408
County of Kern	8062	A	661 326-2054	21350
County of Kern	8399	A	661 631-6346	24767
County of Kern	8322	D	661 363-8910	23651
County of Kern	8111	D	661 868-2000	22996
Crestwood Behavioral Hlth Inc	8322	D	661 363-8127	23762
Crestwood Behavioral Hlth Inc	8069	C	661 363-6711	22015
Crystal Organic Farms LLC	0191	B	661 845-5200	332
Csub Nursing Class of 2006	7389	D	408 219-5914	17118
CW Welding Service Inc	5094	D	661 399-5422	8008
Days Inn Bakersfield	7011	C	661 324-6666	12516
Delmart Cold Storage Co Inc	4222	D	661 849-8608	4499
Dennis Hyde Construction Inc	1521	D	661 393-1077	1155
Dhv Industries Inc	5085	D	661 392-8948	7847
Diaz Plastering Inc	1742	D	661 244-8228	2875
Dignity Health	8351	D	661 832-8300	24315
Dignity Health	8062	E	661 663-6767	21387
Dignity Health	8062	D	661 632-5279	21393
Dignity Health	8062	B	661 632-5000	21394
Diversified Utility Svcs Inc	1623	B	661 325-3212	1915
Don Kinzel Construction Inc	1751	D	661 322-9105	3030
Donald Valpredo Farming Inc	0161	D	661 858-2245	50
Dv Custom Farming LLC	0191	D	661 858-2888	337
E & B Ntral Resources Mgt Corp (PA)	1311	D	661 679-1714	1022
E and B Natural Resources	1382	D	661 679-1700	1044
Electrcal Instrumentation Intl	1731	B	661 836-9466	2572
Electrical & Instrumentation	1731	C	661 836-9466	2575
Elysium Jennings LLC	1381	C	661 679-1700	1035
Encompass Health Corporation	8361	C	661 323-5500	24517
Engineered Well Svc Intl Inc	1389	C	866 913-6283	1057
Esparza Enterprises Inc (PA)	7363	A	661 831-0002	14851
Esparza Enterprises Inc	7361	D	661 831-0002	14616
Esparza Enterprises Inc	4213	A	661 631-0347	4137
Esys Energy Control Company	5084	D	661 833-1902	7750
Europro Inc (PA)	7299	D	661 615-6610	13743
Evergreen At Lakeport LLC	8051	C	661 871-3133	20416
Excalibur Well Services Corp (PA)	1381	D	661 589-5338	1036
Exeter Packers Inc	4222	C	661 399-0416	4503
Fisher Communications Inc	4833	D	661 327-7955	5791
Flyers Energy LLC	5172	B	661 321-9961	8958
Freeport-Mcmoran Oil & Gas LLC	1311	D	661 322-7600	1023
Fritch Eye Care Medical Center	8011	D	661 665-2020	19479
Frito-Lay North America Inc	5145	D	661 328-6034	8549
Frito-Lay North America Inc	5145	E	661 835-0347	8555
Frontier Mechanical Inc	1711	D	661 589-6203	2216
G4s Secure Solutions (usa)	7381	C	661 834-3454	16651
Garcia Roofing Inc	1761	E	661 325-5736	3160
Gilliam & Sons Inc	1794	D	661 589-0913	3427
Giumarra Vineyards Corporation	0172	D	661 395-7071	145
Glenn E Porter	6331	E	661 615-1500	10356
Glenwood Gardens	8051	B	661 587-0221	20458
Golden Empire Concrete Pdts	1771	D	661 833-4490	3257
Golden Empire Mortgage Inc (PA)	6162	D	661 328-1600	9810
Golden Empire Mortgage Inc (PA)	6162	D	661 328-1600	9811
Golden Empire Transit District (PA)	4111	C	661 869-2438	3658
Golden Living LLC	8051	D	661 323-2894	20467
Golden State Drilling Inc	1381	D	661 589-0730	1037
Good Samaritan Hospital	8062	B	661 399-4461	21431
Goodwill Inds S Centl Cal	8331	E	661 377-0191	24187
Granite Construction Company	1611	C	661 399-3361	1772
Grant Construction Inc	1751	C	661 588-4586	3038
Grayson Service Inc	1389	C	661 589-5444	1061
Grimmway Enterprises Inc	0723	C	661 845-5200	524
Gringteam Inc	7011	C	661 426-7919	12624
Guardsmark LLC	7381	C	661 325-5906	16685
Guinn Corporation	1794	D	661 325-6109	3428
H F Cox Inc (PA)	4213	D	661 366-3236	4189
H P Sears Co Inc	7322	D	661 325-5981	14006
Hall Ambulance Service Inc	4119	D	661 322-8741	3806
Hall Ambulance Service Inc (PA)	4119	D	661 322-8741	3807
Halliburton Company	1389	D	661 393-8111	1062
Henrietta Weill Memorial Child (PA)	8093	D	661 322-1021	22592
Herc Rentals Inc	7359	C	661 392-3661	14511
Heritage Medical Group (PA)	8011	D	661 327-4411	19499
Hillcrest Sheet Metal Inc	1761	D	661 335-1500	3164
Hills Wldg & Engrg Contr Inc	1389	C	661 746-5400	1063
Hoffman Hospice of The Valley	8052	D	661 410-1010	20934
Houchin Blood Services (PA)	8099	D	661 323-4222	22819
Houchin Blood Services	8099	D	661 327-8541	22820
Hps Mechanical Inc (PA)	1711	C	661 397-2121	2228
Hps Plumbing Service Inc	1623	B	661 324-2121	1929
Hunter-La Purisima Corp	8748	D	661 616-0600	27750
Hunting Energy Services Inc	1389	D	661 633-4272	1065
Innovative Engrg Systems Inc (PA)	8711	D	661 381-7800	25747
J G Boswell Company	0131	C	661 327-7721	13
Jamison Childrens Home	8322	D	661 334-3500	23870
Jims Steel Supply LLC	5099	E	661 324-6514	8039
Jims Supply Co Inc (PA)	5051	D	661 324-6514	7284
K S Fabrication & Machine Inc	1623	C	661 617-1700	1940
Kaiser Foundation Hospitals	8011	A	877 524-7373	19542
Kaiser Foundation Hospitals	8062	B	661 395-3000	21491
Kaiser Foundation Hospitals	8011	A	877 524-7373	19544
Kaiser Foundation Hospitals	8011	A	661 337-7160	19545
Kaiser Foundation Hospitals	8011	A	877 524-7373	19546
Kaiser Foundation Hospitals	8011	A	877 524-7373	19549
Kaiser Foundation Hospitals	8062	E	661 398-5011	21497
Kaiser Foundation Hospitals	8062	C	661 334-2020	21511
Kbak TV Channel 29 CBS	4833	D	661 327-7955	5804
Kearn Alternative Care Inc (PA)	8082	B	661 631-2036	22350
Kern Alternative Care Inc	8082	C	661 631-2036	22351
Kern Around Clock Foundation	8741	E	661 324-3221	26917
Kern Cnty Mntal Hlth Child Sys	8052	D	661 868-8300	20937
Kern County Hospital Authority	8062	A	661 326-2102	21532
Kern County Water Agency	4941	D	661 634-1512	6268
Kern Federal Credit Union	6061	D	661 327-9461	9563
Kern Health Systems Inc	8011	D	661 664-5000	19626
Kern Member Insurance Services	6061	E	661 327-9461	9564
Kern Rdlgy Imaging Systems Inc (PA)	8011	C	661 326-9600	19627
Kern Regional Center (PA)	8399	C	661 327-8531	24795
Kern River Co Generation Co	4911	D	661 392-2663	6046
Kern Schools Federal Credit Un (PA)	6061	D	661 833-7900	9565
Kern Security Corporation	7382	C	661 363-6874	16915
Kern Steel Fabrication Inc (PA)	1791	C	661 327-9588	3381
Kindred Healthcare Operating	8051	C	661 872-2121	20562
Kirschenman Enterprises Inc	0191	D	661 366-5736	364
Klassen Corporation (PA)	1542	C	661 327-0875	1576
Klein Denatale Goldner Et Al (PA)	8111	D	661 401-7755	23175
KS Industries LP (PA)	1623	A	661 617-1700	1944
Ksi Engineering Inc	8711	E	661 617-1700	25790
Latara Enterprise Inc	8071	C	661 665-9780	22105
Laztrans Inc	4213	E	661 833-3783	4214
Linnco LLC	1311	A	661 616-3900	1024
Lutrel Trucking Inc	4731	C	661 397-9756	5103
M & S Security Services Inc	7381	D	661 397-9616	16725
M P Vacuum Truck Service (PA)	4953	C	661 393-1151	6412
Managed Care Systems Kern Cnty	6411	D	661 716-7100	10675
Mechanical Industries Inc	1791	C	661 634-9477	3387
Mega Farm Labor Services Inc	7361	C	661 229-8077	14667
Mercies Home (PA)	8351	D	661 832-3424	24348
Mercy HM Svcs A Cal Ltd Partnr	8062	C	661 632-5234	21587
Mistras Group Inc	8711	D	661 829-1192	25825
Mmi Services Inc	1389	C	661 589-9366	1069
Moreland PCF Snoqualmie LLC	6552	D	661 322-1081	11893
Morgan Stanley & Co LLC	6211	D	661 663-8100	9999
Mp Environmental Services Inc (PA)	4953	C	800 458-3036	6422
Nabors Well Services Co	1381	C	661 588-6140	1038
Nabors Well Services Co	1389	B	661 589-3970	1070
Nabors Well Services Co	1389	D	661 392-7668	1072
National Mentor Inc	8399	E	661 387-1000	24811
Nations Petroleum Cal LLC	1382	C	661 387-6402	1045
Ned E Dunphy	8111	D	661 395-1000	23282
Nestle Ice Cream Company	5143	A	661 398-3500	8526
New Advances For People Disabi	8399	D	661 327-0188	24812

Employment Codes: A=Over 500 employees, B=251-500,
C=101-250, D=51-100, E=50

2019 Directory of California
Wholesalers and Services Companies

© Mergent Inc. 1-800-342-5647
1543

GEOGRAPHIC

	SIC	EMP	PHONE	ENTRY #
Newport Hospitality Group Inc	7011	C	661 323-1900	12954
Newport Television LLC	4833	D	661 283-1700	5827
Oakdale Heights Senior Living	8051	E	661 663-9671	20670
Oldenkamp Trucking Inc (PA)	4212	D	661 833-3400	4048
Olive Knolls Christian School	8351	D	661 393-3566	24357
Olympus Power LLC	4911	D	661 393-6885	6065
Omni Family Health (PA)	8011	A	661 459-1900	19732
Opal Fry and Son	0161	E	661 858-2523	74
Optimal Health Services Inc	8082	D	661 393-4483	22382
Optimal Hospice Foundation	8082	C	661 716-4000	22383
OXY USA Inc	1311	C	661 869-8000	1025
Pacific Gas and Electric Co	4911	D	661 398-5918	6095
Pacific Process Systems Inc (PA)	1389	D	661 321-9681	1074
Padre Associates Inc	8711	D	661 829-2686	25863
Pan Pacific Petroleum Co Inc	4213	D	661 589-3200	4242
Panama-Buena Vista Un Schl Dst	7349	B	661 397-2205	14340
Panama-Buena Vista Un Schl Dst	4225	D	661 831-7879	4605
Panorama Park Apts	6513	D	661 325-4047	11092
Parkview Jlian Cnvlescent Hosp	8051	D	661 831-9150	20695
Pavletich Elc Cmmnications Inc (PA)	1731	C	661 589-9473	2677
PCL Industrial Services Inc	1541	B	661 832-3995	1428
Penney Lawn Service Inc	0782	D	661 587-4788	919
Perez Contracting LLC	0762	C	661 399-2700	707
Physicians Automated Lab Inc (DH)	8071	D	661 325-0744	22122
Preferred Brokers Inc (PA)	6531	D	661 836-2345	11677
Progauge Technologies Inc	5084	E	661 392-9600	7787
Pros Incorporated	1389	D	661 589-5400	1076
Prosoft Technology Inc (HQ)	4899	D	661 716-5100	5992
Public Health California Dept	8011	C	661 835-4668	19807
Pyramid Produce Inc	0761	D	661 366-5736	667
Quinn Company	5082	D	661 393-5800	7687
Quinn Group Inc	5083	D	661 393-5800	7709
R Stanley Security Service	7381	D	661 634-9283	16770
Rainbow Ranches Inc	0191	C	661 858-2266	374
Ramsgate Engineering Inc	8711	D	661 392-0050	25888
Re/Max	6531	E	661 616-4040	11708
Re/Max Magic	6531	E	661 616-4040	11711
Regent Assisted Living Inc	8361	D	661 663-8400	24647
Rgis LLC	7389	D	661 827-9195	17435
Rhino Ready Mix Trucking Inc (PA)	4212	D	661 679-3643	4055
Richard K Newman and Assoc Inc (PA)	7213	E	661 634-1130	13553
Rio Bravo Ranch Shop	0291	E	661 872-5050	456
Rncmba Inc	7363	C	661 395-1700	14905
Robert Heely Construction LP (PA)	1623	B	661 617-1400	1974
S A Camp Companies (PA)	5083	E	661 399-4451	7711
S A Camp Pump Company	7699	D	661 399-2976	17981
SA Recycling LLC	4953	D	661 327-3559	6467
Salvation Army	8093	D	661 325-8626	22669
San Dimas Medical Group Inc	8011	D	661 663-4800	19846
San Joaquin Community Hospital (PA)	8062	A	661 395-3000	21706
San Joaquin Val UNI Air Pol	8748	D	209 497-1000	27854
Schlumberger Technology Corp	1389	D	661 864-4750	1077
Seven Oaks Country Club	7997	C	661 664-6404	19044
Sierra International McHy LLC	5093	D	661 327-7073	7992
Sierra Recycling & Dem Inc	1795	D	661 327-7073	3462
Sierra Transport Inc	4212	D	661 836-3166	4063
Silla Automotive LLC	5013	D	661 392-8880	6674
Simmons Construction Inc	1542	E	661 636-1321	1650
Sippi Anne Riverside Ranch LLP	8361	E	661 871-9697	24675
Soli-Bond Inc	1389	D	661 631-1633	1080
Southern Cal Prmnnte Med Group	8011	D	661 398-5085	19906
Southern Cal Prmnnte Med Group	8011	D	661 334-2020	19925
Southern California Gas Co	4924	E	661 399-4431	6165
Southwest Contractors (PA)	1623	C	661 588-0484	1982
Stantec Energy & Resources Inc (DH)	8713	C	661 396-3770	26137
Stantec Holdings Del III Inc (HQ)	6719	C	661 396-3770	12007
State Compensation Insur Fund	6331	C	661 664-4000	10396
State Farm Mutl Auto Insur Co	6411	D	661 324-4077	10787
State Farm Mutl Auto Insur Co	6411	D	661 664-9663	10794
Stockdale Country Club	7997	D	661 832-0310	19063
Sturgeon Services Intl Inc (PA)	6719	E	661 322-4408	12009
Sturgeon Son Grading & Pav Inc (PA)	1794	C	661 322-4408	3439
Sun Pacific Maricopa	0723	B	661 847-1015	570
Sun Pacific Marketing Coop Inc	8742	A	213 612-9957	27476
Sun Pacific Marketing Coop Inc	5148	B	661 847-1015	8734
Sun World International Inc (PA)	0723	A	661 392-5000	572
Sun World International LLC	0191	D	661 392-5000	382
Sunridge Nurseries Inc	0721	C	661 363-8463	468
Sunshine Metal Clad Inc	1742	D	661 366-0575	2964
Surface Pumps Inc (PA)	5084	D	661 393-1545	7808
Surgener Electric Inc	1731	D	661 399-3321	2756
Sycamore Cogeneration Co (PA)	4911	D	661 615-4630	6143
Technosocialworkcom LLC	7374	D	661 617-6601	16188
Texaco Inc	6531	B	661 654-7000	11793
Tj Cross Engineers Inc	8711	C	661 831-8782	25954

	SIC	EMP	PHONE	ENTRY #
Total-Western Inc	1522	D	661 589-5200	1322
Trans-West Security Svcs Inc	7381	C	661 381-2900	16837
Triple E Trucking	4212	E	661 834-0071	4072
Truitt Oilfield Maint Corp	1389	B	661 871-4099	1082
Truxtun Radiology Med Group LP	8071	C	661 325-6200	22152
U S Weatherford L P	1389	D	661 589-9483	1084
UCI Construction Inc	8711	D	661 587-0192	25968
Ulta Salon Cosmt Fragrance Inc	7231	C	661 664-1402	13681
Union Pacific Railroad Company	4011	D	661 321-4604	3633
United States Cold Storage Inc	4222	D	661 832-2653	4513
UPS Ground Freight Inc	4213	D	661 395-9500	4287
Valley Industrial X-Ra	8734	C	661 399-8497	26742
Valley Pacific Petro Svcs Inc	5172	C	661 746-7737	8971
Valley Power Systems Inc	5084	E	661 325-9001	7817
Valley Republic Bank	6022	D	661 371-2000	9493
Valley Sun Mechanical Cnstr	1799	D	661 321-9070	3602
Vaquero Energy Incorporated	1311	E	661 363-7240	1031
Vasindas Around The Clock Care	8361	D	661 395-5820	24709
Verizon Communications Inc	4813	E	661 328-2226	5669
Veterans Health Administration	8011	C	661 632-1871	20082
Veterans Health Administration	8011	B	661 323-8387	20084
Vignolo Farms Inc	0131	C	661 393-1431	16
Vinod Kumar MD	8011	D	661 324-4100	20087
W M Lyles Co	8711	C	661 387-1600	25993
Weatherford International LLC	1389	D	661 587-9753	1086
Western Oilfields Supply Co (PA)	7359	C	661 399-9124	14555
Wholesale Fuels Inc	5172	C	661 327-4900	8974
Winegard Energy Inc	1742	D	661 393-9467	2984
Wm Bolthouse Farms Inc (DH)	0161	A	661 366-7209	89
Work Force Services Inc	7363	C	661 327-5019	14946
Zim Industries Inc	1781	D	661 393-9661	3357

BALDWIN PARK, CA - Los Angeles County

	SIC	EMP	PHONE	ENTRY #
All Direct Mail Services Inc	7331	C	818 833-7773	14041
All Star Automotive Products	5013	D	626 960-5164	6617
American Kal Enterprises Inc (PA)	5072	D	626 338-7308	7574
American Mzhou Dngpo Group Inc	8741	D	626 820-9239	26757
Baldwin Hospitality LLC	7011	D	626 962-6000	12350
Bowers Companies Inc (HQ)	4119	D	562 988-6460	3780
California Lighting Sales Inc (PA)	5063	C	626 775-6000	7343
Cbre Inc	6531	B	626 814-7900	11277
Cedarwood-Young Company (PA)	4953	C	626 962-4047	6371
Cedarwood-Young Company	5093	D	626 962-4047	7973
Cellco Partnership	4812	D	626 472-6196	5344
City of Baldwin Park	8699	C	626 960-1955	25410
County of Los Angeles	8711	C	626 337-1277	25627
Crowner Sheet Metal Pdts Inc	1761	E	626 960-4971	3143
First Avenue Inc	1761	C	626 856-2076	3156
G K Tool Corp	5072	D	626 338-7300	7588
Garden View Care Center Inc	8051	C	626 962-7095	20446
Golden State Habilitation Conv (PA)	8051	B	626 962-3274	20486
Haynes Building Service LLC	7349	C	626 359-6100	14286
Ideal Transit Inc	4111	C	626 448-2690	3659
Kaiser Foundation Hospitals	8062	A	626 851-1011	21481
Nichols Lumber & Hardware Co	5031	D	626 960-4802	6842
Nr 2 Group Inc	4212	E	626 251-6681	4046
Ols Hotels & Resorts LLC	7011	A	626 962-6000	12979
Pepsi-Cola Metro Btlg Co Inc	5149	C	626 338-5531	8849
Pepsico Inc	5145	C	626 338-5531	8565
Phoenix Satellite TV US Inc	4841	E	626 388-1188	5928
R B International Inc (PA)	5084	E	626 357-7652	7790
San Gabriel Transit Inc	4121	C	626 430-3650	3868
SCE Federal Credit Union (PA)	6061	C	626 960-6888	9588
Sierra View Care Holdings LLC	8051	C	626 960-1971	20763
Southern California Edison Co	4911	C	626 543-6093	6121
Tanimura & Antle Inc	0723	B	831 424-6100	577
Tecan Sp Inc	5049	D	626 962-0010	7249
Trinity Health Systems (PA)	8051	C	626 960-1971	20842
United Parcel Service Inc OH	4215	C	626 814-6216	4485
USA Waste of California Inc	4953	D	626 856-1285	6492
Valley Light Industries Inc	8331	C	626 337-6200	24245
Vista Specialty Hosp Cal LP	8062	C	626 388-2700	21911

BALLICO, CA - Merced County

	SIC	EMP	PHONE	ENTRY #
Hilltop Ranch Inc	0723	C	209 874-1875	529

BANNING, CA - Riverside County

	SIC	EMP	PHONE	ENTRY #
Bho LLC	8361	E	951 845-2220	24437
Cancer Federation Inc (PA)	8399	C	951 849-4325	24749
Ferrees Group Home Inc	8361	D	951 849-1927	24527
Green Thumb Produce	5148	C	951 849-4711	8693
H E L P Inc	8322	D	951 922-2305	23827
Poison Spyder Customs Inc	7549	A	951 849-5911	17868
Professional Community MGT Cal	6531	C	951 845-2191	11683
Riverside-San Bernardino (PA)	8093	D	951 849-4761	22667
San Gorgonio Memorial Hospital (PA)	8062	C	951 845-1121	21705

2019 Directory of California
Wholesalers and Services Companies

(P-0000) Products & Services Section entry number
(PA)=Parent Co (HQ)=Headquarters (DH)=Div Headquarters

	SIC	EMP	PHONE	ENTRY #
Silent Valley Club Inc	7033	D	951 849-4501	13468
Strech Plastics Incorporated	5088	E	951 922-2224	7915
Sun Lakes Cntry Club Hmeownrs	8641	D	951 845-2135	25255

BARSTOW, CA - San Bernardino County

	SIC	EMP	PHONE	ENTRY #
Barstow Redevelopment Agency	8748	C	760 256-3531	27655
Bnsf Railway Company	4011	C	760 255-7803	3615
Burrtec Waste Group Inc	4212	D	760 256-2730	3983
Darensburg Roghair & Renier	7011	E	760 256-6891	12512
Economy Inn	7011	E	760 256-5601	12548
Frontier California Inc	4813	D	760 256-3511	5563
Golden Empire Mortgage Inc	6162	D	760 256-3593	9809
Hentrel Greathouse Foundation	8641	D	302 513-4056	25172
Hospital of Barstow Inc	8062	C	760 256-1761	21455
Kbrwyle Tech Solutions LLC	8711	C	760 255-8322	25776
Latara Enterprise Inc	8071	D	760 256-3450	22106
Life Care Centers America Inc	8051	B	760 252-2515	20588
Little Sisters Truck Wash Inc	7542	D	760 253-2277	17828
M V Transportation	4789	C	760 255-3330	5236
Time Warner Cable Inc	4841	D	760 256-3526	5958

BASS LAKE, CA - Madera County

	SIC	EMP	PHONE	ENTRY #
Basslake LLC	7011	D	559 642-3121	12358
Home Away Inc	7011	D	559 642-3121	12695

BAY POINT, CA - Contra Costa County

	SIC	EMP	PHONE	ENTRY #
Ambrose Recreation & Park Dst	7999	D	925 458-1601	19095
Caribbean South Amercn Council	4724	E	925 709-3433	4933
Henkel Corporation	8711	C	925 458-8086	25732
K & S Towing & Transport	8742	D	925 709-0759	27291

BAYSIDE, CA - Humboldt County

	SIC	EMP	PHONE	ENTRY #
O A Outfitting Inc	7999	D	707 498-2917	19210

BEALE AFB, CA - Yuba County

	SIC	EMP	PHONE	ENTRY #
US Dept of the Air Force	8011	D	530 634-4738	20038

BEAR VALLEY, CA - Calaveras County

	SIC	EMP	PHONE	ENTRY #
Bear Valley Ski Co	7999	B	209 753-2301	19108

BEAUMONT, CA - Riverside County

	SIC	EMP	PHONE	ENTRY #
Anderson Chrnesky Strl Stl Inc	1791	D	951 769-5700	3359
Arrow USA	5087	D	951 845-6144	7881
Beaumont Unified School Dst	4151	A	951 845-3010	3908
Bogh Engineering Inc	1771	D	951 845-5130	3227
California Oak Valley Golf	7992	E	951 769-9771	18692
Cellco Partnership	4812	D	951 769-0985	5304
Charlee Family Care	8361	D	951 845-3588	24462
Childhelp Inc	8361	C	951 845-6737	24463

BELL, CA - Los Angeles County

	SIC	EMP	PHONE	ENTRY #
4g Wireless Inc	4813	D	562 928-2972	5430
Affiliated Temporary Help	7363	B	323 771-1383	14810
Bernard Perrin Supowitz Inc	5141	E	323 981-2800	8384
Briarcrest Nursing Center Inc	8051	C	562 927-2641	20265
City of Bell	8322	C	323 773-1596	23577
El Aviso Magazine	5192	B	323 586-9199	9112
Fam LLC	5136	D	323 888-7755	8258
Human Services Association (PA)	8621	D	562 806-5400	25019
Jwch Institute Inc	8733	D	323 562-5813	26630
Omega Moulding West LLC	5023	C	323 261-3510	6780

BELL GARDENS, CA - Los Angeles County

	SIC	EMP	PHONE	ENTRY #
Anitsa Inc	7211	C	213 237-0533	13483
Auchante Inc	6531	D	562 231-1880	11225
Bell Gardens Bicycle Club Inc	7999	A	562 806-4646	19109
Bicycle Casino LP	7011	A	562 806-4646	12385
C T and F Inc	1731	C	562 927-2339	2535
Del Rio Sanitarium Inc	8051	C	562 927-6586	20371
WEI-Chuan USA Inc (PA)	5142	C	323 587-2101	8509

BELLFLOWER, CA - Los Angeles County

	SIC	EMP	PHONE	ENTRY #
Advent Securities Investments (PA)	6211	E	562 920-5467	9912
Bio-Mdcal Applications Cal Inc	8092	D	562 920-2070	22466
Empire Enterprises Inc	4119	C	562 529-2676	3791
Empire Transportation	4141	C	562 529-2676	3888
Estrella Inc	8051	C	562 925-6418	20412
Habitat For Humanity of Greate	8399	E	310 323-4663	24786
Harbor Health Care Inc	8361	D	562 866-7054	24549
Hollywood Sports Park LLC	7389	D	562 867-9600	17224
Jwch Institute Inc	8099	D	562 867-7999	22826
Kaiser Foundation Hospitals	8062	A	562 461-3000	21484
Kaiser Foundation Hospitals	6324	D	562 461-3084	10257
Leroy Durbin	6531	D	562 531-2001	11564
Life Care Centers America Inc	8051	D	562 867-1761	20586
Produce Company	5148	C	310 508-7760	8720
Rebecca Terley	8051	D	562 925-4252	20717
Verizon Communications Inc	4899	C	562 804-0354	6005
Young Mens Chrstn Assc Gr L B	8641	D	562 925-1292	25335

BELMONT, CA - San Mateo County

	SIC	EMP	PHONE	ENTRY #
Belmont Oaks Academy	8351	D	650 593-6175	24265
County of San Mateo	8322	C	650 802-6470	23739
Cw Healthcare Inc	7363	E	510 636-9000	14847
Island Hospitality MGT LLC	7011	D	650 591-8600	12785
Namasta Inc	7997	E	650 591-3639	18982
Nikon Precision Inc (DH)	5084	D	650 508-4674	7780
Oracle Systems Corporation	7372	B	650 654-7606	15817
Ringcentral Inc (PA)	7374	D	650 472-4100	16172
Silverado Senior Living Inc	8059	D	650 226-8017	21208
Sunrise Senior Living LLC	8051	D	650 654-9700	20829
Tectura Corporation (PA)	7379	D	650 273-4249	16510
Telecare Corporation	8063	D	650 817-9070	21990
Ten-X LLC	6531	A	800 793-6107	11787
Westlake Development Group LLC	8741	D	650 579-1010	27095
Woodmont Realty Advisors Inc	6371	D	650 592-3960	10495
Wyndham International Inc	7011	E	650 591-8600	13429

BELVEDERE, CA - Marin County

	SIC	EMP	PHONE	ENTRY #
Pacific Union Co	6531	D	415 789-8686	11651

BELVEDERE TIBURON, CA - Marin County

	SIC	EMP	PHONE	ENTRY #
Accenture LLP	8742	C	415 537-5860	27107
Digital Foundry Inc	7379	E	415 789-1600	16348
Magave Tequila Inc	5182	E	415 515-3536	9051
Marcolin USA Inc	5048	C	415 383-6348	7236
Marin Cnvlscent Rhbltton Hosp	8051	D	415 435-4554	20609
Melissa Bradley RE Inc	6531	E	415 435-2705	11604
Pharmacy Temps Inc	7363	E	415 459-5211	14890
Tiburon Hotel LLC	7011	D	415 435-5996	13326
Tiburon Peninsula Club Inc	7997	E	415 789-7900	19071
Vital Farmland Holdings LLC	7389	D	415 465-2400	17571

BENICIA, CA - Solano County

	SIC	EMP	PHONE	ENTRY #
1-800 Radiator & A/C (PA)	5013	D	707 747-7400	6616
All-Points Petroleum LLC	5172	D	707 745-1116	8948
American Civil Const	1611	D	707 746-8028	1718
American Civil Constrs LLC	1629	C	707 746-8028	2006
Americas Lemonade Stand Inc	7389	C	707 745-1274	17000
Anthony Trevino	1752	D	707 747-4776	3094
Awt Construction Group Inc	1521	D	707 746-7500	1121
Benicia Plumbing Inc	1711	D	707 745-2930	2140
Biagi Bros Inc	4213	D	707 745-8115	4108
C E Toland & Son	1799	D	707 747-1000	3498
Califrnia Erctors Bay Area Inc	1791	C	707 746-1990	3369
Clean Harbors Envmtl Svcs Inc	4953	C	707 747-6699	6380
Clean Hrbors Es Indus Svcs Inc	7699	D	707 745-1581	17938
Csu Holding Company	6719	E	707 746-0353	11972
DC Solar Solutions Inc	1711	E	925 203-1088	2183
Delta Tech Service Inc (PA)	7349	D	707 745-2080	14252
Durkee Drayage Company	4214	D	510 970-7550	4345
F3 & Associates Inc (PA)	8713	D	707 748-4300	26129
Fedex Ground Package Sys Inc	4215	D	800 463-3339	4417
Flatiron West Inc	1622	C	707 742-6000	1877
Henry Wine Group LLC (HQ)	5182	D	707 745-8500	9049
Herc Rentals Inc	7359	E	707 747-4444	14512
High End Development Inc	1799	D	925 687-2540	3533
Innovel Solutions Inc	4731	D	707 748-1940	5091
Inter-Rail Trnspt Nshville LLC	4789	D	707 746-1695	5230
J P Consulting	8742	E	707 747-4800	27284
Mdr Inc	8711	D	707 750-5376	25815
Mistras Group Inc	8734	E	707 746-5870	26717
Molecule Labs Inc	8742	D	714 892-3133	27351
Pepsi-Cola Metro Btlg Co Inc	4225	C	707 746-5404	4608
Plan-It Interactive Inc (PA)	7299	E	707 752-6010	13766
Ponder Environmental Svcs Inc (PA)	8748	D	707 748-7775	27824
Safway Services LP	5082	C	707 745-2000	7694
Solano Pacific Corporation	6531	D	707 745-6000	11770
Underground Cnstr Co Inc	4931	C	707 746-8800	6188
Unico Industrial Service Co (PA)	7699	D	707 736-8787	18000
Unico Mechanical Corp	5084	D	707 745-4540	7814
United Site Services Cal Inc	4953	E	707 747-2810	6486
Western Sun Enterprises Inc	1731	C	707 748-2542	2788

BERKELEY, CA - Alameda County

	SIC	EMP	PHONE	ENTRY #
A Better Way Inc (PA)	8399	C	510 601-0203	24727
A T Associates Inc	8059	E	510 649-6670	20976
Ala Costa Center Program For (PA)	8351	D	510 527-2550	24262
Altcare Cedar Creek LLC	8361	C	510 527-7282	24414
Andrew M Jordan Inc	1794	D	510 999-6000	3414
Annies Homegrown Inc	5149	D	510 558-7500	8752
Backroads (PA)	4725	B	510 527-1555	4963
Barra LLC (HQ)	7372	D	510 548-5442	15603
Berkeley 75 Hsing Partners LP	6531	D	510 705-1488	11238
Berkeley Cement Inc	1771	C	510 525-8175	3224
Berkeley Repertory Theatre (PA)	7922	D	510 204-8901	18345

Employment Codes: A=Over 500 employees, B=251-500,
C=101-250, D=51-100, E=50

2019 Directory of California
Wholesalers and Services Companies

© Mergent Inc. 1-800-342-5647

1545

GEOGRAPHIC

	SIC	EMP	PHONE	ENTRY #
Berkeley Student Coop Inc	7041	D	510 848-1936	13473
Berkeley Symphony Orchestra	7929	E	510 841-2800	18426
Berkeley Unified School Dst	4151	E	510 644-6182	3909
Boykin Mgt Co Ltd Lblty Co	7011	B	510 548-7920	12394
Building Opportunities **(PA)**	8322	C	510 649-1930	23521
California Shakespeare Theater	7922	A	510 548-3422	18351
Chaparral Foundation	8051	D	510 848-8774	20308
City of Berkeley	8721	A	510 981-6750	26165
Claremont Ht Prpts Ltd Partnr	7011	A	510 843-3000	12463
Clark Booker T **(PA)**	7349	E	510 482-8900	14216
Community Partners Intl	6732	C	510 225-9676	12076
DSM Biomedical Inc	8731	C	510 841-8800	26355
Earth Island Institute Inc	8699	D	510 859-9100	25418
Els	8748	D	510 549-2929	27716
Endsight	7379	D	510 655-6500	16358
Fmr LLC	6282	C	800 225-6447	10078
Gtxcel Inc	7371	D	800 609-8994	15193
Homegrown Natural Foods Inc	5141	D	510 558-7500	8413
Hornblower Yachts LLC	4489	D	916 446-1185	4718
Hotel Durant A Ltd Partnership	7011	D	510 845-8981	12724
Icygen LLC	7373	D	510 540-7122	15975
Inclusive Cmnty Resources LLC	8331	C	510 981-8115	24194
Ingram Publisher Services Inc	5192	D	510 528-1444	9116
Institute For Eductl Therapy	8331	E	831 457-1207	24195
International House	7021	C	510 642-9490	13440
Internet-Journals LLC	7379	D	510 665-1200	16406
Interntional Cmpt Science Inst	8733	E	510 643-9153	26626
Interstate Hotels Resorts Inc	8741	D	510 843-3000	26899
ISI Inspection Services Inc	7389	D	510 986-1157	17253
ISI Inspection Services Inc **(PA)**	7389	D	510 900-2101	17254
Jewish Fmly & Cmnty Svcs E Bay **(PA)**	8322	D	510 704-7475	23877
L J Kruse Co	1711	D	510 644-0260	2254
Lawrence Berkeley National Lab	8071	A	510 486-5111	22107
Lifelong Medical Care **(PA)**	8011	E	510 704-6010	19650
LOreal Usa Inc	5122	C	510 548-0130	8188
Mason-Mcduffie Real Estate Inc	6531	D	510 705-8611	11588
McKesson Corporation	5122	D	510 666-0854	8192
Moore Iacofano Goltsman Inc **(PA)**	8748	D	510 845-7549	27794
New Bridge Foundation Inc	8322	D	510 548-7270	23933
New Bridge Foundation Inc	8069	D	510 548-7270	22037
O C Jones & Sons Inc **(PA)**	1611	C	510 526-3424	1828
O C Sailing Club Inc	7999	D	510 843-4200	19211
Outfront Media LLC	7312	D	510 527-3350	13930
Pacific Steel Casting Co LLC	5051	B	510 558-2283	7295
Partners For Community Access	8322	D	510 558-6700	23960
Permanente Medical Group Inc	6324	D	510 559-5119	10296
Permanente Medical Group Inc	8011	D	510 559-5338	19778
Pillsbury Winthrop Shaw	8111	C	415 983-1865	23330
Research Triangle Institute	8742	D	510 849-4942	27424
Sanhyd Inc	8051	D	510 843-2131	20746
Satellite First Communities LP **(PA)**	6513	D	510 647-0700	11111
Shattuck Health Care Inc	8051	D	510 665-2800	20758
Sierra Nevada Brewing Co	5181	D	510 647-3439	9026
Sigma Kappa Sorority	7041	D	510 551-9142	13481
Sun Light & Power	7389	D	510 845-2997	17492
Surgery Center of Alta Bates **(HQ)**	8062	A	510 204-4444	21796
Surgery Center of Alta Bates	8011	E	510 204-4411	19955
Surgery Center of Alta Bates	8011	D	510 204-1591	19956
Sutter Health	8071	C	510 204-1591	22150
Toolworks Inc	8322	B	510 649-1322	24089
Toot Sweets Ltd **(PA)**	5149	E	510 526-0610	8886
United States Dept of Energy	8733	A	510 486-4000	26668
United States Dept of Energy	8731	A	510 486-4936	26479
University California Berkeley	8011	B	510 642-2000	20035
Westpost Berkeley LLC	7011	D	510 548-7920	13395
Westward Hospitality MGT	7011	D	510 548-7920	13396
Winnarainbow Inc **(PA)**	7032	E	510 525-4304	13458
Young MNS Chrstn Assn of E Bay	8641	D	510 486-8400	25358
Young MNS Chrstn Assn of E Bay	8641	D	510 848-9092	25359
Young MNS Chrstn Assn of E Bay	8641	C	510 848-9622	25360
Young MNS Chrstn Assn of E Bay	8641	D	510 526-2146	25361
Young MNS Chrstn Assn of E Bay	8351	A	510 644-6290	24404
Young MNS Chrstn Assn of E Bay	8641	D	510 848-6800	25364
Young MNS Chrstn Assn of E Bay	8641	D	510 559-2090	25365

BERMUDA DUNES, CA - Riverside County

	SIC	EMP	PHONE	ENTRY #
Bermuda Dunes Country Club	7997	E	760 360-2481	18864
Bermuda Dunes Learning Ctr Inc	8351	E	760 772-7127	24266
Cockrell Electric Inc	1731	D	760 864-6233	2542
Desert Cncpts Ldscpg Maint Inc	0781	D	760 200-9007	749
Earth Systems Southwest **(HQ)**	8711	D	760 345-1588	25651
Hort Tech Inc	0782	C	760 360-9000	860
KDI Elements	1743	D	760 345-9933	3000
Turf Star Inc	5083	D	760 772-3575	7715
Vantage Plaster & Drywall	1742	D	760 345-3622	2974
Vintage Associates Inc	0782	C	760 772-3673	958

BEVERLY HILLS, CA - Los Angeles County

	SIC	EMP	PHONE	ENTRY #
Academy Foundation **(HQ)**	7819	D	310 247-3000	18176
Academy Mpic Arts & Sciences **(PA)**	8621	D	310 247-3000	24992
Active Lawyers Referral Svc	8999	D	310 247-0425	27916
Advance Building Maintenance	7349	B	310 247-0077	14181
Aeroflot Russian Airlines	4512	D	323 272-4861	4756
Agency For Performing Arts Inc **(PA)**	7922	C	310 557-9049	18341
American Corporation	5015	D	310 274-1800	6701
American Health Connection	7389	B	424 226-0420	16999
Amtrow Group Inc	8742	D	310 557-0857	27134
Anderson Associates Staffing **(PA)**	7363	C	323 930-3170	14816
APA Incorporated	8742	C	310 888-4200	27139
Baker Winokur	8743	D	310 248-6169	27540
Beauty Recognized LP	7231	D	310 278-7646	13648
Beck International Inc	1541	B	310 281-2980	1377
Belvedere Hotel Partnership	7011	D	310 551-2888	12368
Belvedere Partnership	7011	B	310 551-2888	12369
Bentley Health Care Inc	8742	D	310 967-3300	27160
Beverly Hills Lingual Inst	7389	E	323 651-5000	17032
Beverly Hills Polc Ofcrs Assoc	8621	D	310 288-1755	24999
Beverly Radiology Med Group **(PA)**	8011	C	310 975-1500	19323
Bhrac LLC	7514	D	310 862-1933	17629
Bloom Hergott Diemer Cook LLC	8111	D	310 859-6800	22950
Brillstein Entrmt Partners LLC **(PA)**	7812	B	310 205-5100	18026
Bwr Public Relations	8743	D	310 248-6100	27544
Canessa Investments N V	6799	E	310 273-8543	12209
Cardivsclr Mdcl Grp of Sthrn	8011	D	310 278-3400	19349
Casden Builders LP	6512	E	310 274-5553	10860
Casden Company LLC	6552	D	310 274-5553	11863
Casewise Systems Inc **(DH)**	5045	D	424 284-4101	7023
Cedars-Sinai Medical Center	8062	C	310 385-3400	21306
Charles & Cynthia Eberly Inc	6513	D	323 937-6468	11001
City of Beverly Hills	7521	B	310 285-2552	17682
Coldwell Bnkr Residential Brkg	6531	D	310 273-3113	11353
Collective MGT Group LLC	8741	D	323 655-8585	26814
Condor Productions	7819	D	310 449-3000	18185
Cznd Inc	7929	D	323 378-6505	18428
Defy Media LLC	7311	D	310 360-4141	13815
Dosse Entertainment Mgmt	8741	D	323 366-9173	26844
Douglas Elliman Real Estate	6531	E	310 595-3888	11407
E H Summit Inc	7011	D	310 273-0300	12545
Finn Holding Corporation **(PA)**	4449	A	310 712-1850	4705
G Katen Partners Ltd Lblty Co	4731	A	424 354-3241	5068
Gersh Agency Inc **(PA)**	7922	D	310 274-6611	18368
Ggwh LLC	7011	E	310 786-1700	12604
Global Horizons Inc	7361	B	310 234-8475	14627
Gores Group LLC **(PA)**	6211	D	310 209-3010	9960
Granite Escrow Services	6099	D	310 288-0110	9685
Griffin Slr Management Inc	8741	D	310 270-4031	26879
Hair Fashion Inc	7231	D	310 274-0851	13661
Hilltop Securities Inc	6211	E	800 765-2200	9962
Honeymoon Real Estate LP	7011	D	310 277-5221	12698
Hong Kong & Shanghai Hotels	7011	D	310 551-2888	12699
Hyatt Vacation Ownership Inc	6531	D	310 285-0990	11508
Insomniac Inc	7929	D	323 874-7020	18442
Insomniac Holdings LLC	7929	C	323 874-7020	18443
Js Tamers Inc	6531	E	323 609-4101	11538
Kate Somerville Holdings LLC **(HQ)**	5122	D	323 655-4170	8185
Keller Wllams Rlty Bvrly Hills	6531	D	310 432-6400	11545
Kennedy-Wilson Inc **(PA)**	6531	C	310 887-6400	11546
Kpmg LLP	8721	E	310 273-2770	26236
La Peer Surgery Center LLC	8011	D	310 360-9119	19639
Lfk Law	8111	D	310 300-8464	23214
Linden Crest Surgery Center	8011	D	310 601-3900	19654
Live Nation Entertainment Inc	7389	D	323 462-4785	17298
Live Nation Entertainment Inc **(PA)**	7389	C	310 867-7000	17299
Live Nation Worldwide Inc	7922	A	310 867-7000	18382
M L Stern & Co LLC **(DH)**	6211	C	323 658-4400	9973
Magic Workforce Solutions LLC	8743	A	310 246-6153	27563
Marcus Buckingham Company	8742	D	323 302-9810	27317
Massachusetts Mutl Lf Insur Co	6311	D	323 965-6339	10139
Mayer Associates	6513	D	310 274-5553	11063
Mediaplatform Inc	7812	D	310 909-8410	18077
Medical Group Bverly Hills Inc **(PA)**	8011	E	310 385-3200	19675
Medical Group Bverly Hills Inc	8011	D	310 247-4646	19676
Merrill Lynch Pierce Fenner	6211	E	310 858-1500	9977
Metro-Goldwyn-Mayer Inc **(DH)**	7812	B	310 449-3000	18080
MGM and Ua Services Company	8999	A	310 449-3000	27944
Montage Hotels & Resorts LLC	7011	B	310 499-4199	12937
Morgan Stanley & Co LLC	6211	D	310 285-4800	10004
Mufg Union Bank National Assn	6021	D	310 550-6522	9356
N S B N Investments LLC	6799	D	310 273-2501	12247
Nelson Shelton & Associates	6531	C	310 271-2229	11624
Next Management LLC	8742	E	323 782-0038	27368
Nextpoint Inc **(PA)**	4813	D	310 360-5904	5614

2019 Directory of California
Wholesalers and Services Companies

(P-0000) Products & Services Section entry number
(PA)=Parent Co (HQ)=Headquarters (DH)=Div Headquarters

	SIC	EMP	PHONE	ENTRY #
Nourmand & Associates	6531	E	310 274-4000	11636
Omninet Twin Towers Gp LLC	6531	E	310 300-4100	11641
Omninet Twin Towers LP	6531	E	310 300-4110	11642
Orion Pictures Corporation	7812	A	310 449-3000	18088
Paradigm Music LLC (PA)	7922	D	310 288-8000	18392
Park Hotels & Resorts Inc	7011	C	310 415-3340	13030
Participant Channel Inc	4833	D	310 550-7715	5832
Participant Media LLC (PA)	7812	D	310 550-5100	18092
Playboy Enterprises Inc (PA)	7812	D	310 424-1800	18095
Porter Ranch Development Co	1531	D	323 655-7330	1357
Premier Exec Solutions Inc	8748	E	310 989-9925	27825
Project Boat Holdings LLC	6719	A	310 712-1850	12001
Promote Media LP	8742	D	323 433-7950	27405
Protected Outcomes Corporation	7381	D	203 545-9565	16767
Protravel International LLC	4724	D	310 271-9566	4950
Radnet Management Inc	8741	D	323 549-3000	27009
Raffles Lrmitage Beverly Hills	7011	C	310 278-3344	13096
Raines Law Group LLP	8111	E	310 440-4100	23347
Rbc Capital Markets LLC	6211	E	310 273-7600	10010
Regis Corporation	7231	E	310 274-8791	13670
Revel Travel Service Inc	4724	D	310 553-5555	4951
Rodeo Realty Inc (PA)	6531	D	818 349-9997	11739
Row Management Ltd Inc	6531	C	310 887-3671	11745
S J S Link International Inc (PA)	5142	E	310 860-7666	8504
Sajahtera Inc	7011	A	310 276-2251	13163
Shapell Industries LLC (HQ)	6552	D	323 655-7330	11915
Skidmore Owings & Merrill LLP	8712	C	310 651-9924	26108
Skin Health Experts Medic	8093	D	310 623-6869	22679
Sony Music Entertainment Inc	5099	C	310 272-2555	8059
SOS Security LLC	7381	D	310 859-8248	16832
Specialty Surg Ctr Beverly Hil	8011	D	310 659-6333	19931
Star Lax LLC	7514	C	310 642-4500	17648
Starpoint Property MGT LLC	6531	C	310 247-0550	11778
Stockcross Financial Svcs Inc (PA)	6211	E	800 993-2015	10015
Studio 71 LP	7313	C	323 370-1500	13956
Sunrise Senior Living Inc	8051	D	650 326-1108	20802
Sunrise Senior Living Inc	8051	D	310 274-4479	20805
Telemedicine Corp	8099	E	888 472-2853	22894
Telestar Consulting Inc	8742	E	310 748-0008	27485
Thomas Edward Companies (PA)	7011	E	310 859-9366	13325
Tiffanys Liu	8322	D	415 644-0846	24087
Tower Hematology Oncology Medi	8011	D	310 888-8680	20009
Travel Syndicate	4724	D	818 297-9979	4955
Treepeople Inc	0783	D	818 753-4600	981
UBS Financial Services Inc	6211	D	310 274-8441	10025
Universal Home Care Inc	8082	C	323 653-9222	22442
Universe Holdings Dev Co LLC	6531	E	310 785-0077	11807
Weinstein Company LLC	7812	D	424 204-4800	18167
Weintraub Tobin Chediak	8111	D	310 858-7888	23430
Wells Fargo Bank National Assn	6021	C	310 285-5817	9408
West Coast Storm Inc (PA)	8744	E	909 890-5700	27610
William Morris Endeavor	7922	B	310 285-9000	18414
William Morris Endeavor En (HQ)	7922	C	310 285-9000	18415
Wilner Klein Siegel	8111	E	310 550-4595	23436
Zillionaire Empress Danielle B	6722	A	310 461-9923	12056

BIG BEAR CITY, CA - San Bernardino County

	SIC	EMP	PHONE	ENTRY #
Big Bear City Cmnty Svcs Dst (PA)	4952	D	909 585-2565	6320

BIG BEAR LAKE, CA - San Bernardino County

	SIC	EMP	PHONE	ENTRY #
Bear Vly Cmnty Healthcare Dst (PA)	8062	C	909 866-6501	21298
Golden State Water Company	4911	E	909 866-4678	6038
Pacific Snow Valley Resort LLC	7011	D	909 866-3121	13004
Snow Summit Ski Corporation (PA)	7011	A	909 866-5766	13245

BIG CREEK, CA - Fresno County

	SIC	EMP	PHONE	ENTRY #
Southern California Edison Co	4911	C	559 893-3611	6115
Southern California Edison Co	4911	C	559 893-2037	6119

BIG SUR, CA - Monterey County

	SIC	EMP	PHONE	ENTRY #
48123 CA Investors LLC	7011	C	831 667-2331	12294
Tr Big Sur Management LLC	7011	E	831 667-4212	13336

BIGGS, CA - Butte County

	SIC	EMP	PHONE	ENTRY #
Chuck Jones Flying Service (PA)	0721	E	530 868-5798	461
Red Top Rice Growers	0723	E	530 868-5975	558
Sun West Wild Rice Facility	0112	E	530 868-5188	7

BISHOP, CA - Inyo County

	SIC	EMP	PHONE	ENTRY #
Bishop Paiute Gaming Corp	7999	C	760 872-6005	19111
Bishop Waste Disposal Inc	4953	E	760 872-6561	6358
Eastern Sierra Transit Auth	4131	E	760 872-1901	3877
Fedex Freight Corporation	4213	D	760 873-8655	4154
Fedex Ground Package Sys Inc	4213	C	800 463-3339	4172
High Country Lumber Inc	5031	E	760 873-5874	6831
Inyo Mono Advcts Fr Cmmnty Act (PA)	8399	D	760 873-8557	24791
Northern Inyo Healthcare Dst	8062	B	760 873-5811	21609

	SIC	EMP	PHONE	ENTRY #
SCE Eastern Hydro Division	4911	D	760 873-0767	6106
Southern California Edison Co	4911	C	760 873-0715	6117
Toiyabe Indian Health Prj Inc (PA)	8021	C	760 873-8461	20140
Triad Homes Assoc	8711	D	760 873-4273	25959
United Parcel Service Inc OH	4215	C	760 872-7661	4449

BLOOMINGTON, CA - San Bernardino County

	SIC	EMP	PHONE	ENTRY #
Accurate Delivery Systems Inc	4212	D	951 823-8870	3965
Acts For Children (PA)	8361	D	909 877-5499	24406
C M C Steel Fabricators Inc	1791	D	909 873-3060	3367
Calmex Engineering Inc	1771	D	909 546-1311	3230
Chiro Inc (PA)	5087	D	909 879-1160	7884
Distribution Alternatives Inc	4225	C	909 673-1000	4549
Empire Oil Co	5172	D	909 877-0226	8957
Fedex Ground Package Sys Inc	4513	A	800 463-3339	4839
Flyers Energy LLC	5172	C	909 877-2441	8959
Ftdi West Inc	4225	D	909 473-1111	4559
Inland Valley Cnstr Co Inc	1531	D	909 875-2112	1344
Kinder Mrgan Enrgy Partners LP	4619	E	909 873-5100	4926
Lineage Logistics Holdings LLC	4214	A	909 874-1200	4357
MCM Construction Inc	1622	C	909 875-0533	1885
Optimum Inc (PA)	8711	E	909 990-0767	25855
Revchem Composites Inc (PA)	5033	D	909 877-8477	6926
Roberts Lumber Sales Inc	5031	D	909 350-9164	6858
Santana Concrete	1771	D	909 421-2218	3321
Social Science Service Center	8069	D	909 421-7120	22050
Team West Contracting Corp	1629	E	951 340-3426	2066
Unified Aircraft Services Inc (PA)	4783	D	909 877-0535	5212
Union Pacific Railroad Company	4011	D	909 685-2710	3629
UPS Freight Services Inc	4213	D	909 879-7400	4285
Vance Corporation	1611	E	909 355-4333	1867
Verizon Communications Inc	7389	A	909 421-5053	17564

BLUE JAY, CA - San Bernardino County

	SIC	EMP	PHONE	ENTRY #
Alpine Camp Conference Ctr Inc	7999	D	909 337-6287	19093
Cbsrr Inc	6531	D	909 336-2131	11286

BLUE LAKE, CA - Humboldt County

	SIC	EMP	PHONE	ENTRY #
Blue Lake Casino	7011	E	707 668-5101	12390

BLYTHE, CA - Riverside County

	SIC	EMP	PHONE	ENTRY #
Aztec Harvesting	0761	A	760 922-7348	639
Barnes and Berger	0722	E	760 922-6136	474
Blythe Nursing Care Center	8051	D	760 922-8176	20263
Fisher Ranch LLC	0723	D	760 922-4151	516
Hayday Farms Inc	0139	D	760 922-4713	25
Palo Verde Health Care Dst	8062	C	760 922-4115	21625
Palo Verde Hospital Assn	8062	C	760 922-4115	21626
Palo Verde Irrigation District	4971	D	760 922-3144	6561
Xpo Logistics Freight Inc	4213	D	760 922-8538	4319

BODEGA BAY, CA - Sonoma County

	SIC	EMP	PHONE	ENTRY #
Bbcert	8742	E	480 220-3799	27155
Bodega Harbour Homeowners Assn	8641	D	707 875-3519	25100
NAPA Valley Lodge LP	7011	D	707 875-3525	12949

BOLINAS, CA - Marin County

	SIC	EMP	PHONE	ENTRY #
Commonweal	8322	D	415 868-0970	23593

BONITA, CA - San Diego County

	SIC	EMP	PHONE	ENTRY #
Child Development Assoc Inc (PA)	8351	C	619 427-4411	24282
Crockett & Coinc	7992	D	619 267-1103	18702
John Collins Co Inc	6513	D	818 227-2190	11037
Kaiser Foundation Hospitals	8062	D	619 640-6405	21514
McMillin RE & Mrtg Co Inc (PA)	6531	D	619 475-0233	11599
Paradise Valley Hospital	8082	D	619 472-7474	22389

BONSALL, CA - San Diego County

	SIC	EMP	PHONE	ENTRY #
Cunningham Group Inc	8742	D	303 295-1982	27208

BORON, CA - Kern County

	SIC	EMP	PHONE	ENTRY #
Kjc Operating Company	4911	C	760 762-5562	6047
Rio Tinto Minerals Inc	1241	C	760 762-7121	1010

BORREGO SPRINGS, CA - San Diego County

	SIC	EMP	PHONE	ENTRY #
Borrego Cmnty Hlth Foundation (PA)	8011	C	760 767-5051	19325
Copley Press Inc	7011	C	760 767-0100	12484
Rams Hill Country Club	7997	D	760 767-4259	19006

BOULDER CREEK, CA - Santa Cruz County

	SIC	EMP	PHONE	ENTRY #
Easter Seals Inc	7032	D	831 338-3383	13449

BOULEVARD, CA - San Diego County

	SIC	EMP	PHONE	ENTRY #
La Posta Casino	7011	C	619 824-4100	12830

BRAWLEY, CA - Imperial County

	SIC	EMP	PHONE	ENTRY #
Border Valley Trading Ltd	5191	D	760 344-6700	9074
Campesinos Unidos Inc (PA)	8748	C	760 370-5100	27674
Clinicas De Slud Del Peblo Inc (PA)	8011	D	760 344-9951	19390
Clinicas De Slud Del Peblo Inc	8011	D	760 344-6471	19391

Employment Codes: A=Over 500 employees, B=251-500,
C=101-250, D=51-100, E=50

2019 Directory of California
Wholesalers and Services Companies

© Mergent Inc. 1-800-342-5647

1547

GEOGRAPHIC

Company	SIC	EMP	PHONE	ENTRY #
Dacare Inc **(PA)**	8322	D	760 344-4654	23765
Esparza Enterprises Inc	0762	B	760 344-2031	691
Grimmway Enterprises Inc	7538	C	760 344-0204	17765
Irby Construction Company	1623	D	760 344-4478	1931
Kelomar Inc	0161	D	760 344-5253	64
Michael W Morgan	0161	E	760 344-5253	68
Pacific Sun Labor	0761	D	760 556-5085	664
Pioneers Mem Healthcare Dst **(PA)**	8062	A	760 351-3333	21650
Planters Hay Inc	5191	C	760 344-0620	9092
Rothfleisch Ranches Inc	0762	A	760 344-1819	711
Royal Convalescent Hospital	8051	D	760 344-5431	20732

BREA, CA - Orange County

Company	SIC	EMP	PHONE	ENTRY #
4wall Entertainment Inc	7922	C	702 263-3858	18336
Acosta Inc	5141	C	714 988-1500	8370
Aer Technologies Inc	7699	B	714 871-7357	17927
Air Treatment Corporation **(PA)**	5075	D	909 869-7975	7642
Albertsons LLC	4225	A	714 990-8200	4528
Allan Automatic Sprinkler Corp	1711	D	714 993-9500	2099
American Financial Network Inc **(PA)**	6162	C	909 606-3905	9771
American Sanitary Supply Inc	5087	E	714 632-3010	7879
Americold Logistics LLC	4222	A	714 993-3533	4492
Anatec International Inc **(HQ)**	8711	D	949 498-3350	25536
Apollo Electric	1731	D	714 256-8414	2511
Audiobahn Inc	5065	C	714 988-0400	7443
Bank America National Assn	6162	D	949 474-8801	9779
Bergman Kprs LLC **(PA)**	1542	C	714 924-7000	1480
Blaine Convention Services Inc	7389	A	714 522-8270	17034
Brookdale Senior Living Inc	8361	D	714 671-7898	24442
Burns & McDonnell Inc	8711	D	714 256-1595	25584
California Automobile Insur Co	6331	A	714 232-8669	10342
Carrier Totaline **(PA)**	5084	D	714 578-5200	7738
Cellco Partnership	4812	D	714 256-6015	5334
Charles Schwab Corporation	6211	D	714 385-6000	9927
City of Brea	8744	D	714 990-7650	27581
Cmre Financial Services Inc	7322	B	714 528-3200	13997
CNA Financial Corporation	6411	C	714 255-2200	10587
Contact Security Inc	7381	C	714 572-6760	16615
Contract Services Group Inc	7349	C	714 582-1800	14225
Core Communications Group LLC	6531	D	714 729-8404	11379
Cosco Fire Protection Inc	1711	C	714 989-1800	2173
Diversfied Cmmnctions Svcs Inc	4813	D	562 696-9660	5549
Document Proc Solutions Inc **(PA)**	7374	D	714 482-2060	16119
Edwards Brea 10 West	7832	E	714 672-4136	18286
Emergency Ambulance Service	4119	D	714 990-1331	3790
Evangelical Christian Cr Un	6062	D	714 671-5700	9633
Evangelical Christian Cr Un **(PA)**	6062	D	714 671-5700	9634
Fit Electronics Inc **(HQ)**	8731	D	714 988-9388	26366
Griffith Company **(PA)**	1611	D	714 984-5500	1787
Hardage Group of Companies	7011	D	714 579-3200	12645
Hon Hai Precision Indust Ltd	5045	D	714 988-9388	7057
Intercontinental Exchange Inc **(HQ)**	6231	B	770 857-4700	10048
Isys Solutions Inc	8742	D	714 521-7656	27282
Jdf Construction Inc	1521	E	714 526-1120	1180
Kaiser Foundation Hospitals	8011	D	714 672-5100	19532
Kehe Distributors LLC	5149	B	714 255-4600	8817
Kindred Healthcare Oper Inc	8051	D	714 529-6842	20556
Kirkhill Aircraft Parts Co **(PA)**	5088	C	714 223-5400	7907
Kirkhill Aircraft Parts Co	5088	C	714 223-5400	7908
Kprs Construction Services Inc **(PA)**	1542	D	714 672-0800	1577
Leidos Inc	8731	D	714 257-6400	26402
Leidos Engineering LLC	8711	D	714 257-6400	25795
Louis Wurth and Company **(DH)**	5072	D	714 529-1771	7596
Mddr Inc	1711	C	714 792-1993	2276
Mercury Casualty Company **(HQ)**	6331	A	323 937-1060	10371
Mercury Insurance Company	6331	D	714 671-6700	10373
Mercury Insurance Company	6331	D	714 255-5000	10376
Merrill Lynch Pierce Fenner	6221	D	714 257-4400	10046
Monoprice Inc **(HQ)**	5099	C	909 989-6887	8044
New Dream Network LLC **(PA)**	4813	D	626 644-9466	5612
New York Life Insurance Co	6411	D	714 255-5100	10703
Norcal Inc	1751	C	714 224-3949	3052
Norcal Inc	1751	C	714 224-3949	3053
Northstar Dem & Remediation LP **(DH)**	1795	C	714 672-3500	3459
Orora Packaging Solutions	5113	C	714 984-2300	8119
Otb Acquisition LLC	7011	C	520 458-0540	12988
P B C Pavers Inc	1721	C	714 278-0488	2463
Pacific Western Sales **(PA)**	5199	C	714 572-6730	9244
Park Hotels & Resorts Inc	7011	D	714 990-6000	13020
Peterson Bros Contruction Inc	1771	A	714 278-0488	3307
Premier Medical Transport Inc	4731	D	888 353-9556	5145
Priority Building Services LLC	7349	B	714 255-2940	14355
Radiometer America Inc **(HQ)**	5047	D	800 736-0600	7214
Renal Treatment Ctrs - Cal Inc	8092	D	714 990-0110	22485
Sears Roebuck and Co	7699	C	714 256-7328	17986
Solugenix Corporation **(PA)**	8748	D	866 749-7658	27863

Company	SIC	EMP	PHONE	ENTRY #
Specialty Risk Services Inc	6411	D	714 674-1000	10776
Springhuse Manor Care Hlth Svc	8361	D	714 671-7898	24682
Strategic Enlace Inc	8742	D	714 256-8648	27472
Sully-Miller Contracting Co **(DH)**	1611	B	714 578-9600	1856
Sunshine Clearing Corporation	7361	E	714 829-0273	14772
Superior Machining Mfg Co Inc	5084	C	714 529-6000	7806
Systems and Software Entps LLC **(DH)**	7371	D	714 854-8600	15487
Team Finish Inc	1771	D	714 671-9190	3335
The Nevell Group Inc **(PA)**	1542	C	714 579-7501	1673
Tiger Electric Inc **(PA)**	1731	D	714 529-8061	2768
Travel Store	4724	D	714 529-1947	4953
Travelers Property Cslty Corp	6411	C	714 671-8000	10804
Tri-Tech Logistics LLC	4731	C	855 373-7049	5184
V A Anderson Enterprises Inc **(PA)**	7389	D	714 990-6100	17555
Viewsonic Corporation **(PA)**	5045	C	909 444-8888	7127
Walters Wholesale Electric Co	5063	C	714 784-1900	7402
West Coast Prime Meats LLC	5147	C	714 255-8560	8635
Win-Dor Inc **(PA)**	1751	C	714 576-2030	3091
Windsor Capital Group Inc	7011	D	714 990-6000	13407
Xdimensional Technologies Inc	7373	D	714 672-8960	16078

BRENTWOOD, CA - Contra Costa County

Company	SIC	EMP	PHONE	ENTRY #
American Mdsg Specialists Inc	7319	B	925 516-3220	13965
Avalon Staffing LLC	7361	D	925 626-7138	14572
Banyan Solutions Inc	7363	D	650 766-9338	14823
Bay Standard Inc	5085	D	925 634-1181	7837
Bay Standard Manufacturing Inc **(PA)**	5072	E	925 634-1181	7580
Cellco Partnership	4812	D	925 626-3480	5310
Ellison Framing Inc	1751	D	925 516-9269	3031
Groundworks Inc	1771	D	925 513-0300	3262
Hot Line Construction Inc	1731	B	925 634-9333	2608
New York Life Insurance Co	6311	D	925 809-7020	10140
Nines Restaurant	8742	D	925 516-3413	27371
Pacific Communications Assoc	8748	E	925 634-1203	27818
Premier Floor Care Inc **(PA)**	7349	D	925 679-4901	14354
Robert Cecchini Inc	0161	D	925 634-4400	77
Rodda Electric Inc **(PA)**	1711	D	925 240-6024	2340
T&C Roofing Inc	1761	D	925 513-8463	3204
Thorpe Design Inc	1711	D	925 634-0787	2386
V Development Inc	1522	D	925 634-8890	1324

BRISBANE, CA - San Mateo County

Company	SIC	EMP	PHONE	ENTRY #
Bi-Rite Restaurant Sup Co Inc	5141	B	415 656-0187	8385
Caredx Inc **(PA)**	8071	C	415 287-2300	22066
Childcare Careers LLC	7363	A	650 372-0211	14831
Covenant Aviation Security LLC	7381	A	650 219-3473	16618
Dhl Supply Chain (usa)	4731	D	415 531-0596	5044
Edward B Ward & Company Inc **(DH)**	5075	E	415 330-6600	7646
Expeditors Intl Wash Inc	4731	E	415 657-3600	5055
Fedex Corporation	7389	C	415 657-0403	17170
Frito-Lay North America Inc	5145	D	415 467-1860	8553
FW Spencer & Son Inc	1711	C	415 468-5000	2217
Globalenglish Corporation **(PA)**	4813	C	425 868-0271	5571
Johnson Cntrls SEC Sltions LLC	7382	D	650 634-9000	16911
Kinder Mrgan Lqds Trminals LLC	4226	D	415 467-8107	4681
Ktsf Channel 26	4833	E	415 467-6397	5816
Kuehne + Nagel Inc	4731	E	415 656-4100	5098
Lincoln Television Inc	4833	D	415 468-2626	5821
Netease Information Tech Corp	7371	D	415 612-7866	15302
Norman S Wright Mech Eqp Corp **(PA)**	5075	D	415 467-7600	7655
Nsw Real Estate Holdings LLC	6531	D	415 467-7600	11638
Oakville Produce Partners LLC	5148	C	415 647-2991	8711
Pitney Bowes Presort Svcs Inc	7389	D	415 468-1660	17402
Progressive Corporation	6331	D	440 461-5000	10386
Sage Hospitality Resources LLC	7011	D	650 589-1600	13162
Shoppingcom Inc	7374	C	650 616-6500	16177
Unity Biotechnology Inc	8731	D	650 416-1192	26483
Vox Network Solutions Inc	8748	C	650 989-1000	27905
Xojet Inc **(PA)**	4581	C	650 594-6300	4924
Y M International Inc **(PA)**	7389	C	415 467-3888	17600

BROOKS, CA - Yolo County

Company	SIC	EMP	PHONE	ENTRY #
Cache Creek Casino Resort	7011	A	530 796-3118	12417

BROWNSVILLE, CA - Yuba County

Company	SIC	EMP	PHONE	ENTRY #
Sutter North Med Foundation	8011	D	530 675-1245	19993

BUELLTON, CA - Santa Barbara County

Company	SIC	EMP	PHONE	ENTRY #
American Medical Response Inc	4119	C	805 688-6550	3763
Excelta Corporation **(PA)**	5072	D	805 686-4686	7587
Kang Family Partners LLC	7011	C	805 688-1000	12800

BUENA PARK, CA - Orange County

Company	SIC	EMP	PHONE	ENTRY #
A J Parent Company Inc **(PA)**	7389	D	714 521-1100	16970
Abad Foam Inc	5199	E	714 994-2223	9191
Access Business Group Intl LLC	7389	C	800 879-2732	16978
Allstate Building Maintenance	7349	D	714 739-8080	14187

Mergent email: customerrelations@mergent.com

2019 Directory of California
Wholesalers and Services Companies

1548

(P-0000) Products & Services Section entry number
(PA)=Parent Co (HQ)=Headquarters (DH)=Div Headquarters

	SIC	EMP	PHONE	ENTRY #
Amada America Inc (HQ)	5084	D	714 739-2111	7725
Amada Capital Corporation	7359	D	714 739-2111	14471
American Wht Mssn In Sthrn	8322	D	714 522-4599	23480
AT&T Services Inc	4813	D	714 992-3359	5500
AT&T Services Inc	4813	D	510 732-0830	5503
Automatic Data Processing Inc	7374	C	714 690-7000	16085
Beach and La Mirada Car Wash	7542	E	714 994-1099	17802
Bitech-Ace A Joint Venture	1771	D	714 521-1477	3225
Borbon Incorporated	1721	D	714 994-0170	2424
Buena Park Medical Group Inc (PA)	8011	D	714 994-5290	19331
Buena Park Police Association	8631	D	714 562-3901	25055
Cal Fresco LLC	5148	C	714 690-7700	8645
Cambium Business Group Inc (PA)	5021	C	714 670-1111	6716
Center of Rehabilitation	8051	C	714 826-2330	20296
Communications Supply Corp	4899	D	714 670-7711	5975
Continental Exch Solutions Inc (HQ)	6099	D	714 522-7044	9677
Data Specialties Inc (PA)	1731	C	714 523-8489	2562
ECB Corp (PA)	1711	D	714 385-8900	2194
Edco Disposal Corporation Inc	4953	C	714 522-3577	6394
Fibertron Corporation	5065	D	714 670-7711	7477
Fueling and Service Tech Inc	5084	D	714 523-0194	7752
Golden Hotel LLC	7011	D	714 739-5600	12607
Hochiki America Corporation	5063	C	714 522-2246	7364
Houdini Inc	4225	D	714 228-4406	4575
Islamic Relief USA	8322	D	714 676-1300	23867
JC Penney Corporation Inc	4225	D	714 523-6558	4582
Knotts Berry Farm LLC	7011	D	714 995-1111	12820
Korean Community Services Inc	8322	E	714 527-6561	23885
Legacy Farms LLC	5148	C	714 736-1800	8701
Noritsu America Corporation (HQ)	5043	C	714 521-9040	6946
Oasis Brands Inc	5113	D	540 658-2830	8113
Openpopcom Inc (PA)	8748	D	714 249-7044	27814
Orora North America	5113	C	714 562-6002	8117
Orora Packaging Solutions (HQ)	5113	D	714 562-6000	8118
Pacific Chemical Dist Corp (HQ)	4226	D	714 521-7161	4685
Park Hotels & Resorts Inc	7011	C	714 739-5600	13035
Partners Information Tech Inc (HQ)	7379	D	714 736-4487	16451
Primary Freight Services Inc (PA)	4731	C	310 635-3000	5147
Royal Crest Building Maint	7349	E	714 562-5034	14370
States Logistics Services Inc	4731	C	714 523-1276	5174
States Logistics Services Inc (PA)	4225	C	714 521-6520	4636
Tawa Services Inc (PA)	5149	C	714 521-8899	8884
Team Spirit Realty Inc	6531	E	714 562-0404	11786
Tech Systems Inc	5065	C	714 523-5404	7552
Ted Ford Jones Inc (PA)	7538	C	714 521-3110	17788
Uniti Bank (PA)	6029	D	888 733-2599	9519
Uniwell Corporation	7011	C	714 522-7000	13355
Vsa & Associates Inc (PA)	8711	C	562 698-2468	25991
VWR International LLC	5049	E	714 220-2615	7250
Walong Marketing Inc (PA)	5149	D	714 670-8899	8901
Wayne Perry Inc	1799	C	714 826-0352	3607
West Coast Sand and Gravel Inc (PA)	5032	D	714 522-0282	6914
Yamaha Corporation of America (HQ)	5099	B	714 522-9011	8068

BURBANK, CA - Los Angeles County

	SIC	EMP	PHONE	ENTRY #
24 Hour Fitness Usa Inc	8099	E	818 531-0257	22722
A Its Laugh Productions Inc	7812	D	818 848-8787	18008
A-1 Hospice Care Inc	8082	D	818 237-2700	22182
ABC Cable Networks Group	7822	C	818 560-4365	18234
ABC Cable Networks Group (DH)	4832	C	818 460-7477	5688
ABC Family Worldwide Inc (HQ)	7812	B	818 560-1000	18009
Access Hollywood	4833	C	818 840-4444	5765
Ace Industrial Supply Inc (PA)	1521	E	818 252-1981	1110
ACT Lighting Inc	5063	A	818 707-0884	7324
Adcom Interactive Media Inc	7379	D	800 296-7104	16304
Allianz Globl Risks US Insur (DH)	6331	C	818 260-7500	10330
Allianz Underwriters Insur Co	6331	C	818 260-7500	10332
Altria Group Distribution Co	5159	C	804 274-2000	8909
Altria Group Distribution Co	5194	D	626 792-2900	9181
Amberfin Limited	5045	E	818 768-8948	7004
American Multi-Cinema Inc	7832	D	818 953-4020	18257
and Syndicated Productions Inc	7812	D	818 308-5200	18015
Andrews International Inc	7381	C	818 260-9586	16569
Andrews International Inc	7381	C	805 409-4160	16570
Andrews International Inc	7381	A	818 487-4060	16571
Andrews International Inc	7381	C	626 407-2290	16572
Ane Productions Inc	7812	D	818 972-0777	18016
Angeles Los Equestrian Center	7999	C	818 840-9063	19097
Aptiv Digital Inc	7372	D	818 295-6789	15590
Aramark Unf & Career AP LLC	7218	D	818 973-3700	13584
Aramark Unf & Career AP LLC (DH)	7218	C	818 973-3700	13586
Ardwin Inc	4213	C	818 767-7777	4100
Artesia Healthcare Inc	8051	D	818 843-1771	20235
Atlantic Recording Corp	7389	B	818 238-6800	17017
Atlas Digital LLC (PA)	7812	D	323 762-2626	18020
Avis Rent A Car System Inc	7514	D	818 566-3001	17628

	SIC	EMP	PHONE	ENTRY #
AWH Burbank Hotel LLC	7011	C	813 843-6000	12343
Belmont Village LP	6513	D	818 972-2405	10985
Blufocus Inc	7371	D	818 294-7695	15031
Bonanza Productions Inc	7929	A	818 954-4212	18427
Borrmann Metal Center (PA)	5051	D	818 846-7171	7262
Boulevard Entertainment Inc	7389	C	818 840-6969	17039
Bryant Ranch Prepack	5122	E	818 764-7225	8149
Buena Vista International Inc (HQ)	7822	E	818 560-1000	18236
Buena Vista Television (DH)	7383	C	818 560-1878	16954
Burbank Dental Laboratory Inc	5047	C	818 841-2256	7169
Burbank Plg & Zoning Div of	8748	E	818 238-5250	27664
Burbank Television Entps LLC	4833	C	818 954-6000	5769
Bvs Entertainment Inc (DH)	7812	E	818 846-6917	18028
C D Payroll Inc	8721	D	818 848-1562	26157
Callan Management Corporation	7382	B	818 846-2215	16881
Cast & Crew Payroll LLC (PA)	8721	C	818 848-6022	26159
CBS Interactive Inc	7319	C	415 344-1813	13969
Cellco Partnership	4812	D	818 842-2722	5343
Chase Credit Systems Inc	7371	C	818 762-6262	15055
Check Disc Labs	8742	D	818 847-2255	27191
Cheque Guard Inc	7371	C	818 563-9335	15057
CIT Bank NA	6021	D	818 525-3760	9315
Citizens Business Bank	6022	D	818 843-0707	9435
City of Burbank	4931	B	818 238-3550	6181
Clp Resources Inc	7363	D	818 260-9190	14840
Cmp Film & Design Burbank LLC	8743	D	818 729-0800	27549
Come Land Maint Svc Co Inc	7349	A	818 567-2455	14222
Commodity Resource Envmtl Inc (PA)	5093	D	818 843-2811	7975
Consolidated Elec Distrs Inc	5063	D	626 345-0000	7350
Cookie Jar Entrmt USA Inc	7812	C	818 955-5400	18034
County of Los Angeles	8322	C	818 557-4164	23685
Cw Network LLC (PA)	4833	C	818 977-2500	5781
Deluxe Entrmt Svcs Group Inc (PA)	7929	D	818 565-3600	18430
Deluxe Laboratories Inc (DH)	7819	A	323 462-6171	18187
Deluxe Media Services	7374	B	818 526-3700	16117
Disney Enterprises Inc (HQ)	7812	C	818 560-1000	18042
Disney Enterprises Inc	7812	B	818 560-3692	18043
Disney Incorporated (DH)	7812	C	818 560-1000	18044
Disney Interactive Studios Inc	7371	C	818 553-5000	15113
Disney Interfinance Corp	7822	C	818 560-1000	18237
Disney Regional Entrmt Inc (HQ)	7999	C	818 560-1000	19159
Disneyland International (DH)	7996	C	818 560-1000	18798
Edgewise Media Services Inc (PA)	5065	D	714 919-2020	7469
Electrosonic Inc (DH)	8711	C	818 333-3600	25657
Emerson Elementary	8641	D	818 558-5419	25155
Emmis Communications Corp	4832	C	818 238-6705	5710
Enbio Corp	8742	C	818 953-9976	27225
Entertainment Partners (PA)	8721	B	818 955-6000	26190
Esc Entertainment Inc	7819	C	818 954-1018	18191
Estrella Communications Inc	4833	D	818 260-5700	5789
Executive Fitness Management	7991	E	818 259-6753	18597
Facey Medical Foundation	8031	C	818 861-7831	20148
Fact Foundation	7389	D	818 729-8105	17159
Final Film	7336	C	323 467-0700	14113
Firemans Fund Insurance Co	6331	C	818 953-6533	10354
Foto-Kem Industries Inc (PA)	7819	B	818 846-3102	18192
Foto-Kem Industries Inc	7819	D	818 846-3102	18193
Frasco Inc (PA)	7381	D	818 848-3888	16649
Front Porch Communities & Svcs	8059	D	818 729-8100	21074
Gat - Arln Ground Support Inc	4729	C	818 847-9127	4991
Gentle Giant Studios Inc	7389	D	818 504-3555	17186
GL Nemirow Inc	7311	D	818 562-9433	13834
Global Entertainment Inds Inc	1799	D	818 567-0000	3526
Grc Electric Inc	1731	D	818 242-9891	2592
Guardsmark LLC	7381	C	818 841-0288	16682
Guardsmark LLC	7381	C	818 841-0288	16688
Guardsmark LLC	7381	C	818 841-0288	16692
Hertz Corporation	7514	E	818 997-0414	17640
Hertz Corporation	7514	C	818 569-6900	17644
Historic TW Inc	7812	E	818 954-3096	18061
Iheartcommunications Inc	4832	D	818 846-0029	5726
IKEA Purchasing Svcs US Inc	8741	B	818 841-3500	26891
Image IV Systems Inc (PA)	5044	C	323 849-3043	6960
Information Tech Partners Inc	7379	D	800 789-7487	16395
International Fmly Entrmt Inc (DH)	4841	C	818 560-1000	5922
J H Maddocks Photography	7384	D	818 842-7150	16961
Jake Hey Incorporated	7384	C	323 856-5280	16962
Jetblue Airways Corporation	4512	D	718 286-7900	4786
Jim & Doug Carters Automotive	7521	E	818 842-5702	17689
Johnson Cntrls SEC Sltions LLC	7382	C	818 428-6669	16908
JP Allen Inc	6513	E	818 841-4770	11040
JP Allen Extended Stay	7011	E	818 841-4770	12793
Kan-Di-Ki LLC (PA)	8071	C	818 549-1880	22101
Kaza Azteca America Inc	4833	C	818 241-5400	5803
Kcetlink (PA)	4833	C	747 201-5000	5805

Employment Codes: A=Over 500 employees, B=251-500,
C=101-250, D=51-100, E=50

2019 Directory of California
Wholesalers and Services Companies

© Mergent Inc. 1-800-342-5647
1549

GEOGRAPHIC

Name	SIC	EMP	PHONE	ENTRY #
Korea Tchnlgy Cmmnications USA	7382	C	213 381-0061	16918
Kpwr Inc	4832	D	818 953-4200	5736
Krca Television LLC	4833	C	818 563-5722	5813
Lakeside Golf Club	7992	D	818 984-0601	18726
Lawyers Title Company (HQ)	6361	E	818 767-0425	10465
Lbi Media Inc	4832	B	818 729-5316	5740
Le Bleu Chateau Inc	8361	E	818 843-3141	24576
Le Crochet By Saro Inc (PA)	5023	E	818 846-3314	6772
Liberman Broadcasting Inc (PA)	4832	D	818 729-5300	5742
Logix Federal Credit Union (PA)	6061	C	888 718-5328	9567
Los Angeles Equestrian Center	0752	D	818 840-9063	630
Louie Almeida & Settler (PA)	8111	D	818 461-9559	23229
M-N-Z Janitorial Services Inc	7349	C	323 851-4115	14309
Mel Bernie and Company Inc (PA)	5094	D	818 841-1928	8010
Mel Bernie and Company Inc	5137	C	818 841-1928	8320
Mis Sciences Corp	4813	C	818 847-0213	5601
Modern Videofilm Inc (PA)	7819	C	818 840-1700	18202
Movies Anywhere LLC	7829	C	818 560-0038	18252
NBC Universal Inc	4833	C	818 260-5746	5826
New Deal Studios Inc	7819	D	310 578-9929	18206
NW Entertainment Inc (PA)	7812	D	818 295-5000	18087
One K Studios LLC	7336	E	818 531-3800	14124
Outlook Amusements Inc	7379	C	818 433-3800	16448
P Murphy & Associates Inc	7371	C	818 841-2002	15339
Pacific Homes Foundation	8059	D	818 729-8106	21180
Performance Designed Pdts LLC (HQ)	5092	D	323 234-9911	7959
Petrol Advertising Inc	7311	D	323 644-3720	13878
PHF II Burbank LLC	7011	D	818 843-6000	13059
Pixelogic Media Partners LLC	7819	C	818 861-2001	18208
Playboy Entrmt Group Inc (HQ)	7812	C	323 276-4000	18096
Point360	7819	C	818 556-5700	18209
Power 106 Radio	4832	D	818 953-4200	5749
Prdctions N Fremantle Amer Inc (DH)	7922	D	818 748-1100	18395
Producer -Writers Guild	6371	D	818 846-1015	10491
Providence Health & Services F	8062	A	818 843-5111	21665
Providence Health System	8062	A	818 843-5111	21671
Providence Health System	6733	C	818 846-8141	12124
Rgis LLC	7389	C	248 651-2511	17438
Roundabout Entertainment Inc	7812	C	818 842-9300	18111
Rudy Carrillo Drywall Inc	1742	D	818 841-2011	2952
Ryan Herco Products Corp (DH)	5074	C	818 841-1141	7635
Sag- Aftra Federal	6061	D	818 562-3400	9585
Sca Enterprises Inc (PA)	7389	C	818 845-7621	17459
Screen Actors Guild - American	6371	C	818 954-9400	10493
Secure Net Alliance	7381	E	818 848-4900	16782
Shadkor Inc	7216	D	818 953-4627	13569
Shamrock Plus Inc	6211	E	818 845-4444	10013
Shc Burbank II LLC	7011	D	818 843-6000	13213
Spark Unlimited Inc	7371	D	818 788-1005	15468
Spire Concessions LLC	7011	D	818 843-6000	13255
Stereo D LLC	7819	B	818 861-3100	18220
Stumbaugh & Associates Inc (PA)	1799	D	818 240-1627	3588
Survival Insurance Inc	6411	C	818 565-1584	10798
Technicolor Inc	7384	B	818 260-4577	16968
Technicolor New Media Inc	7812	E	818 480-5100	18131
Technicolor Thomson Group	7819	B	818 260-3600	18229
Terminix Intl Co Ltd Partnr	7342	D	818 972-2037	14158
The Team Companies LLC (PA)	8721	D	818 558-3261	26302
Therapeutic Associates Inc	8069	D	818 748-4900	22055
Therapeutic Associates Inc	8049	D	818 843-5111	20207
Thyssenkrupp Elevator Corp	5084	D	818 847-2568	7811
Tidavater Inc	7389	C	818 848-4151	17511
Time Warner Cable Entps LLC	7812	D	818 972-0808	18132
Time Warner Cable Entps LLC	4841	C	818 953-3283	5950
Touchstone Television Prod LLC (PA)	7812	E	323 671-5116	18134
Trailblazer Technologies	7389	D	818 848-6500	17517
Tri-Tech Restoration Co Inc	1541	D	818 565-3900	1446
TTT West Coast Inc	7812	C	818 972-0500	18137
Turner Broadcasting System Inc	7812	E	818 977-5452	18138
Turner Techtronics Inc (PA)	7378	C	818 973-1060	16296
Turtle Entertainment America	7929	E	818 861-7315	18469
Unx Inc A Delaware Corp	7371	D	818 333-3200	15516
Ver Sales Inc (PA)	5051	D	818 567-3000	7322
Vintage Senior Management Inc	8322	A	818 954-9500	24110
Wad Productions Inc	7812	D	818 260-5673	18152
Walt Disney Company	4833	B	818 295-3134	5848
Walt Disney Company	4833	D	818 560-1268	5849
Walt Disney Company	7929	D	818 567-5590	18474
Walt Disney Company	7996	C	818 553-7333	18813
Walt Disney Company	4833	B	818 460-6655	5850
Walt Disney Company	4833	A	818 560-1000	5851
Walt Disney Company (PA)	4833	A	818 560-1000	5852
Walt Disney Company	4833	B	818 560-1000	5853
Walt Disney Pictures and TV	7829	D	818 560-1000	18255
Walt Disney Records Direct (DH)	7812	A	818 560-1000	18154
Warner Bros Consumer Pdts Inc (DH)	8748	C	818 954-7980	27908
Warner Bros Distributing Inc	8741	C	818 954-6000	27089
Warner Bros Entertainment Inc	7812	C	818 954-1817	18155
Warner Bros Entertainment Inc	7812	B	818 954-7232	18156
Warner Bros Entertainment Inc	7812	C	818 954-3000	18157
Warner Bros Entertainment Inc	7812	C	818 954-5301	18158
Warner Bros Entertainment Inc	7812	C	818 954-6000	18159
Warner Bros Entertainment Inc (DH)	7812	A	818 954-6000	18160
Warner Bros Entertainment Inc	7812	C	818 954-3000	18161
Warner Bros Entertainment Inc	7812	C	818 954-2181	18162
Warner Bros Home Entrmt Inc (DH)	7812	D	818 954-6000	18163
Warner Bros Intl TV Dist Inc	7812	D	818 954-6000	18164
Warner Bros Records Inc (DH)	7389	B	818 846-9090	17580
Warner Bros Transatlantic Inc (DH)	7822	A	818 977-0018	18249
Warner Bros Transatlantic Inc	7822	A	818 977-6384	18250
Warner Bros Transatlantic Inc	7822	A	818 972-0777	18251
Warner Brothers Studios	7812	A	818 954-5000	18165
Wdpt Film Distribution LLC	5065	C	818 560-1000	7561
Westwind Media Inc	7812	D	818 972-9000	18168
Westwind Studios LLC	7812	E	818 972-9000	18169
William F Kellogg Corporation	5088	D	818 845-7455	7920
Wonderland Music Company Inc	6794	D	818 840-1671	12147
Xerox Corporation	7334	D	818 848-8676	14095
Young Mens Christian (PA)	8641	D	818 845-8551	25317

BURLINGAME, CA - San Mateo County

Name	SIC	EMP	PHONE	ENTRY #
24 Hour Fitness Usa Inc	7991	E	650 343-7922	18563
Abx Engineering Inc	5065	D	650 552-2300	7433
Acumen LLC	7373	C	650 558-8882	15909
Airline Coach Service Inc (PA)	4111	C	650 697-7733	3636
Alain Pinel Realtors Inc	6531	D	650 375-1111	11200
Allen Drywall & Associates	1742	D	650 579-0664	2840
Amato Industries Incorporated	4119	D	650 697-5548	3743
American Carequest Inc (PA)	8082	C	415 885-3324	22219
American Med	4119	D	650 235-1333	3747
American Medical Response	4119	D	650 235-1333	3757
AMS Relocation Incorporated	4214	D	650 697-3530	4330
AT&T Services Inc	4813	C	650 579-5266	5493
Burlingame Senior Care LLC	8059	B	650 692-3758	21025
California Teachers Assn (PA)	8621	C	650 697-1400	25006
Carr Mc Clellan Ingersoll Thom (PA)	8111	D	650 342-9600	22971
City of Burlingame	1611	E	650 558-7670	1739
Coldwell Bnkr Residential Brkg	6531	D	650 558-4200	11351
Comcast Corporation	4841	D	650 689-5392	5871
Crystal Springs Golf Partners	7997	C	650 342-4188	18907
Cushman & Wakefield Inc	6531	E	650 347-3700	11389
Disney Construction Inc	1611	D	650 689-5149	1759
Environmental Chemical Corp (PA)	8711	D	650 347-1555	25670
Epitomics Inc (HQ)	8731	D	650 583-6688	26363
Gringteam Inc	7011	C	650 344-5500	12629
Guardsmark LLC	7381	C	650 685-2400	16690
Guardsmark LLC	7381	C	650 652-9130	16691
Hamilton Partners	8742	C	650 347-8800	27256
Hanergy Holding America Inc	4911	B	650 288-3722	6041
Harbor View Hotels Inc	7011	D	650 340-8500	12644
Host Hotels & Resorts LP	7011	D	650 347-1234	12705
Host Hotels & Resorts LP	7011	D	650 692-9100	12709
Iasco (PA)	7363	B	707 252-3522	14861
Jacobs Consultancy Inc	8748	C	650 579-7722	27758
Jbs International Inc	8733	D	650 373-4900	26628
Jeremiah Phillips LLC	4212	C	650 697-7733	4028
Jet Airways of India Inc	4512	D	650 762-2345	4785
JS International Shipg Corp (PA)	4731	C	650 697-3963	5093
Kindred Healthcare Operating	8069	B	650 697-1865	22028
Kotobuki-Ya Inc	4111	D	650 344-7955	3663
Ksi Corp	4731	D	650 952-0815	5097
M H Podell Company (PA)	6552	D	415 296-8800	11888
Marriott International Inc	7011	C	650 692-9100	12908
Mid-Peninsula Roofing Inc	1761	D	650 375-7850	3179
Morgan Stanley & Co LLC	6211	D	650 340-6550	10001
OH My Green Inc	5149	D	650 989-8181	8842
Oritz Corporation (PA)	5147	C	650 692-8000	8623
Palcare Inc	8351	E	650 340-1289	24364
Park Hotels & Resorts Inc	7011	C	650 342-4600	13032
Partners and Advocates	8322	D	650 312-0730	23959
Peninsula Womens Health (PA)	8011	E	650 692-3818	19757
Personal Protective Svcs Inc (PA)	7381	D	650 344-3302	16756
Prime Time Athletic Club Inc	7991	D	650 204-3662	18643
Pro Unlimited Inc	8741	C	650 344-1099	26995
Provident Mrtg Cpitl Assoc Inc	6162	A	650 652-1300	9850
Randstad Professionals Us LLC	7361	C	650 343-5111	14714
Robert Meuschke Company Inc	1721	E	650 342-3993	2475
Safway Services LP	5082	E	650 652-9255	7693
Sage Software Inc	7372	C	650 579-3628	15844
San Mateo Healthcare & Wellnes	8051	C	650 692-3758	20742
Sky Chefs Inc	4225	C	650 652-7886	4631

2019 Directory of California
Wholesalers and Services Companies

(P-0000) Products & Services Section entry number
(PA)=Parent Co (HQ)=Headquarters (DH)=Div Headquarters

	SIC	EMP	PHONE	ENTRY #
Stonesfair Financial Corp	6513	D	650 347-0442	11119
Stonesfair Management LLC (PA)	6531	D	650 401-3810	11780
Street and Sewer Yard Corp	4952	E	650 696-7260	6331
Sunkist Enterprises	5072	D	650 347-3900	7605
Synagro West LLC	8748	D	650 652-6531	27873
Tata Communications Amer Inc	7389	D	650 262-0004	17496
Transiris Corporation	8742	D	650 303-3495	27494
Trivad Inc	5045	C	650 286-1086	7121
Virgin America Inc (HQ)	4512	C	877 359-8474	4814
Walter E McGuire RE Inc	6531	D	650 348-0222	11819
Wedriveu Holdings LLC	7361	D	650 579-5800	14797

BURNEY, CA - Shasta County

	SIC	EMP	PHONE	ENTRY #
Dicalite Minerals Corp	7699	D	530 335-5451	17944
Hat Creek Cnstr & Mtls Inc (PA)	1629	E	530 335-5501	2038
Pit River Health Service Inc (PA)	8099	D	530 335-3651	22860
Pit River Tribal Council	8011	D	530 335-3651	19792
Pit River Tribal Council	7999	D	530 335-2334	19217

BUTTONWILLOW, CA - Kern County

	SIC	EMP	PHONE	ENTRY #
Choice Hotels Intl Inc	7011	D	661 764-5207	12456

BYRON, CA - Contra Costa County

	SIC	EMP	PHONE	ENTRY #
G3 Enterprises Inc	4731	C	209 341-3441	5070
New Discovery Inc	7997	D	925 783-6613	18986
New Discovery Inc	7992	D	925 634-0505	18740
Pacific Coast Ldscp MGT Inc	0781	D	925 513-2310	774
San Luis Dlta-Mendota Wtr Auth	4971	D	209 835-2593	6564
Simoni & Massoni Farms	0115	E	925 634-2304	9

CABAZON, CA - Riverside County

	SIC	EMP	PHONE	ENTRY #
Casino Morongo	7996	D	951 849-3080	18791
Matich Corporation	1611	E	951 849-8280	1815
Nestle Waters North Amer Inc	5149	C	951 572-4600	8834

CALABASAS, CA - Los Angeles County

	SIC	EMP	PHONE	ENTRY #
Abbyson Living Corp	5021	B	805 465-5500	6705
Able Cable Inc (PA)	7629	D	818 223-3600	17901
AIA Holdings Inc (PA)	6351	D	818 222-4999	10420
All Motorists Insurance Agency	6411	C	818 880-9070	10513
Amawaterways LLC (PA)	4783	C	800 626-0126	5205
American Travel Solutions LLC	4724	D	818 359-6514	4931
Anchor Loans LP	6798	C	310 395-0010	12152
Apex Development Inc	1522	D	818 887-0400	1263
Arcs Commercial Mortgage Co LP (DH)	6162	C	818 676-3274	9778
Asana Integrated Medical Group	8322	D	888 212-7463	23491
Asgn Incorporated (PA)	7361	D	818 878-7900	14570
Atlas Database Software Corp (PA)	7371	D	818 340-7080	15006
Avanquest North America LLC (HQ)	7371	D	818 591-9600	15010
Boys and Girls Club	7997	E	818 225-8406	18871
Brightview Companies LLC (DH)	1629	D	818 223-3500	2014
Brightview Golf Maint Inc (DH)	1629	D	818 223-8500	2016
Brightview Landscape Dev Inc (DH)	0781	E	818 223-8500	734
Calabasas Country Club	7997	D	818 222-8111	18878
Cartel Marketing Inc	6411	C	818 483-1130	10579
Center For Civic Education (PA)	8733	C	818 591-9321	26609
Central Purchasing LLC (PA)	5085	B	805 388-1000	7843
Coldwell Bnkr Residential Brkg	6531	D	818 222-0023	11358
Countrywide Capital Mkts LLC (DH)	6162	C	818 225-3000	9793
Countrywide Financial Corp (HQ)	6162	A	818 225-3000	9794
Countrywide Securities Corp	6211	B	818 225-3000	9944
Custom Tours Inc	4729	D	310 274-8819	4987
Danerica Enterprises Inc	7299	D	818 774-1813	13737
Davis Research LLC	8732	C	818 591-2408	26509
Dts Inc (HQ)	7819	C	818 436-1000	18189
Ellie Mae Inc	7371	B	818 223-2000	15134
Endocrine Sciences Inc	8071	D	818 880-8040	22082
Exterior Solutions Inc	5033	D	310 400-3510	6924
Galaxy Building Systems Inc	7349	C	818 340-6557	14271
Grant & Weber (PA)	7322	C	818 878-7700	14005
Hearthstone Inc	6282	D	818 385-0005	10087
Idrive Inc	7379	D	818 594-5972	16392
Informa Research Services Inc (DH)	8742	D	818 880-8877	27273
Knight-Calabasas LLC (PA)	7997	D	818 222-3200	18942
Lantz Security Systems Inc	7382	C	818 871-0193	16919
Las Virgenes Municipal Wtr Dst	4941	C	818 251-2100	6270
Litigation Rsrces of America-CA (PA)	7389	D	818 878-9227	17297
M S E Enterprises Inc (PA)	6531	D	818 223-3500	11577
Marcus & Millichap Capitl Corp	6531	E	818 212-2250	11583
Marcus Millichap Reis Nev Inc	6531	D	650 494-1400	11585
Marcus Mllchap RE Inv Svcs Inc (HQ)	6531	E	818 212-2250	11586
Monte Nido Residential Ctr LLC	8361	C	818 457-9958	24606
Mrca Fire Division	8641	E	818 880-4752	25203
New View Landscape Inc	0782	D	818 222-8972	908
Nowher Partners LLC	5149	D	818 857-3366	8841
PNC Bank National Association	8742	D	818 880-3300	27396
Prolifics Inc (DH)	7379	B	212 267-7722	16464

	SIC	EMP	PHONE	ENTRY #
Prolifics Testing Inc	7371	D	925 485-9535	15382
Quantum Solutions Inc	7379	E	818 577-4555	16466
Rainbow Camp Inc	7999	E	310 456-3066	19221
Red Peak Group LLC	8742	D	818 222-7762	27420
Rodeo Realty Inc	6531	D	818 657-4609	11741
Rpmc Inc (PA)	8743	D	818 222-7762	27571
Sedgwick Claims MGT Svcs Inc	6411	C	818 591-9444	10768
Small Business Advertising Inc	7319	E	818 262-8923	13983
T M Mian & Associates Inc	7011	D	818 591-2300	13317
Top Seed Tennis Academy Inc	7999	D	818 222-2782	19247
Unifax Insurance Systems Inc	6411	D	818 591-9800	10808
Valleycrest Ldscp Maint Vcc	0781	E	800 466-8510	793
Western General Holding Co (PA)	6331	C	818 880-9070	10414
Western General Insurance Co	6331	C	818 880-9070	10415
Worxsitehr Insur Solutions Inc	6411	D	877 479-3591	10839

CALABASAS HILLS, CA - Los Angeles County

	SIC	EMP	PHONE	ENTRY #
Helmet House Inc (PA)	5136	D	800 421-7247	8263

CALEXICO, CA - Imperial County

	SIC	EMP	PHONE	ENTRY #
Adventures In Hospitality Inc	7997	D	760 356-2806	18818
ARC - Imperial Valley	8093	D	760 768-1944	22505
California Super Market	4225	D	760 357-3065	4536
Coppel Corporation	5021	D	760 357-3707	6719
Martech Medical Products Inc	8011	C	215 256-8833	19671
R L Jones-San Diego Inc (PA)	4731	D	760 357-3177	5153
R L Jones-San Diego Inc	4731	D	760 357-0140	5154
Service Container Company LLC	7389	D	858 391-7344	17466
Sstmas Y Aranda Eqpos Hdrlicos	5084	E	619 245-4502	7804
Technicolor HM Entrmt Svcs Inc	7819	B	760 357-3372	18225
U S Xpress Inc	4213	C	760 768-6707	4284

CALIENTE, CA - Kern County

	SIC	EMP	PHONE	ENTRY #
James McCutcheon	1522	E	661 867-1810	1292

CALIFORNIA CITY, CA - Kern County

	SIC	EMP	PHONE	ENTRY #
Corecivic Inc	8744	C	760 373-1764	27584

CALIMESA, CA - Riverside County

	SIC	EMP	PHONE	ENTRY #
Tommy Gun Plastering Inc	1742	D	909 795-9966	2969

CALIPATRIA, CA - Imperial County

	SIC	EMP	PHONE	ENTRY #
Brandt Co Inc	0211	D	760 348-2295	396
Calenergy LLC	1731	B	402 231-1527	2536
Frank Barraza	0761	D	760 348-7363	649
Superior Cattle Feeders LLC (PA)	0211	D	760 348-2218	398

CALISTOGA, CA - Napa County

	SIC	EMP	PHONE	ENTRY #
Calistoga Spa Inc	7991	D	707 942-6269	18584
Enzennauer Vineyard Managment	0762	D	707 433-0532	690
Mv Hospitality Inc	7991	E	707 942-6877	18636
Schramsberg Vineyards Company	0172	E	707 942-4558	177
Spa Partners Inc	7991	E	707 942-5789	18658

CALPELLA, CA - Mendocino County

	SIC	EMP	PHONE	ENTRY #
Mendocino Forest Pdts Co LLC	5031	D	707 485-6800	6841
Mendocino Forest Pdts Co LLC	5099	D	707 620-2961	8043

CAMARILLO, CA - Ventura County

	SIC	EMP	PHONE	ENTRY #
Aecom C&E Inc	8711	D	805 388-3775	25506
Affiliated Communications Inc	7389	E	805 650-4949	16987
Airport Connection Inc	4111	C	805 389-8196	3637
All Control Cleaning Inc	7349	C	805 987-4210	14185
American Airlines Inc	4512	C	805 988-0407	4774
Applied Engineering MGT Corp	7371	C	805 484-1909	14991
Arconix/Usa Inc	5065	D	805 388-2525	7440
AT&T Corp	4812	C	805 445-6562	5282
Atria Senior Living Group Inc	8361	D	805 482-9771	24425
Automatic Data Processing Inc	7374	C	805 383-8630	16087
Bml Industries Inc	5063	D	805 388-6800	7339
Boskovich Farms Inc	0161	B	805 987-1443	39
C & C Boats Inc	4499	E	805 445-9456	4753
Camarillo Healthcare Center	8741	A	805 482-9805	26796
Camarillo Ranch Foundation	7389	D	805 389-8182	17052
Casa Pacifica Centers (PA)	8322	C	805 482-3260	23530
Channel Islands Young Mens Ch	8641	D	805 484-0423	25131
CIT Bank NA	6021	C	805 465-1053	9311
Coast Farms Inc	0161	C	805 383-0455	44
Coastal Grading and Excavating	1794	E	805 445-6433	3419
County of Ventura	8322	A	805 654-5529	23759
Crown Golf Properties LP	8742	D	909 481-6663	27206
Data Exchange Corporation (PA)	5045	C	805 388-1711	7033
DB Roberts Inc	5085	D	805 988-4882	7846
Delicate Productions Inc (PA)	7922	D	415 484-1174	18363
Dex Corporation	8711	C	805 388-1711	25643
Dial Security (PA)	7382	C	805 389-6700	16887
Dignity Health	8062	B	805 384-8071	21372
Dignity Health	8062	C	805 389-5800	21388

Employment Codes: A=Over 500 employees, B=251-500,
C=101-250, D=51-100, E=50

2019 Directory of California
Wholesalers and Services Companies

© Mergent Inc. 1-800-342-5647

1551

GEOGRAPHIC

Company	SIC	EMP	PHONE	ENTRY #
DP Technology Corp (PA)	7371	D	805 388-6000	15118
Edwards Theatres Circuit Inc	7832	D	805 383-8866	18298
Electronic Clearing House Inc (HQ)	7372	D	805 419-8700	15665
Eurasia Power LLC	5065	E	805 383-1234	7473
Golden State Medical Supply	5099	D	805 477-8966	8033
Holthouse Carlin Van Trigt LLP	8721	D	805 374-8555	26220
Houweling Nurseries Oxnard Inc	5141	B	805 488-8832	8414
Institute For Applied Behavior	8049	C	805 987-5886	20182
Interface Community (PA)	8322	E	805 485-6114	23861
Jpmorgan Chase Bank Nat Assn	7389	C	805 482-2902	17266
Juvenile Justice Division Cal	8741	B	805 485-7951	26912
Kaiser Foundation Hospitals	8011	A	888 515-3500	19548
Kaiser Foundation Hospitals	6324	D	805 482-0707	10267
Las Posas Club Inc	7997	D	805 482-1811	18956
Las Posas Country Club	7997	D	805 482-4518	18957
Leisure Village Association	8641	D	805 484-2861	25189
Logix Development Corporation	7371	D	888 505-6449	15264
Market Scan Info Systems Inc (PA)	7371	C	805 823-4258	15271
Meathead Movers Inc	4213	D	805 437-5100	4228
Michael Baker Jr Inc	8711	D	805 383-3373	25819
Nallatech Inc	5065	D	805 383-8997	7513
Northrop Grumman Systems Corp	7373	D	805 987-9739	16020
Oasis Technology Inc	7373	D	805 445-4833	16024
Odu-Usa Inc (HQ)	5065	D	805 484-0540	7518
Omniupdate Inc	7371	D	805 484-9400	15327
Pacific Earth Resources (PA)	0181	D	805 986-8277	291
People Creating Success Inc	8011	C	805 644-9480	19758
Red Blossom Sales Inc (PA)	0171	A	805 686-4747	114
Rincon Pacific LLC	0171	D	805 986-8806	118
Saalex Corp (PA)	8711	D	805 482-1070	25899
Salem Media Group Inc (PA)	4832	C	805 987-0400	5750
Solimar Farms Inc	0171	D	805 986-8806	122
Spanish Hills Country Club (PA)	7997	C	805 389-1644	19053
Sunrise Senior Living LLC	8051	D	805 388-8086	20830
Technclor Vdocassette Mich Inc (DH)	7819	B	805 445-1122	18223
Technicolor Inc (DH)	7819	D	805 445-1122	18224
Technicolor HM Entrmt Svcs Inc (DH)	7819	B	805 445-1122	18227
Technicolor Thomson Group	7819	A	805 445-1122	18231
Telecare Corporation	8063	D	805 383-3669	21986
Telecare Las Posadas	8093	D	805 383-3669	22697
Teledyne Scentific Imaging LLC	8731	C	805 373-4979	26472
Tommy Bahama Group Inc	7389	C	805 482-8868	17512
Uribe Trucking Inc	4214	D	805 483-1125	4383
Ventura County Fire Department	8641	E	805 389-9710	25274
Vitas Healthcare Corporation	8052	D	805 437-2100	20970
Voice Print International LLC (PA)	7374	D	805 389-5200	16200
Wilshire Health and Cmnty Svcs	8361	D	805 484-2777	24725

CAMBRIA, CA - San Luis Obispo County

Company	SIC	EMP	PHONE	ENTRY #
Moonstone Management Corp (PA)	6531	C	805 927-4200	11613
Pacific Cambria Inc	7011	D	805 927-6114	12995

CAMERON PARK, CA - El Dorado County

Company	SIC	EMP	PHONE	ENTRY #
Americas Flood Services Inc	6411	D	916 636-9460	10523
Cameron Park Country Club Inc	7997	D	530 672-9840	18882
Hemington Landscape Svcs Inc	0782	D	530 677-9290	859
McClone Construction Company	1521	C	559 431-9411	1198

CAMP PENDLETON, CA - San Diego County

Company	SIC	EMP	PHONE	ENTRY #
Lion-Vallen Ltd Partnership	8741	E	760 385-4885	26935
Marine Corps United States	7011	E	760 430-4709	12876

CAMPBELL, CA - Santa Clara County

Company	SIC	EMP	PHONE	ENTRY #
Adorno Construction Inc	1771	D	408 369-8675	3212
Aicent Inc	7379	C	408 324-1316	16309
All Seasons Homecare	8082	D	408 378-0900	22211
B C C S Inc (PA)	1542	C	408 379-5500	1471
Barracuda Networks Inc (HQ)	7372	C	408 342-5400	15604
Bio-Reference Laboratories Inc	8071	C	408 341-8600	22062
Campbell Hhg Hotel Dev LP	7011	E	408 626-9590	12423
Cape Clear Software Inc	7371	D	408 879-7365	15049
Cdnetworks Inc (DH)	4813	D	408 228-3379	5529
Cem Builders Inc	8711	E	408 395-1490	25603
Century 21 Alpha LLC	6531	D	408 369-2000	11291
Charles Culberson Inc	1742	C	650 335-4730	2865
Classic Car Wash Inc (PA)	7542	C	408 371-2414	17810
Comglobal Systems Inc (DH)	7373	D	619 321-6000	15936
Content Guru Inc	4813	D	408 559-3988	5538
Daleys Drywall and Taping Inc	1742	A	408 378-9500	2871
Dentistat Inc	8742	D	408 376-0336	27214
Douglas Ross Construction Inc	1522	D	408 429-7700	1281
Duran Human Capital Partners	7361	E	408 540-0070	14603
Durham School Services L P	4151	C	408 377-6655	3915
Farmers Group Inc	6411	D	408 557-1100	10618
Fernandes & Sons Gen Contrs	7363	D	408 626-9090	14853
Fierce Wombat Games Inc	7374	E	650 996-2910	16129
Groupware Technology Inc (PA)	7373	E	408 540-0090	15968

Company	SIC	EMP	PHONE	ENTRY #
Intrepid Security Solutions	7382	E	855 379-2223	16906
Kaiser Foundation Hospitals	8011	D	408 871-6500	19610
Knights of Columbus	8641	C	408 371-1531	25180
Largo Concrete Inc	1771	A	408 874-2500	3281
Lark Avenue Car Wash	7542	D	408 377-2525	17824
LLP Moss Adams	8721	C	408 369-2400	26251
Martina Landscape Inc	0782	D	408 871-8800	895
Masudas Landscape Services	0781	D	408 379-7100	769
Maxonic Inc	7379	C	408 739-4900	16424
Merrill Gardens LLC	6513	D	408 370-6431	11071
Mission Vlla Alzhmers Rsidence	8361	E	408 559-8301	24604
Monster Mechanical Inc	1711	D	408 727-8362	2282
Netnow	4813	B	408 370-0425	5610
Netpolarity Inc	7361	B	408 971-1100	14671
Odyssey Healthcare Inc	8051	D	408 626-4868	20679
On-Site Manager Inc (HQ)	7389	E	866 266-7483	17368
Online Technical Services Inc (PA)	7361	E	408 378-1100	14681
Panzura Inc	7373	D	408 457-8504	16029
Perspecta Engineering Inc	7373	D	408 961-3250	16031
Rainmaker Systems Inc	8741	C	408 659-1800	27011
Saama Technologies Inc (PA)	7371	C	408 371-1900	15421
Sandis Civil Engineers (PA)	8713	D	408 636-0900	26135
Senior Living Solutions LLC	8052	C	408 385-1835	20956
Signature Building Maint Inc	7349	D	408 377-8066	14390
Silver Creek Home Owners	8741	E	408 559-1977	27029
SIM Investment Corporation (PA)	7991	B	408 874-0610	18651
Skyhigh Networks Inc	7382	D	408 564-0278	16943
SR Freeman Inc	1751	D	408 364-2200	3082
Streamray Inc	7929	B	408 745-5449	18468
Subacute Chld Hosp Cal Inc	8069	D	408 558-3644	22052
Telecmmnctons MGT Slutions Inc	1731	D	408 866-5495	2764
TownePlace Suites	7011	D	408 370-4510	13334
Uplift Family Services (PA)	8361	D	408 379-3790	24704
Vencore Svcs & Solutions Inc	7373	E	408 961-3200	16072
Wells Fargo Bank National Assn	6021	D	408 378-8155	9392
West Valley Cnstr Co Inc (PA)	1623	C	408 371-5510	2003

CAMPO, CA - San Diego County

Company	SIC	EMP	PHONE	ENTRY #
Campo Band Missions Indians	7993	B	619 938-6000	18781
Mountain Hlth & Cmnty Svcs Inc (PA)	8011	D	619 478-5311	19702

CANOGA PARK, CA - Los Angeles County

Company	SIC	EMP	PHONE	ENTRY #
24 Hour Fitness Usa Inc	7991	D	818 887-2582	18565
A Yafa Pen Company	5112	E	818 704-8888	8074
Aegis Treatment Centers LLC (PA)	8093	E	818 206-0360	22497
American Landscape Inc	0781	C	818 999-2041	727
American Landscape Management (PA)	0781	B	818 999-2041	728
Apn Business Resources Inc	8742	D	818 717-9980	27141
Azimc Investments Inc (HQ)	5013	C	818 678-6571	6625
Bay Clubs Inc	7997	D	818 884-5034	18857
Benjamin Kurzban Son Ctrl Inc	1531	E	347 227-3425	1331
Boeing Company	8711	E	818 466-8800	25572
Bubbla Inc	5199	E	818 884-2000	9200
Buyers Consultation Svc Inc (PA)	5065	E	818 341-4820	7453
Canew Inc	8072	C	818 703-5100	22163
Canoga Park Worksource Center	7361	E	818 596-4448	14583
Catholic Charities of La Inc	8322	E	818 883-6015	23534
Cellco Partnership	4812	D	818 715-9143	5379
Computrition Inc (HQ)	7371	C	818 961-3999	15074
Golden State West Valley	8051	C	818 348-8422	20488
Green Thumb International Inc	5193	D	818 340-6400	9136
Heritage Landscape Inc	0781	C	818 999-2041	760
Hmi Associates Inc	7381	C	818 887-6800	16697
Jones & Jones MGT Group Inc	6513	C	818 594-0019	11039
Landcare USA LLC	0782	C	818 346-7552	886
Leisure Care LLC	8052	D	818 713-0900	20938
Mailmark Enterprises LLC	7331	D	818 407-0660	14052
Mark Land Electric Inc	1731	D	818 883-5110	2634
New Start Home Health Care Inc	8322	C	818 665-7898	23938
Northeast Valley Health Corp	8099	D	818 340-3570	22848
NRG Clean Power Inc	4911	E	818 444-2020	6060
One Call Medical Inc	8742	D	818 346-8700	27376
P-Cove Enterprises Inc	7373	D	818 341-1101	16027
Richard Huetter Inc	5013	D	818 700-8001	6670
Right Choice In-Home Care Inc	8082	A	818 836-6001	22406
Rte Enterprises Inc	1721	D	818 999-5300	2477
Shield Security Inc	7381	E	818 239-5800	16824
Software Dynamics Incorporated	7373	D	818 992-3299	16054
Southern California Mtl Hdlg	5084	D	818 349-1220	7801
Super Garden Centers Inc	5193	E	818 348-9266	9167
T & T Solutions Inc	7379	D	818 676-1786	16501
T M P Inc	5136	D	818 718-1222	8279
West Valley Jewish Cmnty Ctr	7999	D	818 348-0048	19261
Westwood Insurance Agency (DH)	6411	D	818 990-9715	10830

Mergent email: customerrelations@mergent.com
1552

2019 Directory of California
Wholesalers and Services Companies

(P-0000) Products & Services Section entry number
(PA)=Parent Co (HQ)=Headquarters (DH)=Div Headquarters

CANYON COUNTRY, CA - Los Angeles County

Name	SIC	EMP	PHONE	ENTRY #
County of Los Angeles	6371	D	661 298-3406	10483
Design Masonry Inc	1741	D	661 252-2784	2802
Jencor Door and Trim Inc	1751	E	661 251-8161	3046

CANYON LAKE, CA - Riverside County

Name	SIC	EMP	PHONE	ENTRY #
A Caregiver LLC	8082	E	951 676-4190	22180
Canyon Lk Property Owners Assn	8641	D	951 244-6841	25127
Cbabr Inc (PA)	6531	D	951 640-7056	11274
My Choice Inhome Care LLC	8082	D	951 244-8770	22371

CAPISTRANO BEACH, CA - Orange County

Name	SIC	EMP	PHONE	ENTRY #
Capistrano Beach Extended	8051	D	949 496-5786	20285
Golden Living LLC	8051	D	949 496-5786	20475
National Rtrement Partners Inc (PA)	6411	D	949 488-8726	10698
Soto Company Inc	0782	D	949 493-9403	942

CAPITOLA, CA - Santa Cruz County

Name	SIC	EMP	PHONE	ENTRY #
AT&T Corp	4812	D	831 465-6771	5286
Bay Federal Credit Union (PA)	6061	C	831 479-6000	9541
CA Ste Atom Assoc Intr-Ins Bur	7549	D	831 824-9128	17855
Cellco Partnership	4812	D	831 475-3100	5324
Coldwell Bnkr Residential Brkg	6531	D	831 462-9000	11352
Covenant Care LLC	8051	D	831 476-0770	20335
Housing Athrty of The Cnty of	6531	D	831 454-9455	11505
Profile of Santa Cruz	7361	D	831 479-0393	14704

CARLSBAD, CA - San Diego County

Name	SIC	EMP	PHONE	ENTRY #
24 Hour Fitness Usa Inc	7991	D	760 918-4790	18549
24 Hour Fitness Usa Inc	7991	D	760 602-5001	18550
4g Wireless Inc	4813	D	760 828-2543	5435
Abtech Technologies Inc	7379	D	760 827-5100	16302
Active Motif Inc (PA)	8731	C	760 431-1263	26311
Adicio Inc	4813	D	760 602-9502	5443
Advanced Commercial Corporatio	6722	C	760 431-8500	12020
Alogent Holdings Inc	7371	D	760 410-9000	14973
Applied Biosystems LLC (DH)	7372	C	650 638-5000	15588
Arlo Technologies Inc (HQ)	7382	B	408 890-3900	16874
Arnel Development Company	1522	D	760 599-6111	1264
Autogenomics Inc	8731	D	760 477-2248	26334
Aviara Fsrc Associates Limited	7011	A	760 603-6800	12341
Aviara Resort Associates (PA)	7011	A	760 448-1234	12342
Bomel Construction Co Inc	1541	C	760 431-6360	1379
Brehm Communities (PA)	1521	D	760 448-2420	1126
Brehm Communities LLC (PA)	1521	D	760 448-2420	1127
Brightview Landscapes LLC	0781	F	760 438-3551	743
Buffini & Company (PA)	8331	C	760 827-2100	24158
Business Intelligence	8742	E	858 452-8200	27176
Buzztime Inc	4833	C	760 476-1976	5770
By Referral Only Inc	8748	D	760 707-1300	27667
Calatlantic Group Inc	1521	C	760 602-6824	1134
Calatlantic Group Inc	1531	C	760 931-4414	1333
California Bistro At Fo	7011	D	760 603-3700	12419
Callaway Golf Ball Oprtons Inc	5091	A	760 931-1771	7924
Canon Solutions America Inc	7389	D	760 438-6990	17053
Carlsbad Inn Vactn Condo Ownrs	8641	D	760 434-7542	25128
Carlsbad Municipal Water Dst	4941	E	760 438-2722	6219
Carlsbad Surgery Center LLC	8093	D	760 448-2488	22517
Carollo Engineers Inc	8711	C	858 505-1020	25595
CAV Inc	4119	D	760 729-5199	3784
CDM SMITH INC	8711	D	760 438-7755	25599
Cellco Partnership	4812	D	760 720-8400	5326
Cellmatics	7373	E	760 692-2424	15929
Chambers Belt Company	5139	D	760 602-9688	8348
Chopra Cntre For Wll-Being LLC	7999	D	760 494-1600	19124
Cierra Wireless	8711	C	760 476-8700	25609
Clark Richardson and Biskup	8711	D	760 496-3714	25617
Coast Environmental Inc	7389	D	760 929-9570	17090
Coast Waste Management	4953	C	760 753-9412	6381
Cofa Media Group LLC	4813	D	877 293-2007	5534
Colorescience Inc	5122	C	866 426-5673	8163
Community Interface Services	8322	D	760 729-3866	23608
Continuing Lf Communities LLC (PA)	7361	C	760 704-6400	14591
Corporate Visions Inc	8742	D	760 458-0914	27202
Deepak Chopra LLC	7991	E	760 494-1600	18593
Demaria Landtech	0782	E	858 481-5500	823
Electronic Entrmt Design & RES	8732	D	760 579-7100	26514
Electronic Online Systems Intl	7373	D	760 431-8400	15952
Encina Wastewater Authority	4952	D	760 438-3941	6322
Enviance Inc (HQ)	7371	D	760 496-0200	15139
Fashioncraft Floors Inc (PA)	1752	E	714 255-8400	3102
Federal Express Corporation	7389	C	800 463-3339	17165
Ferguson Salon Management	7231	E	760 434-4141	13656
Ferguson Salon Management Inc	7231	D	760 434-5008	13657
First Community Bancorp	6021	D	858 756-3023	9345
Fmt Consultants LLC (PA)	7379	D	844 369-4593	16366

Name	SIC	EMP	PHONE	ENTRY #
Four Seasons Resort Aviara	7992	D	760 603-6900	18714
Franconnect LLC	7373	C	760 720-5354	15959
Front Porch Communities	8059	C	760 729-4983	21071
Genmark Diagnostics Inc (PA)	8071	C	760 448-4300	22088
Genoptix Inc (PA)	8071	C	760 268-6200	22093
Genoptix Inc	8071	B	760 268-6200	22094
Glenview Assisted Living LLP	8099	E	760 704-6800	22808
Global Domains International	4813	E	760 602-3000	5570
Grand Pacific Carlsbad Ht LP	7011	B	760 827-2400	12613
Grand Pacific Resorts Inc	7389	C	760 431-8500	17200
Grand Pacific Resorts Inc (PA)	6531	C	760 431-8500	11489
Grand Pacific Resorts Svcs LP	7011	D	760 431-8500	12614
H M Electronics Inc (PA)	5065	B	858 535-6000	7485
Hansen Icc LLC	8721	D	760 268-7299	26215
Hay House Inc (PA)	5192	D	760 431-7695	9114
Hilton Garden Inns MGT LLC	7011	D	760 476-0800	12663
Hit Portfolio II NTC Trs LP	7011	D	760 431-9399	12686
Hyatt Coporation As Agent of B	7011	D	760 603-6851	12745
Ibis Biosciences Inc	8731	C	760 476-3200	26380
Ibs Interprit Inc (PA)	7371	C	760 268-7299	15208
Integral Senior Living LLC (PA)	6513	B	760 547-2863	11033
Interior Specialists Inc (HQ)	1752	D	760 929-6700	3109
Interstate Hotels Resorts Inc	8741	D	760 476-0800	26896
Intravas Inc	8742	D	760 650-4040	27281
Ipitek Inc	1731	D	760 438-1010	2614
Jazzercise Inc	7991	D	760 476-1750	18615
Jefferson California Congress	8641	D	760 331-5500	25176
Jenny Craig Inc (HQ)	7299	D	760 696-4000	13753
Jenny Craig Wght Loss Ctrs Inc (DH)	7299	C	760 696-4000	13754
Jet Source Inc	4581	D	760 438-0877	4896
Kaiser Foundation Hospitals	8011	C	760 931-4228	19621
Kendal Floral Supply LLC (PA)	5193	D	760 431-4910	9143
La Costa Limousine (PA)	4119	D	760 438-4455	3815
Lassens Ali Leads Club (PA)	8611	D	760 434-3761	24965
Lawinfocom Inc	7372	D	760 510-3000	15741
Lc Trs Inc	7011	A	760 438-9111	12844
Legoland California LLC	7996	B	760 918-5346	18803
Lg Display America Inc	5065	E	760 692-0900	7501
Mardx Diagnostics Inc	5047	D	760 929-0500	7188
Marriott International Inc	7011	A	760 431-9399	12880
Medsphere Systems Corporation (PA)	8742	D	760 692-3700	27335
National Assn Mus Mrchants Inc	8611	D	760 438-8001	24970
Navigate Biopharma Svcs Inc	8733	C	866 992-4939	26642
North Coast Home Care Inc	8082	D	760 260-8700	22373
Nossaman LLP	8111	D	760 918-0500	23292
Ntent Inc	7371	D	760 930-7600	15319
NTN Buzztime Inc (PA)	4833	D	760 438-7400	5830
Optumrx Inc	6324	B	760 804-2399	10287
Ostendo Technologies Inc (PA)	8731	D	760 710-3003	26427
Pacific Western Bank	6021	D	760 918-2469	9364
Pavigym America Corp	5023	C	858 414-8624	6781
Physical Rhbltation Netwrk LLC (PA)	8049	D	760 931-8310	20193
Planet Group Inc	7373	C	402 491-3560	16034
Prana Living LLC (HQ)	5136	D	866 915-6457	8274
Premiere Financial	6282	D	760 518-5034	10105
Prescott Companies (PA)	6531	E	760 634-4700	11679
Prescription Solutions	8742	A	760 804-2370	27398
Product Slingshot Inc	8742	D	760 929-9380	27403
Proficio Inc (PA)	5045	E	800 779-5042	7094
Providence Seminars Inc	8742	D	760 827-2100	27410
Pulse-Link Inc	8731	D	760 448-4690	26442
Quality Childrens Services (PA)	8351	C	760 942-3433	24374
R Q Construction Inc	1541	C	760 477-1199	1430
Rancho Leonero Resort	7011	E	760 438-2905	13100
Really Likeable People Inc	5139	E	760 431-5577	8367
Registry Network Inc (PA)	7363	C	760 966-3700	14902
Rialto Bioenergy Facility LLC	8711	C	760 436-8870	25893
Richard Realty Group Inc	6531	D	760 603-8377	11733
Riolo Transportation Inc	4789	C	760 729-4405	5243
Rockstar San Diego	7374	C	760 929-0700	16173
Rowan Incorporated	1731	D	760 692-0700	2717
Rq Construction LLC	1541	C	760 631-7707	1431
Safc Carlsbad Inc	8733	C	760 710-6100	26656
Sambreel Services LLC	7371	E	760 266-5090	15424
San Diego Gas & Electric Co	4939	C	760 438-6200	6201
Search Engine Optimization Inc	7389	D	760 929-0039	17463
Sethi Management Inc	8741	C	760 692-5288	27026
Sierra Wireless America Inc (HQ)	4812	D	760 444-5650	5415
Signet Armorlite Inc (DH)	8099	B	760 744-4000	22885
Sound Technologies Inc	5047	D	760 918-9626	7219
Source 44 LLC	8748	C	877 916-6337	27866
South Cone Inc	5139	C	760 431-2300	8368
Southern Cal Prmnnte Med Group	6324	A	619 528-5000	10319
Steelpoint Capital Partners LP	6799	C	858 764-8700	12268
Sunrise Senior Living LLC	8051	D	760 930-0060	20818

GEOGRAPHIC

Company	SIC	EMP	PHONE	ENTRY #
Supercuts Admnistrative Office (PA)	7231	C	760 753-5543	13673
Synteracthcr Inc (DH)	8731	B	760 268-8200	26464
Synteracthcr Corporation (HQ)	8731	B	760 268-8200	26465
Synteracthcr Holdings Corp (PA)	8731	B	760 268-8200	26466
Tamarack Bch Condo Owners Assn	8641	E	760 729-3500	25265
Technology Associates EC Inc	8742	D	760 765-5275	27481
Tri City Emergency Med Group	8721	E	760 439-1963	26304
Triton Management Services LLC	8741	D	760 431-9911	27069
Two Jinn Inc (PA)	7389	C	760 431-9911	17526
Unite Eurotherapy Inc	5122	D	760 585-1800	8215
Valley Radiology Consultants (PA)	8071	D	619 797-8248	22156
Vertical Search Works Inc	7311	C	212 967-9502	13916
Villas De Carlsbad Ltd A Cali	8361	E	760 434-7116	24715
Viscent Orthpd Solutions LLC (DH)	8011	E	214 501-0180	20089
Wells Fargo Home Mortgage Inc	6162	B	760 603-7000	9865
West Inn & Suites LLC	7011	D	760 448-4500	13389
Westliving Management LLC (PA)	8361	D	760 602-5850	24720
Weston Solutions Inc	8731	D	760 795-6900	26493

CARMEL, CA - Monterey County

Company	SIC	EMP	PHONE	ENTRY #
Alain Pinel Realtors	6531	D	831 622-1040	11193
B S I Holdings Inc	1742	A	831 622-1840	2848
Bayview Properties Inc	7011	D	831 624-1841	12362
Carmel Mission Inn	7011	D	831 624-1841	12428
Carmel Valley Ranch	7011	D	831 625-9500	12429
Carmel Vly Mrtg Borrower LLC	7011	D	831 625-9500	12430
Highlands Inn Inc	7011	C	831 620-1234	12658
Highlands Inn Investors II LP	7011	B	831 624-3801	12659
Kagan Capital Management Inc	6282	D	831 624-1536	10092
Mission Ranch Inc (PA)	7011	E	831 624-6436	12930
Monterey Pacific Inc (PA)	0762	C	831 678-4845	701
Northern CA Cngrgtnl Rtmt	8059	C	831 624-1281	21167
Preserve Golf Club Inc	7992	D	831 620-6871	18746
Quail Lodge Inc	7011	C	831 624-1581	13087
Santa Lucia Preserve Company	7997	D	831 620-6760	19034
Stewardship Company LLC	8741	C	831 620-6700	27048
Tehama Golf Club LLC	7997	D	831 622-2200	19066
Trevi Partners A Calif LP	7011	C	831 624-1841	13343
Wyndham International Inc	7011	C	831 625-9500	13426

CARMEL VALLEY, CA - Monterey County

Company	SIC	EMP	PHONE	ENTRY #
Douglas Ranch LLC	0291	E	949 500-7009	448
Keller Williams Realty	6531	D	831 622-6200	11539

CARMICHAEL, CA - Sacramento County

Company	SIC	EMP	PHONE	ENTRY #
Acct Holdings LLC	7389	A	916 971-1981	16981
AEgis of Carmichael	8361	D	916 972-1313	24410
Aegis Senior Communities LLC	8051	B	916 972-1313	20220
Atria Senior Living Group Inc	8361	D	916 488-5722	24430
Cal Sierra Construction Inc	1623	D	916 416-7901	1902
Carmichael Care Inc	8051	C	916 483-8103	20290
Carmichael Recreation & Pk Dst	8322	C	916 485-5322	23528
Crestwood Behavioral Hlth Inc	8063	D	916 977-0949	21950
Diez & Leis RE Group Inc	6531	D	916 487-4287	11400
Dignity Health	8062	A	916 537-5151	21371
Dignity Health	8062	A	916 537-5000	21379
Eskaton (PA)	6512	A	916 334-0296	10874
Eskaton Properties Inc	8051	A	916 974-2060	20407
Eskaton Properties Inc	8051	D	916 331-8513	20408
Eskaton Properties Inc (PA)	8051	A	916 334-0810	20411
Eskaton Properties Inc	8361	C	916 974-2000	24523
Fairwood Associates Apts	6513	D	916 944-0152	11016
H B J Corporation	1742	A	707 333-7066	2891
Helios Healthcare LLC	8051	C	916 482-0465	20522
Horizon West Inc	8051	D	916 488-8601	20533
Mission Oaks Recreation Pk Dst	8399	D	916 488-2810	24807
Pacific Cities Management Inc (PA)	6531	D	916 348-1188	11645
SSC Carmichael Operating Co LP	8051	D	916 485-4793	20775
Sunbridge Brittany Rehab Centr	8051	D	916 484-1393	20787
Sunrise Senior Living Inc	8051	D	916 485-4500	20810
Walnut Whtney Cnvalescent Hosp	8051	D	916 488-8601	20874
Wenmat Inc	8699	D	916 485-0714	25483

CARPINTERIA, CA - Santa Barbara County

Company	SIC	EMP	PHONE	ENTRY #
Agilent Technologies Inc	5122	C	805 566-6655	8138
Beacon West Energy Group LLC	8711	D	805 816-2790	25560
Brand Flower Farms Inc (PA)	5193	C	805 684-5531	9126
Carpinteria Motor Inn Inc	7011	E	805 684-0473	12433
CP Opco LLC	7359	D	805 566-3566	14496
Gallup & Stribling Orchids LLC	0181	E	805 684-1998	260
Hollandia Produce LP	0182	C	805 684-8739	314
International Spt Science Assn	7999	E	805 745-8111	19189
Jimenez Nursery Inc	0181	D	805 684-7955	271
Johannes Flowers Inc	0181	D	805 684-5686	272
Myriad Flowers International	0181	D	805 684-8079	286
Ocean Breeze International	0181	D	805 684-1747	288
Plan Member Financial Corp	6282	D	800 874-6910	10104

Company	SIC	EMP	PHONE	ENTRY #
Procore Technologies Inc (PA)	7371	C	866 477-6267	15379
Sunshine Floral Inc	5193	D	805 684-1177	9165
Ucp Work Inc (PA)	8331	C	805 566-9000	24240
Valley Flowers Inc	5193	D	805 684-6651	9173
Westland Orchids Inc	5193	E	805 684-1436	9179

CARSON, CA - Los Angeles County

Company	SIC	EMP	PHONE	ENTRY #
Advanced Cleanup Tech Inc (PA)	8744	C	310 763-1423	27574
Aegis Ambulance Service Inc (PA)	4119	D	626 685-9410	3741
Agility Logistics Corp	4731	D	310 507-6700	4997
Alameda Corridor Engrg Team	8711	D	310 816-0460	25523
Alliedbarton Security Svcs LLC	7381	C	310 324-1219	16551
Ampam Parks Mechanical Inc	1711	A	310 835-1532	2118
Anheuser-Busch LLC	5181	C	310 761-4600	8979
Anschutz So Calif Sports Compl	7941	C	310 630-2000	18506
Apw International Inc	5013	C	310 884-5003	6620
Apw Knox-Seeman Warehouse Inc (HQ)	5013	C	310 604-4373	6621
Aramark Services Inc	7389	D	310 635-5000	17009
Ashland LLC	5169	D	310 223-3505	8918
AT&T Corp.	4812	C	310 225-3028	5268
Auto Parts Warehouse Inc (PA)	5013	E	800 913-6119	6623
Bakkavor Foods Usa Inc (DH)	5149	B	704 522-1977	8759
BP West Coast Products LLC	1311	A	310 816-8787	1014
BP West Coast Products LLC	5171	C	310 549-6204	8941
Calko Transport Company Inc.	4214	D	310 816-0602	4335
Carson Operating Company LLC	7011	D	310 830-9200	12434
Carson Senior Assisted Living	8361	D	310 830-4010	24453
Cellco Partnership	4812	D	310 329-9325	5370
Cintas Corporation No 2	7299	D	310 635-8713	13727
Cirrus Enterprises LLC	5162	D	310 204-6159	8912
City Fashion Express Inc	4731	D	310 223-1010	5033
City of Carson	8322	D	310 835-0212	23578
Clay Dunn Enterprises Inc	1711	C	310 549-1698	2162
Clipper Corporation (PA)	5046	E	310 533-8585	7133
Color Spot Nurseries Inc	5193	D	310 549-7470	9130
County of Los Angeles	8631	C	310 847-4018	25059
County Santtn Dist 2 of La Co	4959	B	310 830-2400	6536
Custom Goods LLC (PA)	4225	E	310 241-6700	4543
Dmf Inc	5063	D	323 934-7779	7354
Durham School Services L P	4151	C	310 767-5820	3914
East Crson II Hsing Prtners LP	6531	C	310 522-9606	11416
Epson America Inc	4225	C	562 290-5855	4553
Fedex Ground Package Sys Inc	4213	C	800 463-3339	4170
Fortress Resources LLC (PA)	7538	C	562 633-9951	17760
Grand View Geranium Grdns Inc	0181	D	310 217-0490	264
H D Smith LLC	5122	D	310 641-1885	8175
H Rauvel Inc (PA)	4225	D	310 604-0060	4570
Hanjin Transportation Co Ltd	4731	D	310 522-5030	5080
Harry Group Inc	4731	D	310 631-9646	5083
Harvard Grand Inv Inc A Cal	6799	D	310 513-7560	12230
Hellmann Wrldwide Lgistics Inc	4731	E	310 847-4600	5086
Herc Rentals Inc	7359	E	310 233-5000	14510
Human Potential Cons LLC	8744	C	310 756-1560	27593
JB Dental Supply Co Inc (PA)	5047	C	310 202-8055	7185
Kaiser Foundation Hospitals	8093	D	310 513-6707	22604
Kinder Mrgan Enrgy Partners LP	4226	E	310 518-7700	4680
Klx Inc	5088	C	310 900-1300	7909
Kole Imports	5199	D	310 834-0004	9228
Liberty Mutual Insurance Co	6331	C	781 740-1920	10369
Long-Lok Fasteners Corporation	5072	E	310 667-4200	7595
Mainfreight Inc (HQ)	4731	D	310 900-1974	5105
Margate Construction Inc	1623	C	310 830-8610	1952
Mayor West Coast LLC	4212	E	424 221-5229	4040
MB Landscaping & Nursery Inc	5193	D	310 965-1923	9146
Merchants Bank California N A	6021	D	310 549-4350	9352
Mhx Inc	4731	D	800 234-2098	5110
Multiquip Inc (DH)	5063	B	310 537-3700	7379
Nnr Global Logistics USA Inc	4731	C	310 357-2100	5122
North American Security Inc.	7381	B	310 630-4840	16741
North Amrcn SEC Invstgtons Inc.	7381	B	323 634-1911	16742
Nova Ortho-Med Inc (PA)	5047	E	310 352-3600	7197
Phoenix Engineering Co Inc	7363	D	310 532-1134	14891
Quik Pick Express LLC	4731	C	310 763-3000	5152
Schafer Bros Trnsf Pano Movers (PA)	4225	D	310 835-7231	4629
Scotts Labor Leasing Co Inc	7361	C	310 835-8388	14754
Secrom Inc.	8059	D	310 830-4010	21205
Sony Electronics Inc.	5064	C	310 835-6121	7429
Southwind Foods LLC (PA)	5146	D	323 262-8222	8602
Spectra I California.	1731	C	310 835-0808	2738
Ssf Imported Auto Parts LLC.	5013	D	310 782-8859	6676
Sunstone Hotel Investors LLC	7011	C	310 830-9200	13296
Swayzers Incorporated	7349	D	323 979-7223	14405
Tabletops Unlimited Inc (PA)	5023	D	310 549-6000	6790
Total Trnsp & Dist Inc	4214	D	310 603-0467	4378
Tri-Modal Dist Svcs Inc (PA)	4214	D	310 522-5506	4381
Triple B Forwarders Inc (PA)	4731	C	310 604-5840	5187

Mergent email: customerrelations@mergent.com
1554

2019 Directory of California
Wholesalers and Services Companies

(P-0000) Products & Services Section entry number
(PA)=Parent Co (HQ)=Headquarters (DH)=Div Headquarters

	SIC	EMP	PHONE	ENTRY #
Watson Cogeneration Co Inc	4911	D	310 816-8100	6148
Western Star Trnsp LLC	4213	C	310 605-1300	4303
Yusen Logistics Americas Inc	4731	C	310 518-3008	5204

CARUTHERS, CA - Fresno County

	SIC	EMP	PHONE	ENTRY #
Charanjit Singh Batth	0173	D	559 864-9421	185
Fresno Cnty Sprntndent Schools	4151	D	559 644-1000	3937
H & R Gunlund Ranches Inc	0172	C	559 864-8186	147
Hammer Down Davila Cnstr	1522	D	559 864-2001	1287
Karam Bath	0172	E	559 864-3868	152
Pacific Boring Incorporated	1781	E	559 864-9444	3355

CASPAR, CA - Mendocino County

	SIC	EMP	PHONE	ENTRY #
Caspar Community	8322	E	707 964-4997	23531

CASTRO VALLEY, CA - Alameda County

	SIC	EMP	PHONE	ENTRY #
ABC Phones North Carolina Inc	4812	D	510 314-0981	5256
American Building Service Inc	7349	D	510 483-5120	14193
Baywood Court (PA)	8082	D	510 733-2102	22234
Coldwell Bankers Residential	6531	D	510 583-5400	11345
East Bay Regional Park Dst	7999	D	510 881-1833	19163
Eden Labs Med Group Inc	8011	E	510 537-1234	19453
Eden Township Hospital Dst	8062	A	510 538-2031	21400
Ku Kyoung	8051	C	510 582-2765	20571
Mason-Mcduffie Real Estate Inc	6531	E	510 886-7511	11591
Mekwus Solar Energy	4931	D	510 731-4134	6184
Online Energy LLC	5084	C	510 583-0091	7781
Ras Management Inc (PA)	4225	E	510 727-1800	4624
Redwood Convalescent Hospital	8059	C	510 537-8848	21194
Solar Company Inc	1711	D	510 888-9488	2360
Valley Pinte Nursing Rehab Ctr	8361	E	510 538-8464	24706

CASTROVILLE, CA - Monterey County

	SIC	EMP	PHONE	ENTRY #
Ajax Portable Services	7359	E	831 384-5000	14469
Brady Company/Central Cal	1742	C	831 633-3315	2852
California Artichoke & Vegetab	0723	D	831 633-2144	499
Giannas Baking Company	5149	D	831 633-3700	8796
National Custom Packing Inc	0723	E	831 724-2026	545
Ocean Mist Farming Company (PA)	0161	C	831 633-2144	72
Randazzo Enterprises Inc	1795	D	831 633-4420	3460
USA Waste of California Inc	4212	C	831 384-4860	4078
Valley Pride Inc (PA)	0761	B	831 633-5883	676
Vps Companies Inc	5142	E	831 633-4011	8508

CATHEDRAL CITY, CA - Riverside County

	SIC	EMP	PHONE	ENTRY #
American Golf Corporation	7997	D	702 431-2191	18833
Big Lgue Dreams Consulting LLC	7032	C	760 324-5600	13446
Briar Golf LP	7999	D	760 328-6571	19114
Crystal Chrysler Plymuth Dodge	7538	D	760 324-9375	17758
Daniel Robert Knowlton	8111	D	760 265-5293	23020
Desert Princess Home	7997	E	760 322-1655	18912
Desert Prncess Homeowners Assn	8641	D	760 322-1907	25151
Heartland Payment Systems Inc	7389	D	760 324-0133	17218

CAZADERO, CA - Sonoma County

	SIC	EMP	PHONE	ENTRY #
Camp Royaneh Boy Scout	8641	D	707 632-5291	25126

CEDAR GLEN, CA - San Bernardino County

	SIC	EMP	PHONE	ENTRY #
San Bernardino Mtns Wildlife	0279	E	909 226-6189	446

CEDARVILLE, CA - Modoc County

	SIC	EMP	PHONE	ENTRY #
Surprise Valley Health Care Di	8062	D	530 279-6111	21797

CERES, CA - Stanislaus County

	SIC	EMP	PHONE	ENTRY #
Bertolottis Ceres Disposal	4953	D	209 537-8000	6352
Chateaux Framing Inc	1751	C	209 537-6799	3020
Dan Avila and Sons	0161	D	209 495-3899	46
Dbi Beverage Inc	5181	C	209 524-2477	8989
Irish Construction	1623	D	209 576-8766	1936
Mark One Corporation	8059	E	209 537-4581	21151
Procter & Gamble Distrg LLC	5169	B	209 538-3987	8935
Ram Mechanical Inc	1711	D	209 531-9155	2327
Sutter Health	8062	C	209 538-1733	21826
Timmerman Starlite Trckg Inc	4213	D	209 538-1706	4278
United Parcel Service Inc OH	4215	C	800 742-5877	4451
West Coast Grape Farming Inc	0762	A	209 538-3131	721

CERRITOS, CA - Los Angeles County

	SIC	EMP	PHONE	ENTRY #
A & D Hauling Services Inc	4212	D	310 514-8969	3957
Access Info MGT Shred Svcs LLC	8741	D	805 529-6866	26744
Achem Industry America Inc (PA)	5085	E	562 802-0998	7824
All Care Industries Inc	7349	D	562 623-4009	14184
Amkotron Inc	7378	D	562 921-3330	16276
Apex Computer Systems Inc	7378	E	562 926-6820	16277
Aspen Youth Inc	8322	E	562 567-5507	23494
Astro Realty Inc	6531	D	562 924-3381	11223
Atkinson And Ly Rd & Rm Lw (PA)	8111	C	562 653-3200	22924
Audio Visual Headquarters (DH)	7359	E	310 603-0652	14474
Auditboard Inc (PA)	7371	E	877 769-5444	15009

	SIC	EMP	PHONE	ENTRY #
Auto Insurance Specialists LLC (DH)	6411	C	562 345-6247	10553
Avalon A Cerritos	8322	E	562 865-9500	23500
Bunzl Usa Inc	5113	D	314 997-5959	8097
Caremore Health Plan (HQ)	8011	D	562 622-2950	19353
Cea-Pack Services Inc	4215	C	562 407-0660	4394
Cellco Partnership	4812	C	562 809-5650	5330
College Hospital Inc (PA)	8063	A	562 924-9581	21941
Community Family Guidance Ctr (PA)	8093	D	562 865-6444	22536
Complete Office California Inc	5021	C	714 880-1222	6718
Crest Financial Corporation (DH)	6411	C	562 733-6500	10596
David Levy Co Inc	5065	E	562 404-9998	7464
Firm A Chugh Professional Corp	8111	C	562 229-1220	23066
First Choice Bank (HQ)	6021	D	562 345-9092	9448
Global Med Services Inc	8082	E	562 207-6970	22302
Healthview Inc	8361	E	562 468-0136	24559
Hometown Buffet Inc	7299	D	562 402-8307	13748
Iron Mountain Info MGT LLC	4226	D	714 526-0916	4679
Kaiser Foundation Hospitals	8011	A	800 823-4040	19547
Management Trust Assn Inc	8742	C	562 926-3372	27314
Memorex Products Inc	5064	C	562 653-2800	7420
Microtek Lab Inc (HQ)	5044	C	310 687-5823	6969
Midway International Inc	5199	E	562 921-2255	9236
Mulhearn	6531	C	562 860-2443	11622
O E C Shipg Los Angeles Inc	4731	E	562 926-7186	5125
Oocl (usa) Inc	4731	D	562 499-2600	5129
Pioneer Medical Group Inc	8099	D	562 229-0902	22859
Poliseek Ais Insur Sltions Inc	6411	C	866 480-7335	10732
Private Medical-Care Inc	6324	C	562 924-8311	10302
Razor USA LLC (PA)	5091	C	562 345-6000	7936
Royal Plywood Company LLC (PA)	5031	C	562 404-2989	6861
Secure One Data Solutions LLC	7374	E	562 924-7056	16176
Southern Glazers Wine	5182	B	562 926-2000	9056
Spectrum MGT Holdg Co LLC	4841	D	562 677-0228	5937
Sun West Mortgage Company Inc (PA)	6162	D	800 453-7884	9861
Temp Unlimited LLC	7363	D	562 860-3340	14920
Tenet Healthsystem Medical	8062	A	562 531-2550	21853
Thyssenkrupp Elevator Corp	7699	E	323 278-9888	17998
Trinitycare LLC (PA)	8082	D	818 709-4221	22440
Uaw-Lbor Emplyment Trning Corp (PA)	7361	C	562 989-7700	14789
United Parcel Service Inc OH	4215	C	562 404-3236	4467
Uquality Automotive Pdts Corp (PA)	5013	E	562 282-2888	6681
Usaco Service Corp	7629	C	562 483-8747	17918
Wells Fargo Bank National Assn	6021	A	562 924-1616	9406
Young Systems Corporation	5044	D	562 921-2256	6994
Zero Energy Contracting Inc	1711	C	626 701-3180	2415
Zero Energy Contracting LLC	1711	D	626 701-3180	2416

CHATSWORTH, CA - Los Angeles County

	SIC	EMP	PHONE	ENTRY #
101communications Holdings LLC (HQ)	7313	D	818 734-1520	13932
A I T Development Corp	1521	D	818 407-5533	1107
Accunex Inc	1731	E	818 882-5858	2500
Adco Container Company	5085	E	818 998-2565	7825
All Tmperatures Controlled Inc	1711	D	818 882-1478	2098
Allstate Imaging Inc (PA)	5044	D	818 678-4550	6949
American Industrial Supply	5085	C	818 841-7788	7827
American Technical Svcs Inc	8711	D	818 590-7784	25534
Atlantic Optical Co Inc	5048	D	818 407-1890	7233
Brewster Marble Co Inc	1743	D	818 834-2195	2988
California Resources Corp (PA)	1382	C	888 848-4754	1040
Cardinal Cartridge Inc	8999	D	818 727-9740	27924
Cbol Corporation	5065	C	818 704-8200	7458
Child Care Resource Center Inc (PA)	8322	C	818 717-1000	23558
Child Care Resource Center Inc	8322	B	661 255-2474	23559
Chubb US Holding Inc	6411	C	818 428-3600	10585
CIT Bank National Association	6021	C	818 885-9065	9321
Comet Electric Inc	1731	C	818 340-0965	2547
Cpcc Inc	8059	D	818 882-3200	21052
Crunch Fitness	7991	D	805 522-5454	18591
Danish Environment Inc	7349	D	818 992-6722	14249
Develop Point Education	7299	E	805 624-6171	13740
Diamond Products LLC (PA)	5199	C	818 772-0100	9211
Dolphin Imaging Systems LLC	7371	C	818 435-1368	15115
Eisenberg International Corp (PA)	5136	D	818 365-8161	8257
Eurodent Inc	8072	D	818 832-1325	22167
Fromer Inc	1521	C	818 341-3896	1166
Genesis Tech Partners LLC	7699	C	800 950-2647	17947
Golden State Health Ctrs Inc	8059	D	818 882-8233	21098
Green Scene Landscape Inc	0782	D	818 280-0420	850
Guardian National Inc	7381	E	800 700-1467	16674
Joerns LLC (HQ)	5047	C	800 966-6662	7186
Lennox Industries Inc	5075	C	818 739-1616	7653
Logistical Support LLC	5088	C	818 341-3344	7911
Los Angeles County MTA	4111	C	213 922-6308	3667
Marotto Corporation	7349	B	818 775-0320	14313
Minilec Service Inc	7622	E	818 341-1125	17885
Mj Star-Lite Inc	1731	E	818 717-0834	2649

GEOGRAPHIC

Company	SIC	EMP	PHONE	ENTRY #
Multi-Pak Corporation	7389	D	818 709-0508	17338
National Notary Association	8621	C	818 739-4071	25029
Nestle Waters North Amer Inc	5149	D	818 349-9201	8835
NNA Insurance Services	6411	C	818 739-4071	10717
NNA Services	8621	C	818 739-4071	25030
Nna Services LLC	7389	C	818 739-4071	17356
OBryant Electric Inc	1731	C	818 407-1986	2666
On-Site Lasermedic Corporation (PA)	7378	D	818 775-9111	16290
Oncore Manufacturing LLC (HQ)	8711	A	818 734-6500	25853
Ontic Engineering and Mfg Inc (HQ)	5088	B	818 678-6555	7912
Pacific Toxicology Labs	8734	D	818 598-3110	26726
Patterson Dental Supply Inc	7371	E	818 435-1368	15347
Pd Liquidation	5199	C	818 772-0100	9248
Piege Co (PA)	5136	C	818 727-9100	8273
Platinum Group Companies Inc (PA)	6719	C	818 721-3800	12000
Premier America Credit Union (PA)	6062	C	818 772-4000	9644
Printful Inc	7384	D	818 351-7181	16965
Printing Technology Inc	5085	C	818 576-9220	7865
PS Development Corporation	1731	D	818 340-0965	2688
R M B Packaging Co Inc	5199	E	818 998-0658	9255
Rancho San Antonio Boys HM Inc (PA)	8361	D	818 882-6400	24642
Red Pointe Roofing LP	1761	D	818 998-3857	3195
Regency Enterprises Inc (PA)	5063	B	818 901-0255	7388
Retail Services Wis Corp	7389	E	818 772-4969	17432
Ricoh Usa Inc	5044	E	818 294-8601	6976
Ronco Inventions LLC (PA)	5023	C	800 486-1806	6785
Rubicon Corporation America	6531	E	818 765-2001	11747
Sage Electric Company	1731	D	818 718-9080	2720
Service Genius Los Angeles Inc	1711	D	818 200-3379	2354
Seven One Inc	7389	D	818 904-3435	17468
Sexy Hair Concepts	5131	D	800 848-3383	8242
Silver Strand	1751	E	818 701-9707	3079
Sliding Door Company (PA)	1751	D	818 997-7855	3080
Southern California Gas Co	4922	B	818 701-2592	6153
Spectrum MGT Holdg Co LLC	4841	C	818 700-6126	5940
Staffchex Inc	7361	A	818 709-6100	14769
Summerville Senior Living Inc	6513	D	818 341-2552	11121
Suttles Plumbing & Mech Corp	1711	D	818 718-9779	2380
Telesis Community Credit Union (PA)	6061	D	818 885-1226	9597
Terminix Intl Co Ltd Partnr	7342	D	818 361-1191	14161
Trendex Corporation	1542	D	818 407-9600	1676
Tuttle Family Enterprises Inc	7349	D	818 534-2566	14412
United Cp/S Chldrns Fndn La	8361	C	818 998-8755	24703
US Interstate Distrg Inc	4813	D	818 678-4592	5658
Verizon Communications Inc	4813	C	818 388-8549	5671
West Coast Coupon Inc	7319	E	818 341-2400	13987
West-Spec Partners	5085	E	818 725-7000	7877

CHERRY VALLEY, CA - Riverside County

Company	SIC	EMP	PHONE	ENTRY #
David-Kleis Inc	8051	C	951 845-1166	20368
Little Peoples	8361	D	951 849-1959	24580
Little Peoples World Inc	8361	E	951 845-8367	24581

CHESTER, CA - Plumas County

Company	SIC	EMP	PHONE	ENTRY #
Chester Public Utility Dst	4939	D	530 258-2171	6195
Seneca Healthcare District	8011	D	530 258-1977	19876
Seneca Healthcare District (PA)	8062	C	530 258-2151	21740

CHICO, CA - Butte County

Company	SIC	EMP	PHONE	ENTRY #
11 Main Inc	4813	C	530 892-9191	5428
Addus Healthcare Inc	8082	E	530 566-0405	22199
Agreserves Inc	0173	D	530 343-5365	184
Ampla Health	8011	D	530 342-4395	19288
ARC of Butte County (PA)	8322	C	530 891-5865	23485
Associated Pension Cons Inc (PA)	6411	D	530 343-4233	10548
AT&T Corp	4812	C	530 891-2025	5281
Auctiva Corporation	8748	D	530 894-7400	27651
B A M I Inc	7991	E	530 343-5678	18575
Baney Corporation	7011	D	530 899-9090	12351
Bank America National Assn	6021	D	530 891-7019	9283
BCM Construction Company Inc	1541	E	530 342-1722	1375
Boys & Girls Clubs of N Vly	8641	D	530 899-0335	25107
Buildcom Inc	5074	B	800 375-3403	7612
Butte Home Health Inc	8082	C	530 895-0462	22244
Caldwell Ventures LLC	8051	D	530 899-0814	20280
Caminar	8093	D	530 343-4421	22515
Catamount Broadcasting of Chic (PA)	4833	C	530 893-2424	5772
Cellco Partnership	4812	D	530 892-6900	5331
Chico Area Recreation & Pk Dst (PA)	7999	D	530 895-4711	19123
Chico Csu	8099	D	530 898-3917	22765
Chico Csu Research Foundation	8641	A	530 898-6811	25137
Chico Electric Inc	1731	D	530 891-1933	2540
Chico Immdate Care Med Ctr Inc (PA)	8011	D	530 891-1676	19374
Cleanrite Inc (PA)	1799	D	530 891-0333	3505
Cloudpeople Global	7371	E	530 591-7028	15066
County of Butte	8093	B	530 891-2850	22540

Company	SIC	EMP	PHONE	ENTRY #
Cummings-Violich Inc	0762	D	530 894-5494	684
Dfa of California	8699	C	530 345-5077	25417
Digital Path Inc	4813	E	800 676-7284	5547
Enloe Hospt-Phys Thrpy	8062	C	530 891-7300	21411
Enloe Medical Center	8062	D	530 332-4111	21412
Enloe Medical Center	8011	B	530 332-7522	19461
Enloe Medical Center	8082	B	530 332-6050	22293
Enloe Medical Center	8049	D	530 332-6138	20174
Enloe Medical Center	8062	C	530 332-6400	21413
Enloe Medical Center	8011	B	530 332-6000	19462
Evergreen At Chico LLC	8051	C	530 342-4885	20414
Fair Trade Corner Inc	0723	E	530 566-1405	514
Far Northern Coordinating Coun	8322	D	530 895-8633	23803
Farmers International Inc	0173	E	530 566-1405	188
Federal Express Corporation	4513	C	800 463-3339	4819
Fedex Ground Package Sys Inc	4213	C	800 463-3339	4171
First Responder Ems Inc	4119	C	530 897-6345	3796
First Rsponder Emrgncy Med Svc	4119	C	530 891-4357	3797
Gas Transmission Systems Inc	8711	C	530 893-6711	25701
Golden Living LLC	8051	D	530 343-6084	20484
Gonzales Enterprises Inc	5136	C	530 343-8725	8262
Helios Healthcare LLC	8059	C	530 345-1306	21107
Heritage One Carpentry Inc	5031	C	530 345-6622	6829
Hignell Incorporated	6513	D	530 345-1965	11031
Hmclause Inc	0181	D	530 713-5838	268
Holdrege Kull Consulting Engr	8711	D	530 894-2487	25738
Home Health Care Management (PA)	8082	D	530 343-0727	22323
Hotel Diamond	7011	E	530 893-3100	12723
Interwest Insurance Svcs LLC	6411	C	530 895-1010	10656
Jeff Stover Inc	7991	D	530 345-9427	18616
Mangrove Medical Group	8011	E	530 345-0064	19666
Mission Linen Supply	7213	C	530 342-4110	13542
Modern Building Inc	1541	D	530 891-4533	1422
Mooney Farms	0723	E	530 899-2661	543
Morrison MGT Specialists Inc	8741	D	530 332-7557	26951
North State Radiology	8011	E	530 898-0504	19717
Northern Cal Yuth Fmly Prgrams (PA)	8322	D	530 893-2316	23943
Northern Vly Indian Hlth Inc	8021	D	530 896-9400	20131
Nph Medical Services	7361	D	530 899-2255	14675
Pacific Gas and Electric Co	4924	C	530 894-4739	6160
Rgis LLC	7389	D	530 898-1015	17442
Rhc Equipment LLC	1542	D	530 892-1918	1630
Riverside Cnvalescent Hosp Inc (PA)	8059	D	530 343-5595	21197
Riverside Health Care Corp (PA)	8059	D	530 897-5100	21199
Roy Carrington Inc	7361	C	530 893-2100	14748
RSC Associates Inc (PA)	6531	C	530 893-8228	11746
Selig Construction Corp	1521	E	530 893-5898	1232
Sierra Landscape & Maintenance	0781	C	530 895-0263	788
Stansbury Hm Preservation Assn	8412	E	530 895-3848	24915
Sungard Bi-Tech Inc (DH)	7371	E	530 891-5281	15483
Terraces Retirement Community	8361	C	530 894-1010	24696
Travidia Inc (PA)	7372	C	530 343-6400	15880
Tri Counties Bank (HQ)	6029	D	530 898-0300	9517
Unitedhealth Group Inc	6324	B	530 879-8251	10326
Veterans Health Administration	8011	D	530 879-5000	20067
Victor Cmnty Support Svcs Inc (PA)	8093	C	530 893-0758	22712
Women Health Center (PA)	8093	B	530 891-1917	22718
Work Truck Solutions Inc	7379	D	855 987-4544	16534

CHINO, CA - San Bernardino County

Company	SIC	EMP	PHONE	ENTRY #
Acepex Management Corporation	8741	B	909 591-1999	26745
Advantage Pntg Solutions Inc	1721	D	951 739-9204	2419
Am-TEC Total Security Inc (PA)	7382	D	909 573-4678	16872
American Beef Packers Inc	0751	C	909 628-4888	623
Angels In Motion LLC	8082	D	909 590-9102	22224
Applied P & Ch Laboratory Sout	8731	C	909 590-1828	26322
Arrow Wire & Cable Inc (PA)	5063	E	909 282-1940	7334
Aspects Furniture Mfg Inc	5021	D	909 606-5806	6710
Baronhr LLC	7361	C	909 517-3800	14575
Canyon Ridge Hospital Inc	8063	D	909 590-3700	21937
Carlisle Construction Mtls Inc	5033	D	909 591-7425	6922
Cellco Partnership	4812	C	909 591-9740	5386
Century 21 Home Realtors (PA)	6531	D	909 591-0158	11301
Chino Grading Inc	1794	D	909 364-8667	3418
Chino Medical Group Inc	8011	D	909 591-6446	19381
Chino Rdological Registry Corp	8062	D	909 591-6688	21321
City of Chino	4959	D	909 591-9843	6531
Cls Landscape Management Inc	0783	B	909 628-3005	970
Concept Green Enrgy Sltons Inc	7389	A	855 459-6535	17097
Consolidated Plastics Corp (PA)	5162	D	909 393-8222	8913
Core Group Inc (PA)	7389	C	909 438-2626	17101
Correctons Rhbltation Cal Dept	8062	C	909 597-1821	21344
Custom Bilt Holdings LLC	5084	D	909 664-1587	7745
DL Long Landscaping Inc	0781	C	909 628-5531	750
Donovan Golf Courses MGT	7992	E	714 528-6400	18709
Duke Pacific Inc	1761	D	909 591-0191	3150

Mergent email: customerrelations@mergent.com
1556

2019 Directory of California
Wholesalers and Services Companies

(P-0000) Products & Services Section entry number
(PA)=Parent Co (HQ)=Headquarters (DH)=Div Headquarters

Company	SIC	EMP	PHONE	ENTRY #
El & El Wood Products Corp (PA)	5031	C	909 591-0339	6821
El Prado Golf Course LP	7992	D	909 597-1751	18711
Farmers Group Inc	6411	D	909 839-2020	10617
Fisher Scientific Company LLC	5049	D	909 393-2100	7243
Flatiron West Inc	1622	D	909 597-8413	1878
Gano Excel (usa) Inc	5149	D	626 338-8081	8795
Gardner Trucking Inc	4213	D	909 563-5606	4183
Generation Construction Inc	1542	C	909 923-2077	1534
Gentek Media Inc	5045	E	909 476-3818	7055
Gilbert Service Corp	4214	D	909 393-7575	4347
Harrington Industrial Plas LLC (HQ)	5074	D	909 597-8641	7627
Inland Empire Utilities Agency (PA)	4941	D	909 993-1600	6264
Interior Experts General Bldrs	1742	D	909 203-4922	2897
June A Grothe Construction Inc	1542	D	909 993-9393	1569
Kaiser Foundation Hospitals	6324	D	888 750-0036	10246
Koury Engrg Tstg & Insptn	7389	D	310 851-8685	17280
McKesson Medical-Surgical Inc	5047	D	800 767-6339	7189
Microtel Computer Systems Inc	7379	D	626 839-6038	16427
Mission Linen Supply	7213	B	909 393-5589	13547
Motivational Marketing Inc	7389	B	909 517-2200	17336
Navy Exchange Service Command	4225	C	909 517-2640	4598
Omnia Italian Design Inc	5021	C	909 393-4400	6732
Prestige Autotech Corporation	5013	E	909 627-6411	6666
Public Investment Corporation	6552	C	310 451-5227	11908
Quetico LLC (PA)	5199	D	909 628-6200	9254
R & B Reinforcing Steel Corp	1791	C	909 591-1726	3393
Ralison International Inc	5093	E	909 393-0008	7988
RDM Electric Co Inc	1731	D	909 591-0990	2695
Redwood Products Chino Inc	5031	D	909 923-5656	6856
Rocky Packaging Solution Inc (PA)	5199	E	909 591-3331	9257
SA Recycling LLC	4953	D	909 622-3337	6468
Salem Christian Homes Inc (PA)	8361	D	909 614-0575	24661
Savant Construction Inc	1542	D	909 614-4300	1640
Schneider Electric Usa Inc	4225	C	909 438-2295	4630
Skate Enterprises Inc	7999	C	562 924-0911	19238
South Coast Childrens Soc Inc	8322	C	909 364-9788	24060
Spanish Trils Girl Scout Cncl	8322	E	909 627-2609	24063
Tactical Lgistic Solutions Inc	4225	D	909 464-2813	4639
Threshold Technologies Inc	4581	D	909 606-1666	4920
Universal Packg Systems Inc	4225	C	909 517-2442	4646
US Elogistics Service Corp	4225	D	732 881-6606	4651
USA Waste of California Inc	4953	D	909 590-1793	6495
Veritas Health Services Inc	8062	A	909 464-8600	21897
Wp Electric Communications Inc	1731	E	909 606-3510	2792
Year Round Landscape Maint Inc	0782	E	909 597-7734	964
Yoshimura Research & Dev Amer	5013	D	909 628-4722	6688

CHINO HILLS, CA - San Bernardino County

Company	SIC	EMP	PHONE	ENTRY #
American Financial Network Inc	6282	D	909 287-7585	10054
Ayres Group	7011	D	909 631-2922	12345
Bank America National Assn	6021	D	909 393-3002	9293
Bates Sample Case Company Inc	7389	D	951 371-4922	17027
Beachside Realtors	1799	D	909 606-1299	3493
Big Lgue Drams Chino Hills LLC	7941	D	909 287-6900	18509
Boys Republic (PA)	8361	C	909 902-6690	24438
Ch Market Center Inc	6531	D	909 628-9100	11311
CIT Bank NA	6021	D	909 631-2560	9304
Flatiron Electric Group Inc	1731	E	714 228-9631	2587
Harkins Theatres Inc	7832	D	909 627-8010	18302
Los Serranos Golf Club	7992	C	909 597-1769	18729
Optima Network Services Inc (DH)	8999	D	305 599-1800	27947
Positive Solution Staffing LLC	7361	C	909 606-7512	14695
Prh Pro Inc	5085	C	714 510-7226	7864
SSC Construction Inc	8711	D	951 278-1177	25923
USA Truck Inc	4213	D	909 334-1406	4296
West Hills Golf Associates	7997	E	714 528-6400	19085

CHOWCHILLA, CA - Madera County

Company	SIC	EMP	PHONE	ENTRY #
Agriland Holding Inc	0179	D	559 665-2100	232
Anderson Pump Company	4941	D	559 665-4477	6209
Avalon Care Ctr - Chwchla LLC	8051	D	559 665-4826	20246
Case Vlott Cattle	0241	E	559 665-7399	408
Chowchilla Mem Hlth Care Dst (PA)	8051	D	559 665-3781	20311
J & R Debenedetto Orchards Inc	0762	D	559 665-1712	695
Madera Community Hospital	8062	C	559 665-3768	21573
Seaman Nurseries Inc	0721	C	559 665-1860	467
Vlot Brothers Trucking Co Inc	0241	C	559 665-7399	426
Winnresidential Ltd Partnr	6513	B	559 665-9600	11143

CHUALAR, CA - Monterey County

Company	SIC	EMP	PHONE	ENTRY #
C & G Farms Inc	0161	C	831 679-2978	40
P & P Agrilabor	7361	D	831 679-2307	14684

CHULA VISTA, CA - San Diego County

Company	SIC	EMP	PHONE	ENTRY #
24 Hour Fitness Usa Inc	7991	C	619 425-6600	18558
Aetna Health California Inc	6324	D	619 656-3104	10176
ARC Starlight Center	8322	D	619 427-7524	23486
Armando C Ibarra CPA	8721	D	619 422-1348	26143
At Your Svc Htg & Coolg LLC	1542	D	602 550-6946	1470
Bayview Hospital and Mental	8063	C	619 426-6311	21926
California American Water Co	4941	D	619 656-2400	6212
California Baking Company	5149	B	619 591-8289	8763
Call Center Services Intl LLC	7389	D	858 427-8500	17051
Care Plus North of San Diego	7361	D	619 421-0807	14584
CDI Marine Company LLC	8711	E	619 407-4010	25597
Cellco Partnership	4812	D	619 216-5840	5355
Citibank National Association	6021	C	619 870-0609	9331
Citigroup Inc	6021	C	619 498-3158	9336
Community Health Group	8011	C	800 224-7766	19397
Coronado Financial Corp	6531	E	619 946-1900	11385
Cox Communications Cal LLC	4841	B	619 263-9251	5896
Culinary Hispanic Foods Inc	5149	A	619 955-6101	8783
Dirt Cheap Demolition Inc	1795	E	619 426-9598	3452
Econa Corp	8721	E	619 722-6555	26187
Episcopal Community	8322	D	619 228-2800	23789
FJ Willert Contracting Co	1794	C	619 421-1980	3425
Fredericka Manor	8361	D	619 422-9271	24534
Front Porch Communities	8059	C	619 427-2777	21073
George G Sharp Inc	8711	D	619 425-4211	25710
Global Exprnce Specialists Inc	7389	C	619 498-6300	17193
Healthcare MGT Systems Inc (PA)	8051	C	619 521-9641	20519
Heartland Meat Company Inc	5147	D	619 407-3668	8618
Home Carpet Investment Inc (PA)	1752	D	619 262-8040	3106
J C Towing Inc	7549	C	619 429-1492	17864
Knight-Swift Trnsp Hldings Inc	4213	D	619 671-0588	4209
Loyda Yu Real Estate Inc	6531	D	619 475-7777	11571
McMillin RE & Mrtg Co Inc	6531	D	619 422-4500	11600
Metropolitan Area Advisory Com (PA)	8331	D	619 426-3595	24204
Metropolitan Area Advisory Com	8331	C	619 420-8981	24206
Nitai Partners Inc	7371	D	855 879-2847	15311
Pacific Coast Truck and Whse (PA)	5013	E	619 661-5451	6662
Pacific Spanish Network Inc	4832	C	619 427-6323	5746
Phoenix Intl Holdings Inc	7389	C	619 207-0871	17397
Plastiflex Company Inc (HQ)	7389	C	619 662-8792	17404
Prosciento Inc	8731	C	619 427-1300	26441
Quality Coast Incorporated	7349	E	619 443-9192	14361
Racelegal Com	8699	E	619 265-8159	25453
Samsung International Inc (DH)	5065	E	619 671-6859	7537
San Diego Country Club Inc	7997	D	619 422-8895	19025
San Diego Gas & Electric Co	4922	C	800 411-7343	6152
Scripps Health	8049	C	619 862-6600	20203
Scripps Health	8062	A	619 691-7000	21731
Sharp Chula Vista Medical Ctr	8062	A	619 502-5800	21745
Sharp Healthcare	8051	C	858 499-2000	20757
Sonora Trade Company Inc	5199	C	619 878-5848	9261
South Bay Community Services	8322	C	619 420-3620	24057
Southcoast Welding & Mfg LLC	7692	B	619 429-1337	17925
Sunrise Senior Living LLC	8051	D	619 470-2220	20819
Sweetwater Authority (PA)	4941	C	619 422-8395	6315
Syzygy Technologies Inc	8711	D	619 297-0970	25938
Tenet Healthsystem Medical	8063	D	619 426-6310	21992
Traffic Tech Inc	4731	C	800 396-2531	5182
United Parcel Service Inc OH	4215	C	619 482-8119	4479
United Sttes Olympic Committee	7941	E	619 656-1500	18536
Veterans Health Administration	8011	C	619 409-1600	20070
Village Club	7999	E	619 425-3333	19256
YMCA of San Diego County	8641	D	619 422-8068	25307

CITRUS HEIGHTS, CA - Sacramento County

Company	SIC	EMP	PHONE	ENTRY #
A Community For Peace	8399	D	916 728-5613	24728
Accountable Health Staff Inc	7361	B	916 286-7667	14566
Always Home Nursing Svc Inc	8082	C	916 989-6420	22215
Anka Behavioral Health Inc	8099	D	916 722-3700	22733
Cellco Partnership	4812	D	916 536-0440	5382
Crossroads Diversfd Svcs Inc	7361	D	916 676-2540	14596
Cypress Garden At Citrus Hts	8052	E	916 729-2722	20927
Deacon Construction - Cal	1542	D	916 969-0900	1514
Deacon Holdings Inc (PA)	1542	D	916 969-0900	1516
Dignity Health	8011	D	916 536-2420	19444
Farmers Group Inc	6411	D	916 727-4600	10621
Hcr Manorcare Med Svcs Fla LLC	8051	C	916 967-2929	20510
Itc Srvice Group Acqsition LLC (PA)	8748	E	877 370-4482	27757
J R Roberts Corp (HQ)	1542	D	916 729-5600	1560
J R Roberts Enterprises Inc	1542	C	916 729-5600	1561
Kings Casino Management Corp	7999	B	916 560-4405	19194
L W Roth Insurance Agency	8611	D	916 721-6273	24964
Lifetouch Inc	7221	C	916 535-7733	13640
Paradise Oaks Youth Services	8322	D	916 725-7182	23958
Probe Information Services Inc	7381	C	916 676-1826	16763
Progrssive Employment Concepts (PA)	8331	D	916 723-3112	24223
SD Deacon Corp California	1542	D	916 969-0900	1642
Sunrise Food Ministry	8322	D	916 965-5431	24079
Terra Nova Counseling (PA)	8322	D	916 344-0249	24085

GEOGRAPHIC

Company	SIC	EMP	PHONE	ENTRY #
Travelmasters Inc	4724	E	916 722-1648	4956
Zikko Inc	4214	C	916 949-8989	4391

CITY OF INDUSTRY, CA - Los Angeles County

Company	SIC	EMP	PHONE	ENTRY #
Abacus Business Capital Inc	5141	E	909 594-8080	8369
Acme Furniture Industry Inc (PA)	5021	D	626 964-3456	6706
Advanced Industrial Cmpt Inc (PA)	5045	D	909 895-8989	6998
Air Tiger Express (usa) Inc	4731	E	626 965-8647	4999
Airgas Safety Inc	5084	D	562 699-5239	7721
Alaska Diesel Electric	7539	C	626 934-6211	17791
Allied Entertainment Group Inc (PA)	7812	B	626 330-0600	18013
America Chung Nam (group) (PA)	5093	C	909 839-8383	7966
America Chung Nam LLC (HQ)	5093	C	909 839-8383	7967
American AC Distrs LLC	1711	D	407 850-0147	2103
American Ace International Co	5141	C	626 937-6116	8379
American Future Tech Corp	5045	C	888 462-3899	7005
American Multi-Cinema Inc	7832	D	626 810-7949	18269
American Paper & Plastics Inc	5113	C	626 444-0000	8093
Anning-Johnson Company	1742	E	626 369-7131	2845
Apw Construction Inc	1799	D	626 855-1720	3488
Arakelian Enterprises Inc	4953	B	626 336-3636	6341
Arakelian Enterprises Inc (PA)	4953	C	626 336-3636	6344
ARC Document Solutions Inc	7334	D	626 333-7005	14078
Arconic Global Fas & Rings Inc	5085	D	626 968-3831	7829
Assa Abloy Rsdential Group Inc	5072	B	626 369-4718	7578
B & K Electric Wholesale (PA)	5063	D	626 965-5040	7335
Boiling Point Rest Sca Inc	7361	B	626 551-5181	14578
California Access Scaffold LLC	1799	D	310 324-3388	3499
California Country Club	7997	D	626 333-4571	18879
Carrara Marble Co Amer Inc (PA)	5032	D	626 961-6010	6878
Chefs Warehouse Westcoast LLC (HQ)	5141	D	626 465-4200	8389
China Yngxin Phrmceuticals Inc	5047	A	626 581-9098	7175
CIT Bank National Association	6021	D	626 435-2260	9322
City of Industry Disposal Co	4953	E	626 336-5439	6374
Classic Distrg & Bev Group Inc	5181	B	626 934-3700	8986
Closet World Inc	1751	B	626 855-0846	3021
Commercial Lbr & Pallet Co Inc	5031	C	626 968-0631	6817
County of Los Angeles	8741	B	562 908-8400	26831
County of Los Angeles	8322	C	626 854-4987	23673
Cyberpower Inc	5045	C	626 813-7730	7030
D & D Wholesale Distrs Inc	5148	D	626 333-2111	8662
Dacor Holdings Inc	8734	C	626 626-4461	26691
Dean Socal LLC	5143	C	951 734-3950	8519
Delta Creative Inc	5092	C	800 423-4135	7950
E-Sceptre Inc	8731	D	888 350-8989	26357
Eforcity Corp - Nfm	5065	D	626 442-3168	7470
El Encanto Healthcare & Rehab	8051	C	626 336-1274	20386
Elmco Sales Inc (PA)	5074	D	626 855-4831	7613
Elmco/Duddy Inc (HQ)	5074	E	626 333-9942	7614
Essendant Co	5112	C	626 961-0011	8079
Estes Express Lines Inc	4213	D	626 333-9090	4140
Ettv America Corp	4841	C	626 581-8899	5912
Ever Win International Corp	5065	E	626 810-8218	7474
Federal Express Corporation	4215	C	800 463-3339	4412
Ferguson Enterprises Inc	5074	D	626 965-0724	7618
Finance America Mortgage LLC	6162	B	562 478-4664	9804
Fiserv Inc	7374	C	909 595-9074	16132
Foria International Inc (PA)	5136	C	626 912-8836	8260
Fortune Dynamic Inc	5139	D	909 979-8318	8357
Freshpoint Inc	5148	C	626 855-1400	8680
Freshpoint Southern Cal Inc	5148	C	626 855-1400	8682
Frito-Lay North America Inc	5145	B	626 855-1300	8547
Frize Corporation	1541	D	800 834-2127	1398
Furniture America Cal Inc (PA)	5021	D	909 718-7276	6722
Gale Lina Inc	5122	D	909 595-8898	8169
GBT Inc	5045	D	626 854-9338	7052
Gels Logistics Inc	4731	D	909 610-2277	5072
Golden Bridge Intl Group	4731	D	626 968-8229	5076
Graycon Inc	1711	E	626 961-9640	2222
Halbert Brothers Inc	4214	D	626 913-1800	4349
Haralambos Beverage Company (PA)	5181	C	562 347-4300	9000
Hikvision USA Inc (HQ)	7382	C	909 895-0400	16901
Home Organizers Inc	1751	A	562 699-9945	3043
J P Original Corp (PA)	5139	D	626 839-4300	8359
Kaiser Foundation Hospitals	8011	A	562 463-4377	19550
Kellwood Company LLC	5136	C	626 934-4133	8265
Kellwood Company LLC	5137	C	626 934-4155	8312
Klm Management Company	5143	C	626 330-3479	8523
Lasertech Computer Distr Inc	5045	C	626 435-2800	7069
Lee & Ro Inc (PA)	8711	E	626 912-3391	25794
Leon Chien Corp	6162	D	626 964-8302	9826
Liberty Glove Inc (PA)	5099	E	909 595-2992	8042
Loretta Lima Trnsp Corp	4213	D	626 330-5517	4217
Los Altos Food Products Inc	5143	C	626 330-6555	8524
MA Laboratories Inc	8731	D	626 820-8988	26413
Magnell Associate Inc (DH)	5045	C	626 271-9700	7073
Magnell Associate Inc	5045	D	626 271-1580	7074
Majestic Industry Hills LLC	7011	B	626 810-4455	12869
Majestic Industry Hills LLC (PA)	7011	A	562 692-9581	12870
Markwins Beauty Products Inc	5122	D	909 595-8898	8190
Marquez Brothers Entps Inc	5141	C	626 330-3310	8423
Max Group Corporation (PA)	5045	D	626 935-0050	7076
Mercado Latino Inc (PA)	5141	D	626 333-6862	8430
Micro-Technology Concepts Inc	5045	D	626 839-6800	7079
Mohan Dialysis Center Industry	8092	D	626 333-3801	22483
Morrow-Meadows Corporation (PA)	1731	A	858 974-3650	2652
MSI Computer Corp (HQ)	5045	D	626 913-0828	7081
Mtc Direct Inc (PA)	5045	D	626 839-6800	7082
Mtc Worldwide Corp	5045	D	626 839-6800	7083
Mtm & Thomasville Co	1542	D	626 934-1112	1597
Nafta Shoes Inc	7251	D	626 369-9681	13686
New Century Media Corp	5099	E	562 695-1000	8048
New Century Science & Tech	5091	D	626 581-5500	7935
Norman Fox & Co (PA)	5169	D	626 581-5600	8933
OTasty Foods Inc	5141	D	626 330-1229	8438
Performance Food Group Inc	5141	D	800 697-7662	8441
Performance Sheets LLC	1761	C	626 333-0195	3185
Port Logistics Group Inc	4214	D	909 839-5901	4367
Port Logistics Group Inc	4731	B	626 330-1300	5144
Potter Roemer LLC (HQ)	5031	C	626 855-4890	6855
Poundex Associates Corporation	5021	D	909 444-5878	6735
Prime Global Solutions Inc (PA)	4731	D	800 424-7746	5148
Private Label Pc LLC	5045	C	626 965-8686	7093
Pruithealth Inc	8059	E	626 810-5567	21190
Public Hlth Fndation Entps Inc (PA)	8641	A	800 201-7320	25226
Quartz Logistics Inc	4731	D	626 606-2001	5151
Quest Components Inc	5065	E	626 333-5858	7529
Quinn Shepherd Machinery	5082	B	562 463-6000	7691
Qy Research Inc	8742	D	626 295-2442	27416
Rongcheng Trading LLC	5147	C	626 338-1090	8629
Royal Crown Enterprises Inc (PA)	5149	D	626 854-8080	8863
Rutland Tool & Supply Co (HQ)	5085	D	562 566-5000	7868
Snap-On Incorporated	5072	C	626 965-0668	7603
Solestage Inc	7373	E	909 576-1309	16055
South Bay Freight System LLC (PA)	4731	D	626 271-9800	5173
Southern California Gas Co	4924	D	213 244-1200	6168
Swatfame Inc (PA)	5137	B	626 961-7928	8337
Sweda Company LLC	5094	C	626 357-9999	8013
Tf Courier Inc	4215	D	214 560-9000	4436
Thunder Group Inc (PA)	5023	E	626 935-1605	6792
Time Warner Cable Inc	4841	D	626 705-7482	5957
Topocean Consolidation Service (PA)	4731	D	562 908-1688	5181
U C L Incorporated (PA)	4213	D	323 235-0099	4283
Unical Aviation Inc (PA)	5088	C	909 348-1700	7917
Unical Enterprises Inc	5045	D	626 965-5588	7124
United Pumping Service Inc	4212	D	626 961-9326	4075
US Air Conditioning Distrs LLC	5075	D	626 854-0429	7660
US Bankcard Services Inc	7389	D	888 888-8872	17553
Valley Management Services	8741	B	626 333-1243	27081
W Diamond Supply Co (DH)	5023	D	909 859-8939	6803
Waterhill Ltd	5021	E	626 369-6828	6743
Yale/Chase Eqp & Svcs Inc (PA)	5084	C	562 463-8000	7822
Zerep Management Corporation	4953	D	626 961-6291	6528
Zmodo Technology Corp Ltd	5065	A	217 903-5673	7570

CLAREMONT, CA - Los Angeles County

Company	SIC	EMP	PHONE	ENTRY #
Ben Bollinger Productions Inc	7922	D	909 626-3296	18344
Bluebridge Professional Svcs	8082	D	909 625-6151	22237
Citigroup Global Markets Inc	6211	D	909 625-0781	9939
Claremont Star LP	7011	E	909 482-0124	12464
Claremont Tennis Club	7997	C	909 625-9515	18892
Corey Nursery Co Inc (PA)	5193	D	909 621-6886	9131
Epitome Enterprises LLC	7371	D	909 625-4728	15142
Front Porch Communities	8059	C	909 626-1227	21072
Guillen Electric Company Inc	1731	E	909 480-3915	2595
HDR Engineering Inc	8711	D	909 626-0967	25730
Hotline Telecommunications (PA)	1731	D	909 593-6575	2609
Kaiser Foundation Hospitals	8062	B	888 750-0036	21522
Lovely Living Homecare	8082	D	909 625-7999	22360
Pilgrim Place In Claremont (PA)	8059	D	909 399-5500	21186
Pilgrim Place In Claremont	7231	D	909 621-9581	13668
Pomona College	7331	C	909 621-8000	14058
Pomona Valley Hospital Med Ctr	8062	A	909 865-9104	21653
Pomona Valley Hospital Med Ctr	8049	D	909 621-7956	20196
Pomona Valley Hospital Med Ctr	8062	A	909 865-9977	21654
Rancho Santa Ana Botanic Grdn	8422	D	909 625-8767	24934
Therapak LLC (DH)	5047	D	909 267-2000	7223
Tierra Del Sol Foundation	7999	D	909 626-8301	19245
Trinity Youth Services (PA)	8361	D	909 980-4755	24700
Visiting Nurse Associ	8082	D	909 621-3961	22446
Western Feld Invstigations Inc (PA)	7375	D	800 999-9589	16261

Mergent email: customerrelations@mergent.com
1558
2019 Directory of California
Wholesalers and Services Companies
(P-0000) Products & Services Section entry number
(PA)=Parent Co (HQ)=Headquarters (DH)=Div Headquarters

	SIC	EMP	PHONE	ENTRY #

CLARKSBURG, CA - Yolo County

	SIC	EMP	PHONE	ENTRY #
Vino Farms Inc	0191	C	916 775-4095	393

CLAYTON, CA - Contra Costa County

American Golf Corporation	7997	D	925 672-9737	18837

CLEARLAKE, CA - Lake County

Adventist Health Clearlake (HQ)	8062	B	707 994-6486	21263
Adventist Health System/West	8011	C	707 995-4888	19269
Adventist Health System/West	8062	E	707 995-4500	21267
Adventist Health System/West	8011	B	707 994-6486	19270
Advintist Hlth Clearlake Hosp	8062	B	707 994-6486	21269
Vindra Inc	8051	D	707 994-7738	20866

CLEARLAKE OAKS, CA - Lake County

Shannon Ranches Inc	8742	C	707 998-9656	27447

CLOVERDALE, CA - Sonoma County

Ensign Cloverdale LLC	8051	D	707 894-5201	20394
Pacific States Industries Inc	5031	C	707 894-4242	6849
Redwood Credit Union	6061	C	800 479-7928	9581
Star H-R	7361	A	707 894-4404	14771

CLOVIS, CA - Fresno County

Agrian Inc (PA)	7379	D	559 437-5700	16308
Agriculture and Priority Pollu (PA)	8734	E	559 275-2175	26681
AT&T Corp.	4813	D	559 294-5431	5462
Blair Engineering Inc (PA)	8711	A	559 326-1400	25569
Borunda Private SEC Patrol Inc	7381	E	559 299-2662	16585
Bowie Enterprises	7542	D	559 292-6565	17805
C2 Financial Corporation	6282	C	559 824-2300	10065
Cellco Partnership	4812	C	559 325-1420	5363
Central Valley Community Bank (HQ)	6022	C	559 323-3384	9431
Central Valley Indian Hlth Inc (PA)	8011	C	559 299-2578	19367
Clovis Custom Drywall Inc	1742	E	559 297-7073	2867
Clovis Unified School District	7911	B	559 327-3900	18332
County of Fresno	8322	D	559 600-5127	23639
Craftman Concrete	1521	D	559 298-8864	1150
Death Valley 49ers Inc	8699	D	559 297-5691	25415
Elite Landscaping Inc	0782	C	559 292-7760	835
Floyd Johnston Cnstr Co Inc	1623	D	559 299-7373	1918
Fresno Cmnty Hosp & Med Ctr	8062	D	559 324-4000	21421
George Browns Sports Club (PA)	7991	D	559 297-8656	18603
Golden Living LLC	8051	D	559 299-2591	20477
Graham Concrete Cnstr Inc	1771	D	559 292-6571	3260
Guarantee Real Estate Corp	6531	D	559 321-6040	11497
Hodges Electric Inc	1731	E	559 298-5533	2607
Kaiser Foundation Hospitals	6324	D	559 324-5100	10237
Kings Credit Services	7322	D	559 322-2550	14011
Krazan & Associates (PA)	8748	D	559 348-2200	27767
Labor One Inc	0761	D	559 430-4202	658
Ladell Inc	1711	E	559 650-2000	2256
Niacc-Avitech Technologies Inc (PA)	7699	D	559 291-2500	17964
Peachwood Medical Group Clovis	8011	D	559 324-6200	19756
Pk Autobody Inc	7532	E	559 298-9691	17732
Regent Assisted Living Inc	8361	D	559 325-8400	24650
Tri-Star Drywall Lp	1742	D	559 299-9858	2973
Valleywide Construction Inc	1521	C	559 834-6212	1253
Vibra Healthcare LLC	8062	D	559 325-5601	21904
Westech Systems Inc	1731	D	559 298-5237	2787
Willow Creek Hralthcare Ctr LLC	8051	A	559 323-6200	20892
Willow Creek Hralthcare Ctr LLC	8051	D	559 323-6200	20893

COACHELLA, CA - Riverside County

29 Palms Enterprises Corp	7999	A	760 775-5566	19089
Coachella Valley Water Dst (PA)	4941	C	760 398-2651	6229
Desert Valley Date Inc	0723	D	760 398-0999	506
Downtown Metro	4812	E	760 398-3310	5405
Esparza Enterprises Inc	7361	A	760 398-0349	14617
L&D Farm Labor	0761	E	760 408-6311	657
Primetime International Inc	5148	D	760 399-4166	8718
SA Recycling LLC	4953	D	760 391-5591	6465
Sun and Sands Enterprises LLC (PA)	0161	D	760 399-4278	83
Sun World International Inc	0723	B	760 398-9300	573
Sunline Transit Agency	4119	C	760 972-4059	3852
Teserra (PA)	1799	D	760 340-9000	3592
Valley Pride Inc	0722	D	760 398-1353	487

COALINGA, CA - Fresno County

Califrnia Dept State Hospitals	8063	B	559 935-4300	21931
Coalinga Dstngished Cmnty Care	8051	D	559 935-5939	20317
Coalinga Regional Medical Cent	8062	C	559 935-6400	21329
Harris Farms Inc	0191	E	559 884-2203	351
Harris Farms Inc	0191	D	559 935-0717	352
Harris Farms Inc	0191	B	559 884-2477	353
Harris Woolf Cal Almonds LLC (PA)	0723	C	559 884-2147	528

COARSEGOLD, CA - Madera County

Chukchansi Gold Resort Casino	7011	A	866 794-6946	12459
Wb Electric Inc	1731	D	408 842-7911	2784
Yosemite Lakes Owners Assn	8641	D	559 658-7466	25316

COLMA, CA - San Mateo County

Cypress Funeral Services Inc	7261	C	650 550-8808	13688
Lucky Chances Inc	7999	A	650 758-2237	19200
Precision Auto Detailing LLC	7542	D	650 992-9775	17835

COLTON, CA - San Bernardino County

A-Z Bus Sales Inc (PA)	5012	D	951 781-7188	6570
Arrowhead Regional Medical Ctr	8062	A	909 580-1000	21291
Bob Hubbard Horse Trnsp Inc (PA)	4212	E	951 369-3770	3980
Brithinee Electric	5063	D	909 825-7971	7340
C E P	8011	D	909 580-1456	19336
Cardinal Health Inc	5122	D	909 824-1820	8151
CBS Radio Inc	4832	C	909 825-9525	5702
Charter Hospice Inc	8052	C	909 825-2969	20920
Colton Joint Unified Schl Dst	8351	D	909 876-4240	24298
Cornerstone Hospice Cal LLC	8082	D	909 872-8100	22278
County of San Bernardino	8071	C	909 580-1000	22074
GATX Corporation	4789	D	909 825-3043	5226
Greenpath Recovery West Inc	5093	D	909 954-0686	7980
Inland Eye Inst Med Group Inc (PA)	8011	D	909 825-3425	19511
Kaiser Foundation Hospitals	6733	A	909 427-5521	12108
King Equipment LLC	7353	D	909 986-5300	14444
Medlin Development	0782	E	909 825-5296	896
Pacific Vision Services Inc	8042	D	909 824-6090	20159
Premier Medical Trnsp Inc	4119	D	909 433-3939	3830
Reche Cyn Rhbliation Hlth Ctr	8051	B	909 370-4411	20718
Republic Services Inc	4953	E	909 370-3377	6451
SA Recycling LLC	4953	D	909 825-1662	6470
Sisters of Soul (sos) Youth	8611	D	909 533-4889	24982
Southern Cal Prmnnte Med Group	8011	E	909 370-2501	19913
Sprouts Farmers Market Inc	4225	C	888 577-7688	4634
Superior Masonry Walls Ltd	1741	D	909 370-1800	2825
Valley Ob Gyn Medical Group	8011	E	909 580-6333	20045
Van Dyk Tank Lines Inc	4212	E	951 682-5000	4084
VFW Post 6476	8641	D	909 754-3828	25277
Western Healthcare Management	8051	C	909 824-1530	20884
Westrux International Inc	4731	D	909 825-5121	5200

COLUMBIA, CA - Tuolumne County

Twain Harte Horsemen	8641	D	209 601-5585	25270
Zephyr River Expeditions Inc	7999	D	800 431-3636	19265

COLUSA, CA - Colusa County

Childrens Services	8322	D	530 458-0300	23571
Colusa Cnty Sbstnce Abuse Svcs	8322	D	530 458-0520	23592
Colusa Indian Cmnty Council	8399	A	530 458-6572	24753
Colusa Regional Medical Center	8741	C	530 458-5821	26815
New Colusa Indian Bingo	7999	B	530 458-8844	19208
Premier Mushrooms LP (PA)	5148	C	530 458-2700	8717
Premier Mushrooms LP	0182	C	530 458-2700	321

COMMERCE, CA - Los Angeles County

4 Earth Farms Inc (PA)	5148	D	323 201-5800	8636
Acco Engineered Systems Inc	7623	D	323 727-7765	17889
Acco Engineered Systems Inc	7389	E	323 201-0931	16980
Adj Products LLC (PA)	5063	C	323 582-2650	7325
Altamed Health Services Corp (PA)	8011	C	323 725-8751	19279
American De Rosa Lamparts LLC (PA)	5063	D	800 777-4440	7328
American Security Force Inc	7381	C	323 722-8585	16567
Arden-Mayfair Inc	4225	E	310 638-2842	4531
Ashland LLC	5169	D	323 767-1300	8919
Associated Landscape	7389	D	714 558-6100	17014
Bctc Corporation	5137	D	323 888-9388	8288
Ben Myerson Candy Co Inc (PA)	5182	B	800 331-2829	9034
Bnsf Railway Company	4011	C	323 869-3002	3616
Buy Fresh Produce Inc	5148	D	323 796-0127	8644
California Commerce Club Inc	7011	A	323 721-2100	12421
California Produce Wholsalers	5148	E	562 776-5770	8649
Califrnia Intermodal Assoc Inc (PA)	4213	D	323 562-7788	4114
Cellco Partnership	4812	D	323 725-9750	5398
Celluphone LLC	5065	C	323 727-9131	7461
Ceramic Decorating Company Inc	7389	E	323 268-5135	17067
Challenge Dairy Products Inc	5143	E	323 724-3130	8516
CIT Bank National Association	6021	D	323 838-6881	9327
City of Commerce	7999	B	323 722-4805	19127
Commerce Center Theatres	7832	D	323 722-5577	18283
County of Los Angeles	8399	D	323 869-7063	24768
County of Los Angeles	8322	B	323 889-3405	23657
D J American Supply Inc	5099	C	323 582-2600	8024
Dart International A Corp (HQ)	4214	C	323 264-8746	4342
East Los Angeles Community Un (PA)	6153	E	323 721-1655	9737
East Los Angeles Mental Hlth	8093	D	323 725-1337	22572

Employment Codes: A=Over 500 employees, B=251-500,
C=101-250, D=51-100, E=50

2019 Directory of California
Wholesalers and Services Companies

© Mergent Inc. 1-800-342-5647

1559

GEOGRAPHIC

Company	SIC	EMP	PHONE	ENTRY #
EDS West LLC	4212	D	323 887-7367	4009
El Guapo Spices Inc **(PA)**	5149	D	213 312-1300	8786
Elkay Plastics Co Inc **(PA)**	5113	D	323 722-7073	8101
Ernest Packaging **(PA)**	5199	C	800 233-7788	9215
Evans Dedicated Systems Inc **(PA)**	4213	C	323 725-2928	4147
Express Messenger Systems Inc	4215	D	323 725-2100	4400
Farwest Insulation Contracting	1742	E	310 634-2800	2883
Fedex Smartpost Inc	4215	D	323 888-8879	4419
Fox Luggage Inc	5099	D	323 588-1688	8030
Gehr Development Corporation **(HQ)**	6512	D	323 728-5558	10882
Gibson Overseas Inc	5023	A	323 832-8900	6764
Glamour Industries Co	5122	B	323 728-2999	8170
Gold Coast Ingredients Inc	5149	D	323 724-8935	8799
Grocers Specialty Company **(DH)**	5141	E	323 264-5200	8412
Haldeman Inc	1711	E	323 726-7011	2226
Hkf Inc **(PA)**	5075	B	323 225-1318	7651
Innovo Azteca Apparel Inc	5131	D	323 837-3700	8227
Interstate Electric Co Inc **(PA)**	5046	D	323 724-0420	7137
Interstate Meat & Provision	5142	D	323 838-9400	8491
Ivo Wall Experts Inc	1742	D	323 246-4026	2899
Iworks Us Inc	1791	D	323 278-8363	3378
Jfc International Inc **(HQ)**	5149	C	323 721-6100	8812
Jfc International Inc	5149	C	323 721-6900	8813
Justman Packaging & Display	5046	D	323 728-8888	7142
LA Impact	7389	D	323 869-6874	17284
Malibu Design Group	5137	E	323 271-1700	8318
Maravilla Foundation **(PA)**	8641	D	323 721-4162	25196
Meridian Textiles Inc **(PA)**	5131	D	323 869-5700	8232
Mexican Amrcn Oprtnty Fndation	8322	D	323 890-1555	23922
Michelson Laboratories Inc **(PA)**	8734	D	562 928-0553	26713
Miken Sales Inc **(PA)**	5137	D	323 266-2560	8322
Milspec Industries Inc **(DH)**	5072	D	213 680-9690	7598
Nora Lighting Inc	5063	D	800 686-6672	7382
Nurses Internet Staffing Svcs **(PA)**	7361	C	323 720-9900	14678
Packaging Manufacturing Inc	5199	C	619 498-9199	9245
Parsec Inc	4789	A	323 268-5011	5240
Penny Lane Centers	8399	C	323 318-9960	24826
Pixior LLC **(PA)**	7389	D	323 721-2221	17403
Printing Inds Assn Suthern Cal	8611	D	323 728-9500	24973
Progressive Produce LLC **(HQ)**	5148	C	323 890-8100	8723
Prudential Overall Supply	7218	D	323 724-4888	13612
Prudential Overall Supply	7218	D	323 722-0636	13617
PWS Holdings LLC	5087	D	323 721-8832	7896
Ramcar Batteries Inc	5013	E	323 726-1212	6668
Reading Entertainment Inc **(HQ)**	7832	D	213 235-2226	18312
Rolled Steel Products Corp **(PA)**	5051	D	323 723-8836	7310
Screamline Investment Corp **(PA)**	4725	C	323 201-0114	4980
Securitas SEC Svcs USA Inc	7381	C	323 832-9074	16807
Seiu United Healthcare Workers	8631	E	323 734-8399	25080
Shason Inc **(PA)**	5131	D	323 269-6666	8243
Shims Bargain Inc	1541	C	323 726-8800	1433
Smart & Final Stores Inc **(PA)**	5141	B	323 869-7500	8453
Solemnity Personnel	7361	E	323 718-3979	14764
Starline Tours Hollywood Inc	4725	D	323 262-1114	4981
Streamline Shippers Assn Inc **(PA)**	8611	C	323 271-3800	24985
Sun Coast Merchandise Corp	5099	C	323 720-9700	8060
Telacu Industries Inc **(HQ)**	6162	E	323 721-1655	9862
Tpg La Commerce LLC	7011	D	401 946-4600	13335
Unified Grocers Inc **(DH)**	5141	A	323 264-5200	8474
Union Pacific Railroad Company	4011	D	213 446-1900	3631
Uniserve Facilities Svcs Corp **(PA)**	7349	B	213 533-1000	14414
United Insurance Company	6411	E	323 869-9381	10810
United Parcel Service Inc OH	7389	B	323 837-1220	17536
Univar USA Inc	5169	C	323 727-7005	8938
Veritiv Operating Company	5113	C	323 725-3700	8134
W2005 Wyn Hotels LP	7011	D	323 887-8100	13376
Waste Mgt Collectn & Recycl	4953	C	626 960-7551	6515
Wood Environment &	8711	D	323 889-5300	26005
Wyndham International Inc	7011	D	323 887-4331	13427
Zemarc Corporation **(PA)**	5084	E	323 721-5598	7823

COMPTON, CA - Los Angeles County

Company	SIC	EMP	PHONE	ENTRY #
Advanced Logistics MGT Inc	4213	E	310 638-0715	4095
All Phase Business Supplies	5112	E	310 631-1900	8075
Apex Logistics Intl Inc **(PA)**	4731	D	310 665-0288	5010
Appliance Recycling Ctrs Amer	4953	D	310 223-2800	6338
Asbury Environmental Services **(PA)**	4212	D	310 886-3400	3975
Auto Expressions LLC	5013	D	310 639-0666	6622
Az/CFS West Inc	4226	D	310 898-2090	4665
Beauchamp Distributing Company	5181	D	310 639-5320	8982
Benettis Italia Inc	5021	D	310 537-8036	6711
Blake H Brown Inc **(DH)**	5084	D	310 764-0110	7732
Bst Enterprises Inc	5013	D	310 638-1222	6628
Cal-State Steel Corporation	1791	C	310 632-2772	3368
CCC Property Holdings LLC	6719	C	310 609-1957	11968
Celebrity Casinos Inc	7011	B	310 631-3838	12445

Company	SIC	EMP	PHONE	ENTRY #
Cintas Corporation No 3	7218	D	310 725-2850	13602
City of Compton	7999	D	310 635-3484	19128
Color Ad Inc	7311	E	310 632-5500	13804
Colosseum Athletics Corp	5136	D	310 667-8341	8253
Concrete Tie Industries Inc	5032	D	310 886-1000	6882
Contractors Cargo Company **(PA)**	4213	C	310 609-1957	4118
Cordelia Lighting Inc	5063	C	310 886-3490	7351
County of Los Angeles	8099	D	310 885-2100	22773
County of Los Angeles	8099	D	310 668-6845	22774
County of Los Angeles	8111	D	310 603-7483	22999
County of Los Angeles	8111	D	310 603-7271	23001
County of Los Angeles	8322	D	310 603-7311	23682
County Santtn Dist 2 of La Co	4959	D	310 638-1161	6537
Crew Inc	1794	D	310 608-6860	3421
Decky Co Inc **(PA)**	5136	D	310 608-2726	8254
Demenno Kerdoon	1382	C	310 537-7100	1043
Demenno-Kerdoon	4212	B	310 898-3848	4002
Dependable Aircargo Ex Inc	4731	C	310 537-2000	5042
Dhx-Dependable Hawaiian Ex Inc **(PA)**	4731	C	310 537-2000	5046
Dna Specialty Inc	5013	D	310 767-4070	6635
Dnow LP	4226	D	310 900-3900	4673
Dti Inc	4212	D	310 635-9002	4008
Element Mtrls Tech HB Inc	8734	D	310 632-8500	26695
Evox Productions LLC **(PA)**	7371	D	310 605-1400	15154
Express Messenger Systems Inc	4215	D	800 359-2959	4406
F R T International Inc **(PA)**	4225	C	310 604-8208	4555
Florence Filter Corporation	5075	D	310 637-1137	7648
FNS Customs Brokers Inc	4731	E	310 667-4880	5065
General Petroleum Corporation **(DH)**	5172	C	562 983-7300	8961
Geodis Logistics LLC	4225	C	310 604-8185	4563
Global Mail Inc	4731	C	310 735-0800	5074
Gourmet Foods Inc **(PA)**	5141	D	310 632-3300	8410
Hydroprocessing Associates LLC	7389	E	310 667-6456	17228
Industrial Valco Inc **(PA)**	5085	E	310 635-0711	7852
Interstate Foods Inc	5144	C	310 635-0426	8533
Jack Rubin & Sons Inc **(PA)**	5051	D	310 635-5407	7282
JAM Industries Inc	4225	D	310 254-0300	4580
Kawai America Corporation **(HQ)**	5099	E	310 631-1771	8041
Knight Transportation Inc	4213	C	888 549-7802	4205
Los Angeles County Health Svc	8011	E	310 763-2244	19661
Lynwood Developmental Care	8059	D	310 764-2023	21146
M M Fab Inc	5131	D	310 763-3800	8231
Mitsubishi Warehouse Cal Corp	4225	D	310 886-5500	4595
Monico Alloys Inc **(PA)**	5051	D	310 928-0168	7291
Nabors Well Services Co	1389	C	310 639-7074	1071
National Retail Trnsp Inc	4213	D	310 605-3777	4233
New Pride Corporation	7534	E	310 631-7000	17749
Newport Apparel Corporation **(PA)**	5137	D	310 605-1900	8326
Ocean Knight Shipping Inc	4731	C	310 885-3388	5126
Pacific Lighting Mfr Inc	5063	D	310 327-7711	7384
Pasha Group	4731	C	310 735-0952	5137
Petrochem Insulation Inc	1742	C	310 638-6663	2938
Pitney Bowes Presort Svcs Inc	7389	C	310 763-4615	17401
Port Logistics Group Inc	4214	C	310 669-2551	4366
Progressive Trnsp Svcs Inc	5085	D	510 268-3776	7866
Purolator International Inc	4731	D	650 871-7075	5150
Quality Production Svcs Inc	1742	D	310 406-3350	2944
RPM Mechanical - A Joint Ventr	1711	D	858 565-4131	2342
Southern California Edison Co	4911	C	310 608-5029	6130
St George Whsng Trckg Cal Inc **(DH)**	4225	D	310 764-4395	4635
Star View Chldrn Fmly Srvcs	8322	D	310 868-5379	24074
Stk International Inc	5092	D	310 720-1277	7962
Tap Operating Co LLC	5013	A	310 900-5500	6678
Tap Worldwide LLC **(PA)**	5013	A	310 900-5500	6679
Transport Express Inc	4214	D	310 898-2000	4379
Uma Enterprises Inc **(PA)**	5023	C	310 631-1166	6797
United Fabricare Supply Inc **(PA)**	5087	D	310 886-3790	7900
USA Waste of California Inc	4953	D	310 763-8500	6498
Vanguard Lgistics Svcs USA Inc	4225	D	310 637-3700	4653
Viharas Group Inc	6722	D	310 537-6700	12051
Wenzlau Engineering Inc	5065	D	310 604-3400	7562
World Wide Technology Inc	5045	E	310 537-8335	7130

CONCORD, CA - Contra Costa County

Company	SIC	EMP	PHONE	ENTRY #
Admiral Security Services Inc	7382	B	888 471-1128	16868
ADT Security Corporation	7382	E	925 251-9088	16869
Agostini and Associates Inc	7363	E	925 691-7300	14811
Albert D Seeno Cnstr Co Inc	1531	D	925 671-7711	1329
Alsco Inc	7213	C	707 751-0652	13501
American Brdge/Fluor Entps Inc	1622	C	510 808-4623	1873
American Medical Response	4119	C	925 454-6000	3752
American Medical Response Inc	4119	C	925 602-1300	3758
American National Red Cross	8322	E	925 603-7400	23476
Anka Behavioral Health Inc **(PA)**	8093	C	925 825-4700	22504
Apria Healthcare LLC	5047	D	925 827-8800	7157
Aptim Corp	8711	A	925 288-2011	25540

2019 Directory of California
Wholesalers and Services Companies

(P-0000) Products & Services Section entry number
(PA)=Parent Co (HQ)=Headquarters (DH)=Div Headquarters

Company	SIC	EMP	PHONE	ENTRY #
Aramark Unf & Career AP LLC	7218	D	925 827-3782	13592
Ascent Services Group Inc	7363	B	925 627-4900	14819
Asrc Industrial Services LLC (HQ)	7363	C	707 644-7455	14820
Assetmark Inc (HQ)	6282	E	925 521-1040	10057
AT&T Corp	4813	D	925 356-6204	5451
AT&T Services Inc	4813	D	925 671-1902	5501
AT&T Services Inc	4813	B	925 671-1059	5507
Athens Insurance Service Inc	6411	C	925 826-1000	10550
Ausenco PSI LLC (HQ)	8711	D	925 939-4420	25554
Ausenco USA Inc (HQ)	8711	D	925 939-4420	25555
Bay Alarm Company (PA)	1731	D	925 935-1100	2517
Bay Area Seating Service Inc	7999	B	925 671-4000	19106
Bay Area/Diablo Petroleum Co	5172	C	925 228-2222	8951
Bay Cities Pav & Grading Inc	1794	C	925 687-6666	3415
Bay Medic Transportation Inc	4119	D	800 689-9511	3775
Bayside Insulation & Cnstr	1542	D	925 288-8960	1474
Brenden Theatre Corporation (PA)	7832	C	925 677-0462	18275
Building Services/System Inc	6512	D	925 688-1234	10859
California Ticketscom Inc	7922	C	925 671-4000	18352
Carlton Senior Living Inc	6552	D	925 935-1660	11862
Carone & Company Inc	1794	D	925 602-8800	3417
CDM SMITH INC	8711	D	617 452-6000	25600
City of Concord	7922	B	925 692-2400	18357
City of Concord	7992	D	925 686-6262	18694
Clyde Miles Cnstr Co Inc	1521	D	925 427-4473	1145
Coldwell Bnkr Residential Brkg (DH)	6531	D	925 275-3000	11350
Comcast Corporation	4841	B	925 271-9794	5888
Compumail Information Svcs Inc	7389	D	925 689-7100	17095
Concord Hotel LLC	7011	D	925 521-3751	12482
Concord Jet Service Inc (PA)	7359	E	925 682-4830	14489
Connexsys Engineering Inc	8711	E	510 243-2050	25620
Contra Costa Vet Med Emrgcy CL	0742	E	925 798-5830	600
Contra Costa Water District (PA)	4941	C	925 688-8000	6232
Cooper Vali & Associates Inc (DH)	8711	D	510 446-8301	25623
County of Contra Costa	7349	D	925 646-5877	14231
County of Contra Costa	8093	C	925 646-5480	22541
Courtyards At Pine Creek Inc	8361	E	925 798-3900	24484
Cowell Homeowners Association (PA)	8641	D	925 825-0250	25144
Customer Loyalty Builders Inc	8742	D	888 478-7787	27209
D A McCosker Construction Co	1611	D	925 686-1780	1754
D C Taylor Co	1761	E	925 603-1100	3146
Dave Calhoun and Assoc LLC (PA)	7349	C	925 688-1234	14251
Delta Personnel Services Inc	7381	D	925 356-3034	16629
Denova Home Sales Inc	6531	D	925 852-0545	11397
Dianne Adair Day Care Centers (PA)	8351	D	925 429-3232	24314
Edgewater Plumbing of Benicia	1711	E	707 747-9204	2198
Edgewood Partners Insur Ctr	6411	C	415 356-3900	10610
Edgewood Prtners Insur Ctr Inc (PA)	6411	D	415 356-3900	10612
Eichleay Engineers Inc	8711	B	925 689-7000	25654
Eichleay Inc (PA)	8711	C	925 689-7000	25656
Electric Tech Construction Inc	1623	D	925 849-5324	1916
Encore Inc	7999	E	925 932-1033	19167
Enterprise Roofing Service Inc	1761	D	925 689-8100	3154
Ernie & Sons Scaffolding	1799	C	925 446-4442	3514
Fidelity Nat HM Warranty Co	6351	D	925 356-0194	10428
First American Title Insur Co	6531	D	925 356-7000	11451
First American Title Insur Co	6361	D	925 798-2800	10461
First Student Inc	4142	D	925 676-1976	3897
Futures Explored	8322	D	925 332-7183	23819
General Electric Company	8711	D	925 602-5950	25706
Gilbane Aecom JV	8744	D	925 946-3100	27592
Gilbane Federal (DH)	8711	C	925 946-3100	25714
Gilbane Smcc LLC	1542	D	925 946-3100	1535
Goldman Avram	8741	D	925 275-3000	26874
Gonsalves & Santucci Inc (PA)	1771	A	925 685-6799	3259
Gonsalves & Santucci Inc	1791	C	707 745-5019	3375
Harris & Associates Inc (PA)	8711	D	925 827-4900	25722
Hemming Morse LLP (PA)	8721	D	415 836-4000	26217
Homecare Professionals Inc	8082	D	925 215-1214	22332
Jacobs Engineering Group Inc	8711	D	925 356-3900	25758
James C Jenkins Insur Svc Inc	6411	C	925 798-3334	10658
Janus Corporation (PA)	1799	D	925 969-9200	3536
John Muir Behavioral Hlth Ctr	8063	C	925 674-4100	21958
John Muir Health	8062	A	925 692-5600	21463
John Muir Health	8062	A	925 682-8200	21468
John Muir Physician Network	8062	A	925 682-8200	21471
John Muir Physician Network	8062	A	925 674-2200	21474
Jopari Solutions Inc	7389	D	925 459-5200	17264
Kindred Healthcare Oper Inc	8051	C	925 692-5886	20554
Kissito Health Case Inc	8082	C	925 689-9222	22355
Kyocera Dcment Sltons Amer Inc	5044	D	925 849-3300	6968
Land Home Financial Svcs Inc (PA)	6162	E	925 676-7038	9824
Leisure Planet	7999	D	925 687-4386	19195
Lemore Transportation Inc (PA)	4213	D	925 689-6444	4215
Lescure Company Inc	1711	D	925 283-2528	2262
McE Corporation (PA)	1611	D	925 803-4111	1817
Microbiology & Qulty Assoc Inc	8733	E	925 288-1400	26639
Mike McCall Landscape Inc	0782	C	925 363-8100	898
Mike Roses Auto Body Inc	7532	E	925 686-1739	17730
Montclair Hotels Mb LLC	7011	D	925 687-5500	12939
New Way LLC	8361	D	925 688-1520	24610
Nextel Communications Inc	4812	D	925 682-2355	5413
Office Movers Inc	4214	E	408 254-5010	4363
Overmiller Inc	7699	D	925 798-2122	17967
Pace Inc	1742	D	925 602-0900	2930
Pacific Gas and Electric Co	4911	D	925 676-0948	6076
Pacific Gas and Electric Co	4911	D	925 674-6305	6081
Pacific Service Credit Union (PA)	6061	D	888 858-6878	9579
Pacificdental Benefits Inc (PA)	6324	C	925 363-6000	10292
Parc Management LLC	7999	A	925 609-1364	19214
Patriot Contract Services LLC	4412	B	925 296-2000	4699
Peppermill Casinos Inc	7011	C	925 671-7111	13058
Planned Prnthod Shst-Dblo Inc (PA)	8093	E	925 676-0300	22648
Precision Television Inc	7622	D	925 825-5296	17886
Ricoh Usa Inc	5044	C	925 988-4000	6982
Seecon Built Homes Inc	6552	D	925 671-7711	11914
Service Hospitality LLC	7011	D	925 566-8820	13206
Shelter Inc (PA)	8322	D	925 335-0698	24049
Sierra Bay Contractors Inc	1541	E	925 671-7711	1434
Stonebrook Convalescent Center	8051	C	925 689-7457	20783
Summit Building Services Inc	7349	D	925 827-9500	14402
Sutter Vsting Nrse Assn Hspice	8082	D	925 677-4250	22431
Swift Worldwide Inc (PA)	4213	C	510 351-7949	4273
Swinerton Builders Inc	1521	D	925 602-6400	1244
Swinerton Incorporated	1522	D	925 689-2336	1318
Telstar Instruments (PA)	1731	C	925 671-2888	2765
Tranquility Incorporated	8059	C	925 825-4280	21230
Travis Credit Union	6061	B	800 877-8328	9600
Ufcw & Employers Trust LLC (PA)	6733	C	800 552-2400	12129
United Behavioral Health	6324	C	925 246-1343	10323
United Parcel Service Inc OH	4215	C	925 689-6584	4472
URS Group Inc	8711	D	925 446-3800	25977
Valley Relocation and Storage (PA)	4214	C	925 230-2025	4385
Value-Centered Solutions Inc	8742	E	510 662-3333	27505
Versa Engineering & Tech Inc (PA)	8711	D	925 405-4505	25990
Veterinary Surgical Associates (PA)	0742	C	925 827-1777	618
Vwi Concord LLC	7011	C	925 827-2000	13371
Wells Fargo Bank National Assn	6021	D	925 746-3718	9388
Willow Pass Hlth Care Ctr Inc	8082	D	925 689-9222	22464
Windsor Convalescent	8051	C	925 689-2266	20897
Young MNS Chrstn Assn of E Bay	8641	A	925 609-7971	25355
Youth Homes Incorporated	8361	D	925 933-2627	24726
Yupana Inc	8711	E	925 482-0657	26015
Zero Waste Solutions Inc	8744	C	925 270-3339	27612
Zwicker & Associates PC	8111	C	925 689-7070	23452

COPPEROPOLIS, CA - Calaveras County

Company	SIC	EMP	PHONE	ENTRY #
Commercial Site Imprvs Inc	1794	E	209 785-1920	3420
Meridian Gold Inc	1041	C	209 785-3222	1006

CORCORAN, CA - Kings County

Company	SIC	EMP	PHONE	ENTRY #
Corcoran District Hospital	8062	D	559 992-3300	21343
Gilkey Farms Inc	0131	D	559 992-2136	12
Hansen Equipment Company LLC	0762	E	559 992-3111	694
Hansen Ranches	0191	D	559 992-3111	350
J G Boswell Company	0723	D	559 992-2141	531
J G Boswell Company	0131	B	559 992-5141	14
Jason Proctor Trnsp Co	4119	E	559 992-1767	3810
Vista Verde Farms Inc	0721	D	559 992-3111	470

CORNING, CA - Tehama County

Company	SIC	EMP	PHONE	ENTRY #
Andersncttonwood Disposal Svcs	4212	D	530 824-4700	3971
Omega Waste Management Inc	8742	D	530 824-1890	27374
Paskenta Band Nomlaki Indians	7011	B	530 528-3500	13049

CORONA, CA - Riverside County

Company	SIC	EMP	PHONE	ENTRY #
ABC School Equipment Inc	5049	D	951 817-2200	7239
Ability Counts Inc (PA)	8331	D	951 734-6595	24144
Acm Technologies Inc (PA)	5044	D	951 738-9898	6948
Advanced Communication Service	7389	C	909 210-9328	16986
Ae & Associates LLC	8748	C	951 278-3477	27621
Agile Sourcing Partners Inc	4939	C	951 279-4154	6194
AK Constructors Inc	1542	D	951 280-0269	1461
All American Asphalt (PA)	1611	A	951 736-7600	1714
All American Asphalt	1611	C	951 736-7617	1715
All American Asphalt	1611	D	951 736-7617	1716
All American Service & Sups	7699	C	951 736-3880	17930
Amec Fster Wheler E C Svcs Inc	8711	C	951 273-7400	25529
American Electric Supply Inc (PA)	5063	C	951 734-7910	7329
Amerisourcebergen Corporation	5122	C	951 493-2339	8140
Amerisourcebergen Drug Corp	5122	C	951 371-2000	8143
ARC Fastener Supply & Mfg	5085	D	909 481-8171	7828

Employment Codes: A=Over 500 employees, B=251-500,
C=101-250, D=51-100, E=50

2019 Directory of California
Wholesalers and Services Companies

© Mergent Inc. 1-800-342-5647
1561

	SIC	EMP	PHONE	ENTRY #
Arizona Pipeline Company	1623	C	951 270-3100	1893
Auto Buyline Systems Inc (PA)	5012	E	909 881-7828	6579
Beador Construction Co Inc	1611	D	951 674-7352	1729
Brookdale Senior Living Inc	8059	D	951 808-9387	21022
C & R Systems Inc (PA)	1731	D	951 270-0255	2533
Calatlantic Group Inc	1521	D	951 898-5500	1135
Cannon Fabrication Inc	1761	D	951 278-1830	3132
Canyon Insulation Inc	1742	D	951 278-9200	2860
Cellco Partnership	4812	D	951 549-6400	5332
Cellco Partnership	4812	D	951 898-0980	5341
Championship Golf Services Inc	7992	C	951 272-4340	18693
Chief Protective Services Inc	7381	C	951 738-0881	16602
Chilis 898 Corona	8741	D	951 734-7275	26802
Citizens Business Bank	6029	E	951 808-8940	9499
City of Corona	8743	C	951 279-3647	27548
City of Corona	4939	D	951 736-2266	6196
Combustion Associates Inc	4911	E	951 272-6999	6021
Comcast Corporation	4841	D	951 268-9378	5877
Community Access Network	8322	D	951 279-1333	23594
Compass Bank	6029	B	951 279-7071	9501
Core-Mark Corona 2	5141	E	800 622-1206	8393
Corona Clipper Inc	5072	C	951 737-6515	7584
Couts Heating & Cooling Inc	1711	D	951 278-5560	2175
De La Torre Landscape & Maint	0782	C	951 549-3525	820
Downs Fuel Transport Inc	5172	C	951 256-8286	8954
DR Horton Inc	1531	E	951 272-9000	1337
Eagle Glen Country Club LLC	7992	D	951 272-4653	18710
Ebs Concrete Inc	1771	E	951 279-6869	3252
Ebs General Engineering Inc	1611	D	951 279-6869	1762
Empire Demolition Inc	1771	D	909 393-8300	3253
Excel Landscape Inc	0782	C	951 735-9650	839
Express Cable Communication	4841	D	951 272-2029	5913
F M Tarbell Co	6531	C	951 280-6040	11432
Fennel Inc	1751	D	951 284-2020	3035
Fire Sprinkler Systems Inc (PA)	1711	D	800 915-3473	2211
First Student Inc	4173	C	951 736-3234	3953
Fst Sand & Gravel Inc	5032	E	951 277-8440	6893
Fullmer Cattle Nthrn Cal LLC	0212	C	909 597-3274	399
Green River Golf Corporation	7992	D	714 970-8411	18716
H & H Transportation LLC	4213	D	951 817-2300	4188
Halo Unlimted Inc	8099	D	714 692-2270	22810
Hardwood Creations (PA)	1751	D	714 674-0527	3040
Hillcrest Contracting Inc	1611	D	951 273-9600	1791
Hoffman Concrete Company Inc	1771	E	951 372-8333	3265
HP Communications Inc	1623	C	951 572-1200	1928
JJ Mac Intyre Co Inc (PA)	7322	C	951 898-4300	14010
K&B Electric LLC	8711	C	951 808-9501	25773
K&B Engineering	8711	C	951 808-9501	25774
Kaiser Foundation Hospitals	8099	D	866 984-7483	22827
Kaiser Foundation Hospitals	6733	A	866 984-7483	12109
Kec Engineering	1611	C	951 734-3010	1800
La Steel Services Inc	1791	E	951 393-2013	3383
Laurence-Hovenier Inc	1751	C	951 736-2990	3049
LDI Mechanical Inc (PA)	1711	C	951 340-9685	2259
Lennar Homes Inc	1531	C	951 739-0267	1350
Lexani Wheel Corporation	5013	C	951 808-4220	6655
Live Media LLC	7929	E	951 279-8877	18446
M E Nollkamper Inc (PA)	8742	E	951 737-9300	27310
Management Trust Assn Inc	6733	C	951 694-1758	12114
Marie Cllender Wholesalers Inc	5142	D	951 737-6760	8495
Marriott International Inc	7011	C	951 371-0107	12897
Minka Lighting Inc (PA)	5063	D	951 735-9220	7377
Mission Ambulance Inc	4119	D	951 272-2200	3823
Monster Energy Company (DH)	5149	C	951 739-6200	8829
More Truck Lines Inc	4212	D	951 371-6673	4042
Multi Mechanical Inc	1711	D	714 632-7404	2285
National Distribution Services	5099	D	951 739-2400	8047
Nep Group Inc	7812	E	951 279-8877	18082
Pacific Shores Masonry	1741	E	951 371-8550	2820
Pacwest Instrument Labs Inc	7699	D	951 737-0790	17969
Paramount Bldg Solutions LLC	7349	C	951 272-4001	14343
Parcell Steel Corp Inc	1791	C	951 471-3200	3390
Peaceful Hearts Home Care Inc	8082	D	951 541-9343	22391
Peoples Choice Staffing Inc	7361	C	951 735-0550	14692
Peppermint Ridge (PA)	8361	D	951 273-7320	24629
Ply Gem Pacific Windows Corp	5031	D	951 272-1300	6854
Preferred Insulation Contrs (PA)	1799	D	951 735-3725	3567
Primary Provider MGT Co Inc (PA)	8741	C	951 280-7700	26993
Pro Building Maintenance Inc	7349	C	951 279-3386	14356
Pro Group Inc	6531	C	951 271-3000	11681
Provident Group Crown Pnte LLC	6513	D	951 737-7482	11100
Quadramed Corporation	7322	A	951 736-6290	14019
Quality Wall Systems Inc	1742	D	951 739-4409	2945
R W Lyall & Company Inc (DH)	1382	C	951 270-1500	1047
Ranch House Doors Inc	1751	D	951 278-2884	3065
Reliable Interiors Inc	8741	C	951 371-3390	27014
Remax All Stars Realty	6531	D	951 739-4000	11727
Rosen Electronics LLC (DH)	5099	D	951 898-9808	8055
Rugby Laboratories Inc (DH)	5122	D	951 270-1400	8208
Ryland Hmes Inlnd Empire Cstmr	1521	D	951 273-3473	1228
Smart Energy Solar Inc	1711	C	800 405-1978	2359
So Cal Sandbags Inc	5085	D	951 277-3404	7871
South Coast Logistics	4214	E	714 894-4744	4373
St Joseph Health Per Care Svcs	8082	D	800 365-1110	22424
Sun Rich Fresh Foods USA Inc (HQ)	0723	D	951 735-3800	571
Superior Construction Inc	1521	D	951 808-8780	1242
Superior Paving Company Inc	1611	D	951 739-9200	1857
T W R Framing	7361	D	951 279-2000	14773
Talco Plastics Inc (PA)	4953	D	951 531-2000	6481
Team Dykspra (PA)	7542	D	951 898-6482	17840
Thyde Inc (PA)	7389	C	951 817-2300	17510
Titan Sheet Metal Inc	1761	C	951 372-1362	3208
Troy Lee Designs LLC (PA)	5091	C	951 371-5219	7940
TWR Enterprises Inc	1751	C	951 279-2000	3087
U Gym LLC	7991	D	951 808-3850	18672
Uhs-Corona Inc (HQ)	8062	A	951 737-4343	21865
Uhs-Corona Inc	8093	C	951 736-7200	22704
US Foods Inc	5141	C	951 256-2400	8478
US Foods Inc	5149	C	800 888-3147	8892
US Foods Inc	5149	C	951 582-8500	8893
US Foods Inc	5149	C	951 256-2400	8899
US Green Building Council -	6732	D	818 621-4880	12086
US Home Corporation	1531	E	951 817-3500	1361
USA Waste of California Inc	4953	C	800 423-9986	6491
Valente Concrete	1771	D	951 279-2221	3341
Veg-Fresh Farms LLC	5148	C	800 422-5535	8742
VIP Transport Inc	4213	E	951 272-3700	4300
Vipstore USA Co	5199	B	626 934-7800	9269
Volt Telecom Group Inc	8748	C	800 548-6602	27903
Volt Telecom Group Inc	8748	C	951 493-8900	27904
West Hills Construction Inc	1541	E	800 515-5270	1450
Wurms Janitorial Service Inc	7349	D	951 582-0003	14429
X-Act Finish & Trim Inc	1751	D	951 582-9229	3092
Yuneec USA Inc	5065	D	855 284-8888	7568

CORONA DEL MAR, CA - Orange County

	SIC	EMP	PHONE	ENTRY #
Balboa Yacht Club	7997	E	949 673-3515	18854
Broker Solutions Inc	6162	D	800 450-2010	9782
CIT Bank NA	6021	D	949 675-2890	9318
Crown Cove Senior Care Cmnty	8361	D	949 760-2800	24499
Delta Max	7379	E	949 759-8529	16346
Pacific Cleaning Service Inc	7349	E	949 829-8790	14338
Service Corp International	6531	D	949 644-2700	11759

CORONADO, CA - San Diego County

	SIC	EMP	PHONE	ENTRY #
51st St & 8th Ave Corp	7011	A	619 424-4000	12296
City of Coronado	7999	D	619 522-7342	19129
City of Coronado	4931	D	619 522-7380	6182
El Cordova Hotel	7011	D	619 435-4131	12551
Four Sisters Inns	7011	C	619 437-1900	12589
GK Management Co Inc	6531	D	619 437-1777	11483
Hotel Del Coronado LP	7011	D	619 522-8011	12722
Ksl Resorts Hotel Del Coronado	7011	D	619 435-6611	12822
L-O Coronado Hotel Inc	7011	A	619 435-6611	12825
Loews Corporation	8111	B	619 424-4000	23226
Mariner Systems Inc (PA)	7389	D	305 266-7255	17311
R3 Strategic Support Group Inc	8742	D	800 418-2040	27417
Star & Crescent Boat Company (PA)	4489	E	619 234-4111	4721

CORTE MADERA, CA - Marin County

	SIC	EMP	PHONE	ENTRY #
Alain Pinel Realtors Inc	6531	D	415 755-1111	11195
American Pacific Mortgage Corp	6163	E	415 891-8706	9872
Bay Clubs Inc	7997	D	415 945-3000	18856
Cellco Partnership	4812	D	415 924-9084	5327
Jackovics Enterprises Inc (PA)	7991	C	415 348-6377	18614
Marin Municipal Water District (PA)	4941	D	415 945-1455	6278
Stage II Inc	7389	E	415 285-8400	17482
Tommy Bahama Group Inc	7389	C	415 737-0400	17513

COSTA MESA, CA - Orange County

	SIC	EMP	PHONE	ENTRY #
24 Hour Fitness Usa Inc	8099	E	949 610-0651	22723
24 Hour Fitness Usa Inc	7991	D	949 650-3600	18555
2ndgear LLC (DH)	7377	C	714 702-1023	16274
ABC Bus Inc	5012	D	714 444-5888	6571
Accent Service Company Inc	7349	D	877 611-0131	14178
Accredited Nursing Services	8082	D	714 973-1234	22194
Adopt-A-Highway Maintenance	1611	C	800 200-0003	1712
Advantage Ground Trnsp Corp	4119	D	714 557-2465	3690
Alfreds Pictures Frames Inc	7389	C	714 434-4838	16990
All-Rite Leasing Company Inc	7349	B	714 530-7074	14186
Altametrics LLC	5045	C	800 676-1281	7002
Amen Clinics Inc A Med Corp (PA)	8071	E	888 564-2700	22060

Mergent email: customerrelations@mergent.com
1562

2019 Directory of California
Wholesalers and Services Companies

(P-0000) Products & Services Section entry number
(PA)=Parent Co (HQ)=Headquarters (DH)=Div Headquarters

	SIC	EMP	PHONE	ENTRY #
American Reprographics Co LLC	7334	C	714 751-2680	14075
Americash	6162	E	714 994-7554	9776
Amica Mutual Insurance Company	6331	D	877 972-6422	10338
Andrew L Youngquist Cnstr Inc	1542	D	949 862-5611	1466
ARC Document Solutions Inc	7334	D	949 660-1150	14079
Arnel Interior Corp	8741	B	714 481-5100	26764
Arta Western Medical Group	6321	C	949 260-6575	10158
Auto Club Enterprises (PA)	6321	A	714 850-5111	10159
Automobile Club Southern Cal	6411	C	714 885-1343	10555
Ayres Group (PA)	7011	D	714 540-6060	12346
Balboa Capital Corporation (PA)	6141	C	949 756-0800	9704
Bdo Usa LLP	8721	D	714 957-3200	26150
Benco Dental Supply Co	5047	D	714 424-0977	7161
Benq America Corp (HQ)	5045	D	714 559-4900	7017
Boyd & Associates	7381	C	714 835-5423	16588
Bright Bristol Street LLC	7011	D	714 557-3000	12400
Brookfeld Sthland Holdings LLC	1521	C	714 427-6868	1129
Caliber Bodyworks Texas Inc	7532	C	714 436-5010	17714
California Ticketscom Inc (DH)	7922	D	714 327-5400	18353
Califrnia Dept State Hospitals	8063	A	714 957-5000	21932
Canon Solutions America Inc	5044	D	949 753-4200	6955
Cardflex Inc	7389	D	714 361-1900	17055
Carecredit LLC	7389	C	800 300-3046	17059
Casanova Pndrill Pblicidad Inc (PA)	7311	C	949 474-5001	13803
Cellco Partnership	4812	C	714 427-0733	5316
Center For Better Health and	8099	D	714 751-8110	22759
Central Parking System Inc	7521	D	714 751-2855	17679
Chargers Football Company LLC (PA)	7941	D	619 280-2121	18514
Citizens Financial Svcs Inc	7359	D	714 751-6100	14487
Coit Services Inc	7216	E	949 760-0760	13564
Competent Care Inc	8082	D	714 545-4818	22274
Cooksey Toolen Gage Duffy (PA)	8111	C	714 431-1100	22988
Countryside Inn-Corona LP	7011	D	714 549-0300	12487
County of Orange	4581	C	949 252-5006	4884
Creative Design Cons Inc (PA)	7389	D	714 641-4868	17110
Crisp Enterprises Inc (PA)	7334	D	714 668-5955	14083
Cyber Technology LLC (PA)	6411	E	614 207-2955	10601
Dechert LLP	8111	C	949 442-6000	23026
Deloitte & Touche LLP	8721	A	714 436-7419	26179
Deloitte Consulting LLP	8742	A	714 436-7100	27213
Developmental Svcs Cal Dept	8331	A	714 957-5151	24179
Donahue Schrber Rlty Group Inc (PA)	6531	D	714 545-1400	11405
Donahue Schriber Rlty Group LP (PA)	6512	D	714 545-1400	10869
Dwiw Inc	0782	E	949 574-7147	833
EBA & M Corporation (PA)	6324	D	714 668-8920	10202
Edward Straling	1731	E	760 887-3673	2569
Edwards Theatres Circuit Inc	7832	D	714 428-0962	18288
El Pollo Loco Holdings Inc (PA)	6794	C	714 599-5000	12137
Elite Tek Services Inc	7379	D	714 881-5301	16356
Empire Leasing Inc	1751	D	949 646-7400	3032
Emulex Corporate Services Corp	8741	D	714 662-5600	26847
Ensign Group Inc	8051	D	949 642-0387	20395
Experian Info Solutions Inc (DH)	7323	A	714 830-7000	14036
Experian Mktg Solutions LLC	8748	A	714 830-7000	27725
EZ Lube LLC (PA)	7549	D	714 556-1312	17861
Federal Express Corporation	4513	D	800 463-3339	4823
Flagstar Bancorp Inc	6099	C	714 549-9100	9683
Food & Agriculture Cal Dept	7999	D	714 751-3247	19176
Food Sales West Inc (PA)	5141	D	714 966-2900	8405
Geek Squad Inc	7379	D	714 434-0132	16381
General Electric Company	6159	C	714 434-4111	9758
Global Business Solutions Inc	7379	B	714 257-1488	16385
Golden Living LLC	8051	D	949 642-0387	20463
Gtt Communications (mp) Inc	8748	D	714 327-2000	27742
Hanley Wood Mkt Intelligence (HQ)	8732	C	714 540-8500	26526
Hanley Wood Mkt Intelligence (PA)	8748	C	714 540-8500	27744
HB Parkco Construction Inc (PA)	1771	B	714 444-1441	3264
Host Hotels & Resorts LP	7011	D	714 957-1100	12711
Human Options Inc	8322	E	949 757-3635	23846
Independent Options	8322	D	714 434-1175	23854
Inhouseit Inc	7378	D	949 660-5655	16288
Insight Investments LLC (HQ)	7377	C	714 939-2300	16275
Integrated Behavioral Hlth Inc	8099	D	714 442-4150	22825
International Bus Mchs Corp	7379	B	714 327-3501	16403
Jabez Building Services Inc	7349	D	714 776-7705	14293
Janico Building Maintenance	7349	B	714 444-4339	14295
JD Power (HQ)	8732	C	714 621-6200	26535
Jpmorgan Chase Bank Nat Assn	7389	C	949 429-6071	17265
K Line America Inc	4412	E	714 861-5000	4698
Koce-TV Foundation	4833	D	714 241-4100	5811
Kyocera International Inc	5065	E	714 428-3600	7498
Latham & Watkins LLP	8111	C	714 540-1235	23189
Lawrence B Bonas Company	1721	D	714 668-5250	2454
Lewis Brsbois Bsgard Smith LLP	8111	D	714 545-6015	23208
Livetime Software Inc	7372	E	415 905-4009	15744

	SIC	EMP	PHONE	ENTRY #
Lombardy Holdings Inc (PA)	1623	C	951 808-4550	1950
Maersk Inc	4731	D	714 428-5500	5104
Manatt Phelps & Phillips LLP	8111	E	714 371-2500	23237
Materials Marketing	8742	D	949 729-9881	27322
Maxgen Energy Services Corp	4932	B	714 908-5266	6192
Medical Eye Services Inc	6411	D	714 619-4660	10689
Mesa Cnsld Wtr Dst Imprv Corp (PA)	4941	D	949 631-1200	6279
Mesa Verde Convalescent Hosp	8051	C	949 548-5584	20643
Mesa Verde Country Club	7997	C	714 549-0377	18972
Mesa Verde Partners	7992	D	714 540-7500	18733
Meyers Research LLC	8732	D	714 619-7800	26544
Michael Maguire & Associates	6411	E	714 435-7500	10692
Mobilitie Investments III LLC	4813	C	877 999-7070	5602
Morgan Lewis & Bockius LLP	8111	C	949 399-7000	23262
Mt Supply Inc (DH)	5085	C	800 938-6658	7861
National Safety Services	8748	E	714 679-9118	27799
Nds Americas Inc (DH)	4841	D	714 434-2100	5923
New Vista Behavioral Health	8399	D	949 284-0095	24813
Newma Garris Gilmo + Partne I	8712	D	949 756-0818	26100
Newport Sbacute Healthcare Ctr	8051	C	949 642-1974	20660
North American Acceptance Corp	6141	C	714 868-3195	9725
Nwp Services Corporation (HQ)	7372	C	949 253-2500	15787
Olson & Assoc	7379	D	714 878-6649	16439
One Town Center Associates LLC	6512	E	714 435-2100	10924
Orange Cnty Sprntndent Schools	8351	D	949 650-2506	24361
Orange County Plst Co Inc	1742	C	714 957-1971	2928
Ovations Fanfare	8741	D	714 708-1880	26970
Pacific Mercantile Bank (HQ)	6022	E	714 438-2500	9472
Park Hotels & Resorts Inc	7011	B	714 540-7000	13039
Parkco Building Company	1542	D	714 444-1441	1610
Paul Hastings LLP	8111	D	714 668-6200	23314
Paul Hastings LLP	8111	C	714 668-6200	23315
Payoff Inc	6141	D	949 430-0630	9726
PDC Capital Group LLC	6552	D	866 500-8550	11907
Pivot Interiors Inc	1731	D	949 988-5400	2681
Planned Parenthood Federation	8093	D	949 548-8830	22643
Plexicor Inc (PA)	7382	E	714 918-8700	16927
Pmd Industries Inc	1731	E	949 222-0999	2682
Powerplant Mint Spcialists Inc	1629	C	714 427-6900	2056
Precise Fit Limited One LLC	7361	B	310 824-1800	14696
Profit Recovery Partners LLC	8748	D	949 851-2777	27826
R S I Insurance Brokers Inc (PA)	6411	D	714 546-6616	10754
Remax Metro Inc	6531	D	714 557-2544	11729
Resources Connection Inc	8742	D	714 430-6550	27426
Restaurant In A Box Llc	7371	E	800 676-1281	15408
Rosanna Inc	7011	C	714 751-5100	13138
Rromeo Corporation	8741	D	714 640-3800	27019
Rutan & Tucker LLP (PA)	8111	D	714 641-5100	23363
Seaview Industries	7389	E	714 957-5073	17465
Secova Inc	8742	C	714 384-0530	27442
Secova Eservices Inc (HQ)	8742	D	714 384-0655	27443
Sheppard Mullin Richter	8111	D	714 513-5100	23381
Silverado Senior Living Inc	8059	D	949 945-0189	21211
Site Crew Inc	7349	B	714 668-0100	14392
Smith & Sons Investment Co	6531	E	949 646-9648	11766
Snell & Wilmer LLP	8111	C	714 427-7000	23392
Solopoint Solutions Inc	8711	D	714 708-3639	25917
South Coast Plaza LLC (PA)	6512	D	714 546-0110	10948
South Coast Plaza LLC	6512	E	714 435-2000	10949
South Coast Repertory Inc	7922	D	714 708-5500	18405
South Coast Westin Hotel Co	7011	D	714 540-2500	13249
Southern California Mar Assn	7538	D	714 850-4004	17786
Sure Haven Inc	8069	A	949 467-9213	22053
Syspro Impact Software Inc	5045	C	714 437-1000	7114
T Boyer Company	1731	E	949 642-2431	2759
Talon Executive Services Inc	7382	E	714 434-7476	16947
Telecare Corporation	8063	D	714 361-6760	21975
Ticketscom LLC (DH)	7922	E	714 327-5400	18410
Tk Carsites Inc	7371	D	714 937-1239	15505
Transprttion Brkg Spclists Inc	4212	B	714 754-4230	4071
Tsi	7349	D	949 515-7800	14411
Ultralink LLC	6311	C	714 427-5500	10150
United Infrstrcture Prjcts Inc	8711	D	949 310-0092	25969
University California Irvine	8011	E	949 646-2267	20034
Upgradedetect Inc (PA)	5045	D	949 460-9000	7125
US Hotel and Resort MGT Inc	7011	D	949 650-2988	13360
UTC Fire SEC Americas Corp Inc	7371	D	949 737-7800	15519
Valassis Communications Inc	7331	D	714 751-4006	14067
Variations In Stone Inc	1741	D	949 438-8337	2826
Villa Pacific Contractors Inc	1741	E	714 850-1640	2827
Viva Life Science Inc	5122	D	949 645-6100	8220
Volcom LLC	5136	C	949 646-2175	8282
Volcom LLC (HQ)	7389	C	949 646-2175	17575
Waddell & Reed Inc	6211	D	714 437-7510	10034
Warmington Homes (PA)	1531	C	714 434-4435	1364

Employment Codes: A=Over 500 employees, B=251-500,
C=101-250, D=51-100, E=50

2019 Directory of California
Wholesalers and Services Companies

© Mergent Inc. 1-800-342-5647

1563

GEOGRAPHIC

Name	SIC	EMP	PHONE	ENTRY #
Warmington Residential Cal Inc	1521	C	714 557-5511	1258
Westar Capital Assoc II LLC	6799	A	714 481-5160	12281
Woodruff Spradlin & Smart	8111	D	714 558-7000	23447
Wyndham International Inc	7011	D	714 751-5100	13428

COTATI, CA - Sonoma County

Name	SIC	EMP	PHONE	ENTRY #
21st Century Health Club (PA)	8093	D	707 795-0400	22495
Mike Brown Electric Co	1731	D	707 792-8100	2648
Stockham Construction Inc	1751	B	707 664-0945	3083

COTTONWOOD, CA - Shasta County

Name	SIC	EMP	PHONE	ENTRY #
All Pro Drywall	1742	E	530 722-5182	2839
County of Shasta	8641	D	530 347-6276	25143
M & M Enterprises	0811	D	530 347-3238	992
Shasta Livestock Auction Yard	5154	D	530 347-3793	8907

COURTLAND, CA - Sacramento County

Name	SIC	EMP	PHONE	ENTRY #
Delta Breeze Farming Inc	0191	C	916 775-2055	334

COVELO, CA - Mendocino County

Name	SIC	EMP	PHONE	ENTRY #
Covelo Indian Community Center	6531	D	707 983-8478	11387
Round Valley Indian Health Ctr	8011	D	707 983-6182	19831

COVINA, CA - Los Angeles County

Name	SIC	EMP	PHONE	ENTRY #
A-1 Event & Party Rentals	7299	D	626 967-0500	13713
Accu-Count Inventory Svcs Inc	7389	D	805 231-6310	16982
Acf Components & Fasteners Inc	5072	C	949 833-0506	7571
Altamed Health Services Corp	6321	D	626 214-1480	10156
American Multi-Cinema Inc	7832	D	626 974-8624	18260
Baltazar Construction Inc	1771	E	626 339-8620	3220
Bowlero Corp	7933	D	626 339-1286	18481
Briteworks Inc	7349	D	626 337-0099	14204
Brutoco Engrg & Cnstr Inc	1611	C	909 350-3535	1733
Cal Empire Engineering Inc	1795	E	626 915-8030	3447
Central Health Plan Cal Inc	8082	A	626 938-7120	22262
Century 21 Masters	6531	D	626 732-6184	11307
Charter Behavioral Health Syst	8063	D	626 966-1632	21939
Citrus Valley Medical Ctr Inc	8062	A	626 858-8515	21323
Citrus Valley Medical Ctr Inc	8062	A	626 331-7331	21325
Citrus Vly Hlth Partners Inc (PA)	8741	A	626 331-7331	26807
Citrus Vly Hlth Partners Inc	8099	A	626 732-3100	22767
Coldwell Banker Town & Country	6531	D	626 966-3688	11344
Covina Rehabilitation Center	8051	C	626 967-3874	20358
Cruz Hoffstetter LLC	7389	D	626 915-5621	17116
Cwf Inc	7359	D	626 967-0500	14498
Davita Magan Management Inc (DH)	8011	C	626 331-6411	19429
Dynamic Realty Corp	6531	D	626 931-3200	11412
Golden Empire Mortgage Inc	6162	D	626 967-3236	9808
Grand Auto Care	7538	E	626 331-8390	17764
Home Capital Group	6162	D	626 331-4213	9814
K-Fed Mutual Holding Company	6712	C	626 339-9663	11954
Keller Williams Realty	6531	D	626 384-2803	11540
Lereta LLC (PA)	6211	B	626 543-1765	9971
Los Angeles Engineering Inc	8711	C	626 869-1400	25801
Masonic Homes of California	8361	D	626 251-2200	24595
Mohan Dialysis Ctr of Covina	8092	D	626 859-2522	22484
Outsource Testing Inc	8748	D	909 592-8898	27816
Park Hotels & Resorts Inc	7011	D	626 915-3441	13029
Rgis LLC	7389	D	626 974-4841	17443
Rowland Convalescent Hosp Inc	8051	D	626 967-2741	20731
San Gabriel Childrens Ctr Inc	8361	D	626 859-2089	24666
Securitas SEC Svcs USA Inc	7381	C	571 321-0913	16791
Staff Today Incorporated	7363	C	800 928-5561	14915
Think Together	8351	A	626 373-2311	24392
Vitas Healthcare Corp Cal	8082	D	626 918-2273	22455
Wood Castle Construction Inc	1521	E	626 966-8600	1260

CRESCENT CITY, CA - Del Norte County

Name	SIC	EMP	PHONE	ENTRY #
County of Del Norte	8399	C	707 464-3191	24766
Del Norte Workforce Center	8331	E	707 464-8347	24178
Elk Valley Casino Inc	7011	C	707 464-1020	12555
Full Spectrum Services Inc	8322	E	707 465-1460	23818
Leavitt Group Enterprises Inc	6411	C	707 465-6508	10670
North Shore Investment Inc	8051	D	707 464-6151	20663
Snoozie Shavings Inc (PA)	4213	A	707 464-6186	4265
Sutter Coast Hospital (HQ)	8062	C	707 464-8511	21801

CROCKETT, CA - Contra Costa County

Name	SIC	EMP	PHONE	ENTRY #
Sugar Workers Local 1	8631	B	510 787-1676	25083

CUDAHY, CA - Los Angeles County

Name	SIC	EMP	PHONE	ENTRY #
County of Los Angeles	8399	C	323 560-5001	24769
Kaiser Foundation Hospitals	8062	D	323 562-6400	21500
Mistras Group Inc	8711	D	323 583-1653	25826
Southern Cal Prmnnte Med Group	8011	E	323 562-6459	19922

CULVER CITY, CA - Los Angeles County

Name	SIC	EMP	PHONE	ENTRY #
A-1 Electric Service Co Inc	1731	D	310 204-1077	2496
Access Spclty Animal Hospitals	0742	D	310 558-6100	592
Advanced Medical Reviews Inc	7363	D	310 575-0900	14809
Alpine Interiors Corporation (PA)	5023	D	310 390-7639	6746
Anonymous Content LLC (PA)	7812	D	310 558-6000	18017
Avoca Productions Inc	7812	D	310 244-4000	18022
Cadforce Inc	7389	A	310 876-1800	17045
California Clinical Trials	6411	C	310 945-1780	10571
Carat N Amer Dntsu Ageis Ntwrk	7319	C	310 255-1000	13968
Century Wilshire Inc	7011	D	310 558-9400	12446
CIT Bank NA	6021	D	310 390-7745	9312
CIT Bank NA	6021	D	310 559-7222	9313
Clutter Inc (PA)	7299	C	800 805-4023	13730
Columbia Pictures Inds Inc (DH)	7812	C	310 244-4000	18033
Common Area Maint Svcs Inc (PA)	7349	D	310 390-3552	14223
Companion Hospice and	8082	D	310 338-1257	22271
Compulaw LLC	7371	E	310 553-3355	15069
Computer Consulting (PA)	4813	A	310 568-5600	5535
Crp Centinela LP	7011	C	901 821-4117	12503
Cuningham Group Arch Inc	8712	E	310 895-2200	26039
D K Fortune & Associates Inc	8059	C	310 391-7266	21057
Didi Hirsch Psychiatric Svc (PA)	8322	C	310 390-6612	23771
Digital Kitchen LLC	7812	E	310 499-9255	18041
Dual Diagnosis Trtmnt Ctr Inc	8093	C	424 207-2220	22571
Exceptional Chld Foundation (PA)	8331	C	310 204-3300	24182
Exceptional Chld Foundation	8331	C	310 204-3300	24183
Exodus Recovery Inc (PA)	8093	D	310 945-3350	22576
Exodus Recovery Ctr At Brotman (PA)	8069	D	310 253-9494	22021
Force-Oakleaf LP	7011	D	310 484-7000	12580
Gardner Neurologic Orthopedic	8741	D	310 649-5824	26867
Genex (HQ)	7371	C	424 672-9500	15175
GK Management Co Inc (PA)	6531	C	310 204-2050	11481
GK Management Co Inc	6531	C	310 204-2050	11482
GK Management Co Inc	6513	D	310 836-1812	11027
Globecast America Incorporated (HQ)	4841	D	310 845-3900	5918
Goldrich & Kest Industries LLC (PA)	6552	A	310 204-2050	11877
Goldrichkest (PA)	6552	B	310 204-2050	11878
Hellmuth Obata & Kassabaum Inc	8712	E	310 838-9555	26058
Hlw Corp	7542	E	310 838-7100	17817
Hok Group Inc	8712	C	310 838-9555	26066
Investment Tech Group Inc	6211	C	310 216-6777	9965
Ipsos Otx Corporation (HQ)	8732	C	310 736-3400	26532
Jeopardy Productions Inc	7812	C	310 244-8855	18065
Jesse Lee Group Inc	8741	D	510 351-3700	26906
Kaercher Campbell Associate In	6411	C	310 556-1900	10661
Kovel/Fuller LLC	7311	C	310 841-4444	13856
L A Services Inc	1711	E	310 838-0408	2253
Lax Plaza Hotel	7011	C	310 902-2202	12842
Liveoffice LLC	7372	D	877 253-2793	15743
LMS Corporation	7389	C	310 641-4222	17300
Maker Studios Inc (HQ)	7929	C	310 606-2182	18450
Marycrest Manor	8059	D	310 838-2778	21154
Max Leather	5199	C	310 841-6990	9234
Midnight Snack LP	8741	E	310 202-1470	26945
Mike Diamond Plumbing Inc (PA)	1711	D	310 838-6197	2281
Morphosis Architects	8712	D	310 453-2247	26096
Nanthealth Inc (HQ)	7373	D	310 883-1300	16009
Nantmobile LLC	7371	C	310 883-7888	15299
Nantworks LLC (PA)	7373	D	310 883-1300	16010
Nfl Properties LLC	7922	B	310 840-4635	18389
Office of Child Development	8351	D	310 842-4230	24356
Omelet LLC (PA)	7311	D	213 427-6400	13872
Oracle Corporation	7372	B	310 258-7500	15812
Pacifica Hotel & Conference Ce	7011	C	310 649-1776	13007
Paychex Inc	8721	D	310 338-7900	26268
Pine Data Processing Inc	7374	C	310 815-5700	16164
Prestige Security Service Inc	7381	B	310 670-5999	16761
Prime Focus North America Inc (HQ)	7819	D	323 461-7887	18212
Property Management Assoc Inc (PA)	6531	C	323 295-2000	11688
Psychemedics Corporation	8734	D	310 216-7776	26728
Punch Studio LLC (PA)	5112	C	310 390-9900	8087
Quadra Productions Inc	7812	C	310 244-1234	18102
Quadrix Information Tech Inc	8748	E	424 603-2140	27830
Reading International Inc (PA)	7832	C	213 235-2240	18316
Reliable Health Care Svcs Inc	7363	E	310 397-2229	14903
Rick Solomon Enterprises Inc (PA)	5136	C	310 280-3700	8276
Roe Holdings LLC	7311	C	310 559-9222	13893
Roman Cath Arch of Los Angels	7261	E	310 836-5500	13694
Roundup Media LLC	7311	C	310 841-2366	13895
Scopely Inc (PA)	7372	C	323 400-6618	15849
Security Indust Spcialists Inc (PA)	7381	C	310 215-5100	16817
Servicon Systems Inc (PA)	8744	A	310 204-5400	27604
Social Studies School Service	5049	D	310 839-2436	7248
Solano County Mental Health	8322	E	707 428-1131	24054
Sony Pictures Entrmt Inc	7812	B	310 840-8000	18120
Sony Pictures Entrmt Inc	7929	B	310 202-1234	18466

Mergent email: customerrelations@mergent.com
1564

2019 Directory of California
Wholesalers and Services Companies

(P-0000) Products & Services Section entry number
(PA)=Parent Co (HQ)=Headquarters (DH)=Div Headquarters

	SIC	EMP	PHONE	ENTRY #
Sony Pictures Entrmt Inc (DH)	7812	A	310 244-4000	18121
Sony Pictures Imageworks Inc	7374	A	310 840-8000	16180
Sony Pictures Television Inc (DH)	7812	B	310 244-7625	18123
Southern Cal Halthcare Sys Inc	8062	A	310 836-7000	21760
Stan Tashman & Associates Inc	8741	A	310 460-7600	27045
Starwood Hotel	7011	D	310 641-7740	13266
Steel House Inc	7311	C	310 773-3331	13905
Syska & Hennessy Engineers Inc	8711	D	310 312-0200	25936
Topanga Productions Inc	7812	E	310 244-4000	18133
Topson Downs California Inc (PA)	5137	C	310 558-0300	8339
Transwestern Corp Pointe LLC	6531	D	310 642-1001	11799
Tristar Television Music Inc	7922	E	310 244-4000	18411
Triton Media Group LLC	4832	D	661 294-9000	5757
U S Private Protection SEC Inc	7381	C	310 301-0010	16842
United Refrigeration Inc	5078	C	310 204-2500	7667
Uproxx Media Group Inc (PA)	4899	C	310 424-2080	6003
Virgin Fish Inc (PA)	4119	C	310 391-6161	3857
West Publishing Corporation	7373	C	424 243-2100	16077
Westside Childrens Center Inc	8351	C	310 846-4100	24399
X Prize Foundation Inc	8399	E	310 741-4880	24861
Yoga Works Inc (HQ)	7991	E	310 664-6470	18677
Yogaworks Inc (PA)	7991	E	310 664-6470	18678
Zb National Association	6021	C	310 258-9300	9412
Zoic Inc	7812	C	310 838-0770	18173

CUPERTINO, CA - Santa Clara County

	SIC	EMP	PHONE	ENTRY #
Aemetis Inc (PA)	8731	C	408 213-0940	26313
California Dental Arts LLC	8072	D	408 255-1020	22162
Ch Cupertino Owner LLC	7011	C	408 253-8900	12447
Corinthian Intl Prkg Svcs Inc	7299	B	408 867-7275	13733
CRC Health Corporate (DH)	8093	D	408 367-0044	22564
CRC Health Corporation (DH)	8069	D	877 272-8668	22014
CRC Health Group Inc (HQ)	8099	D	877 272-8668	22781
Cupertino Healthcare	8051	D	408 253-9034	20364
Cupertino Lessee LLC	7011	C	908 253-8900	12505
Digital Keystone Inc	7373	E	650 938-7301	15943
Digite Inc	7371	D	408 418-3834	15110
Ecrio Inc	7372	C	408 973-7290	15659
Esq Business Services Inc (PA)	7372	D	925 734-9800	15672
Ewing-Foley Inc (PA)	5065	E	408 342-1201	7475
Forge-Vidovich Motel Limited	7011	D	408 996-7700	12581
Forum Healthcare Center	8051	C	650 944-0200	20436
Ggec America Inc	5065	D	714 750-2280	7483
Howard Fischer Associates Inc	7361	D	408 374-0580	14638
Huawei Enterprise USA Inc	4813	D	408 394-4295	5580
Ice Center Enterprises LLC	7999	D	510 604-8878	19185
Knova Software Inc (HQ)	7372	D	408 863-5800	15732
Lanwave Technology Inc	8711	D	408 253-3883	25793
Max Sportsters Inc	8741	E	408 446-8330	26939
Mist Systems Inc	7373	C	408 326-0346	16004
Next Issue Media LLC (PA)	7389	D	650 521-5151	17353
Panasonic Corp North America	8731	C	408 861-3900	26431
Pleasant View Convalescent Hos	8059	C	408 253-9034	21188
Rancho San Antonio Retirement	8361	B	650 265-2637	24643
Referral Realty Inc	6531	D	408 996-8100	11722
Self-Help For Elderly	8322	D	408 873-1183	24041
Silver Lake Partners II LP	6726	C	408 454-4732	12067
Stevens Creek Quarry Inc (PA)	1611	D	408 253-2512	1854
Sugarcrm Inc (PA)	7371	C	408 454-6900	15482
Sunny Retirement Home	8059	C	408 454-5600	21226
Trend Micro Incorporated	5045	D	408 257-1500	7119
Z & M Associates Inc	6531	D	408 996-8100	11844
Zend Technologies Usa Inc	7371	C	408 253-8800	15557

CUTLER, CA - Tulare County

	SIC	EMP	PHONE	ENTRY #
Penas Disposal Inc	4953	D	559 528-3909	6427
Wawona Packing Co LLC	0723	A	559 528-4000	585
Wawona Packing Co LLC	7389	B	559 528-4699	17583

CYPRESS, CA - Orange County

	SIC	EMP	PHONE	ENTRY #
Alltrade Tools LLC	5072	E	310 522-9008	7572
American Honda Finance Corp	6141	D	714 816-8110	9702
Apple Eght Hospitality MGT Inc	7011	D	714 827-1010	12327
Asplundh Tree Expert LLC	0783	C	714 893-2405	968
B2b Staffing Services Inc	7363	B	714 243-4104	14822
Barcott Frank A SEC Invstgtons	7381	C	714 891-8556	16578
Beacon Health Options Inc	8322	C	714 763-2405	23504
Cal Southern United Food	6371	C	714 220-2297	10477
Caliber Capital Group LLC	6282	A	714 507-1998	10067
Cellco Partnership	4812	C	714 899-4690	5376
Christie Dgtal Systems USA Inc (DH)	5043	D	714 527-7056	6941
Clarion Corporation America (DH)	5064	D	310 327-9100	7410
Consoldted Med Bo-Analysis Inc (PA)	8071	D	714 657-7369	22069
Cypress Ctr For Fmly Medicine	8011	D	562 799-4801	19424
Cypress Education Foundation	8641	D	714 220-6900	25149
Daiwa Corporation	5091	D	562 375-6800	7926

	SIC	EMP	PHONE	ENTRY #
DAndrea Graphic Corportion	7336	D	310 642-0260	14110
Dean Goodman Inc	6531	D	714 229-8999	11396
Focus Diagnostics Inc	8071	B	714 220-1900	22085
Focus Technologies Holding Co	8071	A	800 838-4548	22086
Forest Lawn Memorial-Park Assn	6553	D	714 828-3131	11941
Fujifilm North America Corp	5043	C	714 372-4200	6942
Global Exprnce Specialists Inc	7389	D	562 370-1500	17191
Healthsmart Management Service	6411	D	714 947-8600	10645
Hoyu America Co	5122	D	714 230-3000	8178
Hybrid Promotions LLC (PA)	5136	C	714 952-3866	8264
J Perez Associates Inc (PA)	1799	D	562 801-5397	3535
Jvc Americas Corp	7622	E	714 527-7500	17883
Marriott International Inc	7011	C	714 209-6586	12881
Mercury Defense Systems Inc (HQ)	7374	D	714 898-8200	16156
Mitsubishi Electric Us Inc (DH)	1796	C	714 220-2500	3473
Mitsubishi Motors Cr Amer Inc (DH)	6141	B	714 799-4730	9722
Money Mailer LLC (PA)	7331	C	714 889-3800	14054
Pacific Pioneer Insur Group (PA)	6411	C	714 228-7888	10726
Pacificare Health Systems LLC (HQ)	6324	A	714 952-1121	10291
Paragon Partners Ltd (PA)	8748	D	714 379-3376	27819
Pick-A-Part Auto Wrecking	5093	C	559 485-3071	7987
Pilot Painting & Construction	1721	D	714 229-5900	2465
Plumbing Piping & Cnstr Inc	1711	D	714 821-0490	2313
Premier Disp & Exhibits Inc (PA)	7389	D	562 431-2731	17407
Riphagen & Bullerdick Inc	6531	E	714 763-2100	11734
Scientific Applications & RES (PA)	8731	D	714 828-1465	26450
Siemens Industry Inc	5063	C	714 761-2200	7396
Siemens Product Life Mgmt Sftw	7371	C	714 952-6500	15445
Silliker Labs Group Inc	8734	E	714 226-0000	26732
Sitonit Seating Inc	5021	C	714 995-4800	6737
Spectrum MGT Holdg Co LLC	4841	D	714 657-1040	5932
Spectrum MGT Holdg Co LLC	4841	C	714 657-1060	5941
Uhc of California (DH)	6324	A	714 952-1121	10322
United Chinese American Genera (PA)	6411	C	714 228-7800	10809
United Exchange Corp (DH)	7389	C	562 977-4500	17532
Unitedhealth Group Inc	6324	D	952 936-1300	10325
Ushio America Inc (HQ)	5063	D	714 236-8600	7400
Valueoptions of California	6411	C	800 228-1286	10821
Viad Corp	7389	D	562 370-1500	17566
Wcct Global Inc (PA)	8733	D	714 668-1500	26672
Western Overseas Corporation (PA)	4731	E	562 985-0616	5199
Yamaha Motor Corporation USA (HQ)	5088	B	714 761-7300	7921

DALY CITY, CA - San Mateo County

	SIC	EMP	PHONE	ENTRY #
ABS-Cbn International (DH)	4841	C	800 527-2820	5856
American General Life Insur	6411	D	650 994-6679	10520
Bay Area Pdatric Med Group Inc (PA)	8011	C	650 992-4200	19314
Bdp Bowl Inc	7933	E	650 878-0300	18480
Casbn Investment Inc	6531	D	650 991-2800	11270
Catholic Chrts Cyo Archdiocs	4151	C	650 757-2110	3910
City of Daly City	8711	D	650 991-8064	25610
Forte Enterprises Inc (PA)	8741	C	650 994-3200	26862
Genesys Telecom Labs Inc (HQ)	7372	C	650 466-1100	15691
Gerson Baker & Associates	6513	D	650 756-0969	11026
Hillcrest Senior Housing Corp	1522	B	650 757-1737	1289
Kaiser Foundation Hospitals	6324	D	650 301-5860	10247
Lake Merced Golf & Country CLB	7997	D	650 755-2233	18953
Larry Blair Realtor	6531	E	650 991-5261	11559
Mission Villa LLC	8361	D	650 756-1995	24603
Nurse Providers Inc	7361	A	650 992-8559	14676
Oracle Systems Corporation	7372	D	650 506-8648	15816
Pacific Gas and Electric Co	4911	C	650 755-1236	6086
Permanente Medical Group Inc	8011	D	650 301-5860	19788
Reneson Hotels Inc (PA)	7011	D	650 449-5353	13115
Rgis LLC	7389	C	650 757-6770	17446
Roman Catholic Archdiocese of	6553	D	650 756-2060	11947
San Mateo Cnty Pub Hlth Clinic	8093	B	650 301-8600	22676
Seton Medical Center (HQ)	8062	A	650 992-4000	21742
Seton Medical Center	8062	A	650 992-4000	21744
Spinecare Medical Group Inc	8011	C	650 985-7500	19935
St Francis Hts Convalescent	8059	D	650 755-9515	21222
West Lake Touchless Car Wash	7542	E	650 992-5344	17843
Westlake Nail Spa	7991	D	650 994-7777	18674

DANA POINT, CA - Orange County

	SIC	EMP	PHONE	ENTRY #
Altera Real Estate	6531	B	949 547-7351	11209
Cph Monarch Hotel LLC	7011	A	949 234-3200	12497
Ergs Aim Hotel Realty LLC	7011	D	949 661-1100	12562
Gringteam Inc	7011	D	949 661-1100	12630
Mark R Eggen Construction Inc	1521	E	949 661-2674	1196
Monarch Beach Golf Links (HQ)	7992	D	949 240-8247	18737
Pangea Corporation	8999	E	949 443-0666	27951
Pop-Tent Inc	7311	D	949 313-7160	13082
Prutel Joint Venture	7011	A	949 240-2000	13082
Ritz-Carlton Hotel Company LLC	7011	B	949 240-5020	13127
Sunrise Senior Living Inc	8051	D	949 234-3000	20804

Employment Codes: A=Over 500 employees, B=251-500,
C=101-250, D=51-100, E=50

2019 Directory of California
Wholesalers and Services Companies

© Mergent Inc. 1-800-342-5647

1565

GEOGRAPHIC

DANVILLE, CA - Contra Costa County

	SIC	EMP	PHONE	ENTRY #
2 G Fitness LLC	7991	D	925 838-9200	18546
Ameritac Inc (PA)	8744	D	925 743-8398	27577
Architrends Inc	8711	D	925 648-8800	25543
Bara Infoware Inc (PA)	8711	D	925 790-0130	25559
Blackhawk Country Club	7997	C	925 736-6500	18869
Braddock & Logan Group II LP	6552	C	925 736-4000	11857
Braddock & Logan Services Inc	1542	C	925 736-4000	1483
Brookfeld Bay Area Hldings LLC	6552	D	925 743-8000	11859
Creekside Comet Education Fund	6732	D	925 314-2000	12077
Cubix Construction Company (PA)	1541	D	925 314-0770	1389
Danville Long-Term Care Inc	8051	D	925 837-4566	20365
Danville Village Skilled Nursn	8051	D	925 837-4566	20366
DW Morgan LLC	4731	D	925 460-2700	5050
Empire Realty Associates Inc	6531	D	925 217-5000	11420
James E Roberts-Obayashi Corp	1522	C	925 820-0600	1291
Pacific Union Homes Inc (PA)	6552	C	925 314-3800	11903
Patelco Credit Union	6062	D	925 785-9487	9643
Reutlinger Community	8322	C	925 964-2062	23995
Stratcitycom LLC	7372	D	408 858-0006	15865
Sunrise Senior Living LLC	8051	D	925 309-4178	20813
Tenet Healthsystem Medical	8011	B	925 275-8303	19999

DAVENPORT, CA - Santa Cruz County

	SIC	EMP	PHONE	ENTRY #
Swanton Berry Farms Inc	0191	E	831 425-8919	383

DAVIS, CA - Yolo County

	SIC	EMP	PHONE	ENTRY #
Brown and Caldwell	8711	D	530 747-0650	25581
Communicare Health Centers	8011	C	530 758-2060	19395
Cvf Capital Partners Inc	6799	C	530 757-7004	12219
Davis Community Clinic (PA)	8011	C	530 758-2060	19428
Davis Hallmark Partnership	7011	E	530 753-3320	12514
Doug Arnold Real Estate Inc (PA)	6531	E	530 758-3080	11406
Draios Inc	7371	D	916 521-3802	15119
Harpers Model Home Maintenance	7349	D	916 335-0282	14285
Hmclause Inc (DH)	0181	C	800 320-4672	267
Hmclause Inc	8731	D	530 747-3235	26377
Ikes Landscaping & Maintenance	0782	D	530 758-1698	861
Kaiser Foundation Hospitals	8011	E	530 757-7100	19606
Mariner Health Care Inc	8051	C	530 756-1800	20618
Novozymes Inc (DH)	8732	D	530 757-8100	26554
Novozymes Us Inc	6719	A	530 757-8100	11995
Omni Consulting Group LLP	8742	D	530 750-5199	27375
Pacific Gas and Electric Co	4911	B	530 757-5803	6091
Pacific Retirement Svcs Inc	8361	C	530 753-1450	24623
Schilling Robotics LLC	8711	D	530 753-6718	25905
Sciots Tract Association	8641	D	530 753-5219	25243
Sutter Health	8011	C	530 747-0389	19958
Sutter Health	8062	B	530 757-5111	21806
Sutter Health	8062	C	530 750-5904	21814
Sutter Health	8062	C	530 750-5888	21834
Sutter Hlth Scrmnto Sierra Reg	8011	A	530 747-5010	19986
Sutter Hlth Scrmnto Sierra Reg	8062	B	530 756-6440	21837
Tera Investments Inc	6799	E	530 753-7129	12274
Travis Credit Union	6061	B	707 449-4000	9598
Ucd Recreation Hall	7999	D	530 752-6071	19252
University California Davis	8011	D	530 752-2300	20031
West Yost & Associates Inc (PA)	8711	D	530 756-5905	25996
Woodland Healthcare	8062	D	530 756-2364	21919
Yolo Hospice Inc (PA)	8082	D	530 758-5566	22465

DEATH VALLEY, CA - Inyo County

	SIC	EMP	PHONE	ENTRY #
Xanterra Parks & Resorts Inc	7011	C	760 786-2345	13431

DEL MAR, CA - San Diego County

	SIC	EMP	PHONE	ENTRY #
Aecom Energy & Cnstr Inc	1611	B	858 481-9502	1713
Automobile Club Southern Cal	6411	C	858 481-7181	10557
Brightertech Incorporated	4813	E	310 909-4940	5523
Brookfield Homes of California	1521	E	858 481-8500	1130
Brookfield Homes Pacific Inc (HQ)	1521	D	858 481-8500	1131
Crest Beverage Company Inc	5181	D	858 452-2300	8988
Davidson Communities (PA)	6552	E	858 259-8500	11870
Del Mar Thoroughbred Club	7948	B	858 755-1141	18539
Hive Tech Gurus Incorporated	4813	E	323 445-1770	5577
Humetrix Inc	8742	E	858 259-8987	27267
JP Morgan Securities LLC	6211	D	310 201-2693	9967
Lee Johnson	8059	C	858 481-4411	21133
Lhoberge Lessee Inc	7011	C	858 259-1515	12852
Liquid Investments Inc (PA)	5181	D	858 509-8510	9009
Mesa Distributing Coinc (HQ)	5181	D	858 452-2300	9014
Sunstone Durante LLC	7011	C	858 792-5200	13292
Ws Hdm LLC	7011	D	858 792-5200	13419

DEL REY, CA - Fresno County

	SIC	EMP	PHONE	ENTRY #
Chooljian & Sons Inc (PA)	0723	D	559 888-2031	503

DELANO, CA - Kern County

	SIC	EMP	PHONE	ENTRY #
City of Delano	7992	E	661 721-3350	18695
Coronel Construction Inc	1521	D	661 725-4400	1148
County of Kern	8322	D	661 721-5134	23650
Covanta Delano Inc	4911	C	661 792-3067	6024
Delano Dst Sklled Nrsing Fclty	8051	C	661 720-2100	20373
Hronis Inc A California Corp (PA)	0174	D	661 725-2503	206
Innovel Solutions Inc	4731	A	661 721-5910	5092
Jorge Pimental Diaz	0761	C	661 344-5139	656
Loup Logistics Company	4731	A	661 370-4341	5102
M Caratan Inc (PA)	0172	C	661 725-2566	159
M Caratan Inc	0172	C	661 725-1777	160
Monarch Nut Company LLC	0723	C	661 725-6458	541
Munger Bros LLC	0179	A	661 721-0390	238
P C A Farm Management LLC	0762	C	661 720-2400	705
Pandol & Sons	0172	A	661 725-3755	165
Pandol Bros Inc (PA)	5148	C	661 725-3755	8715
Tero Tek International Inc (PA)	8711	D	661 725-1135	25944
Triple R Transportation Inc	4119	C	661 725-6494	3854
Vista Verde Farms	5149	E	661 720-9733	8900
Wonderful Citrus Packing LLC (HQ)	0723	B	661 720-2400	589
Wonderful Company LLC	0174	B	661 720-2400	211

DELHI, CA - Merced County

	SIC	EMP	PHONE	ENTRY #
Califrnia Psychtric Trnsitions	8011	D	209 667-9304	19344
Richard Swanson Inc	0173	D	209 632-3883	195

DENAIR, CA - Stanislaus County

	SIC	EMP	PHONE	ENTRY #
Hamlow Ranches Inc	0175	E	209 632-2873	218
J Crecelius Inc	0191	D	209 883-4826	357
Montpelier Orchards MGT Co Inc	0723	E	209 883-4079	542
Valley Fresh Foods Inc	0252	D	209 669-5510	436

DESERT HOT SPRINGS, CA - Riverside County

	SIC	EMP	PHONE	ENTRY #
Desert Hot Springs Real Proper	6512	D	760 329-6000	10867
Desert Springs Hotel	6512	E	760 251-3399	10868
Paragon Industries Inc	1743	C	760 898-4716	3006
Whatever It Takes Inc	7011	E	760 329-6000	13397

DIABLO, CA - Contra Costa County

	SIC	EMP	PHONE	ENTRY #
Diablo Country Club	7997	D	925 837-4221	18914
Diablo Country Club	7997	E	925 837-4221	18915

DIAMOND BAR, CA - Los Angeles County

	SIC	EMP	PHONE	ENTRY #
24-Hour Med Staffing Svcs LLC	7363	C	909 895-8960	14805
Allstate Insurance Company	6331	A	909 612-5504	10333
American Golf Corporation	7997	D	909 861-5757	18836
Avnet Inc	5065	B	760 946-5030	7448
E-N Realty II	6531	E	909 597-1736	11413
F M Tarbell Co	6531	D	909 861-3100	11436
First Team RE - Orange Cnty	6531	D	909 861-1380	11456
Futurenet Technologies Corp	7371	C	909 396-4000	15173
Graybar Electric Company Inc	5063	A	909 451-4300	7362
Insperity Inc	8742	D	909 569-1000	27275
Kaiser Foundation Hospitals	8011	A	800 780-1277	19553
Legally Yours LLC	8111	C	909 396-7200	23200
Liferay Inc (PA)	7373	D	877 543-3729	15996
March International Inc	1629	E	909 821-5128	2044
Mitsuba Corporation	5045	D	909 374-2631	7080
Modrine Limited	7371	D	213 269-5466	15289
Motech Americas LLC	8731	B	302 451-7500	26420
Oak Creek LP	7011	D	909 860-5440	12966
Point of View Inc	7371	D	909 860-0705	15366
Providian Staffing Corporation (PA)	7361	A	909 598-9099	14707
Qtc Mdcal Group Inc A Med Corp	8099	A	800 260-1515	22868
Republic Document Management (PA)	8111	D	909 718-1421	23353
Residential Bancorp (PA)	6162	D	330 499-8333	9855
Schneider Electric Usa Inc	5063	D	909 612-5400	7392
South Coast Air Qulty MGT Dst (PA)	8748	A	909 396-2000	27868
Specialty Equipment Mkt Assn (PA)	8611	C	909 396-0289	24984
Tetra Tech Bas Inc (HQ)	8711	D	909 860-7777	25948
Transport Drivers Inc	7363	B	800 497-6345	14923
Travelers Indemnity Company	6411	C	909 612-3000	10802

DIAMOND SPRINGS, CA - El Dorado County

	SIC	EMP	PHONE	ENTRY #
Cook Cabinets Inc	1751	D	530 621-0851	3023
County of El Dorado	4953	D	530 626-4141	6384
El Dorado County Transit Auth	4111	D	530 642-5383	3648
Johnsen Construction Inc	1771	D	530 642-2123	3274
Snowline Hspc Eldorado Cnty	8052	C	916 817-2338	20959
Snowline Hspice El Dorado Cnty	8052	C	530 621-7820	20960

DINUBA, CA - Tulare County

	SIC	EMP	PHONE	ENTRY #
Adventist Health System	8011	A	559 595-9890	19268
Calpine Containers Inc	5113	D	559 591-6555	8099
College Operations LLC	8351	E	559 353-0576	24297
Dinuba Medical Clinic (PA)	8011	D	559 591-1820	19445

2019 Directory of California
Wholesalers and Services Companies

(P-0000) Products & Services Section entry number
(PA)=Parent Co (HQ)=Headquarters (DH)=Div Headquarters

	SIC	EMP	PHONE	ENTRY #
Fruit Patch Sales LLC	5148	B	559 591-1170	8685
Gillette Citrus Company	0723	C	559 626-4236	518
Kaweah Delta Health Care Dst	8062	C	559 591-5513	21527
Mikaelian & Sons Inc	0161	C	559 591-6324	69
New Covenant Care of Dinuba	8051	D	559 591-3300	20659
Patterson Dental Supply Inc	5047	C	559 595-1450	7206
Valley Labor Service Inc	7361	D	559 591-5591	14794

DIXON, CA - Solano County

	SIC	EMP	PHONE	ENTRY #
Button Transportation Inc	4213	C	707 678-1983	4113
Cardinal Health Inc	5122	C	530 406-3600	8153
Carlisle Construction Mtls Inc	5033	D	707 678-6900	6923
Century 21 Dstnctive Prpts Inc	6531	D	707 678-6451	11296
First Northern Bank of Dixon (HQ)	6022	D	707 678-4422	9449
First Student Inc	4111	D	707 678-8679	3649
John Stewart Company	6531	D	707 676-5660	11534
Mayoral Bros	0761	B	707 693-9111	660
Recology Inc	4953	D	916 379-3300	6436

DOS PALOS, CA - Merced County

	SIC	EMP	PHONE	ENTRY #
Clark Bros Farming Inc	0131	E	209 392-6144	11
Dos Palos Memorial Hosp Inc	8011	D	209 392-6121	19448

DOWNEY, CA - Los Angeles County

	SIC	EMP	PHONE	ENTRY #
American Financial Network Inc	6282	D	562 861-1414	10053
ARC Los Angles Orange Counties (PA)	8331	D	562 803-1556	24147
AT&T Corp	4812	D	562 923-3032	5298
Cantamar Property MGT Inc	6531	E	562 862-4470	11264
Cellco Partnership	4812	D	562 401-1045	5361
Central Refill Pharmaceuticals	5122	D	562 401-4214	8162
Century 21 A Better Svc Rlty	6531	D	562 287-0230	11289
Christian Kirkwood Schools (PA)	8351	D	562 862-4251	24295
City of Downey	7922	D	562 861-8211	18358
Coldwell Bnkr First Class Rlty	6531	D	323 721-7430	11347
Companion Hospice Care LLC	8082	C	562 944-2711	22272
Companion Hospice LLC	8082	D	562 944-2711	22273
Conrad A Cox	8011	E	562 927-0033	19404
County of Los Angeles	8322	C	562 401-9413	23656
County of Los Angeles	8093	A	562 401-7088	22546
County of Los Angeles	8322	B	562 940-2476	23684
Covenant Care California LLC	8051	D	562 923-9301	20336
Downey Community Health Center	8051	D	562 862-6506	20379
El Camino Children & Fmly Svcs	8322	E	562 364-1258	23782
Farwest Corrosion Control Co (PA)	1799	C	310 532-9524	3516
Financial Partners Credit Un (PA)	6061	D	562 904-3000	9552
First Family Homes	6531	E	562 862-7373	11453
Healthcare Ctr of Downey LLC	8051	C	562 869-0978	20517
Intero Real Estate Svcs Inc	6531	D	562 861-7242	11518
Kaiser Foundation Hospitals	8062	B	562 657-9000	21482
Kaiser Foundation Hospitals	8011	A	800 823-4040	19551
Kaiser Foundation Hospitals	8011	A	800 823-4040	19555
Kaiser Foundation Hospitals	6324	D	562 622-4190	10266
Kpwr Radio LLC	7389	C	562 745-2300	17281
Lakewood Park Health Center (PA)	7389	D	562 869-0978	17289
Liberty Ambulance LLC	4119	D	562 741-6230	3818
Liberty Utilities Pk Wtr Corp (DH)	4941	D	562 923-0711	6271
Los Amigos Country Club Inc	7997	D	562 923-9696	18961
Los Angeles Cty Rnch Los Amgos	8052	A	562 385-7111	20939
Macerich Company	6512	E	562 861-9233	10908
Mental Hlth Cnvlscent Svcs Inc	8051	B	562 869-0978	20642
Mike Campbell & Associates Ltd	4222	A	626 369-3981	4509
Mullahey Chevrolet Inc	7532	E	714 871-2545	17731
Newwest Mortgage Company	6163	D	562 861-8393	9899
Omniment Industries Inc (PA)	1711	C	562 923-9660	2295
Omniteam Inc	5078	C	562 923-9660	7663
Park Hotels & Resorts Inc	7011	D	562 861-1900	13034
Pih Health Hospital - Downey	8062	A	562 698-0811	21646
Pih Health Hospital - Whitti	8062	A	562 904-5482	21648
Pioneer Medical Group Inc	8011	D	562 862-2775	19791
Prestige Too Auto Body Inc	7532	E	310 787-8852	17735
Prudential 24 Hour Real Estate	6531	D	562 861-7257	11690
Ralphs Grocery Company	4225	D	562 633-0830	4620
Ralphs Grocery Company	4225	D	562 869-2042	4622
Rancho Los Amigos Nationa	8322	B	562 401-7111	23980
Rancho Los Amigos Nationa	8322	A	562 401-7111	23981
Rancho Los Amigos Nationa	8322	B	562 401-7266	23982
Rancho Los Amigos Nationa (PA)	8322	D	562 401-7111	23983
Rancho Research Institute	8733	C	562 401-8111	26653
Rockview Dairies Inc (PA)	5149	D	562 927-5511	8861
Rrm Construction Inc	1522	E	562 440-3539	1313
Santa Paula Water Works Ltd	6719	D	562 923-0711	12004
Sialic Contractors Corporation	1611	D	562 803-9977	1849
Southern Cal Prmnnte Med Group	6324	A	562 657-2200	10320
Southern California Alcohol An (PA)	8093	D	562 923-4545	22684
Southern California Gas Co	4924	E	562 803-7453	6175
Southland Credit Union	6062	D	562 862-6831	9656

	SIC	EMP	PHONE	ENTRY #
Spectrum MGT Holdg Co LLC	4841	D	562 372-4008	5939
Steve Roberson	6531	D	562 927-2626	11779
Sunbridge Healthcare LLC	8052	C	562 869-2567	20966
USF Reddaway Inc	4213	C	562 923-0648	4297
Westar Manufacturing Inc	1799	D	562 633-0581	3610
Young Mens Chrstn Assn of La	8322	D	562 862-4201	24137
Young Mens Chrstn Assn of La	8641	D	562 862-4201	25346

DUARTE, CA - Los Angeles County

	SIC	EMP	PHONE	ENTRY #
Baxco Pharmaceutical Inc	5122	C	909 595-0826	8144
Beckman Research Inst Hope	8733	C	626 359-8111	26596
Begroup	8051	D	626 359-9371	20258
Bershtel Enterprises LLC (PA)	7389	C	626 301-9214	17030
Cal Southern Presbt Homes	8051	D	626 359-8141	20278
Cal Southern Presbt Homes	6513	C	626 357-1632	10996
City Hope National Medical Ctr	8062	A	626 256-4673	21328
ESP Group Ltd	5137	D	626 301-0280	8302
Event Guard Services Inc	7381	C	626 531-6772	16640
General Electric Company	7378	C	626 359-7988	16286
Integrated Mech Systems Inc	1711	E	626 446-1864	2237
Kf Community Care LLC	8059	C	626 357-3207	21124
Maryvale Day Care Center	8351	C	626 357-1514	24345
Monrovia Convalescent Hospital	8059	D	626 359-6618	21159
Paris Blues Inc (PA)	6719	D	310 605-2000	11998
Royal Terrace Healthcare	8051	D	626 256-4654	20733
SA Recycling LLC	4953	D	626 359-5815	6462
Santa Teresita Inc (PA)	8062	B	626 359-3243	21722
United Hauling Corp	7513	D	626 358-9417	17618
Westminster Gardens	8059	D	626 359-2571	21254

DUBLIN, CA - Alameda County

	SIC	EMP	PHONE	ENTRY #
4g Wireless Inc	4813	D	925 307-8990	5431
AMS Electric Inc	1731	D	925 961-1600	2509
AT&T Corp	7389	B	925 560-5011	17015
Bay Area News Group E Bay LLC (HQ)	7319	D	925 302-1683	13966
Callidus Software Inc (HQ)	7371	C	925 251-2200	15047
Care Options Management Plans	8082	D	925 551-3227	22247
Challenge Dairy Products Inc (HQ)	5143	D	925 828-6160	8517
Corelynx Inc	7371	C	877 267-3599	15079
Corizon Health Inc	8011	C	925 551-6500	19406
Desilva Gates Construction LP (PA)	1611	D	925 361-1380	1758
Develpment Dimensions Intl Inc	8742	B	925 361-4246	27215
Dublin Hstrcal Prsrvation Assn	8412	D	925 785-2898	24881
Dublin San Ramon Services Dst (PA)	4941	C	925 875-2276	6239
Epicor Software Corporation	7372	C	925 361-9900	15670
Franklin Tmpleton Inv Svcs LLC	6282	C	925 875-2619	10084
Gateway Landscape Cnstr Inc	0782	D	925 875-0000	846
Gettler-Ryan Inc (PA)	1799	D	925 551-7555	3525
New Home Professionals	6531	C	925 556-1555	11626
Oracle Taleo LLC	7372	A	925 452-3000	15823
Pacific Sttes Envmtl Cntrs Inc	1542	E	925 803-4333	1608
Rakon America LLC	5065	A	847 930-5100	7532
Rgis LLC	7389	B	925 829-2875	17439
Saba Software Inc (PA)	7372	C	877 722-2101	15843
Sansa Technology LLC	8731	E	866 204-3710	26449
Service King Paint & Body LLC	7532	C	925 301-8481	17741
T and D Communications Inc (PA)	7371	D	510 824-0010	15488
Trevi Partners A Calif LP (HQ)	7011	D	925 828-7750	13342
Water & Sewer Service	1623	D	925 828-8524	1999

DURHAM, CA - Butte County

	SIC	EMP	PHONE	ENTRY #
Chico Produce Inc (PA)	5148	C	530 893-0596	8653
Fedex Ground Package Sys Inc	4213	C	800 463-3339	4169

E RNCHO DMNGZ, CA - Los Angeles County

	SIC	EMP	PHONE	ENTRY #
Murray Plumbing and Htg Corp (PA)	1711	A	310 637-1500	2287

EARLIMART, CA - Tulare County

	SIC	EMP	PHONE	ENTRY #
Vincent V Zaninovich & Sons	0172	D	661 849-2613	183

EARP, CA - San Bernardino County

	SIC	EMP	PHONE	ENTRY #
Colorado River Adventures Inc (PA)	7033	C	760 663-3737	13462

EAST PALO ALTO, CA - Santa Clara County

	SIC	EMP	PHONE	ENTRY #
Burr Pilger Mayer Inc	8721	E	650 855-6800	26156
Cintas Corporation No 3	7218	D	650 589-4300	13605
County of San Mateo	8322	D	650 853-3139	23737
Dla Piper LLP (us)	8111	B	650 833-2000	23045
Dla Piper LLP (us)	8111	B	650 833-2000	23047
Drew Health Foundation	8399	E	650 328-1619	24775
Duff & Phelps LLC	8742	D	650 798-5500	27220
East Palo Alto Hotel Dev Inc	7011	C	650 566-1200	12546
East Palo Alto Y M C A	8641	D	650 328-9622	25153
Facial Reconstructive Surgery	8011	E	650 328-0511	19468
Four Seasons Hotel Inc	7011	A	650 566-1200	12588
Golf & Tennis Pro Shop Inc	7999	D	650 600-5200	19179
Greenberg Traurig LLP	8111	D	650 328-8500	23113
Hggc LLC (PA)	7371	B	650 321-4910	15199

Employment Codes: A=Over 500 employees, B=251-500,
C=101-250, D=51-100, E=50

2019 Directory of California
Wholesalers and Services Companies

© Mergent Inc. 1-800-342-5647
1567

GEOGRAPHIC

Name	SIC	EMP	PHONE	ENTRY #
Ropes & Gray LLP	8111	D	650 617-4000	23361
Roto-Rooter Services Company	7699	D	650 322-2366	17979
South Cnty Cmnty Hlth Ctr Inc (PA)	8099	D	650 330-7407	22887
Zadaonet	4813	D	650 556-6377	5681

EASTVALE, CA - Riverside County

Name	SIC	EMP	PHONE	ENTRY #
Cellco Partnership	4812	D	951 361-1850	5317
Dejuno Corporation	5199	D	909 230-6744	9210
DSC Logistics Inc	4212	D	909 605-7233	4007
Dz Trading Ltd	5099	C	951 479-5700	8028
Meiko America Inc	4225	D	951 360-0281	4593
Mentor Media (usa) Sup	8741	D	909 930-0800	26943
UPS Ground Freight Inc	4213	D	951 361-1300	4289
WW Grainger Inc	5085	C	951 727-2300	7878

EDGEWOOD, CA - Siskiyou County

Name	SIC	EMP	PHONE	ENTRY #
Siskiyou Development Company	7011	D	530 938-2731	13231

EDISON, CA - Kern County

Name	SIC	EMP	PHONE	ENTRY #
Giumarra Farms Inc	0134	D	661 395-7000	18
Giumarra Vineyards Corporation (PA)	0172	B	661 395-7000	146
Johnston Farms	0134	D	661 366-3201	19
Kirschenman Enterprises Sls LP	7389	B	661 366-5736	17276
Kirschenman Packing Inc	0723	C	661 366-5736	534

EDWARDS, CA - Kern County

Name	SIC	EMP	PHONE	ENTRY #
Jt3 LLC	8711	A	661 277-4900	25772
US Dept of the Air Force	4899	C	661 277-3030	6004
US Dept of the Air Force	8731	D	661 275-5410	26486

EDWARDS AFB, CA - Kern County

Name	SIC	EMP	PHONE	ENTRY #
GE Aviation Systems LLC	4581	D	661 277-7308	4892

EL CAJON, CA - San Diego County

Name	SIC	EMP	PHONE	ENTRY #
A Better Solution In Home Care	8082	C	619 447-1528	22178
Aeromedevac Inc	8742	D	619 284-7910	27117
AJM Packaging Corporation	5199	D	619 448-4007	9192
American Residential Svcs LLC	1711	D	858 292-4452	2110
Anthony P Garofalo A Dental	8021	D	619 440-0071	20110
ARC of San Diego	8399	C	619 448-2415	24738
Artimex Iron Company Inc	1791	C	619 444-3155	3360
Automotive Service Council	8699	D	800 810-4272	25395
Baechler Investigative Svcs	7381	D	619 464-5600	16576
Builders Firstsource	5031	E	619 440-7711	6810
C Team Construction Inc	1771	D	619 579-6572	3228
California Shtmtl Works Inc	1541	D	619 562-7010	1384
Care With Dignity Healthcare	8051	D	619 447-1020	20287
Cass Construction Inc (PA)	1623	C	619 590-0929	1904
Cellco Partnership	4812	D	619 596-7201	5328
Country Hills Health Care Inc	8051	C	619 441-8745	20325
Countywide Mech Systems Inc	1711	C	619 449-9900	2174
Cox Communications Cal LLC	4841	B	619 562-9820	5894
Demko Drywall & Demolition Co	1742	C	619 590-0025	2873
Division 8 Inc	1793	E	619 741-7552	3404
Edwards Theatres Circuit Inc	7832	D	619 660-3460	18289
El Cajon Motors (PA)	7515	D	619 579-8888	17653
El Cajon Plumbing & Htg Sup Co	5075	D	619 449-7300	7647
El Cajon Vly Convalescent Ctr	8051	C	619 440-1211	20385
Eldorado Care Center LP	8051	B	619 440-1211	20388
Eugene N Townsend	7532	D	619 442-8807	17719
Executive Protection Agency K-	7381	E	619 442-5771	16643
F R Ghianni Enterprises Inc	1521	D	619 279-1073	1163
Fox Factory Holding Corp	5013	A	619 768-1800	6641
G M A C-One Source Realty	6531	F	619 405-6231	11476
Gardner Pool Company Inc (PA)	1799	D	619 593-8880	3524
Global Check Service	7389	C	619 449-5150	17189
Granite Hills Healthcare	8051	C	619 447-1020	20496
Grossmont-Cuyamaca Community	8641	D	619 644-7684	25170
Hamann Construction	1541	D	619 440-7424	1405
Helix Water District	4941	D	619 596-3860	6262
Home Guiding Hands Corporation (PA)	8361	B	619 938-2850	24565
J P Witherow Roofing Company	1761	D	619 297-4701	3168
Jeffrey Pine Holdings LLC	8051	D	619 442-0544	20549
K T A Construction Inc	1623	D	619 562-9464	1941
Kaiser Foundation Hospitals	8062	E	619 528-5000	21499
Kaiser Foundation Hospitals	8062	E	619 528-5000	21501
Koch-Armstrong General Engrg	8711	D	619 561-2005	25786
La Maestra Family Clinic Inc	8011	D	619 280-1105	19634
Lundstrom & Associates Inc	8711	E	619 641-5900	25803
Madison Care Center LLC	8051	D	619 444-1107	20606
Magnolia Special Care Center	8052	D	619 442-8826	20940
McAlister Institute For Treat (PA)	8093	C	619 442-0277	22617
McClintock Enterprises Inc	4141	C	619 579-5300	3890
Nan McKay and Associates Inc	8742	C	619 258-1855	27357
National Public Safety	7381	D	619 401-9431	16737
Neighborhood Healthcare	8011	D	619 440-2751	19706
Newport Diversified Inc	7389	C	619 449-7800	17352

Name	SIC	EMP	PHONE	ENTRY #
Our Lady of Grace P T G	7389	E	619 466-0055	17379
Pacific Production Plumbing (PA)	1711	E	951 509-3100	2302
Paradise Electric Inc	1731	D	619 449-4141	2675
Parkside Special Care Center	8051	C	619 442-7744	20694
Plum Healthcare Group LLC	8051	C	619 873-2500	20708
Premier Golf Properties LP	7992	D	619 442-9891	18745
Professionals Choice Sport	5191	D	619 873-1100	9093
R & R Mechanical Contrs Inc	1711	D	619 449-9900	2323
R D S Unlimited Inc	1751	E	619 443-0221	3063
S C Tile Company Inc	1743	E	619 669-1575	3009
San Diego Aerospace Museum	8412	D	619 258-1221	24903
San Diego Blood Bank	8099	C	619 441-1804	22875
Schilling Paradise Corp	1623	D	619 449-4141	1979
Seal Electric Inc	1731	D	619 449-7323	2727
Sears Roebuck and Co	7629	C	619 590-3812	17911
Sharp Healthcare	8011	D	619 442-0844	19882
Somerset Special Care Center	8052	D	619 442-0245	20961
Southern Cal Prmnnte Med Group	8011	E	619 528-5000	19915
St Madeleine Sophies Center	8331	D	619 442-5129	24233
Steve Duich Inc	1771	E	619 444-6118	3331
Sunshine Communications Inc	1731	C	619 448-7600	2753
Sycuan Casino	7999	A	619 445-6002	19243
The Pines Ltd	6513	C	619 447-1880	11125
Thomas J Hoban (PA)	6531	E	619 442-1665	11795
Thyssenkrupp Elevator Corp	7699	D	619 569-7220	17997
Tony Gomez Tree Service	0783	C	619 593-1552	979
Toyotalift Inc (PA)	5084	E	619 562-5438	7812
University Mechanical & (DH)	1711	D	619 956-2500	2392
USA Waste of California Inc	4953	D	619 596-5117	6494
Victoria Post Acute Care	8059	C	619 440-5005	21246
Walter Anderson Plumbing Inc	1711	E	619 449-7646	2403
Waste Management Cal Inc	4953	D	619 596-5100	6511
Way Cool Homecare Inc	8082	E	619 444-3200	22462
West Coast AC Co Inc	1711	C	619 561-8000	2406
Xl Staffing Inc	7361	C	619 579-0442	14800

EL CENTRO, CA - Imperial County

Name	SIC	EMP	PHONE	ENTRY #
Accentcare Home Health	8082	E	760 352-4022	22188
All Star Seed (PA)	0723	D	760 482-9400	490
ARC - Imperial Valley (PA)	8322	C	760 352-0180	23483
Canon Solutions America Inc	5044	C	800 323-4827	6952
Cellco Partnership	4812	D	760 337-5508	5377
City of El Centro	1611	C	760 337-4505	1740
County of Imperial	8099	C	760 482-4441	22771
County of Imperial	8322	C	760 336-3581	23645
County of Imperial	8093	D	760 482-4120	22545
El Centro Regional Medical Ctr (PA)	8062	A	760 339-7100	21403
Granite Construction Inc	1611	C	760 337-3030	1779
Hay Kuhn Inc	5199	E	760 353-0124	9223
I N C Builders Inc	7363	A	760 352-4200	14860
Imperial County Behavioral HLT	8093	D	760 482-2149	22598
Imperial Irrigation District	4931	C	760 339-9800	6183
Noblesse Oblige Inc	0722	A	760 353-3336	482
Original Sid Blackman Plbg Inc	1711	D	760 352-3632	2301
Schaefer Ambulance Service Inc	4119	C	760 353-3380	3844
Securitas SEC Svcs USA Inc	7381	C	760 353-8177	16794
Time Warner Cable Inc	4841	D	760 335-4800	5961
United Families Inc (PA)	8322	C	760 336-8922	24104
United Parcel Service Inc OH	4215	D	858 541-2336	4443
Valencia Bros Inc	1771	D	760 353-2168	3340
Wilbur-Ellis Company LLC	5191	D	760 352-2847	9106

EL CERRITO, CA - Contra Costa County

Name	SIC	EMP	PHONE	ENTRY #
Berkeley Clinic Auxuillary	8699	D	510 525-7844	25398
Berkeley Country Club	7997	C	510 233-7550	18863
Shields Nursing Centers Inc	8051	D	510 525-3212	20761
West Coast Childrens Center	8011	E	510 269-9030	20095

EL DORADO, CA - El Dorado County

Name	SIC	EMP	PHONE	ENTRY #
Conforti Plumbing Inc	1711	A	530 622-0202	2168

EL DORADO HILLS, CA - El Dorado County

Name	SIC	EMP	PHONE	ENTRY #
Action Home Nursing Services	8082	D	530 756-2600	22197
Amdocs Inc	7371	B	916 934-7000	14978
Amdocs Bcs Inc	7371	B	916 934-7000	14979
Bayview Engrg & Cnstr Co Inc	1711	D	916 939-8986	2137
California Physicians Service	6324	B	916 350-7800	10187
CBS Maxpreps Inc	4813	E	530 676-6440	5528
Coldwell Bnkr Rsdntial RE Svcs	6531	D	916 933-1155	11364
Comerit Inc	7379	C	888 556-5990	16328
Consensus Orthopedics Inc	5047	D	916 355-7110	7176
Dorado Software Inc	7371	D	916 673-1100	15116
Dst Output California Inc	7378	D	916 939-4617	16282
El Dorado Hills County Wtr Dst	4941	D	916 933-6623	6249
Frank Gates Service Company	8742	D	916 934-0812	27241
G R Helm Inc	7363	D	916 933-9697	14856
Infinite Technologies Inc (PA)	8711	D	916 987-3261	25743

2019 Directory of California
Wholesalers and Services Companies

(P-0000) Products & Services Section entry number
(PA)=Parent Co (HQ)=Headquarters (DH)=Div Headquarters

	SIC	EMP	PHONE	ENTRY #
Marshall Medical Center	8062	C	916 933-2273	21580
O1 Communications Inc	4813	C	888 444-1111	5615
Patra Corporation (PA)	6311	C	415 595-9987	10143
Patrick K Willis Company Inc	7389	B	800 398-6480	17393
R Systems Inc (HQ)	7379	C	916 939-9696	16469
Response 1 Medical Staffing	7361	C	916 932-0430	14723
Roebbelen Construction Inc	1542	D	916 939-4000	1634
Roebbelen Contracting Inc	1542	B	916 939-4000	1635
School Innovations Achievement (PA)	7372	D	916 933-2290	15848
Securecom Inc	1731	E	916 628-2855	2728
Sequoia Insurance Company	6411	C	916 933-9524	10772
Serrano Associates LLC	7997	D	916 939-3333	19041
Serrano Country Club Inc	7997	C	916 933-5005	19042
Sierra Equipment Leasing Inc	7359	E	925 676-7300	14545
Suds Car Wash Inc	7542	C	916 673-6300	17839
V3 Electric Inc	1711	C	916 597-2627	2393
Weckworth Construction Co Inc	1731	D	916 939-6636	2785
Wyndgate Technologies	7379	D	916 404-8400	16535

EL GRANADA, CA - San Mateo County

	SIC	EMP	PHONE	ENTRY #
Indyne	8621	D	805 606-0664	25020
Range Generation Next LLC	8748	E	310 647-9438	27837

EL MACERO, CA - Yolo County

	SIC	EMP	PHONE	ENTRY #
El Macero Country Club Inc	7997	D	530 753-3363	18920

EL MONTE, CA - Los Angeles County

	SIC	EMP	PHONE	ENTRY #
Access Services	4111	D	213 270-6000	3635
Ahm Gemch Inc	8062	C	626 579-7777	21270
Altamed Health Services Corp	8099	C	323 889-7847	22726
Altamed Health Services Corp	8011	A	877 462-2582	19280
Atlanta Seafoods LLC	5146	D	626 626-4900	8570
Bangkit (usa) Inc	5112	D	626 672-0888	8076
California Schl Employees Assn	7363	B	626 258-3300	14827
Cathay Bank (HQ)	6022	C	626 279-3698	9424
Center Medical Company	8011	E	626 575-7500	19362
County of Los Angeles	8322	C	626 575-4059	23654
County of Los Angeles	8361	C	626 455-4700	24481
Dang Quinten	4899	D	626 429-6332	5978
Davita Medical Management LLC	8011	D	626 444-0333	19432
Eighty One Enterprise Inc	5137	E	626 371-1980	8301
El Monte Community Credit Un	6062	D	626 444-0501	9632
El Monte Convalescent Hospital	8059	D	626 442-1500	21060
ERs SEC Alarm Systems Inc	5063	D	626 579-2525	7360
Exterran Inc	7353	D	626 455-0739	14439
Firefighter Cancer Support Ntw	8322	E	866 994-3276	23806
First Student Inc	4111	D	626 448-9446	3650
Foundation For Early Childhood (PA)	8322	D	626 572-5107	23808
Georgia Atkison Snf LLC	8051	C	626 444-2535	20453
Gibralter Convalescent Hosp	8059	D	626 443-9425	21082
Hope Hse For Mltple Hndicapped (PA)	8361	D	626 443-1313	24566
Insul Acoustics Inc	1742	C	323 686-2670	2896
K T Lucky Co Inc	5149	D	626 579-7272	8816
Nijjar Realty Inc (PA)	6531	D	626 575-0062	11629
Optics Laboratory Inc	8071	D	626 350-1926	22118
Pacific Coast Drum Company	5085	D	626 443-3096	7862
Public Hlth Fndation Entps Inc	8099	C	626 856-6618	22866
R and L Lopez Associates Inc (PA)	8711	D	626 336-9655	25883
Ramona Care Center Inc	8051	D	626 442-5721	20715
Retail Services Wis Corp	7389	D	626 288-1200	17429
Rio Hondo Community Dev Corp	8399	D	626 401-2784	24831
S & S Portable Services Inc	7359	D	626 967-9300	14541
S & S Rent-A-Fence Inc	7359	D	818 896-7710	14542
SA Recycling LLC	4953	D	626 444-9530	6466
Sabu Enterprises Inc	8059	E	626 443-1351	21201
San Gabriel Transit Inc (PA)	4111	C	626 258-1310	3715
San Gabriel Valley Water Co (PA)	4941	C	626 448-6183	6304
San Gbriel Vly Cnvlescent Hosp	8063	D	626 401-1557	21971
Southland Transit Inc (PA)	4119	C	626 258-1310	3849
Triple-E Machinery Moving Inc	4213	D	626 444-1137	4282
Turn Around Communications Inc	1623	D	626 443-2400	1989
Wells Fargo Bank National Assn	6021	B	626 312-3006	9389
Wells Fargo Bank National Assn	6021	C	626 573-1338	9395
Wgg Enterprises Inc	1742	C	626 442-5493	2982
Yew Bio-Pharm Group Inc	0811	D	626 401-9588	996

EL NIDO, CA - Merced County

	SIC	EMP	PHONE	ENTRY #
Standard Cattle LLC	5154	C	559 693-1977	8908

EL PORTAL, CA - Mariposa County

	SIC	EMP	PHONE	ENTRY #
Yosemite Management Group LLC (PA)	7011	D	209 379-2817	13435

EL SEGUNDO, CA - Los Angeles County

	SIC	EMP	PHONE	ENTRY #
24hr Homecare LLC (PA)	8082	D	310 906-3683	22175
A-Mark Precious Metals Inc (PA)	5094	C	310 587-1477	8000
Accenture LLP	8742	B	310 726-2700	27106
Advantage Sales & Mktg Inc	5141	C	310 321-6869	8373

	SIC	EMP	PHONE	ENTRY #
Aerospace Corporation (PA)	8733	A	310 336-5000	26578
After-Party2 Inc	7359	D	310 535-3660	14467
Air Force US Dept of	8733	B	310 336-5000	26585
Air New Zealand Limited	4512	D	310 648-7000	4759
Altech Services Inc	7363	D	888 725-8324	14813
American Golf Corporation (PA)	7997	C	310 664-4000	18829
Arinwine Arcft Maint Svcs LLC	4581	D	310 338-0063	4872
Asset Athene Management L P (HQ)	8741	D	310 698-4444	26768
Avanti Health System LLC	8742	B	310 356-0550	27146
BMC Group Inc	8111	D	310 321-5555	22951
Booz Allen Hamilton Inc	8711	D	310 524-1557	25573
Bshh II LLC	7011	E	310 356-4587	12408
Bshh II LLC	7011	E	310 356-4577	12409
BT Americas Inc	5065	D	646 487-7400	7452
California Physicians Service	6324	C	310 744-2668	10188
Carson Kurtzman Consultants (DH)	8111	C	310 823-9000	22973
Cathay Pacific Airways Limited	4729	D	310 615-1113	4986
Cbre Inc	6531	C	310 363-4900	11280
Century Pk Capitl Partners LLC (PA)	6726	C	310 867-2210	12059
Cetera Financial Group Inc (PA)	7389	C	866 489-3100	17069
Citigroup Global Markets Inc	6211	D	310 727-9533	9931
City National Bank	6021	C	310 297-6606	9340
Cls Trnsprttion Los Angles LLC (HQ)	4119	C	310 414-8189	3785
Columbus Tech & Svcs Inc (PA)	8711	B	310 356-5600	25618
Continental 155 5th Corp	6531	E	310 640-1520	11377
Core Nutrition LLC	5149	D	310 640-0500	8774
Core Nutrition LLC	5149	E	310 640-0500	8775
CSC Consulting Inc	7379	D	310 563-2062	16337
David & Goliath LLC	7311	C	310 445-5200	13809
Davita Inc	8092	D	310 536-2400	22471
Davita Medical Management LLC (HQ)	8011	A	310 354-4200	19433
Daz Systems LLC (DH)	7371	D	310 640-1300	15096
Dedicated Media Inc (PA)	7311	C	310 524-9400	13814
Dfds International Corporation	4731	D	310 414-1516	5043
Directv Inc	4841	A	888 388-4249	5898
Directv Enterprises LLC	4841	C	310 535-5000	5900
Directv Group Holdings LLC (HQ)	4841	C	310 964-5000	5903
Directv Group Inc (DH)	4841	C	310 964-5000	5904
Directv International Inc (DH)	4841	C	310 964-6460	5905
Diverse Journeys Inc (PA)	8322	D	310 643-7403	23773
Doubletree By Hilton Hotel	7011	C	310 322-0999	12539
Edwards Technologies Inc	1731	D	310 536-7070	2570
El Segundo Eductl Foundation	8399	B	310 615-2650	24779
Empire Chauffeur Service Ltd	4212	D	310 414-8189	4011
En Pointe Technologies Sls LLC	5045	C	310 337-6151	7041
Enterprise Services LLC	7374	C	310 331-1074	16127
Enthusiast Network Inc (PA)	4731	B	310 531-9900	5053
Ernst & Young LLP	8721	C	310 725-1764	26192
European Hotl Invstrs of CA	7011	E	310 322-0999	12566
Experian Info Solutions Inc	8742	C	310 343-6700	27230
F&E Aircraft Maintenance (PA)	4581	C	310 338-0063	4890
Fc El Segundo LLC	7011	E	702 439-7945	12571
Federal Express Corporation	7389	B	800 463-3339	17166
Forsythe Technology LLC	7379	D	424 217-6500	16369
Frito-Lay North America Inc	5145	E	310 322-5001	8561
Fujitsu America Inc	7373	C	310 563-7000	15964
Fujitsu Glovia Inc (HQ)	7371	C	310 563-7000	15171
Gbp Intermediate Corp (DH)	6719	A	424 254-9774	11979
Gbp Parent Corp (HQ)	6719	A	424 254-9774	11980
Glovia Inc	7371	C	310 563-7000	15182
Governmentjobscom Inc	7372	C	310 426-6304	15694
Guthy-Renker LLC (PA)	5099	D	760 773-9022	8035
Hco Holding I Corporation (HQ)	6719	A	323 583-5000	11985
Hilton El Segundo LLC	7011	D	310 726-0100	12660
Hilton Garden Inns MGT LLC	7011	D	310 726-0100	12664
Hit Portfolio I NTC Trs LP	7011	E	310 333-0888	12685
Hypermedia Systems Inc	7379	D	213 452-6731	16391
Ibftech Inc	7361	D	424 217-8010	14642
Ignited LLC (PA)	7311	C	310 773-3100	13845
Infineon Tech Americas Corp	8721	A	310 726-8000	26228
Infonet Services Corporation	4225	A	310 335-2600	4578
Infonet Services Corporation (DH)	4813	A	310 335-2859	5585
Infrascale Inc	5045	C	310 878-2621	7062
Internet Brands Inc (PA)	7374	C	310 280-4000	16149
Irise (PA)	7371	D	800 556-0399	15237
Ispace Inc	7379	D	310 563-3800	16410
Jackson Tull Chrtred Engineers	7373	E	310 658-2132	15986
Jalux Americas Inc (HQ)	7359	E	310 524-1000	14518
Japan Airlines Co Ltd	4724	C	310 607-2305	4941
Kleinpartners Capital Corp	6799	B	310 426-2055	12237
Konami Digital Entrmt Inc (DH)	7372	D	310 220-8100	15733
Kyocera International Inc	5043	D	310 647-2805	6945
L E Coppersmith Inc (PA)	4731	D	310 607-8000	5100
L E Coppersmith Inc	4731	D	310 607-8000	5101
Leidos Inc	8731	C	310 524-3134	26403

Employment Codes: A=Over 500 employees, B=251-500,
C=101-250, D=51-100, E=50

2019 Directory of California
Wholesalers and Services Companies

© Mergent Inc. 1-800-342-5647
1569

GEOGRAPHIC

	SIC	EMP	PHONE	ENTRY #
Login Consulting Services Inc	7379	D	310 607-9091	16422
Los Angeles Lakers Inc	7941	C	310 426-6000	18525
Los Angeles Kings Hockey CLB LP	7941	C	310 535-4502	18527
Manduka LLC (HQ)	5091	E	310 426-1495	7933
Mantech International Corp	7373	D	310 765-9324	16002
Marketwire Inc (HQ)	7383	D	310 765-3200	16957
Marriott International Inc	7011	C	310 333-0888	12892
Marriott International Inc	7011	C	310 322-0700	12898
Mattel Toy Company	5092	A	310 252-2357	7956
Matthews Retail Group Inc	6531	D	866 889-0550	11594
Michael Sullivan & Assoc LLP	8111	C	310 337-4480	23252
Mission Critical Tech Inc	7371	E	310 246-4455	15285
Mullin TBG Insur Agcy Svcs LLC (DH)	6411	C	310 203-8770	10697
Nagra Usa Inc (HQ)	5084	D	310 335-5225	7776
National Air Cargo Inc	4731	D	310 662-4766	5114
National Planning Corporation	6141	D	800 881-7174	9724
Nippon Express USA Inc	4731	D	310 535-7200	5120
NRG El Segundo Operations Inc	4911	D	310 615-6344	6061
Oceanx LLC (HQ)	7389	D	310 774-4088	17367
Oracle Corporation	7372	C	310 343-7405	15813
Oracle Systems Corporation	7372	C	818 817-2900	15815
Orbital Sciences Corporation	8731	B	703 406-5000	26425
Osata Enterprises Inc	5139	D	310 297-1550	8364
Pacific Theaters Inc	7832	D	310 607-0007	18309
Patterson Dental Supply Inc	5047	D	310 426-3100	7204
Pcm Sales Inc (HQ)	5045	C	310 354-5600	7089
Peopleware Technical Resources	7361	D	310 640-2406	14693
Performance Team LLC (PA)	4731	C	562 345-2200	5142
Pinnacle Travel Services LLC	4724	C	310 414-1787	4947
Plumb Tech Inc	1711	D	310 322-4925	2312
Primary Color Systems Corp	7335	C	310 841-0250	14098
Prodege LLC (PA)	7371	D	310 294-9599	15380
Professional Janitorial Svc	7349	E	310 410-1452	14357
Prologic Rdmption Slutions Inc (PA)	7389	A	310 322-7774	17416
Prosum Inc (PA)	7374	D	310 404-1545	16168
Pt Gaming LLC	7011	A	323 260-5060	13083
Radica Enterprises Ltd	5092	D	310 252-2000	7960
Rainier Financial Group LLC	8742	E	310 335-9200	27418
Raytheon Command and Control	5065	E	714 446-3232	7534
Raytheon Company	8711	C	310 647-9438	25891
Rhythm and Hues Inc (PA)	7812	D	310 448-7500	18109
Rjt Compuquest Inc (PA)	7379	B	310 378-6666	16473
Rpd Hotels 18 LLC (PA)	7011	A	213 746-1531	13148
Rubicon B Hacienda LLC	7011	D	424 290-5000	13151
Rubicon B Hacienda LLC	7011	D	424 290-5555	13152
Rydek Eletronics LLC	7361	D	310 641-9800	14749
Saviynt Inc (PA)	8742	C	310 641-1664	27440
SC Harp El Segundo LLC	7011	D	310 322-0999	13195
Scope Seven LLC	5099	D	310 220-3939	8058
Securitas Critical Infrastruct	7381	A	310 426-3300	16786
Sierra Systems Inc (PA)	8742	C	310 536-6288	27448
Singapore Airlines Limited	4512	C	310 647-1922	4797
Softscript Inc	7338	A	310 451-2110	14134
Source Interlink Media LLC	7371	D	310 531-9394	15467
Spectrum MGT Holdg Co LLC	4841	D	310 647-3000	5943
Square Enix Inc	5045	D	310 846-0400	7110
Stampscom Inc (PA)	7331	A	310 482-5800	14063
TBG Insurance Services Corp	6411	B	310 203-8770	10799
Tecolote Research Inc	8742	C	310 640-4700	27482
Telenet Voip Inc	7629	D	310 253-9000	17915
Ten Publishing Media LLC (PA)	7819	C	310 531-9900	18232
Time Warner Cable Entps LLC	4841	A	469 665-7735	5949
Trace3 Inc	8742	D	310 220-0164	27492
Transportation Management LLC	4212	E	310 524-1555	4070
Tri-Star Ccw Management L P	7011	D	310 322-0999	13345
Tri-Union Seafoods LLC (DH)	5146	D	858 558-9662	8608
Vagabond Inn Corporation (HQ)	7011	D	213 284-7533	13362
Vision Tech Solutions LLC	7371	D	310 656-3100	15530
Wash Mltfmily Ldry Systems LLC (PA)	7215	C	310 643-8491	13562
Westport Capital Partners LLC	6799	D	310 294-1234	12283
Whelan Security Co	7381	B	310 343-8628	16857
Wpromote LLC (PA)	8742	D	310 421-4844	27524
Xceed Financial Credit Union (PA)	6061	D	800 932-8222	9618
Your Man Tours Inc (DH)	4725	D	310 649-3820	4985
Your Man Tours Inc	8699	D	513 772-4411	25489

EL SOBRANTE, CA - Contra Costa County

	SIC	EMP	PHONE	ENTRY #
D & H Landscaping Inc	0782	D	510 223-6597	816
Greenridge Senior Care	8361	C	510 758-9600	24544
Ppm Real Estate Inc	6531	D	510 758-5636	11676

EL TORO, CA - Orange County

	SIC	EMP	PHONE	ENTRY #
Certainteed Gypsum Inc	5031	E	949 282-5300	6814
Cohen Richard Ldscp & Cnstr	0782	E	949 768-0599	814
Frito-Lay North America Inc	5145	D	949 586-4644	8558
Hallmark Rehabilitation GP LLC	8322	A	949 282-5900	23828

	SIC	EMP	PHONE	ENTRY #
Sunset Landscape Maintenance	0782	D	949 455-4636	946

ELK GROVE, CA - Sacramento County

	SIC	EMP	PHONE	ENTRY #
Alldata LLC	7372	D	916 684-5200	15579
Banner Bank	6021	D	916 685-6546	9298
Bennathon Corp (PA)	1542	D	916 405-2100	1479
Bradshaw Veterinary Clinic	0742	D	916 685-2494	598
Brookdale Senior Living Inc	8051	D	916 683-1881	20272
California Family Health LLC	7991	E	916 685-3355	18583
Cardinal Health Inc	5122	C	916 372-9880	8152
Carlton Senior Living Inc	6531	E	916 714-2404	11267
Comprehensive SEC Svcs Inc (PA)	7381	D	916 683-3605	16614
Concrete North Inc	1771	D	209 745-7400	3241
Cosumnes Community Svcs Dst	7999	B	916 405-7150	19152
County of Sacramento	8744	C	916 874-1927	27588
Customcare Home Hlth Svcs Inc	8082	D	916 714-1155	22282
Dominion International Inc	7011	D	916 683-9545	12537
Elk Grove Adult Cmnty Training	8611	D	916 431-3162	24956
Elk Grove Park District	7999	B	916 685-9502	19166
Emerald Site Services Inc	1794	D	916 685-7211	3423
Farmers Mrchants Bnk Centl Cal	6022	C	916 394-3200	9446
Kaiser Foundation Hospitals	6324	D	916 544-6000	10224
Lifestyles Senior Housing Man	8322	D	916 714-3755	23899
Matheson Fast Freight Inc (HQ)	4213	D	916 686-4600	4222
OC Communications Inc (PA)	4841	C	916 686-3700	5924
Pacific Excavation Inc	1794	D	916 686-2800	3437
Professional Bureau of Collect	7322	C	916 685-3399	14018
Provident Fincl Holdings Inc	6162	D	916 709-3257	9848
R & A Painting Inc	1721	D	916 688-3955	2469
Rhodes Retail Services Inc	8742	D	916 714-9233	27428
River Oak Center For Children	8049	D	916 226-2800	20201
Sacramento Reg Co Sanit Dist	4952	B	916 875-9000	6327
Sacramento Yolo Cnty Mosquito	4959	D	916 685-1022	6549
Saia Motor Freight Line LLC	4213	E	916 690-8417	4256
Spare-Time Inc	7997	D	916 859-5910	19058
Sutter Health	8011	D	916 691-5900	19963
Sutter Health	8062	C	916 455-8137	21816
Sutter Health	8062	A	916 544-5423	21819
Sutter Health	8062	B	916 691-5900	21827
Tim Paxins Pacific Excavation	1794	E	916 686-2800	3443
Valley-HI Country Club	7997	E	916 684-2120	19076

EMERYVILLE, CA - Alameda County

	SIC	EMP	PHONE	ENTRY #
Agilysys Inc	5045	E	702 759-4879	7001
Aguatierra Associates Inc (PA)	8744	D	510 450-6000	27575
Alpha-Winfield Contractors Inc	1521	D	510 652-4712	1113
APM Terminals Pacific Ltd	4731	B	510 992-6430	5012
Armstrong Installation Service	1721	D	408 777-1234	2423
Art Supply Enterprises Inc (PA)	5199	C	510 428-9011	9196
Barry Bishop	8111	D	510 596-0888	22936
Behavioral Intervention Assn	7363	E	510 652-7445	14824
Berkeley Lights Inc (PA)	8733	D	510 898-1433	26597
Berkeley Research Group LLC (PA)	8748	C	510 285-3300	27657
Broadmoor Hotel	7011	D	415 673-8445	12404
Cell Design Labs Inc	5122	E	510 398-0501	8161
Cep America LLC	8011	C	510 350-2691	19370
Chiron Corporation	8099	D	510 655-8730	22766
Clif Bar & Company (PA)	5149	C	510 596-6300	8769
Daniel Loria Novartis	8069	C	510 655-8729	22016
E2 Consulting Engineers Inc	8711	B	510 652-1164	25650
Ernest Gallo Clinic & RES Ctr	8732	C	510 985-3856	26516
Exponential Interactive Inc (HQ)	7311	D	510 250-5500	13828
Federal Express Corporation	4212	C	800 463-3339	4012
Fort James Corporation	8741	C	510 594-4900	26861
Giampolini & Co	1721	D	415 673-1236	2442
Gracenote Inc (DH)	7371	D	510 428-7200	15187
Grifols Diagnstc Solutions Inc (HQ)	8071	C	323 225-2221	22095
Grill Recording Studio	7389	D	510 531-4351	17204
International Bus Mchs Corp	7379	D	510 652-6700	16404
Leidos Inc	8731	D	510 428-2550	26405
Location Labs Inc	7371	D	510 601-7012	15261
Mirixa Corporation	7389	D	510 596-3000	17331
Mobitv Inc	4813	D	510 981-1303	5604
Nmi Holdings Inc	6351	B	855 530-6642	10432
Onebody Inc	8082	D	510 285-2000	22380
Pacific Hotel Management LLC	7011	C	510 547-7888	12999
Pixar	7812	B	510 922-3000	18094
Ramboll Environ US Corporation	8748	D	510 655-7400	27835
Ratcliff Architects	8712	D	510 899-6400	26103
Real Estate America Inc	6531	D	510 594-3100	11714
Rlj Hgn Emeryville Lessee LP	7041	D	510 658-9300	13480
Rljhgn Emeryville Lessee LP	7011	D	510 658-9300	13134
Santen Incorporated	8733	D	415 268-9100	26658
Sutter Vsting Nrse Assn Hspice (HQ)	8082	E	866 652-9178	22430
Tubemogul Inc	7372	D	510 653-0126	15883
University California Berkeley	8733	A	510 495-2490	26670

2019 Directory of California
Wholesalers and Services Companies

(P-0000) Products & Services Section entry number
(PA)=Parent Co (HQ)=Headquarters (DH)=Div Headquarters

	SIC	EMP	PHONE	ENTRY #
Young MNS Chrstn Assn of E Bay	8641	D	510 601-8674	25357

ENCINITAS, CA - San Diego County

	SIC	EMP	PHONE	ENTRY #
Ad Results Media LLC	7313	D	858 480-5223	13933
Benex LLC	5087	D	310 675-6200	7883
Burtech Pipeline Incorporated	1623	D	760 634-2822	1899
Cellco Partnership	4812	D	760 642-0430	5340
Cielo Azul Inc	0782	D	855 863-8503	812
City of Encinitas	1611	E	760 633-2800	1741
Cloudtrigger Inc	8742	D	858 367-5272	27195
Coldwell Banker	6531	D	760 753-5616	11329
Crown Hardware Inc	5072	C	760 334-0300	7586
Dudek (PA)	8711	D	760 942-5147	25647
Dudek	8711	B	760 942-5147	25648
Five Star Quality Care Inc	8361	E	760 479-1818	24529
Hcr Manorcare Med Svcs Fla LLC	8051	D	760 944-0331	20514
J Robert Echter	0181	E	760 436-0188	270
JC Resorts LLC	8741	D	760 944-1936	26904
New Earth Enterprises Inc	0782	C	760 942-1298	906
Nixon Inc (PA)	5094	C	760 944-0900	8012
North Coast Presbyterian Ch	8351	D	760 753-2535	24353
Olivenhain Municipal Water Dst	4941	D	760 753-6466	6292
Perfect Workout Inc (PA)	7991	D	949 943-7281	18639
R N Priority Nursing Service	7361	D	760 635-7776	14711
Rancho Santa Fe Protective Svc	7381	E	760 433-8887	16771
San Diego Hebrew Homes (PA)	8051	C	760 942-2695	20738
Scripps Health	8062	D	760 753-8413	21726
Scripps Health	8062	C	760 479-3900	21729
Scripps Health	8062	D	760 753-6501	21730
Scripps Health	8011	D	760 633-6915	19867
Sethi Management Inc	7011	D	760 652-4010	13207
Silverado Senior Living Inc	8059	D	760 270-9917	21214
Ycg LLC	8748	D	760 230-8016	27913
YMCA of San Diego County	8641	D	858 292-4034	25298
Zephyr Partners Re-LLC	6531	E	858 558-3650	11846

ENCINO, CA - Los Angeles County

	SIC	EMP	PHONE	ENTRY #
A-Able Inc (PA)	7342	D	323 658-5779	14135
Actual Reality Pictures Inc	6531	E	818 325-8800	11190
Adept Consumer Testing Inc	8732	E	310 279-4600	26498
Allen Edwards Beauty Salon (PA)	7231	D	818 981-7711	13645
Anello SEC & Consulting LLC	8748	D	818 632-3277	27642
Answer Financial Inc (HQ)	7389	C	818 644-4000	17005
Automobile Club Southern Cal	8699	E	818 997-6230	25383
Ballard Rosenberg Golper Sav (PA)	8111	D	818 508-3700	22930
Brite Media LLC	7313	C	818 826-5790	13938
Burkshire Has A Way Home Servc	6531	D	818 501-4800	11253
C M A Alliance	6411	E	818 981-0800	10567
Cellco Partnership	4812	D	818 990-4610	5354
Childrens Hospital Los Angeles	8062	C	818 728-4930	21314
CIT Bank NA	6021	D	818 817-5320	9310
Concrete Holding Co Cal Inc	6719	B	818 788-4228	11971
D3publisher of America Inc	7372	D	310 268-0820	15644
Elizabeth Glaser Pedia	8099	A	310 231-0400	22799
Encino Center Car Wash Inc	7542	E	818 788-6300	17814
Encino Hospital Medical Center	8062	B	818 995-5000	21409
Encino Trzana Regional Med Ctr	8062	E	818 995-5000	21410
Graypay LLC	7372	D	818 387-6735	15695
Hemar Rousso & Heald L L P	8111	D	818 501-3800	23128
Holthouse Carlin Van Trigt LLP	8721	D	818 849-3140	26221
Israel Pops Orchestra	7929	E	818 343-6450	18444
Kramer-Wilson Company Inc (PA)	6331	C	818 760-0800	10365
Kravitz Investment Svcs Inc	6282	D	818 995-6100	10093
KSL Media Inc	7319	C	212 468-3395	13975
Life Alert Emergency Response (PA)	7382	C	800 247-0000	16921
Lmno Productions Inc	7812	C	818 995-5555	18072
Lodgen Lacher Golditch Sard	8721	E	818 783-0570	26254
Max Mri Imaging Inc (PA)	8071	E	818 382-2220	22109
Max/Mr Imaging Inc	8071	D	818 382-2220	22110
Merrill Lynch Pierce Fenner	6211	D	818 528-7809	9976
Merrill Lynch Pierce Fenner	6211	D	818 528-7800	9978
Nations Capital Group LLC	6153	E	818 793-2050	9743
Ols Hotels & Resorts LLC (PA)	7011	A	818 905-8280	12978
One Silver Serve Inc	8744	E	818 995-6444	27602
Orchard Horror Film LLC	7929	E	212 203-6147	18453
Orthopedic Consultants (PA)	8011	D	818 788-7343	19739
Pearlman Borska & Wax LLP (PA)	8111	D	818 501-4343	23321
Price Associates	8111	E	818 995-9216	23336
Price Law Group A Prof Corp (PA)	8111	D	818 995-4540	23337
Ralphs Grocery Company	4225	C	818 345-6882	4621
Reprints Desk Inc	7375	D	310 477-0354	16246
Republic Indemnity Company Cal	6331	C	818 990-9860	10388
Republic Indemnity Company of (DH)	6331	C	818 990-9860	10389
Rodeo Realty Inc	6531	D	818 285-3700	11737
Schweizer Rena	6531	D	818 501-7100	11755
Southern Cal Stone Ctr LLC	8011	D	818 784-8975	19926

	SIC	EMP	PHONE	ENTRY #
Specity Srgical Ctr Encino LP	8011	D	310 659-6333	19933
State Farm Mutl Auto Insur Co	6411	D	818 849-5126	10781
Sunrise Senior Living Inc	8051	E	818 346-9046	20801
Survey Sampling Intl LLC	8732	C	866 872-4006	26568
Umpqua Inc	6021	D	818 385-1362	9374
Uniworld River Cruises Inc	4725	C	818 382-2322	4983
Valuation Concepts LLC	6531	D	818 812-6233	11811
Vitas Healthcare Corp Cal	8082	D	818 760-2273	22458
Wagner Jacobson Brokerage Inc	6531	E	323 872-1636	11817
Working With Autism	8093	D	818 501-4240	22719

ESCALON, CA - San Joaquin County

	SIC	EMP	PHONE	ENTRY #
Dan R Costa Inc	0191	C	209 234-2004	333
Noralco Inc	0723	C	209 551-4545	548

ESCONDIDO, CA - San Diego County

	SIC	EMP	PHONE	ENTRY #
4g Wireless Inc	4813	D	760 705-7133	5434
A & G Grove Service	0722	D	760 728-5447	471
American Pride Gen Engrg Inc	8711	E	760 736-4056	25532
ARS National Services Inc (PA)	7322	C	800 456-5053	13991
ARS West LLC	7549	D	760 480-6631	17850
Associate Mechanical Contrs	1711	D	760 294-3517	2131
AT&T Services Inc	4813	D	760 489-3519	5499
AT&T Services Inc	4813	B	760 489-3187	5509
Baker Distributing Company LLC	5075	D	760 708-4201	7644
Bergelectric Corp	1731	A	760 746-1003	2520
Blanchard Training and Dev Inc (PA)	8742	D	760 489-5005	27163
Blanchardcoachingcom Inc	8331	B	760 489-5005	24157
Bmt Scientific Marine Svcs Inc (HQ)	8711	D	760 737-3505	25570
Cal Southern Presbt Homes	8361	C	760 747-4306	24446
Cal Southern Presbt Homes	8361	C	760 737-5110	24447
Cal Southern Sound Image Inc (PA)	5065	D	760 737-3900	7455
California Healthcare	6411	C	760 520-1333	10573
Central State Pre-School	8351	E	760 432-2499	24275
Chicago Title & Escrow	6361	D	760 746-3882	10437
Chicago Title Insurance Co	6361	D	760 546-1000	10444
Choa Hope LLC	7011	E	712 277-4101	12455
Christiansen Amusements Corp	7999	D	760 735-8542	19125
Concrete Concepts Inc	1771	D	760 737-5470	3239
Conrad Acceptance Corporation	6153	D	760 735-5000	9736
Conrad Credit Corporation	7322	C	760 735-5000	14000
Construction Tstg & Engrg Inc (PA)	8711	D	760 746-4955	25621
Covenant Care California LLC	8051	D	760 745-1288	20351
Davey Tree Surgery Company	0783	D	760 975-0225	973
Eleven Western Builders Inc (PA)	1542	C	760 796-6346	1527
Elizabeth Hospice Inc (PA)	8082	C	760 737-2050	22291
Emeritus Corporation	6513	E	760 741-3055	11012
Ensign Group Inc	8051	E	760 746-0303	20399
Erickson-Hall Construction Co (PA)	1542	C	760 796-7700	1530
Garrick Motors Inc	7538	C	760 489-2656	17761
George Richard	1541	D	619 805-6751	1400
Graybill Medical Group Inc (PA)	8011	C	866 228-2236	19488
Henry Avocado Corporation (PA)	0179	D	760 745-6632	236
Hidden Valley Mvg & Stor Inc (PA)	4214	D	602 252-7800	4351
Hmt Electric Inc	1731	D	858 458-9771	2606
In & Out Car Wash Inc	7542	E	619 316-8492	17818
Innovative Drywall Systems Inc	1742	D	760 743-0331	2895
Integrity Healthcare Services	8082	D	760 432-9811	22344
Interfaith Community Svcs Inc	8322	D	760 489-6380	23862
J & P Financial Inc (PA)	6163	E	760 738-9000	9889
JR Filanc Cnstr Co Inc (PA)	1623	D	760 941-7130	1939
Kaiser Foundation Hospitals	8011	A	442 281-5000	19552
Kaiser Foundation Hospitals	8011	D	760 739-3000	19554
Kaiser Foundation Hospitals	8011	E	619 528-5000	19605
Landcare USA LLC	0782	D	760 747-1174	877
Las Villas Del Norte	8051	D	760 741-1047	20576
Laser Electric Inc	1731	E	760 658-6626	2628
Learning Services Corporation	8093	E	760 746-3223	22611
Legacy Partners Limited Inc	1611	D	760 747-2711	1806
Life Care Centers America Inc	8051	C	760 741-6109	20583
Lincoln Witt Mercury	7538	D	760 233-3333	17770
Marathon General Inc	1611	D	760 738-9714	1812
Master Design Drywall Inc	1742	C	760 480-9001	2914
Meadowbrook Village Christian	8361	C	760 746-2500	24598
Medley Communications Inc	1731	D	760 294-4579	2644
Mek Escondido LLC	8051	D	760 747-0430	20639
Mountain Meadow Mushrooms Inc	0182	D	760 749-1201	318
Mountain Shadows Support Group (PA)	8052	C	760 743-3714	20944
Neighborhood Healthcare (PA)	8011	A	760 520-8372	19705
Neighborhood Healthcare	8011	D	760 737-2000	19707
Oj Insulation LP	1742	E	760 839-3200	2925
Pacific Structures Cnstr Inc	1771	E	740 480-4133	3303
Pacific Western Bank	6021	C	760 432-1350	9363
Pacific Western Bank	6021	D	760 432-1100	9366
Pack & Crate Services Inc	4214	E	760 737-6893	4364
Palomar Gem & Mineral Club	7997	D	760 743-0809	18999

Employment Codes: A=Over 500 employees, B=251-500,
C=101-250, D=51-100, E=50

2019 Directory of California
Wholesalers and Services Companies

© Mergent Inc. 1-800-342-5647
1571

GEOGRAPHIC

	SIC	EMP	PHONE	ENTRY #
Palomar Health	8062	B	858 675-5360	21627
Palomar Health	8062	A	760 739-3000	21628
Palomar Health Technology Inc (PA)	8062	C	442 281-5000	21630
Par Electrical Contractors Inc	1731	D	760 291-1192	2672
Physical Therapy Hand Ctrs Inc (PA)	8049	D	760 294-9800	20194
Physical Therapy Hand Ctrs Inc	8049	E	760 233-9655	20195
Pine Tree Lumber Company LP (PA)	5031	D	760 745-0411	6852
Pinery LLC	0811	D	858 675-3575	994
Polestar Labs Inc	5047	C	760 480-2600	7209
Pro Scape Inc	0782	E	760 480-1544	924
Prowall Lath and Plaster	1742	D	760 480-9001	2943
Rapid Product Dev Group Inc	8748	C	760 703-5770	27838
Red Hawk Fire & SEC CA Inc	1731	D	760 233-9787	2699
Redwood Elderlink Scph	8361	B	760 480-1030	24644
Rio Vista Ventures LLC (PA)	5141	E	760 480-8502	8448
Rocky Coast Builders Inc	1751	D	760 489-7770	3068
Romero General Cnstr Corp	1611	C	760 489-8412	1843
Saber Plumbing Inc	1711	D	760 480-5716	2345
Salazar Labor Contracting	0761	C	760 746-0805	672
San Diego County Water Auth	4941	C	760 480-1991	6302
San Diego Gas & Electric Co	4939	B	760 432-5885	6202
Sbrm Inc (PA)	7349	D	760 480-0208	14379
Scripps Health	8011	C	760 806-5700	19868
Service Master Industries Inc	7389	C	760 480-0208	17467
Silverado Senior Living Inc	8059	D	760 456-5137	21213
Sound-Crete Contracting	5082	C	760 291-1240	7695
Southern Cal Prmnnte Med Group	8011	E	760 839-7200	19921
Southland Paving Inc	1771	D	760 747-6895	3328
Southwest General Contrs Inc	5082	C	760 480-8747	7696
Structures West Inc	1771	D	760 737-2349	3332
Sunrize Staging Inc	1799	D	760 743-2043	3589
Surecraft Door and Hdwr Inc	1751	C	760 737-2120	3085
Sylvester Roofing Company Inc	1761	E	760 743-0048	3203
The For Califo Cente	8412	C	760 839-4138	24918
TNT Grading Inc	1611	C	760 736-4054	1861
Tpd Dell Dios	8322	E	760 741-2888	24091
Transmrcan Mling Flfllment Inc	7331	D	760 745-5343	14066
Tri-Ad Actuaries Inc	6411	C	760 743-7555	10805
Valle Vsta Cnvlescent Hosp Inc	8059	D	760 745-1288	21243
Veterans Health Administration	8011	D	760 745-2000	20071
Welk Group Inc (PA)	7011	B	760 749-3000	13386
West Escondido Healthcare LLC	8051	D	760 746-0303	20883
Western Rim Constructors Inc	1611	E	760 489-4328	1870
Westmed Ambulance Inc	4119	B	310 219-1779	3861
Wier Construction Corporation	1542	E	760 743-6776	1703
William Brammer	5148	C	760 746-6006	8748
X3 Management Services Inc	8748	D	760 597-9336	27912
YMCA of San Diego County	8641	B	760 745-7490	25296
Zoological Society San Diego	8422	A	760 747-8702	24938

ESPARTO, CA - Yolo County

	SIC	EMP	PHONE	ENTRY #
R H Phillips Inc (HQ)	0172	C	530 757-5557	166

ETIWANDA, CA - San Bernardino County

	SIC	EMP	PHONE	ENTRY #
C M C Steel Fabricators Inc	1791	C	909 899-9993	3366

ETNA, CA - Siskiyou County

	SIC	EMP	PHONE	ENTRY #
Etna Police Activities League	8322	C	530 467-3400	23790

EUREKA, CA - Humboldt County

	SIC	EMP	PHONE	ENTRY #
Best Western Bayshore Inn	7011	E	707 268-8005	12371
California Dept Transportation	8748	B	707 445-6600	27671
Changing Tides Family Services (PA)	8351	D	707 444-8293	24278
Coast Central Credit Union (PA)	6061	D	707 445-8801	9546
Correctons Rhbltation Cal Dept	8322	D	707 445-6520	23618
County of Humboldt	8322	B	707 445-6180	23644
County of Humboldt	8093	C	707 476-4054	22544
E G Ayers Distributing Inc	5141	D	707 445-2077	8403
Eureka Rehab & Wellness Center	8051	D	707 445-3261	20413
Forest Products Distrs Inc	5031	D	707 443-7024	6823
Fred H Lundblade Jr	6512	D	707 442-8049	10879
Ghd Inc	8711	E	707 443-8326	25712
Granada Healthcre & Rehab Cntr	8059	D	707 443-1627	21100
Hospice of Humboldt Inc (PA)	8093	D	707 445-8443	22596
Humboldt Commnty Accss Resrc	8322	D	707 443-7077	23848
Humboldt Senior Resource Ctr (PA)	8322	C	707 443-9747	23849
Humboldt Yacht Club	7997	D	707 443-1469	18936
Institute For Wildlife Studies (PA)	8641	E	707 822-4258	25175
Keenan & Associates	6411	E	707 268-1616	10664
Laco Associates (PA)	8711	E	707 443-5054	25792
McMurray & Sons Inc (PA)	1761	D	707 443-3088	3178
Mission Linen Supply	7213	D	707 443-8681	13537
Nor-Wall Inc (PA)	7997	E	707 445-5445	18988
North Coast Cleaning Services	7349	E	707 269-0838	14333
Pacific Choice Seafood Company	5146	B	707 442-2981	8591
Pacific Gas and Electric Co	4911	D	707 444-0700	6084
Pacific Rehabilitation & Wel	8051	D	707 443-9767	20686

	SIC	EMP	PHONE	ENTRY #
Redwood Coast Regional	8322	E	707 445-0893	23986
Seaview Hlthcre & Rehab Ctr LL	8361	D	707 443-5668	24669
Securitas SEC Svcs USA Inc	7381	D	707 445-5463	16800
Security Nat Mstr Holdg Co LLC (PA)	6162	C	707 442-2818	9857
Shaw & Petersen Insurance Inc	6411	E	707 443-0845	10773
Shn Consulting Engin (PA)	8711	D	707 441-8855	25910
Six Rivers National Bank (HQ)	6021	D	707 443-8400	9372
Six Rivers Planned Parenthood	8399	D	707 442-5700	24841
St Joseph Health System	8011	D	707 443-9371	19937
St Joseph Hospital (PA)	8062	D	707 445-8121	21779
St Joseph Hospital	8062	A	707 268-0190	21780
St Joseph Hospital of Eureka	8062	A	707 445-8121	21781
State Compensation Insur Fund	6331	C	707 443-9721	10407
Veterans Health Administration	8011	B	707 442-5335	20068
Wayne Maples Plumbing & Htg	1711	D	707 445-2500	2404
Western Living Concepts Inc (PA)	8361	E	707 443-3000	24719

EXETER, CA - Tulare County

	SIC	EMP	PHONE	ENTRY #
Badger Farming Company Inc	0174	D	559 592-5520	202
Best Western International Inc	7011	D	559 592-8118	12374
Bowsmith Inc (PA)	7218	D	559 592-9485	13597
Boys Grls Clubs of Squoias Inc	8641	E	559 592-4074	25117
Exeter Engineering Inc	0723	D	559 592-3161	510
Exeter Packers Inc (PA)	0723	A	559 592-5168	511
Exeter-Ivanhoe Citrus Assn	0723	D	559 592-3141	513
Farmers Insurance Exchange	6411	B	559 594-4144	10624
Frontier California Inc	4813	C	559 592-2100	5567
Kaweah Dlta Hlth Care Dst Gild	8099	C	559 592-7300	22829
Kaweah Dlta Hlth Care Dst Gild	8011	C	559 592-7128	19623
Randstad North America Inc	7363	A	559 592-6700	14898
Redding Tree Growers Corp	0851	D	559 594-9299	1000
San Joaquin Valley Railroad Co	4011	C	559 592-1857	3624
Sequoia Enterprises Inc	5148	D	559 592-9455	8728
Sequoia Orange Co Inc (PA)	0723	D	559 592-9455	567
Sun Pacific Farming Coop Inc (PA)	0762	D	559 592-7121	713
Venida Packing Company	4783	C	559 592-2816	5213

FAIR OAKS, CA - Sacramento County

	SIC	EMP	PHONE	ENTRY #
Atlaz Inc	7371	D	415 671-6142	15007
Burger Rhbltation Systems Inc	8049	D	916 863-5785	20168
Clarklift-West Inc	5084	C	916 381-5674	7741
Coldwell Bnkr Residential Brkg	6531	D	916 966-8200	11356
Eskaton Properties Inc	8051	D	916 965-4663	20409
Lyon Realty	6531	C	916 962-0111	11574
North Ridge Country Club	7997	D	916 967-5717	18990
Sunset Pet Hospital Inc (PA)	0742	D	916 967-7768	609
Wightman Enterprises Inc	7363	D	916 961-2959	14945
William L Lyon & Assoc Inc	6531	D	916 535-0356	11834

FAIRFAX, CA - Marin County

	SIC	EMP	PHONE	ENTRY #
Meadow Club	7997	D	415 453-3274	18969
Melissa Bradley RE Inc	6531	D	415 485-4300	11606

FAIRFIELD, CA - Solano County

	SIC	EMP	PHONE	ENTRY #
Andrews Group Inc (PA)	1711	D	707 422-4844	2122
Anheuser-Busch LLC	5084	B	707 429-7595	7727
AT&T Services Inc	4813	D	707 428-2512	5494
B R Funsten & Co	5023	D	707 863-8300	6749
Blood Centers of Pacific	8099	E	707 428-6001	22749
Brand Services Inc	5082	E	707 603-3400	7669
Calbee North America LLC	5142	C	707 427-2500	8489
Caliber Home Loans Inc	6162	B	707 432-1000	9786
Century 21	6531	E	707 429-2121	11288
Certified Coatings Company	1721	C	707 639-4414	2428
City of Fairfield	6512	C	707 428-7435	10865
Coastal Select Insurance Co	6411	E	707 863-3700	10589
Community Housing Opport (PA)	8748	E	530 757-4444	27694
Community Housing Opport	8741	E	707 759-6043	26816
Copart	5012	E	707 863-0297	6583
Corey Delta Constructors Inc	1711	D	925 370-9808	2171
County of Solano	8322	D	707 784-8400	23744
County of Solano	8322	C	707 784-7600	23745
County of Solano	8052	D	707 784-2080	20926
Delta One Security Inc	7381	D	707 425-9346	16628
Directv Group Inc	4841	C	707 452-7409	5901
Fairfield Nursing & Rehab Ctr	8051	D	707 425-0623	20421
Fairfield-Suisun Sewer Dst	4953	C	707 429-8930	6399
First Priority Financial Inc	6162	B	707 432-1000	9806
Frank-Lin Distillers Pdts Ltd (PA)	5182	C	408 259-8900	9044
Frontier Title Co (PA)	6361	E	707 427-5400	10463
Gaw Van Male Smith Myers	8111	D	707 425-1250	23089
Geovera Specialty Insurance Co	6411	E	707 863-3700	10635
Green Valley Country Club	7997	D	707 864-1101	18932
Hd Supply Construction Supply	5072	D	707 863-8282	7590
Hotel NAPA II Opco LP	7011	E	707 863-0300	12729
Jpmorgan Chase Bank Nat Assn	6021	C	707 864-4700	9348
Kaiser Foundation Hospitals	8011	A	707 427-4000	19556

Mergent email: customerrelations@mergent.com
1572

2019 Directory of California
Wholesalers and Services Companies

(P-0000) Products & Services Section entry number
(PA)=Parent Co (HQ)=Headquarters (DH)=Div Headquarters

Company	SIC	EMP	PHONE	ENTRY #
Kiewit Corporation	1542	D	707 439-7300	1574
Laborers Funds Administrative **(PA)**	8631	C	707 864-2800	25068
Lanza Vineyards Inc	0172	E	707 864-0730	158
Loyalton At Rancho Solano	8361	D	707 425-3588	24589
Meyer Corporation US	5023	D	707 399-2100	6776
Muehlnan Certifed Coatings Inc	1799	C	707 639-4414	3554
New Desserts Inc	5149	D	415 780-6860	8838
Northbay Healthcare Corp **(PA)**	8062	C	707 646-5000	21606
Northbay Healthcare Group **(PA)**	8062	A	707 646-5000	21607
Northern CA Retiredd Ofcrs	8361	C	707 432-1200	24612
Northstate Plastering Inc	1771	D	707 207-0950	3296
Pacific Gas and Electric Co	4911	D	415 973-7000	6067
Partnership Health Plan Cal	6324	B	707 863-4100	10293
Permanente Medical Group Inc	6324	E	707 427-4000	10298
Petersen-Dean Inc	1761	E	707 469-7470	3187
Petersen-Dean Commercial Inc	1761	C	707 469-7470	3189
Private Industry Cncl Slno Cty **(PA)**	7361	E	707 864-3370	14701
S & S Tool & Supply Inc **(PA)**	5085	D	925 313-0360	7869
Solano Family & Chld Council	8351	D	707 863-3950	24383
Solano Garbage Company Inc	4953	C	707 437-8900	6477
Solano Gateway Realty Inc **(PA)**	6531	E	707 422-1725	11769
Solano Regional Medical Group **(PA)**	8011	C	707 426-3911	19895
Transportation California Dept	1611	D	707 428-2031	1864
Travis Credit Union	6061	B	707 449-4000	9607
Tri-Valley Supply Inc **(PA)**	5033	D	707 469-7470	6932
United Parcel Service Inc OH	4215	C	707 864-8200	4450
Valley Inventory Service Inc	7389	D	707 422-6050	17557
Villara Corporation	1761	E	707 863-8222	3209
West Coast Contractors Inc	1542	C	541 267-7689	1698
Westgate Cnstr & Maint Inc	1542	D	707 208-5763	1699
Wind River Enterprises Inc	5012	D	707 864-1040	6614

FALLBROOK, CA - San Diego County

Company	SIC	EMP	PHONE	ENTRY #
County of San Diego	8322	D	866 262-9881	23722
Elston Masonry Inc	1741	D	760 728-3593	2805
Executive Landscape Inc	0782	C	760 731-9036	840
Fallbrook Fire Protection Dst	7389	D	760 723-2010	17162
Fallbrook Public Utility Dst	4941	D	760 728-1125	6254
Fallbrook Sklled Nrsing Fcilty	8051	D	760 728-2330	20423
Garich Inc	7361	A	951 302-4750	14625
Garys Construction Inc	4959	C	760 639-4456	6541
Hamilton Family Ranch	0174	D	760 728-1358	205
Hines Horticulture Inc	5193	B	760 723-1500	9140
Kendall Farms LP	0181	E	760 731-0681	274
Little Sisters Truck Wash Inc **(PA)**	7542	D	760 731-3170	17829
N G A Associates	6512	E	760 726-4015	10917
New Visa Health Services Inc	8059	B	760 723-0053	21163
Olive Hill Greenhouses	0181	D	760 728-4596	290
Pala Band of Mission Indians	7929	C	760 207-2603	18455
Pala Mesa Limited Partnership	7011	C	760 728-5881	13013
Petes Connection Inc	4841	E	760 723-1972	5926
Rainbow Municipal Water Dst	4941	E	760 728-1178	6296
Southwest Construction Co Inc	1771	D	760 728-4460	3329
Straub - Brutoco A Joint Ventr	1531	C	760 414-9000	1359
Sycamore Cc Inc	7997	D	760 451-3700	19065
William C Arterberry	0179	D	760 728-9096	240

FARMINGTON, CA - San Joaquin County

Company	SIC	EMP	PHONE	ENTRY #
Brightview Tree Company	0811	D	209 886-5511	990
Pleasant Valley Farms **(PA)**	0751	D	209 886-1000	624

FELTON, CA - Santa Cruz County

Company	SIC	EMP	PHONE	ENTRY #
Cupertino Electric Inc	1731	A	408 808-8260	2556
Granite Construction Inc	1611	D	831 335-3445	1784

FILLMORE, CA - Ventura County

Company	SIC	EMP	PHONE	ENTRY #
B & R Farm Labor Contractor	7361	C	805 524-1346	14574
Brightview Tree Company	0811	C	714 546-7975	988
California Watercress Inc **(PA)**	0161	D	805 524-4808	41
Fillmore Convalescent Ctr LLC	8059	D	805 524-0083	21066
Magana Labor Services Inc	7361	C	805 524-0446	14666
Moon Mountain Farms LLC	0191	E	805 521-1742	371
Wilmay Inc	7389	D	805 524-2603	17596
Wonderful Citrus Packing LLC	0174	D	805 525-3818	210

FIREBAUGH, CA - Fresno County

Company	SIC	EMP	PHONE	ENTRY #
Empresas Del Bosque Inc	0191	B	209 364-6428	342
Hall Company	0191	D	209 364-0070	348
Hammonds Ranch Inc	0191	D	209 364-6185	349
I S A Contracting Svcs Inc	0722	A	559 659-1080	478
J & J Farms	0191	E	559 659-1457	355
JR Simplot Company	5191	D	209 659-2033	9080
Oxford Farms Inc	0762	E	559 659-3033	704
Panoche Water District	4971	E	209 364-6136	6562
R & N Packing Co	0191	C	209 364-6101	555
Thomason Tractor Co California	5083	C	559 659-2039	7714
Tri-State AG Inc	4961	D	209 364-6185	6552

Company	SIC	EMP	PHONE	ENTRY #
Vaquero Farms Inc	0191	D	559 659-2790	391

FISH CAMP, CA - Mariposa County

Company	SIC	EMP	PHONE	ENTRY #
DNC Prks Resorts At Tenaya Inc **(DH)**	7011	D	877 247-9241	12531

FIVE POINTS, CA - Fresno County

Company	SIC	EMP	PHONE	ENTRY #
ATI Machinery Inc	5083	E	559 884-2471	7700
Britz Fertilizers Inc	5191	D	559 884-2421	9076
Coelho West Custom Farming	0191	D	559 884-2566	331
Nutrien AG Solutions Inc	5191	E	559 884-6010	9090
Telesis Onion Co	0723	E	559 884-2441	580

FOLSOM, CA - Sacramento County

Company	SIC	EMP	PHONE	ENTRY #
24 Hour Fitness Usa Inc	7991	E	916 984-1924	18547
Agreeya Solutions Inc **(PA)**	8742	D	916 294-0075	27120
Benefit & Risk Management Svcs	6411	C	916 467-1200	10561
Brookdale Senior Living Inc	8059	D	916 983-9300	21020
Burger Physcl Therapy Svcs Inc **(HQ)**	8049	C	916 983-5900	20165
Burger Physical Therapy	8049	E	916 983-5900	20166
Burger Rhbilitation Systems Inc **(PA)**	8049	C	800 900-8491	20169
Califrnia Ind Sys Oprator Corp	8742	C	916 608-7000	27180
Califrnia Ind Sys Oprator Corp **(PA)**	4911	A	916 351-4400	6013
Cellco Partnership	4812	D	212 395-1000	5313
Cellco Partnership	4812	B	916 357-1000	5367
Central Valley Community Bank	6022	E	916 985-8700	9430
Chicago Title Insurance Co	6361	E	916 985-0300	10442
City of Folsom	7999	D	916 355-7285	19130
Csac Excess Insurance Auth	6411	C	916 850-7300	10598
Dager Corporation **(PA)**	7231	D	916 989-4229	13652
Dignity Health	8062	C	916 983-7400	21368
Dignity Health	8062	B	916 983-7400	21380
Dignity Health	8011	D	916 983-7988	19443
Dokken Engineering **(PA)**	8711	D	916 858-0642	25646
Ea Consulting Inc	7379	E	916 357-6767	16353
Elliott Homes Inc **(PA)**	1521	C	916 984-1300	1160
Emergency Med Group of Folsom	8011	D	916 983-7470	19459
Erepublic Inc **(PA)**	7389	C	916 932-1300	17155
Eurofins Air Toxics LLC	8734	D	916 985-1000	26701
Flt Inc	7538	C	916 355-1500	17759
Folsom Recreation Corp	7933	D	916 983-4411	18488
FPI Management Inc **(PA)**	6531	E	916 357-5300	11472
Green Acres Nursery & Sup LLC	5083	D	916 782-2273	7703
HDR Engineering Inc	8742	D	916 817-4700	27261
HDR/Cardno Entrix Joint Ventr	8711	D	916 817-4700	25731
Hoshall Corporation	7231	E	916 987-1995	13662
Inductive Automation LLC	8742	D	800 266-7798	27271
Kaiser Foundation Hospitals	8011	A	916 986-4178	19559
Kaiser Foundation Hospitals	8011	C	916 817-5200	19609
Kindred Healthcare Operating	8051	C	916 351-9151	20563
Lake Natoma Lodging LP	7011	D	916 351-1500	12834
Liberty American Mortgage Corp **(PA)**	6163	D	916 780-3000	9892
Liberty Mutual Insurance Co	6411	C	916 294-9518	10672
Location Services LLC **(PA)**	4789	D	800 588-0097	5234
Lyon Real Estate	6531	D	916 355-7000	11573
Matthew Burns	1542	D	209 676-4940	1589
Maximus Inc	8742	D	916 673-2175	27324
Maximus Inc	8742	E	916 673-4162	27325
Mercury Insurance Company	6331	D	916 353-4859	10374
Meridian Knwldge Solutions LLC	8742	D	913 985-9625	27340
Morton & Pitalo Inc **(PA)**	8711	D	916 984-7621	25833
Norcal Gold Inc	6531	E	916 984-8778	11634
Objective Systems Integrators **(HQ)**	7371	E	916 467-1500	15324
Powerschool Group LLC **(HQ)**	7372	C	916 288-1636	15835
Related Technologies Inc	7371	C	916 357-5900	15403
Retail Pro International Inc	7371	C	916 605-7200	15409
Retail Services & Systems Inc	8748	D	916 984-6923	27843
Safe Credit Union **(PA)**	6062	C	916 979-7233	9647
Safe Credit Union	6062	C	916 979-7233	9648
Sierra Pacific Mortgage Co Inc **(PA)**	6162	A	916 932-1700	9859
Spare-Time Inc	7997	D	916 983-9180	19054
Sparta Consulting Inc	7379	B	916 985-0300	16492
Taxresources Inc **(PA)**	8721	C	877 369-7827	26301
Toshiba Memory America Inc	8731	E	916 986-4007	26475
Trimark Operations Center	8748	D	916 357-5970	27890
Vibra Hospital Sacramento LLC	8062	C	916 351-9151	21909
Visio Integ Profe LLC **(HQ)**	8742	D	916 985-9625	27514
Visionary Integration **(PA)**	6719	D	916 985-9625	12017
VPD IV Inc **(PA)**	7822	D	916 605-1500	18247

FONTANA, CA - San Bernardino County

Company	SIC	EMP	PHONE	ENTRY #
ABF Freight System Inc	4213	C	909 355-9805	4094
Advanced Environmental Inc	4212	E	909 356-9025	3968
Advanced Sterlization	4225	D	909 350-6987	4524
American Asphalt South Inc	1611	D	909 427-8276	1717
American Bolt & Screw Mfg Corp **(PA)**	5072	C	909 390-0522	7573
AMS Paving Inc **(PA)**	1611	E	909 357-0711	1721
Anfinson Lumber Sales Inc **(PA)**	5031	D	951 681-4707	6808

Employment Codes: A=Over 500 employees, B=251-500,
C=101-250, D=51-100, E=50

2019 Directory of California
Wholesalers and Services Companies

© Mergent Inc. 1-800-342-5647
1573

GEOGRAPHIC

Company	SIC	EMP	PHONE	ENTRY #
Apex Bulk Commodities Inc	6221	D	909 854-9991	10044
Aqua-Serv Engineers Inc (HQ)	5169	D	951 681-9696	8917
Auto Strap Transport LLC (PA)	4731	C	909 795-4088	5014
Automotive Sup Co Southern Cal (PA)	5013	D	909 428-9072	6624
B&B Industrial Services Inc	1741	D	909 428-3167	2796
Blue Rose Concrete Contrs Inc	1771	C	909 823-6190	3226
Boyd Flotation Inc	5021	D	909 357-6400	6713
Budway Enterprises Inc (PA)	4213	D	909 463-0500	4111
Burrtec Waste Industries Inc (HQ)	4953	C	909 429-4200	6362
California Speedway Corp	7948	E	909 429-5000	18537
Cattrac Construction Inc	1629	D	909 355-1146	2021
Central Reinforcing Corp	1791	D	909 773-0840	3370
Complete Logistics Company	4212	C	909 427-9800	3995
Conco Pumping	1771	D	909 350-0503	3238
Costco Wholesale Corporation	5199	C	909 823-8270	9209
Cox Automotive Inc	5012	A	404 843-5000	6585
CRST International Inc	4213	C	909 829-1313	4119
D W Powell Construction Inc	1611	E	909 356-8880	1755
Dalton Trucking Inc (PA)	4212	C	909 823-0663	3997
Daniel Gerard Worldwide Inc	5051	D	951 361-1111	7268
Defenders Trnsp Svcs Inc	4731	C	909 854-7000	5040
Desert Coastal Transport Inc (PA)	4213	D	909 357-3395	4128
Dhl Supply Chain (usa)	4225	E	909 350-6976	4545
Dispatch Transportation LLC	7359	C	909 355-5531	14500
Dispatch Trucking LLC (PA)	4731	D	909 355-5531	5047
Elegance Wood Products Inc	5023	D	909 484-7676	6759
Estes Express Lines Inc	4213	D	909 427-9850	4139
Express Contractors Inc	7217	D	951 360-6500	13578
Fedex Freight West Inc	4213	B	909 357-3555	4163
Flash Transport Inc	4213	D	909 829-1369	4178
Fontana Resources At Work	8331	C	909 428-3833	24184
Friends Group Express Inc	4213	D	909 346-6814	4181
General Motors LLC	4225	D	951 361-6302	4561
Hanks Inc	4212	D	909 350-8365	4018
Hartman Industries	5051	D	909 428-0114	7279
Hawk Transportation Inc	4213	D	800 709-4295	4191
Heartland Express Inc Iowa	4213	E	319 626-3600	4192
Hsn LLC	4225	D	909 349-2600	4577
Hub Group Trucking Inc	4212	B	909 770-8950	4022
Inland Cc Inc	1771	C	909 355-1318	3267
Inland Empire Utilities Agency	4941	D	909 993-1600	6265
Inland Kenworth (us) Inc (HQ)	5012	D	909 823-9955	6597
James Hardie Building Pdts Inc	5031	C	909 355-6500	6836
Jones Bold Security Inc	7381	D	562 316-6552	16708
Kaden Cash LLC	7929	E	818 714-4665	18445
Kaiser Foundation Hospitals	8011	C	909 609-3800	19536
Kaiser Foundation Hospitals	8011	A	866 205-3595	19558
Kaiser Foundation Hospitals	8011	D	909 427-5000	19597
Kaiser Foundation Hospitals	6324	D	909 427-3910	10265
Kds Printing and Packaging Inc	7389	E	909 770-5400	17270
Little Sisters Truck Wash Inc	7542	D	909 549-1862	17827
Los Angeles Truck Centers LLC	5012	C	909 510-4000	6602
Maxzone Vehicle Lighting Corp (HQ)	5013	E	909 822-3288	6656
McCollisters Trnsp Group Inc	4214	D	909 428-5700	4359
McGuire Contracting Inc	1771	D	909 357-1200	3285
Naumann/Hobbs Material	5084	C	909 427-0125	7778
Network Global Logistics LLC	4513	C	888 285-7447	4845
No Shnacks Inc	8741	E	909 293-8747	26961
Norco Ranch Inc (DH)	0252	B	951 737-6735	433
NY Transport Inc	4213	D	909 355-9832	4237
Orwick Fresh Foods Inc	5149	E	909 985-5604	8843
Patrick Industries Inc	5032	C	909 350-4440	6904
Pointdirect Transport Inc	4731	D	909 371-0837	5143
Pro Loaders Inc (PA)	4731	C	909 355-5531	5149
Rail Delivery Services Inc	4212	D	909 355-4100	4054
Romark Logistics of California	4225	D	909 356-5600	4626
San Gabriel Valley Water Co	4941	D	909 822-2201	6305
Schneider National Inc	4731	C	909 574-2165	5162
Sierra Lakes Golf Club	7992	D	909 350-2500	18762
Slater Inc	1629	D	909 822-6800	2064
Southern Cal Prmnnte Med Group	8062	E	909 427-5000	21762
Stantru Resources Inc	1541	D	909 587-1441	1437
State Farm Mutl Auto Insur Co	6411	D	909 349-2050	10786
STC Netcom Inc (PA)	1731	D	951 685-8181	2745
Sun Mar Management Services	8741	D	909 822-8066	27050
Tire Centers West LLC	5014	C	909 854-1200	6697
Tonys Express Inc (PA)	4213	D	909 427-8700	4280
Tst Inc	4212	D	310 835-0115	4073
Tst Inc	5093	D	909 590-1098	7999
United Facilities Inc	4225	E	951 685-7030	4644
United Family Care Inc (PA)	8011	C	909 874-1679	20018
Utility Trailer Sales of S CA (PA)	5012	C	877 275-4887	6612
Valori Sand & Gravel Company	5032	C	909 350-3000	6912
Vineyard Plastering Inc	1742	E	909 357-3701	2975
Vpet Usa Inc (PA)	5162	D	909 605-1668	8915

Company	SIC	EMP	PHONE	ENTRY #
Werner Enterprises Inc	4213	E	909 823-5803	4302
West Valley Manufacturing LLC	4953	C	909 899-5501	6524
Western Freight Carrier Inc	4731	D	909 357-1011	5198
Western PCF Crane & Eqp LLC (DH)	7353	D	562 286-6618	14462
Weyerhaeuser Company	5031	D	909 877-6100	6873
Windrow Earth Transport Inc	1629	E	909 355-5531	2074
Wsp USA Inc	8742	D	909 427-9166	27525
Xpo Logistics Freight Inc	4213	C	951 685-1244	4322

FOOTHILL RANCH, CA - Orange County

Company	SIC	EMP	PHONE	ENTRY #
Debisys Inc (PA)	6099	D	949 699-1401	9679
Frito-Lay North America Inc	5145	C	925 734-3100	8546
Frontech N Fujitsu Amer Inc (DH)	7373	D	949 855-5500	15960
Global Solutions Integration	8711	D	949 307-1849	25716
Guthy-Renker LLC	7389	C	949 454-1400	17206
Hampton Products Intl Corp (PA)	5072	D	949 472-4256	7589
Ibaset Inc	8748	D	949 598-5200	27751
Ibaset Federal Services LLC (PA)	7371	D	949 598-5200	15207
Image Options	7319	C	949 586-7665	13974
Kaiser Foundation Hospitals	8011	A	800 922-2000	19557
Kawasaki Motors Corp USA (HQ)	5012	B	949 837-4683	6601
Loandepotcom LLC (PA)	6162	A	949 474-1322	9829
Mrt Inc	7331	E	949 348-2292	14056
Nth Degree Inc	7389	E	714 734-4155	17362
Professional Community MGT Cal (PA)	6531	D	800 369-7260	11682
Professional Community MGT Cal	6514	D	949 768-7261	11153
Sgii Inc	5122	C	949 521-6161	8209
Skilled Healthcare LLC (DH)	8051	C	949 282-5800	20767
Solutions 2 Go LLC	5092	D	949 825-7700	7961
Sun Healthcare Group Inc (DH)	8011	D	949 255-7100	19954
Tae Technologies Inc (PA)	8731	C	949 830-2117	26468
Team Makena LLC (PA)	5047	D	949 474-1753	7221
Venus Group Inc	5023	D	949 609-1299	6802
Ytel Inc	7371	D	800 382-4913	15555

FOREST RANCH, CA - Butte County

Company	SIC	EMP	PHONE	ENTRY #
Sierra Cascade Blueberries	0171	E	530 894-8728	121

FORT BRAGG, CA - Mendocino County

Company	SIC	EMP	PHONE	ENTRY #
Caito Fisheries Inc (PA)	5146	D	707 964-6368	8573
Mendocino Coast Clinics Inc	8093	D	707 964-1251	22619
Mendocino Coast District Hosp (PA)	8062	B	707 961-1234	21585
Mendocino Coast District Hosp	8062	C	707 961-4736	21586
Mendocino Railway	4731	C	707 964-6371	5108
Mendocino Transit Authority	4111	D	707 462-1422	3681
Redwood Coast Seniors Inc	8322	D	707 964-0443	23987
Sherwood Oaks Enterprises	8051	D	707 964-6333	20759
Tradewinds Lodge (PA)	7011	D	707 964-4761	13338
Waste MGT Collectn & Recycl	4953	D	707 462-0210	6517

FORT IRWIN, CA - San Bernardino County

Company	SIC	EMP	PHONE	ENTRY #
Dyncorp International LLC	4581	D	817 224-8200	4887
Family Mrale Wlfare Recreation	7997	D	760 380-3493	18922
Iap World Services Inc	8744	B	760 380-6772	27595
Leidos Inc	8731	D	910 574-4597	26410
Raytheon Company	7629	B	760 386-2572	17908
Solution One Industries Inc	4225	D	254 702-7329	4632

FORTUNA, CA - Humboldt County

Company	SIC	EMP	PHONE	ENTRY #
Reaching For Independence Inc	8399	D	707 725-9010	24830
Redwood Memorial Hosp Fortuna (PA)	8062	C	707 725-7327	21685
St Luke Hlthcr & Rehab Ctr LL	8051	D	707 725-4467	20779

FOSTER CITY, CA - San Mateo County

Company	SIC	EMP	PHONE	ENTRY #
American Infrastructure Mlp Fu	8748	D	650 854-6000	27638
Applied Underwriters Inc	6411	E	415 656-5000	10540
Arena Solutions Inc (PA)	7371	D	650 513-3500	14998
B B & K Fund Services Inc	6211	E	650 571-5800	9915
B B & K Holdings (PA)	6282	E	650 571-5800	10060
Bailard Inc (HQ)	6282	E	650 571-5800	10061
Bayshore Ambulance Inc (PA)	4119	D	650 525-9700	3776
Brightedge Technologies Inc (PA)	7371	C	800 578-8023	15036
City of Foster City	7999	D	650 286-3380	19131
Csg Consultants Inc (PA)	8711	E	650 522-2500	25632
Cybersource Corporation (HQ)	7374	C	650 432-7350	16113
Ecker Consumer Recruiting Inc (PA)	8732	E	650 871-6800	26513
Emeter Corporation	7371	D	650 227-7770	15137
Emove Express Company	7374	D	650 377-0913	16123
Founders Management II Corp	7011	B	650 570-5700	12583
Global Ground Automation Inc	5084	D	201 293-4900	7754
Gridgain Systems Inc	7389	C	650 241-2281	17202
Guidewire Software Inc (PA)	7372	C	650 357-9100	15700
Hilton Garden In San Mateo	7011	D	650 522-9000	12661
Ic Compliance LLC (PA)	7371	A	650 378-4150	15209
Interactive Data Corporation	6289	C	510 266-6000	10125
International Bus Mchs Corp	7379	B	800 426-4968	16405
Legacy Prtners Residential Inc (PA)	8741	C	650 571-2250	26931

2019 Directory of California
Wholesalers and Services Companies

(P-0000) Products & Services Section entry number
(PA)=Parent Co (HQ)=Headquarters (DH)=Div Headquarters

	SIC	EMP	PHONE	ENTRY #
Menlo Gateway Inc	6514	D	650 356-2900	11149
Midpen Housing Corporation	6552	B	650 356-2900	11892
Midpen Resident Services Corp	6514	D	650 356-2965	11151
Oracle Corporation	7372	B	650 678-3612	15800
Pacific Partners MGT Svcs Inc	8741	D	650 358-5804	26972
Peninsula Jewish Community Ctr	8322	C	650 212-7522	23966
Peter H Mattson & Co Inc	8731	D	650 356-2500	26437
Qualys Inc (PA)	7371	C	650 801-6100	15389
Quinstreet Inc (PA)	7389	E	650 578-7700	17421
Sanzaru Games Inc	7371	C	650 312-1000	15426
SCI Corp	7349	D	650 578-1142	14380
Scientific Concepts Inc	7699	B	650 578-1142	17985
Sonifi Solutions Inc	4841	C	650 752-1980	5931
Sony Corporation of America	7371	C	650 655-8000	15465
Sony Interactive Entrmt LLC (DH)	7389	C	310 981-1500	17477
Steelwave Inc (PA)	6552	C	650 571-2200	11920
Steelwave LLC	6552	A	650 571-2200	11922
USB Solarcity Master Tenant	6719	D	650 963-5693	12015
Vb Golf LLC	7992	D	650 573-7888	18775
Verinata Health Inc	8731	D	650 632-1680	26489
Visa USA Inc (HQ)	7389	C	650 432-3200	17568
Wiline Networks Inc (PA)	4813	E	888 494-5463	5678

FOUNTAIN VALLEY, CA - Orange County

	SIC	EMP	PHONE	ENTRY #
B T B Events Inc	8743	D	714 415-3313	27539
Bell Private Security Inc	7381	D	714 964-9381	16582
Boys Girls CLB Huntington Vly (PA)	8641	C	714 531-2582	25111
Brightview Landscape Dev Inc	1711	B	714 546-7975	2149
Carmel Vlg Rtirement Residence	6513	D	714 962-6667	10999
Ceridian Tax Service Inc	8721	B	714 963-1311	26163
Command Security Corporation	7381	C	714 557-9355	16608
D-Link Systems Incorporated	5045	C	714 885-6000	7032
Edinger Medical Group Inc (PA)	8011	D	714 965-2500	19454
Forty Four Group LLC	7311	D	949 407-6360	13831
Fountain Valley Body Works M2	7532	D	714 751-8812	17722
Fountain Valley Regl Hospl	8062	A	714 966-7200	21418
Fountain Valley School Dst	7349	D	714 668-5882	14268
Hcr Manorcare Med Svcs Fla LLC	8051	D	714 241-9800	20509
His Passion Inc	8082	E	800 760-6389	22320
Hyundai Atver Tlmtics Amer Inc	7371	D	949 381-6000	15206
Hyundai Motor America (HQ)	6141	B	714 965-3000	9717
Jmg Security Systems Inc	1731	D	714 545-8882	2619
Longwood Management Corp	8361	D	714 962-5531	24583
Memorial Healthtec Labratories	8731	A	714 962-4677	26416
Memorialcare Surgical Center A	8062	D	714 369-1100	21584
Mile Square Golf Course	7992	C	714 962-5541	18735
Mitsubishi Materials USA Corp (HQ)	5085	E	714 352-6100	7860
Mobis Parts America (HQ)	5012	D	786 515-1101	6605
Norco Hills Car Wash	7542	E	951 279-4398	17833
Noritz America Corporation (HQ)	5075	D	714 433-2905	7654
Orange Coast Memorial Med Ctr (HQ)	8062	D	714 378-7000	21615
Orange County Sanitation (PA)	4953	A	714 962-2411	6425
Pan-Pacific Mechanical LLC (PA)	1711	C	949 474-9170	2305
Rcsn Inc	7361	C	714 965-0244	14715
Service King Holdings LLC	7532	D	714 962-2600	17740
Spec Services Inc	8711	D	714 963-8077	25920
Spec Services Inc (PA)	8711	D	714 963-8077	25921
St Jude Hospital Yorba Linda	8011	C	714 665-1797	19942
Stephouse Recovery Center	8322	D	714 394-3494	24076

FOWLER, CA - Fresno County

	SIC	EMP	PHONE	ENTRY #
Bedrosian Farms Inc	0172	E	559 834-5981	131
Fowler Convalescent Hospital	8059	E	559 834-2542	21067
Fowler Labor Service Inc	7361	B	559 834-3723	14622
Gahvejian Enterprises Inc	5113	E	559 834-5956	8103
Golden Living LLC	8051	D	559 834-2542	20462
Kandarian Agri Enterprises	0172	C	559 834-1501	151
Trius Trucking Inc	4731	D	559 834-4000	5189

FREMONT, CA - Alameda County

	SIC	EMP	PHONE	ENTRY #
24 Hour Fitness Usa Inc	7991	E	510 795-6666	18548
314e Corporation	7371	D	510 371-6736	14949
Abode Services (PA)	8322	D	510 657-7409	23457
Ace Financial Services Inc	6411	D	510 790-4600	10509
Ace USA	6411	D	510 790-4695	10510
Actividentity Corporation	7374	C	510 574-0100	16083
Aegis Asssted Living Prpts LLC	8361	E	510 739-1515	24408
Aegis Senior Communities LLC	8082	E	510 739-0909	22205
Aer Electronics Inc (PA)	4953	D	510 300-0500	6335
Agama Solutions Inc	8742	C	510 796-9300	27118
Alameda County Water District (PA)	4941	D	510 668-4200	6206
Alom Technologies Corporation (PA)	7389	D	510 360-3600	16993
Amax Engineering Corporation (PA)	5045	C	510 651-8886	7003
American Bldg Maint Co of III	7349	E	510 573-1618	14190
American Portwell Tech Inc (PA)	5045	D	510 403-3399	7006
AMS Ventures Inc	8742	D	301 980-5087	27133

	SIC	EMP	PHONE	ENTRY #
Anaspec Inc (HQ)	8731	E	800 452-5530	26320
Angioscore Inc	5047	C	510 933-7900	7153
Anka Behavioral Health Inc	8099	D	510 494-1567	22734
Apptivo Inc	7371	C	650 906-1034	14994
Arcsoft Inc (PA)	7371	D	510 440-9901	14995
Ardenbrook Inc (PA)	6531	D	510 797-7980	11216
Ashok Thummalachetty	8748	C	510 687-9797	27644
Asi Computer Technologies Inc (PA)	5045	C	510 226-8000	7009
Asterias Biotherapeutics Inc	8731	C	510 456-3800	26330
Asus Computer International	5045	C	510 739-3777	7010
AT&T Services Inc	4813	C	510 791-6605	5498
Atlas Security & Patrol Inc	7381	E	510 791-7380	16574
Avar Construction Inc	1611	D	510 354-2000	1727
Avar Construction Systems Inc (PA)	1622	E	510 354-2000	1875
Aver Information Inc	5045	E	408 263-3828	7013
AVI Systems Inc	5065	C	415 915-2070	7444
Bayside Interiors Inc (PA)	1742	C	510 438-9171	2849
BFI Waste Systems N Amer Inc	4953	D	510 657-1350	6357
Bigbyte Corporation	7378	D	510 249-1100	16279
Blocka Construction Inc	1711	D	510 657-3686	2145
By-The-Bay Investments Inc	6799	B	510 793-2581	12207
C & C Security Patrol Inc (PA)	7381	C	510 713-1260	16594
C J Health Services Inc	8051	D	510 793-3000	20277
Cal Coast Financial Inc	6163	D	510 683-9850	9874
Cal Coast Financial Corp (PA)	6531	D	510 683-9850	11260
Cancer Prevention Inst Cal (PA)	8733	C	510 608-5000	26603
Celestix Networks Inc	7373	D	510 668-0700	15928
Cellco Partnership	4812	C	510 490-3800	5333
Chrisp Company (PA)	1611	C	510 656-2840	1738
City of Fremont	8412	C	510 791-4196	24872
City of Fremont	8712	C	510 494-4460	26036
Club Sport of Fremont	7389	C	510 226-8500	17087
Cognitiveclouds Software Inc	7371	D	415 234-3611	15068
Coldwell Bnkr Residential Brkg	6531	D	510 608-7600	11362
Concentrix Corporation	7379	C	510 668-3717	16331
Concessionaires Urban Park	7999	C	530 529-1596	19150
Crestwood Behavioral Hlth Inc	8361	C	510 651-1244	24495
Crestwood Behavioral Hlth Inc	8361	C	510 793-8383	24497
CSC Covansys Corporation	7371	C	510 304-3400	15088
D F Rios Construction Inc	1751	C	510 226-7467	3026
Dcm Limited	7379	C	510 494-2321	16340
Dcm Technologies Inc	7371	D	510 791-2182	15097
Del Contes Landscaping Inc	0782	D	510 353-6030	822
Delta America Ltd (HQ)	5065	C	510 668-5100	7466
Delta Electronics Americas Ltd (DH)	5065	D	510 668-5100	7467
DMS Facility Services Inc	7349	A	510 656-9400	14253
Dryco Construction Inc (PA)	1611	C	510 438-6500	1761
E & E Co Ltd (PA)	5023	C	510 490-9788	6758
Edata Solutions Inc	7374	A	510 574-5380	16121
Education California Dept	8351	B	510 794-3666	24317
Electronics For Imaging Inc (PA)	7371	E	650 357-3500	15132
Elliott Laboratories Inc	8734	C	510 440-9500	26697
EMR Cpr LLC	7373	B	408 471-6804	15954
Etouch Systems Corp	7379	A	510 795-4800	16361
Eurogentec North America Inc	8748	C	510 791-9560	27724
Everest Consulting Group Inc	7371	C	510 494-8440	15149
Forsys Inc	7379	C	408 409-2567	16368
Fremont Ambltory Srgery Ctr LP	8011	D	510 456-4600	19477
Fremont Bank (HQ)	6022	C	510 505-5226	9460
Fremont Candle Lighters	8699	C	510 796-0595	25423
Fremont Marriott	7011	C	510 413-3700	12591
Fremont Sports Inc	7933	E	510 656-4411	18490
Fremont Unified School Dst	7349	D	510 657-0761	14269
Genmark Automation (DH)	5084	D	510 897-3400	7753
Globalways Inc (PA)	7379	D	510 580-1974	16387
Golden N-Life Diamite Intl Inc (PA)	5122	D	510 651-0405	8172
Greenbriar Management Company	6531	D	510 497-8200	11490
Growith Inc	1711	D	805 650-6650	2224
Hackerearth Inc	7371	C	650 461-4192	15196
Homelegance Inc	5021	C	510 933-6888	6725
Hyve Solutions Corporation (HQ)	7374	A	855 869-6873	16142
Infinity Nurses Care Inc	7363	D	510 713-8892	14862
Instant Systems Inc	7371	D	510 657-8100	15218
ISE Labs Inc	8734	E	510 687-2500	26710
ISE Labs Inc (DH)	8734	C	510 687-2500	26711
ISS Facility Services Inc	7349	B	650 593-9774	14292
Ists Worldwide Inc	7379	C	510 794-1400	16411
Jiangsu Juwang Info Tech Co (PA)	7371	D	510 967-3729	15242
John J Maguire DDS	8021	D	213 740-6462	20119
Jonce Thomas Construction Co	1751	E	510 657-7171	3047
Kaiser Foundation Hospitals	8011	B	510 248-3000	19613
Kidango Inc	8351	D	510 494-9601	24332
Kositch Enterprises Inc	1731	C	510 657-4460	2626
Land Services Landscape Contrs	6552	D	510 656-8101	11884
Leisure Sports Inc	7991	C	510 226-8500	18625

Employment Codes: A=Over 500 employees, B=251-500,
C=101-250, D=51-100, E=50

2019 Directory of California
Wholesalers and Services Companies

© Mergent Inc. 1-800-342-5647
1575

G E O G R A P H I C

Company	SIC	EMP	PHONE	ENTRY #
Lipman Insur Admnistrators Inc (PA)	6371	D	510 796-4676	10486
Luxar Tech Inc	4813	C	408 835-2551	5594
Luxera Inc	7349	E	510 456-7690	14308
Magnum Drywall Inc	1742	D	510 979-0420	2911
Mariner Health Care Inc	8051	C	510 792-3743	20611
Marriott International Inc	7011	C	510 413-3700	12887
Med Staffing LLC	7363	E	510 795-0114	14879
Merrill Gardens	6514	D	510 790-1645	11150
Metabyte Inc	7379	D	510 405-1117	16425
Milan Corporation	1761	E	510 656-6400	3180
Milestone Technologies Inc (PA)	7373	C	510 651-2454	16003
Myoscience Inc	8748	E	510 933-1500	27797
National Technical Systems Inc	8711	E	510 578-3500	25842
Neptune Management Corporation	7261	D	510 797-2269	13691
Net Express	7373	D	510 887-4395	16011
Netversant - Silicon Vly Inc (PA)	1731	C	510 771-1200	2660
New Image Landscape Company	0782	D	510 226-9191	907
Nidek Incorporated	5048	E	510 226-5700	7238
Novariant Inc (PA)	8711	D	510 933-4800	25847
OES Equipment LLC (PA)	7359	D	510 284-1900	14530
On Lok Senior Health Services	6324	E	510 249-2700	10286
Oplink Communications Inc (DH)	4899	C	510 933-7200	5990
Overton Security Services Inc	7381	C	510 791-7380	16751
Pacific Gas and Electric Co	4911	C	510 770-2025	6083
Pacific Royal Group	5199	D	510 200-2993	9243
Page Front Catering	5087	D	408 406-8487	7893
Pall Fortebio LLC	8731	D	650 322-1360	26428
Pape Material Handling Inc	5084	C	510 659-4100	7783
Park Cntl Care Rhblitation Ctr	8051	D	510 797-5300	20693
Patel Brothers Inc	8741	C	510 590-6914	26982
Penguin Computing Inc (DH)	5045	D	415 954-2800	7090
Permanente Medical Group Inc	8011	A	510 248-3000	19766
Phihong USA Corp (HQ)	5045	D	510 445-0100	7091
PJs Lumber Inc	5031	C	510 743-5300	6853
Priyo Inc	7371	E	408 248-2507	15375
Prospance Inc (PA)	7371	D	925 415-2394	15384
Prudential CA Realty	6531	C	510 487-6088	11691
Psychiatric Solutions Inc	8011	C	510 796-1100	19804
PW Stephens Envmtl Inc	1799	D	510 651-9506	3572
Pyramid Painting Inc	1721	E	650 903-9791	2468
Quadrant Components Inc	5045	D	510 656-9988	7096
Ravenswood Solutions	7373	D	650 241-3661	16040
Raymond Handling Concepts Corp (DH)	7699	D	510 745-7500	17976
Red Hawk Fire & SEC CA Inc	1731	D	510 438-1300	2696
Remax Active Realty	6531	D	510 505-1660	11726
Retirement Lf Care Communities	8361	D	510 505-0555	24652
RK Electric Inc	1731	C	510 580-2850	2711
Rk Logistics Group Inc (PA)	4731	D	408 942-8107	5157
Robert Half International Inc	7361	A	510 744-6486	14728
S & M Moving Systems	4213	D	510 497-2300	4254
San Jose Arena Management LLC	8741	D	510 623-7200	27021
Sansei Gardens Inc	0782	C	510 226-9191	934
Scholastic Book Fairs Inc	5192	D	510 771-1700	9120
Select Hotels Group LLC	7011	E	510 623-6000	13203
Seneca Family of Agencies	8322	D	510 226-6180	24043
Serrato-Mcdermott Inc	5013	D	510 656-6233	6673
Sierra Living Concepts Inc	5023	D	510 402-4906	6786
Sigmaways Inc	8742	D	510 573-4208	27449
Skylite Networks	7371	D	403 934-9349	15450
Smart Software Tstg Solutions	8748	D	833 778-7872	27862
Softsol Resources Inc (HQ)	7371	C	510 824-2000	15459
Sonata Software North Amer Inc (HQ)	7371	D	510 791-7220	15464
Sportvision Inc	7812	E	510 736-2925	18124
SRS Consulting Inc	7379	D	510 252-0625	16494
Startup Farms Intl LLC	7371	B	510 440-0110	15472
Strategic Security Services	6289	D	510 623-2355	10126
Sun Innovations Inc	8731	E	510 573-3913	26461
Sunnyvale Fluid Sys Tech Inc	5085	E	510 933-2500	7874
Superior Automatic Sprnklr Co	1711	D	408 946-7272	2379
Sysco San Francisco Inc (HQ)	5141	A	510 226-3000	8470
T-Mobile Usa Inc	4812	C	510 797-8290	5418
Technology Credit Union	6062	D	408 467-2385	9658
Three Way Logistics Inc (PA)	4731	D	408 748-3929	5179
Tri-City Health Center (PA)	8011	D	510 770-8040	20012
Tyan Computer Corporation	5045	D	510 651-8868	7123
U-Haul Co of California (DH)	7513	C	800 528-0463	17617
Underwriters Laboratories Inc	8734	B	510 771-1000	26738
United Mfg Assembly Inc	8734	D	510 490-1065	26741
United Parcel Service Inc OH	7389	B	800 742-5877	17543
Unitek Inc	7373	D	510 623-8544	16070
Unitek Information Systems Inc (PA)	7379	D	510 249-1060	16521
US Merchant Systems LLC	5065	C	877 432-8871	7558
Vasona Management Inc	1521	D	510 413-0091	1255
Verizon Bus Netwrk Svcs Inc	7376	D	510 497-2500	16273
Vertisystem Inc	7373	C	510 794-8099	16073

Company	SIC	EMP	PHONE	ENTRY #
Via Communications Inc	8731	C	510 687-4650	26491
Via Technologies Inc	5065	D	510 683-3300	7560
Vince Solutions (PA)	8742	D	510 432-0852	27513
Walters & Wolf Glass Company (PA)	1793	C	510 490-1115	3412
Walters & Wolf Interiors (PA)	1751	C	415 243-9400	3089
Washington Outpatient	8062	D	510 791-5374	21912
Washington Township	8062	A	510 797-3342	21913
Wells Fargo Bank National Assn	6021	D	510 792-3512	9397
Wells Fargo Bank National Assn	6021	C	415 222-6834	9402
Wells Fargo Bank National Assn	6021	B	510 745-5025	9407
Western Precooling Systems (PA)	0723	C	510 656-2220	586
Windsor Convalescent	8051	C	510 793-7222	20898
Winward International Inc (PA)	5193	D	510 487-8686	9180
YC Cable Usa Inc (HQ)	7389	D	510 824-2788	17602

FRENCH CAMP, CA - San Joaquin County

Company	SIC	EMP	PHONE	ENTRY #
County of San Joaquin	8322	D	209 468-6966	23731
Fresno Truck Center	5012	C	209 983-2400	6594
Health Plan of San Joaquin	6324	D	209 942-6300	10212
Healthy Beginnings French Camp	8011	D	209 468-6147	19495
Interstate Con Pmpg Co Inc	1771	D	209 983-3092	3269
San Joaquin General Hospital	8062	A	209 468-6000	21707
San Joaquin General Hospital	8062	C	209 468-6000	21708
Silva Trucking Inc	4212	E	209 982-1114	4064

FRESNO, CA - Fresno County

Company	SIC	EMP	PHONE	ENTRY #
A Colmenero Plastering Inc	1742	D	559 435-3606	2834
A J Excavation Inc	1611	C	559 408-5908	1711
A Plus In Home Care	8082	D	559 224-9442	22181
Aaron Dowling Incorporated	8111	D	559 432-4500	22904
ABM Janitorial Services Inc	7349	B	559 276-9096	14172
Access Capital Services Inc (PA)	7322	D	559 627-5221	13988
Activision Blizzard Inc	4225	C	310 431-4000	4522
Aecom Global II LLC	8711	C	559 347-5669	25515
Agri Valley Services	8721	D	559 253-0104	26142
All Commercial Landscape Svc	0782	E	559 453-1670	795
Allen Spees Family Homes	8361	E	559 432-3664	24413
Alliant Educational Foundation	8093	D	559 456-2777	22501
Allied Electric Motor Svc Inc (PA)	5063	D	559 486-4222	7327
Amdal In-Home Care Inc	8059	D	559 227-1701	20988
American All Risk Loss Adm	8742	C	559 277-4960	27128
American Baptist Homes of West	8361	C	559 439-4770	24415
American Fidelity Assurance Co	6411	D	559 230-2107	10519
American Paving Co	1611	E	559 268-9886	1719
Ameripride Services Inc	7218	D	559 266-0627	13582
Anthony Lambe	5013	D	559 268-0709	6618
Aramark Unf & Career AP LLC	7213	C	559 291-6631	13517
ARC Fresno/Madera Counties (PA)	8331	C	559 226-6268	24146
Archer-Daniels-Midland Company	5149	C	559 233-6262	8754
Arise LLC	7999	D	559 485-0881	19100
Arise Construction Inc	1711	D	559 449-8989	2126
Art Piccadilly Shaw LLC (PA)	7011	B	559 348-5520	12334
Art Piccadilly Shaw LLC	7011	D	559 375-7760	12335
Art Piccadilly Shaw LLC	7011	C	559 224-4200	12336
Arthur J Gallagher & Co	6411	C	559 436-0833	10546
Ashwood Construction Inc	1522	E	559 253-7240	1265
Asist Inc	8082	D	559 251-7701	22231
AT&T Services Inc	4813	B	559 454-3597	5476
B T & T Travel Inc	4724	C	559 237-9410	4932
Baker Mnock Jensen A Prof Corp	8111	C	559 432-5400	22929
Baloian Packing Co Inc (PA)	0161	D	559 485-9200	35
Baloian Packing Co Inc	0161	D	559 441-7043	36
Bank America National Assn	6021	D	559 445-7731	9280
BFI Waste Services LLC	4953	D	559 275-1551	6354
Bill Nlson Gen Engrg Cnstr Inc	1623	D	559 439-1756	1897
Bio-Mdical Applications RI Inc	8092	D	559 221-6311	22469
Bowie Enterprises (PA)	7542	D	559 227-6221	17804
Bowie Enterprises	7549	D	559 227-3400	17853
Bradford Messenger Service	7389	D	559 252-0775	17041
Brix Group Inc (PA)	5065	D	559 457-4700	7451
Broder Bros Co	5136	D	559 233-9900	8251
BSK Associates	8711	D	559 497-2888	25583
Buckingham Property Management	7299	D	559 322-1105	13722
Burford Family Farming Co LP (PA)	0191	C	559 431-0902	326
C&S Wholesale Grocers Inc	5141	B	559 442-4700	8386
Calif Stat Univ Fres Foun	8699	D	559 278-0850	25403
California Cancer Assctes	8011	D	559 447-4949	19339
California Eye Institute	8011	C	559 449-5000	19340
California Hlth Collaborative (PA)	7389	D	559 221-6315	17047
California HM For The Aged Inc	8059	C	559 255-8414	21028
Campos Family Farms LLC	0191	D	559 275-3000	329
Cardinal Health Inc	5122	D	559 448-0788	8155
Cardiovascular Consultants Hea	8011	D	559 432-4303	19348
Carrollco Inc	1521	E	559 396-3939	1142
CBS Radio Inc	4832	C	559 490-0106	5699
Cellco Partnership	4812	D	559 454-0803	5315

	SIC	EMP	PHONE	ENTRY #
Cellco Partnership	4812	D	559 451-0556	5329
Central Cal Nikkei Foundation	8361	D	559 237-4006	24460
Central California Blood Ctr	8099	D	559 389-5433	22761
Central California Blood Ctr	8099	D	559 324-1211	22762
Central California Blood Ctr (PA)	8099	D	559 389-5433	22763
Central California Ear Nose	8011	E	559 432-3724	19364
Central California Faculty Med (PA)	8011	D	559 453-5200	19365
Central Freight Lines Inc	4212	D	559 233-5559	3989
Central Valley Cmnty Bancorp (PA)	6022	C	559 298-1775	9428
Central Valley Community Bank	6029	C	559 298-1775	9498
Central Vly Chld Svcs Netwrk	8322	D	559 456-1100	23552
Central Vly Yng MNS Chrn Assoc	8641	E	559 225-9191	25129
Century Adanalian & Vasquez	6531	D	559 244-6000	11309
Champagne Landscape Nurs Inc	0782	D	559 277-8188	811
Change Healthcare Tech LLC	7389	D	559 455-4000	17070
Charles McMurray Co (PA)	5072	C	559 292-5751	7583
Charlies Enterprises	5148	C	559 445-8600	8652
Cherry Avenue Auction Inc	7389	E	559 266-9856	17073
Chicago Title Company	6361	D	559 451-3700	10441
Citigroup Global Markets Inc	6211	E	559 438-2542	9937
City of Fresno	4111	B	559 621-7433	3642
City of Fresno	4941	C	559 621-5300	6222
City of Fresno	7389	D	559 445-8200	17077
Claude Laval Corporation	5084	D	559 255-1601	7742
Clay Miranda Trucking Inc	4212	D	559 275-6250	3991
Clinica Sierra Vista	8322	D	559 457-6900	23589
Clinica Sierra Vista	8011	D	559 457-5292	19389
Club One Casino Inc	7011	B	559 497-3000	12469
Comcast Corporation	4841	D	559 718-9917	5880
Community Hospitals Centl Cal	7374	C	559 459-2916	16106
Community Hospitals Centl Cal (PA)	8062	A	559 459-6000	21334
Community Hospitals Centl Cal	8062	A	559 459-6000	21335
Community Integrated Work Prog	8331	E	559 276-8564	24168
Community Medical Center	8062	C	559 222-7416	21336
Community Medical Center	8062	D	559 447-4050	21337
Community Medical Centers	8062	C	559 320-2200	21338
Community Medical Centers	8062	D	559 447-4000	21339
Comprehensive Youth Ser	8322	D	559 229-3561	23614
Congregation of Poor Sisters	8361	D	559 237-3444	24474
Contemporary Services Corp	7381	C	559 225-9325	16616
Copper River Country Club LP (PA)	7997	D	559 434-5200	18899
County of Fresno	8111	D	559 600-3420	22994
County of Fresno	8322	D	559 600-3800	23638
County of Fresno	8111	D	559 600-3546	22995
County of Fresno	8093	D	559 600-4600	22542
County of Fresno	8621	C	559 600-3534	25014
County of Fresno	8322	C	559 600-3996	23640
County of Fresno	8322	C	559 488-3275	23641
Covenant Care California LLC	8051	D	559 251-8463	20345
Crestwood Behavioral Hlth Inc	8063	D	559 445-9094	21947
D E F Express Corporation	4213	D	559 264-0500	4121
Dairyamerica Inc (PA)	5143	D	559 251-0992	8518
Darden Architects Inc	8712	D	559 448-8051	26041
De Benedetto Farms Inc	0173	D	559 276-2400	186
Decipher Inc (HQ)	8732	D	559 436-6940	26510
Deloitte & Touche LLP	8721	D	559 449-6300	26182
Diamond Intl Investment LLC	7011	D	559 226-2200	12519
Diamond Learning Center Inc	8322	D	559 241-0580	23770
Dibuduo Dfendis Insur Brks LLC (PA)	6411	D	559 432-0222	10605
Diversified Transport Systems	4225	E	559 268-2760	4550
Donaghy Sales Inc	5181	C	559 486-0901	8993
Donahue Schriber Rlty Group LP	6512	D	714 545-1400	10870
Donald P Dick AC Inc (PA)	1711	D	559 255-1644	2187
Douglas L Myovich Trucking Inc	4212	D	559 233-8242	4006
E & S Rsidential Care Svcs LLC	8361	D	559 275-3555	24511
East Bay Clarklift Inc	5084	D	559 268-6621	7747
Educational Employees Cr Un (PA)	6061	C	559 437-7700	9549
Educational Employees Cr Un	6062	D	559 896-0222	9631
Electric Motor Shop	5063	D	559 233-1153	7357
Electronic Recyclers	4953	D	253 736-2627	6396
Electronic Recyclers Intl Inc (PA)	4953	C	800 374-3473	6397
Elim Alzheimers & Rehab	8051	D	559 320-2200	20389
Elitecare Medical Staffing LLC	7361	D	559 438-7700	14610
Energy Experts International	8748	C	559 449-1124	27718
Enterprise Holdings Inc	7514	D	559 261-9221	17632
Environment Control	7349	E	559 456-9791	14259
Exceptnal Prents Unlimited Inc	8322	D	559 229-2000	23791
Express Messenger Systems Inc	4215	D	559 277-4910	4409
Eye Medical Clinic Fresno Inc	8011	D	559 486-5000	19464
Eye Q Vision Care (PA)	8011	D	559 486-2000	19465
F & F Contracting Inc	0761	C	559 276-2418	646
Family Mdcine Rsidency Program	8062	D	559 499-6450	21414
Famous Software LLC (PA)	7371	D	559 438-3600	15156
Fedex Freight West Inc	4213	C	559 266-0732	4162
Ferguson Enterprises Inc	5074	E	559 253-2900	7619
Fig Garden Golf Course Inc	7997	D	559 439-2928	18924
Five Star Quality Care Inc	8051	C	559 446-6226	20434
Fort Wash Golf & Cntry CLB	7997	D	559 434-1702	18926
Fort Washington Parent Assoc	8641	D	559 327-6600	25156
Foster Poultry Farms	0254	A	559 265-2000	442
Foster Poultry Farms	0254	A	559 442-3771	443
Four CS Service Inc	1761	D	559 237-3990	3158
Fowler Packing Company Inc	0723	C	559 834-5911	517
Freshko Produce Services Inc	5148	C	559 497-7000	8678
Fresno Airport Hotels LLC	7011	D	559 252-3611	12593
Fresno Auto Dealers Auction	5012	C	559 268-8051	6592
Fresno Beverage Company Inc	5181	C	559 650-1500	8996
Fresno Cmnty Hosp & Med Ctr (HQ)	8062	A	559 459-6000	21422
Fresno Cnty Economic Opportunt	8322	A	559 263-1000	23810
Fresno Cnty Economic Opportunt (PA)	8322	A	559 263-1010	23811
Fresno Cnty Economic Opportunt	7389	B	559 263-1013	17176
Fresno Cnty Economic Opportunt	8322	D	559 485-3733	23812
Fresno County Private Security	7381	D	559 233-9800	16650
Fresno County Rural Trnst Agcy (PA)	4111	D	559 233-6789	3657
Fresno Heart Hospital LLC	8062	B	559 433-8000	21423
Fresno Heritage Partners	8361	E	559 446-6226	24535
Fresno Hotel Partners LP	7011	D	559 224-4040	12594
Fresno Irrigation District	4971	D	559 233-7161	6554
Fresno Metro Flood Ctrl Dst	7389	D	559 456-3292	17177
Fresno Plumbing & Heating Inc (PA)	1711	C	559 294-0200	2215
Fresno Rescue Mission Inc (PA)	8322	E	559 268-0839	23813
Fresno Roofing Co Inc	1761	D	559 255-8377	3159
Fresno Skilled Nursing	8051	D	559 268-5361	20440
Fresno Surgery Center LP (PA)	8062	C	559 431-8000	21424
Fresno Truck Center	5012	D	559 486-4310	6593
Fresno Unified School District	7349	C	559 457-3074	14270
Fresnos Chaffee Zoo Corp	8422	C	559 498-5910	24929
Frito-Lay North America Inc	5145	C	559 226-8153	8550
Frontier California Inc	4812	D	559 224-9222	5408
Gateway Auto Sales & Lsg Inc	5012	D	800 921-4336	6595
Geil Enterprises Inc (PA)	7381	C	559 495-3000	16664
Gene A Garcia Construction	1521	E	559 352-6173	1170
General Coatings Corporation	1721	C	559 495-4004	2440
GLad Entertainment Inc (PA)	7999	D	559 292-9000	19178
Golden Cross Care II Inc	8051	D	559 268-3023	20459
Golden Living LLC	8051	D	559 237-8377	20461
Golden Living LLC	8051	D	559 275-4785	20465
Golden Living LLC	8051	D	559 222-4807	20476
Golden Living LLC	8059	D	559 486-4433	21093
Golden Living LLC	8051	D	559 227-5383	20478
Golden Living LLC	8059	D	559 227-4063	21094
Golden State Plastering	5032	D	559 439-3920	6895
Graham-Prewett Inc	1761	E	559 291-3741	3161
Granite Construction Company	1611	C	559 441-5700	1778
Granville Homes Inc	1521	D	559 268-2000	1174
Greyhound Lines Inc	4131	C	559 268-1829	3878
Guarantee Real Estate	6531	D	559 650-6030	11496
Guarantee Real Estate Corp	6531	D	559 431-8600	11498
Guardsmark LLC	7381	C	559 243-1217	16687
Harris Construction Co Inc	1542	D	559 251-0301	1543
Health Comp Administrators (PA)	6411	C	559 499-2450	10643
Healthcare California	8082	D	559 243-9990	22315
Healthcare Centre of Fresno	8069	C	559 268-5361	22023
Healthcomp	6411	B	559 499-2450	10644
Heartland Opportunity Ctr Inc (PA)	8331	D	559 674-4521	24189
HI Fresno Hospitality LLC	7011	D	559 233-6650	12657
Hinds Hospice (PA)	8322	C	559 674-0407	23839
Howe Electric Construction Inc	1731	C	559 255-8992	2610
Hub Intrntional Insur Svcs Inc	6411	C	559 447-4600	10648
Hydratech LLC (HQ)	7699	D	559 233-0876	17955
Iheartcommunications Inc	4832	C	559 230-4300	5723
Inland Star Dist Ctrs Inc (PA)	4213	D	559 237-2052	4196
Intrade Industries Inc (PA)	4231	D	559 274-9877	4693
Ipsos Public Affairs Inc	8732	C	559 451-2820	26533
J & D Meat Company	5149	C	559 445-1123	8809
J M C International LLC	1542	E	559 256-1300	1559
J M Equipment Company Inc	5082	E	559 233-0187	7683
Jacks Car Wash 3	7542	D	559 438-8201	17819
James G Parker Insurance Assoc (PA)	6411	D	559 222-7722	10659
JMS Realtors Ltd (PA)	6531	C	559 490-1500	11531
Jorgensen & Sons Inc (PA)	5099	D	559 268-6241	8040
K W P H Enterprises	4119	B	559 443-5900	3812
Kaiser Foundation Hospitals	6324	C	559 448-4555	10223
Kaiser Foundation Hospitals	8062	A	559 448-4500	21521
Kaiser Foundation Hospitals	8011	A	559 448-4500	19620
Kaiser Radiology	8071	D	559 448-5541	22100
Karsyn Construction Inc	1542	D	559 271-2900	1571
Keisers Holdings LLC	7991	D	559 265-4700	18617
Kenyon Construction Inc	1742	D	559 277-5645	2905
Keolis Transit America Inc	4111	D	559 621-5783	3661

Employment Codes: A=Over 500 employees, B=251-500,
C=101-250, D=51-100, E=50

2019 Directory of California
Wholesalers and Services Companies

© Mergent Inc. 1-800-342-5647
1577

GEOGRAPHIC

Company	SIC	EMP	PHONE	ENTRY #
Kertel Communications Inc (HQ)	1731	D	559 432-5800	2624
Kfsn Television LLC	4833	C	559 442-1170	5806
Kftv	4833	D	559 222-2121	5807
Kid Iq 24 Hr Childcare	8351	D	310 492-3037	24331
Kimberlite Corporation (PA)	7382	C	559 264-9730	16917
Kings River Conservation Dst	8999	D	559 237-5567	27938
Kisco Senior Living LLC	6513	D	559 449-8070	11046
Kleinfelder Inc	8711	D	559 486-0750	25783
Kmph Fox 26	4833	C	559 255-2600	5809
Knight-Swift Trnsp Hldings Inc	4213	D	559 441-0340	4207
Kraft Heinz Foods Company	5149	E	559 499-5300	8820
Krm Risk Management Svcs Inc	8741	D	559 277-4800	26923
Kroeker Inc	1795	C	559 237-3764	3456
L A S Transportation Inc	4213	D	559 264-6583	4210
Labor Fnders of The Palm Bches	7363	D	559 221-2023	14870
Lamoures Inc (PA)	7211	D	559 264-0241	13487
Lang Richert & Patch	8111	E	559 228-6700	23183
Lassley Enterprises Inc	6513	E	559 226-4300	11050
Leisure Care LLC	8361	D	559 434-1237	24578
Lily Holdings LLC	8051	D	559 222-4807	20592
Linkus Enterprises LLC	1623	B	559 256-6600	1948
Lozano Smith LLP	8111	C	559 431-5600	23232
Lozano Smith A Prof Corp (PA)	8111	C	559 431-5600	23233
Lyles Diversified Inc (PA)	1623	B	559 441-1900	1951
M & L Plumbing Co Inc	1711	E	559 291-5525	2271
Major Transportation Svcs Inc	4213	E	559 485-5949	4218
Manning Gardens Inc	8051	E	559 834-2586	20607
Manning Gardens Care Ctr Inc	8051	D	559 834-2586	20608
Matson Alarm Co Inc	1731	D	559 438-8000	2637
McCormick Barstow Shepprd Wayt (PA)	8111	C	559 433-1300	23242
McCutcheon Enterprises Inc	0172	D	559 864-3200	161
Melos Plst Lthg & Drywall	1742	D	559 237-0028	2916
Mesa Energy Systems Inc	1711	D	559 277-7900	2279
Midland Express Credit LLC	8742	D	800 961-3904	27347
Millmens Local 1496	8631	E	559 275-8676	25070
Mirabella Farms Inc	0172	D	559 237-4495	162
Mission Linen Supply	7213	D	559 268-0647	13538
Moore Twining Associates Inc (PA)	8734	D	559 268-7021	26719
Morgan Stanley & Co LLC	6211	E	559 431-5900	9996
Morrison MGT Specialists Inc	8099	C	559 459-6449	22843
Muniservices LLC (DH)	8742	C	800 800-8181	27352
Netafim Irrigation Inc (HQ)	5083	D	559 453-6800	7707
Nevocal Enterprises Inc	1442	D	559 277-0700	1095
New England Shtmtl Works Inc	8711	D	559 268-7375	25845
New York Life Insurance Co	6411	D	559 447-3900	10707
New York Life Insurance Co	6411	D	559 447-3900	10715
Newport Television LLC	7922	C	559 761-0243	18388
Nexstar Broadcasting Inc	4833	C	559 222-2411	5828
Nicole Pttrson Crt Rprting LLC	8111	E	559 400-2407	23286
Noble Credit Union (PA)	6061	E	559 252-5000	9575
North Pt Hlth Wellness Ctr LLC	8051	D	559 320-2200	20662
North West Learning Center	8351	E	559 228-3057	24354
Northwest Medical Group Inc	8011	D	559 271-6302	19724
Northwest Physicians Med Group	8011	D	559 271-6370	19725
Olam Americas Inc (DH)	0723	A	559 447-1390	550
Olam West Coast Inc (DH)	0723	C	559 447-1390	551
Omni Womens Hlth Med Group Inc	8011	D	559 441-4271	19733
Organic Pastures Dairy Co LLC	0241	E	559 846-9732	424
P K B Investments Inc	8742	C	559 243-1224	27385
Paccar Leasing Corporation	7513	C	559 268-4344	17606
Pacific Gas and Electric Co	4911	B	559 268-2868	6072
Pacific Grain & Foods LLC (PA)	5153	C	559 276-2580	8906
Pactiv LLC	5199	C	559 251-7351	9246
Pape Trucks Inc	7538	D	559 268-4344	17775
Park Inn By Radisson	7011	D	559 226-2200	13044
Park Inn By Readisson Fresno	7011	D	559 226-2200	13045
Patton Sheet Metal Works Inc	1761	E	559 486-5222	3183
Paychex Inc	8721	D	559 432-1100	26265
PDM Steel Service Centers	5051	E	559 442-1410	7298
Pearson Realty (PA)	6531	D	559 432-6200	11668
Permanente Medical Group Inc	8011	D	559 448-4500	19759
Piccadilly Hospitality LLC	7011	E	559 348-5520	13061
Principal Financial Group Inc	6311	D	559 261-2000	10145
Producers Dairy Foods Inc (PA)	5142	C	559 264-6583	8498
Professional Exchange Svc	7389	E	559 229-6249	17413
Promesa Behavioral Health (PA)	8361	C	559 439-5437	24638
Protosource Corporation	7374	D	559 490-8600	16169
Prudential Overall Supply	7218	D	559 264-8231	13618
Quest Diagnostics Incorporated	8071	D	559 438-2893	22132
Quiring Corporation	1542	D	559 432-2800	1621
Quiring General LLC	1542	D	559 432-2800	1622
R Fellen Inc	8051	D	559 233-6248	20714
Rainbow - Brite Indus Svcs LLC	7349	D	559 925-2580	14362
Randstad North America Inc	7363	C	559 297-0054	14896
Reading and Beyond	8641	D	559 840-1068	25227

Company	SIC	EMP	PHONE	ENTRY #
Real Time Information Svcs Inc	7363	E	559 222-9400	14900
Recyclers I Electronic	4953	D	317 522-1414	6447
Rescue Children Inc	8322	E	559 268-1123	23991
Residence Inn By Marriott	7011	D	559 222-8900	13118
Rex More Elec Contrs Engineers	1731	D	559 294-1300	2705
Rgis LLC	7389	D	559 224-5898	17444
Riverside Nursery & Ldscp Inc	5193	D	559 275-1891	9161
Ron D & Shelley N Horn	0172	E	559 834-2118	171
Royal Express Inc (PA)	4214	C	559 272-3500	4369
SA Recycling LLC	4953	D	559 237-6677	6464
Saint Agnes Med Providers Inc	8099	D	559 435-2630	22871
Saint Agnes Medical Center (HQ)	8062	A	559 450-3000	21693
Saladinos Inc (PA)	5141	C	559 271-3700	8451
San Joaquin Country Club	7997	D	559 439-3483	19028
San Joaquin Figs Inc	0723	E	559 224-4492	564
San Joaquin Val UNI Air Pol (PA)	8748	D	559 230-6000	27853
San Joaquin Valley A P C D	8748	D	559 230-6000	27855
San Joaquin Valley Intergrp	8699	D	559 856-0559	25458
San Joaquin Valley Rehabili (HQ)	8093	B	559 436-3600	22675
Sante Health System Inc (PA)	6321	D	559 228-5400	10172
Scrip Advantage Inc	7389	D	559 320-0052	17462
Securitas SEC Svcs USA Inc	7381	C	559 221-2302	16790
Servi-Tech Controls Inc (PA)	1711	D	559 264-6679	2353
Shaw Hospitality Group Inc	7011	D	559 224-4040	13212
Shaws Strctures Unlimited Inc	1541	E	559 275-3475	1432
Sierra Bancorp	6022	C	559 449-8145	9487
Sierra Pacific Development	6552	D	559 256-1300	11917
Sierra Pacific Ortho	8011	C	559 256-5200	19891
Signature Flight Support Corp	4581	D	559 981-2490	4909
Simone Fruit Co Inc	0723	D	559 275-1368	568
Smartway Express Inc	4731	C	559 272-3500	5170
Smg Holdings Inc	7389	B	559 445-8100	17474
Social Vocational Services Inc	8361	C	559 443-7119	24678
Spirit of Woman of California	8093	D	559 233-4353	22687
State Compensation Insur Fund	6331	B	559 433-2700	10401
Steven G Fogg MD	8011	D	559 449-5010	19948
Strategic Mechanical Inc	1711	D	559 291-1952	2373
Sunland Insurance Agency	6411	A	559 251-7861	10797
Sunrise Senior Living LLC	8051	D	559 325-8170	20825
T Royal Management (PA)	6531	D	559 447-9887	11783
Target Corporation	4226	C	559 431-0104	4689
Telesis Onion Co (PA)	0161	D	559 884-2441	86
Terry Tuell Concrete Inc	1771	D	559 431-0812	3336
Teter LLP (PA)	8711	E	559 437-0887	25945
Thomas M Obinson Jr	6531	D	559 432-6200	11796
Torres Fence Co Inc	1799	E	559 237-4141	3596
Trinity Home Health Svcs Inc	8082	D	559 450-5112	22439
Turn Behavioral Hlth Svcs Inc	8093	D	559 264-7521	22703
Turner Security Systems Inc	7381	C	559 486-3466	16840
Tutor Perini/Zachry/Parsons	1629	E	559 385-7025	2071
Twilight Haven	8051	D	559 251-8417	20844
Ultimate Creations LLC	6799	D	559 221-4936	12278
Unifirst Corporation	7218	D	559 233-0400	13626
Union Pacific Railroad Company	4011	C	559 443-2244	3628
United Crbrl Plsy of Cntrl CA (PA)	8399	E	559 221-8272	24852
United States Cold Storage Inc	4222	E	559 237-6145	4515
Universal Field Services Inc	1629	D	559 453-2901	2072
Univision Radio Inc	4832	E	559 430-8500	5761
Univision Television Group Inc	4833	D	559 222-2121	5844
Uniwell Corporation	6552	D	559 268-1000	11933
Uniwell Fresno Hotel LLC	7011	D	559 268-1000	13356
UPS Ground Freight Inc	4213	D	559 445-9010	4286
Urology Assoc of Cen Cal	8011	D	559 321-2800	20037
US Property Group Inc	6512	E	559 227-1901	10958
USA Waste of California Inc	4953	D	559 834-9151	6496
USI Insurance Services Nat Inc	6411	D	559 666-2001	10815
Utility Trlr Sls of Centl Cal	5084	E	559 237-2001	7815
Valley Fig Growers	0723	E	559 237-3893	582
Valley Healthcare Center LLC	8051	D	559 251-7161	20850
Valley Healthcare Center LLC	8051	C	559 251-7161	20851
Valley Physicians Alliance	8741	D	559 538-3000	27082
Valley Teen Ranch	8361	D	559 437-1144	24707
Valley Transportation Inc (PA)	4212	D	559 266-6674	4083
Veritiv Operating Company	5113	D	559 268-0467	8129
Veterans Health Administration	8062	A	559 225-6100	21903
Veterans Health Administration	8011	A	559 225-6100	20062
Veterans Home Cal - Fresno	8051	D	559 493-4400	20857
Vibra Healthcare LLC	8062	D	559 436-3600	21906
Victus Group Inc	8741	C	559 429-8080	27086
Vision Care Center (PA)	8011	C	559 486-2000	20090
Volt Management Corp	7363	C	559 435-1255	14936
Vucovich Inc (PA)	5083	D	559 486-8020	7717
W M Lyles Co (HQ)	1623	B	559 441-1900	1998
Well Being Group Inc	8082	D	559 432-3737	22463
West Air Inc	4513	D	559 454-7843	4853

Mergent email: customerrelations@mergent.com

1578

2019 Directory of California
Wholesalers and Services Companies

(P-0000) Products & Services Section entry number
(PA)=Parent Co (HQ)=Headquarters (DH)=Div Headquarters

Company	SIC	EMP	PHONE	ENTRY #
Westcare California Inc (HQ)	8361	D	559 251-4800	24718
Western Building Materials Co (PA)	1742	D	559 454-8500	2980
Wild Electric Incorporated	1731	D	559 251-7770	2789
Windham At Saint Agnes	6513	D	559 449-8070	11142
Winegard Energy Inc	1742	D	559 441-0243	2983
Winnresidential Ltd Partnr	7513	B	559 435-3434	17620
Wish I Ah Care Center Inc	8051	C	559 855-2211	20909
Wish-I-Ah Hlthcre & Wellness	8051	D	559 855-2211	20910
Wish-I-Ah Skilled Nursing	8051	C	949 285-8859	20911
Wm B Saleh Co	1721	D	559 255-2046	2494
Wm Michael Stemler Inc	6411	C	559 228-4144	10835
Woolf Farming Co Cal Inc (PA)	0191	A	559 945-9292	395
Xobee Networks Inc	4813	D	559 579-1300	5679
Xpo Logistics Freight Inc	4213	D	559 485-1164	4312
Xpo Logistics Supply Chain Inc	4731	D	559 408-7951	5201
Zumwalt Construction Inc	1542	D	559 252-1000	1709

FRIANT, CA - Fresno County

Company	SIC	EMP	PHONE	ENTRY #
Table Mountain Casino	7011	A	559 822-7777	13320

FULLERTON, CA - Orange County

Company	SIC	EMP	PHONE	ENTRY #
A1 Building Management Inc	7349	C	714 447-3800	14166
Alpha Swimming Pool & Spa	7389	D	714 879-4667	16995
Altura Comm Solutions LLC (DH)	5065	D	714 948-8400	7435
American Golf Corporation	7992	D	714 672-6800	18685
American Multi-Cinema Inc	7832	E	714 992-6961	18264
AMS American Mech Svcs MD Inc	1711	D	714 888-6820	2119
Anaheim Park Hotel	7011	C	714 992-1700	12322
Anderson Air Conditioning LP	1711	D	714 998-6850	2121
Ans World Service Inc	4789	D	714 441-2400	5219
Arconic Global Fas & Rings Inc	5085	D	714 871-1550	7833
Associated Students Californi	8641	D	657 278-2468	25093
Bakery Ex Southern Cal LLC	5149	D	714 446-9470	8758
C & L Refrigeration Corp	1711	C	800 901-4822	2152
Cardservice International Inc	7389	D	714 773-1778	17057
Catalina Enterprise Inc	8748	D	949 637-3091	27676
Cellco Partnership	4812	C	714 449-0715	5391
City of Fullerton	8742	C	714 738-6897	27193
Corecare I I I	8361	C	714 256-8000	24476
Corecare V A Cal Ltd Partnr	8051	C	714 256-1000	20324
County of Orange	8111	E	714 626-3700	23004
Dunlap Property Group Inc	6531	D	714 879-0111	11411
Elliott Auto Supply Co Inc	5013	D	310 527-2500	6638
Excel Construction Svcs Inc (PA)	1541	D	714 680-9200	1397
Federal Express Corporation	4513	C	800 463-3339	4832
Florence Crittenton Services	8361	B	714 680-9000	24530
Geek Squad Inc	7379	C	800 433-5778	16379
Gordon Lane Convalescent Hosp	8062	D	714 879-7301	21435
Harte Hanks Inc	4225	D	210 829-9000	4571
Harte-Hanks Direct Mail/Califo	7331	C	714 738-5478	14045
Henry Bros Electronics Inc	7373	C	714 525-4350	15971
Hidden Villa Ranch Produce Inc	5144	B	714 680-3447	8532
Hot Dogger Tours Inc	4142	C	714 988-4088	3899
Huoyen International Inc	7011	D	714 635-9000	12743
Integrated Parcel Network	4215	B	714 278-6100	4420
Jcv Inc	1742	E	714 871-2007	2902
John G Shipley	6531	D	714 626-2000	11533
Loewy Enterprises	5148	D	323 726-3838	8704
Merritt Hospitality LLC	7011	D	714 738-7800	12923
NTS Technical Systems	8734	C	714 998-4351	26725
Opus Bank	6029	C	714 578-7500	9515
Opus Inspection Inc	7371	D	714 999-6727	15335
Orange Pacific Plumbing Inc	1711	D	714 992-4547	2300
Orora Packaging Solutions	5113	C	714 278-6000	8122
Orora Packaging Solutions	5113	D	714 773-0124	8123
Pavilion At Sunny Hills	8051	C	714 992-5701	20699
Prestige Sales II LLC	5149	D	714 632-8020	8857
Progressive Floor Covering Inc	1752	E	714 213-8805	3115
Quaker Oats Company	4225	E	714 526-8800	4617
Raytheon Command and Control (HQ)	5065	A	714 446-3118	7535
Real Estate Image Inc	7331	D	714 502-3900	14061
Romach LLC	5063	D	805 378-1174	7390
Rosary Academy Parent Council	8641	D	714 879-6302	25228
RPM Consolidated Services Inc (PA)	4225	D	714 388-3500	4627
Sage Behavior Services Inc	8063	D	714 773-0077	21970
Salon Lujon Inc	7231	D	714 738-1882	13671
Salon Technique	7299	E	714 871-4247	13772
Southern California Edison Co	4911	D	714 870-3225	6122
Spectrum MGT Holdg Co LLC	4841	D	714 871-2643	5938
St Joseph Health System	8062	D	714 992-3000	21776
St Jude Hospital (DH)	8062	A	714 871-3280	21786
St Jude Hospital	8011	A	714 992-3057	19940
St Jude Hospital Yorba Linda (PA)	8742	D	714 449-4800	27466
Sun Haven Care Inc	8051	D	714 870-0060	20784
Superior Wall Systems Inc	1742	B	714 278-0000	2966
Swinford Electric Inc	1731	E	714 578-8888	2757

Company	SIC	EMP	PHONE	ENTRY #
Tf Courier Inc	4215	D	714 888-1452	4435
Therapy For Kids Inc	8049	E	714 870-6116	20209
Trendsettah Usa Inc	5099	D	888 775-4881	8064
TW Services Inc	4789	B	714 441-2400	5250
UPS Ground Freight Inc	4213	D	866 372-5619	4295
US Foods Inc	5149	C	714 449-9990	8894
Veg Land Sales Inc (PA)	5141	D	714 871-6712	8485
Veg-Land Inc	4221	E	714 871-6712	4491
Viele & Sons Inc	5141	D	714 447-3663	8486
Ware Disposal Inc	4953	C	714 834-0234	6507
Westview Services Inc	8322	D	714 879-3980	24132
Windsor Gardns Healthcare Cntr	8051	C	714 871-6020	20903
Womens Trnstnal Living Ctr Inc	8331	E	714 992-1939	24250
Wyndham International Inc	7011	D	714 992-1700	13423
YMCA of North Orange County	8641	D	714 879-9622	25292
Young Mens Chrstn Assn Orange	8641	D	714 879-9622	25350

FULTON, CA - Sonoma County

Company	SIC	EMP	PHONE	ENTRY #
Bacchus Vineyard MGT LLC	8741	D	707 837-8304	26772

GALT, CA - Sacramento County

Company	SIC	EMP	PHONE	ENTRY #
Building Material Distrs Inc (PA)	5031	C	209 745-3001	6813
City of Galt	7999	D	209 366-7180	19132
Dry Creek Lath & Plaster Inc	1742	D	209 367-8607	2877
Eliseo Esparza Delgadillo	0761	E	209 745-3937	645
Galt Joint Union School Dst	8351	E	209 745-1546	24323
Golden Living LLC	8082	D	209 745-1537	22303
Gonzales Salvador Labor Contrs	0761	D	209 745-2223	651
Keb Keb Magic Clown	7999	D	916 369-6054	19192
Norogachi Construction Inc/CA	1742	D	916 236-4201	2922
Travis James Watts	0191	C	209 810-6159	388
Western Star Nurseries LLC	5193	E	209 744-2552	9178

GARBERVILLE, CA - Humboldt County

Company	SIC	EMP	PHONE	ENTRY #
Southern Hmbldt Cmnty Dst Hosp	8062	D	707 923-3921	21766
Southern Humboldt Comm Hlth Cr	8062	D	707 923-3925	21767

GARDEN GROVE, CA - Orange County

Company	SIC	EMP	PHONE	ENTRY #
Aaron Thomas Company Inc (PA)	7389	C	714 894-4468	16972
Abbey-Properties LLC (PA)	6512	D	562 435-2100	10847
Accutherm Refrigeraton Inc	1711	D	714 766-7800	2084
Act Home Health Inc	8082	D	714 560-0800	22196
Acxiom Corporation	7375	E	714 636-3093	16207
AGR Group Inc	8742	A	714 245-7151	27119
Alta Care Center LLC	8059	C	714 530-6322	20986
Audio Visual MGT Solutions	8741	C	714 590-8755	26770
Bank America National Assn	6021	E	714 973-8495	9289
Best Valet Parking Corporation	7299	D	800 708-2538	13721
Boys Grls Clubs Grdn Grove Inc	8641	C	714 537-8833	25115
Chapman Hbr Sklled Nrsing Care	8051	D	714 971-5517	20309
Community Action Partnershi (PA)	8322	D	714 897-6670	23595
Compass Group Usa Inc	7359	C	714 899-2520	14488
Complete Relocation Svcs Inc	4214	D	714 901-7411	4337
Consoldted Med Bo-Analysis Inc	8071	C	714 467-0240	22071
Customfab Inc	7389	C	714 891-9119	17120
Elrob Inc	5065	C	714 230-6100	7472
Envise Inc	1711	D	714 901-5800	2203
G Brothers Construction Inc	1742	E	714 590-3070	2887
Garden Grove Convales	8059	C	714 638-9470	21079
Garden Grove Unified Schl Dst	8351	D	714 663-6437	24324
Goodwin Ammonia Company	4225	D	714 894-0531	4567
Hansol Goldpoint LLC	4731	D	714 594-5073	5081
Healthcare System 2000	8011	D	714 899-2000	19493
Hyatt Corporation As Agent O	7011	B	714 750-1234	12749
Informative Research (PA)	7323	E	714 638-2855	14038
Janitorial Equipment Svcs Inc	7349	D	951 205-8937	14296
Kaiser Foundation Hospitals	8011	D	714 741-3448	19528
Kenneth Corp	8062	A	714 537-5160	21531
M M Direct Marketing Inc	7331	B	714 265-4100	14051
Mastroianni Family Entps Ltd	7299	D	310 952-1700	13757
Mitsubishi Electric Us Inc	5065	D	714 934-5300	7509
OfficeMax Incorporated	4225	D	951 485-9353	4603
Ohi Resort Hotels LLC	7011	D	714 867-5555	12975
Orange County Trnsp Auth	4111	A	714 560-6282	3693
Our Watch	8082	D	714 897-1022	22385
Pacific Exteriors Inc	1742	D	714 265-1998	2932
Pacific Haven Convalescent HM	8059	D	714 534-1942	21179
Pacific Rim Resources Srch	7361	C	714 638-0307	14686
Party Pantry Garden Room	7299	E	714 899-0626	13765
Pathfinder Health Inc	8082	C	714 636-5649	22390
Prime Health Care Svcs Grdn Gr	8062	B	714 537-5160	21655
Progressive Power Group Inc	1711	E	714 899-2300	2320
Protect-US	7381	C	714 721-8127	16766
Public Bell Inc	7371	D	818 396-1675	15386
Quail Engineering Inc	1611	E	714 636-0612	1839
R J Daum Construction Co (PA)	1542	C	714 894-4300	1623
RJ Allen Inc	7353	D	714 539-1022	14456

GEOGRAPHIC

	SIC	EMP	PHONE	ENTRY #
Schlumberger Technology Corp	1389	D	714 379-7332	1078
Sherton Grdn Grove Anheim S Ht	7011	D	714 703-8400	13221
South West Sun Solar Inc	5074	E	714 582-3909	7637
Southland Industries (PA)	1711	E	800 613-6240	2370
Southland Industries	1711	C	714 901-5800	2371
Spectrum MGT Holdg Co LLC	4841	D	714 903-4000	5942
Stonebridge McWhinney LLC	7011	E	714 703-8800	13284
Tekworks Inc	4813	D	877 835-9675	5652
Teletrac Inc (HQ)	4899	D	714 897-0877	5999
Video Vice Data Communications	4899	B	714 897-6300	6006
Western Transit Systems Inc	4121	D	949 515-0188	3873

GARDEN VALLEY, CA - El Dorado County

	SIC	EMP	PHONE	ENTRY #
Buckland Vineyard Management (PA)	8741	D	530 333-1534	26788

GARDENA, CA - Los Angeles County

	SIC	EMP	PHONE	ENTRY #
Acme Metals LLC	5051	D	310 329-2263	7251
Action Force Security	7381	E	310 715-6053	16543
Administrative Svcs Coop Inc	8742	C	310 715-1968	27114
American Guard Services Inc (PA)	7381	B	310 645-6200	16564
American Residential Svcs LLC	1711	E	310 808-0279	2108
AMG Construction Group	1611	D	800 310-2609	1720
Arena Painting Contractors Inc	1721	D	310 316-2446	2422
Aries Filterworks	5085	E	323 262-1600	7836
Bank America National Assn	6021	D	800 432-1000	9291
Behavioral Health Services Inc (PA)	8322	E	310 679-9031	23505
Best Contracting Services Inc (PA)	1761	B	310 328-9176	3128
Brentwood Medical Tech Corp	5047	B	800 624-8950	7168
Brightview Landscape Svcs Inc	0781	C	310 327-8700	742
California Supply Inc (PA)	5113	C	310 532-2500	8098
California Waste Services LLC	4953	C	310 538-5998	6365
Canon Bus Solutions-West Inc	5044	B	310 217-3000	6951
Ceridian LLC	8721	C	310 719-7400	26162
Charles E Thomas Company Inc (PA)	1542	D	310 323-6730	1501
City of Gardena	4111	D	310 324-1475	3643
Classic Tile & Mosaic Inc (PA)	5032	D	310 538-9605	6881
Claud Townsley Inc	1761	D	310 527-6770	3138
Cleanstreet	4959	C	310 329-3078	6533
CM Laundry LLC	7219	C	310 436-6170	13630
Cns Logistics Inc	4731	D	562 229-1133	5034
Colich Sons	1623	C	323 770-2920	1910
Comprehensive Dist Svcs Inc	4789	C	310 523-1546	5221
Counseling and Research Assoc (PA)	8361	C	310 715-2020	24477
Duggan & Associates Inc	1721	C	323 965-1502	2433
Eagle Security Service Inc	7381	C	310 532-1626	16635
El Dorado Enterprises Inc	7011	A	310 719-9800	12552
FARaday&future Inc	8711	A	424 276-7616	25680
Fedex Freight Corporation	4213	B	310 323-5230	4156
First Student Inc	4151	C	310 715-6122	3929
First Student Inc	4151	D	310 769-2400	3936
Gardena Flores Inc	8051	D	310 323-4570	20447
Gardena Hospital LP	8062	A	310 532-4200	21425
Gfk Custom Research LLC	8732	C	310 527-2100	26523
Gina B Ltd Inc	5023	D	310 366-7926	6765
Global Paratransit Inc	4119	B	310 715-7550	3803
Global Stainless Supply	5051	B	310 525-1865	7276
Greater South Bay Area HM Hlth	8082	E	310 329-4835	22308
Guardsmark LLC	7381	C	310 522-9603	16677
Harbor Distributing LLC	5181	B	310 538-5483	9002
Health Care Investments Inc	8051	C	310 323-3194	20516
Houston Salem Inc	5137	E	310 719-7004	8307
Image First Healthcre Lndry Sp	7218	C	310 819-1463	13609
JH Bryant Jr Inc (PA)	1541	E	310 532-1840	1410
Jk Imaging Ltd	5043	D	310 755-6848	6944
John S Meek Company Inc	1629	D	310 830-6323	2042
Jomar Industries Inc	7389	E	323 770-0505	17262
JS Real Estate Prpts Inc	1791	D	310 856-6868	3379
Jumpstart Games Inc	7371	D	424 645-4311	15245
Kaiser Foundation Hospitals	8011	A	800 780-1230	19560
Kaiser Foundation Hospitals	8062	E	310 517-2956	21503
Konica Minolta Business Soluti	5044	E	310 214-6696	6967
Landcare USA LLC	0782	D	310 719-1008	881
Landcare USA LLC	0782	C	310 354-1520	883
Legions Protective Svcs LLC	7381	C	310 819-8881	16718
Los Angeles Unified School Dst	7349	C	310 808-1500	14307
M&M Asseet Management Gnl	6513	D	310 769-6669	11061
Magnetika Inc (PA)	5063	D	310 527-8100	7374
Martin Bros/Marcowall Inc (PA)	1742	C	310 532-5335	2912
MGA Healthcare California Inc	7363	D	310 324-5591	14884
MGT Industries Inc	8741	D	310 324-3152	26944
Monark LP	6513	D	310 769-6669	11079
Mufg Union Bank National Assn	6021	D	310 354-4700	9359
Navigant Cymetrix Corporation	8741	C	424 201-6300	26955
Nippon Travel Agency Amer Inc	4724	D	310 768-1817	4944
Nippon Travel Agency PCF Inc (DH)	4724	D	310 768-0017	4945
Northrop Grumman Federal Cr Un (PA)	6062	D	310 808-4000	9642

	SIC	EMP	PHONE	ENTRY #
Nri Usa LLC	4731	D	323 345-6456	5124
Nygard Inc	5137	D	310 776-8900	8328
Oxgord Incorporated	5199	C	800 221-0718	9239
Phoenix Textile Inc (PA)	5131	D	310 715-7090	8235
Premier Tile & Marble	1743	D	310 516-1712	3008
Ps2 (PA)	1721	D	310 243-2980	2467
Pulp Studio Incorporated (PA)	7336	D	310 815-4999	14127
R Haupt Roofing Construction	1761	E	310 515-9709	3192
Radford Alexander Corporation	4212	D	310 523-2555	4053
Radiant Services Corp (PA)	7211	C	310 327-6300	13489
Rancho California Landscaping	0782	D	310 768-1680	927
Raymak Automotive Inc	7538	E	310 329-8910	17780
Republic Services Inc	4953	D	310 527-6980	6452
Roadex America Inc	4731	D	310 878-9800	5158
Schumacher Cargo Logistics Inc (PA)	4731	D	562 408-6677	5163
Servexo	7381	E	323 527-9994	16820
Silverline Construction Inc	1542	C	310 464-8314	1649
SMS Transportation	8111	D	310 527-9200	23391
SOS Metals Inc (DH)	5093	C	310 217-8848	7997
South Bay Auto Auction	5012	C	310 719-2000	6608
Southern Cal Maid Svc Crpt Clg	7349	D	310 675-0585	14397
Stefan Merli Plastering Co Inc (PA)	1771	D	310 323-0404	3330
Tireco Inc (PA)	5014	C	310 767-7990	6698
United Guard Security Inc	7381	C	310 881-2984	16843
United Parcel Service Inc OH	4215	B	310 217-2646	4455
US Foods International LLC	5141	D	310 515-2189	8482
Usfi Inc	5141	D	310 768-1937	8483
Valley of Sun Cosmetics LLC	5122	C	310 327-9062	8216
Vernon Autoparts Inc	7539	D	323 249-7545	17799
W F Hayward Co (PA)	1742	D	310 532-9501	2977
Washington Oma Ir Works Inc (PA)	1799	D	310 327-8660	3606
West Coast Maintenance Inc	7349	D	310 324-2511	14427
World Service West	4581	D	310 538-7000	4922
Wrag-Time Air Freight Inc (PA)	4213	B	800 586-9701	4307
Wsa Group Inc (PA)	7381	E	310 743-3000	16861
XCEL Mechanical Systems Inc	1711	C	310 660-0090	2413
Yrc Inc	4213	C	310 404-2221	4325

GERBER, CA - Tehama County

	SIC	EMP	PHONE	ENTRY #
Haleakala Ranch LLC	0291	E	530 529-6651	450

GEYSERVILLE, CA - Sonoma County

	SIC	EMP	PHONE	ENTRY #
Redwood Empire Vineyard Mgt	0762	D	707 857-3401	709
River Rock Entertainment Auth	7011	A	707 857-2777	13132
Robert Young Family Ltd Partnr	0762	D	707 433-3228	710
Vimark Inc	0762	D	707 857-3588	717
Vinwood Cellars Inc	5182	E	707 857-4011	9060

GILROY, CA - Santa Clara County

	SIC	EMP	PHONE	ENTRY #
Advance Services Inc	7631	A	408 767-2797	17919
Aspen Grove Apartments LLC	6513	D	408 848-6400	10981
Bert E Jessup Transportation	4213	D	408 848-3390	4103
Cellco Partnership	4812	C	408 846-5170	5345
Christopher Ranch LLC (PA)	0139	C	408 847-1100	21
Cleaning Services	7699	D	408 778-9251	17940
Communty Slns For Chldrn Fmls (PA)	8322	C	408 779-2113	23610
Countryside Mushrooms Inc	0182	D	408 683-2748	310
Covenant Care California LLC	8051	C	408 842-9311	20349
Daleo Inc	1623	D	408 846-9621	1913
Eagle Ridge Golf Cntry CLB LLC	7997	C	408 846-4531	18916
Faith T & B Plating Inc	7389	C	408 986-1226	17161
G B Group Inc (PA)	1522	D	408 848-8118	1286
Gilroy Fitness Inc (PA)	7991	E	408 848-1234	18604
Gilroy Gardens Family Theme Pk	7996	C	408 840-7100	18801
Headstart Nursery Inc (PA)	5193	D	408 842-3030	9139
Infosoft Inc	8748	E	408 659-4326	27752
Intero Real Estate Services	6531	C	408 848-8400	11516
Learning Services Corporation	8093	E	408 848-4379	22612
Leonard Anthony Valenti Inc	0782	D	408 848-9688	892
Mariner Health Care Inc	8051	C	408 842-9311	20612
Melo Concrete Construction	1771	D	408 842-3484	3287
Nestle Usa Inc	5143	D	408 846-6892	8527
Noah Concrete Corporation	1771	D	408 842-7211	3294
Odd Fellow-Rebekah Chld HM Cal (PA)	8361	D	408 846-2100	24614
Oj Insulation LP	1742	D	408 842-6315	2924
PSC Industrial Outsourcing LP	4959	D	831 635-0220	6545
PSG Fencing Corporation (PA)	1799	C	831 726-2002	3570
PSI Fire	7371	E	408 842-9308	15385
Recology South Valley (HQ)	4953	D	408 842-3358	6443
Renn Transportation Inc	4213	D	408 842-3545	4251
Rfid Textile Services Inc	7218	D	408 840-7504	13620
Saint Louise Hospital	8062	B	408 848-2000	21696
Syngenta Seeds Inc	5191	E	408 847-4242	9101
Trees Apartments LLC	6513	D	408 848-6400	11128
Uesugi Farms Inc (PA)	0161	D	408 842-1294	88
Verity Health System Cal Inc	8062	D	408 848-2000	21900

Mergent email: customerrelations@mergent.com
1580

2019 Directory of California
Wholesalers and Services Companies

(P-0000) Products & Services Section entry number
(PA)=Parent Co (HQ)=Headquarters (DH)=Div Headquarters

	SIC	EMP	PHONE	ENTRY #
Work2future Foundation	8331	C	408 758-3477	24253

GLEN ELLEN, CA - Sonoma County

	SIC	EMP	PHONE	ENTRY #
Servico Building Maint Co	7349	D	707 935-1224	14387

GLENDALE, CA - Los Angeles County

	SIC	EMP	PHONE	ENTRY #
24 Hour Fitness Usa Inc	7991	D	818 247-4334	18559
A J R Trucking Inc	4212	D	562 989-9555	3961
Abc Inc	4833	B	818 863-7801	5763
Access Integrated Healthcare	8059	D	866 460-7465	20979
Across Systems Inc	5045	D	877 922-7677	6996
Active Measure Inc	8732	D	818 237-8417	26496
Adventist Health System/West	8062	E	818 409-8540	21266
Aerospace Corporation	8733	D	818 952-6075	26582
Amco Foods Inc	8742	B	818 247-4716	27126
American Realty Centre Inc	6531	D	323 666-6111	11212
Amgen Distribution Inc	4213	D	760 989-4424	4099
ARC Document Solutions Inc	7334	C	818 242-6555	14077
Armenian Amrcn Cuncil On Aging	8322	E	818 241-8690	23488
Arthur J Gallagher & Co	6411	C	818 539-2300	10544
Assign Corporation	7379	C	818 247-7100	16315
Atkinson-Baker Inc (PA)	7338	C	818 551-7300	14132
Automated Systems America Inc	7699	D	877 500-0002	17936
Avery Corp	8731	D	626 304-2000	26335
Bank America National Assn	6021	D	800 432-1000	9284
Bartholomew Barry & Associates	8111	D	818 543-4000	22937
Begroup (PA)	8059	D	818 638-4563	21003
Buena Ventura Care Center Inc	8059	D	818 247-4476	21024
Bunim-Murray Productions	7812	C	818 756-5100	18027
Cal Southern Presbt Homes (PA)	6513	D	818 247-0420	10993
Cal Southern Presbt Homes	6513	C	818 244-7219	10994
Cal Southern Presbt Homes	6513	D	818 247-0420	10995
California Credit Union (PA)	6062	C	818 291-6700	9625
Califrnia Insur Guarantee Assn	6399	C	818 844-4300	10497
Camble Center	8331	D	818 242-2434	24162
Caroline Promotions Inc	8743	D	818 507-7666	27546
Caspian Commercial Plbg Inc	1711	D	818 649-2500	2157
Cbre Inc	6531	D	818 502-6700	11281
Cellco Partnership	4812	D	818 500-7779	5335
Chandler Convalescent Hospital	8051	D	818 240-1610	20307
Chicago Title and Trust Co	6361	E	818 548-0222	10438
Childrens Hospital Los Angeles	8069	C	323 361-2215	22006
Cigna Healthcare Cal Inc (DH)	6324	D	818 500-6262	10195
Cinovation Inc	7812	D	818 246-3160	18031
CIT Bank NA	6021	D	818 502-8400	9307
City of Glendale	8711	D	818 548-3945	25611
City of Glendale	7941	D	818 548-3950	18515
City of Glendale	4911	B	818 548-3300	6017
City of Glendale	4911	E	818 548-3980	6018
City of Glendale	4941	C	818 548-2011	6223
Coinmach Corporation (PA)	7215	D	818 637-4300	13558
Comprehensive Community Health	8082	E	818 265-2264	22276
Compspec Inc	8742	D	818 551-4200	27198
Country Villa Service Corp	8051	D	818 246-5516	20329
Countrywide Home Loans Inc	6162	D	818 550-8700	9796
CT Lien Solution	8742	C	818 662-4100	27207
David N Schultz Inc (PA)	6531	C	818 240-1070	11394
Dish Network Corporation	4841	E	818 334-8740	5907
Disney Interactive Studios Inc	7371	D	818 560-1000	15112
Disney Research Pittsburgh	8731	C	412 623-1800	26354
Dma Claims Inc (PA)	6411	D	323 342-6800	10606
Dma Claims Inc	6411	D	323 342-6800	10608
Dreamworks Animation LLC	7812	D	818 695-5000	18045
Dreamworks Animation Pubg LLC	7812	B	818 695-5000	18046
Drinks Holdings Inc	5182	C	310 441-8400	9040
Durini Luis Carlos Estrada	7389	E	502 474-3112	17142
Dwa Holdings LLC (HQ)	7812	D	818 695-5000	18048
Dwa Nova LLC	7372	D	818 695-5000	15658
E Z Staffing Inc (PA)	7361	B	818 845-2500	14605
Easter Seals Southern Cal Inc	8399	D	818 551-0128	24777
Emeritus Corporation	8052	E	818 246-7457	20931
Equity Title Company (DH)	6361	D	818 291-4400	10450
Front Porch Communities (PA)	8059	D	818 729-8100	21070
General Networks Corporation	7379	D	818 249-1962	16384
Ggis Insurance Services Inc	6411	C	818 553-2110	10636
Glendale Adventist Medical Ctr	8082	E	818 409-8379	22301
Glendale Adventist Medical Ctr (HQ)	8062	A	818 409-8000	21426
Glendale Associates Ltd	6512	D	818 246-6737	10884
Glendale Eye Medical Group	8011	D	818 956-1010	19483
Glendale Eye Medical Group (PA)	8011	D	818 956-1010	19484
Glendale Healthcare Center	8051	D	818 246-5516	20456
Glenhaven Healthcare LLC	8099	D	818 240-6720	22807
Glenoaks Convalescent Hosp LP	8062	D	818 240-4300	21428
Global Asylum Incorporated	7812	E	323 850-1214	18056
Global Exprnce Specialists Inc	7389	D	818 638-5959	17192
Goway Travel Inc	4724	D	800 810-3687	4937
Granville Glendale Inc	8741	D	818 550-0472	26876
Griffith Pk Rhbltation Ctr LLC	8051	D	818 845-8507	20497
Gsa Design Inc	7389	C	818 241-2558	17205
H L Moe Co Inc (PA)	1711	C	818 572-2100	2225
Health Net Inc	6324	C	818 543-9037	10205
Hemodialysis Inc (PA)	8092	C	818 500-8736	22477
Howroyd-Wright Emplymnt Agcy (HQ)	7361	D	818 240-8688	14639
Howroyd-Wright Emplymnt Agcy	7361	D	818 240-8688	14640
Hutchinson & Bloodgood LLP (PA)	8721	C	818 637-5000	26225
Institute For Multicultural	8748	D	818 240-4311	27753
Interstate Rhbltation Svcs LLC (PA)	8049	C	818 244-5656	20187
Jimmys Fashions	7389	E	818 790-8932	17260
Johnson & Johnson Pistaccios	0139	E	818 242-7853	27
JP Allen Extended Stay (PA)	7011	D	818 956-0202	12794
Kaiser Foundation Hospitals	8011	A	800 954-8000	19562
Kaiser Foundation Hospitals	8011	E	818 552-3000	19601
Kennard Development Group	1522	E	818 241-0800	1298
Kradjian Importing Company Inc (PA)	5149	D	818 502-1313	8818
Ksm Healthcare Inc	8051	D	818 242-1183	20570
L A Commercial Group Inc (PA)	7322	D	818 551-6800	14012
Legalzoomcom Inc (DH)	8111	B	323 962-8660	23202
Longwood Management Corp	8059	D	818 246-7174	21140
Los Angeles Federal Credit Un (PA)	6061	D	818 242-8640	9568
Lounge 22 LLC (PA)	7359	D	818 502-0700	14522
Mader News Inc	5192	D	818 551-5000	9117
Mariner Health Care Inc	8051	C	818 246-5677	20619
Modern Videofilm Inc	7819	D	818 637-6800	18201
Mv Transportation Inc	4111	D	818 409-3387	3685
National Teleconsultants Inc	8711	C	818 265-4400	25843
Neopets Inc	4813	E	818 551-4338	5609
New York Life Insurance Co	6411	D	818 662-7500	10705
Next Venture Inc	1542	D	818 637-2888	1601
Nurses Tuch HM Hlth Prvder Inc	8082	E	818 500-4877	22375
Oakmont Country Club	7997	C	818 542-4260	18992
Oel/Hhh Inc	8712	D	818 246-6050	26102
Old Republic Title Company	6361	A	818 240-1936	10468
Parexel International Corp	8731	C	818 254-7076	26432
Patterson Ritner Lockwood (PA)	8111	D	818 241-8001	23313
PCL Construction Services Inc	1542	C	818 246-3481	1612
Pegasus Home Health Care A CA	8082	D	818 551-1932	22392
Pegasus Maritime Inc	4731	D	714 728-8565	5139
Pinnacle Electrical Svcs Inc	8748	D	818 241-6009	27822
Pinnacle Networking Svcs Inc	1731	D	818 241-6009	2680
Pkf Certif Pub Accts A Prof (PA)	8721	C	818 630-7630	26272
Prestige Preschools Inc (PA)	8351	D	818 957-1170	24373
Primary Critical Care Medical	8011	C	818 847-9950	19796
Principal Financial Group Inc	6311	D	818 243-7141	10144
PS Business Parks Inc (PA)	6798	D	818 244-8080	12184
PS Business Parks LP	6531	D	818 244-8080	11696
PS Partners III Ltd	4225	C	818 244-8080	4614
Public Storage (PA)	6798	C	818 244-8080	12185
Public Storage Prpts IV Ltd	4225	D	818 244-8080	4615
Public Storage Prpts Xviii Inc	4225	D	818 244-8080	4616
Ralphs Grocery Company	4225	D	818 549-0035	4618
Real Good Food Company LLC	5149	C	909 744-0073	8858
RES-Care Inc	8052	C	818 637-7727	20950
Rev Enterprises	7381	E	818 551-7111	16773
Rose International Inc	7371	C	636 812-4000	15418
Safeco Insurance Company Amer	6411	C	818 956-4250	10763
Salem Media Group Inc	4832	D	818 956-5254	5751
Sitv Inc	4833	D	323 317-9534	5837
Smg Holdings Inc	6512	D	310 432-2893	10943
Sodexo Inc	8742	D	818 952-2201	27460
Software Management Cons Inc (PA)	7379	B	818 240-3177	16489
Spad Holdings LLC	7991	D	818 552-2027	18665
State Compensation Insur Fund	6331	C	213 576-7335	10402
State Compensation Insur Fund	6331	C	323 266-5551	10403
State Compensation Insur Fund	6331	C	888 782-8338	10405
Sunbelt Controls Inc (HQ)	1731	B	818 244-6571	2751
Systech Solutions Inc (PA)	7371	C	818 550-9690	15486
Tacori Enterprises	5094	D	818 863-1536	8014
Tmp Worldwide Advertising & Co	7311	D	818 539-2000	13910
Tri-Tech Internet Services Inc	7375	E	818 548-5400	16254
Ucc Direct Services Inc	7374	D	818 662-4100	16193
United Merchant Svcs Cal Inc	5044	D	818 246-6767	6986
Universal Studios Inc	7812	C	818 262-4301	18142
Univision Communications Inc	4832	C	818 484-7399	5760
UNUM Life Insurance Co Amer	6411	C	818 291-4739	10812
Usc Verdugo Hills Hospital LLC	8062	A	818 790-7100	21891
Usc Vrdugo Hlls Hosp Foundation (PA)	8062	B	800 872-2273	21892
Verdugo Hills Urgent Care Mg	8011	D	818 241-4331	20055
Verdugo Mental Health	8093	D	818 244-7257	22709
Viking Equipment Corp.	1795	D	818 500-9447	3467
Walt Disney Company	4833	B	818 544-5009	5847
Walt Disney Company	7996	A	818 544-6500	18812

Employment Codes: A=Over 500 employees, B=251-500,
C=101-250, D=51-100, E=50

2019 Directory of California
Wholesalers and Services Companies

© Mergent Inc. 1-800-342-5647

1581

GEOGRAPHIC

	SIC	EMP	PHONE	ENTRY #
Walt Disney Company	7812	C	818 553-4222	18153
Walt Disney Imagineering (DH)	7819	A	818 544-6500	18233
Wfg National Title Insur Co (PA)	6361	D	818 476-4000	10474
Yellowpagescom LLC (HQ)	7389	B	818 937-5500	17603
Young Mens Chrstn Assoc Gndl	8641	C	818 484-8256	25352

GLENDORA, CA - Los Angeles County

	SIC	EMP	PHONE	ENTRY #
Americas Christian Credit Un (PA)	6062	D	626 208-5400	9621
Automobile Club Southern Cal	8699	E	626 963-8531	25386
Building Elctronic Contrls Inc (PA)	1731	E	909 305-1600	2531
Care Unlimited Health Systems	8082	D	626 332-3767	22252
Cliftonlarsonallen LLP	8721	C	626 857-7300	26167
Community Convalescent Hospita	8051	D	626 963-6091	20322
CPC Services Inc	5032	D	626 852-6200	6884
East Valley Glendora Hosp LLC	8062	D	626 852-5000	21399
Foothill Hospital-Morris L Jo (PA)	8062	D	626 857-3145	21417
Glendora Country Club	7997	D	626 335-4051	18928
Harbor Glen Care Center	8051	D	626 963-7531	20505
National Hot Rod Association (PA)	7948	C	626 914-4761	18541
National Link Incorporated	5044	D	909 670-1900	6971
Oakdale Memorial Park (PA)	6553	D	626 335-0281	11946
Right Choice A Health Care	7361	B	626 335-1318	14724
San Gabriel Childrens Ctr Inc (PA)	8322	D	626 859-2089	24022
Seidner-Miller Automotive Inc	7538	E	909 394-3500	17783
Spectrum MGT Holdg Co LLC	4841	D	626 857-1075	5934
Ulta Salon Cosmt Fragrance Inc	7231	C	909 592-5393	13680
Venue Management Systems Inc	7381	A	626 445-6000	16853
Village Glen Apartments	6513	D	626 963-4575	11134

GOLD RIVER, CA - Sacramento County

	SIC	EMP	PHONE	ENTRY #
California Dept Fish Wildlife	7032	C	916 358-2900	13447
Centene Corporation	6324	D	314 505-6689	10191
Ehealthinsurance Services Inc	7371	C	916 608-6101	15128
Eskaton	8361	D	916 852-7900	24520
Hartford Fire Insurance Co	6411	B	916 294-1000	10641
Health Net Inc	6324	B	916 935-3520	10206
Health Net Cmnty Solutions Inc	8011	D	800 675-6110	19490
Performance Tech Partners LLC	7379	C	800 787-4143	16454
Practice Wares Inc	5047	E	916 526-2674	7211
Premier Pools and Spas Lp (PA)	1799	D	916 852-0223	3568
Salu Beauty Inc	8621	D	916 475-1400	25039
Spare-Time Inc	7997	D	916 859-5910	19055
Spare-Time Inc	7997	E	916 638-7001	19057
Synergex International Corp	7372	D	916 635-7300	15871
USA Waste of California Inc (HQ)	4953	C	916 387-1400	6490

GOLETA, CA - Santa Barbara County

	SIC	EMP	PHONE	ENTRY #
6500 Hllister Ave Partners LLC	6512	D	805 722-1362	10845
Aecom Global II LLC	8711	D	805 692-0600	25510
Asplundh Tree Expert Co	0783	D	805 964-9216	966
AT&T Corp.	4812	D	805 562-0121	5275
Cathedral Oaks Tennis Swim Ath	7997	D	805 964-7762	18885
Community Action Commsn Santa (PA)	8399	E	805 964-8857	24757
Community West Bank	6021	D	805 692-5821	9342
Cottage Health System	8062	A	805 967-3411	21348
Devereux Foundation	8093	B	805 968-2525	22567
Devereux Foundation	6733	B	805 968-2525	12094
Ergomotion Inc	5021	D	805 979-9400	6721
Flir Commercial Systems Inc (HQ)	5065	A	805 964-9797	7478
Gamma PHI Beta Sorority Inc	7041	D	805 968-4221	13475
Givens John	0161	D	805 964-4477	59
Glen Annie Golf Club	7992	D	805 968-6400	18715
Goleta Hhg Hotel Dev LP	7011	D	805 562-5996	12610
Intercontinental Hotels Group	7011	D	805 964-6241	12771
Intouch Technologies Inc (PA)	7372	B	805 562-8686	15717
Juniper Networks Inc	7373	D	805 880-2000	15988
Khp III Goleta LLC	7011	D	805 964-6241	12808
Kitson Landscape MGT Inc	0782	D	805 681-9460	873
L3 Maripro Inc	8711	D	805 683-3881	25791
Las Cumbres Observatory Global	8733	E	805 880-1600	26632
Lastline Inc	7372	C	805 456-7075	15739
Millenium Athletic Club LLc	7991	D	805 562-3845	18632
One Call Plumber Goleta	7299	D	805 284-0441	13760
Raytheon Company	7389	D	805 562-2941	17425
Santa Barbara Airbus	4119	D	805 964-7759	3842
Santa Barbara Trnsp Corp (HQ)	4151	D	805 681-8355	3944
Schulte Ranches	0191	D	805 563-0821	379
Securitas SEC Svcs USA Inc	7381	C	805 967-8987	16799
Sitestuff Yardi Systems I (PA)	8742	D	805 966-3666	27451
Southern California Edison Co	4911	D	805 683-5291	6131
Toyon Research Corporation (PA)	8711	D	805 968-6787	25956
Transphorm Inc (PA)	8731	D	805 456-1300	26476
United Parcel Service Inc OH	4215	C	805 964-7848	4473
Verizon South Inc	4813	D	805 681-8527	5673
Waterfall Resort	7011	D	805 879-3780	13381

GONZALES, CA - Monterey County

	SIC	EMP	PHONE	ENTRY #
Alicia Arroyo Inc	0761	C	831 675-2850	637
Bulmaro Castro Contractors	7361	C	831 675-2927	14579
George Amaral Ranches Inc	0161	D	831 679-2977	56
Granite Construction Inc	1611	D	831 763-5595	1783
L & J Farms Caraccioli LLC	0191	C	831 675-7901	365
RC Packing LLC	0722	B	831 675-0308	485
Silva Farms LLC (PA)	0161	B	831 675-2327	82

GOSHEN, CA - Tulare County

	SIC	EMP	PHONE	ENTRY #
Western Milling LLC (HQ)	5191	C	559 302-1000	9103

GRANADA HILLS, CA - Los Angeles County

	SIC	EMP	PHONE	ENTRY #
A Cori Partnership	8059	D	818 368-2802	20975
Aegis Senior Communities LLC	8082	D	818 363-3373	22208
Atlas Security Inc	7382	E	323 876-1401	16876
Brad Watkins Masonry Inc	1741	D	818 360-3796	2800
C21 Peak	6531	C	818 363-1717	11259
Errama Trucking Company Inc	4213	E	818 381-3341	4136
Global Work Group LLC	8742	D	424 220-9994	27247
Granada Hlls Convalescent Hosp	8051	D	818 891-1745	20491
Jag Framing Inc	1751	D	818 822-7110	3044
James I Miller	0742	E	818 363-7444	603
Kaiser Foundation Hospitals.	8011	A	818 832-7200	19561
Longwood Management Corp	8051	D	818 360-1864	20598
Medical Investment Co.	8059	D	818 360-1003	21157
Metropolitan Water District	4941	D	818 368-3731	6283
Park Regency Inc	6531	D	818 363-6116	11662
PS National Inc	7361	B	818 366-1300	14708
San Fernando City of Inc	8093	D	818 832-2400	22671
Siracusa Enterprises Inc	7361	D	818 831-1130	14760
Valley Properties Inc.	6512	D	818 360-3430	10959

GRAND TERRACE, CA - San Bernardino County

	SIC	EMP	PHONE	ENTRY #
Grand Terrace Care Center	8051	D	909 825-5221	20494
James McMinn Inc	1611	E	909 514-1231	1796
Keystone NPS LLC (DH)	8399	D	909 633-6354	24797
Peace Offics For A Grn Envirn	1799	E	951 824-7705	3566
West Coast Arborists Inc	0783	E	909 783-6544	983

GRANITE BAY, CA - Placer County

	SIC	EMP	PHONE	ENTRY #
Allen L Bender Inc	1542	C	916 372-2190	1462
Bushnell Gardens	5193	D	916 791-4199	9127
C & C Construction Inc	1542	E	916 434-5280	1491
Granite Bay Golf Club	7997	C	916 791-5379	18931
Green Valley Security Inc	7381	D	916 797-4058	16665
Paramount Equity Mortgage LLC	6162	D	916 290-9999	9843
Tricks Gymnastic Inc (PA)	7999	D	916 791-4496	19249
United States Pony Clubs	7997	D	916 791-1223	19075
Village At Granite Bay	8361	D	916 789-0326	24712
Williams Keller Realty	6531	D	916 774-6700	11835

GRASS VALLEY, CA - Nevada County

	SIC	EMP	PHONE	ENTRY #
Alta Sierra Country Club Inc	7997	E	530 273-2041	18823
Beam Vacuums California Inc	1731	E	916 564-3279	2518
Blue Eagle Contracting Inc	4212	D	530 272-0287	3979
Briarpatch Coop Nev Cnty Inc	8699	C	530 272-5333	25400
Byers Enterprises Inc	1761	D	530 272-7777	3131
Durham School Services L P	4151	D	530 273-7282	3918
Golden Empire Convalescent Hos	8062	C	530 273-1316	21429
Grass Valley LLC	8361	D	530 272-1055	24543
Hansen Bros Enterprises (PA)	1442	D	530 273-3100	1093
Hills Flat Lumber Co (PA)	1731	D	530 273-6171	2605
Hospice of Foothills (PA)	8082	D	530 272-5739	22336
JM Streamline Inc	1542	D	530 272-6806	1564
Meadow View Manor Inc	8051	D	530 272-2273	20635
Networked Insurance Agents LLC	6411	C	800 682-8476	10699
Nevada County Behavioral Hlth	8093	E	530 265-1450	22623
Nevada Irrigation District (PA)	4971	C	530 273-6185	6559
Pacific Gas and Electric Co	4911	D	530 477-3245	6074
Pride Industries	8331	D	530 477-1832	24221
Sierra Nevada Memorial Hm Care	8082	D	530 274-6350	22418
Springhill Manor Rehabilitatio	8059	E	530 273-7247	21219
Tim Mello Construction	1521	L	530 205-8588	1246
USA Waste of California Inc	4212	E	530 274-3090	4080
Victor Cmnty Support Svcs Inc	8999	C	530 273-2244	27961

GREENBRAE, CA - Marin County

	SIC	EMP	PHONE	ENTRY #
County of Marin	8093	D	415 448-1500	22550
Northern California Presbyteri	8059	D	415 464-1767	21168
Ocadian Care Centers LLC	8051	D	415 461-9700	20675
Petroleum Sales Inc	1311	D	415 256-1600	1026
Ross Valley Homes Inc	8052	D	415 461-2300	20952

GREENFIELD, CA - Monterey County

	SIC	EMP	PHONE	ENTRY #
Azcona Harvesting LLC	0722	C	831 674-2526	473
Neil Bassetti Farms	0161	E	831 674-2040	71

Mergent email: customerrelations@mergent.com
1582

2019 Directory of California
Wholesalers and Services Companies

(P-0000) Products & Services Section entry number
(PA)=Parent Co (HQ)=Headquarters (DH)=Div Headquarters

	SIC	EMP	PHONE	ENTRY #
Southern Mnterey Cnty Mem Hosp	8062	C	831 674-0112	21769
Southern Mntrrey Cnty Lbor Sup	0761	D	831 674-2727	675

GREENVILLE, CA - Plumas County

	SIC	EMP	PHONE	ENTRY #
Indian Valley Health Care Dist	8062	D	530 284-7191	21457

GRIDLEY, CA - Butte County

	SIC	EMP	PHONE	ENTRY #
Gridley Packing Inc	0723	C	530 846-3753	520
Hovlid Skilled Nursing	8051	E	530 846-9065	20538
Orchard Hospital	8062	C	530 846-9000	21618
Stapleton - Spence Packing Co (PA)	5149	C	408 297-8815	8871
Wild Goose Storage Inc	4922	D	530 846-7350	6154

GROVELAND, CA - Tuolumne County

	SIC	EMP	PHONE	ENTRY #
Evergreen Dstntion Hldings LLC	7011	D	209 379-2606	12568
Pine Mountain Lake Association (PA)	8641	C	209 962-4080	25216
Thousand Trails Inc	7033	E	209 962-0100	13469

GROVER BEACH, CA - San Luis Obispo County

	SIC	EMP	PHONE	ENTRY #
Regatta Tropicals Ltd (PA)	5148	D	805 473-1320	8724

GUADALUPE, CA - Santa Barbara County

	SIC	EMP	PHONE	ENTRY #
Ball Horticultural Company	0181	C	805 343-2723	243
Byrd Harvest Inc	0722	B	805 343-1608	475
Community Action Commsn Santa	8399	C	805 343-0615	24755
Freitas Brothers	0161	C	805 343-3134	52

GUALALA, CA - Mendocino County

	SIC	EMP	PHONE	ENTRY #
Redwood Coast Medical Services (PA)	8011	E	707 884-1721	19816

GUERNEVILLE, CA - Sonoma County

	SIC	EMP	PHONE	ENTRY #
Dawn Ranch Lodge & Rd Hse Rest	7011	D	707 869-0656	12515
Russian River Health Center	8011	E	707 869-2849	19832
West County Health Centers Inc	8011	D	707 869-2849	20096

GUSTINE, CA - Merced County

	SIC	EMP	PHONE	ENTRY #
Andersen Nut Company	0723	E	209 854-6820	493

HACIENDA HEIGHTS, CA - Los Angeles County

	SIC	EMP	PHONE	ENTRY #
Berkshire Hattaway Home Servcs	6531	D	626 913-2808	11239
Care Associates Inc	8361	D	626 330-4048	24451
Courtyard By Marriott	7011	D	626 965-1700	12491
CSX Corporation	4011	C	626 336-1377	3619
Good Deal Insurance Services	6411	D	626 275-6795	10637
Soto Provision Inc	5023	D	626 458-4600	6788

HALF MOON BAY, CA - San Mateo County

	SIC	EMP	PHONE	ENTRY #
Bay City Flower Co (PA)	5193	B	650 726-5535	9125
Bay City Flower Co	0181	C	650 712-8147	246
Bre Diamond Hotel LLC	7011	D	650 712-7000	12396
Coastside Senior Housing Limit	6531	E	415 355-7100	11326
Coldwell Banker	6531	E	650 726-1100	11331
Giusti Farms LLC	0161	D	650 726-9221	58
Half Moon Bay Lodge	7011	E	650 726-9000	12636
Harbor Fuel Dock	4493	D	650 726-4419	4749
Home Helpers San Mateo County	8082	D	650 532-3122	22324
Lesley Foundation	8748	D	650 726-4888	27774
Ocean Colony Partners LLC	6552	C	650 726-5764	11900
Ocean Links Corporation	7992	E	650 726-1800	18742
Pacific Beach House LLC (PA)	7011	D	650 712-0220	12994
Pacifica Hotel Company	7011	E	650 726-9000	13009
Rocket Farms Inc (PA)	0181	C	800 227-5229	296

HANFORD, CA - Kings County

	SIC	EMP	PHONE	ENTRY #
All Health Services Corp (PA)	7361	D	559 583-9101	14568
B & R Tevelde	0241	D	559 583-1277	406
Central Valley General Hosp (HQ)	8062	B	559 583-2100	21307
City Hanford Public Imprv Corp	1623	D	559 585-2550	1908
County of Kings	6321	C	559 584-1411	10163
County of Kings	8322	C	559 852-4316	23652
Danell Custom Harvesting LLC	0722	C	559 582-1251	476
Educational Employees Cr Un	6062	E	559 587-4460	9630
Hacienda Rehabilitation & Heal	8051	C	559 582-9221	20503
Hanford Community Hospital (HQ)	8062	A	559 582-9000	21438
Hanford Joint Un High Schl Dst	8322	D	559 583-5905	23830
High Plains Ranch LLC (PA)	0241	C	559 583-1277	415
Kings Community Action O (PA)	8322	D	559 582-4386	23882
Kings Rehabilitation Center (PA)	8322	D	559 582-9234	23883
Kings View	8093	D	559 582-9307	22608
Lone Oak Farms	0191	C	559 583-1277	367
Marquez Brothers Intl Inc	5141	C	559 584-8000	8426
Mission Medical Entps Inc	8051	C	559 582-2871	20647
Mission Medical Entps Inc	8051	D	559 582-4414	20648
Randstad North America Inc	7363	C	559 582-2700	14897
Smith Residential Care Fcilty (PA)	8082	D	559 584-8451	22420
Texture Specialties Inc	1791	E	559 904-6047	3401
Veterinary Pharmaceuticals Inc	5122	D	559 582-6800	8218
Western Health Resources	8742	E	559 537-2860	27521
Wilshire Hlth & Cmnty Svcs Inc	8059	D	559 582-4414	21259

HAPPY CAMP, CA - Siskiyou County

	SIC	EMP	PHONE	ENTRY #
Happy Camp Chamber Commerce	8611	E	530 493-2900	24960

HARBOR CITY, CA - Los Angeles County

	SIC	EMP	PHONE	ENTRY #
Bennett Enterprises A CA	0782	D	310 534-3543	804
Del AMO Insurance Services	6411	D	310 534-3444	10603
Kaiser Foundation Hospitals	8011	A	310 325-5111	19595
Southern Cal Prmnnte Med Group	8011	D	800 780-1230	19910

HAT CREEK, CA - Shasta County

	SIC	EMP	PHONE	ENTRY #
United States Forest Service	0851	E	530 335-4103	1001

HAWAIIAN GARDENS, CA - Los Angeles County

	SIC	EMP	PHONE	ENTRY #
Cypress Garden Villas	6513	D	562 860-9260	11006
Hawaiian Gardens Casino	7011	A	562 860-5887	12647
Howard Contracting Inc	1794	E	562 596-2969	3429
Richmond Plastering Inc	1742	E	562 924-4202	2949
Total Building Care Inc	1542	D	562 467-8333	1675

HAWTHORNE, CA - Los Angeles County

	SIC	EMP	PHONE	ENTRY #
2300 West El Secundo LP	6531	D	310 769-6669	11185
7days Inc	5065	C	424 255-5872	7432
Advanced Air LLC	4522	E	310 676-4673	4855
Argon Enterprises Inc	6531	D	310 349-8777	11220
Axminster Medical Group Inc (PA)	8011	D	310 670-3255	19313
Ayres Group	7011	D	310 220-6447	12344
Blue Chip Moving and Stor Inc	4213	D	323 463-6888	4110
Calhot Illinios LLC	7011	C	310 536-9800	12418
Eastbiz Corporation (PA)	7999	D	310 212-7134	19165
Federal Express Corporation	4513	C	800 463-3339	4821
Hawthorne Healthcare	8051	D	310 679-9732	20506
Inspectorate America Corp	7389	C	800 424-0099	17242
Longwood Management Corp	8051	C	310 679-1461	20597
Los Angeles Guild LLC	8742	C	323 733-5033	27306
Marriott International Inc	7011	C	310 725-9696	12899
Pb Car Movers	7389	D	310 283-2741	17394
Roofing Supply Group LLC	5033	D	424 269-7330	6927
Sandhurst Convales Grp Ltd A	8051	E	310 675-3304	20745
Schnierow Dental Care	8021	E	310 377-6453	20136
Seems Plumbing Co Inc	1711	E	310 297-4969	2352
Servicon Systems Inc	1771	A	310 970-0700	3324
Skyone Federal Credit Union (PA)	6061	D	310 491-7500	9593
South Bay Rgonal Pub Comm Auth	4899	E	310 973-1802	5995
Tech Flex Package	7336	E	323 241-1800	14129
Thinkom Solutions Inc	4899	C	310 371-5486	6001
Tricor America Inc	4731	C	310 676-0800	5185
Trident Labs LLC	8072	C	310 915-9121	22174
Wilshire Hlth & Cmnty Svcs Inc	8059	D	310 679-9732	21258
Windsor Gardens	8051	D	310 675-3304	20901
Xdbs Corporation	8732	D	302 566-3006	26577
Zaharoni Holdings	8741	E	310 297-9722	27102

HAYWARD, CA - Alameda County

	SIC	EMP	PHONE	ENTRY #
24 Hour Fitness Usa Inc	7991	D	510 264-3275	18570
American Asp Repr Rsrfcing Inc (PA)	1771	D	510 723-0280	3213
American Messaging Svcs LLC	4813	C	510 889-2300	5447
American Residential Svcs LLC	1711	D	510 657-7601	2114
American Synergy Asbestos Remo	1799	D	510 444-2333	3484
American Technologies Inc	1799	D	510 429-5000	3485
Ameriflight LLC	4512	D	510 569-6000	4776
Andrew Chekene Enterprises Inc	1521	C	650 588-1001	1118
Anning-Johnson Company	1742	C	510 670-0100	2844
Aramark Unf & Career AP LLC	7218	C	510 487-1855	13591
Arborwell Inc (PA)	0783	C	510 881-4260	965
ARC of Alameda County	8331	C	510 582-8151	24149
Arcus Biosciences Inc	8731	C	510 694-6200	26326
Aurora Algae Inc	8731	D	510 266-5000	26333
Axis Services Inc	1522	C	510 732-6111	1267
Bassard Convalescent & Med Hm (PA)	8059	D	510 537-6700	21002
Bay Valley Medical Group Inc (PA)	8011	D	510 785-5000	19318
Berkeley Farms LLC (DH)	5143	B	510 265-8600	8513
Bess Testlab Inc	1623	E	408 988-0101	1896
Big Joe California North Inc (PA)	5084	C	510 785-6900	7731
Bigham Taylor Roofing Corp	1761	D	510 886-0197	3130
Blue River Seafood Inc	5146	D	510 300-6800	8571
Boyett Construction Inc (PA)	1742	D	510 264-9100	2851
Brightview Landscape Svcs Inc	0781	E	510 487-4826	736
Brook Furniture Rental Inc	7359	E	510 487-4440	14482
Bruml Management LLC	5137	E	800 733-3629	8290
California Golden Realty	6531	A	408 822-6000	11263
California Hydronics Corp (PA)	5075	D	510 293-1993	7645
Casa Sandoval LLC	6513	D	510 727-1700	11000
Casey-Fogli Con Contrs Inc	1771	D	510 887-0837	3231
Cell-Crete Corporation	1771	D	510 471-7257	3232
Centimark Corporation	1761	D	510 921-5500	3135
Chapel of Chimes (DH)	6553	D	510 471-3363	11939
Chipman Corporation	4213	D	510 748-8787	4117

Employment Codes: A=Over 500 employees, B=251-500,
C=101-250, D=51-100, E=50

2019 Directory of California
Wholesalers and Services Companies

© Mergent Inc. 1-800-342-5647
1583

GEOGRAPHIC

Company	SIC	EMP	PHONE	ENTRY #
Cintas Corporation No 3	7218	D	510 352-6330	13601
Classic Soft Trim Inc	5199	D	510 782-4911	9207
Cnet Technology Corporation (HQ)	5065	C	408 392-9966	7462
Comcast Corporation	4841	D	510 266-3200	5876
Commercial Rfrgn Spcalists LLC (HQ)	1711	D	510 784-8990	2167
Community Integrated Work Prog	8322	E	510 487-9768	23607
Controlled Contamination Svcs	7349	D	510 728-1106	14227
Core-Mark International Inc	5149	C	510 487-3000	8779
County of Alameda	1611	B	510 670-5455	1746
County of Alameda	8331	E	510 670-5700	24173
Cox Automotive Inc	5012	B	510 786-4500	6586
Custom Commercial Dry Clrs Inc (PA)	7216	D	510 723-1000	13565
D S P Service Inc	7349	E	510 782-2200	14247
D W Nicholson Corporation (PA)	1711	C	510 887-0900	2179
Dhl Supply Chain (usa)	4225	D	510 784-7360	4546
Double D Transportation Co	4212	D	510 783-2335	4005
Dt Floormasters Inc	1752	D	510 476-1900	3101
Durham School Services L P	4151	C	510 887-6005	3917
E W C H Inc	8051	D	510 783-4811	20380
Eagle Systems Intl Inc	1711	B	510 259-1700	2193
Earle M Jorgensen Company	5051	D	510 487-2700	7271
Early Transportation Services	4213	D	510 324-1119	4134
Eden Area Regnl Occupational P	8331	D	510 293-2900	24180
Eden Housing Inc (PA)	1522	D	510 582-1460	1282
Eden Housing Management Inc (PA)	6531	E	510 582-1460	11417
Eden West Rehabilitation	8051	D	510 783-4811	20383
Fba Inc (PA)	8711	E	510 265-1888	25681
Fedex Freight Corporation	4213	B	510 895-0440	4157
Felson Companies Inc	6531	D	510 538-1150	11444
Felson Management Corp (PA)	6531	E	510 538-1150	11445
Foam Distributors Incorporated	5199	D	510 441-8377	9217
Forensic Analytical Spc Inc (PA)	8734	C	510 887-8828	26702
Foster Dairy Farms	5143	E	510 783-1270	8521
Gallo Sales Company Inc (DH)	5182	C	510 476-5000	9046
Gco Inc (PA)	5074	E	510 786-3333	7625
Gel Pak LLC	7336	D	510 576-2220	14115
Glen Alpine Building Svcs Inc	7349	D	510 582-7400	14277
Gourmet Foods	5141	D	510 887-0340	8409
H U S D Maintenance Operation	7349	D	510 784-2666	14283
Hayward Area Recreation Pkdist	8041	E	510 881-6700	20154
Hayward Area Recreation Pkdist	7992	E	510 317-2300	18717
Hayward Area Recreation Pkdist	4225	D	510 881-6750	4573
Hayward Police Officers Assn	8631	E	510 293-7207	25060
Hayward Sisters Hospital (HQ)	8062	A	510 264-4000	21441
HEs Transportation Svcs Inc	4731	E	510 783-6100	5087
Hillsdale Group L P	8059	D	510 538-3866	21114
Imp Foods Inc	5146	D	510 429-4600	8577
Intarcia Therapeutics Inc	8731	D	510 782-7800	26384
Jagpreet Enterprises Inc	5149	C	510 336-8376	8811
Johnson Cntrls SEC Sltions LLC	7382	D	510 246-2862	16912
Jon K Takata Corporation (PA)	8322	D	510 315-5400	23878
Kaiser Foundation Hospitals	6324	D	510 454-1000	10231
Kaiser Foundation Hospitals	8011	A	510 678-4000	19607
Katherine Bousson	7999	D	510 582-1166	19191
Keeco LLC (PA)	5023	D	510 324-8800	6770
Kissito Health Care Inc	8082	D	510 582-8311	22354
Kuehne + Nagel Inc	4225	D	510 785-0555	4583
Kwan Wo Ironworks Inc	1791	C	415 822-9628	3382
L & W Supply Corporation	5032	D	510 429-8003	6899
Lansing Mall Ltd Partnership	6512	E	510 782-3527	10905
LBC Mundial Corporation (HQ)	4513	D	650 873-0750	4841
Leggett & Platt Incorporated	7319	D	510 487-8063	13976
Lifetouch Nat Schl Studios Inc	7221	E	510 293-1818	13641
Lloyd W Aubry Co Inc (PA)	1796	D	510 732-9038	3472
Marelich Mechanical Co Inc (HQ)	1711	D	510 785-5500	2273
Mariner Health Care Inc	8051	D	510 538-4424	20621
Mariner Health Care Inc	8051	C	510 785-2880	20622
Metric Equipment Sales Inc	5065	D	510 264-0887	7507
Monument Security Inc	7381	D	510 430-3540	16734
Mygrant Glass Company Inc (PA)	5013	E	510 785-4360	6660
Nor-Cal Moving Services (PA)	4214	C	510 371-4942	4361
Northstar Contg Group Inc (DH)	1799	D	510 491-1330	3558
Oakhurst Industries Inc	5141	D	510 265-2400	8437
Omnicare Inc	5122	D	510 293-9663	8200
Pacheco Brothers Gardening Inc (PA)	0781	D	510 732-6330	773
Pacific Cheese Co Inc (PA)	5143	D	510 784-8800	8528
Pacific Gas and Electric Co	4924	B	510 784-3253	6159
Predicine Inc	8011	E	650 300-2188	19795
R F Macdonald Co (PA)	5084	C	510 784-0110	7791
R2g Enterprises Inc	1761	C	510 489-6218	3193
Restec Contractors Inc	1799	D	510 670-0100	3577
RJS & Associates Inc	1771	C	510 670-9111	3315
Roadstar Trucking Inc	4212	D	510 487-2404	4056
Rural/Metro Corporation	4119	C	510 266-0885	3837
Safeco Door & Hardware Inc	1793	D	510 429-4768	3410

Company	SIC	EMP	PHONE	ENTRY #
Serpico Landscaping Inc	0782	E	510 293-0341	936
Siemens Industry Inc	5063	B	510 783-6000	7394
Siemens Industry Inc	5084	C	510 783-6000	7796
Signet Testing Labs Inc (HQ)	8734	C	510 887-8484	26731
Solcom Inc	1623	B	510 940-2490	1980
SOS Security Incorporated	7381	C	510 782-4900	16831
Spectrum Community Services (PA)	8322	D	510 881-0300	24064
St Francis Extended Care Inc	8059	D	510 785-3630	21221
St Michael Convalescent Hosp	8051	D	510 782-8424	20780
Starzz Management Services (PA)	8741	D	510 632-5533	27047
Stonebrae LP	7997	D	510 728-7878	19064
TCI Aluminum/North Inc	5051	D	510 786-3750	7319
Telecare Corporation	8063	C	510 582-7676	21983
Thyssenkrupp Elevator Corp	5084	E	510 476-1900	7810
Tiburcio Vasquez Hlth Ctr Inc	8011	D	510 471-5907	20007
Tps Aviation Inc (PA)	5088	C	510 475-1010	7916
Tricor America Inc	4513	C	510 293-3960	4847
Ultraex LLC	4215	D	510 723-3760	4440
Ultraex Inc	4513	D	800 882-1000	4848
Underwriters Laboratories Inc	8734	C	408 754-6500	26739
Urban Trading Software Inc	7372	E	877 633-6171	15887
USA Waste of California Inc	4953	D	831 384-5000	6504
Ustov Inc	5141	E	510 781-1818	8484
Vista Universal Inc (PA)	7349	E	510 785-6166	14425
Vitalant	8099	C	510 785-9554	22900
Wagan Corporation	5013	E	510 471-9221	6684
Wells Fargo Bank National Assn	6021	B	510 266-0595	9398
Windsor Gardens Healthcare C	8059	C	510 582-4636	21260
Xpo Logistics Freight Inc	4213	C	510 785-6920	4321
Yrc Inc	4213	D	510 783-7010	4324

HEALDSBURG, CA - Sonoma County

Company	SIC	EMP	PHONE	ENTRY #
Alliance Medical Center Inc	8011	D	707 431-8234	19273
Clendenen Vineyard MGT LLC	0172	D	707 473-0881	137
Corporate Soul LLC	7299	B	707 431-7781	13734
E & J Gallo Winery	0172	D	707 431-5400	142
E & M Electric and McHy Inc (PA)	5084	D	707 433-5578	7746
H2 Hotel LLC	7011	D	707 431-2202	12635
Healdsburg Dist Hosp Rehab Svc	6324	D	707 433-9150	10203
Hotel Healdsburg (PA)	7011	D	707 431-2800	12725
Hotel Healdsburg	7011	D	707 922-5399	12726
Klein Foods Inc	0172	D	707 431-1533	154
Madrona Mnr Wine Cntry Inn	7011	D	707 433-4231	12868
Metier Ltd	7379	D	707 546-9300	16426
North Sonoma County Hosp Dst	8062	C	707 431-6500	21605
Scheid Vineyards Inc	0172	D	707 433-1858	176
Social Finance Inc	6163	B	707 473-9889	9908
Syar Industries Inc	5032	D	707 433-3366	6907
Vino Farms Inc	0762	D	707 433-8241	719

HEBER, CA - Imperial County

Company	SIC	EMP	PHONE	ENTRY #
C S Transport Inc	4212	D	760 666-5661	3985
Ormat Nevada Inc	4939	E	760 353-8200	6200
Ralph Collazo Packing Inc	7389	D	760 353-0856	17424

HELENDALE, CA - San Bernardino County

Company	SIC	EMP	PHONE	ENTRY #
Silver Lakes Association	8641	D	760 245-1606	25251

HELM, CA - Fresno County

Company	SIC	EMP	PHONE	ENTRY #
Terranova Ranch Inc	0191	E	559 866-5644	386
Wilbur-Ellis Company LLC	5191	D	559 866-5667	9104

HEMET, CA - Riverside County

Company	SIC	EMP	PHONE	ENTRY #
American Medical Response Inc	4119	C	951 658-2826	3760
American Medical Response Inc	4119	C	951 765-3900	3766
Anka Behavioral Health Inc	6411	C	951 929-2744	10527
Apex Healthcare Med Ctr Inc (PA)	8049	D	951 765-0700	20163
Bank America National Assn	6021	E	951 929-8614	9290
Brookdale Senior Living Inc	8059	D	951 744-9861	21021
Caring Companions Home	8082	D	951 765-1441	22255
Casa-Pacifica Inc	8361	B	951 658-3369	24456
Casa-Pacifica Inc	8361	D	951 766-5116	24457
Devonshire Care Center LLC	8051	D	951 925-2571	20376
Hcr Manorcare Med Svcs Fla LLC	8051	C	951 925-9171	20511
Hemet Valley Imaging Med Group (PA)	8011	D	951 925-6537	19496
Johnre Care LLC	8051	D	951 658-6374	20550
Lake Hemet Municipal Wtr Dst (PA)	4941	D	951 927-1816	6269
Lpsh Holdings Inc	1711	A	951 926-1176	2269
Meadowbrook Convalescent Hosp	8361	D	951 658-2293	24597
Miramonte Enterprises LLC	8051	C	951 658-9441	20645
Pama Management Co	8741	E	951 929-0340	26978
Physicians For Healthy Hospita (PA)	8062	D	951 652-2811	21642
Physicians For Healthy Hospita	8062	C	951 652-2811	21644
Primerica Life Insurance Co	6411	C	951 652-6190	10742
Ramona Community Services Corp (HQ)	8082	C	951 658-9288	22402
Ramona Rehabilitation and Post	8062	D	951 652-0011	21682
Southland Arthritis Osteo	8011	E	951 672-1866	19928

Mergent email: customerrelations@mergent.com
1584

2019 Directory of California
Wholesalers and Services Companies

(P-0000) Products & Services Section entry number
(PA)=Parent Co (HQ)=Headquarters (DH)=Div Headquarters

	SIC	EMP	PHONE	ENTRY #
Spectrum MGT Holdg Co LLC	4841	D	951 260-3143	5933
Sunrise Senior Living LLC	8051	D	951 929-5988	20831
The For Valley Resource Center (PA)	8331	E	951 766-8659	24236
Time Warner Cable Inc	4841	D	951 306-3117	5955
Trilar Management Group	8741	C	951 925-2021	27068
Ulta Beauty Inc	7231	C	951 652-2966	13679
Valley Rsrce Ctr For Retarded	8399	D	951 766-8659	24856

HERCULES, CA - Contra Costa County

	SIC	EMP	PHONE	ENTRY #
Blize Healthcare Cal Inc	8082	D	800 343-2549	22236
Hercules Fitness	7991	E	510 724-2900	18608
Mechanics Bank	6022	D	510 741-7545	9466
Security Pacific RE Brkg	6531	D	510 245-9901	11758
Shields Nursing Centers Inc (PA)	8051	C	510 724-9911	20760
Watkin & Bortolussi Inc	0782	D	415 453-4675	960

HERLONG, CA - Lassen County

	SIC	EMP	PHONE	ENTRY #
Aecom Global II LLC	8711	D	530 827-2406	25514

HERMOSA BEACH, CA - Los Angeles County

	SIC	EMP	PHONE	ENTRY #
24 Hour Fitness Worldwide Inc	7991	E	310 374-4524	18572
All Environmental Inc	8748	C	310 798-4255	27633
AT&T Corp.	4812	D	310 303-3888	5270
CIT Bank NA	6021	D	310 372-8473	9306
Gps Flyers	8742	D	951 588-7777	27251
Liminex Inc	7371	D	310 963-3031	15259
Marlin Equity Partners LLC (PA)	6282	D	310 364-0100	10095
Marlin Equity Partners III LP (PA)	6799	C	310 364-0100	12242
Perverted Jstice Fundation Inc	6732	D	310 910-9380	12083
Southbay Website Design LLC	7374	D	310 370-4043	16181
Sunrise Senior Living LLC	8051	E	310 937-0959	20817

HESPERIA, CA - San Bernardino County

	SIC	EMP	PHONE	ENTRY #
Arizona Pipeline Company (PA)	1623	B	760 244-8212	1892
Ascon Recycling Co	4953	C	760 948-1538	6347
Best Way Disposal Co Inc	4953	D	760 244-9773	6353
Caremark Rx LLC	8011	E	760 948-6606	19351
Cellco Partnership	4812	D	760 662-5914	5362
Desert Recycling Inc	4953	E	760 948-3122	6388
Flyers Energy LLC	5171	D	760 949-3356	8943
Foremost Healthcare Centers	6513	E	760 244-5579	11020
Foremost Operations LLC	8361	D	760 244-5579	24532
Hesperia Senior Living LLC	8361	D	760 244-5579	24561
High Dsert Ptent Care Svcs LLC	8011	D	760 956-4150	19501
Jesse Alexander Transport	4789	D	760 669-0379	5233
Lake Arrowhead Cmnty Svcs Dst	8399	E	909 337-6395	24799
Ortiz Asphalt Paving Inc	1611	E	951 966-7060	1830
Total Renal Care Inc	8092	D	760 947-7405	22494
Victor Valley Moose Lodge No	8641	C	760 244-1808	25278

HICKMAN, CA - Stanislaus County

	SIC	EMP	PHONE	ENTRY #
Dave Wilson Nursery Inc (PA)	0181	E	209 874-1821	252
Foster Dairy Farms	7699	C	209 874-9605	17945
Frantz Wholesale Nursery LLC	0181	C	209 874-1459	259

HIDDEN VALLEY LAKE, CA - Lake County

	SIC	EMP	PHONE	ENTRY #
Hidden Valley Lake Association (PA)	8641	D	707 987-3146	25173

HIGHLAND, CA - San Bernardino County

	SIC	EMP	PHONE	ENTRY #
Beaver Medical Group LP (HQ)	8011	C	909 425-3321	19321
Cedar Holdings LLC	8051	D	909 862-0611	20294
Century 21 Showcase Inc	6531	D	909 936-9334	11308
County of San Bernardino	8351	E	909 425-0785	24309
East Valley Water District	4941	D	909 889-9501	6247
Immanuel Baptist Cruch	8351	D	909 862-6641	24328
Kcb Towers Inc	1791	D	909 862-0322	3380
Kindred Healthcare Oper Inc	8051	C	909 862-0611	20557
San Manuel Indian Bingo Casino (PA)	7999	A	909 864-5050	19231
YMCA of East Valley	8641	E	909 425-9622	25291

HILLSBOROUGH, CA - San Mateo County

	SIC	EMP	PHONE	ENTRY #
Burlingame Country Club	7997	D	650 696-8100	18876
Camaro Cleaners Corp (PA)	7216	D	650 343-4296	13563
John Plane Construction Inc	1542	C	415 468-0555	1567
Synctruck LLC	4215	C	415 450-0447	4431

HOLLISTER, CA - San Benito County

	SIC	EMP	PHONE	ENTRY #
Alpha Teknova Inc	8731	D	831 637-1100	26318
American Electrical Svcs Inc	1731	C	831 638-1737	2506
American Medical Response Inc	4119	C	831 636-9391	3767
Bhandal Bros Inc	4213	E	831 728-2691	4105
Bhandal Bros Trucking Inc	4213	D	831 728-2691	4106
Chamberlains Children Ctr Inc	8361	D	831 636-2121	24461
Guerra Nut Shelling Company	0723	D	831 637-4471	527
Hollister Process Service	7389	E	831 634-1479	17223
Infinity Staffing Service	7363	D	831 638-0360	14863
R and R Labor Inc	0761	B	831 638-0290	668
San Benito Health Care Dst (PA)	8062	B	831 637-5711	21702

	SIC	EMP	PHONE	ENTRY #
San Benito Htg & Shtmtl Inc	1711	D	831 637-1112	2347
San Juan Oaks LLC	7992	D	831 636-6113	18756
Woltcom Inc	1731	C	831 638-4900	2790

HOLLYWOOD, CA - Los Angeles County

	SIC	EMP	PHONE	ENTRY #
Battery Marketing Inc	7311	D	323 467-7267	13796
Car Park Inc	7521	C	323 462-6060	17677
Cellco Partnership	4812	D	323 465-0640	5371
Deep Focus Inc	8742	A	323 790-5340	27211
Loews Hollywood Hotel LLC	7011	B	323 450-2235	12860

HOLT, CA - San Joaquin County

	SIC	EMP	PHONE	ENTRY #
Victoria Island Farms	0191	D	209 465-5609	392

HOLTVILLE, CA - Imperial County

	SIC	EMP	PHONE	ENTRY #
Black Dog Farms of California	0161	C	760 356-2951	37
Five Star Packing LLC	0761	A	760 356-4103	647
Grimmway Farms	0191	D	760 356-2513	347
John Grizzle Farming	0191	E	760 356-4381	361
Ormesa LLC	4911	D	760 356-3020	6066
Sunharbor Management LLC	8361	E	760 356-1262	24692

HOMELAND, CA - Riverside County

	SIC	EMP	PHONE	ENTRY #
Harvest V Citizens Patrol	7381	C	951 926-9763	16695

HOMEWOOD, CA - Placer County

	SIC	EMP	PHONE	ENTRY #
Homewood Village Resorts LLC	7011	E	530 525-2992	12697

HOOPA, CA - Humboldt County

	SIC	EMP	PHONE	ENTRY #
Klma W Medical Center	8093	D	530 625-4114	22606

HOPLAND, CA - Mendocino County

	SIC	EMP	PHONE	ENTRY #
Hopland Band Pomo Indians Inc	7999	C	707 744-1395	19182
Hopland Band Pomo Indians Inc (PA)	8699	D	707 472-2100	25429

HORNITOS, CA - Mariposa County

	SIC	EMP	PHONE	ENTRY #
Hornitos Telephone Co	4813	D	608 831-1000	5578

HUGHSON, CA - Stanislaus County

	SIC	EMP	PHONE	ENTRY #
Alderwoods (delaware) Inc	6553	E	209 883-0411	11938
Community Hospice Inc	8052	E	209 578-6380	20923
Duarte Nursery Inc (PA)	0181	B	209 531-0351	255
Grower Direct Nut Company Inc	0723	E	209 883-4890	525
Lakewood Mem Pk Fnrl Svcs Inc	6553	D	209 883-4465	11945
Samaritan Village Inc	8322	C	209 883-3212	24009

HUNTINGTON BEACH, CA - Orange County

	SIC	EMP	PHONE	ENTRY #
2nd Floor Main Street Concepts	6513	E	714 969-9000	10969
A Growing Concern Landscapes	0781	D	714 843-5137	724
Ace Parking Management Inc	7521	C	714 845-8000	17673
AES Huntington Beach LLC	4911	E	714 374-1476	6009
Aire-Rite AC & Rfrgn Inc	1711	D	714 895-2338	2094
Alltek Company U S A Inc	5084	E	714 375-9785	7724
American Golf Corporation	7997	D	714 536-8866	18835
American Golf Corporation	7997	D	714 846-1364	18841
Americare Medservices Inc (PA)	4119	C	310 632-5047	3772
AMG Huntington Beach LLC	8711	D	714 894-9802	25535
Applied Computer Solutions (HQ)	7371	C	714 861-2200	14990
Aramark Facility Services LLC	7349	E	714 372-0683	14198
AT&T Corp.	4812	D	714 965-4685	5260
Bartco Lighting Inc	5063	D	714 230-3200	7336
Beachside Realtors (PA)	6531	B	714 969-6100	11233
Captured Sea Inc	1542	D	714 856-3358	1497
Cellco Partnership	4812	D	714 847-8799	5365
Child Development Incorporated	6531	D	714 842-4064	11315
Childrens Hospital Los Angeles	8021	B	714 841-4990	20114
Cinemark Usa Inc	7832	D	714 373-4545	18280
Coastal Traffic Systems Inc	5063	D	714 641-3744	7347
Coastline Cnstr & Awng Co Inc	1521	D	714 891-9798	1146
Cogar International Enrgy Corp (PA)	1731	E	626 494-8157	2543
Confie Seguros Inc (HQ)	6411	C	714 252-2500	10593
Custom Building Products Inc	1521	E	562 598-8808	1151
Dix Metals Inc	5051	C	714 677-0777	7269
Douglas Fir Holdings LLC	8051	C	714 842-5551	20378
Element Mtrls Tech HB Inc (DH)	8734	C	714 892-1961	26696
First Team RE - Orange Cnty	6531	D	714 965-2244	11461
Flw Inc	5064	E	714 751-7512	7416
Freeway Insurance (PA)	6411	C	714 252-2500	10631
Friedman Professional Mgt Co	8011	D	714 842-1426	19478
Galkos Construction Inc (PA)	7299	D	714 373-8545	13746
GBI Tile & Stone Inc (PA)	5032	E	949 567-1880	6894
Geosyntec Consultants Inc	8641	D	714 969-0800	25160
Glen Beverly Laboratories Inc	8621	D	714 848-5777	25016
Grani Installation Inc (PA)	1542	D	714 898-0441	1537
Harbor Distributing LLC (HQ)	5181	C	714 933-2400	9001
HB Healthcare Associates LLC	8051	D	714 887-0144	20507
Hobbs Herder Advertising	7311	D	800 999-6090	13838
Horsemen Inc	7381	D	714 847-4243	16698
Huntington Bch Cnvlescent Hosp	8051	B	714 847-3515	20539

Employment Codes: A=Over 500 employees, B=251-500,
C=101-250, D=51-100, E=50

2019 Directory of California
Wholesalers and Services Companies

© Mergent Inc. 1-800-342-5647

1585

GEOGRAPHIC

	SIC	EMP	PHONE	ENTRY #
Huntington Beach Commnty Clinc	8011	C	714 847-4222	19505
I Hot Leads	7374	D	714 960-8028	16143
Icallfirst	4813	D	808 557-9299	5583
Ics Professional Services Inc	1752	C	714 868-3900	3108
Innocean Wrldwide Americas LLC (HQ)	7311	C	714 861-5200	13846
K W K Trucking Inc	4212	C	714 791-7928	4032
Kings Seafood Company LLC	5146	D	714 793-1177	8580
Landmark Health LLC	8082	B	253 394-2566	22357
Managed Health Network	6324	C	714 934-5519	10280
Marblewest Inc	1743	E	714 847-6472	3003
MCB-Cjs LLC	8742	C	714 230-3600	27327
Medical Diagnostic	8059	C	714 841-2273	21156
Merrill Gardens LLC	6513	C	714 842-6569	11070
Michaelson Connor & Boul (PA)	8742	C	714 230-3600	27346
Mortgage Fax Inc	7323	C	714 899-2656	14039
Nakase Brothers Wholesale Nurs (PA)	5193	D	949 855-4388	9150
Netball America Inc	7389	E	949 307-4455	17348
New Port Orthopedic Institute	8011	C	949 722-5071	19709
No Ordinary Moments Inc	8082	C	714 848-3800	22372
Nuvision Fincl Federal Cr Un (PA)	6061	C	714 375-8000	9576
Orange County Sanitation	4952	C	714 962-2411	6326
Pachinko World Inc	7993	C	714 895-7772	18786
Pacific Aquascape Inc	1799	D	714 481-7260	3559
Pacific City Hotel LLC	7011	B	714 698-6100	12996
Paul Maurer Company	7999	D	714 231-8241	19216
Portermatt Electric Inc	1731	C	714 596-8788	2685
Primal Elements Inc	5122	C	714 899-0757	8207
Prime Hlthcare Hntngton Bch	8062	B	714 843-5000	21663
PW Stephens Envmtl Inc (PA)	1799	D	714 892-2028	3571
Pyro-Comm Systems Inc (PA)	1731	C	714 902-8000	2689
R C Hotels Inc	7011	C	714 891-0123	13090
Rainbow Disposal Co Inc (HQ)	4953	C	714 847-3581	6432
Rainbow Transfer Recycling	4953	C	714 847-5818	6433
RC Wendt Painting Inc	1721	C	714 960-2700	2472
Reliable Wholesale Lumber Inc (PA)	5031	D	714 848-8222	6857
Restaurant Depot	5141	E	714 378-3535	8447
Restaurant Depot LLC	5142	C	714 378-3535	8502
Ricoh Usa Inc	5044	E	714 396-0568	6977
Russell Fisher Partnership	7542	E	714 842-4453	17837
Russell Fisher Partnership (PA)	7542	C	909 930-5420	17838
Sea Breeze Health Care Inc	8051	C	714 847-9671	20750
Shekinah Inc	8111	E	714 475-5460	23376
Sho-Air International Inc (PA)	4731	E	949 476-9111	5168
Skyhill Financial Inc	6531	C	714 657-3938	11765
Soroptmist Intl Huntington Bch	7389	E	714 271-9305	17478
Southern Cal Prmnnte Med Group	8011	E	714 841-7293	19914
Staff Pro Inc (PA)	7382	A	714 230-7200	16945
Star Real Estate	6531	D	714 500-3300	11775
Thomas Crane and Trckg Co Inc	1629	E	562 592-2837	2068
Trilogy Financial Services Inc (PA)	7389	D	714 843-9977	17522
Tscm Corporation	7349	D	714 841-1988	14410
Two Roads Prof Resources Inc	7363	C	714 901-3804	14927
Unison Electric	1731	E	714 375-5915	2774
United Medical Imaging Inc	8011	C	714 843-6255	20020
United States Technical Svcs	7379	C	714 374-6300	16520
Unitedhealth Group Inc	6324	B	714 969-9050	10324
Waterfront Hotel LLC	7011	B	714 845-8000	13382

HUNTINGTON PARK, CA - Los Angeles County

	SIC	EMP	PHONE	ENTRY #
Aircraft Xray Laboratories Inc	8734	D	323 587-0164	26682
All Care Medical Group Inc	8011	D	408 278-3550	19271
AT&T Corp	4812	D	323 589-7045	5271
Cellco Partnership	4899	D	323 826-9880	5974
Chhp Management LLC	8062	D	323 583-1931	21313
Covenant Care California LLC	8051	C	323 589-5941	20344
D2j Inc	7389	D	323 589-1374	17123
First Community Investments	6531	D	951 238-8322	11452
Huntington Pk Police League	8322	D	323 584-6254	23850
Living Opportunities MGT Co	6513	C	323 589-5956	11056
Mexican Amrcn Oprtnty Fndation	8351	E	323 588-7320	24349
Pledge Insurance Brokerage	6411	D	323 588-0223	10731
Powerhouse Realty Inc	6531	D	323 562-7777	11675
Prajin 1 Stop Distributors Inc (PA)	5099	E	323 395-5302	8050
Saroyan Lumber Company Inc (PA)	5031	D	800 624-9309	6862

HURON, CA - Fresno County

	SIC	EMP	PHONE	ENTRY #
California Valley Land Co Inc (PA)	0721	D	559 945-9292	460
Dick Anderson & Sons Farming	0191	C	559 945-2511	335
Dole Fresh Vegetables Inc	0723	D	559 945-2591	507
Dresick Farms Inc (PA)	0161	D	559 945-2513	51
Royal Packing Dcf	0161	D	559 945-2537	78
West Cotton AG Management Inc	0762	C	559 945-2511	722

IDYLLWILD, CA - Riverside County

	SIC	EMP	PHONE	ENTRY #
Guided Discoveries Inc	7032	E	951 659-6062	13450

IMPERIAL, CA - Imperial County

	SIC	EMP	PHONE	ENTRY #
County of Imperial	1611	D	760 355-1748	1749
Empire Southwest LLC	5082	B	760 545-6200	7674
Imperial Irrigation District (PA)	4911	A	800 303-7756	6044
Imperial Irrigation District	4971	B	760 339-9220	6556
Nutrien AG Solutions Inc	5191	D	760 355-1133	9088
Western Meat Processors Inc	0212	E	760 355-1175	402

IMPERIAL BEACH, CA - San Diego County

	SIC	EMP	PHONE	ENTRY #
Boys Girls CLB Imperial Beach	8641	D	619 424-2266	25112
Comprhnsive Trning Systems Inc	8331	E	619 424-6650	24169
Intervec Phoenix Travel Club	7997	C	828 728-5287	18939
Jpmorgan Chase Bank Nat Assn	6029	E	619 424-8197	9509
Sodexo Operations LLC	7349	D	619 429-5692	14395

INDEPENDENCE, CA - Inyo County

	SIC	EMP	PHONE	ENTRY #
County of Inyo	7513	D	760 878-0292	17605
Eastern California Museum (PA)	8412	B	760 878-0292	24882
Los Angeles Dept Wtr & Pwr	4941	A	760 878-2156	6275
Sheriffs Offices	8111	D	760 878-0383	23382

INDIAN WELLS, CA - Riverside County

	SIC	EMP	PHONE	ENTRY #
Coldwell Bnkr Residential Brkg	6531	D	760 771-5454	11360
Dhccnp	7997	D	760 340-4646	18913
El Dorado Country Club	7997	C	760 346-8081	18919
Hit Portfolio I Misc Trs LLC	7011	B	760 341-1000	12680
Indian Wells Country Club Inc	7997	D	760 345-2561	18937
Indian Wells Resort Hotel	7011	E	760 345-6466	12762
Lh Indian Wells Operating LLC	7011	C	760 341-2200	12848
Renaissance Hotel Operating Co	7011	A	760 773-4444	13113
Renaissnce Esmralda Resort Spa	7011	A	760 773-4444	13114
Reserve Club	7997	C	760 674-2222	19013
Toscana Country Club Inc	7997	C	760 404-1444	19073
Troon Golf LLC	8741	C	760 346-4653	27070
Vintage Club (PA)	7997	E	760 346-5566	19079
Vintage Club	7997	D	760 340-0500	19080
Vintage Club Master Assn Inc	8641	D	760 340-0500	25283

INDIO, CA - Riverside County

	SIC	EMP	PHONE	ENTRY #
Cabazon Band Mission Indians	7011	A	760 342-5000	12416
Coachella Vly Rescue Mission	8322	E	760 347-3512	23590
Commercial Lighting Inds Inc	5063	D	800 755-0155	7348
County of Riverside	8011	D	760 863-8283	19422
County of Riverside	8361	D	760 863-7600	24482
County of Riverside	7999	D	760 863-8247	19154
Desert Recreation District (PA)	7999	D	760 347-3484	19157
Easia Golf Investment LLC	6799	D	760 775-2000	12221
East Valley Tourist Dev Auth	7999	A	760 342-5000	19164
Elite Anywhere Corp	4731	D	917 860-9247	5052
Fc Landscape Inc	0781	D	760 347-6600	755
Frontier California Inc	4813	D	760 342-0500	5561
Granite Construction Company	1611	B	760 775-7500	1773
HMS Agricultural Corporation	6531	D	760 347-2335	11504
Indio Hlthcare Wllness Ctr LLC	8051	D	760 347-6000	20542
JB Finish Inc	1751	D	760 342-6300	3045
John F Kennedy Memorial Hosp	8062	A	760 347-6191	21462
Kaiser Foundation Hospitals	8011	A	866 984-7483	19563
Kirkpatrick Ldscpg Svcs Inc	0782	C	760 347-6926	872
Lb Hills Golf Club LLC	7992	D	760 775-2000	18727
Marthas Village & Kitchen	8322	D	760 347-4741	23911
Oasis Mental Health Trtmnt Ctr	8063	C	760 863-8609	21968
P H B Contracting Inc	1742	C	760 347-7290	2929
Plantation Golf Club Inc	7997	D	760 775-3688	19003
Triangle Distributing Co	5181	D	760 347-4052	9030
Valley Medical Trnsp LLC	4119	D	760 501-8929	3856

INGLEWOOD, CA - Los Angeles County

	SIC	EMP	PHONE	ENTRY #
Aero Port Services Inc (PA)	7382	D	310 623-8230	16871
After-Party2 Inc (HQ)	7359	C	310 202-0011	14466
Air-Sea Forwarders Inc (PA)	4731	D	310 216-1616	5000
Alamo Rental (us) Inc	7514	D	310 649-2242	17621
American Eagle Pro	7381	D	310 412-0019	16562
American Nursing Home MGT Inc	8748	D	310 672-1012	27639
American Service Industries	7382	D	323 779-4000	16873
Ao Freight Corporation (PA)	4731	E	310 419-8833	5008
Apollo Couriers Inc (PA)	4215	D	310 337-0377	4393
Beckett Enterprise	8742	E	310 686-3817	27159
Big 5 Sporting Goods Corp	7999	B	323 755-2663	19110
California Credit Union	6062	D	310 671-1080	9626
Centinela Skilled Nursing and	8051	D	310 674-3216	20297
Centinela Sklld Nrsng & Wllnss	8051	D	310 674-3216	20298
Centinela Valley Care Center	8361	C	310 674-3216	24459
Century Skill Care	8051	D	310 672-1012	20301
Cfhs Holdings Inc	8062	A	310 673-4640	21310
City of Inglewood	7999	D	310 412-5370	19133
CP Opco LLC (HQ)	7299	A	310 966-4900	13735
Dolphin Hkg Ltd (PA)	5199	D	310 215-3356	9212

2019 Directory of California
Wholesalers and Services Companies

(P-0000) Products & Services Section entry number
(PA)=Parent Co (HQ)=Headquarters (DH)=Div Headquarters

	SIC	EMP	PHONE	ENTRY #
Eldorado Community Service Ctr	8011	D	424 227-7971	19457
Forum Enterprises Inc	7929	E	310 330-7300	18434
Gelshmal Enterprises LLC	5043	E	310 672-9090	6943
Goodman Food Products Inc (PA)	5141	C	310 674-3180	8408
Holiday Meat & Provision Corp	5147	C	310 674-0541	8619
Inglewood Meadows Kbs LP	6513	C	310 820-4888	11032
Inglewood Unified School Dst	8351	D	310 419-2691	24329
Interdent Inc (HQ)	8021	D	310 765-2400	20117
Interdent Service Corporation (DH)	8021	E	310 765-2400	20118
J Robert Scott Inc (PA)	5131	C	310 659-4910	8228
Kaiser Foundation Hospitals	8011	B	310 419-3303	19619
Mariner Health Care Inc	8051	C	310 677-9114	20616
Motel 6 Operating LP	7011	D	310 419-1234	12945
Prime Healthcare Centinela LLC	8062	A	310 673-4660	21657
Prime International Security	7381	C	310 670-4565	16762
RHO Chem LLC (DH)	4959	E	323 776-6234	6546
Royal Airline Linen Inc	7211	D	310 677-9885	13490
Sea-Air International Inc	4731	D	310 338-0778	5164
Smith Coleman Inc	6531	E	310 671-8271	11767
UPS Worldwide Logistics Inc	4731	C	310 673-7661	5195
Usas Express International	4731	D	310 645-2313	5196
Watts Health Foundation Inc (HQ)	8052	B	310 424-2220	20971
West Cntinela Vly Care Ctr Inc	8051	D	310 674-3216	20882

IONE, CA - Amador County

	SIC	EMP	PHONE	ENTRY #
Concessionaires Urban Park	7999	E	209 763-5121	19148
Concessionaires Urban Park	7999	D	209 763-5166	19149
Parks and Recreation Cal Dept	7999	E	209 763-5121	19215

IRVINE, CA - Orange County

	SIC	EMP	PHONE	ENTRY #
1105 Media Inc	4899	C	949 265-1520	5968
4g Wireless Inc (PA)	4812	C	949 748-6100	5255
7 Layers Inc	8711	D	949 716-6512	25490
A & H Communications Inc	1623	C	949 250-4555	1889
ABS Consulting Inc	8711	D	714 734-4242	25496
Absg Consulting Inc	8748	D	714 734-4242	27617
Accretive Solutions Inc (HQ)	8721	A	312 994-4600	26141
Accurate Background LLC (PA)	7375	B	800 784-3911	16206
Ace Parking Management Inc	7521	C	949 727-1470	17668
Acme Television Holdings LLC	4833	B	714 245-9499	5766
Action Property Management Inc (PA)	6514	D	949 450-0202	11146
Activision Blizzard Inc	7372	C	949 955-1380	15568
Adams Streeter Civil Engineers	8711	D	949 474-2330	25501
Advantage Sales & Mktg Inc (PA)	5141	C	949 797-2900	8374
Advantage Sales & Mktg LLC (HQ)	8732	C	949 797-2900	26499
Agendia Inc	8093	C	949 540-6300	22498
Agility Holdings Inc (DH)	4731	D	714 617-6300	4996
Ahtna-CDM JV	1541	E	714 824-3470	1372
Ahtna-CDM Smith JV	8748	D	714 824-3471	27630
Aids Svcs Fndation Orange Cnty	8322	D	949 809-5700	23465
Alcone Marketing Group Inc (HQ)	7311	C	949 595-5322	13791
Alecto Healthcare Services LLC (PA)	8062	A	323 938-3161	21277
Aleks Corporation	7372	C	714 245-7191	15576
All Environmental Inc	8748	D	949 752-9300	27632
Allen Matkins Leck Gmble	8111	D	949 553-1313	22911
Allergan Sales LLC (DH)	5122	A	862 261-7000	8139
Alliance Healthcare Svcs Inc (DH)	8071	C	949 242-5300	22058
Alorica Inc (PA)	7374	D	949 527-4600	16084
Alton Irvine Inc	5021	D	949 428-4141	6708
American Express Travel	4724	D	949 453-7123	4930
American Funds Service Company	6289	E	949 975-5000	10124
American Golf Corporation	7997	D	949 786-1224	18828
American Interbanc Mrtg LLC	6162	E	714 957-9430	9772
American Liberty Capital Corp	6163	C	949 623-0288	9871
American Medical Tech Inc	5047	D	949 553-0359	7151
Americor Funding Inc	7299	C	866 333-8686	13715
Ameripath Mortgage Corporation	6162	C	949 753-9211	9777
Ampronix Inc	5047	D	949 273-8000	7152
Ancca Corporation	1742	D	949 553-0084	2843
Anderson & Howard Electric Inc	1731	C	949 250-4555	2510
Andrew Lauren Company Inc	7389	C	949 861-4222	17003
Anheuser-Busch LLC	5181	C	949 263-9270	8980
Applied Geokinetics	8711	D	949 502-5353	25539
Aptim Corp	8711	D	949 261-6441	25541
Arbitech LLC	5045	D	949 376-6650	7008
Arcules Inc	7371	D	949 439-0053	14997
Argent Management Co LLC	6531	D	949 777-4070	11218
Argent Management LLC (PA)	6531	B	949 777-4000	11219
Aria Group Incorporated	8711	D	949 475-2915	25544
Arthur J Gallagher & Co	6411	E	949 349-9800	10543
Artistic Maintenance Inc	0782	C	949 733-8690	801
Ashley Home Care Services LLC	8082	E	323 286-2831	22230
Ashley Management Group	8742	E	949 754-3120	27143
Asics America Corporation (HQ)	5139	C	949 453-8888	8343
Aspect Software Inc	7372	E	408 595-5002	15593
Assi Security (PA)	1731	D	949 955-0244	2512

	SIC	EMP	PHONE	ENTRY #
AT&T Corp	4812	D	949 559-1457	5272
AT&T Corp	4812	D	949 622-8240	5294
AT&T Datacomm LLC	4813	E	714 675-9752	5469
Aten Technology Inc	5045	D	949 428-1111	7011
Atkinson Construction Inc	1611	B	303 410-2540	1726
Atlas Hospitality Group	6531	D	949 622-3400	11224
Atria Senior Living Group Inc	8741	D	949 786-5665	26769
Auctioncom Inc	6531	C	800 499-6199	11226
Auctioncom LLC (PA)	6531	C	949 859-2777	11227
Automatic Data Processing Inc	7374	C	949 751-0360	16092
Autoweb Inc (PA)	7375	C	949 225-4500	16209
Avalonbay Communities Inc	6531	E	949 955-6200	11228
Avaya Inc	4813	C	949 225-5678	5519
Avnet Inc	5065	C	949 789-4100	7445
Axiom Memory Solutions Inc	5045	D	949 581-1450	7014
Axonics Modulation Tech Inc	8731	D	949 396-6322	26337
Ayco Company LP	6282	C	949 955-1544	10059
Aztec Engineering Group Inc	8711	D	951 471-6190	25557
Bankruptcy MGT Solutions Inc (PA)	8111	D	949 222-1212	22932
BDS Marketing LLC (DH)	7311	C	800 234-4237	13798
BDS Solutions Group LLC (DH)	7311	A	949 472-6700	13799
Bear Stearns Companies LLC	6162	A	949 856-8300	9780
Beneficial Administration Inc	6411	D	949 756-1000	10560
Bergelectric Corp	1731	D	949 250-7005	2522
Berger Kahn	8111	E	310 821-9000	22942
Berkshire Mortgage Fin Corp	6162	D	949 754-6300	9781
Best Best & Krieger LLP	8111	E	949 263-2600	22945
Best Life and Health Insur Co	6311	D	949 253-4080	10131
Bigrentz Inc	7353	D	855 999-5438	14437
Black & Veatch Corporation	8711	A	913 458-2000	25568
Blb Resources Inc (PA)	8742	C	949 261-9155	27164
Blizzard Entertainment Inc (HQ)	7372	C	949 955-1380	15612
Bogart Construction Inc	1542	D	949 453-1400	1482
Bomel Construction Co Inc (PA)	1541	D	714 921-1660	1380
Brady Vorwerck Rydr & Cspno (PA)	8111	D	480 456-9888	22958
Brandrep Inc	8742	E	800 405-7119	27171
Brer Affiliates LLC (DH)	6794	C	949 794-7900	12134
Bridgwter Consulting Group Inc	8742	D	949 535-1755	27172
Brinderson LP (HQ)	8711	C	714 466-7100	25577
Brinderson LP	8711	D	714 466-7100	25578
Brooker Associates	0783	D	949 559-4877	969
Brown and Streza LLP	8742	D	949 453-2900	27174
Bryan Cave Lighton Paisner LLP	8111	D	949 223-7000	22962
Buchalter Nemer A Prof Corp	8111	D	714 549-5150	22964
Burleigh Point Ltd (DH)	6531	C	949 428-3200	11254
C T Corporation System	8111	D	925 287-9801	22967
Cal Southern Illumination	5063	E	949 622-3000	7342
Cal Southern Presbt Homes	6513	C	949 854-9500	10992
Calatlantic Group Inc	1521	C	949 789-1600	1137
Calatlantic Group Inc	1521	D	949 789-1600	1139
Calico Building Services Inc	7349	C	949 380-8707	14207
California First Nat Bancorp (PA)	6021	D	949 255-0500	9299
California First National Bank	6029	D	949 255-0500	9497
California Pacific Homes Inc (PA)	1531	D	949 833-6000	1334
Calteck USA Inc	7539	E	949 786-4854	17792
Cannon Cochran MGT Svcs Inc	6411	C	949 474-6500	10576
Canon Solutions America Inc	5084	D	800 333-6395	7737
Canon USA Inc	5043	B	949 753-4000	6940
Cap Diagnostics LLC	8071	D	714 966-1221	22064
Cape Environmental MGT Inc	8744	B	949 236-3000	27579
Capital Group Companies Inc	6282	D	949 975-5000	10072
Capital Research and MGT Co	6282	D	949 975-5000	10074
Carfinance Capital LLC	6799	A	800 900-5150	12210
Carpenter Fund Manager Gp LLC	6021	C	949 261-8888	9301
CDM SMITH INC	8711	D	949 752-5452	25598
Cellco Partnership	4812	A	949 286-7000	5319
Center For Atism Rlted Dsrders	8093	E	949 203-8872	22521
Centex Homes Inc	1521	C	949 453-0113	1144
Cfp Fire Protection Inc	1711	D	949 338-4280	2159
Cgtech (PA)	7373	E	949 753-1050	15931
Chambers Group Inc	8748	E	949 261-5414	27684
Child Development Incorporated	8351	A	949 725-0961	24285
Child Development Incorporated	8351	A	949 854-5060	24286
Childrens Hospital Orange Cnty	8062	A	949 387-2586	21318
Cie Digital Labs LLC (PA)	7319	D	949 381-6200	13971
Citigroup Global Markets Inc	6211	D	949 955-7500	9935
Citigroup Inc	6021	D	949 726-5124	9335
City of Irvine	8742	D	949 724-7600	27194
City of Irvine	7999	D	949 724-7740	19134
City of Irvine	8621	D	949 724-7101	25010
City of Irvine	7999	D	949 724-6728	19135
City of Irvine	8322	D	949 724-6900	23579
CK Franchising Inc (DH)	8082	D	800 498-8144	22264
Clark Cnstr Group-California	1541	B	714 754-0764	1387
Clark Cnstr Grup-California LP	1542	B	714 429-9779	1507

Employment Codes: A=Over 500 employees, B=251-500,
C=101-250, D=51-100, E=50

2019 Directory of California
Wholesalers and Services Companies

© Mergent Inc. 1-800-342-5647

1587

GEOGRAPHIC

Company	SIC	EMP	PHONE	ENTRY #
Clearpath Lending	6163	C	949 502-3577	9876
Coast To Coast Bus Eqp Inc (PA)	5044	D	949 457-7300	6956
Cofiroute Usa LLC	4785	C	949 754-0198	5215
Column Five Media LLC (PA)	7336	E	949 614-0759	14105
Commerce Velocity LLC	7372	C	949 756-8950	15632
Commercial Landscape Svc	0781	D	949 660-8655	748
Commonwealth Equity Svcs LLP	7291	D	949 336-6440	13703
Commonwealth Land Title Co	6361	D	949 460-4500	10448
Connect Your Home LLC	1542	D	949 777-0100	1509
Connotate Technologies Inc	7371	E	949 270-1916	15077
Consoldted Fire Protection LLC (HQ)	7389	A	949 727-3277	17099
Consumer Portfolio Svcs Inc	6141	C	949 788-5695	9707
Consumer Portfolio Svcs Inc	6141	D	949 753-6800	9708
Contec Microelectronics USA	5045	D	949 250-4025	7025
Corelogic Inc	6531	E	714 250-6400	11382
Corelogic Credco LLC (HQ)	7323	C	949 214-1000	14033
Corner Products Company	5065	C	800 876-8889	7463
Corporate Risk Hldings III Inc	7389	A	949 428-5839	17102
Corvel Corporation (PA)	8741	C	949 851-1473	26821
Corvel Enterprise Comp Inc	6411	C	949 851-1473	10595
Council On Aging - S Cali Inc	8322	D	714 479-0107	23620
Courtney Inc (PA)	1799	D	949 222-2050	3507
Cox Communications Inc	4841	D	949 546-1000	5893
Creative Maintenance Systems	7349	D	949 852-2871	14235
Crescent Staffing Inc (PA)	7371	C	949 724-0304	15085
Crestmont Capital LLC	6799	C	800 949-0401	12218
Critchfeld Mech Inc Sthern Cal	1711	D	949 390-2900	2176
Crowdstrike Holdings Inc (PA)	7379	D	888 512-8906	16336
Crowell & Moring LLP	8111	E	949 263-8400	23015
Cushman & Wakefield Cal Inc	6531	E	949 474-4004	11391
Custom Business Solutions Inc (PA)	5044	D	949 380-7674	6958
Customer Srvc Dlvry Pltfrm Crp	7379	E	717 896-8489	16339
Cwpfl Inc	7389	E	714 564-7900	17122
Cybercoders Inc	7361	C	949 885-5151	14599
Cylance Inc (PA)	7372	C	949 375-3380	15643
D P S Inc	1721	D	714 564-7900	2431
Dal-Tile Corporation	5032	D	949 260-0488	6885
Database Marketing Group Inc	7331	B	714 727-0800	14043
Davita Inc	8092	B	949 930-4400	22470
Deacon Corp	1542	D	949 222-9060	1515
Decision Ready Solutions Inc	6162	E	949 400-1126	9798
Decision Toolbox Inc	8748	D	562 377-5600	27704
Decton Inc	7361	C	949 851-0111	14600
Delta Galil USA Inc	5137	D	949 296-0380	8298
Denken Solutions Inc	7371	C	949 630-5263	15102
Developers Surety Indemnity Co (DH)	6351	D	949 263-3300	10426
Dharne & Company	7379	D	949 293-5675	16347
Digital Map Products Inc	4899	D	949 333-5111	5979
Dkn Hotel LLC (PA)	7011	B	714 427-4320	12529
DOT Leasing Company	5111	C	949 474-1100	8069
Duke Energy Corporation	4911	C	949 727-7434	6027
Dyntek Inc (PA)	7379	D	949 271-6700	16352
Dzyne Technologies Inc	8711	D	703 454-0704	25649
Edison Capital (DH)	4911	D	909 594-3789	6031
Edwards Lifesciences LLC (HQ)	8011	A	949 250-2500	19455
Edwards Theatres Circuit Inc	7832	D	949 854-8811	18299
Ekedal Concrete Inc	1741	D	949 720-8011	2804
Elevate Property Services LP	6519	E	562 219-2101	11170
Elite Security Services Inc	7381	B	949 222-2203	16638
Empcc Inc	1721	D	714 564-7900	2434
Enclarity Inc	7374	D	949 614-8110	16124
Eon Reality Inc (PA)	5045	E	949 460-2000	7044
Ephesoft Inc (PA)	5045	D	949 335-5335	7045
Equinox-76th Street Inc	7991	D	949 296-1700	18596
Equinox-76th Street Inc	8049	B	949 975-8400	20175
Equistar Irvine Company LLC	7011	D	949 833-3331	12560
Eri Economic Research Inst Inc	7372	D	800 627-3697	15671
Ernst & Young LLP	8721	B	949 794-2300	26197
Ernst & Young LLP	8721	C	949 838-3300	26198
Es Engineering Inc	8748	D	714 919-6500	27723
Es Engineering Services LLC	8711	D	949 988-3500	25676
Essex Properties LLC	6531	D	949 798-8100	11422
European Hotl Invstrs of CA (PA)	7011	D	949 474-7368	12567
Eveg Inc	7371	E	844 221-3359	15148
Evisions Inc (PA)	7371	D	949 833-1384	15153
Eworkplace Solutions Inc	5045	C	949 583-1646	7047
Experian Info Solutions Inc	7323	C	949 567-3731	14037
Exult Inc	8742	A	949 856-8800	27232
F M Tarbell Co	6531	E	714 639-0677	11437
F M Tarbell Co	6531	D	949 559-8451	11438
Fao ROC Holdings LLC	5092	C	949 900-6501	7951
Far West Management Corp (PA)	6531	D	949 863-1757	11443
Federal Express Corporation	7389	B	800 463-3339	17168
Federal Express Corporation	4512	C	949 862-4500	4783
Fedex Freight Corporation	4213	D	800 706-1687	4160
Festival Fun Parks LLC	7999	D	949 559-8336	19173
Ficcadenti & Waggoner Consul (PA)	8711	D	949 474-0502	25683
Fieldstone Communities Inc	1521	E	949 790-5400	1164
Fieldstone Communities Inc (PA)	1531	C	949 790-5400	1339
Finance America LLC (PA)	6162	C	949 440-1000	9803
First Amercn Prof RE Svcs Inc (PA)	6531	C	714 250-1400	11449
First Team RE - Orange Cnty (PA)	6531	C	888 236-1943	11460
Firstservice Residential (HQ)	6531	C	949 448-6000	11467
Fisher & Paykel Healthcare Inc	5047	C	949 453-4000	7180
Fisher & Phillips LLP	8111	D	949 851-2424	23071
Flagship Credit Acceptance LLC	7389	C	949 748-7172	17173
Fluor Enterprises Inc	8711	D	949 349-2000	25687
Fnc Inc	7371	D	714 866-1099	15164
Footh The / Easte Trans Corri	1611	D	949 754-3400	1764
Ford Motor Company	8111	B	949 341-5800	23079
Ford Motor Land Dev Corp	8711	B	949 242-6606	25690
Fostering Executive Leadership	8742	D	949 651-6250	27240
Fox Head Inc (PA)	5136	C	888 369-7223	8261
Fragomen Del Rey Bernse	8111	D	949 660-3504	23082
Francisco Emilio Assoc Law Off	8111	D	949 474-2222	23084
Frank D Yelian MD PC	8011	E	949 788-1133	19475
Full Circle Wireless Inc	5065	D	949 783-7979	7480
Fuscoe Engineering Inc (PA)	8711	D	949 474-1960	25696
G4s Justice Services LLC	7382	C	800 589-6003	16898
GA Services LLC	7379	E	949 752-6515	16374
Gallup Inc	8742	C	949 474-2700	27244
Gdr Group Inc	7379	D	949 453-8818	16376
Genea Energy Partners Inc	7373	D	714 694-0536	15966
General Electric Company	6159	C	949 838-3043	9759
General Tool Inc	5085	D	949 261-2322	7849
Genpact Mortgage Services Inc (HQ)	6162	D	949 417-5131	9807
Georg Fischer LLC (DH)	5051	C	714 731-8800	7274
Ghost Management Group LLC	7313	C	949 870-1400	13946
Gibson Dunn & Crutcher LLP	8111	C	949 451-3800	23092
Gkk Corporation (PA)	8712	C	949 250-1500	26050
Global Ascent Inc	7389	E	714 930-6860	17188
Global Debt Management LLC (PA)	7389	D	949 825-7800	17190
Global Eagle Entertainment Inc	7812	C	949 608-8700	18057
Global Language Solutions LLC	7389	D	949 798-1400	17195
Glovis America Inc (HQ)	4731	D	714 435-2960	5075
Go2 Systems Inc	7375	D	949 553-0800	16226
Golden Hotels Ltd Partnership	7011	C	949 833-2770	12608
Goodman North America LLC	6531	D	949 407-0100	11488
Gordian Medical Inc	5047	B	714 556-0200	7182
Gordon Rees Sclly Mnskhani LLP	8111	D	949 255-6950	23105
Gradient Engineers Inc	8711	D	949 477-0555	25718
Greenberg Traurig LLP	8111	D	949 732-6500	23114
Greens Group Inc	7011	C	949 829-4902	12619
Greystar Management Svcs LP	8741	B	949 705-0010	26877
Griffin Technology LLC (HQ)	5065	D	615 399-7000	7484
Hardesty LLC (PA)	7361	E	949 407-6625	14634
Harmony Escrow Inc	6531	D	949 474-1134	11499
Harris & Associates Inc	8711	D	949 655-3900	25721
Hcp Inc (PA)	6798	D	949 407-0700	12164
HDR Engineering Inc	8711	C	714 730-2300	25726
Healthcare MGT Partners LLC	8741	B	949 263-8620	26885
HEI Irvine LLC	7011	E	949 553-8332	12651
Hensel Phlps Grnte Hngr JV	1542	C	949 852-0111	1552
Heritage Indemnity Company	6331	D	303 987-5500	10361
Hireright LLC (HQ)	7375	C	949 428-5800	16230
Hit Portfolio I Misc Trs LLC	7011	B	949 975-1234	12679
Hntb Corporation	8711	D	949 460-1700	25736
Hoag Memorial Hospital Presbt	8062	A	949 764-4624	21452
Holthouse Carlin Van Trigt LLP	8721	D	714 361-7600	26222
Home Franchise Concepts LLC (PA)	1771	D	949 404-1100	3266
HPM Construction	1542	D	949 474-9170	1556
Huitt - Zollars Inc	8713	E	949 988-5815	26130
Human Options Inc (PA)	8322	D	949 737-5242	23847
Hunsaker & Assoc Irvine Inc (PA)	8711	D	949 583-1010	25740
Hyland Software Inc	7371	D	949 242-3100	15204
Hyundai Capital America (DH)	6141	D	714 965-3000	9716
Icat Logistics Inc	4731	D	310 884-5923	5090
Icf Jones & Stokes Inc	8742	D	949 333-6600	27269
Idexx Reference Labs Inc	8071	E	949 477-2840	22097
Ignite Health LLC (PA)	7311	C	949 861-3200	13844
Impac Mortgage Corp	6162	B	949 475-3600	9817
Impac Mortgage Holdings Inc (PA)	6798	A	949 475-3600	12166
Impac Secured Assets Corp	6733	C	949 475-3600	12097
Indemnity Company California (DH)	6351	D	949 263-3300	10429
Inductors Inc	5065	E	949 623-2460	7493
Ingram Micro Inc (HQ)	5045	A	714 566-1000	7063
Insco Insurance Services Inc (HQ)	6411	D	949 797-9243	10650
Insituform Technologies LLC	1623	E	714 724-2324	1930
Interactive Media Holdings (DH)	7311	D	949 861-8888	13848
Intercontinental Hotels Group	7011	C	949 863-1999	12766

Mergent email: customerrelations@mergent.com

1588

2019 Directory of California
Wholesalers and Services Companies

(P-0000) Products & Services Section entry number
(PA)=Parent Co (HQ)=Headquarters (DH)=Div Headquarters

	SIC	EMP	PHONE	ENTRY #
Intercontinental Hotels Group	7011	D	949 863-1999	12773
Interior Office Solutions Inc (PA)	7389	E	949 724-9444	17244
International Toy Inc	5092	E	949 333-3777	7952
Interstate Hotels Resorts Inc	8741	C	949 833-9999	26900
Interwall Dev Systems Inc	1742	D	949 553-9102	2898
Intratek Computer Inc	7379	B	949 334-4200	16407
Ipass Inc	7373	D	650 232-4100	15985
Irvine APT Communities LP (HQ)	6513	C	949 720-5600	11035
Irvine Company LLC	8699	D	949 653-5300	25434
Irvine Ranch Water District (PA)	4941	C	949 453-5300	6266
Irvine Ranch Water District	4941	C	949 453-5300	6267
Irvine Technology Corporation	7361	C	714 445-2624	14653
Irvine Unified School Distict	4151	D	949 936-5300	3938
Irvine Valencia Growers	0179	D	949 936-8000	237
Isotis Orthobiologics Inc	8731	D	949 595-8710	26387
Ixos Software Inc (PA)	5045	D	949 784-8000	7065
J Baron Inc	6531	D	949 451-1200	11525
J5 Infrastructure Partners LLC	4812	D	949 299-5258	5410
Jackson Demarco Tidus Peter (PA)	8111	D	949 752-8585	23148
Jacobs Engineering Group Inc	8711	D	949 224-7585	25756
Jacobs Field Svcs N Amer Inc	1629	C	949 224-7585	2040
Jacobs Project Management Co	8711	D	949 224-7695	25765
Jacobus Consulting (PA)	8742	E	949 727-0720	27287
James R Glidewell Dental	8072	A	800 411-9723	22169
Jeff Tracy Inc	1711	E	949 582-0877	2243
Jeffrey Rome & Associates	8712	D	949 760-3929	26071
Jelight Company Inc	5063	D	949 380-8774	7367
Jetsuite Inc (PA)	4522	C	949 892-4300	4861
JF Shea Construction Inc	1521	C	949 526-8792	1182
Jnr Inc	8742	D	949 476-2788	27289
Johnson Cntrls SEC Sltions LLC	7382	C	714 223-2300	16913
Jones Day Limited Partnership	8111	D	949 851-3939	23154
Jones Lang Lsalle Americas Inc	6282	C	949 296-3600	10091
Jonset Corporation	4959	D	949 551-5151	6542
K Hovnanian Companies Cal Inc (HQ)	1521	D	714 368-4500	1187
Kaiser Foundation Hospitals	8062	C	949 262-5780	21475
Kaiser Foundation Hospitals	6733	B	949 932-5000	12110
Kasdan Smnds Riley Vaughan LLP (PA)	8111	D	949 851-9000	23160
Keating Dental Arts Inc	8072	D	949 955-2100	22171
Keystone PCF Property MGT Inc (PA)	6531	D	949 833-2600	11549
Kieckhafer Schiffer & Co LLP (PA)	8721	E	949 250-3900	26235
Kilroy Realty LP	6531	D	949 788-1200	11550
Kite Electric Inc	1731	C	949 380-7471	2625
Knobbe Martens Olson Bear LLP (PA)	8111	B	949 760-0404	23177
Koeller Nbker Crlson Hluck LLP (PA)	8111	D	949 864-3400	23179
Kofax Inc (PA)	7371	B	949 783-1000	15250
Kore1 Inc	7379	D	949 706-6990	16418
Kronos Incorporated	7372	D	800 580-7374	15737
Ksm Marketing Inc	7389	C	949 597-2222	17282
Ktgy Group Inc (PA)	8712	D	949 851-2133	26077
L S A Associates Inc (PA)	8748	C	949 553-0666	27769
La Jolla Group Inc	7389	D	949 428-2800	17286
Landmark Event Staffing	7381	A	714 293-4248	16714
Lawyers Title Insurance Corp	6361	C	949 223-5575	10466
Lba Inc (PA)	8742	C	949 833-0400	27299
Lba Realty Fund III - III LLC	6798	D	949 833-0400	12170
Lba Realty LLC (PA)	6531	E	949 833-0400	11560
Lba Rlty Fund I-Company IV LLC	6798	D	949 955-9321	12171
Lee & Associates Coml RE Svcs (PA)	6531	E	949 727-1200	11562
Legacy Prtners Residential Inc	8741	B	949 930-6600	26930
Leighton and Associates Inc (PA)	8748	D	949 250-1421	27773
Leighton Group Inc (PA)	8744	B	949 477-4040	27599
Liberty Dental Plan Cal Inc	6324	B	949 223-0007	10277
Liberty Dental Plan Nevada Inc	6324	D	888 703-6999	10278
Liberty Mutual Insurance Co.	6411	C	310 316-9428	10671
Lineage Logistics Holdings LLC (PA)	4222	C	800 678-7271	4507
Lineage Logistics Holdings LLC	4214	A	909 433-3100	4356
Lineage Logistics Icm LLC	4222	C	972 462-0042	4508
Linksys LLC (DH)	5065	B	949 270-8500	7504
Livescribe Inc	5045	E	503 290-4029	7072
LLP Moss Adams	8721	E	949 221-4000	26252
Loan Administration Netwrk Inc	7361	D	949 752-5246	14663
Local Corporation (PA)	7311	D	949 784-0800	13857
LPA Inc (PA)	8712	C	949 261-1001	26084
Luther Burbank Corporation	6029	D	949 428-8043	9510
M F Salta Co Inc (PA)	8742	D	562 421-2512	27311
Malcolm & Cisneros A Law Corp	8111	C	949 252-1039	23236
Marriott International Inc.	7011	B	949 724-3606	12888
Maruchan Inc	4225	D	949 789-2300	4591
Mazda Research & Dev of N Amer.	8711	A	949 852-8898	25813
MBK Real Estate Companies	6531	E	949 789-8300	11596
MBK Real Estate Ltd A Calfor (HQ)	6531	D	949 789-8300	11597
McDermott Will & Emery LLP Inc	8111	D	949 757-7165	23244
McKinley Equipment Corporation (PA)	5084	D	800 770-6094	7773
Mds Consulting (PA)	8711	D	949 251-8821	25816
Mechanics Bank	6141	B	855 272-2886	9721
Medata Inc (PA)	7372	D	714 918-1310	15754
Mercer (us) Inc	8742	D	949 222-1300	27338
Merchsource LLC	5092	D	800 374-2744	7957
Merrill Lynch Pierce Fenner	6211	D	949 859-2900	9989
Mesa Energy Systems Inc (HQ)	1711	C	949 460-0460	2278
Mesa Properties GP	7011	D	949 857-1905	12924
Mhh Holdings Inc	5149	C	949 651-9903	8825
Michael Madden Co Inc	5113	D	800 834-6248	8110
Microsoft Corporation	7372	C	949 263-3000	15762
Mind Research Institute	8733	C	949 345-8700	26641
Mirion Technologies Gds Inc (HQ)	8734	C	949 419-1000	26715
Mission Energy Holding Company	6719	A	949 752-5588	11993
Mission Hills Mortgage Corp (HQ)	6163	C	714 972-3832	9896
Mjp Empire Inc (PA)	1721	B	714 564-7900	2460
Mobilenet Services Inc (PA)	8711	C	949 951-4444	25828
Mobilityware Inc	7371	D	949 788-9900	15288
Monarch Healthcare A Medical (HQ)	8011	D	949 923-3200	19699
Montage Hotels & Resorts LLC (PA)	7011	B	949 715-5002	12938
Montrose Envmtl Group Inc (PA)	8748	D	949 988-3500	27792
Morgan Stanley	6211	D	949 809-1200	9994
Mtc Financial Inc	6733	E	949 252-8300	12116
Murtaugh Myer Nlson Trglia LLP	8111	D	949 794-4000	23279
Mve + Partners Inc (PA)	8712	D	949 809-3388	26097
Nationwide Funding LLC	6159	E	949 679-3600	9761
Netapp Inc	7373	C	949 754-6600	16012
Network Capital Funding Corp (PA)	6162	B	949 442-0060	9836
Neudesic LLC (PA)	7379	C	949 754-4500	16433
Neuintel LLC (PA)	7371	C	949 625-6117	15305
New York Life Insurance Co	6411	D	949 797-2400	10708
Newport Meat Southern Cal Inc	5147	C	949 399-4200	8622
Newport Pacific Capital Co Inc (PA)	6531	D	949 852-5575	11628
Newton Softed Inc	8748	E	949 396-6192	27800
Nexa Technologies Inc (HQ)	7371	D	972 590-8669	15307
Nexgenix Inc (PA)	7371	B	714 665-6240	15308
Nextgen Healthcare Inc (PA)	7372	C	949 255-2600	15782
Nextgen Healthcare Info System (HQ)	7371	D	949 255-2600	15309
Nihon Kohden America Inc (HQ)	5047	D	949 580-1555	7196
Nikken Global Inc (HQ)	5087	C	949 789-2000	7891
Ninyo & Moore Geotechnical	8748	D	949 753-7070	27803
Nitto Avecia Pharma Services (PA)	8734	D	949 951-4425	26722
Nnn Realty Investors LLC	6799	B	714 667-8252	12249
North Amercn Science Assoc Inc	8734	D	949 951-3110	26723
Northstar Technology Corp (PA)	7371	C	949 788-0738	15316
Nossaman LLP	8111	E	949 833-7800	23294
NRLL LLC	6799	E	949 768-7777	12251
Nrp Holding Co Inc (PA)	6719	C	949 583-1000	11996
Ntrust Infotech Inc	7372	D	562 207-1600	15785
NW Manor Community Partners LP	6552	D	714 662-5565	11898
Ocmbc Inc	6162	D	714 479-0999	9837
One 3 Two Inc	5137	C	949 596-8400	8329
Operation Technology Inc (PA)	7371	D	949 462-0100	15332
Optima Mortgage Corporation	6162	D	714 389-4650	9840
Optumrx Inc (DH)	6324	B	714 825-3600	10288
Ora Pacific Regional Field Off	7389	D	949 608-2907	17373
Oracle Corp	8999	A	650 506-7000	27948
Oracle Systems Corporation	7372	D	949 224-1000	15821
Oracle Systems Corporation	7372	B	949 623-9460	15822
Orange County Produce LLC	0171	D	949 451-0880	111
Orangepeople LLC	8999	D	949 535-1308	27949
Orchard Holdings Group Inc	6531	C	949 502-8300	11644
Ortiz Enterprises Incorporated (PA)	1611	D	949 753-1414	1831
OSI Digital Inc	7379	E	949 724-8300	16447
Owl Companies (PA)	8331	A	949 797-2000	24215
Owl Education and Training	8331	A	949 797-2000	24216
Pacific Dental Services Llc (PA)	8021	B	714 845-8500	20132
Pacific Pharma Inc	5122	A	714 246-4600	8201
Pacific Premier Bank (HQ)	6022	C	714 431-4000	9473
Pacific Symphony	7929	C	714 755-5788	18454
Paciolan LLC (HQ)	7372	D	949 476-2050	15824
Palumbo Lawyers LLP (PA)	8111	D	949 442-0300	23308
Pan American Bank Fsb	6035	B	949 224-1917	9528
Paramount Equity Mortgage LLC	6162	C	916 290-9999	9844
Park Hotels & Resorts Inc	7011	B	949 553-8332	13038
Parking Concepts Inc	7389	B	949 752-5558	17387
Passco Companies LLC (PA)	6531	D	949 442-1000	11665
Pathway Capital Management LP (PA)	8741	D	949 622-1000	26983
Patric Communications Inc (PA)	1731	D	619 579-2898	2676
Patron Solutions LLC	7372	C	949 823-1700	15826
Payne & Fears LLP (PA)	8111	D	949 851-1101	23320
Pennymac Financial Svcs Inc	8742	A	949 341-0020	27391
Pension Administrators Inc (PA)	7331	C	949 253-4080	14057
Peoples Choice Home (PA)	6162	D	949 494-6167	9845
Philips Medical Systems Clevel	5047	D	949 699-2300	7208
Physician Weblink of Cal (HQ)	8741	C	949 923-3201	26986

Employment Codes: A=Over 500 employees, B=251-500,
C=101-250, D=51-100, E=50

2019 Directory of California
Wholesalers and Services Companies

© Mergent Inc. 1-800-342-5647

1589

GEOGRAPHIC

Company	SIC	EMP	PHONE	ENTRY #
Piercey Management Svcs Inc (PA)	8741	D	949 379-3701	26987
Ponderosa Electric Inc	1731	D	949 253-3100	2684
Post Modern Edit LLC (PA)	7812	D	949 608-8700	18098
Precept Inc (DH)	6411	D	949 955-1430	10735
Prelude Systems Inc (PA)	7379	C	949 208-7126	16461
Premier Office Centers LLC (PA)	7389	E	949 253-4616	17408
Pricewaterhousecoopers LLP	8721	B	949 437-5200	26274
Prime Tech Cabinets Inc	1751	C	714 558-4837	3059
Primecare Quality HM Care Inc	1521	D	949 681-3515	1218
Proove Medical Labs Inc	8071	C	949 427-5303	22127
Propath Inc	1522	E	949 341-8000	1308
Proview Advanced Solutions Inc	6411	D	949 752-2484	10745
Prudential Insur Co of Amer	6411	E	949 440-5300	10746
Prudential Overall Supply (PA)	7218	C	949 250-4855	13613
Pts Staffing Solutions	7361	C	949 268-4000	14710
Qbe First Insurance Agency Inc	6411	B	949 206-6200	10750
Quadion LLC	6282	A	714 546-0994	10107
Quest Group (PA)	5099	D	949 585-0111	8051
Quest Intl Monitor Svc Inc (PA)	7378	D	949 581-9900	16291
Quovera Inc	8748	E	949 224-3825	27834
Racquet Club of Irvine	7997	D	949 786-3000	19005
Railpros Inc (PA)	8711	D	714 734-8765	25887
Railpros Field Services	7389	E	877 315-0513	17423
Rakworx Inc	7378	C	949 215-1362	16292
Ramboll Environ US Corporation	8748	D	949 261-5151	27836
Ramboll US Corporation	8999	E	949 798-3604	27957
Rand Technology LLC (PA)	5065	D	949 255-5700	7533
Ranscapes Inc	7349	E	866 883-9297	14363
Redhill Group Inc	8732	D	949 752-5900	26561
Rels LLC	6531	A	949 214-1000	11725
Renal Treatment Ctrs - Cal Inc	8092	D	949 930-6882	22486
Renovo Solutions LLC	8741	B	714 599-7969	27015
Residence Mutual Insurance Co	6331	D	949 724-9402	10390
Residnce Inn By Mrriott Irvine	7011	D	949 380-3000	13122
Resolve Systems LLC (PA)	7371	D	949 325-0120	15405
Resources Connection Inc (PA)	8742	A	714 430-6400	27427
Resources Connection LLC (HQ)	7361	D	714 430-6400	14722
Result Group Inc	7373	D	480 777-7130	16043
Ricoh Usa Inc	5044	D	949 225-2300	6983
RMS Group Inc	1542	D	714 373-4882	1632
Robert Half International Inc	7361	D	949 476-3199	14741
Robert Kinsella Inc	5141	D	949 453-9533	8450
Rockefeller Group Dev Corp	6552	D	949 468-1800	11910
Roland Dga Corporation (HQ)	5045	C	949 727-2100	7098
Rose International Inc	8748	E	636 812-4000	27847
RSM US LLP	8721	D	949 255-6500	26283
Ryland Homes of Texas Inc	1531	C	805 367-3800	1358
S E O P Inc	8742	C	949 682-7906	27436
S K & A Information Svcs Inc (DH)	8732	D	949 476-2051	26563
S W P T X Inc	1721	C	714 564-7900	2478
Safe-Guard Products Intl LLC	6411	D	800 742-7896	10762
Sage Software Inc	7375	D	949 753-1222	16249
Sage Software Holdings Inc (HQ)	7372	B	866 530-7243	15845
San Joaquin Hills Transporttn (PA)	1611	D	949 754-3400	1845
Sand Canyon Corporation (HQ)	6163	D	949 727-9425	9906
Sand Canyon LLC	7992	D	949 551-2560	18757
Savala Equipment Company Inc (PA)	7353	D	949 552-1859	14457
Savoy Contractors Group Inc	1521	C	949 753-1919	1230
SBE Contracting	1731	E	714 544-5066	2725
SCC Acquisitions Inc	6552	C	949 777-4000	11913
Sea Breeze Financial Services (PA)	6162	E	949 223-9700	9856
Sean P OConnor	8111	D	949 851-7323	23369
Second Harvest Food	8322	D	949 653-2900	24037
Secureauth Corporation (PA)	7371	D	949 777-6959	15434
Sema Construction Inc	1622	N	949 330-4300	1888
Sentinel Monitoring Corp (HQ)	7382	C	949 453-1550	16940
Sentinel Offender Services LLC (PA)	7382	D	949 453-1550	16941
Seven Resorts Inc (PA)	7011	B	949 588-7100	13208
Sfn Group Inc	7363	D	949 727-8500	14912
Shady Canyon Golf Club Inc	7997	C	949 856-7000	19045
Shiftpixy Inc	7371	E	949 207-7184	15443
Shimano North Amer Holdg Inc (HQ)	5091	C	949 951-5003	7938
Shlemmer+algaze+associ (PA)	8711	D	949 724-8958	25909
Signature Resources Insurance	6411	D	949 930-2400	10774
Silverado Bellingham LLC	8082	D	949 240-7200	22419
Silverado Energy Company	4911	B	949 752-5588	6109
Silverado Senior Living Inc (PA)	8059	D	949 240-7200	21209
Silverado Senior Living Holdin	8361	A	949 240-7200	24674
Singerlewak LLP	8721	D	949 261-8600	26294
Sitelite Holdings Inc	7379	C	949 265-6200	16484
Smart Energy Systems LLC (PA)	7371	C	909 703-9609	15452
Smart Energy Systems LLC	7371	D	909 703-9609	15453
Smart Systems Technologies (PA)	4911	D	949 367-9375	6111
SMC Networks Inc (HQ)	5045	D	949 679-8029	7104
Smile Brands Group Inc (PA)	8741	D	714 668-1300	27032
Snyder Langston L P	1542	D	949 863-9200	1654
Sony Electronics Inc.	7812	C	714 508-7634	18118
Southern Cal Prmnnte Med Group	8011	D	949 262-5780	19905
Southern California Edison Co	4911	C	949 587-5416	6133
Southern Implants Inc	8741	C	949 273-8505	27042
Spad Holdings LLC	7991	D	949 733-0473	18662
Specialty Surgical Centers	8011	E	949 341-3499	19932
Spectrum Hotel Group LLC	7011	D	949 471-8888	13252
Spectrum Hotel Group LLC	7011	D	949 471-8888	13253
Spectrum Information Svcs LLC (PA)	7331	D	949 752-7070	14062
Sph-Irvine LLC	8011	E	949 833-1432	19934
Spireon Inc (PA)	4214	C	800 557-1449	4375
Sprint Corporation	4812	B	949 748-3353	5416
Ssinfotek Inc.	7373	E	949 732-3100	16059
St Andrews Children Center	8351	E	949 651-0198	24385
Stantec Arch & Engrg PC	8711	C	949 923-6000	25927
Stantec Architecture Inc	8712	C	949 923-6000	26112
Stantec Consulting Svcs Inc	8712	C	949 923-6000	26115
Startel Corporation (PA)	7371	D	949 863-8700	15471
State Farm Mutl Auto Insur Co	6411	D	309 766-2311	10789
State Group LLC	8742	B	949 612-2879	27468
Steelwave Inc	6552	C	949 863-0390	11921
Stratacare Llc	7371	A	949 743-1200	15477
Strategic Financial Group	6411	E	949 622-7200	10795
Strategy Companion Corp.	7372	D	714 460-8398	15867
Strategy For Water & Land Reso	8731	E	949 572-3034	26460
Stratham Homes Inc	1522	D	949 833-1554	1317
Strawberry Farms Golf Club LLC	7992	D	949 551-2560	18768
Student Government Associat.	4724	C	949 824-5547	4952
Student Works Painting Inc	1721	B	714 564-7900	2485
Stussy Inc	5136	D	949 474-9255	8278
Success Strategies Inst Inc	8331	D	949 721-6808	24235
Sullivancurtismonroe Insurance (PA)	8742	C	800 427-3253	27474
Sun Ten Labs Liquidation Co	5149	D	949 587-0509	8875
Sunscape Eyewear Inc	5099	D	949 553-0590	8061
Sunstone Center Crt Lessee Inc	7011	C	949 382-4000	13291
Sunstone Hotel Investors Inc (PA)	6798	E	949 330-4000	12188
Sunstone Ocean Lessee Inc	7011	B	949 382-4000	13306
Sunwest Bank (DH)	6022	E	714 730-4441	9489
Synoptek Inc (PA)	7379	D	949 241-8600	16499
Tanaka Farms	5149	D	949 653-2100	8883
Tantra Lake Partners LP	6513	C	949 756-5959	11123
Tanvex Biopharma Usa Inc (PA)	8731	D	858 210-4100	26470
Taylor Morrison California LLC	6552	C	949 341-1200	11928
Tcg Software Services Inc.	7371	E	714 665-6200	15495
Team Post-Op Inc (DH)	5047	D	949 253-5500	7222
Temporary Staffing Union	8631	A	714 728-5186	25084
Testamerica Laboratories Inc	8734	C	949 261-1022	26733
Tetra Tech Inc	8711	D	949 263-0846	25946
Tetra Tech Inc	8711	D	949 809-5000	25947
Texxis Limited	7371	E	213 631-3547	15500
Thomas Gallaway Corporation (PA)	5045	D	949 716-9500	7115
Tonner Hills Hsing Partners LP	1522	E	949 263-8676	1320
Toshiba Bus Solutions USA Inc (DH)	7629	C	949 462-6000	17917
Toshiba Education Center	8732	D	949 583-3000	26571
Total Renal Care Inc.	8092	D	949 930-6882	22492
Trace3 LLC (PA)	8742	D	949 333-2300	27493
Tradesmen International LLC	8741	D	949 588-3280	27065
TRC Solutions Inc (DH)	8748	C	949 753-0101	27888
Tressler LLP	8111	C	949 336-1200	23411
Tri Pointe Contractors LP (HQ)	1531	D	949 478-8600	1360
Tri Pointe Homes Inc (HQ)	1522	C	949 438-1400	1323
Trimark Raygal LLC	7389	D	949 474-1000	17524
True Air Mechanical Inc	1711	C	888 316-0642	2390
Truesdail Laboratories Inc	8731	E	714 730-6239	26478
Turner Techtronics Inc.	7378	D	949 724-1339	16295
TW Security Corp (DH)	5045	C	949 932-1000	7122
Tyler Palmieri Wiener	8111	D	949 851-9400	23417
UFS International LLC	7389	C	714 713-6311	17531
Uniglobe Travel West Inc (PA)	4724	D	949 623-9000	4957
Unisys Corporation	7373	A	949 380-5000	16069
United Agribusiness League (PA)	8611	E	800 223-4590	24987
United Cerebral Palsy Assoc.	8322	C	949 333-6400	24101
Universal Card Inc.	7389	B	949 861-4000	17547
Universal Care Inc (PA)	8093	D	562 424-6200	22707
University Cal Irvine Med Cent.	8099	B	714 456-5678	22899
University California Irvine	8731	D	949 824-2819	26484
Upstanding LLC	7372	C	949 788-9900	15886
US Best Repair Service Inc.	1521	C	888 750-2378	1252
USI South Coast	6411	D	949 790-9200	10820
V G Carelli International Corp	7389	E	310 247-8410	17556
Velapoint LLC	6411	C	877 434-1904	10824
Velocitel Rf Inc.	8711	D	949 809-4999	25989
Velocity Tech Solutions Inc.	7374	D	949 417-0260	16196
Venture Pacific Tools Inc	5072	D	949 475-5505	7607

Mergent email: customerrelations@mergent.com
1590

2019 Directory of California
Wholesalers and Services Companies

(P-0000) Products & Services Section entry number
(PA)=Parent Co (HQ)=Headquarters (DH)=Div Headquarters

	SIC	EMP	PHONE	ENTRY #
Viant Technology LLC **(DH)**	7319	C	949 861-8888	13986
Victory Foam Inc **(PA)**	5199	D	949 474-0690	9268
Villa Balboa Community Assoc	8641	D	949 450-1515	25281
Vinculums Services Inc	8748	C	949 783-3552	27902
Vision Solutions Inc **(PA)**	7371	D	949 253-6500	15529
Vision Solutions Inc	7379	D	949 253-6500	16528
Voit Development Manager Inc	6552	D	949 851-5110	11935
Vpm Management Inc	8741	C	949 863-1500	27088
W Brown & Assc Property & Csu	6411	D	949 851-2060	10825
Ware Malcomb **(PA)**	8712	C	949 660-9128	26119
Warmington Homes	1531	D	949 679-3100	1365
Warrior Custom Golf Inc **(PA)**	5091	C	949 699-2499	7942
Waste MGT Collectn Recycl Inc	4953	C	949 451-2600	6520
WD Partners Inc	8712	E	949 753-7676	26120
Wells Fargo Dealer Svcs Inc **(DH)**	6141	B	949 727-1002	9728
West Coast Consulting LLC **(PA)**	7372	D	949 250-4102	15891
Western Alliance Bank	6029	D	949 222-0855	9521
Western Growers Association **(PA)**	8611	C	949 863-1005	24991
Western Medical Management LLC	8741	E	949 260-6575	27093
Western National Contractors	8741	D	949 862-6200	27094
Western National Properties **(PA)**	1522	C	949 862-6200	1326
Western National Securities **(PA)**	6531	C	949 862-6200	11829
Western United Insurance Co	6411	C	800 959-9842	10829
Whiting-Turner Contracting Co	1542	E	949 863-0800	1702
Wimberly Allison Tong Goo Inc	8712	D	949 574-8500	26124
Wnc Housing LP	6799	E	714 662-5565	12285
Wolf Firm A Law Corporation	8111	D	949 720-9200	23444
Wood Environment &	8711	D	949 642-0245	26003
Woodbridge Village Association	8641	D	949 786-1800	25286
Wyndham Irvn-Orange Cnty Arprt	8741	D	949 863-1999	27100
Wynne Systems Inc **(DH)**	7371	D	949 224-6300	15551
Xavor Corporation	7379	D	949 529-7372	16537
Zippy Usa Inc	5063	D	949 366-9525	7405
Zymo Research Corp **(PA)**	8731	D	949 679-1190	26495

IRWINDALE, CA - Los Angeles County

	SIC	EMP	PHONE	ENTRY #
Agritec International Ltd	5099	E	626 812-7200	8016
American Med	4119	B	626 633-4600	3746
Arminak & Associates LLC	5199	C	626 358-4804	9195
Best Overnite Express Inc **(PA)**	4212	C	626 256-6340	3978
Bonneville Steel Inc	1791	D	866 956-8323	3365
Brightview Companies LLC	0781	C	626 574-3940	733
Calibre International LLC **(PA)**	8743	C	626 969-4660	27545
Central Garden & Pet Company	5199	C	626 334-9301	9205
Church & Larsen Inc	1742	C	626 303-8741	2866
Ds Services of America Inc	5149	C	626 472-7201	8785
East San Gbriel Vly Consortium	4119	D	626 960-3964	3788
Eggleston Youth Centers Inc **(PA)**	8322	C	626 480-8107	23781
Essilor Laboratories Amer Inc	5048	C	626 969-6181	7234
Gc Services Ltd Partnership	7322	C	626 851-8227	14004
Health Valley Foods Inc	5149	B	626 334-3241	8804
Mariposa Landscapes Inc **(PA)**	0782	C	626 960-0196	894
Mee Industries Inc	0711	C	626 359-4550	459
Metro One Telecom Inc	7311	C	626 337-8100	13868
Mountain Gear Corporation	5136	C	626 851-2488	8270
Neovia Logistics Dist LP	4731	C	626 359-4500	5117
Pacific Wine Distributors Inc	4212	D	626 471-9997	4049
Phfe Wic Program	8322	C	626 856-6650	23970
Pierre Landscape Inc	0781	C	818 373-0023	777
Public Hlth Fndation Entps Inc	8099	C	626 856-6600	22863
Service Solutions Group LLC	7629	D	626 960-9390	17912
Sinecera Inc	7389	D	626 962-1087	17471
Southern California Edison Co	4911	C	626 543-8081	6114
Southern California Edison Co	4911	E	626 815-7296	6127
Southern California Edison Co	4911	C	626 633-3070	6134
Southern California Edison Co	4911	C	626 814-4212	6136
Superior Communications **(PA)**	5065	C	877 522-4727	7548
Turbo Wholesale Tires Inc **(PA)**	5014	A	626 856-1400	6700
United Site Services Cal Inc **(PA)**	7359	D	626 462-9110	14552
Western Paving Contractors Inc	1611	D	626 338-7889	1869
Wor International Inc	5136	E	626 812-8888	8283

ISLETON, CA - Sacramento County

	SIC	EMP	PHONE	ENTRY #
Kay Dix Inc	0175	E	916 776-1701	221

IVANHOE, CA - Tulare County

	SIC	EMP	PHONE	ENTRY #
Family Healthcare Network	8011	C	559 798-1877	19471
Klink Citrus Association	0723	C	559 798-1881	535

JACKSON, CA - Amador County

	SIC	EMP	PHONE	ENTRY #
Amador Tlmne Cmnty Action Agcy **(PA)**	8399	C	209 296-2785	24732
Amador-Tolumne Cmnty Resources	8399	D	209 223-1485	24734
Apria Healthcare LLC	8099	C	209 223-7727	22736
AT&T Services Inc	4813	C	209 223-0012	5475
Farms of Amador	8699	D	209 257-0112	25422
Sita Ram LLC	7011	D	209 223-0211	13232
Sutter Amador Hospital **(HQ)**	8062	B	209 223-7500	21798

	SIC	EMP	PHONE	ENTRY #
Sutter Health	8011	C	209 223-5445	19962
Sutter Hlth Scrmnto Sierra Reg	8011	A	209 223-7540	19987
Tutera Group Inc	8361	D	209 223-2231	24702
Xp Power LLC	5065	D	209 267-1630	7567

JAMESTOWN, CA - Tuolumne County

	SIC	EMP	PHONE	ENTRY #
Chicken Ranch Bingo & Casino	7999	C	209 984-3000	19122
Diestel Turkey Ranch	0253	C	209 984-0826	437

JAMUL, CA - San Diego County

	SIC	EMP	PHONE	ENTRY #
Poltex Company Inc	7371	D	619 669-1846	15370
Spectrum Security Services Inc **(PA)**	7382	C	619 669-6660	16944
Steele Canyon Golf Club Corp **(PA)**	7992	C	619 441-6900	18765

JULIAN, CA - San Diego County

	SIC	EMP	PHONE	ENTRY #
Borrego Cmnty Hlth Foundation	8011	B	760 765-1223	19324
YMCA of San Diego County	8641	E	760 765-0642	25302

JURUPA VALLEY, CA - Riverside County

	SIC	EMP	PHONE	ENTRY #
Deluxe Auto Carriers Inc	4212	D	909 746-0900	4001
Optimum Con Fundations USA Inc	1771	D	877 212-7994	3298
Pavement Recycling Systems Inc **(PA)**	5093	C	951 682-1091	7986

KEENE, CA - Kern County

	SIC	EMP	PHONE	ENTRY #
United Farm Workers America **(PA)**	8631	C	661 822-5571	25086

KELSEY, CA - El Dorado County

	SIC	EMP	PHONE	ENTRY #
California Teachers Assn	8621	D	530 622-8013	25005

KELSEYVILLE, CA - Lake County

	SIC	EMP	PHONE	ENTRY #
BT Holdings Inc	0175	E	707 279-4317	215

KENTFIELD, CA - Marin County

	SIC	EMP	PHONE	ENTRY #
1125 Sir Francis Drake Bouleva	8069	C	415 456-9680	21994
Marin General Hospital	8062	A	415 925-7000	21576

KENWOOD, CA - Sonoma County

	SIC	EMP	PHONE	ENTRY #
Arthur Kunde & Sons Inc	0762	C	707 833-5501	681
Dirt Farmer & Co Inc	0172	D	707 833-2054	139
Palo Alto Vineyard MGT LLC	0761	D	707 996-7725	665

KERMAN, CA - Fresno County

	SIC	EMP	PHONE	ENTRY #
Acemi Nursery Inc	0174	D	559 842-7766	199
Hall AG Enterprises Inc	0761	C	559 846-7360	652
Hall Management Corp	8741	A	559 846-7382	26883
Kerman Telephone Co	4813	D	559 846-4954	5591
Kermantelnet Internet Service	4813	D	559 842-2223	5592
Sebastian Enterprises Inc **(PA)**	4813	C	559 946-4954	5639

KERNVILLE, CA - Kern County

	SIC	EMP	PHONE	ENTRY #
Eagle Rafting	4489	C	760 376-3648	4715

KETTLEMAN CITY, CA - Kings County

	SIC	EMP	PHONE	ENTRY #
Chemical Waste Management Inc	4953	D	559 386-9711	6372
Keenan Farms Inc	0173	D	559 945-1400	191

KEYES, CA - Stanislaus County

	SIC	EMP	PHONE	ENTRY #
A L Gilbert Company	5153	D	209 537-0766	8903

KING CITY, CA - Monterey County

	SIC	EMP	PHONE	ENTRY #
Anthony Harvesting Inc	0722	C	831 385-6460	472
El Camino Labor LLC	0761	D	831 809-9537	643
Fresh Farms Inc	0161	E	831 385-3285	53
L A Hearne Company **(PA)**	5191	D	831 385-5441	9082
Rava Ranches Inc	0291	E	831 385-3285	455
San Bernabe Vineyards	0172	D	831 385-4897	172
Southern Mnterey Cnty Mem Hosp **(PA)**	8062	B	831 385-6000	21768

KINGS BEACH, CA - Placer County

	SIC	EMP	PHONE	ENTRY #
Robert Morken Construction	1521	E	530 386-1512	1227

KINGS CANYON NATIONA, CA - Tulare County

	SIC	EMP	PHONE	ENTRY #
Montecito Sequoia Inc	7011	D	559 565-3388	12940

KINGSBURG, CA - Fresno County

	SIC	EMP	PHONE	ENTRY #
Design Machine and Mfg	7699	E	559 897-7374	17943
Enns Packing Company Inc	0175	E	559 897-7700	216
Kingsburg Apple Packers Inc	5148	B	559 897-5132	8699
Kingsburg Apple Partners LP	0175	D	559 897-5132	222
Mike Jensen Farms	0175	C	559 897-4192	226
Peterson Family Inc	0175	D	559 897-5064	227
Sun-Maid Growers California **(PA)**	5149	A	559 897-6235	8876
Sun-Maid Growers California	5149	B	559 897-8900	8877
Sunbridge Care Entps W Inc	8051	C	559 897-5881	20788
Sunbridge Care Entps W LLC	8051	A	559 897-5881	20789
Van Beurden Insurance Svcs Inc **(PA)**	6411	D	559 634-7125	10822
Wildwood Express	4213	E	559 805-3237	4304

KIRKWOOD, CA - Alpine County

	SIC	EMP	PHONE	ENTRY #
Mountain Springs Kirkwood LLC	7011	C	209 258-6000	12946

Employment Codes: A=Over 500 employees, B=251-500,
C=101-250, D=51-100, E=50

2019 Directory of California
Wholesalers and Services Companies

© Mergent Inc. 1-800-342-5647
1591

G
E
O
G
R
A
P
H
I
C

	SIC	EMP	PHONE	ENTRY #

KNIGHTS LANDING, CA - Yolo County

	SIC	EMP	PHONE	ENTRY #
Cattail Farms Inc	0112	D	916 207-6580	4

KORBEL, CA - Humboldt County

	SIC	EMP	PHONE	ENTRY #
Green Diamond Resource Company	0811	D	707 668-4400	991

LA CANADA, CA - Los Angeles County

	SIC	EMP	PHONE	ENTRY #
Child Educational Center	8351	D	818 354-3418	24287
Crescenta-Canada YMCA (PA)	8641	B	818 790-0123	25146
Dilbeck Inc (PA)	6531	D	818 790-6774	11401
La Canada Flintridge Cntry CLB	7997	D	818 790-0611	18944

LA CANADA FLINTRIDGE, CA - Los Angeles County

	SIC	EMP	PHONE	ENTRY #
Allen Lund Company LLC (HQ)	4731	D	818 790-1110	5002
Allen Lund Corporation (PA)	4731	E	818 790-8412	5004
Cal Tech Emplyees Fderal Cr Un (PA)	6061	D	818 952-4444	9542
California Peo Home	8361	D	626 300-0400	24449
Holmes Body Shop (PA)	7532	D	626 795-6447	17726
J&R Fleet Services LLC	7538	D	909 820-7000	17768

LA CRESCENTA, CA - Los Angeles County

	SIC	EMP	PHONE	ENTRY #
Century 21 Crest	6531	D	818 248-9100	11295
Dilbeck Inc	6531	D	818 248-2248	11402
EAM Enterprises Inc (PA)	6531	B	818 248-9100	11414
Mariner Health Care Inc	8051	D	818 957-0850	20629
Neardata Inc	8742	D	818 249-2469	27362

LA GRANGE, CA - Stanislaus County

	SIC	EMP	PHONE	ENTRY #
Green Tree Nursery	5193	E	209 874-9100	9137

LA HABRA, CA - Orange County

	SIC	EMP	PHONE	ENTRY #
Add2net Inc (PA)	7379	E	714 521-8150	16305
Albertsons LLC	4225	D	714 578-4670	4527
American First Credit Union (PA)	6061	D	562 691-1112	9539
Applied Language Solutions LLC	7389	C	800 579-5010	17008
Cellco Partnership	4812	D	562 694-8630	5321
City of La Habra	8322	E	562 905-9708	23580
Corner Bakery Store	5149	E	714 459-1420	8780
Haircutters	7241	D	562 690-2217	13685
Infinity Metals Inc	5051	E	562 697-8826	7281
Jayasinghe Medical Group Inc (PA)	8011	D	562 267-7000	19518
JKB Corporation	1771	E	562 905-3477	3272
JWdangelo Company Inc	5087	E	562 690-1000	7888
Life Care Centers America Inc	8051	D	562 690-0852	20579
Mary and Friends	8361	C	562 691-1575	24591
Peerless Maintenance Service	7349	B	714 871-3380	14347
Seasons	8361	D	562 691-1200	24668
Shinsuke Clifford Yamamoto	0782	D	714 992-5783	938
Southwest Inspection and Tstg	7389	D	562 941-2990	17480
Westridge Golf Inc	7992	D	562 690-4200	18778

LA HABRA HEIGHTS, CA - Orange County

	SIC	EMP	PHONE	ENTRY #
Hacienda Golf Club	7997	D	562 694-1081	18933
R Navarro Landscape Services	0782	D	562 690-6414	926

LA JOLLA, CA - San Diego County

	SIC	EMP	PHONE	ENTRY #
A Ursgi-Bmdc Joint Venture	8711	D	858 812-9292	25492
Advance Health Solutions LLC	8082	D	858 876-0136	22203
Aegis Software Inc	7319	E	858 551-1652	13964
Altium Inc (HQ)	7371	D	858 864-1661	14976
Altium LLC	7372	D	800 544-4186	15580
Bartell Hotels	7011	D	858 453-5500	12357
Bh Partn A Calif Limit Partne	7011	D	858 453-4420	12384
Birch Aquarium At Scripps	8422	E	858 534-4109	24925
Cal Southern Presbt Homes	8361	C	858 454-4201	24445
Califrnia Inst For Bmdical RES	8733	C	858 242-1000	26601
Chateau La Jolla Inn	7011	E	858 459-4451	12450
Citigroup Global Markets Inc	6211	D	858 456-4900	9936
Cloisters of La Jolla Inc	8051	D	858 459-4361	20315
Covenant Care La Jolla LLC	8051	C	858 453-5810	20355
Cripts Health Care	8011	E	858 554-8646	19423
CSS Holdings Inc	7371	D	888 884-9224	15090
Destination Residences LLC	7299	B	858 550-1000	13739
Dewhurst & Associates	1521	D	858 456-5345	1156
Edgewave Inc	7372	D	800 782-3762	15660
Everyone Counts Inc	7371	D	858 427-4673	15151
Fairway Technologies Inc	7379	D	858 454-4471	16365
Fargo Colonial LLC	7011	D	858 454-2181	12570
Front Porch Communities	6513	D	858 454-2151	11022
Gary Mary W Wireless Hlth Inst	8733	E	858 412-8600	26620
Geneohm Sciences Inc	8731	C	201 847-5824	26369
Glaxosmithkline LLC	5122	E	858 260-5900	8171
Hensel Phelps Construction Co	1542	D	619 544-6828	1551
Hotel La Jolla	7011	D	858 459-0261	12727
Impact Assessment Inc	8731	D	858 459-0142	26381
Institute For La Jolla	8733	C	858 752-6500	26625
J Craig Venter Institute Inc (PA)	8733	B	301 795-7000	26627
Joshua J Bodenstadt CPA A Prof	8721	E	858 642-5050	26232

	SIC	EMP	PHONE	ENTRY #
La Jolla Bch & Tennis CLB Inc (PA)	7997	C	858 454-7126	18946
La Jolla Bch & Tennis CLB Inc	7011	C	858 459-8271	12828
La Jolla Country Club Inc	7997	C	858 454-9601	18947
La Jolla Cove Hotel & Motel	7011	D	858 459-2621	12829
La Jolla Nurses Home Care	7361	C	858 454-9339	14660
La Jolla Orthopaedic	8011	D	858 657-0055	19632
Lav Hotel Corp	7011	C	858 454-0771	12839
Lavine Lofgren Morris Engelb	8721	E	858 455-1200	26245
Lawrence Family Jewish Commu (PA)	8399	C	858 362-1144	24800
Leidos Inc	8731	B	858 826-6000	26406
Machintel Corporation	7311	D	617 517-3090	13860
Marriott International Inc	7011	B	858 587-1414	12889
Merrill Lynch Pierce Fenner	6211	D	858 456-3600	9990
Mfw Partners	6512	E	858 454-8857	10912
Mountain-Pacific Financial (PA)	6531	D	858 456-8420	11616
Museum Cntmprary Art San Diego (PA)	8412	C	858 454-3541	24892
National Marine Fisheries Svc	8731	C	858 546-7081	26421
North County Ob-Gyn Med Group (PA)	8011	D	858 453-0753	19716
Northwestern Mutl Fincl Netwrk (PA)	6411	D	619 234-3111	10720
Park Hotels & Resorts Inc	7011	E	858 450-4569	13024
Professional Health Tech	8011	D	858 449-1599	19797
Robert Half International Inc	7361	D	888 744-9202	14735
Sanford Burnham Prebys Medical (PA)	8733	A	858 795-5000	26657
Scripps Clinic Carmel Valley	8011	B	858 554-8096	19861
Scripps Clinic Medical Group	8011	D	858 554-9606	19862
Scripps Dialasys Inc (PA)	8011	E	619 453-9070	19863
Scripps Health	8062	B	858 455-9100	21733
Scripps Health	8062	C	800 727-4777	21735
Scripps Health	8641	C	858 452-1279	25246
Scripps Health	8011	D	858 458-5100	19869
Scripps Health	8011	C	858 626-5200	19870
Scripps Health	8062	D	858 626-6150	21736
Scripps Health	8011	D	858 554-8892	19871
Scripps Health	8011	D	858 554-9469	19872
Scripps Health	8062	C	858 626-4123	21737
Scripps Health	8731	C	858 652-5504	26451
Scripps Memorial Hospitals	8062	D	858 450-4481	21738
Scripps Research Institute (PA)	8733	D	858 784-1000	26659
Sk Sanctuary Day Spa Salon LLC	7991	E	858 459-2400	18653
Synthetic Genomics Inc (DH)	8731	C	858 754-2900	26467
Theat and Arts Found of San Di	8641	C	858 623-3366	25268
Tom Hom Investment Corp	6512	E	858 456-5000	10956
Torreyana Grille	7011	D	858 558-1500	13333
UBS Financial Services Inc	7389	D	858 454-9181	17529
University Cal San Diego	7374	B	858 534-5000	16195
University Cal San Diego	8062	B	858 657-7000	21879
Vaco Lajolla LLC	7361	D	858 642-0000	14791
Wells Fargo Bank National Assn	6021	A	858 454-0362	9390
Wells Fargo Clearing Svcs LLC	6211	E	858 456-7706	10038
Westmont Living Inc (PA)	8361	C	858 456-1233	24722
Willis Allen Real Estate (PA)	6531	E	858 459-4033	11836
Willis Insurance Svcs Cal Inc	6311	D	858 678-2000	10152
YMCA of San Diego County	8641	C	858 453-3483	25294

LA MESA, CA - San Diego County

	SIC	EMP	PHONE	ENTRY #
Abbood Zeyad	8711	E	619 212-2820	25494
Age Advantage HM Care Svcs	8059	D	619 449-5900	20982
Anthonys Fish Grotto	5146	D	619 713-1853	8569
Automobile Club Southern Cal	8699	D	619 464-7001	25394
Bh-SD Opco LLC	8063	D	619 465-4411	21930
Brady Company/San Diego Inc	1742	B	619 462-2600	2854
Brady Socal Incorporated	1742	D	619 462-2600	2855
C & D Towing Specialists Inc (PA)	7549	D	619 463-8697	17854
Cal West General Engrg Inc	7359	E	619 469-5811	14484
California Coast Credit Union	6062	D	858 495-1600	9624
Center Glass Co No 3	1793	D	619 469-6181	3403
City of La Mesa	1611	E	619 667-1450	1742
Coldwell Banker	6531	D	619 460-6600	11328
Comprehensive Autism Ctr Inc	8049	D	951 813-4035	20172
Custom Medical Products Inc	5047	C	619 461-2068	7177
Davis Framing Inc	1751	D	619 463-2394	3028
Excel Home Health Inc	8082	E	619 460-6622	22294
Grossmont Hospital Corporation (HQ)	8062	A	619 740-6000	21436
Grossmont Hospital Corporation	8062	C	619 667-1900	21437
Grossmont Shopping Center Co	6512	D	619 465-2900	10887
Healthcare Group	8361	D	619 463-0281	24557
Helix Healthcare Inc	8063	B	619 465-4411	21957
Helix Water District (PA)	4941	C	619 466-0585	6261
Helm Management Co (PA)	6531	D	619 589-6222	11502
Home Instead Senior Care	8082	E	619 460-6622	22328
Kaiser Foundation Hospitals	8011	A	619 528-5000	19564
Kaiser Foundation Hospitals	8062	E	619 528-5000	21496
Kensington Agency Inc	7363	E	619 280-6993	14869
La Mesa Health Care Center	8059	E	619 465-1313	21132
La Mesa Intrnl Mdc Mdcl Gr	8011	E	619 460-4050	19638
La Mesa Lions Club	8641	D	619 469-9988	25182

Mergent email: customerrelations@mergent.com

1592

2019 Directory of California
Wholesalers and Services Companies

(P-0000) Products & Services Section entry number
(PA)=Parent Co (HQ)=Headquarters (DH)=Div Headquarters

	SIC	EMP	PHONE	ENTRY #
Life Gnerations Healthcare LLC	8051	C	619 460-2330	20589
Perry & Shaw Inc	8711	D	619 390-6500	25874
Pvcc Inc (PA)	6512	D	619 463-4040	10929
Razavi Corporation	8051	D	619 465-8010	20716
San Diego Mortgage & RE	6531	E	619 334-7779	11752
Scripps Health	8011	D	619 670-5400	19865
Senior Care Inc	8052	C	619 928-5644	20954
Sharp Healthcare	8011	D	619 460-6200	19887
Umpqua Bank	6022	D	619 668-5159	9492
YMCA of San Diego County	8641	D	619 464-1323	25297

LA MIRADA, CA - Los Angeles County

	SIC	EMP	PHONE	ENTRY #
Aecom Energy & Cnstr Inc	8711	C	714 228-4300	25508
American Financial Network Inc	8742	D	562 926-2401	27129
American Golf Corporation	7992	D	562 943-7123	18683
B S A Partners	7011	D	714 523-2800	12348
Beven-Herron Inc	1761	D	714 523-5870	3129
Bravo Tech Inc	4812	E	714 230-8333	5301
Compremex LLC	4215	C	714 739-1348	4396
Dynamex Operations West Inc	4215	E	714 994-1615	4398
E T Horn Company (PA)	5169	D	714 523-8050	8926
Eagle High Reach Equipment LLC	7359	D	619 265-2637	14501
Estes Express Lines Inc	4213	C	714 994-3770	4138
Estes Express Lines Inc	4213	D	714 523-1122	4146
Far East Broadcasting Co Inc	4832	D	562 947-4651	5717
Georgia-Pacific LLC	5093	C	562 926-8888	7977
Green Wave Ingredients Inc	5122	E	562 207-9770	8173
H&E Equipment Services Inc	7359	C	714 522-6590	14507
Healthpointe Medical Group Inc (PA)	8011	D	714 956-2663	19494
Katana Racing Inc (PA)	5013	C	562 977-8565	6651
Life Care Centers America Inc	8051	D	562 943-7156	20580
Life Care Centers America Inc	8051	D	562 947-8691	20581
Life Care Centers America Inc	8051	D	562 943-7156	20585
Makita USA Inc (HQ)	5072	C	714 522-8088	7597
Mejico Express Inc (PA)	4513	C	714 690-8300	4842
Nittany Lion Landscaping Inc	0782	D	714 635-1788	911
Northeast Protective Svcs Inc	7381	D	800 577-0899	16744
Norwalk La Mirada Unif	8621	D	714 521-0970	25031
Physical Distribution Svc Inc (PA)	4225	D	323 881-0886	4611
Precision Relocation Inc	4214	C	714 690-9344	4368
Reliance Steel & Aluminum Co	5051	C	714 736-4800	7307
Southern Cal Spcialty Care Inc (DH)	8062	D	562 944-1900	21765
Special Dispatch Cal Inc (PA)	4214	D	714 521-8200	4374
Stainless Stl Fabricators Inc.	5084	D	714 739-9904	7805
Sunstone Hotel Investors LLC	7011	C	714 739-8500	13294
Tiffany Dale Inc (PA)	5023	D	714 739-2700	6793
Tomarco Contractor Spc Inc (PA)	5072	D	714 523-1771	7606
US Foods Inc	5141	D	714 670-3500	8480
US Foods Inc	5141	E	714 670-3500	8481
US Foods Inc	5149	C	714 670-3500	8897
Veritiv Operating Company	5113	C	714 690-4000	8130
Winco Industries Company	5087	E	562 926-5600	7903
Wow Party Rental Inc	7359	D	714 367-3380	14558

LA PALMA, CA - Orange County

	SIC	EMP	PHONE	ENTRY #
Applecare Medical MGT LLC	8741	C	714 443-4507	26762
Arco Envmtl Remediation LLC	8742	D	714 523-5674	27142
Automatic Data Processing Inc	7374	D	714 994-2000	16094
Commercial Carriers Insur Agcy	6331	C	562 404-4900	10347
Dr Fresh LLC	5122	D	714 690-1573	8166
Kaiser Foundation Hospitals	8011	E	714 562-3420	19600
La Palma Hospital Medical Ctr	8062	B	714 670-7400	21544
Pacific Bay Lending Group	6163	D	714 367-5125	9900
Parsons Corporation	1629	C	714 562-5725	2054
Slade Gorton & Co Inc	5146	D	714 676-4200	8601
Sunrise Senior Living LLC	8051	D	714 739-8111	20826
Tech Knowledge Associates LLC	7699	D	714 735-3810	17994
Travelers Club Luggage Inc	5099	D	714 523-8808	8062
Veritiv Operating Company	5113	B	714 690-6600	8135

LA PUENTE, CA - Los Angeles County

	SIC	EMP	PHONE	ENTRY #
Alert Insulation Company Inc	1742	D	626 961-9113	2838
Apw Construction (PA)	1622	D	626 820-0812	1874
Arakelian Enterprises Inc	4953	D	818 768-1477	6343
Arrow Disposal Services Inc	4953	E	626 336-2255	6345
Athens Disposal Company Inc (PA)	4953	B	626 336-3636	6348
Cacique Inc	5143	C	626 961-3399	8514
Cal-Lift Inc	5084	D	562 566-1400	7736
Ldla Clothing LLC	5137	D	323 312-2805	8314
Plaza De La Raza Child Develop (PA)	8351	D	562 776-1301	24371
Powell Works Inc	5084	B	909 861-6699	7784
San Gabriel Vly Training Ctr (PA)	8331	D	626 330-3185	24226
Wave Plastic Surgery Ctr Inc	8011	B	626 964-7788	20093

LA QUINTA, CA - Riverside County

	SIC	EMP	PHONE	ENTRY #
Adams Learning Center	8351	E	760 777-4260	24260
Cartwright Termite & Pest Ctrl	7342	E	760 771-6091	14138
Chapman Golf Development LLC	7997	D	760 564-8723	18887
CIT Bank NA	6021	D	760 771-3498	9302
Deser Sands Unifi Schoo Distr	8351	D	760 777-4200	24313
Imperial Irrigation District	4939	C	760 398-5811	6197
Interiors By Linda	7389	E	760 341-9651	17246
Ksl II Mngement Operations LLC	8741	D	760 564-8000	26924
La Quinta Country Club	7997	D	760 564-4151	18948
Lqr Property LLC	7011	C	760 564-4111	12865
Madison Club Owners Assn	7992	D	760 777-9320	18732
Professional Golf MGT LLC	8741	D	760 564-0804	26999
Silver Rock Resort Golf Club	7992	D	760 777-8884	18763
TD Desert Dev Ltd Partnr (HQ)	6552	C	760 777-1001	11929
Tradition Golf Club Associates	7992	D	760 564-3355	18772
Trilogy Golf At La Quinta	7992	D	760 771-0707	18774

LA VERNE, CA - Los Angeles County

	SIC	EMP	PHONE	ENTRY #
American Eagle Services Inc	7363	D	574 859-2055	14814
Automobile Club Southern Cal	8699	C	909 392-1444	25392
Brethren Hillcrest Homes	8361	C	909 593-4917	24439
David and Margaret Home Inc	8361	C	909 596-5921	24500
Haaker Equipment Company (PA)	5012	C	909 542-0800	6596
Haynes Family Programs Inc	8361	C	909 593-2581	24556
J C French & Company	1721	D	909 596-1423	2447
Jet Delivery Inc (PA)	4215	D	800 716-7177	4421
Mass Electric Construction Co	1731	C	800 933-6322	2636
Metropolitan Water District	4941	B	909 593-7474	6284
Onemain Holdings Inc	6282	C	909 392-5578	10100
Peter Kiewit Sons Inc	1611	C	909 962-6001	1838
Steve and Beth Chaput	7349	C	909 596-9994	14401
Tofasco of America Inc (PA)	8741	C	909 392-8282	27063

LADERA RANCH, CA - Orange County

	SIC	EMP	PHONE	ENTRY #
AT&T Corp.	4812	D	949 364-4052	5269
Xqawesome Inc	8331	C	949 929-9622	24254

LAFAYETTE, CA - Contra Costa County

	SIC	EMP	PHONE	ENTRY #
Advanced Acoustics	1742	E	925 299-0515	2836
Arthur J Gallagher & Co	6411	E	925 299-1112	10547
Cellco Partnership	4812	C	925 472-0487	5360
Child Day School (PA)	8351	D	925 284-7092	24281
Clubsport San Ramon LLC	7991	C	925 283-4000	18587
Eden Housing Inc	1522	D	925 297-4297	1283
Independent Quality Care Inc	8059	D	925 284-5544	21120
Murphy McKay & Associates Inc	7379	D	925 283-9555	16429
Optimum Solutions Group LLC	7372	C	415 954-7100	15791
Prestige Car Wash Lafayette LP	7542	C	925 283-1190	17836
Rate Is Low	6162	E	925 299-9364	9853
Techexcel Inc (PA)	7371	D	925 871-3900	15497

LAGUNA BEACH, CA - Orange County

	SIC	EMP	PHONE	ENTRY #
Baja Life Online Partners	7371	E	949 376-4619	15018
C & B Delivery Services	4225	D	909 623-4708	4534
Esolar Inc (DH)	1629	D	818 303-9500	2031
Festival of Arts Laguna Beach	7999	D	949 494-1145	19174
Home Express Delivery Svc LLC	4731	A	949 715-9844	5088
JC Resorts LLC	8741	B	949 376-2779	26903
Laguna Bch Golf Bnglow Vlg LLC	0291	E	949 499-2271	451
Laguna Bch Golf Bnglow Vlg LLC	7992	D	949 499-2271	18725
Laguna Playhouse (PA)	7922	C	949 497-2787	18379
Landmark Hotels LLC	7011	C	949 640-5040	12836
National Film Laboratories	7819	C	323 466-0281	18204
Oc Accessories LLC	7389	D	949 229-2410	17365
Pacific Housing Management (PA)	6531	D	714 508-1777	11646
Seaside Laguna Inn & Suites	7011	D	949 494-9717	13201
South Coast Water District (PA)	4941	D	949 499-4555	6314
Spencer Recovery Centers Inc (PA)	8093	D	949 376-3705	22686

LAGUNA HILLS, CA - Orange County

	SIC	EMP	PHONE	ENTRY #
Age Well Senior Services Inc (PA)	8322	D	949 855-8033	23463
Altec Products Inc (PA)	7389	D	949 727-1248	16997
American Capital Group Inc	6159	D	949 271-5800	9752
Atrilogy Solutions Group Inc (PA)	8748	E	949 777-4700	27650
Automobile Club Southern Cal	8699	E	949 951-1400	25391
Bel Esprit Builders Inc	1542	E	949 709-3500	1477
Birtcher/Aetna Laguna Hills	6513	D	949 458-2311	10988
California Limousines	4119	C	949 581-7531	3782
Care Plus Home Care Inc	8082	C	949 716-2273	22249
Care Plus Nursing Services Inc	8082	C	949 600-7194	22250
Cirrus Health II LP	8011	C	949 855-0562	19382
Dva Renal Healthcare Inc	8092	D	949 588-9211	22474
F M Tarbell Co	6531	D	949 830-6030	11433
Factory R D	5049	C	949 900-3460	7242
Gate Three Healthcare LLC	8361	C	949 770-3348	24538
Hardrock Tile & Marble Inc	1741	D	714 282-1766	2809
Harvest Small Business Fin LLC	6163	D	949 446-8683	9886
Herren Enterprises Inc.	4119	D	949 951-1666	3808
Hillview Acres	8361	D	714 694-2828	24563

Employment Codes: A=Over 500 employees, B=251-500,
C=101-250, D=51-100, E=50

2019 Directory of California
Wholesalers and Services Companies

© Mergent Inc. 1-800-342-5647
1593

Company	SIC	EMP	PHONE	ENTRY #
Hines Nurseries LLC	5193	D	602 254-2831	9141
Jamboree Realty Corp **(PA)**	6531	C	949 380-0300	11529
Kennedy Pipeline Company	1623	D	949 380-8363	1943
Laguna Hills Hotel Dev Ventr	7011	D	949 586-5000	12832
Laguna Woods Golf Club	7997	E	949 597-4336	18951
Magarro Farms	0723	D	949 859-6506	538
Marginpoint **(PA)**	8742	D	949 766-9933	27318
Metron-Athene Inc **(PA)**	7371	D	949 588-5757	15280
Muller-Ing-Gateway LLC	6512	D	951 687-2900	10915
Nms Data Inc	8748	E	949 472-2700	27804
Parallax Capital Partners LLC **(PA)**	6726	C	949 296-4800	12065
Professional Community MGT Cal	6531	C	949 597-4200	11685
Rye Electric Inc	1731	D	949 441-0545	2718
Saddle Corp **(PA)**	1799	D	949 589-3422	3579
Saddleback Memorial Med Ctr **(HQ)**	8062	A	949 837-4500	21692
Saddleback Memorial Med Ctr	8071	D	949 452-3405	22138
South County Orthopedic Specia	8011	D	949 586-3200	19899
Sun Coast Gen Insur Agcy Inc	6411	D	949 768-1132	10796
Sunrise Senior Living Inc	8051	D	949 581-6111	20809
Support Associates Inc	8744	C	949 595-4379	27606
Tech Mahindra (americas) Inc	7371	D	949 462-0640	15496
Tom Ray Industries Inc	5023	D	949 380-8333	6794
Varsity Contractors Inc	7349	D	949 586-8283	14424
Villageway Management Inc	6531	D	949 450-1515	11813

LAGUNA NIGUEL, CA - Orange County

Company	SIC	EMP	PHONE	ENTRY #
Aegis Senior Communities LLC	8361	E	949 496-8080	24411
Birtcher Andrson Property Svcs **(PA)**	6531	D	949 831-0707	11243
Bitfone Corporation **(PA)**	7371	E	949 234-7000	15027
California Title Company **(PA)**	6361	D	949 582-8709	10436
Cellco Partnership	4812	D	949 831-3955	5388
E Tradeshowgirlscom	7389	D	949 661-4177	17144
Enterprise Rent-A-Car	7514	D	949 373-9350	17635
First Team RE - Orange Cnty	6531	D	949 240-7979	11463
Focus 360 Inc	7371	D	949 234-0008	15165
Mission Internal Med Group Inc	8011	D	949 364-3605	19692
Moulton Niguel Water **(PA)**	4941	D	949 831-2500	6289
Pacific Line Clean-Up Inc	1799	C	949 348-0245	3561
Pacific Monarch Resorts Inc	6531	E	949 228-1396	11648
Rancho Niguel Dental Group	8021	E	949 249-4180	20133
Spearman Clubs Inc **(PA)**	7999	D	949 496-2070	19240

LAGUNA WOODS, CA - Orange County

Company	SIC	EMP	PHONE	ENTRY #
Countryside Inn-Corona LP	7011	D	949 588-0131	12486
Laguna Woods Village	6531	A	949 597-4267	11556
Professional Community MGT Cal	6531	C	949 206-0580	11684
Rainbow Realty Corporation	6531	D	949 770-9626	11700
Withrow Phrm & Hlth Spc Lab	5122	D	323 721-4281	8222

LAKE ARROWHEAD, CA - San Bernardino County

Company	SIC	EMP	PHONE	ENTRY #
Lake Arrwhead Rsort Oprtor Inc **(HQ)**	7011	C	909 336-1511	12833
Mountains Community Hosp Fndtn	8062	C	909 336-3651	21603
RE Max All Cities Lk Arrowhead	6531	E	909 337-6111	11706

LAKE ELSINORE, CA - Riverside County

Company	SIC	EMP	PHONE	ENTRY #
AAA Restoration Inc	1799	E	951 471-5828	3479
Castle & Cooke Inc	1522	A	951 245-0476	1273
Chief Trnsp & Engrg Contrs Inc	1611	D	951 258-6607	1737
County of Riverside	8322	D	951 245-3060	23708
County of Riverside	8322	D	951 245-3100	23711
Division Three Cnstr Svcs	1542	D	951 609-3043	1521
Elsinore Vly Municpl Wtr Dst **(PA)**	4941	D	951 674-3146	6253
F M Tarbell Co	6531	D	951 471-5333	11427
F M Tarbell Co	6531	D	951 471-5333	11439
Gbc Concrete Masnry Cnstr Inc	1741	C	951 245-2355	2808
Hakes Sash & Door Inc	1751	C	951 674-2414	3039
JD Miller Construction Inc	1721	E	951 471-3513	2450
Lake Elsinore Unified Schl Dst	8351	D	951 253-7091	24337
Near-Cal Corp	1542	E	951 245-5400	1600
Onemain Holdings Inc	6162	C	951 245-5029	9839
Pacific Clay Products Inc	5032	C	661 857-1401	6902
Perfection Glass Inc	1793	E	951 674-0240	3407
Prime Communications LP	4813	D	951 253-3304	5630
Sci Inc	1771	D	951 245-7511	3322
Service Transport Inc	4214	D	951 403-3464	4372
Timeshare Relief Inc	6541	C	951 525-1539	11849
Volume Services Inc	7999	D	951 245-9995	19260
West Coast Ltg & Enrgy Inc	1731	D	951 296-0680	2786

LAKE FOREST, CA - Orange County

Company	SIC	EMP	PHONE	ENTRY #
24 Hour Fitness Usa Inc	7991	D	949 830-4213	18562
Advanced Protection Inds Inc	7382	E	800 662-1711	16870
AMF Bowling Centers Inc	7933	E	949 770-0055	18479
Apria Healthcare Group Inc **(HQ)**	8082	D	949 639-2000	22226
Apria Healthcare LLC	8099	C	949 639-2000	22737
Apria Healthcare LLC **(DH)**	5047	B	949 639-2163	7156
Arb Inc **(HQ)**	1629	C	949 598-9242	2008

Company	SIC	EMP	PHONE	ENTRY #
Atria Senior Living Inc	8361	D	805 370-5400	24424
Aveva Software LLC **(DH)**	7373	B	949 727-3200	15919
Beech Street Corporation **(DH)**	8741	B	949 672-1000	26779
Cellco Partnership	4812	D	949 472-0700	5350
Chapel Funding Corporation	6162	C	949 580-1800	9791
Commercial Indus Design Co Inc	5045	C	949 273-6199	7024
Digital Networks Group Inc	7373	D	949 428-6333	15944
Dove Ceilings Inc **(PA)**	1742	E	949 597-1794	2876
Eagle Community Credit Union **(PA)**	6062	D	949 588-9400	9629
El Toro Water Distr Public Fac **(PA)**	4941	D	949 837-1662	6252
Environmental Resolutions Inc	8748	B	949 457-8950	27721
Environments For Learning Inc **(PA)**	8351	C	949 855-5630	24319
Freedom Village Healthcare Ctr	8051	D	949 472-4733	20438
Golden West Custom WD Shutters	5099	E	949 951-0600	8034
Great Destinations Inc	8742	D	949 667-9401	27254
Gypsum Contractors Inc	1742	E	949 340-9100	2890
Heinaman Contract Glazing Inc **(PA)**	1799	C	949 587-0266	3531
Infor (us) Inc	7372	C	678 319-8000	15710
Insight Health Corp **(DH)**	8069	E	877 566-6500	22026
Inspiria Inc **(PA)**	8711	D	949 206-0606	25748
Insulectro **(PA)**	5065	D	949 587-3200	7494
Intertek Group Inc	8734	D	949 448-4100	26706
Intertek Testing Svcs NA Inc	8734	D	949 448-4100	26707
Intertek Testing Svcs NA Inc	7389	D	949 349-1684	17249
Itek Services Inc	7379	D	949 770-4835	16414
Juniper Rock Corporation	1423	B	949 500-1797	1089
Lake Forest LI Master Homeown	8641	D	949 586-0860	25185
Life Care Centers America Inc	8051	C	949 380-9380	20584
Mike Rovner Construction Inc	8741	C	949 458-1562	26947
Molly Maid	7349	D	949 367-9400	14326
Nakase Brothers Wholesale Nurs	5193	C	949 855-4388	9151
Natures Image Inc	0781	C	949 680-4400	771
Nelson Moving & Storage Inc	4213	E	949 582-0380	4234
Panasonic	5064	C	949 581-0661	7421
Panasonic Avionics Corporation	8711	D	949 472-2376	25864
Panasonic Avionics Corporation **(DH)**	8711	D	949 672-2000	25865
Parsons Government Svcs Inc **(HQ)**	8731	D	949 768-8161	26433
Performance Building Services	7349	C	949 364-4364	14349
Primoris Services Corporation	1623	B	949 598-9242	1971
Quantum Technologies Inc	1311	C	949 399-4500	1027
RJP Construction & Painting **(PA)**	1721	D	949 707-5449	2474
Ses LLC	7371	A	949 727-3200	15440
Streamline Finishes Inc	1542	D	949 600-8964	1659
Toshiba Amer Bus Solutions Inc **(DH)**	5044	B	949 462-6000	6984
US Real Estate Services Inc	6531	D	949 598-9920	11808
Vadnais Trenchless Svcs Inc	1623	B	858 550-1460	1993
Validus Group Inc	7361	D	949 457-7606	14792
Vintage Design Inc **(PA)**	1752	D	714 974-4822	3119
W B Starr Inc	0782	D	949 770-8835	959
Wonderware Corporation **(DH)**	5045	B	949 727-3200	7129
Xpo Logistics Freight Inc	4213	D	949 581-9030	4317

LAKE ISABELLA, CA - Kern County

Company	SIC	EMP	PHONE	ENTRY #
Kern River Tours Inc	7999	D	760 379-4616	19193
Kern Valley Hosp Foundation **(PA)**	8062	B	760 379-2681	21533

LAKE VIEW TERRACE, CA - Los Angeles County

Company	SIC	EMP	PHONE	ENTRY #
Phoenix Houses Los Angeles Inc	8361	D	818 686-3000	24631

LAKEPORT, CA - Lake County

Company	SIC	EMP	PHONE	ENTRY #
County Lake Health Services	8621	D	707 263-1090	25013
Evergreen At Lakeport LLC **(PA)**	8051	D	707 263-6382	20415
Konocti Vista Casino **(PA)**	7011	C	707 262-1900	12821
Lake Cnty Trbal Hlth Cnsortium	8021	D	707 263-8382	20123
People Services Inc **(PA)**	8361	D	707 263-3810	24628
Sequoia Senior Solutions Inc	8322	D	707 263-3070	24046
Sutter Health	8011	D	707 263-6885	19964
Sutter Health	8031	C	707 263-3520	20150
Sutter Health	8011	D	707 263-6885	19977
Sutter Lakeside Hospital **(HQ)**	8062	B	707 262-5000	21841
Windflower Holdings LLC	8051	D	707 263-6101	20895
Xpo Enterprise Services Inc	4213	C	916 399-8291	4308

LAKESHORE, CA - Fresno County

Company	SIC	EMP	PHONE	ENTRY #
China Peak Mountain Resort LLC	7011	D	559 233-2500	12453

LAKESIDE, CA - San Diego County

Company	SIC	EMP	PHONE	ENTRY #
A M Ortega Construction Inc **(PA)**	1731	C	619 390-1988	2495
Barona Creek Golf Club	7992	D	619 387-7018	18687
Barona Resort & Casino	7011	A	619 443-2300	12352
Buds & Son Trucking Inc	4212	D	619 443-4200	3981
Clauss Construction	1795	D	619 390-4940	3449
Errecas Inc	1794	D	619 390-6400	3424
Global Power Group Inc **(PA)**	1731	D	619 579-1221	2591
Johnson Finch & McClure Cnstr **(PA)**	1799	C	619 938-9727	3540
Lakeside Fire Protection Dst	7389	D	619 390-2350	17287
Lakeside Tax & Financial Svcs	7389	D	619 561-2681	17288

	SIC	EMP	PHONE	ENTRY #
LLC Brewer Crane	7353	D	619 390-8252	14445
Marco Crane & Rigging Co	7353	D	619 938-8080	14447
Minshew Brothers Stl Cnstr Inc	1541	C	619 561-5700	1421
Nicholas Grant Corporation	1611	D	619 390-3900	1826
Pacific Green Landscape Inc	0782	C	619 390-1546	915
Rdo Construction Equipment Co	7353	D	619 443-3758	14455
Standard Drywall Inc (HQ)	1742	B	619 443-7034	2962
Towne Construction Inc	1742	D	619 390-4557	2972
Turning Point For God	7922	D	619 258-3600	18412
Unyeway Inc	8331	D	619 562-6330	24243
Wagner Construction Co (PA)	1771	C	619 873-2160	3343
Williams & Sons Masonry Inc	1741	D	619 443-1751	2830

LAKEWOOD, CA - Los Angeles County

	SIC	EMP	PHONE	ENTRY #
Admiral Home Health Inc	8082	D	562 421-0777	22202
American Golf Corporation	7992	E	562 421-0550	18681
Berro Management	6531	D	562 432-3444	11240
Cal Bowl Enterprises LLC	7933	E	562 421-8448	18485
Caremore Medical Group Inc	6321	B	562 622-2900	10162
Center For Dscovery Adoloscent	8069	E	562 425-6404	22003
Contractor Warehouse	1542	D	562 633-1428	1510
County of Los Angeles	8322	B	562 497-3500	23660
Discovery Practice Management	8011	E	562 425-6404	19446
Lakewood Cerritos Dental Ctr	8021	D	562 860-0388	20124
Nationwide Theatres Corp	7933	D	562 421-8448	18496
Pacific Theaters Inc	7832	D	562 634-1183	18310
Rainbow Properties Inc	6531	D	323 562-0730	11699
Tarzana Treatment Centers Inc	8093	C	562 428-4111	22693
Tenet Healthsystem Medical	8011	A	562 531-2550	20000
Time Warner Cable Inc	4841	C	424 529-6011	5956
Young Mens Chrstn Assc Gr L B	8641	D	562 272-4884	25333
Young Mens Chrstn Assc Gr L B	8641	D	562 425-7431	25336

LAMONT, CA - Kern County

	SIC	EMP	PHONE	ENTRY #
Community Action Partnr Kern	8399	D	661 845-3901	24760
Grimmway Enterprises Inc	5148	B	661 845-3758	8694
Maxco Supply Inc	5113	D	559 646-6700	8109

LANCASTER, CA - Los Angeles County

	SIC	EMP	PHONE	ENTRY #
Aecom	8712	C	661 266-0802	26018
Allied Risk Management Inc	7381	D	661 305-0455	16548
American Med Rspnse Sthern Cal	4119	A	661 945-9310	3751
Antelope Valley Foundation	8322	E	661 945-7290	23481
Antelope Valley Hospital Inc	8011	D	661 949-1550	19298
Antelope Valley Hospital Inc	8011	C	661 726-6180	19299
Antelope Valley Hospital Inc (PA)	8062	A	661 949-5000	21289
Antelope Valley Medical Group	8011	E	661 945-2783	19300
Antelope Vly Dom Vlnce Council (PA)	8322	D	661 723-7772	23482
Antelope Vly Retirement HM Inc	8059	D	661 948-7501	20993
Antelope Vly Retirement HM Inc	8059	C	661 949-5524	20994
Antelope Vly Schl Trnsp Agcy	4151	C	661 945-3621	3907
BDR Industries Inc (PA)	4841	D	661 940-8554	5857
C D R Enterprises Inc	1742	D	661 940-0344	2857
California Traffic Safety Inst	8748	D	661 940-1907	27673
Cellco Partnership	4812	D	661 726-4762	5396
Counseling and Research Assoc	8361	D	661 726-5500	24478
County of Los Angeles	8322	B	661 940-4181	23655
County of Los Angeles	8322	C	661 723-4051	23658
County of Los Angeles	8322	C	661 948-2320	23662
County of Los Angeles	8711	C	661 723-6088	25626
County of Los Angeles	8011	A	661 948-8581	19413
County of Los Angeles	8093	D	661 524-2005	22549
Daniel O Mongiano MD A PR	8011	E	661 951-9195	19426
Desert Haven Enterprises Inc (PA)	0782	A	661 948-8402	825
Desert Haven Enterprises Inc	0782	B	661 948-8402	826
Easter Seals Southern Cal Inc	8399	E	661 723-3414	24778
Esna Corporation	6163	E	661 206-6010	9882
Excel Contractors Inc	1521	D	661 942-6944	1162
Fidelity National Title Co	6361	E	818 881-7800	10452
Frito-Lay North America Inc	5145	C	661 951-1399	8551
Gene Wheeler Farms Inc	0191	C	661 951-2100	344
Go Get Em Inc	7382	D	702 985-5637	16899
Granite Construction Company	1611	C	661 726-4447	1776
Hartwig Realty Inc (PA)	6531	D	661 948-8424	11500
Hathaway-Sycamores Chld Fam Sv	8361	A	661 942-5749	24553
High Desert Med Corp A Med Grp (PA)	8011	D	661 945-5984	19500
High Desert Phoenix	7999	E	661 547-5630	19181
Iheartcommunications Inc	4832	D	661 942-1268	5728
Kaiser Foundation Hospitals	8062	C	661 726-2500	21478
Kaiser Foundation Hospitals	8062	B	661 949-5000	21492
Kaiser Foundation Hospitals	8011	A	661 951-0070	19566
Keolis Transit America Inc	4111	D	661 341-3910	3662
La County High Desert Hlth Sys	8011	B	661 945-8461	19631
Lancaster Comm Svcs Fndtn	7538	D	661 723-6230	17769
Lancaster Crdlgy Med Group Inc (PA)	8011	D	661 726-3058	19641
Lancaster Jethawks	7997	D	661 726-5400	18955

	SIC	EMP	PHONE	ENTRY #
Lantz Security Systems Inc (PA)	7381	D	661 949-3565	16716
Metropolitan Dst Private SEC	7381	D	661 942-3999	16731
Michaels Stores Inc	5199	C	661 951-3500	9235
Mission Linen Supply	7213	D	661 948-5051	13544
Nibbelink Masonry Cnstr Corp	1741	D	661 948-7859	2818
North La County Regional Ctr	8748	D	661 945-6761	27806
Opsec Specialized Protection	7381	D	661 942-3999	16750
Penny Lane Centers	8399	C	661 274-0770	24827
Rich Meiers Landscaping Inc (PA)	0781	D	661 723-2220	782
SA Recycling LLC	4953	C	661 723-1383	6469
Sarah Elizabeth Treusdell	8093	E	661 949-0131	22677
Simulations Plus Inc (PA)	7373	D	661 723-7723	16052
Spiral Technology Inc	8711	D	661 723-3148	25922
Sygma Network Inc	5149	C	661 723-0405	8880
Tarzana Treatment Centers Inc	8093	D	661 726-2630	22695
United Parcel Service Inc OH	4215	C	800 828-8264	4463
United Way Inc	8399	C	661 874-4288	24853
V Troth Inc	6531	D	661 948-4646	11810
Warner Media LLC	4841	D	661 344-1546	5966
West Antlope Vly Hstorical Soc	8412	D	661 945-5369	24921
Wilshire Insurance Company	6411	E	661 940-7300	10831

LARKSPUR, CA - Marin County

	SIC	EMP	PHONE	ENTRY #
All California Mortgage Inc (PA)	6162	D	415 925-5225	9769
Courtyard By Marriott	7011	D	415 925-1800	12490
Golden Gate	4785	C	415 455-2000	5216
Hospice By Bay (PA)	8082	C	415 927-2273	22334
Lilien LLC (HQ)	7373	E	415 389-7500	15998
ONeill Beverages Co LLC (PA)	0172	D	844 825-6600	164
Power Factors LLC	5045	D	415 299-7448	7092
Sysorex USA (HQ)	7373	D	415 389-7500	16062

LATHROP, CA - San Joaquin County

	SIC	EMP	PHONE	ENTRY #
Cunha Draying Inc	4213	D	209 858-1400	4120
Elma Electronic Inc	5065	E	209 858-2411	7471
Global Building Services Inc	8999	B	209 858-9501	27929
Knight-Swift Trnsp Hldings Inc	4213	D	209 858-1630	4206
Mid Valley Plastering Inc	1742	B	209 858-9766	2919
Nbccat Corp	7539	D	209 858-0283	17796
Performant Recovery Inc	7322	C	209 858-3500	14016
Super Store Industries	5149	B	209 858-3365	8878
UPS Ground Freight Inc	4213	D	209 858-5095	4288

LATON, CA - Fresno County

	SIC	EMP	PHONE	ENTRY #
Zonneveld Dairies Inc	0241	D	559 923-4546	428
Zonneveld Farms	0241	D	559 923-4546	429

LAWNDALE, CA - Los Angeles County

	SIC	EMP	PHONE	ENTRY #
Advanced Veterinary Care Ctr	0742	D	310 542-8018	595
Alondra Golf Course Inc	7992	D	310 217-9915	18680
Lawndale Healthcare & Wellness	8051	D	310 679-3344	20577
McCarthy Framing Construction	1751	D	310 219-3038	3051
Southwestern Orthpd Med Corp	8011	E	562 803-0600	19929
Ultimate Maintenance Svcs Inc	7349	E	310 542-1474	14413

LE GRAND, CA - Merced County

	SIC	EMP	PHONE	ENTRY #
J Marchini & Son Inc	0191	D	559 665-2944	359
J Marchini & Son Inc	0161	D	559 665-9710	62
Marchini Inc	0191	E	209 389-4566	370

LEBEC, CA - Kern County

	SIC	EMP	PHONE	ENTRY #
Schneider National Inc	4213	C	661 858-1031	4260
Tejon Ranch Co (PA)	0173	D	661 248-3000	196

LEMON GROVE, CA - San Diego County

	SIC	EMP	PHONE	ENTRY #
Aztec Landscaping Inc (PA)	0782	C	619 464-3303	802
Developmental Svcs Continuum	8361	D	619 460-7333	24504
Monte Vista Retirement Lodge	6513	D	619 465-1331	11081
Pacific Sthwest Structures Inc	1771	C	619 469-2323	3301
San Diego Recyling Inc	4953	B	619 287-7555	6473
Thompson Building Mtls Inc	5032	E	619 287-9410	6908

LEMOORE, CA - Kings County

	SIC	EMP	PHONE	ENTRY #
Bennett & Bennett Inc (PA)	1711	E	559 582-9336	2141
City of Lemoore	4953	E	559 924-6744	6375
R & D Leasing Inc	7359	D	559 924-1276	14539
Santa Rosa Rnchria Gaming Comm	7929	D	559 924-6948	18461
Superior Truck Lines Inc	4213	E	559 924-6418	4271
Tachi Palace Hotel & Casino	7011	A	559 924-7751	13321
United States Dept of Navy	8062	A	559 998-4201	21868
United States Dept of Navy	8062	A	559 998-4481	21869
United States Dept of Navy	8062	B	559 998-2894	21872
Wood Bros Inc	1629	D	559 924-7715	2075

LINCOLN, CA - Placer County

	SIC	EMP	PHONE	ENTRY #
B Z Plumbing Company Inc	1711	C	916 645-1600	2133
Calhoun Construction Inc	1521	C	916 434-8356	1140
Catta Verdera Country Club	7997	D	916 645-7200	18886

GEOGRAPHIC

Company	SIC	EMP	PHONE	ENTRY #
Clubcorp Usa Inc	7992	E	916 434-9100	18698
Crstb Partners LLC	7992	C	916 645-7200	18703
Gdsa-Lincoln Inc (PA)	7629	D	916 645-8961	17904
Gold Hill Grange No 326	8641	D	916 645-3605	25167
Kaiser Foundation Hospitals	8011	A	916 543-5153	19565
Lincoln Hills Golf Club	7992	E	916 543-9200	18728
Raylee Electric	1731	E	916 408-7556	2693
RE Max Advantage	6531	D	800 247-4200	11705
Rocklin Power Investors LP	4911	D	916 645-3383	6101
Ulta Beauty Inc	7231	C	916 581-4121	13676
United Auburn Indian Community	7011	A	916 408-7777	13353
Verifone Inc	4225	D	916 408-4900	4654
Weygandt & Associates	7699	E	916 543-0431	18007

LINDEN, CA - San Joaquin County

Company	SIC	EMP	PHONE	ENTRY #
Duarte Nursery Inc	0181	B	209 887-3409	254
Normans Nursery Inc	5193	C	209 887-2033	9153

LINDSAY, CA - Tulare County

Company	SIC	EMP	PHONE	ENTRY #
Acmpc California 3 LLC	0174	C	559 591-6140	200
Cal Citrus Packing Co	0723	D	559 562-2536	498
California Silver-Agriculture	0851	E	559 562-3795	997
Friant Water Authority (PA)	4941	D	559 562-6305	6255
Friant Water Users Association	4941	D	559 562-6305	6256
Lindsay Fruit Company LLC	7389	D	559 562-1327	17296
Lo Bue Bros Inc	0723	C	559 562-6367	537
Padilla Farm Labor Inc	0174	C	559 562-1166	208
Sheldon Ranches	0191	D	559 562-3978	381
Suntreat Pkg Shipg A Ltd Prtnr	4783	C	559 562-4991	5210
Verizon Communications Inc	8748	D	559 562-0000	27897

LITTLE LAKE, CA - Inyo County

Company	SIC	EMP	PHONE	ENTRY #
Cgp Holdings LLC	4961	D	760 764-1300	6551
Coso Operating Company LLC	4911	D	760 764-1300	6023

LITTLE RIVER, CA - Mendocino County

Company	SIC	EMP	PHONE	ENTRY #
Little River Inn Inc	7011	D	707 937-5942	12857

LITTLEROCK, CA - Los Angeles County

Company	SIC	EMP	PHONE	ENTRY #
Ascon Recycle Company	4953	E	661 533-0154	6346

LIVE OAK, CA - Sutter County

Company	SIC	EMP	PHONE	ENTRY #
Malloy Orchards Inc	0175	C	530 695-1861	224
Micheli Farms Inc	0175	E	530 695-9022	225
Smith Ranch	0175	E	530 695-2521	230
Sunset Moulding Co	5031	D	530 695-3379	6867
Wilbur Packing Company Inc	0723	B	530 671-4911	587

LIVERMORE, CA - Alameda County

Company	SIC	EMP	PHONE	ENTRY #
5 Star Pool Plaster Inc	1541	D	209 599-3111	1369
Aeronautical Radio Inc	4812	D	925 294-8400	5258
All-Guard Alarm Systems Inc (PA)	1731	D	800 255-4273	2505
Altamont Infrastructure Co	4911	D	925 245-5500	6012
American Med	4119	C	510 895-7600	3748
Amsnet Inc (PA)	7373	E	925 245-6100	15912
Aqua Gunite Inc	1799	E	408 271-2782	3489
Aragon Commercial Ldscpg Inc	0782	C	408 998-0600	798
Architectural GL & Alum Co Inc (PA)	5051	C	925 583-2460	7258
Brock LLC (PA)	4731	D	925 371-2184	5020
Califrnias Gnite Pool Plst Inc	1799	D	925 960-9500	3501
Care Solution Associates LLC	8082	D	925 443-1000	22251
Cattlemens	7299	D	925 447-1224	13725
Cellco Partnership	4812	D	925 245-0494	5307
City of Livermore	1629	D	925 960-8100	2023
Clark Pest Ctrl Stockton Inc	7342	D	925 449-6203	14146
CMS Llnl	7819	D	925 422-5584	18183
Comcast of California/Colo	4812	D	925 424-0273	5400
Cosco Fire Protection Inc	1731	D	925 455-2751	2552
Country Builders Inc	1522	C	925 373-1020	1277
Custom Product Dev Corp	1761	D	925 960-0577	3145
Davey Tree Surgery Company (HQ)	0783	A	925 443-1723	972
Eurofins Food	8731	A	609 452-4440	26364
Fault Line Plumbing	1711	D	925 443-6450	2207
Fbd Vanguard Construction Inc	8741	C	925 245-1300	26858
Fields Construction Services	7349	D	925 294-8183	14264
For Hospital Committee	8741	D	925 447-7000	26860
Goodfellow Bros California LLC	1521	B	925 245-2111	1172
Green Ridge Services LLC	4911	D	925 245-5500	6040
GSE Construction Company Inc	1611	D	925 447-0292	1789
GSe Construction Company Inc (PA)	1623	C	925 447-0292	1923
Harris Rebar Northern Cal Inc	1791	D	925 373-0733	3376
Haskell Company (inc)	1541	C	925 960-1815	1406
High Summit LLC	7539	E	925 605-2900	17795
Hilton Garden Inns MGT LLC	7011	E	925 292-2000	12665
Insidesalescom Inc	7372	C	385 207-7252	15713
J & M Inc	1623	E	925 724-0300	1937
J Redfern Inc	0782	C	925 371-3300	863
Jacobs Engineering Group Inc	1542	D	925 423-7564	1562

Company	SIC	EMP	PHONE	ENTRY #
JF Shea Construction Inc	1521	C	925 245-3660	1185
Jpa Landscape & Cnstr Inc	0782	D	925 960-9602	871
Kenyon Construction Inc	1771	B	925 371-8102	3279
Kier & Wright Civil ENGrs&srvy	8713	E	925 245-8788	26131
Kindred Healthcare Oper Inc	8051	D	925 443-1800	20558
Kinetics Mechanical Svc Inc	1711	D	925 245-6200	2252
Lawrence Livermore NA	8699	A	925 422-1100	25438
Leisure Care LLC	6513	C	925 371-2300	11052
Livermore Area Rcration Pk Dst	7999	C	925 373-5700	19196
Livermore Area Rcration Pk Dst (PA)	7999	B	925 373-5700	19197
Livermore Snior Lving Assoc LP	6719	E	925 371-2300	11990
Livermore Valley Tennis Club	7991	C	925 443-7700	18626
LJ Walch Co Inc	5088	C	925 449-9252	7910
McGrath Rentcorp	7359	D	925 453-3312	14524
McGrath Rentcorp	5084	C	877 221-2813	7771
McGrath Rentcorp (PA)	5084	C	925 606-9200	7772
Mch Electric Inc (PA)	1731	D	209 835-9755	2640
Mike Champlin	1721	D	925 961-1004	2459
Mountain Cascade Inc (PA)	1623	C	925 373-8370	1958
Mthuron Inc	1743	C	925 932-4101	3005
National Security Tech LLC	8711	D	925 960-2500	25841
Nestle Waters North Amer Inc	5149	D	925 294-7720	8836
North Valley Construction Inc	1799	D	925 373-1246	3557
Pacific Gas and Electric Co	4911	C	925 373-2623	6090
Packaging Innovators LLC	5113	C	925 371-2000	8126
Pen-Cal Administrators Inc	8741	D	925 251-3400	26984
Performance Contracting Inc	1541	E	925 273-3800	1429
Performant Financial Corp (PA)	7375	D	925 960-4800	16240
Performant Recovery Inc (HQ)	7322	C	209 858-3994	14017
Performant Technologies Inc	6282	C	925 960-4800	10103
Permanente Medical Group Inc	8011	D	925 243-2600	19780
Peterson Painting Inc	1721	E	925 455-5864	2464
Pinamar LLC	7359	D	925 243-8979	14536
Point One Elec Systems Inc	1731	D	925 667-2935	2683
Poppy Ridge Inc	7992	D	925 456-8229	18744
Prevent Life Safety Svcs Inc	7389	E	925 667-2088	17409
Produce Exchange Incorporated (DH)	5148	D	925 454-8700	8721
Pta California Cong P A S Elem	8641	E	925 606-4700	25220
Puronics Retail Services Inc	1711	D	925 456-7000	2321
Puronics Water Systems Inc	5074	C	925 456-7000	7634
Republic Svcs Vsco Rd Landfill	5064	D	925 447-0491	7427
Rjms Corporation (PA)	5084	D	510 675-0500	7794
Roma Food Enterprises Inc	5149	D	800 233-6211	8862
Sanact Inc (PA)	7699	C	510 483-2324	17982
Seaside Rfrigerated Trnspt Inc (PA)	4213	D	510 732-0472	4263
Selex Inc (PA)	1799	D	707 836-8836	3582
Sidjon Corporation	7011	D	925 606-6135	13225
Smp Construction & Maint Inc (PA)	1542	D	925 961-9012	1653
Sosa Granite & Marble Inc	1743	E	925 373-7675	3011
Sutter Health	8099	C	925 371-3800	22892
Tao Mechanical Ltd	1711	E	925 447-5220	2381
Tennyson Electric Inc	1731	E	925 606-1038	2766
Tgcon Inc (HQ)	8711	C	925 449-5764	25950
The National Food Lab LLC	8733	C	925 828-1440	26666
Uncle Credit Union (PA)	6061	D	925 447-5001	9612
Unified Grocers Inc	5141	C	323 264-5200	8476
United States Dept of Energy	8731	A	925 422-1100	26480
US Foods Inc	5141	B	925 606-3525	8479
Valleycare Hospital Corp (DH)	8011	D	925 447-7000	20046
Veritiv Operating Company	5084	C	925 245-6075	7818
Veterans Health Administration	8011	B	925 447-2560	20077
Waxies Enterprises Inc	5087	E	925 454-2900	7902

LIVINGSTON, CA - Merced County

Company	SIC	EMP	PHONE	ENTRY #
E & J Gallo Winery	0762	D	209 394-6271	686
Foster Poultry Farms	0254	A	209 394-7901	440
Livingston Community Health	8011	C	209 394-7913	19655
Quail H Farms LLC	0139	A	209 394-8001	28
Yagi Bros Inc	0139	D	209 394-7311	31

LLANO, CA - Los Angeles County

Company	SIC	EMP	PHONE	ENTRY #
Crystal Aire Country Club Golf	7997	E	661 944-2112	18906

LODI, CA - San Joaquin County

Company	SIC	EMP	PHONE	ENTRY #
Alexander Delu	0172	D	209 334-6660	128
Anka Behavioral Health Inc	8099	D	209 982-4697	22732
Bjj Company LLC (PA)	4213	D	209 941-8361	4109
Boething Treeland Farms Inc	0811	D	209 727-3741	986
Calfornia Fruit Exchange LLC (PA)	5148	C	209 365-2340	8648
City Rise Inc (PA)	7389	D	209 333-0807	17085
Clark Pest Ctrl Stockton Inc (PA)	7342	D	209 368-7152	14140
Crescent Court Nursing Home	8059	E	209 367-7400	21053
Diede Construction Inc	1542	D	209 369-8255	1520
ED Safety Services Inc	1611	C	209 333-0807	1763
Evergreen Company Inc	7389	D	916 257-5994	17157
F & H Construction (PA)	1542	D	209 931-3738	1531

Mergent email: customerrelations@mergent.com
1596

2019 Directory of California
Wholesalers and Services Companies

(P-0000) Products & Services Section entry number
(PA)=Parent Co (HQ)=Headquarters (DH) Div Headquarters

	SIC	EMP	PHONE	ENTRY #
Ford Construction Company Inc	1629	D	209 333-1116	2032
Frank C Alegre Trucking Inc (PA)	4213	C	209 334-2112	4179
Golden Living LLC	8051	D	209 368-0693	20470
Greg H Carpenter Concrete Inc	1771	E	209 367-4224	3261
Gross Convalescent Hospital	8051	D	209 334-3760	20498
J & L Collections Services Inc	7322	D	800 481-6006	14009
J Rivera Associates Inc	8999	D	415 617-5660	27935
John H Kautz Farms	0721	E	209 334-4786	463
Jose Vramontes	0191	E	209 810-5384	362
Lithia Automotive Group Inc	7549	E	209 956-6500	17865
Lodi Development Inc	6552	E	209 367-7600	11885
Lodi Memorial Hosp Assn Inc (HQ)	8062	A	209 334-3411	21557
Lodi Memorial Hosp Assn Inc	8062	E	209 339-7583	21558
Lodi Memorial Hosp Assn Inc	8011	C	209 333-3100	19657
Lodi Unified School District	7349	C	209 331-7181	14305
Lodi Unified School District	4151	C	209 331-7169	3940
Mv Transportation Inc	4111	D	209 339-1972	3687
Odyssey Landscaping Co Inc	1771	E	209 369-6197	3297
Pacific Coast Producers	7389	B	209 365-9982	17383
R DS For Healthcare	8049	E	209 333-2115	20198
Rdr Builders LP	1522	E	209 368-7561	1310
River Maid Land Co A Cal Ll (PA)	0723	B	209 369-3586	561
Schryver Med Sls & Mktg LLC	8071	C	303 459-8150	22146
Sg Personnel LLC	0181	E	209 369-3018	300
Spare-Time Inc	7933	C	209 371-0241	18498
Sutter Health	8062	C	209 366-2007	21810
Sutter Health	8011	C	209 334-3333	19975
Sutter Home Winery Inc	7389	C	707 963-5928	17493
T & T Trucking Inc (PA)	4213	C	800 692-3457	4274
Teresi Trucking LLC (PA)	4213	D	209 368-2472	4276
Tiger Lines LLC (HQ)	4213	D	209 334-4100	4277
Valley Landscaping & Maint Inc	0782	C	209 334-3659	956
Vienna Convalescent Hospital	8051	C	209 368-7141	20859
Vino Farms Inc (PA)	0762	E	209 334-6975	718
Vino Farms LLC	5182	C	209 334-6975	9058
Westrec Marina Management Inc	4493	D	209 369-1041	4752

LOLETA, CA - Humboldt County

	SIC	EMP	PHONE	ENTRY #
Bear River Casino	7011	B	707 733-9644	12365

LOMA LINDA, CA - San Bernardino County

	SIC	EMP	PHONE	ENTRY #
ABI Document Support Svcs LLC	7389	D	909 793-0613	16975
Brookdale Snior Lving Cmmnties	8059	D	909 796-5421	21023
Chancellor Hlth Care Cal I Inc (PA)	8059	D	909 796-0235	21036
Faculty Physcans Srgeons Llusm	8011	D	909 558-4000	19469
Heritage Health Care Inc	8051	D	909 796-0216	20526
Laren D Tan MD	8011	D	909 558-4444	19643
Linda Loma Univ Hlth Care (HQ)	8062	D	909 558-2806	21555
Linda Loma Univ Hlth Care	8011	C	909 558-2851	19651
Linda Loma Univ Hlth Care (PA)	8011	A	909 558-4729	19652
Linda Loma Univ Hlth Care	8011	C	909 558-2840	19653
Loma Linda - Inland Empire C	8062	C	909 651-5832	21559
Loma Linda University Med Ctr	8062	C	909 558-2100	21560
Loma Linda University Med Ctr (DH)	8062	A	909 558-4000	21561
Loma Linda University Med Ctr	8062	C	909 558-8244	21562
Loma Linda University Med Ctr	8062	C	909 558-4216	21564
Loma Linda University Med Ctr	8082	C	909 558-3096	22359
Loma Linda University Med Ctr	8062	C	909 796-0167	21565
Loma Linda University Med Ctr	8011	A	877 558-6248	19659
Mountain View Child Care Inc (PA)	8062	B	909 796-6915	21602
South Coast Childrens Soc Inc	8322	C	909 478-3377	24059
Universal Self Storage	4225	E	951 206-5263	4647
Veterans Health Administration	8011	A	909 825-7084	20078

LOMITA, CA - Los Angeles County

	SIC	EMP	PHONE	ENTRY #
Aaxis Pharmaceuticals Inc	5047	C	424 263-5294	7147
City of Lomita	4941	E	310 325-9830	6224
Industry Events	7993	E	310 834-3422	18783
Kaiser Foundation Hospitals	8011	A	310 325-6542	19567
Kaiser Foundation Hospitals	8093	C	424 251-7000	22600
Lomita Verde Inc	8059	D	310 325-1970	21137
Long Beach Investment Group	6162	E	562 595-7277	9830
Torrance Amateur Rdo Assn Inc	8699	E	310 245-0989	25475
Travers Tree Service Inc	0783	E	310 545-5816	980

LOMPOC, CA - Santa Barbara County

	SIC	EMP	PHONE	ENTRY #
Aerospace Corporation	8733	D	805 320-9599	26580
Air Force US Dept of	8741	D	805 606-5355	26751
Carnahan Occupational Therapy	8093	E	805 737-1604	22518
Channel Islands Young Mens Ch	8641	D	805 736-3483	25130
Coasthills Credit Union (PA)	6062	C	805 733-7600	9628
Family Service Agency	8322	E	805 735-4376	23797
Ghc of Lompoc LLC	8093	C	805 735-4010	22583
Imerys Minerals California Inc	1481	B	805 736-1221	1100
Imerys Minerals California Inc (DH)	1499	D	805 736-1221	1104
Jay Fisher Farms Inc	0161	E	805 735-1598	63
Kbrwyle Tech Solutions LLC	4899	B	805 734-2982	5986

	SIC	EMP	PHONE	ENTRY #
Life Optons Vctnal Rsource Ctr (PA)	8322	C	805 735-3428	23893
Lompoc Valley Medical Center (PA)	8062	A	805 737-3300	21566
Lompoc Valley Medical Center	8059	C	805 736-3466	21138
Ocean View Flowers LLC	0181	C	800 736-5608	289
Santa Barbara County of	8322	C	805 737-7080	24027
Santa Barbara Farms LLC (PA)	0161	C	805 736-9776	80
Transitions - Mental Hlth Assn	8093	D	805 865-1940	22699
Valley Medical Group of Lompoc	8011	D	805 736-1253	20044
Vandenberg Afb Child Care	8351	E	805 606-1555	24396
Velazquez Packing Inc	0761	C	805 735-6477	677
Zikakis Auto Holdings LLC (PA)	7532	E	805 736-4595	17747

LONE PINE, CA - Inyo County

	SIC	EMP	PHONE	ENTRY #
Southern Inyo Healthcare Dst	8051	C	760 876-5501	20773

LONG BARN, CA - Tuolumne County

	SIC	EMP	PHONE	ENTRY #
Silicon Valley Monterey Bay Co	7032	D	209 965-3432	13454

LONG BEACH, CA - Los Angeles County

	SIC	EMP	PHONE	ENTRY #
1130 W La Palma Ave Inc	8051	D	562 930-0777	20214
4g Wireless Inc	4813	D	562 432-7744	5438
A-Throne Co Inc	7359	D	562 981-1197	14464
Abbey Management Company LLC	6719	C	562 243-2100	11960
Abilty First	8361	C	562 426-6161	24405
Ace Relocation Systems Inc	4212	E	310 632-2800	3967
Acom Solutions Inc (PA)	7373	E	562 424-7899	15907
Advanced Medical MGT Inc	8741	C	562 766-2000	26749
Advertising Consultants Inc (PA)	7319	C	310 233-2750	13963
Aecom Global II LLC	8748	C	310 343-6977	27624
AES Alamitos LLC	4911	D	562 493-7891	6008
AES Southland LLC	4911	D	562 430-8685	6010
Agilon Health Inc	6324	C	562 256-3800	10178
Alamitos-Belmont Rehab Inc	8051	D	562 434-8421	20225
Alpert & Alpert Iron & Met Inc	5051	C	562 624-8833	7253
Als Services Usa Corp	8734	C	562 597-3932	26683
American Corporate SEC Inc (PA)	7381	D	562 216-7440	16560
American Golf Corporation	7992	E	562 494-4424	18682
American Textile Maint Co	7213	D	562 438-7656	13504
American Textile Maint Co	7213	D	562 438-1126	13505
American Textile Maint Co	7218	C	562 424-1607	13581
AON Consulting Inc	6411	C	562 496-2888	10534
APL Logistics Ltd	4412	C	310 548-8700	4695
Apriso Corporation	7373	C	562 951-8000	15913
Aquarium of Pacific	8422	D	562 590-3100	24922
Aquarium of Pacific (PA)	8422	B	562 590-3100	24923
Argus Management Company LLC	8744	B	562 299-5200	27578
Armada Trucking Group Inc	4212	D	800 620-8592	3974
Arts and Services For Disabled	8322	E	562 377-0302	23490
Associated Students California	8641	B	562 985-4994	25094
Association For Retarded (PA)	8331	C	562 597-7716	24154
Atlantic Express Trnsp	4119	C	562 997-6868	3773
Atlantic Mem Healthcare Assoc (PA)	8051	C	562 424-8101	20240
Auto Insur Spcialists-Long Bch	6411	C	562 496-2888	10552
Bank America National Assn	6021	E	562 624-4330	9285
Behavioral Health Services Inc	8322	C	562 599-4194	23506
Belmont Athletic Club	7997	D	562 438-3816	18862
Bragg Investment Company Inc (PA)	7389	A	562 984-2400	17042
Bret Boylan Property Mgt	8741	E	562 437-7886	26785
Brittany House LLC	8361	D	562 421-4717	24440
Brittney House	8082	D	562 421-4717	22242
C O T S Inc (PA)	4119	C	714 751-5466	3781
C S I Patrol Services	7381	C	562 981-8988	16595
California Broadcast Ctr LLC	4841	C	310 233-2425	5859
California Repertory Company	7922	E	562 985-7891	18350
California Resources Corp	1311	C	562 624-3400	1017
California Traffic Control	7389	C	562 595-7575	17050
Califrnia Rsurces Long Bch Inc	1389	C	562 624-3204	1053
Camp Fire USA Long Beach Cncl	8641	E	562 421-2725	25125
Career Transition Center	8331	C	562 570-9675	24163
Careonsite Inc (PA)	8011	E	562 437-0831	19355
Carfax Studios	7299	D	562 377-0223	13724
Carnival Corporation	4724	A	562 843-5569	4934
Carnival Corporation	4724	A	562 901-3232	4935
Casey Company (PA)	5172	C	562 436-9685	8952
Catalina Channel Express Inc	4491	C	562 435-8686	4725
Catalina Channel Express Inc	4489	C	562 495-3565	4713
CE Allencompany Inc	1629	E	562 989-6100	2022
Century 21 Beachside	6531	D	562 430-2121	11293
Century 21 Landmark Properties	6531	E	562 422-0911	11303
Charles Drew Univ Mdcine Scnce	8351	C	310 605-0164	24279
Charter Cmmnctons Oprating LLC	4841	B	310 971-4001	5861
Childnet Youth & Fmly Svcs Inc (PA)	8322	C	562 498-5500	23564
Childnet Youth & Fmly Svcs Inc	8361	D	562 492-9983	24464
Childrens Clinic serving Chl	8011	B	562 264-4638	19375
Chlb LLC	8063	D	562 997-2000	21940
Choura Venue Services	7299	D	562 426-0555	13726

Company	SIC	EMP	PHONE	ENTRY #
Circle Marina Car Wash Inc	7542	E	562 494-4698	17809
CIT Bank NA	6021	D	562 433-0972	9309
Citadel Security Inc	7381	C	562 248-2300	16603
City of Long Beach	7389	B	562 570-7298	17078
City of Long Beach	7538	D	562 570-2828	17757
City of Long Beach	8111	D	562 570-5423	22978
City of Long Beach	4959	C	562 570-2890	6532
City of Long Beach	4932	C	562 570-2000	6189
City of Long Beach	4581	C	562 570-2600	4877
City of Long Beach	7389	B	562 436-3636	17079
City of Long Beach	8111	D	562 570-6919	22979
City of Long Beach	1611	B	562 570-6383	1743
City of Long Beach	4941	C	562 570-2390	6225
Cmac Construction Company	1623	D	562 435-5611	1909
Coast Carwash LP	7542	E	562 961-5555	17811
Coastal Alliance Holdings Inc	6531	C	562 370-1000	11325
Coastal Closeouts Inc	7389	C	323 589-7900	17091
Coastal Cmnty Senior Care LLC	8082	C	562 596-4884	22265
Code America Inc	7361	D	562 502-7365	14589
Cogent Financial Group	6153	D	562 985-1388	9735
College Park Realty Inc	6531	E	562 982-0300	11368
Columbia Specialty Company Inc (PA)	1711	D	562 634-6425	2164
Comcast Corporation	4841	D	800 240-3640	5882
Commercial Protective Svcs Inc	7381	A	310 515-5290	16612
Community Hospital Long Beach	8062	A	562 494-0600	21333
Compulink Management Ctr Inc	7372	C	562 988-1688	15635
Conservation Corps Long Beach	8331	C	562 986-1249	24170
Continental Graphics Corp (HQ)	7336	C	714 503-4200	14107
Continental Graphics Corp	8711	D	714 503-4200	25622
Corridor Recycling Inc	4953	D	310 835-3849	6383
Cosco Agencies (los Angeles) (DH)	4731	D	213 689-6700	5037
Country Villa Blmnt Hght Hlth	8059	D	562 597-8817	21045
Country Villa Service Corp	8741	D	562 597-8817	26824
County of Los Angeles	4941	C	213 367-3176	6233
County of Los Angeles	8011	C	562 599-9200	19416
Covenant Care California LLC	8051	C	562 426-0394	20339
Covenant Care California LLC	8051	C	562 427-7493	20342
Covenant Industries Inc	7361	C	951 808-3708	14593
CPS Security Solutions Inc (PA)	7381	C	310 818-1030	16619
Crane Co	5085	C	562 426-2531	7844
Daylight Transport LLC (PA)	4213	D	310 507-8200	4122
Demler Armstrong & Rowland LLP	8111	E	562 597-0029	23029
Denso Pdts & Svcs Americas Inc (DH)	5013	C	310 834-6352	6633
Dhs Member Services	8021	E	562 595-5151	20115
Dignity Health	8062	A	562 491-9000	21376
Douglas W Jackson MD	8011	D	562 424-6666	19449
Dream Home Care Inc	8361	D	562 595-9021	24507
Duthie Electric Service Corp	7629	E	562 790-1772	17903
Easy Care Mso LLC	8099	B	562 676-9600	22797
Ecamsecure	7382	D	888 246-0556	16890
Edge Systems LLC (PA)	5047	C	800 603-4996	7178
Edgewater Convalescent Hosp	8051	D	562 434-0974	20384
Edwards Theatres Circuit Inc	7832	D	562 429-3321	18294
Eichleay Inc	8711	C	562 256-8600	25655
Elements Behavioral Health Inc (PA)	8093	C	562 741-6470	22574
Elite Craftsman (PA)	7349	C	562 989-3511	14256
Envent Corporation (PA)	8748	C	562 997-9465	27720
Epcm Prof Svc Partners LLC	8748	D	562 936-1000	27722
Eric D Feldman MD Inc	8011	E	562 424-6666	19463
Eversoft Inc (PA)	5074	D	562 495-7766	7616
Fabric Barn	5131	C	562 494-3450	8226
Faith Com Inc (PA)	8748	D	562 719-9300	27727
Family Plg Assoc Med Group	7389	D	562 595-5653	17163
Family Plg Assoc Med Group (PA)	8011	D	213 738-7283	19472
Farmers Merchants Bnk Long Bch (HQ)	6022	C	562 437-0011	9444
Federal Express Corporation	4513	C	800 463-3339	4836
Federal Express Corporation	4513	C	562 522-4014	4837
Fire and Police	8611	E	562 961-0066	24957
First Team RE - Orange Cnty	6531	D	562 346-5088	11462
First Transit Inc	4111	D	310 515-8270	3653
Foasberg Laundry & Clrs Inc (PA)	7213	D	562 426-7345	13530
Forest Lawn Memorial-Park Assn	6553	D	562 424-1631	11943
Formula One Systems Inc (HQ)	7371	D	562 424-7899	15167
Foss Maritime Co Inc	4492	D	562 435-0171	4746
Foss Maritime Company	4412	C	562 435-0171	4697
Free Conferencing Corporation	4813	C	562 437-1411	5560
Fresenius Med Care Long Beach	8092	E	562 432-4444	22476
Garcia Juarez Construction Inc (PA)	8711	D	951 657-3535	25698
Glenn E Thomas Company Inc	7538	D	562 426-5111	17763
Goodwill Srvng The Ppl of Sthr (PA)	7389	D	562 435-3411	17197
Greater Alarm Company Inc (DH)	1731	C	949 474-0555	2593
Guidance Center (PA)	8093	D	562 595-1159	22589
Gulfstream Aerospace Corp GA	8711	A	562 420-1818	25719
Hanjin Shipping Co Ltd	4499	A	201 291-4600	4754
Harbor Diesel and Eqp Inc	5084	D	562 591-5665	7755
Healthcare Partners LLC	8011	D	562 304-2100	19491
Healthcare Partners LLC	8099	D	562 429-2473	22813
Healthcare Partners LLC	8011	B	562 988-7000	19492
Healthcare Services Group Inc	8999	A	562 494-7939	27932
Healthsmart Pacific Inc (PA)	8062	A	562 595-1911	21447
HEI Long Beach LLC	7011	C	562 983-3400	12652
Hellmann Wrldwide Lgistics Inc	4731	D	310 847-4600	5085
HFS Concepts 4 Inc	8712	E	562 424-1720	26059
Hillcrest Cnvalescent Hosp Inc	8059	C	323 636-3462	21111
Hit Portfolio I Misc Trs LLC	7011	B	562 432-0161	12677
Hospitlity Fcsed Solutions Inc	8712	D	562 424-1720	26068
Howard CDM	1521	E	562 427-4124	1179
Human Touch LLC	5021	D	562 426-8700	6726
Hutchison Corporation	1742	D	310 763-7991	2893
ICI Enterprises Inc	8331	D	562 989-7715	24193
Intelsat US LLC	4899	C	310 525-5500	5983
Intercommunity Care Centers	8051	C	562 427-8915	20546
International Garment Finisher	7218	D	562 983-7400	13610
International Trnsp Svc (HQ)	4491	C	562 435-7781	4727
Intertrend Communications Inc	7311	D	562 733-1888	13849
Intex Recreation Corp	5021	D	310 549-1846	6728
Intex Recreation Corp (PA)	5091	D	310 549-5400	7932
Intex Recreation Corp	6512	C	310 549-5400	10900
Iqa Solutions Inc	8711	D	562 420-1000	25752
Jacobs Civil Inc	8711	D	310 847-2500	25754
Jacobs Engineering Group Inc	8711	D	310 847-2500	25759
Jewish Community Ctr Long Bch	8322	C	562 426-7601	23872
Jfe Shoji Trade America Inc (DH)	5051	D	562 637-3500	7283
Jvckenwood USA Corporation (HQ)	5064	C	310 639-9000	7419
K2 Industrial Services Inc	7389	E	562 624-5800	17268
Kazarian/Jewett Inc	1541	E	562 594-5927	1413
Keesal Young Logan A Prof Corp (PA)	8111	D	562 436-2000	23166
Kenny Pabst	6531	E	562 439-2147	11548
Kevcomp Inc	8711	D	562 423-3028	25778
Kindercare Learning Ctrs LLC	8351	D	562 961-8882	24336
Kirkhill Rubber Company	5085	D	562 803-1117	7854
Km Industrial Inc	7349	D	562 786-6200	14299
Kpff Inc	8711	D	562 437-9100	25788
L A Cstm AP & Promotions Inc (PA)	5136	C	562 595-1770	8266
Laugh Factory Inc	8699	D	562 495-2844	25436
Lb Funding LLC	7011	D	562 983-3400	12843
Ld Products Inc	5045	C	562 986-6940	7070
Life Steps Foundation Inc	8322	D	562 426-0751	23895
Lite Solar Corp	1711	C	562 256-1249	2265
Long Bch Museum Art Foundation	8412	D	562 439-2119	24888
Long Beach Behavioral Health U	8099	D	310 221-6336	22835
Long Beach Care Center Inc	8051	C	562 426-6141	20596
Long Beach Cmnty Action Partnr	8399	C	562 216-4600	24802
Long Beach Cmnty College Dst	4225	A	562 938-4291	4587
Long Beach Day Nursery	8351	E	562 421-1488	24341
Long Beach Memorial Med Ctr (HQ)	8062	A	562 933-2000	21567
Long Beach Public Trnsp Co	4111	B	562 591-2301	3664
Long Beach Public Trnsp Co (PA)	4111	D	562 591-8753	3665
Long Beach Public Trnsp Co	4111	D	562 591-8753	3666
Long Beach Unified School Dst	7361	A	562 491-1281	14664
Long Beach Unified School Dst	4151	D	562 426-6176	3941
Long Beach Unified School Dst	7349	C	562 997-7550	14306
Long Beach Unified School Dst	7389	A	562 493-3596	17301
Long Beach Yacht Club	7997	D	562 598-9401	18959
Longwood Management Corp	8059	D	562 432-5751	21145
Loofs Lite A Line	7993	E	562 436-2978	18784
M O Dion & Sons Inc (PA)	5172	D	562 432-3946	8966
M P O Inc (HQ)	5122	D	562 628-1007	8189
M4 Wind Services Inc	8999	D	562 981-7797	27940
Macro-Pro Inc (PA)	7389	C	562 595-0900	17307
Maintenance Staff Inc	7349	A	562 493-3982	14311
Mangan Inc (PA)	8711	D	310 835-8080	25810
Maritzcx Research LLC	8732	A	310 525-1300	26542
Marlora Investments LLC	8051	D	562 494-3311	20631
Marriott International Inc	7011	C	562 425-5210	12894
Marriott International Inc	7011	C	562 595-0909	12902
Matrix Environmental Inc	1799	D	562 236-2704	3549
Matrix Industries Inc	1799	B	562 236-2700	3550
Matus International Inc	4731	C	562 435-5200	5107
Med-Legal LLC	8111	D	626 653-5160	23248
Medasend Biomedical Inc (PA)	8099	C	800 200-3581	22838
Memor Ortho Surgic Group A M	8011	D	562 424-6666	19680
Memorial Counseling Assoc Inc	8011	D	562 961-0155	19681
Memorial Psychiatric Hlth Svcs	8011	E	562 494-9243	19683
Mental Health Amer Los Angeles	8322	D	562 437-6717	23919
Merritt Hospitality LLC	7011	C	562 983-3400	12922
Metropower Inc	1731	D	562 305-9617	2647
Michael McCarthy	7381	E	310 800-5367	16732
Mida Industries Inc	7349	C	562 616-1020	14323
Midnite Air Corp (HQ)	4513	D	310 910-9199	4844

2019 Directory of California
Wholesalers and Services Companies

(P-0000) Products & Services Section entry number
(PA)=Parent Co (HQ)=Headquarters (DH)=Div Headquarters

Company	SIC	EMP	PHONE	ENTRY #
Milco Constructors Inc	1629	E	562 595-1977	2045
Mistras Group Inc	8734	D	562 597-3932	26716
Moffatt & Nichol	8711	D	562 426-9551	25831
Molina Healthcare Inc	6324	B	310 221-3031	10284
Molina Healthcare Inc (PA)	8011	A	562 435-3666	19697
Molina Healthcare Inc	8099	B	562 435-3666	22842
Molina Healthcare California	8011	C	800 526-8196	19698
Molina Healthcare of Californi	6321	A	562 435-3666	10169
Motion Theory Inc	7336	C	310 396-9433	14122
Muni-Fed Energy Inc	1711	E	714 321-3346	2286
Museum of Latin American Art	8412	E	562 437-1689	24894
Neonatal Medical Assoc Inc	8011	B	562 933-8100	19708
New Alliance Insurance Brokers	6411	E	424 205-6700	10700
Nhca Inc	7011	C	310 519-8200	12956
Noble/Utah Long Beach LLC	7011	D	562 436-3000	12960
NRC Environmental Services Inc	4953	D	562 432-1304	6424
Ocean Blue Envmtl Svcs Inc (PA)	4212	D	562 624-4120	4047
Olive Crest	8361	D	562 216-8841	24618
Olympix Fitness LLC	7991	D	562 366-4600	18638
Onewest Bank NA	6035	D	562 433-0971	9526
Oocl (usa) Inc	4731	D	562 499-2600	5128
Opex Communications Inc	4813	E	562 968-5420	5618
Oshyn Inc	7374	D	213 483-1770	16163
Overland Pacific & Cutler LLC (PA)	7389	D	562 429-9391	17380
P2s Inc	8711	C	562 497-2999	25857
Pacific Care Inc	8082	D	562 494-6500	22386
Pacific Gtwy Wrkfrce Prtnr Inc	7361	E	562 570-3700	14685
Pacific Occptnal Medicine Svcs	8062	E	562 997-2290	21622
Pacific Palms Healthcare LLC	8082	D	562 433-6791	22388
Pacific Shores Med Group Inc (PA)	8011	D	562 590-0345	19743
Palm Harbor Residency LP	8059	D	562 595-4551	21182
Palmcrest Grand Care Ctr Inc	8051	D	562 595-4551	20689
Palp Inc	1611	C	562 599-5841	1832
Parwood Preservation LP	6531	D	562 531-7880	11664
Pbi-Birkenwald Market Eqp Inc (PA)	5046	E	562 595-4785	7144
Pegasus Building Svcs Co Inc (PA)	7349	B	562 961-1998	14348
Penske Truck Leasing Co LP	7513	D	310 327-3116	17611
Perona Langer Beck A Prof Corp	8111	D	562 426-6155	23325
Phillips Steel Company	5051	E	562 435-7571	7301
Platt Security Systems Inc	7381	D	562 986-4484	16758
Polar Tankers Inc (DH)	4424	D	562 388-1400	4703
Porchlight Inc	8059	D	562 989-5100	21189
Port of Long Bch Employees CLB	8631	B	562 590-4102	25073
Posca Brothers Dental Lab	8072	D	562 427-1811	22173
Pponext Inc	8099	B	888 446-6098	22862
Praxair Inc	5084	D	562 427-0099	7786
Preferred Construction Co Inc	1542	D	714 630-3004	1619
Premier Insite Group Inc	7361	D	562 741-5018	14699
Premier Nursing Services Inc (PA)	7361	A	562 437-4313	14700
Primus Pipe and Tube Inc (DH)	5051	D	562 808-8000	7302
Prindle Decker & Amaro LLP (PA)	8111	D	562 436-3946	23339
Psav Holdings LLC	7359	A	562 366-0138	14537
PSC Industrial Outsourcing LP	4953	D	562 997-6000	6431
Qualfax Inc	7389	D	562 988-1272	17419
Queensbay Hotel LLC (PA)	7011	C	562 628-0625	13088
Queensbay Hotel LLC	7011	D	562 481-3910	13089
R G Vanderweil Engineers LLP	8711	C	562 256-8623	25884
R L Klein & Associates	7363	D	562 427-5577	14895
Rance King Properties Inc (PA)	6513	C	562 240-1000	11106
Rdc-S111 Inc (PA)	8712	D	562 628-8000	26105
Recovery Place Inc	8069	D	954 200-8308	22042
Redbarn Pet Products Inc (PA)	5199	D	562 495-7315	9256
Regency Oaks Care Center	8051	D	562 498-3368	20720
Rehabilitation California Dept	8322	E	562 422-8325	23990
Resource Environmental Inc	1542	D	562 468-7000	1629
Restaurant Depot LLC	5142	D	562 634-6771	8503
Retirement Housing Foundation (PA)	6531	D	562 257-5100	11731
Reynolds Health Industries	8059	D	562 591-7621	21195
Rmd Group Inc	8742	B	562 866-9288	27430
RMS Foundation Inc	7011	A	562 435-3511	13135
Ronald J Lemieux Assoc Law Off	8111	D	562 375-0095	23358
Roux Associates Inc	8748	D	562 446-8600	27848
Ruffin Hotel Corp of Cal	7011	B	562 425-5210	13153
Runa Hr Holdings Inc	7371	D	562 883-3546	15420
Safe Refuge	8361	D	562 987-5722	24659
Salvation Army (HQ)	8322	C	562 491-8464	24005
Santa Monica Rhf Housing Inc (PA)	6513	D	562 257-5100	11110
Save Queen LLC	7011	D	562 435-3511	13193
Scan California Management Co	6324	A	562 989-5100	10306
Scan Group (PA)	6324	B	562 308-2733	10307
Securitas SEC Svcs USA Inc	7381	C	562 427-2737	16809
Senior Care (PA)	6324	A	562 989-5100	10309
Senior Care	6324	D	562 492-9878	10310
Shelton Construction Company	1611	D	714 903-7853	1848
Shield Security Inc	7381	B	562 283-1100	16825
Shimadzu Precision Instrs Inc (DH)	5088	D	562 420-6226	7914
Shipco Transport Inc	4731	D	562 295-2900	5167
Shoreline Holdings Inc (PA)	1731	C	562 498-6444	2733
Signature Flight Support Corp	4581	D	562 997-0700	4912
Smg Holdings Inc	6512	D	562 499-7611	10945
Southern California Edison Co	4911	B	562 491-3803	6139
Spectacor Management Group	6512	B	562 436-3636	10951
Ssa Containers Inc	4491	D	206 520-0304	4737
Ssa Marine Inc	4491	E	562 983-1001	4738
St Mary Medical Center (HQ)	8062	A	562 491-9000	21787
Star Brite Building Maint	7349	B	562 988-2829	14400
Starlight International Ltd LP	5122	D	562 439-5740	8212
State Farm Mutl Auto Insur Co	6411	D	310 642-3300	10785
Sterile Proc Svcs Amer LLC	7389	D	562 428-5858	17487
Steuber Corporation (PA)	5046	D	310 632-8255	7146
Sunbridge Harbor View	8051	D	562 989-9907	20790
Sunbridge Healthcare LLC	8052	D	562 981-9392	20965
Synergy Health North Amer Inc	7213	D	562 428-5858	13554
Ta Chen International Inc (HQ)	5051	C	562 808-8000	7318
Talent & Acquisition LLC	7371	D	213 742-1972	15489
Tarzana Treatment Centers Inc	8093	E	562 218-1868	22694
Telecare Corporation	8063	D	562 630-8672	21980
Telecare Corporation	8063	C	562 634-9534	21981
Telecare La Step Down	8093	E	562 216-4900	22696
Tell Steel Inc	5051	D	562 435-4826	7320
The Designory Inc (HQ)	7336	C	562 624-0200	14130
Total Intermodal Services Inc (PA)	4491	D	562 427-6300	4742
Toyota Logistics Services	7549	B	562 437-6767	17878
Transcendent Security Services	7381	D	562 850-3313	16838
Trinity Health Systems	8051	D	562 437-2797	20841
Tristar Insurance Group Inc (PA)	6331	A	562 495-6600	10412
Turelk Inc (PA)	1542	C	310 835-3736	1681
Twining Inc (PA)	8734	D	562 426-3355	26736
Ultimate Construction Inc	1751	C	562 633-3389	3088
United El Segundo Inc (PA)	5172	D	310 323-3992	8970
Universal Protection Svc LP	7381	D	562 981-5700	16846
Urban Commons Queensway LLC	7011	A	562 499-1611	13358
US Skillserve Inc (PA)	8741	D	562 930-0777	27076
USA Waste of California Inc	4953	D	310 830-7100	6497
Vanguard Lgistics Svcs USA Inc (HQ)	4731	D	310 847-3000	5197
Ventura Transfer Company (PA)	4213	D	310 549-1660	4299
Veolia Es Waste-To-Energy Inc	4953	D	562 436-0636	6506
Verizon Communications Inc	4813	C	562 496-0288	5665
Veterans Affrs LNG Bch Hlthre	8011	D	562 826-8000	20057
Villa De La Mar Inc	8059	E	562 494-5001	21247
Villa Serena Healthcare Center	8051	D	562 437-2797	20862
Virginia Country Club	7997	D	562 427-0924	19081
Vista Cove Care Center At Long	8051	D	562 426-4461	20868
W A Rasic Cnstr Co Inc (PA)	1623	C	562 928-6111	1997
Walter Voss Cynthia RE Max	6531	D	562 434-5980	11822
Warren E&P Inc	5172	D	877 587-9494	8973
Wells Hse Hspice Fundation Inc	8051	D	714 952-3795	20879
Western Exterminator Company	7342	E	310 835-3513	14163
Weyerhaeuser Company	0811	D	562 983-6589	995
William H Warden III MD	8011	D	562 424-6666	20103
Windes Inc (PA)	8721	D	562 435-1191	26307
Wm Wireless Inc	4812	E	562 633-9288	5427
Women Infant & Children	8322	D	562 570-4228	24134
World Trade Ctr Ht Assoc Ltd	7011	C	562 983-3400	13418
Xerox Education Services LLC (DH)	5044	D	310 830-9847	6993
Yhb Long Beach LLC	7011	D	562 597-4401	13433
Young Mens Christian Associat	8641	D	562 624-2376	25331
Young Mens Chrstn Assc Gr L B	8641	B	562 596-3394	25334
Young Mens Chrstn Assc Gr L B	8641	D	562 423-0491	25337
Young Mens Chrstn Assc Gr L B	8641	D	562 423-0491	25338
Young Mens Chrstn Assc Gr L B	8641	D	562 633-0106	25339

LOOMIS, CA - Placer County

Company	SIC	EMP	PHONE	ENTRY #
Abshear Landscape Development	0781	E	916 660-1617	725
Jls Environmental Services Inc	8744	D	916 660-1525	27598
McCuen Construction Inc (PA)	1542	E	916 652-7824	1592
Online Communications Inc	1731	C	916 652-7253	2668
Sierra Wes Drywall Inc (PA)	1742	B	916 652-4491	2958
VCA Animal Hospitals Inc	0742	E	916 652-5816	612
Wilkie Masonry Inc	1741	E	916 652-0118	2829

LOS ALAMITOS, CA - Orange County

Company	SIC	EMP	PHONE	ENTRY #
Advantage Plumbing Group Inc	1711	D	714 898-6020	2086
Alamitos Enterprises LLC (PA)	7549	D	562 596-1827	17846
Apfeld & Neal Insurance Svcs	6411	E	714 821-7041	10538
Barrys Security Services Inc	7381	C	562 493-7007	16580
Benchmark Internet Group LLC	7379	D	562 286-6820	16316
Carol Electric Company Inc	1731	D	562 431-1870	2538
College Park Realty Inc (PA)	6531	D	562 594-6753	11367
Dynalectric Company	1731	C	714 236-2242	2567
Friedas Inc	5148	D	714 733-7655	8683

Employment Codes: A=Over 500 employees, B=251-500,
C=101-250, D=51-100, E=50

2019 Directory of California
Wholesalers and Services Companies

© Mergent Inc. 1-800-342-5647

1599

GEOGRAPHIC

Company	SIC	EMP	PHONE	ENTRY #
Fruit Guys	5148	D	714 826-2993	8684
General Services Cal Dept	7374	D	562 342-7212	16137
Goodman Group Inc	8051	D	562 596-5561	20490
Hansen Adkins Auto Trnspt Inc (PA)	4213	A	562 430-4100	4190
Katella Properties	8051	C	562 596-5561	20552
Kdc Inc (HQ)	1731	C	714 828-7000	2623
Lakewood South Car Wash LLC	7542	E	562 430-4975	17822
Los Alamitos Medical Ctr Inc (HQ)	8062	A	714 826-6400	21570
Los Almtos Hmodialysis Ctr Inc	8092	D	562 426-8881	22482
Marinow Harry MD Facs Inc	8011	E	562 430-3561	19668
Mggb Inc	8711	C	714 226-0520	25818
Millie and Severson Inc	1541	D	562 493-3611	1420
Mulligan Limited	6732	C	714 484-6799	12080
Mulligan Limited (PA)	7996	D	714 484-6799	18806
Severson Group Incorporated (PA)	1542	D	562 493-3611	1644
Southland Credit Union (PA)	6062	D	562 862-6831	9655
Ssl Robotics LLC	8711	C	626 296-1373	25926
Sure Forming Systems Inc	1771	E	562 598-6348	3334
Tenet Healthsystem Medical	8011	A	805 546-7698	20001
Thermo Power Industries	1742	E	562 799-0087	2968
Trojan Professional Svcs Inc	7375	D	714 816-7169	16255
US Bank National Association	6021	E	562 795-7520	9375
Utblo Inc	6719	C	562 493-3664	12016

LOS ALTOS, CA - Santa Clara County

Company	SIC	EMP	PHONE	ENTRY #
Adobe Animal Hospital Inc	0742	D	650 948-9661	593
Alain Pinel Realtors Inc	6531	D	650 941-1111	11202
American Baptist Homes of West	8059	C	650 948-8000	20991
Coldwell Banker Affiliates	6531	D	650 941-7040	11332
Covenant Care California LLC	8051	C	650 941-5255	20353
Guardsmark LLC	7381	C	800 238-5878	16684
Iqtalent Partners LLC	7361	C	888 501-4787	14652
Kisco Senior Living LLC	6513	E	650 948-7337	11048
Los Altos Golf and Country CLB	7997	D	650 947-3100	18960
Midpeninsul Rgnl Opn Sp	8999	D	650 691-1200	27945
Mw2 Consulting LLC	8742	D	408 573-6310	27355
Netcube Systems Inc	7372	D	650 862-7858	15775
Netskope Inc	7371	D	800 979-6988	15303
Older Adults Care Management (PA)	8322	C	650 329-1411	23949
Palo Alto Medical Foundation	8011	D	650 254-5200	19750
R J Dailey Construction Co	1521	D	650 948-5196	1221
Robertson Piper Management LLC	8742	C	650 625-8333	27432
Roman Cthlic Bishp of San Jose	6553	A	833 304-0763	11948
State Farm Mutl Auto Insur Co	6411	D	650 694-6767	10782
The David Lcile Pckard Fndtion	8699	D	650 917-7167	25473
Toyota Research Institute Inc	8733	D	703 231-6680	26667

LOS ALTOS HILLS, CA - Santa Clara County

Company	SIC	EMP	PHONE	ENTRY #
Footh-De Anza Commun Colleg Di	4832	D	650 949-7260	5719
Idea Travel Company	4724	A	650 948-0207	4939

LOS ANGELES, CA - Los Angeles County

Company	SIC	EMP	PHONE	ENTRY #
120 South Los Angeles Street H	7011	D	213 629-1200	12287
1755 Efm 1 LLC	6531	D	323 231-4174	11184
180a LLC	7311	C	310 382-1400	13783
24 Hour Fitness Usa Inc	7991	D	310 553-7600	18551
3dna Corp (PA)	7371	D	213 394-4623	14950
417 Stockton St LLC	7011	D	323 327-9656	12291
4g Wireless Inc	4813	D	310 429-9048	5432
4g Wireless Inc	4813	D	323 679-9991	5433
4wall Entertainment Inc	7922	D	818 252-7481	18337
5 Design Inc	8712	D	323 308-3558	26016
550 Flower St Operations LLC	7011	C	213 892-8080	12297
6417 Selma Hotel LLC	7011	C	323 844-6417	12299
711 Hope LP	6519	C	213 365-5000	11162
800 Degrees LLC	8741	E	310 443-1911	26743
834 W Arrow Highway LP	8052	D	213 355-1024	20914
901 West Olympic Blvd LP	7011	C	347 992-5707	12301
A Buchalter Professional Corp (PA)	8111	C	213 891-0700	22903
A Community of Friends	6513	C	213 480-0809	10971
A F Gilmore Company	6531	D	323 939-1191	11186
A Filml Inc	7819	D	213 977-8600	18175
A M S Partnership (PA)	6552	D	310 312-6698	11851
A S E C International Inc	7374	A	803 939-4809	16082
A Touch of Kindness	8322	D	323 997-6500	23454
A World Fit For Kids	8742	C	213 387-7712	27104
A&E Television Networks LLC	4841	C	310 201-6015	5855
AA Autmtive Personnel Svcs Inc	7549	C	310 914-3012	17844
Aaaza Inc	7311	D	213 380-8333	13786
Aab Water Company Inc	4941	D	559 497-2700	6205
Abba Bail Bonds (PA)	7389	E	213 680-1400	16973
ABC Cable Networks Group	4832	C	323 860-5900	5689
Abilityfirst	8322	D	213 748-7309	23456
ABM Distributors Inc	7812	D	310 401-0434	18010
ABM Industries Incorporated	7349	E	323 720-4020	14170
ABM Janitorial Services Inc	6211	A	213 384-0600	9911
ABM Parking Services	7521	D	213 955-7945	17661
Abode Communities	6531	C	213 629-2702	11189
Absolute Towing-Hollenbeck Div	7549	E	323 225-9294	17845
Aca Financial Guaranty Corp	6163	D	323 255-3583	9867
Access Finance Inc	7389	E	310 826-4000	16979
Accor Corp	7011	C	310 278-5444	12304
Accurate Courier Services Inc.	4212	D	310 481-3937	3964
Accurate Services Inc	6099	C	323 906-1000	9667
Ace Beverage Co	5181	C	323 266-6238	8975
Acetech Construction Inc.	8711	E	213 637-4702	25498
Aceteck Roofing Co Inc	1761	E	323 231-6060	3121
Aci International (PA)	5139	D	310 889-3400	8342
ACS Security Industries Inc	7382	C	310 475-9016	16867
Action Property Management Inc.	8641	C	800 400-2284	25090
Adcolony Inc.	7371	C	650 625-1262	14964
Added Value LLC (DH)	8732	C	323 254-4326	26497
Adee Plumbing and Heating Inc (PA)	1711	D	323 296-8787	2085
Adeste Program Company	8351	B	213 251-3551	24261
Adexa Inc (PA)	7372	E	310 642-2100	15571
Adir International LLC	4225	D	213 386-4412	4523
Adlink Cable Advertising LLC	7311	C	310 477-3994	13787
Admarketing Inc	7311	D	310 203-8400	13788
Admiralty Partners Inc	6799	D	310 471-3772	12198
Advanced Digital Services Inc (PA)	7812	C	323 962-8585	18011
Advantage Produce Inc.	5148	E	213 627-2777	8638
Aecom (PA)	8711	C	213 593-8000	25505
Aecom C&E Inc.	8742	C	213 593-8100	27115
Aecom E&C Holdings Inc (DH)	8711	C	213 593-8000	25507
Aecom Energy & Cnstr Inc (DH)	1622	C	213 593-8100	1872
Aecom Global II LLC (HQ)	8711	C	213 593-8100	25511
Aecom Global II LLC	8748	C	213 996-2200	27623
Aecom Services Inc (HQ)	8712	C	213 593-8000	26019
Aecom Technical Services Inc (HQ)	8748	D	213 593-8000	27625
Aecom Usa Inc	8748	C	213 330-7200	27626
Aecom Usa Inc	8748	C	213 593-8000	27628
AEG Global Partnerships LLC	8742	E	213 763-7700	27116
AEG Management Lacc LLC	8741	C	213 741-1151	26750
AEG Presents LLC (DH)	7922	C	323 930-5700	18340
Aero-Engines Inc.	7699	D	323 663-3961	17928
Aerotransporte De Carge Union	4512	B	310 649-0069	4757
Aesthetic Maintenance Corp	7349	E	213 353-1525	14183
African American Unity Center	8322	D	323 789-7300	23461
Aftershock La Studios Inc.	7371	C	650 450-9660	14970
AG Facilities Operations LLC	8059	A	323 651-1808	20980
Agencycom LLC	7372	C	415 817-3800	15575
Aids Project Los Angeles (PA)	8322	C	213 201-1600	23464
Air Lease Corporation (PA)	7359	D	310 553-0555	14468
Airgas Usa LLC	5084	C	323 568-2244	7722
Airport Century Inn	7011	C	310 649-4000	12309
Airpush Inc	7311	C	877 944-2490	13790
Ajit Healthcare Inc	8741	D	213 484-0510	26752
Akin Gump Strauss	8111	C	310 229-1000	22906
Alameda Produce Market LLC	6531	C	213 221-3400	11204
Alaska Airlines Inc	4512	C	310 925-2409	4761
Alexandria Care Center LLC	8059	C	323 660-1800	20985
All Area Plumbing Inc	1711	C	323 939-9990	2097
All Nation Security Svcs Inc (PA)	7381	C	213 769-4510	16546
Allaquaria LLC	5199	D	310 645-1107	9193
Alldayeveryday Productions LLC	7812	E	323 556-6200	18012
Allen Matkins Leck Gmble (PA)	8111	B	213 622-5555	22910
Alliance For Housing & Healing (PA)	8052	D	323 344-4885	20915
Alliance Ground Intl LLC	4581	C	310 646-2446	4870
Alliancebernstein LP	6722	D	310 286-6000	12021
Allied Refrigeration Inc	5075	C	310 202-2220	7643
Alliedbarton Security Svcs LLC	7381	B	800 418-6423	16558
Allstate Construction Co.	1521	E	310 652-6942	1112
Alsco Inc.	7213	C	323 465-5111	13494
Alston & Bird LLP	8111	C	213 626-8830	22912
Alta Healthcare System LLC (HQ)	8399	C	323 267-0477	24731
Alta Hospitals System LLC	8062	C	323 267-0477	21279
Alta Hospitals System LLC (HQ)	8062	C	310 943-4500	21281
Altamed Health Services Corp	8011	D	323 980-4466	19276
Altamed Health Services Corp	8011	E	323 980-4000	19281
Altegra Health	8742	D	310 776-4001	27124
Altoon Partners LLP (PA)	8712	D	213 225-1900	26022
Altour International Inc	4724	C	310 571-6000	4928
Altour International Inc (PA)	4724	C	310 571-6000	4929
Alzheimers Greater Los Angeles	8322	D	323 938-3379	23471
Amada Enterprises Inc.	8051	C	323 757-1881	20229
Amanecer Cmnty Counseling Svc	8093	D	213 481-7464	22503
Amcap Fund Inc	6722	B	213 486-9200	12022
American Airlines Inc	4512	C	310 215-7054	4768
American Airlines Inc.	4512	C	213 935-6045	4770
American Airlines Inc.	4512	B	310 646-0093	4771
American Airlines Inc.	4512	C	310 646-3013	4773

Name	SIC	EMP	PHONE	ENTRY #
American Care Givers Westwood	8322	D	310 208-8005	23472
American Contrs Indemnity Co (DH)	6351	C	213 330-1309	10421
American Funds Distrs Inc (DH)	6722	C	213 486-9200	12023
American Golf Corporation	7997	C	310 476-2411	18830
American Heart Association Inc	8621	E	213 291-7000	24995
American Home Assurance Co	6331	B	213 689-3500	10336
American Intl Group Inc	6399	B	213 689-3500	10496
American Multi-Cinema Inc	7832	E	310 228-5500	18267
American Mutual Fund Inc	6722	C	213 486-9200	12024
American Realty Advisors	6798	D	818 545-1152	12150
American Red Cross	8322	D	310 445-9900	23478
American Red Cross La Chapter (PA)	8322	B	310 445-9900	23479
American Reprographics Co LLC	7334	D	213 745-3145	14071
American Textile Maint Co	7213	E	213 749-4433	13503
American Textile Maint Co	7213	C	323 735-1661	13506
American Voice Mail Inc (PA)	4812	E	310 478-4949	5259
Americantours Intl LLC (HQ)	4725	C	310 641-9953	4961
Amgreen Solar and Electrics	1711	E	213 388-5647	2117
Amgreen Solutions Inc	8742	E	213 388-5647	27131
AMS - Exotic LLC	5148	D	213 612-5888	8639
Analytic US Market Neutral Off	6211	D	213 688-3015	9913
Andersen Tax LLC	7291	C	213 593-2300	13701
Anderson Kayne Capital	6282	B	800 231-7414	10056
Anderson Kayne Inv MGT Inc (PA)	8742	D	310 556-2721	27135
Anderson McPharlin Conners LLP (PA)	8111	D	213 688-0080	22916
Angel Care Home Health Inc	8082	E	818 248-8811	22222
Angeles Home Health Care Inc	8082	A	213 487-5131	22223
Angelus Western Ppr Fibers Inc	5093	D	213 623-9221	7969
Anschutz Entrmt Group Inc (HQ)	7929	C	213 337-5052	18418
Anschutz Film Group	1742	A	310 887-1000	2846
Ant Farm LLC	7819	C	323 850-0700	18178
AON Consulting Inc	6411	D	818 506-4300	10528
AON Risk Svcs Companies Inc	6411	C	213 630-3200	10537
Apla Health & Wellness	8011	D	213 201-1546	19301
App Wholesale LLC	5149	B	323 980-3746	8753
Appetize Technologies Inc	7372	C	877 559-4225	15585
Apumac LLC	5065	C	888 248-7775	7439
Aramark Facility Services LLC	7349	C	213 740-8968	14197
Aramark Services Inc	7219	C	323 587-7661	13629
Aramark Spt & Entrmt Group LLC	7929	C	213 740-1224	18420
Aramark Unf & Career AP LLC	7218	C	323 266-0555	13589
ARC Mid-Cities Inc	8331	C	310 329-9272	24148
Arclight Cinema Company	7832	C	323 464-1465	18272
Arent Fox LLP	8111	C	213 629-7400	22918
Ares Management LP (PA)	6722	C	310 201-4100	12025
Ares Management LLC (HQ)	6799	C	310 201-4100	12199
Ares Management LLC	6722	C	310 201-4100	12026
Arko Foods International Inc (PA)	5141	D	323 257-1888	8382
Armand Hammer Museum	8412	C	310 443-7000	24864
Armanino LLP	8721	C	310 478-4148	26144
Arnies Supplies Service Ltd	7699	D	323 263-1696	17935
Arnold Porter Kaye Scholer LLP	8111	C	310 788-1000	22922
Aroma Spa & Sports LLC	7999	EMP	213 387-2111	19102
Arroyo Vsta Fmly Hlth Fndation (PA)	8011	C	323 254-5221	19305
Arthrtis Fundation PCF Reg Inc	8641	E	323 954-5760	25092
Artist Silva Management LLC (PA)	8741	C	323 856-8222	26766
Artwear Inc	5136	C	310 217-1393	8249
Arup North America Limited	8711	C	310 578-4182	25548
Arya Group Inc	1521	E	310 446-7000	1120
Arya Ice Cream Distrg Co Inc	5143	D	323 234-2994	8512
Asbestos Instant Response Inc	1799	D	323 733-0508	3490
Ascot Hotel LP	7011	C	310 476-6411	12337
Asia Pacific Capital	6726	D	213 628-8800	12057
Asian PCF Hlth Care Ventr Inc (PA)	8399	C	323 644-3880	24739
Assist 65 Plus	7389	E	323 557-4426	17013
Associated Entrmt Releasing (PA)	7812	E	323 934-7044	18019
Associated Press	7383	D	213 626-1200	16952
Associated Students UCLA (PA)	8399	B	310 825-4321	24742
Associated Students UCLA	8399	C	310 794-0242	24743
Associated Students UCLA	8011	A	310 825-9451	19310
AT&T Corp	4812	D	310 473-3649	5273
AT&T Corp	4813	D	213 787-0055	5452
AT&T Corp	4812	D	310 659-7600	5296
AT&T Corp	4813	D	213 787-0055	5467
AT&T Services Inc	4813	A	213 975-4089	5487
AT&T Services Inc	4813	E	213 741-3111	5495
AT&T Services Inc	4813	B	323 468-6813	5511
Atelier Ace LLC	7336	C	503 546-6836	14100
Athicon	8711	E	213 454-0662	25551
Attn Inc	7313	C	323 413-2878	13935
Aurora Resurgence Fund LP	6722	A	310 551-0101	12027
Authority Tax Services LLC	7389	D	213 486-5135	17019
Authorized Taxi Cab	7382	C	323 776-5324	16877
Automatic Data Processing Inc	7374	D	800 225-5237	16097
Automobile Club Southern Cal (PA)	6411	C	213 741-3686	10554
Autry Museum of American West	8412	C	323 667-2000	24866
Avida Caregivers Inc	8082	A	323 498-1500	22233
Avongard Products USa Ltd	7819	E	310 319-2300	18179
Axa Advisors LLC	6282	D	213 251-1600	10058
Axaio Industries LLC	4813	E	323 504-1074	5520
B F Management	6531	D	323 931-7776	11230
Babyfirst Americas LLC	7371	D	310 442-9853	15017
Bachelor Productions Inc	7812	D	310 567-9249	18023
Bain & Company Inc	8742	D	310 229-3000	27150
Baker Keener & Nahra	8111	E	213 241-0900	22925
Baker & Hostetler LLP	8111	D	310 820-8800	22926
Ballard Spahr LLP	8111	D	424 204-4400	22931
Bamko Inc	7312	C	310 470-5859	13926
Banamex USA Bancorp (DH)	6712	C	310 203-3440	11952
Banc California National Assn	6021	E	310 286-0710	9278
Bank America National Assn	6021	D	310 384-4562	9288
Bank Leumi USA	6021	D	323 966-4700	9295
Bank of Hope (HQ)	6021	C	213 639-1700	9296
Bank of Tokyo Ltd	6029	A	213 488-3700	9495
Barclays Capital Inc	6211	D	310 481-4100	9917
Barlow Group (PA)	8069	C	213 250-4200	21997
Barlow Respiratory Hospital (PA)	8069	C	213 250-4200	21998
Barnes & Thornburg LLP	8111	C	310 284-3880	22934
Barrys Bootcamp Holdings LLC (PA)	5091	B	270 535-5005	7922
Bbcn Bank	6022	E	213 389-5550	9421
Behringer Harvard Wilshire Blv	7011	D	310 475-8711	12366
Beitler & Associates Inc (PA)	6531	C	310 820-2955	11236
Bel-Air Country Club	7997	C	310 472-9563	18861
Belmont Village LP	6513	E	323 874-7711	10987
Bender/Helper Impact Inc (PA)	8743	D	310 473-4147	27542
Beres Consulting	8611	D	310 476-9941	24945
Berg Lacquer Co (PA)	5198	D	323 261-8114	9188
Bergelectric Corp (PA)	1731	D	310 337-1377	2519
Bestway Recycling Company Inc (PA)	5093	D	323 588-8157	7971
Bet Tzedek	8111	D	323 939-0506	22946
Better Life Produce Inc	5148	E	213 623-0640	8641
Beverly Blvd Leaseco LLC	7011	D	310 278-5444	12380
Beverly Hills Country Club	6552	C	310 836-4400	11856
Beverly Hills Luxury Hotel LLC	7011	B	310 274-9999	12381
Beverly Sunstone Hills LLC	7011	D	310 228-4100	12382
Beverly West Health Care Inc	8051	D	323 938-2451	20262
Beverlywood Realty Inc	6531	E	310 836-8322	11242
Bienvenidos Childrens Center (PA)	8322	C	213 785-5906	23512
Big3 Basketball LLC	7941	D	213 417-2013	18512
Biomat Usa Inc	8099	A	310 772-7777	22743
Biomat Usa Inc (DH)	8099	E	323 225-2221	22744
Bird Mrlla Bxer Wlpert A Prof	8111	D	310 201-2100	22947
Black Canyon Capital LLC	8741	C	310 272-1800	26781
Blackstone Consulting Inc (PA)	8742	C	310 826-4389	27162
Blair Television Inc	7812	D	714 537-5923	18024
Blank Rome LLP	8111	D	424 239-3400	22948
Bloom David Law Offices of	8111	E	323 938-5248	22949
Bls Lmsine Svc Los Angeles Inc (PA)	4119	B	323 644-7166	3779
BLT & Associates Inc	7336	C	323 860-4000	14101
Blue Cross & Blue Shield Mich	6324	C	323 782-3046	10181
Blue Planet International Inc	5137	E	323 526-9999	8289
Blx Group LLC	6282	D	213 612-2400	10063
Bonne Bridge Muell Okeef & (PA)	8111	D	213 480-1900	22953
Bonneville International Corp	4832	E	323 634-1800	5692
Bonnie Brae Cnvlscent Hosp Inc (PA)	8059	D	213 483-8144	21011
Booz Allen Hamilton Inc	8742	D	310 297-2100	27166
Booz Allen Hamilton Inc	8742	D	213 620-1900	27168
Boston Consulting Group Inc	8742	D	213 621-2772	27169
Boy Scouts of America (PA)	8641	C	213 353-9879	25102
Braille Institute America Inc (PA)	8322	C	323 663-1111	23517
Breitbart News Network LLC	7313	D	424 371-0585	13937
Breitburn GP LLC	1311	A	213 225-5900	1016
Brentwood Bmdical RES Inst Inc	8733	C	310 312-1554	26598
Brentwood Country Club	7997	C	310 451-8011	18873
Brier Oak On Sunset LLC	8059	C	323 663-3951	21016
Brinks Incorporated	7381	C	818 503-8630	16589
Brinks Incorporated	7381	E	323 262-2646	16593
Brisam Lax (de) LLC	7011	C	310 649-5151	12402
Broadreach Capitl Partners LLC	6799	A	310 691-5760	12204
Broadview Inc	8051	E	323 221-9174	20270
Brookfield Dtla Fund Office	6798	D	213 626-3300	12154
Browning Apartments	6513	E	213 252-8847	10991
Bsm UNI	5146	E	213 626-2557	8572
Buck Global LLC	8999	D	310 282-8232	27922
Buckingham Affrdbl Aprtmnts LP	8741	D	424 273-6162	26787
Buena Ventura Care Center Inc (PA)	8051	D	323 268-0106	20273
Bungalow 16 Entertainment LLC	5094	E	310 226-7870	8004
Bunker Hill Club Inc	8641	D	213 620-9662	25120
Burke Williams & Sorensen LLP (PA)	8111	D	213 236-0600	22965
Burlington Convalescent Hosp (PA)	8051	D	213 381-5585	20275

Employment Codes: A=Over 500 employees, B=251-500,
C=101-250, D=51-100, E=50

2019 Directory of California
Wholesalers and Services Companies

© Mergent Inc. 1-800-342-5647

1601

Company	SIC	EMP	PHONE	ENTRY #
Burlington Convalescent Hosp	8051	D	323 295-7737	20276
Burn 60 LLC	7991	E	310 476-5656	18582
Burton-Way House Ltd A CA	7011	C	310 273-2222	12411
Burton-Way House Ltd A CA (PA)	7011	C	310 552-6623	12412
Busa Servicing Inc (DH)	6022	D	310 203-3400	9422
Busa Servicing Inc	6022	C	800 222-1234	9423
BV General Inc	8059	D	323 651-0043	21026
C P Document Technologies LLC (PA)	5065	D	213 617-4040	7454
C&C Jewelry Mfg Inc	5094	D	213 623-6800	8005
C-Air International Inc	4731	D	310 695-3400	5023
Caa Sports LLC (HQ)	7941	D	424 288-2000	18513
Caffeine Productions	7812	D	323 860-8111	18029
Cal Southern Assn Governments (PA)	8748	C	213 236-1800	27668
Caliber Holdings Corporation	7532	D	323 913-4000	17718
California Assn Realtors Inc (PA)	8611	C	213 739-8200	24947
California Club	8641	C	213 622-1391	25122
California Cmnty Foundation (PA)	6732	C	213 413-4130	12074
California Credit Union	6061	D	213 975-1254	9545
California Cryobank Inc (PA)	8099	D	310 443-5244	22754
California Endowment (PA)	8399	D	800 449-4149	24746
California Fair Plan Assn	6411	D	213 487-0111	10572
California Pav Grading Co Inc	1611	D	323 372-5920	1735
California Rain Company Inc	5137	D	213 623-6061	8291
California State Univ Aux Svcs	8741	A	323 343-2531	26795
California Suncare Inc	5122	D	310 578-4400	8150
California Transit Inc	4111	D	323 234-8750	3640
Califrnia Hosp Med Ctr Fndtion	8062	A	213 748-2411	21304
Califrnia Scnce Ctr Foundation	8412	B	213 744-2545	24867
Call To Action LLC (PA)	6799	D	310 996-7200	12208
Callisonrtkl Inc	8712	C	213 627-7373	26029
Callisonrtkl Inc	8712	C	213 633-6000	26030
Camp Bow Wow Franchising Inc	0742	D	310 571-6500	599
Canton Food Co Inc	5141	C	213 688-7707	8387
Cantor Fitzgerald L P	6211	D	310 282-6500	9921
Canvas Worldwide LLC	7313	C	424 303-4300	13939
Canyon Partners Incorporated (HQ)	6211	D	310 272-1000	9922
Cap-Mpt (PA)	6351	C	213 473-8600	10425
Capital Brands LLC (HQ)	5149	C	310 996-7200	8766
Capital Drywall LP	1742	C	909 599-6818	2862
Capital Group Companies Inc	6282	B	310 996-6238	10069
Capital Group Companies Inc (PA)	6282	A	213 486-9200	10070
Capital Guardian Trust Company (HQ)	6733	D	213 486-9200	12089
Capital Research and MGT Co (HQ)	6282	B	213 486-9200	10073
Capitol Records LLC	7389	A	213 462-6252	17054
Captain Marketing Inc	8742	D	310 402-9709	27181
Cara Communications Corp	7812	E	310 442-5600	18030
Career Group Inc (PA)	7361	A	310 277-8188	14585
Carleton Booker Marketing Inc	8742	D	510 999-1682	27183
Carmichael International Svc (DH)	4731	D	213 353-0800	5025
Carpenters Southwest ADM Corp (PA)	7011	D	213 386-8590	12432
Caruso MGT Ltd A Cal Ltd Prtnr	6531	D	323 900-8100	11269
Casa Dscanso Convalescent Hosp	8744	C	323 225-5991	27580
Catasys Inc (PA)	8063	D	310 444-4300	21938
Cathay Bank	8741	B	213 687-1300	26799
Cathay Bank	6022	D	213 896-0098	9426
Cathedral Center of St Paul	8699	D	213 482-2040	25407
Catholic Charities of La Inc (PA)	8733	D	213 251-3400	26607
Catholic Charities of La Inc	8322	D	213 251-3400	23535
CB Richard Ellis RE Svcs LLC	6531	D	213 613-3333	11273
CB Richard Ellis Strategic Par	6799	D	213 614-6862	12212
CB Richard Ellis Strtgc Prtnrs	6512	D	213 683-4200	10861
Cbest Inc	8069	D	310 445-2378	22002
Cbre Inc (HQ)	6726	C	213 613-3333	12058
Cbre Inc	6531	D	310 550-2500	11282
Cbre Global Investors LLC (DH)	8742	C	213 683-4200	27185
Cbre Group Inc (PA)	6531	C	213 613-3333	11285
Cbre Services Inc	8742	C	213 613-3333	27187
CBS Broadcasting Inc	8711	D	323 575-2345	25596
CBS Corporation	4833	D	323 575-2345	5775
CBS Radio Inc	4832	D	323 525-0980	5701
CBS Radio Inc	4832	D	323 930-1067	5703
CBS Radio Inc	4832	C	323 930-7580	5704
Cdsnet LLC	8748	D	310 981-9500	27678
Cecico Inc	5137	D	323 269-7000	8292
Cedars-Sinai Medical Center	8011	C	310 824-3664	19359
Cedars-Sinai Medical Center	8011	B	310 423-3849	19360
Cedars-Sinai Medical Center	8011	A	323 866-8483	19361
Cellco Partnership	4812	D	310 659-0775	5366
Cellco Partnership	4812	D	213 738-9771	5369
Cellular Palace Inc	5065	D	310 278-2007	7460
Cels Enterprises Inc (PA)	5139	D	310 838-0280	8347
Center Thtre Group Los Angeles (PA)	7922	C	213 972-7344	18354
Centurion Security Inc	7381	C	818 755-0202	16600
Century 21 Beverlywood Realty	6531	D	310 836-8321	11294
Century City Primary Care	8011	E	310 553-3189	19369
Century Plaza Garage	7521	C	310 226-7495	17681
Century Properties Owners Assn	6531	E	310 272-8580	11310
Certified Aviation Svcs LLC	4581	D	310 338-1224	4876
Cha Hollywood Medical Ctr LP (PA)	8062	A	213 413-3000	21311
Chance Group LLC	5137	E	310 343-3766	8293
Charles Dunn Co Inc	6531	D	213 481-1800	11312
Charles Dunn RE Svcs Inc (PA)	6531	D	213 270-6200	11313
Charter Realty Group Inc (PA)	6531	D	310 826-3174	11314
Chase Care Center Inc	8059	C	323 935-8490	21038
Chicago Title Company	6361	D	213 488-4375	10440
Childrens Bureau Southern Cal (PA)	8361	C	213 342-0100	24465
Childrens Hospital Los (PA)	8011	D	323 361-2336	19377
Childrens Hospital Los Angeles	8062	C	323 361-2153	21315
Childrens Hospital Los Angeles (PA)	8069	D	323 660-2450	22005
Childrens Hospital Los Angeles	8011	B	323 361-2119	19379
Childrens Hospital Los Angeles	8733	B	323 361-2751	26613
Childrens Hospital Los Angeles	8062	D	323 660-2450	21317
Childrens Hospital Los Angeles	8069	C	323 361-5702	22007
Childrens Inst Los Angeles	8322	A	213 383-2765	23568
Childrens Inst Los Angeles (PA)	8733	A	213 385-5100	26614
Childrens Institute Inc (PA)	8322	B	213 385-5100	23569
China Airlines Ltd (HQ)	4512	C	310 646-4233	4778
Chinatown Service Center (PA)	8331	C	213 808-1700	24166
Chinese Laundry Inc	5139	E	310 945-3299	8349
Chiquita Brands Intl Inc	5148	D	213 488-0925	8654
Chodorow De Castro West	8111	D	310 478-2541	22975
Christmas Bonus Fund of The Pl	6733	D	213 385-6161	12091
Chrome River Technologies Inc (PA)	7371	D	323 857-5800	15058
Chsp Trs Los Angeles LLC	7011	D	213 624-0000	12458
Churchill MGT Group Corp	6282	E	877 937-7110	10075
Cim Group LP (PA)	6531	D	323 860-4900	11318
Cinelease Inc (HQ)	7819	D	855 441-5500	18182
Cinepolis Luxury Cinemas	7832	C	323 556-6340	18282
Cinnabar	7336	C	818 842-8190	14103
Cinnabar California Inc	7336	D	818 842-8190	14104
CIT Bank NA	6021	D	310 475-4594	9305
CIT Bank NA	6021	D	310 477-0546	9314
CIT Bank National Association	6021	D	310 820-9650	9324
Citadel Group Solutions Inc	7373	D	310 649-7500	15932
Citigroup Global Markets Inc	6211	C	213 486-8811	9930
City National Bank (DH)	6021	B	310 888-6000	9337
City National SEC Svcs Inc	7381	D	310 641-6666	16604
City of Los Angeles	8711	A	213 978-0259	25612
City of Los Angeles	8111	C	213 978-4049	22980
City of Los Angeles	8412	D	213 473-0800	24873
City of Los Angeles	8712	D	213 485-4282	26037
City of Los Angeles	8699	D	213 202-5500	25411
City of Los Angeles	7349	D	213 847-2799	14210
City of Los Angeles	8111	A	213 978-8100	22981
City of Los Angeles	7032	E	323 467-7193	13448
CJ America Inc (HQ)	5149	C	213 427-5566	8768
Classic Couriers Inc (PA)	4215	D	323 461-3741	4395
Classic Protection Inc	7381	E	213 742-1238	16606
Clearview Capital LLC	6799	A	310 806-9555	12215
Cliftonlarsonallen LLP	8721	D	310 273-2501	26168
Clinic Inc (PA)	8093	D	323 730-1920	22532
Clinica Msr Oscar A Romero (PA)	8011	D	213 989-7700	19385
Clinica Popular Medical Group	8011	E	213 381-7175	19386
Club Assist North America Inc (PA)	5013	D	213 388-4333	6630
Club Assist US LLC	5013	C	213 388-4333	6631
Cmts LLC	8741	C	310 215-0237	26813
Cnn America Inc	4841	D	323 993-5000	5863
Coast Citrus Distributors	5148	C	213 955-3444	8658
Coast Produce Company (PA)	5148	C	213 955-4900	8660
Cohen Brown MGT Group Inc (PA)	8742	D	310 966-1001	27197
Cohnreznick LLP	8721	E	310 477-3722	26170
Collins Avenue LLC	4833	E	323 930-6633	5779
Colony Capitl Inv Advisors LLC	6799	D	310 282-8820	12216
Colony Management Inc	6531	D	310 282-8820	11374
Colony Northstar Inc	6531	D	310 882-7230	11375
Comcast Cble Cmmunications LLC	4841	E	310 216-3500	5866
Comcast Cble Cmmunications LLC	4841	C	310 216-3686	5869
Comcast Corporation	4841	D	323 993-8000	5887
Command Security Corporation	7381	A	310 981-4530	16610
Commercial Coating Company Inc	1611	D	323 256-1331	1745
Commercial Property Management (PA)	6513	D	213 739-2000	11003
Commodity Forwarders Inc (DH)	4731	D	310 348-8855	5035
Community Build Inc (PA)	8641	D	323 290-6560	25140
Community Partners (PA)	8399	D	213 346-3200	24765
Community Redevelopment Agency (PA)	8748	C	213 977-1600	27695
Complex Studios	7389	E	310 477-1938	17094
Comprehensive Cmnty Hlth Ctr	8011	E	323 344-4144	19402
Concession Management Svcs Inc	7999	C	310 846-5830	19146
Constellation Newenergy Inc	4911	D	213 576-6001	6022
Coopertive Amrcn Physcians Inc (PA)	8621	D	213 473-8600	25012

Mergent email: customerrelations@mergent.com

1602

2019 Directory of California
Wholesalers and Services Companies

(P-0000) Products & Services Section entry number
(PA)=Parent Co (HQ)=Headquarters (DH)=Div Headquarters

Company	SIC	EMP	PHONE	ENTRY #
Cordoba Corporation	7373	D	213 895-0224	15937
Cornerstone Research Inc	8732	D	213 553-2500	26507
Corp of Church of Christ Ld St	7641	C	323 268-7281	17921
Corporate Building Svcs Inc	7349	C	213 252-0999	14228
Corridor Capital LLC (PA)	6799	C	310 442-7000	12217
Country Villa East LP	8059	C	323 939-3184	21046
Country Villa Imperial LLC	8051	C	323 666-1544	20328
Country Villa Service Corp	8741	C	323 666-1544	26822
Country Villa Service Corp	8741	C	323 734-5600	26826
Country Villa Service Corp	8741	C	310 574-3733	26827
Country Villa Service Corp	8741	C	323 734-9122	26828
Country Villa Terrace (PA)	8059	D	323 653-3980	21048
Country Villa Terrace	8059	E	323 939-3184	21049
County of Los Angeles	8099	D	213 739-2360	22772
County of Los Angeles	7375	C	213 974-0515	16215
County of Los Angeles	8069	A	213 974-7284	22012
County of Los Angeles	8062	C	310 668-4545	21353
County of Los Angeles	8361	D	323 226-8611	24479
County of Los Angeles	8011	B	323 226-6221	19411
County of Los Angeles	8011	B	213 744-3677	19412
County of Los Angeles	8322	C	818 374-2161	23663
County of Los Angeles	8111	C	323 226-8998	22997
County of Los Angeles	7336	A	213 922-6210	14108
County of Los Angeles	8721	C	323 267-2136	26173
County of Los Angeles	8322	C	213 974-9331	23664
County of Los Angeles	8621	A	213 240-8412	25015
County of Los Angeles	8322	B	323 586-7263	23666
County of Los Angeles	8093	D	323 769-7800	22547
County of Los Angeles	8322	C	323 226-8511	23667
County of Los Angeles	8069	A	323 226-3468	22013
County of Los Angeles	8322	D	213 351-5600	23668
County of Los Angeles	8322	C	323 727-1639	23669
County of Los Angeles	8322	B	213 744-5601	23671
County of Los Angeles	8099	D	213 351-7800	22776
County of Los Angeles	8062	C	323 226-6021	21354
County of Los Angeles	8412	D	323 857-6000	24879
County of Los Angeles	8099	D	213 240-7780	22778
County of Los Angeles	8111	C	213 974-2811	23000
County of Los Angeles	8322	D	323 780-2185	23678
County of Los Angeles	8322	A	213 351-7257	23680
County of Los Angeles	8322	D	323 586-6469	23681
County of Los Angeles	1611	C	626 458-1700	1751
County of Los Angeles	7389	C	323 267-2771	17104
County of Los Angeles	8062	B	213 473-6100	21355
County of Los Angeles	4789	C	213 974-4561	5222
County of Los Angeles	4941	C	213 974-8301	6235
Covenant House California	8361	C	323 461-3131	24485
Covington & Burling LLP	8111	B	424 332-4800	23012
Cox Castle & Nicholson LLP (PA)	8111	C	310 284-2200	23013
CP Opco LLC	7359	D	209 524-1966	14493
CP Opco LLC	7359	D	310 966-4900	14494
Create Music Group Inc	7389	D	310 623-0696	17109
Creative Artists Agency LLC (PA)	7922	A	424 288-2000	18361
Creative Channel Services LLC (HQ)	7311	D	310 482-6500	13805
Creative Circle LLC (DH)	7361	D	323 930-2333	14594
Credit Ssse Securities USA LLC	6211	D	213 253-2600	9945
Crenshaw YMCA	8641	C	323 290-9113	25145
Crestline Hotels & Resorts Inc	7011	C	213 629-1200	12499
Crestline Hotels & Resorts LLC	8741	D	213 624-0000	26834
Crew Creative Advertising LLC	7311	C	310 451-3225	13806
Crime Impact Security Patrol	7381	D	323 296-6406	16621
Crown Building Maintenance Co	7349	E	213 765-7800	14241
Crown Energy Services Inc	7349	A	213 765-7800	14242
Crown Transportation Inc	4119	D	310 737-0888	3787
Crowne Plaza Lax LLC	7011	C	310 258-1321	12502
Crystal Cruises LLC (DH)	4481	C	310 785-9300	4707
Crystal Stairs Inc (PA)	8322	B	323 299-8998	23764
Crystal Valet Parking Inc	7299	D	323 663-7275	13736
Culinary Services America Inc	7363	E	323 965-7582	14846
Culver City Roofing Company	1761	D	323 930-1311	3144
Culver West Health Center LLC	8059	D	310 390-9506	21054
Cumulus Intrmdate Holdings Inc	4832	D	310 840-4900	5707
Curatel LLC	4813	B	213 427-7411	5542
Custom Hotel LLC	7011	D	310 645-0400	12506
Cyberdefender Corporation	7371	B	323 449-0774	15092
Cybrex Consulting Inc	7372	D	513 999-2109	15642
DA Davidson & Co	6211	B	213 620-1850	9948
Dailey & Associates	7311	D	310 360-3100	13808
Daily Journal Corporation	7313	E	213 229-5500	13941
Dailylook Inc	7389	D	888 888-6645	17124
Daiwa House California Inc	1521	B	310 228-5675	1152
Daniel J Edelman Inc	8743	D	323 857-9100	27552
Daniel J Edelman Inc	7313	D	323 857-9100	13943
Danning Gill Damnd Kollitz LLP	8111	D	310 277-0077	23021
Daqri LLC (PA)	7371	D	213 375-8830	15093
Davalan Sales Inc	5148	C	213 623-2500	8663
David Evans Enterprises Inc	8711	A	213 337-3680	25640
Davie Brown Entertainment Inc	7922	D	310 979-1980	18362
Davis Wright Tremaine LLP	8111	D	213 633-6800	23025
Daviselen Advertising Inc (PA)	7311	C	213 688-7000	13810
Dechert LLP	8111	C	213 489-1357	23027
Decurion Corporation (PA)	7832	D	310 659-9432	18285
Defined Contribution Trust Fun	6733	D	213 385-6161	12092
Deloitte & Touche LLP	8721	A	213 688-0800	26177
Deloitte & Touche LLP	8721	C	213 688-0800	26184
Delta Air Lines Inc	4731	D	310 646-9614	5041
Delta Air Lines Inc	4512	D	323 417-7374	4779
Delta Floral Distributors Inc	5193	C	323 751-8116	9133
Deluxe Digital Dist Inc	7819	E	818 260-6202	18186
Deluxe Media Services LLC	7812	A	323 462-6171	18039
Dentons US LLP	8111	C	213 623-9300	23035
Dentons US LLP	8111	C	213 688-1000	23036
Dependable Highway Express Inc (PA)	4213	B	323 526-2200	4126
Design Collection Inc	5131	D	323 277-9200	8225
Desmond Mail Delivery Service	4212	D	323 262-1085	4004
Destination Shuttle Svcs LLC	4111	D	310 338-9466	3645
Deutsch La Inc	7311	D	310 862-3000	13817
Deutsche Bank National Tr Co (DH)	6111	D	213 620-8200	9693
Dfusion Software Inc	7371	E	323 617-5577	15105
Digital Domain 30 Inc (PA)	7812	D	310 314-2800	18040
Digital Media Management LLC	8741	D	323 378-6505	26840
Dignity Health	8062	B	213 484-7111	21367
Dignity Health	8062	A	213 748-2411	21378
Direct Partners Inc (HQ)	7311	D	310 482-4200	13820
Directors Guild America Inc (PA)	7819	C	310 289-2000	18188
Disability Rights California	8111	D	213 213-8000	23041
Discovery Communications Inc (PA)	4899	B	310 975-5906	5980
Diversified RE Packaging Corp	8748	A	310 855-1946	27706
Diversified Transportation LLC	4111	D	310 981-9500	3646
Dla Piper LLP (us)	8111	D	213 330-7700	23044
Dla Piper LLP (us)	8111	D	310 595-3000	23046
Dlr Group Inc	8712	C	626 796-8230	26044
Dlr Group Inc (HQ)	8712	C	213 800-9400	26045
Docler Media LLC (DH)	7374	D	424 777-3999	16118
Document Technologies LLC	7389	D	213 892-9000	17136
Doheny Eye Institute	8733	C	323 442-6682	26616
Domestic Linen Supply Co Inc (HQ)	7213	E	213 749-6300	13529
Dominguez Firm Inc	8111	D	213 388-7788	23050
Donald T Sterling Corporation	7011	D	310 275-5575	12538
Dorani Limited	7371	D	213 355-7230	15117
Double G Productions Ltd	7929	C	310 479-0978	18431
Doubleline Capital LP	7389	C	213 633-8200	17138
Drew Child Dev Corp Inc (PA)	8322	C	323 249-2950	23774
Drinker Biddle & Reath LLP	8111	C	310 229-1282	23054
Drive Thru Technology Inc	7382	C	323 576-1400	16889
Dti Services Inc (PA)	7379	C	213 670-1100	16351
Dual Diagnosis Trtmnt Ctr Inc	8071	C	424 289-9031	22080
Duckpunk Productions Inc	7812	C	310 836-3818	18047
Duff & Phelps LLC	8742	D	213 270-2300	27221
Dya Assoc	6552	C	323 364-4270	11872
Dykema Gossett PLLC	8111	D	213 457-1800	23058
E & C Fashion Inc	7389	B	323 262-0099	17143
E H Summit Inc (PA)	7011	C	310 476-6571	12544
E L Payne Heating Company	1711	E	310 275-5331	2192
E-Times Corporation Ltd	7375	B	213 452-6720	16219
Ea Mobile Inc	4812	B	310 754-7125	5407
Earle M Jorgensen Company	5051	D	323 567-1122	7272
Earth Technology Corp USA	4953	A	213 593-8000	6390
Earthbound Productions LLC	7812	D	504 734-3337	18049
East L A Remarkable Citizens (PA)	8322	D	323 223-3079	23777
Eastside Group Corporation	7381	C	213 368-9777	16636
Eaton Corporation	5063	B	818 409-0200	7355
EC Group Inc (PA)	5021	C	310 815-2700	6720
Eclipse Berry Farms LLC	0171	D	310 207-7879	97
Economic Dev Corp of La County	8748	E	213 622-4300	27713
Edge Financial Inc	7291	E	323 857-5809	13704
Edgemine Inc	5137	C	323 267-8222	8300
Efilm LLC	7812	C	323 463-7041	18050
Eharmony Inc (PA)	7299	C	424 258-1199	13741
Ejm Kyrene LLC (PA)	1531	E	310 278-1830	1338
El Al Israel Airlines Ltd	4729	C	323 852-1252	4988
El Pas-Los Angles Lmsne Ex Inc	4142	E	213 623-2323	3895
Eladh LP	8062	D	323 268-5514	21404
Elevate Services Inc (PA)	8748	B	310 853-8448	27715
Elite Information Group Inc (DH)	7373	B	323 642-5200	15953
Elvis Schoenberg Production	7922	E	323 344-1745	18364
Emerald Trans Los Angeles LLC	4212	E	323 277-2500	4010
Emerik Hotel Corp	7011	D	213 748-1291	12558
Emery Smith Laboratories Inc	8734	C	213 745-5333	26699
Emmi Inc	5094	D	213 622-7234	8009

GEOGRAPHIC

Company	SIC	EMP	PHONE	ENTRY #
Emmis Publishing Corporation	5192	D	323 801-0100	9113
Emp III Inc	6799	D	323 231-4174	12223
Emser International LLC (PA)	5032	D	323 650-2000	6891
End-Time Message & Support	6799	E	323 756-6252	12225
Englekirk Institutional Inc (PA)	8711	E	323 733-2640	25668
Englekirk Structural Engineers (PA)	8711	E	323 733-6673	25669
Engstrom Lipscomb and Lack A (PA)	8111	D	310 552-3800	23060
Entertainment & Sports Today	4833	D	213 388-9050	5783
Entertinment Studios Media Inc (PA)	7929	D	310 277-3500	18432
Entravsion Communications Corp	4833	D	323 900-6100	5785
Epstein Becker & Green PC	8111	D	310 556-8861	23061
Equator LLC (HQ)	7371	C	310 469-9500	15143
Equicare Medical Supply Inc	8051	D	213 385-1715	20406
Eric Jones Customs Brokerage	4731	E	310 348-3777	5054
Ernst & Young LLP	8721	A	213 977-3200	26191
Espn Inc	4841	B	212 456-7439	5911
Essential Access Health (PA)	8399	D	213 386-5614	24780
Ethiopian World Federation	8399	E	323 844-1826	24781
Evergreen Cleaning Systems Inc	7349	D	213 386-3260	14260
Evgo Services LLC	7549	D	310 954-2900	17860
Evolve Growth Initiatives LLC	8361	D	424 281-5000	24526
Evoq Properties Inc	6531	D	213 988-8890	11424
Excellence Ventures Inc	7389	D	323 262-6800	17158
Expeditors Intl Wash Inc	4731	D	310 343-6200	5057
Expeditors Intl Wash Inc	4731	C	310 343-6200	5058
F O C Electronics Corporation	5064	E	213 625-5775	7415
Facter Direct Ltd	7389	D	323 634-1999	17160
Fame Assistance Corporation	8748	D	323 373-7720	27728
Far East Home Care Inc	8082	C	949 673-3100	22297
Farmers Group Inc	6311	D	213 615-2500	10135
Farmers Group Inc	6411	D	818 249-3000	10620
Farmers Insurance Fed Cred UNI (PA)	6061	C	323 209-6000	9551
Fc Metropolitan Lofts Inc	6552	D	213 488-0010	11875
Fcs Medical Corporation	8031	D	323 317-9200	20149
Fcti Inc (PA)	6099	D	310 405-0022	9681
Federal Deposit Insurance Corp	6399	C	323 545-9260	10500
Federal Express Corporation	4213	D	800 463-3339	4150
Federal Rsrve Bnk San Frncisco	6011	A	213 683-2300	9274
Fedex Office & Print Svcs Inc	7334	D	213 892-1700	14089
Fei Enterprises Inc	1731	C	323 937-0856	2583
Fender Digital LLC (HQ)	7371	D	323 462-2198	15159
Festival Management Corp (PA)	6531	D	310 665-9610	11446
Fifth & Sunset Enterprises LLC	7359	D	310 979-0212	14505
Fiji Water Company LLC (HQ)	5149	E	310 966-5700	8789
Film Payroll Services Inc (PA)	8721	D	310 440-9600	26204
Fire Insurance Exchange (PA)	6411	A	323 932-3200	10630
Firefighters First Credit Un (PA)	6061	C	323 254-1700	9553
First Capitol Consulting Inc	8742	D	213 382-1115	27236
First Choice Bank	6022	D	213 617-0082	9447
First City Credit Union (PA)	6061	C	213 482-3477	9554
First Entertainment Credit Un (PA)	6061	D	323 851-3673	9555
First Fire Systems Inc (PA)	7382	D	310 559-0900	16896
First Legal Support Svcs LLC (PA)	8111	D	213 250-1111	23068
First Regional Bancorp	6022	B	310 552-1776	9450
First Republic Bank	6022	C	213 239-8883	9454
First Republic Bank	6029	D	310 712-1888	9503
Five Star Transportation Inc	4729	E	310 348-0820	4990
Floorgate Inc	1752	D	323 478-2000	3103
FM Seoul Bang Song Inc	4832	E	323 525-1650	5718
Foley & Lardner LLP	8111	C	213 972-4500	23076
Fonda & Frazer LLP (PA)	8111	D	310 553-3320	23078
Forest Lawn Memorial-Park Assn	6553	D	323 254-7251	11942
Fortress Investment Group LLC	6722	D	310 228-3030	12037
Fortuna Enterprises LP	7011	B	310 410-4000	12582
Four Points By Sheraton	7011	D	310 645-4600	12585
Fox Inc (DH)	4833	A	310 369-1000	5792
Fox Animation Studios Inc	7812	B	323 857-8800	18054
Fox Broadcasting Company (DH)	4833	C	310 369-1000	5793
Fox BSB Holdco Inc	7941	A	323 224-1500	18518
Fox Networks Group Inc	4841	C	310 369-5104	5914
Fox Networks Group Inc (DH)	4841	D	310 369-9369	5915
Fox Rent A Car Inc (PA)	7514	E	310 342-5155	17637
Fox Television Stations Inc (DH)	4833	B	310 584-2000	5794
Fragomen Del Rey Bernse	8111	E	310 820-3322	23081
Frandzel Share Robins Bloom Lc	8111	D	323 852-1000	23085
Fred Leeds Properties	6513	E	310 826-2466	11021
Freeman Freeman & Smiley (PA)	8111	D	310 398-6100	23086
Freshology Inc	5149	D	818 847-1888	8791
Friends of The Los Angeles	8399	C	323 653-0440	24783
Front Line MGT Group Inc	8741	D	310 209-3100	26865
Front Porch Communities	8051	C	323 661-1128	20441
Fti Consulting Inc	8711	D	213 689-1200	25693
Fuel TV	4833	D	310 444-8564	5795
Full Throttle	7389	C	323 474-8417	17178
Fulwider and Patton LLP	8111	D	310 824-5555	23087
Fund Services Advisors Inc	6282	E	213 612-2196	10085
Futuredontics Inc (PA)	8742	C	310 215-6400	27243
Fx Networks LLC	4841	C	310 369-1000	5916
G B & P Citrus Co Inc (PA)	6512	D	213 312-1380	10881
G J Sullivan Co Inc	6411	D	213 626-1000	10632
G M Floral Company	5193	C	213 489-7055	9135
G4s Secure Solutions (usa)	7381	B	323 938-9100	16652
Gabriella Foundation	7911	D	213 365-2491	18334
Gaju Market Corporation	5199	C	213 382-9444	9219
Gamefly Inc (PA)	7379	C	310 568-8224	16375
Garda CL West Inc (DH)	7381	B	213 383-3611	16661
Garden Crest Convalesce	8051	D	323 663-8281	20445
Garden Grove Advanced Imaging	8071	C	310 445-2800	22087
Garment Industry Laundry	7218	C	323 752-8335	13608
Gartner Inc	8732	C	310 479-2108	26521
Gary Lask	8011	D	310 825-0631	19480
Gateway Security Inc	7381	A	310 410-0790	16663
Gateways Hosp Mental Hlth Ctr	8063	D	323 644-2026	21954
Gateways Hosp Mental Hlth Ctr (PA)	8063	D	323 644-2000	21955
Gehry Partners LLP	8712	C	310 482-3000	26046
Gelfand Rennert & Feldman LLP (PA)	7389	C	310 553-1707	17183
General Services Cal Dept	8712	D	213 897-3995	26048
General Services Cal Dept	7349	D	213 897-2241	14275
Genesis Healthcare Corporation	8051	D	310 391-8266	20450
Gentlecare Transport Inc	4119	D	323 662-8777	3800
Gentry Group LLC	7929	E	310 968-5399	18435
Genzyme Corporation	8734	C	310 482-5000	26703
Getty Images Inc	7389	D	323 202-4200	17187
Gibbs Giden Locher	8111	D	310 552-3400	23090
Gibson Dunn & Crutcher LLP (PA)	8111	B	213 229-7000	23093
Gibson Dunn & Crutcher LLP	8111	D	310 552-8500	23094
Gilbert Klly Crwley Jnnett LLP (PA)	8111	D	213 615-7000	23096
Gils Distributing Service (PA)	7319	C	213 627-0539	13973
Gipson Hoffman & Pancione A	8111	D	310 556-4660	23097
Girardi & Keese (PA)	8111	D	213 977-0211	23098
Girardi and Keefe	6512	D	213 489-5330	10883
Girl Scuts Greater Los Angeles (PA)	8641	C	626 677-2200	25164
Giroux Glass Inc (PA)	1793	C	213 747-7406	3405
Giumarra Bros Fruit Co Inc (PA)	5148	D	213 627-2900	8689
Glaser Weil Fink Jacobs (PA)	8111	C	310 553-3000	23099
Global Management Company LLC	8742	D	323 261-8114	27246
Global Nurses Online Inc	7361	D	310 306-2760	14628
Global Reach 18 Inc (PA)	6726	D	310 203-5850	12061
Global Staffing Inc	7361	C	303 451-5602	14629
Gold Parent LP	6211	A	310 954-0444	9957
Golden International	6799	A	213 628-1388	12229
Golden State Mutl Lf Insur Co (PA)	6311	D	713 526-4361	10136
Goldman Sachs & Co	6211	C	310 407-5700	9959
Goldstar Hlthcr Cntr of Chtswr	8059	C	818 882-8233	21099
Gonzalez Barba Enterprises	4731	E	323 233-7995	5078
Good Samaritan Hospital (PA)	8062	C	213 977-2121	21432
Good Samaritan Hospital Aux	8011	A	213 977-2121	19486
Goodwin Procter LLP	8111	D	213 426-2500	23102
Gordon Edelstein Krepack Gr	8111	E	213 739-7000	23103
Gordon Rees Sclly Mnskhani LLP	8111	D	213 576-5000	23107
Gores Norment Holdings Inc	6719	C	310 209-3010	11983
Grand Park Convalescent Hosp	8051	D	213 382-7315	20493
Grand Performances	7389	D	213 687-2190	17201
Grant Thornton LLP	8721	E	213 627-1717	26207
Grant Thornton LLP	8721	D	213 627-1717	26209
Great American Insurance Co	6331	D	323 937-8600	10358
Great American Insurance Co	6331	C	213 430-4300	10359
Great Western Bancorp Inc	6022	B	213 622-1895	9461
Greater Los Angeles Agency	8322	C	323 478-8000	23826
Greater Los Angeles Zoo Assn	8399	D	323 644-4200	24785
Green Equity Investors III L P	6211	A	310 954-0444	9961
Green Farms Inc	5148	B	858 831-7701	8691
Green Farms Inc (PA)	5148	C	213 747-4411	8692
Green Glusk Field Clama & Mach	8111	C	310 553-3610	23110
Green Hasson & Janks LLP	8721	C	310 873-1600	26211
Greenberg Traurig LLP	8111	D	310 586-7708	23112
Greenland US Consulting Inc	1531	D	213 362-9300	1341
Greenspire LLC	8742	D	310 477-7686	27255
Greenway Arts Alliance Inc	7922	D	323 655-7679	18370
Greybor Medical Transportation	4119	E	213 250-4444	3805
Greyhound Lines Inc	4173	B	213 629-8400	3954
Grifols Biologicals Inc	4225	B	323 255-2221	4568
Grifols Shared Svcs N Amer Inc (HQ)	5122	C	323 225-2221	8174
Grill On The Alley The Inc	7389	A	323 856-5530	17203
Grosslight Insurance Inc	6411	D	310 473-9611	10638
Gruen Associates	8712	D	323 937-4270	26053
Guardian Eagle Security Inc	7381	B	888 990-0002	16673
Guardian Rehabilitation Hosp	8059	D	323 930-4815	21102
Guardians of The Los Angeles	8051	D	310 479-2468	20499
Guardsmark LLC	7381	C	310 287-3103	16678

Mergent email: customerrelations@mergent.com
1604

2019 Directory of California
Wholesalers and Services Companies

(P-0000) Products & Services Section entry number
(PA)=Parent Co (HQ)=Headquarters (DH)=Div Headquarters

	SIC	EMP	PHONE	ENTRY #
Gursey Schneider & Co LLC (PA)	8721	D	310 552-0960	26213
Gva Enterprises Inc (PA)	8059	D	213 484-0510	21103
Gva Enterprises Inc.	8051	D	213 484-0784	20500
Gvs Italy	5051	D	424 382-4343	7277
H & K Abouaf Corporation	8082	D	310 393-1282	22309
H D S I Managment	6512	E	323 231-1104	10889
H2 Wellness Incorporated	7372	D	310 362-1888	15701
Haight Brown & Bonesteel LLP (PA)	8111	D	213 542-8000	23119
Hall Windsor	8361	D	213 383-1547	24545
Hamburger Home	1521	D	213 637-5000	1176
Hamburger Home (PA)	8361	D	323 876-0550	24546
Hana Commercial Finance Inc	6153	D	213 240-1234	9740
Hana Financial Inc (PA)	7359	D	213 240-1234	14508
Hancock Pk Rhblitation Ctr LLC	8051	C	323 937-4860	20504
Hanil Development Inc	6553	E	213 387-0111	11944
Hanin Federal Credit Union (PA)	6061	E	213 368-9000	9560
Hanmi Bank (HQ)	6022	C	213 382-2200	9462
Hannam Chain USA Inc (PA)	5046	C	213 382-2922	7135
Harris Stockwell (PA)	8111	E	310 277-6669	23123
Harrys Auto Body Inc	7532	D	323 933-4600	17725
Hartford Fire Insurance Co	6411	C	213 452-5179	10642
Hatchbeauty Products LLC (PA)	5122	D	310 396-7070	8176
Hathaway Resource Center	8322	E	323 837-0838	23831
Hathaway-Sycamores Chld Fam Sv	8361	D	323 257-9600	24552
Hawaiian Airlines Inc	4512	D	310 417-1677	4784
Hazens Investment LLC	7011	B	310 642-1111	12650
HDR Architecture Inc	8711	D	626 584-1700	25724
HDR Engineering Inc	8742	C	626 584-1700	27259
Hdsi Management Inc (PA)	6531	D	323 231-1104	11501
Health Link Medi Van	4789	D	310 981-9500	5227
Height Brown and Bonesteel	8111	D	213 241-0900	23127
Helloworld Travel Svcs USA Inc	4724	D	310 535-1000	4938
Herbalife Intl Amer Inc (DH)	5122	B	213 745-0500	8177
Here Films	8748	E	310 806-4288	27746
Here Media Inc (PA)	4813	D	310 806-4288	5576
Highland Park Skilled Nursing	8051	D	323 254-6125	20530
Hill Farrer & Burrill	8111	D	213 620-0460	23130
Hillcrest Country Club	7997	C	310 553-8911	18935
Hinerfeld-Ward Inc	1521	D	310 842-7929	1178
Hinshaw & Culbertson LLP	8111	D	213 680-2800	23131
Hirsh Inc	1389	E	213 622-9441	1064
Historical Soc Centinela Vly	8412	B	310 649-6272	24885
Hit Portfolio I Misc Trs LLC	7011	C	323 656-1234	12673
Hks Inc	8712	D	310 788-7700	26060
Hntb Corporation	8711	D	213 403-1000	25734
Hob Entertainment LLC (DH)	7929	C	323 769-4600	18439
Holland & Knight LLP	8111	D	213 896-2400	23133
Holland Flower Market Inc (PA)	5193	C	213 627-9900	9142
Hollywood Community Hospital M	8062	C	323 462-2271	21453
Hollywood Medical Center LP	8062	A	213 413-3000	21454
Hollywood Mental Health Center	8093	D	323 769-6100	22594
Hollywood Rntals Prod Svcs LLC (PA)	7819	C	818 407-7800	18196
Hollywood Standard LLC	7011	C	323 822-3111	12694
Holthouse Carlin Van Trigt LLP (PA)	8721	C	310 477-5551	26223
Homeboy Industries (PA)	8322	B	323 526-1254	23840
Homeland Housewares LLC	5064	D	310 996-7200	7418
Hong Kong & Shanghai Banking	6081	D	213 626-2460	9663
Honk Technologies Inc	4729	D	800 979-3162	4992
Horizon Media Inc	7311	C	310 282-0909	13839
Hospital Assn Southern Cal (PA)	8399	D	213 347-2002	24789
Host Hotels & Resorts LP	7011	D	310 216-5858	12713
Houlihan Lokey Inc (PA)	6282	B	310 788-5200	10089
House of Blues Concerts Inc (DH)	7929	C	323 769-4977	18440
Hpt Trs Ihg-2 Inc	7011	D	310 642-7500	12736
Hsbc Business Credit (usa)	6029	D	213 553-8089	9506
Hsbc Finance Corporation	6029	C	213 628-8167	9508
Hudson Pacific Properties Inc (PA)	6798	D	310 445-5700	12165
Hueston Hennigan LLP	8111	D	213 788-4340	23137
Hulu LLC	4813	A	888 631-4858	5581
Humnit Hotel At Lax LLC	7011	D	424 702-1234	12741
Hunton Andrews Kurth LLP	8111	D	213 532-2000	23140
Hustle Digital Inc	7389	E	310 882-2680	17227
Hwn Mariposa Associates LLC	1531	D	310 478-8757	1343
Hyatt Corporation	7011	B	312 750-1234	12747
Hyde Park Convalescent Hosp	8051	E	323 753-1354	20540
Hyperloop Technologies Inc	4789	C	213 800-3270	5228
Hyrian LLC	7361	C	212 590-2567	14641
I D Property Corporation	6531	D	213 625-0100	11509
I Mean It Creative Inc	7311	E	310 287-1000	13842
Ias Administrations Inc	8399	D	323 953-3490	24790
Ibisworld Inc (DH)	8732	D	800 330-3772	26529
Icarus Fuel Services US Corp	4581	D	310 417-0124	4894
Icon Exposure Inc	7384	D	323 933-1666	16960
Ideal Program Services Inc	8322	D	323 296-2255	23851
IDS Real Estate Group (PA)	6531	D	213 627-9937	11511
If Live LLC (PA)	7812	D	323 957-6868	18062
Ignition Creative LLC	7812	D	310 315-6300	18063
Ihg Management (maryland) LLC	7011	C	310 642-7500	12760
Image of California Inc (PA)	7335	D	213 896-0039	14097
Imaginary Forces LLC (PA)	7812	D	323 957-6868	18064
Imaging Technologies Group LLC	5112	E	310 638-2500	8082
Imax Corporation (HQ)	7819	D	310 255-5500	18197
Imperial Capital Group LLC (PA)	6211	D	310 246-3700	9963
Imperial Capital LLC (PA)	6211	D	310 246-3700	9964
Imperial Mridian Companies Inc	7359	D	310 447-3460	14516
Imperial Parking Industries (PA)	7521	D	323 651-5588	17688
Infinity Broadcasting Corp Cal	4832	D	323 936-5784	5730
Infinity Care of East LA	8051	D	323 261-8108	20543
Insignia/Esg Ht Partners Inc (DH)	6512	D	310 765-2600	10899
Institute For Applied Behavior (PA)	8049	C	310 649-0499	20181
Integrated Decision Systems	7373	D	310 954-5530	15979
Integrated Trnsp Svcs Inc	4119	D	310 553-5060	3809
Interbake Foods LLC	5149	D	213 484-8161	8805
Intercare Therapy Inc	8049	C	323 866-1880	20184
Interior Office Solutions Inc	7389	E	310 726-9067	17245
Interlink	6159	C	310 734-1499	9760
International Creative Mgt Inc (HQ)	7922	C	310 550-4000	18373
International Creative MGT Inc	7922	C	310 550-4000	18374
International Design Services	8711	D	323 662-3963	25751
International Fdn For Korea Un	7389	B	213 550-2182	17247
International Inst Los Angeles (PA)	8322	D	323 224-3800	23863
International Marine Pdts Inc (HQ)	5146	D	213 893-6123	8578
International Media Group Inc	4833	D	310 478-1818	5801
International Medical Corps (PA)	8322	D	310 826-7800	23864
Internet Corp For Assigned Nam (PA)	7373	D	310 823-9358	15982
Interstate Hotels Resorts Inc	7011	C	213 617-1133	12776
Interstate Hotels Resorts Inc	7011	B	213 624-1000	12777
Investors Capital MGT Group	8741	D	310 553-5175	26902
Irell & Manella LLP (PA)	8111	D	310 277-1010	23142
Irell & Manella LLP.	8111	D	213 620-1555	23144
Irp Lax Hotel LLC	7011	C	310 645-4600	12780
Irwin Naturals	5122	D	310 306-3636	8179
Israel Discount Bank New York	6022	C	213 861-6440	9464
Ivie McNeill Wyatt A Prof Law	8111	E	213 489-0028	23146
Ivy Realty	6531	E	213 386-8888	11524
Iw Group (PA)	7311	D	310 289-5500	13851
J Alexander Investments Inc (PA)	6726	D	213 687-8400	12064
J Brand Holdings LLC	6719	D	212 228-8181	11988
J C Entertainment Ltg Svcs Inc	7922	D	818 252-7481	18375
J H Synder Co LLC	6531	D	323 857-5546	11526
J M Carden Sprinkler Co Inc	1711	D	323 258-8300	2239
J P H Consulting Inc (PA)	8051	C	323 934-5660	20547
J P H Consulting Inc.	8051	C	323 934-5660	20548
J Paul Getty Trust	8732	D	310 440-7325	26534
J2 Cloud Services LLC (HQ)	4822	D	323 860-9200	5684
J2 Global Inc (PA)	4822	D	323 860-9200	5685
Jack Engle & Co (PA)	5093	D	323 589-8111	7981
Jack Morton Worldwide Inc	7311	D	310 967-2400	13853
Jack Nadel Inc (PA)	8742	D	310 815-2600	27285
Jackoway Tyreman Wertheimer Au	8111	D	310 553-0305	23147
Jacobs Engineering Group Inc	8711	C	213 362-4336	25762
Jalmar Properties Inc (PA)	6531	E	310 207-8481	11528
Jameson Properties Co Inc	6512	E	213 487-3770	10902
Jarrow Formulas Inc (PA)	5122	D	310 204-6936	8182
JE Williams Trucking Inc	4213	E	406 248-7397	4198
Jean Mart Inc	5137	D	323 752-7775	8309
Jeffer Mngels Btlr Mtchell LLP (PA)	8111	C	310 203-8080	23149
Jefferies LLC	6211	D	310 445-1199	9966
Jenkins Gales & Martinez Inc	8741	D	310 645-0561	26905
Jetro Cash and Carry Entps LLC	5181	D	323 964-1200	9005
Jetro Holdings LLC	5046	C	213 516-0301	7140
Jewish Cmnty Fndn of (PA)	8641	B	323 761-8700	25177
Jewish Family Svc Los Angeles (PA)	8621	D	323 761-8800	25022
Jewish Family Svc Los Angeles	8322	E	323 937-5900	23875
Jewish Vocational Services (PA)	8331	E	323 761-8888	24197
Jhp Produce Inc	5148	D	213 627-1093	8698
Jim Henson Company Inc (PA)	7812	D	323 856-6680	18066
Jj Grand Hotel	7011	D	213 383-3000	12791
John Hancock Life Insur Co USA (DH)	7389	A	213 689-0813	17261
John Stewart Company	6531	E	213 787-2700	11535
Johnson Fain Inc	8712	D	323 224-6000	26072
Jonair Services LLC	4522	D	310 529-5482	4862
Jonathan Club (PA)	8641	B	213 624-0881	25178
Jones Day Limited Partnership	7389	D	213 489-3939	17263
Jones Lang La Salle	6798	D	213 239-6000	12168
Jules and Associates Inc	7359	D	213 362-5600	14520
Julio Gonzalez	8748	D	310 310-4055	27761
Jwmcc Limited Partnership	7011	B	310 277-1234	12796
K A Associates Inc	6211	C	310 556-2721	9968
K&L Gates LLP	8111	E	310 552-5000	23158

GEOGRAPHIC

Name	SIC	EMP	PHONE	ENTRY #
Kaa Design Group Inc	8712	D	310 821-1400	26073
Kaiser Foundation Hospitals	8062	D	323 783-4011	21479
Kaiser Foundation Hospitals	8011	A	323 857-2000	19535
Kaiser Foundation Hospitals	6324	D	800 954-8000	10221
Kaiser Foundation Hospitals	6324	D	800 954-8000	10232
Kaiser Foundation Hospitals	6733	E	323 881-5516	12105
Kaiser Foundation Hospitals	8093	C	323 298-3300	22602
Kaiser Foundation Hospitals	8063	C	213 580-7200	21959
Kaiser Foundation Hospitals	8062	E	800 954-8000	21520
Kajima Construction Svcs Inc	1541	E	323 269-0020	1412
Kal Krishnan Consulting Svcs (PA)	8741	D	510 893-3500	26915
Kash Apparel LLC	5137	D	213 747-8885	8310
Katten Muchin Rosenman LLP	8111	C	310 788-4498	23161
Katten Muchin Rosenman LLP	8111	C	310 788-4400	23163
Katz Media Group Inc	8748	D	323 966-5000	27763
Kaufman and Broad Limited	1531	C	310 231-4000	1345
Kava Holdings Inc (PA)	7011	B	310 472-1211	12801
Kayne Anderson Rudni	6722	C	310 229-9260	12040
KB Home (PA)	6351	C	310 231-4000	10430
KB Home Coastal Inc	1531	C	310 231-4000	1346
KB Home Grater Los Angeles Inc (HQ)	1521	D	310 231-4000	1188
Kbsa Inc	1531	D	310 231-4000	1347
Keck Hospital of Usc	8062	D	800 872-2273	21529
Kedren Community Hlth Ctr Inc	8322	C	323 524-0634	23881
Kedren Community Hlth Ctr Inc (PA)	8063	B	323 233-0425	21960
Keiro Nursing Home	8062	C	323 276-5700	21530
Keiro Services	8741	B	213 873-5700	26916
Kelley Drye & Warren LLP	8111	C	310 712-6100	23168
Kennedy Care Center	8059	D	323 651-0043	21123
Kenneth Brdwick Intr Dsgns Inc	7389	D	310 274-9999	17272
Keolis Transit America Inc (DH)	4119	E	310 981-9500	3813
Kerlan-Jobe Orthopedic Clinic (PA)	8011	D	310 665-7200	19625
Ketchum Incorporated	8743	D	310 437-2600	27558
Kevin Holubowski LLC	8399	C	310 908-6542	24796
Kf Sunray LLC	8059	D	323 734-2171	21126
Kfco Inc	4212	C	310 441-2483	4035
Kilroy Realty Corporation (PA)	6798	D	310 481-8400	12169
Kim Chong	7389	D	323 581-4700	17274
Kindred Healthcare Operating	8062	B	310 642-0325	21539
King Hlmes Ptrno Berliner LLP	8111	E	310 282-8989	23172
Kings Pawnshop	6163	D	213 383-5555	9890
Kingsley Apartments	6513	D	323 666-8862	11042
Kintetsu Enterprises	8741	D	213 687-2000	26920
Kintetsu Enterprises Co Amer	7011	D	213 617-2000	12817
Kl Cutting Service Inc	7219	C	213 742-9001	13635
Km Fresno Investors LLC	6799	E	323 556-6600	12238
Knet TV	4833	E	323 469-5638	5810
Kommonwealth Inc	5139	E	310 278-7328	8360
Koram Insurance Center Inc	6411	D	323 660-1000	10669
Korean Air Lines Co Ltd	4512	C	310 646-4866	4789
Korean Airlines	4512	C	310 417-5294	4790
Korean Airlines Co Ltd	4512	C	310 410-2000	4791
Korean Health Education (PA)	8322	D	213 427-4000	23886
Koreatown Youth and Cmnty Ctr (PA)	8322	D	213 365-7400	23887
Korn/Ferry International (PA)	8742	C	310 552-1834	27295
Kos-USA	5137	D	213 747-2591	8313
Kpff Inc	8711	D	310 665-1536	25787
Kpmg LLP	8721	D	703 286-8175	26239
Kpmg LLP	8721	A	212 758-9700	26240
Ktgy Group Inc	8712	E	310 394-2625	26078
Kusc Radio	4832	E	213 225-7400	5739
L & T Meat Co	5142	D	323 262-2815	8494
L and R Auto Parks Inc	7521	C	213 784-3018	17690
L J Trucking USA	4213	A	323 469-9663	4211
L R Investment Company	7521	D	213 627-8211	17691
La Asociacion Nacional Pro Per	8322	B	213 202-5900	23888
La Cienega Associates	6531	C	310 854-0071	11555
La Follette Johnson De Haas (PA)	8111	C	213 426-3600	23181
La Hotel Venture LLC	7011	B	213 617-1133	12827
La Inc Convention Vistors Bur	7389	D	213 236-2301	17285
La Laser Center Pc Cpmc	8011	D	310 446-4400	19633
La Live Properties LLC	7922	E	213 763-7700	18378
LA Sports Properties Inc	7941	C	213 742-7500	18523
La Vida Mltispecialty Med Ctrs	8011	D	213 765-7500	19640
Laaco Ltd (PA)	6519	C	213 622-1254	11175
Lac Usc Medical Center	8062	C	323 226-7858	21545
Ladas & Parry LLP	8111	E	323 934-2300	23182
Laguna Country Mart Ltd Inc	6512	E	310 826-5635	10904
Lakewood Manor North Inc	8051	D	213 380-9175	20575
Lamp Inc	8361	C	213 488-9559	24574
Langdon Wilson International (PA)	8712	E	213 250-1086	26079
Language Weaver Inc	7371	D	310 437-7300	15254
Larchmont Radiology Med Group	8011	D	213 483-5953	19642
Latham & Watkins LLP (PA)	8111	A	213 485-1234	23187
Latham & Watkins LLP	8111	D	213 891-7108	23188
Latham & Watkins LLP	8111	C	213 891-1200	23190
Lathrop & Gage LLP	8111	D	310 789-4600	23192
Lax Hospitality LP	7011	C	310 670-9000	12840
Lax Hotel Ventures LLC	7011	E	310 645-4600	12841
Lax International Service Ctr	7389	D	310 337-8764	17292
LAX Wheel Refinishing Inc	5013	C	323 269-1484	6654
Lax-C Inc	5141	E	323 343-9000	8420
Lear Capital Inc	6211	D	310 571-0190	9969
Led Global LLC	1711	D	917 921-4315	2260
Legacy Partners Hollywood	6513	C	949 930-7706	11051
Legend3d Inc	7812	D	858 793-4420	18067
LEK Consulting LLC	8742	D	310 209-9800	27303
Lendlease US Construction Inc	8741	D	213 430-4660	26932
Lenlyn Limited Which Will Do B (HQ)	6099	D	310 417-3432	9687
Leo A Daly Company	8712	D	213 627-9300	26081
Leo A Daly Company	8712	D	213 533-8855	26082
Level Four Business MGT LLC	8748	E	310 914-1600	27775
Levy Prmium Fdsrvice Ltd Prtnr	1541	D	213 742-7867	1418
Lewis Brsbois Bsgard Smith LLP	8111	D	213 250-1800	23204
Lewis Brsbois Bsgard Smith LLP (PA)	8111	A	213 250-1800	23206
Lewis P C Jackson	8111	D	213 689-0404	23213
Lgh Digital Media Inc	7812	E	323 469-3986	18068
Libsource LLC	8741	C	323 852-1083	26934
Lieberman RES Worldwide LLC (PA)	8732	C	310 553-0550	26539
Lifesigns Now (PA)	7389	B	323 550-4210	17295
Lifetime Entrmt Svcs LLC	4833	C	310 556-7500	5820
Lighthouse Healthcare Ctr LLC	8051	C	323 564-4461	20591
Linden Center	8063	D	213 251-8226	21963
Liner LLP	8111	C	310 500-3500	23216
Linne Entertainment LLC	7812	E	213 425-1146	18069
Linquest Corporation (PA)	8711	C	323 924-1600	25797
Lippin Group Inc (PA)	8743	E	323 965-1990	27562
Little Citizens Schools Inc	8351	D	323 732-1212	24340
Little Tokyo Service Center (PA)	8322	C	213 473-3003	23901
Live Nation Entertainment Inc	7929	D	323 468-1160	18447
Live Nation Entertainment Inc	7922	D	213 639-6178	18380
Live Nation Worldwide Inc	7922	C	323 966-5066	18381
Livhome Inc (PA)	8082	A	800 807-5854	22358
LLP Locke Lord	8111	C	213 485-1500	23220
LLP Mayer Brown	8111	C	213 229-9500	23223
LLP Robins Kaplan	8111	C	310 552-0130	23224
Lmb Mortgage Services Inc	6162	C	310 348-6800	9827
Local Initiative Health Author	6324	A	213 694-1250	10279
Lockton Companies LLC- Pacifi (HQ)	6411	B	213 689-0500	10674
Loeb & Loeb LLP (PA)	8111	C	310 282-2000	23225
Longwood Management Corp	8059	D	323 735-5146	21139
Longwood Management Corp	8059	D	323 737-7778	21141
Longwood Management Corp	8059	C	213 382-8461	21142
Longwood Management Corp	8051	E	323 933-1560	20601
Longwood Manor	8051	C	323 935-1157	20602
Lookout Productions LLC	7812	E	310 408-5687	18073
Los Angeles 2024 Exploratory	7997	A	310 407-0539	18962
Los Angeles Airport Peace Offc	8641	C	310 242-5218	25193
Los Angeles Athletic Club Inc	7991	C	213 625-2211	18627
Los Angeles Cardiology Assoc (PA)	8011	D	213 977-0419	19660
Los Angeles Chmber Orchstra	7929	D	213 622-7001	18448
Los Angeles Cnty Dev Svc Fndtn	8099	C	213 383-1300	22836
Los Angeles Cnty Mseum of Art	8412	C	323 857-6000	24889
Los Angeles Conven and Exh	6512	B	213 741-1151	10907
Los Angeles Country Club	7997	C	310 276-6104	18963
Los Angeles County Bar Assn (PA)	8621	D	213 627-2727	25025
Los Angeles County MTA	4111	C	213 922-5887	3668
Los Angeles County MTA	4111	C	213 922-6301	3669
Los Angeles County MTA	4111	B	213 922-6203	3670
Los Angeles County MTA	4111	C	213 922-6202	3671
Los Angeles County MTA (PA)	4111	A	323 466-3876	3672
Los Angeles County MTA	4111	C	213 922-6207	3673
Los Angeles County MTA	4111	B	213 533-1506	3675
Los Angeles County MTA	4111	C	213 922-5012	3676
Los Angeles County MTA	4111	C	213 244-6783	3678
Los Angeles County MTA	4111	C	213 626-4455	3679
Los Angeles Dept Wtr & Pwr	4941	A	323 256-8079	6273
Los Angeles Dept Wtr & Pwr (PA)	4941	C	213 367-4211	6276
Los Angeles Dept Wtr & Pwr	4911	D	213 367-4211	6050
Los Angeles Dept Wtr & Pwr	4941	C	213 367-5706	6277
Los Angeles Dodgers LLC	7941	A	323 224-1507	18524
Los Angeles Free Clinic (PA)	8011	B	323 653-8622	19662
Los Angeles Free Clinic	8011	D	323 653-8622	19663
Los Angeles Job Corps	8331	C	213 748-0135	24201
Los Angeles Lgbt Center (PA)	8399	C	323 993-7618	24803
Los Angeles Mem Coliseum Comm	8699	B	213 747-7111	25440
Los Angeles Mission Inc (PA)	8361	D	213 629-1227	24584
Los Angeles Orphans Home Soc (HQ)	8361	C	323 463-2119	24586
Los Angeles Philharmonic Assn (PA)	7929	A	213 972-7300	18449
Los Angeles Police Command	8699	B	877 275-5273	25441

Company	SIC	EMP	PHONE	ENTRY #
Los Angeles Rubber Company (PA)	5063	D	323 263-4131	7372
Los Angeles SEC National (PA)	8322	E	323 651-2930	23903
Los Angeles Senior Citizen	6513	D	310 271-9670	11060
Los Angeles Unified School Dst	7378	C	213 485-3691	16289
Los Angeles Unified School Dst	8641	C	323 753-3175	25194
Los Angeles Unified School Dst	8351	D	323 939-7322	24342
Los Angeles Unified School Dst	7374	A	213 847-6911	16152
Los Angeles Unified School Dst	8322	C	213 739-5600	23904
Los Angeles Unified School Dst	8322	C	310 258-2000	23905
Los Angeles World Airports (PA)	4581	C	310 646-7911	4898
Los Angles Area Chmber Cmmerce	8611	D	213 580-7500	24966
Los Angles Child Gdance Clinic (PA)	8322	C	323 373-2400	23907
Los Angles Clippers Foundation	8742	D	213 742-7555	27307
Los Angles Cnsrvtion Corps Inc (PA)	7363	D	213 362-9000	14873
Los Angles Cnty Employees Assn	8631	D	213 368-8660	25069
Los Angles Kings Hockey CLB LP (PA)	7941	C	888 546-4752	18528
Los Angles Trism Convention Bd (PA)	7389	E	213 624-7300	17304
Los Angles Universal Preschool	8351	C	213 416-1200	24343
Lotus Communications Corp (PA)	4832	D	323 512-2225	5744
Lotus Interworks Inc	8742	C	310 442-3330	27308
Louis Luskin & Sons Inc	1711	D	323 938-5142	2266
Lowcom LLC	7311	C	213 408-0080	13859
Lowe Enterprises Inc.	6531	C	310 820-6661	11569
Lowe Enterprises Inc (PA)	6531	C	310 820-6661	11570
Lowe Enterprises Inc.	6552	D	310 820-6661	11886
Lowe Enterprises RE Group	6552	D	310 820-6661	11887
Loyola Marymount University	4832	D	310 338-2866	5745
Lq Management LLC	7011	D	310 645-2200	12864
Lrw Investments LLC	7521	D	310 337-1944	17693
Lucky Strike Entertainment LLC	7933	D	818 933-3752	18492
Lufthnsa Crgo Aktngesellschaft	4512	C	310 242-2590	4792
Lumina Healthcare LLC (PA)	8082	D	888 958-6462	22361
Lusive Decor	8748	E	323 227-9207	27778
Lynberg & Watkins A Prof Corp (PA)	8111	E	213 624-8700	23234
M & S Acquisition Corporation (PA)	6531	C	213 385-1515	11576
M Arthur Gensler Jr Assoc Inc.	8712	C	213 927-3600	26090
M-E Engineers Inc	8711	D	310 842-8700	25804
Macdonald Mott Group Inc	8711	D	323 903-4100	25805
Macerich Company	6531	D	310 474-5940	11579
Made In USA Foundation Inc	8641	E	310 623-3872	25195
Mafab Inc (PA)	6719	D	714 893-0551	11991
Magnolia Eductl RES Foundation (PA)	8399	D	714 892-5066	24804
Magnolia Ventures Ltd	7389	D	213 389-6900	17309
Management Tech Consulting LLC	8748	D	323 851-5008	27780
Manchster Mnor Cnvlescent Hosp	8059	D	323 753-1789	21150
Mandalay Sports Entrmt LLC (PA)	7941	D	323 549-4300	18529
Manning Kass Ellrod Ram Trestr (PA)	8111	C	213 624-6900	23238
Manufacturers Bank (DH)	6029	C	213 489-6200	9511
Marcum LLP	8721	C	310 432-7400	26257
Mariner Health Care Inc	8051	D	323 665-1185	20617
Marland Co LP	0174	E	213 614-6171	207
Marmol Radziner	8712	D	310 826-6222	26092
Marriott International Inc	7011	B	310 337-2800	12882
Marriott International Inc.	7011	A	310 641-5700	12884
Marriott International Inc.	7011	C	213 284-3862	12907
Marsh & McLennan Companies Inc	6411	D	213 346-5555	10682
Martin AC Partners Inc	8712	C	213 683-1900	26093
Martin Associates Group Inc (PA)	8711	D	213 483-6490	25812
Martin Lther King/Drew Med Ctr	8011	D	310 773-4926	19672
Masa Trucking Co	4214	E	310 329-1567	4358
Massage Place	7299	C	310 204-3004	13756
Matrix Aviation Services Inc	4729	C	310 337-3037	4993
Matrix Institute On Addictions (PA)	8069	D	310 478-6006	22035
Maxim Healthcare Services Inc.	8082	C	323 937-9410	22364
Maxus USA	8999	A	323 202-4650	27942
Mayesh Wholesale Florist Inc (PA)	5193	C	310 342-0980	9145
Mayfair Hotel	7011	D	213 484-9789	12915
McDermott Will & Emery LLP Inc	8111	C	310 277-4110	23243
McGuirewoods LLP	8111	D	310 315-8200	23245
MCI Communications Svcs Inc	4813	C	213 625-1005	5595
McKinsey & Company Inc	8742	E	424 249-1000	27329
McKool Smith Hennigan	8111	D	213 694-1200	23246
Mechanical Drives Co (PA)	5085	D	323 263-4131	7858
Med-Life Ambulance Services	4119	D	818 242-1785	3820
Media Temple Inc	4813	C	877 578-4000	5596
Mediabrands Worldwide Inc	7319	B	323 370-8000	13977
Medical Management Cons Inc (PA)	7363	E	310 659-3835	14881
Medical Support Services	7363	D	323 860-7994	14882
Mellano & Co (PA)	5193	B	213 622-0796	9147
Memory To Go	5045	D	310 446-0111	7078
Mendelsohn/Zien Advg LLC	7311	D	310 444-1990	13866
Mercer (us) Inc	8742	C	213 346-2200	27336
Merchant of Tennis Inc	7389	D	310 855-1946	17320
Mercury Air Cargo Inc (HQ)	4581	C	310 258-6100	4902
Mercury General Corporation (PA)	6331	D	323 937-1060	10372
Mercury Insurance Company (HQ)	6331	C	323 937-1060	10377
Mercury Insurance Services LLC	6331	A	323 937-1060	10380
Mercury Mailing Systems Inc	7331	D	323 730-0307	14053
Merlot Film Productions Inc.	7812	C	323 575-2906	18078
Merrill Lynch Pierce Fenner.	6211	C	310 407-3900	9986
Metro Service South Inc	7349	D	310 995-8950	14322
Metrolux Theatres	7822	D	310 858-2800	18240
Metropolis Hotel MGT LLC	7011	C	213 683-4855	12925
Metropolitan Water District	4971	A	213 217-6667	6558
Mexican American Legal Defense (PA)	8111	D	213 629-2512	23250
Mgh Corporation	8361	E	323 754-1408	24600
Michael A Meczka	8732	E	310 670-4824	26545
Mid Century Insurance Company	6331	C	323 932-7116	10382
Mid Cities Assn Retarded Ctzns (PA)	8331	D	310 537-4510	24207
Mid Rckland Imging Prtners Inc (HQ)	8071	C	310 445-2800	22111
Mid Wilshire Health Care Ctr	8051	D	213 483-9921	20644
Midnight Mission (PA)	8641	D	213 624-9258	25198
Midnite Air Corp.	4513	E	310 330-2300	4843
Midway Rent A Car Inc	7514	D	310 445-4355	17645
Millennia Holdings Inc	8742	D	213 252-1230	27348
Millennium Alarm Systems Inc (PA)	7382	E	310 337-1108	16923
Miniluxe Inc	7231	D	424 442-1630	13665
Minority Aids Project Inc.	8322	D	323 936-4949	23925
Mintie Corporation (PA)	7349	D	323 225-4111	14324
Miramax Film Ny LLC	7812	D	310 409-4321	18081
Mission Beverage Co (HQ)	5181	C	323 266-6238	9015
Mitchell Silberberg Knupp LLP (PA)	8111	C	310 312-2000	23257
Mitsui & Co (usa) Inc	5051	D	213 896-1100	7290
Miyako Hotels	7011	D	213 617-2000	12933
Mocean LLC	7374	C	310 481-0808	16161
Modern Button Company of Cal	5131	E	213 747-7431	8233
Mogannam and Whalen Med Corp (PA)	8322	E	213 622-6010	23926
Monarch Landscape Holdings LLC (PA)	0782	C	213 816-1750	901
Monarchy Diamond Inc	1499	B	213 924-1161	1105
Morgan Lewis & Bockius LLP	8111	C	213 612-2500	23263
Morgan Lewis & Bockius LLP	8111	C	213 612-2500	23265
Morgan Creek Productions (PA)	7822	D	310 432-4848	18241
Morgan Services Inc	7213	D	213 485-9666	13548
Morgans Hotel Group MGT LLC	7011	C	323 650-8999	12943
Morris Polich & Purdy LLP (PA)	8111	D	213 891-9100	23266
Morrison & Foerster LLP	8111	C	213 892-5200	23270
Mortgage Capital Assoc Inc	6162	D	310 477-6877	9833
Mortgage Capital Partners Inc	6162	D	310 295-2900	9834
Motion Picture and TV Fund	8062	C	310 231-3000	21599
Mpower Communications Corp (DH)	4813	D	866 699-8242	5606
Ms Bubbles Inc (PA)	5137	D	323 544-0300	8324
MSS Nurses Registry Inc	7363	D	323 467-5717	14885
Mufg Americas Leasing Corp (DH)	7359	D	213 488-3700	14528
Mufg Bank Ltd	6029	D	213 488-3700	9513
Mufg Union Bank Foundation	6022	A	213 236-5000	9467
Mufg Union Bank National Assn	6021	E	213 972-5500	9354
Mufg Union Bank National Assn	6021	D	213 312-4500	9358
Muir-Chase Plumbing Co Inc.	1711	C	818 500-1940	2284
Mulholland SEC & Patrol Inc	7381	B	818 755-0202	16736
Mulroses Usa Inc	0181	D	213 489-1761	285
Munger Tolles & Olson LLP	8111	C	213 683-9100	23274
Munger Tolles Olson Foundation (PA)	8111	B	213 683-9100	23275
Murchison & Cumming LLP (PA)	8111	D	213 623-7400	23277
Murphy OBrien Inc	8743	D	310 453-2539	27564
Museum Associates	8412	B	323 857-6172	24891
Museum of Contemporary Art (PA)	8412	C	213 626-6222	24893
Musick Peeler & Garrett LLP (PA)	8111	C	213 629-7600	23280
Mutual Trading Co Inc (DH)	5149	C	213 626-9458	8831
Mv Medical Management	8742	C	323 257-7637	27353
Mystic Inc (PA)	5137	D	213 746-8538	8325
Mza Events Inc (PA)	7389	E	213 201-1348	17342
Nadel Inc (PA)	8712	C	310 826-2100	26098
National Cble Cmmnications LLC	7319	D	310 231-0745	13978
National Ecnomic RES Assoc Inc	8732	C	213 346-3000	26548
National Genetics Institute	8071	C	310 996-6610	22115
National Research Group Inc.	8732	B	323 817-2000	26549
Nationwide Legal LLC (PA)	8111	D	213 249-9999	23281
Nationwide Theatres Corp (HQ)	7833	D	310 657-8420	18329
Natural History Museum of Los	8412	B	213 763-3442	24895
Navigant Consulting Inc	8742	D	213 452-4516	27360
Nb Enterprises & Dist Inc	8741	D	866 216-1515	26956
NBBJ LP	8712	C	213 243-3333	26099
Nederlander of California Inc	6512	E	323 468-1700	10918
Ner Precious Metals Inc.	5094	D	213 489-1549	8011
Network Automation Inc	7372	E	213 738-1700	15777
Network Management Group Inc (PA)	8741	C	323 263-2632	26957
Neuberg Nuberg Importers Group	5023	E	800 832-2742	6777
New Crew Production Corp	7389	C	323 234-8880	17349
New Directions Inc (PA)	8322	D	310 914-4045	23934
New Dream Network LLC	4813	D	323 375-3842	5613

Employment Codes: A=Over 500 employees, B=251-500,
C=101-250, D=51-100, E=50

2019 Directory of California
Wholesalers and Services Companies

© Mergent Inc. 1-800-342-5647

1607

GEOGRAPHIC

Company	SIC	EMP	PHONE	ENTRY #
New Economics For Women (PA)	8322	D	213 483-2060	23935
New Figueroa Hotel Inc	7011	D	213 627-8971	12952
New Global Telecom Inc	7389	D	213 489-3708	17350
New Image Emrgncy Shltr (PA)	8322	C	562 983-7289	23937
New Regency Productions Inc (PA)	7812	C	310 369-8300	18085
New Vista Health Services	8059	C	310 477-5501	21164
New York Life Insurance Co	6411	E	323 782-3000	10714
Newsways Services Inc	5192	C	323 258-6000	9118
Nexstar Digital LLC	7311	D	310 971-9300	13870
Nextel Communications Inc	4812	D	323 290-2400	5412
Ngs Group Inc	5149	D	323 735-1700	8839
Nielsen Company (us) LLC	8732	B	323 817-2000	26550
Nielsen Company (us) LLC	8732	C	323 462-0050	26552
Nixon Peabody LLP	8111	D	213 629-6000	23288
North Pacific Resources Inc	5146	D	206 676-3828	8585
Northeast Community Clinic	8011	D	323 373-9400	19719
Northern Trust Company	6021	E	310 282-3800	9361
Northrop Grumman Systems Corp	7389	B	310 556-4911	17359
Nossaman LLP (PA)	8111	D	213 612-7800	23291
Notellage Corporation	8059	E	323 257-8151	21170
Now Medical Services Inc	7363	D	310 479-4520	14888
Nowcom Corporation	7379	D	323 938-6449	16435
Nrea-TRC 711 LLC	7011	C	213 488-3500	12965
Nri Usa LLC (PA)	4731	D	323 345-6456	5123
Ntt Data Services Corporation	7376	D	310 342-3200	16271
Nuevo Amnecer Latino Chld Svcs (PA)	8322	D	323 720-9951	23947
Numero Uno Market	6799	D	323 231-9403	12252
Numero Uno Market	6799	D	213 381-1734	12253
O & S Holdings LLC	6552	E	310 207-8600	11899
Oak Paper Products Co Inc (PA)	5113	C	323 268-0507	8112
Oaks Diagnostics Inc (PA)	8011	D	310 855-0035	19727
Oaktree Capital Management LP (HQ)	6282	C	213 830-6300	10099
Oaktree Holdings Inc	6799	A	213 830-6300	12254
Oaktree Real Estate Opportunit	6531	A	213 830-6300	11640
Oaktree Strategic Income LLC	7389	A	213 830-6300	17364
Oberman Tivoli & Pickert Inc	7373	C	310 440-9600	16025
Oblong Industries Inc (PA)	7371	C	213 683-8863	15325
Ocean Breeze Manufacturing	7389	D	323 586-8760	17366
Ocean Group Inc (PA)	5146	D	213 622-3677	8586
Ocm Real Estate Opportunities	6799	A	213 830-6300	12255
Odesus Inc (PA)	7379	D	310 473-4600	16438
Ods Technologies LP	4833	C	310 242-9400	5831
Olympia Convalescent Hospital	8059	C	213 487-3000	21173
Olympia Health Care LLC	8062	A	323 938-3161	21614
Olympus Adhc Inc	8351	E	310 572-7272	24358
Omega/Cinema Props Inc	7819	D	323 466-8201	18207
OMelveny & Myers LLP (PA)	8111	A	213 430-6000	23296
OMelveny & Myers LLP	8111	C	310 553-6700	23298
Omni Hotels Corporation	7011	C	213 617-3300	12984
On Central Realty Inc	6531	B	323 543-8500	11643
One Legal Inc	7389	D	213 617-1212	17369
Onelegacy	8099	C	213 229-5600	22852
Onelegacy (PA)	8099	C	213 625-0665	22853
Onemarket Network LLC (HQ)	7373	C	415 638-9868	16026
Oneunited Bank	6022	D	323 295-3381	9468
Onsite Consulting LLC	8748	D	323 401-3190	27812
Op Bancorp	6022	D	213 892-9999	9469
Ore-Cal Corp (PA)	5146	D	213 623-8493	8588
Organic & Sustainable Buty Inc	7231	E	310 815-8201	13666
Organztion Amrcn Kdaly Edctors	8699	E	310 441-3555	25449
Orrick Hrrington Sutcliffe LLP	8111	C	213 629-2020	23304
Orthopaedic Hospital (PA)	8062	C	213 742-1000	21620
Otis Elevator Company	5084	E	323 342-4500	7782
Otts Asia	6799	C	562 259-3447	12256
Our Alchemy LLC (PA)	7829	C	310 893-6289	18253
Overseenet (PA)	7311	C	213 408-0080	13876
Oxford Palace Hotel	7011	D	213 382-7756	12992
P-Wave Holdings LLC	6799	A	310 209-3010	12257
P8ge Consulting Inc	8748	E	310 666-2301	27817
Pachulski Stang Zehl Jones LLP (PA)	8111	D	310 277-6910	23306
Pacific Asian Consortm Emplymn	8322	D	213 989-3228	23955
Pacific Asian Consortm Emplymn (PA)	8331	C	213 353-3982	24217
Pacific Aviation Corporation (PA)	4581	C	310 646-4015	4903
Pacific Capital Companies LLC	6159	D	800 583-3015	9762
Pacific Equities Captl	6519	D	310 477-5300	11180
Pacific Health Corporation	8062	B	714 619-7797	21621
Pacific Indemnity Company	6411	D	213 622-2334	10725
Pacific Paper Converting Inc (PA)	5113	D	323 888-1330	8125
Pacific Premier Bank	6022	D	213 626-0085	9474
Pacific Theaters Inc (PA)	7832	C	310 657-8420	18308
Pacific Theatres Entrmt Corp (HQ)	7832	D	310 659-9432	18311
Pacific Trellis Fruit LLC (PA)	5148	C	323 859-9600	8714
Pacific Western Bank	6022	C	213 430-7000	9475
Pacific Western Bank	6022	E	310 996-9100	9476
Pacifica Hosts Inc	7011	D	310 670-9000	13006

Company	SIC	EMP	PHONE	ENTRY #
Packard Realty Inc	7011	D	310 649-5151	13011
Paladin Realty Partners LLC (PA)	6531	E	310 914-2410	11658
Pamc Ltd (PA)	8062	A	213 624-8411	21631
Panasonic Corp North America	5064	C	323 436-3500	7422
Para Los Ninos	8351	C	213 623-3942	24366
Paracelsus Los Angeles Comm	8062	C	323 267-0477	21633
Paradigm Industries Inc	7389	D	310 965-1900	17385
Paragon Textiles Inc	5137	D	310 323-7500	8330
Paramount Pictures Corporation (HQ)	7812	A	323 956-5000	18090
Paramount Television Service	7812	A	323 956-5000	18091
Paramunt Contrs Developers Inc	6531	E	323 464-7050	11661
Park n Fly Inc	7521	D	310 417-3566	17695
Parker Milliken Clark OHar	8111	D	818 784-8087	23310
Parker Stanbury LLP (PA)	8111	D	619 528-1259	23311
Parking Company of America	7521	D	562 862-2118	17696
Parking Concepts Inc	7521	E	310 208-1611	17697
Parking Concepts Inc	7521	E	213 746-5764	17698
Parking Concepts Inc	7521	E	213 623-2661	17700
Parking Network Inc	1799	C	213 613-1500	3563
Parsec Inc	4789	D	323 276-3116	5241
Pasadena Model Railroad Club	7997	D	323 222-1718	19001
Passprt Accept Fclty Los Angel	7389	D	323 460-4811	17392
Pathways La (PA)	8322	E	213 427-2700	23964
Paul Hastings LLP (PA)	8111	C	213 683-6000	23316
Payden and Rygel (PA)	6282	C	213 625-1900	10102
Pbms Inc	7349	D	213 386-2552	14345
Pcs Link Inc	8748	B	949 655-5000	27820
Pcs Property Managmnt LLC	6531	C	310 231-1000	11667
Peach Inc	4215	C	323 654-2333	4426
Pediatric & Family Medical Ctr	8093	C	213 342-3325	22639
Pegasus Squire Inc	7379	D	866 208-6837	16453
Penny Roofing Company	1761	E	323 731-5424	3184
Penske Media Corporation (PA)	7313	D	310 321-5000	13952
Penske Truck Leasing Co LP	7513	E	213 628-1255	17610
People Assisting Homeless	8322	C	323 644-2216	23968
People Coordinated Services (PA)	8399	D	323 735-1231	24828
Performing Arts Center of La C	7922	D	213 972-7211	18393
Phenomenon Mktg & Entrmt LLC (PA)	8742	D	323 648-4000	27395
Philippine Airlines	4512	D	310 646-1981	4794
Philmont Management Inc	1542	D	213 380-0159	1615
Phoenix Textile Inc	7389	D	213 239-9640	17398
Pico Cleaner Inc (PA)	7216	D	310 274-2431	13567
Pico Rents Inc	7359	D	310 275-9431	14535
Pillsbury Winthrop Shaw	8111	C	213 488-7100	23329
Pircher Nichols & Meeks (PA)	8111	C	310 201-0132	23333
Pixelmags Inc	7371	D	310 598-7303	15363
Planned Parenthood Los Angeles (PA)	8093	D	213 284-3200	22645
Plasma Collection Centers Inc	8099	C	323 441-7720	22861
Plaza De La Raza Child Develop	8351	D	323 224-1788	24369
Plb Management LLC	6513	E	323 549-5400	11098
PLD Enterprises Inc	5146	D	213 626-4444	8594
Pmk-Bnc Inc (PA)	8743	C	310 854-0455	27568
Pmk-Bnc Inc	8743	E	310 854-4800	27569
Point360 (PA)	7819	C	818 565-1400	18210
Polsinelli PC	8111	D	310 556-1801	23335
Pomwonderful LLC (DH)	5149	C	310 966-5800	8853
Post Group Inc (PA)	7819	C	323 462-2300	18211
Pounce Consulting Inc	7379	C	714 774-3500	16457
Precise Air Systems Inc	1711	D	818 240-1737	2316
Preciseq Inc	7379	D	310 709-6094	16460
Premier Healthcare Svcs LLC (HQ)	7361	C	626 204-7930	14698
Premier Management Company (PA)	8721	D	310 286-3074	26273
Prg Parking Century LLC	7521	D	310 642-0947	17703
Prime Administration LLC	6798	A	323 549-7155	12181
Pro-Wash Inc	7215	D	323 756-6000	13561
Proactive Risk Management Inc	8741	D	213 840-8856	26998
Professional Produce	5148	D	323 277-1550	8722
Professional Security Cons (PA)	7381	C	310 207-7729	16764
Proland Property Managmnt LLC (PA)	6531	D	213 738-8175	11686
Promo Shop Inc (PA)	8742	D	310 821-1780	27404
Proskauer Rose LLP	8111	C	310 557-2900	23342
Prospect Enterprises Inc (PA)	5146	C	213 599-5700	8596
Prospect Medical Holdings Inc (PA)	8011	C	310 943-4500	19799
Protiviti Inc	8742	D	213 327-1400	27409
Prototypes Centers For Innov	8322	C	213 542-3838	23978
Proven Solutions Inc	7361	D	310 933-4544	14706
PS Arts	8748	E	310 586-1017	27829
Psomas (PA)	8713	C	213 223-1400	26134
Public Communications Svcs Inc	4813	C	310 231-1000	5631
Public Counsel	8111	D	213 385-2977	23343
Public Health California Dept	8011	D	213 620-6160	19806
Public Hlth Fndation Entps Inc	8641	C	323 263-0262	25224
Public Hlth Fndation Entps Inc	8099	C	323 733-9381	22865
Public Security Inc	7381	E	323 293-9884	16769
Qre Operating LLC	1382	C	213 225-5900	1046

2019 Directory of California
Wholesalers and Services Companies

(P-0000) Products & Services Section entry number
(PA)=Parent Co (HQ)=Headquarters (DH)=Div Headquarters

Company	SIC	EMP	PHONE	ENTRY #
Quake City Casuals Inc	5136	C	213 746-0540	8275
Qualified Blling Cllctions LLC	7322	C	323 556-3470	14020
Queen of Angels Hollywood Pres	8062	A	213 413-3000	21677
Queenscare Health Centers	8011	D	323 780-4510	19810
Queenscare Health Centers	8011	D	323 644-6180	19811
Quick Systems Inc	1711	E	702 335-3574	2322
Quigly-Simpson Heppelwhite Inc	7311	C	310 996-5800	13885
Quinn Emanuel Urquhart (PA)	8111	B	213 443-3000	23346
R & B Realty Group	6513	D	323 851-3450	11101
R & B Realty Group LP	6531	A	310 478-1021	11698
R & R Electric	1731	E	310 785-0288	2690
R F R Corporation	6552	D	800 346-7663	11909
R W Zant Co (PA)	5147	C	323 980-5457	8625
Radar Medical Systems Inc	8999	D	440 337-9521	27956
Radiology Department Cal Hosp	8011	E	213 742-5840	19813
Radisson Hotel At Usc	7011	C	213 748-4141	13092
Radix Textile Inc	5131	D	323 234-1667	8237
Radlax Gateway Hotel LLC	7011	B	310 670-9000	13095
Radleys	7812	E	310 765-2223	18103
Radnet Inc (PA)	8071	C	310 445-2800	22133
Raleigh Enterprises Inc (PA)	7011	C	310 899-8900	13097
Raleigh Enterprises Inc	7819	C	323 466-3111	18214
Ralphs Grocery Company	4225	A	310 637-1101	4619
Ramcast Ornamental Sup Co Inc (PA)	5051	C	323 585-1625	7303
Ramsey-Shilling Residential RE	6531	D	323 851-5512	11702
Randall Mc-Anany Company	1721	D	310 822-3344	2471
Ranker Inc	7311	E	323 782-1448	13886
Rapp Worldwide Inc	7311	D	310 563-7200	13887
Rayv Inc	7373	E	310 600-2959	16041
Rbb Architects Inc (PA)	8712	D	310 479-1473	26104
Reaume and Associates Inc	8711	D	310 398-5768	25892
Red Hawk Fire & SEC CA Inc (HQ)	1731	D	818 683-1500	2698
Reed Smith LLP	8111	C	213 457-8000	23349
Regent Worldwide Sales LLC	7812	E	310 806-4288	18105
Rehabltion Cntre of Bvrly Hlls	8051	C	323 782-1500	20721
Reliance Media Works Vfx Inc	7819	E	818 557-7333	18215
Reliance Steel & Aluminum Co (PA)	5051	D	213 687-7700	7304
Religious Technology Center	6794	D	323 663-3258	12141
Relx Inc	7375	D	213 627-1130	16245
Remington Hotel Corporation	7011	A	310 553-6561	13109
Resolution Economics Group LLC (PA)	8748	D	310 275-9137	27842
Restaurant Depot LLC	5181	C	323 964-1220	9022
Revenue Frontier LLC	7319	D	310 584-9200	13982
Revolt Media and Tv LLC	4833	C	323 645-3000	5833
Rey-Crest Roofg Waterproofing	1799	D	323 257-9329	3578
Rheumatology Diagnostics Lab	8071	D	310 253-5455	22137
Richard J Metz MD Inc	8011	E	310 553-3189	19824
Richards Watson & Gershon PC (PA)	8111	C	213 626-8484	23354
Richards Group Inc	7311	C	214 891-5700	13892
Riot Games Inc (DH)	7371	C	310 828-7953	15414
Rnc Capital Management LLC	6282	D	310 477-6543	10111
Robert Consl Englekirk Strctrl (PA)	8711	C	323 733-6673	25895
Robert Half International Inc	7361	D	213 270-6731	14726
Robert Kaufman Co Inc (PA)	5131	C	310 538-3482	8238
Robert Kaufman Co Inc	5131	E	310 538-3482	8239
Rock-It Cargo USA LLC	4731	C	310 410-0935	5160
Rocket Smog Inc	7538	D	310 590-7664	17781
Rockport ADM Svcs LLC	8051	D	323 223-3441	20730
Rockport ADM Svcs LLC (PA)	8742	D	323 330-6500	27433
Rodeo Realty Inc	6531	D	310 873-0100	11736
Rodgers Security Service Inc	7381	C	310 684-3016	16776
Rogers Poultry Co (PA)	5144	C	323 585-0802	8539
Roland Corporation US (HQ)	5099	C	323 890-3700	8054
Romex Textiles Inc (PA)	5131	E	213 749-9090	8240
Roosevelt Hotel LLC	7011	C	323 466-7000	13136
Rosano Partners	6531	E	213 802-0300	11744
Rp Realty Partners LLC	6512	E	310 207-6990	10930
Rubicon Project Inc (PA)	7311	C	310 207-0272	13896
Ruby Creek Resources	8742	E	212 671-0404	27434
Rutherford Co Inc (PA)	1742	D	323 666-5284	2953
S L G G Consulting Group LLC (PA)	8721	C	310 477-3924	26285
S W K Properties LLC (PA)	8741	D	213 383-9204	27020
SA Recycling LLC	4953	D	323 564-5601	6456
Saatchi & Saatchi N Amer Inc	7311	C	310 437-2500	13899
Saban Brands LLC (HQ)	8742	D	310 557-5230	27437
Sac International Steel Inc (PA)	5051	D	323 232-2467	7312
Saehan Bank (PA)	6022	E	213 368-7700	9484
Sag-Aftra Foundation	8631	E	323 549-6708	25074
Saint Justin Education Fu	8399	D	323 221-3400	24835
Salt of Earth Productions Inc	7389	C	818 399-1860	17451
Saltzburg Ray & Bergman LLP	8111	C	310 481-6700	23364
Salvation Army	8322	E	213 484-0772	24006
Salvation Army Residences Inc	8322	D	213 553-3273	24008
Sam Jung USA Inc	5131	D	323 231-0811	8241
Samaritan Imaging Center	8071	A	213 977-2140	22139
San Vicente Hospital	8062	D	323 930-1040	21713
Santa Mnica Wlshire Imging LLC	8071	E	323 549-3055	22141
Santa Monica Bay Physicians He (PA)	8011	D	310 417-5900	19859
Santa Monica Express Inc	4212	D	310 458-6000	4060
Santee Systems Services II	8322	D	323 445-0044	24035
Santee Systems Services II LL	7991	E	323 445-0044	18650
Sbb Roofing Inc (PA)	1761	C	323 254-2888	3199
SBE Hotel Group LLC	6799	D	323 655-8000	12265
Sbehg 465 S La Cienega LLC	7011	B	310 247-0400	13194
Scalelab LLC	7812	C	310 526-7524	18113
Schaefer Ambulance Service Inc (PA)	4119	D	323 469-1473	3843
Schindler Elevator Corporation	7699	D	310 785-9775	17983
Schirmer Fire Protection Eng	6411	D	213 630-2020	10765
Schmidt Phyllis MD Corporation	8062	A	213 613-1163	21724
Scottel Voice & Data Inc	7629	C	310 737-7300	17910
Scv Facilities Services	7349	D	310 803-4588	14381
SDI Media USA Inc (DH)	7812	D	323 602-5455	18115
Sea Win Inc	5146	E	213 688-2899	8599
Search Agency Inc (PA)	7311	D	310 582-5700	13901
Season Produce Co Inc	5148	B	213 689-0008	8727
Seaworld Global Logistics	4731	B	310 208-9488	5166
Secom International (PA)	7373	D	310 641-1290	16047
Secret Charm LLC (PA)	5137	B	213 742-7744	8333
Secure Nursing Service Inc	7361	B	213 736-6771	14757
Securitas SEC Svcs USA Inc	7381	C	213 580-8825	16808
Securitech Security Services	7381	C	213 387-5050	16815
Sega Entertainment USA Inc	7993	D	909 987-4263	18789
Seiu Local 2015	8631	C	213 985-0384	25077
Seiu Local 721	8631	D	213 368-8660	25078
Senior Keiro Health Care	8361	D	323 263-9651	24670
Sentinel Acqstion Holdings Inc	7371	A	310 201-4100	15437
Serrano Covalescent Hospital	8051	D	323 465-2106	20753
Service Parking Corporation	7521	D	323 851-2416	17706
ServiceMaster Company LLC	7349	D	760 298-7001	14385
Seven Licensing Company LLC	5137	D	323 881-0308	8334
Seyfarth Shaw LLP	8111	C	213 270-9600	23372
Seyfarth Shaw LLP	8111	C	310 277-7200	23373
Shadow Animation LLC	7812	E	323 466-7771	18116
Shapiro-Gilman-Shandler Co (PA)	5148	C	213 593-1200	8730
Sharon Care Center LLC	8051	C	323 655-2023	20756
Sharp Guard Services Inc	7381	A	213 739-1900	16821
Shawmut Woodworking & Sup Inc	1542	C	323 602-1000	1645
Shed Media US Inc	7313	D	323 904-4680	13955
Sheppard Mullin Richter (PA)	8111	B	213 620-1780	23377
Sheppard Mullin Richter	8111	D	310 228-3700	23380
Sheraton Corporation	7011	B	310 642-1111	13216
Shields For Families (PA)	8069	D	323 242-5000	22046
Shilpark Paint Corporation (PA)	5198	D	323 732-7093	9189
Showa Marine Inc (PA)	5146	D	213 627-4091	8600
Shriners Hspitals For Children	8069	B	213 388-3151	22047
Sia Engineering (usa) Inc	8711	D	310 693-7108	25911
Signature Consultants LLC	7748	D	310 229-5731	27859
Silv Communication Inc	8748	D	213 381-7999	27861
Silver Cinemas Acquisition Co (PA)	7832	D	310 473-6701	18321
Silver Fredman A Prof Law Corp	8111	E	310 556-2356	23387
Silverado Senior Living Inc	8059	D	323 984-7313	21216
Simpson & Simpson	8741	D	213 736-6664	27030
Sinai Temple	7261	C	323 469-6000	13698
Singerlewak LLP (PA)	8721	C	310 477-3924	26293
Sisters of Nzareth Los Angeles	8361	D	310 839-2361	24676
Sitrick Brincko Group LLC	8742	D	310 788-2850	27452
Six Continents Hotels Inc	7011	D	213 748-1291	13235
Six Point Harness	7819	E	323 462-3344	18217
Skadden Arps Slate Meagher & F	8111	C	213 687-5000	23390
Skanska-Rados A Joint Venture	1611	D	213 978-0600	1851
Skidmore Owings & Merrill LLP	8712	C	213 996-8366	26109
Skilled Healthcare LLC	8051	D	323 663-3951	20768
Skirball Cultural Center	8412	C	310 440-4500	24913
Sky Zone LLC (HQ)	7929	D	310 734-0300	18463
Skyline Healthcare & Wellness	8051	D	323 665-1185	20769
Skypower Holdings LLC	1711	C	323 860-4900	2358
SM 10000 Property LLC	6552	D	305 374-5700	11919
Smith-Emery Company (PA)	8742	D	213 745-5312	27457
SMS Transportation Svcs Inc	4111	D	213 489-5367	3727
Smuk Inc	7812	C	323 904-4680	18117
Sobel Ross H Law Offices	8111	E	310 788-8995	23393
Sobol Philip A MD P C Inc	8011	E	310 649-5894	19893
Society of St Vincent De (PA)	8699	D	323 224-6280	25466
Solheim Lutheran Home	8361	C	323 257-7518	24679
Solver Inc	5045	E	310 691-5300	7105
Sonicocom Inc	7379	D	213 291-0475	16491
Sony Pictures Entrmt Inc	7929	B	310 244-3558	18467
Sony Pictures Studios Inc	7812	B	310 244-4000	18122
South Bay Senior Services Inc	8082	D	310 338-8558	22421
South Bay Vlla Preservation LP	6513	D	310 516-7325	11116

Employment Codes: A=Over 500 employees, B=251-500, C=101-250, D=51-100, E=50

© Mergent Inc. 1-800-342-5647

Name	SIC	EMP	PHONE	ENTRY #
South Baylo University	8093	C	213 387-2414	22681
South Central Family Hlth Ctr	8011	D	323 908-4200	19898
South Central Los	8399	C	213 744-7000	24842
South China Sheet Metal Inc	1711	D	323 225-1522	2367
South Cntl Heath & Rehab Prog	8093	D	323 751-2677	22683
Southern Building Maint Inc	7349	D	213 598-7071	14396
Southern Cal Pipe Trades ADM **(PA)**	6733	D	213 385-6161	12127
Southern Cal Prmnnte Med Group	8011	D	323 857-2000	19909
Southern Cal Prmnnte Med Group	8011	D	323 783-5455	19911
Southern Cal Prmnnte Med Group	8011	B	323 783-4893	19912
Southern Cal Rgional Rail Auth	4111	B	213 452-0200	3730
Southern California Gas Co **(DH)**	4924	C	213 244-1200	6163
Southern California Gas Tower	4924	D	213 244-1200	6177
Southwest Airlines Co	4512	D	310 665-5700	4802
Southwest Rgnal Rncil Crpnters **(PA)**	8631	E	213 385-1457	25082
Sp Plus Corporation	7521	D	213 488-3100	17707
Special Needs Network	8069	E	323 291-7100	22051
Special Service For Groups Inc **(PA)**	8331	A	213 368-1888	24232
Special Service For Groups Inc	8399	D	213 620-5713	24845
Sprinkles Cupcakes Inc	1541	C	310 657-4102	1436
Spus7 Miami Acc LP	6726	E	213 683-4200	12070
Squire Patton Boggs (us) LLP	8111	D	213 624-2500	23395
Srht Property Mgmt Co	8741	D	213 683-0522	27044
SRK Global Consulting	7379	D	310 295-2524	16493
St Annes Maternity Home	8361	C	213 381-2931	24683
St Barnabas Senior Center of L	8322	D	213 388-4444	24067
St Johns Well Child **(PA)**	8021	D	323 541-1600	20138
St Vincent Senior Citizn Nutr **(PA)**	8621	D	213 484-7775	25043
Standard Chartered Bank	6022	C	626 639-8000	9488
Standard Hollywood Lessee LLC	7011	C	323 822-3102	13261
Standard-Southern Corporation	4222	D	213 624-1831	4510
Standard-Southern Corporation	4222	D	213 624-1831	4511
Standard-Southern Corporation	4222	D	213 624-1831	4512
Star Fabrics Inc **(PA)**	5131	D	213 688-2871	8245
Starline Tours Hollywood Inc **(PA)**	4725	D	323 463-3333	4982
Starwood Htls & Rsrts Wrldwde	7011	C	310 208-8765	13274
Starwood Htls & Rsrts Wrldwde	7011	A	213 624-1000	13275
Starwood Htls & Rsrts Wrldwde	7011	C	323 798-1300	13279
State Bar of California	8621	B	213 765-1000	25045
State Farm Mutl Auto Insur Co	6411	B	309 766-2311	10780
State Farm Mutl Auto Insur Co	6411	D	323 852-6868	10793
Steiny and Company Inc **(PA)**	1731	D	626 962-1055	2746
Steiny and Company Inc	1731	C	213 382-2331	2747
Steptoe & Johnson LLP	8111	E	213 439-9400	23399
Sterling Westwood Inc	7216	D	310 287-2431	13570
Steve Beattie Inc	1721	D	310 454-1786	2484
Stjohn God Rtirement Care Ctr	8051	C	323 731-0641	20782
Stockbridge/Sbe Holdings LLC	7011	A	323 655-8000	13282
Stone Tree Landscape Corp	0782	E	323 965-0944	945
Storybots Inc	7371	D	310 314-4394	15474
Straight Lander Inc	8741	D	323 337-9075	27049
Stroock & Stroock & Lavan LLP	8111	C	310 556-5800	23402
Study US Research Inst Inc	8733	D	213 840-9575	26664
Stutman Trster Glatt Prof Corp	8111	D	310 228-5600	23403
Stv Architects Inc	8712	D	213 482-9444	26117
Success Healthcare 1 LLC **(PA)**	8082	A	213 989-6100	22428
Suffolk Construction Co Inc	1542	D	949 453-9400	1661
Sullivan & Cromwell LLP	8111	D	310 712-6600	23404
SunAmerica Hsng Fnd 1071	6512	C	310 772-6000	10952
SunAmerica Inc **(HQ)**	6091	A	310 772-6000	9666
SunAmerica Investments Inc **(DH)**	8741	D	310 772-6000	27053
SunAmerica Investments Inc	6722	C	310 772-6000	12047
Sunrise Brands LLC **(PA)**	5137	E	323 780-8250	8336
Sunrise Senior Living Inc	8051	D	310 437-7178	20806
Sunset Tower Hotel LLC	7011	D	323 654-7100	13289
Sunstone Hotel Investors Inc	7011	C	310 215-1000	13293
Sunstone Hotel Investors LLC	7011	C	310 649-1400	13300
Sunstone Hotel Properties Inc	7011	D	310 228-4100	13303
Superbalife International LLC	5122	D	310 553-7400	8213
Svi Lax LLC	7011	D	310 281-0300	13309
Svn International Corp	6531	D	310 979-0800	11782
Swinerton Builders	1542	D	213 896-3400	1664
Swiss Port Corp	8744	B	310 417-0258	27607
Swissport Cargo Services LP	4581	A	310 910-9541	4914
Swissport Usa Inc	4581	B	310 345-1986	4916
Swissport Usa Inc	4581	D	310 910-9560	4918
Sycamore Park Care Center LLC	8059	D	323 223-3441	21227
Sydell Hotels LLC	7011	C	213 381-7411	13314
Synermed	8741	D	213 626-4556	27056
T C R Limited Partnership	7514	C	310 645-1881	17649
T C W Realty Fund VI	6798	D	213 683-4200	12189
T Points Inc	7219	E	323 846-9176	13638
Takenaka Partners LLC **(PA)**	6211	E	213 593-4011	10017
Tanner Mainstain Blatt & Gly	8721	D	310 446-2700	26300
Tarrant Apparel Group	5137	C	323 780-8250	8338

Name	SIC	EMP	PHONE	ENTRY #
Tbwa Chiat/Day Inc	7389	D	310 305-5000	17497
Tbwa Worldwide Inc	7311	C	310 305-4400	13909
Tcw Funds Management Inc	6211	A	213 244-0000	10019
Tcw Group Inc **(PA)**	6282	B	213 244-0000	10116
Tcw Value Added Ltd Partnr	6733	D	213 244-0000	12128
Team-One Emplyment Spclsts LLC	7361	A	310 481-4480	14775
Technclor Crative Svcs USA Inc **(DH)**	7819	B	818 260-3800	18221
Technclor Crative Svcs USA Inc.	7819	C	323 467-1244	18222
Technicolor Thomson Group	7819	A	323 817-6600	18228
Telaflora LLC	5193	B	310 231-9199	9169
Tele-Car Couriers Inc	4215	D	877 910-1313	4432
Temple Israel of Hollywood **(PA)**	7261	D	323 876-8330	13700
Temple Park Convalescent Hosp	8059	D	213 380-2035	21228
Tender Home Healthcare Inc	8082	D	323 466-2345	22433
Tenet Health Systems Norris	8062	B	323 865-3000	21851
Tessie Clvland Cmnty Svcs Corp	8322	D	323 586-7333	24086
The Gray-Line Tours Company	4142	D	323 463-3333	3904
The Orthopedic Institute of	8011	A	213 977-2010	20005
The Teecor Group Inc	1799	D	213 632-2350	3593
Think Passenger Inc **(PA)**	7371	D	323 556-5400	15501
Thinkwell Group Inc	7922	D	818 333-3444	18408
Thompson Coburn LLP	8111	B	310 282-2500	23409
Thoreau Janitorial Svcs Inc	7349	C	310 822-8017	14406
Time Inc.	7313	C	310 268-7200	13959
Time Warner Cable Entps LLC	4841	C	323 993-7076	5948
Time Warner Cable Inc	4841	B	323 993-8000	5959
Tinco Sheet Metal Inc.	1761	D	323 263-0511	3207
Tishman Construction Corp Cal	8741	D	213 542-6400	27062
TNT USA Inc	4513	D	310 242-9700	4846
Tom Malloy Corporation **(PA)**	5082	C	310 327-5554	7697
Topa Berkeley Ltd	6531	D	310 203-9199	11797
Topa Insurance Company **(HQ)**	6399	C	310 201-0451	10505
Topa Management Company **(PA)**	6512	C	310 203-9199	10957
Total Professional Network	7361	D	213 382-5550	14783
Tpg Reflections II LLC	6513	D	213 613-1900	11127
Tps Parking Management LLC	7521	D	310 846-4747	17708
Trading Financial Credit LLC **(PA)**	6141	E	213 375-3113	9727
Trailer Park Inc	7311	D	310 845-8400	13911
Trailer Park Inc **(PA)**	7311	D	310 845-3000	13912
Trams Inc **(DH)**	7373	D	310 641-8726	16066
Trans West Investigations Inc	7381	D	213 381-1500	16836
Transamerica Securities Sales	6211	D	213 741-7702	10022
Transmerica Fincl Advisors Inc	6211	C	213 741-7702	10023
Transmrica Occidental Lf Insur **(DH)**	6311	A	213 742-2111	10148
Travel Store **(PA)**	4724	D	310 575-5540	4954
Triage Entertainment Inc	7812	D	310 417-4800	18135
Trifecta Multimedia LLC **(PA)**	7379	E	626 355-1303	16517
Trope and Trope LLP	8111	D	323 879-2726	23412
Troygould PC	8111	D	310 553-4441	23415
Truck Underwriters Association **(DH)**	8621	A	323 932-3200	25047
Truconnect Communications **(PA)**	4813	C	800 430-0443	5656
True Rate Insurance Agency Inc **(PA)**	6411	E	323 735-1600	10807
Trz Holdings II Inc	6531	B	213 955-7170	11805
Tucker Ellis LLP	8111	D	213 430-3400	23416
Tumbleweed Educational Entps	7999	C	310 444-3232	19251
Turner Broadcasting System Inc	4832	D	310 788-6767	5759
Turner Construction Company	1521	D	213 891-3000	1251
Twentieth Century Fox Home E **(DH)**	7812	A	310 369-1000	18139
Twentieth Cntury Fox Film Corp **(DH)**	7812	D	310 369-1000	18140
Twentieth Cntury Fox Intl Corp **(DH)**	7822	B	310 969-5300	18244
Twenty Mile Productions LLC	7929	C	412 251-0767	18470
Tzippy Care Inc	8059	D	323 737-7778	21235
Uaw-Lbor Emplyment Trning Corp	7361	C	323 730-7900	14788
UBS Financial Services Inc	6211	C	213 972-1511	10024
Uc Regents	8011	D	310 301-8777	20016
Ucla Copy Services	7334	E	310 794-6371	14093
Ucla Foundation	6732	B	310 794-3193	12084
Ucla Health System	8011	D	310 825-9111	20017
Ucla Health System Auxiliary	8082	A	310 267-4327	22441
Ucla Marina Center	7999	D	310 825-3671	19253
Umina Bros Inc **(PA)**	5148	D	213 622-9206	8739
UNI Hosiery Co Inc **(PA)**	5136	C	213 228-0100	8281
Unified Grocers Inc	5143	D	323 232-6124	8530
Uniserve Facilities Svcs Corp	7349	A	310 440-6747	14415
Unitas Global LLC **(PA)**	7374	D	213 785-6200	16194
United Airlines Inc	4512	C	310 342-8086	4806
United Airlines Inc	4512	B	310 258-3319	4809
United Artists Productions Inc	7822	C	310 449-3000	18245
United Artists Television Corp	7822	C	310 449-3000	18246
United Convalescent Facilities	8059	D	626 629-6950	21236
United Cp/S Chldrns Fndn La	8322	D	323 737-0303	24103
United Express Messengers Inc	7389	D	310 261-2000	17533
United Fabrics Intl Inc	5131	D	213 749-8200	8247
United Food and Commercial **(PA)**	8631	D	213 487-7070	25087
United Ind Taxi Drivers **(PA)**	4121	D	323 462-1088	3871

	SIC	EMP	PHONE	ENTRY #
United Independent Taxi Co	4121	E	213 385-2227	3872
United Parcel Service Inc OH	4215	C	310 474-0019	4460
United Parcel Service Inc OH	4215	A	323 729-6762	4478
United States Attorneys	8111	C	213 894-2400	23419
United States Fire Insur Co	6411	D	213 797-3100	10811
United Talent Agency LLC	8742	B	310 385-2800	27501
United Teachers-Los Angeles	8631	D	213 487-5560	25088
United Way Inc (PA)	8399	D	213 808-6220	24854
Unity Courier Service Inc (PA)	4215	A	323 255-9800	4487
Universal Studios Company LLC	7812	C	310 235-4749	18148
University Cal Los Angeles	8062	A	310 825-0640	21874
University Cal Los Angeles	8062	A	310 825-9111	21877
University Credit Union	6061	C	310 477-6628	9615
University Southern California	8062	A	323 442-8500	21888
University Southern California	8011	D	213 743-5339	20036
University Student Union Inc	7389	C	323 343-2450	17551
URS Group Inc	8711	D	213 996-2200	25974
URS Group Inc	8711	D	213 996-2200	25976
US Army Corps of Engineers	8711	D	213 452-3967	25985
US International Media LLC (PA)	7319	D	310 482-6700	13985
US Metro Group Inc	7349	A	213 382-6435	14423
US Telepacific Corp (HQ)	4813	E	866 699-8242	5659
Usc Care Medical Group Inc	8062	D	323 442-5100	21890
Usc Credit Union	6061	C	213 821-7100	9616
Usc Emergency Medicine Assoc	8011	D	323 226-6667	20039
Usc Institute For Neuroimaging	8011	C	323 442-7246	20040
Usc Shoah Fndn Inst For Visual	8699	D	213 740-6001	25479
Usc Surgeons Incorporated	8011	C	323 442-5910	20041
Uscb Inc	7322	D	213 387-6181	14025
Uscb Inc (PA)	7322	D	213 985-2111	14026
USI Insurance Services Nat Inc	6411	C	213 253-6700	10816
Vacation and Holiday Benefit F	6733	D	213 385-6161	12130
Val-Pro Inc	5148	D	213 689-0844	8741
Valet Parking Svc A Cal Partnr (PA)	7521	A	323 465-5873	17710
Valetor Inc	7216	E	323 654-1271	13571
Valley Couriers Inc (PA)	4212	A	818 591-2212	4082
Vancrest Construction Corp	1542	E	323 256-0011	1692
Vayan Marketing Group LLC	8742	E	310 943-4990	27509
VCA Animal Hospitals Inc (DH)	0742	C	310 571-6500	613
VCA Antech Inc	0742	B	310 207-0781	614
VCA Inc	0742	C	310 473-2951	616
Veatch Carlson Grogan & Nelson	8111	E	213 381-2861	23420
Vector Security Inc	1731	D	323 224-6700	2779
Vendor Direct Solutions LLC	8741	C	213 362-5622	27084
Verifi Inc	8742	D	323 655-5789	27510
Veritiv Operating Company	5113	C	310 527-3000	8133
Verizon Business Global LLC	4813	D	909 466-5633	5664
Verizon Communications Inc	7389	A	213 330-2556	17565
Verizon Digital Media Svcs Inc (HQ)	7379	D	310 396-7400	16525
Versa Products Inc (PA)	5021	D	310 353-7100	6741
Veterans Health Administration	8011	A	310 478-3711	20059
Veterans Health Administration	8011	C	213 253-2677	20083
Via Care Cmnty Hlth Ctr Inc	8011	D	323 268-9191	20086
Viacom Consumer Products Inc	6794	E	323 956-5634	12146
Viacom Networks	7812	A	310 752-8000	18151
Vicar Operating Inc (DH)	0742	C	310 571-6500	620
VIP Tours of California Inc	4725	D	310 216-7507	4984
Virgil Sntrium Cnvlescent Hosp	8051	C	323 665-5793	20867
Visionaire Group Inc	7311	D	310 823-1800	13917
Visionstar Inc	8742	D	213 387-3700	27515
Vista Anglina Hsing Prtners LP	6531	E	213 482-4718	11814
Viva Group Inc	6513	D	310 449-6400	11138
Vivid Solution	7389	D	310 498-2559	17572
Volume Services Inc	7999	D	323 644-6038	19258
Volunteers of Amer Los Angeles	8322	C	323 780-3770	24116
Vxi Global Solutions LLC (PA)	7389	A	213 739-4720	17576
W Los Angeles	7011	B	310 208-8765	13372
W Scott Bllard Dsign Arch Inc	7389	E	323 386-4740	17577
Walker & Dunlop Inc	6162	D	301 215-5500	9864
Walter J Conn & Associates	8712	D	213 683-0500	26118
Wardlow 2 LP (PA)	7699	D	562 432-8066	18005
Warren Drye Kelley	8111	D	310 712-6100	23426
Washington Enterprises 3 LLC	8051	D	323 731-0861	20875
Wasserman Media Group LLC (PA)	8742	C	310 407-0200	27519
Watts Health Foundation Inc	6733	B	323 357-6688	12132
Watts Healthcare Corporation	8011	C	323 241-1780	20091
Watts Healthcare Corporation (PA)	8011	C	323 564-4331	20092
Watts Labor Community Action	8322	C	323 563-5639	24128
We See Dragons LLC	7379	C	310 361-5700	16530
We Team Security Firm Inc	7381	D	800 745-9051	16856
Wealth Educators Inc	8741	C	310 623-9145	27091
Wedbush Securities Inc (HQ)	6211	B	213 688-8000	10035
Weingart Center Association	8322	C	213 622-6359	24130
Weitz & Luxenberg PC	8111	D	310 247-0921	23432
Wells Fargo Bank Ltd	6021	D	213 253-6227	9379

	SIC	EMP	PHONE	ENTRY #
Wells Fargo Bank NA	6021	C	213 628-2251	9380
Wells Fargo Clearing Svcs LLC	6211	E	213 486-5200	10036
West Coast Ambulance Corp	4119	C	310 435-1862	3858
West Corporation	7389	C	310 481-7878	17587
West Hotel Partners LP (PA)	7011	C	310 477-3593	13387
West Oahu Mall Associates	6798	E	310 276-1290	12192
West Side Rehab Corporation	6512	C	323 231-4174	10961
Western Exterminator Company	7342	D	310 274-9244	14162
Westfield LLC (DH)	6512	B	813 926-4600	10963
Westfield America Inc (HQ)	6512	C	310 478-4456	10964
Westfield America Ltd Partnr	6552	C	310 478-4456	11937
Westfield America Ltd Partnr	6512	B	310 277-3898	10965
Westlake Health Care Center	8051	C	805 494-1233	20887
Westlake Services LLC (PA)	6159	C	323 692-8800	9766
Westpoint Marketing Intl Inc	7389	D	323 233-0233	17593
Westside Jewish Cmnty Ctr Inc (PA)	8399	C	323 938-2531	24859
Weststar Cinemas Inc	7832	D	323 461-3331	18323
Westwood Healthcare Center LP	8051	D	310 826-0821	20890
Wga West Inc	7313	D	323 782-4512	13962
Whb Corporation	7011	A	213 624-1011	13398
White & Case LLP	8111	C	213 687-9655	23434
White Carnival LLC	8741	E	310 914-1600	27097
White Memorial Med Group Inc (PA)	8011	D	323 987-1300	20102
White Memorial Medical Center (HQ)	8062	A	323 268-5000	21916
Whiting-Turner Contracting Co	1542	C	213 310-7900	1701
WI Spa LLC	7991	E	213 487-2700	18675
Wiemar Distributors Inc	5148	D	213 747-7036	8747
Will Perkins Inc	8712	C	213 270-8400	26121
William Morris Endeavor	7922	B	310 285-9000	18413
Wilmer Cutler Pick Hale Dorr	8111	C	213 443-5300	23435
Wilshire Center Dental Group	8021	E	213 386-3336	20145
Wilshire Consumer Credit	6141	E	323 692-8585	9729
Wilshire Country Club	7997	D	323 934-6050	19087
Wilson Elser Moskowitz	8111	C	213 443-5100	23437
Windsor Gardens Convalescnt	8051	D	323 937-5466	20902
Windstar Capital Advisors	6282	C	310 505-3720	10123
Winterthur U S Holdings Inc	6411	D	213 228-0281	10832
Wood Smith Henning Berman LLP (PA)	8111	E	310 481-7600	23446
Workmens Auto Insurance Co	6331	D	213 742-8700	10417
Worldlink LLC (PA)	7389	D	323 866-5900	17599
Worldwide Flight Services Inc	4581	C	310 646-7510	4923
Worldwide Flight Services Inc	4512	C	310 342-7830	4815
Worldwide Holdings Inc (PA)	6411	D	213 236-4500	10838
Worldwide Security Associates (HQ)	7381	B	310 743-3000	16860
Worleyparsons Group Inc	8711	B	610 855-2000	26008
Woundco Holdings Inc	7352	B	310 551-0101	14436
Wrap News Inc	7383	E	424 248-0612	16959
Writers Guild America West Inc	8631	C	323 951-4000	25089
Written On My Skin LLC	7812	E	312 504-5100	18170
Wsp USA Inc	8711	E	212 465-5000	26012
Xpo Logistics Freight Inc	4213	C	213 744-0664	4318
Yeshiva Rau Isacsohn Academy	8351	C	323 549-3170	24401
Yf Art Holdings Gp LLC	6719	A	678 441-1400	12018
York Hlthcare Wllness Cntre LP	8051	D	323 254-3407	20912
Young Mens Chrstn Assn of La (PA)	8641	D	213 351-2256	25342
Young Mens Chrstn Assn of La	8641	E	310 216-9036	25343
Young Mens Chrstn Assn of La	8641	C	323 467-4161	25345
Young Mens Chrstn Assn of La	8641	D	213 624-2348	25347
Young Mens Chrstn Assn of La	8641	C	323 295-4280	25366
Young Womens Christian Assoc	8641	C	323 295-4280	25366
Youngs Market Company LLC	5182	B	213 629-3929	9068
Yucaipa Companies LLC (PA)	8748	C	310 789-7200	27914
Yue Feng Inc	8322	D	310 253-9795	24142
Yuen Yee Laundry & Cleaners	7211	D	323 734-7205	13491
Yukevich / Cvanaugh A Law Corp (PA)	8111	D	213 362-7777	23449
Z Valet Inc	7299	C	323 954-3700	13782
Zabin Industries Inc (PA)	5131	D	213 749-1215	8248
Zastrow Construction Inc	1522	D	323 478-1956	1328
Zefr Inc	7812	D	310 392-3555	18172
Zestfinance Inc	7371	D	323 450-3000	15559
Ziffren B B F G-L S&C Fnd	8111	C	310 552-3388	23451
Zimmer Gunsul	8712	D	213 617-1901	26125
Zurich American Insurance Co	6411	C	213 270-0600	10841

LOS BANOS, CA - Merced County

	SIC	EMP	PHONE	ENTRY #
Al Barcellos Et	0131	E	209 826-2636	10
Bowles Farming Co Inc	0191	E	209 827-3000	325
David Santos Farming	7389	D	209 826-1065	17125
Facilities Operation and Trnsp	4151	D	209 826-1936	3922
Hobby Lobby Stores Inc	7389	D	209 829-1807	17222
Kings View Work Experience Ctr	6321	E	209 826-8118	10167
McElvany Inc	1623	D	209 826-1102	1954
New Bthny Rsdntl CRE&sklld	8361	D	209 827-8933	24609
Para & Palli Inc	8051	D	209 826-0790	20691
Ranchwood Contractors Inc	1542	D	209 826-6200	1625
Sutter Health	8641	C	209 827-4866	25259
Wolfsen Incorporated	0131	C	209 827-7700	17

Employment Codes: A=Over 500 employees, B=251-500,
C=101-250, D=51-100, E=50

2019 Directory of California
Wholesalers and Services Companies

© Mergent Inc. 1-800-342-5647

1611

GEOGRAPHIC

LOS GATOS, CA - Santa Clara County

	SIC	EMP	PHONE	ENTRY #
Accel Biotech LLC	8711	D	408 354-1700	25497
Addison-Penzak Jewish Communit	7991	C	408 358-3636	18573
Alain Pinel Realtors Inc	6531	D	408 358-1111	11197
American Baptist Homes of West	8059	C	408 357-1100	20992
Audrey Adams MD	8011	E	408 354-2114	19312
Auto World Car Wash LLC	7542	A	408 345-6532	17801
Butter Paddle	7389	D	408 395-1678	17044
Calvary Baptist Ch Los Gatos	8351	D	408 356-5126	24272
Caresouth Home Health Svcs LLC	8082	E	408 378-6131	22254
Coldwell Bnkr Rsdential RE LLC	6531	D	408 355-1500	11363
Courtside Tennis Club	7997	D	408 395-7111	18904
Episcopal Senior Communities	8361	C	408 354-0211	24519
Golden Living LLC	8059	D	408 356-8136	21089
Golden Living LLC	8051	D	408 356-9151	20481
Good Samaritan Hospital LP	8062	C	408 356-4111	21434
Infogain Corporation **(PA)**	7379	C	408 355-6000	16393
Inner Circle Entertainment	5145	D	415 693-0777	8563
Intellicus Tech Pvt Ltd	7373	D	408 213-3314	15980
Joie De Vivre Hospitality LLC	1731	A	408 335-1700	2621
La Rinconada Country Club Inc **(PA)**	7997	D	408 395-4181	18949
NC Fit Inc	7991	D	408 910-6748	18637
Netflix Inc	7841	A	408 540-3700	18330
Netflix Inc **(PA)**	7841	C	408 540-3700	18331
Netline Corporation **(PA)**	8742	D	408 374-4200	27365
Roku Inc **(PA)**	4841	B	408 556-9040	5929
SA Photonics Inc	8748	D	408 560-3500	27850
Sanco Pipelines Incorporated	1623	E	408 377-2793	1978
Santa Clara County of	7999	C	408 355-2200	19233
Santa Clara Valley Water	4941	D	408 395-8121	6309
Sierra Nevada Corporation	8711	C	408 395-2004	25914
Sierra Weatherization Co Inc	7311	D	408 354-1900	13903
Stratford School Inc	8351	D	408 371-3020	24387
Sutter Health	8641	C	408 523-3900	25260
Tenet Healthsystem Medical	8062	A	408 378-6131	21856
Therapy In Your Home O TP TS	8082	D	408 358-0201	22435
Trevi Partners A Calif LP	7011	D	408 395-7070	13341
Triple Hs Inc **(PA)**	8748	D	408 458-3200	27891
Uplift Family Services	8093	D	408 379-3790	22708
Verizon Wireless Inc	4812	C	408 354-6374	5426

LOS OSOS, CA - San Luis Obispo County

	SIC	EMP	PHONE	ENTRY #
Cellco Partnership	4812	D	805 596-2300	5314

LOST HILLS, CA - Kern County

	SIC	EMP	PHONE	ENTRY #
Roll Properties Intl Inc	6799	C	661 797-6500	12263
Wonderful Orchards LLC	0173	C	661 797-6400	198

LOTUS, CA - El Dorado County

	SIC	EMP	PHONE	ENTRY #
Adventure Connection Inc	7999	D	530 626-7385	19091

LOWER LAKE, CA - Lake County

	SIC	EMP	PHONE	ENTRY #
Barrick Gold Corporation	1041	D	707 995-6070	1004
Epidendio Construction Inc	1771	E	707 994-5100	3254

LOYALTON, CA - Sierra County

	SIC	EMP	PHONE	ENTRY #
Eastern Plumas Health Care	8051	D	530 993-1225	20382

LUCERNE VALLEY, CA - San Bernardino County

	SIC	EMP	PHONE	ENTRY #
Specialty Minerals Inc	1422	C	760 248-5300	1087
SS Hert Trucking Inc **(PA)**	4213	E	760 248-9327	4267

LYNWOOD, CA - Los Angeles County

	SIC	EMP	PHONE	ENTRY #
ADM Furniture Inc	5021	D	310 762-2800	6707
Country Villa Service Corp	8051	D	310 537-2500	20331
Jones Lumber Company Inc	5031	D	323 564-6656	6838
Kaiser Foundation Hospitals	8011	A	310 604-5700	19568
Legacy Frames	5065	D	310 537-4210	7499
Marlinda Management Inc **(PA)**	8059	C	310 638-6691	21152
Midas Express Los Angeles Inc	4225	C	310 609-0366	4594
South Cntl Heatlh & Rehab Prog	8093	D	310 667-4070	22682
Southern CA Hlth & Rhbltn Prg	8011	C	310 631-8004	19900
Southern Cal Prmnnte Med Group	8011	D	310 604-5700	19908
St Francis Medical Center **(HQ)**	8011	C	310 900-8900	19936
Verity Health System Cal Inc	8062	D	310 900-2000	21901
Verity Health System Cal Inc	8062	A	310 900-8900	21902
Via Trading Corporation	5199	D	877 202-3616	9267

LYTLE CREEK, CA - San Bernardino County

	SIC	EMP	PHONE	ENTRY #
Burlingame Industries Inc	7033	C	909 887-7038	13460

MACDOEL, CA - Siskiyou County

	SIC	EMP	PHONE	ENTRY #
Plant Sciences Inc	5193	E	530 398-4042	9157

MADERA, CA - Madera County

	SIC	EMP	PHONE	ENTRY #
Agri-World Cooperative	0762	E	559 673-1306	680
Avalon Care Ctr - Madera LLC	8051	D	559 673-9278	20247
Berry & Berry Inc **(PA)**	1521	D	559 674-2491	1122
Camarena Health	8011	D	559 664-4000	19345
Comcast Corporation	4841	D	559 474-4194	5879
Community Action Prtnrshp **(PA)**	8351	C	559 673-9173	24300
Costa View Farms	0241	E	559 675-3131	409
County of Los Angeles	8322	C	559 675-7739	23688
County of Madera	7549	D	559 675-7811	17858
Eurodrip USA Inc	5083	D	559 674-2670	7702
First Student Inc	4151	C	559 661-7433	3935
Fresno-Madera Federal Land	6111	D	559 674-2437	9696
Golden Living LLC	8059	D	559 673-9278	21091
Iest Family Farms	0241	D	559 674-9417	417
Kronos Foods Corp	5149	D	559 674-4445	8821
Lamanuzzi & Pantaleo LLC **(PA)**	0172	D	559 432-3170	156
Lion Raisins Inc	0191	C	559 662-8686	366
Madera Cnty Bhvioral Hlth Svcs	8093	C	559 673-3508	22616
Madera Community Hospital	8062	C	559 675-5530	21572
Madera Community Hospital **(PA)**	8062	B	559 675-5555	21574
Madera Convalescent Hospital **(PA)**	8051	C	559 673-9228	20605
Madera Private Security Patrol	7381	D	559 662-1546	16726
Mid Valley Labor Services Inc	7361	B	559 661-6390	14669
Our House Residential Care Ctr	8059	D	559 674-8670	21177
Pediatric Physical Rehab Clnc	8093	E	559 353-6130	22640
Ready Roast Nut Company LLC **(PA)**	0723	D	559 661-1696	557
Resource Rfrral Child Care Dev	8322	E	559 673-9173	23994
Richard Iest Dairy Inc	0139	D	559 673-2635	29
S & J Ranches LLC	0723	D	559 437-2600	562
Span Construction & Engrg Inc **(PA)**	1542	D	559 661-1111	1658
Stellar Distributing Inc	5148	B	559 664-8400	8732
Talley Transportation	4212	D	559 673-9013	4068
Valley Childrens Healthcare	8011	A	559 353-3000	20042
Valley Childrens Hospital	8062	C	559 353-6425	21893
Valley Childrens Hospital **(PA)**	8062	A	559 353-3000	21894
Valley Productions Inc	7389	E	559 661-6121	17558

MALIBU, CA - Los Angeles County

	SIC	EMP	PHONE	ENTRY #
California Fuji International	7992	E	818 889-6680	18691
County of Los Angeles	8322	C	818 889-1353	23687
Creating Arts Company	7922	E	310 804-0223	18360
Curtco Publishing LLC **(PA)**	7313	D	310 589-7700	13940
Dun & Bradstreet Emerging **(DH)**	7389	C	310 456-8271	17141
Fitness Ridge Malibu LLC	7011	D	818 874-1300	12576
Grasshopper House LLC	8093	C	310 589-2880	22586
Hrl Laboratories LLC	8733	B	310 317-5000	26622
Malibu Conference Center Inc	6512	B	818 889-6440	10909
Malibu Realty Inc	6531	E	310 457-5124	11581
Marmalade LLC	7389	E	310 317-4242	17312
Mbipch LLC	7011	D	310 456-6444	12916
Monte Nido Residential Ctr LLC **(PA)**	8082	D	310 457-9958	22369
Parks and Recreation Cal Dept	8412	D	310 456-8432	24899
Phifactor Technologies LLC	8071	D	424 234-9494	22121
Pritchett Rapf and Associates	6531	D	310 456-6771	11680
Snb Corporation	8322	C	310 457-9111	24051
Sobaliving Llc	8099	E	800 595-3803	22886
Sothebys Intl Rlty Inc	6531	E	310 456-6431	11771
Tall Pony Productions Inc	7812	C	310 456-7495	18130
Terra Coastal Properties Inc	6531	E	310 457-2534	11790
Westmed Ambulance Inc	4119	C	310 456-3830	3860

MAMMOTH LAKES, CA - Mono County

	SIC	EMP	PHONE	ENTRY #
Horizons 4 Condominiums Inc	8641	D	760 934-6779	25174
Mammoth Mountain Lake Corp	7032	B	760 934-2571	13452
Mammoth Mountain Ski Area LLC **(DH)**	7011	B	760 934-2571	12872
Snowcreek Property Management	6531	E	760 934-3333	11768
Southern Mono Healthcare Dst	8062	B	760 934-3311	21770

MANHATTAN BEACH, CA - Los Angeles County

	SIC	EMP	PHONE	ENTRY #
1334 Partners LP	7997	D	310 546-5656	18814
Access To Loans For Learning	6163	E	310 979-4700	9868
Adventureplex	7991	E	310 546-7708	18574
Aerospace Corporation	8733	B	310 336-1025	26581
CIT Bank NA	6021	D	310 727-5660	9303
Comstock Crosser Assoc Dev Inc	6552	E	310 546-5781	11866
Connectx Inc	7379	E	310 702-8686	16332
Dalaklis McKeown Entertainment	7812	D	310 545-0120	18037
Ebc Inc **(PA)**	1521	D	310 753-6407	1159
Emergent Medical Associates **(PA)**	8011	D	310 379-2134	19460
Frys Electronics Inc	5045	C	310 364-3797	7049
GBS Financial Corp	7389	D	310 937-0073	17181
Global Holdings Inc	6719	C	818 905-6000	11981
Guru Denim LLC **(DH)**	5137	C	323 266-3072	8304
Host Hotels & Resorts LP	7011	D	310 546-7511	12714
Human Touch Home Health	8082	C	424 247-8165	22339
Indigo Hospitality Management	8742	E	310 787-7795	27270
Investlinc Group LLC **(PA)**	7389	D	310 997-0580	17251
Jag Professional Services Inc	8748	C	310 945-5648	27759
Kinecta Alternative Fin **(HQ)**	6099	D	310 538-2242	9686

Company	SIC	EMP	PHONE	ENTRY #
Kinecta Federal Credit Union (PA)	6061	C	310 643-5400	9566
M & E Technical Services L L C (PA)	8744	D	256 964-6486	27600
Mbs Equipment Company (PA)	7819	D	310 558-3100	18200
Pancreatic Cancr Actn Netwrk I (PA)	8099	C	310 725-0025	22856
Puttin On Productions Corp	7812	E	310 546-5544	18101
Re/Max Beach Cities Realty Mar	6531	C	310 376-2225	11710
Solartis LLC	7371	C	310 251-4861	15461
Sunstone Hotel Properties Inc	7011	D	310 546-7627	13304
Trilogy Squaw Spa LLC	7231	E	310 760-0044	13675
Vantage Oncology LLC (HQ)	8011	B	310 335-4000	20048
Western America Properties LLC	6531	D	310 374-4381	11828

MANTECA, CA - San Joaquin County

Company	SIC	EMP	PHONE	ENTRY #
1st Light Energy Inc (PA)	1799	E	209 824-5500	3478
AT&T Corp.	4813	D	209 956-8324	5453
B R Funsten & Co	5023	D	209 825-5375	6748
Bay Area Cnstr Framers Inc	1751	C	925 454-8514	3018
Cen Cal Plastering Inc	1742	D	209 858-1045	2864
Clearpath Management Group Inc (PA)	7363	B	209 239-8700	14832
Clearpath Workforce MGT Inc	7363	D	209 239-8700	14833
Compass Bank	6022	B	209 239-1381	9437
Cool Roofing Systems Inc (PA)	1761	D	209 825-0818	3142
Doctors Hospital Manteca Inc	8069	D	209 823-3111	22018
Ecologic Brands Inc	5199	E	209 239-3600	9213
Ford Motor Company	5013	C	209 824-6600	6640
Frontier California Inc.	4813	D	209 239-4128	5565
J M Equipment Company Inc (PA)	7359	D	209 522-3271	14517
Kaiser Foundation Hospitals	8062	A	209 825-3700	21515
Kaiser Manteca Medical Office	8071	C	209 825-3700	22099
Kamps Company	7363	C	209 823-8924	14868
Karma Inc.	8051	C	209 239-1222	20551
Merrill Gardens LLC	6513	D	209 823-0164	11075
Pgande	8611	D	209 942-1745	24972
Priority 1 Warehousing Inc (PA)	4225	D	209 824-8876	4613
Propane Transport Service Inc	4212	C	209 823-8005	4050
S K S Enterprises Inc (PA)	0252	D	209 599-4095	434
South San Jquin Irrigation Dst	4971	D	209 249-4600	6567
Stockton Cardiology Medical Gr	8011	D	209 824-1555	19950
Tenet Healthsystem Medical	8062	B	209 823-3111	21854
Transforce Inc	7363	E	209 952-2573	14922
United Parcel Service Inc OH	4513	C	209 944-5932	4851
Valley Oak Dental Group	8021	D	209 823-9341	20142
Valley Oaks Residential	8322	D	209 239-3244	24108
Van Groningen & Sons Inc	0191	B	209 982-5248	390
Villara Corporation	1711	D	209 824-1082	2400
Western Repacking Lllp	7389	D	916 668-8443	17592

MARCH ARB, CA - Riverside County

Company	SIC	EMP	PHONE	ENTRY #
Taft Broadcasting Company LLC	7812	D	951 413-2337	18129

MARICOPA, CA - Kern County

Company	SIC	EMP	PHONE	ENTRY #
Aera Energy LLC	1381	D	661 665-3200	1033
Luis Esparza Services Inc	7361	B	661 766-2344	14665

MARINA, CA - Monterey County

Company	SIC	EMP	PHONE	ENTRY #
American Medical Response Inc	4119	C	831 718-9555	3765
Collins Electrical Company Inc	1731	D	831 384-0114	2546
Monterey Rgional Waste MGT Dst	4953	C	831 384-5313	6421

MARINA DEL REY, CA - Los Angeles County

Company	SIC	EMP	PHONE	ENTRY #
Al Anwa USA Incorporated	7011	C	310 301-2000	12310
ARINC Incorporated	8711	D	310 301-9040	25545
Berger Kahn (PA)	8111	D	310 578-6800	22941
Calatlantic Group Inc	1521	D	310 821-9843	1138
Can-Do	8322	D	646 228-7049	23525
Cfhs Holdings Inc	8062	A	310 823-8911	21308
Cfhs Holdings Inc	8062	A	310 448-7800	21309
CIT Bank National Association	6021	D	310 577-6142	9325
Diagnostic and Interventio	8011	D	310 574-0400	19441
Executive Network Entps Inc (PA)	4119	D	310 447-2759	3793
Fedex Office & Print Svcs Inc	7334	E	310 827-2297	14087
Four Medica Inc	4899	D	310 348-4100	5982
Gebbs Software Intl Inc	7379	E	201 227-0088	16377
Guidance Solutions Inc	7375	E	310 754-4000	16229
Host Hotels & Resorts LP	7011	D	310 301-3000	12715
Igotchu Inc.	7382	D	818 987-1699	16905
International Mgt Systems	8748	D	310 822-2022	27755
Laaco Ltd	7997	D	310 823-4567	18950
Liquidate Direct LLC	7373	E	800 750-7617	15999
Marina Auto Body Shop Inc	7532	E	310 822-6615	17729
Marina City Club LP A Cali	6513	C	310 822-0611	11062
Marina Del Rey Hospital	8062	A	310 823-8911	21577
Modern Parking Inc	7521	D	310 821-1081	17694
Post Modern Edit LLC	7812	D	310 396-7375	18097
R & B Realty Group	6513	D	310 751-4545	11103
Regional Investment & MGT LLC	1522	E	310 821-1945	1312
Ritz-Carlton Marina Del Rey	7011	D	310 823-1700	13131

Company	SIC	EMP	PHONE	ENTRY #
Skylar Film Studios LLC	7819	C	424 653-8902	18218
Sony Dadc New Mdia Sltions Inc	7822	C	310 760-8500	18243
Textplus Inc	4812	D	424 272-0296	5421
Thirdwave Technology Services	7378	E	310 563-2160	16294
Trendshift LLC	7371	D	866 644-8877	15511
Trotta Associates	8732	C	310 306-6866	26574
USA Travel Services LLC	8699	A	207 899-8803	25478
USG Enterprises Inc	4489	D	310 827-2220	4722
Veba Administrators Inc	6411	E	310 577-1444	10823
Washington Inn LLC	7011	D	310 821-4455	13380
Williamson Enterprises Inc	7532	D	310 822-6615	17745

MARIPOSA, CA - Mariposa County

Company	SIC	EMP	PHONE	ENTRY #
John C Fremont Healthcare Dst	8062	C	209 966-3631	21461
Ponderosa Enterprises (PA)	7011	E	209 742-7777	13072

MARSHALL, CA - Marin County

Company	SIC	EMP	PHONE	ENTRY #
Nicks Cove Inc.	7011	D	415 663-1033	12957

MARTINEZ, CA - Contra Costa County

Company	SIC	EMP	PHONE	ENTRY #
Alhambra Convalescent Hosp LLC	8051	D	925 228-2020	20226
Baja Construction Co Inc (PA)	1791	D	925 229-0732	3361
Bay Area/Diablo Petroleum Co (HQ)	5172	C	925 228-2222	8950
Braddock & Logan Inc	6513	D	925 229-1747	10989
Brightview Landscape Svcs Inc	0781	D	925 957-8831	738
Careonsite Inc	8011	D	562 437-0381	19354
Central Contra Costa Sanit	4952	D	925 228-9500	6321
Contra Costa Electric Inc (DH)	1731	B	925 229-4250	2550
County of Contra Costa	8322	C	925 313-4000	23633
County of Contra Costa	1611	C	925 313-2000	1747
County of Contra Costa	7349	D	925 313-7052	14232
County of Contra Costa	8322	C	866 901-3212	23634
County of Contra Costa	8322	C	925 313-1500	23635
County of Contra Costa	8062	C	925 370-5000	21349
Dynalectric Company	1731	C	415 487-4700	2568
Dynamic Maintenance Svcs Inc	7349	D	925 228-7434	14254
Engineering/Remdtn Rsrcs Grp (PA)	4959	C	925 839-2200	6539
Gregg Drilling LLC.	1781	D	925 313-5800	3351
Gregg Drilling & Testing Inc.	1781	D	925 313-5800	3352
Kaiser Foundation Hospitals	6733	C	925 372-1000	12104
Legacy and Nursing Rehab	8322	D	925 228-8383	23892
Nalco Company LLC	5169	D	925 957-9720	8932
National Railroad Pass Corp	4011	A	925 335-5180	3620
Parsons Government Svcs Inc.	8711	D	925 313-3217	25868
Permanente Medical Group Inc	8011	D	925 372-1000	19764
Plant Maintenance Inc.	7363	C	925 228-3285	14892
Power Engineers Incorporated	8711	D	925 372-9284	25877
R M Harris Company Inc	1622	D	925 335-3000	1887
RE Milano Plumbing Corp	1711	E	925 500-1372	2332
Telfer Oil Company (PA)	1611	D	925 228-1515	1860
Terracare Associates LLC	8742	C	925 374-0060	27486
Thrive Support Services Inc	8082	E	925 682-2273	22437
Waters Moving & Storage Inc	4214	D	925 372-0914	4389
YWCA Contra Costa/Sacramento (PA)	8322	D	925 372-4213	24143

MARYSVILLE, CA - Yuba County

Company	SIC	EMP	PHONE	ENTRY #
Advantage Framing Solutions	1542	E	530 742-7660	1456
Alliance Wall Systems Inc	1742	E	530 740-7800	2841
Childrens Protective Services	8322	D	530 749-6311	23570
County of Yuba	6552	D	530 749-5470	11867
County of Yuba	8322	C	530 749-7550	23760
Frank M Booth Inc (PA)	8711	C	530 742-7134	25692
Fremont Hospital	8062	A	530 751-4000	21419
Marysvlle Nrsing Rehab Ctr LLC	8051	D	530 742-7311	20633
Melon Holdings LLC	8051	D	530 742-7311	20641
Pacific Gas and Electric Co	4911	B	530 742-3251	6070
Peach Tree Healthcare	8011	D	530 749-3242	19755
Recology Yuba-Sutter	4953	D	530 743-6933	6446
Rideout Memorial Hospital (HQ)	8062	A	530 749-4416	21686
US Dept of the Air Force	8062	B	530 634-4839	21889
Yuba Community College Dst	8322	D	530 788-0973	24141

MATHER, CA - Sacramento County

Company	SIC	EMP	PHONE	ENTRY #
Bloodsource Inc (PA)	8099	B	916 456-1500	22750
Mather Aviation LLC (PA)	4581	D	916 364-4711	4900
Reynen & Bardis Construction (PA)	1521	D	916 366-3665	1224
Sutter Health	8051	D	916 454-8200	20835
Veterans Health Administration	8011	D	916 366-5427	20061
Veterans Health Administration	8011	B	916 843-7000	20076
Volunteers of America Inc	8322	C	609 877-2665	24124

MAYWOOD, CA - Los Angeles County

Company	SIC	EMP	PHONE	ENTRY #
Food Express Inc	4212	E	323 589-1417	4014
Jack H Caldwell & Sons Inc	5148	D	323 589-4008	8697
Keeney Truck Lines Inc	4212	E	323 589-3231	4033
Maywood Halthcare Wellness Ctr	8051	D	323 560-0720	20634
R G Canning Enterprises Inc	7389	C	323 560-7469	17422

GEOGRAPHIC

Company	SIC	EMP	PHONE	ENTRY #
Tapia Enterprises Inc (PA)	5141	D	323 560-7415	8473

MC FARLAND, CA - Kern County

Company	SIC	EMP	PHONE	ENTRY #
A G Hacienda Incorporated	4212	B	661 792-2418	3960
Armando Gonzalez Contracting	0761	B	661 792-3785	638
Community Action Partnr Kern	8322	D	661 792-1066	23598
Etchegaray Farms LLC	0214	E	661 393-0920	405
Flores Labor Contracting	0761	D	661 792-3061	648
Geo Group Inc	8741	C	661 792-2731	26869
Jakov P Dulcich & Sons	0172	C	661 792-6360	149
LS Farms LLC	0191	B	661 792-3192	368
Renteria Santiago J Farm Labo	7361	D	661 792-0052	14721
Sandrini Farms	0172	D	661 792-3192	173

MC KITTRICK, CA - Kern County

Company	SIC	EMP	PHONE	ENTRY #
Dwaynes Engineering & Cnstr	1389	D	661 762-7261	1056

MCCLELLAN, CA - Sacramento County

Company	SIC	EMP	PHONE	ENTRY #
AAR Manufacturing Inc	7629	D	916 830-7011	17899
AAR Manufacturing Inc	7629	D	800 422-2213	17900
Califrnia Shock Truma A Rescue (PA)	4522	D	916 921-4000	4857
Global Blue Dvbe Inc	7376	D	916 632-2583	16269
Lionsgate Ht & Conference Ctr	7011	D	916 643-6222	12856
Mansion Hospitality Services	8742	D	916 643-6222	27315
McClellan Business Park LLC	8742	D	916 965-7100	27328
McClellan Facilities Svcs LLC	6512	D	916 965-7100	10910

MCCLELLAN, CA - Sacramento County

Company	SIC	EMP	PHONE	ENTRY #
McClellan Hospitality Svcs LLC	7011	D	916 965-7100	12918

MCCLELLAN, CA - Sacramento County

Company	SIC	EMP	PHONE	ENTRY #
Monument Security Inc (PA)	7381	C	916 564-4234	16735
Sbm Management Services LP	7349	B	866 855-2211	14377
Sbm Site Services LLC (PA)	7349	A	916 922-7600	14378
Siemens Mobility Inc	7538	D	916 621-2700	17784
Sunergy California LLC	5074	E	916 550-5370	7639
Villara Corporation (PA)	1711	B	916 646-2700	2398
Villara Corporation	1711	D	916 646-2222	2401

MCKINLEYVILLE, CA - Humboldt County

Company	SIC	EMP	PHONE	ENTRY #
Kernen Construction	1541	D	707 826-8686	1416

MECCA, CA - Riverside County

Company	SIC	EMP	PHONE	ENTRY #
Richard Bagdasarian Inc	0172	D	760 396-2168	167

MENDOCINO, CA - Mendocino County

Company	SIC	EMP	PHONE	ENTRY #
Big River Ltd-Design	7011	D	707 937-5615	12386
Mendocino Hotel & Resort Corp	7011	D	707 937-0511	12919
Sweetwater Gardens Inc	7991	E	707 937-4140	18669

MENDOTA, CA - Fresno County

Company	SIC	EMP	PHONE	ENTRY #
Pomwonderful LLC	5149	D	310 966-5800	8854
S & S Ranch Inc	0721	D	559 655-3491	466
S Stamoules Inc	0723	A	559 655-9777	563

MENIFEE, CA - Riverside County

Company	SIC	EMP	PHONE	ENTRY #
Bedon Construction Inc	8711	D	951 246-9005	25565
F M Tarbell Co	6531	D	951 301-5932	11434
Mackenzie Landscape A Cal Corp	0782	D	951 679-5477	893
Valley Pacific Concrete Inc	1771	C	951 672-6151	3342

MENLO PARK, CA - San Mateo County

Company	SIC	EMP	PHONE	ENTRY #
Alain Pinel Realtors Inc	6531	D	650 462-1111	11203
Allstate Research and Plg Ctr	6411	D	650 833-6200	10516
Atrium Capital Corp	6211	A	650 233-7878	9914
Avitas Systems Inc	7389	D	650 233-3900	17023
Barclays Capital Inc	6799	D	650 289-6000	12200
Boardvantage Inc (HQ)	8741	D	212 401-8700	26783
Bodega Bay Associates	7011	D	650 330-8888	12391
Boys & Girls CLB of Peninsula	7997	D	650 322-6255	18870
Cal Care Inc	8741	C	650 325-8600	26792
Caprion Proteomics USA LLC	8733	E	650 470-2300	26605
Carr & Ferrell	8111	D	650 812-3400	22969
Carr & Ferrell LLP (PA)	8111	D	650 812-3400	22970
Cataphora Inc (PA)	7371	D	650 622-9840	15052
Citigroup Global Markets Inc	6211	C	650 926-7600	9940
Coldwell Banker	6531	D	650 324-4456	11330
Cornerstone Research Inc (PA)	8748	D	650 853-1660	27699
Critchfield Mechanical Inc	1711	B	650 321-7801	2177
Exponent Inc (PA)	8711	C	650 326-9400	25678
Facebook Inc (PA)	7375	A	650 543-4800	16224
First Republic Bank	6022	C	650 233-8880	9453
First Republic Bank	6029	C	650 470-8888	9505
Gachina Landscape MGT Inc	0782	B	650 853-0400	844
Geological Survey US Dept	8731	D	650 329-5229	26374
Hewlett Wlliam Flora Fndation	8699	D	650 234-4500	25428
Hines Interests Ltd Partnr	6531	C	650 518-6139	11503
Intuit Inc	7372	C	650 944-6000	15722
Katerra Inc (PA)	1389	D	650 422-3572	1068

Company	SIC	EMP	PHONE	ENTRY #
Kind Homecare Inc	8082	D	888 885-5463	22353
Kleiner Prkins Cfeld Byers LLC (PA)	6799	C	650 233-2750	12236
Kohlberg Kravis Roberts Co LP	6799	D	650 233-6560	12239
Kranz & Assoc Holdings LLC	8721	D	650 854-4400	26244
Lafayette Park Hotel Corp (PA)	7011	B	650 330-8888	12831
Latham & Watkins LLP	8111	C	650 328-4600	23184
Lifemoves (PA)	8322	E	650 685-5880	23898
Lovazzano Mechanical Inc	1711	D	650 367-6216	2267
Mc Graw Commercial Insur Svc (PA)	6411	D	650 780-4800	10687
Menlo Med Clinic A Med Corp	8011	C	650 498-6500	19685
Merrill Lynch Pierce Fenner	6211	C	650 473-7888	9975
Merrill Lynch Pierce Fenner	6211	C	650 473-7888	9983
Morningside Corecare Assoc LP	8051	C	650 854-5600	20653
Nasdaq Inc	8741	C	510 705-8951	26954
Novo Construction Inc (PA)	1542	C	650 701-1500	1603
Nuance Communications Inc	7371	C	650 847-0000	15321
Oak Hill Capital Partners LP	8082	A	650 234-0500	22377
OMelveny & Myers LLP	8111	C	650 473-2600	23299
Orrick Hrrington Sutcliffe LLP	8111	D	650 614-7400	23302
Orrick Hrrington Sutcliffe LLP	8111	C	650 614-7454	23303
Pan-Pacific Mechanical LLC	1711	A	650 561-8810	2306
Peninsula Volunteers Inc (PA)	8322	E	650 326-0665	23967
Peninsula World Travel LLC (PA)	4724	E	650 328-2030	4946
Personalis Inc	8731	D	650 752-1300	26436
Protiviti Inc (HQ)	8742	D	650 234-6000	27408
Quicken Inc	7371	C	650 564-3399	15392
Robert Half International Inc (PA)	7363	D	650 234-6000	14907
Robert Half International Inc	7361	C	650 234-6000	14738
Robert Half International Inc	7361	C	650 234-6000	14739
Robert Half International Inc	7361	C	650 234-6000	14740
Rosewood Hotels & Resorts LLC	7011	C	650 561-1500	13141
S R I C B I	8748	D	650 859-4865	27849
Sequoia Capital Operations LLC	6799	D	650 854-3927	12266
Silver Lake Partners LP (PA)	6726	D	650 233-8120	12066
Space Systems/Loral LLC	4225	D	650 852-4000	4633
SRI International (PA)	8733	A	650 859-2000	26661
Stamos Capital Partners LP	6282	D	650 233-5000	10114
Stanford Park Hotel	7011	C	650 322-1234	13264
Strategic Bus Insights Inc (PA)	8742	D	650 859-4600	27471
Strivr Labs Inc	7371	D	650 656-9987	15480
Tcmi Inc (PA)	6799	E	650 614-8200	12272
United Parcel Service Inc OH	4215	C	650 952-5200	4477
Uplift Inc	8742	D	844 257-5400	27502
Veterans Health Administration	8011	A	650 614-9997	20079
Vitesse LLC	7374	A	650 543-4800	16198
Western Allied Mechanical Inc	1711	C	650 326-8290	2408
Winston & Strawn LLP	8111	B	650 858-6500	23443

MENTONE, CA - San Bernardino County

Company	SIC	EMP	PHONE	ENTRY #
International Paving Svcs Inc	1611	D	909 794-2101	1792
Nice Avenue LLC	8051	D	909 794-1189	20661

MERCED, CA - Merced County

Company	SIC	EMP	PHONE	ENTRY #
Avalon Care Cen	8051	D	209 723-1056	20242
Avalon Care Center - Merced	8051	D	209 722-6231	20244
Bear Creek Manor	6513	E	209 723-4674	10983
Bloodsource Inc	8099	D	209 724-0428	22751
Central Valley Concrete Inc (PA)	4212	C	209 723-8846	3990
CF Merced La Sierra LLC	8051	D	209 723-4224	20302
Country Villa Service Corp	8322	D	209 723-2911	23624
County of Merced	8331	D	209 724-2000	24174
Culver-Melin Enterprises	7349	D	209 726-9182	14244
Dedicated Management Group LLC	7389	C	209 385-0694	17127
Fuentes Farms Ag Inc	7361	B	209 722-7201	14623
Golden Living LLC	8059	D	209 722-6231	21095
Golden Valley Health Centers (PA)	8093	A	209 383-1848	22584
Golden Valley Health Centers	8093	D	209 383-5871	22585
Guardco Security Services	7381	D	209 723-4273	16672
Holiday Inn Express Merced	7011	D	209 383-0333	12691
Madera Convalescent Hospital	8063	D	209 723-8814	21964
Madera Convalescent Hospital	8059	C	209 723-2911	21147
Mater Misericordiae Hospital (PA)	8062	A	209 564-5000	21582
McLane/Pacific Inc	5141	B	209 725-2500	8429
Merced Irrigation District (PA)	4911	E	209 722-5761	6052
Merced Irrigation District	4971	C	209 722-2719	6557
Merced School Employees F C U (PA)	6061	D	209 383-5550	9569
Merced Transportation Company	4151	D	209 384-2575	3942
Mercy HM Svcs A Cal Ltd Partnr	8062	B	209 564-4200	21591
Mobley Enterprises Inc	7349	D	209 726-9190	14325
N & S Tractor Co (PA)	7699	D	209 383-5888	17963
Paul Pietrzyk	1742	E	209 726-5034	2937
Promesa Behavioral Health	8361	D	209 725-3114	24637
Travis Credit Union	6061	B	209 723-0732	9604
Via Adventures Inc (PA)	4142	E	209 384-1315	3906
WLMD (PA)	1799	C	209 723-9120	3612

2019 Directory of California
Wholesalers and Services Companies

(P-0000) Products & Services Section entry number
(PA)=Parent Co (HQ)=Headquarters (DH)=Div Headquarters

	SIC	EMP	PHONE	ENTRY #

MERIDIAN, CA - Sutter County

	SIC	EMP	PHONE	ENTRY #
Colusa Produce Corporation	5149	D	530 696-0121	8771

MIDDLETOWN, CA - Lake County

	SIC	EMP	PHONE	ENTRY #
Cpn Wild Horse Geothermal LLC	4911	B	707 431-6229	6025
Gr Hardester LLC	6798	C	707 987-2325	12163
Heart Consciousness Church (PA)	7041	C	707 987-2477	13476
Northern California Power Agcy	4911	D	707 987-2381	6058

MILL VALLEY, CA - Marin County

	SIC	EMP	PHONE	ENTRY #
Adventres Rlling Cross-Country	7032	C	415 332-5075	13442
City of Mill Valley	7999	E	415 383-1370	19136
City of Mill Valley	1611	C	415 388-4033	1744
First Marin Realty Inc	6531	D	415 383-9393	11454
First Republic Bank	6022	C	415 389-0880	9451
Joseph Cozza Salon Inc (PA)	7231	D	415 433-3030	13663
Kabler Construction Svcs Inc	8742	E	415 888-8812	27292
Marin Horizon School Inc	8351	E	415 388-8408	24344
Melissa Bradley RE Inc	6531	D	415 388-5113	11601
Sequoia Residential Funding	6153	D	415 389-7373	9748
The Redwoods A Cmnty Seniors	8361	C	415 383-2741	24697
Unified Teldata Inc	5065	D	415 888-8940	7556
Van Acker Cnstr Assoc Inc	1521	D	415 383-5589	1254
Wisdom University	8699	D	415 259-7122	25486

MILLBRAE, CA - San Mateo County

	SIC	EMP	PHONE	ENTRY #
A & C Health Care Services Inc	8011	C	650 689-5784	19266
El Rancho Motel Inc	7011	C	650 588-8500	12553
Hillsdale Group LP	8059	E	650 742-9150	21113
Magnolia of Millbrae Inc	8361	D	650 697-7700	24590
Millbrae Racquet Club	7997	D	650 583-4345	18975
Millbrae Serra Sanitarium	8059	C	650 697-8386	21158
Millbrae Wcp Hotel II LLC	7011	E	650 443-5500	12929
Starwood Hotels & Resorts	7011	D	650 692-6363	13271
Trans World Maintenance Inc	1721	D	650 455-2450	2487
Western Host Inc (PA)	7389	E	650 692-3500	17591

MILPITAS, CA - Santa Clara County

	SIC	EMP	PHONE	ENTRY #
3k Technologies LLC	7371	C	408 716-5900	14951
Abbyy USA Software House Inc (DH)	7371	C	408 457-9777	14957
Abzooba Inc	7371	C	650 453-8760	14958
Advantech Corporation (HQ)	5045	D	408 519-3800	6999
Aerohive Networks Inc (PA)	7373	A	408 510-6100	15910
Alhambra/Sierra Springs	5149	D	408 727-1067	8750
American Golf Corporation	7997	E	408 262-8813	18838
Anjaneyap Inc	8742	C	408 922-9690	27137
Arena Stuart Rentals Inc	7359	C	408 856-3232	14473
At Road Inc (HQ)	7373	B	510 668-1638	15916
Automatic Data Processing Inc	7374	B	408 876-6600	16093
B H R Operations LLC	7011	D	408 321-9500	12347
B T Mancini Co Inc (PA)	1752	B	408 942-7900	3095
Bizcom Electronics Inc (HQ)	5045	C	408 262-7877	7018
Bottomley Distributing Co Inc	5181	D	408 945-0660	8983
Boys & Girls Club Silicon Vly	8322	D	408 957-9685	23516
Bre Select Hotels Oper LLC	7011	D	408 719-1313	12397
Bright Horizons Chld Ctrs LLC	8351	C	408 853-2196	24269
Browning-Ferris Industries LLC	4953	D	408 262-1401	6361
California Wireless Solutions	4812	D	408 771-1249	5302
Cellco Partnership	4812	D	408 263-1960	5349
Cetecom Inc (DH)	8748	D	408 586-6200	27682
Cg2 Inc	8733	D	407 737-8800	26611
Clark Pest Ctrl Stockton Inc	7342	D	408 945-3600	14145
Clement Support Services Inc	5051	C	408 227-1171	7265
Cni Thl Ops LLC	7011	D	408 943-0600	12472
Command Security Corporation	7381	C	510 623-2355	16609
Composite Software (HQ)	7372	D	800 553-6387	15633
Coyote Creek Consulting Inc	7379	D	408 383-9200	16334
Creative Labs Inc (DH)	5045	C	408 428-6600	7026
Custom Drywall Inc	1742	D	408 263-1616	2869
Daylight Foods Inc	5148	C	408 284-7300	8664
Decision Minds	7374	C	408 309-8051	16116
Devcon Construction Inc (PA)	1541	B	408 942-8200	1391
Dga Services Inc (PA)	4214	D	408 232-4800	4343
Dsp Group Inc (PA)	7371	D	408 986-4300	15121
Elo Touch Solutions Inc (HQ)	5045	C	408 597-8000	7040
Enquero Inc	7373	C	408 406-3203	15955
Estuate Inc	7371	D	408 946-0002	15146
Fieldserver Technologies	4932	E	408 262-2299	6191
Fireeye Inc (PA)	7372	C	408 321-6300	15677
First Call Nursing Svcs Inc	7361	C	408 262-1533	14621
Flextronics Intl USA Inc	4813	C	408 576-6769	5559
Fresh Lifelines For Youth Inc	8322	D	408 263-2630	23809
Frontrange Holding Inc	7372	B	408 601-2800	15686
General Dynmics Mssion Systems	5045	D	954 846-3400	7053
H V Welker Co Inc	1752	D	408 263-4400	3104
Haworth Inc	5021	D	408 262-6400	6724

	SIC	EMP	PHONE	ENTRY #
Homefrst Svcs Santa Clara Cnty	8322	C	408 539-2100	23842
Humane Society Silicon Valley	8699	D	408 262-2133	25430
Idc Technologies Inc (PA)	7361	D	408 376-0212	14643
Interntional Disposal Corp Cal	4953	D	408 945-2802	6408
Iron Mountain Fulfillment (HQ)	7331	E	408 945-1600	14047
Jag Software Inc	5045	C	408 262-0572	7066
Kaiser Foundation Hospitals	8011	E	408 945-2900	19598
Knights of Columbus	8699	D	408 262-6609	25435
Lightwaves 2020 Inc	8731	E	408 503-8888	26412
Lite-On Inc (HQ)	5065	E	408 946-4873	7505
Lite-On Sales and Dist Inc	5045	D	510 687-1800	7071
Loomis Armored Us Inc	7381	D	408 273-1101	16721
Macronix America Inc (HQ)	5065	D	408 262-8887	7506
Marketshare Inc (PA)	7312	D	408 262-0677	13927
Mega Professional Intl	7371	D	408 946-1500	15276
Messagesolution Inc	7374	D	408 383-0100	16157
Moschip Semiconductor Tech USA	5065	C	408 737-7141	7511
Nanolab Technologies Inc (PA)	8734	D	408 433-3320	26720
New Solar Incorporated	8741	E	888 886-0103	26959
Nikewoman	5139	E	408 942-6457	8363
Northland Control Systems Inc (PA)	1731	D	510 226-1015	2664
NTS It Care Inc	7371	C	408 480-4083	15320
Ohana Partners Inc (PA)	7359	D	408 856-3232	14531
Oracle America Inc	7372	B	408 635-3072	15795
Pacific Gas and Electric Co	4911	D	408 945-6215	6093
Park Hotels & Resorts Inc	7011	D	408 942-0400	13019
Permanente Medical Group Inc	8011	D	408 945-2900	19767
Preston Pipelines Inc (PA)	1623	C	408 262-1418	1969
Preston Pipelines Inc A Cal	1623	B	408 262-6989	1970
Promise Technology Inc	5045	D	408 228-1400	7095
Prudential Overall Supply	7218	D	408 719-0886	13616
Quantros Inc (PA)	7371	D	408 957-3300	15391
R S Software India Limited	7379	D	408 382-1200	16468
R&M USA Inc	5065	D	408 945-6626	7531
Reading Partners	8322	D	408 945-5720	23984
Saint-Joseph Home Health	8099	E	408 244-5488	22872
Sandisk LLC	8742	C	408 801-1000	27439
Sankara Eye Foundation USA	8699	E	408 456-0555	25459
Semi	8611	C	408 943-6900	24981
SGS North America Inc	8734	D	408 588-0200	26730
SJ Distributors Inc (PA)	5142	C	888 988-2328	8505
Sonicwall Inc (PA)	7373	D	800 509-1265	16056
Spidercloud Wireless (HQ)	4899	D	408 567-9165	5997
Spike Technologies Inc	7373	E	408 410-0624	16058
Ss8 Networks Inc (PA)	4899	C	408 894-8400	5998
Stellartech Research Corp (PA)	8731	C	408 331-3134	26459
Tcg Builders Inc	1542	E	408 321-6450	1670
Technical Temps Inc	7361	D	408 956-8256	14777
Universal Site Services Inc (PA)	7349	C	800 647-9337	14422
Vitas Healthcare Corp Cal	8082	D	408 964-6800	22451
Winmax Systems Corporation	7371	C	408 894-9000	15546
Xcerra Corporation	5065	C	408 635-4300	7566
XI Construction Corporation (PA)	1542	D	408 240-6000	1708
Ziontech Solutions Inc	7379	D	408 434-6001	16539
ZI Technologies Inc (PA)	7371	E	408 240-8989	15561

MIRA LOMA, CA - Riverside County

	SIC	EMP	PHONE	ENTRY #
Act Fulfillment Inc	4225	C	909 930-9083	4521
Adesa Corporation LLC	5012	E	951 361-9400	6574
Big League Dreams Jurupa LLC	7941	C	951 685-6900	18508
C P S Express (HQ)	4212	D	951 685-1041	3984
Ceva Logistics US Inc	4226	E	951 332-3202	4668
Complete Food Service Inc	5149	D	951 685-8490	8772
Galassos Bakery (PA)	5149	C	951 360-1211	8794
Galleano Enterprises Inc	0172	D	951 685-5376	144
Geodis Logistics LLC	4225	D	951 571-2481	4566
Hino Motors Mfg USA Inc	5013	C	951 727-0286	6646
Knight-Swift Trnsp Hldings Inc	4213	D	951 360-0130	4208
Le Vecke Corporation (PA)	5181	D	951 681-8600	9008
Lineage Logistics LLC	4222	E	951 360-7970	4506
Olivet International Inc (PA)	5099	C	951 681-8888	8049
RSI Professional Cab Solutions	1751	C	909 614-2900	3070
S P Richards Company	5112	C	951 681-3114	8089
Southwest Material Hdlg Inc (PA)	5084	C	951 727-0477	7803
Time and Alarm Systems (PA)	1731	D	951 685-1761	2769
Toll Global Fwdg Scs USA Inc	4731	D	951 360-8310	5180
Total Trnsp Logistics Inc	4213	D	951 360-9521	4281
Triways Inc	4214	D	951 361-4840	4382
Ttx Company	4789	B	951 685-0158	5249
United Parcel Service Inc OH	7389	B	951 749-3400	17542

MIRAMONTE, CA - Fresno County

	SIC	EMP	PHONE	ENTRY #
Hume Lake Christian Camps Inc	7032	D	559 305-7770	13451

MISSION HILLS, CA - Los Angeles County

	SIC	EMP	PHONE	ENTRY #
Accentcare Home Health Cal Inc	8082	E	818 528-8855	22190

Employment Codes: A=Over 500 employees, B=251-500,
C=101-250, D=51-100, E=50

2019 Directory of California
Wholesalers and Services Companies

© Mergent Inc. 1-800-342-5647

1615

GEOGRAPHIC

Company	SIC	EMP	PHONE	ENTRY #
Ararat Home of Los Angeles	8059	C	818 837-1800	20995
Ararat Home of Los Angeles (PA)	8059	B	818 365-3000	20996
Best Friends Animal Society	8699	B	818 643-3989	25399
Clean King Laundry Systems Inc	7215	E	818 363-5500	13557
Ecola Services Inc	7342	C	818 920-7301	14150
El Nido Family Centers (PA)	8322	C	818 830-3646	23785
Facey Medical Foundation (PA)	8099	C	818 365-9531	22803
Facey Medical Foundation	8099	C	818 837-5677	22804
Facey Medical Foundation	8011	C	818 365-9531	19467
Greater Valley Medical Group (PA)	8093	B	818 838-4500	22588
Hemodialysis Inc	8092	E	818 365-6961	22478
Jade Inc	1742	D	818 365-7137	2901
Kaiser Foundation Hospitals	6324	C	888 778-5000	10229
Laboratory Corporation America	8071	C	818 361-7089	22102
Los Angeles Unified School Dst	8331	C	818 365-9645	24202
National Business Group Inc (PA)	7353	C	818 221-6000	14449
National Cnstr Rentals Inc (HQ)	7359	C	818 221-6000	14529
Providence Health & Svcs - Ore	8062	B	818 365-8051	21668
Providence Health System	8011	A	818 898-4530	19800
Providence Health System	8062	D	818 898-4561	21669
Providence Holy Cross (PA)	8062	D	818 365-8051	21674

MISSION VIEJO, CA - Orange County

Company	SIC	EMP	PHONE	ENTRY #
Associated Realtors	6531	D	949 813-1888	11222
Auxiliary of Mission	8062	D	949 364-1400	21293
Black Dot Wireless LLC	4812	D	949 502-3800	5300
Centex Homes Inc	1521	C	949 453-0113	1143
CIT Bank NA	6021	D	949 347-7014	9316
CIT Bank NA	6021	D	949 598-9621	9317
Claim Jumper Restaurant	1542	C	949 461-7170	1505
Coldwell Banker Residential RE (DH)	6531	B	949 367-1800	11342
Coldwell Bnkr Rsdntial Re Svcs (PA)	6531	D	949 367-1800	11365
Community Orthopedic Medical	8011	C	949 348-4000	19401
Cs Concrete Solutions Inc	1771	D	949 285-3122	3243
Ctek Solutions Inc	7334	C	949 614-0700	14084
Cynergistek Inc (PA)	7334	C	949 614-0700	14085
Edwards Theatres Circuit Inc	7832	C	949 582-4078	18290
Ensign Services Inc	8051	C	949 487-9500	20403
Ensign Southland LLC	8051	C	949 487-9500	20404
Fitness International LLC	7991	E	949 421-6082	18601
Foundstone Inc	7372	C	949 297-5600	15684
Golda & I Chocolatiers Inc	5149	D	949 660-9581	8800
Greenleaf Paper Products	5113	D	949 348-0048	8107
Home Instead Senior Care	8082	E	949 347-6767	22331
James Hardie Building Pdts Inc (DH)	5031	C	949 348-1800	6835
Jewish Home For The Aging of O	8361	D	949 364-0010	24569
Lake Mission Viejo Association	8641	D	949 770-1313	25186
Lauras House	8322	D	949 361-3775	23891
Law Enforcement Officers Inc	7382	C	855 477-3536	16920
Mimg Medical Management LLC	8741	D	949 282-1600	26948
Mission Hosp Regional Med Ctr (PA)	8062	A	949 364-1400	21594
Mission Internal Med Group Inc	8011	C	949 364-3570	19690
Mission Internal Med Group Inc	8011	C	949 364-6559	19691
Mission Viejo Country Club	7997	C	949 582-1550	18977
Olympus America Inc	5047	C	949 466-3548	7199
Orange County Royale Convlscnt	8062	D	949 458-6346	21616
Paydarfar Industries Inc	5045	C	949 481-3267	7088
Philip DAmato Racing LLC	7948	D	949 830-7027	18543
Planned Prnthood Mar Monte Inc	8093	D	949 768-3643	22652
Prestige Auto Collision Inc	7532	D	949 470-6031	17734
Quest Diagnostics Incorporated	8071	B	949 728-4235	22131
Rock Canyon Healthcare Inc	8059	B	949 487-9500	21200
Saddleback Vly	7997	D	949 586-1234	19023
Southern Cal Prmnnte Med Group	8099	D	949 376-8619	22888
St Jude Hospital Yorba Linda	8011	E	949 365-2492	19941
St Vincent De Paul Vlg Inc	8699	C	619 233-8500	25470
Standardbearer Insur Co Ltd	8051	B	949 487-9500	20781
Sunrise Senior Living LLC	8051	C	949 582-2010	20816
Swiss RE America Holding Corp	6311	E	858 485-5018	10146
Technicon Design Corporation	7389	C	949 218-1300	17499
Vintage Senior Living Corp	6513	D	949 364-6210	11136
Vocational Visions	8331	C	949 837-7280	24247
Wakunaga of America Co Ltd (HQ)	5122	D	949 855-2776	8221
Young Mens Chrstn Assn Orange	8641	D	949 859-9622	25351

MODESTO, CA - Stanislaus County

Company	SIC	EMP	PHONE	ENTRY #
Acme Construction Company Inc	1541	D	209 523-2674	1370
Addus Healthcare Inc	8082	D	209 526-8451	22198
Aderholt Specialty Company Inc	1742	D	209 526-2000	2835
Almond Board of California	8611	E	209 549-8262	24942
Aramark Unf & Career AP LLC	7218	D	209 368-9785	13583
Arcadia Health Services Inc	8082	D	209 572-7650	22229
Arete Hotels LLC	7011	D	209 602-7952	12332
Avalon Care Center - Modesto	8051	D	209 526-1775	20245
Avalon Care Ctr - Modesto LLC	8051	D	209 529-0516	20248
Basic Resources Inc (PA)	1611	E	209 521-9771	1728

Company	SIC	EMP	PHONE	ENTRY #
Bethel Retirement Community	8059	D	209 577-1901	21010
Beyer Park Villas LLC	8361	D	209 236-1900	24436
BJs Restaurants Inc	5094	C	209 526-8850	8003
Blue Diamond Growers	0723	C	209 545-6221	496
Brenden Theatre Corporation	7832	D	209 491-7770	18274
C & S Draperies Inc	7217	C	209 466-5371	13573
C L Bryant Inc	5171	C	209 566-5000	8942
California Forensic Med Group	8011	D	209 525-5670	19341
Cellco Partnership	4812	D	209 543-6500	5368
Central Valley Autism Project	8322	D	209 521-4791	23551
Central Valley Party Supply	7359	E	209 569-0399	14485
Central Vly Specialty Hosp Inc	8051	D	209 248-7700	20300
Charles Fenley Enterprises	7542	E	209 523-2832	17808
Childrens Crisis Cntr Stanisl	8322	D	209 577-4413	23566
Clark Pest Ctrl Stockton Inc	7342	D	209 524-6384	14141
Co Team Staffing	7363	D	209 578-4286	14841
Comcast Corporation	4841	D	209 222-3656	5874
Communication Consultants (PA)	8748	D	209 869-5206	27693
Community Hospice Inc (PA)	8052	C	209 578-6300	20922
County of Stanislaus	4959	C	209 525-4130	6534
County of Stanislaus	8062	A	209 525-7000	21360
County of Stanislaus	8322	D	209 558-8828	23747
County of Stanislaus	8322	C	209 567-4120	23748
County of Stanislaus	8322	C	209 558-7377	23749
County of Stanislaus	8322	C	209 558-9675	23750
County of Stanislaus	8399	D	209 525-6225	24773
County of Stanislaus	8093	C	209 525-7423	22559
County of Stanislaus	8322	D	209 558-2500	23751
County of Stanislaus	8331	C	209 558-2100	24177
Covenant Care California LLC	8059	C	209 521-2094	21050
Crestwood Behavioral Hlth Inc	8063	C	209 526-8050	21945
Curtis Legal Group A Professi	8111	E	209 521-1800	23017
D A Wood Construction Inc	8711	D	209 491-4970	25638
D C Vient Inc (PA)	1721	B	209 578-1224	2430
Dal-Tile Corporation	5032	C	209 543-0924	6889
De Hart Plumbing Htg & A Inc	1711	E	209 523-4578	2184
Del Rio Golf & Country Club	7997	C	209 341-2414	18910
Delta Blood Bank	8099	D	209 943-3830	22782
Delta Brands Inc	5181	D	209 522-9044	8992
Dependable Highway Express Inc	4213	C	209 342-0184	4125
Directline Technologies Inc	8732	C	209 491-2020	26512
Doctors Med Ctr Modesto Inc (HQ)	8062	D	209 578-1211	21397
DOT Foods Inc	5141	D	209 581-9090	8401
E & J Gallo Inc	7373	D	209 287-1716	15949
Eastside Management Co Inc	0762	C	209 578-9852	688
Ed Rocha Livestock Trnsp Inc	4213	C	209 538-1302	4135
English Oaks Convalescent	8051	C	209 577-1001	20393
Enviro Tech Chemical Svcs Inc (PA)	5169	C	209 581-9576	8927
Fig Holdings LLC	8051	D	209 524-4817	20428
Fitness Evolution	7991	D	209 545-9055	18600
Foster Dairy Farms (PA)	0241	A	209 576-3400	412
Foster Dairy Products Distrg (PA)	5143	A	209 576-3400	8522
Frito-Lay North America Inc	5145	C	209 544-5424	8560
G3 Enterprises Inc (PA)	4731	C	209 341-7515	5069
G3 Enterprises Inc	4731	C	209 341-4045	5071
General Petroleum Corporation	5171	C	209 537-1056	8944
Golden Living LLC	8059	C	209 529-0516	21088
Golden Living LLC	8051	C	209 548-0318	20480
Graham Packaging Company LP	5199	C	209 572-5187	9221
Gringteam Inc	7011	B	209 526-6000	12627
Grover Landscape Services Inc	0181	D	209 545-4401	265
Hamilton and Dillon Elc Inc	1731	D	209 529-6292	2599
Howard Training Center (PA)	8331	D	209 538-2431	24192
Kaiser Foundation Hospitals	8011	A	209 735-5000	19569
Kaiser Foundation Hospitals	8011	A	209 735-5000	19571
Kaiser Foundation Hospitals	6324	D	855 268-4096	10253
Kaiser Foundation Hospitals	6324	D	209 557-1000	10269
Khatri Inc	7011	E	209 576-1481	12806
Kissito Health Case Inc	8051	C	209 524-4817	20567
Kiwanis International Inc	8641	D	209 578-1448	25179
McHenry Bowl Inc	7933	E	209 571-2695	18495
McHenry Medical Group Inc	8011	D	209 577-3388	19673
Medamerica Billing Svcs Inc (HQ)	8721	D	209 491-7710	26259
Medex Pratice Solutions Inc	8721	D	209 845-1346	26260
Mocse Federal Credit Union	6061	D	209 572-3600	9573
Modesto Court Room Inc	7997	D	209 577-1060	18978
Modesto Hospitality LLC	7011	C	209 526-6000	12934
Modesto Hospitality Lessee LLC	7011	D	209 526-6000	12935
Modesto Industrial Elec Co Inc (PA)	1731	C	209 495-1597	2651
Modesto Irrigation District	4911	B	209 526-7563	6054
Modesto Irrigation District (PA)	4911	C	209 526-7337	6055
Modesto Irrigation District	4911	B	209 526-7373	6056
Modesto Wstewater Trtmnt Plant	4953	D	209 577-5300	6419
Montpelier Nut Company Inc (PA)	5145	D	209 566-9084	8564
Mtc Distributing (PA)	5194	C	209 523-6449	9185

Mergent email: customerrelations@mergent.com
1616

2019 Directory of California
Wholesalers and Services Companies

(P-0000) Products & Services Section entry number
(PA)=Parent Co (HQ)=Headquarters (DH)=Div Headquarters

Name	SIC	EMP	PHONE	ENTRY #
Muscolino Inventory Svc Inc	7389	E	209 576-8469	17340
Mve Inc (PA)	8711	D	209 526-4214	25836
Ontel Security Services Inc	7381	D	209 521-0200	16749
Pacific Gas and Electric Co	4911	E	209 576-6636	6087
Pacwend Inc	8741	D	209 577-6690	26976
Pacwend III Inc	8741	D	209 577-6690	26977
Paratransit Incorporated	4119	C	209 522-2300	3829
Pegasus Risk Management Inc (PA)	6411	D	209 574-2800	10728
Pepsi-Cola Metro Btlg Co Inc	4225	C	209 557-5100	4607
Permanente Medical Group Inc	6324	D	209 735-5000	10300
Radnet Management Inc	8741	D	209 524-6800	27008
Regent Assisted Living Inc	8361	D	209 491-0800	24648
Riverside Health Care Corp	8059	D	209 523-5667	21198
Salon-Salon	7231	D	209 571-3500	13672
Satellite Healthcare Inc	8092	C	209 578-0691	22488
Sawyers Heating & AC	1711	D	209 416-7700	2348
Scotts Plant Service Co	0782	D	209 545-0903	935
Seca Eqp Removal & Dismantle	1795	E	209 543-1600	3461
Slakey Brothers Inc	5051	E	209 556-1100	7314
Solecon Industrial Contrs Inc	1711	D	209 572-7390	2364
Sportsmen of Stanislaus Inc	7991	D	209 578-5801	18668
Squab Producers Calif Inc	5144	D	209 537-4744	8540
Stanislaus County Police	8322	C	209 529-9121	24072
Stanislaus Farm Supply Company (PA)	5191	D	209 538-7070	9100
Stanislaus Surgical Hosp LLC (PA)	8062	C	209 572-2700	21795
Stellar Group Incorporated	5078	D	209 549-0899	7666
Sterling Mktg & Fincl Corp	8742	E	209 593-1140	27470
Storer Transportation Service (PA)	4141	B	209 521-8250	3892
Sutter Central Vly Hospitals (HQ)	8062	C	209 526-4500	21800
Sutter Central Vly Hospitals	4522	E	209 526-4500	4866
Sutter Gould Med Foundation (PA)	8011	E	209 948-5940	19957
Sutter Health	8062	C	209 524-1211	21825
Sutter Health	8011	D	209 522-0146	19972
Sysco Central California Inc	5141	B	209 527-7700	8465
T-Mobile Usa Inc	4812	C	209 529-0539	5419
Tcb Industrial Inc (PA)	1541	C	209 571-0569	1443
United Sttes Intrmdal Svcs LLC	4731	C	209 341-4045	5191
US Foods Inc	5149	C	209 572-2882	8895
Valley First Credit Union (PA)	6061	D	209 549-8511	9617
Valley Mtn Regional Ctr Inc	8361	D	209 529-2626	24705
Wells Fargo Bank National Assn	6021	D	209 578-6810	9384
Wondertreats Inc	5199	B	209 521-8881	9272
Woodside Group Inc	6162	E	209 579-2030	9866
Yosemite Meat Company Inc	4222	D	209 524-5117	4519

MOFFETT FIELD, CA - Santa Clara County

Name	SIC	EMP	PHONE	ENTRY #
Bay Area Envmtl Res Inst	8733	D	707 938-9387	26595
Millennium Engrg Integration	8711	D	703 413-7750	25823

MOJAVE, CA - Kern County

Name	SIC	EMP	PHONE	ENTRY #
Golden Queen Mining Co LLC	1041	C	661 824-4300	1005
La Department Water and Power	4939	D	661 824-7900	6198
Ridgetop Energy LLC	4911	E	661 822-2400	6100
Virgin Galactic LLC (DH)	4789	C	562 384-4400	5251

MONROVIA, CA - Los Angeles County

Name	SIC	EMP	PHONE	ENTRY #
Adams & Barnes Inc	6531	E	626 358-1858	11191
Alakor Healthcare LLC	8062	C	626 408-9800	21275
Amatel Inc (PA)	8748	E	323 801-0199	27636
Arch Bay Holdings LLC	6719	D	949 679-2400	11963
California Business Bureau Inc (PA)	7322	C	626 303-1515	13994
Country Villa Service Corp	8741	C	626 358-4547	26825
Creative Housing & Services	6513	C	626 403-5454	11005
Ctour Holiday LLC	7999	B	323 261-8811	19156
Facility Operations Plus	8741	D	800 789-9608	26855
Federal Deposit Insurance Corp	6399	D	626 359-7152	10498
Garden View Inc	0781	E	626 303-4043	756
H C Olsen Cnstr Co Inc	1541	D	626 359-8900	1403
Harris Corporation	8711	B	626 584-4527	25723
Imperial Project Inc	7929	D	310 671-3263	18441
Kentmaster Mfg Co Inc (PA)	5084	E	626 359-8888	7760
Krikorian Premiere Theatre LLC	7832	C	626 305-7469	18303
Leekilpatrick Management Inc	8742	D	818 500-9631	27301
Linear Industries Ltd (PA)	5085	D	626 303-1130	7856
M T M & M Inc	7353	D	626 445-2922	14446
Monrovia Health Center	8011	D	626 256-1600	19700
MWH Americas Inc	8711	C	626 386-1100	25838
Parasoft Corporation (PA)	5045	E	626 256-3680	7087
Pih Health Hospital - Whitti	8062	B	626 357-6876	21647
Sage Hospitality Resources LLC	7011	D	626 357-5211	13161
Santa Anita Family Young	8331	D	626 359-9244	24228
SM Broadway Corp	6798	D	626 301-1198	12187
Southern California Edison Co	4911	D	626 303-8480	6116
St Baldricks Foundation Inc (PA)	8621	D	626 792-8247	25042
Trap	7389	D	626 572-5610	17520
Visionfund International	7389	D	626 303-8811	17569

Name	SIC	EMP	PHONE	ENTRY #
Vivopools Inc	7389	D	818 952-2121	17573
Vivopools LLC	7389	D	888 702-8486	17574
Webasto Charging Systems Inc (DH)	5013	D	626 415-4000	6686
World Class Distribution Inc	4225	C	909 574-4140	4662
World Vision International (HQ)	8699	C	626 303-8811	25487
Worleyparsons Group Inc	8711	B	626 803-9000	26007
Yang Ming America Corporation	4731	D	626 782-9797	5203

MONTCLAIR, CA - San Bernardino County

Name	SIC	EMP	PHONE	ENTRY #
A Plus Senior Care Inc	8322	E	909 989-2563	23453
Acepex Management Corporation	8744	C	909 625-6900	27573
Aragon Construction Inc	1542	D	909 621-2200	1467
Community Convalescent Center	8051	D	909 621-4751	20321
Converse Inc	5139	C	909 625-6655	8351
Cramer Painting Inc	1721	E	909 397-5770	2429
E M S Trading Inc	5139	E	909 581-7800	8354
Foundation For Dance Education	7911	D	909 482-1590	18333
Medicrest of California 1	8051	D	909 626-1294	20638
Mission Drive-In Theatre Co	7833	D	909 465-9219	18328
Omnitrans Inc	4111	C	909 379-7100	3692
Oparc (PA)	8331	E	909 982-4090	24213
Pomona Valley Motorcycles Inc	7699	D	909 981-9500	17972
Pomona Valley Workshop (PA)	8331	D	909 624-3555	24219
Prime Healthcare Svcs III LLC (DH)	8062	C	909 625-5411	21661
US Skillserve Inc	8051	C	909 621-4751	20847

MONTEBELLO, CA - Los Angeles County

Name	SIC	EMP	PHONE	ENTRY #
2253 Apparel Inc (PA)	5137	D	323 837-9800	8284
Allied Building Products Corp	5033	D	323 721-9011	6918
American Multi-Cinema Inc	7832	E	323 722-4583	18270
AMF Bowling Centers Inc	7933	E	323 728-9161	18477
Beverly Community Hosp Assn	8062	B	323 889-2452	21299
Beverly Community Hosp Assn (PA)	8062	C	323 726-1222	21300
Beverly Community Hosp Assn	8062	A	323 725-1519	21301
California Creations Inc	5021	E	323 722-9832	6715
Davita Medical Management LLC	8011	D	323 720-1144	19431
Eastwestproto Inc	4119	C	888 535-5728	3789
Fast Deer Bus Chrtr Incrprtion	4142	C	323 201-8988	3896
Ford Motor Company	4225	C	323 267-6121	4558
Honolulu Freight Service (PA)	4731	E	323 887-6777	5089
Hubbard Iron Doors Inc	5051	C	323 724-6500	7280
Katzkin Leather Inc (PA)	5199	C	323 725-1243	9226
Lockheed Martin Government Ser	7379	E	323 721-6979	16420
Marquez Brothers Intl Inc	5141	D	323 722-8103	8425
Mexican Amrcn Oprtnty Fndation (PA)	8322	D	323 890-9600	23921
Montebello School Transportion	4151	D	323 887-7900	3943
Montebello Transit	4111	D	323 887-4600	3683
Montebello Unified School	7349	D	323 887-2140	14327
Old Dominion Freight Line Inc	4213	C	323 725-3400	4240
Orora Packaging Solutions	5113	C	323 832-2000	8121
Paladin Eastside Services Inc	8361	D	323 890-0180	24624
Rio Hndo Sbcute Nrsing Ctr LLC	8051	C	323 838-5915	20722
SA Recycling LLC	4953	C	323 723-8327	6463
Source Logistics Center Corp	4731	C	323 887-3884	5172
Star Scrap Metal Company Inc	4953	D	562 921-5045	6479
Votum Staffing Inc	7361	B	310 499-4902	14796
Worldwide Intgrted Rsurces Inc	5087	D	323 838-8938	7904

MONTEREY, CA - Monterey County

Name	SIC	EMP	PHONE	ENTRY #
1000 Aguajito Op Co LLC	7011	D	831 373-6141	12286
Aramark Spt & Entrmt Group LLC	7929	C	831 648-9809	18421
AT&T Inc	4812	D	831 642-0100	5297
AT&T Services Inc	4813	D	831 394-2690	5473
AT&T Services Inc	4813	D	831 649-2029	5483
Augustine Consulting Inc (PA)	8711	D	831 920-1754	25553
Ave Maria Convalescent Hosp	8051	D	831 373-1216	20251
Bayview Properties Inc	7011	D	831 655-7650	12361
Bayview Properties Inc (PA)	7011	D	831 394-3321	12363
California Capital Insur Co (PA)	6331	C	831 233-5500	10343
Casa Munras Hotel LLC	7011	D	831 375-2411	12436
Cellco Partnership	4812	D	831 644-0858	5308
Central Coast Cmnty Hlth Care	8059	C	831 372-6668	21035
Central Coast Cmnty Hlth Care	8082	B	831 648-4200	22259
Central Coast Vna & Hospice (PA)	8082	C	831 372-6668	22260
Classic Park Lane Partnership	6513	D	831 373-0101	11002
Classic Riverdale Inc	7011	D	831 373-0101	12466
Classic Rsdence Mgt Ltd Partnr	7011	D	831 373-0101	12467
Clum Morford Distributing (PA)	7389	D	831 333-1100	17088
Columbia Hospitality Inc	7011	D	831 646-8900	12475
Columbia Hospitality Inc	7011	D	831 373-5700	12476
Columbia Hospitality Inc	7011	E	831 373-8000	12477
Comcast Corporation	4841	D	831 657-6095	5889
Community Caregivers Inc	8082	D	831 645-1434	22268
Community Human Services (PA)	8322	C	831 658-3811	23606
Custom House Hotel LP	7011	D	831 649-4511	12507
Cypress Hlthcare Partners LLC (PA)	8011	C	831 649-1000	19425

Employment Codes: A=Over 500 employees, B=251-500,
C=101-250, D=51-100, E=50

2019 Directory of California
Wholesalers and Services Companies

© Mergent Inc. 1-800-342-5647
1617

GEOGRAPHIC

	SIC	EMP	PHONE	ENTRY #
Data Recognition Corporation	8748	E	831 393-0700	27703
Del Mar French Laundry	7211	E	831 375-9597	13485
DMC Construction Incorporated	1542	D	831 656-1600	1522
Employnet Inc	7361	A	831 316-1814	14614
Entravsion Communications Corp	4833	C	831 333-9736	5784
Federal Express Corporation	4513	D	800 463-3339	4824
First Alarm	1731	A	831 649-1111	2584
Granite Construction Inc	1611	D	831 657-1700	1780
Healthcare Pathways Management	8082	D	831 373-1111	22316
Hit Portfolio I Misc Trs LLC	7011	B	831 372-1234	12678
Hospital of Community (HQ)	8069	A	831 624-5311	22025
Hyatt Hotels Management Corp	7011	B	831 372-1234	12755
Language Line Services Inc (DH)	7389	D	800 752-6096	17290
Mangold Property Management	6531	D	831 372-1338	11582
Michael Bruington	1521	E	831 663-1772	1202
Montage Health	8011	A	831 625-4821	19701
Montage Health (PA)	8741	A	831 625-4830	26949
Monterey Bay Aqar Foundation (PA)	8422	C	831 648-4800	24933
Monterey Credit Union (PA)	6062	D	831 647-1000	9641
Monterey Dental Group	8021	C	831 373-3068	20128
Monterey One Water (PA)	4952	D	831 372-3367	6323
Monterey Peninsula Dntl Group	8021	D	831 373-3068	20129
Monterey Peninsula Hospital	8062	E	831 373-0924	21597
Monterey Pines Sklld Nursg Fac	8051	D	831 373-3716	20652
Monterey Plaza Ht Ltd Partnr	7011	B	800 334-3999	12941
Ocean Park Hotels Inc (PA)	7011	B	805 544-0812	12970
Ocean Park Hotels Inc.	7011	C	831 373-6141	12971
P Monterey LP	8361	D	831 250-6159	24621
Pacific Gas and Electric Co	4911	E	831 648-3231	6082
Pacific Parking & Valet LLC	4959	C	831 646-0426	6544
Pater Digintas Inc	8051	E	831 624-1875	20698
Portfolio Hotels & Resorts LLC	7011	B	831 375-2411	13074
Pro Act LLC	5148	D	831 655-4250	8719
Procall Solutions Inc	7389	C	800 733-9675	17411
Product Development Corp (PA)	7389	C	831 333-1100	17412
Robert Half International Inc	7361	C	831 241-9042	14729
Salinas Valley Memorial Hlthca	8011	B	831 884-5048	19838
San Carlos Associates Ltd	7011	C	831 649-4234	13166
Sequoia Insurance Company (HQ)	6331	C	831 655-9612	10393
Southwest Correctional Medical	8093	C	831 641-3298	22685
Stocker & Allaire Inc	1521	E	831 375-1890	1240
Sunrise Senior Living Inc	8051	C	831 643-2400	20811
Tele-Interpreters LLC	7389	B	800 811-7881	17502
Triad Broadcasting Company (PA)	4832	C	831 655-6350	5755
United Parcel Service Inc OH	4215	C	831 757-6294	4469
United States Dept of Navy	8731	D	831 656-4613	26482
V I P Associates Inc (PA)	7011	E	831 646-1549	13361
Visiting Nurse Association	8082	D	831 385-1014	22447
Windsor Monterey Care Ctr LLC	8059	D	831 373-2731	21261
Zhg Inc	7011	D	831 394-3321	13436

MONTEREY PARK, CA - Los Angeles County

	SIC	EMP	PHONE	ENTRY #
Ahmc Garfield Medical Ctr LP	8051	C	626 573-2222	20222
American Multi-Cinema Inc	7832	D	626 407-0240	18259
American Reprographics Co LLC	7334	D	626 289-5021	14073
Arroyo Developmental Services	8322	D	626 307-2240	23489
Care 1st Health Plan (PA)	8099	C	323 889-6638	22757
Cathay Bank	6022	D	626 588-1911	9425
Childrens Law Center Cal (PA)	8111	C	323 980-8700	22974
City of Monterey Park	7999	D	626 307-1388	19137
County of Los Angeles	8322	C	323 265-1804	23661
East West Bank	6036	D	626 280-1688	9533
F & A Federal Credit Union	6061	D	323 268-1226	9550
Guard-Systems Inc (PA)	7381	A	626 443-0031	16668
Guard-Systems Inc	7381	B	323 881-6711	16670
Guard-Systems Inc	7381	B	323 881-6715	16671
Heritage Manor Inc	8051	D	626 573-3141	20527
Innovations Building Svcs LLC	7349	D	323 787-6068	14289
JC Foodservice Inc (PA)	5046	C	626 299-3800	7138
Lincoln Plaza Hotel Inc	7011	D	626 571-8818	12855
Merchants Building Maint Co (PA)	7349	D	323 881-6701	14318
Merchants Building Maint Co	7349	C	323 881-8902	14321
Monterey Park Hospital	8062	C	626 570-9000	21596
Monterey Pk Convalescent Hosp	8059	C	626 280-0280	21160
Ntt Data Inc	7373	D	213 228-2500	16021
Roque Development and Inv	8711	D	626 427-9077	25896
Southern California Gas Co	4924	B	213 244-1200	6166
Southern California Gas Co	4924	C	213 244-1200	6174
State Compensation Insur Fund	6331	C	323 266-5000	10411
Synermed	8011	C	216 406-2845	19997
Syntelesys Inc	7622	E	323 859-2160	17888
Union Technology Corp (PA)	5065	E	323 266-6871	7557
United Parcel Service Inc OH	7389	A	626 280-8012	17540
Uti Leak Seekers	1623	D	323 724-0081	1992
Wah Hung Intl McHy Inc.	5012	D	323 263-3513	6613

MONTROSE, CA - Los Angeles County

	SIC	EMP	PHONE	ENTRY #
Golden Living LLC	8059	D	818 249-3925	21085
Great Wstn Cnvlescent Hosp Inc	8059	C	818 248-6856	21101

MOORPARK, CA - Ventura County

	SIC	EMP	PHONE	ENTRY #
Ace Floor Co Inc	1752	D	805 955-9000	3093
Cardservice International Inc (HQ)	7389	B	805 648-1425	17058
Cimatron Gibbs LLC	7371	D	805 523-0004	15060
Citrus North Venture	7011	D	256 428-2000	12461
City of Moorpark	8322	D	805 517-6261	23581
Donovan Bros Golf LLC	7992	D	805 531-9300	18707
Dynalectric Company	1731	C	805 517-1253	2565
EBM Janitorial Services Inc	7349	D	805 523-3700	14255
Fiserv Inc.	7374	D	805 532-9100	16135
Gemmm Corp	6531	D	805 267-2700	11477
Harold Jones Landscape Inc	0781	E	805 582-7443	758
Kretek International Inc (DH)	5194	D	805 531-8888	9184
Lane Stuart Company LLC	6531	D	805 553-9562	11557
Lifetech Resources LLC	5122	E	818 885-1199	8187
Malibu Canyon Ldscp & Maint	0781	D	805 523-2676	766
Mike Rovner Construction Inc (PA)	1521	D	805 584-5961	1204
Muranaka Farm	0161	C	805 529-0201	70
Ned L Webster Concrete Cnstr	1771	D	805 529-4900	3292
Pacific Rim Realty Group	6531	E	805 553-9562	11650
Pindler & Pindler Inc (PA)	5131	D	805 531-9090	8236
Prudential Overall Supply	7213	C	805 529-0833	13550
Raycon Environmental Cnstr	1799	E	805 955-9000	3575
Testequity LLC (PA)	7629	C	805 498-9933	17916
Wall Systems Inc	1742	D	805 523-9091	2978
Xp Systems Corporation (HQ)	7373	C	805 532-9100	16079

MORAGA, CA - Contra Costa County

	SIC	EMP	PHONE	ENTRY #
Engineered Forest Products LLC	6799	D	925 376-0881	12226
Moraga Cntry CLB Hmowners Assn	7997	D	925 376-2600	18981
Pioneer Health Care Services	8741	D	925 631-9100	26988
Sunrise Senior Living Inc	8051	D	510 531-7190	20797

MORENO VALLEY, CA - Riverside County

	SIC	EMP	PHONE	ENTRY #
Atsugi Kokusai Kanko USA Inc	7997	D	951 924-4444	18851
Bluegill Technologies LLC	7382	D	877 765-2770	16879
Community Health Systems Inc	8011	C	951 571-2300	19398
County of Riverside	8011	D	951 486-4000	19419
County of Riverside	8011	D	951 486-4000	19421
Integrted Care Communities Inc	8051	E	951 243-3837	20545
Kaiser Foundation Hospitals	6733	E	951 601-6174	12106
Kaiser Foundation Hospitals	8011	B	951 243-0811	19618
National Construction & Maint	1542	E	909 888-7042	1599
National Lgal Studies Inst Inc	7389	E	951 653-4240	17344
Parenthood of Planned	8093	D	951 222-3101	22635
Plaza Hand Carwash Inc	7542	E	951 697-4420	17834
Retail Services Wis Corp	7389	D	951 653-1472	17428
Ritchie Plumbing Inc	1711	C	949 709-7575	2338
Riverside University Health	8062	A	951 486-4000	21691
Spectrum MGT Holdg Co LLC	4841	C	951 571-8738	5947
Think Together	8351	A	951 571-9944	24393
Waste MGT Collectn & Recycl	4953	C	951 242-0421	6514
Waste MGT Collectn & Recycl	4953	D	909 242-0421	6518

MORGAN HILL, CA - Santa Clara County

	SIC	EMP	PHONE	ENTRY #
Aragen Bioscience Inc	8731	E	408 779-1700	26325
Cal Color Growers LLC	5193	D	408 778-0835	9128
Child Development Incorporated (PA)	8351	E	408 556-7300	24284
City of Morgan Hill	8748	D	408 776-7333	27686
Coyote Creek Golf Club	7992	D	408 463-1400	18701
Del Monaco Specialty Foods Inc.	5141	D	408 500-4100	8400
Fresh Pick Produce	5099	C	408 315-4612	8031
George Chiala Farms Inc	0161	C	408 778-0562	57
Hillview Convalescent Hospital	8051	E	408 779-3633	20531
Institute LLC	7992	E	408 782-7101	18722
Irish Construction	1623	D	408 612-8440	1934
K R Anderson Inc (PA)	5169	C	408 825-1800	8930
Kawahara Nursery Inc.	0181	C	408 779-2400	273
Lusamerica Foods Inc (PA)	5146	D	408 294-6622	8582
Medallion Landscape MGT Inc (PA)	0781	D	408 782-7500	770
Micro-Mechanics Inc	5065	E	408 779-2927	7508
Monterey Mushrooms Inc.	0182	B	408 779-4191	316
Monument Construction Inc	0782	D	408 778-1350	902
Operating Engineers Loca	8711	C	408 782-9803	25854
Pacific Metro LLC (PA)	5199	B	408 201-5000	9242
Pacific States Industries Inc	5031	D	408 779-7354	6850
Prism Electronics Corp (PA)	5065	E	408 778-7050	7526
Psynergy Programs Inc	8361	D	408 776-0422	24639
Reinhardt Roofing Inc	1761	D	510 713-7014	3196
Royal Oaks Enterprises Inc.	0182	E	408 779-2362	322
Sakata Seed America Inc (HQ)	5191	D	408 778-7758	9095
Santa Clara County of	8361	D	408 201-7600	24667

Mergent email: customerrelations@mergent.com

1618

2019 Directory of California
Wholesalers and Services Companies

(P-0000) Products & Services Section entry number
(PA)=Parent Co (HQ)=Headquarters (DH)=Div Headquarters

Company	SIC	EMP	PHONE	ENTRY #
South County Housing Corp (PA)	6531	E	510 582-1460	11772
Town Cats Morgan Hill Rescue	0752	E	408 779-5761	634
Youngs Market Company LLC	5182	D	408 782-3121	9066

MORRO BAY, CA - San Luis Obispo County

Company	SIC	EMP	PHONE	ENTRY #
Compass Health Inc	8059	C	805 772-7372	21042
Mission Linen Supply	7213	E	805 772-4451	13534
Morro Bay Public Works	1611	D	805 772-6261	1821
Smile Housing Corporation	8093	D	805 772-6066	22680

MOSS BEACH, CA - San Mateo County

Company	SIC	EMP	PHONE	ENTRY #
Friends Fitzgerald Mar Reserve	8399	D	650 728-3584	24782
Seton Medical Center	8062	C	650 563-7100	21743

MOSS LANDING, CA - Monterey County

Company	SIC	EMP	PHONE	ENTRY #
Capurro Marketing LLC	5148	D	831 728-1767	8651
Dobler & Sons LLC	0161	B	831 724-6727	49
Dynegy Moss Landing LLC	4911	D	831 633-6618	6028
Monterey Bay Aquarium RES Inst	8731	C	831 775-1700	26419
Moss Landing Marine Labs	8071	D	831 771-4400	22112

MOUNT HERMON, CA - Santa Cruz County

Company	SIC	EMP	PHONE	ENTRY #
Mount Hermon Association Inc (PA)	7032	D	831 335-4466	13453

MOUNT SHASTA, CA - Siskiyou County

Company	SIC	EMP	PHONE	ENTRY #
County of Siskiyou	8093	D	530 918-7200	22558
Mercy HM Svcs A Cal Ltd Partnr	8062	B	530 926-6111	21589
Siskiyou Lake Golf Resort Inc	7992	D	530 926-3030	18764
Siskiyou Opportunity Center (PA)	8331	C	530 926-4698	24229
Wholesale Solar Inc	1711	D	800 472-1142	2410

MOUNTAIN PASS, CA - San Bernardino County

Company	SIC	EMP	PHONE	ENTRY #
Chevron Mining Inc	1221	B	760 856-7625	1008
Mp Mine Operations LLC	1481	C	702 277-0848	1101

MOUNTAIN VIEW, CA - Santa Clara County

Company	SIC	EMP	PHONE	ENTRY #
23andme Inc (PA)	7375	B	650 961-7152	16205
24 Hour Fitness Usa Inc	7991	E	650 941-2268	18568
500 Startups Incubator LLC (PA)	8748	C	650 743-4738	27614
500 Startups Management Co LLC	6799	C	650 743-4738	12195
Achievo Corporation (PA)	7371	D	925 498-8864	14961
Addepar Inc (PA)	7371	D	855 464-6268	14965
Aera Technology Inc	7371	C	408 524-2222	14968
Alphabet Inc (PA)	7371	D	650 253-0000	14975
American Century Inv MGT Inc	6282	C	650 965-8300	10052
Apigee Corporation	7371	C	408 343-7300	14989
Apteligent Inc	7372	D	415 371-1402	15589
Argo Ai LLC (HQ)	7371	D	412 709-6992	14999
Artificial Solutions Inc	7371	D	650 943-2325	15001
Assure Consulting Inc	8748	D	650 966-1967	27646
AT&T Corp	4813	D	415 276-0039	5466
AT&T Services Inc	4813	C	650 960-2255	5484
Atrenta Inc (HQ)	7371	D	408 453-3333	15008
Axcient Inc (HQ)	7371	D	650 314-7300	15013
Balboa Enterprises Inc	8051	C	650 961-6161	20255
Bdna Corporation (PA)	7372	D	650 625-9530	15605
Bella Terra Technologies Inc	4899	D	650 316-6660	5969
Bionetics Corporation	8731	E	650 604-5327	26341
Blue Coat LLC	7372	A	408 220-2200	15613
Blue Coat Systems LLC (HQ)	7373	D	650 527-8000	15921
Blue Jeans Network Inc (PA)	4899	D	408 550-2828	5970
Boeing Company	8711	B	650 316-3732	25571
Branderscom Inc (PA)	5199	D	650 292-2752	9198
CA Ste Atom Assoc Intr-Ins Bur	6411	D	650 623-3200	10568
Camino Real Group LLC	7011	E	650 964-1700	12422
Ceva Inc	6794	D	650 417-7900	12135
Channel Intelligence Inc (DH)	4813	D	321 939-5600	5530
Chronicle LLC	7382	D	650 214-5199	16882
Churchill Downs Incorporated	7948	A	502 638-3879	18538
Clearwell Systems Inc	7372	C	877 253-2793	15630
Coherent Inc	8732	D	408 764-4000	26505
Computer History Museum	8412	D	650 810-1010	24874
Coursera Inc (PA)	7371	D	650 963-9884	15082
Covenant Care California LLC	8062	D	650 964-0543	21361
Cumulus Networks Inc (PA)	7372	C	650 383-6700	15641
Cushman & Wakefield Inc	7349	C	408 664-5403	14245
Devxcom Inc	4813	E	650 390-6553	5545
Dg Architects Inc (PA)	8712	D	650 943-1660	26043
Driveai Inc	7372	C	650 729-0499	15654
Egnyte Inc (PA)	7371	D	650 968-4018	15127
Ehealth Inc (PA)	6411	D	650 584-2700	10613
Ehealthinsurance Services Inc (HQ)	6411	D	650 584-2700	10614
El Camino Hospital	8322	C	650 988-7444	23783
El Camino Hospital	8092	D	650 940-7310	22475
El Camino Hospital	8069	C	650 988-4825	22019
El Camino Hospital Auxiliary	8082	A	650 940-7214	22290
El Camino Surgery Center LLC	8062	D	650 961-1200	21402
Elance Inc (HQ)	7311	C	650 316-7500	13823
Elasticsearch Inc (PA)	7371	D	650 458-2620	15131
Fenwick & West LLP (PA)	8111	B	650 988-8500	23064
First Technology Federal Cr Un (PA)	6061	D	855 855-8805	9556
General Dynamics Advanced Info	8711	A	650 966-2000	25705
Gigya Inc (HQ)	7371	D	650 353-7230	15178
Google Fiber Inc (DH)	4813	D	650 253-0000	5572
Google International LLC (DH)	4813	D	650 253-0000	5573
Google LLC (HQ)	7371	C	650 253-0000	15186
Google LLC	7375	D	650 253-7323	16227
Google Payment Corp	7389	E	650 253-0000	17198
Group Avantica Inc	7371	B	650 248-9678	15192
Healthpocket Inc	6321	D	800 984-8015	10165
Iap World Services Inc	8744	D	650 604-0451	27594
Intellisync Corporation (HQ)	7371	D	650 625-2185	15226
Intermedia Holdings Inc (PA)	7379	D	650 641-4000	16401
Intuit Inc (PA)	7372	D	650 944-6000	15718
Intuit Inc	7372	C	650 944-6000	15719
Intuit Inc	7372	C	650 944-6000	15720
Jacobs Technology Inc	8711	E	650 604-5946	25767
Kaiser Foundation Hospitals	8062	D	650 903-3000	21507
Kaiser Med Clinic	8011	C	650 903-2103	19622
Khan Academy Inc	7372	D	650 336-5426	15728
Kindred Healthcare Oper Inc	8062	C	650 962-6000	21535
Loon LLC	7389	C	310 625-3449	17302
Lozano Inc	7542	C	650 941-0590	17830
Mindsource Inc	7371	D	650 314-6400	15282
Mobileiron Inc (PA)	7372	C	650 919-8100	15767
Moog Inc	8711	D	650 210-9000	25832
Motorola Solutions Inc	7371	C	650 318-3200	15295
Mozilla Corporation (HQ)	7373	B	650 903-0800	16007
Mp Shoreline Assoc Ltd Partnr	6513	E	650 966-1327	11082
Nagra Usa Inc	5084	C	310 335-5225	7775
Nebula Inc	8731	D	650 539-9900	26422
Neuropace Inc	8731	D	650 237-2700	26423
Northrop Grumman Systems Corp	7373	C	650 604-6056	16019
OGrady Paving Inc	1611	C	650 966-1926	1829
Palo Alto Medical Foundation	8011	D	408 739-6000	19753
Perkstreet Financial Inc	8742	E	978 801-1177	27392
Planprescriber Inc	6411	B	650 584-2700	10730
Polaris Building Maintenance	7349	D	650 964-9400	14352
Polaris Wireless Inc	7371	D	408 492-8900	15368
Project Consulting Specialists	8748	E	650 265-2400	27827
Quintiles Pacific Incorporated (HQ)	8732	E	650 567-2000	26558
Quora Inc	7375	E	650 485-2464	16243
Quotient Technology Inc (PA)	7319	C	650 605-4600	13981
Quova Inc	8748	D	650 965-2898	27832
Redis Labs Inc	7371	D	415 930-9666	15401
Rhythmone LLC	7371	D	650 961-9024	15411
Samsung Electronics Amer Inc	5065	A	650 210-1000	7536
Samsung Research America Inc (DH)	8731	D	408 544-5700	26447
Sectek Inc	7382	D	650 604-1785	16934
Sequoia Retail Systems Inc (DH)	7371	D	650 237-9000	15438
Service By Medallion	7349	B	650 625-1010	14384
Seti Institute	8733	C	650 961-6633	26660
Siemens AG	8711	C	650 969-9112	25912
Siemens Med Solutions USA Inc	5047	B	650 694-5747	7218
Silicon Vly Cmnty Foundation	8641	C	650 450-5400	25250
Soaprojects Inc (PA)	8742	C	650 960-9900	27459
Spotcues Inc	5045	A	408 435-2700	7109
Symantec Corporation (PA)	7379	B	650 527-8000	16496
Synopsys Inc (PA)	7372	B	650 584-5000	15872
Synplicity Inc (HQ)	7372	C	650 584-5000	15874
Tabula Inc	5065	B	408 986-9140	7550
Takara Bio Usa Inc	8731	C	650 919-7300	26469
Thoits Insurance Service Inc	6411	C	408 792-5400	10800
Thomson Reuters (legal) Inc	8748	D	650 210-1900	27884
Tidebreak Inc	7372	D	650 289-9869	7116
Tintri Inc	7375	B	650 810-8200	16253
Travelzoo Usa Inc	7313	D	650 316-6956	13960
Treasure Data Inc	7371	D	866 899-5386	15510
Tvu Networks Corporation (PA)	4833	D	650 969-6732	5843
Upwork Global Inc	8621	E	650 316-7500	25049
Veritas Technologies LLC (HQ)	7371	D	650 933-1000	15523
Veritas US Inc	7371	C	650 933-1000	15524
Viewray Technologies Inc	5047	D	650 252-0920	7230
Villa Siena	8059	D	650 961-6484	21248
Vimo Inc (PA)	8748	C	650 618-4600	27901
Waterline Data Science Inc	7371	D	650 868-4409	15542
Wing Aviation LLC	4513	D	650 260-8170	4854
Xad Inc	8742	C	650 386-6867	27528
YMCA of Silicon Valley	8641	B	650 969-9622	25121
Yub Inc	7374	C	650 265-7316	16201
Zelos Consulting LLC	8748	E	650 968-2881	27915
Zonare Medical Systems Inc	8733	D	650 230-2800	26679

GEOGRAPHIC

	SIC	EMP	PHONE	ENTRY #

MURPHYS, CA - Calaveras County

	SIC	EMP	PHONE	ENTRY #
Kautz Vineyards Inc (PA)	0172	D	209 728-1251	153

MURRIETA, CA - Riverside County

	SIC	EMP	PHONE	ENTRY #
Alta Loma Assisted Living LLC	8322	D	909 481-2600	23470
Bear Creek Golf Club Inc	7997	D	951 677-8621	18859
Bear Creek Partners LLC	7997	D	951 677-8621	18860
Bowlero Corp	7933	E	951 698-2202	18484
Carson Capital Corp (PA)	5012	A	951 684-9585	6581
Cell Site Management Group LLC	4812	E	800 906-9778	5303
Community Health Network LLC	8082	D	951 265-8281	22269
Elite Enfrcment SEC Sltons Inc	7381	E	866 354-8308	16637
F M Tarbell Co	6531	E	951 677-3565	11428
Faith Quality Auto Body Inc	7532	D	951 698-8215	17720
First American Card Service	7389	E	951 677-8720	17172
Golden Living LLC	8322	D	951 600-4640	23824
Goodman Manufacturing Co LP	5075	B	951 304-7402	7649
Inzunza Real Estate Inc	6531	E	951 544-8801	11523
Jpi Development Group Inc	1711	D	951 973-7680	2246
Legacy Tile and Stone Inc	1743	E	951 296-1096	3002
Monique Suraci	7991	D	951 677-8111	18633
Mulligan Ltd A Cal Ltd Partnr	7996	D	951 696-9696	18807
My Kids Dentist	8021	B	951 600-1062	20130
National Bus Invstigations Inc	7389	D	951 677-3500	17343
Oak Grove Inst Foundation Inc (PA)	8011	B	951 677-5599	19726
Ptac Rail Ranch Elem School	8641	D	951 696-1404	25223
Rancho Physical Therapy Inc (PA)	8049	C	951 696-9353	20200
Reading International Inc	7832	E	951 696-7045	18313
S I J Inc	1751	E	951 304-9444	3071
Sanborn Theatres Inc	7832	D	909 296-9728	18320
Scga Golf Course MGT Inc	7992	D	951 677-7446	18760
SI Inc	1751	E	951 304-9444	3076
Skywest Airlines Inc	4512	D	951 600-9181	4799
South Coast Piering Inc	1542	D	800 922-2488	1657
Southwest Healthcare Sys Aux	8062	E	800 404-6627	21771
Southwest Healthcare Sys Aux (HQ)	8062	B	951 696-6000	21772
Temecula Valley Drywall Inc	1742	D	951 600-1742	2967
Utah Pacific Construction Co	1623	E	951 677-9876	1991
Your Way Fumigation Inc	7342	D	951 699-9116	14165

NAPA, CA - Napa County

	SIC	EMP	PHONE	ENTRY #
Back Street Fitness Inc	7991	E	707 254-7200	18576
Barrel Ten Quarter Circle Inc	5182	B	707 265-4000	9032
Bell Products Inc	1711	D	707 255-1811	2139
California Odd Fellows (PA)	6513	D	707 257-7885	10997
California Odd Fellows	6513	D	707 257-7885	10998
Califrnia Dept State Hospitals	8063	A	707 253-5000	21933
Carneros Inn LLC	7011	B	707 299-4880	12431
Cello & Maudru Cnstr Co Inc	1542	E	707 257-0454	1499
Chardonnay/ Club Shakespeare	7997	D	707 257-1900	18888
Child Start Inc (PA)	8351	C	707 252-8931	24289
City of NAPA	4131	E	707 255-7631	3876
Collabria Care	8082	D	707 258-9080	22266
Comcast Corporation	4841	D	707 266-7012	5881
County of NAPA	8322	D	707 253-4625	23695
County of NAPA	8322	E	707 253-4361	23696
County of NAPA	8093	B	707 253-4461	22552
Dickenson Peatman & Fogarty A (PA)	8111	E	707 252-7122	23037
Doctors Company	8011	D	707 226-0289	19447
Doctors Company Insurance Svcs	6351	B	707 226-0100	10427
Doctors Management Company (HQ)	6411	C	707 226-0100	10609
DOD Constructors A JV	1629	D	707 265-1100	2025
DOD Fueling Constructors A JV	1629	D	707 265-1100	2026
DOD Marine Constructors A JV	1629	D	707 265-1100	2027
Dolce International / NAPA LLC	7011	B	707 257-0200	12534
Domaine Carneros Ltd	0172	D	707 257-0101	140
Folio Wine Company LLC (PA)	5182	C	707 254-9885	9042
Folio Wine Company LLC	5182	D	707 256-2757	9043
GD Nielson Construction Inc	1623	D	707 253-8774	1919
GF Carneros Tenant LLC	7231	E	707 299-4900	13660
Golden Living LLC	8059	D	707 255-6060	21086
Guardsmark LLC	7381	C	415 898-9022	16681
Hired Hands Inc	7361	C	707 265-6400	14636
IA Lodging NAPA Solano Trs LLC	7011	D	707 253-8600	12759
Infinex Investments Inc	6282	D	707 927-3578	10090
JD Wesson & Associates Inc	7389	D	707 255-8667	17257
Kaiser Foundation Hospitals	6733	C	707 258-2500	12107
La Tavola LLC (PA)	7213	D	707 257-3358	13532
LLP Moss Adams	8742	D	707 224-4001	27305
Lodgeworks LP	7011	D	707 690-9800	12859
Melissa Bradley RE Inc	6531	D	707 258-3900	11602
Meritage Resort LLC	7011	B	707 251-1900	12921
NAPA Es Leasing LLC	7011	D	707 253-9540	12948
NAPA Golf Associates LLC	7997	D	707 257-1900	18983
NAPA Nursing Center Inc	8051	C	707 257-0931	20658
NAPA Sanitation District	4952	E	707 254-9231	6324

	SIC	EMP	PHONE	ENTRY #
NAPA Sunrise Rotary Club Inc	8641	D	707 257-9564	25205
NAPA Valley Country Club	7997	D	707 252-1111	18984
NAPA Valley PSI Inc	8331	D	707 255-0177	24208
NAPA Valley Wine Train LLC (HQ)	7999	C	707 253-2160	19207
Napastyle Inc (PA)	7313	E	707 251-5100	13949
North Bay Developmental (PA)	8331	D	707 256-1224	24211
Nova ATL Elc A Joint Ventr	1629	D	707 265-1100	2050
Nova Brink A Joint Venture	1629	D	707 265-1100	2051
Nova Group Inc	1623	C	707 265-1100	1960
Nova Grp Inc -Obayashi Corp A	1623	E	707 265-1116	1961
Nova Lane Constructors A JV	1629	D	707 265-1100	2052
Nova-Cpf Inc	1623	C	707 257-3200	1962
Nova/Tic Gov Proj JV	1623	C	707 257-3200	1963
Ole Health	8011	E	707 254-1770	19730
On The Move	8399	E	707 251-9432	24817
Park Hotels & Resorts Inc	7011	D	707 253-9540	13025
Peck & Hiller Company	1771	D	707 258-8800	3304
Pina Vineyard Management LLC	0762	E	707 944-2229	708
Piners Nursing Home Inc	8051	D	707 224-7925	20701
Queen of Valley Medical Center (DH)	8062	A	707 252-4411	21679
Retreat & Conference Center	7299	E	707 252-3810	13771
Seguin Mreau NAPA Coperage Inc	5085	D	707 252-3408	7870
Sheehan Construction Inc	1521	B	707 603-2610	1236
Silverado Resort and Spa	7997	A	707 257-0200	19049
Silverado Rsort Svcs Group LLC	7011	B	707 257-0200	13228
Stagecoach Vineyards	0172	D	707 255-5459	178
Sunstone Hotel Investors LLC	7011	D	707 253-8600	13298
Tahoe Lake Partners LLC	6552	D	707 255-9890	11927
Tailored Living Choices LLC	1799	C	707 259-0526	3590
Travis Credit Union	6061	B	800 877-8328	9601
Treasury Wine Estates Americas	5182	C	707 259-4500	9057
United Parcel Service Inc OH	4215	C	707 224-1205	4453
US Advisor LLC	6798	D	707 253-9953	12191
Verasa Management LLC	7011	D	707 257-1800	13367
Walsh Vineyards Management Inc	6531	C	707 255-1650	11818
Wells Fargo Bank National Assn	6021	D	707 259-5552	9387
Winiarski Management Inc	5182	D	707 944-2020	9063

NATIONAL CITY, CA - San Diego County

	SIC	EMP	PHONE	ENTRY #
Builders Firstsource Inc	5031	E	619 425-6660	6811
Castle Manor Inc	8051	D	619 791-7900	20292
Centro De Salud De La	8322	D	619 477-0165	23554
Del Mar Holding LLC	5147	A	313 659-7300	8615
Ehmcke Sheet Metal Corp	1761	D	619 477-6484	3152
Fornaca Inc (PA)	7532	C	866 308-9461	17721
Framing Associates Inc	1522	C	619 336-9991	1285
Ghazal & Sons Inc (PA)	5113	C	619 474-6677	8106
Greenwalds Autobody Frameworks (PA)	7532	D	619 477-2600	17724
Hardisty Construction Administ	1542	D	619 245-6828	1541
Harvest Meat Company Inc (HQ)	5147	D	619 477-0185	8617
Horizons Adult Day Health Care	8099	D	619 474-1822	22818
Imaginative Horizons Inc	8051	D	619 477-1176	20541
Maniflo Money Exchange Inc	6099	D	619 434-7200	9688
McKinley Plaza LLC	8741	D	619 405-6307	26940
Motivational Systems Inc (PA)	7336	D	619 474-8246	14123
Nms Management Inc	7349	D	619 425-0440	14331
Paradise Valley Hospital (PA)	8062	A	619 470-4100	21634
Paradise Vly Hlth Care Ctr Inc	8051	D	619 470-6700	20692
Plaza Manor Preservation LP	6531	A	619 475-2125	11673
San Diego Unified Port Dst	4491	C	619 686-6200	4734
San Diego-Imperial	8322	D	619 336-6600	24013
Sand Dollar Holdings Inc (PA)	5147	D	619 477-0185	8630
Six Continents Hotels Inc	7011	D	619 474-2800	13240
South Bay Sand Blasting and Ta	7699	D	619 238-8338	17989
St Pauls Episcopal Home Inc	8361	D	619 232-2996	24686
Sureride Charter Inc	4142	C	619 336-9200	3903
US Foods Inc	5149	C	619 474-6525	8898
Westair Gases & Equipment Inc	5084	D	619 474-0079	7820
Windsor Healthcare Management	8051	C	619 474-6741	20904

NEEDLES, CA - San Bernardino County

	SIC	EMP	PHONE	ENTRY #
Colorado River Medical Center	8011	D	760 326-4531	19394
Havasu Landing Casino (PA)	7011	D	760 858-5380	12646
International Assoc of Machini	8631	E	760 326-7048	25062
Lifepoint Health Inc	8062	C	760 326-7100	21554

NEVADA CITY, CA - Nevada County

	SIC	EMP	PHONE	ENTRY #
Milhous Feed	5191	C	530 292-3242	9086
Mountain Valley Child and Fami	8052	C	530 265-9057	20945
Northern Queen Inc	7011	D	530 265-4492	12962
Patrick Dean Bryan	1799	D	530 273-5484	3565
Robinson & Sons	0212	D	530 265-5844	401
Telestream LLC (PA)	7371	D	530 470-1300	15498
Tri Counties Bank	6029	D	530 478-6001	9518

NEWARK, CA - Alameda County

	SIC	EMP	PHONE	ENTRY #
Advanced Cell Diagnostics Inc	8731	D	510 576-8800	26312

2019 Directory of California
Wholesalers and Services Companies

(P-0000) Products & Services Section entry number
(PA)=Parent Co (HQ)=Headquarters (DH)=Div Headquarters

Company	SIC	EMP	PHONE	ENTRY #
Alliance Bay Funding Inc	6531	D	510 742-6600	11205
America Shredding	7389	D	702 262-3607	16998
Apn Software Services Inc (PA)	7379	C	510 623-5050	16312
Bay Advanced Technologies LLC	5084	D	510 857-0900	7729
Bioclinca (PA)	7371	C	415 817-8900	15025
Bioclinca	8731	E	503 284-3334	26339
Cargill Incorporated	5169	C	510 797-1820	8922
Central Business Solutions Inc (PA)	7379	D	510 573-5500	16325
Courtesy Security Inc	7381	D	888 572-5545	16617
D&A Enterprises	5141	B	510 445-1600	8399
Elitegroup Cmpt Systems Inc	5045	C	510 226-7333	7039
Everest Silicon Valley MGT LP	8741	D	510 494-8800	26853
Fitness 2000 Inc	7991	E	510 791-2481	18599
Hardage Investments Inc	6512	D	510 795-1200	10892
Innovated Packaging Company	7389	D	510 713-3560	17238
Integrated Pkg & Crating Svcs	4783	E	510 745-8180	5209
Intelliswift Software Inc (PA)	7371	C	510 490-9240	15225
Itrenew Inc (HQ)	7379	E	408 744-9600	16415
Javelin Logistics Company Inc	4225	C	800 577-1060	4581
Javelin Logistics Corporation (PA)	4214	E	510 795-7287	4353
Kutir Corporation	7373	E	510 402-4526	15994
Lancashire Group Incorporated	8742	B	510 792-9384	27298
Marriott International Inc	7011	C	510 657-4600	12901
Membrane Technology & RES Inc (PA)	8731	D	650 328-2228	26415
Mickwee Group Inc	7389	D	510 651-5527	17329
Moving Solutions Inc	4214	C	408 920-0110	4360
Mshift Inc	7371	E	408 437-2740	15296
National Distribution Agcy Inc (HQ)	4225	D	510 487-6226	4597
Nefab Packaging West LLC	7389	D	408 678-2516	17346
Newark Courtyard By Marriott	7011	D	510 792-5200	12953
Oak Harbor Freight Lines Inc	4213	D	510 608-8841	4238
Oatey Supply Chain Svcs Inc	5074	D	510 797-4677	7631
Palo Alto Egg and Food Svc Co	5141	E	510 456-2420	8440
Payment Processing Inc	7371	C	510 795-2290	15348
Perlegen Sciences Inc	8731	C	650 625-4500	26435
Risk Management Solutions Inc (DH)	6794	D	510 505-2500	12142
Roseryan Inc	8721	D	510 456-3056	26281
Second Chance Inc (PA)	8322	E	510 792-4357	24036
Shotspotter Inc	7372	D	510 794-3100	15851
Special Dispatch Cal Inc	4213	D	510 713-0300	4266
Stomper Co Inc	1795	D	510 574-0570	3464
Tegile Systems Inc	8731	C	510 791-7900	26471
Triple Ring Technologies Inc	8742	E	510 592-3000	27498
Valassis Direct Mail Inc	7331	C	510 505-6500	14068
Vm Services Inc (DH)	7371	C	510 744-3720	15533
Worldpac Inc (DH)	5013	C	510 742-8900	6687
Xtraplus Corporation	5045	D	510 897-1890	7131
Zenith Infotech Limited	7373	D	510 687-1943	16080
Zws/ABS Joint Venture LLC	7349	D	510 461-1433	14430

NEWBURY PARK, CA - Ventura County

Company	SIC	EMP	PHONE	ENTRY #
Area Housing Authority (PA)	6531	E	805 480-9991	11217
BMW Designworks	5013	D	503 614-3403	6627
Carnegie Agency Inc	6411	E	805 445-1470	10578
Compulink Business Systems Inc	7372	D	805 446-2050	15634
Conejo Pacific Technologies	1541	D	805 498-5315	1388
Giant Bicycle Inc (DH)	5091	D	805 267-4600	7930
Graymeta Inc	7379	E	855 202-2270	16388
Hawaiian Hotels & Resorts Inc	7011	D	805 480-0052	12648
Hearst Communications Inc	4841	B	805 375-3121	5919
Isolutecom Inc (PA)	7372	E	805 498-6259	15725
Mary Hlth SCK Cnvlscnt &NRsng	8051	D	805 498-3644	20632
McKesson Medical-Surgical Inc	5047	B	805 375-8800	7190
People Creating Success Inc (PA)	8059	D	805 375-9222	21185
Perillo Industries Inc	5065	E	805 498-9838	7524
Time Warner Cable Inc	4841	B	805 214-1353	5953
Timothy Everitt	8049	D	805 214-9933	20210
United Parcel Service Inc OH	4215	C	805 375-1832	4476
United Payment Services Inc	7389	B	866 886-4833	17545
Weldlogic Inc	7692	D	805 375-1670	17926

NEWHALL, CA - Los Angeles County

Company	SIC	EMP	PHONE	ENTRY #
Calex Engineering Inc	1794	D	661 254-1866	3416
Hollenbeck Palms	8361	C	323 263-6195	24564
N V Landscape Inc	0782	D	661 286-8888	904
Santa Clarita Athletic Club	7991	D	661 255-3365	18649
Valencia Health Care Inc	8059	D	661 254-2425	21242

NEWMAN, CA - Stanislaus County

Company	SIC	EMP	PHONE	ENTRY #
Avalon Care Ctr - Newman LLC	8051	D	209 862-2862	20249
Cerutti Bros Inc	0161	C	209 862-2249	42
Dimare Enterprises (PA)	0161	D	209 827-2900	48
Golden Living LLC	8051	D	209 862-2862	20485
Superior Truck Lines Inc (PA)	4213	D	209 862-9430	4272

NEWPORT BEACH, CA - Orange County

Company	SIC	EMP	PHONE	ENTRY #
10632 Bolsa Avenue LP	6513	D	949 673-1221	10967
A White and Yellow Cab Inc	4121	C	714 258-1000	3863
Absolute Return Portfolio	6722	A	800 800-7646	12019
Accelerize Inc (PA)	7371	D	949 515-2141	14959
Accentcare Home Health Cal Inc	8082	D	949 250-0133	22193
Alamo Rental (us) Inc	7514	E	949 852-0403	17622
Alight (us) LLC	8742	C	949 725-4500	27123
Alliant Insurance Services Inc (PA)	6411	C	949 756-0271	10514
Allianz Globl Invstors Amer LP (HQ)	6282	D	949 219-2200	10050
Allied Lube Texas LP (PA)	7549	D	949 486-4008	17848
Amarik Properties Inc (PA)	6531	E	714 505-5200	11210
Ambassador Gaming Inc	7999	C	714 969-8730	19094
America Consulting Group LLC	8742	C	714 390-3105	27127
Andersonpenna Partners Inc	8742	D	949 428-1500	27136
Anne M Kent MD	8011	D	949 650-7100	19297
Applebee Leasing Inc	7389	D	818 612-6218	17007
Avalon At Newport LLC	8361	D	949 631-3555	24432
Baid Vivek	4813	D	888 550-8553	5521
Balboa Bay Club Inc (HQ)	7997	B	949 645-5000	18853
Barcelo Enterprises Inc	0181	D	760 728-3444	245
Bassenian/Lagoni Architects	8712	D	949 553-9100	26027
Beacon Accunting Resources LLC	8742	E	949 981-5946	27156
Beacon Healthcare Services	8063	D	949 650-9750	21927
Beacon Resources LLC	8742	E	949 955-1773	27157
Ben Bennett Inc (PA)	8059	C	949 209-9712	21005
Big Canyon Country Club	7997	C	949 644-5404	18865
Bremer Whyte Brown Omeara LLP (PA)	8111	C	949 221-1000	22960
Buchanan Fund I LLC	6799	D	949 721-1414	12206
Buchanan Street Partners LP	6531	D	949 721-1414	11252
C B Coast Newport Properties	6531	D	949 644-1600	11256
Call & Jensen APC	8111	E	949 717-3000	22968
Canadian Imperial Bank	6021	D	949 759-4718	9300
Cbre Global Investors LLC	8742	B	949 725-8500	27186
Cemak Trucking Inc (PA)	4212	D	949 253-2800	3987
Centurion Security Svcs Inc (PA)	7381	D	949 474-0444	16601
Childrens Hospital Orange Cnty	8351	A	949 631-2062	24293
Citivest Inc	6531	D	949 474-0440	11320
Citizens Business Bank	6022	D	949 440-5200	9433
Clean Energy	4924	A	949 437-1000	6157
Clean Energy Fuels Corp (PA)	4932	C	949 437-1000	6190
Core Realty Holdings LLC (PA)	6798	D	949 863-1031	12156
Core Realty Holdings MGT Inc	6531	D	949 863-1031	11380
Cws Apartment Homes LLC (PA)	6531	B	949 640-4200	11392
Dans Landscape Service Inc	0782	D	714 241-9501	818
Dansk Enterprises Inc	7381	D	714 751-0347	16626
Dentons US LLP	8111	C	949 732-3700	23031
Donald Lucky LLC	8741	C	949 752-0647	26843
Downtown SD Ventures LLC	7999	D	619 231-9200	19160
Dpr Construction Inc	1542	E	949 955-3771	1524
Dream Home Estates Inc	6531	E	949 415-4646	11410
Duxford Financial Inc	6162	E	949 471-2010	9800
Edwards Theatres Circuit Inc (DH)	7832	C	949 640-4600	18293
Emery Financial Inc (PA)	6163	D	949 219-0640	9881
Entrepreneurial Capital Corp	6512	D	949 809-3900	10873
ESA P Prtfolio Oper Lessee LLC	7011	E	949 851-2711	12563
Eureka Realty Partners Inc (PA)	6552	B	949 224-4100	11874
Excel Academy	8699	D	949 387-7822	25420
Executive Express Inc (PA)	4215	E	949 852-0450	4399
Fallon Land Company Inc	5051	E	213 880-1279	7273
Festival Fun Parks LLC	7999	C	954 921-1411	19170
Festival Fun Parks LLC	7996	E	949 261-0404	18800
Fidelity National Fincl Inc	6411	D	949 622-5000	10628
First Team RE - Orange Cnty	6531	D	949 759-5747	11459
Five Star Quality Care Inc	8051	C	949 642-8044	20429
Global Risk MGT Solutions LLC	7375	C	949 759-8500	16225
Harbor Health Systems LLC	8099	D	949 273-7020	22811
Health Information Partners	8059	C	949 261-5000	21106
Healthcare Cost Solutions Inc	8721	D	949 721-2795	26216
Heat Waves LLC	7371	C	323 753-8441	15197
Hit Portfolio I Misc Trs LLC	7011	D	949 729-1234	12681
Hoag Memorial Hospital Presbt (PA)	8062	A	949 764-4624	21451
Host Hotels & Resorts LP	7011	D	949 640-4000	12703
Host Hotels & Resorts LP	7011	D	949 854-4500	12712
Houalla Enterprises Ltd	1542	D	949 515-4350	1555
International Bay Clubs LLC (PA)	7997	B	949 645-5000	18938
Internet Booking Agencycom Inc	7361	B	949 673-7707	14650
Interstate Hotels Resorts Inc	8741	D	949 783-2500	26895
Irell & Manella LLP	8111	D	949 760-0991	23143
Iron Mountain Incorporated	4226	D	562 345-6900	4678
Irvine Eastgate Office II LLC	6798	A	949 720-2000	12167
James R Glidewell Dental (PA)	8072	A	949 440-2600	22170
Jwc Construction Inc	1522	E	949 252-2107	1295
Kalpana LLC (PA)	7011	B	949 610-8200	12798
Koll Management Services Inc	6531	D	949 833-3030	11553
Kollwood Golf Operating LP	7992	B	949 833-3025	18724
La Habra Villa	8361	D	714 529-1697	24573

Employment Codes: A=Over 500 employees, B=251-500,
C=101-250, D=51-100, E=50

2019 Directory of California
Wholesalers and Services Companies

© Mergent Inc. 1-800-342-5647
1621

	SIC	EMP	PHONE	ENTRY #
Labmed Partners	8742	E	949 242-9925	27297
Lbs Financial Credit Union	6111	D	714 893-5111	9698
Lee Hong Degerman Kang	8111	D	949 250-9954	23196
Lee & Associates Realty Group	6531	E	949 724-1000	11563
Leisure Care Inc	6513	E	949 645-6833	11053
Lennar Partners of Los Angeles (PA)	7389	E	949 885-8500	17294
Lionakis	8711	C	949 955-1919	25798
LLP Locke Lord	8111	D	949 423-2100	23221
Lyon Promenade LLC	1531	E	949 252-9101	1352
M Arthur Gensler Jr Assoc Inc	8712	D	949 863-9434	26091
Makar Properties LLC (PA)	6552	A	949 255-1100	11889
Marriotts Newport Coast Villa	7011	D	949 464-6000	12911
McCarthy Bldg Companies Inc	1542	B	949 851-8383	1590
McCarthy Bldg Companies Inc	1542	D	949 851-8383	1591
Merrill Lynch Pierce Fenner	6211	C	949 467-3760	9981
Mesa Management Inc	6531	E	949 851-0995	11610
Message Broadcastcom LLC	7389	E	949 428-3111	17326
Meyer Properties Corp (PA)	6552	D	949 862-0500	11891
Mf Services Company LLC (HQ)	8742	D	949 474-5800	27345
Mig Management Services LLC	8741	D	949 474-5800	26946
Mobilitie Services LLC	4813	B	877 999-7070	5603
Montrenes Financial Svcs Inc	7389	E	562 795-0450	17335
Morgan Stanley	6282	D	949 760-2440	10097
Mscsoftware Corporation (HQ)	7372	C	714 540-8900	15769
Mscsoftware Corporation	7373	B	714 540-8900	16008
Mulechain Inc	4212	D	888 456-8881	4043
Multipoint Wireless LLC	8711	E	714 262-4172	25835
National Liquidators	5091	E	949 631-6715	7934
National Therapeutic Svcs Inc (PA)	8093	D	866 311-0003	22621
Newmark & Company RE Inc	6531	D	949 608-2000	11627
Newmeyer & Dillion LLP (PA)	8111	C	949 854-7000	23284
Newport Beach Country Club Inc	7997	D	949 644-9550	18987
Newport Beach Orthopedic Inst	8011	D	949 722-7038	19710
Newport Beach Surgery Ctr LLC	8011	C	949 631-0988	19711
Newport Diagnostic Center Inc (PA)	8071	D	949 760-3025	22116
Newport Fmly Mdcne/A Med Group	8011	D	949 644-1025	19712
Newport Harbor Radiology Assoc	8011	D	949 721-8191	19713
Olen Commercial Realty Corp	6512	B	949 644-6536	10922
Olen Residential Realty Corp (HQ)	1522	D	949 644-6536	1304
OMelveny & Myers LLP	8111	C	949 760-9600	23297
Pacific Bay Properties (PA)	1521	E	949 440-7200	1211
Pacific Club (PA)	7997	D	949 955-1123	18996
Pacific Hotel Management Inc	7011	C	949 608-1091	13002
Pacific Investment MGT Co LLC (DH)	6282	C	949 720-6000	10101
Pacific Life & Annuity Company	6311	A	949 219-3011	10142
Pacific Life Global Funding	6153	D	949 219-3011	9744
Pacific Monarch Resorts Inc (PA)	6531	D	949 609-2400	11649
Palace Entertainment Inc (DH)	7999	E	949 261-0404	19213
Panattoni Development Co Inc (PA)	6531	D	916 381-1561	11659
Park Newport Ltd (PA)	6513	D	949 644-1900	11093
Pimco Funds Distribution Co	6722	B	949 720-4761	12044
Pyramid Peak Corporation	6799	D	949 769-8600	12261
Qw Media International LLC	7313	E	949 200-4616	13954
R Mc Closkey Insurance Agency	6411	C	949 223-8100	10753
REO World Inc	6722	D	949 478-8000	12046
Research Affiliates Capital LP	6282	D	949 325-8700	10109
Research Affiliates LLC	6282	D	949 325-8700	10110
Riverside Research Institute	8733	E	949 631-0107	26655
Roth Capital Partners LLC (PA)	6211	D	800 678-9147	10012
Scicon Technologies Corp	8711	C	949 252-1341	25907
Signature Services	6512	D	949 851-9391	10942
Sleepy Giant Entertainment Inc	7371	C	949 464-7986	15451
Sleepy Giant Entertainment Inc	7929	D	714 460-4113	18464
Solve Healthcare Corporation (PA)	8748	D	949 891-0300	27864
Sound Mind and Body Inc	7991	C	206 547-2706	18654
Squar Milner Peterson (PA)	8721	D	949 222-2999	26297
SSC Newport Beach Oper Co LP	8051	C	949 642-8044	20776
Stradling Yocca Carlson & Raut (PA)	8111	C	949 725-4000	23400
Surterre Properties Inc (PA)	6512	C	949 717-7100	10953
Synnexxus LLC	8111	E	714 933-4500	23405
T-Force Inc (PA)	8748	D	949 208-1527	27875
Tad Group LLC	7382	C	949 476-3601	16946
Thrifty Rent-A-Car System Inc	7514	E	949 757-0659	17651
Toni & Guy Hairdressing (PA)	7231	D	949 721-1666	13674
Tribeworx LLC	7372	D	800 949-3432	15881
True Investments LLC	6799	E	949 258-9720	12277
Twenty4seven Hotels Corp	8741	A	949 734-6400	27011
Tz Holdings LP	7372	D	949 719-2200	15884
U Gym LLC (PA)	7991	D	714 668-0911	18673
UBS Financial Services Inc	6211	C	949 760-5308	10028
Uka LLC	7011	E	949 610-8000	13352
United Cpitl Fncl Advisers LLC	6282	D	949 999-8500	10119
Universal Space Lines Inc	8711	D	215 328-9130	25971
US Lines LLC (DH)	8611	D	714 751-3333	24988
Ventage Senior Housing	6513	E	949 631-3555	11131

	SIC	EMP	PHONE	ENTRY #
Vital Express Inc	4789	E	330 777-5450	5252
Voit Real Estate Services Lp	6531	C	949 644-8648	11816
West Dermatology Med MGT Inc	8011	C	909 793-3000	20098
Whitaker Welness Institute In	8011	D	949 851-1550	20101
William Lyon Homes (PA)	1531	C	949 833-3600	1367
William Lyon Homes Inc (HQ)	1531	D	949 833-3600	1368
Windjammer Capital Invstr III	6211	A	949 706-9989	10042
Windjmmer Capitl Investors LLC (PA)	6799	D	949 706-9989	12284
Wj Newport LLC	7011	C	949 476-2001	13414
Wright Finlay & Zak LLP	8111	D	949 477-5050	23448
Ymarketing LLC	8742	D	714 545-2550	27529
Young Mens Chrstn Assn Orange	8641	D	949 642-9990	25349
Your Practice Online LLC	4813	C	877 388-8569	5680

NEWPORT COAST, CA - Orange County

	SIC	EMP	PHONE	ENTRY #
Pricemetrix Usa Inc	7374	E	714 357-6192	16167
Resort At Pelican Hill LLC	7011	C	949 467-6800	13123

NIPOMO, CA - San Luis Obispo County

	SIC	EMP	PHONE	ENTRY #
American Golf Corporation	7997	D	805 343-1214	18834
Community Health Centers (PA)	8011	C	805 929-3211	19396
Integrity Management Svcs Inc	7349	C	805 238-0905	14291
Jj Fisher Construction Inc	1611	D	805 723-5220	1797
L J T Flowers Inc	0181	D	805 310-6036	279
Pre Con Industries Inc	1751	E	805 481-7305	3057

NIPTON, CA - San Bernardino County

	SIC	EMP	PHONE	ENTRY #
Primm Valley Golf Club	7992	D	702 679-5509	18747

NORCO, CA - Riverside County

	SIC	EMP	PHONE	ENTRY #
American Tech Service	8711	D	951 372-9664	25533
Anna Corporation	1721	D	951 736-6037	2420
Bonanza Plumbing Inc (PA)	1711	D	951 360-8262	2147
Cal West Underground Inc	1629	D	951 371-6775	2020
Cal-West Nurseries Inc	0782	C	951 270-0667	808
Car Spa Inc	7549	E	951 279-1422	17856
City of Norco	4941	D	951 270-5632	6226
City of Norco	8748	D	951 270-5617	27687
County of Riverside	8322	E	951 272-5400	23706
CSRA LLC	7371	D	951 898-3015	15089
CSRA Systems & Solutions LLC	7379	E	951 735-3300	16338
F J Hoover Plumbing Inc	1711	D	951 360-8262	2205
Guy Yocom Construction Inc (PA)	1771	C	951 284-3456	3263
Hampton Inn Norco Corona North	7011	D	951 279-1111	12638
Hci Inc (HQ)	1623	B	951 520-4200	1924
Hoyt Roofs Inc	1761	E	714 632-3939	3166
Industrial Masonry Inc	1741	D	951 284-0251	2811
Janus Corporation	1799	E	951 479-0700	3537
JIT Corporation	5065	D	805 238-5000	7495
Kerdus Plastering Inc	1742	C	951 272-6720	2907
Luberski Inc	5144	D	951 271-3866	8535
Norco Fire Department	6371	A	951 737-8097	10490
North Orange Coast Pntg Inc	1721	D	951 279-2694	2462
Royal West Drywall Inc	1742	D	951 271-4600	2951

NORDEN, CA - Nevada County

	SIC	EMP	PHONE	ENTRY #
Sugar Bowl Corporation	7999	D	530 426-9000	19242

NORTH FORK, CA - Madera County

	SIC	EMP	PHONE	ENTRY #
Mono Nation	8322	D	559 877-2450	23927

NORTH HIGHLANDS, CA - Sacramento County

	SIC	EMP	PHONE	ENTRY #
AAA Drain Patrol	1711	E	916 348-3098	2082
Capital City Drywall Inc	1742	D	916 331-9200	2861
Eagle Lath & Plaster Inc	1542	D	916 925-1435	1526
Energetic Pntg & Drywall Inc (PA)	1742	D	916 488-8455	2881
Heritage 1 Window and Building	5031	C	916 481-5030	6828
Heritage Interests LLC (PA)	1751	D	916 481-5030	3041
Heritage One Door and Building	5031	D	916 481-5030	6830
Homeq Servicing Corporation (DH)	6162	A	916 339-6192	9815
Kenyon Construction Inc	1742	C	916 514-9502	2906
Lund Construction Co	8711	C	916 344-5800	25802
Lund Equipment LP	1611	E	916 344-5800	1807
MCM Construction Inc (PA)	1622	D	916 334-1221	1884
Mission Courier Inc	7389	D	916 484-1992	17332
Pacific Coast Supply LLC	5031	C	916 481-2220	6847
Pacific Coast Supply LLC (HQ)	5031	C	916 971-2301	6848
Paragon Coml Bldg Maint Inc	7349	D	916 334-8801	14342
Pride Industries	8331	D	916 334-5415	24222
Recycling Industries Inc	4953	D	916 452-3961	6448
Rick H Hitch Plastering Inc	1742	D	916 334-3591	2950
Security Contractor Svcs Inc (PA)	5039	D	916 338-4200	6936
U S Army Corps of Engineers	8711	D	916 925-7001	25966

NORTH HILLS, CA - Los Angeles County

	SIC	EMP	PHONE	ENTRY #
Brentwood Cmmncations Intl Inc	7812	E	818 333-3680	18025
Dynamo Aviation Inc	4581	D	818 785-9561	4886
Living Colors Inc	1721	D	818 893-5068	2455

2019 Directory of California
Wholesalers and Services Companies

(P-0000) Products & Services Section entry number
(PA)=Parent Co (HQ)=Headquarters (DH)=Div Headquarters

	SIC	EMP	PHONE	ENTRY #
Penny Lane Centers **(PA)**	8399	B	818 892-3423	24818
Penny Lane Centers	8399	C	818 892-3423	24819
Penny Lane Centers	8399	C	818 892-3423	24820
Penny Lane Centers	8399	C	818 892-3423	24822
Penny Lane Centers	8399	C	818 892-1112	24823
Penny Lane Centers	8399	C	818 892-3423	24824
Plummer Vlg Preservation LP	6513	D	818 891-0646	11099
Prn Ambulance LLC	4119	B	818 810-3600	3832
Veterans Health Administration	8011	C	818 895-9311	20073
Veterans Health Administration	8011	A	818 891-7711	20075
Veterans Health Administration	8011	C	818 895-9449	20080
Walker & Zanger Inc **(PA)**	5032	D	818 280-8300	6913

NORTH HOLLYWOOD, CA - Los Angeles County

	SIC	EMP	PHONE	ENTRY #
1658 Camden LLC	6513	E	818 769-1944	10968
51 Minds Entertainment LLC	7929	D	323 466-9200	18417
Academy TV Arts & Sciences	8621	D	818 754-2800	24993
Advanced Cable Technologies	1623	E	818 262-6484	1890
Alpha Systems Fire Protection	5099	E	323 227-0700	8017
Ambulnz Health LLC	4119	B	877 311-5555	3744
American Solar Solution Inc	1521	D	877 946-8855	1115
Andy Gump Inc	7359	D	818 255-0650	14472
Arriaga Usa Inc	1743	D	818 982-9559	2987
Arriaga Usa Inc **(PA)**	5032	C	818 982-9559	6876
AT&T Corp.	4812	D	818 506-9118	5295
Bento Box Entertainment LLC	7929	B	818 333-7700	18425
Break Floor Productions LLC **(PA)**	7922	E	818 432-1234	18346
California Credit Union	6061	D	818 291-5434	9544
Cats USA Inc	7342	D	818 506-1000	14139
CB Associates Inc	7322	E	424 777-8214	13995
Center For Autism Related Svcs	8748	E	323 850-7177	27680
Century National Properties **(PA)**	6512	D	818 760-0880	10862
Century Theatres Inc	7833	D	818 508-1943	18327
Chapman/Leonard Studio Eqp Inc **(PA)**	7819	C	323 877-5309	18181
Circulating Air Inc **(PA)**	1711	D	818 764-0530	2160
Coastal Tile Inc.	1743	D	818 988-6134	2991
Coldwater Care Center LLC	8051	D	818 766-6105	20319
Cri-Help Inc **(PA)**	8361	C	818 985-8323	24498
Emergency Technologies Inc	5063	D	818 765-4421	7359
Eqal Inc	7311	C	818 276-6300	13826
Four Seasons Healthcare	8051	D	818 985-1814	20437
Golden Care Inc	8059	D	818 763-6275	21083
Hillsdale Group LP	8059	D	818 623-2170	21112
Hollywood Health System Inc	8082	D	323 662-3731	22321
Hollywood Spa Inc	7991	E	323 464-0445	18609
Horizon Actuarial Services LLC	8742	D	818 691-2000	27264
Insurance Auto Auctions Inc	5012	D	818 487-2222	6598
IPC Healthcare Inc **(DH)**	8011	D	888 447-2362	19515
Jackson Shrub Supply Inc.	7819	D	818 982-0100	18198
Japanese Assistance Netwrk Inc	7389	B	818 505-6080	17256
JC Party Rentals Inc	7359	D	818 765-4819	14519
Jessica Cosmetics Intl Inc.	5122	D	818 759-1050	8183
Jewish Family Svc Los Angeles	8322	D	818 984-0276	23874
Kaiser Foundation Hospitals	8011	A	888 778-5000	19570
Kaiser Foundation Hospitals	6324	D	818 503-7082	10268
M Gaw Inc	1799	D	818 503-7997	3546
Mariner Health Care Inc	8051	D	818 985-5990	20628
Mark Herzog & Company Inc	7812	D	818 762-4640	18075
Messenger Express **(PA)**	4215	C	213 614-0475	4424
Midway Rent A Car Inc.	7515	C	818 985-9770	17657
Mikado Hotels Inc	7011	E	818 763-9141	12927
Morigon Technologies LLC	5047	E	818 764-8880	7194
O P I Products Inc **(HQ)**	5087	D	818 759-8688	7892
On-Scene Security Services Inc	7381	E	661 263-2343	16748
Pie Town Productions Inc	7812	C	818 255-9300	18093
Pierce Brothers **(DH)**	7261	D	818 763-9121	13693
Pilgrim Operations LLC	5043	B	818 478-4500	6947
Power Generation Entps Inc	5084	D	818 484-8550	7785
Protection Specialists	7381	B	818 503-1306	16768
Rio Vista Development Company **(PA)**	7011	C	818 980-8000	13124
Rodin & Co Inc	1721	D	818 358-3427	2476
Sada Systems Inc	7379	C	818 766-2400	16475
Silverscreen Healthcare Inc	8051	D	818 763-8247	20766
SLC Operating Ltd Partnership	7299	D	818 980-1212	13775
Southern California Golf Assn **(PA)**	8611	D	818 980-3630	24983
Stark Services	7374	D	818 985-2003	16182
Toner Supply USA Inc	5045	E	818 504-6540	7117
Trinity Health Systems	8059	D	818 983-0103	21231
Universal Studios Inc	7812	D	818 753-0000	18143
Universal Studios Company LLC **(DH)**	7812	C	818 777-1000	18146
Valley Community Healthcare	8011	B	818 763-8836	20043
Valley Vista Nursing and Trans	8051	C	818 763-6275	20853
Valley Wholesale Supply Corp **(PA)**	5023	D	818 769-5656	6800
Volunteers of Amer Los Angeles	8322	D	818 764-8722	24114
Volunteers of Amer Los Angeles	8322	C	818 769-3617	24121
Volunteers of Amer Los Angeles	8322	E	818 506-0597	24122

	SIC	EMP	PHONE	ENTRY #
Western Costume Leasing	7299	D	818 760-0900	13781
Western General Agency Inc	6411	D	818 766-6500	10828
Western Magnesite Inc.	1799	E	818 255-1150	3611
Woods Maintenance Services Inc	1799	C	818 764-2515	3613
Young Mens Chrstn Assn of La	8351	A	818 763-5126	24402

NORTHRIDGE, CA - Los Angeles County

	SIC	EMP	PHONE	ENTRY #
1-800-4-insure Insurance Svcs	6411	C	818 701-3733	10506
3m/Pharmaceuticals	1741	D	818 341-1300	2795
Alliant Tchsystems Oprtons LLC	8731	D	818 887-8195	26316
Apex Group	8741	C	818 885-0513	26761
Arete Associates **(PA)**	8731	C	818 885-2200	26328
Assisted Home Recovery Inc **(PA)**	7361	C	818 894-8117	14571
Automobile Club Southern Cal	8699	D	818 993-1616	25388
Bellis Steel Company Inc **(PA)**	1791	D	818 886-5601	3363
Child and Family Guidance Ctr **(PA)**	8093	C	818 739-5140	22528
Child and Family Guidance Ctr	8093	E	818 830-0200	22529
Choosing Independence Inc	8741	C	818 257-0323	26803
Contemporary Services Corp **(PA)**	7361	C	818 885-5150	14590
Discount Tire Ctr	7539	D	818 993-4758	17793
Elite & Associates	1761	D	805 582-0353	3153
Eminence Home Health Care Inc	8082	E	818 830-7113	22292
Extreme Telecom Inc.	4813	C	818 902-4821	5558
First Nationwide Mortgage Corp	6163	C	818 209-3134	9883
Friends of Family	8322	E	818 988-4430	23816
Heritage Provider Network Inc **(PA)**	8621	A	818 654-3461	25018
Holman Family Counseling Inc **(PA)**	8049	D	818 704-1444	20178
Ikano Communications Inc **(PA)**	7374	D	801 924-0900	16144
Lakeside Systems Inc	8741	A	866 654-3471	26927
Lansing Mall Ltd Partnership	6512	D	818 885-9700	10906
M K H Inc	7542	D	818 882-9274	17831
Mikuni American Corporation **(HQ)**	5013	C	310 676-0522	6658
Move Inc	6531	C	818 701-0012	11617
MSC Chatsworth	5099	C	818 718-7696	8046
Musclebound Inc **(PA)**	7991	B	818 349-0123	18635
National Center On Deafness	8322	D	818 677-2054	23929
Northwest Excavating Inc.	7353	D	818 349-5861	14451
Omega Security Services & Cons	7381	C	818 831-1100	16747
Pacific Theaters	7829	D	818 501-5121	18254
PHI Delta Theta Inc	7041	E	818 885-9940	13479
Pinnacle Estate Properties **(PA)**	6531	C	818 993-4707	11670
Porter Valley Country Club	7997	C	818 360-1071	19004
Production Special Events Svcs	7922	E	818 831-5326	18397
Prudential California Realty	6531	E	818 993-8900	11692
Rashman Corporation	5087	D	818 993-3030	7897
Regal Medical Group Inc **(PA)**	8621	A	818 654-3400	25038
Retail Services Wis Corp	7389	D	818 407-2680	17433
Rodeo Realty Inc.	6531	D	818 349-9997	11740
Ryder Integrated Logistics Inc.	7513	C	818 701-9332	17613
San Frnndo Vly Intrfith Cncil	8399	C	818 885-5220	24839
Securitas SEC Svcs USA Inc	7381	C	818 891-0458	16813
Shapell Industries LLC	1521	E	818 366-1132	1233
Southern California Mtl Hdlg	5084	D	805 650-6000	7800
Spad Holdings LLC	7991	B	818 772-8900	18664
Sunrise Senior Living LLC	8051	D	818 886-1616	20815
Telecom Evolutions LLC	7389	E	818 264-4400	17504
Teutonic Holdings LLC	7375	C	818 264-4400	16252
Tri - Star Win Coverings Inc	5023	E	818 718-3188	6795
University Student Union of CA.	8641	B	818 677-2251	25272
Valley Hospital Medical Center **(HQ)**	8062	B	818 885-8500	21895
Village At Northridge	8361	D	818 514-4497	24713
World Private Security Inc	7381	C	818 894-1800	16859

NORWALK, CA - Los Angeles County

	SIC	EMP	PHONE	ENTRY #
American Multi-Cinema Inc	7832	E	562 864-6206	18266
Aquirecorps Norwalk Auto Auctn	5012	C	562 864-7464	6578
Coast Plaza Doctors Hospital **(PA)**	8062	D	562 868-3751	21330
County of Los Angeles	7374	A	562 462-2094	16108
County of Los Angeles	8322	C	562 807-7860	23679
Cph Hospital Management LLC	8082	A	562 838-3751	22340
El Clasificado	7313	D	323 837-4095	13945
Elena Villa Healthcare Center	8059	D	562 868-0591	21061
Faro Services Inc	4225	C	562 483-7799	4556
Front Porch Communities & Svcs	8059	C	562 868-9761	21075
Granville Hotel Corp	7011	C	562 863-5555	12616
Joes Sweeping Inc	4953	C	562 929-4344	6409
Jwch Institute Inc.	8733	D	562 281-0306	26631
Kaiser Foundation Hospitals	8011	A	562 807-6100	19572
Kerber Bros Inc	1799	D	562 921-3447	3543
Life Care Centers America Inc	8051	D	562 921-6624	20587
Lj Distributors Inc	5148	D	562 229-7660	8703
Norwalk Community Hospital	8062	D	562 863-4763	21610
Norwalk Meadows Nursing Ctr LP	8051	C	562 864-2541	20665
Norwalk Transit System	4111	D	562 929-5550	3691
Pedestal Capital II LLC	6799	D	562 863-5555	12258
Tap Ram Reinforcing Inc.	1791	D	562 484-0859	3400

GEOGRAPHIC

Company	SIC	EMP	PHONE	ENTRY #
Tvb (usa) Inc (DH)	4841	E	562 345-9871	5962
Weber Distribution Warehouses	4225	E	562 404-9996	4658
West Central Produce Inc	5148	B	213 629-3600	8746

NOVATO, CA - Marin County

Company	SIC	EMP	PHONE	ENTRY #
Activision Blizzard Inc	7372	C	415 881-9100	15566
Atria Senior Living Group Inc	8361	E	415 892-0944	24429
Automatic Data Processing Inc	7374	C	415 899-7300	16091
Bank of Marin Bancorp (PA)	6022	C	415 763-4520	9414
Bear Flag Marketing Corp	8082	C	415 899-8466	22235
Biomarin Inc	5047	A	415 761-8600	7163
Birkenstock Usa Lp (DH)	5139	D	415 884-3200	8345
Brayton Purcell APC (PA)	8111	C	415 898-1555	22959
Buck Inst For RES On Aging (PA)	8733	C	415 209-2000	26599
Cellmark Inc (DH)	5099	D	415 927-1700	8022
Charles Schwab Corporation	6211	D	415 294-3503	9928
Charming Trim & Packaging	5131	A	415 302-7021	8223
Comet Building Maintenance Inc	0781	D	415 383-1035	747
County of Marin	7374	C	415 499-7060	16109
Drivesavers Inc	7375	D	415 382-2000	16218
Griffin Group LLC (PA)	8741	D	415 892-4569	26878
Horizon Pharmaceutical LLC (HQ)	8733	D	415 408-6200	26621
Indian Valley Golf Club Inc	7992	E	415 897-1118	18721
Interntnal Prnsrance Assoc LLC	6411	E	415 223-5548	10654
Jaylaneentertainment Corp	7313	D	707 820-2773	13947
Johann B Garovi	1622	D	415 898-1801	1882
Kaiser Foundation Hospitals	8062	E	415 899-7400	21506
King Security Services Inc	7381	A	415 556-5464	16711
L & L Logic and Logistics LP	5139	E	707 795-2475	8361
Marin Airporter Inc	4131	D	415 884-2878	3880
Marin Community Clinic	8011	D	415 448-1500	19667
Marin Country Club Inc	7997	D	415 382-6700	18967
Marin County Sart Program	8063	D	415 892-1628	21965
Marin Humane Society	8699	D	415 883-4621	25442
Melissa Bradley RE Inc	6531	D	415 209-1000	11605
Navitas LLC	5149	D	415 883-8116	8832
North Marin Water District (PA)	4941	E	415 897-4133	6290
Novato Fire Protection Dist	7389	D	415 878-2690	17360
Novato Healthcare Center LLC	8051	C	415 897-6161	20666
Pacific Inptient Med Group Inc	8011	D	415 485-8824	19742
Permanente Medical Group Inc	8011	D	415 209-2444	19775
Permanente Medical Group Inc	8011	D	415 899-7400	19776
Radiant Logic Inc	7371	D	415 209-6800	15393
Scene7 Inc	7371	D	415 506-6000	15432
Stonetree Golf LLC	7992	E	415 209-6744	18767
Sutter Health	8062	C	415 897-8495	21822
Sutter Health	8062	C	415 602-5380	21835
Sutter West Bay Hospitals (HQ)	8062	B	415 209-1300	21848
Tennis Everyone Incorporated	7997	D	415 897-2185	19067
Thompson Builders Corporation	1522	C	415 456-8972	1319
Tile West Inc (PA)	1743	D	415 382-7550	3012
Viscomm Inc (PA)	7375	D	415 454-7191	16259
Visual Concepts Entertainment	7371	D	415 479-3634	15531
W Bradley Electric Inc (PA)	1731	E	415 898-1400	2781
Willis Lease Finance Corp (PA)	7359	D	415 408-4700	14557
Winery Exchange Inc (PA)	5182	E	415 382-6900	9062
Young Mens Christian Assoc SF	8641	D	415 883-9622	25329

OAK HILLS, CA - San Bernardino County

Company	SIC	EMP	PHONE	ENTRY #
Double Eagle Trnsp Corp	4213	C	760 956-3770	4130
Little Sisters Truck Wash Inc	7542	D	760 947-4448	17826

OAK VIEW, CA - Ventura County

Company	SIC	EMP	PHONE	ENTRY #
Casablanca Alzheimers Resid	8361	D	805 649-5143	24458

OAKDALE, CA - Stanislaus County

Company	SIC	EMP	PHONE	ENTRY #
Alldrin Brothers Inc	0723	E	855 667-4231	491
Amerine Systems Incorporated	0781	E	209 847-5968	729
Central Valley AG Trnspt Inc	0723	D	209 544-9246	502
Damrell Nelson Schrimp Pall	8111	E	209 848-3500	23019
Gcu Trucking Inc	4213	D	209 845-2117	4185
Gilton Resource Recovery	4953	D	209 527-3781	6403
Gilton Solid Waste MGT Inc	4953	C	209 527-3781	6404
Mozingo Construction Inc	1794	E	209 848-0160	3436
Oak Valley Hospital District (HQ)	8062	B	209 847-3011	21611
Oakdale Golf and Country Club	7997	D	209 847-2984	18991
Oakdale Irrgtion Dst Fing Corp	4941	D	209 847-0341	6291
Premier Valley Inc (PA)	6531	D	209 847-6111	11678
Ross F Carroll Inc	8711	E	209 848-5959	25897

OAKHURST, CA - Madera County

Company	SIC	EMP	PHONE	ENTRY #
Associated Koi Clubs America	7997	D	949 650-5225	18850
Camarena Health	8011	D	559 642-6724	19346
Kaiser Foundation Hospitals	6324	D	559 658-8388	10240
Oakhurst Skilled Nursing Welln	8051	D	559 683-2244	20671
Sierra Masonic Association	8641	D	559 683-7713	25249
Sierra Tel Cmmunications Group	4813	D	559 683-7777	5642
Sierra Tel Cmmunications Group (PA)	4813	D	559 683-4611	5643
Sierra Telephone Company Inc	4813	C	559 683-4611	5644
State Farm Mutl Auto Insur Co	6411	D	559 683-3467	10790

OAKLAND, CA - Alameda County

Company	SIC	EMP	PHONE	ENTRY #
A T Associates Inc	8059	D	510 261-8564	20977
A3 Labs LLC	8731	E	925 274-8503	26308
ABC Security Service Inc (PA)	7381	D	510 436-0666	16542
ABF Freight System Inc	4213	D	510 533-8575	4091
ABM Facility Services Inc (DH)	7349	D	510 251-0381	14169
Absg Consulting Inc	8748	E	510 508-6289	27616
Ace Parking Management Inc	7521	C	510 589-2313	17663
Ace Parking Management Inc	7521	C	510 272-9788	17666
Ace Parking Management Inc	7521	C	510 251-0509	17667
Aecom Technical Services Inc	8711	C	510 834-4304	25516
Aecom-TSE Joint Venture	8711	D	510 285-6639	25520
Alameda Cnty Cmnty Fd Bnk Inc	8322	D	510 635-3663	23466
Alameda County Employees Retir	6371	D	510 628-3000	10475
Alameda Health System (PA)	8062	A	510 437-4800	21276
Alameda-Contra Costa Trnst Dst (PA)	4111	A	510 891-4777	3638
Alameda-Contra Costa Trnst Dst	4173	C	510 577-8816	3949
Alaska Airlines Inc	4512	C	510 577-5813	4763
Allied Fire Protection	1711	C	510 533-5516	2100
Altenheim Inc	6513	D	510 530-4013	10975
American Automobile Assctn	8699	C	510 350-2042	25379
American Baptist Homes of West	8361	C	510 654-7172	24416
American National Red Cross	8099	C	510 594-5100	22730
American President Lines LLC	4731	C	510 272-3990	5006
Aperian Global Inc (PA)	8742	D	628 222-3773	27140
Aramark Unf & Career AP LLC	7218	C	510 835-9285	13588
Asian Community Mental Hlth Bd	8093	D	510 869-6000	22508
Asian Health Services	8011	C	510 986-0601	19306
Asian Health Services (PA)	8011	C	510 986-6800	19307
Associated Internal Medicine (PA)	8011	C	510 465-6700	19308
AT&T Services Inc	4813	C	510 645-7684	5514
AT&T Services Inc	4813	C	510 645-4507	5516
Athletics Investment Group LLC (PA)	7941	C	510 638-4900	18507
Avis Rent A Car System Inc	7514	D	510 577-6360	17625
B&C Transit Inc (PA)	8711	D	510 483-3560	25558
Balfour Beatty Cnstr LLC	1542	D	510 903-2060	1472
Bay Alarm Company	8732	C	510 452-3211	26502
Bay Area Community Svcs Inc (PA)	8322	E	510 613-0330	23502
Belcampo Group Inc (PA)	0279	D	510 250-7810	445
Beneficial State Bank (HQ)	6029	D	510 550-8420	9496
Berry & Berry Law Firm	8111	D	510 250-0200	22943
Bonita House Inc	8322	D	510 923-0180	23515
Boornazian Jensen & Garthe A	8111	D	510 834-4350	22954
Brightcurrent Inc	7389	D	877 896-3306	17043
Brilliance Investment LLC	7011	D	510 568-1880	12401
Brita Products Company	5074	D	510 271-7000	7611
Broadway Mech - Contrs Inc	1711	C	510 746-4000	2151
Brown & Toland Medical Group (PA)	8011	C	415 972-4162	19329
Burnham Brown A Prof Corp	8111	C	510 444-6800	22966
C/O Uc San Francisco (PA)	8741	C	858 534-7323	26791
Calidad Industries Inc	8331	D	510 534-6666	24160
California Cereal Products Inc (PA)	5153	D	510 452-4500	8905
California Child Care Resourc	8322	E	510 658-0381	23522
California Motorcycle Club	7997	D	510 534-6222	18880
California Nurses Association (PA)	8621	C	510 273-2200	25004
California Waste Solutions Inc	4953	D	408 292-0830	6366
Califrnia Hlth Care Foundation (PA)	8641	D	510 891-3963	25124
Califrnia Leag Cnsrvtion Vters (PA)	8651	D	510 271-0900	25369
Califrnia-Nevada Methdst Homes (PA)	8361	D	510 893-8989	24450
Califrnia-Nevada Methdst Homes	8059	C	510 835-5511	21030
Carpenter Funds	6733	D	510 633-0333	12090
Cartridge Family Inc	5112	C	510 658-0400	8077
Cass Inc (PA)	5093	C	510 893-6476	7972
Catholic Charities of The Dioc (PA)	8322	D	510 768-3100	23538
Cellco Partnership	4812	D	510 267-0731	5356
Center For Elders Independence	6324	C	510 433-1150	10192
Center To Promote Healthcare A (PA)	8099	D	510 834-1000	22760
Central Parking Corporation	7521	D	510 832-7227	17678
Cgi Technologies Solutions Inc	7379	D	510 238-5300	16326
Ch2m Hill Inc	8711	C	510 604-4144	25606
Chapel of Chimes	7261	E	510 654-1288	13687
Charles Pankow Bldrs Ltd A Cal	1542	D	510 893-5170	1503
Childrens Hosp Oakland Res Inst	8733	D	510 450-7600	26612
Childrens Hospotal & Research (PA)	8062	A	510 428-3000	21319
Christian Church Homes	6531	C	510 893-2998	11317
Christopher Ransom Corporation (PA)	6726	C	510 345-9144	12060
Cim/Oakland City Center LLC	7011	C	510 451-4000	12460
City of Oakland	8322	B	510 238-6796	23582
City of Oakland	7999	E	510 238-3494	19138
City of Oakland	7999	D	510 268-9000	19139
Civicorps	4953	C	510 992-7800	6379
Claremont Country Club	7997	D	510 653-6789	18891

2019 Directory of California
Wholesalers and Services Companies

(P-0000) Products & Services Section entry number
(PA)=Parent Co (HQ)=Headquarters (DH)=Div Headquarters

Company	SIC	EMP	PHONE	ENTRY #
Claremont House Incorporated	8361	D	510 658-9266	24471
Clorox Services Company (HQ)	8741	D	510 271-7000	26812
Cohen Ventures Inc (PA)	8748	D	510 482-4420	27691
Computer Sciences Corporation	7379	D	510 645-3000	16330
Comrade Inc	7389	D	510 277-3400	17096
Condon-Johnson & Assoc Inc (PA)	1771	E	510 636-2100	3242
Consolidated Cleaning Services	7349	D	510 663-2585	14224
Covenant Care California LLC	8051	D	510 261-2628	20341
Covia Communities	8361	C	510 835-4700	24487
Creative Energy Foods Inc	5149	D	510 638-8668	8781
Crucible	8322	D	510 444-0919	23763
Custom Alloy Scrap Sales Inc (HQ)	5093	E	510 893-6476	7976
David Darroch	8111	D	510 835-9100	23023
Dealey Renton and Associates	6411	D	510 465-3090	10602
Destiny Arts Center	7999	E	510 597-1619	19158
District Council DC (PA)	8322	D	510 638-7600	23772
Dnv GL Energy Insights USA Inc	8748	E	510 891-0446	27707
Donahue Gallager Woods LLP (PA)	8111	D	415 381-4161	23051
Dorado Network Systems Corp	7372	C	650 227-7300	15652
Dreisbach Enterprises Inc (PA)	6519	C	510 533-6600	11168
Dreyers Grand Ice Cream Hold (DH)	5143	C	510 652-8187	8520
East Bay Asian Local Dev Corp	6513	C	510 267-1917	11010
East Bay Asian Youth Center	8322	E	510 533-1092	23776
East Bay Btncal Zoological Soc	7999	D	510 632-9525	19162
East Bay Community Foundation	8399	D	510 836-3223	24776
East Bay Foundation Grad Med	8099	D	510 437-4197	22794
East Bay Municipal Utility Dst	4941	D	866 403-2683	6241
East Bay Municipl Utility Distr	4941	D	866 403-2683	6242
East Bay Municipl Utility Distr	4953	D	866 403-2683	6391
East Bay Municipl Utilty Distr (PA)	4941	A	866 403-2683	6245
East Bay Municipl Utility Distr	4941	D	510 287-0760	6246
EBSC LP	8011	D	510 547-2244	19452
Encompass Health Corporation	8069	D	510 547-2244	22020
Engie Services US Inc (HQ)	8711	D	844 678-3772	25663
Environmental Health Hazard	8734	D	510 622-3200	26700
Fair Trade USA	8733	D	510 663-5260	26619
Family Bridges Inc	8322	C	510 839-2270	23794
Family Paths Inc (PA)	8093	D	510 893-9230	22578
Family Support Services	8322	D	510 204-2443	23799
Federal Express Corporation	4215	B	510 382-2344	4414
Federal Express Corporation	4513	D	510 465-5209	4825
Federal Express Corporation	4513	D	800 463-3339	4826
Fidelity Roof Company (PA)	1761	D	510 547-6330	3155
First Place For Youth (PA)	8322	E	510 272-0979	23807
First Transit Inc	4111	D	510 535-9192	3654
First Transit Inc	4111	D	510 437-8990	3655
Fitzgrald Abbott Beardsley LLP	8111	D	510 451-3300	23072
Fluid Inc (DH)	7371	D	877 343-3240	15163
Fruitvale Long Term Care LLC	8051	D	510 261-5613	20443
Future State	7379	D	925 956-4200	16373
General Services Cal Dept	8712	D	510 622-3101	26047
George E Masker Inc	1721	D	510 568-1206	2441
Geosyntec Consultants Inc	8711	E	510 836-3034	25711
Give Something Back Inc (PA)	5112	D	800 261-2619	8081
Golden State Warriors LLC	7941	D	510 986-2200	18519
Green Planet 21 Inc (PA)	5093	E	510 873-8777	7979
Grubb Co Inc	6531	D	510 339-0400	11494
GSC Logistics Inc (PA)	4214	C	510 844-3700	4348
Gt Nexus Inc (DH)	4813	D	510 808-2222	5574
Guardsmark LLC	7381	C	510 562-7606	16683
H2c2 & Associates Inc (PA)	1542	E	510 267-6181	1540
Hanna Brophy Mac Lean Mc Ale (PA)	8111	E	510 839-1180	23120
Hans Technologies Inc	1629	D	510 464-8018	2037
Hapag-Lloyd (america) LLC	4731	E	510 251-8405	5082
Health Care Workers Union (PA)	6512	C	510 251-1250	10894
Health Net California Inc	6324	B	510 465-9600	10208
Herc Rentals Inc	7359	C	510 633-2040	14513
High Street Hand Car Wash Inc	7549	D	510 536-4333	17862
Highcom Security Services	7381	D	510 893-7600	16696
Hntb-Gerwick JV	8712	D	510 839-8972	26064
Homewood Suites Management LLC	7011	E	510 663-2700	12696
Horizon Beverage Company	5181	D	510 465-2212	9003
Horizon Beverage Company LP	5181	D	510 465-2212	9004
Hospice & Home Health of E Bay	8082	C	510 632-4390	22333
IAC Publishing LLC	4813	D	510 985-7400	5582
IAC Search & Media Inc (HQ)	7375	C	510 985-7400	16231
Imperial Parking (us) LLC	7521	E	510 382-2140	17687
Independent Quality Care Inc	8059	D	510 836-3677	21119
Institute On Aging	8059	D	510 536-3377	21122
Intelliguard Security Services	7381	C	510 547-7656	16700
Interactive Solutions Inc (HQ)	7372	D	510 214-9002	15716
Itron Inc	1731	A	510 844-2800	2615
Jacobs Project Management Co	8742	D	510 457-2436	27286
Jaqui Foundation Inc	8999	E	510 562-4721	27936
Jetblue Airways Corporation	4512	D	510 381-1369	4787
K G O T V News Bureau	4832	D	510 451-4772	5731
Kaiser Foundation Hospital	8082	E	510 752-6295	22348
Kaiser Foundation Hospitals	8011	A	510 752-1000	19529
Kaiser Foundation Hospitals (HQ)	8062	C	510 271-6611	21483
Kaiser Foundation Hospitals	8062	A	510 752-1000	21485
Kaiser Foundation Hospitals	6324	D	510 752-7864	10222
Kaiser Foundation Hospitals	8011	A	510 987-1000	19599
Kaiser Foundation Hospitals	8062	B	510 891-3400	21510
Kaiser Foundation Hospitals	6324	D	510 251-0121	10256
Kaiser Fundation Hlth Plan Inc (PA)	6324	B	510 271-5800	10272
Kaiser Fundation Hlth Plan Inc	6324	D	510 752-7644	10273
Kaiser Fundation Hlth Plan Inc	6324	D	510 987-2255	10275
Kaiser Group Holdings Inc	8711	D	510 419-6000	25775
Kaiser Hlth Plan Asset MGT Inc	8741	E	510 271-5910	26914
Kaiser Permanente	8062	D	510 450-2109	21526
Kaiser Permanente Admin H	6324	C	559 448-4405	10276
Kaiserair Inc (PA)	5172	C	510 569-9622	8965
Katten Muchin Rosenman LLP	8111	D	415 360-5444	23162
Kazan McClain Satterley &	8111	D	877 995-6372	23165
Kids Overcoming LLC	8082	D	415 748-8052	22352
Kiewit Infrastructure West Co	1611	D	510 452-1400	1801
Ktgy Group Inc	8712	E	510 463-2097	26076
Ktvu Partnership Inc	4833	C	510 834-1212	5817
La Clinica De La Raza Inc	8011	C	510 535-6300	19628
La Clinica De La Raza Inc	8021	D	510 535-4700	20121
La Clinica De La Raza Inc	8011	C	510 535-6200	19630
Lake Merritt Hotel Associates	1522	E	510 832-2300	1300
Lapham Company Inc	6531	D	510 531-6000	11558
Laughlin Falbo Levy Moresi LLP (PA)	8111	D	510 628-0496	23193
Lazar Landscape Design & Cnstr	0781	D	510 444-5195	764
Lehar Sales Co	5144	D	510 465-3255	8534
Leidos Inc	8731	D	510 466-7138	26409
Lincoln (PA)	8093	D	510 273-4700	22613
Lincoln Child Center	8699	C	510 531-3111	25439
Lion Creek Senior Housing Part	6531	D	510 878-9120	11565
LN Curtis and Sons (PA)	5087	D	510 839-5111	7889
Lucid Design Group Inc	7373	D	510 907-0400	16000
M Arthur Gensler Jr Assoc Inc	8712	D	510 625-7400	26089
Magnetic Imaging Affilates	8071	D	510 204-1820	22108
Mariner Health Care Inc	8051	D	510 261-5200	20626
Marriott Foundation For People	8331	D	510 834-4700	24203
Marriott Hotels & Resorts	7011	D	510 451-4000	12879
Mason-Mcduffie Real Estate Inc	6531	D	510 834-2010	11592
Matson Navigation Company Inc (HQ)	4424	C	510 628-4000	4700
Mbh Enterprises Inc	5045	D	510 302-6680	7077
Medical Insurance Exchange Cal	6411	D	510 596-4935	10690
Meditab Software Inc	7372	D	510 632-2021	15756
Menke & Associates Inc (PA)	8748	D	415 362-5200	27785
Mercy Retirement and Care Ctr	8361	C	510 534-8540	24599
Meyers Nave Riback Silver & (PA)	8111	C	510 351-4300	23251
Michael Baker Intl Inc	8711	C	510 879-0950	25820
Moc Products Company Inc	7549	D	510 635-1230	17867
Monarch Place Piedmont LLC	8361	C	510 658-9266	24605
Monterey Mechanical Co (PA)	1629	E	510 632-3173	2047
Morgan Stanley & Co LLC	6211	D	510 839-8080	10000
Mufg Union Bank National Assn	6021	D	510 891-2495	9360
Multivision Inc (HQ)	7389	D	510 740-5600	17339
Museum of Childrens Art	7999	E	510 465-8770	19206
Nancy Smith Construction Inc	1522	E	510 923-1671	1302
National Rental (us) Inc	7514	D	510 877-4507	17646
Native American Health Ctr Inc (PA)	8011	D	510 535-4400	19704
Navis Holdings LLC	7371	D	510 267-5000	15300
Noble Tower Preservation LP	6531	D	510 444-5228	11633
Noodle Analytics Inc	7371	D	415 412-2139	15414
North Star Emergency Svcs Inc	4119	D	510 452-3400	3826
Northgate Ter Cmnty Partner LP	6531	E	510 465-9346	11635
Nt Sunset Inc	8733	E	510 420-3772	26644
O C Jones & Sons Inc	8748	D	510 663-6911	27808
Oakland Healthcare & Wellness	8051	C	323 330-6572	20672
Oakland Mrtime Spport Svcs Inc	4493	E	510 868-1005	4750
Oakland Museum of California	8412	D	510 318-8400	24897
Oakland Private Industry Counc	8331	D	510 768-4400	24212
Oakland Public Education Fund	6732	D	510 221-6968	12081
Oakland Unified School Dst	7349	D	510 535-2717	14335
Ocadian Care Centers LLC	8051	D	510 832-3222	20674
Officeworks Inc	7361	D	510 444-2161	14679
Opinion Dynamics Corp Fla Inc	8742	D	510 444-5050	27383
Otis Elevator Intl Inc	1796	D	510 874-5129	3474
Outsource Consulting Svcs Inc (PA)	7361	D	510 986-0686	14683
Pacific Gas and Electric Co	4911	D	510 450-5744	6071
Pacific Union Intl Inc	6531	B	510 338-1379	11654
Pacific Union Residental Brkg	6531	D	510 339-6460	11656
Pandora Media Inc (PA)	4832	C	510 451-4100	5748
Paradigm Staffing Solutions	7361	E	510 663-7860	14687
Paramount Theatre of Arts Inc	6512	D	510 893-2300	10926

Employment Codes: A=Over 500 employees, B=251-500,
C=101-250, D=51-100, E=50

2019 Directory of California
Wholesalers and Services Companies

© Mergent Inc. 1-800-342-5647

1625

GEOGRAPHIC

	SIC	EMP	PHONE	ENTRY #
Park Hotels & Resorts Inc	7011	C	510 635-5000	13023
Park Plaza Hotel	7011	E	510 635-5300	13046
Pasha Hawaii Trnspt Lines LLC	4424	D	510 271-1400	4701
Pasta Shop	5149	D	510 250-6005	8847
Paylocity Holding Corporation	7372	D	847 956-4850	15828
Peace Action West (PA)	8651	E	510 830-3600	25372
Permanente Federation LLC	8742	D	510 625-6920	27393
Permanente Medical Group Inc	8011	D	510 752-1000	19765
Permanente Medical Group Inc (DH)	8099	B	866 858-2226	22858
Permanente Medical Group Inc	8011	D	510 625-6262	19783
Permanente Medical Group Inc	8011	D	510 752-1190	19784
Phillips & Assoc Law Offs PC	8111	D	510 464-8040	23327
Playworks Education Energized (PA)	7999	E	510 893-4180	19218
Porrey Pines Bank Inc	6021	B	510 899-7500	9369
Port Dept City of Oakland (PA)	4491	B	510 627-1100	4731
Port Dept City of Oakland	4581	C	510 563-3300	4905
Prevention Institute	8742	D	510 444-4133	27399
Proactive Bus Solutions Inc	8741	C	510 302-0120	26997
Professonal Technical SEC Svcs	7381	B	510 645-9200	16765
Providence Health & Svcs - Ore	8062	B	510 444-0839	21667
Public Health Institute	8733	A	510 285-5500	26651
Ramsell Public Health Rx LLC	6411	D	510 587-2600	10756
Rcc Facility Incorporated	8059	D	510 658-2041	21192
Rdp Acquisition Company	8732	B	510 652-8187	26560
Regional Center of E Bay Inc	8322	C	510 383-1200	23989
Restaurant Depot LLC	5142	C	510 628-0600	8501
Ricoh Usa Inc	5044	E	510 839-6399	6981
Rmt Landscape Contractors Inc	0782	E	510 568-3208	932
Robert Half MGT Resources	8742	E	510 271-0910	27431
Rockyou Inc (PA)	7375	D	415 580-6400	16248
Rory V Parker	7381	C	510 595-5543	16777
Salestar LLC (PA)	5045	D	510 637-4700	7099
San Francisco Bay Area Rapid	4111	E	510 464-6000	3706
San Francisco Bay Area Rapid	4111	D	510 834-1297	3707
San Francisco Bay Area Rapid	4111	C	510 464-6126	3708
San Francisco Bay Area Rapid (PA)	4111	B	510 464-6000	3710
San Francisco Bay Area Rapid	4111	A	510 286-2893	3712
San Francisco Bay Area Rapid	4111	D	510 464-7000	3713
San Francisco Bay Area Rapid	4111	C	510 464-6000	3714
Schnitzer Steel Industries Inc	5093	D	510 444-3919	7991
Sea West Cast Gard Fdral Cr Un (PA)	6061	C	510 568-4100	9591
Sea-Logix LLC	4213	D	510 271-1400	4261
Securitas SEC Svcs USA Inc	7381	C	925 746-0552	16805
Security Central Inc	7699	D	510 652-2477	17988
Sedgwick Claims MGT Svcs Inc	6411	E	510 302-3000	10769
SEIU Local 1021	0761	C	510 350-9811	674
Seiu United Healthcare Workers (PA)	8631	C	510 251-1250	25079
Service King Holdings LLC	7532	C	510 562-9650	17738
Shimmick Construction Co Inc (HQ)	1629	C	510 777-5000	2061
Sierra Club (PA)	8641	C	415 977-5500	25248
Silverado Contractors Inc (PA)	1795	D	510 658-9960	3463
Simpson Gumpertz & Heger Inc	8711	C	510 835-0705	25916
Society of St Vincent (PA)	8699	D	510 638-7600	25465
Solar Spectrum LLC	1711	B	844 777-6527	2362
Southwest Airlines Co	4512	C	510 563-1000	4800
Southwest Airlines Co	4512	C	510 563-1234	4803
Spectrum Credit Union	6061	C	510 251-6000	9594
SSC Oakland Excell Oper Co LP	8051	D	510 261-5200	20777
Standard Iron & Metals Co	5093	E	510 535-0222	7998
State Compensation Insur Fund	6331	C	510 577-3000	10397
Sterling Hsa Inc	7389	E	800 617-4729	17488
Stuart Lovett	8011	D	510 444-0790	19953
Sunrise Senior Living LLC	8051	D	303 410-0500	20821
Sutter Health	8011	B	510 547-2244	19968
Sutter Health	8011	C	510 869-8777	19969
Sutter Health	5122	C	510 869-8835	8214
Swissport Fueling Inc	5172	D	510 562-1701	8968
T25cl Entertainment LLC	7812	C	951 308-2040	18128
Ted Jacob Engrg Group Inc (PA)	8711	D	510 763-4880	25941
Teecom	8711	D	510 337-2800	25942
Telecare Corporation	8063	C	510 261-9191	21982
Telecare Corporation	8063	C	510 535-5115	21991
Telecom Inc	7389	D	510 873-8283	17505
Tree Sculpture Group	0782	D	510 562-4000	949
Tucson Hotels LP	7011	B	510 658-9300	13347
Turner Construction Company	1542	E	510 267-8100	1684
United Parcel Service Inc OH	4215	C	510 813-5662	4466
URS Group Inc	8711	C	510 893-3600	25972
URS Group Inc	8711	D	415 896-5858	25973
URS Group Inc	8711	D	415 896-5858	25981
URS-Gei Joint Venture	8711	E	510 874-3051	25983
Veterans Health Administration	8011	B	510 267-7820	20065
Volunteers of America Greater	8322	C	510 663-4546	24125
Wallis Fashions Inc	7389	C	510 763-8018	17578
Waste MGT of Alameda Cnty (HQ)	4953	A	510 613-8710	6521

	SIC	EMP	PHONE	ENTRY #
Waterfront Plaza Hotel LLC	7011	D	510 836-3800	13383
Waypoint Real Estate Group LLC	6531	D	510 250-2200	11824
Wells & Bennett Realtors (PA)	6531	D	510 531-7000	11826
Wells Fargo Bank National Assn	6021	D	510 530-3095	9405
Wendel Rosen Black & Dean LLP (PA)	8111	D	510 834-6600	23433
West Oakland Health Council	8093	C	510 835-9610	22715
Westcoast Childrens Clinic	8093	C	510 269-9030	22716
Wested	8733	D	510 302-4200	26673
Willow Tree Nursing Center	8059	D	510 261-2628	21256
Wipfli LLP	8742	D	510 768-0066	27523
Wood Environment &	8711	C	510 663-4100	26004
Workers Compensation (PA)	6331	C	888 229-2472	10416
Xantrion Incorporated	7379	E	510 272-4701	16536
Young MNS Chrstn Assn of E Bay	8641	D	510 654-9622	25353
Young MNS Chrstn Assn of E Bay	8641	A	510 451-8039	25356
Zillow Group Inc	7374	A	415 836-6760	16202

OAKLEY, CA - Contra Costa County

	SIC	EMP	PHONE	ENTRY #
Coldwell Banker Amaral & Assoc	6531	D	925 439-7400	11333
Flordo Oakley Hall	6512	C	925 625-4076	10876
Foundation Constructors Inc (PA)	1629	D	925 754-6633	2033

OCCIDENTAL, CA - Sonoma County

	SIC	EMP	PHONE	ENTRY #
Alliance Rdwods Cnfrnce Grunds	7032	D	707 874-3507	13444
Westminster Woods Camp & Confe	7032	E	707 874-2426	13457

OCEANO, CA - San Luis Obispo County

	SIC	EMP	PHONE	ENTRY #
Phelan & Taylor Produce Co	0723	C	805 489-2413	554

OCEANSIDE, CA - San Diego County

	SIC	EMP	PHONE	ENTRY #
Aegis Asssted Living Prpts LLC	8361	D	760 806-3600	24409
Allied Swiss Limited	6512	C	760 941-1702	10850
American Golf Corporation	7997	D	760 757-2100	18839
AT&T Services Inc	4813	C	760 722-7261	5505
Bergensons Property Svcs Inc	7349	A	760 631-5111	14200
Brother Benno Foundation Inc (PA)	8361	D	760 439-1244	24444
Business and Support Services	8021	D	760 725-5187	20112
Business and Support Services	8351	E	760 725-2817	24270
Central Indiana Hdwr Co Inc (PA)	5072	C	317 558-5700	7582
Cinemastar Luxury Theaters	7832	B	760 945-2500	18281
CK Enterprises Inc	7389	D	760 967-8863	17086
County of San Diego	8322	C	760 754-3456	23725
Cox Automotive Inc	5012	B	760 754-3600	6588
Cox California Telcom LLC	4899	C	760 966-0447	5977
E R I T Inc (PA)	8361	D	760 433-6024	24512
E R I T Inc	8361	C	760 721-1706	24513
El Camino Rental	7359	E	760 722-7368	14502
Future Energy Corporation	1742	D	760 477-9700	2885
Gfp Oceanside Block 21 LLC	7011	D	760 722-1003	12603
Go-Staff Inc	7361	A	760 730-8520	14630
Goodwill Inds San Diego Cnty	8699	B	760 806-7670	25424
Impact Solutions LLC	7361	E	760 231-0450	14645
Infrastructure Engrg Corp	8711	E	760 529-0795	25745
La Cantina Doors Inc	5039	E	888 221-0141	6934
Labor Ready Inc	7363	C	760 433-4980	14871
Laconstructora Co Inc	1521	E	760 439-7686	1190
Marine Corps United States	8069	A	760 725-1304	22034
McAlister Institute For Treat	8093	C	760 726-4451	22618
Mellano & Co	5193	C	760 433-9550	9148
Merrill Gardens LLC	6513	D	760 414-9880	11072
Mission Linen Supply	7213	C	760 757-9099	13533
Mold Testing and Inspection	7389	D	760 643-1834	17334
Monterey Financial Svcs Inc (PA)	6141	C	760 639-3500	9723
Nitto Denko Technical Corp	8732	D	760 435-7011	26553
North Coast Surgery Center	8093	D	760 940-0997	22624
North County Transit District (PA)	4111	C	760 966-6500	3690
Ocean Holiday LP	7011	C	760 231-7000	12969
Oceans Eleven Casino	7011	B	760 439-6988	12974
Oceanside Lifeguards	7999	D	760 435-4500	19212
OConnell Landscape Maint Inc	0782	E	760 630-4963	913
Pacific Marine Credit Union (PA)	6061	C	760 430-7511	9578
Pardee Tree Nursery	5193	D	760 630-5400	9156
Pendleton Farms	0171	C	760 754-2359	112
Pepperjam LLC	7371	C	760 585-7150	15350
Primeco Painting & Cnstr	1721	D	760 967-8278	2466
R & R Profession	8049	C	760 754-9020	20197
Rancho Del Oro Ldscp Maint Inc	0781	D	760 726-0215	781
S and R Towing Inc (PA)	7549	E	760 722-6686	17870
San Diego Coastl Med Group Inc	8099	C	760 901-5259	22876
Scripps Health	8011	D	760 901-5200	19873
Service Corp International	6553	D	760 754-6600	11951
Shieldx Networks Inc	7371	E	760 724-2700	15442
Smart & Final Stores LLC	5141	D	760 726-7274	8458
Suja Life LLC	5149	C	855 879-7852	8873
Sundance Natural Foods Company	0179	E	760 945-9898	239
Superior Support Services Inc	8741	B	559 458-0507	27054
Tri City Orthopedic Sgy & Mdcl	8011	E	760 724-9000	20011

Mergent email: customerrelations@mergent.com

2019 Directory of California
Wholesalers and Services Companies

(P-0000) Products & Services Section entry number
(PA)=Parent Co (HQ)=Headquarters (DH)=Div Headquarters

1626

Company	SIC	EMP	PHONE	ENTRY #
Tri-City Hospital District (PA)	8062	A	760 724-8411	21861
Veridiam Allied Swiss	8748	D	760 941-1702	27896
Waste Management Cal Inc	4953	D	760 439-2824	6513
World Mark of Oceanside	7011	D	760 721-0890	13417
YMCA of San Diego County	8641	D	760 754-6042	25293
YMCA of San Diego County	8641	D	760 758-0808	25305
YMCA of San Diego County	8641	D	760 757-8270	25306

OJAI, CA - Ventura County

Company	SIC	EMP	PHONE	ENTRY #
ARC of Ventura County Inc	8093	D	805 650-8611	22506
Coldwell Banker Property Shop	6531	D	805 646-7288	11337
Community Memorial Health Sys	8062	C	805 646-1401	21342
Gables of Ojai LLC	6513	D	805 646-1446	11025
Hotrollergirl Productions	7941	D	530 521-2745	18520
Krishnmrti Foundation of Amer (PA)	6732	E	805 646-2726	12079
Mf Daily Oxnard Ranch Partnr	7992	E	805 646-5633	18734
Ojai Raptor Center	0752	D	805 649-6884	631
Ojai Valley Inn Golf Course	7011	A	805 646-2420	12976
Ovis Llc	7011	A	805 646-5511	12991

OLIVEHURST, CA - Yuba County

Company	SIC	EMP	PHONE	ENTRY #
Ampla Health	8011	D	530 743-4614	19289
Lindhurst Dental Clinic	8021	E	530 743-4614	20126
Naumes Inc	0181	E	530 743-2055	287
Nordic Industries Inc	1629	D	530 742-7124	2048
Nordic/Great Lakes E&I JV	1629	D	530 742-7124	2049
Rodgz Farm Labor Contg LLC	0761	D	530 329-8403	671
Shoei Foods USA Inc	5141	D	530 742-7866	8452

OLYMPIC VALLEY, CA - Placer County

Company	SIC	EMP	PHONE	ENTRY #
Bruce Olson Construction Inc	1521	C	530 581-1087	1132
Cncml A California Ltd Partnr	7011	D	530 583-1578	12471
Squaw Valley Development Co (HQ)	7011	D	530 452-6985	13258
Squaw Valley Ski Corporation (DH)	7011	C	530 583-6985	13259

ONTARIO, CA - San Bernardino County

Company	SIC	EMP	PHONE	ENTRY #
3M Company	4225	C	909 974-3004	4520
A-1 Delivery Co	4212	D	909 444-1220	3962
Accentcare Home Health Cal Inc	8082	D	909 605-7000	22191
ACI Construction Company Inc	8711	E	909 391-4477	25499
Aecom Technical Services Inc	8711	E	909 554-5000	25517
Air Control Systems Inc	1711	E	909 786-4230	2089
Alaska Airlines Inc	4512	C	800 426-0333	4760
AMC Entertainment Inc	7832	E	909 476-1288	18256
American Fidelity Assurance Co	6411	D	909 941-1175	10518
American Financial Network Inc	8742	C	951 582-2655	27130
Americold Logistics LLC	4222	E	909 390-4950	4495
Ameriwest Industries Inc	5072	E	909 930-1898	7575
Artistic Maintenance Inc	0782	E	909 390-5156	800
AT&T Corp	4812	D	909 930-6508	5266
Atchesons Express Inc	4212	E	714 808-9199	3976
Automotive Tstg & Dev Svcs Inc (PA)	7549	C	909 390-1100	17851
Avis Rent A Car System Inc	7514	D	909 974-2192	17623
Beauty 21 Cosmetics Inc	5122	C	909 945-2220	8146
Behavoral Autism Therapies LLC (PA)	8322	C	909 483-5000	23509
Bella Vista Healthcare Center	8051	D	909 985-2731	20259
Biagi Bros Inc	4213	C	909 390-6910	4107
Bio-Med Services Inc	8099	D	909 235-4400	22742
Blumenthal Distributing Inc (PA)	5021	C	909 930-2000	6712
Boshart Automotive Tstg Svcs	7389	D	909 466-1602	17038
BP Industries Incorporated	5023	D	909 481-0227	6751
C E B M Inc	7349	E	909 975-4440	14205
CA Station Management Inc	1623	C	909 245-6251	1901
Calico Brands Inc	5199	E	909 930-5000	9201
Canon Solutions America Inc	5044	D	909 390-7400	6953
Cardinal Health Inc	5122	D	909 605-0900	8157
CAT Logistics Inc	4225	D	909 390-1920	4539
Cbre Inc	6531	D	909 418-2000	11284
Celestica LLC	5065	B	909 418-6986	7459
Centimark Corporation	1761	E	909 652-9280	3134
Chino Valley Sawdust Inc	4953	D	909 947-5983	6373
Chino-Pacific Warehouse Corp (PA)	4225	D	909 545-8100	4540
Cintas Corporation No 3	7213	C	909 930-9096	13525
Cintas Corporation No 3	7218	D	909 390-4912	13604
Citizens Business Bank (HQ)	6022	C	909 980-4030	9432
Coastal Pacific Fd Distrs Inc	5141	C	909 947-2066	8391
Comfort Systems Usa Inc	1711	D	909 390-6677	2166
Concord Foods Inc (PA)	5141	D	909 975-2000	8392
Contemporary Services Corp	7376	D	909 740-3834	16265
Converse Inc	5139	C	909 974-5695	8353
Country Inn &SUite By Carlson	7011	E	909 937-6000	12485
CU Direct Corporation (PA)	7371	C	909 481-2300	15091
Customized Dist Svcs Inc	8742	D	909 947-0084	27210
Dal-Tile Corporation	5032	D	909 390-7000	6888
Damao Luggage Intl Inc	5099	A	909 923-6531	8025
David Evans and Associates Inc	8711	E	909 481-5750	25639
Dennis Foland Inc	5099	D	909 930-9900	8027

Company	SIC	EMP	PHONE	ENTRY #
Dependable Highway Express Inc	4213	D	909 923-0065	4124
Dhl Supply Chain (usa)	4225	D	623 907-2338	4547
Directv LLC	4841	D	909 509-4790	5899
Diversity Bus Solutions Inc	7361	C	909 395-0243	14602
Dlt Growers Inc	0181	E	909 947-8198	253
Dominos Pizza LLC	4226	C	909 390-1990	4674
Dpi Specialty Foods West Inc (DH)	5141	C	909 975-1019	8402
Edc Service Corporation (del)	6099	D	909 390-4747	9680
Electrolux Home Products Inc	5064	D	909 605-9448	7413
Emser Tile LLC	1743	D	909 974-1600	2996
F M Tarbell Co	6531	D	951 270-1022	11440
F R T International Inc	4731	C	909 390-4892	5062
Federal Express Corporation	7389	B	800 463-3339	17169
Federal Express Corporation	4513	D	909 390-3237	4831
Fedex Supply Chain	4225	D	909 605-9210	4557
Fortune Avenue Foods Inc	5141	D	909 930-5989	8407
Fuji Natural Foods Inc (HQ)	0182	D	909 947-1008	312
Fullmer Construction	1541	C	909 947-9467	1399
Gardner Trucking Inc (HQ)	4213	B	909 563-5606	4184
General Electric Company	7699	B	909 605-7603	17946
Genuine Parts Distributors	5013	C	562 692-9034	6642
Gold Star Foods Inc (PA)	5142	C	909 843-9600	8490
Gregg Electric Inc	1731	C	909 983-1794	2594
Gringteam Inc	7011	B	909 605-4222	12622
Grove Lumber & Bldg Sups Inc (PA)	5031	C	909 947-0277	6825
Guard-Systems Inc	7381	B	909 947-5400	16669
Hci Systems Inc (PA)	1731	E	909 628-7773	2602
HHS Communications Inc	1731	D	909 230-5170	2603
HMC Group (PA)	8712	D	909 989-9979	26062
HMC Group	8712	D	909 980-8058	26063
Hospital Business Services Inc	7389	C	909 235-4400	17226
Hub Construction Spc Inc	5082	E	909 947-4669	7682
Hub Group Trucking Inc	4212	C	951 693-9813	4023
Iapmo Research and Testing Inc (HQ)	8611	D	909 472-4100	24961
Impact Logistics	7361	E	909 937-9035	14644
Industrial Labor MGT Group Inc	7361	C	323 582-4100	14648
Inland Christian Home Inc	8051	C	909 395-9322	20544
Inland Empire Chapter-Assn of	8699	D	512 478-9000	25432
Inqbrands Inc	7379	D	909 390-7788	16397
Intercontinental Hotels Group	7011	C	909 930-5555	12774
International Assoc of Plmbng (PA)	8611	C	909 472-4100	24963
Island Hospitality MGT LLC	7011	E	909 937-6788	12784
Jack Jones Trucking Inc	4212	D	909 456-2500	4026
Jacobs Engineering Group Inc	8711	D	909 974-2700	25760
Jeeva Corp	1731	E	909 238-4073	2617
Jett Pro Line Maintenance Inc (PA)	4581	D	909 980-0552	4897
K A R Construction Inc	1771	D	909 988-5054	3278
Kaiser Foundation Hospitals	8011	A	909 724-5000	19573
Kaiser Foundation Hospitals	6324	D	888 750-0036	10241
Kaman Industrial Tech Corp	5085	E	909 390-7919	7853
Keystone Automotive Inds Inc	5013	D	909 986-4586	6652
Kf Ontario Healthcare Inc	8059	E	909 984-6713	21125
Kindred Healthcare Oper Inc	8062	B	909 391-0333	21538
Lanting Hay Dealer Inc	5191	D	909 563-5601	9084
Las Vegas / LA Express Inc (PA)	4213	C	909 972-3100	4213
Lee & Assoc Comm Real Est Svcs	6531	E	909 989-7771	11561
Liberty Hardware Mfg Corp	5072	D	909 605-2300	7594
Liberty Mutual Insurance Co	6331	D	909 476-6688	10367
Los Angeles World Airports	4581	D	909 544-5490	4899
Main Street Fibers Inc	4953	D	909 986-6310	6414
Majestic Terminal Services Inc	4141	D	909 937-2580	3889
Marriott International Inc	7011	C	909 937-6788	12895
Mazar Corp	7381	D	909 292-8269	16729
McIntyre Company (PA)	1791	D	909 962-6322	3386
Menifee Management Corp	7997	D	951 672-4824	18970
Menzies Aviation (texas) Inc	4581	D	909 937-3998	4901
Michael Baker Intl Inc	8748	E	909 974-4900	27788
Mills Corporation	6512	D	909 484-8300	10913
Mission Landscape Service	0782	D	909 947-7290	899
Mondelez Global LLC	5149	D	909 605-0140	8828
Myers Power Products Inc (PA)	5063	C	909 923-1800	7380
NAFTA Distributors	5141	E	909 605-7515	8433
National Distribution Centers	4731	D	909 390-5696	5115
National Employee Benefits LLC	8742	D	877 778-8330	27358
National General Insurance Co	6331	D	909 944-8085	10383
Nationwide Trans Inc (PA)	4731	D	909 355-3211	5116
Nordstrom Inc	4225	B	909 390-1040	4600
North American Med MGT Cal Inc (DH)	8741	D	909 605-8000	26964
Ontario Convention Center Corp	7389	D	909 937-3000	17370
Ontario Health Educatn Co Inc	8082	E	951 817-8553	22381
Ontario Montclar Sch Dist Food	8099	D	909 930-6360	22855
Ontario Refrigeration Svc Inc (PA)	1711	C	909 984-2771	2298
Optec Displays Inc	5046	D	626 369-7188	7143
Oregon PCF Bldg Pdts Maple Inc	5031	C	909 627-4043	6845
Otto International Inc (PA)	5136	E	909 937-1998	8272

Employment Codes: A=Over 500 employees, B=251-500,
C=101-250, D=51-100, E=50

2019 Directory of California
Wholesalers and Services Companies

© Mergent Inc. 1-800-342-5647
1627

GEOGRAPHIC

Company	SIC	EMP	PHONE	ENTRY #
Owens & Minor Inc	5047	D	909 944-2100	7202
Paat & Kimmel Development Inc	1542	D	909 315-8074	1605
Pacific Rebar Inc	1791	D	909 984-7199	3389
Paramount Restyling Auto Inc (PA)	5013	D	909 781-6492	6663
Park Hotels & Resorts Inc	7011	C	909 980-3420	13026
Park Hotels & Resorts Inc	7011	C	909 980-0400	13036
Patton Sales Corp (PA)	5051	C	909 988-0661	7296
Penske Logistics LLC	4213	A	800 529-6531	4243
Pentel of America Ltd	5112	E	909 975-2200	8086
Pepper Tree Motel	7011	E	909 988-2646	13057
Prize Proz	8742	E	909 509-8600	27402
Pro-Med Hlth Care Administrator	8741	D	909 932-1045	26996
R & B Wholesale Distrs Inc (PA)	5064	C	909 230-5400	7426
Rahf IV Grove LP	6513	E	216 621-6060	11105
Raymond Handling Solutions Inc	5084	D	909 930-9399	7793
Redlands Employment Services	7361	B	951 688-0083	14719
Ridgeside Construction Inc	1521	D	909 218-7593	1226
Ruuhwa Dann and Associates Inc	4953	C	909 467-4800	6454
San Dimas Luggage Company	5099	C	909 510-8820	8057
Scandia Recreation Centers	7993	D	909 390-3092	18788
Sears Roebuck and Co	7699	C	909 390-4210	17987
Securitas SEC Svcs USA Inc	7381	D	909 974-3160	16793
Shii LLC	6531	E	909 354-8000	11764
Sigmanet Inc (HQ)	5045	C	909 230-7500	7102
Signal 88 LLC	7381	A	714 713-5306	16827
Smg Food and Beverage LLC (PA)	7389	D	909 937-3000	17473
Solar Link International Inc	5085	C	909 605-7789	7872
Southtown Industrial Park	6512	E	909 947-3768	10950
Spectrum MGT Holdg Co LLC	4841	D	909 821-8159	5945
SS Heritage Inn Ontario LLC	7011	D	909 937-5000	13260
Synnex Corporation	4225	C	909 923-8900	4638
Target Corporation	4226	C	909 937-5500	4687
Taylored Services LLC (DH)	4225	D	909 510-4800	4641
Taylored Services Holdings LLC (HQ)	4731	D	909 510-4800	5177
Taylored Svcs Parent Co Inc (PA)	4731	D	909 510-4800	5178
Tcm Group LLC	8741	E	909 527-8580	27058
Technicolor HM Entrmt Svcs Inc	7819	D	909 974-2016	18226
Technicolor Thomson Group	7819	B	909 974-2222	18230
Test-Rite Products Corp (DH)	5023	D	909 605-9899	6791
Texas Home Health America LP (PA)	8049	D	972 201-3800	20206
Todays Vi LLC	7011	D	909 980-2200	13331
Tokai Intl Holdings Inc (PA)	6719	E	909 930-5000	12010
Toyo Tire USA Corp.	5014	E	562 431-6502	6699
Transport Drivers Inc	7363	C	909 937-3312	14924
Turbine Repair Services LLC (PA)	7699	D	909 947-2256	17999
Ua Galaxy Los Cerritos	7832	D	562 865-6499	18322
Uline Inc	5199	D	909 605-7090	9264
Ultra Solutions LLC	5047	E	909 628-1778	7227
Unifirst Corporation	7218	C	909 390-8670	13625
United Parcel Service Inc OH	7389	A	909 974-7250	17538
United Parcel Service Inc OH	4513	C	909 974-7190	4852
United Parcel Service Inc OH	4215	D	909 974-7000	4482
United Road Towing Inc	7549	C	909 923-6100	17879
URS Group Inc	8711	D	909 980-4000	25975
US Elogistics Service Corp	4225	D	732 357-6665	4650
US Merchants Fincl Group Inc	7389	C	909 923-3388	17554
UST Development Inc	4812	C	626 205-1123	5425
Verizon New York Inc	5065	D	909 481-7897	7559
Vertex Coatings Inc	1721	D	909 923-5795	2490
Vitco Distributors Inc	5113	D	909 355-1300	8136
Vitran Logistics Inc	4225	D	909 972-3100	4655
Wade & Lowe A Prof Corp (PA)	8111	D	909 483-6700	23423
Waxies Enterprises Inc	5087	C	909 942-3100	7901
Xpo Logistics Supply Chain Inc	4731	D	909 975-6300	5202
Xtreme Security Services Inc	7381	E	909 390-6818	16862

ORANGE, CA - Orange County

Company	SIC	EMP	PHONE	ENTRY #
ABF Freight System Inc	4213	E	714 974-2485	4092
Adair Enterprises	7922	D	714 998-5551	18338
Aecom Usa Inc	8748	D	714 567-2501	27629
Aerospace Corporation	8733	B	714 248-1194	26579
Alan Smith Pool Plastering Inc	1742	D	714 628-9494	2837
Alignment Health Plan	6324	D	323 728-7232	10180
Alignment Healthcare USA LLC (PA)	8099	D	844 310-2247	22725
All Seasons Framing Corp	1751	E	714 634-2324	3015
All-Pro Remodeling	1521	D	714 288-1314	1111
Alliance Funding Group	7819	D	800 978-8817	18177
Alliedbarton Security Svcs LLC	7381	C	626 213-3100	16549
Alliedbarton Security Svcs LLC	7381	C	714 260-0805	16559
American Advisors Group (PA)	6282	E	866 948-0003	10051
American Contractors Inc	1711	D	714 282-5700	2104
American Intgrted Rsources Inc	8741	D	714 921-4100	26756
American Multi-Cinema Inc	7832	D	714 769-4288	18263
American Residential Svcs LLC	1711	D	714 634-1826	2115
American Technologies Inc (PA)	1521	C	714 283-9990	1116
Ameripride Services Inc	7213	E	714 385-8991	13511
Ameriquest Capital Corporation (PA)	6163	B	714 564-0600	9873
Amerisourcebergen Corporation	8741	C	610 727-7000	26758
Amerisourcebergen Corporation	8741	C	714 704-4407	26759
Anaheim Ca LLC	7011	D	714 634-4500	12320
Arbormed Inc (PA)	8099	C	714 689-1500	22738
Architects Orange	8712	C	714 639-9860	26023
Ashunya Inc	7371	D	714 385-1900	15004
Atc Services Inc	8712	B	213 593-8100	26024
Avanti Agency Corporation	7389	B	714 935-0900	17021
B C Rentals Inc	5084	D	714 974-1190	7728
Bapko Metal Inc	1791	D	714 639-9380	3362
Beks Acquisition Inc	1781	E	714 744-2990	3348
Bergen Brunswig Drug Company	5122	A	714 385-4000	8147
Bernel Inc	1711	C	714 778-6070	2142
Boyle Engineering Corporation (HQ)	8711	D	949 476-3300	25574
Boyle Engineering Corporation	8711	D	714 543-5274	25575
Cal/Pac Paintings & Coatings	1721	D	714 628-1514	2427
Calnev Pipe Line LLC	8711	C	714 560-4400	25588
Cashcall Inc	6141	A	949 752-4600	9705
Cellco Partnership	4812	D	714 921-5130	5309
Cellco Partnership	4812	D	714 564-0050	5322
Center For Indvdual and Fam Th	8322	C	714 558-9266	23548
Chapman Global Medical Center	8062	B	714 633-0011	21312
Chapman University	7389	C	714 997-6821	17071
Childrens Healthcare Cal	8011	A	714 997-3000	19376
Childrens Healthcare Cal (PA)	8069	A	714 997-3000	22004
Childrens Hospital Orange Cnty	8069	D	714 997-3000	22008
Childrens Hospital Orange Cnty	8069	B	949 365-2416	22009
Choc Health Alliance	6324	C	714 565-5100	10193
Choic Admini Insur Servi	6411	B	714 542-4200	10582
Cik Power Distributors LLC	8741	D	714 938-0297	26804
Cirtech Inc	7389	E	714 921-0860	17074
Citigroup Inc	6162	D	714 938-0748	9792
City of Orange	8322	D	714 744-7264	23583
City of Orange	7999	E	714 744-7272	19140
Cleveland Marble LP	1741	D	714 998-3280	2801
Cleveland Wrecking Company (DH)	1795	D	626 967-4287	3450
Cmf Inc	1761	D	714 637-2409	3139
Coastal Building Services Inc.	7349	B	714 775-2855	14220
Cobb Waterblasting Inc	7349	D	714 769-2622	14221
Colonial Home Care Svcs Inc	8082	C	714 289-7220	22267
Companion Home Hlth & Hospice	8082	C	714 560-8177	22270
Comppartners Inc	8082	D	949 253-3111	22275
Conexis Bneft Admnistrators LP (HQ)	6411	C	714 835-5006	10592
Cornerstone Family Svcs LLC	8082	C	714 744-3800	22277
County of Orange	8322	C	714 704-8000	23700
County of Orange	8322	D	714 935-6435	23702
County Whl Elc Co Los Angeles	5063	D	714 633-3801	7352
Cruz Modular Inc (PA)	4214	D	714 283-2890	4340
De Par Inc	8734	D	714 771-6900	26692
Destination Science LLC	8748	C	714 289-9100	27705
Doctors of Affiliated	8741	D	714 539-3100	26842
Dynamic Auto Images Inc	7542	B	714 981-4367	17813
Electronic Commerce LLC	6159	D	800 770-5520	9756
Elite Nursing Services Inc	7361	E	714 919-7898	14609
Elliott Auto Supply Co Inc	5013	E	800 278-6394	6637
Emergency Medicine Specialist	8062	D	714 543-9811	21408
Enterprise Rent-A-Car (DH)	7515	D	657 221-4400	17654
Ergs Aim Hotel Realty LLC	7011	D	714 938-1111	12561
ESA P Prtfolio Oper Lessee LLC	7011	D	714 639-8608	12564
Fedex Freight Corporation	4231	C	714 637-9346	4691
Ford Plastering Inc	1771	B	714 921-0624	3255
Frick Paper Company	5113	C	323 726-8200	8102
Geek Squad Inc	7379	D	714 938-0380	16382
General Coatings Corporation	1721	C	858 587-1277	2438
General Underground	1711	D	714 632-8646	2220
Handyman Connection	7299	E	714 288-0077	13747
Harvest Landscape Entps Inc	0782	C	714 693-8100	856
Hill Brothers Chemical Company (PA)	5169	C	714 998-8800	8928
Hit Portfolio II Trs LLC	7011	C	714 938-1111	12687
Holmes & Narver Inc (HQ)	8711	D	714 567-2400	25739
Honeywell International Inc	5063	E	714 283-0110	7365
Interior Electric Incorporated	1731	D	714 771-9098	2613
Investment Concepts Inc (PA)	6552	C	714 283-5800	11881
Jack P Selman	8712	D	714 639-9860	26070
Jezowski & Markel Contrs Inc	1771	C	714 978-2222	3271
John Jory Corporation (PA)	1742	B	714 279-7901	2903
K & S Air Conditioning Inc	1711	C	714 685-0077	2248
K T W Productions Inc.	5023	A	714 685-0428	6769
Kaiser Foundation Hospitals	6324	D	714 748-7622	10259
Kaiser Foundation Hospitals	6324	D	888 988-2800	10270
Kings Seafood Company LLC	5146	D	714 771-6655	8581
Kondaur Capital Corporation (PA)	6162	C	714 352-2038	9822
Larkin Leasing Inc	1623	D	714 528-3232	1945
Leaf Commercial Capital Inc	8742	E	866 219-7924	27300

(P-0000) Products & Services Section entry number
(PA)=Parent Co (HQ)=Headquarters (DH)=Div Headquarters

	SIC	EMP	PHONE	ENTRY #
Leonard Chaidez Inc	0783	D	714 279-8173	975
Liberty Mutual Insurance Co	6331	C	714 937-1400	10368
Lonestar Sierra LLC	5085	C	866 575-5680	7857
Lres Corporation (PA)	6531	D	714 520-5737	11572
Lucky Strike Entertainment LLC	7933	D	248 374-3420	18494
M S International Inc (PA)	5032	B	714 685-7500	6901
Madden Corporation	7389	D	714 922-1670	17308
Main Street Specialty Surgery	8062	D	714 704-1900	21575
Maintech Incorporated	7371	C	714 921-8000	15269
Manufacturing Solutions Inc (PA)	8741	B	714 453-0100	26937
Marina Landscape Inc	0781	D	714 939-6600	767
Mark 1 Mortgage Corporation (PA)	6163	E	714 752-5700	9894
Marne Construction Inc	1771	D	714 935-0995	3284
Martin Integrated Systems	1742	D	714 998-9100	2913
Matrix Service Inc	1623	D	714 289-4419	1953
MB Coatings Inc	7389	D	714 625-2118	17316
Medical Specialties Managers	8742	C	714 571-5000	27334
Merical LLC	7389	D	714 283-9551	17325
Meyer Coatings Inc	1721	E	714 467-4600	2457
Miller Environmental Inc	1795	D	714 385-0099	3457
Monroe Operations LLC	8069	C	714 288-0872	22036
Mx Courier Systems Inc	7389	E	714 288-8622	17341
Nestle Waters North Amer Inc	5149	D	714 532-6220	8833
Newport Ch International LLC (PA)	5093	D	714 572-8881	7985
Nexinfo Solutions Inc	5045	E	714 368-1452	7084
Omega Insurance Services	6411	E	714 973-0311	10723
Optisource Technologies Inc	7334	E	714 288-0825	14091
Orange Children & Parents	8351	C	714 639-4000	24360
Orange Coast Masonry Acquisit	1741	D	714 538-4386	2819
Orange County Association (PA)	8621	D	714 547-7559	25032
Orange County Health Auth	8621	D	714 246-8500	25033
Orange County Trnsp Auth (PA)	4111	B	714 636-7433	3694
Orange County Trnsp Auth	4111	A	714 999-1726	3695
Orange Healthcare & Wellness	8051	C	714 633-3568	20681
P & D Consultants Inc (HQ)	8711	E	714 835-4447	25856
P H S Management Group (PA)	8742	D	714 547-7551	27384
P J Video Services Inc	7812	D	714 705-6088	18089
Padilla Construction Company	1742	C	714 685-8500	2936
Pavilion Surgery Center LLC	8011	D	714 744-8850	19754
Pentron Clinical Tech LLC	8071	D	203 265-7397	22120
Planned Parenthood/Orange and (PA)	8093	C	714 633-6373	22647
Platinum Strands Salon	7231	D	714 532-2633	13669
Prospect Medical Systems Inc (HQ)	8741	C	714 667-8156	27002
Providence Speech Hearing Ctr	8093	E	714 639-4990	22656
Raymond Group (PA)	8741	D	714 771-7670	27012
Red Hawk Fire & SEC CA Inc	1731	C	714 685-8100	2697
Red Pointe Roofing LP (PA)	1761	D	714 685-0010	3194
Rehabltation Inst Southern Cal (PA)	8093	C	714 633-7400	22660
Retail Services Wis Corp	7389	D	714 637-3431	17431
Rfid Textile Services Inc	7218	C	714 998-6109	13619
Rick Hamm Construction Inc	1611	D	714 532-0815	1841
Rika Corporation	1791	D	949 830-9050	3395
RJ Noble Company (PA)	1611	C	714 637-1550	1842
Robert Half International Inc	7361	C	714 450-9838	14730
Roger L Crumley MD Inc	8011	E	714 456-5750	19830
Roth Staffing Companies LP (PA)	7363	D	714 939-8600	14908
SA Recycling LLC (PA)	5093	C	714 632-2000	7990
Sanders & Wohrman Corporation	1721	D	714 919-0446	2479
Sas Institute Inc	7372	D	949 250-9999	15847
Schryver Med Sls & Mktg LLC	8071	D	303 459-8160	22145
Securitas Critical Infrastruct	7381	A	310 817-2177	16784
Sfpp LP (DH)	4613	C	714 560-4400	4925
Shade Structures Inc	1799	B	714 427-6981	3584
Signature Flooring Inc	1752	D	714 558-9200	3117
Solari Enterprises Inc	6512	C	714 282-2520	10946
Southern Counties Oil Co (PA)	5171	C	714 744-7140	8946
Ssae 16 Professionals LLP	8721	D	866 480-9485	26298
St Joseph Hospital of Orange (DH)	8062	A	714 633-9111	21782
St Joseph Hospital of Orange	8062	A	714 771-8037	21783
States Drawer Box Spc LLC	5031	D	714 744-4247	6866
Steger Inc	1721	E	714 974-4383	2483
Stoneriver Inc	7371	B	714 705-8227	15473
Sunnyslope Tree Farm Inc	5193	D	714 532-1440	9164
Tiller Constructors Partnr Inc	1542	D	714 771-5600	1674
Transportation Chrtr Svcs Inc	4142	E	714 396-0346	3905
Unisource Discovery LLC (PA)	8111	D	888 248-0020	23418
United Spectrum Inc	1799	E	714 283-1010	3599
Universal Cylinder Exch Inc	8999	D	714 744-1036	27960
University California Irvine	8011	A	714 456-6170	20032
University California Irvine	8062	A	714 456-6011	21886
University California Irvine	8062	A	714 456-5558	21887
Valori Sand & Gravel Company (PA)	5032	D	714 637-0104	6911
Van Grow Jack S MD	8011	D	714 564-3300	20047
Vandorpe Chou Associates Inc	8711	E	714 978-9780	25987
Village Nurseries Whl LLC (PA)	5193	E	714 279-3100	9174

	SIC	EMP	PHONE	ENTRY #
Volt Management Corp	7363	B	714 921-7460	14933
Volt Management Corp	7363	C	714 921-8800	14937
W Corporation	8748	C	714 532-8800	27907
Walswrth Frnklin Bevins McCall (PA)	8111	D	714 634-2522	23425
West Coast Firestopping Inc	1799	D	714 935-1104	3609
West Corporation	7389	D	949 294-2801	17588
Western Dental Services Inc (PA)	8021	B	714 480-3000	20144
Western Pacific Distrg LLC	5032	C	714 974-6837	6915
Word & Brown Insurance	8741	C	714 567-4398	27098
Wsp USA Inc	8711	D	714 973-4880	26011
Xpo Logistics Freight Inc	4213	A	714 282-7717	4315
Young Mens Christn Assn Orange	8641	D	714 771-1287	25332
Zettler Components Inc (PA)	5065	C	949 831-5000	7569

ORANGE COVE, CA - Fresno County

	SIC	EMP	PHONE	ENTRY #
Booth Ranches LLC	0291	D	559 626-4472	447
Cecelia Packing Corporation	0723	C	559 626-5000	501
Nnncc Ranch	7389	D	559 626-4890	17357
United Health Ctrs San Joaquin	8093	D	559 626-4031	22706

ORANGEVALE, CA - Sacramento County

	SIC	EMP	PHONE	ENTRY #
Fountainwood Residential Care	8361	D	916 988-2200	24533
Summerville At Hazel Creek LLC	8361	A	916 988-7901	24689

ORCUTT, CA - Santa Barbara County

	SIC	EMP	PHONE	ENTRY #
Orcutt Lions Club	8699	D	805 937-0158	25448
Spiess Construction Co Inc	1623	D	805 937-5859	1983

ORINDA, CA - Contra Costa County

	SIC	EMP	PHONE	ENTRY #
Agemark Corporation (PA)	8051	C	925 257-4671	20221
First Republic Bank	6022	C	925 254-8993	9455
Miramnte High Schl Parents CLB	8399	D	925 280-3965	24806
Orinda Convalescent Hospital	8059	D	925 254-6500	21176
Orinda Country Club	7997	D	925 254-4313	18995
Van Inn II Inc (PA)	8051	D	510 548-6600	20855

ORLAND, CA - Glenn County

	SIC	EMP	PHONE	ENTRY #
City of Orland (PA)	4941	E	530 865-1610	6227
Glenn County Office Education	8351	D	530 865-1145	24325
Lassen Land Co	0762	E	530 865-7676	697
Omega Walnut Inc	0723	E	530 865-0136	552
Tepa Ec LLC (PA)	8711	D	719 596-8114	25943

OROSI, CA - Tulare County

	SIC	EMP	PHONE	ENTRY #
Abe-El Produce	0161	B	559 528-3030	32
Mountain View AG Services Inc	0761	A	559 528-6004	661

OROVILLE, CA - Butte County

	SIC	EMP	PHONE	ENTRY #
1000 Executive Parkway LLC	8051	C	530 533-7335	20213
Artists of River Town	8621	D	530 534-7690	24997
Butte County Office Education	8699	B	530 532-5786	25401
County of Butte	8322	C	530 538-7661	23626
County of Butte	8322	B	530 538-7721	23627
County of Butte	8322	A	530 538-7572	23629
County of Butte	8322	B	530 538-6802	23630
County of Butte	8322	A	530 538-7711	23631
Evergreen At Oroville LLC	8051	D	530 533-7335	20417
Feather Rver Recreation Pk Dst	7999	D	530 533-2011	19169
Mooretown Rancheria	7993	A	530 533-3885	18785
Mooretown Rancheria (PA)	7999	E	530 533-3625	19204
Oroville Hospital (PA)	8062	A	530 533-8500	21619
Oroville Hospital	8049	D	530 538-8700	20191
Oroville Internal Meds Group	8011	E	530 538-3171	19738
Peter J Wolk MD	8011	E	530 544-6517	19790
Recology Inc	4953	C	530 533-5868	6438
Shadowbrook Health Care Inc	8051	D	530 534-1353	20755
South Feather Water & Pwr Agcy (PA)	4971	D	530 533-4578	6566
The For Work Training Center	8331	E	530 534-1112	24237
Tyme Maidu Tribe-Berry Creek	7011	D	530 538-4560	13351
Youth For Change	8322	D	530 538-8347	24140

OXNARD, CA - Ventura County

	SIC	EMP	PHONE	ENTRY #
AG Rx (PA)	5191	D	805 487-0696	9071
Alliedbarton Security Svcs LLC	7381	D	805 983-1204	16553
Apria Healthcare LLC	7352	C	805 278-6700	14431
Aptos Berry Farms Inc	0171	D	831 726-3256	90
Arizona Channel Isla	7999	D	480 788-0755	19101
Ava Enterprises Inc	5064	E	805 988-0192	7409
Ayala Drywall	1742	E	805 487-3392	2847
Best Western Oxnard Inn	7011	E	805 483-9581	12375
Blois Construction Inc	1623	C	805 485-0011	1898
Boskovich Farms Inc (PA)	0723	C	805 487-2299	497
Boyd & Associates	7381	C	805 988-8298	16586
Calatlantic Group Inc	1521	D	805 379-6600	1136
California Resources Prod Corp	1311	D	805 483-8017	1018
Channel Islnds Vgtble Frms Inc (PA)	0182	C	805 984-1910	309
Chicago Title Insurance Co	6361	D	805 656-1300	10443
Child Development Resources of (PA)	8322	C	805 485-7878	23562

Employment Codes: A=Over 500 employees, B=251-500,
C=101-250, D=51-100, E=50

2019 Directory of California
Wholesalers and Services Companies

© Mergent Inc. 1-800-342-5647

1629

GEOGRAPHIC

	SIC	EMP	PHONE	ENTRY #
Chiquita Fresh North Amer LLC	0179	B	954 924-5642	233
City Impact Inc	8322	D	805 983-3636	23575
City of Oxnard	8322	D	805 385-8019	23584
City of Oxnard	4941	D	805 385-8136	6228
City of Oxnard	7996	D	805 385-7950	18793
City of Oxnard	7992	D	805 983-4653	18696
Clinicas Del Camino Real Inc	8093	D	805 487-5351	22533
Coalition For Family Harmony	8322	D	805 983-6014	23591
Conroy Farms Inc.	0171	B	805 981-0537	95
County of Ventura	8322	C	805 385-8654	23757
County of Ventura	8351	E	805 240-2701	24311
Courtyard Oxnard	7011	D	805 988-3600	12495
Covenant Care California LLC	8051	C	805 488-3696	20343
Covenant Players (PA)	7922	C	805 486-7155	18359
Dataprose Inc	7374	D	805 278-7430	16114
Deardorff-Jackson Co	5148	E	805 487-7801	8665
Dignity Health	8062	A	805 988-2500	21391
Dw Berry Farms LLC	0191	B	805 795-8403	338
Etchandy Farms LLC	0171	D	805 983-4700	98
Fame Systems Inc	7349	E	805 485-0808	14263
Family Circle Inc	8322	D	805 385-4180	23795
Federal Express Corporation	4513	D	800 463-3339	4833
Fedex Ground Package Sys Inc	4213	D	800 463-3339	4174
Fresh Venture Farms LLC	0161	D	805 754-4449	55
G P M M Money Centers Inc	6099	E	619 288-7607	9684
Gama Berry Farms LLC	0171	D	805 483-1000	100
Geek Squad Inc	7379	D	805 278-9555	16378
Gibbs International Inc (PA)	7538	C	805 485-0551	17762
Gill Transport LLC	4213	B	805 240-1979	4186
Gills Onions LLC	5148	C	805 240-1983	8688
Glenwood Corporation	8051	D	805 983-0305	20457
Gmh Inc	7623	E	805 485-1410	17895
Golden Living LLC	8051	D	805 983-0305	20468
Grolink Plant Company Inc (PA)	5193	C	805 984-7958	9138
H & F Grain Farms LLC	8748	D	805 754-4449	27743
HE Julien & Associates Inc	0782	E	805 488-8342	857
High Tide and Green Grass Inc.	7992	D	805 981-8722	18720
ICI Services Corporation	8711	B	805 988-3210	25741
Insurance Services Amercn LLC	6411	D	805 981-2220	10651
Js Hospitality Group LLC	7011	D	805 988-3600	12795
Jsl Technologies Inc	8711	D	805 985-7700	25771
Kaiser Foundation Hospitals	8011	A	888 515-3500	19574
Kaiser Foundation Hospitals	8011	A	805 988-6300	19576
Kindred Healthcare Oper Inc	8059	D	805 487-7840	21128
Koxr Spanish Radio	4832	E	805 487-0444	5735
Labaya Beachcomber LP	7532	E	805 278-6688	17727
Las Islas Family Med Group PC	8011	D	805 385-8662	19644
Marathon Land Inc (PA)	0181	C	805 488-3585	281
Mariz Berry Farms	0171	C	805 981-9908	107
Maxim Healthcare Services Inc	7363	A	805 278-4593	14876
Merrill Lynch Pierce Fenner	6211	C	800 964-5182	9982
Milwood Healthcare Inc	6512	D	626 274-4345	10914
Mission Linen Supply	7213	D	805 485-6794	13539
Mission Produce Inc.	5148	D	805 981-3650	8705
New York Life Insurance Co	6411	E	805 656-4598	10713
Nordman Cormany Hair & Compton	8111	C	805 485-1000	23290
Oceanview Produce Company	0161	D	805 488-6401	73
Olde Thompson Inc	5023	C	800 827-1565	6779
Oxnard Manor Healthcare Ctr LP	8051	D	805 983-0324	20684
Oxnard Perfrmn Arts & Convtn	7389	E	805 486-2424	17381
Pacific Building Maint Inc (PA)	7349	D	805 642-0214	14337
Pacific Coast Produce Inc	5148	D	805 240-3385	8712
Pacific Labor Services Inc	7021	E	805 488-4625	13441
Pleasant Valley Flowers Inc	0182	B	805 986-2776	320
Pyramid Flowers Inc	0181	C	805 382-8070	293
Quinn Company	5082	D	805 485-2171	7688
Quinn Group Inc	5083	D	805 485-2171	7708
Ramco Enterprises LP	0723	A	805 469-9328	556
Recp Cy Oxnard LLC	7011	C	805 604-7527	13102
Recp RI Oxnard LLC	7011	C	805 278-2200	13103
Reiter Affl Companies LLC (PA)	0171	E	805 483-1000	117
Republic Services Inc.	4953	D	805 385-8060	6453
Rescue Mission Alliance (PA)	8699	D	805 487-1234	25454
Rescue Mission Alliance	8099	E	805 201-4341	22870
River Ridge Farms Inc	0181	D	805 647-6880	295
River Ridge Golf Club	7997	D	805 981-8724	19016
SA Recycling LLC	4953	D	805 486-7525	6461
Safeguard Business Systems Inc.	5112	D	805 486-9769	8090
San Miguel Produce Inc	0161	B	805 488-0981	79
Santa Rosa Berry Farms LLC	0171	B	805 981-3060	120
Saticoy Lemon Association	8611	C	805 654-6543	24980
Scarborough Farms Inc	0161	C	805 483-9113	81
Scorpion Athc Booster CLB Inc	8641	E	805 482-2005	25244
Sea View Medical Group Inc	8099	D	805 373-5781	22883
Seaboard Produce Distrs Inc	5083	D	805 981-8001	7712

	SIC	EMP	PHONE	ENTRY #
Seminis Inc (DH)	8731	B	805 485-7317	26453
Seminis Vegetable Seeds Inc (DH)	5191	A	855 733-3834	9098
State Compensation Insur Fund	6321	B	888 782-8338	10173
Sunrise Ranch	0181	D	805 488-0813	304
Sunshine Floral LLC	5193	D	805 982-8822	9166
Superior Fruit LLC	0171	C	805 485-2519	123
Synectic Solutions Inc (PA)	7379	D	805 483-4800	16497
Sysco Ventura Inc	5141	B	805 205-7000	8472
Systems Application & Tech Inc.	8711	D	805 487-7373	25937
T M Mian & Associates Inc	7011	D	805 983-8600	13318
Tanimura & Antle Inc	4225	D	805 483-2358	4640
Topstar Floral Inc.	0181	E	805 984-7972	306
Toro Enterprises Inc.	1611	D	805 483-4515	1862
Tradewind Seafood Inc	5146	E	805 483-8555	8606
Tri County Regional Center	8049	D	805 485-3177	20211
Venco Western Inc (PA)	0782	C	805 981-2400	957
Ventura Cnty Council On Aging	8322	D	805 986-1424	24109
Ventura County Hematology (PA)	8011	E	805 485-8709	20051
Verizon Communications Inc.	7361	A	805 988-5760	14795
Veterans Health Administration	8011	B	805 983-6384	20072
Volt Management Corp	7363	C	805 485-0506	14941
West Flower Growers	0181	D	805 488-0814	308
Western Precooling Systems	7359	D	805 486-6371	14556
Windsor Capital Group Inc	7011	D	805 988-0627	13402
Wonderful Citrus Packing LLC	0723	D	805 988-1456	590
Workrite Uniform Company Inc (DH)	7218	C	805 483-0175	13628

PACHECO, CA - Contra Costa County

	SIC	EMP	PHONE	ENTRY #
Hertz Corporation	7514	D	925 680-0316	17642
Pleasant Hl Byshore Dspsal Inc	4953	C	925 685-4711	6429
Universal Bldg Svcs & Sup Co	7349	C	925 934-5533	14419

PACIFIC GROVE, CA - Monterey County

	SIC	EMP	PHONE	ENTRY #
Aramark Services Inc	7011	C	831 372-8016	12331
Covia Communities	8361	D	831 373-3111	24488
Gateway Ctr of Monterey Cnty (PA)	8361	D	831 372-8002	24539
K&M Construction	1522	D	831 643-2819	1296
Pacific Grove Aslmar Oper Corp	7011	D	831 372-8016	12997
Pacific Grove Cnvalescent Hosp	8059	D	831 375-2695	21178
Rotary CLB PCF Grove Char Fund	7997	D	831 372-3877	19020

PACIFIC PALISADES, CA - Los Angeles County

	SIC	EMP	PHONE	ENTRY #
Atria Senior Living Inc	8361	D	310 573-9545	24423
Bel-Air Bay Club Ltd	8641	C	310 230-4700	25099
Fusionzone Automotive Inc	7379	E	888 576-1136	16371
Get Heal Inc	7363	D	310 528-4957	14858
Lighthouse Capital Funding	6799	E	310 230-8335	12240
Palisades Optimist Foundation	8641	D	310 454-4111	25211
Santa Monica Bay Physcians	8011	D	310 459-2363	19858
State Farm Mutl Auto Insur Co	6411	D	310 454-0349	10792

PACIFICA, CA - San Mateo County

	SIC	EMP	PHONE	ENTRY #
Cal-Pacific Construction Inc	1542	E	650 557-1238	1495
City of Pacifica-Vallemar	8351	D	650 738-7466	24296
Little Giant Bldg Maint Inc	7349	C	415 508-0282	14304
Ortega Elementary Pto.	8641	D	650 738-6670	25209
Pacific Engineering Builders	1542	D	650 557-1238	1607
Pacifica Care Center	8051	C	650 355-5622	20687
Pacifica Linda Mar Inc	8051	D	650 359-4800	20688
Pyramid Alternatives Inc (PA)	8093	E	650 355-8787	22658

PACOIMA, CA - Los Angeles County

	SIC	EMP	PHONE	ENTRY #
County of Los Angeles	8011	C	818 896-1903	19415
CPI Luxury Group	5094	D	818 249-9888	8007
Global Bakeries Inc	5149	D	818 896-0525	8797
Global Emergency Road Svc LLC	4119	E	818 518-1166	3802
Gonzalez Management Co Inc	8741	D	818 485-0596	26875
Hathaway-Sycamores Chld Fam Sv	8361	D	818 897-1766	24551
Hillview Mental Health Center	8093	D	818 896-1161	22593
Hope of Valley Rescue Mission	8322	D	818 392-0020	23844
Looney Bins Inc (PA)	4953	D	818 485-8200	6410
Northeast Valley Health Corp	8011	D	818 896-0531	19721
Phillips Plywood Co Inc	5031	D	818 897-7736	6851
Scenic Route Inc	1799	E	818 896-6006	3580
Volunteers of Amer Los Angeles	8322	C	818 834-9097	24115
Volunteers of Amer Los Angeles	8322	C	818 834-8957	24123
Wetzel & Sons Moving and Stor.	4214	D	818 890-0992	4390
Xpo Logistics Freight Inc.	4213	C	818 890-2095	4314

PALA, CA - San Diego County

	SIC	EMP	PHONE	ENTRY #
Pala Casino Spa & Resort	7011	A	760 510-5100	13012

PALM DESERT, CA - Riverside County

	SIC	EMP	PHONE	ENTRY #
Ambiente Enterprises Inc	8082	C	760 674-1905	22218
American Golf Corporation	7997	E	760 568-9311	18843
Atria Senior Living Group Inc	8361	D	760 341-0890	24431
Bank America National Assn	8741	C	760 636-7500	26773
Bighorn Golf Club	7997	C	760 773-2468	18867

2019 Directory of California
Wholesalers and Services Companies

(P-0000) Products & Services Section entry number
(PA)=Parent Co (HQ)=Headquarters (DH)=Div Headquarters

Company	SIC	EMP	PHONE	ENTRY #
California Closet Co O	1799	D	760 773-4784	3500
CJ Construction & Dev Inc	1522	D	760 247-6868	1274
Claro Pool Services Inc	1799	D	760 341-3377	3504
Coachella Valley Water Dst	4941	C	760 398-2651	6230
Coachella Valley Water Dst	4941	C	760 398-2651	6231
Coldwell Bnkr Residential Brkg	6531	D	760 776-9898	11359
Cora Constructors Inc	8711	E	760 674-3201	25624
Cove Electric Inc	1731	D	760 568-9924	2553
Danny Mahagna Shapprie	7929	E	760 341-5070	18429
Dave Williams Plbg & Elec Inc	1711	D	760 296-1397	2182
Desert Falls Country Club Inc	7997	D	760 340-5646	18911
Desert Resort Management	6531	D	760 831-0172	11398
Desert Television LLC	4833	D	760 343-5700	5782
Desert Willow Golf Resort Inc	7992	D	760 346-0015	18706
Desertarc	8322	B	760 346-1611	23768
Destination Residences LLC	7011	E	760 346-4647	12518
Dlo Enterprises Inc	7381	D	760 346-8033	16631
Emerald Brook LLC	7033	E	760 345-4770	13466
Enterprise Rent-A-Car	7514	C	760 772-0281	17633
Entravsion Communications Corp	4833	D	760 568-3636	5786
F M Tarbell Co	6531	E	760 346-7405	11441
Family YMCA of Desert	8322	D	760 423-5860	23802
First Team RE - Orange Cnty	6531	D	760 340-9911	11455
Friends of Cultural Center Inc	7922	C	760 346-6505	18367
Gary Cardiff Enterprises Inc	4119	D	760 568-1403	3799
Host Hotels & Resorts LP	7011	C	760 341-2211	12706
Kaiser Foundation Hospitals	8011	A	800 777-1256	19575
Kaiser Foundation Hospitals	8011	A	866 984-7483	19578
Kaiser Foundation Hospitals	6324	D	760 360-1475	10242
Lakes Country Club Assn Inc **(PA)**	7997	B	760 568-5423	18954
Leighton Group Inc	8621	C	760 776-4192	25023
Living Desert	8422	C	760 346-5694	24930
Marrakesh Management Corp	6531	E	760 568-2688	11587
Marriott International Inc	7011	C	760 776-0050	12891
Marriott Rsrts Hspitality Corp	7011	D	760 779-1200	12910
Marriotts Shadow Ridge	7011	D	760 674-2600	12912
Oasis Palm Dsert Hmowners Assn	7997	D	760 345-5661	18993
Odyssey Healthcare Inc	8059	E	760 674-0066	21172
Oj Insulation LP	1742	D	760 200-4343	2926
Olive Crest	8361	D	760 341-8507	24617
Palm Desert Greens Association	8641	D	760 346-8005	25212
Palm Dsert Rcrtl Fclities Corp	7997	D	760 346-0015	18998
Paul Williams Tile Co Inc	1743	D	760 772-7440	3007
Platinum Landscape Inc	0781	C	760 200-3673	778
Premier Residential Svcs LLC	7299	C	760 773-4081	13769
Quarry At La Quinta Inc **(PA)**	7992	D	760 777-1100	18749
Renova Energy Corp	1711	E	760 568-3413	2336
Resort Parking Services Inc	7521	C	760 328-4041	17705
Securitas SEC Svcs USA Inc	7381	C	559 221-2302	16803
Shamrock-Hostmark Palm Desrt	7011	D	760 340-6600	13211
Spectrum MGT Holdg Co LLC	4841	C	760 340-2225	5944
Sun City Palm Dsert Cmnty Assn **(PA)**	8641	D	760 200-2100	25254
Sunrise Desert Partners	6552	C	760 404-1280	11925
Sunrise Desert Partners **(PA)**	6552	C	760 772-7227	11926
Sunrise Senior Living Inc	8051	D	760 340-5999	20796
Sunrise Senior Living LLC	8051	D	760 346-5420	20833
Toscana Homes LP	1522	E	760 772-7227	1321
Toscana Land LLC	6552	E	760 772-7200	11930
United Brothers Concrete Inc	1771	C	760 346-1013	3338
Visitng Nurse Assn Inlnd CNT	8082	C	760 346-3982	22449
Watermark Rtrment Cmmnties Inc	8051	D	760 346-5420	20877
West Coast Turf **(PA)**	0181	E	760 340-7300	307
West Ville Palm Desert	6512	E	760 346-2121	10962
Westin Desert Willow	7011	D	760 636-7003	13392

PALM SPRINGS, CA - Riverside County

Company	SIC	EMP	PHONE	ENTRY #
A & A Home Care Services	8082	D	760 416-6769	22176
A A A Five Star Adventures	7997	E	760 320-1500	18816
Agua Caliente Development Auth	6531	D	760 699-6800	11192
Agua Clnte Band Chilla Indians **(PA)**	8699	C	760 699-6800	25375
Agua Clnte Band Chilla Indians	7011	A	800 854-1279	12308
American Medical Response Inc	4119	C	760 883-5000	3764
Angel View Inc	8361	E	760 322-2440	24417
Brudvik Inc **(PA)**	1731	D	760 320-4429	2529
California Nursing and Rehab	8051	C	760 325-2937	20282
Cardinal Health Inc	5047	C	951 360-2199	7171
Carefusion Corporation	8099	D	760 778-7200	22758
Casa Real Estate Ltd Partnr	7011	C	760 320-4117	12437
City of Palm Springs	4581	D	760 318-3800	4879
Cnrc LLC	8051	C	760 325-2937	20316
Coldwell Bnkr Residential Brkg	6531	C	760 325-4500	11355
Colony Palms Hotel LLC	7011	C	760 969-1800	12474
County of Riverside Department	8099	D	760 320-1048	22779
Crestline Hotels & Resorts LLC	7011	C	760 322-6000	12500
Desert Aids Project **(PA)**	8322	D	760 323-2118	23767
Desert Air Conditioning Inc	1761	E	760 323-3383	3149

Company	SIC	EMP	PHONE	ENTRY #
Desert Arts Center	8412	D	760 323-7973	24880
Desert Medical Group Inc **(PA)**	8011	C	760 320-8814	19436
Desert Medical Group Inc	8011	C	760 323-8657	19437
Desert Regional Med Ctr Inc **(HQ)**	8062	A	760 323-6511	21364
Desert Regional Med Ctr Inc	8069	C	760 323-6640	22017
Desert Water Agency Fing Corp	4941	D	760 323-4971	6238
Diamond Resorts LLC	7011	D	760 866-1800	12521
Ensign Palm I LLC	8051	D	760 323-2638	20402
Federal Express Corporation	4512	C	800 463-3339	4782
First Student Inc	4151	D	760 320-4659	3926
Five Star Quality Care Inc	8741	D	760 327-8541	26859
HHC Trs Portsmouth LLC	7011	D	760 322-6000	12654
Hilton Resort Palm Springs	7011	C	760 320-6868	12667
Hyatt Hotels Management Corp	7011	D	760 322-9000	12753
Interstate Hotels Resorts Inc	8741	C	760 322-7000	26897
Jack Parker Corp	7011	C	760 770-5000	12787
Joseph Dipuzo	7212	E	760 325-1200	13492
Kaiser Foundation Hospitals	6324	D	866 370-1942	10260
Kittridge Hotels & Resorts LLC	7011	D	760 325-9676	12818
Loandepotcom LLC	6162	A	760 797-6000	9828
M C Builder Corp	1721	E	760 323-8010	2456
Mesquite Golf & Cntry CLB Corp	7999	E	760 323-9377	19202
Morrison MGT Specialists Inc	8741	C	760 323-6296	26950
Mount San Jacinto Win Pk Auth	7999	D	760 325-1449	19205
Palm Springs Art Museum Inc	8412	C	760 322-4800	24898
Palm Springs Disposal Services	4953	C	760 327-1351	6426
R P S Resort Corp	7011	C	760 327-8311	13091
Remington Hotel Corporation	7011	D	760 322-6000	13108
Riviera Reincarnate LLC	7011	D	760 327-8311	13133
S S W Mechanical Cnstr Inc	1711	C	760 327-1481	2344
San Gorgonio Memorial Hospital	8093	D	760 656-2251	22674
Seven Lakes Hm Assn Cntry CLB	7997	E	760 328-2695	19043
Smg Holdings Inc	8742	C	760 325-6611	27456
Smoke Tree Inc	7011	D	760 327-1221	13244
Spa Resort Casino **(PA)**	7011	A	888 999-1995	13251
Springs Ambulance Service Inc	4119	D	760 883-5000	3850
Sunrise Senior Living LLC	8051	D	760 322-3444	20828
Temalpakh Inc	1542	D	760 770-5778	1672
United Airlines Inc	4512	C	760 778-5690	4811
United Parcel Service Inc OH	4215	B	760 325-1762	4444
VCA Desert Animal Hospitals	0742	D	760 778-9999	615
Walters Family Partnership	7011	C	760 320-6868	13378
Wyndham International Inc	7011	D	760 322-6000	13424

PALMDALE, CA - Los Angeles County

Company	SIC	EMP	PHONE	ENTRY #
Antelope Valley Country Club	7997	C	661 947-3142	18846
Antelope Valley Mall	6512	C	661 266-9150	10853
Cellco Partnership	4812	D	661 274-2112	5364
Child and Family Guidance Ctr	8093	D	661 265-8627	22527
Child Care Resource Center Inc	8322	E	661 723-3246	23560
City of Palmdale	7349	C	661 267-5338	14211
Colsa Corporation	8731	C	661 273-3859	26349
County of Los Angeles	1611	C	661 947-7173	1750
Csi Electrical Contractors Inc	1731	D	661 723-0869	2554
Delta Scientific Corporation **(PA)**	7382	C	661 575-1100	16886
Forest City Rental Prpts Corp	6512	D	661 266-9150	10877
Jacobs Engineering Group Inc	8711	D	661 275-5685	25757
Lou Bozigian	6531	D	661 948-4737	11568
Palmdale Center For Pain MGT	8011	E	661 267-6876	19747
Palmdale Resort Inc	7011	E	661 947-8055	13014
Palmdale Water District	4941	D	661 947-4111	6295
Palmdale Womans Club	7299	D	661 266-3008	13763
Penny Lane Centers	8399	C	818 892-3423	24825
People Creating Success Inc	8322	D	661 225-9700	23969
Primerica Life Insurance Co	6411	D	661 947-9070	10741
Sunstone Hotel Investors LLC	7011	C	661 267-6587	13295
Tarzana Treatment Centers Inc	8093	C	818 654-3815	22691
Vista Home Health Service Inc	8082	D	818 701-1877	22450
Waste Management Cal Inc	4953	D	661 947-7197	6512
Xi Enterprise Inc	7991	D	661 266-3200	18676

PALO ALTO, CA - Santa Clara County

Company	SIC	EMP	PHONE	ENTRY #
4290 El Camino Properties LP	7011	C	650 857-0787	12293
Abilities United **(PA)**	8322	C	650 494-0550	23455
Actian Corporation **(PA)**	7373	D	650 587-5500	15908
Adaptive Insights Inc **(HQ)**	7372	C	650 528-7500	15570
Affymax Research Institute	8733	E	650 812-8700	26584
Alain Pinel Realtors Inc	6531	C	650 323-1111	11201
Allana Buick & Bers Inc **(PA)**	8711	D	650 543-5600	25527
Ariba Inc **(DH)**	7372	C	650 849-4000	15592
Arnold Porter Kaye Scholer LLP	8111	C	650 319-4500	22921
Avenidas **(PA)**	8322	C	650 289-5400	23501
Azumio Inc **(PA)**	7371	C	719 310-3774	15014
Baker & McKenzie LLP	8111	C	650 856-2400	22928
Beauty Bazar Inc	7231	D	650 326-8522	13647
Beneficent Technology Inc	7389	E	650 644-3400	17029

GEOGRAPHIC

Company	SIC	EMP	PHONE	ENTRY #
Bex Portfolio LLC	7389	D	650 494-3700	17033
Billcom Inc	7372	C	650 353-3301	15609
Bml Works Na LLC	8741	D	650 268-8305	26782
Bpr Properties Berkeley LLC	6512	C	650 424-1400	10857
Broadrach Cpitl Prtners Fund I	6722	A	650 331-2500	12032
Broadreach Capitl Partners LLC (PA)	6211	A	650 331-2500	9919
Cambridge Design Partnr Inc	8711	D	650 387-7812	25589
Capiot Software Inc	7379	C	650 766-2469	16323
Cardic Arithmias	8011	E	650 617-8100	19347
Cc-Palo Alto Inc	8052	C	650 853-5000	20919
Cellco Partnership	4812	D	650 323-6127	5392
Channing House	8059	D	650 327-0950	21037
City of Palo Alto	7389	D	650 329-2598	17080
Cloudera Inc (PA)	7371	C	650 362-0488	15065
Community Housing Inc	8361	E	650 328-3300	24473
Cooley LLP (PA)	8111	B	650 843-5000	22990
Cooley LLP	8111	C	650 843-5124	22991
Covenant Care California LLC	8051	D	415 327-0511	20338
Danger Inc	4813	C	650 323-9700	5543
Datasafe Inc	4226	E	650 875-3800	4672
Declara Inc	7379	D	650 800-7695	16342
Dentons US LLP	8111	D	650 798-0300	23030
Document Technologies LLC	7389	D	650 485-2705	17137
E3 Healthcare Management LLC	8741	D	650 324-0600	26845
Electric Power RES Inst Inc (PA)	8731	A	650 855-2000	26359
Eprisolutions Inc	8711	D	650 855-8900	25671
Ernst & Young LLP	8721	C	650 496-1600	26194
Essential Products Inc	7371	D	650 300-0000	15145
Essex Management Corporation (HQ)	6798	D	650 494-3700	12161
F-Secure Inc	5045	E	888 432-8233	7048
Family & Children Services	8322	D	650 326-6576	23792
Ferrado Garden Court LLC	7011	D	650 543-2224	12573
Fiorano Software Inc	7372	B	650 326-1136	15676
Foley & Lardner LLP	8111	C	650 856-3700	23074
Garden Court Hotel	7011	D	650 322-9000	12597
Genomic Health Inc	8071	B	650 269-0545	22091
Genpact LLC	8748	E	203 690-9308	27736
Gibson Dunn & Crutcher LLP	8111	B	650 849-5300	23091
Gordon Betty Moore Foundation	8641	D	650 213-3000	25169
Gordon E Btty I More Fundation	8748	D	650 213-3000	27741
Harris Mycfo Inc	8742	D	480 348-7725	27257
Haynes and Boone LLP	8111	D	650 687-8800	23126
Hercules Capital Inc (PA)	6799	D	650 289-3060	12232
Hewlett Packard	7371	A	650 857-1501	15198
Hewlett Packard Enterprise Co (PA)	7372	C	650 687-5817	15705
Houzz Inc (PA)	7371	D	650 326-3000	15201
Hyatt Hotels Management Corp	7011	B	650 352-1234	12754
Ideo LP	7389	C	650 289-3400	17230
Ideo LP (PA)	7336	C	650 289-3400	14117
Instart Logic Inc	7371	D	888 418-5044	15219
Intapp Inc (PA)	7372	C	650 852-0400	15714
Integral Development Corp (PA)	7372	D	650 424-4500	15715
Intellectsoft LLC	7371	C	650 300-4335	15224
Intellectual Ventures LLC	8741	B	650 941-1330	26894
Joguru Inc	4725	D	855 526-4332	4971
Jones Day Limited Partnership	8111	D	650 739-3955	23155
Kawela One LLC	8111	D	650 843-5000	23164
Kirkland & Ellis LLP	8111	A	650 852-9131	23173
Leland Stanford Junior Univ	8732	C	650 723-6254	26537
Leland Stanford Junior Univ	8062	E	650 723-2997	21547
Leland Stanford Junior Univ	8099	C	650 723-5548	22833
Leland Stanford Junior Univ	8732	B	650 723-7546	26538
Leland Stanford Junior Univ	8062	A	650 725-2377	21548
Leland Stanford Junior Univ	8062	A	650 723-4000	21549
Leland Stanford Junior Univ	8011	D	650 725-4416	19647
Leland Stanford Junior Univ	8062	A	650 725-4617	21550
Leland Stanford Junior Univ	8733	D	650 723-4733	26636
LLP Mayer Brown	8111	A	650 331-2000	23222
Lowenstein Sandler LLP	8111	E	650 433-5800	23231
Lucile Packard Childrens Hosp	8069	D	650 321-2545	22030
Lucile Packard Childrens Hosp	8069	E	650 736-4089	22031
Lucile Salter Packard Chil (PA)	8069	C	650 497-8000	22032
Lucile Salter Packard Chil	8999	B	650 736-4030	27939
Luminar Technologies Inc	8733	D	626 629-8686	26637
Machine Zone Inc (PA)	7371	D	650 320-1678	15267
Maximus Holdings Inc	7372	A	650 935-9500	15748
Mc Graw Insurance Services Co	6411	D	650 780-4800	10688
McKinsey & Company Inc	8742	C	650 494-6262	27331
Mercury Interactive LLC (HQ)	7372	B	650 857-1501	15757
Merrill Lynch Pierce Fenner	6211	D	650 842-2440	9979
Metricstream Inc (PA)	7372	C	650 620-2900	15758
Metricus Inc	7389	D	650 328-2500	17328
Morgan Lewis & Bockius LLP	8111	D	650 843-4000	23261
Morrison & Foerster LLP	8111	B	650 813-5600	23268
Nest Labs Inc (DH)	5065	D	650 331-1127	7514
Norwest Venture Partners VI LP	6799	D	650 289-2243	12250
Npario Inc	7371	C	650 461-9696	15318
Nuevacare LLC	8051	D	650 396-3596	20667
Oak Creek Apartments	6513	E	650 327-1600	11086
Odyssey Telecorp Inc	4813	C	650 470-7505	5616
Oshman Family Jewish Cmnty Ctr	8322	C	650 223-8700	23954
Pacific Hotel Dev Ventr LP	7011	D	650 347-8260	12998
Pacific Hotel Management LLC	7011	B	650 328-2800	13001
Pacific Specialty Insurance Co	6411	C	650 780-4800	10727
Packard Childrens Hlth Aliance	8011	D	650 497-8000	19744
Packard Medical Group Inc	8011	D	650 724-3637	19745
Pahc Apartments Inc	6513	E	650 321-9709	11091
Palantir Technologies Inc (PA)	7371	C	650 815-0200	15342
Palantir Usg Inc (HQ)	7371	C	650 815-0200	15343
Palmetto Hospitality	7011	E	650 843-0795	13015
Palo Alto Commons	8361	D	650 320-8626	24626
Palo Alto Family Y M C A	8641	E	650 856-9622	25213
Palo Alto Hills Golf An	7299	D	650 948-1800	13764
Palo Alto Medical Clinic	8011	E	650 321-4121	19748
Palo Alto Medical Foundation (HQ)	8011	A	650 321-4121	19749
Palo Alto Medical Foundation	8731	E	650 326-8120	26429
Palo Alto Research Center Inc	8731	C	650 812-4000	26430
Palo Alto Vterans Inst For RES	8733	C	650 858-3970	26646
Paloras Corporation	8742	D	650 440-7663	27387
Paul Hastings LLP	8111	C	650 320-1800	23319
Paycycle Inc	4813	D	866 729-2925	5623
Perkins Coie LLP	8111	C	415 725-1313	23322
Pillsbury Winthrop Shaw	8111	C	650 233-4500	23332
Precision Ideo Inc	7389	B	650 688-3400	17406
Primerica Life Insurance Co	6411	D	650 323-2554	10740
Quovera Inc (PA)	8748	C	650 691-0114	27833
R H O Capital Partners Inc	6799	E	650 463-0300	12262
Robert Half International Inc	7361	D	650 812-9790	14744
Sap Labs LLC	7371	D	650 849-4000	15427
Sap Labs LLC (DH)	7371	D	650 849-4000	15428
Sharethis Inc (PA)	7311	C	650 641-0191	13902
Shopping Center Mgt Corp	6512	D	650 617-8234	10938
Sidley Austin LLP	8111	D	650 565-7000	23385
Sidley Austin LLP	8111	C	650 565-7000	23386
Simpson Thacher & Bartlett LLP	8111	C	650 251-5000	23389
Skoll Foundation	8699	E	650 331-1031	25463
Skype Inc	4813	D	650 493-7900	5646
Smartek21 LLC	7379	C	650 617-3221	16486
Solaredge Technologies Inc	5063	B	650 320-7695	7398
Space Systems/Loral LLC (DH)	4899	C	650 852-7320	5996
Spieker Companies Inc (PA)	6531	C	650 968-2660	11774
Stanford Federal Credit Union (PA)	6061	D	650 725-1000	9595
Stanford Health Care	8062	A	650 736-7844	21793
Stanford Health Care Primary	8011	D	650 723-6963	19943
Stanford Hospital and Clinics	8062	A	650 213-8360	21794
Stratford School Inc (PA)	8351	E	650 493-1151	24388
Striim Inc	7371	E	425 894-1998	15479
Suning Cmmerce R D Ctr USA Inc	8732	D	650 834-9800	26567
Sutter Health	8011	C	650 853-2975	19960
Sutter Health	8011	C	650 853-2904	19978
Swaminatha Mahadevan MD	8011	D	650 723-6576	19996
Talview Inc	7379	C	510 227-8227	16504
Tcv Management 2004 LLC	8741	C	650 614-8200	27059
Technology Credit Union	6062	D	650 326-6445	9660
Teris LLC (PA)	7374	D	650 213-9922	16189
Teris-Bay Area LLC	8111	D	650 213-9922	23406
Tibco Software Inc (HQ)	7371	C	650 846-1000	15504
Total Quality Maintenance Inc	7349	C	650 846-4700	14408
Uber Technologies Inc	7375	C	832 610-0359	16257
Veterans Health Administration	8011	A	650 493-5000	20064
Vinson & Elkins LLP	8111	C	650 617-8400	23421
Vmware Inc	7371	C	650 427-2100	15534
Vmware Inc (DH)	7371	C	650 427-5000	15535
Vmware Inc	7371	C	650 812-8200	15536
Watercourse Way	7299	C	650 462-2000	13779
Willow Garage Inc	8731	D	650 322-2584	26494
Wilson Sonsini Goodrich & Rosa (PA)	8111	A	650 493-9300	23439
Womble Bond Dickinson (us) LLP	8111	C	408 720-8300	23445
Xcelmobility Inc	7372	D	650 320-1728	15897
Xerox Corporation	5044	D	650 813-6787	6989
Xerox Corporation	5044	C	650 813-7138	6991

PALO CEDRO, CA - Shasta County

Company	SIC	EMP	PHONE	ENTRY #
Rotary International	8641	D	530 547-5272	25229

PALOS VERDES ESTATES, CA - Los Angeles County

Company	SIC	EMP	PHONE	ENTRY #
Malaga Bank Fsb (HQ)	6035	D	310 375-9000	9525
Malaga Financial Corporation (PA)	6036	D	310 375-9000	9536
Palos Verdes Beach & Athc CLB	7997	D	310 375-8777	19000
Plantasia Inc	0782	D	310 375-0387	922
Seibo LLC (PA)	7819	D	310 465-1700	18216

Company	SIC	EMP	PHONE	ENTRY #

PALOS VERDES PENINSU, CA - Los Angeles County

Company	SIC	EMP	PHONE	ENTRY #
County of Los Angeles	8062	B	310 222-2401	21352

PANORAMA CITY, CA - Los Angeles County

Company	SIC	EMP	PHONE	ENTRY #
American Protection Group Inc (PA)	7381	C	818 279-2433	16566
Cellco Partnership	4812	D	818 920-4848	5337
Creative Technology Group Inc (DH)	7389	D	818 779-2400	17111
Deanco Healthcare LLC	8063	A	818 787-2222	21952
E2 Corp	7373	D	818 904-5660	15950
Ensign Group Inc	8051	C	818 893-6385	20396
Golden Living LLC	8059	D	818 893-6385	21084
Import Collection (PA)	5199	D	818 782-3060	9224
Kaiser Foundation Hospitals	8062	A	818 375-2000	21488
Kaiser Foundation Hospitals	6324	D	818 375-2028	10230
Leigh Jerry California Inc (PA)	5137	A	818 909-6200	8315
Leonid M Glosman DDS A D	8021	D	818 989-2400	20125
Panorama Community Hospital	8062	E	818 787-2222	21632
Panorama Madows Nursing Ctr LP	8051	D	818 894-5707	20690
Qmadix Inc	5065	D	818 988-4300	7527
Rahf IV Casa Panorama LP	6513	E	216 621-6060	11104
Southern Cal Prmnnte Med Group	6324	D	800 272-3500	10312
Zodax LP (PA)	5023	D	818 785-5626	6804

PARADISE, CA - Butte County

Company	SIC	EMP	PHONE	ENTRY #
Butte Primary Care Med Group	8011	D	530 877-0762	19334
California Vocations Inc	8059	C	530 877-0937	21029
County of Butte	8322	B	530 872-6328	23628
Feather River Hospital (PA)	8062	A	530 877-9361	21415
Feather River Hospital	8062	D	530 872-3378	21416
Feather River Hospital	5047	C	530 876-7216	7179
Sunbridge Paradise Rhblttn Ctr	8051	D	530 872-3200	20792
Tegtmeier Associates Inc	6512	D	530 872-7700	10955
USA Waste of California Inc	4953	D	530 877-2777	6499
Youth For Change (PA)	8322	C	530 877-8187	24139

PARAMOUNT, CA - Los Angeles County

Company	SIC	EMP	PHONE	ENTRY #
Advanced Industrial Svcs Inc	1721	D	562 940-8305	2418
Aramark Unf & Career AP LLC	7213	D	323 774-4216	13515
Asphalt Management Inc	1771	E	562 630-6811	3216
Aylesva Inc	5139	C	562 688-0592	8344
Braun Linen Service Inc (PA)	7213	C	909 623-2678	13519
Calmet Inc (PA)	4953	C	323 721-8120	6368
Cfr Rinkens LLC (PA)	4731	D	310 639-7725	5030
Cort Business Services Corp	7359	D	562 582-1515	14490
Don Brandel Plumbing Inc	1711	E	562 408-0400	2186
Goldenpark LLC	7011	D	562 863-5555	12609
M & J Seafood Company Inc	5146	D	562 529-2786	8583
MB Herzog Electric Inc	1731	C	562 531-2002	2639
Modern Dev Co A Ltd Partnr	7389	D	949 646-6400	17333
Mountain Valley Express Co Inc	4731	C	562 630-5500	5113
Mv Transportation Inc	4789	D	562 790-8642	5237
Paramount Convalescent Group	8059	D	562 634-6895	21183
Paramunt Madows Nursing Ctr LP	8741	D	562 531-0990	26979
Premier Mailing Inc	7331	E	562 408-2134	14059
Promise Hosp E Los Angeles LP	8062	B	562 531-3110	21664
Reliable Energy Management Inc	1711	D	562 984-5511	2335
Schaefer Mary-Judith	1799	C	562 634-3164	3581
Telecare Corporation	8063	C	562 633-5111	21989
Total-Western Inc (HQ)	1389	E	562 220-1450	1081
Triage Partners LLC	7379	D	562 634-0058	16515
Vernon Security Inc	7382	D	562 790-8993	16949
Vss Sales Inc (PA)	7699	D	562 630-0606	18004

PARKER DAM, CA - San Bernardino County

Company	SIC	EMP	PHONE	ENTRY #
Black Meadow Landing	7011	D	760 663-4901	12388

PARLIER, CA - Fresno County

Company	SIC	EMP	PHONE	ENTRY #
Kozuki Farming Inc	0175	D	559 646-2652	223
Maxco Supply Inc (PA)	5113	C	559 646-8449	8108
United Health Ctrs San Joaquin (PA)	8093	B	559 646-6618	22705

PASADENA, CA - Los Angeles County

Company	SIC	EMP	PHONE	ENTRY #
24 Hour Fitness Usa Inc	7991	D	626 795-7121	18552
A P H Technological Consulting	8711	E	626 796-0331	25491
Aah Hudson LP	6513	A	626 794-9179	10972
Ab/SW 70 S Lake Owner LLC	6519	E	650 571-2200	11164
Access Pacific Inc	1542	E	626 792-0616	1455
Accredited Nursing Services	8051	D	626 573-1234	20219
Algos Inc A Medical Corp (PA)	8093	D	626 696-1400	22500
Amadeus Salon (PA)	7231	D	626 795-0969	13646
American Multi-Cinema Inc	7832	D	626 585-8900	18265
American Multimedia TV USA	4833	D	626 466-1038	5767
American Union Fincl Svcs Inc	6141	C	714 619-2520	9703
Amstar/Davidson Robles LLC	7011	D	626 577-1000	12319
Annandale Golf Club	7997	C	626 796-6125	18845
AON Consulting Inc	6411	D	626 683-5200	10535
Are- Maryland No 31 LLC	6512	E	626 578-0777	10855

Company	SIC	EMP	PHONE	ENTRY #
Arroyo Seco Medical Group (PA)	8011	D	626 795-7556	19304
Art & Logic Inc	7373	D	818 500-1933	15915
Arts Elegance Inc (PA)	5094	D	626 405-1522	8001
AT&T Corp	4812	D	626 396-0100	5274
AT&T Services Inc	4813	D	626 578-4168	5486
Atk Space Systems Inc	8731	D	626 351-0205	26331
Aurora Las Encinas LLC	8063	C	626 795-9901	21925
Ayzenberg Group Inc	7311	D	626 584-4070	13794
B Jacqueline and Assoc Inc	7371	B	626 844-1400	15015
Black Knght RE Data Sltons LLC	6531	C	626 808-9000	11244
Blue Chip Stamps	5051	A	626 585-6700	7261
Bluebeam Inc (PA)	7371	C	626 788-4100	15030
Boston Brick & Stone Inc	1741	E	626 269-2622	2799
Brighton Convalescent Center	8059	D	626 798-9124	21017
Brookfield Dtla Fund Office	7011	D	626 792-2727	12406
C W Driver Incorporated (PA)	1542	D	626 351-8800	1492
California Convalescent Hosptl	8051	D	626 793-5114	20281
California Credits Group LLC	7389	E	626 584-9800	17046
California Institute Tech	8731	C	626 395-8700	26345
California Linen Services Inc	7213	D	626 564-4576	13521
Camellia Gardens Care Ctr	8051	D	626 798-6777	20284
Carnegie Institution Wash	8733	D	626 577-1122	26606
Casecentral Inc (DH)	7389	D	415 989-2300	17060
Cellco Partnership	4812	D	626 395-0956	5346
Century 21 Golden Realty (PA)	6531	D	626 797-6680	11299
Charles Pankow Bldrs Ltd A Cal (PA)	1542	E	626 304-1190	1502
CIT Bank NA (HQ)	6021	D	626 859-5400	9319
Citizens Business Bank	6022	E	626 577-1700	9434
City of Pasadena	7349	D	626 744-4311	14212
City of Pasadena	7992	D	626 543-4708	18697
Community Hlth Alance Pasadena (PA)	8062	D	626 398-6300	21331
Congress Med Surgery Ctr LLC	8011	D	626 396-8100	19403
County of Los Angeles	8322	D	626 356-5281	23653
County of Los Angeles	8099	D	626 229-3825	22775
County of Los Angeles	8322	D	626 356-5281	23683
Cpo Commerce LLC	5072	C	626 585-3600	7585
D & C Care Center Inc	8059	D	626 798-1175	21056
Dallas Union Hotel Inc	6798	C	626 356-1000	12157
David Ross Inc	8051	D	323 684-7673	20367
Dilbeck Inc	6531	C	626 584-0101	11404
Diversified Health Svcs Del	8361	E	626 798-6753	24505
Dowling Advisory Group	8742	D	626 319-1369	27217
Dy-Dee Service Pasadena Inc	7219	D	626 792-6183	13631
Dydee Service of Pasedena	7219	D	626 240-0115	13632
E Z Data Inc (HQ)	7371	D	626 585-3505	15124
East West Bank (HQ)	6022	B	626 768-6000	9440
Econnections Inc	8741	C	626 307-6200	26846
Electric Svc & Sup Co Pasadena	1731	D	626 795-8641	2573
Emmis Communications Corp	4832	C	626 484-4440	5711
Employee Benefits Security ADM	6371	D	626 229-1000	10485
Energy Innovations Inc	8731	D	626 585-6900	26361
Fed Air Security Corporation	7382	D	626 535-2200	16892
Financial Healthcare Services	8742	E	626 356-7950	27235
Founders Healthcare LLC	8082	D	626 683-5401	22300
Front Porch Communities & Svcs	8361	C	626 796-8162	24536
Garda CL West Inc	7381	D	800 883-8305	16662
Gates of Spain Wibel	7231	E	626 441-3078	13659
Gem Transitional Care Center	8051	D	626 737-0560	20449
Gemalto Cogent Inc (DH)	7373	D	626 325-9600	15965
Glenn Building Services Inc	7349	D	626 398-8000	14278
Golden Cross Care Inc	8051	D	626 791-1948	20460
Golds Gym International Inc	7991	D	626 304-1133	18605
Gonzalez/Goodale Architects	8712	D	626 568-1428	26051
Good Works LLC	8082	D	626 584-8130	22306
Gourmets Fresh Pasta	5149	D	626 798-0841	8802
Grandcare Health Services LLC (PA)	8082	C	866 554-2447	22307
Green Dot Corporation (PA)	6141	C	626 765-2000	9714
Greensoft Technology Inc	7374	C	323 254-5961	16139
Grizzard Cmmncations Group Inc	7311	D	818 543-1315	13837
Gs1 Group Inc	7381	D	626 510-6384	16666
Gsg Associates Inc	8741	D	626 585-1808	26882
Guidance Software Inc (HQ)	7372	C	626 229-9191	15699
Hahn & Hahn LLP	8111	D	626 796-9123	23118
Hathaway-Sycamores Chld Fam Sv (PA)	8361	D	626 395-7100	24555
Hertz Claim Management Corp	7514	D	626 296-4760	17639
Hillsides	8361	B	323 254-2274	24562
Holthouse Carlin Van Trigt LLP	8721	D	626 243-5100	26219
Home Care of America Inc	8082	D	626 309-7696	22322
Hunt Ortmann Palffy Nieves	8111	E	626 440-5200	23138
Huntington Ambltry Surg Ctr	8011	E	626 229-8999	19504
Huntington Care LLC	8082	B	877 405-6990	22340
Huntington Hospital	8062	A	626 397-5000	21456
Huntington Med Res Institutes	8733	D	626 397-5804	26623
Huntington Otptent Surgery Ctr	8011	D	626 535-2434	19506
Huntington Reprodctve Ctr Inc (PA)	8011	E	626 204-9699	19507

	SIC	EMP	PHONE	ENTRY #
Idealab Holdings LLC **(PA)**	6799	A	626 585-6900	12233
Imagescan Inc	7374	D	626 844-2050	16145
Integro USA Inc	6411	E	626 795-9000	10652
Inter-Con Investigators Inc	7381	D	626 535-2200	16701
Inter-Con Security Systems Inc **(PA)**	7381	C	626 535-2200	16702
Interntional Un Oper Engineers	8631	E	626 792-2519	25065
Interprsnal Dvlpmntal Fclttors	8322	D	626 793-8967	23866
Invitation Homes	6512	D	805 372-2900	10901
Ion Media Networks Inc	4833	E	818 953-7193	5802
Ironwrker Emplyees Beneft Corp	6733	D	626 792-7337	12100
Jacobs Atcs Fema A Joint Ventr	8711	D	571 218-1115	25753
Jacobs Engineering Company	8711	A	626 449-2171	25755
Jacobs Engineering Group Inc	1629	D	626 578-3500	2039
Jacobs Engineering Inc **(HQ)**	8711	D	626 578-3500	25763
Jacobs International Ltd Inc	8711	B	626 578-3500	25764
Jpmorgan Chase Bank Nat Assn	6021	D	626 795-5177	9349
Kaiser Foundation Hospitals	6324	E	626 405-5000	10218
Kaiser Foundation Hospitals	8011	E	626 440-5639	19602
Kaiser Foundation Hospitals	8062	B	626 440-5659	21518
Kids Klub Care Centers Inc **(PA)**	8351	D	626 795-2501	24333
Kidspace A Prticipatory Museum	8412	D	626 449-9144	24886
Kinemetrics Inc **(DH)**	8711	D	626 795-2220	25781
La Asociacion Nacional Pro Per **(PA)**	8322	A	626 564-1988	23889
Land Design Consultants Inc	8748	D	626 578-7000	27770
Langham Hotels Pacific Corp	7011	D	617 451-1900	12837
Law Crossing **(PA)**	8331	D	626 243-1801	24199
Law School Financial Inc	6111	C	626 243-1800	9697
Legacy Healthcare Center LLC	8099	D	626 798-0558	22832
Lender Processing Services Inc	7374	D	626 808-9000	16151
Linden Optometry A Prof Corp	8042	D	323 681-5678	20158
Los Angeles Cnty Emp Retiremnt **(PA)**	6371	B	626 564-6000	10487
Madison Radiology Med Group	8011	D	626 793-8189	19665
Marianne Frostig Center **(PA)**	8621	E	626 791-1255	25026
Maxim Planning Group	8748	D	818 425-4343	27783
Merrill Lynch Pierce Fenner	6163	D	626 304-1596	9895
Merrill Lynch Pierce Fenner	6221	D	626 844-8500	10047
Mhh Holdings Inc	5149	D	626 744-9370	8826
Monte Vista Grove Homes	8361	D	626 796-6135	24607
Morgan Stanley	6211	D	626 405-9313	9992
Msj Healthcare LLC	8082	E	818 244-8446	22370
Msla Management LLC	8748	C	626 824-6020	27796
Myers Capital Partners LLC	6211	E	626 568-1398	10006
Myinternetservicescom LLC	4813	D	213 256-0575	5607
Norton Simon Museum	8412	D	626 449-6840	24896
Nrt Commercial Utah LLC	6531	D	626 449-5222	11637
Odona Central Security Inc	7381	C	323 728-8818	16746
Old Republic Contractors Ins	6411	D	626 683-5200	10721
Openx Technologies Inc **(DH)**	7311	D	855 673-6948	13874
Operating Engineers Funds Inc **(PA)**	6733	C	866 400-5200	12118
Pacific Clinics Foundation	8322	D	626 796-3453	23956
Pacific Huntington Hotel Corp	7011	A	626 568-3900	13003
Pacific Program/Design Managem	8741	D	626 440-2000	26973
Pacifica Services Inc	8711	D	626 405-0131	25862
Pardee Homes **(DH)**	6552	D	310 955-3100	11905
Park Hotels & Resorts Inc	7011	C	626 577-1000	13027
Park Marino Convalescent Ctr	8059	E	626 463-4105	21184
Parsons Constructors Inc.	8741	A	626 440-2000	26980
Parsons Corporation **(PA)**	1629	A	626 440-2000	2053
Parsons Engrg Science Inc **(DH)**	8711	B	626 440-2000	25866
Parsons Government Svcs Inc **(HQ)**	8711	B	626 440-2000	25867
Parsons Gvrnment Svcs Intl Inc.	1542	D	626 440-6000	1611
Parsons Project Services Inc	1541	C	626 440-4000	1427
Parsons Services Company	8711	A	626 440-2000	25870
Parsons Technical Services Inc.	8711	D	626 440-3998	25871
Parsons Wtr Infrastructure Inc.	8711	D	626 440-7000	25872
Pasadena Baking Co	5149	E	626 796-5093	8846
Pasadena Billing Associates	8721	D	626 795-6596	26264
Pasadena Center Operating Co	7389	C	626 795-9311	17391
Pasadena Child Dev Assoc Inc	8093	D	626 793-7350	22637
Pasadena Child Development Ass	8322	D	626 793-7350	23961
Pasadena Cyto Pathology Lab.	8062	B	626 397-8616	21636
Pasadena Hospital Assn Ltd **(PA)**	8062	A	626 397-5000	21637
Pasadena Hospital Assn Ltd	8051	E	626 397-3322	20696
Pasadena Hotel Dev Ventr LP	7011	D	626 449-4000	13047
Pasadena Humane Society	8699	D	626 792-7151	25450
Pasadena Madows Nursing Ctr LP	8051	D	626 796-1103	20697
Pasadena Rbles Acquisition LLC	7011	D	626 577-1000	13048
Permits Today LLC	7389	D	626 585-2931	17396
Physician Assoc San Gabriel	6324	C	626 817-8300	10301
PNC Bank National Association	6021	D	626 432-4500	9367
PNC Bank National Association	6021	D	626 351-2211	9368
Pollard Crnert Crwford Stevens	8111	E	626 793-4440	23334
Prima Royale Enterprises Ltd	5139	D	626 960-8388	8365
Prime Clinical Systems **(PA)**	7371	D	626 449-1705	15374
Principles Inc **(PA)**	8093	D	323 681-2575	22654

	SIC	EMP	PHONE	ENTRY #
Ptsi Managed Services Inc	8711	D	626 440-3118	25880
Ralphs Grocery Company	4225	D	626 793-7480	4623
Real Property Systems Inc	6531	C	760 243-1143	11716
Regency Park Senior Living Inc	8361	D	626 396-4911	24645
Regency Park Senior Living Inc	6531	D	626 568-2020	11723
Restaurant Depot LLC	5142	C	626 744-0204	8500
Robert C Hamilton	8361	D	626 794-4103	24655
Robert Half International Inc	7361	D	626 463-2037	14742
Rockley Photonics Inc **(HQ)**	7371	D	626 304-9960	15417
Rose Bowl Aquatics Center	7997	D	626 564-0330	19019
Rosemary Childrens Services **(PA)**	8361	C	626 844-3033	24656
Rt Pasad Hotel Partners LP	7011	D	626 403-7600	13149
Saiful/Bouquet Con Stru Eng **(PA)**	8711	D	626 304-2616	25900
Sedgwick Claims MGT Svcs Inc.	6411	D	626 568-1415	10767
Seville Construction Svcs Inc	8742	D	626 204-0800	27446
Seville Group **(PA)**	8741	D	626 395-7474	27027
Sierra Lobo Inc	8711	C	626 510-6340	25913
Sigma Investment Holdings LLC	1629	E	626 398-3098	2062
Slch Inc **(PA)**	8051	E	626 798-0558	20770
Smith Brothers Restaurant Inc	8741	D	626 577-2400	27034
Snap Technologies Inc	8742	D	626 585-6900	27458
Southern Cal Prmnnte Med Group **(PA)**	6324	D	626 405-5704	10317
Special Events Staffing	7361	A	626 296-6771	14766
Ssl Robotics LLC **(DH)**	8711	D	626 296-1373	25924
Ssl Robotics LLC	8711	D	626 296-1373	25925
Stantec Architecture Inc	8712	C	626 796-9141	26113
Stantec Consulting Svcs Inc	8711	D	626 796-9141	25931
Strategic Staffing Svcs Inc	8742	A	818 248-0049	27473
Sun Pacific Marketing Coop Inc **(PA)**	5148	A	213 612-9957	8733
Swca Incorporated	8748	D	626 240-0587	27872
Synopsys Inc	7372	D	626 795-9101	15873
Tetra Tech Executive Svcs Inc.	7361	C	626 470-2400	14779
Tetra Tech Nus Inc	8748	D	412 921-7090	27883
Tetra Tech Technical Services	8711	C	626 351-4664	25949
Ticor Title Insurance Company **(DH)**	6361	D	616 302-3121	10473
Tokio Marine Management Inc	6411	D	626 568-7600	10801
Torres Construction Corp **(PA)**	1541	D	323 257-7460	1445
Trinus Corporation	7371	E	818 246-1143	15512
Ttg Engineers **(PA)**	8711	C	626 463-2800	25962
Two Palms Nursing Center Inc	8059	E	626 798-8991	21232
Two Palms Nursing Center Inc	8059	D	626 796-1103	21233
Two Palms Nursing Center Inc	8059	D	323 681-4615	21234
UBS Financial Services Inc.	7389	E	626 449-1501	17530
Unified Valet Parking Inc	7521	D	818 822-5807	17709
United Couriers Inc **(DH)**	4512	C	213 383-3611	4813
Unity SEC & Protective Svc	7381	D	323 695-7234	16844
Universal Accounts Inc	7322	D	626 356-7900	14024
Valley Hunt Club	8641	D	626 793-7134	25273
Vincent Hayley Enterprises	8059	D	626 398-8182	21249
Voch Inc	8059	D	626 798-1111	21252
Wescom Central Credit Union **(PA)**	6062	B	888 493-7266	9662
Wescom Holdings LLC **(HQ)**	6411	D	888 493-7266	10827
Western Asset Core Plus	6722	D	626 844-9400	12054
Western Asset MGT Co LLC **(HQ)**	6722	D	626 844-9265	12055
Western Asset Mrtg Capitl Corp	6798	A	626 844-9400	12194
Worleyparsons Group Inc	8711	B	626 440-7000	26009
Zenith Health Care	6531	D	626 578-0460	11845

PASO ROBLES, CA - San Luis Obispo County

	SIC	EMP	PHONE	ENTRY #
Ameripride Services Inc	7213	D	805 239-9449	13507
AT&T Services Inc	4813	C	805 237-9503	5481
Cellco Partnership	4812	C	805 237-8200	5339
County of Los Angeles	8322	C	805 237-3110	23670
Dave Spurr Excavating Inc	1794	E	805 238-0834	3422
Emeritus Corporation	6513	E	805 239-1313	11013
Iqms **(PA)**	7371	C	805 227-1122	15235
Marsh Consulting Group	7389	D	239 433-5500	17314
Mge Underground Inc	1623	D	805 238-3510	1956
Michael Dusi Trucking Inc	4213	D	805 237-9499	4230
Omega 2 Alpha Services LLC	8742	D	805 610-2249	27373
Paso Robles Inn LLC	7011	D	805 238-2660	13050
Paso Robles Tank - Brown-Minne **(PA)**	1791	D	805 227-1641	3391
Pearce Services LLC **(HQ)**	1623	E	805 237-7480	1968
RE Max Parkside Real Estate	6531	D	805 239-3310	11707
Special Service Contrs Inc	1799	D	805 227-1081	3587
Treasury Wine Estates Americas	0172	C	805 237-6000	180
Union Pacific Railroad Company	4011	D	805 286-5851	3627
Villa Paseo Senior Residences	6513	D	805 227-4588	11132

PATTERSON, CA - Stanislaus County

	SIC	EMP	PHONE	ENTRY #
Del Puerto Health Care Dst	8011	D	209 892-9100	19434
Designed MBL Systems Inds Inc	1542	C	209 892-6298	1518
Diablo Grande Ltd Partnership	6552	D	209 892-7421	11871
Lucich Santos Farms	0191	C	209 892-6500	369
Traina Dried Fruit Inc	5149	C	209 892-5472	8887

2019 Directory of California
Wholesalers and Services Companies

(P-0000) Products & Services Section entry number
(PA)=Parent Co (HQ)=Headquarters (DH)=Div Headquarters

	SIC	EMP	PHONE	ENTRY #

PATTON, CA - San Bernardino County

	SIC	EMP	PHONE	ENTRY #
Califrnia Dept State Hospitals	8063	A	909 425-7000	21934

PAUMA VALLEY, CA - San Diego County

	SIC	EMP	PHONE	ENTRY #
Pauma Band of Mission Indians	7011	B	760 742-2177	13051
Pauma Valley Country Club	7997	D	760 742-1230	19002
T - Y Nursery Inc	5193	C	760 742-2151	9168

PEBBLE BEACH, CA - Monterey County

	SIC	EMP	PHONE	ENTRY #
California Golf Association	8611	D	831 625-4653	24950
Czech Commerce Ltd	5169	D	831 649-4633	8924
I Cypress Company	7011	A	831 649-8500	12757
I Cypress Company (PA)	7011	A	831 647-7500	12758
Lone Cypress Company LLC	7011	A	831 624-3811	12861
Lone Cypress Company LLC	7997	D	831 625-8507	18958
Monterey Peninsula Country CLB	7997	C	831 373-1556	18980
Pebble Bch Resrt Co DBA Lone C (PA)	7011	C	831 647-7500	13053
Poppy Hills Inc	7992	E	831 625-1513	18743

PENN VALLEY, CA - Nevada County

	SIC	EMP	PHONE	ENTRY #
Lake Wildwood Association	8641	C	530 432-1152	25188

PENRYN, CA - Placer County

	SIC	EMP	PHONE	ENTRY #
Sinclair Concrete	1771	D	916 663-0303	3326

PERRIS, CA - Riverside County

	SIC	EMP	PHONE	ENTRY #
4g Wireless Inc	4813	D	951 210-7980	5436
American Airlines Group Inc	4512	A	310 251-9184	4775
Basic Occpational Training Ctr	8399	C	951 657-8028	24744
Big Lgue Dreams Consulting LLC	7941	C	619 846-8855	18510
County of Riverside	8322	D	951 443-2262	23707
Dropzone Waterpark	7999	C	951 210-1600	19161
Eastern Municipal Water Dst (PA)	4941	B	951 928-3777	6248
Global Plastics Inc	5093	C	951 657-5466	7978
Griswold Industries	5085	C	951 657-1718	7850
Herca Telecomm Services Inc	5082	C	951 940-5941	7678
Integrity Rebar Placers	1791	C	951 696-6843	3377
Jeff Carpenter Inc	1794	D	951 657-5115	3431
Mamco Inc (PA)	1611	C	951 776-9300	1810
Oak Grove Inst Foundation Inc	0291	B	951 238-6022	453
Pacific Hydrotech Corporation	8711	C	951 943-8803	25860
Pacific Restoration Group Inc	0781	E	951 940-6069	775
Perris Valley Cmnty Hosp LLC (PA)	8062	B	951 436-5000	21640
Silver Creek Industries Inc	1542	C	951 943-5393	1648
SR Bray LLC	7359	E	951 436-2920	14546
United Material Handling Inc	4225	D	951 657-4900	4645
Village Nurseries Whl LLC	5193	C	951 657-3940	9176

PESCADERO, CA - San Mateo County

	SIC	EMP	PHONE	ENTRY #
Joie De Vivre Hospitality LLC	8741	D	650 879-1100	26911
King-Reynolds Ventures LLC	7389	D	650 879-2136	17275
Pescadero Conservation Aliance	8641	C	650 879-1441	25215

PETALUMA, CA - Sonoma County

	SIC	EMP	PHONE	ENTRY #
AB Closing Corporation	7361	D	707 766-1777	14562
Allianz Globl Risks US Insur	6331	B	415 899-3758	10331
Allianz Technology America Inc	7379	C	415 899-2713	16310
American Insurance Company Inc	6331	A	415 899-2000	10337
Arntz Builders Inc	1541	E	415 382-1188	1374
Associated Indemnity Corp	6311	A	415 899-2000	10128
Braden Partners LP A Calif (HQ)	8082	C	415 893-1518	22238
Clover-Stornetta Farms Inc (PA)	5149	C	707 769-3282	8770
Club One At Petaluma	7997	D	707 766-8080	18896
County Engineers Assn Cal	8711	D	707 762-3492	25625
Courseco Inc (PA)	7992	A	707 763-0335	18700
Crocodile Bay Lodge	7021	C	707 559-7990	13439
Crosscheck Inc (PA)	7389	C	707 665-2100	17114
Evergreen At Petaluma LLC	8051	C	707 763-6887	20418
Exchange Bank	6022	D	707 762-5555	9442
Federal Express Corporation	4513	D	800 463-3339	4817
Fedex Freight West Inc	4213	E	707 778-3191	4164
Firemans Fund Insurance Co (HQ)	6331	A	415 899-2000	10352
First California Mrtg Co II	6162	D	415 209-0910	9805
Fishman Supply Company	5087	D	707 763-8161	7886
Golden Living LLC	8051	D	707 763-4109	20473
Incom Mechanical Inc	1711	D	707 586-0511	2231
Intelisys Inc	8742	D	800 615-8330	27276
Kaiser Foundation Hospitals	8062	E	707 765-3900	21505
Legacy Marketing Group (PA)	8742	C	707 778-8638	27302
Marketlive Inc	7374	C	707 780-1600	16154
Midstate Construction Corp	1521	D	707 762-3200	1203
Molecular Bioproducts Inc	5049	D	707 762-6689	7245
Morris Distributing Inc	5181	D	707 769-7294	9016
National Surety Corporation	6351	A	415 899-2000	10431
NMN Construction Inc	1771	D	707 763-6981	3293
North Bay Construction Inc	1611	D	707 283-0093	1827
Oak Knoll Convalescent Center	8051	D	707 778-8686	20668

	SIC	EMP	PHONE	ENTRY #
Optio Solutions LLC	7322	C	800 360-2827	14014
Pacific Gas and Electric Co	4911	E	707 765-5118	6073
Permanente Medical Group Inc	8011	D	707 765-3900	19779
Petaluma Health Center Inc	8011	B	707 559-7500	19789
Photo TLC Inc	7384	C	415 462-0010	16963
Point Reyes Bird Observator	8699	D	415 868-0371	25452
Point Reyes Bird Observatory	8733	D	707 781-2555	26648
Praetorian USA	7299	D	707 780-8020	13768
Pure Luxury Limousine Service	4119	C	800 626-5466	3833
Redwood Building Maint Co	7349	D	707 782-9100	14364
Reichardt Duck Farm Inc	0259	D	707 762-6314	444
Rooster Run Golf Club Inc	7992	E	707 778-1211	18753
San Francisco Reinsurance Co	6321	D	415 899-2000	10170
San Frncsco North/Petaluma KOA	7033	C	707 763-1492	13467
Securitas SEC Svcs USA Inc	7381	C	707 586-1393	16798
Soligent Distribution LLC (HQ)	5065	D	707 992-3100	7543
Sonoma Cnty Ind Living Skills	8361	D	707 765-8444	24680
Sonoma Hotel Partners LP	7011	D	707 283-2888	13247
Sonoma Technology Inc	8748	D	707 665-9900	27865
Srm Alliance Hospital Services (PA)	8062	B	707 778-1111	21773
St Joseph Health System	8062	E	707 778-2505	21777
Star H-R (PA)	7363	A	707 762-4447	14916
Sunrise Farms LLC	5144	C	707 778-6450	8541
Sunrise of Petaluma	8361	D	707 776-2885	24694
Sunrise Senior Living Inc	8051	C	707 776-2885	20798
Sunset Aviation LLC (PA)	4581	E	707 775-2786	4913
Team Ghilotti Inc	1611	E	707 763-8700	1859
Transportation California Dept	1611	C	707 762-6641	1863
Trestles Holdings LLC	6719	D	707 778-8686	12013
United Cmps Cnfrences Retreats (PA)	7032	D	707 762-3220	13456
United Parcel Service Inc OH	4215	C	650 952-5200	4471
USI Insurance Services Nat Inc	6411	D	707 769-2900	10814

PICO RIVERA, CA - Los Angeles County

	SIC	EMP	PHONE	ENTRY #
ABF Freight System Inc	4213	E	323 773-2580	4090
Altamed Health Services Corp	8011	D	562 949-6069	19278
Altamed Health Services Corp	8099	D	562 949-8717	22727
Amini Innovation Corp	5021	C	562 222-2500	6709
AP Express LLC	4731	C	562 236-2250	5009
AP Express International LLC	4789	C	562 236-2250	5220
Aurora World Inc	5092	C	562 205-1222	7944
Benzara Inc	5023	C	562 633-7612	6750
California Hispanic Com	8069	C	562 942-9625	22000
Cellco Partnership	4812	C	562 942-8527	5399
Century 21 Excellence	6531	E	562 948-4553	11297
Chalmers Corporation	1541	D	562 948-4850	1385
Cintas Corporation No 3	7213	C	562 368-3200	13524
Clarklift Los Angeles Inc	5084	C	562 949-1006	7740
Daniels Western Mt Packers Inc	5147	C	562 948-2254	8614
Fedex Office & Print Svcs Inc	4215	C	562 942-1953	4418
Grm Information MGT Services	8741	E	562 373-9000	26880
Grm Information MGT Svcs Inc	8741	D	562 373-9000	26881
Herb Thyme Farm Inc	0139	D	603 542-3690	26
Howards Appliances Inc	4225	D	626 288-4010	4576
Ionics Altrpure Wtr Crparation	5149	D	562 948-2188	8807
Krikorian Premiere Theatre LLC	7832	D	562 205-3456	18305
L I Metal Systems	1761	E	562 948-5950	3171
Level 9 Security Services	7381	E	562 949-7180	16719
Los Angeles Unified School Dst	7389	D	562 654-9007	17303
Lucky Installations	1761	E	562 948-5950	3175
Manhole Adjusting Contrs Inc	1611	E	323 725-1387	1811
Mariner Health Care Inc	8051	D	562 942-7019	20623
Noble Rents Inc	7353	D	855 767-4424	14450
Pacific Logistics Corp (PA)	4731	C	562 478-4700	5131
Partschannel Inc	5013	E	562 654-3400	6664
Public Hlth Fndation Entps Inc	8099	C	562 801-2323	22864
Rivera Sanitarium Inc	8051	D	562 949-2591	20724
Riviera Nursing & Conva	8051	C	562 806-2576	20729
Rolo Transportation Company	4212	D	562 463-1440	4057
Santa Teresa Conv Hospital	8062	D	562 948-1961	21721
Sectran Security Incorporated (PA)	7381	C	562 948-1446	16781
Three Sons Inc	5147	D	562 801-4100	8631
Unisource Solutions Inc (PA)	5021	C	562 654-3500	6738
United Pacific Waste	4953	D	562 699-7600	6485
United Rentals North Amer Inc	7359	C	562 695-0748	14551
UPS Ground Freight Inc	4213	D	562 801-1300	4293
Wm Recycle America LLC	4953	D	562 948-3888	6526
Your Executive Solutions	7361	A	562 388-4150	14802

PIEDMONT, CA - Alameda County

	SIC	EMP	PHONE	ENTRY #
Boyscout of America	8641	D	510 547-4493	25118
Kinemed Inc	8731	D	510 655-6525	26390
Linda Beach Coop Pre-School	8351	E	510 547-4432	24338

PINE GROVE, CA - Amador County

	SIC	EMP	PHONE	ENTRY #
Volcano Communications Company (PA)	4813	D	209 296-7502	5674

GEOGRAPHIC

Employment Codes: A=Over 500 employees, B=251-500,
C=101-250, D=51-100, E=50

2019 Directory of California
Wholesalers and Services Companies

© Mergent Inc. 1-800-342-5647
1635

	SIC	EMP	PHONE	ENTRY #
Volcano Vision Inc	4841	C	209 296-2288	5964

PINECREST, CA - Tuolumne County

	SIC	EMP	PHONE	ENTRY #
Dodge Ridge Corporation	7011	B	209 536-5300	12533

PINOLE, CA - Contra Costa County

	SIC	EMP	PHONE	ENTRY #
Geek Squad Inc	7379	D	800 433-5778	16380
Kaiser Foundation Hospitals	8011	A	510 243-4000	19577
Pathway To Choices Inc	8322	D	510 724-9044	23963
Pinole Assisted Living Cmnty	6513	D	510 758-1122	11096
Pinole Senior Center	8322	D	510 724-9800	23971
State Farm Mutl Auto Insur Co	6411	D	510 222-1102	10784

PIONEER, CA - Amador County

	SIC	EMP	PHONE	ENTRY #
Pacific Gas and Electric Co	4911	D	209 295-2651	6094

PIRU, CA - Ventura County

	SIC	EMP	PHONE	ENTRY #
La Verne Nursery Inc	0181	D	805 521-0111	280

PISMO BEACH, CA - San Luis Obispo County

	SIC	EMP	PHONE	ENTRY #
Castlblack Pismo Bch Owner LLC	7011	E	805 773-6020	12438
Castleblack Owner Holdings LLC	8741	E	805 773-6020	26798
Pacific Gas and Electric Co	4911	D	805 773-6109	6089
Pismo Beach Athletic Club	7991	E	805 773-3011	18641
Pismo Coast Village Inc	7011	D	805 773-1811	13068
T I C Hotels Inc	7011	D	805 773-4671	13316

PITTSBURG, CA - Contra Costa County

	SIC	EMP	PHONE	ENTRY #
A T Associates Inc (PA)	8059	D	925 808-6540	20978
Allied Food Distributors Inc	5149	D	925 432-1625	8751
Arb Inc	4225	E	925 432-3649	4530
Comcast Corporation	4841	D	925 432-0500	5883
Concord Iron Works Inc	1791	E	925 432-0136	3374
Durham School Services L P	4151	C	925 686-3391	3919
First Baptist Head Start	8351	D	925 473-2000	24321
G&K Services LLC	7218	E	925 427-4401	13607
Hydrochem LLC	7349	D	925 432-1749	14288
La Clinica De La Raza Inc	8021	C	925 431-1250	20122
Lincoln Child Center Inc	8361	D	925 521-1270	24579
McCampbell Analytical Inc	8734	D	925 252-9262	26712
Pittsburg Care Center Ltd	8051	E	925 432-3831	20702
Pittsburg Skilled Nursing	8051	D	925 808-6540	20703
Ravig Inc	5045	D	925 526-1234	7097
Redwood Painting Co Inc	1721	C	925 432-4500	2473
Rfid Corporation	7213	C	925 473-9978	13551
SSC Pittsburg Operating Co LP	8059	A	925 427-4444	21220
State Preschool	8351	E	925 473-4380	24386

PLACENTIA, CA - Orange County

	SIC	EMP	PHONE	ENTRY #
Alta Vista Country Club LLC	7997	D	714 524-1591	18824
Bejac Corporation (PA)	5084	D	714 528-6224	7730
City Service Contracting Inc (PA)	1799	D	714 632-6610	3503
Clima-Tech Inc	7623	D	909 613-5513	17892
Customline Professional	7336	B	714 996-1333	14109
Elljay Acoustics Inc	1742	D	714 961-1173	2880
Facility Solutions Group Inc	5063	C	714 993-3966	7361
GD Heil Inc	1795	C	714 687-9100	3453
Hardy Window Company (PA)	5031	C	714 996-1807	6826
Interface Rehab Inc	8049	A	714 646-8300	20185
Linda Placentia-Yorba	4225	D	714 985-8775	4585
Linda Yorba Water District (PA)	4941	D	714 701-3000	6272
Micon Construction Cal Inc	1542	D	714 666-0203	1595
Osscim Inc	1761	E	714 680-0015	3182
Premier Auto W Covina LLC	7538	D	626 858-7202	17778
Residence Inn By Marriott	7011	D	714 996-0555	13120
SGF Produce Holding Corp	5148	B	714 630-6292	8729
So California Ventures Ltd	1542	D	714 524-0021	1655
Spad Holdings LLC	7991	E	714 993-6003	18661
Sunrise Growers Inc (HQ)	5148	A	714 630-2170	8737
Tct Circuit Supply Inc	5085	D	714 644-9700	7875
Tenet Healthsystem Medical	8069	B	714 993-2000	22054
Total Woman	7991	D	714 993-6003	18671

PLACERVILLE, CA - El Dorado County

	SIC	EMP	PHONE	ENTRY #
Centene Corporation	6324	D	530 626-5773	10190
Consortm On Reachng Excellnce	8748	E	510 540-4200	27697
County of El Dorado	8063	D	530 621-6210	21942
County of El Dorado	7349	D	530 621-5845	14233
County of El Dorado	8322	D	530 642-7130	23637
El Dorado County Health Dept	8011	D	530 621-6100	19456
El Dorado Irrigation District	4941	B	530 622-4513	6250
El Dorado Savings Bank (PA)	6035	D	530 622-1492	9523
El Dorado Water & Shower Svc	4941	E	530 622-8995	6251
Elder Options (PA)	8322	E	530 626-6939	23786
ERA Realty Center	6531	D	530 295-2900	11421
Gladiolus Holdings LLC	8051	D	530 622-3400	20455
Gold Country Health Center Inc (PA)	8399	C	530 621-1100	24784
Hangtown Knnel CLB Plcrvlle CA	0752	D	530 622-4867	629

	SIC	EMP	PHONE	ENTRY #
Harmony Home Health LLC	8082	D	916 933-9777	22310
Help At Home Inc	8322	D	916 933-9050	23834
Innovative Education MGT Inc	8741	C	530 295-3566	26893
Lyon Realty	6519	C	530 295-4444	11176
Marshall Medical Center (PA)	8062	A	530 622-1441	21581
Mother Lode Rehabilit	8361	C	530 622-4848	24608
NPS Marketing	8742	B	916 941-5510	27372
Pacific Gas and Electric Co	4911	E	530 621-7237	6077
Placervlle Pnes Cnvlscent Hosp	8059	C	530 622-3400	21187
Progress House Inc (PA)	8361	D	530 626-9240	24636
Quality In-Hmecare Specialists	8082	D	530 303-3477	22400
Shingle Sprng Trbal Gming Auth	7999	A	530 677-7000	19237
Summitview Child Treatment Ctr	8361	E	530 644-2412	24690
USDA Forest Service	0851	D	530 626-1546	1002
W F Hayward Co	1742	D	530 303-3030	2976
Western Slope Health Center	8051	D	530 622-6842	20885

PLAYA DEL REY, CA - Los Angeles County

	SIC	EMP	PHONE	ENTRY #
Automate Parking Inc	7521	D	310 674-3396	17676
Los Angeles Dept Wtr & Pwr	4939	C	310 524-8500	6199
Parking Concepts Inc	7521	D	310 322-5008	17701

PLAYA VISTA, CA - Los Angeles County

	SIC	EMP	PHONE	ENTRY #
1on1 LLC	7372	E	310 448-5376	15563
72andsunny LLC	7311	C	310 215-9009	13784
Belkin International Inc (DH)	5065	B	310 751-5100	7450
Chownow Inc	7372	D	888 707-2469	15626
Fullscreen Inc (HQ)	7311	D	310 202-3333	13832
Lee Burkhart Liu Inc (PA)	8712	D	310 829-2249	26080
Linksys LLC	5065	C	310 751-5100	7503
Lowermybills, Inc.	7375	D	310 348-6800	16238
Microsoft Corporation	7372	D	213 806-7300	15763
Phelps Group	7311	C	310 752-4400	13879
Pop Media Networks LLC (DH)	7929	D	323 856-4000	18456
Ryot Corp	7336	D	323 356-1787	14128

PLEASANT GROVE, CA - Sutter County

	SIC	EMP	PHONE	ENTRY #
Holt of California (HQ)	5082	C	916 991-8200	7679
Sysco Sacramento Inc	5141	B	916 275-2714	8468
Withrow Cattle	0241	D	916 780-0364	427

PLEASANT HILL, CA - Contra Costa County

	SIC	EMP	PHONE	ENTRY #
Accentcare Home Health Cal Inc	8082	D	925 356-6066	22189
Aegis Senior Communities LLC	8082	D	925 588-7030	22206
Ascendantfx Capital USA Inc	6099	D	201 633-4667	9669
AT&T Corp.	4812	D	925 603-9476	5261
Brighter Beginnings (PA)	8322	D	510 903-7503	23519
Carlton Senior Living	8082	D	925 935-1001	22256
Choice In Aging (PA)	8093	D	925 682-6330	22530
Contra Costa Country Club	7997	D	925 798-7135	18898
Controlco (PA)	5084	D	800 800-7126	7743
Courtyard Management Corp	7011	E	925 691-1444	12493
Crestwood Behavioral Hlth Inc	8063	D	925 938-8050	21951
Diablo Vly College Foundation (PA)	7389	D	925 685-1230	17132
Dreamctchers Empwerment Netwrk	8361	C	925 935-6630	24509
East Bay Connection Inc	4111	E	925 609-1920	3647
John Muir Health	8062	A	925 952-2887	21464
John Muir Physician Network	8062	A	925 685-0843	21470
Mark Scott Construction Inc (PA)	1542	E	925 944-0502	1587
Marriott International Inc	7011	C	925 689-1010	12905
Maxim Services Ltd Inc	7349	D	925 969-1907	14315
Mc Namara Dodge Ney Beatt (PA)	8111	D	925 939-5330	23241
Quest Diagnostics Incorporated	8071	B	925 687-2514	22130
Solo W-2 Inc	8742	C	925 680-0200	27461
Young MNS Chrstn Assn of E Bay	8641	D	925 687-8900	25354

PLEASANTON, CA - Alameda County

	SIC	EMP	PHONE	ENTRY #
1st United Services Credit Un (PA)	6061	D	800 649-0193	9537
ABM Elctrcal Ltg Solutions Inc	7349	D	408 399-3030	14167
ABM Janitorial Services Inc	7349	B	925 924-0270	14173
Acosta Inc	5141	D	925 600-3500	8371
Advantage Sales & Marketing	5141	C	925 463-5600	8372
Advantage Sales & Mktg LLC	5141	C	925 463-5600	8375
Aegis Enterprises Inc.	1711	D	925 417-5550	2087
Alain Pinel Realtors Inc	6531	D	925 251-1111	11199
Alameda County AG Fair Assn	7999	D	925 426-7600	19092
Alliance Information Technolog (PA)	7371	D	925 462-9787	14972
American Baptist Homes of West (HQ)	6513	D	925 924-7100	10977
American Property Management	7011	C	925 463-8000	12316
Anixter Inc	5063	E	925 469-8500	7333
AOC Technologies Inc.	5051	B	925 875-0808	7257
Automatic Data Processing Inc	7374	D	925 251-5300	16095
Axis Community Health Inc	8093	D	925 462-1755	22509
Bay Vista Senior Housing	8741	C	925 924-7100	26776
Better Living Brands LLC	7389	C	888 723-3929	17031
Black Tie Transportation LLC	4119	C	925 847-0747	3778
Blackhawk Network Inc (DH)	6099	A	925 226-9990	9672

Mergent email: customerrelations@mergent.com
1636

2019 Directory of California
Wholesalers and Services Companies

(P-0000) Products & Services Section entry number
(PA)=Parent Co (HQ)=Headquarters (DH)=Div Headquarters

Company	SIC	EMP	PHONE	ENTRY #
Blackhawk Network Holdings Inc (HQ)	6099	B	925 226-9990	9673
Blackrock Logistics Inc	4731	C	925 523-3878	5017
Boeing Company	8731	D	925 398-7664	26342
Bricsnet FM America Inc	7379	D	202 756-1840	16321
Brightview Landscape Svcs Inc	0781	D	925 924-8900	741
Buxton Consulting	8748	D	925 467-0700	27666
Calatlantic Group Inc	1531	E	925 847-8700	1332
Caliber Home Loans Inc	6162	D	925 417-3491	9785
California and Nevada IBEW/Nec	1731	D	925 828-6322	2537
Califrnia Yuth Soccer Assn Inc	8699	D	925 426-5437	25404
Can-AM Plumbing Inc	1711	C	925 846-1833	2156
Castlewood Country Club	7997	C	925 846-2871	18884
Ce2 Kleinfelder JV	8711	D	925 463-7301	25601
Center Cnslng Edctn & Crisis	8322	D	925 462-1755	23546
Citimortgage Inc	6211	E	925 730-3800	9942
Citrusbits Inc	7371	E	925 452-6012	15062
CJ Model Home Maintenance Inc	7349	D	925 485-3280	14215
Clorox Services Company	8741	D	925 425-6748	26811
Cognix Automation Inc	7373	E	925 464-8822	15935
Commerce West Insurance Co	6141	D	925 730-6400	9706
Construction Testing Services (PA)	8741	E	925 462-5151	26818
Conti Life Comm Plea LLC	7389	D	925 227-6800	17100
Convergint Technologies LLC	7382	E	510 300-2800	16885
Convo Communications LLC	4899	C	925 227-5500	5976
Corporate Visions Inc (PA)	8742	D	415 464-4400	27201
Crossmark Inc	5141	B	925 463-3555	8398
Dahlin Group Inc (PA)	8712	D	925 251-7200	26040
Dan Lofgren	7349	D	925 846-6632	14248
Deloitte & Touche LLP	8721	C	415 782-4020	26183
Dimension Data North Amer Inc	7373	D	925 226-8378	15946
Dublin San Ramon Services Dst	4941	D	925 846-4565	6240
E-Loan Inc (DH)	6163	A	925 847-6200	9880
Elavon Inc	7375	B	925 734-8939	16222
Ellie Mae Inc (PA)	7372	C	925 227-7000	15666
Ernst & Young LLP	8721	C	925 734-6388	26202
Et Capital Solar Partners USA	8741	E	925 460-9898	26850
Evidentio Inc (HQ)	7371	C	855 933-1337	15152
Excel Building Services LLC	7349	A	925 474-1080	14261
Farmers Group Inc	6411	B	925 847-3100	10619
Federal Express Corporation	7389	D	800 463-3339	17167
Ford Motor Company	6141	D	925 351-6205	9712
Fusion Mphc Holding Corp	7372	C	925 201-2500	15687
Gatan Inc (HQ)	8711	D	925 463-0200	25702
Glass Pak Inc	4783	D	707 207-0400	5208
Global Software Resources Inc (PA)	7379	E	925 249-2200	16386
Gtt Communications (mp) Inc (DH)	4813	C	925 201-2500	5575
Guardian Computer Support	7378	C	925 251-8800	16287
Guardsmark LLC	7381	B	925 484-4412	16676
Hitachi High Tech Amer Inc	5065	D	925 218-2800	7488
Humangood (PA)	8059	D	602 906-4024	21116
Impact Group LLC	5141	D	925 327-7322	8416
Jpmorgan Xign Corporation	8721	D	925 469-9446	26233
Kaiser Foundation Hospitals	8062	D	925 598-2799	21493
Kaiser Foundation Hospitals	8062	D	925 847-5000	21509
Kaiser Fundation Hlth Plan Inc	6324	D	510 271-5800	10274
Kiewit Infrastructure West Co	1611	D	925 462-1088	1802
Kleinfelder Inc	8711	D	925 484-1700	25784
Kraft Heinz Foods Company	5149	B	925 469-0057	8819
Leisure Sports Inc	6719	B	925 942-6301	11989
Mackay Smps Cvil Engineers Inc (PA)	8711	D	925 416-1790	25809
Market Smart Inc	5141	D	925 846-6237	8422
Martin ATI-AC Inc (PA)	8712	D	925 648-8800	26094
Mason-Mcduffie Real Estate Inc	6531	D	925 734-5000	11593
Maxplore Technologies Inc	7371	D	925 621-1400	15275
McM Partners Inc	6531	D	925 463-9500	11598
Meadowbrook Meat Company Inc	5142	D	252 985-7200	8496
Megapath Cloud Company LLC (PA)	4813	D	925 201-2500	5597
Megapath Inc (PA)	4813	D	877 611-6342	5600
Mission Peak Orthopedics	8011	D	510 797-3933	19694
North American Title Co Inc	6361	D	925 399-3000	10467
Nucompass Mobility Svcs Inc (PA)	7389	D	925 734-3434	17363
Oc IV A California LP	7538	E	925 734-5800	17774
On-Time AC & Htg Inc (PA)	1711	D	925 598-1911	2296
Oracle America Inc	7372	C	925 694-3314	15794
Oracle Corporation	7372	B	877 767-2253	15809
Oracle Systems Corporation	7372	B	925 694-3000	15820
Patelco Credit Union (PA)	6061	C	800 358-8228	9580
Philips Hlthcare Infrmtics Inc (DH)	7371	C	650 293-2300	15357
Pinnacle Document Systems (PA)	5044	D	925 417-8400	6973
Pleasant Canyon Hotel Inc	7011	E	925 847-0535	13070
Pleasanton Project Owner LLC	7011	D	925 847-7592	13071
Pleasanton Unified School Dst	7336	C	925 462-5500	14125
Plex Systems Inc	7374	D	248 391-8001	16166
Product Quality Partners Inc	7379	D	925 484-6491	16463
Psinapse Technology Ltd	7361	D	925 225-0400	14709
Pulte Home Company LLC	1521	D	925 249-3200	1219
Pyramid Advisors LLC	7011	D	925 847-6000	13084
Quality Auto Craft Inc	7538	A	925 426-0120	17779
Roche Molecular Systems Inc (DH)	8731	B	925 730-8000	26446
Rs Calibration Services Inc	7699	E	925 462-4217	17980
Ruby Hill Golf Club LLC	7992	D	925 417-5840	18754
S&J Stadtler Inc	6531	B	925 847-8900	11751
Sabah International Inc (HQ)	1731	D	925 463-0431	2719
Safe America Credit Union (PA)	6061	D	925 734-4111	9583
Safetraces Inc	7371	C	925 398-8985	15422
Schneider Electric Usa Inc	5063	C	925 462-0986	7391
Servicemax Inc (DH)	7371	C	925 965-7859	15439
Sheraton Operating	7011	B	925 463-3330	13219
Shooter & Butts Inc	0781	E	925 460-5155	787
Signature Properties Inc	6552	D	925 463-1122	11918
Simbol Inc (PA)	8731	D	925 226-7400	26456
Simpson Strong-Tie Intl Inc	5051	D	925 560-9000	7313
Six Continents Hotels Inc	7011	D	925 847-6000	13238
Smartzip Analytics Inc (PA)	8742	D	925 218-1900	27455
Spacetone Acoustics Inc	1742	E	925 931-0749	2960
Specialty Risk Services Inc	6411	C	877 809-9478	10777
Spring Bioscience Corp	8071	A	925 474-8463	22149
State Compensation Insur Fund	6331	C	925 523-5000	10409
State Compensation Insur Fund	6331	C	888 782-8338	10410
Sun-Maid Growers California	0172	E	800 752-9277	179
Sunbelt Controls Inc	7623	E	925 660-3900	17897
Sunol Vly Golf & Recreation Co	7992	D	925 862-2404	18770
Telecom Technology Svcs Inc	8748	C	925 224-7812	27878
Terminix Intl Co Ltd Partnr	7342	C	925 460-5063	14159
The For Hospital Committee (DH)	8741	B	925 847-3000	27061
Toll Brothers Inc	1521	D	925 855-0260	1248
Toolwire Inc	7371	D	925 227-8500	15506
Total Renal Care Inc	8092	E	925 737-0120	22491
Transbay Fire Protection Inc (PA)	1796	E	925 846-9484	3476
Trevi Partners A Calif LP (PA)	7011	C	925 225-4000	13344
Unchained Labs (PA)	8071	E	925 587-9800	22153
Unisource Packaging Inc	5113	C	925 227-6000	8128
Veeva Systems Inc (PA)	7372	C	925 452-6500	15888
Wastexperts Incorporated	8741	D	925 484-1057	27090
Wavestrong Inc	7373	D	925 549-2882	16075
Wells Fargo Bank National Assn	6021	D	925 463-1983	9400
West Valley Engineering Inc	7361	D	925 416-9707	14798
Workday Inc (PA)	7371	C	925 951-9000	15548
Youngs Market Company LLC	5182	B	510 475-2200	9067
Zenith Insurance Company	6311	D	925 460-0600	10153

PLS VRDS PNSL, CA - Los Angeles County

Company	SIC	EMP	PHONE	ENTRY #
Aichinger International Inc	5012	D	310 375-1533	6576
Episcopal Communities & Servic	8051	D	310 544-2204	20405

PLYMOUTH, CA - Amador County

Company	SIC	EMP	PHONE	ENTRY #
Borjon Iscander	0761	C	209 245-6289	640

POINT ARENA, CA - Mendocino County

Company	SIC	EMP	PHONE	ENTRY #
Manchester Band Pomo Indians	8322	D	707 882-2788	23909

POINT REYES STATION, CA - Marin County

Company	SIC	EMP	PHONE	ENTRY #
Pacific Slope Tree Coop Inc	0783	E	415 663-1300	977

POINT RICHMOND, CA - Contra Costa County

Company	SIC	EMP	PHONE	ENTRY #
Hartmann Studios Inc (HQ)	7389	C	510 232-5030	17209

POMONA, CA - Los Angeles County

Company	SIC	EMP	PHONE	ENTRY #
American National Red Cross	8099	A	909 859-7006	22731
Anka Behavioral Health Inc	8011	D	909 622-8217	19296
Behavioral Health Services Inc	8322	D	909 865-2336	23507
Braun Linen Service Inc	7211	D	909 623-2678	13484
Cal Poly Pomona Foundation Inc (PA)	8699	A	909 869-2950	25402
Casa Colin Comprehensive	8093	C	909 596-7733	22519
Casa Colina Inc (PA)	8322	A	909 596-7733	23529
Casa Colina Hospital and Cente (HQ)	8062	B	909 596-7733	21305
Central Reference Lab Inc	8071	C	909 861-6966	22067
Centrescapes Inc	0782	D	909 392-3303	810
Chino Valley Healthcare Center	8051	D	909 628-1245	20310
Circle Wood Services Inc	8741	D	909 784-0733	26805
City of Pomona	8399	D	909 397-5506	24752
City of Pomona	4953	C	909 620-2361	6376
Coan Construction Co Inc	1771	D	909 868-6812	3235
Commercial Door Company Inc	1751	D	714 529-2179	3022
Continental Agency Inc	4731	D	909 595-8884	5036
Coptic Clinics	8011	D	562 900-2692	19405
Country Oaks Partners LLC	8051	D	909 622-1067	20327
County of Los Angeles	8111	C	909 620-3330	22998
County of Los Angeles	7992	D	909 629-1166	18699
County of Los Angeles	8322	D	909 469-4500	23674
Dedicated Fleet Systems Inc (PA)	4212	D	909 590-8209	4000
DJ Scheffler Inc (PA)	1741	E	909 595-2924	2803

Employment Codes: A=Over 500 employees, B=251-500,
C=101-250, D=51-100, E=50

2019 Directory of California
Wholesalers and Services Companies

© Mergent Inc. 1-800-342-5647

1637

GEOGRAPHIC

	SIC	EMP	PHONE	ENTRY #
Eastman Music Company (PA)	5099	D	909 868-1777	8029
Fairplex Enterprises Inc	7999	D	909 623-3111	19168
Ferguson Enterprises Inc	5074	C	909 364-8700	7621
Ferguson Fire Fabrication Inc (DH)	5074	D	909 517-3085	7624
Frank S Smith Masonry Inc	1741	D	909 468-0525	2807
Furniture Trnsp Systems	4731	D	909 869-1200	5067
Genesis Healthcare Corporation	8051	E	909 622-1069	20451
Genesis Healthcare Corporation	8051	D	909 628-6024	20452
Healthright 360	8322	D	909 624-1233	23833
Henkels & McCoy Inc	1623	B	909 517-3011	1925
Henkels & McCoy Inc	1623	D	909 590-8419	1926
Howard Roofing Company Inc	1761	D	909 622-5598	3165
Hsbc Finance Corporation	6141	A	909 623-3355	9715
Inland Valley Partners LLC	8049	C	909 623-7100	20180
Inter Valley Pool Supply Inc	5091	D	626 969-5657	7931
Inter-Valley Health Plan Inc	6324	D	909 623-6333	10215
J & E Private Security Corp	7381	C	909 594-1111	16706
Jeff Kerber Pool Plst Inc	1799	B	909 465-0677	3539
K K W Trucking Inc (PA)	4213	B	909 869-1200	4200
Keith T Kusunis MD	8093	D	909 469-9494	22605
Landmark Medical Services Inc	8063	C	909 593-2585	21962
Latara Enterprise Inc (PA)	8071	C	909 623-9301	22104
LDI Transportation Inc	4214	D	909 620-7001	4354
Lee Jennings Target Ex Inc (PA)	4212	C	909 868-1040	4036
Lexmar Distribution Inc	4213	D	909 620-7001	4216
Longwood Management Corp	6513	D	818 884-7100	11058
Los Angeles County Fair Assn (PA)	7999	B	909 623-3111	19199
Master Disposal Co	4953	E	626 444-6789	6417
Merchants Building Maint Co	7349	C	909 622-8260	14320
MJB Partners LLC	8051	C	909 623-2481	20649
Murcor Inc	6531	C	909 623-4001	11623
Myers Tire Supply Dist Inc	5013	D	602 233-1037	6659
NW Packaging LLC (PA)	5199	D	909 706-3627	9238
PHD Marketing Inc	5199	D	909 620-1000	9249
Pomona Community Health Center	8621	D	909 630-7927	25037
Pomona Housing Partners LP	6531	E	909 622-1010	11674
Pomona Valley Hospital Med Ctr (PA)	8062	A	909 865-9500	21652
Pomona Valley Hospital Med Ctr	8069	C	909 865-9700	22038
Rfid Textile Services Inc	7213	D	909 623-5135	13552
Rwp Transfer Inc	5099	E	909 868-6882	8056
San Gabriel/Pomona Valleys	8322	B	909 620-7722	24023
Schaefer Ambulance Service Inc	4119	D	626 333-4533	3845
Second Image National LLC	7335	D	909 445-8080	14099
Securitas SEC Svcs USA Inc	7381	C	909 865-4356	16806
Siemens Industry Inc	5063	D	909 627-6141	7395
Southern California Edison Co	4911	D	909 469-0251	6128
Spectra Company	1741	C	909 599-0760	2824
Spiniello Companies	1623	D	909 629-1000	1984
Starwood Htls & Rsrts Wrldwde	7011	C	909 622-2220	13280
T McGee Electric Inc	1731	D	909 591-6461	2760
Tri City Mental Health Center	8093	D	909 784-3200	22700
Ultimate Removal Inc	1795	C	909 524-0800	3466
Valley Nurses	8049	D	714 549-2512	20212
W Why W Enterprises Inc	4214	D	626 969-4292	4388
Whitefield Medical Lab Inc (PA)	8071	E	909 625-2114	22160
Yamamoto of Orient Inc (HQ)	5149	C	909 594-7356	8902

PORT HUENEME, CA - Ventura County

	SIC	EMP	PHONE	ENTRY #
Advantedge Technology Inc	8711	D	805 488-0405	25504
Alion Science and Tech Corp	8711	D	805 488-8761	25526
Cecos	8711	E	805 982-5400	25602
Interntional Longshore Whse Un	7361	D	805 488-2944	14651
Oxnard Beach Hotel LP	7011	E	805 488-6560	12993
Pride Industries	1522	C	805 985-8481	1307
United States Dept of Navy	8011	A	805 982-6392	20024
United States Dept of Navy	8011	A	805 982-6370	20026
Waggoners Trucking	4213	D	800 999-9097	4301

PORTER RANCH, CA - Los Angeles County

	SIC	EMP	PHONE	ENTRY #
Coast To Coast Realty	6531	D	818 360-2609	11324
Infogen Labs Inc	7379	D	818 825-5024	16394

PORTERVILLE, CA - Tulare County

	SIC	EMP	PHONE	ENTRY #
Baird-Neece Packing Corp	0723	C	559 784-3393	494
Bank of Sierra (HQ)	6022	C	559 782-4300	9416
Developmental Svcs Cal Dept	8051	A	559 782-2222	20375
E M Tharp Inc (PA)	5012	D	559 782-5800	6591
E W Merritt Farms (PA)	0191	D	559 784-8916	339
Exeter Packers Inc	0723	C	559 784-8820	512
Family Healthcare Network	8011	B	559 781-7242	19470
Fern Oaks Frms A Cal Gen Prtnr	0241	E	559 684-8220	411
Foster Farms LLC	0252	B	559 793-5501	431
Gaithers Family Home	8059	C	559 781-0301	21078
Good Shepherd Lutheran Hm of W (PA)	8361	D	559 791-2000	24542
Mitch Brown Construction Inc	1629	D	559 781-6389	2046
Moyles Central Vly Hlth Care	8051	C	559 782-1509	20657

	SIC	EMP	PHONE	ENTRY #
Nuvi Global	5047	A	559 306-2646	7198
Propak Logistics Inc	7699	D	559 782-8696	17973
R & G Enterprises	0722	C	559 781-1351	484
River Island Country Club Inc	7997	D	559 781-2917	19015
Salvador Martinez	0761	C	559 781-5150	673
Sierra Valley Rehab Center	8059	C	559 784-7375	21207
Sierra View Dst Hosp Leag Inc (PA)	8011	C	559 784-1110	19892
Sierra View Local Hospital Dst	8062	B	559 781-7877	21755
Sun Villa Inc	8051	C	559 784-6644	20786
Tharp Truck Rental Inc (PA)	7699	C	559 782-5800	17996
Tule River Indian Hlth Ctr Inc	8093	D	559 784-2316	22701
Valley Careidence Opco LLC	8051	D	559 784-8371	20849
Wescordon Incorporated (PA)	8051	C	559 784-8371	20880

PORTOLA, CA - Plumas County

	SIC	EMP	PHONE	ENTRY #
Eastern Plumas Health Care (PA)	8099	C	530 832-4277	22796
R Joy Inc	8711	D	530 832-5760	25885

PORTOLA VALLEY, CA - San Mateo County

	SIC	EMP	PHONE	ENTRY #
Boething Treeland Farms Inc	0811	A	650 851-4770	984
Intuit Inc	7372	C	650 944-2840	15721
McClenahan Pest Control Inc	7342	E	650 326-8781	14154
Pointspeed Inc	7379	D	650 638-3720	16456
SP McClenahan Co	0783	D	650 326-8781	978

PORTOLA VALLY, CA - San Mateo County

	SIC	EMP	PHONE	ENTRY #
Semans Communications (PA)	1731	D	650 529-9984	2729

POTRERO, CA - San Diego County

	SIC	EMP	PHONE	ENTRY #
Rancho De Sus Ninos Inc	8361	D	619 661-9232	24641

POTTER VALLEY, CA - Mendocino County

	SIC	EMP	PHONE	ENTRY #
McFadden Farm	0112	E	707 743-1122	6

POWAY, CA - San Diego County

	SIC	EMP	PHONE	ENTRY #
Arch Health Partners Inc (HQ)	8062	D	858 675-3100	21290
Bay City Equipment Inds Inc	5063	D	619 938-8200	7337
Benchmark Landscape Inc	0782	C	858 513-7190	803
Braswells Villa Monte Vista	8059	C	858 487-6242	21013
Brieck Restoration Inc	1521	E	858 679-9928	1128
Centre Care Management Co LLC	8011	C	858 613-6255	19368
Chef Works Inc (PA)	5136	C	858 643-5600	8252
Climatec LLC	1731	E	858 391-7000	2541
Community Dev Inst Head Start	8351	D	858 668-2985	24302
Concrete Images International	1771	D	858 676-1253	3240
Corodata Corporation (PA)	4226	C	858 748-1100	4670
Corovan Corporation (PA)	4214	C	858 762-8100	4338
Corovan Moving & Storage Co (HQ)	4214	C	858 748-1100	4339
D and D Concrete Cnstr Inc	1771	D	619 518-9737	3244
Decision Sciences Intl Corp	5065	C	858 571-1900	7465
Desert View Auto Auctions Inc (PA)	5012	C	760 788-6955	6590
Diazyme Laboratories Inc	8071	C	858 455-4754	22076
Eappraiseit LLC (PA)	6531	D	800 281-6200	11415
Electronic Control Systems LLC	1731	C	858 513-1911	2576
Ems Construction Inc	1542	C	858 679-8292	1528
Geico General Insurance Co	6411	B	858 848-8200	10634
Generation Contracting & Emerg	1521	E	858 679-9928	1171
Hubb Systems LLC	7373	C	510 865-9100	15973
Ickler Electric Corporation	1731	E	858 486-1585	2611
Information Systems Labs Inc (PA)	8711	D	858 535-9680	25744
Intelligent Automation Corp	8711	E	858 679-4140	25749
Jinx Inc	5092	D	888 546-9266	7954
Kiewit Infrastructure West Co	1622	A	360 693-1478	1883
Law Offices of Thomas W	8111	C	858 883-2000	23195
Lorber Greenfield & Polito LLP (PA)	8111	E	858 486-6757	23228
Maderas Golf Club	7992	D	858 451-8100	18731
Palomar Health	8062	B	858 613-4000	21629
Palomar Health	8072	C	858 613-4000	22172
Pkl Services Inc	7699	C	858 679-1755	17971
Pomerado Operations LLC	8051	D	858 487-6242	20711
Prestige Concrete	1771	D	858 679-2772	3309
Provoast Automation Controls (PA)	5084	D	858 748-2237	7788
Quality Reinforcing Inc	1791	C	858 748-8400	3392
Rutledge Claims Management Inc	6411	D	858 883-2000	10760
San Diego Bay Area Elc Inc	1731	D	858 748-2060	2721
Sysco San Diego Inc	5141	B	858 513-7300	8469
T G T Enterprises Inc	7331	C	858 413-0300	14064
Tekworks Inc (PA)	7389	C	858 668-1705	17500
Trepco Imports & Dist Ltd	5194	E	619 690-7999	9187
Wr Chavez Construction Inc	1542	D	858 375-2100	1705

QUINCY, CA - Plumas County

	SIC	EMP	PHONE	ENTRY #
Artimisa & Co	8711	D	530 283-3700	25547
Plumas District Hospital (PA)	8062	C	530 283-2121	21651
Plumas District Hospital	8011	C	530 283-0650	19793
Plumas Rural Services	8322	D	530 283-2725	23973
Sierra Cscade Fmly Opprtnities (PA)	8351	C	530 283-1242	24381

2019 Directory of California
Wholesalers and Services Companies

(P-0000) Products & Services Section entry number
(PA)=Parent Co (HQ)=Headquarters (DH)=Div Headquarters

RAMONA, CA - San Diego County

Company	SIC	EMP	PHONE	ENTRY #
Burch Construction Company Inc	1542	E	760 788-9370	1489
Famous Ramona Water Inc	5149	E	760 789-0174	8788
Prudential California Realty	6531	D	858 487-3520	11694
San Diego Country Estates Assn	8641	C	760 789-3788	25234
Spe Go Holdings Inc	7997	E	858 638-0672	19059
Triton Logistics Corporation	4731	D	619 822-8832	5188
United Power Contractors Inc	1623	C	760 735-8028	1990
Unyeway Inc (PA)	8331	D	760 789-5960	24242

RANCHO CORDOVA, CA - Sacramento County

Company	SIC	EMP	PHONE	ENTRY #
A B C D Associates	8051	C	916 363-4843	20217
ABI Document Support Svcs LLC	7389	E	909 793-0613	16974
Accentcare HM Hlth Scrmnto Inc	8082	D	916 852-5888	22187
Ad Land Venture LP	0782	C	916 853-9015	794
AmeriGas Propane LP	5172	C	916 852-7400	8949
AT&T Services Inc	4813	C	916 638-6096	5491
Bergelectric Corp	1731	D	916 636-1880	2521
Bissell Brothers Janitorial	7349	D	916 635-1852	14202
Capital Engineering Cons Inc (PA)	8711	D	916 851-3500	25590
Child Support Svcs Cal Dept (DH)	8322	D	916 464-5000	23563
Clark Pest Ctrl Stockton Inc	7342	E	916 635-7770	14147
Corelogic Inc	7323	D	916 431-2146	14032
Courtyard Management Corp	7011	C	916 638-3800	12494
D7 Roofing Services Inc	1761	D	916 447-2175	3147
Dignity Health	8062	C	916 861-1100	21366
Dignity Health	8062	C	916 851-2153	21373
Dignity Health	4225	E	916 851-3800	4548
Dignity Health Med Foundation	8099	A	916 379-2840	22787
Dignity Health Med Foundation (HQ)	8062	C	916 379-2840	21395
Ducks Unlimited Inc	0971	C	916 852-2000	1003
Educational Credit MGT Corp	6111	B	800 367-1590	9694
Enterprise Services LLC	7374	A	916 636-1000	16125
Fine Chemicals Holdings Corp	6719	B	916 357-6880	11976
Franklin Tmpleton Inv Svcs LLC	6282	C	650 312-2000	10083
Franklin Tmpleton Inv Svcs LLC (DH)	6211	A	916 463-1500	9953
Gei Consultants Inc	8711	D	916 631-4500	25704
General Electric Company	6153	C	916 286-8020	9739
General Environmental	7389	D	916 351-0980	17184
General Pool & Spa Supply Inc (PA)	5091	D	916 853-2401	7929
Harelson Mechanical Inc	1796	D	916 386-2586	3471
Health Net Federal Svcs LLC (DH)	6324	A	916 935-5000	10210
Heritage Community Credit Un	6061	E	916 364-1700	9562
Home Instead Senior Care	8082	D	916 920-2273	22326
Infor (us) Inc	7372	C	916 921-0883	15711
Judson Enterprises Inc (PA)	1522	B	916 596-6721	1293
Kaiser Foundation Hospitals	6324	E	916 631-3088	10233
Keenan & Associates	6411	C	916 858-2981	10666
Kleinfelder	8711	D	916 366-1701	25785
Kls Air Express Inc (PA)	4731	D	916 857-6305	5094
Landcare USA LLC	0782	D	916 635-0936	884
Lennar Homes Inc	1531	C	916 517-4950	1349
LLP Moss Adams	8721	C	916 503-8100	26247
Lyle Company	8748	C	916 266-7000	27779
Maximus Inc	8082	C	916 364-6610	22365
McKesson Corporation	5122	D	916 636-8700	8194
Michael Baker Intl Inc	8748	D	916 361-8384	27786
Mitchell Jones Concrete Inc	1771	C	916 638-6870	3289
Nehemiah Construction Inc	1611	E	707 746-6815	1825
Nevada Republic Electric N Inc	1731	C	916 294-0140	2661
Nightingale Vantagemed Corp (HQ)	7372	D	916 638-4744	15783
North State Elec Contrs Inc	1731	D	916 572-0571	2663
Pacific Coast Companies Inc	7389	C	916 631-6500	17382
Paramount Equity Mortgage LLC	6162	C	916 290-9999	9842
Permanente Medical Group Inc	8011	C	916 631-3000	19787
Pick Pull Auto Dismantling Inc (HQ)	5015	E	916 689-2000	6703
PR Rancho Hotel LLC	7011	D	916 638-4141	13079
Presidio Hotel Group LLC	7011	D	916 631-7500	13080
Rci Electric Inc	1731	D	916 858-8000	2694
Ricoh Usa Inc	5044	C	916 638-3333	6974
River City Auto Recovery Inc	7389	D	916 851-1100	17447
Robert Half International Inc	7361	D	916 852-1705	14733
Ron Nurss Inc	1771	D	916 631-9761	3318
Russell Mechanical Inc	1711	D	916 635-2522	2343
Scott Silva Concrete Inc	1771	D	916 859-0593	3323
Select Hotels Group LLC	7011	E	916 638-4141	13204
Sierra PCF HM & Comfort Inc	5075	D	916 638-0543	7656
Sunsystem Technology LLC (PA)	8731	B	916 671-3351	26463
Superior Vision Services Inc (PA)	6324	E	916 859-6218	10321
Technology Services Cal Dept	7374	E	916 464-3747	16187
Tetra Tech Ec Inc	8748	A	916 852-8300	27882
Tri Tool Inc (PA)	5084	C	916 288-6100	7813
True North Ar LLC	7361	D	916 369-9850	14787
Two Rivers Demolition Inc	1795	D	916 638-6775	3465
Universal Site Services Inc	7349	D	916 635-1122	14421

Company	SIC	EMP	PHONE	ENTRY #
Urata & Sons Concrete Inc	1771	C	916 638-5364	3339
USI Insurance Services Nat Inc	6411	C	916 589-8000	10817
Varis LLC	8742	D	916 294-0860	27507
Verizon Bus Netwrk Svcs Inc	4813	C	916 779-5600	5661
Vision Service Plan	6324	A	916 851-5000	10327
Vsp Holding Company Inc	6324	D	916 851-5000	10328
Wells Fargo Coml Dist Fin LLC	6153	D	916 636-2020	9750
William E Heinselman	8711	E	916 920-0220	26001

RANCHO CUCAMONGA, CA - San Bernardino County

Company	SIC	EMP	PHONE	ENTRY #
24 Hour Fitness Usa Inc	7991	D	909 944-1000	18553
ABM Janitorial Services Inc	7349	C	909 987-3700	14175
Adrianas Insurance Svcs Inc (PA)	6411	D	909 291-4040	10511
Agent Franchise LLC	6321	C	949 930-5025	10155
Allmark Inc (PA)	6531	D	909 989-7556	11208
Aloft Ontario-Rancho Cucamonga	7011	D	909 484-2018	12314
American Med	4119	C	909 948-1714	3749
Apex Staffing Service	7363	E	909 941-0267	14817
Arrowhead Central Credit Union (PA)	6061	B	866 212-4333	9540
Artic Mechanical Inc (PA)	1711	D	909 980-2539	2129
Assistance League Foothill Com	8399	C	909 987-2813	24740
AT&T Corp.	4812	C	909 646-9644	5265
Automatic Data Processing Inc	7374	C	800 225-5237	16086
Automobile Club Southern Cal	6411	C	909 980-0233	10556
Bear Vly Fbrcators Stl Sup Inc	1541	C	760 247-5381	1376
Bowlero Corp	7933	E	909 945-9392	18483
Bradshaw International Inc (HQ)	5023	B	909 476-3884	6752
Branlyn Prominence Inc (PA)	8082	D	909 476-9030	22240
Bunzl Retail Services LLC	5113	D	909 476-2457	8096
C A Hofmann Construction Inc	1742	E	909 484-5888	2856
California Empire Bancorp Inc	6162	E	909 484-7988	9788
Ccna Vons Athletes For Life	8699	D	805 453-2499	25408
CDM Constructors Inc	1623	C	909 579-3500	1906
Century 21 Home Realtors	6531	D	909 980-8000	11302
Cerenzia Foods Inc	5141	D	909 989-4000	8388
Childrens Btq At Stevens Hope	5137	D	909 256-0100	8294
CMC Fontana Steel	1791	D	909 899-9993	3371
CMC Rebar	1791	D	909 899-9993	3372
Collection Technology Inc	7322	D	800 743-4284	13999
Corvel Corporation	6411	C	909 257-3700	10594
County of San Bernardino	8322	D	909 945-4000	23718
CU Cooperative Systems Inc (PA)	6099	B	909 948-2500	9678
Cucamonga Valley Water Dst	4941	D	909 987-2591	6237
Davis Brothers Framing Inc	1751	C	909 944-4899	3027
Empire Estates Inc	6531	D	909 980-3100	11419
Etiwanda Historical Society	8412	D	909 899-8432	24883
Evolution Fresh Inc (HQ)	5148	D	800 794-9986	8675
Excellnce of Inland Empire Inc	6531	C	909 758-4311	11425
Falken Tire Holdings Inc	5014	C	800 723-2553	6690
Fenagh Engineering & Tstg LLC	7389	E	925 462-5151	17171
Fox Transportation Inc (PA)	8748	C	909 291-4646	27731
Frito-Lay North America Inc	5145	B	909 941-6214	8548
Frontier California Inc	4212	D	909 941-4068	4017
Gamut Construction Company Inc	6799	D	909 948-0500	12228
General Coatings Corporation	1721	C	909 204-4150	2437
General Motors LLC	4225	C	800 521-7300	4560
Gentex Corporation	8731	C	909 481-7667	26373
Giti Tire (usa) Ltd (DH)	5014	C	909 527-8800	6691
Hibshman Trading Corporation	5137	D	909 581-1800	8306
Hoffman Southwest Corp	7699	D	909 397-0567	17951
Honeyville Inc	4221	D	909 980-9500	4489
Infinity Service Group Inc	1711	D	909 466-6237	2234
Inland Empire Health Plan (PA)	6321	A	909 890-2000	10166
Inland Empire Real Estate	6531	E	909 944-2070	11513
Inland Empire Utilities Agency	4941	D	909 993-1755	6263
J B Hunt Transport Inc	4213	C	909 466-5361	4197
JB Upland Ltd Liability Co	8742	E	909 944-5456	27288
Jones/Covey Group Incorporated	1799	D	888 972-7581	3541
Just Mortgage Inc	6162	C	562 908-5000	9821
Kaiser Foundation Hospitals	8011	A	888 750-0036	19540
Kings Seafood Company LLC	5146	D	909 803-1280	8579
Knd Development 55 LLC	8062	D	909 581-6400	21542
L & R Distributors Inc	5131	B	909 980-3807	8229
Ledesma & Meyer Cnstr Co Inc	1542	D	909 297-1100	1579
Ledesma & Meyer Dev Inc	8741	D	909 476-0590	26929
Lexxiom Inc	8741	B	909 481-2536	26933
M & G Jewelers Inc	7631	C	909 989-2929	17920
Majesty One Properties Inc	6531	D	909 980-8000	11580
McGuire Talent Inc	7922	D	909 527-7006	18386
Miracle Home Health Agency	8082	E	562 653-0668	22367
Msblous LLC	4225	D	909 929-9689	4596
National Cmnty Renaissance Cal (PA)	6552	D	909 483-2444	11895
National Community Renaissance (PA)	7041	D	909 483-2444	13477
National Mentor Inc	8331	D	909 483-2505	24209
Nationwide Guard Services Inc	7381	D	909 608-1112	16739
Network Intgrtion Partners Inc	7373	D	909 919-2800	16017

GEOGRAPHIC

	SIC	EMP	PHONE	ENTRY #
Newco Distributors Inc	5191	D	909 291-2240	9087
Nongshim America Inc **(HQ)**	5141	C	909 481-3698	8435
Novatime Technology Inc **(HQ)**	7361	D	909 895-8100	14674
NRG California South LP	4911	C	909 899-7241	6059
Pacific Cycle Inc	4225	E	909 481-5613	4604
Pacific West Corporation **(PA)**	7379	D	515 270-8181	16449
Par Electrical Contractors Inc	1731	D	909 854-2880	2673
Paradise Building Services	7349	D	909 399-0707	14341
Penwal Industries Inc	1542	D	909 466-1555	1613
Perris Valley Cmnty Hosp LLC	8062	C	909 581-6400	21641
Priority One Med Trnspt Inc **(PA)**	4119	C	909 948-4400	3831
Professnal Elec Cnstr Svcs Inc	1731	C	909 373-4100	2687
Promed Hlth Care Admnistrators	8011	D	909 932-1045	19798
Provident Savings Bank	6162	E	909 484-6286	9851
Puratos Corporation	4221	D	909 484-1312	4490
R M A Group Inc **(PA)**	8711	D	909 980-6096	25886
Rancho Ccamonga Cmnty Hosp LLC	8062	C	909 581-6400	21683
Rancho Pacific Electric Inc	1731	E	909 476-1022	2692
Red Hill Country Club	7997	D	909 982-1358	19011
Replanet LLC	4953	D	909 980-1203	6450
Rwc Enterprises Inc	8711	E	909 373-4100	25898
Ryder Truck Rental Inc	7513	C	909 980-5084	17616
San Antonio Community Hospital	8062	E	909 948-8000	21700
Schoolsfirst Federal Credit Un	0291	C	800 462-8328	457
Sheraton Corporation	7011	B	909 204-6100	13218
Sherman Security	7381	C	909 941-4167	16822
Smith International Inc	1389	C	909 906-7900	1079
Southwire Company LLC	5063	C	909 989-2888	7399
Starco Group Inc	7389	D	909 989-9898	17484
Starwood Hotels & Resorts	7011	C	909 484-2018	13267
Steno Employment Services Inc	7363	A	909 476-1404	14917
Sumitomo Rubber North Amer Inc **(HQ)**	5014	D	909 466-1116	6695
Sunrise Senior Living Inc	8051	D	909 941-3001	20795
Superior Elec Mech & Plbg Inc	1731	B	909 357-9400	2755
Supershuttle International Inc	4111	C	909 944-2606	3732
Tamo Inc	4213	E	909 803-1030	4275
Tech Packaging Inc	5199	D	909 243-7047	9263
TMT Industries Inc	4213	E	909 493-3441	4279
Treeline and Associates	8742	D	909 476-2757	27496
TRL Systems Incorporated	1731	D	909 390-8392	2771
US Tournament Golf Ltd Lblty	8742	E	909 987-6695	27503
Vavrinek Trine Day & Co LLP **(PA)**	8721	C	909 466-4410	26306
Vehicle Accessory Center LLC	5013	C	909 987-8237	6682
Vocational Imprv Program Inc **(PA)**	8331	C	909 483-5924	24246
Weber Distribution Warehouses	4225	E	909 481-1600	4657
West End Yung MNS Chrstn Assn	8641	D	909 477-2780	25285
Yellow Jacket Drlg Svcs LLC	1781	D	909 989-8563	3356

RANCHO DOMINGUEZ, CA - Los Angeles County

	SIC	EMP	PHONE	ENTRY #
Advanced Fresh Concepts Corp **(PA)**	6794	D	310 604-3630	12133
Afc Distribution Corp	5141	E	310 604-3630	8378
Allied High Tech Products Inc	5085	D	310 635-2466	7826
Calpipe Industries LLC **(HQ)**	5051	C	562 803-4388	7264
Cds Moving Equipment Inc **(PA)**	5084	D	310 631-1100	7739
Eco Flow Transportation LLC	4731	D	310 816-0260	5051
Heavy Load Transfer LLC	4212	D	310 816-0260	4021
Iap West Inc	5013	D	310 667-9720	6647
Kw International Inc	4731	D	310 747-1380	5099
Kw International Inc	4226	B	213 703-6914	4683
Mariak Industries Inc	5023	B	310 661-4400	6775
Mover Services Inc	1799	E	310 868-5143	3552
Neway Packaging Corp **(PA)**	5113	D	602 454-9000	8111
Nippon Ex Nec Lgstics Amer Inc	4212	D	310 604-6100	4045
Pacific Lighting Mfr Inc	5063	D	310 327-7711	7385
Premium Trnsp Svcs Inc **(PA)**	4731	C	310 816-0260	5146
R R Donnelley & Sons Company	7331	E	310 784-8485	14600
Samsung Electronics Amer Inc	5064	C	310 537-7000	7428
Seeds of Change Inc	5191	C	310 764-7700	9097
Soc Pathology Medical Group	8011	D	310 225-3220	19894
Union Supply Group Inc **(PA)**	5141	C	310 603-8899	8477
Unis LLC	4225	D	310 747-7388	4642
Westcoast Warehousing LLC	4225	E	310 537-9958	4659

RANCHO MIRAGE, CA - Riverside County

	SIC	EMP	PHONE	ENTRY #
Agua Clnte Band Chilla Indians	7011	A	760 321-2000	12307
Annenberg Foundation Trust **(PA)**	6733	D	760 202-2222	12088
Betty Ford Center **(HQ)**	8069	C	760 773-4100	21999
Blx Group Inc	0181	D	760 776-6622	247
Brookdale Senior Living Inc	8059	D	760 340-5999	21018
Brookdale Senior Living Inc	8059	D	760 346-7772	21019
Cellco Partnership	4812	D	760 568-5542	5348
Charlie W Shaeffer Jr MD	8011	D	760 346-0642	19373
Childrens Museum of Desert	8412	E	760 321-0602	24870
Club of Sunrise Country	7997	D	760 328-6549	18895
Community Blood Bank Inc	8099	D	760 773-4190	22769
Country Villa Rancho	8322	D	760 340-0053	23622

	SIC	EMP	PHONE	ENTRY #
Country Villa Service Corp	7389	D	760 340-0053	17103
Desert Cardiology Consultants	8011	D	760 346-0642	19435
Desert Orthopdc Center A Mdcl **(PA)**	8011	D	760 568-2684	19438
Dual Diagnosis Trtmnt Inc	8099	C	949 324-4531	22793
Eisenhower Medical Center **(PA)**	8062	A	760 340-3911	21401
Janet K Hartzler MD	8011	D	760 340-3937	19517
Mission Hills Country Club Inc	7997	C	760 324-9400	18976
Mission Hills Senior Living	8361	D	760 770-7737	24602
Morningside Community Assn	8641	D	760 328-3323	25202
Omni Hotels Corporation	7011	B	760 568-2727	12981
Osf International Inc	5149	D	760 341-5600	8844
Outpatnt Eye Srgry Ctr of Dsrt	8011	E	760 340-3937	19740
Protect-For-Less Security Svcs	7382	C	760 343-1192	16929
Ritz-Carlton Hotel Company LLC	7011	B	760 321-8282	13126
Ritz-Carlton Hotel Company LLC	7011	B	760 321-8282	13130
Spa Cas Palmas	7991	E	760 836-3106	18655
Springs Club Inc	7997	D	760 328-0254	19061
Starwood Htls & Rsrts Wrldwde	7011	B	760 328-5955	13276
Thunderbird Country Club	7997	D	760 328-2161	19070
Windermere Real Estate East	6531	D	760 568-2568	11840

RANCHO MURIETA, CA - Sacramento County

	SIC	EMP	PHONE	ENTRY #
Empire Golf Inc **(PA)**	7992	D	916 314-3150	18712
Energy Store of California Inc	1711	D	916 825-8751	2201
Rancho Murieta Country Club	7997	D	916 354-2400	19008
Whiting Construction Inc	1771	D	916 354-2756	3346

RANCHO PALOS VERDES, CA - Los Angeles County

	SIC	EMP	PHONE	ENTRY #
American Golf Corporation	7997	D	310 377-7370	18840
Artists Studio Gallery	7999	D	424 206-9902	19104
Belmont Village LP	6513	D	310 377-9977	10986
Carpet Solutions	7217	E	310 886-3800	13574
CIT Bank National Association	6021	D	310 265-1656	9328
Inman Spinosa & Buchan Inc	6531	D	310 519-1080	11514
Long Point Development LLC	7011	A	310 265-2800	12863
Los Verdes MNS Golf Cntry CLB	7992	D	310 377-7370	18730
Normandie Club LP	7999	A	310 352-3486	19209
Re/Max Plos Vrdes Rlty / Exces	6531	E	310 541-5224	11713
Vh Property Corp	7992	B	310 303-3210	18776
Wells Fargo Bank National Assn	6021	D	310 831-0632	9401

RANCHO SANTA FE, CA - San Diego County

	SIC	EMP	PHONE	ENTRY #
A W Properties West LLC	1521	D	858 832-1462	1109
Bridges Club At Rancho SA	8641	C	858 759-7200	25119
Clubcorp Usa Inc	7997	C	858 756-2471	18897
Crosby National Golf Club LLC	7997	D	858 756-6310	18905
Del Mar Country Club Inc	7997	D	858 759-5500	18908
Fairbanks Ranch Cntry CLB Inc	7997	C	858 259-8811	18921
Farms Golf Club Inc	7997	D	858 756-5585	18923
First National Bank	6021	B	858 756-3023	9346
HCC Investors LLC	7997	C	858 759-7200	18934
Helen Woodward Animal Center **(PA)**	8699	D	858 756-4117	25427
Huntington Hotel Company	7011	B	858 756-1131	12742
Pacific Western Bank	6021	B	858 756-3023	9362
Rancho Santa Fe Association A	7997	D	858 756-1182	19009
Rancho Valencia Resort	7011	B	858 756-1123	13101
Willis Allen Real Estate	6531	E	858 756-2444	11837

RANCHO SANTA MARGARI, CA - Orange County

	SIC	EMP	PHONE	ENTRY #
Aliso Mechanical Incorporated	1711	C	949 544-1601	2096
Foundation 9 Entertainment Inc **(PA)**	7372	C	949 698-1500	15683
Jct Company LLC	1711	C	949 589-2021	2242
Safe Harbor Intl Relief	8399	E	949 858-6786	24834
Wendt Landscape Services Inc	0782	D	949 589-8680	961

RCHO STA MARG, CA - Orange County

	SIC	EMP	PHONE	ENTRY #
C-21 Super Stars	6531	D	949 389-1600	11258
Capital Invstmnts Vntures Corp **(PA)**	8621	C	949 858-0647	25008
Fakouri Electrical Engrg Inc	7378	C	949 888-2400	16284
Hackney Electric Inc **(PA)**	1731	D	949 264-4000	2598
Jipc Management Inc	8741	A	949 916-2000	26908
Kisco Senior Living LLC	6513	D	949 888-2250	11045
Nucourse Distribution Inc	5065	D	866 655-4366	7516
Padi Americas Inc	8621	C	949 858-7234	25035
Park Landscape Maintenance **(PA)**	0782	B	949 546-8300	916
Park West Rescom Inc	0782	C	949 546-8300	917
Santa Margarita Water District **(PA)**	4941	D	949 459-6400	6310
Santa Margarita Water District	4941	D	949 459-6400	6311
Sarco Inc	5065	E	949 888-5548	7539
Virtium LLC	7379	C	949 888-2444	16526
Wags & Wiggles Dog Daycare LLC **(PA)**	0752	D	949 635-9655	635

RED BLUFF, CA - Tehama County

	SIC	EMP	PHONE	ENTRY #
Bio Industries Inc	0711	E	530 529-3290	458
Brentwood Skill Nursng & Rehab	8059	D	530 527-2046	21014
Business Connections	7361	D	530 527-6229	14580
Concessionaires Urban Park **(PA)**	7999	B	530 529-1512	19147

Mergent email: customerrelations@mergent.com

1640

2019 Directory of California
Wholesalers and Services Companies

(P-0000) Products & Services Section entry number
(PA)=Parent Co (HQ)=Headquarters (DH)=Div Headquarters

Company	SIC	EMP	PHONE	ENTRY #
County of Tehama	8322	C	530 527-5631	23752
County of Tehama	8322	D	530 527-4052	23753
Lassen Hse Assisted Living LLC	8361	E	530 529-2900	24575
Lassen Medical Group Inc (PA)	8011	D	530 527-0414	19645
Pactiv LLC	5199	D	530 529-3340	9247
St Elizabeth Community Hosp (HQ)	8062	D	530 529-7760	21774
United Sttes Bowl Congress Inc	7933	D	530 527-9049	18501

REDDING, CA - Shasta County

Company	SIC	EMP	PHONE	ENTRY #
Addus Healthcare Inc	8049	D	530 247-0858	20161
Airgas Inc	5084	B	530 241-1544	7719
Alexandria Clayton	7373	C	530 262-5961	15911
Ameripride Services Inc	7213	E	530 242-0564	13508
Aramark Unf & Career AP LLC	7218	D	530 241-6433	13587
Best Western Hilltop Inn	7011	E	530 221-6100	12372
Big Lgue Dreams Consulting LLC	7997	C	530 223-1177	18866
Bridge Bay Resort & Marina	7011	D	530 275-3021	12399
California Oregon Broadcasting (HQ)	4833	D	530 243-7777	5771
California Physicians Service	6324	C	530 351-6115	10186
Califrnia Physcn Reimbursement	6411	D	530 241-0473	10574
Cardinal Health Inc	5122	D	530 225-8735	8156
Care Options Management Plans (PA)	8082	D	530 242-8580	22248
CB C&C Properties/Comm Di Inc	6531	D	530 221-7551	11272
Ch2m Hill Inc	8711	C	530 243-5832	25604
Charter Cmmnctons Oprating LLC	4841	E	530 241-7352	5862
Class Act Hair & Nail Salon	7231	C	530 223-3442	13650
Copper Ridge Care Center	8051	C	530 222-2273	20323
County of Shasta	6371	C	530 225-5000	10484
County of Shasta	8322	D	530 225-5554	23742
County of Shasta	8111	D	530 245-6300	23008
County of Shasta	8351	E	530 225-2999	24310
Crestwood Behavioral Hlth Inc	8361	D	530 221-0976	24494
David Civalier MD Inc	8011	D	530 244-4034	19427
Dignity Health	8062	C	530 225-6345	21381
Donor Network West	8099	D	510 418-0336	22792
Far Northern Coordinating Coun (PA)	8322	D	530 222-4791	23804
Federal Express Corporation	4513	C	800 463-3339	4827
Fedex Ground Package Sys Inc	4213	E	800 463-3339	4165
Foothill Distributing Co Inc	5181	C	530 243-3932	8995
Forestry and Fire Protection	0851	C	530 225-2418	998
Golden Living LLC	8059	D	530 241-6756	21092
Hfrm II Inc (PA)	6512	B	530 242-2010	10895
Interim Assiited Care of Nort	8082	D	530 722-1530	22346
Interim Hlthcare Nthrn Cal Inc (PA)	8082	B	530 221-1300	22347
James D Tate MD	8011	D	530 225-8710	19516
JF Shea Construction Inc	1521	D	530 246-4292	1181
Kaidan Hospitality LP	7011	D	530 221-8700	12797
Kindred Nursing Centers W LLC	8051	D	530 243-6317	20565
Lassen Canyon Nursery Inc (PA)	5141	C	530 223-1075	8419
MD Imaging Inc A Prof Med Corp	8011	D	530 243-1249	19674
Medical Home Specialists Inc	7363	C	530 226-5577	14880
Mercy Foundation North	8099	D	530 247-3424	22840
Mercy HM Svcs A Cal Ltd Partnr (HQ)	8062	A	530 225-6000	21588
Mercy HM Svcs A Cal Ltd Partnr	8011	B	530 225-6000	19686
Mercy HM Svcs A Cal Ltd Partnr	8082	D	530 245-4070	22366
Meyers Earthwork Inc	1794	D	530 365-8858	3434
Muse Concrete Contractors Inc	1611	D	530 226-5151	1822
Nichols Melburg Rossetto Assoc (PA)	8712	E	530 222-3300	26101
North State Security Inc	7381	D	530 243-0295	16743
Northern California Hlth Care	8082	D	530 223-2332	22374
Northern California Rehab	8062	C	530 246-9000	21608
Northern Valley Catholic Socia	8322	D	530 241-0552	23946
Northstar Senior Living Inc	8741	A	530 242-8300	26965
Oakdale Heights MGT Corp (PA)	6513	B	530 222-6797	11087
Ocadian Care Centers LLC	8051	C	530 246-9000	20673
Pacific Gas and Electric Co	4911	C	530 365-7672	6079
Parenthood of Planned	8093	D	530 351-7100	22636
Patients Hospital	8062	D	530 225-8700	21638
Peerless Building Maint Inc	7349	D	530 222-6369	14346
Pre-Employcom	7381	D	800 300-1821	16759
Pre-Employcom	7381	D	530 378-7680	16760
Prime Healthcare Services	8062	A	530 244-5400	21658
Prime Healthcare Servs Sh	8062	A	530 244-5458	21659
Redding Aero Enterprises Inc	4111	D	530 224-2300	3698
Redding Bank of Commerce (HQ)	6021	D	530 224-7355	9370
Redding Drywall Systems Inc	1742	E	530 222-8767	2946
Redding Family Medicine Assoc	8011	E	530 244-4907	19814
Redding Pathologists Lab (PA)	8011	C	530 225-8050	19815
Redding Pathologists Lab	8071	D	530 225-8050	22134
Redding Rancheria (PA)	7011	D	530 225-8979	13106
Redding Rancheria	8099	D	530 224-2700	22869
Riverview Golf and Country CLB	7997	D	530 224-2254	19017
Roy E Ladd Inc	1611	E	530 241-6102	1844
Sac River Outfitters	7999	D	530 275-3500	19228
Securitas SEC Svcs USA Inc	7381	D	530 245-0256	16795
Sefnco Communications Inc	4899	D	530 338-2460	5994

Company	SIC	EMP	PHONE	ENTRY #
Set Free Services Inc	8742	D	530 243-3373	27445
Sfn Group Inc	7363	C	530 222-3434	14913
Shasta Convalescent Center	8059	C	530 222-3630	21206
Shasta County Head Start Child (PA)	8351	E	530 241-1036	24380
Shasta Lake Resorts LP	7999	D	209 785-3300	19236
Sierra Oaks Senior Living	8361	D	530 241-5100	24673
Slideco Recreation Inc	7996	D	530 246-9550	18811
State Compensation Insur Fund	6331	D	888 782-8338	10399
Steve Manning Construction Inc	1611	D	530 222-0810	1853
Tenet Healthsystem Medical	8082	D	530 222-1992	22434
Thom Sharon & G Enterprises	8082	E	530 226-8350	22436
Tierra Oaks Golf Club Inc	7997	D	530 275-0795	19072
Transportation California Dept	0782	C	530 225-3349	948
Turtle Bay Exploration Park	8412	E	530 243-4282	24919
Utility Tree Service LLC (DH)	0783	C	530 226-0330	982
VCA Inc	0742	C	530 224-2200	617
Veterans Affairs Cal Dept	8051	C	530 224-3300	20856
Veterans Health Administration	8011	B	530 226-7555	20063
Vibra Healthcare LLC	8062	D	530 246-9000	21905
Walsh Group Inc	7997	D	530 221-4405	19084
Willow Sprngs Alzhmrs Spcl Cr	8361	E	530 242-0654	24724
Win River Hotel Corporation	7011	E	530 226-5111	13400
Win-River Resort & Casino	7999	B	530 243-3377	19262
Yaley Enterprises Inc	5099	E	530 365-5252	8067
Youth For Change	8322	D	530 605-1520	24138

REDLANDS, CA - San Bernardino County

Company	SIC	EMP	PHONE	ENTRY #
ABI Attorneys Service Inc (PA)	7334	D	909 793-0613	14069
AG Redlands LLC	8059	C	909 793-2678	20981
American Baptist Homes of West	6513	C	909 335-3077	10976
American Baptist Homes of West	8059	C	909 793-1233	20990
American Med	4119	C	909 793-7676	3745
Ash Holdings LLC	8051	D	909 793-2609	20236
Assistance League of Redlands	8399	C	909 792-2675	24741
Beaver Medical Clinic Inc (PA)	8011	C	909 793-3311	19320
Becton Dickinson and Company	5047	C	909 748-7300	7160
Bon Appetit Management Co	8742	C	909 748-8970	27165
Braswell Col Care Redlands CA	8059	C	909 792-6050	21012
Central Svc Ctr & Exec Offs	7389	E	909 307-6555	17064
Citigroup Inc	6021	D	909 335-0547	9334
City of Redlands	4953	E	909 798-7525	6377
Coldwell Banker RE Corp	6531	D	909 792-4147	11340
Contain-A-Way Inc	4953	B	909 796-2860	6382
Countryside Inn-Corona LP	8741	E	909 335-9024	26829
David Ollis Landscape Dev Inc	0782	C	909 307-1911	819
DSC Logistics Inc	4213	D	909 363-4354	4132
Enerpath Services Inc	1731	D	909 335-1699	2579
Epic Management LP (PA)	8741	C	909 799-1818	26849
First American Title Insur Co	6361	C	909 889-0311	10457
Geodis Logistics LLC	4225	D	909 801-3145	4564
Girl Scuts San Grgonio Council (PA)	8641	C	909 307-6555	25165
Haralambos Beverage Company	5181	C	909 307-1777	8999
Harvest Facility Holdings LP	6513	C	909 793-8691	11029
Hr Mission Commons Fc 5183	8361	D	909 793-8691	24567
Hydro Tek Systems Inc	5087	D	909 799-9222	7887
Inland Hlth Org of So Cal (HQ)	8011	E	909 335-7171	19512
Jonbec Care Incorporated (PA)	8052	D	909 798-4003	20936
Kaiser Foundation Hospitals	8011	D	888 750-0036	19531
Kuehne + Nagel Inc	4225	D	909 574-2300	4584
L Lyon Distributing Inc	7389	E	909 798-7129	17283
Larry Jacinto Construction Inc	1611	D	909 794-2151	1805
Larry Jacinto Farming Inc	0762	D	909 794-2276	696
Layne Christensen Company	8748	C	909 390-2833	27771
Lois Lauer Realty	6531	C	909 748-7000	11566
Loma Linda University	8011	D	909 558-6422	19658
Loma Linda University Med Ctr	8062	B	909 558-9275	21563
Loma Linda Vet Association For	8641	C	909 583-6250	25191
M Block & Sons Inc	4225	C	909 335-6684	4588
Mountain Top Comm Svcs LLC	8748	E	909 798-4400	27795
Mountain West Financial Inc (PA)	6162	B	909 793-1500	9835
Option One Home Med Eqp Inc	7352	C	909 478-5413	14435
P & R Paper Supply Co Inc (PA)	5113	C	909 389-1811	8124
Pacific Maintenance Svcs Inc	7349	C	909 793-7111	14339
Performance Team Frt Sys Inc	7389	D	801 301-1732	17395
Performance Team Frt Sys Inc	4731	C	424 358-6943	5141
Plum Healthcare Group LLC	7389	D	909 793-2609	17405
Plumbing Systems West Inc	1711	D	909 794-3823	2314
Prime-Line Products Company (PA)	5072	B	909 887-8118	7600
Pro-Craft Construction Inc	1711	D	909 790-5222	2318
R J M Construction Inc	1542	E	909 794-8853	1624
Redlands Cmnty Hosp Foundation	8059	C	909 793-1382	21193
Redlands Community Hospital (PA)	8062	D	909 335-5500	21684
Redlands Country Club	7997	D	909 793-2661	19012
Redlands Foothill Groves	0723	D	909 793-2164	559
Redlands Ford Inc	7532	D	909 793-3211	17737
RHS Corp	8741	A	909 335-5500	27018

GEOGRAPHIC

	SIC	EMP	PHONE	ENTRY #
Safely Home	8082	D	909 370-0343	22409
Silverscreen Healthcare Inc	8059	C	909 793-1382	21217
Soren McAdam Christianson LLP	8721	D	909 798-2222	26296
Southern California Gas Co	4924	B	909 335-7802	6167
Spectra Premium (usa) Corp	5013	D	951 653-0640	6675
Study Tapes	7812	D	909 792-0111	18127
Tarbell Financial Corporation	6531	D	909 335-0750	11785
United Road Towing Inc	7549	D	909 798-4863	17880
Westcor Construction of Cal	1521	C	909 796-8900	1259
YMCA of East Valley (PA)	8641	C	909 798-9622	25289

REDONDO BEACH, CA - Los Angeles County

	SIC	EMP	PHONE	ENTRY #
4g Wireless Inc	4813	D	310 376-2299	5437
Aamcom LLC	4813	E	310 318-8100	5440
Aerospace Corporation	8733	D	310 374-8866	26583
Axiom Home Warranty LLC	6351	C	844 562-9466	10422
Beach Cities Health District	8399	C	310 318-7939	24745
Beachsports Inc	7032	E	310 372-2202	13445
Bicara Ltd	5147	B	310 316-6222	8611
California Subshine Inc	7389	D	310 374-4900	17049
Catalina Events Inc	8743	E	310 925-6986	27547
Corporate Production Designs	7812	E	310 937-9663	18035
Craft Resources Inc	7363	C	310 937-3744	14845
D & W LLC	7011	D	310 345-0075	12511
Dsd Trucking Inc (PA)	4581	D	310 338-3395	4885
Fire Safe Systems Inc	1711	D	310 542-0585	2210
Heartland Payment Systems LLC	7389	D	424 247-8521	17215
Hpt Trs Ihg-2 Inc	7011	B	310 318-8888	12737
K & P Janitorial Services	7349	C	310 540-8878	14297
Leidos Inc	8731	D	310 791-9671	26398
Leight Sales Co Inc	5072	C	310 223-1000	7593
Map Cargo Global Logistics (PA)	4731	D	310 297-8300	5106
Max Sommers Real Estate	6531	E	310 560-1499	11595
Multax Systems Inc (PA)	8711	C	310 379-8398	25834
Muscle Improvement Inc	7991	C	310 374-5522	18634
NBC Consulting Inc	8742	E	310 798-5000	27361
New-Jack Industries Inc	7381	B	310 297-3605	16740
Nzg Specialties Inc (PA)	5141	D	310 216-7575	8436
Portofino Hotel Partners LP	7011	C	310 379-8481	13075
Reign Accessories Inc	8741	E	310 297-6400	27013
Reproductive Ptnr Med Grp Inc (PA)	8011	E	310 318-3010	19818
Riviera Finance of Texas Inc (PA)	6153	C	310 540-3993	9747
Scat Enterprises Inc	5013	D	310 370-5501	6672
Silverado Senior Living Inc	8051	D	424 257-6418	20765
Sport Center Fitness Inc	7991	D	310 376-9443	18667
Stevens Global Logistics Inc (PA)	4731	D	310 216-5645	5175
Thor Inc (PA)	7361	D	310 727-1777	14780
Thor Group Inc (PA)	7361	E	310 727-1777	14781
Transportation Concept Inc	4111	D	323 268-2202	3736
Trcf Redondo LLC	7011	E	310 536-1209	13340
Wedgewood Inc (PA)	6799	C	310 640-3070	12280
Westwind Engineering Inc	8711	C	310 831-3454	25997
Westwind Engineering Inc	8711	C	310 831-3454	25998

REDWOOD CITY, CA - San Mateo County

	SIC	EMP	PHONE	ENTRY #
ABC Bus Inc	5012	D	650 368-3364	6572
Accor Bus & Leisure N Amer LLC	7011	C	650 598-9000	12303
Acxiom Corporation	7375	D	650 356-3400	16208
Adaptive Spectrum and Signal A	4813	D	650 264-2667	5442
Amobee Inc (DH)	7311	D	650 353-4399	13792
Anomali Incorporated	7371	D	408 800-4050	14988
Ascend Clinical LLC (PA)	8071	D	650 780-5500	22061
Assocted Lrng Lngage Spcialist (PA)	8748	D	650 631-9999	27645
AT&T Corp	4813	D	650 780-1005	5456
Automatic Data Processing Inc	7374	C	800 225-5237	16090
Badgeville Inc	7372	E	650 323-6668	15602
Bay Brokerage Inc	5141	E	650 413-1721	8383
Bay Clubs Inc	7991	D	650 593-1112	18578
Betterworks Systems Inc	7372	C	650 656-9013	15607
Bkf Engineers (PA)	8711	C	650 482-6300	25567
Bluevine Capital Inc	6153	D	888 216-9619	9734
Box Inc (PA)	7372	C	877 729-4269	15615
Broadvision Inc	7372	D	650 331-1000	15617
Brookdale Lving Cmmunities Inc	8051	D	650 366-3900	20271
Buildingminds Inc	7371	E	973 397-6510	15040
C3 Iot Inc	7372	C	650 503-2200	15618
Cake Corporation	7371	D	650 215-7777	15045
Cardiodx Inc	8071	C	650 475-2788	22065
Care 2	8699	C	650 622-0860	25405
Chapel of Chimes	6553	D	650 349-4411	11940
Child Care Coordinating Counsi	8322	E	650 517-1400	23557
Clp Resources Inc	7363	C	650 261-2100	14837
Community Gatepath	8322	C	650 259-8500	23603
Coretechs Staffing Inc	7371	D	650 363-7960	15080
County of San Mateo	8322	C	650 599-7336	23734
County of San Mateo	8741	C	650 363-4915	26832

	SIC	EMP	PHONE	ENTRY #
County of San Mateo	8741	E	650 363-4343	26833
County of San Mateo	8999	C	650 363-4548	27926
County of San Mateo	8322	D	650 363-1910	23738
County of San Mateo	7033	D	650 363-4020	13463
County of San Mateo	8322	C	650 363-4244	23741
Covington & Burling LLP	8111	C	650 632-4700	23010
Crystal Dynamics Inc	7372	D	650 421-7600	15640
Cyara Solutions Corp	5045	C	650 549-8522	7028
Dealix Corporation	5012	C	650 599-5500	6589
Delphix Corp (PA)	7372	E	650 494-1645	15646
Des Architects + Engineers Inc	8712	C	650 364-6453	26042
Digital Insight Corporation (HQ)	7375	C	818 879-1010	16217
Diva Systems Corporation	4841	C	650 779-3000	5910
Dpr Construction Inc (PA)	1541	A	650 474-1450	1393
Dpr Construction A Gen Partnr (HQ)	1541	A	650 474-1450	1396
E A Com Inc	7371	C	650 628-1500	15123
El Concilio San Mateo Cnty Inc	8322	E	650 373-1080	23784
Electronic Arts Inc (PA)	7372	B	650 628-1500	15664
Equilar Inc	7389	C	877 441-6090	17154
Equinix Inc (PA)	6798	C	650 598-6000	12160
Equinix (us) Enterprises Inc (HQ)	4899	C	650 598-6363	5981
Ernst & Young LLP	8721	C	650 802-4500	26220
Evernote Corporation (PA)	4813	D	650 216-7700	5557
Fish & Richardson PC	8111	D	650 839-5070	23069
Flo Health Inc	7371		510 303-9307	15162
French Redwood Inc	7011	C	650 598-9000	12592
Genium Inc	7371	C	415 240-0442	15176
Genomic Health Inc (PA)	8071	C	650 556-9300	22090
Genomic Health Inc	8071	B	650 556-9300	22092
Glint Inc	7374	D	650 817-7240	16138
Goodwill Industrs of San Franc	8331	C	650 556-9700	24188
Granite Rock Co	1611	B	650 869-3370	1786
Green Again Ldscpg & Con Inc	0782	C	650 368-9304	849
Guardant Health Inc	8071	C	855 698-8887	22096
Gunderson Dettmer Stough Ville (PA)	8111	C	650 321-2400	23117
Heartflow Inc (PA)	7373	C	650 241-1221	15970
Heartland Payment Systems LLC	7389	C	650 678-2824	17212
I2c Inc	5045	B	650 480-5222	7060
Imperva Inc (PA)	7371	C	650 345-9000	15212
Impossible Foods Inc (PA)	5141	D	650 461-4385	8417
Inflection LLC	7374	C	650 618-9910	16146
Inflection Risk Solutions LLC	7374	E	650 618-9910	16147
Informatica LLC (DH)	7372	C	650 385-5000	15712
Interana Inc	7371		844 426-4678	15228
Ipass Inc (PA)	4813	C	650 232-4100	5589
Isheriff Inc	7371	C	650 412-4300	15240
Itco Solutions Inc	7379	B	650 367-0514	16413
Kainos Home & Training Ctr	8322	E	650 361-1355	23880
Kaiser Foundation Hospitals	8011	A	650 299-2000	19593
Kaspick & Co LLC (DH)	8742	D	650 585-4100	27293
Keenan & Associates	6411	D	650 306-0616	10662
Lydia C Gonzalez	8322	E	650 299-4707	23908
Mid-Peninsula Tyrella Corp (PA)	6513	D	650 299-8000	11078
Motiga Inc	7371	D	425 748-8509	15293
Multiven Inc	7379	E	408 828-2715	16428
Oracle America Inc	5045	D	800 633-0584	7086
Oracle Corporation (PA)	7379	A	650 506-7000	16443
Oracle Systems Corporation	7372	B	650 506-0300	15819
Oracle Systems Corporation (HQ)	7379	A	650 506-7000	16444
Origin Systems Inc	7371	B	650 628-1500	15337
Paxata Inc	7372	D	650 542-7897	15827
Perfect World Entrmt Inc	7371	C	650 590-7700	15351
Permanente Medical Group Inc	8011	D	650 299-2000	19769
Permanente Medical Group Inc	8011	D	650 299-2015	19770
Permanente Medical Group Inc	6324	D	650 598-2852	10295
Picture It On Canvas Inc	7384	C	858 679-1200	16964
Pierry Inc (PA)	7372	E	800 860-7953	15830
Provident Credit Union (PA)	6062	C	650 508-0300	9645
Pubmatic Inc	7311	D	650 351-9162	13883
Quinn Emanuel Urquhart	8111	C	650 801-5000	23345
Reach Fitness Club	7991	D	650 327-3224	18644
Reputationcom Inc (PA)	7382	C	650 381-3056	16932
Reynolds Cleaning Services Inc	7349	C	650 599-0202	14366
Robert Bosch Start-Up Pltfm NA	7371	E	248 876-6430	15415
Rocket Fuel Inc (HQ)	7379	C	650 595-1300	16474
Ropers Majeski Kohn Bentley (PA)	8111	D	650 364-8200	23359
S J Amoroso Cnstr Co Inc (PA)	1542	B	650 654-1900	1638
San Mateo Credit Union (PA)	6062	D	650 363-1725	9651
Seiler LLP (PA)	8721	C	650 365-4646	26288
Selligent Inc (HQ)	7373	D	650 421-4200	16049
Senior Companions At Home	8322	E	650 364-1265	24044
Sequoia Adrc LP	8322	D	650 364-5504	24045
Sequoia Health Services (HQ)	8062	D	650 369-5811	21741
Shopkick Inc	7371	D	650 763-8727	15444
Shutterfly Inc (PA)	7384	C	650 610-5200	16966

2019 Directory of California
Wholesalers and Services Companies

(P-0000) Products & Services Section entry number
(PA)=Parent Co (HQ)=Headquarters (DH)=Div Headquarters

	SIC	EMP	PHONE	ENTRY #
Silicon Valley Clean Water	4952	D	650 591-7121	6328
Skire Inc	7371	D	650 289-2600	15449
Talend Inc (HQ)	7373	D	650 539-3200	16064
Telecare Corporation	8063	C	650 367-1890	21987
Tradebeam Inc	7379	D	650 653-4800	16514
Trilliant Incorporated	8748	D	650 204-5050	27889
Trilliant Networks Inc (PA)	7389	D	650 204-5050	17521
Trion Worlds, Inc.	7372	B	650 631-9800	15882
Truebeck Construction Inc (PA)	1542	E	650 227-1957	1679
Turn Inc (PA)	7319	C	650 353-4399	13984
Verity Health System Cal Inc	8062	B	310 900-8900	21898
Verity Health System Cal Inc	8062	C	650 551-6507	21899
W Bradley Electric Inc	1731	C	650 701-1502	2780
W L Butler Construction Inc (PA)	1542	E	650 361-1270	1694
Water Heaters Only Inc	5064	D	650 368-9998	7431
Weil Gotshal & Manges LLP	8111	C	650 802-3000	23428
WL Butler Inc	1522	C	650 361-1270	1327
Yodlee Inc (HQ)	8742	D	650 980-3600	27530
Zb Rehab Staffing Inc	7363	D	650 396-2207	14947
Zyme Solutions Inc (PA)	7375	D	650 585-2258	16263

REDWOOD VALLEY, CA - Mendocino County

	SIC	EMP	PHONE	ENTRY #
Consolidated Tribal Health Prj	8093	D	707 485-5115	22538
Redwood Valley Industrial Park	4225	D	707 485-8766	4625

REEDLEY, CA - Fresno County

	SIC	EMP	PHONE	ENTRY #
Cal Packing & Storage LP	4222	D	559 638-2929	4497
Golden Living LLC	8051	D	559 638-3577	20479
Moonlight Packing Corporation (PA)	5148	C	559 638-7799	8707
Moya Juan Farm Labor Services	0761	D	559 638-9498	662
Paragon Health & Rehab CT	8093	E	559 638-3578	22632
Rio Vista Ventures LLC	5141	E	559 897-6730	8449
Sierra View Homes	8051	C	559 637-2256	20764
Trinity Fruit Packing Company	0723	C	559 743-3913	581
Trinity Packing Company Inc	7389	B	559 743-3913	17525
Verizon Communications Inc.	4813	C	559 637-0204	5667
Youngstown Grape Distrs Inc	0723	C	559 638-2271	591

RESEDA, CA - Los Angeles County

	SIC	EMP	PHONE	ENTRY #
Advanced Bioservices LLC (PA)	8741	D	818 342-0100	26748
Alumatec Inc	1381	D	818 609-7460	1034
Auto Body Management Inc	7532	E	818 888-7654	17712
Chase Group Llc	8742	D	818 708-3533	27189
Fabulous & Company LLC	7231	E	818 261-7242	13654
GK Management Co Inc	6531	D	818 705-8834	11484
Honda R&D Americas Inc	8732	E	818 345-7922	26528
Longwood Management Corp	8062	D	818 881-7414	21569
Los Angles Jewish HM For Aging (PA)	8051	B	818 774-3000	20603
Los Angles Jewish HM For Aging	8051	B	818 774-3000	20604
Mid Vlley Racquetball Athc CLB	7997	C	818 705-6500	18974
Spa Dreams	7991	D	818 298-1120	18656
Verizon Communications Inc.	7389	A	818 438-1104	17563
West Valley Family YMCA	8351	C	818 774-2840	24398
Woodland Care Center LLC	8059	C	818 881-4540	21262

RIALTO, CA - San Bernardino County

	SIC	EMP	PHONE	ENTRY #
B & B Plastics Recyclers Inc (PA)	5093	D	909 829-3606	7970
Burlingame Industries Inc (PA)	7033	D	909 355-7000	13459
Caremark Rx Inc	8011	D	909 822-1164	19350
Clem-Trans Inc	4212	E	909 877-4450	3992
Confire J P A	7389	D	909 356-2375	17098
Crestview Cnvalescent Hosp Inc	8051	C	909 877-1361	20362
Filter Recycling Services Inc (PA)	4953	C	909 873-4141	6400
Geodis Logistics LLC	4225	D	909 240-6298	4565
Mercy Air Tri-County LLC	4522	C	909 829-1051	4864
Mesa Counselling	8742	E	909 421-9301	27342
Molina Healthcare Inc	8011	C	909 546-7116	19696
Ptr Group Inc	8741	E	951 965-1822	27006
Robert Clapper Cnstr Svcs Inc	1542	D	909 829-3688	1633
Sierra Lathing Company Inc	1742	C	909 421-0211	2957
Simple Luxuries LLC	1771	E	310 627-6514	3325
So-Cal Strl Stl Fbrication Inc	1791	E	909 877-1299	3398
State Pipe & Supply Inc	5051	E	909 356-5670	7316
State Pipe & Supply Inc (DH)	5051	D	909 877-9999	7317
Sudhakar Company International	1611	D	909 879-2933	1855
Vista Cove Care Ctr - Rialto	8051	D	909 877-1361	20869

RICHGROVE, CA - Tulare County

	SIC	EMP	PHONE	ENTRY #
Vincent B Zaninovich Sons Inc	0172	A	661 720-9031	182

RICHMOND, CA - Contra Costa County

	SIC	EMP	PHONE	ENTRY #
Alsco Inc	7213	D	510 237-9634	13493
Alta Vista Solutions	8711	C	510 594-0510	25528
Alten Construction Inc	1542	D	510 234-4200	1464
Ameripride Services Inc	7213	E	800 748-6178	13512
Aquatic Science Center	8731	E	510 746-7334	26324
AT&T Corp	4813	D	510 965-9714	5465

	SIC	EMP	PHONE	ENTRY #
Bay Area Beverage Co	5182	C	510 965-6120	9033
Bay Area Distributing Coinc	5181	E	510 232-8554	8981
Bay Cities Crane & Rigging Inc (PA)	7359	E	510 232-7222	14477
Bay City Mechanical Inc	1711	C	510 233-7000	2136
Ben Myerson Candy Co Inc	5182	D	510 236-2233	9035
BP West Coast Products LLC	1311	B	510 231-4724	1015
Brand Services LLC	1799	D	510 231-9640	3495
Brookside Community Health Ctr	8011	E	510 215-5001	19328
C Overaa & Co (PA)	1541	C	510 234-0926	1382
Califrnia Atism Foundation Inc (PA)	8399	C	510 758-0433	24748
Cardinal Health Inc	5122	D	510 232-2030	8154
Century Theatres Inc	7833	D	510 758-9626	18326
Chevron Energy Technology Co (HQ)	8711	D	510 242-5059	25608
Chevron Investor Inc	8741	D	510 242-3000	26801
City of Richmond	7999	D	510 620-6788	19141
Contra Costa ARC	8361	D	510 233-7303	24475
Ctc Food International Inc (PA)	5149	E	650 873-7600	8782
Dahl-Beck Electric Co	5063	D	510 237-2325	7353
Department Health Care Svcs	8071	C	510 412-3700	22075
Diversified Health Svcs Del (PA)	8059	C	510 231-6200	21059
East Bay Municipl Utilty Distr	4941	C	866 403-2683	6243
Ecology Control Industries	4959	D	510 235-1393	6538
First Student Inc	4151	C	510 237-6677	3923
First Student Inc	4151	D	510 237-6365	3931
Foss Maritime Company	4412	D	510 307-4271	4696
Gardeners Guild Inc	0782	C	415 457-0400	845
Hartmann Studios Incorporated	7389	C	510 232-5030	17210
Hotel Mac Restaurant Inc	7011	E	510 233-0576	12728
Hydrox Properties Xii LLC	6512	D	510 262-7200	10897
Inter-Rail Trnspt Nshville LLC	4789	D	510 231-2744	5229
International Delicacies	5149	C	510 669-2444	8806
Kaiser Foundation Hospitals	8011	B	510 307-1500	19534
Levin-Richmond Terminal Corp	4491	D	510 232-4422	4728
Macdonald Housing Partners LP	6531	E	510 620-0865	11578
New Ngc Inc	5093	C	510 234-6745	7984
Oliver & Company Inc	1542	D	510 412-9090	1604
Pacific Hotel Management LLC	7011	C	510 262-0700	13000
Palecek Imports Inc (PA)	5021	C	510 236-7730	6734
Permanente Medical Group Inc	8011	D	510 231-5406	19771
Public Health California Dept	8011	C	510 412-1502	19808
Richmond Country Club	7997	D	510 231-2241	19014
Richmond Rescue Mission (PA)	8322	D	510 215-4555	23997
Richmond Sanitary Service Inc (HQ)	4959	C	510 262-7100	6547
Richmond Wholesale Meat Co	5147	D	510 233-5111	8627
Rubber Dust Inc (PA)	7534	D	510 237-6344	17750
Rubicon Enterprises Inc	7349	C	510 235-1516	14371
Rubicon Programs Incorporated (PA)	7349	D	510 235-1516	14372
S P R E Inc	6531	D	510 222-8340	11750
San Francisco Bay Area Rapid	4111	C	510 233-6848	3709
San Francisco Bay Area Rapid	4111	D	510 233-7444	3711
Sangamo Therapeutics Inc (PA)	8731	C	510 970-6000	26448
Sims Group USA Corporation (DH)	5093	D	510 412-5300	7994
Sims Group USA Corporation	5093	C	510 236-0606	7995
Stalker Software Inc	7372	E	415 569-2280	15864
Sunpower Corporation Systems (DH)	1711	D	510 260-8200	2375
T F Louderback Inc (PA)	5181	C	510 965-6120	9028
United Parcel Service Inc OH	4215	C	510 262-2338	4445
Universal Bldg Svcs & Sup Co (PA)	7349	D	510 527-1078	14418
Vicor Inc	7373	D	510 621-2000	16074
Vila Construction Co.	1542	D	510 236-9111	1693
West Countra Costa Youth Svcs (PA)	8322	D	510 412-5647	24131
West County Resource Recovery	4953	E	510 231-4200	6523
WR Forde Associates Inc	1611	D	415 924-3072	1871
Young MNS Chrstn Assn of E Bay	8351	A	510 223-7000	24403
Young MNS Chrstn Assn of E Bay	8641	B	510 412-5647	25362
Young MNS Chrstn Assn of E Bay	8641	C	510 222-9622	25363

RICHVALE, CA - Butte County

	SIC	EMP	PHONE	ENTRY #
Bianchi Ag Services Inc (PA)	5083	C	530 882-4575	7701

RIDGECREST, CA - Kern County

	SIC	EMP	PHONE	ENTRY #
Altaone Federal Credit Union (PA)	6061	C	760 371-7000	9538
Community Action Partnr Kern	8399	C	760 371-1469	24762
Desert Area Resources Training	8399	D	760 375-8494	24774
Drummond Medical Group Inc	8011	C	760 446-4571	19450
Golden Living LLC	8082	D	760 446-3591	22305
Great Western Hotels Corp	7011	E	760 446-6543	12617
Jacobs Technology Inc	8711	D	760 446-7084	25766
Jacobs Technology Inc	8711	C	760 446-1549	25768
L3 Technologies Inc	7373	D	760 375-0390	15995
Leidos Inc	7374	B	858 826-7670	16150
Navy Exchange Service Command	7041	D	760 939-8681	13478
New Directions Tech Inc (PA)	7373	D	760 384-2444	16018
Peekay Investments Prpts LLC	7011	E	714 403-1923	13055
Poulin Corporation (PA)	6799	C	760 375-6531	12260
Pre Con Industries Inc	1742	D	760 499-6176	2940

Employment Codes: A=Over 500 employees, B=251-500,
C=101-250, D=51-100, E=50

2019 Directory of California
Wholesalers and Services Companies

© Mergent Inc. 1-800-342-5647

1643

Company	SIC	EMP	PHONE	ENTRY #
Ridgecrest Regional Hospital	8011	B	760 499-7260	19826
Ridgecrest Regional Hospital (PA)	8062	D	760 446-3551	21687

RIO LINDA, CA - Sacramento County

Company	SIC	EMP	PHONE	ENTRY #
KRC Builders Incorporated	1751	D	916 417-1200	3048
U S Army Corps of Engineers	8711	D	916 649-0133	25965

RIO VISTA, CA - Solano County

Company	SIC	EMP	PHONE	ENTRY #
California Vegetable Spc Inc	5148	D	707 374-2111	8650
Lindsay Transportation	5084	C	707 374-6800	7762
Paul Graham Drilling & Svc Co	1381	D	707 374-5123	1039
Trilogy Rio Vista	1541	D	707 374-1100	1447

RIPON, CA - San Joaquin County

Company	SIC	EMP	PHONE	ENTRY #
Brocchini Farms Inc	0172	E	209 599-4229	132
Cheema Freightlines LLC	4731	D	209 599-0777	5032
Fishers Nursery	5193	D	209 599-3412	9134
Gico Management	5145	D	209 599-7131	8562
Jim Aartman Inc (PA)	4212	C	209 599-5066	4029
Lassen Canyon Nursery Inc	0171	E	209 599-7777	106
Nulaid Foods Inc (PA)	5144	D	209 599-2121	8537
Nushake Inc	1761	D	209 239-8616	3181
V&V Farm Labor Contractor	0191	D	209 599-4834	389

RIVERBANK, CA - Stanislaus County

Company	SIC	EMP	PHONE	ENTRY #
Econtactlive Inc	7389	D	209 548-4300	17146
LMC West Inc	5084	E	209 869-0144	7763
Onemain Holdings Inc	6162	C	209 869-8030	9838
Valley West Health Care Inc	8051	D	209 869-2569	20854

RIVERDALE, CA - Fresno County

Company	SIC	EMP	PHONE	ENTRY #
Ayala Corporation	7361	C	559 867-5700	14573
Linda Terra Farms (PA)	0213	C	559 867-3473	403
Maddox Dairy LLC	0241	D	559 867-3545	419
Maddox Dairy A Ltd Partnership (PA)	0241	D	559 867-3545	420
Maddox Dairy A Ltd Partnership	0241	E	559 867-4457	421
Maddox Dairy A Ltd Partnership	0241	D	559 866-5624	422
Terra Linda Farms 1	0191	E	559 867-3400	385

RIVERSIDE, CA - Riverside County

Company	SIC	EMP	PHONE	ENTRY #
20/20 Plumbing & Heating Inc	1711	C	951 396-2020	2076
A F V W Health Center	8051	B	951 697-2025	20218
A-Check America Inc (PA)	7323	C	951 750-1501	14028
A-Check America Inc	7323	D	800 872-2677	14029
Abbey Partner VI	6531	E	951 785-8800	11188
Ace Cash Express Inc	6099	C	951 509-3506	9668
Adkison Engineers Inc	8711	D	951 688-0241	25502
Adventist Media Center Inc (PA)	7922	D	805 955-7777	18339
Air Force Village West Inc	8051	B	951 697-2000	20223
Albert A Webb Associates (PA)	8711	C	951 686-1070	25524
Allied Steel Co Inc	1791	D	951 241-7000	3358
Alliedbarton Security Svcs LLC	7381	D	951 801-7300	16550
Alta Interiors Inc	1742	D	951 784-1400	2842
Alta Vista Healthcare and Well	8011	C	951 688-8200	19275
Altura Credit Union (PA)	6062	D	888 883-7228	9620
Always There Live In Care LLC	8082	D	888 606-8880	22216
American Dntl Partners of Cal	8021	C	951 689-5031	20108
American Medical Response (DH)	4119	C	951 782-5200	3756
American Reprographics Co LLC	7334	C	951 686-0530	14076
American Residential Svcs LLC	1711	D	951 341-9371	2112
Anheuser-Busch	5181	C	951 782-3935	8978
Apria Healthcare LLC	8082	D	951 320-1100	22227
Arakelian Enterprises Inc	4953	C	951 342-3300	6342
AT&T Corp	4812	C	951 275-8801	5280
AT&T Services Inc	4813	C	951 369-2282	5482
Automobile Club Southern Cal	8699	D	951 684-4250	25390
B & B Nurseries Inc	5193	D	951 352-8383	9124
Babcock Laboratories Inc	8734	D	951 653-3351	26684
Banquet Facilities	7299	E	951 360-2081	13719
Barrys Security Services Inc (PA)	7381	C	951 789-7575	16579
Bedrock Company	1771	D	951 273-1931	3222
Behavioral Health Resources	8063	C	951 275-8400	21929
Bens Asphalt & Maint Co Inc	1611	E	951 248-1103	1731
Best Best & Krieger LLP (PA)	8111	C	951 686-1450	22944
Bio-Mdcal Applications Cal Inc	8092	C	951 343-7700	22468
Blazing Industrial Steel Inc	1791	D	951 360-8340	3364
Bledsoe Masonry Inc	1741	D	951 360-6140	2798
Blue Banner Company Inc (PA)	0723	D	951 682-6183	495
Bright Expectations Inc	8082	E	951 360-2070	22241
Bx Construction LLC	1521	D	951 509-9412	1133
California Citrus Cooperative	0174	C	951 683-4045	204
Canyon Crest Country Club Inc	7997	D	951 274-7900	18883
Career Dev Inst For Excptnl	6552	E	951 337-3678	11861
Carolyn E Wylie Center	8351	D	951 683-5193	24274
Cellco Partnership	4812	D	951 697-3035	5311
Champion Electric Inc	1731	D	951 276-9619	2539
Citibank National Association	6021	C	800 627-3999	9330
City National Bank	6021	E	951 276-8800	9338
City of Riverside	7389	D	951 346-4700	17081
Clpf - Sycamore	6531	D	212 883-2500	11323
Community Care Rehab Ctr LLC	8051	C	951 680-6500	20320
Community Med Group of Rvrside	8011	C	951 274-3414	19399
Complete Coach Works (HQ)	7549	B	951 682-2557	17857
Corona - College Heights Ora	0723	B	951 359-6451	504
County of Riverside	8111	C	951 955-6000	23005
County of Riverside	8011	D	951 955-0840	19418
County of Riverside	8399	D	951 358-5306	24771
County of Riverside	8011	D	951 358-6000	19420
County of Riverside	8322	C	951 955-3100	23710
County of Riverside	8322	D	951 275-8783	23712
County of Riverside	8322	D	951 697-4699	23713
County of Riverside	7379	E	951 486-7700	16333
County of Riverside	8322	A	951 955-0905	23714
County of Riverside	8322	D	951 358-4415	23715
County of Riverside	1521	D	951 955-4800	1149
County of Riverside	8331	D	951 955-3100	24175
County of Riverside Department (PA)	8699	D	951 358-5000	25413
Cove Builders Inc	1522	C	714 436-2973	1278
Cox Automotive Inc	5012	A	951 689-6000	6587
Craftsman Lath and Plaster Inc	1751	B	951 685-9922	3024
Crest Steel Corporation	5051	D	310 830-2651	7267
Cross Country Healthcare Inc	7361	B	951 786-7683	14595
Cypress Gardens Convalescent H	8059	C	951 688-3643	21055
Del Mar Plastering Inc	1742	D	951 343-5955	2872
Digiquest Corp	5045	D	951 776-4344	7037
Dmcg Inc (PA)	7389	D	951 683-9685	17133
Dynamic Plumbing Commercial	1711	D	951 343-1200	2190
Dynamic Plumbing Systems Inc	1711	D	951 343-1200	2191
E Business Solutions Inc	7311	C	800 660-2669	13822
Edwards Theatres Circuit Inc	7832	D	951 361-1917	18287
Elias Elliott Lampasi Fehn (PA)	8021	D	951 689-5031	20116
Elite Electric	1731	C	951 681-5811	2577
Empire Company LLC	5031	C	951 742-5273	6822
Encore Senior Living III LLC	6513	E	951 360-1616	11014
Entrepreneurial Hospitality	7389	C	951 346-4700	17152
Erlanger Distribution Ctr Inc	5199	E	951 784-5147	9214
Etairos Consulting	7379	E	844 219-7027	16359
Far West Electric Inc	1731	D	909 684-8661	2582
Fencecorp Inc (HQ)	1799	B	951 686-3170	3517
Fenceworks Inc (PA)	1799	C	951 788-5620	3519
Festival Fun Parks LLC	7996	D	951 785-3000	18799
FS Commercial Landscape Inc (PA)	0782	C	951 360-7070	843
G4s Secure Solutions (usa)	7381	B	951 341-3000	16653
Ghossain & Truelock Entps Inc	7349	D	951 781-9345	14276
Gless Ranch Inc (PA)	0762	E	951 780-8458	693
Gonzales Painting Corp	1721	D	951 214-6400	2444
Guard Force International Inc	7382	E	512 296-0316	16900
Guardsmark LLC	7381	B	909 989-5345	16693
Haider Spine Ctr Med Group Inc	8011	D	951 413-0200	19489
Hal Hays Construction Inc (PA)	1541	C	951 369-1008	1404
Hamblins Bdy Pnt Frame Sp Inc	7538	D	951 689-8440	17766
Harbor Pipe and Steel Inc	5051	C	951 369-3990	7278
Herman Weissker Inc (HQ)	1623	C	951 826-8800	1927
High-Light Electric Inc	1731	D	951 352-9646	2604
Historic Mission Inn Corp	7011	B	951 784-0300	12671
Hit Portfolio I Misc Trs LLC	7011	B	909 240-9526	12674
Honey Flower Holdings LLC	8051	C	951 351-2800	20532
Hy-Tech Tile Inc	1752	C	951 788-0550	3107
Iheartcommunications Inc	4832	D	951 684-1992	5722
Index Fresh Inc (PA)	5148	D	909 877-0999	8696
Inland Inspections Consulting	7389	E	951 697-1000	17236
J Ginger Masonry LP (PA)	1741	B	951 688-5050	2812
J M V B Inc	1721	C	714 288-9797	2448
Jaguar Computer Systems Inc	5045	E	951 273-7950	7067
John L Ginger Masonry Inc	1741	C	951 688-5050	2815
Johnson Cntrls SEC Sltions LLC	7382	C	951 787-0420	16909
Johnson Machinery Co (PA)	5082	C	951 686-4560	7684
Kadena Pacific Inc	1542	E	951 990-7865	1570
Kaiser Foundation Hospitals	8011	A	951 248-4000	19579
Kaiser Foundation Hospitals	8011	A	866 984-7483	19580
Kaiser Foundation Hospitals	8011	A	951 353-2000	19615
Kana Pipeline Inc	1623	D	714 986-1400	1942
Keenan & Associates	6411	D	951 788-0330	10665
Keller Williams Realty	6531	E	951 215-0787	11543
Kindred Healthcare Operating	8059	C	951 688-8200	21129
Kleinfelder Inc	8748	D	951 801-3681	27764
Knollwood Psychiatric and Chem	8063	D	951 275-8400	21961
Kpc Group LLC (PA)	8742	C	951 782-8812	27296
Liberty Landscaping Inc	0781	D	951 683-2999	765
Lozano Plumbing Services Inc	1711	C	951 683-4840	2268
M & M Interiors Inc	1542	C	951 279-9535	1583
M & M Plumbing Inc	1711	D	951 354-5388	2272

Mergent email: customerrelations@mergent.com

1644

2019 Directory of California
Wholesalers and Services Companies

(P-0000) Products & Services Section entry number
(PA)=Parent Co (HQ)=Headquarters (DH)=Div Headquarters

	SIC	EMP	PHONE	ENTRY #
Magnolia Rhblttion Nursing Ctr	8059	D	951 688-4321	21149
Main Electric Supply Co LLC	5063	D	951 784-2900	7376
McKesson Corporation	5122	D	951 686-3575	8191
Metropolitan Water District	4941	E	951 688-5672	6281
Metropolitan Water District	4941	E	951 780-1511	6286
Mfi Recovery Center (PA)	8093	D	951 683-6596	22620
Mgb Construction Inc	1611	C	951 342-0303	1819
ML Electricworks Inc	1731	D	951 687-5078	2650
Mount Rbdoux Convalescent Hosp	8051	C	951 681-2200	20654
National Paving Company Inc	1611	D	951 369-1332	1824
Neal Trucking Inc	4212	D	951 685-5048	4044
New York Life Insurance Co	6311	D	951 354-2094	10141
Officeworks Inc	7361	D	951 784-2534	14680
Olive Grove Retirement Resort	6513	C	951 687-2241	11090
Onrad Inc	8741	D	800 848-5876	26967
Orangetree Convalescent Hosp	8062	C	951 785-6060	21617
Pacific Tank Lines Inc	4923	D	951 680-1900	6155
Parkview Cmnty Hosp Med Ctr	8062	A	951 354-7404	21635
Paychex Inc	8721	E	951 682-6100	26267
Peggs Company Inc (PA)	7699	D	253 584-9548	17970
Pepsi-Cola Metro Btlg Co Inc	5078	B	951 697-3200	7664
Perry Coast Construction Inc	1542	C	951 774-0677	1614
Pharmerica Long-Term Care LLC	5122	D	951 784-1616	8205
Pinnacle Rvrside Hspitality LP	7011	C	951 784-8000	13066
Plan-It Life Inc	8322	D	951 742-7561	23972
Ppc Enterprises Inc	1711	C	951 354-5402	2315
Precise Distribution Inc	4225	E	951 367-1037	4612
Prestige Gunite California Inc	1771	E	909 276-9096	3310
Professnal Cmmnctons Netwrk LP (PA)	7389	E	951 275-9149	17414
Provident Savings Bank (HQ)	6035	D	951 782-6177	9529
Provident Savings Bank	6035	D	951 686-6060	9530
Provident Savings Bank LLC	6022	D	951 686-6060	9480
Prudential Overall Supply	7218	C	951 687-0440	13614
Psychiatric Solutions Inc	8011	C	951 789-4405	19805
R&S Carpet Services Inc	5023	D	909 740-6645	6784
Raincross Hospitality Corp (PA)	7299	D	951 346-4700	13770
Rancho Jurupa Park	7999	E	951 684-7032	19222
Rcr Plumbing and Mech Inc (PA)	1711	C	951 371-5000	2331
Rdo Construction Equipment Co	5083	E	951 778-3700	7710
Real Estate California Dept	6531	D	951 715-0130	11715
Realty One Group Inc	6531	D	951 565-8105	11720
Recycler Core Company Inc	5013	D	951 276-1687	6669
Regional Connector Constrs	1521	E	951 368-6400	1223
Reid & Helly	8111	D	951 682-1771	23352
Rhf Plymouth Tower	8361	D	951 248-0456	24653
Rls Electrical Contrs Inc	1731	E	951 688-8049	2709
Riverside Care Inc	8051	C	951 683-7111	20725
Riverside Cmnty Hlth Systems (DH)	8062	D	951 788-3000	21688
Riverside County Flood Control	8999	E	951 955-1200	27958
Riverside Dialysis Center	8092	E	951 682-2700	22487
Riverside Equities LLC	8051	D	951 688-2222	20726
Riverside Healthcare System LP	8062	A	951 788-3000	21689
Riverside Medical Clinic Inc	8011	B	951 683-6370	19827
Riverside Medical Clinic Inc (PA)	8011	B	951 683-6370	19828
Riverside Sanitarium LLC	8051	D	951 684-7701	20728
Riverside Scrap Ir & Met Corp (PA)	5093	E	951 686-2120	7989
Riverside Transit Agency (PA)	4111	B	951 565-5000	3699
Riverside University Health (PA)	8062	D	951 358-5000	21690
Robert Half International Inc	7361	D	951 779-9081	14732
Roberts & Associates Inc	8082	D	951 727-4357	22407
Rogan Building Services Inc	7349	E	951 248-1261	14368
Roy E Whitehead Inc	1751	D	951 682-1490	3069
Secure Transportation Company	4119	C	951 737-7300	3847
Security California Bancorp	6712	C	951 368-2265	11958
Skanska USA Civil West Rocky M (DH)	1629	D	970 565-8000	2063
Skanska USA Cvil W Cal Dst Inc (DH)	1611	A	951 684-5360	1850
Sky Scan Satelite Systems	4841	D	909 322-1393	5930
Solcius LLC	1711	B	951 772-0030	2363
South Coast Concrete Cnstr	1771	E	951 351-7777	3327
South Coast Health Wellness	8051	D	951 686-9001	20772
Southern Cal Prmnnte Med Group	6324	B	866 984-7483	10314
Southern California Fleet Svc	7538	C	951 272-8655	17785
Southern Glazers Wine	5182	E	951 274-2420	9053
Springboard Solutions LLC	8748	C	951 779-7739	27870
State Compensation Insur Fund	6331	C	888 782-8338	10408
Stronghold Engineering Inc (PA)	1542	D	951 684-9303	1660
Sun Mar Management Services	8051	D	951 687-3842	20785
Sunrise Senior Living LLC	8051	D	951 785-1200	20834
Sunstone Hotel Management Inc	7011	D	951 784-8000	13301
Sysco Riverside Inc	5141	B	951 601-5300	8467
T C H P Inc	8051	D	951 687-7330	20837
T S J Elec Communications Inc	1731	D	951 785-0921	2761
Team Truck Dismantling Inc	5015	D	951 685-6744	6704
Thompson & Colegate LLP	8111	E	951 682-5550	23408
Ticor Title Company California	6361	E	951 509-0211	10472

	SIC	EMP	PHONE	ENTRY #
Toad 1350	4832	E	951 369-1350	5754
Tony R Crisalli Inc	7353	E	951 727-0110	14459
Top Priority Couriers Inc (PA)	4215	D	951 781-1000	4437
Trugreen Limited Partnership	0782	E	951 231-2760	953
UBS Financial Services Inc	7389	E	951 684-6300	17528
Ucr Botany and Plant Sciences	6732	E	951 827-5133	12085
Unique Carpets Ltd	5023	D	951 352-8125	6798
United Service Tech Inc	7699	D	714 224-1406	18002
University Cal Riverside	8732	D	951 827-4801	26575
USA Fact Inc (PA)	8742	D	951 656-7800	27504
USDA Forest Service	8731	D	951 680-1560	26487
Van Daele Development Corp	1531	C	951 354-6800	1362
Venvest Ballard Inc	1711	D	951 276-9744	2397
Verizon Business Global LLC	4841	E	951 653-4482	5963
Veterinary Service Inc	5047	D	951 328-4900	7228
Villa Convalescent Hosp Inc	8051	D	951 689-5788	20860
Visitng Nurse Assn Inlnd CNT (PA)	8082	A	951 413-1200	22448
Vista Behavioral Health Inc	8063	D	800 992-0901	21993
Vista Pacifica Enterprises Inc (PA)	8051	C	951 682-4833	20871
Vista Pacifica Enterprises Inc	8059	C	951 682-4867	21251
Vitas Healthcare Corp Cal	8082	D	909 386-6000	22454
Volt Management Corp	7363	D	951 789-8133	14939
Waterman Convalescent Hospital	8069	D	951 681-2200	22057
West Coast Drywall & Co Inc	1742	B	951 778-3592	2979
West Coast Interiors Inc	1721	A	951 778-3592	2491
West Riverside Veterinary Hosp	0742	E	951 686-2242	621
West States Skanska Inc	1623	C	970 565-4903	2002
Westcoe Realtors Inc	6531	D	951 784-2500	11827
Westview Services Inc	8999	D	951 343-2356	27962
Wilmon Corporation	8051	D	951 685-7474	20894
Windsor Capital Group Inc	7011	D	951 276-1200	13412
Z-Best Concrete Inc	1771	D	951 774-1870	3347

RLLNG HLS EST, CA - Los Angeles County

	SIC	EMP	PHONE	ENTRY #
Citigroup Global Markets Inc	6211	D	310 544-3600	9938
Cox California Telcom LLC	4813	D	310 377-1800	5539
Das Global Capital Corp	8732	D	702 967-1688	26508
Dincloud Inc	7372	D	310 929-1101	15648
Jack Kramer Club	7997	D	310 326-4404	18940
Metropolitan Water District	4941	A	310 832-6106	6287
Natural Health Trends Corp	8099	D	310 541-0888	22845
Regal Cinemas Inc	7832	D	310 544-3042	18318
Rolling Hlls Esttes Tennis CLB	7999	D	310 541-4585	19226
Seatech Consulting Group Inc	7379	E	310 356-6828	16479
Spalding Srgcl Ctr of Bvrly Hl	8011	C	949 863-0022	19930
Sqa Services Inc	8742	B	310 544-6888	27465

ROCKLIN, CA - Placer County

	SIC	EMP	PHONE	ENTRY #
American Hlthcare ADM Svcs Inc	8099	B	916 773-7227	22728
Brower Mechanical Inc	7623	D	530 749-0808	17890
Builders & Tradesmens	6411	D	916 772-9200	10566
Builders & Tradesmens Insur	6311	D	916 772-9200	10132
Casa De Santa Fe of Rocklin	8059	D	916 435-8800	21034
Cellco Partnership	4812	D	916 408-7958	5342
Cha-Dor Realty	5031	D	916 624-0627	6815
Csdvrs LLC (PA)	7389	C	727 443-1218	17117
Data Control Corporation	7373	D	916 774-4000	15939
Ecorp Consulting Inc (PA)	8742	D	916 782-9100	27223
Educational Media Foundation (PA)	4832	B	916 251-1600	5709
Federal Express Corporation	4512	C	800 463-3339	4781
Financial Pacific Insurance Co	6411	D	916 630-5000	10629
First Technology Federal Cr Un	6061	C	855 855-8805	9557
Great Lakes E & I/ Inquip JV	1629	D	805 687-2007	2036
Habitat Rstration Sciences Inc	0782	E	916 408-2990	855
Horizon West Healthcare Inc (HQ)	8051	D	916 624-6230	20535
Infinity Energy Inc	1711	D	916 474-4723	2233
Jemtown Inc	7542	D	916 315-0555	17820
Jkf Auto Service Inc	7542	D	916 315-0555	17821
JR Perce Plbg Inc Sacramento	1711	D	916 434-9554	2247
Kitchen Mart Inc	1521	D	916 315-3535	1189
Kniesels Auto Collision Center	5013	D	916 315-8888	6653
L&H Airco LLC	1711	D	916 677-1000	2255
La Voie & Sons Construction	8741	D	916 408-6900	26926
MA Steiner Construction Inc	1541	D	916 988-6300	1419
Marksys LLC	8742	D	916 745-4883	27321
Oracle Corporation	7372	B	916 435-8342	15808
Oracle Corporation	7372	B	916 315-3500	15814
Pacific Secured Equities Inc	8742	D	916 677-2500	27386
Precision Medical Products Inc	8011	D	573 474-9302	19794
Purple Language Services Co	7812	C	916 435-8216	18100
Quality Telecom Consultants (PA)	1623	D	916 315-0500	1972
Road Safety Inc	7389	D	916 543-4600	17448
Rruff-Rocklin Residents Unite	8641	E	415 806-2778	25230
SE Scher Corporation	7361	D	916 632-1363	14756
Security On-Site Services Inc	7382	C	916 988-6500	16938
Sierra View Landscape Inc	0782	E	916 408-2990	940

Employment Codes: A=Over 500 employees, B=251-500,
C=101-250, D=51-100, E=50

2019 Directory of California
Wholesalers and Services Companies

© Mergent Inc. 1-800-342-5647

1645

GEOGRAPHIC

Company	SIC	EMP	PHONE	ENTRY #
SMA Solar Technology Amer LLC (HQ)	5065	D	916 625-0870	7542
Sonoran Roofing Inc (PA)	1761	C	916 624-1080	3200
Stantec Consulting Svcs Inc	8712	D	916 773-8100	26114
Star Inc	8322	C	916 632-8407	24073
Strikes Unlimited Inc	7933	D	916 626-3600	18500
Sunrise Senior Living LLC	8051	D	916 632-3003	20832
Surveillance Systems	5065	E	800 508-6981	7549
Swan Engineering Inc	1794	D	916 474-5299	3441
Trane US Inc	5075	C	916 577-1100	7657
United Natural Foods Inc	5149	C	916 625-4100	8890
United Natural Foods West Inc (HQ)	5149	B	401 528-8634	8891
Wpcs Intrntional-Suisun Cy Inc	1731	D	916 624-1300	2793
Zentek Corporation	7371	D	916 749-3610	15558

ROHNERT PARK, CA - Sonoma County

Company	SIC	EMP	PHONE	ENTRY #
24 Hour Fitness Usa Inc	8099	E	707 536-0048	22721
Animal Care Center	0742	D	707 584-4343	596
Artizen Incorporated	7371	C	650 261-9400	15002
Calif Institute Human Ser	8742	D	707 664-2416	27178
Catati Rohnert Park Inc	7389	C	707 792-4531	17062
Codding Construction Co	1542	E	707 795-3550	1508
Cve Nb Contracting Group Inc	8744	E	707 584-1900	27589
Emt LLC (PA)	6798	D	707 584-5123	12159
Exchange Bank	6022	B	707 584-7300	9443
Federted Indans Grton Rncheria	7011	B	707 588-7100	12572
Herc Rentals Inc	7359	D	707 586-6491	14509
Kaiser Foundation Hospitals	6324	C	707 206-3000	10254
Kisco Senior Living LLC	6513	D	707 585-1800	11047
Lemo USA Inc	5065	D	707 206-3700	7500
Merrill Gardens LLC	6513	C	707 585-7878	11068
North Bay Eye Assoc A Med Corp	8011	A	707 206-0849	19714
OHagin Manufacturing LLC	1711	E	707 872-3620	2293
OHagins Inc	1711	D	707 303-3660	2294
Pace Supply Corp (PA)	5074	D	707 755-2499	7632
Red Condor Inc	7371	D	707 569-7419	15400
State Farm Fire and Cslty Co	6411	B	707 588-6011	10779

ROMOLAND, CA - Riverside County

Company	SIC	EMP	PHONE	ENTRY #
Southern California Gas Co	4924	D	213 244-1200	6169

ROSAMOND, CA - Kern County

Company	SIC	EMP	PHONE	ENTRY #
Catalina Solar Lessee LLC	4911	A	888 903-6926	6016
Tapia Farms	0191	E	661 256-4401	384

ROSEMEAD, CA - Los Angeles County

Company	SIC	EMP	PHONE	ENTRY #
Anka Behavioral Health Inc	8999	D	626 573-5902	27918
Cathay Bank	6022	C	626 452-1582	9427
Cox Automotive Inc	5012	C	626 573-8001	6584
Del Mar Convalescent Hospital	8062	D	626 288-8353	21363
Doubletree Hotel	7011	D	323 722-8800	12541
Durham School Services L P	4151	C	626 573-3769	3920
Edison International (PA)	4911	A	626 302-2222	6032
Edison Mission Energy (DH)	4911	E	626 302-5778	6033
Edison Mssion Midwest Holdings	4911	A	626 302-2222	6034
Ensign Group Inc	8051	D	626 607-2400	20400
Ensign Group Inc	8051	C	626 287-0438	20401
Herald Christian Health Center (PA)	8011	D	626 286-8700	19498
Irish Communication Company (DH)	1623	D	626 288-6170	1932
Irish Construction (HQ)	1623	D	626 288-8530	1933
K&I International Trade Inc	5021	E	312 766-1848	6730
Landcare USA LLC	0782	D	310 354-1520	882
Longwood Management Corp	8051	D	626 280-2293	20599
Longwood Management Corp	8051	C	626 280-4820	20600
Los Angeles Orphan Asylum Inc	8361	C	323 283-9311	24585
Maryvale	8361	C	626 280-6510	24592
Maryvale Day Care Center (PA)	8351	C	626 280-6511	24346
Monterey Healthcare & Wellness	8051	D	626 280-3220	20651
Psychiatric Solutions Inc	8093	D	626 286-1191	22657
Southern California Edison Co (HQ)	4911	A	626 302-1212	6113
Southern California Edison Co	4911	C	626 302-5101	6120
Southern California Edison Co	4911	C	626 302-1212	6124
Southern California Edison Co	4911	D	714 895-0488	6129
Southern California Edison Co	4911	D	626 302-0530	6141
Sun Mar Management Services	8741	D	626 288-8353	27051
Sunny Cal Adhc Inc	8322	D	626 307-7772	24078

ROSEVILLE, CA - Placer County

Company	SIC	EMP	PHONE	ENTRY #
10up Inc	7373	D	888 571-7130	15905
Aardvark Staffing Inc	7363	E	916 774-7115	14807
Abso	7361	C	800 943-2589	14563
Adventist Health System/West (PA)	8062	B	916 781-2000	21265
American Pacific Mortgage Corp (PA)	6162	C	916 960-1325	9774
Cal Consoldated Communications	4813	D	916 786-6141	5525
California Rural Indian Health	8399	D	916 437-0104	24747
California Sun Centers Inc	7299	D	916 789-9767	13723
Cellco Partnership	4812	D	916 786-6151	5318
Century 21 Haley & Associates	6531	D	916 782-1500	11300

Company	SIC	EMP	PHONE	ENTRY #
Century Theatres Inc	7833	D	916 797-3466	18325
Certent Inc (PA)	7371	C	925 730-4300	15054
Chicago Title Insurance Co	6361	B	916 783-7195	10445
Claims Management Inc	6411	C	916 631-1250	10586
Clark & Sullivan Builders Inc	1542	C	916 338-7707	1506
CLC Incorporated (PA)	7361	E	916 789-7600	14587
Clearcapitalcom Inc	6531	D	530 582-5011	11322
Clearcaptions LLC	4813	E	866 868-8695	5532
Cliftonlarsonallen LLP	8721	B	916 784-7800	26166
Clp Resources Inc	7363	D	916 788-0300	14836
Cokeva Inc	7378	C	916 462-6001	16280
Coldwell Banker RE Corp	6531	E	408 981-7200	11339
Crocus Holdings LLC	8051	D	916 782-1238	20363
D Augustine & Associates	7311	D	916 774-9600	13807
Denios Roseville Farmers	7389	C	916 782-2704	17130
Dignity Health Med Foundation	8099	D	916 787-0404	22788
Directapps Inc (PA)	7379	C	916 787-2200	16350
Dwayne Nash Industries Inc	1761	C	916 253-1900	3151
Dynamic Staffing Inc (PA)	7361	C	916 773-3900	14604
Enterprise Rent-A-Car Compan (DH)	7515	E	916 787-4500	17655
Erickson Construction LP	1751	C	916 774-1100	3034
Ernst & Young LLP	8721	C	916 218-1900	26201
Eskaton Properties Inc	8361	D	916 334-0810	24522
Esl Technologies Inc	7378	B	916 677-4500	16283
Federal Deposit Insurance Corp	6399	C	916 789-8580	10501
Flexcare LLC	7363	A	866 564-3589	14854
Flintco Pacific Inc	8711	D	916 757-1000	25684
Fmr LLC	6282	C	916 784-3649	10079
Fraternal Order Eagles 1582	6512	C	916 782-2694	10878
Genuent Usa LLC	7371	D	916 772-3700	15177
Global Touchpoints Inc	7371	D	916 878-5954	15180
Golden State Collision Centers	7532	C	916 772-1666	17723
Hewlett Packard Enterprise Co	7372	C	916 786-8000	15704
Horizon West Healthcare Inc	8069	D	916 782-1238	22024
Hotel Contracting Services Inc	7011	D	916 865-4204	12721
Huppe Landscape Company Inc (HQ)	0781	D	916 784-7666	761
Industrial Container Services	5085	C	916 781-2775	7851
Intech Mechanical Company LLC	1711	C	916 797-4900	2236
Intercare Holdings Insur Svcs	6411	B	916 677-2500	10653
Iptor Supply Chain Systems USA (DH)	7371	C	916 542-2820	15234
Kaiser Foundation Hospitals	8062	C	916 746-3937	21476
Kaiser Foundation Hospitals	8011	C	916 784-4000	19608
Kaiser Foundation Hospitals	6324	C	916 784-4050	10239
Kaiser Foundation Hospitals	8062	A	916 784-4000	21519
Lancaster Burns Cnstr Inc	1742	C	916 624-8404	2909
Med-Data Incorporated	8721	D	916 771-1362	26258
Merchant Valley Corporation	7389	C	916 786-7227	17321
Neptune Management Corporation	7261	D	916 771-5300	13692
New York Life Insurance Co	6411	D	916 774-6200	10710
Nortech Waste LLC	4953	C	916 645-5230	6423
Northern California Power Agcy (PA)	4911	D	916 781-3636	6057
Olivieri Enterprises LP	1751	C	916 791-7857	3054
Parchment Inc	7389	C	480 719-1646	17386
Patterson Dental Supply Inc	5047	C	916 780-5100	7205
Permanente Medical Group Inc	8011	D	916 784-4000	19777
Pinnacle Builders Inc	1521	B	916 372-5000	1216
Pinnacle Telecom Inc (PA)	7373	E	916 426-1000	16032
Polycomp Administrative Svcs	6411	E	916 773-3480	10733
Precision Framing Inc	1751	B	916 791-7464	3058
Premiere Agency of California	6411	C	916 784-1008	10738
Pride Industries (PA)	4226	C	916 788-2100	4686
Production Framing Inc	1751	D	916 978-2843	3060
Production Framing Systems Inc (PA)	1751	C	916 978-2888	3061
Project Go Incorporated	1799	C	916 782-3443	3569
Psomas	8711	C	916 788-8122	25879
Quest Media & Supplies Inc (PA)	7373	C	916 338-7070	16038
Reeve-Knight Construction Inc	1542	D	916 786-5112	1628
River Rock Equipment LLC	6719	D	916 791-1609	12002
Roseville Sportworld Inc	7999	D	916 783-8550	19227
Roseville Towne Place Suites	7011	D	916 782-2232	13140
Rountree Plumbing and Htg Inc	1711	D	650 298-0300	2341
S P Thomas Co of Northern Cal (PA)	6552	D	916 786-2040	11912
Safe Credit Union	6061	E	916 979-7233	9584
Sierra Care Rehabilitation Ctr	8051	D	916 782-3188	20762
Sierra Hills Care Center Inc	8052	D	916 782-7007	20958
Sierra View Country Club	7997	D	916 782-3741	19047
Sign of Dove	6513	C	916 786-3277	11113
Spare-Time Inc	7997	D	916 782-2600	19056
Specialty Steel Service Co Inc (HQ)	5051	C	916 771-4737	7315
Sun City Rsvlle Cmnty Assn Inc (PA)	7992	C	916 774-3880	18769
Sunrise Retirement Villa	6513	D	916 786-3277	11122
Sutter Health	8011	C	916 797-4725	19959
Sutter Health	8062	D	916 797-4715	21813
Sutter Health	8071	D	916 784-2277	22151
Sutter Health	8011	D	916 797-4700	19983

	SIC	EMP	PHONE	ENTRY #
Sutter Hlth Scrmnto Sierra Reg	8062	A	916 781-1000	21839
Sutter Roseville Medical Ctr	8062	A	916 781-1000	21843
Sutter Rsvlle Med Ctr Fndation	8062	A	916 781-1000	21844
Tasq Technology Inc	6099	B	916 632-7600	9690
Tech-Ed Networks Inc	7379	C	916 784-2005	16507
Teleplan Service Solutions Inc	7378	D	916 677-4500	16293
Union Pacific Corporation	4011	A	916 789-5311	3626
Union Pacific Railroad Company	4011	D	916 789-5930	3630
Union Pacific Railroad Company	4011	C	916 789-6055	3632
United Building Maint Inc	7349	C	916 772-8101	14416
United States Info Systems Inc	1731	C	845 353-9224	2775
USA Multifamily Management	6531	C	916 773-6060	11809
USA Properties Fund Inc (PA)	6552	D	916 773-6060	11934
Varis LLC (PA)	8742	C	916 294-0860	27508
Vexillum Inc	4911	C	916 218-3815	6147
Vibrantcare Outpatient Rehab (PA)	8093	D	916 782-1212	22711
Volt Management Corp	7363	D	916 923-0454	14938
Walt Disney Company	4832	D	916 780-1470	5762
Waterhouse Management Corp	6515	C	916 772-4918	11160
Wells Fargo Bank National Assn	6021	D	916 724-2982	9391
Wells Fargo Bank National Assn	6021	D	916 774-2249	9394
Wells Fargo Home Mortgage Inc	6021	E	916 782-2221	9409
West Safety	7389	E	514 340-3314	17589
Westmont Living Inc	8361	B	916 786-3277	24721

ROSS, CA - Marin County

	SIC	EMP	PHONE	ENTRY #
Pacific Union Intl Inc	6531	B	415 461-8686	11653

ROWLAND HEIGHTS, CA - Los Angeles County

	SIC	EMP	PHONE	ENTRY #
Angeles Contractor Inc (PA)	1541	D	714 523-1021	1373
Bowie Limited	7371	D	716 610-2480	15032
Ruiteng Internet Technology Co	7374	C	302 597-7438	16174

ROYAL OAKS, CA - Santa Cruz County

	SIC	EMP	PHONE	ENTRY #
Falcon Trading Company (PA)	5149	C	831 786-7000	8787
Gino Rinaldi Inc	1743	D	831 761-0195	2998
Kelvin Hildebrand Inc	4212	E	831 768-9104	4034
Monterey Mushrooms Inc	0182	A	831 728-8300	317

RUTHERFORD, CA - Napa County

	SIC	EMP	PHONE	ENTRY #
Amer Zoetrope Research LLC	8732	C	707 963-9230	26500
Terre Du Soleil Ltd	7011	B	707 963-1211	13323
Vyborny Vineyard Management	0762	D	707 944-9135	720

SACRAMENTO, CA - Sacramento County

	SIC	EMP	PHONE	ENTRY #
15th & L Investors LLC	7011	D	916 267-6805	12289
A Meissners Hhld & Indus Svc	5084	D	916 920-2121	7718
A Teichert & Son Inc (HQ)	5032	C	916 484-3011	6874
A1 Protective Services LLC	7381	E	916 421-3000	16541
AAA Signs Inc	7534	D	916 568-3456	17748
Abacus Service Corporation	7371	B	916 288-8948	14956
ABF Freight System Inc	4213	A	916 428-3531	4093
Accenture LLP	8742	C	916 557-2200	27111
Access Dental Plan (PA)	8021	D	916 922-5000	20106
Access Info MGT Shred Svcs LLC	4226	D	925 461-5352	4664
Ace High Entertainnment LLC	7941	E	916 243-5515	18502
Adesa Corporation LLC	5012	C	916 388-8899	6573
Administrative Systems Inc	7389	D	916 563-1121	16985
Advanced HM Hlth & Hospice Inc	8021	D	916 978-0744	20107
Advanced Home Health Inc	8082	D	916 978-0744	22204
Aecom Global II LLC	8711	B	916 679-2000	25512
Aecom Global II LLC	8748	C	916 679-8700	27622
Aecom Technology Corporation	8711	D	916 414-5800	25519
After Market Group Inc (HQ)	5047	D	916 361-1687	7150
Agamerica Fcb (PA)	6111	D	651 282-8800	9692
Air Systems Service & Cnstr	1711	C	916 368-0336	2091
Airco Mechanical Inc (PA)	1711	C	916 381-4523	2092
Alcal Specialty Contg Inc (DH)	1761	D	916 929-3100	3123
All West Coachlines Inc	4142	D	916 423-4000	3893
Alliedbarton Security Svcs LLC	7381	C	916 489-8280	16552
Alsco Inc	7213	C	916 454-5545	13502
Alston Construction Co Inc (PA)	1542	D	916 340-2400	1463
Amador Stage Lines Inc	4141	D	916 444-7880	3887
American Building Supply Inc (HQ)	5031	C	916 503-4100	6806
American Dream	1521	D	916 613-4917	1114
American Institute Research	8733	B	916 286-8800	26591
American Medical Response	4119	B	916 563-0600	3753
American Patriot Security	7381	D	916 706-2449	16565
American Reprographics Co LLC	7334	D	916 443-1322	14072
American Water Works Co Inc	4941	D	916 568-4236	6208
Amerisourcebergen Drug Corp	5122	C	916 830-4500	8142
Anixter Inc	5063	C	916 563-7560	7330
AON Consulting Inc	6411	D	800 558-0655	10529
Apexcare Inc (PA)	8082	A	916 924-9111	22225
Apple Hospitality Reit Inc	7011	D	916 568-5400	12328
Applewood Care Center	8051	E	916 446-2506	20232
Apria Healthcare LLC	5047	C	530 677-2713	7155

	SIC	EMP	PHONE	ENTRY #
Aramark Unf & Career AP LLC	7218	B	916 286-4100	13585
Aramark Uniform Services	7218	D	916 286-4100	13596
Arden Hills Country Club Inc	7997	D	916 482-6111	18849
Arraycon LLC (PA)	1711	E	916 925-0201	2127
Arreolas Complete Ldscp Svc	0782	E	916 387-6777	799
Asbury Pk Nrsing Rhblttion Ctr	8059	C	916 649-2000	21000
Asian Community Center of Sac (PA)	8322	C	916 394-6399	23493
Assuredpartners Inc	6411	D	916 443-0200	10549
AT&T Corp	4813	B	916 830-5000	5461
AT&T Services Inc	4813	C	916 972-2248	5485
AT&T Services Inc	4813	C	916 453-6267	5504
AT&T Services Inc	4813	C	916 972-2423	5506
Atkinson Youth Services Inc	8322	D	916 927-1863	23498
Atkinson Youth Services Inc	8361	D	916 257-0637	24422
Atlas Disposal Industries LLC	4953	D	916 455-2800	6349
Auburn Constructors Inc	1629	D	916 924-0344	2009
Avis Rent A Car System Inc	7514	C	916 922-5601	17626
B & G Delivery System Inc	4212	C	916 921-4401	3977
B B & T Management Corp	5031	C	916 428-8060	6809
Baco Realty Corporation	7381	D	916 974-9898	16575
Bagatelos Glass Systems Inc (PA)	1793	D	916 364-3600	3402
Bank America National Assn	8741	C	916 326-3161	26774
Banner Bank	6022	D	916 648-2100	9419
Barnum & Celillo Electric Inc (PA)	1731	D	916 646-4661	2516
Bayer Protective Services Inc	7382	C	916 486-5800	16878
Benetech Inc (PA)	6411	D	916 484-6811	10562
Benetech Inc	6411	E	916 484-6811	10563
BEST Consulting Inc	8052	C	916 448-2050	20917
Bickmore and Associates Inc (DH)	6411	D	916 244-1100	10565
Bloodsource Inc	8099	E	916 488-1701	22752
Bohm Law Group Inc (PA)	8111	E	916 927-5574	22952
Bradford & Barthel LLP (PA)	8111	D	916 569-0790	22957
Briarwood Health Care Inc	8059	D	916 383-2741	21015
Brightview Landscape Svcs Inc	0781	D	916 381-2800	740
Brinks Incorporated	7381	C	916 452-5279	16590
Broadway Sacramento (PA)	7922	C	916 446-5880	18348
Brunswick Corner Partnership	6531	E	916 649-7500	11251
Burgett Incorporated	5099	D	916 567-9999	8021
Buzz Oates Management Services	6531	E	916 381-3843	11255
C & S Wholesale Grocers Inc	4225	B	916 383-5275	4535
C A H H S	8611	D	916 552-7507	24946
Cali Hsg Finance Agcy	8748	D	916 326-8627	27669
California American Water Co	4941	E	916 568-4216	6214
California Association O (PA)	8621	D	916 443-7401	25000
California Chamber Commerce (PA)	8611	D	916 444-6670	24949
California Cmplte CNT Cnsus	8733	D	916 852-2020	26600
California Dental Association (PA)	8621	C	916 443-0505	25001
California Dept Tax & Fee ADM	7291	D	800 400-7115	13702
California Govrnmnt Opr Agncy	6371	A	800 228-5453	10479
California Health Benefit Exch	8621	D	916 228-8210	25002
California Medical Association (PA)	8621	D	916 444-5532	25003
California Pavement Maint Inc	1611	D	916 381-8033	1736
California Public Employees Ret	6371	C	916 795-3000	10480
California Public Emplyees Ret (DH)	6371	D	916 795-3000	10481
Califrnia High Speed Rail Auth	4011	D	916 324-1541	3618
Califrnia Hlth Humn Srvcs Agcy	7374	B	916 739-7640	16102
Califrnia State Employees Assn (PA)	8631	D	916 444-8134	25058
Calstars	8721	E	916 445-0211	26158
Calvey Incorporated	5113	D	916 681-4800	8100
Capital Athletic Club Inc	7991	D	916 442-3927	18585
Capital Commercial Flrg Inc	1752	E	916 569-1960	3097
Capital Public Radio Inc	4832	E	916 278-8900	5696
Capitol Casino	7999	C	916 446-0700	19119
Capitol Corporate Services	8732	E	916 444-6787	26503
Capitol Regency LLC	7011	B	916 443-1234	12426
Careability Health Svcs Corp	8082	D	916 479-8554	22253
Cares Community Health	8011	C	916 443-3299	19356
Carescope LLC	8322	E	916 780-1384	23527
Carlton Senior Living Inc	8361	C	916 971-4800	24452
Carrier Corporation	7623	C	916 928-9500	17891
Case Dealer Holding Co LLC	5082	C	916 649-0096	7672
Cathedral Pioneer Church Homes (PA)	8051	D	916 442-4906	20293
Cbre Inc	6531	D	916 446-6800	11275
CBS Radio Inc	4832	C	916 923-6800	5705
Cellco Partnership	4812	C	916 331-6833	5347
Cellco Partnership	4812	E	916 419-6200	5358
Central Anesthesia Service	8011	D	916 481-6800	19363
Central Freight Lines Inc	4213	C	800 782-5036	4115
Central Parking System Inc	7521	C	916 441-1074	17680
Century Stadium	7832	D	916 922-4241	18277
Ceva Freight LLC	4731	C	916 379-6000	5028
Cgl Companies LLC	8712	D	916 678-7890	26032
Ch2m Hill Inc	8712	A	916 920-0300	26033
Ch2m Hill Inc	8712	D	916 920-0300	25605
Ch2m Hill Inc	8711	A	916 920-0300	25605
Ch2m Hill Constructors Inc	1623	B	916 920-0212	1907

Employment Codes: A=Over 500 employees, B=251-500,
C=101-250, D=51-100, E=50

2019 Directory of California
Wholesalers and Services Companies

© Mergent Inc. 1-800-342-5647
1647

	SIC	EMP	PHONE	ENTRY #
Channel 40 Inc	4833	C	916 454-4422	5777
Chem Quip Inc	5091	D	800 821-1678	7925
Chemical Dependency Recovery	5169	E	916 482-1132	8923
Child Action Inc **(PA)**	8351	B	916 369-4460	24280
Childrens Recvg Hm Sacramento	8361	C	916 482-2370	24468
Choice Medical Group Inc	8093	C	916 483-2885	22531
Cintas Corporation No 3	7218	C	916 419-8519	13603
Citigroup Global Markets Inc	6211	E	916 567-2056	9932
Clark Pest Ctrl Stockton Inc	7342	D	916 925-7000	14142
Coact Designworks	8712	E	916 930-5900	26038
Coldwell Banker	6531	D	916 447-5900	11327
Colliers Intl Prperty Cons Inc	6531	D	916 929-5999	11371
Columbia Woodlake LLC	7011	D	206 728-9063	12478
Comcast Corporation	4841	D	916 459-2964	5870
Comcast Corporation	4841	B	916 830-6790	5884
Confi-Chek Inc **(PA)**	7375	D	800 718-8997	16212
Consultnts In Edctl Per Skills **(PA)**	8322	A	916 348-1890	23616
Cook Realty Inc	6531	C	916 451-6702	11378
Cooperative Personnel Services **(PA)**	8742	C	916 263-3600	27200
Corporation of The President	8331	D	916 482-1480	24172
Corporation Service Company	7349	D	302 636-5400	14229
Correctons Rhbltation Cal Dept	7374	C	916 358-2319	16107
County of Sacramento	7376	B	916 874-7752	16266
County of Sacramento	1622	C	916 875-2711	1876
County of Sacramento	8051	D	916 875-0900	20333
County of Sacramento	8111	C	916 874-5411	23006
County of Sacramento	7349	D	916 874-0746	14234
County of Sacramento	7996	D	916 363-8383	18795
County of Sacramento	8322	C	916 875-4467	23716
Covenant Care California LLC	8051	D	916 391-6011	20346
Creative Design Interiors Inc **(PA)**	1752	D	916 641-1121	3098
Crestwood Behavioral Hlth Inc	8063	D	916 452-1431	21946
Crocker Art Museum Association	8699	D	916 808-7000	25414
Crossroads Facility Svcs Inc	7349	D	916 568-5230	14236
Crown Building Maintenance Co	7349	A	916 920-9556	14237
Cuneo Black Ward Missler A Law	8111	E	916 363-8822	23016
Cusa AWC LLC	4111	E	916 423-4000	3644
Cy Sac Operator LLC	7011	D	916 455-6800	12510
D & J Plumbing Inc	1711	D	916 922-4888	2178
Dairy Council of California **(PA)**	8748	E	949 756-7892	27702
Dal Cais Inc	1542	C	916 381-8080	1512
Dave Gross Enterprises Inc	1799	D	916 388-2000	3509
DC Transport Inc	4213	D	916 438-0888	4123
Ddso Inc **(PA)**	8322	D	916 456-5166	23766
Dealertrack Collte Manag Servi	7379	C	916 368-5300	16341
Del Paso Country Club	7997	C	916 489-3681	18909
Delegata Corporation	7373	D	916 609-5400	15942
Delta Dental of California	6324	A	916 853-7373	10201
Dentists Insurance Company **(HQ)**	6411	C	916 443-4567	10604
Desilva Gates Construction LP	1611	C	916 386-9708	1757
Develop Disabilities Svc Org	8322	D	916 973-1951	23769
DFI Technologies LLC	5045	D	916 568-1234	7036
Dialysis Clinic Inc	8092	C	916 453-0803	22473
Diepenbrock Elkin LLP	8111	D	916 492-5000	23038
Dignity Health	8062	E	916 681-1600	21370
Dignity Health	8011	C	916 667-0000	19442
Dignity Health	8062	C	916 423-5940	21385
Dignity Health	8062	D	916 453-4545	21386
Dignity Health	8062	A	916 423-3000	21389
Dignity Health	8071	A	916 453-4453	22078
Dignity Health Med Foundation	8099	D	916 681-6300	22784
Dimare Fresh	5148	B	916 921-6302	8666
Disability Rights California **(PA)**	8111	D	916 488-9950	23042
Dish Network Corporation	4841	E	916 381-5084	5909
Dominguez Landscape Svcs Inc	0782	D	916 381-8855	830
Domus Construction & Design	1521	E	916 381-7500	1157
Dongalen Enterprises Inc **(PA)**	5162	C	916 422-3110	8914
Doumit Communication Inc	1611	D	916 362-3519	1760
Downey Brand LLP **(PA)**	8111	C	916 444-1000	23052
Dpr Construction Inc	1542	B	916 568-3434	1523
Dpr Construction A Gen Partnr	1541	D	916 568-3434	1395
Dreyer Bbich Bccola Cllham LLP	8111	D	916 379-3500	23053
Drywall Works Inc	1742	D	916 383-6667	2878
Easter Seal Soc Superior Cal **(PA)**	8099	C	916 485-6711	22795
Easun Inc	7011	C	916 929-8855	12547
Eclipse Solutions Inc	7379	C	916 565-8090	16354
Edaw Inc	0781	C	916 414-5800	753
Edward E Straine CPA	8721	D	916 646-6464	26188
Ehealthwirecom Inc	8099	D	916 924-8092	22798
Elegant Surfaces	5032	D	209 823-9388	6890
Elica Health Centers	8011	D	916 454-2345	19458
Elite Power Inc	1731	D	916 739-1580	2578
Elizabethan Inn Associates LP	7011	E	916 448-1300	12554
Elk Grove Unified School Dst	4151	C	916 686-7733	3921
Elliott Benson Market Research	8732	E	916 325-1670	26515

	SIC	EMP	PHONE	ENTRY #
Els Investments	0781	C	916 388-0308	754
Employment Dev Cal Dept	7361	A	916 654-7867	14613
Energy Salvage Inc	8741	E	916 737-8640	26848
Entercom Communications Corp	4832	C	916 766-5000	5712
Entercom Communications Corp	4832	C	916 334-7777	5714
Enterprise Rent-A-Car Compan	7514	D	916 576-3164	17636
Entravsion Communications Corp	4832	E	916 646-4000	5715
Entravsion Communications Corp	4833	E	916 648-6029	5787
Environmental Protection Agcy	4959	D	916 324-7572	6540
Environmental Systems Research	5045	D	916 448-2412	7043
Eskaton Lodge	8361	A	916 789-0326	24521
Eskaton Properties Inc	8051	C	916 393-2550	20410
Essendant Co	5112	C	916 344-6707	8080
Essex Property Trust Inc	6798	D	916 381-0345	12162
Ethan Conrad Properties Inc	6512	D	916 779-1000	10875
Eugene Burger Management Corp	8741	C	916 443-6637	26852
Excel Managed Care Disa	8742	D	916 944-7185	27229
Express Messenger Systems Inc	4215	D	916 921-6016	4408
Federal Express Corporation	4513	D	916 361-5500	4834
Federico Beauty Institute	7231	E	916 929-4242	13655
First Responder Ems Inc	4119	C	916 381-3780	3795
First US Community Credit Un **(PA)**	6061	D	916 576-5700	9558
Fischer Tile and Marble Inc	1743	C	916 452-1426	2997
Foundtion For Cal Cmnty Cllges **(PA)**	8611	D	916 325-4300	24958
Frank Carson Ldscp & Maint Inc	0782	C	916 856-5400	842
Frys Electronics Inc	8748	B	916 286-5800	27732
Fusion Real Estate Network Inc	6531	D	916 448-3174	11475
G&K Services Inc	7218	D	916 381-5500	13606
Gat - Arln Ground Support Inc	4581	B	916 923-2349	4891
Gccfc 2005-Gg5 Y St Ltd Partnr	7011	D	916 455-6800	12599
Geico Corporation	6411	D	707 448-7172	10633
General Prod A Cal Ltd Partnr **(PA)**	5148	C	916 441-6431	8687
General Services Cal Dept	7349	D	916 845-4942	14273
General Services Cal Dept	8711	B	916 657-9960	25707
General Services Cal Dept	8711	B	916 657-9903	25708
General Services Cal Dept	7349	A	916 445-4566	14274
Girl Scouts Heart Central Cal	8641	D	916 452-9181	25161
Gold Country Management Inc	6531	D	916 929-3003	11486
Golden 1 Credit Union **(PA)**	6062	B	916 732-2900	9636
Golden Coast Cnstr Restoration	1542	D	916 955-7461	1536
Golden Pacific Bancorp Inc **(PA)**	6712	D	916 444-2450	11953
Golden Pond LP	8361	E	916 369-8967	24541
Golden West Packg Group LLC **(PA)**	6719	B	404 345-8365	11982
Goodwill Industries of Sacrame	8699	E	916 331-0237	25425
Gordon & Schwenkmeyer Inc	7389	C	916 569-1740	17199
Gordon Rees Sclly Mnskhani LLP	8111	D	916 830-6900	23104
Granite Construction Company	1629	D	916 855-4400	2035
Granite Construction Inc	1611	D	916 855-4495	1781
Greater Sacramento Sur	8093	D	916 929-7229	22587
Gringteam Inc	7011	D	916 929-8855	12626
Growing Company Inc	0782	D	916 379-9088	852
Gudgel Roofing Inc	1761	E	916 387-6900	3162
Guild Mortgage Company	6163	C	916 486-6257	9885
H & D Electric	1731	B	916 332-0794	2596
H C C S Inc	8051	D	916 454-5752	20501
Halstead Partnership	6512	D	916 830-8000	10891
Hammel Green & Abrahamson Inc	8712	D	916 787-5100	26054
Hank Fisher Properties Inc	8361	C	916 447-4444	24548
Hank Fisher Properties Inc **(PA)**	6513	D	916 485-1441	11028
Hank Fisher Properties Inc	8059	D	916 921-1970	21104
Hanson Bridgett LLP	8111	E	916 442-3333	23121
Harold E Nutter Inc **(PA)**	1731	E	916 334-4343	2600
Harris & Sloan Consulting	8748	E	916 921-2800	27745
HDR Engineering Inc	8711	D	916 564-4214	25729
Health By Design	8082	E	916 974-3322	22312
Heartland Payment Systems LLC	7389	D	916 844-9548	17217
Helping Hearts Foundation Inc	8361	D	916 368-7200	24560
Hendrickson Truck Lines Inc	4213	C	916 387-9614	4193
Hendrickson Trucking Inc	4213	B	916 387-9614	4194
Henwood Energy Services Inc **(DH)**	8711	C	916 955-6031	25733
Heritage Community Credit Un **(PA)**	6061	D	916 364-1700	9561
Hilary A Brodie MD PHD	8011	D	916 734-3744	19502
Honeywell International Inc	7382	D	916 923-7851	16903
Horizon West Inc	8051	D	916 331-4590	20534
Howe Community Center	7999	E	916 927-3802	19184
Hub Intrntional Insur Svcs Inc	6411	D	916 974-7800	10647
Hunt Convenience Stores LLC	8741	E	916 383-4868	26890
Hurley Construction Inc	1522	D	916 446-7599	1290
Huttig Building Products Inc	5031	D	916 383-3721	6834
Hylton Security Inc	7381	C	916 442-1000	16699
Iconic Chronicles Magazine LLC	5192	D	707 712-2097	9115
Iheartcommunications Inc	4832	C	916 929-5325	5727
Iheartcommunications Inc	4832	D	916 929-5325	5729
Inland Business Machines Inc **(DH)**	7699	D	916 928-0770	17958
Innovative Maint Solutions Inc	1711	C	916 568-1400	2235

Mergent email: customerrelations@mergent.com
1648

2019 Directory of California
Wholesalers and Services Companies

(P-0000) Products & Services Section entry number
(PA)=Parent Co (HQ)=Headquarters (DH)=Div Headquarters

Company	SIC	EMP	PHONE	ENTRY #
Inter-State Oil Co (PA)	5172	D	916 457-6572	8962
Internal Mdcine Rsdncy Affairs	8621	D	916 734-7080	25021
Interntional Un Oper Engineers (PA)	8631	D	916 444-6880	25066
Interstate Fuel Systems Inc	5172	D	916 457-6572	8963
Interstate Hotels Resorts Inc	7011	C	916 922-4700	12779
Interwest Insurance Svcs LLC (PA)	6411	C	916 488-3100	10655
Iunlimited Incorporated	7381	C	916 218-6198	16705
Iuoe Sttonary Engineers Lcl 39	8631	E	916 928-0399	25067
J and J Wall Baking Co Inc	5142	D	916 381-1410	8492
J B Company	1542	D	929 929-3003	1558
Jackson Construction (PA)	1541	E	916 381-8113	1409
Jarka Enterprises Inc	1799	D	916 491-6180	3538
Jensen Enterprises Inc	5039	D	916 992-8301	6933
Jerry S Powell MD	8011	D	916 734-5959	19519
Jetro Cash and Carry Entps LLC	5141	D	916 492-2305	8418
JJR Enterprises Inc (PA)	7629	D	916 363-2666	17905
Jma Investments Ltd	0782	D	916 685-1355	870
John F Otto Inc	1542	C	916 441-6870	1565
John Jackson Masonry	1741	D	916 381-8021	2814
John Stewart Company	6513	C	415 345-4400	11038
Juniper Networks Inc	7373	D	916 503-1593	15989
Justice California Department	8748	A	916 324-5039	27762
Kaiser Foundation Hospitals	8062	D	916 973-5000	21494
Kaiser Foundation Hospitals	8011	D	916 688-2000	19612
Kaiser Foundation Hospitals	8062	C	916 525-6300	21523
Khanna Entps - II Ltd Partnr	7011	C	916 338-5800	12805
Kindred Healthcare Oper Inc	8051	D	916 454-5752	20555
Kindred Healthcare Oper Inc	8059	D	916 457-6521	21127
Kings Arena Ltd Partnership	7941	D	916 928-0000	18522
Kojenov Arkadi Nilovich	4731	E	916 718-1790	5095
Kpmg LLP	8721	C	916 448-4700	26242
Kronick Moskovitz Tiedemann (PA)	8111	D	916 321-4500	23180
Kvie Inc (PA)	4833	D	916 929-5843	5818
Kxtv Inc	4833	C	916 441-2345	5819
La Familia Counseling Center	8322	D	916 452-3601	23890
Landmark Healthcare Svcs Inc (DH)	8041	C	800 638-4557	20155
Lawnman II Inc	0782	D	916 739-1420	891
Lawson Mechanical Contractors (PA)	1711	D	916 381-5000	2257
LDI Mechanical Inc	1711	E	916 361-3925	2258
League of California Cities (PA)	8743	D	916 658-8200	27560
Leo A Daly Company	8712	D	916 564-3259	26083
Lewis-Goetz and Company Inc	5085	D	916 366-9340	7855
Lexisnexis Courtlink Inc	8621	C	425 974-5000	25024
Liberty Mutual Insurance Co	6331	B	916 564-1792	10370
Lighthouse Living Services (PA)	8322	D	916 454-4381	23900
Lionakis (PA)	8711	C	916 558-1901	25799
LLP Downey Brand	8111	D	775 329-5900	23218
Loomis Armored Us LLC	7381	D	916 441-1091	16723
Lpa Insurance Agency Inc	7372	D	916 286-7850	15745
Lpas Inc	8712	D	916 443-0335	26086
Lukenbill Enterprises	4512	D	916 454-2400	4793
Lumens LLC (HQ)	5063	D	916 444-5585	7373
Luppen and Hawley Inc	1711	C	916 456-7831	2270
Lupton Excavation Inc	1794	D	916 387-1104	3433
Lyon Realty (PA)	6531	A	916 574-8800	11575
Lyons Security Service Inc	7381	D	916 925-9667	16724
M K S Construction Inc	1521	C	916 446-2521	1193
M7 Builders LLC	1531	E	916 317-3529	1353
Macdonald Mott LLC	8711	D	916 399-0580	25808
Macias Gini & OConnell LLP (PA)	8721	D	916 928-4600	26255
Macys Inc	4226	D	916 373-0333	4684
Mariner Health Care Inc	8051	C	916 422-4825	20614
Mariner Health Care Inc	8051	C	916 481-5500	20630
Mark Diversified Inc	1542	E	916 923-6275	1586
Mark H Leibenhaut MD	8011	D	916 454-6600	19670
Mark III Construction (PA)	1731	D	916 381-8080	2633
Markstein Bev Co Sacramento	5181	D	916 920-3911	9010
Marquee Fire Protection (PA)	1711	D	916 641-7997	2274
Marques Pipeline Inc	8711	E	916 923-3434	25811
Marticus Electric Inc	1731	D	916 368-2186	2635
Martin Brothers Construction (PA)	1611	D	916 386-1600	1813
Matheny Sars Linkert Jaime LLP	8111	D	916 978-3434	23239
Matheson Fast Freight Inc	4213	D	209 342-0184	4221
Matheson Trucking Inc (PA)	4213	E	916 685-2330	4223
May-Han Electric Inc	1731	D	916 929-0150	2638
McClatchy Company	8999	A	916 321-1941	27943
McKinley Park Care Center	8062	D	916 452-3592	21583
McWong Envmtl & Enrgy Group	8748	E	916 371-8080	27784
Mec International LLC	8711	C	415 866-4497	25817
Medical Couriers Inc	4215	D	916 452-5700	4422
Medstar LLC	4119	D	916 669-0550	3822
Mek Norwood Pines LLC	8051	D	916 922-7177	20640
Mercy HM Svcs A Cal Ltd Partnr	8062	A	916 453-4545	21590
Mercy Housing California Xxvi	6531	D	916 414-4400	11607
Meringcarson Holdings (PA)	7311	D	916 441-0571	13867
Mexican Amrcn Alcoholism Progr (PA)	8322	D	916 394-2320	23920
Mission Linen Supply	7213	C	916 423-3179	13535
Mission Linen Supply	7213	C	916 423-3135	13545
Montessori Learning Commons (PA)	8351	D	916 444-7786	24350
Morgan Stanley & Co LLC	6211	E	916 444-8041	9995
Morton Golf LLC	7992	D	916 481-4653	18738
Mounting Systems Inc	1711	D	916 374-8872	2283
Mueller Pet Medical Center	0742	E	916 428-9202	605
Mutual Assist Network Del Paso (PA)	8322	E	916 927-7694	23928
Myers & Sons Construction LP	1611	C	916 283-9950	1823
National Security Industries	7382	B	916 779-0640	16924
Nehemiah Progressive Housing D	6552	D	916 231-1999	11896
New West Partitions	1742	C	916 456-8365	2921
Nissan North America Inc	4225	D	916 920-4712	4599
Nmi Industrial Holdings Inc	8711	D	916 635-7030	25846
North Wind Cnstr Svcs LLC	1521	D	916 333-3015	1209
Northern California Cardiology (PA)	8011	D	916 733-1788	19723
Northern California Inlliance (PA)	8322	C	916 381-1300	23945
Northwest Staffing Resources	7361	A	916 960-2668	14673
Nv5 Inc (DH)	8711	D	916 641-9100	25849
Nv5 Inc	8711	D	916 641-9100	25851
Oates Buzz Enterprises	6512	D	916 381-3600	10921
Office Depot Inc	5044	D	916 927-0171	6972
Office of The Legislative Coun	4812	B	916 341-8708	5414
Office of The Legislative Coun	8748	A	916 445-3796	27810
Ogilvy Pub Rltons Wrldwide Inc	8743	D	916 231-7700	27566
Oleander Holdings LLC	8051	D	916 331-4590	20680
Oregon PCF Bldg Pdts Calif Inc	5031	D	916 381-8051	6844
Original Petes Pizza Inc	6794	E	916 442-6770	12139
Orrick Hrrington Sutcliffe LLP	8111	D	916 447-9200	23305
Owen & Company	6411	D	916 923-2700	10724
Pacific Civil & Strl Cons LLC	8711	D	916 421-1000	25859
Pacific Coast Trnsp Svcs Inc	4789	D	916 266-5300	5239
Pacific Fresh Sea Food Company (HQ)	5142	C	916 419-5500	8497
Pacific Frnsic Psychlogy Assoc	8093	D	925 253-3111	22631
Pacific Legal Foundation (PA)	8111	D	916 419-7111	23307
Pacific Sea Food Co Inc	5146	D	916 419-5500	8592
Pacific West Lath & Plaster	1742	E	916 329-9028	2935
Paladin Prtction Spcalists Inc	7381	C	916 331-3175	16753
Pape Machinery Inc	5082	D	916 922-7181	7685
Paramount Bldg Solutions LLC	1542	C	916 564-4102	1609
Parasec Incorporated (PA)	8111	D	916 576-7000	23309
Paratransit Incorporated (PA)	4119	C	916 429-2009	3828
Parc Specialty Contractors	1799	D	916 992-5405	3562
Parker Landscape Dev Inc	0781	E	916 383-4071	776
Parsons Brnckrhoff Hldings Inc	8742	D	916 567-2500	27388
Patricks Construction Clean-Up	1629	D	916 452-5495	2055
PDQ Automatic Transm Parts Inc	7537	D	916 681-7701	17753
Performance Warehouse Co	5013	D	916 920-2221	6665
Permanente Medical Group Inc	8011	D	916 688-2055	19760
Perry-Smith LLP	8721	D	916 441-1000	26270
Personlzed Hmcare Hmmaker Agcy	8082	D	916 979-4975	22394
Pinelands Preservation Inc	0782	D	609 703-0359	921
Pinsetters Inc	7933	D	916 488-7545	18497
Pioneer Towers Rhf Partners LP	6513	E	916 443-6548	11097
Planned Parenthood Federation	8093	D	916 446-5247	22644
Positive Option Family Service (PA)	8322	D	916 973-2838	23975
Precision Home Care LLC	8322	D	916 749-4051	23976
Pricewaterhousecoopers LLP	8721	D	916 930-8100	26277
Pride Industries	8999	C	916 649-9499	27955
Primrose Alzheimers Living	8361	D	916 392-3510	24635
Procida Landscape Inc	0782	D	916 387-5296	925
Professnal Ldscp Solutions Inc	0781	E	916 424-3815	780
Protege Builders Inc	1751	E	916 825-8478	3062
Prs/Roebbelen JV	1542	D	916 641-0324	1620
Psychiatric Solutions Inc	8011	C	916 288-0300	19803
Psychiatric Solutions Inc	8063	D	916 489-3336	21969
Public Consulting Group Inc	8742	D	916 565-8090	27411
Public Employees Retirement	6371	B	916 795-3400	10492
Pulmonary Medicine Assoc	8011	D	916 733-5040	19809
Quality Group Homes Inc	1521	C	916 930-0066	1220
Quality Inv Prpts Scrmento LLC	7374	D	916 679-2100	16170
Ragingwire Data Centers Inc (DH)	7376	B	916 286-3000	16172
Ram Commercial Enterprises Inc	6531	E	916 429-1205	11701
Rcb Corporation (PA)	6022	D	916 567-2600	9482
Rdo Vermeer LLC	5082	D	916 643-0999	7692
Reading International Inc	7832	A	916 442-0985	18315
Recp/Wndsor Scramento Ventr LP	7011	D	916 455-6800	13104
Regal Cinemas Inc	7832	D	916 419-0205	18317
Remax Gold	6531	D	916 609-2800	11728
Republic Electric Inc	1731	D	916 294-0140	2701
Republic Electric West Inc	1731	D	916 294-0140	2702
Rescue Concrete Inc	1771	D	916 852-2400	3313
Research of America	7374	C	916 443-4722	16171
Retail Services Wis Corp	7389	C	916 485-3427	17430

Employment Codes: A=Over 500 employees, B=251-500,
C=101-250, D=51-100, E=50

2019 Directory of California
Wholesalers and Services Companies

© Mergent Inc. 1-800-342-5647
1649

GEOGRAPHIC

Company	SIC	EMP	PHONE	ENTRY #
Retinal Consultants Inc (PA)	8011	D	916 454-4861	19821
Rex Moore Group Inc	1731	B	916 372-1300	2703
Rex More Elec Contrs Engineers (PA)	1731	A	916 372-1300	2704
Rex More Elec Contrs Engineers	1731	D	510 785-1300	2706
Rgis LLC	7389	D	916 387-9692	17437
River City Bank (HQ)	6022	D	916 567-2600	9483
River Oak Center For Children (PA)	8093	C	916 609-5100	22666
River Oak Center For Children	8059	D	916 550-5600	21196
Riverside Health Care Corp	8051	D	916 446-2506	20727
Rose & Kindel Grayling	8399	C	916 441-1034	24833
Royal Plywood Company LLC	5031	D	916 386-9873	6860
Runyon Saltzman Inc	7311	D	916 446-9900	13897
S L H C C Inc	8051	E	916 457-6521	20734
S&W Seed Company (PA)	0139	E	559 884-2535	30
Saccani Distributing Company	5181	D	916 441-0213	9024
Sacramento Area Emerg Housing (PA)	8322	E	916 454-2120	24001
Sacramento Area Sewer District (PA)	4953	B	916 876-6000	6472
Sacramento Childrens Home	8361	D	916 927-5059	24657
Sacramento Childrens Home (PA)	8361	C	916 452-3981	24658
Sacramento Chinese Community S	8322	C	916 442-4228	24002
Sacramento County Off Educatn	8322	E	916 875-0300	24003
Sacramento County Water Agency	4941	D	916 874-6851	6298
Sacramento Credit Union (PA)	6062	D	916 444-6070	9646
Sacramento Cy Unified Schl Dst (PA)	8641	B	916 643-7400	25232
Sacramento Ear Nose & Throat (PA)	8011	D	916 736-3399	19833
Sacramento Employement & Train	8331	C	916 263-3800	24224
Sacramento Employement & Train (PA)	8331	C	916 263-3800	24225
Sacramento Harness Association	8611	D	916 239-4040	24976
Sacramento Hotel Partners LLC	7011	D	916 326-5000	13158
Sacramento Loaves & Fishes (PA)	8322	D	916 446-0874	24004
Sacramento Municpl Utility Dst (PA)	4911	A	916 452-3211	6102
Sacramento Municpl Utility Dst	4911	A	916 452-3211	6103
Sacramento Municpl Utility Dst	7539	A	916 452-3211	17797
Sacramento Municpl Utility Dst	4911	D	916 732-5155	6104
Sacramento Municpl Utility Dst	4911	B	916 732-5616	6105
Sacramento Operating Co LP	8051	C	916 422-4825	20736
Sacramento Reg Co Sanit Dist (PA)	4959	A	916 876-6000	6548
Sacramento Regional Trnst Dist (PA)	4111	A	916 726-2877	3700
Sacramento Regional Trnst Dist	4111	C	916 321-2800	3701
Sacramento Regional Trnst Dist	4173	C	916 869-8611	3955
Sacramento Suburban Water Dst	4941	D	916 972-7171	6299
Sacramento Suburban Water Dst	4941	D	916 972-7171	6300
Sacramento Theatrical Ltg Ltd	7922	D	916 447-3258	18400
Sacramento Zoological Society	8422	E	916 808-5888	24935
Sacramnto Forty Niner Trvl Plz	7011	C	916 927-4774	13159
Sacramnto Hsing Rdvlpment Agcy	6411	D	916 440-1376	10761
Sacramnto Mtro A Qulty MGT Dst	8748	D	916 874-4800	27851
Sacramnto Ntiv Amercn Hlth Ctr	8011	C	916 341-0575	19834
Sacremento Eductn Readng Lions	8641	D	916 228-2219	25233
Safelite Fulfillment Inc	7536	D	916 442-4715	17752
Saia Inc	4213	A	916 483-8331	4255
Saint Claires Nursing Ctr LLC	8051	C	916 392-4440	20737
Salvation Army	8399	D	916 563-3700	24836
Sandwich Spot (PA)	7011	D	916 492-2613	13185
Scandia Sports Inc	7999	E	916 331-5757	19235
Schetter Electric Inc (PA)	1731	D	916 446-2521	2726
Schools Financial Credit Union (PA)	6062	C	916 569-5400	9653
Scott A Porter Prof Corp	8111	D	916 929-1481	23368
Securitas SEC Svcs USA Inc	7381	C	916 564-2009	16788
Securitas SEC Svcs USA Inc	7381	C	916 569-4500	16801
Sedgwick Claims MGT Svcs Inc	6411	C	916 568-7394	10770
Sheraton Corporation	7011	B	916 447-1700	13217
Shermn-Lehr Cstm Tile Wrks Inc	1743	D	916 386-0417	3010
Shri Sidhi Vinayaka Hotel Inc	7011	C	855 922-5252	13224
Shriners Hspitals For Children	8069	B	916 453-2050	22048
Shriners Hspitals For Children	8069	B	916 453-2000	22049
Sierra Bookkeeping & Tax Svc	8721	D	916 349-7610	26291
Sierra Forever Families	8322	D	916 368-5114	24050
Sierra Waste Transport Inc	4789	E	916 386-9937	5246
Simas Floor Co Inc (PA)	1752	C	916 452-4933	3118
Singley Enterprises (PA)	5031	E	866 890-1776	6865
Sitoa	4121	D	916 444-0008	3870
Six Flags Entertainment Corp	7996	B	916 924-3747	18810
Sky Park Gardens Assisted	8361	D	916 422-5650	24677
Skyles Insurance Agency	6411	E	916 361-9585	10775
Skyslope Inc	7379	D	916 833-2390	16485
Smart Management & Companies	8741	B	916 392-3000	27031
Southgate Glass & Screen Inc (PA)	5039	E	916 476-8396	6937
Southgate Glass & Screen Inc	5039	E	916 476-8396	6938
Southgate Recreation & Pk Dst	8322	E	916 421-7275	24062
Southwest Dealer Services Inc	7389	C	925 753-0696	17479
Spare-Time Inc	7991	D	916 649-0909	18666
Spectrum Services Group Inc	8748	D	916 760-7913	27869
Spencer Building Maintenance	7349	B	916 922-1900	14399
Ssmb Pacific Holding Co Inc	5012	D	916 371-3372	6611
St Vncent De Paul Bltmore Inc	8322	C	916 485-3482	24070
Stanford Youth Solutions (PA)	8399	D	916 344-0199	24846
Stantec Consulting Svcs Inc	8711	E	916 924-8844	25932
Starwest Botanicals Inc (PA)	5149	D	916 638-8100	8872
Starwood Hotels & Resorts	7011	C	916 447-1700	13268
State Compensation Insur Fund	6331	B	916 924-5100	10406
Stericycle Comm Solutions Inc	7389	D	888 370-6711	17485
Stommel Inc (PA)	1731	E	916 646-6626	2748
Stradling Yocca Carlson & Raut	8111	C	916 449-2350	23401
Strategies For Change	8093	D	916 395-3552	22688
Stratgies To Empwer People Inc (PA)	8052	E	916 679-1527	20963
Stucco Works Inc	1742	B	916 383-6699	2963
Students of Associated	8351	D	916 278-6216	24389
Sunrise Senior Living LLC	8051	E	916 486-0200	20820
Supershuttle International Inc	4111	D	916 648-2500	3733
Support For Home Inc	1521	E	530 792-8484	1243
Surety West Logistics Inc	4731	D	800 761-2551	5176
Surgical Care Affiliate	8721	E	916 529-4590	26299
Surgical Staff Inc	7363	C	916 444-4424	14918
Sutter Club Inc	8641	D	916 442-0456	25256
Sutter Health	8062	C	916 733-1025	21803
Sutter Health	8062	C	916 733-9588	21805
Sutter Health	8011	C	916 262-9400	19965
Sutter Health	8062	C	916 566-4819	21818
Sutter Health	8011	C	916 262-9414	19966
Sutter Health	8011	A	916 646-8300	19967
Sutter Health	8062	B	916 887-0000	21823
Sutter Health (PA)	8062	A	916 733-8800	21824
Sutter Health	8062	D	916 733-8133	21828
Sutter Health	8011	D	916 451-3344	19979
Sutter Health	8011	C	916 453-5955	19980
Sutter Health	8062	C	916 731-5672	21831
Sutter Health	8062	B	916 454-6747	21833
Sutter Health	8011	D	916 262-9456	19984
Sutter Health	8641	B	916 551-9550	25263
Sutter Health At Work	8011	D	916 565-8607	19985
Sutter Hlth Rhabilitation Svcs	8322	D	916 733-3040	24081
Sutter Hlth Scrmnto Sierra Reg	8099	A	916 733-7080	22893
Sutter Hlth Scrmnto Sierra Reg (HQ)	8062	B	916 733-8800	21836
Sutter Hlth Scrmnto Sierra Reg	8062	B	916 454-2222	21838
Sutter Hlth Scrmnto Sierra Reg	8322	D	916 446-3100	24082
Sutter Hlth Scrmnto Sierra Reg	8062	A	916 733-3095	21840
Sutter Medical Foundation	8049	A	916 924-7764	20205
Sutter Physician Services (HQ)	8742	A	916 854-6600	27478
Sutter Valley Med Foundation (PA)	8062	A	916 887-7122	21847
Swinerton Builders Hc	1542	C	916 383-4825	1665
System Integrators Inc (HQ)	7373	C	916 830-2400	16063
T M Cobb Company	5031	D	916 381-7330	6868
Tammi R James MD	8011	E	916 383-6783	19998
Technology Services Cal Dept (DH)	7379	D	916 319-9223	16509
Teichert/Great Lakes E&I JV	1629	D	916 484-3011	2067
Tele-Direct Communications	7389	D	916 348-2170	17501
Terkensha Associates Inc	8322	D	916 922-9868	24084
Terracina Meadows Apts	6513	E	916 419-0925	11124
Textron Aviation Inc	4581	D	916 929-5656	4919
Tf Courier Inc	4215	D	916 379-0708	4433
The Executive Office of	8731	D	916 322-2318	26474
The For Sacramento Society	8699	D	916 383-7387	25474
Therapeutic Pathways Inc	8049	D	916 489-1376	20208
Thunder Mountain Enterprises (PA)	1799	D	916 381-3400	3594
Tierra Del Oro Girl Scout Cnsl	8641	D	916 452-9174	25269
Timber Works Construction Inc	1521	C	916 786-6666	1247
Tlcs Inc	8322	D	916 441-0123	24088
Tradewinds Partnership	7011	D	916 333-5239	13339
Training Toward Self Reliance	8322	E	916 442-8877	24093
Travis Credit Union	6061	B	916 443-1446	9603
Tricorp Construction Inc (PA)	1542	D	916 779-8010	1677
Trinity Fresh Distribution LLC	5149	D	916 714-7368	8888
Trinity Technology Group Inc	7373	D	916 779-0201	16067
Tucson Hotels LP	7011	C	916 446-0100	13348
Tucson Hotels LP	7011	C	916 446-0100	13349
Turner Construction Company	1542	D	916 444-4421	1683
Turner Construction Company	1542	D	916 444-4421	1687
Turning Point Cmnty Programs	8361	D	916 393-1222	24701
U C Med Humn Rsrces Aplcat Svc	8062	D	916 734-5916	21863
UBS Financial Services Inc	6211	E	916 648-7200	10029
Uc Davis Health System (PA)	8011	D	916 734-1000	20015
Ucd Mc Home Care Services	8741	C	916 734-2458	27072
Unifirst Corporation	7213	E	916 929-3766	13555
United Airlines Inc	4729	C	916 877-3002	4994
United Parcel Service Inc OH	4215	D	916 373-4089	4454
United Parcel Service Inc OH	4215	C	916 857-0311	4486
Universal Limousine & Trnsp Co	4119	C	916 361-5466	3855
Universal Network Dev Corp (PA)	8748	D	916 475-1200	27892
University California Davis	8011	E	916 734-2846	20030

2019 Directory of California
Wholesalers and Services Companies

(P-0000) Products & Services Section entry number
(PA)=Parent Co (HQ)=Headquarters (DH)=Div Headquarters

	SIC	EMP	PHONE	ENTRY #
University California Davis	8062	A	916 734-3141	21883
University California Davis	8062	A	916 734-2011	21884
University California Davis	8062	A	916 734-5113	21885
URS Group Inc	8711	D	916 679-2000	25979
US Army Corps of Engineers	8711	A	916 557-7490	25984
US Loan Auditors LLC	8721	D	916 248-8625	26305
USA Valet Parking LLC	7299	E	916 792-1055	13778
USA Waste of California Inc	4953	D	916 379-0500	6488
USA Waste of California Inc	4212	C	916 379-2611	4077
V S N F Inc	8051	D	916 452-6631	20848
Valley Can	8399	E	916 273-4890	24855
Valley Communications Inc (PA)	1731	D	916 349-7300	2776
Valley Health Care Systems Inc	7361	C	916 505-4112	14793
Vanir Construction MGT Inc (PA)	8741	D	916 444-3700	27083
Vasko Electric Inc	1731	D	916 568-7700	2777
Veritiv Operating Company	5113	D	916 283-2160	8131
Verizon Bus Netwrk Svcs Inc	4813	C	916 569-5999	5662
Veterans Affairs Cal Dept	8748	B	916 653-2535	27898
Village Nurseries Whl LLC	5193	B	916 993-2292	9175
Villara Corporation	1711	D	916 364-9370	2399
Visions Unlimited (PA)	8093	C	916 394-0800	22713
Vitas Healthcare Corp Cal	8082	D	916 925-7010	22452
Volunteers of America Greater (PA)	8322	D	916 265-3400	24126
W H C Inc	8051	D	916 927-9300	20873
Water Resources Cal Dept	7375	E	916 324-3812	16260
Watson Contractors Inc	1541	D	916 481-6293	1449
Wdc Explrtion Wells Holdg Corp	1623	C	916 419-6043	2001
WEAVE Incorporated (PA)	7363	C	916 448-2321	14943
Weintraub Tobin Chediak (PA)	8111	E	916 558-6000	23431
Wellhead Electric Company Inc	4911	E	916 447-5171	6149
Wells Fargo Bank National Assn	6021	E	916 440-4570	9399
Wellspace Health (PA)	8093	D	916 325-5556	22714
Western Health Advantage	6321	C	916 567-1950	10174
Western States Fire Protection	1711	C	916 924-1631	2409
Western States Info Netwrk Inc	8733	D	916 263-1180	26677
Whgca LLC	7011	D	916 922-4700	13399
William L Lyon & Assoc Inc	6531	C	916 447-7878	11833
Wilmor & Sons Plumbing & Cnstr	1711	D	916 381-9114	2411
Winter Care Center Sacramento	8051	C	916 922-8855	20908
Wireless Store Inc	4899	C	916 206-3600	6007
Wmk Sacramento LLC	7011	D	916 929-8855	13415
Wood Rodgers Inc (PA)	8711	C	916 341-7760	26006
Xerox Corporation	5044	D	916 444-8100	6990
XI Construction Corporation	1521	D	916 282-2900	1261
Xpo Logistics Freight Inc	4213	D	916 399-8291	4316
Yrc Inc	4213	D	916 371-4555	4326
Zimmerman Roofing Inc	1761	D	916 454-3667	3211
Zoel Holding Company Inc	7361	C	916 646-3100	14804

SAINT HELENA, CA - Napa County

	SIC	EMP	PHONE	ENTRY #
Chappellet Vineyard	0172	E	707 286-4219	134
E & J Gallo Winery	8748	E	707 967-9284	27708
Hall Wines LLC	5182	D	707 967-2626	9048
Jack Neal & Son Inc	0172	C	707 963-7303	148
Mitchell Vineyards LLC	0762	D	707 963-7050	700
Nissen Vineyard Services Inc	0762	D	707 963-3480	703
Penterman Farming Co LLC	0762	D	707 967-9977	706
Rios Farming Company LLC	0172	C	707 965-2587	169
Silverado Orchards (PA)	6513	D	707 963-1461	11114
St Helena Hospital (PA)	8062	A	707 963-1882	21775
T and M Agricultural Svcs LLC	0762	D	707 963-3330	714
Taylor Bailey Inc	1542	D	707 967-8090	1668

SALIDA, CA - Stanislaus County

	SIC	EMP	PHONE	ENTRY #
Royce Corporation (PA)	7342	D	209 545-0789	14156
Western Drywall Inc	1742	D	209 847-6401	2981

SALINAS, CA - Monterey County

	SIC	EMP	PHONE	ENTRY #
Adobe Packing Company (PA)	0723	C	831 753-6195	488
American Farms LLC	0139	D	831 424-1815	20
Americold Logistics LLC	4222	E	831 424-1537	4494
Ameripride Services Inc	7213	C	800 882-5326	13513
ASset Private Security Inc	7381	C	831 809-9779	16573
BFI Waste Systems N Amer Inc	4953	C	831 775-3850	6356
Blazer Wilkinson LP	5148	B	831 455-3700	8642
Califrnia Frnsic Med Group Inc	8011	C	831 755-3886	19343
Carmel Valley Packing Inc	0723	C	831 771-8860	500
Central Coast Cooling LLC	4222	D	831 422-7265	4498
Central Coast Vna & Hospice	8082	D	831 758-8243	22261
Christensen & Giannini LLC	0161	D	831 449-2494	43
Church Brothers LLC (PA)	5148	D	831 796-1000	8656
City of Salinas	7349	D	831 758-7233	14213
Corral De Tierra Country Club	7997	D	831 484-1325	18901
Corral Del Tierra	7997	D	831 372-6244	18902
County of Monterey	7389	D	831 755-4944	17106
County of Monterey	7389	D	831 755-5027	17107

	SIC	EMP	PHONE	ENTRY #
County of Monterey	8399	E	831 755-4500	24770
County of Monterey	8062	A	831 755-4201	21356
County of Monterey	8011	E	831 769-8800	19417
County of Monterey	8699	B	831 755-3700	25412
County of Monterey	8322	A	831 755-3500	23694
County of Monterey	8744	C	831 755-3782	27587
County of Monterey	1611	B	831 755-4800	1753
Cowles California Media Co	4833	D	831 422-3500	5780
DArrigo Broscoof California (PA)	0161	E	831 455-4500	47
Dassels Petroleum Inc	5172	E	831 636-5100	8953
Elioco Produce Inc	0761	C	831 424-5450	644
Employnet Inc	7361	A	831 233-9999	14615
Foothill Estates Inc	6552	D	831 422-7819	11876
Fresh Leaf Farms LLC (DH)	0161	E	831 422-7405	54
Gieg Chevron LLC	7542	C	831 755-8000	17816
Growers Company Inc	7361	D	831 424-3850	14633
Growers Express LLC (PA)	5148	B	831 757-9951	8695
Growers Street Cooling	0723	C	831 424-2929	526
Growers Transplanting Inc (HQ)	0182	C	831 449-3440	313
Guardsmark LLC	7381	C	831 769-8981	16689
Hearst Stations Inc	4833	D	831 758-8888	5797
Helios Healthcare LLC	8051	A	831 449-1515	20523
Henry Hibino Farms	0161	D	831 757-3081	61
Higard Farms LLC	0191	C	831 753-5982	354
Hilltown Packing Co Inc	0723	B	831 784-1931	530
Hope Services	8331	C	831 455-4940	24190
Interim Inc	8999	C	831 754-3838	27934
J Waters Inc	7381	E	831 424-1946	16707
Jensco Inc	1731	E	831 422-7819	2618
Jlg Harvesting Inc	0723	B	831 422-7871	532
Kindred Healthcare Oper Inc	8051	C	831 424-8072	20560
Kysmet Security & Patrol Inc	7381	C	831 710-2425	16712
M V Transportation	4789	C	831 373-1395	5235
Mann Packing Co Inc (DH)	0723	B	831 422-7405	539
Massolo Trucking LLC (PA)	4212	C	831 424-7205	4038
Matsui Nursery Inc (PA)	0181	D	831 422-6433	283
Mission Linen Supply	7213	C	831 424-1707	13536
Mission Linen Supply	7218	C	831 424-1753	13611
Mission Linen Supply	7213	C	831 375-2491	13543
Monterey County Office Educatn	8732	D	831 755-0324	26547
Monterey-Salinas Transit Corp	4131	C	831 754-2804	3881
Natividad Medical Center	8062	A	831 755-4111	21604
Newstar Fresh Foods LLC	0723	D	831 758-7800	546
Newstar Fresh Foods LLC (PA)	0723	C	888 782-7220	547
Noland Hamerly Etienne (PA)	8111	E	831 372-7525	23289
Nunes Company Inc (PA)	5148	E	831 751-7510	8710
Nunes Cooling Inc	0723	E	831 751-7510	549
Nutrien AG Solutions Inc	5191	C	831 757-5391	9091
Odd Fellow-Rebekah Chld HM Cal	8361	D	831 775-0348	24615
Old Republic Title Company	6361	C	831 757-8051	10469
Pacific Intl Vgetable Mktg Inc (PA)	5148	D	831 422-3745	8713
Pemer Packing Co Inc	7361	A	831 758-8586	14690
Planned Parenthood Mar Monte (PA)	8093	C	831 373-1709	22646
Plant Tape Usa Inc	0721	E	831 455-2255	465
Porter Construction Co Inc	1521	C	831 455-3020	1217
Pre Con Industries Inc	8741	E	805 345-3147	26990
Premium Packing Inc	0722	C	831 443-6855	483
Quinn Group Inc	5082	D	831 758-8461	7690
Quinn Lift Inc	5084	A	831 758-4086	7789
Rabobank National Association	6022	C	831 422-6642	9481
Rancho Salinas Packing Inc	0761	C	831 758-3624	670
Red Blossom Sales Inc	0191	A	831 751-9169	376
Reegs Inc	1522	D	831 455-7931	1311
Rh Framing Inc	1751	C	831 759-8860	3066
River Ranch Fresh Foods LLC (HQ)	5148	D	831 758-1390	8725
Rocket Farms Herbs Inc	0191	B	562 340-5108	377
S&P Global Inc	6282	C	831 393-6044	10112
Salinas Med Mngt Srvcs Org Inc	8011	C	831 751-7070	19836
Salinas Valley Medical Clinic	8011	B	831 424-7389	19837
Salinas Valley Memorial Hlthca	8062	A	831 759-3236	21697
Salinas Valley Memorial Hlthca (PA)	8062	A	831 757-4333	21698
Salinas Valley Memorial Hlthca	8069	A	831 757-3041	22043
Salinas Valley Memorial Hlthca	8062	B	831 757-7880	21699
Scheid Vineyards Cal Inc	0172	D	831 385-4801	174
Scheid Vineyards Inc (PA)	0172	D	310 301-1555	175
Securitas SEC Svcs USA Inc	7381	A	831 444-9607	16804
Seed Dynamics Inc	0723	D	831 424-1177	566
Sg Personnel LLC	0181	A	831 444-0523	299
SMD Logistics Inc	4731	C	831 758-5300	5171
Sturdy Oil Company	5172	C	831 970-9897	8967
Superior Contracting Corp	1742	E	831 757-1089	2965
Sysco San Francisco Inc	5141	C	831 771-5000	8471
Tanimura Antle Fresh Foods Inc (PA)	0161	C	831 455-2950	84
Tanimura Brothers	6211	D	831 424-0841	10018
Taylor Farms California Inc (HQ)	0723	E	831 754-0471	578

Employment Codes: A=Over 500 employees, B=251-500,
C=101-250, D=51-100, E=50

2019 Directory of California
Wholesalers and Services Companies

© Mergent Inc. 1-800-342-5647
1651

GEOGRAPHIC

	SIC	EMP	PHONE	ENTRY #
Taylor Fresh Foods Inc (PA)	0723	C	831 676-9023	579
United Parcel Service Inc OH	4215	C	831 758-9112	4446
UPS Ground Freight Inc	4213	D	831 751-0262	4292
USA Waste of California Inc	4953	D	831 754-2500	6500
Vals Plumbing and Heating Inc	1711	D	831 424-1633	2396
Vegetable Growers Supply Co (PA)	5199	E	831 759-4600	9266
Villa Serra Corporation	6513	D	831 754-5532	11133
Wilbur-Ellis Company LLC	5191	D	831 422-6473	9107
Windsor Convalescent	8051	C	831 424-0687	20899
Windsor Rdge Rhblttion Ctr LLC	8093	D	831 449-1515	22717
Windsor Skyline Care Ctr LLC	8051	D	831 449-5496	20905
Xpo Logistics Freight Inc	4213	D	831 758-8874	4313

SAN ANDREAS, CA - Calaveras County

	SIC	EMP	PHONE	ENTRY #
Avalon Care Center	8051	C	209 754-3823	20243
Calaveras County Water Dst	4941	D	209 754-3543	6210
County of Calaveras	8322	D	209 754-6402	23632
Dignity Health	8062	D	209 754-3521	21384
Mark Twain Medical Center (HQ)	8062	C	209 754-3521	21578
Mark Twain Medical Center	8062	B	209 754-1487	21579
Resource Connection of Amador (PA)	8322	D	209 754-3114	23992
Rite of Pass Athl Trai Cent	8361	C	209 736-4500	24654

SAN ARDO, CA - Monterey County

	SIC	EMP	PHONE	ENTRY #
PSC Industrial Outsourcing LP	4212	D	831 627-2595	4051

SAN BERNARDINO, CA - San Bernardino County

	SIC	EMP	PHONE	ENTRY #
Alliance Fc	8699	E	909 784-0005	25377
Allied Building Products Corp	5031	E	909 796-6926	6805
American Force Private SEC Inc	7381	D	909 384-9820	16563
Arrowhead Convalescent Home	8051	D	909 886-4731	20234
Assoc For Retarded Citizens	8331	C	909 884-6484	24153
AT&T Corp	4813	D	909 381-7729	5463
Aviation & Defense Inc	4581	C	909 382-3487	4874
Baron Pool Plst Sthern Cal Inc	1799	D	909 792-8891	3491
Barrett Business Services Inc	7361	A	909 890-3633	14576
Bear Trucking Inc	4214	D	909 799-1616	4332
Blood Bank of San Bernardino A (PA)	8099	B	909 885-6503	22747
Bnsf Railway Company	4011	C	909 386-4002	3614
Brennan Electric Inc	1731	C	909 772-2263	2527
Brickley Construction Co Inc	1799	E	909 888-2010	3496
Budget Electrical Contrs Inc	1731	C	909 381-2646	2530
California Title Co Nthrn Cal	6361	D	909 825-8800	10434
Care Tech Inc	8051	D	909 882-2965	20286
Caston Inc	1742	C	909 381-1619	2863
Cellco Partnership	4812	C	909 381-0576	5381
Community Action Prtnship Sb C	8399	C	909 723-1500	24764
Community Hosp San Bernardino (HQ)	8062	B	909 887-6333	21332
Copier Source Inc (PA)	5044	C	909 890-4040	6957
Cornerstone Medical Group	8041	E	909 890-4353	20153
Correctons Rhbltation Cal Dept	8322	C	909 806-3516	23619
County of San Bernardino	8322	D	909 891-3300	23717
County of San Bernardino	8351	D	909 387-5455	24307
County of San Bernardino	8351	D	909 387-2363	24308
County of San Bernardino	8361	D	909 387-0535	24483
County of San Bernardino	8721	C	909 386-8818	26174
D M Electric Inc	1731	D	909 888-8639	2559
Daart Engineering Company Inc	1711	D	909 888-8696	2181
Del Rosa Villa Inc	8051	D	909 885-3261	20372
Dish Network Corporation	4841	D	909 381-4767	5906
DSC Logistics Inc	4731	B	540 377-2302	5048
Eagle Systems Inc	4213	C	909 386-4343	4133
Empire Disposal LLC	4953	E	909 797-9125	6398
Far West Inc	8051	D	909 884-4781	20426
Fedex Freight Corporation	4213	C	909 887-3970	4153
First Hotels International Inc	7011	C	909 884-9364	12575
First Student Inc	4151	C	909 383-1640	3925
First Student Inc	4151	C	909 383-7104	3928
Fischer Inc	1711	C	909 881-2910	2212
Garda CL West Inc	7381	E	909 574-2676	16660
Gate City Beverage Distrs (PA)	5181	B	909 799-0281	8997
Gerdau Reinforcing Steel	5051	D	909 713-1130	7275
Gresham Savage Nolan & Tilden (PA)	8111	D	619 794-0050	23116
Help For The Hurting Inc	8322	D	909 796-4222	23835
Hillcrest Care Inc	8059	D	909 882-2965	21110
Hub Construction Spc Inc (PA)	7359	E	909 889-0161	14515
Inland Bhavioral Hlth Svcs Inc (PA)	8099	D	909 881-6146	22823
Inland Cnties Regional Ctr Inc (PA)	8741	D	909 890-3000	26892
Inland Empire Health Plan	6324	B	866 228-4347	10214
Inland Empre 66ers Bsebll CLB	7941	C	909 888-9922	18521
Institute For Bhvoral Hlth Inc	8099	B	909 289-1041	22824
Iron Workers Local 433	6733	E	909 884-5500	12099
J G Golfing Enterprises Inc	7992	C	909 885-2414	18723
Jenco Productions Inc (PA)	7389	C	909 381-9453	17258
Job Options Incorporated	7219	A	909 890-4612	13634
Kaiser Foundation Hospitals	6324	D	888 750-0036	10245

	SIC	EMP	PHONE	ENTRY #
Kohls Corporation	5199	A	909 382-4300	9227
Konica Minolta Business Soluti	5044	D	909 824-2000	6966
L & L Nursery Supply Inc (PA)	5191	C	909 591-0461	9081
Lane Winpak Inc (HQ)	5199	D	909 386-1762	9229
Legacy Vulcan LLC	1442	E	909 875-1150	1094
Lewis Brsbois Bsgard Smith LLP	8111	E	909 387-1130	23210
Llu Advntist Hlth Sciences Ctr	8011	E	909 558-4386	19656
Lucky Farms Inc	0161	D	909 799-6688	67
Marna Health Services Inc	8059	D	909 882-2965	21153
Matich Corporation (PA)	1611	D	909 382-7400	1814
Maxim Healthcare Services Inc	7363	B	951 684-4148	14877
Metropolitan Water District	4941	E	909 890-3776	6280
Michael P Byko DDS A Prof Corp (PA)	8021	D	909 888-7817	20127
Michael Reyes	1542	C	909 444-0120	1594
Midnight Auto Recycling LLC	5093	E	909 884-5308	7983
NTS Technical Systems	8734	D	909 382-2360	26724
Omnitrans Inc	8361	C	909 383-1680	24620
On Trac Overhead Door Co Inc	1751	C	909 799-8555	3055
Original Mowbrays Tree Svc Inc (PA)	0783	C	909 383-7009	976
Pacific Airworks Group LLC	8711	D	909 815-7012	25858
Pathway Inc	8322	D	909 890-1070	23962
Plott Management Co	8051	D	909 883-0288	20705
Property Insight	6512	C	909 876-6505	10928
Roofing Wholesale Co Inc	5033	D	909 825-8440	6929
S&E Gourmet Cuts Inc	5145	C	909 370-0155	8567
Sac Health System (PA)	8021	D	909 382-7100	20134
Safety Security Patrol LLC	7381	D	909 888-7778	16780
San Bernardino California City (PA)	8111	B	909 384-7272	23365
San Bernardino California City	8611	D	909 384-5111	24977
San Bernardino Care Company	8059	D	909 884-4781	21202
San Bernardino City Unf School	7349	C	909 388-6100	14374
San Bernardino City Unf School	8351	D	909 388-6307	24376
San Bernardino City Unf School	8099	D	909 881-8000	22873
San Bernardino Hilton (HQ)	7011	C	909 889-0133	13165
San Bernardino Med Group Inc (PA)	8011	C	909 883-8611	19840
San Bernardino Symphony	7929	C	909 381-5388	18457
San Brnrdino Pub Emplyees Assn	8631	E	909 386-1260	25075
Soffietti Co	5072	D	909 907-2277	7604
Southern California Gas Co	4924	C	909 335-7941	6173
Spectrum MGT Holdg Co LLC	4841	D	909 918-6972	5936
Springleaf Fincl Holdings LLC	8742	C	909 796-1603	27462
Sprint Communications Co LP	4813	D	909 382-6030	5649
Stavatti Industries Ltd	1041	D	651 238-5369	1007
Terminix Intl Co Ltd Partnr	7342	E	909 332-2479	14160
Think Together	8351	A	909 723-1400	24391
United Medical Management Inc	8059	C	909 886-5291	21239
Universal	7349	D	909 882-5337	14417
Vibra Hosp San Bernardino LLC	8062	C	909 473-1233	21908
Vna Hospice & Pllatve Cre S CA	8082	C	909 384-0737	22460
Vna Hospice & Pllatve Cre S CA (PA)	8082	C	909 624-3574	22461
Waterman Convalescent Hospital (PA)	8051	C	909 882-1215	20876
Wsp USA Inc	8711	D	909 888-1106	26014
Xavier Plumbing and Mech Inc	1711	D	909 883-9426	2412
YMCA of East Valley	8641	E	909 881-9622	25290

SAN BRUNO, CA - San Mateo County

	SIC	EMP	PHONE	ENTRY #
Artichoke Joes Inc	7999	B	650 589-8812	19103
Honeywell International Inc	5045	D	650 918-3229	7058
Kaiser Foundation Hospitals	6324	D	650 742-2100	10250
Ksi Corp (PA)	4731	D	650 952-0815	5096
La Petite Baleen Inc	7991	C	650 588-7665	18624
Latino Commission On Alcohol (PA)	8093	E	650 244-1444	22610
Permanente Medical Group Inc	8011	C	650 742-2100	19761
Premier Source LLC	8733	E	415 349-2010	26649
Provident Funding Assoc LP (PA)	6162	E	650 652-1300	9849
Qumu Inc	7372	C	650 396-8530	15839
Responsys Inc (DH)	7371	C	650 745-1700	15407
Sapho Inc	7371	C	650 597-2746	15429
Skypark Inc	7299	D	650 875-6655	13774
Spiritual Direction	8322	E	650 952-9456	24065
Staffing Specialists Intl	8082	E	650 737-0777	22427
United Airlines Inc	4512	C	650 634-2468	4805
Vantagepoint Management Inc (PA)	6799	C	650 866-3100	12279
Vantagepoint Venture Partners	6722	D	650 866-3100	12050

SAN CARLOS, CA - San Mateo County

	SIC	EMP	PHONE	ENTRY #
A G Paceman Inc	6519	D	650 592-7282	11163
Broadway By Bay	7922	C	650 579-5565	18347
Check Point Software Tech Inc (HQ)	7372	C	650 628-2000	15625
Coldwell Banker	6411	D	650 596-5400	10590
Commercial Mechanical Svc Inc (PA)	7623	E	650 610-8440	17893
D & J Tile Company Inc	1743	D	650 632-4000	2992
Duckys of San Carlos Inc	7542	D	650 637-1301	17812
Emagined Security Inc	7382	E	415 944-2977	16891
George P Johnson Company	5199	C	650 226-0600	9220
Global Meddata Inc	8099	D	650 369-9734	22809

2019 Directory of California
Wholesalers and Services Companies

(P-0000) Products & Services Section entry number
(PA)=Parent Co (HQ)=Headquarters (DH)=Div Headquarters

Company	SIC	EMP	PHONE	ENTRY #
Helix Holdings I LLC	8731	D	415 805-3360	26375
Helix Opco LLC	8731	D	415 805-3360	26376
Inside Source Inc (PA)	5021	D	650 508-9101	6727
Ira Services Inc	6733	C	650 593-2221	12098
Lifestreet Corporation	5199	D	650 508-2220	9231
Lyngso Garden Materials Inc	5032	E	650 364-1730	6900
Marklogic Corporation (PA)	7371	C	650 655-2300	15273
Maxx Metals Inc	5051	D	650 654-1500	7289
Morrow-Meadows Corporation	1731	C	510 562-1980	2653
Natera Inc (PA)	8071	C	650 249-9090	22114
Peninsula Crrdor Jint Pwers Bd	4111	C	650 508-6200	3697
Peninsula Custom Homes Inc	1521	C	650 574-0241	1214
Professional Insur Assoc Inc (PA)	6411	E	650 592-7333	10743
Purcell-Murray Company Inc (PA)	5074	D	415 468-6620	7633
Recology San Mateo County	4953	C	650 595-3900	6442
Revjet	7372	C	650 508-2215	15842
Rudolph and Sletten Inc (HQ)	1542	D	650 216-3600	1637
San Mateo County Transit Dst (PA)	4111	C	650 508-6200	3718
San Mateo County Transit Dst	4173	C	650 508-6412	3956
Sb Group Us Inc	6282	D	650 562-8110	10113
Sb Product Group LLC	1731	C	650 562-8221	2724
Starvista	8322	C	650 591-9623	24075
Universal General Builders	8711	C	650 591-3104	25970
VCA Animal Hospitals Inc	0742	E	650 631-7400	611

SAN CLEMENTE, CA - Orange County

Company	SIC	EMP	PHONE	ENTRY #
Advanced Mp Technology Inc (PA)	5065	C	949 492-6589	7434
American Corrective Counseling	8322	B	949 369-6210	23473
Asociacon De Bomberos Del Esta	8611	D	949 355-4249	24943
Bemus Landscape Inc	1629	B	714 557-7910	2012
Brad Rambo & Associates Inc (PA)	5136	C	949 366-9911	8250
Buyefficient LLC	5046	D	949 382-3129	7132
Cellco Partnership	4812	D	949 488-9990	5397
Dealersocket Inc (PA)	7371	D	949 900-0300	15098
Dual Diagnosis Trtmnt Ctr Inc (PA)	8093	C	949 276-5553	22570
Evolution Hospitality LLC (PA)	8741	C	949 325-1350	26854
GCI Construction Inc	1611	E	714 957-0233	1765
Golf Investment LLC (PA)	7997	D	949 498-6604	18930
HCA Inc	8062	C	949 496-1122	21443
Heritage Golf Group LLC	7992	D	949 369-6226	18719
Internet Marketing Assn Inc	8742	C	949 443-9300	27279
Julius Steve Construction Inc	1541	E	949 369-7820	1411
Keenan & Associates	6411	D	949 940-1760	10668
Matsushita International Corp (PA)	6799	C	949 498-1000	12243
Mega Mail Mall Inc	6512	E	888 998-6245	10911
Metagenics Inc	5122	D	800 692-9400	8198
Pacific Golf & Country Club	7997	D	949 498-6604	18997
Partner Hero Inc	7389	E	888 968-2767	17388
Rainbow Sandals Inc	5139	E	949 276-4431	8366
Regenesis Bioremediation Pdts (PA)	8748	E	949 366-8000	27841
Sambazon Inc (PA)	5148	D	877 726-2296	8726
San Clemente Medical Ctr LLC	8062	B	949 496-1122	21703
San Clemente Villas By Sea	8361	C	949 489-3400	24664
San Diego Gas & Electric Co	4931	E	949 361-8090	6187
Southern California Edison Co	4911	A	949 368-2881	6123
Speedy Locksmith	7699	D	760 439-5000	17991

SAN DIEGO, CA - San Diego County

Company	SIC	EMP	PHONE	ENTRY #
1835 Columbia Street LP	7011	D	619 564-3993	12290
24 Hour Fitness Usa Inc	7991	E	619 294-2424	18564
24 Hour Fitness Usa Inc	7991	E	858 538-4400	18569
5th Avenue Partners LLC	7011	B	619 515-3000	12298
8110 Aero Holding LLC	7011	C	858 277-8888	12300
A C Rentals LLC	1711	E	858 271-8571	2080
A Caos Medical Corporation	8082	D	800 362-2731	22179
A J Esprit	7011	E	619 223-8171	12302
A O Reed & Co	1711	B	858 565-4131	2081
A-Star Staffing Inc	7361	C	619 574-7600	14561
Aat Torrey Reserve 6 LLC	6512	D	858 350-2600	10846
Aba Holdings LLC	6719	C	858 565-4131	11959
Abacus Data Systems Inc (HQ)	7371	D	858 452-4280	14955
ABC Home Health Care Llc	8082	D	858 455-5000	22183
Abe Entercom Holdings LLC	4832	D	619 291-9797	5690
ABM Parking Services (PA)	7521	C	619 235-4500	17662
Accentcare Inc	8082	A	858 576-7410	22186
Accentcare Home Health Cal Inc	8082	C	858 576-7410	22192
Accenture Federal Services LLC	8742	C	619 574-2400	27105
Access Nurses Inc	7361	D	858 458-4400	14565
Accumen Inc (PA)	8082	D	858 777-8160	22195
Ace Parking Management Inc	7521	C	858 552-0237	17664
Ace Parking Management Inc	7521	C	619 238-4765	17669
Ace Parking Management Inc (PA)	7521	E	619 233-6624	17671
Ace Parking Management Inc	7521	D	619 230-0003	17674
Ace Parking Management Inc	7521	C	619 232-1234	17675
Ace Relocation Systems Inc (PA)	4212	D	858 677-5500	3966
Acea Biosciences Inc	8731	D	858 724-0928	26309
Achates Power Inc	8731	D	858 535-9920	26310
Acon Laboratories Inc (PA)	5047	D	858 875-8000	7148
Activcare Living Inc (PA)	8741	C	858 565-4424	26746
Adaptamed LLC	7371	C	877 478-7773	14963
Adesa Corporation LLC	5012	C	619 661-5565	6575
Administrative Services SD	4121	E	619 398-2314	3864
Adminstrtive Office of US Crts	8322	C	619 557-6650	23460
Advanced Lighting Concepts Inc	5063	E	858 521-0233	7326
Advanced Rehabilitation Tech	5047	D	858 621-5959	7149
Advanced Rsrvation Systems Inc	7379	C	858 300-8600	16306
Advanced Test Equipment Corp	7359	D	858 558-6500	14465
Aecom Technical Services Inc	8711	D	619 610-7600	25518
Aewestjv	8712	E	619 233-1023	26021
Affinity Auto Programs Inc	7389	C	858 643-9324	16988
Affinity Development Group Inc	8699	C	858 643-9324	25374
Affordable Engrg Svcs Inc	8711	D	973 890-8915	25522
Affymetrix Inc	8731	C	858 642-2058	26314
Age Concerns Inc	8322	B	619 544-1622	23462
AIG Direct Insurance Svcs Inc	6411	B	858 309-3000	10512
Airgas Inc	5084	C	858 279-8200	7720
Airgas Usa LLC	5169	C	858 279-8200	8916
AJW Restoration Services LLC	1542	E	858 429-5641	1460
Akela Pharma Inc	8733	E	512 391-3525	26587
Alaska Airlines Inc	4512	C	619 238-2042	4762
Aldridge Pite LLP	8111	C	858 750-7700	22908
All Star Glass Inc (PA)	7536	E	619 275-3343	17751
All Star Maintenance Inc	1799	D	858 259-0900	3482
All Stars	1799	D	858 259-0900	3483
All System Personnel Mgmt	8741	E	858 674-4090	26754
All Valley Home Hlth Care Inc	8082	D	619 276-8001	22212
Allegis Residential Svcs Inc	8741	D	858 430-5700	26755
Alliant Insurance Services Inc	6411	D	619 238-1828	10515
Allied Gardens Towing Inc (HQ)	7549	D	619 563-4060	17847
Alliedbarton Security Svcs LLC	7381	B	858 874-8200	16557
Allstar Commercial Cleaning	7699	E	858 715-0500	17931
Alorica Customer Care Inc	7389	A	619 298-7103	16994
Alpha Mechanical Inc	1711	D	858 278-3500	2101
Alpha Mechanical Inc (PA)	1711	D	858 278-3500	2102
Alpha Project For Homeless (PA)	8322	D	619 542-1877	23468
Alsco Inc	7213	C	619 234-7291	13496
Alta-Dena Certified Dairy LLC	5143	D	858 292-6930	8511
Alvarado Hospital LLC (DH)	8062	A	619 287-3270	21282
Alvizia Landscape Co LLC	0782	C	619 661-6557	796
Amber Financial Group LLC (PA)	6162	C	858 487-7209	9770
America West Airlines Inc	4512	E	619 231-7340	4764
American Airlines Inc	4512	E	619 574-0615	4772
American Electronic Warfare As	8711	C	858 524-6119	25530
American Freightways LP	4213	D	866 326-5902	4097
American Institute of Aeronaut	8733	D	619 545-3736	26590
American Internet Mortgage Inc	6162	C	888 411-4246	9773
American Intl Group Inc	6411	A	619 682-4058	10521
American Medical Response Inc	4119	C	858 492-3500	3761
American Medical Response Inc	4119	A	858 492-8111	3762
American Multi-Cinema Inc	7832	E	619 296-0370	18258
American Multi-Cinema Inc	7832	D	619 296-2737	18268
American National Red Cross	8322	D	858 309-1200	23477
American Nwland Communities LP (PA)	6552	C	858 455-7503	11854
American Prprty-Mnagement Corp	7011	C	619 232-3121	12317
American Red Cross San Diego (PA)	8399	D	858 309-1200	24736
American Residential Svcs LLC	1711	D	858 457-5547	2107
American Residential Svcs LLC	1711	D	858 677-5445	2109
American Spclty Hlth Group Inc (HQ)	8082	B	858 754-2000	22221
American Specialty Health Inc (PA)	6411	B	858 754-2000	10522
American Sunrise Inc	7371	C	858 610-4766	14980
American Technologies Inc	8748	D	858 530-2400	27640
Amn Healthcare Inc (HQ)	8011	C	858 792-0711	19287
Amn Healthcare Services Inc	8049	A	858 792-0711	20162
Amn Healthcare Services Inc (PA)	7363	C	866 871-8519	14815
Amsec LLC	8731	B	858 522-6319	26319
Anchor General Insurance Agcy	6411	C	858 527-3600	10525
Andrew and Williamson Sales Co (PA)	5148	D	619 661-6000	8640
Andrew M Golden MD	8011	D	619 528-5342	19293
Anesthesia Service Med Group	8011	E	858 277-4767	19295
Anixter Inc	5063	E	858 571-6571	7331
Anixter Inc	5087	C	800 854-2088	7880
Anova Food LLC	5146	C	858 715-4000	8568
Antimite Associates Inc	7342	C	619 231-2900	14137
Apex Mechanical Systems Inc.	1711	D	858 536-8700	2123
Appfolio Inc	7372	A	866 648-1536	15587
Apple Nine Hospitality MGT	7011	D	858 573-0700	12330
Applied Molecular Evolution (HQ)	8731	E	858 597-4990	26321
Apria Healthcare LLC	7352	D	858 653-6800	14432
Aquaclean Janitorial	7349	D	858 537-9090	14196
Aramark Unf & Career AP LLC	7213	C	858 550-1131	13516
Aramark Unf & Career AP LLC	7218	C	858 550-5200	13593

Company	SIC	EMP	PHONE	ENTRY #
ARC of San Diego (PA)	8399	A	619 685-1175	24737
Archer Western Contractors LLC	1611	D	858 715-7200	1724
Armed Forces Officials Assn	8621	E	858 672-1438	24996
Arrowhead Gen Insur Agcy Inc (DH)	6331	C	619 881-8600	10339
Arrowhead Management Company (DH)	6411	D	800 669-1889	10541
Artiano Shinoff Abed (PA)	8111	D	619 232-3122	22923
Ashford Trs Nickel LLC	8741	D	619 260-0111	26767
ASI Hastings Inc	1711	C	619 590-9300	2130
Asset Marketing Systems Insu	8742	C	888 303-8755	27144
Associated Students San Diego (PA)	8699	A	619 594-0234	25382
Assocted Third Pty Admnstrtors	6371	C	619 358-8140	10476
At Your Home Familycare	7299	C	858 625-0406	13717
AT&T Corp	4812	D	858 693-0815	5288
AT&T Services Inc	4813	C	619 515-5100	5471
AT&T Services Inc	4813	C	858 886-2762	5479
AT&T Services Inc	4813	B	858 495-3907	5508
Ata Engineering Inc (PA)	8711	D	858 480-2000	25550
Atk Space Systems Inc	8733	B	858 621-5700	26594
Atkins North America Inc	8711	D	858 874-1810	25552
Atlas Construction Supply Inc (PA)	5032	D	858 277-2100	6877
Atlas General Insur Svcs LLC	6411	C	858 529-6700	10551
Atyr Pharma Inc	8731	D	858 731-8389	26332
Audatex North America Inc (DH)	7372	C	858 946-1900	15597
Aurora Behavioral Health Care	8063	C	858 487-3200	21924
Aurora Healthcare Inc	8062	E	858 487-3200	21292
Ausgar Technologies Inc	8711	C	855 428-7427	25556
Austin Veum Rbbins Prtners Inc (PA)	8712	D	619 231-1960	26025
Autism Otrach Southern Cal LLC	8322	D	619 795-9925	23499
Automatic Data Processing Inc	7374	D	619 293-4800	16098
Automation Engrg Systems Inc	7373	D	858 967-8650	15918
AV Builder Corp (PA)	1522	D	858 622-9200	1266
Avia Tech LLC	7311	D	858 777-5000	13793
Aviva Systems Biology Corp (PA)	8731	D	858 552-6979	26336
Avnet Inc	5065	B	858 385-7500	7449
Awarepoint Corporation (PA)	7371	C	858 345-5000	15012
Axa Advisors LLC	6311	D	619 239-0018	10130
Axa Equitable Life Insur Co	6411	D	858 552-1234	10558
Aya Healthcare Inc (PA)	7363	D	858 458-4410	14821
Babcock & Brown Elec MGT LLC	8742	C	858 587-5820	27149
Bahia Sternwheelers Inc	4489	E	858 539-7720	4709
Bainbridge Inc (PA)	8742	D	858 638-1800	27152
Baja Freight Forwarders Inc (PA)	4731	C	619 671-3100	5015
Bakbone Software Inc (DH)	7371	D	858 450-9009	15019
Baker & Taylor LLC	5192	C	858 457-2500	9109
Bald Eagle Security Svcs Inc	7381	D	619 230-0022	16577
Banner Bank	6022	E	619 243-7900	9420
Barrett Business Services Inc	8111	A	858 314-1100	22935
Bartell Hotels	7011	C	619 224-3411	12353
Bartell Hotels	7011	C	619 222-6440	12354
Bartell Hotels	7011	E	858 581-3500	12355
Bartell Hotels	7011	D	619 222-0561	12356
Basile Construction Inc	1623	E	858 278-2739	1895
Bay Area Credit Service LLC	6062	A	858 653-3824	9622
Bay City Television Inc (PA)	4833	D	858 279-6666	5768
Bay Club Hotel and Marina A C	7011	D	619 224-8888	12360
Bdo Usa LLP	8721	D	858 404-9200	26148
Being Fit Inc (PA)	7991	D	858 549-3456	18579
Being Fit Inc	7991	D	858 483-9294	18580
Belmont Village LP	8059	D	858 486-5020	21004
Belville Enterprises Inc	8011	D	858 652-6960	19322
Ben F Smith Inc	1771	C	858 271-4320	3223
Berkshire Hathaway Homestates	6411	D	619 686-8424	10564
Bernardo Hts Healthcare Inc	8059	D	858 673-0101	21007
Beston Development	7011	D	619 232-6315	12379
Bh Partn A Calif Limit Partne (PA)	7011	B	858 539-7635	12383
Bill Howe Plumbing Inc	1711	D	800 245-5469	2144
Binding Site Inc (PA)	5047	D	858 453-9177	7162
Biocept Inc	8731	D	858 320-8200	26338
Biomed Realty LP (HQ)	6798	E	858 485-9840	12153
Biomedicure LLC	8731	D	858 586-1888	26340
Biosite Inc	5047	D	510 683-9063	7165
Biotheranostics Inc (PA)	8071	D	877 886-6739	22063
Blue Box Opco LLC (PA)	5092	D	800 840-4916	7947
Blue-Grace Logistics LLC	4731	D	858 427-5093	5019
Bmr 21 Erie St LLC	6531	D	858 485-9840	11247
Bmv Direct II LP	8748	D	858 485-9840	27660
Bonded Inc (PA)	7217	D	858 576-8400	13572
Booz Allen Hamilton Inc	8742	D	619 725-6500	27167
Boykin Mgt Co Ltd Lblty Co	7011	E	619 299-6633	12393
Bps Bioscience Inc	8731	E	858 202-1401	26343
Brady Gce II	8711	D	858 496-0500	25576
Braemar Partnership	7011	B	858 488-1081	12395
Brandes Inv Partners Inc (PA)	6722	C	858 755-0239	12031
Bridge Group Hh Inc	6719	C	858 455-5000	11967
Bright Event Rentals LLC	7359	A	858 496-9700	14480
Brightcloud Inc	7382	C	858 652-4803	16880
Brighton Gardens Inc	8051	D	858 259-2222	20266
Brighton Health Alliance (PA)	8051	D	619 461-0376	20267
Brighton Place San Diego	8051	C	619 263-2166	20269
Brightview Landscape Dev Inc	1629	B	858 458-9900	2017
Brightview Landscape Svcs Inc	0781	C	858 458-1900	737
Brinks Incorporated	7381	C	619 263-6615	16591
Bristol Hotel	7011	D	619 232-6141	12403
Broadcast Co of Americas LLC (PA)	4832	C	858 453-0658	5695
Broadway Typewriter Co Inc	5045	D	800 998-9199	7020
Brokerage Lgstics Slutions Inc	4731	C	619 671-0276	5021
Brown and Caldwell	8711	D	858 514-8822	25582
Bullup Inc	7371	E	566 997-2543	15041
Business and Support Services	7999	A	858 577-1061	19115
Butterwick Dr Kimberly Jane MD	8011	D	858 657-1002	19335
Bycor General Contractors Inc	1542	D	858 587-1901	1490
Byrom-Davey Inc	1629	E	858 513-7199	2018
C N L Hotel Del Partners LP	7011	D	619 522-8299	12414
C2 Financial Corporation	6282	C	858 220-2112	10066
Ca Inc	7372	C	631 342-6000	15620
Cableconn Industries Inc	5063	D	858 571-7111	7341
Cabrillo Gen Insur Agcy Inc	6411	C	858 244-0550	10569
Caci Inc - Federal	7373	E	619 881-6000	15923
Cactus Recycling Inc (PA)	4953	C	619 661-1283	6363
Cal Pinnacle Mltary Cmmunities	8741	D	619 764-5087	26793
Calderon Building Maintenance	7349	C	619 269-5940	14206
California Air Cartage Inc (PA)	4512	C	619 291-8544	4777
California American Water Co (HQ)	4941	D	619 409-7703	6211
California Club Lucky Lady	7011	E	619 287-6690	12420
California Coast Credit Union (PA)	6062	C	858 495-1600	9623
California Coast Credit Union	6061	C	858 495-1600	9543
California Comfort Systems USA	1711	B	858 564-1100	2153
California Forensic Med Group	8099	C	858 694-4690	22755
California Home Care Inc	8082	C	619 521-5858	22245
California Marine Cleaning Inc (PA)	4953	C	619 231-8788	6364
California Title Company	6361	D	619 516-5227	10435
Califrnia Rgional Intranet Inc	4813	D	858 974-5080	5526
Calpine Energy Solutions LLC (DH)	4931	D	877 273-6772	6180
Calworks Partnr Conference	6732	E	858 292-2900	12075
Cameron Intrstate Pipeline LLC	1623	C	619 696-3110	1903
Canji Inc	8733	D	858 597-0177	26604
Canteen Vending - San Diego	5145	D	619 527-1900	8544
Capital Plus Financial Corp	6162	E	619 744-1900	9789
Captiva Software Corporation (DH)	7373	D	858 320-1000	15926
Cardinal Health 200 LLC	5047	C	951 686-8900	7172
Cardinal Point Captains Inc	7363	C	760 438-7361	14829
Care Medical Trnsp Inc	7363	C	858 653-4520	14830
Care With Dignity Healthcare (PA)	8051	C	858 278-4750	20288
Carefusion Solutions LLC (DH)	5047	A	858 617-2100	7173
Carrier Johnson (PA)	8712	D	619 236-9462	26031
Casa De Las Campanas Inc (PA)	8361	C	858 451-9152	24455
Casas - Comprehensive	8699	D	858 292-2900	25406
Casas International Brkg Inc (PA)	4225	C	619 661-6162	4537
Cask Technologies LLC (PA)	7371	C	858 458-9951	15051
Caster Family Enterprises Inc	6799	C	619 287-8893	12211
Catalent San Diego Inc	8734	C	858 805-6383	26688
Catalina Solar 2 LLC	4911	A	888 903-6926	6015
Catholic Charities Diocese San	8322	E	619 287-9454	23533
Cbiz Mayor Hoffman Mechan (PA)	8721	D	858 795-2000	26160
Cbre Inc	6531	C	858 546-4600	11283
Celgene Corporation	5122	C	858 677-0034	8160
Cellco Partnership	4812	D	858 625-7751	5336
Cellco Partnership	4812	D	858 614-0011	5385
Cellco Partnership	4812	C	858 618-2100	5395
Cement Cutting Inc	1771	D	619 296-9592	3233
Center For Autsm Rsrch Evltn	8093	C	858 444-8823	22522
Center For Sustainable Energy	8748	C	858 244-1177	27681
Central Garden & Pet Company	5199	D	858 695-0743	9203
Century 21 Able Inc	6531	D	858 450-2100	11290
Century Contract Services Inc	7349	C	858 672-4118	14209
Certified Air Conditioning Inc	1711	C	858 292-5740	2158
Chaduxtt JV	8711	D	619 525-7188	25607
Chadwick Center For Children &	8011	E	858 966-5814	19371
Champion Signs Incorporated	7336	E	858 751-2900	14102
Charles Schwab Corporation	6211	D	858 523-2454	9929
Chicago Title Company	6361	C	619 230-6340	10439
Chief San Diego Hotel LLC	7011	D	619 239-2400	12452
Children of Rainbow Inc (PA)	8351	C	619 615-0652	24290
Children of The Rainbow Head	8351	C	619 266-7311	24291
Childrens Angelcare Aid Intl	8322	C	619 795-6234	23565
Childrens Specialist of San D (PA)	8011	B	858 576-1700	19380
Christian and Wakefield (PA)	6531	C	619 236-1555	11316
Chromalloy San Diego Corp	7699	C	858 877-2800	17937
Chubb US Holding Inc	6411	C	619 563-2400	10584
CIC Research Inc	8732	D	858 637-4000	26504

Company	SIC	EMP	PHONE	ENTRY #
Cintas Corporation No 3	7218	C	619 239-1001	13600
Cintiva Financial Corporation	6163	D	877 246-8482	9875
Citigroup Global Markets Inc	6211	D	858 597-7777	9933
City Leasing & Rentals	7515	C	619 276-6171	17652
City National Bank	6021	D	619 645-6100	9339
City of San Diego	8748	E	619 533-3012	27688
City of San Diego	8069	D	619 533-6518	22010
City of San Diego	8711	C	858 627-3210	25614
Citywide Plumbing Heating	1711	E	619 231-2022	2161
Clairemont Healthcare	8051	D	858 278-4750	20313
Clean Enviroment	7349	D	619 521-0543	14217
Clearbalance Holdings LLC	6719	E	858 535-0870	11969
Clinapps Inc	7371	D	858 866-0228	15064
Clinicomp International Inc (PA)	7373	D	858 546-8202	15933
Closingcorp Inc	7379	D	858 551-1500	16327
CNA Surety Corporation	6411	D	619 682-3550	10588
Coast Citrus Distributors (PA)	5148	D	619 661-7950	8657
Coastal Marine Services Inc (PA)	1799	E	619 291-8176	3506
Coastal Transport Co Inc	4212	E	619 584-1055	3993
Coffman Specialties Inc (PA)	1771	C	858 536-3100	3237
Cognitive Medical Systems Inc	7371	D	858 509-4949	15067
Cohn Wholesale Fruit & Grocery (PA)	5148	C	619 528-1113	8661
Colliers Intl Prperty Cons Inc	6531	E	858 455-1515	11370
Collwood Ter Stellar Care Inc	8059	D	619 287-2920	21040
Colrich Communities Inc	6552	D	858 350-7672	11865
Colt Services Inc	7217	D	858 271-9910	13576
Commercial Finance & L	6029	D	858 866-8525	9500
Communction Wlrg Spcalists Inc	1731	D	858 278-4545	2548
Community Clinics Hlth Netwrk	8621	E	619 542-4300	25011
Competitive Edge RES Comm Inc	8732	D	619 702-2372	26506
Competitor Group Events Inc	8743	E	858 450-6510	27550
Comprehensive Enviro	8711	E	619 294-9400	25619
Comps Inc	7375	C	858 658-0576	16211
Computer Proc Unlimited Inc	7371	D	858 530-0875	15070
Conam Management Corporation (PA)	6531	C	858 614-7200	11376
Concerro Inc (DH)	7371	D	858 882-8500	15076
Considine & Considine An Acco	8721	D	619 231-1977	26172
Consolidated Elec Distrs Inc	5063	D	858 268-1020	7349
Contrlled Cntmination Svcs LLC	7349	C	888 263-9886	14226
Cooley LLP	8111	C	858 550-6000	22992
Copley Press Inc	7372	C	619 718-5200	15637
Corecivic Inc	8744	C	619 661-9119	27583
Corinthian Title Company Inc	6361	D	619 299-4800	10449
Correctional Services Corp LLC	8744	C	858 566-9816	27586
Cortel Inc	4812	C	650 703-7217	5401
Cosco Fire Protection Inc	1711	D	858 444-2000	2172
Costar Group Inc	6531	C	858 458-4900	11386
County of San Diego	8322	D	858 694-5141	23721
County of San Diego	8322	D	858 495-5537	23723
County of San Diego	8322	D	619 515-8202	23724
County of San Diego	8111	D	619 531-4040	23007
County of San Diego	8748	C	619 236-2191	27701
County of San Diego	8062	E	858 694-2895	21357
County of San Diego	8063	B	619 692-8200	21943
County of San Diego	8322	D	619 563-2765	23727
County of San Diego	8099	D	619 531-4521	22780
County of San Diego	8322	D	619 236-8725	23728
County Sandiego Dept Chldspprt	8322	B	619 578-6660	23761
Courtyard By Marriott	7011	D	619 291-5720	12488
Courtyard-Central	7011	D	858 573-0700	12496
Covance Inc	8731	C	858 352-2300	26351
Cox Communications Inc	4841	D	858 715-4500	5891
Cox Communications Cal LLC	4841	B	619 262-1122	5895
CP Opco LLC	7359	D	858 496-9700	14492
CPM Ltd Inc (PA)	7363	A	619 237-9900	14844
Crash Inc Short Term I	8093	D	619 282-7274	22562
Creative Nail Design Inc	7231	C	760 599-2900	13651
Credit Solutions Corp	6141	C	858 650-0812	9709
Crestline Funding Corporation	6162	E	949 863-8600	9797
Cricket Communications LLC (DH)	4812	D	858 882-6000	5402
Cricket Indiana Property Co	4812	D	858 587-2648	5403
Crown Building Maintenance Co	7349	C	858 560-5785	14240
Crown Plaza SD	7011	D	619 297-1101	12501
Csi Financial Services LLC	8741	E	858 200-9200	26836
CSRA LLC	7376	A	619 225-2600	16267
Cubic Corporation	7373	A	858 277-6780	15938
Cubic Global Defense Inc	8711	D	858 277-8760	25633
Cusa Gcbs LLC	4725	C	619 266-7365	4969
Customzed Svcs Admnstrtors Inc	6411	C	858 810-2000	10599
Cutting Edge Drywall Inc	1742	E	858 408-0870	2870
Cy Gaslamp LLC	7011	D	619 544-1004	12509
D & K Engineering (PA)	8711	C	858 451-8999	25637
Dal-Tile Corporation	5032	D	858 571-0283	6886
Dart Neuroscience LLC	8731	C	858 736-3060	26352
Davenport Development Corp	1752	E	858 300-3333	3099
Davis Trucking LLC (PA)	4212	E	619 229-9997	3999
Daw Industries Inc	5099	E	858 622-4955	8026
Daybreak Game Company LLC	7371	B	858 239-0500	15095
Daymark Realty Advisors Inc	6531	B	714 975-2999	11395
De Anza Campland LLC (PA)	7033	D	858 581-4200	13464
De Anza Land & Leisure Corp	7832	E	619 423-2727	18284
Decisionlogic LLC	7372	D	858 586-0202	15645
Defenseweb Technologies Inc	7379	D	858 272-8505	16343
Dehart Inc	1799	D	858 695-0882	3510
Del Rey Systems and Tech Inc (PA)	7379	D	858 874-8992	16344
Delimex Holdings Inc	6719	A	619 210-2700	11974
Deloitte & Touche LLP	8721	C	619 232-6500	26178
Delta Dental of California	6324	B	619 683-2549	10199
Delta-T Group LLC	8082	C	619 543-0556	22283
Dentons US LLP	8111	D	619 595-5400	23032
Dentons US LLP	8111	B	619 236-1414	23033
Diamondrock San Dego Tnant LLC	7011	C	619 239-4500	12522
Dietz Glmor Chazen A Prof Corp (PA)	8111	E	858 565-0269	23039
Digitalmojo Inc (PA)	4813	D	800 413-5916	5548
Dimension Development Two LLC	7011	D	619 233-8408	12523
Dimension Development Two LLC	7011	D	858 485-9250	12524
Directions In Research Inc (PA)	8732	B	619 299-5883	26511
Distinctive Concrete Inc	1771	E	858 277-9707	3249
Dla Piper LLP (us)	8111	C	619 699-2700	23048
Dla Piper LLP (us)	8111	C	858 677-1400	23049
DMS Facility Services LLC	8711	C	858 560-4191	25645
Dollar Thrifty Auto Group Inc	7514	A	619 298-7635	17630
Donahue Schriber Rlty Group LP	6512	C	858 793-5757	10872
Doubletree By Hilton Hotel	7011	D	619 881-6900	12540
Downtown San Diego Partnr Inc (PA)	8611	C	619 234-0201	24953
Downtown San Diego Partnr Inc	8611	D	619 234-8400	24954
Dpr Construction Inc	1541	B	858 646-0757	1394
DR Systems Inc	8071	C	858 625-3344	22079
Drain Patrol	1711	D	858 560-1137	2189
Dreamscape Ldscp & Maint Inc	0781	E	619 583-4439	751
Duckor Spradling Metzger	8111	D	619 209-3000	23057
Dynalectric Company	1731	D	858 712-4700	2566
Dyncorp	7373	C	619 522-2222	15948
Ealliant LLC	8748	E	619 255-9344	27710
Eastern Goldfields Inc	8742	C	619 497-2555	27222
Eastrdge Prsonnel of Las Vegas (PA)	7361	E	619 260-2000	14608
Edaw Inc	0781	D	619 233-1454	752
Edf Msschstts Spnsor Mmber LLC	4911	A	888 903-6926	6029
Edf Renewables Inc (PA)	1711	C	858 521-3300	2197
Edf Renewables Services Inc (HQ)	7539	D	858 521-3575	17794
Edf Rnwbles Asset Holdings Inc	4911	A	888 903-6926	6030
Edmin Open Systems Inc (PA)	7379	D	858 712-9341	16355
Edwards Theatres Circuit Inc	7832	D	858 635-7716	18291
Einstein Industries Inc	7371	C	858 459-1182	15130
Elavon Inc	7375	A	954 776-7990	16221
Electra Owners Assoc	8611	C	619 236-3310	24955
Elevate Credit Inc	6141	C	817 928-1500	9710
Elite Maintenance Services Inc	7349	D	619 516-7000	14257
Elite Show Services Inc	7381	A	619 574-1589	16639
Elk Hills Power LLC	4911	C	661 763-2730	6035
Embassy Suites Management LLC	7011	C	858 453-0400	12557
Emcor Fclities Svcs N Amer Inc	1711	C	858 712-4700	2199
Emerald Connect LLC (HQ)	7374	D	800 233-2834	16122
Emerald Textiles LLC	7211	B	619 330-7077	13486
Emeritus Corporation	8051	E	858 292-8044	20391
Employment & Community Options	8331	C	858 565-9870	24181
Empyr Incorporated	7299	C	888 664-5669	13742
Encore Capital Group Inc (PA)	6153	D	877 445-4581	9738
Encore Semi Inc	8711	C	858 225-4993	25660
Engility LLC	8711	C	858 552-9500	25665
Enginring Sftwr Sys Sltons Inc (PA)	8711	D	619 338-0380	25667
Enterprise Rent-A-Car	7514	C	619 297-0311	17634
Enterprise Services LLC	7374	B	619 817-3851	16126
Envoy Air Inc	4581	E	619 260-9069	4888
Epic Sciences Inc	8071	D	858 356-6610	22083
Epicenter Live Inc	7922	C	424 235-4835	18366
Eplica Inc (PA)	7363	C	619 260-2000	14850
Epsilon Mission Solutions Inc	8711	D	619 702-1700	25672
Epsilon Systems Solutions Inc	8711	D	619 702-1700	25673
Epsilon Systems Solutions Inc (PA)	8711	D	619 702-1700	25674
Equitable Variable Lf Insur Co	6311	D	619 239-0018	10134
Ernst & Young LLP	8721	C	858 535-7200	26196
Escalate Inc (DH)	7371	B	858 457-3888	15144
Eset LLC (HQ)	5045	C	619 876-5400	7046
Esquire Landscape Inc	0782	E	858 530-2949	838
Etc Building & Design Inc (PA)	7389	C	858 554-1150	17156
Evergreen Distributors Inc (PA)	0181	E	858 481-0622	257
Evotek Inc (PA)	7379	D	858 362-5083	16363
EW Scripps Company	4833	D	619 237-1010	5790
Examone World Wide Inc	8099	D	619 299-3926	22802

Employment Codes: A=Over 500 employees, B=251-500,
C=101-250, D=51-100, E=50

2019 Directory of California
Wholesalers and Services Companies

© Mergent Inc. 1-800-342-5647

1655

GEOGRAPHIC

Company	SIC	EMP	PHONE	ENTRY #
Exp US Services Inc	8711	D	858 597-0555	25677
Expeditors Intl Wash Inc	4731	D	619 710-1900	5059
Exprescom LLC	5064	D	619 271-0531	7414
EZ Acceptance Inc	7359	C	858 278-8351	14504
Fairfield Development Inc (PA)	1522	D	858 457-2123	1284
Faith Jones & Associates Inc (PA)	8082	D	619 297-9601	22296
Falconwood Inc	7378	D	619 297-9080	16285
Family Hlth Ctrs San Diego Inc (PA)	8093	D	619 515-2303	22577
Federal Dfenders San Diego Inc (PA)	8111	D	619 234-8467	23063
Federal Express Corporation	4513	C	800 463-3339	4818
Federal Express Corporation	4731	C	800 463-3339	5063
Fedex Freight Corporation	4213	D	619 710-0268	4155
Fedex Ground Package Sys Inc	4215	C	800 463-3339	4415
Fedex Ground Package Sys Inc	4513	C	800 463-3339	4838
Fenton Scripps Landing LLC	6513	D	858 586-0206	11018
Ferguson Enterprises Inc	5074	C	619 515-0300	7620
Ferring Research Institute Inc	8731	D	858 657-1400	26365
Fieno Inc	0723	D	760 352-2996	515
Figi Acquisition Company LLC	5199	C	800 678-3444	9216
Firemans Fund Insurance Co	6331	C	858 492-3019	10353
First Allied Securities Inc (PA)	6211	D	619 702-9600	9951
First American Title Insur Co	6361	D	619 238-1776	10456
First National Bank (PA)	6733	D	619 233-5588	12095
First Republic Bank	6022	C	619 238-9088	9456
Firstat Nursing Services Inc	8082	C	619 220-7600	22298
Fish & Richardson PC	8111	C	858 678-5070	23070
Fitness International LLC	7991	E	858 550-5912	18602
Five Star Quality Care Inc	8051	B	858 673-6300	20433
Foley & Lardner LLP	8111	D	858 847-6700	23077
Forensic Analytical	8748	D	858 859-3322	27730
Forward Slope Incorporated	8711	D	619 299-4400	25691
Foshay Electric Coinc	1731	C	858 277-7676	2588
Foster Wheeler Energy Svcs Inc	1796	E	800 500-1993	3470
Fragomen Del Rey Bernse	8111	D	858 793-1600	23080
Frank Sciarrino Marble G	5032	D	858 695-8030	6892
Friends Chbad Lbvtch San Diego (PA)	8322	E	619 265-7700	23815
Front Porch Communities	6513	B	858 274-4110	11023
Fuji Food Products Inc	5149	C	619 268-3118	8793
G & L Penasquitos Inc	8322	D	858 538-0802	23820
G2 Software Systems Inc	8711	D	619 222-8025	25697
G4s Secure Solutions USA Inc	7381	C	619 295-2394	16655
G5 Global Partners Ix LLC	7011	D	619 291-6500	12595
G7 Productivity Systems	7372	D	858 675-1095	15688
Gafcon Inc (PA)	8741	D	858 875-0010	26866
Garich Inc (PA)	7361	B	858 453-1331	14624
Garrad Hassan America Inc (DH)	8711	D	858 836-3370	25699
Gary R Edwards Inc	7389	D	619 299-8700	17180
Gaslamp Hotel Management Inc	7011	C	619 234-0977	12598
General Atomics (HQ)	8731	A	858 455-2810	26370
General Atomics	8731	D	858 676-7100	26371
General Atomics	8731	C	858 455-4000	26372
General Coatings Corporation (PA)	1721	C	858 587-1277	2439
General Dynamics Info Tech Inc	7379	E	619 881-8989	16383
Genesis Healthcare Partners PC	8093	C	619 230-0400	22581
Genesis Healthcare Partners PC (PA)	8093	C	858 810-7200	22582
Genomedx Biosciences Corp	8071	D	888 975-4540	22089
Gentry Associates LLC	7011	D	619 296-0057	12601
Geocon Consultants Inc (PA)	8748	C	858 558-6900	27737
Geocon Incorporated	8711	D	858 558-6900	25709
Gerdau Reinforcing Steel (DH)	1541	E	858 737-7700	1401
Gerwend Enterprises Inc	8744	C	619 254-5018	27591
Girl Scts Sn Diego-Imprl Cncl (PA)	8641	C	619 610-0751	25163
Gkk Corporation	8712	D	619 398-0215	26049
Glenn A Rick Engrg & Dev Co (PA)	8711	C	619 291-0708	25715
Global Dev Strategies Inc	7699	D	858 408-1173	17948
Gmg Stone Inc	1743	E	619 258-6899	2999
GMI Building Services Inc	7349	C	858 279-6262	14281
Gms Janitorial Services Inc	7349	D	858 569-6009	14282
Goforth & Marti (PA)	5021	D	951 684-0870	6723
Gold Coast Design Inc	1721	D	619 574-0111	2443
Golden Eagle Insurance Corp (DH)	6331	C	619 744-6000	10357
Golden Hour Data Systems Inc	4731	C	858 768-2500	5077
Goodman Manufacturing Co LP	5075	B	858 569-1715	7650
Gordon Rees Sclly Mnskhani LLP	8111	D	619 696-6700	23108
Gordon Rees Sclly Mnskhani LLP	8111	D	415 986-5900	23109
Grand Del Mar Resort LP	7011	A	858 314-2000	12612
Grant Thornton LLP	8721	C	858 704-8000	26210
Great Western Wind Energy LLC	4911	A	888 903-6926	6039
Greater San Diego AC Co Inc	1711	C	619 469-7818	2223
Greencycle US Holding Inc (DH)	6719	D	858 677-0884	11984
Greenwood Holdings LLC	7011	D	619 299-6633	12620
Gringteam Inc	7011	C	858 485-4145	12621
Gringteam Inc	7011	B	619 297-5466	12628
Grisworld Real Estate MGT (PA)	6531	D	858 597-6100	11493
GS Levine Insurance Svcs Inc	6411	D	858 481-8692	10639
Guaranteed Rate Inc	6162	C	760 310-6008	9812
Guard Management Inc	7381	A	858 279-8282	16667
Guardsmark LLC	7381	C	858 499-0025	16686
H & R Accounts Inc	7371	D	619 819-8844	15195
H C T Inc	7011	B	619 224-1234	12633
Hampstead Lafayette Hotel LLC	7011	E	619 296-2101	12637
Handlery Hotels Inc	7011	C	415 781-4550	12640
Harbor View Hotel Ventures LLC	7011	D	619 239-6800	12643
Harmonium Inc (PA)	8351	C	858 684-3080	24326
Harper Construction Co Inc (PA)	1542	C	619 233-7900	1542
Harper Mechanical Contrs LLC	5046	C	619 543-1296	7136
Harte-Hnks Mkt Intlligence Inc (PA)	7374	C	858 450-1667	16141
Harvey Inc	1542	C	858 769-4000	1544
Havas Formula LLC	8743	D	619 234-0345	27555
Hawthorne Machinery Co (PA)	7353	C	858 674-7000	14442
Hawthorne Machinery Co (HQ)	7353	C	858 674-7000	14443
Hawthorne Machinery Co	7538	D	858 674-7000	17767
Hawthorne Machinery Co	5082	C	858 974-6800	7677
Hazard Construction Company	1622	A	858 587-3600	1881
HDR Engineering Inc	8711	D	619 231-4865	25727
HDR Engineering Inc	8742	E	858 712-8400	27258
HDR Environmental Ope	8712	D	858 712-8400	26056
Health Source Staffing Inc	8082	D	619 220-8044	22314
Healthstream Inc	7372	B	800 733-8737	15702
HEI Mission Valley LP	7011	C	619 299-2729	12653
Hensel Phelps Construction Co	1542	D	858 266-7979	1549
Herring Broadcasting Company	4833	E	858 270-6900	5798
Herring Networks Inc	4833	C	858 270-6900	5799
Herzog Contracting Corp	1799	A	619 849-6990	3532
HG Fenton Company	6513	D	619 400-0120	11030
Hhlp San Diego Lessee LLC	7011	C	619 446-3000	12655
Hibrid Home LLC	1711	C	844 442-7431	2227
Higgs Fletcher & Mack Llp	8111	C	619 236-1551	23129
High Ridge Wind LLC	4911	A	888 903-6926	6042
Historical Properties Inc (PA)	7011	D	619 230-8417	12672
Hit Portfolio I Misc Trs LLC	7011	C	619 849-1234	12684
Hitachi Vantara Corporation	5045	C	858 537-3000	7056
Hob Entertainment LLC	7929	C	619 299-2583	18438
Holiday Inn Rncho Bernardo LLC	7011	D	858 485-6530	12693
Home Instead Senior Care	8082	D	858 277-3722	22325
Hornblower Yachts Inc	4489	C	619 686-8700	4717
Hornblower Yachts Inc	8742	C	619 234-8687	27265
Host Hotels & Resorts Inc	7011	C	619 232-1234	12702
Host Hotels & Resorts LP	7011	D	619 692-3800	12704
Host Hotels & Resorts LP	7011	D	619 291-2900	12707
Host International Inc	7011	C	619 231-5100	12717
Hotel Circle Inn & Suites	7011	E	619 851-6800	12719
Hotel Circle Property LLC	7011	B	619 291-7131	12720
Hotel Managers Group Llc	8741	C	858 673-1534	26887
Hoya Corporation	5048	C	858 309-6050	7235
HP Capital LLC	8742	D	858 753-8486	27266
Hronopoulos	8741	C	619 237-6161	26888
Hst Lessee Boston LLC	7011	C	619 692-2255	12739
Hst Lessee San Diego LP	7011	B	619 291-2900	12740
Hudson Ranch Power I LLC	4911	A	858 509-0150	6043
Huntleigh USA Corporation	4581	D	619 231-8111	4893
Hyatt Hotels Management Corp	7011	B	858 552-1234	12752
Icw Group Holdings Inc (PA)	6331	C	858 350-2400	10362
Icw Valencia LLC	6512	D	858 350-2600	10898
ID Analytics LLC	7382	C	858 312-6200	16904
Idun Pharmaceuticals Inc	8733	C	858 622-3000	26624
Igo Medical Group A Med Corp (PA)	8011	D	858 455-7520	19508
Iheartcommunications Inc	4832	B	858 522-5547	5724
Iheartcommunications Inc	4832	D	858 292-2000	5725
Imageware Systems Inc (PA)	7372	D	858 673-8600	15708
Imaging Hlthcare Spcalists LLC	8734	C	619 229-2299	26705
Imaging Hlthcare Spcalists LLC (PA)	8011	D	619 295-9729	19509
IMS Recycling Services Inc (PA)	4953	D	619 231-2521	6407
Independa Inc	7373	E	800 815-7829	15977
Independent Options Inc	8361	C	858 598-5260	24568
Indevia Accounting Inc	8721	C	858 450-2981	26227
Indus Technology Inc	8711	C	619 299-2555	25742
Indyme Solutions LLC	8999	E	858 268-0717	27933
Ingenium Technologies Corp	8711	D	858 227-4422	25746
Innovasystems Intl LLC	7371	C	619 955-5890	15215
Innovasystems Intl LLC (PA)	7371	D	619 756-6500	15216
Innovtive Emplyee Slutions Inc	8721	A	858 715-5100	26229
Inova Diagnostics Inc (HQ)	8731	B	858 586-9900	26383
Inseego North America LLC (DH)	7373	D	541 685-9045	15978
Insurance Company of West (HQ)	6331	C	858 350-2400	10363
Integrits Corporation (PA)	7379	E	858 300-1600	16398
Inter Con Security Inc	8742	D	619 523-0291	27277
Interactivate Inc	7379	D	619 814-1999	16400
Intercontinental Hotels Group	7011	D	619 727-4000	12767
Interlab Inc	5049	E	619 302-3095	7244

2019 Directory of California
Wholesalers and Services Companies
(P-0000) Products & Services Section entry number
(PA)=Parent Co (HQ)=Headquarters (DH)=Div Headquarters

Company	SIC	EMP	PHONE	ENTRY #
International Industrial Park	6726	D	858 623-9000	12063
Interntional Pet Sups Dist Inc	5199	D	858 453-7845	9225
Interntnal Rscue Committee Inc	8322	D	619 641-7510	23865
Interstate Btry San Diego Inc	5013	E	858 790-8244	6648
Interstate Electronics Corp	7373	D	858 552-9500	15983
Intertek USA Inc	8734	D	858 558-2599	26708
Intuit Inc	7372	B	858 215-8000	15723
Ips Group Inc (PA)	4899	D	858 404-0607	5984
Iq Pipeline LLC	7363	D	858 483-7400	14865
Isaac Fair Corporation	7371	D	858 369-8000	15238
Iserve Residential Lending LLC	6162	D	858 486-4169	9819
J B Hunt Transport Svcs Inc	4789	B	619 230-0054	5232
J D L Motor Express	4212	D	619 232-6136	4025
J Gelt Corporation	8322	E	619 424-8181	23868
J Harris Sim Inc (PA)	1611	D	858 437-0190	1794
J W Floor Covering Inc (PA)	1752	C	858 536-8565	3111
J5th LLC	7011	D	619 487-1200	12786
Ja Automation & Control LLC	5084	E	619 661-2591	7759
Jackson & Blanc	1711	C	858 831-7900	2241
Jacobs Cshman San Diego Fd Bnk	8322	E	858 527-1419	23869
Jaynes Corporation California	1542	C	619 233-4080	1563
JC Resorts Inn	7011	D	858 487-0700	12788
Jck Hotels LLC	7011	D	858 635-5566	12789
Jetblue Airways Corporation	4512	D	619 725-0807	4788
Jetmore Wind LLC	4911	A	888 903-6926	6045
Jetro Holdings LLC	5046	C	858 564-0466	7139
Jewish Family Svc San Diego (PA)	8322	D	858 637-3000	23876
JM Driver LLC	7371	D	855 596-9832	15243
Joe Canpagna	6531	D	619 222-0555	11532
Johnson Cntrls SEC Sltons LLC	7382	C	561 988-3600	16910
Jones Day Limited Partnership	8111	D	858 314-1200	23153
Jones Sign Co Inc	5046	D	858 569-1400	7141
Jpmorgan Chase Bank Nat Assn	7389	C	858 605-3300	17267
Jr Construction Inc	1542	D	858 505-4760	1568
Juan Lopez	1521	D	619 428-3138	1186
June Group LLC	7363	D	858 450-4290	14867
K Tech Security & Protect Svc	7381	D	619 858-5832	16709
Ka Management Inc	8741	D	858 404-6080	26913
Kaiser Foundation Hospitals	6733	B	619 662-5107	12102
Kaiser Foundation Hospitals	8011	D	619 542-7210	19525
Kaiser Foundation Hospitals	6733	A	619 528-5888	12103
Kaiser Foundation Hospitals	8062	D	619 528-2583	21487
Kaiser Foundation Hospitals	6324	D	619 528-5000	10226
Kaiser Foundation Hospitals	6324	D	619 528-5000	10227
Kaiser Foundation Hospitals	8011	A	858 847-3500	19581
Kaiser Foundation Hospitals	8011	A	858 502-1350	19582
Kaiser Foundation Hospitals	8093	C	858 573-0090	22601
Kaiser Foundation Hospitals	8062	A	619 641-4663	21495
Kaiser Foundation Hospitals	8011	E	858 573-0299	19604
Kalpana LLC	7011	C	619 543-9000	12799
Kbm Fclity Sltons Holdings LLC	7349	B	858 467-0202	14298
Kesari Hospitality LLC	7011	D	619 298-1291	12803
Kforce Inc	7361	C	858 550-1645	14657
Khp II San Diego Hotel LLC (PA)	7011	C	619 515-3000	12807
Kifm Smooth Jazz 981 Inc	4832	C	619 297-3698	5733
Kimball Tirey & St John LLP (PA)	8111	D	619 234-1690	23170
Kimley-Horn and Associates Inc	8711	D	619 234-9411	25780
Kinder Mrgan Lqds Trminals LLC	4922	D	619 283-6511	6151
Kindred Healthcare Oper Inc	8069	C	502 596-7300	22027
Kineticom Inc (PA)	7361	D	619 330-3100	14658
Kings Inn Hotel San Diego	7011	D	619 297-2231	12815
Kintera Inc (HQ)	7372	D	858 795-3000	15730
Kleinfelder Inc (HQ)	8711	C	619 831-4600	25782
Kleinfelder Associates	8748	A	619 831-4600	27765
Knox Attorney Service Inc (PA)	8111	C	619 233-9700	23178
Koam Engineering Systems Inc	7373	C	858 292-0922	15992
Kobey Corporation Inc (PA)	7389	D	619 523-2700	17277
Kone Inc	7699	D	858 578-5100	17960
Kpmg LLP	8721	C	858 750-7100	26237
Kratos Tech Trning Sltions Inc (HQ)	7372	C	858 812-7300	15736
Kros-Wise	8748	C	619 223-1980	27768
Kswb Inc	4833	D	858 492-9269	5815
Kyriba Corp (HQ)	7372	E	858 210-3560	15738
L & W Supply Corporation	5032	E	858 627-0811	6898
L A Swikard Inc	0782	C	858 408-3700	874
L C C H Associates Inc	8059	E	858 565-4424	21131
L3 Technologies Inc	4899	D	858 623-6513	5987
La Jolla Pharmaceutical Co (PA)	8731	C	858 207-4264	26393
La Jolla Village Towers 500	8051	D	858 646-7700	20572
La Maestra Family Clinic Inc	8011	D	619 280-4213	19635
La Maestra Family Clinic Inc	8011	D	619 501-1235	19636
La Maestra Family Clinic Inc (PA)	8011	C	619 584-1612	19637
La Puerta	8641	E	619 696-3466	25183
Laboratory Specialty Gases	5084	D	619 234-6060	7761
Landcare USA LLC	0782	C	858 453-1755	885
Largo Concrete Inc	1521	C	619 356-2142	1191
Lawyers Title Company	6361	D	858 650-3900	10464
Ledcor CMI Inc	1541	D	602 595-3017	1417
Ledcor Management Services Inc	8741	E	858 527-6400	26928
Legal Aid Society of San Diego (PA)	8111	E	619 262-1872	23197
Legal Recovery Law Offices Inc	8111	D	619 275-4001	23198
Leidos Inc	8731	B	858 826-5552	26397
Leidos Inc	8731	C	858 535-4499	26399
Leidos Inc	8731	C	703 676-4300	26400
Leidos Inc	8731	D	858 826-9416	26401
Leidos Inc	8731	D	858 826-6616	26404
Leidos Inc	8731	D	858 826-6000	26407
Leidos Inc	8731	D	858 826-7129	26408
Leidos Engineering LLC	8711	D	858 826-6000	25796
Leidos Engrg & Sciences LLC	8731	D	619 542-3130	26411
Lenore John & Co (PA)	5149	C	619 232-6136	8824
Leonards Carpet Service Inc	1771	E	858 453-9525	3282
Lewis Brsbois Bsgard Smith LLP	8111	D	619 233-1006	23207
Lge Electrical Sales Inc	5063	B	408 379-8568	7371
Lho Mssion Bay Rsie Lessee Inc	7011	B	619 276-4010	12850
Liberty Station Hhg Hotel LP	7011	D	619 221-1900	12853
Liberty Station Hhg Hotel LP	7011	D	619 222-0500	12854
Life Cycle Engineering Inc	7349	D	619 785-5990	14303
Lifetouch Portrait Studios Inc	7221	E	858 693-9197	13642
Lightbridge Hospice LLC	8069	D	858 458-2992	22029
Lincoln Mariners Assoc Ltd	6513	D	619 225-1473	11055
Linda Vista Manor Inc	8051	C	858 278-8121	20593
Lindbergh Parking Inc	7521	C	619 291-1508	17692
Lloyd Pest Control Co (PA)	7342	C	619 298-9865	14152
LLP Moss Adams	8721	D	858 627-1400	26253
Local Media San Diego LLC	4832	D	858 888-7000	5743
Locator Services Inc	7381	D	619 229-6100	16720
Lockheed Martin Orincon Corp (HQ)	7371	C	858 455-5530	15262
Locums Unlimited LLC	8049	B	619 550-3763	20189
Lodge At Torrey Pines Partners	7011	B	858 550-3908	12908
Logility Inc	7371	D	858 565-4238	15263
Loma Riviera Community Assn	8641	D	619 224-1313	25192
Loomis Armored Us LLC	7381	D	619 232-5106	16722
Lpl Holdings Inc (HQ)	6211	D	858 450-9606	9972
Luth Research Inc (PA)	8732	B	619 234-5884	26541
Lynup Corporation	8742	D	858 207-4610	27309
M4dev LLC	7011	D	619 696-6300	12867
Mabie Marketing Group Inc	7389	C	858 279-5585	17306
Magnesite Specialties Inc	1752	E	858 578-4186	3113
Magnus Security	7381	E	619 546-7789	16727
Management Trust Assn Inc	6733	C	858 547-4373	12113
Manas Hospitality LLC	7011	E	619 298-1291	12873
Manchester Grand Resorts LP	7011	A	619 232-1234	12874
Mantech International Corp	7373	C	858 492-9938	16001
Mantech Systems Engrg Corp	8748	D	858 292-9000	27781
Mapp Digital Us LLC	8742	D	619 295-1856	27316
Marika Group Inc	5137	C	858 537-5300	8319
Marine Band San Diego	7929	C	619 524-1754	18451
Marriott International Inc	7011	D	858 523-1700	12883
Marriott International Inc	7011	D	619 831-0225	12886
Marriott International Inc	7011	D	858 587-1770	12893
Marriott International Inc	7011	C	858 278-2100	12903
Marriott International Inc	7011	D	619 831-0224	12909
Marsh & McLennan Agency LLC	6411	C	858 457-3414	10681
Martinez Farms Inc	0181	B	619 661-6571	282
Mason-West Inc	5084	E	619 226-8253	7767
MAT Parcel Express Inc (PA)	4212	D	619 849-9600	4039
Mbp Land LLC	7011	D	619 291-5720	12917
McAfee Inc	7372	D	858 967-2342	15749
McKesson Ptent Care Sltons Inc (HQ)	8099	D	412 507-0077	22837
McKinnon Broadcasting Company (HQ)	4833	C	858 571-5151	5823
McKinnon Publishing Company	4833	A	858 571-5151	5824
McKowskis Maint Systems Inc	7349	D	619 269-4600	14316
McMillin Communities Inc (PA)	6799	D	619 561-5275	12244
McMillin Companies LLC (PA)	6799	D	619 477-4117	12245
McMillin Construction Svcs LP	1521	E	619 477-4170	1200
McMillin Management Svcs LP (HQ)	6722	C	619 477-4117	12042
MCR Printing and Packg Corp	4225	C	619 488-3012	4592
Mea Digital Worx LLC	7311	E	619 238-8923	13863
Meals-On-Wheels Grtr Sn Diego (PA)	8322	C	619 260-6110	23918
Media All Stars Inc	7389	D	858 300-9600	17317
Medical Management Cons Inc	8742	A	858 587-0609	27332
Medical Transcription Billing	7372	A	800 869-3700	15755
Medimpact Hlthcare Systems Inc (HQ)	8621	A	858 566-2727	25027
Meeting Services Inc	7359	D	858 348-0100	14525
Merchants Building Maint Co	7349	B	858 455-0163	14319
Mercury Insurance Company	6331	C	858 694-4100	10378
Meridian Rack & Pinion Inc	5013	D	858 587-8777	6657
Merit Technologies LLC	8742	D	858 623-9800	27341
Merrill Gardens LLC	6513	D	619 961-4990	11069

Employment Codes: A=Over 500 employees, B=251-500, C=101-250, D=51-100, E=50

2019 Directory of California
Wholesalers and Services Companies

© Mergent Inc. 1-800-342-5647

1657

GEOGRAPHIC

Company	SIC	EMP	PHONE	ENTRY #
Merrill Lynch Pierce Fenner	6211	C	619 699-3700	9984
Merritt Hawkins & Assoc LLC (HQ)	7363	C	858 792-0711	14883
Merry X-Ray Chemical Corp (PA)	5047	C	858 565-4472	7192
Message Center Communication	7389	E	858 974-7419	17327
Messenger Express	4215	D	858 550-1400	4425
Metron Incorporated	8742	E	858 792-8904	27343
Metropolitan Area Advisory Com	8331	B	619 255-7284	24205
MHS Customer Service Inc	7361	D	858 695-2151	14668
Michael Baker Intl Inc	8748	D	858 453-3602	27787
Michael S Duffy Sr Do Inc	8011	D	619 461-3717	19688
Microconstants Inc	8731	E	858 652-4600	26417
Microsoft Corporation	7372	D	619 849-5872	15760
Midland Credit Management Inc (HQ)	6153	A	877 240-2377	9742
Millennium Health LLC (PA)	8734	B	877 451-3534	26714
Milo Wind Project LLC	4911	D	888 903-6926	6053
Mintz Levin Cohn Ferris GL	8111	D	858 314-1500	23256
Miramar Ford Truck Sales Inc	5012	D	619 272-5340	6604
Miramar Transportation Inc	4731	D	858 693-0071	5112
Mirnavseh Inc	7371	D	858 335-2470	15284
Mirum Inc	7336	C	619 237-5552	14121
Mission Federal Credit Union (PA)	6061	A	858 546-2184	9571
Mission Federal Services LLC (PA)	6061	C	858 524-2850	9572
Mission Hills Healthcare Inc	8051	D	619 297-4086	20646
Mission Hills Post Acute Care	8361	D	619 297-4484	24601
Mission Valley Ht Operator Inc	7011	D	619 291-5720	12932
Mission Valley Hts Surgery Ctr	8011	D	619 291-3737	19695
Mitchell International Inc (HQ)	7371	C	858 368-7000	15286
Mlim Holdings LLC	6719	A	619 299-3131	11994
Molecular Bioproducts Inc (DH)	4953	C	858 453-7551	6420
Molina Healthcare Inc	8099	B	858 614-1580	22841
Mopar Enterprises	7331	D	858 492-1123	14055
Morgan Stanley	6211	E	858 597-7777	9993
Morgan Stanley & Co LLC	6211	D	619 236-1331	9998
Morrison & Foerster LLP	8111	C	858 720-5100	23267
Mosaic	8741	D	858 397-2261	26953
Motorola Mobility LLC	5065	D	858 455-1500	7512
Mr Copy Inc (DH)	5044	D	858 573-6300	6970
Mufg Union Bank National Assn	6021	D	619 230-4666	9357
Multimodal Esquer Inc	4213	D	619 710-0477	4232
Musicmatch Inc	7372	C	858 485-4300	15771
My Office Inc	1799	D	858 549-6700	3555
Narven Enterprises Inc	7011	C	619 239-2261	12950
National Air Inc	1711	C	619 299-2500	2289
National Railroad Pass Corp	4011	D	619 239-9989	3621
Nationl Medcl Assn Comp Health	8093	D	619 231-9300	22622
Naval Coating Inc	1799	C	619 234-8366	3556
Naval Fac Eng Cmmd SW Wrkng CA	8711	D	619 532-1158	25844
Neighborhood House Association	8351	D	619 262-8199	24352
Neighborhood House Association (PA)	8322	B	858 715-2642	23930
Neighborhood House Association	8322	E	619 527-1287	23931
Neighborhood House Association	8322	D	619 263-7761	23932
Neil Dymott Frank McFall	8111	C	619 238-1712	23283
Nestwise LLC	7389	B	855 444-6378	17347
New Bi US Gaming LLC	7372	D	858 592-2472	15778
New Day Staffing Inc	7363	C	619 481-5400	14887
New Way Landscape & Tree Svcs	0782	C	858 505-8300	909
New York Life Insurance Co	6411	C	858 623-8600	10711
Newland Group Inc (PA)	6552	E	858 455-7503	11897
Newland Real Estate Group LLC (HQ)	6282	D	858 455-7503	10098
Next Image Medical Inc (PA)	8742	D	858 847-9185	27367
Nielsen Claritas Inc	7371	B	858 622-0800	15310
Nielsen Company (us) LLC	8732	C	858 677-9542	26551
Ninyo & Moore Geotechnical (PA)	8748	D	858 576-1000	27802
Nnj Services Inc	6531	C	858 550-7900	11632
Noiro West LLC	7011	C	619 819-6620	12961
Norman Industrial Mtls Inc	5051	E	858 277-8200	7294
Northrop Grumman Systems Corp	7371	B	858 514-0400	15315
Northrop Grumman Systems Corp	8731	A	858 592-3000	26424
Novartis Institut	8733	D	858 812-1976	26643
Nphase LLC	4899	D	312 577-1650	5989
Ntrepid Corporation	8741	D	800 921-2414	26966
Ntrepid LLC	7379	D	858 866-1309	16436
Nu Flow America Inc (PA)	1711	D	619 275-9130	2291
Nurlogic Design Inc (DH)	7373	D	858 455-7570	16022
Nursefinders LLC (HQ)	7361	C	858 314-7427	14677
Nv5 Inc	8711	C	858 385-0500	25850
Oak Valley Hotel LLC	7011	D	619 297-1101	12967
Oasis Repower LLC	4911	A	888 903-6926	6064
Odyssey Healthcare Inc	8082	D	858 565-2499	22378
Old Globe Theatre	7922	B	619 234-5623	18390
Old Town Fmly Hospitality Corp	7011	C	619 246-8010	12977
Old Town Trlley Turs San Diego	4725	D	619 298-8687	4974
Olivermcmillan LLC (DH)	6552	D	619 321-1111	11901
Omni Hotels Corporation	7011	B	619 231-6664	12982
Onsolve LLC	7371	C	858 724-1200	15329
Operation Samahan Inc	8011	C	619 477-4451	19737
Oracle America Inc	7372	D	858 625-5044	15796
Oracle Corporation	7372	C	858 202-0648	15804
Organovo Holdings Inc (PA)	8731	D	858 224-1000	26426
Overseas Service Corporation	8999	C	858 408-0751	27950
P & A Holdings Inc (PA)	6712	C	619 233-3522	11957
P J J Enterprises Inc	7359	D	619 232-6136	14532
Pacific Building Group	1742	D	858 552-0600	2931
Pacific Building Group (PA)	1542	C	858 552-0600	1606
Pacific Event Productions Inc (PA)	7299	C	858 458-9908	13761
Pacific Gas Turbine Center LLC	7699	C	858 877-2910	17968
Pacific Marine Dev Corp	8711	E	760 593-9138	25861
Pacific Medical Buildings LP	6531	D	858 794-1900	11647
Pacific Rim Mech Contrs Inc (PA)	1711	B	858 974-6500	2304
Pacific Western Bank	6021	D	858 436-3500	9365
Pacifica Companies LLC (PA)	6798	D	619 296-9000	12178
Pacifica Health and Medical	7299	C	619 688-1848	13762
Pacifica Hotel Company	7011	C	619 221-8000	13008
Pacifica Katie Avenue LLC	8732	D	619 296-9000	26556
Pacifica San Jose LP	7011	D	619 296-9000	13010
Pacira Pharmaceuticals Inc	5122	B	858 625-2424	8202
Packard Hospitality Group LLC	8741	C	858 277-4305	26975
Packetvideo Corporation (DH)	7371	D	858 731-5300	15341
Padres LP	7941	A	619 795-5000	18530
Pan Pcfic Htels Rsrts Amer Inc	7011	B	619 239-4500	13016
Pan-Pacific Mechanical LLC	1711	C	858 764-2464	2307
Panasonic Corp North America	5064	E	619 661-1134	7423
Panasonic Corp North America	5064	E	619 661-1134	7425
Paradigm Information Services	8999	D	858 693-6115	27952
Paradise Lessee Inc	7011	B	858 274-4630	13017
Paramount Export Company	5148	D	858 452-8101	8716
Pardee Homes	6552	E	858 259-6390	11904
Parenthood of Planned (PA)	8093	D	619 881-4500	22634
Park Hotels & Resorts Inc	7011	B	619 276-4010	13021
Parma Management Co Inc	6531	C	858 457-4999	11663
Parpro Holdings Co Ltd	6719	C	619 498-9004	11999
Parsons Government Svcs Inc	8711	B	619 685-0085	25869
Partners Risk Specialists	8999	E	619 326-0840	27953
Patenaude & Felix A Prof Corp (PA)	8111	D	858 244-7600	23312
Patientsafe Solutions Inc (PA)	7371	D	858 746-3100	15345
Paul Hastings LLP	8111	D	858 458-3000	23317
Paxvax Inc	8731	E	858 450-9595	26434
Paychex Inc	8721	D	858 547-2920	26266
Paychex Benefit Tech Inc	4813	C	800 322-7292	5622
Payrollingcom Corp	8721	E	858 866-2626	26269
Pbp Hotel LLC	6552	D	619 881-6900	11906
PCI Collections Inc	7322	B	619 595-3114	14015
Perfect Bar LLC	5149	D	866 628-8548	8852
Petco Animal Supplies Inc (DH)	0752	B	858 453-7845	632
Petti Kohn Ingrassia & L P R Co	8111	D	310 649-5772	23326
Phamatech Incorporated	8734	C	858 643-5555	26727
Pharmerica Long-Term Care LLC	5122	C	858 537-9374	8204
Phone Ware Inc	7389	B	858 530-8550	17399
Physician Management Group Inc	8741	C	858 309-6300	26985
Pinnacle 1617 LLC	7011	E	619 239-9600	13065
Piveg Inc	5141	C	858 436-3070	8445
Pivot Technology Solutions Ltd	7379	A	647 788-2034	16455
Plaza Home Mortgage Inc (PA)	6162	E	858 346-1200	9846
Point Loma Convalescent Hosp	8051	C	619 224-4141	20709
Point Loma Rhblitation Ctr LLC	8051	C	619 224-4141	20710
Polexis Inc	7371	D	858 812-7300	15369
Polypeptide Labs San Diego LLC	8731	D	858 408-0808	26439
Poor Sisters of Nazareth of SA	8361	D	619 563-0480	24632
Pre Con Industries Inc	1742	D	805 928-3397	2939
Precision Toxicology LLC	8071	D	800 635-6901	22124
Predicate Logic Inc (PA)	8711	D	858 715-0100	25878
Preferred Employers Insur Co	6411	D	619 688-3900	10736
Preferred Hlthcare Rgistry Inc	7361	C	800 787-6787	14697
Preferred Valet Parking LLC	7521	E	619 233-7275	17702
Premier Dealer Services Inc	6411	D	858 810-1700	10737
Premier Hlthcare Solutions Inc	8741	B	858 569-8629	26991
Premier Management Company	8082	E	619 582-5168	22397
Presidio Components Inc	5065	C	858 578-9390	7525
Pricewaterhousecoopers LLP	8721	D	858 677-2400	26276
Pro Specialties Group Inc	5199	D	858 541-1100	9252
Professional Maint Systems Inc	7349	A	619 276-1150	14358
Progenity Inc (PA)	8071	C	760 494-1555	22126
Progressive Computing LLC	7371	D	858 707-0707	15381
Project Concern International (PA)	8611	C	858 279-9690	24974
Project Design Consultants	8748	D	619 235-6471	27828
Project Management Institute	8741	C	760 458-6198	27000
Property Management Cons (PA)	6531	E	858 485-9811	11689
Propulsion Controls Engrg (PA)	7699	D	619 235-0961	17974
Protec Association Services (PA)	7349	C	858 569-1080	14360
Psychiatric Ctrs At San Diego (PA)	8011	D	619 528-4600	19802

Mergent email: customerrelations@mergent.com

1658

2019 Directory of California
Wholesalers and Services Companies

(P-0000) Products & Services Section entry number
(PA)=Parent Co (HQ)=Headquarters (DH)=Div Headquarters

Company	SIC	EMP	PHONE	ENTRY #
Ptac Carmel Valley Mid School	8641	D	858 481-8221	25222
Qualcomm International Inc (HQ)	6794	A	858 587-1121	12140
Quality Claims Management Corp	6411	D	619 450-8600	10752
Quality Loan Service Corp	6733	B	619 645-7711	12125
Quality Plus Auto Parts Inc	5013	E	619 424-9991	6667
Quartus Engineering Inc (PA)	8711	D	858 875-6000	25882
R & V Management Corporation	8741	D	619 429-3305	27007
Radiation Medical Group Inc (PA)	8011	E	619 220-4100	19812
Rady Childrens Hosp & Hlth Ctr (PA)	8069	A	858 576-1700	22040
Rady Chld Hospital-San Diego	8069	A	858 966-6795	22041
Rady Chld Hospital-San Diego (HQ)	8062	A	858 576-1700	21681
Rady Chld Hospital-San Diego	8741	D	858 966-5833	27010
Rain Bird Corporation	4971	D	619 661-4493	6563
Rancho Bernardo Golf Club	7997	D	858 487-1134	19007
Rancho Bernardo Partners Ltd	7011	D	858 451-6600	13099
Randstad Technologies LP	7379	D	619 798-7300	16470
Raphaels Party Rentals Inc (PA)	7359	C	858 444-1692	14540
Raytheon Company	8711	C	858 455-9741	25890
RB Anglers Club	7997	D	858 487-6484	19010
Reading International Inc	7832	D	858 207-2606	18314
Real Time Logic Inc	7373	D	858 812-7300	16042
Realtor Sfr Green	6531	E	858 488-4090	11718
Recon Environmental Inc (PA)	8748	D	619 308-9333	27839
Redwood Bridge Club	7999	D	619 296-4274	19224
Redwood Healthcare Staffing	7363	D	619 238-4180	14901
Regency Hill Associates	6513	D	619 281-5200	11107
Regulus Therapeutics Inc	8733	D	858 202-6300	26654
Relational Investors LLC	6282	D	858 704-3333	10108
Relationedge LLC	7375	C	858 451-4665	16244
Renovate America Inc	7371	C	858 605-5333	15404
Renty LLC	4119	E	858 560-0066	3834
Reputation Impression LLC	8742	D	858 633-4500	27422
Rescue Agency Pub Benefit LLC (PA)	7311	D	619 231-7555	13891
Residence Inn By Marriott	7011	D	858 673-1900	13121
Residntial Alzheimers Care Inc	8741	C	858 565-4424	27016
Resort Procomm Inc	8742	D	858 866-6280	27425
Resource Management Group Inc (PA)	4731	D	858 677-0884	5155
Rett Inc	7338	D	619 231-0403	14133
Reuben H Fleet Science Center	8412	C	619 238-1233	24900
Reyes Holdings LLC	6211	B	858 452-2300	10011
Rhino Building Services Inc	7349	C	858 455-1440	14367
Riosoft Holdings Inc	7371	E	858 529-5005	15413
Robbins Geller Rudman Dowd LLP (PA)	8111	B	619 231-1058	23355
Robinsn Clgne Rsn Shpr Dvs Inc	8111	D	619 338-4060	23356
Rokstad Power Corp	5063	E	888 310-8830	7389
Rore Inc (PA)	1542	D	858 404-7393	1636
Rosemont Media LLC	7311	E	858 200-0044	13894
Rossin Steel Inc	5051	C	619 656-9200	7311
Royal Hospitality Incorporated	7011	D	858 278-0800	13143
Rp Scs Wsd Hotel LLC	7011	D	619 398-3020	13144
RPC Old Town Avenue Owner LLC	7011	D	619 299-7400	13146
RPC Old Town Jefferson	7011	D	619 725-4221	13147
Rt Sd-Denver LP	7011	E	858 278-2100	13150
Rural/Metro San Diego Inc	4119	D	619 280-6060	3839
Rx Pro Health LLC	7363	A	858 369-4050	14909
SA Recycling LLC	4953	D	619 238-6740	6455
SA Recycling LLC	4953	D	714 632-2000	6471
Sackett National Holdings Inc	8742	D	866 834-6242	27438
Sadie Rose Baking Co	5149	D	858 831-0290	8864
Salvation Army	8361	D	858 279-1100	24662
Salvation Army	7991	B	619 269-1404	18647
San Dego Cnty Rgnal Arprt Auth (PA)	4581	C	619 400-2400	4907
San Dego Cnty Rgnal Arprt Auth	4581	C	619 400-2404	4908
San Dego Cnvntion Ctr Corp Inc (PA)	6512	D	619 525-5000	10931
San Dego Mrrott Marquis Marina	7011	E	301 380-3000	13167
San Dego Soc of Ntural History	8412	D	619 232-3821	24902
San Diego Arcft Carier Museum	8412	C	619 544-9600	24904
San Diego Assn Governments (PA)	8611	B	619 699-1900	24978
San Diego Blood Bank (PA)	8099	C	619 296-6393	22874
San Diego Car Accident Lawyers	7389	E	858 201-4178	17452
San Diego Cemetery Assn	7261	D	858 453-2121	13697
San Diego Center For Children (PA)	8059	D	858 277-9550	21203
San Diego Community Hsing Corp	8748	C	619 527-4633	27852
San Diego Composites Inc	8711	D	858 751-0450	25902
San Diego County Credit Union (PA)	6062	C	877 732-2848	9649
San Diego County Employees Ret	8631	D	619 515-6800	25076
San Diego County Water Auth (PA)	4941	B	858 522-6600	6301
San Diego Diagnstc Radlgy Medi (PA)	8011	D	858 565-6328	19841
San Diego Family Care (PA)	8011	D	858 279-0925	19842
San Diego Family Care	8099	D	619 563-0250	22877
San Diego Family Housing LLC	8699	B	858 874-8100	25455
San Diego Farah Partners	7011	E	619 239-2261	13168
San Diego Gas & Electric Co (DH)	4931	C	619 696-2000	6186
San Diego Gas & Electric Co	4939	C	619 699-1018	6203
San Diego Gulls Hockey CLB LLC	7999	D	619 359-4700	19229
San Diego Hbr Excursions Inc	1629	D	619 234-4111	2059
San Diego Hospice	8082	A	619 688-1600	22410
San Diego Hotel Company LLC	7011	C	619 696-0234	13169
San Diego Hotel Lease LLC	7011	C	619 446-3000	13170
San Diego Humane Soc & Spca	8699	D	619 299-7012	25456
San Diego Imaging - Chula Vist (PA)	8011	D	858 565-0950	19843
San Diego Land Systems	0781	E	858 558-0542	784
San Diego Lesbian Gay Bisexu	8322	E	619 692-2077	24011
San Diego Lessee LLC	7011	C	619 297-5466	13171
San Diego Med Svcs Entp LLC	4119	B	619 280-6060	3840
San Diego Messenger Inc	4215	E	858 514-8866	4429
San Diego Metro Trnst Sys	4111	A	619 231-1466	3702
San Diego Metropolitan Cr Un (PA)	6062	D	619 297-4835	9650
San Diego Museum of Art	8412	D	619 696-1971	24905
San Diego Opera Association (PA)	7922	E	619 232-7636	18401
San Diego Orthopaedic Associat	8011	D	619 299-8500	19844
San Diego Pathologists Medical (PA)	8011	C	619 297-4012	19845
San Diego Rescue Mission Inc (PA)	8399	D	619 819-1880	24837
San Diego Sheraton Corporation	7011	A	619 291-6400	13172
San Diego State University	4832	D	619 594-1515	5752
San Diego Symphony Orchestra	7929	D	619 235-0800	18458
San Diego Testing Engineers	8711	D	858 715-5800	25903
San Diego Theatres Inc	6512	C	619 615-4000	10932
San Diego Tourism Authority (PA)	7389	D	619 232-3101	17453
San Diego Transit Corporation (PA)	4111	D	619 238-0100	3703
San Diego Transit Corporation	4111	D	619 238-0100	3704
San Diego Trolley Inc	4111	D	619 595-4933	3705
San Diego Unified Port Dst	4491	D	619 686-6585	4735
San Diego Unified Port Dst (PA)	4491	C	619 686-6200	4736
San Diego Unified School Dst	7349	D	858 627-7130	14375
San Diego Youth Services Inc (PA)	8322	D	619 221-8600	24012
San Diego-Imperial Council (PA)	8641	E	619 294-3806	25235
San Diego-Imperial Counties De (PA)	8322	B	858 576-2996	24014
San Miguel Hospital Assn	8062	D	619 297-2251	21711
Sandm San Dego Mrriott Del Mar	7011	A	858 523-1700	13184
Santaluz Club Inc	7997	C	858 759-3120	19036
Saturn Electric Inc	1731	E	858 271-4100	2723
SC Wright Construction Inc	8711	B	619 698-6909	25904
Scalematrix Holdings Inc	7379	D	888 349-9994	16477
Schmidt Fire Protection Co Inc	1711	D	858 279-6122	2349
Schroff Inc	7629	C	858 740-2400	17909
Science Applications Intl Corp	7379	D	703 676-4300	16478
Science Applications Intl Corp	7373	A	858 826-3061	16045
Science Applications Intl Corp	7373	B	858 826-6000	16046
Scripps Clinic	8062	C	858 794-1250	21725
Scripps Clinic Foundation	8741	A	858 554-9000	27024
Scripps Health	8011	D	858 622-9076	19864
Scripps Health	8062	D	619 294-8111	21727
Scripps Health	8641	C	858 678-6966	25245
Scripps Health	8051	C	858 657-4218	20749
Scripps Health	8062	B	858 271-9770	21728
Scripps Health	8099	B	619 245-2350	22882
Scripps Health (PA)	8062	A	800 727-4777	21732
Scripps Health	8011	B	858 292-4211	19866
Scripps Health	8062	B	619 294-8111	21734
Scripps Health	8082	B	858 764-3000	22412
Scripps Health	8011	B	858 784-5888	19874
Scripps Health	8093	C	858 794-0160	22678
Scripps Mercy Hospital	8062	D	619 294-8111	21739
Scst Inc (PA)	8734	D	619 280-4321	26729
SD Hotel Circle LLC	7011	D	619 881-6800	13196
SD Sports MDCne&fmly Hlth Cntr	8011	D	619 229-3910	19875
SD Stadium Hotel LLC	7011	D	858 278-9300	13197
SE San Diego Hotel LLC	7011	D	619 515-3000	13198
SE Scher Corporation	7361	D	858 546-8300	14755
Seacoast Commerce Bank (HQ)	6022	D	858 432-7000	9486
Sealaska Envmtl Svcs LLC	8748	D	619 564-8329	27857
Search Optics LLC (PA)	8742	C	858 678-0707	27441
Sears Home Imprv Pdts Inc	1521	D	858 790-7721	1231
Secure Transportation Co Inc	4789	D	858 790-3958	5245
Securitas Critical Infrastruct	7381	A	858 560-0448	16783
Securitas Electronic SEC Inc	7382	D	858 812-7349	16935
Securitas SEC Svcs USA Inc	7381	C	619 641-0049	16796
Security On-Demand Inc	7373	E	858 563-5655	16048
Seltzer Caplan McMahon (PA)	8111	C	619 685-3003	23370
Semantic Ai Inc (PA)	7373	D	619 222-4050	16050
Sempra Energy (PA)	4932	A	619 696-2000	6193
Sempra Energy	4911	A	619 696-2000	6107
Sempra Energy Global Entps	4924	A	619 696-2000	6162
Sempra Energy International (HQ)	4911	A	619 696-2000	6108
Senior Care Inc	8052	C	619 817-8855	20955
Senomyx Inc	8731	D	858 646-8300	26454
Sentek Consulting Inc	7379	D	619 543-9550	16481
Sequenom Inc (HQ)	8731	D	858 202-9000	26455
Sequenom Center For Molecular	8071	B	858 202-9051	22147

Employment Codes: A=Over 500 employees, B=251-500,
C=101-250, D=51-100, E=50

2019 Directory of California
Wholesalers and Services Companies

© Mergent Inc. 1-800-342-5647

1659

	SIC	EMP	PHONE	ENTRY #
Serco Inc	8711	C	858 569-8979	25908
Servi-Tek Inc	7349	B	858 638-7735	14383
Service King Holdings LLC	7532	D	619 219-3927	17739
Serving Seniors (PA)	8322	D	619 235-6572	24048
Seven Seas Associates LLC	7011	D	619 291-1300	13209
Sharp Chula Vista Medical Ctr	8062	D	858 499-5150	21746
Sharp Community Medical Group	8621	C	858 499-4525	25041
Sharp Health Plan	6324	D	858 499-8300	10311
Sharp Healthcare	8011	D	619 398-2988	19880
Sharp Healthcare	8011	D	619 284-1400	19881
Sharp Healthcare	8062	D	858 939-5434	21747
Sharp Healthcare (PA)	8062	A	858 499-4000	21748
Sharp Healthcare	8011	C	619 446-1575	19883
Sharp Healthcare	8011	D	858 653-6100	19884
Sharp Healthcare	8062	C	858 627-5152	21749
Sharp Healthcare	8082	D	858 541-4850	22416
Sharp Healthcare	8011	D	858 616-8411	19885
Sharp Healthcare	8062	D	858 621-4010	21751
Sharp Healthcare	8011	D	800 827-4277	19886
Sharp Healthcare	8011	D	858 616-8200	19888
Sharp Mary Birch H	8062	D	858 939-3400	21752
Sharp McDonald Center	8069	A	858 637-6920	22045
Sharp Memorial Hospital (HQ)	8062	A	858 939-3636	21753
Sharp Memorial Hospital	8063	C	858 278-4110	21972
SHe Manages Properties Inc (PA)	6531	D	619 291-6300	11761
Shelter Pointe LLC	4493	C	619 221-8000	4751
Sheppard Mullin Richter	8111	D	619 338-6500	23378
Sheraton Htl San Diego Msn Vly	7011	D	619 321-4602	13220
Sherwood Mechanical Inc	1711	D	858 679-3000	2356
Shinwoo P&C Usa Inc	7389	A	619 407-7164	17469
Shoreline Land Care Inc	0782	D	858 560-8555	939
Show Call Productions Inc	7922	B	619 602-0656	18404
Siemens Industry Inc	5084	D	858 693-8711	7797
Signal Pharmaceuticals LLC	5122	C	858 795-4700	8210
Simplex Time Recorder LLC	1731	D	858 740-0100	2734
Simpson Delmore and Greene LLP (PA)	8111	E	619 515-1194	23388
Sinclair Companies	7011	C	619 238-1818	13230
Six Continents Hotels Inc	7011	D	619 232-3861	13237
Six Continents Hotels Inc	7011	D	619 795-4000	13239
Skylight Halthcare Systems Inc	8742	D	858 523-3700	27453
Slate Creek Wind Project LLC	4911	A	888 903-6926	6110
Smart & Final Stores LLC	5141	D	858 268-2400	8455
Smart & Final Stores LLC	5141	D	858 270-8200	8456
Smart & Final Stores LLC	5141	D	619 523-3640	8457
Smart & Final Stores LLC	5141	D	619 291-8287	8459
Smartdrive Systems Inc (PA)	7371	D	858 225-5550	15454
Socal Services Inc	7361	C	858 453-1331	14763
Socal Sportsnet LLC	7929	A	619 795-5000	18465
Social Advocates For Y	8322	C	619 283-9624	24052
Softhq	7379	E	858 658-9200	16488
Soleil Communications LLC	8732	D	619 624-2888	26566
Solomon Ward Sdnwurm Smith LLP	8111	D	619 231-0303	23394
Solpac Inc	1542	D	619 296-6247	1656
Solpac Construction Inc	8741	C	619 296-6247	27040
Solute Inc	8711	D	619 224-2810	25918
Sorrento Therapeutics Inc (PA)	8731	C	858 203-4100	26457
Souldriver Lessee Inc	7011	D	619 819-9500	13248
Southbay Sndblst & Tank Clg	7699	D	619 238-8338	17990
Southern Cal Prmnnte Med Group	6324	D	858 974-1000	10313
Southern Cal Prmnnte Med Group	8011	D	619 528-5000	19907
Southern Cal Prmnnte Med Group	8011	E	619 516-6000	19920
Southern California Car Transf	4789	D	858 586-0006	5247
Southern California Physicia	8741	D	858 824-7000	27041
Southern Glazers Wine	5182	C	858 537-3912	9054
Southland Electric Inc	1731	D	858 634-5050	2736
Southland Technology Inc	5045	D	858 694-0932	7107
Southwest Airlines Co	4512	B	619 231-7345	4801
Southwestern Artists Assn	8412	E	619 232-3522	24914
Southwestern Yacht Club Inc	7997	E	619 222-0438	19052
Sovereign Capitl MGT Group Inc	6531	A	619 294-8989	11773
Specialty Textile Services LLC	5131	D	619 476-8750	8244
Spectrum Prof Staffing Inc	7363	C	800 644-1150	14914
Spinning Spur Wind Three LLC	4911	A	858 521-3319	6142
Spreadtrum Cmmncations USA Inc	8731	D	858 546-0895	26458
St Pauls Episcopal Home Inc	8361	D	619 239-2097	24684
St Pauls Episcopal Home Inc	8361	D	619 239-8687	24685
Staccato Communications Inc	7389	D	858 812-0981	17481
Staff Pro Inc	7381	C	619 544-1774	16835
Stanley M Kirkpatrick MD	8011	E	858 966-5855	19944
Star Laundry Services Inc	7219	C	619 572-1009	13637
Starwood Hotels & Resorts	7011	C	619 239-2200	13273
Starwood Htls & Rsrts Wrldwde	7011	D	619 239-9600	13281
State Compensation Insur Fund	6331	B	888 782-8338	10400
Station Venture Operations LP	4833	D	619 231-3939	5839
Steren Electronics Intl LLC (PA)	5065	D	800 266-3333	7545
Stewart Enterprises Inc	7261	E	858 453-2121	13699
Stewart Title California Inc (DH)	6361	C	619 692-1600	10471
Strata Information Group Inc	7379	D	619 296-0170	16495
Strategic Data Systems	7373	C	619 546-7200	16060
Strategic Insights Inc	7372	D	858 452-7500	15866
Strategic Operations Inc	7389	C	858 244-0559	17489
Strategic Property Management	6531	D	619 295-2211	11781
Stu Segall Productions Inc	7812	C	858 974-8988	18126
Student Movers Inc	4214	D	303 296-0600	4377
Stx Wireless Operations LLC	4812	A	858 882-6000	5417
Sullinovo	4959	C	619 260-1432	6550
Sullivan Moving & Storage (HQ)	4213	E	858 874-2600	4270
Sun Pharmaceuticals Inc	8731	C	858 380-8865	26462
Sunbelt Towing Inc (PA)	7549	D	619 297-8697	17874
Sundance Financial Inc	6552	E	619 298-9877	11924
Sunstone Hotel Investors LLC	7011	D	619 239-6171	13297
Sunstone Top Gun LLC	7011	D	858 453-0400	13307
Sunstone Top Gun Lessee Inc	7011	D	949 330-4000	13308
Superior Envmtl Svcs Inc	7349	E	619 462-7079	14404
Supplypro Inc (PA)	5084	D	858 587-6400	7807
Supreme Court United States	8322	C	619 557-7149	24080
Survivalcave Inc	5149	E	800 719-7650	8879
Swinerton Bldrs Pacific R	1542	D	619 954-8011	1663
Swinerton Builders	1541	D	858 622-4040	1440
Swvp Del Mar Hotel LLC	7011	C	858 481-5900	13311
Symitar Systems Inc	7371	C	619 542-6700	15484
Synergy Health Ast LLC (DH)	8742	D	858 586-1166	27480
Sysintelli Inc	7371	C	858 271-1600	15485
T B Penick & Sons Inc (PA)	1541	C	858 558-1800	1441
T I C Hotels Inc	7011	E	619 238-7577	13315
T-12 Three LLC	7011	B	619 702-3000	13319
T3w Business Solutions Inc	8741	D	619 298-0888	27057
Tachyon Inc	4813	E	858 882-8108	5650
Tactical Engrg & Analis Inc (PA)	7379	C	858 573-9869	16533
Takeda California Inc	8733	C	858 622-8528	26665
Tangoe Inc	7372	C	858 452-6800	15876
Tapestry Solutions Inc (HQ)	7371	C	858 503-1990	15491
Tax Compliance Inc	7371	C	858 547-4100	15494
Tcp Global Corporation (PA)	5198	D	858 909-2110	9190
Tealium Inc (PA)	7374	D	858 779-1344	16186
Team Risk MGT Strategies LLC	8748	A	877 767-8728	27877
Techflow Inc (PA)	8744	C	858 412-8000	27608
Teg Staffing Inc	7361	A	619 260-2000	14778
Tegp Inc	7363	D	619 584-3408	14919
Telecare Corporation	8063	D	619 275-8000	21978
Telecare Corporation	8063	D	619 692-8225	21985
Telisimo International Corp	4813	A	619 325-1593	5653
Teradata Corporation	7379	A	858 485-1220	16511
Teris LLC	7374	E	619 231-3282	16190
Terra Vista Management Inc	6531	C	858 581-4200	11791
Tesi Investment Company LLC	7011	D	619 224-3254	13324
Tetra Tech Inc	8742	D	619 525-7188	27487
Tetra Tech Ec Inc	8748	D	619 234-8690	27881
Tf Courier Inc	4215	D	888 541-2965	4434
Therastaff Inc	7363	C	858 569-7555	14921
Thorsnes Bartolotta & McGuire	8111	D	619 236-9363	23410
Thurston Martin H DDS Ms	8021	E	858 676-5010	20139
Tiburon Inc	7373	D	858 799-7000	16065
Tic Hotels Inc	7011	E	619 238-7577	13327
Tic World-Wide Corp	7011	D	619 233-7500	13328
Tillster Inc (PA)	7379	D	858 784-0800	16513
Time Warner Cable Inc	4841	D	619 346-4573	5951
Time Warner Cable Inc	4841	B	858 695-3220	5954
Time Warner Cable Inc	4841	B	858 695-3110	5960
Tomatoes Extraordinaire Inc	5148	C	619 295-3172	8738
Top of Market	8741	B	619 234-4867	27064
Torrey Aat Point LLC	6798	D	858 350-2600	12190
Torrey Pines Bank (HQ)	6022	A	858 523-4600	9491
Toward Maximum Independence (PA)	8322	C	858 467-0600	24090
Toyota Logistics Services	7549	C	619 531-0157	17876
Trandes Corp	8711	C	619 398-0464	25957
Transpak Inc	4783	D	858 292-9094	5211
Transwest San Diego	4214	B	858 450-0707	4380
Treefrog Developments Inc	5099	D	619 324-7755	8063
Trellisware Technologies Inc	4812	D	858 753-1600	5422
Trendsource Inc	8732	C	619 718-7467	26573
Trex Partners LLC	6719	C	858 646-5300	12014
Trigild International Inc	7011	D	619 291-6500	13346
Trilink Biotechnologies LLC	8731	D	858 546-0004	26477
Trilogy Financial Services Inc	7389	E	858 755-6696	17523
Triton Structural Concrete Inc	1542	C	858 866-2450	1678
Troutman Sanders LLP	8111	D	858 509-6000	23413
Troxel Cycling & Fitness LLC	5091	D	858 587-7720	7939
Tru Green Landcare Inc	0782	B	602 276-4311	952
Tum Yeto Inc	5091	E	619 232-7523	7941

Mergent email: customerrelations@mergent.com

1660

2019 Directory of California
Wholesalers and Services Companies

(P-0000) Products & Services Section entry number
(PA)=Parent Co (HQ)=Headquarters (DH)=Div Headquarters

Company	SIC	EMP	PHONE	ENTRY #
Turelk Inc	1542	D	858 633-8085	1680
Turn Behavioral Hlth Svcs Inc (PA)	8093	D	858 573-2600	22702
Turner Construction Company	1542	D	858 320-4040	1686
Tuv Sud America Inc	8734	D	858 546-3999	26735
Twin Oaks Power LP (HQ)	4911	D	619 696-2034	6145
Tyler Bluff Wind Project LLC	4911	A	888 903-6926	6146
U S Mbile Wrless Cmmunications (PA)	4812	C	858 537-0709	5424
UBS Financial Services Inc	6211	C	619 236-0460	10026
Ucsd Healthcare	8099	D	858 657-7105	22897
Ulta Beauty Inc	7231	C	858 581-9003	13678
Underground Elephant Inc	7311	D	800 466-4178	13913
Unifirst Corporation	7218	D	619 263-6116	13624
Union Pan Asian Communities (PA)	8322	D	619 232-6454	24100
United Airlines Inc	4512	C	619 692-3310	4808
United Behavioral Health	8741	D	619 641-6800	27073
United Cerebral Palsy Assn San (PA)	8699	C	858 495-3155	25477
United Development Group Inc	6552	E	858 244-0900	11932
United Parcel Service Inc OH	4215	C	858 455-8800	4459
United Parcel Service Inc OH	4215	C	909 279-5111	4465
United States Dept of Navy	7363	C	619 524-1069	14928
United States Dept of Navy	8011	A	619 532-6397	20021
United States Dept of Navy	8011	D	619 532-8953	20022
United States Dept of Navy	8011	B	619 556-8210	20023
United States Dept of Navy	8062	D	619 532-6400	21870
United States Dept of Navy	8731	E	619 532-1897	26481
United States Dept of Navy	8011	D	619 532-7400	20025
United States Dept of Navy	8011	D	619 767-6592	20027
United Svcs Amer Federal Cr Un (PA)	6061	D	858 831-8100	9614
Univers of Calif San Diego Hs	8062	D	619 543-3713	21873
University Cal San Diego	8062	A	619 543-6654	21878
Univision Television Group Inc	4833	E	858 576-1999	5846
Up N Down Scaffold Company Inc (PA)	1799	D	619 266-0542	3600
UPS Store Inc (HQ)	7389	C	858 455-8800	17552
Upwind Blade Solutions Inc	7699	C	866 927-3142	18003
Urban Corps of San Diego	8331	C	619 235-6884	24244
US Bank National Association	6021	D	619 744-2140	9376
US Grant Hotel Ventures LLC	7011	D	619 744-2007	13359
Valiant Integrated Services	8611	B	858 277-6780	24989
Vanguard Resources Corp	8744	D	858 336-7147	27609
Vanpike Inc (PA)	7363	C	858 453-1331	14931
Vastek Inc	7389	C	925 948-5701	17559
Vector Resources Inc	8711	E	858 546-1014	25988
Vencore Inc	8748	E	571 313-6000	27894
Verance Corporation	8732	D	858 202-2800	26576
Verizon Connect Nwf Inc	7371	C	858 450-3245	15525
Vertex Phrmctcals San Dego LLC (HQ)	8731	C	858 404-6600	26490
Veterans EZ Info Inc	8748	C	866 839-1329	27899
Veterans Health Administration	8021	B	858 552-7525	20143
Veterans Health Administration	8011	B	619 400-5000	20074
Veterans Medical Research Fund	8641	C	858 642-3080	25276
Veterinary Practice Assoc Inc	8093	C	949 833-9020	22710
Viacyte Inc	8733	D	858 455-3708	26671
Vibra Healthcare LLC	8062	C	619 260-8300	21907
Vibra Hospital San Diego LLC	8062	D	619 260-8300	21910
Victory Pharma Inc	5122	C	858 720-4500	8219
Vietnam Veterans of San Diego (PA)	8641	D	619 497-0142	25279
Vietnms-Mrcan Yuth Alance Corp	8641	E	619 320-8292	25280
Villa Rancho Brno Hlth Cr LLC	8051	C	858 672-3900	20861
Villas De Carlsbad Ltd A Cali (PA)	8361	C	858 565-4424	24714
Vista Hill Foundation	8322	D	619 266-0166	24113
Vista Hill Foundation (PA)	8621	E	585 514-5100	25052
Vistage International Inc (PA)	8742	C	858 523-6800	27516
Visual Pak San Diego LLC	7389	C	847 689-1000	17570
Vitas Healthcare Corp Cal	8082	D	619 680-4400	22457
Vitro LLC	7311	D	619 234-0408	13918
Vitrorobertson LLC	7311	D	619 234-0408	13919
Volt Management Corp	7363	C	858 576-3140	14934
Volt Management Corp	7363	C	858 578-0920	14935
Volume Services Inc	7999	D	619 525-5800	19259
VT Milcom Inc	8711	D	619 424-9024	25992
W-Emerald LLC	7011	D	619 239-4500	13374
Wamc Company Inc (PA)	6513	D	858 454-2753	11139
Warfighter & Family Services	7389	D	619 556-7168	17579
Washington Inventory Service (DH)	7389	C	858 565-8111	17581
Washington Inventory Service	7389	D	619 461-8198	17582
Water Resources Control Bd Cal	8611	D	619 521-3010	24990
Watermark Rtrment Cmmnties Inc	6531	D	858 597-8000	11823
Wawanesa General Insurance Co	6331	B	619 285-6020	10413
Webb Sunrise Inc	5199	E	619 220-7050	9271
Wells Fargo Bank National Assn	6021	D	858 622-6958	9386
Wermers Multi-Family Corp	1522	C	858 535-1475	1325
Westair Gases & Equipment Inc (PA)	5084	E	866 937-8247	7821
Westcore Delta LLC	6799	D	858 625-4100	12282
Western Pump Inc (PA)	7699	D	619 239-9988	18006
Westgroup Kona Kai LLC	7997	D	619 221-8000	19086
Westgroup San Diego Associates	7011	B	858 274-4630	13391
Wheatland Wind Project LLC	4911	A	888 903-6926	6150
Whiskey Girl	8741	D	619 236-1616	27096
White Digital Media Inc	5192	C	760 827-7800	9122
Whittier Inst For Diabetes	8733	D	877 944-8843	26678
William M Perkins Company Inc (PA)	1721	E	619 236-0343	2492
Willmark Cmmnties Univ Vlg Inc (PA)	6513	C	858 271-0582	11140
Wilmark Management Services (PA)	6531	D	858 271-0583	11839
Wilson Sonsini Goodrich & Rosa	8111	C	858 350-2300	23438
Wilson Turner Kosmo LLP	8111	D	619 236-9600	23441
Win Time Ltd (PA)	7011	D	858 695-2300	13401
Wind River Systems Inc	7372	D	858 824-3100	15893
Wingert Grebing Brubaker & Jus	8111	D	619 232-8151	23442
Wirtz Qulty Installations Inc	1741	D	858 569-3816	2832
Wirtz Tile & Stone Inc	1752	D	858 569-3816	3120
Wmbe Payrolling Inc	7361	D	858 810-3000	14799
Wme Bi LLC	7372	D	877 592-2472	15894
Wmk Office San Diego LLC (PA)	5021	C	858 569-4700	6745
Woodfin Suite Hotels LLC	7011	A	858 314-7910	13416
Wordsmart Corporation	7372	D	858 565-8068	15895
Wright Broadband Group Inc	8748	D	858 362-0380	27911
Ws Mmv Hotel LLC	7011	D	619 692-3800	13420
Wtw Delaware Holdings LLC	8742	D	858 523-5500	27527
Ww San Diego Harbor Island LLC	7011	C	619 291-6700	13422
Wyndham International Inc	7011	D	619 239-4500	13425
Xcite Steps Corp	8052	C	858 722-1948	20972
Xpo Logistics Freight Inc	4213	E	858 569-8921	4311
YMCA of San Diego County (PA)	8641	C	858 292-9622	25295
YMCA of San Diego County	8641	D	619 281-8313	25299
YMCA of San Diego County	8641	D	619 226-8888	25300
YMCA of San Diego County	8641	C	619 521-3055	25301
YMCA of San Diego County	8641	C	619 298-3576	25303
YMCA Youth & Family Services	8641	C	619 543-9850	25315
Z57 Inc (DH)	7311	C	858 623-5577	13923
Zb National Association	6021	E	858 793-7400	9411
Zeetogroup LLC	7311	C	888 771-9194	13924
Zenith Insurance Company	6331	D	619 299-6252	10419
Zmicro Inc (PA)	7373	D	858 831-7000	16081
Zoological Society San Diego (PA)	8422	A	619 231-1515	24937
Zoological Society San Diego	8422	D	619 744-3325	24939
Zs Associates Inc	8742	D	858 677-2200	27535

SAN DIMAS, CA - Los Angeles County

Company	SIC	EMP	PHONE	ENTRY #
AON Consulting Inc	6411	D	800 815-1823	10532
Associations of United Nurses (PA)	8631	D	909 599-8622	25054
AT&T Corp	4812	D	626 912-0600	5267
Automatic Data Processing Inc	7374	C	909 592-6411	16089
Automatic Data Processing Inc	7374	C	800 225-5237	16096
Christian Community Credit Un (PA)	6062	D	626 915-7551	9627
Custom Cooler Inc	5078	C	909 592-1111	7662
Davita Magan Management Inc	8011	D	909 592-9712	19430
Festival Fun Parks LLC	5091	A	909 802-2200	7928
Golden State Water Company (HQ)	4941	D	909 394-3600	6258
Golden State Water Company	4941	D	909 394-3600	6259
I P S Services Inc	8093	D	909 305-0250	22597
Imobile LLC	4813	A	909 599-8822	5584
Kaiser Foundation Hospitals	8062	D	909 394-2530	21486
L Barrios & Associates Inc	0782	E	626 960-2934	875
Legal Solutions Holdings Inc	8111	C	800 244-3495	23199
McKinley Childrens Center Inc (PA)	8361	C	909 599-1227	24596
McKinley Home Foundation	8399	D	909 599-1227	24805
ML Prior Inc	8111	C	626 653-5160	23258
National Credit Industries Inc	6163	D	626 967-4355	9898
New York Life Insurance Co	6411	D	909 305-6500	10716
Pacific Systems Interiors Inc	1742	C	310 436-6820	2934
Pacific W Space Cmmnctions Inc	1623	D	909 592-4321	1966
Prime Healthcare-San Dimas LLC	8062	B	909 599-6811	21662
Progressive Corporation	6331	D	626 232-1540	10385
Qtc Management Inc (DH)	8099	C	800 260-1515	22867
San Dimas Golf Inc	7997	D	909 599-8486	19026
San Dimas Retirement Center (PA)	6513	D	909 599-8441	11109
Second Image National LLC (PA)	7334	C	800 229-7477	14092
Southern Cal Prmnnte Med Group	6324	E	909 394-2505	10318
Southern California Edison Co	4911	C	909 592-3757	6137
Southern California Gas Co	4923	A	909 305-8297	6156
Wellpoint Inc	6311	C	805 375-1605	10151

SAN FERNANDO, CA - Los Angeles County

Company	SIC	EMP	PHONE	ENTRY #
All State Association Inc	8611	C	877 425-2558	24941
Bank America National Assn	6021	D	818 898-3033	9286
Bernards Builders Inc	1522	B	818 898-1521	1268
Brightview Landscape Dev Inc	1711	D	818 838-4700	2148
Cacho Landscape Maintenance Co	0782	E	818 365-0773	807
County of Los Angeles	8011	D	818 837-6969	19409
Environments Plus (PA)	1799	D	805 375-5727	3513
First Student Inc	4151	C	818 896-0333	3934

GEOGRAPHIC

Company	SIC	EMP	PHONE	ENTRY #
Frontier California Inc	4813	C	818 365-0542	5564
Industrial Stitchtech Inc	7389	C	818 361-6319	17233
Jme Inc (PA)	5063	D	201 896-8600	7368
Masterserv Inc	1711	E	818 356-4602	2275
Mv Transportation Inc	4111	D	323 666-0856	3684
Northeast Valley Health Corp (PA)	8322	D	818 898-1388	23942
Northeast Valley Health Corp	8011	D	818 365-8086	19720
Pepsi-Cola Metro Btlg Co Inc	5149	C	818 898-3829	8850
Prg (california) Inc	7812	E	818 252-2600	18099
Stan Winston Inc	7819	D	818 782-0870	18219
Tyan Inc	7381	D	818 785-5831	16841
Universal Mail Delivery Svc (PA)	4212	D	818 997-7531	4076
Wild Side West (PA)	7336	D	818 837-5000	14131

SAN FRANCISCO, CA - San Francisco County

Company	SIC	EMP	PHONE	ENTRY #
1life Healthcare Inc	8099	D	415 644-5265	22720
3scale Inc	7382	E	415 349-5187	16864
3vr Security Inc	7382	D	415 513-4577	16865
425 North Point Street LLC	7011	D	800 648-4626	12292
42nd Street Moon	7922	E	415 255-8207	18335
495 Geary LLC	7011	C	415 775-4700	12295
500 Startups Incubator LLC	8748	C	415 974-6343	27613
A Ruiz Cnstr Co & Assoc Inc	1542	E	415 647-4010	1452
A Smwm California Corporation	8712	D	415 546-0400	26017
A T Kearney Inc	8742	C	415 490-4000	27103
A1 Protective Services Inc	7381	D	415 467-7200	16540
ABB Enterprise Software Inc	7372	C	415 527-2850	15564
ABC Cable Networks Group	4833	C	415 954-7911	5764
Able Services Inc	8711	D	800 461-9577	25495
ABS Capital Partners III LP	6799	D	415 617-2800	12196
Accenture LLP	8742	B	415 537-5000	27108
Access Public Relations LLC	8743	C	415 904-7070	27536
Accor Services US LLC (DH)	7011	A	415 772-5000	12306
Accountants 4 Contract	8721	D	415 781-8644	26140
Ace Parking Management Inc	7521	D	415 345-8354	17665
Ace Parking Management Inc	7521	D	415 749-1949	17670
Active Wellness LLC	8741	A	415 741-3300	26747
Addiction RES & Trtmnt Inc	8093	D	415 928-7800	22496
Adg Corporation	6799	E	415 864-4090	12197
Adivo Associates LLC	8742	D	415 992-1449	27113
Adobe Systems Incorporated	7372	A	415 832-2000	15573
Adroll Inc (PA)	7311	D	877 723-7655	13789
Advantis Global Inc (PA)	7379	C	415 850-1500	16307
Advent Software Inc (HQ)	7371	C	415 543-7696	14967
Aecom Global II LLC	8711	D	415 774-2700	25513
Aetna Health California Inc	6324	D	415 645-8200	10175
Affirm Inc	6153	C	415 984-0490	9730
Air France (air Nationale)	4512	A	415 877-0179	4758
Airbnb Inc (PA)	7041	A	415 800-5959	13471
Airco Mechanical Inc	1711	C	415 982-4726	2093
Akin Gump Strauss Hauer & Fel	8111	C	415 765-9500	22907
Akqa Inc (HQ)	8742	B	415 645-9400	27121
Alain Pinel Realtors Inc	6531	D	415 814-6690	11194
Alcatraz Cruises LLC	4725	C	415 981-7625	4960
Alegrecare Inc	8082	B	415 974-3530	22210
All Hallows Preservation LP	6513	A	415 285-3909	10974
Allen Matkins Leck Gmble	8111	D	415 837-1515	22909
Allied Medical Service of Cal	4119	E	415 931-1400	3742
Almavia of San Francisco	8051	D	415 337-1339	20228
Alois LLC	7361	D	215 297-4492	14569
Alsco Inc	7213	C	415 648-9266	13497
Alta Equipment Leasing Company	7359	D	415 875-1000	14470
Alvarez & Marsal Holdings LLC	8742	C	415 490-2300	27125
Amber Holdings Inc	7371	A	415 765-6500	14977
AMD Trading Company Inc	5199	C	415 391-0601	9194
American Academy of Opthalmlgy (PA)	8621	C	415 561-8500	24994
American Bldg Maint Co-West (HQ)	7349	C	415 733-4000	14191
American Building Maint Co NY	7349	A	415 733-4000	14192
American Conservatory	7922	C	415 749-2228	18342
American Conservatory	7922	A	415 749-2228	18343
American Conservatory Theater	7299	C	415 439-2379	13714
American Gen Lf Insur Co Del	6311	B	415 836-2700	10127
American Legal Copy-Or LLC	7334	D	415 777-4449	14070
American Marketing Systems Inc	6531	C	800 747-7784	11211
American Medical Response	4119	D	415 922-9400	3754
American Multi-Cinema Inc	7832	E	415 674-4630	18261
American National Red Cross	8322	C	415 427-8134	23475
Ammunition LLC	8742	C	415 632-1170	27132
Amoeba Music Inc	7389	D	415 831-1200	17001
Amplify Education Inc	7371	D	562 209-7875	14982
Amzn Mobile LLC	7371	B	925 348-4580	14983
Anaplan Inc (PA)	7379	C	415 742-8199	16931
Andatha International Inc (PA)	8111	D	415 398-8600	22915
Anderson Rowe & Buckley Inc	1711	D	415 282-1625	2120
Animoto LLC	7371	D	415 987-3139	14985
Annie App Inc (DH)	7371	D	844 277-2664	14987
Annuzzi Concrete Service Inc	1611	E	415 468-2795	1722
Anvil Builders Inc	1611	C	415 285-5000	1723
AON Benfield Fac Inc	6321	C	415 486-6900	10157
AON Consulting Inc	6411	D	800 283-1667	10531
AON Consulting Inc	6411	D	415 486-6226	10533
AON Consulting & Insur Svcs	6411	D	415 486-7500	10536
Apic Hotels Group LLC (HQ)	7011	C	415 692-1502	12326
Appdirect Inc (PA)	7372	D	415 852-3924	15582
Appdynamics LLC (HQ)	7372	C	415 442-8400	15583
Appsflyer Ltd	7313	D	415 636-9430	13934
Appster Inc	7371	D	415 926-2741	14993
AR Preservation LP	6513	D	415 776-2151	10979
Aramark Unf & Career AP LLC	7213	C	415 244-8332	13518
Arb Inc	1542	E	415 206-1015	1468
ARC Document Solutions Inc	7334	E	415 495-8700	14080
ARC San Francisco (PA)	8331	C	415 255-7200	24150
Arctouch LLC	7371	C	415 944-2000	14996
Argonaut Hotel	7011	C	415 563-0800	12333
Aria Systems Inc (PA)	7372	C	415 852-7250	15591
Arlene Keller MD	8011	E	415 923-3598	19303
Arnold & Porter LLP	8111	B	818 788-8081	22919
Arnold & Porter PC	8111	D	415 434-1600	22920
Arnold Palmer Golf MGT LLC	8741	D	415 561-4670	26765
Arriba Juntos (PA)	8331	D	415 487-3240	24151
Arroyo & Coates Inc	6531	D	415 445-7800	11221
Arthur J Gallagher & Co	6411	C	415 546-9300	10545
Arup North America Limited (DH)	8711	C	415 957-9445	25549
Arxan Technologies Inc (PA)	7379	D	415 247-0900	16313
Ascendify Corporation	7371	E	415 528-5503	15003
Asia Foundation (PA)	8733	D	415 982-4640	26593
Asian Art Museum Found San Fra	8412	C	415 581-3500	24865
Aspen Apts I	6513	D	415 673-5879	10980
Aspiranet	8361	D	415 759-3690	24420
Aspiriant LLC	7389	E	415 371-7800	17012
Astoria Software	7372	E	415 956-3917	15594
AT&T Corp	4812	D	415 970-8520	5262
AT&T Corp	4813	A	415 442-2600	5449
AT&T Corp	8743	C	415 442-5900	27538
AT&T Services Inc	4813	C	415 545-9051	5474
AT&T Services Inc	4813	D	415 545-9058	5489
AT&T Services Inc	4813	B	415 394-3000	5497
AT&T Services Inc	4813	C	415 774-1957	5502
Atel Capital Group (PA)	6159	D	800 543-2835	9753
Atel Corporation	7389	D	415 989-8800	17016
Atkins North America Inc	8748	E	916 325-4800	27649
Atlassian Inc (DH)	7372	C	415 701-1110	15595
Augmedix Inc	7389	D	855 720-2929	17018
Autodesk Inc	7372	D	415 356-0700	15598
Automatic Data Processing Inc	7374	E	800 225-5237	16088
Automattic Inc	4813	D	877 273-3049	5518
Avalon Golden Gate LLC	8361	D	415 664-6264	24433
Avolent Inc	7372	D	415 553-6400	15601
Axa Advisors LLC	8742	C	415 276-2100	27147
Ayoob & Peery Plumbing Co Inc	1711	D	415 550-0975	2132
B F C Inc	1731	C	415 495-3085	2514
Ba Leasing & Capital Corp (DH)	7359	C	415 765-1804	14475
Baart Behavioral Hlth Svcs Inc	8093	D	415 928-7800	22510
Baart Community Healthcare	8093	D	415 928-7800	22511
Baaz Inc	7371	D	408 621-6912	15016
Babcock & Brown Holdings Inc (HQ)	6211	D	415 512-1515	9916
Babcock & Brown Latin America	6159	D	415 512-1515	9754
Babycenter LLC (DH)	7299	E	415 537-0900	13718
Bain & Company Inc	8742	C	415 627-1000	27151
Baker & McKenzie LLP	8111	C	415 576-3000	22927
Baker Places Inc	8093	D	415 503-3137	22512
Baker Places Inc (PA)	8361	C	415 864-4655	24434
Banc America Lsg & Capitl LLC (DH)	6159	C	415 765-7349	9755
Bank America National Assn	6021	E	800 432-1000	9281
Bank America National Assn	6021	C	415 913-5891	9282
Bank America National Assn	8732	D	415 913-3438	26501
Bank of Orient (HQ)	6022	C	415 338-0651	9415
BANK OF THE WEST (HQ)	6022	A	415 765-4800	9418
Bankamerica Financial Inc	6153	D	415 622-3521	9733
Bar Architects	8712	D	415 293-5700	26026
Bar Asscation of San Francisco (PA)	8621	D	415 982-1600	24998
Barger & Wolen LLP	8111	E	415 434-2800	22933
Bartko Zankel Tarrant & Mil	8111	C	415 956-1900	22938
Bauers Intelligent Trnsp Inc (PA)	4119	C	415 522-1212	3774
Bavaria Holdings Inc	6719	A	415 418-2900	11964
Bay Area Air Quality (PA)	8748	B	415 749-4900	27656
Bay Area Video Coalition Inc	7819	D	415 861-3282	18180
Bay Bread LLC	5149	D	415 440-0356	8760
Bay Club Golden Gateway LLC	7997	D	415 616-8800	18855
Bay Club Holdings III LLC	7999	D	415 433-2936	19107
Bay Grove Capital Group LLC (PA)	6722	E	415 229-7953	12028

Mergent email: customerrelations@mergent.com
1662
2019 Directory of California
Wholesalers and Services Companies
(P-0000) Products & Services Section entry number
(PA)=Parent Co (HQ)=Headquarters (DH)=Div Headquarters

Company	SIC	EMP	PHONE	ENTRY #
Bay West Shwplace Invstors LLC (PA)	6512	D	415 490-5800	10856
Bayorg	8422	D	415 623-5300	24924
Bayspring Medical Group A Pro	8011	E	415 674-2600	19319
Bayview Hunters Point Foundati (PA)	8699	D	415 468-5100	25396
Bayview Hunters Point Y M C A	8641	D	415 822-7728	25097
Bayview Preservation LP	6513	A	415 285-7344	10982
Bbam Arcft Holdings 137 Labuan	7359	D	415 267-1600	14478
Bbam US LP	6211	B	415 267-1600	9918
BBDO Worldwide Inc	7311	D	415 808-6200	13797
Bcci Construction Company (PA)	1542	C	415 817-5100	1475
Bdo Usa LLP	8721	C	415 397-7900	26147
Beats Music LLC	7372	D	415 590-5104	15606
Beauties of Life Inc	7371	C	415 297-6765	15022
Bechtel Capital MGT Corp	8741	A	415 768-1234	26778
Bechtel Energy Corporation	8711	D	415 768-1234	25561
Bechtel Enterprises Holdings (HQ)	8711	D	415 768-1234	25562
Bechtel Entps Holdings Inc	1542	B	415 768-6745	1476
Bechtel Global Energy Inc	8711	D	415 768-1234	25563
Bechtel Group Inc (PA)	1629	D	415 768-1234	2010
Bechtel Intl Systems Inc (DH)	8711	D	415 768-1234	25564
Beresford Corp	0174	C	415 981-7386	203
Beresford Corporation	7011	D	415 673-9900	12370
Best Western Hotel Tomo	7011	E	415 921-4000	12373
Billing Services Plus DBA Apex	7349	D	415 604-3515	14201
Birst Inc	7371	B	415 766-4800	15026
Bite Communications LLC (HQ)	8742	D	415 365-0222	27161
Bittorrent Inc	7371	E	408 641-4219	15028
Black Bear Security Services	7381	C	415 559-5159	16583
Blackrock Funds III	6722	D	415 597-2000	12029
Blackrock Global Investors	6282	A	415 670-2000	10062
Blackrock Holdco 2 Inc	6531	D	415 678-2000	11245
Blackrock Instnl Tr Nat Assn (HQ)	6722	A	415 597-2000	12030
Blackstone Technology Group (PA)	8748	D	415 837-1400	27658
Bleacher Report Inc	7374	D	415 777-5505	16099
Bleacher Report Inc	7822	C	415 777-5505	18235
Blood Centers of Pacific (PA)	8099	C	415 567-6400	22748
Bloomberg LP	7383	D	415 912-2960	16953
Blue and Gold Fleet	4489	D	415 705-8200	4710
Blue Bus Tours LLC	7999	D	415 353-5310	19113
Blue Earth Inc (PA)	6719	C	702 608-5476	11965
Bmr Apps Inc	7379	D	954 651-1412	16319
Bohemian Club (PA)	8641	C	415 885-2440	25101
Bongmi Inc	5047	E	415 823-8595	7166
Bonhams Bttrflds Actneers Corp (DH)	7389	D	415 861-7500	17036
Bonhams Corporation	7389	D	415 861-7500	17037
Bonneville International Corp	4832	D	415 764-1021	5693
Bonneville International Corp	4832	E	415 777-0965	5694
Boutique Air Inc	4522	B	415 449-0505	4856
Bpaz Holdings 6 LLC	6719	D	415 295-8080	11966
Bracket Global LLC	7371	D	415 293-1340	15034
Brad Miller	8742	D	415 986-5400	27170
Brady Company	7379	D	415 644-0836	16320
Brandnet Inc	8748	D	415 216-4152	27662
Bre/Japantown Owner LLC	7011	D	415 922-3200	12398
Bridge Housing Acquisition	6512	D	415 989-1111	10858
Bridge Housing Corporation (PA)	6552	D	415 989-1111	11858
Brience Inc (DH)	7371	D	415 974-5300	15035
Brighterion Inc	7371	D	415 986-5600	15037
Broadmoor Hotel (PA)	6513	C	415 776-7034	10990
Broadmoor Hotel	7011	D	415 673-2511	12405
Broadreach Capitl Partners LLC	6799	A	415 354-4640	12205
Brown & Toland Medical Group	8011	A	415 752-8038	19330
Bryan Cave Lighton Paisner LLP	8111	E	415 675-3400	22961
Btig LLC (PA)	6211	D	415 248-2200	9920
Build Group Inc (PA)	1542	C	415 367-9399	1487
Burr Pilger Mayer (PA)	8721	C	415 421-5757	26154
Business For Scial Rspnsbility (PA)	8742	D	415 984-3200	27175
Business Services Network	7331	C	415 282-8161	14042
Bynd LLC	7371	D	415 944-2293	15043
CA Ste Atom Assoc Intr-Ins Bur	6331	A	415 565-2012	10340
Cadreon LLC	7311	C	415 262-5900	13801
Cadreon LLC	7311	C	415 262-5900	13802
Cahill Contractors Inc (PA)	1542	D	415 986-0600	1493
Cahill Contractors Inc	1542	D	415 986-0600	1494
Cai International Inc (PA)	7359	D	415 788-0100	14483
California Academy Sciences (PA)	8422	A	415 379-8000	24926
California Child Care Resource (PA)	8322	D	415 882-0234	23523
California Club of CA	8641	D	415 474-3516	25123
California Dept Rehabilitation	7361	D	415 904-7100	14581
California Pacific CA	8062	E	415 345-0940	21302
California Pacific Medical Ctr	8062	D	415 600-1378	21303
California Parking Company (PA)	6519	D	415 781-4896	11165
California Physicians Service (PA)	6324	A	415 229-5000	10185
California Shellfish Co Inc	5146	B	707 542-9490	8574
Califrnia PCF Med Ctr Fndation (PA)	8733	D	415 600-4400	26602
Callan LLC (PA)	6282	C	415 974-5060	10068
Campaign Monitor USA Inc	7371	D	888 533-8098	15048
Canon Solutions America Inc	5044	D	415 743-7300	6954
Canterbury Hotel Corp	7011	C	415 345-3200	12425
Capcom Entertainment Inc	5092	D	650 350-6500	7948
Capcom U S A Inc (HQ)	5092	C	650 350-6500	7949
Capgemini America Inc	7379	D	415 796-6777	16322
Capital Group Companies Inc	6282	B	213 486-1698	10071
Caranythingcom Inc	8742	D	916 781-4344	27182
Carat	7319	D	415 541-2700	13967
Carbonfive Incorporated	7371	D	415 546-0500	15050
Caritas Management Corporation	6531	B	415 647-7191	11265
Carlton Hotel Properties LP	7011	C	415 673-0242	12427
Carmel Partners Inc (PA)	6531	C	415 273-2900	11268
Carroll Burdick Mc Donough LLP (PA)	8111	C	415 989-5900	22972
Casey Securities Inc (PA)	6211	D	415 544-5030	9923
Cassidy Trly Prop MGT Sn Frncs	6531	D	415 781-8100	11271
Castlight Health Inc (PA)	7374	D	415 829-1400	16103
Catholic Chrts Cyo Archdiocs	8322	D	415 743-0017	23539
Catholic Chrts Cyo Archdiocs	8322	D	415 405-2000	23540
Catholic Chrts Cyo Archdiocs	8322	D	415 334-5550	23541
Catholic Chrts Cyo Archdiocs	8322	D	415 553-8700	23542
Catholic Chrts Cyo Archdiocs (PA)	8322	D	415 972-1200	23543
Caviar Inc (HQ)	8322	D	888 978-5619	23545
Cb-1 Hotel	7011	D	415 633-3838	12443
CBS Broadcasting Inc	4833	B	415 765-0928	5773
CBS Broadcasting Inc	4832	C	415 765-4097	5697
CBS Corporation	4832	D	415 765-4000	5698
CBS Interactive Inc (DH)	7319	A	415 344-2000	13970
CBS Radio Inc	4832	C	415 765-4097	5700
Cdc San Francisco LLC	7011	D	415 616-6512	12444
Celerity Consulting Group Inc (PA)	8742	D	415 986-8850	27188
Cellco Partnership	4812	D	415 402-0640	5351
Cellco Partnership	4812	D	415 695-8400	5373
Cellco Partnership	4812	D	415 351-1700	5383
Central Gardens Inc	8051	C	415 567-2967	20299
Centro Inc	7373	C	415 788-6190	15930
Cesar Chavez Student Center	6512	C	415 338-7362	10863
Cesars Productions	7389	E	415 821-1156	17068
Cfgi LLC	8721	C	415 670-9041	26164
Changeorg Inc	7375	D	415 817-1840	16210
Charles Schwab Corporation (PA)	6211	C	415 667-7000	9925
Charolais Care V Inc	8082	C	415 921-5038	22263
Chesapeake Lodging Trust	7011	D	415 296-2900	12451
Chikpea Inc	8748	E	888 342-3828	27685
Childrens Creativity Museum	8412	D	415 820-3320	24869
Childrens Cuncil San Francisco (PA)	8322	C	415 343-3378	23567
Childrens Day School	8351	E	415 861-5432	24292
Chinese Cnsld Benevolent Assn	8641	D	415 982-6000	25138
Chinese Hospital Association (PA)	8062	D	415 982-2400	21320
Chirag Hospitality Inc	7011	D	415 922-0244	12454
Chong Partners Architecher Inc	8712	C	613 995-8210	26035
Chronicle Broadcasting Co	4833	B	415 561-8000	5778
Chsp Trs Fisherman Wharf LLC	7011	C	415 563-1234	12457
Chubb US Holding Inc	6411	D	415 547-4400	10583
Cie Games LLC	7371	E	415 800-6100	15059
Cigna Healthcare Cal Inc	6324	D	415 374-2500	10194
Citibank FSB (HQ)	6035	B	415 627-6000	9522
Citibank National Association	6021	C	415 431-6940	9332
Citigroup Inc	6211	D	415 617-8524	9941
Citiscape Prprty MGT Group LLC	6531	D	415 674-1440	11319
City & County of San Francisco	8322	C	415 553-1706	23573
City & County of San Francisco	7922	D	415 621-6600	18355
City & County of San Francisco	4941	A	415 551-3000	6221
City & County of San Francisco	7922	D	415 621-6600	18356
City & County of San Francisco	8412	D	415 581-3500	24871
City & County of San Francisco	8062	A	415 206-8000	21326
City & County of San Francisco	8621	C	415 557-4713	25009
City & County of San Francisco	8111	C	415 554-4700	22976
City & County of San Francisco	8111	C	415 553-1752	22977
City & County of San Francisco	8322	D	415 753-7561	23574
City & County of San Francisco	8741	C	415 554-4799	26808
City Club LLC	7997	D	415 362-2480	18890
City Impact	8699	E	415 292-1770	25409
Clean Power Finance Inc	7699	C	899 525-2123	17939
Clean-A-Rama Maint Svc LLC	7349	D	415 495-5298	14218
Clearesult Consulting Inc	8748	D	415 848-1250	27689
Clearslide Inc (DH)	7372	D	877 360-3366	15629
Click Labs Inc	7371	A	415 658-5227	15063
Climate Corporation (DH)	0762	D	415 363-0500	683
Cloudflare Inc (PA)	7382	D	650 319-8930	16883
Clp Resources Inc	7363	E	415 508-0910	14834
Club Quarters San Francisco	7011	D	415 268-3606	12470
Clyde & Co US LLP	8111	D	415 365-9800	22983
CM Wind Down Topco Inc	4832	D	415 995-6800	5706

GEOGRAPHIC

	SIC	EMP	PHONE	ENTRY #
Cnet Networks Inc	7373	A	415 344-2000	15934
CNX Media Inc	7812	D	415 229-8300	18032
Coblentz Patch Duffy Bass LLP	8111	D	510 655-4598	22984
Code and Theory LLC	5199	D	415 839-6455	9208
Code For America Labs Inc	8742	D	415 625-9633	27196
Coinbase Inc (PA)	6099	D	415 275-2890	9674
Coldwell Bnkr Residential Brkg	6531	D	415 447-8800	11354
Collabrus Inc	8721	C	415 288-1826	26171
Collectivehealth Inc	6411	B	650 376-3804	10591
Collier Warehouse Inc	5031	E	415 920-9720	6816
Colliers International	6531	E	415 788-3100	11369
Comca Sport Net Bay Area	4841	C	415 896-2557	5864
Comcast Cble Cmmunications LLC	4841	C	415 715-0524	5867
Comcast Corporation	4841	C	415 665-5507	5872
Comcast Corporation	4841	C	415 835-5700	5885
Comfort California Inc	7011	E	415 928-5000	12479
Compass Family Services	8351	D	415 644-0504	24303
Compass Family Services	8351	D	415 644-0504	24304
Compass Family Services	8322	C	415 644-0504	23611
Compass Family Services	8322	C	415 644-0504	23612
Compass Family Services	8322	C	415 644-0504	23613
Computer Resources Group Inc	7371	C	415 398-3535	15071
Conduit Inc	4813	C	650 340-1550	5536
Conrad Imports Inc	5023	D	415 626-3303	6755
Conservation Liquidation	8999	D	415 676-5000	27925
Consumer Credit Counseling Svc (PA)	7299	D	415 788-0288	13732
Converse Inc	5139	C	415 433-1174	8350
Converseai Inc (HQ)	7371	C	415 919-7891	15078
Convoy Inc	7378	E	415 403-2770	16281
Cooley LLP	8111	D	415 693-2000	22989
Cooper Pugeda Management Inc	8741	E	415 543-6251	26819
Cooper White & Cooper LLP (PA)	8111	C	415 433-1900	22993
Corelogic Inc	6531	E	714 250-6400	11381
Cornell Companies Inc	8744	D	415 346-9769	27585
Cornerstone Cnsulting Tech Inc	8748	E	415 705-7800	27698
Cornerstone Hotel Management (DH)	8741	D	415 397-5572	26820
Cornerstone Research Inc	8748	D	415 229-8100	27700
Corportion of Fine Arts Mseums	8412	D	415 750-3600	24875
Corportion of Fine Arts Mseums	8412	C	415 750-3600	24876
Corportion of Fine Arts Mseums	8412	C	415 750-3600	24877
Corportion of Fine Arts Mseums (PA)	8412	C	415 750-3600	24878
Costless Maintenance Svcs Co	7349	D	415 550-8819	14230
Coverity LLC (HQ)	7371	D	415 321-5200	15083
Covia Communities	8361	C	415 776-0500	24490
Covington & Burling LLP	8111	E	415 591-6000	23011
CP Development Co LLC	6552	D	415 995-1770	11868
Craftworks Rest Breweries Inc	7389	E	415 292-5800	17108
Crane Acquisition Inc	7342	C	415 922-1666	14149
Creativebug LLC	7371	C	415 325-5926	15084
Credit Karma Inc (PA)	7389	C	415 510-5059	17113
Credit Suisse (usa) Inc	6211	D	415 249-2100	9946
Credit Suisse (usa) Inc	6211	E	415 678-3940	9947
Credo Mobile Inc	4813	D	415 369-2000	5541
Creedence Lessee LLC	7011	D	415 561-1100	12498
Crestline Hotels & Resorts LLC	8741	C	415 775-7555	26835
Cross Link Inc	4492	D	415 495-3191	4745
Crosscap Media Services Inc (PA)	7371	D	415 217-8860	15086
Crowell & Moring LLP	8111	D	415 986-2800	23014
Crown Building Maintenance Co	7349	B	303 680-3713	14239
Crunch LLC	7991	C	415 495-1939	18590
Cupertino Electric Inc	1731	D	415 970-3400	2558
Current Tv LLC	7389	C	415 995-8328	17119
Cusa Fi LLC	4142	C	415 642-9400	3894
Cushman & Wakefield Cal Inc (DH)	6531	C	408 275-6730	11390
Cutler Group LP	7389	E	415 645-6745	17121
Cvpartners Inc (HQ)	7361	C	415 543-8600	14598
Cyber Policy	6411	C	877 626-9991	10600
Cybernet Entertainment LLC (PA)	7812	D	415 865-0230	18036
Cypress Security LLC (PA)	7381	C	866 345-1277	16623
Daniel J Edelman Inc	8743	D	415 222-9944	27551
Dannis Wlver Klley A Prof Corp (PA)	8111	D	415 543-4111	23022
Davis Wright Tremaine LLP	8111	D	415 276-6500	23024
Davis Ziff Publishing Inc	4813	C	415 551-4800	5544
Dcp Jl Triton Sf LLC	7011	E	844 808-0290	12517
DDB Worldwide	7311	C	415 732-3600	13813
Decarta Inc	7371	D	408 294-8400	15099
Dechert LLP	8111	D	415 262-4500	23028
Decimal Inc	7389	D	855 980-6612	17126
Degenkolb Engineers (PA)	8711	C	415 392-6952	25641
Delancey Street Foundation (PA)	8361	B	415 957-9800	24502
Deloitte & Touche LLP	8721	B	415 783-4000	26180
Deloitte Consulting LLP	8742	D	510 251-4400	27212
Deloitte Tax LLP	8721	B	415 783-4000	26185
Delta Dental of California (PA)	6324	B	415 972-8300	10200
Demand Chain Inc	5045	D	800 466-3786	7035

	SIC	EMP	PHONE	ENTRY #
Demandbase Inc (PA)	7372	D	415 683-2660	15647
Dena Corp	7371	D	415 375-3170	15101
Dentons US LLP	8111	C	415 882-5000	23034
Destination Moon LP	7336	D	415 675-7777	14111
Deutsche Bank Tr Co Americas	6211	C	415 617-4200	9949
Deutsche Inv MGT Americas Inc	6282	E	415 648-9408	10076
Dewolf Realty Co Inc	8741	D	415 221-2032	26838
Dhap Digital Inc	7371	E	415 962-4900	15106
Dhl Express (usa) Inc	4513	D	415 826-7338	4816
Dietrich Post Co Inc	5112	E	510 596-0080	8078
Digital Realty Trust Inc (PA)	7379	C	415 738-6500	16349
Digital Realty Trust LP	6798	A	415 738-6500	12158
Digitalist USA Ltd	7373	A	949 278-1354	15945
Digitalthink Inc (DH)	8742	C	415 625-4000	27216
Dignity Health	8062	B	415 438-5500	21375
Dignity Health (PA)	8062	C	415 438-5500	21377
Dignity Health	8062	A	415 668-1000	21392
Directorate of Mwr Fmd Usag	8741	D	210 466-1376	26841
Discount Builders Supply	5031	D	415 285-2800	6820
Distil Networks Inc	7382	C	415 423-0831	16888
Docker Inc (PA)	7371	D	800 764-4847	15114
Doctor On Demand Inc	7372	D	415 935-4447	15650
Document Technologies LLC	7389	C	415 495-4100	17135
Docusign Inc (PA)	7372	B	415 489-4940	15651
Dodge & Cox	6722	C	415 981-1710	12034
Dolby Labs Licensing Corp	6794	C	415 558-0200	12136
Doremus & Company	7311	E	415 273-7800	13821
Doubledutch Inc (PA)	7372	D	800 748-9024	15653
Dpk Consulting	8742	D	415 495-7772	27218
Dppm Inc	6531	D	415 695-7707	11409
Drinker Biddle & Reath LLP	8111	C	415 591-7500	23055
Driver Inc	7372	D	415 999-4960	15655
Dropbox Inc (PA)	7372	C	415 857-6800	15656
Duane Morris LLP	8111	D	415 957-3000	23056
Duff & Phelps LLC	7389	D	415 693-5000	17140
Dun & Bradstreet Inc	7323	C	415 343-6540	14034
Earls Organic	5148	D	415 824-7419	8673
East West Bank	6022	C	415 391-8912	9441
Eastrdge Prsonnel of Las Vegas	7361	D	415 248-2567	14607
Eco Bay Services Inc	8748	D	415 643-7777	27712
Edaw Inc (HQ)	6552	C	415 955-2800	11873
Edgewood Ctr For Childrens (PA)	8361	B	415 681-3211	24514
Efront Financial Solutions Inc	7371	D	415 653-3239	15126
Egomotion Inc	7372	E	415 849-4662	15662
Eileen Nottoli	8111	D	415 837-1515	23059
Eis Group Inc	7372	D	415 402-2622	15663
Elaine Null	7389	C	415 345-4428	17147
Eleven Inc	7311	D	415 707-1111	13824
Elizabeth Larson	6531	D	415 409-7300	11418
Ellation Inc (PA)	7371	D	415 796-3560	15133
Embarcadero Inn Associates	7011	D	415 495-2100	12556
Embassador Private Securities	6211	D	415 822-8811	9950
Emerge Digital Inc	7379	D	415 839-5055	16357
Emergent Ventures Intl Inc	8748	D	415 655-6617	27717
Emotiv Systems Inc	7993	E	415 503-3601	18782
Encore Cnsmr Capitl Fund II LP (PA)	6799	D	415 296-9850	12224
Encore Fund LP	6722	D	415 676-4000	12035
Energy Livermore Off US Dept	8733	D	415 648-3878	26617
Enertis Solar Inc	8711	E	415 400-5271	25662
Engage Technologies Inc	7371	B	415 829-1400	15138
Entercom Communications Corp	4832	C	610 660-5610	5713
Environmental Science Assoc (PA)	8731	D	415 896-5900	26362
Envivio Inc	4813	C	650 243-2700	5554
Envoy Inc	7371	D	415 787-7871	15140
Episcopal Comm Svc San Fran (PA)	8322	C	415 487-3300	23788
Epocrates Inc (HQ)	8099	E	650 227-1700	22800
Equal Access International	1731	D	415 561-4884	2580
Equinox Holdings Inc	7991	B	415 243-0492	18594
Equinox-76th Street Inc	7991	D	415 398-0747	18595
Ernst & Young LLP	8721	B	415 894-8000	26193
Ernst & Young LLP	8721	A	415 894-8000	26203
Esurance Insurance Svcs Inc (HQ)	6411	C	415 875-4500	10615
Eventbrite Inc	7379	C	415 692-7779	16362
Everest Wtrprfing Rstrtion Inc	7299	D	415 282-9800	13744
Everwise Corporation	8742	D	888 250-6219	27228
Evidera Archimedes Inc	6411	D	415 490-0400	10616
Evolent Health Inc	8099	B	571 389-6000	22801
Execushield Inc	7381	D	415 508-0825	16642
Executives Outlet Inc	7991	E	415 433-6044	18598
Exigen (usa) Inc (PA)	7371	A	415 402-2600	15155
Exploratorium (PA)	8412	B	415 528-4462	24884
Express Messenger Systems Inc	4215	D	415 495-7300	4410
Exyte US LLC	8711	E	415 621-1199	25679
Family Svc Agcy San Francisco (PA)	7363	D	415 474-7310	14852
Farallon Capital Partners LP (PA)	6722	D	415 421-2132	12036

Mergent email: customerrelations@mergent.com

1664

2019 Directory of California
Wholesalers and Services Companies

(P-0000) Products & Services Section entry number
(PA)=Parent Co (HQ)=Headquarters (DH)=Div Headquarters

	SIC	EMP	PHONE	ENTRY #
Fastly Inc (PA)	7371	D	415 488-6329	15157
Fcb Worldwide Inc	7311	A	415 820-8545	13829
Fcb Worldwide Inc	7311	A	415 820-8000	13830
Federal Deposit Insurance Corp	6399	C	415 546-0160	10499
Federal Express Corporation	4513	C	800 463-3339	4835
Federal Hm Ln Bnk San Frncisco (PA)	6111	B	415 616-1000	9695
Federal Insurance Company	6411	D	415 273-6300	10627
Federal Rsrve Bnk San Frncisco (HQ)	6011	A	415 974-2000	9273
Fenton Communications Inc	8743	E	415 255-1946	27553
Fenty Beauty LLC	5122	C	818 973-2709	8167
Fenwick & West LLP	8111	C	415 875-2300	23065
Ferguson Enterprises Inc	5074	D	408 441-7276	7617
Figure Eight Technologies Inc	7374	D	415 471-1920	16130
Fillmore Marketplace LP	6531	E	415 921-6514	11447
Financialforcecom Inc (DH)	7371	D	866 743-2220	15161
Finastra Merchant Services Inc (PA)	6099	D	415 277-9900	9682
Fine Line Group Inc	1542	E	415 777-4070	1532
First Databank Inc	7374	D	650 588-5454	16131
First Page Sage LLC	8742	D	415 624-3526	27237
First Republic Bank	6029	D	415 392-1400	9502
First Republic Bank	6022	C	415 392-3888	9452
First Republic Bank	6022	C	415 564-8881	9457
First Republic Bank	6022	C	415 487-0888	9458
First Republic Bank	6022	C	415 975-3877	9459
First Republic Bank (PA)	6029	B	415 392-1400	9504
First Student Inc	4151	B	415 647-9012	3930
Firstcall	7381	C	415 781-4300	16647
Fleischman Field Research Inc	8732	C	415 398-4140	26517
Fleishman-Hillard Inc	8743	E	415 318-4000	27554
Flexport Inc (PA)	4789	C	415 231-5252	5225
Florence Villa Hotel	7011	D	415 397-7700	12578
Florence Villa Hotel LLC	7011	D	415 397-7700	12579
Flurish Inc	6141	D	855 253-6387	9711
Flynn Industries Inc (PA)	0181	D	415 776-7337	258
Flynn Properties Inc	6531	E	415 835-0225	11470
Foley & Lardner LLP	8111	D	415 434-4484	23075
Forex Capital Markets LLC	6211	D	415 343-4874	9952
Forgerock Inc (PA)	7372	D	415 599-1100	15679
Forgerock US Inc (HQ)	7372	D	415 599-1100	15680
Formation Inc	7372	D	650 257-2277	15681
Fort Mason Center	8999	D	415 345-7500	27928
Fortress Investment Group LLC	6722	D	415 284-7400	12038
Forward Management LLC	6282	D	415 869-6300	10080
Four Seasons Hotel Inc	7011	A	415 633-3441	12587
France Telecom RES & Dev LLC	8732	D	415 284-9765	26518
Franciscan Lines Inc	4119	C	415 642-9400	3798
Francisco Partners LP (HQ)	7373	C	415 418-2900	15958
Francisco Partners MGT LP (PA)	6799	E	415 418-2900	12227
Frank Rimerman & Co LLP	8721	D	415 439-1144	26205
Freckle Education Inc	7371	E	215 896-9896	15168
Free Stream Media Corp (PA)	5199	D	415 889-6404	9218
Fremont Mutual Funds Inc	6211	D	800 548-4539	9954
Fremont Properties Inc	6512	E	415 284-8500	10880
Fremont Realty Capital LP	6519	D	415 284-8665	11173
Frog Design Inc (DH)	7336	C	415 442-4804	14114
Frontapp Inc	7372	D	415 680-3048	15685
Fti Consulting Inc	8748	D	415 283-4200	27733
Fujitsu America Inc	7373	C	408 992-3561	15963
Fundbox Inc	6159	C	415 509-1343	9757
Funding Circle Usa Inc	6141	D	855 385-5356	9713
Fuse Project LLC	8748	D	415 908-1492	27734
Fusionstorm	8748	C	415 623-2626	27735
G2 Direct and Digital	7371	E	415 421-1000	15174
G4s Secure Solutions USA Inc	7381	C	415 591-0780	16656
Galleria Park Associates LLC	7011	D	415 781-3060	12596
Gastroenterology Division	8011	E	415 206-8823	19481
Gcl Solar Energy Inc	1711	D	415 362-2601	2218
Geary Darling Lessee Inc	7011	C	415 292-0100	12600
Genstar Capital LP	6211	A	415 834-2350	9955
Geographic Expeditions Inc	4724	D	415 922-0448	4936
Getaround Inc (PA)	7514	C	866 438-2768	17638
Gfk Custom Research LLC	8732	D	415 398-2812	26522
GI GP IV LLC (PA)	6211	E	415 688-4800	9956
Giant Creative Strategy Llc	7311	C	415 655-5200	13833
Gibson Dunn & Crutcher LLP	8111	D	415 393-8200	23095
Gic Real Estate Inc (HQ)	6531	D	415 229-1800	11480
Giga Omni Media Inc	7383	D	415 974-6355	16955
Gigsurf Inc	7361	B	415 894-2445	14626
Glass Lewis & Co LLC (HQ)	8732	D	415 678-4110	26524
Global Innovation Partners LLC	7389	D	650 233-3600	17194
Global USA Green Card	8111	D	415 915-4151	23101
Glu Mobile Inc (PA)	7371	C	415 800-6100	15183
GM Cruise LLC (HQ)	4119	D	415 335-4097	3804
Gmg Janitorial Inc	7349	C	415 642-2100	14280
Go West Holdings LLC	7389	C	888 670-0080	17196

	SIC	EMP	PHONE	ENTRY #
Go West Tours Inc (PA)	4725	E	415 837-0154	4970
Gobig Inc	7373	E	415 513-3029	15967
Golden Bear Rest Assn LLC	8611	E	415 227-8660	24959
Golden Gate Brdg Hwy & Transpo (PA)	4785	C	415 921-5858	5217
Golden Gate Capitol	8748	B	415 983-2700	27740
Golden Gate Nat Prks Cnsrvancy (PA)	8999	D	415 561-3000	27931
Golden Gate Regional Ctr Inc (PA)	8322	C	415 546-9222	23822
Golden Gate Scnic Stmship Corp	4489	E	415 901-5249	4716
Golden Living LLC	8051	D	415 563-0565	20466
Goldman Sachs & Co	6211	C	415 393-7500	9958
Good Eggs Inc	5144	E	415 483-7344	8531
Goodby Slverstein Partners Inc	7311	C	415 392-0669	13835
Gordon Rees Sclly Mnskhani LLP (PA)	8111	B	415 986-5900	23106
Gould Evans P C	8712	D	415 503-1411	26052
Grand View Research Inc	8742	E	415 349-0058	27252
Granite Solutions Groupe Inc	7361	C	415 963-3999	14632
Grant Thornton LLP	8721	C	415 986-3900	26206
Great American Music Hall	7922	E	415 885-0750	18369
Gree International Inc	7371	C	415 409-5159	15189
Gree International Entrmt Inc	7371	C	415 409-5200	15190
Green Tortoise Adventure Trvl	4142	D	415 834-1000	3898
Greenberg Traurig LLP	8111	D	415 655-1300	23111
Greene Rdvsky Maloney Share LP	8111	D	415 981-1400	23115
Greentree Property MGT Inc	6512	E	415 347-8600	10886
Grid Net Inc (PA)	7371	D	415 872-5097	15191
Groundwork Open Source Inc	7375	D	415 992-4500	16228
Guardsmark LLC	7381	B	415 956-6070	16680
Guidebook Inc (PA)	7371	D	650 319-7233	15194
H&R Block Inc	7291	E	415 441-2666	13708
Habenicht & Howlett A Corp	1793	D	415 824-7040	3406
Hackerone Inc (PA)	7374	D	415 891-0777	16140
Hall Capital Partners LLC (PA)	6282	D	415 288-0544	10086
Hamilton Families	8322	D	415 409-2100	23829
Handlery Hotels Inc	7011	C	415 781-7800	12639
Hands-On Mobile Americas Inc (PA)	7373	E	415 580-6400	15969
Hanson Bridgett LLP (PA)	8111	B	415 543-2055	23122
Harley Ellis Devereaux Corp	8712	D	415 981-2345	26055
Harrison Drywall Inc	1742	E	415 821-9584	2892
Hart Howerton Ltd (PA)	0781	D	415 439-2200	759
Hartford Casualty Insurance Co	6331	A	415 836-4800	10360
Hassard Bonnington LLP (PA)	8111	D	415 288-9800	23125
Hatfield Inc	7291	E	415 802-8635	13709
Hathaway Dinwiddie Cnstr Co	1542	B	415 986-2718	1546
Hathaway Dinwiddie Cnstr Group (PA)	1542	B	415 986-2718	1547
Haven Engineering Inc	4731	E	888 838-3868	5084
Hawaii Parent Corp	6726	E	415 263-3660	12062
HDR Architecture Inc	8711	D	415 546-4242	25725
HDR Engineering Inc	8742	D	415 546-4200	27260
Hearsay Social Inc (PA)	7372	D	888 990-3777	15703
Heartland Payment Systems Inc	7389	D	415 518-4810	17219
Hebrew Home For Aged Disabled	8051	A	415 334-2500	20521
Heffernan Insurance Brokers	6411	C	800 829-9996	10646
Hellman & Friedman Capital IV	6799	E	415 788-5111	12231
Hellmuth Obata & Kassabaum Inc (DH)	8712	C	415 243-0555	26057
Henry Broadcasting Co	4832	E	415 285-1133	5720
Henry J Kaiser Fmly Foundation (PA)	6732	C	650 854-9400	12078
Herrero Builders Incorporated (PA)	1541	A	415 824-7675	1407
Highmark Capital Management	6282	D	800 582-4734	10088
Hill & Knowlton Strategies LLC	8743	D	415 281-7120	27556
Hilton San Francisco Fincl Dst	7011	E	415 433-6600	12668
Hines Gs Properties Inc	6552	E	415 982-6200	11880
Hinttech Inc	8748	C	415 874-3200	27748
Hirschfeld Kraemer LLP (PA)	8111	E	415 835-9000	23132
Hit Portfolio I Misc Trs LLC	7011	A	415 788-1234	12675
Hit Portfolio I Misc Trs LLC	7011	A	415 788-1234	12683
Hks Architects Inc	8712	E	415 356-3800	26061
Hok Group Inc	8712	C	415 243-0555	26065
Holland & Knight LLP	8111	E	415 743-6900	23134
Holzmueller Corporation	7359	E	415 826-8383	14514
Homebridge Inc	8322	B	415 255-2079	23841
Homeless Prenatal Program	8322	E	415 546-6756	23843
Homestar Systems Inc	7379	D	415 694-6000	16390
Honeybook Inc	7371	D	770 403-9234	15200
Hood & Strong LLP (PA)	8721	D	415 781-0793	26224
Horn Group Inc	7311	E	415 905-4000	13840
Hornberger Worstell Assoc Inc	8712	E	415 391-1080	26067
Hornblower Yachts LLC (PA)	4489	C	415 788-8866	4719
Host Hotels & Resorts Inc	7011	E	415 775-7555	12701
Host Hotels & Resorts LP	7011	E	415 896-1600	12708
Hotel Nikko San Francisco Inc	7011	B	415 394-1111	12730
Hotel Tonight Inc (PA)	7011	D	800 208-2949	12731
Hotel Whitcomb	7011	D	415 626-8000	12732
Hotwire Inc	4813	C	415 645-7350	5579
House of Air LLC	7999	D	415 345-9675	19183
Howard Hughes Medical Inst	8731	C	415 476-9668	26379

Employment Codes: A=Over 500 employees, B=251-500,
C=101-250, D=51-100, E=50

2019 Directory of California
Wholesalers and Services Companies

© Mergent Inc. 1-800-342-5647

1665

GEOGRAPHIC

Company	SIC	EMP	PHONE	ENTRY #
Huckleberry Youth Programs Inc (PA)	8322	D	415 668-2622	23845
Humanitycom Inc	7371	E	415 230-0108	15202
Hunton Andrews Kurth LLP	8111	D	415 975-3700	23139
Huntsman Architectural Group (PA)	8712	D	415 394-1212	26069
Huskies Lessee LLC	7011	B	415 392-7755	12744
Hvsf Transition LLC	7311	D	415 477-1999	13841
Hyatt Corporation	7011	B	415 848-6050	12748
Ic BP III Holdings Xii LLC	6531	D	415 549-5054	11510
Ic BP III Holdings Xv LLC	6519	E	415 273-4250	11174
Ideo LP	7389	D	415 615-5000	17231
Ifwe Inc (HQ)	7372	C	415 946-1850	15707
Iheartcommunications Inc	4832	B	415 975-5555	5721
Ihms (sf) LLC	7011	C	415 781-5555	12761
Impact Destinations & Events	7299	E	415 766-4170	13750
Imperial Parking (us) LLC	7521	A	415 495-3909	17684
Indus Corporation	7371	D	415 202-1830	15213
Indus Light & Magic (vanco) LL	7699	D	415 292-4671	17957
Industrial Grwth Partners V LP	6719	D	415 882-4550	11987
Influxdata Inc	7389	C	415 295-1901	17234
Ingenio Inc	4813	C	415 248-4000	5586
Ingenio LLC	7389	D	415 992-8218	17235
Inkling Systems Inc	8742	D	415 975-4420	27274
Insideview Technologies Inc	5045	C	415 728-9309	7064
Insikt Inc	7389	D	415 391-2431	17241
Institute For Health & Healing	8062	E	415 600-3503	21459
Institute For One World Health	7991	E	650 392-2510	18613
Institute On Aging	8322	D	415 600-2690	23858
Institute On Aging (PA)	8322	D	415 750-4101	23859
Insurance Services Office Inc	7375	B	415 874-4361	16232
Integrated Clg Solutions Inc	7349	E	415 821-6757	14290
Intercntnntal Ht Group Rsurces	7011	B	415 771-9000	12764
Intercom Inc	7371	B	831 920-7088	15229
Intercontinental Hotels	7011	C	415 616-6500	12765
Intercontinental Hotels Group	7011	C	415 626-6103	12768
Intercontinental Hotels Group	7011	D	415 398-8900	12770
Intercontinental Hotels Group	7011	E	415 409-4600	12772
International Bus Mchs Corp	5044	C	415 545-4747	6963
Internet Archive	7375	C	415 561-6767	16233
Internet Escrow Services Inc	6531	D	888 511-8600	11515
Interpacific Group Inc	8721	A	415 442-0711	26230
Interstate Hotels Resorts Inc	7011	C	415 362-5500	12775
Interstellar Inc	8741	D	415 598-0346	26901
Invitae Corporation (PA)	8734	D	415 374-7782	26709
Isyndicate Inc	7375	D	415 896-1900	16234
Ita Group Inc	8742	C	415 277-3200	27283
J Walter Thompson USA LLC	7311	D	415 268-5555	13852
Japanese Cmnty Youth Council (PA)	8399	D	415 202-7905	24792
Jeffer Mngels Btlr Mtchell LLP	8111	D	415 398-8080	23150
Jetro Cash and Carry Entps LLC	5147	D	415 920-2888	8620
Jewis Vocational & Counseling	8331	D	415 391-3600	24196
Jewish Community Fedrtn San Fr (PA)	8399	D	415 777-0411	24793
Jewish Family and Chld Svcs (PA)	8322	B	415 449-1200	23873
Jewish Senior Living Group	6513	D	415 562-2600	11036
Jh Capital Partners LP	6799	E	415 364-0300	12235
Jillians San Francisco CA	7389	D	415 369-6100	17259
Jmt Charitable Foundation	8721	D	415 974-6000	26231
Jn Projects Inc	7299	D	415 766-0273	13755
John Paul USA (PA)	7363	D	415 905-6088	14866
John Stewart Company (PA)	6531	D	213 833-1860	11536
Joie De Vivre Hospitality LLC (PA)	8741	E	415 835-0300	26909
Joie De Vivre Hospitality LLC	8741	D	415 986-2000	26910
Jones Lang Lasalle Inc	6531	C	415 395-4900	11537
Joyent Inc	7379	C	415 400-0600	16416
Joyride Coffee Distrs LLC	5149	D	718 841-7206	8815
Jumpshot Inc	7371	D	415 212-9250	15244
K&L Gates LLP	8111	D	415 882-8200	23157
K&L Gates LLP	8111	D	415 249-1000	23159
Kabam Inc (HQ)	7371	D	604 256-0054	15246
Kaiser Foundation Hospitals	6324	D	415 833-2616	10217
Kaiser Foundation Hospitals	8011	A	415 833-2000	19530
Kaiser Foundation Hospitals	8011	C	415 833-9688	19596
Kaiser Foundation Hospitals	8011	A	415 833-2000	19617
Kaiser Med Security Services	7381	D	415 833-3683	16710
Kallidus Inc	7371	C	877 554-2176	15247
Kane & Finkel LLC	7311	C	415 777-4990	13854
Kcbs News Radio 74	4832	D	415 765-4112	5732
Keep Truckin Inc (PA)	7371	E	855 434-3564	15249
Keker and Van Nest LLP	8111	D	415 391-5400	23167
Kennedy/Jenks Consultants Inc (PA)	8711	D	415 243-2150	25777
Kenshoo Inc (HQ)	8742	C	877 536-7462	27294
Ketchum Incorporated	8743	D	415 984-6100	27559
Kfi	8741	E	415 956-9812	26918
Kgo Television Inc	4833	C	415 954-7777	5808
Kid Stock Inc	7922	D	415 753-3737	18377
Kilroy Realty LP	6531	D	415 243-8803	11551
Kimpton Hotel & Rest Group LLC	7011	D	415 885-2500	12809
Kimpton Hotel & Rest Group LLC (HQ)	7011	D	415 397-5572	12810
Kimpton Hotel & Rest Group LLC	7011	C	415 397-7720	12811
Kimpton Hotel & Rest Group LLC	7011	D	415 561-1100	12812
Kimpton Hotel & Rest Group LLC	7011	D	415 561-1111	12813
Kimpton Hotel & Rest Group LLC	8741	D	415 292-0100	26919
Kindred Healthcare Oper Inc	8051	D	415 922-5085	20561
Kindred Healthcare Oper Inc	8062	C	415 566-1200	21537
Kindred Nursing Centers W LLC	8093	C	415 673-8405	22607
King & Spalding LLP	8111	B	415 318-1200	23171
Kinsale Holdings Inc	5122	C	415 400-2600	8186
Kipp Foundation	8399	C	415 399-1556	24798
Kirkland & Ellis LLP	8111	C	415 439-1400	23174
Kisco Senior Living LLC	8741	D	415 664-6264	26921
KMD Architects (PA)	8712	D	415 398-5191	26075
Kms Fishermans Wharf LP	7011	C	415 561-1100	12819
Kong Inc	7371	E	415 754-9283	15251
Kountable Inc	7389	D	310 613-5481	17729
Kpff Inc	8711	D	415 989-1004	25789
Kpisoft Inc	7372	D	415 439-5228	15734
Kpmg LLP	8721	E	415 963-5100	26238
Kqed Inc (PA)	4833	B	415 864-2000	5812
Kraft & Kennedy Inc	7373	D	415 956-4000	15993
L-O Soma Hotel Inc	7011	B	415 974-6400	12826
La Salle Apartments	6513	D	415 647-0607	11049
Landor Associates Intl Ltd (DH)	7336	C	415 365-1700	14118
Lateral Designs Inc	7336	C	415 847-6618	14119
Latham & Watkins LLP	8111	C	415 391-0600	23191
Launch Media Inc (HQ)	4813	C	310 593-6152	5593
Lawson Roofing Co Inc	1761	D	415 285-1661	3172
Leadstack Inc	7361	D	628 200-3063	14662
Leemah Electronics Inc	4911	C	415 394-1288	6048
Leerink Partners LLC	6211	D	800 778-1164	9970
Legend Merchant Group Inc	7389	E	415 957-9555	17293
Legion Corporation	7381	C	800 750-0062	16717
Lendingclub Asset MGT LLC	6163	D	415 632-5600	9891
Lendingclub Corporation (PA)	6153	D	415 632-5600	9741
Level-It Installations Ltd	1542	E	604 942-2022	1581
Lever Inc	7371	D	415 458-2731	15257
Levin and Simes	8111	E	415 426-3000	23203
Lewis & Taylor LLC	7349	C	415 781-3496	14302
Lewis Brsbois Bsgard Smith LLP	8111	C	415 362-2580	23209
Lewis P C Jackson	8111	C	415 394-9400	23212
Lewis PR Inc (DH)	8743	D	415 432-2400	27561
Liberty Mutual Insurance Co	6331	C	415 957-1175	10366
Licensale Inc	6794	D	604 681-6888	12138
Lieff Cabraser Heimann & (PA)	8111	C	415 788-0245	23215
Lightbend Inc	7371	D	877 989-7372	15258
Linardos Enterprises Inc	8742	D	415 644-0827	27304
Linden Research Inc	7371	B	415 243-9000	15260
Lithium Technologies LLC (PA)	7372	D	415 757-3100	15742
Little Sisters of Poor	8361	C	415 751-6510	24582
Littler Mendelson PC (PA)	8111	B	415 433-1940	23217
Live Nation Merchandise Inc (HQ)	5199	E	415 247-7400	9232
Livevox Inc (PA)	8748	D	415 671-6000	27776
LLP Locke Lord	8111	C	415 318-8800	23219
LLP Moss Adams	8721	C	415 956-1500	26250
Lockheed Martin Corporation	8711	C	415 402-0406	25800
Long & Levit LLP	8111	E	415 397-2222	23227
Low Ball & Lynch A Prof Corp (PA)	8111	D	415 981-6630	23230
Loyal3 Holdings Inc	7389	D	415 981-0700	17305
Lucasfilm Ltd LLC (HQ)	7812	C	415 623-1000	18074
Lumetra Healthcare Solutions	8748	C	415 677-2000	27777
Luxor Cabs Inc	4121	D	415 282-4141	3866
Lyft Inc (PA)	4119	B	415 230-2905	3819
Lynch Gilardi & Grummer LLP	8111	C	415 397-2800	23235
M & H Realty Partners LP	6799	D	415 693-9000	12241
M Arthur Gensler Jr Assoc Inc (PA)	8712	B	415 433-3700	26088
M Squared Consulting Inc (HQ)	8742	C	415 391-1038	27312
M T C Holdings (DH)	4491	C	912 651-4000	4729
Macarthur Transit Community	1521	C	415 989-1111	1194
Macfarlane Partners LLC (PA)	6722	D	415 356-2500	12041
Macqurie Arcft Lsg Svcs US Inc	7359	C	415 829-6600	14523
Malcolm Drilling Company Inc (PA)	1799	C	415 901-4400	3548
Marcum LLP	8721	C	415 543-6900	26256
Marcus & Millichap Real Estate	6531	E	415 391-9220	11584
Mariadb Usa Inc	5045	D	847 562-9000	7075
Marin Software Incorporated (PA)	7374	C	415 399-2580	16153
Marines Memorial Association	8641	C	415 673-6672	25197
Marketbridge Corp	8742	D	240 752-1800	27319
Marketwatch Inc (DH)	7383	D	415 439-6400	16956
Markmonitor Holdings Inc	7371	B	415 278-8400	15274
Markmonitor Inc (DH)	7379	D	415 278-8400	16423
Maroevich OShea & Coghlan	6411	D	415 957-0600	10678
Marriot Courtyard	7011	E	415 775-1103	12877

Mergent email: customerrelations@mergent.com
1666
2019 Directory of California
Wholesalers and Services Companies
(P-0000) Products & Services Section entry number
(PA)=Parent Co (HQ)=Headquarters (DH)=Div Headquarters

Company	SIC	EMP	PHONE	ENTRY #
Marriott International Inc	7011	D	415 947-0700	12885
Marriott International Inc	7011	D	415 989-3500	12900
Marriott International Inc (PA)	7011	D	415 929-2030	12906
Marsh & McLennan Agency LLC	6411	D	415 243-4160	10680
Marsh USA Inc	6411	D	415 743-8000	10683
Mason Street Opco LLC	7011	A	415 772-5000	12914
Masonic Homes of California (PA)	8361	B	415 776-7000	24593
Massdrop Inc	8748	D	415 340-2999	27782
Maverick Hotel Partners LLC	8741	D	415 655-9526	26938
Maximus Real Estate Partners	6519	D	415 584-4832	11177
Maxson Young Assoc Inc	6411	C	415 228-6400	10685
Maynard Cooper & Gale PC	8111	C	415 704-7433	23240
Mazzetti Inc (PA)	8711	E	415 362-3266	25814
McCann World Group Inc (PA)	7311	D	415 262-5500	13861
McCann-Erickson Corporation (HQ)	7311	D	415 348-5600	13862
McCann-Erickson Usa Inc	8732	C	415 262-5600	26543
McKesson Corporation (PA)	5122	A	415 983-8300	8196
McKinsey & Company Inc	8742	B	415 981-0250	27330
McMillan Data Cmmnications Inc	1731	D	415 826-5100	2641
McMillan Electric	1731	D	415 826-5100	2642
MD P Foundation Inc	8322	C	415 552-0240	23913
MDE Electric Company Inc	1731	E	415 552-2500	2643
Meals On Whels San Frncsco Inc	8322	E	415 920-1111	23917
Meany Wilson L P	6552	D	415 905-5300	11890
Medidata Solutions Inc	8733	C	415 295-4300	26638
Mekanism Inc (PA)	7311	D	415 908-4000	13865
Meltwater News US Inc (DH)	7383	D	415 829-5900	16958
Memsql Inc (PA)	7371	E	855 463-6775	15277
Mercer (us) Inc	8742	C	415 743-8700	27337
Mercer Health & Benefits LLC	8742	D	415 743-8751	27339
Merchant Services Inc (PA)	7374	B	817 725-0900	16155
Mercy Hsing California Xxxiv	6513	D	415 503-0816	11066
Meridian Industrial Trust	6798	D	415 281-3900	12175
Meridian Management Group	6531	C	415 434-9700	11608
Merlin Securities LLC	6211	D	415 848-0269	9974
Merrill Lynch Pierce Fenner	6211	E	415 274-7000	9988
Metromile Inc (PA)	6331	D	888 244-1702	10381
Metropolitan Club	7997	D	415 673-0600	18973
Metropolitan Elec Cnstr Inc	1731	D	415 642-3000	2646
Metropolitan Life Insur Co	6411	B	415 536-1065	10691
Metropolitan Trnsp Comm (PA)	4111	C	415 778-6700	3682
Michael Cardellini	8711	E	415 243-8400	25822
Micro Holding Corp	7374	A	415 788-5111	16158
Microsoft Corporation	7372	C	415 972-6400	15764
Midokura USA Inc	7371	E	888 512-0460	15281
Mile Post Properties LLC	7011	D	415 673-4711	12928
Milliman Inc	8999	E	415 403-1333	27946
Minami Tamaki LLP	8111	E	415 788-9000	23255
Mindfull Body	7999	D	415 931-2639	19203
Minimalisms Inc	7389	D	415 309-3108	17330
Mission Neighborhood Hlth Ctr (PA)	8011	C	415 552-3870	19693
Mission Pets Inc	5199	D	415 904-9914	9237
Mission Stuart Ht Partners LLC	7011	D	415 278-3700	12931
Mitchell Engineering	1794	E	415 227-1040	3435
Mithun Inc	8621	D	415 956-0688	25028
Mizuho Securities USA Inc	6211	D	415 268-5500	9991
Mjus LLC (fka Mindjet Llc)	7372	D	415 229-4344	15766
Mma Renewable Ventures LLC	5074	D	415 229-8817	7630
Mobpartner Inc	7312	D	650 300-6388	13928
Moffitt H C Hospital	8062	C	415 476-1000	21595
Monitise Americas Inc	7371	D	415 526-7900	15291
Monroe Residence Club	6513	D	415 771-9119	11080
Mons Viridis Llc	4813	D	415 297-6765	5605
Moov Corporation	7371	C	877 666-8932	15292
Morgan Lewis & Bockius LLP	8111	A	415 393-2000	23260
Morgan Lewis & Bockius LLP	8111	B	415 442-1000	23264
Morgan Stanley & Co LLC	6211	D	415 693-6000	10005
Morgans Hotel Group MGT LLC	7011	C	415 775-4700	12944
Morrison & Foerster LLP	8111	E	925 295-3300	23269
Morrison & Foerster LLP (PA)	8111	B	415 268-7000	23271
Morrison & Foerster LLP	8111	B	415 268-7178	23272
Motion Math Inc	7371	C	415 590-2961	15294
Mufg Union Bank National Assn (DH)	6021	A	415 705-7000	9353
Mulesoft Inc	7372	A	415 229-2009	15770
Munger Tolles Olson Foundation	8111	E	415 512-4000	23276
Murphy (PA)	8111	D	415 788-1900	23278
MWH Americas Inc	8711	D	415 430-1800	25839
Mxb Battery Operations LP	8641	D	415 230-8000	25204
Mya Systems Inc	7361	E	877 679-0952	14670
Mypointscom LLC (HQ)	7311	D	415 615-1100	13869
National Assn Ltr Carriers	8631	B	415 362-0214	25072
National Council Negro Women	8699	D	415 564-4153	25445
Ncc Group Inc (HQ)	7379	D	415 268-9300	16431
Ncircle Network Security Inc (DH)	7371	D	415 625-5900	15301
Netsource Inc	7361	D	415 831-3681	14672
Nevin Levy LLP A Partnership	6531	D	415 800-5770	11625
New Civic Company Ltd	6799	C	415 986-1668	12248
New Paradigm Productions Inc (PA)	7812	D	415 924-8000	18084
New Relic Inc (PA)	7372	C	650 777-7600	15780
New York Life Insurance Co	6411	E	415 393-6060	10709
Nexant Inc (PA)	8748	D	415 369-1000	27801
Nexstar Broadcasting Inc	4833	B	415 441-4444	5829
Nextdoorcom Inc	8399	D	415 236-0000	24815
Nibbi Bros Associates Inc	1522	C	415 863-1820	1303
Nicolaides Fink Thorpe Michael	8111	D	415 745-3778	23285
Nielsen Mobile LLC (DH)	7389	C	917 435-9301	17354
Ninth House Inc	8331	E	612 339-0927	24210
Nitro Software Inc	7371	C	415 632-4894	15312
Nixon Peabody LLP	8111	C	415 984-8200	23287
No More Dirt Inc	7349	D	415 821-6757	14332
Nob Hill Properties Inc	7011	B	415 474-5400	12958
Nomura Securities Intl Inc	6211	B	415 445-3831	10007
Norcal Mutual Insurance Co (PA)	6411	B	415 397-9703	10718
Norcal Painters Inc	1721	D	415 566-6800	2461
Northern California Institute	8399	B	415 750-6954	24816
Northern California Presbyteri	8051	B	415 922-9700	20664
Nossaman LLP	8111	B	415 398-3600	23293
Novogradac and Co LLP	8721	D	415 356-8000	26262
NRG Energy Inc	4911	D	415 255-8105	6062
Nuna Incorporated	7371	D	415 942-5200	15322
Nyse Arca Inc	6231	B	415 393-4000	10049
Obscura Digital Incorporated	7313	E	415 227-9979	13950
Ocean Park Health Center	8011	D	415 753-8100	19728
Ogletree Deakins Nash Smoak	8111	D	415 442-4810	23295
Okabe International Inc (PA)	4725	E	415 921-0808	4973
Okta Inc (PA)	7371	C	888 722-7871	15326
Olympic Club (PA)	8641	B	415 345-5100	25207
OMelveny & Myers LLP	8111	C	415 984-8700	23300
Omni Hotels Corporation	7011	B	415 677-9494	12983
On Lok Inc	8011	D	415 292-8888	19734
On Lok Senior Health Services (PA)	6324	A	415 292-8888	10285
On24 Inc (PA)	7372	B	877 202-9599	15789
Onboardiq Inc	7375	E	480 433-1197	16239
One Embarcadero Center Venture	6798	D	415 772-0700	12177
One Medical Group Inc (PA)	8011	C	415 578-3100	19735
One Medical Group Inc	8011	C	415 529-4522	19736
One Nob Hill Associates LLC	7011	D	415 392-3434	12985
One Workplace L Ferrari LLC	5021	E	415 357-2200	6733
One Workplace L Ferrari LLC	8744	D	415 357-2200	27603
One10 LLC	8742	D	415 398-3534	27379
One10 LLC	8742	D	415 844-2200	27380
Open Harbor Inc	8742	D	650 413-4200	27381
Opentable Inc (HQ)	7389	C	415 344-4200	17371
Opentv Inc (DH)	7372	C	415 962-5000	15790
Opswat Inc (PA)	7371	D	415 590-7300	15333
Optimizely Inc (PA)	7371	C	415 376-4598	15334
Oracle America Inc	7372	D	415 908-3609	15793
Oracle Corporation	7372	C	415 402-7200	15807
Orange Silicon Valley	8748	D	415 243-1500	27815
Orchard International Group (PA)	7011	D	415 362-8878	12987
Organic Inc (HQ)	7379	C	415 581-5300	16446
Organic Holdings Inc	7311	B	415 581-5300	13875
Orrick Hrrington Sutcliffe LLP (PA)	8111	C	415 773-5700	23301
Osterhout Group Inc	7389	E	415 644-4000	17378
Otis Elevator Company	7699	D	415 546-0880	17966
Otr Global LLC	8732	E	415 675-7660	26525
Oum & Co LLP (PA)	8721	D	415 434-3744	26263
Outcast Agency LLC	8743	C	415 392-8282	27567
Pac-12 Enteprises LLC	7313	C	415 580-4200	13951
Pacific Bell Telephone Company (HQ)	4813	A	415 542-9000	5619
Pacific Eagle Holdings Corp	6512	D	415 398-2473	10925
Pacific Energy Fuels Company	4924	A	415 973-8200	6158
Pacific Eye Associated Inc	8011	D	415 923-3007	19741
Pacific Gas and Electric Co (HQ)	4911	A	415 973-7000	6068
Pacific Gas and Electric Co	4911	B	415 695-3513	6092
Pacific Gas and Electric Co	4924	D	415 973-8089	6161
Pacific Growth Equities LLC	6211	D	415 274-6800	10008
Pacific Park Management	8741	D	415 440-4840	26971
Pacific Structures Inc (PA)	1771	D	415 970-5434	3302
Pacific Union Club	8641	D	415 775-1234	25210
Pacific Union Co	6531	D	415 474-6600	11652
Pacific Union RE Group (DH)	6531	D	415 929-7100	11655
Paganini Electric Corporation	1731	C	415 575-3900	2671
Pagerduty Inc (PA)	4899	D	650 989-2965	5991
Paragon Real Estate Group	6531	D	415 323-4066	11660
Parenthood of Planned	8641	D	415 821-1282	25214
Paribas Asset Management Inc	6082	D	415 772-1300	9664
Pariveda Solutions Inc	7373	C	415 946-6100	16030
Park Hotels & Resorts Inc	7011	B	415 771-1400	13022
Park Hotels & Resorts Inc	7011	B	415 392-8000	13028

GEOGRAPHIC

	SIC	EMP	PHONE	ENTRY #
Park Hotels & Resorts Inc	7011	D	415 771-1400	13040
Parkmerced Investors LLC	7359	E	877 243-5544	14534
Parkside Lending LLC	6211	D	415 771-3700	10009
Parsons Corporation	1611	D	415 490-2400	1834
Parthenon DCS Holdings LLC	8741	A	925 960-4800	26981
Patreon Inc	7371	D	415 967-2735	15346
Pattern Energy Group LP (PA)	4911	D	415 283-4000	6097
Pattern Renewables 2 LP	1711	C	415 283-4000	2308
Paul Hastings LLP	8111	D	415 856-7000	23318
Pccp LLC (PA)	6798	D	415 732-7645	12179
People Center Inc	7372	E	781 864-1232	15829
Pepsi-Cola Metro Btlg Co Inc	5149	D	415 206-7400	8851
Pereira & ODell LLC (PA)	7311	D	415 284-9916	13877
Perkins Coie LLP	8111	E	415 344-7000	23324
Permanente Medical Group Inc	8062	D	415 833-2000	21639
Permanente Medical Group Inc	6324	C	415 833-2000	10297
Pets Unlimited	8699	C	415 563-6700	25451
PG&e Capital LLC	8742	B	415 321-4600	27394
PG&e Corporation (PA)	4931	C	415 973-1000	6185
Phacil Inc	7371	A	415 901-1600	15356
PHF Ruby LLC	7011	C	415 885-4700	13060
Philippine Airlines Inc	4512	C	415 217-3100	4795
Philotic Inc	7371	D	510 730-1740	15358
Picsart Inc	7371	D	415 757-6800	15359
Pier 39 Limited Partnership (PA)	6512	C	415 705-5500	10927
Pillsbury Winthrop Shaw	8111	C	415 983-1000	23328
Pillsbury Winthrop Shaw	8111	B	415 983-1075	23331
Pine & Powell Partners LLC	7011	D	415 989-3500	13064
Pinterest Inc (PA)	7375	B	650 561-5407	16241
Pioneer Square Hotel Company	7011	E	415 346-2323	13067
Pivotal Software Inc (HQ)	7371	C	415 777-4868	15361
Plaid Inc	7375	C	415 799-1354	16242
Planet Labs Inc (PA)	7374	D	415 829-3313	16165
Planetout Inc (HQ)	4813	E	415 834-6500	5628
Playwrights Foundation Inc	7922	D	415 626-2176	18394
Plivo Inc (PA)	4813	D	415 758-3659	5629
Polaris Research & Development	8748	D	415 777-3229	27823
Pomeroy Rcrtion Rhbltation Ctr (PA)	8322	C	415 665-4100	23974
Post Street Renaissance	7011	B	415 563-0303	13078
Postman Inc	7371	D	415 796-6470	15371
Postmates Inc (PA)	4789	C	800 882-6106	5242
Powerreviews Oc LLC	7371	D	415 315-9208	15372
Practice Fusion Inc (PA)	7371	D	415 346-7700	15373
Praetorian Group (PA)	7379	E	415 962-8310	16458
Presidio Wealth Management LLC	6282	E	415 449-2500	10106
Pricewaterhousecoopers LLP	8721	B	415 498-5000	26278
Primitive Logic Inc	7373	D	415 391-8080	16035
Prn LLC (HQ)	7371	D	415 805-2525	15376
Proday Co	7313	C	517 980-1362	13953
Progress Foundation	8641	D	415 553-3100	25217
Progress Glass Co Inc (PA)	1793	C	415 824-7040	3408
Project Open Hand (PA)	8322	D	415 292-3400	23977
Prologis Inc (PA)	6798	A	415 394-9000	12182
Prologis LP (HQ)	6798	B	415 394-9000	12183
Prophet Brand Strategy (PA)	8742	E	415 677-0909	27406
Prosper Funding LLC	6153	C	415 593-5400	9746
Prosper Marketplace Inc (PA)	6163	C	415 593-5400	9904
Prudential California Realty	6531	D	415 664-9400	11693
Prudential Insur Co of Amer	6411	D	415 398-7310	10747
Prudential Insur Co of Amer	6324	D	415 486-3050	10303
Prudential Realty Corp	6531	D	415 566-9800	11695
Ps24 Inc	8741	D	415 834-5105	27005
Public Policy Institute Cal (PA)	8611	D	415 291-4400	24975
PWC STRategy& (us) LLC	8742	C	415 498-5000	27412
Quadriga Inc	7371	D	650 270-6326	15388
Quality Planning Corporation	8742	D	415 369-0707	27415
Quantcast Corporation (PA)	7371	D	800 293-5706	15390
Quest Software Inc	7372	D	415 373-2222	15837
Quicksilver Delivery Inc	7389	C	415 431-1600	17420
Quinn Emanuel Urquhart	8111	E	415 875-6600	23344
Quri Inc	8732	E	415 413-0100	26559
R & S Investments (PA)	6722	D	415 591-2700	12045
Radisson Ht Fishermans Wharf	7011	D	415 392-6700	13094
Rainbow Wtrprofing Restoration	1799	C	415 641-1578	3574
Rainforest Qa Inc	7371	C	650 866-1407	15394
Randstad North America Inc	7363	C	415 397-3384	14899
Ranger Pipelines Incorporated	1623	C	415 822-3700	1973
Rappi Inc	4215	B	347 740-4824	4428
RE Barren Ridge 1 LLC	4911	C	415 675-1500	6099
RE La Mesa LLC	1629	D	415 675-1500	2058
Real Estate Equity Exchange	6162	D	415 992-4200	9854
Rec Center	5091	C	415 831-6818	7937
Reciprocity Inc	7371	E	415 851-8667	15399
Recology Inc (PA)	4953	D	415 875-1000	6434
Recology Inc	4953	D	415 330-1300	6435
Recology Inc	4953	D	415 970-1582	6437
Recology Inc	4953	C	415 330-1400	6439
Recology San Francisco	4953	C	415 468-1752	6441
Recurve Inc	7623	D	510 540-4860	17896
Red Sky Interactive	7311	C	415 430-3200	13890
Redfin Corporation	6531	B	206 340-8794	11721
Reed Smith LLP	8111	D	415 659-5964	23348
Reed Smith LLP	8111	C	415 543-8700	23350
Reed Smith LLP	8111	C	415 543-8700	23351
Reliable Caregivers Inc	8082	C	415 436-0100	22403
Reneson Hotels Inc	7011	C	415 621-7001	13116
Rentjuice Corporation	4813	D	415 376-0369	5634
Republic Indemnity Co Amer	6331	D	415 981-3200	10387
Resmex Partners LLC	7389	E	415 440-2737	17427
Respond 2 LLC	7812	C	415 398-4200	18108
Restaurant Depot LLC	5181	C	415 920-2888	9021
Retailnext Inc	8732	C	408 298-2585	26562
Rfj Corporation	1742	D	415 824-6890	2947
Rhythmone LLC (HQ)	4813	D	415 655-1450	5635
Richard J Mendoza Inc	6331	D	415 644-0180	10391
Richmond Area Mlt-Services Inc	8093	D	415 392-4453	22661
Richmond Area Mlt-Services Inc	8093	D	415 800-0699	22662
Richmond Area Mlt-Services Inc	8093	D	415 689-5662	22663
Richmond Area Mlt-Services Inc	8093	D	415 579-3021	22664
Richmond Area Mlt-Services Inc (PA)	8093	D	415 800-0699	22665
Richmond Dst Neighborhood Cntr (PA)	8322	D	415 751-6600	23996
Ricoh Usa Inc	5044	D	415 733-5600	6975
Ricoh Usa Inc	5044	D	415 392-6850	6979
Riivos Inc	1731	D	415 813-1840	2708
Ritz-Carlton Hotel Company LLC	7011	B	415 781-9000	13125
Ritz-Carlton Hotel Company LLC	7011	B	415 773-6168	13129
Riviera Partners LLC (PA)	8742	D	877 748-4372	27429
RMR Construction Company	1542	C	415 647-0884	1631
Robert Half International Inc	7361	D	415 434-2429	14727
Robert Half International Inc	7361	C	415 434-1900	14736
Ropes & Gray LLP	8111	C	415 315-6300	23360
Rosendin Electric Inc	1731	D	415 495-9300	2715
Rosendin Electric Inc	1731	A	415 495-9300	2716
Rp/Kinetic Parc 55 Owner LLC	7011	C	415 392-8000	13145
Rpx Corporation (HQ)	6794	D	866 779-7641	12143
RSM US LLP	8721	D	415 848-5300	26282
Ruth Barajas	8322	E	415 977-6949	24000
Ryder Truck Rental Inc	7513	C	415 285-0756	17614
S F Auto Parts Whse Inc	5013	D	415 255-0115	6671
Saarman Construction Ltd	1522	C	415 749-2700	1314
Sagan Systems Inc	7371	D	650 387-8485	15423
Saint Francis Memorial Hosp (HQ)	8062	A	415 353-6000	21694
Salesforcecom Inc	7372	A	415 901-7000	15846
Salesforcecom Foundation	4813	C	800 667-6389	5638
Salesian Boys and Girls Club	7997	D	415 397-3068	19024
Salon Media Group Inc (PA)	7375	D	415 870-7566	16250
Salt Lake Hotel Associates LP (PA)	7011	C	415 397-5572	13164
Salvation Army	8361	D	415 643-8000	24663
Salvation Army Glden State Div (PA)	8322	D	415 553-3500	24007
San Francisco City & County	8322	D	415 695-5660	24016
San Francisco Aids Foundation (PA)	8322	D	415 487-3000	24017
San Francisco Ballet Assn	7922	C	415 865-2000	18402
San Francisco City & County	8322	D	415 356-2700	24018
San Francisco City & County	8322	D	415 356-2700	24019
San Francisco City & County	7539	C	415 550-4600	17798
San Francisco City Clinic	8093	D	415 487-5500	22673
San Francisco Federal Cr Un (PA)	6061	D	415 775-5377	9586
San Francisco Fertility Ctrs	8011	D	415 834-3000	19847
San Francisco Food Bank	8322	D	415 282-1900	24020
San Francisco Foundation	7389	C	415 733-8500	17454
San Francisco Health Authority (PA)	8621	D	415 615-4407	25040
San Francisco Hotel Associates	7011	C	415 392-4666	13173
San Francisco Hotel Group LLC	7011	C	415 276-9888	13174
San Francisco Ladies Protecti	8361	D	415 931-3136	24665
San Francisco Meritime N H P	8412	D	415 561-7000	24906
San Francisco Museum Modrn Art (PA)	8412	B	415 357-4035	24907
San Francisco Opera Assn	7922	A	415 861-4008	18403
San Francisco Partclr Cncl Sct	8322	D	415 255-3525	24021
San Francisco Radio Assets LLC (DH)	4832	C	415 216-1300	5753
San Francisco Symphony Inc (PA)	7929	B	415 552-8000	18459
San Francisco Tennis Club	7991	D	415 777-9000	18648
San Francisco Travel Assn	7389	D	415 974-6900	17455
San Francisco Zoological Soc	7999	C	415 753-7080	19230
San Frncsco Econ Oprtnty Cncl	8399	C	415 749-3798	24838
San Frncsco Mrtime Nat Pk Assn (PA)	8412	E	415 561-6662	24908
Sauce Labs Inc (PA)	7373	D	415 946-1117	16044
Scott Street Senior Housing Co	8052	C	415 345-5083	20953
Scribd Inc	7375	D	415 896-9890	16251
SD Squared North America Ltd	7371	C	650 721-1158	15433
Securitas SEC Svcs USA Inc	7381	C	510 568-6818	16792

Mergent email: customerrelations@mergent.com

1668

2019 Directory of California
Wholesalers and Services Companies

(P-0000) Products & Services Section entry number
(PA)=Parent Co (HQ)=Headquarters (DH)=Div Headquarters

	SIC	EMP	PHONE	ENTRY #
Sega of America Inc	5045	C	415 701-6000	7101
Seiler LLP	8721	C	415 392-2123	26289
Selectquote Insurance Services **(PA)**	6411	C	415 543-7338	10771
Self-Help For Elderly	8322	D	415 391-3843	24039
Self-Help For Elderly **(PA)**	8322	C	415 677-7600	24040
Sendme Inc	4813	D	415 978-9504	5641
Sentient Technologies USA LLC	7371	E	415 422-9886	15436
Severson & Werson A Prof Corp	8111	D	415 398-3344	23371
Seyfarth Shaw LLP	8111	D	415 397-2823	23374
Sfd Partners LLC	7011	B	415 392-7755	13210
Sfi 2365 Iron Point LLC	6512	E	415 395-9701	10935
Sfi Carlsbad LLC	6512	E	415 395-9701	10936
Sfo Airporter Inc	4111	D	415 495-3909	3725
Sfusd Building Ground	7349	D	415 695-5508	14389
Sfusd Jrotc Brigade	7371	D	415 242-2546	15441
Sharespost Inc	6719	D	800 279-7754	12005
Sharper Future	8011	D	415 297-6767	19889
Shartsis Friese LLP	8111	C	415 421-6500	23375
Shea Labagh Dobberstein Cpa **(PA)**	8721	E	415 731-0100	26290
Sheedy Drayage Co **(PA)**	7353	C	415 648-7171	14458
Shell Vacations LLC	8741	C	415 441-7100	27028
Shenyang Zhong Yi Tin-Plating	6512	C	415 788-2280	10937
Sheppard Mullin Richter	8111	D	415 434-9100	23379
Sheraton Corporation	7011	B	415 362-5500	13215
Shift Technologies Inc	5012	D	415 800-2038	6607
Shook Hardy & Bacon LLP	8111	D	415 544-1900	23383
Shorenstein Company LLC	6512	E	415 772-7000	10939
Shorenstein Properties LLC **(PA)**	6512	C	415 772-7000	10940
Shoreview Preservation LP	6513	D	415 647-6922	11112
Showpad Inc **(HQ)**	7379	B	415 800-2033	16483
Sideman & Bancroft LLP	8111	D	415 392-1960	23384
Sift Science Inc	7371	D	415 882-7709	15446
Sight Machine Inc	7372	D	888 461-5739	15852
Signaldemand Inc	7371	E	415 356-0800	15447
Silver Lake Partners II LP	6726	C	415 293-4355	12068
Simpler Postage Inc **(PA)**	4731	D	408 915-0063	5169
Simpson Gumpertz & Heger Inc	8711	C	415 495-3700	25915
Situs Holdings LLC	6799	B	415 374-2820	12267
Skidmore Owings & Merrill LLP	8712	C	415 981-1555	26107
Skyblue Sewing Manufacturing	7389	E	415 777-9978	17472
Skyline Commercial Interiors **(PA)**	1542	D	415 908-1020	1652
Slack Technologies Inc **(PA)**	7372	C	415 579-9153	15853
Smg Holdings Inc	6512	C	650 738-8737	10944
Smith-Emery San Francisco Inc	7389	C	415 647-7326	17475
Smithgroup Inc	8712	D	415 227-0100	26110
Smithgroup Inc	8712	C	313 442-8351	26111
Snapdocs Inc	7371	E	415 967-0136	15457
Soc/General Services/Bpm	8741	D	415 703-5341	27036
Social Finance Inc **(PA)**	6163	C	415 697-2049	9907
Socialize Inc	7372	E	415 529-4019	15856
Society For San Francisco	8699	C	415 554-3000	25464
Socratic Technologies Inc **(PA)**	8732	D	415 430-2200	26565
Sodexo Management Inc	8741	D	925 325-9657	27037
Soiree Valet Parking Service	7299	C	415 284-9700	13776
Solutionset LLC	7311	C	415 367-6300	13904
Soma Surgicenter	8062	E	415 641-6889	21758
Sony Electronics Inc	7812	B	415 833-4796	18119
South Market Child Care Inc	8351	D	415 820-3500	24384
Southbourne Inc	7011	C	415 781-5555	13250
Spigit Inc	7372	D	855 774-4480	15859
Splunk Inc	7372	C	415 848-8400	15860
Spus7 235 Pine LP	6726	C	231 683-4200	12069
Square Inc **(PA)**	7372	E	415 375-3176	15861
Squaretrade Inc **(DH)**	6399	C	415 541-1000	10504
Squire Patton Boggs (us) LLP	8111	C	415 954-0334	23396
SRI **(PA)**	6163	C	415 989-5363	9909
St Anthony Foundation **(PA)**	8322	E	415 241-2600	24066
St Francis Yacht Club	7997	C	415 563-6363	19062
St Marys Med Ctr Foundation	8062	A	415 668-1000	21789
Stackla Inc	7372	D	415 528-4910	15863
Stadtner Co Inc	1731	E	415 752-2850	2744
Standard Pacific Capital LLC	6211	E	415 352-7100	10014
Standard Poors Fincl Svcs LLC	6282	D	415 371-5000	10115
Stanford Hotels Corporation **(PA)**	7011	E	415 398-3333	13263
Stantec Arch & Engrg PC	8711	D	415 882-9500	25928
Stantec Architecture Inc	8711	D	415 882-9500	25929
Stantec Consulting Svcs Inc	8711	D	415 882-9500	25933
Starwood Hotels & Resorts	7011	D	415 777-5300	13269
Starwood Hotels & Resorts	7011	C	415 284-4000	13272
Starwood Htls & Rsrts Wrldwde	7011	C	415 284-4049	13277
Starwood Htls & Rsrts Wrldwde	7011	C	415 512-1111	13278
State Bar of California **(PA)**	8621	B	415 538-2000	25044
State Compensation Insur Fund **(PA)**	6331	C	888 782-8338	10394
Steele Cis LLC	8111	B	415 692-5000	23397
Steelriver Infrastructure Fund **(HQ)**	4924	C	415 291-2200	6179
Stein & Lubin LLP	8111	E	415 981-0550	23398
Sterling Consulting Group LLC	8742	D	415 248-7900	27469
Steve Silver Productions Inc	7922	D	415 421-4284	18406
Stone & Youngberg LLC **(PA)**	6211	C	415 445-2300	10016
Strevus Inc	7372	D	415 704-8182	15868
Stripe Inc	7373	A	888 963-8955	16061
Stryder Corp	7372	D	415 981-8400	15869
Stubhub Inc **(HQ)**	7374	D	415 222-8400	16183
Successor To San Francisco	8748	D	415 749-2400	27871
Sunday Bazaar Inc	5023	C	415 621-0764	6789
Sunrise Senior Living Inc	8051	D	415 664-6264	20807
Sunset Scavenger Company	4953	B	415 330-1300	6480
Sutter Bay Hospitals **(HQ)**	8062	A	415 600-6000	21799
Sutter Health	8062	B	415 600-7034	21804
Sutter Health	8742	B	415 600-3311	27477
Sutter Health	8062	B	415 345-0100	21809
Sutter Health	8062	C	415 731-6300	21811
Sutter Health	8062	C	415 600-0110	21812
Sutter Health	8062	A	415 600-1020	21817
Sutter Health	8062	A	415 600-0140	21820
Sutter Health	8062	A	415 600-4280	21821
Sutter Health	8011	E	415 647-8600	19981
Sutter Vsting Nrse Assn Hspice	8082	D	415 600-6200	22429
Swander Pace Capital LLC **(PA)**	8742	A	415 477-8500	27479
Swinerton Builders **(HQ)**	1541	C	415 421-2980	1439
Swinerton Incorporated **(PA)**	1542	C	415 421-2980	1666
Swirl Inc	7311	D	415 276-8300	13907
Switchfly Inc **(PA)**	5045	D	415 541-9100	7113
Syapse Inc	7372	D	650 924-1461	15870
Sypartners LLC **(HQ)**	8748	D	415 536-6600	27874
T Y Lin International **(HQ)**	8711	D	415 291-3700	25939
T-Mobile Usa Inc	4812	C	415 440-5370	5420
Tacit Knowledge Inc	7379	D	415 694-4322	16502
Tactivos Inc	4813	D	415 687-2501	5651
Talentburst Inc	7389	C	415 813-4011	17495
Talix Inc	7372	D	628 220-3885	15875
Tapjoy Inc **(PA)**	7311	C	415 766-6900	13908
Tariff Building Associates LP **(PA)**	6512	C	415 397-5572	10954
Taulia Inc **(PA)**	7371	C	415 376-8280	15492
Techlink Systems Inc **(PA)**	7361	B	415 732-7580	14776
Techsoup Global Inc	8641	C	800 659-3579	25266
Tegsco LLC	7549	D	415 575-2340	17875
Telegraph Hill Partners Invest **(PA)**	8742	E	415 765-6980	27483
Tenderloin Housing Clinic Inc	8099	C	415 771-2427	22895
Tenderloin Housing Clinic Inc **(PA)**	6531	C	415 771-9850	11789
Textainer Equipment Mgt US Ltd **(DH)**	7359	D	415 434-0551	14547
Textainer Group Holdings Ltd **(HQ)**	8741	D	415 434-0551	27060
Textainer Eqp Income Fund II LP	7359	D	415 434-0551	14548
The Charles Schwab Trust Co **(HQ)**	6211	E	415 371-0518	10020
Thermasource LLC **(PA)**	8711	D	707 523-2960	25951
Thiel Capital LLC **(PA)**	8742	D	415 567-7360	27488
Third & Mission Associates LLC	6531	E	415 341-8457	11794
Thismoment Inc	7371	C	415 200-4730	15502
Thoma Bravo LLC	6799	B	415 263-3660	12275
Thomas Weisel Partners LLC **(DH)**	6211	D	415 364-2500	10021
Thomson Reuters (legal) Inc	8748	D	415 344-6000	27885
Thomson Reuters (markets) LLC	7389	C	415 677-2500	17508
Thornton Tomasetti	8711	D	415 365-6900	25953
Thousandeyes Inc **(PA)**	7372	D	415 513-4526	15878
Ticketweb LLC	7999	E	415 901-0210	19244
Tides Inc **(PA)**	8399	C	415 561-6400	24849
Tides Center	7011	C	415 359-9401	13329
Tides Network	8399	D	415 561-6400	24850
Time Inc	7313	D	415 982-5000	13958
Tm Financial Forensics LLC **(PA)**	8748	E	415 692-6350	27886
Todays Hotel Corporation **(PA)**	7011	C	415 441-4000	13330
Tonal Systems Inc	7999	D	855 698-6625	19246
Toolworks Inc **(PA)**	8331	D	415 733-0990	24238
Topdown Consulting Inc	8742	D	888 644-8445	27491
Topgolf Media LLC **(HQ)**	7999	D	214 377-0615	19248
Topica Inc	4813	D	415 344-0800	5655
Towns End Studios LLC	7371	A	415 802-7936	15507
Tpg Sixth Street Partners LLC	6282	C	415 743-1500	10117
Tradeshift Holdings Inc **(HQ)**	6719	D	800 381-3585	12011
Transamerica Cbo I Inc	6282	D	415 983-4000	10118
Transamerica Intl Holdings	6719	C	415 983-4000	12012
TransMontaigne PDT Svcs LLC	4789	B	415 576-2000	5248
Treadwell & Rollo Inc **(DH)**	8711	C	415 955-9040	25958
Treeline Staffing	7361	E	415 819-7195	14784
Triage Consulting Group **(PA)**	8742	D	415 512-9400	27497
Trinity Capital Corporation **(DH)**	6159	D	415 956-5174	9764
Triton Cont Intl Inc N Amer **(DH)**	7353	D	415 956-6311	14460
Troutman Sanders LLP	8111	D	415 477-5700	23414
Trulia Inc **(HQ)**	7374	D	415 648-4358	16191
Trustarc Inc	7379	D	415 520-3400	16518

Name	SIC	EMP	PHONE	ENTRY #
Tunein Inc	4832	C	650 319-7100	5758
Turk & Eddy Associates LP	6513	D	415 474-6524	11130
Turner Construction Company	1542	D	415 705-8900	1685
Twilio Inc (PA)	4812	C	415 390-2337	5423
Twitch Interactive Inc	4813	A	415 919-5000	5657
Twitter Inc (PA)	7375	C	415 222-9670	16256
TY Lin International Group (PA)	8711	C	415 291-3700	25963
U C S F School of Dentistry	8021	E	415 476-5609	20141
Ubi Soft Entertainment	7929	D	415 547-4000	18471
UBS Financial Services Inc	6211	C	415 954-6700	10027
UBS Financial Services Inc	6211	C	415 398-6400	10030
UBS Financial Services Inc	6211	C	415 398-6400	10031
UBS Securities LLC	6211	C	415 352-5650	10032
Ucsf Aids Health Project	8322	C	415 476-6445	24099
United Behavioral Health (HQ)	8741	C	415 547-1403	27074
United Biosource LLC	0762	D	415 293-1340	715
United California Glass & Door	7699	C	415 824-8500	18001
United Parcel Service Inc OH	4215	C	415 252-4564	4457
United Way of Bay Area (PA)	8322	C	415 808-4300	24105
Universal Paragon Corporation (PA)	7011	B	415 468-6676	13354
Universal Protection Svc LP	7381	C	415 759-5056	16849
University Cal San Francisco	8733	D	415 476-9000	26669
University Cal San Francisco	8062	A	415 476-7000	21880
University Cal San Francisco	8062	E	415 476-1611	21881
University Cal San Francisco	8011	D	415 353-3155	20029
University Cal San Francisco	8062	B	415 567-6600	21882
UPS Supply Chain Solutions Inc	4731	D	650 635-2693	5192
UPS Supply Chain Solutions Inc	4225	E	415 775-6644	4649
URS Holdings Inc (DH)	8711	B	415 774-2700	25982
Usag Ansbach Financial MGT Div	8741	D	210 466-1376	27077
Usag Rheinland Pfalz Fincl MGT	8741	D	210 466-1376	27078
Usag Vicenza Italy Dmwr F M D	8741	D	210 466-1376	27079
Usag Wiesbaden Fincl MGT Div	8741	D	210 466-1376	27080
USI Insurance Services Nat Inc	6411	C	628 201-9001	10818
Ustream Inc	4813	D	415 489-9400	5660
Van Ness Hotel Inc	7011	D	415 673-4711	13364
Van Sark Inc	5021	D	415 362-5888	6739
Vector Talent II LLC	6726	A	415 293-5000	12072
Vegiworks Inc	5148	D	415 643-8686	8743
Venables/Bell & Partners LLC	7311	C	415 288-3300	13915
Vendini Inc (PA)	7371	D	415 693-9611	15521
Veritable Vegetable Inc	5148	D	415 641-3500	8744
Veritiv Operating Company	5113	D	415 586-9160	8132
Verizon Business Global LLC	4813	D	415 606-3621	5663
Verticalresponse Inc	8742	C	866 683-7842	27511
Vestek Systems Inc (DH)	7375	D	415 344-6000	16258
Veterans Health Administration	8011	A	415 750-2009	20066
Vida Health Inc	7371	D	408 203-7959	15527
Viking Asset Management LLC	6282	A	415 981-5300	10120
Vinson & Elkins LLP	8111	C	415 979-6900	23422
Vintrust Inc	4226	E	877 846-8787	4690
Viscira LLC	5045	D	415 848-8010	7128
Viva Soma Lessee Inc	8741	A	415 974-6400	27087
Vladigor Investment Inc	7542	D	415 558-9274	17842
Volta Charging LLC	7312	D	888 264-2208	13931
Volume Services Inc	7999	D	415 972-1500	19257
VSC Sports Inc	8748	D	415 820-3525	27906
W R Hambrecht Co Inc (PA)	6211	D	415 551-8600	10033
W S B & Associates Inc	7381	D	510 444-6266	16854
W S B & Associates Inc (PA)	7381	D	415 843-3510	16855
Wachovia A Division Wells F	6021	A	415 571-2832	9377
Walkme Inc (HQ)	7371	D	855 492-5563	15540
Walkup Melodia Kelly	8111	E	415 981-7210	23424
Walt Disney Family Museum	8412	D	415 345-6800	24920
Walter E McGuire RE Inc (PA)	6531	B	415 929-1500	11820
Walter E McGuire RE Inc	6531	E	415 296-0123	11821
Warwick California Corporation	7011	D	415 992-3809	13379
Watchit Media Inc	7812	C	702 740-1700	18166
Weber Shandwick	8743	D	415 262-5600	27572
Webpass Inc	4813	D	415 233-4100	5676
Weisscomm Group Ltd (PA)	8748	D	415 362-5018	27909
Wells Fargo & Company (PA)	6021	C	866 249-3302	9378
Wells Fargo Asset Management	6722	B	415 396-8000	12052
Wells Fargo Bank National Assn	6021	E	415 396-6267	9382
Wells Fargo Bank National Assn	6021	B	415 396-6161	9383
Wells Fargo Bank National Assn	6021	B	415 777-9497	9393
Wells Fargo Bank National Assn	6021	A	415 394-4021	9404
Wells Fargo Clearing Svcs LLC	6211	C	415 291-1200	10037
Wells Fargo Intl Bond CIT	6722	C	415 396-4943	12053
Wells Fargo Securities LLC	6211	D	415 645-0800	10041
Wentworth Hauser & Violich Inc	6282	D	415 981-6911	10121
Wested (PA)	8733	C	415 565-3000	26675
Wested	8733	C	415 565-3000	26676
Western Alliance Bank	6029	D	415 230-4834	9520
Western Messenger Service Inc	4212	C	415 487-4229	4087
Westside Lodge	8399	E	415 864-1515	24860
Weststar Marine Services Inc	4499	C	415 495-3191	4755
Wetherby Asset Management	6282	D	415 399-9159	10122
Wfc Holdings LLC (HQ)	6021	C	415 396-7392	9410
Wideorbit Inc (PA)	7371	C	415 675-6700	15545
Wikimedia Foundation Inc	8699	C	415 839-6885	25484
Wilbur-Ellis Company LLC (DH)	5191	B	415 772-4000	9105
Wildenradt-Mcmurray Inc	5072	D	510 835-5500	7609
Will Perkins Inc	8712	D	415 856-3000	26122
William McGann MD	8011	D	415 221-0665	20104
Wilson Sonsini Goodrich & Rosa	8111	D	415 947-2000	23440
Woodruff-Sawyer & Co (PA)	6411	C	415 391-2141	10837
Workforcelogic	7371	D	707 939-4300	15549
Workshare Technology Inc	7371	C	415 590-7700	15550
Wsp USA Buildings Inc	8711	D	415 398-3833	26010
Wsp USA Inc	8711	D	415 243-4600	26013
Wtw Delaware Holdings LLC	8742	D	415 733-4100	27526
Wu Yee Childrens Services	8351	D	415 677-0100	24400
Wu Yee Childrens Services	8999	D	415 677-0100	27964
Xamarin Inc (PA)	7371	C	855 926-2746	15552
Xl Construction Corporation	1542	D	408 240-6312	1707
Xoom Corporation	6099	C	415 777-4800	9691
Yellow Cab Cooperative Inc	4121	D	415 333-3333	3875
Yelp Inc (PA)	7375	D	415 908-3801	16262
Yhb San Francisco LLC	7011	D	415 421-7500	13434
Youappi Inc	8742	D	646 854-3390	27531
Young & Rubicam Inc	7311	C	415 882-0600	13921
Young Brdcstg of San Francisco	4833	D	415 441-4444	5854
Young Dowlin L	0174	E	760 397-4104	212
Young Electric Co	1731	C	415 648-3355	2794
Young Mens Christian Assnsf	8641	D	415 447-9622	25318
Young Mens Christian Assoc SF	8641	D	415 831-4093	25321
Young Mens Christian Assoc SF	8641	D	415 447-9602	25322
Young Mens Christian Assoc SF (PA)	8641	E	415 777-9622	25324
Young Mens Christian Assoc SF	8641	D	415 666-9622	25325
Young Mens Christian Assoc SF	8641	D	415 957-9622	25326
Young Mens Christian Assoc SF	8641	D	415 885-0460	25327
Young Mens Christian Assoc SF	8641	D	415 752-0790	25328
Yourpeople Inc	6411	A	415 798-9086	10840
Yume Inc (HQ)	7311	D	650 591-9400	13922
Zapier Inc	7371	D	770 988-0633	15556
Zelle Hofmann Voelbel Masn LLP	8111	E	415 693-0700	23450
Zendesk Inc (PA)	7372	C	415 418-7506	15899
Zenpayroll Inc (PA)	7372	B	800 936-0383	15900
Zignal Labs Inc	7371	D	415 683-7871	15560
Zinio Systems Inc	7372	D	415 494-2700	15901
Zoe Holding Company Inc	8999	C	415 421-4900	27965
Zoosk Inc (PA)	4813	D	415 728-9543	5682
Zurich American Insurance Co	6411	C	415 538-7100	10842
Zvents Inc	7311	E	408 376-7346	13925
Zynga Inc (PA)	7374	C	855 449-9642	16203
Airport Commisions	4581	A	650 821-5000	4869
Alliance Ground Intl LLC	4581	C	650 821-0855	4871
American Airlines Inc	4512	A	650 877-6000	4767
Sfo Shuttle Bus Inc	4111	C	650 877-0430	3726
Signature Flight Support Corp	4581	C	650 877-6800	4910
Singapore Airlines Cargo Pte	4512	A	650 876-7363	4796
Swissport Usa Inc	4581	D	650 821-6220	4915
Swissport Usa Inc	4581	C	571 214-7068	4917
Thrifty Car Rental	7514	C	877 283-0898	17650
United Airlines Inc	4512	C	650 634-4209	4804
United Airlines Inc	4512	C	650 634-7800	4807
United Airlines Inc	4512	C	650 634-4469	4810
United Airlines Inc	4512	C	650 634-2772	4812

SAN GABRIEL, CA - Los Angeles County

Name	SIC	EMP	PHONE	ENTRY #
Alderwood Inc	8059	D	626 289-4439	20984
Cal Southern Services	7213	D	626 281-5942	13520
Country Villa Service Corp	8059	D	626 285-2165	21047
Facey Medical Foundation	8099	D	626 576-0800	22806
Fernview Convalescent Hospital	8051	D	626 285-3131	20427
Information & Referral Fed Los	7299	D	626 350-1841	13751
Life Care Centers America Inc	8051	D	626 289-5365	20582
Longwood Management Corp	8059	D	626 289-3763	21144
Normans Nursery Inc (PA)	5193	E	626 285-9795	9152
Park Cleaners Inc (PA)	7213	D	626 281-5942	13549
Park Hotels & Resorts Inc	7011	C	626 270-2700	13037
Pine Grove Healthcare	8051	D	626 285-3131	20700
San Gabriel Ambulatory Sugery	8011	A	626 300-5300	19848
San Gabriel Country Club	7997	D	626 287-9671	19027
San Gabriel Nursery and Flor (PA)	0181	D	626 286-0787	298
San Gbriel Vly Med Ctr Fndtion	8062	A	626 289-5454	21704
San Marino Manor	8059	E	626 446-5263	21204
Temple City Youth Dev Fund	8641	D	626 548-5085	25267

Mergent email: customerrelations@mergent.com
1670

2019 Directory of California
Wholesalers and Services Companies

(P-0000) Products & Services Section entry number
(PA)=Parent Co (HQ)=Headquarters (DH)=Div Headquarters

	SIC	EMP	PHONE	ENTRY #

SAN GERONIMO, CA - Marin County

Company	SIC	EMP	PHONE	ENTRY #
National Golf Properties Inc	7997	D	415 488-4030	18985

SAN JACINTO, CA - Riverside County

Company	SIC	EMP	PHONE	ENTRY #
Healthcare MGT Systems Inc	8051	D	951 654-9347	20520
Matthews International Corp	7699	E	951 654-9123	17962
Millenia Development	1521	E	951 660-5691	1206
Physicians For Healthy Hospita	8062	C	951 652-2811	21645
Riverside-San Bernardino	8011	D	951 654-0803	19829
Soboba Band Luiseno Indians	7389	A	951 665-1000	17476
Valley Wide Recreation Pk Dst (PA)	7999	D	951 654-1505	19255

SAN JOAQUIN, CA - Fresno County

Company	SIC	EMP	PHONE	ENTRY #
Standard Cattle LLC	0751	D	559 693-1977	625

SAN JOSE, CA - Santa Clara County

Company	SIC	EMP	PHONE	ENTRY #
22nd Century Technologies Inc	7371	D	866 537-9191	14948
24 7ai Inc (PA)	7379	C	650 385-2247	16299
4 CS Council	8351	C	408 487-0747	24255
40 Hrs Inc	7361	A	408 414-0158	14559
4d Inc	7371	C	408 557-4600	14952
8x8 Inc (PA)	4813	C	408 727-1885	5439
A & A Mechanical Contractors	1711	D	408 225-1321	2077
A A A Furnace AC Co	1711	D	408 293-4717	2079
A C Freight Systems Inc (PA)	4213	C	408 392-8900	4088
A Is For Apple Inc	8049	C	877 991-0009	20160
A10 Networks Inc (PA)	7373	A	408 325-8668	15906
Abbott Stringham An	8721	D	408 377-8700	26139
ABF Freight System Inc	4213	E	408 435-8550	4089
Able Exterminators Inc	7342	D	408 251-6500	14136
Accenture LLP	8742	C	408 817-2100	27109
Accenture LLP	8742	C	650 213-2000	27110
Ace Parking Management Inc	7521	D	408 437-2185	17672
Acer America Corporation (DH)	7379	D	408 533-7700	16303
Achiever Christian Pre-Schl &	8351	E	408 264-2345	24257
Acronics Systems Inc	8711	C	408 432-0888	25500
Action Day Nrseries Prmry Plus	8351	E	408 266-8952	24259
Adminstrtive Office of US Crts	8322	D	408 535-5200	23459
Adobe Inc (PA)	7372	A	408 536-6000	15572
Advantage Logistics Inc	4731	C	408 943-6300	4995
Advent Group Ministries Inc	8361	D	408 281-0708	24407
Aecom Usa Inc	8748	C	408 392-0670	27627
Aedis Architects (PA)	8712	E	949 496-6191	26020
Aeris Communications Inc (PA)	4813	D	408 557-1900	5444
Aerospace & Marine Intl	8999	E	408 360-0440	27917
Airdrome Orchards Inc (PA)	0174	E	408 297-6461	201
Airgas Usa LLC	5084	D	408 998-6380	7723
Alfa Tech Cnslting Engners Inc (PA)	8711	D	408 487-1200	25525
All Fab Prcsion Sheetmetal Inc	1761	D	408 279-1099	3124
Alldragon International Inc	7371	E	408 410-6248	14971
Alliance Credit Union (PA)	6062	D	408 445-3386	9619
Allied Landscape Svcs S Inc	0781	D	408 310-8476	726
Alliedbarton Security Svcs LLC	7381	B	408 954-8274	16556
Almaden Golf & Country Club	7997	D	408 323-4812	18821
Almaden Valley Athletic Club	7997	D	408 445-4900	18822
Alsco Inc	7213	C	408 279-2345	13500
American Airlines Inc	4512	D	408 291-3800	4766
American Cancer Soc Cal Div	8399	E	408 265-5535	24735
American Funding	6163	D	408 269-4238	9870
American Metal & Iron Inc	5093	C	408 452-0777	7968
American Residential Svcs LLC	1711	D	650 856-1612	2111
American Residential Svcs LLC	7699	D	408 435-3810	17932
American Tire Distributors	5014	C	408 435-3340	6689
Amtel Inc	8748	E	408 615-0522	27641
Andrian Inc	1799	E	408 434-0730	3486
AON Consulting Inc	8742	C	408 321-2500	27138
Aopen America Incorporated	5045	D	408 586-1200	7007
Apria Healthcare LLC	7352	D	949 639-2163	14433
Apx Inc (PA)	8748	E	408 517-2100	27643
Aqualine Piping Inc	1711	D	408 745-7100	2125
Aquinas Corporation	8051	D	408 248-7100	20233
Aramark Spt & Entrmt Group LLC	7929	D	408 999-5735	18419
Aramark Unf & Career AP LLC	7213	D	408 243-9824	13514
Arcadia Management Service Co	6531	E	408 286-4440	11215
Ariosa Diagnostics Inc	8731	C	408 229-7500	26329
Asian Amercn Recovery Svcs Inc	8069	D	408 271-3900	21996
Associated Students Cdc	8351	D	408 924-6988	24264
AT&T Corp	4812	D	408 729-8400	5292
AT&T Corp	4812	D	408 871-3870	5293
AT&T Services Inc	4813	C	408 554-3335	5496
AT&T Services Inc	4813	D	408 973-7504	5515
Atlantic Aviation Svc	4581	E	408 297-7552	4873
Atria Senior Living Group Inc	8361	D	408 266-1660	24428
Automation Anywhere Inc (PA)	5045	D	888 484-3535	7012
Avnet Inc	5065	D	408 501-3925	7447
Bad Boys Bail Bonds Inc (PA)	7389	D	408 298-3333	17025

Company	SIC	EMP	PHONE	ENTRY #
Barbaccia Properties	6515	D	408 225-1010	11157
Bay Area Surgical MGT LLC	8011	E	408 297-3432	19315
Baynote Inc	5045	D	866 921-0919	7016
Bdo Usa LLP	8721	D	408 278-0220	26149
Bea Systems Inc (HQ)	7371	A	650 506-7000	15021
Beacon Roofing Supply Inc	5033	D	408 293-5947	6919
Bell Integrator Inc (PA)	7373	A	650 943-2415	15920
Belmont Bruns Construction Inc	1542	D	408 977-1708	1478
Biarca Inc (PA)	7379	D	408 564-4465	16318
Big Bulb Ideas Inc	7371	E	408 888-2346	15024
Biggs Cardosa Associates Inc (PA)	8711	D	408 296-5515	25566
Bill Brown Construction Co	1522	D	408 297-3738	1269
Bill Brown Construction Co	1521	D	408 297-3738	1123
Bizmatics Inc (PA)	7372	C	408 873-3030	15610
Blach Construction Company (PA)	1541	D	408 244-7100	1378
Blackarrow Inc (HQ)	7371	D	408 642-6400	15029
Blaine Tech Services Inc (PA)	8748	D	408 573-0555	27659
Blossom Valley Cnstr Inc	0782	D	408 993-0766	805
Brandvia Alliance Inc	5199	D	408 955-0500	9199
Breakout Prison Outreach	8322	D	408 702-2405	23518
Brilliant General Maintinc	7349	C	408 287-6708	14203
Brinks Incorporated	7381	D	408 436-7717	16592
Bristlecone Incorporated	7371	A	650 386-4000	15038
Brocade Cmmnctions Systems Inc	8748	A	408 333-4300	27663
Brookdale Lving Cmmunities Inc	8361	C	408 445-7770	24441
Burr Pilger Mayer Inc	8721	E	408 961-6355	26155
Business Furn Solutions Inc (PA)	5021	C	408 325-3100	6714
C & O Painting Inc	1721	E	408 279-8011	2425
C H Reynolds Electric Inc	1731	B	408 436-9280	2534
C R S Drywall Inc	1742	C	408 998-4360	2858
Cadence Design Systems Inc (PA)	7372	A	408 943-1234	15621
Cadent Inc	7373	C	408 470-1000	15924
Caliber Bodyworks Texas Inc	7532	C	408 972-0300	17716
California Drywall Co (PA)	1742	C	408 292-7500	2859
California Schl Employees Assn (PA)	8631	C	408 473-1000	25057
California United Mech Inc (PA)	1711	B	408 232-9000	2155
California Waste Solutions Inc (PA)	4953	D	510 832-8111	6367
California Water Service Co (HQ)	4941	C	408 367-8200	6215
Cambium Networks Inc	4899	C	847 640-3809	5972
Careage Inc	8051	E	408 238-9751	20289
Carlton Senior Living Inc	6411	D	408 972-1400	10577
Casavina Foundation Corp	8051	C	408 238-9751	20291
Catholic Charities	8011	C	408 468-0100	19358
Catholic Charities of Santa CL (PA)	8322	C	408 468-0100	23536
Cavendish Kinetics Inc	5065	C	408 627-4504	7457
Cbre Inc	6531	D	408 453-7400	11279
Cbsj Financial Corporation	7322	D	408 792-4600	13996
Ccintegration Inc (PA)	8731	E	408 228-1314	26346
Center For Employment Training (PA)	8331	D	408 287-7924	24164
Central Valley Clinic Inc	8093	E	408 885-5400	22523
Ch2m Hill Inc	8712	E	408 436-4936	26034
Challenger Schools	8351	D	408 723-0111	24276
Challenger Schools	8351	D	408 266-7073	24277
Chelbay Schuler & Chelbay (PA)	6371	D	408 288-4400	10482
Chester C Lehmann Co Inc (PA)	5063	D	408 293-5818	7345
Choices For Children (PA)	8351	D	408 297-3295	24284
Christian Counseling Centers	8322	D	408 559-1115	23572
Cintas Corporation No 2	7218	C	408 292-6700	13598
Ciphercloud Inc (PA)	7372	D	408 519-6930	15627
Ciphermax Inc (PA)	8742	D	408 382-6500	27192
Cisco Ironport Systems LLC (HQ)	7372	B	650 989-6500	15628
Cisco Systems Capital Corp (HQ)	7389	C	610 386-5870	17075
Cisco Webex LLC (HQ)	7389	A	408 435-7000	17076
City II Enterprises Inc	0782	E	408 275-1200	813
City of San Jose	7389	B	408 277-5277	17082
City of San Jose	8422	D	408 794-6400	24927
City of San Jose	4581	B	408 392-3600	4880
City of San Jose	7011	C	408 226-6765	12462
Ckl Construction Inc	1522	D	408 244-7042	1275
Clarion Hotel San Jose Airport	7011	D	408 453-5340	12465
Classic Custom Vacations Inc	4725	C	800 221-3949	4965
Classic Parking Inc	7521	B	408 278-1444	17683
Classic Vacations LLC	4725	C	800 221-3949	4966
Coassure Inc	8748	D	408 244-0400	27690
Coast Insulation Contrs Inc (DH)	1742	D	386 304-2222	2868
Cohesity Inc (PA)	7389	D	408 645-0041	17093
Coldwell Banker Prof Group	6531	D	408 383-1044	11336
Coldwell Banker RE LLC	6531	D	408 491-1600	11341
Colliers Parrish Intl Inc	6531	D	408 282-3800	11372
Comcast Corporation	4841	C	408 216-2878	5878
Command Security Corporation	7381	D	650 574-0911	16611
Commonwealth Central Credit Un (PA)	6061	D	408 531-3100	9547
Complete Genomics Inc	8733	B	650 943-2800	26615
Computer Task Group Inc	7371	C	408 573-6070	15072
Computer Task Group Inc	7371	B	800 992-5350	15073

Employment Codes: A=Over 500 employees, B=251-500,
C=101-250, D=51-100, E=50

2019 Directory of California
Wholesalers and Services Companies

© Mergent Inc. 1-800-342-5647

1671

GEOGRAPHIC

Company	SIC	EMP	PHONE	ENTRY #
Corventis Inc (PA)	7375	D	408 790-9300	16214
County Building Materials Inc	5031	D	408 274-4920	6819
Creative Security Company Inc	7381	B	408 295-2600	16620
Crestwood Behavioral Hlth Inc	8361	D	408 275-1067	24493
Cse Holdings Inc (DH)	5087	C	408 436-1907	7885
Cupertino Electric Inc (PA)	1731	B	408 808-8000	2557
Customized Performance Inc	7349	C	408 437-1720	14246
Cws Utility Services Corp	8611	B	408 367-8200	24952
Dapcon Inc	1721	D	408 573-7200	2432
De Mattei Construction Inc	1521	D	408 295-7516	1153
Della Maggiore Tile Inc	1743	D	408 286-3991	2993
Deloitte & Touche LLP	8721	B	408 704-4000	26181
Deloitte Tax LLP	8721	B	408 704-4000	26186
Developmental Svcs Cal Dept	8052	A	408 451-6000	20928
DH Smith Company Inc	1742	D	408 532-7617	2874
Diablo Landscape Inc	0782	D	408 487-9620	827
Digex Inc	4813	C	408 468-5000	5546
Dinyari Construction Inc	1522	E	408 289-5400	1280
Dma Claims Inc	6411	D	800 649-7602	10607
Doudell Trucking Company (PA)	4213	C	408 263-7300	4131
Dpr Construction Inc	1541	E	408 370-2322	1392
Dt Research Inc (PA)	8731	D	408 934-6220	26356
Dtex Systems Inc	7371	E	408 418-3786	15122
Durham School Services	4151	D	408 448-0740	3913
Eah Elena Gardens LP	6513	B	415 295-8840	11009
Echelon Security Inc	8748	E	408 436-8844	27711
ECi Corporation A Corp Nev (PA)	6162	D	408 941-9268	9801
Econosoft Inc	7371	D	408 442-3663	15125
Edges Electrical Group LLC (HQ)	5063	D	408 293-5818	7356
Edgewater Networks Inc	4813	D	408 351-7200	5553
Ees Residential Group Homes	8361	D	408 265-8780	24515
Einfochips Inc (HQ)	7371	C	408 496-1882	15129
Ek Health Services Inc (PA)	8742	D	408 973-0888	27224
El Camino Hospital	8071	C	650 940-7000	22081
Electric Cloud Inc (PA)	5045	D	408 419-4300	7038
Empress Care Center	8059	D	408 287-0616	21063
Energy Livermore Off US Dept	8733	B	408 267-1413	26618
Ensighten Inc (HQ)	8742	D	650 249-4712	27226
Epicentro Advertising Mktg Svc	7311	E	408 453-0353	13825
Eric Stark Interiors Inc	1742	D	408 441-6136	2882
Ericsson Inc	7373	A	408 597-3600	15956
Ernst & Young LLP	8721	A	408 947-5500	26195
Estes Express Lines Inc	4213	E	408 286-3894	4141
Etrigue Corporation	7371	E	408 490-2900	15147
European Paving Designs Inc	1721	D	408 283-5230	2435
Exis Inc	5065	E	408 944-4600	7476
Facility Masters Inc (PA)	7349	B	408 436-9090	14262
Fair Isaac Corporation (PA)	8748	B	408 535-1500	27726
Family and Children Services	8748	D	408 292-9353	27729
Fcs Software Solutions Limited	7371	D	408 324-1203	15158
Federal Express Corporation	4215	C	800 463-3339	4413
Fedex Ground Package Sys Inc	4213	A	800 463-3339	4175
Fertility & Reproductive	8011	D	408 358-2500	19473
First Alarm SEC & Patrol Inc (PA)	7381	C	408 866-1111	16645
Fluor Enterprises Inc	8711	C	408 256-0853	25686
Fluor Facility & Plant Svcs	7349	C	408 256-1333	14266
Fnti Fidelity Nat Tech Imagin	7379	E	408 942-1780	16367
Foothill Health Center Inc	8011	C	408 729-4290	19474
Force10 Networks Inc	7373	A	707 665-4400	15957
Forescout Technologies Inc (PA)	7371	C	408 213-3191	15166
Foundtion For Hispanic Educatn (PA)	8641	D	408 585-5022	25157
Four Points San Jose Downtown	7011	E	408 282-8800	12586
Fourth Street Bowl	7933	E	408 453-5555	18489
FPI Management Inc	8741	C	408 267-3952	26863
Frito-Lay North America Inc	5145	D	559 312-8553	8552
Frontiir Corporation	4813	C	510 996-2071	5568
Fujitsu America Inc	7373	D	408 746-8419	15962
Fusionone Inc	7371	D	408 282-1200	15172
Gaia Interactive Inc	4813	C	408 573-8800	5569
Galli Produce Company	5148	D	408 436-6100	8686
Garden City Inc	7999	A	408 244-3333	19177
Gardner Family Care Corp	8093	C	408 935-3906	22579
Gct Semiconductor Inc (PA)	5065	C	408 434-6040	7482
Gda Technologies Inc (HQ)	8711	D	408 753-1191	25703
General George W Sliney Basha	8641	D	408 296-3423	25159
George M Robinson & Co (PA)	1711	D	510 632-7017	2221
Giarretto Institute	8322	E	408 453-7616	23821
Gilbane Building Company	8741	D	408 660-4400	26871
Glenrock Group	7997	D	408 323-9900	18929
Global Industry Analysts Inc	8732	A	408 528-9966	26525
Global Infotech Corporation	8748	A	408 567-0600	27739
Globallogic Inc (PA)	7371	C	408 273-8900	15181
Golden Living LLC	8051	C	408 923-7232	20474
Golden Living LLC	8361	E	408 255-5555	24540
Good Samaritan Hospital LP (DH)	8062	A	408 559-2011	21433
Goodwill of Silicon Valley (PA)	7363	D	408 998-5774	14859
Graham Contractors Inc	1611	E	408 293-9516	1769
Grand Intelligence LLC	7371	D	408 954-7368	15188
Grant Thornton LLP	8721	E	408 275-9000	26208
Green Valley Corporation (PA)	1542	E	408 287-0246	1538
Greenbriar Homes Communities	1531	D	510 497-8200	1340
Greenwaste Recovery Inc	4953	E	408 283-4804	6405
Greenwaste Recovery Inc (PA)	4953	D	408 283-4800	6406
Greystone Plastering Inc	1742	D	408 298-5934	2889
Gringteam Inc	7011	B	408 453-4000	12623
Guavus Inc (HQ)	7372	D	650 243-3400	15697
Gypsum Dry Wall Supply Co	5099	E	408 993-9710	8037
H M H Engineers	8711	D	408 487-2200	25720
H&H Resolution LLC	7322	D	408 362-2293	14007
Hacienda Involved Parent Staff	8641	D	408 535-6259	25171
Harding Mktg Cmmunications Inc (PA)	7336	D	408 345-4545	14116
Hayes Mansion Conference Ctr	7011	C	408 226-3200	12649
HCA Inc	8062	C	408 729-2801	21442
Hd Supply Construction Supply	5072	E	408 428-2000	7591
Health & Rehabilitation Center	8051	E	408 377-9275	20515
Health Trust (PA)	8621	D	408 513-8700	25017
Heavenly Construction Inc	1799	C	408 723-4954	3530
Hensel Phelps Construction Co	1542	C	408 452-1800	1550
Heritage Bank of Commerce (HQ)	6022	C	408 947-6900	9463
Herman Health Care Center	8051	D	408 269-0701	20528
Herman Sanitarium	8051	C	408 269-0701	20529
Hetrosys LLC	8748	D	408 270-0240	27747
Hid Global Safe Inc	7373	D	408 453-1008	15972
Hit Portfolio I Misc Trs LLC	7011	B	408 453-3006	12682
Hoffman Agency (PA)	8743	D	408 286-2611	27557
Home Port Inc	6514	D	408 377-4134	11148
Homeguard Incorporated (PA)	7342	D	408 993-1900	14151
Hope Services (PA)	8331	E	408 284-2850	24191
Hopkins & Carley A Law Corp (PA)	8111	D	408 286-9800	23136
Host International Inc	7011	C	408 294-1702	12716
Hsbc Finance Corporation	6029	D	408 796-3600	9507
Hyatt Equities LLC	7011	B	408 993-1234	12750
Hypergrid Inc	7371	D	650 316-5524	15205
Ice Delivery Systems Inc	4212	C	408 640-4625	4024
Icom Mechanical Inc	1711	C	408 292-4968	2230
Ics Integrated Comm Systems	1731	D	408 491-6000	2612
Imerys Filtration Minerals Inc (DH)	1499	E	805 562-0200	1103
Immersion Medical Inc	8111	C	408 467-1900	23141
Incline Incorporated	7361	D	408 454-1140	14646
Incube Labs LLC (PA)	6799	D	408 457-3700	12234
Indian Hlth Ctr Snta Clara Vly	8011	C	408 445-3400	19510
Indosys Corporation	7361	C	408 705-1953	14647
Insite Digestive Health Care	8011	C	408 471-2222	19514
Inspira Inc	7371	C	408 247-9500	15217
Integra Telecom Inc	7389	D	408 758-7700	17243
International Bus Mchs Corp	7371	A	408 463-2000	15230
International Bus Mchs Corp	5044	C	408 452-4800	6964
International Bus Mchs Corp	8731	B	408 927-1080	26386
Intero Real Estate Svcs Inc	6531	C	408 574-5000	11520
Intero Real Estate Svcs Inc	6531	E	408 558-3600	11521
Invesmart Inc	6411	D	408 961-2800	10657
Iscs Inc	7371	C	408 362-3000	15239
Italent Corporation (PA)	7379	D	408 496-6200	16412
Itron Networked Solutions Inc (HQ)	4899	B	669 770-4000	5985
Ixsystems Inc (PA)	7372	D	408 943-4100	15726
J & J Air Conditioning Inc	1711	D	408 920-0662	2238
J T R Company Inc (PA)	5122	D	408 975-7733	8180
J T R Company Inc	4225	E	408 293-3272	4579
Jabil Silver Creek Inc (HQ)	7692	C	669 255-2900	17924
Jacobs Engineering Group Inc	8711	A	408 995-3257	25761
Jan Marini Skin Research Inc	5122	C	408 620-3600	8181
Jensen Corp Landscape Contr	0782	C	408 446-4881	866
Jensen Corporate Holdings Inc (PA)	0782	C	408 446-1118	867
Jensen Landscape Services Inc	0782	C	408 446-1118	868
Jeppesen Dataplan Inc	7375	C	408 961-2825	16235
JF Shea Construction Inc	1521	B	408 225-1475	1184
John A Maida Enterprises	5112	E	408 254-3100	8083
John F Dmingue Attorney At Law	8111	C	408 591-5180	23151
Johns Dog Food Distributing	5149	D	408 275-1943	8814
Johnson Service Group Inc	6512	A	408 728-9510	10903
Josephines Prof Staffing (PA)	7361	C	408 943-0111	14655
Kaiser Foundation Hospitals	8082	A	408 361-2100	22349
Kaiser Foundation Hospitals	8062	B	408 972-6010	21489
Kaiser Foundation Hospitals	8011	D	408 972-7000	19592
Kaiser Foundation Hospitals	8011	C	408 972-3000	19616
Kaiser Foundation Hospitals	8062	D	408 972-3376	21516
Kaiser Foundation Hospitals	8062	C	408 972-6700	21517
Keenan & Associates	6411	E	408 441-0754	10667
Kidango Inc	8099	C	408 297-9044	22830
Kinder Mrgan Lqds Trminals LLC	4226	D	408 435-7399	4682

Mergent email: customerrelations@mergent.com
1672

2019 Directory of California
Wholesalers and Services Companies

(P-0000) Products & Services Section entry number
(PA)=Parent Co (HQ)=Headquarters (DH)=Div Headquarters

Company	SIC	EMP	PHONE	ENTRY #
Kindred Healthcare Inc	8062	D	408 261-6943	21534
Kranem Corporation	7372	C	650 319-6743	15735
Krty Ltd A Cal Ltd Partnr	4832	E	408 293-8030	5737
Kusumoto Farms	0171	D	408 927-8348	103
Lab-Gistics LLC	8731	C	650 309-2627	26394
Labcyte Inc (PA)	8731	C	408 747-2000	26395
Landcare USA LLC	0782	D	408 727-4099	887
Landmark Protection Inc	5136	B	408 293-6300	8267
Lark Avenue Car Wash	7542	D	408 371-2565	17823
Lavante Inc	7372	E	408 754-1410	15740
Lee Bros Foodservices Inc (PA)	5141	C	408 275-0700	8421
Leed International LLC	8748	E	650 861-7883	27772
Legacy Transportation Svcs Inc (PA)	4214	C	408 294-9800	4355
Lg Display America Inc (HQ)	5065	D	408 350-0190	7502
Liberty Healthcare of Oklahoma	8051	D	408 532-7677	20578
Lightbeam Power Company Gridle	1623	D	800 696-7114	1946
Lightbeam Pwr Gridley Main LLC	1623	D	800 696-7114	1947
Lincoln Glen Manor	8059	D	408 267-1492	21136
Logitech Ice At San Jose	7999	E	408 279-6000	19198
Loglogic Inc	7371	C	408 215-5900	15265
LPA Inc	8712	C	408 780-7200	26085
Lwi Financial Inc	6282	D	408 260-3100	10094
Lynx Software Technologies Inc (PA)	7372	D	408 979-3900	15746
M Arthur Gensler Jr Assoc Inc	8712	E	408 885-8100	26087
M K Technical Services Inc	7363	E	408 528-0401	14874
Macdonald Mott LLC	8711	D	408 321-5900	25807
Magma Design Automation Inc (HQ)	7371	B	408 565-7500	15268
Mariner Health Care Inc	8051	D	408 298-3950	20613
Mariner Health Care Inc	8051	D	408 377-9275	20625
Marquez Brothers Advg Agcy	7389	D	408 960-2700	17313
Marquez Brothers Intl Inc (PA)	5141	C	408 960-2700	8424
Marsh USA Inc	6411	D	408 467-5600	10684
Maxim Healthcare Services Inc	7363	B	408 914-7478	14875
McCall Gym Group Inc (PA)	7991	D	408 271-2416	18631
McManis Faulkner A Prof Corp	8111	E	408 279-8700	23247
ME Fox & Company Inc	5181	C	408 435-8510	9013
Meals On Wheels-The Health Tr	8322	E	408 961-9870	23916
Megapath Group Inc (HQ)	4813	C	408 952-6400	5598
Megapath Group Inc	4813	C	408 324-1353	5599
Meriwest Credit Union (PA)	6061	C	408 363-3200	9570
Merrill Lynch Pierce Fenner	6211	E	408 283-3000	9985
MGM Drywall Inc	1742	D	408 292-4085	2917
Mission Truck Sales	7515	D	408 436-2920	17658
Mobica US Inc	7373	A	650 450-6654	16005
Mobile Hm Communities of Amer (PA)	6515	C	408 279-5200	11158
Mobilygen Corporation	5065	D	408 601-1000	7510
Mochanin LLC	7374	D	408 432-7259	16162
Momentum For Mental Health	8399	D	408 261-7777	24808
Montavista Software LLC (DH)	7372	C	408 572-8000	15768
Monterey Bay Masonry Inc	1741	E	408 289-8295	2817
Morgan Stanley & Co LLC	6211	D	408 947-2200	10003
Mt Eden Nursery Co Inc (PA)	6519	E	408 213-5777	11178
Mt Hamilton Grange	8399	D	408 513-5528	24810
N A Aricent Inc	7371	D	408 324-1800	15297
ND Systems Inc	7319	D	408 776-0085	13979
Nds Surgical Imaging LLC	5047	C	408 776-0085	7195
Neals Janitorial Service	7349	E	408 271-9944	14329
Netapp Inc	7373	C	408 822-3803	16016
Netcontinuum Inc	7382	D	408 961-5600	16925
Netronix Integration Inc (PA)	1731	D	408 573-1444	2659
New Age Electric Inc	1731	E	408 279-8787	2662
New York Life Insurance Co	6411	D	408 392-9782	10706
Nexenta Systems Inc	7372	C	408 791-3341	15781
Nexsentio Inc	7349	D	408 392-9249	14330
Next Door Sltons To Dom Vlence	8399	D	408 279-2962	24814
Nor-Cal Moving Services	4214	D	408 954-1175	4362
Normandin Auto Brokers	5012	D	408 266-2824	6606
Normandins	7538	C	877 330-0391	17773
Northwest Landscape Maint Co	0782	E	408 298-6489	912
Nsg Technology Inc	7629	B	408 547-8700	17906
Nth Connect Telecom Inc	7389	E	408 922-0800	17361
Nu Horizons Electronics Corp	5065	E	408 946-4154	7515
Numbers Only Inc	7379	C	408 689-7258	16437
Nutanix Inc (PA)	7371	A	408 216-8360	15323
Nuvoton Technology Corp Amer	5065	D	408 544-1718	7517
O C McDonald Co Inc	1711	C	408 295-2182	2292
Ocadian Care Centers LLC	8051	E	408 295-2665	20677
OConnor Hospital	8062	D	408 947-2929	21612
OConnor Hospital	8062	A	408 947-2500	21613
OConnor Imaging Med Group Inc	8011	D	408 947-2992	19729
Oocl (usa) Inc	4731	D	408 576-6543	5127
Ooyala Inc (HQ)	7371	C	650 961-3400	15330
Opera San Jose Inc	7922	D	408 437-4450	18391
Operatix Inc	8742	D	408 332-5796	27382
Oracle Corporation	7372	B	408 276-3822	15803
Oracle Corporation	7372	B	408 390-8623	15806
Oracle Corporation	7372	B	925 694-6258	15810
Outfront Media Inc	7312	C	408 457-0111	13929
Outreach & Escort Inc (PA)	4111	D	408 678-8585	3696
Pacific Groservice Inc	5194	B	408 727-4826	9186
Pacific West Security Inc	7382	D	801 748-1034	16926
Packet Design Inc	7371	D	408 490-1000	15340
Panasonic Corp North America	5064	D	201 348-7000	7424
Parsons Corporation	1611	D	626 440-2000	1835
Pathway Society	8093	E	408 244-1834	22638
Paypal Inc (HQ)	4813	C	877 981-2163	5624
Paypal Holdings Inc (PA)	4813	C	408 967-1000	5625
Pdf Solutions Inc (PA)	7371	E	408 280-7900	15349
Pds Tech Inc	7361	A	408 916-4848	14688
Penske Automotive Group Inc	7513	E	408 293-7688	17609
Pentech Financial Services Inc (PA)	6159	D	408 879-2200	9763
Permanente Medical Group Inc	8011	D	408 972-6883	19763
Pernixdata Inc	7371	D	408 724-8413	15352
Petalon Landscape MGT Inc	0782	D	408 453-3998	920
Phase 3 Communications Inc	1731	D	408 946-9011	2679
Physical Rehabilitation Netwrk	8049	E	408 570-0510	20192
Piedmont Transfer & Storage	4213	E	408 288-5600	4244
Pillar Data Systems Inc	7372	B	408 503-4000	15831
Pittsburg Wholesale Groc Inc (PA)	5141	C	916 372-7772	8444
Pivot Systems Inc	7371	C	408 435-1000	15360
Pixim Inc	7373	D	650 934-0550	16033
Planned Prnthood Mar Monte Inc	8093	C	408 287-7529	22650
Planned Prnthood Mar Monte Inc (PA)	8093	D	408 287-7532	22651
Platinum Facilities Services	7349	C	408 998-9004	14351
Platinum Roofing Inc	1761	D	408 280-5028	3190
Playmar Inc	5032	C	408 324-1930	6905
Plda Inc	6519	C	408 273-4528	11181
Plum Healthcare Group LLC	8051	D	408 998-8447	20707
Plx Technology Inc	7372	C	408 435-7400	15832
Polaris Networks Incorporated	7371	D	408 625-7273	15367
Pricewaterhousecoopers LLP	8721	A	408 817-3700	26275
Procera Networks Inc (HQ)	7371	D	510 230-2777	15377
Prolinx Services Inc	7361	D	408 689-5777	14705
Propel Software Corporation	7379	C	408 571-6300	16465
Property Maintenance Company (PA)	7349	C	408 297-7849	14359
Proxim Wireless Corporation	8732	C	408 383-7600	26557
Pulse Secure LLC (HQ)	7371	D	408 372-9600	15387
Q Analysts LLC (PA)	8742	D	408 907-8500	27413
Qal Affiliate Inc	6531	E	408 238-5111	11697
Qct LLC	7373	A	510 270-6111	16036
Quail Hill Investments Inc	6798	C	408 978-9000	12186
Quantum Corporation (PA)	8731	B	408 944-4000	26443
Quest Dgnstics Clncal Labs Inc	8071	A	408 975-1015	22128
R E Cuddie Co	1752	E	408 998-1250	3116
R L Safety Inc	8322	E	408 557-0887	23979
R-Bros Painting Inc	1721	E	408 291-6820	2470
Race Street Foods Inc (PA)	5144	D	408 294-6161	8538
Radonich Corp	1731	E	408 275-8888	2691
Railway Distributing Inc (PA)	5032	E	408 280-7623	6906
Ranch Golf Club	7992	D	408 270-0557	18750
Rando AAA Hvac Inc	1711	E	408 293-4717	2328
Rawitser Golf Shop Mike	7992	E	408 441-4653	18751
Resonate Inc (PA)	7371	C	408 545-5500	15406
Responselogix Inc	8741	C	408 220-6505	27017
Restaurant Depot LLC	5142	C	408 344-0107	8499
Retailnext Inc (PA)	7371	C	408 884-2162	15410
RFI Enterprises Inc (PA)	1731	D	408 298-5400	2707
Rgis LLC	7389	D	408 243-9141	17440
Robert Half International Inc	7361	C	408 961-2975	14725
Robert Half International Inc	7361	C	408 293-8611	14734
Robinson and Wood Inc	8111	D	408 298-7120	23357
Ron Filice Enterprises Inc	6411	E	408 294-0477	10759
Rosendin Electric Inc (PA)	1731	A	408 286-2800	2712
Rosendin Electric Inc	1731	A	408 321-2200	2714
Rossi Hamerslough Reishchl &	8111	D	408 244-4570	23362
Royal Coach Tours (PA)	4142	C	408 279-4801	3901
Royalty Tours	4725	E	408 279-4801	4977
RSM US LLP	8721	C	408 572-4440	26284
Rural/Metro Corporation	4119	C	888 876-0740	3838
S J General Building Maint	7349	D	408 392-0800	14373
Sage Intacct Inc (HQ)	7379	C	408 878-0900	16476
Salas OBrien Engineers Inc (PA)	8711	E	408 282-1500	25901
Samsung SDS America Inc	7371	C	408 638-8800	15425
Samsung Semiconductor Inc (DH)	5065	C	408 544-4000	7538
San Andreas Regional Center (PA)	8322	C	408 374-9960	24010
San Jose Airport Garden Hotel	7011	D	408 793-3300	13175
San Jose Airport Hotel LLC	7011	D	408 793-3939	13178
San Jose Chld Discovery Museum	8412	D	408 298-5437	24909
San Jose Conservation Corps	8331	C	408 283-7171	24227
San Jose Country Club	7997	D	408 258-4901	19029

Employment Codes: A=Over 500 employees, B=251-500,
C=101-250, D=51-100, E=50

2019 Directory of California
Wholesalers and Services Companies

© Mergent Inc. 1-800-342-5647
1673

GEOGRAPHIC

Company	SIC	EMP	PHONE	ENTRY #
San Jose Fairmont Lessee LLC	7011	B	408 998-1900	13177
San Jose Lessee LLC	7011	D	408 453-4000	13178
San Jose Medical Systems Lp	8062	A	408 259-5000	21709
San Jose Museum of Art Assn	8412	D	408 271-6840	24910
San Jose Redevelopment Agency	8748	C	408 535-8500	27856
San Jose Sharks LLC	7941	D	408 999-6810	18534
San Jose Silicon Valley Cham	8611	D	408 291-5250	24979
San Jose State University	8011	E	408 924-1000	19849
San Jose Surgical Supply Inc (PA)	5047	E	408 293-9033	7216
San Jose Water Company (HQ)	4941	C	408 288-5314	6306
San Jose Water Company	4941	C	408 298-0364	6307
San Joses Healthcare & Well	8051	D	408 295-2665	20739
Santa Clara County of	8322	D	408 435-2000	24030
Santa Clara Cnty Fderal Cr Un (PA)	6061	C	408 282-0700	9587
Santa Clara County of	8111	A	408 792-2704	23367
Santa Clara County of	8721	C	408 885-7200	26286
Santa Clara County of	8062	E	408 885-6818	21717
Santa Clara County of	7322	D	408 282-3200	14022
Santa Clara County of	8322	D	408 435-2111	24031
Santa Clara County of	8011	D	408 792-5680	19853
Santa Clara County of	8721	C	408 885-7354	26287
Santa Clara Valley Corporation	7349	D	408 947-1100	14376
Santa Clara Valley Medical Ctr.	8011	B	408 885-6300	19854
Santa Clara Valley Medical Ctr.	8099	A	408 885-5730	22881
Santa Clara Valley Medical Ctr (PA)	8062	B	408 885-5000	21718
Santa Clara Valley Trnsp Auth (PA)	4111	A	408 321-2300	3721
Santa Clara Valley Trnsp Auth	4111	C	408 321-5559	3722
Santa Clara Valley Trnsp Auth	4131	B	408 321-5555	3882
Santa Clara Valley Water (PA)	4941	D	408 265-2600	6308
Santa Teresa Golf Club	7992	D	408 225-2650	18759
Santana Row Hotel Partners LP	7011	C	408 551-0010	13191
Saratoga Capital Inc	7011	D	408 286-1000	13192
Sarpa-Feldman Enterprises Inc	7389	D	408 982-1790	17458
Satellite Healthcare Inc (PA)	8092	D	650 404-3600	22489
Satellite Healthcare Inc	8092	D	408 258-8720	22490
SCC ESA Dept of Risk Mgmt	6411	D	408 441-4207	10764
Schaper Construction Inc (PA)	1721	D	408 437-0337	2480
Schwager Davis Inc	1629	C	408 281-9300	2060
SE Scher Corporation	7363	A	408 844-0772	14911
Second Harvest Food Bank (PA)	8322	E	408 266-8866	24038
Service Workers Local 715 (PA)	8631	D	408 678-3300	25081
Sezzo Labs Inc.	7373	E	408 562-0081	16051
Sharks Sports & Entrmt LLC	7941	A	408 287-7070	18535
Sierra Lumber Co	1751	C	408 286-7071	3077
Sigma Networks Inc	4813	C	408 876-4002	5645
Significant Cleaning Svcs LLC	7349	D	408 559-5959	14391
Silicon Valley Hwang LLC	7011	D	408 452-0200	13227
Silicon Valley Mechanical Inc	1711	D	408 943-0380	2357
Silicon Vly Educatn Foundation	8399	A	408 790-9400	24840
Silicon Vly SEC & Patrol Inc (PA)	7381	C	408 267-1539	16828
Siliconware Usa Inc (DH)	5065	E	408 573-5000	7541
Silver Creek Vly Cntry CLB Inc	7997	C	408 239-5775	19048
Silver Shield Security	7381	C	408 435-1111	16829
SIM Investment Corporation	7991	D	408 445-3310	18652
Sims Group USA Corporation	5093	D	408 494-4242	7993
Sj Hotel Manager LLC	7011	D	401 946-4600	13241
Sjb Child Development Centers (PA)	8351	C	408 538-0200	24382
Sjsu Foundation	8699	A	408 924-1410	25462
SJW Group (PA)	4941	B	408 279-7800	6312
Sk Hynix America Inc (HQ)	5045	D	408 232-8000	7103
Skybox Security Inc (PA)	7382	C	408 441-8060	16942
Slakey Brothers Inc	5074	E	408 494-0460	7636
Smashon Inc	7379	E	855 762-7466	16487
SMC Corporation of America	5084	E	408 943-9600	7799
Soleeva Energy Inc	1711	D	408 396-4954	2365
Somansa Technologies Inc	5045	D	408 297-1234	7106
Sourcewise	8322	D	408 350-3200	24055
South Bay Airport Shuttle	4111	D	408 225-4444	3729
South Bay Regl Public Safety T	8331	E	408 270-6494	24231
South Bay Senior Solutions Inc	8082	D	408 370-6360	22422
South Valley Plumbing Inc	1711	C	408 265-5566	2369
Southern Glazers Wine	5182	D	408 750-3540	9055
Sperasoft Inc	7371	B	408 715-6615	15469
Sprig Electric Co (PA)	1731	C	408 298-3134	2739
SSC San Jose Operating Co LP	8051	D	408 249-0344	20778
Staffing Solutions Inc	7361	D	408 980-9000	14770
Stanford Health Care	8062	A	408 426-4900	21791
Starlight Management Group	7011	D	408 334-7456	13265
State Compensation Insur Fund	6331	C	888 782-8338	10398
Steinberg Architects (PA)	8712	D	408 295-5446	26116
Structural Integrity Assoc Inc (PA)	8711	D	408 978-8200	25934
Student Trnsp Amer Inc	4119	D	408 998-8275	3851
Student Un San Jose State Univ	8699	D	408 924-6405	25472
Suddath Relo Sys of No CA	4213	D	408 288-3030	4268
Suddath Relocation Systems of	4213	E	904 858-1273	4269
Suez Wts Systems Usa Inc	5074	D	408 360-5900	7638
Sumitomo Electric Device Innov	5065	D	408 232-9500	7547
Summit Hr Worldwide Inc	8742	D	408 884-7100	27475
Sun Basket Inc (PA)	8322	C	408 669-4418	24077
Sunrise Senior Living Inc	8051	D	408 223-1312	20808
Sunrun Installation Svcs Inc	1711	A	408 746-3062	2378
Super Talent Technology Corp	5045	A	408 957-8133	7111
Synchronoss Technologies Inc	1731	B	800 575-7606	2758
Syniverse Technologies LLC	7379	C	408 324-1830	16498
Systech Integrators Inc	7379	C	408 441-2700	16500
Talent Space Inc	7361	D	408 330-1900	14774
Tamtron Corporation (DH)	7371	D	408 323-3303	15490
Taos Mountain LLC (PA)	7379	B	408 324-2800	16505
Team San Jose	7389	A	408 295-9600	17498
Tech Museum of Innovation (PA)	8412	A	408 795-6116	24916
Tech Museum of Innovation	8412	A	408 795-6168	24917
Techaisle LLC	8732	E	408 253-4416	26569
Technology Credit Union	6062	D	408 467-2382	9657
Technology Credit Union (PA)	6062	D	408 451-9111	9659
Ted Cooper/Cooper Industries	0782	E	408 358-3060	947
Terry Meyer	6531	D	408 723-3300	11792
Thomas Mark & Company Inc (PA)	8711	D	408 453-5373	25952
Threatmetrix Inc	7371	C	408 200-5700	15503
Topbuild Services Group Corp	1799	D	408 882-0411	3595
Toshiba Memory America Inc (DH)	5065	C	408 526-2400	7554
Tradecom Med Transcription Inc	5047	D	408 225-9200	7225
Traditions Golf LLC	7992	D	408 323-5200	18773
Traffic Management Inc.	7389	E	877 763-5999	17515
Transpak Inc (PA)	7389	C	408 254-0500	17519
Tranzeal Inc.	8742	D	408 834-8711	27495
Tredence Inc (PA)	8732	C	408 819-2336	26572
Trim Tech Industries Inc	5031	D	408 573-4514	6870
Tsmc North America (HQ)	8742	C	408 382-8000	27500
Tumi Inc.	5099	D	408 244-6512	8065
Tupaz Day Care Services Inc.	8322	D	408 377-1622	24097
Tupaz Homes LLC	1521	D	408 377-1622	1250
TV 36	4833	E	408 953-3636	5842
U S Perma Inc.	1743	E	408 436-0600	3014
UBS Financial Services Inc	7389	E	408 282-8402	17527
Underwriters Laboratories Inc	8734	B	248 427-5300	26737
Underwriters Laboratories Inc	8734	C	408 493-9910	26740
Unifirst Corporation	7218	D	408 297-8101	13627
Unilab Corporation	8071	B	408 927-8331	22155
Unish Corporation	7379	E	408 708-9300	16519
United Administrative Services	6371	C	408 288-4400	10494
United Parcel Service Inc OH	4215	B	408 291-2942	4456
United Site Services Cal Inc.	7359	C	408 295-2263	14553
United Temp Services Inc.	7361	D	408 472-4309	14790
Univar USA Inc.	5169	D	408 435-8649	8939
Universal Bldg Svcs & Sup Co	7349	C	408 995-5111	14420
Univision Television Group Inc	4833	D	415 538-8000	5845
URS Group Inc	8711	D	408 297-9585	25980
User Zoom Inc.	7371	D	408 533-8619	15517
Valin Corporation (PA)	5084	D	408 730-9850	7816
Valley US Inc.	7379	D	408 260-7342	16523
Vat Incorporated (DH)	5085	E	781 935-1446	7876
Ventrum LLC	7379	D	510 304-0852	16524
Verity Medical Foundation (HQ)	8011	D	408 278-3000	20056
Viaworld Advanced Products	5072	D	408 597-7051	7608
Vidhwan Inc (PA)	8742	C	408 289-8200	27512
Vidhwan Inc.	7371	C	408 521-0167	15528
Villages Golf and Country Club	7997	C	408 274-4400	19078
Virident Systems Inc.	8731	C	408 573-5000	26492
Virtual Instruments Corp.	7379	D	408 579-4000	16527
Visualon Inc.	7372	C	408 645-6618	15890
Vivente 1 Inc	6514	D	408 279-2706	11155
Vivente 2 Inc	6514	D	408 279-2706	11156
Vn Home Health Care LP	8082	D	408 998-0550	22459
Vormetric Inc (HQ)	7379	D	408 433-6000	16529
Vss Monitoring Inc (HQ)	4813	C	408 585-6800	5675
Waste Connections Cal Inc (DH)	4953	C	408 282-4400	6509
Watlow Electric Mfg Co	8711	D	408 776-6646	25995
Watson Carton	8399	D	408 979-9618	24857
Wells Fargo Bank National Assn	6021	E	408 998-3714	9385
West Coast Legal Service Inc	7389	E	408 938-6520	17586
West Hotel Partners LP	7011	C	408 947-4450	13388
West San Crlos Ht Partners LLC	7011	D	408 998-0400	13390
Western Alliance Bank	6022	D	408 423-8500	9494
Westwind Enterprises Ltd (PA)	6515	C	408 998-8444	11161
Whitehat Security Inc	7379	D	408 343-8300	16532
Willow Glen Hsing Partners LP	6531	E	408 267-7252	11838
Willow Glen Villa A	6513	D	408 266-1660	11141
Winbond Electronics Corp Amer	5065	D	408 943-6666	7564
Winchester Mystery House LLC	7999	D	408 247-2101	19263
Work2future Foundation	8331	C	408 794-1234	24251

Mergent email: customerrelations@mergent.com
1674

2019 Directory of California
Wholesalers and Services Companies

(P-0000) Products & Services Section entry number
(PA)=Parent Co (HQ)=Headquarters (DH)=Div Headquarters

Company	SIC	EMP	PHONE	ENTRY #
Work2future Foundation	8331	C	408 216-6202	24252
WW Grainger Inc	5063	C	408 432-8200	7403
Wyndham International Inc	7011	C	408 451-3050	13430
Xerox Corporation	7378	C	408 953-2700	16298
Xpo Logistics Freight Inc	4213	D	408 435-3876	4310
Yang C Park	7361	D	408 260-8066	14801
Yellow Cab Company Peninsula	4121	C	408 739-1234	3874
YMCA of Silicon Valley	8641	B	650 493-9622	25310
YMCA of Silicon Valley	8641	C	408 298-1717	25311
YMCA of Silicon Valley	8641	C	408 226-9622	25313
YMCA of The Mid-Peninsula Inc	8641	B	650 493-9622	25314
Yosh Enterprises Inc	7381	B	408 287-4411	16863
Young Womens Christian Associ	8641	C	408 295-4011	25367
Yuja Inc	7372	C	888 257-2278	15898
Zanker Road Resource MGT Ltd	4953	D	408 457-1189	6527
Zell Associates Inc (PA)	6211	D	408 978-1950	10043
Zenith Talent Corporation	7361	C	844 467-2300	14803
Zone24x7 Inc (PA)	7371	B	408 268-8589	15562
Zscaler Inc (PA)	7372	C	408 533-0288	15902

SAN JUAN BAUTISTA, CA - San Benito County

Company	SIC	EMP	PHONE	ENTRY #
Anthony Botelho	0175	D	831 623-4228	213
Christopher Ranch LLC	5148	D	831 636-8722	8655
Earthbound Farm LLC (DH)	0723	A	831 623-7880	508
Seminis Inc	8731	D	831 623-4554	26452

SAN JUAN CAPISTRANO, CA - Orange County

Company	SIC	EMP	PHONE	ENTRY #
Action Sports Retailer	7389	D	949 226-5744	16983
Atria Senior Living Group Inc	8361	C	949 661-1220	24426
Birtcher Andrson Investors LLC	6799	E	949 545-0526	12202
Carparts Technologies	7372	C	949 488-8860	15622
Celera Corporation (HQ)	8733	D	510 749-4200	26608
Coastal Mirage Landscapes	0781	D	949 496-7070	746
Cox Communications Inc	4813	C	949 240-1212	5540
Diamondpeo LLC	7361	C	714 728-5186	14601
Emerald Expositions LLC (HQ)	7389	B	949 226-5700	17151
Ip Access International	7379	E	949 655-1000	16408
Kaiser Foundation Hospitals	6324	D	888 988-2800	10264
Marbella Country Club	7997	C	949 248-3700	18965
Marbella Golf & Country Club	7997	C	949 248-3700	18966
Medusind Solutions Inc (HQ)	7389	A	949 240-8895	17318
Merit Logistics LLC	4731	A	949 481-0685	5109
Nichols Inst Reference Labs (DH)	8071	A	949 728-4000	22117
Pioneer Sands LLC	1446	D	949 728-0171	1097
PRC Builders Inc	1522	D	949 529-7011	1306
Rancho Mission Viejo LLC (PA)	6531	D	949 240-3363	11703
San Juan Golf Inc	7992	E	949 493-1167	18755
Solag Incorporated	4953	D	949 728-1206	6476
Southern Cal Prmnnte Med Group	8011	E	949 234-2139	19917
Sunrise Senior Living LLC	8051	D	949 248-8855	20827

SAN LEANDRO, CA - Alameda County

Company	SIC	EMP	PHONE	ENTRY #
14766 Wash Ave Operations LLC	8059	A	510 352-2211	20973
A-Para Transit Corp	4119	C	510 562-5500	3739
Aa/Acme Locksmiths Inc	1731	C	510 483-6584	2498
Acco Engineered Systems Inc	1711	C	510 346-4300	2083
Alameda County Industries Inc	4953	E	510 357-7282	6336
Alco Iron & Metal Co (PA)	5093	D	510 562-1107	7965
Alemeda County Industries LLC	4953	D	510 357-7282	6337
American Medical Response Inc	4119	C	415 794-9204	3769
American Residential Svcs LLC	1711	D	510 729-6227	2113
Apple Inns Inc	7011	E	510 895-1311	12329
Apria Healthcare LLC	8082	D	510 346-4000	22228
ARC of Alameda County (PA)	8322	C	510 357-3569	23484
Aviation Port Services LLc	4491	D	510 636-8790	4724
Avis Rent A Car System Inc	7514	C	510 562-8828	17624
Bae Sys Sierra Detroit Allison (DH)	7538	D	510 635-8991	17755
Bay Area Installations Inc (PA)	1799	D	510 895-8196	3492
Bluewater Envmtl Svcs Inc	1799	D	510 346-8800	3494
Buckeye Fire Equipment Company	5084	B	510 483-1815	7734
Carlton Senior Living	6531	D	510 636-0660	11266
Cinemark 16 Bayfair	7832	C	510 276-9684	18279
Cintas Corporation No 3	7299	E	510 352-6330	13728
Cnh Industrial America LLC	5082	E	510 351-2015	7673
Coast Counties Truck & Eqp Co	5012	C	510 568-6933	6582
County of Alameda	8011	C	510 481-4141	19407
Crossroad Services Inc	7389	B	510 895-5055	17115
Cummins Pacific LLC	5084	B	510 351-6101	7744
Dal-Tile Corporation	5032	D	510 357-6197	6887
Datapark Inc	7373	D	510 483-7275	15941
Dependable Highway Express Inc	4225	E	510 357-2223	4544
Dependable Highway Express Inc	4213	D	510 357-2223	4127
Dhx-Dependable Hawaiian Ex Inc	4731	C	510 686-2600	5045
Dunbar Armored Inc	7381	D	510 569-7400	16634
East Bay Innovations	7389	D	510 618-1580	17145
Engility LLC	8711	C	510 357-4610	25664
Estes Express Lines Inc	4213	D	510 635-0165	4142
Fayaka Airways LLC	4522	C	800 771-5489	4859
Federal Express Corporation	4513	C	510 347-2430	4822
Fedex Freight West Inc	4213	D	650 244-9522	4161
Fidelity Home Energy Inc	1711	D	858 220-7784	2209
Frank Ghiglione Inc (PA)	4212	C	510 483-7000	4015
Frank Ghiglione Inc	4212	D	510 483-2063	4016
Galena Equipment Rental LLC	7353	E	510 638-8100	14440
H A Bowen Electric Inc	1731	D	510 483-0500	2597
Hilton Garden Inn	7011	D	510 346-5533	12662
Independent Electric Sup Inc (DH)	5063	C	510 877-9850	7366
J R Pierce Plumbing Company	1711	D	510 483-5473	2240
K/P LLC	7331	E	510 614-7800	14048
Kaimanu Outrigger Canoe Club	7999	D	510 895-0435	19190
Kaiser Foundation Hospitals	8011	A	510 454-1000	19584
Kindred Healthcare Oper Inc	8062	D	510 357-8300	21536
Kissito Health Case Inc	8082	C	510 357-4015	22356
KMA Emergency Services Inc	4119	D	510 614-1420	3814
Koffler Elec Mech Apprts Repai	5063	D	510 567-0630	7370
Kp LLC	7331	D	510 346-0729	14049
Kp LLC	7331	C	510 614-7800	14050
L3 Applied Technologies Inc	8731	D	510 577-7100	26392
Laboratory Corporation America	8071	D	510 635-4555	22103
Landmark Event Staffing	7363	A	510 632-9000	14872
Marymount Villa LLC	8052	C	510 895-5007	20941
Medical Couriers Inc	4215	D	650 872-1144	4423
Monarch Bay Golf Resort	7992	D	510 895-2162	18736
Mv Transportation Inc	4119	C	510 351-1603	3824
N V Heathorn Inc	1711	D	510 569-9100	2288
Nan Fang Dist Group Inc	5084	D	510 297-5382	7777
Osisoft LLC (PA)	7371	B	510 297-5800	15338
Pacific Coast Container Inc (PA)	4789	C	510 346-6100	5238
Penhall Company	1771	D	510 357-8810	3305
Permanente Medical Group Inc	8011	A	510 454-1000	19772
Peterson Machinery Co (PA)	7629	D	541 302-9199	17907
Providnce All STS Subacute LLC	8051	C	510 481-3200	20712
Ransome Company	1542	E	510 686-9900	1626
Roofing Constructors Inc	1761	C	415 648-6472	3197
Royal Ambulance Inc	4119	C	510 568-6161	3836
Royal Investigation Patrol Inc	7381	C	510 352-6800	16778
Saia Motor Freight Line LLC	4213	C	510 347-6890	4258
San Francisco Bay Area Councl	8641	C	510 577-9000	25236
San Leandro Healthcare Center	8051	C	510 357-4015	20740
San Leandro Hospital LP	8062	B	510 357-6500	21710
San Leandro Surgery Center Lt	8011	D	510 276-2800	19850
Schryver Med Sls & Mktg LLC	8071	C	303 371-0073	22144
Service Lathing Company	1742	E	510 483-9732	2956
Silman Venture Corporation (PA)	1541	D	510 347-4800	1435
Ssmb Pacific Holding Co Inc (HQ)	5012	C	510 836-6100	6609
St Francis Electric Inc	1731	D	510 639-0639	2742
St Francis Electric LLC	1731	D	510 750-8271	2743
State Roofing Systems Inc	1761	C	510 317-1477	3201
Stepping Stn Grwth Ctr Fr Chld	8331	C	510 568-3331	24234
Subacute Trtmnt Adolescnt Reha (PA)	8093	D	510 352-9200	22689
Sunbridge Healthcare LLC	8052	D	510 352-2211	20967
Sutter Health	8052	C	510 618-5200	20968
Sutter Vsting Nrse Assn Hspice	8051	D	510 618-5277	20836
Telecare Corporation	8063	C	510 895-5502	21976
Telecare Corporation	8063	D	510 352-9690	21984
Thyssenkrupp Elevator Corp	5084	D	510 476-1900	7809
Trinet Group Inc (PA)	7361	C	510 352-5000	14786
TRM Corporation (PA)	1743	C	510 895-2700	3013
True Wrld Fods San Frncsco LLC	5146	D	510 352-8140	8610
Unity Courier Service Inc	7389	D	510 568-8890	17546
Vanguard Legato A Cal Corp	5021	C	510 351-3333	6740
Waste MGT of Alameda Cnty	4953	D	510 638-2303	6522
Webers Quality Meats Inc	5147	C	510 635-9892	8634
Westates Mechanical Corp Inc	1711	D	510 635-9830	2407
Westmed Ambulance	4119	D	510 401-5420	3859
Wild Karma Inc	8051	B	510 639-9088	20891

SAN LORENZO, CA - Alameda County

Company	SIC	EMP	PHONE	ENTRY #
Directv Group Inc	4841	C	510 481-1324	5902
Echo Landscape	0782	D	510 481-8614	834
Oakland Pallet Company Inc (PA)	5031	C	510 278-1291	6843
Too Good Gourmet Inc (PA)	5149	D	510 317-8150	8885
Wells Fargo Bank National Assn	6021	E	510 276-0875	9396

SAN LUIS OBISPO, CA - San Luis Obispo County

Company	SIC	EMP	PHONE	ENTRY #
American West	4213	E	805 926-2800	4098
American West Worldwide Ex Inc (PA)	4214	D	800 788-4534	4329
Amir Ahmad MD	8011	D	805 545-8100	19286
Amk Foodservices Inc	5141	C	805 544-7600	8380
Associated Students Inc (PA)	8322	D	805 756-1281	23497
Associated Students Inc	8999	D	805 756-1281	27920
Aviation Consultants Inc (PA)	8741	D	805 548-1300	26771

© Mergent Inc. 1-800-342-5647

GEOGRAPHIC

	SIC	EMP	PHONE	ENTRY #
Bank of Sierra	6021	D	805 541-0400	9297
Bayshore Healthcare Inc	8051	C	805 544-5100	20257
Boeing Company	4581	D	805 606-6340	4875
Cal Poly Corporation	7021	D	805 756-1587	13438
Cal Poly Corporation	8741	C	805 756-1131	26794
Cannon Corporation (PA)	8713	D	805 544-7407	26128
Cellco Partnership	4812	D	805 549-6260	5393
Community Action Partnership	8322	B	805 541-4122	23596
Community Action Partnership (PA)	8322	D	805 544-4355	23597
Compass Health Inc	8059	D	805 543-0210	21041
Correctons Rhbltation Cal Dept	8093	A	805 547-7900	22539
County of San Luis Obispo	8062	C	805 781-4800	21358
County of San Luis Obispo	8322	C	805 781-5437	23732
County of San Luis Obispo	8093	D	805 781-4700	22555
County of San Luis Obispo	8322	B	805 781-1864	23733
County of San Luis Obispo	8711	C	805 781-5258	25630
Courtyard By Marriott	7011	D	805 786-4200	12489
Drug & Alcohol Services of	8093	D	805 781-4275	22568
Enercon Services Inc	8711	D	805 242-0600	25661
Experts Exchange LLC	7379	D	805 787-0603	16364
Family Care Network Inc (PA)	8351	D	805 503-6240	24320
First American Title Insur Co	6361	E	805 543-8900	10459
French Hosp Med Ctr Foundation (HQ)	8062	B	805 543-5353	21420
Harvest Management Sub LLC	8361	A	805 543-0187	24550
Kci Environmental Inc	8999	E	805 543-3311	27937
Kennedy Club Fitness	7991	D	805 781-3488	18619
King Ventures	6552	C	805 544-4444	11883
Ksby Communications Inc	4833	D	805 541-6666	5814
Life Steps Foundation Inc	8322	D	805 549-0150	23896
Lindamood-Bell Lrng Processes (PA)	8351	C	805 541-3836	24339
Martin Resorts Inc (PA)	7011	B	805 545-7900	12913
Meathead Movers Inc	4213	D	805 541-4285	4226
Meathead Movers Inc	4213	D	805 544-6328	4227
Merrill Lynch Pierce Fenner	6211	E	661 802-0764	9980
Mindbody Inc (PA)	7374	D	877 755-4279	16159
Morris Grritano Insur Agcy Inc	6411	D	805 543-6887	10696
National Assn Ltr Carriers	8631	B	805 543-7329	25071
Nipomo Dial A Ride	4119	D	805 929-2881	3825
Ocean View Manor LP	6519	D	805 781-3088	11179
Oddworld Inhabitants Inc	7372	D	805 503-3000	15788
Pain Management Specialists PC	8011	E	805 544-7246	19746
Pathpoint	8331	D	805 782-8890	24218
Pickford Realty Inc	6531	D	805 782-6000	11669
Q S San Luis Obispo LP	7011	E	805 541-5001	13086
Rew Inc	6324	D	805 541-1308	10304
Rrm Design Group (PA)	8712	D	805 549-0442	26106
San Luis Ambulance Service Inc	4119	C	805 543-2626	3841
San Luis Obispo Cnty Frm Inc (PA)	5191	D	805 543-3751	9096
San Luis Obispo Golf	7997	D	805 543-3400	19030
San Luis Obispo Regional	4111	D	805 781-4465	3717
San Luis Physical Therapy (PA)	8049	E	805 788-0805	20202
Sealant Systems International	5014	D	805 489-0490	6694
Sesloc Federal Credit Union (PA)	6061	D	805 543-1816	9592
Sierra Vista Hospital Inc (HQ)	8062	A	805 546-7600	21756
Specialty Construction Inc	1731	D	805 543-1706	2737
SRI International	8733	C	805 542-9330	26662
Sunrun Installation Svcs Inc (HQ)	1731	C	415 580-6900	2752
Sycamore Mineral Spring Resort	7011	D	805 595-7302	13313
Thoma Electric Inc	1731	D	805 543-3850	2767
Transitions - Mental Hlth Assn (PA)	8322	D	805 540-6500	24094
Trust Automation Inc	8711	D	805 544-0761	25960
Ultrex Management Services (PA)	5044	D	805 783-1234	6985
United Cerebral Palsy Assoc of	8399	D	805 543-2039	24851
United Parcel Service Inc OH	4215	C	801 973-3400	4470
USA Staffing Inc	7363	D	805 269-2677	14929
Verizon Communications Inc	4813	C	805 441-4001	5668
Veterans Health Administration	8011	D	805 543-1233	20060
Villa La Esperanza LP	1531	D	805 781-3088	1363
Village Pacific Mgt Group	8051	D	805 543-2350	20863
Village Pacific Mgt Group (PA)	8051	D	805 543-2300	20864
Vitalant	8099	D	805 543-1077	22901
Vitalant	8099	D	831 751-1993	22902
Voloagri Inc	5191	D	805 547-9391	9102
Weatherford International LLC	1389	D	805 781-3580	1085
Wells Fargo Bank National Assn	6021	D	805 541-0143	9403

SAN MARCOS, CA - San Diego County

	SIC	EMP	PHONE	ENTRY #
American Concrete	1771	D	760 471-9907	3214
American Homes Trust	6798	D	619 694-7821	12149
Americare Hlth Retirement Inc	6512	D	760 744-4484	10852
Associated Students Inc	7041	E	760 750-4990	13472
AT&T Corp	4812	D	760 752-3273	5284
Beaudry R V San Marcos Inc	7549	C	760 736-8800	17852
Birth Choice of San Marco	8322	D	760 744-1313	23514
Care Choice Health Systems Inc	8059	D	760 798-4508	21033
Casa De Amparo (PA)	8361	D	760 754-5500	24454

	SIC	EMP	PHONE	ENTRY #
Cellco Partnership	4812	D	760 738-0088	5323
Chateau Lake San Marcos Homeow	8641	D	760 471-0083	25136
Chatham Inc	5094	E	800 222-2002	8006
Citizens Development Corp (PA)	7997	D	760 744-0120	18889
Community Catalysts California	8331	E	760 471-3700	24167
Control Air Conditioning Corp	7623	C	760 744-2727	17894
Corkys Pest Control Inc	7342	C	760 432-8801	14148
Diamond Environmental Svcs LP	7359	D	760 744-7191	14499
Doose Landscape Incorporated	0782	D	760 591-4500	831
Duke Financial Co Inc	7231	C	858 694-1215	13653
Edco Waste & Recycl Svcs Inc (HQ)	4953	D	760 744-2700	6395
Edwards Theatres Circuit Inc	7832	D	760 471-3734	18295
Fresh Origins LLC	0139	B	760 736-4072	22
Golden Door Properties LLC	7011	C	760 744-5777	12606
Hollandia Dairy Inc (PA)	0241	C	760 744-3222	416
Home Improvement Company Inc	1799	E	760 744-4840	3534
Iron Law Inc (PA)	8111	D	844 476-6529	23145
Kindred Healthcare Oper Inc	8051	C	760 471-2986	20559
KRC Equipment LLC	5083	D	760 744-1036	7704
La Provence Inc	5149	C	760 736-3299	8822
M Bar C Construction Inc	1791	C	760 744-4131	3385
Markstein Beverage Co	5181	C	760 744-9100	9011
Naumann/Hobbs Material	5084	C	858 207-6274	7779
North County Health Prj Inc (PA)	8011	C	760 736-6755	19715
Olympus Building Services Inc	8744	A	760 750-4629	27601
Orora North America	5113	D	760 510-7170	8114
Orora North America	5113	D	760 510-7000	8116
Paramount Trnsp Systems Inc (PA)	4731	E	760 510-7979	5134
Plant Source Inc	5193	E	760 743-7743	9158
Plum Healthcare Group LLC (PA)	8051	D	760 471-0388	20706
Primary Care Assod Med Group (PA)	8741	D	760 471-7505	26992
Rancho Physical Therapy Inc	8049	C	760 752-1011	20199
Rehab West Inc	6411	D	619 518-3710	10757
Rose Thompson Company	0181	C	760 736-6020	297
San Diego-Imperial Counties De	8322	D	760 736-1200	24015
San Marcos Caterers Inc	7011	C	760 744-0120	13179
San Marcos Operating Co LP	8051	D	760 471-2986	20741
San Marcos Unified School Dst	8351	D	760 752-1252	24377
Shasta Landscaping Inc	0782	D	760 744-6551	937
Southern Contracting Company	1731	C	760 744-0760	2735
Tel Tech Plus Inc	1731	E	760 510-1323	2763
Ulta Salon Cosmt Fragrance Inc	7231	C	760 744-0853	13683
Village Square Nursing Center	8051	C	760 471-2986	20865
Welk Resort Group Inc (PA)	6531	E	760 652-4913	11825
Woodspear Properties (PA)	6513	E	760 761-4340	11145

SAN MARINO, CA - Los Angeles County

	SIC	EMP	PHONE	ENTRY #
D&D Equipment Rental LLC	7353	E	562 595-4555	14438
Tricor Entertainment Inc	7812	C	626 282-5184	18136

SAN MARTIN, CA - Santa Clara County

	SIC	EMP	PHONE	ENTRY #
Cordevalle Golf Club LLC	7997	C	408 695-4500	18900

SAN MATEO, CA - San Mateo County

	SIC	EMP	PHONE	ENTRY #
AAA Travel	6331	E	650 572-5600	10329
Aauw Action Fund Inc	8699	D	650 574-9160	25373
Abd Insurance & Fincl Svcs Inc (PA)	6411	D	650 488-8565	10508
Aceva Technologies Inc	7323	C	650 227-5500	14030
Addus Healthcare Inc	8082	B	650 638-7943	22200
AF Software Holdings Inc	6719	B	888 317-3395	11961
AF Software Parent Inc	6719	B	888 317-3395	11962
Alain Pinel Realtors Inc	6531	D	650 548-1111	11196
Alfresco Software Inc (PA)	7372	C	888 317-3395	15577
Alienvault LLC (DH)	7372	C	650 713-3333	15578
Allegis Group Inc	7363	C	650 425-6950	14812
Allen Lund Company LLC	4731	D	650 358-9454	5003
Alliance Hospital Services	8082	E	650 697-6900	22213
Andreini & Company (PA)	6411	D	650 573-1111	10526
Apttus Corporation (PA)	7373	C	650 445-7700	15914
Archives Management Corp (PA)	8741	C	650 544-2200	26763
Aryaka Networks Inc (PA)	8743	D	408 273-8420	27537
Assista Hlthcare Prfssnals LLC	8322	C	650 393-4293	23496
Atrium Plaza LLC	7011	C	650 653-6000	12340
Barrett Business Services Inc	8741	A	650 653-7588	26775
Bay Area Senior Services Inc	8322	C	650 579-5500	23503
Bay Meadows Racing Association	8611	C	650 573-4500	24944
Belectric Inc (HQ)	1629	D	510 896-3940	2011
Bertram Capital Management LLC	6799	B	650 358-5000	12201
Big Oak Hardwood Floor Co Inc	1752	D	650 591-8651	3096
Borland Software Corporation	7372	A	650 286-1900	15614
C9 Edge Inc	5045	D	650 561-7855	7021
C9 Inc	7371	D	650 561-7855	15044
CA Ste Atom Assoc Intr-Ins Bur	6331	D	650 572-5600	10341
California Casualty Mgt Co (HQ)	6331	C	650 574-4000	10344
California Envmtl Hlth Assn	8748	D	650 363-4726	27672
Califrnia CPA Edcatn Foundation	8621	D	800 922-5272	25007

(P-0000) Products & Services Section entry number
(PA)=Parent Co (HQ)=Headquarters (DH)=Div Headquarters

	SIC	EMP	PHONE	ENTRY #
Califrnia Cslty Indemnity Exch (PA)	6331	C	650 574-4000	10346
Camico Mutual Insurance Co (PA)	6411	C	650 378-6874	10575
Cellarstone Inc (PA)	7379	D	650 242-0008	16324
Center For Learning and	8322	B	800 538-8365	23549
Cir	8731	C	650 574-6900	26348
City of San Mateo	7349	D	650 522-7300	14214
Clarizen Inc	8741	C	866 502-9813	26810
Coldwell Bnkr Residential Brkg	6531	D	650 558-6800	11348
County of San Mateo	8322	C	650 312-5327	23735
County of San Mateo	8322	B	650 312-8887	23736
County of San Mateo	8093	D	650 372-8540	22556
County of San Mateo	8322	C	650 312-8803	23740
Coupa Software Incorporated (PA)	7372	C	650 931-3200	15639
Daniel J Edelman Inc	7313	D	650 762-2800	13942
David D Bohannon Organization (PA)	6512	D	650 345-8222	10866
Demandtec LLC	7371	B	914 499-1900	15100
Device Anywhere	7371	D	650 655-6400	15103
Digital Chocolate Inc	7371	D	650 372-1600	15108
Drawbridge Inc	8742	D	650 513-2323	27219
Endorse Corp	5045	A	617 470-8332	7042
Engagio Inc	7372	E	650 265-2264	15667
Ero-Tech Corp	7822	D	415 468-5600	18238
Essex Property Trust Inc (PA)	6513	C	650 655-7800	11015
Essex Queen Anne LLC	6519	D	650 849-1600	11171
Fce Benefit Administrators Inc (PA)	6411	C	650 341-0306	10625
Fhar Fmly Hsing Adult Rsources	8322	D	650 573-3341	23805
Fifty Peninsula Partners	6513	D	650 344-8200	11019
First Student Inc	4151	D	650 685-8245	3924
Franklin Advisers Inc (HQ)	6282	A	650 312-2000	10081
Franklin Resources Inc (PA)	6722	D	650 312-2000	12039
Franklin Templeton Svcs LLC	6282	A	650 312-3000	10082
Freedom Financial Network LLC (PA)	7299	D	650 393-6619	13745
Gengo Inc	7389	E	650 585-4390	17185
Glenborough LLC (PA)	6531	D	650 343-9300	11485
Golden Gate Regional Ctr Inc	8322	D	650 574-9232	23823
Inclin Inc	8731	D	650 961-3422	26382
Infogroup Inc	7331	C	650 389-0700	14046
Instill Corporation	7371	C	650 645-2600	15220
Institute For Humn Social Dev (PA)	8351	D	650 871-5613	24330
Intelpeer Cloud Cmmnctions LLC	4813	C	650 525-9200	5588
Ip International Inc	7379	E	650 403-7800	16409
Isearch Media LLC	7311	D	415 358-0882	13850
Island Hospitality MGT LLC	7011	D	650 574-4700	12782
Jobvite Inc	8742	D	650 376-7200	27290
John Gore Organization Inc	7922	D	650 340-0469	18376
Judy Madrigal & Associates Inc	8011	A	650 873-3444	19522
Kaiser Foundation Hospitals	8011	A	650 358-7000	19583
Kurt Meiswinkel Inc	1742	E	650 344-7200	2908
La Joie Jerry	8741	E	650 375-1808	26925
Lattice Engines Inc (PA)	7379	D	877 460-0010	16419
Lisi Inc (PA)	6411	C	650 348-4131	10673
Logictier Inc	7379	D	650 235-6600	16421
Marketo Inc (DH)	7371	C	650 376-2300	15272
Medallia Inc (PA)	7372	C	650 321-3000	15753
Milestone Topco Inc (HQ)	6719	A	650 376-2300	11992
Mission Hospice & HM Care Inc (PA)	8699	D	650 554-1000	25444
Movoto LLC	6531	D	888 766-8686	11620
N Model Inc (PA)	7371	D	650 610-4600	15298
National Fncl Srvcs Cnsrtm LLC	8742	D	650 572-2872	27359
NC Interactive LLC	7372	D	650 393-2200	15772
Netsuite Inc (DH)	7372	C	650 627-1000	15776
New York Life Insurance Co	6411	B	650 571-1220	10702
Nlyte Software Americas Ltd (DH)	7372	D	650 561-8200	15784
Nursing & Rehab At Home	8082	D	650 286-4272	22376
Open Text Inc (HQ)	7371	D	650 645-3000	15331
Opya Inc	8093	D	650 931-6300	22628
Oracle Systems Corporation	7372	C	650 506-6780	15818
Peninsula Community Foundation	6732	D	650 358-9369	12082
Peninsula Family Service (PA)	8351	B	650 403-4300	24367
People Science Inc	7361	E	888 924-1004	14691
Permanente Medical Group Inc	8011	D	650 358-7000	19781
Personlized Buty Discovery Inc (PA)	7231	D	888 769-4526	13667
Prometheus RE Group Inc (PA)	6531	C	650 931-3400	11687
Raiser Senior Services LLC	8361	D	650 342-4106	24640
Rapid Solutions Consulting LLC	7371	E	415 226-1131	15396
Reflektion Inc (PA)	7371	E	650 293-0800	15402
Research Libraries Group Inc	7375	D	650 288-1288	16247
Robert Half International Inc	7361	E	650 574-8200	14737
San Mateo Cnty Expo Fair Assn	7999	E	650 574-3247	19232
San Mateo County Community	4833	D	650 574-6586	5836
San Mateo Credit Union	6062	C	650 363-1725	9652
Satmetrix Systems Inc (PA)	7371	D	650 227-8300	15430
Scott Place Associates	6531	C	650 345-8222	11756
Securitas SEC Svcs USA Inc	7382	C	650 358-1556	16936
Sequoia Bnefits Insur Svcs LLC	8742	D	650 369-0200	27444

	SIC	EMP	PHONE	ENTRY #
Smile Family Inc	7371	D	727 771-3641	15455
Snaplogic Inc (PA)	7372	C	888 494-1570	15855
Snowflake Computing Inc (PA)	7371	D	844 766-9355	15458
Sociable Labs Inc	7374	E	415 225-8740	16178
State Farm Mutl Auto Insur Co	6411	D	650 345-3571	10788
Strands Inc A Delaware Corp	7371	E	541 753-4426	15475
Strands Labs Inc	7371	E	415 398-4333	15476
Sunrise Senior Living Inc	8051	D	650 558-8555	20799
Sutter Health	8011	C	650 262-4262	19973
Tano Capital LLC	6799	E	650 212-0330	12270
Telesys Software	7371	E	650 522-9922	15499
Templeton Franklin Intl Tr	6722	C	650 312-2000	12048
Ten-X LLC	6531	B	949 609-5376	11788
Tesla Energy Operations Inc (HQ)	1711	A	650 638-1028	2383
Total Airport Services LLC	4581	C	650 358-0144	4921
Trident Capital Inc (PA)	6799	C	650 289-4400	12276
Tunari Corp Inc	7371	D	650 249-6740	15514
Veterinary Surgical Associates	8011	D	650 696-8196	20085
Vindicia Inc	7372	C	650 264-4700	15889
Wageworks Inc (PA)	8742	C	650 577-5200	27518
Westlake Development Group LLC (PA)	6512	D	650 579-1010	10966
Westlake Realty Group Inc (PA)	6531	D	650 579-1010	11830
Wise Commerce Inc	7371	D	855 469-4737	15547
Young Mens Christian Assoc SF	8641	C	650 286-9622	25323
Zs Associates Inc	7389	C	650 762-7800	17604
Zuora Inc (PA)	7372	B	800 425-1281	15903

SAN PABLO, CA - Contra Costa County

	SIC	EMP	PHONE	ENTRY #
C Overaa & Co	1541	C	510 235-0540	1383
Creekside Healthcare Ctr	8051	E	510 235-5514	20360
East Bay Nephrology	8011	E	510 235-1057	19451
Grancare LLC	8051	B	510 232-5945	20492
Lytton Rancheria	7999	A	510 215-7888	19201
Making Waves Education Program (PA)	6733	C	510 237-3434	12111
Mariner Health Care Inc	8051	C	510 232-5945	20615
Promab Biotechnologies Inc	8731	C	510 860-4615	26440
San Pablo Healthcare	8051	C	510 235-3720	20743

SAN PEDRO, CA - Los Angeles County

	SIC	EMP	PHONE	ENTRY #
Advent Resources Inc	7372	D	310 241-1500	15574
APM Terminals Pacific LLC	4731	E	310 221-4000	5011
APM Terminals Pacific LLC (DH)	4491	C	704 571-2768	4723
AT&T Corp	4812	D	310 547-0400	5276
Beach Cities Invest & Protctn	7381	B	310 322-4724	16581
Bombard Mar & Resort MGT Svcs (PA)	4489	B	310 519-7971	4711
Boys and Girls Clubs of The La (PA)	8641	D	310 833-1322	25108
Boys and Girls Clubs of The La	8641	D	310 833-1322	25109
Bridges At Sn Pdro Pnnsla Hspt	8093	D	310 514-5359	22514
Catalina Channel Express Inc (HQ)	4489	D	310 519-7971	4712
City of Los Angeles	4491	C	310 732-7681	4726
Comprehensive Child Dev Inc	8351	D	310 514-4998	24305
Gs Brothers Inc (PA)	0782	C	310 833-1369	853
Healthview Inc (PA)	8361	C	310 547-3341	24558
Isabel Garreton Inc (PA)	5137	C	310 833-7768	8308
Little Sisters The Poor of La	8051	D	310 548-0625	20594
Meristar San Pedro Hilton LLC	7011	C	310 514-3344	12920
Nippon Express USA Inc	4731	D	310 532-6300	5119
Performance Team Frt Sys Inc	4225	C	310 241-4100	4610
PLD Enterprises Inc (PA)	5146	D	310 547-3366	8595
Procel Temporary Services Inc	7363	B	310 372-0560	14894
Proficient LLC	7011	D	310 519-8200	13081
Providence Health & Services S	8062	D	310 832-3311	21666
Providence Health System	8062	A	310 832-3311	21670
Providence Health System	8062	D	310 514-5270	21672
San Pedro Convalescent HM Inc	8051	D	310 832-6431	20744
Seacrest Convalescent Hosp Inc	8051	D	310 833-3526	20751
So Cal Ship Services	4489	D	310 519-8411	4720
Spf Capital Real Estate LLC	7011	D	310 519-8200	13254
Ssa Pacific Inc	4491	D	310 833-9606	4740
Star Fisheries (PA)	5146	D	310 832-8395	8605
Tri-Marine Fish Company LLC	5146	D	310 547-1144	8607
Tri-Marine Fishing MGT LLC	8741	E	310 547-1144	27066
Tri-State Employment Svc Inc	7361	B	310 521-9616	14785
Y & S Enterprises Inc (PA)	7532	E	310 548-1120	17746
Yusen Terminals LLC (DH)	4491	D	310 548-8000	4744

SAN QUENTIN, CA - Marin County

	SIC	EMP	PHONE	ENTRY #
Distillery Inc	7372	D	415 505-5446	15649

SAN RAFAEL, CA - Marin County

	SIC	EMP	PHONE	ENTRY #
Adolph Gasser Inc	5043	C	415 495-3852	6939
Aldersly Retirement Center	6513	D	415 453-9271	10973
Arcadia Services Inc	7363	D	248 352-7530	14818
AT&T Corp	4812	D	415 721-1470	5285
Autodesk Inc (PA)	7372	B	415 507-5000	15599
Autodesk Inc	7372	C	415 507-5000	15600
Bank of Marin	6022	D	415 472-2265	9413

Employment Codes: A=Over 500 employees, B=251-500,
C=101-250, D=51-100, E=50

2019 Directory of California
Wholesalers and Services Companies

© Mergent Inc. 1-800-342-5647
1677

GEOGRAPHIC

Company	SIC	EMP	PHONE	ENTRY #
Bernard Osher Marin Jewish Com	8322	C	415 444-8000	23510
Bradley Melissa Real Estate	6531	D	415 459-1010	11249
Buckelew Programs (PA)	8322	C	415 457-6964	23520
Cal-Coast Healthcare Inc	8051	D	415 479-5149	20279
Casa Allegra Community Svcs	8742	D	415 499-1116	27184
Catholic Chrts Cyo Archdiocs	8322	B	415 507-2000	23544
Cellco Partnership	4812	D	415 258-8404	5357
Center Point Inc (PA)	8322	D	415 492-4444	23550
Central Payment Co LLC	7389	D	415 462-8335	17063
CF San Rafael LLC	8051	D	415 479-5161	20303
Clp Resources Inc	7363	E	415 446-7000	14838
Comcast California Ix Inc	4841	D	215 286-3345	5865
Community Action Marin	8093	C	415 459-6330	22535
County of Marin	8322	B	415 499-6970	23690
County of Marin	8711	D	415 499-7877	25628
De Mello Roofing Inc	1761	D	415 456-0741	3148
Dutra Dredging Company (HQ)	1629	D	415 721-2131	2028
Dutra Group (PA)	1629	D	415 258-6876	2029
Dutra Manson JV	1629	D	415 258-6876	2030
E C Wise Inc (PA)	7374	D	415 355-9473	16120
Eah Inc (PA)	6514	D	415 258-1800	11147
Edgewood Partners Insur Ctr	6411	D	415 456-4323	10611
Enterprise Events Group Inc	8742	C	415 499-4444	27227
Equator Coffees LLC	5046	D	415 485-2213	7134
Fair Isaac International Corp (HQ)	7372	A	415 446-6000	15674
Family Svcs Agcy Marin Cnty (PA)	8322	D	415 491-5700	23801
Frank Howard Allen Fincl Corp	6531	D	415 456-3000	11473
Ghilotti Bros Inc	1611	B	415 454-7011	1766
Gilardi & Co LLC	8741	D	415 461-0410	26870
Golden Gate Bridge High	4785	A	415 457-3110	5218
Golden Gate Nat Prks Cnsrvancy	8999	D	415 785-4787	27930
Guide Dogs For Blind Inc (PA)	0752	E	415 499-4000	628
Herbs Pool Service Inc	7389	D	415 479-4040	17220
Hospitality Ventures MGT LLC	7011	D	415 499-9222	12700
Icf Consulting Group Inc	8742	A	703 934-3000	27268
Independent Quality Care Inc	8059	D	415 479-1230	21117
Innovative Sleep Centers Inc	8011	D	415 927-4990	19513
Interactive Med Specialists	7363	D	415 472-4204	14864
Jacksons Hardware Inc	5072	D	415 870-4083	7592
Jerry Thompson & Sons Pntg Inc	1721	C	415 454-1500	2452
Kaiser Foundation Hospitals	8011	A	415 444-2000	19533
Kaiser Foundation Hospitals	6324	D	415 444-3522	10220
Kindred Nursing Centers W LLC	8062	D	415 456-7170	21541
Kisco Senior Living LLC	6513	D	415 491-1935	11043
Knight-Calabasas LLC	7997	D	415 453-4940	18943
Lifehouse Inc (PA)	8322	D	415 472-2373	23897
Lucas Digital Ltd (DH)	7922	B	415 258-2000	18383
Managed Health Network (DH)	6324	B	415 460-8168	10281
Managed Health Network	6324	A	510 620-6143	10282
Marin Airporter Inc (PA)	4111	D	415 256-8833	3680
Marin Clean Energy	4911	D	415 464-6028	6051
Marin Sanitary Service (PA)	4953	D	415 456-2601	6416
Marin Snior Crdnting Cncil Inc	8322	D	415 454-0964	23910
Mariner Health Care Inc	8051	D	415 479-3610	20624
Mhn Government Services LLC	8322	C	916 294-4941	23923
Mhn Services	6324	A	415 460-8300	10283
Michael B Mayock Inc	1742	D	415 456-9306	2918
Mighty Leaf Tea	5149	D	415 491-2650	8827
Mill Valley Refuse Service Inc	4953	D	415 457-2287	6418
Millsap Degnan & Assoc Inc	8711	D	415 472-4244	25824
Mountain Play Association	7922	E	415 383-1100	18387
Northgate Care Center	8059	D	415 479-1230	21169
Ocadian Care Centers LLC	8051	D	415 499-1000	20676
Pasha Group (PA)	4731	B	415 927-6400	5136
Pasha Hawaii Trnspt Lines LLC (PA)	4449	C	415 927-6400	4706
Penske Automotive Group Inc	7513	E	415 492-1922	17608
Permanente Medical Group Inc	8011	D	415 444-2000	19773
Pf West LLC	7991	C	415 479-9600	18640
Phoenix American Incorporated (PA)	4841	D	415 485-4500	5927
Powerhouse Building Inc	1771	D	415 446-0188	3308
Quaker Pet Group Inc	5199	D	415 721-7400	9253
R C Roberts & Co (PA)	6515	C	415 456-8600	11159
Rafael Convalescent Hospital	8059	C	415 479-5000	21191
Redhill Towing & Autobody	7549	D	415 456-8943	17869
Redhorse Constructors Inc	1521	D	415 492-2020	1222
Richard Shames MD	8011	D	415 388-0456	19825
San Rafael Hillcrest LLC	7011	D	415 479-8800	13182
San Rafael Rock Quarry LLC (HQ)	1429	D	415 459-7740	1090
Sea-Logix LLC (DH)	4213	D	415 927-6400	4262
Sisters of Nazareth	8059	D	415 479-8282	21218
Starwood Hotels & Resorts	7011	C	415 479-8800	13270
Urban Painting Inc	1721	D	415 485-1130	2489
Valentine Corporation	1799	E	415 453-3732	3601
Villa Marin Homeowners Assn	8641	C	415 499-8711	25282
Warren Security Systems Inc	7382	E	415 456-7034	16951

Company	SIC	EMP	PHONE	ENTRY #
Whitegold Solutions Inc	7379	E	415 456-4493	16531
Young Mens Christian Assnsf	8641	C	415 459-9622	25319
Young Mens Christian Assoc SF	8641	B	415 492-9622	25330

SAN RAMON, CA - Contra Costa County

Company	SIC	EMP	PHONE	ENTRY #
24 Hour Fitness Usa Inc (HQ)	7991	C	925 543-3100	18556
24 Hour Fitness Usa Inc	7991	D	916 722-7588	18560
24 Hour Fitness Worldwide Inc (PA)	7991	C	925 543-3100	18571
A D Bilich Inc	6162	E	925 820-5557	9767
A S A P Professional Services	7361	C	800 303-2727	14560
Accela Inc (PA)	7372	C	925 659-3200	15565
Accelon Inc	7361	E	925 216-5735	14564
Accountnow Inc	8742	A	925 498-1800	27112
Aetna Health California Inc (DH)	6324	C	925 543-9223	10177
Alexander Properties Company	6512	E	925 866-0100	10848
AMP Technologies LLC (PA)	7371	C	877 442-2824	14981
AMR Appraisals Inc	6531	D	925 400-6066	11213
Annabel Investment Company	6552	D	925 866-0100	11855
Armanino LLP (PA)	8721	C	925 790-2600	26145
Arrand Properties LLC	1521	E	925 289-1032	1119
AT&T Corp	4813	C	415 394-3000	5457
AT&T Corp	4812	D	925 327-7100	5291
AT&T Corp	4813	D	925 275-8048	5458
AT&T Corp	4813	A	925 823-5388	5459
AT&T Services	4813	D	925 901-9318	5470
AT&T Services Inc	4813	A	925 821-1443	5488
AT&T Services Inc	4813	D	415 823-0993	5513
Athoc Inc (DH)	7371	D	925 242-5660	15005
Atlas Lift Tech Inc	8099	D	415 283-1804	22739
Baco Realty Corporation	4225	D	925 275-0100	4532
Bara Construction Services	1531	E	925 790-0130	1330
Bay Area Techworkers (PA)	7361	D	925 359-2200	14577
Bishop Ranch Veterinary Center (PA)	0742	D	925 743-9300	597
Bridges At Gale Ranch LLC	7997	D	925 735-4253	18874
Brilliant Sftwr Solutions Inc	7373	D	510 742-5120	15922
Carlson Barbee & Gibson Inc	8711	D	925 866-0322	25592
Castro Valley Health Inc	8082	C	510 690-1930	22257
Cellco Partnership	4812	D	925 743-9327	5353
Chevron Investor Inc (HQ)	6799	B	925 842-1000	12214
Chevron USA Inc	1311	D	925 842-0855	1021
Clubspan San Ramon LLC (PA)	7991	B	925 735-1182	18588
Cmg Financial Services	7389	D	925 983-3073	17089
Cmg Mortgage Inc (PA)	6163	B	619 554-1327	9877
Commerce Home Mortgage Inc (HQ)	6163	D	925 830-1500	9878
Concessionaires Urban Park	7999	C	530 529-1513	19151
Digicentury Corporation	7371	D	408 213-0146	15107
Donor Network West (PA)	8099	C	925 480-3100	22791
Enpower Management Corp	4911	E	925 244-1100	6036
Express System Intermodal Inc	4731	C	801 302-6625	5060
Expressworks International LLC (PA)	8742	C	925 244-0900	27231
Ferreira Service Inc (PA)	1711	D	925 831-9330	2208
Five9 Inc (PA)	7372	C	925 201-2000	15678
G4s Secure Solutions (usa)	7381	C	925 543-0008	16654
GE Digital LLC (HQ)	7372	B	925 242-6200	15689
General Electric Company	7372	D	925 242-6200	15690
Good Technology Corporation (HQ)	7371	C	408 352-9102	15185
Gorilla Tech Americas Inc	8742	C	925 365-1161	27250
Greystone Homes Inc	1521	C	925 242-0811	1175
Hill Physicians Med Group Inc (PA)	8011	B	800 445-5747	19503
Hit Portfolio I Misc Trs LLC	7011	B	925 743-1882	12676
Independent Quality Care Inc (PA)	8059	D	925 855-0881	21118
International Bus Mchs Corp	8742	C	925 277-5000	27278
Jaroth Inc	1731	C	925 553-3650	2616
Kaiser Foundation Hospitals	8011	A	925 244-7600	19585
KB Home South Bay Inc	1522	D	925 983-2500	1297
Kindercare Education LLC	8351	D	925 824-0267	24335
Legacy Mech & Enrgy Svcs Inc	1711	D	925 820-6938	2261
Lindquist LLP (PA)	8721	D	925 277-9100	26246
Lucile Salter Packard Chil	8011	D	925 277-7550	19664
Macdonald Mott Group Inc	8711	D	925 469-8010	25806
Mason McDuffie Mortgage Corp (PA)	6162	D	925 242-4400	9831
Millennial Brands LLC (PA)	5139	D	866 938-4806	8362
Mountain Retreat Incorporated	6552	D	925 838-7780	11894
Mt View Apartments LLC	6513	D	925 866-8429	11083
Native Sons Landscaping Inc	0782	E	925 837-8175	905
Netpace Inc	7379	D	925 543-7760	16432
New York Life Insurance Co	6411	D	415 999-9576	10712
Old Republic HM Protection Inc	6411	B	925 866-1500	10722
Pacifica Reflections	1531	E	925 275-9800	1356
Parkway Apartments LLC	6513	D	925 866-8429	11094
Pinnacle Funding Group Inc	6163	E	925 552-5302	9903
Plus Group Inc	7361	D	925 831-8551	14694
Primed MGT Consulting Svcs Inc	8741	B	925 327-6710	26994
Procter & Gamble Distrg LLC	5169	D	925 867-4900	8936
Protiviti Inc	8742	D	415 402-3663	27407
Reproductive Science Center	8011	D	925 867-1800	19819

Mergent email: customerrelations@mergent.com
1678

2019 Directory of California
Wholesalers and Services Companies

(P-0000) Products & Services Section entry number
(PA)=Parent Co (HQ)=Headquarters (DH)=Div Headquarters

Company	SIC	EMP	PHONE	ENTRY #
Robert Half International Inc	7361	E	925 913-1000	14745
Rose International	8748	C	636 812-4000	27846
RW Lynch Co Inc (PA)	7311	D	925 837-3877	13898
Safe Security Inc	7382	B	925 830-4777	16933
San Ramon Regional Med Ctr LLC	8062	A	925 275-9200	21712
Seacastle Inc	7359	D	925 480-3000	14543
Security Alarm Fing Entps Inc	7382	D	925 830-4786	16937
Shapell Inc	7992	D	925 735-4253	18761
Sirva Inc	4213	C	925 824-3109	4264
Splash Swim School Inc	7999	E	925 838-7946	19241
Spruce Technology Inc	7371	D	925 415-8160	15470
Summerhill Construction Co	1521	E	925 244-7520	1241
Surplus Line Association Cal	8611	D	415 434-4900	24986
T W M Industries	6726	A	925 866-1156	12071
Tracy Trujillo MD	8011	E	925 838-6511	20010
United Parcel Service Inc OH	4215	C	800 833-9943	4483
Universal Protection Svc LP	7381	D	805 496-4401	16845
Unocal Corporation (HQ)	1311	B	310 726-7600	1030
V A Anderson Enterprises Inc	7334	D	925 866-6150	14094
Vyshnavi Information Techn	7371	C	408 454-6218	15539
Warmington Homes	1531	C	925 866-6700	1366
Webly Systems Inc	7389	E	888 444-6400	17584
Wurldtech Security Tech Ltd	5065	D	604 669-6674	7565

SAN SIMEON, CA - San Luis Obispo County

Company	SIC	EMP	PHONE	ENTRY #
Cavalier Inn Inc	7011	D	805 927-4688	12440
Cavalier Inn Incorporated	7011	D	805 927-6444	12441

SAN YSIDRO, CA - San Diego County

Company	SIC	EMP	PHONE	ENTRY #
Centro De Salud De La (PA)	8093	D	619 428-4463	22526
Nigal Inc (PA)	4822	D	619 428-5051	5686

SANGER, CA - Fresno County

Company	SIC	EMP	PHONE	ENTRY #
Cal Custom Tile	1743	D	559 875-1460	2989
Chooljian Bros Packing Co Inc	5149	E	559 875-5501	8767
Farmex Land Management Inc	7389	C	559 875-7181	17164
Gerawan Farming Partners Inc	0721	B	559 787-8780	462
Golden Living LLC	8059	D	559 875-6501	21096
Gongs Market of Sanger Inc (PA)	6512	E	559 875-5576	10885
Pitman Family Farms (PA)	0191	D	559 875-9300	373
Suma Fruit Intl USA Inc	0723	E	559 875-5000	569
Virginia Sarabian	0175	E	559 493-2900	231
Wine Group Inc	5182	D	559 638-3511	9061

SANTA ANA, CA - Orange County

Company	SIC	EMP	PHONE	ENTRY #
2100 Trust LLC (PA)	6733	C	877 469-7344	12087
5 Diamond Protection Inc	6512	D	949 466-1367	10844
Adtek Engineering Service	8711	C	800 451-0782	25503
Advanced Clnroom McRclean Corp	7349	C	714 751-1152	14182
Affiliated Funding Corporation	6163	D	714 619-3100	9869
Alan B Whitson Company Inc	8742	A	949 955-1200	27122
Aldoc Inc	1711	D	714 836-8477	2095
Allied Anesthesia Med Group	8011	D	951 830-9816	19274
Allied Building Products Corp	5033	E	714 647-9792	6916
Aluminum Precision Pdts Inc (PA)	5051	C	714 546-8125	7254
Alvaradosmith A Prof Corp (PA)	8111	C	714 852-6800	22914
Alzheimers Care Since 1983	8082	E	714 641-0959	22217
AM Products Inc	5051	E	714 662-4454	7255
America West Airlines Inc	4512	D	949 852-5471	4765
American Airlines Inc	4512	C	949 852-5470	4769
American Concrete Cutting Inc	1795	D	714 547-7181	3445
American Leak Detection Inc	1711	E	714 836-8477	2106
American National Red Cross	8322	E	714 481-5300	23474
American-1 Airtight SEC Co	7381	E	714 997-0605	16568
Aramark Unf & Career AP LLC	7218	D	714 545-4877	13590
Architectural Coatings Inc	1721	E	714 701-1360	2421
Assurant Inc	6311	B	714 571-3900	10129
Atlas International Inc	5074	E	714 622-1550	7610
B-Per Electronic Inc	4812	D	626 912-0600	5299
Banc California National Assn (HQ)	6021	D	877 770-2262	9277
Banc of California Inc (PA)	6021	C	855 361-2262	9279
Barry McPherson Inc	6411	C	425 343-5000	10559
Beacon Sales Acquisition Inc	5033	C	714 288-1974	6920
Behr Process Sales Company	8743	C	714 545-7101	27541
Blind Childrens Lrng Ctr Inc	8351	E	714 573-8888	24267
Blower-Dempsay Corporation (PA)	5199	C	714 481-3800	9197
Brethren Inc	5099	E	714 836-4800	8020
Brightview Landscape Dev Inc	0781	D	714 546-7843	735
Brightview Landscape Svcs Inc	0781	D	714 546-7843	739
Bsnap LLC	6162	D	657 269-4410	9783
Bureau Veritas North Amer Inc	8748	D	714 431-4100	27665
California Anesthesia Asso Med	8011	D	800 888-2186	19338
Calvary Church Santa Ana Inc	8351	C	714 973-4800	24273
Carollo Engineers Inc	8711	D	714 540-4300	25594
Carrasco Heleo	7349	C	714 639-1759	14208
Cellco Partnership	4812	D	714 775-0600	5394
Celmol Inc	5199	D	714 259-1000	9202
Cemtek Environmental Inc	8748	E	714 437-7100	27679
Certified Trnsp Svcs Inc	4151	D	714 835-8676	3911
Chamson Management Inc	7011	D	714 751-2400	12449
Charles W Bowers Museum Corp	8412	D	714 567-3600	24868
Chroma Systems	7217	D	714 557-8480	13575
Clear World Communications	4813	B	714 445-3900	5531
Clinica Medica Familiar	8011	D	714 541-0870	19384
Collectors Universe Inc (PA)	7699	D	949 567-1234	17941
Colton Real Estate Group (PA)	6519	D	949 475-4200	11167
Compwest Insurance Company	6331	D	714 641-9500	10348
Continental Currency Svcs Inc (HQ)	6099	E	714 569-0300	9675
Continental Currency Svcs Inc (PA)	6099	D	714 569-0300	9676
Contractors Flrg Svc Cal Inc	5023	C	714 556-6100	6756
County of Orange	8071	E	714 834-8385	22073
County of Orange	4953	D	714 834-4000	6385
County of Orange	8651	E	714 567-7500	25370
County of Orange	8322	D	714 834-8899	23701
County of Orange	8052	A	714 834-6021	20925
Covenant Care California LLC	8051	C	714 554-9700	20352
CP Opco LLC	7359	D	714 540-6111	14497
CRC Health Corporate	8093	D	714 542-3581	22563
Crown Building Maintenance Co	7349	E	714 434-9494	14238
Crown Facility Solutions	7349	E	657 266-0821	14243
Data Trace Info Svcs LLC (HQ)	8999	D	714 250-6700	27927
Debtmerica LLC	7299	D	714 389-4200	13738
Dekra-Lite Industries Inc	7389	D	714 630-0705	17129
Deutsche Bank National Tr Co	6733	D	714 247-6000	12093
Deutsche Bank National Tr Co	6091	D	714 247-6054	9665
Dgwb Inc	7311	D	714 881-2300	13818
Dgwb Ventures LLC	7311	D	714 881-2308	13819
Dhs Consulting Inc	8741	D	714 276-1135	26839
Discovery Scnce Ctr Ornge Cnty	7996	D	866 552-2823	18796
Dish Network Corporation	4841	E	714 424-0503	5908
Donovan Golf Courses MGT (PA)	7992	C	714 554-0672	18708
DOT Printer Inc	4225	D	949 752-7730	4551
Duplo USA Corporation (PA)	5044	C	949 752-8222	6959
Durham School Services L P	4173	C	714 542-8989	3952
Edwards Theatres Circuit Inc	7832	D	714 557-5701	18292
Embee Processing LLC	8711	B	714 546-9842	25658
Empire Building Services Inc	7349	E	714 836-7700	14258
Ephonamationcom Inc	7389	C	714 560-1000	17153
Experian Corporation	7323	A	714 830-7000	14035
F M Tarbell Co (HQ)	6531	C	714 972-0988	11431
F R A L P	7261	D	714 633-1442	13690
Family Assessment Cnslng Edctn	8322	E	714 447-9024	23793
Financial Statement Svcs Inc (PA)	7331	C	714 436-3326	14044
First American Financial Corp (PA)	6361	C	714 250-3000	10453
First American Mortgage Svcs	6361	B	714 250-4210	10454
First American Title Insur Co (HQ)	6361	C	800 854-3643	10455
First American Title Insur Co	6361	C	714 800-3000	10460
First American Title Insur Co	6361	A	714 250-4000	10462
First American Trust Company (HQ)	6282	D	714 560-7856	10077
First Student Inc	4151	D	714 850-7578	3933
Fishel Company	1623	C	714 668-9268	1917
French Park Care Center	8051	C	714 973-1656	20439
Fresh Grill LLC	5149	C	714 444-2126	8790
G W Maintenance Inc (PA)	5085	D	714 541-2211	7848
Gamboa Service Inc	7349	D	714 966-5325	14272
Goglanian Bakeries Inc (HQ)	5149	B	714 549-1524	8798
Goodwill Inds Orange Cnty Cal	8331	C	714 754-7808	24186
Gps Painting Wallcovering Inc	1721	D	714 730-8904	2445
Grants Landscape Services Inc	0782	D	714 444-1903	848
Gringteam Inc	7011	C	714 825-3333	12625
Guardsmark LLC (DH)	7381	C	714 619-9700	16679
Hardy & Harper Inc	1611	E	714 444-1851	1790
Hart King Coldren A Prof Corp	8111	D	714 432-8700	23124
Harveys Industries Inc	5137	D	714 277-4700	8305
Health Resources Corp	8062	B	714 754-5454	21444
Healthcare Partners LLC	8099	E	714 964-6229	22814
Hirsch Electronics LLC	5065	C	949 250-8888	7487
Hntb Corporation	8711	D	714 460-1600	25735
Hntb Gerwick Water Solutions	8711	D	714 460-1600	25737
Hollins Schechter A Prof Corp	8111	D	714 558-9119	23135
Honeywell International Inc	5075	C	714 796-7500	7652
Idondemand Inc	7373	B	415 200-4546	15976
Indvls	8742	E	818 703-3855	27272
Innovative Cnstr Solutions	8744	C	714 893-6366	27597
Integrus LLC	5044	D	714 547-9500	6962
Intergro Rehab Service	8049	C	714 901-4200	20186
IPC (usa) Inc (HQ)	5172	D	949 648-5600	8964
IRC Technologies Inc (PA)	1761	D	949 476-8626	3167
Jhc Investment Inc	7011	D	714 751-2400	12790
Jmac Lending Inc	6141	D	949 390-2688	9718
John M Frank Construction Inc	1542	D	714 210-3600	1566
Johnson La Follette	8111	D	714 558-7008	23152

Employment Codes: A=Over 500 employees, B=251-500,
C=101-250, D=51-100, E=50

2019 Directory of California
Wholesalers and Services Companies

© Mergent Inc. 1-800-342-5647
1679

GEOGRAPHIC

Company	SIC	EMP	PHONE	ENTRY #
Kaiser Foundation Hospitals	8011	A	714 223-2606	19586
Kaiser Foundation Hospitals	6324	D	888 988-2800	10244
Kaiser Foundation Hospitals	6324	E	714 967-4700	10271
Kingspan Light & Air LLC	1761	C	714 540-8950	3170
Klein-Testan-Brundo	8111	E	714 245-8888	23176
Knox Services LLC (PA)	7334	C	714 479-1650	14090
Kpc Healthcare Inc	8062	B	714 800-1919	21543
Kya Services LLC	1752	E	714 659-6476	3112
L&T Staffing Inc (PA)	7361	D	714 558-1821	14659
La Boxing Franchise Corp	7991	C	714 668-0911	18623
Landcare USA LLC	0782	D	949 559-7771	876
Landmark Services Inc	7349	D	714 547-6308	14300
Latham & Watkins LLP	8111	B	714 755-8288	23185
Lenox Financial Mortgage Corp	6162	C	949 428-5100	9825
Lisi Inc	6399	D	714 460-5153	10503
Lloyd Pest Control Co	7342	E	714 979-6021	14153
Loan Now	6141	D	714 352-2250	9719
M & A Mortgage Inc	6163	D	714 560-1970	9893
Macro-Z-Technology Company (PA)	1611	D	714 564-1130	1809
Madison Materials	4953	D	714 664-0159	6413
Main Electric Supply Co LLC (PA)	5063	D	949 833-3052	7375
Managed Homecare Inc	8082	E	951 341-0782	22362
Marriott International Inc	7011	C	714 545-5261	12904
Medical Network Inc	8741	D	949 863-0022	26942
Melmet Steven J Law Ofc	8111	D	949 263-1000	23249
Merchants Building Maint Co	7349	B	714 973-9422	14317
Mercy House Living Centers	8611	C	714 836-7188	24968
Metropro Road Services Inc (PA)	7549	D	714 556-7600	17866
Midori Landscape Inc	0782	D	714 751-8792	897
Mission Ldscp Companies Inc	0782	C	714 545-9962	900
Moms Orange County	8082	E	714 972-2610	22368
Montrose Envmtl Group Inc	8748	A	714 332-8646	27793
Moore Law Group A Prof Corp	8111	D	714 431-2000	23259
Moorefield Construction Inc (PA)	1542	D	714 972-0700	1596
Morgan Stanley & Co LLC	6211	D	714 836-5181	9997
Morrison Landscaping Inc	5052	E	714 571-0455	7323
Mpl Enterprises Inc	0782	D	714 545-1717	903
Mw Partners	8742	D	949 705-0682	27354
Newmark & Company RE Inc	8742	D	714 667-8252	27366
Nieves Landscape Inc	0782	C	714 835-7332	910
North River Ranch LLC	0171	E	714 556-6244	110
Nova Plumbing Inc	1711	C	714 556-6682	2290
NRG Power Inc	1731	D	714 424-6484	2665
Oc 405 Partners Joint Venture	1622	D	858 251-2200	1886
Oc Engineering	8711	D	714 667-3212	25852
OC Special Events SEC Inc	7381	C	714 541-4111	16745
Odyssey Healthcare Inc	8051	D	714 245-7420	20678
Olive Crest (PA)	8361	B	714 543-5437	24619
Oneoc (PA)	8699	D	714 953-5757	25447
Optima Tax Relief LLC	7291	C	714 361-4636	13711
Orange Cast Title Southern Cal (PA)	7389	D	714 558-2836	17374
Orange County Cncl Bsa (PA)	8641	D	714 546-4990	25208
Orange County Employees Retir	6722	D	714 558-6200	12043
Orange County Head Start (PA)	8351	D	714 241-8920	24362
Orange County Health Care Agcy	8621	D	714 568-5683	25034
Orange County Royale Convlscnt (PA)	8059	B	714 546-6450	21175
Orange County Services Inc	1711	E	714 541-9753	2299
Orange Countys Credit Union (PA)	6061	C	714 755-5900	9577
Orange Courier Inc	7389	B	714 384-3600	17376
Orangewood Foundation	8322	D	714 619-0200	23953
Orchid MPS	5047	D	714 549-9203	7200
Pacific Eastern Intl Pdts	5199	D	714 538-3434	9241
Pacific Foods & Dist Inc	5149	D	714 547-0787	8845
Pacific Rim Contractors Inc	1742	D	714 641-7380	2933
Pacific Rim Mech Contrs Inc	1711	D	714 285-2600	2303
Pacifica Hiorange LP	7011	D	714 556-3838	13005
Pacificare Dental	6324	C	661 631-8613	10289
Pacificare Health Plan Admin (DH)	6324	B	714 825-5200	10290
Partners Capital Group Inc (PA)	7389	D	949 916-3900	17389
Patrol Masters Inc	7381	C	714 426-2526	16754
Pds Tech Inc	7361	D	214 647-9600	14689
Phoenix House Orange County	8361	D	714 953-9373	24630
Pipe Restoration Inc	1711	E	714 564-7600	2310
Pipeline Restoration Plumbing	1711	D	714 957-5836	2311
Platinum Equity Partners Inc	7532	C	714 444-3100	17733
Ponderosa Builders Inc	7349	A	714 434-9494	14353
Pps Parking Inc	7299	A	949 223-8707	13767
Prospect Medical Group Inc (HQ)	8741	D	714 796-5900	27001
Psomas	8713	C	714 751-7373	26132
Pta CA Cngrss of Parnts Tchrs	8641	D	714 836-2700	25218
Q S H Properties Inc	7011	D	714 957-9200	13085
Rainbow Home Care Services	8082	D	714 544-8070	22401
Ralph D Mitzel Inc	7353	D	714 554-4745	14454
Reed Thomas Company Inc	1794	D	714 558-7691	3438
Reputation Management Cons Inc	8742	D	949 682-7906	27423

Company	SIC	EMP	PHONE	ENTRY #
Rgis LLC	7389	D	714 541-1431	17445
Rice Drywall Inc	1742	D	714 543-5400	2948
RPM Transportation Inc (HQ)	4213	C	714 388-3500	4253
S W K Properties LLC	7011	C	714 481-6300	13157
SA Recycling LLC	4953	D	714 667-7898	6458
Santa Ana City of	7361	E	714 565-2600	14752
Santa Ana Country Club	7997	D	714 556-3000	19031
Santa Ana Police Officers Assn	8699	A	714 836-1211	25460
Santa Ana Radiology Center	8011	D	714 835-6055	19852
Santa Ana Unified School Dst	8099	D	714 431-1900	22879
Satellite Management Co (PA)	6531	C	714 558-2411	11754
Schoolsfirst Federal Credit Un (PA)	6061	B	714 258-4000	9589
Scottish American Insurance (PA)	6411	D	714 550-5050	10766
Script To Screen	7812	D	714 558-3287	18114
Service First Contractors	1542	E	714 573-2200	1643
ServiceMaster Company LLC	7349	C	714 245-1465	14386
Shield Security Inc (DH)	7381	B	714 210-1501	16823
Silverwood Landscape Cnstr Inc	0782	D	714 427-6134	941
Simons Wholesale Bakery Inc	5149	E	714 259-0855	8868
Skeffington Enterprises Inc	6719	D	714 540-1700	12006
South Coast Fencing Center	1799	D	714 549-2946	3586
South Coast Stone Paving	1611	D	714 835-0258	1852
Southern Cal Blldog Rescue Inc	8699	E	714 381-7691	25469
Southern Cal Prmnnte Med Group	8011	D	714 967-4760	19919
Southern Cal Spcialty Care Inc	8062	C	714 564-7800	21764
Southern California Edison Co	4911	C	714 973-5481	6125
Southland Integrated Svcs Inc (PA)	8399	D	714 558-6009	24843
Southwest Express LLC	4212	D	949 474-5038	4066
Southwest Landscape Inc	0782	D	714 545-1084	943
Spectrum Security Services Inc	7381	D	714 542-9600	16833
St Joseph Heritage Med Group	8062	C	714 633-1011	21778
State Compensation Insur Fund	6331	B	714 565-5000	10395
Stearns Lending LLC (HQ)	6162	D	714 513-7777	9860
Sterling Plumbing Inc	1711	D	714 641-5480	2372
Sukut Construction LLC	1623	D	714 540-5351	1986
Sukut Construction Inc (PA)	1794	D	714 540-5351	3440
Sun Electric LP	1731	D	714 210-3744	2750
Sundance Construction Inc	1751	C	714 437-0802	3084
Systems Paving Inc (PA)	1611	D	949 263-8301	1858
Taber Company Inc	5031	D	714 543-7100	6869
Tait Environmental Svcs Inc (PA)	1799	D	714 560-8200	3591
Tarbell Financial Corporation (PA)	6163	D	714 972-0988	9910
Technology Resource Center Inc	7379	D	714 542-1004	16508
Tecta America Southern Cal Inc (DH)	1761	E	714 973-6233	3205
Templo Calvario Cmnty Dev Corp	8399	D	714 543-3711	24848
Ten Enthusiast Network LLC	5192	C	714 709-9021	9121
Tenet Healthsystem Medical	8062	A	714 966-8191	21852
Terra Pacific Landscape (HQ)	0781	D	714 567-0177	791
Tmx Engineering LLC	8711	D	714 641-5884	25955
Town & Country Manor of The Ch	8051	C	714 547-7581	20840
Towne Inc	7331	D	714 540-3095	14065
Trans-Pak Incorporated	7389	D	310 618-6937	17518
Transit Air Cargo Inc	4731	D	714 571-0393	5183
Trilogy Realty Group Inc	6531	D	937 206-0725	11801
Tristar Risk Management	6411	D	714 543-0700	10806
United Petrochemicals Inc	5169	D	949 629-8736	8937
Universal Protection Svc LP (HQ)	7381	C	714 619-9700	16848
Universal Services America LP (DH)	7381	D	714 619-9700	16850
University California Irvine	8011	D	714 480-2443	20033
USA Waste of California Inc	4953	D	714 637-3010	6503
Utility Systems Science (PA)	7371	D	714 542-1004	15520
Veros Credit LLC (PA)	6153	D	714 415-6185	9749
Visiting Nrse Assn Orange Cnty (PA)	8082	D	949 263-4700	22445
Volkswagen South Coast	7538	D	657 231-5600	17790
Volunteers of Amer Los Angeles	8322	D	714 426-9834	24120
Waste MGT Collectn Recycl Inc	7353	D	714 637-3010	14461
Waymakers (PA)	8322	D	714 492-1010	24129
West Coast Aviation Svcs LLC (PA)	8742	E	949 852-8340	27520
Western Medical Center Aux (HQ)	8062	C	714 835-3555	21915
White Cap Construction Supply	5082	A	949 794-5300	7698
William Hzmlhlch Archtects Inc	8712	D	949 250-0607	26123
Windsor Capital Group Inc	7011	D	714 241-3800	13411
Wm Vandergeest Landscape Care	0782	D	714 545-8432	962
Womens Law Center	8322	D	714 667-1038	24136
Xerox Corporation	5044	B	714 565-1100	6992
XI Fire Protection Co (PA)	1711	D	714 554-6132	2414

SANTA BARBARA, CA - Santa Barbara County

Company	SIC	EMP	PHONE	ENTRY #
1260 Bb Property LLC	7011	B	805 969-2261	12288
Advanced Dental Imaging LLC	8072	E	805 687-5571	22161
Agilysys Inc	5045	C	805 692-6339	7000
American Baptist Homes of West	6513	D	805 687-1571	10978
American Indian Health & Svcs	8099	E	805 681-7356	22729
Appfolio Inc (HQ)	7372	C	805 364-6093	15586
Applied Research Assoc Inc	8731	D	805 962-4810	26323
Arcana Corporation	7389	E	805 882-1305	17010

Mergent email: customerrelations@mergent.com
1680

2019 Directory of California
Wholesalers and Services Companies

(P-0000) Products & Services Section entry number
(PA)=Parent Co (HQ)=Headquarters (DH)=Div Headquarters

Name	SIC	EMP	PHONE	ENTRY #
Ascar Inc	7379	D	805 966-3331	16314
Bartlett Pringle & Wolf LLP	8721	E	805 564-2103	26146
Beach Motel Partners Ltd	7011	D	800 755-0222	12364
BFI Waste Systems N Amer Inc	4953	D	805 965-5248	6355
Birnam Wood Golf Club	7997	C	805 969-2223	18868
Blue Casa Communications Inc	4813	E	805 966-1669	5522
Brightview Golf Maint Inc	1629	E	805 968-6400	2015
Butler America LLC (HQ)	8711	A	805 880-1965	25585
Butler International Inc (PA)	7363	C	805 882-2200	14825
Butler Service Group Inc (HQ)	7363	D	201 891-5312	14826
Caesar and Seider Insur Svcs (PA)	6411	D	805 682-2571	10570
Caliber Home Loans Inc	6162	C	805 883-6800	9787
California Convalescent Hosp	8059	D	805 682-1355	21027
Cellco Partnership	4812	D	805 569-2525	5389
Channel Islands Young Mens Ch	8641	C	805 687-7727	25132
Channel Islands Young Mens Ch	8641	D	805 969-3288	25133
Chicago Title Insurance Co (HQ)	6361	C	805 565-6900	10446
Child Abuse Lstening Mediation	8322	E	805 965-2376	23556
Cicileo Landscapes	0781	E	805 967-3939	745
Classified Advertising	5192	C	805 564-5200	9110
Cliff View Terrace Inc	8361	C	805 682-7443	24472
Coldwell Banker Premier Prpts	6531	C	805 565-2200	11335
Cottage Care Center	8062	C	805 682-7111	21345
Cottage Health (PA)	8062	A	805 682-7111	21346
County of Santa Barbara Alcoho	8093	D	805 681-4093	22557
Covenant Care California LLC	8051	C	805 964-4871	20347
Cox Communications Inc	4841	C	805 681-6600	5892
Curvature LLC (DH)	5045	B	800 230-6638	7027
Dennis Allen Associates (PA)	1521	D	805 884-8777	1154
El Capitan Canyon LLC	7033	D	805 685-3887	13465
Employbridge LLC (HQ)	7363	C	805 882-2200	14849
Encina Pepper Tree Joint Ventr (PA)	7011	D	805 687-5511	12559
Evangelical Covenant Church	8361	D	805 687-0701	24525
Evans Hardy & Young Inc	7311	E	805 963-5841	13827
Family Svc Agcy Santa Barbara	8322	D	805 965-1001	23800
Fastclick Inc	7319	D	805 689-9839	13972
Fess Prker-Red Lion Gen Partnr	7011	B	805 564-4333	12574
Frank Schipper Construction Co	1542	E	805 963-4359	1533
Front Prch Cmmunities/Services	8059	C	805 687-0793	21076
Goleta Valley Cottage Hospital	8062	B	805 681-6468	21430
Granite Construction Company	1611	C	805 964-9951	1774
Green Hills Software Inc (PA)	7372	C	805 965-6044	15696
H D G Associates	7011	D	805 963-0744	12634
Help Unlmted Personnel Svc Inc	8082	C	805 962-4646	22317
Helping Hands Sanctuary of Ida	8051	C	805 687-6651	20524
Hillside House Inc	8052	D	805 687-4818	20933
Hub Intrntional Insur Svcs Inc	6411	D	805 682-2571	10649
International Alliance Thea	8631	D	805 898-0442	25061
Jacob Stern & Sons Inc (PA)	5169	D	805 565-4532	8929
JM Roofing Company Inc	1761	D	805 966-3696	3169
John Kenney Construction Inc	1771	D	805 884-1579	3273
Jordanos Inc (PA)	5181	C	805 964-0611	9006
Kamunity Properties (PA)	6513	E	805 682-5008	11041
Kenneth P Slaught Inc	6531	E	805 962-8989	11547
La Cumbre Country Club	7997	D	805 687-2421	18945
Lacolina Jr High CA Congress O	8641	D	805 967-4506	25184
Logicmonitor Inc (PA)	7375	C	805 617-3884	16237
Los Prietos Boys Camp	8361	D	805 692-1750	24588
Marborg Industries	4953	D	805 963-1852	6415
Master Clean USA Inc	7349	E	805 681-0950	14314
Meathead Movers Inc	4213	D	805 966-6328	4229
Mentor Worldwide Inc	5047	D	805 681-6000	7191
Mercer Global Securities LLC	6282	D	805 565-1681	10096
Mission Linen Supply	7213	E	805 962-7687	13541
Mission Security and Patrol	7381	D	805 899-3039	16733
MNS Engineers Inc (PA)	8711	D	805 962-6921	25827
Modular Systems Inc	6531	D	805 963-9350	11612
Montecito Country Club Inc	7997	D	805 969-0800	18979
Montecito Fire Protection Dst	8641	E	805 969-7762	25200
Montecito Retirement Assn	8051	B	805 329-9011	20650
Morgans Hotel Group LLC	7011	C	805 969-2203	12942
Mufg Union Bank National Assn	6021	D	805 564-6410	9355
Mullen & Henzell LLP	8111	E	805 966-1501	23273
Nevins-Adams Properties Inc (PA)	6512	C	805 963-2884	10919
New York Life Insurance Co	6411	D	805 898-7625	10704
Nhr Newco Holdings LLC (HQ)	5045	C	805 964-9975	7085
One Call Plumber Santa Barbara	1711	D	805 364-6337	2297
Pacific Centrex Services Inc	4813	D	818 623-2300	5620
Park Hotels & Resorts Inc	7011	B	805 564-4333	13018
Pitts & Bachmann Realtors Inc	6531	E	805 963-1391	11671
Planned Prnthood Cal Cntl Cast (PA)	8093	D	805 963-2445	22649
Price Postel and Parma LLP	8111	C	805 962-0011	23338
Qad Inc (PA)	7372	C	805 566-6000	15836
R M Matovu Memorial	8062	E	412 337-5975	21680
Real Time Staffing Services	7361	D	805 882-2200	14718
Rightscale Inc (PA)	7371	D	805 560-4164	15412
Ritz-Carlton Hotel Company LLC	7011	A	301 547-4700	13128
Roman Cath Arch of Los Angels	7261	A	805 687-8811	13695
Ronald L Wolfe & Assoc Inc	6531	E	805 964-6770	11743
S B C Senior Care Inc	8082	D	805 560-6995	22408
San Marcos Kids Helpng Kids FN	8641	C	800 659-6411	25237
San Ysidro Bb Property LLC	7011	D	805 969-5046	13183
Sansum Clinic (PA)	8011	D	805 681-7700	19851
Sansum Clinic	8082	E	805 682-6507	22411
Santa Barbara City of	4725	D	805 962-6464	4978
Santa Barbara Athletic CLB Inc	7997	D	805 966-6147	19032
Santa Barbara City of	7389	C	805 564-5485	17456
Santa Barbara Cottage Hospital	8062	A	805 569-7367	21714
Santa Barbara Cottage Hospital (PA)	8062	D	805 682-7111	21715
Santa Barbara County of	8322	B	805 882-3700	24025
Santa Barbara County of	8099	D	805 681-5100	22880
Santa Barbara County of	8322	D	805 884-1600	24028
Santa Barbara County of	8322	C	866 901-3212	24029
Santa Barbara Fabricare Inc	7216	E	805 963-6677	13568
Santa Barbara Metro Trnst Dst (PA)	4111	D	805 963-3364	3720
Santa Barbara Museum	8412	D	805 682-4711	24911
Santa Barbara Museum of Art (PA)	8412	D	805 963-4364	24912
Santa Barbara PC Users Group	7389	E	805 964-5411	17457
Santa Barbara San Luis Obispo	6321	C	800 421-2560	10171
Santa Barbra Cttge Hsptl	8071	B	805 569-7224	22140
Santa Brbara Zlgcal Foundation	8422	C	805 962-1673	24936
Select Temporaries LLC (DH)	7361	D	805 882-2200	14758
Smith Broadcasting Group Inc (PA)	8741	D	805 965-0400	27033
Smith Broadcasting Group Inc	4833	D	805 882-3933	5838
Specialty Team Plastering Inc	1742	C	805 966-3858	2961
Stantec Consulting Svcs Inc	8713	D	805 963-9532	26136
Sutter Health	8011	D	805 966-1600	19974
Tempest Telecom Solutions LLC (PA)	8748	D	805 879-4800	27879
The Valley Club of Montecito	7997	E	805 969-2215	19068
Tnci Operating Company LLC (HQ)	4813	D	800 800-8400	5654
Towbes Group Inc (PA)	6552	D	805 962-2121	11931
Town & Country Event Rentals	7389	B	805 770-5729	17514
Trackr Inc	7371	D	855 981-1690	15508
Tri-Counties Association F (PA)	8322	C	805 962-7881	24096
Trueblue Inc	7363	E	805 963-5370	14926
Ucp Work Inc	8699	C	805 962-6699	25476
United Paradyne Corporation	8741	D	805 734-2359	27075
United Seal Coating Slurryseal	1542	D	805 563-4922	1690
United States Marines Youth Fd	8641	C	805 967-7990	25271
Upham Hotel	7011	E	805 962-0058	13357
URS Group Inc	8711	D	805 964-6010	25978
US Data Management LLC (PA)	7379	C	888 231-0816	16522
Valencia Tree Landscape	0781	E	805 965-4244	792
Vetronix Sales Corporation	5013	C	805 966-2000	6683
Visiting Care & Companions Inc	8082	C	805 690-6202	22444
Visiting Nurse & Hospice Care (PA)	8621	C	805 965-5555	25050
W J Griffin Inc	5193	C	805 683-5639	9177
Wayne R Kidder	8011	C	805 967-6993	20094
Yardi Systems Inc (PA)	7371	B	805 699-2040	15554

SANTA CLARA, CA - Santa Clara County

Name	SIC	EMP	PHONE	ENTRY #
2wire Inc (DH)	4813	C	408 235-5500	5429
6wind Usa Inc	7371	D	408 816-1366	14954
Acalvio Technologies Inc	7382	C	408 931-6160	16866
Accel North America Inc	5045	C	408 514-5199	6995
Access Systems Americas Inc	7371	A	408 400-3000	14960
Accion Labs Us Inc	8734	A	408 970-9809	26680
Advance Staffing Inc	7363	B	408 205-6154	14808
Alliance Roofing Company Inc (PA)	1761	E	800 579-2595	3125
Alpha Net Consulting LLC	7371	C	408 330-0896	14974
Altaba Inc	4813	C	408 349-5080	5446
Alventive Inc (PA)	7372	C	408 969-8000	15581
American Reprographics Co LLC	7334	D	408 295-5770	14074
Anderson PCF Engrg Cnstr Inc	1629	D	408 970-9900	2007
Aramark Spt & Entrmt Group LLC	7929	D	408 748-7030	18422
Aricent US Inc (DH)	7371	E	408 329-7400	15000
Arrow Electronics Inc	5065	C	631 847-2918	7441
Asiainfo-Linkage Inc	4813	A	408 970-9788	5448
AT&T Corp	4813	C	408 980-2004	5464
Atac (PA)	7373	C	408 736-2822	15917
Atypon Systems LLC (PA)	7372	C	408 988-1240	15596
Avaya Inc (HQ)	7389	C	908 953-6000	17022
B A Technolinks Corporation	8742	D	408 940-5921	27148
Backweb Technologies Inc	5045	E	408 933-1700	7015
Bandai Namco Entrmt Amer Inc	5092	C	408 235-2000	7946
Bay Clubs Inc	7991	D	408 738-2582	18577
Bay Counties Waste Svcs Inc	4953	D	408 565-9900	6351
Big Switch Networks Inc (PA)	7372	C	650 322-6510	15608
Bill Wilson Center (PA)	8322	D	408 243-0222	23513
Biltmore Hotel	7011	D	408 988-8411	12387
Bramasol Inc	5045	D	408 831-0046	7019

GEOGRAPHIC

	SIC	EMP	PHONE	ENTRY #
Buckles-Smith Electric Company **(PA)**	5084	D	408 280-7777	7735
Build Group Inc	1542	D	408 986-8711	1488
Burdick Painting	1799	D	408 567-1330	3497
Bytemobile Inc	4899	B	408 327-7700	5971
Byton North America Corp	8731	C	408 966-5078	26344
Ca Inc	7372	C	800 225-5224	15619
Calculi Corporation	7373	E	408 970-0007	15925
California Eastern Labs Inc **(PA)**	5065	D	408 919-2500	7456
Cavisson Systems Inc	8748	B	800 701-6125	27677
Cedar Fair LP	7996	C	408 988-1776	18792
Centrify Corporation **(PA)**	7371	C	669 444-5200	15053
Church of Vly Rtrment Hmes Inc	8361	D	408 241-7750	24470
Citrix Systems Inc	7371	C	408 790-8000	15061
City of Santa Clara	1799	D	408 615-3770	3502
City of Santa Clara	4911	E	408 615-2300	6019
City of Santa Clara	4911	C	408 615-2046	6020
Coast Personnel Services Inc **(PA)**	7361	A	408 653-2100	14588
Coastal Paving Incorporated	1771	D	408 988-5559	3236
Colortokens Inc	7372	E	408 341-6030	15631
Community Home Partners LLC	8052	D	408 985-5252	20921
Complete Millwork Services Inc	5031	D	408 567-9664	6818
Covenant Care California LLC	8051	D	408 248-3736	20340
Cybercsi Inc	5045	C	408 727-2900	7029
Dan Connolly Inc	7381	D	408 241-0910	16625
Data Domain LLC	7373	A	408 980-4800	15940
Datastax Inc **(PA)**	7374	C	650 389-6000	16115
Decathlon Club Inc	7991	C	408 738-2582	18592
Dewmobile USA Inc	7371	E	408 550-2818	15104
Dialog Semiconductor Inc	5065	C	408 327-8800	7468
Digital Guardian Inc	7371	B	408 716-4200	15109
Dimension Data Cloud Solutions **(HQ)**	7371	D	408 567-2000	15111
Direct Flow Medical Inc **(PA)**	8099	D	707 576-0420	22789
Dolan Concrete Construction	1771	D	408 869-3250	3250
Drain Doctor	1711	E	408 970-3800	2188
Droisys Inc **(PA)**	7373	B	408 874-8333	15947
Eag Inc **(HQ)**	8734	C	408 454-4600	26694
Eag Holdings LLC	8748	A	408 530-3500	27709
Elcor Electric Inc	1731	C	408 986-1320	2571
Electric USA	1731	E	800 921-1151	2574
Emagia Corporation	7389	E	408 654-6575	17150
Embrane Inc	7371	E	408 550-2700	15136
Enterprise Solutions Inc	8748	C	408 727-3627	27719
Environmental Systems Inc **(PA)**	1711	D	408 980-1711	2202
Ericsson Inc	4813	A	408 750-5000	5555
Everett Basham	4813	D	408 261-3000	5556
Fast Pro Inc	5013	D	408 566-0200	6639
Fedex Freight Corporation	4212	E	408 988-2111	4013
Filemaker Inc **(HQ)**	7372	C	408 987-7000	15675
Firm A Chugh Professional Corp	8111	E	408 970-0100	23067
Flair Building Services Inc	7349	D	408 987-4040	14265
Forest Park Cabana Club	7997	D	408 244-1884	18925
Forty Niners Football Co LLC	7941	D	408 562-4949	18517
Fragomen Del Rey Bernse	8111	D	408 919-0600	23083
Frontech N Fujitsu Amer Inc	7371	D	408 982-3697	15170
Gigamon Inc **(HQ)**	7372	C	408 831-4000	15692
Granite Construction Company	1611	C	408 327-7000	1777
Hathaway Dinwiddie Cnstr Co	1542	D	415 986-2718	1545
Hathaway Dinwiddie Cnstr Group	6512	D	408 988-4200	10893
Hcl Finance Inc **(PA)**	6162	C	408 845-9035	9813
Hertz Corporation	7514	D	408 450-6025	17641
Honeywell International Inc	5065	D	408 986-8200	7490
Hortonworks Inc **(PA)**	7372	A	408 916-4121	15706
Hostmark Investors Ltd Partnr	8741	C	408 330-0001	26886
Hpt Trs Ihg-2 Inc	7011	D	408 241-9305	12734
Hudson Tchmart Cmmerce Ctr LLC	6512	D	408 451-4440	10896
Hyatt Regency Santa Clara	7011	D	408 200-1234	12756
Idaptive LLC	7371	C	669 444-5400	15210
Immigration Voice	6733	D	408 204-2200	12096
In Home Health Inc	8082	C	408 986-8160	22341
Innova Solutions Inc	7379	C	408 889-2020	16396
Innovative Silicon Inc	7389	D	408 572-8700	17240
INTEL Corporation	7371	C	503 696-8080	15222
Intel Media Inc	4841	B	408 765-0063	5921
Intellipro Group Inc	7379	B	408 200-9891	16399
International Bus Mchs Corp	7379	A	408 850-8999	16402
Ip Infusion Inc **(HQ)**	7373	D	408 400-1900	15984
Irdeto Usa Inc **(DH)**	7371	D	760 268-7299	15236
Ironclad Security Services Inc	7381	D	408 773-2800	16704
J & J Acoustics Inc	1742	C	408 275-9255	2900
J M K Investments Inc **(PA)**	6531	D	408 249-2500	11527
Jamcracker Inc	4813	E	408 496-5500	5590
Joseph J Albanese Inc	1771	A	408 727-5700	3275
Kaiser Foundation Hospitals	8062	A	408 851-1000	21525
Kana Software Inc **(HQ)**	7372	D	650 614-8300	15727
Kazeon Systems Inc	7371	D	650 641-8100	15248
Keypoint Credit Union **(PA)**	6062	C	408 731-4100	9638
Keypoint Credit Union	6062	C	408 562-7011	9639
KG Oldco Inc **(HQ)**	7373	E	408 980-8550	15991
Kier & Wright Civil ENGrs&srvy **(PA)**	8711	D	408 727-6665	25779
Kno Inc	7372	D	408 844-8120	15731
Laxmi Group Inc	7371	D	408 329-7733	15255
Leantaas Inc	7371	D	650 409-3501	15256
Legrande Affaire Inc	4119	C	408 988-4884	3817
Lombardo Diamnd Core Drlg Inc	1771	D	408 727-7922	3283
Lucid Vr Inc	7371	D	408 391-1065	15266
Mapr Technologies Inc **(PA)**	7371	B	408 914-2390	15270
Marianis Inn & Restaurant	7011	C	408 243-0312	12875
McAfee LLC **(HQ)**	7372	C	888 847-8766	15750
McAfee Finance 2 LLC	7372	A	888 847-8766	15751
McAfee Security LLC	7372	A	866 622-3911	15752
Mera Software Services Inc	7371	A	415 513-6401	15278
Microsoft Corporation	7372	D	408 987-9608	15765
Mission Trail Wste Systems Inc	4212	D	408 727-5365	4041
Mojo Networks Inc **(PA)**	7371	D	650 961-1111	15290
Move Inc **(HQ)**	6531	B	408 558-7100	11618
Move Sales Inc **(DH)**	7299	D	805 557-2300	13759
Msr Hotels & Resorts Inc	7011	D	408 496-6400	12947
National Rental (us) Inc	7514	D	408 492-0501	17647
Navisite LLC	4813	E	408 965-9000	5608
Net Optics Inc	7372	E	408 737-7777	15774
Net4site LLC	8742	D	408 427-3004	27363
Netbase Solutions Inc **(PA)**	8742	E	650 810-2100	27364
Ni Ki Cruz LLC	8742	D	408 332-7616	27370
Nominum Inc **(HQ)**	7371	E	650 381-6000	15313
Norland Group	7379	D	408 855-8255	16434
O2 Micro Inc	7373	D	408 987-5920	16023
One Diversified LLC	8748	D	408 969-1972	27811
Onebill Software Inc	7371	D	844 462-7638	15328
Ontario Airport Hotel Corp	7011	D	408 562-6709	12986
Opallios Inc	8748	E	408 769-4594	27813
Oracle America Inc	7372	C	408 276-4300	15792
Oracle America Inc	7371	C	408 276-3331	15336
Oracle America Inc	7372	C	408 276-7534	15797
Oracle Corporation	7372	B	408 421-2890	15801
Oracle Corporation	7372	C	408 276-5552	15802
Oracle Corporation	7372	B	650 506-9864	15805
Owens Corning Sales LLC	5033	B	408 235-1351	6925
Pactron	7379	D	408 329-5500	16450
PDM Steel Service Centers	5051	C	408 988-3000	7297
Persistent Systems Inc **(HQ)**	7371	D	408 216-7010	15353
Persistent Tlcom Solutions Inc	7371	E	408 216-7010	15354
Playspan LLC	6153	E	408 617-9155	9745
Plaza Suites	7011	D	408 748-9800	13069
Posh Bagel Inc **(PA)**	5149	D	408 980-8451	8855
Posh Bakery Inc	5149	C	408 980-8451	8856
Priority Dispatch Service Inc	4215	D	408 400-3860	4427
Processweaver Inc	7371	D	888 932-8373	15378
Punctus Temporis Translations	7389	E	510 309-0888	17418
Radiabeam Technologies LLC	8733	E	310 822-5845	26652
Recology Los Altos	4953	D	650 961-8044	6440
Redwood Electric Group Inc **(PA)**	1731	A	707 451-7348	2700
Restivo Enterprises	4119	D	408 988-4884	3835
Rivio Inc	4813	E	408 653-4400	5636
Robert A Bothman Inc **(PA)**	1771	C	408 279-2277	3317
Royal Glass Company Inc	1793	D	408 969-0444	3409
Rsa Security LLC	7371	C	650 529-9992	15419
SA Technologies Inc **(PA)**	7361	D	408 400-3900	14750
Safeway Stores Incorporated	1542	D	408 719-9460	1639
San Francisco Forty Niners	6719	C	408 562-4949	12003
San Francisco Forty Niners **(PA)**	7941	C	408 562-4949	18533
Santa Clara Tenant Corp	7011	C	408 496-6400	13186
Santa Clara Vngard Booster CLB	8641	E	408 727-5532	25239
Santa Clara Womens Club	7997	D	408 246-8000	19033
Serene Ast LLC **(HQ)**	7379	D	408 986-8544	16482
Serrano Electric Inc	1731	E	408 986-1570	2730
Sharedata Inc	7372	C	408 490-2500	15850
Silicon Valley Bank **(HQ)**	6029	A	408 654-7400	9516
Simco Electronics **(PA)**	7629	D	408 734-9750	17914
Soft Machines Inc	7373	D	408 969-0215	16053
Software Ag Inc	7372	C	408 490-5300	15857
Solidcore Systems Inc **(DH)**	7371	D	408 387-8400	15462
Solix Technologies Inc **(PA)**	7371	D	408 654-6446	15463
Sonic Solutions Holdings Inc	7372	B	408 562-8400	15858
Soundhound Inc **(PA)**	7371	D	408 441-3200	15466
South Bay Historical RR Soc	8699	E	408 243-3969	25468
Spec Personnel LLC	7361	C	408 727-8000	14765
Special Home Needs	8052	D	408 985-8666	20962
Sra Oss Inc	7372	C	408 855-8200	15862
Stanford Hotels Corporation	7011	D	408 330-0001	13262
Stmicroelectronics Inc	5065	C	408 452-8585	7546

Mergent email: customerrelations@mergent.com
1682

2019 Directory of California
Wholesalers and Services Companies

(P-0000) Products & Services Section entry number
(PA)=Parent Co (HQ)=Headquarters (DH)=Div Headquarters

Company	SIC	EMP	PHONE	ENTRY #
Sunset Building Maintenance Inc	7349	E	408 727-3408	14403
Sutter Health	8011	B	408 524-5952	19961
Svb Financial Group (PA)	6022		408 654-7400	9490
Tata America Intl Corp	7379	D	408 569-5845	16506
Tavant Technologies Inc (PA)	7371	D	408 519-5400	15493
Teen Challenge Norwestcal Nev	8322	D	408 703-2001	24083
Tekever Corporation	7372	D	408 730-2617	15877
Telenav Inc	8742	B	360 765-0058	27484
Tensilica Inc (HQ)	6794	D	408 986-8000	12144
Thermal Mechanical	1711	D	408 988-8744	2384
Tiger Analytics LLC	8732	D	408 508-4430	26570
TLC of Bay Area Inc	8051	D	408 988-7667	20838
Trianz Inc (HQ)	7379	C	408 387-5800	16516
Tusa Inc (PA)	7378	C	888 848-3749	16297
United Marble & Granite Inc	5032	C	408 347-3300	6910
Valley Process Systems Inc	1711	D	408 261-1277	2395
Valley Water Proofing Inc	1799	D	408 985-7701	3603
Verint Americas Inc	7371	D	408 830-5400	15522
Webyog Inc	7371	C	408 512-1434	15544
Wescon Technology Inc	7373	C	408 727-8818	16076
Wincere Inc	7379	C	408 841-4355	16533
Worldwide Ground Transportatio	4119	D	408 727-0000	3862
Xyka Inc	7371	E	408 340-1923	15553
Yes Videocom Inc (PA)	7812	B	408 907-7600	18171
YMCA of Silicon Valley (PA)	8641	D	408 351-6400	25309

SANTA CLARITA, CA - Los Angeles County

Company	SIC	EMP	PHONE	ENTRY #
American Health Services LLC	8011	C	661 254-6630	19285
Applied Companies	8711	E	661 257-0090	25538
AT&T Corp	4812	C	661 297-1720	5277
Broadspire	4813	D	213 785-8043	5524
Canon Recruiting Group LLC	7363	B	661 252-7400	14828
Castaic Lk Wtr Agcy Fing Corp (PA)	4941	D	661 259-2737	6220
Child & Family Center	8322	C	661 259-9439	23555
Community Therapies	8049	E	661 945-7878	20171
Curtiss-Wright Controls	8711	C	661 257-4430	25635
Curtiss-Wright Controls (DH)	8711	C	661 702-1494	25636
De Oliviera Concrete Inc	1771	D	661 252-7522	3246
Facey Medical Foundation	8099	D	661 250-5225	22805
Facey Medical Foundation	8011	D	661 513-2100	19466
Friendly Valley Recrtl Assn	8322	E	661 252-3223	23814
Gierahn Dry Wall Inc	1742	E	661 257-7900	2888
Henry Mayo Newhall Mem Hosp	8099	D	661 253-8227	22816
Honda Performance Dev Inc	7549	D	661 294-7300	17863
Hope of Valley Mission	8093	E	661 673-5951	22595
Internet Security Systems Inc	7371	C	661 296-5752	15232
Kaiser Foundation Hospitals	8011	A	888 778-5000	19587
Kaiser Foundation Hospitals	8011	D	661 222-2323	19614
Los Angeles Residential Comm F	8361	D	661 296-8636	24587
Marathon Industries Inc	5012	C	661 286-1520	6603
Midwest Enviromental Control	8731	E	661 255-0722	26418
Mountasia Family Fun Center	7996	E	661 253-4386	18805
Mountasia of Santa Clarita	7299	D	661 253-4386	13758
NTS Technical Systems	8748	D	661 259-8184	27807
Oceanside Hlthcare Stffing Inc	8099	C	213 503-5649	22851
Partsearch Technologies Inc	5065	E	661 257-7700	7523
Paul Mitchell John Systems (PA)	5122	E	310 248-3888	8203
Petersen-Dean Inc	1761	D	661 254-3322	3186
Princess Cruise Lines Ltd	4724	A	661 753-2291	4948
Princess Cruise Lines Ltd (HQ)	4481	A	661 753-0000	4708
RE/Max of Valencia Inc (PA)	6531	C	661 255-2650	11712
Robinson Ranch Golf LLC	7992	C	818 885-0599	18752
S C Security Inc	7381	E	661 251-6999	16779
Santa Clarita City of	4131	B	661 294-1287	3883
Santa Clarita City of	7999	D	661 284-1423	19234
Santa Clarita Concrete	1771	E	661 252-2012	3320
Santa Clarita Health Care Assn (PA)	8741	D	661 253-8000	27022
Santa Clarita Interiors Inc	1791	D	661 253-0861	3396
Santa Clarita Valley Bldrs Inc	1751	C	661 295-6722	3074
Santa Clarita Vlly Cmmtt Aging	8322	D	661 259-9444	24032
Sheldon Mechanical Corporation	1711	D	661 286-1361	2355
Southern Cal Prmnnte Med Group	8062	D	661 290-3100	21761
Southern Cal Prmnnte Med Group	8011	E	661 222-2150	19924
Universal Wood Moulding Inc (PA)	5023	E	661 362-6262	6799
USA Waste of California Inc	4953	D	661 259-2398	6502

SANTA CRUZ, CA - Santa Cruz County

Company	SIC	EMP	PHONE	ENTRY #
(a) Tool Shed Inc (PA)	7359	D	831 477-7133	14463
7th Avenue Center LLC	8063	D	831 476-1700	21921
Alliance Member Services Inc	8699	D	831 459-0980	25378
American Medical Response	4119	D	831 423-7030	3755
Associated Pathology Med Group	8011	D	831 462-7625	19309
Bastille Networks Inc	7371	E	800 530-3341	15020
Benchmark-Tech Corporation	7389	D	831 475-5600	17028
Bontadelli Inc	5148	D	831 423-8572	8643
California Certified Organic	8611	D	831 423-2263	24948
Camp Recovery Centers LLP	8093	D	831 438-1868	22516
Canyon View Capital Inc	6798	D	831 480-6335	12155
Capitola Care Center Inc	8059	D	831 477-0329	21032
Cellco Partnership	4812	D	831 421-0753	5380
Chaminade Ltd	7011	C	831 475-5600	12448
Coldwell Bnkr Residential Brkg	6531	D	831 420-2628	11361
Cruz Veterinary Hospital	0742	D	831 475-5400	601
David Lyng & Associates Inc	6531	D	831 429-5700	11393
Derjian Associates Inc (PA)	8741	C	831 423-4111	26837
Dignity Health	8062	A	831 462-7700	21383
Dignity Health Med Foundation	8099	D	831 475-8834	22785
Dominican Hospital Foundation	8361	C	831 457-7057	24506
Dominican Hospital Foundation (HQ)	8062	C	831 462-7700	21398
Dominican Oaks Corporation	6513	D	831 462-6257	11007
First American Title Insur Co (HQ)	6361	C	831 426-5000	10458
Forever Firewood Inc (PA)	1761	E	831 461-0634	3157
Friends Santa Cruz State Parks	8641	D	831 429-1840	25158
Front St Inc	8059	C	831 420-0120	21077
His Manna Inc	8742	D	831 423-5515	27263
Janus of Santa Cruz	8322	D	831 462-1060	23871
Lho Santa Cruz One Lesse Inc	7011	C	831 475-5600	12851
Lifespan Inc	8399	D	831 469-4900	24801
Mariner Health Care Inc	8051	D	831 475-6323	20620
Moose International Inc	8641	C	831 438-1817	25201
National Security Industries	7381	B	831 425-2052	16738
Nicholas B Macy Dvm	0742	D	831 475-5400	608
Palo Alto Med Fndtion STA Cruz	8062	A	831 458-5670	21624
Performance Food Group Inc	5141	D	831 462-2400	8442
Pfyffer Associates Inc	0161	E	831 423-8572	76
Regent Assisted Living Inc	8361	D	831 459-8400	24649
Rope Partner Inc	5085	C	831 460-9448	7867
Santa Cruz County of	7374	D	831 454-2030	16175
Santa Cruz County Symphony	7929	E	831 462-0553	18460
Santa Cruz Hotel Associates	7011	D	831 426-4330	13187
Santa Cruz Medical Foundation (HQ)	8011	D	831 458-5537	19857
Santa Cruz Metro Trnst Dst	4131	D	831 469-1954	3884
Santa Cruz Seaside Company (PA)	7996	B	831 423-5590	18808
Santa Cruz Westside Elc Inc	1731	D	831 469-8888	2722
Skills Center Inc (PA)	8331	D	831 421-9900	24230
Smartrevenuecom Inc	8732	B	203 733-9156	26564
Stagnaro Brothers Seafood Inc	5146	D	831 423-1188	8603
Sutter Health	8641	C	831 458-6310	25257
Sutter Health	8062	E	831 477-3600	21829
Sutter Health	8641	C	831 458-5500	25261
Sutter Maternity & Surgery Ctr	8062	C	831 477-2200	21842
Trowbridge Enterprises (PA)	5112	C	831 476-3815	8091
Two Pore Guys System Inc	7373	D	821 420-0710	16068
United Natural Foods Inc	5149	C	831 462-5870	8889
United Parcel Service Inc OH	4215	C	831 425-1054	4481
Visiting Nurse Association of (DH)	8621	D	831 477-2600	25051
Well Within Spa	1799	D	831 458-9355	3608
Western Med Assoc Med Group (PA)	8011	D	831 475-1111	20100

SANTA FE SPRINGS, CA - Los Angeles County

Company	SIC	EMP	PHONE	ENTRY #
All-City Management Svcs Inc	8748	A	310 202-8284	27634
Alliedbarton Security Svcs LLC	7381	B	562 906-4800	16554
American Rlction Logistics Inc	4214	D	562 229-3600	4328
B & E Convalescent Center Inc (PA)	8059	D	562 923-9449	21001
Barr Engineering Inc	1711	D	562 944-1722	2135
Bekins Moving Solutions Inc (PA)	4214	D	562 356-9460	4333
Brenntag Pacific Inc (DH)	5169	C	562 903-9626	8921
Cadnchev Inc	5015	D	562 944-6422	6702
California Lab Sciences LLC	8734	B	562 758-6900	26687
Central Garden & Pet Company	5199	C	562 926-5252	9204
Coa Inc (PA)	5021	C	562 944-7899	6717
Coast Alum & Architectural Inc (PA)	5051	C	562 946-6061	7266
Coast Iron & Steel Co	1791	E	562 946-4421	3373
Commodity Distribution Service	8748	E	562 777-9969	27692
County of Los Angeles	8322	B	562 903-5000	23659
Crescent Healthcare Inc (DH)	8082	C	714 520-6300	22281
Crown Fence Co	1799	C	562 864-5177	3508
Csi Electrical Contractors Inc (PA)	1731	C	562 946-0700	2555
Custom Companies Inc	4731	D	310 672-8800	5039
Cypress Security LLC	7381	D	562 222-4197	16624
Disabled Amrcn Vtrans Dept Cal (PA)	8641	D	562 404-1266	25152
E Jordan Brookes Co Inc (PA)	5049	D	562 968-2100	7241
El Monte Rents Inc (HQ)	7519	C	562 404-9300	17659
Electric Sales Unlimited	5063	E	562 463-8300	7358
Ellison Machinery Co (DH)	5084	D	562 949-8311	7748
Ellison Technologies Inc	5084	D	562 949-8311	7749
Ethosenergy Field Services LLC (DH)	1389	D	310 639-3523	1058
Federal Express Corporation	4513	D	800 463-3339	4829
Field Foundation	1389	E	562 921-3567	1059
Fuji Food Products Inc (PA)	5149	D	562 404-2590	8792
Galleher LLC (PA)	5023	C	562 944-8885	6762
Gatehouse Msi LLC	1751	E	562 623-3000	3037

GEOGRAPHIC

Company	SIC	EMP	PHONE	ENTRY #
Georgia-Pacific LLC	5113	B	562 861-6226	8105
Gold Tree Inc	8742	D	562 801-0218	27249
Griffith Company	1611	D	562 929-1128	1788
Haringa Inc **(PA)**	7389	D	800 499-9991	17207
Harris L Woods Elec Contr	1731	D	562 945-8751	2601
Healthfirst Medical Group Inc **(PA)**	8093	E	562 949-9328	22590
Holbrook Construction Inc	1542	D	714 523-1150	1554
Horner-Halleher Holding Co **(PA)**	5023	C	562 944-8885	6767
Igt Global Solutions Corp	7999	D	562 946-9922	19188
Integrated Office Tech LLC **(PA)**	5044	D	562 236-9200	6961
Interntonal Win Treatments Inc **(PA)**	5023	A	562 236-2120	6768
Janus Et Cie **(PA)**	5021	C	310 601-2908	6729
Johnson Controls	7382	C	562 405-3817	16914
Jvc Americas Corp	7622	D	562 463-8110	17884
Kbl Group International Ltd	5137	E	562 699-9995	8311
Kemp Bros Construction Inc	1541	E	562 236-5000	1414
Kiewit Corporation	1542	D	907 222-9350	1575
Kiewit Infrastructure West Co	1611	D	562 946-1816	1803
Kloeckner Metals Corporation	5051	D	562 906-2020	7286
Kloeckner Metals Corporation	5051	E	562 906-2020	7287
L Tech Network Services Inc	1731	D	562 222-1121	2627
LA Specialty Produce Co **(PA)**	5148	B	562 741-2200	8700
Lakin Tire West Incorporated **(PA)**	5014	C	562 802-2752	6693
Landcare USA LLC	0782	C	714 936-9512	880
Larsen Supply Co **(PA)**	5074	C	562 698-0731	7628
Leed Electric Inc	1731	D	562 270-9500	2630
Los Angeles Center For Alcohol **(PA)**	8093	D	562 906-2676	22614
Masonry Concepts Inc	1741	D	562 802-3700	2816
Material Handling Supply Inc **(HQ)**	5084	C	562 921-7715	7768
Matt Construction Corporation **(PA)**	8742	D	562 903-2277	27323
Matt-Colombo A Joint Venture	1542	D	562 903-2277	1588
Maxon Lift Corporation	5084	D	562 464-0099	7769
McKesson Corporation	5122	C	562 463-2100	8193
MCP Industries Inc	5169	D	562 944-5511	8931
Memo Scaffolding Inc	1799	D	562 404-8600	3551
Mias Fashion Mfg Co Inc	5137	B	562 906-1060	8321
Millennia Stainless Inc	5085	D	562 946-3545	7859
Morrison Concrete Inc	1771	E	562 802-1450	3291
Nelson & Associates Inc	5063	D	562 921-4423	7381
New Cingular Wireless Svcs Inc	4812	D	562 941-6422	5411
Newport Diversified Inc	7389	C	562 921-4359	17351
Ninos Latino Unidos FSA	8361	D	562 801-5454	24611
Norman International Inc	5023	D	562 946-0420	6778
Northstar Contg Group Inc	1795	D	714 639-7600	3458
Ob Usa Inc	5181	C	213 465-4876	9018
Oil Well Service Company **(PA)**	1389	C	562 612-0600	1073
Pacific Clinics	8093	D	562 949-8455	22630
Partitions Installation Inc	1799	D	562 207-9868	3564
Penny Lane Centers	8399	C	562 903-4135	24821
Performance Team Frt Sys Inc	4225	D	562 741-1300	4609
Porteous Enterprises Inc	5072	C	310 549-9180	7599
Pro-Tech Design & Mfg Inc	7389	D	562 207-1680	17410
Production Delivery Svcs Inc	4213	D	562 777-0060	4246
Raymond Handling Solutions Inc **(DH)**	5084	C	562 944-8067	7792
Rebar Engineering Inc	1791	C	562 946-2461	3394
Reliance Steel & Aluminum Co	5051	D	562 695-0467	7306
Reliance Steel & Aluminum Co	5051	D	562 944-3322	7309
Rentokil North America Inc	5191	D	562 802-2238	9094
Rockey Murata Landscaping	0781	D	562 921-3210	783
Royal Paper Corp **(PA)**	5113	D	562 903-9030	8127
Ryder Truck Rental Inc	7513	D	562 921-0033	17615
S E Pipe Line Construction Co	1623	D	562 868-9771	1976
Scorpio Enterprises	1711	D	562 946-9464	2350
Seaboard Corporation	0213	B	806 435-5935	404
Sequel Contractors Inc	1611	E	562 802-7227	1847
Sfadia Inc	1731	D	323 622-1930	2732
Shoring Engineers	1799	D	562 944-9331	3585
Sohnen Barry As Co Trustee	6733	E	562 946-3531	12126
Sohnen Enterprises Inc **(PA)**	7622	E	562 903-4957	17887
Solaris Paper Inc	5093	C	562 653-1680	7996
Southeast Area Social Services	8322	E	562 946-2237	24061
Southern California Edison Co	4911	D	562 903-3191	6138
Spicers Paper Inc **(HQ)**	5111	C	562 698-1189	8071
Strand Energy Company	1311	D	562 944-9580	1029
Swann Communications USA Inc	5045	D	562 777-2551	7112
TA Industries Inc **(PA)**	5074	D	562 466-1000	7640
Talley Inc **(PA)**	5065	C	562 906-8000	7551
Telecntric Communications Intl	7389	D	562 906-2555	17503
Think Together	7991	A	562 236-3835	18670
Trail Lines Inc	4212	D	562 758-6980	4069
Tri-West Ltd **(PA)**	5023	C	562 692-9166	6796
Triangle Distributing Co **(PA)**	5181	D	562 699-3424	9029
Troyer Contracting Company Inc	1799	D	562 944-6452	3598
Twin Med LLC **(PA)**	5047	A	323 582-9900	7226
Ugm Citatah Inc **(PA)**	5032	C	562 921-9549	6909
Ultradot Media	7313	D	562 906-0737	13961
Universal Asphalt Co Inc	1611	E	562 941-0201	1866
Valverde Construction Inc	1623	D	562 906-1826	1995
Valvoline International Inc	7549	E	562 906-6200	17881
Van King & Storage Inc **(PA)**	4212	D	562 921-0555	4085
Van King & Storage Inc	4225	E	562 921-0555	4652
Van Torrance & Storage Company **(PA)**	4214	D	562 567-2100	4386
Verizon Network Integration	4813	C	562 903-7953	5672
Warren Distributing Inc	5013	D	562 789-3360	6685
Weber Distribution LLC **(PA)**	4222	B	855 469-3237	4518
West Pacific Medical Lab LLC **(PA)**	8071	D	818 773-9771	22159
Western Allied Service Company	7623	B	562 941-3243	17898
Western Exterminator Company	7342	D	562 802-2238	14164
Whittier Equipment Rentals	1623	D	562 863-0641	2004
Wismettac Asian Foods Inc **(DH)**	5141	C	562 802-1900	8488
Xpo Logistics Freight Inc	4213	C	562 946-8331	4323
Xtra Department Inc	8741	D	562 462-3800	27101

SANTA MARIA, CA - Santa Barbara County

Company	SIC	EMP	PHONE	ENTRY #
Aardex Inc	1542	D	805 928-7600	1453
Agro-Jal Farms Inc	0723	D	805 928-2682	489
Ais Construction Company	1542	D	805 928-9467	1459
Arbor Medical Group Inc **(PA)**	8011	D	805 614-7591	19302
Big F Company Inc	5191	D	805 928-2333	9073
Blackjack Farms De La Costa CN	0191	C	805 347-1333	324
Boca Mesa Incorporated	8748	D	805 934-9470	27661
Brannon Inc	1541	C	805 621-5000	1381
Buona Terra Farming Co Inc	8741	D	805 614-9229	26789
Caci Nss Inc	5045	C	703 841-7800	7022
Cal Gran Theatres LLC	7832	E	805 934-1582	18276
Cardenas Bros Farming Company	0171	D	805 928-1559	92
Central Coast Distributing LLC	5181	D	805 922-2108	8985
Central Coast Pub Safety Inc	7381	D	805 556-4450	16599
Certified Frt Logistics Inc **(PA)**	4213	C	805 925-9900	4116
CJJ Farming Inc	0171	E	805 739-1723	94
Community Action Commsn Santa	8399	B	805 614-0786	24756
Community Action Commsn Santa	8399	D	805 922-2243	24758
Community Health Ctrs Cntrl **(PA)**	8322	D	805 346-3900	23604
Country Oaks Care Center Inc	8051	D	805 922-6657	20326
Darensberries LLC	0171	C	805 937-8000	96
Diani Building Corp **(PA)**	1542	D	805 925-9533	1519
Dignity Health	8062	B	805 739-3000	21369
Dignity Health	8082	C	805 739-3830	22285
Dignity Health	8051	D	805 739-3650	20377
Dignity Health	8062	A	805 739-3100	21390
Eagle Resources Inc	7361	D	805 922-0000	14606
Edwards Theatres Circuit Inc	7832	D	805 347-1164	18301
Employment Dev Cal Dept	7361	D	805 614-1550	14612
Ensign Group Inc	8361	C	805 925-8713	24518
Express Messenger Systems Inc	4215	C	800 488-2829	4404
Festival Fun Parks LLC	7999	C	805 922-1574	19171
First Transit	4111	C	805 925-5254	3652
Foothill Packing Inc	5141	B	805 925-7900	8406
Freshway Farms LLC	0171	C	805 349-7170	99
Frey Farming & Tpsry Vineyards	0762	D	805 937-1542	692
Frontier California Inc	4813	D	805 925-0000	5562
Glad-A-Way Gardens Inc	0181	D	805 938-0569	261
Good Samaritan Shelter	8322	D	805 346-8185	23825
Greka Inc	1241	C	805 347-8700	1009
H & R Block Inc	7291	D	805 349-9266	13706
Hardy Diagnostics **(PA)**	5047	B	805 346-2766	7183
Hunter Realty Inc	6531	D	805 346-8688	11507
Hvi Cat Canyon Inc	1389	C	805 621-5800	1066
KG Berry Farms LLC	0191	C	805 680-6751	363
Kimberly Care Center Inc	8051	D	805 925-8877	20553
La Palma Farms Inc	5191	D	805 928-2333	9083
Lacuesta Farming Inc	0171	D	805 349-1940	104
Larrabee Brothrs Distribtng Co	5181	D	805 922-2108	9007
Laurel Labor Services Inc	7361	D	805 928-0113	14661
Los Dos Valles Harvstg & Pkg	0722	C	805 739-1688	480
Meathead Movers	4213	D	805 349-8000	4224
Mendoza Farms Inc	0171	E	805 352-1070	108
Merrill Gardens LLC	6513	D	805 310-4102	11073
Mesa Vineyard Management Inc	0762	D	805 925-7200	698
Mission Linen Supply	7213	D	805 922-3579	13546
New Century Farms	0762	D	805 928-2333	702
New Hope Harvesting LLC	0722	D	805 478-4469	481
Nursecore Management Svcs LLC	8361	A	805 938-7660	24613
Nutrien AG Solutions Inc	5191	D	805 922-5848	9089
Optimum Cx LLC	7389	C	805 922-2999	17372
PC Mechanical Inc	1389	E	805 925-2888	1075
Peoples Self-Help Housing Corp	8748	D	805 349-9341	27821
Plantel Nurseries Inc	5193	B	805 349-8952	9159
Premier Drywall	1742	D	805 928-3397	2941
Primus Group Inc **(PA)**	8742	D	805 922-0055	27401
Quinn Company	5082	D	805 925-8611	7689

Mergent email: customerrelations@mergent.com
1684

2019 Directory of California
Wholesalers and Services Companies

(P-0000) Products & Services Section entry number
(PA)=Parent Co (HQ)=Headquarters (DH)=Div Headquarters

Company	SIC	EMP	PHONE	ENTRY #
Radisson Hotel Santa Maria	7011	D	805 928-8000	13093
Ramco Enterprises LP	7361	A	805 922-9888	14712
Rancho Laguna Farms LLC	0191	D	805 925-7805	375
Red Blossom Sales Inc	0171	B	805 349-9404	113
Reiter Affl Companies LLC	0171	C	805 925-8577	115
RMR Inc (PA)	1771	D	805 928-4013	3316
Safari Harvstg & Farming LLC	0191	B	805 925-2600	378
Santa Barbara Cottage Hospital	8062	C	805 346-7135	21716
Santa Barbara County of	8322	C	805 614-1550	24026
Santa Barbara County of	8111	E	805 346-7540	23366
Santa Barbara Trnsp Corp	4151	D	805 928-0402	3945
Santa Maria Hotel Corp	7011	D	805 928-6000	13188
Santa Maria Valley YMCA	8641	C	805 937-8521	25240
Segura Enterprises Inc	7381	D	805 349-0550	16819
Shepard Eye Center	8011	E	805 925-2637	19890
Skylstad-Schoelen Co Inc	7349	D	805 349-0503	14393
Smith Packing Inc	5199	C	805 343-0329	9260
Social Advocates For Youth (PA)	8322	E	805 928-1707	24053
Sturgeon Son Grading & Pav Inc	8711	C	805 938-0618	25935
Sunberry Growers Inc	5148	A	805 922-9888	8735
Teixeira Farms Inc	0161	C	805 928-3801	85
Tetra Tech Inc	8748	D	805 739-2600	27880
Transitions - Mental Hlth Assn	8093	D	805 614-4940	22698
Tri Valley Vegetable Harvstg	0722	D	805 928-2727	486
Tri-Counties Association F	8621	D	805 922-4640	25046
Ulta Beauty Inc	7231	C	805 825-0093	13677
Union Asphalt Inc	4212	D	805 922-3551	4074
United Parcel Service Inc OH	4215	C	805 922-7851	4474
Valley Garbage Rubbish Co Inc	4953	D	805 614-1131	6505
Vtc Enterprises (PA)	8331	B	805 928-5000	24248
White Hills Vineyard Ranc	0762	D	805 934-1986	723

SANTA MONICA, CA - Los Angeles County

Company	SIC	EMP	PHONE	ENTRY #
19 Entertainment Worldwide LLC	7929	D	310 777-1940	18416
1nteger LLC	7299	E	424 320-2977	13712
24 Hour Fitness Usa Inc	7991	D	310 450-4464	18561
525 Studios Inc	7819	D	310 525-1234	18174
Accor Services US LLC	7011	B	310 319-3122	12305
Activision Blizzard Inc	7371	C	310 581-4700	14962
Activision Blizzard Inc (PA)	7372	C	310 255-2000	15567
Activision Publishing Inc (HQ)	7372	A	310 255-2000	15569
Air Force US Dept of	8733	B	310 393-0411	26586
Alisam Oxnard Operating	6512	C	310 877-7179	10849
American Retirement Corp	8051	C	310 399-3227	20230
Apex Machine Works Inc	8711	D	310 393-5987	25537
Arizona and 21st Corp	8059	D	310 829-5377	20998
Artisan Entertainment Inc	7812	A	310 449-9200	18018
Artisan Pictures Inc	5099	C	310 449-9200	8018
Attendant Care Referrals Inc	8082	D	310 399-2904	22232
Basis Worldwide	7311	E	424 261-2354	13795
Beach Club	7997	D	310 395-3254	18858
Beachbody LLC (PA)	7313	B	310 883-9000	13936
Berkeley E Convalescent Hosp	8059	C	310 829-5377	21006
Blue Devils Lessee LLC	7011	C	310 399-9344	12389
Box Bros Corp	7389	E	310 394-8660	17040
Boys Grls CLB Snta Monica Inc	8641	D	310 361-8500	25114
Brighter Inc	8021	D	888 230-4413	20111
Bryan Cave Lighton Paisner LLP	8111	C	310 576-2100	22963
Businesscom Inc	8742	D	310 586-4000	27177
By The Blue Sea LLC	7011	B	310 458-0030	12413
C W Hotels Ltd	7011	C	310 395-9700	12415
C/O Uc San Francisco	8011	D	310 794-1841	19337
Caliber Bodyworks Texas Inc	7532	D	310 392-7662	17713
Callfire Inc	7371	D	213 221-2289	15046
Callison LLC	8712	C	310 394-8460	26028
Campus Explorer Inc	4813	D	310 574-2243	5527
Capital Oversight Inc (PA)	8748	B	310 453-8000	27675
Casestack Inc (PA)	4731	C	310 473-8885	5026
CBS Television Distribution (PA)	8741	A	310 264-3300	26800
Cedar Management LLC	6531	D	310 396-3100	11287
Century Finance Incorporated	6162	D	310 281-3081	9790
Childrens Hospital Los Angeles	8011	C	310 820-8608	19378
CIT Bank NA	6021	D	310 452-3802	9308
CIT Bank National Association	6021	C	310 394-1640	9323
CIT Bank National Association	6021	D	310 829-4477	9326
Clare Foundation Inc (PA)	8322	D	310 314-6200	23587
Clare Foundation Inc	8322	D	310 314-6200	23588
Coastal Health Care Inc	8051	D	310 828-5596	20318
Colfin Esh Funding LLC	6722	B	310 282-8820	12033
Company 3 Inc	7819	D	310 255-6600	18184
Connexity Inc (HQ)	4813	C	310 571-1235	5537
Converse Inc	5139	D	310 451-0314	8352
Cornerstone Ondemand Inc (PA)	7372	C	310 752-0200	15638
Counter Brands LLC (PA)	5122	D	310 828-0111	8164
County of Los Angeles	8322	D	310 266-3711	23675
Cwgp Limited Partnership	7011	D	310 395-9700	12508

Company	SIC	EMP	PHONE	ENTRY #
Cypress Creek Holdings LLC	4911	D	310 581-6299	6026
David King Convalescent Hosp	8059	D	310 451-9706	21058
Dcp Rights LLC	7812	E	310 255-4600	18038
Disability Group Inc	8111	B	310 829-5100	23040
Douglas Emmett Realty Fund 199	6531	D	310 255-7700	11408
Dtrs Santa Monica LLC	7011	B	310 458-6700	12543
Ecompanies LLC	4813	E	310 586-4000	5552
Edmunds Holding Company (PA)	7375	A	310 309-6300	16220
Edmundscom Inc (HQ)	7313	A	310 309-6300	13944
Edward Thomas Hospitality Corp	7011	B	310 458-0030	12550
Ellie Fashion Group Inc	7389	D	818 355-3812	17149
Emperors Clg Trdtnl Orntl Mdc	8049	C	310 453-8383	20173
Entitlement LLC	7929	E	224 336-2669	18433
Entravsion Communications Corp (PA)	4833	C	310 447-3870	5788
Epochcom LLC	7374	C	310 664-5700	16128
Et Whitehall Seascape LLC	7011	C	310 581-5533	12565
Executive Network Entps Inc	4119	D	310 457-8822	3792
Friends of Max Rose LLC	7812	D	424 901-1260	18055
Game Show Network LLC (DH)	4841	C	310 255-6800	5917
Genius Products Inc	5099	C	310 453-1222	8032
Georgian Hotel	7011	D	310 395-9945	12602
Global Futures Exch & Trdg Co	6221	D	818 996-0401	10045
Global-Dining Inc California	8741	C	310 576-9922	26873
Good Shepherd Health Care Ce	8051	D	310 451-4809	20489
Gumbiner Savett Inc CPA	6512	D	310 828-9798	10888
Guthy-Renker LLC	5099	D	310 581-6250	8036
Hct Packaging Inc (PA)	7389	C	310 260-7680	17211
Hirsch/Bedner Intl Inc (PA)	7389	C	310 829-9087	17221
Home Box Office Inc	4841	D	310 382-3000	5920
Hulu LLC (PA)	4833	C	310 571-4700	5800
Ice Specialty Entrmt Inc (PA)	7999	C	310 899-3889	19186
Imagestat Corporation	5045	C	310 392-1100	7061
Innovative Artists Talent Agny (PA)	7922	C	310 656-0400	18372
Interactive Data Corporation	7371	D	310 664-2500	15227
Jackson National Life Insur Co	6311	D	310 899-7900	10137
Jakks Sales Corporation	5092	E	424 268-9444	7953
John M Adams Jr MD	8011	D	310 829-2663	19520
John Wayne Institute For Ctr	8733	C	310 449-5253	26629
Jonathan Club	7997	C	310 393-9245	18941
Jurlique Hlistic Skin Care Inc (PA)	7231	D	914 998-8800	13664
K-Micro Inc	5045	D	310 442-3200	7068
Kcrw Foundation Inc	8399	D	310 450-5183	24794
Kfa LLP	8712	D	310 399-7975	26074
Kingcom(us) LLC (HQ)	7372	C	424 744-5697	15729
Kite Pharma Inc (HQ)	8731	C	310 824-9999	26391
Kor Hotel Groups Inc	8741	C	310 309-8066	26922
Leaf Group Ltd (PA)	7313	C	310 656-6253	13948
Les Kelley Family Health Ctr	8011	D	310 319-4700	19649
Lightcrest LLC	7373	E	888 320-8495	15997
Lions Gate Entertainment Inc (HQ)	7812	D	310 449-9200	18070
Lions Gate Films Inc	7812	C	310 449-9200	18071
Luma Pictures Inc	7819	C	310 888-8738	18199
M&C Hotel Interests Inc	7011	C	310 399-9344	12866
Macerich Company (PA)	6798	C	310 394-6000	12172
Maguire Properties Twr 17 LLC	6798	C	310 857-1100	12173
MBK Real Estate Ltd A Califor	6513	E	310 399-3227	11065
Media Vntures Entrmt Group LLC	7812	E	310 260-3171	18076
Medicl Imgng Ctr of Southrn CA	8011	D	310 829-9788	19677
Mens Apparel Guild In Cal Inc	8611	C	310 857-7500	24967
Mercury Insurance Company	6331	C	310 451-4943	10375
Method Studios LLC	7812	C	310 434-6500	18079
Milken Family Foundation	8641	C	310 570-4800	25199
Milken Institute	8733	E	310 570-4600	26640
Miller & Associates LLP	8111	D	310 315-1100	23254
Millward Brown LLC	8732	D	310 309-3352	26546
Morgan Stanley & Co LLC	6211	D	310 319-5200	10002
Morley Construction Company (HQ)	1771	D	310 399-1600	3290
MSC Service Co	8721	D	310 399-1600	26261
Msd Capital LP	6799	D	310 458-3600	12246
National Apartment Flrg LLC	1752	D	800 773-6904	3114
Natural Rsrces Def Council Inc	8641	D	310 434-2300	25206
Neg Operations LLC	7819	C	310 777-1940	18205
Nms Properties Inc	6531	D	310 475-7600	11631
Ocean Avenue LLC	7011	B	310 576-7777	12968
Ocean Park Community Center	8748	D	310 828-6717	27809
Ocean Park Community Center	8322	D	310 450-0650	23948
Ogilvy & Mather Worldwide Inc	7311	D	310 280-2200	13871
Palisades Media Group Inc (PA)	7319	C	310 564-5400	13980
Pandora Media Inc	4832	B	424 653-6803	5747
Partos Agency LLC	7389	D	310 458-7800	17390
Patientpop Inc	7372	D	844 487-8399	15825
Perkins Coie LLP	8111	D	310 788-9900	23323
Perr & Knight Inc (PA)	6411	D	310 230-9339	10729
Pk Nevada LLC	6531	E	310 255-0025	11672
Platinum Clg Indianapolis LLC	7349	B	310 584-8000	14350

Employment Codes: A=Over 500 employees, B=251-500,
C=101-250, D=51-100, E=50

2019 Directory of California
Wholesalers and Services Companies

© Mergent Inc. 1-800-342-5647
1685

GEOGRAPHIC

Company	SIC	EMP	PHONE	ENTRY #
Playhaven LLC	7371	E	310 308-9668	15364
Playtika Santa Monica LLC	7993	C	310 622-7380	18787
Porter Crispin & LLC Bogusky	7311	C	305 859-2070	13881
Postaer Rubin and Associates (PA)	7311	C	310 394-4000	13882
Providence St Johns Hlth Ctr	8062	B	310 829-6562	21675
Provident Financial Management	8741	D	310 282-0477	27004
Realdefense LLC	7382	D	310 693-5935	16931
Red Bull Distribution Co Inc (HQ)	5149	D	916 515-3501	8859
Red Interactive Agency LLC (PA)	7311	D	310 399-4242	13889
Reilly Worldwide Inc	7812	E	310 449-4065	18106
Remote Control Productions Inc (PA)	7812	E	310 260-0171	18107
Revolution Studios Dist Co LP (PA)	7822	D	310 255-7000	18242
Rick Weiss New Hope Apartments	6513	E	310 395-1026	11108
Right At Home	8082	D	310 313-0600	22405
Rightpoint Consulting LLC	7379	C	310 451-4619	16471
Rock Paper Scissors LLC	7812	E	310 586-0600	18110
Roscoe Real Estate Ltd Partnr	7011	D	310 260-7500	13139
Rustic Canyon Group LLC	6799	D	310 998-8000	12264
S F Broadcasting of Wisconsin	4833	C	310 586-2410	5834
Saint Jhns Hlth Ctr Foundation	8011	C	310 315-6111	19835
Saint Jhns Hlth Ctr Foundation	8351	D	310 829-5511	24375
Saint Jhns Hlth Ctr Foundation	8062	B	310 829-8970	21695
Santa Monica City of	4131	D	310 451-5444	3885
Santa Monica Amusements LLC	7996	B	310 451-9641	18809
Santa Monica Bay Womens Club	8699	E	310 395-1308	25461
Santa Monica City of	8351	D	310 399-5865	24379
Santa Monica City of	6512	E	310 458-8551	10933
Santa Monica Hotel Owner LLC	7011	C	310 395-3332	13189
Santa Monica Hsr Ltd Partnr	7011	C	310 395-3332	13190
Santa Monica Orthopedic (PA)	8011	D	310 315-2018	19860
Santa Monica Seafood Company	5146	D	310 393-5244	8598
Screen Gems-EMI Music Inc	7389	E	310 586-2700	17461
Seaside Hotel Lessee Inc	7389	C	310 260-7500	17464
Second Street Corporation	7011	D	310 394-5454	13202
Shore Hotel	7011	D	310 458-1515	13223
Snap Inc (PA)	7371	D	310 399-3339	15456
Society6 LLC	7374	E	310 394-6400	16179
Solarreserve LLC	4911	D	310 315-2200	6112
SOS Security Incorporated	7381	D	310 392-9600	16830
Spilo Worldwide Inc	5087	D	213 687-8600	7898
Step Up On Second Street Inc (PA)	8699	D	310 394-6889	25471
Stephen B Meisel MD PC	8011	D	310 828-8843	19946
Stephen B Meisel MD A Med Corp (HQ)	8011	D	310 828-8843	19947
Storquest Self Storage (HQ)	4225	D	310 451-2130	4637
Taskus Inc (PA)	7374	E	888 400-8275	16185
Taslimi Construction Co Inc	1542	D	310 447-3000	1667
Tennenbaum Capitl Partners LLC (HQ)	6799	D	310 566-1000	12273
Tennis Channel Inc (HQ)	7922	D	310 392-1920	18407
Threshold Digital Research Lab	8742	E	310 452-8885	27489
Tigerconnect	7379	D	310 401-1820	16512
Tonopah Solar Energy LLC	1711	D	310 315-2200	2388
Truecar Inc (PA)	7299	C	800 200-2000	13777
TV Guide Entrmt Group LLC	5064	D	310 360-1441	7430
Ty Investment Inc	7997	D	619 448-4242	19074
Ucla Healthcare	8062	D	310 319-4560	21864
Universal Mus Investments Inc (HQ)	7389	D	818 577-4700	17548
Universal Music Group Inc (HQ)	7389	D	310 865-4000	17549
Universal Music Group Inc	7929	D	310 865-4000	18472
Universal Studios Company LLC	7812	D	310 865-5000	18149
University Cal Los Angeles	8062	A	310 319-4000	21876
US Credit Bancorp Inc	6162	D	310 829-2112	9863
US Small Cpitl Value Portfolio	6722	D	310 395-8005	12049
Van Etten Suzumoto Becket LLP	8742	D	310 315-8284	27506
Venice Family Clinic	8011	C	310 392-8636	20050
Verizon Communications Inc	7389	D	310 315-7597	17561
Verizon Communications Inc	4813	B	310 319-6148	5670
Vista Del Mar Child Fmly Svcs	8361	B	310 836-1223	24716
Watt Properties Inc (PA)	6552	D	310 314-2430	11936
Wells Fargo Capital Fin Inc (DH)	7389	C	310 453-7300	17585
Wells Fargo Capital Fin LLC (DH)	6159	D	310 453-7300	9765
William Warren Group Inc (PA)	7513	D	310 451-2130	17619
Wilshire Animal Hospital	0742	E	310 828-4587	622
Wilshire Associates Inc (PA)	8742	C	310 451-3051	27522
Windsor Capital Group Inc	7011	D	310 566-1100	13403
Windsor Capital Group Inc	7011	D	310 566-1100	13404
Windsor Capital Group Inc	7011	D	209 577-3825	13405
Windsor Capital Group Inc	7011	D	209 577-3825	13406
Windsor Capital Group Inc	7011	D	310 566-1100	13409
Windsor Capital Group Inc	7011	D	310 566-1100	13410
Xerox Corporation	5044	D	310 526-3940	6988
Ziprecruiter Inc	8742	A	800 557-9015	27533

SANTA PAULA, CA - Ventura County

Company	SIC	EMP	PHONE	ENTRY #
Calavo Growers Inc (PA)	5148	C	805 525-1245	8646
Calavo Growers Inc	4783	D	805 525-5511	5206
Carbon California Company LLC	1311	D	805 933-1901	1020
Coastal Harvesting Inc	0761	B	805 525-6250	641
Fenceworks Inc	1799	C	661 265-0082	3520
Hayward Baker Inc	1799	D	805 933-1331	3528
Knights of Columbus	8641	C	805 525-7810	25181
Limoneira Company (PA)	0723	C	805 525-5541	536
Marin Labor Services	0761	C	805 525-7730	659
Raycon Construction Inc	1741	E	805 525-5256	2822
Rey Con Construction Inc	1771	C	805 525-8134	3314
Santa Clara Vly Job Career Ctr	7361	D	805 933-8300	14753
Saticoy Lemon Association (PA)	0723	D	805 654-6500	565
Time Warner Cable Inc	4841	D	888 892-2253	5952
Ventura County Medical Center	8011	D	805 933-8600	20052
Vista Cove Care Center	8059	D	805 525-7134	21250

SANTA ROSA, CA - Sonoma County

Company	SIC	EMP	PHONE	ENTRY #
Advanced Surgery Institute LLC	8011	C	707 528-6331	19267
Airport Club	7997	C	707 528-2582	18820
Alain Pinel Realtors Inc	6531	D	707 636-3800	11198
Allied Building Products Corp	5033	E	707 584-7599	6917
Allison Dowdy	6531	D	707 303-3472	11207
Alsco Inc	7213	D	707 523-3311	13499
Amaturo Sonoma Media Group LLC	4832	C	707 543-0126	5691
American Agcredit Flca (PA)	6159	D	707 545-1200	9751
American Automobile Assctn	6331	C	707 566-4000	10334
American Med Resp Amblnc Svc	4119	C	707 536-0400	3750
Apria Healthcare LLC	7352	D	707 543-0979	14434
Argonaut Constructors	1611	C	707 542-4862	1725
Ashley Ltc Inc	8051	C	707 528-2100	20237
AT&T Services Inc	4813	D	707 545-5000	5492
Atech Logistics Inc	4731	C	707 526-1910	5013
Atech Warehousing & Dist Inc (PA)	4213	D	707 526-1910	4102
Aurora Behavioral Health	8063	D	707 800-7700	21923
Balletto Ranch Inc (PA)	0161	D	707 568-2455	34
Bavarian Lion Company Cal (PA)	7011	D	707 545-8530	12359
Blood Bank of Redwoods (PA)	8099	C	707 545-1222	22746
Boys & Girls Clubs Cent Sonoma	8641	D	707 528-7977	25105
Boys & Girls Clubs of Marin A	8641	D	707 769-5322	25106
Burbank Housing Dev Corp	6552	D	707 526-9782	11860
Burr Pilger Mayer	8721	D	707 544-4078	26153
California American Water Co	4941	E	707 542-1717	6213
California Human Dev Corp (PA)	8331	C	707 523-1155	24161
Canine Cmpnons For Indpendence (PA)	0752	D	707 577-1700	626
Carlilemacy Inc	8741	E	707 542-6451	25591
Cellco Partnership	4812	D	707 525-5010	5390
Century 21 Les Ryan Realty	6531	D	707 577-7777	11305
Childrens Vlg of Sonoma Cnty	8361	E	707 566-7044	24469
City Towel & Dust Service Inc	7213	E	707 542-0391	13527
Claimremedi Inc	7323	D	707 827-1274	14031
Clp Resources Inc	7363	E	707 569-0200	14835
Community Action Partnership O	8399	C	707 544-0120	24759
Community Chld Cre Cncl Sonoma (PA)	8351	D	707 522-1413	24301
Council On Aging Svcs For SRS (PA)	8322	C	707 525-0143	23621
County of Sonoma	8063	C	707 565-4850	21944
County of Sonoma	7374	C	707 527-2911	16110
County of Sonoma	8111	C	707 565-2209	23009
County of Sonoma	8322	C	707 527-2641	23746
County of Sonoma	7374	C	707 527-2911	16111
Covia Communities	8361	B	707 538-8400	24489
CPI International	5049	D	707 521-6327	7240
Creekside Cnvalescent Hosp Inc	8051	C	707 544-7750	20359
Creekside Rehab and Behavioral	8051	C	707 524-7030	20361
Dennett Tile & Stone Inc	1743	E	707 541-3700	2994
Deposition Sciences Inc	8731	D	707 573-6700	26353
Devincenzi Concrete Cnstr	1771	E	707 568-4370	3248
Driven Performance Brands Inc (PA)	5013	C	707 544-4761	6636
Drug Abuse Alternatives Center (PA)	8322	C	707 544-3295	23775
Drug Abuse Alternatives Center	8093	E	707 571-2233	22569
Dura Metrics Inc (PA)	8072	D	707 546-5138	22166
Electric Lightwa	7389	D	707 284-4000	17148
Ensign Group Inc	8051	C	707 525-1250	20398
Epic Ventures Inc (PA)	5182	E	831 219-9100	9041
Exchange Bank (HQ)	6036	D	707 524-3000	9534
Exchange Bank	6021	D	707 524-3399	9344
F Korbel & Bros	4581	C	707 525-1875	4889
Famand Inc	1711	D	707 255-9295	2206
Finley Swim Center	7999	E	707 543-3760	19175
First Alarm SEC & Patrol Inc	7382	B	707 584-1110	16895
Flyers Energy LLC	5172	D	707 546-0766	8960
Fountain Grove Golf & Athc CLB	7992	D	707 521-3207	18713
Fountaingrove Inn LLC	7011	D	707 578-6101	12584
Frank Howard Allen Fincl Corp	6531	D	707 523-3000	11474
Gallaher Construction Inc	1521	E	707 535-3200	1169
Ghd Inc	8711	D	707 523-1010	25713
Ghilotti Construction Co Inc (PA)	1629	C	707 585-1221	2034
Golden Living LLC	8051	D	707 546-0471	20471
Heartland Payment Systems LLC	7389	D	707 338-0510	17214

Company	SIC	EMP	PHONE	ENTRY #
Hired Hand Home Care	8082	C	707 575-4700	22319
Humane Society Sonoma County (PA)	8699	D	707 542-0882	25431
Icon Design and Display Inc	7389	D	707 284-3400	17229
Individuals Now	8322	D	707 544-3299	23855
Inoxpa USA Inc	5084	B	707 585-3900	7757
Jackson Family Wines Inc	5182	C	415 819-0301	9050
Jlp Landscape Contracting	0782	E	707 526-6285	869
Joe Lunardi Electric Inc	1731	D	707 823-2129	2620
Johnson Controls	1711	D	707 578-3212	2245
Johnson Controls	8711	D	707 546-3042	25770
K G Walters Cnstr Co Inc	1629	D	707 527-9968	2043
Kaiser Foundation Hospitals	8011	A	707 393-4000	19526
Kaiser Foundation Hospitals	6324	D	707 571-3835	10251
Kaiser Foundation Hospitals	6324	D	707 393-4033	10252
Keith Development Corporation	6552	D	707 528-8703	11882
Klh Consulting Inc	8748	D	707 575-9986	27766
La Tortilla Factory Inc (PA)	5149	B	707 586-4000	8823
Landesign Cnstr & Maint Inc	0782	D	707 578-2657	889
Loring Smart Roast Inc	5084	D	707 526-7215	7764
Luther Burbank Mem Foundation	7922	D	707 546-3600	18384
Luther Burbank Savings (HQ)	6036	E	707 578-9216	9535
Manor Bell L P	1531	D	707 526-9782	1354
Mark E Jacobson M D	8011	D	707 571-4022	19669
Mayacama Golf Club LLC	7997	C	707 569-2900	18968
Melissa Bradley RE Inc	6531	D	707 536-0888	11603
Mendocino Forest Pdts Co LLC (PA)	5031	B	707 620-2961	6840
Mission Car Wash	7542	E	707 537-2040	17832
Murphy-True Inc	1542	D	707 576-7337	1598
Neese Inc	4121	E	707 544-4444	3867
Noble Aew Vineyard Creek LLC	7011	D	707 284-1234	12959
Nordby Construction Co	1542	E	707 526-4500	1602
North American Cinemas Inc	7832	B	707 571-1412	18307
North Coast Fisheries LLC	5146	D	707 579-0679	8584
Northwest Insurance Agency	6411	D	707 573-1300	10719
Oakmont Golf Club Inc (PA)	7992	D	707 538-2454	18741
Occidental Cnty Sanitation Dst	4952	D	707 547-1900	6325
One Main Financial Services	8742	C	707 546-5162	27378
Optima Building Services Maint	7349	D	707 586-6640	14336
Orenda Center	8093	D	707 565-7450	22629
Pacific Gas and Electric Co	4911	C	800 756-7243	6075
Parenthood of Planned	8093	D	707 527-7656	22633
Pepsi-Cola Metro Btlg Co Inc	5149	D	707 535-4560	8848
Permanente Medical Group Inc	8011	D	707 393-4000	19762
Primrose Alzheimers Living (PA)	8361	E	707 568-4355	24633
Primrose Alzheimers Living	8361	E	707 578-8360	24634
Pw Jade LLC	8082	D	707 843-5192	22399
Realogy Holdings Corp	6531	B	707 284-1111	11717
Redwood Credit Union (PA)	6061	C	707 545-4000	9582
Redwood Empir	4953	D	707 586-5533	6449
Redwood Empire Ice Oprtons LLC (PA)	7999	D	707 546-7147	19225
Redwood Regional Medical Group (PA)	8071	D	707 525-4080	22135
Redwood Toxicology Lab Inc	8071	D	707 577-7958	22136
Richard Hancock Inc	1751	D	707 528-4900	3067
Roman Cthlic Bshp of Snta Rosa	8399	C	707 528-8712	24832
Saint Joseph Home Care Network	8361	D	707 206-9124	24660
Santa Rosa & Sonoma Co Real Es	6531	E	707 524-1124	11753
Santa Rosa Community Hlth Ctrs (PA)	8322	C	707 547-2422	24033
Santa Rosa Dental Group	8021	D	707 545-0944	20135
Santa Rosa Golf & Country Club	7997	D	707 546-3485	19035
Santa Rosa Memorial Hospital (DH)	8062	A	707 546-3210	21719
Santa Rosa Radiology Med Group (PA)	8071	E	707 546-4062	22142
Santa Rosa Surgery Center LP	8062	D	707 575-5831	21720
Security One Inc	7381	D	800 778-3017	16818
Sonoma County Airport Ex Inc	4111	D	707 837-8700	3728
Sonoma County Humane Society	0752	E	707 542-0882	633
Sonoma County Indian Health PR (PA)	8011	C	707 521-4545	19896
Sonoma County Water Agency	4941	C	707 526-5370	6313
Sonoma Grapevines Inc (PA)	5193	D	707 542-5521	9162
Sonoma Vly Cnty Sanitation Dst	4952	C	707 547-1900	6329
Sotoyome Medical Building LLC	6512	D	707 525-4000	10947
Ss Skikos Incorporated	4214	D	707 575-3000	4376
Steven N Ledson	1521	D	707 537-3810	1239
Summit Technology Group Inc	1731	E	707 542-4773	2749
Sunrise Senior Living Inc	8051	E	707 575-7503	20812
Sutter Health	8062	C	707 526-1800	21807
Sutter Health	8062	C	707 535-5600	21815
Sutter Health	8062	B	707 545-2255	21830
Sutter Health	8062	C	707 523-7253	21832
Sutter Med Group of Redwoods	8011	D	707 546-2788	19989
United Parcel Service Inc OH	7389	A	678 339-3171	17535
UPS Ground Freight Inc	4213	D	707 526-1910	4290
Venture Design Services Inc	7389	D	707 524-8368	17560
Veterans Health Administration	8011	D	707 570-3800	20069
Victor Treatment Centers Inc	8361	C	707 360-1509	24711
Vintage Wine Estates Inc (PA)	5182	C	877 289-9463	9059

Company	SIC	EMP	PHONE	ENTRY #
Vintners Inn	7011	D	707 575-7350	13369
West County Trnsp Agcy	4111	C	707 206-9988	3738
Windsor Redwoods LP	7389	D	707 526-1020	17597
Winzler & Kelly	8711	D	707 523-1010	26002
Woodmont Real Estate Svcs LP	8999	B	707 569-0582	27963
Wright Contracting LLC	1542	D	707 528-1172	1706
Xpo Logistics Freight Inc	4213	D	707 584-0211	4320
Y W C A of Sonoma County	8641	E	707 546-9922	25288
Youngs Market Company LLC	5182	D	707 584-5170	9069

SANTA ROSA VALLEY, CA - Ventura County

Company	SIC	EMP	PHONE	ENTRY #
Tucker Electric Corporation	1731	E	818 426-7645	2772

SANTA YNEZ, CA - Santa Barbara County

Company	SIC	EMP	PHONE	ENTRY #
Channel Islands Young Mens Ch	8641	D	805 686-2037	25135
Chumash Casino Resort (HQ)	7999	C	805 686-0855	19126

SANTEE, CA - San Diego County

Company	SIC	EMP	PHONE	ENTRY #
A & D Fire Protection Inc	1711	D	619 258-7697	2078
AT&T Corp	4812	D	619 448-1798	5263
Aztec Sheet Metal Inc	1761	D	619 937-0005	3126
C & M Transfer San Diego Inc	4214	D	619 562-6111	4334
Catania Hijar Corporation	1623	C	800 400-3401	1905
Challenger Sheet Metal Inc	1761	D	619 596-8040	3136
Hd Supply Inc	4212	D	800 431-3000	4020
International Thermoproducts	5084	E	619 562-7001	7758
J Vitale Landscape & Maint	0782	D	619 938-2435	864
Life Gnerations Healthcare LLC	8059	D	619 449-5555	21135
Pacific Western Bank	6022	D	619 562-6400	9477
Padre Dam Municipal Water Dst (PA)	4941	D	619 258-4617	6294
Ra Hughes Enterprises In	1711	E	619 390-4880	2326
Santee Senior Retirement Com	8322	C	619 955-0901	24034
Scantibodies Clinical Lab Inc	8071	E	866 249-1212	22143
T C Construction Company Inc	1623	C	619 448-4560	1987
Tarpy Heating & Air	1711	E	619 485-3311	2382
Torres General Inc	1521	D	619 448-8900	1249
Tower Glass Inc	1793	D	619 596-6199	3411
YMCA of San Diego County	8641	D	619 449-9622	25304

SARATOGA, CA - Santa Clara County

Company	SIC	EMP	PHONE	ENTRY #
Action Day Nrseries Prmry Plus	8351	D	408 370-0350	24258
Club At Los Gatos Inc	7991	D	408 867-5110	18586
Intero Real Estate Svcs Inc	6531	D	408 741-1600	11517
Montalvo Association	8422	D	408 961-5800	24932
Odd Fellows Home California	8361	B	408 741-7100	24616
Our Lady of Fatima Villa Inc	8051	D	408 741-2950	20683
Precious Enterprises Inc	8351	D	408 265-2226	24372
Preston Wynne Spa Inc	7991	D	408 741-1750	18642
Progressive Sub-Acute Care	8069	C	408 378-8875	22039
Saratoga Court Inc	6514	D	408 866-1392	11154
Stage 4 Solutions Incorporated	8742	E	408 868-9739	27467
YMCA of Silicon Valley	8699	C	408 370-1877	25488

SAUGUS, CA - Los Angeles County

Company	SIC	EMP	PHONE	ENTRY #
Desert Star Co	5169	E	661 259-5848	8925
Pleasantview Industries Inc	8093	D	661 296-6700	22653

SAUSALITO, CA - Marin County

Company	SIC	EMP	PHONE	ENTRY #
Aperio Group LLC	7389	D	415 339-4300	17006
Butler Shine Stern Prtners LLC	7311	C	415 331-6049	13800
Casa Madrona Hotel and Spa LLC	7011	D	415 332-0502	12435
Cavallo Point LLC (PA)	7011	D	415 339-4700	12442
Coastal International Inc (PA)	7389	A	415 339-1700	17092
Comcast Corporation	4841	D	415 367-4153	5875
County of Marin	8322	B	415 332-6158	23689
Gate Five Group LLC	5023	C	415 339-9500	6763
Lexington Associates Inc (PA)	6513	D	415 332-8500	11054
Marine Mammal Center (PA)	0742	E	415 339-0430	604
Naturebridge	8699	D	415 332-5771	25446
Qlm Consulting Inc	8742	E	415 331-9292	27414
Steelriver Infrasructure Part (PA)	6719	C	415 512-1515	12008
Swa Group (PA)	0781	C	415 332-5100	790
U S Army Corps of Engineers	8711	D	415 289-3067	25967
Ubics Inc	7371	C	415 289-1400	15515
Wested	8733	D	415 289-2300	26674

SCOTIA, CA - Humboldt County

Company	SIC	EMP	PHONE	ENTRY #
Humboldt Redwood Company LLC (HQ)	5031	B	707 764-4472	6833

SCOTTS VALLEY, CA - Santa Cruz County

Company	SIC	EMP	PHONE	ENTRY #
Ava The Rabbit Haven Inc	8748	D	831 600-7479	27652
Bellavista Landscape Svcs Inc	0781	D	831 461-1761	731
Bfp Fire Protection Inc	1711	D	831 461-1100	2143
Hospice of Santa Cruz County (PA)	8082	C	831 430-3000	22337
Inn At Scotts Valley LLC	7011	D	831 440-1000	12763
MBK Real Estate Ltd A Calfor	6513	D	831 438-7533	11064
R W Garcia Co Inc (PA)	5145	E	408 287-4616	8566
Roi Communications Inc (PA)	8748	D	831 430-0170	27845

Employment Codes: A=Over 500 employees, B=251-500,
C=101-250, D=51-100, E=50

2019 Directory of California
Wholesalers and Services Companies

© Mergent Inc. 1-800-342-5647

1687

GEOGRAPHIC

Company	SIC	EMP	PHONE	ENTRY #
West Interactive Services Corp	4822	D	888 527-5225	5687
Zero Motorcycles Inc	5012	D	831 438-3500	6615

SEAL BEACH, CA - Orange County

Company	SIC	EMP	PHONE	ENTRY #
Autism Partnership Inc	8742	D	562 431-9293	27145
Bakercorp (DH)	7359	C	562 430-6262	14476
Califrn/Nvada Developments LLC	6519	C	714 677-5721	11166
Country Villa Service Corp	8322	D	562 598-2477	23623
Countryside Inn-Corona LP	8741	E	562 596-8330	26830
Encore Aerospace LLC	1799	D	562 344-1700	3512
Farmers Merchants Bnk Long Bch	6022	D	562 430-4724	9445
First Team RE - Orange Cnty	6531	C	562 596-9911	11458
Fisheries Resource Vlntr Corps	8742	E	562 596-9261	27238
Golden Living LLC	8059	D	562 598-2477	21090
Golden Rain Foundation	8011	D	562 493-9581	19485
Healthnet California Inc	6324	D	562 598-4043	10213
Kendrick Construction Services	1541	D	562 546-0200	1415
Limbach Company LP	1711	C	714 653-7000	2263
National Product Services LLC	8743	E	562 594-8206	27565
Olson Company LLC (PA)	1521	C	562 596-4770	1210
Olson Urban Housing LLC	6552	D	562 596-4770	11902
P2f Holdings	5199	D	562 296-1055	9240
Pasha Distribution Svcs LLC	4731	D	714 889-2460	5135
Saga Seal Co Ltd	7011	D	562 493-7501	13160
Samedan Oil Corporation	1311	B	661 319-5038	1028
Strlng Path Medcl Corp	7549	E	562 799-8900	17873
Sunrise Senior Living Inc	8051	D	562 594-5788	20800
Tenet Healthsystem Medical	8011	D	562 493-9581	20002
Tyr Sport Inc	5137	D	562 430-1380	8340
Wells Fargo Clearing Svcs LLC	6211	E	562 594-1220	10039

SEASIDE, CA - Monterey County

Company	SIC	EMP	PHONE	ENTRY #
Bsl Golf Corp	7992	C	831 899-7271	18690
County Monterey Social Svcs	8322	D	831 899-8001	23625
Morale Welfare Recreation Fund	8399	C	831 242-6631	24809
Sodexo Operations LLC	8741	D	831 582-3838	27039
Tucson Hotels LP	7011	C	831 393-1115	13350

SEBASTOPOL, CA - Sonoma County

Company	SIC	EMP	PHONE	ENTRY #
Apple Vly Cnvalescent Hosp Inc	8051	C	707 823-7675	20231
Camp Recovery Centers LP	8069	A	707 823-3385	22001
County of Sonoma	8062	C	707 823-8511	21359
Seaver International	7379	D	707 291-4929	16480
Sebastopol Rifle & Pistol Club	7997	D	707 824-0184	19039
TLC Child & Family Services (PA)	8361	D	707 823-7300	24699
Weeks Drilling and Pump Co (PA)	1711	E	707 823-3184	2405

SELMA, CA - Fresno County

Company	SIC	EMP	PHONE	ENTRY #
Adventist Medical Center-Selma	8062	B	559 891-1000	21268
Bethel Lutheran Home Inc	8059	D	559 896-4900	21009
Circle K Ranch	0172	D	559 834-1571	135
Dragados/Flatiron Joint Ventr	1542	D	559 847-5388	1525
Jane McClurg	0172	D	559 834-3080	150
Kaiser Foundation Hospitals	6324	D	559 898-6000	10258
Robert Alves Farms Inc	0172	D	559 896-3309	170
Selma Portuguese Azorian Assn	8322	E	559 896-2508	24042
Serimian M S D L Ranch	0191	E	559 896-1517	380

SHAFTER, CA - Kern County

Company	SIC	EMP	PHONE	ENTRY #
Baker Hghes Olfld Oprtions LLC	1389	E	661 834-9654	1048
Baker Hughes A GE Company LLC	1389	D	661 831-7686	1050
Bps Supply Group (PA)	5051	D	661 589-9141	7263
Cummings Vacuum Service Inc	1389	D	661 746-1786	1055
Delmart Farms Inc	0172	D	661 746-2148	138
Farm Pump & Irrigation Co Inc (PA)	5084	C	661 589-6901	7751
Garlic Company	0139	C	661 393-4212	23
Grimmway Enterprises Inc	0723	C	661 393-3320	521
Grimmway Enterprises Inc	0191	B	661 399-0844	346
J D Rush Company Inc (HQ)	6733	C	661 392-1900	12101
Lufkin Industries LLC	5084	D	661 746-0030	7765
Standard Industries Inc	5033	D	661 387-1100	6931
Tryad Service Corporation	1389	D	661 391-1524	1083
Varner Family Ltd Partnership (PA)	6733	D	661 399-1163	12131
Wonderful Orchards LLC (HQ)	0173	C	661 399-4456	197

SHELL BEACH, CA - San Luis Obispo County

Company	SIC	EMP	PHONE	ENTRY #
Dolphin Bay Ht & Residence Inc	7011	D	805 773-4300	12535
La Bonne Vie Inc	7991	D	805 773-5003	18622

SHERMAN OAKS, CA - Los Angeles County

Company	SIC	EMP	PHONE	ENTRY #
Adhei Enterprises Inc	7349	E	818 788-7680	14180
Ansira Partners Inc	7389	D	818 461-6100	17004
Arclight Cinema Company	7832	D	818 501-0753	18271
Azubu North America Inc	5092	E	310 759-9529	7945
Barazani Outdoors Inc	0781	D	818 701-6977	730
Baseline Consulting Group Inc	8742	E	818 906-7638	27153
Beating Wall Street Inc (PA)	8742	E	818 332-9696	27158
Blue Chip Inventory Service	7389	D	818 461-1765	17035

Company	SIC	EMP	PHONE	ENTRY #
Branded Entrmt Netwrk Inc (PA)	7335	C	310 342-1500	14096
Bright Pharmaceutical Services	5122	D	818 981-9100	8148
Campanile II LP	5149	B	323 939-6813	8764
Care Inc	8052	E	818 232-7940	20918
Coldwell Banker RE Corp	6531	D	818 995-2424	11338
Crowe LLP	8721	C	818 501-5200	26176
Dynamic Home Care Service Inc (PA)	8082	C	818 981-4446	22288
Fedelity National Title Co Org	6361	D	818 758-6849	10451
Filmquest Pictures Corporation	7812	D	818 905-1006	18053
Frank N Magid Associates Inc	8732	D	818 263-3300	26519
Frank N Magid Associates Inc	8732	D	818 263-3300	26520
Golden State Health Ctrs Inc (PA)	8051	D	818 385-3200	20487
Help Group West (PA)	8093	C	818 781-0360	22591
Highpoint Productions Inc	7812	D	818 728-7600	18060
Homebridge Financial Services	6163	A	818 981-0606	9887
Ideal Products LLC	7299	E	818 217-2574	13749
Investors MGT Tr RE Group Inc (PA)	6513	C	818 784-4700	11034
Lucky Strike Entertainment LLC	7933	C	818 933-0872	18493
Malka Communications Group Inc	8999	E	818 239-4431	27941
Mega Appraisers Inc	7389	A	818 246-7370	17319
Metro Home Loan Inc	6162	D	818 461-9840	9832
Moss & Company (PA)	6531	D	310 453-0911	11614
Motion Picture Assn Amer Inc (PA)	8611	C	818 995-6600	24969
Mpc Productions	7929	C	310 418-8115	18452
Neurobrands LLC	5149	C	310 393-6444	8837
Nexcare Collaborative (PA)	8322	E	818 907-0322	23939
Organic Affinity LLC	5065	D	801 870-7433	7520
P& JP Brokerage LLC	4731	E	310 801-9707	5130
Pk Management LLC	8741	B	818 808-0600	26989
Premiere Radio Network Inc (DH)	7922	C	818 377-5300	18396
Prime Healthcare Services - Sh	8742	A	818 981-7111	27400
Prime Healthcare Svcs II LLC	8062	B	818 981-7111	21660
Project Six	7389	D	818 781-0360	17415
Prudential Insur Co of Amer	6411	E	818 990-2122	10748
Reel Security California Inc	7381	D	818 928-4737	16772
Rodeo Realty Inc	6531	D	818 986-7300	11735
Royal Specialty Undwrt Inc	6331	D	818 922-6700	10392
Serviz Inc	7299	E	818 381-4826	13773
Seymour Gale & Associates	5137	E	213 622-5361	8335
Sherman Oaks Health System	8062	D	818 981-7111	21754
Silicon Valley Bank	6021	E	818 382-2600	9371
Sunrise Delivery Service Inc	4215	D	323 464-5121	4430
Tharpe & Howell (PA)	8111	D	714 437-4900	23407
Thoughtful Media Group Inc	7313	D	818 465-7500	13957
Triton Media Group LLC (PA)	4832	A	323 290-6900	5756
Unlimited SEC Specialists Inc	7381	C	877 310-4877	16851
Vubiquity Inc	7822	C	818 526-5000	18248
Vubiquity Holdings Inc (PA)	4841	C	818 526-5000	5965
WERM Investments LLC	7929	E	213 627-8070	18475

SHERWOOD FOREST, CA - Los Angeles County

Company	SIC	EMP	PHONE	ENTRY #
Slade Industrial Landscape Inc	0781	D	818 885-1916	789

SHINGLE SPRINGS, CA - El Dorado County

Company	SIC	EMP	PHONE	ENTRY #
County of El Dorado	8322	C	530 621-5625	23636
Salutary Sports Clubs Inc	7991	E	530 677-5705	18646
Straight Line Roofing & Cnstr	1761	E	530 672-9995	3202

SIGNAL HILL, CA - Los Angeles County

Company	SIC	EMP	PHONE	ENTRY #
2h Construction Inc	1542	D	562 424-5567	1451
Ajr Trucking Inc	4212	C	562 989-9555	3970
American Tile Brick Veneer Inc	1743	E	562 595-9293	2986
Edco Disposal Corporation Inc (PA)	4953	C	619 287-7555	6393
Fenderscape Inc	0782	C	562 988-2228	841
First American Team Realty Inc (PA)	6531	C	562 427-7765	11450
Goldsmith Construction Co Inc	1771	E	562 595-5975	3258
Gregg Drilling LLC (PA)	1781	D	562 427-6899	3350
Gregg Drilling & Testing Inc (PA)	1799	D	562 427-6899	3527
Intertek USA Inc	7389	E	562 494-4999	17250
Lovco Construction Inc	1794	C	562 595-1601	3432
Nsv International Corp	5013	D	562 438-3836	6661
Optimal Hospice Foundation	8052	C	562 494-7687	20947
Professional Parking (PA)	7521	C	714 722-0242	17704
SCCH	8741	D	562 494-5188	27023
Traffic Management Inc (PA)	7389	C	562 595-4278	17516
Viking Office Products Inc (HQ)	5112	B	562 490-1000	8092
Walters Wholesale Electric Co (HQ)	5063	E	562 988-3100	7401
Wannajob Inc	7363	D	562 426-5272	14942

SILVERADO, CA - Orange County

Company	SIC	EMP	PHONE	ENTRY #
Inside Outdoors Foundation	8322	C	714 708-3885	23857

SIMI VALLEY, CA - Ventura County

Company	SIC	EMP	PHONE	ENTRY #
Aerovironment Inc	8711	D	626 357-9983	25521
Aerovironment Inc	8611	D	805 581-2187	24940
American GNC Corporation	8711	E	805 582-0582	25531
American Golf Corporation	7997	E	805 522-0803	18844

	SIC	EMP	PHONE	ENTRY #
American Golf Corporation	7992	D	805 527-9663	18684
American Technologies Inc	1521	E	818 700-5060	1117
American Vision Windows Inc	7699	C	805 582-1833	17933
Anjana Software Solutions Inc	7371	D	805 583-0121	14986
ARC Industries	8361	D	805 520-0399	24418
Arconic Global Fas & Rings Inc (HQ)	5085	C	805 527-3600	7832
AT&T Corp	4812	D	805 583-9483	5287
B & M Contractors Inc	1771	D	805 581-5480	3218
B S Hand & Sons Inc	1771	E	818 983-1155	3219
Bank America National Assn	6153	D	805 520-5100	9732
Bestitcom Inc (PA)	7379	D	602 667-5613	16317
Big Sky Country Club LLC	7992	D	805 522-4653	18688
Boys & Girls Club Simi Vly Inc	8641	E	805 527-4437	25104
Cardservice International Inc	7389	A	800 217-4622	17056
Cellco Partnership	4812	D	805 955-9035	5378
CFS Tax Software	7372	D	805 522-1157	15624
Chase Group Llc	8742	D	805 522-9155	27190
CM Concrete Inc	1771	C	805 520-8100	3234
Cobalt Construction Company	1522	D	805 577-6222	1276
Collectech Systems Inc (DH)	7322	C	818 597-7500	13998
Computerized Management	7363	D	805 522-5999	14842
Computerized Mgt Svcs Inc	8741	D	805 522-5940	26817
Dbi Services Inc	1623	D	805 523-7114	1914
Edwards Theatres Circuit Inc	7832	D	805 526-4329	18300
Engility LLC	8711	A	703 633-8300	25666
Facey Medical Foundation	8031	C	805 206-2000	20147
First & La Realty Corp (PA)	6531	D	805 581-0021	11448
Genesis Home Health Inc	7363	E	805 520-7100	14857
GI Industries	4953	D	805 522-2150	6402
Golden State Water Company	4941	E	805 583-6400	6260
Hewitt and Canfield Cnstr Inc	1751	D	805 522-2426	3042
Home Instead Senior Care	8082	C	805 577-0926	22327
Johnson Controls Inc	5065	D	805 522-5555	7496
Kaiser Foundation Hospitals	6324	D	888 515-3500	10263
Kidney Center Inc	8092	C	805 433-7777	22481
Kids N Things Inc (PA)	8351	D	805 522-1011	24334
Landcare USA LLC	0782	C	805 520-9394	878
LBC Inc	1761	D	805 581-1068	3173
Mortgage Corp America Inc	6163	D	805 582-2220	9897
Nfp Property & Casualty Svcs	8742	E	805 579-1900	27369
North Star Building Maint Inc	7349	D	805 518-0417	14334
Official Police Garage Assn of	4492	A	805 624-0572	4747
Posada Royale Hotel & Suites	7011	E	805 584-6300	13077
PW Gillibrand Co Inc	1446	D	805 526-2195	1098
Q L P Inc	5063	E	805 579-0440	7387
Qualitylogic Inc (PA)	8748	C	805 531-9030	27831
Rancho Simi Recreation Pk Dst (PA)	7999	D	805 584-4400	19223
Rand Medical Billing Inc	8721	D	805 578-8300	26280
Ronald Reagan Presidential	8412	D	805 522-2977	24901
SA Recycling LLC	4953	D	805 483-0512	6457
Sdj General Partnership	6512	D	805 582-3200	10934
Second Opinion Med Grp Inc	6324	D	805 496-4315	10308
Shopper Inc	5046	B	805 527-6700	7145
Sierra Vista Family Medical	8099	D	805 582-4000	22884
Simi Radiology & Imaging	8742	D	805 522-5978	27450
Simi Vly Hosp & Hlth Care Svcs (HQ)	8049	D	805 955-6000	20204
Simi West Inc	7011	C	805 583-2000	13229
Smart Living Company (PA)	5199	E	805 578-5500	9259
Specialized Landscape MGT Svcs	0782	D	805 520-7590	944
Troop Real Estate Inc (PA)	6531	A	805 581-3200	11804
United Parcel Service Inc OH	7389	D	866 553-1069	17544
Vickie Lobello	8699	D	805 750-2327	25480
Vintage Senior Housing LLC	6513	B	805 583-3500	11135
Volutone LLC (PA)	7382	D	805 520-8500	16950
Warner Media LLC	4841	D	805 421-4467	5967
Wsm Investments LLC	6794	D	818 332-4600	12148
Xavient Info Systems Inc	7372	A	805 955-4111	15896
Young Mens Christian Asso	7999	D	805 583-5338	19264

SMITH RIVER, CA - Del Norte County

	SIC	EMP	PHONE	ENTRY #
Reservation Ranch (PA)	7011	C	707 487-3516	13117
Smith River Lucky 7 Casino	7011	C	707 487-7777	13243

SNELLING, CA - Merced County

	SIC	EMP	PHONE	ENTRY #
JS Homen Trucking Inc	4212	D	209 723-9559	4031

SODA SPRINGS, CA - Nevada County

	SIC	EMP	PHONE	ENTRY #
Boreal Ridge Corporation	7011	C	530 426-1012	12392
Royal Gorge Nordic Ski Resort (PA)	7011	C	530 426-3871	13142

SOLANA BEACH, CA - San Diego County

	SIC	EMP	PHONE	ENTRY #
All-Pro Bail Bonds Inc (PA)	7389	D	858 481-1200	16991
American Golf Corporation	7997	C	858 755-6768	18826
BNC Real Estate (PA)	6531	B	858 481-3000	11248
Boys Grls Clubs of San Deguito (PA)	8641	D	858 755-9371	25116
Builders Firstsource Inc	5031	D	858 755-0246	6812
Child Development Center	8351	E	858 794-7160	24283

	SIC	EMP	PHONE	ENTRY #
Daley & Heft Attorneys	8111	E	858 755-5666	23018
Daviselen Advertising Inc	7311	D	858 847-0789	13811
Healthfusion Holdings Inc (HQ)	6719	D	858 523-2120	11986
Merlin Global Services LLC	4522	C	904 305-9559	4865
National Insurance Housing	8748	D	800 550-1911	27798
Onehealth Solutions Inc	7379	D	858 947-6333	16441
Senior Resource Group LLC	8361	D	858 519-0890	24671
Smart & Final Stores LLC	5141	D	858 350-7900	8460
Srg Management LLC	8741	D	858 792-9300	27043
Warren Auto De Mexico LLC	5199	D	858 794-7947	9270

SOLEDAD, CA - Monterey County

	SIC	EMP	PHONE	ENTRY #
Costa Sons	0161	E	831 678-0799	45
Dole Fresh Vegetables Inc	5148	C	831 678-5030	8668
Kvl Holdings Inc (PA)	0172	E	831 678-2132	155
Robertas Labor Contracting	7361	B	831 678-8176	14747
Sandoval Brothers Inc	7361	D	831 678-1465	14751
Soledad Cmnty Hlth Care Dst	8051	D	831 678-2462	20771
Valley Farm Management Inc	0762	D	831 678-1592	716
Vasquez Brothers Inc	0723	D	831 678-8894	583

SOLVANG, CA - Santa Barbara County

	SIC	EMP	PHONE	ENTRY #
Alisal Properties (PA)	7032	C	805 688-6411	13443
Cottage Health	8062	D	805 688-6432	21347
MWH Americas Inc	8711	D	805 683-2409	25837
National Hospitality LLC	7011	D	805 688-8000	12951
Pacific Western Bank	6022	C	805 688-6644	9478
Santa Ynez Valley Cottage Hosp	8062	D	805 688-6431	21723

SOMIS, CA - Ventura County

	SIC	EMP	PHONE	ENTRY #
Coast Nurseries Inc (PA)	0181	C	805 386-4253	251
Saticoy Country Club	7997	D	805 647-1153	19038
Venegas Farming LLC	0761	E	805 529-5038	678

SONOMA, CA - Sonoma County

	SIC	EMP	PHONE	ENTRY #
Appellation Tours Inc	4725	E	707 938-9390	4962
Artisan Bakers	5149	D	707 939-1765	8755
AV Brands Inc	5182	E	410 884-9463	9031
Bright Event Rentals LLC	7359	C	310 202-0011	14481
Broderick Gen Enginneering Inc	1611	E	707 996-7809	1732
Clarbec Inc	0172	E	707 996-4012	136
CP Opco LLC	7359	D	707 253-2332	14491
CP Opco LLC	7359	D	650 652-0300	14495
Credit Bureau NAPA County Inc	7322	D	707 940-3000	14001
Diageo North America Inc	5182	D	707 939-6200	9037
Don Sebastiani & Sons Internat (PA)	5182	D	707 933-1704	9039
Emeritus Corporation	8052	D	707 996-7101	20930
Enterprise Vineyards	0172	E	707 996-6513	143
Freixenet Usa Inc	5182	D	707 996-7256	9045
Golden Living LLC	8051	D	707 938-1096	20483
Grega Brooke Sra	6531	E	707 938-3362	11491
Marriott International Inc	7011	D	707 935-6600	12903
Merrill Gardens LLC	6513	D	707 996-7101	11074
North Counties Drywall Inc	1742	D	707 996-0198	2923
On My Own Indepedent Living	8059	D	707 938-9156	21174
Pacific Union Intl Inc	6163	A	707 934-2300	9901
Renaissance Hotel Holdings Inc	7011	D	707 935-6600	13112
Smisc Holdings	7948	E	707 938-8448	18544
Sonoma Hotel Operator Inc	7011	C	707 938-9000	13246
Sonoma Valley Health Care Dst (PA)	8062	B	707 935-5000	21759
Sonoma Valley Womans Club	8641	D	707 938-8313	25252
Speedway Sonoma LLC	7948	D	707 938-8448	18545
Swiss Hotel Group Inc	7011	D	707 938-2884	13310
V Sangiacomo & Sons	0172	C	707 938-5503	181
Vintage Senior Management Inc	6513	A	707 595-0009	11137

SONORA, CA - Tuolumne County

	SIC	EMP	PHONE	ENTRY #
Adventist Health Sonora (HQ)	8062	A	209 532-5000	21264
Aladdin Sonora Motor Inn	7011	E	209 533-4971	12311
Amador Tlmne Cmnty Action Agcy	8399	E	209 533-1397	24733
Avalon Care Ctr - Sonora LLC	8051	C	209 533-2500	20250
Condor Earth Technologies Inc (PA)	8748	C	209 532-0361	27696
County of Tuolumne	7374	B	209 533-5561	16112
County of Tuolumne	8322	C	209 533-5711	23754
Diestel Turkey Ranch (PA)	0253	C	209 532-4950	438
Front Porch Inc (PA)	7371	D	209 288-5500	15169
Golden Living LLC	8059	C	209 533-2500	21087
Kingsview Corp	8093	D	209 533-6245	22609
Sonora Retirement Center Inc	8361	E	209 588-0373	24681
Tuolumne Utilities District	4941	D	209 532-5536	6316
Watch Resources Inc (PA)	8322	D	209 533-0510	24127

SOQUEL, CA - Santa Cruz County

	SIC	EMP	PHONE	ENTRY #
Balance4kids	8641	D	831 464-8669	25096
Bask Jewelry Inc	5094	E	831 479-8849	8002
Bay Photo Inc	7221	C	831 475-6090	13639
Federal Express Corporation	4215	D	800 463-3339	4411

GEOGRAPHIC

	SIC	EMP	PHONE	ENTRY #
Sutter Health	8641	B	831 458-6272	25258
Trailer Park Inc	7033	D	831 462-3271	13470

SOUTH EL MONTE, CA - Los Angeles County

	SIC	EMP	PHONE	ENTRY #
Ahmc Healthcare Inc	8062	A	626 579-7777	21273
American Wrecking Inc	1795	D	626 350-8303	3446
Bali Construction Inc	1623	D	626 442-8003	1894
California Med Response Inc	4119	C	562 968-1818	3783
Commonwealth International	7381	E	626 279-9201	16613
Fresh Air Environmental Svcs	1799	D	323 913-1965	3522
Gama Contracting Services Inc	5082	C	626 442-7200	7676
Jetworld Inc	5012	C	626 448-0150	6600
Leader Industries Inc	4119	C	626 575-0880	3816
Lincoln Training Center and RE	8331	D	626 442-0621	24200
Out of Shell LLC	1541	C	626 401-1923	1426
Statewide Pest Control Co Inc (PA)	7342	C	626 443-2847	14157
Ted Levine Drum Co (PA)	7699	D	626 579-1084	17995

SOUTH GATE, CA - Los Angeles County

	SIC	EMP	PHONE	ENTRY #
AT&T Corp	4813	D	323 568-2006	5450
Castle Dental	8021	E	323 567-1227	20113
Century 21 A Better Svc Rlty	6411	D	562 806-1000	10580
County of Los Angeles	8099	D	562 861-0316	22777
Daily Saw Service Inc	5085	E	323 564-1791	7845
Dickson Testing Co Inc (DH)	8734	D	562 862-8378	26693
Eppink of California Inc	1751	E	562 633-1275	3033
Far West Inc	8051	D	323 564-7761	20425
Herbert Malarkey Roofing Co	1761	D	562 806-8000	3163
Interior Rmoval Specialist Inc	1795	D	323 357-6900	3455
Koos Manufacturing Inc	7389	A	323 249-1000	17278
Meribear Productions Inc	7389	D	310 204-5353	17323
Pan Pacific Petroleum Co Inc (PA)	4213	B	562 928-0100	4241
Pcs Mobile Solutions LLC	4813	D	323 567-2490	5627
Privilege International Inc	5021	C	323 585-0777	6736
Pws Inc (PA)	5087	D	323 721-8832	7895
Quality Carriers Inc	4213	D	800 282-2031	4248
Rick Studer	4213	E	323 357-1720	4252
Samuel J Piazza & Son Inc (PA)	4214	D	323 357-1999	4370
Scott Jacks DDS Inc	8021	C	323 564-2444	20137

SOUTH LAKE TAHOE, CA - El Dorado County

	SIC	EMP	PHONE	ENTRY #
ABC Phones North Carolina Inc	4812	D	530 541-9500	5257
Algonquin Power and Utilities	1731	B	530 543-5288	2504
Barton Hospital	8062	A	530 543-5685	21297
Belmont Corporation	7011	D	530 542-1101	12367
California Land Mgt Svcs Corp	7033	E	530 544-5994	13461
California Tahoe Conservancy	8999	D	530 542-5580	27923
City of South Lake Tahoe	7999	D	530 542-6056	19142
Healthcare Barton System (PA)	8062	A	530 541-3420	21445
Healthcare Barton System	8062	E	530 543-5685	21446
Lake Tahoe Secret Witness	7381	D	530 541-6800	16713
Liberty Utlties Clpeco Elc LLC	4911	D	800 782-2506	6049
Marriott Grand Residence	7011	B	530 542-8400	12878
Park Hotels & Resorts Inc	7011	D	530 543-2126	13031
Park Hotels & Resorts Inc	7011	E	530 541-6122	13043
Roppongi-Tahoe Lp A Californi	7011	C	530 544-5400	13137
Saa Sierra Programs LLC	8641	D	530 541-1244	25231
Soroptomist Intl Tahoe Sierra	8699	E	530 573-1657	25467
South Tahoe Public Utility Dst	4952	C	530 544-6474	6330
South Tahoe Refuse Co	4953	D	530 541-5105	6478
Steven P Abelow MD	8011	D	530 544-8033	19949
Tahoe Beach & Ski Club	7011	D	530 541-6220	13322
Tahoe Seasons Resort Time Inte	6531	C	530 541-6700	11784
United Parcel Service Inc OH	7389	B	800 742-5877	17539

SOUTH PASADENA, CA - Los Angeles County

	SIC	EMP	PHONE	ENTRY #
Anderson Burton Construction	1542	D	626 441-2464	1465
Cccc Growth Fund LLC	6799	D	626 441-8770	12213
Collins Cllins Muir Stwart LLP	8111	E	626 243-1100	22985
Hospice Cheers	8082	D	626 799-2727	22335
Omni Ventures Group Llc	6719	D	510 384-1033	11997
Stargate Films Inc	7812	D	626 403-8403	18125
Total Education Solutions Inc (PA)	8748	A	323 341-5580	27887
Young Mens Chrstn Assn of La	8641	D	626 799-9119	25341
Young Mens Chrstn Assn of La	8641	D	323 682-2147	25348

SOUTH SAN FRANCISCO, CA - San Mateo County

	SIC	EMP	PHONE	ENTRY #
23andme Inc	7375	B	510 381-7237	16204
ABM Aviation Inc	4581	B	650 872-5400	4867
Abp Liquidating Corp	5148	E	650 871-7689	8637
Aeroground Inc (DH)	4581	A	650 266-6965	4868
Ageis Living	8361	E	650 952-6100	24412
Allogene Therapeutics Inc	8731	D	650 457-2700	26317
American Etc Inc	7211	B	650 873-5353	13482
Andrews Air Corporation	4731	C	650 871-4747	5007
Andrighetto Produce Inc	1799	D	650 588-0930	3487
Apria Healthcare LLC	5047	D	650 588-9744	7154

	SIC	EMP	PHONE	ENTRY #
Aramark Unf & Career AP LLC	7218	D	650 244-9332	13595
Ashbury Market Inc	5149	C	650 952-8889	8757
Asian Amercn Recovery Svcs Inc (PA)	8322	C	650 243-4888	23492
Avis Rent A Car System Inc	7514	D	650 616-0150	17627
Balliet Bros Construction Corp	1542	E	650 871-9000	1473
California Cryobank Inc	8099	B	650 635-1420	22753
Califrnia Golf CLB San Frncsco	7997	D	650 588-9021	18881
Centra Freight Services Inc (PA)	4783	D	650 873-8147	5207
Coast Citrus Distributors	5148	E	650 588-0707	8659
Comfort Suites	7011	D	650 589-7100	12481
Comparenetworks Inc (PA)	8731	D	650 873-9031	26350
Complete Linen Svc	7213	D	650 873-1221	13528
Cooper & Jackson Inc	8734	C	408 437-2750	26690
Core-Mark Holding Company Inc (PA)	5141	C	650 589-9445	8394
Core-Mark International Inc (HQ)	5141	D	650 589-9445	8395
Core-Mark Midcontinent Inc (DH)	5194	C	650 589-9445	9183
Counsyl Inc	8071	B	888 268-6795	22072
Crown Energy Services Inc	8711	A	415 546-6534	25631
Datasafe Inc (PA)	4226	E	650 875-3800	4671
Dbi Beverage San Francisco	5181	C	415 643-9900	8990
Decker Elc Co Inc Elec Contrs	1731	D	650 635-1390	2563
Discharge Resource Group	7363	C	650 877-8111	14848
Djont/Cmb Ssf Leasing LLC	7011	D	650 589-3400	12528
Double Day Office Services Inc	4214	E	650 872-6600	4344
Elan Drug Delivery Inc	8731	D	770 531-8100	26358
Emerald Cloud Lab Inc	8731	D	650 257-7554	26360
Expeditors Intl Wash Inc	4731	C	919 489-7431	5056
Express Messenger Systems Inc	4215	C	650 553-4001	4407
Fedex Ground Package Sys Inc	4215	E	800 463-3339	4416
Fluidigm Corporation (PA)	8731	C	650 266-6000	26367
Freeman Expositions LLC	7389	D	650 878-6023	17175
Geodis Wilson Usa Inc	4731	C	650 692-9850	5073
Grosvenor Properties Ltd	7011	C	650 873-3200	12631
Hertz Corporation	7514	D	650 624-6391	17643
Hoem & Associates Inc	1752	D	650 871-5194	3105
Imperial Parking (us) LLC	7521	D	650 871-5423	17685
Inter-City Cleaners	7216	C	650 875-9200	13566
Italfoods Inc	5149	C	650 873-2640	8808
Jacobs Farm/Del Cabo Inc	0191	C	650 827-1133	360
Janssen Alzheimer Immunothera	8731	D	650 794-2500	26388
JMB Construction Inc	1623	D	650 267-5300	1938
Kaiser Foundation Hospitals	8011	A	650 742-2000	19611
L B C Holdings U S A Corp (PA)	4724	C	650 873-0750	4943
Larkspur Hsptality Dev MGT LLC	7011	D	650 872-1515	12838
Legalmatchcom (PA)	8111	E	415 946-0800	23201
Mad Dog Express Inc (PA)	4212	D	650 588-1900	4037
Master Roofing Systems Inc	1761	D	415 407-4450	3176
Matagrano Inc	5181	D	650 829-4829	9012
Medical Care Professionals	8051	D	650 583-9898	20637
Monster Inc (PA)	5099	B	415 840-2000	8045
Panalpina Inc	4731	E	650 825-3036	5132
Park Hotels & Resorts Inc	7011	D	650 589-3400	13042
Pathways Home Health	8099	D	650 634-0133	22857
Peeters Transportation Co	4214	E	800 356-5877	4365
Peking Handicraft Inc (PA)	5023	C	650 871-3788	6782
Peninou French Ldry & Clrs Inc (PA)	7219	D	800 392-2532	13636
Peninsula Family Service	8322	C	650 952-6848	23965
Pennisula Pthlogists Med Group	8071	C	650 616-2940	22119
Permanente Medical Group Inc	6324	D	650 827-6500	10294
Pribuss Engineering Inc	1711	D	650 588-0447	2317
Prothena Biosciences Inc	8733	C	650 837-8550	26650
Quality Systems Installations	1799	D	650 875-9000	3573
Raven Biotechnologies Inc	8731	D	650 624-2600	26444
San Mateo County Transit Dst	4111	B	650 588-4860	3719
San Mateo Health Commission	8099	D	650 616-0050	22878
Schenker Inc	4731	D	650 745-3000	5161
Seafus Corporation	7349	E	415 584-6100	14382
Sfo Airporter Inc (PA)	4111	D	650 246-2734	3724
Shaw Bakers LLC	5149	D	650 273-1440	8867
Ssf Imported Auto Parts LLC (DH)	5013	D	800 203-9287	6677
Steven Engineering Inc	5085	C	650 588-9200	7873
Successfactors Inc (DH)	7371	C	650 212-1296	15481
Tosoh Bioscience Inc	5047	D	650 615-4900	7224
Tri Counties Bank	6021	C	650 583-8450	9373
Tricor International	4731	D	650 877-3678	5186
Trinity Building Services	7349	B	650 873-2121	14409
U-2 Home Entertainment Inc	5065	D	650 871-8118	7555
United Parcel Service Inc	4215	D	650 737-3737	4442
University Cal San Francisco	4225	D	510 987-0700	4648
UPS Supply Chain Solutions Inc	4731	E	650 875-8300	5194
Valgenesis Inc	5045	D	510 445-0505	7126
Veracyte Inc	8071	C	650 243-6300	22158
Yrc Worldwide Inc	4213	D	650 952-1112	4327
Zipline International Inc	8742	C	415 993-0604	27532

Mergent email: customerrelations@mergent.com
1690

2019 Directory of California
Wholesalers and Services Companies

(P-0000) Products & Services Section entry number
(PA)=Parent Co (HQ)=Headquarters (DH)=Div Headquarters

SPRING VALLEY, CA - San Diego County

Name	SIC	EMP	PHONE	ENTRY #
A Better Life Together Inc	8082	D	619 741-1548	22177
B-Spring Valley LLC	8051	D	619 797-3991	20253
Brighton Place East Inc	8051	D	619 461-3222	20268
Brightview Landscapes LLC	0781	D	619 644-8584	744
Burns and Sons Trucking Inc	4212	D	619 460-5394	3982
Casper Company	1795	C	619 589-6001	3448
Commercial Indus Roofg Co Inc	1761	D	619 465-3737	3140
County of San Diego	8322	D	619 479-1832	23726
Covenant Rtirement Communities	8059	C	619 479-4790	21051
D A V Industries	8641	D	619 337-9244	25150
Encompass Fmly Phy Med Grp Inc (PA)	8031	D	619 660-6212	20146
Evangelical Covenant Church	8361	D	619 931-1114	24524
Greenbrier Lawn Tree Exprt Co	0782	C	619 469-8720	851
Hugo Alonso Inc	1541	E	619 660-6255	1408
Irish Construction	1623	C	619 713-1991	1935
J&M Keystone Inc	7217	D	619 466-9876	13579
Layfield USA Corporation (DH)	1799	C	619 562-1200	3545
Mt Miquel Covenant Village	8059	C	619 479-4790	21162
Otay Water District	4941	D	619 670-2222	6293
Pnc Inc	5147	D	619 713-2278	8624
Robinson Company Contrs Inc	1711	D	619 697-6040	2339
Roofing Wholesale Co Inc	5033	E	619 287-7600	6928
Socal Coatings Inc	1721	D	619 660-5395	2482
Treebeard Landscape Inc	0782	D	619 697-8302	950

STANFORD, CA - Santa Clara County

Name	SIC	EMP	PHONE	ENTRY #
Associated Students Stanford (PA)	8641	D	650 723-4331	25095
General Electric Company	4911	C	650 725-0516	6037
Hoover Institution	7389	C	650 723-0603	17225
Howard Hughes Medical Inst	8731	E	650 725-8252	26378
Imperial Parking (us) LLC	7521	E	650 724-4309	17686
Leland Stanford Junior Univ	4832	C	650 725-4868	5741
Leland Stanford Junior Univ	8011	D	650 723-7863	19646
Leland Stanford Junior Univ	8733	C	650 723-4150	26633
Leland Stanford Junior Univ	8641	C	650 723-2021	25190
Leland Stanford Junior Univ	1731	C	650 723-9633	2631
Leland Stanford Junior Univ	8733	C	650 723-0107	26634
Leland Stanford Junior Univ	8733	C	650 724-8899	26635
Leland Stanford Junior Univ	8062	A	650 725-2386	21551
Leland Stanford Junior Univ	8062	A	650 725-6127	21552
Leland Stanford Junior Univ	8011	D	650 723-0821	19648
Leland Stanford Junior Univ	8062	A	650 723-4000	21553
Lucile Salter Packard Chil	8069	C	650 723-5791	22033
Palo Alto Community Child Care	8351	C	650 855-9828	24365
Stanford Health Care	8062	A	650 723-4000	21790
Stanford Health Care (HQ)	8062	A	650 723-4000	21792
Stanford Law Schl Off Fncl Aid	7389	D	650 723-9247	17483
Stanford Management Company	8741	C	650 721-2200	27046
Stanford Univ Frman Spgli Inst	8733	C	650 723-8681	26663
Stanford Univ Med Ctr Aux	8322	B	650 723-6636	24071

STANTON, CA - Orange County

Name	SIC	EMP	PHONE	ENTRY #
California Friends Homes	8361	B	714 530-9100	24448
Denver D Darling Inc	1541	C	714 761-8299	1390
Great Scott Tree Service Inc (PA)	0783	C	714 826-1750	974
Haulaway Storage Cntrs Inc	4225	A	800 826-9040	4572
Johnson & Turner Painting Co	1721	E	714 828-8282	2453
Muth Development Co Inc	6512	C	714 527-2239	10916
USS Cal Builders Inc	1542	C	714 828-4882	1691

STEVENSON RANCH, CA - Los Angeles County

Name	SIC	EMP	PHONE	ENTRY #
AT&T Corp	4812	D	661 799-0800	5279
Century Bankcard Services	7389	D	818 700-3100	17066
Global Building Services Inc (PA)	7349	A	661 288-5733	14279

STEVINSON, CA - Merced County

Name	SIC	EMP	PHONE	ENTRY #
Frank J Gomes Dairy A Califo	0241	D	209 669-7978	413
James J Stevinson A Corp (PA)	0241	E	209 632-1681	418
Stevinson Ranch-Savannah GP	7992	D	209 668-8200	18766

STOCKTON, CA - San Joaquin County

Name	SIC	EMP	PHONE	ENTRY #
3900 West Lane Bowl Inc	7933	E	209 466-6100	18476
A G Spanos Management Inc	6531	E	209 478-7954	11187
ABM Janitorial Services Inc	7349	C	209 983-3923	14176
AC Square Inc	8748	C	650 293-2730	27618
Ace Tomato Company Inc	0161	D	209 982-0734	33
Acrt Pacific LLC	8748	B	330 945-7500	27620
Alsha Academy	7021	D	310 908-1962	13437
American Automobile Assctn	8699	E	209 952-4100	25381
American Building Supply	5031	D	209 941-8852	6807
American Cstm Private SEC Inc	7381	D	209 369-1200	16561
American Golf Corporation	7997	E	209 477-4653	18831
American Medical Response West	4119	B	209 948-5136	3770
Ameripride Services Inc	7213	E	209 982-0020	13510
Anand Software Inc	7371	D	209 287-1708	14984
Antonini Freight Express Inc (PA)	4212	C	209 466-4900	3972

Name	SIC	EMP	PHONE	ENTRY #
Aryzta LLC	5149	E	209 469-4920	8756
Ashley Lane Cherry Orchards LP	0175	E	209 546-0426	214
Auto Town Inc	7538	D	209 473-2513	17754
Bank of Stockton (HQ)	6022	C	209 929-1600	9417
Best Western Plus-Heritage Inn	7011	E	209 474-3301	12376
Bockmon & Woody Elc Co Inc	1731	C	209 464-4878	2524
Boretech Resrce Recovry Engine	5084	D	209 373-2588	7733
Borgens & Borgens Inc	7381	D	209 547-2980	16584
Brightview Companies LLC	0781	C	209 993-9277	732
Brookside Country Club	7997	D	209 956-6200	18875
Burlingame Industries Inc	5033	D	209 464-9001	6921
California Guard Inc	7381	D	209 465-8420	16596
California Materials Inc	4212	E	209 472-7422	3986
California Security Cons	7381	C	209 465-8420	16598
California Water Service Co	4941	D	209 547-7900	6217
Canepas Car Wash (PA)	7542	D	209 948-1636	17806
Caraustar Industries Inc	4953	C	209 476-7710	6369
Caremark Rx LLC	8011	C	209 957-7050	19352
Castlehill Properties Inc (PA)	7011	D	209 472-9800	12439
Catholic Charities Diocese (PA)	8322	D	209 444-5900	23532
Chicago Title Insurance Co	6541	D	209 952-5500	11847
Childrens Home of Stockton	8361	D	209 466-0853	24466
Clark Pest Ctrl Stockton Inc	7342	E	209 474-3204	14144
Coastal Pacific Fd Distrs Inc (PA)	5141	C	909 947-2066	8390
Collins Electrical Company Inc (PA)	1731	B	209 466-3691	2544
Comcast Corporation	4841	C	209 955-6521	5886
Comfort Air Inc	1711	D	209 466-4601	2165
Communication Svc For Deaf Inc	8399	E	209 475-5000	24754
Community Medical Centers Inc	8011	D	209 944-4700	19400
Community Medical Centers Inc (PA)	8093	D	209 373-2800	22537
Compass Bank	6022	B	209 473-6925	9438
Compass Bank	6022	B	209 939-3288	9439
County of San Joaquin	8322	B	209 468-2601	23729
County of San Joaquin	8322	D	209 468-4100	23730
County of San Joaquin	8093	B	209 468-8750	22554
County of San Joaquin	8399	D	209 468-3021	24772
County of San Joaquin	8331	C	209 468-3500	24176
Covenant Care California LLC	8051	C	209 477-5252	20337
Covey Auto Express Inc (PA)	7549	C	253 826-0461	17859
Creative Child Care Inc (PA)	8351	B	209 941-9100	24312
Cumulus Intrmdate Holdings Inc	4832	C	209 766-5103	5708
D S S Company	1623	E	209 948-0302	1912
Dameron Hospital Association (PA)	8062	A	209 944-5550	21362
Dbi Beverage San Joaquin	5181	D	209 948-9400	8991
Delta Blood Bank (HQ)	8099	D	800 244-6794	22783
Delta Hawkeye Security Inc	7381	D	209 957-3333	16627
Delta Hlth Care MGT Svcs Corp (PA)	8093	D	209 444-8300	22566
Designers LLC (PA)	7217	D	209 982-0600	13577
Dfa of California	7389	D	209 465-2289	17131
Dignity Health	8071	C	209 467-6430	22077
Dignity Health	8082	D	209 943-4663	22286
Dorfman-Pacific Co (HQ)	5136	C	209 982-1400	8255
Dreamctchers Empwerment Netwrk (PA)	8361	A	209 478-5291	24508
Dreamctchers Empwerment Netwrk	8361	A	209 477-4817	24510
Dynamex Inc	4215	D	209 464-7008	4397
E D D 2100	6321	D	209 941-6501	10164
E J Williams Property MGT	6513	C	209 473-4022	11008
Embarcadero Homes Assn Inc	8641	D	954 776-2611	25154
Employment Training Academy	8699	E	209 475-1529	25419
Estes Express Lines Inc	4213	D	209 982-1841	4144
Exel N Amercn Logistics Inc	4222	A	209 942-0102	4501
Exel N Amercn Logistics Inc	4222	A	209 932-2400	4502
Express Messenger Systems Inc	4215	D	209 234-8255	4401
Express Messenger Systems Inc	4215	D	209 234-8255	4402
Family Resource & Referral Ctr	8322	D	209 948-1553	23796
Farmington Fresh Sales LLC (PA)	0175	C	209 983-9700	217
Federal Express Corporation	4513	E	800 463-3339	4828
Fedex Freight Corporation	4213	D	209 466-7726	4159
First Alarm SEC & Patrol Inc	7382	B	209 473-1110	16893
First Amercn Title of Stockton (PA)	6541	D	209 929-4800	11848
First Student Inc	4151	D	209 466-7737	3927
Five Star Quality Care Inc	8082	E	209 951-6500	22299
Five Star Quality Care Inc	8051	D	209 466-2066	20430
Franke Con J Electric Inc	1731	D	209 462-0717	2589
Friends Outside	8322	C	209 955-0701	23817
Frontier Land Companies	1521	E	209 957-8112	1167
Fsq Rio Las Palmas Business Tr	6513	E	209 957-4711	11024
Fuel Delivery Services Inc	4213	D	209 751-2185	4182
G and L Brock Cnstr Co Inc	1794	E	209 931-3626	3426
Golden Living LLC	8051	D	707 546-0471	20464
Golden Living LLC	8051	D	209 466-3522	20482
Golden State Lumber Inc	5031	C	209 234-7700	6824
Greyhound Lines Inc	4513	E	209 466-3568	4840
Groupe Development Associates	6552	D	209 473-6000	11879
Grupe Company (PA)	6531	D	209 473-6000	11495

Company	SIC	EMP	PHONE	ENTRY #
Grupe Dev Companynorthern Cal	1531	C	209 473-6000	1342
Grupe Properties Co	4225	E	209 956-7885	4569
H and H Drug Stores Inc	5099	D	209 931-5200	8038
Heritage Land Company Inc	0181	E	209 444-1700	266
Holistic Approach Inc	7361	D	209 956-7050	14637
Holt of California	5082	D	209 462-3660	7681
Hospice of San Joaquin	8051	D	209 957-3888	20537
In Shape Management Company	7991	B	209 472-2231	18610
In-Shape Health Clubs LLC (PA)	7991	E	209 472-2231	18611
Inreach Internet LLC (HQ)	4813	D	888 467-3224	5587
International Longshoremens	8631	D	209 464-1827	25064
Interstate Truck Center LLC (PA)	5012	D	209 944-5821	6599
Its Technologies Logistics LLC	4789	D	209 460-6023	5231
J & P Solari	0175		209 931-1765	220
John Aguilar & Company Inc	4212	D	209 546-0171	4030
Jpmorgan Chase Bank Nat Assn	6035	A	209 460-2888	9524
Kaiser Foundation Hospitals	8062	C	209 476-3101	21524
Kimberlite Corporation	7382	D	209 948-2551	16916
Kindred Nursing Centers W LLC	8051	C	209 957-4539	20566
Lafaltte Rhbilitation Care Ctr	8051	D	209 466-2066	20574
Lincoln School Bus Trnsp	4131	C	209 953-8596	3879
Lithia Motors Inc	7538	C	209 956-1930	17771
LLP Moss Adams	8721	E	209 955-6100	26249
Mariner Health Care Inc	8051	C	209 466-2066	20627
Mark Scott Construction Inc	1522	D	209 982-0502	1301
Martin-Brower Company LLC	5141	C	209 466-2980	8427
Maxim Crane Works LP	7353	C	209 464-7635	14448
Meadowood Hlth Rehabilitation	8051	B	209 956-3444	20636
Mexican Heritg Ctr Gallery Inc	8412	D	209 969-9306	24890
Mgd Inc (PA)	6513	D	209 955-0535	11077
Mid State Steel Erection (PA)	1791	D	209 464-9497	3388
Midstate Barrier Inc	1611	D	209 944-9565	1820
Morada Produce Company LP	0723	A	209 546-0426	544
Mountain Valley Express Co Inc (PA)	4213	D	209 823-2168	4231
Mv Transportation Inc	4111	D	209 547-7879	3686
New Stockton Poultry Inc	5144	E	209 466-1952	8536
OConner Woods A California	6513	C	209 956-3400	11088
OConnor Woods Housing Corp	6513	D	209 955-3400	11089
Pacific Coast Services Inc	8082	A	209 956-2532	22387
Pacific Gas and Electric Co	4911	D	209 942-1787	6088
Pacific Metro Electric Inc	1731	D	209 939-3222	2669
Pacific State Bancorp	6035	D	209 870-3214	9527
PDM Steel Service Centers (HQ)	5051	D	209 943-0555	7299
PDM Steel Service Centers	5051	C	209 234-0548	7300
Pearl Crop Inc (PA)	0723	D	209 808-7575	553
Permanente Medical Group Inc	8011	D	209 476-3737	19785
Permanente Medical Group Inc	8011	E	209 476-2000	19786
Pinasco Plumbing & Heating Inc	1711	E	209 463-7793	2309
Progressive Services Inc	1761	D	209 824-2837	3191
Reeve Trucking Company Inc (PA)	4213	D	209 948-4061	4249
Reliance Intermodal Inc	5141	D	209 946-0200	8446
Retirement Housing Foundation	6531	D	209 466-4341	11732
Sahargun Plumbing Inc	1711	D	209 474-2611	2346
Salvation Army	8093	D	209 466-3871	22670
San Joaquin Cnty Aging & Commu	8322	C	209 468-9455	24024
San Joaquin Regional Trnst Dst	4111	C	209 948-5566	3716
Scan-Vino LLC (PA)	4213	D	209 931-3570	4259
Schuff Steel Company	1791	D	209 938-0869	3397
Securitas SEC Svcs USA Inc	7381	C	209 943-1401	16789
Sierra Health Services LLC	8721	E	209 956-7725	26292
Signode Industrial Group LLC	5084	D	209 931-0917	7798
Smg	8744	B	209 937-7433	27605
Southwest Traders Incorporated	5141	C	209 462-1607	8461
St Joseph Community Home Care	8082	D	209 478-9547	22423
St Joseph Surgery Center LP	8011	D	209 467-6316	19938
St Josephs Med Ctr Stockton	8062	A	209 943-2000	21784
St Josephs Medical Center	8062	C	209 943-2000	21785
Standard Industries Inc	5033	E	209 242-5000	6930
State Compensation Insur Fund	6331	C	888 782-8338	10404
Stockton Cardiology Medical Gr (PA)	8011	E	209 994-5750	19951
Stockton Congregational Home	8361	D	209 466-4341	24687
Stockton Edson Healthcare Corp	8059	D	209 948-8762	21224
Stockton Hotel Ltd	7011	D	209 957-9090	13283
Stockton Orthpd Med Group Inc	8011	E	209 948-1641	19952
Stockton Port District	4491	D	209 946-0246	4741
Stone Bros Management (PA)	6552	D	209 478-1791	11923
Storer Transportation	4111	D	209 644-5100	3731
Sugar Transport of The NW	4212	D	209 931-3587	4067
Sunbridge Healthcare LLC	8051	D	209 477-4817	20791
Sygma Network Inc	5141	C	209 932-5300	8464
Table Community Foudation	8641	D	209 951-1753	25264
Thompson & Rich Crane Service	7389	E	209 465-3161	17507
Tire & Wheel Master Inc	5014	C	209 465-9000	6696
Tranquilmoney Inc	5045	D	800 979-6739	7118
Unified Grocers Inc	5141	C	209 931-1990	8475
Unifirst Corporation	7218	E	209 941-8364	13623
United Cerebral Palsy Assoc (PA)	8621	C	209 956-0290	25048
United Cerebral Palsy Associat	8069	C	209 956-0295	22056
United Rentals North Amer Inc	7359	D	209 948-9500	14550
University of Pacific	7999	A	209 946-2030	19254
US Security Associates Inc	7381	C	209 476-7062	16852
USA Waste of California Inc	4212	E	209 946-5721	4079
USG Interiors LLC	5031	D	209 466-4636	6871
Valley Cmnty Counseling Svcs (PA)	8322	D	209 956-4240	24106
Valley Mtn Regional Ctr Inc (PA)	8322	C	209 473-0951	24107
Valley Wholesale Drug Co LLC	5122	D	209 466-0131	8217
Van De Pol Enterprises Inc (PA)	5172	D	209 465-3421	8972
Villa Real Inc	8748	D	209 460-5069	27900
Village West Yacht Club	7997	D	209 478-8992	19077
Volt Management Corp	7363	C	209 952-5627	14940
Westland Hotel Corporation	7011	E	209 931-3131	13394
Williams Tank Lines (PA)	4213	D	209 944-5613	4305
Wm Michael Stemler Inc (PA)	6411	D	209 948-8483	10834
Womens Center-Youth Fmly Svcs (PA)	8322	C	209 941-2611	24135
World Class Distribution Inc	4225	C	909 574-4140	4661
Wtmg Inc (PA)	7349	D	209 954-1599	14428
Xpo Logistics Freight Inc	4213	D	209 983-8285	4309
YMCA of San Joaquin County	8641	D	209 472-9622	25308
Yuen SOO Benevolent Assn	8641	C	209 464-3048	25368
Zeiter Eye Medical Group Inc (PA)	8011	D	209 366-0446	20105

STRATFORD, CA - Kings County

Company	SIC	EMP	PHONE	ENTRY #
Crisp Warehouse Inc	0723	D	559 947-9221	505
Stone Land Company (PA)	0131	D	559 947-3185	15

STRATHMORE, CA - Tulare County

Company	SIC	EMP	PHONE	ENTRY #
Golden Valley Citrus Inc	0723	D	559 568-1768	519
Lopez Harvesting	0722	D	559 568-2553	479

STUDIO CITY, CA - Los Angeles County

Company	SIC	EMP	PHONE	ENTRY #
American Private Duty Inc	8082	D	818 386-6358	22220
Blayne Pacelli	6531	D	310 383-6281	11246
CBS Broadcasting Inc	4833	B	818 655-2000	5774
Cellco Partnership	4812	D	818 980-4200	5359
Commercial Prgrm Systems Inc (PA)	7379	C	818 308-8560	16329
Crown Media United States LLC (DH)	4841	D	818 755-2400	5897
Dpr Holdings LLC	6719	E	323 761-9829	11975
Dream Lounge Inc	5136	A	213 688-7888	8256
Enrichment Eductl Experiences	8351	D	818 989-7509	24318
Everett Mall 01 LLC	6519	E	818 505-6777	11172
Fort Hill Construction (PA)	1521	D	323 661-7425	1165
Gavin De Becker & Associates	8742	C	818 760-4213	27245
High Technology Video Inc	7819	C	323 969-9822	18195
Jpmorgan Chase Bank Nat Assn	6021	E	818 763-7343	9350
Longwood Management Corp	8059	C	818 980-8200	21143
Motion Pcture Hlth Wlfare Fund	6371	C	818 769-0007	10488
Motion Picture Industry Plans	6371	C	818 769-0007	10489
Music Collective LLC	7819	E	818 508-3303	18203
Northridge 07 A LLC	6512	E	818 505-6777	10920
Radford Studio Center Inc	7922	B	818 655-5000	18398
Ranch Hand Entertainment Inc	7812	D	612 396-2632	18104
Rodeo Realty Inc	6531	C	818 308-8273	11738
Sierra Vista 16 A LLC	6512	E	818 505-6777	10941
Sportsmens Lodge Hotel LLC	7011	C	818 769-4700	13256
Sunrise Senior Living LLC	8051	C	818 505-8484	20824
Universal Studios Inc	7812	C	818 777-2351	18144
Wurzel Landscape Maintenance	0782	E	818 762-8653	963

SUISUN CITY, CA - Solano County

Company	SIC	EMP	PHONE	ENTRY #
Cement Mason Health & Welfare	8399	D	707 864-3300	24751
Dropcar Inc	4813	D	707 421-1300	5551
E B Stone & Son Inc	5191	D	707 426-2500	9078
Hal-Mar-Jac Enterprises	7381	C	415 467-1470	16694
Redevelopment Agency of The Ci	8748	D	707 421-7309	27840
Walker Communications Inc	1731	D	707 421-1300	2782

SUN CITY, CA - Riverside County

Company	SIC	EMP	PHONE	ENTRY #
Compass Bank	6021	B	951 672-4829	9343
Physicians For Healthy Hospita	8062	B	951 679-8888	21643
Sun City Rhf Housing Inc	8361	D	951 679-2391	24691
United Parcel Service Inc OH	4513	C	951 928-5221	4850

SUN VALLEY, CA - Los Angeles County

Company	SIC	EMP	PHONE	ENTRY #
Aadlen Brothers Auto Wrecking (PA)	5093	D	323 875-1400	7964
Alcorn Fence Company (PA)	1799	C	818 983-0650	3481
Araco Enterprises LLC	4953	B	818 767-0675	6339
Arakelian Enterprises Inc	4953	C	818 768-0689	6340
Arakelian Enterprises Inc	4212	C	818 768-1492	3973
Arcadia Transit Inc	4111	E	818 252-0630	3639
Beacon Roofing Supply Inc	5085	C	818 768-4661	7838
Browning-Ferris Industries Inc	4953	C	818 790-5410	6360
Ceramic Tile Art Inc	1743	D	818 767-9088	2990

Mergent email: customerrelations@mergent.com
1692

2019 Directory of California
Wholesalers and Services Companies

(P-0000) Products & Services Section entry number
(PA)=Parent Co (HQ)=Headquarters (DH)=Div Headquarters

Company	SIC	EMP	PHONE	ENTRY #
Coast To Coast Water Damage	7349	E	818 255-3323	14219
Crown Disposal Company Inc	4953	C	818 767-0675	6387
CSC Auto Salv Dismantling Inc	4731	D	818 532-4624	5038
Daybreak Care Center (PA)	8361	E	818 504-6154	24501
Dazian LLC	5131	D	818 287-3800	8224
Estes Express Lines Inc	4213	D	818 504-4155	4143
Express Messenger Systems Inc	4215	C	818 504-9043	4405
Fathers of St Charles	6513	C	818 768-6500	11017
Federal Express Corporation	4512	C	800 463-3339	4780
Fedex Freight Corporation	4213	D	818 899-1141	4158
Fedex Ground Package Sys Inc	4213	D	800 463-3339	4177
Hawker Pacific Aerospace	7699	B	818 765-6201	17949
JP Motorsports Inc	4119	D	818 381-8313	3811
LA Hydro-Jet Rooter Svc Inc	7699	D	818 768-4225	17961
Landco	0782	D	818 612-0118	888
Los Angeles County MTA	4111	B	213 922-6215	3674
Los Angeles Dept Wtr & Pwr	4941	A	213 367-1342	6274
Mission Valley Bancorp	6712	C	818 394-2300	11956
Mountain View Child Care Inc	8351	C	818 252-5863	24351
Nicola International Inc	5149	C	818 767-1133	8840
Norman Industrial Mtls Inc (PA)	5051	B	818 729-3333	7293
Northeast Valley Health Corp	8099	D	818 432-4400	22849
Option Care Home Care Inc	8082	D	818 351-3000	22384
Pacific Pavingstone Inc	1771	C	818 244-4000	3300
Pacifica of Valley Corporation	8062	A	818 767-3310	21623
PBM Maintenance Corp	7349	B	818 771-1100	14344
Pena Grading & Demolition Inc	1611	C	818 768-5202	1837
Penske Truck Rental Inc	7513	E	818 718-2536	17612
PRI Medical Technologies Inc (DH)	5047	D	818 394-2800	7212
Pro Ponds West Inc	0781	D	818 244-4000	779
Quixote Studios LLC	7519	D	818 252-7722	17660
Rawlings Mechanical Corp (PA)	1711	D	323 875-2040	2330
Refrigeration Hdwr Sup Corp	5078	E	818 768-3636	7665
Reliable Carriers Inc	4213	E	818 252-6400	4250
REM Optical Company Inc	5049	C	818 504-3950	7247
Rose Brand Wipers Inc	7922	D	818 505-6290	18399
SA Recycling LLC	4953	D	323 875-2520	6459
San Gabriel Transit Inc	4121	D	818 771-0374	3869
Serra Community Med Clinic Inc	8011	C	818 768-3000	19878
Serra Medical Clinic Inc	8011	C	818 768-3000	19879
Smg Stone Company Inc	1741	D	818 767-0000	2823
Smokehouse Pet Products Inc	5149	E	818 771-0181	8869
Sugar Foods Corporation	7389	C	818 768-7900	17490
Sugar Foods Corporation	7389	D	818 768-7900	17491
Svd Inc	5143	D	818 504-1775	8529
Title Records Inc	6541	D	818 767-9610	11850
USA Waste of California Inc	4953	D	818 252-3112	6489
Waste Management Cal Inc (HQ)	4953	C	877 836-6526	6510
Wet (PA)	7389	D	818 769-6200	17594

SUNLAND, CA - Los Angeles County

Company	SIC	EMP	PHONE	ENTRY #
Brightview Tree Company	0811	C	818 951-5500	987
New Vista Health Services	8059	C	818 352-1421	21165
P R N Convalescent Hospital	8051	D	818 352-3158	20685
Patriot Brokerage LLC	4731	D	910 227-4142	5138
Shadow Hlls Cnvlscent Hosp Inc	8051	D	818 352-4438	20754
Tierra Del Sol Foundation (PA)	8361	C	818 352-1419	24698
Wimer Construction	1542	E	818 848-0400	1704

SUNNYVALE, CA - Santa Clara County

Company	SIC	EMP	PHONE	ENTRY #
Al-Tar Services Inc	7699	D	866 522-3499	17929
Alvarion Inc (HQ)	5065	E	650 314-2500	7436
AT&T Corp	8999	D	650 960-2313	27921
Avenuesocial Inc	7371	C	510 275-4485	15011
Backproject Corporation	5047	D	408 730-1111	7159
Belmont Village LP	6513	D	408 720-8498	10984
Bmi Imaging Systems Inc (PA)	7374	C	916 924-6666	16100
Broadsoft Contact Center Inc	7371	E	408 338-0900	15039
Cashedge Inc	7389	D	408 541-3900	17061
Chelsio Communications Inc	7371	C	408 962-3600	15056
City of Sunnyvale	7041	D	408 730-7451	13474
City of Sunnyvale	7389	D	408 730-7510	17083
Clover Network Inc	4813	D	650 210-7888	5533
Coadna Holdings Inc (HQ)	6719	D	408 736-1100	11970
Compvue Inc	7371	D	408 892-9909	15075
Comtel Systems Technology	1731	D	408 543-5600	2549
Contactual Inc	7372	E	650 292-2408	15636
Crowdstrike Inc (HQ)	7379	C	888 512-8906	16335
Cyphort Inc	5045	E	408 841-4665	7031
De Anza Square Shopping Center	1531	D	408 738-4444	1335
Drchrono Inc	7371	E	650 600-2079	15120
Druva Inc (HQ)	7372	D	650 241-3501	15657
Egain Corporation (PA)	7372	C	408 636-4500	15661
Entco LLC (DH)	7372	B	312 580-9100	15668
Enterprise Signal Inc	7372	D	877 256-8303	15669
Evergent Technologies Inc	7371	D	408 718-5453	15150
Exablox Corporation	7375	D	408 773-8477	16223
Executive Inn Inc	7011	D	408 245-5330	12569
Federal Express Corporation	4513	D	800 463-3339	4820
Financial Engines LLC (HQ)	8742	C	408 498-6000	27234
Fiserv Inc	7374	D	408 242-3011	16134
Fortinet Inc (PA)	7372	C	408 235-7700	15682
Fujitsu America Inc (DH)	7373	B	408 746-6000	15961
Fujitsu Computer Pdts Amer Inc (HQ)	5045	B	408 746-7000	7050
Fujitsu Electronics Amer Inc (DH)	8711	D	408 737-5600	25695
Fujitsu Laboratories Amer Inc (DH)	8731	D	408 530-4500	26368
Future Dial Incorporated	7379	D	408 245-8880	16372
Ghc of Sunnyvale LLC	8059	C	408 738-4880	21081
Giva Inc	7371	D	408 260-9000	15179
Goodman Usa Inc	8011	D	408 329-5400	19487
Guck Ariba	7372	C	650 390-1445	15698
Hcl America Inc (DH)	7376	D	408 733-0480	16270
Hcr Manorcare Med Svcs Fla LLC	8051	D	408 735-7200	20512
Headstrong Corporation	7379	D	408 732-8700	16389
Honeywell International Inc	5065	E	408 962-2000	7489
Horizon Technologies Inc	5045	C	408 733-1530	7059
Hpt Trs Ihg-2 Inc	7011	E	408 745-1515	12738
Idec Corporation (HQ)	5065	D	408 747-0550	7492
Illumio Inc	7371	C	669 800-5000	15211
Indium Software Inc	7372	C	408 501-8844	15709
Inko Industrial Corporation	7374	D	408 830-1040	16148
Innopath Software Inc (PA)	7371	D	408 962-9200	15214
Intertrust Technologies Corp (HQ)	7371	C	408 616-1600	15233
Ipolipo Inc	7372	D	408 916-5290	15724
Island Hospitality MGT LLC	7011	D	408 720-1000	12781
Island Hospitality MGT LLC	7011	D	408 720-8893	12783
Jfrog Inc (PA)	7371	D	408 329-1540	15241
Joie De Vivre Hospitality Inc	7011	D	408 738-0500	12792
Juniper Networks Inc	7373	A	408 745-2000	15987
Juniper Networks Inc	7373	A	888 586-4737	15990
Kaiser Foundation Hospitals	8011	A	408 851-1000	19589
Level 10 Construction LP	1542	C	408 747-5000	1580
Linkedin Corporation (HQ)	7375	C	650 687-3600	16236
Luxn Inc	4899	D	408 213-7437	5988
Microsoft Corporation	7372	C	650 964-7200	15759
Microsoft Corporation	7372	C	650 693-1009	15761
Mlslistings Inc	8742	D	408 874-0200	27349
Mocana Corporation	7374	D	415 617-0055	16160
Moreno & Associates Inc	7349	D	408 924-0353	14328
Mp Morse Court Associates	6514	D	408 734-9442	11152
Netapp Inc	7373	C	408 822-3402	16013
Netapp Inc	7373	C	408 419-5301	16015
Nuance Communications Inc	7372	C	781 565-5000	15786
Ooma Inc (PA)	4813	C	650 566-6600	5617
Opal Soft Inc	7379	D	408 267-2211	16442
Oracle Corporation	7372	B	650 607-5402	15799
Osram Opto Semiconductors Inc	5065	D	408 588-3800	7521
Osram Opto Semiconductors Inc (HQ)	5065	E	408 962-3736	7522
Palo Alto Medical Foundation	8011	D	408 730-4390	19751
Palo Alto Medical Foundation	8011	D	408 524-5900	19752
Panasas Inc (PA)	7371	D	408 215-6800	15344
Pareto Networks Inc	4813	C	877 727-8020	5621
Parkinsons Institute	8733	D	800 786-2958	26647
Personagraph Corporation	7371	D	408 616-1600	15355
Pivotcloud Inc	7371	E	408 475-6090	15362
Playphone Inc (PA)	7371	D	408 261-6200	15565
Plug & Play LLC	6799	C	408 524-1400	12259
Polaris Home Care LLC	8082	D	408 400-7020	22396
Polyvore Inc	5199	D	650 968-1195	9250
Positea Inv & Pub Relations	8743	E	408 736-1120	27570
Proofpoint Inc (PA)	7371	C	408 517-4710	15383
Qsolv Inc	7373	C	408 429-0918	16037
Qubera Solutions Inc	7379	E	650 294-4460	16467
Real-Time Innovations Inc	7371	D	408 990-7400	15398
Redseal Inc	7372	C	408 641-2200	15841
Ruckus Wireless Inc (HQ)	4813	C	650 265-4200	5637
S R H H Inc	7011	E	408 247-0800	13156
SC Builders Inc (PA)	1542	D	408 328-0688	1641
Screen Spe Usa LLC (DH)	5065	C	408 523-9140	7540
Selvi-Vidovich LP	7011	D	408 720-8500	13205
Sendmail Inc	4813	D	510 594-5400	5640
Sensity Systems Inc (HQ)	8748	D	408 841-4200	27858
Silicon Valley Exec Netwrk	8748	A	408 746-5803	27860
Siliconsage Construction Inc	1522	C	408 916-3205	1316
Software AG Usa Inc	7371	C	703 860-5050	15460
Star One Credit Union (PA)	6061	C	408 543-5202	9596
Stormgeo (DH)	8999	C	408 731-8600	27959
Streamvector Inc	7371	D	760 203-3257	15478
Sunnyside Gardens	8361	D	408 730-4070	24693
Sunnyvale Healthcare Center	8051	D	408 245-8070	20794
Sunnyvale Sof-X Owner L P	7011	E	408 542-8264	13288

Employment Codes: A=Over 500 employees, B=251-500,
C=101-250, D=51-100, E=50

2019 Directory of California
Wholesalers and Services Companies

© Mergent Inc. 1-800-342-5647

1693

GEOGRAPHIC

	SIC	EMP	PHONE	ENTRY #
Sunrise Senior Living LLC	8051	D	408 749-8600	20822
Supportcom Inc (PA)	7374	D	650 556-9440	16184
Sutter Health	8011	C	408 733-4380	19976
Teraburst Networks Inc	4899	C	408 400-4100	6000
Texas Instruments Sunnyvale	7389	E	408 541-9900	17506
Toyota-Sunnyvale Inc (PA)	7538	C	408 245-6640	17789
Tri-Power Group Inc	4899	D	925 583-8200	6002
UPS Ground Freight Inc	4213	D	408 400-0595	4291
US Interactive Delaware	7311	C	408 863-7500	13914
US Interactive Delaware (PA)	8711	C	408 863-7500	25986
W L Hickey Sons Inc	1711	C	408 736-4938	2402
W2005 New Cntury Ht Prtflio LP	7011	D	408 745-6000	13375
Waste Connections Cal Inc	4953	C	408 752-8530	6508
West Valley Engineering Inc (PA)	7363	D	408 735-1420	14944
Westak International Sales Inc (HQ)	5065	C	408 734-8686	7563
Wm ONeill Lath and Plst Corp	1742	E	408 329-1413	2985
Xoriant Corporation (PA)	7379	C	408 743-4400	16538
Zspace Inc	5063	D	408 498-4050	7406
Zyrion Inc	7372	D	408 524-7424	15904

SUNOL, CA - Alameda County

	SIC	EMP	PHONE	ENTRY #
Brightview Tree Company	0811	D	925 862-2485	989
Save Our Sunol	8641	D	925 862-2263	25242

SUSANVILLE, CA - Lassen County

	SIC	EMP	PHONE	ENTRY #
Banner Health	8062	C	530 251-3147	21295
Banner Lassen Medical Center	8062	C	530 252-2000	21296
Diamond Mountain Casino	7011	C	530 252-1100	12520
Golden 1 Credit Union	6062	C	530 251-0205	9637
Honey Lake Hospice Inc	5047	D	530 257-3137	7184
Northeastern Rur Hlth Clinics (PA)	8011	D	530 251-5000	19722
Sierra-Cascade Nursery Inc (PA)	0181	B	530 254-6867	302

SUTTER CREEK, CA - Amador County

	SIC	EMP	PHONE	ENTRY #
Amador Water Agency	4941	D	209 223-3018	6207
American Legion Ambulance Svc	8641	D	209 223-2963	25091
Resource Connection of Amador	8322	D	209 223-7685	23993

SYLMAR, CA - Los Angeles County

	SIC	EMP	PHONE	ENTRY #
A A Gonzalez Inc	1742	D	818 367-2242	2833
Allied Beverage LLC	5078	B	818 493-6400	7661
Allied Company Holdings Inc (PA)	5181	D	818 493-6400	8977
American Residential Svcs LLC	1711	D	818 833-6677	2116
Aramark Unf & Career AP LLC	7218	D	818 364-8272	13594
Astoria Convalescent Hospital	8051	C	818 367-5881	20238
Becho Inc	1611	D	818 362-8391	1730
Build Rehabilitation Inds (PA)	8331	D	818 485-8560	24159
Canyon Properties III LLC	8059	D	818 890-0430	21031
County of Los Angeles	8062	D	818 364-1555	21351
County of Los Angeles	8361	D	818 364-2011	24480
Desert Mechanical Inc	1711	A	702 873-7333	2185
Fisk Electric Company	1731	C	818 884-1166	2586
Foothill Waste Reclamation Inc	4953	C	818 897-5099	6401
G and E Healthcare Svcs LLC	8051	C	818 367-5881	20444
Garda CL Technical Svcs Inc	7381	D	818 362-7011	16659
Golden State Health Ctrs Inc	8063	D	818 834-5082	21956
Lopez Canyon Landfill	4953	C	818 834-5122	6411
Morrison MGT Specialists Inc	8741	D	818 364-4219	26952
Mountain View Cnvalescent Hosp.	8051	E	818 367-1033	20655
Oak Springs Nursery Inc	4971	D	818 367-5832	6560
Olive View-Ucla Medical Center (PA)	8011	D	818 364-1555	19731
Olive View/Ucla Education &	8733	D	818 364-3434	26645
Pearson Dental Supplies Inc (PA)	5047	D	818 362-2600	7207
Quality Long Term Care Nev Inc	8051	D	818 361-0191	20713
Quinn Company	5082	D	818 767-7171	7686
Reyes Coca-Cola Bottling LLC	5149	D	818 362-4307	8860
Schindler Elevator Corporation	7699	C	818 336-3000	17984
Security Paving Company Inc (PA)	1611	C	818 362-9200	1846
Sigue Corporation (PA)	7389	D	818 837-5939	17470
Spears Manufacturing Co (PA)	5083	C	818 364-1611	7713
Superior Gunite (PA)	1771	C	818 896-9199	3333
Sylmar Hlth Rehabilitation Ctr	8063	C	818 834-5082	21974
Tony Marquez Pool Plst Inc	1742	D	818 833-5872	2970
Tri-Signal Integration Inc (PA)	1731	D	818 566-8558	2770
Tutor Perini Corporation (PA)	1542	C	818 362-8391	1688
Tutor-Saliba Corporation (HQ)	1542	D	818 362-8391	1689
United Cp/S Chldrns Fndn La	8059	D	818 364-5911	21237
United Parcel Service Inc.	4215	D	800 742-5877	4441
University Cal Los Angeles	8062	A	818 364-1555	21875
Wildlife Waystation	8699	E	818 899-5201	25485
Winning Performance Pdts Inc	7389	E	818 367-1041	17598

TAFT, CA - Kern County

	SIC	EMP	PHONE	ENTRY #
Alloy Construction Inc	1629	D	661 203-2592	2005
Braun Electric Company Inc	1731	C	661 763-1531	2526
County of Kern	8322	D	661 763-1535	23649
County of Kern	7999	E	661 763-4246	19153

	SIC	EMP	PHONE	ENTRY #
Gene Watson Construction A CA	1389	A	661 763-5254	1060
General Production Svc Cal Inc	1623	C	661 765-5330	1920
Geo Group Inc	8744	B	661 763-2510	27590
Jerry Melton & Sons Cnstr	1389	A	661 765-5546	1067
Mashburn Trnsp Svcs Inc	4213	C	661 763-5724	4220
Providence Service Corporation	8093	E	661 765-7025	22655
Taft College Children Center	8351	E	661 763-7850	24390
Taft Production Company	1241	D	661 765-7194	1011
Watkins Construction Co Inc	1623	D	661 763-5395	2000
West Side District Hospital	8062	C	805 763-4211	21914

TAHOE CITY, CA - Placer County

	SIC	EMP	PHONE	ENTRY #
Bruce Olson Construction Inc	1522	D	530 581-1087	1271
Granlibakken Management Co Ltd	7011	D	800 543-3221	12615
John Brink General Contractor	1611	E	530 583-2005	1798
Pepper Tree Inn	7011	D	530 583-3711	13056
Sunnyside Resort	7011	D	530 583-7200	13287

TARZANA, CA - Los Angeles County

	SIC	EMP	PHONE	ENTRY #
Advanced Medical Placement	8399	C	818 996-9812	24729
Airey Enterprises LLC	5088	E	818 530-3362	7905
AMI-Hti Tarzana Encino Joint V	8062	A	818 881-0800	21284
Amisub of California Inc (DH)	8062	A	818 881-0800	21286
Attorney Recovery Systems Inc (PA)	7322	D	818 774-1420	13992
Blue Sky Services Inc	4731	C	818 609-8779	5018
Braemar Country Club Inc	7997	C	323 873-6880	18872
Drum Security Service Inc	7381	D	818 708-7914	16633
El Caballero Country Club	7997	C	818 654-3000	18918
Guardnow Inc (PA)	7381	E	877 482-7366	16675
Institute For Applied Behavior	8049	C	818 881-1933	20183
JB Partners Group Inc.	6531	C	818 668-8201	11530
National Organization of.	8099	C	800 489-0210	22844
Nurturing Tots Inc	8351	D	818 996-1602	24355
Providence Tarzana Medical Ctr	8062	A	818 881-0800	21676
Shapp International Trdg Inc	5031	C	818 348-3000	6863
Sinanian Development Inc	1542	D	818 990-9666	1651
Tarzana Treatment Centers Inc (PA)	8093	C	818 996-1051	22692
Wasserman Comden & Casselman (PA)	8111	D	323 872-0995	23427
Zohar Construction Inc	1521	D	818 609-7473	1262

TECATE, CA - San Diego County

	SIC	EMP	PHONE	ENTRY #
Temarry Recycling Inc	4953	D	619 270-9453	6482

TEHACHAPI, CA - Kern County

	SIC	EMP	PHONE	ENTRY #
Bear Valley Springs Assn	8641	C	661 821-5537	25098
Galice Inc	7389	D	323 731-8200	17179
Pjbs Holdings Inc (PA)	4953	D	661 822-5273	6428
Selecta Products Inc (PA)	5063	D	661 823-7050	7393
Tehachapi Vly Healthcare Dst (PA)	8399	C	661 750-4848	24847
Worldwind Services LLC	1731	D	661 822-4877	2791

TEMECULA, CA - Riverside County

	SIC	EMP	PHONE	ENTRY #
Altaf Zahid Engineering Svcs	7389	E	760 481-9072	16996
Bank America National Assn	6021	D	951 676-4114	9294
Bbk Performance Inc.	5013	D	951 296-1771	6626
Berkadia Commercial Mrtg LLC	6531	D	951 506-2787	11237
Calavo Growers Inc.	5148	E	951 676-7331	8647
Cellco Partnership	4812	C	951 296-3499	5305
Charles Schwab Corporation	7389	C	951 587-2840	17072
County of Riverside	8322	C	951 600-6500	23709
Cutting Edge Staffing Inc	7361	C	951 587-0550	14597
Eco Farm Field Inc	0762	C	951 676-4047	689
Eco Farms Avocados Inc (PA)	0723	D	951 694-3013	509
Eco Farms Sales Inc (PA)	5148	D	951 694-3013	8674
Edwards Theatres Circuit Inc	7832	D	951 296-0144	18297
F M Tarbell Co	6531	C	951 303-0307	11435
Fff Enterprises Inc (PA)	5122	B	951 296-2500	8168
Freedom Solar Services	1711	D	951 696-9506	2213
Homeland Security Services Inc	7382	B	714 956-2200	16902
HRP Capital Inc.	8741	D	951 676-0171	26889
Inland Erosion Control Svcs	1794	D	951 301-8334	3430
Inland Valley Business and Com	8699	D	951 378-5316	25433
Irri-Scape Construction Inc.	0782	D	951 694-6936	862
Kaiser Foundation Hospitals	6324	D	866 984-7483	10228
Kelly Moses Floors	1743	E	951 296-5147	3001
Kenedco Inc	7389	D	951 699-9339	17271
Lewis Brsbois Bsgard Smith LLP	8111	D	951 252-6150	23205
MBK Senior Living LLC	8059	D	951 506-5555	21155
McCusker Enterprises Inc	8351	D	951 699-9777	24347
McMillan Farm Management	8741	C	951 676-2045	26941
McMillin Communities Inc	1521	A	951 506-3303	1199
Medley Communications Inc (PA)	1731	C	951 245-5200	2645
Michael Baker Intl Inc	8711	D	951 676-8042	25821
Miles Construction Group Inc	1521	E	951 260-2504	1205
Neighborhood Healthcare	8099	C	951 225-6400	22846
Oreq Corporation	8741	E	951 296-5076	26969
Partners In Leadership LLC (HQ)	8742	D	951 694-5596	27389

Mergent email: customerrelations@mergent.com
1694

2019 Directory of California
Wholesalers and Services Companies

(P-0000) Products & Services Section entry number
(PA)=Parent Co (HQ)=Headquarters (DH)=Div Headquarters

	SIC	EMP	PHONE	ENTRY #
Partners In Leadership Interme **(PA)**	8742	D	951 506-6878	27390
Pechanga Development Corp	7011	A	951 695-4655	13054
Peed Equipment Company	7353	E	951 657-0900	14453
Phs / Mwa **(HQ)**	4581	E	950 695-1008	4904
Ponte Vineyard Inn	7011	D	951 587-6688	13073
Primerica Financial Svcs Inc	6411	D	951 695-4325	10739
Professional Hospital Sup Inc **(HQ)**	5047	A	951 699-5000	7213
Pslq Inc	1522	D	951 795-4260	1309
Raintree Systems Inc	7371	D	951 252-9400	15395
Rancho California Water Dst **(PA)**	4941	C	951 296-6900	6297
Rancho West Landscape	0782	E	951 301-3979	928
Rancon Real Estate Corporation **(PA)**	6531	D	951 677-1800	11704
Responsible Med Solutions Corp	8011	E	951 308-0024	19820
Richard Burns MD	8011	D	951 296-9300	19823
RR Donnelley & Sons Company	5112	D	951 296-2890	8088
Sears Roebuck and Co	7549	D	951 719-3528	17871
Securitas SEC Svcs USA Inc	7381	C	951 676-3954	16802
Sft Realty Galway Downs LLC	6531	D	951 232-1880	11760
Sierra Pacific Farms Inc **(PA)**	0762	D	951 699-9980	712
Solex Contracting Inc	1623	D	951 308-1706	1981
Southern California Tele Co **(PA)**	4813	C	951 693-1880	5647
Southwest Traders Incorporated **(PA)**	5141	C	951 699-7800	8462
Spectrum MGT Holdg Co LLC	4841	D	951 587-8660	5935
Springleaf Fincl Holdings LLC	8742	C	951 296-0135	27463
T B Penick & Sons Inc	1521	C	951 719-1492	1245
Talentscale LLC	8711	D	951 744-0053	25940
Temecula Valley Unified School	4151	B	951 695-7110	3946
Walz Group LLC **(HQ)**	7371	D	951 491-6800	15541
Wedgewood Hspitality Group Inc	7299	E	951 491-8110	13780
Wholesale Air-Time Inc	4813	E	951 693-1880	5677
Windsor Capital Group Inc	7011	D	951 676-5656	13408

TEMPLE CITY, CA - Los Angeles County

	SIC	EMP	PHONE	ENTRY #
Community Care Adhc Inc	8322	D	626 614-8999	23601
Fran-Jom Inc	8059	D	626 443-3028	21068
Golden State Health Ctrs Inc	8059	C	626 579-0310	21097
Santa Anita Convalescent Hospi	8051	C	626 579-0310	20747
Temple Garden Homes Inc	8361	E	626 286-6408	24695
Western Tear-Off & Disposal	1761	D	626 443-9984	3210

TEMPLETON, CA - San Luis Obispo County

	SIC	EMP	PHONE	ENTRY #
Grants Custom Cabinets	1521	C	805 466-9680	1173
Mesa Vineyard Management Inc **(PA)**	0762	D	805 434-4100	699
Pacific Coast Supply LLC	5031	D	805 434-4800	6846
Pacific Gas and Electric Co	4911	D	805 434-4418	6096
Twin Cities Community Hosp Inc	8011	B	805 434-3500	20014
Wilshire Health and Cmnty Svcs	8059	D	805 434-3035	21257

TERRA BELLA, CA - Tulare County

	SIC	EMP	PHONE	ENTRY #
Setton Pstchio Terra Bella Inc **(HQ)**	5149	D	559 535-6050	8866
Sierra Forest Products	5031	C	559 535-4893	6864

THERMAL, CA - Riverside County

	SIC	EMP	PHONE	ENTRY #
Drake Larson Ranchs	0172	C	760 399-5494	141
Golden Acres Farms	0161	E	760 399-1923	60
Golden State Herbs **(PA)**	0181	E	760 342-7117	263
Gomez Farm Labor Contg Inc	0761	D	760 399-1994	650
Interntnal Pvment Slutions Inc	1771	D	909 794-2101	3268
James Fedor Masonry Inc	1741	D	760 772-3036	2813
Kono Farms Incorporated	0161	C	760 397-7110	65
North Shore Greenhouses Inc	0182	C	760 397-0400	319
Red Earth Casino	7011	C	760 395-1200	13105
Torres-Martinez	7011	C	760 395-1200	13332
West Coast Aggregate Supply	1442	E	760 342-7598	1096

THOUSAND OAKS, CA - Ventura County

	SIC	EMP	PHONE	ENTRY #
A P R Inc	7363	C	805 379-3400	14806
American Golf Corporation	7997	D	805 495-5407	18827
American Services and Products	7349	D	805 375-2858	14194
Amgen Pharmaceuticals Inc	8733	A	805 447-1000	26592
Bauer Hockey Inc	5091	B	818 782-6445	7923
Bead Society	8699	C	805 495-2550	25397
Bob Dillon Construction Inc	1751	C	805 495-2607	3019
Bright Horizons Chld Ctrs LLC	8351	C	805 447-6793	24268
California Kidney Med Group	8011	C	805 497-7775	19342
Calleguas Municipal Water Dict	4941	D	805 526-9323	6218
Cellco Partnership	4812	D	805 376-8917	5312
Change Hlthcare Operations LLC	7374	D	805 777-7773	16105
Cigna Healthcare Cal Inc	6324	C	805 230-8300	10196
CIT Bank NA	6021	D	805 379-5520	9320
Citigroup Inc	6021	D	805 557-0930	9333
Conejo Valley Unified Schl Dst	8351	D	805 496-9035	24306
Conejo Valley Unified Schl Dst	8641	C	805 492-3531	25141
Countrywide Home Loans Inc **(DH)**	6162	A	818 225-3000	9795
Durham School Services L P	4151	D	805 495-8338	3916
Edo LLC	8711	C	914 641-2000	25652
Elms Sanitarium Inc	8051	D	818 240-6720	20390

	SIC	EMP	PHONE	ENTRY #
Enhanced Landscape MGT Inc	0782	D	805 557-2737	837
Fedex Office & Print Svcs Inc	7334	E	805 379-1552	14086
Five Star Quality Care Inc	8051	C	805 492-2444	20432
Floyd Skeren & Kelly LLP **(PA)**	8111	D	818 206-9222	23073
Gemmm Corp **(PA)**	6531	D	805 496-0555	11479
Kaiser Foundation Hospitals	8011	A	888 515-3500	19588
Kaiser Foundation Hospitals	8011	A	888 515-3500	19590
Kaiser Foundation Hospitals	6324	D	888 515-3500	10262
Kevin Persons Inc	0781	D	805 371-8746	763
Los Robles Bank	6022	D	805 373-6763	9465
Los Robles Hospital & Med Ctr **(DH)**	8062	D	805 497-2727	21571
Management Trust Assn Inc	6733	C	805 496-5514	12112
Meathead Movers Inc	4213	D	805 496-1416	4225
Miramed Global Services Inc	8748	C	805 277-1017	27790
Mv Transportation Inc	4111	D	805 557-7372	3688
R T Framing Corporation	1751	D	805 496-3985	3064
Red Pocket Inc	4813	D	888 993-3888	5633
Retail Services & Systems Inc	8748	D	805 494-0108	27844
S A Cali-U Acoustics Inc	1742	D	805 376-9300	2954
Sherwood Country Club	7997	C	805 496-3036	19046
Sherwood Development Company **(PA)**	6552	E	805 496-1833	11916
Southern Cal Orthpd Inst LP	8011	D	805 497-7015	19901
Southern California Edison Co	4911	C	818 999-1880	6126
Staff Assistance Inc **(PA)**	7361	B	818 894-7879	14767
Staff Assistance Inc	7361	B	805 371-9980	14768
Star of California	8099	D	805 379-1401	22889
Tecom Industries Incorporated	5065	C	805 267-0100	7553
Teledyne Scentific Imaging LLC **(HQ)**	8731	D	805 373-4545	26473
Thousand Oaks Surgical Hosp LP	8062	D	805 777-7750	21857
Ventu Park LLC	7011	D	805 716-4200	13365
Ventura County Office Educatn	8641	D	805 495-7037	25275
Young Mens Christian Asso	8641	D	805 523-7613	25320
Zs Associates Inc	8742	D	805 413-5900	27534

THOUSAND PALMS, CA - Riverside County

	SIC	EMP	PHONE	ENTRY #
CBS Corporation	4833	D	760 343-5700	5776
Club At Shnndoah Sprng Vlg Inc	7997	E	760 343-3497	18893
Gate City Beverage Distrs	5181	B	760 775-5483	8998
Gulf- California Broadcast Co	4833	C	760 773-0342	5796
Jacobsson Engrg Cnstr Inc	1611	D	760 345-8700	1795
Kincaid Industries Inc	1711	D	760 343-5457	2250
Little Sisters Truck Wash Inc	7542	D	760 343-3448	17825
Readylink Inc	7361	D	760 343-7000	14716
Readylink Healthcare	7361	D	760 343-7000	14717
San Val Corp **(PA)**	0781	B	760 346-3999	785
Sunline Transit Agency **(PA)**	4131	C	760 343-3456	3886
Vorwaller & Brooks Inc	1521	D	760 262-6300	1257

TIPTON, CA - Tulare County

	SIC	EMP	PHONE	ENTRY #
Bosman Dairy LLC	0241	C	559 752-7018	407
Mendes Calf Ranch	0211	D	559 688-4708	397
Sunkist Growers Inc	0723	C	909 983-9811	574
Sunkist Growers Inc	0723	C	559 752-4256	575

TOLLHOUSE, CA - Fresno County

	SIC	EMP	PHONE	ENTRY #
Duleys Landscape Inc	0782	E	559 855-5090	832

TOLUCA LAKE, CA - Los Angeles County

	SIC	EMP	PHONE	ENTRY #
James B Branch Inc **(PA)**	4214	E	818 765-3521	4352
Wells Fargo Bank National Assn	6021	E	818 766-7172	9381

TOPANGA, CA - Los Angeles County

	SIC	EMP	PHONE	ENTRY #
Rock-It Cargo USA LLC	4731	D	310 455-1900	5159

TOPAZ, CA - Mono County

	SIC	EMP	PHONE	ENTRY #
Northern Mono Chamber Commerce	8611	E	530 208-6078	24971

TORRANCE, CA - Los Angeles County

	SIC	EMP	PHONE	ENTRY #
A L S Industries Inc **(PA)**	5092	E	310 532-9262	7943
ACS Communications Inc	1731	E	310 767-2145	2501
Act 1 Group Inc **(PA)**	7361	D	310 532-1529	14567
Active Storage Inc	7389	E	818 709-1133	16984
Adia LLC	8082	C	310 370-0555	22201
Aestiva Software Inc	7371	E	310 697-0338	14969
Ait Worldwide Logistics Inc	4731	D	310 538-4383	5001
All In One Inc	8741	C	310 538-3374	26753
All South Bay Central Office	8699	D	310 618-1180	25376
Allied Digital Services LLC **(HQ)**	7376	D	310 431-2375	16264
Allied Protection Services Inc	7381	D	310 330-8314	16547
Alpine Electronics America Inc	5064	C	310 783-7391	7407
Alpine Electronics America Inc **(HQ)**	5064	C	310 326-8000	7408
Alpine Village	6512	D	310 327-4384	10851
American Honda Finance Corp **(DH)**	6141	C	310 972-2239	9701
American Honda Motor Co Inc **(HQ)**	5012	A	310 783-2000	6577
American Multi-Cinema Inc	7832	C	310 326-5011	18262
Ana Trading Corp USA **(DH)**	5084	C	310 542-2500	7726
Arconic Global Fas & Rings Inc	5085	D	310 784-0700	7830
Arconic Global Fas & Rings Inc	5085	B	310 530-2220	7831

Employment Codes: A=Over 500 employees, B=251-500,
C=101-250, D=51-100, E=50

2019 Directory of California
Wholesalers and Services Companies

© Mergent Inc. 1-800-342-5647
1695

Company	SIC	EMP	PHONE	ENTRY #
Arconic Global Fas & Rings Inc	5085	E	310 530-2220	7834
Arconic Global Fas & Rings Inc	5085	A	310 530-2220	7835
Automobile Club Southern Cal	8699	D	310 325-3111	25384
Bankcard Services (PA)	7389	C	213 365-1122	17026
Bayco Financial Corporation (PA)	6531	D	310 378-8181	11232
Binex Line Corp (PA)	4731	D	310 416-8600	5016
Bioscreen Testing Services Inc (PA)	8734	D	602 277-1154	26686
Bowman and Brooke LLP	8111	D	310 768-3068	22956
BQE Software Inc	7372	D	310 602-4020	15616
Breast Diagnostic Center	8011	E	310 517-4709	19326
Breville Usa Inc	5023	E	310 755-3000	6753
Bright Event Rentals LLC (PA)	7359	C	310 202-0011	14479
Burdette De Cock Inc	8082	C	310 542-0563	22243
C H Robinson Intl Inc	4731	D	310 763-6080	5022
California Mfg Tech Consulting	8742	D	310 263-3060	27179
California Yacht Marina Inc (PA)	4493	E	310 534-8436	4748
CCH Incorporated	7374	B	310 800-9800	16104
Cellco Partnership	4812	C	310 891-6991	5306
Century 21 Amber Realty Inc	6531	C	310 625-4363	11292
Century 21 Exclusive Realtors	6531	C	310 373-5252	11298
Ceva Freight LLC	4731	D	310 972-5500	5027
Ceva Logistics LLC	4731	B	310 223-6500	5029
CH Robinson Freight Svcs Ltd	4731	E	310 515-7755	5031
Charles M Kamiya and Sons Inc	6411	D	310 781-2066	10581
Choura Events	7359	C	310 320-6200	14486
Citigroup Global Markets Inc	6211	E	310 540-9511	9934
City of Torrance	7999	D	310 781-6901	19143
Compex Legal Services Inc (PA)	8111	C	310 782-1801	22987
Contemporary Services Corp	7382	C	310 320-8418	16884
Continental Dntl Ceramics Inc	8072	E	310 618-8821	22164
Contract Recruiting Inc (PA)	7361	D	310 792-7100	14592
County of Los Angeles	8011	D	310 222-4220	19410
County of Los Angeles	5122	D	310 222-2357	8165
County of Los Angeles	8111	D	310 222-3552	23002
Credit Card Services Inc (PA)	7389	D	213 365-1122	17112
Crenshaw Bowling	7933	E	310 326-5120	18487
Ctc Group Inc (DH)	7011	C	310 540-0500	12504
Del AMO Construction	1542	D	310 378-6203	1517
Del AMO Diagnostic Center	8093	E	310 316-2424	22565
Del AMO Grdns Cnvlscnt Hosp &	8051	D	310 378-4233	20369
Del AMO Hospital Inc	8063	B	310 530-1151	21953
Delta Computer Consulting	7379	C	310 541-9440	16345
Dicaperl Corporation (DH)	1499	D	610 667-6640	1102
Divergent Technologies Inc	8711	D	310 339-1186	25644
Docmagic Inc	7389	D	800 649-1362	17134
DTM Services Inc (PA)	4731	D	310 521-1200	5049
Earlwood LLC	8051	D	310 371-1228	20381
Easy Ride Transportation	4789	D	424 999-8830	5224
Electronic Data Care Inc	7373	D	310 791-2600	15951
Emax Laboratories Inc	8734	E	310 618-8889	26698
Express Imaging Services Inc	4226	D	888 846-8804	4675
First Evang Lutheran Ch & Schl	8351	D	310 320-9920	24322
Fns Inc (PA)	4731	D	661 615-2300	5064
Freedom Staff Leasing Inc	7363	B	310 834-6621	14855
Frito-Lay North America Inc	8741	C	310 224-5600	26864
Fujitsu Ten Corp of America	5064	C	310 327-2151	7417
G & H Dental Arts Inc (PA)	8072	C	310 214-8007	22168
Gable House Inc	7933	D	310 378-2265	18491
Gdf Parent LLC	7389	D	714 743-7209	17182
Gerber Ambulance Company Inc	4119	C	310 542-6464	3801
Geri Care Inc	8051	D	310 320-0961	20454
Geri-Care II Inc	8059	C	310 328-0812	21080
Global Accents Inc	5023	C	310 639-2600	6766
Good Sports Plus Ltd	7371	B	310 671-4400	15184
Goodridge Usa Inc (DH)	5013	D	310 533-1924	6643
Harbor Building Services	7349	D	310 320-2966	14284
Harbor Developmental Disabilit	8399	C	310 540-1711	24787
Harbor-Cla Med Ctr Dept Srgery	8062	D	310 222-2701	21439
Harbor-Ucla Med Foundation Inc (PA)	8741	D	310 222-5015	26884
Harbor-Ucla Medical Center	8062	A	310 222-2345	21440
Holiday Inn Hotel Torrance	7011	C	310 781-9100	12692
Hunt Enterprises Inc	6531	C	310 325-1496	11506
I C Class Components Corp (PA)	5065	C	310 539-5500	7491
Imperial Cfs Inc	4226	E	310 768-8188	4676
Industrial Parts Depot LLC (HQ)	5084	D	310 530-1900	7756
Intercontinental Hotels Group	7011	D	310 781-9100	12769
Janet Hilton	6411	D	310 851-7200	10660
Jtb Americas Ltd (HQ)	4724	D	310 303-3750	4942
Kaiser Foundation Hospitals	6324	D	800 780-1230	10261
Keenan & Associates (HQ)	6411	B	310 212-3344	10663
Keller Williams Realty	6531	B	310 375-3511	11541
Kingdom Express Inc	4213	D	310 258-0900	4202
Kintetsu Enterprises Co Amer (HQ)	7011	C	310 782-9300	12816
Kobata Growers Inc (PA)	0181	D	310 323-0662	277
Lifecare Systems Inc	8051	C	310 540-7676	20590
Lisi Aerospace North Amer Inc (DH)	4225	A	310 326-8110	4586
Little Company Mary Hospital	8062	A	310 540-7676	21556
Long Beach Golden Sails Inc	7011	D	562 596-1631	12862
Longwood Management Inc	6513	D	310 370-5828	11059
Los Angeles Bio Med RES Inst	8732	E	310 222-3604	26540
Los Defensores Inc	7311	E	310 519-4050	13858
Mariner Health Care Inc	8051	D	310 371-4628	20610
Maritzcx Research LLC	4725	D	310 783-4300	4972
Mednax Inc	8011	C	310 375-7172	19678
Menemsha Development Group Inc (PA)	1542	C	310 676-6591	1593
Metroplex Theatres LLC	7832	A	310 856-1270	18306
Mighty Enterprises Inc	5084	D	310 516-7478	7774
Milestone Hospice	8052	C	310 782-1177	20942
Mishima Foods USA Inc (PA)	5141	D	310 787-1533	8432
Nippon Express USA Inc	4731	E	310 532-6300	5118
Nissin Intl Trnspt USA Inc (HQ)	4731	E	310 222-8500	5121
Organic Inc	7379	D	310 543-4600	16445
Oriental Motor USA Corporation (DH)	5063	C	310 715-3300	7383
Pacific Echo Inc	5085	D	310 539-1822	7863
Pacific Home Works Inc	1799	C	310 781-3012	3560
Panalpina Inc	4731	D	310 819-4060	5133
Partner Assessment Corporation (PA)	8711	C	800 419-4923	25873
Pediatric Therapy Network	8093	D	310 328-0276	22641
Pentel of America Ltd (HQ)	5112	C	310 320-3831	8085
Performance Team Frt Sys Inc	4731	D	562 345-2200	5140
Physical Optics Corporation (PA)	8731	C	310 320-3088	26438
Physicians Choice HM Hlth Inc	8082	E	310 793-1616	22395
Pioneer Theatres Inc	7389	C	310 532-8183	17400
Platinum Empire Group Inc	7363	C	310 821-5888	14893
Polypeptide Laboratories Inc (DH)	8071	D	310 782-3569	22123
Providence Health System	8011	A	310 376-9474	19801
Providence Health System	6733	C	310 543-5900	12122
Providence Health System	6733	D	310 370-5895	12123
Providence Health System	8062	A	310 530-3800	21673
Providence Health System	8082	D	310 370-5895	22398
Providence Health System	8741	C	310 303-6970	27003
PS Environmental Svcs Inc	7389	D	310 373-6259	17417
PSC Industrial Outsourcing LP	7699	C	310 325-1600	17975
Pta California Congress of Par	8641	D	310 328-3100	25221
Public Hlth Fndation Entps Inc	8641	C	310 320-5215	25225
Quinstar Technology Inc	5065	D	310 320-1111	7530
R C I Enterprises Inc	5049	E	310 370-5900	7246
Rapiscan Systems Inc	7382	C	310 978-1457	16930
Resource Collection Inc	7349	A	310 219-3272	14365
Restaurant Depot LLC	5181	D	310 516-7400	9020
Riad Adoumie MD	8011	D	310 373-6864	19822
Rmi International Inc	7381	D	310 781-6768	16775
Robert Half International Inc	7361	D	310 719-1400	14743
Roy Jorgensen Associates Inc	7349	D	310 468-2478	14369
Ryans Express Trnsp Svcs Inc (PA)	4142	C	310 219-2960	3902
Sakura Finetek USA Inc (HQ)	5047	C	310 972-7800	7215
Salson Logistics Inc	4789	C	310 328-6800	5244
Sanyo Denki America Inc (HQ)	5045	C	310 783-5400	7100
Securitas SEC Svcs USA Inc	7381	D	310 787-0747	16810
Securitas SEC Svcs USA Inc	7381	C	714 385-9745	16811
Shimadzu Precision Instrs Inc	5047	C	310 217-8855	7217
Silicon Prime Technologies Inc	7371	E	310 279-0222	15448
Simplehuman LLC (PA)	5023	D	310 436-2250	6787
Six Continents Hotels Inc	7011	D	310 371-8525	13233
Six Continents Hotels Inc	7011	C	310 781-9100	13236
Smart Choice Investments Inc	7361	D	310 944-6985	14761
Sonic Industries Inc	8711	C	310 532-8382	25919
South Bay Family Medical Group	8011	D	310 378-2234	19897
Space Age Metal Products Inc	5045	C	310 539-5500	7108
Special Service For Groups Inc	8399	D	310 323-6887	24844
Stanley R Klein MD Facs Inc	8011	E	310 373-6864	19945
Star View Adolescent Center	8063	D	310 373-4556	21973
Sun Chlorella USA Corp	5149	D	310 891-0600	8874
Sunnyside Rhblttion Nrsing Ctr	8051	D	310 320-4130	20793
Supershuttle Los Angeles Inc	4111	C	310 222-5500	3734
Supershuttle Orange County Inc	4111	B	310 222-5500	3735
Sweis Inc (PA)	5087	C	310 375-0558	7899
Taisei Construction Corp (HQ)	1541	D	714 886-1530	1442
Topwin Corporation (PA)	5136	D	310 325-2255	8280
Toro Nursery Inc	5193	D	310 715-1982	9170
Torrance Care Center West Inc	8051	C	310 370-4561	20839
Torrance Health Assn Inc (PA)	8062	A	310 325-9110	21858
Torrance Memorial Medical Ctr (HQ)	8062	A	310 325-9110	21859
Torrance Surgery Center LP	8011	A	310 986-2005	20008
Total Management Svcs Amer Inc	7361	E	310 328-0867	14782
Tower Energy Group (PA)	5172	D	310 538-8000	8969
Toyota Logistics Services (DH)	7549	D	310 618-5009	17877
Trendnet Inc (PA)	5045	D	310 961-5500	7120
Ttik Inc (PA)	7382	D	310 303-3600	16948
Unified Inv Programs Inc (PA)	8099	D	310 782-1878	22898

Mergent email: customerrelations@mergent.com

1696

2019 Directory of California
Wholesalers and Services Companies

(P-0000) Products & Services Section entry number
(PA)=Parent Co (HQ)=Headquarters (DH)=Div Headquarters

	SIC	EMP	PHONE	ENTRY #
Unify Financial Federal Cr Un (PA)	6061	D	310 536-5000	9613
United Parcel Service Inc OH	4215	D	800 742-5877	4447
UPS Supply Chain Solutions Inc	4731	C	310 404-2719	5193
Vector Resources Inc (PA)	1731	C	310 436-1000	2778
Virco Inc (HQ)	5021	D	310 533-0474	6742
Vitas Healthcare Corp Cal	8082	D	310 324-2273	22456
Volt Management Corp	7363	C	310 316-8523	14932
Walker Advertising LLC	7311	E	310 519-4050	13920
Windsor Gardens	8051	D	562 422-9219	20900
Xld Group LLC	7011	D	310 316-3636	13432

TRABUCO CANYON, CA - Orange County

	SIC	EMP	PHONE	ENTRY #
Coto De Caza Golf Club Inc	7941	C	949 766-7886	18516
Coto De Caza Golf Racquet CLB	7997	C	949 858-4100	18903
Davlor Company	1542	D	949 244-9748	1513

TRACY, CA - San Joaquin County

	SIC	EMP	PHONE	ENTRY #
American Engrg Contrs Inc	1731	C	209 229-1591	2507
Arconic Global Fas & Rings Inc	5072	D	209 839-3005	7576
Arnaudo Bros Transport Inc (PA)	0191	D	209 835-0406	323
Bossard North America	5085	D	562 906-2003	7841
Boys & Girls Club of Tracy (PA)	8641	E	209 832-2582	25103
Brookdale Senior Living Inc	8361	D	209 835-1000	24443
Cascade Logistics LLC	4225	D	209 832-4205	4538
Crosslink Prof Tax Sltions LLC (PA)	7371	D	209 835-1360	15087
D and S Landscaping Inc	0782	C	925 455-4630	817
DSC Logistics Inc	4225	D	209 362-2232	4552
Ed Thoming & Sons Inc	0173	D	209 835-2792	187
Es3 LLC	4225	E	209 832-4205	4554
Faith Enterprises Inc	8051	E	209 835-6034	20422
Glassfab Tempering Svcs Inc (PA)	8748	D	209 229-1060	27738
Head Start Child Dev Cncil Inc	8351	C	209 832-7844	24327
Home Depot USA Inc	4225	D	209 835-5133	4574
Imobile LLC	4812	B	209 833-6757	5409
In-Shape Health Clubs LLC	7991	C	209 836-2504	18612
Jesse Lee Group Inc	8741	C	209 832-2273	26907
Kaiser Foundation Hospitals	8011	A	209 839-3200	19538
Kaiser Foundation Hospitals	6324	D	209 832-6339	10249
McLane Company Inc	5141	C	209 221-7500	8428
Myra Investment and Dev Corp	6798	D	209 834-2343	12176
Owens & Minor Inc	5047	D	209 833-4600	7203
Pacific Medical Inc (PA)	7389	C	800 726-9180	17384
Safeway Stores Incorporated	4225	B	209 833-4700	4628
Tracy Bancshares Inc	6035	D	209 836-5111	9531
Tracy Dlta Solid Waste Mgt Inc	4953	D	209 835-0601	6483
Tracy Interfaith Ministries	8322	D	209 836-5424	24092
Tracy Sutter Community Hosp	8062	B	209 835-1500	21860
United Facilities Inc	4225	E	209 839-8051	4643
United States Cold Storage Inc	4222	E	209 835-2653	4516
We Care Day Care & Pre School	8351	D	209 832-4072	24397
Yrc Inc	4789	C	209 833-1300	5254

TRANQUILLITY, CA - Fresno County

	SIC	EMP	PHONE	ENTRY #
Don Gragnani Farms	0191	D	559 693-4352	336

TRAVER, CA - Tulare County

	SIC	EMP	PHONE	ENTRY #
Foster Poultry Farms	5191	A	559 457-6509	9079

TRAVIS AFB, CA - Solano County

	SIC	EMP	PHONE	ENTRY #
US Airforce Band of Golden W	7929	E	707 424-2263	18473

TRINIDAD, CA - Humboldt County

	SIC	EMP	PHONE	ENTRY #
Cher-Ae Heights Indian Cmnty	7999	C	707 677-3611	19121

TRONA, CA - San Bernardino County

	SIC	EMP	PHONE	ENTRY #
Searles Valley Minerals Inc	1479	A	760 372-2259	1099

TRUCKEE, CA - Nevada County

	SIC	EMP	PHONE	ENTRY #
Charles Schwab Corporation	6211	D	530 448-8038	9926
Clearcapitalcom Inc	6531	C	530 550-2500	11321
Hyatt Corporation	7011	B	530 562-3900	12746
Lahontan Golf Club	7997	C	530 550-2400	18952
Martis Camp Club	8322	B	530 550-6000	23912
Tahoe Donner Golf Course Inc	7992	D	530 587-9455	18771
Tahoe Forest Hospital District	8062	C	530 582-3277	21849
Tahoe Forest Hospital District (PA)	8062	A	530 587-6011	21850
Tahoe Trcke Unfd Sch Dis Fincn	8748	D	530 582-7630	27876
Tahoe-Truckee Sanitation Agcy	4952	D	530 587-2525	6332
Trimont Land Company (DH)	6531	B	530 562-1010	11802
Truckee Dnner Rcreation Pk Dst	7999	D	530 582-7720	19250
Truckee Donner Pub Utly Dist F	4911	D	530 587-3896	6144
Western Nevada Supply Co	5074	C	530 582-5009	7641

TUJUNGA, CA - Los Angeles County

	SIC	EMP	PHONE	ENTRY #
Crescenta-Canada YMCA	8641	E	818 352-3255	25147
Oakview Convalescent Hospital	8059	E	818 352-4426	21171
Sun Mar Management Services	8741	D	818 352-1454	27052
Volunteers of Amer Los Angeles	8322	C	818 352-5974	24119

TULARE, CA - Tulare County

	SIC	EMP	PHONE	ENTRY #
Altura Centers For Health	8011	D	559 686-9097	19283
Amdal In-Home Care Inc (PA)	8059	E	559 686-6611	20987
Central California Tr	8733	D	559 686-4973	26610
City of Tulare	4953	D	559 684-4200	6378
Curti Family Inc	0241	D	559 688-8323	410
Dan Freitas Electric	1731	D	559 686-9572	2561
Darrell L Green Inc	4214	D	559 688-0686	4341
Faulkner Trucking Inc	4213	D	559 684-9298	4149
Kings County Truck Lines (HQ)	4213	C	559 686-2857	4203
Kloeckner Metals Corporation	5051	C	559 688-7980	7288
Klx Inc	4213	D	559 684-1037	4204
M & T Calf Ranch	0212	D	559 686-7663	400
Moyles Central Vly Hlth Care (PA)	8051	B	559 688-0288	20656
Moyles Health Care Inc	8059	A	559 686-1601	21161
Nielsens Creamery (PA)	0241	D	559 686-4744	423
Porterville Sheltered Workshop	5047	D	559 684-9168	7210
SA Recycling LLC	4953	D	559 688-0271	6460
Tulare Local Health Care Dst	8062	A	559 685-3462	21862
Tulare Nrsing Rhbltation Hosp	8051	C	559 686-8581	20843
Turnupseed Electric Service	1731	D	559 686-1541	2773
United States Cold Storage Inc	4222	E	559 686-1110	4514
Vander Weerd General Cnstr	1794	D	559 688-1099	3444

TULELAKE, CA - Siskiyou County

	SIC	EMP	PHONE	ENTRY #
Lava Beds National Monuments	8699	E	530 667-2282	25437

TUOLUMNE, CA - Tuolumne County

	SIC	EMP	PHONE	ENTRY #
Black Oak Casino	7999	D	209 928-9300	19112
Silver Spur Christian Camp	7032	D	209 928-4248	13455
Tuolumne City Inv Grp II LP	6513	E	209 928-1567	11129
Tuolumne Me-Wuk Indian	8011	D	209 928-5400	20013

TURLOCK, CA - Stanislaus County

	SIC	EMP	PHONE	ENTRY #
American Medical Response Inc	4119	C	209 567-4030	3759
Aspiranet	8361	D	209 669-2582	24421
Aspiranet	8322	D	209 667-0327	23495
Associated Feed & Supply Co (PA)	5191	C	209 667-2708	9072
Border Valley Trading Ltd (PA)	5191	D	209 669-6000	9075
Cellco Partnership	4812	D	209 668-9579	5352
Central California Faculty Med	8099	B	209 620-6937	22764
Central Valley Cheese Inc	5143	D	209 664-1080	8515
Covenant Care California LLC	8051	C	209 632-3821	20348
Covenant Rtirement Communities	8361	C	209 632-9976	24486
Creative Alternatives	8361	C	209 668-9361	24491
Crimetek Security	7381	B	209 668-6208	16622
Emanuel Medical Center Inc	8062	C	209 667-5600	21405
Emanuel Medical Center Inc (DH)	8062	A	209 667-4200	21406
Emanuel Medical Center Inc	8062	C	209 664-2520	21407
Foster Poultry Farms	0254	D	209 668-5922	441
Freshpoint Central California	5148	C	209 216-0200	8681
Gemperle Enterprises	0252	D	209 667-2651	432
Humphrey Plumbing Inc	1711	D	209 634-4626	2229
Joe L Coelho Inc	4213	E	209 667-2676	4199
LJC Construction Inc	1761	D	209 668-2700	3174
Machado & Sons Cnstr Inc	1521	E	209 632-5260	1195
Mickey Wall Painting Inc	1721	E	209 669-0557	2458
Northern Rfrigerated Trnsp Inc (PA)	4213	C	209 664-3800	4236
Poppy State Express Inc	4213	D	209 664-3950	4245
Ruan	4212	D	209 634-4928	4059
Select Harvest Usa LLC (PA)	5159	D	209 668-2471	8910
Sodexo Management Inc	8741	D	209 667-3634	27038
Swanson Farms	0253	D	209 667-2002	439
Thorsens Inc	1761	D	209 524-5296	3206
Turlock Dairy & Rfrng Inc	5083	D	209 667-6455	7716
Turlock Irrigation District (PA)	8631	C	209 883-8222	25085
Turlock Irrigation District	4971	B	209 883-8300	6568
Ulta Salon Cosmt Fragrance Inc	7231	C	209 664-1725	13682
Valley Fresh Foods Inc	0252	D	209 669-5600	435
Winton Ireland Strom & Green (PA)	6411	D	209 667-0995	10833
Yosemite Farm Credit Aca (PA)	6111	D	209 667-2366	9700

TUSTIN, CA - Orange County

	SIC	EMP	PHONE	ENTRY #
A P R Consulting Inc	7379	A	714 544-3696	16301
AB Cellular Holding LLC	4813	A	562 468-6846	5441
ABM Elctrcal Ltg Solutions Inc	7349	D	866 226-2838	14168
Absolute Exhibits Inc (PA)	7389	D	714 685-2800	16977
Advantage Waypoint LLC	5141	D	717 424-4973	8376
AJ Kirkwood & Associates Inc	1731	D	714 505-1977	2502
All Care Services Inc	8322	D	714 669-1148	23467
All Counties Courier Inc	4215	C	949 224-0900	4392
Alta Hospitals System LLC	8062	A	714 619-7700	21280
Ansar Gallery	5141	C	949 220-0000	8381
Apollo Agencies Inc (PA)	6411	C	714 832-2100	10539
Arq LLC	8711	D	888 384-0971	25546
AT&T Corp	4812	D	714 258-8290	5264

Employment Codes: A=Over 500 employees, B=251-500,
C=101-250, D=51-100, E=50

2019 Directory of California
Wholesalers and Services Companies

© Mergent Inc. 1-800-342-5647
1697

GEOGRAPHIC

	SIC	EMP	PHONE	ENTRY #
Autocrib Inc	7389	C	714 274-0400	17020
Briggs Electric Inc **(PA)**	1731	D	714 544-2500	2528
Broker Solutions Inc **(PA)**	8742	A	800 450-2010	27173
Caliber Bodyworks Texas Inc	7532	D	714 665-3905	17715
Canon Medical Systems USA Inc **(DH)**	5047	B	714 730-5000	7170
Centrl Territrl Salvation Army	8322	D	714 832-7100	23553
Corland Companies **(PA)**	6531	D	714 573-7780	11384
Cosmopro West Inc	8082	E	714 258-8301	22279
Crown Golf Properties LP	8742	C	714 730-1611	27205
Day Star Fixtures	1751	E	714 838-4613	3029
Encompass Health Corporation	8093	C	714 832-9200	22575
Executive Personnel Services	7361	B	714 310-9506	14618
First Team RE - Orange Cnty	6531	C	714 544-5456	11464
Foundation Building Mtls LLC **(HQ)**	1742	D	714 380-3127	2884
General Procurement Inc **(PA)**	5045	E	949 679-7960	7054
Hanford Hotels LLC	7011	C	714 210-0400	12641
Health South Tustin Rehab Hosp	8322	C	714 832-9200	23832
Hmwc Cpas & Business Advisors	8721	C	714 505-9000	26218
Hotel Adventures LLC	7011	D	714 730-7717	12718
I L S West Inc	8721	E	714 505-7530	26226
Innovative Medical Solutions	7699	C	714 505-7070	17959
Innovtive Scntfic Slutions Inc	7361	C	714 508-8620	14649
Integrium LLC **(PA)**	8731	D	714 541-5591	26385
Internet Blueprint Inc	7371	E	714 673-6000	15231
Kaiser Foundation Hospitals	8011	A	888 988-2800	19591
Key Inn Ltd A Cal Ltd Partnr	7011	E	714 832-3220	12804
Kinship Center	8322	C	714 979-2365	23884
Ledra Brands Inc	5023	D	714 259-9959	6773
Logomark Inc	5199	C	714 675-6100	9233
Lsf9 Cypress Holdings LLC	5039	A	714 380-3127	6935
M & S Trading Inc	5136	C	714 241-7190	8269
Management Trust Assn Inc **(PA)**	6733	C	714 285-2626	12115
Oracle Corporation	7372	C	713 654-0919	15798
Orange County Dept Education	8741	A	714 730-7301	26968
Portellus Inc	7372	C	949 250-9600	15834
Pphm Inc	5122	C	714 508-6100	8206
Pramira Inc	7379	C	800 678-1169	16459
R Ranch Market	0291	A	714 573-1182	454
RES-Care Inc	8082	D	800 707-8781	22404
RJN Investigations Inc	7381	D	951 686-7638	16774
Sanyo Foods Corp America	7997	C	714 730-1611	19037
Schick Moving & Storage Co **(PA)**	4214	D	714 731-5500	4371
Schoolsfirst Federal Credit Un	6061	C	714 258-4000	9590
Silverado Senior Living Inc	8059	D	657 888-5752	21215
Southern Cal Prmnnte Med Group	6324	D	714 734-4500	10316
Star Real Estate	6531	C	714 731-3777	11776
Steadfast Management Co Inc	6513	C	714 542-2229	11117
Sterling Collision Center LLC **(PA)**	7532	D	714 259-1111	17744
Superior Sod I LP	0181	C	909 923-5068	305
Transpacific Management Svc	6531	D	714 285-2626	11798
Trinity Brdcstg Netwrk Inc	4833	C	714 665-3619	5840
Trinity Christian Center of SA **(PA)**	4833	C	714 665-3619	5841
Turbo Data Systems Inc **(PA)**	7374	E	714 573-5757	16192
Tustin Care Center Corp	8052	D	714 832-6780	20969
Wood Gutmann Bogart Insur Brkg	6411	C	714 505-7000	10836
Woodbridge Glass Inc	1793	C	714 838-4444	3413
Worldstage Inc **(PA)**	8741	C	714 508-1858	27099
Youngs Holdings Inc **(PA)**	5182	C	714 368-4615	9064
Youngs Market Company LLC **(HQ)**	5182	B	800 317-6150	9065

TWENTYNINE PALMS, CA - San Bernardino County

	SIC	EMP	PHONE	ENTRY #
Business and Support Services	7997	D	760 830-6873	18877
Mark Clemons	4213	C	760 361-1531	4219
United States Dept of Navy	8062	B	760 830-2190	21871

TWIN BRIDGES, CA - El Dorado County

	SIC	EMP	PHONE	ENTRY #
Sierra At Taho Ski Resorts	7011	E	530 659-7519	13226

UKIAH, CA - Mendocino County

	SIC	EMP	PHONE	ENTRY #
Berryman Health Inc	8059	D	707 462-8864	21008
Century 21 Les Ryan Realty **(PA)**	6531	D	707 468-0423	11304
Community Care Management Corp **(PA)**	8322	E	707 468-9347	23602
County of Mendocino	4581	D	707 463-4363	4883
County of Mendocino	8322	B	707 463-2437	23691
County of Mendocino	1611	C	707 463-4363	1752
County of Mendocino	8093	C	707 463-4396	22551
Fedex Ground Package Sys Inc	4213	D	800 463-3339	4168
Ford Street Project Inc	8361	E	707 462-1934	24531
Granite Construction Inc	1611	C	707 467-4100	1782
Hildreth Farm Incorporated	0175	D	707 462-0648	219
Horizon West Healthcare Inc	8051	D	707 462-1436	20536
Lake County Home Loans	6162	E	707 462-4000	9823
Mayfield Equipment Company **(PA)**	5083	D	707 462-2404	7706
Mendocino Cmnty Hlth Clnic Inc **(PA)**	8011	C	707 468-1010	19684
Mendocino Forest Pdts Co LLC	5031	C	707 468-1431	6839
Mendocino Redwood Company LLC **(PA)**	0811	B	707 463-5110	993

	SIC	EMP	PHONE	ENTRY #
National Veterinary Assoc Inc	0742	D	707 462-8625	606
Redwood Coast Regional **(PA)**	8322	B	707 462-3832	23985
Redwood Community Services **(PA)**	8322	C	707 467-2000	23988
Redwood Empire Packing Inc	0723	C	707 462-5521	560
Redwood Health Club **(PA)**	7991	D	707 468-0441	18645
Redwood Regional Medical Group	8011	D	707 463-3636	19817
Savings Bank Mendocino County **(PA)**	6022	C	707 462-6613	9485
Sequoia Senior Solutions Inc	8322	D	707 621-9235	24047
SERVPRO of Mendocino	7349	E	707 462-3848	14388
Ukiah Adventist Hospital **(HQ)**	8062	B	707 462-3111	21866
Ukiah Adventist Hospital	8062	C	707 462-3111	21867
Ukiah SC Transportation	4151	D	707 463-5234	3947
Ukiah Vly Assn For Hbilitation **(PA)**	8331	C	707 468-8824	24241
United Parcel Service Inc OH	4215	C	707 468-5481	4468
Valley View Sklled Nursing Ctr	8051	D	707 462-1436	20852
Waste MGT Collectn & Recycl	4953	D	707 462-0210	6519

UNION CITY, CA - Alameda County

	SIC	EMP	PHONE	ENTRY #
AAA Restaurant Fire Ctrl Inc	7389	D	510 786-9555	16971
Anixter Inc	5063	D	510 477-2400	7332
Basquez Tiburcio Health Center	8093	C	510 471-5907	22513
Best Contracting Services Inc	1761	D	510 886-7240	3127
Buffalo Distribution	5139	E	510 475-9810	8346
Cal-West Concrete Cutting Inc **(PA)**	1771	D	510 656-0253	3229
Cellco Partnership	4812	C	510 324-5740	5374
Child Family & Cmnty Svcs Inc	8351	C	510 796-9512	24288
Corinthian Realty LLC	6531	C	510 487-8653	11383
CSC Serviceworks Holdings Inc	7215	C	510 429-0900	13559
Dust Networks Inc	4812	C	510 400-2900	5406
Excel Moving Services	4214	C	800 392-3596	4346
Finezi Inc	7361	C	510 790-4768	14620
Forward Air Inc	4731	E	415 570-6040	5066
Freshpoint Inc	5148	C	510 476-5900	8679
Genesis Logistics Inc	4225	D	510 476-0790	4562
Graybar Electric Company Inc	5063	D	925 557-3000	7363
Intero Real Estate Svcs Inc	6531	D	510 489-8989	11519
Interstate Hotels Resorts Inc	7011	C	510 489-2200	12778
Iron Mountain Incorporated	7382	D	510 798-6387	16907
Kaiser Foundation Hospitals	6324	D	510 675-5777	10216
Kaiser Foundation Hospitals	8011	A	510 675-4010	19539
Kaiser Foundation Hospitals	6324	C	510 675-2170	10248
Masonic Homes of California	8361	B	510 441-3700	24594
Mercado Latino Inc	5141	E	510 475-5500	8431
Mission Linen Supply	7213	C	510 429-7305	13540
Oracle Corporation	7372	C	510 471-6971	15811
Orora Packaging Solutions	5113	D	510 487-1211	8120
Permanente Medical Group Inc	6324	C	510 675-4010	10299
Pregis LLC	5199	E	510 404-1360	9251
Purebeauty Inc	5087	C	510 477-7950	7894
Qng Inc	5065	D	480 330-3804	7528
Reliance Steel & Aluminum Co	5051	C	510 476-4400	7305
Rki Instruments Inc **(PA)**	5084	C	510 441-5656	7795
Southern Glazers Wine	5182	B	510 477-5500	9052
Specialized Laundry Svcs Inc	7218	C	510 487-8297	13621
Tiburcio Vasquez Hlth Ctr Inc **(PA)**	8011	E	510 471-5880	20006
Tournesol Siteworks LLC **(PA)**	1799	D	800 542-2282	3597
Tri-City Economic Dev Corp	4953	C	510 429-8030	6484
Ultimo Software Solutions Inc	7372	C	408 943-1490	15885
Union Sanitary District	4952	C	510 477-7500	6333
United States Pipe Fndry LLC	4619	C	510 441-5810	4927

UNIVERSAL CITY, CA - Los Angeles County

	SIC	EMP	PHONE	ENTRY #
Amblin/Reliance Holding Co LLC	7812	D	818 733-6272	18014
Hilton Los Angles Universal Cy	7011	B	818 506-2500	12666
Hilton Universal Hotel	7011	B	818 506-2500	12669
Latham & Watkins LLP	8111	B	818 753-5000	23186
Lh Universal Operating LLC	7011	B	818 980-1212	12849
NBC Subsidiary (knbc-Tv) LLC	4833	C	818 684-5746	5825
Shen Zhen New World II LLC	7011	B	818 980-1212	13214
Sprint Communications Co LP	4813	E	818 755-7100	5648
Sun Hill Properties Inc **(HQ)**	7011	B	818 506-2500	13286
Universal City Studios LLC **(DH)**	7812	D	800 864-8377	18141
Universal Music Group Inc	7389	C	818 286-4000	17550
Universal Stdios Licensing Inc	6794	C	818 762-6284	12145
Universal Studios Company LLC	7812	B	818 622-4455	18145
Universal Studios Company LLC	7812	C	818 777-1000	18147

UPLAND, CA - San Bernardino County

	SIC	EMP	PHONE	ENTRY #
Allied Prof Nursing Care	8082	D	909 949-1066	22214
Apex Parks Group LLC	7999	D	909 981-5251	19098
Azalea & Rose Co	0181	E	909 949-2442	242
B & L Consulting LLC	8748	D	682 238-6994	27654
Bms Parent Inc **(PA)**	8721	D	909 981-2341	26151
Bni Enterprises Inc	8743	A	909 305-1818	27543
C P Construction Co Inc	1623	E	909 981-1091	1900
California Ldscp & Design Inc	0782	C	909 949-1601	809

Mergent email: customerrelations@mergent.com
1698

2019 Directory of California
Wholesalers and Services Companies

(P-0000) Products & Services Section entry number
(PA)=Parent Co (HQ)=Headquarters (DH)=Div Headquarters

UPLAND, CA (continued)

Company	SIC	EMP	PHONE	ENTRY #
California Skateparks	7389	C	909 949-1601	17048
Camstar International Inc	5072	D	909 931-2540	7581
Cascade Drilling LP	1781	E	909 946-1605	3349
Diamond Ridge Corporation	6162	C	909 949-0605	9799
F M Tarbell Co	6531	C	909 982-8881	11442
Firstsight Vision Services Inc (DH)	8042	D	909 920-5008	20157
Firstsrvce Rsidential Cal Inc (DH)	6531	D	909 981-4131	11468
Future Energy Corporation (PA)	1742	C	800 985-0733	2886
Garrett J Gentry Gen Engrg Inc	8711	D	909 693-3391	25700
Golden Eagle Moving Svcs Inc	4213	D	909 946-7655	4187
Hamilton Brwart Insur Agcy LLC	6411	D	909 920-3250	10640
Hardcore Skateparks Inc	7996	C	909 949-1601	18802
Holliday Rock Co Inc (PA)	5032	D	909 982-1553	6897
Inland Empire Therapy Provider (PA)	8049	D	909 985-7905	20179
Inland Valley Drug & Alcohol (PA)	8322	D	909 932-1069	23856
Inland-Metro Services Inc	7389	D	909 373-6810	17237
JAS Pacific	8711	C	909 605-7777	25769
Kanopy Insurance Center LLC	6399	C	877 513-2434	10502
Largo Concrete Inc	1771	A	909 981-7844	3280
Lewis Companies (PA)	1531	B	909 985-0971	1351
Master Lightning SEC Solutions	7381	D	310 419-2915	16728
Mgr Services Inc	6531	D	909 981-4466	11611
Mladen Buntich Cnstr Co Inc	1623	D	909 920-9977	1957
Mountain View Physical Therapy	8049	D	909 949-6235	20190
Park Place Ford LLC	7538	D	909 946-5555	17776
Perry Floor Systems Inc	1771	D	909 949-1211	3306
Re/Max LLC	6531	E	303 770-5531	11709
Reach Out West End	8399	D	909 982-8641	24829
San Antonio Regional Hospital (PA)	8062	A	909 985-2811	21701
Sela Healthcare Inc (PA)	8051	C	909 985-1981	20752
Serec Entertainment LLC	5072	D	626 893-0600	7601
Shield Security Inc	7381	B	909 920-1173	16826
Sneary Construction Inc	1742	E	909 982-1833	2959
Soltis Golf Incorporated	1629	D	909 822-7000	2065
Upland Community Care Inc	8059	D	909 985-1903	21240
Vci Construction LLC (HQ)	1623	D	909 946-0905	1996
Victoria Place Community Assn	8699	D	909 981-4131	25481
Walton Electric Corporation	1731	D	909 981-5051	2783
West End Yung MNS Christn Assn	8641	D	909 946-6120	25284

UPPER LAKE, CA - Lake County

Company	SIC	EMP	PHONE	ENTRY #
Running Creek Casino	7011	C	707 275-9209	13154

VACAVILLE, CA - Solano County

Company	SIC	EMP	PHONE	ENTRY #
AFA Constrctn Grp/Cal Inc JV	1542	D	707 446-7996	1457
Albertsons LLC	4225	B	707 446-5922	4526
Allied Framers Inc	1751	C	707 452-7050	3017
Blue Mountain Cnstr Svcs Inc	1711	C	800 889-2085	2146
Brenden Theatre Corporation	7832	D	707 469-0180	18273
Citadel Roofing & Solar	1761	C	707 446-5500	3137
City of Vacaville	8322	D	707 449-6122	23585
City of Vacaville	8711	B	707 449-5170	25615
Clark Pest Ctrl Stockton Inc	7342	E	707 446-9748	14143
Contemprary Hstrical Vhcl Assn	8641	D	707 448-7266	25142
County of Solano	4941	D	707 451-6090	6236
General Electric Company	1731	D	707 469-8346	2590
Hearn Enterprise Inc (PA)	1799	C	707 446-5467	3529
International Brthrhd of Elctr (PA)	8631	D	707 452-2700	25063
Kaiser Foundation Hospitals	8011	A	707 624-4000	19537
Kaiser Foundation Hospitals	6324	E	707 624-4000	10234
Kuic Inc	4832	D	707 446-0200	5738
M&G Duravent Inc	4225	B	800 835-4429	4589
Mariani Packing Co Inc (PA)	0723	B	707 452-2800	540
Mark Garcia	7349	D	707 446-4529	14312
Master Drywall Inc	1742	C	707 448-8659	2915
Maximum Fitness LLC	7991	E	707 447-0606	18630
Mental Health California Dept	8063	D	707 449-6504	21966
Merrill Gardens LLC	6531	D	707 447-7496	11609
Mv Transportation Inc	4111	D	707 446-5573	3689
Navy Federal Credit Union	6061	C	888 842-6328	9574
No Barriers	8322	D	707 451-1947	23940
North Bay Distribution Inc	5136	D	707 450-1219	8271
North Bay Distribution Inc (PA)	4225	D	707 452-9984	4601
Par Electrical Contractors Inc	1731	D	707 693-1237	2674
Recology Vacaville Solano	4953	D	707 448-2945	6444
Solano Irrigation District	4971	D	707 448-6847	6565
Stars Recreation Center LP	7933	E	707 455-7827	18499
Sutter Regional Med Foundation	8011	D	707 454-5800	19995
Taylor Structures Inc	1542	D	707 499-6870	1669
Travis Credit Union (PA)	6061	B	707 449-4000	9602
Travis Credit Union	6061	B	707 449-4000	9606
Travis Credit Union	6061	B	707 449-4000	9609
Triumph Protection Group Inc	7381	C	800 224-0286	16839
Vacaville Condolescent and Reh	7363	C	707 449-8000	14930
Vacavlle Cnvalescent Rehab Ctr	8059	D	707 449-8000	21241
Valyria LLC (HQ)	5023	D	707 452-0600	6801

Company	SIC	EMP	PHONE	ENTRY #
Winsor House Compalessant	8051	D	707 448-6458	20907

VALENCIA, CA - Los Angeles County

Company	SIC	EMP	PHONE	ENTRY #
AAA Elctrcal Cmmunications Inc (PA)	1731	C	800 892-4784	2499
Academy Swim Club	7997	D	661 702-8585	18817
Advanced Dcument Solutions Inc (PA)	8713	E	661 251-0337	26126
Advantage Media Services Inc	4225	D	661 705-7588	4525
Ai Inc/CSC Grou	7381	D	661 775-8400	16544
Alfred E Mann Foundation (PA)	8733	D	661 702-6700	26588
Amerisourcebergen Drug Corp	5122	C	661 257-6400	8141
Applied Companies RE LLC	6512	E	661 257-0090	10854
Atk Audiotek	1731	D	661 705-3700	2513
Avita Medical Americas LLC	5047	D	661 367-9170	7158
Behavioral Learning Center Inc	8322	D	661 254-7086	23508
Bel Air Lighting Inc (PA)	5063	C	818 768-5511	7338
C A Rasmussen Inc (PA)	1629	E	661 367-9040	2019
California Strl Concepts Inc	1542	C	661 257-6903	1496
Cardinal Health Inc	5122	C	661 295-6100	8158
CC Wellness LLC (HQ)	5122	D	661 295-1700	8159
Cellco Partnership	4812	C	661 286-2399	5375
Cintas Corporation No 3	7213	D	661 310-7400	13526
Circle W Enterprises Inc	5063	E	661 257-2400	7346
Curtiss-Wright Controls (DH)	8711	D	626 851-3100	25634
Discoverready LLC	8111	D	661 284-6401	23043
Efs West	8711	E	661 705-8200	25653
Encore Media Services Inc	7819	D	661 705-1323	18190
Falcon Aerospace Holdings LLC	8741	A	661 775-7200	26857
Fidelity Security Services Inc	7381	C	661 295-5007	16644
Fpk Security Inc	7381	B	661 702-9091	16648
Gothic Landscaping Inc (PA)	0782	C	661 257-1266	847
Gothic Landscaping Inc	0781	B	661 257-5085	757
Green Convergence (PA)	5074	D	661 491-5111	7626
Henry Mayo Newhall Mem Hlth	8062	D	661 253-8000	21448
Henry Mayo Newhall Mem Hosp	8011	A	661 253-8112	19497
Henry Mayo Newhall Mem Hosp (PA)	8062	A	661 253-8000	21449
Heritage Golf Group Inc	7992	D	661 254-4401	18718
Hoffman Texas Inc	7699	E	661 257-9200	17952
Hrd Aero Systems Inc	7699	D	661 295-0670	17953
Hrd Aero Systems Inc (PA)	7699	C	661 295-0670	17954
Hyatt Hotels Management Corp	7011	C	661 799-1234	12751
Ice Station Valencia L L C	7999	D	661 775-8686	19187
Image 2000 Inc	7699	E	818 781-2200	17956
Iron Mountain Incorporated	4226	D	661 775-9008	4677
JT Wimsatt Contg Co Inc (PA)	1771	D	661 775-8090	3276
Jyg Concrete Construction Inc	1771	C	661 600-0337	3277
King Monster Inc	6531	D	661 253-3000	11552
Klm Orthotic Laboratories Inc	5047	D	661 295-2600	7187
Krg Technologies Inc	7371	A	661 257-9967	15252
Landscape Development Inc (PA)	0782	B	661 295-1970	890
Magic Mountain LLC	7922	B	661 255-4100	18385
Market Tech Media Corporation	7336	D	661 257-4745	14120
Mercury Insurance Company	6331	D	661 291-6470	10379
N Qiagen Amercn Holdings Inc (HQ)	5122	C	800 426-8157	8199
Nutec Enterprises Inc	6531	D	661 287-3200	11639
Oakridge Landscape Inc (PA)	0721	E	661 295-7228	464
Ocean Park Hotels Inc	7011	D	661 284-3200	12972
Ocean Park Hotels Mmex LLC	7011	E	661 284-2101	12973
Princess Cruises and Tours Inc	4724	A	206 336-6000	4949
Pyramid Enterprises Inc (PA)	7999	D	661 702-1420	19219
Quest Dgnstics Clncal Labs Inc	8071	B	661 964-6582	22129
Realty Executives	6531	C	661 286-8600	11719
Regent Aerospace Corporation (PA)	1799	C	661 257-3000	3576
Rgis LLC	7389	D	661 702-8987	17441
Sage Staffing Consultants Inc (PA)	7363	C	661 254-4026	14910
Santa Clarita Medical Group	8011	E	661 255-6802	19855
Scicon Technologies Corp (PA)	8711	D	661 295-8630	25906
Scorpion Design LLC	7311	A	661 702-0100	13900
Southern California Gas Co	4924	D	800 427-2200	6176
Spad Holdings LLC	7991	D	661 286-0229	18660
Specialty Laboratories Inc (DH)	8071	A	661 799-6543	22148
Star Nail Products Inc	5122	D	661 257-3376	8211
Stellar Microelectronics Inc	5065	C	661 775-3500	7544
Summer Systems Inc	1542	D	661 257-4419	1662
Sunkist Growers Inc (PA)	5148	C	661 290-8900	8736
Sunrise Senior Living Inc	8051	D	661 253-3551	20803
Sunvair Aerospace Group Inc (PA)	7699	D	661 294-3777	17992
Trianim Health Services Inc	8099	D	818 362-6882	22896
Ultraviolet Devices Inc	5075	D	661 295-8140	7659
Vista Valencia Group Inc	6531	E	661 255-4600	11815
Volunteers of Amer Los Angeles	8322	D	661 290-2829	24118
Way Forward Technology Inc	7371	E	661 286-2769	15543
Wesco Aircraft Hardware Corp (HQ)	5088	B	661 775-7200	7918
Wesco Aircraft Hardware Corp	5088	B	661 775-7200	7919
Wesco Aircraft Holdings Inc (PA)	8741	D	661 775-7200	27092
Weslar Inc	1751	D	661 702-1362	3090
William S Hart Pony & Softball	8748	D	661 254-9780	27910

GEOGRAPHIC

Employment Codes: A=Over 500 employees, B=251-500,
C=101-250, D=51-100, E=50

2019 Directory of California
Wholesalers and Services Companies

© Mergent Inc. 1-800-342-5647
1699

Company	SIC	EMP	PHONE	ENTRY #
Young Mens Chrstn Assn of La	8641	C	661 253-3593	25344

VALLEJO, CA - Solano County

Company	SIC	EMP	PHONE	ENTRY #
Blu Homes Inc	1521	C	415 625-0809	1124
City of Vallejo	7996	B	707 644-4000	18794
Cooper Crane & Rigging Inc (PA)	1629	D	707 765-4646	2024
Crestwood Behavioral Hlth Inc	8361	C	707 552-0215	24496
Crestwood Behavioral Hlth Inc	8063	D	707 558-1777	21948
Crestwood Behavioral Hlth Inc	8063	D	707 552-0215	21949
CSRA LLC	7376	C	703 876-1026	16268
Emeritus Corporation	8052	E	707 552-3336	20929
Empres Financial Services LLC	8051	D	707 643-2793	20392
Execusheld Prtection Group LLC	7381	D	707 439-6351	16641
Getright Ventures Inc	6163	D	510 402-4816	9884
Greater Vallejo Recreation Dst	7999	C	707 648-4600	19180
H & R Block Inc	7291	C	707 643-1856	13707
Helios Healthcare LLC	8059	C	707 644-7401	21108
J B Laquindanum & Associates	7291	E	707 648-0501	13710
James-Timec International	1629	E	707 642-2222	2041
Jeffco Painting & Coating Inc	1721	D	707 562-1900	2451
Kaiser Foundation Hospitals	6324	D	707 645-2720	10219
Kaiser Foundation Hospitals	8062	A	707 651-1000	21512
La Clinica De La Raza Inc	8011	B	707 556-8100	19629
M F Maher Inc	1611	D	707 552-2774	1808
Medic Ambulance Service Inc (PA)	4119	C	707 644-1761	3821
Merrill Gardens LLC	6513	C	707 553-2698	11067
Michaels Trnsp Svc Inc	4141	D	707 674-6013	3891
Milestones Adult Dev Ctr	8322	C	707 644-0464	23924
Milestones of Development Inc	8052	D	707 644-0496	20943
Permanente Medical Group Inc	8011	D	707 765-3930	19782
R & R Maher Cnstr Co Inc	1771	C	707 552-0330	3311
Recology Vallejo (HQ)	4953	C	707 552-3110	6445
San Pablo Lodge 43	8641	D	707 642-1391	25238
Sutter Solano Medical Center (HQ)	8062	A	707 554-4444	21845
Syar Industries Inc	1422	D	707 643-3261	1088
Teamross Inc	7538	D	707 643-9000	17787
Timec Acquisitions Inc (DH)	1629	A	707 642-2222	2069
Timec Companies Inc (DH)	1629	B	707 642-2222	2070
Total Renal Care Inc	8092	A	707 556-3637	22493
Travis Credit Union	6061	B	800 877-8328	9599
United Parcel Service Inc OH	4215	C	707 252-4560	4458
Valle Sanit and Flood Contr Di	8748	D	707 644-8949	27893
Veterans Health Administration	8011	B	707 562-8200	20058

VALLEY CENTER, CA - San Diego County

Company	SIC	EMP	PHONE	ENTRY #
Caesars Entrtnment Oprting Inc	7999	A	760 751-3100	19117
Indian Health Council (PA)	8611	D	760 749-1410	24962
San Psqual Band Mssion Indians	7011	B	760 291-5500	13180
San Psqual Csino Dev Group Inc	7011	E	760 291-5500	13181
Survival Systems Intl Inc (PA)	7699	D	760 749-6800	17993
Valley Center Municipal	4941	D	760 735-4500	6317
Valley Center Municpl Wtr Dst	4952	D	760 735-4500	6334

VALLEY SPRINGS, CA - Calaveras County

Company	SIC	EMP	PHONE	ENTRY #
Bolin Builders Inc	1521	E	209 772-9721	1125

VALLEY VILLAGE, CA - Los Angeles County

Company	SIC	EMP	PHONE	ENTRY #
Afm & Sag-Aftra Intellectual	7389	D	818 255-7980	16989
Douglas Steel Supply Inc (PA)	5051	D	323 587-7676	7270
Eam Inc (PA)	7514	D	213 342-1760	17631
Executive Financial HM Ln Corp	6162	E	818 285-5626	9802

VAN NUYS, CA - Los Angeles County

Company	SIC	EMP	PHONE	ENTRY #
1370 Realty Corp	6531	C	818 817-0092	11182
14545 Friar LLC	6512	D	818 817-0082	10843
16700 Roscoe Associates LLC	7997	D	818 989-2300	18815
AG Air Conditioning & Htg Inc	1711	E	818 988-5388	2088
Airespring Inc	4813	C	818 786-8990	5445
All Valley Washer Service Inc	7215	D	818 787-1100	13556
Allen Medical Group Inc	8011	E	818 698-8444	19272
Alta Healthcare System LLC	8399	C	818 787-1511	24730
Alta Hollywood Community Hsptl	8063	D	818 787-1511	21922
American Merchant Center Inc	6153	D	818 947-1700	9731
American Prof Ambulance Corp	4119	C	818 996-2200	3771
Apprentice & Journeymen Traini	1711	D	818 464-4579	2124
Apprentice & Journeymen Trn Tr	8331	D	323 636-9871	24145
Apu Inc (PA)	5013	D	661 948-2880	6619
ARC Document Solutions Inc	7334	C	818 908-0222	14081
Arrow Tools Fas & Saw Inc	5072	E	818 780-1464	7577
AT&T Corp	4813	D	818 374-6458	5454
AT&T Corp	4813	D	818 373-6896	5455
AT&T Corp	8748	D	818 997-5998	27647
Barazani Pave Stone Inc	1741	C	818 701-6977	2797
Berkley Vly Cnvlscent Hosp Inc	8051	B	818 786-0020	20261
Broadstreet Solar Inc	1711	E	818 206-1464	2150
Bubbles Devine Bakeries Inc	5149	D	818 786-1700	8761
C B B Z S Inc	1721	D	818 908-1900	2426

Company	SIC	EMP	PHONE	ENTRY #
Caine & Weiner Company Inc (PA)	7322	D	818 226-6000	13993
California Contrs Sups Inc	5082	D	818 785-8823	7670
California Survey Res Svcs	7374	C	818 780-2777	16101
Carlisle Research Corporation	7373	D	818 785-8677	15927
Cbre Inc	6531	D	818 907-4600	11278
Century-National Insurance Co (HQ)	6311	B	818 760-0880	10133
Checker Cab Co	4121	D	818 488-5088	3865
City of Los Angeles	8711	A	818 756-8022	25613
City of Los Angeles	4581	D	818 908-5950	4878
Clay Lacy Aviation Inc (PA)	4581	B	818 989-2900	4881
Command International SEC Svcs	7381	D	818 997-1666	16607
County of Los Angeles	8322	C	818 362-6437	23672
County of Los Angeles	8322	D	818 374-2000	23676
County of Los Angeles	8111	D	818 374-2406	23003
Courtyard Plaza	8051	E	818 780-5005	20334
Dee Sign Co	7389	D	818 904-3400	17128
Dfs Flooring Inc (PA)	1752	C	818 374-5200	3100
Diversfied Envmtl Ctalysts Inc (PA)	5013	D	818 994-1958	6634
Ds Services of America Inc	5149	D	818 787-9397	8784
E & S International Entps Inc (PA)	5064	D	818 887-0700	7412
Elite Aviation LLC	4522	D	818 988-5387	4858
Energy Enterprises USA Inc (PA)	1711	D	424 339-0005	2200
Exandal Corporation	5141	C	818 705-9497	8404
Factory 2-U Import Export Inc	5137	D	323 587-9900	8303
Ferguson Enterprises Inc	5074	E	818 786-9720	7623
Financial Information Network	7371	D	818 782-0331	15160
Five Star Quality Care Inc	8051	D	818 997-1841	20431
Fusefx LLC	7819	D	818 237-5052	18194
George M Rajacich MD PC	8011	E	818 787-2020	19482
Golden Living LLC	8082	D	805 494-4949	22304
Grand Valley Health Care Ctr	8051	C	818 786-3470	20495
Grht Inc	5199	D	323 873-6393	9222
Grobstein Horwath & Co	8721	D	818 501-5200	26212
Hamburger Home	8361	C	818 980-3200	24547
Health Advocates LLC	8399	C	818 995-9500	24788
Health Entps Lf Long Plan	8082	B	818 654-0330	22313
Helinet Aviation Services LLC (PA)	7812	C	818 902-0229	18059
Hemacare Corporation (PA)	8099	C	818 986-3883	22815
Hi-TEC Sports Usa Inc (DH)	5139	D	209 545-1111	8358
Icon Media Direct Inc (PA)	7311	D	818 995-6400	13843
Incare Dme	8099	D	818 582-1016	22822
Interviewing Service Amer LLC (PA)	8732	C	818 989-1044	26531
Jet Edge International LLC	4522	D	818 442-0096	4860
K Automotive Distributors (PA)	5013	D	818 988-1500	6650
Keolis Transit America Inc	4111	C	818 616-5254	3660
Kincaid & Decker Inc (PA)	5023	C	818 785-1528	6771
L A Party Rents Inc	7359	D	818 989-4300	14521
Lees Maintenance Service Inc	7349	B	818 988-6644	14301
Longwood Management Corp	6513	C	818 781-6348	11057
Los Angeles Police Credit Un (PA)	6062	C	818 787-6520	9640
Los Angeles Unified School Dst	8093	B	818 997-2640	22615
Love Lifted US Youth Services	7991	D	818 471-0594	18628
M Network Television Inc	4833	C	818 756-5150	5822
M P M & Associates Inc	1542	D	818 708-9676	1584
Maguire Aviation Group LLC	4522	E	818 989-2300	4863
ME and ME Inc	7363	C	818 891-0197	14878
Merabi & Sons LLC	6798	C	818 817-0006	12174
Mercury Messenger Service Inc	7389	E	818 989-3115	17322
Mesa Energy Systems Inc	1711	C	818 756-0500	2280
MGA Entertainment Inc (PA)	5092	B	818 894-2525	7958
Microlease Inc (DH)	7359	D	866 520-0200	14527
Momentous Insurance Brkg Inc	6411	D	818 933-2700	10694
Moulton Logistics Management (PA)	7389	D	818 997-1800	17337
Mp Aero LLC	1799	D	818 901-9828	3553
Nat Sim Corp	5112	D	818 705-3131	8084
National Commercial Services	7322	D	818 701-4400	14013
Nep Group Inc	7812	D	412 423-1354	18083
Normand/Wlshire Rtrment Ht Inc	6513	D	818 373-5429	11084
North La County Regional Ctr (PA)	8748	B	818 778-1900	27805
Onegeneration	8322	D	818 708-6625	23950
Parkwood Landscape Maint Inc	0782	E	818 988-9677	918
Pride Collision Centers Inc (PA)	7532	C	818 909-0660	17736
Primex Clinical Labs Inc (PA)	8071	C	818 779-0496	22125
Prudential Insur Co of Amer	6411	D	818 901-0028	10749
Regency Fire Protection Inc	1711	D	818 982-0126	2334
Reliable Gardens Inc	0782	D	818 904-9801	929
Restaurant Depot LLC	5181	C	818 376-7687	9023
Richmond American Homes	1521	E	818 908-3267	1225
Rite Way Enterprises	4731	C	818 376-6960	5156
Rotorcraft Support Inc	4581	D	818 997-7667	4906
S D Property Management Inc	6531	D	323 658-7990	11749
S G D Enterprises	0782	C	323 658-1047	933
San Fernando Valley Community (PA)	8093	A	818 901-4830	22672
Security America Inc	7381	D	310 532-0121	16816
Shalev Senior Living	8361	E	818 780-4808	24672

	SIC	EMP	PHONE	ENTRY #
Sharf Woodward & Associates	7361	D	818 989-2200	14759
Signature Flight Support Corp	4581	D	818 464-9500	4911
Six Continents Hotels Inc	7011	D	818 989-5010	13234
SMA Builders Inc	1521	E	818 994-8306	1238
Southern Cal Orthpd Inst LP	8011	C	818 901-6600	19902
Southern Cal Orthpd Inst LP (PA)	8011	C	818 901-6600	19904
Sylmark Inc (PA)	8741	D	818 217-2000	27055
T & R Painting Construction	1721	C	818 779-3800	2486
Titan Solar Construction	1711	C	866 575-1211	2387
Touch-Up Inc	1742	C	818 994-6166	2971
Town & Country Event Rentals (PA)	7359	B	818 908-4211	14549
Transtar Industries Inc.	5013	E	818 785-2000	6680
United Parcel Service Inc OH	4215	C	404 828-6000	4464
Valley Clark Plbg & Htg Co Inc (PA)	1711	D	818 782-1047	2394
Valley Presbyterian Hospital	8062	A	818 782-6600	21896
Van Nuys Care Center Inc.	8059	D	818 343-0700	21245
Weinstein Construction Corp.	1542	E	818 782-4000	1697
Wolfe Trucking Inc.	4213	C	818 376-6960	4306
Woodley Lakes Golf Course.	7992	D	818 780-6886	18780
Young Mens Chrstn Assn of La	8641	E	818 989-3800	25340

VANDENBERG AFB, CA - Santa Barbara County

	SIC	EMP	PHONE	ENTRY #
Indyne Inc	8744	A	805 606-7225	27596
Range Generation Next LLC	8711	D	310 647-9438	25889
Securitas Critical Infrastruct	7381	A	805 685-1100	16785

VENICE, CA - Los Angeles County

	SIC	EMP	PHONE	ENTRY #
1524 Abbot Kinney LLC	6531	D	310 907-6517	11183
Bully Pictures Inc (PA)	7922	C	310 395-6500	18349
DDB Worldwide	7311	D	310 907-1500	13812
Globalex Corporation	7372	D	310 593-4833	15693
Host Hotels & Resorts LP	7011	D	310 823-1700	12710
Intrinsik Envmtl Sciences Inc	8748	D	310 392-6462	27756
Los Angeles County MTA	4111	C	310 392-8636	3677
Mad Dogg Athletics Inc (PA)	5137	C	310 823-7008	8317
Outrigger Hotels Hawaii	7011	D	310 301-2000	12989
Parking Concepts Inc	7521	C	310 821-1081	17699
Prologue Films (PA)	7336	E	310 589-9090	14126
Safe Harbor Treatment Cen	8093	E	949 645-1026	22668
Southern California Gas Co	4924	D	310 823-7945	6172
St Joseph Center	8322	C	310 396-6468	24068
Trg Inc	6531	D	310 396-6750	11800
Venice Family Clinic (PA)	8011	D	310 664-7703	20049

VENTURA, CA - Ventura County

	SIC	EMP	PHONE	ENTRY #
A M Ortega Construction Inc	1521	D	951 360-1352	1108
Agi Holding Corp (PA)	7997	D	805 667-4100	18819
Alsco Inc	7213	D	805 650-6578	13495
American Landscape Management	0782	E	805 647-5077	797
Arb Inc	1623	A	805 643-4188	1891
ARC of Ventura County Inc	8093	C	805 644-0880	22507
Asplundh Tree Expert LLC	0783	D	805 641-0528	967
Automobile Club Southern Cal	8699	D	805 644-7171	25385
Bentley-Simonson Inc.	1311	D	805 650-2794	1012
Beverly Health Care Corp (PA)	8741	E	805 642-1736	26780
Boyd & Associates (PA)	7381	C	818 752-1888	16587
Brokaw Nursery LLC	0181	D	805 647-2262	248
Buenaventura Medical Group (PA)	8011	B	805 477-6000	19332
Buenaventura Medical Group	8011	D	805 477-6220	19333
C D Lyon Construction Inc (PA)	8711	D	805 653-0173	25586
C J Vandergeest Ldscp Care Inc.	0782	D	805 650-0726	806
Cabrillo Economic Dev Corp (PA)	1522	D	805 659-3791	1272
California Forensic Med Group	8099	D	805 654-3343	22756
Catholic Charities of Santa CL	8322	D	805 643-4694	23537
Cellco Partnership	4812	D	805 650-0410	5338
Central Courier LLC	4212	D	805 654-1145	3988
Channel Islands Young Mens Ch	8641	C	805 484-0423	25134
Clinicas Del Camino Real Inc (PA)	8093	D	805 647-6322	22534
Clocktower Inn	7011	D	805 652-0141	12468
Coastal View Halthcare Ctr LLC.	8059	D	805 642-4101	21039
Community Mem HSP/Sn Benua	8062	D	805 652-5072	21340
Community Memorial Health Sys (PA)	8062	A	805 652-5011	21341
Cornell Corrections Cal Inc (DH)	8322	B	805 644-8700	23617
County of Ventura	8322	C	805 654-2561	23755
County of Ventura	8322	D	805 654-3456	23756
County of Ventura	8721	D	805 654-3152	26175
County of Ventura	8322	A	805 652-6000	23758
D S R Inc	7699	D	805 275-0039	17942
Dcor LLC (PA)	1382	D	805 535-2000	1041
Dcor LLC	1382	D	805 576-1200	1042
Del Mar Seafoods Inc.	5146	C	805 850-0421	8575
Dialysis Centers Ventura Cnty	8092	D	805 658-9211	22472
E & M Concrete Construction	1771	D	805 658-2888	3251
E J Harrison & Sons Inc.	4953	C	805 647-1414	6389
E&S Financial Group Inc	6163	D	805 644-1621	9879
Evans/Sipes Inc (PA)	6531	C	805 644-1242	11423

	SIC	EMP	PHONE	ENTRY #
Fedex Office & Print Svcs Inc	7334	D	805 339-2000	14088
Florida Beauty Flora Inc	7231	B	805 642-1633	13658
Fpl LLC	7011	D	805 643-6144	12590
G W Surfaces (PA)	1799	C	805 642-5004	3523
Golden Living LLC	8051	D	805 642-1736	20469
GPA Technologies Inc	8711	D	805 643-7878	25717
Hailwood Inc.	6512	D	805 487-4981	10890
Harbor Island Hotel Group LP	7011	D	805 658-1212	12642
Hbe Corporation	1542	E	805 641-1305	1548
Interact Pmti Inc (PA)	8711	C	805 658-5600	25750
J L S Concrete Pumping Inc	1771	D	805 643-0766	3270
Johnson Controls	1711	D	805 642-0366	2244
Kaiser Foundation Hospitals	6324	C	888 515-3500	10243
Kingledon Inc	7011	C	805 643-6000	12814
Kkzz 1590	4832	E	805 289-1400	5734
L A Fitness Intl LLC	7991	D	805 289-9907	18621
Livingston Mem Vna Hlth Corp	8741	C	805 642-0239	26936
Offshore Crane & Service Co (PA)	7353	D	805 648-3348	14452
Oilfield Electric Company	1731	D	805 648-3131	2667
Ojai Ambulance Inc	4119	E	805 653-9111	3827
Ost Trucks and Cranes Inc	7389	D	805 643-9963	17377
Pier Pont Hotel LP	7011	E	805 643-6144	13062
Pierpont Inn Inc	7011	D	805 643-0245	13063
Plowboy Landscapes Inc	0782	D	805 643-4966	923
Registration Ctrl Systems Inc (PA)	7389	C	805 654-0171	17426
Retail Services Wis Corp	7389	D	805 644-5422	17434
Rgis LLC	7389	C	805 644-0454	17436
Sam Hill & Sons Inc	1623	E	805 620-0828	1977
Saticoy Lemon Association	0174	D	805 654-6500	209
Securitas SEC Svcs USA Inc	7381	C	805 650-6285	16787
Sigma Services Inc (PA)	1542	D	805 642-8377	1647
Snapdragon Place 1 LP	6513	D	805 659-3791	11115
SRS Protection Inc.	7381	D	805 744-7122	16834
Star of California (PA)	8099	C	805 644-7823	22891
Taft Electric Company (PA)	1731	D	805 642-0121	2762
Tidwell Excav Acquisition Inc	1794	D	805 647-4707	3442
Trade Desk Inc (PA)	7371	D	805 585-3434	15509
Triunfo Public Facilities Corp.	4939	D	805 658-4605	6204
United Parcel Service Inc OH	4215	C	805 642-6784	4484
Ventura County Credit Union (PA)	6062	D	805 477-4000	9661
Ventura County Lemon Coops	0723	D	805 385-3345	584
Ventura County Medical Center (PA)	8011	C	805 652-6000	20053
Ventura County Medical Center.	8011	D	805 652-6201	20054
Ventura Hsptality Partners LLC	7011	C	805 648-2100	13366
Ventura Medical Management LLC	8741	B	805 477-6220	27085
Ventura Streets Dept	1521	D	805 652-4515	1256
Veternary Med Srgcal Group Inc	0742	D	805 339-2290	619
Victoria Care Center.	8051	D	805 642-1736	20858
Vista Steel Co Inc.	1629	E	805 653-1189	2073
West Ventura Family Care Ctr.	8011	D	805 641-5620	20099
Willow Farms LLC	0191	D	805 647-0720	394

VERNON, CA - Los Angeles County

	SIC	EMP	PHONE	ENTRY #
A A A Packing and Shipping Inc	4212	E	626 310-7787	3959
A-1 Express Delivery Service (PA)	4212	E	323 585-4440	3963
Adir International LLC	1541	C	213 639-7716	1371
Americold Logistics LLC	4222	D	323 581-0025	4496
B Boston & Associates Inc (PA)	5137	C	323 264-3915	8285
Bcbg Max Azria Group LLC	5137	D	323 589-2224	8286
Bcbg Max Azria Group LLC (HQ)	5137	B	323 589-2224	8287
Bnsf Railway Company	4011	C	323 267-4133	3617
California Farms Meat Co Inc	5147	D	323 581-3663	8613
City Fibers Inc (PA)	5093	C	323 583-1013	7974
City Fibers Inc	4225	D	323 583-1013	4541
City of Los Angeles	4173	D	213 485-4981	3951
Claudia Richard Inc.	5137	C	323 264-3915	8295
Collected Group Company LLC	5137	E	323 277-3900	8296
Comak Trading Inc A Cal Corp	5137	C	323 261-3404	8297
Completely Fresh Foods Inc	5149	C	323 722-9136	8773
Core-Mark International Inc.	5149	C	323 583-6531	8777
Country Floors America LLC (PA)	5032	D	310 657-0510	6883
DOT-Line Transportation Inc	4213	D	877 900-7768	4129
Dutch LLC (DH)	5137	C	323 277-3900	8299
Famma Group Inc (PA)	5136	D	323 826-9600	8259
Fedex Freight Corporation	4213	D	323 269-9800	4151
Golden West Trading Inc.	5147	D	323 581-3663	8616
Gourmet Specialties Inc	5148	D	323 587-1734	8690
Greatwide Logistics Svcs LLC	4731	D	323 268-7100	5079
H & N Foods International Inc (HQ)	5146	C	323 586-9300	8576
Jordana Cosmetics Corporation	5122	D	323 589-5625	8184
Joseph T Ryerson & Son Inc.	5051	D	323 267-6000	7285
Kaiser Foundation Hospitals	8062	D	323 264-4310	21490
Kellytoy Worldwide Inc.	5092	D	323 923-1300	7955
Kenan Advantage Group Inc	4213	D	323 582-3778	4201
Lafayette Textile Inds LLC	5131	D	323 264-2212	8230
Lineage Logistics LLC	4222	C	323 583-3163	4505

Employment Codes: A=Over 500 employees, B=251-500,
C=101-250, D=51-100, E=50

2019 Directory of California
Wholesalers and Services Companies

© Mergent Inc. 1-800-342-5647

1701

GEOGRAPHIC

	SIC	EMP	PHONE	ENTRY #
Los Angeles Junction Rlwy Co	4013	E	323 277-2004	3634
Los Angeles Regional Food Bank	8322	C	323 234-3030	23902
Lymi Inc (PA)	5137	D	213 434-2772	8316
Macsei Industries Corporation	5147	D	323 233-7864	8621
Martys Cutting Inc	7389	C	323 582-5758	17315
Mola Inc	5137	C	323 582-0088	8323
Morgan Fabrics Corporation (PA)	5131	C	323 583-9981	8234
Natures Produce Company	5148	D	323 235-4343	8708
Nydj Apparel LLC	5137	C	323 581-9040	8327
Ocean Queen 87 Inc	5146	E	323 585-1200	8587
Orient Fisheries Inc	5146	D	323 588-4185	8589
Pacific American Fish Co Inc (PA)	5146	B	323 319-1551	8590
Palisades Ranch Inc	5141	D	323 581-6161	8439
Rancho Foods Inc	5147	C	323 585-0503	8626
Red Chamber Co (PA)	5146	D	323 234-9000	8597
Reliance Steel & Aluminum Co	5051	C	323 583-6111	7308
Rggd Inc (PA)	5099	D	323 581-6617	8053
Rite-Way Meat Packers Inc	5147	D	323 826-2144	8628
Robin K	5137	D	323 235-5152	8331
Rose & Shore Inc	7389	D	323 826-2144	17450
Saia Motor Freight Line LLC	4213	D	323 277-2880	4257
Same Swim LLC	5137	D	323 582-2588	8332
Shims Bargain Inc (PA)	5199	D	323 881-0099	9258
Showroom Interiors LLC	7359	C	323 348-1551	14544
Soex West Usa LLC	5136	B	323 264-8300	8277
Soofer Co Inc	5149	C	323 234-6666	8870
Stone Blue Inc	7218	D	323 277-0008	13622
Tadin Inc	5149	D	213 406-8880	8881
Tama Trading Company	5149	D	213 748-8262	8882
True Wrld Fods Los Angeles LLC	5146	D	323 846-3300	8609
United Parcel Service Inc OH	4513	B	323 260-8957	4849
V & L Produce Inc	5148	C	323 589-3125	8740
Vernon Central Warehouse Inc	4214	C	323 234-2200	4387
Vernon Truck Wash Inc	7542	C	323 267-0706	17841
Wayne Provision Co Inc (PA)	5147	D	323 277-5888	8633
West Pico Distributors LLC	5141	D	323 586-9050	8487
West Pico Foods Inc	5142	C	323 586-9050	8510
Wm Healthcare Solutions Inc	4953	C	713 328-7350	6525
World Variety Produce Inc	5148	B	800 588-0151	8749
Young Bae Fashions Inc	5137	D	323 583-8684	8341

VICTOR, CA - San Joaquin County

	SIC	EMP	PHONE	ENTRY #
Victor Treatment Centers Inc	8361	C	209 340-7900	24710

VICTORVILLE, CA - San Bernardino County

	SIC	EMP	PHONE	ENTRY #
Branlyn Prominence Inc	8082	C	760 843-5655	22239
Cambrian Homecare Inc	8082	D	760 955-2250	22246
Cemex Cnstr Mtls PCF LLC	5032	C	760 381-7600	6880
Charter Cmmnctons Oprating LLC	4841	C	760 452-8609	5860
Coldwell Banker Home Source	6531	D	760 684-8100	11334
Comav Technical Services LLC	4581	C	760 530-2400	4882
County of San Bernardino	8322	D	760 843-5100	23719
Desert Valley Hospital Inc (DH)	8062	D	760 241-8000	21365
Desert Valley Med Group Inc	8011	D	760 245-2474	19439
Desert Valley Med Group Inc (PA)	8011	B	760 241-8000	19440
Desert View Funeral Home	7261	E	760 244-0007	13689
E & T Foods Inc	0291	B	760 843-7730	449
Faith Electric LLC	1731	D	909 767-2682	2581
Green Tree Capital LP	7011	D	760 245-3461	12618
Hartwick & Hand Inc (PA)	4212	D	760 245-1666	4019
Heritage Medical Group	8099	C	760 956-1286	22817
Heritage Senior Care Inc	8082	D	800 562-2734	22318
In Shape Health Club	8099	E	760 381-1200	22821
Innovative Bus Partnerships	8059	E	760 243-2229	21121
Interntnal Arospc Coatings Inc	4581	C	760 246-1651	4895
Jamboor Medical Corporation	8092	C	760 241-8063	22480
Joseph A Foroosh Dental Corp (PA)	8021	D	760 241-3336	20120
Kaiser Foundation Hospitals	6324	D	888 750-0036	10225
Keller Williams Realty	6531	D	760 951-5242	11542
Knolls Convalescent Hospital (PA)	8051	C	760 245-5361	20568
Knolls Convalescent Hospital	8051	D	760 245-6477	20569
Knolls West Enterprise	8361	D	760 245-0107	24572
Knolls West Post Acute LLC	8059	D	760 245-5361	21130
L & S Investment Co Inc	7011	D	760 245-3461	12824
Landforce Express Corporation	4213	C	760 843-7839	4212
Lee-Victorville Hotel Corp	7011	C	760 245-3461	12846
Odyssey Healthcare Inc	8082	D	760 241-7044	22379
Peoples Care Inc	8082	C	760 962-1900	22393
Psomas	8713	E	760 843-5700	26133
Securitas SEC Svcs USA Inc	7381	C	760 245-1915	16812
Sonshine Collision Services	7532	D	760 243-3185	17742
Sonshine North Autobody	7532	D	760 245-3183	17743
Southern California Edison Co	4911	D	760 951-3242	6140
Southwest Gas Corporation	4924	D	760 951-4000	6178
Spring Valley Lake Country CLB	7997	D	760 245-5356	19060
Spring Valley Post Acute LLC	8051	C	760 245-6477	20774

	SIC	EMP	PHONE	ENTRY #
Springleaf Fincl Holdings LLC	8742	C	760 241-1451	27464
Sterling-Ase Ltd Partnership	6513	C	760 951-9507	11118
Stress Relief Services	7011	D	760 241-7472	13285
Super Care Inc	5047	D	760 245-2034	7220
Telecare Corporation	8063	D	760 245-8837	21977
United California Realty Inc	6531	D	760 949-4040	11806
United Parcel Service Inc	7389	A	760 241-5540	17534
Valley Bulk Inc	4213	D	760 843-0574	4298
Verizon Communications Inc	4813	C	760 245-0409	5666
Victorvlle Trsure Holdings LLC	7011	D	760 245-6565	13368

VIEW PARK, CA - Los Angeles County

	SIC	EMP	PHONE	ENTRY #
Hathaway-Sycamores Chld Fam Sv	8361	D	323 733-0322	24554

VILLA PARK, CA - Orange County

	SIC	EMP	PHONE	ENTRY #
School Portraits By Kranz	7221	D	714 545-1775	13643
Tropical Plaza Nursery Inc	0782	D	714 998-4100	951

VINA, CA - Tehama County

	SIC	EMP	PHONE	ENTRY #
Andersen & Sons Shelling Inc	0723	D	530 839-2236	492

VISALIA, CA - Tulare County

	SIC	EMP	PHONE	ENTRY #
ABM Janitorial Services Inc	7349	D	559 651-1612	14171
Agriholding Inc (PA)	4731	D	559 738-5880	4998
Agsource Services LLC	0761	E	559 735-9700	636
Allen Development Partners LLC (PA)	6552	D	559 732-5425	11852
American Incorporated	1711	B	559 651-1776	2105
Bacci Glinn Physcl Therapy Inc	8049	E	559 733-2478	20164
Bank America National Assn	6021	E	800 432-1000	9287
Beethoven Holdings Inc	6531	C	559 733-4100	11235
Bethesda Lthran Cmmunities Inc	8361	D	559 636-6300	24435
Bowie Enterprises	7542	D	559 732-2988	17803
California Coml Solar Inc	1711	D	559 667-9200	2154
Central Valley Community Bank	6022	D	559 625-8733	9429
Central Vly Regional Ctr Inc	8093	C	559 738-2200	22524
Chicago Title Insurance Co	6361	D	559 733-3814	10447
Cigna Healthcare Cal Inc	6324	B	559 738-2000	10197
City of Visalia	7389	D	559 713-4000	17084
Comcast Cble Cmmunications LLC	4841	D	559 253-4050	5868
Dae-IL Usa Inc	5013	D	559 651-5170	6632
Delta Nrsing Rhbilitation Hosp	8051	D	559 625-4003	20374
Donald Lawrence Fulbright Co	1531	D	559 625-0762	1336
E & M AG Svc Inc A Cal Corp	0762	E	559 627-2724	687
Family Healthcare Network	8049	C	559 734-1939	20176
Family Services	8699	E	559 741-7310	25421
Family Services Tulare County	8322	D	559 732-1970	23798
Far West Inc	8051	D	559 627-1241	20424
Far West Inc	8059	C	559 733-0901	21065
Federal Express Corporation	4513	C	800 463-3339	4830
Financial Credit Network Inc (PA)	7322	E	559 733-7550	14003
Frito-Lay North America Inc	5145	C	559 651-1334	8559
GAF Holdings Inc	6719	B	559 734-3333	11978
Georgia-Pacific LLC	5113	C	559 651-5500	8104
Grosvenor Visalia Associates	7011	D	559 651-5000	12632
Heilind Electronics Inc	5065	D	559 651-0168	7486
Indian River Transport Co	4213	B	209 664-0456	4195
J & S Farm	0191	D	559 308-0294	356
J A Contracting Inc	0761	B	559 733-4865	653
Jacobs Tree Specialist Inc	0761	C	559 639-7138	654
Kaweah Delta Health Care Dst (PA)	8062	A	559 624-2000	21528
Kaweah Dlta Hlth Care Dst Gild	8099	C	559 624-3100	22828
Kaweah Dlta Hlth Care Dst Gild	8011	C	559 624-4800	19624
Keller Williams Realty Inc	6531	D	559 636-1235	11544
Kern 2008 Cmnty Partners LP	1522	D	559 651-3559	1299
L E Cooke Co	0181	C	559 732-9146	278
Lamp Liter Associates	7011	D	559 733-4328	12835
Lawrence Tractor Coinc (PA)	5083	D	559 734-7406	7705
Michael SD Nagatini	8011	D	559 738-7502	19689
Morgan Kleppe & Nash	6411	D	559 733-1181	10693
OConnor Pest Control Visalia	7342	D	559 732-3436	10695
Orange Belt Stages (PA)	4142	D	559 366-4853	14155
Phillips Farms	0175	E	559 733-4408	3900
Quad Knopf Inc (PA)	8711	E	559 798-1871	228
Quail Park Retirement Village	8052	D	559 733-0440	25881
Red One - PSI Joint Ventr LLC	1542	E	559 624-3500	20948
Robert Quintero Labor Contg	7361	E	559 772-8264	1627
Self Help Enterprises (PA)	8641	D	559 732-6954	14746
Sequoia Beverage Company LP	5181	D	559 651-1000	25247
Sequoia Regional Cancer Center	8069	C	559 651-2444	9025
State Farm Fire and Cslty Co	6411	D	559 624-3000	22044
Tim Hofer Inc	7349	C	559 625-4330	10778
Tucoemas Federal Credit Union (PA)	6061	D	559 732-6676	14407
Tucoemas Federal Credit Union	6061	D	559 737-5900	9610
Tulare Cnty Chld Care Home Edu	8351	D	559 429-7094	9611
Tulare Cty Trng Ctr Hndcpd	8331	D	559 651-0247	24395
Turning Point Central Cal Inc	8322	E	559 651-3683	24239
			559 627-1490	24098

2019 Directory of California
Wholesalers and Services Companies

(P-0000) Products & Services Section entry number
(PA)=Parent Co (HQ)=Headquarters (DH)=Div Headquarters

	SIC	EMP	PHONE	ENTRY #
United Parcel Service Inc OH	4215	D	559 651-7690	4480
USA Waste of California Inc	4953	D	559 741-1766	6487
USA Waste of California Inc	4953	D	559 834-4070	6501
Valley Sweet LLC	4222	D	559 686-3381	4517
Visalia Country Club	7997	D	559 734-3733	19082
Visalia Medical Clinic Inc (PA)	8011	B	559 733-5222	20088
Visalia Unified School Dst	8322	C	559 730-7871	24111
Viscamar LLC	7011	D	559 636-1111	13370
Welcome Group Management LLC	7011	D	310 378-6666	13385
Westgate Gardens Care Center	8051	C	559 733-0901	20886
Wonderful Citrus Packing LLC	0723	D	559 798-3100	588

VISTA, CA - San Diego County

	SIC	EMP	PHONE	ENTRY #
Access Biologicals LLC	5122	D	760 597-9749	8137
All-Pro Bail Bonds Inc	7389	D	760 941-4100	16992
Altman Specialty Plants Inc (PA)	5193	A	800 348-4881	9123
American Faucet Coatings Corp	5023	E	760 598-5895	6747
Apical Industries Inc	5088	C	760 724-5300	7906
ARS American Residential (HQ)	1711	D	760 941-7000	2128
Bachem Americas Inc	5169	D	760 597-8820	8920
Bent Tree Nursing Center Inc	8051	C	760 945-3033	20260
Biomedical Life Systems Inc	5047	D	760 727-5600	7164
Caldwell Banker Inc	6531	D	760 941-6888	11261
Cassidy Medical Group Inc (PA)	8011	D	760 630-5487	19357
City of Vista	7999	C	760 940-9283	19144
Cols Inc	4119	C	714 720-6100	3786
Demaria Landtech Inc	0782	E	858 481-5500	824
Deployment Solutions LLC	1731	E	317 281-9682	2564
Easyturf Inc (DH)	1799	D	760 745-7026	3511
Epitec Inc	7371	A	760 650-2515	15141
Exagen Diagnostics Inc	8071	D	505 272-7966	22084
Excel Mdular Scaffold Lsg Corp	1799	A	760 598-0050	3515
Experienced Home Care Registry	8082	D	760 724-0880	22295
Festival Fun Parks LLC	7999	D	760 945-9474	19172
Frito-Lay North America Inc	5145	D	760 727-6022	8557
Habitat Rstration Sciences Inc (PA)	0782	D	760 479-4210	854
Heaviland Enterprises Inc (PA)	0782	C	760 598-7065	858
HMS Construction Inc (PA)	1781	D	760 727-9808	3353
I Pwlc Inc	0781	D	760 630-0231	762
Industrial Coml Systems Inc	1711	C	760 300-4094	2232
Jeld-Wen Inc	5031	B	760 597-4201	6837
Jwc Construction Inc (PA)	1522	E	760 727-2494	1294
Kids First Foundation	8361	C	760 631-7550	24570
Kids First Foundation	8361	C	760 631-7550	24571
Krikorian Premiere Theatre LLC	7832	C	760 945-7469	18304
Lee-Mar Aquarium & Pet Sups	5199	D	760 727-1300	9230
Leidos Inc	8731	C	858 826-9090	26396
Life Care Centers America Inc	8059	C	760 724-8222	21134
McCain Inc (DH)	5084	C	760 727-8100	7770
Minegar Contracting Inc	1771	E	760 598-5001	3288
Neal Electric Corp (HQ)	1731	D	858 513-2525	2658
Neostyle Eyewear Corporation	5048	C	760 305-4004	7237
New Haven Youth Fmly Svcs Inc	8322	C	760 630-4060	23936
Novo Engineering Inc (PA)	8711	D	760 598-6686	25848
Orion Construction Corporation	1623	D	760 597-9660	1964
Pac West Land Care Inc	0782	D	760 630-0231	914
Pave-Tech Inc	1611	E	760 727-8700	1836
Pleasant Care of Vista	8051	C	760 945-3033	20704
Plug Connection Inc	0181	D	760 631-0992	292
Ponto Nursery Inc	5193	D	760 724-6003	9160
Production Plus Plumbing Inc	1711	C	760 597-0235	2319
Prudential Overall Supply	7218	D	760 727-7163	13615
Rancho Vista Health Center	8052	C	760 941-1480	20949
Ready America Inc (PA)	5099	D	760 295-0234	8052
Regency Centers LP	8051	A	760 724-9795	20719
Rescom Services Inc	0782	D	760 930-3900	930
Roto Rooter Plumbing & Drain S	7699	E	951 658-8541	17978
Scripps Health	8051	B	760 806-9263	20748
Sharp Healthcare	8062	D	760 806-5600	21750
Sherpaul Corporation	8082	D	760 639-6472	22417
Sierra Pacific West Inc	1542	D	760 599-0755	1646
Sol Transportation Inc	4119	E	760 720-4327	3848
Spa Havens LP	7991	C	760 945-2055	18657
Tri-City Home Care Services	8082	C	760 940-5800	22438
United Floral Exchange Inc	5193	D	760 597-1940	9171
US Foods Inc	5199	B	760 599-6200	9265
USA Bouquet LLC	5193	D	800 878-9909	9172
Vadnais Trenchless Svcs Inc	1623	D	858 550-1460	1994
Vista Care Group LLC (PA)	8322	D	760 295-3900	24112
Vista Community Clinic (PA)	8031	A	760 631-5000	20151
Vista Community Clinic	8031	E	760 631-5030	20152
Vista Irrigation District	4971	D	760 597-3100	6569
Vista Knoll Inc	8051	D	760 630-2273	20870
Vista Valley Country Club	7997	D	760 758-2800	19083
Vista Woods Health Assoc LLC	8051	C	760 630-2273	20872
Western Concrete Pumping Inc (PA)	1771	D	760 598-7855	3345

	SIC	EMP	PHONE	ENTRY #
Winners Only Inc	5021	C	760 599-0300	6744

WALNUT, CA - Los Angeles County

	SIC	EMP	PHONE	ENTRY #
Able Hands Inc	8082	D	626 965-2233	22184
Adesso Inc	5045	C	909 839-2929	6997
Amerifreight Inc	4225	A	909 839-2600	4529
Bulk Transportation (PA)	4213	C	909 594-2855	4112
Caliber Bodyworks Texas Inc	7532	E	909 598-1113	17717
Capacity LLC	4226	C	732 745-7770	4666
Clarion Construction Inc	1541	E	909 598-4060	1386
Command Delivery Systems Inc (PA)	4212	D	909 444-1475	3994
Concept Enterprises Inc	5064	C	626 968-8827	7411
East Lion Corporation	5139	E	626 912-1818	8355
Emeritus Corporation	8052	E	909 595-5030	20932
Extra Express (cerritos) Inc	4731	E	714 985-6000	5061
Fiserv Inc	7374	D	909 598-8700	16133
Fiserv Inc	7374	D	909 595-9074	16136
Forever Link International Inc	5139	E	877 839-9899	8356
JF Shea Construction Inc	1521	E	909 594-0998	1183
Kelly Paper Company (HQ)	5111	E	909 859-8200	8070
Kent Daniels & Associates Inc	7361	D	626 859-5018	14656
Los Angeles Royal Vista Golf C	7997	D	909 595-7471	18964
M & R Joint Venture Electrical	1731	D	909 598-7700	2632
Nestle Dreyers Ice Cream Co	5143	C	909 595-0677	8525
Oparc	8322	D	909 598-8055	23951
Patina Freight Inc	4225	C	909 444-1025	4606
Ronsin Photocopy Inc (PA)	7389	D	909 594-5995	17449
Seapassion Logistics Inc	4731	D	562 907-4300	5165
Shea Homes Arizona Ltd Partnr	6531	D	909 594-9500	11762
Shea Homes At Montage LLC	1521	D	909 594-9500	1234
Shea Homes Lmtd Partnership A (HQ)	1521	E	909 594-9500	1235
Shea Homes Vantis LLC	1522	D	909 594-9500	1315
Shipbycom LLC	4212	D	626 271-9800	4061
Sysco Los Angeles Inc	5141	A	909 595-9595	8466
Unis LLC (PA)	4731	C	909 839-2600	5190
United Riggers & Erectors Inc (PA)	1796	C	909 978-0400	3477
Vistancia Marketing LLC	8742	D	909 594-9500	27517
Walnut Valley Unified Schl Dst	8699	D	909 595-1261	25482
Walnut Valley Water District	4941	D	909 595-7554	6318

WALNUT CREEK, CA - Contra Costa County

	SIC	EMP	PHONE	ENTRY #
24 Hour Fitness Usa Inc	7991	D	925 930-7900	18567
741 Studios LLC	7379	C	925 407-2063	16300
A F Evans Company Inc	7389	D	925 937-1700	16969
Advanced Software Design Inc	7371	D	925 975-0691	14966
Alliedbarton Security Svcs LLC	7381	B	510 839-4041	16555
Amen Clinics Inc A Med Corp	8011	E	650 416-7830	19284
American Automobile	6411	D	925 279-2300	10517
American Automobile Assctn	8699	B	510 596-3669	25380
American Automobile Associatio	6331	D	510 596-3669	10335
American Financial Network Inc	6282	D	925 705-7710	10055
Amerit Fleet Solutions Inc (HQ)	7549	D	877 512-6374	17849
Anderson & Martella Inc	1796	E	925 934-3831	3468
Anesthesia Business Cons Inc	8011	D	925 951-1366	19294
Appery LLC	7372	C	925 602-5504	15584
Archer Norris A Prof Law Corp (PA)	8111	C	925 930-6000	22917
Argonaut Kensington Associates	8322	D	925 943-1121	23487
Ashford Trs Nickel LLC (PA)	7011	D	925 934-2500	12338
AT&T Services Inc	4813	B	510 836-6889	5490
AT&T Services Inc	4813	B	925 943-4383	5510
Atria Senior Living Group Inc	8361	D	925 938-6611	24427
Axiom Global Technologies Inc	8748	C	925 393-5800	27653
Barcelon Associates MGT Corp	6531	C	925 627-7000	11231
Bay Imaging Cons Med Group Inc (PA)	8011	D	925 296-7150	19316
Bay Medical Management LLC	8011	C	925 296-7150	19317
BDS Plumbing Inc	1711	D	925 939-1004	2138
Bentley Systems Incorporated	7371	D	925 933-2525	15023
Berding & Weil LLP (PA)	8111	D	925 838-2090	22939
Bowles & Verna	8111	E	925 935-3300	22955
Bpg Storage Solutions Inc	8741	D	562 467-2000	26784
Bridge Partners Inc (PA)	6799	D	925 256-9448	12203
Brosamer & Wall Inc	8711	C	925 932-7900	25577
Brosamer & Wall LLC	6531	E	925 932-7900	11250
Brown and Caldwell (PA)	8711	C	925 937-9010	25580
C C Connection Inc	6531	D	925 937-0100	11257
C2 Financial Corporation	6282	C	925 938-1300	10064
California Physicians Service	6324	C	925 927-7419	10184
California State Automobile (HQ)	6331	A	925 287-7600	10345
Carollo Engineers Inc (PA)	8711	D	925 932-1710	25593
Caswell Bay Inc	8082	D	925 933-8181	22258
Century Vision Developers Inc	1542	E	925 588-7390	1500
Colliers Parrish Intl Inc	6531	D	925 279-1050	11373
Comerica Bank	6021	D	925 941-1900	9341
Covia Affordable Communities	8051	D	925 956-7400	20357
Csaa Insurance Exchange (PA)	6411	C	800 922-8228	10597
Cytosport Holdings Inc	6719	C	707 751-3942	11973

Employment Codes: A=Over 500 employees, B=251-500,
C=101-250, D=51-100, E=50

2019 Directory of California
Wholesalers and Services Companies

© Mergent Inc. 1-800-342-5647
1703

	SIC	EMP	PHONE	ENTRY #
Davidon Five Star Corp	6799	D	925 945-8000	12220
Diablo Realty Inc	6531	E	925 933-9300	11399
East Bay Municipl Utility Distr	4941	D	866 403-2683	6244
Engineered Soil Repairs Inc	1741	D	408 297-2150	2806
Ericksen Arbuthnot Kilduff (PA)	8111	D	925 947-1702	23062
Erm-West Inc (DH)	8711	D	925 946-0455	25675
Exadel Inc (PA)	7372	D	925 363-9510	15673
Factory Mutual Insurance Co	6331	C	925 934-2200	10349
Fehr & Peers (PA)	8711	D	925 977-3200	25682
First Alarm SEC & Patrol Inc	7382	B	925 295-1260	16894
Fugro USA Land Inc	8711	E	925 256-6070	25694
Galloway Lucchese Everson	8111	E	925 930-9090	23088
Glaspy & Glaspy A Prof Corp	8111	E	408 279-8844	23100
Golden Rain Foundation (PA)	6531	E	925 988-7700	11487
Golden Rain Foundation	8641	B	925 988-7800	25168
Hagen Streiff Newton Oshiro	8721	E	925 941-1050	26214
Harvest Technical Service Inc	7361	C	925 937-4874	14635
Hcr Manorcare Med Svcs Fla LLC	8051	C	925 274-1325	20508
Hcr Manorcare Med Svcs Fla LLC	8051	C	925 975-5000	20513
HDR Engineering Inc	8711	D	925 974-2500	25728
Heartland Payment Systems LLC	7389	D	925 360-3258	17216
Home Instead Senior Care	8082	D	510 686-9940	22330
Interstate Hotels Resorts Inc	8741	C	925 934-2500	26898
Izt Mortgage Inc (PA)	6163	E	925 946-1858	9888
John Muir Health (PA)	8062	A	925 947-4449	21465
John Muir Health	8062	E	925 947-5300	21466
John Muir Health	8062	A	925 939-3000	21467
John Muir Physician Network	8062	A	925 952-2701	21469
John Muir Physician Network	8062	A	925 296-9700	21472
John Muir Physician Network	8062	B	925 939-3000	21473
Kaiser Foundation Hospitals	8062	A	925 906-2380	21480
Kaiser Foundation Hospitals	8093	A	925 295-4145	22599
Kaiser Foundation Hospitals	8011	A	925 295-4000	19594
Kaiser Foundation Hospitals	8062	A	925 906-2000	21508
Kaiser Foundation Hospitals	6324	D	925 926-3000	10236
Kilpatrick Twnsend Stckton LLP	8111	C	925 472-5000	23169
Kimco Staffing Services Inc	8099	A	925 256-3132	22831
Kpmg LLP	8721	E	925 946-1300	26241
Kropa Realty	6531	E	925 937-4040	11554
Kugga Inc	7371	D	925 639-0721	15253
Leisure Sports Inc	7011	B	925 938-3058	12847
Lindsay Wildlife Museum	8412	D	925 935-1978	24887
Malikco LLC	7372	E	925 974-3555	15747
Mason-Mcduffie Real Estate Inc	6531	D	925 932-1000	11589
Meals On Wheels Diablo Region (PA)	8322	D	925 937-8311	23915
Mechanics Bank (DH)	6029	C	800 797-6324	9512
Mechanics Bank	6712	D	925 934-1601	11955
Merrill Lynch Pierce Fenner	6211	D	925 945-4800	9987
Miller Starr & Regalia A Pro (PA)	8111	D	925 935-9400	23253
Moffatt & Nichol	8711	E	925 944-5411	25829
Moffatt & Nichol	8711	E	510 645-1238	25830
Mp Tice Oaks Associates A CA	6531	D	650 356-2976	11621
Muir Labs	8071	B	925 947-3335	22113
Muir Orthopedic Specialists	8011	C	925 939-8585	19703
Newport Group Inc (PA)	8741	C	925 328-4540	26960
Northern Cal Ret Clks-Emp Fund	6733	C	925 746-7530	12117
Olympic Investors Ltd	7997	D	925 322-8996	18994
One Planet Ops Inc (PA)	7311	C	925 983-2800	13873
Pacific Cast Bnkers Bancshares (PA)	6022	D	415 399-1900	9470
Pacific Coast Bankers Bank	6022	D	415 399-1900	9471
Permanente Medical Group Inc	8011	A	925 906-2000	19774
Professnal Creer Placementscom	7361	E	415 615-0688	14702
Qwest Corporation	4813	D	925 974-4908	5632
R R Donnelley & Sons Company	4011	E	925 951-1320	3623
Recurrent Energy LLC (HQ)	1711	D	415 956-3168	2333
Robert Half International Inc	7361	D	925 930-7766	14731
Savvius Inc (HQ)	7371	D	925 937-3200	15431
SEC Pac Inc	6531	D	925 938-9200	11757
Sequoia Surgical Center LP	8011	E	925 935-6700	19877
Signature Painting & Cnstr Inc	1721	E	925 287-0444	2481
Stantec Consulting Svcs Inc	8711	C	925 627-4500	25930
Sunrise Senior Living LLC	8051	E	925 932-3500	20814
Tactical Telesolutions Inc	7389	C	415 788-8808	17494
Thomas Wirig Doll & Co Cpas	8721	D	925 939-2500	26303
Tony La Russas Animal RES Fnd	0742	D	925 256-1273	610
Travelers Property Cslty Corp	6411	B	925 945-4000	10803
Tryfacta Inc	7371	B	408 419-9200	15513
USI Insurance Services Nat	6411	D	925 988-1700	10813
Vitas Healthcare Corp Cal	8082	D	925 930-9373	22453
Waste Mgt Collectn & Recycl	4212	C	925 935-8900	4086
West Unfied Cmmnctons Svcs Inc	7389	D	925 988-7112	17590
Windsor Capital Group Inc	7011	C	925 934-2000	13413
XI Specialty Insurance Corp	6351	D	925 942-6142	10433
Yapstone Inc (PA)	7389	C	866 289-5977	17601
Ydesign Group LLC (PA)	5063	E	866 842-6209	7404

WALNUT GROVE, CA - Sacramento County

	SIC	EMP	PHONE	ENTRY #
Ryde Hotel LLC	7011	E	916 776-1318	13155

WASCO, CA - Kern County

	SIC	EMP	PHONE	ENTRY #
Community Action Partnr Kern	8351	D	661 758-0129	24299
Community Support Options Inc	8322	C	661 758-5331	23609
D J Farm Management	0762	E	661 792-6222	685
Darr & Pitcairn AG Inc	0722	C	661 758-5156	477
Demler Egg Ranch	0252	E	661 758-4577	430
Early Morning LLC	0181	D	503 912-5261	256
R Mora Farm Labor	0761	C	661 746-2858	669
South Valley Almond Co LLC	5159	C	661 391-9000	8911

WATERFORD, CA - Stanislaus County

	SIC	EMP	PHONE	ENTRY #
Frazier Nut Farms Inc	0173	E	209 522-1406	189

WATSONVILLE, CA - Santa Cruz County

	SIC	EMP	PHONE	ENTRY #
3-Way Farms (PA)	0181	E	831 722-0748	241
A & I Trucking Inc (PA)	4212	E	831 763-7805	3958
Amar Transportation Inc (PA)	4213	C	831 728-8209	4096
Ameri-Kleen	7349	B	831 722-8888	14188
California Pajarosa	0181	E	831 722-6374	249
California Pajarosa Floral	5193	E	831 722-6374	9129
Camflor Inc	0181	C	831 726-1330	250
CB North LLC	0191	A	831 786-1642	330
CBS Farms LLC	0171	C	831 724-0700	93
Cellco Partnership	4812	D	831 786-0267	5320
CF Watsonville LLC	8051	D	831 724-7505	20304
CF Watsonville East LLC	8051	D	310 574-3733	20305
CF Watsonville West LLC	8051	D	831 724-7505	20306
Community Action Brd of Snt Cr	8641	D	831 724-0206	25139
Community Bridges	8322	C	831 724-2024	23600
Couch Distributing Company Inc	5181	C	831 724-0649	8987
Driscolls Inc (PA)	5148	D	831 424-0506	8670
Driscolls Inc	5148	D	800 871-3333	8671
Edward J Kelly	0191	E	831 724-0832	340
Elkhorn Berry Farms LLC	0191	D	831 722-2472	341
Elyxir Distributing LLC	5181	E	831 761-6400	8994
Encompass Community Services	8322	B	831 724-3885	23787
Fedex Ground Package Sys Inc	4213	D	800 463-3339	4176
Field Fresh Farms LLC	5148	D	831 722-1422	8677
Fitz Fresh Inc	0182	E	831 763-4440	311
G I L C Inc	1521	E	831 724-1011	1168
Granit-Bayashi 2 A Joint Ventr	1623	D	831 724-1011	1922
Granit-Bayashi 3 A Joint Ventr	1611	E	831 724-1011	1770
Granite Construction Company (HQ)	1611	C	831 724-1011	1771
Granite Construction Inc (PA)	1622	C	831 724-1011	1880
Granite Rock Co (PA)	1442	D	831 768-2000	1091
Guy George	0171	E	831 728-2410	101
Hospice of Santa Cruz County	8082	D	831 430-3000	22338
International Almond Exchange	0173	E	831 728-4534	190
Jacobs Farm/Del Cabo Inc	4212	C	831 460-3500	4027
Kitayama Bros Inc	0181	D	831 722-2912	275
Kitayama Brothers Inc	0181	D	831 722-8118	276
Maggiora Bros Drilling Inc (PA)	1781	D	831 724-1338	3354
Marty Franich Leasing Co	7515	E	831 724-2463	17656
Miguel Ramos	0291	D	831 761-9941	452
Monte Vsta Mem Schlrship Assoc	8748	E	831 722-8178	27791
Monterey Bay Acadamy Laundry	7211	D	831 728-1481	13488
Monterey Bay Bouquet Acquisit	5193	C	831 786-2700	9149
Monterey Mushrooms Inc (PA)	0182	E	831 763-5300	315
Morgan Farm LLC	0171	D	831 726-5120	109
Oceanside Laundry LLC	7215	D	831 722-4358	13560
Pajaro Valley Greenhouses (PA)	5193	E	831 722-2773	9155
Pajaro Valley Prevntn & Studen	8322	D	831 728-6445	23957
Pt Logistics Inc	4212	E	831 728-4535	4052
Ramco Enterprises LP	7361	A	831 722-3370	14713
Reiter Affl Companies LLC	0171	D	831 786-4244	116
Rio Mesa Farms LLC	0171	D	831 728-1965	119
Salud Para La Gente	8011	C	831 728-0222	19839
Santa Cruz County of	8011	D	831 763-8400	19856
Santa Cruz Metro	4111	B	831 426-6080	3723
Suncrest Nurseries Inc	5193	D	831 728-2595	9163
Superior Foods Inc	5142	D	831 728-3691	8506
T T Miyasaka Inc	0171	D	831 722-3871	124
Uyeda Farm	0171	E	831 722-6345	125
Uyematsu Inc	0171	D	831 724-2200	126
Vps Companies Inc (PA)	5142	D	831 724-7551	8507
Waste Mgt Collectn & Recycl	4953	D	831 768-9505	6516
Watsonville Coast Produce Inc	5148	D	831 722-3851	8745
West Coast Hospitals Inc	8059	D	831 722-3581	21253

WEAVERVILLE, CA - Trinity County

	SIC	EMP	PHONE	ENTRY #
Mountain Comm Hlth Cre Dist	8062	C	530 623-5541	21600
Mountain Comm Hlth Cre Dist (PA)	8062	C	530 623-5541	21601

Mergent email: customerrelations@mergent.com
1704

2019 Directory of California
Wholesalers and Services Companies

(P-0000) Products & Services Section entry number
(PA)=Parent Co (HQ)=Headquarters (DH)=Div Headquarters

	SIC	EMP	PHONE	ENTRY #

WEED, CA - Siskiyou County

	SIC	EMP	PHONE	ENTRY #
Lassen Canyon Nursery Inc	0171	D	530 938-4720	105
Personnel Preference Inc	7363	C	530 938-3909	14889
Roseburg Forest Products Co	5031	C	530 938-2721	6859

WEST COVINA, CA - Los Angeles County

	SIC	EMP	PHONE	ENTRY #
Assisted Home Recovery Inc	8999	D	626 915-5595	27919
Big Lgue Dreams Consulting LLC	7941	C	626 839-1100	18511
BKK Corporation (PA)	4953	D	626 965-0911	6359
Bowlero Corp	7933	D	626 960-3636	18482
Certified Nursing Registry Inc	7361	C	626 912-1877	14586
Citrus Valley Hospice	8051	D	626 859-2263	20312
Citrus Valley Medical Ctr Inc (PA)	8062	A	626 962-4011	21322
Citrus Valley Medical Ctr Inc	8062	A	626 963-8411	21324
Citrus Vly Hlth Partners Inc	8011	B	626 962-4011	19383
Clara Baldwin Stocker Home	8051	E	626 962-7151	20314
Concorde Battery Corporation	4225	C	626 962-4006	4542
Covina Bowl Inc	7933	D	626 339-1286	18486
Doctors Hospital W Covina Inc	8062	C	626 338-8481	21396
East Valley Cmnty Hlth Ctr Inc (PA)	8093	D	626 919-3402	22573
Eastland Tower Partnership	6519	E	626 858-2000	11169
Foothill Transit Service Corp (PA)	4111	D	626 967-3147	3656
Futuro Infantil Hispano Ffa	8361	E	626 339-1824	24537
Golden Living LLC	8051	D	626 962-3368	20472
Harris & Ruth Painting Contg (PA)	1721	D	626 960-4004	2446
In Home Health Inc	8082	D	419 254-7841	22342
Jpmorgan Chase Bank Nat Assn	6021	D	626 919-3129	9351
Kaiser Foundation Hospitals	8062	A	866 319-4269	21502
Lead Staffing Corporation	8049	C	800 928-5561	20188
Matrix Group International Inc	1521	D	626 960-6205	1197
Paul Calvo and Company	6531	E	626 814-8000	11666
Queen of Valley Hospital	8062	A	626 962-4011	21678
Regent Assisted Living Inc	8361	D	626 332-3344	24646
RM Galicia Inc	7322	C	626 813-6200	14021
Rp Automotive Inc (PA)	7538	C	626 430-9011	17782
Schoolwires Inc	4899	D	626 974-7600	5993
Solugenix Corporation	7379	C	866 749-7658	16490
South Hills Country Club	7997	D	626 339-1231	19051
Southern Cal Prmnnte Med Group	6324	C	626 960-4844	10315
Southern Cal Spcialty Care Inc	8062	D	626 339-5451	21763
Universal Bank (PA)	6035	C	626 854-2818	9532
Volunteers of Amer Los Angeles	8322	C	626 337-9878	24117
West Covina Medical Clinic Inc (PA)	8011	C	626 960-8614	20097
Wicoro Inc (HQ)	8059	E	626 962-4489	21255

WEST HILLS, CA - Los Angeles County

	SIC	EMP	PHONE	ENTRY #
Care 4 U LLC	8322	D	818 593-7911	23526
Childrens Home Southern Cal (PA)	8361	E	818 592-2960	24467
Damon Electrical	1731	D	818 426-3450	2560
Dlh Davinci LLC	8072	D	818 703-5100	22165
Electro Rent Corporation (PA)	7359	C	818 786-2525	14503
Hvantage Technologies Inc	7371	D	818 661-6301	15203
Unilab Corporation (HQ)	8071	B	818 737-6000	22154

WEST HOLLYWOOD, CA - Los Angeles County

	SIC	EMP	PHONE	ENTRY #
24 Hour Fitness Usa Inc	7991	E	310 652-7440	18554
AT&T Corp	4812	D	323 874-7000	5290
Atlas Entertainment Inc	7812	E	310 786-4900	18021
Auto Club Enterprises	6321	B	310 914-8500	10160
Black & White TV Inc	7622	D	310 855-1040	17882
Cellco Partnership	4812	D	323 603-0369	5372
Coldwer Banker Previews	6531	C	310 278-9470	11366
Cpe Hr Inc	8742	D	310 270-9800	27203
Cpe Peo Inc	7363	D	310 385-1000	14843
Crunch LLC	7991	D	323 654-4550	18589
Endemol	7922	D	310 860-9914	18365
Funny or Die Inc	7379	E	650 461-3929	16370
Graphic Orb Inc	8742	D	310 967-2350	27253
Harpo Inc	7922	D	312 633-1000	18371
Harpo Productions Inc	7812	D	312 633-1000	18058
Hmbl LLC	7011	D	323 656-0800	12688
Hob Entertainment LLC	7929	C	323 848-5100	18437
Le Montrose Hotel	7011	D	310 855-1115	12845
Modani Los Angeles LLC	5021	E	310 652-2323	6731
Modern Hr Inc	8742	B	310 270-9800	27350
N Compass International Inc	8742	C	323 785-1700	27356
Neonroots LLC	7372	C	310 907-9210	15773
Ols Hotels & Resorts LP	7011	C	310 855-1115	12980
Outrigger Hotels Hawaii	7011	D	323 491-9015	12990
Own LLC	4841	C	323 602-5500	5925
Quixote Mm LLC	7819	E	323 851-5030	18213
Quixote Studios LLC (PA)	7359	E	323 851-5030	14538
Rsa Films Inc (PA)	7812	D	310 659-1577	18112
S&F Management Company LLC (PA)	8051	D	310 385-1090	20735
Snf Management	8741	D	310 385-1090	27035
Suissa Miller Advertising LLC	7311	D	310 392-9666	13906

	SIC	EMP	PHONE	ENTRY #
Super Photo Laboratory Inc	7384	D	323 512-0247	16967
Ticketmaster Entertainment LLC	7922	A	800 653-8000	18409
Valadon Hotel LLC	7011	D	310 854-1114	13363
W-Bel Age LLC	7011	D	310 854-1111	13373
White Rabbit Partners Inc	8361	C	310 975-1450	24723

WEST SACRAMENTO, CA - Yolo County

	SIC	EMP	PHONE	ENTRY #
A Csg-Nova Joint Venture	1611	D	916 371-7303	1710
ABM Janitorial Services Inc	7349	B	916 374-1739	14174
AEP Span Inc	1761	D	916 372-0933	3122
Ahtna Government Services Corp	1542	D	916 372-2000	1458
American Metals Corporation (HQ)	5051	C	916 371-7700	7256
ASC Profiles LLC (DH)	5051	D	916 372-6851	7259
AT&T Services Inc	4813	C	916 376-2006	5517
Aus Decking Inc	1771	D	916 373-5320	3217
Big City Access Inc (PA)	5082	D	916 428-4090	7668
Blazona Concrete Cnstr Inc	1542	D	916 375-8337	1481
Brown Construction Inc	1542	D	916 374-8616	1485
Burger Rhblitation Systems Inc	8049	D	916 617-2400	20167
Bytheways Manufacturing Inc	5023	B	916 453-1212	6754
Califor State Teach Retire Sys (DH)	6371	C	800 228-5453	10478
California Correctnl Peace Ofc (PA)	8631	C	916 372-6060	25056
California School Boards Assn	8611	D	800 266-3382	24951
California Sierra Express Inc	4731	C	916 375-7070	5024
Capay Incorporated (PA)	5149	D	530 796-0730	8765
Capital Beverage Company (PA)	5181	C	916 371-8164	8984
Cgi Technologies Solutions Inc	8731	E	916 281-3200	26347
Cirks Construction Inc	1542	D	916 362-5460	1504
Collins Electrical Company Inc	1731	C	209 466-3691	2545
Core-Mark International Inc	5149	C	509 535-9768	8778
Core-Mark Sacramento 2	5141	E	866 791-4210	8396
Creative Living Options Inc	8361	C	916 372-2102	24492
Dbi Beverage Sacramento (HQ)	5182	D	916 373-5700	9036
Dennis Blazona Construction	1771	D	916 375-8337	3247
Dependable Highway Express Inc	4212	E	916 374-0782	4003
Devine & Son Trucking Co Inc (PA)	4449	C	559 486-7440	4704
Farm Fresh To You (PA)	0191	C	916 303-7145	343
Fredericksen Tank Lines Inc (PA)	4213	D	916 371-4960	4180
Frito-Lay North America Inc	5145	C	916 372-5400	8554
Holt of California	5082	C	916 373-4100	7680
Idexx Reference Labs Inc	8071	C	916 372-4200	22098
Jacmar Ddc LLC	5149	D	916 372-9795	8810
McKesson Corporation	5122	C	916 372-3655	8195
Nor-Cal Beverage Co Inc (PA)	5181	B	916 372-0600	9017
Nor-Cal Pipeline Services	1623	D	530 673-3886	1959
Nor-Cal Produce Inc	5148	C	916 373-0830	8709
Oak Harbor Freight Lines Inc	4213	D	916 371-3960	4239
Occupnl Urgnt Care Hlth Syst	8099	B	916 374-4600	22850
Pacific Gas and Electric Co	4911	C	916 375-5005	6069
Parts	7513	D	916 371-3115	17607
PC World Corp (PA)	4813	C	240 855-8988	5626
Pittsburg Wholesale Groc Inc	5141	D	916 372-7772	8443
Psi3g Inc	5023	D	916 803-2879	6783
Quad/Graphics Inc	7311	C	916 371-9500	13884
Ramos Oil Co Inc (PA)	5171	D	916 371-2570	8945
Redstone Print & Mail Inc	8742	D	916 318-6450	27421
River Bend Nursing Home Inc	8051	D	916 371-1890	20723
River Cy Basbal Inv Group LLC (PA)	7941	D	916 376-4700	18531
River Cy Geoprofessionals Inc	8711	D	916 372-1434	25894
Rural Cmnty Assistance Corp (PA)	8322	D	916 447-2854	23999
Sacramento River Cats Baseball	7941	E	916 376-4700	18532
Sacramento Television Stns Inc (DH)	4833	C	916 374-1452	5835
Sacramento-Yolo Port District	4491	C	916 371-8000	4733
Serving Seniors LLC	8082	D	916 372-9640	22415
Siemens Industry Inc	7629	D	916 371-2600	17913
Ssa Pacific Inc	4491	D	916 374-1866	4739
Testamerica Laboratories Inc	8734	D	916 373-5600	26734
Tonys Fine Foods (HQ)	5147	B	916 374-4000	8632
Tricor America Inc	4215	C	916 371-1704	4439
Triton Tower Inc (PA)	1623	D	916 375-8546	1988
U S Army Corps of Engineers	8711	D	916 557-7491	25964
United Parcel Service Inc OH	4215	D	916 373-4076	4452
UPS Ground Freight Inc	4213	D	916 371-9101	4294
Valley Toxicology Service Inc	8071	D	916 371-5440	22157
Vss International Inc (HQ)	1611	D	916 373-1500	1868
Wallace-Kuhl Investments LLC (PA)	8711	D	916 372-1434	25994
Walton Engineering Inc	1799	D	916 372-1888	3605
Youngs Market Company LLC	5182	E	916 617-4402	9070

WESTLAKE VILLAGE, CA - Ventura County

	SIC	EMP	PHONE	ENTRY #
5 Nine Group Inc	7371	C	805 880-2948	14953
Adelson Testan Brundo Novel (PA)	8111	E	805 604-1816	22905
Allen Construction Inc	1751	C	818 879-5334	3016
Allied Interstate Inc (DH)	7322	A	818 575-5400	13990
Alston & Bird LLP	8111	B	202 239-3673	22913
Amgreen-Karena Ht Partnr Ltd (PA)	7011	D	818 707-9494	12318

GEOGRAPHIC

Company	SIC	EMP	PHONE	ENTRY #
AP Global Inc	5065	D	818 707-3167	7438
Appraiser Loft LLC	6531	E	858 832-8334	11214
Bana Home Loan Servicing	6021	A	213 345-7975	9276
Bankcard USA Merchant Srvc	5044	D	818 597-7000	6950
Baxter Healthcare Corporation	5122	A	805 372-3000	8145
Blue Cross of California (DH)	6324	C	805 557-6050	10182
Burton-Way House Ltd A CA	7011	C	805 214-8075	12410
California Coml Inv Group Inc	8748	E	805 495-8400	27670
Castle & Cooke Calaveras Inc	1542	A	310 208-3636	1498
Citibank National Association	6021	C	805 497-7361	9329
Coastal Radiation Oncology Med	8011	D	805 494-4483	19393
Conversant LLC (HQ)	7375	C	818 575-4500	16213
Cornerstone Healthcare Inc	8052	C	805 777-1133	20924
Country Floral Supply Inc (PA)	5193	D	805 520-8026	9132
Dennis M McCoy & Sons Inc (PA)	1611	D	818 874-3872	1756
Digital Insight Corporation	7375	C	818 879-1010	16216
Dilbeck Inc.	6531	E	805 379-1880	11403
Dole Food Company Inc (HQ)	0179	D	818 874-4000	234
Dole Fresh Fruit Company (DH)	5148	B	818 874-4000	8667
Dole Holding Company LLC	0179	A	818 879-6600	235
Dole Holdings Inc (PA)	5148	D	818 879-6600	8669
Elite Airways LLC	4729	C	805 496-3334	4989
Ernst & Young LLP	8721	D	805 778-7000	26199
Fdsi Logistics LLC	8742	D	818 971-3300	27233
Frontier California Inc.	5065	A	805 372-6000	7479
Frontier California Inc.	4813	C	805 372-6000	5566
G4s Secure Solutions USA Inc	7381	C	818 889-1113	16658
Gemmm Corp	6531	C	818 522-0740	11478
General Home Medical Sup Inc	5047	C	805 449-1559	7181
Greystripe Incorporated	7311	C	415 644-1702	13836
Hanover Builders Inc	1521	E	818 706-2279	1177
High Road Program (PA)	8322	D	805 497-8800	23838
Integrated Dynmc Solutions Inc	7371	E	818 707-8797	15221
Intellirisk Management Corp	7322	E	818 575-5400	14008
International Advisors LLC	8748	D	497 961-7988	27754
Ipayment Inc (DH)	7389	D	212 802-7200	17252
Jackie Hoofring	7361	E	818 961-7272	14654
JD Power	8732	B	805 418-8000	26536
Jri Inc.	5065	E	818 706-2424	7497
Lantz Security Systems Inc	7381	B	805 496-5775	16715
Mannkind Corporation (PA)	8731	C	818 661-5000	26414
Mediaplex Inc (DH)	7311	D	818 575-4500	13864
Microfinancial Incorporated	7359	C	805 367-8900	14526
Move Co	6531	C	805 557-2300	11619
Mws Precision Wire Inds Inc	5051	D	818 991-8553	7292
National Builder Services Inc	7363	D	714 634-7800	14886
North Ranch Country Club	7997	C	818 889-3531	18989
Ownit Mortgage Solutions Inc	6162	B	513 872-6922	9841
Pacific Compensation Insur Co	6331	C	818 575-8500	10384
Pds Tech Inc	7379	A	805 418-9862	16452
Pleasant Holidays LLC (HQ)	4725	C	818 991-3390	4976
Pmt Crdit Risk Trnsf Tr 2015-1	6733	C	818 224-7028	12119
Pmt Crdit Risk Trnsf Tr 2015-2	6733	C	818 224-7442	12120
Pmt Issuer Trust - Fmsr	6798	C	818 224-7028	12180
Pnmac Gmsr Issuer Trust	6733	A	818 746-2271	12121
Premium Rock Drywall Inc	1742	D	818 676-3350	2942
Pyj V A California Ltd Partnr	7992	D	805 495-8437	18748
Registry Monitoring Ins Srvcs	6531	C	800 400-4924	11724
Remax Olson	6531	D	805 267-4929	11730
Rwr Homes Inc (PA)	6552	D	805 413-1792	11911
Sdg Enterprises	1711	D	805 777-7978	2351
Securitas SEC Svcs USA Inc	7381	B	818 706-4909	16797
Securitas SEC Svcs USA Inc	7381	C	818 706-6800	16814
Select Home Care	8082	D	805 777-3855	22413
Sky Court USA Inc.	7011	C	805 497-9991	13242
Smith Bros (PA)	1751	D	805 449-2841	3081
Southern Cal Orthpd Inst LP	8011	D	818 901-6600	19903
Spad Holdings LLC	7991	D	805 496-9978	18659
Sunrise Senior Living LLC	8051	D	805 557-1100	20823
Swvp Westlake LLC	7011	C	805 557-1234	13312
Thousand Oaks Prtg & Spc Inc	7389	C	818 706-8330	17509
Triplecurve LLC	8742	D	855 874-2878	27499
Troop Real Estate Inc.	6531	D	805 402-3028	11803
United Cp/S Chldrns Fndn La	8322	E	805 494-1141	24102
United Parcel Service Inc OH	7389	A	818 735-0945	17541
University Cal Los Angeles	8011	A	805 494-6920	20028
Velocity Commercial Capitl LLC	6531	E	818 532-3700	11812
Verizon Communications Inc	7389	D	805 390-5417	17562
Warner Pacific Insur Svcs Inc (PA)	6411	C	408 298-4049	10826
Westlake Village Inn	7011	D	818 889-0230	13393
WF Cinema Holdings LP	7832	E	805 379-8966	18324
Young Estates	6531	D	805 446-1800	11842
Young Realtors	6531	D	805 497-0947	11843

WESTMINSTER, CA - Orange County

Company	SIC	EMP	PHONE	ENTRY #
Abrazar Inc	8322	D	714 893-3581	23458
Anderson News LLC	5192	D	714 892-7766	9108
B & E Farms Inc	0171	E	714 893-8166	91
Co D L Pham MD	8011	E	714 531-2091	19392
Consoldted Med Bo-Analysis Inc	8071	D	714 657-7389	22070
County of Orange	8322	D	714 896-7188	23697
County of Orange	8322	D	714 896-7500	23699
Edco Drywall Inc	1742	E	714 799-9886	2879
Extended Care Hosp Westminster	8051	C	714 891-2769	20420
Ferguson Enterprises Inc	5074	C	714 893-1936	7622
Helping Hands Sanctuary of Ida	8051	D	714 892-6686	20525
Kindred Hospital-Westminster	8062	B	714 372-3014	21540
Lbs Financial Credit Union (PA)	6111	C	562 598-9007	9699
Maxwell Petersen Associates	8742	E	714 230-3150	27326
Memorial Promptcare Medical Gr (PA)	8011	E	714 891-9008	19682
National Fail Safe Inc	1731	C	562 493-5447	2656
New CAM Commerce Solutions LLC	7372	D	714 338-0200	15779
Orange County One Stop Center	7361	D	714 241-4900	14682
Pyramid Logistics Services Inc (PA)	4213	D	714 903-2600	4247
Snowbounders Ski Club	7997	D	714 892-4897	19050
Southern California Edison Co	4911	C	714 934-0838	6118
Southern California Edison Co	4911	B	714 895-0420	6132
Southern California Edison Co	4911	C	714 895-0163	6135
Sunrise Plumbing & Mech Inc	1711	E	562 424-0332	2377
Thompson Family Farms LLC	0191	E	714 848-7536	387
Vina Holdings Inc	8082	D	714 622-5334	22443
Westminster Housing Parteners	6531	E	714 891-3000	11831
Westview Services Inc	8331	D	714 418-2090	24249

WHEATLAND, CA - Yuba County

Company	SIC	EMP	PHONE	ENTRY #
Northern California Inalliance	8322	C	530 633-9695	23944
Wheatland School District	6531	D	530 633-3135	11832

WHITTIER, CA - Los Angeles County

Company	SIC	EMP	PHONE	ENTRY #
24 Hour Fitness Usa Inc.	7991	D	562 943-3771	18566
Ahmc Whittier Hosp Med Ctr LP	8062	A	562 945-3561	21274
Asian Rehabilitation Svc Inc (PA)	8331	D	562 632-1141	24152
Assocted Reproduction Svcs Inc	7334	C	562 696-1181	14082
Beachside Realtors	6531	D	562 947-7834	11234
Bright Health Physicians (PA)	8011	C	562 947-8478	19327
Caldwell Realty	6531	C	562 907-5655	11262
Capc Inc	8399	C	562 693-8826	24750
Cellco Partnership	4812	D	562 789-0911	5384
Cintas Corporation No 3	7213	C	562 692-8741	13523
City of Whittier	8322	D	562 567-9446	23586
Complete Landscape Care Inc	0782	C	562 946-4441	815
County of Los Angeles	8322	C	562 908-3119	23665
County of Los Angeles	4151	C	562 945-2581	3912
County Santtn Dist 2 of La Co (PA)	4959	A	562 699-7411	6535
County Santtn Dist 2 of La Co	4953	C	562 699-5204	6386
Credit Union Southern Cal (PA)	6061	E	562 698-8326	9548
Cypress College Foundation	8641	D	714 484-7128	25148
Del Rio Health Care Inc	8051	C	562 947-5221	20370
Ensign Group Inc	8051	C	562 947-7817	20397
Fedex Freight Corporation	4231	B	800 288-0743	4692
Freedom Painting Inc	1721	E	562 696-0785	2436
Friendly Hills Country Club	7997	C	562 698-0331	18927
Ghg Properties LLC	7011	D	562 945-8511	12605
Gourmet India Food Company LLC	5149	D	562 698-9763	8801
Grand Supercenter Inc	5141	D	562 318-3451	8411
Helpline Youth Counseling (PA)	8322	E	562 273-0722	23837
In2vision Programs LLC	8322	D	562 789-8888	23852
Inclusion Services LLC	8322	C	562 945-2000	23853
Intercommunity Child	8322	C	562 692-0383	23860
Intercommunity Dialysis Svcs	8092	E	562 696-1841	22479
Interhealth Corp (PA)	8062	A	562 698-0811	21460
Interhealth Services Inc (HQ)	8082	D	562 698-0811	22345
International Home Mortgage	6162	D	562 945-7753	9818
J P Carroll Co Inc	1721	D	323 660-9230	2449
John Shannon Mc Gee Co Inc	5063	E	562 789-1777	7369
Kaiser Foundation Hospitals	8062	E	866 340-5974	21513
League of Wmen Voters Whittier	8651	E	562 947-5818	25371
Longwood Management Corp	8062	D	562 693-5240	21568
Magnell Associate Inc	4225	C	626 271-1420	4590
Mercedes Diaz Homes Inc	1521	D	562 945-4576	1201
Merrill Gardens LLC	6513	D	562 693-0505	11076
NLc Enterprises Incorporated	7389	E	562 693-3590	17355
Oltmans Construction Co (PA)	1541	D	562 948-4242	1424
Oltmans Investment Company	6512	E	562 948-4242	10923
Orchard - Post Acute Care Ctr	8051	A	562 693-7701	20682
Peoples Care Inc.	8351	D	562 320-0174	24368
Pep Boys Manny Moe Jack of Cal	7538	E	562 908-4400	17777
Pih Health Hospital - Whittier (PA)	8062	A	562 698-0811	21649
Plaza De La Raza Child Develop	8351	D	562 695-1070	24370
Rio Hondo Education Consortium	8322	C	562 945-0150	23998
Rose Hills Company (HQ)	6553	A	562 699-0921	11949
Rose Hills Holdings Corp (PA)	6553	A	562 699-0921	11950

2019 Directory of California
Wholesalers and Services Companies

(P-0000) Products & Services Section entry number
(PA)=Parent Co (HQ)=Headquarters (DH)=Div Headquarters

	SIC	EMP	PHONE	ENTRY #
Rose Hills Mortuary Inc	7261	A	562 699-0921	13696
S CA University Hlth Sciences	8041	E	562 947-8755	20156
Sanitation Districts	4953	A	562 908-4288	6474
Sas Entertainment Partners Inc	7929	E	213 400-1901	18462
Secure Transportation Co Inc (PA)	4119	C	562 941-0107	3846
Southern California Gas Co	4924	D	562 803-3341	6171
Southern California Mtl Hdlg (DH)	5084	C	562 949-1006	7802
Southern Fresh Prod Provs Inc	5148	D	562 236-2784	8731
Summerville Senior Living Inc	6513	D	562 943-3724	11120
Transportation California Dept	1611	C	562 692-0823	1865
Whittier Hospital Med Ctr Inc	8062	C	562 945-3561	21917

WILDOMAR, CA - Riverside County

	SIC	EMP	PHONE	ENTRY #
Asr Constructors Inc	1542	B	951 779-6580	1469
Classic Installs Inc	1796	D	951 678-9906	3469
Coldwell Banker and Associates (PA)	6211	D	951 304-2900	9943
Diverscape Inc	0782	D	951 245-1686	828
Heartland Payment Systems LLC	7389	D	909 609-1836	17213
Inland Vly Rgional Med Ctr Inc (HQ)	8062	C	951 677-1111	21458
Kaiser Foundation Hospitals	8062	E	951 353-2000	21498
Kilcrew Productions	7389	D	619 564-2080	17273
Lake Elsinore Unified Schl Dst	4151	C	951 253-7830	3939
S Taylor Construction Inc	1521	C	310 291-4505	1229
Sunpro Solar Inc	1711	D	951 678-7733	2376

WILLIAMS, CA - Colusa County

	SIC	EMP	PHONE	ENTRY #
ACC-Gwg LLC	8748	D	530 473-2827	27619
Elvira Sandoval	7361	C	530 473-5718	14611
La Grande Farm	0161	D	530 473-5923	66
Valley West Health Care Inc (PA)	8059	D	530 473-5321	21244
Viking Pools LLC	1799	E	530 473-5319	3604

WILLITS, CA - Mendocino County

	SIC	EMP	PHONE	ENTRY #
Brooktrails Lodge LLC	7011	D	707 459-1596	12407
Ensign Willits LLC	8059	D	707 459-5592	21064
Sherwood Valley Rancheria	7011	D	707 459-7330	13222
Shusters Transportation Inc	4212	D	707 459-4131	4062
Solid Wastes of Willits Inc (PA)	4212	D	707 459-4845	4065
Willits Hospital Inc	8062	B	707 459-6801	21918
Willits Seniors Inc	8322	D	707 459-6826	24133

WILLOW CREEK, CA - Humboldt County

	SIC	EMP	PHONE	ENTRY #
Northcoast Childrens Services	8322	D	530 629-2283	23941

WILLOWS, CA - Glenn County

	SIC	EMP	PHONE	ENTRY #
County of Glenn	8099	D	530 934-6582	22770
County of Glenn	1611	C	530 934-6530	1748
County of Glenn	8322	D	530 934-6453	23642
County of Glenn	8322	C	530 934-6514	23643
County of Glenn	8093	D	530 934-6582	22543
Glenn Cnty Humn Resource Agcy	8331	C	530 934-6510	24185
Glenn Cnty Plg Pub Works Agcy	1611	C	530 934-6541	1768
Glenn Medical Center Inc	8062	D	530 934-4681	21427
Glenn-Colusa Irrigation Dst (PA)	4971	D	530 934-8881	6555
Kumar Hotels Inc	7011	D	530 934-8900	12823
Sunbridge Healthcare LLC	8052	D	530 934-2834	20964

WILMINGTON, CA - Los Angeles County

	SIC	EMP	PHONE	ENTRY #
Ajc Sandblasting Inc	1799	D	562 436-3606	3480
American Integrated Svcs Inc (PA)	8744	E	310 522-1168	27576
Anderson Hay & Grain Co Inc	5153	C	310 518-2935	8904
Boys and Girls Clubs of The La	8641	D	310 833-1322	25110
Ccc2931 LLC	4226	D	562 590-8591	4667
City of Los Angeles	4173	B	310 732-3550	3950
Conglobal Industries LLC	4226	D	310 518-2850	4669
County of Los Angeles	8011	D	310 518-8800	19414
E Street Cold Logistics LLC (PA)	4222	E	310 233-7300	4500
Estes Express Lines Inc	4213	D	310 549-7306	4145
Fast Lane Transportation Inc (PA)	4213	D	562 435-3000	4148
Harbor Industrial Services	7353	D	310 522-1193	14441
Icpk Corporation	5141	D	310 830-8020	8415
Konoike-Pacific California Inc (HQ)	4222	D	310 518-1000	4504
Los Angeles Unified School Dst	8322	C	310 518-1128	23906
Marine Technical Services Inc	7389	D	310 549-8030	17310
MCM Construction Inc	1771	D	310 549-9207	3286
Pacific Harbor Line Inc (HQ)	4011	C	310 834-4594	3622
Pacific Sea Food Co Inc	5146	E	310 835-4343	8593
Pasha Stevedoring Terminals LP	4491	E	310 223-2006	4730
Pasha Stevedoring Terminals LP	4424	E	415 927-6353	4702
Potential Industries Inc (PA)	4953	C	310 807-4466	6430
Praxair Inc	5169	D	562 983-2100	8934
South Bay Ctr For Counseling	8322	C	310 414-2090	24058
Star Fisheries	5146	C	310 549-4992	8604
Trapac LLC (HQ)	4491	E	310 513-1572	4743
Wwl Vehicle Svcs Americas Inc	4225	C	310 835-8806	4663

WINCHESTER, CA - Riverside County

	SIC	EMP	PHONE	ENTRY #
Help Hospitalized Veterans II	8322	D	951 926-4500	23836

	SIC	EMP	PHONE	ENTRY #
Metropolitan Water District	4941	C	760 663-4911	6282
Metropolitan Water District	4941	D	951 926-7095	6285
Metropolitan Water District	4941	D	951 926-1501	6288
Mind Dragon Inc	8748	E	877 367-6060	27789
Skywest Airlines Inc	4512	D	951 926-9511	4798

WINDSOR, CA - Sonoma County

	SIC	EMP	PHONE	ENTRY #
Arete Associates	8731	D	818 885-2200	26327
Cali Calmecac Language Academy	8641	D	707 837-7747	25121
Fedex Ground Package Sys Inc	4213	C	800 463-3339	4173
Happy Pet Co	0742	E	707 586-8660	602
Landcare USA LLC	0782	D	707 836-1460	879
North Bay Construction Inc	1771	E	707 836-8500	3295
Petersen Builders Inc	1521	E	707 838-3035	1215
Richards Grove Saralees Vinyrd	0172	D	707 837-9200	168
Robert A Hall	7363	D	707 837-8564	14906
Selex Inc	1799	D	707 836-8836	3583
Shook & Waller Cnstr Inc	1751	D	707 578-3933	3075
Windsor Golf Club Inc	7992	D	707 838-7888	18779

WINNETKA, CA - Los Angeles County

	SIC	EMP	PHONE	ENTRY #
David W Golen	4212	D	213 716-0706	3998
Memon Aamir	7381	E	818 339-8810	16730
Valley Village (PA)	8361	D	818 587-9450	24708

WINTERHAVEN, CA - Imperial County

	SIC	EMP	PHONE	ENTRY #
Quechan Indian Tribe	7999	B	760 572-2413	19220

WINTERS, CA - Yolo County

	SIC	EMP	PHONE	ENTRY #
Button & Turkovich	0191	D	530 795-2090	327
Mariani Nut Company Inc (PA)	0173	C	530 795-3311	192
Mariani Nut Company Inc	0173	D	530 795-2225	193
Ramos Orchards	0173	D	530 795-4748	194
Terra Firma Farm Corp	0161	E	530 795-2473	87

WINTON, CA - Merced County

	SIC	EMP	PHONE	ENTRY #
Cederlind Farms LP	0172	D	209 606-8586	133
Central Valley Oprtnty Ctr Inc (PA)	8331	C	209 357-0062	24165
P H Ranch Inc	0241	E	209 358-5111	425

WOODBRIDGE, CA - San Joaquin County

	SIC	EMP	PHONE	ENTRY #
The Woodbridge Golf Cntry CLB	7997	D	209 369-2371	19069

WOODLAKE, CA - Tulare County

	SIC	EMP	PHONE	ENTRY #
Gold Coast Farms LLC	0181	E	559 564-6316	262
Pete Santellan	0761	C	559 564-3748	666

WOODLAND, CA - Yolo County

	SIC	EMP	PHONE	ENTRY #
Alcohol DRG Program Yolo Cnty	8093	E	530 666-8650	22499
Apria Healthcare LLC	8099	D	530 669-6441	22735
AT&T Corp.	4812	D	530 661-7724	5289
B E Giovannetti & Sons (PA)	0111	D	530 662-1729	1
Broward Builders Inc	1542	D	530 666-5635	1484
Butterfield Electric Inc (PA)	1731	C	530 666-2116	2532
Campos Dmetrio Frm Labor Contr	7361	D	530 662-4143	14582
City of Woodland	7999	C	530 661-5878	19145
City of Woodland	8744	C	530 661-5962	27582
City of Woodland	8711	C	530 661-5961	25616
County of Yolo	8093	D	530 666-8630	22561
CPI Econco Division (DH)	7629	D	530 662-7553	17902
Dignity Health	8062	C	530 666-8828	21382
E & E Co Ltd	1521	B	530 669-5991	1158
E & E Co Ltd	5023	C	530 669-5991	6757
Half Moon Fruit & Produce Co (PA)	0112	D	530 662-1727	5
Home Instead Senior Care	8082	E	707 678-2005	22329
Interpac Technologies Inc	7389	D	530 662-6363	17248
J H Meek & Sons Inc	0191	E	530 662-1106	358
Joe Heidrick Enterprises Inc	0115	C	530 662-2339	8
Liberty Packing Company LLC (PA)	5148	E	209 826-7100	8702
Mann Lake Ltd	5191	E	530 662-4061	9085
Monsanto Company	5148	B	530 669-6224	8706
Muller Ranch LLC	0111	D	530 662-0015	2
North American Health Care	8741	D	530 662-9193	26962
Northern Vly Indian Hlth Inc	8063	D	530 661-4400	21967
Nugget Market Inc	4225	C	530 662-5479	4602
Omar Orozco	0761	D	530 723-0849	663
Oscar Valero	0191	E	530 668-4342	372
Palm Grdns Rsdntial Care Fclty	8361	E	530 661-0574	24625
Payne Brothers Ranches	0161	D	530 662-2354	75
Seminis Vegetable Seeds Inc	5191	E	530 669-6903	9099
Sierra Entertainment	4011	E	530 666-9646	3625
St Johns Retirement Village (PA)	8059	E	530 662-9674	21223
Summer House Inc (PA)	8361	D	530 662-8493	24688
Sunfoods LLC (HQ)	5141	D	530 661-1923	8463
Sutter Health	8011	B	530 406-5600	19970
Sutter Health	8011	C	530 406-5600	19971
Sutter Hlth Scrmnto Sierra Reg	8011	A	530 406-5616	19988
Target Corporation	4226	B	530 666-3705	4688

Employment Codes: A=Over 500 employees, B=251-500,
C=101-250, D=51-100, E=50

2019 Directory of California
Wholesalers and Services Companies

© Mergent Inc. 1-800-342-5647

1707

GEOGRAPHIC

	SIC	EMP	PHONE	ENTRY #
Tc Property Mgt A Californi	6799	D	530 666-5799	12271
Travis Credit Union	6061	B	800 877-8328	9608
United Health Systems Inc	8051	C	530 662-9161	20846
Woodland Healthcare	8062	C	530 668-2600	21920
Woodland Jint Unified Schl Dst	4151	E	530 662-0201	3948
Woodland Residential Services	6513	D	530 419-0059	11144
Woodland Swim Team Bosters CLB	8641	D	530 662-9783	25287

WOODLAND HILLS, CA - Los Angeles County

	SIC	EMP	PHONE	ENTRY #
21st Century Insurance Company (DH)	6411	A	877 310-5687	10507
21st Century Lf & Hlth Co Inc (PA)	6321	C	818 887-4436	10154
7410 Woodman Avenue LLC	6513	D	805 496-4336	10970
8020 Consulting LLC	8748	E	818 523-3201	27615
Advanced Critical Care Emerge	0742	D	818 887-2262	594
All Action Security Inc	7381	D	800 482-7371	16545
Alliant Asset MGT Co LLC (PA)	6531	D	818 668-2805	11206
Allied Industries Inc (PA)	8748	C	818 781-2490	27635
Amwins Insurance Brkg Cal LLC (HQ)	6411	D	818 772-1774	10524
Andwin (PA)	5113	C	818 999-2828	8094
AON Consulting Inc	6411	D	562 345-4700	10530
Arrow Electronics Inc	5065	A	818 932-1022	7442
Assertive Security Services &	7382	A	818 888-2405	16875
Associated Foreign Exch Inc (HQ)	6099	D	888 307-2339	9670
Assocted Fgn Exch Holdings Inc (PA)	6099	D	818 386-2702	9671
Automobile Club Southern Cal	8699	E	818 883-2660	25389
Avnet Inc	5065	D	818 594-8310	7446
B C Life & Health Insurance Co	6321	D	818 703-2345	10161
B Riley Financial Inc (PA)	7389	C	818 884-3737	17024
Bank America National Assn	6021	C	818 577-2000	9292
Benefitvision Inc	8331	D	818 348-3100	24156
Blackline Systems Inc (HQ)	7372	C	818 746-4700	15611
Blh Construction Company	1522	C	818 905-3837	1270
Boething Treeland Farms Inc (PA)	0811	D	818 883-1222	985
California Physicians Service	6351	D	818 228-2010	10424
California Physicians Service	6324	B	818 598-8000	10189
California Preferred Bldrs Inc	1521	E	818 402-3345	1141
Canoga Hotel Corporation	7011	C	818 595-1000	12424
Canter/Edwards Enterprises (PA)	7231	E	818 887-7330	13649
Center For Autism & (PA)	8049	C	818 345-2345	20170
Centrelink Insur & Fincl Svcs	7389	D	818 587-2001	17065
Child Development Institute	8322	D	818 888-4559	23561
Classmates Media Corporation	7299	B	818 287-3600	13729
Cohnreznick LLP	8721	C	818 205-2600	26169
Conduit Lngage Specialists Inc	7299	D	859 299-3178	13731
Corptax LLC	7371	C	818 316-2400	15081
Courtyard Management Corp	7011	D	818 999-2200	12492
Creative Events Enterprises	8742	C	818 610-7000	27204
Custom Design Co Inc	1542	E	818 507-5959	1511
Dassault Systemes Americas	7371	C	818 999-2500	15094
Digital Communications Network (PA)	4812	D	818 227-3333	5404
Dunn & Berger Inc	8082	B	818 986-1234	22287
Environmental Construction Inc	1542	D	818 449-8920	1529
Ev Ray Inc	5023	E	818 346-5381	6760
Factory Mutual Insurance Co	6331	D	818 227-2200	10350
Farmers Group Inc (HQ)	6331	A	323 932-3200	10351
Farmers Group Inc	6411	A	805 583-7400	10622
Farmers Insurance Exchange (DH)	6411	A	323 932-3200	10623
Federal Insurance Company	6411	D	818 596-6100	10626
Film Roman Llc	7812	C	818 748-4000	18051
Film Roman LLC	7812	C	818 748-4000	18052
First Interstate Security Inc	7381	D	818 995-6664	16646
Firstfed Financial Corp	6021	A	562 618-0573	9347
Fountain Court Essex	6531	E	818 227-2100	11471
Goetzman Group Inc (PA)	8742	D	818 595-1112	27248
Greystar Management Svcs LP	6531	B	818 596-2180	11492
Guarachi Wine Partners Inc	5182	C	818 225-5100	9047
Harris Direct	7389	D	818 357-2040	17208
Health Net Inc (HQ)	6324	C	818 676-6000	10204
Health Net California Inc (DH)	6324	C	818 676-6775	10207
Health Net Community Solutions	6324	D	818 676-6000	10209
Health Net Life Insurance Co	6324	C	800 865-6288	10211
Hilton Woodland Hills & Towers	7011	C	818 595-1000	12670
Hsbc Finance Corporation	6162	B	818 999-9175	9816
IDS Inc	4724	D	855 997-7437	4940
Image Entertainment Inc (DH)	7822	D	818 407-9100	18239
Infinite Home Health Inc	8082	D	818 888-7772	22343
Innovative Merch Solutions LLC	7389	C	818 936-7800	17239
Intelex Systems Inc	7371	D	818 518-1100	15223
Inter/Media Time Buying Corp (PA)	7311	E	818 995-1455	13847
Interstate Protective Services	7381	D	818 995-6664	16703
John Alden Life Insurance Co	6311	D	818 595-7600	10138
Joseph C Sansone Company (PA)	8111	D	818 226-3400	23156
Kaiser Foundation Hospitals	8062	A	818 719-2000	21477
Kaiser Foundation Hospitals	8062	E	818 592-3100	21504
Kaiser Foundation Hospitals	6324	D	888 515-3500	10238
Kellogg Andlson Accntancy Corp (PA)	8721	D	818 971-5100	26234

	SIC	EMP	PHONE	ENTRY #
Kern Organization Inc	7311	D	818 703-8775	13855
Kpmg LLP	8721	E	818 227-6900	26243
Law Offices Berglund & Johnson (PA)	8111	D	951 276-4783	23194
Lewis Marenstein Wicke Sherwin	8111	E	818 703-6000	23211
Lifecare Assurance Company	6321	C	818 887-4436	10168
LLP Moss Adams	8721	D	818 577-1822	26248
Markel Corp	6411	B	818 595-0600	10676
Markel West Inc	6411	E	818 595-0600	10677
Marriott International	7011	C	818 887-4800	12896
Mediscan Diagnostic Svcs LLC	8099	D	818 758-4224	22839
Medpoint Management	8011	E	818 702-0100	19679
Memeged Tevuot Shemesh (PA)	1711	C	866 575-1211	2277
Metropolitan Marketing Inc (PA)	8742	D	909 620-5083	27344
Motion Picture and TV Fund (PA)	8062	A	818 876-1777	21598
Netapp Inc	7373	C	818 227-5025	16014
Netzero Inc (DH)	7371	C	805 418-2000	15304
Neversoft Entertainment Inc	7371	C	818 610-4100	15306
New Mediscan II LLC	8099	D	866 758-4224	22847
Nmms Twin Peaks LLC	6531	C	818 710-6100	11630
Novastar Post Inc	7812	D	323 467-5020	18086
Omnikron Systems Inc	7379	C	818 591-7890	16440
Pacific Lodge Youth Services	8361	C	818 347-1577	24622
Pacific Protection Services	7381	C	818 313-9369	16752
Panavision Inc (PA)	7359	B	818 316-1000	14533
Physicians Choice LLC	8721	D	818 340-9988	26271
Pinnacle Contracting Corp	1542	E	818 888-6548	1616
Poms & Assoc Insur Brks Inc (PA)	6411	D	818 449-9300	10734
Pro-Tek Consulting (PA)	7379	C	805 807-5571	16462
Prober & Raphael A Law Corp	8111	D	818 227-0100	23341
Propertyplus Insur Agcy Inc	6411	A	818 432-2640	10744
Pta CA Congress of Parents	8641	E	818 340-6700	25219
Qbi LLC (PA)	8721	D	818 594-4900	26279
Qualified Benefits Inc	6411	E	818 594-4900	10751
R & B Realty Group	6513	D	818 710-5400	11102
Ramkade Insurance Services	6411	D	818 444-1340	10755
Reachlocal Inc (HQ)	7311	D	818 274-0260	13888
Real Software Systems LLC (PA)	7372	D	818 313-8000	15840
Realty Alliance Inc	6163	D	818 610-0080	9905
Ricoh Usa Inc	5044	D	213 629-1838	6978
Ricoh Usa Inc	5044	D	818 703-0265	6980
Rodeo Realty Inc	6531	D	818 999-2030	11742
Russon Financial Services Inc	8742	D	818 999-2800	27435
Santa Monica Mntins Trils Cncil	8641	D	818 222-4531	25241
Scherzer International Corp (PA)	7389	D	818 227-2770	17460
Singerlewak LLP	8721	D	818 999-3924	26295
Skyhigh Woodland Hills LLC	7999	D	805 484-6300	19239
Solar Energy LLC	1711	D	818 449-5816	2361
Southern Cal Prmnnte Med Group	8011	E	818 592-3038	19923
Spad Holdings LLC	7991	D	818 710-7606	18663
State Farm Mutl Auto Insur Co	6411	D	818 887-1060	10791
Talon International Inc (PA)	5131	D	818 444-4100	8246
TI Limited LLC (PA)	7372	D	323 877-5991	15879
Top Tier Consulting	8742	D	818 338-2121	27490
Topanga Villas Company	6513	D	818 884-8017	11126
Tr Warner Center LP	7011	B	818 887-4800	13337
Truck Underwriters Association	6311	A	323 932-3200	10149
United Cp/S Chldrns Fndn La	8059	D	818 782-2211	21238
United Ribbon Company Inc	5044	D	818 716-1515	6987
Universal Mus Group Hldngs Inc	5099	A	317 871-0319	8066
Universal Protection Svc LP	7381	D	818 227-1240	16847
USI of Southern California Ins	6411	E	818 251-3000	10819
Viking River Cruises Inc (HQ)	4724	D	818 227-1234	4958
W M Klorman Construction Corp	1542	D	818 591-5969	1695
Wells Fargo Clearing Svcs LLC	6211	D	818 226-2222	10040
West Valley Area Squad Club	8399	C	818 888-0980	24858
Wham-O Inc	5092	A	818 963-4200	7963
Willits Perpetual LLC	7389	D	818 668-6800	17595
Zenith Insurance Company (DH)	6331	B	818 713-1000	10418

WOODSIDE, CA - San Mateo County

	SIC	EMP	PHONE	ENTRY #
Ecullet Inc	4953	D	650 493-7300	6392
Filoli Center	8422	D	650 364-8300	24928
Skyline Consulting Group	8742	C	650 529-3455	27454

WRIGHTWOOD, CA - San Bernardino County

	SIC	EMP	PHONE	ENTRY #
MHRP Resort Inc	7011	D	760 249-5808	12926
Mountain High Resort Assoc LLC	6531	A	760 249-5808	11615

YORBA LINDA, CA - Orange County

	SIC	EMP	PHONE	ENTRY #
AJ Oster West LLC	5051	D	714 692-1000	7252
Alliance Rvrside Hsptality LLC	7011	E	949 229-3168	12313
Ambreen Enterprises Inc	8748	D	909 620-1339	27637
American Golf Corporation	7997	D	714 779-2461	18832
American Transport Inc	6162	D	714 567-8000	9775
Black Gold Golf Club	7992	D	714 961-0060	18689
Brewsters Automotive Inc	7538	D	714 528-4683	17756

2019 Directory of California
Wholesalers and Services Companies

(P-0000) Products & Services Section entry number
(PA)=Parent Co (HQ)=Headquarters (DH)=Div Headquarters

	SIC	EMP	PHONE	ENTRY #
Coldwell Bnkr Residential Brkg	6531	E	714 832-0020	11357
Dsh West Inc	7336	D	714 692-8777	14112
Eastern Star Homes California **(PA)**	8322	D	714 986-2380	23780
First Team RE - Orange Cnty	6531	D	714 223-2143	11457
Food Management Associates Inc	8742	E	714 694-2828	27239
Force Framing Inc	1751	E	714 970-3888	3036
Hulk Construction	1795	D	714 701-9458	3454
IMG **(PA)**	7389	E	714 974-1700	17232
Kaiser Foundation Hospitals	8011	E	714 685-3520	19603
Loma Vista Nursery	5193	D	714 779-5583	9144
Mesa Contracting Corporation	1611	C	714 974-7300	1818
Nasser Company Inc **(PA)**	5141	C	714 279-2100	8434
Professnal Rgistry Netwrk Corp	7361	C	714 394-4071	14703
Reeves Tractor Service Inc	1611	D	714 692-4020	1840
Robert Moreno Insurance Svcs	6411	C	714 525-5168	10758
Southern Cal Prmnnte Med Group	8011	E	714 685-3520	19918
St Jude Heritage Medical Group	8011	C	714 528-4211	19939
Ta-Kai Home Care Inc	8082	D	714 393-4586	22432
V-Tek Systems Corporation	7373	D	909 396-5355	16071
Vident	5047	D	714 221-6700	7229
Yorba Properties Corp	6531	D	714 777-5112	11841

YOSEMITE NTPK, CA - Mariposa County

	SIC	EMP	PHONE	ENTRY #
DNC Prks Rsrts At Yosemite Inc	7011	A	209 372-1001	12532

YOUNTVILLE, CA - Napa County

	SIC	EMP	PHONE	ENTRY #
Bazan Mario AG Services & Vine	0172	D	707 945-0718	130
French Laundry Restaurant Corp **(PA)**	7219	D	707 944-0167	13633
Remington Ldging Hsptality LLC	7011	A	877 932-5333	13110
Vintners Golf Club	7992	E	707 944-1992	18777

YREKA, CA - Siskiyou County

	SIC	EMP	PHONE	ENTRY #
Belcampo Group Inc	7299	D	530 842-5200	13720
County of Siskiyou	8322	D	530 841-2700	23743
RCO Reforesting Inc	0851	E	530 842-7647	999
Siskiyou Hospital Inc	8062	B	530 842-4121	21757

YUBA CITY, CA - Sutter County

	SIC	EMP	PHONE	ENTRY #
Alta Cal Regional Ctr Inc	8322	B	530 674-3070	23469
Ampla Health **(PA)**	8021	C	530 674-4261	20109
AT&T Corp	4812	D	530 822-2700	5283
Bi-County Ambulance Service	4119	E	530 674-2780	3777
Bianchi Ag Services Inc	0762	D	530 923-7675	682
Butte Basin Management Co	8741	E	530 674-2060	26790
Butte-Yb-Stter Wtr Qlty Cltion	4221	D	530 673-5131	4488
Calpine Corporation	4911	E	530 821-2075	6014
Cellco Partnership	4812	D	530 674-8007	5387
County of Sutter	8093	C	530 822-7250	22560
E Center	8351	C	530 634-1200	24316
Express Personnel Services	7361	D	530 671-9202	14619

	SIC	EMP	PHONE	ENTRY #
Freemont Rideout Health Group	8011	D	530 751-4000	19476
Frito-Lay North America Inc	5145	C	530 671-7854	8545
Gene M Accito	0139	D	530 674-3179	24
Golden 1 Credit Union	6062	C	877 465-3361	9635
Guava Holdings LLC	8069	E	530 671-0550	22022
Hilbers Inc	1542	D	530 673-2947	1553
Lamon Construction Company Inc	1542	E	530 671-1370	1578
New Legend Inc	4213	C	530 674-3100	4235
Northgate Terrace Apts	6513	D	530 671-2026	11085
R B Spencer Inc	1711	D	530 674-8307	2325
Sacramento Packing Inc **(PA)**	0175	E	530 671-4488	229
Sears Roebuck and Co	7549	D	530 751-4628	17872
Sierra Central Credit Union **(PA)**	6062	D	530 671-3009	9654
Sierra Gold Nurseries Inc	0181	D	530 674-1145	301
Sutter Health	8011	C	530 749-3585	19982
Sutter N Med Group A Prof Corp **(PA)**	8011	C	530 749-3661	19990
Sutter North Med Foundation **(PA)**	8011	C	530 741-1300	19991
Sutter North Med Foundation	8011	D	530 749-3635	19992
Sutter North Med Foundation	8011	D	530 749-3450	19994
Sutter Surgical Hospital N Vly	8062	C	530 749-5700	21846
Thiara Sukhwant	0721	E	530 673-1581	469
Tri County Respite Care Svc	8322	D	530 755-3500	24095
Trueblue Inc	7363	C	530 755-3291	14925
United Com Serve	8051	D	530 790-3000	20845
United Landscape Resource Inc	0782	C	530 671-1029	955
Valley Aggregate Transport Inc	4212	D	530 821-2600	4081
Virga Investment Property	6512	C	530 755-4409	10960
Yuba City Nursing & Rehab LLC	8051	D	530 671-0550	20913
Yuba City Racquet Club Inc	7997	D	530 673-6900	19088
Yuba City Unified School	8399	A	530 822-7601	24862

YUCAIPA, CA - San Bernardino County

	SIC	EMP	PHONE	ENTRY #
Avenue H LLC	8051	D	909 795-2476	20252
B B G Management Group **(PA)**	5145	D	909 797-9581	8543
Braswells Yucaipa Valley C	8051	D	909 795-2476	20264
Calimesa Operations LLC	8051	C	909 795-2421	20283
Cedar Operations LLC	8051	C	909 790-2273	20295
Kad Paving Company	1611	D	909 790-3366	1799
Winegardner Masonry Inc	1741	E	909 795-9711	2831
Yucaipa Valley Water District **(PA)**	4941	D	909 797-5117	6319

YUCCA VALLEY, CA - San Bernardino County

	SIC	EMP	PHONE	ENTRY #
A & W Maintenance	1521	D	310 619-8694	1106
A-1 Elite Painting Inc	1721	E	760 365-6702	2417
Catalyst Development Corp	7372	E	760 228-9653	15623
County of San Bernardino	8322	D	760 228-5234	23720
Desert Manor Care Center LP	8361	D	760 365-0717	24503
Hi-Desert Mem Hlth Care Dst **(PA)**	8062	D	760 820-9229	21450

Employment Codes: A=Over 500 employees, B=251-500,
C=101-250, D=51-100, E=50

2019 Directory of California
Wholesalers and Services Companies

© Mergent Inc. 1-800-342-5647

1709

GEOGRAPHIC